D0597182

Cassell's [A] new

A German and English Dictionary

COMPILED FROM THE
BEST AUTHORITIES IN BOTH LANGUAGES

REVISED AND CONSIDERABLY ENLARGED
BY

KARL BREUL
M.A., Litt.D. (Cambridge), Ph.D. (Berlin)
SCHRÖDER PROFESSOR OF GERMAN
in the University of Cambridge

CASSELL AND COMPANY, LTD
London, Toronto, Melbourne and Sydney

First published	*September*	1909
Reprinted	*August*	1910
"	*August*	1911
"	*February*	1913
"	*June*	1914
"	*August*	1916
"	*January*	1919
"	*February*	1921
"	*January*	1923
"	*April*	1924
"	*September*	1926
"	*January*	1928
"	*January*	1929
"	*July*	1930
"	*November*	1931

Printed in Great Britain

PREFACE

TO THE REVISED EDITION

AMONG the smaller dictionaries of the English and German languages Cassell's German Dictionary, compiled by Miss E. Weir, has for many years been held in well-deserved esteem by English and American students of German, and even been used by several of the latest German dictionary writers. When the publishers asked me to revise the book, originally published in 1888, I undertook the laborious task in the hope of being able to correct a number of actual mistakes, and to add many important words and phrases that had either been overlooked or had recently come into existence. But, especially, I wished to make several general improvements which would materially enhance its practical usefulness, and make it, if possible, the best English-German dictionary in one volume at a moderate price, a book comparable, in its more limited sphere, to the new Grieb-Schröer, Flügel-Schmidt-Tanger, and the small Muret. To the accomplishment of this task nearly all my leisure hours during the last eight years have been devoted, but I am only too conscious that I have not been able fully to realise the aim which I had set before me. I shall at all times be sincerely grateful for notifications of mistakes or important omissions—the only way in which those who use a book of this kind can to some extent repay the compiler for the onerous work he has performed in their interest.

Only the principal accent of the German words has been given, and this, it is hoped, will be found helpful. As the book will in all probability be mainly used by English-speaking students—although not addressed to them exclusively—it did not seem to be equally important to indicate the accentuation of the English words. For the same reason the vocabulary of the German-English part is somewhat fuller than that of the English-German portion. In the former, besides the stock of ordinary words that are bound to appear in both parts, many German dialectal terms (*e.g. Deern*, *man*, *Marjell*, *Fluh*, etc.) are introduced, as well as the most common German slang expressions—such as occur in every modern German book or newspaper, and are frequently heard in educated families—while there was no necessity to give them in the English-German part. All reasonable assistance for writing German composition, up to an advanced stage, has, however, been given, and it will be found that the idioms of both languages have been treated with particular fulness for a book of this size.

In compiling this new edition the best modern dictionaries of English and German have been consulted, above all the admirable Muret-Sanders, in the compilation of which I myself had for some time a modest share. The nature of this monumental work precludes all thoughts of comparison or rivalry. Also the excellent works of Flügel, Flügel-Schmidt-Tanger, Grieb-Schröer, the small Muret (in 2 vols.), Heyne, Paul, Kluge, Heintze, Saalfeld; the New English Dictionary, Cassell, Webster, Annandale, Chambers, Skeat, and many others, were frequently consulted, and rarely without profit. A comparison of these valuable works with the books enumerated by Miss Weir as her chief authorities shows at a glance the great strides made in the field of English and German lexicography since the publication of the first edition in 1888.

The chief points in which the present edition differs from the original are the following:—

Not only have numerous mistakes and misprints been corrected, and many thousands of new words and phrases been added, but a large number of the old renderings have been corrected and re-arranged. Words etymologically connected have, as a rule, been grouped under the same heading, while in many cases homonyms of different origin, which had been confused in the former edition, have now for the first time been separated. The forms of all the strong and irregular verbs, besides appearing in the Indexes, have been entered in their alphabetical place in the main part of the Dictionary.

In the German-English part the German accentuation has been indicated. In the English-German part, and in the lists of the German strong and irregular verbs, the latest official spelling of 1902 (as adopted by Germany, Austria, and Switzerland) is given. This spelling, which will probably be generally adopted in the future, (*Efeu*, *Tür*, *gibt*, *imstande sein*) has hitherto not appeared in any other English-German dictionary. Wherever the spelling of German words in Part I. and Part II. disagrees, the spelling of Part II. should be followed. The spelling of Part I., however, is the one which until now is found in nearly every ordinary German book.

A great improvement on the old edition is the insertion, in brackets, of the case required in particular phrases by German prepositions that take more than one case. The want of such information is the frequent cause of mistakes in German composition, and the way to avoid these common errors is not always readily discovered even in larger dictionaries. The prepositions required in connection with certain nouns have as a rule been added (*e.g. Ehrfurcht* (*vor*), *Hoffnung* (*auf*), *Lust* (*zu*), *Abneigung* (*gegen*), etc.). The cases have been added in all such reflexive verbs as do not take the accusative, *e.g. sich denken*, *sich einbilden*, *sich verschaffen*. The somewhat misleading *etwas* and *jemand* have been replaced by the terms *eine S.*, *einer S.* and *einen*, *einem*. In the English-German part great care has been bestowed upon the rendering of foreign terms by their German equivalents. In conformity with the moderate principles of the "Allgemeiner Deutscher Sprachverein," German renderings are generally given alone or in the first place, where in the previous edition the English word had merely been rendered by a German homonym.

Among the new words and phrases inserted will be found many thousands of idiomatic phrases, well-known proverbs that have no literal equivalent in the other language, and familiar quotations; many ordinary dialectal and colloquial expressions, and a number of German slang terms in common use that often prove puzzling to English students. There will also be found the chief new cycling and motoring terms, ordinary military, postal, railway, tennis, historical, geographical, phonetic and linguistic expressions, newspaper terms and advertisements, the chief technical terms of commerce, education, literature, and art. Space was gained for the very numerous additions by the omission of some lengthy translations of unimportant Biblical passages, some little used and obsolete words, vulgarisms and rare scientific and technical terms. In many cases space was saved by the suppression of compounds the formation of which presented no difficulty and the component parts of which were given under their separate headings, *e.g.* "butter-dish" *Butterschale*, "water-melon" *Wassermelone*, etc. On the other hand, "butterfly" *Schmetterling*, "waterlily" *Wasserrose*, had, of course, to be given, as well as words in which one part of the compound is inflected in German, such as "sunflower" *Sonnenblume*, "woman-hater" *Frauenhasser*, *Weiberfeind*, "goose-quill" *Gänsefeder*, etc. Thus, while compounds such as *Apfelbaum*, *Buchmacher*, *Öllampe*, or "breadfruit tree," "house door," "tiger-cat," and many others could safely be omitted, words such as *Sündflut*, *Maultier*, *Heerstrasse* or "ladybird," "titmouse," "wormwood," and others are given. Accurate information as to the best German pronunciation is given in the books by Viëtor, Siebs, Johannson, and others (see p. ix) which are cheap and easily accessible. The appendix to the original edition, containing a synopsis of the changes introduced into German orthography in 1880, has been omitted, as it is now quite out of date. Students should consult the little official Prussian spelling-book, and the handy and cheap works by Duden and Sarrazin, the full titles of which are given below. For fuller information on all these works, and for a synopsis of the chief difficulties of German pronunciation, students may refer to my book on the "Teaching of Modern Foreign Languages" (Cambridge: University Press. Fourth Edition, 1909). In dividing up words the combination ſt is now considered inseparable, hence ne'ſteln, trö'ſten, etc. In case of doubt concerning the best spelling of certain English words I have often been guided by the "Rules for Compositors and Readers," at the University Press, Oxford, by H. Hart, London and Oxford, ^{20}1907.

The very full indexes of names (including the chief colloquial forms of proper names) and abbreviations, and the lists of strong and irregular verbs in both parts, are for the most part new, and will, it is hoped, greatly add to the usefulness of the book. The insertion and explanation of some important German "kenningar," such as *der grosse Schweiger*, *der rote Prinz*, *die rote Erde*, *der eiserne Kanzler*, *der alte Fritz*, or terms such as *Erlkönig*, *Rübezahl*, *Königsleutnant*, *Schildbürger*, *Buxtehude*, etc., will probably be welcome additions. In this way, although in the briefest possible manner, some common German and English *realia* could be explained.

In conclusion, there remains for me the pleasant duty to render my heartiest thanks to many old pupils and kind friends who, by sending me contributions, or in some other way, have assisted me in my work. Among my friends and colleagues my thanks are due to Professors Fiedler, Herford, Napier, Marshall Ward, and to Messrs. Chas. Elsden, G. Morier-Hinde, Yule Oldham, S. Ruhemann, O. Siepmann, Francis Storr, Josiah Walker. Of former pupils I gratefully mention the names of the Misses G. M. Parry, H. Sollas, and J. Burne, and of Messrs. H. Brown, E. C. Quiggin, Thomas Rea, and F. E. Sandbach. I am particularly indebted to my friends and former pupils Mr. E. Bullough, and, above all, to Miss Minna Steele Smith, Head Lecturer in Modern Languages at Newnham College, who have with the greatest care assisted me in the revision of part of the proofs. Much that is good in the book is due to the assistance received from these various kind helpers, while I must alone be responsible for its shortcomings. My thanks are also due to the great pains bestowed on its production by the printers of Cambridge, U.S.A., and the care and resourcefulness of their able press reader. I now dismiss my book from the quiet study into the bustling world and its manifold claims on it with the parting words of the good old Sir Richard Ros:

"Goo, litle book, God sende the good passage . . .
And specially lete this be thi prayere
Vnto hem all that the wil rede or here,
Wher thou art wrong, after ther helpe to calle,
The to correcte in eny parte or alle."

Cambridge, 1906.

A large number of minor corrections and improvements have been made in this reprint, and all the misprints noticed have been corrected. I shall be grateful to any users of this book who will kindly either point out to me actual mistakes, or call my attention to important omissions (for a book of this size), in order to enable me to introduce further improvements into subsequent editions. My thanks are due to Professor Walter Rippmann, M.A., Mr. Francis E. Sandbach, M.A., Ph.D., Mr. E. C. Quiggin, M.A., Ph.D., Mr. Thomas Rea, M.A., Mr. G. Morier-Hinde, M.A., Mr. A. Henry, M.A., Mr. E. Barry, M.A., and Mr. G. W. Bullen for kindly sending me corrections and suggestions.

K. B.

Cambridge,
10, Cranmer Road,
Easter, 1909.

EXPLANATION OF METHOD

Grouping of Words into Articles. Words etymologically related and having an initial syllable or syllables in common are grouped under this initial syllable or syllables. The completion of each word, the suffixes and second components, being printed in full-faced type, readily catch the eye, thus obviating any difficulty which the breaking up of the words might otherwise present. Words formed by terminations—derivative words—come first in each group in alphabetical order, the compounds following in the same order, but separated from them by the abbreviation *Comp.* (for Compound).* No attempt has been made to distinguish between *primary* derivatives (such as Kunst, Blume, Himmel) and *secondary* (as trinkbar, Spieler, lieblich), such distinctions being deemed beyond the province of a work like the present.

Use of Brackets. When a prefix, suffix, or component of a word is enclosed in brackets it is to be understood as signifying that the unbracketed word is a synonym by itself, and when taken with the bracketed word or syllable forms another synonym, which may be used in the same sense as that in which the unbracketed word is used: thus (Blut-)Ader signifies that Ader and Blutader are both equivalents in a certain sense of the English word "vein" in the same way, (ein)tauchen, to dip; (er)läßlich, venial; electric(al), elektrisch; crook(ed)-backed, buckelig, etc., etc. But if a word or phrase enclosed in brackets in one language be followed by a word or phrase enclosed in brackets in the other language, the contents of the one bracket are to be understood as translating the contents of the other: for example, *to do good* (*evil*), Gutes (Böses) tun, where Böses is the translation of the bracketed "*evil*," and the phrase Böses tun of the phrase *to do evil*. When a German word or words enclosed in brackets is followed by no bracketed word or words in English, the contents of the bracket are for the purpose of showing the case required by the German verb it accompanies, or for some other grammatical purpose; thus, when *to court* is to be rendered by (einer Person) den Hof machen, (einer Person) is inserted for the purpose of informing the student that, although the English verb governs the accusative case, the German requires the dative; in the same way, *to court* is further defined as sich (um eine S.) bewerben, in order to exhibit the fact that in this sense of *court* the German equivalent is followed by the accusative with um. In the German-English division (einem etwas) is employed as a short way of saying that the verb to which it is joined governs the dative of the person and the accusative of the thing.

Punctuation. When several synonyms are given, all answering to one sense of a word, they are separated by commas, whilst those representing different senses are separated by semicolons; thus—Fall, decay, ruin, downfall; case (*Gram.*)—*decay, ruin, downfall*, being all synonyms of Fall in one sense, are only separated from one another by commas, but they are separated from *case*, which represents a wholly different sense, by a semicolon. A phrase, on the other hand, even when exhibited in wholly different senses, has the different renderings divided only by commas; before each new sense, however, in the English-German part an explanatory word or phrase is inserted in parentheses: as—to break down, im Abnehmen sein (*as a p.'s health*), durchfallen (*at an examination*), umwerfen (*as a carriage*), or—to come round (recover), sich erholen (change one's opinion) schwanken, sich bedenken, sich anders besinnen, (return, as an anniversary) wiederkehren, (return, as a term) fällig werden, (change, as the wind) sich drehen, etc.

* English words given under *Comp.* are not always written as compounds.

English Synonyms, or Explanations of German Words.

In Part II., or the English-German division of the work, every new sense in which a word is taken is either preceded by an English synonym* in Roman type in parentheses, as—to doom (sentence) verurteilen; (destine) bestimmen—or followed by some explanatory word or phrase in italics in parentheses, as—to do, erweisen (*kindness*)—or—to drivel, geifern (*as infants*)—in place of a synonym, a word is occasionally preceded by an explanatory clause in italics, as—to drink (*of beasts*) saufen—which denotes that *drink*, when expressing the action of a beast, is translated by saufen and not by trinken, which is the word employed in the case of human beings.†

Gender of German Nouns shown by accompanying Article or Adjective.

The gender of German substantives in this part, too, is shown by the accompanying article der, die, das; but when an adjective is given with the substantive the article is usually omitted and the gender shown by the termination of the adjective, as, *dry measure*, trockenes Maß; *dry cough*, trockener Husten.

The term Particle.

The term *part.* (for particle) has been employed throughout to denote a class of words—so numerous in the German language—which, while possessing a certain force, have no precise syntactical relation to the other words in a sentence. This is the only particular in which the ordinary terminology of English grammarians has been departed from.

Similarly spelt Words are numbered.

Words differing in meaning and origin, but spelt alike, are numbered, so that no difficulty can arise owing to their separation for etymological reasons under different heads.

For an explanation of abbreviations, see Abbreviations (p. xiv).

* These words are, of course, only approximately synonymous.

† It is, of course, to be understood that where a synonym of, say, an adjective is explained, the substantive, etc., corresponding to this adjective, and included in the same article, is not in general separately explained: as—**Pleasant**, *adj.*, freundlich (*as a room*); (lively) munter, etc.; **-ness**, *s.*, die Freundlichkeit; die Munterkeit.

SOME GERMAN BOOKS USEFUL FOR REFERENCE *

I. Larger German-English and English-German General Dictionaries :—

1. *Muret-Sanders.* Encyklopädisches Englisch-Deutsches und Deutsch-Englisches Wörterbuch. Four Vols. Berlin. 1891-1902. Abridged Edition. Two Vols. Berlin, London. 1900. Revised Edition, 1908.
2. *Felix Flügel.* Allgemeines Englisch-Deutsches und Deutsch-Englisches Wörterbuch. Three Vols. Braunschweig. 1891.
3. *Flügel-Schmidt-Tanger.* A Dictionary of the English and German Languages for Home and School. Two Vols. Braunschweig, London, New York. 1896.
4. *Grieb-Schröer.* Englisch-Deutsches und Deutsch-Englisches Wörterbuch. Two Vols. Stuttgart. 1894–1902.
5. *Thieme-Kellner.* Neues und vollständiges Handwörterbuch der englischen und deutschen Sprache. Two Vols. Braunschweig. 1902–1905.

II. Special Dictionaries (English and German).

6. *F. W. Eitzen.* Wörterbuch der Handelssprache. Two Vols. Leipzig. 1893–1902.
7. *Gustav Eger.* Technologisches Wörterbuch in englischer und deutscher Sprache. Two Vols. Braunschweig. 1882–1884.

III. German-German Dictionaries, etc. †

8. *Moriz Heyne.* Deutsches Wörterbuch. Three Vols. Leipzig. 1890–95. (There is also an abridged edition of this work in one volume. 1896.)
9. *Herm. Paul.* Deutsches Wörterbuch. One Vol. Halle. 1897. [2]1908.
10. *Friedr. Kluge.* Etymologisches Wörterbuch der deutschen Sprache. Strassburg. [6]1899.‡
11. *Albert Heintze.* Deutscher Sprachhort. Ein Stil-Wörterbuch. Leipzig. 1900.
12. *Otto Sarrazin.* Verdeutschungs-Wörterbuch. Berlin. [3]1906.
13. *Günther A. Saalfeld.* Fremd-und Verdeutschungs-Wörterbuch. Berlin. 1898.
14. Regeln für die deutsche Rechtschreibung nebst Wörterverzeichnis. Neue Bearbeitung. Berlin. 1902.
15. *Konrad Duden.* Orthographisches Wörterbuch der deutschen Sprache. Leipzig. [7]1902.
16. *Otto Sarrazin.* Wörterbuch für eine deutsche Einheitsschreibung. Berlin. [3]1906.
17. *Eberhard-Lyon.* Synonymisches Handwörterbuch der deutschen Sprache. Leipzig. [15]1896.
18. *Otto Ladendorf.* Historisches Schlagwörterbuch. Strassburg and Berlin. 1906.
19. *Borchardt-Wustmann.* Die sprichwörtlichen Redensarten im deutschen Volksmunde nach Sinn und Ursprung erläutert. Leipzig. [5]1895.
20. *Arnold Genthe.* Deutsches Slang. Eine Sammlung familiärer Ausdrücke und Redensarten. Strassburg. 1892.
21. *Georg Büchmann.* Geflügelte Worte. Der Citatenschatz des deutschen Volkes gesammelt und erläutert. Berlin. [16]1889 (there are later editions).

IV. Pronunciation.

22. *W. Viëtor.* Die Aussprache des Schriftdeutschen. Leipzig. [5]1901.
23. *Theod. Siebs.* Grundzüge der Bühnenaussprache. Berlin, etc. [2]1904.
24. *Theod. Siebs.* Deutsche Bühnenaussprache. Berlin, etc. [2]1901. (A fuller treatise than No. 23.)
25. *Arwid Johannson.* Phonetics of the New High German Language. Manchester, Leipzig. 1906.

* The English and American dictionaries consulted for the present book, *e.g.* the New English Dictionary, Cassell, Webster, Annandale, Chambers, Skeat, and others are too well known to require the full titles to be given in this place.

† For older and larger books, *e.g.* the still unfinished dictionary of the brothers Grimm and their successors, the works of Daniel Sanders, etc., I refer to my "Handy Bibliographical Guide to the Study of the German language and literature, for the use of students and teachers of German." London. 1895; pp. 48 *sqq.*

‡ [6]1899 means that the sixth edition was published in 1899.

ABBREVIATIONS

Abkürzungen

a.	see v.a.
abbr.	*abbreviation, abbreviated*, Abkürzung, abgekürzt.
Acc.	*accusative* (case), Akkusativ.
Acoust.	*acoustics*, Akustik.
adj.	*adjective*, Adjektiv Eigenschaftswort.
adv.	*adverb*, Adverbium, Nebenwort, Umstandswort.
Agr.	*agriculture*, Landwirtschaft.
Alg.	*algebra, term in algebra*, Algebra, algebraischer Ausdruck.
Amer	*Americanism*, Amerikanismus.
anal.	*analogous*, analog, analogisch.
Anat.	*anatomy*, Anatomie.
Arch.	*architecture*, Architektur.
Arith.	*arithmetic*, Arithmetik.
art.	*article*, Artikel, Geschlechtswort.
Art.	(the fine) *arts*, die schönen Künste.
Artil.	*artillery*, Artillerie, Geschützkunst.
Astr.	*astronomy*, Astronomie, Sternkunde.
Astrol.	*astrology*, Astrologie, Sterndeuterei.
aux. v.	*auxiliary verb*, Hülfszeitwort.
B.	*Bible, biblical*, Bibel, biblisch.
Bak.	*baking*, in der Bäckerei gebräuchliches Wort.
Bill.	*Billiards*, Billardspiel
Bookb.	*bookbinding*, Buchbinderei
Books.	*bookselling* (trade), Buchhandel
Bot.	*botany*, Pflanzenkunde, Botanik.
Brew.	*brewing, brewery*, Brauerei.
Build.	*building*, Bauwesen.
Butch.	*butcher*, Fleischer, Metzger.
Cal. Prin.	*calico-Printing*, Kattun-Druckerei.
C. L.	*commercial language*, kaufmännischer Ausdruck.
Cards.	*cardplaying*, Kartenspiel.
Carr.	*carriages, &c.*, Fuhrwesen.
Carp.	*carpentry*, Zimmermannskunst.
Chem.	*chemistry*, Chemie, Scheidekunst.
Chron.	*chronology*, Chronologie, Zeitrechnung.
coll.	*colloquialism*, Ausdruck der gewöhnlichen Umgangssprache.
comp.	*comparative* (degree), Steigerungsform.
Comp(s)	*compound word(s)*, zusammengesetztes Wort (zusammengesetzte Wörter).
Conch.	*conchology*, Konchyliologie, Schaltierkunde.
Conf.	*confectionery*, Zuckerbäckerei.
conj.	*conjunction*, Konjunktion, Bindewort.
Cook.	*cookery*, Kochkunst.
Coop.	*cooperage*, Böttcherei.
Crick.	*Cricket*, Schlagballspiel.
Danc.	*dancing*, Tanzkunst.
Dat.	*dative* (case), Dativ, Wemfall.
def.	*definite*, bestimmt.
dem.	*demonstrative*, demonstrativ, hinweisend.
dial.	*dialectal*, dialektisch, mundartlich.
dim.	*diminutive*, Diminutiv, Verkleinerungswort.
Dipl.	*diplomacy*, Diplomatie.
Draw.	*drawing*, Zeichenkunst, Zeichnen.
Dyer.	*dyer, dyeing*, Färber, Färberei.
Dyn.	*dynamics*, Dynamik, Kraftlehre.
Eccl.	*ecclesiastical*, kirchlich; *ecclesiastical history*, Kirchengeschichte.
Elect.	*electricity*, Elektrizität.
Ellipt.	*elliptical(ly)*, elliptisch, (auslassungsweise).
Engr.	*engraving*, Gravierkunst.
Ent.	*entomology*, Entomologie, Insektenkunde.
f.	*substantive of the feminine gender*, weibliches Hauptwort.
fam.	*familiar(ly)*, familiär, vertraulich.
Farr.	*farriery*, Hufschmiedehandwerk.
Fenc.	*fencing*, Fechtkunst.
fig.	*figuratively*, bildlich, figürlich.
Firew.	*fireworks*, Feuerwerk.
Fort.	*fortification*, Befestigungskunst.
Found.	*foundry, foundry-work*, Gießerei.
Forg.	*forging*, Hammerschmiedekunst.
Freem.	*freemasonry*, Freimaurerei.
Furr.	*furriery*, Kürschnerei.
Gen.	*genitive* (case), Genitiv, Wesfall.
gen'lly.	*generally*, gewöhnlich.

Geog. *geography*, Geographie, Erdbeschreibung.
Geol. *geology*, Geologie, Erdbeschaffenheit.
Geom. *geometry*, Geometrie.
Gild. *gilding*, Vergolderkunst.
Glassw. *glassworks*, Glashütte.
Gram. *grammar*, Grammatik.
Gun. *gunnery*, Geschützkunst.
Gymn. *gymnastics*, Gymnastik.
h. haben, *to have.*
Her. *heraldry*, Heraldik, Wappenkunst.
Hist. *history*, Geschichte.
Horol. *horology*, Uhrmacherkunst.
Hort. *horticulture*, Gärtnerei.
Hydr. *hydraulics*, Hydraulik; *hydrostatics*, Hydrostatik, Wasserwägekunst.
Icht. *ichthyology*, Fischkunde.
imp. *impersonal(ly)*, unpersönlich.
imperat. *imperative* (mood), Imperativ.
ind. *indefinite*, unbestimmt, unbestimmend.
indec. *indeclinable*, undeklinierbar, unveränderlich.
insep. *inseparable*, unzertrennlich.
int. *interjection*, Interjektion, Empfindungslaut.
inter. *interrogative*, fragend, Fragewort.
inv. *invariable*, unveränderlich.
ir. *irregular* (*strong*), unregelmäßig (stark).
iron. *ironical(ly)*, ironisch.
Jew. *Jewish*, jüdisch.
Join. *joinery*, Tischlerei.
Law. *law-term*, juristischer Ausdruck.
lit. *literally*, buchstäblich.
Locom. *locomotive*, Lokomotive.
Log. *logic*, Logik.
m. *substantive of the masculine gender*, männliches Hauptwort.
Mach. *machinery*, Maschinenwesen.
Magnet. *magnetism*, Magnetismus.
Manuf. *manufacture(s)*, Fabrik, Manufaktur.
Mas. *masonry*, Maurerarbeit.
Math. *mathematics*, Mathematik.
Mech. *mechanics*, Mechanik, Bewegungslehre, Triebwerkslehre.
Med. *medicine*, Medizin, Heilkunde.
Metall. *metallurgy*, Metallurgie, Hüttenwesen.
Meteor. *meteorology*, Meteorologie.
Mil. *military term*, militärisch, Soldatensprache.
Mill. *miller*, *milling*, Müller, Mühlwesen.
Min. *mining*, Bergbau; *mineralogy*, Mineralogie.
Mint. *minting*, Münzwesen.
Mollusc. *mollusca*, Mollusken, Weichtiere.
Mus. *music*, Musik, Tonkunst.
Myth. *mythology*, Mythologie.
n. *substantive of the neuter gender*, sächliches Hauptwort; see subst. n.; also v.n.
Nat. Hist. *natural history*, Naturgeschichte.
Naut. *nautical term*, *nautical affairs*, Schifferausdruck, Seewesen.
Nav. *naval term*, Marineausdruck.
Opt. *optics*, Optik.
opp. (*in*) *opposition* (*to*), (im) Gegensatz (zu).
Org. *organ*, Orgel.
Orn. *ornithology*, Ornithologie.
p. *present participle*, Partizipium der Gegenwart.
p.p. *past participle*, Partizipium der Vergangenheit.
Paint. *painting*, Malerei.
Pap. *paper-manufacture*, Papierfabrikation.
Parl. *parliament*, *parliamentary expression*, Parlament, Parlamentsausdruck.
part. *particle*, Partikel.
pers. *personal*, persönlich.
Persp. *perspective*, Perspektive.
Pharm. *pharmacy*, Pharmazie.
Phil. *philosophy*, Philosophie.
Philol. *Philology*, Philologie.
Phren. *phrenology*, Phrenologie.
Phys. *physics*, Physik.
Physiol. *physiology*, Physiologie.
pl. *plural*, Mehrzahl; *noun in the plural*, Substantiv im Plural.
Pneum. *pneumatics*, Pneumatik.
Poet. *poetry*, Poesie, Dichtkunst.
Pol. *politics*, Politik.
poss. *possessive*, besitzanzeigend.
Pott. *pottery*, Töpferei.
pres. *present tense*, gegenwärtige Zeit.
Print. *printing*, Druckerei.
pron. *pronoun*, Fürwort.
prov. *provincialism*, Provinzialismus.
Prov. *proverb*, Sprichwort.
prep. *preposition*, Präposition, Verhältniswort.
q. v. *quod vide*, siehe dies.
r. *reflective* (verb), Reflexivum.
Railw. *railways*, Eisenbahnwesen.
reg. *regular* (*weak*), regelmäßig (schwach).
Rel. *religion*, Religion.
Rhet. *rhetoric*, Rhetorik, Redekunst.
R. C. *Roman Catholic religion*, katholische Religion.
s. *substantive* (in the 2nd part), Substantiv (im zweiten Teile).

Saddl.	*saddlery*, Sattlerei.
Saltw.	*saltworks*, Salzsiederei.
Sculp.	*sculpture*, Bildhauerkunst.
Semp.	*sempstress*, *sewing*, Näherin, Näherei.
see	*see* or =, siehe oder gleich.
sep.	*separable*, trennbar.
Sew.-mach.	*sewing-machine*, Nähmaschine.
Shipb.	*shipbuilding*, Schiffsbaukunde.
Shoem.	*shoemaking*, Schuhmacherei.
sing.	*singular*, Einzahl.
sl.	*slang*, Slang.
Smith,	*smith*, *smith's work*, Schmied, Schmiedehandwerk.
Spin.	*spinning*, Spinnerei.
Sport,	*sport*, Jagdwesen.
subst. n.	*indicates the infinitive used as substantive when it is necessary to distinguish it from* n. = v.n., bezeichnet den substantivisch gebrauchten Infinitiv, wo er vom *n.*=*v.n.* zu unterscheiden ist.
Sug.-ref.	*sugar-refining*, Raffinieren des Zuckers.
sup.	*superlative* (degree), Superlativ.
Surg.	*surgery*, Chirurgie.
Surv(ey)	*surveying*, *civil engineering*, Feldmeßkunst, Ingenieurkunst.
T.	*technical term*, Kunstausdruck.
Tail.	*tailoring*, Schneiderei.
Tan(n)	*tanning*, Lohgerberei.
Tech.	*technology*, Technologie.
Tele.	*telegraphy*, *electric telegraph*, Telegraphie, elektrischer Telegraph.
Theat.	*theatre*, Theater, Schauspiel.
Theol.	*theelogy*, Theologie Gottesgelehrsamkeit.
Turn.	*turning*, Drechslerei.
Typ.	*typography*, Typographie.
Univ.	*university*, Universität, Hochschulausdruck.
v.a.	*active* or *transitive verb*, tätiges oder transitives Zeitwort.
v.aux.	*auxiliary verb*, Hilfszeitwort.
v.imp.	*impersonal verb*, unpersönliches Zeitwort.
v.n.	*neuter* or *intransitive verb*, neutrales oder intransitives Zeitwort.
v.r.	*reflective verb*, Reflexivum.
Vap.	*vapour*, *steam*, Dampf.
Vet.	*veterinary art*, Tierarzneikunde.
vulg.	*vulgar*, gemein.
Weav.	*weaving*, Weberei.
Zool.	*zoology*, Zoologie, Tierkunde.
Zooph.	*zoophytes*, Zoophyten, Pflanzentiere.

= stands for *equality*, *the same as*, gleich.

A
GERMAN-ENGLISH DICTIONARY

A, a, A, a; **das A (des A(s), die As)** the letter A; the note A *or* La; **A dur,** (*the key of*) A major; **A moll,** (*the key of*) A minor; **diese Melodie geht aus A dur,** this tune is in La *or* in A major; **A=Saite,** the A-string (*of a violin*); *in commercial language still often used for* **zu, à fünf Prozent,** at five per cent.; **er kann A und B nicht unterscheiden** (*prov.*) he does not know a great B from a bull's foot; **ich bin das A und das O** (*bibl.*) I am alpha and omega (*i. e.* the beginning and the end); **von A bis Z,** from the beginning to the end, at full length, exhaustively, fully; **wer A gesagt hat, muß auch B sagen** (*prov.*), he who has begun a thing must go on with it; having started a thing you must be prepared for the less agreeable consequences; in for a penny, in for a pound; *abbr. for* **am, an,** *etc.* **a. Rh.** *or* **a. Rhein = am Rhein,** on the Rhine; **a. L. = an der Lahn,** on the Lahn (*e. g.* **Marburg a. L.**); **a. O.** *or* **a. d. Oder = an der Oder,** on the Oder (*e. g.* **Frankfurt a. O.**); **a. S. = an der Saale,** on the Saale (*e. g.* **Halle a. S.**); **a. D. = außer Dienst(en),** retired on half pay; **a. a. O. =** *either* **am angeführten Orte,** in the above-mentioned place, loco citato, see above; *or* **am andern Orte,** in another place; *or* **an andern Orten,** in some other places, elsewhere; **=a** *or* **=ach** *at the end of river names denotes* water, stream, *e. g.* **Salza, Salzach, Schwarza, Steinach; a=a' machen** (*of children*), to perform.

Aa, Aach, Ach, *f.* rivulet, stream (*dial.*).

Aak, *n.* (**—s** *or* **es,** *pl.* **—e**) *or f.* (*pl.* **—en**), a flat-bottomed lighter used on the Rhine.

Aal, *m.* (**—es,** *pl.* **—e,** *dialectic* **Äle**) eel; a wrong fold in cloth; **Aal blau (gekocht),** boiled eel; **er entschlüpft wie ein —,** he's as slippery as an eel; **den — beim Schwanz abstreifen,** to begin at the wrong end (*prov.*). *Comp.* **—artig,** eel-shaped, anguilliform. **—baum,** *m.* upright honeysuckle. **—beere,** *f.* black currant. **—butte,** *f.* eel-pout, burbot. **—fang,** *m.* catching of eels; time and place where eels are caught. **—lege,** *f.* eel-dam, eel-weir. **—mutter,** *f.* the viviparous blenny. **—puppe,** *f.*, **—quaste,** *f.* a bundle of bulrushes used for catching eels. **—quappe,** *f.*, **—raupe,** *f. see* **—butte. —reuse,** *f.* eel-pot, basket in which eels are caught. **—schlange,** *f.* conger eel. **—streif,** *m.* black streak on the back of an eel *or* of a dun-coloured horse. **—streifig,** *adj.*, eel-backed. **—wehr,** *f. see* **—lege. —wels,** *m.* silurus.

Aa'len, *v.a. & n.* to catch *or* fish for eels.

Aap, *n.* (**—es,** *pl.* **—en**) mizzen-stay-sail.

Aar, *m.* (**—es,** *pl.* **—e**) *in older German the usual word for an* eagle; *the word is now poetic,* **Adler** *being the prose term. As the second part of compounds* **Aar** *often denotes merely* a large bird of prey. *Comp.* **—weihe,** *m. & f.* a kind of kite.

Aas, *n.* (**—es,** *pl.* **Äser**) carcass; carrion; lure, bait; **ein — an die Angel stecken,** to bait a hook; **wo ein Aas ist, da sammeln sich die Adler** (*bibl. & prov.*) wherever the carcass is there will the eagles be gathered together. **—haft, —ig,** ugly; dirty; carrion-like. *Comp.* **—blatter,** *f.* plague-blister, pock. **—käfer,** *m.* horse-beetle, dung-beetle. **—kopf,** *m.* (*Arch.*) flayed head of an ox *or* ram *as ornament on Doric pillars.* **—pocke,** *f. see* **—blatter.**

Aa'sen, *v.* I. *a.* to flesh (*hides*); to bait (*a hook or snare*). II. *n.* to browse, to graze (*of deer*); to feed on carrion.

Ab (*pronounce* **ap,** *also in compounds*). I. *adv.* off; down; away from; from; exit; **Maria — (***for* **Maria geht —),** exit Mary (*stage direction*); **— heute,** (*Comm.*) from to-day; **— Bremen,** (*Comm.*) (*freight*) from Bremen; **von hier —,** from here; **von nun —,** henceforth; **vom ersten Oktober —,** on and after the first of October; **weit —,** far off; **Hut —!** off with your hat! **Bajonett —!** (*stress on* **ab**) (*mil.*) unfix bayonets! **Gewehr —!** (*stress on* **ab**) (*mil.*) ground arms! **hiervon geht —,** deduct; **— an Unkosten,** charges to be deducted; **vom Wege — sein,** to be astray; **— und zu',** (*local*) to and fro, backward and forward, off and on; (*temporal*) now and then, sometimes; **— und an',** now and then, sometimes; **Strom —** (*stress on* **ab,** *usually spelt* **stromab**), down stream; **Berg —,** down hill; **auf und —,** up and down; **eine Mark auf oder —,** a mark more or less; **ich bin ganz —,** I am quite exhausted (*colloq.*); **kurz —,** abruptly, shortly; **— nach Kassel,** off and away, away with you (*colloq.*). II. *Separable prefix. When employed as a prefix* **ab** *implies* separation from, deviation from, disinclination to, *and sometimes* participation in, similitude; *in many verbs it denotes* to tire one by the repeated action of the verb, to do a thing out and out, *e. g.* **einen abherzen, abküssen, sich ablaufen,** *taking the accent and being pronounced* **ap.** *Words beginning with a vowel after* **ab** *must be pronounced with the glottal stop. If a compound verb beginning with* **ab** *is not given in the following lists, look under the simple verb.*

Ab'ächzen, *v.r.* to pine away, to exhaust oneself with sighing and moaning.

Ab'ackern, *v.a.* to separate by ploughing; to take away by ploughing.

Ab'änder—lich, *adj.* alterable. **—ung,** *f.* alteration; variation; modification.

Ab'ändern, *v.a.* to alter, to change; to vary, to modify.

Ab'ängst—en, (*poetic & archaic, now usually*) **—igen,** *v.* I. *a.* to alarm, distress; **einem etwas —,** to extort s.th. from s.o. by frightening. II. *r.* to be in great anxiety *or* alarm.

Ab'ankern, *v.a.* to unmoor.

Ab'arbeiten, *v.* I. *a.* to work off (*a debt*); to get (*a ship*) afloat *or* off; to wear out (*an implement, a horse, &c.*); **sich —,** to work hard, to exert oneself greatly; **das Gröbste —,** to rough-hew. II. *n.* (*aux.* **h.**) (*of wine, etc.*) to cease fermenting.

Ab'art, *f.* (*pl.* **—en**) degeneracy; degenerate race *or* breed; species, variety (*Nat. Hist.*).

Ab'art—en, *v.n.* (*aux.* **f.**) to degenerate; to vary. **—ung,** *f.* degeneration.

Ab'äschern, Ab'eschern, *v.* I. *a.* to scour with ashes. II. *r.* to exert oneself greatly *or* to the utmost, *or* to worry oneself.

Ab'ästen, *v.a.* to cut off branches, lop, trim; **abgeästete Weide,** pollard willow.

Ab'ätzen, *v.a.* to eat away, remove by caustics.
Ab'äugeln, *v.a.* to obtain by ogling; to spy out (*the track*); **die Richtung einer Mauer —,** to gauge the line of a wall with the eye.
Ab'backen, *ir. v.* I. *a.* to bake fully; to bake in too hot an oven; to mark a line with small posts. II. *n.* (*aux.* **h.**) to finish baking.
Ab'baden, *v.* I. *a.* to bathe, to wash thoroughly; to wash away, to get rid of. II. *n.* (*aux.* **h.**) to finish bathing.
Ab'bähen, *v.a.* to foment thoroughly.
Ab'baken, *v.a.* to set buoys, to mark by beacons.
Ab'balgen, *v.* I. *a.* to skin. II. *r.* to tire oneself by wrestling *or* boxing.
Ab'bangen, *v.a.;* **einem etwas —,** to extort something by fear from someone.
Ab'bau, *m.* (**—es**) work(ing); mine-digging; mining.
Ab'bauen, *v.a.* to remove, finish, *or* demolish a building; to work a mine; to exhaust *or* drain a mine; to abandon a mine; to pay off with the produce of a mine the expense of working it.
Ab'beeren, *v.a.* to strip of berries.
Ab'befehlen, *ir.v.a.* to countermand; **die Parade ist abbefohlen,** the review has been countermanded.
Ab'behalten, *ir.v.a.;* **den Hut —,** to remain uncovered.
Ab'beißen, *ir.v.a.* to bite off; **sich die Nägel —,** to bite one's nails; **sich vor Lachen die Zunge —,** to split one's sides with laughing; **er hat aller Scham den Kopf abgebissen,** he is past all shame.
Ab'beizen, *v.a.* to remove by caustics; to macerate, to dress (*skins*).
Ab'bekommen, *ir.v.a.* to partake of, to get a share of, to come in for; **etwas —,** to get (blows); **er hat in der Schlacht nichts —,** he has not been hit in the battle; to remove, get loose *or* off; **er kann den Stiefel nicht —,** he is unable to get off his boot.
Ab'berufen, *ir.v.a.* to call home, to recall; to appeal to a higher court (*archaic*) (*Law*); **einen Prozeß —,** to change the venue, remove a cause from one court to another.
Ab'bestell—en, *v.a.* & *n.* to countermand. **—ung,** *f.* counter-order.
Ab'beten, *v.a.* to recount in prayer; to avert, *or* atone for by praying; to pray off, pray mechanically; **den Rosenkranz —,** to tell one's beads.
Ab'betteln, *v.a.;* **einem etwas —,** to obtain s.th. from some one by begging.
Ab'bezahlen, *v.a.* to pay off *or* in full; to discharge (*a debt*); to liquidate; **er zahlt seine Schulden in jährlichen Raten ab,** he pays his debts in yearly instalments.
Ab'biegen, *ir.v.* I. *a.* to bend off, turn aside; to propagate by layers; **sich —,** to diverge. II. *n.* (*aux.* **s.**) to turn off, aside.
Ab'bild, *n.* (**—es,** *pl.* **—er**) copy; image.
Ab'bild—en, *v.* I. *a.* to portray; to paint *or* model from; to delineate; to describe. II. *r.* to be reflected; **der Himmel bildet sich im Meere ab,** the sky is reflected in the sea. **—ung,** *f.* representation; illustration; picture; image.
Ab'billigen, *v.a.;* **einem etwas —,** to refuse something to someone (*arch.*)
Ab'bimsen, *v.a.* to smooth with pumice-stone.
Ab'binden, *ir.v.a.* to unbind; to detach by binding (*warts, etc.*); to wean (**ein Kalb von der Kuh —**); to castrate; to hoop (*a cask*). *In Swiss German it is used figuratively for* to settle briefly *or* to say briefly; **kurz abgebunden,** in short.
Ab'bitt—e, *f.* (*pl.* **—en**) apology; deprecation; **—e thun,** to ask a man's pardon, to apologize.
Ab'bitten, *ir.v.a.* to apologize for; to deprecate, beg off; **einem etwas —,** to apologize to someone for something; to obtain by begging (*rare*).
Ab'blasen, *ir.v.* I. *a.* to blow off or away; to blow (*a horn, etc.*); to sound (*the hours*). II. *n.* (*aux.* **h.**) to cease blowing; **den Soldaten —,** to sound a retreat.
Ab'blassen, *v.n.* (*aux.* **s.**) to fade.
Ab'blatten, *v.a.* to pluck off leaves.
Ab'blattern, *v.n.* (*aux.* **h.**) to scale off (*of the skin in small-pox*).
Ab'blätter—n, *v.* I. *a.* to strip of leaves. II. *r.* & *n.* (*aux.* **h.**) to lose the leaves; to exfoliate; to peel off. **—ung,** *f.* exfoliation.
Ab'bläuen, *v.a.* to blue (*of linen*).
Ab'bleichen, I. *v.a.* to bleach duly. II. *ir.v.n.* (*aux.* **s.**) to fade, grow pale.
Ab'bleuen (*wrongly* **Ab'bläuen,** *not connected with* **blau**), to thrash, to give a thorough beating, to beat black and blue.
Ab'blitzen, *v.n.* (*aux.* **s.**) to flash off; to miss fire; (*aux.* **h.**) to cease flashing (*coll.*); **sie ließ ihn —,** he met with a rebuff from her (*coll.*); **einen — lassen,** to give some one the slip.
Ab'blühen, *v.n.* (*aux.* **s.** & **h.**) to drop the blossom, to cease blooming; to droop, fade, fall (*of flowers*); **die Nelken haben abgeblüht,** the carnations have done blossoming, are over.
Ab'bohnen, *v.a.* to polish, to rub.
Ab'bohr—en, *v.* I. *a.* to bore quite through. II. *n.* (*aux.* **h.**) to finish boring. **—er,** *m.* auger for finishing the boring of a hole.
Ab'borgen, *v.a.* (**einem etwas**) to borrow from.
Ab'bosse(l)n, *v.a.* to emboss, to model in wax.
Ab'brand, *m.* (**—es,** *pl.* **Abbrände**) waste of metals (*in testing, etc.*), *or* of chalk (*in burning*).
Ab'brändler, *m.* (**—s,** *pl.* **—**) one that has lost everything by fire (*dial.*).
Ab'brassen, *v.a.* to brace (*the yards*); to fill the sails after they have been braced back (*Naut.*).
Ab'brauchen, *v.a.* to wear out *or* off.
Ab'brausen, *v.n.* (*aux.* **h.**) to cease fermenting; to cease storming.
Ab'brech—en, *ir.v.a.* & *n.* (*aux.* **s.** & **h.**) to break, break off, snap; to break up; to demolish, dismantle, pull down; to abate, deduct; to pluck, gather (*fruit, flowers, etc.*); **einen Briefwechsel —en,** to break off a correspondence; **jede Minute, die ich der Arbeit —en kann,** every moment I can snatch from work; **ein Wort —en,** to divide a word; **abgebrochene Worte,** broken utterances; **wir wollen davon —en,** no more of that, let us drop the subject; **kurz —en,** to cut short, interrupt suddenly; **ein Gerüst —en,** to take down a scaffolding; **die Glieder —en,** to break off (*the files*), to diminish the front (*Milit.*); **das Lager —en,** to break up the camp; **Zelte —en,** to strike the tents; **die Brücke eines Schiffes —en,** to cast off the gangway; **die Ballen —en,** to knock off the balls (*Typ.*); **einem Pferde die Eisen —en,** to unshoe a horse; **den Mast —en,** to carry away the mast; **wir können uns nichts —en lassen,** we can abate nothing, allow no discount, take nothing off; **einem in der Bezahlung —en,** to cut one's pay short; **sich** (*dat.*) **etwas —en,** to deny oneself, deprive o.s. of; **er bricht sich sogar an der Nahrung ab,** he even stints himself in food. **—ung,** *f.* taking down, demolition.
Ab'brennen, *ir.v.* I. *a.* to burn off; to burn down; to set on fire; to fire off; to cleanse by fire; to temper (*steel, etc.*); to calcine; **ein Schiff rein —,** to burn (*weeds, &c.*) off the bottom of a ship. II. *n.* (*aux.* **s.**) to be burnt down; to be damaged by fire; to go off; to cease burning, go out; **Abgebrannte,** people burned out of house and home; **ein Feuerwerk —,** to let off fireworks; **er hat auf mich abgebrannt,** he has fired at me; **das**

Zündkraut ist abgebrannt, the powder has flashed in the pan; **ich bin abgebrannt,** I am penniless, cleaned out, stumped (*fam.*).

Abbreviatu'r, *f.* abbreviation. *Comp.* **—schrift,** *f.* shorthand (*writing*).

Ab'bring—en, *ir.v.a.* to get off, out, away, afloat; to divert; to drive out of one's head; to dissuade; **vom rechten Wege—en,** to mislead; **davon lasse ich mich nicht —en,** I will not be dissuaded from it; **es ist eine Grille von ihm, von der man ihn nicht —en kann,** it is one of his whims which there is no driving out of his head. **—ung,** *f.* bringing off; **—ungs=kosten eines Schiffes,** charges for getting a vessel off.

Ab'brocken, *v.a.* to crumble off, to break off small pieces.

Ab'bröckeln, *v.a.* to crumble away; to peel off.

Ab'bruch, *m.* (**—es,** *pl.* **Abbrüche**) the act of breaking off, pulling down; damage, injury, loss; rupture; discontinuance (*of relations*); the thing broken off; the place where a house, etc., has been pulled down or fallen; deduction, discount; abatement (*in price*); a break (*in type*); **— thun,** to damage, to be prejudicial to, to injure, to impede; **sich** (*dat.*) **selbst — thun,** to deprive oneself of; **ein Haus auf den — verkaufen,** to sell the materials of a house that is to be pulled down; **ein sofortiger — diplomatischer Beziehungen,** an immediate breaking off of diplomatic relations.

Ab'brüchig, *adj.* brittle; derogatory; prejudicial.

Ab'brühen, *v.a.*, so scald, to seethe.

Ab'bürsten, *v.a.* to brush off, brush clean.

Ab'büß—en, *v.a.*, to atone for, to expiate; **mit Geld —en,** to make amends by paying a fine. **—ung,** *f.* atonement, expiation.

Abc, (**Abece'**), *n.* abc, alphabet; (*fig.*) the first rudiments; **zum — gehörig,** belonging to the alphabet; **nach dem —,** alphabetically; **einem das — beibringen,** to teach one his letters. *Comp.* **—buch,** *n.* spelling-book, first primer, elementary book, horn-book. **—schüler, —schütz,** *m.* abecedarian, alphabetarian, primer boy, tyro.

Ab'cirkeln, *see* **Abzirkeln.**

Ab'dach—en, to take off the roof; to slope, slant; **eine Mauer —en,** to cope a wall; **sich —en,** to slope off, to shelve. **—ig,** *adj.* sloping. **—ung,** *f.* unroofing; slope, descent; talus, glacis, scarp. *Comp.* **—ungs=winkel,** *m.* angle of inclination.

Ab'dächig, *adj.* sloping.

Ab'dämmen, *v.a.* to dam up, off; to embank.

Ab'dampfen, *v.n.* (*aux.* **s.**) to evaporate; to cease to evaporate; *fam.* = **abfahren, abreisen.**

Ab'dämpfen, *v.a.* to cause to evaporate.

Ab'dank—en, *v.* I. *a.* to dismiss from service; to discharge; to disband; to lay up (*a ship*); **ein abgedankter Offizier,** a disbanded officer, a half-pay officer; **zur Strafe —en,** to cashier; **das Schiffsvolk —en,** to pay off a crew. II. *n.* (*aux.* **h.**) to resign, to retire, to quit the service, to abdicate; **der Nachtwächter dankt ab,** the watchman calls for the last time at break of day; **ein Schiff —en,** to declare a vessel unseaworthy; **bei einer Leiche —en,** to deliver a funeral oration. **—ung,** *f.* resignation, abdication; dismission, discharge, disbanding; funeral oration (*obs.*).

Ab'darben, *v.a.* to deprive of, stint in; **sich etwas —,** to deny oneself something, pinch oneself; **er darbt sich die besten Bissen für sie ab,** he saves the best pieces for her.

Ab'darren, *v.a.* to dry, kiln-dry (*malt, etc.*).

Ab'deck—en, *v.a.* to uncover; to unroof; to flay (*arch.*); to clear (*the table*). **—er,** *m.* (**—ers,** *pl.* **—er**) flayer. **—erei',** *f.* (*pl.* **—erei'en**) (*operation of*) flaying; knacker's-yard.

Ab'deichen, *v.a.* to dam up *or* in; to dike off.

Ab'dielen, *v.a.* to separate by boards; to floor.

Ab'dienen, *v.a.* to pay off by service: to obtain by serving; to finish by serving; **der Freiwillige dient sein Jahr ab,** the volunteer serves his year.

Ab'dingen, *ir.v.a.* to beat down in bargaining; to cheapen (*by haggling*); to dismiss an apprentice; **einem etwas —,** to hire s.th. from one; to obtain s.th. from s.o. by negotiating; to bargain one out of a thing; **wir haben den Preis zu fünfzehn Mark abgedungen,** we have agreed upon fifteen marks for the price; **sich** (*dat.*) **etwas — lassen,** to allow an abatement; **ich habe mir nichts — lassen,** I have made no allowance.

Ab'disputieren, *v.a.* to gain by dispute; **sich —,** to tire oneself with discussing.

Ab'donnern, *v.* I. *a.* to thunder forth. II. *n.* (*aux.* **h.**) to cease thundering; **das Gewitter donnert sich ab,** the thunderclaps of the storm grow weaker and weaker.

Ab'drängen, *v.a.* to force away; **einem etwas —,** to extort s.th. from s.o.

Ab'drechseln, *v.a.* to turn off, to separate by turning; to turn (*as on a lathe*).

Ab'drehen, *v.a.* to twist off; to turn off (*gas, etc.*).

Ab'dreschen, *ir.v.a.* to thrash off; to thrash; to finish thrashing; **abgedroschen,** *p.p.* & *adj.* trite, vulgar; **es war alles vorher abgedroschen,** it was preconcerted; **abgedroschene Gedanken,** hackneyed ideas; **abgedroschene Phrasen,** commonplace and empty phrases.

Ab'dringen, *ir.v.a.* to force away; **einem etwas —,** to extort, wring a thing from one.

Ab'drohen, *v.a.*; **einem etwas —,** to extort s.th. from s.o. by threats.

Ab'druck, *m.* (**—(e)s,** *pl.* **Abdrücke**) impression; copy-print; single copy; stamp, stamping; fossil remains, fossil; mark; the act of pulling the trigger; the trigger; **ein Gyps—,** a plaster-cast; **abermaliger —,** reprint; **— vor der Schrift,** proof-impression, proof-print. *Comp.* **—s=recht,** *n.* (**—(e)s, —e**) copyright.

Ab'drucken, *v.a.* to print, to imprint, to stamp; to print off.

Ab'drücken, *v.* I. *a.* to separate, loosen *or* set free by pressing; to pull the trigger, to fire off (*a gun*); **es drückt mir das Herz ab,** it breaks my heart. II. *n.* (*aux.* **h.**) to weigh anchor.

Ab'dunkeln, *v.* I. *a.* to change a light colour into a darker one. II. *n.* to assume a darker colour.

Ab'dunsten, *v.n.* (*aux.* **s.**) to evaporate.

Ab'dünst—en, *v.a.* to convert into steam, to cause to evaporate. **—ung,** *f.* evaporation. *Comp.* **—ungs=haus,** *n.* drying-house.

Ab'eb(e)nen, *v.a.* to level, make even.

Ab'ecken, *v.a.* to take off corners; to dent, scallop; **abgeeckter Krystall,** spiculated crystal.

Ab'eifern, *v.r.* to worry oneself; to exhaust oneself by zeal, eagerness, *or* anger.

Ab'eisen, *v.* I. *a.* to clear from ice. II. *n.* (*aux.* **h.**) to thaw; **es hat abgeeist,** the ice is gone.

A'bend, *m.* (**—s,** *pl.* **—e**) evening; eve; the west (*especially in biblical language*); **diesen Abend,** this evening; **heute abend,** to-night; **auf heute abend,** for this evening; **gestern abend,** yesterday night; **morgen abend,** to-morrow night; **alle abend** *or* **Abende,** every evening; **am heiligen —,** on Christmas eve; **— des Lebens,** decline of life; **der Wind weht aus —,** there is a west wind; **es wird —,** it is getting dark; **am —, zu —, auf den —,** in the evening; **zu — essen,** to sup; **guten —,** good evening; **gegen —,** towards evening; westwards, occidental (*bibl. & high style; technic lang.*). **—lich,** *adj.* evening; western. **—s,** *adv.* in the evening, of an evening; **es ist noch nicht aller Tage —** *or* **man soll den Tag nicht vor dem — loben,** (*prov.*) we have not yet seen the last of it; don't whistle before you are out of the wood. *Comp.* **—andacht,** *f.* evening devotion, prayers; vespers. **—blatt,** *n.* evening (news)paper. **—brot,** *n.*, **—essen,** *n.* supper. **—dämmerung,** *f.* evening twilight, dusk. **—falter,** *m.* (—s, *pl.* —) hawk-moth. **—gang,** *m.* evening walk; westerly lode. **—gegend,** *f.* west. **—gesellschaft,** *f.* evening party, dinner party; **große —gesellschaft,** rout. **—land,** *n.* occident. **—länder,** *m.* inhabitant of the west; man from the west. **—ländisch,** *adj.* occidental, belonging to the west. **—mahl,** *usually* **das heilige —mahl,** the Lord's supper; the holy communion; **das —mahl nehmen,** to partake of the Lord's supper, to communicate; **das —mahl reichen,** to administer the sacrament. **—mahls=gast,** *m.* communicant. **—mahls=kelch,** *m.* a chalice, communion-cup. **—mahlzeit,** *f.* supper. **—pfauen=auge,** *n.* ocellate sphinx. **—punkt,** *m.* the true west, west-point (*Astr.*). **—regen,** *m.* the latter rain (*B.*). **—rot,** *n.*, **—röte,** *f.* evening glow, sunset glow. **—sonne,** *f.* setting sun. **—sonnen=schein,** *m.* light of the setting sun. **—ständchen,** *n.* serenade. **—stern,** *m.* evening star, Venus, Hesperus. **—stillstand,** *m.* evening station (*Astr.*). **—tau,** *m.* night dew. **—tisch,** *m.*; **der arme Student hat den —tisch bei uns,** the poor student has supper with us. **—trunk,** *m.* evening draught; (*coll.*) nightcap. **—wärts,** *adv.* westerly, westwards. **—weite,** *f.* western amplitude (*Astr.*). **—wind,** *m.* evening wind; west wind, zephyr.

A'benteuer, *n.* (—s, *pl.* —) adventure. **—(e)n,** to live the life of an adventurer, to seek adventures. **—er,** (**A'benteurer**), *m.* adventurer; knight-errant. **—erin,** (**A'benteurerin**), *f.* adventuress. **—lich,** I. *adj.* adventurous; wonderful; strange, odd; quixotic, romantic; fantastic. II. *adv.* adventurously, etc. **—lichkeit,** *f.* adventurousness; romance, quixotism; strangeness; **—lichkeiten,** *pl.* strange things.

A'ber, I. *adv.* again, once more; **tausend und — tausend,** thousands and thousands (*lit.* a thousand and another thousand). *In some cpds.* **Aber** *denotes* ill, a bad kind of (*cp.* **Ab** *in* **Abgott, Abgunst**). II. *conj.* but; **nein —,** I say (*expression of astonishment*); **nun —,** but now; say; **—, —!** but alas! III. *subst.n.* an objection; **die Sache hat ein —,** there is a but in the question; **die Wenns und die —s,** the conditions and objections, the difficulties in the way; **ein Wenn und ein — haben,** to make some objection or other. *Comp.* **—acht,** *f.* renewed and increased ban, double-ban (*archaic*). **—glaube,** *m.* superstition. **—gläubisch,** *adj.* & *adv.* superstitiously. **—gläubigkeit,** *f.* superstitiousness. **—malig,** *adj.* reiterated, repeated. **—mals,** *adv.* again, once more. **—saat,** *f.* second sowing. **—klug,** *adj.* silly (*rare*). **—weise,** *adj.* foolish. **—witz,** *m.* false, strained wit; craziness; absurdity; imbecility. **—witzig,** *adj.* & *adv.* crazy, foolish; **—witzig reden,** to rave, to dote. **—wille,** *m.* disinclination, ill-will.

Ab'erkenn—en, *ir.v.a.*; **einem etwas —,** to deprive s.o. of s.th. by a judicial sentence; to set aside a plea. **—ung,** *f.* abjudication, dispossession by judicial decree; **—ung der bürgerlichen Ehrenrechte,** deprivation of civil rights.

Ab'ernten, *v.* I. *a.* to reap, to harvest. II. *n.* (*aux.* **h.**) to finish reaping.

Ab'erobern, *v.a.*; **einem etwas —,** to wrest something by conquest from someone.

A'berraute, *f.* (*fr. abrotonum*) southernwood.

Ab'eschern, *v.r.*, *see* **Abäschern.**

Ab'essen, *ir.v.* I. *a.* to eat off, up, to clear (*a plate*), to leave nothing on (*the table*); to sit out (*a long dinner*); **einen Knochen —,** to pick a bone. II. *n.* (*aux.* **h.**), to finish eating; **abgegessen haben,** to have done eating, to rise from the table.

Ab'fach—en, *v.a.* to partition, to divide into compartments; to classify. **—ung,** *f.* division into compartments; ranging on shelves, etc.; classification.

Ab'fädeln, *v.a.* to shred (*beans, etc.*).

Ab'fahr—en, *ir.v.* I. *a.* to break by driving against; to cart away; to make a road *or* a track by driving over; to wear out by driving; to overdrive; **ein Rad —en,** to drive a wheel off; **der Doktor hat seine Krankenbesuche abgefahren,** the doctor has driven round to see his patients. II. *n.* (*aux.* **s.**), to set off, to depart; to start; to put to sea; to slip off, to glide; **fahr ab!** be gone! (*vulg.*); **der Zug fährt um 3 Uhr ab,** the train starts at three o'clock; **er fuhr sehr übel ab,** he got off badly, got the worst of it. **—t,** *f.* (*pl.* **—ten**) departure; starting time. **—ts=ort,** *m.* place of departure. **—ts=perron,** *m.* platform from which the train starts. **—ts=zeit,** *f.* time of departure.

Ab'fall, *m.* (**—es,** *pl.* **Abfälle**) slope, descent; falling off; apostasy; defection, revolt; short-weight, loss in weight; escapement; fall of water; *pl.* waste, refuse, clippings, shreds, cuttings, scraps, combings, offal; **der — einer Farbe,** fading of a colour; **— zwischen zwei Dingen,** contrast between two things; **— des Laubes,** fall of the leaves; **— der Niederlande,** revolt of the Netherlands. *Comp.* **—händler,** *m.* seller of offal. **—s=röhre,** *f.* waste pipe.

Ab'fallen, *ir.v.n.* (*aux.* **s.**) to fall off; to slope; to decrease, to decay; to desert, to revolt; to fade; to fall back (*Mil.*); to lose flesh; to go to waste; to contrast strongly; **fall ab!** ease the helm (*Naut.*); **es fällt dabei nicht viel ab,** there is little profit to be made out of, by it; **Sie ließ ihn —,** (*colloq.*) she snubbed him, she gave him the cold shoulder; she gave him the slip; **der Abgefallene,** the apostate; **von Gott —,** to become recreant to God; **er ist vom Glauben abgefallen,** he has apostatized; **das Schiff fiel vom Striche ab,** the ship fell from her course; **abfallende Qualität,** inferior quality, "off" quality.

Ab'fällig, *adj.* falling off; shelving, sloping; decaying; disapproving, dissenting; ready to desert; disloyal, rebellious (*archaic*); **— werden,** to revolt; **vom Glauben — werden,** to turn apostate; **sich — (über einen) äußern,** to criticise unfavourably, to cut up; **einen — bescheiden,** to give a negative answer to s.o., to refuse, to decline a request.

Ab'fangen, *ir.v.a.* to catch, snatch from; to prop; to stab, to kill game (*wounded, with the hunting knife*); **das Wasser —,** to turn off water; **Kunden —,** to catch customers, to entice away customers.

Ab'färben, *v. n.* (*aux.* **h.**) to lose colour; to finish dyeing; to stain; **abgefärbt,** *p.p.* & *adj.* faded, discoloured; **das Tuch hat rot abgefärbt,** the cloth has come off red (*upon something*); **es färbt nicht ab,** the dye does not come off.

Ab'fasern, *v.* I. *a.* to take off the fibres. II. *r.* & *n.* (*aux.* **h.**) to lose the fibre; to unravel.

Ab'faß—en, *v.a.* to sort *or* separate; to weigh out (*articles*); to bend, weld (*iron*); to compose, to write; to draw up; (*fam.*) to catch, to seize, to arrest; **in bündigen Ausdrücken abgefaßt,** couched in concise terms; **laß dich ja nicht dabei —en,** beware of being caught while you do it. **—er,** *m.* (**—ers**) one who draws up (*a statement, etc.*); editor; writer. **—ung,** *f.* composition, style, wording; drawing up, penning, writing.

Ab'fasten, *v.a.* to atone for by fasting; **sich —,** to fast to exhaustion; **abgefastet,** *p.p.* & *adj.* exhausted with fasting; famished with hunger.

Ab'faulen, *v.n.* (*aux.* **s.**) to rot and fall off.
Ab'fechten, *ir.v.a.* to get by fighting; **sich —,** to fight to exhaustion; **sich im Sprechen mit den Händen —,** to gesticulate in speaking.
Ab'federn, *v.* I. *a.* to pluck (*feathers*). II. *n.* to lose the feathers, moult.
Ab'fegen, *v.a.* to sweep off; **Staub —,** to dust; **—de Mittel,** detergents; **der abgefegte Bast eines Hirsches,** the peel of a deer's horn.
Ab'feilschen, *v.a.* to cheapen (*by haggling*), to haggle, to beat down; to obtain by haggling.
Ab'fertig—en, *v.a.* to finish; to despatch, to expedite; to forward; to dismiss; **kurz —en,** to send about one's business, to treat curtly, to snub. **—er,** *m.* (**—ers,** *pl.* **—er**) sender, despatcher. **—ung,** *f.* act of finishing; despatch; clearance, expedition, smart rejoinder; reproof, snub; dismissal. *Comp.* **—ungs=schein,** *m.* customs declaration; permit. **—ungs=stelle,** *f.* despatch office.
Ab'fetten, *v.a.* to skim off the fat; to grease.
Ab'feuchten, *v.n.* (*aux.* **h.**) to dry up.
Ab'feuer—n, *v.a.* to fire off, to discharge; **abgefeuert!** fire! (*Mil.*). **—ung,** *f.* discharge, firing, etc.; **—ung der Geschütze,** cannonade; **unter —ung der Kanonen,** guns saluting.
Ab'fiedeln, *v.a.* to fiddle off.
Ab'fiedern, *v.* I. *a.* to clip *or* break off the edges of glass. II. *n.* *see* **Abfedern.**
Ab'find—en, *ir.v.* I. *a.* to satisfy, to compound with (*creditors*); to pay off; to portion; **abgefundene Prinzen,** appanaged princes. II. *r.* to come to terms (**mit einem,** with someone), to be quits (with someone); **sich gütlich mit einem —,** to settle things amicably with someone. **—ung,** *f.* act of satisfying; settlement; composition, compromise. *Comp.* **—ungs=geld,** *n.*, **—ungs=summe,** *f.* money paid to get clear of all claims; sum in full of all demands; composition, compensation; appanage.
Ab'fingern, *v.a.* to reckon with the fingers; to thumb over; to finger *or* play (*a tune*).
Ab'fischen, *v.* I. *a.* to empty (*a pond*) by fishing; **das Beste —,** to take the cream of; **einem etwas —,** to cheat one out of a thing. II. *n.* (*aux.* **h.**) to finish fishing.
Ab'flachen, *v.a.* to flatten gradually, to shoal, to level, to slope; to become dull (*as trade*).
Ab'flau—en, *v.a.* to wash (*ore*); to rinse (*linen*). *Comp.* **—faß,** *n.* buddle.
Ab'flechten, *ir.v.a.* to unplait, untwist.
Ab'flehen, *v.a.* (**einem etwas**) to obtain by imploring.
Ab'fleisch—en, *v.a.* to flay; to pick the flesh (*from the bone*). *Comp.* **—eisen, —messer,** *n.* fleshing-knife, flaying-knife.
Ab'fliegen, *ir.v.n.* (*aux.* **s.**) to fly off.
Ab'fließen, *ir.v.n.* (*aux.* **s.**) to run off, to flow off *or* down; to ebb.
Ab'flößen, *v.a.* to make to float away; to float down a river.
Ab'flug, *m.* flight, departure (*of migratory birds*).
Ab'flügeln, *v.* I. *a.* to deprive of wings.
Ab'fluß, *m.* (**—sses,** *pl.* **Abflüsse**) flowing off; ebb; discharge, defluxion (*Med.*); refuse-fluid. **— des Geldes,** efflux *or* drain of money. *Comp.* **—graben,** *m.* drain. **—röhre,** *f.* waste pipe, gutter.
Ab'folg—e, *f.* succession, sequence. **—en,** *v.n.* (*aux.* **s.**) *see* **Verabfolgen.**
Ab'foltern, *v.a.* to extort from; **einem ein Geständnis —,** to extort a confession from someone by torturing.
Ab'forder—n, *v.a.* to call away; (**einem etwas**) to demand from, make a claim against; **einem Rechenschaft —n,** to call one to account. **—ung,** *f.* a demand from; recall.
Ab'form, *f.* (*pl.* **—en**) form, mould.
Ab'formen, *v.a.* to mould, to form from a mould; **einen Schuh —,** to take a shoe off the last.
Ab'forschen, *v.a.* (**einem etwas**) to search out, to ascertain by pumping.
Ab'forsten, *v.a.* to cut down, to root up (*a forest*).
Ab'fragen, *v.a.* to inquire of, to ascertain by inquiring; **einem Kinde die Grammatik —,** to hear a child's grammar.
Ab'fressen, *ir.v.a.* to eat off, to browse; to consume; **der Gram frißt ihm das Herz ab,** grief gnaws his heart.
Ab'frieren, *ir.v.n.* (*aux.* **s.**) to be bitten off by cold, to be half frozen; **er hat sich die Zehen abgefroren** *or* **die Zehen sind ihm abgefroren,** his toes are frost-bitten.
Ab'fügen, *v.a.* to smooth off, to plane smooth.
Ab'fuhr, *f.* removal *or* transportation (*of goods*); carting off, carriage; disabling (*of an antagonist*) (*students' slang*). **—lohn,** *m.* cartage, carriage. **—wagen,** *m.* dust cart, mud cart, night cart.
Ab'führ—en, *v.a.* to lead away; to carry off, down, away; to export; to mislead; to purge; to draw wire; to snub; to discharge a debt, put to one's credit; **er wurde in Gewahrsam abgeführt,** he was removed into custody; **diese Arznei führt zu stark ab,** this medicine is too strong an aperient; (*fam.*) **er ist schon abgeführt worden,** he has got his answer; **den habe ich glänzend abgeführt,** I have beaten him hollow. **—end,** *p. & adj.* purgative, aperient; **—ende Muskeln,** abductor muscles. **—ung,** *f.* removal, carrying off; evacuation; purgation; **—ung einer Schuld,** wiping off of a debt. *Comp.* **—(ungs)=mittel,** *n.* aperient. **—ungs=röhre,** *f.* waste-pipe.
Ab'füllen, *v.a.* to fill out; to draw off (*wine*); **Wein auf Flaschen —,** to bottle wine.
Ab'furchen, *v.a.* to divide by furrows.
Ab'fütter—n, *v.a.* to feed, to fodder. **—ung,** *f.* feeding, the last feed at night; great evening party, rout (*coll.*).
Ab'gabe, *f.* (*pl.* **—n**) tax, tribute, duty; draft, bill of exchange; delivery, place of delivery (*South German*). **—n,** *pl.* fees, dues. *Comp.* **—pflichtig,** *adj.* liable to taxes, assessable, taxable. **—n=frei,** *adj.* duty-free, free of taxes. **—n=wesen,** *n.* (*state of*) imposts and taxes.
Ab'gähren, *ir.v.n.* (*aux.* **h.**) to cease fermenting.
Ab'gang, *m.* (**—es,** *pl.* **Abgänge**) departure; deduction; tare; sale; decease; loss; exit; (*arch.*) want; miscarriage (*Med.*); *pl.* scrapings, filings; **guten — haben,** to have a ready sale; **es findet keinen —,** there is no sale for it, it is a drug in the market; **nach — der männlichen Linie,** failing heirs male; **in — kommen,** to fall into disuse; to decay. *Comp.* **—s=rechnung,** *f.* note of tare, tare-account.
Ab'gäng—ig, *adj.* going off, departing; saleable; excremental; declining; sloping, uneven; deteriorating; missing (*of papers, etc.*); shabby. **—ling,** *m.* waste matter; abortion. **—sel,** *n.* refuse, clippings.
Ab'gaukeln, *v.a.* (**einem etwas**) to obtain by juggling.
Ab'geben, *ir. v.* I. *a.* to give, to deliver; to deliver up; to furnish a contingent; to give (*an opinion*); to pay (*taxes*); to draw (*a bill*); to be good for; to transfer; **einen Wechsel, eine Tratte auf einen —,** to draw on one, to give a cheque *or* draft on one; **dies ist für Sie abgegeben,** this has been left for you; **einen Soldaten von einem Regiment zu einem andern —,** to draft a soldier from one regiment to another; **er hätte einen guten Arzt abgegeben,** he would have made a good doctor; **er kann einen Zeugen —,** he can bear witness; **einem eins —,** to give one a cutting reply, to give

one a blow; einem etwas —, to share with one; es wird wohl etwas —, something is sure to happen; jetzt giebt es aber etwas ab, we (you) are in for it now; einen Narren —, to play the fool. II. *r.* sich mit jemand(em) —, to frequent one's company; mit dem Menschen gebe ich mich nicht ab, I won't have anything to do with that fellow; sich mit etwas —, to occupy oneself with a matter; er giebt sich viel mit den neueren Sprachen ab, he spends a great deal of his time on modern languages. III. *n.* (*aux.* h.) to deal (*cards*) for the last time.

Ab'gebrannt, *p.p. of* **ab'brennen** *& adj.* burnt out; (*fam.*) without money, out of cash, stumped. *See* **Abbrennen.**

Ab'gebrochen, *p.p. & adj.* broken off; abrupt. *See* **Abbrechen.** —**heit,** *f.* abruptness.

Ab'gebrüht, *p.p. & adj.* (*colloq.*) insensible (*to*); er ist gegen Schande —, he does not care for disgrace, he has no feeling of shame whatsoever.

Ab'gedacht, *p.p. & adj.* sloping.

Ab'gedroschen, *p.p. & adj.* trite. *See* **Abdreschen.**

Ab'gefeimt (**Abgefäumt** *is less good*), *p.p.* (*of the now obsolete* **abfeimen,** to skim (off), to scum) *& adj.* crafty, cunning, knowing; ein —er Bösewicht, an arch-rogue, an out and out rascal.

Ab'gegriffen, *p.p. of* **ab'greifen** *& adj.* worn by thumbing; —e Münze, worn coin; —es Gebetbuch, well-worn prayer-book.

Ab'gehen, *ir.v.* I. *n.* (*aux.* s.) to go off, to depart, to start; to swerve; to go astray; to deviate, digress; to relinquish; to come off, wear off; to make one's exit; to pass (*Med.*); to be in want; to be missing; to lose; to sell, to find purchasers; wann geht die Post ab? when does the post go? davon kann ich nicht —, I must insist on that; vom Preise —, to lower the price; geht nichts vom Preise ab? is there no reduction? is this your last price? der Pfad geht links ab, the path goes off to the left; er läßt sich nichts —, he denies himself nothing; von der Schule —, to leave school; von einem Amte —, to resign an office; er ist abgegangen worden, he has been dismissed (*coll.*); mit Tode —, to depart this life; das Rad ging ab, the wheel came off; die Farbe ging ab, the colour faded, came off; es sind ihm Würmer abgegangen, he has passed worms; mir gehen dafür die Kenntnisse ab, I am wanting in the knowledge required for that; geht mir dadurch etwas ab? am I the worse for it? es soll ihr nichts —, she shall want for nothing; Shylock geht ab, exit Shylock; es wird übel —, it will turn out badly; das Konzert ging gut ab, the concert went off well; die Leibesfrucht ging ihr ab, she had a miscarriage; hiervon geht ab, discount (*in an account*), deduct; abgehen lassen, to send off, to run. II. *a.* to wear out by walking; to measure by steps.

Ab'gehoben, *p.p. & adj.* taken off; —e Dividenden, dividends collected *or* cashed.

Ab'geizen, *v.a.* to get by avarice; sich etwas —, to starve oneself through avarice.

Ab'gelagert, *p.p. & adj.* seasoned; —e Zigarren, matured, well-seasoned cigars.

Ab'gelaufen, *p.p. & adj.* expired; due, payable.

Ab'gelebt, *p.p. & adj.* decrepit; faded; worn out; blasé. —**heit,** *f.* decrepitude.

Ab'gelegen, *p.p. & adj.* remote, distant; —er Wein, wine long laid down. —**heit,** *f.* remoteness, isolation.

Ab'geleitet, *p.p. & adj.* derived (*Mus. & Gram.*).

Ab'gemacht, *p.p. & interj.* settled, agreed, all right, that's a bargain!

Ab'gemessen, I. *p.p. & adj.* measured; slow; formal. II. *adv.* with careful adjustment. —**heit,** *f.* regularity, exactitude.

Ab'geneigt, *p.p. & adj.* disinclined, averse. —**heit,** *f.* disinclination, repugnance.

Ab'genutzt, *adj.* worn out, used up; stale; threadbare.

Ab'geordnete, *m.* (—n, *pl.* —n) deputy, delegate member (*of a senate*), political representative; ein —er, a member. *Comp.* —n=haus, house of representatives, chamber of deputies; das preußische —n Haus, the Prussian Chamber of Deputies, the Prussian House of Commons *or* Representatives.

Ab'gerannt, *p.p. of* **ab'rennen.**

Ab'gerben, *v.a.* to tan off; to beat.

Ab'gerechnet, *p.p.* deducted; — davon, setting aside; not to speak of.

Ab'gerissen, *p.p. of* **ab'reißen** *& adj.* torn, ragged, shabby.

Ab'gesagt, *p.p. & adj.* declared (*enemy*).

Ab'gesandt, *p.p. of* **absenden.** —**e,** *m.* (—en, *pl.* —en) ambassador; ein —er, an ambassador. —e *or* —in, *f.* ambassadress.

Ab'gesang, *m.* (—(e)s, *pl.* Abgesänge) *a technical term in the lang. of the mastersingers denoting* the latter portion of a stanza, *the former half being called* Aufgesang.

Ab'geschieden, *p.p. & adj.* solitary; secluded; separate; defunct; dead; —er Geist *or* —e Seele, departed spirit. —**heit,** seclusion, secuded spot; solitude, privacy, retirement.

Ab'geschliffen, *p.p. & adj.* polished; refined, polite. —**heit,** *f.* refinement, elegance of manners.

Ab'geschlossen, *p.p. & adj.* retired, secluded; concluded; exclusive; closed, settled. —**heit,** *f.* seclusion.

Ab'geschmackt, *adj.* tasteless, insipid; absurd; in bad taste. —**heit,** *f.* absurdity; insipidity; bad taste, bad breeding.

Ab'gesehen, *p.p.*; — von, without regard to; apart from; — davon daß, without mentioning that; — auf, (*acc.*) intended for; das war auf mich —, that was a cut at me.

Ab'gesinnt, *adj.* averse, unfavourably disposed (*obs.*).

Ab'gesondert, *p.p. & adj.* separated; separate; distinct; retired; insulated (*Phys.*); —e Feuchtigkeit, secretion (*Med.*).

Ab'gespannt, *p.p. & adj.* slackened, debilitated, tired, low. —**heit,** *f.* exhaustion; debility; seediness; lowness of spirits.

Ab'gestanden, *p.p. & adj.* stale; dead (*wine*).

Ab'gestempelt, *p.p. & adj.* stamped; defaced, blackened.

Ab'gestorben, *p.p. & adj.* dead; der Gesellschaft —, lost to society.

Ab'gestumpft, *p.p. & adj.* blunted; dull.

Ab'gestutzt, *p.p. & adj.* cropped; truncate (*Bot.*).

Ab'getakelt, *p.p. & adj.* unrigged, without rigging.

Ab'gethan, *p.p. & adj.* done (*away*) with, settled, over.

Ab'getragen, *p.p. & adj.* worn out, threadbare.

Ab'getrieben, *p.p. & adj.* worn out, tired out, jaded; ein —er Gaul, a jade.

Ab'gewandt, *p.p. of* **ab'wenden.**

Ab'gewinnen, *ir.v.a.* to win from; einem den Vorteil —, to get the better of one; einem den Vorsprung —, to get the start of, to steal a march upon; die Luft, den Wind —, to gain the wind; einer Sache Geschmack —, to get a taste for a thing; sich (*dat.*) mit Mühe etwas —, to prevail upon oneself after a struggle.

Ab'gewöhnen, *v.* I. *a.* (einem etwas) to disaccustom, to wean from, to break of. II. *r.* to break oneself of, to give up (*a habit, etc.*); sich (*dat.*) das Rauchen —, to give up smoking.

Ab'gezirkelt, *p.p. & adj.* ruled with compasses; —es Benehmen, stiffish behaviour.

Ab'gezogen, *p.p. & adj.* far off, remote;

deducted (*C.L.*); abstract (*Philos.*); —**er Begriff**, abstract idea; —**es Gewicht**, stamped *or* standard weight.
Ab'gieren, *v.* I. *a.* to obtain by importunity. II. *n.* to sheer off *or* away (*Naut.*).
Ab'gieß—en, *ir.v.a.* to pour off; to decant; to cast. —**er**, *m.* caster, moulder. —**ung**, *f.* decanting; casting.
Ab'glanz, *m.* (—**es**) reflected splendour; reflection.
Ab'glätten, *v.* I. *a.* to smooth, to polish. II. *r.* (**Menschen**) **glätten sich ab**, (*men*) become polished, well-mannered.
Ab'gleich—en, *ir.v.a.* to equalize; to level (*rare*); **Rechnungen —en**, to square accounts. —**ung**, *f.* levelling; equalization; adjustment. *Comp.* —**ungs=wage**, *f.* adjusting-scale. —**zirkel**, *m.* a divider (*T.*).
Ab'gleiten, *ir.v.n.* (*aux.* **s.**) to slip *or* glide off; **abgleitender Rhythmus**, dactylic rhythm.
Ab'glimmen, *i.r.v.n.* (*aux.* **s.**) to cease to glow.
Ab'glitschen, *v.n.* (*fam.*) *see* **Abgleiten.**
Ab'glühen, *v.a.* to make red-hot, heat thoroughly; to mull (*wine*).
Ab'—gott, *m.* (—**gottes**, *pl.* **Abgötter**) idol; **einen zu seinem —gott machen**, to idolise a p. —**göttin**, *f.* (*female*) idol. *Comp.* —**gott=schlange**, *f.* boa constrictor.
Abgött—erei', *f.* idolatry. —**isch** (**ab'göttisch**), *adj. & adv.* idolatrous; —**isch lieben**, to idolize.
Ab'graben, *ir.v.a.* to dig off; to furnish with a trench; to lower by digging; to separate by a ditch; to drain.
Ab'grämen, *v.r.* to pine away with grief.
Ab'grasen, *v.a.* to graze (*a field*); to cut grass.
Ab'greifen, *ir.v.a.* to wear out by constant handling; **abgegriffene Bücher**, well-thumbed volumes.
Ab'grenzen, *v.a.* to fix the limits of; **gegen den Himmel scharf abgegrenzt**, sharply outlined against the sky.
Ab'grund, *m.* (—**es**, *pl.* **Abgründe**) abyss, precipice.
Ab'gründ—en, *v.a.* to prove to the bottom; to groove. —**lich**, *adj.* precipitous.
Ab'grünen, *v.n.* (*aux.* **h.**) to cease to be verdant; **die Bäume grünen ab**, the leaves are changing.
Ab'gucken, *v.a.* (**einem etwas**) to learn from looking at someone stealthily.
Ab'gunst, *f.* ill-will, envy, spite.
Ab'günstig, *adj.* spiteful, envious, grudging; **er ist mir —**, he has no goodwill towards me.
Ab'gurgeln, *v.a.; etwas —*, to remove by gargling; **ein Lied —**, to sing from the throat, to murder a song.
Ab'gürten, *v.a.* to ungird; to unsaddle.
Ab'guß, *m.* (—(**ss**)**es**, *pl.* **Abgüsse**) pouring off; casting, founding; cast; sink; lower part of a tobacco pipe, stem.
Ab'haaren, *v.* I. *a.* to take off hair. II. *n.* (*aux.* **h.**) to lose hair; **der Muff haart ab**, the hairs are falling out of the muff.
Ab'haben, *ir.v.a.* to have a part of; to have off; **etwas — wollen**, to wish to come in for a share; **den Hut —**, to have the hat off; **dafür soll er schon etwas —**, he is sure to be punished for it.
Ab'hacken, *v.a.* to chop off.
Ab'hadern, *v.a.* (**einem etwas**) to extort from by dispute.
Ab'hageln, *v.* I. *a.* to beat down as hail; **es hat die Blüten abgehagelt**, the hail has beaten off the blossoms. II. *n. sometimes refl.* (*aux.* **h.**) to cease hailing.
Ab'haken, *v.a.* to unhook.
Ab'halt—en, *ir.v.* I. *a.* to hold off; to restrain; to ward off; to hinder; to hold (*the assizes*); **lassen Sie sich nicht —en**, don't be deterred, don't let me hinder you; **Lehrstunden richtig —en**, to give, to take lessons regularly. II. *n.* (*aux.* **h.**) **vom Lande —en**, to bear off from the land. —**er**, *m.* guy (*Naut.*). —**ung**, *f.* hindrance, impediment, hindering, impeding.
Ab'hand—el=n, *v.a.* to settle; to bargain for; to beat down in bargaining; to treat of, to debate, discuss; **einem etwas —eln**, to purchase something of a person. —**l=ung**, *f.* discussion; treatise, essay; negotiation.
Abhan'den, *adj.* not at hand, mislaid, lost; — **kommen**, to get lost; — **gekommen sein**, to be missing; **das Buch ist mir — gekommen**, I have lost the book.
Ab'hang, *m.* (—**es**, *pl.* **Abhänge**) slope, declivity.
[1]**Ab'häng—en**, *ir.v.n.* to hang down; to incline; to hang at a distance from; to depend on; **es hängt von Umständen ab**, it depends on circumstances. —**ig**, *adj.* sloping, declivitous; depending, dependent on, subject to; —**ige Fläche**, inclined plane. —**igkeit**, *f.* slope, declivity; dependence.
[2]**Ab'hängen**, *v.a.* to unhang; to take off *or* down.
Ab'harken, *v.a.* to remove with a rake.
Ab'härmen, *v.r.* to languish; to pine away (*from grief*); **sich — über eine Sache**, to grieve at a thing.
Ab'härten, *v.* I. *a.* to harden. II. *r.* to inure oneself (*to fatigue, etc.*).
Ab'harzen, *v.a.* to take the resin from (*a tree*).
Ab'haschen, *v.a.;* (**einem etwas**) —, to snatch (s.th. from s.o.).
Ab'haspeln, *v.a.* to unwind from a reel; to play or recite quickly and without any expression and feeling (*a piece of music, a poem*).
Ab'hauen, *ir.v.a.* to cut off, to cut down.
Ab'häufen, **Abhäufeln**, *v.a.* to separate into small heaps.
Ab'häuten, *v.* I. *a.* to skin. II. *n.* (*aux.* **h.**) to cast the skin.
Ab'heben, *ir.v.* I. *a.* to lift off; to uncover; to contrast, to bring out in relief; to cut (*cards*); **wer hebt ab?** whose turn is it to cut? **eine Kanone —**, to dismount a gun; **Rahm —**, to skim the cream. II. *r.* to detach itself, to be contrasted, to be brought into relief; **die helle Gestalt hebt sich auf dem dunkeln Hintergrunde vorteilhaft ab**, the light figure is set off to advantage against the dark background.
Ab'hefteln, **Abheften**, *v.a.* to loosen; to unhook; to unbind.
Ab'heilen, *v.n.* (*aux.* **s.**) to heal completely.
Ab'helfen, *ir.v.n.* (*aux.* **h.** *dat.*) to help down from; to remedy; to supply (*a want*); **dem ist nicht abzuhelfen**, that cannot be helped; **einer Schwierigkeit —**, to remove a difficulty; **einem Fehler —**, to correct a fault; **Beschwerden** (*dat.*) —, to redress grievances.
Ab'herzen, *v.a.* to hug to one's heart's content, to smother with kisses (*fam.*).
Ab'hetzen, *v.* I. *a.* to tire by hunting; to run down (*a stag, etc.*); **einem etwas —**, to worry one out of a thing. II. *r.* to tire oneself out, to weary; to give o.s. a lot of trouble.
Ab'heucheln, *v.a.;* **einem etwas —**, to obtain s.th. from s.o. by hypocrisy.
Ab'heulen, *v.* I. *a.* to howl. II. *r.* (*fam.*) to weary oneself with howling.
Ab'hexen, *v.a.;* **einem etwas —**, to get s.th. from s.o. by witchcraft.
Ab'hinken, *v.n.* (*aux.* **s.**) to limp off *or* away.
Ab'hobeln, *v.a.* to smooth with a plane; to plane.
Ab'hold, *adj.* disinclined, unfavourable; unfriendly.
Ab'holen, *v.a.* to fetch off, away; to fetch; to haul, get off (*Naut.*); **einen — lassen**, to send for one; **ich will Sie bei Ihrem Vater —**, I will call for you at your father's; **der Wagen wird mich —**, the carriage will come for me.

Ab'holz, *n.* (—es) chips of wood; dead wood.
Ab'holzen, *v.a.* to cut down, to clear of timber (*a wood*).
Ab'horchen, *v.a.;* **einem etwas —**, to learn s.th. from s.o. by listening.
Ab'hör—en, *v.a.* to learn by hearing; **Rechnungen —en**, to audit accounts; **die Zeugen —en**, to examine witnesses (*judicially*); **Zeugen gegen einander —en**, to confront witnesses. **—ung**, *f.* hearing; trial, examination.
Ab'hub, *m.* (—es) remains of a meal; broken meat; offal; dross; cut (*at cards*); — (**der bürgerlichen Gesellschaft**), offscum, roughscuff. *Comp.* **—kiste**, *f.* rake (*Min.*).
Ab'hudeln, *v.a.* to worry; to perform badly.
Ab'huld, *f.* dislike (*obs.*).
Ab'hülfe, *f.* redress, relief.
Ab'hülsen, *v.a.* to shell; to blanch (*almonds*).
Ab'hüpfen, *v.n.* (*aux.* **f.**) to hop away.
Ab'hüten, *v.a.* to graze.
Abicht, (**Ä'big**) *adj.* turned, on the wrong side, left (*Techn.*).
Ab'irr—en, *v.n.* (*aux.* **f.**) to lose one's way; to deviate, to err. **—ung**, *f.* deviation; aberration (*Opt.*).
Abiturie'nt, *m.* (**—en**, *pl.* **—en**), boy of the top form of a large secondary school (**Gymnasium, Realschule**) who is going in for his leaving-certificate examination (**Maturitätsprüfung, Reifeprüfung**). **—en=proletaria't**, *n.* academic proletariate. **—en=prüfung**, *f.* leaving-certificate examination in the best secondary boys' schools.
Ab'jachern, *v.r.* to get out of breath by over-exertion, to run hard (*coll.*).
Ab'jagen, *v.a.* to over-ride, over-drive; to walk down, stalk (*game*); **einem etwas —**, to rescue, recover something from a person; **sich —**, to overexert oneself, to exert oneself greatly.
Ab'jochen, *v.a.* to unyoke.
Abjurie'ren, *v.a.* to deny formally (*under an oath*).
Ab'kälten, *v. a.* to cool; **Wein —**, to ice wine.
Ab'kämmen, *v.a.* to comb off; to shoot off the crest of a parapet.
Ab'kämpfen, *v.a.;* **einem etwas —**, to get s.th. from s.o. by fighting.
Ab'kanten, *v.a.* to take off the corners; to take off the selvage.
Ab'kanzeln, *v.a.;* **einen —**, to rebuke a p. from the pulpit; to give a p. a good scolding (*coll.*).
Ab'kappen, *v.a.* to unhood; to cut off, lop, dock.
Ab'kargen, *v.a.;* **einem etwas —**, to stint one of s.th.
Ab'karren, *v.* I. *a.* to remove in a cart. II. *n.* (*aux.* **f.**) to go in a cart (*rare*).
Ab'karten, *v.a.* to concert, to plot; **ein abgekartetes Spiel**, a preconcerted game.
Ab'kasteien, *v.r.* to exhaust oneself by mortifications.
Ab'kauen, *v.a.* to separate by chewing; to bite off; **sich die Nägel —**, to bite one's nails.
Ab'kauf, *m.* (—s, *pl.* **Abkäufe**) purchase, the act of purchasing; act of buying off (*a claim, etc.*).
Ab'kaufen, *v.a.;* **einem etwas —**, to buy s.th. from s.o.
Ab'käuf—er, *m.* purchaser. **—lich**, *adj.* redeemable; purchasable.
Ab'kehlen, *v.a.* to cut the throat; to flute, to groove.
Ab'kehr, *f.* (*no pl.*) the turning away, renunciation; alienation, estrangement; — **von Gott**, backsliding; — **von der Sünde**, desistance from sin, conversion.
Ab'kehr—en, *v.a.* to turn away; to distract, divert; to brush away; **ein abgekehrter Besen**, a broom worn to the stump; **sich von einem —en**, to turn from one, withdraw one's assistance from a p.; to turn one's back upon. **—er**, *m.* (—ers, *pl.* **—er**) sweeper. **—icht**, *m.* (—ichts) sweepings.
Ab'keilen, *v.a.* to separate, *or* cleave by a wedge; **einem etwas —**, to buy s.th. from s.o. (*vulg.*).
Ab'keltern, *v.a.* to press (*wine*).
Ab'ketten, *v.a.* to unchain.
Ab'klabastern, *v.r.* to exert oneself, to toil hard (*coll.*).
Ab'klaftern, *v.a.* to fathom; to cord (*wood*).
Ab'klagen, *v.a.;* **einem etwas —**, to get from one by lamenting, *or* by a lawsuit.
Ab'klammern, *v.a.* to unpeg.
Ab'klang, *m.* (—s, *pl.* **Ab'klänge**) dissonance; echo.
Ab'klär—en, *v.a.* to clear, to clarify; **sich —en**, to grow clear. **—ung**, *f.* clarification. **—ungs=gefäß**, *n.* decanting vessel, decanter.
Ab'klatsch, *m.* (—es, *pl.* —e) cast, impression; copy, press copy; proof.
Ab'klatschen, *v.a.* to print off (*a proof sheet, a medal, etc.*); to dab; to stereotype; to copy; to slap, smack (*vulg.*); to refuse (*in dancing*).
Ab'klecksen, *v.a.* to copy in a scrawling manner.
Ab'kleiden, *v.a.* to undress; to partition off; **die Taue —**, to take off the service (*Naut.*).
Ab'klemmen, *v.a.* to pinch off.
Ab'klettern, *v.a.* to climb down.
Ab'klimpern, *v.a.* to play badly, to strum off (*a tune*).
Ab'klopfen, *v.a.* to beat, to knock off; to beat up; to thrash, to beat soundly; **einen Probebogen —**, to strike off a proof sheet.
Ab'knabbern, *v.a.* to nibble off, to pick (*a bone*).
Ab'knallen, *v.* I. *n.* (*aux.* **f.**) to explode. II. *a.* **eine Flinte —**, to fire off a gun (*coll.*).
Ab'knappen, Ab'knapsen, *v.a.* to break off in little bits; to stint; **einem am Lohne —**, to curtail one's wages.
Ab'knauserei, *f.* stinting.
Ab'kneifen, *ir. v.a.* to pinch (*or* to rip) off; **den Wind —**, to haul the wind; to ply to windward; **einem Schiffe den Wind —**, to take the wind out of a ship's sails; to gain the wind (*or* the weather-gage) of a ship.
Ab'kneipen, *v.a.* to pinch off. *See* **Abkneifen.**
Ab'knicken, *v.a.* to crack, snap off; to wring off.
Ab'knöpfbar, *adj.* removable.
Ab'knöpfen, *v.a.* to unbutton; to take off the buttons; **einem etwas —**, to take something away from someone without his noticing it (*coll.*).
Ab'knüpfen, *v.a.* to unbind, to undo.
Ab'knutschen, *v.a.* to smother with caresses (*coll.*).
Ab'kochen, *v.* I. *a.* to boil down; to decoct; to elixate; **Milch —**, to scald milk; **Früchte langsam —**, to stew fruit; **abgekochter Trank**, decoction. II. *n.* (*aux.* **h.**) to finish cooking.
Ab'kommandieren, *v.a.* to order off, to detach; **er ist zur großen Armee abkommandiert**, he has joined the majority (*fam.*).
Ab'komme, *see* **Abkömmling.**
Ab'kommen, I. *ir.v.n.* (*aux.* **f.**) to come away, to deviate; to get away; to swerve; to digress; to be descended from; to fall into disuse; to go out of fashion; to fall to leeward; **vom Wege —**, to lose the way; **können Sie wohl eine Viertelstunde —?** can you get away (*or* be spared) a quarter of an hour? **ich bin davon abgekommen**, I have given it up; **ich bin von meiner früheren Ansicht abgekommen**, I have altered my former opinion; **mit jemand —**, to come to an understanding with one; **er kann —**, we can do without him. II. *subst. n.* falling into disuse; origin, descent; composition, agreement; **ein — treffen**, to come to an agreement. **—schaft**, *f.* offspring, posterity.
Ab'kömmlich, *adj.* able to get away, not wanted, disposable, disengaged.
Ab'kömmling, *m.* (—s, *pl.* —e) descendant.

Ab'konterfeien, *v.a.* (*fam.*) to take the likeness of; to portray.
Ab'köpfen, *v.a.* to decapitate; to top, poll (*trees*).
Ab'koppeln, *v.a.* to uncouple, unleash (*dogs*).
Ab'kosen, *v.a.*; **einem etwas —,** to get s.th. from s.o. by wheedling.
Ab'kosten, *v.a.* to take away by tasting.
Ab'kramen, *v.a.* to remove, to clear away.
Ab'kratzen, *v.a.* to scrape, to scratch off; **sich die Schuhe —,** to scrape one's shoes; **kratz ab!** get away! (*coll.*).
Ab'kreischen, *v.r.* to grow hoarse by screaming.
Ab'kreisen, *v.* I. *a.* to divide by a circle; to encircle. II. *n.* (*aux.* **ſ.**) to fly off with a circular motion. **—d,** *adj.* eccentrical.
Ab'kriegen, *v.a.* (**einem etwas**) to obtain by making war; to get; to remove, get off (*vulg.*); **etwas —,** to get a reprimand; to get a beating.
Ab'kritzeln, *v.a.* to scribble off, copy scribblingly.
Ab'kröschen, *v.a.* to fry, roast; **das Öl —,** to clarify (*Typ.*).
Ab'krümeln, *v.a.* & *n.* (*aux.* **ſ.**) to crumble off.
Ab'krümmen, *v.a.* to bend down, to crook; to fire off.
Ab'kugeln, *v.a.* to bowl off; to vote, to reckon by ballot.
Ab'kühl—en, *v.a.* & *n.* (*aux.* **ſ.**) to cool; **sich —en,** to refresh oneself, to cool down. **—ung,** *f.* cooling; refrigeration; refreshment. *Comp.* **—faß,** *n.* cooling vat.
Ab'künd—en, *usually* **—igen,** *v.a.* to publish from the pulpit; to proclaim, announce; to resign (*Law*). **—igung,** *f.* proclamation, publishing; publishing of the banns; notice, warning.
Ab'kunft, *f.* (*pl.* **Ab'künfte**) descent, parentage, origin; breed, race; agreement; **von niedriger —,** of low origin.
Ab'küpfen, Abkuppen, *v.a.* to cut the top, to nip off; to lop.
Ab'kuranzen, *v.a.* to give a good scolding (*coll.*).
Ab'kürz—en, *v.a.* to shorten; to abridge; to abbreviate; to lessen, curtail; to reduce to a lower term (*Arith.*). **—er,** *m.* abridger, epitomist. **—ung,** *f.* abbreviation; abridgment; reduction (*of fractions, etc.*); **—ung im Schreiben,** shorthand.
Ab'küssen, *v.a.* to kiss away (*e.g.* **Thränen**); to kiss again and again, to kiss to one's heart's content.
Ab'lad—en, *ir. v. a.* to unload; to discharge (*cargo*). **—er,** *m.* (**—ers,** *pl.* **—er**) unloader. **—ung,** *f.* unloading, discharging. *Comp.* **—e=ort, e=platz,** *m.*, **e=stelle,** *f.* place of discharge; port.
Ab'lag—e, *f.* (*pl.* **—en**) laying aside; compensation to children instead of inheritance; assignment to separate use (*Law*); place of deposit; a yard; **Rechnungs—e,** rendering of accounts. **—er,** *n.* resting-place; haunt; bed, deposit; privilege of liege lords of resting for refreshment at any tenant's house.
Ab'lager—n, *v.* I. *a.* to deposit; to separate from and encamp elsewhere; to remove from a storehouse; to store up; **abgelagerte Cigarren,** well-seasoned (*or* matured) cigars. II. *n.* & *r.* to settle. **—er=ung,** *f.* deposit; deposition (*Geol.*); furrow. **—er=ungs=stelle,** *f.* (**für Schutt**) refuse-ground.
Ab'landen, *v.n.* (*aux.* **h.**) to depart, to set sail.
Ab'langen, *v.a.* to reach down; **er kann es —,** it is within his reach.
Ab'längen, *v.a.* to cut the proper length *or* in lengths; to dig lengthways.
Ab'laschen, *v.a.* to blaze (*trees*). to blaze out (*a path*).
Ab'laß, *m.* (**—sses,** *pl.* **Abläſſe**) letting off, draining; drain; sluice; intermission; (**des Papstes**) indulgence, remission of punishment; **ohne —,** incessantly; **vollkommener —,** plenary indulgence. *Comp.* **—brief,** *m.* letter of indulgence; dispensation. **—geld,** *n.* shrove-money. **—hahn,** *m.* delivery cock; blow-off cock. **—handel,** *m.* selling of indulgences. **—krämer, —prediger,** *m.* vendor, preacher of indulgences. **—woche,** week of Corpus Christi day, Corpus Christi week. **—zettel,** *m.* ticket of indulgence.
Ab'lassen, *ir.v.* I. *a.* to drain, let off; to decant; to rack (*wine*); to launch (*a vessel*); to unbend (*a bow*); to anneal (*steel*); to reduce (*in price*); **auf beiden Seiten etwas —,** to split the difference; **ein Faß —,** to broach a cask. II. *n.* (*aux.* **h.**) to leave off, to desist.
Ab'lativ, *m.* (**—s,** *pl.* **—e**) ablative.
Ab'latten, *v.a.* to take off the laths.
Ab'lauern, *v.a.* to lurk, watch for; to obtain, learn by watching; **dem Wilde die Fährte —,** to spy out the track of the game.
Ab'lauf, *m.* (**—es**) running off; lapse, expiration (*of time, of a treaty, etc.*); wane; apophyge (*Arch.*), gutter; issue (*of a matter*); ebb; **— eines Wechsels,** maturity of a bill. Comp. **—(s)=frist,** *f.* (**eines Wechsels**), time (*or* term) of payment. **—(s)=loch,** *n.* venthole, outlet. **—(s)=rinne,** *f.* a sink. **—(s)=röhre,** *f.* a waste-pipe.
Ab'laufen, *ir.v.* I. *n.* (*aux.* **ſ.**) to run down; to run off *or* astray; to set off, to depart; to elapse, to expire; to become due; to start (*racers*); to issue; **das Wasser läuft ab,** the tide turns, ebbs; **das Licht läuft ab,** the candle gutters; **die Uhr ist abgelaufen,** the watch has run down; **deine Uhr ist abgelaufen,** your sand has run out, your hour is come (*poet.*); **— lassen,** to parry a thrust; to answer sharply, to set down; to start (*races*); to launch (*a ship*) to despatch (*a letter*). II. *a.* to wear off by running; to attain by running; to get the better of; **sich die Hörner —,** to sow one's wild oats; **das habe ich (mir) längst an den Schuhen abgelaufen,** I knew that long ago.
Ab'läufer, *m.* (**—s,** *pl.* **—**) that which runs off; spool; thread out of place (*Weav.*).
Ab'laugen, *v.a.* to wash out the lye; to steep in lye.
Ab'läugnen. *See* **Ab'leugnen.**
Ab'lauschen, *v.a.* to learn by listening; to lurk, lie in wait for.
Ab'laut, *m.* (**—es,** *pl.* **—e**) vowel-gradation, ablaut (*a regular change of vowels, usually radical, in forms of the same word and in etymologically connected words*).
Ab'lauten, *v.a.* to change the (*radical*) vowel; **ablautende Zeitwörter,** strong verbs.
Ab'läuten, *v.a.* to ring the bell for the train to start; **der Zug wird gleich abgeläutet,** the bell for the train will be rung in a minute.
Ab'läutern, *v.a.* to clear, to clarify; to refine (*sugar*); to filter; to wash (*ore*).
Ab'leben, I. *v.n.* (*aux.* **ſ.**) to die; to become decrepit. II. *subst. n.* decease, demise, death.
Ab'lecken, *v.a.* to lick off.
Ab'ledern, *v.a.* to skin; to unbuff (*pl. no hammers, etc.*); to beat.
Ab'leg—en, I. *v.a.* to put, take off to lay off, down, aside (*garments, arms, a burden, etc.*); to slough off (*skin, etc.*); to give up (*habits*); **Rechenschaft —en,** to render an account, to account; **die Kleider —en,** to undress; **Rechnung —en,** to submit accounts, to give in an account, to account; **einen Eid —en,** to take an oath; **Zeugnis —en,** to bear witness; **ein Bekenntnis —en,** to make a confession; **die Kinderschuhe —en,** to be no longer a child; **Bitte, legen Sie ab,** pray take off your things!; **eine Schuld —en,** to pay a debt; **Nelken —en,** to layer pinks; **Karten —en,** to throw out cards; **Arbeiter —en,** to pay off

workmen. II. *v.n.* (*aux.* **h.**) to be delivered of young; to put out to sea; to decline, fail. **—er,** *m.* (**—ers,** *pl.* **—er**) layer; scion; a cub; sprig, shoot. **—ung,** *f.* laying off, giving up, rendering; layering; profession of faith; swearing, taking of an oath. *Comp.* **—e=fehler,** *m.* wrong letter, misprint. **—e=span,** *m.* distributing rule (*Typ.*).

Ab'lehn—en, *v.a.* to lean, turn aside; to remove; to keep off, avert; to decline, excuse oneself. **—ung,** *f.* declining, refusal.

Ab'leiern, *v.a.* to perform on the lyre; to drawl, to deliver mechanically (*a speech, an air*).

Ab'leihen, *ir.v.a.;* **einem etwas —,** to borrow s.th. from s.o.

Ab'leist—en, I. *v.a.;* **einen Eid —en,** to take an oath (*in due form*); to pass, to serve (*e. g.* **das Militärjahr,** the year of military service). II. *subst.n.;* **—en der Dienstpflicht,** performing the military service. **—ung,** *f.* serving.

Ab'leitbar, *adj.* capable of being turned aside, drainable; deducible, derivable.

Ab'leit—en, *v.a.* to divert, lead away; to mislead; to draw off, drain; to trace back; to derive; to deduce; to let off, escape. **—er,** *m.* conductor; conduit-pipe, channel; **Blitz—er,** lightning-conductor; **ein Nicht—er,** a non-conductor. **—ung,** *f.* a leading off; diversion (*of a stream, etc.*); derivation. *Comp.* **—ungs=rinne,** *f.* sewer, drain. **—ungs=silbe,** *f.* derivation syllable, suffix.

Ab'lenk—en, *v.* I. *a.* to divert; to avert; to parry; to turn away. II. *n.* (*aux.* **h.**) to turn off; to swerve. **—ung,** *f.* diversion; **einen —ungs-angriff machen,** to effect a diversion (*Mil.*).

Ab'lernen, *v.a.;* **einem etwas —,** to imitate, to learn s.th. from s.o. by looking at him.

Ab'lesen, *ir.v.a.* to read off; to read aloud, over; to pick off, to gather; **vom Blatt —,** to read at sight; **ein Buch —,** to wear out a book by reading.

Ab'leugn—en, *v.a.* to deny, disown, disclaim. **—er,** *m.* denier. **—ung,** *f.* denial, disavowal.

Ab'lichten, *v.a.* to give a lighter shade to; to clear (*woods*).

Ab'liefer—n, *v.a.* to deliver (*over, up*); to consign. **—ung,** *f.* delivery; issue (*of provisions*); **nach erfolgter —ung,** after delivery, when delivered. *Comp.* **—ungs=schein,** *m.* certificate of delivery. **—ungs=tag,** *m.* day fixed for delivery. **—ungs=termin,** *m.*, **—ungs=zeit,** *f.* settling day.

Ab'liegen, *ir.v.* I. *n.* (*aux.* **s.**) to lie at a distance, to be remote; (*aux.* **h.**) to lie until mellow, to grow mature; to settle, to clear; **ein abgelegener Weg,** bypath. II. *r.* to get rubbed off with lying (*the hair, etc.*).

Ab'listen, *v.a.;* **einem etwas —,** to obtain s.th. by cunning from s.o.

Ab'locken, *v.a.* to entice away; to obtain by flattery, to lure from; **einem etwas —,** to coax one out of a thing; **einem Thränen —,** to draw tears from one.

Ab'lockern, *v.a.* to loosen (*earth round roots*).

Ab'lohnen, *v.a.* to pay off; to discharge.

Ab'löschen, *v.a.* to cool, quench; to slake (*lime*); to temper (*iron*); to wipe, blot out.

Ab'lös—en, *v.* I. *a.* to loosen, unloose; to cut off, to sever; to take off; to detach; to commute (*a penalty*); to set a watch; to relieve (*guard*); to redeem (*a pledge*), buy up; **ablösende Mittel,** resolvents, pectorals (*Med.*). II. *r.* to be detached; to peel, drop off; to succeed in turn, alternate, relieve one another. **—(s)lich,** *adj. & adv.* capable of being untied; redeemable. **—ung,** *f.* loosening; amputation; relief, relieving guard; ransom; redemption.

Ab'löten, *v.a.* to unsolder.

Ab'luchsen (*also* **Ablugsen** *and* **Abluxen**), *v.a.* to learn by lurking; **einem etwas —,** to swindle one out of a thing (*coll.*).

Ab'lügen, *ir.v.a.* to deny by lying; **einem etwas —,** to get s.th. from s.o. by lying.

Ab'mach—en, *v.a.* to undo, to loosen; to detach; to finish; to settle, arrange definitely; **eine Schuld —,** to discharge a debt; **ein Geschäft —,** to settle a business, to transact a business; **das ist ei'n —,** that goes all in one, that makes one job of it; **das ist abgemacht!** agreed! it's a bargain! done!; **abgemacht,** in order (*Comm.*). **—ung,** *f.* arrangement, settlement; stipulation, agreement; adjustment.

Ab'magern, *v.n.* (*aux.* **s.**) to grow lean; **abgemagert,** *p.p. & adj.* emaciated.

Ab'mähen, *v.a.* to mow, to cut off, down.

Ab'mahlen (*p.p.* **abgemahlen**), *v.a.* to grind thoroughly, to finish grinding.

Ab'mahn—en, *v.a.* to dissuade from, to warn against. **—end,** *p. & adj.* dissuasive. **—ung,** *f.* dissuasion.

Ab'malen, *v.a.* to paint, to portray, to copy, to depict, describe; **sich — lassen,** to have one's portrait painted (*fam.*); **laß dich —!** nonsense, bosh! (*coll.*).

Ab'mangeln, *v.* I. *a.* to mangle thoroughly. II. *n.* (*aux.* **h.**) to finish mangling.

Ab'marachen, *v.r.* to overexert oneself, to tire oneself out (*coll.*).

Ab'märgeln, *see* **Abmergeln.**

Ab'marken, *v.a.* to mark out, to lay out (*a field*).

Ab'markten, *v.a.;* **davon läßt sich nichts —,** nothing can be deducted from this.

Ab'marsch, *m.* (**—es,** *pl.* **Abmärsche**) departure; marching off, march. **—ieren,** *v.n.* (*aux.* **s.**) to march off; **Mann für Mann —ieren,** to file off.

Ab'martern, *v.a.* to torment; **einem etwas —,** to extort s.th. from s.o. (by tormenting him).

Ab'maß, *n.* the measure of a thing, dimension.

Ab'matt—en, *v.a.* to fatigue, to weary out; **ganz abgemattet,** quite knocked up. **—ung,** *f.* harassing, tiring; weariness, exhaustion.

Ab'meiern, *v.a.* to turn out of a farm; to dispossess a person (*coll.*).

Ab'meischen, *v.a.* to mash duly (*Brew.*).

Ab'meißeln, *v.a.* to chisel off *or* out.

Ab'mergeln, *v.a.* to waste, to emaciate; **ein abgemergelter Mensch,** a worn-out individual, a man without strength or savour.

Ab'merken, *v.a.* to observe, to perceive; to learn by observing; **einem etwas —,** to learn s.th. by observing a p.

Ab'mess—en, *ir.v.a.* to measure off; to measure, to gauge; to survey; to suit, make to suit; to compare; **er mißt seine Ausdrücke nicht ab,** he uses unmeasured language; **andere nach sich selbst —en,** to judge of others by oneself; **die Zeit —en,** to apportion time, to time; **einen Vers —en,** to scan a verse; **das ist nicht abzumessen,** that cannot be gauged, there is no standard for that. **—er,** *m.* (**—ers,** *pl.* **—er**) measurer, surveyor. **—ung,** *f.* measurement; adjustment; survey.

Ab'metzen, *v.a.* to take a peck of grain (*as payment for grinding*), to take the miller's toll.

Ab'miet—en, *v.a.* to hire from; to farm. **—er,** *m.* (**—ers,** *pl.* **—er**) lessee, hirer, tenant.

Ab'minder—n, *v.a.* to diminish, to lessen. **—ung,** *f.* diminution, lessening; reduction.

Ab'misten, *v.a.* to clear of manure.

Ab'modeln, *v.a.* to form after a model; to copy.

Ab'moosen, *v.a.* to clear of *or* free from moss.

Ab'müden, *v.a. & r.* to tire out.

Ab'mühen, *v.r.* to make great exertions, to labour, to drudge, to slave.

Ab'murksen (*or* **Abmucksen**), *v.a.;* **einen —,** to kill one secretly, to make away with one; to despatch a p.; (*coll.; especially said ironically of murders in sensational dramas*).

Ab'müßigen (*sometimes pronounced with short* ü), *v.* I. *a.* **einen —**, to cause s.o. to take leisure, to disturb anyone; to detain one (*from his occupation*); **einem etwas —**, to extort s.th. from s.o. II. *r.* to find time *or* leisure; **ich kann mir die Zeit nicht —**, I cannot spare the time from my work *or* business.

Ab'muster—n, *v.a.* to pay off (*a crew*). **—ung**, *f.* paying off (*of the crew*).

Ab'nagen, *v.a.* to gnaw off, to gnaw; **sein Verlust nagt ihm das Herz ab**, his loss preys on him.

Ab'nahme, *f.* (*pl.* **—n**) the taking off, down; diminution, decline; decay; wane (*of the moon*); ebb; amputation; sale; **die — vom Kreuze**, the Descent from the Cross; **— einer Rechnung**, auditing an account; **— eines Eides**, the administering of an oath; **— der Tage**, the shortening of the days; **in — geraten**, to fall into disuse, to decay.

Ab'nehm—en, *ir.v.* I. *a.* to take off; to amputate; to cut (*cards*); to gather (*fruit*); to buy (*goods*); to examine, audit (*an account*); to skim (*cream*); to wean (*a calf*); to call off (*dogs*); **wollen Sie nicht abnehmen?** will you not take off your things?; **den Hut —en vor**, to take off one's hat to; **aus etwas —en**, to perceive *or* judge from, to conclude; **daraus kann ich —en**, from that I can gather; **einem einen Eid —en**, to administer an oath to a person; **die Maschen —en**, to narrow; **einem ein Versprechen —en**, to obtain a promise from s.o.; **die Ruderpinne —en**, to unship the tiller; **einem etwas —en**, to exempt, remove one from, take from one, relieve one of; **einem Geld —en**, to gain money from one. II. *n.* (*aux.* **h.**) to wane; to decrease; to sink, to be lowered; to fail; to shorten; **die Preise sind im —en**, prices are going down; **der Wein nimmt ab**, the wine deteriorates; **der Mond nimmt ab**, the moon is waning; **es nimmt mit ihm sichtbar ab**, he is going downhill rapidly; **sich abnehmen lassen**, to have one's photograph taken (*coll.*); **—ende Reihe**, diminishing series. **—er**, *m.* (**—ers**, *pl.* **—er**) buyer, purchaser, customer.

Ab'neig—en, *v.* I. *a.* to turn away; to bend down; to incline, decline; to avert; to render averse. II. *r.* to turn aside from; to incline, to diverge; **sich abneigende Linien**, divergent lines. **—ung**, *f.* a turning aside; disinclination, aversion; declination; divergence; **eine (natürliche) —ung (gegen einen)**, a natural antipathy.

Ab'nieten, *v.a.* to unrivet (*T.*).

Abno'rm, *adj.* abnormal, irregular, exceptional; exorbitant.

Ab'nötigen, *v.a.*; **einem etwas —**, to force s.th. from s.o.; to extort from, elicit.

Ab'nutz—en, (*sometimes* **Abnütz—en**), *v.a.* to use; to have the usufruct of; to wear out by use. **—er**, *m.* (**—ers**) usufructuary. **—ung**, *f.* the wear and tear; wearing out; usufruct.

Abonn—eme'nt, *n.* (**—s**, *pl.* **—s**) subscription to (*journals*); **aus dem —ement treten**, to drop one's subscription. **—s=karte**, *f.* subscriber's ticket, season ticket. **—en't**, *m.* (**—en'ten**, *pl.* **—en'ten**) subscriber. **—en'tin**, *f.* (*pl.* **—en'=tinnen**) lady subscriber. **—ie'ren**, *v.a.* & *r.* to subscribe to (**auf eine S.**).

Ab'ordn—en, *v.a.* to delegate, depute; to countermand. **—er**, *m.* constituent, voter. **—ung**, *f.* delegation, deputation; committee.

Ab'orgeln, *v.a.* to play off on the (*barrel-*) organ.

Ab'ort, *m.* (**—es**) remote, retired place; (*water-*) closet, W.C., privy.

Abortie'ren, *v.n.* (*aux.* **h.**) to have an abortion, to abort, to miscarry.

Abo'rtus, *m.* abortion, miscarriage.

Ab'pacht—en, *v.a.* to farm; to rent a farm. **—er** (*or* **Ab'pächter**), *m.* (**—ers**, *pl.* **Abpächter**) farmer, lessee of a farm.

Ab'packen, *v.a.* to take off (*the packages*); to unload, to discharge.

Ab'passen, *v.a.* to measure, to proportion, to square; to make to fit; to watch for; to time well *or* ill.

Ab'peinigen, *v.a.*; **einem etwas —**, to extort something from one by torment.

Ab'peitschen, *v.a.* to whip soundly; to whip off.

Ab'pellen, *v.a.* to peel off (*potatoes; coll.*).

Ab'pelzen, *v.a.* to beat (*skins*); to thrash.

Ab'pfählen, *v.a.* to pale, enclose with palings.

Ab'pfänden, *v.a.* to seize by law, distrain.

Ab'pfarren, *v.a.* to separate from one parish and attach to another.

Ab'pfeifen, *ir.v.a.* to whistle (*a tune*).

Ab'pflöcken, *v.a.* to mark with pegs; to unpeg and take down from the lines (*linen*).

Ab'pflücken, *v.a.* to pluck off, gather; to pluck.

Ab'pflügen, *v.a.* to plough off.

Ab'picken, *v.a.* to peck off.

Ab'placken, Abplagen, *v.a.*; **einem etwas —**, to extort from; to worry one out of; **sich —**, to tire oneself out, worry oneself to death.

Ab'platt—en, *v.a.* to flatten. **—ung**, *f.* flattening; **die —ung der Erde**, the oblateness of the earth at the poles.

Ab'plätten, *v.a.* to smooth.

Ab'plätzen, *v.a.* to blaze (*trees*); to loosen by blasting, to cause to burst.

Ab'pochen, *v.a.* to knock off; to beat.

Ab'prägen, *v.a.* to stamp, to coin; to stamp a copy.

Ab'prall—en, *v.n.* (*aux.* **f.**) to rebound. **—ung**, *f.* recoil, rebound. *Comp.* **—ungs=winkel**, *m.* angle of reflection.

Ab'prellen, *v.a.* to make rebound.

Ab'pressen, *v.a.* to press sufficiently; to press off; **einem etwas —**, to extort s.th. from s.o.

Ab'prossen, *v.a.* to bite off the buds (*Hunt.*).

Ab'protzen, *v.a.* to unlimber (a gun); **protzt ab!** action!

Ab'prozessieren, *v.a.*; **einem etwas —**, to get s.th. from s.o. by a lawsuit.

Ab'prügeln, *v.a.* to beat soundly; to cudgel.

Ab'pulen, *v.a.* to gnaw off (*bones; coll.*).

Ab'putzen, *v.a.* to cleanse, to clean, to polish; to snuff (*a candle*); to rub down (*a horse*); to plaster, to roughcast (*a wall*); to scrape (*cables*); **einen wacker —**, to reprimand one smartly (*vulg.*); **sich die Zähne —**, to clean one's teeth.

Ab'quälen, *v.a.* to torment; **einem etwas —**, to torment one out of a thing; **sich —**, to exert oneself, to toil hard; to worry oneself.

Ab'querlen, *v.a.* to beat up, to mill, to froth.

Ab'quetschen, *v.a.* to crush, squeeze off.

Ab'quicken, *v.a.* to refine with mercury (*metals*); to cool after melting.

Ab'rackern, *v.r.* to toil hard (*coll.*).

Ab'raff—en, *v.a.* to snatch away; to tie up in sheaves. **—t**, *m.* & *n.* (**—es**) corn grist purloined from the mill, *or* by the miller (*fam.*).

A'braham, *m.*; **in —s Schoß sitzen**, to be in Abraham's bosom, to enjoy ease and prosperity. *Comp.* **—s=baum**, *m.* Abraham's balm, chaste-tree (*see* **Keuschbaum**).

Ab'rahmen, *v.a.* to take off the cream, to skim; to take off the frame; **abgerahmte Milch**, skimmed milk, skim-milk.

Ab'rainen, *v.a.* to separate fields by ridges, *or* landmarks on which grass is suffered to grow; to balk off.

Ab'rändeln, Abränden, *v.a.* to take off the margin *or* edge; to clip (*money*).

Ab'ranken, *v.a.* to prune (*a vine*); **sich —,** to stray away; **die Zweige ranken sich ab,** the boughs are straying from the trellis.

Ab'rasen, *v.a.* to browse; to cut the grass.

Ab'rasen, *v.a. usually r.* to cease raging; **der Sturm hat sich abgerast,** the storm has ceased raging, the storm is over.

Ab'rat—en, *ir.v.a.* to dissuade from, advise against; **er rät mir von meinem Vorhaben ab,** he dissuades me from my purpose; **einem seine Gedanken —en,** to guess *or* divine one's thoughts. **—ung,** *f.* dissuasion.

Ab'rauch—en, *v.n.* (*aux.* **s.**) to evaporate, to exhale. *Comp.* **—schale,** *f.* evaporating dish.

Ab'räuchern, *v.a.* to smoke thoroughly.

Ab'raufen, *v.a.* to pull off, to tear off; **sich —,** to come to blows, to fight with all one's might, to scuffle.

Ab'raum, *m.* (**—s**) rubbish; clearing away (*of wood*); chips, loppings of wood; shelf (*Min.*).

Ab'räum—en, *v.a.* to clear, to remove; **den Tisch —en,** to clear away (*the tea things, etc.*). **—ung,** *f.* removal, clearance; forest clearing.

Ab'raupen, *v.a.* to clear of caterpillars.

Ab'rechen, *v.a.* to rake off.

Ab'rechn—en, *v.a. & n.* to settle accounts; to deduct, subtract; to make allowance for; **sein Vorurteil abgerechnet ist er &c.,** making allowance for his prejudice he is, etc.; **einige Stellen abgerechnet,** with the exception of a few passages. **—ung,** *f.* settlement (*of accounts*); deduction; discount; **auf —ung,** on account; **—ung halten,** to balance accounts. *Comp.* **—ungs=tag,** *m.* settling-day, day of liquidation, audit day.

Ab'recht—e, *f.* wrong side (of cloth). **—en,** *v.a.* to dress the wrong side of cloth. **—s,** *adv.* on (*or*) to the wrong side; wrong side outwards, *see* **Verkehrt.**

Ab'rede, *f.* (*pl.* **—n**) agreement; denial; **—treffen** *or* (*obs.*) **nehmen,** to concert together, stipulate, agree, make an appointment; **ich bin es** (*genit.*) **nicht in —,** I do not deny it; *now usually:* **in — stellen,** to dispute, to deny; **ich stelle das nicht in —,** I do not deny it; **das ist wider die —,** that is against our agreement.

Ab'reden, *v.* I. *a.*; **eine S. —,** to agree upon, to appoint, concert a th.; **einem —,** to dissuade one from; **abgeredetermaßen,** according to arrangement; **eine abgeredete Sache,** a settled affair; **ich will dabei weder zureden noch —,** I will say nothing either way. II. *r.* to fatigue oneself by talking; to talk one's fill.

Ab'regnen, *v.* I. *a.* to beat off by raining. II. *r. & n. imper.* to cease raining; **es hat sich abgeregnet,** it has ceased raining.

Ab'reib—en, *ir.v.a.* to rub, to rub off; to grind (*colours*), to wear by friction; **reiben Sie mich tüchtig ab,** rub me down well!; **sich —en,** to chafe; **die Schuhe —en,** to scrape *or* wipe one's shoes. **—ung,** *f.* rubbing down; friction (*Med.*).

Ab'reichen, *v.a.* to reach down; to reach; to grasp.

Ab'reise, *f.* departure.

Ab'reisen, *v.n.* (*aux.* **s.**) to set out, to start, to depart; **—en nach** (*dat.*), to set out for, leave for.

Ab'reiß—en, *ir.v.* I. *n.* (*aux.* **s.**) to break off; to tear; **abgerissene Sätze,** disconnected phrases; **meine Geduld reißt ab,** I lose all patience. II. *a.* to tear, break, pull, wrench off; to pull down; to wear out; to come to an end (*coll.*); to draw a plan of; to sketch; to force (*a lock*); **das reißt ja gar nicht ab,** there is no end of it (*coll.*); **er sieht sehr abgerissen aus,** he looks very much out at elbows. **—er,** *m.* one who tears off; sketcher; tracing-machine. **—ung,** *f.* avulsion; sudden break (*Mus.*). *Comp.* **—kalender,** *m.* sheet calendar, calendar in slips.

Ab'reiten, *ir.v.* I. *n.* (*aux.* **s.**) to ride away; to ride along *or* past (*a line of troops*). II. *a.* to break (*a horse*); to wear by riding; to override; to lose by riding (*as a shoe*); to make the horse cast a shoe.

Ab'rennen, *ir.v.* I. *a.* to knock off in running; **einem etwas —,** to get a thing from one by running; **einen —,** to tire a p. by walking too fast. II. *n.* (*aux.* **s.**) to run away. III. *r.* to fatigue oneself by running.

Ab'richt—en, *v.a.* to adjust, to measure exactly; to level; to regulate; to train, to teach tricks, to break in (*an animal*); **ein Schiff —en,** to fit a ship for sea; **ein gut abgerichteter Hund,** a dog well in hand. **—er,** *m.* a trainer; one who levels, *etc.* **—ung,** *f.* the act of training; training, breaking in, drill. *Comp.* **—hammer,** *m.* straightening hammer. **—peitsche,** *f.* schooling whip (*Vet.*). **—stab, —stock,** *m.* straightening anvil. **—wagen,** *m.* break, brake.

Ab'riegeln, *v.a.* to bolt the door; **sich —,** to bolt one's door.

Ab'rieseln, *v.n.* (*aux.* **s.**) to flow down gently; to drizzle down; to trickle down.

Ab'rind—en, *v.a.* to bark, peel, strip off the rind; to take off the crust. **—ig,** *adj.* having a gaping rind *or* crust; without bark *or* crust.

Ab'ringen, *ir.v.a.* to gain by wrestling; to twist off; **einem etwas —,** to wrest s.th. from s.o., to wring (*concessions, a confession, etc.*); **sich —,** to wrestle to exhaustion; **sich im Todeskampfe —,** to wrestle, struggle with death; to writhe with agony; **sich** (*dat.*) **die Haut von den Händen —,** to wring one's hands in despair.

Ab'rinnen, *ir.v.n.* (*aux.* **s.**) to run off, flow down.

Ab'riß, *m.* (**—(ss)es,** *pl.* **—(ss)e**) hasty sketch; plan; draught; abstract, summary; outlines, first sketch.

Ab'ritt, *m.* (**—es,** *pl.* **—e**) departure on horseback, the riding away, the start.

Ab'rohren, *v.a.* to clear of reeds, to remove the reeds from (*a pond, lake*).

Ab'rollen, *v.* I. *a.* to roll away, off, down; to transport goods from the railway-station to the town; to unroll; to unfold; to mangle; **ein Tau —,** to pay out cable. II. *n.* (*aux.* **s.** & **h.**) to roll, run down; to finish mangling.

Ab'rosten, *v.n.* (*aux.* **s.**) to rust off.

Ab'rücken, *v.n.* to move off, displace, remove; **die Zeilen —,** to begin with a new line.

Ab'rudern, *v.n.* (*aux.* **s.**) to row off; **sich —,** to tire oneself by rowing.

Ab'ruf, *m.* (**—s**) recall; calling away; proclamation. **—bar,** *adj.* that can be called away; within call.

Ab'ruf—en, *ir. v. a.* to call away *or* off; to recall; **einen —en lassen,** to have a p. called away from his work, to send for one. **—ung,** *f.* proclamation; recall. *Comp.* **—ungs=schreiben,** *n.* letter of recall. **—ungs=schuß,** *m.* signal of recall.

Ab'rüffeln, *v.a.* to reprimand severely (*coll.*).

Ab'rühren, *v.a.* to beat up, to stir; **Eier —,** to beat up eggs.

Ab'ründen, Abrunden, *v.a.* to round off, make round; to round (*periods in writing*).

Ab'rupfen, *v.a.* to pluck off.

Ab'rüst—en, *v.a.* to take down a scaffolding; to disarm; to demobilize (*troops, an army*). **—ung,** *f.* reduction of the army, disarmament; **allgemeine —ung,** universal disarmament.

Ab'rutschen, *v.n.* (*aux.* **s.**) to slip off, to glide down; to sneak off, to leave (*by train*) (*coll.*); to die (*coll. & vulg.*).

Ab'rütteln, *v.a.* to shake off.

Ab'säbeln, *v.a.* to cut off with a sword, sabre off; to cut off clumsily (*bread, meat, as if with a sword*).

Ab'sacken, *v.* I. *a.* to unload; to divide into

sacks. II. *n.* (*aux.* h.) to drop down with the stream *or* tide (*Naut.*).

Ab'sage, *f.* countermanding, counter-order; disowning; renunciation; refusal (*of an invitation*); defiance, challenge, renunciation of friendship (*obs.*).

Ab'sag—en, *v.* I. *a.* to countermand, to retract; to refuse; **eine Einladung —en,** to recall an invitation; **einen Besuch —en lassen,** to send word that one is unable to call at the appointed time; **ich ließ ihm die heutige Stunde —en,** I sent him word not to come to his lesson today; **falls Sie mir nicht —en,** unless I hear from you to the contrary; **einem die Freundschaft —en,** to break with a man; **ein abgesagter Feind,** a declared enemy; a sworn enemy, an open foe. II. *n.* (*aux.* h.) to renounce. **—ung,** *f. see* **Absage.**

Ab'sägen, *v.a.* to saw off.

Ab'sahnen, *v.a.* to skim off the cream.

Ab'satteln, *v.* I. *a.* to unsaddle (*a horse*); to unseat, unhorse (*a rider*). II. *n.* (*aux.* h.) to dismount.

Ab'satz, *m.* (**—es,** *pl.* **Absätze**) pause, stop, intermission; pause in music; stanza (*in song*); break in an inclined plane; sale, market, vent; period, break (*Typ.*); stanza; deposit (*Chem.*); heel (*of a shoe*); ledge; knot, joint (*Bot.*); landing place (*on a staircase*); shelf (*of a mountain*); paragraph; contrast; terrace (*of a vineyard*); **ein Glas ohne — austrinken,** to empty a glass at one draught; **lesen Sie bis zum nächsten —,** read as far as the next paragraph; **in Absätzen,** at intervals, intermittently, by fits and starts; **der — der zweiten Treppe,** the second floor landing. *Comp.* **—gebiet,** *n.* market (*for the sale of goods*). **—kanal,** *m.* channel (*Comm.*). **—leder,** *n.* heel piece (*of a shoe*). **—pflöcke,** *pl.* heel-pegs. **—quelle,** *f.* market (*Comm.*). **—weise,** *adv.* intermittently, by intervals.

Ab'sätzig, *adj.* having breaks or stops; intermissive, interrupted; faulty (*of a stratum*); inferior (*of wool*).

Ab'saugen, *ir.v.a.* to suck off; to weaken by sucking; to suck dry.

Ab'säugen, *v.a.* to suckle; to wean; to inarch, to graft by approach (*Hort.*).

Ab'schab—en, *v.a.* to scrape off, to rub off; to wear out *or* threadbare; to scrape, to grave (*a ship's bottom*); **schab ab!** get away! (*fam.*). **abgeschabt,** *p.p. & adj.* shabby, threadbare. **—sel,** *n.* (**—s**) parings, shavings, shreds.

Ab'schach, *n.* (*now* **Ab'zugsschach**), check by discovery (*a move by which a piece is unmasked which unexpectedly menaces the hostile king*).

Ab'schachern, *v.a.;* (**einem etwas**) to bargain from, get by higgling.

Ab'schaff—en, *v.a.* to abolish, repeal, abrogate, annul; to do away with; to dismiss, discharge, disband; to remove, supersede; to give up keeping; to suppress (*an office*). **—ung,** *f.* doing away with, discharging; giving up; abrogation (*of a law*); abolition (*of slavery, etc.*); **—ung von Mißbräuchen,** reformation of abuses. *Comp.* **—bar,** *adj.* abolishable, removable; abatable (*Law*). **—barkeit,** *f.* removability, possibility of abolishing.

Ab'scha(c)keln, *v.a.* to fleet *or* shift, to ease (*a tackle*).

Ab'schäkern, *v.a.;* **einem etwas —,** to get s.th. from a p. by playing tricks, trick a p. out of a th.

Ab'schäl—en, *v.a.* to peel, to pare; to shell; to blanch; to bark; to excorticate; to cut off the crust; **sich —en,** to peel off. *Comp.* **—schaufel,** *f.* turf-spade, turf-cutter.

Ab'schärfen, *v.a.* to blunt; to sharpen off; to chamfer; to pare off.

Ab'scharr—en, *v.a.* to scrape; to scratch off. **—icht, —sel,** *n.* scrapings.

Ab'schatt—en, *v.a.* to shadow out; to sketch; to shade (*a drawing*); to adumbrate. **—ung,** *f.* sketch, outline; silhouette.

Ab'schätz—en, *v.a.* to estimate, value; to appraise, tax; to depreciate. **—er,** *m.* appraiser. **—ig,** *adj.* contemptible (= **geringschätzig**). **—ung,** *f.* valuation.

Ab'schauern, *v.a.* to partition off.

Ab'schauern, *v.r.* to cease raining.

Ab'schaufeln, *v.a.* to shovel off.

Ab'schaum, *m.* (**—s**) scum, dross, refuse, dregs, **— der Gesellschaft,** dregs of society.

Ab'schäumen, *v.a.* to scum, to skim.

Ab'scheeren, *see* **Abscheren.**

Ab'scheid—en, *ir.v.* I. *a.* to separate; to seclude, divide off; to portion (*children, i.e.* to give children their portion and to exclude them from all future claims, *Law*); to refine (*metals*). II. **—en,** *n.* (*aux.* f.) to depart; **von der Welt—en,** to depart this life, to breathe one's last; **die Abgeschiedenen,** the departed. III. **—en,** *subst.n.* (**—ens**) death, decease; parting; separation. **—er,** *m.* a refiner. **—ung,** *f.* parting, separating; death.

Ab'scheren (Ab'scheeren), *ir.v.a.* to shear, to shave off, to cut off; to separate by a partition.

Ab'scheu, *m.* (**—s**) aversion, abhorrence; abomination; loathing, disgust; object of aversion; **ich habe (einen) — vor ihm,** I loathe the very sight of him. **—lich,** (*pron.* **abscheu'lich**) *adj.* abominable, detestable; horrible; loathsome; *& adv.* **das war recht —lich von Ihnen,** that was really very bad of you. **—lichkeit,** *f.* abominableness; abomination; atrocity.

Ab'scheuern, *v.a.* to scour off; clear away.

Ab'schichten, *v.a.* to divide into rows; to portion, pay off (*Law*).

Ab'schicken, *v.a.* to send, to send off; to depute.

Ab'schieben, *ir.v.* I. *a.* to shove off; **etwas von sich —,** to back out of a th., to exculpate oneself; **er will es von sich — und mir zuschieben,** he wants to clear himself and throw the blame on me; **einen —,** to knock down more pins than another (*at skittles*); to get away, to withdraw (*vulg.*); **schieb ab!** get away! (*vulg.*). II. *n.* (*aux.* h.) to shed the milk teeth.

Ab'schied, *m.* (**—(e)s,** *pl.* **—e**) discharge, dismissal; departure; leave; adieu, good-bye, farewell, parting; certificate; recess (*Law*); **— nehmen,** to bid farewell, to take leave; **hinter der Thür — nehmen,** to take French leave; **einem den — geben,** to dismiss, discharge a person; **einem Offizier den — geben,** to cashier an officer; **um seinen — einkommen,** to send in one's resignation; **der — des Gerichts ist dahin ausgefallen,** the sentence of the court was. *Comp.* **—s=auftritt,** *m.* farewell appearance, farewell performance. **—s=geschenk,** *n.* parting-gift. **—s=gesuch,** *n.* resignation; sending in of one's papers (*Mil.*). **—s=rede,** *f.* valedictory address. **—s=trunk,** *m.* parting-cup. **—s=zeugnis,** *n.* testimonial on leaving; leaving certificate.

Ab'schiefern, *v.a. & r.* to peel off in flakes.

Ab'schienen, *v.a.* to put in splints; to take off splints; to rim (*a wheel*); to measure out (*a mine*); to take off the rails (*Railw.*).

Ab'schießen, *ir.v.* I. *a.* to shoot off (*a leg, etc.*); to fire off, discharge; to shoot down, hit; to out-shoot; to shoot (*an arrow*). II. *n.* (*aux.* h.) to cease shooting; (*aux.* f.) to slide, shoot down; to fade, to rush away, to dart off; **den Vogel —,** to win the prize, to do the best, to carry away the bell.

Ab'schiffen, *v.* I. *a.* to ship. II. *n.* (*aux.* f.) to set sail.

Ab'schilder—n, *v.a.* to paint, depict (*obs. & poet.*), **—ung,** *f.* description, picture (*obs.*).

Ab'schinden, *ir. v.* I. *a.* to skin. II. *r.* to exert o.s. to the utmost; to fag o.s. to death.

Ab'schirren, *v.a.* to unharness.
Ab'schlachten, *v.a.* to slaughter, to kill (*animals for food*).
Ab'schlag, *m.* (—(e)s, *pl.* Abschläge) what is beaten *or* hewn off, fragments; rebound; diminution; fall in price; contrast; repulse; refusal, outlet, vent; **es ist ein großer —,** it differs widely; **auf —,** in part payment; on account; **das Brot ist in — gekommen,** bread is down; **mit — verkaufen,** to sell at a reduced price.
Ab'schlag—en, *ir.v.* I. *a.* to beat off; to strike; to cast (*a medal, etc.*); to refuse, reject; to repulse, repel; to dam off; **einem den Kopf —en,** to strike off a man's head; **einen Pferdeschweif —en,** to dock a horse's tail; **ein Zelt —en,** to strike a tent; **eine Brücke —en,** to break up a bridge; **eine Bettstelle —en,** to take down a bedstead; **die Segel —en,** to unreef the sails; **einen Angriff —,** to repel an attack; **den Dritten —,** a German running game; **einen Stoß —en,** to parry a thrust; **einem etwas rund —en,** to give one a flat refusal; **Sie dürfen es mir nicht —en,** I will take no refusal; **Wasser —en,** to make water. II. *n.* (*aux.* **s.**) to abate, decline, fall off; to fly back, to rebound; **die Kuh schlägt ab,** the cow gives less milk; **die Kälte schlägt ab,** the cold abates. *Comp.* **—s=anleihe,** *f.* money lent to be paid back by instalments. **—s=zahlung,** *f.* part-payment, payment on account, instalment.
Ab'schläg—ig, *adj.* containing a refusal; negative; brittle; **—ige Antwort,** *f.* refusal. **—lich,** *adj.* in part payment, on account.
Ab'schlämmen (Ab'schlammen), *v.a.* to clear of mud.
Ab'schlängeln, *v.r.* to meander, wind away; to leave quietly, to slink away (*coll.*).
Ab'schleichen, *ir.v.* I. *a.* (**einem etwas**) to get by sneaking. II. *v.n.* & *r.* to slink away.
[1]**Ab'schleif—en,** *ir.v.* I. *a.* to grind off; to wear away; to polish; to whet, sharpen. II. *r.* to improve one's manners. **—er,** *m.* polisher. **—sel,** *n.* grindings, shreds; cutler's dust.
[2]**Ab'schleifen,** *v.a.* to carry away on a sledge; to wear out (*clothes, etc.*) by dragging.
Ab'schleimen, *v.a.* to rid of slime; to clean fish.
Ab'schleißen, *v.a.* to wear out.
Ab'schlendern, *v.n.* (*aux* **s.**) to saunter off.
Ab'schlenkern, *v.a.* to shake off.
Ab'schleudern, *v.* I. *a.* to throw off with a sling; to shake off. II. *n.* (*aux.* **s.**) to fly off.
Abschlichten, *v.a.* to smooth, polish off (*with a plane, file, etc.*).
Ab'schließ—en, *ir.v.* I. *a.* to separate by locking up; to lock off, up; to close, settle (*a bargain, etc.*); to unlock, unchain, unfetter (*prisoners, etc.; rare*); to seclude; to wind up, to balance (*accounts, etc.*); **einen Vertrag —en,** to sign, close an agreement; **sich —en,** to seclude oneself; **abgeschlossen leben,** to live in seclusion. II. *n.* (*aux.* **h.**) **—en über eine S.** to decide upon a th. **—end,** *p.* & *adj.* definitive, final. **—lich,** *adj.* & *adv.* positive, final, definitive. **—ung,** *f.* locking, making up; seclusion; settling (*of accounts, etc.*).
Ab'schlüpfen, *v.n.* (*aux.* **s.**) to slip off; to slide down.
Ab'schlürfen, *v.a.* to sip off.
Ab'schluß, *m.* (—sses, *pl.* Abschlüsse) closing; close, conclusion; winding up; settlement. *Comp.* **—note,** *f.* note of sale; contract. **—protokoll,** *n.* recess, minutes. **—prüfung,** *f.* leaving examination (*at the end of a six years' course at a* Realschule, Progymnasium, *or* Realprogymnasium). **—rechnung,** *f.* balance of account, final account. **—zettel,** *m.* broker's contract, broker's note.
Ab'schmack, *m.* (—es) bad taste (*of wine, etc.*).

Ab'schmatzen, *v.a.* to kiss heartily, to smother with kisses (*fam.*).
Ab'schmausen, *v.* I. *a.* to eat up (*greedily*). II. *n.* (*aux.* **h.**) to have done feasting.
Ab'schmecken, *v.* I. *a.* to know by tasting. II. *n.* (*aux.* **h.**) to have a bad taste.
Ab'schmeckig, *adj.* ill-favoured, unsavoury.
Ab'schmeicheln, *v.a.* (**einem etwas**) to obtain by flattery, coax out of.
Ab'schmeißen, *ir.v.a.* (*vulg.*) *see* **Abwerfen.**
Ab'schmelz—en, I., *ir.v.n.* (*aux.* **s.**) to melt off, away, *or* down. II. *reg. v.a.* to separate by melting; to clarify; to melt off. *Comp.* **—=draht,** *m.* fusible wire.
Ab'schmieren, *v.* I. *a.* to grease; to transcribe negligently; to pirate; to thrash (*vulg.*). II. *n.* (*aux.* **h.**) to give off grease, to stain.
Ab'schmutzen, *v.n.* (*aux.* **h.**) to soil, to allow the dirt to come off; to blot (*Typ.*).
Ab'schnallen, *v.a.* to unbuckle.
Ab'schnappen, *v.* I. *n.* (*aux.* **s.**) to snap; to stop suddenly. II. *a.* to snap off; to leave suddenly (*coll.*); to lock, to bolt.
Ab'schneid—en, *ir.v.* I. *a.* to cut off; to clip; to crop, poll; to deprive of; to settle (*accounts by tallies*); to cut out (*a paper pattern*); **die Zufuhr —en,** to cut off the supplies; **einem den Weg —en,** to stop a man's passage, communication; **einem das Wort —en,** to stop one short; **einem die Ehre —en,** to injure one's reputation; **einem die Kehle —en,** to cut a person's throat. II. *n.* (*aux.* **h.**) to form a contrast, to differ. **—ung,** *f.* cutting off; recision; nipping; amputation.
Ab'schneien, *v.r.imp.;* **es hat sich abgeschneit,** it has ceased snowing.
Ab'schnellen, *v.* I. *a.* to jerk off. II. *n.* (*aux.* **s.**) to fly off with a jerk.
Ab'schnippen, *v.a.* to clip, snip off; to trim (*the beard*).
Ab'schnipfeln, *v.a.* to cut off small pieces (*coll.*).
Ab'schnitt, *m.* (—es, *pl.* —e) cut; segment; section; paragraph; division; cæsura; epoch; period; musical section; a pattern (*cut out*); entrenchment, trench, retreat; balance paid in addition. *Comp.* **—s=linie,** *f.* cutting line (*Typ.*); line of section (*Math.*). **—s=winkel,** *m.* angle of a segment. **—s=zeichen,** *n.* section (§).
Ab'schnitzel (Abschnipfel), *n.* (—s, *pl.* —) snippings, clippings, shavings.
Ab'schnitzeln, *v.a.* to cut into chips, chip, whittle away.
Ab'schnüren, to unlace; to detach by tying; to measure out, lay out, separate with the line.
Ab'schnurren, *v.* I. *a.* to obtain by begging. II. *n.* (*aux.* **s.**) to rattle, whirr off; slink away (*coll.*)
Ab'schöpfen, *v.a.* to scoop off, to skim, to scum.
Ab'schoß, (*with short* **o**) *m.* emigration tax; legacy tax; offshoot.
Ab'schrägen, *v.a.* to plane off; to slope, slant; to bevel.
Ab'schrammen, *v.n.* to scratch off, to scar; to slip off *or* away, to bolt (*coll.*); to die (*coll.*).
Ab'schrapen (*dial.* **Ab'schrappen**), *v.a.* to scrape off.
Ab'schrauben, *v.a.* to unscrew, to screw off.
Ab'schrecken, *v.a.* to frighten, scare away; **einen von . . . —,** to deter one from . . . by fear; to discourage; to sprinkle hot things with a liquid; **er läßt sich leicht —,** he is easily intimidated; **abgeschrecktes Wasser,** lukewarm water. **—d,** *p.* & *adj.* serving as a warning; horrible, forbidding; **ein —des Beispiel,** a warning (*against*).
Ab'schreib—en, *ir.v.a.* to write out, transcribe, copy; to wear out by writing; to countermand; to put off; to deduct; to carry to one's credit. **—er,** *m.* (—ers, *pl.* —er) copier, copyist; plagiarist. **—erei',** *f.* plagiarism. **—ung,** *f.*

copying, transcribing; transcription. *Comp.* —**e=gebühr**, *f.* copying fee.

Ab'schreien, *ir.v.* I. *a.* to cry, proclaim; **einem etwas** —, to get a thing from one by crying. II. *r.* to fatigue oneself by screaming; **sich die Kehle** —, to scream oneself hoarse.

Ab'schreiten, *ir.v.* I. *a.* to measure by steps, to pace; to pass along, to walk past. II. *n.* (*aux.* **s.**) to step aside, to stalk away; to swerve; to digress.

Ab'schrift, *f.* (*pl.* —**en**) copy, transcript; **eine** — **nehmen**, to take a copy; **eine beglaubigte** —, an attested copy. —**lich**, *adj. & adv.* as a copy, copied out.

Ab'schröpfen, *v.a.* to cut off with a sickle; to cup, to weaken by cupping; to strip, to rob (*rare*).

Ab'schroten, *v.a.* to roll down; to saw off; to grind coarsely; to divert (*a water-course*).

Ab'schuppen, *v.* I. *a.* to scale. II. *r.* to scale off; to chap. III. *subst.n.* desquamation.

Ab'schürfen, *v.* I. *a.* to scrape off; to take off the scurf (*of or from a wound*). II. *r.* **sich die Haut** —, to tear one's skin, to scratch one's skin.

Ab'schuß, *m.* (—(ss)es, *pl.* **Abschüsse**) rushing down, fall (of water); slope, descent.

Ab'schüssig, *adj.* declivitous, steep. —**keit**, *f.* declivity, steepness.

Ab'schütteln, *v.a.* to shake off; to shake violently.

Ab'schütt—en, *v.a.* to pour off; to throw, pour out (*corn, etc., from a sack*). —**sel**, *n.* (—**sels**) wind-falls, wind-fallen fruit (*rare*).

Ab'schützen, *v.a.* to stop by a flood-gate; to let off; to drain (*ponds, etc.*); to shut off (*steam, etc.*); to stop (*an engine*).

Ab'schwäch—en, *v.* I. *a.* to weaken; to lessen, to diminish; to attenuate, to soften down. II. *r.* to diminish, to decrease, to fall off. —**ung**, *f.* weakening, softening; decrease, diminution.

Ab'schwänzeln, *v.a.* (**einem etwas**) to get by coaxing (*vulg.*).

Ab'schwären, *ir.v.n.* (*aux.* **s.**) to fall off by ulceration; (*aux.* **h.**) to cease festering; **es ist mir ein Nagel abgeschworen**, one of my nails has festered and come off.

Ab'schwärmen, *v.* I. *n.* (*aux.* **h.**) to swarm for the last time (*of bees*); (*aux.* **s.**) to fly off (*in swarms*). II. *r.* to fatigue oneself by revelry.

Ab'schwarten, *v.a.* to peel off the sward, skin *or* rind (*of ham, etc.*); to square (*timber*).

Ab'schwärzen, *v.* I. *n.* (*aux.* **h.**) to lose black colour. II. *a.* to blacken, smut.

Ab'schwatzen, *v.a.*; **einem etwas** —, to talk one out of s.th.

Ab'schwefeln, *v.a.* to clear from sulphur; to impregnate with sulphur.

Ab'schweif, *m.* (—(e)s) digression, deviation.

Ab'schweif—en, *v.* I. *n.* (*aux.* **s.**) to digress; to deviate. II. *a.* to wash; to rinse; to scallop. —**end**, *p. & adj.* digressive. —**ung**, *f.* digression, deviation; **ohne** —**ung**, directly, to the point.

Ab'schweißen, *v.a.* to smooth *or* fashion iron by heating and hammering it.

Ab'schwemmen, *v.a.* to cause to swim off, to float; to wash away; to purify by washing *or* rinsing; to flush; **Pferde** —, to ride horses into the water.

Ab'schwenken, *v.* I. *a.* to cleanse by rinsing. II. *r.* to turn aside; to wheel off *or* aside; **rechts (links) abgeschwenkt!** right (left) wheel!

Ab'schwindeln, *v.a.*; **einem etwas** —, to get a thing from a person by swindling.

Ab'schwingen, *ir. v.* I. *a.* to shake off; to clean by shaking; to winnow. II. *r.* to swing oneself down.

Ab'schwirren, *v.a.* to go off (*or* away) with a shrill sound; to get away, to bolt (off) (*coll.*)

Ab'schwitzen, *v.* I. *a.* to remove by sweating (*a disease, superabundant flesh, etc.*). II. *r.* to weaken oneself by sweating; to exhaust o.s.

Ab'schwören, *ir.v.a.* to deny by oath; to abjure; **einem etwas** —, to deprive one of something by an oath.

Ab'schwung, *m.* (*pl.* **Abschwünge**), act of leaping down, somersault, somerset (*Gymn.*).

Ab'segeln, *v.* I. *n.* (*aux.* **s.**) to set sail, sail away; **vom Winde** —, to bear off. II. *a.* **sie segelten die Masten ab**, the masts were carried away *or* sprung.

Ab'sehbar, I. *adj. & adv.* visible; within sight; conceivable; **in absehbarer Zeit**, within a measurable (*or* reasonable) space of time.

Ab'sehen, I. *ir.v.a. & n.* to look away from; to perceive; to watch an opportunity; to see to the end of; to conceive; to aim at; **davon abgesehen**, apart from this consideration; **einem etwas an den Augen** —, to anticipate one's wishes, divine one's thoughts; **es ist schwer abzusehen**, it is hard to foresee *or* to imagine; **da ist gar kein Ende abzusehen**, there is no prospect of an end; **das war auf mich abgesehen**, that was a hit at me; **ist es darauf abgesehen?** is that the object?; **einem etwas** —, to learn s.th. by looking at *or* on s.o.; **das hast du von deinem Nebenmann abgesehen**, you have copied that from your neighbour. II. *subst.n.* a looking away from; design, purpose; the sight upon the barrel of a gun *or* upon an optical instrument.

Ab'seide, *f.* floss-silk, refuse of silk.

Ab'seif—en, *v.a.* to wash out soap; to clean with soap. —**ung**, *f.* washing out the soap; cleaning with soap.

Ab'seigern, *v.a.* to measure depth (*with a plummet*); to separate silver from copper.

Ab'seihen, *v.a.* to strain, filter.

Ab'sein, I. *ir.v.n.* (*aux.* **s.**) to be off, away; to be broken off; to be abolished (*Law*); **wir sind noch weit ab**, we are still at a great distance; **ich bin ganz ab**, I am thoroughly tired, I am quite exhausted, I am out of breath, I am knocked up (*coll.*). II. *subst.n.* the being off, the absence; the state of exhaustion.

[1]**Ab'seite**, *f.* vault, wing (*of an edifice*); aisle (*of a church*).

[2]**Ab'seite**, *f.* off side, part farther off, reverse (*of a coin*).

Absei'ten, *prep.* from any one's side, on the part of (*obs. Law*); — **meiner**, for my part, as for me (*obs.*).

Ab'seits, I. *adv.* aside, apart, aloof; — **vom Wege**, away from the road; — **von der großen Heerstraße**, away from the beaten track. II. *prep.* — **der Straße**, off from the street.

Ab'send—en, *ir.v.a.* to send away, to despatch; to depute; to detach (*Mil.*). —**er**, *m.* sender, consignor; shipper; despatcher. —**ung**, *f.* sending off, despatching, despatch; conveyance, shipping.

Ab'sengen, *v.a.* to singe off, to burn slightly.

Ab'senk—en, *v.a.* to sink (*a shaft*); to layer *or* set plants. —**er**, *m.* layer, slip.

Absentie'ren, *v.r.* to absent oneself.

Ab'setz—bar, *adj.* removable; deposable; salable.

Ab'setz—en, *v.* I. *a.* to set down; to deposit; to remove (*from office*); to depose (*a king*); to cashier (*an officer*); to dismiss, to discard, to discharge; to bring forth (*clandestinely*); to wean; to pick out with contrasting colours; to set up in type; to break off; to throw off, to unhorse; **Waaren** —**en**, to dispose of goods, to sell goods; **setzt ab!** ground arms! II. *n.* (*aux.* **h.**) to put off (*from shore*); to settle (*of liquids*); to contrast (*of colours*); to discontinue, to stop, to pause, to begin a new line; to be faulty (*Min.*); to finish composing (*Typ.*); to take the glass from the mouth, to stop drinking; **das Gestein setzt ab**, the rock cracks, breaks; **er trank die ganze Flasche aus, ohne einmal abzusetzen**, he emptied the whole bottle at one draught. III. *imp.* to result in. IV. *subst. n.* fault (*in a stratum*); deposition; subsidence (*of waters*); hesitation (*in speaking, etc.*). **—ung**, *f.* deposition (*of sediment*); removal (*from office*); composition (*Mus. & Typ.*); **—ung des Oxyds**, oxidisation. *Comp.* **—tisch**, *m.* side-table.

Ab'sicht, *f.* (*pl.* **—en**) view; design, purpose, end, aim; **ohne —**, unintentionally; **in der besten —**, with the best intention; **es ist der — gemäß**, it answers the purpose; it is in accordance with the intention; **in — auf**, (*with acc.*) with a view to, in reference to, as to. *Comp.* **—s=los**, I. *adj.* unpremeditated. II. *adv.* unintentionally.

Ab'sichtlich & **Absicht'lich**, *adj.* & *adv.* intentional, deliberate, premeditate, purposely. **—keit**, *f.* (*twofold accentuation as in* **absicht=lich**) premeditation, preconcerted design.

Ab'sickern, *v.n.* (*aux.* **s.**) to trickle down.

Ab'sieben, *v.a.* to sift off.

Ab'sieden, *ir.v.a.* to seethe, to boil; **einen Trank —**, to make a decoction, to decoct.

Ab'singen, *ir.v.* I. *a.* to sing off; to chant; to recite. II. *r.* to exhaust oneself with singing. III. *n.* (*aux.* **h.**) to sing to the end, finish singing.

Ab'sitzen, *ir.v.* I. *n.* (*aux.* **h.**) to sit away from; (*aux.* **s.**) to dismount. II. *a.*; **eine Schuld —**, to pay a debt by remaining in prison.

Ab'solden, *v.a.* to pay the full salary; to pay off.

Absolu't, *adj.* & *adv.* absolute; unconditional.

Absolutio'n, *f.* absolution; **einem die — ertei=len**, to give the absolution to some one.

Absoluti'smus, *m.* absolutism.

Absolvie'ren, *v.a.* to absolve, to acquit; to finish, complete (*one's studies at college*).

Ab'sonder—bar, *adj.* separable. **—lich**, *adj.* separable; separated, apart.

Abson'derlich, *adj.* peculiar, singular, odd, bizarre; *adv.* principally, chiefly, expressly. **—keit**, *f.* singularity, peculiarity, oddness, oddity.

Ab'sonder—n, *v.a.* to separate, to divide; to detach; to secrete (*Med.*); to abstract (*ideas*); **sich —n**, to separate, seclude oneself; **ein Kind —n**, to portion off a child (*Law*). **—ung**, *f.* separation, division; seclusion; sequestration; abstraction; secretion (*Med.*); individualisation; jointed structure (*of rocks*); isolation (*Phys.*). *Comp.* **—ungs=vermögen**, *n.* power of abstraction; power of secreting (*Med.*). **—ungs=zeichen**, *n.* sign of separation.

Ab'sonnig, *adj.* out of the sun, shady (*rare*).

Absorbie'rend, *p.* & *adj.* absorbing; **—e Mittel**, absorbents.

Ab'sorgen, *v.r.* to wear away with anxiety.

Absorptio'n, *f* (*pl.* **—en**) absorption; electrification.

Ab'spalten, *v.* I. *a.* to split off. II. *n.* (*aux.* **s.**) to get separated by splitting.

[1]**Ab'spannen**, *v.a.* to unbend; to slacken (*a drum, etc.*); to relax; to unyoke; to unharness; to exhaust utterly; **den Hahn —**, to uncock (*a pistol*); **ein Gezelt —**, to strike a tent. **abgespannt**, *p.p.* & *adj.* tired out; seedy.

[2]**Ab'spannen**, *v.a.* to entice (*away*), to seduce, to cause to be disaffected (*obs.*).

Ab'spänstig, **Ab'spenstig**, *adj.* alienated, disloyal; **— machen**, to seduce from allegiance; **einem eine Person — machen**, to alienate the affections of a p. from; **— werden**, to desert; to become disaffected.

Ab'sparen, *v.a.* to spare from; **ich will es mir am Munde —**, I will pinch myself (in food) for it.

Ab'speisen, *v.* I. *n.* (*aux.* **h.**) to finish a meal. II. *a.* to clear (*a plate, a tree, etc.*) by eating; to feed, entertain; **einen mit leeren Worten —**, to put one off with fair words; **einen kurz —**, to cut one short.

Ab'spenstig, *see* **Abspänstig**.

Ab'sperr—en, *v.a.* to barricade; to exclude; to separate, to lock off; to isolate. **—ung**, *f.* act of barring; separation; isolation; solitary confinement; exclusion. **—ungs=system**, *n.* prohibitive system; system of solitary confinement. *Comp.* **—hahn**, *m.* stop-cock (*of the boiler*).

Ab'spiegel—n, *v.* I. *a.* to reflect (*as from a mirror*). II. *r.* to be mirrored *or* reflected. **—ung**, *f.* reflection.

Ab'spielen, *v.a.* to play (*off*) a tune; to wear out with playing; to pay off by playing (*cards, etc.*); **vom Blatte —**, to play at sight (*Mus.*).

Ab'spinnen, *ir.v.* I. *a.* to spin off; to pay a debt by spinning. II. *n.* (*aux.* **h.**) to finish spinning.

Ab'spitzen, *v.a.* to take off the point, to blunt; to cut, make (*a pen*), to point (*ends of the hair*).

Ab'splittern, *v.* I. *n.* (*aux.* **s.**) to splinter, to come off in splinters. II. *a.* to splinter off. III. *r.* to exfoliate.

Ab'spotten, *v.a.*; **einen —**, to ridicule a p. (*obs.*); **einem etwas —**, to get a th. by deriding a p.

Ab'sprache, *f.* (*usually* **Abrede**) agreement, convention.

Ab'sprech—en, *ir.v.* I. *a.* (**einem etwas**) to give a sentence against, to pronounce sentence of deprivation; to give up (*Med.*); to gainsay, deny, refuse; **einem alle Hoffnung —en**, to take away all hope from one; **einem das Leben —en**, to condemn s.o. to death; **die Ärzte haben ihm das Leben abgesprochen**, the doctors have given him up; **eine Sache —en**, to talk over a matter; **Talent kann man ihm nicht —en**, there is no denying that he has talent; **ich spreche es Ihnen nicht ab**, I do not dispute it with you. II. *n.* (*aux.* **h.**) to decide; to decide hastily; to dogmatize on; **über (eine S.) —en**, to give a decided *or* unfavourable opinion upon. **—end**, *p.* & *adj.* dogmatical, unfavourable; **—end urteilen über einen** *or* **eine Sache**, to pronounce an adverse criticism on s.o. or s.th. **—erisch**, *adj.* decisive, magisterial; dogmatic; unfavourable.

Ab'sprengen, *v.* I. *a.* to cause to fly off; to burst, to blow up with gunpowder; to chip; to cut off from the bulk of the army, to drive off from the herd. II. *n.* (*aux.* **s.**) to gallop off.

Ab'springen, *ir.v.* I. *n.* (*aux.* **s.**) to leap off *or* down; to jump off; to snap off; to chip off; to crack off (*as paint*); to gape, warp; to rebound; to desert, change (*one's party*); to shift (*from one subject to another*); to shuffle, to prevaricate; **von einem Versprechen —**, to retract a promise. II. *r.* to fatigue o.s. by jumping, to tire o.s. with leaping.

Ab'spritzen, *v.* I. *a.* to squirt off. II. *n.* (*aux.* **s.**) to spirt back; to set out for a trip (*stud. sl.*).

Ab'sproß, *m.* (**—(ss)es**, *pl.* **—(ss)en**) (*rare, see* **Absprößling**); result.

Ab'spross—en, *v.n.* (*usually* **Ab'stammen**) (*aux.* **s.**) to be descended from.

Ab'sprößling, *m.* (**—s**, *pl.* **—e**) offspring, descendant.

Ab'spruch, *m.* (*pl.* **Absprüche**) a sentence, verdict, final decision; **— des Lebens**, sentence of death, doom.

Ab'sprung, *m.* (**—(e)s**, *pl.* **Absprünge**) a leap; leaping off; double (*of a hare*); snapping (*of a spring, etc.*); digression; falling off; contrast; disparity; renunciation of a claim. *Comp.* **—s=winkel**, *m.* angle of reflection.

Ab'spulen, *v.a.* to wind off from the reel, to unreel, to unspool.

Ab'spül—en, *v.a.* to wash; to rinse; to wash off, up. **—icht**, *n.* hogwash; dishwater. **—ung**, *f.* (*act of*) rinsing, washing, washing up (*of tea things, etc.*); ablution.

Ab'stählen, *v.a.* to steel; to harden (**gegen**, against).

Ab'stamm—en, *v.n.* (*aux.* **s.**) to descend, to be derived from, to come of; to derive, to be derived from (*Gram.*); derivation, etymology; **aus der Stadt Hannover —end**, a native of the town of Hanover. **—ung**, *f.* descent, parentage; extraction, source; birth, blood; **von guter —ung**, of (*good*) family; **von edler —ung**, of noble birth. *Comp.* **—ungs=lehre**, *f.* theory of descent, origin of species; theory of derivation. **—ungs=tafel**, *f.* pedigree, genealogical table.

Ab'stampfen, *v.a.* to stamp off; to wear out by stamping; to pound thoroughly.

Ab'stand, *m.* (—es, *pl.* **Abstände**) distance; interval, space; difference, disparity; **greller —**, contrast; renunciation, renouncement, cession, abandonment; **von einer Sache — nehmen** (*or* **thun** (*obs.*)) to desist from a th., to renounce, to give up. *Comp.* **—s=geld**, *n.* money paid to a person who desists from a claim. **—s=punkt**, *m.* apsis. **—s=winkel**, *m.* angle of elongation.

Ab'ständig, *adj.* spoiled (*by old age or too long keeping*), grown worse; dead, dried up, stale, tasteless, musty, flat.

Ab'statten, *v.a.* to pay (*in a complimentary sense*); to give, make, discharge, render; **einen Besuch —**, to pay a visit; **einen Gruß —**, to deliver a compliment; **seine Schuldigkeit —**, to pay one's debt; to pay one's respects; **Bericht —**, to report; **Zeugnis —**, to bear witness; **Dank —**, to render *or* to return thanks; **einen Besuch —**, to make a call, to pay a visit; **einem seinen Glückwunsch —**, to offer one's congratulations to s.o., to congratulate one.

Ab'staub—en, **Ab'stäub—en**, *v.a.* to wipe off the dust, to dust. **—er**, *m.* one that dusts, duster; feather-broom, dusting brush.

Ab'stech—en, *ir.v.* I. *a.* to bring down with a thrust; to stab, to pierce, to stick; to unhorse; to defeat (*in a students' duel, sl.*); to carry off the ring (*at tilting*); to slope; to escarp (*Mil.*); to mark out; to draw off (*water*); to train; to outdo; to over-trump; **Heu —en**, to pitch down *or* to unload hay; **Rasen —en**, to cut sods; **ein Schwein —en**, to stick a pig; **ein Muster —en**, to prick a pattern on paper; **eine Zeichnung —en**, to engrave a drawing; **einem Schiffe —en**, to take the wind out of another ship's sails. II. *n.* (*aux.* **s.**) to sheer off (*Naut.*); (*aux.* **h.**) to contrast; **diese Farbe sticht von der andern zu sehr ab**, this colour contrasts too strongly with the other; **sie sticht gegen dich ab**, she is a good foil to you. **—er**, *m.* little excursion, trip, ramble; digression; one that marks out; **auf der Reise machten sie einen —er von drei Meilen, um ihn zu besuchen**, on their journey they went three miles out of their way to visit him. *Comp.* **—eisen**, *n.* spud; scuffling hoe; scraper; turf-spade. **—messer**, *n.* butcher's knife. **—pflug**, *m.* breast-plough.

Ab'steck—en, *v.a.* to unpin, to unpeg; to undo, to unfasten (*hair*); to mark out; **ein Lager —en**, to mark out, peg out, stake off a camp; **ein Kalb —en**, to wean a calf. *Comp.* **—eisen**, *n.* iron pole, picket. **—kette**, *f.* surveyor's chain. **—leine**, *f. or* **—schnur**, *f.* measuring line, marking cord.

Ab'stehen, *ir.v.* I. *n.* (*aux.* **h.**) to stand off from; to stand out, stick out; (*aux.* **s.**) to grow flat (*as beer*); to decay, fade, die away; **— von**, to desist from, relinquish, give up; **einem** *or* **von einem —**, to desert, withdraw from, leave one unassisted (*rare*). II. *a.* to concede, to yield, to relinquish, give up, resign (*rare*). **—d**, *p. & adj.* distant; expanding (*Bot.*); **—de Ohren**, standing out ears, sticking out ears.

Ab'stehlen, *ir.v.a.* to steal away; to learn by stealth; **einem etwas —**, to steal s.th. from s.o.

Ab'steifen, *v.* I. *a.* to stiffen; to prop, to underprop. II. *n.* (*aux.* **s.**) to grow stiff.

Ab'steig—en, *ir.v.n.* (*aux.* **s.**) to descend, to alight; to dismount; to put up (*at an inn, etc.*). **—end**, *p. & adj.* descending; **—ender Rhythmus**, descending rhythm, trochaic *or* dactylic rhythm (*see* **Abgleitend**). **—ung**, *f.* descending; alighting; descent; descension (*Astr.*). *Comp.* **—e=quartier**, *n.* resting place, place where to put up, night quarters, temporary lodging; billet (*Mil.*).

Ab'stell—en, *v.a.* to put away; to put down (*a burden, etc.*); to abolish; to remedy, redress; to remove (*nuisances, etc.*); to mix with yeast; to season, flavour (*beer*); to stop, throw out of gear. *Comp.* **—hahn**, *m.* regulator tap.

Ab'stemmen, *v.a.* to chisel off.

Ab'stempeln, *v.a.* to stamp.

Ab'sterben, I. *ir.v.n.* (*aux.* **s.**) to die away *or* out, to wither, to perish; to fade away; to become paralysed, benumbed; to mortify; **meine Eltern sind mir sehr früh abgestorben**, I lost my parents when very young; **der Welt —**, to withdraw from the world; **allen Vergnügungen abgestorben sein**, to be dead to all pleasures. II. *subst.n.* death, mortification, atrophy; decay; extinction.

Ab'stich, *m.* a copy, pattern pricked off; what is dug *or* cut off; contrast.

Ab'stieg, *m.* descent, climb down.

Ab'stimm—en, *v.* I. *a.* to tune; **gut abgestimmte Glocken**, well tuned bells; to lower the pitch; to outvote (= **überstimmen**; *dial.*). II. *n.* (*aux.* **h.**) to give one's vote, to record one's vote, to vote; **einem —en**, to disagree, dissent from (*dial.*); **über etwas —en lassen** to put a th. to the vote; **geheim durch Stimmzettel —en**, to vote by ballot. **—ig**, *adj.* discordant, dissonant; disagreeing (*in opinion*). **—ung**, *f.* act of voting; suffrage; division, show of hands; dissonance; **der Antrag wurde zur —ung gebracht**, the motion was put to the vote; **durch —ung gefaßter Beschluß**, resolution; grace (*Univ.*); **sich der —ung enthalten**, to abstain from voting; **geheime —ung**, voting by ballot; **namentliche —ung**, poll, polling; **—ung durch Hammelsprung**, division.

Ab'stocken, *v.a.* to hive a new swarm of bees.

Ab'stöpseln, *v.a.* to uncork, to unstop.

Ab'stoß—en, *ir. v.* I. *a.* to knock off, to thrust off; to scrape, plane; to rub off; to strike short; to play staccato; to repulse; to break; **es wird ihm das Herz —en**, it will break his heart; **sich die Hörner —en**, to sow one's wild oats; **eine Schuld —en**, to pay off a debt; **die Bienen —en**, to kill the bees and take their honey; **Zähne —en**, to shed one's teeth. II. *n.* (*aux.* **h.**) to push off, to shear off, to get clear of the shore, to set sail. **—end**, *adj.* repulsive, repugnant; **sich abstoßende (Naturen)**, antipathetic (natures); repellant. **—ung**, *f.* act of repelling; repulsion. *Comp.* **—zeichen**, & **—ungs=zeichen**, *n.* staccato sign (*Mus.*).

Ab'strafen, *v.a.* to punish, chastise (*thoroughly*).

Abstrahie'ren, *v.a.* to abstract.

Ab'strahl, *m.* (—s, *pl.* —en) a reflected ray; splendour.

Ab'strahl—en, *v.* I. *a.* to reflect. II. *n.* (*aux.* **h.**) to be reflected. **—ung**, *f.* reflection. **—ungs=winkel**, *m.* angle of reflection.

Abstra'kt, *adj. & adv.* abstract; **—er Begriff**, abstract idea, abstraction.

Ab'strängen, *v.a.* to unharness (*horses*).

Ab'strapazieren, *v.* I. *a.* (**eine Sache**) to wear

out. II. *r.* to fag o.s.; to toil hard; to work o.s. to death.
Ab'ſtreben, *v.n.* (*aux.* **h.**) to strive to get loose *or* away (*from the centre*); **die —de Kraft,** *f.* (**Abſtrebekraft**) centrifugal force.
Ab'ſtreich—en, *ir. v.* I. *a.* to wipe, strike off; to scrape off; to strop (*a razor*); to beat (*a field*) for game. II. *n.* (*aux.* **ſ.**) to sneak away; to quit the nest. *Comp.* **—holz,** *n.* straight edge.
Ab'ſtreifen, *v.* I. *a.* to strip off; to skin; to slip, draw off; to lay aside; to do away with. II. *n.* (*aux.* **ſ.**) to wander, to roam; to digress; to glance off.
Ab'ſtreiten, *ir.v.a.* to dispute; to deny; **einem etwas —,** to obtain something from one by dispute; **das laſſe ich mir nicht —,** I won't be argued out of that.
Ab'ſtrich, *m.* (**—s,** *pl.* **—e**) act of skimming; reduction, diminution; that which is taken off, skimmings; litharge.
Ab'ſtricken, *v.a.* to knit off (*the stitches on a needle*); to loose, untie.
Ab'ſtriegeln, *v.a.* to curry, rub down (*a horse*).
Ab'ſtrömen, *v.* I. *a.* to float *or* wash away down a stream. II. *n.* (*aux.* **ſ.**) to flow off rapidly; to drift away; (*fig.*) to disperse, to become scattered; **ab= und zu=ſtrömen,** to ebb and flow.
Abſtru's, *adj. & adv.* abstruse.
Ab'ſtückeln, *v.a.* to break down in small pieces.
Ab'ſtudieren, *v.r.* to tire o.s. out by studying.
Ab'ſtuf—en, *v.* I. *a.* to break off (*of ore*); to separate by gradations, graduate; to shade off. II. *n.* (*aux.* **ſ.**) to be shaded, to be graduated. **—ung,** *f.* gradation, graduation; shade.
Ab'ſtumpf—en, *v.a.* to blunt; to dull; to stupefy; **ein abgeſtumpfter Kegel,** a truncated cone. **—end,** *p. & adj.* obtundent, blunting, dulling. **—ung,** *f.* blunting; dulling.
Ab'ſtürmen, *v.* I. *n.* to rush off in the greatest hurry. II. *v.r.* to have done storming, to calm down, to abate.
Ab'ſturz, *m.* (**—es,** *pl.* **Abſtürze**) rapid fall; precipice.
Ab'ſtürzen, *v.* I. *a.* to precipitate; **ſich den Hals —,** to break one's neck by falling. II. *n.* (*aux.* **ſ.**) to fall down headlong.
Ab'ſtutzen, *v.a.* to lop; to poll; to dock, cut; to shear (*cloth*). **abgeſtutzt,** *p.p. & adj.* truncate.
Ab'ſtützen, *v.a.* to prop, shore up (*a ship*).
Ab'ſuchen, *v.a.* to search all over; to search and take; to pick off, from.
Ab'ſud, *m.* (**—(e)s,** *pl.* **—e**) decoction; extract.
Ab'ſudeln, *v.a.* to transcribe negligently, to copy (*a picture*) daubingly.
Ab'ſumpfen, *v.a.* to drain (*marshes*).
Abſu'rd, *adj.* absurd; inconsistent, irrational. **—itä't,** *m.* (*pl.* **—itä'ten**) absurdity.
Abt, *m.* (**—es,** *pl.* **Äbte**) abbot; **den — reiten laſſen,** to be merry without constraint; **ein weltlicher —,** a lay abbot; **infulierter —,** mitred abbot; **Würde eines —es,** abbotship, abbacy; **der Kaiſer und der —,** (*well known poem by Bürger, adaptation of*) King John and the Abbot of Canterbury. **—ei',** *f.* (*pl.* **—ei'en**) abbey (*building*); abbacy (*office*). **—ei'lich,** *adj.* abbatial.
Ab'tafeln, *v.n.* (*aux.* **h.**) to finish dining.
Ab'täfeln, *v.a.* to wainscot.
Ab'takeln, *v.a.* to unrig, dismantle; **ein abgetakeltes Frauenzimmer,** a faded beauty (*coll.*).
Ab'tanzen, *v.* I. *a.* (*e.g.* **einen Walzer**) to dance. II. *n.* to dance off *or* down; to get off (*coll.*).
Ab'tauen, *v.a. & n.* (*aux.* **ſ.**) to thaw off.
Ab'taumeln, *v.n.* (*aux.* **ſ.**) to reel, stagger away.
Ab'tauſchen, *v.a.* to exchange; to barter.
Ab'teil, *m.* share; appanage; compartment (*of a railway carriage*).
Ab'teilen, *v.a.* to divide, to share; to classify; to portion off; to partition off; to divide into degrees; to separate into lots; **Kinder —,** to pay off children, to give children their due share (*Law*).
Ab'teilung (*less good* **Abtei'lung**), *f.* division; separation (*from*); division (*of an army*); set (*of a form in school*); classification, section, division (*of a subject, etc.*); compartment (*of a railway carriage*). *Comp.* **—ungs=zeichen,** *n.* hyphen; mark of separation.
Ab'teuf—en, *v.a.*; **einen Schaft —en,** to sink *or* deepen a shaft *or* pit. **—er,** *m.* pitman.
Ab'thun, *ir.v.a.* to take, put off; to lay aside; to abolish; to settle; to despatch; to kill, to execute; **ſich ſeines Glaubens —,** to free o.s. from one's faith; to renounce; (= **ſich abgewöhnen**) to give up, **er hat ſich den Trunk abgethan,** he has given up drinking (*poet.*); **die Hand von einem —,** to abandon one; **etwas geſchwind —,** to huddle up a thing; **eine abgethane Sache,** a settled affair.
Äb't—in (*pl.* **—innen**), **Äbtiſ'ſin** (*pl.* **—nen**), *f.* abbess. **—lich,** *adj.* as an abbot, belonging to an abbot, abbatial.
Ab'toben, *v.* I. *n.* to rage *or* cease raging. II. *a.* **einem etwas —,** to bully one out of a thing.
Ab'tön—en, *v.a.* to shade. **—ung,** *f.* shading; shade.
Ab'töt—en, *v.a.* to kill, deaden; to mortify (*inclinations, etc.*). **—ung,** *f.* mortification.
Ab'trab, *m.* (**—(e)s**) detachment (*of cavalry*).
Ab'traben, *v.n.* (*aux.* **ſ.**) to trot off.
Ab'trag, *m.* (**—(e)s,** *pl.* **Abträge**) payment; compensation; what is carried off; damage; **einem — thun,** to injure one (*rare*).
Ab'trag—en, *ir.v.a.* to carry away; to pull down; to level; to clear (*the table*); to pay (*debts*); to sketch, to brace; to wear out (*clothes*). **—ung,** *f.* carrying off, demolition; dismantling (*of a fort*); levelling (*of a hill, etc.*); payment, liquidation.
Ab'trauern, *v.* I. *n.* (*aux.* **h.**) to put off mourning. II. *r.* to pine away with grief.
Ab'träufeln, *v.n.* (*aux.* **ſ.**) to trickle down.
Ab'treib—en, *ir.v.* I. *a.* to drive off; to repel, repulse; to overdrive, to jade (*horses*); **ein abgetriebener Gaul,** a jade; **ein Kind —en,** to procure abortion; **einen von einem Gute —en,** to dispossess one of his estate; **—ende Mittel** (**Abtreibe=Mittel**), abortive medicines. II. *n.* (*aux.* **ſ.**) to drift off. **—er,** *m.* refiner of metals. **—ung,** *f.* (**der Leibesfrucht**) miscarriage procured by an unlawful operation.
Ab'trenn—bar, —lich, *adj.* separable.
Ab'trenn—en, *v.a.* to separate; to disunite; to unrip. **—ung,** *f.* separation; ripping off.
Ab'treppen, *v.a.* to build like a staircase (*a wall, etc.*).
Ab'tret—en, *ir.v.* I. *a.* to tread off; to form by treading; to wear out by walking; to pace out; to relinquish, resign; to transfer; to abandon; **er trat ſeinem Neffen die Regierung ab,** he resigned in favour of his nephew; **einem etwas —en,** to yield up a right to one; **einen noch nicht fälligen Wechſel —en,** to discount a bill. II. *n.* (*aux.* **ſ.**) to retire; to withdraw; to make one's exit; to quit, to secede from; **ſie hieß ihn —en,** she ordered him to retire; **tritt ab,** exit; **treten ab,** exeunt (*stage direction*); **tretet ab** *or* **abgetreten!** break ranks!; **von Amte —en,** to resign an office; **bei einem —en,** to alight, stop at a p.'s house; **ſich —en** *or* **ſich die Füße —en,** to scrape one's boots (*before entering a house*), to wipe the dirt off one's shoes. **—er,** *m.* ceder, resigner, transferrer; scraper. **—ung,** *f.* treading off *or* out; cession; abdication, withdrawal; surrender; exit; **derjenige, an den die —ung geſchieht,** assignee. **—ungs=ſchrift,** *f.*, *or* **ungs=urkunde,** *f.* deed of cession, instrument of conveyance, assignment.

Ab'trieb, *m.* (—**es**) driving off *or* away; driving the cattle down fr. the Alps (*dial.*); cutting down, felling (*For.*); refusal (*Law*); **ich habe ihm den — versprochen,** I promised to give him the refusal of it. *Comp.* —**s=recht,** right of refusal, prior right of purchase.
Ab'triefen, *ir.v.n.* (*aux.* **s.**) to trickle down, drip.
Ab'trift, *f.* right of pasturage, common; drift, leeway (*Naut.*).
Ab'trinken, *ir.v.a.* to drink off; to drink a small quantity (*from a glass*); to sip off.
Ab'tritt, *m.* (—**s,** *pl.* —**e**) withdrawal; abdication, renunciation; cession, abandonment; exit; death; alighting; privy, water-closet (*vulg.*); step (*before a door*); grass trodden down by deer, abatures, foiling; **seinen — nehmen,** to withdraw, to retire (*obs.*).
Ab'trocknen, *v.* I. *a.* to wipe dry; to dry; to drain. II. *n.* (*aux.* **s.**) to dry up, wither away.
Ab'trollen, *v.n. & r.* (*aux.* **s.**) to slip away, to pack off.
Ab'trommeln, *v.* I. *a.* to drum off; to publish by beat of drum; to drum; **ein Stück auf dem Klavier —,** to hammer (*or* bang) away a piece of music on the piano. II. *n.* (*with* **h.**) to cease drumming; to beat the tattoo.
Ab'tropf—en, Ab'tröpfeln, *v.n.* (*aux.* **s.**) to trickle down; —**en lassen,** to drain; **Schmalz rc. auf den Braten am Spieße —en lassen,** to baste roast meat. *Comp.* —**bank,** *f.* plate-drainer.
Ab'trotzen, *v.a.* (**einem etwas**) to bully out of.
Ab'trumpfen, *v.a.* to trump; **einem eine Karte —,** to take a man's card by a higher trump; **einen —,** to snap one up, snub one; to give a p. a set-down or rebuff.
Ab'trünnig, *adj.* faithless, recreant; disloyal, rebellious; — **werden,** to revolt, to desert; to turn apostate; — **machen,** to seduce, draw off (*from a cause, etc.*); **von der Religion —,** apostate; **der —e,** deserter, recreant, renegade, apostate; turncoat. —**keit,** *f.* disloyalty; desertion; apostasy.
Ab'tummeln, *v.* I. *a.* to fatigue (*a horse*) by a hard ride. II. *r.* to fatigue oneself.
Ab'tünchen, *v.a.* to whitewash all over.
Ab'tupfen, *v.a.* to dry up (*spots, etc.*).
Ab'urteilen, *v.a. & n.* (*aux.* **h.**) to decide finally; to decide against; **einem etwas —,** to dispossess a p. (*by a judgment*).
Ab'verdienen, *v.a.* to earn by service; **eine Schuld —,** to work off a debt.
Ab'verlangen, *v.a.*; **einem etwas —,** to ask s.o. for s.th., to demand s.th. from s.o.
Ab'vermieten, *v.a.*; **ein Zimmer an einen Aftermieter —,** to sublet a room.
Ab'vieren, *v.a.* to square; to polish; to veer (*Naut.*).
Ab'visieren, *v.a.* to measure (*standing timber, etc.*); to sight out, to survey, to gauge.
Ab'wachen, *v.* I. *a.* to watch for. II. *r.* to weary oneself by watching or sitting up.
Ab'wackeln, *v.* I. *a.* to shake off; to cudgel. II. *n.* (*aux.* **s.**) to waddle away, off.
Ab'wachsen, *ir.v.n.* (*aux.* **s.**) to decrease; to take another direction in growing.
Ab'wäg—en, *reg. & ir.v.a.* to weigh; to weigh out; to compute elevations; to level; **gegen einander —en,** to counterbalance. —**ung,** *f.* weighing; levelling. *Comp.* —**e=kunst,** *f.* art of levelling.
Ab'walken, *v.a.* to mill (*cloth*); to thrash (*vulg.*).
Ab'wallen, *v.n.* (*aux.* **s.**) to float down in ringlets (*of curls*).
Ab'walzen, *v.* I. *a.* to make even, smooth with a roller. II. *r.* to tire oneself waltzing. III. *n.* (*aux.* **s.**) to go off waltzing, to go away (*coll.*).
Ab'wälzen, *v.a.* to roll off; **die Beschuldigung von sich —,** to shift the blame from one's own shoulders, to exculpate oneself by throwing the blame upon others.
Ab'wamsen, *v.a.* to beat soundly, to administer a thorough drubbing (*vulg.*).
Ab'wandel—bar, I. *adj.* declinable, capable of being inflected, capable of inflection. II. *v.a.* to conjugate, to decline. —**ung,** *f.* (*usually* **Abwandlung**) inflection; declension, conjugation.
Ab'wandeln, *v.* I. *a.* to inflect; to decline (*nouns*), to conjugate (*verbs*). II. *r.* to be inflected; **dies Zeitwort wandelt sich regelmäßig ab,** this verb is conjugated regularly, is weak.
Ab'wandern, *v.n.* (*aux.* **s.**) to depart, to wander away.
Ab'wanken, *v.n.* (*aux.* **s.**) to totter away; to decline from the right way.
Ab'wart—en, *v.a.* to wait for; to await; to watch for; to tend; to attend to; **er kann nichts —en,** he is always in a hurry; **ich will Sie da —en,** I will wait for you there; **seine Zeit —en,** to bide one's time; **den Regen —en,** to wait till it has stopped raining, till the rain is over. —**ung,** *f.* waiting for; attendance on, nursing.
Ab'wärts, *prep. & adv.* downward; downwards; aside; — **des Flusses,** down the stream; — **fahren,** to descend (*a river*); to go down stream; **mit ihm geht 's —,** he is on the decline (*health*), his affairs are going from bad to worse (*business*).
Ab'wasch—en, *ir.v.a.* to wash; to wash off; to clear by washing. —**ung,** *f.* washing off *or* away; ablution; lotion. *Comp.* —**becken,** *n.* a wash-hand-basin.
Ab'wässern, *v.a.* to water, to soak; to drain; **eine Schwelle —,** to slope a threshold so as to let the rain fall off.
Ab'weben, *ir.v.a.* to finish weaving; to work off by weaving.
Ab'wechsel—n, *v.* I. *a.* to exchange; to vary; to modulate (*the voice*). II. *n.* (*aux.* **h.**) to do alternately, to alternate; to intermit (*as a fever*). —**nd,** I. *p. & adj.* changeable; intermittent; alternate. II. *adv.* by turns, alternately. —**ung,** *f.* exchange; change; vicissitude; alternation; modulation (*Mus.*); variety; **zur —ung,** for a change. —**ungsweise,** *adv.* alternately.
Ab'weg, *m.* (—(**e**)**s,** *pl.* —**e**) by-way, by-path; wrong way. —**e suchen,** to try shifts; **auf —e führen,** to misguide, to seduce; **auf —e geraten,** to go astray. —**s,** *adv.* out of the way, aside. —**sam,** *adj. & adv.* out of the way; devious.
Ab'wehen, *v.* I. *a.* to blow off, away. II. *n.* (*aux.* **s.**) to blow over; to blow from.
Ab'wehr, *f.* fence; defence; repulse; guard, parry. *Comp.* —**mittel,** *n.* means of defence, preventive.
Ab'wehr—en, *v.a.* to fence, ward off; to avert; **er läßt sich nicht —en,** he won't be kept off, won't be rebuffed. —**ung,** *f.* act of parrying, warding off; protection from.
Ab'weichen, I. *v.a.* to soften; to detach by soaking. II. *v.n.* (*aux.* **s.**) to grow soft and fall off.
Ab'weich—en, *ir.v.n.* (*aux.* **s.**) to deviate, swerve; to diverge; to digress; to depart from; to pass, elapse; to decline, deflect (*as the magnetic needle*); **von der Wahrheit —en,** to swerve from the truth; **er weicht keinen Fingerbreit ab,** he will not abate an inch, retract a word; **wir weichen sehr von einander ab,** we differ widely; **im abgewichenen Jahre,** last year (*obs.*). —**end,** *adj. & adv.* varying; irregular; oblique; devious; —**ende Sonnenuhr,** declinator, azimuth-dial. —**ung,** *f.* deviation, variation; deflection; declination; divergence; exception; softening.
Ab'weiden, *v.a.* to feed on, to graze (*a meadow*);

to feed (*a flock*); **die Alp ist abgeweidet,** the mountain pastures are grazed quite bare.

Ab'weinen, *v.* I. *a.* to expiate by tears. II. *r.* to cry one's eyes out.

Ab'weis—en, *ir.v.a.* to refuse admittance to, to reject, send away; to refuse; to repulse, beat back; to nonsuit, to dismiss (*a case; Law*); **kurz —en,** to send one about one's business; **er läßt sich nicht —en,** he will take no refusal; **einen Wechsel —en,** to protest *or* to dishonour a bill. **—ung,** *f.* refusal, rejection; disavowal; protestation, non-acceptance; non-suit. *Comp.* **—ungs=bescheid; —ungs=bescheid erhalten,** to be non-suited.

Abweißen, *v.* I. *a.* to whitewash, whiten. II. *n.* (*aux.* **h.**) to lose whiteness (*obs.*).

Ab'welken, *v.* I. *a.* to wither, to cause to shrivel. II. *n.* (*aux.* **s.**) to wither off.

Ab'wend—bar *or* **—lich,** *adj.* preventible.

Ab'wend—en, *reg. & ir. v.* I. *a.* to avert, prevent; to ward off, parry; **das wolle Gott —en,** God forbid. II. *r.* to turn away from; to desert. **—ig,** *adj.* alienated, estranged, averse; **—ig machen,** to alienate, to divert from, to seduce; **einem etwas —ig machen,** to deprive one of a thing. **—ung,** *f.* averting; parrying; ward; alienation.

Ab'werfen, *ir.v.a.* to throw, cast, fling, knock off; to yield (*a profit*); to knock down; to throw (*a horseman*); to cast, shed (*feathers, skin, etc.*); to outthrow; **Junge —,** to whelp.

Ab'wesen, *obs. subst. n., see* **Abwesenheit. —d,** *adj.* absent; **geistes—d,** absent-minded, lost in thought. **—heit,** *f.* absence; absenteeism; alibi (*Law*).

Ab'wetten, *v.a.;* **einem etwas —,** to gain s.th. from s.o. by betting.

Ab'wettern, *v.n. & r.* (*aux.* **h.**) to cease thundering and lightening.

Ab'wetzen, *v.a.* to blunt, to rub off (*the point*); to wear out by whetting; to whet.

Ab'wichsen, *v.a.* to polish with wax; to cudgel thoroughly (*vulg.*).

Ab'wickeln, *v.a.* to wind off, to unroll; to wind up (*a business*).

Ab'wiegeln, *v.a.* to pacify, to appease.

Ab'wiegen, *see* **Ab'wägen.**

Ab'wimmeln, *v.a.* to manage to get rid of s.th. *or* s.o. (*coll.*).

Ab'winden, *ir.v.a.* to unwind, untwist; to reel off; to let down by a pulley (*goods*).

Ab'winken, *v.a.* to warn off by a nod or beck, to beckon not to take any notice. (*colloq. p. part.* **abgewunken; ich habe abgewunken,** I have declined, I have said no (*coll.*).)

Ab'wirtschaften, *v.* I. *a.* to ruin by bad management, to mismanage. II. *n. & r.* to get ruined by bad management.

Ab'wisch—en, *v.* I. *a.* to wipe off, wipe; **den Staub —en,** to dust; **sich —en,** to wipe oneself clean. II. *n.* (*aux.* **s.**) to steal away (*vulg.*). **—er,** *m.* one who wipes, dusts; duster. **—ung,** *f.* wiping up *or* off. *Comp.* **—lappen,** *m.*, **—tuch,** *n.* duster, dish-cloth.

Ab'wittern, *v.* I. *a.* to scent out. II. *n.* (*aux.* **h.**) to cease thundering; (*aux.* **s.**) to decompose and fall off (*from the action of the atmosphere*).

Ab'wuchern, *v.a.* (**einem etwas**) to obtain by usury.

Ab'wurf, *m.* (—**s**, *pl.* **Abwürfe**) a throwing down, off, away; refuse; offal; produce, proceeds; last throw (*at dice*).

Ab'würf—eln, *v.a.* to cast more than another; (**einem etwas**) to win at dice. **—ig,** *adj.* inclined to kick (*of a horse*).

Ab'würgen, *v.a.* to throttle; to kill.

Ab'wüten, *v.n. & r.* (*aux.* **h.**) to cease raging.

Ab'zahl—en, *v.a.* to pay off; to discharge; **einen —en,** to pay one out. **—ung,** *f.* payment in full.

Ab'zählen, *v.a.* to count out, off; to subtract; to number, reckon; to put in a heap (*Print.*); **ich kann es mir an den Fingern —,** that I can easily conceive, my senses tell me as much.

Ab'zahnen, *v.* I. *n.* (*aux.* **h.**) to shed the milk teeth. II. *a.* to take off with the tooth-plane, to indent.

Ab'zanken, *v.a.* to obtain by quarrelling; to scold.

Ab'zapfen, *v.a.* to tap; to draw off; to bottle, to cheat; **Blut —,** to bleed.

Ab'zaubern, *v.a.* (**einem etwas**) to get by witchcraft, to charm out of.

Ab'zäumen, *v.a.* to take off the bridle.

Ab'zäunen, *v.a.* to fence in; to separate by a fence.

Ab'zehnten, *v.a.* to pay tithes; to levy tithes.

Ab'zehr—en, *v.* I. *a.* to waste, consume; **eine Schuldforderung —en,** to pay oneself by living at the debtor's expense. II. *n. & r.* (*aux.* **s.**) to waste away. **—end,** *p. & adj.* wasting, consumptive; **—ende Krankheit,** an emaciating disease; atrophy. **—ung,** *f.* emaciation; consumption.

Ab'zeichen, *n.* (—**s**, *pl.* —) mark of distinction; badge; mole; *pl.* insignia.

Ab'zeichn—en, *v.a.* to sketch, to draw; to copy a drawing; to mark off; **sich am Horizont —en,** to stand out against the horizon. **—ung,** *f.* copied drawing; sketch; plan.

Ab'zerren, *v.a.;* **einem etwas —,** to wrest a thing from one.

Ab'zetteln, *v.a.* to unwarp.

Ab'zieh—en, *ir.v.* I. *a.* to draw, pull, take off; to turn off, to divert, to dissuade; to abstract; to subtract, deduct; to distil, rectify; to drain; to clear (*soup, etc.*), to skim; to rack off (*wine, etc.*); to tap, to bottle, to decant; to blanch (*almonds*); to smooth; to whet, sharpen; to straighten; to size, adjust (*a weight*); to divert (*attention*); to boil out (*colour*); to lower (*wages*); **den Hut, die Kleider —en,** to take off one's hat, one's clothes; **die Kopfhaut —en,** to scalp; **einen Druckbogen —en,** to pull, take off a proof; **ein abgezogener Begriff,** an abstract idea; **abgezogene Wasser,** distilled waters. II. *n.* (*aux.* **s.**) to retire, retreat; to go off guard, be relieved (*Mil.*); to retire with disgrace; to leave service; **aus der Festung —en,** to evacuate (*a stronghold*); **von (der) Wache —en,** to come off guard, to be relieved; **heimlich —en,** to slink away; **sein Gönner zieht die Hand von ihm ab,** his patron withdraws his aid; **mit einer langen Nase —en,** to be baulked in one's design (*coll.*). **—end,** *p. & adj.;* **der —ende,** subtractor. **—er,** *m.* (—**ers**, *pl.* —**er**) one who draws off; abductor. **—ung,** *f.* drawing, moving off; distillation; diversion; subtraction; abstraction. *Comp.* **—blase,** *f.* alembic. **—bogen,** *m.* tympan-sheet. **—bild,** *n.* metachromotype (*Typ.*). **—eisen,** *n.* scraper; hackle (*for flax, etc.*). **—feile,** *f.* smoothing file. **—flasche,** *f.* retort. **—kolben,** *m.* alembic. **—leder,** *n.* razor-strop. **—muskel,** *m.* abductor (*Anat.*). **—pflug,** *m.* draining-plough. **—presse,** *f.* proof-press. **—stein,** *m.* hone. **—zahl,** *f.* number to be subtracted, subtrahend. **—zeug,** *n.* distilling utensils.

Ab'zielen, *v.* I. *n.* (*aux.* **h.**) **auf etwas —,** to aim at s.th., to tend to s.th. II. *a.* to strive for.

Ab'zirkeln, *v.* I. *a.* to measure *or* delineate with compasses; to define strictly. II. *n.* to be ridiculously nice *or* measured in one's behaviour.

Ab'zucht, *f.* (*pl.* **Abzüchte**) breed, race; conduit, sewer; channel (*Found.*).

Ab'zug, *m.* (—**s**, *pl.* **Abzüge**) departure, retreat; scum; proof-impression; trigger; drain, conduit; outlet; deduction; **— am Gewicht,** tare; **zum —e blasen,** to sound the retreat; **den — nehmen,** to retire; **nach — der Kosten,** expenses deducted; **ohne —,** clear. *Comp.*

—s=bogen, *m.* proof-sheet. —s=graben, *m.* drain. —s=schach, *n.* check by discovery; *see* Abschach. —s=schleuse, *f.* culvert. —s=zahl, *f.* minuend. —s=ziegel, *m.* draining tile. —s=zoll, *m.* emigration fine.

Ab'zupfen, *v.a.* to pull off.

Ab'zwacken, *v.a.* to pinch off; einem etwas —, to squeeze *or* extort something from one in a mean way, to snap away.

Ab'zwecken, *v.* I. *n.* & *a.* (etwas, auf eine S.) to aim at. II. *a.* to unpeg.

Ab'zweig—en, *v.a.* to branch off. —ung, *f.* (*act of*) lopping, pruning; (des Weges) deviation, branching off.

Ab'zwicken, *v.a.* to pinch off.

Ab'zwingen, *ir.v.a.* to obtain by force; einem etwas —, to extort a thing from a person.

Ab'zwirnen, *v.a.* to wind off thread.

Aca'cie, *see* Akazie.

Academie', *rc.*, *see* Akademie, *rc.*

Accaparie'ren, *v.a.* to engross, to forestall.

Acce'nt, *m.* (*also spelt* Akze'nt) (—s, *pl.* —e) accent; scharfer —, acute accent; tiefer —, grave accent; gedehnter —, circumflex accent; gestoßener —, acute accent; geschleifter —, circumflex accent; zweigipfliger —, fluctuating accent, intermittent accent, accent points; dynamischer —, dynamic *or* stress accent; chromatischer —, musical *or* pitch accent; exspiratorischer —, dynamic *or* stress accent; Satz—, sandhi. —u=ie'ren, *v.a.* to accentuate.

Acce'pt, *n.* (—s, *pl.* —e) acceptance (*of a bill*). —a'nt, *m.* (—anten, *pl.* —anten) accepter. —ie'ren, *v.a.* to accept, honour (*a bill of exchange*).

Accessi'st, *m.* (—en, *pl.* —en) attendant; unpaid assistant, supernumerary (*in an office*).

Acces'sit, *n.* (*pl.* —e) second best premium.

Accesso'risch, *adj.* accessory, accessorial.

Ac'cidens, *n.* (*pl.* Accide'ntien *and* Accide'nzien); accident; additional profits, occasional emoluments.

Accis'bar, *adj.* excisable.

Acci'se, excise; —e nehmen von, —e legen auf, to levy an excise on. *Comp.* —einnehmer, —bedienter, —beamter, *m.* exciseman. —frei, *adj.* free of excise duty. —zettel, *m.* permit, excise bill.

Acclimatisie'ren, *v.* I. *a.* to accustom to a climate, to acclimatise, naturalize. II. *r.*; sich leicht —, to become easily acclimatized, settled.

Accomodie'ren, *v.a.* to render damaged goods salable; sich (einer Sache, den Verhältnissen) —, to accommodate, reconcile oneself to.

Acco'rd, *m.* (—es, *pl.* —e) accord (*Mus.*); chord; compact; contract; settlement; auf —, in —, by the job, by contract; mit — einnehmen, to take by capitulation. —ie'ren, *v.* I. *n.* (*aux.* h.) to accord (*Mus.*); to be correct; —ieren über, to agree upon, to bargain; —ieren wegen, to compound for. II. *a.* to grant; to make agree. *Comp.* —arbeit, *f.* piece-work. —lohn, *m.* payment by contract.

Accredit—ie'ren, *v.a.* to open a credit account; to accredit. —i'v, *n.* (—ivs) letter of credit.

Accura't, *adj.* accurate, exact; particular; economical. —e'sse, *f.* exactness, accuracy.

A'ccusativ, *m.* (—s, *pl.* —e) accusative.

Ach! *int.* alas! ah!

Acha't, *m.* (—s, *pl.* —e) agate. —en, *adj.* of agate. *Comp.* —dattel, *f.* agatine.

A'chel, *f. see* Blutegel.

Ach'se, *f.* (*pl.* —n) axle, axletree; axis; per —, auf der —, by land-carriage; by waggon *or* car. *Comp.* —n=büchse, *f.* axle-box. —n=neigung, *f.* obliquity of the ecliptic. —n=nagel, *m.* linch-pin. —n=riegel, *m.* transom, cross-timber. —n=ring, *m.* iron-ring. —n=schraube, *f.* axle-nut.

Ach'sel, *f.* (*pl.* —n) shoulder; die Achseln zucken, to shrug the shoulders; über die — ansehen, to scorn, look down upon; auf beiden —n tragen, to favour both sides; auf die leichte — nehmen, to treat lightly; die —n hängen, to be out of sorts. *Comp.* —band, *n.* shoulder knot. —bein, *n.* upper bone of the arm. —drüse, *f.* axillary gland. —fleck, *m.*, —stück, *n.* gusset, shoulder-piece. —grube, —höhle, *f.* armpit. —hemd, *n.* sleeveless shirt. —klappe, *f.* shoulder-strap, shoulder-piece; *pl.* wings. —naht, *f.* shoulder-seam (*of a dress, etc.*). —röhre, *f. see* —bein. —rote, *f.* fiddle hung over the back of the mediæval travelling minstrel (*obs.*). —stück, *n.*, *see* —klappe. —träger, *m.* time-server; hypocrite. —troddel, *f.* epaulette. —zucken, *n.* shrug of the shoulders.

Acht, *num. adj.* (*sometimes* Achte *if the numeral stands predicatively;* es sind ihrer acht(e)) eight; — Tage, a sennight; a week; heute über — Tage, this day week; binnen — Tagen, within a week; halb —, half past seven; mit —en fahren, to drive a coach and eight; der, die, das, —e, the eighth. —el, *n.* (—els, *pl.* —el) eighth part; quaver (*Mus.*); arc of 45 degrees; octavo. —ens, *adv.* eighthly. —er, *m.* (—ers, *pl.* —er) anything consisting of eight parts; an eighth; figure eight. *Comp.* —=blätterig, *adj.* octopetalous. —eck, *n.* octagon. —eckig, *adj.* octagonal. —e=halb, seven and a half. —el=form, —el=größe, *f.* octavo size. —ender, *m.* stag having eight branches to his antlers. —er=lei, *adv.* of eight kinds. —fach, —fältig, *adj.* & *adv.* eight-fold. —flach, *n.* octahedron. —jährig, *adj.* eight years old. —klang, (*Mus.*) octave. —mal, *adj.* eight times. —riemer, *m.* an eight (*a race boat*). —seitig, *adj.* octagonal. —silbig, *adj.* octosyllabic. —spännig, *adj.* yoked with eight horses. —schildig, *adj.* having eight quarterings in the coat of arms, etc. —tägig, *adj.* weekly, for a week; for eight days. —undvierzig, *num. adj.* forty-eight; ein alter —undvierziger, a man who took part in the revolution of 1848. —wöchentlich, *adj.* every second month. —zehn, *num. adj.* eighteen. —zehnte, *num. adj.* eighteenth. —zeilig, *adj.* of eight lines; octave (*poet.*). —zig, *num. adj.* eighty; ein —ziger, an octogenarian. —zig=jährig, *m.* octogenarian. —zigste, *num. adj.* eightieth.

[1]Acht, *f.* (*no pl.*) attention, care, heed; in — nehmen, to take care of; to observe, mind; — geben auf, (*with acc.*) to mark; to pay attention to, to be careful concerning; gebt —, mark ye!; sich (*acc.*) in — nehmen, to take care, beware; ich nehme mich vor ihm in Acht, I beware of him. —bar, *adj.* respectable. —barkeit, *f.* respectability. —sam, *adj.* mindful, attentive. —samkeit, *f.* attention; heedfulness. *Comp.* —ens=wert, *see* —ungs=wert. —los, *adj.* negligent, inattentive. —losigkeit, *f.* inattention, heedlessness.

[2]Acht, *f.* ban, outlawry; — und Bann, outlawry and excommunication; in die — verfallen, to become outlawed; einen in die — erklären, to put s.o. under the ban, to proscribe one, to outlaw one. *Comp.* —brief, *m.* writ of proscription. —(s)=erklärung, *f.* outlawing.

Ächt, *see* Echt.

Ach't—en, *v. a.* & *n.* to regard, to esteem; to deem; to pay attention to; dessen ungeachtet, nevertheless, regardless of this. —ung, *f.* attention; esteem, respect, regard; hab —ung! have a care!; —ung! attention! (*Mil.*); den Gesetzen —ung verschaffen, to vindicate the law; vor einem —ung hegen, to hold one in high esteem; einem —ung einflößen, to inspire one with respect; seine —ung bezeigen, to pay one's respects; —ung geben auf (*acc.*), to pay attention to. —ung=einflößend, *adj.* imposing. —ungs=bezeugung, *f.* tribute of respect. —ungs=los, *adj.* disrespectful. —ungs=voll, *adj.* respectful. —ungs=wert, —ungs=würdig, *adj.* respectable, estimable. —ungs=widrig, *adj.* disrespectful, irreverent.

Äch't—en, *v.a.* to outlaw, proscribe; geächtet und gebannt, outlawed (*by the state*) and excommunicated (*by the church*). —er, *m.* man outlawed, outlaw. —ung, *f.* outlawing, proscription.

Ach'ter, *prep. and adv.* aft (*Naut.*).

Äch'zen, *v.n.* to groan heavily.

A'cker, *m.* (—s, *pl.* Äcker) field, arable land; soil; acre (*square measure, pl.* die Acker); ein fetter —, a rich soil; den — bauen, bestellen, to till the ground. *Comp.* —bau, *m.* agriculture. —bauer, *m.* husbandman. —bau=schule, *f.* school of agriculture. —beet, *n.* ridge (*in a field*). —bestellung, *f.* tillage. —galle, barren tract, *or* patch (*in a field*). —gaul, *m.* farm-horse. —geld, *n.* land tax; farm-expenses. —gesetz, *n.* agrarian law. —hof, *m.* farm; farm-yard; farm-house. —knecht, *m.* farm labourer. —land, *n.* arable land. —lohn, *m.* labourer's wages. —mann, *m.* husbandman. —männchen, *n.* water-wagtail. —rain, *m.* ridge between fields. —vieh, *n.* draught cattle. —walze, *f.* roller. —wirt=schaft, *f.* agriculture. —zeug, *n.* agricultural implements. *Before most botanical terms,* Acker = field, wild, *or* corn. —baldrian, *m.* great wild valerian. —ehrenpreis, *m.* chickweed. —hollunder, *m.* dwarf-elder. —grindkraut, *n.* meadow-scabious. —klee, *m.* hare's-foot clover. —klette, *f.* prickly parsnip. —minze, *f.* mountain calamint. —raute, *f.* fumitory. —senf, *m.* charlock. —spargel, *m.* pearlwort. —waldmeister, *m.* woodroof.

A'ckern, *v.a.* to till, to plough.

Act, *m. see* Akt.

Ac'te, *f. see* Akte.

Ac'tie, *f. see* Aktie.

Acti'v, *adj. see* Aktiv.

Actua'r, *m. see* Aktuar.

A'dams—feige, *f.* Egyptian fig, sycamore. —apfel, *m.* Adam's apple, thyroid cartilage.

Addie'ren, *a.* to add, to sum up.

Ade', I. *int.* farewell! II. *subst. n.* farewell, adieu.

A'debar, A'debär, *m.* stork (*dial.*).

A'del, *m.* (—s) nobility; nobleness; vom —, of noble birth; der niedere —, the gentry. —ig, adlig, *adj.* noble. —schaft, *f.* aristocracy. *Comp.* —s=brief, *m.* patent of nobility. —s=buch, *n.* peerage-book. —stand, *m.* the nobility; in den —stand erheben, to ennoble, raise to the rank of a peer *or* knight. —sucht, *f.* tufthunting, love of titles, etc. —süchtig, *adj.* tuft-hunting.

A'deln, *v.a.* to ennoble; to dignify; to give worth to.

Ade'pt, *m.* adept, one expert in alchemy (*lit.: one who has found* viz. *the panacea*).

A'der, *f.* (*pl.* —n) vein; lode; streak, grain (*in wood*); die goldene —, hemorrhoids; zur — lassen, to bleed; eine dichterische —, a poetical vein; es ist keine gute — an ihm, there is no good in him; er hat keine — von seinem Vater, he is wholly unlike his father. —ig, *see* Äderig. *Comp.* —bruch, *m.* varicocele. —gebäude, *n.* venous system. —geflecht, —gewebe, *n.* vascular plexus. —gewächs, *n.* polypus. —haut, *f.* choroid. —knoten, —kropf, *m.* varicose vein. —laß, *m.* blood-letting. —laß=eisen, *n.* lancet, phleme. —laß=kunst, *f.* phlebotomy. —laß=schnäpper, *m.* lancet. —presse, *f.* tourniquet. —rippig, *adj.* nerved (*Bot.*). —schlag, *m.* beat of the pulse. —wasser, *n.* lymph.

Ä'der—chen, *n.* (—chens, *pl.* —chen) little vein. —ig, *adj.* veined, full of veins.

Ä'dern, *v.a.* to grain, vein (*wood, etc.*).

Adieu', I. *int.* farewell. II. *subst.n.* farewell.

Adje's, *int.* (*coll.*) = Ade, Adieu.

Adju'nkt, *m.* (—en, *pl.* —en) assistant, colleague; deputy.

Adjustie'ren, *v.a.* to adjust, regulate; sich —, to adjust oneself; to dress properly.

Ad'ler, *m.* (—s, *pl.* —) eagle; junger —, eaglet; doppelter —, two-headed eagle; der weibliche —, female eagle; der — kreischt, the eagle screams. *Comp.* —ähnlich, *adj.* aquiline. —blume, *f.* columbine. —eule, *f.* eagle-owl. —fisch, *m.* sea-eagle (*Icht.*). —fittig, *m.* eagle's pinion. —geier, *m.* bald eagle. —holz, *n.* a species of agallochum, Amboyna wood. —horst, *m.* aerie, eyrie, eyry. —jüng=ling, *m.* young eagle. —kraut, *n.* female fern. —nase, *f.* aquiline nose. —orden, *m.* order of the Eagle; Ritter des schwarzen (*or* roten) Adler=ordens, Knight of the Black (*or* Red) Eagle. —stein, *m.* aetite.

Administrie'ren, *v.a.* to administer.

Admira'l, *m.* (—s, *pl.* —ale, *better than* —äle) admiral. —itä't, *f.* admiralty. —schaft machen, to sail in company. *Comp.* —itäts=gericht, *n.* Board (*or* Court) of Admiralty; Vorsitzender des —itäts=gerichts, First Lord of the Admiralty. —s=brief, *m.* sailing orders. —s=rat, *m.* admiralty. —s=schiff, *n.* flag-ship.

Adopt—ie'ren, *v.a.* to adopt. —i'v, *adj.* adoptive, adopted; (*in compounds, e.g.* —i'v=tochter, *f.* adopted daughter, *etc.*).

Adre'ss—e, *f.* (*pl.* —en) address; direction; place of residence; firm (*C. L.*); an die —e von, per —e, care of. —a't, *m.* (—a'ten, *pl.* —a'ten) person addressed; person recommended; the drawee. *Comp.* —(ß)=buch, *n.*, —(ß)=kalen=der, *m.* directory. —(ß)=bureau, *n.* registry office, enquiry office. —(ß)=zettel, *m.* label.

Adress—ie'ren, *v.a.* to address; to consign; er hat mich an Sie —iert, he has directed *or* sent me to you, recommended me to you.

Adve'nt, *m.* (—s) advent. *Comp.* —s=vogel, *m.* ember goose. —s=zeit, *f.* advent season.

Advoka't, *m.* (—en, *pl.* —en) barrister, advocate. —u'r, *f.* advocacy. *Comp.* —en=gebüh=ren, *pl.* lawyer's fees.

Advozie'ren, *v.n.* (*aux.* h.) to follow the law.

A'ero— (*trisyllabic; only used in compounds*). —dyna'mik, *f.* aerodynamics (*Physics*). —dyna'misch, *adj.* aerodynamic (*Physics*). —li'th, *m. pl.* aerolite. —nau'tik, *f.* aeronautics. —sta't, *m.* air-balloon. —sta'tik, *f.* aerostatics. —sta'tisch, *adj.* aerostatic.

Äff'—en, *v.a.* to mock, make a fool of, to ape. —erei', *f.* chaff; mimicry. —isch, *adj.* apish. —in, *f.* (*pl.* —innen) she-ape.

Aff'e, *m.* (—n, *pl.* —n) ape, monkey; crane (*Mech.*); knapsack (*soldiers' sl.*); einen —n an einem gefressen haben, to be infatuated with a person; seinem —n Zucker geben, to be extravagantly merry (*coll.*); sich einen (kleinen) —n kaufen, to get tipsy (*sl.*). *Comp.* —n=artig, *adj.* monkeyish. —n=fratze, *f.*, —n=gesicht, *n.* monkeyish grimace. —n=ge=schlecht, *n.* quadrumana. —n=jung, *adj.* very young; das —njunge Blut, the young ninny (*joc.*). —n=liebe, *f.* blind partiality (*for one's children*). —n=nase, *f.* flat nose. —n=pinscher, *m.* pug. —n=schande, *f.* very great shame, scandal (*sl.*). —n=schwanz, *m.* ape's tail; droll fellow. —n=stein, *m.* monkey bezoar. —n=weibchen, *n.* she-ape.

Affe'kt, *m.* (—s, *pl.* —e) emotion, passion, affection. —ionie'rt, *adj. see* Geneigt. *Comp.* —ions=preis, *m.* fancy-price. —los, *adj.* dispassionate. —losigkeit, *f.* apathy; calmness.

Affekt—ie'ren, *v.a.* to affect. —ie'rt, *p.p. & adj.* affected; das —ierte Wesen, affectation.

Affhol'der, Afhol'der, *m.* guelder rose.

Afficie'ren, *see* **Affizie'ren.**
Af'fig, *adj.* apish, silly, foolish.
Affiliie'rt, *adj.* affiliated.
Affizier'bar, *adj.* sensitive, irritable.
Affizie'ren, *v.a.* to affect.
Affodi'll, *m.* **Affodi'll=lilie,** *f.* daffodil.
Affrica'ta, Affrika'te, affricate (*a consonant diphthong, e. g.* **z, pf**).
Afrika'nder, *m.* Africander, inhabitant of South Africa born of white parents.
Af't'er, I. *m.* (**—s,** *pl.* **—**) buttocks; anus; residuum. II. *prep. & adj.* (*used in comp.* = after, behind; similar, approaching to; inferior; spurious, sham, mock). **—arzt,** *m.* quack. **—bier,** *n.* swipes. **—bildung,** *f.* deterioration; malformation; false culture. **—binde,** *f.* T-bandage (*Surg.*). **—blättchen,** *n.* stipula. **—bürge,** *m.* second surety. **—darm,** *m.* rectum. **—einsetzung,** *f.* entail. **—erbe,** *m.* substitute heir. **—gelehrsamkeit,** *f.* sham erudition. **—kind,** *n.* posthumous child. **—klaue,** *f.* hind-claw. **—kohlen,** *pl.* coal-dust; cinders. **—könig,** *m.* pretender (*to a crown*). **—kugel,** *f.* spheroid. **—lehn,** *n.* mesne tenure, under-fief. **—lehre,** *f.* heterodoxy. **—mahd,** *f.* second swath. **—mehl,** *n.* pollards. **—miete,** *f.* sub-letting; subtenancy. **—mieter,** *m.* undertenant. **—moose,** *pl.* sea-weeds. **—muse,** *f.* false muse, wrong ideal of poetry. **—pacht,** *f.* sub-lease; under-tenancy. **—rede,** *f.* calumny. **—sprache,** *f.* jargon; slang; calumny. **—vermieter,** *m.* sub-letter (*of houses*). **—weisheit,** *f.* sophistry, philosophism. **—welt,** *f.* posterity. **—zeit,** *f.* the future. **—zins,** *m.* compound interest.
Aga't, *m.* (**—s,** *pl.* **—e**) *see* **Acha't.**
Age'nde, *f.* (*pl.* **—n**) liturgy, ritual, office-book; duty to be done; memorandum-book, tablets.
Age'nt, *m.* (**—en,** *pl.* **—en**) agent. **—u'r,** *f.* agency.
Ägi'de, *f.* (*pl.* **—n**) ægis; shelter, protection.
Agie'ren, *v.a. & n.* (*aux.* **h.**) to act.
A'gio, *n.* agio; exchange; premium. **—ta'ge,** *f.* stock-jobbing. **—teu'r,** *m.* stock-jobber. *Comp.* **—conto,** *n.* agio-account.
A'glei, *see* **Akelei.**
Agna't, *m.* (**—en,** *pl.* **—en**) paternal relation.
Agra'ffe, *f.* brooch, clasp.
Agra'r—, (*in compounds*) agrarian.
Agra'rier, *m.* agrarian, agriculturist.
Agra'risch, *adj.* agrarian.
Agrono'misch, *adj.* dealing with farming; **—e Schrift,** treatise on farming.
A'gtstein, *m. see* **Bernstein.**
Ah, *interj.* ah; oho, pooh!
Aha', *interj.* (*denoting realisation of an expectation*) aha; there, you see.
A'hle, *f.* (*pl.* **—n**) awl, pricker, bodkin.
A'hm, *f.* ship's draught *marked on stern-post* (*Naut.*). **—en,** *v.a.* to gauge (*a cask*). **—er,** *m.* gauger. **—ing,** *f. see* **Ahm** (*Naut.*).
Ahn, *m.* (**—s, —en,** *pl.* **—en**) grandfather, ancestor; *pl.* ancestors, forefathers, primogenitors; **von vierzehn —en,** of fourteen descents, *or* with fourteen quarterings. **—e** *or* **—in,** (*rare*) grandmother, ancestress. **—lich,** *adj.* ancestral. *Comp.* **—en=probe,** *f.* proof of ancestry. **—en=recht,** *n.* privilege of birth, ancestral right. **—en=reihe,** *f.* pedigree. **—en=stolz,** I. *m.* pride of birth; II. *adj.* proud of birth. **—frau,** *f. see* **Ahnin.** **—herr,** *m. see* **Ahn.** **—herrlich,** *adj.* ancestral.
A'hnd—en, *v.a.* to revenge, requite (*a wrong*); sometimes = **ahnen.** **—ung,** *f.* resentment, requital; revenge.
Ä'hneln, *v.n.* to bear a likeness to, to look like, to be like; **sie ähnelt ihrer Mutter,** she looks much like her mother.
A'hn—en, *v.a. & n.* (*aux.* **h.**) to have a presentiment of; to suspect, surmise; **es —t mir nichts Gutes,** I have a foreboding of evil; **—en lassen,** to cause a foreboding, to foreshadow; **der Knabe ließ den Mann —en,** the boy gave promise of the man. **—ung,** *f.* foreboding, presentiment; **keine —ung!** no, not by any means! (*sl.*); **keine blasse —ung von einer Sache haben,** to have not the faintest notion of a thing *or* how to do a thing. *Comp.* **—ungs=los,** *adj.* without misgiving or presentiment; unsuspecting. **—ungs=schwer,** full of presentiment, portentous. **—ungs=voll,** *adj.* bodeful, foreboding; mistrustful.
Ä'hnlich, *adj.* similar, like, resembling; analogous to; **er sieht seinem Bruder sehr —,** he looks very much like his brother; **das sieht ihm —,** that is just like him; **— machen,** to assimilate. **—keit,** *f.* resemblance, similarity, likeness; analogy. *Comp.* **—keits=associa=tion,** *f.* association by similarity.
A'horn, *m.* (**—s,** *pl.* **—e**) maple.
Ä'hr—chen, *n.* spicula (*Bot.*). **—e,** *f.* (*pl.* **—en**) ear of corn; **die taube —e,** tare. **—en lesen,** to glean. **—ig,** *adj.* (*in compounds, e. g.* **kurz=ährig**) having short ears *or* spikes. *Comp.* **—en=ständig,** *adj.* spicate.
Ä'hren, *v.a. & n.* to form into ears, spike; to glean; to plough before sowing.
Ai'chen, *v.a.* to gauge, *see* **Eichen.**
A'is (*two syllables*), *n.* A sharp (*Mus.*).
Akadem—ie', *f.* (*pl.* **—ie'en**) academy; university. **—iker** (*pron.* **akade̅'miker**), *m.* (**—ikers,** *pl.* **—iker**) academician; Platonist. **—isch** (*pron.* **akade̅'misch**), *adj.* academic; **—isches Viertel,** *n.* quarter of an hour's allowance (*German university lectures begin at a quarter past the full hour*).
Aka'zie, *f.* (*pl.* **—en**) acacia, locust tree.
A'kelei, *f.* whiting; columbine; whitlow.
Akro'stich—on, *n.* (*pl.* **—a**) acrostic.
Akt, *m.* (**—es,** *pl.* **—e**) act; deed, document, legal instrument (*see* **Akte**); pose, position, attitude (*of a model*); whole figure of a nude model (*Sculp. Paint.*); **von einer Sache — nehmen,** to take a written certificate of a fact; to take note of a fact (*coll.*). *Comp.* **—zeichnen,** *n.* drawing after a nude model.
Ak'te, *f.* (*pl.* **—n**) act; deed, bill, document; (*pl.*) public papers, reports; **etwas zu den —n legen,** to pigeon-hole, to shelve a th. *Comp.* **—n=mensch,** *m.* bureaucrat, red-tapist. **—n=stück,** *n.* official document, deed.
Ak't—ie, *f.* (*pl.* **—ien**) share, fund, stock. **—ionä'r,** *m.* (**—ionä'rs,** *pl.* **—ionä're**) shareholder. *Comp.* **—ien=abschnitt,** *m.* coupon. **—ien=gesellschaft,** *f.* joint-stock company. **—ien=händler,** *m.* stock-jobber. **—ien=inhaber,** *m.* shareholder.
Aktio'n, *f.* battle, encounter (*obs.*). *Comp.* **—s=radius,** *m.* sphere of action (*of a war-ship until it wants fresh coal*).
Akti'v, *adj.* active; effective; actual; **er ist bei dem Korps Borussia —,** he is just now a member of the students' club Borussia. **—a,** (*pl.*) assets, outstanding debts. **—itä't,** *f.* activity. *Comp.* **—handel,** *m.* export trade. **—schulden,** *pl. see* **—a.** **—stand,** *m.* assets; effective condition (*Mil.*).
Aktua'r, *m.* (*pl.* **—e**) actuary.
Aku'st—ik, *f.* acoustics. **—isch,** *adj.* acoustic.
Alaba'ster, *m.* (**—s**) alabaster. **—n,** *adj.* of alabaster.
A'lant, *m.* chub; elecampane. *Comp.* **—beere,** *f.* black currant.
Ala'rm, *m.* alarm; **— blasen** *or* **— schlagen,** to sound an alarm, beat to arms; **blinder —,** false alarm. *Comp.* **—glocke,** *f.* alarm-bell, tocsin. **—kanone,** *f.* signal-gun. **—quartiere,** *n. pl.* alarm-quarters, quarters near the enemy. **—signal,** *n.* alarm-signal; signal light, beacon.
Alarmie'ren, *v.a.* to alarm, to beat up.

Alau'n, *m.* (—s) alum. **—en,** *adj.* of alum. **—ig,** *see* **—artig.** *Comp.* **—artig, —haltig,** *adj.* aluminous.

Alau'nen, *v.a.* to impregnate with alum.

Alb, *see* **Alm, Alp, Alpe.**

Alb, *m.* (—(e)s, *pl.* —en) elf (*Mythol.*).

A'lbe, *f.* (*pl.* —n) white poplar (*Bot.*); ablet (*Ichth.*).

A'lber (*obs.*), **—n,** *adj.* & *adv.* silly, foolish, simple; weak-minded; absurd; **—nes Zeug,** nonsense; stuff and nonsense. **—ei',** *f.* *usually* **—n=heit,** *f.* (*pl.* **—n=heiten**) silliness; absurdity; silly action. **—ig,** *adj.* = **albern.**

A'lbum, *n.* blank book, scrap book; album for photographs *or* postage stamps.

Albumi'n, *n.* albumin(e), albumen.

Alexandri'n—er, *m.* (—ers, *pl.* —er); Alexandrine (*verse of twelve syllables*). **—isch,** *adj.* & *adv.* Alexandrian; Alexandrine.

A'lfanz, *m.* foolery, idle talk. **—er,** *m.* silly fellow. **—e=rei',** *f.* tomfoolery; **—ereien treiben,** to play foolish tricks. **—ig,** *adj.* silly, sham.

A'lgebra, *f.* algebra. **—isch,** *adj.* algebraical.

A'lge, *f.* sea-weed. **—n=artig,** *adj.* algal (*Bot.*).

Alime'nt, *n.* alimony. *Comp.* **—atio'n,** *f.* alimentation. **—en=geld,** *n.* allowance for alimony.

Alimentie'ren, *v.a.* to maintain (*Law*).

Alk, *m.* auk (*Orn.*).

A'lkohol, *n.* (—(e)s, *pl.* —e) alcohol. **—haltig,** *adj.* alcoholic. **—iker,** *m.* a man given to taking too much alcohol. **—isch,** *adj.* alcoholic. **—isie'ren,** *v.* to alcoholize.

A'lkoven, *m.* (—s, *pl.* —) alcove, recess in a room.

All, I. *n.* (—s) the universe. II. *adj.* (—er, —e, —es) *used collectively,* all, entire, whole; *used distributively,* every, each, any, all; **—e, sie —e,** all of them; **—e Menschen,** all men, everybody; **—e beide,** both of them; **auf —e Fälle,** in any case; **auf —e Weise,** by all means, in every possible way; **—e drei Tage,** every third day; **—e Tage,** every day; **—e Welt,** the whole world; everybody; **ohne —e Ursache,** without any cause; **ohne —en Zweifel,** undoubtedly; **vor —en Dingen,** above all, first of all; **—e und jede Hoffnung,** all and every hope; **bei —edem,** for all that; *used substantively;* **—es,** everything; everybody; **—es rannte dahin,** all people were running there; **über —es,** above all things; **um —es in der Welt,** for any sake, for the whole world; **—es war entzückt,** every one was delighted, charmed; **er ist —es in —em,** he is all in all (**bei,** with); **er ist —en —es,** he is all things to all men; **er kann —es,** he can do anything, is good at everything; **—es aufbieten,** to strain every nerve; **es ist —es eins,** it is all the same; **—es Mögliche,** all that is possible; **—e für einen und einer für —e,** jointly and separately, collectively and individually, with oneness of interest, solidarity; **—es durch einander,** higgledy-piggledy; **—es in allem genommen,** taking one thing with another; **—es, nur nicht,** anything rather than, anything but; **—es was,** all that, whatsoever. III. **—e,** *adv.* all gone, all spent, at an end, exhausted; **das Geld ist —e,** the money is spent (*coll.*); **es ist —e mit ihm,** it is all up with him, he is done for (*coll.*); **ich bin ganz —e,** I am quite exhausted (*coll.*); **—e werden,** to be spent, to run out; **die Dummen werden nicht —e,** there is no end of fools (*prov.*). **—heit,** *f.* sum of all, totality, universality; greatest extension (*of a term*). *Comp.* (**All** *in comp. generally* = universally; all; *prefixed to adverbs it is sometimes archaic and often causes no appreciable change of meaning*). **—bekannt,** *adj.* notorious. **—bereits,** *adv.* already. **—da, —dort,** *adv.* there. **—dieweil,** *conj.* whereas. **—eigen,** *adj.*; **—eigenes Gut,** freehold. **—ein,** *see* **Allein.** **—erba'rmer,** *m.* the All-merciful. **—geber,** *m.* God, Giver of all. **—gefällig,** *adj.* time-serving, politic, pleasing both sides. **—gegenwart,** *f.* omnipresence. **—gegenwärtig,** *adj.* omnipresent. **—gemach,** *adv.* gradually. **—gemein,** *adj.* & *adv.* universal, general; **im —gemeinen,** in general; **ein —gemeines Mittel,** specific; **man sagt es —gemein,** it is commonly reported. **—gemein=begriff,** *m.* general concept. **—gerecht,** *adj.* all-just, all-righteous. **—gewaltig,** *adj.* all-powerful; omnipotent. **—götterei,** *f.* pantheism. **—gütig,** *adj.* all-bountiful, most kind. **—heil,** *n.*, **—heil=mittel,** *n.* panacea, sovereign remedy. **—hier,** *adv.* here. **—jährlich,** *adj.* annual; *adv.* annually, every year. **—macht,** *f.* omnipotence. **—mächtig,** *adj.* omnipotent. **—mählich** (*bad spellings:* **allmälich, allmälig**) *adj.* & *adv.* by degrees, gradual. **—monatlich,** *adj.* & *adv.* monthly, every month. **—nächtlich,** *adj.* & *adv.* nightly, every night. **—seitig,** *adj.* universal; versatile; **—seitig erwägen,** to look at on all sides; **—seitige Bildung,** liberal education. **—stund,** *adv.* at all times, always. **—tägig, —täglich,** *adj.* daily; common; commonplace; ordinary; **—tägliches Fieber,** quotidian fever. **—tags=kleid,** *n.* every-day dress. **—tags=mensch,** *m.* commonplace fellow. **—tags=welt,** *f.* work-a-day world. **—tags=worte,** *n.pl.* household words. **—waltend,** *adj.* all-governing, sovereign, all-ruling. **—vater,** *m.* father of all (*God; often applied to Wodan*). **—weise,** *adj.* all-wise. **—weisheit,** *f.* supreme wisdom. **—wissend,** *adj.* omniscient. **—wissenheit,** *f.* omniscience. **—wisserei,** *f.* pretension to know everything. **—wo,** *adv.* where. **—wöchentlich,** *adj.* & *adv.* happening every week, hebdomadal; weekly, hebdomadary. **—zu,** *adv.* too, much too, quite too. **—zugleich,** *adv.* all together. **—zumal,** *adv.* all at once; all together.

Alle, *in comp.*; **—das; trotz —dem und —dem,** for all that and all that. **—mal,** *adv.* always; yet, still, of course; **ein für —mal,** once for all; **—mal wenn,** whenever. **—n=falls,** *adv.* in any case, at all events; by chance, possibly, perhaps. **—n=fallsig,** *adj.* casual, eventual. **—nt=halben,** *adv.* everywhere, in all places. **—sammt,** *adv.* altogether. **—wege,** *adv.* everywhere; always; quite; in every way, surely, undoubtedly. **—weile,** *adv.* always; just now. **—zeit,** *adv.* always; at all times.

Allee', *f.* (*pl.* —n) alley, walk, avenue.

Allegor—ie', *f.* (*pl.* —ie'en) allegory. **allego'risch,** *adj.* & *adv.* allegorical. **—isie'ren,** *v.a.* & *v.n.* to allegorize.

Allei'n, I. *indec. adj.* & *adv.* alone, sole, single; solitary, apart, by one's self; **dies — würde hinreichen,** this alone would suffice. II. *adv.* only, merely; **nicht — . . . sondern 2c.,** not only . . . but, *etc.* III. *conj.* only, but; **ich wollte es gern thun, — ich konnte nicht,** I wished to do it, but I could not. **—ig,** *adj.* & *adv.* exclusive, only, unique; **der —ige Gott,** the one God; **für seinen —igen Gebrauch,** for his separate *or* private use. **—igkeit,** *f.* solitariness, aloneness, sole existence. *Comp.* **—besitz,** *m.* exclusive possession, absolute property. **—gespräch,** *n.* soliloquy. **—handel,** *m.* exclusive trade, monopoly. **—herr,** *m.* autocrat. **—herrschaft,** *f.* undivided sway, absolute monarchy. **—herrscher,** *m.* absolute monarch, autocrat. **—rheder,** *m.* sole owner (*of a ship*). **—seligmachend,** *adj.* only saving, having the sole disposal of the means of grace; **der —seligmachende Glaube,** the (*only*) true faith, the orthodox faith, strict orthodoxy. **—spiel,** *n.* solo.

Aller, *gen. pl. of* All (*in comp. with the sup.* = of all; *with titles* = most; *the accent falls in most cases on the second part of the compound, e.g.* allerdi'ngs); **—christlichst**, *adj.* most Christian; Se. Majestät der —christlichste König, His most Christian Majesty (*a title officially given to the King of France*). **—dings**, *adv.* to be sure, of course, by all means, indeed; it is true. **—erst**, *adj. & adv.* first of all; zu —erst, first and foremost, originally. **—hand**, *indec. adj.* (*orig. gen. plur.* = of all hands), of all sorts and kinds, diverse, sundry; —hand Hochachtung! I say, that is excellent! (*sl.*). **—heiligen**, *pl.* All-Saints; All-Saints-Day. **—heiligste**, *n.* holy of holies. **—lei**, I. *indec. adj. see* —hand. II. *n.* medley, hodge-podge. **—liebst**, *adj.* dearest; best-beloved; delightful; charming. **—manns=harnisch**, *m.* long-rooted, wild, broad garlic. **—maßen**, I. *adv.* in every way, entirely. II. *conj.* since (*obs.*). **—meist**, I. *adj.* most of all, most part. II. *adv.* especially, chiefly. **—nächst**, I. *adj.* the very next. II. *adv.* close, hard by; immediately. **—seelen**, *pl.* All Souls' (*Day*). **—seits**, *adv.* on all sides; from all parts; altogether. **—wärts**, *adv.* everywhere. **—welts=freund**, *m.* everybody's friend.

Allia'nz, *f.* (*pl.* —en) alliance, league.

Alliie'r—en, *v.a.* to ally, unite; die —ten, the allies.

All'mende, *f.* common (*pasture land*) (*dial.*).

Allopa'th, *m.* (—en, *pl.* —en) allopathist.

A'lm, *f.* pasture land on the mountain-side (*dial.*).

Al'manach, *m.* (—s, *pl.* —e) almanac.

A'lmosen, *n.* (—s, *pl.* —) alms; um ein — bitten, to ask for a charity. **—ie'r**, *m.* (—iers, *pl.* —iere) almoner. *Comp.* **—amt**, *n.* almonry; alms-house. **—büchse**, *f.* poor box. **—empfänger**, *m.* pauper, alms-receiver. **—pfleger**, *m.* guardian of the poor, almoner. **—spende**, *f.* distribution of alms.

A'loe, *f.* (*pl.* —(e)n) aloe; aloes. **—tisch**, *adj.* aloetic. *Comp.* **—auszug**, *m.* extract of aloes.

1**Alp**, *m.* (—es, *pl.* —e), *orig.* elf, bad spirit; nightmare; incubus. *Comp.* **—drücken**, *n.* nightmare. **—männchen**, hobgoblin. **—schoß**, *m.* fairystone. **—zopf**, *m.* plica polonica.

2**Alp**, *f.* (*pl.* —en), mountain; hilly tract of country; (*pl.*) mountain pasturages; Alps; die Schwäbische *or* rauhe —, a hilly tract in the south of Würtemberg; jenseits der —en, transalpine; diesseits der —en, cisalpine. **—i'n**, **—i'nisch**, *adj.* alpine. *Comp.* **—balsam**, *m.* dwarf-rose-bay. **—en=bewohner**, *m.* dweller on the Alps. **—en=birke**, *f.* dwarf birch. **—en=dohle**, *f.* hermit crow. **—en=kiefer**, *f.* mountain pine. **—en=klub**, *m.* Alpine club. **—en=maus**, **—en=ratte**, marmot. **—=rose**, *f.* alpine rose, rhododendron. **—en=stock**, *m.* climbing pole; alpenstick.

Ä'lpler, *m.* dweller on the Alps; Swiss cowherd. **—in**, *f.* dairy woman (*on the Alps*).

Alphabe't, *n.* (—s, *pl.* —e) alphabet. **—isch**, *adj. & adv.* alphabetical, alphabetically. **—isie'ren**, *v.a.* to arrange in alphabetical order.

Alrau'n, *m.* (—es, *pl.* —e) mandrake. **—e**, (Alru'ne), *f.* mandrake (*mandragora*). **—en=wurzel**, *f.* mandrake (*mandragora officinalis*).

Als, *conj. in comparisons*, than, as; *demonstratively*, as, in the capacity *or* character of; *in an explanatory sense*, als (*or* als da sind) *denotes* as, such as, for example; *as an expletive before relatives*, — welche, which; *after a negative*, but, except, other than; *noting past time*, when, as, as soon as; *before* daß *with inverted clause* = *an inf. of the finite verb in the clause; as mere copulative*, as; größer — er, taller than he; so kalt — (*better:* wie) Eis, as cold as ice; ich — Vater, I as father; die kostbaren Metalle — Gold, the precious metals, such as gold; — Entschuldigung, by way of excuse; nichts —, nothing but; kein Fürst — er, no prince except him; er thut nichts — spielen, he does nothing but play; — er kam, when he came; zu gut, — daß man es wegwerfen sollte, too good to be thrown away; zu klug, — daß er das nicht merken sollte, too clever not to notice that; sowohl er — ich, he as well as I. —(s)o, *see* Also. *Comp.* (*with accent on the second part, e.g.* alsba'ld). **—bald**, *adv.* as soon as; forthwith, thereupon, presently, at once, immediately. **—dann**, *adv.* then.

Al'so, I. *adv.* so, thus, so much, so far; die Sache verhält sich —, the matter stands thus. II. *conj.* therefore, consequently; ich ging — hin, I went accordingly; Sie wollen — nicht? You won't, then? *Comp.* **—bald**, *see* Alsbald.

Alt, *adj. & adv.* (*comp.* älter; *sup.* ältest) old; ancient, antique, long established; stale; bad, unpleasant (*dial.*); er ist so — wie ich, he is my age; er ist immer der —e, he is still the same; es bleibt beim —en, there will be no change; das ist etwas —es, that is nothing new; — thun, to assume a knowing air; — werden, to grow old; die —en, the ancients; meine —en, my forefathers; my seniors; das —e, old thing; ich bleibe beim —en, I stick to the old way; mein —er, my old friend; old fellow, old chap; my principal; my father, my governor (*sl.*); der alte Fritz, *i.e.* King Frederick II. of Prussia; —er, *see* Alter. *Comp.* **—backen**, *adj.* stale. **—bekannt**, *adj.* long-known. **—ehrwürdig**, *adj.* time-honoured. **—en=teil**, *n.* reservation of property made by an old person making over his estate to an heir; sich aufs —enteil zurückziehen, to withdraw from actual participation in a business or in general affairs. **—flicker**, *m.* cobbler. **—fränkisch**, *adj.* old Franconian; antiquated. **—gesell**, *m.* foreman; old bachelor (*rare*). **—gläubig**, *adj.* orthodox. **—hochdeutsch**, *adj.* Old High German. **—katho'lisch**, Old Catholic (*since* 1871). **—klug**, *adj.* knowing, precocious. **—land=ammann**, *m.* late high bailiff. **—meister**, elder, senior master, patriarch, *e.g.* Goethe, Haydn. **—modisch**, *adj.* out of fashion, old-fashioned. **—mutter**, *f.* grandmother. **—=nordisch**, *adj.* Old Norse. **—philologe**, *m.* philologist (*or* scholar) versed in ancient languages; classical scholar. **—reichskanzler**, *m.* First Chancellor of the (new German) Empire, *i.e.*, Prince Bismarck. **—vater**, *m.* grandfather, progenitor, patriarch. **—väterlich**, *adj.* ancestral, primitive, old. **—verjährt**, *adj.*; —verjährtes Eigentum, prescriptive property. **—vertraut**, *adj.* of long acquaintance. **—vordern**, *pl.* ancestors. **—weiberhaft**, **—weiber=mäßig**, *adj.* anile. **—weiber=sommer**, *m.* Indian summer, gossamer.

Alt, *m.* (—(e)s, *pl.* —e) alto, counter (*or* second) tenor. **—i'st**, *m.* counter-tenor singer. **—i'stin**, *f.* contralto singer. *Comp.* **—geige**, *f. see* Bratsche. **—schlüssel**, *m.* **—zeichen**, *n.* alto-clef. **—stimme**, *f.* counter-tenor.

Altā'n, *m.* (—s, *pl.* —e) balcony; platform; gallery.

Altā'r, *m.* (—s, *pl.* —e & Altä're) altar. *Comp.* **—blatt**, *n.* altar piece. **—buch**, *n.* office-book (*Eccl.*). **—diener**, *m.* priest ministering at the altar; acolyte. **—kelch**, *m.* chalice. **—platz**, *m.*, **—stätte**, *f.* chancel.

Ält—e, *f.* oldness (*obs.*). **—er**, *adj. compar. of* Alt, older, elder. **—er=lich** (*usually* elterlich) *adj.* parental. **—ern**, *pl. see* Eltern. **—est**, *adj. superlat. of* alt, oldest, most ancient. **—este**, *m. & f.* senior, elder; die —esten, the elders (*B.*). **—lich**, *adj. and adv.* elderly, oldish. *Comp.* **—er=mutter**, *f.* great-grandmother, ancestress. **—ern=los** (*usually*

elternlos) *adj.* orphaned, parentless. **—er=vater,** *m.* great-grandfather, ancestor, patriarch. **—esten=amt,** *n.*, **—esten=würde,** *f.* eldership. **—esten=recht,** *n.* right of primogeniture.

A'lter, *n.* (—s) age, old age; antiquity; epoch, age; **das blühende —,** the prime of life; **man sieht ihm sein — nicht an,** he does not look his age; **bis in das späteste —,** to the last, to the latest period of one's existence; **vor —s, von —s her,** of old, anciently; **— schützt vor Thorheit nicht,** the old ones too are sometimes foolish (*prov.*). **—tum,** *n.* (**—tums,** *pl.* **—tümer**) antiquity. **—tümelei',** *f.* antiquarianism. **—tümler,** *m.* antiquary; dabbler in antiquities. **—tümlich,** *adj. & adv.* antique, ancient. *Comp.* **—s=erlaß,** *m.* exemption because of age. **—s=folge,** *f.* seniority. **—s=genoß,** *m.*, **—s=genossin,** *f.* one having the same age as another; of the same age; contemporary. **—s=schwach,** *adj.* decrepit. **—s=schwäche,** *f.* weakness of old age. **—s=stufe,** *f.* stage of life. **—tums=forscher,** *m.* antiquary. **—tums=gesellschaft,** *f.* antiquarian society. **—tums=kunde,** *f.* archæology. **—tums=stück,** *n.* antique. **—s=versicherung, —s=versorgung,** *f.* old age pension (*scheme*), old age insurance. **—tums=wissenschaft,** *f.* knowledge (*or* science) of antiquity *or* antiquities; archæology.

Alteratio'n, *f.* emotion, anger.

Alterie'ren, *v.* I. *a.* to affect, alter, influence; to excite, annoy. II. *refl.* to get excited, to become vexed.

A'ltern, *v.n.* (*aux.* **h.**) to become old, age; to decline, decay.

Altrui'smus, *m.* altruism.

Alumn—ā't, *n.* boarding-school connected with a day-school. **—us,** *m.* (*pl.* **—i**) boarder.

Alveo'l—e, *f.* alveole. **—a'r,** *adj.* alveolary

Alveola'rlaut, *m.* alveolar continuant (*viz. a consonant formed by pressing the point of the tongue against the ridge above the upper teeth, hence a kind of dental*).

Am (= **an dem**) *see* **An; wer ist — Spiele?** whose turn is it to play?; **— Ende,** after all, in short; abbreviated **a.** *e.g.* **Frankfurt a. M.** = **Frankfurt am Main,** F. on the Main. *It forms the superlative of the adverb.* **— besten,** best; **— ehesten,** soonest; **ich bin — besten daran,** I have the best of it; **— aller=ersten,** at the very first.

Amalgā'm, —a, *n.* amalgam. **—ie'ren,** *v.a.* to amalgamate.

Amara'nt, *m.* (—s, *pl.* **—en**) amaranth. **—en,** *adj.* amaranthine.

Amazō'ne, *f.* (*pl.* **—n**) amazon; virago; horsewoman, female equestrian. *Comp.* **—n=kleid,** *n.* lady's riding-habit. **—n=stein,** *m.* Amazonite (species of felspar).

A'mbe, *f.* (*pl.* **—n**) combination of two numbers; two lucky numbers drawn, double prize.

A'mber, *m.* (—s) amber; **grauer —,** ambergris. **—i'ne,** *f.* ambreine. (*For cpds. see* **Ambra.**)

A'mboß, *m.* (**—sses,** *pl.* **—sse**) anvil; incus (*Anat.*). **Hand—,** small anvil. *Comp.* **—bahn,** *f.* face of the anvil. **—schmied,** *m.* blacksmith.

A'mbra, *m.* (—s) *see* **Amber.** *Comp.* **—baum,** *m.* sweet-gum. **—duft,** *m.* perfume of amber, fragrant-odour. **—fett,** *n.* ambreine. **—holz,** *n.* species of sandalwood. **—kugel,** *f.* musk-ball. **—öl,** *n.* oil of amber. **—staude,** *f* amber tree *or* plant.

Ambro's—ia, *n.* ambrosia. **—isch,** *adj.* ambrosial; fragrant, delicious.

Ambrosia'nisch, *adj.* Ambrosian (*Eccles.*).

A'meise, *f.* (*pl.* **—n**) ant, emmet. *Comp.* **—n=bär, —n=fresser, —n=jäger,** *m.* ant-bear, ant-eater. **—n=ei,** *n.* ant's-egg. **—n=haufen,** *m.* ant-hill. **—n=kriechen,** *n.*, **—n=laufen,** *n.*, **—n=schauder,** *m.* formication. **—n=jungfer,** *f.*, **—n=löwe,** *m.* lion-ant. **—n=säure,** *f.* formic acid.

A'mel— (*in comp.*). **—korn,** *m.* a kind of spelt *or* German wheat. **—mehl,** *n.* starch; spelt flour.

A'melung, *m.* descendant of (*the East Gothic king*) Amala; *especially:* follower of Dietrich von Bern, noble Goth. **—enlied,** *n.* cycle of epic songs on Dietrich von Bern and his Gothic thanes.

Am'mann, *m.* (—s, *pl.* **Ammänner**) magistrate; bailiff (*in Switzerland and parts of Germany*).

A'mme, *f.* (*pl.* **—n**) nurse, wet-nurse; **zur — thun,** to put (*out*) to nurse. *Comp.* **—n=märchen,** *n.* nursery tale. **—n=stube,** *f.* nursery.

A'mmer, *f.* (*pl.* **—n**) yellow-hammer (*Orn.*).

Ammonia'k, *n.* ammonia; **salzsaures —,** chloride of ammonium: **schwefelsaures —,** sulphate of ammonia. **—a'lisch,** *adj.* ammoniacal. *Comp.* **—gas,** *n.* gaseous ammonia, ammoniac(al) gas.

A'mmonshorn, *n.* (—(e)s, *pl.* **Ammonshörner**) ammonite.

Amnesie', *f.* loss of memory.

Amnestie', *f.* (*pl.* **—n**) amnesty; (*political*) pardon. *Comp.* **—dekret,** *n.* act of oblivion.

Amore'tte, *m.* little Cupid; *pl.* loves, amoretti.

Amo'rph, *adj.* shapeless.

Amort—ie'ren, —isie'ren, *v.a.* to liquidate, pay off (*debts*); to buy up (*annuities, etc.*). **—isatio'n,** *f.* legal extinction, liquidation. *Comp.* **—isatio'ns=fonds,** *m.* sinking-fund.

A'mpel, *f.* (*pl.* **—n**) hanging lamp.

A'mpfer, *m.* (—s) sorrel, dock.

Amphi'bie, *f.* (*pl.* **—n**) amphibious animal. **n=haft,** *adj. & adv.* amphibious.

Amputie'ren, *v.a.* to amputate.

A'mse, Emse, *see* **Ameise.**

A'msel, *f.* (*pl.* **—n**) blackbird. **Wasser—,** *f.* ousel.

A'mt, *n.* (**—es,** *pl.* **Ämter**) any responsible situation, office, charge, place, employment, official position, board, court, council; administration; jurisdiction; domain, sphere of duty; concern; guild; ecclesiastical duty; ministry; mass; place of public business; **ein öffentliches — bekleiden** *or* **inne haben,** to fill a public office; **das Auswärtige —,** *n.* the Foreign Office; **einem —e vorstehen,** to hold *or* fill an office; **einen seines —es entsetzen,** to deprive one of his situation; **kraft meines —es,** by virtue of my office; **von —es wegen,** ex officio, officially; **sein — antreten,** to come into office, to enter upon one's functions; **seines —es walten** (*or* **warten**), to perform the duties of one's office, to officiate; **das hohe — verrichten, halten,** to administer the sacraments, to say mass (*Rom. Cath.*); **es ist meines —es nicht,** it is not in my province, it is not my business. **—lich,** *adj. & adv.* official, ministerial. *Comp.* **—los,** *adj. & adv.* out of office; out of employment; private. **—mann,** *m.* magistrate; bailiff; domain judge, steward. **—mannschaft,** *f.* bailiwick; jurisdiction *or* dignity of an amtmann. **—meister,** *m.* master of a guild. **—s=alter,** *n.* seniority in office. **—s=ansehen,** *n.* official authority. **—s=befehl,** *m.* official order. **—s=beförderung,** *f.* official promotion. **—s=bericht,** *m.* official report. **—s=bescheid,** *m.* sentence, decree. **—s=bewerber,** *m.* candidate (*for an office*). **—s=bezirk,** *m.* extent of jurisdiction. **—s=blatt,** *n.* official gazette. **—s=buch,** *n.* official register, court-roll. **—s=bruder,** *m.* colleague. **—s=diener,** *m.* serjeant, beadle, usher. **—s=dorf,** *n.* village of a jurisdiction. **—s=eid,** *m.* oath of office; **den —seid ablegen,** to be sworn into office; **etwas auf den —seid nehmen,** to make a declaration, deposition on one's oath of office. —s=folge, *f.* rotation of office; —s=folge leisten, to obey the orders of a magistrate *or* bailiff. —s=frohne, *f.* statute labour, socage. —s=führung, *f.* administration. —s=gebühr, *f.* (*usually in the pl.*) fees due to an official. —s=gebührlich, *adj.* official. —s=gefälle, *pl.* domain revenues; fees of office. —s=genoß, *m.* colleague. —s=gericht, *n.* lower court, police (*or* district) court. —s=geschäft, *n.*, —s=handlung, *f.* official function; (*Theol.*) ministration. —s=hau'pt=mann, *m.* high constable of a district, supreme bailiff. —s=kleidung, *f.* official costume; pontificals, robes, gown, *etc.* —s=kreis, *m.* district. —s=lade, *f.* corporation chest. —s=mäßig, *adj.* official, professional. —s=richter, *m.* district-judge. —s=schild, *n.* badge of office. —(s)=stube, *f.* court-house, magistrate's room, office. —s=tag, court-day. —s=tracht, *f.* robes of office, official attire. —s=verrichtung, *f.* performing of an official duty; —s=verrichtungen versehen, to officiate. —s=vertreter, *m.* deputy in office. —s=verwalter, *m.* substitute. —s=verweser, *m.* deputy-administrator. —s=vogt, *m.* bailiff; justiciary; beadle; tipstaff. —s=vogtei', *f.* stewardship; bailiwick. —s=vorgänger, *m.* predecessor in office. —s=wohnung, *f.* official residence, lodgings of an official.

Ämtchen, *n.* (*dimin. of* Amt); — bringen Käppchen, office brings profit (*prov.*).

Amüsan't, *adj.* & *adv.* amusing.

Amüsie'ren, *v.a.* & *refl.* to amuse; to enjoy (*oneself*).

An, I. *prep.* at; at *or* to the edge of; by, close by; against; along; to; towards, near; near to, not far from; as far as, up to; till; on, upon, with; in (*very often with verbs, e.g.* glauben — eine Sache, Freude finden — einer Sache); of; about; by means of; in respect to, in the way of; by reason of. ***Used with dat.*** 1. *when signifying rest or motion within a place* (*in answer to the question* wo? where?); 2. *when denoting a point of time* (*in answer to* wann? when?); 3. *after verbs expressive of delight, want, doubt, recognition, anger, etc.;* 4. *after such adj.'s as* arm, poor; reich, rich; krank, sick; ähnlich, like; stark, strong; schwach, weak, *etc.;* 5. *in answer to* woran, on, in, of what, *etc.;* 6. *in answer to* an wem? to whom, whose? — der Thüre, at the door; am Leben, alive; am Tode sein, to be at the point of death; Professor — der Universität, professor at the university; das liegt — Ihnen, that is your fault; — seinem Finger, on his finger; am Wege, on the way, along the road; am Bord, *or* — Bord, on board; am Sonntag, on Sunday; am Schiff zu liefern, to be delivered at the ship's side (*C. L.*); rächen —, to revenge on; der Hut hängt — der Wand, the hat hangs on the wall; — einem Orte, in a place; am rechten Orte (*or* recht am Ort), in the right place; — der Themse, on the Thames; — der Grenze, upon the frontier; es ist nichts — der Sache, there is no truth in it; diese Bemerkung ist nicht — ihrer Stelle, this remark is not applicable, not à-propos; am Morgen, in the morning; — meiner Statt, in my place; wäre ich — Ihrer Stelle, if I were you, in your place; es ist nichts — ihm, he is a worthless fellow; — sich *or* — und für sich, in the abstract, in itself; das Unternehmen — sich hat wenig Schwierigkeit, the undertaking in itself presents few difficulties; sie hat viele Fehler — sich, she has many faults; so viel — mir ist, as far as lies in my power; — der Hand führen, to lead by the hand; — einer Stadt vorbeikommen, to pass a town; — der Küste hin, along the coast; ich nehme mir ein Beispiel —, I take example by; thue — mir wie ich — dir, do by me as I do by you; — seinen Blicken &c., by his looks, *etc.* (*to perceive, know by*); einem am Herzen liegen, to be near one's heart, dear to one; er starb — einem Fieber, he died of a fever; es ist — der Zeit, it is about the time, the time has come; die Reihe (*or* es) ist — mir, it is my turn; es ist — dem, daß er abreist, he is on the eve of departure; ist es — dem? is that so? ***Used with acc.*** *signifying* 1. *progression or motion towards a place or thing* (*in answer to* wohin? where to?); 2. *expressing duration of time* (*in answer to,* bis wann? to what time, *etc.*?); 3. *after verbs of believing and remembering;* 4. *in answer to the question* an wen? an was? to whom? to what? *for other relations see idioms;* nun ging es — ein Arbeiten, they now set to work; seine Tochter — einen Kaufmann verheiraten, to marry his daughter to a merchant; er gewöhnte sich — eine spärliche Kost, he accustomed himself to a frugal diet; ich ging — die Thür, I went to the door; — die Gewehre! to arms! fall in! (*Mil.*); wenn die Reihe — mich kommt, when it comes to my turn; when my turn comes; bis — das Ende (*or* bis ans Ende), to the end; bis — die Schultern, up to the shoulders; — die Thüre klopfen, to knock at the door; ich dachte — Sie, I was thinking of you; ich glaube nicht — Gespenster, I don't believe in ghosts; ich schreibe — ihn, I write to him; der Brief ist — Sie, the letter is for you; vom Morgen bis — den Abend, from morning till evening; es kostet — die vierzehn Mark, it costs nearly (*or* about) fourteen marks; es waren — vierhundert Zuschauer da, there were about four hundred spectators; es ging — ein Prügeln, they came to blows. II. *adv.* on, onward; along; up, along upward; close to, adjoining; von heute —, from this day forth; von nun —, henceforth; oben —, up above; unten —, below, at the end; berg—, uphill; himmel—, heavenwards; neben—, close by; (*in* berga'n, himmela'n, nebena'n, an *takes the stress*). III. *Separable prefix, meaning* at, to, on, *etc.* *In case a possible compound is not given in the following lists, look under the simple word.*

Anachore't, *m.* (—en, *pl.* —en) anchoret, anchorite.

An'ackern, *v.a.* to earth (*potatoes*).

Analo'g (—isch *rare*), *adj.* analogous. —ie', *f.* (*pl.* —ie'en) analogy.

Analy'—se, *f.* analysis. —sie'ren, *v.a.* to analyse; (*Gramm.*) to parse. —tik, *f.* analytics. —tisch, *adj.* analytical.

A'nanas, *f.* pineapple. *Comp.* —bowle, *f.* light hock flavoured with pineapple slices (*in a large punch-bowl*).

An'arbeiten, *v.a.* to join on to; gegen einen —, to oppose one.

Anarch—ie', *f.* (*pl.* —ie'en) anarchy. —isch (*pron.* ana'rchisch), *adj.* anarchical. —i'st, *m.* anarchist.

An'arten, *v.n.* (*aux.* s.) to become natural to; (einem) angeartet, inborn, connate.

Anathe'm (—s, *pl.* —e), **Ana'thema** (—s, *pl.* —ta), *n.* anathema.

An'atmen, *v.a.* to breathe upon.

Anatom—ie', *f.* anatomy. —iker (*pron.* Anato'miker), *m.* (—ikers, *pl.* —iker) anatomist. —ie'ren, *v.a.* to dissect. —isch (*pron.* anato'misch), *adj.* anatomical.

An'äugeln, *v.a.* to ogle, leer at; to look at tenderly.

An'backen, *v.* I. *a.* to stick to, cause to adhere (*by baking*). II. *n.* (*aux.* h.) to cleave, stick *or* adhere to by baking.

An'bahnen, *v.a.* to break a way for (*reforms*).

An'ballen, *v.r.* to clod, ball, clot.

An'bändeln, *v.n.;* **mit einer** *or* **einem —,** to make friends with, to flirt with.
An'bannen, *v.a.* to bewitch, inflict by witchcraft; **wie angebannt,** as if spell-bound.
An'bau, *m.* (**—s,** *pl.* **An'bauten**) cultivation, culture; settlement, wing, addition (*to a building*); outhouse. **—bar, —lich,** *adj.* cultivable.
An'bau—en, *v.a.* to till, to cultivate; to add to by building; **sich—en,** to establish oneself, to settle. **—er,** *m.* (**—ers,** *pl.* **—er**) cultivator; settler.
An'befehlen, *ir.v.a.* to enjoin; to command, to order; to recommend, give in charge to.
An'beginn, *m.* earliest beginning, origin.
An'behalten, *ir.v.a.* to keep on.
Anbei', *adv.* annexed, enclosed; **— folgt,** herewith you receive; please find enclosed.
An'beißen, *ir.v.* I. *a.* to bite at; to take a bite of, eat. II. *n.* to bite, nibble; to swallow a bait; **auf eine Sache —,** to take the bait (*fig.*).
An'belangen, *v.a.* to relate to, to concern; **was mich anbelangt,** as for me, for my part.
An'bellen, *v.a.* to bark at, yelp at; to snarl at.
An'bequemen, *v.a.* to accommodate *or* adapt to; **sich der Laune jemandes —,** to fall in with some one's humour.
An'beraumen, *v.a.* to fix, to appoint (**eine Frist, einen Termin;** *it is not connected with* **Raum,** *m.*).
An'beregt, *adj.* aforesaid, above mentioned (*Law*).
An'bet—en, *v.a.* to adore, worship, idolize. **—er,** *m.* (**—ers,** *pl.* **—er**) adorer, admirer, lover. **—ung,** *f.* adoration. *Comp.* **—ungs=würdig,** *adj.* adorable.
An'betreffen, *ir.v.a.* to concern, refer to. **—d,** *p. & adj.* concerning, as for.
An'betteln, *v.a.* to beg of; to annoy by begging.
An'biedern, *v.n. & r.;* **sich bei** (*or* **mit**) **einem —,** to obtrude oneself, to intrude on a p., to make friends with a p. (*coll.*).
An'biegen, *ir.v.a.* to annex; to bend towards; to subjoin. **angebogen** *often* = **anbei.**
An'biet—en, *ir.v.* I. *a.* to offer, proffer, propose; **der Herr bot mir seine Dienste an,** the gentleman offered me his services; **eine Gelegenheit bietet sich an,** an opportunity offers itself. II. *n.* (*aux.* **h.**) to start a price (*at auctions*). **angeboten,** *p.p. & adj.* offered; letter (*Comm.*). **—ung,** *f.* offer. *Comp.* **—ungs=preis,** *m.* starting price (*at auctions*).
An'binden, *ir.v.* I. *a.* to tie on *or* to; to tie up (*Hort.*); to strap; to moor; **einen Bären —,** to contract a debt (*slang*); **einen (zum Geburtstage) —,** to make one a (*birthday*) present (*rare*); **ein Kalb —,** to wean a calf; **am Fuße —,** to tether; **ein Buch (einem andern) —,** to bind up a book (*with another*). II. *n.* (*aux.* **h.**) **mit einem —,** to enter into relations with; to pick a quarrel with; **kurz angebunden sein (mit einem),** to be blunt, bluff, abrupt, brusque; to cut one short, to rebuff one, to give one a sharp answer.
An'blasen, *ir.v.a.* to blow at, upon; to blow up (*fire*); to inflame; to sound; **die Jagd —,** to sound the signal for the chase; **einen —,** to rebuke a p. sharply (*sl.*).
An'blick, *m.* (**—s**) look; view, sight; aspect, appearance; **beim ersten —,** at first sight.
An'blicken, *v.a.* to look at, look in the face, view.
An'blinz—eln, —en, *v.a.* to leer at, to blink *or* wink at.
An'blitzen, *v.a.* to cast a furious look upon, to dart a look upon; to throw a ray on.
Anblöken, Anblö'cken, *v.a.* to bleat at; to bellow, growl at.
An'bohren, *v.a.* to bore, pierce; to tap (*casks*).
An'brausen, *v.a. & n.* (*aux.* **h.**) to rush at *or* on.
An'brechen, *ir.v.* I. *a.* to broach; to open; to break; to cut (*a loaf, etc.*). II. *n.* (*aux.* **s.**) to enter upon, begin; to break, to dawn; to begin to rot; **bei —dem Tage,** at day-break.
An'brennen, *ir.v.* I. *a.* to light, to kindle; to set fire to; to mark by burning; **— lassen,** to burn (*meat, etc.*); **das Licht ist angebrannt,** the candle is partly burnt; **die Speisen sind angebrannt,** the food is burnt. II. *n.* (*aux.* **s.**) to catch fire; to kindle; **nichts — lassen,** to be very active (*prov.*).
An'bringbar, *adj. & adv.* salable, marketable.
An'bring—en, I. *ir.v.a.* to bring about, in *or* on; to bring to bear; to put in operation, set to work; to apply; to construct, fix, put up; to dispose of; to invest, to place, settle (*children, etc.*); to sell; to pass off; to depose; to lodge information against; **ich kann die nassen Kleider nicht —en,** I cannot get my wet clothes on; **eine Tochter —en,** to marry a daughter; **einen Sohn —en,** to settle *or* to find a place for a son; **Geld —en,** to place money; **Wechsel —en,** to negotiate bills; **die Hunde —en,** to set on the dogs; **ein Wort —en,** to put in a word; **für voll —en,** to pass as current; **wohl angebracht,** seasonable, apt; **ein wohl angebrachter Stoß,** a home thrust. II. *subst. n.* denunciation; business. **—er,** *m.* (**—ers,** *pl.* **—er**), **—in,** *f.* (*pl.* **—innen**) informer, tell-tale; accuser.
An'bruch, *m.* (**—(e)s,** *pl.* **Anbrüche**) break, beginning; first act *or* break; opening; rot, mould; decay; **— des Tages,** day-break; **— der Nacht,** night-fall.
An'brüchig, *adj. & adv.* beginning to break; rotten, spoilt, mouldy.
An'brühen, *v.a.* to scald, soak (*with hot water*); to infuse, steep.
An'brüllen, *v.a.* to bellow, roar at.
An'brummen, *v.a.* to growl at; to scold.
An'brüten, *v.a.* to begin to hatch; **angebrütete Eier,** addled eggs.
Ancho've, Ancho'vis, *see* **Anschovis.**
An'dacht, *f.* (*pl.* **—en**) devotion; **seine — verrichten,** to say one's prayers, attend to one's devotions. *Comp.* **—s=los,** irreverent, undevout. **—s=losigkeit,** *f.* want of devotion. **—s=übungen,** devotional exercises. **—s=voll,** *adj.* devotional, devout.
Andächtelei', *f.* (*pl.* **—en**) bigotry; hypocrisy; religious nonsense.
An'dächt—eln, *v.n.* to affect devotion, to be over-pious; to act the hypocrite. **—ler** (**—lers,** *pl.* **—ler**), **—lerin,** (*pl.* **—lerinnen**) devotionist, devotee, hypocrite. **—lerisch,** *adj.* bigoted, goody-goody.
An'dächtig, *adj. & adv.* devout; devotional, pious; **sie hörte — zu,** she listened with all her heart, with close attention.
An'dämmen, *v.a.* to dam up.
An'dauern, *v.n.* to continue, to last.
An'denken, *n.* (**—s,** *pl.* **—**) remembrance; keepsake, memento, token; memory; **zum — an ihn,** in remembrance, in memory of him; **seligen —s,** of blessed memory; **das — eines Heiligen feiern,** to keep a saint's day, to commemorate a saint.
An'der, *adj.* other, else, different; second, next; *used substantively or as pron.* (**der, die, das —e, ein —er, eine —e, ein —es,** *or* **andrer, andre, andres,** *but* **anderm, andern**) any one else, anything else, some one else; **kein —er,** no one else; **nichts —es,** nothing else; **einen Tag um den —n,** every other day; **einmal über das —e,** repeatedly; **eins um das —e,** alternately, by turns; **eins ins —e gerechnet,** taking one with another; **selb —,** myself and another, we two; **unter —en,** among other things; **ein —er, eine —,** another; **einer oder der —e,** some one or another; **das ist**

etwas —es, that's a different thing, that alters the case; —e Kleider anziehen, to change (one's clothes); das —e Ufer, the opposite shore; die —e Seite (der Münze), the reverse (of a coin); die —e Seite (des Tuches), the wrong side (of cloth); —es *or* —en Sinnes werden, to change one's mind; —e Saiten aufziehen, to alter one's behaviour; to come down a peg. —s, *see* Anders. *Comp.* —lei, *indec. adj.* of another kind. —n=falls, *adv.* otherwise, else, in the contrary case. —n=teils, *adv.* on the other hand. —seits, *adv.* on the other side. —t=halb, *see* Anderthalb. —=wärtig, *adj.* of *or* in another place. —wärts, *adv.* elsewhere. —weit, *adv.* in another place; at another time; otherwise; —weite Folge, second continuation. —weitig, *adj.* from another quarter; done in another way *or* at another time; further, furthermore; —weitige Hülfe erwarten, to expect help from another quarter.

An'ders, *adv.* otherwise; else; differently; under other circumstances; nichts — als, nothing but; irgendwo —, somewhere else; etwas, was —, something else; — werden, to change; sich — besinnen, to change one's mind; ich kann nicht —, ich muß lachen, I cannot help laughing; nicht —, exactly so, just so; wenn —, wo —, if indeed, provided; wenn — nicht, unless. *Comp.* —gläubiger, *m.* a dissenter, heretic; one holding a different (*religious*) opinion, heterodox. —wo, *adv.* elsewhere. —woher, *adv.* from some other place. —wohin, *adv.* elsewhere, to another place.

An'derthalb, Anderthal'b, *adj.* one and a half (*lit. the second* (*only*) *half*); — Pfund, a pound and a half. —ig, *adj.* sesquialteral, one and a half times as many.

Än'der—n, *v.a.* to alter, change; sich —n, to alter, vary, reform, change; to change one's mind; das läßt sich nicht —n, there is no help for it. —bar, *adj. & adv.* alterable, capable of modification. —ei', *f.* (*pl.* —ei'en) useless *or* too frequent change. —ung, *f.* change, alteration, variation.

An'deut—en, *v.a.* to signify, point out, indicate; to typify; to intimate. —ung, *f.* intimation; signification; suggestion.

An'dichten, *v.a.;* einem etwas —, to attribute, to impute falsely s.th. to s.o.

An'donnern, *v.a.* to thunder at; er stand wie angedonnert, he stood like one thunderstruck.

An'drang, *m.* (—es) pressing forward, pressure; competition; congestion (*Med.*); crowd, press.

An'drängen, *v.a.* to crowd, press to *or* against; sich an die Großen —, to thrust oneself on great people.

Andre'as—kreuz, *n.* St. Andrew's cross, saltier cross, Scotch cross. —nacht, *f.* night preceding St. Andrew's day. —tag, *m.* St. Andrew's day (*Nov. 30*).

An'drechseln, *v.a.* to turn, fit, adapt to; einem etwas —, to sell s.th. too dear to s.o. (*coll.*).

An'drehen, *v.* I. *a.* to fix on by turning; to screw on; einem eine Nase —, to hoax one; die Wanten —, to set up the top-mast shrouds. II. to bring about, to set going.

An'dring—en, *ir.v.a.* & *n.* (*aux.* s.) to press on *or* against; to push *or* urge forward; to rush upon (gegen); to charge (*Mil.*). —end, *p.* & *adj.* urgent, pressing; pathetic. —lich, *adj.* importunate, pressing.

An'droh—en, *v.a.;* einem etwas —en, to menace, threaten s.o with s.th. —ung, *f.* threat, menace.

An'drücken, *v.a.* to press close to *or* against.

Andu'rch, *adv.* hereby, by this, enclosed (*Law*).

An'eifern, *v.a.* to urge on, incite, stimulate.

An'eignen, *v.r.* to appropriate; to adapt; to assimilate; sich (*dat.*) Gewohnheiten —, to contract habits; —de Verwandtschaft, approximating affinity (*Chem.*); sich (*dat.*) die Meinungen anderer —, to adopt the opinions of others.

Aneinan'der, *adv.* together; to *or* against one another. *Comp.* —fügen, *v.a.* to join.

Anekdo'te, *f.* (*pl.* —n) anecdote.

An'ekeln, *v.a.* & *imp.* to disgust.

An'empfehlen, *ir.v.a.* to recommend.

An'empfind—en, *v.n.* to assume the feelings of others. —ung, *f.* adoption of the sentiments of others; true appreciation; feine —ung für Schönheiten fremder Litteratur, a fine appreciation of the beauties of foreign literature.

An'erbe, I. *m.* (—n, *pl.* —n) heir-apparent; next heir. II. *n.* (—s) heritage.

An'erben, *v.a.* to transmit by inheritance; to inherit.

An'erbiet—en, I. *ir.v.a.* to offer. II. —en, *n.*, —ung, *f.* offer, proffer.

An'erkanntermaßen, *adv.* confessedly.

An'erkenn—bar, —lich, *adj.* & *adv.* recognizable; that may be acknowledged.

An'erkenn—en, *ir.v.a.* to recognize, appreciate; to own, acknowledge (*sep.; but sometimes used insep.* ich anerkenne, *which should not be imitated*); nicht —en, to disown; ich erkenne an, I acknowledge, admit. —t=nis, *f.* & *n.* acknowledgment; clear perception (*of a truth, etc.*). —ung, *f.* acknowledgment; acceptation (*Comm.*); recognition. —ungs=wert, *adj.* worthy of recognition, commendable.

An'erschaffen, I. *ir.v.a.* to imprint *or* implant in. II. *p.p.* & *adj.* innate.

An'fachen, *v.a.* to blow into a flame; to kindle.

An'fädeln, *v.a.* to string to, to thread.

An'fahrbar, *adj.* accessible (*shore*), fit for landing.

An'fahr—en, *ir.v.* I. *n.* (*aux.* s.) to drive up to; to arrive; to drive, to strike against; to put in (*at a port*); to descend a shaft; bei einem —en, to drive up to and stop at one's house; angefahren kommen, to arrive in a carriage, to arrive. II. *a.* to carry *or* bring near, up *or* to; to land; to address angrily, rudely; man muß die Leute nicht so —en, one must not fly at people like that; was wollen Sie? fuhr er mich an, what do you want? he asked me gruffly. —t, *f.* (*pl.* —ten) approach, arrival; (*Min.*) going to work; landing-place, place of arrival. *Comp.* —schacht, *m.* descending, down-cast shaft (*Min.*).

An'fall, *m.* (—s, *pl.* Anfälle) onset, attack, shock, assault; fit; paroxysm; fall against, on; *pl.* yearly returns; — eines Gutes, accession to an inheritance; künftige Anfälle, inheritance in reversion; die Anfälle (an Vogelherden) the perching-sticks. *Comp.* —s=recht, *n.* right of inheriting, reversion.

An'fallen, *ir.v.* I. *n.* to fall against *or* towards; to fall to (*Law, of property*). II. *a.* to fall on, assail, attack, assault; to invade (ein Land).

An'fällig, *adj.* reversionary; inherited.

An'fang, *m.* (—s, *pl.* Anfänge) commencement; beginning; spring (*of an arch*); von — an, from the very first; er hat die Anfänge dieser Wissenschaft inne, he is well grounded in the rudiments of this science; gleich zu —, at the very beginning; aller — ist schwer, the first step is all the difficulty (*prov.*). —s, *adv.* in the beginning; gleich —s, at the very beginning. *Comp.* —s=buchstabe, initial letter. —s=gefühl, *n.* inceptive feeling (*Phil.*). —s=gründe, *pl.* rudiments, first principles, elements. —s=geschwindigkeit, initial speed; muzzle velocity (*Artill.*).

An'fangen, *ir.v.* I. *a.* to begin, commence; to set about, take up; to be occupied with, do; was wollen Sie heute —? what are you going to do to-day? was soll ich —? what am I to do? ein Geschäft —, to set up as a tradesman; mit ihm ist nichts anzufangen, there is no doing anything with him; etwas verkehrt —, to begin something at the wrong end; ich weiß nichts damit anzufangen, I do not know what to make of it; sagen Sie mir, wie Sie das —, tell me how you manage that. II. *n.* (*aux.* h.) to begin, originate. III. sich —, to begin (*obsol.*).

An'fäng—er, *m.* (—ers, *pl.* —er), —erin, *f.* beginner, tyro. —lich, I. *adj.* incipient, original. II. *adv.* at first.

An'fassen, *v.a.* to take hold of, to seize; to set about; to touch (*a chessman*); faßt an! bear a hand!; falsch —, to bungle; etwas beim rechten Ende *or* Zipfel —, to go the right way to work, to set about a thing in the right way; Perlen —, to string beads.

An'faulen, *v.n.* (*aux.* s.) to begin to rot. angefault, *p.p.* & *adj.* rotten, decayed.

An'fechtbar, *adj.* & *adv.* controvertible, disputable, open to controversy *or* doubt.

An'fecht—en, *ir.v.a.* to attack, to assail; to trouble; to tempt; to contest; was ficht dich an? what is the matter with you? was ficht mich das an? what is that to me? —ung, *f.* attacking, contesting; attack; opposition; vexation; (*Theol.*) temptation.

An'feilen, *v.a.* to begin filing; to file (*a point*).

An'feind—en, *v.a.* to bear ill will to, to show enmity to. —ung, *f.* persecution; enmity, hostility.

An'fertig—en, *v.a.* to make, manufacture, to get up. —ung, *f.* making, manufacturing, preparation.

An'fesseln, *v.a.* to fetter, shackle, chain (*to*); enchain (*fig.*).

An'feuchten, *v.a.* to moisten, to wet.

An'fetten, *v.a.* to mix with grease; to baste.

An'feuern, *v.* I. *a.* to set on fire, to heat; to inflame, fire, animate, encourage, excite. II. *n.* (*aux.* h.) to begin firing.

An'firnissen, *v.a.* to varnish over.

An'flammen, *v.a.* to inflame; to sear; to animate.

An'flattern, *v.n.* to flutter up, to come on fluttering.

An'flecken, *v.a.* to put on a patch.

An'fleh—en, *v.a.* to implore. —ung, *f.* supplication.

An'fletschen, *v.a.* to grin at, show the teeth to.

An'flicken, *v.a.* to patch, sew on to; to patch up.

An'fliegen, *ir.v.n.* (*aux.* s.) to fly to *or* against; es fliegt ihm alles an, he succeeds easily in everything; die Krankheit ist ihm wie angeflogen, that illness attacked him very suddenly; ihm sind einige theologische Kenntnisse angeflogen, he has picked up a smattering of divinity.

An'fließen, *ir.v.n.* (*aux.* s.) to flow towards; to wash, to run by; to rise, swell.

An'flöß—en, *v.a.* to float to; to cause to drift to. —ung, *f.* a floating to; alluvium.

An'fluchen, *v.a.* to call down a curse on, to curse at, to meet with curses.

An'flug, *m.* (—s, *pl.* Anflüge) flight; flying to *or* against; sudden approach; tinge; smattering; copse; — von Röte, slight blush; — von Narrheit, fit of folly.

An'fluß, *m.* (—sses, *pl.* Anflüsse) flowing on, towards *or* against; swelling; flow, rise (*of the tide*); alluvial deposit.

An'fluten, *v.n.* (*aux.* s.) to rush on (*as a flood*).

An'forder—(e)n, *v.a.* to demand as due, to claim. —ung, *f.* claim, demand; pretension.

An'frage, *f.* (*pl.* —n) enquiry; demand; auf —, on inquiry, on application.

An'fragen, *reg.* (& *ir.*) *v.n.* (*aux.* h.) to ask in passing, to put a question, to ask.

An'fress—en, *ir.v.a.* to gnaw; to corrode; ein angefressener Zahn, a decayed tooth. —end, *adj.* corrosive, corroding. —ung, *f.* corrosion, erosion.

An'freunden, *v.r.*; sich mit einem —, to become intimate with s.o., to enter upon friendly relations with s.o. (*coll.*).

An'frieren, *ir.v.n.* (*aux.* s.) to freeze; to freeze fast to.

An'frisch—en, *v.a.* to freshen, to refresh; to revive, reduce (*metals*); to animate, stimulate, arouse; eine Pumpe —en, to pour water down a pump. angefrischt, *p.p.* & *adj.* spirited. —er, *m.* refiner (*Metal.*). —ung, *f.* refreshment; touching up (*a picture*); reduction (*of metals*); encouragement. *Comp.* —ofen, *m.* refining furnace.

An'fuge, *f.* (*pl.* —n) an inserted leaf; rider (*to a proposition*); in der —, enclosed (*obs.*).

An'fugen, *v.a.* to fit on to.

An'fügen, *v.a.* to join to; to add to, to subjoin.

An'fühlen, *v.a.* to touch, to feel; to know by the feel; sich —, to feel; es fühlt sich weich an, it feels soft.

An'fuhr, *f.* (*pl.* —en) conveying, transporting, transport.

An'führbar, *adj.* adducible; what may be quoted.

An'führ—en, *v.a.* to lead on; to bring up to *or* near; to head, conduct, lead; to guide, direct; to quote, cite; to allege, adduce; to train; to hoax, dupe, cheat, trick, take in; eine Meute —en, to hunt (*a pack of hounds*); am angeführten Orte (*abbrev.* a. a. O.) *loco citato*, in the before-mentioned place *or* passage, see above; angeführt! caught! taken in!; —er, *m.* (—ers, *pl.* —er) leader, general, commander-in-chief; ringleader; instructor; cheat. —erei', *f.* hoaxing, imposition. —ung, *f.* command (*of an army*), leadership; quotation; allegation, pleading; hoaxing, taking in, deception; training; falsche —ung, misquotation. *Comp.* —ungs=zeichen, *n.* sign of quotation, quotation mark, inverted comma.

An'füllen, *v.a.* to fill, replenish; to cram.

An'funkeln, *v.a.* to sparkle upon.

An'furt, *f.* (*pl.* —en) landing-place, wharf, quay.

An'gabe, *f.* (*pl.* —n) declaration; account; estimate; sketch, plan; assertion; earnest-money, deposit; denunciation; nach —, according to statement; nach seiner —, according to him.

An'gaffen, *v.a.* to gape at, to gaze at.

An'gähnen, *v.a.* to yawn in one's face; to yawn at.

An'gang, *m.* coming near, advance, approach; feindlicher —, hostile approach, attack.

An'gängig, *adj.* permissible, permitted, feasible; es ist nicht —, it is not possible, it will not do.

An'geb—en, *ir.v.* I. *a.* to begin to give (*obs.*); to assign (*a reason*); to declare, make a statement, give an account of; to mention; to estimate; to denounce; to inform against; to instance; to give in advance, give in part payment; to suggest; to sketch, plan; sich —en, to denounce oneself; to accuse oneself; den Ton —en, to give the keynote, to lead the fashion; Gründe —en, to specify reasons; Waren —en, to enter goods at the custom-house; die Melodie —en, to start, raise the tune; seinen Namen —en, to give *or* send in one's name; sein Alter —, to state one's age; sein Spiel —en, to call (*the points in*) one's game. II. *n.* (*aux.* h.) to deal first (*at cards*); to follow suit. —er, *m.* (—ers, *pl.* —er) stater, declarer; informer; talebearer; author; first dealer (*cards*). —erei', *f.* (*pl.* —erei'en) informing, talebearing, informer's trade. —erisch, *adj.* informing, sneaky. —lich, *adj.* & *adv.* alleged; pretended, ostensible; nominal; der —liche Preis, the price quoted; —licher Maßen, —lichermaßen, *adv.* in the manner stated; ein —licher Kaufmann, a person calling himself *or* supposed to be a merchant. *Comp.* —s=liste, *f.* ship's manifest.

An'gebinde, *n.* (—s, *pl.* —) gift, (*birthday*) present.

An'geboren, *adj.* inborn, innate; connate.

An'gebot, *n.* (—es, *pl.* —e) (*first*) offer; first bid; — und Nachfrage, supply and demand.

An'gedeihen, *ir.v.n.*; einem etwas — lassen, to confer s.th. upon s.o., grant s.th. to s.o.

An'gedenken, *see* Andenken.

An'gehänge, *n.* (—s, *pl.* —) appendage, amulet; pendant.

An'gehen, *ir.v.* I. *a.* to approach; to apply to, to solicit; to concern, have to do with, be related to; mit Bitten —, to approach with entreaties, to beseech, to memorialise; einen —, to concern; was geht's mich an? what's that to me? er geht mich nichts an, he is nothing to me; er hat uns um eine Unterstützung angegangen, he has applied to us for support; ich wurde von ihm um eine milde Gabe angegangen, I was asked by him for a charity. II. *n.* (*aux.* s.) to begin, commence; to begin to take root; to grow; to catch fire; to spoil *or* rot, to go on (*of clothes*); to be practicable; to be endurable; das geht nicht an *or* so geht's nicht an, that won't do; der Verlust wird wohl noch —, the loss will not be so great after all. —d, I. *adj.* beginning; bei —der Nacht, at nightfall, dusk; ein —der Soldat, a young soldier, a (*raw*) recruit; ein —der Professor, a scholar on the way to become a professor; ein —der Student, a freshman; —de Schönheit, budding beauty; ein —der Dreißiger, a man just turned of thirty. II. *prep.* concerning, as for; mich —d, as for me. —ds, *adv.* at first; in the beginning.

An'geheiratet, *adj.* connected by *or* on account of marriage; ein —er Vetter, a cousin by marriage.

An'geheitert, *adj.* slightly tipsy.

An'gehör—en, *v.n.* (*aux.* s.) to belong to, to appertain. —ig, *adj.* & *adv.* belonging to; related to; seine —igen, *pl.* his relations, his people.

An'geklagt—e(r), *m.* (—en, *pl.* —en) a man accused, defendant. —er! defendant!

An'gel, *m.* (—s, *pl.* —n) (*obs.*) & (*usually*) *f.* (*pl.* —n) sting of bees; hinge; pole (*of the earth*); fishing-rod; tang (*of a knife, sword, etc.*); pivot; mantrap; aus den —n heben, to take off the hinges; zwischen Thür und — stecken, to be in a sad dilemma, in a fix; to be about to leave, in a hurry. *Comp.* —förmig, *adj.* barbed, hooked. —haken, *m.* fishing-hook. —kreis, *m.* polar circle. —locke, *f.* lovelock. —punkt, *m.* cardinal-point; pole (*of the earth*). —rute, *f.* fishing-rod. —schmied, *m.* maker of fishing-tackle. —schnur, *f.* fishing-line. —stern, *m.* pole-star, polar star, lode-star (*obs.*). —tugend, *f.* cardinal virtue. —weit, *adj.* & *adv.* (*hinges*) wide open.

An'geld, *n.* (—es, *pl.* —er) earnest-money; money in advance; first part-payment.

An'gelegen, *p.p.* & *adj.* adjacent; important; sich (*dat.*) — sein lassen, to pay attention to, interest oneself in, take to heart; ich lasse es mir — sein, I make it my business. —heit, *f.* (*pl.* —heiten) concern, affair, business; transaction; Minister der auswärtigen —heiten, minister for foreign affairs; Secretary of State for Foreign Affairs (*in England*). —t=lich, *adj.* & *adv.* pressing, urgent.

An'geln, *v.a.* to angle, to fish (nach, for); to fish with the line; sich (*dat.*) einen —, to take a p. to task (*sl.*); sie sucht ihn zu —, she wishes to secure him (*as a suitor and future husband*) (*coll.*)

An'geloben, *v.a.* to vow; to promise solemnly.

An'gelöbnis, *n.* (—sses, *pl.* —sse) vow, solemn protestation.

An'gemessen, *p.p.* of anmessen & *adj.* adapted to, in keeping with; proper; suitable, conformable. —heit, *f.* propriety; correspondence, suitableness, fitness.

An'genehm, *adj.* & *adv.* acceptable, agreeable, pleasing, grateful; „Herr X." „Sehr —," "Mr. X." "Very pleased to see him."

An'genommen, *see* Annehmen.

An'ger, *m.* (—s, *pl.* —) grassy place, green; mead, meadow, pasture, paddock.

An'gesagt, *p.p.* & *adj.* announced, appointed.

An'geschnäuselt, *adj.* slightly tipsy (*sl.*).

An'geschossen, *p.p.* of anschießen & *adj.* smitten, love-sick (*coll.*); —er Eber, a wounded wild boar.

An'gesehen, *p.p.* of ansehen & *adj.* respected, of consequence; esteemed; distinguished.

An'gesessen, *adj.* settled; resident, residing.

An'gesicht, *n.* (—s, *pl.* —er) face; countenance; presence; von —, by sight; von — zu —, face to face; ins —, to one's face. —s, *prep.* (*gen.*) in face of, in view of, considering; immediately on (*receiving, seeing, etc.*).

An'gestammt, *adj.* (durch Abstammung ererbt) hereditary, ancestral; natural, innate; customary (*sl.*).

An'gethan, *p.p.* of anthun, clad; adapted.

An'gewöhn—en, *v.a.* (einem etwas) to accustom, inure to; sich —en, to accustom oneself to. —ung, *f.* accustoming *or* inuring to; —ung übler Sitten, contracting of bad habits.

An'gewohnheit, *f.* (*pl.* —en) custom, use, habit; aus —, from habit.

An'gieren, *v.a.* to look at greedily *or* longingly; to sheer up (*Naut.*).

An'gießen, *ir.v.a.* to pour at *or* on; to cast on, join by casting; to water; to asperse (*prov.*); das Kleid sitzt wie angegossen, the dress fits like a glove, fits tight.

An'glanz, *m.* (—es) reflection, lustre *or* glare (*cast on a body*).

An'glänzen, *v.n.* to shine, glance, cast a glance on; to glare on; to favour (*luck*).

An'gleich—en, *ir.v.a.* to assimilate. —ung, *f* assimilation.

Anglici'st, see Anglist.

An'glieder—n, *v.a.* to join by links, attach to, combine with. —ung, *f.* combination with (an, *acc.*).

Anglika'nisch, *adj.* Anglican; die —e Kirche, the Anglican Church, the Church of England.

An'glimmen, *ir.v.n.* (*aux.* s.) to kindle, to catch fire slowly; to kindle.

Anglisie'ren, *v.a.* to anglicise; Pferde —, to dock (*the tails of*) horses.

Angli'st, *m.* student *or* teacher of English philology. —ik, *f.* English philology.

Anglo= *in compounds*, Anglo-, *e. g.* Anglo=Norma'nne, Anglo-Norman.

Angloma'n—e, *m.* anglomaniac. —ie', *f.* anglomania.

An'glotzen, *v.a.* to stare at, glare on.

An'glühen, *v.* I. *a.* to heat to a glow; to mull (*wine*); to dye with glowing colour; to look on with glowing eyes. II. *n.* (*aux.* s.) to begin to glow. angeglüht, *p.p.* & *adj.* heated to redness; red-hot.

An'greifbar, *adj.* assailable; open to criticism.

An'greif—en, *ir.v.* I. *a.* to handle, touch; to feel; to lay hands on, seize; to undertake, to set about; to attack; to dispute, impugn, assail; to offend, insult; to affect injuriously; to weaken, exhaust; ein Land —en, to attack a country; meine Nerven sind sehr angegriffen, my nerves are quite unstrung; etwas verkehrt —en, to set to work the wrong way; meine Augen sind angegriffen, my eyes are tired, sind sehr angegriffen, are much affected. II. *r.* to exert o.s.; **es greift sich weich an,** it feels soft; **er hat sich sehr angegriffen,** he has been very free with his money; he has been very munificent (*coll.*). **—end,** *adj.* offensive, aggressive; tiring, exhausting; **der —ende Teil,** the assailants. **—er,** *m.* (**—ers,** *pl.* **—er**) aggressor, assailant. **—lich,** *adj.* touchable; tangible, assailable.

An'grenzen, *v.n.* (*aux.* **s.**) to border upon, to confine : to adjoin. **—d,** *p. & adj.* adjacent; **—d an** (*accus.*) contiguous to.

An'griff, *m.* (**—s,** *pl.* **—e**) attack, assault; commencement; invasion; handling; handle; **zum — blasen,** to sound the charge; **dem ersten — standhalten,** to bear the brunt; **einen neuen — machen,** to return to the charge; **in — nehmen,** to take hold of; to begin; **— am Deckel,** thumb-piece (*Typ.*). *Comp.* **—s=bündnis,** *n.* offensive alliance. **s=krieg,** *m.* offensive war. **—s=linie,** *m.* line of attack. **—s=weise,** I. *f.* mode of attack. II. *adv.* offensively; **—sweise zu Werke gehen,** to act on the offensive.

An'grinsen, *v.a.* to grin at *or* on.

An'gst, *f.* (*pl.* **Ängste**), anguish; anxiety, fear; **Todes—,** pangs of death, agony; **in — geraten,** to take alarm; **einem — machen,** to alarm one; *used as adj. or adv., and usually spelt* **angst,** *e.g.* **mir ist —,** I am afraid (**vor,** of); **mir wird —,** I am getting uneasy; **ihm wurde — und bange,** he got into a terrible state of fear. *Comp.* **—geschrei,** *n.* cry of terror *or* anguish. **—meier,** *m.* coward, poltroon (*coll.*). **—röhre,** *f.* top hat (*vulg.*) **—schweiß,** *m.* cold sweat. **—voll,** *adj.* fearful; painful.

Än'gst—en (*obs. & poet.*), **—igen,** *v.a.* to alarm, distress, render anxious; to worry; **sich —igen** (**über eine Sache**), to fret, be uneasy *or* alarmed (about s.th.). **—lich,** *adj. & adv.* anxious, uneasy, distressed; nervous, timid; scrupulous. **—lichkeit,** *f.* anxiety, alarm; nervousness; timidity; scrupulousness.

An'gucken, *v.a.* to look at, peep at.

An'gürten, *v.a.* to gird on.

An'guß, *m.* (**—sses,** *pl.* **Angüsse**) a piece cast on.

An'haben, *ir.v.a.* to have on, to be dressed in; **einem etwas —,** to harm one; to lay anything to one's charge; **sie konnten ihm nichts —,** they could get no hold upon him, find nothing against him, could not do him any harm.

An'hacken, *v.a.* to begin to chop, hack *or* cut; to begin hoeing.

An'haften, *v.n.* (*aux.* **h.**) to adhere to, to be connected with.

An'häkeln, *v. a.* to fasten with little hooks; to clasp.

An'haken, *v.a.* to hook to, to grapple; to grasp.

An'haltern, *v.a.* to fasten by a halter; to tether to.

An'halt, *m.* (**—es,** *pl.* **—e**) stopping, pause, stay; railway station (*dial.*); hold, support. **—sam,** *adj.* persevering, persistent; uninterrupted. **—samkeit,** *f.* perseverance. *Comp.* **—(e)=punkt,** *m.* stopping-place; station; fulcrum. **—s=punkt,** *m.* fact which would help to form a conviction; **keine —s=punkte für eine Vermutung haben,** to be without any actual proofs of a supposition, without anything to go by in making a conjecture. **—(e)=seil,** *n.* headfast.

An'halt—en, I. *ir.v.a.* to check, stop, pull up; to hold to, make faithful to; to seize; to restrain, control; **sich —en** (**an einer S.**), to seize and cling to, to hold on (*by*); **einen zum Zahlen —en,** to urge one to payment, to dun a p. II. *ir.v.n.* (*aux.* **h.**) to stop, halt, draw up; to continue, persevere; to persist in, to stick to; **—en um,** to sue for; **er hat um sie** *or* **ihre Hand angehalten,** he asked her in marriage. III. *subst. n.* stopping; stoppage; clinging to; solicitation, *etc.* **—end,** *p. & adj.* continuous, lasting; persevering; adhesive; **—endes Arzneimittel,** astringent; **—ender Fleiß,** assiduity.

An'hang, *m.* (**—es,** *pl.* **Anhänge**) appendix, supplement, addition, codicil; appendage; postscript; followers, adherents, party.

An'hangen, *ir.v.n.* (*aux.* **s.**) to hang on *or* upon; to adhere to; (*aux.* **h.**) to stick to, to hold by.

An'häng—en, *v.a.* to hang on *or* fasten to; to attach, append, affix; to add, subjoin; to bestow; **der Katze die Schelle —en,** to bell the cat; **einem etwas —en,** to cast a slur (*or* an aspersion) on one, fasten upon one something disagreeable; **einem eine Krankheit —en,** to infect one with a disease (*coll.*); **sich —en,** to adhere to, force oneself on. **—er,** *m.* (**—ers,** *pl.* **—er**) partisan, adherent; hanger-on. **—erei',** *f.* inclination to hang to; partisanship. **—ig,** *adj. & adv.* adherent; cleaving to; importunate; **—iger Prozeß,** pending lawsuit; **eine Klage, einen Prozeß —ig machen,** to bring an action against; **und was dem —ig ist,** with its appurtenances. **—lich,** *adj.* attached to, faithful. **—lichkeit,** *f.* adherence; attachment, constancy. **—sel,** *n.* (**—sels,** *pl.* **—sel**) appendage; appendix; amulet.

An'haspen, *v.a.* to fasten with iron hooks.

An'hauch, *m.* (**—es**) breath (*of wind*); afflation; slight tint; touch.

An'hauchen, *v.a.* to breathe upon. **angehaucht,** *p.p. & adj.* inspired by; **künstlerisch angehaucht,** with the touch of an artist, being something of an artist.

An'hauen, *ir.v.a.* to strike upon; to begin to chop, hew *or* cut; to whip on; to jerk up.

An'häufeln, *v.a.* to gather into small heaps; to hoe.

An'häuf—en, *v.a.* to heap up; to accumulate. **—er,** *m.* (**—ers,** *pl.* **—er**) accumulator. **—ung,** accumulation; aggregation (*Geol.*).

An'heb—en, *ir.v.* I. *a.* to heave up *or* towards: to commence. II. *n.* (*aux.* **h.**) to begin. **—er,** *m.* (**—ers,** *pl.* **—er**) beginner, author, instigator.

An'heften, *v.a.* to fasten to, to affix; to sew, baste *or* pin to *or* on; **unten —,** to stitch down; **einem etwas —,** to cast a slur on a p.

An'heilen, *v.* I. *a.* to join by healing. II. *n.* (*aux.* **s.**) to heal up, to unite in healing; **der Knochen ist gut angeheilt,** the bone has become well consolidated.

Anhei'm, *adv.* at home, in one's house; to one's share; **— fallen,** to fall to, to devolve on; **— geben, — stellen,** to leave to, to place in the keeping of; **sie stellt es dir —,** she leaves it to you; **dem Urteile eines andern — stellen,** to submit to the judgment of another; **stelle das Weitere dem Himmel —,** leave the rest to God *or* in the hands of God. *Comp.* **—fall,** *m.* devolution.

An'heimeln, *v.a.* to remind one (*or* to put one in mind) of home. **—d,** *p.p. & adj.* comfortable.

An'heischig, *adj.* bound; pledged; **sich** (*accus.*) **— machen,** to pledge oneself, to promise.

Anhe'r, *adv.* hither. to this place; **bis —,** hitherto.

An'herrschen, *v.a.* to talk to a p. in an imperious tone; to hector.

An'hetz—en, *v.a.* to begin to hunt; to set on; to incite, stimulate. **—er,** *m.* (**—ers,** *pl.* **—er**), **—erin,** *f.* (*pl.* **—erinnen**) incitor, instigator. **—erei',** *f.*, **—ung,** *f.* setting on, incitation, instigation.

An'heucheln, *v.a.* to put on, feign.

An'heulen, *v.a.* to howl at, to cry at.

An'hexen, *v.a.* to inflict by witchcraft, to bewitch.

An'hieb, *m.* (**—(e)s,** *pl.* **—e**) place where wood is felled; the first stroke (*fenc.*); **auf —,** at the first attempt, at once (*coll.*).

An'höhe, *f.* (*pl.* **—n**) high ground, eminence, hill, knoll.

An'hol—en, *v.a.* to haul tight. *Comp.* **—tau,** *n.* hawser.
An'hör—en, *v.a.* to hear, to listen to; to perceive by listening; **das läßt sich —en,** that is worth considering; **man hört ihm den Ausländer an,** one can tell by his accent that he is a foreigner. **—ung,** *f.* audience, hearing; hearing (*of witnesses, etc.*).
Ani'l, *m.* (—s) indigo. **—säure,** *f.* anilic acid.
Anili'n, *n.* aniline. **—farben,** *f. pl.* aniline (*or* coal-tar) colours, dyes.
Anima'l—ien, *pl.* animal bodies; animal food. **—isch,** *adj. & adv.* animal; beastly.
Animie'r—en, *v.a.* to excite, encourage, urge. **—t,** *adj.;* **—te Stimmung,** high spirits.
A'nimus, *m.* mind; **einen — haben,** to have a mind (*coll.*).
Ani's, *m.* (—ses) anise; anise-seed. *Comp.* **—blatt,** *n.* seringa. **—holz,** *n.* aniseed wood. **—likö'r,** *m.* anisette. **—zucker,** *m.* sugared anise.
Ani'tzo, Ani'tzt (*obs.*) *see* **Jetzt.**
An'jagen, *v.* I. *a.* to give chase to; to slip (*hounds*) at, to set on; to impel to greater speed. II. *n.* (*aux.* **s.**) *or* **angejagt kommen,** to come at full gallop, rush up *or* on.
Anje'tz—o, —t, *adv.* now, at present (*obs.*).
An'jochen, *v.a.* to yoke to, to put to the yoke.
An'kämpfen, *v.a.* (**gegen einen** *or* **eine Sache**) to struggle against *or* with; to combat.
An'kauf, *m.* (—s, *pl.* **Ankäufe**) purchase; buying.
An'kaufen, *v.* I. *a.* to purchase, buy, buy up. II. *r.* to buy lands, settle in a place.
An'ker, *m.* (—s, *pl.* —) anker; cramp-iron, brace; anchor; grapnel; **vor — gehen, den — auswerfen, — werfen,** to cast anchor, to anchor; **dem — mehr Tau ausstechen,** to pay out more cable; **der — greift zu,** the anchor bites; **der — ist triftig, der — setzt durch,** the anchor drags; **einen Sturm vor — aushalten,** to ride out a storm (at anchor); **den** *or* **die — lichten,** to weigh anchor; **vor — liegen,** to ride at anchor. *Comp.* **—boje,** *f.*, **—flott,** *n.* buoy; beacon. **—fliege,** *f.*, **flügel,** *m.* fluke of an anchor. **—geld,** *n.* harbour-dues. **—grund,** *m.* anchorage. **—haken,** *m.* cat-hook. **—haspel,** *m. & f.* capstan. **—loch,** *n.* eye of an anchor. **—rute,** *f.*, **schaft,** *m.* shank of an anchor. **—tau,** *n.* cable. **—winde,** *f.* windlass, capstan. **—zeichen,** *n.* sea-mark.
A'nkern, *v.a. & n.* to anchor; to ride at anchor.
An'ketten, *v.a.* to chain; to enchain; **sich an einen —,** to stick to, attach oneself to a p.
An'kitten, *v.a.* to cement, to fasten with putty.
An'klag—bar, *adj. & adv.* indictable. **—e,** *f.* (*pl.* **—en**) accusation; impeachment, arraignment. *Comp.* **—e=akte,** *f.* bill of indictment. **—e=bank,** *f.* dock. **—e=fall,** *m.* accusative case. **—e=prozeß,** *m.* prosecution. **—e=schrift,** *f.* bill of indictment, accusation. **—e=stand, —e=zustand,** *m.* state of being accused, indicted; **einen in —e=zustand versetzen,** to accuse s. o.
An'klagen, *v.a.* to accuse; **öffentlich —,** to impeach, to indict; **auf Leib und Leben —,** to accuse of a capital crime; **der Angeklagte,** the accused, defendant.
An'kläger, *m.* (—s, *pl.* —), **—in,** *f.* (*pl.* **—innen**) accuser; plaintiff, complainant; informer. **—isch,** *adj.* prone to accuse. **—ischerseits,** *adv.* on the part of the plaintiff.
An'klammern, *v.* I. *a.* to fasten with cramps. II. *r.* **sich an eine Sache —,** to cling to a thing.
An'klang, *m.* (—s, *pl.* **Anklänge**) accord, harmony; concord; sympathy; approbation; **der Vorschlag fand keinen —,** the proposal met with no approval, was not supported.
Ankleben, *v.* I. *n.* to stick to. II. *a.* to glue *or* paste on, up, *or* to; to stick together. **—d,** *p. & adj.* inherent, adhesive.

2

An'kleid—en, *v.* I. *a.* to put on clothes, to attire. II. *r.* to dress (oneself). *Comp.* **—e=zimmer,** *n.* dressing-room; vestry (*eccles.*).
An'kleistern, *v.a.* to paste, to paste to, on, up.
An'klingeln, *v.* I. *n.* to ring the bell; **bei einem —,** to sound, sift one; (*coll.*). II. *a.* to announce by ringing; **angeklingelt kommen,** to arrive in a carriage *or* sledge (*bells being fastened to the vehicles and to the horses*).
An'klingen, *ir.v.* I. *n.* (*aux.* **h.**) to begin to sound; to accord in sound; **etwas klingt mir an,** something strikes my ear (*poet.*). II. *a.* to clink (*glasses*). III. *reg.v.a.* to cause to tinkle (*glasses*).
An'klopf—en, *v.* I. *n.* to knock at, to knock; to sound. II. *a.* to fasten by hammering. **—er,** *m.* (—ers, *pl.* —er) person knocking.
An'knöpfen, *v.a.* to button (to *or* on).
An'knüpf—en, *v.a.* to tie, join, fasten with a knot; to begin, enter into; **Verbindungen —en,** to form connections, begin a correspondence with; **ein Gespräch wieder —en,** to resume a conversation; **eine Bekanntschaft wieder —en,** to resume an acquaintance. *Comp.* **—ungs=punkt,** *m.* point of contact, point or interest in common, starting point, connecting link.
An'knurren, *v.a.* to growl, snarl at.
An'kommen, *ir.v.* I. *a.* to befall, come upon; **es kam mich (mir) eine Lust an,** I took a fancy to; **der Schlaf kam mich an,** I grew drowsy; **es kam mich (mir) eine Furcht an,** I was seized with fear; **was kommt ihn an?** what ails him? **es kommt mich (mir) schwer an,** it is hard on me; I find it hard. II. *n.* (*aux.* **s.**) to come to *or* near, to approach; to arrive; to fall in with (*Naut.*); to reach, overtake; to obtain a place, be established; to get on, succeed; to depend on, be determined by; to concern; to import, matter; **bei einem wohl, übel —,** to be well, ill received by one; **da kommen Sie schön an,** you will meet with a nice reception! (*iron.*); **bei mir kommt man damit nicht an,** that will not do for me; **gut —,** to be well situated, settled; **auf etwas (einen) —,** to depend on; **es auf etwas (einen) — lassen,** to run the risk, to leave it to some one's decision; **ich lasse es auf das Äußerste —,** I will push the matter to extremities; **das Fenster, worauf es mir ankam,** the window which concerned me; **es kommt auf sein Leben an,** his life is at stake; **darauf kommt es an,** that is the point; **es kommt darauf an, zu wissen, &c.,** the question is, to know, *etc.*; **wir wollen es darauf — lassen,** we will take our chance; **es soll mir nicht auf ein paar Mark —,** I shall not mind a few shillings; **es kommt ihm auf einen Tag nicht an,** he is not particular to a day; **es kommt nichts darauf an,** no matter, it matters little. **—d,** *p.;* **—der Zug,** train coming in.
An'kömm—lich, *adj.* accessible (*rare*). **—ling,** *m.* (**—lings,** *pl.* **—linge**) new-comer, stranger; novice.
An'kontrahieren, *v.a.* to challenge for a duel (*sl.*).
An'köpfen, *v.a.* to head (*pins*).
An'kränkeln, *v.a.* to sickly over; **von des Gedankens Blässe angekränkelt,** sicklied over with the pale east of thought.
An'kreiden, *v.a.* to chalk up, note with chalk; **etwas — lassen,** to have something entered into the account book, to go without paying (*sl.*); **das werde ich ihm —,** I shall make him pay for that! (*sl.*).
An'kriechen, *ir.v.n.* (*aux.* **s.**) to approach by creeping; **angekrochen kommen,** to creep up.
An'künd—en, —igen, *v.a.* to announce; to advertise; to declare, proclaim. **—iger,** *m.* (**—igers,** *pl.* **—iger**) announcer. **—igung,** *f.* declaration, proclamation, announcement.

An'kunft, *f.* arrival, advent; origin, descent (*obs.*).

An'lachen, *v.a.* to laugh at, to look at laughingly, to smile upon; to favour.

An'lächeln, *v.a.* to smile at *or* upon.

An'lage, *f.* (*pl.* **—n**) a laying out; plan, arrangement; rough sketch; pleasure-ground, (*pl.*) grounds, park, promenade; talent, ability; natural tendency; predisposition; capital; thing annexed, appendix; foundation-works, groundwork; **— zur Gicht,** a tendency to gout; **aus der — werden Sie ersehen,** you will see by the annexed. *Comp.* **—kapita'l,** *n.* funds, stock, business-capital. **—kosten,** *pl.* cost of construction. **—papier,** *n.* investment-paper, investment-stock.

An'land—en, *v.* I. *n.* (*aux.* **s.**) to land, to disembark, to get ashore. II. *a.* to put (*a boat*) on shore. **—ung,** *f.* landing.

An'lände, *f.* landing-place (*obs.*).

An'langen, *v.* I. *n.* (*aux.* **s.**) to arrive at, to reach. II. *a.* to concern, to relate to. **—d,** *p. used as prep.* concerning; as for.

An'laß, *m.* (**—sses,** *pl.* **Anlässe**) letting in; appearance; cause, occasion, motive; **es hat allen — dazu,** it seems very probable; **ohne allen —,** without the slightest reason *or* provocation; **zu einem Gerüchte — geben,** to give occasion to a rumour, to raise a report.

An'lassen, *ir.v.* I. *a.* to leave on; to let loose, let go; to temper; to set agoing; to receive, treat; to turn on (*water, steam, mills, etc.*); **er hat ihn scharf angelassen,** he has given him a sharp rebuke. II. *r.* to appear; to promise; **ein junger Mensch, der sich gut anläßt,** a promising youth; **die Sache läßt sich nicht übel an,** the matter is getting on very well so far; **das Wetter läßt sich gut an,** the weather is fine.

An'läßlich, *prep.* (*with genit.*) à propos of; on the occasion of.

An'lauf, *m.* (**—(e)s,** *pl.* **Anläufe**) start, run; rise; onset, attack; concourse, crowd; apophyge (*Arch.*); **er nahm einen — zum Springen,** he took a run before leaping; **der — des Wassers,** the rising of the water.

An'laufen, *ir.v.* I. *n.* (*aux.* **s.**) to run up to, to rush against; to attack (*obs.*); to begin to run; to rise, swell; to get dim, rusty, mouldy; **übel —,** to run a bad chance, to be badly received; **die Fläche läuft sanft an,** the plain rises with a gentle slope; **in diesem Keller läuft alles an,** everything grows mouldy, rusty in this cellar; **schwarz — lassen,** to make black; **Stahl blau — lassen,** to make steel blue. II. *a.* to solicit, importune; to attack (*obs.*).

An'laut, *m.* (**—s,** *pl.* **—e**) initial sound, letter *or* letters (*Gramm.*); **im —,** initially, when initial (*Gramm.*).

An'lauten, *v.n.* to begin with a sound, letter *or* letters; **das Wort lautet mit E an,** the initial letter of the word is E. **—d,** *adj. & adv.* initial(ly) (*Gram.*).

An'läuten, *v.a.* to ring the bell (*as a signal to commence work*); to ring.

An'leg—en, I. *v.a.* to lay *or* put on, against, to; to apply; to lay out, plan; to plot; to sketch; **Holz —en,** to put wood (*on the fire*); **einem Ketten —en,** to chain one; **Reifen —en,** to hoop (*casks, etc.*); **das Gewehr —en,** to take aim at; **legt an!** present! (*Mil.*); **Feuer —en,** to set fire to; **angelegte Feuer,** incendiary fires; **Hand —en,** to take in hand, give a hand; **etwas mit einem —en,** to concert, plan s.th.; **ein Kleid, Trauer —en,** to put on a dress, mourning; **Geld —en,** to invest money; **Zeit —en,** to employ time; **eine Stadt, 2c., —en,** to found, establish a town, etc.; **eine Kolonie —en,** to plant a colony; **einem Pferde den Zaum —en,** to bridle a horse; **die letzte Hand —en,** to give the finishing touch **to (an** *acc.*); **er legte es darauf an,** he made it his object. II. *r.* to lean against; to adhere to; to board (*a ship*). III. *n.* (*aux.* **h.**) to land, to lie to; to lie alongside; **—en auf** (*acc.*) to take aim at. **—ung,** *f.* the putting on; laying out, planning; establishment; employment, investment (*of capital*). *Comp.* **—e=marken,** *pl.* markers. **—e=schloß,** *n.* padlock.

An'leh(e)n, *n.* (**—s,** *pl.* **—**) loan (*obs.*).

An'lehn—e, *f.* (*pl.* **—en**) a rest, the back of a chair, *etc.* *Comp.* **—punkt,** *m.* point of support (*Mil.*).

An'lehnen, *v.a. & r.* to lean against; **die Thüre —,** to leave the door ajar.

An'leihe, *f.* (*pl.* **—n**) loan; **eine — machen,** to raise a loan.

An'leimen, *v.a.* to glue on; (*Geol.*) to agglutinate (*Gram.*).

An'leit—en, *v.a.* to guide to, to conduct; to instruct; to train; to introduce (*to a study, etc.*). **—ung,** *f.* guidance; methodical instruction; introduction; method; primer.

An'lernen, *v.a.* to acquire by study; to train, instruct.

An'liegen, I. *ir.v.n.* to lie close to, to join, to border on; to fit well (*of clothes*); to stand to, steer (*Naut.*); to concern; **sich** (*dat.*) **angelegen sein lassen,** to bestow care upon, to have at heart; **einem —,** to urge *or* solicit a p.; **—de Winkel,** adjacent angles. II. *subst.n.* adjacency; concern, object of interest; anxiety, cause of solicitude; desire, wish, aim; request.

An'lock—en, *v.a.* to allure, to attract, to entice. **—end,** *p. & adj.* attractive, alluring. **—er,** *m.* (**—ers,** *pl.* **—er**) enticer. **—erin,** *f.* (*pl.* **—erinnen**) flirt, coquette. **—ung,** *f.* enticement.

An'löten, *v.a.* to solder to.

An'lügen, *ir.v.a.* to tell s.o. an impudent falsehood.

An'luven, *v.n.* to go to windward, to luff.

An'machen, *v.* I. *a.* to fasten, fix, join to, *or* on; to light (*a fire*); to mix; to adulterate; **einen Salat —,** to dress a salad; **mit Gewürz —,** to spice; **Farben —,** to temper colours; **Kalk —,** to slack lime. II. *r.* **sich an einen machen,** to accost one; to approach one, to make up to one, to insinuate o.s. into one's favour.

An'mahnen, *v.a.* to exhort, to admonish; to animate, urge on; to dun (*a debtor*) (*rare*).

An'malen, *v.a.* to paint; to give a coat of paint.

An'marsch, *m.* (**—es,** *pl.* **Anmärsche**) advance (*of an army*).

An'marschieren, *v.n.* (*aux.* **s.**) to advance, to march on *or* up.

An'maß—en, *v.r.* to claim, pretend to; to usurp, arrogate; to presume; **was maßest du dir an?** what do you presume? **—end,** *p. & adj.* arrogant; **nicht —end,** unassuming. **—lich,** *adj. & adv.* assumable, presumptive; arrogant. **—ung,** *f.* presumption; usurpation; arrogance; **kühne —ung,** insolence. *Comp.* **—ungs=voll,** *adj.* full of arrogance; very presumptuous.

An'melden, *v.a.* to announce; to notify; to report, to usher in; **sich — lassen,** to have oneself announced; to send in one's name; **sich zu etwas —,** to offer oneself for, apply for.

An'merk—en, *v.a.* to perceive, observe, notice; to note, write down. **—er,** *m.* (**—ers,** *pl.* **—er**) observer; annotator. **—lich,** *adj. & adv.* observable. **—ung,** *f.* remark, observation; note, annotation. *Comp.* **—e=buch,** *n.* notebook. **—ens=wert,** *adj.* worthy of note.

An'messen, *ir.v.a.* to measure, take the measure for; to fit, suit, adapt; **einem einen Rock —,** to take a p.'s measure for a coat. **angemessen,** *p.p. & adj.* suitable, proper.

Anmi't, *adv.* herewith (*rare*).

An'mut, *f.* agreeableness; charm, grace, gracefulness; sweetness, amenity. **—ig,** *adj.* pleasant, charming; graceful; gracious. *Comp.* **—los,** *adj.* devoid of grace, lacking in grace, unpleasing. **—s=voll,** *adj. see* **—ig.**

An'muten, *v.a. see* **Zu'muten.** **—ung,** *f.* expectation of what a person can do, demand; *see* **Zumutung.**

An'nagen, *v.a.* to begin to gnaw at; to nibble at.

An'nähen, *v.a.* to sew on.

An'näher—n, *v.* I. *a.* to approximate, bring near. II. *r.* to approach. III. *n.* (*aux.* **f.**) to approach, draw near. **—nd,** I. *p. & adj.* approximative; contiguous. II. *adv.* approximate, by approximation. **—ung,** *f.* approximation; approach; advance. *Comp.* **—ungs=graben,** *m.* approach, parallel (*Fort.*). **—ungs=kraft,** *f.* centripetal force. **—ungs=linie,** *f.* line of approach (*Fort.*); asymptote. **—ungs=punkt,** *m.* point of approximation.

An'nahme, *f.* (*pl.* **—n**) taking; acceptance; engagement (*of a servant*); adoption (*of opinions; of children*); acceptation; assumption, postulation; **die — eines Wechsels verweigern,** to dishonour a bill; **wegen nicht erfolgter —,** for non-acceptance; **einem Wechsel eine willige — bereiten,** to meet, duly honour a bill.

Anna'len, *pl.* annals. **—i'stik,** *f.* writing of annals.

Anna'ten, *pl.* (*Rom. Cath. Church*) first fruits.

An'nehmbar, *adj.* acceptable, admissible.

An'nehm—en, *ir.v.a.* to take, to receive; to close with; to admit; to take into one's service; to retain, employ; to suppose, take for granted; to undertake (*a commission*); to take up (*a challenge*); to admit as true; to take (*colour, impression, polish, etc.*); to embrace (*a faith, etc.*); to honour, accept (*a bill*); to agree to (*a condition, etc.*); to assume (*a character; a form, etc.*); to contract (*habits*); to embrace (*an opinion*); **nicht —en,** to reject; **die Fährte —en,** to catch the scent; **an Kindes Statt —en,** to adopt; **sich einer Sache —en,** to interest oneself in, take up a thing; **sich einer Person —en,** to interest oneself for, espouse the cause of, assist a person; **Vernunft —,** to listen to reason; **sich** (*dat.*) **etwas —en,** to apply to oneself; **das brauchst du dir nicht anzunehmen,** you need not apply that to yourself; **der König hat sich seiner angenommen,** the king has taken care of him *or* the king has espoused his cause; **angenommen,** assuming (*that*); **angenommene Freundlichkeit,** assumed friendliness. **—er,** *m.* (**—ers,** *pl.* **—er**) accepter. **—lich,** *adj. & adv.* acceptable; agreeable; assumable. **—lichkeit,** *f.* acceptableness; pleasantness; pleasure, charm; amenity; comforts.

An'neigen, *v.* I. *a.* to incline towards; **sich —,** to lean against. II. *n.* to converge; **—de Linien,** convergent lines.

Annektie'r—en, *v.a.* to annex, to take away. **—ung,** *f.* annexation.

A'nno (*Lat. ablative case of annus, 'year'*) in the year; **—To'bak,** antediluvian, in days long gone by (*coll.*).

Anno'ch, *adv.* as yet.

Anno'nce, *f.* (*pl.* **—n**) advertisement.

Annullie'r—en, *v.a.* to annul, nullify, cancel; to annihilate, defeat. **—ung,** *f.* nullification, cancelling, annulment; defeating.

An'öden, *v.a.* to molest, tease, bore (*sl.*).

Anomal—ie', *f.* (*pl.* **—ie'en**) anomaly. **—isch** (*pron.* **anomā'lisch**), *adj. & adv.* anomalous.

Anony'm, *adj. & adv.* anonymous.

An'ordn—en, *v.a.* to order; to regulate, arrange; to appoint; to marshal, to institute. **—er,** *m.* (**—ers,** *pl.* **—er**) arranger; director; disposer, compiler. **—ung,** *f.* arrangement; regulation; preparation; instruction; **—ungen treffen,** to make preparations.

An'packen, *v.a.* to grasp, to seize; to attack.

An'pappen, *v.a.* to paste on, up *or* to.

An'passen, *v.* I. *n.* (*aux.* **f.**) to fit, to suit. II. *a.* to make to fit; to adapt; **sich** (*acc.*) **den Verhältnissen —,** to accommodate o.s. to circumstances. **—d,** *p. & adj.* well-fitting; fit, suitable, appropriate to.

An'pfählen, *v.a.* to prop; to pale up, to empale.

An'pfeifen, *v.a.* to whistle at; to hiss at.

An'pflanz—en, *v.a.* to form a plantation; to plant; to cultivate; **sich —en,** to settle. **—er,** *m.* (**—ers,** *pl.* **—er**) planter, settler, colonist. **—ung,** *f.* plantation, planting; *pl.* improvements.

An'pflöcken, *v.a.* to fasten with pegs; to stretch (*a canvas*).

An'pflügen, *v.* I. *n.* to plough against. II. *a. & n.* to begin to plough, to open a furrow.

An'pichen, *v.a.* to pitch; to stick to with pitch.

An'pfropfen, *v.a.* to graft; to glut, gorge (*vulg.*).

An'pinseln, *v.a.* to daub *or* paint coarsely.

An'pochen, *v.a.* to knock, knock at loudly.

An'poltern, *v.* I. *n.* (*aux.* **h.**) to knock violently at (**an**), to rattle at. II. (*aux.* **f.**) **er ist angepoltert** *or* **er kam angepoltert,** he came up in a swaggering *or* in a noisy manner.

An'posaunen, *v.a.* to announce with the trumpet; to puff.

An'prall, *m.* (**—s**) act of bounding against; forcible impact; bruise. *Comp.* **—(s)=winkel,** *m.* angle of reflection.

An'prallen, *v.n.* (*aux.* **f.**) to bound against.

An'preisen, *ir.v.a.* to recommend, praise.

An'pressen, *v.a.* to press *or* squeeze against.

An'proben, An'probieren, *v.a.* to try on, fit on.

An'prosten, *v.a.;* **einen —,** to drink to a person, to pledge a p., saying **Prost** (*sl.*).

An'pumpen, *v.a.* to borrow money of a p., to squeeze money out of a p. (*sl.*).

An'putz, *m.* (**—es**) dress, finery; dressing. **—en,** *v.* I. *a.* to dress out, bedizen. II. *r.* to dress up; to deck oneself out.

An'quick—en, *v.a.* to amalgamate (*metals*). **—ung,** *f.* amalgamation.

An'racken, *v.a.* to fasten the yards with a parrel (*Naut.*).

An'rammen, *v.a.* to fasten by ramming, ram tight.

An'ranken, *v.a.* to fasten by tendrils, to twine round, clasp.

An'ranzen, *v.a.;* **einen —,** to give one a severe scolding, to rebuke, to speak harshly to a p.

An'raten, *ir.v.a.;* **einem etwas —,** to advise, recommend s.th. to s.o.

An'rauchen, *v.a.* to begin to smoke, to light (*a pipe*); to smoke for the first time (*a new pipe*); to season by smoking; to smoke brown; **eine Pfeife —,** to season *or* colour a pipe. **angeraucht,** *p.p. & adj.* smoke-coloured; seasoned.

An'räuchern, *v.a.* to smoke a little; to drive smoke *or* perfume against; to fumigate.

An'rauschen, *v.n.* to rush up; **angerauscht kommen,** to come up with a rustle.

An'rechnen, *v.a.;* **einem etwas —,** to charge something to someone, or a person with something; to reckon; to rate; to impute, to attribute to; **Sie haben es mir zu hoch angerechnet,** you have overcharged me for it; **ich rechne ihm diesen Dienst sehr hoch an,** I value greatly the service he has done me.

An'recht, *n.* (**—es,** *pl.* **—e**) claim, right; **ein — auf eine Sache haben,** to have right to, a title *or* claim to a thing.

An'rede, (*pl.* **—n**) *f.* address, harangue, allocution; apostrophe (*Rhet.*).

An'red—en, *v.a.* to speak to, to accost; to harangue; to accuse; **einem etwas —en,** to persuade one to (*do* or *buy a thing*) *Comp.* **—e=fall,** *m.* vocative case.

An'reg—en, *v.a.* to stir up; to incite; to stimulate; to allude to, make mention of; **angeregte Unterhaltung,** animated conversation.

—**end**, stimulating, interesting, suggestive. —**ung**, *f.* the alluding to; stimulus, incitation, stimulation, stirring up; hint, mentioning; **in —ung bringen**, to allude to, touch upon; to mention, suggest; **auf —ung von**, at the instigation *or* suggestion of; **etwas bei einem wieder in —ung bringen**, to remind one of s.th.; **geistige —**, intellectual stimulus.

An'reiben, *ir.v.a.* to begin to rub; to get, to give by rubbing; to rub against.

An'reihen, *v.* I. *a.* to string; to file; to arrange in sequence; to baste on. II. *r.* to follow; to join; to rank with; **sich — lassen**, to be placed in the same rank with; **an diesen Satz lassen sich eine Menge Folgerungen —**, numerous deductions result from this proposition.

An'reim, *m.* alliteration (*metre*).

An'reißen, *ir.v.a.* to tear off; to begin to tear, break *or* cut; to make a first sketch.

An'reiten, *ir. v.* I. *n.* (*aux.* **s.**) to ride towards; to ride against; to stop *or* alight; **er kam angeritten**, he rode up. II. *a.* to break in (*a horse*); to ride up to; to charge.

An'reiz, *m.* (—**es**, *pl.* —**ungen**) incitement, motive, incentive.

An'reiz—en, *v.a.* to incite, induce (**zu**, to); **einen zum Bösen —en**, to entice one to do wrong. —**end**, *p.* & *adv.* attractive. —**er**, *m.* (—**ers**, *pl.* —**er**) instigator. —**ung**, *f.* instigation; incentive; provocation, encouragement.

An'rempeln, *v.a.*; **einen —**, to jostle against a p. on purpose; to pick a quarrel with a p. (*coll.*).

An'rennen, *reg.* & *ir.v.* I. *a.* to rush upon, to assail. II. *n.* (*aux.* **s.**) to run against; to start with a run; **angerannt kommen**, to come running, to come in great haste; **übel —**, to meet with a bad reception, to catch a Tartar; **da bist du mal schön angerannt**, there you have caught it hot (*sl.*).

An'richte, *f.* (*pl.* —**n**) dresser.

An'richt—en, *v.a.* to prepare; to cook; to dish up; to regulate; to produce, cause; **es ist angerichtet**, dinner, supper is served; **was hast du angerichtet?** what have you done? **da haben Sie was Schönes angerichtet**, you have put in your foot nicely (*coll.*). —**ung**, *f.* dressing, preparation, *etc.*; detent (*Horol.*). *Comp.* —**kunst**, *see* **Kochkunst**. —**löffel**, *m.* ladle. —**schüssel**, *f.* platter, dish. —**tisch**, *m.* kitchen table, dresser.

An'riechen, *ir.v.* I. *n.* to emit a smell. II. *a.* to smell at; **einem etwas —**, to know by the smell of a p.; **ich habe ihm den Tabak angerochen**, I perceived that he smelt of tobacco.

An'ringen, *ir.v.n.* (*aux.* **h.**) to struggle (*against*)

An'rinnen, *ir.v.n.* (*aux.* **s.**) to run against (*of water, etc.*); to run *or* flow near.

An'ritt, *m.* (—**es**) approach on horseback; first ride; cavalry charge. *Comp.* —**s=geld**, *n.* earnest money paid to troopers for an outfit.

An'ritzen, *v.a.* to slit, scratch a little.

An'rollen, *v.* I. *a.* to roll against. II. *n.* (*aux.* **s.**) to approach rolling, to roll up *or* on.

An'rosten, *v.n.* (*aux.* **s.**) to rust (*on*); to begin to rust.

An'rüchig, *adj.* notorious; infamous; disreputable. —**keit**, *f.* notoriety, disrepute.

An'rücken, *v.* I. *n.* (*aux.* **s.**) to approach; to advance. II. *a.* to move *or* bring near to.

An'rudern, *v.n.* to row against; to row up, approach rowing.

An'ruf, *m.* (—**s**) call, shout; appeal; summons.

An'ruf—en, *ir.v.a.* to call to; to challenge; to invoke, implore; to appeal to; to hail (*a ship*); to call up (*Telegr.*); to ring up (*Telephon.*); **zum Zeugen —en**, to call to witness. —**er**, *m.* (—**ers**, *pl.* —**er**) appellant. —**ung**, *f.* calling to, appealing to; appeal; invocation. *Comp.* —**ungs=gericht**, *n.* court of appeal. —**ungs=richter**, *m.* judge of appeals.

An'rühren, *v.a.* to touch; to touch upon; to mix; **angerührte Farben**, mixed colours; **jemandes guten Namen —**, to hurt a man's reputation.

An'rüsten, *v.a.* to arm, prepare for.

Ans, *abbr.* of **an das**.

An'säen, *v.a.* to sow (*for the first time*), to begin to sow.

An'sage, *f.* (*pl.* —**n**) notification, announcement; summons; message.

An'sag—en, *v.a.* to bring word to; to announce, notify, give notice of, intimate; to summon; **Sie sagen an**, it is your turn to call; **sag(e) an!** speak! say on! tell me! **sich —en**, to announce an intended visit; **sich —en lassen**, to send in one's name (*as a visitor*). —**er**, *m.* (—**ers**, *pl.* —**er**) notifier, messenger. —**ung**, *f.* notification. *Comp.* —**e=zettel**, *m.* written notice.

An'sägen, *v.a.* to begin to saw; to saw a little.

An'sammeln, *v.a.* to collect, accumulate; **sich —**, to collect, gather.

An'sammlung, *f.* accumulation. *Comp.* —**s=apparat**, *m.* condenser.

An'sässig, *adj.* settled in a place, domiciled; **er hat sich — gemacht**, he has taken up his abode. —**keit**, *f.* domiciliation; right of settlement.

An'satz, *m.* (—**es**, *pl.* **Ansätze**) putting to *or* upon; deposit, crust; mouthpiece (*of a wind-instrument*); method of blowing (*a flute, etc.*); touch (*on the piano*); attack, onset; start; rate, charge; disposition, tendency; statement (*Arith.*); estimate; leaf (*of a table*); reinforce, patent breach (*of a gun*); (*pl.*) charges, items. *Comp.* —**größe**, *f.* differential quantity; **die —größen suchen**, to differentiate. —**preis**, *m.* taxation. —**rechnung**, *f.* differential calculus. —**rohr**, *n.*, —**röhre**, *f.* adjutage; mouth and nose (*as organs of speech; Phonet.*).

An'saugen, *ir.v.* I. *n.* (*aux.* **h.**) to (*begin to*) suck. II. *a.* to suck. III. *r.* to attach oneself by sucking; to take (*of leeches*).

An'säuseln, *v.a.* to breathe gently on, to play around (*of wind, etc.*); **angesäuselt**, tipsy (*sl.*).

An'sausen, *v.n.* to come storming, to approach noisily; **angesaust kommen = ansausen**.

[1]**An'schaff—en**, *v.a.* to provide; to procure; to furnish with; **er hat sich das Buch angeschafft**, he has bought that book. —**er**, *m.* (—**ers**, *pl.* —**er**) procurer, provider; remitter; overseer. —**ung**, *f.* procuring, *etc.*; provision; remittance; —**ung des Hausgerätes**, the purchase of furniture.

[2]**An'schaffen**, *ir.v.a.* to create with *or* in; to imprint on; **das ist ihm angeschaffen**, that is innate in him.

An'schäften, *v.a.* to provide with a stock or handle; to mount (*put a stock to*) a gun; to put tops to boots.

An'schälen, *v.a.* to begin to peel *or* pare.

An'schau—en, I. *v.a.* to look at; to contemplate. II. *subst. n.* looking at; aspect. —**end**, *p.* & *adj.* intuitive; contemplative; —**ende Erkenntnis**, intuitive knowledge. —**er**, *m.* (—**ers**, *pl.* —**er**) looker-on; contemplator. —**lich**, *adj.* & *adv.* intuitive; perceptual, intuitively evident; clear; **die Sache ist —lich klar**, the thing is self-evident. —**ung**, *f.* view; perception; observation; contemplation; **zur —ung bringen**, to demonstrate; exhibit. *Comp.* —**ungs=begriff**, *m.* intuitive idea. —**ungs=bild**, conversation picture. —**ungs=erkenntnis**, *f.* intuitive knowledge. —**ungs=unterricht**, *m.* intuitive method of instruction, pictorial instruction, object lessons. —**ungs=vermögen**, *n.* power of intuition.

An'schein, *m.* (—**s**) appearance; likelihood; show; **dem — nach**, apparently; **den — haben**, to appear as if; **allem — nach**, to all appearance; **sich** (*dat.*) **den — geben**, to assume the appearance.

An'schein—en, *ir.v.* I. *a.* to shine upon. II. *n.* (*aux.* **h.**) to appear. **—end,** *p. & adj.;* **eine —ende Gefahr,** an apparent danger.

An'schellen, *v.a. & n.* to ring the bell.

An'schicken, *v.r.;* **sich zu etwas —,** to prepare for; to get ready; to begin, set about; to be disposed for; **er schickte sich gut dazu an,** he set about in the right way.

An'schieb—en, *ir. v.* I. *a.* to shove *or* push against. II. *n.* (*aux.* **h.**) to have first bowl (*at skittles*). **—er,** *m.* one that shoves; additional leaf (*of a table*). **—sel,** *n.* (**—sels**) appendage, supplement.

An'schielen, *v.a.*, to squint at; to look at askant; to cast a sidelong glance at; to ogle.

An'schieß—en, I. *ir.v.a.* to wound by shooting; to fire a gun for the first time; to add (*as a supplement, etc.*); to sew in (*sleeves, etc.*); **ein angeschoßner Eber,** a wild boar wounded by a shot; **angeschossen,** wounded; somewhat tipsy (*sl.*); cracked *or* smitten; lovesick. II. *ir.v.n. aux.* **s.**) to rush along; to rush against; to shoot forth; to be adjacent to; **zu Krystallen —en,** to crystallize; (*aux.* **h.**) to shoot first, begin shooting; to shoot against; **wer schießt an?** who has the first shot? III. *subst.n. see* **—ung.** **—ung,** *f.* crystallisation. *Comp.* **—kessel,** *m.* filler. **—pinsel,** *m.* gilding brush.

An'schiffen, *v.* I. *n.* (*aux.* **s.**) to approach in a vessel; to touch at; to ground. II. *a.* to ship to.

An'schimmeln, *v.n.* (*aux.* **s.**) to grow mouldy.

An'schirren, *v.a.* to harness.

An'schlag, *m.* (**—s,** *pl.* **Anschläge**) striking against, stroke; place struck against; striking (*of a clock*); affixing, posting up; placard, poster; touch (*of a player*); butt (*of a gun*); clapper; embrasure; calculation, computation; estimate, valuation; tariff; plot, design; rabbet (*of a door*); surf; game of tag *or* touch; advice; **das Haus ist im —e,** the house is advertised for sale; **in — bringen,** to take into consideration; **seine Kosten in — bringen,** to calculate *or* charge expenses; **im —e halten,** to point (*a gun*), to present (*a rifle*); **einen geheimen — gegen einen machen,** to conspire against one; **einen leichten — haben,** to have a light touch (*Mus.*). *Comp.* **—faden,** *m.* basting thread. **—zettel,** *m.* placard, poster.

An'schlagen, I. *ir.v.a.* to strike against, upon *or* at; to knock at; to sound; to affix, post up, placard; to nail on; to estimate, value; to splice (*a rope*); to bend (*sails*); to ring *or* toll (*bells*); to put up for sale; to baste to *or* on; **Feuer —,** to strike fire; **Stunden —,** to strike the hours; **— auf,** to rate (*at*), to tax; **den Ton —,** to give the key note; **das Klavier —,** to touch the piano; **das Gewehr —,** to take aim at; **zum Verkaufe —,** to put up for sale. II. *ir.v.n.* to strike *or* fall against; to begin to strike; (*of dogs*) to bark, to bay; (*of birds*) to sing; to take effect, to operate; to succeed; to begin to rot; **es schlägt gut bei ihm an,** it agrees with him. III. *subst. n.* striking (*against, etc.*); ripple.

An'schläg—er, *m.* (**—ers,** *pl.* **—er**) who *or* which strikes; hammer (*in a piano*); projector, designer. **—ig,** *adj.* inventive, ingenious, full of devices; **ein —iger Kopf,** a resourceful person.

An'schlämmen, *v.a. & r.* to fill with mud; to form of mud; to grow muddy.

An'schleichen, *ir.v.* I. *n.* (*aux.* **s.**) to creep *or* sneak near; to come on slowly. II. *r.* to creep up to.

[1]**An'schleifen,** *v.a.* to drag towards; to bring on a sledge; to drag to a place; to bring up (*sl.*); to fasten with a (*slip-*)knot.

[2]**An'schleifen,** *ir.v.a.* to begin to grind; to grind to a point, sharpen.

An'schlendern, *v.n.* (*also* **angeschlendert kommen**), to come sauntering on.

An'schleppen, *v.a.* to drag along; to bring up (*sl.*).

An'schließen, *ir.v.* I. *a.* to fasten with a lock; to chain to; to annex, join on, enclose. II. *r.* to join, attach oneself to; to follow; **sich völlig —,** to go heart and hand with; **rechts angeschlossen!** close to the right! (*Mil.*). III. *n.* (*aux.* **h.**) to fit close.

An'schluß, *m.* (**—sses,** *pl.* **Anschlüsse**) a joining, accession, addition; thing annexed, enclosure; junction, correspondence (*of trains*); fit (*of clothes*); **den — versäumen,** to miss one's train; **— an einen Zug haben,** to meet another train; **keinen — haben,** to meet no other train, to go no farther; **er findet keinen —,** he finds no companion, nobody will join him. *Comp.* **—bahn,** junction railway, branch line.

An'schmachten, *v.a.;* **einen —,** to look at s.o. in a languishing manner.

An'schmecken, *v.* I. *a.* to taste. II. *n.* (*aux.* **h.**) to scent (*the game*).

An'schmeißen, *ir.v.* I. *a.* to dash, *or* throw, against. II. *n.* (*aux.* **h.**) to begin to throw.

An'schmelzen, *reg. & ir.v.* I. *a.* to begin to melt *or* smelt; to fasten by smelting. II. *n.* (*aux.* **s.**) to begin to melt; to adhere by melting.

An'schmieden, *v.a.* to fasten to by forging; to chain, to fetter.

An'schmiegen, *v.* I. *a.* to bend *or* press to; to adapt. II. *r.* to cling to; to nestle to (*one*); to conform to.

An'schmieren, *v.a.* to smear; to daub; to cheat (*coll.*); to adulterate (*wine*); *see* **Aufschmieren.**

An'schmunzeln, *v.a.;* **einen —,** to smirk at s.o.

An'schnallen, *v.a.* to buckle on; **sich etwas —,** to get hold of s.th., procure s.th. (*sl.*).

An'schnarchen, *v.a.* to snarl at; to snap at.

An'schnauben, An'schnauzen, *v.* I. *n.* (*aux.* **s.**) to come puffing and blowing. II. *a.* to snort at; to snub; to assail with angry words, address gruffly.

An'schneiden, *ir.v.a.* to begin to cut *or* carve, to give the first cut to; to fit by cutting; to cut, to notch.

An'schnellen, *v.* I. *a.* to jerk against. II. *n.* (*aux.* **s.**) to fly against.

An'schnitt, *m.* (**—es,** *pl.* **—e**) cut, first cut; the act of cutting into *or* first; notch.

An'schnüffeln, *v.a.* to smell at (*of dogs*).

An'schnüren, *v.a.* to lace to, to fasten with a string *or* cord.

Anscho'v—e, —is, *f.* (*pl.* **—en**) anchovy.

An'schrauben, *v.a.* to screw on, to screw up.

An'schreib—en, *ir.v.a.* to write on; to write, note *or* put down; to enter, charge to; to ascribe to; **angeschrieben stehen,** to be in a certain estimation (**bei einem,** with one); **übel angeschrieben sein,** to stand in bad repute, to be in (some one's) bad books; **nichts —en lassen,** to buy nothing on credit. **—er,** *m.* (**—ers,** *pl.* **—er**) marker. *Comp.* **—e=buch,** *n.* note-book, household book, account book. **—e=tafel,** *f.* tablet, note-book.

An'schreien, *ir.v.a.* to scream *or* call at; to hail; to talk gruffly *or* angrily at.

An'schreiten, *ir.v.n.* (*aux.* **s.**) to stride up to.

An'schrote, *f.* (*pl.* **—n**) selvage, list.

An'schroten, *v.a.* to roll near; to form the selvage.

An'schub, *m.* (**—s,** *pl.* **Anschübe**) first shove, first throw; anything added.

An'schuhen, *v.a.* to shoe.

An'schuldigen, *v.a.* to accuse of; to charge with; **einen eines Diebstahls —,** to charge one with theft.

An'schüren, *v.a.* to stir up, to rake; to excite; to inflame; to foment (*a quarrel*).

An'schuß, *m.* (**—sses,** *pl.* **Anschüsse**) shooting first; rheumatic attack; crystallisation; rush.

An'schütten, *v.a.* to pour out against; to heap up against; to fill.

An'schwänzeln, *v. n.* (*aux.* **s.**) to approach

wagging the tail *or* wriggling; to approach fawningly; to come like a dandy.

An'schwänzen, *v.a.* to sprinkle.

An'schwärz—en, *v.a.* to blacken; to calumniate. **—er,** *m.* (**—ers,** *pl.* **—er**) slanderer. **—ung,** *f.* calumny, backbiting.

An'schwatzen, *v.a.;* **einem etwas —,** to talk one into (*doing, taking or buying*).

An'schweben, *v.n.* (*aux.* **s.**) to approach hovering, fly towards.

An'schwefeln, *v.a.* to fumigate with sulphur.

An'schweißen, *v.a.* to weld (to); to braze; to wound (*Sport*).

An'schwellen, *reg. & ir. v.a. & n.* (*aux.* **s.**) to swell, to increase by swelling. **—d,** *p. adj. & adv.* crescendo (*Mus.*).

An'schwemm—en, *v.a.* to cause to float; to float towards; to form by alluvium; to deposit alluvium. **—ung,** *f.* floating down *or* on; alluvium, alluvial deposit. *Comp.* **—ungs=recht,** *n.* right to alluvial earth.

An'schwimmen, *ir.v.n.* (*aux.* **s.**) to swim up to.

An'schwirren, *v.n.* to come, arrive (*coll.*).

An'segeln, *v.* I. *n.* (*aux.* **s.**) to sail near *or* up to, to run foul of a ship. II. *a.* **einen Hafen —,** to touch at a port.

An'seh—en, I. *ir.v.a.* to look at *or* upon; to see; to regard, consider; to respect, esteem; **einem etwas —en,** to perceive something in, recognize as characteristic of one; **man sieht es ihm nicht an,** he does not look (*like*) it; **man sieht es ihm gleich an, wes Geistes Kind er ist,** you can read his character in his face; **ich sah ihn für seinen Bruder an,** I took him for his brother; **—en für, als,** to consider, to take for; **etwas mit —en,** to witness, to look on with toleration, suffer, let pass; **ein sehr angesehener Mann,** a man of high repute; **einen über die Achsel —en,** to look down on one; **er wird dafür angesehen werden,** he will be punished for it. II. *subst.n.* looking at; appearance, aspect; consideration, authority, consequence; esteem, respect; **sich ein —en geben,** to give oneself airs; **allem —en nach,** to all appearance; **vor Gott gilt kein —en der Person,** God is no respecter of persons. **—n=lich,** *adj. & adv.* important, considerable; stately, portly; eminent, conspicuous; fine-looking; **die —nlichsten Männer der Stadt,** the principal *or* most important citizens. **—n=lichkeit,** *f.* importance; dignity; stateliness; conspicuousness. **—ung,** *f.* looking at, viewing; consideration; **in —ung,** seeing that, whereas (*Law*); **in —ung seines Fleißes,** in consideration of his diligence; **in —ung der Ausführung,** with regard to execution.

An'sengen, *v.a.* to singe *or* burn a little, begin to singe.

An'setz—en, I. *v.a.* to put to *or* near; to join; to apply; to add to, affix, join on; to fix, establish; to form; to sew to; to charge in a bill; to rate, tax; to appoint (*a day, etc.*); to begin to; to set (*trees, etc.*); **Land —,** to wash earth to the shore; **er wollte den Dolch —en,** he was about to stab; **den Becher —,** to put the goblet to the lips; **Rost —en,** to gather rust; **Deckel an Bücher —en,** to glue the covers on books; **die Feder —en,** to take up one's pen; **den Spaten —en,** to begin to dig; **eine Ladung —en,** to ram down (*a gun-charge*); **zum öffentlichen Verkauf —en,** to put up for sale. II. *v.r.* to settle down; to stick to, be deposited. III. *v.n.* (*aux.* **h.**) to take a run (*before leaping*); to try; to begin; to thrive; to sprout; to make an onset. IV. *subst. n.* efflorescence (*Chem.*); juxtaposition; welding of steel with iron; **das —en neuen Stoffes,** the apposition of new matter. **—er,** *m.* (**—ers,** *pl.* **—er**) driving-bolt; rammer. **—ung,** *f.* the act of applying, putting near *or* to; the thing put near *or* added; application; apposition; juxtaposition; prothesis (*Surg.*). *Comp.* **—blatt,** *n.* fly-leaf (*Typ.*).

An'sicht, *f.* (*pl.* **—en**) looking at; sight, view, prospect; opinion, notion, view; **ein Mann von beschränkten —en,** a man of narrow views; **bei — dieses,** on receipt of this; **zu Ihrer gütigen —,** for your kind inspection, on approval. **—ig,** *adj.;* **—ig werden** (*usually with gen., rarely with acc.*) to get sight of. *Comp.* **—s=postkarte,** *f.* postcard with view of the place from which it is sent, illustrated postcard. **—sendung,** *f.* consignment for inspection *or* approval (*Comm.*). **—s=seite,** *f.* front, forepart. **—s=tafel,** *f.* table, summary (*of history, etc., given on a single sheet*).

An'siedelei', *f.* (*pl.* **—en**) settlement.

An'sied—el=n, *v.* I. *a.* to settle, colonise. II. *r.* to settle, establish oneself. **—l=er,** *m.* (**—lers,** *pl.* **—ler**) settler, colonist. **—el=ung,** *f.* colonisation; colony, settlement.

An'sinnen, *ir.v.a.* to desire, require of; **einem etwas —,** to demand s.th. from s.o.; to impute.

An'sintern, *v.n.* (*aux.* **s.**) to form stalactite-like deposits.

An'sitz, *m.* (**—es,** *pl.* **—e**) settled abode, domicile; landed property.

An'sitzen, *ir.v.n.* (*aux.* **h.**) to sit close to; to stick, adhere to; to be domiciled, settled.

An'spann, *m.* (**—es**), **—e,** *f.* draught-cattle; team.

An'spann—en, *v.a.* to yoke to, to put to; to stretch; to strain; to exert; to bend (*sails*); **er ließ —en,** he ordered the carriage to be got ready. **—ung,** *f.* harnessing, yoking; exertion, straining.

An'speien, *ir.v.a.* to spit on *or* upon.

Anspiel, *n.* (**—s,** *pl.* **—e**) innings.

An'spiel—en, *v.* I. *n.* (*aux.* **h.**) to begin to play; to play first; to allude to. II. *a.* to lead a suit, a card; to try (*a musical instrument*). **—ung,** *f.* allusion (**auf eine S.,** to a th.).

An'spießen, *v.a.* to pierce with a spear; to impale; to spit (*meat*).

An'spinnen, *ir.v.* I. *a.* to join by spinning, to spin together; to contrive, plot, hatch; to begin. II. *r.* to originate, to spin to; **etwas spinnt sich an zwischen den beiden,** an affection is springing up between these two.

An'spitzen, *v.a.* to point, to furnish with a point, to sharpen (*a pencil*).

An'spornen, *v.a.* to spur, spur on.

An'sprache, *f.* (*pl.* **—n**) address, speech; appeal; tone (*of an instrument*); claim (*Law*).

An'sprechen, *ir.v.* I. *n.* (*aux.* **h.**) to sound, emit a sound; **bei einem —,** to call on one (*rare*). II. *a.* to address; to appeal to; to interest, to please; to touch (*the heart, etc.*); to claim; to call; **einen um etwas —,** to beg s.th. of s.o., to ask s.o. for s.th. **—d,** *part.* prepossessing; plausible; **eine —de Vermutung,** a plausible conjecture; **sie hat etwas sehr —des in ihrem Äußeren,** she has a most engaging appearance.

An'sprengen, *v.* I. *a.* to put, force to a gallop; to force against; to explode against; to begin to explode; to besprinkle. II. *n.* (*aux.* **s.**) to gallop up *or* on.

An'springen, *ir.v.n.* (*aux.* **s.**) to begin to spring *or* crack; to crack *or* bounce against; **angesprungen kommen,** to come running *or* leaping along; (*aux.* **h.**) to begin to run, leap; to take the first leap; **er ließ das Pferd links —,** he made the horse lead with the off foot.

An'spritzen, *v.a.* to squirt at, besprinkle.

An'spruch, *m.* (**—s,** *pl.* **Ansprüche**) address; claim, title, pretension; **— haben auf eine S.,** to be entitled to a th.; **— machen auf, in — nehmen,** to claim, demand, pretend to, to come in for, to occupy, to tax; **es nimmt meine Zeit zu sehr in —,** it takes up too much of my time.

Comp. —s=los, *adj.* & *adv.* unassuming, modest. —s=losigkeit, *f.* modesty. —s=voll, *adj.* full of pretension, presumptuous.

An'spül—en, *v.* I. *n.* (*aux.* h.) to flow against, wash. II. *a.* to wash against, to carry on to, to deposit. —ung, *f.* the washing on of earth; alluvium.

An'spulen, *v.a.* to reel (*thread*, *cotton*, *etc.*).

An'stacheln, *v.a.* to fix *or* fasten to; to goad on.

An'stählen, *v.a.* to point with steel.

An'stalt, *f.* (*pl.* —en) preparation, arrangement; institution, establishment; place of education, school; ich habe —en getroffen meine Stelle ihm abzutreten, I have made arrangements for resigning my appointment in his favour; höhere Lehr—en, secondary schools.

An'stammen, *v.n.* to descend by race *or* blood; ein angestammtes Gut, an hereditary estate; mein angestammter Platz, my usual place (*coll.*).

An'stand, *m.* (—es, *pl.* Anstände) stand, station (*Sport*); delay, pause, respite; objection; scruple; bearing, demeanour, behaviour; propriety, decorum; grace, pleasing deportment; carriage (*of a horse*); — nehmen, to hesitate, doubt, pause; Anstände gegen eine Rechnung beibringen, to object to items in a bill; der edle —, the noble bearing, dignity; ohne —, unhesitatingly. *Comp.* —s=besuch, *m.* formal call, set visit. —s=brief, *m.* letter of respite *or* grace (*Comm.*). —s=dame, *f.* chaperon. —s=halber, *adv.* for decency's sake. —s=los, *adj.* unhesitating. —s=rock, *m.* presentation-suit (*men*); petticoat (*women*). —s=röckchen, *n.* small woollen petticoat. —s=rolle, *f.* part of noble parent (*Theat.*). —s=voll, *adj.* well-behaved, seemly. —s=widrig, *adj.* indecorous; indecent; improper.

An'ständig, *adj.* & *adv.* proper, decorous; respectable; reasonable; suitable; good (*coll.*); eine —e Cigarre, a good cigar (*coll.*); es schneit ganz —, there is a great deal of snow (*coll.*). —keit, *f.* (*pl.* —keiten) decency, propriety; suitableness.

An'stapeln, *v.a.* to pile up.

An'starren, *v.a.* to stare at, to gaze at.

Ansta'tt, *prep.* (*gen.*) instead of, in the place of.

An'staunen, *v.a.* to gaze at with astonishment. *Comp.* —s=wert, —s=würdig, *adj.* astonishing, wonderful, worthy of admiration, admirable.

An'stechen, *ir.v.* I. *a.* to prick, to pierce; to broach, to tap (ein Faß Wein); to stitch to, fix (*with a pointed instrument*); to jeer, provoke. II. *n.* angestochen kommen, to come stalking along (*vulg.*); kommen Sie wieder damit angestochen? do you come with this again? are you still harping on the same string? (*vulg.*).

An'steck—en, *v.a.* to stick on, to put on; to pin *or* fasten on; to light (*a candle*); to set on fire, kindle; to spit (*meat*); to infect, to taint; angestecktes Obst, tainted fruit; angesteckt von, infected with; er ist von den Masern angesteckt worden, he has caught the measles; Lachen steckt an, laughing is catching. —end, *p.* & *adj.* contagious; infectious. —ung, *f.* kindling; infection; contagion; fastening on. *Comp.* —ärmel, *pl.* sham-sleeves. —bohrer, *m.* piercer. —e=gift, *n.*, —ungs=stoff, *m.* infectious matter, virus.

An'stehen, *ir.v.n.* (*aux.* h. & s.) to stand near *or* by; to be appointed *or* fixed; to hesitate, scruple; to last, remain; einem —, to become, to suit, to fit, to please; eine Schuld — lassen, to defer payment of a debt; — lassen, to let be, to defer, delay, grant a respite, forbear; mit einem —, to join in an enterprise; um etwas —, *see* Anhalten; es stand nicht lange an, so sah ich, 2c., it was not long before I saw, *etc.*; es stund nur an eine kleine Weil, it was only a short time (before); ich habe nicht angestanden ihm zu sagen, I have not hesitated to tell him; es steht ihr alles wohl an, all she says and does is in good taste; das steht mir nicht an, that does not please me; was steht dir von meinen Sachen an? which of my things would you like to have?

An'steigen, *ir.v.n.* (*aux.* s.) to mount, ascend; angestiegen kommen, to come stalking along.

An'stell—en, *v.* I. *a.* to place, put near *or* to, to post, assign parts *or* positions to; to place, appoint, employ; to arrange; to get up, give (*a banquet*, *etc.*); to set in operation; to undertake; to make (*an experiment*); to draw (*a comparison*); to do, cause (*mischief*, *etc.*); to contrive; to institute, set up; ich weiß nicht, wie ich es —en soll, I don't know how I am to set about it. II. *r.* to lie in wait (*Sport*); to behave; to feign, pretend; to fuss; zu etwas sich —en, to set about a th.; sich —en als ob, to pretend to be, act as if; er stellte sich jämmerlich an, he cut a miserable figure; stell dich nicht an! do not make a fuss! er stellt sich wohl dazu an, he sets about it in good style. —er, *m.* (—ers, *pl.* —er) employer, appointer (*to a place*); author, instigator. —ig, *adj.* & *adv.* handy, able, adroit, fit. —ung, *f.* act of appointing, arranging, *etc.*; appointment, post.

An'stemmen, *v.a.* to stem, push, press against.

An'sterben, *ir.v.n.* (*aux.* s.) to devolve on; das ist ihm angestorben, that has fallen to him by death, he has inherited it.

An'steuern, *v.a.* to steer towards, to make for.

An'stich, *m.* (—s) act of piercing *or* broaching; the first draught from a freshly broached cask (*of beer*); frischer —, a fresh glass of beer (*from a new cask*); puncture (*of fruit by insects*).

An'sticken, *v.a.* to embroider; to stitch on.

An'stieben, *ir.v.n.* (*aux.* s.) to be driven along, drift *or* fly (*as dust*).

An'stiefeln, *v.a.* & *r.* to put on boots; angestiefelt kommen, to come striding along (*coll.*)

An'stieren, *v.a.* to stare fixedly at.

An'stift—en, *v.* I. *a.* to cause, set on foot; to plot; to incite, instigate; to stir up; to suborn. II. *subst.n.* (—ens), —ung, *f.* instigation, machination; the suborning; contriving; —ung einer Feuersbrunst, incendiary. —er, *m.* (—ers, *pl.* —er) originator (*of a plot*), causer; instigator; suborner.

An'stimm—en, *v.a.* to begin to sing *or* sound; to strike up; to give the key-note; tune (*fiddle*). —ung, *f.* the striking up; intonation; tuning.

An'stoß, *m.* (—es, *pl.* Anstöße) a striking against, shock, impulse, impulsion; attack, paroxysm; stammering; scandal, offence; ohne — erklären, to expound fluently and without hesitation; — nehmen an (einer S.), to take offence at, be scandalised by (a th.); Stein des —es, stumbling-block; — am Brode, kissing-crust.

An'stoß—en, *ir.v.* I. *a.* to strike, push, knock against; to touch, clink (*glasses*); to join; to nudge; to attack (*of a disease*); to fine-draw; to give offence; angestoßenes Obst, bruised fruit. II. *n.* (*aux.* h.) to run, dash, stumble against; to touch, abut, border on; mit den Gläsern —en, to touch glasses; wir stießen auf seine Gesundheit an, we drank to his health; mit dem Kopfe —en an *or* wider, to knock one's head against; mit der Zunge *or* im Reden —en, to hesitate, stammer; —en wider, gegen, to offend, shock; bei einem —en, to scandalise s.o.; nur nicht —en! beware of giving offence! —end, *p.* & *adj.* contiguous, adjoining; das —ende Zimmer, the adjoining room.

An'stößig, *adj.* & *adv.* scandalous, offensive, shocking, indecent, causing scandal, objection able; bruised, decaying; stumbling (*of horses*). **—keit**, *f.* impropriety; offensiveness; indelicacy, indecency.

An'strahlen, *v.a.* to cast rays on, to beam upon.

An'strängen, *v.a.* to fasten to *or* with cords; **die Pferde —**, to put the horses to.

An'streb—en, *v.n.* (*aux.* **h.**); **gegen etwas —en**, to strive against a th. *Comp.* **—e=kraft**, *f.* centripetal force.

An'strecken, *v.a.* to strain, stretch (*to*).

An'streiche, *f.* paint, water *or* oil colour.

An'streich—en, *ir.v.a.* to paint, daub over; to mark *or* underline (*a passage in a book, etc.*); **mit Theer —en**, to tar; **weiß —en**, to whitewash; **eine Geige —en**, to begin to play on a violin; to try a fiddle; **einem etwas —en**, to make one pay for s.th., to punish s.o. (*coll.*). **—er**, *m.* (**—ers**, *pl.* **—er**) house-painter.

An'streifen, *v.n.* (*aux.* **h.** & **s.**) to graze, rub against, touch lightly in passing.

An'streng—en, *v.* I. *a.* to force; to strain; to stretch; **alle Kräfte —en**, to strain every nerve; **eine —ende Arbeit**, a work requiring great exertion; **einen —en**, to fatigue a person; **der kleine Druck strengt die Augen sehr an**, small print is very trying to the eyes; **den Geist —en**, to exert the mind. II. *r.* to exert oneself; to tax one's energies, strive, make every effort; **sich über die Maßen —en**, to over-exert oneself. **—ung**, *f.* exertion, effort; strain; struggle.

An'strich, *m.* (**—s**, *pl.* **—e**) a painting *or* daubing over; coat of paint; tint, colour; varnish, gloss, colouring; tinge, shade, slight admixture; air, appearance; **einer Sache einen guten — geben**, to gloss a matter over, make it appear its best; to palliate a thing; **ein — von Gelehrsamkeit**, a smattering of learning; **ein — von Schwermut**, a dash, an air of melancholy.

An'stricken, *v.a.* to knit on to; **Strümpfe —**, to foot stockings.

An'strömen, *v.* I. *n.* (*aux.* **s.**) to flow towards; to advance, flow near; to flock together, crowd towards; **— an (ein Ufer)**, to wash. II. *a.* to deposit, wash up on.

An'stück—eln, **—en**, *v.a.* to piece, to patch. **—ung**, *f.* patch; piece added.

An'stülpen, *v.a.* to new-top (*boots*).

An'sturm, *m.* (**—s**, *pl.* **Anstürme**) rushing up, attack, onset, charge, assault.

An'stürmen, *v.n.* (*aux.* **s.**) to rush along; (*with* **auf, an, gegen, wider, 2c.**) to attack violently, to storm, assail.

An'sturz, *m.* (**—es**, *pl.* **Anstürze**) violent onset, charge; shock, collision.

An'stürzen, *v.* I. *a.* to throw up against. II. *n.* (*aux.* **s.**) to rush against; to tumble against; **angestürzt kommen**, to come on with a rush, to come up in great haste and excitement; to charge; to fall violently against.

An'stützen, *v.a.* to prop up; **sich —**, to lean against, support oneself on.

An'such—en, I. *v.n.* (*aux.* **h.**) to ask, sue, apply (**um etwas**, for something); to solicit, request, petition; to make a requisition. II. *subst. n.* solicitation, petition; application, requisition; **auf —en von**, at the suit of, upon the application of. **—end**, *p.* & *adj.* supplicatory; **der —ende**, the petitioner. **—er**, *m.* (**—ers**, *pl.* **—er**) one who solicits; petitioner, suitor (*rare*). **—ung**, *f.* application, requisition, suit, request; instigation. *Comp.* **—s=schreiben**, **—ungs=schreiben**, *n.* letter of request, requisition.

Antagoni'stisch, *adj.* & *adv.* antagonistic.

An'takeln, *v.a.* to rig, to equip (*a ship*).

An'tanzen, *v.n.* (*aux.* **h.**) to lead off in dancing; (*aux.* **s.**) to approach dancing; to strike against in dancing; **er kam angetanzt**, he came (*sl.*).

An'tappen, *v.* I. *n.* (*aux.* **s.**) to grope at; to knock against. II. *a.* to take hold of awkwardly.

An'tasten, *v.a.* to touch, to handle; to attack; to question, impugn, dispute; to hurt, injure (*one's reputation, etc.*); to infringe (*on one's rights*); **einen —**, to lay hands on one.

An'taumeln, *v.n.* (*aux.* **s.**) to tumble, reel up, stagger against; to approach staggering.

An'teil, *m.* (**—s**, *pl.* **—e**) portion, share; dividend; lot; sympathy, interest; **— haben an einer S.**, to participate in a th.; **— nehmen an**, to take an interest in, sympathize with, participate in. *Comp.* **—haber**, *m.*, **—in**, *f.* participator, partaker; shareholder. **—los**, *adj.* & *adv.* neutral; indifferent; unsympathetic. **—mäßig**, *adj.* & *adv.* proportionate, according to one's share. **—schein**, *m.*, **—s=verschreibung**, *f.* share.

An'thun, *ir.v.a.* to put on, don; to do to, inflict, offer, show; to bewitch; **einem Gutes (Böses) —**, to benefit (injure) a p.; **sich** (*dat.*) **ein Leid** (*or* **Leides**) **—**, to lay violent hands on oneself; **sich Zwang —**, to constrain oneself; **sich eine Güte —**, to allow oneself a pleasure; **das Mädchen hat es ihm angethan**, the girl has quite charmed him; **einem Gewalt —**, to offer violence to one; **einem Schande —**, to bring disgrace on one; **Strafe —**, to inflict punishment; **einem** *or* **einer S. Ehre —**, to do honour to a p. *or* a th.; **einen Hafen —**, to make, touch at a port. **angethan**, *p.p.* & *adj.* clad, attired.

Anti— in many compounds corresponding to the English anti-, *e. g.* **Antichrist**, **Antisemit**, **antiseptisch**, **Antistrophe**, *etc.*

An'ti—christlich, *adj.* & *adv.* antichristian. **—kritik**, *f.* reply to a criticism. **—pathie'**, *f.* (*pl.* **—pathie'en**) antipathy. **—penu'ltima**, *f.* antepenult. **—the'se**, *f.* (*pl.* **—the'sen**) antithesis.

Anti'k, *adj.* antique. **—e**, *f.* (*pl.* **—en**) an antique; antiquity. *Comp.* **—en=händler**, *m.* dealer in antiquities *or* curiosities.

Antimo'n, **—ium**, *n.* antimony (**Spießglanz**).

An'tippen, *v.a.* to touch lightly, tap; touch upon in talking, mention briefly (*coll.*).

Anti'q—ua, *f.* Roman type (*Typ.*). **—ua'r**, *m.* (**—ua'rs**, *pl.* **—ua're**) antiquary; second-hand bookseller; dealer in antiques *or* curiosities. **—uaria't**, *n.* business of a dealer in old books *or* art-curiosities; second-hand book shop. **—ua'risch**, *adj.* second-hand; archæological, antiquarian. **—uitä't**, *see* **Antiquität**. *Comp.* **—ua=schrift**, *f.* Roman type.

Antiquie'ren, *v.n.* to become antiquated.

Antiquitä't, *f.* antiquity. *Comp.* **—en=kenner**, **—en=sammler**, *m.* collector of antiquities *or* curiosities; virtuoso. **—en=laden**, *m.*, **—en=handlung**, *f.* old curiosity shop.

An'tlitz, *n.* (**—es**, *pl.* **—e**) countenance; face. *Comp.* **—seite**, *f.* front-side (*Arch.*).

An'toben, *v.n.* (*aux.* **h.**) to thunder against; (*aux.* **s.**) to come on blustering *or* raging.

An'traben, *v.n.* (*aux.* **s.**) to trot up to; to trot on; **angetrabt kommen**, to come trotting up.

An'trag, *m.* (**—s**, *pl.* **Anträge**) offer, tender, proposal; proposition, motion (*in Parliament, etc.*); **einen — stellen**, to make a motion, to move (*Parliam.*); **einen — unterstützen**, to second a motion; (**einer Dame**) **einen — machen**, to propose (to a lady). *Comp.* **—steller**, *m.* mover (*of an address, resolution*).

An'tragen, *ir.v.a.* to carry, bring near to, up to; to propose, offer, tender; **es wurde ihm ein Amt angetragen**, an appointment was offered to him; **auf etwas —**, to move, make a motion, to request, desire; **es wurde auf die Bildung eines Ausschusses angetragen**, a motion was made for going into committee *or* that a committee should be appointed.

An'trauen, *v.a.* to marry (*a woman to a man*), to unite in marriage.

An'treffen, *ir.v.* I. *a.* to light upon; to concern; **auf frischer That —**, to take in the act; ich traf ihn zufällig an, I met him by chance. II. *n.* to meet and strike against.

An'treib—en, *ir.v.* I. *a.* to drive, push on; to urge on, incite; **vom Hunger angetrieben,** impelled by hunger; **die Planken —en,** to wring the planks (*Ship.*); **die Reife —en,** to hoop a cask. II. *n.* (*aux.* **f.**) to drive, drift against; to float to, on, against. **—er,** *m.* (**—ers,** *pl.* **—er**) inciter, impeller, whipper-in. **—ung,** *f.* incitation; driving on.

An'treten, *ir.v.* I. *a.* to tread on *or* down; to enter upon; to begin; to set out on (*a journey*); to take possession of; to go up to, approach, come upon (*a person*) (*poet.*); to take up a position; **ein Amt —,** to enter on duty; **einen Beweis —,** to undertake to prove. II. *n.* (*aux.* **f.**) to step up for; to begin; **zum Tanze —,** to take one's place (*for dancing*); to fall in (*Mil.*); **angetreten!** fall in! (*Mil.*); **— zum Appell!** fall in for calling roll!

An'trieb, *m.* (**—s,** *pl.* **—e**) the floating, *or* driving against; impulse; incitement, stimulus; instigation; inclination; motive; **aus natürlichem —e,** instinctively; **aus freiem —e,** of one's own accord; **aus eigenem —e,** spontaneously, of one's own initiative.

An'trinken, *ir.v.* I. *n* (*aux.* **h.**) to drink first, begin to drink. II. *r.* to get tipsy. **angetrunken,** *p.p. & adj.* tipsy.

An'tritt, *m.* (**—s,** *pl.* **—e**) amble (*of a horse*); entrance on, accession to, assuming of; setting out, start; commencement; first step (*of a staircase*); anteroom; dais; footstep (*Typ.*). *Comp.* **—s=audienz,** *f.* audience of reception. **—s=geld,** *n.* admission, entrance money. **—s=predigt,** *f.* inaugural sermon. **—s=rede,** *f.* inaugural speech. **—s=schmaus,** *m.* installation banquet. **—s=vorlesung,** *f.* inaugural lecture.

An'trocknen, *v.n.* (*aux.* **f.**) to begin to dry; to dry and adhere.

Ant'wort, *f.* (*pl.* **—en**) answer, reply; **er ist gleich mit einer — da,** he is good at repartee; **sie blieb ihm keine — schuldig,** she was quite a match for him; **zur — geben,** to answer; **Rede und — geben über,** to account for; **eine abschlägige —,** a refusal; **keine — ist auch eine —,** silence means assent *or* gives consent (*prov.*). **—lich,** *adj. & adv.* in reply, as an answer. *Comp.* **—gesang,** *m.* alternate chant. **—karte,** *f.* reply (post-)card. **—schreiben,** *n.* written reply, answer in writing. **—weise,** *adv.* catechetically.

Ant'wort—en, *v.a. & n.* to answer, reply; **einem auf seine Frage —en,** to answer one's question. **—er,** *m.* (**—ers,** *pl.* **—er**) respondent (*Law*); answerer.

An'üben, *v.r.* (*dat.*) to acquire by practice.

An'ulken, *v.a.;* **einen —,** to accost one mockingly; to make sport of a p. (*especially in a street or a public place*) (*sl.*).

An'verloben, *v.a.* to betroth to a p.

An'vermählen, *v.a.* to marry to a p.

An'versuchen, *v.a.* to fit, try on (*a dress*).

An'vertrau—en, *v.a.* to confide, entrust to, give in charge; **sich einem —en,** to unbosom *or* to entrust oneself to a person. **—t,** *p.p. & adj.* entrusted to, consigned to; **—tes Geld,** trust money, deposit.

An'verwandt, *adj.* related, akin; *especially in the phrase* **anverwandt und zugethan,** related and devoted to.

An'wachs, *m.* (—(**f**)**es**) increase, growth, swelling, accretion, increment.

An'wachsen, *ir.v.n.* (*aux.* **f.**) to grow upon *or* to; to adhere to; to grow up, to grow together; to swell, to rise (*rivers*); to accumulate, augment; **die angewachsene Haut des Auges,** the conjunctiva (*Anat.*); **das Pferd ist angewachsen,** the horse is hide-bound.

2*

An'wackeln, *v.n.* to toddle on; **angewackelt kommen,** to come toddling on (*coll.*).

An'wall—en, *v.n.* (*aux.* **f.**) to roll near (*like waves*). **—ung,** *f.* rolling on; crowding near; fit, paroxysm.

An'walt, *m.* (**—es,** *pl.* **—e,** *also* **Anwälte**) lawyer, attorney, solicitor; agent; **— der Gläubiger,** official assignee. **— einer Stadt,** syndic. **—schaft,** *f.* agency, attorneyship, proctorship. *Comp.* **—s=gebühr,** *f.* attorney's fees, agent's fees.

An'walzen, *v.n.* to begin to waltz, to waltz first; to level or press with a roller (*earth*).

An'wälzen, *v.a.* to roll against, on *or* to.

An'wand—eln, *v.* I. *n.* (*aux.* **f.**) to walk up to, to approach slowly. II. *a. imp.* to befall come over, come upon; to attack, to seize (*of illness, etc.*); **was wandelte dich an?** what came over you, what was the matter with you, what did you think of? **es wandelte ihn eine Ahnung an,** a presentiment came over him: **es wandelte mich eine Ohnmacht an,** I was seized with a fainting fit. **—l=ung,** *f.* seizure; fit, paroxysm; touch (*of pity, etc.*), slight attack; inclination to.

An'wanken, *v.n.* (*aux* **f.**) to totter up *or* against.

An'wärmen, *v.a.* to heat *or* warm a little; to begin to heat.

An'wart—en, *v.n.* (*aux.* **h.**) (*with* **auf eine S.**) to wait for; to be the owner in expectancy. **—schaft,** *f.* reversion; expectancy; **er hat die —schaft auf seines Vaters Amt,** he has the reversion of his father's office. **—schaftlich,** *adj. & adv.* reversionary.

An'wärter, *m.* reversioner, expectant, candidate. *See* **Civil—, Militär—.**

An'wässern, *v.a.* to irrigate, to moisten.

An'weben, *reg. & ir.v.a.* to weave on to.

An'wedeln, *v.a.* to fan; to wag the tail at.

An'wehen, *v.a.* to drift against; to blow towards, upon, against; to seize upon, fall on, come over; **Entsetzen wehte ihn an,** horror seized him.

An'weichen, *v.a.* to soften a little, steep, soak.

An'weis—en, *ir.v.a.* to assign, allot; to point out, show; to designate, appoint; to instruct, direct; to admonish; to refer (**auf einen,** to one); **sich —en lassen,** to take directions *or* advice; **man hat mich auf Sie angewiesen,** I have been directed to apply to you; **er wurde auf sich selbst angewiesen,** he was thrown on his own resources; **ich werde Ihnen Ihr Geld —,** I shall give you a cheque for your money; **die Beamten sind angewiesen,** the officials have instructions to. **—er,** *m.* (**—ers,** *pl.* **—er**) director; instructor; adviser; assigner. **—ung,** *f.* assignment; direction, injunction; cheque, bill of exchange; advice; method, course; **in einer —ung festgesetzt,** secured by deed of assignment; **methodische —,** systematic instruction.

An'wendbar, *adj. & adv.* applicable; practicable; available. **—keit,** *f.* applicability; availability.

An'wend—en, *reg. & ir. v. a.* to employ, use make use of; **—en auf eine S.,** to apply to a th.; **viele Mühe bei etwas —en,** to bestow much pains on a thing; **Vorsicht —en,** to take precaution; **angewandte Wissenschaften,** applied sciences; **angewandte und abgezogene Begriffe,** concrete and abstract ideas; **angewandte Chemie,** experimental chemistry; **—en zu einem Zwecke,** to employ for a purpose; **Schmeichelei ist bei mir nicht gut angewandt,** flattery is lost upon me. **—ung,** *f.* application; practice; employment; **—ung auf einen bestimmten Fall,** application to a special case; **in der —ung,** in practice.

An'werb—en, *ir. v.* I. *n.* (*aux.* **h.**) (**um etwas**) to sue for, solicit. II. *a.* to raise, levy troops;

ein Angeworbener, a recruit; sich—en lassen, to enlist; Soldaten sollen angeworben werden, men are to be enrolled for active service. —er, *m.* recruiting officer *or* sergeant. —ung, *f.* enlistment, enrolment, levying, levy.

An'werfen, *ir.v.* I. *n.* (*aux.* h.) to have the first throw, begin to throw. II. *a.* to throw at; to throw on (*clothes, etc.*); Kalk —, to roughcast.

An'wesen, *n.* the being present, presence (*obs.*); abode; property; estate, farm, house. —d, *p.* & *adj.* present; jeder —de, every one present; die —den, those present, the audience; hochgeehrte—de! (ladies and) gentlemen! —heit, *f.* presence.

An'wetzen, *v.a.* to begin to whet, to whet; *see* Anschleifen.

An'widern, *v.a.* to disgust; sich angewidert fühlen, to feel disgusted.

An'wimmern, *v.* I. *a.* to address whiningly. II. *n.* (*aux.* s.) to approach whining.

An'winden, *ir. v.a.* to draw up, put to by means of a windlass.

An'winken, *v.a.* to wink at; to beckon to; to ease the sheets of fore and aft sails (*Naut.*).

An'winseln, *v.a.* to whine at, to moan at.

An'wirbeln, *v.* I. *a.* to fasten by turning a peg; to fasten by a turnbolt. II. *n.* (*aux.* s.) to whirl, spin against.

An'wohn—en, *v.n.* (*aux.* h.) to live near, close by; to be present to, to attend (= beiwohnen); einer Vorstellung —en, to be present at a representation. —er, *m.* (—ers, *pl.* —er) neighbour; dweller near (*a river*); borderer.

An'wuchs, *m.* (—(s)es, *pl.* Anwüchse) growth; increase; increment; accretion; junger —, young copse.

An'wünschen, *v.a.*; einem etwas —, to wish something to happen to one; to adopt (*Law*); er wünschte mir viel Gutes an, he wished that much good might befall me; sie wünschte ihm Böses an, she wished him evil, she imprecated him.

An'wurf, *m.* (—s, *pl.* Anwürfe) a throwing, *or* laying on; dashing (*with mortar*); deposit, alluvium; first throw; hasp (*of a trunk, etc.*); selvage.

An'würfeln, *v.n.* to begin to throw; to have the first throw (*with dice*).

An'wurzeln, *v.n.* (*aux.* s.) to strike root; to be rooted to the ground.

An'zahl, *f.* number, quantity, multitude.

An'zahlen, *v.a.* to pay on account; to pay a first instalment.

An'zählen, *v.a.* to begin to count; to reckon, to count, to tell.

An'zapf—en, *v.a.* to broach, tap (*a cask, etc.*); to tap (*Med.*); to nettle, badger, chaff (*vulg.*); to pump (*coll.*); einen —en, to get s.th. (money, a secret, *etc.*) out of a person, to pump a p. (*coll.*); to pick a quarrel with s.o. (*coll.*). —ung, *f.* personal attack (*coll.*).

An'zaubern, *v.a.* to fascinate, bewitch; to root to the spot by witchcraft; to bring on one by sorcery. angezaubert, *p.p.* & *adj.* spellbound.

An'zäumen, *v.a.* to bridle, put on a bridle.

An'zeichen, *n.* (—s, *pl.* —) symptom, sign; token; augury, omen; foreboding.

An'zeichnen, *v.a.* to mark, note; to make a note of; to signal; einem etwas —, to put to one's account, attribute to; to make one pay for s.th. (*coll.*).

An'zeige, *f.* (*pl.* —n) notice, intimation; advertisement; announcement; declaration; indication; symptom; proof; gerichtliche —, denunciation, information against; eine — machen *or* thun, to file a declaration. *Comp.* —amt, *n.* enquiry-office; registry-office. —blatt, *n.* advertiser; advertisement sheet *or* journal. —brief, *m.* letter of intimation *or* information, circular.

An'zeig—en, *v.a.* to announce, to notify; to advertise; to point out; to indicate; to augur; to signify, lead to a supposition; to declare (*value, etc.*); to give a receipt for (*C. L.*); to advise (*C. L.*); einem etwas —en, to inform *or* apprise one of a thing; einen —en, to denounce (*a criminal*); öffentlich —en, to proclaim. angezeigt, *p.p.* & *adj.* (*lit.:* pointed out as the proper thing to do), advisable, necessary; er hielt es für angezeigt, he deemed it prudent. —end, *p.* & *adj.*; —ende Fürwörter, demonstrative pronouns; besitz—ende Fürwörter, possessive pronouns. —er, *m.* (—ers, *pl.* —er) one who points out; advertiser; informer; exponent (*Math.*). —ung, *f.* informing; advertising; information (*against*).

An'zettel, *m.* warp, weft, woof.

An'zettel—n, *v.a.* to set up a web; to weave a plot. —ung, *f.* setting up of a web; plotting. —er, *m.* (—ers, *pl.* —er), —in, *f.* (*pl.* —innen) plotter, contriver of a plot.

An'zieh—en, *ir. v.* I. *a.* to draw, pull (*on, in, etc.*); to draw tight, tighten, screw; put on clothes, dress; to make the first move (*at a game*); to haul home (*Naut.*); to suck up, imbibe (*as a sponge*); to attract; to quote, cite; to stretch; to drive home (*a screw*); to breed, raise (*cattle, etc.*); to cultivate, train (*trees, etc.*); to draw in (*the reins*); sich (*acc.*) —en, to dress, attire o.s.; sich (*dat.*) etwas —en, to apply something to oneself; einen neuen Menschen —, to turn over a new leaf (*prov.*); angezogene Stellen, passages referred to, quotations. II. *n.* (*aux.* h.) to draw; to stick, hold fast (*as glue, etc.*); to begin to draw; to take effect; die Prügel ziehen an, every stroke tells; der Nagel zieht an, the nail draws, takes firm hold; (*aux.* s.) to draw, *or* march on, near, to approach; to enter upon service, upon office; to rise (*in price*); das Heer kam angezogen, the army came marching on. —end, *p.* & *adj. see* —en; attractive; interesting; —ende Kraft, power of attraction; —ende Mittel, astringent medicines. —er, *m.* (—ers, *pl.* —er) shoe-horn; ringer (*of a bell*); adductor (*Anat.*). —ung, *f.* attraction; quoting, citing; natürliche —ung, gravitation. *Comp.* —ungs=kraft, *f.* (force of) attractive power, attraction. —ungs=los, *adj.* unattractive. —ungs=punkt, *m.* centre of attraction. —zimmer, *n.* dressing-room.

An'zischen, *v.a.* to hiss at.

An'zucht, *f.* (*pl.* Anzüchte) breeding; cultivation; nursery; sewer; breed. *Comp.*—schweine, *pl.* breeding-pigs.

An'zuckern, *v.a.* to sprinkle with sugar.

An'zug, *m.* (—s, *pl.* Anzüge) a drawing near, approach; getting, putting on (*of clothes*); dressing; dress, apparel, clothes; accoutrements; costume, toilet; first move; entrance upon duties; taper; ein — Spitzen, a set of lace; der Feind ist im —e, the enemy is approaching; es ist etwas im —, there is something in the wind; es ist ein Gewitter im —, a storm is coming on. *Comp.* —s=geld, *n.* entrance-money; tax paid by strangers for permission to reside in a place. —s=tag, *m.* day of entering upon duty.

An'züglich, *adj.* & *adv.* sarcastic, severe; personal; offensive, abusive; seien Sie nicht —, don't be personal. —keit, *f.* sarcasm, invective; offensiveness; personal remarks.

An'zünd—en, *v.a.* to kindle, light (*a fire, etc.*); to ignite, set on fire; to inflame. —er, *m.* (—ers, *pl.* —er) incendiary; lighter, kindler; fusee. —ung, *f.* ignition, act of kindling.

An'zwängen, *v.a.* to squeeze *or* force against; to force on (*clothes, etc.*).

An'zwecken, *v.a.* to tack, nail, *or* peg on.

A'olsharfe, *f.* Æolian harp. *See Index of Names.*

Ao'rt—a, *f.* aorta. *Comp.* —en=kammer, *f.* left ventricle of the heart.

Apath—ie', *f.* (*pl.* —ie'en) apathy. **—isch** (*pron.* **apa'thisch**) *adj.* & *adv.* apathetic.

Ap'fel, *m.* (—s, *pl.* Äpfel) *dim.* **Äpfelchen, Äpflein**, *n.* apple; **ich muß in den sauern — beißen**, I must grin and bear it, I must swallow the bitter pill (*prov.*); **der — fällt nicht weit vom Stamm**, like sire like son (*prov.*). *Comp.* **—äther**, *m.* malic ether. **—blech**, *n.* apple-roaster. **—brei**, *m.* apple sauce. **—förmig**, *adj.* spheroidal. **—garten**, *m.* orchard. **—gelee**, *n.* apple jelly. **—grau**, *adj.* dapple-gray. **—gröbs**, *m.*, **—häuschen**, *n.* core of an apple. **—kammer**, *f.* apple loft. **—kern**, *m.* apple pip. **—kuchen**, *m.* apple tart. **—most**, *m.* cider. **—mus**, *n.* apple-sauce. **—rose**, *f.* dog-rose. **—säure**, *f.* malic acid. **—schale**, *f.* apple paring, apple-peel. **—scheibe**, *f.* apple slice. **—schimmel**, *m.* dapple-gray horse. **—schnitt**, *m.*, **—schnitz**, *m.* slice of apple. **—schnitzchen**, *pl.* apple fritters. **—staude**, *f.* dwarf apple-tree. **—stecher**, *m.* apple-scoop. **—torte**, *f.* apple tart. **—wein**, *m.* cider.

Apfelsi'ne, *f.* (*pl.* —n) orange.

Apica'l, Apika'l, *adj.* apical; **—e Bildung**, narrowing of the mouth brought about by the front rim (apex) of the tongue touching the ridge above the upper teeth to produce 'apical' sounds, *i. e.* certain dental consonants (*Phonet.*).

Apo— (*does not take the stress in the following compounds:*) **—kryphisch**, *adj.* apocryphal; **—kryphische Bücher**, Apocrypha. **—log**, *m.* (—logen, *pl.* —logen) apologue. **—loge't**, *m.* (—logeten, *pl.* —logeten) apologist. **—physe**, *f.* apophysis (*Bot.*). **—stat**, *m.* (—staten, *pl.* —staten) apostate. **—stem**, *n.* (—stemes, *pl.* —steme) aposteme, abscess. **—stroph**, *m.* (—strophs, *pl.* —strophe) apostrophe. **—strophe**, *f.* (*pl.* —strophen) address, harangue. **—theose**, *f.* apotheosis.

Apo'st—el, *m.* (—els, *pl.* —el) apostle; large jug with the picture of the apostles (*obs.*). **—o'lisch**, *see* Apostolisch. *Comp.* **—el=amt**, *n.* apostleship. **—el=geschichte**, *f.* Acts of the Apostles, the Acts. **—el=salbe**, *f.* ointment composed of twelve ingredients.

Aposto'lisch, *adj.* & *adv.* apostolic; **das —e Glaubensbekenntnis**, the Apostles' Creed; **der —e Stuhl**, the apostolic see, the see of Rome; **die —en Väter**, the apostolic fathers.

Apothe'k—e, *f.* (*pl.* —en) apothecary's shop, dispensary, chemist's shop. **—er**, *m.* (—ers, *pl.* —er) chemist, druggist; apothecary. *Comp.* **—er=buch**, *n.* pharmacopœia. **—er=garten**, *m.* herb garden. **—er=gewicht**, *n.* troy weight. **—er=kunst**, *f.* pharmacy. **—er=topf**, *m.* gallipot. **—er=taxe**, *f.* fixed price of drugs. **—er=waren**, *pl.* drugs. **—er=wissenschaft**, *f.* science of pharmaceutics.

Appara't, *m.* (—s, *pl.* —e) apparatus.

Appe'll, *m.* (—s, *pl.* —e) roll-call; inspection (*of boots, rifles*); call; alarm; **— haben**, to be obedient (*of dogs*); **— blasen**, to sound the alarm; **zum — antreten**, to fall in for calling roll. **—a'nt**, *m.* (—a'nten, *pl.* —a'nten) appellant. **—a't**, *m.* (—a'ten, *pl.* —a'ten) defendant, appellee. **—atio'n**, *f.* appeal (*Law*); **er legte —ation ein**, he gave notice of appeal; **seine —ation wurde für unzulässig erklärt**, it was decided that he had no right of appeal. *Comp.* **—ations=freiheit**, *f.* right of appeal. **—ations=gericht**, *n.* court of appeal. **—ations=klage**, *f.* action upon appeal. **—ations=richter**, *m.* judge of appeals.

Appellie'ren, *v.a.* to appeal (*to a higher court*); **— an einen Gerichtshof**, to appeal to a court.

Apperceptio'n, *f.* (*pl.* —en) apperception. *Comp.* **—s=verbindung**, apperceptive combination.

Appeti't, *m.* (—s) appetite. **—lich**, *adj.* dainty; appetising. **—los**, *adj.* devoid of appetite.

Applaudie'ren, *v.a.* & *n.* to applaud.

Applicatu'r, *f.* (*pl.* —en) fingering (*Mus.*).

Appli—cie'ren, —zie'ren, *v.a.* to apply, bestow.

Apportie'ren, *v.a.* to retrieve.

Appret—ie'ren, *v.a.* to dress, finish. **—u'r**, *f.* dressing; finish.

Apriko'se, *f.* (*pl.* —n) apricot. *Comp.* **—n=baum**, *m.* apricot tree. **—n=pfirsich**, *m.* nectarine.

Apri'l, *m.* (—s) April; **einen in den — schicken**, to make an April fool of one; **ist der — feucht und naß, so füllt er dem Bauer Scheun' und Faß**, when April blows his horn, 't is good for hay and corn (*prov.*). *Comp.* **—glück**, *n.* vicissitude of fortune.

Apsi'de, *f.* (*pl.* —n) apsis (*Astr.*).

Aquare'll, *n.* a water-colours drawing. *Comp.* **—maler**, *m.* painter in water-colours. **—ie'ren**, *v.a.* to paint in water-colours.

Äquatio'n, *f.* equation. **—or**, *m.* (*pron.* **Äqua'=tor**) equator, equinoctial circle *or* line, the line.

Aquavit', *m.* (—s) aqua vitæ.

Äquilibri'st, *m.* (—en, *pl.* —en) rope-dancer.

Ar'beit, *f.* (*pl.* —en) work, labour, toil; result of labour; performance, composition; employment; fermentation; **eingelegte —**, inlaid work, marqueterie; **erhabene —**, embossed, raised work, relief; **getriebene —**, chasing; **Hand—**, needle-work; **es ist in der —**, it is in hand, is being made; **bei der — sein**, to be quick at one's work; **sich an die — machen**, to set to work; **Hand an die — legen**, to set to work, put one's hand to; **von seiner Hände — leben**, to live by manual labour; **(Hand)—en**, *pl.* hand-made articles; **schriftliche —en**, compositions, essays. **—sam**, *adj.* & *adv.* laborious, industrious. **—samkeit**, *f.* industry, diligence. **—selig**, *adj.* labour-loving, toilsome. *Comp.* **—geber**, *m.*, **—geberin**, *f.* employer. **—nehmer**, *m.* workman, labourer, clerk. **—nehmerin**, *f.* woman who does paid work; working woman, factory girl. **—s=ameise**, *f.* working emmet. **—s=beutel**, *m.* work-bag. **—s=biene**, *f.* working bee. **—scheu** & **—s=scheu**, I. *adj.* work-shirking, idle, lazy. II. *f.* laziness. **—s=einstellung**, *f.* strike. **—s=fähig**, *adj.* able-bodied, capable of working. **—s=gedränge**, *n.* press of work. **—s=gerüst**, *n.* scaffolding. **—s=gesellschaft**, *f.* working party; gang of workmen. **—s=haus**, work-house; penitentiary. **—s=kästchen**, *n.* work-box; tool-box. **—s=kammer**, *f.* laboratory. **—s=korb**, *m.* work-basket. **—s=lohn**, *m.* wages, pay for work. **—s=loch**, *n.* man-hole (*in boilers, etc.*); working *or* lading hole (*Glass-w.*). **—s=mann**, *m.* workman. **—s=nachweis=stelle**, *f.* place where information as to work wanted is gratuitously given to workmen. **—s=sperre**, *f.* lock-out. **—s=tisch**, *m.* work-table. **—s=unfähig**, *adj.* incapable of working. **—s=vogt**, *m.* overseer; clerk of works; gauger. **—s=zeit**, *f.* work-hours, working hours, time. **—s=zeug**, *n.* tools.

Ar'beit—en, *v.* I. *a.* to cultivate (*land*); to work, execute, fashion; **sich hindurch —en**, to work one's way through; **sich immer tiefer in die Wut hinein —en**, to work oneself into a rage; **ein Schiff über eine Bank —en**, to force a ship over a sandbank; **sich krank —en**, to knock oneself up with work. II. *n.* (*aux.* **h.**) to toil, labour; to ferment; to work (*as a machine*); **—en an einer S.**, to be busy with, employed on; **—en mit**, to transact business with; **ich —e daran**, I am at it; **das Schiff —et**, the ship labours; **es —et sich schlecht**, work progresses badly. **—er**, *m.* (—ers, *pl.* —er) worker, workman, labourer; **der —er ist seines Lohnes wert**, every labourer is worthy of his hire (*prov.*) **—er=ausstand**, *m.* strike. **—er=frage**, *f.* question of the working classes, social question. —**erin**, *f.* (—**erinnen**) working woman, female labourer, factory girl. —**er=schaft**, *f.* working men, working class. —**er=schutz**, *m.* protection of labour. —**er=sperre**, *f.* lock-out. —**er=stand**, *m.* working class, labouring classes. —**er=verein**, *m.* workmen's club *or* union. **er=wohnungen**, *f. pl.* artisans' dwellings.

Archai'stisch, *adj.* archaic.

Archäo—lo'g, *m.* (—**logen**, *pl.* —**logen**) archeologist. —**lo'gisch**, *adj.* archeological.

Arche, *f.* (*pl.* —**n**) ark; sounding board, air-chest of an organ.

Ar'chi— (*in comp.*) —**dia'conus**, *m.* arch-deacon. —**pe'l**, *m.* (—**pe'ls**) archipelago. —**te'kt**, *m.* (—**te'kten**, *pl.* —**te'kten**) architect. —**tekto'nisch**, *adj.* & *adv.* architectural. —**tektu'r**, *f.* (*pl.* —**tektu'ren**) architecture.

Archime'disch, *adj.* Archimedean; —**e Schraube**, screw-propeller, Archimedean screw.

Architra'v, *m.* (—**s**, *pl.* —**e**) architrave.

Archi'v, *n.* (—**es**, *pl.* —**e**) archives. —**a'r**, *m.* (—**ars**, *pl.* —**are**) keeper of the archives, registrar; Master of the Rolls. *Comp.* —**gebäude**, *n.* record office.

Arg, I. *adj.* & *adv.* (**ärger**, **ärgst**) bad, mischievous, wicked; gross; severe; deceitful; utter, arch, arrant; hard, sad; **ich hatte nichts —es dabei**, I meant no harm by it; **im ärgsten Falle**, if the worst come to the worst; **er denkt von jedermann —es**, he thinks ill of every one; **einen —en Fehler begehen**, to commit a grave error; **ein —er Tabaksraucher**, an inveterate smoker; **das ist zu —**, that is too bad; **es wird immer ärger**, things go from bad to worse; **man hat ihn sehr — mißhandelt**, he has been very badly used, cruelly treated; **zu — mit einem verfahren**, to be too severe with one. II. *subst.n.* **es ist kein — an (in) ihm**, there is no deceit in him; **ohne —**, undesigning; **die Welt liegt im —en**, this is a wicked world; **bei euch liegt noch alles im —en**, you are still far behind (*with your affairs or preparations*). —**heit**, *f.* wickedness, malice. *Comp.* —**list**, *f.* cunning, craftiness, deceit; artifice, intrigue. —**listig**, *adj.* & *adv.* cunning, crafty, deceitful. —**los**, *adj.* & *adv.* innocent, guileless; harmless; unsuspecting. —**losigkeit**, *f.* harmlessness; guilelessness. —**sinnig**, *adj.* & *adv.* suspicious; malicious (*rare*). —**wille**, *m.* ill-will, mischievousness, malice (*rare*). —**wohn**, *m.* (*no pl.*) mistrust, suspicion; jealousy; surmise; —**wohn hegen gegen einen**, to suspect a p. —**wohnen**, *usually* —**wöhnen**, *v.a.* to suspect, mistrust. —**wöhnisch**, *adj.* & *adv.* suspicious, distrustful; jealous.

Argo'n, *n.* argon (*Chem.*).

Är'ger, *m.* (—**s**) vexation; anger, chagrin; spite; **einem zum —**, in spite of one. —**lich**, *adj.* & *adv.* annoying, vexatious, provoking; easily annoyed; angry, vexed, put out; snappish, crusty; scandalous; **auf einen** *or* **eine S. —lich sein**, to be irritated at a p. *or* a th.

Är'ger—n, *v.a.* to annoy, vex, put out of temper, irritate; to scandalise; to offend; **sich —n**, to take offence, lose one's temper, fret, worry oneself. —**nis**, *n.* (—**sses**, *pl.* —**sse**) scandal; offence; vexation, anger, annoyance; **ein —nis nehmen an einer S.**, to be scandalised at a thing; —**nis geben**, to cause annoyance, to shock the feelings, to hurt.

A'rie, *f.* (*pl.* —**n**) tune, air, song (*Mus.*).

Aristokra't, *m.* (—**en**, *pl.* —**en**) aristocrat. —**ie'**, *f.* aristocracy. —**isch**, *adj.* aristocratic.

Arithmet—i'k, *f.* arithmetic. —**iker** (*pr.* —**me'tiker**), *m.* (—**ikers**, *pl.* —**iker**) arithmetician. —**isch** (*pr.* —**me'tisch**), *adj.* & *adv.* arithmetical.

Arkebusie'r, *m.* arquebusier (*xvii. cent. foot soldier*).

Ark'tisch, *adj.* & *adv.* arctic, northern, towards the North Pole.

Arm, (**ärmer**, **ärmst**) *adj.* & *adv.* poor, needy; meagre, scanty; barren; miserable; despicable; **ein —er**, a poor man; **die —en**, the poor; **die verschämten —en**, poor people that are ashamed to beg, the deserving poor; —**e Ritter**, fritters; **ein —er Sünder**, a poor wretch; a condemned criminal; **ich —er! ich —e!** unfortunate wretch that I am! — **an einer S.**, destitute of, void of, poor in a th.; — **an Schönheit**, wanting in beauty. —**selig**, *adj.* & *adv.* poor, needy; paltry, wretched, miserable; despicable. —**seligkeit**, *f.* wretchedness, misery; paltriness —**ut**, *f.* indigence, poverty; the poor. *Comp.* —**en=anstalt**, *f.* almshouse; charity-school; institution (for poor people). —**en=gesetz**, *n.* poor law. —**en=haus**, *n.* almshouse, poor-house. —**en=kasse**, *f.* poor-box; relief-fund. —**en=pflege**, *f.* care of the poor, charity organization. —**en=pfleger**, *m.* relieving officer; overseer of the poor; almoner. —**en=schule**, *f.* charity-school, free-school. —**en=steuer**, *f.* poor-rate. —**e=sünder=Blume**, *f.* wild chicory. —**e=sünder=Gesicht**, *n.* mien of a criminal. —**e=sünder=Glöcklein**, *n.* knell rung for an execution, passing bell. —**e=sünder=Karren**, *m.* the hangman's cart. —**e=sünder=Stuhl**, *m.* stool of repentance. —**en=vogt**, *m.*, —**en=vorsteher**, *m.* overseer of the poor; poor-law guardian. —**en=wesen**, *n.* system of providing for the poor, charity organisation.

Arm, *m.* (—**es**, *pl.* —**e**) arm; fore-leg (*of a beast*); beam (*of scales*); branch (*of a candlestick*); shaft (*of a barrow, carriage, etc.*); arm (*of a chair*); shank (*of scissors, etc.*); leg (*of tongs*); — **der Segelstange**, yard-arm; **einem unter die —e greifen**, to help one (*coll.*); **mit freien —en**, unpinioned; **die —e übereinander schlagen**, to fold one's arms; **der weltliche —**, the secular arm. *Comp.* —**ader**, *see* —**blutader**. —**band**, *n.* bracelet. —**binde**, *f.* sling. —**blatt**, *n.* preserver. —**blutader**, *f.* brachial artery. —**bruch**, *m.* fracture of the arm. —**brust**, *f.* (*pl.* **Armbrüste**) cross-bow. —**brust=schütze**, *m.* archer. —**geflecht**, *n.* brachial plexus. —**geige**, *f.* tenor viol. —**geschmeide**, *n.* armlets, bracelets. —**heber**, *m.* brachial levator. —**höhle**, *f.* armpit. —**holz**, *n.* pommel. —**korb**, *m.* basket with a handle. —**lehne**, *f.* elbow-rest. —**leuchter**, *m.* chandelier, branched candlestick. —**los**, *adj.* without arms. —**nerv**, *m.* brachial nerve. —**schiene**, *f.* armlet; radius; splint; turner's arm-rest. —**spange**, *f.* bangle. —**sessel**, *m.*, —**stuhl**, *m.* arm-chair, easy chair.

Armatu'r, *f.* (*pl.* —**en**) armament, equipment.

Armee', *f.* (*pl.* —**en**) army. *Comp.* —**befehl**, *m.* order issued by the commander-in-chief, general order. —**bericht**, *m.* army report, bulletin, despatch. —**corps**, *m.* army corps (*consisting in Germany of 2* **Divisionen** *or 4* **Brigaden**). —**lieferant**, *m.* army contractor.

Är'mel, *m.* (—**s**, *pl.* —) sleeve; **mit aufgestülpten —n**, with tucked-up sleeves; **die — zurückschlagen**, to turn up the cuffs, *or* sleeves; **auf den — heften**, to tell a fib to (*coll.*); **etwas** (*acc.*) **aus dem — schütteln**, to do a thing off-hand *or* to do a thing with the greatest ease. *Comp.* —**holz**, *n.* sleeve-board for ironing. —**loch**, *n.* sleevehole. —**meer**, *n.* English Channel.

Är'm—er, *see* **Arm**, *adj.* —**lich**, *adj.* & *adv.* poorish, needy, poor, miserable, scanty; pitiful. —**lichkeit**, *f.* poverty, scantiness.

Armie'r—en, *v.a.* to equip (*a vessel*); to arm (*a magnet*). —**ung**, *f.* armament, equipment.

Aro'ma, *n.* (—**s**) aroma. —**tisch** (*pr.* **aroma'tisch**) *adj.* & *adv.* aromatic. —**tisie'ren**, *v.a.* to perfume, render aromatic.

A'rrack, **A'rrak**, **A'rak**, *m.* (—**s**) arrack, rack.

Arrest', *m.* (—**es**, *pl.* —**e**) arrest; attachment;

mit — belegen, to seize; **— anlegen**, to sequestrate. **—a'nt**, *m.* (**—anten**, *pl.* **—anten**) prisoner.

Arretie'ren, *v.a.* to arrest.

Ar'sch, *m.* (**—es**, *pl.* **Ärsche**) arse, hind part, posterior, bottom, backside, breech (*vulg.*). *Comp.* **—backe**, *f.* buttock (*vulg.*). **—leder**, *n.* breech leather of miners. **—lings**, *also* **ärschlings = rücklings, rückwärts.**

Arse'nik, *n.* (**—s**) arsenic; **gediegenes —**, native arsenic. **—alisch**, *adj.* arsenical. *Comp.* **—blei**, *n.* arseniate of lead. **—butter**, *f.* chloride of arsenic. **—kalk**, *m.* arseniate of lime. **—kies**, *m.* arsenical pyrites. **—könig**, *m.* regulus of arsenic. **—rubin**, *m.* red orpiment. **—sauer**, *adj.* consisting of *or* containing arsenic; **—saures Salz**, *n.* arseniate. **—vitriol**, *m.* sulphate of arsenic. **—wasserstoffgas**, *n.* arseniureted hydrogen gas.

¹**Art**, *f.* (*pl.* **—en**) kind, species, sort; race, breed; nature; manner; method, way; mood (*Gram.*); propriety; good-breeding; **eine — Pflanzen**, a species of plants; **einzig in seiner —**, unique; **aus der — schlagen**, to degenerate, to vary from a type; **— läßt nicht von —**, what is bred in the bone comes not out of the flesh; **die Fortpflanzung der —**, the propagation of the species; **von göttlicher —**, of divine origin; **die — des Bodens**, the nature of the soil; **das ist bloß eine Redens—**, that is only a figure of speech, a way of talking; **auf diese —**, in this way, at this rate; **der — Leute**, such people; **ein guter Mann nach seiner —**, a good fellow in his way; **es ist auf gewisse — schon geschehen**, it is in a manner done already; **es hat keine —**, it is not polite, seemly; **er hat keine —, er hat keine Lebens—**, he has no manners. **—ig**, *adj.* good, well-behaved; polite, courteous, civil, kind, friendly; nice, agreeable, pleasing; **sei —ig!** be good! *as suffix;* —like, resembling (*as* **Balladen—ig**, in ballad style; **gut—ig**, good-natured; **bös—ig**, malicious). **—igkeit**, *f.* (*pl.* **—igkeiten**) good behaviour; politeness, courtesy, civility, kindness; civil speech; prettiness, comeliness; niceness (*of manners*); **er hat ihr allerlei —igkeiten gesagt**, he said a number of pretty things to her, paid her many compliments. *Comp.* **—name**, *m.* specific name.

²**Art**, *f.* ploughing; arable land. **—bar**, *adj.* arable. *Comp.* **—lohn**, *m.* wages for tillage.

Art—en, *v.* I. *n.* (*aux.* **h.**) to acquire, assume a certain quality, to thrive; **—en nach**, to resemble, take after; **gut geartet**, of good disposition (*of children*). II. *a.* to impart, transmit a quality *or* nature to; to modify. **—ung**, *f.* formation, modification.

Arti'kel, *m.* (**—s**, *pl.* **—**) article; part; item, entry; point of faith. *Comp.* **—briefe**, *m.* articles of war; ship's articles (*Naut.*). **—weise**, *adv.* article by article, item by item.

Arte'sisch, *adj.* artesian; **ein —er Brunnen**, an artesian well.

Artikul—atio'n, *f.* articulation. **—ie'ren**, *v.a.* to articulate (*a skeleton*); to pronounce distinctly, articulate.

Ar'tiller—ie, *f.* artillery; gunnery; **leichte —ie**, flying artillery; **reitende —ie**, horse artillery. **—i'st**, *m.* (**—isten**, *pl.* **—isten**) artilleryman, gunner. *Comp.* **—ie=park**, *m.* train of artillery, artillery-park. **—ie=schießplatz**, *m.* gunnery-practising ground. **—ie=wagen**, *m.* tumbler.

Ar'tischocke, *f.* (*pl.* **—n**) artichoke.

A'rum, *m.* arum, cuckoo-pintle, bare-mint.

Arz(e)nei', *f.* (*pl.* **—en**) medicine, physic; **eine bewährte — verordnen, verschreiben**, to prescribe a specific. **—lich**, *adj.* & *adv.* medicinal. *Comp.* **—bereiter**, *m.* apothecary. **—bereitungs=kunst**, *f.* pharmaceutics; pharmacy. **—buch**, *n.* pharmacopœia. **—formel**, *f.* recipe. **—glas**, *n.* phial. **—händler**, *m.* druggist, chemist. **—kästchen**, *n.* medicine chest. **—kräuter**, *pl.* simples. **—kunde**, *f.*, **—kunst**, *f.* pharmacy, medicine. **—mittel**, *n.* remedy. **—mittel=lehre**, *f.* pharmaceutics, pharmacology. **—schrank**, *m.* medicine chest. **—trank**, *m.* draught. **—verschreibung**, *f.* recipe, prescription. **—wein**, *m.* medicated wine. **—wissenschaft**, *f.* science of medicine. **—zettel**, *m.* label; prescription.

Arzt, *m.* (**—es**, *pl.* **Ärzte**) doctor, physician, medical man. *Comp.* **—gebühr**, *f.* (*pl.* **—gebühren**) doctor's fee.

Ärztin, *f.* (**—nen**) doctoress, lady-physician.

Ä'rztlich, *adj.* & *adv.* medical.

¹**As**, *n.* A flat (*Mus.*); **—=Dur**, A flat major; **—=Moll**, A flat minor.

²**As, Aß**, *n.* (**—sses**, *pl.* **—sse**), ace (*cards*); grain (*a weight*).

A'sant, *m.* (**—s**); **wohlriechender —**, benzoin; **stinkender —**, asafœtida.

Asbe'st, *m.* asbestos, asbestus; **gemeiner —**, rockwood. **—artig**, *adj.* asbestine.

Asce't, Aske't, *m.* (**—en**, *pl.* **—en**). **—iker**, *m.* (**—ikers**, *pl.* **—iker**) ascetic. **—isch**, *adj.* & *adv.* ascetic.

Asch—e, *f.* ashes; **glimmende —e**, embers; **in —e legen, zu —e verbrennen**, to burn to ashes, to reduce to ashes; **in —e verwandeln**, to calcine; **er hat —e**, he has much money, is very well off (*sl.*). **—icht** (*obs.*), **—ig**, *adj.* ashy. *Comp.* **—blei**, *n. see* **Wismut.** **—bleich**, *adj.* ashy-pale. **—en=becher**, *m.* ash-tray. **—en=behälter**, *m.* ash-pan, ash-pit. **—en=brödel**, *n.* (& *f.*) slut; scullion; Cinderella. **—en=fall**, *m.* ash-pit. **—en=farbig**, *adj.* ashy (*in colour*). **—en=grube**, *f.* ash-pit. **—en=kasten**, *m.* dust-bin, ash-box. **—en=krug**, *m.* funeral urn. **—en=lauge**, *f.* lye of wood ashes. **—en=pflanze**, *f.* cineraria. **—en=salz**, *n.* potassium carbonate. **—en=sieb**, *n.* cinder-sifter. **—urne**, *f.* (funeral) urn. **—en=zieher**, *m.* tourmaline. **—er=Mittwoch**, *m.* Ash-Wednesday. **—farbe**, *f.* ash-colour. **—grau**, *adj.* ashy (in colour). **bis ins —e**, ever so long; beyond all measure, past all conceptions (*sl.*).

Ä'scher, *m.* slack-lime.

Ä'schern, *v.a.* to reduce to ashes; to bestrew with ashes; to slacken (*a hide*).

A'se, *m.* (*pl.* **—n**) & **A'sin**, *f.* (*pl.* **—nen**) asa, *name of the old German gods and goddesses.*

Aspe'kt, *m.* aspects, configuration (*Astron.*).

Aspir—a'nt, *m.* **—a'ntin**, *f.* aspirant, candidate for a post. **—a'ta**, **—a'te**, aspirated stop (th ph kh ; dh bh gh). **—atio'n**, *f.* aspiration.

Aspirie'ren, *v.a.* to aspirate, to sound the aspirated stop.

Aß', *n. see* **As.**

A'ßen, Ä'ßen, *v.n.* (*aux.* **h.**) to graze (*of deer*).

Assekur—a'nt, *m.* (**—anten**, *pl.* **—anten**) insurer. **—a'nz**, *f.* (*pl.* **—anzen**) insurance, assurance; **die —anz validiert auf M.**, the insurance is effected on M. **—a't**, *m.* (**—aten**, *pl.* **—aten**) person insured. **—a'tor**, *m.* (**—ators**, *pl.* **—ator**) assurer, insurer. *Comp.* **—anz=police**, *f.* policy of insurance. **—anz=prämie**, *f.* premium on a policy.

Assekur—ie'ren, *v. a.* & *n.* to insure. **—ier=ba'r**, *adj.* insurable.

A'ssel, *f.* woodlouse.

Asse'ss—or, *m.* (*pl.* **—o'ren**) assessor; judge lateral, assistant judge.

Assigna'nt, *m.* drawer, giver of a draft.

Assigna't, *m.* (**—en**, *pl.* **—en**) drawee. **—e**, *f.* assignat.

Assignie'ren, *v.a.* to assign, to draw.

Assi'sen, *pl.* assizes. *Comp.* **—gericht**, *n.*, **—gerichtshof**, *m.* court of assizes.

Assiste'nt, *m.* (**—en**, *pl.* **—en**) assistant; clerk.

Associé', *m.* (**—s**, *pl.* **—s**) partner: **wirklicher**

—, active, working partner; **stiller** —, sleeping partner.
Associie'ren, *v.a.* to associate; **ich habe mich mit ihm associiert**, I have entered into partnership with him.
Assona'nz, *f.* assonance.
Assonie'ren, *v.n.* to assonate.
Assort—ie'ren, *v.a.* to assort, to sort. **—ime'nt**, *n.* assortment (*Comm.*).
Ast, *m.* (—es, *pl.* Äste) bough, branch; knot (*in wood*); **sich** (*dat.*) **einen — lachen**, to split with laughter, to laugh excessively (*sl.*). *Comp.* **—loch**, *n.* knothole. **—werk**, *n.* branches (*of a tree*).
As'ter, *f.* (*pl.* —n) aster, China aster.
Äst—chen, *n.* (—chens, *pl.* —chen) twig, small bough. **—ig**, *adj.* branching; knotty, gnarled. **—ling**, *m.* (—lings, *pl.* —linge) young bird that has left the nest.
Ästhe't—ik, *f.* æsthetics. **—iker**, *m.* (—ikers, *pl.* —iker) æsthetician, lover (student, professor) of æsthetics. **—isch**, *adj. & adv.* æsthetic.
Astro—lo'g, *m.* (—logen, *pl.* —logen) astrologer. **—logie'**, *f.* astrology. **—lo'gisch**, *adj.* astrological. **—nom**, *m.* (—nomen, *pl.* —nomen) astronomer. **—nomie'**, *f.* astronomy. **—no'misch**, *adj.* astronomical.
Asy'l, *n.* (—s, *pl.* —e) asylum, sanctuary.
A't—em, *m.* (—ems) breath, respiration; spirit; **kurzer —em**, shortness of breath; **schwerer —em**, asthma; **—em holen, —em schöpfen**, (**—em ziehen**, *obs.*) to draw breath, to breathe; **den —em an sich halten**, to hold one's breath; **außer —em**, breathless; **ein Pferd wieder zu —em kommen lassen**, to let a horse get its wind; **wieder zu —em kommen**, to recover breath. **—em=bar**, *adj.* breathable. *Comp.* **—em=los**, *adj.* breathless. **—em=losigkeit**, *f.* breathlessness. **—em=zug**, *m.* breath, respiration; **einen tiefen —emzug thun**, to draw a deep breath; **der letzte —emzug**, the last gasp.
At'm—en, I. *v.a. & n.* to breathe; **schwer —en**, to gasp. II. *subst. n.* act of breathing. **—ung**, *f.* respiration. **—ungs=geräusch**, *n.* respiratory murmur. **—ungs=organe**, *pl.* organs of respiration *or* breathing.
Athe—i'smus, *m.* atheism. **—i'st**, *m.* (—isten, *pl.* —isten) atheist. **—isterei'**, *f. see* —ismus.
Ä'ther, *m.* (—s) ether; sky. **—isch** (*pr.* äthe'risch), *adj.* ethereal; **—ische Öle**, *pl.* ethereal oils (*Phys.*); **—ische Stoffe**, imponderables.
Athlet', *m.* (—en, *pl.* —en) athlete. **—isch**, *adj. & adv.* athletic.
At'las, *m.* (—(ss)es, *pl.* —(ss)e *and* **Atla'nten**) atlas. *Comp.* **—format**, *n.* atlas folio.
At'laß, *usually* **At'las**, *m.* (—(ss)es, *pl.* —(ss)e) satin. **—(ss)en**, *adj.* made of satin. *Comp.* **—band**, *n.* satin ribbon. **—brocat, —brokat**, *m.* brocaded satin.
Ato'm, *n.* atom, particle. **—i'st**, *m.* atomist. **—i'stisch**, *adj.* atomic (-al) (*Chem.*).
Atmosphär'—e, *f.* (*pl.* —en) atmosphere. **—isch**, *adj.* atmospheric.
Ätsch, Ätsch! (*long* ä) that serves you right! (*exclamation of mockery*).
Atta'cke, *f.* charge; **Gewehr zur — rechts!** prepare to charge! (*Mil.*)
Attent—at', *n.* (—ates, *pl.* —ate) attempt on a man's life, outrage. **—äter**, *m.* he who did it; culprit (*humorous*). **—a'ten**, *v.a.* to attempt an attentat (*coll.*).
Attest't, —a't, *n.* (—es, *pl.* —e) certificate. **—ie'ren**, *v.a.* to attest, certify.
At'tich, *m.* (—s, *pl.* —e) dwarf-elder.
Attra'penmöbel, *n.* furniture serving a double purpose.
A'tzel, *f.* (*pl.* —n) magpie (*obsol.*) *see* **Elster**.
Ätz'—bar, *adj.* etchable, that may be eaten by an acid; corrosive. *Comp.* **—druck**, *m.* etching. **—grund**, *m.* etching ground. **—kalk**, *m.* quick-lime. **—kraft**, *f.* causticity, corrosive power. **—kunst**, *f.* the art of etching (*on copper, etc.*). **—manier**, *f.* aqua-fortis style. **—mittel**, *n.* corrosive. **—nadel**, *f.* etching needle. **—pulver**, *n.* corrosive powder. **—stein**, *m.* lunar caustic. **—stoff**, *m.* caustic. **—wasser**, *n.* solution of aqua-fortis for etching; caustic solution. **—zeichnung**, *f.* etching.
Atz'—en, *v.a.* to feed (*obs.*). **—ung**, *f.* feeding, food.
Ätz'—en, *v.a.* to feed, bait; to bite, corrode (*as an acid*); (*Surg.*) to cauterize; to etch (*on copper, etc.*). **—ung**, *f.* cauterizing; etching.
Au! oh (*exclamation of physical pain, also of mockery after hearing a bad joke*). **Au weh!** oh, oh!
Auch, *conj. & adv.* also, too; even; likewise; *after* **wer, was, welcher, wie, ꝛc.** = ever, soever; **ohne — nur zu fragen**, without so much as asking; — **nicht**, neither, nor . . . either; **nicht nur . . . sondern —**, not only . . . but also; **und wenn — schon, wenn — gleich**, even though, although; **wo —**, wheresoever; **wer es — sei**, whoever he (it) may be; **aber —**, but, but yet; **und mag er — noch so reich sein**, let him be ever so rich; **dieser Ring ist schön, — kostet er viel**, this ring is handsome and well it may be, for it costs a great deal; **wenn es nur jetzt — Zeit ist**, if it be not already too late; **und wenn er — bezahlt**, and even if he pay; **willst du es — thun?** will you be sure to do it? **bist du — glücklich?** are you really happy? **das wäre — an der Zeit!** it is, I think, high time indeed! **es geschehe wann es — wolle**, whenever it may happen; **so sehr er — lachte**, however much he laughed; — **noch**, still; **so groß —, so oft —**, as great, as often as.
Auctio'n, *f. see* **Auktion**.
Audi—e'nz, *f.* (*pl.* —enzen) audience; hearing; reception; **zur —enz kommen**, to be admitted to an audience. **—teu'r**, *m.* (—teurs, *pl.* —teurs) officer of justice (*Mil.*). **—tor**, *m.* (*pron.* **Audi'tor**, *pl.* **Audito'ren**) judge advocate. **—toria't**, *n.* (—toria'ts) office and duties of a judge advocate, of a military justiciary. **—to'rium**, *n.* (—to'riums) lecture-room; people (*students, etc.*) attending a lecture. *Comp.* **—e'nz=saal**, *m.*, **—e'nz=zimmer**, *n.* presence chamber.
Au'e, *f.* (*pl.* —n) brook (*obs.*); fertile plain, meadow (*watered by a brook*); pasture.
Au'er—, (*m.*) *Comp.* **—hahn**, *m.*, **—huhn**, *n.* mountain (*or* heath) cock; capercaillie. **der —hahn balzt**, the capercaillie plays. **—hahnbalz**, *f.* pairing time of the mountain cock. **—henne**, *f.* mountain hen. **—ochs**, *m.* urus, bison; aurochs (*fossil*)
Auf, I. *prep.* ***With dat.*** *signifying rest, or limited motion in a place;* on, upon; in; of; at; by; — **der Erde liegen**, to lie on the ground; — **der Flöte spielen**, to play on the flute; **die Ente schwimmt — dem Teiche**, the duck swims on the pond; — **der Erde**, on the earth; — **der Stelle**, on the spot, immediately; — **der Reise sein**, to be on one's way, on a journey, travelling; — **einem Berge gehen**, to walk about on a mountain, along the ridge of a mountain; — **der Straße**, in the street; — **seinem Zimmer**, in his room; — **der Flotte dienen**, to serve in the navy; — **dieser Welt**, in this world; — **dem Markte**, in the market; — **der Hochschule** (up) at the university; **es hat nichts — sich**, it is of no consequence; **viel — sich haben**, to be of great importance; — **dem Lande wohnen**, to live in the country; — **einem Auge blind**, blind of an eye; — **einem Balle**, at a ball; — **seiner Seite**, at his side, on his side; **die Ehre ist ganz — meiner Seite**, the honour is all for

me; — **dem nächsten Wege**, by the nearest way. ***With acc.*** *when signifying motion to a place, or change; or when used not locally, but metaphorically;* on; in; of; immediately after; at; by; to, for; all but, up to; towards; up; — **einen Berg steigen**, to climb a mountain; **stellen Sie die Lampe — den Tisch**, place the lamp on the table; — **Rechnung**, on account; **sich verlassen —**, to depend on; — **Anfrage**, on application, on inquiry; — **meine Ehre**, upon my honour; — **Königswort**, upon my royal word; — **keinen Fall**, on no account; — **deutsch**, in German; — **'s neue**, a new; — **'s eheste**, as soon as possible; — **'s beste**, in the best possible way; — **diese Art**, in this way, at this rate; **er ist stolz — seine Kinder**, he is proud of his children; — **das Essen spazieren gehen**, to walk after dinner; **er beging eine Thorheit — die andere**, he committed one folly after another; — **jeden Fall**, in any case, at all events; — **einmal**, all at once; — **einen Blick**, at a glance; — **einen Zug**, at one draught; — **ein Haar**, to a T., very accurately; — **die Post geben**, to post; — **die Post gehen**, to go to the post; — **die Universität gehen**, to go to the University, to go up; — **einen zeigen**, to point to one; **wir schoben es — den Abend auf**, we put it off to the evening; — **eine gewisse Entfernung**, to a certain distance; **fünf Pfund — den Quadratzoll**, 5 lbs. to the square inch; — **jemandes Gesundheit trinken**, to drink to a person's (good) health; **ich bin — morgen eingeladen**, I have an invitation for to-morrow; **es geht — Leben und Tod**, it is a matter of life and death; **alle bis — einen**, all but one; — **Befehl des Königs**, by order of the king; **es geht — neun**, it is getting on to nine; **ein Viertel — eins**, a quarter past twelve; **drei Viertel — vier**, a quarter to four; **bis — weiteren Befehl**, until further orders; — **einen Baum steigen**, to climb up a tree; **er hat ihn — Pistolen gefordert**, he challenged him to a duel with pistols; **das geht — meine Kosten**, I pay for that; — **Wache ziehen**, to mount guard; — **die Jagd ausgehen**, to go hunting; **so viel — die Person**, so much per head; — **die Seite schaffen**, to lay aside; to do away with. II. *adv.* up, upwards; open, awake; — **oder ab**, up or down, more or less; — **und nieder**, up and down; apeak (*Naut.*); **Trepp(en) —, Trepp(en) ab**, upstairs and downstairs; **was soll ich denn so spät — sein?** why am I to stay up so late? **von Jugend —**, from (*my, his, her, etc.*) youth; **Berg —**, up hill. III. *conj.* — **daß**, in order that (*archaic, elevated style*), that not, lest. IV. *interj.* —, up! arise! **Auf'** = *before many verbs:* up, on, upon; un-, open; afresh, anew. *It is a separable prefix, e.g.* **aufbieten, ich biete auf, aufgeboten.** *In case a possible compound is not given in the following lists see under the simple word.*

Auf'ächzen, *v.n.* to groan, sigh heavily.

Auf'ackern, *v.a.* to plough up.

Auf'arbeiten, *v.a.* to work (*a lock, etc.*) open; to use up; **sich —**, to work one's way up.

Auf'atmen, *v.n.* (*aux.* **h.**) to draw a deep breath (*of relief*), to breathe again.

Auf'ätzen, *v.a.* to open by corrosives.

Auf'backen, *reg. & ir.v.a.* to rebake; to use up in baking.

Auf'bahren, *v.a.* to put on the bier.

Auf'ballen, *v.a.* to pile *or* put up in bales.

Auf'bau, *m.* (—(e)s, *pl.* —ten) building; elevation; erection; superstructure.

Auf'bauen, *v.a.* to erect, build up; to rebuild.

Auf'bäumen, *v.a.* to beam, to wind up; **sich —**, to rear up.

Auf'bauschen, *v.* I. *a.* to puff out the cheeks; **eine Sache —**, to puff up a th., make too much of, exaggerate a th. II. *n.* to bag (*of clothes*).

Auf'begehren, *v.n.* to start up in anger; to remonstrate in an angry manner.

Auf'behalten, *ir.v.a.* to keep on (*one's hat*); to keep in store; **sich** (*dat.*) —, to reserve for o.s.

Auf'beißen, *ir.v.a.* to open by biting; to crack (*nuts, etc.*).

Auf'bekommen, *ir.v.a.* to get on; to get open; to get, receive (*a task, etc.*).

Auf'bersten, *reg. & ir.v.n.* (*aux.* **s.**) to burst open; to crack, chap; to gape, split.

Auf'besser—n, *v.a.* to improve, raise (*salaries*); to mend, patch (*clothes*). **—ung,** *f.* amelioration, improvement, raising (*of salaries*).

Auf'betten, *v.a.* to put up a bed, to make a bed anew.

Auf'bewahr—en, *v.a.* to put by, store up; to stow away; to reserve; to preserve, keep; **dieses Obst läßt sich nicht —en**, this fruit does not keep (well). **—er,** *m.* (**—ers**, *pl.* **—er**) *m.* storer, one that lays up. **—ung,** *f.* storage; preserving; keeping; storing away.

Auf'biegen, *ir.v.a.* to bend up; to unfold.

Auf'bieten, *ir.v.a.* to cite, to summon; to call up, order out, call for service; to proclaim; to give notice of; to exert, put forth; **ein Brautpaar —**, to publish banns of marriage; **sie wurden gestern zum erstenmale öffentlich aufgeboten**, yesterday their banns of marriage were read out for the first time; **sie bot alle ihre Reize auf**, she displayed all her charms; **alles —**, to strain every nerve, to make every possible endeavour.

Auf'binden, *ir.v.a.* to tie on, fasten on; to tie up, tuck up, truss up; to untie, unbind; **einem etwas** *or* **einen Bären —**, to impose upon a person, hoax one, to make a person believe (*a falsehood*), to tell a fib; to green one (*coll.*).

Auf'blähen, *v.a.* to puff up, swell; to inflate.

Auf'blasen, *ir.v.a.* to blow up, inflate; to blow (*a bubble*); to blow open; to raise (*dust*); to rouse by blowing (*a horn, etc.*); **eins —**, to sound a flourish with trumpets; **zum Tanze —**, to strike up *or* accompany a dance (*with a wind instrument*).

Auf'blättern, *v.a.* to open, turn over the leaves of a book; to look up (*a word, a passage*); **sich —**, to expand, to open out.

Auf'bleiben, *ir.v.n.* (*aux.* **s.**) to remain open; to sit up, remain up.

Auf'blick, *m.* upward glance; — **zu Gott**, lifting up the eyes, *or* one's thoughts, to God.

Auf'blicken, *v.n.* (*aux.* **h.**) to look upwards; to flash, glitter up, appear in gleams.

Auf'blühen, *v.n.* (*aux.* **s.**) to come into bloom; to open; to begin to flourish, flourish; **eine —de Schönheit**, a budding beauty.

Auf'brämen, *v.a.* to adorn with trimming.

Auf'brassen, *v.a.* to bring to, heave to (*Naut.*).

Auf'braten, *ir.v.a.* to roast again, to broil; to consume in roasting.

Auf'brauchen, *v.a.* to use up, waste, consume.

Auf'brausen, *v.n.* (*aux.* **h.** & **s.**) to rush up, (*begin to*) roar; to effervesce; to ferment; to get into a rage. **—d,** *p. & adj.* passionate, irritable; boisterous; effervescent.

Auf'brechen, I. *ir.v.a.* to break open, up; to brittle, eviscerate (*a stag*); to stir in the vat (*Brew.*); **Land —**, to cut off the sward of land. II. *v.n.* (*aux.* **s.**) to burst open, to open; to burst; to rise from table; to start, decamp, depart. III. *subst. n.* breaking open *or* up; piercing (*of a canal*); bursting (*of an ulcer*).

Auf'breiten, *v.a.* to spread, stretch out; **das Tischtuch —**, to lay the cloth; **das Erz —**, to clean the ore.

Auf'bremsen, *v.a.;* **einem einen —**, to give a man a blow, to strike one (*sl.*).

Auf'brennen, *ir.v.* I. *a.* to burn up, consume; to

brand; to scald (*clothes*). II. *n.* (*aux.* s.) to burn up suddenly; to kindle.
Auf'bring—en, *ir.v.a.* to raise; to bring up; to rear; to introduce (*a fashion, etc.*); to levy, collect (*troops, etc.*); to bring round, restore to health; to raise (*means*); to defray (*expenses*); to bring forth, utter; to produce (*witnesses*); to hazard, broach (*an opinion*); to capture, bring in (*a prize, Naut.*); to irritate, enrage, provoke, excite; **aufgebracht werden,** to get angry, to fly into a passion. **—er,** *m.* (**—ers,** *pl.* **—er**) captor (*Naut.*).
Auf'brodeln, *v.n.* (*aux.* s.) to bubble up.
Auf'bruch, *m.* (**—s,** *pl.* **Aufbrüche**) act of breaking up; rising from table; departure; decampment (*Mil.*); brittling (*of deer, etc.*); breaking up (*Agric.*); **zum — blasen,** to sound the march.
Auf'brummen, *v.a.;* **einem etwas —,** to put s.th. upon a p.; **einem einen dummen Jungen —,** to call one a silly boy (*with the intention of calling one out to a duel*) (*stud. slang*).
Auf'bürden, *v.a.* to impose a burden; **einem etwas —,** to attribute *or* lay s.th. to one's charge.
Auf'bürsten, *v.a.* to brush up, make trim.
Auf'damen, *v.a.* to crown a man (*at draughts*).
Auf'dämmen, *v.a.* to dam up.
Auf'dämmern, *v.n.* (*aux.* s.) to dawn; **eine Ahnung dämmerte ihm auf,** it dawned upon him.
Auf'dampfen, *v.n.* (*aux.* s.) to rise in steam; to evaporate.
Auf'decken, *v.a.* to spread (*a table-cloth*); to uncover; to disclose, reveal, expose.
Auf'dingen, *reg. & ir.v.a.* to bind apprentice, to indenture, to apprentice.
Auf'donnern, *v.* I. *n.* (*aux.* s.) to open with great noise. II. *a.* to awake by thundering. III. *refl.* **sich —,** to dress showily *or* vulgarly. **aufgedonnert,** *p.p. & adj.* tricked out *or* dressed out showily (*colloq.*).
Auf'drängen, *v.* I. *a.* to open by pressure; to push open. II. *r.* **sich einem —,** to obtrude oneself upon, to intrude; **Gedanken, die sich dem Gemüte —,** thoughts that force themselves upon the mind.
Auf'drehen, *v.a.* to screw open; to unscrew; to turn (*a cock*); to screw to; to untwist, unravel.
Auf'dring—en, *ir.v.a.* to press upon, urge on; to obtrude; **sich—en,** to intrude. **—er,** *m.* (**—ers,** *pl.* **—er**) intruder; importunate person. **—lich,** *adj. & adv.* importunate; obtrusive. **—lichkeit,** *f.* (*pl.* **—lichkeiten**) importunity, obtrusiveness. **—ung,** *f.* obtrusion, intrusion.
Auf'dröseln, *v.a.* to untwine, untwist.
Auf'druck, *m.* (**—(e)s,** *pl.* **Aufdrücke**) surcharge (*of postage stamps*).
Auf'drucken, *v.a.* to impress, imprint; to set to, affix (*a seal*); to use up in printing; to surcharge (*a postage stamp*).
Auf'drücken, *v.a.* to press open; to break up; to press on, to stamp on; to imprint.
Auf'dunsen, *v.n.* (*aux.* s.) to be swelled up, bloated. **aufgedunsen,** *p.p. & adj.* puffed up; bloated; turgid (*of style*).
Aufeinan'der, *adv.* one upon another, one after another. *Comp.* **—folge,** *f.* succession, series. **—folgend,** *adj. & adv.* consecutive. **—stoßen,** *n.* collision, clashing together, conflict. **—treiben,** *n.* running foul of another ship (*Naut.*).
Auf'eisen, *v.* I. *a.* to break ice; to clear away ice. II. *n.* (*aux.* h. & s.) to thaw.
Auf'enthalt, *m.* (**—s,** *pl.* **—e**) stay, abode; sojourn; haunt; delay, hinderance; demurrage (*Naut.*). *Comp.* **—s=karte,** *f.* **—s=schein,** *m.* certificate of permission to reside (*in a foreign town*). **—s=ort,** *m.* dwelling, place of residence, abode, resort; domicile (*Law*). **—s=zeit,** *f.* period of sojourn, stay (*in a place*).
Auf'erbauen, *v.a.* to erect; to edify (*poet.*).
Auf'erlegen, *v.a.;* **einem etwas —,** to lay one under an obligation; to enjoin s.th. on a p.; to impose (*taxes*); **sich Zwang —,** to force oneself.
Auf'ersteh—en, *ir.v.n.* (*aux.* s.) to rise up; to rise from the dead. **auferstanden,** *p.p. & adj.* risen. **—ung,** *f.* resurrection. *Comp.* **—ungs=fest,** *n.* Easter. **—ungs=tag,** *m.* Day of Resurrection, Easter-Day.
Auf'erwachen, *v.n.* (*aux.* s.) to awake, wake up.
Auf'erweck—en, *v.a.* to wake; to raise from the dead. **—ung,** *f.* resuscitation.
Auf'erziehen, *ir.v.a.* to rear, train, bring up.
Auf'fädeln, *v.a.* to string (*beads*); to untwist, unravel; to baste (*folds*).
Auf'fahr—en, *ir.v.* I. *n.* (*aux.* s.) to ascend; to drive up; to mount, rise, fly up; to start up; to fly open; to run, drive against; to run upon, run aground; to get into a passion. II. *a.* to drive open; to raise (*a road, garden, etc.*); to cut up a road (*by driving*); to mount (*guns*); to pile on (*dishes on the table*). **—end,** *p.*, **—erisch,** *adj.* passionate, vehement; irritable. **—t,** *f.* (*pl.* **—ten**) ascending, ascension; ascent; driving up; rising ground.
Auf'fallen, *ir.v.* I. *n.* (*aux.* s.) to fall upon; to fall open; **einem —,** to strike, astonish, to shock, to offend; **auf etwas —,** to light on (*of birds, etc.*); **es fiel uns allen auf,** it struck us all (*as strange*). II. *a. & r.* to hurt, wound by falling. **—d,** *p.*, **auffällig,** *adj. & adv.* striking, extraordinary; shocking; **—d gekleidet,** showily dressed; **sein Betragen war sehr —d,** his conduct gave occasion to much remark, his behaviour was very strange.
Auf'falten, *v.a.* to unfold; to fold up.
Auf'fang—en, *ir.v.a.* to catch while in motion; to snap, snatch up; to collect (*rain-water*); to intercept; **einem Schiffe den Wind —en,** to take the wind out of a ship's sails; **wo haben Sie das aufgefangen?** where did you pick that up? *Comp.* **—e=glas,** *n.* object-glass. **—e=stange,** *f.* lightning conductor.
Auf'färben, *v.a.* to re-dye, to dip afresh.
Auf'faß—en, *v.a.* to collect; to catch (*rain-water, etc.*); to string (*beads*); to take up (*a dropped stitch*); to comprehend, conceive, take in; **schwer —en,** to be dull *or* slow of apprehension; **eine Rolle gut —en,** to grasp the character, a part (*in acting*) well. **—ung,** *f.* act of grasping; comprehension. *Comp.* **—ungs=kraft,** *f.* power of comprehension, perceptive faculty.
Auf'feilen, *v.a.* to open by filing; to file anew.
Auf'finden, *ir.v.a.* to find out; to seek out.
Auf'flackern, *v.n.* (*aux.* s.) to flare up.
Auf'flammen, *v.n.* (*aux.* s.) to flame up, break into a flame; to blaze.
Auf'flechten, *ir.v.a.* to plait, braid up; to twist up; to unplait, untwist, ravel out.
Auf'fliegen, *ir.v.a.* (*aux.* s.) to fly upwards; to perch (*as a bird*); to ascend; to end in smoke; to fly open (*of doors, etc.*); to explode; **— lassen,** to blow up; **einen Drachen — lassen,** to fly a kite.
Auf'flug, *m.* (**—s,** *pl.* **Aufflüge**) flying *or* flight upwards; ascent (*of a balloon*).
Auf'forderer, *m.* (**—s,** *pl.* **—**) summoner; challenger.
Auf'forder—n, *v.a.* to summon; to challenge; to invite, ask; **das heißt aufgefordert!** this language is equivalent to a challenge; **—nde Blicke,** inviting, challenging, provocative glances; **darf ich Sie zum Tanze —n?** may I have the pleasure of dancing with you? **man forderte ihn auf ein Lied zu singen,** he was called on for a song. **—ung,** *f.* invitation; challenge; citation, summons; **eine Rechts—ung erlassen,** to issue a writ, a summons. *Comp.* **—ungs=schreiben,** *n.* summons.

Auf'formen, *v.a.* to put on a form; to turn up the brim of a hat.
Auf'forst—en, *v.a.* to afforest, to plant trees on waste land. **—ung,** *f.* afforesting, afforestation.
Auf'fressen, *ir.v.a.* (*of beasts*) to eat up; to devour, consume; to corrode.
Auf'frischen, *v.a.* to freshen up, renew; to touch up (*Paint.*); to awaken, revive (*memory, grief, etc.*); to inspirit.
Auf'führbar, *adj.* that may be erected; that may be represented, acted.
Auf'führ—en, *v.a.* to lead up; to establish; to represent, perform, act (*a play, etc.*); to execute, play (*a piece, Mus.*); to build up, erect; to mount (*guns on a battery, etc.*); to mount guard, post a sentry; to enter (*to one's account*); to produce (*witnesses*); to specify (*in a list, etc.*); to lead off (*a dance*); **sich —en,** to conduct oneself, to act, to behave. **—ung,** *f.* leading up; introduction; performance, representation; erection, building up (*of an obelisk, etc.*); posting (*of a sentry*); mounting (*of guns*); adducing (*of reasons*); production (*of witnesses*); conduct; **gute —ung,** good manners, good behaviour, good conduct.
Auf'füll—en, *v.a.* to fill up; to refill. *Comp.* **—wein,** *m.* wine for filling up casks.
Auf'futtern, *v.a.* to batten (*Carp.*).
Auf'füttern, *v.a.* to spend in feeding; to rear by feeding, to feed up, to bring up by hand.
Auf'gabe, *f.* (*pl.* **—n**) proposition, problem; putting (*of a riddle*); statement; task, exercise, problem, lesson (*school*); business, mission (*of life*); act of posting a letter (**— auf die Post**); surrender (*of a town*); resignation (*of an office*); giving up; command, order, advice (*C. L.*); **laut —,** as per advice; **unter —,** with advice; **nach —,** according to statement.
Auf'gabeln, *v.a.* to pick up with a fork; to fish, ferret out; **wo haben Sie den aufgegabelt,** where did you come across that fellow? (*coll.*)
Auf'gähren, *v.n.* (*aux.* **h.** & **s.**) to rise (*in fermentation*); to ferment anew.
Auf'gang, *m.* (**—es,** *pl.* **Aufgänge**) rise, rising, ascension (*of stars, sun, etc.*); ascent; east; consumption, spending; **Sonnen—,** sunrise.
Auf'geb—en, *ir.v.a.* to give, hand up; to post (*a letter*); to give up, surrender; to abandon, relinquish (*a principle, a cause, etc.*); to resign (*an office*); to drop (*an acquaintance*); to relinquish (*a claim*); to give up (*a riddle; a game; the ghost; a patient; a habit*); **einem etwas —en,** to set one a task, to propose, propound (*a riddle, a problem*), to advise, order, give notice of (*C. L.*); **bitte, geben Sie den Brief auf,** please post the letter; **das Spiel —en,** to throw up the cards. **—er,** *m.* (**—ers,** *pl.* **—er**) propounder (*of a riddle*), one that resigns, delivers, *etc.*
Auf'geblasen, *p.p.* & *adj.* puffed up; arrogant, haughty; *see* **Aufblasen.** **—heit,** *f.* conceit, self-sufficiency; arrogance; inflation (*of style*).
Auf'gebot, *n.* (**—es,** *pl.* **—e**) summons; public call; publication (*of banns*); calling out (*of troops*); **dies ist das erste —,** this is the first time the banns are published, the first time of asking; **allgemeines —,** levy en masse.
Auf'gebracht, *p.p.* & *adj. see* **Aufbringen;** enraged, angry (**über eine S.,** at a th.).
Auf'gedinge, *n.* (**—s,** *pl.* **—**) the binding and indenture of an apprentice together with the premium.
Auf'gedonnert, *p.p.* & *adj. see* **Aufdonnern** (**sich —**); to be decked out in an exaggerated way and without taste, tricked out (*coll.*).
Auf'gedunsen, *v.a.* (*v.n.*) inflated, puffed.
Auf'gehen, *ir.v.n.* (*aux.* **s.**) to rise (*of dough; of the sun, etc.*); to evaporate; to open (*as a door*); to break (*as an abscess*); to come loose, untie, untwist; to uncurl; to break up (*of ice*); to come up (*of plants*); to open, expand; to be spent, consumed; to be contained without a remainder (*mathem.*); to be merged, disappear; to go on (*of a hat, etc.*); **Ihr Hutband ist aufgegangen,** your bonnet strings have come undone; **der Mond ist aufgegangen,** the moon is up; **jetzt geht mir ein Licht auf,** now the matter becomes clear, I begin to comprehend; **es ging mir ein neuer Stern auf,** a new life dawned for me; **der Frost geht auf,** it begins to thaw; **in Rauch —,** to end in smoke; **in Feuer —,** to be consumed by fire; **er läßt viel —,** he spends a great deal; **drei in fünfzehn geht auf,** fifteen can be divided by three without a remainder; **5 geht nicht in 9 auf,** 9 cannot be divided by 5 without a remainder; **eine Rechnung — lassen,** to strike a balance; **wechselseitige Schulden — lassen,** to set off mutual debts; **— in,** to coincide with; **ihr Glück geht i dem ihrer Tochter auf,** her happiness is bound up in her daughter's; **Preußen geht fortan in Deutschland auf,** from this day on Prussia is merged in Germany.
Auf'geklärt, *p.p.* & *adj. see* **Aufklären;** enlightened, cultivated; civilized; liberal-minded. **—heit,** *f.* enlightenment.
Auf'geknöpft, *p.p.* & *adj.* easily accessible, talkative (*coll.*).
Auf'gekratzt, *p.p.* & *adj.* in good spirits (*coll.*).
Auf'geld, *n.* (**—es,** *pl.* **—er**) premium (*C. L.*); deposit, earnest money.
Auf'gelegt, *p.p.* & *adj.* disposed; inclined; **gut — sein,** to be in good humour, in a happy mood; **er ist zum Singen nicht gut —,** he is not in a singing mood.
Auf'geräumt, *p.p.* & *adj.* in high spirits; **nicht — sein,** to be in bad spirits; to be depressed, gloomy. **—heit,** *f.* cheerfulness, gaiety.
Auf'gesang, *m.* (**—s,** *pl.* **Aufgesänge**), the former part of a stanza clearly consisting of two portions, the latter being called **Abgesang.** The — is usually subdivided into two equal portions called **Stollen.**
Auf'geschaut! *int.* look out! look up! take courage!
Auf'geweckt, *p.p.* & *adj.* intelligent, bright; lively.
Auf'geworfen, *p.p.* & *adj. see* **Aufwerfen; eine —e Nase,** a turned-up nose.
Auf'gießen, *ir.v.a.* to pour upon; to infuse; **der Thee ist schon aufgegossen,** the tea is made.
Auf'gleiten, *v.n.;* **—der Rhythmus,** anapaestic rhythm; *see* **Aufsteigender Rhythmus.**
Auf'grab—en, *ir.v.a.* to dig up; to trench. **—ung,** *f.* a digging up; trenching.
Auf'greifen, *ir.v.a.* to snatch up; to take up.
Auf'gürten, *v.a.* to gird up, tuck up; to girth on (*a saddle, etc.*); to ungird.
Auf'guß, *m.* (**—sses,** *pl.* **Aufgüsse**) infusion; pouring on. *Comp.* **—tierchen,** *pl.* infusoria; **zu den —tierchen gehörend,** infusorial.
Auf'haben, *ir.v.a.* to have on, to wear; to have open; to bear on the head; to have to do, to have as a task; **zu viel —,** to be overburdened; **hast du heute viel auf?** have you got much home work to-day? **die Sache hat nichts auf sich,** the matter is of no consequence.
Auf'hacken, *v.a.* to hew open; to hoe up, loosen with a hoe; to peck, pick up.
Auf'haken, *v.a.* to unhook, to hook up.
Auf'halsen, *v.* I. *a.;* **einem etwas —,** to load one with; to put on to; impute to. II. *r.* to saddle oneself with; to incur.
Auf'halt—en, *ir.v.a.* to hold up *or* forth; to stop, arrest; to retard; to put a stop to; to sustain, keep up; to keep open; to detain, to delay; **den Feind —en,** to keep off the enemy; **sich bei Kleinigkeiten —en,** to stand upon *or* dwell on trifles; **halte dich bei solchen Kleinigkeiten**

nicht auf, don't lose your time with such trifles; **sich —en,** to stop (*in a place*); **sich bei einem —en,** to stay at a person's house; **A.N. hält sich jetzt in O. auf,** A. N. is now (a) resident in O.; **sich über etwas —en,** to find fault with, to make game of; **sich bei Worten —en,** to stick to, dwell on words. **—er,** *m.* (**—ers,** *pl.* **—er**) stopper, detainer; catch (*of a lock*); guyrope (*Naut.*); breeching (*of harness*); retardation (*Mus.*); any instrument for stopping. **—erei,** *f.* faultfinding, scoffing. **—ung,** *f.* hindrance, delay, detention; stopping, stay; detent.

Auf'häng—en, *v.a.* to hang up; to hang; **einem etwas —en,** to palm off a thing on one, impose upon one, to infect one with (*a disease*) (*vulg.*). *Comp.* **—e=boden,** *m.* drying place. **—e=muskel,** *f.* suspensory muscle. **—e=schnüre,** *pl.* drying-ropes.

Auf'haschen, *v.a.* to catch up; **Neuigkeiten —,** to pick up news.

Auf'haspeln, *v.a.* to wind, reel (*thread, etc.*); to wind up, twist up; **sich von der Erde wieder —,** to rise slowly from the ground (*coll.*); **sich wieder —,** to recover slowly from an illness (*coll.*).

Auf'häufeln, *v.a.* to form into small heaps; to earth up.

Auf'häuf—en, I. *v.a.* to heap *or* store up; **sich —en,** to accumulate, to become congested. II. **—en,** *subst. n.*, **—ung,** *f.* a heaping up, accumulation.

Auf'heb—en, I. *ir.v.a.* to lift, raise, take up; to pick up; to weigh (*anchor*); to arrest, apprehend; to break up; to raise (*a siege*); to keep, reserve, preserve, store away, provide for; to suspend (*the free list in theatres, etc.*); to repeal, annul (*a law, etc.*); to suspend from action, destroy the force of; to hold up (*the hand*); to do away with (*punishments, etc.*); to finish, end (*a game; a quarrel, etc.*); to put an end to (*friendship, etc.*); to reduce (*fractions*); **das Parlament —en,** to dissolve parliament; **die Tafel wurde aufgehoben,** the guests rose from table; **einen Verbrecher —en,** to arrest a criminal; **ein Kloster —en,** to suppress a convent; **Handelsgenossenschaft —en,** to dissolve partnership; **Stillschweigen —en,** to break silence; **er ist gut aufgehoben,** he is well taken care of; **das Kind ist bei uns sehr gut aufgehoben,** the child is in good hands with us; **der Richter hat den Vertrag aufgehoben,** the judge declared the agreement null and void; **ein Urteil —en,** to quash a judgment; **sich gegenseitig —en,** to compensate, to destroy each other; **aufgeschoben ist nicht aufgehoben,** postponed is not abandoned; forbearance is not acquittance (*prov.*); **zu einer Sache aufgehoben sein,** to be destined for a th. II. *subst.n.* lifting (*up*); **beim —en der Hände,** on a show of hands; **viel —ens wegen Kleinigkeiten,** much ado about nothing; **machen Sie doch davon kein —ens,** please don't make a fuss about it. **—er,** *m.* (**—ers,** *pl.* **—er**) elevator; *see* **—emuskel.** **—ung,** *f.* the lifting *or* taking up; elevation; abrogation; suspension; suppression; removal (*of restrictions*); raising (*of the host; of a siege*); breaking up, dissolution; ending; *see* **—en**; **bei —ung der Tafel,** when the cloth was removed, at the conclusion of the meal; **—ung eines Befehls,** repeal of an order; **—ung einer Klage,** non-suit; **—ung einer Versammlung,** dissolution. *Comp.* **—e=binde,** *f.* suspensory bandage (*Surg.*). **—e=muskel,** *m.* levator (*Anat.*). **—ungs=gericht,** *n.* court of cassation.

Auf'heften, *v.a.* to pin, tie up; to stitch upon, fasten to; to unpin, undo, unclasp; **einem etwas —,** to palm s.th. off on one.

Auf'heiter—n, *v.a.* to make clear, brighten; to cheer up, enliven; **sich —n,** to grow bright, pleasant; to clear up. **—ung,** *f.* enlivenment, cheering up; clearing up.

Auf'helf—en, *ir.v.a.;* **einem —en,** to help s.o. up; to aid, to succour. **—er,** *m.* (**—ers,** *pl.* **—er**) one who helps another; a cord to help a p. to sit up in bed.

Auf'hell—en, *v.a.* to clear, to brighten up; to clarify; to light up; to elucidate; to enlighten; to heighten (*a tint*); **sich —en,** to clear up (*of weather*), to settle (*of liquors*). **—ung,** *f.* clarification; brightening; heightening (*of a tint*); elucidation, explanation; enlightenment; clearing up.

Auf'henken, *v.a.* to hang up, hang (*obs.*).

Auf'hetz—en, *v.a.* to rouse, start (*game, etc.*); to stir up, incite, instigate. **—er,** *m.* (**—ers,** *pl.* **—er**) instigator. **—ung,** *f.* instigation, incitement.

Auf'hilfe, *f.* help, aid, assistance, succour.

Auf'hissen, *v.a.* to hoist up (*sails, a flag, etc.*).

Auf'hocken, *v.* I. *r.;* **sich etwas —,** to take on one's back. II. *n.* (*aux.* **h.**) to get, hang on one's back.

Auf'hol—en, *v.a.* to fetch *or* draw up; to haul up *or* in; to bring (*a ship*) close to the wind; to draw up the threads of a warp. **—er,** *m.* (**—ers,** *pl.* **—er**) relieving tackle; halliard (*of a stay-sail*).

Auf'horchen, *v.n.* (*aux.* **h.**) to prick up one's ears; to listen attentively; **hoch —,** to listen with the very greatest attention.

Auf'hören, I. *v.n.* (*aux.* **h.**) to listen attentively; to cease, stop, end, give over; **zu zahlen —,** to suspend payment; **zu handeln —,** to give up business; **hör' doch nur auf!** pray stop! have done! **da hört doch alles auf!** (*coll.* **da hört (sich) denn doch Verschiedenes auf!**) that beats everything, that is indeed too much; **in Geldsachen hört die Gemütlichkeit auf** money matters must be taken seriously, business is business. II. *subst. n.* cessation; **ohne —,** incessantly.

Auf'hülfe, *see* **Aufhilfe.**

Auf'hüpfen, *v.n.* (*aux.* **s.**) to bound into the air.

Auf'husten, *v.* I. *a.* to cough up (*blood, etc.*). II. *n.* (*aux.* **h.**) to cough aloud.

Auf'jagen, *v.a.* to start, rouse (*game, etc.*); to raise (*dust, etc.*); **einen —,** to hunt one up.

Auf'jammern, *v.* I. *n.* (*aux.* **h.**) to wail, set up a lamentation. II. *a.* to rouse by wailing.

Auf'jauchzen, Auf'jubeln, *v.* I. *n.* (*aux.* **h.**) to shout aloud for joy. II. *a.* to rouse with shouts.

Auf'kämmen, *v.a.* to comb anew *or* up (*the hair*); to dress (*a wig*); to re-cog (*the wheels of a machine*).

Auf'kappen, *v.a.* to hood (*a hawk*).

Auf'kauf, *m.* (**—s,** *pl.* **Aufkäufe**) buying up, purchase on speculation. **—en,** *v.a.* to buy up; to forestall. **—ung,** *f.* buying up; forestalling.

Auf'käufer, *m.* (**—s,** *pl.***—**) forestaller, engrosser.

Auf'kegeln, *v.a.* to pile up (*cannon balls*).

Auf'keimen, *v.n.* (*aux.* **s.**) to sprout, germinate, bud, spring up. **—d,** *p. & adj.* dawning, budding; young, fresh.

Auf'kett—eln, —en, *v.a.* to unchain, unfasten, open.

Auf'kippen, *v.a. & n.* (*aux.* **s.**) to tilt up.

Auf'kitten, *v.a.* to fasten on with cement.

Auf'klaffen, *v.n.* (*aux.* **h.**) to gape; to open out widely; to become torn.

Auf'klär—en (Auf'klaren), *v.a.* to clear up; to elucidate; to enlighten, instruct, inform; to clarify; **sich —en,** to clear up (*of weather*), to brighten (*of the countenance, etc.*); **das Wetter klärt (klart) sich auf,** the weather is clearing up. **—er,** *m.* (**—ers,** *pl.* **—er**) clearer up (*of a mystery, etc.*); finer (*of wine*); instructor, enlightener, apostle of culture. **—erei',** *f.*,

—**icht**, *n.* sham-enlightenment. —**ung**, *f.* clearing up; explanation; clarification; enlightenment. —**ungs=sucht**, *f.*, —**ungs=wut**, *f.* mania for enlightenment.

Auf'klauben, *v.a.* to pick up; to open by picking with the fingers.

Auf—kleben, I. *v.a.* to paste on; to fasten. II. *v.n.* (*aux.* **h.**) to adhere, to stick. III. *subst. n.* paperhanging (*act of*).

Auf'klecksen, *v.a.* to daub on colours.

Auf'klinken, *v.a.* to unlatch (*a door*).

Auf'klopfen, *v.a.* to open by knocking; to fasten by hammering; **einen** —, to arouse s.o. (*from sleep*) by knocking; to tease (*hair, wool, etc. of a mattress, etc.*).

Auf'knacken, *v.a.* to crack open (*nuts, etc.*).

Auf'knöpfen, *v.a.* to unbutton; to button up.

Auf'knüpfen, *v.a.* to tie, bind up; to string up, hang (*a criminal*); to untie, undo a knot.

Auf'kochen, *v.* I. *a.* to boil up, warm up, boil again. II. *n.* (*aux.* **h.**) to boil, bubble up.

Auf'kommen, I. *ir.v.n.* (*aux.* **s.**) to rise, get up; to come up; to recover (*from illness*); to prevail; to come into fashion; to prosper, get on in the world; — **lassen**, to give rise *or* scope to; to allow to rise and to spread; to suffer; **wir dürfen solche Zweifel nicht — lassen**, we must prevent the rise of such doubts; **den Fluß** —, to come, go, row, sail up the river; **das Schiff kommt vor seinem Ruder auf**, the ship answers to her helm. II. *subst. n.* getting up, *etc.*; recovery (*from sickness*); introduction (*of a fashion*); rise in the world; sanctioning.

Auf'kömmling, *m.* (—**s**, *pl.* —**e**) upstart, parvenu.

Auf'köpf—en, *v.a.* to head (*pins, etc.*). —**er**, *m.* (—**ers**, *pl.* —**er**) workman who heads pins.

Auf'koppeln, *v.a.* to undo a leash, uncouple.

Auf'krachen, *v.n.* (*aux.* **s.**) to burst open with a crack; to crack.

Auf'krähen, *v.n.* (*aux.* **h.**) to crow aloud, set up a crow.

Auf'krämpeln, **Auf'krempeln**, *v.a.* to bend back, turn up; to card wool a second time.

Auf'krämpen, *v.a.* to turn up the brim of a hat.

Auf'kratz—en, *v.a.* to scratch up, open; to raise the nap of cloth; to card (*wool*); **eine Naht —en**, to smooth down a seam with the nail; **einen** —, to put a p. in good humour (*colloq.*). —**er**, *m.* (—**ers**, *pl.* —**er**) wool-carder.

Auf'kräuseln, *v.a. & r.* to curl up.

Auf'kreischen, *v.n.* (*aux.* **h.**) to raise a scream.

Auf'kriechen, *ir.v.n.* (*aux.* **s.**) to creep upwards.

Auf'kriegen, *v.a.* (*coll.*) *see* **Aufbekommen**.

Auf'krimpen, *v.a.* (*of wind*) to veer round against the sun (*Naut.*).

Auf'kündbar, *adj.* subject to a notice to quit; liable to abolition.

Auf'künd—en, —**igen**, *v.a.*; **einem etwas —en**, to give notice, warning; to recall (*an investment*); to retract (*a statement*); to withdraw (*from an engagement*); to renounce (*a person's friendship*); **mein Wirt hat mir aufgekündigt**, my landlord has given me notice to quit; **die Arbeit (in Massen) —igen**, to strike work; **ohne aufzukündigen**, without previous notice. —**igung**, —**ung**, *f.* warning, notice (*of removal; dismissal; withdrawal, etc.*); —**ung einer Hypothek**, calling in of a mortgage. *Comp.* —**igungs=brief**, *m.* written notice (*to quit, etc.*).

Auf'lachen, *v.a.* (*aux.* **h.**) to burst into a laugh.

Auf'lad—en, *ir.v.a.* to load, put on a load; **einem etwas —en**, to charge, burden one with; **sich** (*dat.*) —**en**, to take upon oneself, to saddle oneself with. —**er**, *m.* (—**ers**, *pl.* —**er**) packer, loader. —**ung**, *f.* act of loading. *Comp.* —**er=lohn**, *m.* payment for loading.

Auf'lage, *f.* (*pl.* —**n**) edition (*of a book*); tax, impost, duty; charity collection; club; meeting; judge's order, injunction; **wie stark ist die neue** —? of how many copies does the new edition consist? **unveränderte** —, reprint; **verbesserte und vermehrte** —, a corrected and enlarged edition; **das Buch hat zwölf —n erlebt**, the book has gone through twelve editions; **einem eine — thun**, to issue a writ against one.

Auf'lagern, *v.a.* to lay in stock, store up.

Auf'lang—en, *v.a.* to hand, reach up. —**er**, *m.* (—**ers**, *pl.* —**er**) futtock (*Naut.*); **verkehrte —er**, top timbers.

Auf'lassen, *ir.v.a.* to allow, cause to rise; to loosen; to leave open; **eine Grube** —, to abandon a mine.

Auf'lauer—n, *v.n.* (*aux.* **h.**) to lie in wait (**einem**, for one). —**er**, *m.* one who lies in wait, spy. —**ung**, *f.* the lying in wait.

Auf'lauf, *m.* (—**es**, *pl.* **Aufläufe**) mob, riotous crowd; riot, uproar; swelling; increase; soufflet, raised pudding; — **der Zinsen**, increase of interest.

Auf'laufen, *ir.v.* I. *n.* (*aux.* **s.**) to rise, run up, swell; **der Dampfer ist aufgelaufen**, the steamer has run aground (ashore); **der Fluß läuft auf**, the river is rising; **das Volk — lassen**, to man the yards. **aufgelaufen**, *p.p. & adj.* inflamed, bloated, swollen. II. *a.* to open *or* make sore by running.

Auf'laufer, *m.* ship's boy.

Auf'läufer, *m.* raised cake *or* pudding; charging man, stoker.

Auf'lavieren, *v.a.* to beat up (*a river, etc.*).

Auf'leben, *v.* I. *n.* (*aux.* **s.**) to be revived; to live again; to be invigorated, cheered up. II. *a.* to touch up, retouch (*a picture*).

Auf'leg—en, *v.a.* to put, lay on, apply; to lay on (*hands, colours, etc.*); to impose, inflict (*a fine : a tax, etc.*); to enjoin (*silence*); to take an in pression of; to publish, issue; to show one's hand (*at cards*); to lay up (*a ship; stores*); to lean (*the elbow*) on; to be disposed *or* in a certain humour; to tender an oath; **ich war nicht dazu (zum Singen, ꝛc.) aufgelegt**, I was not in the mood for it (for singing, etc.); **einem Pferde den Sattel —en**, to saddle a horse; **Bank —en**, to hold the bank (*at faro, etc.*); **wieder —en**, to reprint (*a book*); **einem Pferde das Hufeisen —en**, to shoe a horse; **einem etwas Schändliches —en**, to throw disgrace on one. —**ung**, *f.* application (*of a plaster, etc.*); imposition (*of hands; fines, taxes, etc.*); infliction (*of punishments*); laying up in ordinary (*of a ship*). *Comp.* —**e=geld**, *n.* club money; trades union contributions.

Auf'lehn—en, *v.r.* to lean, lounge, loll (*against*); to rear, prance; (*with* **gegen**) to oppose, resist; to revolt, mutiny. —**ung**, *f.* rearing; lounging; opposition, revolt, mutiny.

Auf'lesen, *ir.v.a.* to glean; to gather *or* pick up.

Auf'leuchten, *v.n.* (*aux.* **h.**) to flash up, rise resplendent, shine.

Auf'lichten, *v.a.* to heighten the lights (*Paint.*).

Auf'liegen, *ir.v.n.* (*aux.* **s.**) to lie, lean on; to be out of service *or* employment; to bear upon (*the bit*); **einem** —, to be incumbent on.

Auf'lockern, *v.a.* to loosen (*earth, etc.*); to shake up (*a featherbed*); to unfix; **sich** —, to get loose.

Auf'lodern, *v.n.* (*aux.* **s.**) to flash, flare up.

Auf'lösbar, *adj. & adv.* soluble. —**keit**, *f.* solubility.

Auf'lös—en, *v.* I. *a.* to resolve, dissolve; to loosen, untie; to solve (*a problem*); to reduce (*fractions*); to resolve (*a discord*); to decompose; to analyse (*Gram. & Chem.*); to break (*a spell*); to break up (*an assembly*); to dissolve (*partnership, marriage, etc.*); to disband (*troops*). II. *r.* to get loose : to melt, dissolve;

to become clear; to die. **—end,** *p. & adj.* solvent; **—ende Mittel,** dissolvents. **—(s)lich,** *see* **—bar. —ung,** *f.* loosening; dissolution, decomposition; solution; analysis; elucidation (*of a mystery*); resolution (*of a discord; of forces*); conversion (*of an equation*); denouement (*of a plot*); dissolution (*of a partnership, etc.*); death; diæresis; **die —ung der Farben im Wasser,** tempering, mixing, dissolving the colours for painting. *Comp.* **—ungs=kunst,** *f.* science of analysis, analytics (*Math.*). **—ungs=lehre,** *f.* analysis (*Logic*). **—ungs=mittel,** *n.* dissolvent, solvent. **—ungs=zeichen,** *n.* natural (*Mus.*).

Auf'machen, *v.a.* to open; to undo, untie; to turn (*the cock of a barrel*); to unlace (*stays*); to begin (*a new set of books, C. L.*); to turn up (*the sleeves, etc.*); to put up (*curtains; an umbrella*); to fix, get ready; **die Havereikosten —,** to settle the average (*C.L.*); **aufgemachtes Leinen,** dressed linen; **sich —,** to rise, get up, to prepare to start; to set out; **sich auf und davon machen,** to run away, to decamp.

Auf'marsch, *m.* (—es, *pl.* **Aufmärsche**) marching up; drawing up (*of troops*). **—ieren,** *v.n.* (*aux.* **s.**) to deploy; to march up; **—ieren lassen,** to draw up.

Auf'merk—en, *v.* I. *a.* to note, distinguish by a mark. II. *n.* (*aux.* **h.**) to attend, give heed to. **—sam,** *adj. & adv.* attentive, mindful, observant; **einen auf eine Sache —sam machen,** to call a person's attention to a th.; to remind a p. of a th. **—samkeit,** *f.* attention; **—samkeit erregen, abziehen,** to attract attention, distract one's attention; **einem eine —samkeit erweisen,** to show one an attention.

Auf'mucken, *v.n.* to object, remonstrate (*coll.*).

Auf'munter—n, *v.a.* to awake, arouse; to encourage, inspirit; to enliven; to urge on, incite; **sich —n,** to cheer up, take courage. **—nd,** *p. & adj.* rousing, encouraging, animating. **—er,** *m.* one who gives encouragement, cheers up. **—ung,** *f.* encouragement, incitement; animation.

Auf'mutzen, *v.a.* to object; **einem etwas —,** to rebuke s.o. because of s.th. (*coll.*).

Auf'näh—en, *v.a.* to sew on; to use up in sewing. **—er,** *m.* luck.

Auf'nahm—e, *f.* taking up; borrowing, loan (*of money*); reception; admission (*into holy orders; to a club, etc.*); advance, improvement, promotion; survey; taking of a photographic picture, sitting, photograph (*Photogr.*); **—e bereiten,** to give a reception; to honour (*a bill, etc.*); **—e an Kindesstatt,** adoption; **in —e sein,** to be in favour; **in —e kommen,** to come into fashion, favour, *etc.*, to prosper; **in —e bringen,** to bring into notice *or* favour; to patronise, forward; **—e finden,** to meet with a good reception. *Comp.* **—e=schein,** *m.* certificate of admission. **—e=fähig,** *adj.* admissible, eligible (*for election, etc.*). **—e=fähigkeit,** *f.* admissibility, eligibility. **—e=prüfung,** *f.* entrance examination. **—e=würdig,** *adj.* worthy of admission.

Auf'nehm—en, *ir.v.a.* to take up; to take in, shelter; to take possession of; to appraise, estimate; to hold, contain; to absorb (*Chem.*); to receive, entertain; to elect; to admit; to draw up (*a statement*); to raise, borrow (*money*); to pick up (*stitches*); to adopt; to survey, map down; **eine Festung —en,** to make a ground-plan of a fortress; **sich in eine Gesellschaft —en lassen,** to become a member of a club, society; **die Fährte —en,** to catch the scent; **es mit einem —en,** to cope with, compete, be a match for; **gut, übel —en,** to take well, ill; **—en für, als,** to look upon, consider as; **in sich** (*acc.*) **—en,** to appropriate, make one's own. **—er,** *m.* receiver, one that takes up.

Auf'nesteln, *v.a.* to unlace, untie, undo.

Auf'notieren, *v.a.* to note down, to charge.

Auf'nötigen, *v.a.*; **einem etwas —,** to force s.th. on one.

Auf'opfer—n, *v.a.* to offer up, sacrifice; to dedicate, devote to. **—nd,** *adj.* sacrificing; devoted. **—ung,** *f.* sacrificing; sacrifice. **—ungs=voll,** *adj.* devoted.

Auf'packen, *v.* I. *a.* to pack up; to make off with (*coll.*); **einem etwas —,** to load *or* saddle one with a th. II. *n.* (*aux.* **h.**) to pack off (*vulg.*).

Auf'palmen, *v.r.* to climb a rope hand over hand.

Auf'pass—en, *v.* I. *a.* to adapt, fit (*a lid; a hat, etc.*). II. *n.* (*aux.* **s.**) to fit; (*aux.* **h.**) to pay attention, attend to; to watch, to spy; **einem —en,** to waylay one; **aufgepaßt!** attention! be attentive! mind! take care! look out! **—er,** *m.* (**—ers,** *pl.* **—er**) watcher; excise officer; overseer; spy.

Auf'pfeifen, *ir.v.a. & n.* to pipe, to play on a pipe; **einen —,** to rouse (wake) by whistling; **einem beständig —,** to dance attendance on one; to be at one's service.

Auf'pflanzen, *v.a.* to set up, erect; to mount (*guns*); to raise (*a standard*); **das Seitengewehr pflanzt auf!** fix swords (bayonets)!; **sich vor jemand —,** to plant oneself before a person.

Auf'pflügen, *v.* I. *a.* to plough up. II. *n.* to strike against in ploughing.

Auf'pfropfen, *v.a.* to ingraft; to rabbet, join.

Auf'platzen, *v.n.* (*aux.* **s.**) to burst open, crack; to tear, split; to come suddenly upon a p.

Auf'plustern, *v.n.*; **sich —,** to ruffle one's feathers (*of birds*).

Auf'polieren, *v.a.* to polish up.

Auf'prägen, *v.a.* to imprint, stamp, impress on.

Auf'prallen, *v.n.* (*aux.* **s.**) to spring up *or* open; to rebound; to bounce against.

Auf'prellen, *v.a.* to toss, jerk up.

Auf'pressen, *v.a.* to press open; to press again; to imprint.

Auf'probieren, *v.a.* to try on (*a hat*).

Auf'protzen, *v.a.* to limber up (*guns*).

Auf'putz, *m.* (**—es**) dressing, decking; finery; ornaments; trimmings.

Auf'putzen, *v.a.* to clean, brush up; to make smart; to dress up, deck out.

Auf'quellen, *ir.v.* I. *a.* to steep, soak in water. II. *n.* (*aux.* **s.**) to bubble, well up; to swell, rise, expand.

Auf'raffen, *v.a.* to rake up; to snatch up, collect hastily; to pick up; **sich —,** to rise quickly, arouse oneself; to set to work energetically; to recover from an illness.

Auf'ragen, *v.n.* (*aux.* **h.**) to jut, tower up.

Auf'rappeln, *v.r.*; **sich —,** to rise quickly, to pull o.s. together. (*coll.*) *see* **sich aufraffen.**

Auf'ranken, *v.n. & r.* to creep up (*Botan.*).

Auf'rauchen, *v.a.* to consume by smoking, to smoke up.

Auf'räum—en, *v.a.* to arrange, put in order; to clear, take away; to thin, reduce in number; to widen (*a hole*); to dredge (*a harbour*); to plunder, empty; **das Lager —en,** to clear out the stock (*C. L.*). **—er,** *m.* (**—ers,** *pl.* **—er**) *see* **Aufreiber, Raumnadel. —ung,** *f.* clearing up, arranging, making tidy.

Auf'rauschen, *v.n.* (*aux.* **s.**) to rush up, fly open; to rise with a rushing noise.

Auf'rechn—en, *v.a.* to reckon up; to put to one's account; to specify (*charges*); **gegenseitig —en,** to balance accounts. **—ung,** *f.* act of reckoning, balancing of accounts.

Auf'recht, *adj. & adv.* upright, erect; straight; **— halten, erhalten,** to maintain (*order*); to support (*a friend*); to uphold (*a doctrine, etc.*); **sich — erhalten,** to sit up, hold oneself up, to keep up one's courage, to maintain one's ground. *Comp.* **—erhaltung,** *f.* maintaining, keeping up, maintenance, preservation. **—halter,** *m.* supporter, sustainer. **—haltung,** *f.* support. **—sehen,** *n.* erect vision. **—sitzend,** *adj.* squat (*Her.*). **—stehend,** *adj.* rampant (*Her.*); upright.

Auf'recken, *v.a.* to lift, to stretch up; to prick up (*the ears*).

Auf'reden, *v.a.*; **einem etwas —,** to press upon a p., persuade; to instigate.

Auf'reg—en, *v.a.* to stir up; to excite; to enrage; to arouse, awake. **—end,** *p. & adj.* exciting; irritant; seditious. **—er,** *m.* (**—ers,** *pl.* **—er**) agitator. **—ung,** *f.* excitement, agitation; tumult.

Auf'reib—en, *ir.v.* I. *a.* to rub on; to rub open; to fret, gall; to scrub; to grind, grate (*sugar, etc.*); to wear away (*by friction*); to destroy, slay; to nap (*cloth*); to knead thoroughly. II. *r.* to worry oneself to death; to run to waste; **sich gegenseitig —en,** to destroy one another. **—er,** *m.* (**—ers,** *pl.* **—er**) boring auger; dough-kneader; scraping instrument. **—ung,** extirpation.

Auf'reichen, *v.a.* to hand up.

Auf'reih—en, *v.a.* to file (*papers*); to string (*beads*). **—ung,** *f.* evolution (*Mil.*).

Auf'reißen, *ir.v.* I. *a.* to tear, rip up, open; to burst, wrench, force open; to fling up, open; to slit, cut; to take up (*a pavement*); to sketch hastily; to nap, tease; to break up (*ground*); **den Mund —,** to gape. II. *n.* (*aux.* **s.**) to split open, burst; to crack, gape; to chap. III. *r.* to get up hastily; to be torn open; **die Wolken rissen sich auf,** the clouds parted.

Auf'reiz—en, *v.a.* to incite, inflame, stir up, provoke. **—ung,** *f.* provocation; instigation; excitation (*Law*).

Auf'rennen, I. *v.a.* to run open. II. *ir.v.n.* (*aux.* **s.**) to run against, aground, on.

Auf'richt—en, *v.a.* to set up, erect; to plant (*a standard*); to right (*a ship*); to found, establish (*schools, etc.*); to contract (*an alliance, friendship, etc.*), to cheer, support, comfort; to raise up, set upright; **den Kopf —en,** to hold up one's head; **sich —en,** to rise, sit upright. **—er,** *m.* (**—ers,** *pl.* **—er**) erector (*muscle*). **—ig,** *adj. & adv.* sincere, candid; open, faithful; honest, genuine; upright; **—ig gesagt,** speaking candidly. **—igkeit,** *f.* uprightness; sincerity, *etc.* **—ung,** *f.* erection; foundation, establishment. *Comp.* **—zug,** *m.* crane for lifting weights.

Auf'riegeln, *v.a.* to unbolt, to unbar.

Auf'riß, *m.* (**—sses,** *pl.* **—sse**) elevation, sketch, draught; construction of figure (*Math.*); **perspektivischer —,** perspective view.

Auf'ritzen, *v.a.* to slit, rip, scratch open; to chap; **leicht aufzuritzen ist das Reich der Geister,** the realm of spirits is easily opened.

Auf'röcheln, *v.n.* to make a rattle in the throat.

Auf'rollen, *v.a. & n.* (*aux.* **s.**) to roll up; to unroll; to mangle.

Auf'rücken, *v.* I. *n.* (*aux.* **s.**) to advance upwards, rise (*in a service*). II. *a.* to push, move up; **einem etwas —,** to reproach one with a th.

Auf'ruf, *m.* (**—s,** *pl.* **—e**) calling up, summons; calling over; appeal to.

Auf'rufen, *ir.v.a.* to summon, call up; to call over (*names*); to invite, ask; to cite.

Auf'ruhr, *m.* (**—s**) tumult, uproar, riot; revolt; mutiny; insurrection. *Comp.* **—akte,** *f.*, **—gesetz,** *n.* riot-act. **—stifter,** *m.* agitator. **—süchtig,** *adj.* seditious.

Auf'rühr—en, *v.a.* to stir up; to provoke (*a tumult*); to mention again, revive (*a quarrel, etc.*). **—er,** *m.* (**—ers,** *pl.* **—er**) rebel, insurgent, rioter; **die —er,** the mutineers. **—erisch,** *adj. & adv.* mutinous, rebellious; seditious; inflammatory.

Auf'rütteln, *v.a.* to shake up; to arouse.

Aufs (Auf's), *abbr. of* **auf das**; **— späteste,** at the latest; **— billigste,** at the cheapest rate; **— Pferd,** to horse!

Auf'sagen, *v.a.* to say, repeat; to unsay, recall; to recant; to countermand; to give notice to quit *or* warning; to refuse; to renounce.

Auf'sägen, *v.a.* to saw open; to saw up.

Auf'samm—eln, *v.a.* to gather up, collect. **—ler,** *m.* (**—lers,** *pl.* **—ler**) collector.

Auf'sässig, Auf'sätzig, *adj.* hostile, inimical; refractory. **—keit,** *f.* obstinacy, hostility.

Auf'satz, *m.* (**—es,** *pl.* **Aufsätze**) anything put *or* placed on another (*as finish, ornament, etc.*); landing (*of a staircase*); ajutage, spout (*of a jet d'eau*); knob; head-dress; course (*of dishes*); service, set (*of china, etc.*); epergne, centre-piece; essay, composition; plan, sketch, design; joint, year's growth; a piece sewed on; top, headpiece (*of a pipe, a mirror, etc.*); cage (*of a windmill*); panel (*Arch.*); **vermischte Aufsätze,** miscellaneous essays.

Auf'schanzen, *v.a.* to trench, throw up (*a mound, etc.*).

Auf'schauen, *v.n.* (*aux.* **h.**) to look upward; to look surprised; to look out, take heed.

Auf'schaufeln, *v.a.* to shovel up; to put new floats *or* paddles (*on a water-wheel, etc.*).

Auf'scheren, *v.a.* to warp; to coil (*a rope*).

Auf'scheuchen, *v.a.* to startle up, scare away.

Auf'schicht—en, *v.a.* to pile up (*timber, etc.*); to put in layers, stratify. **—ung,** *f.* stratification.

Auf'schiebbar, *adj.* that may be postponed.

Auf'schieb—en, *ir.v.a.* to shove, push open; to throw up (*a window*); to postpone; to adjourn, prorogue; to delay, procrastinate. **—ling,** *m.* (**—lings,** *pl.* **—linge**) chantlate (*Arch.*); young tree. **—ung,** *f.* delay; adjournment; respite. *Comp.* **—e=fenster,** *n.* sash-window. **—e=ring,** *m.* umbrella-runner.

Auf'schienen, *v.a.* to fasten up (*as a splint*); to clamp, fasten with iron bands.

Auf'schießen, *ir.v.* I. *a.* to shoot open *or* up; to use up in shooting; to open (*a breach*); to coil (*a rope*). II. *n.* (*aux.* **s.**) to shoot upwards (*of plants, animals, etc.*); to spring up.

Auf'schlag, *m.* (**—es,** *pl.* **Aufschläge**) striking *or* beating upon; impact; trump, turn-up card; upward stroke (*in beating time*); facings (*on a coat*); cuff; top (*of a boot*); advance (*in price*); highest bid (*at auctions*); additional impost *or* duty; young growth of wood; arsis (*Pros.*).

Auf'schlag—en, *ir.v.* I. *a.* to strike up; to strike, beat open; to put up (*a bedstead, etc.*); to rouse by striking; to turn up (*a card; a table; one's dress, trowsers, sleeves, etc.*); to pitch (*a tent*); to face (*clothes*); to line, border (*caps, etc.*); to untwist (*a rope*); to open (*a book*); to look out (*a word, a passage*); to fasten, fix; to pick (*oakum*); to open (*the eyes*); to put on the last; **dumpf —en,** to thud; **einem die Quartiere —en,** beat up one's quarters; to come upon a person unawares; to come down upon a man (*rare*); **einem Pferde die Hufeisen —en,** to shoe a horse; **ein Gelächter —en,** to burst out laughing; **eine Lache —en,** to set up a laugh, to break out into a roar (*or* fit) of laughter; **seine Wohnung —en,** to set up one's habitation. II. *n.* (*aux.* **s.**) to turn up; to spring up; to fall upon violently; to rise in price. *Comp.* **—e=buch,** *n.* book of reference. **—fenster,** *n.* window *or* shutter that forms a table for exposure of goods. **—holz,** *n.* sleeveboard. **—e=tisch,** *m.* folding table.

Auf'schlämmen, Auf'schlemmen, *v.a.* to deposit mud; to squander (*one's fortune*).

Auf'schleudern, *v.a.* to fling upwards.

Auf'schließ—en, *ir.v.* I. *a.* to unlock, open; to elucidate; to disclose. II. *r.* to open. **—er,**

m. (—ers, *pl.* —er) opener; box-keeper; turnkey. —ung, *f.* opening; disclosure.

Auf'schlingen, *ir.v.a.* to fasten with a loop, twine; to untwist; sich —, to twine upward, to creep up.

Auf'schlitzen, *v.a.* to rip, slit up; to slit open, up; aufgeschlitzter Lachs, crimped salmon.

Auf'schluchzen, *v.n.* (*aux.* h.) to burst into sobs, to sob aloud.

Auf'schluß, *m.* (—sses, *pl.* Aufschlüsse) opening up, unlocking; disclosure; information; elucidation; — über eine Sache geben, to explain a th., inform, give the particulars of a matter.

Auf'schmausen, *v.a.* to eat up, to waste by feasting.

Auf'schmettern, *v.* I. *a.* to smash open. II. *n.* (*aux.* s.) to crash, dash against; to yield a loud sound.

Auf'schmieren, *v.a.* to smear on, to spread.

Auf'schminken, *v.a.*; eine Sache —, to adorn a matter with false colours, paint up.

Auf'schmoren, *v.a.* to stew again.

Auf'schnabeln, Auf'schnabelieren, *v.a.* to pick up; to eat up (*coll.*).

Auf'schnappen, *v.* I. *a.* to snap, catch, snatch up; to pick up (*a smattering*). II. *n.* (*aux.* s.) to spring, fly up; to snap (*as a spring*).

Auf'schneid—en, *ir.v.* I. *a.* to cut up, open; to notch; to dissect; to rip up, unrip; ein Buch —en, to cut the leaves of a book. II. *n.* (*aux.* h.) to brag, boast, swagger, talk big, draw the long bow, to exaggerate. —er, *m.* (—ers, *pl.* —er) swaggerer, boaster; exaggerator. —erei', *f.* (*pl.* —ereien) bombast, boasting, gasconade; exaggeration. —ung, *f.* cutting up *or* open.

Auf'schnellen, *v.* I. *a.* to jerk, fling up. II. *n.* (*aux.* s.) to fly up with a jerk.

Auf'schnitt, *m.* (—es, *pl.* —e) cutting open; cut, slit, incision; assay of gold; kalter —, dish consisting of various kinds of cut meat, slices of cold meat; heute giebt es kalten — zum Abendbrot, to-day we shall have cold meat and sausage for supper.

Auf'schnob(b)ern, Auf'schnüffeln, *v.a.* to track by the scent.

Auf'schnüren, *v.a.* to cord up, fasten in *or* on; to lace; to string; to unlace, untie, uncord; sich —, to come undone (*of parcels*).

Auf'schobern, *v.a.* to stack up, put into cocks.

Auf'schöpfen, *v.a.* to scoop *or* ladle up; to drain.

Auf'schößling, *m.* (—s, *pl.* —e) shoot, sprig, scion; stripling, overgrown child; upstart.

Auf'schrauben, *reg. & ir. v.a.* to screw on; to screw open, unscrew; to screw up; to exalt.

Auf'schrecken, I. *v. a.* to startle; to rouse, frighten up. II. *ir.v.n.* (*aux.* s.) to start up.

Auf'schrei, *m.* (—es, *pl.* —e) outcry, shriek, scream, yell, shout.

Auf'schreiben, *ir.v.a.* to write down, take a note of; to enter, to book; to put to one's account; to record; du bist aufgeschrieben, you are in for it (*coll.*).

Auf'schreien, *ir.v.n.* (*aux.* h.) to cry out, scream.

Auf'schrift, *f.* (*pl.* —en) address, direction; superscription; inscription; label (*on goods, bottles, etc.*); signature, endorsement; epitaph.

Auf'schroten, *v.a.* to roll up (*a cask*); to punch open; to widen a hole (*with an auger, etc.*); to grind coarsely.

Auf'schub, *m.* (—s) postponement, deferring; delay; adjournment; respite; Zahlung ohne —, immediate payment; die Sache leidet keinen —, the matter must not be delayed. *Comp.* —s=befehl, *m.* reprieve. —s=brief, *m.* letter of respite.

Auf'schüppen, *v.a.* to throw up with a spade.

Auf'schüren, *v.a.* to stir up, poke.

Auf'schürz—en, *v.a.* to tuck up (*a skirt, etc.*); to ungird, let down; die Segel —en, to furl the sails; sich —en, to tuck up one's clothes. —er, *m.* (—ers, *pl.* —er), —band, *n.* dress-holder, ladies' page.

Auf'schütteln, *v.a.* to shake up, arouse by shaking.

Auf'schütten, *v.a.* to heap *or* throw up; to pour on *or* into; to store up; to raise (*earth*); das Pulver —, to prime a fire arm, (*obs.*) to put powder on the pan of a gun.

Auf'schützen, *v.a.* to open *or* close sluices.

Auf'schwänzen, *v.a.* to truss up (*a horse's tail*); to serve up fish with the tail in the mouth; sich —, to spread the tail (*as peacocks*).

Auf'schwärzen, *v.a.* to blacken afresh.

Auf'schwatzen, *v.a.*; einem etwas —, to palm off a thing upon a person.

Auf'schwellen, I. *v.a.* to cause to swell; to puff out; to animate, encourage. II. *ir.v.n.* (*aux.* s.) to swell; to rise; to surge up; to heave; to tumefy, grow turgid; der Kamm schwillt ihm auf, his blood is rising, he begins to grow proud (*vulg.*).

Auf'schwemme, *f.* landing-place for floatwood.

Auf'schwemm—en, *v.a.* to wash up; to land floatwood; to deposit (*sand, etc.*); to let in the tide. —er, *m.* (—ers, *pl.* —er) workman who lands floatwood.

Auf'schwingen, *ir.v.a.* to swing upwards; to brandish; sich —, to soar upwards.

Auf'schwung, *m.* (—es), swing; soaring; soaring up; flight (*of fancy, etc.*); elevation of soul, rapture; einen neuen — nehmen, to receive a fresh impetus, to rise again.

Auf'seh—en, I. *ir.v.n* (*aux.* h.) to look up, upon. II. *subst. n.* observation; stir, sensation; er wollte alles —en vermeiden, he wished to escape notice; —en erregen, to cause a sensation; die Sache (*or* es) ist nicht wert, daß man so viel —ens davon macht, the matter is not worth making so much fuss about. —er, m. (—ers, *pl.* —er) overseer, inspector; warden; proctor; curator. *Comp.* —er=amt, *n.*, —er=stelle, *f.* inspectorship.

Auf'setz—en, *v.* I. *a.* to set on *or* up; to put *or* pile up; to put on (*a hat; a kettle; a patch, etc.*); to put down, note; to stake; to affix (*a seal*); to crown (*a man at draughts*); to serve up (*dishes*); to fish (*the anchor*); das Besteck —en, to prick the chart (*Naut.*); eine Rechnung —en, to cast an account, draw a bill; eine Schrift —en, to compose, to draw up (*a writ; a memorial, etc.*); die Krone —en, to crown; seinen Kopf —en, to be obstinate about a thing; einem Hörner —en, to cuckold one; bitte, setzen Sie auf, pray put on your hat. II. *r.* to oppose, be refractory; to sit upright; to mount (*on horseback*). III. *n.* (*aux.* h.) to put forth (*shoots, etc.*); —en lassen, to allow to mount; die Zähne der Uhrräder setzen auf, the teeth of the wheels don't catch (*Horol.*). —er, *m.* (—ers, *pl.* —er) one who puts up, loader, *etc.* —erin, *f.* hair-dresser (*rare*). *Comp.* —holz, *n.* baker's fuel. —röhre, *f.* spout. —stunde, *f.* noonday rest from work.

Auf'sicht, *f.* inspection; superintendence; care, charge; control; guardianship, keeping; invigilation (*at an examination*); custody; unter — stehen, to be under control; — führen, to superintend; — führen (bei Prüfungen), to invigilate. *Comp.* —s=behörde, *f.* board of superintendence *or* control. —s=bezirk, *m.* inspector's district. —s=komitee, *n.* visiting committee.

Auf'sieden, *reg. & ir.v.* I. *a. & n.* (*aux.* h. & s.) to boil up. II. *a.* to blanch (*silver*).

Auf'siegeln, *v.a.* to fasten on by sealing; to unseal.

Auf'sitz, *m.* (—es) mounting (*on horseback*); zum — bereit, ready to mount (*Mil.*). *Comp.*

—geld, *n.* pupil's present to his riding-master. —stange, *f.* perch, roost.

Auf'sitzen, I. *ir.v.n.* (*aux.* h.) to sit, rest on; to get aground; to sit up (*at night*); to perch; (*aux.* s.) to mount, take horse; **einem aufgesessen sein,** to bear one ill-will. II. *subst. n.* sitting up; incubation; mounting; **zum — blasen,** to sound to horse (*Mil.*); — **aufgesessen,** to horse! mount! (*Mil.*); **das Ziel — lassen,** to aim just below the mark.

Auf'spannen, *v.a.* to stretch, strain; to bend (*a bow*); to open (*a fan, an umbrella, etc.*); to cock (*a gun*); to string (*an instrument*); to pitch (*a tent*); to spread sails (*Naut.*); to stretch on; **alle Kräfte —,** to use every exertion; **gelindere Saiten —,** to lower one's tone.

Auf'sparen, *v.a.* to save, lay by; to reserve, keep in reserve; to defer, postpone.

Auf'speichern, *v.a.* to store up; to warehouse.

Auf'speisen, *v.a.* to eat up, consume.

Auf'sperr—en, *v.a.* to open wide; to pick (*a lock*); **das Maul —en,** to gape; **er sperrt Mund und Nase auf,** he opens his mouth in wonder and surprise. **—ung,** *f.* opening wide (*of a door, etc.*).

Auf'spielen, *v.a. & n.* (*aux.* h.) to play to; to strike up a tune; to make music; to arouse by playing.

Auf'spießen, *v.a.* to spit; to impale; to run through with a sword; to take on the point of a sword; to head (*pins*).

Auf'sprengen, *v.a.* to burst *or* blow open; to blow up; to sprinkle; to rouse; to set in motion.

Auf'sprießen, *ir.v.n.* (*aux.* s.) to sprout, spring up.

Auf'springen, *ir.v.n.* (*aux.* s.) to leap up, bound; to fly, burst open; to split asunder, crack; to chap; to rebound; to sparkle up. **—d,** *p. & adj.* rampant (*Her.*).

Auf'spritzen, *v.* I. *a.* to squirt up; to blow, spout up (*water*); to open by injections. II. *n.* (*aux.* s.) to splash up.

Auf'sprossen, *v.n.* (*aux.* s.) *see* **Aufsprießen.**

Auf'sprudeln, *v.* I. *a.* to throw up (*water*). II. *n.* (*aux.* s.) to bubble up, boil up.

Auf'sprühen, *v.n.* (*aux.* s.) to sparkle up.

Auf'sprung, *m.* (—es, *pl.* **Aufsprünge**) springing up; bound, leap; bursting, flying open.

Auf'spul—en, *v.a.* to wind on (*a reel, etc.*). **—er,** *m.* (—ers, *pl.* —er), **—erin,** *f.* winder.

Auf'spülen, *v.a.* to wash, rinse up.

Auf'spunden, Auf'spünden, *v.a.* to unbung.

Auf'spüren, *v.a.* to spy *or* trace out, track.

Auf'stacheln, *v.a.* to goad up; to spur, goad on.

Auf'stampfen, *v.* I. *a.* to stamp on; to affix; to stamp open. II. *n.* (*aux.* h.) to stamp.

Auf'stand, *m.* (—es, *pl.* **Aufstände**) move; commotion; getting up, rising, tumult, revolt; sedition, insurrection; leaving service *or* employ (*of tailors, etc.*); **er war der erste, der einen — machte,** he made the first move to go away (*obs.*).

Auf'ständisch, *adj.* seditious, riotous, insurgent, rebellious, revolutionary; **ein —er,** an insurgent, rebel, revolutionist.

Auf'stapeln, *v.a.* to pile up (*wood*).

Auf'stau—en, *v.a.* to stow away; to block; to swell (*water*); **aufgestaute Güter,** stowage. **—ung,** *f.* dammed water, banking.

Auf'stechen, *ir.v.* I. *a.* to fasten on by pinning *or* stitching; to pierce open; to lance (*Surg.*); to stir; to retouch (*an engraving*); to splice (*ropes*); to fork (*hay; meat, etc.*); **ein Wort —,** to cavil at a word; **Halsen und Schoten —,** to ease tacks and sheets; **das Schiff hat sich aufgestochen,** the ship has broken her back. II. *n.* (*aux.* h.) **dicht bei dem Winde —,** to ply to windward.

Auf'steck—en, *v.a.* to set up, fix; to pin up; to affix; to hoist (*a flag*); to fix (*bayonets*); to put up (*curtains*); to dress (*the hair*); to abandon, give up (*coll.*); **ein Licht —en,** to set up a candle; **einem ein Licht —en,** to enlighten a p. *Comp.* **—nadel,** *f.* corking-pin, nursery-pin.

Auf'stehen, *ir.v.n.* (*aux.* s.) to stand up; to rise, get up; to appear, arise (*as a prophet, etc.*); to fly up; to break cover; to right (*of a ship*); to recover (*from an illness*); to rise, revolt; **das Volk steht auf,** the nation rises (*against a tyrant, etc.*); to mutiny (*soldiers against their officers*); to referment; (*aux.* h.) to stand *or* be open; to stand firm upon.

Auf'steifen, *v.a.* to stiffen *or* do up.

Auf'steig—en, I. *ir.v.n.* (*aux.* s.) to ascend, rise, mount; **es stieg ein Gedanke in mir auf,** a thought struck me; **der Teig fängt an aufzusteigen,** the dough is rising; **das Blut stieg ihr ins Gesicht auf,** the blood rushed to her face; **—ender Rhythmus,** ascending rhythm, iambic rhythm; (*for anapæstic, see* **Aufgleitend**). II. *subst.n.* mounting (*a horse, etc.*); ascent; dispersion (*of a fog*); exhalation (*of vapour, etc.*); **das —en der Gebärmutter,** hysterical fit. **—ung,** *f.* ascension (*Astr.*); exhalation (*of vapours, etc.*); **gerade —ung,** right ascension. *Comp.* **—e=riemen,** *pl.* backstraps (*of a carriage*). **—ungs=unterschied,** *m.* ascensional difference.

Auf'stell—en, *v.* I. *a.* to set up; to erect; to range, draw up; to put *or* make up (*a bed, etc.*); to advance (*an opinion*); to set (*a trap*); to expose (*goods for sale*); to post (*sentries*); to bring forward (*instances, etc.*); **eine Behauptung —en,** to make an assertion; **es läßt sich nichts mit ihm —en,** nothing can be done with him. II. *r.* to draw up (*in battle-array, etc.*), form; to stand up (*to dance*). **—ung,** *f.* putting up, arranging, disposition; drawing up, array (*Mil.*); assertion, statement; putting forward, nomination (*of a candidate*). *Comp.* **—spiegel,** *m.* cheval-glass.

Auf'stemmen, *v.a.* to prop up, support; to force open; **sich — auf eine S.,** to lean upon a th.

Auf'steppen, *v.a.* to quilt on.

Auf'sticken, *v.a.* to stitch *or* embroider upon.

Auf'stimmen, *v.a.* to raise the pitch of (*Mus.*).

Auf'stöbern, *v.a.* to start (*game*); to hunt up, find out, light on.

Auf'stöhnen, *v.n.* to groan aloud.

Auf'stören, *v.a.* to rouse up, disturb, startle.

Auf'stoßen, *ir. v.* I. *a.* to knock, kick open; to kick, throw *or* push up; to knock against (**gegen**); to stave (*a cask*); to gall, raise (*the skin*). II. *n.* (*aux.* s.) (**einem**) to rise up (*in the stomach*); to run aground; to meet with, light upon; to happen to; to re-ferment; to turn acid; **das —,** rising of the stomach, eructation, hiccupping; **er leidet viel am —,** he is much disposed to eructation; **da ist mir etwas Seltsames aufgestoßen,** there a strange thing happened to me.

Auf'stößig, *adj.* sick; flat, acid, sour.

Auf'streb—en, *v.n.* (*aux.* s.) to aspire, soar up; to struggle upwards. **—end,** *p. & adj.* aspiring. **—ung,** *f.* aspiring; exertion.

Auf'streich, *m.* (—es, *pl.* —e) public auction, sale (*dial.*).

Auf'streichen, *ir.v.* I. *a.* to lay on; to spread (*butter on bread, etc.*); to stroke up; to strike up; to brush up (*cloth m.*).

Auf'streifen, *v.* I. *a.* to turn, tuck up (*one's cuffs, etc.*); to raise, wound (*the skin*). II. *n.* (*aux.* s.) to graze, touch the surface; to trail, sweep.

Auf'streuen, *v.a.* to strew *or* sprinkle on; to dredge.

Auf'strich, *m.* (—es, *pl.* —e) *see* **Aufstreich;** up-stroke (*of the pen*), up-bow (*Mus. string instrum.*).

Auf'stuf—en, *v.a. & n.* (*aux.* **s.**) to raise *or* rise by degrees. **—ung,** *f.* climax (*Rhet.*); gradation.
Auf'stülpen, *v.a.* to cock (*a hat, etc.*); **eine aufgestülpte Nase,** a turned-up nose.
Auf'stürzen, *v.* I. *a.* to clap on; to turn up. II. *n.* (*aux.* **s.**) to fall violently on *or* against.
Auf'stutzen, *v.* I. *a.* to trim up; to turn up, cock. II. *n.* (*aux.* **h.**) to start.
Auf'stützen, *v.a.* to prop up; **sich —,** to lean upon.
Auf'such—en, *v.a.* to hunt up, seek out; to look out (*a passage, etc.*); to gather; to take the bearings (*Naut.*); to go in quest of. **—ung,** *f.* search.
Auf'summen, *v.n.* (*aux.* **s.**) *& r.* to accumulate, run up.
Auf'tafeln, *v.a.* to dish, serve up; to fold (*the cloth*).
Auf'takeln, *v.a.* to rig (*a ship*); **regelrecht aufgetakelt,** rigged shipshape; **sich —,** to trick oneself out (*coll.*).
Auf'takt, *m.* upward beat (*Mus.*); unaccented syllable (*or* syllables) before the first accent in the metrical line, anacrusis.
Auf'tauchen, *v.n.* (*aux.* **s.**) to emerge, appear, rise to the surface.
Auf'tauen, *v.n.* (*aux.* **s.**) to thaw; to become lively, talkative, to become communicative.
Auf'thun, *ir.v.* I. *a.* to open; to disclose; to put open. II. *r.* to open; to blow (*of flowers*); to clear; to loom, appear on the horizon; **sich —,** to get started *or* established (*clubs, societies*).
Auf'tischen, *v.a.* to set on the table, serve up; **einem etwas —,** to serve, regale one with a th.
Auf'trag, *m.* (—es, *pl.* **Aufträge**) transfer (*of property*); commission; order; errand, message, commission; laying on (*of colours*); **im —e von,** by order of; **sich eines —s entledigen,** to acquit oneself of a task; **einen — ausführen,** to execute a commission. *Comp.* **—s=besorger,** *m.* agent; commissionaire; messenger. **—geber,** *m.* employer; customer. **—s=handel,** *m.* commission business.
Auf'tragen, *ir.v.* I. *a.* to carry up, serve up; to lay on (*colour*); to ink (*the rollers, Typ.*); to draw (*a plan*); to transfer, convey (*property*); to commission; to charge one with (*a duty*); to wear out (*clothes*); **er hat mir viele Grüße an jeden von Ihnen aufgetragen,** he charged me with many greetings to each of you; **einem eine Arbeit —,** to set one a task; **das Abendbrot ist aufgetragen,** supper is served *or* on the table. II. *n.* (*aux.* **h.**) to be bulky, make a p. appear too stout.
Auf'träufeln, *v.n.* (*aux.* **s.**) to drop *or* trickle upon.
Auf'treib—en, *ir.v.* I. *a.* to drive up, cause to rise; to start, dislodge (*a stag, etc.*); to put up (*birds*); to hunt up, to procure (*with difficulty*), to get hold of; to swell up, distend; to raise (*prices; money; dust*); to levy, impress (*troops*); to hunt, rummage out; to drive upon, fasten on. II. *n.* (*aux.* **s.**) to run aground. **—er,** *m.* (—ers, *pl.* —er) beater (*for game*). **—lich,** *adj. & adv.* that may be found with difficulty. *Comp.* **—e=holz,** *n.* roller of a mangle; rolling-pin.
Auf'trennen, *v.* I. *a.* to rip, unrip; to undo. II. *n.* (*aux.* **s.**) to come asunder.
Auf'treten, *ir.v.* I. *a.* to open by treading on, crush open. II. *n.* (*aux.* **s.**) to step up *or* on; to appear, come forward; **er trat als Othello auf,** he appeared in the part of Othello; **als Schriftsteller —,** to come forward as an author; **er ist mit einem Anspruche aufgetreten,** he has advanced a claim; **zum ersten Mal —,** to make one's debut; **gegen einen —,** to rise against one; **als Zeuge —,** to appear as witness; **sanft, leise —,** to act, proceed cautiously, gently; **dies war ihr erstes —,** this was her first public appearance, her debut.
Auf'tritt, *m.* (—s, *pl.* —e) treading on; step, doorstep; horse-block; appearance; scene (*in a play*); scene, event; banquette (*Fort.*); **erster —,** first scene. *Comp.* **—bank,** *f.* treadle (*in lacemaking*).
Auf'trommeln, *v.a.* to beat the reveille, beat up.
Auf'trumpfen, *v.a.* to trump; to snub, snap up.
Auf'tuchen, *v.a.* to furl (*sails, etc.*).
Auf'tupfen, *v.a.* to stop, to dry up (*with towel*); to press down gently (*gold leaves*).
Auf'türmen, *v.a.* to raise (*as high as a tower*), to heap; **sich —,** to tower up. **aufgetürmt,** *p.p. & adj.* high-heaped, towering.
Auf'tuschen, *v.a.* to touch up (*a drawing*) with sepia.
Auf'wachen, *v.n.* (*aux.* **s.**) to awake, wake up.
Auf'wachsen, *ir.v.n.* (*aux.* **s.**) to grow, shoot up.
Auf'wägen, *r. & ir.v.a.* to weigh; to balance; to outweigh; to lift, raise (*by a crane*).
Auf'wall—en, *v.n.* (*aux.* **s.**) to boil up; to rage, foam up; to roll, heave up. **—ung,** *f.* act of boiling up, ebullition; effervescence; emotion; transport.
Auf'walzen, *v.a.* to wind on a cylinder; to put on rollers.
Auf'wälzen, *v.a.* to roll up; **einem etwas —,** to burden one with a th.
Auf'wand, *m.* (—es) expense; expenditure, consumption; display; **den — betreffend,** sumptuary; **viel — machen,** to live at great expense. *Comp.* **—s=gesetz,** *n.* sumptuary law.
Auf'wärmen, *v.a.* to warm up; to bring up again, renew (*a dispute, etc.*).
Auf'wart—en, *v.n.* (*aux.* **h.**) (**einem**) to wait upon, attend on; to wait; to call on, pay one's respects to; to beg (*of dogs*); **kann ich damit —en?** may I offer you some?; **ich will gleich damit —en,** you shall have it directly; **einem oft —en,** to dance attendance on one; **womit kann ich Ihnen —en?** what can I do for you? **—ung,** *f.* waiting, attendance; visit, ceremonious call; **—ung bei Hofe haben,** to be in waiting (*at court*); **—ung bei Hochzeiten,** attendance (*also* music) at weddings; **einem seine —ung machen,** to pay one's respects to a p. *Comp.* **—e=frau,** *f.* waiting woman. **—e=geld,** *n.*, **—e=lohn,** *m.* fee for attendance *or* service.
Auf'wärter, *m.* (—s, *pl.* —) attendant, waiter; steward. **—in,** *f.* waiting maid; waitress; stewardess. *Comp.* **—lohn,** *m.* waiter's fee.
Auf'wärts, *adv.* upwards; **den Fluß —** *or* **strom—,** up stream; **— gerichtet,** erect; **— sehen,** to look up. *Comp.* **—zieher,** *m.* adductor (*muscle*).
Auf'wasch—en, *ir.v.a.* to wash up, away, off; to use up in washing; **sich** (*dat.*) **die Hände —en,** to wash one's hands sore. *Comp.* **—faß,** *n.*, **—kübel,** *m.* tub for washing up in. **—küche,** *f.* scullery. **—wasser,** *n.* dish-water.
Auf'weck—en, *v.a.* to rouse, awake; to animate. **—er,** *m.* (—ers, *pl.* —er) awakener; alarum-clock.
Auf'wehen, *v.* I. *a.* to blow up *or* open; to blow into a blaze. II. *n.* (*aux.* **s.**) to rise.
Auf'weichen, *v.a.* to soften; to soak; to temper (*colours*); to open by softening. **—d,** *p. & adj.* emollient.
Auf'weinen, *v.n.* (*aux.* **h.**) to burst into tears, weep aloud.
Auf'weisen, *ir.v.a.* to show forth, exhibit; to produce.
Auf'wenden, *reg. & ir.v.a.* to spend, expend; **Mühe —,** to bestow pains (**auf eine S.,** on a th.); **vergebliche Worte —,** to waste one's words.
Auf'werfen, *ir.v.a.* to cast up (*earth, a rampart, etc.*); to dig (*a ditch*); to throw open (*a*

door); to throw up (*one's cards; a ball; dice, etc.*); to raise (*bubbles*); to turn up (*one's nose*); **aufgeworfene Lippen,** pouting lips; **einen Zweifel, eine Frage —,** to raise a doubt, start a question; **aufgeworfene Nasenlöcher,** distended nostrils; **sich — zu** (**zum Schützer, &c.**), to set up for; **sich wider** *or* **gegen einen —,** to rise up against one.

Auf'wick—eln, *v.a.* to wind; to put in curl papers; to loosen, let down (*one's hair*); to unfurl (*sails*); to unpaper (*a parcel*); to unswathe (*a child*); **aufgewickelte Seide,** sleave silk. **—ler,** *m.* (**—lers,** *pl.* **—ler**) lapper.

Auf'wieg—eln, *v.a.* to stir up, incite to rebellion. **—elei',** *f.*, **—elung,** *f.* instigation to rebellion. **—ler,** *m.* (**—lers,** *pl.* **—ler**), **—lerin,** *f.* instigator (*to revolt*), mutineer, agitator. **—lerisch,** *adj. & adv.* seditious, mutinous.

Auf'wiegen, *ir.v.a.* to outweigh; to counterbalance; to make up for; to atone for.

Auf'winden, *ir.v.a.* to wind up; to reel; to hoist (*with a windlass*); to untwist, undo; **sich —,** to take a winding course upward.

Auf'wirbeln, *v.* I. *a.* to whirl, twist up; to open by turning a bolt; to wake by drumming. II. *n.* (*aux.* **s.**) to rise whirling.

Auf'wirken, *v.a.* to work up; to knead (*dough*); to undo, unravel; to cut open (*game*).

Auf'wischen, *v.a.* to wipe up; to wipe away, clear.

Auf'wuchern, *v.n.* (*aux.* **s.**) to grow up luxuriantly (of weeds, creepers).

Auf'wühlen, *v.a.* to grub up, root up (*like swine*).

Auf'wurf, *m.* (**—s,** *pl.* **Aufwürfe**) act of throwing up; anything thrown up (*as a rampart, bank, etc.*), ridge.

Auf'zählen, *v.a.* to count down; to reckon up, enumerate, detail; to administer (*stripes, blows*).

Auf'zäumen, *v.a.* to bridle (*a horse*); **ein Pferd beim Schwanze —,** to put the cart before the horse (*coll.*).

Auf'zehr—en, *v.a.* to consume; to waste; to absorb. **—ung,** *f.* consumption, expenditure.

Auf'zeichn—en, *v.a.* to draw upon, sketch, design; to catalogue, make an inventory of; to note down, take a note of; to register; to record. **—er,** *m.* (**—ers,** *pl.* **—er**) one who notes down, takes notes; designer. **—ung,** *f.* note; noting down; account; inventory; **aus den —ungen meines verstorbenen Freundes,** from the papers of my late friend. *Comp.* **—ungs=buch,** *n.* note book.

Auf'zeigen, *v.a.* to show forth, produce, exhibit.

Auf'zieh—en, *ir.v.* I. *a.* to draw up, raise; to draw (*water*); to draw open; to bring up (*children*); to cultivate (*plants*); to rear, breed (*cattle, etc.*); to screw up (*a fiddle-string, etc.*) to warp; to assume (*an air*); to wind up (*a watch*); to open by drawing (*a bolt*); to open (*a sluice-gate*); to mount (*a print, maps, etc.*); to tow up (*a ship*); to undo (*a knot*); to weigh (*anchor*); to set (*a sail*); **gelindere Saiten —en,** to come down a peg, take a lower tone; to draw in, to yield; **andere Saiten —en,** to adopt (*or* to speak in) a different tone; **ein Schloß —en,** to unlock; **einen —en,** to chaff, make fun of a person; **sie zieht mich gern auf,** she is fond of teasing me; **Gestricktes —en,** to rip out knitting. II. *n.* (*aux.* **s.**) to mount guard; to march, move up, go in procession; to draw up; to gather, draw on (*of storms*); to draw to a head (*of ulcers, etc.*); **in Parade —en lassen,** to parade; **lächerlich —en,** to cut a ridiculous figure. **—erei',** *f.* chaffing. *Comp.* **—brücke,** *f.* drawbridge. **—fenster,** *n.* sash-window. **—loch,** *n.* key-hole (*of a watch, etc.*).

Auf'zucken, *v.n.* (*aux.* **h.**) to start convulsively.

Auf'zug, *m.* (**—s,** *pl.* **Aufzüge**) act of drawing up; warp; procession; cortege, suite, train; pageantry, pomp; parade; mounting guard; hoist, crane, windlass; lift; act (*of a play*); elevation, drawing (*of a house, etc.*); appearance-beam (*of a balance*); covey (*of young birds*); equipment; **— zu Pferde,** cavalcade. *Comp.* **—brücke,** *f.* drawbridge. **—s=geld,** *n.* lock charges; cranage.

Auf'züglich, *adj. & adv.* dilatory (*Law*).

Auf'zwängen, *v.a.* to force open by pressing; **einem eine Sache —,** to force a th. upon a p.

Auf'zwingen, *ir.v.a.*; **einem —,** to force on one.

Au'g—e, *n.* (**—es,** *pl.* **—en**); (*dim.* **Äuglein,** eyelet, little eye) eye; face; sight, view; person, soul; guide, leader; bud, germ; pip, spot (*on cards; dice*); eye (*of a needle*); lustre (*of precious stones*); stitch (*in knitting*); anything resembling an eye (*cavities in bread, whey-drops in cheese, grease drops in soup, etc.*); **das rechte —e (eines Pferdes, mit Bezug auf den Reiter),** the off-eye; **das linke —e,** the near-eye; **mit bloßen —en,** with the naked eye; **einem die —en ausstechen,** to put a person's eyes out; **ganz —e und Ohr sein,** to be all attention, to look alive; **in meinen —en,** in my view, in my opinion; **es wird für uns saure —en geben,** we shall meet with a bad reception; **große —en machen,** to open one's eyes in surprise; **die —en gingen ihm über,** his eyes were suffused with tears; **er ist ihm ein Dorn im —e,** he is an eyesore to him; he is a thorn in his side; he annoys him; **mit scheelen —en ansehen,** to look upon with an evil eye; **einem den Daumen aufs —e setzen,** to keep s.o. under one's thumb, to keep one short; **das paßt wie die Faust aufs —e,** it does not fit at all; **einem Sand in die —en streuen,** to throw dust into *or* to cast a mist before one's eye, to deceive a p.; **ein —e zudrücken,** to wink at, connive at; **kein —e zuthun,** not to sleep a wink; **er ist mir aus den —en gekommen,** I have lost sight of him; **aus den —en setzen,** to make light of; **es sieht ihm der Schalk aus den —en,** he looks a rogue; **er ist ihm wie aus den —en geschnitten,** he is as like him as he can be; **es hackt keine Krähe der anderen die —en aus,** there is honour among thieves; **er hat es ihr an den —en abgesehen,** he anticipated her wishes; **er thut alles, was er seiner Frau an den —en absehen kann,** he does everything he can think of to please his wife; **diese Farbe fällt sehr in die —en,** this is a very glaring colour; **jemand ins —e fassen,** to have an eye on one; **eine Sache im —e behalten,** to keep one's eye on something; **es fiel mir sogleich ins —e,** it caught my eye at once; **in die —en fallend,** striking, evident; **in die —en springen,** to stare one in the face; **in die —en stechen,** to suit one's fancy, to tempt one; **unter vier —en,** between two persons, tête à tête; among ourselves; private; **unter vier —en sagen,** to tell in confidence; **—e um —e,** an eye for an eye; **komm' mir nicht wieder vor die —en,** never let me see your face again; **es schwimmt mir vor den —en,** I feel giddy, dizzy; my brain turns; **ich hab' es ihm an den —en angesehen,** I saw it by his face; **ich habe es ihm unter die —en gesagt,** I told it to him, said it to his face; **bei einem das Kalb in die —en schlagen,** to offend a person's susceptibilities; **geh' mir aus den —en!** get out of my sight; **aus den —en, aus dem Sinn,** out of sight, out of mind; **er ist mit einem blauen —e davongekommen,** he got off pretty cheap *or* with but a small loss; **—en rechts!** eyes right! **—en gerade aus!** eyes front! (*Mil.*). *Comp.* **—apfel,** *m.* eyeball. **—bolzen,** *m.* eyebolt (*Naut.*). [*For other compounds of* **Aug,** *see* **Augen—**.]

Äug—eln, *v.* I. *a.* to graft, inoculate, bud. II. *n.* (*aux.* **h.**) to ogle; to look about (*hunt.*). III.

subst.n. grafting, inoculating; ogling; **das —eln mit dem Schilde**, scutcheon-grafting. **—icht**, *adj.* ocellate, eye-spotted. **—ig** (*in comp.*) -eyed, *e.g.* **blau-äugig**, blue-eyed. **—lein**, *n.* little eye; bud (*of a plant*).

Au'gen— (*Comp.*) **—achat**, *m.* cat's eye. **—(blut)ader**, *f.* ophthalmic vein (*Anat.*). **—ähnlich**, *adj.* ocellate, like an eye. **—arzt**, *m.* oculist. **—bad**, *n.* ophthalmic bath, eye-douche. **—bader**, *m.* eye-cup. **—balsam**, *m.* eye-salve. **—beben**, *n.* spasm in the muscles of the eye. **—betrug**, *m.* optical delusion. **—bild**, *n.* visual image. **—blende**, *f.* shying-blind, blinkers. **—blick**, *m.* moment, instant; twinkling; **im —blick**, in a moment; **auf einen —blick**, for a moment; **lichte —blicke**, lucid intervals, moments of consciousness; **in diesem —blicke**, at this moment. **—blick'lich**, I. *adj.* momentary, instantaneous. II. *adv.* instantaneously, on the spot, instantly, forthwith. **—blicks**, *see* **—blicklich**, II. **—blitz**, *m.* glance of the eye. **—blüte**, *f.* pimpernel. **—bogen**, *m.* iris. **—braue** (*less correctly* **—braune**), *f.* eye-brow; **mit hervorragenden —brauen**, beetlebrowed. **—brauen=bogen**, *m.* orbital curve. **—diener**, *m.* eye-server. **—dienst**, *m.* eye-service. **—drüse**, *f.* lachrymal gland. **—dunkelheit**, *f.* dimness of sight. **—entzündung**, *f.* inflammation of the eye; **nasse —entzündung**, blearedness; **die trockene —entzündung**, xerophthalmy. **—fällig**, *adj.* evident, obvious. **—farbe**, *f.* colour of the eyes. **—fell**, *n.* film (*of the eye*). **—feuchtigkeit**, *f.* (**wässerige, glasartige**, aqueous, vitreous) humour of the eye; **krystallene —feuchtigkeit**, crystalline lens. **—fleck**, *m.*, **—mal**, *n.* speck on the eye. **—flimmern**, *n.* twitching (*or* flimmering) of the eye. **—fluß**, *m.* catarrh of the eye. **—förmig**, *adj.* eye-shaped; ocellate. **—geschwulst**, *f.* exophthalmia; swelling of the eye. **—geschwür**, *n.* ægilops, egilops. **—gewölk**, *n.* nebula, film on the eye. **—glas**, *n.* eye-glass; quizzing-glass, monocle. **—glasschleifer**, *m.* lens-grinder. **—grube**, *f.* cavity in the forehead over the eyes. **—haut**, *f.* tunic, *or* coat of the eyes; **harte —haut**, cornea; **braune —haut**, choroid coat; **weiße**, *or* **gemeinschaftliche —haut**, conjunctive membrane. **—höhle**, *f.* orbit, socket (*of the eye*). **—höhlenentzündung**, *f.* orbital inflammation. **—kitzel**, *m.* itching of the eye; sensual gratification of the eye. **—klappe**, *f.* blinkers; patch (*over the eye*). **—kreis**, *m.* orbit. **—leder**, *n. see* **Scheuleder**. **—lehre**, *f.* ophthalmology. **—lid**, *n.* (*pl.* **—lider**) eyelid. **—lider=brand**, *m.* ulcer on the eyelid. **—lider=knorpel**, *m.* tarsus. **—lider=krampf**, *m.* twitching of the eyelid. **—loch**, *n.* opening of the iris, pupil. **—los**, *adj.* blind; eyeless. **—lust**, *f.* pleasure of seeing; delight of the eyes. **—maß**, *n.* judgment of distance, *etc.* by the eye; eye-sight; **ein gutes —maß haben**, to have a sure eye. **—merk**, *n.* view, aim, object; **sein —merk auf eine S. richten**, to aim at a th., to have a th. in view. **—mittel**, *n.* ophthalmic remedy; **—mittel zu äußerlichem Gebrauche**, eye-lotion. **—muskel**, *m.* abductor oculi; muscle of the eye-ball. **—nadeln**, *pl.* needles. **—nerv**, *m.* optic nerve. **—nicht(s)**, *n.* tutty (*Min.*). **—paar**, *n.* pair of eyes. **—pappel**, *f.* spiked mallow. **—pulver**, *n.* anything injurious to the eyes; diamond type; very small *or* illegible handwriting. **—punkt**, *m.* object in view; aim; sight. **—reiz**, *m.* irritation of the eye; *see also* **—lust**. **—ring**, *m.* iris. **—röte**, *f.* xerophthalmia. **—salbe**, *f.* ointment for the eyes. **—schein**, *m.* inspection; personal observation; evidence; appearance; **in —schein nehmen**, to inspect; **dem —schein nach**, to all appearance. **—schein'lich**, *adj.* self-evident, manifest, obvious, apparent; **—scheinlicher Beweis**, ocular demonstration. **—scheinlichkeit**, *f.* obviousness; self-evidence; apparency. **—schirm**, *m.* shade for the eyes. **—schlagader**, *f.* ophthalmic artery. **—schleim**, *m.* rheum. **—schleimfluß**, *m.* ophthalmorrhea. **—schmaus**, *m.* feast for the eyes, delightful sight. **—schnecke**, *f.* spotted snail. **—schwäche**, *f.* weakness of the eyes. **—schwinden**, *n.* atrophy of the eye-ball. **—spiegel**, *m.* speculum oculi, eye-mirror, ophthalmoscope. **—spiel**, *n.* play of the eyes; ogling. **—sprache**, *f.* language of the eyes. **—spritze**, *f.* syringe for the eye. **—sprosse**, *f.* brow-antler. **—staar**, *m.* cataract. **—stechen**, *n.* shooting pains in the eye. **—stein**, *m.* eye-stone; white copperas. **—stern**, *m.* pupil (*of the eye*); favourite, pet, darling. **—tabak**, *m.* eye-snuff. **—täuschung**, *f.* optical illusion. **—träger**, *m.* the bulb through which the germ shoots forth. **—treibend**, *adj.* gemmiparous (*Bot.*). **—triefen**, *n.* running from the eyes; blearedness. **—trockenheit**, *f.* xerophthalmia. **—trost**, *m.* eye-bright (*Bot.*); consolation (*figur.*). **—verdunkelung**, *f.* amaurosis, gutta serena. **—vorfall**, *m.* proptosis, protrusion of the bulb of the eye. **—wassersucht**, *f.* hydrophthalmia. **—weh**, *n.* pain in the eyes, sore eyes. **—weide**, *f.* delight of the eyes; pleasing sight. **—weiß**, *n.* the white of the eye. **—weite**, *f.* eye-shot, range of vision. **—wimper**, *f.* eyelash. **—wink**, *m.* wink. **—winkel**, *m.* corner of the eye, canthus. **—wurzel**, *f.* root of dandelion; root of valerian (*Bot.*). **—zahn**, *m.* eye-tooth, canine tooth. **—zauber**, *m.* fascination. **—zeuge**, *m.* eye-witness. **—zeugnis**, *n.* ocular proof. **—zirkel**, *m.* iris; orbit.

Augurie'ren, *v.a. & n.* (*aux.* **h.**) to augur, predict.

Augu'ri—um, *n.* (**—ums**, *pl.* **—en**), augury, presage.

Augu'st, *m.* (**—s**), August (*the month*). *Comp.* **—hafer**, *m.* early oats. **—hopfen**, *m.* hasty hops. **—kirsche**, *f.* morella cherry. **—pflaume**, *f.* green-gage.

Au'gust, Augustus (*proper name*).

Au'gustin, Augustin, Austin. **—er**, *m.* Austin friar. **—er=kloster**, *n.* monastery of Austin friars. **—er=mönch**, *m.*, **—er=nonne**, *f.* Austin friar, Austin nun. **—er=orden**, *m.* order of Austin friars (*or* nuns). **—isch**, *adj.* Augustinian.

Auktio'n, *f.* (**—en**), auction, public sale; **in die — geben**, to put up for public sale. **—ä'r**, *m.* (**—ärs**, *pl.* **—äre**), **—a'tor**, *m.* (**—ators**, *pl.* **—atoren**) auctioneer. *Comp.* **—s=kommissar**, *m.* broker. **—s=gebühren**, *f.pl.* auction fees.

Auri'kel, *f.* (*pl.* **—n**) auricula, bear's ear (*Bot.*)

Aus, I. *prep.* **With dat.** out of; from; of; by, for; on, upon, on account of; in; **— der Mode**, out of fashion; **— Achtung**, out of respect; **er ist — den Dreißigen**, he is turned of forty; **— vollem Halse schreien**, to scream at the top of one's voice; **was wurde — der Unternehmung?** what was the result of the undertaking? **— Paris kommen**, to come from Paris; **— unserer Mitte**, from amongst us; **— jemandes Betragen schließen**, to conclude from a person's behaviour; **— Erfahrung lernen**, to learn by *or* from experience; **er ist — London gebürtig**, he is a native of London; **— Silber gemacht**, made of silver; **er versteht seinen Beruf — dem Grunde**, he is a thorough master of his profession; **was wird — ihr werden?** what will become of her? **— Ihrem Briefe ersehe ich**, I see by your letter; **— freier Hand**, by free choice, spontaneously; by hand (*of carving, etc.*); **— eigener Wahl**, voluntarily; **ich sehe — den Zeitungen**, I see by the newspapers; **— Haß**, through hatred; —

vielen Ursachen, from many reasons, on many grounds; — **bloßem Verdacht,** on mere suspicion; — **Mangel an,** for want of; — **Liebe,** from love, out of love; — **verschiedenen Gründen,** for many reasons; — **Gehorsam gegen ihn,** in obedience to him; **es war bloß — Scherz gesagt,** it was only said in jest; **bestehen —,** to consist of; — **Vorsatz,** designedly; — **den Augen, — dem Sinn,** out of sight, out of mind. II. *adv. & sep. prefix,* over; out, forth; forward, in front; done with, up with, ended, past; finished; **jahr— jahrei'n,** from one year's end to another; **höre mich —,** hear me out, let me finish; **er weiß weder — noch ein,** he is at his wit's end; he does not know what to do or to say; **und damit ist es —,** and there is an end of the matter; **die Kirche ist —,** church is over; **trinke es —,** drink it up; **es ist — mit ihm,** it is all over with him; **von Grund —,** thoroughly, radically; **Trumpf —!** out with the trump.

Aus— (*separable*) *prefix, denoting* out; thoroughly, sufficiently, to the end. *For possible compounds not found in the following lists, see the simple verbs.*

Aus'ächzen, *v.a.* to groan out, forth (*one's life*).

Aus'ackern, *v.* I. *a.* to plough up; to exhaust land by cultivation. II. *v.n.* to cease ploughing.

Aus'arbeit—en, *v.* I. *a.* to work out; to hollow out; to train; to complete, perfect; to elaborate; to compose, write (*a book, etc.*); to flay (*a beast*). II. *n.* (*aux.* **h.**) to cease working; to cease to ferment. **—er,** *m.* (**—ers,** *pl.* **—er**) elaborator; finisher. **—ung,** *f.* carrying out (*of a plan*); perfecting; finishing touch; elaboration, essay, composition, treatise.

Aus'art, *f.* (*pl.* **—en**) degeneration; degenerated variety (*rare*); variety.

Aus'art—en, *v.n.* (*aux.* **s.**) to degenerate; **die Freiheit artet oft in Anarchie aus,** freedom often degenerates into anarchy. **—ung,** *f.* a degenerating; deterioration.

Aus'ästen, *v.a.* to prune.

Aus'atmen, *v.* I. *a.* to breathe out *or* forth, to exhale. II. *n.* (*aux.* **h.**) to breathe one's last, to expire.

Aus'baden, *v.* I. *a.* to pay, suffer, smart for (*coll.*); **etwas — müssen,** to have to suffer for a th. II. *n.* (*aux.* **h.**) to have done bathing; to bathe sufficiently.

Aus'baggern, *v.a.* to dredge, clear by dredging.

Aus'balgen, Aus'bälgen, *v.a.* to skin; to stuff (*birds, etc.*).

Aus'ballen, *v.a.* to unpack (*bales of goods*).

Aus'ballotieren, *v.a.* to black-ball, vote out.

Aus'bau, *m.* (**—es**) finishing a building; projecting building (*as a shop-front*); extension of cultivation.

Aus'bauch—en, *v.* I. *a.* to cause to bulge; to hollow out. II. *r.* to bulge, project, swell out. **—ung,** *f.* swelling, bulging.

Aus'bauen, *v.a.* to finish a building; to improve, cultivate; to build out; **ausgebaute Kohlengrube,** exhausted coal-pit.

Aus'beding—en, *ir.v.a.* to stipulate; **sich** (*dat.*) **—en,** to reserve to oneself by stipulation. **—ung,** *f.* reservation; stipulation.

Aus'beißen, *ir.v.a.* to bite out; **sich** (*dat.*) **einen Zahn —,** to break out a tooth in biting; **einen —,** to oust a person (*coll.*). **ausgebissen,** *p.p. & adj.* erose (*Bot.*).

Aus'beizen, *v.a.* to remove by caustics; to eat out.

Aus'besser—n, *v.a.* to mend, darn; to repair; to refit (*a ship*); **eine Mauer unterhalb —n,** to underpin a wall; **es wird ausgebessert,** it is undergoing repair. **—er,** *m.* (**—ers,** *pl.* **—er**) one who mends, patcher, darner, cobbler, *etc.* **—ung,** *f.* repair, mending. *Comp.* **—ungskosten,** *pl.* cost of repairs.

Aus'beugen, *see* **Ausbiegen.**

Aus'beut—e, *f.* gain; net profit; share; **—e schließen,** to decide the dividend due to shareholders (*Comm.*). *Comp.* **—e=bogen,** *m.* profit-account.

Aus'beut—en, *v.a.* to draw a profit from, to exploit; **ausgebeutet werden,** to be taken advantage of. **—ung,** *f.* (*of mines*) exploitation; working of a mine; spoliation (*fig.*).

Aus'biegen, *ir.v.* I. *a.* to bend outwards; to bend. II. *n.* (*aux.* **h.**) to turn aside, off; to evade, elude; **einem** *or* **vor einem —,** to make way for a person, give place to one.

Aus'bieten, *ir.v.a.* to offer for sale; to outbid (= **überbieten**); to give notice to quit.

Aus'bildbar, *adj.* capable of development.

Aus'bild—en, *v.a.* to form, develop, cultivate, improve; to finish, perfect; to render accomplished, drill; to mature; **sie ist ganz ausgebildet,** she has finished her education; **sie ist sehr ausgebildet,** she is highly accomplished; **er hat sich in kurzer Zeit sehr ausgebildet,** he improved greatly in a short time; **den Leib —en,** to render the body active and supple, to go in for gymnastics *or* bodily exercises. **—er,** *m.* (**—ers,** *pl.* **—er**) developer; finishing master; improver. **—ung,** *f.* improvement, development; finishing education; culture; **—ung höherer Lehrer,** training of secondary teachers; **—ung von Rekruten,** drilling of recruits; **—ung eines Geschwürs,** a gathering (*Med.*); **—ung des Körpers,** physical training.

Aus'binden, *ir.v.a.* to untie and take out (*of a parcel*); to unbind (*sheets from a book*); to loose; to tie up (*Typ.*); to tie (*a fine specimen*) to the outside of a bundle *or* parcel.

Aus'bitten, *ir.v.a.* to beg for, ask for; to require; **das bitte ich mir aus** *or* **das will ich mir ausgebeten haben,** I must insist on this, I won't suffer that; **darf ich mir —?** may I trouble you for?; **darf ich mir das Salz —?** please pass the salt!; **wir sind heute abend ausgebeten,** we are asked out, *or* we have received an invitation, for to-night.

Aus'blas—en, *ir.v.* I. *a.* to blow out (*a light, etc.*); to empty by blowing, to blow (*an egg*); to blow up, swell by blowing; to publish by sound of trumpet, blaze forth; to blow to the end; to improve (*a flute*) by blowing; **einem das Lebenslicht —en,** to kill one (*coll.*). II. *n.* (*aux.* **h.**) to cease blowing. *Comp.* **—e=hahn,** *m.* blow-off cock (*in steam-engines*).

Aus'bleiben, I. *ir.v.n.* (*aux.* **s.**) to stay away, fail to appear; to be wanting; to be left out (*of a word, etc.*); not to take place; **eine Gelegenheit blieb nicht lange aus,** an opportunity soon presented itself; **der Puls bleibt ihm aus,** his pulse has stopped; **deine Strafe soll nicht —,** you shall not escape punishment; **es sind mehrere Posten ausgeblieben,** several mails are due. II. *subst.n.* non-appearance, absence, non-attendance; non-arrival; — **der Zahlung,** failure in paying.

Aus'bleichen, I. *v.a.* to bleach out (*stains, etc.*). II. *reg. & ir.v.n.* (*aux.* **s.**) to finish bleaching; to grow pale, fade.

Aus'blick, *m.* (**—s**) outlook, prospect, view; **der — in die Zukunft,** the prospect of the future, the outlook.

Aus'blühen, *v.n.* (*aux.* **h.**) to cease flowering; to decay, fade; **die Rosen haben ausgeblüht,** the roses are over.

Aus'bluten, *v.* I. *n.* (*aux.* **h.**) to bleed; to cease bleeding. II. *a.* **das Leben —,** to bleed to death, to die.

Aus'bohren, *v.a.* to bore (*out*); to drill; to cut (*a screw*); to tap (*a cask*); **kugelförmig —,** to chamfer.

Aus'braten, *ir.v.* I. *a.* to roast out *or* suffi-

ciently. II. *n.* (*aux.* ſ.) to be well roasted; to drip in roasting.
Aus′brauſen, *v.n. & refl.* (*aux.* h.) to cease raging, quiet down.
Aus′brech—en, *ir.v.* I. *a.* to break, force out; to vomit; to lop, prune (*trees*); to pluck off; to quarry (*stone*); to shell (*peas, etc.*); **einen Zahn —en,** to draw a tooth. II. *n.* (*aux.* ſ.) to break out (*as fire; a disease; perspiration; sedition, etc.*); to break loose *or* out of prison; to become known; to break forth, burst out; to be cut (*of teeth*); **der Angſtſchweiß brach ihm aus,** he broke into a sweat with terror; **in Thränen —en,** to burst into tears. **—er,** *m.* (**—ers,** *pl.* **—er**) ripping chisel.
Aus′breit—en, *v.* I. *a.* to spread, stretch (*the arms; a cloth; sails; wings; branches; a mantle; a report, etc.*); to extend (*shelter; one's power; the limits of an empire; a business, etc.*); to spread out; to lay (*tablecloth*); to air; to spread abroad, divulge, circulate; to propagate (*vines; mankind; diseases; opinions; the gospel, etc.*); to broaden out; **vor einem —en,** to unfold, display to one. II. *r.* to go into details; to gain ground; to spread; to branch; to spread, make progress; **ſich** (*acc.*) **über eine S. —en,** to enlarge on a subject. **—ung,** *f.* spreading, extension; propagation; diffusion (*of knowledge, etc.*); promulgation. *Comp.* **—ungs=fähigkeit,** *f.* diffusibility. **—ungs=ſucht,** *f.* propagandism.
Aus′brennen, *ir.v.* I. *a.* to burn out; to cauterise; to scale (*a cannon*); to bake, fire (*bricks, etc.*); to remove by burning; to scorch; to burn down. II. *n.* (*aux.* h.) to cease burning, to go out; (*aux.* ſ.) to be consumed inwardly; **ein ausgebrannter Feuerberg,** an extinct volcano.
Aus′bringen, *ir.v.a.* to bring out; to get off; to hatch; to launch; to take out (*stains*); to publish, circulate (*a secret*); to introduce (*a novelty*); **eine Geſundheit —,** to propose a person's health, to toast a person.
Aus′bruch, *m.* (—(e)s, *pl.* Ausbrüche) outbreak, eruption (*of a volcano; of measles, etc.*); explosion; escape (*from prison, etc.*); elopement; flight (*of folly*); outburst (*of passion, etc.*); the purest wine that runs from the tub before the choicest grapes are pressed, wine of the first press; **zum — kommen,** to break out; **ſeine Thränen zum — kommen laſſen,** to give vent to one's tears. *Comp.* **—fieber,** *n.* eruptive fever.
Aus′brühen, *v.a.* to scald (*a vessel*).
Aus′brüten, I. *v.a.* to hatch; to brood over, plot. II. *v.n.* (*aux.* h.) to cease hatching. III. *subst. n.* incubation, hatching; plotting.
Aus′buddeln, *v.a.*, to dig out (*coll.*).
Aus′bügeln, *v.a.* to iron.
Aus′bund, *m.* (—s, *pl.* Ausbünde) selected specimen, pick (*see* Ausbinden); model, pattern; paragon; quintessence; **ſie iſt ein — von Schönheit,** she is a paragon of beauty; **ein — aller Schelme,** an arrant knave, arch rogue; **— von Bosheit,** a regular demon.
Aus′bündig, *adj. & adv.* excellent, exemplary, extraordinary. *adv.* exceedingly, uncommonly; **— gelehrt,** of profound erudition.
Aus′bürſten, *v.a.* to brush out; to dust.
Aus′büßen, *v.a.* to expiate fully, make ample amends for; to plant new shoots in the place of dead ones; to mend (*nets*).
Aus′cult—, *see* Auskult—.
Aus′dampfen, *v.n.* (*aux.* ſ.) to evaporate, exhale; (*aux.* h.) to cease steaming.
Aus′dämpfen, *v.a.* to cause to evaporate; to extinguish (*fire*); to smoke out (*a fox*).
Aus′därmen, *v.a.* to disembowel.
Aus′dauer, *f.* perseverance; persistence; steadiness, endurance.
Aus′dauern, *v.* I. *a.* to endure; to hold out against. II. *n.* (*aux.* h.) to hold out, last; to persevere, be steadfast. **—d,** *p. & adj.* persevering, steadfast; perennial (*Bot.*).
Aus′dehnbar, *adj.* that may be extended, expanded; diffusible; ductile. **—keit,** *f.* expansibility; diffusibility; ductility.
Aus′dehn—en, *v.a.* to extend, enlarge, expand; to dilate; to spread out; **—en auf einen** *or* **eine S.** to extend to s.o. *or* s.th.; **im ausgedehnteſten Sinne,** in the widest sense; **weit ausgedehnt,** widespread; **ſich —en,** to expand, spread, develop. **—end,** *p. & adj.* expansive. **—ung,** *f.* expansion; extension; dimension; extent; comprehension (*of a term*); dilation; **—ung des Herzens,** diastole. *Comp.* **—ungs=kraft,** *f.* expansive force, elasticity.
Aus′denkbar, *adj.* imaginable, conceivable; capable of being reasoned out.
Aus′denken, *ir.v.a.* to contrive, invent, devise; to think out, follow out a train of thought; **ſich —,** to exhaust oneself by thinking; **ſich** (*dat.*) **etwas —,** to imagine; **ich kann mir kein paſſendes Geſchenk für ihn —,** I cannot think of a suitable present for him.
Aus′deut—en, *v.a.* to interpret, explain (*a dream*); to decipher; **übel —en,** to misinterpret. **—ung,** *f.* construction, interpretation.
Aus′dienen, *v.n.* (*aux.* h.) to serve (*out*) one's time; to end a term of service; to become superannuated; **ein ausgedienter Profeſſor,** an emeritus professor; **ein ausgedienter Soldat,** a soldier who has served his time, an old soldier, a veteran.
Aus′drechſeln, *v.a.* to hollow out (*on a lathe*); to mould pottery (*on the wheel*); to finish turning; to elaborate.
Aus′drehen, *v.a.* to turn out, turn off, put out (*a lamp, gas*).
Aus′dreſchen, *ir.v.a.* to thrash out.
Aus′druck, *m.* (—s, *pl.* Ausdrücke) expression; phrase; term; **Geſichts—,** expression of countenance; **ein veralteter —,** an archaism; **ein überladener —,** pleonasm; **Kunſt—,** technical term; **bildlicher —,** figurative term, expression; **verblümter —,** allegorical expression; **mit —,** with expression (*Mus.*). *Comp.* **—s=art,** *f.* style (of expressing oneself). **—s=leer, —s=los,** *adj.* expressionless, devoid of expression. **—s=voll,** *adj. & adv.* expressive.
Aus′drucken, *v.a.* to print in full, print at full length; to express (clearly, *Typ.*); to work off (*a form*).
Aus′drück—en, *v.a.* to press, to squeeze out; to strain, wring; to express, utter; **nicht mit Worten auszudrücken,** inexpressible. **—lich,** *adj. & adv.* express(ly). **—lichkeit,** *f.* expressness (*of instructions, etc.*), explicitness.
Aus′duft—en, *v.n.* (*aux.* ſ.) to exhale (*in perfume*). **—ung,** *f.* exhalation (*from flowers, etc.*); bouquet (*of wine*).
Aus′dulden, *v.* I. *a.* to endure (*sufferings*) to the end. II. *n.* to cease to suffer; **er hat ausgeduldet,** he endured to the end, his sufferings are over; he is dead.
Aus′dunſtbar, *adj.* evaporable. **—keit,** *f.* evaporability.
Aus′dunſten, *v.n.* (*aux.* ſ.) to evaporate, pass off in vapour *or* perspiration.
Aus′dünſt—en, *v.a.* to sweat out; to exhale. **—ung,** *f.* evaporation; effluvium; exhalation; perspiration; **ſchädliche —ungen,** damps, night perspirations; **unmerkliche —ung,** *f.* imperceptible perspiration; **anſteckende —ung,** contagious effluvium.
Auseinan′der, *adv.* asunder, apart; separated. *Comp.* **—bringen, —thun,** *ir.v.a.* to separate, sunder, divide. **—fahren,** *ir.v.n.* (*aux.* ſ.) to start asunder, to separate suddenly; to diverge; **—fahrende Strahlen,** divergent rays. **—legen,**

v.a. to display; to take to pieces; to explain. **—setzen,** *v.a.* to put asunder; to explain, set forth, analyse; **sich mit jemandem —setzen,** to arrange, come to an understanding; compound with a person, to dissolve partnership.

Aus'eisen, *v.a.* to clear of ice; to get out of ice.

Aus'eitern, *v.n.* (*aux.* **h.**) to cease to suppurate; (*aux.* **s.**) to discharge (*matter, pus*).

Aus'erkiesen, Aus'erküren, *v.a.* to choose, select. **auserkoren,** *p.p. & adj.* chosen, elect, selected.

Aus'erlesen, I. *ir.v.a.* to choose, select. II. *p.p. & adj.* choice, picked, select; **sie ist wie —,** she is especially chosen, as it were.

Aus'ersehen, *ir.v.a.* to choose, select, pick out; to destine, to doom.

Aus'erwähl—en, *v.a.* to select, choose out; to predestinate; **ein —tes Gefäß** (*or* **Rüstzeug**), a chosen vessel (*B.*); **die —ten,** the elect; **seine —te,** his love, his intended wife.

Aus'essen, *ir.v.a.* to eat up; to clear a dish; to pay *or* suffer for (*faults*).

Aus'fächsern, *v.a.* to provine; **einen Weinstock —,** to propagate a vine.

Aus'fädeln, *v.a.* to unthread; to unravel, unweave; **sich —,** to ravel out.

Aus'fahr—en, *ir.v.* I. *a.* to deepen, *or* cut up, (*a road*) by driving; to hollow out, rabbet; to export; to take out for a drive; **ein ausgefahrener Weg,** a bad, rutty, bumpy road. II. *n.* (*aux.* **s.**) to drive out (*in a carriage, etc.*); to mount the shaft; to put to sea; to go out of (*as devils from one possessed; B.*); to emerge; to break out (*as an eruption*); to set out (in a hurry); **—ende Lichtstrahlen,** emergent rays; **gegen einen —en,** to break out in anger against one; **der Fuß fuhr mir aus,** my foot slipped. **—t,** *f.* carriage airing; drive; going out (*in a boat*); setting out, excursion; excursion; porte cochère, the opening out (*of a bay or canal*); getting out of the pit. *Comp.* **—schacht,** *m.* upcast shaft.

Aus'fall, *m.* (—(e)s, *pl.* **Ausfälle**) falling out; faling off; prolapsus (*Med.*); shedding (*of grain from the ear*); sally, sortie; pass, lunge; result (*of an enterprise*); deficit; attack; invective. *Comp.* **—gatter,** *n.*, **—(s)=pforte, —(s)=thor,** *n., f.* postern-gate, sally-post.

Aus'fall—en, *ir.v.* I. *n.* (*aux.* **s.**) to fall out; to shed, fall out of the ear; to make a pass, a lunge (**gegen einen,** at one); not to take place; to sally forth, make a sortie; to fall short, prove deficient; to end, turn out, result; **das Bild ist gut ausgefallen,** the picture has turned out well, is a (great) success; **die Zähne fallen ihm aus,** he is losing his teeth; **es fiel gegen ihn aus,** it went against him; **die Schule fällt heute aus,** there is no school to-day. II. *a.* **sich** (*dat.*) **den Arm —en,** to dislocate one's arm by falling. **—end,** *adj.* aggressive; **er wurde —end,** he became personal.

Aus'fällig, *adj.* aggressive, insulting.

Aus—fasern, —fäsern, *v.a.* to unravel.

Aus'fechten, *ir.v.* I. *a.* to fight out. II. *n.* (*aux.* **h.**) to give over fighting.

Aus'federn, *v.n.* (*aux.* **h.**) to moult.

Aus'feg—en, *v.a.* to sweep out, to cleanse (*a well*); to drain (*a person's purse*); to purge. **—sel,** *n.* (—sels) sweepings.

Aus'feilen, *v.a.* to file out; to polish; to trim. **ausgefeilt,** *p.p. & adj.* elaborate.

Aus'fertig—en, *v.a.* to draw up (*a deed, any paper*); to make out (*an appointment; bills, etc.*); to execute (*an order*); to carry out (*a plan*); to equip, fit out; to portion (*children*); to despatch (*business*); **einen Paß —en,** to issue, make out a passport. **—ung,** *f.* despatch (*of business*); execution (*of a deed, etc.*); portioning; equipment; issuing (*of an order*). *Comp.* **—ungs=tag,** *m.* date (*of issue, of despatch*).

Aus'feuern, *v.* I. *a.* to heat thoroughly; to burn out (*Coop.*). II. *n.* (*aux.* **h.**) to cease firing; to lash out; **hinten —,** to kick (*of horses*).

Aus'filzen, *v.a.* to line with felt; to stuff with hair (*saddles, etc.*); to snub, rebuke.

Aus'findbar, *adj.* discoverable; **— machen,** to discover.

Aus'find—en (*us.* **herausfinden**), *ir.v.a.* to find out, discover. **—ig,** *adj. & adv.* (*only with* **machen**); **mache Genossen von gutem Rufe —ig,** seek out associates of good reputation; **ein Mittel —ig machen,** to devise an expedient.

Aus'fischen, *v.a.* to draw fish (*a pond, etc.*): to fish out (*secrets*).

Aus'flammen, *v.a.* to scale (*a gun*).

Aus'flechten, *ir.v.a.* to unplait, untwist; to line with wickerwork; to mend (*hurdles, etc.*).

Aus'flicken, *v.a.* to patch up.

Aus'fliegen, *ir.v.n.* (*aux.* **s.**) to fly out; to escape, run away; to make an excursion; to leave home; **er ist eben erst ausgeflogen,** he has left home for the first time.

Aus'fließen, *ir.v.n.* (*aux.* **s.**) to flow out; to discharge itself; to issue; to emanate.

Aus'fluchen, *v.* I. *a.* to curse. II. *n.* (*aux.* **h.**) to cease cursing.

Aus'flucht, *f.* (*pl.* **Ausflüchte**) flight, act of fleeing; evasion, shift, subterfuge; **bei seiner ersten —,** at his first setting out; **eine elende, kahle —,** a shuffling excuse; **Ausflüchte machen** (*or* **suchen**) to dodge, shuffle, prevaricate.

Aus'flug, *m.* (—s, *pl.* **Ausflüge**) act of flying out, flight; ramble, trip, excursion; first flight (*of young birds*); fledglings; entrance (*to a beehive*); pigeon-hole.

Aus'flügler, *m.* (—s, *pl.* —) excursionist, tripper (*coll.*)

Aus'fluß, *m.* (—(ss)es, *pl.* **Ausflüsse**) a flowing out, sluice; effluence; discharge (*of matter*); outlet, issue, mouth; flux, issue; emanation; exhalation.

Aus'flut, *f.* outlet, waste-weir; channel.

Aus'folg—en, *v.a. & n.*; **einem etwas —en** *or* **—en lassen,** to deliver up a th. to s.o., to have a th. delivered up. *Comp.* **—e=schein,** *m.* bill of delivery.

Aus'forderer, *m.* (—s, *pl.* —) challenger.

Aus'forder—n (*us.* **Herausfordern**), *v.a.* to call out for a duel, to defy; **Trumpf —n,** to lead trumps. **—ung,** *f.* challenge; defiance. *Comp.* **—ungs=brief,** *m.* letter of defiance, written challenge.

Aus'fördern, *v.a.* to dig, get out of, to get up (*Min.*); to effect, produce.

Aus'forsch—en, *v.a.* to enquire after; to search, fish, trace, hunt out; **einen —en,** to pump a person; **jemandes Meinungen —en,** to sound one (*as to his views, etc.*). **—er,** *m.* (—ers, *pl.* —er) investigator; pryer, spy; discoverer. **—ung,** *f.* investigation; sifting; prying out. *Comp.* **—ungs=methode,** *f.* method of investigation.

Aus'frag—en, *reg. & ir.v.a.* to ascertain by questioning; to sound, pump (*a person*). **—er,** *m.* (—ers, *pl.* —er) interrogator. **—erei',** *f.* pumping, sounding (*of a person*).

Aus'fressen, *ir.v.a.* to eat up, consume; to hollow out; to waste; to corrode; to do something forbidden, to make mischief (*coll.*); **was hat er ausgefressen?** what evil has he done? (*coll.*); **der Junge hat wieder einmal etwas ausgefressen,** the boy has again made some mischief (*coll.*).

Aus'frieren, *ir.v.n.* (*aux.* **s.**) to freeze up; to freeze right to the bottom; to be injured by freezing; (*aux.* **h.**) to cease to freeze.

Aus'fuchteln, *v.a.* to belabour (*with the flat of a sword*); to thrash soundly.

Aus'fuhr, *f.* exportation; export trade; **zur —**

geeignet, exportable. *Comp.* **—artikel,** *pl.* export-goods. **—handel,** *m.* export trade. **—prämie,** *f.* drawback (*C. L.*). **—schein,** *m.* bill of sufferance, cocket. **—waaren,** *pl.* exports. **—zoll,** *m.* export duty.

Aus'führbar, *adj.* exportable; practicable, feasible. **—keit,** *f.* practicability.

Aus'führ—en, *v.a.* to export; to transport (*criminals*); to purge; to carry into effect; to execute, carry out; to realise, work out; to fulfil (*an engagement*); **einem etwas —en,** to take s.th. away (*secretly*) from s.o., to pilfer (*coll.*); to prosecute (*a scheme; a lawsuit*); to finish (*a picture, a building*); to pursue (*a subject*); to draw (*a character*); to amplify (*a description*); to play (*a part*); to clean out (*a pond*). **—er,** *m.* (**—ers,** *pl.* **—er**) exporter; finisher; achiever. **—lich** (*pr.* **ausführ'lich**) I. *adj.* detailed, circumstantial; **—liche Erzählung,** a full, true and particular account. II. *adv.* in detail, circumstantially; **—lich schreiben,** to write fully; **ich bin bei Untersuchung des** 2c. **sehr —lich zu Werke gegangen,** I have been very particular in examining, *etc.* completely. **—lichkeit,** *f.* minuteness of detail; prolixity. **—ung,** *f.* carrying on, out; exportation; evacuation (*Med.*); prosecution (*of a scheme, etc.*); execution (*of an order*); realisation (*of a plan*); completion (*of a building, etc.*); performance (*of a play, etc.*); fulfilment (*of a contract, etc.*); **in** *or* **zur —ung bringen,** to put into practice, to carry into effect. *Comp.* **—ungs=gang,** *m.* excretory duct. **—ungs=röhre,** *f.* eduction-pipe (*which carries off expended steam from the cylinder of an engine*).

Aus'füll—en, *v.a.* to fill out; to stuff; to fill; to pour out, to empty; to stop, close; to supply (*a deficit*); to fill up (*time; a form, etc.*); **jemandes Stelle —en,** to supply a person's place. **—end,** *p. & adj.* expletive; **—ende Musik,** ritornello. **—ung,** *f.* act of filling up, out, padding; panelling, *etc. Comp.* **—ungs=partikel,** *f.* expletive particle. **—ungs=silbe,** *f.*, **—ungs=wort,** *n.* expletive.

Aus'fütter—n, *v.a.* to provide with forage; to feed up, fatten; to use up fodder. **—ung,** *f.*; **—ung der Stückpforten,** half-port (*Naut.*).

Aus'gabe, *f.* delivery (*of letters, etc.*); edition (*of a book*); expenditure; issue; distribution; publication, announcement; **in — bringen,** to expend, to charge; **— und Einnahme in Übereinstimmung bringen,** to make both ends meet, to make receipts balance expenses. *Comp.* **—buch,** *n.* cash book. **—rechnung,** *f.* calculation of expenditure.

Aus'gähren, *r. & ir.v.n.* (*aux.* **h.**) to cease fermenting; (*aux.* **s.**) to rise by fermentation.

Aus'gang, *m.* (**—(e)s,** *pl.* **Ausgänge**) act of going out, exit; outlet, vent, issue; passage out; issue, result; catastrophe, denouement; termination, end, close; exodus (*of the children of Israel*); procession (*of the Holy Ghost*); **klingender —,** feminine ending (*Metre*); **stumpfer —,** masculine ending (*Metre*); **einen — machen,** to take a walk; **den — halten,** to be churched; **der Fluß hat drei Ausgänge,** the river branches into three forks. *Comp.* **—s=punkt,** *m.* point of departure, starting-point. **—s=stück,** *n.* finale (*Mus.*). **—s=zettel,** *m.* permit. **—s=zoll,** *m.* export duty.

Aus'gäten, Aus'jäten, *v.a.* to weed out.

Aus'geb—en, *ir.v.* I. *a.* to give out; to distribute (*orders, etc.*); to deliver (*letters*); to deal (*cards*); to issue (*bank-notes; proclamations, etc.*); to spend, lay out (*money*); to give (*the word, Mil.*); to give (*a daughter in marriage*); to give out, pass off for; to set on foot (*a rumour*); to yield (*a profit*); **sich —en,** to spend all one's strength; to run short of money; **sich für adlig —en,** to pass oneself off for a nobleman; **er giebt sich für einen großen Gelehrten aus,** he pretends to be a great scholar. II. *n.* (*aux.* **h.**) to bear, yield, bring in; to yield abundantly; to sound; to give tongue (*as hounds*); **das Korn giebt nicht aus,** the corn falls short. **—er,** *m.* (**—ers,** *pl.* **—er**) distributor; drawer (*of a bill, etc.*); utterer (*of a cheque, etc.*); caterer; dispenser (*of drugs*). **—erin,** *f.* housekeeper. *Comp.* **—e=geld,** *n.* small change; pocket-money.

Aus'gebot, *n.* (**—es,** *pl.* **—e**) setting up for sale; first bid at an auction.

Aus'geburt, *f.* (*pl.* **—en**) offspring, production; abortion; **— der Hölle,** diabolical scheme; hell-born being, fiend.

Aus'gedinge, *n.* reservation, rights reserved.

Aus'gehen, *ir.v.n.* (*aux.* **s.**) to go out; to proceed; to start; to aim at; to fail, come to an end, be exhausted; to be fulfilled (*of dreams, etc.*); to come out (*as stains*); to come off (*as boots*); to fall out (*of hair*); to fade (*of colours*); to go out (*of light, etc.*); to become illegible; to be spent (*of money, etc.*); to result, terminate, end in; to project; to expire (*of time*); to die (*of plants*); to ramify (*Anat.*); to rise (*of dough*); **frei —,** to go free; **einen Befehl — lassen,** to issue a decree; **ein Buch im Druck — lassen,** to publish, edit a book; **er ist leer ausgegangen,** he has gone away empty-handed; **der heilige Geist geht vom Vater und Sohne aus,** the Holy Ghost proceedeth from the Father and the Son; **—de Waaren,** export goods; **ich gehe von dem Grundsatze aus,** I start from the principle that — **auf eine S.,** to aim at s.th.; **auf Bettel —,** to go a-begging; **er ging darauf aus mich zu ärgern,** his object was to annoy me; **sie gingen auf mein Verderben aus,** they plotted my ruin; **er schwatzte, bis ihm der Atem ausging,** he talked till he was out of breath; **die Geduld geht mir aus,** I lose all patience; **das Wort geht auf ein S aus,** the word ends in S; **wie wird diese Sache —?** how will this end?; **—der Winkel,** salient angle.

Aus'gekehlt, *p.p. & adj.* fluted.

Aus'gelassen, *p.p. & adj.* wild, unruly, frolicsome; wanton; extravagant, excessive. **—heit,** *f.* boisterousness; wildness; wantonness.

Aus'gemacht, *p.p. & adj.* settled; determined on, decided; confirmed, undoubted; arrant; **eine —e Wahrheit,** an undeniable truth; **ein —er Schurke,** a confirmed (out-and-out) rascal; **ein —er Kenner,** an undoubted connoisseur, an admitted authority.

Aus'genießen, *ir.v.a.* to enjoy to the utmost.

Aus'genommen, *p.p. & prep.* save, except, with the exception of, barring.

Aus'gepicht, *adj.* pitched out, seasoned; potproof (*fam.*); **—e Kehlen,** well-seasoned throats; **eine —e Gurgel haben,** to be a hard drinker (*coll.*).

Aus'geschnitten, *p.p.* cut out; cut to shape (*of postage stamps*); low-bodied (*dress*).

Aus'gewitzt, *adj.*; **—e Leute,** very clever people.

Aus'gezackt, *p.p.* scalloped (*of postage stamps*).

Aus'gezeichnet, *also pron.* **Ausgezeich'net,** *p.p. & adj.* excellent; distinguished, illustrious.

Aus'giebig, *adj.* plentiful, abundant, rich.

Aus'gieß—en, *ir.v.a.* to pour out; to diffuse, shed; to fill up, load (*a stick with lead*); to vent (*one's anger*); **das Kind mit dem Bade —en,** to throw away the good with the bad, to act without discernment; **sein Herz —en,** to unbosom oneself. **—ung,** *f.* effusion; libation; descent (*or* coming) (*of the Holy Ghost*).

Aus'gipsen, *v.a.* to fill with plaster.

Aus'gleich, *m.* (**—es**) settlement, agreement. **—bar,** *adj.* compensable.

Aus'gleich—en, *ir.v.a.* to make even, to equal

ise; to compensate, make up for (*a loss, etc.*); to level; to settle (*a dispute, etc.*); to balance (*accounts*); **die Mißverständnisse sind ausgeglichen,** the misunderstandings have been arranged; **womit Sie meine Rechnung —en wollen,** balancing thereby my account. **—end,** *p. & adj.* compensatory. **—er,** *m.* (**—ers,** *pl.* **—er**) adjuster; reconciler; comptroller; compensating pendulum. **—ung,** *f.* equalisation, adjustment; balancing, clearing; balance; accommodation, settlement; compensation; levelling; arrangement; **zur —ung dieses Gegenstandes,** in order to close this transaction. *Comp.* **—ungs=münze,** *f.* cash balance, odd money. **—ungs=wage,** *f.* adjusting scale.

Aus'gleiten, *ir.v.n.* (*aux.* **s.**) to slip, slide.

Aus'glimmen, *ir.v.n.* (*aux.* **h.**) to go out gradually.

Aus'glitschen, *v.n.* (*aux.* **s.**) to slip, slide (*coll.*).

Aus'glühen, *v.a.* to heat thoroughly; to anneal.

Aus'graben, *ir.v.a.* to dig up, out; to disinter, exhume; to excavate; to unearth (*a badger*); to grub (*a tree-root*); to engrave, sink.

Aus'gräten, *v.a.* to bone (*a fish*).

Aus'greifen, *ir.v.* I. *a.* to seize, pick out (*of a number*); to handle, feel; to wear out. II. *n.* (*aux.* **h.**) to stretch; to step out (*of horses*).

Aus'gründen, *v.a.* to groove out; to flute; to carve in high relief.

Aus'guck, *m.* look-out (*Naut.*).

Aus'guck—en, *v.a.* to look, peep out. **—er,** *m.* (**—ers,** *pl.* **—er**) look-out man (*Naut.*).

Aus'guß, *m.* (**—(ss)es,** *pl.* **Ausgüsse**) effusion, outpouring; sink; gutter, drain; spout (*of a vessel*). *Comp.* **—pfännchen,** *n.* ingot mould. **—rinnen, —röhren,** *pl.* drain-pipes.

Aus'hacken, *v.a.* to hew, hack out; to scallop; to grub up; to cut up; to rough-hew; to pick out (*the eyes*).

Aus'haken, Aus'häkeln, *v.a.* to unhook, hook out, unclasp.

Aus'halftern, *v.a.* to unhalter; **sich —,** to slip one's neck out of the halter.

Aus'halt—en, *ir.v.* I. *a.* to hold out, endure, bear; to stand (*a test*); to sustain (*a siege*); to weather, ride out (*at anchor*) (*a storm*); to sustain, prolong (*a note*); to withstand (*temptation*); **es ist nicht zum —en,** it is not to be borne; **seine Zeit —en,** to serve one's time. II. *n.* (*aux.* **h.**) to endure; to last; to persevere; to hold out; **dieses Kleid soll noch einen Winter —en,** this dress must last another winter; **in diesem Hause halten die Dienstboten nicht lange aus,** the servants don't stay long in this house. **—er,** *m.* (**—ers,** *pl.* **—er**) note to be sustained (*Mus.*). *Comp.* **—ungs=zeichen,** *n.* pause, corona, hold (*Mus.*).

Aus'händigen, *v.a.* to hand over, deliver up.

Aus'hang, *m.* (**—s**) placard; goods hung out for sale *or* show.

Aus'hangen, *ir.v.n.* (*aux.* **h.**) to hang out, be suspended; **hier hängt nicht viel aus,** no great profit is to be made here *or* by this; there is not much money to be got in this place.

Aus'häng—en, *v.a.* to hang out (*a sign, a flag, etc.*); to post up (*a bill*); to take off its hinges (*a door*); to unship (*a rudder*); to make a show of. *Comp.* **—e=bogen,** *m.* specimen sheet, clean proof, advance-proof, advance sheet (*Typ.*). **—e=schild,** *n.* sign (*of an inn, etc.*); signboard; pretence, false show; **unter dem —eschild freisinniger Gedanken,** under the pretence of liberal ideas. **—e=zettel,** *m.* placard.

Aus'harren, *v.n.* (*aux.* **h.**) to endure to the end, wait, hold out.

Aus'hau, *m.* (**—es**) act of hewing; lopping, pruning; glade.

Aus'hauch, *m.* (**—es**) act of exhaling; exhalation; breath; fume.

Aus'hauchen, *v.* I. *a.* to exhale; **seine Seele —,** to breathe one's last, expire. II. *a.* (*aux.* **h.**) to expire.

Aus'hauen, *ir.v.a.* to hew out; **eine Bildsäule in Marmor —,** to hew out a statue in marble, to carve; to thin (*a forest*); to cut up (*a slaughtered animal*); to lop (*trees*); to engrave (*an inscription*); to flog (*coll.*); **ein ausgehauenes Kohlenfeld,** an exhausted coal-mine.

Aus'häuten, *v.a.* to skin, flay; **sich —,** to cast the skin.

Aus'heb—en, *ir.v.a.* to lift out *or* up; to take up (*a plant, etc.*); to take off the hinges (*of a door, etc.*); to draw out (*with a siphon*); to lift up the detents (*Horol.*); to lift out the form (*Typ.*); to pick out, select; to signalize, distinguish; to draw (*recruits*); to tell off, levy (*soldiers for special duty*); **sich den Arm —en,** to dislocate one's arm; **ein Ausgehobener,** recruit. **—er,** *m.* (**—ers,** *pl.* **—er**) ratch (*Horol.*); a machine for lifting and transplanting; trowel; recruiting officer. **—ung,** *f.* levy, conscription, draft. *Comp.* **—e=span,** *m.* composing-stick (*Typ.*).

Aus'hecken, *v.a.* to hatch; to plot, brew, devise, contrive; **eine Taube heckt keinen Adler aus,** you can't make a silk purse out of a sow's ear (*prov.*).

Aus'heilen, *v.* I. *a.* to heal *or* cure perfectly. II. *n.* to be healed, heal up.

Aus'helf—en, *ir.v.* I. *n.* (*aux.* **h.**) to help out; to aid; to accommodate, supply with. II. *a.* to help off. **—er,** *m.* (**—ers,** *pl.* **—er**), **—in,** *f.* (*pl.* **—innen**) help, helper; occasional assistant.

Aus'hieb, *m.* (**—s,** *pl.* **—e**) what is hewn *or* cut out; opening of shafts. **—meißel,** *m.* hewing chisel.

Aus'hilfe, *see* **Aushülfe.**

Aus'höhl—en, *v.a.* to hollow out; to groove; to chamfer, flute; to excavate; to undermine. **ausgehöhlt,** *p.p. & adj.* striate (*Bot.*). **—ung,** *f.* excavation; grooving; fluting (*of a column, etc.*); **die —ung auf einer Armbrust,** the groove of a crossbow.

Aus'hol—en, *v.* I. *a.*; **einen —en,** to pump one, ascertain by pumping. II. *n.* (*aux.* **h.**) to lift the arm (*for throwing, striking, etc.*); **zu einem Sprunge —en,** to take a run in leaping; **weit —en,** to go far back in narrating anything. **—er,** *m.* (**—ers,** *pl.* **—er**) name of certain ropes (*Naut.*).

Aus'hören, *v.a.* to hear out, to hear to the end.

Aus'hub, *m.* (**—es**) levy, choice.

Aus'hülf—e, Aus'hilf—e, *f.* aid, assistance; stop-gap; accommodation; **ich habe ihn bloß als —e gebraucht,** I have only employed him as a stop-gap. **—s=koch,** *m.* assistant cook. **—s=lehrer,** *m.* teacher engaged for temporary assistance. **—s=schauspieler,** *m.* understudy. **—stellung,** *f.* temporary situation. **—s=weise,** *adv.* as a makeshift, temporarily.

Aus'hülsen, *v.a.* to shell, hull (*peas, etc.*).

Aus'hungern, *v.a.* to starve out; to starve.

Aus'jagen, *v.* I. *a.* to hunt out, expel; to unearth (*a fox*). II. *n.* (*aux.* **s.**) to ride out hard; (*aux.* **h.**) **er hat ausgejagt,** his hunting days are over.

Aus'jäten, *see* **Ausgäten.**

Aus'kämpfen, *v.* I. *a.* to fight out. II. *n.* (*aux.* **h.**) to cease fighting.

Aus'kauen, *v.a.* to chew out, extract by chewing.

Aus'kauf, *m.* (**—es,** *pl* **Auskäufe**) buying out *or* up; outbidding; ransom.

Aus'kaufen, *v.a.* to buy out, buy the whole stock; to forestall; to outbid; **die Zeit —,** to make the most of one's time; **die Gelegenheit —,** to improve the occasion.

Aus'kehl—en, *v a.* to chamfer, to flute. **—ung,** *f.* fluting, grooving; chamfer.

Aus'kehr—en, *v.a.* to sweep out, sweep clean. **—icht,** *n.* (—s) sweepings.

Aus'keilen, *v.* I. *a.* to fit, provide with wedges; to thrash (*vulg.*). II. *r.* & *n.* (*aux.* **h.**) to end in a wedge; **der Gang keilt (sich) aus,** the lode disappears suddenly.

Aus'keltern, *v.a.* to press out (*wine*).

Aus'kerben, *v.a.* to notch, indent; to mill (*the edge of a coin*). **ausgekerbt,** *p.p.* & *adj.* engrailed (*Her.*), serrated; **ein ausgekerbtes Blatt,** a notched leaf.

Aus'kernen, *v.a.* to stone (*fruit*); to take out the kernel; to cull, pick out; to seize on the gist of.

Aus'klagen, *v.a.* to sue for, to demand, prosecute; **sich —,** to tell all one's grievances.

Aus'klatschen, *v.a.* to slap; to hiss off (*the stage*); to condemn (*a play*); to blurt out.

Aus'klauben, *v.a.* to pick out (*with the fingers*); to cull (*ore*); to think out, devise.

Aus'kleben, *v.a.* to stop (*a hole*); to paper; **eine Schachtel mit Papier —,** to line a box with paper.

Aus'kleid—en, *v.* I. *a.* to undress; **—en helfen,** to assist in undressing. II. *r.* to take off one's clothes; to dress up. **—ung,** *f.* act of undressing. *Comp.* **—e=zimmer,** *n.* dressing-room.

Aus'klingeln, *v.a.* to publish by ringing a bell.

Aus'klingen, *ir.v.n.* (*aux.* **h.**) to cease to sound, to die away (*as an echo*); **die Rede klang in ein Hoch aus,** the speech ended with cheers.

Aus'klopfen, *v.a.* to beat out (*as dust*); to clean by beating; to thrash, drub.

Aus'klügeln, *v.a.* to subtilise, to excogitate, to discover by subtilising.

Aus'kneifen, *v.a.* to pinch out; to slip off; to leave secretly, to run away (*coll*).

Aus'knobeln, *v.a.* to settle by dicing; **eine Flasche Wein —,** to settle by throwing dice who is to pay for a bottle of wine.

Aus'kochen, *v.*I. *a.* to extract by boiling; to boil sufficiently; to scald (*a vessel*); **ausgekochtes Fleisch,** meat which has become juiceless by overboiling. II. *n.* (*aux.* **f.**) to boil over *or* away; (*aux.* **h.**) to cease boiling.

Aus'kommen, I. *ir.v.n.* (*aux.* **f.**) to come, go out; to break out (*of fire*); to break out of the shell; to become public, get abroad; to hold good, answer the purpose; to agree, live peaceably with; to make do; **ich kann unmöglich damit —,** I can't possibly manage with so little; **er kommt kaum mit seinen Einkünften aus,** he barely makes both ends meet; **er wird mit dieser Entschuldigung nicht —,** this excuse will not do; **es ist mit ihm nicht auszukommen,** there is no living with him; **ich komme nicht mit der Seide aus,** I shall not have enough silk for it; **ich werde schon mit ihm —,** I shall no doubt manage to get along with him. II. *subst. n.* act of getting out; competence. peaceable intercourse; **ein — treffen,** to come to some agreement, to find ways and means.

Aus'körnen, *v.a.* to pick out the grains.

Aus'kosten, *v.a.* to select by tasting; to taste fully, to experience thoroughly; to consume by tasting.

Aus'kramen, I. *v.a.* to expose for sale; to display, make a parade of; to show up, to let see. II. *subst.n.* ostentatious display.

Aus'kratzen, *v.* I. *a.* to scratch out, erase. II. *n.* (*aux.* **h.**) to cease scratching; (*aux.* **f.**) to run away, to scratch (*vulg.*).

Aus'kriechen, *ir.v.n.* (*aux.* **f.**) to creep out of; to come forth (*from the shell*); **der Wind kriecht aus und ein,** the wind chops about.

Aus'kühlen, *v.a.* & *n.* (*aux.* **f.**) to cool thoroughly.

Auskult—a'nt, *m.* auscultator (*Med.*); young lawyer attending at court; first grade of a barrister (*Law*). **—atio'n,** *f.* auscultation, stethoscopy. **—a'tor,** *m.* = **—ant** (*Law*).

Auskultie'ren, *v.a.* to auscult, to practise auscultation (*Med.*); to listen, to attend (*at a court of law*).

Aus'kund—en, Aus'kundschaft—en, *v.a.* to explore; to discover by spies; to reconnoitre. **—er,** *m.* spy, informer.

Aus'kunft, *f.* (*pl.* **Auskünfte**) way out; means of subsistence; intelligence, information; expedient, resource; **ich fragte ihn um nähere — über, ꝛc.,** I asked him for fuller particulars as to, *etc.* **—ei',** *f.* intelligence-office, inquiry office. *Comp.* **—s=bureau,** *n. see* **Aus'=kunftei. —s=mittel,** *n.* resource, expedient. **—stelle,** *f.* intelligence office.

Aus'künsteln, *v.a.* to invent, contrive (*with too great art*); to elaborate.

Aus'lachen, *v.* I. *a.* to laugh at; to deride, laugh to scorn; **sich —,** to laugh one's fill. II. *n.* (*aux.* **h.**) to cease laughing. *Comp.* **—s=wert, —s=würdig,** *adj.* & *adv.* ridiculous.

Aus'lad—en, *ir.v.a.* to unload, unlade; discharge; to project; **ein Gewehr —en,** to draw the charge from a gun; **sich —en,** to break out, erupt. **—er,** *m.* (**—ers,** *pl.* **—er**) unloader, discharging-rod (*Phys.*). **—ung,** *f.* unloading; drawing (*of a gun charge*); projection (*Arch.*). *Comp.* **—e=kosten,** *pl.* charges for unloading. **—e=lohn,** *m.* tonnage. **—e=ort,** *m.* port of discharge; landing-place, wharf.

Aus'lage, *f.* (*pl.* **—n**) disbursement; outlay, expenses; advance (*C. L.*); stall, bench (*for exposure of wares*); posture of defence, guard (*Fenc.*); **die — wieder erstatten,** to reimburse; **es lohnt die —n nicht,** it does not pay.

Aus'land, *n.* (**—es**), foreign country, foreign parts; **im —e,** abroad; **In= und Aus=land,** country and abroad; **Waaren vom —e,** foreign goods.

Aus'länd—er, *m.* (**—ers,** *pl.* **—er**) foreigner, alien. **—erei',** *f.* predilection for things foreign; affectation of foreign ways. **—isch,** *adj.* foreign, alien; exotic; outlandish.

Aus'langen, *v.n.* (*aux.* **h.**) to be sufficient, to suffice, to do; **zum Streiche —,** to lift up the arm to strike, to aim a blow; **diese Summe wird schwerlich —,** this sum will be scarcely sufficient; **du wirst mit dieser Entschuldigung nicht —,** this excuse will not help you.

Aus'längen, *v.a.* to stretch out, extend.

Aus'laß, *m.* (—(ss)es, *pl.* **Auslässe**) outlet.

Aus'lass—en, *ir.v.a.* to let out, let go; to let off; to give vent to; to melt; to leave out, omit; to overlook; to let out, widen; **seine Wut an einem —en,** to vent one's anger on a person; **ausgelassene Butter,** melted butter; **sich —en,** to express one's mind; **er ließ sich nicht weiter aus,** he did not explain himself further; **ein ausgelassenes Leben,** a riotous, dissolute life; **ein ausgelassenes Lachen,** an unrestrained, boisterous laugh. **—ung,** *f.* letting out; discharge (*from prison, etc.*); leaving out; omission; ellipse, ellipsis (*Rhet.*); elision, expressing an opinion, utterance, remark(s). *Comp.* **—ungs=zeichen,** *n.* apostrophe; mark of elision.

Aus'lauf, *m.* (**—es,** *pl.* **Ausläufe**) running out leakage; effusion; setting sail (*of a ship*); projection; mouth (*of a river*); net profit (*of salt-works*).

Aus'lauf—en, *ir.v.n.* (*aux.* **f.**) to run, flow out; to leak; to discharge itself into; to put to sea, to clear a port; to project (*Arch.*); to spread, run out; to branch out; to diverge; to come to an end; to run down, to cease running (*hourglass*); **der Befehl zum —en,** sailing orders; **die Erbsen laufen aus,** the peas drop out of the pods; **dünn —en,** to taper off; **spitz —en,**

to end in a point; (*aux.* h.) to finish running; **die ganze Sache ist auf einen Scherz ausgelaufen,** the whole matter ended in a joke. II. *a.* to convey away (*in a wheelbarrow*); to go over; **sich —en,** to take plenty of exercise by running about; to wear out *or* widen by running *or* friction. *Comp.* **—e=platz,** *m.* starting place.

Aus'läufer, *m.* (—s, *pl.* —) errand-boy; printer's devil; sucker, runner; spur (*of a mountain chain*); deserter (*Mil.*).

Aus'laugen, *v.a.* to wash in lye; to clear of lye.

Aus'laut, *m.* (—es) terminal sound (*letter or group of letters at the end of a word or a syllable*); **im —,** when final. **—en,** *v.n.* (*aux.* h.) to cease to sound; to end in; **die Wurzelsilbe lautet auf einen Konsonanten aus,** the root-syllable ends in a consonant. **—end,** *p. & adj.* final.

Aus'leben, *v.* I. *a.* to live to the end of; **sich —,** to live out one's nature; **sich voll und ganz —,** to live entirely according to the requirements of one's nature. II. *n.* (*aux.* h.) to cease to live, to die.

Aus'leer—en, *v.a.* to empty; to drain; to clear out (*a room, etc.*); to purge (*Med.*); to drench (*a horse*); **sich** (*dat.*) **das Herz —en,** to pour out one's heart. **—ung,** *f.* emptying out; evacuation (*Med.*); excretion. *Comp.* **—ungs=mittel,** *n.* purgative.

Aus'leg—en, *v.a.* to lay, spread out; to anchor (*a ship*) in the roads; to inlay; to lay out, spend; to explain, expound; (*refl.*) to get into position; to stand upon guard (*fenc.*); **ein Geschützrohr —en,** to dismount a gun; **Soldaten —en,** to change the quarters of soldiers; **eine Stelle falsch —en,** to misinterpret a passage; **etwas zum besten —en,** to put the best construction on a thing; **es wurde ihm als Stolz ausgelegt,** it was set down to his pride; **Geld auf Zinsen —en,** to put money out at interest. **—er,** *m.* (—ers, *pl.* —er) expositor, expounder; commentator; outrigger (*Naut.*). **—ung,** *f.* exposition, construction, interpretation; explanation; exegesis; laying out (*of money*); **die buchstäbliche —ung,** the literal interpretation; **die wahre —ung,** the true construction. *Comp.* **—ungs=kunst,** *f.* art of interpreting texts, hermeneutics. **—ungs=weise,** *adv.* by way of interpretation, exegetically.

Aus'leiden, *ir.v.n.* (*aux.* h.) to suffer to the end; to cease to suffer; **er hat ausgelitten,** his sufferings are over, he is dead.

Aus'leihen, *ir.v.a.* to lend out; to hire out.

Aus'lernen, *v.n.* (*aux.* h.) to finish one's apprenticeship; to finish learning; **man lernt nie aus,** one is never too old to learn; **diese Kunst lernt sich nie aus,** there is always something new to learn in this art. **ausgelernt,** *p.p. & adj.* experienced, practised; **— haben,** to have done learning; to be out of one's time (*as an apprentice*).

Aus'lese, *f.* (*pl.* —n) selection; assortment; elite, flower, the best, the pick; the choicest wine (*of a special kind, e.g.* **Vöslauer —,** superior Vöslau wine).

Aus'les—en, *ir.v.a.* to select, pick out; to sort; to cull (*flowers*); to pick clean; to read through *or* to the end. **—er,** *m.* (—ers, *pl.* —er), **—erin,** *f.* selecter, chooser; sorter.

Aus'lichten, *v.a.* to clear (*a wood*), prune (*trees*).

Aus'liefer—n, *v.a.* to hand over, deliver up. **—ung,** *f.* surrender, extradition (*of a criminal, etc.*); delivery. *Comp.* **—ungs=schein,** *m.* bill of delivery. **—ungs=vertrag,** *m.* extradition treaty.

Aus'liegen, *ir.v.n.* to lie out, to be put out, to be generally accessible.

Aus'lieger, *m.* (—s, *pl.* —) revenue cutter; guard-ship.

3

[1]**Aus'lösch—en,** *v.a.* to put out, extinguish; to efface, obliterate; to erase; to pay off (*a debt*); to blot out (*one's guilt, B.*). **—er,** *m.* (—ers, *pl.* —er) extinguisher (*of a candle*); quencher (*of a fire*). **—lich,** *adj.* that may be erased *or* extinguished. **—ung,** *f.* obliteration; extinction.

[2]**Aus'lösch—en,** *ir.v.n.* (*aux.* f.) to go out, be extinguished; to become illegible; to become extinct, to die; **die Lampe losch aus,** the lamp became extinguished.

Aus'losen, *v.a.* to draw lots for; to raffle.

Aus'lös—en, *v.a.* loosen, draw out, release; to cut out; to redeem, ransom; produce; **einen Arm —en,** to dislocate an arm; **auszulösen,** redeemable. **—ung,** *f.* act of releasing; redeeming; ransom; reimbursement; dislocation; ratch (*Horol.*).

Aus'lüften, *v.a.* to air thoroughly; **sich —,** to take an airing.

Aus'machen, *v.a.* to make out; to take out (*stains*); to shell (*peas, etc.*); to open (*oysters*); to draw (*poultry*); to extinguish (*fire, etc.*); to make up, constitute; to decide, arrange, determine; to settle (*a dispute*); to end (*a lawsuit*); to stipulate; to matter; to draw a cover (*Sport*); to procure, get for another; to discover; to amount to; **einen —,** to scold (*vulg.*); **es macht nichts aus,** it is of no consequence; **wir haben es so ausgemacht,** we have settled the matter thus; **es ist eine ausgemachte Sache,** it is a settled affair; **was hast du mit ihm auszumachen?** what have you to arrange with him?; **für ausgemacht annehmen,** to take for granted; **ausgemacht!** agreed!; **ein ausgemachter Narr, Schelm,** a downright fool, a thorough knave; **er ist ein ausgemachter Schurke,** he is an out and out villain; **einem einen Dienst —,** to procure one employment; **was ist ausgemacht worden?** what has been decided on?; **sie mögen es mit einander —,** let them fight it out between themselves. **—d,** *p. & adj.* constituent; amounting to.

Aus'mahlen, *v.a.* to grind thoroughly.

Aus'malen, *v.a.* to paint; to colour; to illuminate; to finish (*a picture*); **sich** (*dat.*) **etwas —,** to imagine s.th. (*in detail*).

Aus'marsch, *m.* (—es, *pl.* **Ausmärsche**) marching out, departure (*of troops*).

Aus'marschieren, *v.n.* (*aux.* f.) to march out.

Aus'mauern, *v.a.* to line with stones *or* masonry; to wall up.

Aus'mergeln, *v.a.* to emaciate; to exhaust (*land*); to enervate, debilitate; **ein ausgemergelter Wüstling,** a worn-out roué.

Aus'merz—en, *v.a.* to sort, pick, cull out; to reject, remove (*what is bad*); to take away, reject (*Math.*). **—ung,** *f.* abolition, abrogation, elimination, suppression, effacing, proscription, purification.

Aus'meß—en, *ir.v.a.* to measure out; to take the dimensions of; to survey; to gauge; to retail; to apportion. **—er,** *m.* (—ers, *pl.* —er) measurer; surveyor. **—ung,** *f.* measuring, measurement; survey; gauging; **die —ung eines Schiffes nehmen,** to take a ship's bearings.

Aus'mieten, *v.a.* to let out on hire; to dislodge by offering a higher rent; to take a lodging for another outside of one's own house.

Aus'misten, *v.a.* to cast the dung out, to cleanse (*a stable*).

Aus'möblieren, *v.a.* to fit up, furnish.

Aus'münd—en, *v.r. & n.* (*aux.* h.) to empty, discharge itself. **—ung,** *f.* mouth (*of a river*).

Aus'münzen, *v.a.* to coin; **geringer —,** to debase.

Aus'mustern, *v.a.* to discharge, reject (*soldiers*); to cast (*horses*); to discard; to expurgate (*pas-*

sages from a book); **einen Schriftsteller —**, to expurgate an author's writings.

Aus'nähen, *v.a.* to embroider; to stitch; to quilt; to adorn with needlework.

Aus'nahm—e, *f.* (*pl.* **—en**) exception; **ohne —e**, without exception, absolutely. *Comp.* **—e=fall,** *m.* exceptional case. **—gesetz,** *n.* exceptional law. **—s=satz,** *m.* exceptional clause. **—s=weise,** *adv.* by way of exception, exceptionally.

Aus'nehm—en, *ir.v.a.* to take out; to draw (*a fowl; a tooth*); to select; to except, exempt; **er nimmt alles auf Borg aus**, he takes everything on credit; **ausgenommen**, except; **sich —en**, to make a figure, be distinguished; to look, have a certain appearance; **sich schlecht —**, to look bad *or* ill; **diese Farbe nimmt sich sehr gut aus**, this colour looks very well. **—end,** *p. & adj.* rare, exceptional, extraordinary; exquisite. *adv.* exceedingly.

Aus'nutz—en, *v.a.* to wear out; to utilise fully. **—ung,** *f.* utilisation.

Aus'packen, *v.a.* to unpack.

Aus'pappen, *v.a.* to line with pasteboard.

Aus'pfänd—en, *v.a.* to seize, distrain. **—er,** *m.* (**—ers,** *pl.* **—er**) distrainer. **—ung,** *f.* distraint.

Aus'pfarren, *v.a.* to separate from a parish.

Aus'pfeifen, *ir.v.a.* to hiss off the stage (*an actor*); to condemn (*a play*).

Aus'pflastern, *v.a.* to pave (*completely*).

Aus'pflügen, *v.a.* to plough up, turn up in ploughing.

Aus'pichen, *v.a.* to coat the inside with pitch; **ein ausgepichter Magen**, the stomach of an ostrich (*i.e. a strong digestion*).

Aus'pinseln, *v.a.* to paint inside; to efface by painting over.

Auspi'zien, *n.pl.* auspices.

Aus'plätten, *v.a.* to smooth, to iron.

Aus'platzen, *v.n.* (*aux.* **f.**) to burst; to burst out; to blurt out.

Aus'plaudern, *v.a.* to blab, let out (*secrets, etc.*); **sich —**, to have a good talk.

Aus'plünder—n, *v.a.* to empty, strip, desolate by plunder. **—er,** *m.* (**—ers,** *pl.* **—er**) plunderer.

Aus'polstern, *v.a.* to stuff, pad; to line.

Aus'posaunen, *v.a.* to trumpet forth; to make universally known; **seinen eignen Ruhm —**, to blow one's own trumpet.

Aus'prägen, *v.a.* to stamp, impress; to coin.

Aus'predigen, *v.n.* (*aux.* **h.**) to have done preaching, come to the end of a sermon.

Aus'pressen, *v.a.* to crush, squeeze out; to extort, force from.

Aus'proben, *v.a.* to try thoroughly; **Wein —**, to taste wine.

Aus'prügeln, *v.a.* to cudgel soundly.

Aus'pumpen, *v.a.* to pump out; to exhaust (*air*).

Aus'putz, *m.* (**—es**) ornaments; trimming.

Aus'putzen, *v.a.* to clean, cleanse, sweep out; to polish up; to adorn, decorate; to snuff out (*a candle*); to prune (*trees*); to pick (*teeth, etc.*); to sponge (*a cannon*); to rebuke, blow up (*coll.*); **sich —**, to deck oneself out.

Aus'radieren, *v.a.* to scrape out, erase.

Aus'rändeln, Aus'randen, Aus'ränden, *v.a.* to surround with a beading; to jag the edges; **ausgerändete Blätter**, crenated leaves.

Aus'rangieren, *v.a.* to put away as useless; **ausrangierte Kleider**, cast off clothes.

Aus'rasen, *v.n.* (*aux.* **h.**) to cease raging, become quiet; to abate; **der Sturm hat sich ausgerast**, the storm has spent itself.

Aus'rauchen, *v.a.* to consume in smoking; to smoke out (*a fox, etc.*).

Aus'raufen, *v.a.* to pluck, tear out; **er raufte sich** (*dat.*) **die Haare aus**, he tore his hair.

Aus'räum—en, *v.a.* to clear out, away, off; to clean out · to gut (*a house*); **sich** (*dat.*) **die Ohren —en**, to clean one's ears. **—er,** *m.* (**—ers,** *pl.* **—er**) clearer out; gun-pick. **—ung,** *f.* act of clearing out, cleansing *or* removing.

Aus'rechn—en, *v.a.* to cast up (*a sum*); to make a calculation, calculate, compute. **—ung,** *f.* computation, calculation.

Aus'rede, *f.* (*pl.* **—n**) excuse, pretence; **gerichtliche —**, legal quibble; **nichts als —n**, nothing but evasions; **Sie sind nie um eine — verlegen**, you are never at a loss for an excuse.

Aus'reden, *v.* I. *n.* (*aux.* **h.**) to finish speaking, to speak freely; **laß mich —**, let me finish. II. *a.* **einem etwas —**, to dissuade from doing a thing, to talk one out of (*an opinion, etc.*). III. *r.* to excuse oneself from; to exculpate oneself; to have one's say out; **sich mit einem —**, to come to an understanding with a person after a thorough discussion.

Aus'regnen, *v.* I. *a.* to wash out, wash away. II. *r.* (*aux.* **h.**) to cease raining.

Aus'reiben, *ir.v.a.* to rub out, off, away.

Aus'reichen, *v.n.* (*aux.* **h.**) to suffice, do; to last.

Aus'reiß—en, *ir.v.* I. *a.* to pluck, tear out; to pull up; to extract (*a tooth*); **Unkraut —en**, to weed; **aus den Händen —en**, to wrench, snatch out of one's hands. II. *n.* (*aux.* **f.**) to run away, decamp, abscond (*coll.*); to bolt (*of a horse*); to desert (*Mil.*); to fail, be exhausted; to be worn, torn; **ausgerissene Knopflöcher**, worn out button-holes; **ausgerissene Deiche**, broken down dams, dykes. **—er,** *m.* (**—ers,** *pl.* **—er**) deserter; runaway (*coll.*).

Aus'reiten, *ir.v.a. & n.* (*aux.* **h.**) to ride out, take a ride.

Aus'renk—en, *v.a.* to dislocate. **—ung,** *f.* dislocation.

Aus'rennen, *ir.v.* I. *a.* to knock out in running. II. *n.* (*aux.* **h.**) to cease running; (*aux.* **f.**) to start from.

Aus'reuten, *v.a.* to root out, clear, eradicate.

Aus'rheden, *v.a.* to rig, fit out, equip (*a vessel*).

Aus'richt—en, *v.a.* to make straight *or* level; to turn outwards; to execute (*an order*); to deliver (*a message*); to accomplish (*a purpose*); to fulfil (*a bequest, etc.*); to defray (*expenses*); to give (*a dinner, etc.*); to prevail, effect; to rebuke; to calumniate (*obsol.*); **Sie können bei ihm viel —en**, you have great influence with him; **nichts —en**, to labour in vain; **damit ist nichts ausgerichtet**, that is of no avail, won't do; **Sie werden dabei nichts —en**, you won't be able to do anything in the matter; **richten Sie ihm meinen Gruß aus**, give him my kind regards, present my compliments to him; **ich werde es —en**, I shall not fail to do so; **Wild —en**, to draw a cover. **—er,** *m.* (**—ers,** *pl.* **—er**) one that does, executes, *etc.*; discoverer (*of a mine*); executor (*of a will*); defrayer (*of expense*). **—ung,** *f.* giving, getting up (*a banquet, etc.*); defraying (*expenses*); performance, execution, delivery; part of a dowry.

Aus'riefen, *v.a.* to chamfer, flute; to rifle (*the barrel of a gun*).

Aus'ringen, *ir.v.* I. *a.* to wring out; to dislocate; **einem etwas —**, to wrest something from one. II. *n.* (*aux.* **h.**) to finish wrestling; **er hat ausgerungen**, his struggles are over; he is dead.

Aus'rinnen, *ir.v.n.* (*aux.* **f.**) to run, trickle out.

Aus'ritt, *m.* (**—es,** *pl.* **—e**) ride, excursion on horseback; departure.

Aus'roden, *v.a.* to root out, stub up; to clear (*a forest*), prepare (*land*) for tillage.

Aus'rollen, *v.a.* to roll out; to unroll.

Aus'rott—en, *v.a.* to extirpate, exterminate, root out. **—er,** *m.* (**—ers,** *pl.* **—er**) extirpator. **—ung,** *f.* extirpation. Comp. **—ungs=krieg,** *m.* war of extermination.

Aus'rücken, *v.* I. *n.* (*aux.* **f.**) **to march out, to**

move out; aus dem Lager —, to decamp. II. *a.* to throw out of gear; eine Zeile —, to commence a new line (*Typ.*). **ausgerückt,** *p.p. & adj.* out of gear.

Aus'ruf, *m.* (—(e)s, *pl.* —e) cry; outcry; proclamation; public sale; exclamation; interjection.

Aus'ruf—en, *ir.v.* I. *a.* to proclaim; to publish (*banns*); to cry (*for sale*); to publish (*by the town crier*). II. *n.* (*aux.* h.) to cry out, ejaculate, exclaim; to cease crying, calling. **—er,** *m.* (—ers, *pl.* —er) crier, hawker; bellman, town-crier; herald. **—ung,** *f.* act of crying (*for sale*); proclaiming; publishing (*of banns*); cry; exclamation, outcry; **die —ungen der Verkäufer in den Straßen von London,** the cries of London. *Comp.* **—ungs=wort,** *n.* interjection (*Gram.*). **—ungs=zeichen,** *n.* mark of exclamation (*Gram.*).

Aus'ruhen, *v.n. & r.* to rest, take repose; — **von einer Anstrengung,** to rest from *or* after an exertion.

Aus'runden, *v.a.* to round; to round out.

Aus'rupfen, *v.a.* to pluck out.

Aus'rüst—en, *v.a.* to equip, fit out; **ein Kriegsschiff —en,** to fit out a man-of-war; **mit Vernunft ausgerüstet,** endowed with reason. **—er,** *m.* (—ers, *pl.* —er) fitter out, preparer. **—ung,** *f.* fitting out; preparation; outfit, equipment.

Aus'rutschen, *v.n.* (*aux.* s.) to slip, lose one's footing (*coll.*).

Aus'rütteln, *v.a.* to shake out; to shake soundly.

Aus'saat, *f.* (*pl.* —en) sowing; seed; seed-corn; — **in Löcher,** dibbling. *Comp.* **—korb,** *m.* hopper.

Aus'säen, *v.a.* to sow (*seed*); to disseminate (*errors; discord, etc.*).

Aus'sage, *f.* (*pl.* —n) declaration, assertion, statement; deposition; predicate (*Gram.*); **eine gerichtliche — thun,** to give evidence, make a deposition; — **anhören,** to receive an audit (*Law*); **eidliche —,** deposition on oath; **Zeugen—,** evidence; affidavit; **seine — beweisen,** to prove one's statement; **nach — aller,** by all accounts; **auf seine — hin,** from what he says. *Comp.* **—begriff,** *m.* predicate. **—satz,** *m.* affirmative proposition. **—weise,** *f.* mood (*indicative, subjunctive m.*). **—wort,** *n.* word that predicates *or* affirms, verb.

Aus'sagen, *v.a.* to state, declare, assert; to depose, give evidence; to say out *or* entirely; to express; **die Zeitwörter sagen etwas von einem Dinge aus,** verbs affirm something of the subject; **eidlich etwas —,** to make a sworn deposition; **ich mag es nicht —,** I don't like to say it out.

Aus'sägen, *v.a.* to saw out.

Aus'satz, *m.* (—es) leprosy; scab (*in sheep*); tetter (*in horses*); the lead (*Bill.*); show, display (*for sale*).

Aus'sätzig, *adj.* leprous. **—e(r),** *m.* leper.

Aus'saufen, *v.a.* to drink up, to empty.

Aus'saug—en, *ir.v.a.* to suck out; to drain, exhaust, impoverish; **einem Volke das Blut —en,** to eat up a people, to ruin a nation; **ein Kind —en lassen,** to allow a child to suck his (her) fill. **—er,** *m.* (—ers, *pl.* —er) sucker; extortioner; parasite; parasitical plant.

Aus'säugen, *v.* I. *a.* to suckle the full time. II. *n.* (*aux.* h.) to leave off suckling.

Aus'schaben, *v.a.* to scrape out.

Aus'schachteln, *v.a.* to rub inside with shave-grass; to take out of a bandbox; to eliminate.

Aus'schachten, *v.a.* to sink, excavate.

Aus'schäften, *v a.* to pierce a ship for guns.

Aus'schalen, *v.a.* to line with laths, to batten; to lath (*a ceiling*).

Aus'schälen, *v.a.* to shell; to peel; to blanch (*almonds*); to cut out.

Aus'schalt—en, *v.a.* to eliminate; to put out of use *or* circuit. **—er,** *m.* cut out, commutator for breaking contact. **—ung,** *f.* putting out of circuit.

Aus'schämen, *v.r.* to be thoroughly ashamed (*vulg.*); to lose all sense of shame (*obs.*).

Aus'schank, *m.* (—(e)s), retail-license; public house, ale house.

Aus'scharren, *v.* I. *a.* to rake, scratch up *or* out; to dig up; to insult; to drive away by scraping with the feet (*way of expressing discontent*). II. *n.* (*aux.* h.) to fling, kick out; to scrape with the feet.

Aus'scharten, *v.a.* to notch, indent.

Aus'schatt—en, —iren, *v.a.* to shade (*Paint.*).

Aus'schauen, *v.* I. *a.* (*aux.* h.) to look out; (**nach einem,** for one). II. *n.* to look, to have an appearance; **traurig —,** to look sad.

Aus'schaufeln, *v.a.* to scoop, shovel out.

Aus'scheid—en, I. *ir.v.a.* to separate; to reject; to segregate; to secrete (*Med.*); **—ende Gefäße,** secretory vessels. II. *ir.v.n.* (*aux.* s.) to secede, to withdraw from a body of people, a club, a party, etc.; **—en aus einem Verbande,** to leave a society; **—en aus dem Geschäftsbetrieb,** to retire from business. III. *subst.n.* **—ung,** *f.* separation; secession; secretion; **—ungs=organe,** *n.pl.* excretive organs.

Aus'schelten, *ir.v.a.* to reprimand severely, scold; — **wegen einer S.,** to rebuke for a th.

Aus'schenken, *v.a.* to pour, fill out; to help one to (*wine, etc.*); to sell, retail (*liquors*).

Aus'scheuern, *v.a.* to scour out; to wear out by scouring.

Aus'schicken, *v.a.* to send out; to send on an errand; **auf Kommando —,** to detach, draft off (*Mil.*).

Aus'schieben, *ir.v.a.* to shove out; to draw (*bread from the oven*); to draw out, lengthen (*a telescope-table*); to finish (*a game at bowls*).

Aus'schieß—en, I. *ir.v.a.* to shoot out; to shoot for (*a prize*); to improve (*by shooting*); to wear out by shooting; to reject, cast out (*from a number*); to sort; to impose (*the columns, Typ.*); to discharge (*ballast, etc.*); **ein Revier —en,** to shoot all the game in a preserve; **ein Hauptmann wurde ausgeschossen,** a captain was selected (*obs.*). II. *ir.v.n.* (*aux.* s.) to sprout, shoot forth. III. *subst.n.* act of shooting out, *etc.*; rejection; projection of a ship's stem. **—er,** *m.* (—ers, *pl.* —er) sorter (*in paper-mills*). **—ung,** *f. see* **—en,** III.

Aus'schiff—en, *v.* I. *a.* to put on shore, disembark, land; detrain (*Mil.*). **—ung,** *f.* disembarking, disembarkation; detrainment of troops (*Mil.*). II. *n.* (*aux.* s.) to put to sea.

Aus'schimpfen, *v.a.* to scold thoroughly, abuse (*vulg.*).

Aus'schirren, *v.a.* to unharness.

Aus'schlachten, *v.a.* to cut up for sale (*a carcase*); to parcel out, to sell in portions, to retail; to take out the entrails (*of a slaughtered beast*).

Aus'schlafen, *ir.v.* I. *n.* (*aux.* h.) to sleep one's fill *or* enough. II. *a.* to sleep away; **sich —,** *v. refl.* to have one's sleep out, to sleep one's fill; to enjoy a good night's rest; **ausgeschlafen haben,** to have done sleeping; **ausgeschlafen sein,** to be wide awake, to be stirring; **seinen Rausch —,** to sleep oneself sober; **guten Morgen! Ausgeschlafen?** good morning! Did you get a good sleep? (*coll.*).

Aus'schlag, *m.* (—es, *pl.* **Ausschläge**) the first blow; kick (*of horses*); budding, sprouting (*of trees, etc.*); cutaneous eruption, rash, exanthema; exudation (*on a new wall*); lining (*of a carriage, etc.*); border, trimming; turn(ing) of the scale; result, event, end; playing off (*at ball, etc.*); **eine Feder giebt der Wage den —,**

a feather will turn the scale; **der Schlacht den — geben**, to turn the scale, decide the issue of a battle; **die Stimme, die den — giebt, die —gebende Stimme**, the casting vote. *Comp.* **—fäustel**, *m.* hammer used in pounding ore. **—fieber**, *n.* eruptive fever. **—maschi'ne**, *f.* punching machine. **—schuppen**, *f.pl.* raments (*Bot.*). **—s=winkel**, *m.* angle of elongation (*Astr.*).

Aus'schlag—en, I. *ir.v.a.* to strike out, to beat, dash, knock out; to take (*a bedstead*) to pieces; to flatten out; to line; to hang (*with paper or tapestry*); to trim, face (*with fur, etc.*); to untwist, disentangle; to unfold, lay out, spread; to cut out *or* stamp (*paper, leather, etc.*); to notch, indent; to refuse, decline (*an invitation, etc.*); to give up (*an inheritance*); to ward off, parry. II. *ir.v.n.* (*aux.* h.) to strike the first blow; to play off (*a ball*); to lash out (*as horses*); to strike the hour; to incline to one side; to cease to sing (*of nightingales, etc.*); (*aux.* s.) to break out (*in pustules*); to grow moist, be covered with an exudation; to result, turn out; to break out, burst forth; to sprout, bud; **eine ausgeschlagene Stunde**, a full hour. III. *subst.n.* refusal; renunciation (*of a right*); eruption, *etc.* **—end**, *p. & adj.* deciding, decisive.

Aus'schläger, *m.* (—s, *pl.* —), **—in**, *f.* striker; kicker; sorter; server (*of a ball*).

[1]**Aus'schleifen**, *ir.v.a.* to grind down; to take out by grinding; **sich —**, to wear off *or* out.

[2]**Aus'schleifen**, *v.a.* to convey on a drag *or* sledge.

Aus'schleudern, *v.* I. *a.* to hurl forth; to knock out. II. *n.* (*aux.* s.) to swerve, deviate.

Aus'schließ—en, *ir.v.a.* to lock out; to exclude; to excommunicate; to debar from; to justify (*Typ.*); to loosen, unfetter; to except, to exempt; **keiner, keinen ausgeschlossen**, no one excepted, without exception; **sich —en**, to separate oneself, secede. **—end**, *p. & adj.* exclusive; exceptional; excepting; excluding; **sich —end**, disjunctive. **—lich**, I. *adj. & adv.* exclusive; exceptional; **—liches Vorrecht**, exclusive privilege. II. *prep.* exclusive of. **—lichkeit**, *f.* exclusiveness. **—ung**, *f.* exclusion; expulsion; exemption; barring out; privation; excommunication; (*pl.*) justifiers (*Typ.*).

Aus'schluchzen, *v.* I. *a.* to sob out; **sich —**, to sob to one's heart's content. II. *n.* (*aux.* h.) to have done sobbing.

Aus'schlüpfen, *v.n.* (*aux.* s.) to slip out, creep forth.

Aus'schlürfen, *v.a.* to sip up, empty by sipping.

Aus'schluß, *m.* (—(ss)es) exclusion; exception; exemption; **mit — eines einzigen**, with a single exception; **mit — der Öffentlichkeit**, with closed doors.

Aus'schmelzen, I. *v.a.* to extract by smelting; to melt; to fuse. II. *ir.v.n.* (*aux.* s.) to melt out, run out by melting; to dissolve, melt entirely.

Aus'schmieren, *v.a.* to smear (*inside*); to grease; to compile without judgment.

Aus'schmoren, *v.* I. *a.* to get out by stewing. II. *n.* (*aux.* s.) to run out in stewing.

Aus'schmücken, *v.a.* to deck out; to adorn, embellish, decorate.

Aus'schnauben, *v.* I. *a.* to get out by blowing the nose; **sich die Nase —**, to blow one's nose. II. *n.* (*aux.* h.) to recover breath, cease panting.

Aus'schnäuzen, *v.a.* *see* Ausschnauben; to snuff out (*the candle*).

Aus'schneid—en, *ir.v.a.* to cut out; to carve; to cut off; to pink; to castrate; to sell by the yard; to prune. **ausgeschnitten**, *p.p. & adj.* crenate, serrated; low-bodied (*dress*). **—er**, *m.* (—ers, *pl.* —er) cutter out; retail dry goods merchant; **—er von Schattenrissen**, silhouette cutter. **—ung**, *f.* act of cutting out, excision.

Aus'schnitt, *m.* (—(e)s, *pl.* —e) act of cutting out; notch; scallop; cut, slit, piece cut out; **Zeitungs —**, newspaper cutting; sector (*Geom.*); slope (*of a sleeve*); counter foil; crotchet-passage (*in a glacis*); crenelle (*Fort.*); **— eines Fensters**, embrasure; **Leibchen mit viereckigem —**, bodice with open square; **auf den — verkaufen**, to sell by the yard *or* retail. *Comp.* **—handel**, *m.* retail mercery. **—waaren**, *pl.* retail dry goods, retail drapery.

Aus'schnitze(l)n, *v.a.* to carve out, cut out.

Aus'schöpfen, *v.a.* to scoop, ladle, bale out; to empty, drain off; to exhaust; to deal completely with.

Aus'schößling, *m.* (—s, *pl.* —e) sucker, shoot.

Aus'schreib—en, I. *ir.v.a.* to write out; to copy; to pirate, plagiarise; to write to the end, finish (*a letter, etc.*); to convoke (*by writing*); to appoint (*a day, etc.*); to impose (*taxes*); to exact (*contributions*); to proclaim, promulgate; to advertise (*a vacant post*); to write in full; **eine ausgeschriebene Hand**, a fully developed, a current handwriting; **die ausgeschriebene Stimme**, a part of the score written by itself; **sich —en**, to exhaust one's powers of writing (*of literary men*); **er hat sich ausgeschrieben**, he has nothing new to say in his books. II. *ir.v.n.* (*aux.* h.) to cease to write. III. *subst.n.* copy, copying; order; writ; levying (*of taxes, etc.*); promulgation; convocation, *etc.*; **ein —en erlassen**, to issue a proclamation. **—end**, *p. & adj.* convoking, having the power to convoke (*assemblies*). **—er**, *m.* (—ers, *pl.* —er) copyist, transcriber; plagiarist. **—erei'**, *f.* plagiarism. **—ung**, *f. see* —en, III.

Aus'schreien, *ir.v.* I. *a.* to cry out, exclaim; to cry for sale; to proclaim (*as the town crier*); to cry down. II. *n.* (*aux.* h.) to cry out.

Aus'schreit—en, *ir.v.* I. *a.* to pace, step out (*a distance*), traverse. II. *n.* (*aux.* s.) to step out; to go too far, overstep (*reasonable limits*); **man muß weit —en**, it requires a good stride. **—ung**, *f.* excess, extravagance; transgression.

Aus'schroten, *v.a.* to roll up (*a cask out of the cellar, etc.*); to sell by the barrel; to eat, gnaw out; to scoop out.

Aus'schüppen, *v.a.* to scoop out, to shovel out.

Aus'schüren, *v.a.* to rake out.

Aus'schuß, *m.* (—(ss)es, *pl.* Ausschüsse) selection (*of good from bad*); that which is separated (*both the chosen and rejected*); dross, refuse, waste matter; choice *or* best part; élite; committee; board; commission; draught of cast cavalry horses; militia. **— des Pöbels**, the lowest rabble; **die größeren und engeren Ausschüsse**, general and sub-committees; **geschäftsleitender —**, executive committee, board of management; **allgemeiner —**, committee of the whole house. *Comp.* **—bogen**, *m.* waste-sheet; outside sheet. **—gewehre**, *pl.* rejected rifles. **—mitglied**, *n.* member of a board, committee *or* syndicate; syndic. **—papier**, *n.* waste paper, outsides.

Aus'schütten, *v.a.* to pour out, shoot out; to fill up (*a ditch*); to give freely, shed, shower down; **einem sein Herz —**, to unburden one's heart, open one's mind to one; **dem Herrn sein Herz —**, to pour out one's soul before the Lord; **das Kind mit dem Bade —**, to act without discretion, reject the good with the bad; **sich vor Lachen —**, to split one's sides laughing *or* with laughter.

Aus'schwären, *ir.v.n.* (*aux.* s.) to come out by suppuration; (*aux.* h.) to cease to suppurate.

Aus'schwärmen, *v.n.* (*aux.* s.) to swarm out (*as bees*); to form a line of skirmishers, to proceed in extended line (*Mil.*); (*aux.* h.) to settle down, to cease to sow wild oats.

Aus'schwatzen, *v.a.* to blurt, blab out.
Aus'schwefeln, *v.a.* to fumigate with sulphur.
Aus'schweif, *m.* (—es, *pl.* —e) *see* **Umschweif**; slope.
Aus'schweif—en, *v.* I. *a.* to slope; to scallop; to cut out, shape in a slope. II. *n.* (*aux.* **h.**) to roam about; to be prolix; to digress; to exceed, yield to excess; to lead a dissolute life. **ausgeschweift,** *p.p. & adj.* sinuate (*Bot.*). **—end,** *p. & adj.* extravagant; eccentric; dissolute; licentious. **—ung,** *f.* sloping out (*in cutting a dress, etc.*); excess, intemperance; digression (*in speech, obs., now usually* **Abschweifung**); aberration (*of mind*); extravagance (*of imagination, etc.*); debauchery; **große —ungen begehen,** to indulge in great excesses. *Comp.* **—ungs=kreis,** *m.* line of aberration (*Astr.*).
Aus'schweißen, *v.a.* to hammer out, forge; to purify; to sweat out (*Vet.*); to bleed.
Aus'schwemmen, *v.a.* to wash away; to excavate, wear out by washing against; to wash.
Aus'schwenken, *v.a.* to rinse, wash out (*a glass, goblet, etc.*).
Aus'schwingen, *ir.v.a.* to swing, cast swinging; **Flachs —,** to scutch, clean flax; **Getreide —,** to winnow corn (*in a sieve*).
Aus'schwitzen, *v.* I. *a.* to exude; to sweat out, discharge by perspiration; **etwas —,** to forget something (*colloq.*). II. *n.* (*aux.* **s.**) to perspire; (*aux.* **h.**) to cease sweating.
Aus'segeln, *v.n.* (*aux.* **s.**) to sail out of (*a canal, etc.*); to sail away from.
Aus'segnen, *v.a.* to church (*a woman after deliverance*).
Aus'sehen, I. *ir.v.a.* to see out, see to the end (*a play, etc.*); **ein Baumgang, den man nicht — kann,** an avenue that one can't see to the end of; **sich die Augen nach einem —,** to look oneself blind for s.o. II. *ir.v.n.* (*aux.* **h.**) to look (**nach einem,** for one); to look, appear; **er sieht sehr wohl aus,** he looks very well; **er sieht sehr gut aus,** he looks very smart; **wie sieht er aus?** what does he look like?; **die Sache sieht sehr verdächtig aus,** the matter looks very suspicious; **— wie, — als wenn,** to look like, to seem; **es sieht aus, als wenn es regnen wollte,** it looks like rain; **nach etwas recht Vornehmem —,** to have an air of distinction; **sie sieht nicht übel aus,** she is not bad-looking; **da sehe ich schön aus!** I look well, don't I! I am in a nice pickle!; **es sieht nach etwas aus und kostet wenig,** it has a great show and costs little; **wie sieht es mit deinem Bruder aus,** how is your brother (doing)? **es sieht schlimm mit ihm aus,** he is in a bad way. III. *subst.n.* exterior; appearance, look; **ein edles —,** a noble air, look; **nach dem — beurteilen,** to judge by appearances; **er hat ganz das — darnach,** he quite looks it. **—d,** *p. & adj.* **weit —de Pläne,** grand *or* extensive plans; **weit —de Hoffnungen,** remote hopes; **wohl —d,** healthy-looking.
Aus'seimen, *v.a.* to let run, to clarify (*honey*).
Au'ßen, *adv.* out, without; outside; out of doors; abroad; **von — her,** from without; **— vor der Stadt,** outside the town; **nach —,** outwards. *Comp.* **—böschung,** *f.* counterscarp. **—ding,** *n.*, **—gegenstand,** *m.* external object. **—graben,** *m.* avant-fosse. **—linie,** *f.* outer line; outline; (*pl.*) rudiments. **—posten,** *m.* outpost (*Mil.*). **—schläge,** *pl.* outlying fields. **—seite,** *f.* outside; surface, superficies. **—welt,** *f.* outer *or* external world; all objects exterior to us. **—werke,** *pl.* outworks. **—winkel,** *m.* external angle.
Aus'send—en, *ir.v.a.* to send out; to emit. **—ling,** *m.* (—lings, *pl.* —linge) emissary. **—ung,** *f.* act of despatching; mission; emission.
Au'ßer, I. *prep.* ***With dat.***, out of, outside of; without; besides; except; **— dem Hause,** out of doors; **— Dienst,** off duty, retired from active service, on half pay; **du bist — dir,** you are beside yourself, mad, raving; **— unserem Bereiche,** beyond our reach; **— Gebrauch kommen,** to become obsolete, to go out of fashion; **— Kraft gesetzt,** annulled extinct; **— der Zeit,** out of season, untimely; **er ist — Stande 2c.,** he is not in a position, *etc.*; **— Fassung kommen,** to lose all self-possession; **— Zweifel,** beyond all doubt; **niemand — diesen beiden,** no one except these two; **alle — einem,** all but one. ***With gen.*** **— Landes,** out of the country, abroad. ***With acc.*** (*after an active verb of placing*), out of; **— den Schutz der Gesetze stellen,** to place beyond the pale of the law; **— Stand setzen,** to disable, put out of one's power. II. *conj.* except, unless, save, but; **— daß,** except that, save that; **— wenn,** unless. *Comp.* (= *external; outer; extra*) **—amtlich,** *adj. & adv.* non-official, private. **—de'm,** *adv.* besides, moreover, into the bargain; over and above, not to mention. **—ehelich,** *adj.* apart from wedlock, illegitimate. **—halb,** I. *prep.* ***With gen.*** outside, beyond; **—halb der Berufsgeschäfte liegend,** extra-professional. II. *adv.* on the outside, externally. **—o'rdentlich,** *adj. & adv.* extraordinary; unusual, uncommon; exceptional, special, singular; **—ordentlicher** (*pron.* **au'ßerordentlicher**) **Professor,** University lecturer; **—ordentliche Unkosten,** extra charges. **—sinnlich,** *adj.* supersensual, *see* **Übersinnlich. —weltlich,** *adj.* extra-mundane. **—wesentlich,** *adj.* non-essential, accidental, contingent.
Äu'ßer—e, *attrib. adj.* outer, exterior, external, outward; **—e Winkel,** external angles (*Math.*); **—er Winkel,** salient angle (*Fortif.*). **—e(s),** *n.* outward appearance; the surface; the exterior; foreign affairs; **seinem —en nach ist er ein Mann von Stande,** he looks a gentleman; **Minister des —en,** minister of foreign affairs. **—lich,** *adj. & adv.* external, outward; **der —liche Wert einer Münze,** the face value of a coin. **—lichkeit,** *f.* superficialness, externality; (*pl.*) externals. **—st,** I. *adv.* extremely. II. *adj.* extreme, utmost, uttermost; **ich werde mein —stes thun,** I will do my very best; **er wurde aufs —ste gebracht,** he was driven to extremities; **aufs —ste treiben,** to drive to extremities; **eine Sache von —ster Wichtigkeit,** a matter of the greatest importance; **zum —sten schreiten,** to go the greatest lengths. **—ung,** *f.* utterance, assertion, expression; **—ungen der Güte,** deeds of kindness.
Äu'ßer—n, *v.a.* to utter, express, give utterance to; to advance (*an opinion, etc.*); to manifest; **er —te schon früh einen Hang zur Satire,** he early displayed a turn for satire; **sich —n,** to express one's opinion; to make itself felt, to make its appearance (*of a disease, etc.*); **eine Rückwirkung —te sich bald,** a reaction soon took place *or* set in.
Aus'setz—en, *v.* I. *a.* to set out, put out; to display; to eject; to post (*sentries*); to lower, hoist out (*a boat*); to plant out (*trees, etc.*); to make a settlement on; to bequeath; to set (*a task*); to defer; to expose (*to cold, etc.*); to disembark (*troops*); **das Ausgesetzte,** allowance; **etwas (an einer S.) —en,** to take exception to, to find fault with; **daran ist nichts auszusetzen,** there is nothing to find fault with in that; **die Zahlung —en,** to suspend payment; **sich dem Betruge —en,** to lay oneself open to imposition; **die Stimmen —en,** to copy the parts from the score; **einen Bogen —en,** to finish composing a sheet; **die Segel —en,** to set the sails; **die Arbeit —en,** to interrupt *or* stop one's work; **ein Boot —en,** to hoist out *or* lower a boat. II. *n.* (*aux.* **h.**)

to pause, stop, intermit; to have the first move (*at draughts, etc.*); to play off (*Bill.*); to crop out (*Min.*); **seine Arbeit ist vielen Störungen ausgesetzt**, his work is liable to numerous interruptions; **ein —endes Fieber**, an intermittent fever; **der Puls setzt häufig aus**, the pulse frequently stops *or* is very irregular. **—ling**, *m.* (**—lings**, *pl.* **—linge**) foundling, child exposed. **—ung**, *f.* a setting out; exposure; intermission; suspension; ejectment; censure, exception; settlement (*of a pension, etc.*); landing (*of troops*); exposition (*of goods*).

Aus'seufzen, *v.a.* to sigh forth; **sich —**, to sigh one's fill *or* to one's heart's content.

Aus'sicht, *f.* (*pl.* **—en**) prospect, view; expectation; **das Haus hat die — auf den Fluß, die Straße**, the house looks on the river, faces the street; **er hat —en auf eine gute Stelle**, he has hopes of a good appointment; **eine schöne — auf Glück**, a fair chance of happiness. *Comp.* **—s=haus, —s=häuschen**, *n.* belvedere. **—s=turm**, *m.* belvedere tower on the top of a hill *or* mountain; look-out.

Aus'sickern, *v.n.* (*aux.* **s.**) to trickle out, percolate.

Aus'sieden, *ir.v.a.* to extract by boiling.

Aus'sinnen, *ir.v.a.* to excogitate; to concoct.

Aus'sitzen, *ir.v.* I. *n.* (*aux.* **h.**) **mit Waaren —**, to have a stall *or* baskets with goods for sale. II. *a.* **seine Zeit —**, to stay, sit out one's time (*in jail, etc.*).

Aus'söhnbar, *adj.* expiable; reconcilable.

Aus'söhn—en, *v.a.* to expiate; to reconcile; **sich mit einem —en**, to make one's peace with a person, make it up. **—ung**, *f.* atonement; reconciliation.

Aus'sonder—n, *v.a.* to separate, single out; to sort; to select. **—ung**, *f.* separation; selection; excretion (*Med.*).

Aus'sortrn, Aus'sortieren, *v.a.* to sort, cull, separate; to set *or* lay aside.

Aus'späh—en, *v.a.* to spy out. **—er**, *m.* (**—ers**, *pl.* **—er**) spy, scout. **—erei'**, *f.* espionage.

Aus'spann, *m.* (**—es**) baiting-place; stage.

Aus'spann—en, *v.a.* to unharness, unyoke; to set, spread (*sails*); to stretch (*a cord*); to expand, stretch out; to spread out (*nets*); to slacken (*a spring, wire, etc.*); to unframe (*a drawing, etc.*); to relax (*exertions*); to unfold; **die Post spannt hier aus**, the mail changes horses here; **gänzlich —en**, to take a complete rest (*coll.*); **ich will drei Wochen —en**, I will take a three weeks' holiday (*coll.*); **einem etwas —en**, to take something secretly from a p., to help oneself to a th. (*coll.*). **—ung**, *f.* rest from work, relaxation; holiday (*coll.*).

Aus'sparen, *v.a.* to spare; to leave a space to be filled up (*Paint.*); to keep back, to reserve for a special purpose.

Aus'speien, *reg. & ir. v.* I. *a.* to spit forth, out, up. II. *n.* (*aux.* **h.**) to spit, expectorate.

Aus'spend—en, *v.a.* to distribute, dispense; to administer (*the sacrament*). **—ung**, *f.* distribution; administration (*of the sacrament*).

Aus'sperr—en, *v.a.* to spread out, distend; to shut out, exclude; **mit ausgesperrten Beinen gehen, stehen**, to straddle, to stand with the legs wide apart. **ausgesperrt**, *p.p. & adj.* astride; straddling. **—ung**, *f.* exclusion.

Aus'spielen, *v.* I. *a.* to play out; to lead; to play to the end; to improve (*or* wear out) by playing on; to raffle; **dieselbe Farbe wieder —**, to return a lead; **sich —**, to exhaust one's self by playing, not to know what to play next. II. *n.* (*aux.* **h.**) to lead (*at cards*); to play off (*Bill.*); to finish playing; **wer spielt aus?** who begins? who leads?

Aus'spinnen, *ir.v.a.* to get by spinning; to spin out; to lengthen out; to enlarge upon; to devise, imagine, plot.

Aus'spitz—en, *v.a.* to point off, to sharpen; to calculate accurately (*dial.*); **eine ausgespitzte Lüge**, a cunning lie.

Aus'sprach—e, *f.* (*pl.* **—en**) pronunciation, enunciation, accent, utterance; conversation, discussion; utterance; **die deutliche —e der Silben**, the distinct articulation of the syllables; **richtige —e**, correct pronunciation, right accent and enunciation; orthoepy; orthophony; **fremdartige —e**, (foreign) accent; **irische —e**, Irish brogue; **lispelnde —e**, lisping; **eine sächsische —e**, a Saxon accent; **er hatte mit seinem Vater eine volle —e über diesen Gegenstand**, he talked the matter out fully *or* in detail with his father. *Comp.* **—(e)=bezeichnung**, *f.* figuration of sounds, phonetic notation. **—lehre**, *f.* theory of pronunciation. **—lehrer**, *m.* teacher of pronunciation, master of elocution. **—(e)=wörterbuch**, *n.* pronouncing dictionary.

Aus'sprech—en, *ir.v.* I. *a.* to pronounce, articulate; to utter, express; to pronounce, pass sentence on; **nicht ausgesprochen werden**, to be silent, mute (*of a letter*); **nicht auszusprechen**, unutterable; **seine Dankbarkeit —en**, to express one's gratitude. II. *r.* to speak out one's mind; to express one's opinion; to declare oneself (*for or against*); to manifest; to be stamped, expressed (*upon one's face*); to exhaust (*oneself, one's subject*) in speaking. **ausgesprochen**, *p.p. & adj.* pronounced, avowed, strongly marked, decided. III. *n.* (*aux.* **h.**) to finish speaking; to articulate, *etc.* **—bar**, *adj.*, **—lich**, *adj.* expressible, utterable; pronounceable.

Aus'spreiten, Aus'spreizen, *v.a.* to extend, stretch apart; **mit ausgespreizten Beinen**, with straddling legs.

Aus'sprengen, *v.a.* to sprinkle; to spread (*a report*); to blast out; **ein Pferd —**, to put a horse to a gallop.

Aus'springen, *ir.v.* I. *n.* (*aux.* **s.**) to leap out, spring forth; to fly off; to escape; (*aux.* **h.**) to cease springing; **—de Winkel**, salient angles. II. *a.* **sich den Fuß —**, to sprain one's foot; **lassen Sie die Kinder sich —**, let the children run till they are tired, romp to their hearts' content.

Aus'spritzen, *v.* I. *a.* to squirt out; to put out fire (*as an engine*); to syringe; to inject. II. *n.* (*aux.* **s.**) to spurt out.

Aus'sprossen, *v.n.* (*aux.* **s.**) to sprout, shoot forth.

Aus'sprößling, *m.* (**—s**, *pl.* **—e**) offshoot.

Aus'spruch, *m.* (**—(e)s**, *pl.* **Aussprüche**) declaration of opinion; decision, finding, verdict, sentence, award; dictum (*of an authority*); maxim; **— der Geschworenen**, verdict; **— der Schiedsrichter**, award (*of arbitration*); **der Gerichtshof fällte einen — zu Gunsten des Beklagten**, the court decided in favour of the defendant; **den — thun**, to pass sentence on, give a decision.

Aus'sprudeln, *v.* I. *a.* to sputter out. II. *n.* (*aux.* **s.**) to bubble out.

Aus'sprühen, *v.* I. *a.* to emit (*sparks*), vomit forth, cast up (*fire, etc.*). II. *n.* (*aux.* **s.**) to be cast up, to fly out in sparks.

Aus'sprung, *m.* (**—(e)s**, *pl.* **Aussprünge**) a leaping out; projection. *Comp.* **—s=winkel**, *m.* angle of reflection.

Aus'spülen, *v.a.* to rinse out, cleanse by rinsing; to wash away, to undermine (*as a river*).

Aus'spür—en, *v.a.* to track out, trace. **—er**, *m.* (**—ers**, *pl.* **—er**) tracker; detective.

Aus'staffier—en, *v.a.* to dress up, deck out, bedizen; to equip; to trim, edge; to line. **—ung**, *f.* outfit, equipment, trimming; bedizenment.

Aus'stampfen, *v.a.* to tread out (*corn*); to pound, beat out.

Aus'stand, *m.* (**—es**, *pl.* **Ausstände**) strike; outstanding debt; **Arbeiter—**, strike; **verlorene Ausstände**, bad debts.

Aus'ständ—er, *m.* hive of bees that have outlived the winter. **—ig,** *adj.* striking, on strike; in arrears, outstanding.

Aus'statt—en, *v.a.* to provide with; to portion, to settle something on (*a daughter*); to endow; to establish; to equip. **—ung,** *f.* outfit, portion; dowry, wedding trousseau; establishment (*of a son*); **ohne —ung,** portionless, dowerless, unendowed.

Aus'stäuben, *v.a.* to dust, beat out the dust.

Aus'stäupen, *v.a.* to flog soundly; to scourge publicly, expel by whipping (*obs.*).

Aus'stech—en, *ir.v.a.* to cut out (*peat, etc.*); to scuffle (*a walk*); to put out (*the eyes*); to open (*oysters*); to cut out, supplant; to dig (*a ditch*); to pay out (*cable*); **hohl —en,** to carve, engrave in bas-relief; **ein Muster —en,** to prick out a pattern; **ein paar Flaschen Wein mit Freunden —en,** to crack a few bottles of wine with one's friends. **—er,** *m.* (**—ers,** *pl.* **—er**) outrigger; spanker-boom; bowsprit.

Aus'stecken, *v.a.* to hang out, display (*a flag, etc.*); to mark out (*with pegs*); to dibble in; to put out, thrust out.

Aus'steh—en, *ir.v.* I. *n.* (*aux.* **h.** *and* **s.**) to stand out; **mit Waaren —en,** to keep a stall; **—ende Schulden,** outstanding debts; **ich habe Geld —en (auszustehen),** I have money owing to me; **—endes Gehalt,** arrears of salary; (*aux.* **s.**) **die Sammlung steht noch aus,** the collection is not yet made; **die Antwort steht noch aus,** the answer has not yet come to hand; to stand to the end. II. *a.* to endure, undergo, bear; to brook, put up with, endure; **ich kann ihn nicht —en,** I can't bear him. **—lich,** *adj.* bearable, endurable, tolerable.

Aus'steig—en, *ir.v.n.* (*aux.* **s.**) to get *or* walk out; to alight; to disembark; to land; **ausgestiegen sein,** to be set down. *Comp.* **—e=platz,** *m.* arrival platform; landing stage.

Aus'steinen, *v.a.* to pick, take away stones (*from land*); to mark, line, *or* fortify with stones; to stone (*fruit*).

Aus'stell—en, *v.a.* to expose, set out; to exhibit; to lay out (*a corpse in state*); to post (*a sentry*); to expose (*to insult, etc.*); to take exception to, to blame, find fault with; to draw (*a bill of exchange*); **eine Verschreibung —en,** to give a bond; **einen Wechsel —en,** to issue a draft; **ein Vorhaben —en,** to defer the execution of a design. **—er,** *m.* (**—ers,** *pl.* **—er**) exhibitor; drawer (*of a bill*); deponent. **—ung,** *f.* exhibition, show; drawing (*of a bill of exchange*); **—ung von Kunstsachen,** fine-art exhibition; **—ung von Blumen,** flower-show; **—ung auf dem Paradebette,** lying in state; **—ung des Sacraments,** elevation of the Host; **—ungen machen,** to raise objections, find fault with, to criticise. *Comp.* **—ungs=ge'genstand,** *m.* exhibited object, exhibit. **—ungs=lotterie,** *f.* exhibition lottery *or* raffle. **—ungs=saal,** *m.* gallery, exhibition-room. **—ungs=tag,** *m.* date (*of a bill*).

Aus'stemmen, *v.a.* to chisel, gouge out.

Aus'sterb—en, *ir.v.n.* (*aux.* **s.**) to die out; to become extinct (*of a family*); **die Stadt ist wie ausgestorben,** the town is as quiet as the grave; **auf den —e=Etat kommen** *or* **gesetzt werden,** to be destined to die out *or* to be discontinued, to cease.

Aus'steuer, *f.* portion, dowry; trousseau, outfit; gift; endowment.

[1]**Aus'steuern,** *v.n.* (*aux.* **s.**) to steer out of a place.

[2]**Aus'steuern,** *v.a.* to portion, endow; to give as a dowry.

Aus'stich, *m.* best produce of a vineyard, choice wine; jut-window (*Arch.*).

Aus'sticken, *v.a.* to embroider; to fill in (*with needle work*); to finish embroidering.

Aus'stöbern, *v.a.* to rummage out; to drive out, beat up (*game*).

Aus'stocken, *v.a.* to grub up, root out; to clear (*a forest*).

Aus'stopfen, *v.a.* to stuff (*birds; chairs; etc.*).

Aus'stören, *v.a.* to rummage through, search thoroughly.

Aus'stoß, *m.* (**—es,** *pl.* **Ausstöße**) lunge, thrust, pass (*Fenc.*).

Aus'stoßen, *ir.v.* I. *a.* to thrust out, to knock out; to expel; to remove, to relegate; to do away with; to stave in (*the head of a cask*); **das heißt dem Fasse den Boden —,** that means spoiling all at once; to scuffle (*walks*); to expel; to utter; to set (*topsails*); to elide, cut off (*a syllable*); **Gotteslästerungen —,** to utter blasphemies; **einen Seufzer —,** to heave a sigh; **einen Schrei —,** to scream; **Schimpfreden —,** to launch invectives, to abuse; **Verwünschungen —,** to utter imprecations; **einen Fluch —,** to rap out an oath; **einen aus einer Gesellschaft —,** to expel a p. from a club. II. *n.* (*aux.* **h.**) to push first; to make a pass *or* lunge; (*aux.* **s.**) to burst forth.

Aus'strahlen, *v.a. & n.* (*aux.* **h.**) to emit rays, radiate, shine forth.

Aus'streck—en, *v.a.* to reach out, hold out, extend; to stretch out, expand; **sich —en,** to stretch oneself, extend one's length. **—er,** *m.* (**—ers,** *pl.* **—er**) extensor (*muscle*). **—ung,** *f.* extension, stretching. *Comp.* **—muskel,** *m.* *see* **—er.**

Aus'streichen, *ir.v.* I. *a.* to smooth, stroke out; to obliterate, erase, strike out (*a word, name, etc.*); to fill up crevices; to grease (*a cake-tin, etc.*); to flog soundly, to whip out of a place (*obs.*); **viele Ansätze in einer Rechnung —,** to cancel many items in an account; **die Farbe —,** to work (*the ink*) on the table (*Typ.*). II. *n.* (*aux.* **s.**) to roam, rove about; to beat for game; to step out, hasten; to crop out (*Min.*); **einen Vogel — lassen,** to give a bird rise before shooting.

Aus'streifen, *v.* I. *n.* (*aux.* **s.**) to rove, range, wander about. II. *a.* to shred (*beans*).

Aus'streu—en, *v.a.* to scatter abroad, to disseminate; to circulate (*rumours*); **den Samen der Zwietracht —en,** to sow the seeds of discord. **—ung,** *f.* dissemination; circulation.

Aus'strich, *m.* (**—es,** *pl.* **—e**) blotting out, erasure; granular tin.

Aus'ström—en, *v.* I. *a.* to pour forth. II. *n.* (*aux.* **s.**) to stream, issue forth; to emanate; to break forth (*into lamentation, etc.*). **—ung,** *f.* act of flowing out; emanation (*of light*); radiation (*of heat*); current (*of electricity*).

Aus'studieren, *v.* I. *n.* (*aux.* **h.**) to finish one's studies; to get one's degree. II. *a.* to study thoroughly; to study out, devise, ascertain by study. **aus'studiert,** *p.p. & adj.* one who has gone through his University course; one who has studied his subject thoroughly, learned (*e.g.* **ein ausstudierter Jurist,** a learned lawyer).

Aus'stufen, *v.a.* to cut into steps.

Aus'stürzen, *v.* I. *n.* (*aux.* **s.**) to rush out. II. *a.* to throw out.

Aus'suchen, *v.a.* to seek out; to search thoroughly, rummage out; to select, single, pick out; **ausgesuchte Ausdrücke,** choice, well-chosen expressions; studied terms; **ausgesuchte Leckerbissen,** choice dainties; **ausgesuchte Höflichkeit,** special, extraordinary politeness.

Aus'sühnen, *see* **Aussöhnen.**

Aus'süßen, *v.a.* to edulcorate (*Chem.*).

Au'st, *m.* harvest (*dial.*). **—wagen,** *m.* waggon for bringing the crops in (*dial.*).

Aus'täfeln, *v.a.* to wainscot; to batten; to floor.

Aus'tausch, *m.* (**—es**) barter; exchange; interchange (*of commodities, of ideas*). **—en,** *v.a.*

to barter, change, exchange; **das —en der Gedanken,** the interchange of ideas.

Aus'teil—en, *v.a.* to distribute (**unter,** among); to dispense (*favours; alms, etc.*); to divide, apportion (*shares, etc.*); to issue (*orders*); to administer (*the sacrament*); to deal out (*blows*); to serve out (*meat, etc.*). **—end,** *p. & adj.* distributive. **—er,** *m.* (**—ers,** *pl.* **—er**) distributor; dispenser. **—ung,** *f.* distribution; apportionment; administration (*of the sacrament*).

Au'ster, *f.* (*pl.* **—n**) oyster; **—n anstechen, aufmachen,** to open oysters; **—n fangen,** to dredge for oysters. *Comp.* **—bank,** *f.* oyster bed. **—dieb, —vogel,** *m.* oyster-catcher (*Orn.*). **—fang,** *m.*, **—fischerei,** *f.* oyster-dredging; oyster-bank (*the place where oysters are taken*). **—flieber,** *m.* oyster-opener, oyster man. **—lager,** *n. see* **—bank.** **—laich,** *m.* spat. **—messer,** *n.* oyster-knife. **—netz,** *n.* dredge. **—n=grus,** *m.* ostracite. **—pastete,** *f.* oyster patty *or* pie. **—(n)=schale,** *f.* oyster-shell. **—stein,** *m. see* **—n=grus.**

Aus'thun, *ir.v.a.* to pull, take off (*clothes*); to put out (*a light*); to cancel (*debts*); to erase; to invest (*money*); to let, farm out; to send away.

Aus'tiefen, *v.a.* to deepen.

Aus'tilgen, *v.a.* to destroy utterly, exterminate; to eradicate; to efface, obliterate; **durch Reue —,** to wipe out by repentance.

Aus'toben, *v.n.* (*aux.* **h.**) to cease raging, abate in violence; **sich —,** to exhaust one's fury, quiet down.

Aus'tollen, *v.n.* to cease being wild; **sich —,** to romp to one's heart's content.

Aus'tönen, *v.* I. *n.* (*aux.* **h.**) to die away, cease to sound. II. *v.a.* to sound, to breathe forth.

Aus'traben, *v.n.* (*aux.* **s.**) to trot out; **ein Pferd — lassen,** to make a horse trot out, trot his best.

Aus'trag, *m.* (—(e)s, *pl.* **Austräge**) the carrying out; end, issue; decision; arbitration; **eine S. zum — bringen,** to determine, decide a th.; **eine S. gerichtlich zum — bringen,** to go to law; **vor — der Sache,** while the case is pending; **gütlicher —,** amicable arrangement. *Comp.* **—s=gericht,** *n.* a court deciding doubtful matters between the princes of the German Empire.

Aus'tragen, *ir.v.* I. *a.* to carry out; to bear the full time (*of women who are with child*); to carry away; to divulge; to retail (*gossip*); to asperse; to wear out; to decide; to arbitrate; to amount to; **einer, der die Briefe von der Post austrägt,** letter-carrier, postman; **ein nicht ausgetragenes Kind,** a prematurely-born child; **das Bad — müssen,** to pay for (the faults of others); **eine Streitsache durch Schiedsrichter — lassen,** to leave a disputed matter to arbitration; **es trägt die Kosten nicht aus,** it does not cover expenses. II. *n.* (*aux.* **h.**) to yield; to cease bearing (*of trees*).

Aus'träger, *m.* (**—s,** *pl.* **—**), **—in,** *f.* letter-carrier; light porter; tale-bearer; tattler. **—ei',** *f.* tattling; gossip; tale-bearing.

Aus'trauern, *v.n.* (*aux.* **h.**) to mourn the due time; to leave off mourning; to cease to mourn.

Aus'träufeln, *v.a. & n.* (*aux.* **s.**) to drop in small drops, to distil.

Aus'träumen, *v.n.* to cease dreaming; to dream out *or* to the end; **sich** (*dat.*) **etwas —,** to fancy s.th. in one's dream.

Aus'treib—en, *ir.v.a.* to drive out; to eject, expel; to dislodge (*an enemy*); **Schweiß —en,** to cause to perspire; **Teufel —en,** to cast out devils. **—end,** *p. & adj.* expulsive, expelling; **Schweiß—ende Mittel,** sudorifics. **—ung,** *f.* expulsion.

Aus'treten, *ir.v.* I. *a.* to tread out (*grapes, etc.*); to trample out (*fire, etc.*); to wear out, widen by treading; **die Kinderschuhe ausgetreten haben,** to be past the spoon, to be no longer a child; **einem die Schuhe —,** to supplant one, to cut one out. II. *n.* (*aux.* **s.**) to step out; to lead off; to come forth; to withdraw from (*a company*); to secede (*from a church, etc.*); to retire from (*an office, etc.*); to abscond; to desert (*Mil.*); to go somewhere; to protrude (*as in hernia, etc.*); to overflow, break out (*of rivers*); **das ausgetretene Blut,** extravasated blood; **Flüsse sind ausgetreten,** rivers have overflowed their banks; **der Fluß tritt aus den Bergen aus,** the river issues from the mountains.

Aus'trinken, *ir.v.a.* to empty by drinking, to drain (*a glass, etc.*).

Aus'tritt, *m.* (**—s,** *pl.* **—e**) stepping out; emersion (*Astr.*); recession; retiring, retirement (*from an office, etc.*); disappearance, absconding, desertion; protrusion, prolapsus (*Med.*); doorstep; porch; ante-chamber; balcony; **der — aus diesem Leben,** death, departure; **der — des Flusses aus den Bergen,** the issuing of the river from the mountains. *Comp.* **—s=bogen,** *m.* arc of vision. **—s=punkt,** *m.* point of reappearance.

Aus'trockn—en, *v.* I. *a.* to dry (*up*); to season (*timber*); to drain (*a marsh*). II. *n.* (*aux.* **s.**) to dry up. **—end,** *p. & adj.* desiccative. **—ung,** *f.* desiccation; drainage (*of land*).

Aus'trommeln, *v.a.* to publish by beat of drum; to publish, spread abroad; to drum out; to condemn (*a play*) by shuffling and stamping.

Aus'tuschen, *v.a.* to paint, draw in Indian ink.

Aus'üb—en, *v.a.* to practise (*law; medicine, etc.*); to exercise (*authority; privilege, etc.*); to perfect by practice; to execute, carry out; to commit (*crimes, etc.*); **Rache an einem —en,** to take revenge on one. **—end,** *p. & adj.* practising; executive; **—ender Arzt,** practitioner. **—er,** *m.* (**—ers,** *pl.* **—er**) practiser; practitioner; perpetrator. **—lich,** *adj.* practicable; practical, not speculative. **—ung,** *f.* practice (*opp. to theory*); practice (*of one's profession*); exercise (*of privilege*); execution (*of duty*); perfecting by practice; **in —ung bringen,** to put into practice.

Aus'verkauf, *m.* (**—s**) a selling off, clearance sale.

Aus'verkaufen, *v.a.* to sell off, clear a shop; **das Theater war ausverkauft,** all the seats in the theatre were taken.

Aus'wachsen, *ir.v.n.* (*aux.* **s.**) to shoot, grow out, sprout; to grow irregularly; to attain full growth; to crystallise; **er ist hinten ausgewachsen,** he is humpbacked; **ausgewachsenes Fleisch,** proud flesh; **ein ausgewachsenes Mädchen,** a fully grown up girl, a full grown girl; (*aux.* **h.**) to cease to grow.

Aus'wägen, *reg. & ir.v.a.* to weigh out; to sell by weight, to retail; to choose by weight.

Aus'wahl, *f.* choosing; choice, selection; assortment; set; **eine — treffen,** to make a selection; **ohne —,** indiscriminately; **eine — deutscher Lieder,** a selection of German songs.

Aus'wählen, *v.a.* to choose out, select, single out, fix on. **ausgewählt,** *p.p. & adj.* selected, choice; **ausgewählte Soldaten,** picked soldiers (*for special service*); **ausgewählte Gedichte,** selected poems, anthology of poetry.

Aus'walzen, *v.a.* to roll out; to finish a waltz.

Aus'wanderer, *m.* (**—s,** *pl.* **—**) emigrant.

Aus'wander—n, *v.a.* (*aux.* **s.**) to depart, set out; to emigrate; (*aux.* **h.**) to complete one's travels. **—ung,** *f.* emigration.

Aus'wärm—en, *v.a.* to warm thoroughly; to anneal. *Comp.* **—e=ofen,** *m.* annealing furnace.

Aus'warten, *v.a.* to wait to the end, hold out (*obs.*).

Aus'wärt—ig, *adj.* foreign; abroad; outward;

das Ministerium der —igen Angelegenheiten, the Foreign Office; Minister der —igen Angelegenheiten, minister of foreign affairs; ein —iger Freund, a friend abroad, in foreign parts; —iger Berichterstatter, foreign correspondent (*of a newspaper*); Sie waren alle —ige, they all came from foreign parts, they were all aliens. —s, *adv.* outward; outwards; abroad; —s bestimmt, outward bound, destined for abroad; die Spitze des Fußes —s setzen, to turn out the toes. *Comp.* —s=gekehrt, *adj.* addorsed (*Her.*). —s=zieher, *m.* abductor.

Aus'waschen, *ir.v.a.* to wash, to wash up, out; sich —, to wash out (*of colours*).

Aus'wässer—n, *v.a.* to soak, steep (*herrings, etc. so as to remove the salt*). *Comp.* —ungs=linie, *f.* load-waterline.

Aus'wechsel, *m.* (—s) exchange.

Aus'wechsel—n (gegen eine S.), *v.a.* to exchange, to change for a th.; ein ausgewechseltes Kind, a changeling. —ung, *f. see* Auswechsel. *Comp.* —ungs=vertrag, *m.* cartel.

Aus'weg, *m.* (—es, *pl.* —e) way out, issue, outlet; opening; means, remedy, way out of a *or* the difficulty; shift, evasion.

Aus'wehen, *v.a.* to blow out; to waft away.

Aus'weich—en, I. *v.a.* to soften, soak thoroughly; to get out by soaking, softening. II. *ir.v.n.* (*aux.* s.) to turn aside; to give place to, make way for, withdraw (*before another*); to yield; to elude, evade, avoid, shun; to shirk; to modulate, change from one key into another (*Mus.*); einem Stoße —en, to parry a blow. —end, *p. & adj.* evasive. —ung, *f.* act of giving way before, place to; yielding; evasion, avoidance, shirking, *etc.*; elongation (*Surg.; Astr.*); modulation (*Mus.*). *Comp.* —e=platz, *m.* siding (*on a railway*). —e=schiene, *f.* siding-rail; switch. —e=zungen, *pl.* switches, points (*Railw.*).

Aus'weiden, *v.a.* to eviscerate; eine Wiese —, to graze (*cattle*) on a meadow.

Aus'weinen, *v.* I. *a.* to weep, utter, alleviate in weeping; sich die Augen —, to cry one's eyes out; sich —, to cry to one's heart's content, to have a good cry. II. *n.* (*aux.* h.) to cease weeping.

Aus'weis, *m.* (—(s)es, *pl.* —(s)e) statement, tenor, substance, purport; argument, evidence; returns; nach — der Gesetze, according to the tenor of the law, in conformity with the law.

Aus'weis—en, *ir.v.a.* to banish, turn out, expel; to show, prove, decide; die Zeit wird es —en, time will show; sich —en als, to prove oneself to be; sich genügend —en, to give a satisfactory account of oneself; das wird sich —en, the end will show, we shall see. —ung, *f.* turning out, banishment, expulsion. —ungs=befehl, *m.* order of removal, expulsion.

Aus'weit—en, *v.a.* to widen, stretch. *Comp.* —e=holz, *n.* glove-stretcher.

Aus'wendig, *adj. & adv.* outside, outward; by rote, by heart; — lernen, to commit to memory, to learn by heart; — wissen, to know by heart; etwas in= und — können, to know a th. thoroughly.

Aus'werfen, *ir.v.* I. *a.* to throw out; to knock out by throwing; to eject; to vomit; to evacuate (*Med.*); to expectorate; to reject; to disgorge; to cut (*a ditch*); to throw up (*a rampart*); to throw overboard; to hoist out (*a boat*); to cast (*anchor*); to fix (*a salary*); to draw out, set apart (*a sum of money*); to make an entry of, place to one's account; to settle (*an annuity*); das Lot —, to take the soundings. II. *n.* (*aux.* h.) to step high (*of horses*); to oscillate regularly (*Horol.*); to have the first throw.

Aus'wetzen, *v.a.* to whet, grind off; eine Scharte —, to wipe out *or* obliterate a dent, blot, *or* stain; to revenge (*an insult*).

3*

Aus'wickeln, *v.a.* to unfold, unwrap; to disentangle; to develop; sich —, to extricate oneself.

Aus'windeln, *v.a.* to unswathe.

Aus'winden, *ir.v.a.* to wring out; to draw out by a windlass; sich — (aus), to extricate oneself (from).

Aus'wirken, *v.* I. *a.* to work out; to take out; to pare a horse's hoof; to contrive, manage, effect, obtain (*with trouble*); den Teig —, to knead the dough; einen Verhaftungsbefehl gegen einen —, to execute a warrant against, have a warrant served upon a person; sich (*dat.*) etwas —, to obtain s.th. for oneself. II. *n.* (*aux.* h.) to operate fully, to take effect; to cease to work *or* operate.

Aus'wirren, *v.a.* to disentangle, unravel.

Aus'wischen, *v.a.* to wipe out *or* away; to efface, rub out; Staub —, to dust out; eine Kanone —, to sponge out a cannon; sich die Augen —, to wipe one's eyes; einem einen (*or* eins) —, to give one a sudden blow (*coll. also used figuratively*).

Aus'wittern, *v.* I. *a.* to decompose (*by exposure to the air*); to air; to season (*timber, etc.*); to scent out (*game*); to discover; sich —, to swarm round the hive (*of bees*). II. *n.* (*aux.* s.) to be decomposed, acted on by the air; — lassen, to season (*timber*); (*aux.* h.) to cease thundering and lightening.

Aus'wuchern, *v.a.* to despoil by taking usury; sich —, to spread out luxuriantly.

Aus'wuchs, *m.* (—(s)es, *pl.* Auswüchse) sprouting out; excrescence, protuberance; sprout; abuse (*rare*); — an Bäumen, knob, knot; — auf dem Rücken, hunch; — der Knochen, exostosis.

Aus'wühlen, *v.a.* to root up (*as pigs*); to rummage out; to dig, grub out; to undermine, wash away.

Aus'wurf, *m.* (—s, *pl.* Auswürfe) the act of throwing out; ejection; thing cast out; excrement; discharge; expectoration; outcast; refuse, dregs, scum, rubbish; first throw (*at games*); oscillation (*of a pendulum*); waste-paper; flotsam, jetsam. *Comp.* —blatt, *n.*, —bogen, *m.* waste sheet. —münzen, *pl.* scramble-money.

Aus'würf—eln, *v.a.* to raffle for *or* away. —ling, *m.* (—lings, *pl.* —linge) outcast.

Aus'wurzeln, *v.* I. *a.* to uproot, root out. II. *n.* (*aux.* s.) to shoot out roots.

Aus'zack—en, *v.a.* to notch, indent, jag; to engrail (*Her.*); to scallop, vandyke. ausgezackt, *p.p. & adj.* crenate, denticulate; scalloped (*of postage stamps*). —ung, *f.* (das Ausgezackte) indentation; denticulation.

Aus'zahl—en, *v.a.* to pay out, over, away; bar —en, to pay down in cash. —er, *m.* (—ers, *pl.* —er) the person that pays; cashier; paymaster. —ung, *f.* payment.

Aus'zählen, *v.* I. *a.* to count out; to sell piece by piece *or* at retail. II. *n.* (*aux.* h.) to count to the end; to cease to count.

Aus'zähneln, *v.a.* to indent, notch; to tooth a (*watch*) wheel.

Aus'zahnen, *v.* I. *a.* to cut teeth (*in a comb*). II. *n.* (*aux.* h.) to have done teething; das Kind hat ausgezahnt, the child has cut all its teeth.

Aus'zapfen, *v.a.* to retail (*liquor*).

Aus'zechen, *v.* I. *a.* to drink up *or* off. II. *n.* (*aux.* h.) to cease carousing.

Aus'zehnten, *v.a.* to take tithe; to decimate.

Aus'zehr—en, *v.* I. *a.* to consume; eine —ende Krankheit, a wasting disease, consumption; einen —en, to impoverish a person, eat one out of house and home, drain a p. II. *n.* (*aux.* s.) & *r.* to waste away; er zehrt aus, he is in a decline. —ung, *f.* consumption, phthisis; die —ung haben, to be consumptive.

Aus'zeichn—en, *v.a.* to mark out; to distinguish; to treat with distinction; to mark (*goods*); to copy out (*a passage*); to draw out, finish a drawing; **ausgezeichnete Männer,** distinguished men; **ausgezeichnete Tugenden,** eminent virtues; **sich —en,** to distinguish oneself, excel. **ausgezeichnet,** *p.p. & adj.* distinguished, excellent. **—ung,** *f.* distinction; respect, consideration; mark. *Comp.* **—ungs=wert, —ungs=würdig,** *adj.* worthy of distinction *or* of special notice.

Aus'zieh—en, *ir.v.* I. *a.* to draw out, extract; to draw, take off; to make an abstract of (*in writing*); to make out (*an account*); to rifle (*the barrel of a gun*); to extract (*the charge of a gun; the square root, etc.; juices*); to take out (*colours*); to stretch (*clothes, etc.*); **sich —en,** to undress; **einen Zahn —en,** to draw a tooth; **Unkraut —en,** to pull up weeds; **einen —en,** to undress a person; to fleece him; **ich habe diese Stellen aus guten Schriftstellern ausgezogen,** I extracted these passages from the writings of good authors; **den alten Adam** *or* **Menschen —en,** to put off the old man, to turn over a new leaf. II. *n.* (*aux.* **f.**) to remove (*from a house, a town, etc.*); to emigrate; to have the move (*Chess, etc.*); to march out; to take the field (*Mil.*); **er ist vor acht Tagen ausgezogen,** he left his quarters eight days ago. **—er,** *m.* (**—ers,** *pl.* **—er**) epitomist; person *or* thing that takes off *or* out. **—ung,** *f.* act of drawing out; extraction (*Chem.; Math.; Surg.; etc.*); undressing; pulling, taking off. *Comp.* **—stube,** *f.* dressing-room. **—tisch,** *m.* telescope table.

Aus'zier—en, *v.a.* to adorn, decorate, ornament; to bedeck; **das —en eines Schiffes,** the dressing of a ship. **—er,** *m.* (**—ers,** *pl.* **—er**) decorator. **—ung,** *f.* decoration.

Aus'zimmern, *v.a.* to square (*timber*); to line (*a shaft*) with timber work, to brattice; to elaborate.

Aus'zinnen, *v.a.* to line with tin.

Aus'zirkeln, *v.a.* to measure, mark out with compasses; **alles —,** to do everything by rule.

Aus'zischen, *v.a.* to hiss off (*the stage*).

Aus'zug, *m.* (**—s,** *pl.* **Auszüge**) marching, going out *or* off; departure; drawer; leaf (*of a table*); number drawn (*in a lottery*); removal; procession; emigration; extract (*from a book; from flowers, etc.*); abstract, epitome, abridgment; proviso; bill; **der höchste, letzte —,** quintessence; **— der Kinder Israels,** exodus; **in einen — bringen,** to epitomise; **— eines Tisches,** sliding drawer in a table. *Comp.* **—blatt,** *n.* leaf of a telescope table. **—s=graben,** *m.* underditch. **—s=weise,** *adv.* in the form of an extract.

Aus'zupfen, *v.a.* to pluck out; to undo (*knots*); to unravel; to disentangle; **ausgezupfte Leinwand,** lint.

Authenticitä't, *f.* authenticity.

Authen'tisch, *adj.* authentic.

Authentifie'ren, *v.a.* to authenticate.

Auto— (*in comp.*) **—biographie',** *f.* autobiography. **—biogra'phisch,** *adj.* autobiographical. **—dida'kt,** *m.* self-taught person. **—gra'ph,** *m.* autograph; autographical writing; copying machine. **—gra'phisch,** *adj.* autographic. **—kra't,** *m.* autocrat. **—kratie',** *f.* autocracy. **—kra'tisch,** *adj.* autocratic. **—ma't,** *m.* automaton. **—ma'tisch,** *adj.* automatic; **—matische Figuren,** automaton figures. **—nomie',** *f.* the right of self-government, autonomy.

Au'tor, *m.* (**—s,** *pl.* **Auto'ren**) author. **—itä't,** *f.* authority; **die besten —itäten,** the persons best qualified to judge. **—schaft,** *f.* authorship.

Autorisie'ren, *v.a.* to empower, authorise.

Auwe'h, *int.* oh! alas!

Auxilia'r, *adj.* auxiliary.

Ava'l, *n.* written security, surety for payment.

Avalisie'ren, *v.a.* to stand security, go bail.

Avan'ce, *f.* (*pl.* **—n**) advance, money advanced; **mit — verkaufen,** to sell to advantage, at a profit; **mit — bezahlen,** to pay beforehand.

Avanceme'nt, *n.* (**—s,** *pl.* **—s**) preferment, promotion, advance in rank or office.

Avan—cie'ren, *v.* I. *n.* to be promoted; **im Dienste —cieren,** to rise in the service. II. *a.* to advance (*money*); to put on (*clocks, etc.*). **—tageu'r,** *m.* a gentleman cadet, military aspirant.

Avant'garde, *f.* van, vanguard (*Mil.*); van (*Naut.*).

Ava'rie, *see* **Havarie.**

Ave Mari'a, *n.* Ave Maria, Ave Mary. **—=Läuten,** *n.* Angelus (*bell*).

Ave'rs, *m.* (**—es,** *pl.* **—(s)e**), obverse (*of a coin*).

Avi's, Avi'so, *m.* advice, intelligence (*C.L.*). *Comp.* **—brief,** *m.* letter of advice. **—schiff,** *n.* advice-boat, aviso.

Avisie'ren, *v.a.* to advise (*C.L.*).

Avi'sta, *adv.* at sight (*C. L.*).

Axt, *f.* (*pl.* **Äxte**), axe, hatchet. *Comp.* **—blatt,** *n.* axe-blade. **—helm,** *n.* neck of an axe. **—stiel,** *m.* handle of an axe.

A'zen, *v.a.* to feed; to bait, *see* **Ätzen.**

Azimuta'l (*in comp.*) **—kreis,** *m.* vertical circle. **—uhr,** *f.* azimuth dial.

Azu'r, *m.* (**—(e)s,** *no pl.*) azure-stone, azurite, lazulite, lapis lazuli; azure colour. **—n,** *adj.* azure, azury. *Comp.* **—blau,** *adj.* azure.

Azy'mon, Azy'mum, *n.* unleavened bread.

B

B, b, B, b; B-flat (*Mus.*); *a mark depressing the note before which it is placed a semitone lower* (b-flat); **das Quadrat B,** *or* **B-Quadrat,** *a mark* (♮) *rendering the note to which it is prefixed natural;* **das Stück geht aus —moll, —dur,** the piece is in the key of B-flat minor, in the key of B-flat major; *for abbreviations see Index at the end of the German-English part.*

Ba! Bah! *interj.* bah! pooh! pish! pshaw!

Bä! *interj.* baa (*bleating of sheep*).

Baar, *see* **Bar.**

Babbel—ei', *f.* babble; twaddle. **—er,** *m.* (*pron.* **Bab'bler**) (**—ers,** *pl.* **—er**) babbler.

Bab'beln, *v.a.* (*aux.* **h.**) to babble.

Baccalaure—a't, *n.* bachelor's degree; B. A., B. Sc. (*degree of*). **—us,** (*pron.* **Baccalau'reus**) *m.* bachelor (*of arts, etc.*). **—us=würde,** *f.* baccalaureate.

Baccha'nt, *m.* (**—en,** *pl.* **—en**) worshipper of Bacchus; Bacchanal, reveller; travelling scholar, scamp (*obs.*). **—in,** *f.* a priestess of Bacchus; a female bacchanal, bacchante. **—isch,** *adj.* bacchantic, bacchic.

Bac'chus, *often written* **Ba'chus** (*in comp.*). **—feste, Bachana'lien,** *pl.* Bacchanalian feasts, Bacchanalia. **—lied,** *n.* Bacchanalian song, dithyrambic. **—stab,** *m.* thyrsus, thyrse.

Bach, *m.* (**—es,** *pl.* **Bäche,** *dim.* **Bächlein**) brook, stream, rivulet, rill. *Comp.* **—amsel,** *f.* water-ousel, dipper. **—binse,** *f.* bulrush. **—bunge,** *f.* brooklime. **—fahrt,** *f.* water-course; rut, channel made by rain; bed of a brook. **—holder, —holunder,** *m.* guelder-rose. **—krebs,** *m.* cray-fish. **—kresse,** *f.* water-cress. **—mücke,** *f.* crane-fly. **—stelze,** *f.*, **—stelzchen,** *n.* water-wagtail. **—weide,** *f.* crack-willow, osier.

Bach'—e, *f.* (*pl.* **—en**) wild sow. **—er,** *m.* (**—ers,** *pl.* **—er**) wild boar.

Bacil'lus, *see* **Bazillus.**

Back, I. *n.* (**—es,** *pl.* **—e**) (*also f. pl.* **—en**) forecastle (*Naut.*); punt; berth; locker; platter, bowl; mess. II. *adv.* backwards; abaft, aback (*in comp.* = larboard). *Comp.* **—bord,** *m.* larboard; **—bord das Ruder!** port the helm! **—bug,** *m.* larboard bow. **—s=geselle,** *m.* messmate. **—stag,** *m.* backstay. **—s=volk,** *n.* seamen forming a mess.

Back—e, *f.* (*pl.* **—en**), **—en,** *m.* (**—ens,** *pl.* **—en**) cheek; bow (*of a ship*); part of a gunstock; (*pl.*) sidebeams; cheeks; **mit eingefallenen —en,** hollow-cheeked; **dicke —e,** swollen cheek; **die —en vollnehmen,** to talk big; **—en des Bugspriets,** fiddle of the bowsprit. **—ig,** *adj.* (*only in compounds, also* **—bäckig,** *for inst.* **rotbackig, rotbäckig**) cheeked. *Comp.* **—en=ausschnitt,** *m.* cheek-piece (*of a musket*). **—en=bart,** *m.* whiskers. **—en=bärtig,** *adj.* whiskered. **—en=grube,** *f.*, **—en=grübchen,** *n.* dimple in the cheek. **—en=knochen,** *m.* cheekbone. **—en=riemen,** *m.* saddle-breeching. **—en=streich,** *m.* box on the ear, slap in the face. **—en=streif,** *m.* lappet. **—en=stück,** *n.* cheek-piece; headstall of a bridle (*pl.*), side-walls (*of a kiln*). **—en=tasche,** *f.* cheek-pouch (*Anat.*). **—en=tuch,** *n.* muffler. **—en=zahn,** *m.* molar tooth, grinder. **—feige,** *f.*, **—pfeife,** *f.* box on the ear.

Back'—en, *reg. & ir.v.* I. *n.* (*aux.* **h.**) to bake; II. *a.* to bake (*bread, etc.*); to burn, fire (*pottery, tiles*); to dry (*fruit*); to stick (*coll.*); **in einer Pfanne —en,** to fry; **sein Brod ist ihm schon gebacken,** there is a rod in pickle for him. *Comp.* **—apfel,** *m.* baking-apple. **—blech,** *n.* sheet of tin used in baking. **—brett,** *n.* bake-board. **—fisch,** *m.* baked fish; fried fish; girl in her teens, half-grown school-girl, girl that is not yet 'out,' but already past childhood, boarding-school miss, bread-and-butter miss, flapper (*sl.*) **—fleisch,** *n.* meat for a pie; baked meat. **—form,** *f.* cake-tin, patty-pan, pastry-mould. **—koch,** *m.* pastry-cook, confectioner. **—mulde,** *f.* kneading trough. **—obst,** *n.* dried fruit; fruit for baking; baked fruit. **—ofen,** *m.* baker's oven. **—ofen=hitze,** *f.* great heat, extraordinary heat. **—pfanne,** *f.* baking tin; frying pan. **—rädchen,** *n.* paste-cutter. **—schaufel,** *f.* oven peel. **—schüssel,** *f.* pie-dish, baking-dish. **—stein,** *m.* brick, brickbat. **—tag,** *m.* baking day. **—trog,** *m.* kneading trough. **—werk,** *n.* pastry.

Bä'cker, *m.* (**—s,** *pl.* **—**) baker. **—ei',** *f.* (*pl.* **—eien**) bakery; bakehouse. **—in,** *f.* baker's wife. *Comp.* **—krätze,** *f.* baker's itch. **—messer,** *n.* dough knife. **—schabe,** *f.* cockroach.

Bad, *n.* (**—es,** *pl.* **Bäder**) bath; watering-place; (*pl.*) (*mineral*) waters; **das Kind mit dem —e ausschütten,** *see* **Ausschütten; Fuß—,** foot-bath; **Gieß—,** douche; **Regen—,** shower-bath; **Schwimm—,** swimming bath, plunge bath; **Schwitz—,** vapour bath, sweating bath; **Sitz—,** hip-bath; **ins Bad reisen,** to go to a watering-place, go to the seaside; **die Bäder brauchen,** to take the waters. *Comp.* **—e=anstalt,** *f.* baths, bathing-establishment. **—e=anzug,** *m.* bathing costume. **—e=arzt,** *m.* physician at a watering-place. **—e=engel,** *m.* naked person; china doll. **—e=diener,** *m.*, **—e=frau,** *f.* attendant (*at the baths*). **—e=gast,** *m.* visitor at a watering-place. **—e=gerät,** *n.* bath requisites. **—e=häuschen,** *n.* bathing-box. **—e=hose,** *f.* bathing drawers. **—e=kappe,** *f.* bathing (*oilskin*) cap. **—e=knecht,** *m.* attendant at a bath. **—e=kur,** *f.* course of mineral waters. **—e=kutsche,** *f.* bathing machine. **—e=mantel,** *m.* bathing gown. **—e=meister,** *m.* proprietor *or* overseer of baths. **—e=mutter,** *f.* midwife. **—e=ort,** *m.* watering-place, spa. **—e=platz,** *m.* bathing place (*sheds*). **—e=reise,** *f.* journey to a watering-place. **—e=saison,** *f.* bathing season. **—e=schiff,** *n.* boat used in bathing; floating bath. **—e=schwamm,** *m.* bath sponge. **—e=wanne,** *f.* bathing tub. **—e=zimmer,** *n.* bathroom.

Ba'd—en, *v.a. & r.* to bathe; **in Blut —en,** to wallow in blood; **der, die —ende,** the bather. **—er,** *m.* (**—ers,** *pl.* **—er**) bath-keeper; barber-surgeon; bather. **—erei',** *f.* baths.

Baff, *interj.* bang, pop!; **ich bin ganz —,** I am dumbfounded, I do not know what to say (*coll.*).

Bäff'chen, *n.* (**—s,** *pl.* **—**) bands (*of a clergyman, proctor, etc.*).

Baga'ge, *f.* baggage. *Comp.* **—karren,** *m.* baggage-cart *or* waggon. **—wagen,** *m.* baggage waggon.

Bagatel'l—e, *f.* (*pl.* **—en**) trifle. *Comp.* **—gericht,** *n.* base-court. **—klage, —sache,** *f.* petty case (*Law*). **—mäßig,** *adv.* disdainfully, as a trifle. **—schulden,** *pl.* trifling debts.

Bag'ger, *m.* (**—s,** *pl.* **—**) person *or* machine for cleaning out mud, *etc.*, dredger. *Comp.* **—maschine,** *f.* dredging machine, dredging steamer. **—netz,** *n.* dredging net.

Bag'gern, *v.a.* (*aux.* **h.**) to dredge.

Bäh, *interj.* baa (*bleating of sheep*). **—lamm,** *n.* sheep (*nursery word*); a stupid fellow (*sl.*).

Bäh'—en, *v.a.* to foment, stupe, bathe. *Comp.* **—(e)=kraut,** *n.* plant used for fomenting. **—(e)=mittel,** *n.* fomentation.

Bahn, *f.* (*pl.* **—en**) path, pathway, road; railway, railroad; course; orbit; trajectory, track (*of a comet*); face (*of a hammer, plane, anvil, etc.*); groove; breadth (*of fabrics*); **sich** (*dat.*) **— brechen,** to force one's way; **die — brechen,** to break the ice, to beat a path; **zur — gehen,** to go to the station; **auf die — bringen,** to take to the station; to put in the right way, to start, introduce (*a topic*); **— des Lebens, Lebens—,** career, path of life; **Reit—,** riding-school; **Renn—,** race-course; **Gleit—,** slide; **ein seiner —entrückter Stern,** a disorbed star. *Comp.* **—arbeiter,** *m.* navvy. **—brechend,** *adj.* pioneering, epoch-making; **—brechende Arbeit,** pioneer work. **—brecher,** *m.* pioneer. **—brücke,** *f.* railway viaduct, railway bridge. **—fahrt,** *f.* railway journey. **—gleise,** *n.* the railway track, the line. **—hof,** *m.* railway station. **—hofs=inspektor,** *m.* station-master. **—los,** *adj.* pathless, trackless. **—renner,** *m.* path racer (*cycl.*). **—steig,** *m.* platform (*at railway stations*). **—stollen,** *m.* tunnel. **—wärter,** *m.* signal-man, line-keeper.

Bah'nen, *v.a.* to make a pathway; to smooth, prepare (*the way*); to pioneer; **einem den Weg — zu,** to put one in the right way for.

Bah'r—e, *f.* (*pl.* **—en**) bier, barrow, litter. *Comp.* **—recht,** *n.* bleeding of the wounds of a murdered man stretched out on the bier at the approach of the murderer, by means of which, according to popular belief, the personality of the murderer was ascertained. **—tuch,** *n.* pall.

Bai, *f.* (*pl.* **—en**) bay; **eine kleine —,** creek cove. *Comp.* **—salz,** *n.* bay-salt.

Bajone'tt, *n.* (**—s,** *pl.* **—e**) bayonet; (**das**) **— ab!** unfix bayonets! **das — aufsetzen,** to fix bayonets; **das — gefällt!** bayonet in charge! **mit dem — angreifen,** to charge with the bayonet; **mit dem — nehmen,** to carry at the point of the bayonet. **—fechten,** *n.* crossing bayonets (*military drill*).

Bajonettie'ren, *v.a.* to fight with bayonets; to kill with bayonets.

Ba'ke, *f.* (*pl.* **—n**) beacon, buoy. *Comp.* **—n=geld,** *n.* beaconage.

Ba'kel, *m.* (**—s,** *pl.* **—**) stick, cudgel, cane of the schoolmaster (*humor*).

Ba'keljau, *m.* dried salt cod; dried ling. *Comp.* **—fischer,** *m.* banker.

Bakte'ri—e, *f.* bacterium, bactery. **—en=forschung,** *f.*, **—en=kunde,** *f.*, **—ologie',** *f.* bacteriology.

Ba'kteriologisch, *a.* bacteriological.
Bala'nce, *f.* balance, equilibrium.
Balancier', *m.* beam, balance; engine-beam; balance-wheel. **—maschine**, *f.* beam-engine.
Balancie'r—en, *v.a.* to balance. *Comp.* **—schritt**, *m.* goose-step (*Mil.*). **—stange**, *f.* balancing-pole. **—stängelchen**, *pl.* balancers (*Zool.*).
Bald, *adv.* (**eher**, (*obs.*) **bälder; am ehesten**) soon, shortly, directly; almost, nearly; quickly; easily; **er kam —**, he came before long; **ich wäre — gestorben**, I had nearly died; **so — als**, as soon as; as; **es ist — gesagt**, it 's easy talking; **je eher, je lieber**, the sooner, the better; **— so, — so**, now one way, now another; **— heiter, — traurig**, one moment merry, the next sad; **— das eine, — das andere**, first one thing, then another; sometimes this, sometimes that. **—ig**, I. *adj.* early; speedy. II. *adv.* soon. **—igst**, *adv.* as soon as possible.
Bal'dachin, *m.* (—s, *pl.* —e) canopy.
Bäl'de, *f.*; **in —**, soon (*obs.*).
Bal'drian, *m.* valerian. **—säure**, *f.* valeric acid. **—tropfen**, *pl.* valerian essence.
Balg, *m.* (—es, *pl.* **Bälge**) bag; skin, sloughed skin; husk, pod, shell, case, chaff; bellows; cyst; brat, urchin; wretch; **der dicke —**, paunch; **die Bälge treten**, to blow, to work the bellows (*of an organ*). *Comp.* **—blume**, *f.* glumous flower. **—en-deckel**, *m.* upper board of bellows. **—en-linse, —en-niese**, *f.* nozzle of bellows. **—en-luftklappe**, *f.* bellows-valve. **—en-register**, *n.* wind-indicator (*in an organ*). **—en-schwengel**, *m.* bellows-handle. **—en-treter, Bälgetreter**, *m.* organ-blower. **—geschwulst**, *f.* encysted tumour. **—kapsel**, *f.* follicle.
Bal'g—en (**Bäl'g—en**) *v.* I. *a.* to skin. II. *refl.* to cast the skin; to wrestle, fight; to romp. **—er**, *m.* (—ers, *pl.* —er) wrestler, fighter. **—erei'**, *f.* (*pl.* **—ereien**) tussle (*coll.*).
Bal'ken (*obs.* **Bal'ke**), *m.* (—s, *pl.* —) beam, rafter; baulk, ridge between furrows; loft; bar, chevron (*Her.*); bass bar of a violin; **Wasser hat keine —**, water is not planked over (*prov.*); **die — der Kuhbrücke**, orlop-beams (*Naut.*); **— des Gehirns**, corpus callosum cerebri (*Anat.*). *Comp.* **—anker**, *m.* building clamp, brace. **—band**, *n.* dove-tail (*Carp.*). **—brücke**, *f.* wooden bridge. **—decke**, *f.* raftered ceiling. **—gerüst**, *n.* scaffolding. **—gesims**, *n.* cornice. **—lage**, *f.* flooring. **—streif**, *m.* fesse (*Her.*). **—stein**, *m.* corbel. **—stütze**, *f.* **—träger**, *m.* corbel, girder. **—wage**, *f.* steelyard. **—werk**, *n.* wood-work, timbers (*of a building*).
Balko'n, *m.* (—s, *pl.* —e) balcony.
[1]**Ball**, *m.* (—es, *pl.* **Bälle**) ball; globe, sphere; **den — anspielen**, to serve a ball; to play off, lead; **den — im Aufsprunge fangen**, to catch the ball at the bound; **einen — machen**, to pocket, hole a ball (*Bill.*); **ein schön gemachter —**, a good hazard (*Bill.*). **—on, —ot, —otage**, *see* **Ballon, Ballot, Ballotage**. *Comp.* **—förmig**, *adj.* spherical. **—haus**, *n.* tennis *or* racket court, fives court. **—holz**, *n.* bat. **—netz**, *n.*, **—schlägel**, *m.* racket. **—pritsche**, *f.* battledore. **—rose**, *f.* guelder rose. **—schläger**, *m.* racket-player, batter. **—spiel**, *n.* any game at ball, tennis, rackets, fives. **—stock**, *m.* cue; bat.
[2]**Ball**, *m.* (—s, *pl.* **Bälle**) ball, dance; **auf Bälle gehen**, to go to dances. *Comp.* **—dame**, *f.* lady partner at a dance. **—hut**, *m.* opera-hat. **—kleid**, *n.* ball dress.
Balla'de, *f.* (*pl.* —n) ballad, lyric-epic poem of moderate length. *Comp.* **—n-dichter**, *m.* ballad-writer. **—n-dichtung**, *f.* ballad poetry. **—n-jahr**, *n.* year in which Goethe and Schiller composed many of their finest ballads (1796–97). **—n-stil**, *m.* ballad style. **—ton**, *m.* the true ballad style.
Ba'llast *or* **Balla'st**, *m.* (—es) ballast; **den — einschießen**, to take in ballast; **mit —**, in ballast. *Comp.* **—ladung**, *f.* dead freight.
Ba'lle, *f.* cannon ball (*obs.*).
Ballei', *f.* (*pl.* —en) commandery (*Teutonic and other orders*); bailiwick.
Ba'llen, *m.* bundle, bale, package; ten reams (*of paper*); a weight, measure (*for flax, silk, etc.*); palm (*of the hand*); ball (*of the foot*); sole (*of a horse's foot*); button (*of a foil*); ball (*Typ.*); handle (*of a plane*); track, foot-print (*of game*). *Comp.* **—binder**, *m.* packer. **—binder-lohn**, *m.* packing, package. **—degen**, *m.* foil. **—eisen**, *n.* ripping-chisel. **—griff**, *m.*, **—holz**, *n.* ball-stock (*Typ.*). **—knechte**, *pl.* racks (*Typ.*). **—waaren**, *pl.* bale-goods. **—weise**, *adv.* in bales.
Ba'llen, *v.a.* to form into a ball, conglobate; to double up, to clench (*the fist*).
Ba'ller—n, *v.a.* to make a noise; to throw, so shoot. *Comp.* **—büchse**, *f.* pop-gun.
Balle'tt, *n.* (—s, *pl.* —e) ballet. **—tänzer**, *m.*, **—tänzerin**, *f.*, ballet-dancer, figure-girl. **—eu'se**, *f.* = **—tänzerin** (*sl.*).
Ball'horn—en, **—isie'ren**, *v.a.* to alter for the worse, to make pseudo-improvements (*as did the printer Johann Ballhorn*) (*usually* **verballhornisie'ren**).
Balli'stik, *f.* ballistics, science of projectiles.
Ballon', *m.* (—s, *pl.* —s) balloon; globular receiver (*Chem.*); **einen — aufblasen**, to inflate a balloon.
Ballot', *m.* bale of goods; measure of sheets of glass.
Ballot—a'ge, *f.* act of balloting; ballot. **—ie'ren**, *v.n.* (*aux.* **h.**) to vote by ballot.
Bal'sam, *m.* (—s, *pl.* —e) balsam, balm. **—i'ne**, *f.* balsamine. **—isch** (*pron.* **balsa'misch**) *adj.* balmy; fragrant; balsamic. *Comp.* **—apfel**, *m.* balm apple. **—baum**, *m.* balsam tree; balm tree. **—(baum)holz**, *n.* xylobalsamum. **—blüte**, *f.* blossom of the balm tree; balsam blossom; any fragrant blossom. **—duft**, *m.* fragrance. **—duftend**, *adj.* balmy. **—geist**, *m.* spirit of balsam. **—harz**, *n.* balsamic resin. **—kraut**, *n.* any balsamic plant; marvel of Peru.
Balsamie'ren, *v.a.* to embalm, to render fragrant.
Balz, *f.* pairing time (*of capercaillies and several large birds*).
Bal'zen, *v.n.* (*aux.* **h.**) to pair; to play; **der Auerhahn balzt**, the capercaillie plays.
Bam'bus, *m.* (—(ss)es, *pl.* —(ss)e), **—rohr**, *n.* bamboo, bamboo-cane.
Bam'mel, *f.* fear, bait (*sl.*).
Bam'mel, *f.* (*pl.* —n) bob, pendant, tassel.
Bam'meln, *v.n.* to dangle, to hang down (*coll.*).
Bams, *m.* (—(s)es, *pl.* —(s)e) saddle-cushion.
Bam'sen, *v.a.* to beat (*furs*); to hang down.
Bana'l, *adj.* commonplace, trite, banal.
Bana'ne, *f.* (*pl.* —n) banana. **—n-faser**, *f.* plantain-fibre.
Banau's—e, *m.* (—en, *pl.* —en) narrow-minded fellow. **—isch**, *a.* narrow-minded, low thinking.
Ban'co, *see* **Bank**. *Comp.* **—zettel**, *m.* bank bill.
Band, I. *n.* (—es, *pl.* **Bänder**; *dim.* **Bändchen**, a narrow ribbon) band; ribbon; hinge; hoop (*of a cask*); swathe (*of a sheaf*); ligament (*Anat.*); ligature, bandage; tie-beam (*of a roof, etc.*); covered point (*Backg.*); **Schuh—**, shoe-lace; **Zwirn—**, tape; **ein — machen**, to make a point (*Backg.*). II. *n.* (—es, *pl.* —e) tie, bond; (*pl.*) fetters, bonds; **eheliches —**, conjugal tie. III. *m.* (—es, *pl.* **Bände**) volume, tome; binding (*of a book*). **—a'ge**, *f.* (*pl.* **—agen**) bandage; truss. **—agi'st**, *m.* (**—agisten**,

pl. —agisten) truss-maker; bandager, surgeon. —elier, n. (—eliers, pl. —eliere) shoulder-belt, pouch-belt. —ig, adj. striped, streaked. Comp. —acha't, m. onyx, etc. —blume, f. artificial flower; striped pink. —eisen, hoop-iron. —gras, n. ribbon-grass. —haken, m. hasp. —handel, m. ribbon-trade. —kette, f. brace. —krämer, m. haberdasher, ribbon-seller. —macher, m. ribbon-manufacturer; tape-weaver. —messer, n. adze. —nu=deln, pl. ribbon vermicelli. —reif, m. hoop. —schleife, f. favour; cockade. —spinne, f. striped spider. —streif, m. bend (Her.); top-knot. —streifig, adj. banded. —tresse, f. worsted lace. —verlängerung, f. strain (of a ligament). —wurm, m. tape-worm.

Bänd'—chen, n. (—chens, pl. —chen) small ribbon; small volume. Comp. —e=reich, adj. voluminous.

Ban'de, f. (pl. —n) band, company; set, gang; pack; border, edge; stripe; side (of a ship); cushion (Bill.); eine Räuber—, a gang of robbers; lustige —, merry party; platte —, plat-band; ein Schiff auf die — legen, to careen a ship; einen Ball dicht an die — spielen, to leave one's ball under the cushion (Bill.).

Bän'dig, adj. manageable, tame, obedient (rare).

Bän'dig, adj. (in compounds) in . . . volumes, e.g. ein drei—er Roman, a novel in three volumes.

Bän'dig—en, v.a. to restrain; to subdue, master; to break in (a horse). —ung, f. taming, subduing.

Ban'g, —e, (—er, bänger; —st, bängst), adj. & adv. afraid; anxious; —e machen gilt nicht, I am not to be browbeaten, intimidated; bullying goes for nothing; I have lived too near a wood to be frightened by an owl (prov.); es ist mir —(e) um ihn, I fear for him; es ist mir —(e) vor ihm, I am uneasy in his presence; I am afraid of him; wir waren angst und —, we were in great trepidation; uns ist —e, aber wir verzagen nicht, we are perplexed, but not in despair (B.). —igkeit, f. anxiety, fear, dread, uneasiness.

Ban'ge, f. fear (sl.); haben Sie keine —, don't be afraid (sl.).

Ban'g—en, v.n. (aux. h.) & imp. to be afraid; mir —t vor der Zukunft, I am anxious about the future; mir —t davor, I am afraid of it; uns soll nicht —en, we shall not be afraid; ich lasse mir nicht —en, I do not allow myself to be worried.

[1]**Bank**, I. f. (pl. Bänke) bench; seat; sand-bank; reef; bed, layer; board (of a university); banquette, barbette (Fort.); press (Typ.); auf die lange — schieben, to put aside, defer, to keep putting off; die geistliche —, the bench of bishops; die weltliche —, the secular bench (in the old German Diet), the bench of judges, etc.; Dreh—, turning-lathe; Hobel—, carpenter's bench; Fleisch—, butcher's block; Fleischer—, stall, shambles; Fleisch zur — hacken, to cut meat for sale; — am Horizont, cloudy horizon; sich nicht leicht unter die — stecken lassen, not to be easily put down; unter die — liegen, to lie close (dial.); von der — fallen or von der — gefallen sein, to be a bastard, to be an illegitimate child; durch die —, in gross, on an average, all through. Comp. —hobel, m. long plane; grooving plane. —lehne, f. back of a form. —mäßig, adj. negotiable, saleable at the public stalls (butch.). —messer, n. cleaver. —wagen, m. char à bancs.

[2]**Bank**, f. (pl. —en), bank, banking establishment; gambling-bank; Geld in die — legen, to deposit money in the bank; die — sprengen, to break the bank; die — halten, to keep bank. —(e)rott, —ett, etc. see Bankrott, Bankett, &c. —ier, see Banquier. —o, m. & n. bank, bank-money. Comp. —agent, m. exchange-broker. —agio, n. see Agio. —aktie (—actie) f. bank-stock. —aktionär (—actionär) m. holder of bankstock. —an=weisung, f. cheque, bank bill. —bruch, m. bankruptcy; —bruch machen, to fail. —brüchig, adj. bankrupt, insolvent. —buch, n. banking book. —fach, n. banking-line, banking business. —fähig, adj. negotiable, bankable. —gericht, n. chamber of commerce. —gewölbe, n. bank-safe, bullion-vault, safe-deposit. —halter, m. banker. —konto, n. banking account; haben Sie ein —konto bei uns, do you bank with us?; ein —konto eröffnen, to open a credit at a bank. —note, f. bank note; bank bill (Amer.) —noten, pl., —notenausgabe, f. note-issue. —notenpapier, n. currency paper. —noten=umlauf, m. notes in circulation, paper-currency. —papier, n. bankable paper, security. —procura, f. power of attorney to transact banking business. —schein, m. see —note. —schreiber, m. bank-clerk. —werte, pl. negotiable papers. —wesen, n. banking affairs. —zettel, m. bank-note; check. —zet=telbuch, n. check book. —zins, m. rent of a stall.

Bän'kel—gesang, m. ballad-singing; low popular ballad. —krämer, m. hawker, pedlar. —sänger, m. rhymester, itinerant singer, singer of coarse and vulgar ballads in unartistic metre and melody. —sängerei', f. singing of worthless ballads, popular poetry of a sentimental or vulgar character.

Bank(e)ro'tt, I. m. bankruptcy, insolvency, failure. — machen, to fail, break; to become a bankrupt, to smash; betrügerischer —, fraudulent bankruptcy. II. adj. & adv. bankrupt; — werden, to fail. Comp. —befehl, m. fiat in bankruptcy. —s=erklärung, f. declaration (or act) of bankruptcy.

Ban'kert, m. (—s, pl. —e) bastard.

Banke'tt, n. (—s, pl. —e) banquet; bank; banquette (Fort.); side space (Railw.).

Bankie'r, Banquie'r, m. (—s, pl. —s), banker.

Bann, m. (—es) territory, jurisdiction; proscription; public summons; curse, charm; ban; excommunication; kleiner Kirchen—, interdict; in den — thun, to excommunicate, to put under the ban of the church; den — aufheben, to remove an interdict. Comp. —brief, m. interdict. —bulle, f. Pope's bull. —fluch, m. anathema. —strahl, m.; den — strahl schleudern, to fulminate excommunication (gegen einen, against one); to thunder out a bull of excommunication. —spruch, m. excommunication; exorcism. —wasser, n. private fishing pond of a feudal lord. —werk, n. statute labour. —wort, n. exorcising word; exorcism.

Ban'n—en, v.a. to banish, expel; to put under the ban; to forbid, to reserve an exclusive privilege concerning s.th.; to enchant; to conjure up or away; to banish; to fix to a certain place; festgebannt, rooted to the spot, charmed. —er, m. (—ers, pl. —er) exorciser.

Ban'ner, n. (—s, pl. —) banner. Comp. —herr, m. banneret. —leute, pl. armed retainers under a banneret. —träger, m. standard-bearer.

Ban'nig, adj. & adj. extraordinary, very great (sl.).

Banquier, m. see Bankier.

Bans—e, f. and m. (pl. —en) bay, recess (in a barn for sheaves). —er, m. (—ers, pl. —er) workman who piles up sheaves in a barn.

[1]**Bar**, m. (—s, pl. —e), technical name given by the mastersingers to a song of several stanzas composed according to the strict rules laid down by them.

[2]**Bar**, *adj. & adv.* bare, naked, destitute of; pure, unmixed; ready (*of money*). **—e Zahlung**, cash payment; **—er Ertrag**, net proceeds, proceeds in cash; **— bezahlen**, to pay cash; **gegen —**, for cash; **für —e Münze nehmen**, to believe implicitly, to take for gospel; **—es Geld** (*or* **— Geld**), ready money; cash; **—er Unsinn**, sheer nonsense. **—schaft**, *f.* ready money; stock; property. *Comp.* **—beinig**, *adj.* barelegged. **—frost**, *m.* black frost. **—füßer**, *m.* barefooted friar. **—füßele**, *n.* little Miss Barefoot. **—füßig**, *see* **—beinig**. **—häuptig**, *adj. & adv.* bare-headed, unbonnetted, uncovered. **—laufen**, *n.* prisoner's base (*a game*). **—kauf**, *m.* cash-purchase. **—preis**, *m.* cash price; **zu beigefügten —preisen**, at the annexed cash prices. **—schenkler**, *m.* sansculotte. **—sendung**, *f.* consignment of *or* in specie. **—vorschuß**, *m.* cash advance. **—zahlend**, *adj.*; **—zahlende Banken**, specie-, cash-paying banks. **—zahlung**, *f.* payment in cash.

[1]**Bär** (**—en**, *pl.* **—en**) bear; **ein junger —**, bear's cub; **der große —**, the Great Bear, Ursa major; **der große und kleine —**, the Greater and Lesser Bear; **—en anbinden**, to contract debts; **einen —en abbinden**, to pay a debt; **einem einen —en aufbinden**, to hoax one, play one a practical joke; **der — brummt**, the bear growls; **ungeleckter —** unlicked cub, bear; rude fellow (*figur.*). **—in**, *f.* (*pl.* **—innen**) she-bear. *Comp.* **—beißig**, *adj.* quarrelsome, surly. **—en=artig**, *adj.* ursine. **—en=beißer**, *m.* bull-dog. **—en=decke**, *f.* bear-skin cover. **—en=dill**, *see* **Bärwurz**. **—en=fang**, *m.* bear-hunting; bear-trap. **—en=fell**, *n.* bear's skin. **—en=fett**, *n.* bear's grease. **—en=führer**, *m.* bear leader; tutor, cicerone (*sl.*). **—en=fuß**, *m.* arctopas (*Bot.*). **—en=hatz, en=hetze**, *f.* bear-baiting. **—en=haut**, *f.* bear's skin; **auf der —enhaut liegen**, to be lazy. **—en=häuter**, *m.* idler, sluggard. **—en=hüter**, *m.* keeper of bears, caretaker; Bootes (*Astr.*). **—en=kälte**, *f.* extraordinary cold, awful cold (*coll.*). **—en=klau**, *f.* brookursin; acanthus (*Bot.*). **—en=mäßig**, *adj. & adv.* very great, extraordinary (*coll.*). **—en=mütze**, *f.* bearskin cap; busby (*milit.*). **—en=ohr**, *n.* arctotis (*Bot.*). **—en=öhrlein**, *n.* auricula. **—en=pfeife**, *f.* bourdon pipe (*of an organ*). **—en=raupe**, *f.* bear-caterpillar. **—en=wärter**, *m.* bear-keeper. **—en=zwinger**, *m.* bear-garden. **—lapp**, *m.* club-moss, lycopodium. **—winkel**, *m.* lesser periwinkle. **—wurz**, *f.* bear's wort; saxifrage; periwinkle; cowparsnip.

[2]**Bär**, *m.* (**—(e)s**, *pl.* **—en**) = **Eber** (*dial.*).

[3]**Bär**, *m.* (**—s**, *pl.* **—e**) ram(mer), rammer-log.

[4]**Bär**, *m.* (**—(e)s**, *pl.* **—e**) dam (*fortif.*).

Bara'cke, *f.* soldier's hut, barrack; wretched hovel.

Barba'r, *m.* (**—en**, *pl.* **—en**) barbarian. **—ei'**, *f.* barbarity, cruelty; uncivilisation, vandalism. **—en** (*in comp.*) barbarian, *e. g.* **Barba'renschwärme**, *pl.* swarms of barbarians. **—isch**, *adj. & adv.* barbarous; barbarian; cruel; **ich habe —ischen Hunger**, I am fearfully hungry (*colloq.*); **ich bin —isch müde**, I am awfully tired (*colloq.*) **—i'smus**, *m.* barbarism.

[1]**Bar'be**, *f.* (*pl.* **—n**) barbel (*Icht.*); lappets of a cap.

[2]**Bar'be**, *f.* barb, lappet.

Barbie'r, *m.* (**—s**, *pl.* **—e**) barber. *Comp.* **—becken**, *n.* shaving-basin. **—messer**, *n.* razor. **—riemen**, *m.* (razor-)strop. **—stube**, *f.* barber's shop, toilet saloon, shaving and hairdressing saloon. **—toilette**, *f.*, **—zeug**, *n.* shaving case. **—zeichen**, *n.* barber's pole *or* sign.

Barbie'ren, *v.a.* to shave; to fleece, cheat; **sich — lassen**, to get shaved; **einen über den Löffel —**, to dry-shave, to fleece, to cheat a p.

Bar'chent, *m.* (**—s**, *pl.* **—e**) fustian; **feiner, geköperter —**, dimity. **—en**, *adj.* of fustian.

Ba'rd—e, *m.* (**—en**, *pl.* **—en**) bard; minstrel; **zu —en gehörig**, bardic, bardish; **kleiner —e**, bardling. **—ie't**, *m. & n.* (**—ietes**, *pl.* **—iete**) war-song of the ancient Germans; song in this style; a certain kind of patriotic drama written by Klopstock containing songs of the bards (= *old German priests, as Klopstock understood the name*). **—isch**, *adj.* bardic, bardish; **die —ische Lyrik**, bardic lays; *see* **—engebrüll**. **—en=tum**, *n.* period of bardic song; bardic song. *Comp.* **—en=gebrüll**, *n.* roaring of the bards (*said of the exaggerated songs on old German subjects written in the second half of the eighteenth century by followers of Klopstock*). **—en=gesänge**, *pl.* songs of the bards; bardic lays.

Ba're, *f.* bare place in the woods; copse.

Bare'tt, *n.* (**—s**, *pl.* **—e**) cap; cardinal's hat; skull-cap. *Comp.* **—kram**, *m.* haberdashery.

Barg, Bä'rge, *impf. indic. & subj. of* **bergen.**

Ba'riton, *m.* (**—s**, *pl.* **—e**) barytone.

Bark, *f.* bark. **—a'sse**, *f.* long-boat. **—e**, *f.* bark; **die kleinere —e**, lighter, barge.

Bar'laufen, *n.* (prisoner's) base, a running game for boys.

Bä'rm—e, Ba'rm—e, *f.* barm, yeast. *Comp.* **—brod**, *n.* bread baked with yeast.

Barmher'zig, *adj. & adv.* compassionate; charitable; **—er Bruder**, monk hospitaller; **—e Schwester**, sister of mercy *or* charity. **—keit**, *f.* compassion, charity, mercy.

Bä'rmutter, *see* **Gebärmutter.**

Barn, *m.* (**—(e)s**, *pl.* **—e**) crib, manger.

Baro'ck, *adj.* quaint, odd, queer.

Barome't—er, *n.* (*also m.*) (**—ers**, *pl.* **—er**) barometer. **—risch**, *adj.* barometrical. *Comp.* **—er=stand**, *m.* height of the barometer.

Baro'n, *m.* (**—s**, *pl.* **—e**) baron. **—in**, *f.* (*pl* **—innen**), **—esse**, *f.* (*pl.* **—essen**) baroness.

Ba'rre, *f.* bar, ingot; rough whalebone; pole (*of a piano, etc.*). **—n**, *m.* rail; parallel bars (*Gymn.*). *Comp.* **—n=gold**, *n.* gold in ingots. **—n=händler**, *m.* bullion dealer.

Barrie're, (*trisyll.*) barrier, guard, railway-gate; toll-bar.

Bars, Barsch, *m.* (**—es**, *pl.* **—e**) perch (*Icht.*).

Barsch, *adj. & adv.* rough; rude, tart, brusque. **—heit**, *f.* rudeness, roughness.

Barst, Bärste, *imperf. indic. & subj. of* **bersten.**

Bart, *m.* (**—es**, *pl.* **Bärte**, *dim.* **Bärtchen**) beard; comb (*of a cock*); wattles (*of a turkey*); whiskers (*of a cat*); barb (*Bot.*); fin, barb (*of fishes*); choke (*of artichokes*); beard (*of grain*); growth (*on a foul ship*); tail (*of a comet*); beard (*of oysters*); wards (*of a key*); **einen um den — gehen**, to cajole some one; **in den — brummen**, to mutter to oneself; **er lacht in den —**, he laughs in his sleeve; **Schnurr—**, moustache; **Backen—**, whiskers; **einem in den — sagen** *or* **werfen**, to cast in one's teeth; **sich um des Kaisers — streiten**, to quarrel about trifles; to fight for a shadow. **—los**, *adj.* beardless, smooth-faced. *Comp.* **—becken**, *n.* shaving basin. **—binde**, *f.* mustache-trainer. **—geier**, *m.* golden vulture. **—kratzer**, *m.* barber (*coll.*). **—lappen**, *pl.* gills (*Orn.*, *Icht.*). **—männchen**, *n.*, **—meise**, *f.* bearded titmouse. **—moos**, *n.* earthmoss. **—nelke**, *f.* Sweet William (*Bot.*). **—nuß**, *f.* filbert. **—putzer**, *m.*, **—scherer**, *m.* shaver, barber. **—salbe**, *f.*, **—wichse**, *f.* pomade hongroise. **—seife**, *f.* shaving soap. **—weizen**, *m.* bearded wheat. **—zange**, *f.* tweezers.

Ba'rte, *f.* (*pl.* **—n**) broad axe; upper jaw of a whale; unprepared whalebone.

Bär'tel—n, *v.a.* to mill cloth. *Comp.* **—tuch**, *n.* cloth of the first dressing.

Bär'tig, *adj.* bearded.
Ba'rtschen, *pl.* steering oars (*for rafts, etc.*).
Bary't, *m.* baryta. *Comp.* **—haltig,** *adj.* barytiferous.
Basa'lt, *m.* (—(e)s, *pl.* —e) basalt. **—isch,** *adj.* basaltic. *Comp.* **—haltig,** *adj.* basaltic. **—säule,** *f.* basaltic column.
[1]**Ba'se,** *f.* (*pl.* —n, *dim.* **Bäschen,** *n.* little girl cousin, darling cousin); aunt (*obs.*); female cousin. **—nhaft,** *adj.* gossip-like. **—nschaft,** *f.* cousinship; cousins, relatives.
[2]**Ba's—e,** *f.* (*pl.* —en), **—is,** *f.* (*pl.* —en) base; pedestal. **—isch,** *adj.* basic, basal (*Chem.*); radical.
Basie'ren, *v.* I. *a.* to establish, base, ground. II. *n.* to be based, grounded, founded on.
Basi'lie, *f.* (**—n=kraut,** *n.*) basil (*Bot.*).
Basili'sk, *m.* (—en, *pl.* —en) basilisk; cockatrice. *Comp.* **—en=blick,** *m.* basilisk-glance.
[1]**Baß,** *adv.* (*archaic & poetic*) better; (*usually*) very, very much, highly, more, rather, well.
[2]**Baß,** *m.* (—(ss)es, *pl.* **Bässe**) bass; bass-singer; **begleitender, gebundener** —, thorough bass. **—(ss)e't(t),** *n.* small bass viol. **—(ss)i'st,** *m.* (—(ss)isten, *pl.* —(ss)isten) bass-singer. **—(ss)o'n,** *m.* (—(ss)ons, *pl.* —(ss)ons) bassoon. *Comp.* **—bläser,** *m.* bassoon-player, bassoonist. **—geige,** *f.* bass-viol; **kleine —geige,** violoncello; **große —geige,** counter-bass, double-bass. **—pfeife,** *f.* bassoon, fagotto; drone(-pipe) (*of a bagpipe*). **—posaune,** *f.* trombone. **—saite,** *f.* bass-string. **—schlüssel,** *m.* bass clef, bass key. **—spieler,** *m.* violoncellist. **—stimme,** *f.* bass voice; bass part.
Ba'ssermann(i)sch, *adj.*; **—e Gestalten,** *pl.* tattered mob, ragamuffins.
Basse't(t), *m.* a sporting dog; small three-stringed bass viol. **—chen,** *n.* basset(-hound). *Comp.* **—stimme,** *f.* baritone voice (*between tenor and bass*).
Bassi'n, *n.* (—s, *pl.* —s) reservoir; dock; basin.
Ba'st, *m.* & *n.* (—es) inner bark (*of trees, etc.*), liber; husk (*of flax, etc.*); cuticle off a stag's antlers; bast; Indian stuff of silk and bast; skin. **—en,** *adj.* made of bast. *Comp.* **—matte,** *f.* bast mat. **—seide,** *f.* raw silk. **—ulme,** *f.* soft-leaved elm.
Ba'sta, *int.* enough; **und damit —!** and there 's an end of it.
Ba'stard, *m.* (—s, *pl.* —e) bastard; hybrid, mongrel. *Comp.* **—artig,** *adj.* hybrid. **—feile,** *f.* flat file. **—fühlkraut,** *n.* sesban. **—fenster,** *n.* blind window. **—geier,** *m.* white-headed vulture. **—rasse,** *f.* cross-breed. **—spindel,** *m.* spinning-mule (*Mech.*). **—wechsel,** *m.* accommodation bill.
Bastei', Bastio'n, *f.* (*pl.* —en) bastion, bulwark.
Ba'steln, *v.a.* to work carefully, to take great pains about trifles.
Bastonna'de, *f.* (*pl.* —n) bastinado; **die — erhalten,** to be bastinadoed.
Bat, Bäte, *imperf. indic. & subj. of* **bitten.**
Bataill—o'n, *n.* (—ons, *pl.* —one) battalion. *Comp.* **—ons=bureau,** *n.* orderly room. **—ons=chef,** *m.* commander of a battalion, major. **—ons=tambour,** *m.* drum-major.
Bä'ting, *m.* & *f.* (**—s=hölzer,** *pl.*) bitts, bits (*Naut.*); **die große —,** main bitts; **das Ankertau um die —e schlagen,** to bitt the cable. *Comp.* **—s=bolzen,** *pl.* bitt-bolts. **—s=spur,** *f.* step of the bitt-pins.
Bati'st, *m.* (—es, *pl.* —e) cambric. **—en,** *adj.* made of batiste. *Comp.* **—weber,** *m.* manufacturer of cambric.
Batterie', *f.* (*pl.* —en) battery; ordnance; tier of (*naval*) guns; fight, battle (*obsol.*); **eine — Fußartillerie,** a battery of artillery; **fahrende —,** mounted battery; **eine reitende —,** a troop of horse artillery; **eine — errichten,** to raise *or* mount a battery; **offne —,** barbette battery; **verdeckte —,** masked battery. *Comp.* **—geschütz,** *n.* piece of ordnance. **—seite,** *f.* broadside (*of a ship*).
Ba'tzen, *m.* a small German coin now no longer current; **er hat —,** he is well off.
[1]**Bau,** *m.* (—es, *pl.* —e, —ten, *obs.* **Bäue**) building, erection, construction; edifice, structure; working (*of a mine*); fabric (*of the universe*); build, frame, form (*of man and beasts*); kennel, earth, den, burrowing-place; style of architecture; cultivation, culture, agriculture (*especially as suffix*); **Acker—,** agriculture; **Garten—,** horticulture; **Wein—,** cultivation of vines, wine growing; **Berg—,** mining; **die Kirche ist im —(e) begriffen,** the church is being built; **auf den — kommen,** to be condemned to the public works (*as a convict*). **—bar,** *adj.* capable of cultivation; worth working. **—lich,** *adj.* relating to buildings; in good repair; **in —lichem Zustande,** habitable. **—te,** *f. see* **Bau; öffentliche —ten,** public buildings. *Comp.* **—akademie',** *f.* academy of architecture. **—akade'miker,** *m.* pupil (*or* beginning architect) at a school of architecture. **—akko'rd,** *m.* building contract *or* agreement. **—amt,** *n.* board of public works. **—anschlag,** *m.* builder's estimate. **—art,** *f.* style of architecture; construction, structure. **—aufseher,** *m.* inspector of buildings; district surveyor. **—dienst,** *m.*, **—frohne,** *f.* statute service in building. **—fällig,** *adj.* crazy, ruinous, tumble-down; **—fällig werden,** to decay. **—fälligkeit,** *f.* state of decay, dilapidation. **—führer,** *m.* overseer of the building works, young architect. **—gefangener,** *m.* convict employed on public works. **—geräte,** *n.* building utensils. **—gerüst,** *n.* scaffolding. **—gesellschaft,** *f.* building society *or* company. **—gesetz,** *n.* building act; building regulation. **—handwerker,** *m.* building artisan. **—herr,** *m.* proprietor of a house to be erected; member of the Board of Works in a town. **—hof,** *m.* timber yard. **—holz,** *n.* building wood, timber. **—klotz,** *m.* building-block, brick (*for children*). **—kommissio'n,** *f.* Board of Works. **—kosten,** *pl.* expenses of building; cost of working a mine. **—kunst,** *f.* architecture, engineering. **—künstler,** *m.* architect. **—leute,** *pl.* workmen employed on a building. **—meister,** *m.* architect; master-builder. **—rat,** *m.* Board of Works; member of this board; government architect; state (*or* public) surveyor of works *or* buildings; title given to distinguished architects. **—rede,** *f.* carpenter's speech when the woodwork is up. **—riß,** *m.* plan, architect's drawing. **—schule,** *f.* school of civil engineering *or* architecture. **—stätte, —stelle,** *f.* building-ground; site. **—stil,** *m.* style of architecture. **—sucht,** *f.* building mania. **—verwalter,** *m.* clerk of the works; overseer. **—verwaltung,** *f.* Board of Works. **—werk,** *n.* edifice, building. **—wesen,** *n.* architecture, building-department, building concerns. **—zierat,** *m.* architectural ornament.
[2]**Bau,** *interj.*; **—wau,** bow-wow (*barking of dogs*).
Bauch, *m.* (—es, *pl.* **Bäuche**) belly; paunch; bulge; abdomen; **einen — machen,** to bulge out; **sich** (*dat.*) **den — halten,** to hold one's sides (*with laughing*); **auf dem —e liegen,** to lie flat on one's face; **seinem —e fröhnen,** to worship one's belly, to lead a life of gluttony; **fauler —,** sluggard; **ein voller —, ein leerer Kopf,** a fat belly, a lean brain; *in compounds usually* belly- *or* abdominal-. **—ig,** *adj.* bulgy, convex; bellied; ventriculous (*Bot.*). *Comp.* **—bänder,** *pl.* hoops round the middle of a cask. **—bedeckungen, —decken,** *pl.* abdominal integuments. **—bruch,** *m.* rupture. **—brüchig,** *adj.* ruptured. **—bruchband,** *n.*, **—compresse,** *f.* truss. **—decken** (*in comp.*), epigastric.

—diener, *m.* belly-slave, glutton, gourmand. —entzündung, *f.* inflammation of the bowels *or* stomach. —fell, *n.* peritoneum. —fell=entzündung, *f.* peritonitis. —finne, *f.*, —flosse, *f.* ventral fin. —fluß, *m.* diarrhœa; dysentery. —glieder, *pl.* feet (*of birds*), hindfeet (*of beasts*). —gordingen, *pl.* buntlines (*Naut.*). —grimmen, *n.* violent colic; belly-aches, griping. —gurt, *m.* belly-band; roller; surcingle. —kneipen, *n.* gripes. —nervenkrank, *adj.* hypochondriac. —redner, *m.* ventriloquist. —rednerei, *f.* ventriloquism. —riemen, *m. see* —gurt. —ring, *m.* inguinal. —speichel, *m.* gastric juice. —speichel=drüse, *f.* pancreas. —stich, *m.* tapping (*for dropsy*). —weh, *n.* belly-ache, stomach-ache. —windsucht, *f.* tympanitis. —wolle, *f.* underlocks.

Bäu'che, Beu'che, *f.* steep, buck, lye.

Bau'chen, *v.a. & n.* to bulge out.

Bäu'chen, Beu'chen, *v.a.* to buck, soak, steep (*linen*).

Bau'ch—en, *v.a. & n.* to bulge out. —ig, *adj.* (*suffix*) -bellied. —lings, *adv.* lying flat on one's belly. —ung, *f.* protuberance, convexity of a column.

Bau'de, *f.* (*pl.* —n) hut (*in the mountains*, e.g. *in the Riesengebirge*).

Bau'en, *v.* I. *a.* to build; to construct; to till, cultivate; to raise (*flowers, etc.*); to work (*a mine*); to make (*a road*); sich — auf eine S., to be founded on a th., to rest on; wohlgebaut, well made, well-shaped (*of men, etc.*); sich (*dat.*) einen Anzug — lassen, to have a suit made for o.s., to order a new suit (*coll.*). II. *n.* (*aux.* h.) to count upon, rely on (auf einen); Leute, auf die man (Häuser) — kann, people to be thoroughly depended on.

[1]**Bau'er,** *m.* (—s, *pl.* —) one who builds *or* constructs; builder, constructor (*especially as the second part of compound*) *e.g.* Orgelbauer, Schiffsbauer.

[2]**Bau'er,** *m.* (—s & —n, *pl.* —n) husbandman, peasant; wealthy peasant; rustic; boor, clown; knave (*Cards*); pawn (*Chess*). —(n)=schaft, *f.* peasantry. *Comp.* —bengel, *m.* sturdy young rustic; country yokel, lout. —frau, *f.* country-woman; peasant's wife. —lehn, *n.* base tenure; socage. —magd, *f.* farmer's servant. —n=brod, *n.* coarse, black bread. —n=bursch, *m.* country lad, young peasant. —n=dirne, *f.* country lass, peasant girl. —n=flegel, *m.* churl, boor. —n=frohne, *f.* statute labour. —n=gut, *n.* farm. —n=hof, *m.* farm, farm-buildings. —n=kerl, *m.* yokel. —n=kittel, *m.* smock-frock. —(n)=knecht, *m.* farm servant. —n=krieg, *m.* Peasants' War (*esp'lly 1525 in Germany*). —n=schenke, *f.* pot-house. —n=schule, *f.* village school. —schwager, *m. or* —schwägerin, *f.* brother *or* sister of brother- *or* sister-in-law. —n=sitten, *pl.* rustic manners, customs. —spiel, *n.* peasant drama, theatricals acted by peasants (*e.g. the Oberammergauer Passionspiel*). —n=stand, *m.* peasant class, peasantry. —n=tracht, *f.* rustic costume. —n=volk, *n.*, —s=leute, *pl.* peasants, country-folk. —n=wirtschaft, *f.* cottage farm, homestead; agriculture.

[3]**Bau'er,** *n.* (*rarely m.*) (*bird-*)cage; aviary.

Bäu'(e)r—in, *f.* (*pl.* —innen) female peasant, peasant's wife; farmer's wife. —isch (Bäurisch), *adj.* rustic; boorish. —lich (Bäuerlich), *adj.* countrified; rural, country; —liche Spiele, country sports.

Baum, *m.* (—es, *pl.* Bäume, *dim.* Bäumchen, Bäumlein) tree; pole; beam; boom; — der Erkenntnis, tree of the knowledge of good and evil; — des Lebens, Lebens—, tree of life; er sieht den Wald vor (lauter) Bäumen nicht, he does not see the wood for trees; den — erkennt man an den Früchten, such as the tree is such is the fruit; der — fällt nicht auf den ersten Streich, Rome was not built in a day. *Comp.* —achat, *m.* sand agate. —ähnlich, —artig, *adj.* arborescent. —auster, *f.* mangrove oyster. —axt, *f.* felling axe. —bohne, *f.* connarus (*Bot.*). —brand, *m.* blight. —elfe, *f.* dryad, hamadryad. —ente, *f.* black-billed whistling duck. —eule, *f.* little horned owl. —fall, *m.* windfall wood. —farn, *m.* oakfern, polypody. —flechte, *f.* tree-moss. —fraß, *m.* canker (*Min.*). —frosch, *m.* green tree-frog. —gang, *m.* avenue of trees. —gans, *f.* brentgoose; barnacle. —garten, *m.* orchard; tree-nursery. —geist, *m.* dryad. —geländer, *n.* espalier. —grille, *f.* harvest bug; tree cricket. —gruppe, *f.* clump of trees. —hacker, *m.* great black woodpecker. —harz, *n.* resin of trees. —hecke, *f.* hedge-row. —hippe, *f.* bill-hook. —holder, *m.* common black elder. —huhn, *n.* crested curassow. —käfer, *m.* garden beetle. —kahn, *m.* canoe. —klee, *m.* laburnum. —kriecher, —läufer, *m.* tree-creeper (*Orn.*). —kuchen, *m.* pyramidal cake (*baked on a spit and resembling the trunk of a knotty tree*). —kunde, *f.* dendrology. —lang, *adj.* tall, strapping; lanky. —laus, *f.* woodlouse. —lerche, *f.* woodlark. —lilie, *f.* woodbine. —lungenkraut, *n.* tree-moss. —marder, *m.* pine-marten. —messer, *n.* pruning knife; dendrometer. —nuß, *f.* walnut. —nymphe, *f.* wood nymph, dryad. —öl, *n.* olive oil, sweet oil. —pflanzung, *f.* tree-nursery, plantation. —picker, *m.* tree-creeper. —pieper, *m.* wood-lark. —reiter, *m. see* —kriecher, *m.* —rose, *f.* hollyhock. —saft, *m.* sap. —säge, *f.* cross-cut saw, grafting saw. —schere, *f.* garden shears. —schilf, *n.* bamboo. —schlag, *m.* foliage (*Paint.*). —schröter, *m.* stag-beetle. —schule, *f.* tree-nursery. —schwamm, *m.* agaric. —seide, *f.* bombazine. —stamm, *m.* trunk of a tree. —stark, *adj.* very strong, robust. —stein, *m.* dendrolite. —still, *adj.* quite silent, quite still. —stock, *m.* stump. —tau, *n.* guest-rope (*Naut.*). —wachs, *n.* grafting wax. —wanze, *f.* tree-bug. —wärter, *m.* (wood)ranger. —weide, *f.* white willow. —werk, *n.* foliage (*Paint.*). —wolle, *f.* cotton. —wollen, *adj.* made of cotton; —wollene Gaze, tarletan; —wollener Casimir, nankeen. —wollen=docht, *m.* cotton wick. —wollen=fabrik, *f.* cotton mill. —wollen=garn, *n.* cotton yarn. —wollen=streicher, *m.* carder. —wollen=zeug, *n.* cotton-stuff, print, cottons. —wollicht, —wollig, *adj.* cottony. —woll=spinnmaschine, *f.* spinning jenny. —zucht, *f.* arboriculture. —züchter, *m.* arborist. —zunder, *m.* German tinder.

Bäu'm—chen (—chens, *pl.* —chen), —lein, *n.* (—leins, *pl.* —lein) little tree; ‚Wechselt das —chen' spielen, to play at puss in the corner. —icht, *adj.* tree-like. —ig, *adj.* wooded.

Bau'mel, *f.* (*pl.* —n) tassel, pendant.

Bau'meln, *v.n.* (*aux.* h.) to hang dangling, to bob, to swing; der (Kerl) muß —, hang him!

[1]**Bäu'men,** *v.a.* to fasten (*a cart-load of hay with a pole*).

[2]**Bäu'men,** *v.a. & refl.* to rear, to prance; sich —, to stand on hind legs.

Baus—, *also* **Paus—**. —back, *m.* chubby face; blowze. —bäckig, *adj.* chubby-faced.

Bausch, *m.* (—es, *pl.* Bäusche) pad, bolster; bundle; compress (*Surg.*); tuft; roll; in — und Bogen, in the lump, in the gross, wholesale. —ig, *adj.* swelled, distended. *Comp.* —ärmel, *m.* puffed sleeve. —kauf, *m.* (*also* Bauschkauf) purchase in the lump, wholesale purchase. —summe, *f.* (*also* Bauschsumme) average sum, sum total.

Bäuschchen, *n.* (—s, *pl.* —) little pad; pledget, compress.
Bau'schen, *v.n.* (*aux.* h.) to swell out, stick out, puff.
Bauz, Bautz, *int.* smash! bang!
Bay, *see* Bai.
Baza'r, *m.* (—s, *pl.* —e) bazaar; fancy fair.
Bazi'll—us, *m.* (*pl.* —en) bacillus. **—en=kraut**, *n.* basil (*Bot.*).
Be, *inseparable prefix* (*weakened from old* **bi**, *which, when accented, became* **bei**). *It is joined with verbs, and changes an intransitive into a transitive verb* (*e.g.* **antworten auf eine Frage, eine Frage beantworten**) *or changes the object of the action of a transitive verb; it is also used to form transitive verbs from substantives and adjectives. Verbs preceded by this unaccented prefix do not separate it in their conjugation. The glottal stop is clearly heard in all compounds with* **be—** *beginning with a vowel, e.g.* **be=achten.** *For possible compounds not found in the following lists see the simple verbs.*
Bea'bsichtigen, *v.a.* to have in view, aim at, intend; **der beabsichtigte Zweck**, the end in view, the object proposed.
Bea'cht—en, *v.a.* to take heed to, pay attention to; to regard; to take into consideration; **er —ete mich kaum**, he scarcely noticed me. **—ung**, *f.* consideration; notice; regard. *Comp.* **—ens=wert, —ungs=wert**, *adj.* worthy of notice, noticeable.
Bea'ckern, *v.a.* to till, to cultivate.
Bea'mt—e(r), (*obs.* **—ete(r)**), *m.* (**—en**, *pl.* **—en**) functionary; official; public officer. **—en=herrschaft**, *f.* bureaucracy. **—en=verein**, *m.* civil-service association. **—en=zopfigkeit**, *f.* red-tapism.
Beä'ngst—igen (*rarely* **—en**), *v.a.* to make anxious. **—ung**, *f.* anxiety, anguish, uneasiness, disquietude, alarm.
Bea'nlag—en, *v.a.* to endow with talents. **—t**, *p.p.* & *adj.* talented, gifted.
Bea'nspruchen, *v.a.* to advance pretensions, to claim, to lay claim to.
Bea'nstanden, *v.a.* to object to; to contest, appeal against (*a return to Parliament, etc.*).
Bea'ntragen, *v.a.* to move, to propose; **er beantragte**, he proposed.
Bea'ntwort—en, *v.a.* to answer, reply to; **wieder —en**, to rejoin. **—lich**, *adj.* answerable. **—ung**, *f.* answering; answer; **in —ung Ihres Geehrten**, in reply to your favour (*C. L.*).
Bea'rbeitbar, *adj.* that may be worked; that may be treated of.
Bea'rbeit—en, *v.a.* to till, work, cultivate (*land*); to elaborate, produce by labour; to treat, work up (*a subject*); to arrange, adapt; to revise, re-write (*a book*); **einen —en**, to work on, influence a person, to belabour one. **—er**, *m.* (**—ers**, *pl.* **—er**) compiler, author; elaborator; reviser; editor (*of a reprint*). **—ung**, *f.* act of working on *or* at; treatment (*of a subject*); compilation (*of a book*); revision; **sorgfältige —ung**, elaboration.
Bea'rgwohnen, Bea'rgwöhnen, *v.a.* to suspect.
Beau'fsichtig—en, *v.a.* to inspect, overlook, superintend. **—ung**, *f.* invigilation, surveillance; superintendence.
Beau'ftrag—en, *v.a.* to commission, delegate, empower; to charge, instruct; **er beauftragte mich**, he commissioned me. **—te(r)**, *m.*, (*pl.* **Beauftragte(n)**) deputy; commissioner.
Beäu'geln, *v.a.* to ogle.
Beau'genscheinigen, *v.a.* to inspect.
Bebau'en, *v.a.* to build on, cover with buildings; to cultivate, till.
Be'b—en, I. *v.n.* (*aux.* h.) to shiver, quake; to palpitate; to thrill, to quiver; **vor Frost —**, to shake with cold. II. *subst.n.* trembling; tremor; thrill; vibration; tremolo (*Mus.*); **Erd—en**, *n.* earthquake. **—end**, *p.* & *adj.* tremulous; shivering. **—er**, *m.* (**—ers**, *pl.* **—er**) tremolo-stop (*in organs*). *Comp.* **—er=zug**, *m. see* **—er. —köpfchen**, *n.* nodding mandarin.
Be'bern, *v.n.*, to quake, to tremble (*coll.*).
Beblä'tter—n, *v.a.* to cover over with leaves. **—t**, *p.p.* & *adj.* foliate, leafy.
Beblü'men, *v.a.* to flourish, to cover with flowers (*poet.*).
Bebrä'men, *v.a.* to border, trim (*with fur, etc.*).
Bebrü'ten, *v.a.* to hatch; to brood over.
Becassi'ne, *f.* (*pl.* **—n**) snipe.
Be'cher, *m.* (**—s**, *pl.* **—**) beaker, cup, bowl, chalice, goblet; can, mug; tumbler; Crater (*Astr.*); cup, calix (*Bot.*); **Aschen—**, ash-tray; **Tabaks—**, tobacco jar; **Würfel—**, dice-box. *Comp.* **—blume**, *f.* common burnet. **—förmig**, *adj.* cup-shaped. **—held**, *m.* hard drinker. **—spiel**, *n.* jugglery; cup-and-ball. **—stürzer**, *m.* toper, hard drinker.
Be'chern, *v.n.* to tope, tipple, carouse, booze.
Be'cken, *n.* (**—s**, *pl.* **—**) basin; pelvis (*Anat.*); cymbal (*Mus.*); vortex (*of a whirlpool*). *Comp.* **—abweichung**, *f.* malformation of the pelvis. **—eingeweide**, *pl.* pelvic viscera. **—höhle**, *f.* pelvic cavity. **—schläger**, *m.* cymbal-player; brazier.
Beda'ch—en, *v.a.* to roof (*a house*). **—ung**, *f.* roofing.
Beda'cht, I. *m.* (**—es**) consideration; deliberation; **Vor—**, foresight; prudence; **— nehmen auf eine S.**, to take s.th. into consideration; **mit —**, advisedly, carefully; **mit gutem —**, after mature reflection. II. *adj.* intent (*on*), thoughtful (*of*); **auf etwas — sein**, to be intent on a thing, to consider a matter. **—sam**, *adj.* considerate. *Comp.* **—los**, *adj.* & *adv.* inconsiderate.
Bedach'te, *imperf. ind.* & *subj. of* **bede'nken.**
Bedäch'tig, *adj.* & *adv.* circumspect, discreet, prudent; deliberate; considerate. **—keit**, *f.* considerateness; prudence; habit of deliberation.
Bedächt'lich, *adj.* (*obs.*) *see* **Bedächtig.**
Beda'ng, Bedän'ge, *imperf. ind.* & *subj. of* **bedingen.**
Bedan'ken, *v.r.* to return thanks for; to refuse; **sich bei einem Freunde —**, to thank a friend; **dafür bedanke ich mich!** no, thank you, I beg to be excused; I do not want to have it.
Beda'rf, *m.* (**—(e)s**) necessary supply, requirements, requisites; demand (*C. L.*); **— an einer S.**, need of a th., demand for a th.; **mein —**, all I need; **Kriegs—**, material of war. *Comp.* **—s=liste**, *f.* list of requirements, list of things needed.
Bedäuch'te, *imperf. of* **bedünken.**
Bedau'erlich, *adj.* regrettable, deplorable.
Bedau'er—n, I. *v.a.* to pity (**einen wegen**, one for); to deplore, bewail (**eine Sache, jemandes Tod**, a thing, one's death); to compassionate; to regret, be sorry for; **ich —e sehr, daß ich Sie beleidigt habe**, I am extremely sorry for having offended you. II. *subst. n.* sorrow, regret; pity. *Comp.* **—ens=wert, —ens=würdig**, *adj.* deplorable, pitiable, unfortunate, to be regretted.
Bede'ck—en, *v.a.* to cover; to shelter, protect, screen; to escort (*Mil.*); to convoy (*Naut.*); to cover over *or* up; to obscure, hide from view; **Truppen auf dem Rückzuge —en**, to cover the retreat of troops; **der Himmel ist —t (—t sich)**, the sky is (growing) overcast; **sich —en**, to put on one's hat; **bitte, —en Sie sich**, pray, put on your hat; pray, be covered. **—t**, *p.p.* & *adj.*; **Pflanzen mit —ten Samen**, plants with seeds inclosed in a pod; **—te**

Batterie, masked battery; —te Stimme, husky voice (*Mus.*); —ter Gang, covered way (*Fort.*), verandah. —ung, *f.* covering; cover, integument; escort, convoy; breastwork, epaulment (*Fort.*); occultation (*Astr.*); security (*C. L.*). *Comp.* —ungs=schiff, *n.* convoy.

Bede'nk—en, I. *ir.v.a.* to consider, ponder, reflect on; to mind, heed; to care for, bear in mind; to provide for (*in one's will, etc.*); —en Sie, daß Sie es versprochen haben, mind that you have promised it; einen mit etwas —en, to provide one with; sich —en, to deliberate, weigh, consider, to take care of number one; sich anders —en, to change one's mind; sich eines Besseren —en, to think better of a thing. II. *subst. n.* reflection, deliberation, consideration; opinion; hesitation; scruple, doubt, qualm; —en tragen, to have misgivings, to make scruples. —lich, *adj.* doubtful, suspicious; critical; serious; delicate, nice; hazardous. —lichkeit, *f.* scruple, doubtfulness; scrupulousness, nicety; hesitation; timidity; seriousness, critical state; —lichkeiten haben, to have scruples, to scruple. *Comp.* —zeit, *f.* time for reflection.

Bedeu't—en, *v.a.* to inform; to set right, direct, enjoin; to give to understand; to signify, mean, imply; to portend, forebode; to beckon; to be of importance; das hat nichts zu —en, it is of no consequence; was soll das —en? what does this mean? how now? —end, *p. adj. & adv.* considerable; important; full of meaning, significant, weighty; nichts —end, of no consequence. —sam, *adj.* significant. —samkeit, *f.* significance; importance. —ung, *f.* signification, meaning; importance; sign; ein Mann von —ung, a man of high standing, of consequence. *Comp.* —ungs=geschichte, *f.* history of the development of the meaning of words, semasiology. —ungs=leer, *adj.* devoid of meaning, meaningless, trivial, insignificant. —ungs=lehre, *f.* science of the meaning of words, semasiology. —ungs=los, *adj.* meaningless, unimportant, insignificant. —ungs=schwer, *adj.* full of meaning, momentous, of great importance. —ungs=wandel, *m.* change in the meaning of words (*in the development of a language*).

Bedib'bert, *adj.*, intimidated, embarrassed, helpless (*sl.*).

Bedie'n—en, *v.* I. *a.* to serve, wait on; to fill, do the duty of (*an office*); to serve (*guns*); eine Farbe —en, to follow suit (*cards*); nicht —en, to revoke. II. *r.* to help oneself; sich (*acc.*) einer Sache —en, to make use of a thing; sich (*acc.*) einer Gelegenheit —en, to avail oneself of an opportunity; bitte, —en Sie sich, pray, help yourself. —te(r), *m.* servant, footman, flunkey, lackey. —tenhaft, *adj.* servile. —ung, *f.* service, attendance, waiting; servants; household; service (*Artil.*); zu Ihrer —ung, at your command, for your use. —ungs=mannschaft (eines Geschützes), *f.* gunners (*Milit.*). *Comp.* —ten=glocke, *f.* servants' bell. —ten=seele, *f.* cringing soul, servile character. —ten=sitz, *m.* rumble, dickey. —ten=zimmer, *n.* servants' hall.

Bedie'nstete(r), *m.* employé.

Bedi'ng, *m.* (*obs.* Bedi'nge, *n.*) = Bedi'ngung.

Bedi'ng—en, *reg. & ir.v.a.* to stipulate, bargain, agree on *or* for; to settle (*terms, etc.*); to postulate; ein Schiff —en, to charter a vessel. —t, *p.p. & adj.* conditional, qualified; hypothetical; —te Annahme, conditional acceptance; von etwas —t sein, to depend on, be affected by a th. —t=heit, *f.* conditionality. —t=sein, *n.* condition, conditionality, limitation by certain conditions. —ung, *f.* act of stipulating; stipulation, condition, proviso, terms; —ungen einreichen, to make a tender for; unter der —ung, on condition, provided; auf —ungen eingehen, to accept conditions; unter keiner —ung, on no account; unter jeder —ung, in any case. —ungs=los, *adj. & adv.* without condition, unconditional(ly). —ungs=satz, *m.* hypothesis. —ungs=weise, *adv.* conditionally.

Bedrän'g—en, *v.a.* to oppress, grieve, afflict; to press hard. —er, *m.* (—ers, *pl.* —er) oppressor. —t, *p.p. & adj.* in distress, in difficulties. —nis, *f.* (*pl.* —ni(ss)e), —ung, *f.* pressure; oppression; affliction; distress; embarrassment.

Bedräu'en, (*archaic & poetic*) = bedrohen.

Bedrip'pen (Bedrip'peln), *v.a.* to soil (*by dripping*) (*coll.*).

Bedro'h—en, *v.a.* to threaten, menace, grievance. —lich, *adj. & adv.* threatening; —liche Worte, threats, menaces. —ung, *f.* menacing; threat; commination (*Law*).

Bedru'cken, *v.a.* to print on.

Bedrü'ck—en, *v.a.* to press; to oppress, harass, distress. —er, *m.* (—ers, *pl.* —er) oppressor. —ung, *f.* oppression.

Bedun'gen, *p.p. of* bedingen.

Bedü'nken, I. *v.a. imp.* to seem; mich bedünkte, methought, it seemed to me. II. *subst. n.* opinion; meines —s, in my opinion, to my thinking.

Bedup'pen, *v.a.* to intimidate; to cheat (*sl.*).

Bedü'rf—en, *ir.v.* I. *n.* (*aux.* h.) *& imp.* (*gen.*) to be in want of, need, require; es bedarf keines Beweises, no proof is required; der Ruhe —en, to need rest. II. *a.;* Geld —en, to want, need money. —nis, *n.* (—ni(ss)es, *pl.* —ni(ss)e) necessity, requirement; Lebens=—nisse, necessaries of life. —nis=anstalt, *f.* public place of convenience, public lavatory. —tig, *adj.* in need of, wanting; necessitous, poor, needy. —tigkeit, *f.* indigence, want.

Bedu'seln, *v.r.;* sich —, to get tipsy (*sl.*). bedu'=selt, *p.p. & adj.* fuddled, tipsy (*sl.*).

Beeh'ren, *v.a.* to confer an honour on; to honour; das Fest mit seiner Gegenwart —, to honour *or* grace the feast with his presence; ich beehre mich Ihnen anzuzeigen, I have the honour to inform you, *or* to announce to you.

Beei'dig—en (Beei'den), *v.a.* to confirm by oath; to put one on his oath, to swear in (*a person*); —te Aussage, sworn deposition, affidavit —ung, *f.* swearing (*a witness*); attestation (*upon oath*).

Beei'fern, *v.r.* to exert oneself for, to be zealous about; sich für einen —, to enter warmly into a person's interests.

Beei'len, *v.a. & r.* to hurry, hasten, make haste.

Beein'flussen, *v.a.* to influence.

Beein'trächtig—en, *v.a.* to injure, wrong; to prejudice; to encroach upon (*another's rights*); to injure (*a person's reputation*). —end, *p. & adj.* prejudicial, injurious to, infringing upon. —ung, *f.* prejudice; injury; encroachment on.

Beei'sen, *v.a.* to cover with ice.

Bee'ndig—en (Bee'nden), *v.a.* to terminate conclude, bring to an end; to put a stop to. —ung, *f.* termination, finish, close; issue.

Bee'ngen, *v.a.* to cramp; to constrain, contract; to narrow; ich fühlte mich sehr beengt, I felt under great restraint; beengte Luft, close atmosphere.

Bee'rb—en, *v.a.;* einen —en, to be a person's heir, inherit from one; —t sein, to have heirs.

Bee'rdig—en, *v.a.* to bury (*only of human beings*). —ung, *f.* interment, burial. *Comp.* —ungs=feier, *f.* funeral obsequies. —ungs=kosten, *pl.* funeral expenses.

Bee'r—e, *f.* (*pl.* —en) berry. *Comp.* —blau, *n.* bilberry-blue. —en=ähnlich. —en=artig,

—en=förmig, *adj.* berry-like; bacciform (*Bot.*). —en=baum, *m.* American gooseberry. —en=fressend, *adj.* baccivorous. —en=wein, *m.* unpressed wine. —esche, *f.* mountain-ash. —grün, *n.* sap-green; lesser periwinkle (*Bot.*). —wein, *m.* wine from unpressed grapes.

Beet, *n.* (—es, *pl.* —e) border, bed; couch (*of malt*). —en, *v.a.* to divide into beds *or* plots.

Bee'te, *f.* beet, beet-root.

Befä'hig—en, *v.a.* to qualify. —ung, *f.* qualification; capacity; authorisation.

Befa'hl, *imperf. of* befehlen.

Befa'hrbar, *adj.* practicable (*for driving*); navigable.

Befa'hr—en, *ir.v.a.* to travel over, ply on (*a road*); to cover with (*gravel, etc.*); to navigate (*a river*); to fear (*poetic*); ein sehr —ener Weg, a much frequented road; die Küsten —en, to sail along the coasts; —ene Leute, old salts, old tars; eine Grube —en, to descend into a mine. —ung, *f.* navigation; using a road; working of a mine; —ung eines Weges mit Kies, gravelling of a road.

Befa'llen, *ir.v.a. & imp.* to befall, happen; to attack; von einem Sturme — werden, to be overtaken by a storm; von einer Krankheit — werden, to be taken ill.

Befa'ngen, I. *ir.v.a.* to encompass, surround; to comprehend, include, comprise; to engage, to implicate, involve; to overpower; to seize; in einer Verschwörung — sein, to be implicated in a conspiracy; vom Schlafe —, overcome with sleep; in einem Irrtume — sein, to labour under a mistake. II. *p.p. & adj.* embarrassed, disconcerted, put out; restrained (*in manner*), shy, timid; partial; prepossessed, prejudiced, biassed (*in favour of, for*); preoccupied (*with*), engrossed (*in*); —er Kopf, narrow-minded person; ein —er Richter, a corrupt judge; ein —es Ei, an addled egg. —heit, *f.* embarrassment; prejudice, bias.

Befa'ssen, *v.a.* to touch, handle; to comprehend; sich mit etwas —, to occupy oneself with, to enter into, engage in; in sich —, to include; er will sich damit nicht —, he refuses to be concerned in it; — Sie sich mit Ihren eigenen Sachen, mind your own business; niemand befaßt sich gern mit ihm, nobody likes to have anything to do with him.

Befe'hd—en, *v.a.* to make war upon; to attack; sich —en, to be in a state of conflict. —ung, *f.* war; act of making war upon.

Befe'hl, *m.* (—s, *pl.* —e) command, mandate, order; commission (*C.L.*); auf wessen —? by whose orders? ich stehe Ihnen zu —, I am at your service; Tages—, order of the day, general order (*Mil.*); den — übernehmen, to take the command (*Mil.*); Ober—, supreme command (*Mil.*); bis auf weiteren —, till further orders; stets zu —, always at command *or* at your service; gerichtlicher —, warrant; mündlicher, schriftlicher —, verbal, written order: was steht zu Ihrem —? what is your pleasure, what can I get you?; zu —, yes, sir; zu —, Herr Hauptmann, yes, sir; very good, sir; zu —, Herr Sergeant, very good, sergeant; er hat mir strengen — erteilt, he gave me strict orders. —erisch, *adj. & adv.* haughty, overbearing, imperious. *Comp.* —(s)=flagge, *f.* commodore's flag (*Naut.*). —s=form, *f.* imperative mood. —s=haber, *m.* commanding officer; chief. —s=haberisch, *adj.* authoritative; imperious, dictatorial. —s=haberstab, *m.* commander's staff *or* baton. —s=weise, I. *adv.* as a command. II. *f. see* —s=form. —s=widrig, *adj. & adv.* contrary to orders. —s=wort, *n.* word of command. —s=zettel, *m.* bulletin. —wimpel, *m.* broad pennant (*Naut.*).

Befe'hl—en, *ir.v.a.* to order, command; to commit to, commend to the care of; to entrust, to send by a p.; wie Sie —en, as you wish; —en Sie sonst noch etwas, do you wish anything else? have you any other orders?; thue, was ich dir befehle, do as I tell you; Gott befohlen! good bye! God be with you!; sich Gott —en, to commend one's soul to God. —end, *p. & adj.* imperative, dictatorial; die —ende Form, the imperative mood; ein —ender Ton, a tone of authority. —erl(e)s, *n.* little imperious person (*dial.*).

Befe'hl—igen, *v.a.* to command (*a regiment, an army*); —igt von, under the command of, led by.

Befei'nden, *v.a.* to show enmity to, to persecute; er ist mit uns befeindet, he is on bad terms with us.

Befe'stig—en (**Befe'sten**), *v.a.* to fasten, make fast; to pin; to tack; to fortify; to establish; to strengthen; mit Nägeln —en, to nail; da wurden die Gemeinen im Glauben —t, so were the churches established in the faith (*B.*). —ung, *f.* act of fastening; fastening, that which strengthens; fortification. *Comp.* —ungs=kunst, *f.* science of fortification; unterirdische —ungskunst, military mining. —ungs=pfahl, *m.* palisade. —ungs=werke, *n.pl.* defences.

Befeu'cht—en, *v.a.* to dampen, moisten; to water. —ung, *f.* moistening; irrigation.

Befeu'ern, *v.a.* to fire (*with enthusiasm, etc.*).

Be'ffchen, *n.* (—s, *pl.* —) *also* Bä'ffchen, bands (*of a Protestant clergyman, a proctor, etc.*).

Befie'dern, *v.a.* to cover with feathers; to mount an arrow with feathers; sich —, to get feathers.

Befie'hl, Befie'hlst, Befie'hlt, *see* Befe'hlen.

Befi'nd—en, I. *ir.v.a.* to find, deem, consider; es wurde für ratsam befunden, it was deemed advisable; sich —en, to be, to fare, to feel; die Sache —et sich nicht so, that is not the true state of the case; sich in Verlegenheit —en, to be embarrassed; Sie —en sich in einem seltsamen Irrtume, you labour under a strange misapprehension; wie —en Sie sich? how are you?; Sie —en sich doch wohl? you are quite well, I hope?; wir —en uns hier sehr wohl, we are very comfortable here; sich an einem Orte —en, to be (*stationed*) at a place. II. *subst.n.* state of health; condition; the being in a certain place, opinion; nach —en der Sache, as things turn out; nach —en, as you may think fit. —lich, *adj. & adv.* to be found; existing; irgendwo —lich sein, to be somewhere or other; alle in seinem Kabinette —lichen Seltenheiten, all the curiosities contained in his cabinet.

Befle'ck—en, *v.a.* to defile, pollute; to blot, spot, stain; to patch, heel (*shoes, etc.*); jemandes guten Namen —en, to sully a person's reputation. —ung, *f.* stain, spot, blot; staining; contamination, pollution.

Beflei'ß—en, *ir.v.r.*, —igen, *reg.v.r.*; sich einer Sache —igen, to study a subject, devote oneself to, *or* bestow pains upon, it; —ige dich zu gefallen, study (*or* take pains) to please; ich habe mich immer beflissen, I have always sedulously endeavoured; er —igt sich der Kürze, he studies brevity.

Befli'ssen, *p.p. of* befleißen, *adj. & adv.* studious (einer Sache); assiduous, diligent; intent (*upon*), devoted (*to*); ein —er der Rechte, a student of law; ein Handels —er, a clerk, attendant in a shop. —heit, *f.* sedulousness, assiduity. —t=lich, *adv.* sedulously.

Befli'ß, *imperf. of* befleißen.

Befli'ttern, *v.a.* to bespangle, cover with tinsel.

Beflo'ren, *v.a.* to cover with crape; mit beflortem Hute, with crape on his hat.

Beflü'gel—n, *v.a.* to furnish with wings; to

lend wings to, to accelerate, to urge on. **—t,** *p.p. & adj.* winged.

Befóh'le, Befoh'len, *imperf. subj. & p.p. of* **befehlen.**

Befo'lg—en, *v.a.* to obey; to comply with, act up to; to adhere to (*a custom; a principle*). **—ung,** *f.* following, *etc.;* observance of, adherence to (*orders, etc.*).

Befö'rder—er, *m.* (**—ers,** *pl.* **—er**) forwarder (*of letters, etc.*); forwarding agent; promoter; instigator; patron. **—lich,** *adj.* favourable, conducive, furthering, accessary to.

Befö'rder—n, *v.a.* to forward (*letters, goods, etc.*); to despatch (*business*); to further, promote, advance; to assist, advance; to prefer (*to an office*); **zur Reife —n,** to mature. **—ung,** *f.* forwarding (*of goods, etc.*); furthering (*of plans*); promotion; advancement; encouragement.

Befrach't—en, *v.a.* to freight (*a vessel*). **—er,** *m.* (**—ers,** *pl.* **—er**) charterer; freighter; shipper. **—ung,** *f.* freighting.

Befra'g—en, *reg. & ir.v.a.* to interrogate, question, examine; **sich bei einem —en (über eine S. *or* wegen einer S.),** to consult with a person about a th. **—ung,** *f.* questioning, interrogation.

Befrei'—en, *v.a.* to free, set free, liberate; to rescue; to discharge (*troops*); to release (*from obligations*); to acquit (*of charges; of debts*); to disengage; **befreit sein von,** to be exempt from (*taxes; military service, etc.*); **sich von einem —en,** to get rid of a person. **—er,** *m.* (**—ers,** *pl.* **—er**) liberator. **—te(r),** *m.* one who is exempt *or* free. **—ung,** *f.* liberation; deliverance; exemption; disentanglement; immunity, *etc. Comp.* **—ungs=geld,** *n.* ransom. **—ungs=krieg,** *m.* war of independence; **die —ungs=kriege,** *m.pl.* the war(s) of Liberation (*of Germany against Napoleon I., 1813-1815*).

Befrem'd—en, I. *v.a. & imp.* to appear strange, astonish, surprise; **dies —et mich von ihm,** this surprises me in him; **sich —en lassen,** to feel surprised. II. *subst.n.* surprise. **—end,** *p. & adj.*, **—lich,** *adj.* odd, strange, surprising. **—ung,** *f. see* **—en,** II.

Befreun'd—en, *v.a.* to befriend, favour; to connect by friendship; **—et sein mit,** to be the friend of, to be on friendly terms with; **sich —en,** to become friends; **sich —en mit,** to make friends with; reconcile oneself to; **er —ete sich bald mit seiner neuen Lage,** he soon became reconciled to his new situation. **—et,** I. *p.p. & adj.* friendly; allied, akin; **—ete Zahlen,** amicable numbers; **der, die —ete,** friend, relative, connection. II. *adv.* on terms of friendship. **—ung,** *f.* befriending; friendly terms; friendship; affinity, relation.

Befrie'dicht, *adj. hum. for* **befriedigt** (*sl.*).

Befrie'dig—en, *v.a.* to satisfy; to gratify; to appease; **schwer zu —en,** fastidious, dainty; *see* **Einfriedigen. —end,** *p. & adj.* satisfactory. **—ung,** *f.* satisfaction; gratification; fence, enclosure; **—ung gewährend,** satisfactory.

Befru'cht—en, *v.a.* to fructify, fecundate; to fertilise; to impregnate. **—ung,** *f.* fertilisation; impregnation; fecundation, fructification; **verborgene, unmerkliche —ung,** cryptogamy; **—ung der Feigen,** caprification. *Comp.* **—ungs=röhre,** *f.* pistil (*Bot.*).

Befu'g—en, *v.a.* to empower, authorise. **—nis,** *f.* (*pl.* **—ni(ss)e**) authorisation; authority; warrant; powers (*of an envoy, etc.*); faculty; license; **einem —nis erteilen,** to authorise a person; **seine —nisse überschreiten,** to exceed one's powers. **—t,** *p.p. & adj.* authorised; competent; legal, legitimate; **sich für —t halten,** to think oneself entitled (*to*), justified (*in*).

Befüh'l—en, *v.a.* to feel (*the pulse, etc.*); to examine by feeling; to fumble; to handle, maul.

Befum'meln, *v.a.* to cheat (*sl.*); to investigate (*sl.*); to manage, get done (*sl.*).

Befu'nd, *m.* (**—es**) state in which a thing is found; **nach —,** *see* **nach Befinden.** *Comp.* **—bericht,** *m.* report. **—buch,** *n.* inventory; journal. **—schein,** *m.* certificate of the condition of a thing.

Befürch't—en, *v.a.* to fear, to apprehend; to suspect. **—ung,** *f.* fear, apprehension.

Befü'rwort—en, *v.a.* to speak (*or* write) in favour of, recommend; to support, second, advocate. **—ung,** *f.* recommendation, support.

Bega'b—en, *v.a.* to endow; to bestow upon, to give presents to. **—t,** *p.p. & adj.* gifted, talented; endowed. **—ung,** *f.* endowment; (*pl.*) talents.

Bega'ffen, *v.a.* to stare at *or* upon, to gape at.

Bega'ngen (*p.p. of* **begehen**), *adj.* gone *or* walked over; committed; **ein —er Weg,** a beaten track; **ein —er Fehler,** a mistake that has been made, a fault that has been committed.

Begä'ngnis, *n.* (**—(ss)es,** *pl.* **—(ss)e**) celebration, solemnisation; **Leichen—,** funeral.

Bega'nn, Begän'ne (Begön'ne), *imperf. ind. & subj. of* **beginnen.**

Bega'tt—en, *v.r.* to pair; to copulate, to couple. **—ung,** *f.* pairing; copulation; **verborgene —ung,** cryptogamy (*Bot.*). *Comp.* **—ungs=trieb,** *m.* sexual instinct. **—ungs=zeit,** *f.* coupling time; pairing time; time of fecundation (*Bot.*).

Begau'nern, *v.a.* to swindle, take in, cheat.

Bege'b—en, *ir.v.* I. *a.* to negotiate, transfer; to sell; to pass (*a note*); **zu —en,** negotiable (*C. L.*). II. *r.* to betake (*oneself*); to set about (*business, etc.*); **sich zur Ruhe —en,** to go to bed, to rest; **sich auf die Flucht —en,** to take to flight; **sich zu seinem Regiment —en,** to join one's regiment; **sich auf den Weg —en,** to set out (*on one's journey*); **sich in Gefahr —en,** to venture into danger, run the risk; **sich in den Ehestand —en,** to marry; **begieb dich an dein Gebet,** fall to your prayers; **es begab sich, daß,** it fell out, chanced that; **sich einer Sache —en,** to give up, renounce a th., withdraw one's claim to a th.; **ich begebe mich meines Vorteils,** I will forego my advantage. **—enheit,** *f.*, **—nis,** *n.* event, occurrence, adventure. **—ung,** *f.* giving up; negotiation of a bill (*C. L.*).

Bege'gn—en, *v.n.* (*aux.* **f.**) (*dat.*) to meet, meet with, light upon, encounter; to befall, happen, come to pass; to obviate, prevent; **was ist Ihnen —et?** what has happened to you?; **allen Einwürfen zu —en,** to obviate all objections; **jemandes Wünschen —en,** to meet, to anticipate one's wishes; **einem grob —en,** to receive, treat one rudely, harshly; **sich —en,** to concur (*in a wish, etc.*). **—is,** *n.* (**—(ss)es,** *pl.* **—(ss)e**) occurrence, event. **—ung,** *f.* meeting, encounter; treatment, usage.

Bege'h—en, *ir.v.a.* to traverse; to pace off; to frequent (*a road*); to beat (*for game*); to visit, inspect; to celebrate (*a festival*); to commit (*an error, etc.*); **ein Kirchspiel —en,** to perambulate *or* beat the bounds of a parish; **sich —en = sich begatten. —ung,** *f.* celebration, solemnisation; commission, perpetration. *Comp.* **—ungs=sünde,** *f.* sin of commission.

Bege'hr, *m. & n.* (**—s**) desire; **in —,** in demand (*C. L.*); **was ist Ihr —?** what do you want?

Bege'hr—en, I. *v.a.* to long for, desire; want; to hanker after; to crave, demand; **was —en Sie?** what do you want?; **du sollst nicht —en**

deines Nächsten Weib, thou shalt not covet thy neighbour's wife (*B.*); jemandes Tochter zur Ehe —en, to solicit a person's daughter in marriage; was —t man von uns? what is required of us?; Zucker ist wenig —, sugar is flat (*C. L.*); Kaffee ist sehr —t, coffee is in great demand (*C. L.*). II. *subst.n.* desire, demand, request; pretension; auf Ihr —en, at your request, by your desire; was ist Ihr —en? what do you desire? what can I do for you? in what can I serve you? —lich, *adj. & adv.* covetous. —lichkeit, *f.* covetousness; inordinate desire. —ung, *f.* desire, longing for; hankering after. *Comp.* —ens=wert, —ens=würdig, *adj.* desirable.

Begei'fern, *v.a.* to beslobber; to asperse, slander.

Begei'ster—n, *v.a.* to inspire; to animate, fill with enthusiasm; to throw into raptures; von etwas —t sein, to be in raptures with; sich für eine S. —n, to be *or* become enthusiastic about a th. —ung, *f.* inspiration; exaltation, rapture; enthusiasm. —ungs=fähig, *adj.* capable of enthusiasm. —ungs=voll, *adj.* full of enthusiasm; dithyrambic.

Begie'r, *f.*, **—de**, *f.* (*pl.* —den) eager desire; inordinate desire; (*carnal*) appetite, lust, concupiscence. —ig, *adj. & adv.* eager (nach, for); covetous; greedy; lustful; einen —ig machen, to excite a person's desire for, to arouse desire in him; ich bin —ig zu erfahren, ob ꝛc. I am anxious *or* curious to learn if, *etc.* —igkeit, *f.* avidity, eagerness.

Begie'ßen, *ir.v.a.* to water (*plants, etc.*); to sprinkle; to wet, moisten; to baste (*meat*); mit Blei —, to pour lead on, seal up.

Beg(h)i'ne, *see* Beguine.

Begi'nn, *m.* (—es) beginning, origin, commencement.

Begi'nnen, I. *ir.v.a.* to begin, commence; to set about; to do, undertake; was wollen Sie —? what will you do? how do you intend to act? II. *ir.v.n.* (*aux.* h.) to begin, commence; to originate. III. *subst.n.* undertaking, action, enterprise.

Begi'psen, *v.a.* to plaster.

Begi'ttern, *v.a.* to grate, to lattice.

Beglä'nzen, *v.a.* to throw light on, to illumin(at)e; Mondbeglänzt, lit up by the moon.

Begla'sen, *v.a.* to glaze (*see* Verglasen).

Beglau'big—en (*obs.* **Beglau'ben**), *v.a.* to attest, certify; to accredit (*an ambassador*); to confirm (*news*); eine —te Abschrift, an attested copy; sich —en, to prove one's identity. —er, *m.* (—ers, *pl.* —er) certifier; notary. —ung, *f.* accrediting; attestation, verification; zur —ung dessen, in testimony thereof *or* whereof. *Comp.* —ungs=amt, *n.* office of a public notary. —ungs=brief, *m.*, —ungs=schreiben, *n.* credentials. —ungs=eid, *m.* affidavit. —ungs=schein, *m.* certificate.

Beglei'ch—en, *ir.v.a.* to balance, pay, settle (*C. L.*). —ung, *f.*; zur —ung Ihrer Rechnung, in settlement of your bill (*C. L.*).

Beglei't—en, *v.a.* to accompany; to accompany (*Mus.*); to escort; to convoy; eine Dame nach Hause —en, to see a lady home; Schwächen —en das Alter, infirmities attend old age. —er, *m.* (—ers, *pl.* —er) attendant, escort; guide; companion; accompanist (*Mus.*). —ung, *f.* accompanying; attendants; train, retinue; procession; escort, convoy; accompaniment. *Comp.* —adresse, *f.* declaration-form. —erscheinung, *f.* accompanying *or* concomitant phenomenon. —schein, *m.* letter of advice; permit. —stimme, *f.* second (*Mus.*). —ungs=schiff, *n.* convoy; tender, consort. —zettel, *m.* way-bill.

Beglü'ck—en (**Beglü'ckseligen**), *v.a.* to make happy, to bless. —er, *m.* (—ers, *pl.* —er) benefactor, giver of happiness. *Comp.* —wünschen, *v.a.* to congratulate, felicitate. —wünschung, *f.* congratulation.

Begna'd—en, **—igen**, *v.a.* to pardon; to favour, grant favours to. —igung, *f.* pardoning; pardon; amnesty; favour, grace. *Comp.* —igungs=gesuch, *n.* petition for mercy. —igungs=recht, *n.* prerogative of mercy, right to pardon.

Begnü'gen, *v.r.*; sich — (lassen) an einer S., to content oneself with a th.; to be satisfied (*with*), to acquiesce (*in*).

Begö'nne, **Bego'nnen**, *imperf. sub. & p.p. of* begi'nnen.

Bego'ß, **Begö'sse**, **Bego'ssen**, *imperf. ind. & subj. & p.p. of* begie'ßen; wie ein begossener Pudel, shamefaced, dumfounded, abashed, depressed.

Begra'ben, *ir.v.a.* to bury, inter; to conceal; sich in der Einsamkeit —, to bury oneself in solitude; da liegt der Hund —! there's the rub!

Begrä'bnis, *n.* (—(ss)es, *pl.* —(ss)e) burial; funeral; obsequies; burial-place, grave. *Comp.* —feierlichkeiten, —gebräuche, *pl.* funeral rites. —grüfte, *pl.* vaults; catacombs. —lied, *n.* dirge. —platz, *m.* cemetery.

Begra'sen, *v.a.* to cover with grass; to lay down in grass (*land*); to graze; sich —, to be covered with grass; to feed, grow fat; begrast, grassy.

Begrei'f—en, *ir.v.* I. *a.* to touch, feel, handle; to include, comprise; to comprehend, understand, conceive; England wurde nicht mit in den Frieden begriffen, England was not included in the peace; schnell etwas —en, to be quick of comprehension; etwas schwer —en, to be slow; ich —e nicht, wo er bleibt, I cannot imagine where he is; in sich —en, to include, contain; dieses Wort —t mehrere Bedeutungen in sich, this word has several meanings; begriffen sein, to be engaged in, to be about a thing; das Haus ist im Bau(e) begriffen, the house is being built, is in process of construction; in fortwährender Aufregung begriffen, in a state of constant excitement; auf der Reise begriffen sein, to be travelling; über der Arbeit begriffen sein, to be at work; im Anmarsch begriffen sein, to approach, be on the way; beim Anziehen begriffen sein, to be just dressing. II. *r.* to recover, recollect oneself; to be easy of comprehension; das —t sich leicht, that is easily understood. —lich, *adj. & adv.* comprehensible, conceivable; einem etwas —lich machen, to make one understand, make one see a thing. —lichkeit, *f.* conceivability, intelligibility.

Begre'nzbar, *adj.* limitable; definable.

Begre'nz—en, *v.a.* to bound (*countries, etc.*); to limit, circumscribe; to define, limit; jenes Haus —t unsere Aussicht, that house shuts out (*or* obstructs) our view. —t, *p.p. & adj.* bounded; narrow; limited. —t=heit, *f.* limitation; finiteness. —ung, *f.* limitation; limit, bounds.

Begri'ff, *m.* (—s, *pl.* —e) comprehension; conception; idea, notion; concept; extent, circumference; contents; verkehrte —e, crude notions, wrong ideas; einem einen — beibringen, to convey some idea to one; falscher —, misconception; schwer von —en sein, to be dull of apprehension, to be slow, to be a duffer; sich (*dat.*) einen — machen, to form (*for oneself*) a conception; es ist über seine —e, it is beyond his powers of comprehension; that passes his comprehension; ein kurzer —, epitome; im —(e) sein, to be on the point of, in the act of; ich war eben im —(e) ꝛc., I was just going to, *etc.*; ich war im — zu gehen, I was about to go. —lich, *adj.* ideal; abstract; rein —lich, abstract; conceptional; conceptual. *Comp.* **—s=bestimmung,** *f.* definition. **—s=fach,** *n.* category (*Log.*). **—s=vermögen,** *n.* intellectual capacity. **—s=verwechselung,** *f.* confounding of ideas. **—s=verwirrung,** *f.* confusion of ideas. **—s=zergliederung,** *f.* analysis of conceptions.

Begrü'nd—en, *v.a.* to base, found; to prove, make good (*an assertion, etc.*); to offer reasons for; to confirm. **—er,** *m.* (**—ers,** *pl.* **—er**) founder, establisher; originator. **—ung,** *f.* founding; establishment; argument (*of a book*); preamble (*of a bill*); confirmation; proof.

Begrü'nen, *v.a.* to make green; **sich —,** to grow green, to burst into leaf.

Begrü'ß—en, *v.a.* to greet, salute, hail; to welcome. **—ung,** *f.* greeting, salutation; welcome. *Comp.* **—ungs=schuß,** *m.* salute.

Begu'cken, *v.a.* to look at, to peep at (*colloq.*).

Begui'ne, *f.*, (**Beg(h)i'ne,** *f.*) Beguine (*member of an order of females in Holland and Germany, established for devotion and charity*).

Begünstig—en, *v.a.* to favour, befriend; to patronise; **—t von,** favoured by. **—er,** *m.* (**—ers,** *pl.* **—er**) patron; partisan; abettor. **—ung,** *f.* encouragement, patronage; act of favouring.

Begü'rten, *v.a.* to gird.

Begu'tacht—en, *v.a.* to give an opinion on; **—ende Stelle,** body of experts. **—ung,** *f.* formal opinion, expert opinion; examination.

Begü'tert, *adj.* opulent, rich; well to do; **—er Adel,** noble owners of large estates; **ein —er,** a wealthy man; rich landed proprietor.

Begü'tigen, *v.a.* to appease, to propitiate. **—d,** *adv.* soothingly; in an appeasing manner.

Behaa'r—en, *v.a.* to cover with hair; **sich —en,** to get hair. **—t,** *p.p. & adj.* pilose; hirsute.

Behä'big, *adj. & adv.* in easy circumstances; comfortable (= **behaglich**); corpulent, stout (*of persons*); **ein —er alter Herr,** a portly old gentleman.

Beha'ft—en, *v.a.* to burden, charge with, load; to infect, affect with. **—et,** *p.p. & adj.* subject to (*fainting, fits, etc.*); loaded with (*vices, etc.*); afflicted with, affected by (*disease, etc.*); **mit Schulden —et,** deeply in debt; **—ete Güter,** encumbered estates.

Beha'g—en, I. *v.n.* (*aux.* **h.**) (*dat.*) to please, suit; **es —t ihm nicht,** it does not suit him, he does not like it; **sie ließen es sich —en,** they made themselves comfortable, enjoyed themselves. II. *subst.n.* comfort, ease; enjoyment; **—en an einer Sache finden,** to take delight in a thing. **—lich,** *adj. & adv.* comfortable; **er macht es sich —lich,** he takes his ease, makes himself comfortable *or* at home. **—lichkeit,** *f.* comfort, ease; sociability.

Beha'lt—en, I. *ir.v.a.* to retain; to maintain; to carry (*Arith.*); to remember; **im Auge —en,** to keep in view, not to lose sight of; **seine Fassung —en,** to retain one's self-command, to keep one's composure *or* temper; **bei sich —,** to keep to oneself; **Recht —en,** to maintain one's point, to gain one's cause; **für sich —en,** to keep to oneself, to keep secret; **die Oberhand —en,** to maintain the upper hand, to be victorious; **das Feld —en,** to remain master of the battlefield (*Mil.*); **das behält immer seinen Wert,** that will always fetch its price; **an sich —en,** to retain. II. *subst.n.* **das —en und Erlassen der Sünden,** binding and loosing from sin. III. *p.p. & adj.* **ein —enes Schiff,** a ship that has escaped from danger; **wohl —en,** safe and sound; **der —ene Kurs,** the true course; **—ene Güter,** goods in good condition. **—bar,** *adj.* retainable. **—lich** (*usually* **vorbehaltlich**), *prep. with gen.* with reservation of. **—sam,** *adj.* retentive (*of memory*); lasting. **—samkeit,** *f.* retentiveness.

Behä'lt—er, *m.* (**—ers,** *pl.* **—er**) reservoir; receptacle; fish-tank. **—nis,** *n.* (**—ni(ss)es,** *pl.* **—ni(ss)e**) place to store things in and keep them in good condition; cover (*for game*); reservoir; receptacle; box, bin; shrine (*for relics*); cage (*for wild beasts*).

Beha'nd—eln, *v.a.* to handle (*an object, a subject*); to manage; to treat; to manipulate, manage; to dress (*wounds*); to bargain for, to chaffer; **dieser Arzt —elt uns beide,** this physician attends us both; **wie ein kleines Kind —eln,** to treat like a baby; **wie einen Fremden —eln,** to make a stranger of (*one*); **einen redlich —eln,** to deal honestly with one; **sie versteht es, Kinder zu —eln,** she understands the management of (*or* how to manage) children; **eine Waare —eln,** to cheapen, *or* bargain for, an article (*C. L.*). **—lung,** *f.* treatment; management, manipulation; dressing (*of wounds*); bargaining; **ärztliche —lung,** professional medical attendance. **—lungs=art,** *f.* mode of treatment, usage.

Beha'ng, *m.* (**—es,** *pl.* **Behänge**) anything suspended for ornament; hanging(s); appendage; dangling ears (*of dogs*); long hair (*on the feet of horses*); **— der Bäume im Winter,** snow and ice on the trees in the winter. **—en,** *adj.* hung with; having large, hanging ears; **der Hund ist schön —en,** the dog has handsome ears.

Behä'ngen, *ir. & reg. v.a.* to hang (*walls, etc.*); to put up (*curtains, hangings, etc.*); to cover with; to tie (*a hound*) and lead it; to attack, to stick fast to (*game*); **sich mit etwas —,** to deck oneself out with; **sich mit schlechten Leuten —,** to keep bad company.

Beha'rr—en, I. *v.n.* (*aux.* **h.**) to persevere, continue, persist in; to remain firm, steadfast; **auf, bei, in etwas —en,** to persist in, insist upon, continue to do, be steadfast in something; **er beharrte darauf, fünf Mark zu fordern,** he stood out for five marks; **steif auf seinem Sinne —en,** to be obstinate; **wie ich beharre bin ich Knecht,** as soon as I do not move on I become a servant; **fest auf seinem Sinne —,** to stick firmly to one's purpose; **bei seinem Vorsatze —,** to stand to one's resolution. II. *subst.n.* perseverance, persistence; **—en in Ruhe,** permanency, vis inertiæ. **—lich,** *adj. & adv.* persevering, persistent; constant, unyielding, firm; **—licher Fleiß,** assiduity; **—liches Bitten,** importunity; **—licher Eigensinn,** obstinacy, pig-headedness; **ein Mann, der —lich bei seinem Vorsatze bleibt,** a man constant to his purpose. **—lichkeit,** *f.* perseverance, persistence, steadfastness, stability; **—lichkeit führt zum Ziel,** perseverance brings success, everything comes in time to him who can wait (*prov.*). **—ung,** *f. see* **—lichkeit.** *Comp.* **—ungs=vermögen,** *n.* vis inertiæ, inertness; persistence of motion. **—ungs=zustand,** *m.* permanence; persistence; resistance (*of machines*).

Behau'en, *ir.v.a.* to hew; to trim, dress, square (*timber, stone*); to poll, lop (*trees*); to assay (*Min.*); **ein —er Gang,** an exhausted lode.

Behau'pt—en, *v.* I. *a.* to assert; to affirm, avouch; to keep, maintain (*one's station; one's reputation or character; one's opinion, etc.*), to make good, prove (*an assertion, etc.*); to uphold (*the truth*); **das Schlachtfeld —en,** to remain master of the battlefield; **das will ich —en,** that I'll be bound; **zu viel —en,** to overstate one's point, to go too far. II. *r.* to hold one's ground; to make good one's position; to hold up, be firm (*of prices, etc.*). **—end,** *p. & adj.*; **—ender Satz,** affirmative (enunciative) proposition. **—ung,** *f.* assertion, statement; maintaining, upholding (*one's dignity,* *position, etc.*); holding out; **das ist eine bloße —ung,** that is merely an assertion. *Comp.* **—ungs=wort,** *n.* predicate.

Behau'ſ—en, *v.a.* to lodge, house, take in; **ſich —en,** to settle. **—ung,** *f.* lodging; house, home.

Behe'lf, *m.* (**—s,** *pl.* **—e**) expedient, shift; device; excuse; resource.

Behe'lf—en, *ir.v.r.* to manage, contrive; to content oneself (**mit,** with); to have recourse to; **wir —en uns kümmerlich,** we make shift to live; **er mußte ſich mit einer Lüge —en,** he was forced to resort to a lie. **—lich,** *adj.* auxiliary; serviceable; serving as an expedient *or* excuse (*rare*).

Behe'llig—en, *v.a.* to importune, bother. **—ung,** *f.* importunity.

Behe'lm—en, *v.a.* to put on a helmet; to cover with a helmet; **—te Krieger,** soldiers with helmets.

Behe'nd—e, *adj.* & *adv.* handy, agile, nimble; adroit. **—igkeit,** *f.* agility, activity; adroitness; dexterity; lightness.

Behe'rberg—en, I. *v.a.* to lodge, shelter. II. *subst.* **—en,** *n.,* **—ung,** *f.* lodging.

Behe'rrſch—en, *v.a.* to rule over, govern; to be master of; **die Feſtung —t die Stadt,** the fortress commands the city; **wir können die Ereigniſſe des Lebens nicht immer —en,** the events of life are not always under our control; **ſich —en,** to control one's feelings, keep one's temper. **—er,** *m.* (**—ers,** *pl.* **—er**) ruler, master, sovereign, ruler, lord. **—erin,** *f.* mistress, sovereign. **—ung,** *f.* sway, control; domination, mastery.

Behe'rz—igen, *v.a.* to take to heart; to consider well, weigh, ponder. **—igens=wert,** *adj.* worthy of being considered. **—igung,** *f.* the taking to heart; reflection, consideration. **—t,** *p.p.* & *adj.* brave, spirited, courageous, stout-hearted; **—t machen,** to embolden, inspirit; **eine —te Antwort,** a spirited *or* bold reply. **—t=heit,** *f.* spirit, intrepidity.

Behe'x—en, *v.a.* to bewitch. **—ung,** *f.* sorcery, bewitchment.

Behie'lt, *imperf.* of **behalten.**

Behi'lflich, *see* **Behülflich.**

Behi'ndern, *v.a.* to prevent.

Behi'ng (**Behie'ng**) *imperf.* of **behängen.**

Beho'lz—en, *v.a.* to plant with timber, to tend, nurse young trees; to fell (*wood*). **—t,** *p.p.* & *adj.* wooded. *Comp.* **—ungs=gerechtigkeit,** *f.* right of felling timber.

Beho'rchen, *v.a.* to overhear; to eavesdrop.

Behö'rde, *f.* (*pl.* **—n**) magistracy, authority; the authorities; office, court; **die höchſte —,** government; **Gerichts—,** law officers; **Orts—,** local authorities; **Polizei—,** police office.

Beho'ſen, *v.a.* to put into breeches *or* trousers.

Behu'f, *m.* (**—s**) behalf, behoof; use, advantage, benefit; **zu dieſem —,** on this behalf, for this purpose; **zum — der Armen,** for the benefit of the poor. **—s,** *prep.* (*with gen.*) for the purpose of, in order to.

Behu'ft, *p.p.* & *adj.* hoofed.

Behü'lflich, *adj.* useful, serviceable; helpful, **einem — ſein,** to help one, assist, lend one a helping hand; **einem bei Bezahlung ſeiner Schulden — ſein,** to help one to pay his debts.

Behü't—en, *v.a.* to guard (**vor,** against), to preserve, keep (*from*); to watch over, guard, defend, protect; **der Himmel —e mich vor ſolchen Gedanken,** heaven preserve me from harbouring such thoughts; **—e!** no idea! certainly not! far from it!; **—e Gott!** God forbid!; **Gott —e euch! —' dich Gott!** God save you! may God protect you! **—er,** *m.* (**—ers,** *pl.* **—er**), **—erin,** *f.* guardian; protector.

Behu'tſam, *adj.* & *adv.* on one's guard, circumspect, prudent; careful, heedful; wary, cautious. **—keit,** *f.* caution, discretion, circumspection, care; watchfulness, cautiousness.

Bei, I. *prep.* (*with dat.*) about; amidst, among(st); at; with; in possession of; by (*as instrument*); by, upon (*in oaths*); at the house of; during; for; by; in company with; near, by, at the side of; to; on, in case of; under penalty of; in connection with, along with; considering; in spite of; in presence of; **ich habe kein Geld — mir,** I have no money about me; **— alle ſeinem Unglück,** amidst all his misfortunes; **— den Römern,** amongst *or* with the Romans; **er genießt keine große Achtung — uns,** he is not held in very high esteem amongst us; **—m erſten Anblick,** at the first glance, at first sight; **— einem anklopfen,** to knock at a person's door, to make enquiries of a p., to sound a p.; **—m offenen Fenſter ſitzen,** to sit at the open window; **er wohnt — ſeinem Vater,** he lives at his father's; **— Tiſche,** at table; **—m Eſſen,** at one's meal, at dinner; **— Hofe,** at court; **—m Spiele,** at play; **— dieſer Nachricht,** at this news; **— dem Buchhändler,** at the bookseller's; **—m Scheiden,** at parting; **— Sonnenaufgang,** at sunrise; **— der Hand,** at hand, handy; **— ſeinem Worte nehmen,** to take (*one*) at his word; **— der Hochzeit,** at the wedding; **—m Feuer,** by, near the fire; **— Tage,** by day; **— Licht,** by (candle-)light; **— einem aushalten,** to stand by one; **— ſeinem Namen nennen,** to call (*one*) by his name; **— der Hand nehmen,** to take by the hand; **er ergriff ſie — den Haaren,** he seized her by the hair; **—m Himmel, — Gott ſchwören,** to swear by heaven, by God; **— Leibe nicht,** not for your life; by no means, decidedly not; **— weitem beſſer,** better by far; **— ſeinen Lebzeiten,** during his lifetime; **— alle dem,** for all that, notwithstanding; **— ſich überlegen,** to consider in one's own mind; **— Jahren ſein,** to be (*up*) in years; **— hellem Tage,** in broad daylight; **ich war damals — Gelde,** I was well off at that time; **— ſich, — Sinnen bleiben,** to control oneself, to keep in one's senses; **— guter Laune,** in good humour; **nicht — Laune ſein,** to be in bad spirits, out of humour; **nicht — Stimme ſein,** to have no voice; **— Homer,** in Homer; **— Zeiten,** in good time, early, betimes; **— guter Geſundheit,** in good health; **— der Kirche,** near the church; **die Schlacht — Sedan,** the battle of Sedan; **beſiegt — Sedan,** defeated at Sedan; **— Leibesſtrafe,** upon pain of death; **— meiner Seele,** upon my soul; **— meiner Seligkeit,** as I hope to be saved; **— näherer Überlegung,** on second thoughts; **Pfeiler — Pfeiler ſtürzte hin,** pillar upon (*or* after) pillar crashed down; **— einem Glaſe Wein,** over a glass of wine; **— ſich behalten,** to keep to oneself; **— ſich denken,** to think to oneself; **er hat ſtets — dem Prinzen Zutritt,** he has always access to the prince; **ſich — der Polizei beſchweren,** to complain to the police; **das iſt — ihm ganz einerlei,** it is all the same to him; that makes no difference in his case; **— dem Winde ſegeln,** to sail close to the wind; **er hat mich — Heller und Pfennig bezahlt,** he has paid me to the last farthing; **— Gott iſt alles möglich,** with God all things are possible; **— dieſen Verben ſteht der Konjunktiv,** these verbs take the subjunctive; **— uns,** with us, at home, at our house; **er fing —m letzten an,** he began with the last; **— ihm verliere ich die Geduld,** I lose all patience with him; **— offenen Fenſtern ſchlafen,** to sleep with the windows open; **— Gelegenheit,** upon occasion, as opportunity offers; **— Seite,** aside; **—m Leben erhal-**

ten, to preserve, keep alive; — **einander**, together; — **alle dem**, with all that, notwithstanding; **bestellen** —, to order from, through, to bespeak of. II. *adv.* almost, nearly, up to, about; — **sechshundert Mann**, nearly six hundred men; — **sechs Jahr älter**, about six years older. III. *adv. or sep. prefix*, near, near by; beside, in addition; as accessory; as help.

Beia'n, *adv.* close by (*but* **anbei'**, herewith).

Bei'anker, *m.* kedge-anchor.

Bei'behalt—en, *ir.v.a.* to keep on, retain (*in office*); to keep (*at hand*); to keep, retain, preserve. **—ung**, *f.* keeping; retention, continuance.

Bei'biegen, *ir.v.a.* to inclose (*Law*); **bei'gebogen**, inclosed (*Law, C. L.*); **sich** (*dat.*) **etwas** —, to possess oneself of a thing (*colloq.*).

Bei'binden, *ir.v.a.* to bind with, to tie to, to bind up with.

Bei'blatt, *n.* supplement (*to a newspaper or periodical*); extra sheet.

Bei'bote, *m.* (—**n**, *pl.* —**n**) extra messenger.

Bei'bring—en, I. *ir.v.a.* to bring forward; to produce (*witnesses*); to cite (*authorities*); to adduce (*reasons, proofs*); to deal (*blows*); **einem etwas —en**, to impart something to a p., to teach; **Kenntnis —en**, to teach, instruct; **einem einen Begriff —en**, to give one an idea of, convey some notion of; **einem Trost —en**, to comfort a person; **einem eine Wunde —en**, to inflict a wound upon a p.; **dem Feinde eine Niederlage —en**, to inflict a defeat on the enemy; **einem Furcht —en**, to inspire one with fear; **einem Arznei, Gift —en**, to administer medicine to, to poison a person; **einem eine schlimme Meinung von einem andern —en**, to insinuate evil of a person to another. II. *subst.n.*; **—en einer Frau**, wife's marriage portion. **—ung**, *f.* producing, production (*of proofs, etc.*).

Bei'cht—e, *f.* (*pl.* —**en**) confession; **seine —e ablegen**, to confess; **einem (die) —e hören**, to confess a person; **zur —e gehen**, to confess. **—iger**, *m.* (—**igers**, *pl.* —**iger**) father confessor. *Comp.* **—gänger**, *m.*, **—kind**, *n.* penitent, confessant. **—geld**, *n.* shrove-money; confessor's fee. **—geheimnis**, *n.* secret of the confessional. **—siegel**, *n.* seal of confession. **—stuhl**, *m.* confessional; confessional box, *or* chair. **—vater**, *m.* father confessor.

Bei'cht—en, *v.a. & n.* to confess. **—ende**, *m. & f.* penitent, person confessing.

Bei'd—e, *num. adj.* both; **alle —e**, both one and the other; both of them; **keiner von —en**, neither one nor the other; **in —en Fällen**, in either case; **—e für einen und einer für —e**, each for the other; **wir —e**, we two, both of us. **—erlei**, *indec. adj.* of both sorts, of either sort; **—erlei Geschlechts**, of either sex; of common gender. **—es**, *n.* both; **—es, Männer und Frauen**, both men and women. *Comp.* **—er=seitig**, *adj.* on both sides, mutual, reciprocal. **—er=seits**, *adv.* reciprocally, mutually. **—lebig**, *adj.* amphibious.

Bei'drehen, *v.a.* to bring, heave to (*Naut.*).

Bei'drucken, *v.a.* to print (*in addition*), to annex.

Bei'drücken, *v.a.* to affix (*one's seal*) to.

Beieina'nder, *adv.* together.

Bei'erbe, *m.* (—**n**, *pl.* —**n**) co-heir, joint-heir.

Bei'fall, *m.* (—**s**) approbation; applause; **es hat meinen** —, I approve of it; — **winken**, to nod approval; — **finden**, to meet with approval; **stürmischer** —, loud applause, acclamation. *Comp.* **—geber**, *m.* applauder. **—(s)=ruf**, *m.* shout of applause. **—s=bezeigung**, *f.* mark of applause. **—s=trieb**, *m.* love of approbation (*Phren.*).

Bei'fallen, *ir.v.n.* (*aux.* **f.** *dat.*) to come into the mind, to occur to one; **lassen Sie sich nicht — zu sagen**, don't think of saying; **jetzt fällt es mir bei**, now it strikes me, it occurs to me; **einer Person, einer Sache** —, to approve of, *or* applaud, a person *or* thing; **jemandes Meinung** —, to coincide with a person's views; **einem** —, to side with a person.

Bei'fällig, *adj.* incidental; assenting, approving; — **aufnehmen**, to receive with approval; to receive graciously (*of superiors*).

Bei'folgen, *v.n.* (*aux.* **f.**) to follow; to be annexed, inclosed. **—d**, *p. & adj.* inclosed, subjoined.

Bei'füg—en, *v.a.* to add, subjoin, inclose. **—ung**, *f.* addition, annexing; attribute (*Gram.*).

Bei'fuß, *m.* wormwood; artemisia; truss (*of a sail*).

Bei'geben, *ir.v.a.* to add, join to; to appoint (*as an assistant*); to associate (*in an office, an undertaking, etc.*); **klein** —, to come down a peg; to give in, to become submissive, to lower one's pretensions *or* tone, to sing small.

Bei'gehen, *ir.v.n.* (*aux.* **f.**) to go with, be joined to; to occur to; **es ging mir nicht bei, ihn zu beleidigen**, I never thought of offending him; **sich** (*dat.*) — **lassen**, to take into one's head, to imagine, to venture, presume.

Bei'genannt, *p.p. & adj.* surnamed.

Bei'geordnete(r), *m.* assistant to an official.

Bei'gerichte, *n.pl.* entremets, hors d'œuvre; side dishes.

Bei'geschlossen, *p.p. & adj.* inclosed (*of letters*).

Bei'geschmack, Bei'schmack, *m.* (—**s**) taste of something extraneous to the thing itself, aftertaste, smack, flavour, savour.

Bei'gesellen, *v.a.* to associate; **sich einem** —, to associate with, to join one.

Bei'glied, *n.* additional member; small moulding (*Arch.*).

Beihe'r, *adv.* beside, at the side of; besides, moreover; **mit** —, by the way, by the bye.

Bei'hilf—e, Bei'hülf—e, *f.* assistance, aid, succour; **—e an Geld**, subsidy; **—e an Mannschaft**, auxiliary troops. **—lich**, *adj.* helping; subsidiary.

Bei'holen, *v.a.* to haul aft (*the sheets*) (*Nav.*).

Bei'kommen, *ir.v.n.* (*aux.* **f.**) to come at, get at, get near; to come up to, to reach; to be inclosed, annexed; **ihm ist nicht beizukommen**, there is no getting at him, no making an impression on him; **der Festung ist nicht beizukommen**, the fortress is inaccessible; **nicht** —, to fall short of; **hierin kommen wir den Franzosen nicht bei**, in this respect we are inferior to the French; **seinem Schaden (wieder)** —, to repair one's loss. **—d**, *adj.* following; inclosed, annexed; **—d erhalten Sie Faktura**, inclosed please find invoice; **sich** (*dat.*) — **lassen**, to dare, to presume, to imagine; **laß dir nicht** —, don't take it into your head.

Beil, *n.* (—**s**, *pl.* —**e**) hatchet. *Comp.* **—brief**, *m.* builder's certificate; grand bill of sale, register of a ship (*Naut.*). **—eisen**, *n.* bar-iron. **—fertig**, *adj.* ready built, finished all but the rigging. **—förmig**, *adj.* hatchet-shaped. **—kraut**, *n.*, **—pflanze**, *f.* hatchet vetch. **—schnecke**, *f.* Dolabella. **—stein**, *m.* axe-stone, ofite. **—stiel**, *m.* hatchet-helve. **—stock**, *m.* walking-stick with a kind of hatchet at the top (*obs.*). **—träger**, *m.* lictor; halberdier bill-man. **—wurzel**, *f.* common blue iris.

Bei'lage, *f.* (*pl.* —**n**) something added; inclosure, letter inclosed; supplement (*to a newspaper, etc.*); appendix; deposit; **Gemüse mit** —, a dish of vegetables with a slice of meat; **Fleisch mit** —, a dish of meat with vegetables.

Bei'lager, *n.* (—**s**, *pl.* —) nuptials (*old technical term applied to persons of high rank*);

das — halten, to celebrate the nuptials, to consummate the marriage.
Bei'last, *f.* (*pl.* —en) extra freight; seaman's free cargo.
Bei'läuf—er, *m.* (—ers, *pl.* —er) errand-boy, foot-boy; supernumerary. —**ig,** I. *adj.* incidental, parenthetic; approximative; eine —ige Bemerkung, a passing remark; eine —ige Berechnung, a rough calculation. II. *adv.* incidentally, by the way, by the bye; nearly, about.
Bei'leg—en, I. *v.a.* to adjoin, to add; to enclose; to confer (*a title*); to attribute, ascribe to; to attach (*value, importance to*); einem Briefe eine Banknote —en, to enclose a banknote in a letter; einem einen Namen —en, to give a name to, to surname; er besitzt alle die Laster, die man ihm —t, he has all the vices imputed to him; eine beigelegte Eigenschaft, an attribute (*Log.*); Streitigkeiten —en, to settle disputes; sie haben ihren Streit beigelegt, they have made up their quarrel; die Segel —en, *see* Einreffen. II. *n.* to heave to, lie to (*Naut.*); to come round to (*a person's opinion*); frisch —en, to apply oneself zealously to a task (*poet.*). —**ung,** *f.* addition; attribution, imputation; conferring (*of a title, a name, etc.*); adjustment, settlement; deposing; laying to. *Comp.* —ungs=wort, *n.* adjective.
Beilei'de, *adv. in the phrase* — nicht! not for (*your*) life; by no means, on no account whatever.
Bei'leid, *n.* (—es) condolence; einem sein — bezeigen, to condole with one. *Comp.* —s=brief, *m.*, —s=schreiben, *n.* letter of condolence.
Bei'liegen, *ir.v.n.* (*aux.* h.) to lie with; to sleep with; to accompany; to lie to (*Naut.*); —der Brief, the enclosed letter, enclosure.
Beil'ke, *f.*, **Beil'kespiel,** *n.* shovel-board, trucks, spillikins.
Beim, *short for* bei dem.
Bei'mengen, *v.a.* to admix.
Bei'meſſ—en, *ir.v.a.*; einem etwas —en, to attribute, ascribe, impute s.th to s.o., to charge a p. with s.th.; (einer S.) Glauben —en, to believe, to attach *or* give credit to; wenn ich diesen Gerüchten Glauben —en darf, if I may believe these reports; einem gute Absichten —en, to give one credit for good intentions; beizumessen, attributable, imputable. —**ung,** *f.* imputation, attributing to.
Bei'misch—en, *v.a.* to add to a mixture, to mix with, to admix. —**ung,** *f.* admixture; eine geringe —ung von, a sprinkling of.
Bein, *n.* (—s, *pl.* —e) leg; bone; das heilige —, os sacrum; es fuhr (ging) mir durch Mark und —, it cut me to the quick, it sent a thrill through me; Stein und — schwören, to swear most solemnly; zu — werden, to ossify; einem ein — stellen, to trip one up; to make one fall unexpectedly; er ist mir ein Klotz am —, he is always in my way; mit verschränkten —en, cross-legged; er ist gut auf den —en, he is a good walker; auf die —e bringen, to bring up (*children*), to raise (*an army*), to help one, to set one up; einem auf die —e helfen, to give a man a lift; wieder auf die —e kommen, to recover health; auf den —en, on foot, afoot; sind Sie so früh auf den —en? are you up so early?; er ist immer auf den —en, he is always stirring, on the move; ich kann auf keinem —e stehen, I have not a leg to stand on; er steht auf sehr schwachen —en, his affairs are in a shaky condition; sich auf die —e machen, to start, set out, to run away; er machte sich schnell auf die —e, he hastily took to his legs; ich will dir —e machen, I'll make you find your legs; nimm die —e mit! make haste!; sich auf den —en halten, to keep one's footing, to keep on one's legs; kein —! not a bit, by no means, not at all (*sl.*). —**chen,** *n.* ossicle, small bone. —**ern,** *adj.* of bone. —**icht,** *adj.* bony. —**ig,** *adj.* (*suffix*) = legged, as krummbeinig, bandy-legged. —**ling,** *m.* (—lings, *pl.* —linge) leg-hide (*Shoem.*); leg of a stocking. *Comp.* —**ader,** *f.* crural vein. —**ähnlich,** *adj.* osseous; shaped like a leg. —**brech,** *m.* bone-glue; Narthecium ossifragum (*Bot.*). —**brecher,** *m.* osprey. —**bruch,** *n.* fracture of the leg. —**brüchig,** *adj.* broken-legged. —**bruch=lade,** *f.* splinters, cradle for keeping a broken leg in its proper position. —**dürr,** *adj.* exceedingly thin, meagre. —**fäule,** —**fäulnis,** *f.* caries. —**flügel,** *pl.* the talaria (*Myth.*). —**fügung,** *f.* articulation. —**geige,** *f. see* Gambe. —**gerippe,** —**gerüst,** *n.* skeleton. —**geschwulst,** *f.* osseous tumour. —**gewächs,** *n.* exostosis. —**glas,** *n.* alabaster glass. —**gras,** *n. see* —brech. —**harnisch,** *m.* greaves, cuisses. —**hai,** *m.* basking shark. —**haus,** *n.* charnel-house. —**haut,** *f.* periosteum. —**hebel,** —**heber,** *m.* elevator (*Surg.*). —**heil,** *n.* comfrey (*Bot.*). —**höhle,** *f.* bone-socket. —**kleider,** *pl.* trousers. —**kleider=rollen,** *pl.* parts in which women appear in men's clothes (*Theat.*). —**kleider=stoffe,** *pl.* trouserings. —**knopf,** *m.* bone button; condyle. —**lade,** *f.*, —**leder,** *n.* leg of a riding-boot. —**leim,** *m.* bone-glue. —**los,** *adj.* boneless. —**mehl,** *n.* bone-dust. —**säge,** *f.* bone-saw. —**schellen,** *pl.* shackles, fetters. —**schiene,** *f.* splint; (*pl.*) greaves. —**schraube,** *f.* the boot (*torture*). —**schwarz,** *adj.* & *n.* ivory black. —**spat,** *m.* bone spavin. —**well,** *n.*, —**wurz,** *m.* comfrey.
Beina'h, Beina'he, *adv.* almost, nearly, well-nigh; *as prefix of adj.* = sub, *as* —rostfarbig, subferruginous; es ist — einerlei *or* — dasselbe, it is much the same thing; ich wäre — gestorben, I had almost died, I was on the point of dying; — hätte ich es ihr gesagt, I was within an ace of telling her; er wäre — geschlagen, he was all but defeated.
Bei'name, *m.* (—ns, *pl.* —n) surname, epithet; ein spöttischer —, a by-name, nickname; Wilhelm I. mit dem —n der Siegreiche, William I. surnamed the Victorious.
Bei'nerven, *pl.* accessory nerves.
Bei'ordnen, *v.a.* to appoint as assistant *or* adjunct; beigeordnet, coordinate; adjunct.
Bei'pferd, *n.* (—s, *pl.* —e) spare horse; led-horse, reserve *or* relay horse.
Bei'pflicht—en, *v.n.* (*aux.* h.); einem —en, to agree with one in opinion; ich pflichte seinen Meinungen bei, I am of the same opinion, I agree with his views; einer Maßregel —en, to approve of a measure. —**ung,** *f.* consent; assent; approval.
Bei'rat, *m.* (—(e)s, *pl.* Beiräte) advice; (*assistant*) counsellor; juristischer —, legal adviser.
Be=ir'ren, *v.a.* to mislead, confuse; er läßt sich nicht —, he does not allow himself to be disconcerted, he sticks to his opinion.
Beisam'men, *adv.* together; seine Gedanken — haben, to have one's wits about one; — nicht bestehen können, to be incompatible; das — sein, the being together, union.
Bei'sa—ß, Bei'sa—sse, *m.* (—(ss)en, *pl.* —(ss)en) inhabitant of a town or borough who has no rights of citizenship; small farmer; squatter. *Comp.* —(ss)en=recht, *n.* right of settlement.
Bei'satz, *m.* (—es, *pl.* Beisätze) addition; apposition; admixture; er vertraute mir das Geheimnis mit dem —e, daß, he imparted the secret to me, adding, *etc.*; ohne —, unalloyed. *Comp.* —**wort,** *n.* apposition, epithet (*Gramm.*).
Bei'schießen, *ir.v.a.* to contribute, to advance (*money*); to add (= bei'steuern).
Bei'schiff, *n.* cock-boat; tender (*Naut.*).

Bei'schlaf, *m.* (—es) cohabitation, coition; **unehelicher —,** concubinage; fornication.
Bei'schlafen, *ir.v.n.* (*aux.* **h.**) to sleep with.
Bei'schläfer, *m.* bed-fellow, bed-mate.
Bei'schläferin, *f.* concubine.
Bei'schlag, *m.* (—es, *pl.* **Beischläge**) base *or* counterfeit coin.
Bei'schlagen, *ir.v.a.* to add, superadd, subjoin, inclose.
Bei'schließen, *ir.v.a.* to inclose; to add, annex.
Bei'schluß, *m.* (—sses, *pl.* **Beischlüsse**) enclosure; **im — sende ich,** enclosed I send.
Bei'schlüssel, *m.* (—s, *pl.* —) false key.
Bei'schreib—en, I. *ir. v.a.* to write by the side of, on the margin; to add in writing. II. *subst. n.* writ *or* letter appended to the principal one. **—er,** *m.* (—ers, *pl.* —er) assistant clerk *or* writer.
Bei'schrift, *f.* (*pl.* —en) annotation, marginal note; postscript, additional document.
Bei'schuß, *m.* (—sses, *pl.* **Beischüsse**) contribution, additional payment, share; *see* **Beitrag.**
Bei'schüssel, *f.* (*pl.* —n) side-dish, hors d'œuvre; entrée.
Bei'sein, *n.* (—s) presence; **in meinem —,** in my presence; **ohne mein —,** without my being present.
Beisei'te, (*obs.*) **Beisei'ts,** *adv.* aside, apart; in an undertone, stage-whisper (*Theatr.*). — **setzen,** to set aside; forget; **Scherz — !** joking apart! — **bringen,** to purloin.
Bei'setz—en, *v.a.* to put to, set on (*the fire*); to lay aside; to bury, entomb; to add to, to adjoin; **alle Segel —en,** to crowd on all sail. **—ung,** *f.* entombment, burial.
Bei'sitz, *m.* (—es, *pl.* —e) presence at an assembly; right to a seat in council.
Bei'sitz—en, *ir.v.n.* (*aux.* **h.**) to act as assessor to a judge; to sit by; to have a seat in (a committee, *etc.*). **—er,** *m.* (—ers, *pl.* —er) assessor; member of a committee *or* syndicate. *Comp.* **—er=amt,** *n.* assessorship.
Bei'spiel, *n.* example, precedent; **ein — geben,** to set an example; **als — anführen,** to instance; **zum —,** (*abbrev.* **z. B.**) for example, for instance, such as, viz.; **sich** (*dat.*) **ein — nehmen an einem,** to take an example from *or* by a p.; **ein — aufstellen,** to make an example; **ein abschreckendes —,** a warning example. *Comp.* **—los,** *adj. & adv.* unprecedented, unexampled. **—losigkeit,** *f.* matchlessness, singularity, exceptional condition. **—s=weise,** *adv.* by way of instance, for instance.
Bei'springen, *ir.v.n.* (*aux.* **s.**); **einem —,** to hasten to one's aid, to succour, help one.
Bei'ß—en, *ir.v.a. & n.* (*aux.* **h.**) to bite; to prick, sting (*as the conscience*); to burn, bite (*as mustard, pepper*), to itch; to smart; **in eine S. —en,** to take a bite out of something; **nichts zu —en oder zu brechen haben,** to have nothing to eat; to be starving; **in die Angel —en,** to take the bait; **in den saueren Apfel —en,** to swallow the bitter pill; **ins Gras —en,** to bite the dust, to die (*coll.*); **nach einem, einer S. —,** to snap at a person, a thing; **auf die Stange —en,** to champ the bit; **die Zähne zusammen —en,** to gnash the teeth; **ich kann das nicht —en,** I cannot masticate it; **etwas beißt mich,** my skin itches; **es beißt mich in die Augen,** it makes my eyes smart. **—end,** *p. & adj.* pungent, hot, stinging; acrid, caustic; **ein —ender Witz,** a poignant wit; **das —ende dieser Ausdrücke,** the pungency, sarcasm of these expressions; **eine —ende Schreibart,** a keen, sarcastic style; **—ende Kälte,** nipping cold; **auf eine —ende Weise,** sarcastically, bitterly. **—ig,** (*obs.; now usually* **bissig**) *adj. & adv.* snappish. *Comp.* **—beere,** *f.* capsicum. **—kohl,** *m.* beet. **—korb,** *m.* muzzle. **—mittel,** *n.* corrosive. **—rübe,** *f.* red beet. **—wurz,** *f.* pasque flower. **—zahn,** *m.* incisor, cutting tooth. — **zange,** *f.* pincers, nippers.
Bei'stand, *m.* (—es) support, assistance; assistant, helper; second (*in duels*); second *or* consortship; **einem — leisten,** to lend one a helping hand, give one assistance; **rechtlicher —, — vor Gericht,** legal adviser, counsel; **ohne —,** unaided. *Comp.* **—s=gelder,** *pl.* subsidies.
Bei'ständ—er, *m.* (—ers, *pl.* —er) bystander, assistant; ship appointed as second to the flag-ship when in action, consort vessel.
Bei'stechen, *ir.v.n.* (*aux.* **h.**) to sail close-hauled.
Bei'steh—en, *ir.v.n.* (*aux.* **h.**) (**einem**) to stand by (*a friend, etc.*); to aid, succour, help; **alle Segel —en lassen,** to let all sails out; **mit Trost —en,** to comfort; **Gott stehe mir bei!** God help me! **die —enden,** the bystanders, those present. **—er,** *m.* (—ers, *pl.* —er) assistant; abettor; second; *see* **Beistand.**
Bei'steuer, *f.* (*pl.* —n) contribution, subsidy, subvention, pecuniary aid; additional tax; **milde —,** charities, alms.
Bei'steuern, *v.a.* to contribute.
Bei'stimm—en, *v.n.* (*aux.* **h.** *dat.*) to assent to, to agree with; to defer (*to another's judgment*); to join in with; **einem Vorschlage —en,** to accede to a proposition. **—er,** *m.* (—ers, *pl.* —er) assenter. **—ung,** *f.* assent, acquiescence.
Bei'strich, *m.* (—s, *pl.* —e) comma.
Bei'strom, *m.* (—s, *pl.* **Beiströme**) arm, branch of a river.
Bei'tisch, *m.* (—es, *pl.* —e) side table.
Bei'trag, *m.* (—s, *pl.* **Beiträge**) contribution; share; supply; premium (*of insurance, etc.*); **— an Truppen,** contingent; **Beiträge zu einem Buche,** contributions to a book; materials for a book; **als —,** as a contribution, supplementary.
Bei'tragen, *ir.v.a.* to contribute, to bear a share; to contribute towards, conduce to, assist, help (**zu**); **zur Unterstützung einer Anstalt —en,** to contribute towards the support of an institution; **es hat zu meinem Glücke beigetragen,** it has helped to make my fortune; **das trägt nur bei ihn zu erbittern,** that will only serve to embitter him.
Bei'träger, *m.* (—s, *pl.* —) contributor.
Bei'treiben, *ir.v.a. see* **Eintreiben.**
Bei'treten, *ir.v.n.* (*aux.* **s.** *dat.*) to agree to, assent to (*an opinion, a condition*); to enter into (*a treaty, etc.*); to come over to (*a party*); **einem als Teilhaber im Geschäft —,** to enter into partnership with one.
Bei'tritt, *m.* (—s) accession to (**zu**), taking part in; joining (*a society*).
Bei'urteil, *n.* interlocution; interlocutory sentence; injunction (*pending a final decision*).
Bei'wache, *f.*, **Bei'wacht,** *f.* (*pl.* —(e)n) bivouac.
Bei'wagen, *m.* extra-coach (*on a posting line*).
Bei'weg, *m.* (—s, *pl.* —e) by-way, by-road.
Bei'werk, Bei'wesen, *n.* the non-essential part of a work; accessories (*in a painting, etc.*).
Bei'wohn—en, *v.n.* (*aux.* **h.** *dat.*) to be present at, attend (*a meeting, etc.*); to cohabit with, to sleep with; **es wohnt ihm große Klugheit bei,** he is endowed with great sagacity; **einer S. —en,** to be inherent in, to be peculiar to a th. **—ung,** *f.* presence, inherence; cohabitation.
Bei'wort, *n.* adjective (*Gramm.*); epithet (*Rhetor.*); title (*Law*).
Bei'wörtlich, *adj. & adv.* adjectival.
Bei'zählen, *v.a.* to count amongst, number with; **er wurde beigezählt,** he was classed with.
Bei'z—e, *f.* corrosion, maceration; liquor in which anything is steeped *or* macerated; ooze, rot-steep, *etc.*; aqua-fortis; wood-stain; hawking; (*Sport*) **Reiher —,** heron-hawking. *Comp.* **—brühe,** *f.* corrosive mixture; liquor in which anything is steeped. **—kufe,** *f.* tanvat. **—mit=**

tel, *n.* corrosive, mordant, caustic. **—vogel,** *m.* hawk, falcon.

Bei'z—en, *v.a.* to steep, to macerate; to tan, to curry (*hides*); to stain (*wood*); to corrode; to cauterize (*a wound*); to etch (*copper*); to fly (*a hawk*); **Fleisch in Essig —en,** to soak meat in vinegar; **gebeiztes Fleisch,** pickled meat; **gebeiztes Holz,** stained wood. **—end,** *p. & adj.* corrosive, caustic, pungent; **ein —ender Toback,** stringing tobacco (*obs.*).

Bei'zeichen, *n.* counter-mark; additional mark *or* note; sign in music placed before individual notes to mark incidental flats, sharps, *etc.*; symbol of office *or* character (*Myth.*); **ein Wappen ohne —,** a plain coat of arms.

Beizei'ten, *adv.* betimes, early, soon, in good time, in good season. **— aufstehen,** to be an early riser.

Bei'zoll, *m.* extra duty, additional duty.

Bei'zügel, *m.* near-hand rein, left-rein.

Beja'gen, *v.a.* to hunt, shoot over.

Beja'h—en, *v.a.* to answer in the affirmative; **wer schweigt, bejaht,** silence gives consent, means assent; **ein —ender Satz,** an affirmative proposition. **—ung,** *f.* affirmative answer, affirmation, assertion. *Comp.* **—ungs=fall,** *m.*; **im —ungsfall,** in case of an (*answer in the*) affirmative. **—ungs=satz,** *see* **—ender Satz. —ungs=weise,** *adv.* affirmatively.

Beja'hrt, *adj.* aged, stricken in years.

Bejam'mern, *v.a.* to bewail, deplore, bemoan. *Comp.* **—s=wert, —s=würdig,** *adj. & adv.* lamentable, deplorable.

Bejauch'zen, Beju'beln, *v.a.* to receive with exultation; to rejoice *or* exult at.

Bekäm'pfen, *v.a.* to combat, stand up against, do battle with; to attack, oppose (*opinions, etc.*); to overcome, subdue, control (*one's passions, etc.*).

Beka'nnt, *p.p. & adj.* known; **allgemein —,** notorious; **sind Sie in Hannover —?** do you know Hanover? **ich bin hier selbst nicht —,** I am a stranger here myself; **— machen,** to make known, notify, advertise, publish; **das ist mir —,** I know that; **sich — machen,** to make oneself a name; **einen mit jemandem — machen,** to introduce one to a person; **— werden,** to make oneself a name, to acquire a (*great*) reputation; to get abroad, transpire, to become acquainted with; **die Sprache ist ihm ebenso — wie seine Muttersprache,** the language is as familiar to him as his mother tongue; **er hat sich mit den besten deutschen Schriftstellern — gemacht,** he has made himself familiar *or* he is conversant with the best German writers; **er hat es in den Zeitungen — gemacht,** he advertised it in the papers; **er ist wegen seiner Leistungen —,** he is celebrated for his works; **er ist wegen seiner billigen Preise —,** he is noted for his cheap prices; **für — annehmen,** to take for granted. **—e(r),** *m.*, **—e, —in,** *f.* acquaintance. **—heit,** *f.* notoriety; acquaintance. **—lich, (—er=maßen),** *adv.* as is well known, as you know. **—schaft,** *f.* (*pl.* **—schaften**) acquaintance; circle of acquaintance; knowledge, connection. *Comp.* **—machung,** *f.* publication, notification, intimation; public notice, advertisement.

Bekap'pen, *v.a.* to furnish with a cap; to hood (*a hawk*); to cap (*Artil.*); to cap (*the toes of shoes, etc.*); to lop (*trees*); to cope (*a wall*).

Bekehr'bar, *adj.* convertible.

Bekeh'r—en, *v.a.* to convert; **sich —en,** to become converted, to amend, turn over a new leaf. **—er,** *m.* (**—ers,** *pl.* **—er**) proselytiser, converter. **—te(r),** *m.*, **—te,** *f.* convert, proselyte. **—ung,** *f.* conversion. *Comp.* **—ungs=anstalt,** *f.* mission; mission-house. **—ungs=bote,** *m.* missionary; propagandist. **—ungs=geist,** *m.* proselytising spirit. **—ungs=gesandtschaft, —ungs=gesellschaft,** *f.* mission, missionary society. **—ungs=sucht,** *f.*, **—ungs=wut,** *f.* proselytism, propagandism. **—ungs=wesen,** *n.* propaganda.

Beken'n—en, *ir.v.a.* to confess, admit, acknowledge (*sins; a crime; the truth*); to acknowledge (*the receipt of a letter*); **Farbe —en,** to follow suit (*cards*); **—en Sie Farbe!** be candid! throw off the mask, no more disguise! **sich** (*Acc.*) **zu einer That —en,** to acknowledge having done something; **sich schuldig —en,** to plead guilty; **sich zur Schuld —en,** to acknowledge a debt; **sich zu einer Religion —en,** to profess, embrace a religion; **sich zur christlichen Religion —en,** to profess oneself a Christian. **—er,** *m.* (**—ers,** *pl.* **—er**) one who confesses *or* professes (*a religion*); follower; **Eduard der —er,** Edward the Confessor. **—tnis,** *n.* (**—tnisses,** *pl.* **—tnisse**) confession, avowal, acknowledgment; (*religious*) denomination; **Glaubens —tnis,** creed; **das schriftliche —tnis,** recognizance; **das eidliche —tnis,** affidavit. *Comp.* **—tnis=feier,** *f.* sacrament of the Lord's Supper. **—tnis=schriften,** *pl.* symbolic books.

Bekla'g—en, *v.a.* to lament, bewail, deplore; to commiserate; **sich —en,** to complain (**über eine S.,** of a th.; **bei einem,** to a p.). **—te(r),** *m.*, **—te,** *f.* defendant, accused (*in a police-court, etc.*). *Comp.* **—ens=wert, —ens=würdig,** *adj.* lamentable, deplorable.

Beklat'schen, *v.a.* to clap, applaud (*a performer*); **einen —,** to calumniate (*usually* **verklatschen**).

Bekle'ben, *v.* I. *a.* to paste on; to line (*with paper*); to label. II. *n.* (*aux.* **h.**) to stick, adhere.

Bekle'ck—sen, *v.a.* to blot, blotch.

Beklei'ben, *v.n.* to strike *or* take root (*obs.*); to thrive (*rare*); to stick in the mire (*obs.*).

Beklei'd—en, *v.a.* to clothe, dress, array; to drape (*Paint. etc.*); to cover over, to deck (*an altar*); to hang, paper (*a room*); to line, face; to wainscot; to shoe (*an anchor*); to invest (*with authority, an office, etc.*); to occupy (*a post*); to fill, hold (*a situation, etc.*). **—ung,** *f.* clothing, draping, *etc.*; clothes; drapery; lining (*of a mine, a wall, etc.*); inlaying, veneering, facing; hangings; tapestry; mantelpiece; investiture; administration, exercise (*of an office*); **die äußere —ung an einem Schiffe,** bulwarks.

Beklei'stern, *v.a.* to bedaub, besmear; to plaster, paste (*over*); to slur over, palliate.

Beklem'm—en, *v.a.* (*p.p. often* **beklommen,** *which see*) to pinch, straiten; to oppress (*the heart, etc.*); **in —ten Umständen,** in straits, in straitened circumstances. **—ung,** *f.* oppression (*of the chest*); anxiety; anguish (*of the heart*).

Beklom'men, *p.p. & adj.* anxious, uneasy; oppressed in breathing; depressed. **—heit,** *f.* depression; anxiety; oppression (*of the chest*).

Beklop'fen, *v.a.* to beat, tap; to test by knocking, to percuss (*Med.*).

Beklü'gel—n, *v.a.* to criticise, censure, pick holes in (*a book, etc.*); to subtilize. **—ung,** *f.* hypercriticism.

Beknei'p—en, *v.r.*; **sich —,** to get tipsy (*stud. sl.*). **—t,** *p.p. & adj.* tipsy (*stud. sl.*).

Beknur'ren, *v.a.* to snarl at; to grumble at.

Bekom'men, *ir.v.* I. *a.* to get, gain, obtain, have, **kann ich ein Zimmer —?** can I have a room? **es ist nicht zu —,** it is not to be had; **Lust zu etwas —,** to take a fancy to a thing; **ich konnte ihn nicht zu sehen —,** I could not get a sight of him, could not get an interview with him; **Befehle —,** to receive orders; **ich bekomme eine Mark heraus,** I get a shilling change; **sie hat ein Söhnchen —,** she has got a little son; **einen Korb —,** to meet with a repulse, a refusal; **Hunger —,** to grow hungry;

Furcht —, to grow afraid; Wurzel —, to strike *or* take root; Zähne —, to cut teeth; das Land zu Gesichte —, to descry land; eine Krankheit —, to fall ill; eine ansteckende Krankheit —, to catch an infectious illness; den Schnupfen —, to catch cold; wieder —, to recover (*something lost*); etwas fertig —, to get a thing finished; to succeed in doing a thing, to bring about a th.; etwas lieb —, to grow fond of a thing. II. *n.* (*aux.* f.) to agree with one, suit one; wohl bekomm' es Ihnen! much good may it do you! bless you! (*said after sneezing*); diese Speise bekommt mir, this food agrees with me; es wird ihm schlecht —, he will be none the better for it, he will fare badly with it, he will suffer for it; es bekam ihm übel, it cost him dear; ich finde, daß es ihr nicht — ist, I think her the worse for it; sie haben einander endlich —, they have got married at last.

Bekömm'lich, *adj.* salubrious.

Bekomplimentie'ren, *v.a.* to compliment; sich gegenseitig —, *or* einander —, to exchange compliments *or* civilities.

Bekös'tig—en, *v.a.* to provide with food, to board. —**ung,** *f.* boarding, catering; board, diet; worin besteht die —ung? what does the board include? Wohnung und —ung, board and lodging.

Bekräf'tig—en, *v.a.* to strengthen; to affirm, aver, to corroborate, confirm (*one in a view, a statement*); to ratify (*treaties, etc.*). —**ung,** *f.* corroboration, confirmation; affirmation. *Comp.* —**ungs=eid,** *m.* affidavit.

Bekrän'z—en, *v.a.* to wreathe, crown with a garland, festoon. —**ung,** *f.* festooning, crowning.

Bekreu'zen, Bekreu'zigen, *v.a.* to make the sign of the cross upon; to affix one's mark *or* cross to; sich —, to cross oneself.

Bekrie'gen, *v.a.;* einen —, to fight one, make war upon one.

Bekrit't—eln, *v.a.* to carp at, pick holes in. —**ler,** *m.* (—lers, *pl.* —ler) faultfinder, carping critic, caviller.

Bekrit'zeln, *v.a.* to scrawl over, to scribble on.

Bekrus't—en, *v.a.* to incrust; sich —, to get *or* be incrusted. —**ung,** *f.* incrustation.

Beküm'mer—n, *v.* I. *a.* to grieve, afflict, distress, trouble; to seize (*Law*); um *or* über eine Sache —t sein, *also* ob (*obs.*) *or* wegen einer Sache —t sein, to be grieved at, concerned for, anxious about a thing; Schulden halber —n, to distrain. II. *r.* to sorrow, grieve oneself, fret (über, at); to concern oneself about, to care for, mind; to meddle with; —e dich nicht darüber, never mind that; ich —te mich nicht um sie, I took no notice of her; er —t sich um nichts, he cares for nothing; er —t sich gar nicht um mich, he does not care a button about me; he pays not the slightest attention to me; —e dich um dich, mind your own business. —**nis,** *n.* (—nisses, *pl.* —nisse), & *f.* (*pl.* —nisse) solicitude; grief, affliction. —**t,** *p.p.* & *adj.* grieved, afflicted; solicitous, anxious.

Bekun'd—en, *v.a.* to depose, give evidence on oath; to prove, manifest, demonstrate. —**ung,** *f.* manifestation, averment.

Belä'cheln, *v.a.* to smile at.

Bela'chen, *v.a.* to laugh at, ridicule. *Comp.* —**s=wert,** —**s=würdig,** *adj.* & *adv.* ridiculous.

Bela'd—en, *ir.v.a.* to load, freight; to burden. —**ung,** *f.* act of loading.

Bela'g, *m.* (—s, *pl.* Beläge) anything laid on or upon, slice, meat slices, bits of cheese (*on sandwiches*); foil (*of a looking-glass*); fur (*of the tongue, Med.*); Beläge, documents proving something, vouchers (*incorrect spelling instead of* Belege; *see* Beleg).

Bela'ger—n, *v.a.* to besiege, lay siege to; to invest (*a fortress*); to beleaguer (*a garrison*); die —ten, *pl.* the besieged. —**er** (—ers, *pl.* —er) besieger. —**ung,** *f.* siege. *Comp.* —**ungs=batterie,** *f.* siege battery. —**ungs=werke,** *pl.* approaches (*parallels, trenches, etc.*). —**ungs=zustand,** *m.* state of siege; der kleine —ungszustand, the minor state of siege (*in some manufacturing towns with many socialists*).

Bela'ng, *m.* (—s) amount; importance; von —, important; nicht von —, *or* von keinem —, of no account, of no consequence, inconsiderable. *Comp.* —**reich,** *adj.* considerable, weighty, momentous, important.

Belang'bar, *adj.* actionable; to be got at.

Belan'g—en, *v.a.* to concern, belong to; einen gerichtlich —, to take legal proceedings against a person, to proceed against a p. (*at law*); was mich —t, as for me. —**end,** *p.* & *adj.* touching, concerning. —**ung,** *f.* prosecution, suit at law.

Belas'sen, *ir.v.a.* to leave at rest *or* as it was.

Belas't—en, *v.a.* to load, lade, freight; to burden, encumber; to overload, overcharge; to charge to one's account, to debit with; erblich —et sein, to be tainted with a(n) hereditary disease; to be full of ancestral features (*coll.*). —**ung,** *f.* charge; load, burden; debit; erbliche —ung, affliction with a(n) hereditary disease, hereditary habit *or* proclivity, hereditary taint. —**ungs=zeuge,** *m.* witness for the prosecution.

Beläs'tig—en, *v.a.* to burden; to trouble, annoy, bother, molest; to bore, harass; mit Bitten —en, to importune; um Zahlung —en, to dun. —**end,** *p.* & *adj.* burdensome; harassing; importunate; boring; oppressive. —**ung,** *f.* burden; molestation; importunity; a bore.

Belat'ten, *v.a.* to cover with laths; to batten; to rib (*a roof*).

Belau'ben, *v.a.* to cover with leaves; to foliage (*Archit.*); sich —, to burst into leaf.

Belau'ern, *v.a.* to lie in wait, watch for; einen —, to humbug one, take one in.

Belau'f, *m.* (—s) amount, sum; der ganze —, the sum total; bis zum —e von, up to the amount of.

Belau'fen, *ir.v.a.* to walk, go over; to visit, inspect; to cover; sich —en auf, to amount to; (auf) wie hoch beläuft sich das Ganze? what does it all amount to? what is the sum total?

Belau'sch—en, *v.a.* to listen to; to play the spy on; man —t uns, we are overheard, some one is listening. —**er,** *m.* (—ers, *pl.* —er) eavesdropper.

Bel'chen, *m.* round top of a mountain (*dial.* = Berg); der Gebweiler —, the Gebweiler balloon (in Alsatia).

Bele'b—en, *v.a.* to enliven; to animate, invigorate; to cheer; to elevate. —**end,** *p.* & *adj.* enlivening; restorative, cordial; genial; animating. —**t,** *p.p.* & *adj.* lively; bustling. —**theit,** *f.* animation; liveliness. —**ung,** *f.* enlivenment; act of animating. *Comp.* —**ungs=versuche,** *pl.* attempts to restore animation. —**ungs=mittel,** *pl.* restoratives.

Bele'cken, *v.a.* to lick (*over*).

Bele'der—n, *v.a.* to cover with leather; to buff (*the hammers of a piano*). —**ung,** *f.* leathering, buffing (*of a piano*).

Bele'g, *m.* (—es, *pl.* —e) document serving as voucher, voucher; receipt; proof, verification, example; fur, coating (*of the tongue. Med. See* Belag); einen — liefern zu, to furnish evidence of. —**schein,** *m.,* —**stück,** *n.* voucher. —**stelle,** *f.* quotation, citation; evidence, authority.

Bele'g—en, I. *v.a.* to cover, overlay; to lay down (*carpets; turf; boards; stones; tiles; nails, etc.*); to carpet, board, pave, *etc.;* mit Dielen *or* Brettern —, to board; mit Rasen —, to turf; to silver (*a mirror*); to shoe (*a* *wheel*); to hoop (*a cask*); to show proof of, verify; to secure, retain (*a place*); **ein Haus mit Soldaten —en,** to quarter soldiers in a house; **eine Stadt mit Truppen —en,** to garrison a town; **mit Strafe —en,** to inflict a punishment on; **eine Stute —en,** to cover a mare; **mit Fluch —en,** to curse; **mit Arrest —en,** to arrest; **mit Abgaben —en,** to impose taxes on; **mit Beweisen —en,** to demonstrate, show by proofs; **können Sie das —?** can you furnish proof of that? **Geld —en,** to invest capital; **Vorlesungen —en,** to enter one's name for a course of lectures, to pay lecture fees; **eine —te Stimme,** a husky *or* thick voice; **ein —tes Butterbrot,** a sandwich; **seinen Platz —en,** to mark one's place (so as to retain it); **ich habe drei Plätze —t,** I have reserved three seats. II. *adj.* situated. **—ung,** *f.* covering, overlaying, laying down *or* on, *etc.;* the coating (*of a Leyden jar, etc.*); **—ung von Steuern,** taxation; **—ung von Geldern,** investment of capital. *Comp.* **—hölzer,** *pl.* belaying pins, cleats, *etc.* (*Naut.*).

Beleh'n—en, *v.a.* to enfeoff; to invest with. **—te(r),** *m.* vassal. **—ung,** *f.* enfeoffment.

Beleh'r—en, *v.a.* to instruct; to advise; apprise; **sich —en lassen,** to take advice, listen to reason; **laß dich —en,** be advised; **man hat mich eines andern —t,** I am otherwise advised; **(einen) eines Bessern —,** to undeceive, to set right. **—end,** *p. & adj.* instructive; didactic. **—ung,** *f.* instruction; information, advice, correction. *Comp.* **—ungs=gabe,** *f.* talent for imparting instruction.

Belei'bt, *adj.* corpulent, stout, fat; **wohl —,** corpulent; **er wird —,** he is falling into flesh. **—heit,** *f.* corpulence, embonpoint.

Beleib'züchtigen, *v.a.* to settle a life annuity on a person.

Belei'dig—en, *v.a.* to offend; to insult; to shock; to wrong; **gröblich —en,** to outrage; **es —t das Ohr,** it grates on *or* offends the ear; **sich —t fühlen, sich für —t halten,** to feel hurt, insulted. **—end,** *p. & adj.* offensive; disagreeable; insulting. **—er,** *m.* (**—ers,** *pl.* **—er**) offender; insulter. **—te(r),** *m.*, **—te,** *f.* person offended *or* insulted. **—ung,** *f.* offence; insult; affront.

Beleih'bar, *adj.* that may serve as a pledge or a mortgage.

Belei'hen, *see* **Belehnen;** to lend (*Commerc.*); **Wertpapiere —,** to lend on securities.

Belem'mer—n, *v.a.* to befoul; to encumber; to confuse; to cheat, take in (*coll.*); **—nde Güter,** cumbersome goods. **—t,** *p.p. & adj.* cheated; trashy; **das ist —t,** that 's all rubbish (*sl.*).

Belemni't, *m.* (**—en,** *pl.* **—en**) belemnite, fingerstone, thunder-stone.

Bele'sen, *adj.* well-read; **ein —er Mann,** a man of wide reading. **—heit,** *f.* acquaintance with books, book-learning, extensive reading.

Bel=eta'ge, *f.* first floor; **in der —,** on the first floor.

Beleuch't—en, *v.a.* to light (*up*); to illuminate; to illustrate, throw light on; to arrange the light and shade (*in a picture*); to examine closely; **die Sonne —en,** to gild refined gold, to carry coals to Newcastle. **—ung,** *f.* lighting (*of streets, etc.*); illumination; lights (*Paint.*); elucidation, illustration (*of a subject*); examination, inquiry; **freie —ung und Heizung,** no charge for lights and fires; **Abend—ung,** evening glow, sunset glow.

Beleu'mund—en, *v.a.* to bring into (*good or bad*) reputation; **übel —et,** in bad repute.

Bel'fer—er, *m.* (**—ers,** *pl.* **—er**) yelping, snarling dog; snarler. **—in,** *f.* shrew.

Bel'fern, *v.n.* (aux. **h.**) to snarl, yelp; to quarrel, nag.

Belich'tung, *f.* exposure (*Phot.*).

Belie'b—en, I. *v.a.* to like, choose, wish for; to think proper, resolve; **—en Sie noch etwas?** would you like anything else? **—en Sie einzutreten,** please to walk in. II. *v.n. & imp.* (*aux.* **h.**, *dat.*) to please; **was —t Ihnen?** please? what is your pleasure? what do you wish? what will you have? **mir —t es nicht,** I don't like it, don't wish for it; **es —t Ihnen, so zu sagen,** you are pleased to say so; **wie es Ihnen —t,** as you please; **wenn's —t,** if you please; when you like. III. *subst.n.* will, pleasure; **nach —en,** at will, ad libitum (*Mus.*); **ich stelle es in Ihr —en,** I leave it to your discretion; **nach Ihrem —en,** as you please. **—ig,** *adj. & adv.* agreeable, to your liking; **in —iger Größe,** of any size you choose; **nehmen Sie einen —igen Maßstab an,** take any standard you like; **zu jeder —igen Zeit,** at any time that will suit, at any time whatever. **—t,** *p.p. & adj.* favourite; popular; **sich bei einem —t machen,** to ingratiate oneself with a person, to get into a p.'s good books.

Belladon'na, *f.* belladonna, deadly night-shade.

Bel'len, *v.n.* (*aux.* **h.**) to bark, bay, cry; to growl.

Belletri'st, *m.* (**—en,** *pl.* **—en**) literary man; person of literary taste. **—erei',** *f.* pretension to literary knowledge *or* taste. **—isch,** *adj.* relating to belles lettres, belletristic; **—ische Zeitschriften,** literary magazines.

Belo'b—en, *v.a.* to praise, commend. **—ung,** *f.* (*also* **Belo'bigung**) commendation. *Comp.* **—ungs=preis,** *m.* second best premium. **—ungs=schreiben,** *n.* commendatory letter.

Belohn'bar, *adj.* that may be rewarded.

Beloh'n—en, *v.a.* to reward; to recompense; **mit Undank —en,** to treat ungratefully; **schlecht —t,** ill requited. **—end,** *p. & adj.* remunerative. **—er,** *m.* (**—ers,** *pl.* **—er**) rewarder. **—ung,** *f.* reward, recompense; gratuity; premium.

Beluch'sen, *v.a.* to cheat, take in, outwit (*coll.*).

Belü'gen, *ir.v.a.* to deceive by lying; **er belog sie,** he told her a lie.

Belus'tig—en, *v.a.* to divert, amuse, entertain; **sich —en,** to make merry, enjoy oneself. **—end,** *p. & adj.* amusing, diverting. **—er,** *m.* (**—ers,** *pl.* **—er**) merrymaker. **—ung,** *f.* amusement, entertainment, merrymaking.

Bemäch'tig—en, *v.r.* (*gen.*) to take possession of, seize, make oneself master of; **welche Wut —te sich deiner?** what fury possessed you? **sich des Thrones (widerrechtlich) —en,** to usurp the throne. **—ung,** *f.* (*act of*) obtaining possession of; seizure.

Bema'len, *v.a.* to bedaub; to paint (*over*).

Beman'nen, *v.a.* to man (*a ship*).

Bemän'teln, *v.a.* to cloak; to palliate.

Bemas'ten, *v.a.* to furnish with masts.

Bemei'ster—n, *v.a.* (*& r. with gen.*) to make oneself master of, to seize; to subdue, gain the mastery over; to overcome (*difficulties, etc.*); **die Schwierigkeiten des Deutschen —n,** to master the difficulties of the German language. **—ung,** *f.* overcoming (*of difficulties*), mastery.

Bemel'd—en, *v.a.* to mention, to report. **—et,** *p.p. & adj.* aforesaid. *Comp.* **—eter=maßen,** *adv.* as afore said *or* reported.

Bemen'gen, *v.r.* to meddle, intermeddle.

Bemerk'bar, *adj.* perceptible; sensible, noticeable. **—keit,** *f.* perceptibility.

Bemer'k—en, *v.a.* to observe, perceive; to note; to take notice of; to remark; **er that als —te er mich nicht,** he pretended not to see me; he cut me; **wie unten —t,** as noted below; **er —t es sehr übel, daß,** he takes it very ill that. **—lich,** *adj. & adv. see* **—bar; er möchte sich gern —lich machen,** he would fain attract notice; **einem —lich machen,** to observe, hint, point out to one. **—ung,** *f.* observation, remark; note, annotation; **—ungen am Rande**

marginal notes; **nötige —ung nehmen,** to take due note; **sich** (*dat.*) **schriftliche —ungen machen,** to take notes. *Comp.* **—ens=wert, —ens=würdig,** *adj.* worthy of remark, noteworthy. **—ungs=gabe,** *f.* power of observation.

Bemit'leiden, *v.a.* to pity. *Comp.* **—s=würdig,** *adj.* pitiable.

Bemit'telt, *adj.* of means, in easy circumstances, well off, well to do.

Bemo'dert, *adj.* mouldy, covered with mould.

Bemo'geln, *v.a.*; **einen —,** to take a person in, to cheat (*at cards*) (*fam.*).

Bemoo'sen, *v.n.* (*aux.* **s.**) to be overgrown with moss; **ein bemoostes Haupt, bemooster Bursch,** an old student, a student of many terms (*stud. sl.*).

Bemü'h—en, I. *v.a.* to trouble, give trouble; **darf ich Sie darum —en?** may I trouble you for it? II. *v.r.* to take trouble, pains; to strive, endeavour; **—en Sie sich doch nicht,** pray, don't trouble yourself; **sich um einen —en,** to interest oneself on behalf of a person; **—en Sie sich mit mir hinein,** just step in with me; **er —te sich die Sprache zu erlernen,** he took pains to learn the language; **—t sein,** to seek, to struggle. **—end** (= **peinlich**), *adj.* painful, unpleasant, vexing (*dial.*); **eifrigst —t um,** eagerly bent on. III. *subst.n.* **—ung,** *f.* trouble, pains, effort, exertion; **seine —ung wurde ihm vergolten,** he was rewarded for his trouble.

Bemü'ßigen, *v.a.* to induce (*to do, etc.*); *now only used in the phrase* **sich** (*acc.*) **bemüßigt sehen** *or* **fühlen,** to feel induced *or* obliged.

Bemut'tern, *v.a.* to fill a mother's place *or* to be a mother to; **ein junges Mädchen —,** to chaperon a young lady.

Benach'bart, *adj.* neighbouring, adjoining, adjacent.

Benach'richtig—en, *v.a.*; **einen von etwas —en,** to acquaint, apprise, send word, inform, warn one of s.th. **—er,** *m.* (**—ers,** *pl.* **—er**) informant, informer; authority. **—ung,** *f.* communication, notification; intimation; notice; report; advice; **um —ung bitten,** to ask for information *or* instructions. *Comp.* **—ungs=brief,** *m.* letter of advice. **—ungs=wort,** *n.* cautionary word.

Benach'teiligen, *v.a.* to prejudice, to injure.

Bena'g—en, *v.a.* to gnaw, begnaw, benibble. **—t,** *p.p. & adj.* eroded, suberose (*Bot.*).

Benä'hen, *v.a.* to sew round, upon; to patch.

Benam'sen, *v.a.* to name, surname, call (*famil.*).

Bena'nnt, *p.p. & adj.* named; **—e Zahlen,** concrete numbers (*Arithm.*).

Benar'b—en, *v.a.* to scar; **sich —en,** to cicatrize. **—t,** *p.p. & adj.* scarred. **—ung,** *f.* scar.

Be'ne, *adv.*; **sich — thun,** to feast *or* indulge oneself (*sl.*).

Bene'bel—n, *v.a.* to cloud over, wrap in mist; to obscure, to dim, to obfuscate; to intoxicate; **sich —n,** to get slightly tipsy. **—t,** *p.p. & adj.* clouded over; slightly intoxicated.

Bene'bst, *prep.* together with; withal, besides.

Benedei'—en, *v.a.* (*p.p.* (**ge**)**benedeit**) to bless (*rel.* = **segnen**); to glorify. **—ung,** *f.* benediction; glorification.

Benedik'ten=kraut, *n.* herb bennet, avens.

Benedikti'ner, *m.* (**—,** *pl.* **—s**) Benedictine monk. **—in,** *f.* Benedictine nun. *Comp.* **—likör,** *m.* Benedictine.

Benefi'z, *n.* (**—es,** *pl.* **—e**) benefit; (*pl.* **Benefi'zien**) benefice, living. **—ia'nt, —ia't,** *m.* one benefited; beneficiary. *Comp.* **—vorstellung,** *f.* benefit-performance; performance for the benefit of.

Beneh'men, I. *ir.v.a.* to take away; to size (*coins*); (**einem etwas**) **—,** to take away from, deprive of; **einem die Lust zu etwas —,** to spoil one's pleasure in a th.; **einem seinen Irrtum —,** to undeceive, disabuse one of his errors. II. *ir.v.r.* to behave, demean oneself; to act; **sich — mit,** to concert *or* agree with. III. *subst.n.* conduct, behaviour; **das feine —,** good manners, gentlemanly behaviour; **sich mit einem wegen einer Sache in — setzen,** to confer with a person about a thing, to agree with a p. about a th.

Benei'den, *v.a.* (**einen, einen um eine S.,** *or* **wegen einer S., einem etwas**) to envy; **ich beneide Sie um Ihre Kraft,** I envy your strength; **sie — ihn,** they are envious of him. *Comp.* **—s=wert,** *adj.* enviable.

Benen'n—en, *ir.v.a.* to name; to designate; to christen; **einen Tag —en,** to fix a day; **benannte Zahlen,** concrete numbers. **—end** *adj.* denominative. **—ung,** *f.* naming, designation; appellation, denomination; **Brüche unter einerlei —ung bringen,** to reduce fractions to a common denominator; **falsche —ung,** misnomer.

Benet'zen, *v.a.* to wet, to moisten; to sprinkle; **mit Tau —,** to bedew.

Ben'gel, *m.* (**—s,** *pl.* **—**) cudgel, club (*obs.*); billet (*of wood*); bar (*of a printing-press*); clapper (*of a bell*); unmannerly rough fellow; **dummer —,** silly fool; **großer —,** great lout; **kleiner —,** bantling; little urchin. **—ei',** *f.* churlishness, rudeness, boorish trick. **—haft,** *adj.* clownish, boorish, rude.

Benom'men, *past part. of* **benehmen. —heit,** *f.* (be)numbedness, numbness; stupefaction.

Benö'tigen, *v.a.*; **eine S. — & einer S. —,** *usually* **einer S. benötigt sein,** to be in want *or* to stand in need of a th.; **das benötigte Geld,** the necessary money; **benötigten Falls,** in case of need.

Benutz'bar, *adj.* usable.

Benut'z—en, (**Benüt'z—en,**) *v.a.* to make use of, utilize; to profit by (*an occasion, etc.*); to take advantage of (*a person, etc.*); **—e die Gelegenheit,** improve the occasion, embrace your opportunity! **—ung,** *f.* act of using, making use of; use; **freie —ung eines Gartens haben,** to have the run of a garden.

Benz—i'l, *n.* benzile. **—i'n,** *n.* benzine. **—oe** (*pr.* **Be'nzo=e**), *f.* benzoin; (*in comp.*) benzoic. **—oe=harz,** *n.* gum benzoin. **—oe=säure,** *f.* benzoic acid.

Beo'bacht—en, *v.a.* to observe; to watch; to discharge, do (*one's duty, etc.*); to execute (*an order*); to keep (*silence; a festival*); to respect (*laws*); **—ende,** observant; inquiring; **zu —ende Dinge,** things to be observed. **—er,** *m.* (**—ers,** *pl.* **—er**) observer. **—ung,** *f.* observation; observance. *Comp.* **—ungs=heer,** *n.* army of observation.

Beö'len, *v.a.* to oil.

Beor'dern, *v.a.* to order, direct, command.

Bepa'cken, *v.a.* to load.

Bepflan'zen, *v.a.* to plant; **mit Hecken —,** to hedge.

Bepflas'tern, *v.a.* to plaster (*over*); **mit Steinen —,** to pave.

Bepflü'gen, *v.a.* to plough.

Bepin'seln, *v.a.* to touch with the brush; to bedaub.

Bepol'stern, *v.a.* to stuff; to wad; to upholster.

Bepu'dern, *v.a.* to powder.

Beque'm, *adj.* convenient, commodious; comfortable; fitting; opportune; proper; indolent, fond of ease; **er weiß es sich — zu machen,** he knows how to make himself comfortable; **machen Sie es sich —,** make yourself comfortable *or* at home; **wenn es Ihnen — ist,** at your convenience; **ein —er Aufgang,** an easy ascent; **ein —er Sommeranzug,** a comfortably fitting summer suit; **eine —e Gelegenheit,** a good opportunity; **mein Freund ist ein**

sehr —er Mensch, my friend is a somewhat indolent fellow, my friend likes to take it easy; ein —er Hausgenosse, a fellow lodger easy to get on with.

Beque'm—en, *v.* I. *a.* to accommodate, suit. II. *r.* to accommodate oneself, conform, put up with, submit to; to yield to, comply with; ich mußte mich dazu —en, I had to give in to it, to make the best of it; sich nach der Zeit —en, to go with the times. III. *n.* es —t ihm nicht, it does not suit, does not please him. —lichkeit, *f.* convenience; suitability; ease, comfort; indolence; (*place of*) convenience, privy, water-closet. —lichkeits=liebe, *f.* indolence, laziness; love of comfort.

Bequi'cken, *v.a.* to foliate, silver (*mirrors*).

Berah'men, *v.a.* to frame.

Beran'den, Berän'deln, Berän'dern, *v.a.* to give a border *or* edge to; to mill, to edge (*coins*).

Berap'pen, *v.a.* to roughcast, to plaster (*a wall*); to pay (*vulg.*).

Bera'sen, *v.* I. *a.* to cover with grass, to sod. II. *r.* (*aux.* s.) to be overgrown with turf.

Bera't—en, *ir.v.* I. *a.* to furnish with what is necessary, to endow; to counsel, advise (*obs.*); die Welt ist wohl —en, the world is well arranged, is what it should be; Sie sind schlecht —en, you are ill advised; Gott —e dich! God direct you! einen Plan —en, to concert a plan. II. *r.* to take counsel together, to deliberate; er beriet sich mit ihm über die Sache, he conferred with him about the matter. —end, *p. & adj.* consultative, deliberative; eine —ende Stimme haben, to have a voice (*but not a vote*) (*in a council, etc.*). —er, *m.* (—ers, *pl.* —er) adviser, counsellor. —ung, *see* —schlagung; in —ung ziehen, to deliberate.

Bera'tschlag—en, *v.n. & refl.* (*aux.* h.) to deliberate; es wird über die Sache —t, the affair is under consideration; er —te sich mit uns über die zu ergreifenden Maßregeln, he conferred with us as to the steps to be taken. —ung, *f.* consultation, deliberation; conference, council.

Berau'ben, *v.a.* (einen einer Sache) to rob (a p. of a th.); to deprive of; to divest of; to bereave.

Beräu'chern, *v.a.* to perfume (*with incense, etc.*); to smoke (*meat, etc.*); to fumigate, to disinfect; to smoke, smother (*bees, etc.*).

Berau'cht, *p.p. & adj.* smoky, smoke-stained.

Berau'schen, *v.a.* to intoxicate; sich —, to get tipsy.

Ber'beris, Berberit'ze, *f.* barberry.

Bere'chenbar, *adj.* calculable.

Berech'n—en, *v.a.* to compute, calculate to cast up (*an account*); to estimate (auf, at); fremde Münze auf einheimische —en, to reduce foreign coin to the home standard; einem etwas —en, to account to one for, to put to one's account; wir —en diese Waaren zu rc., we charge these goods at, *etc.*; Sie haben mir zu viel —et, you have charged me too much; sich mit einem —en, to settle (*accounts*) with, to reckon with a p.; das läßt sich nicht —en, that is beyond computation, incalculable; wie —en Sie das? how do you make that out? —et, *p.p. & adj.* calculated on; intended, premeditated; das war nicht —et, that was not taken into account; schlecht —et, ill-judged. —er, *m.* (—ers, *pl.* —er) calculator, computer. —ung, *f.* calculation, computation; eine ungefähre —ung, a rough estimate; außer aller —ung, incalculable.

Berech'tig—en, *v.a.* to justify (*one*) in, to entitle (*one*) to; to authorise, empower, warrant; zu Hoffnungen —en, to bid fair; er —t zu den schönsten Hoffnungen, he is a man of much promise, who promises well. —t, *p.p. & adj.* competent, qualified, empowered, entitled (zu, to); bin ich dazu —t oder nicht? am I entitled to it or not? ausschließlich —t, exclusively privileged. —ung, *f.* title, right; qualification; bürgerliche —ung, civil rights; franchise; —ung zum einjährig=freiwilligen Heeresdienst, privilege of one year's military service as a volunteer. *Comp.* —ungs=wesen, *n.* standards and examinations required for admission to certain professions, privileges conferred by special examinations.

Bere'd—en, *v.a.;* einen zu etwas —en, to persuade one to a thing, to talk one over; er wollte sich nicht —en lassen, he was not to be persuaded; man —et die Leute leicht dessen (*usually* zu dem) was sie wünschen, men are easily persuaded to what they desire; etwas —en, to talk a matter over, to consider a th.; sich —en, to persuade oneself; sich mit einem —en, to confer with, deliberate, take council with a person, concert (*a plan*) with one. —sam, *adj.* eloquent. —samkeit, *f.* eloquence; rhetoric. —t, *p.p. adj. & adv.* eloquent; talkative; eine —te Zunge haben, to have a glib tongue, to be a fluent speaker; auf das —t(e)ste, in the most eloquent manner.

Bere'gt, *adj.* (*lit.* stirred up), brought up, mentioned, in question; die —e Sache, the before-mentioned matter, the point in question.

Bereg'nen, *v.a.* to rain on *or* upon.

Berei'ch, *m. & n.* (—s, *pl.* —e) scope, range, reach; compass; sphere; province; außer meinem —e, beyond my reach; not within my ken, not within my province; im —e der Stimme sein, to be within call *or* well within earshot; auf —sweite, *adv.* within reach.

Berei'chern, *v.a.* to enrich; unsere Kenntnisse —, to enlarge our stock of knowledge; sich —, to feather one's nest.

1**Berei'fen,** *v.a.* to cover with hoar-frost.

2**Berei'fen,** *v.a.* to hoop, to rim (*casks*).

Berei'sen, *v.a.* to travel over *or* through a country; to visit, frequent (*fairs, etc.*); — lassen, to have a district visited by commercial travellers, to work by travellers (*C. L.*).

Berei't, *adj.* ready, prepared; — halten, to keep, hold in readiness. —s, *adv.* already; almost (*dial.*). —schaft, *f.* readiness, preparation; Geld in —schaft haben, to have money in hand. *Comp.* —stehend, *adj.* available, disposable. —willig, *adj. & adv.* ready, willing; readily, willingly; die —willige Annahme, due honour, acceptance (*of a bill, etc.*). —willigkeit, *f.* readiness, willingness; allzu große —willigkeit, over-readiness, officiousness.

1**Berei't—en,** *v.a.* to prepare, make ready; to procure; einem den Untergang —en, to work one's ruin; ein Getränk wird daraus —et, a drink is prepared from it. —er, *m.* (—ers, *pl.* —er) preparer. —ung, *f.* preparation; manufacture; dressing.

2**Berei't—en,** *ir.v.a.* to ride over, visit riding (*a country*); to train, break in (*a horse*); beritten, mounted (*Mil.*); broken in. —er, *m.* (—ers, *pl.* —er) rough-rider, horse-breaker, trainer; riding-master. *Comp.* —er=gesellschaft, *f.* company of equestrians. —er=peitsche, *f.* jockey-whip.

Beren'n—en, *ir.v.a.* to invest, blockade; to assault, storm; to run against. —ung, *f.* assault (*of a fortress*).

Bereu'—en, *v.a.* to repent, regret. —ung, *f.* repentance, regret; remorse. *Comp.* —ens=wert, *adj.* regrettable.

Berg, *m.* (—es, *pl.* —e) mountain, hill; unten am —e, at the foot of the mountain; die Haare standen mir zu —e, my hair stood on end; —e versetzen, to remove mountains (*Bibl.*); jenseits des —es sein, to be in the decline of life, going down hill; wir sind noch nicht über den

—, we are not out of the wood *or* round the corner yet; **um diese Zeit ist er sicherlich über alle —e**, by this time he is certainly off and away; **über — und Thal**, across country; (**mit einer Sache**) **hinter dem —e halten**, to dissemble, to be uncommunicative; **hinter dem —e wohnen auch noch Leute**, do not be too clever; **goldene —e versprechen**, to promise wonders; **am —e stehen**, to encounter a difficulty, to come to a stand-still; **da stehen die Ochsen am —e!** there is the rub! **—icht**, *adj.* (*now unusual*) mountain-like. **—ig**, *adj.* mountainous, hilly. *Comp.* (*usually* mountain—, rock—, alpine —, mining —, native —). **—a'b**, *adv.* downhill. **—abhang**, *m.* slope, ascent, declivity. **—ahorn**, *m.* sycamore maple. **—akademie**, *f.* school of mining *or* mines, mining academy. **—alaun**, *m.* rock alum. **—ammer**, *f.* mountain bunting, snowbird. **—amsel**, *f.* ring-ousel; blackbird. **—amt**, *n.* mining office; board of mines. **—a'n** *or* **—au'f**, *adv.* uphill. **—arbeit**, *f.* mining (industry). **—art**, *f.* any metalliferous mineral *or* stratum, matrix of the ore. **—auster**, *f.* rock-oyster. **—balsam**, *m.* naphtha. **—bau**, *m.* mining; working of mines; **einen —bau anstellen**, to open a mine. **—baukunst**, *f.* science of mining; metallurgy. **—beamte(r)**, *m.* mining official. **—beschreiber**, *m.* orologist. **—beschreibung**, *f.* orography, orology. **—bewohner**, *m.* mountaineer, highlander. **—blau**, *n.* ultramarine, lapis lazuli. **—bock**, *m.* mountain-goat, wild goat. **—braun**, *n.* umber. **—buche**, *f.* common-beech. **—dachs**, *m.* marmot. **—distel**, *f.* (**kleine**) mountain saffron; (**große**) cotton thistle. **—dohle**, *f.* Alpine chocard *or* chough. **—dorf**, *n.* mountain-village; mining village. **—drossel**, *f.* singing thrush. **—eben=holz**, *n.* bastard senna. **—e=hoch**, *a.* as high as mountains, extremely high. **—erle**, *f.* grey alder; alpine azerole. **—es=alte**, *m.* mountain sprite (protector of the wild animals). **—e=tief**, *a.* as deep as mountains, extremely deep. **—fahrt**, *f.* excursion into the mountains; voyage up stream. **—falk**, *m.* common stone-falcon. **—fall**, *m.* land-slide, landslip. **—faulbaum**, *m.* alpine buckthorn. **—fein**, *adj.* native (*min.*). **—fertig**, *adj.* sickly, broken-down (*of miners*). **—fett**, *n.* fossil tallow. **—feuer**, *n.* ignis fatuus; signal fire on a mountain. **—fex**, *m.* enthusiastic alpinist (*coll.*). **—fieberwurzel**, *f.* yellow gentian. **—fink**, *m.* brambling, mountain finch. **—flecken**, *m.* small mountain town; mining village. **—fleisch**, *n.* asbestos, mountain cork. **—forelle**, *f.* char. **—freiheit**, *f.* right of mining; privileges of a mountain *or* miner's town. **—fried**, *m.* (*arch.*) (=**Belfried**); donjon. **—gang**, *m.* vein of ore. **—gebrauch**, *m.* mining custom. **—gegenschreiber**, *m.* controller of mines. **—geist**, *m.* mountain-sprite, gnome. **—gelb**, *n.* yellow ochre. **—gericht**, *n.* court for deciding mining causes. **—gerichts=ordnung**, *f.* miners' code. **—gesetz**, *n.* mining law. **—gift**, *n.* arsenic. **—gipfel**, *m.* summit. **—glas**, *n.* rock-crystal. **—glas=artig**, *adj.* crystalliform. **—gras**, *n.* species of bent grass; sweet scented vernal grass; sheep's fescue grass. **—grat**, *m.* mountain-ridge, crest. **—grün**, *n.* lesser periwinkle; mountain green; (**feinstes**) Olympian green (*Min.*). **—gut**, *n.* minerals; fossils. **—haar**, *n.* pliable asbestos. **—hänfling**, *m.* yellow-beaked linnet. **—hahn**, *m.* *see* **Auerhahn**. **—halde**, *f.* mountain-slope, hillside. **—haue**, *f.* pick, pickaxe. **—hauptmann**, *m.* superintendent of a mine *or* mines. **—herr**, *m.* mine-owner. **—holder**, *m.* red-berried elder. **—holz**, *n.* ligniform asbestos, rock-wood, wale. **—huhn**, *n.* red-legged partridge. **—kalk**, *m.* carboniferous limestone. **—karren**, *m.* truck (*used in a mine*). **—katze**, *f.* wild cat; mountain lynx. **—kegel**, *m.* conical (*or* sugar-loaf) mountain. **—keller**, *m.* cellar cut in the rock; name of an inn on a hill. **—kessel**, *m.* deep valley, gorge. **—kette**, *f.* mountain chain, ridge of mountains. **—kiefer**, *f.* mountain pine. **—knappe**, *m.* miner, pitman. **—knappschaft**, *f.* miners' association. **—krank**, *adj.* suffering from the miners' (*or* alpine climbers') disease; = **—fertig**. **—krystall**, *m.* rock-crystal. **—kunde**, *f.* orology; science of mining, metallurgy. **—kundige(r)**, *m.* orologist; expert in mining. **—kupfer**, *n.* native copper. **—land**, *n.* hilly country, upland, highland. **—läufig**, *adj.* & *adv.* in miner fashion, usual amongst miners. **—leder**, *n.* a kind of asbestos, mountain cork; miner's apron. **—lehne**, *f.* mountain slope. **—lette(n)**, *m.* metallic clay. **—leute**, *pl.* miners; mountaineers. **—lilie**, *f.* martagon. **—mann**, *m.* miner; mountaineer; **—mann vom Leder**, actual miner; **—mann von der Feder**, one employed in the office of a mine; **—mann vom Feuer**, smelter. **—männchen**, **—männlein**, *n.* gnome. **—männisch**, *adj.* mining; relating to miners; usual amongst miners. **—manns=treu**, *f.* mountain eryngo. **—maus**, *f.* lem(m)ing. **—mehl**, *n.* fossil dust, marl. **—meise**, *f.* long-tailed titmouse. **—meister**, *m.* surveyor of mines. **—merle**, *f.* ring-ousel. **—milch**, *f.* rock milk, agaric mineral, fossil farina. **—münze**, *f.* calamint. **—nachfahrer**, *m.* inspector of mines. **—nymphe**, *f.* oread, fairy of the hill (*Mythol.*). **—öl**, *n.* petroleum, bitumen. **—ordnung**, *f.* regulation(s) for the mines. **—pech**, *n.* mineral pitch, asphalt. **—pech=erde**, *f.* bituminous earth. **—predigt**, *f.* (*Christ's*) sermon on the mount. **—rat**, *m.* board of mining directors; member of a council of mines. **—ratte**, *f.* marmot. **—recht**, *n.* right of working a mine; mining privilege; miners' code. **—reien**, (**—reigen**, **—reihen**), *m.* alpine melody; miners' song; popular poem (*originally sung by bands of miners*). **—reihe**, *f.* mountain range. **—rose**, *f.* rock-rose (*cistus*); alpine rose, rhododendron. **—rot**, *n.* red ochre. **—rüster**, *f.* common elm; cork-elm (*Ulmus suberosa*). **—rutsch**, *m.* land-slide, land-slip. **—salz**, *n.* rock salt. **—sattel**, *m.* depression in a mountain-ridge. **—schicht**, *f.* layer, stratum; extra work done after hours by miners. **—schichtmeister**, *m.* mining accountant *or* controller, purser. **—schlucht**, *f.* ravine, gorge, glen, cleft. **—schotten**, *pl.* Scotch Highlanders. **—schüler**, *m.* student at a mining academy. **—schwaden**, *pl.* damps (*or* choke) in a mine. **—schwalbe**, *f.* rock swallow. **—schwefel**, *m.* native sulphur. **—segen**, *m.* produce of the mines. **—steiger**, *m.* mountain climber, alpinist. **—storch**, *m.* white-headed vulture. **—straße**, *f.* mountain-road; hilly district between Darmstadt and Heidelberg. **—strom**, *m.* torrent. **—sturz**, *m.* fall of a hill *or* mine; landslip. **—sucht**, *f.* pulmonary disease, miner's consumption. **—sumpf**, *m.* bog (*at the top of a mountain*). **—taube**, *f.* smaller wood pigeon *or* stock-dove. **—teer**, *m.* mineral tar. **—u'nter**, *see* **—ab**. **—ver=walter**, *m.* superintendent of a mine. **—volk**, *n.* mountaineers, highlanders; miners. **—wand**, *f.* precipitous side of a mountain, bluff. **—wardei'n**, *m.* assayer of the mines. **—werk**, *n.* mine; pit; **ein —werk bauen**, to sink, to work a mine. **—werks=aktie**, *f.* share in a mine. **—wesen**, *n.* mining matters. **—wetter**, *n.* fire damps (*in mines*). **—winde**, *f.* fly-honeysuckle. **—wolle**, *f.* mountain flax. **—wort**, *n.* mining term. **—zehnte**, *m.* tithe from the produce of mines. **—zeichen**, *n.* miner's badge (*pick* *crossed by a hammer*). **—zinn,** *n.* native tin. **—zinnober,** *m.* native cinnabar.

Bergamot'te, *f.* (*pl.* **—n**) bergamot. *Comp.* **—n=öl, (Bergamott'öl,)** *n.* essence of bergamot.

Ber'g—en, *ir.v.a.* to save, secure; to save, recover (*shipwrecked goods, etc.*); to conceal; to shade (*Paint.*); **sich —en vor,** to save, conceal oneself from, to flee from; **er ist geborgen,** he is safe; **die Segel —en,** to shorten, take in sail. **—e=** (*in comp.*) = salvage. **—er,** *m.* (**—ers,** *pl.* **—er**) salver, saver; **diebischer —er,** wrecker. **—ung,** *f.* salvage.

Beri'cht, *m.* (**—s,** *pl.* **—e**) report, statement, (*official*) return; intelligence, information; advice (*C. L.*); **— erstatten,** to present *or* hand in a report, to report, to give an account of; **laut —,** according to my report, as per advice. *Comp.* **—abstatter, —erstatter,** *m.* reporter, relater; returning officer (*at elections*). **—erstattung,** *f.* reporting; report, information. **—mäßig,** *adv.* in the form of a report. **—zettel,** *m.* bulletin; notice-paper.

Berich'ten, *v.a.* to inform, to instruct; to report; to order, arrange; to train (*a hawk*); **einen falsch —,** to misinform one; **einem etwas, einem über etwas —,** to report upon, inform of, acquaint with, notify, give notice of; **ich lasse mich —,** I allow myself to be set right *or* to be corrected, I listen to advice, I listen to reason; **einen Kranken —,** to administer the sacrament to a sick person.

Berich'tig—en, *v.a.* to set right, rectify; to arrange; to adjust (*scales*); to settle (*a debt or bill; a dispute*); to correct (*errors; proofs, etc.*). **—igung,** *f.* correction; emendation, rectification; adjustment, settlement; payment.

Berie'chen, *v.a.* to smell, sniff at; to scent (*of dogs*).

Berie'seln, *v.a.* to irrigate.

Berie'fen, Berie'feln, *v.a.* to channel, flute, groove (*Archit.*).

Beri'll, *m.* (**—s,** *pl.* **—e**) *see* **Beryll;** a kind of flannel for printing on.

Berin'det, *p.p. & adj.* covered with bark, crust.

Beri'tt, *m.* (**—es**) district under the care of a mounted inspector; squad (*Mil.*).

Berit'ten (*see* ²**Bereiten**), *adj.* ridden over; mounted, on horseback; **— machen,** to mount (*a force*); **gut —, schlecht —,** well *or* badly mounted *or* horsed; **—e Garde,** horse-guards; **—e Landwehr** *or* **Miliz,** yeomanry.

Ber'kan, *m.* (**—s,** *pl.* **—e**) barracan (*stuff, cloth*).

Berli'n—e, *f.* (*pl.* **—en**) a sort of carriage. *Comp.* **—er=blau,** *n.* prussian blue. **—er=blau=säure,** *f.* prussic acid. **—er=zimmer,** *n.* back room with only one window, darkish room.

Berlo'cke, *f.* (*pl.* **—n**) trinket, knick-knack, charm.

Ber'me, *f.* berm(e) (*Fort.*).

Berna'kelmuschel, *f.* barnacle.

Bern'stein, I. *m.* (**—s**) amber; **schwarzer —,** jet. II. *adj.* (*in comp.*) = amber—. **—en, —ern,** *adj.* made of amber. *Comp.* **—grus,** *n.* amber dust. **—kirsche,** *f.* white-heart cherry. **—kohle,** *f.* residuum of distilled amber. **—koralle,** *f.* amber-bead. **—säure,** *f.* succinic acid. **—spitze,** *f.* amber mouth-piece (*pipe*); amber cigar-holder.

Berser'ker, *m.* berserker, ancient Scandinavian warrior (*frenzied fighter, regardless of wounds*), a person of extreme violence and fury; **eine — Wut,** a frenzied and resistless fury, berserker rage, ungovernable fury (*fig.*).

Ber'st—en, *ir.v.n.* (*aux.* **f.**) to burst, to crack, split, chap. *Comp.* **—gras,** *n.* carex.

Ber'tram, *m.* (**—s**) Spanish pellitory.

Berüch'tig—en, *v.a.* to defame. **—t,** *p.p. & adj.* infamous, ill-famed, noted, notorious.

Berü'cken, *v.a.* to ensnare; to take in, impose upon, cheat; to beguile; to fascinate, charm. **—d,** *p. & adj.* ensnaring, fascinating, charming.

Berück'sichtig—en, *v.a.* to respect; to have regard to; to take into consideration; to consider, bear in mind; to take notice of; **ohne irgend die Richtigkeit zu —en,** without any regard to correctness. **—ung,** *f.* consideration, regard.

Beru'f, *m.* (**—s,** *pl.* **—e**) calling; vocation; profession, business, office, employment; walk of life; province, function; faculty; sphere; **der innere —,** the inward call; divine summons; **seinen — verfehlt haben,** to have missed one's vocation; **es ist mein — nicht,** it is no business of mine; **einem —e gehörig,** professional. **—s=,** (*in comp.*) professional. *Comp.* **—s=mäßig,** *adj. & adv.* professional. **—s=reise,** *f.* official tour. **—s=soldat,** *m.* soldier by profession, professional soldier. **—s=wahl,** *f.* choice of a profession.

Beru'f—en, I. *ir.v.a.* to call; to call together, convoke, convene (**zusammen—en**); to call up (*bad spirits, by excessive boasting, etc.*), to bring ill-luck upon (*by boasting of*); to blame, censure; to call (*Theol.*); **die viel —ene Angelegenheit,** the much discussed affair; **ein —ener Richter,** a qualified judge; **einen zu einem Amte —en,** to appoint a p. to an office, to offer a professorship to a p. (*Univ.*), to call (*a minister*); **sich auf einen —en,** to appeal to, refer to, to make use of a person's name; **darauf darf man sich nicht —en,** that cannot be taken as precedent; **berufe es nicht!** don't forespeak it (*by untimely praise or boast*)!; **unberufen!** let the devil rest! II. *p.p. & adj. see* **Verrufen; wohl —,** of good repute (*poet.*); **ich fühle mich —en,** I feel called upon (*to*). **—er,** *m.* appellant. **—ung,** *f.*, **—ungs=,** (*in comp.*) act of summoning *or* of appealing; call; vocation; appeal. **—ungs=gericht,** *n.* court of appeal. **—ungs=recht,** *n.* patronage, right of nomination.

Beru'h—en, *v.n.* (*aux.* **h.**) to rest; **etwas —en lassen,** to let a thing be, leave a th. alone; **ich will es dabei, darauf —en lassen,** I will be satisfied with that, I will let it pass; **—en auf einer S.,** to be founded on, to depend on; **dies —t auf einem Irrtum,** this is due to a mistake.

Beru'hig—en, *v.a.* to tranquillize, quiet, pacify; to mitigate, assuage (*pain, etc.*); to compose (*the mind; fears, etc.*); to lull; to bridle, curb (*the passions*); **sich —igen,** to make one's mind easy, to compose oneself; **sich bei einer S. —igen,** to be easy in one's mind about a thing, to be satisfied with a thing as it is. **—igend,** *p. & adj.* sedative. **—iger,** *m.* calmer, pacifier. **—igung,** *f.* quieting, calming; ease of mind; pacification.

Berüh'm—en, *v.r.;* **sich einer Sache —en,** to boast *or* brag of a thing. **—t,** *p.p. & adj.* famous, celebrated; **sich —t machen,** to render oneself famous, to make oneself a reputation, to distinguish oneself. **—theit,** *f.* celebrity, renown, distinction; person of fame, lion, star.

Berühr'bar, *adj.* tangible.

Berüh'r—en, *v.a.* to touch, to be contiguous; to touch, to touch upon, allude to; to meddle with; to concern, affect (*one's interests, etc.*); **diese Saite darf nicht —t werden,** this string must not be struck; no allusion is to be made to this subject; **sich —en,** to touch one another. **—end,** *p. & adj.* contiguous; touching; tangent. **—ung,** *f.* contact; act of touching; contiguity; collision; appulse (*Astr.*); reference to (*a subject*); **in —ung kommen,** to come in contact (*with*). *Comp.* **—ungs=association,** *f.* association by contiguity. **—ungs=elektrizität,** *f.* galvanism, voltaic electricity. **—ungs=fläche,** *f.* surface of contact. **—ungs=lehre,** *f.* science of touch, haptics. **—ungs=linie,** *f.* tangent (*Geom.*). **—ungs=punkt,** *m.* point of contact. **—ungs=winkel,** *m.* angle of contact.

Berup'fen, *v.a.* to pluck; **einen —,** to fleece, plunder a p.
Beru'ßen, *v.* I. *a.* to begrime, blacken with soot. II. *n.* (*aux.* **f.**) to grow sooty.
Bery'll, *m.* (—**s**, *pl.* —**e**) beryl; **meergrüner** —, aquamarine. *Comp.* —**erde,** *f.* glucina.
Besab'beln, Besab'bern, *v.a.* & *r.* to beslabber (*coll.*).
Besä'—en, *v.a.* to sow (*a field, etc.*). —**(e)t,** *p.p.* & *adj.* sowed; studded, strewn; **mit Sternen —et,** bespangled with stars, star-spangled.
Besa'g—en, *v.a.* to say; to purport; to prove; **das hat nichts zu —en,** that is not very important; **Ihr Brief —t,** the purport of your letter is; **das —t die Unterschrift,** that is attested by the signature. —**end,** *p.* & *adj.* to the effect, *etc.* —**t,** *p.p.* & *adj.* aforesaid. *Comp.* —**termaßen,** *adv.* as before mentioned.
Besai'ten, *v.a.* to string (*an instrument*); **zart besaitetes Gemüt,** delicately sensitive disposition.
Besa'm—en, *v.* I. *a.* to sow; impregnate. II. *r.* to be propagated by seed; to run to seed. —**t,** *adj.* seeded. —**ung,** *f.* sowing; propagation by seed.
Besa'n, *m.* (—**s**, *pl.* —**e**) mizzen; **den — losmachen,** to set the mizzen. *Comp.* —**baum,** *m.* mizzen-boom. —**bramstange,** *f.* mizzen-top-gallant mast. —**flagge,** *f.* rear-admiral's flag; gallant. —**mars,** *m.* mizzen-top. —**raa,** *f.* mizzen-yard. —**wand,** *f.* mizzen-shroud.
Besänf'tig—en, *v.a.* to allay, assuage; to appease; to soothe; **nicht zu —en,** unappeasable, implacable. —**end,** *adj.* assuasive. —**er,** *m.*, —**erin,** *f.* appeaser, calmer. —**ung,** *f.* allayment; calming, appeasing. *Comp.* —**ungsmittel,** *n.* palliative; sedative, lenitive.
Besa'ß, Besä'ße, *impf.ind.* & *subj.* *of* **besitzen.**
Besa'tz, *m.* (—**es**, *pl.* **Besätze**) trimming (*of a dress, etc.*); border (*of cloth, etc.*); embroidery. —**ung,** *f.* garrison; crew (*of a man-of-war*); wards (*of a lock*); —**ung legen in einen Ort,** to garrison a place. —**ungs-recht,** *n.* right of garrisoning. *Comp.* —**spitze,** *f.* braid, braiding. —**teich,** *m.* stockpond.
Besau'fen, *v.r.*; **sich —,** to get drunk (*vulg.*).
Beschä'dig—en, *v.a.* to injure, damage; to blight, mildew; to wound; **sich —en,** to hurt oneself; **leicht zu —en,** easily damageable. —**er,** *m.* (—**ers**, *pl.* —**er**) causer of damage; one who hurts *or* injures. —**t,** *p.p.* & *adj.* damaged; (*weather*) beaten; **schwer —t,** tipsy (*sl.*). —**ung,** *f.* damage, injury; average (*Naut.*); **frei von —ung,** warranted free from average.
Beschaf'fen, †I. *ir.v.a.* to create. II. *reg. v.a.* to procure, *see* **Anschaffen.** III. *p.p.* & *adj.* constituted; **so ist er —,** it 's the nature of that creature, that 's his nature; **gut —,** in good condition, in good circumstances; **so ist die Welt —,** that 's the way of the world; **wie ist der Weg — ?** what is the condition of the road? **die Sache mag — sein wie sie wolle,** let the matter be as it may; **die Sache ist so —,** the matter stands thus; **— wie es wolle,** of what quality soever. —**heit,** *f.* nature, quality, kind, constitution; condition; disposition; humour; idiosyncrasy, peculiarity; **nach —heit der Umstände,** according to circumstances. *Comp.* —**heits-wort,** *n.* attribute, adjective.
Beschäf'tig—en, *v.a.* to occupy, employ, keep busy, engage. —**t,** *p.p.* & *adj.* busy; occupied with; **bei einem —t sein,** to be in one's employment, to be employed by; **mit etwas —t sein,** to be occupied about *or* with a thing. —**er,** *m.* (—**ers**, *pl.* —**er**) employer. —**ung,** *f.* occupation, business, pursuit; **schwere langweilige —ung,** drudgery.
Becha'len, *v.a.* to furnish with a shell *or* cover; to lath (*a ceiling*); to board (*a floor*); to put a handle to, to haft (*a knife*).
[1]**Beschä'len,** *v.a.* to husk, pare, peel; to bark (*trees*).
[2]**Beschä'l—en,** *v.a.* to cover (*of horses*). —**er,** *m.* (—**ers**, *pl.* —**er**) stallion, stud-horse; stud-groom.
Beschä'm—en, *v.a.* to shame, confuse, disconcert, make ashamed, abash. —**end,** *p.* & *adj.* disgraceful, reflecting shame upon. —**t,** *p.p.* & *adj.* abashed, confused. —**ung,** *f.* confusion, shame; act of making a p. ashamed.
Beschat'ten, *v.a.* to overshadow; to shade.
Beschat'z—en, *v.a.* to assess. —**ung,** *f.* assessment.
Beschau'—en, *v.a.* to view, behold; to inspect, examine; to gaze upon; to contemplate; **näher** *or* **kritisch —,** to criticise, review (*writings*); **sich —en,** to examine oneself, look into one's own heart, *etc.* —**end,** *p.* & *adj.* contemplative; **der —ende,** *see* —**er.** —**er,** *m.* (—**ers**, *pl.* —**er**) looker on, spectator; inspector; searcher (*of a ship*); critic; contemplator. —**lich,** *adj.* & *adv.* perceptible; intuitive; contemplative; meditative. —**ung,** *f.* viewing, looking; examination; inspection; contemplation; **bei näherer —ung,** on closer inspection. *Comp.* —**ens-wert,** *adj.* worthy of observation.
Beschei'd, *m.* (—**es**, *pl.* —**e**) knowledge, accurate information; instructions, directions; answer; award, decision, decree; **um eine S.** (**über eine S., von einer S.**) **— wissen,** to know, to have knowledge *or* intelligence of a thing, to be acquainted with it; **— trinken (einem),** to drink a glass of wine with the proposer, to pledge one; **ich weiß hier keinen —,** I am a stranger here; I don't know what to do, I am quite at sea about this; **in einem Hause — wissen,** to know one's way about a house; **einem — sagen lassen,** to send one word, let one know; **einem von etwas — geben,** to inform one of a thing; **bis auf weiteren —,** till further orders, provisionally.
Beschei'd—en, I. *ir.v.a.* to allot, assign, apportion; to direct, order; **einen über eine Sache —en,** to inform one of a thing; **ich lasse mich —en,** I am open to conviction; **er ist zu seinem Regimente beschieden,** he is ordered to join his regiment; **er beschied mich auf die folgende Woche,** he bade me call on him next week; **einen zu sich —en,** to send for one; **vor Gericht —en,** to summon; **sich —en,** to moderate one's pretensions, resign o. s.; **er weiß sich zu —en,** he knows how to limit his desires, he knows his place; **sich (mit einer Sache,** *or* **in etwas) —en,** to acquiesce in, be satisfied with, concede; **wir —en uns gern,** we concede willingly (*that, etc.*). II. *adj.* & *adv.* modest; discreet; unassuming; moderate. —**enheit,** *f.* modesty; diffidence; discretion; demureness; moderation.
Beschei'n—en, *ir.v.a.* to shine upon, irradiate; **von der Sonne beschienen,** sunny.
Beschei'nig—en, *v.a.* to acquit, receipt; to issue a certificate of; to vouch for; to attest, certify to; **ich will Ihnen den Empfang —en,** I will give you a receipt for it; **hiermit —e ich,** I hereby testify; **ich —e Herrn Z. gern,** I have much pleasure in testifying to Mr. Z. —**ung,** *f.* act of certifying; certificate; voucher; receipt, acquittance.
Beschen'k—en, *v.a.* to present with; **er —te mich mit Schillers Werken,** he made me a present of Schiller's works; **reichlich —t,** laden with gifts *or* presents, richly endowed. —**ung,** *f.* giving away of presents; donation.
Besche'r—en, I. *ir.v.a.* to shave; to shear. II. *reg.v.a.* (**einem etwas**) to give, to bestow upon, to make a present; **zu Weihnachten —en,** to give as a Christmas present *or* gift. —**ung,** *f.* bestowal of gifts; distribution of (*Christmas*) presents; gift, present: **eine schöne —ung!** a

pretty kettle of fish! a pretty business! a fine to-do! a nice mess! **da haben wir die —ung!** that 's where the mischief lies! that 's it! **die ganze —ung,** the whole lot (*coll.*).

Beschi'ck—en, *v.a.* to send for *or* to; to manage; to bring about, to do; to put in order; to till; to tend; to take care of; to alloy (*gold*); to prepare (*ores*); to impregnate; **eine Ausstellung —en,** to exhibit, contribute to an exhibition; **den Reichstag —en,** to send deputies, to return a member to parliament, *etc.*; **ich habe heute nicht viel —t,** I have not done much to-day, I have got through little work to-day. **—ung,** *f.* act of sending delegates for *or* to; deputation of representatives; alloying; alloy; preparation; **—ung des Landes,** tillage. *Comp.* **—ungs=regel,** *f.* alligation (*rule of*).

Beschie'den, *p.p.* (*of* **bescheiden**) & *adv.* allotted, ordered, given.

Beschie'nen, *v.a.* to fix with splinters; to provide with bands of iron; to shoe (*a wheel*); to clout (*the axle-box*); to lay down rails (*Railw.*).

Beschie'ß—en, I. *ir.v.a.* to fire on; to bombard, shell; to prove (*a gun*) by firing it. II. *ir.v.n.* (*aux.* **s.**) to become covered with some deposit (*Chem.*). III. *subst. n.* **—ung,** *f.* cannonading; shelling, bombardment. *Comp.* **—hütte,** *f.* shed for testing guns, *etc.*

Beschiff'bar, *adj.* navigable.

Beschif'fen, *v.a.* to navigate; to ply on (*a river, etc.*); to bepiss (*coll.*).

Beschil'f—en, *v.* I. *a.* to thatch with reeds. II. *n.* (*aux.* **s.**) to be overgrown with reeds. **—t,** *adj.* reeded, reedy, sedgy.

Beschim'pf—en, *v.a.* to insult, to revile; to dishonour; to injure (*a reputation*); to call (*a p.*) names. **—end,** *p. & adj.* derogatory, defamatory; libellous; disgraceful. **—er,** *m.* (**—ers,** *pl.* **—er**) insulter; asperser. **—ung,** *f.* aspersion; affront, insult, outrage; libel; disgrace.

Beschir'm—en, *v.a.* to screen; to protect, shelter. **—er,** *m.* (**—ers,** *pl.* **—er**) protector; shield, shelter. **—ung,** *f.* defence, safeguard.

Beschla'fen, *ir.v.a.* to sleep *or* lie with; **etwas —,** to sleep upon a matter, take a night to consider it (*coll.*).

Beschla'g, *m.* (**—s,** *pl.* **Beschläge**) anything attached to an article by way of ornament *or* as fastening; metal rims, knobs, plates, studs, *etc.*, serving as ornament *or* to strengthen an article; mounting (*of a gun, album, cabinet, etc.*); shoeing (*of a wheel; of a horse*); clasp (*of a book*); ferule (*on a stick*); sheathing (*of a ship*); metal-work (*of a door, etc.*); guard (*of a sword*); mouldiness; damp, humidity; efflorescence (*Chem.*); attachment (*against property of a debtor*); embargo (*on a ship*); sequestration (*of an income*); distraint (*upon goods*); **— der Früchte auf dem Halm,** execution on growing crops; **in — nehmen,** to arrest, to seize judicially; to occupy, engross (*attention, etc*); **mit — belegen,** to issue an attachment against, sequestrate, lay an embargo on, distrain, impress, requisition; **den — aufheben,** to remove an embargo, sequestration, *etc.*; **der — auf das Eigentum eines Schuldners, das in fremden Händen ist,** *or* **— in der Hand eines dritten,** foreign attachment. *Comp.* **—befehl,** *m.* detainer (*Law*). **—bendsel, —bindsel,** *n.*, **—leine,** *f.* furling-line (*Naut.*). **—leger,** *m.* sequestrator, distrainer, seizer. **—legung, -nahme,** *f.* distraint, attachment, seizure, sequestration. **—(e)=tasche,** *f.* farrier's pouch. **—(s)=verwalter, —(s)=verweser,** *m.* sequestrator. **—(e)=zeug,** *n.* farrier's tools.

Beschla'gen, *ir.v.* I. *a.* to hammer, to mount (*a case, a box, a gunstock, etc.*); to sheath (*the bottom of a ship*); to tip (*a stick, boots, etc.*); to clout, to fit with clasps (*a book, etc.*); to furl (*a sail*); to line (*a mine; deer, etc.*); to stock (*a farm*); to square (*timber*); to flatten; to lute (*Chem.*); to secure (*a place, etc.*); to drape; to seize, *see* **in Beschlag nehmen; mit Silber —,** silver-mounted; **ein mit Leder —er Koffer,** leather-covered trunk; **scharf —,** to rough-shoe (*a horse*); **mit Nägeln —,** to stud with nails; **mit einem Deckel —,** to fit with a cover. II. *r. & n.* (*aux.* **s.**) to grow mouldy; to get tarnished; **die Fensterscheiben — sich,** the window panes are dimmed, grow thick (*with moisture*); **in einer Sache gut — sein,** to be well versed in, have a sound knowledge of, be familiar with a thing; **ein —er,** an expert, one well informed.

Beschlei'chen, I. *ir.v.a.* to steal upon, creep up to stealthily; to steal over one; to surprise; to cheat. II. *subst.n.* **das — des Wildes,** deer-stalking.

Beschleu'nig—en, *v.a.* to accelerate, hasten, expedite; to precipitate (*a catastrophe*). **—end,** *p. & adj.* **die —ende Kraft,** the accelerating force. **—ung,** *f.* acceleration; despatch; speed.

Beschlie'ß—en, *ir.v.a.* to close, conclude; to resolve, determine on, decide; to terminate; **etwas mit einander —en,** to agree upon a th. with a person. **beschlo'ssen,** *p.p. & adj.* land-locked; sheltered, closed in; resolved; **es wurde beschlossen,** it was agreed, resolved, carried; **beschlossenermaßen,** as agreed. **—er,** *m.* (**—ers,** *pl.* **—er**), **—erin,** *f.* caterer, house-keeper, steward.

Beschlu'ß, *m.* (**—(ss)es,** *pl.* **Beschlüsse**) close, termination, conclusion; resolve, resolution; decree; locking-up; **es ist unter meinem —e,** I have it under lock and key, it is in my custody; **zum —e,** finally, in conclusion, in short; **Beschlüsse einer Kirchenversammlung,** canons of an ecclesiastical council; **das Parlament faßte diesen —,** the house came to this conclusion, the house passed the following resolution. *Comp.* **—fähig,** *adj.* competent to pass resolutions; **eine —fähige Anzahl,** a quorum; **in —fähiger Anzahl sein,** to be sufficiently numerous to form a house (*Parl.*); to be a quorum. **—fassung,** *f.*, **—nahme,** *f.* determination; decree; passing of a resolution.

Beschmau'sen, *v.a.* to feast at a p.'s expense.

Beschmei'ßen, *ir.v.a.* to fling at; to soil, bedaub; to pelt, to blow (*of flies*).

Beschmie'ren, *v.a.* to besmear; to dirty, daub, bedaub; to grease; to tar; **mit Butter —,** to butter.

Beschmis'sen, *adj.* fly-blown (*see* **Beschmeißen**).

Beschmut'zen, *v.a.* to soil, dirty; to foul (*of fire-arms*).

Beschnei'd—en, *ir.v.a.* to clip; to lop, prune; to pare (*nails*); to circumcise; to curtail; **einem den Gehalt —en,** to cut down a p.'s salary; **(einem) die Gelegenheit —en,** to take away an opportunity; **einem die Flügel —,** to clip one's wings. **—er,** *m.* (**—ers,** *pl.* **—er**) circumciser; cutter, clipper. **—ung,** *f.* circumcision; cutting; clipping.

Beschnei'—en, *v.a.* to cover with snow. **—t,** *p.p. & adj.* snow-covered, snowy.

Beschnit'ten, *p.p. & adj.*; **—e Bäume,** pollards; **—es Geld,** clipped money; **—es Papier,** paper with the edges cut; **ein —er,** a circumcised person.

Beschnüf'feln, *v.a. fig.*; **er beschnüffelt alles,** he pokes *or* thrusts his nose into everything.

Beschnü'ren, *v.a.* to tie, cord; **Raketenhülsen —,** to choke rockets.

Beschö'n(ig)en, *v.a.* to palliate, extenuate; **beschönigende Ausdrücke,** extenuating phrases, euphemistic terms.

Beschrän'k—en, *v.a.* to bound, confine; to limit, circumscribe; to restrict; **sich auf eine S. —en,** to restrict oneself to, to be satisfied with a thing. **—end,** *p. & adj.* restrictive. **—t,** *p.p. & adj.* limited; narrow (*in capacity*); circumscribed (*in means*); **in —tem Sinne,** in a certain *or* restricted sense; **ein —ter Kopf,** a narrow-minded person, a dull mind, a duffer (*coll.*). **—theit,** *f.* narrowness; scantiness; (*intellectual*) dulness, stupidity. **—ung,** *f.* restraint; limit, limitation.

Beschrei'b—en, *ir.v.a.* to write upon, cover with writing; to describe, depict, portray; to describe (*a circle, etc.*); **nicht zu —en,** indescribable. **—end,** *p. & adj.* descriptive; **—ende Zeit,** imperfect tense; **—ender Text,** descriptive letter-press; **—ende Naturwissenschaften,** *i. e.* mineralogy, botany, zoölogy. **—er,** *m.* (**—ers,** *pl.* **—er**) describer. **—lich,** *adj. & adv.* describable. **—ung,** *f.* description; inventory; *in compounds often* —logy *or* —graphy; **—ung des Leibes, der Erde, des Gewässers, der Vögel, der Fische, der Knochen, eines Ortes, der Welt,** physiology, geography, hydrography, ornithology, ichthyography, osteology, topography, cosmography, *etc., etc.*

Beschrei'en, *ir.v.a.* (*in older German sometimes reg.*) to cry about, at (*a thing*); to decry; to disparage; to render notorious; to bewitch, cast a spell on; to over-praise; **— Sie es nicht!** don't crow over it! let the devil rest!; **der weitbeschreite Zauberkünstler,** the far-famed magician (*obs.*).

Beschrei'ten, *ir.v.a.* to walk on, step over; to cross (*a threshold, etc.*); to bestride (*a horse*); **den Rechtsweg —,** to go to law; **das Ehebett —,** to occupy the marriage bed, to consummate one's marriage.

Beschrie'bener=maßen, *adv.* as I have just said, as described, *etc.*

Beschro'ten, *v.a.* to clip the edges, to trim; to curtail, cut down; to nibble.

Beschu'hen, *v.a.* to provide with shoes; **sich —,** to put on one's shoes.

Beschul'dig—en, *v.a.* (**einen einer Sache**) to accuse of, charge with, impute to. **—er,** *m.* (**—ers,** *pl.* **—er**) accuser; plaintiff. **—t,** *p.p. & adj.*; **der —te,** person accused, defendant. **—ung,** *f.* accusation, impeachment.

Beschum'meln, *v.a.* to cheat, to take in (*coll.*).

Beschup'p—en, *v.a.* to cover with scales, to scale; to take in (*coll., see* **Beschummeln**). **—t,** *p.p. & adj.* covered with scales, scaly.

Beschüt'ten, *v.a.* to throw, cast on; to pour over; to cover with.

Beschüt'z—en, *v.a.* to protect, guard, shelter, defend; to favour; to patronise; to fence in. **—er,** *m.* (**—ers,** *pl.* **—er**), **—erin,** *f.* protector; guardian; patron, patroness. **—ung,** *f.* protection, defence; patronage.

Beschwat'zen, *v.a.* to persuade, wheedle, talk over; to slander, speak ill of.

Beschwei'ß—en, *v.a.* to cover with sweat, to cover with blood (*Hunt.*). **—t,** *p.p. & adj.* sweaty, bloody.

Beschwe'r, *f.* (*no pl.*) & *n.* (**—s,** *no pl.*), **—de,** *f.* (*pl.* **—den**) trouble, difficulty; hardship; inconvenience, annoyance; grievance, ground of complaint; complaint, malady; weight; **—de über eine S. führen,** to complain of a th.; **Kopf—den,** headache; **körperliche —den,** bodily complaints *or* troubles; **die —den des Alters,** the infirmities of old age; **Brust —de,** difficulty of breathing. **—lich,** *adj.* troublesome; painful; difficult, hard; cumbersome, inconvenient; importunate; **einem —lich sein, fallen,** to inconvenience, annoy a p., to be a burden to one; **das Gehen fällt ihm —lich,** he walks with difficulty. **—lichkeit,** *f.* troublesomeness; burdensomeness; hardship; inconvenience, trouble; toil; difficulty. **—nis,** *f.* (*pl.* **—nisse**) *see* **—de.** **—t,** *p.p. & adj.* heavy; loaded; encumbered, mortgaged; **—ter Brief,** letter containing money. **—ung,** *f.* burdening, *etc.*; burden; encumbrance, mortgage; trouble. *Comp.* **—de=buch,** *n.* book for entering complaints. **—de=führer,** *m.* complainant. **—de=punkt,** *m.* grievance.

Beschwe'ren, *v.a.* to load, charge, burden; to encumber; to be troublesome to; to clog, lie heavy on (*the stomach*); to bore; to burden (*the memory*); **sich —,** to complain (**bei einem über einen,** to a person of someone).

Beschwi'chtig—en, *v.a.* to still, soothe, appease; to allay; to silence (*conscience*); to hush up; to compose (*a quarrel*). **—er,** *m.* (**—ers,** *pl.* **—er**) soother, calmer, appeaser; composer (*of quarrels*). **—ung,** *f.* lulling, stilling, appeasing; hushing-up. *Comp.* **—ungs=geld,** *n.* hush money.

Beschwö'r—en, *ir.v.a.* to affirm, testify on oath, take one's oath to; to conjure; to exorcise; to conjure, adjure; entreat. **—er,** *m.* (**—ers,** *pl.* **—er**) conjurer; exorcist, magician. **—ung,** *f.* confirmation by oath; exorcism; adjuration, imploring, entreaty. *Comp.* **—ungs=buch,** *n.* conjuring-book. **—ungs=formel,** *f.* form of adjuration; incantation, charm. **—ungs=kunst,** *f.* (*art of*) exorcism; magic, necromancy.

Besee'l—en, *v.a.* to animate; to enliven, inspirit. **—er,** *m.* (**—ers,** *pl.* **—er**) enlivener; animater. **—t,** *p.p. & adj.* animate; having a soul. **—ung,** *f.* animation.

Bese'geln, *v.a.* to navigate, sail (*the ocean, etc.*); **die Küste —,** to coast, sail along the coast; **ein Schiff —,** to fit a ship with sails; to join a ship at sea.

Bese'hen, *ir.v.a.* to look on *or* at; to inspect; to examine; **sich —,** to look at oneself, to look round about (*archaic* = **sich umsehen**); **eine Tracht Prügel —,** to get a sound thrashing (*coll.*); **bei Lichte —,** on closer inspection, viewed in the right light; **sich** (*dat.*) **etwas —,** to visit, view; **zu —,** on view, for inspection.

Besei'tig—en, *v.a.* to put aside; to remove, do away with (*difficulties, etc.*); to put an end to, settle (*disputes, etc.*); to explain away, account for. **—t,** *p.p. & adj.* done away with; on the shelf. **—ung,** *f.* act of putting aside; removal (*of difficulties*); settlement (*of quarrels*).

Bese'ligen, *v.a.* to bless; to make happy.

Be'sen, *m.* (**—s,** *pl.* **—**) besom, broom; housemaid (*stud. sl.*); **neue — kehren gut,** new brooms sweep clean (*prov.*). *Comp.* **—binder,** *m.* broom-maker. **—garde,** *f.* the broom-girls, the housemaids (*stud. sl.*). **—heide,** *f.* *f.* bog-heath. **—reis,** *n.* birch-twig. **—stiel,** *m.* broomstick.

Besen'den, *v.a.* to send for one's vassals (*obs.*); **er besendet sich, er besendet seine Helden,** he summons his thanes (*obs.*).

Besef'sen, *p.p.* (*of* **besitzen**) & *adj.* possessed; **der —e,** demoniac. **—heit,** *f.* possession (*by the evil one*), demoniacal possession; diabolism, demoniacism.

Beset'z—en, *v.a.* to put, lay on; to trim, garnish, border; to set (*with jewels*); to patch (*shoes*); to occupy; to garrison; to man (*a ship*); to mount (*guns*); to stock (*a pond*); to furnish (*a dinner table*); to plant (*with trees*); to mount (*guard*); to fill (*an office*); to fill up (*a vacancy*); to engage (*a place*); to stake, lay money on; to guard (*of cards*); to distribute the parts (*of a play*); **mit Bändern, Spitzen, Pelz —en,** to trim with ribbons, with lace, with fur; **mit Einwohnern —en,** to people; **es war alles —t,** every seat was engaged; **der Abteil ist —t,** the compartment is full; **—t,** engaged (*water closet*); **meine Dame war mit zwei Karten —t,** my queen was guarded by two small cards; **ein gut —tes Stück,** a well cast piece; **jede Stimme war dreimal —t,** each part was sung by three voices; **ein stark —tes Orchester**, a well-filled orchestra. **—ung**, *f.* trimming; bordering, edging; the taking possession of, occupation; the nomination (*to an office*); filling (*of a vacancy*); presentation to (*a living*); distribution (*of parts*), cast (*of a play*); instrumentation (*Mus.*). *Comp.* **—schlägel, —stößel**, *m.* pavior's rammer. **—ungs=recht**, *n.* right of presentation, patronage, advowson.

Beseuf'zen, *v.a.* to sigh over, lament, bemoan.

Besich't—igen, *v.a.* to inspect; to survey; **einen Leichnam von Amtswegen —igen**, to hold an inquest over *or* on a corpse. **—iger**, *m.* (**—igers**, *pl.* **—iger**) inspector, surveyor; viewer, searcher; **sachverständiger —iger**, expert. **—igung**, *f.* inspection, survey; **—igung einer Leiche**, coroner's inquest; visitation. *Comp.* **—igungs=bericht**, *m.* inspector's report. **—igungs=gebühren**, *pl.* surveyor's fees. **—igungs=reise**, *f.* tour of inspection.

Besie'del—n, *v.a.* to colonize; **ein Land —n**, to settle in a country. **—ung**, *f.* colonization.

Besieg'bar, *adj.* conquerable, vanquishable.

Besie'gel—n, *v.a.* to seal, put one's seal to. **—ung**, *f.* sealing (*of a deed*).

Besie'g—en, *v.a.* to vanquish, overcome, conquer, subdue (*passions*); surmount (*difficulties*). **—er**, *m.* (**—ers**, *pl.* **—er**) conqueror, victor. **—ung**, *f.* conquering; conquest.

Be'sing, *m.* (*pl.*—**e**), **Be'singe**, *f.*; **schwarze —**, bilberry, myrtle whortleberry (*also called* **Bickbeere**); **rote —**, red whortleberry.

Besin'gen, *ir.v.a.* to sing, to celebrate in song.

Besin'n—en, I. *ir.v.r.*; **sich (auf eine S.) —en**, to recollect, remember, to call to mind, think of, hit on; **sich eines Bessern —en**, to think better of a th.; **sich eines andern —en**, to change one's mind; **er ist schnell besonnen**, he is quick in taking his resolution; **sich —en (über eine S.)**, to consider, deliberate, reflect; **ohne sich zu —en**, without thinking *or* considering, at once; **sich wieder —en**, to come to oneself again. II. *subst.n.* reflection. **—ung**, *f.* recollection; reflection, consideration, deliberation; **wieder zur —ung kommen**, to recover consciousness; **sie war nicht bei —ung**, she was beside herself, she was unconscious; **er blieb bei —ung**, he retained his consciousness; **einen zur —ung bringen**, to bring one to his senses. *Comp.* **—ungs=los**, *adj.* unconscious; senseless; inconsiderate, rash. **—ungs=losigkeit**, *f.* senselessness, insensibility. **—ung=raubend**, *adj. & adv.* depriving of consciousness *or* reason.

Besi'tz, *m.* (**—es**) possession; property; **in — nehmen** *or* **— ergreifen von einer S.**, to take possession of a th.; **in (den) — setzen**, to put in possession of; **im —e einer S. sein**, to be in possession of a th.; **einen aus dem —e setzen**, to dispossess, expropriate, oust a p. **—tum**, *n.* (**—tums**, *pl.* **Besitztümer**) possession, property. *Comp.* **—anzeigend**, *adj.* possessive (*Gram.*) **—ergreifer**, *m.* occupant, occupier. **—ergreifung**, *f.* occupancy, occupation; seizure; (**widerrechtliche**) usurpation. **—fall**, *m.* genitive case. **—nahme, —nehmung**, *f.* act of taking possession, occupancy. **—stand**, *m.* state of possession; active property (*C. L.*). **—störung**, *f.* disturbance. **—urkunde**, *f.* livery (*Law*).

Besit'z—en, *ir.v.a.* to possess, be in possession of, have; to sit upon; **die Eier sind besessen**, the eggs have been too long set upon, are addled. **—end**, *p. & adj.* **die —enden Klassen**, the moneyed *or* propertied classes. **—er**, *m.* (**—ers**, *pl.* **—er**), **—erin**, *f.* possessor; proprietor; principal (*of a business*); master; owner; occupier; **Grund—er**, land-owner; **den —er wechseln**, to change hands; **selig ist der —er**, possession is nine points of law. **—ung**, *f.* possession, property; manor, estate; (*pl.*) dominions, dependencies.

Besof'fen, *p.p. & adj.* drunk, tipsy (*vulg.*).

Besoh'len, *v.a.* to sole (*shoes, etc.*).

Besol'd—en, *v.a.* to pay; to give a salary to; to have in one's pay; **—ete Truppen**, stipendiary troops. **—ung**, *f.* act of paying (*wages, salary, etc., to*); salary, stipend, pay, wages.

Beson'der, *adj.* particular, peculiar; separate, distinct, especial; odd, strange, singular; **ich habe keine —e Absicht dabei**, I have no particular purpose to effect by it; **ins —e**, in particular; **nichts —es**, nothing particular; **—e Havarie**, particular *or* simple average; **eine —e Wohnung**, a separate lodging; **jeder Teil ins —e**, each several part; **—e Befehle**, special orders; **die —en Eigenschaften einer Pflanze**, the specific qualities of a plant; **die —en Umstände**, the particulars; **meine —e Meinung**, my individual opinion; **das —e**, the concrete (*Log.*); the particular; the extraordinary. **—heit**, *f.* specialty; peculiarity; strangeness, oddness; individuality; (*pl.*) details, particulars. **—s**, *adv.* especially, in particular; apart, separately, severally; peculiarly; extraordinarily, greatly, much.

Beson'nen, *p.p.* (*of* **besinnen**) & *adj.* prudent, circumspect; thoughtful, discreet, considerate; in full possession of one's mental faculties. **—heit**, *f.* prudence, circumspection, thoughtfulness; presence of mind, self-possession; **mit —heit**, discreetly.

Besor'g—en, *v.* I. *a.* to take care of; to provide for; to do, effect; to manage (*a business, etc.*); to execute (*a commission*); to discharge (*functions*); to conduct (*divine service*); **das Beste eines Freundes —en**, to look after a friend's interests. II. *n.* (*aux.* **s.**) to be apprehensive of, anxious about; **er war um uns nicht wenig —t**, he was not a little anxious on our account; **ein —tes Aussehen**, a careworn look, a look of anxiety; **einen —t machen**, to alarm one; **seien Sie ganz ruhig, ich werde es —en**, be quite at ease, I shall see to it. **—er**, *m.* (**—ers**, *pl.* **—er**) manager, conductor; care-taker; executor (*of a commission*); agent. **—lich**, *adj.* anxious, solicitous. **—lichkeit**, *f.* apprehensiveness, fearfulness; fear, anxiety, solicitude. **—nis**, *f.* (*pl.* **—nisse**), care; anxiety, apprehension; superintendence, management; **in —nis geraten**, to become alarmed. **—sam**, *adj.* careful. **—ung**, *f.* the taking care of; care, management; execution, performance; **sie hat die —ung meiner häuslichen Angelegenheiten**, she manages my domestic concerns. *Comp.* **—nis=voll**, *adj.* solicitous; disquieting; apprehensive. **—ungs=gebühren**, *pl.* commission fees.

Bespan'nen, *v.a.* to span; to string (*an instrument*); to put (*horses*) to.

Bespei'en, *ir.v.a.* (*in older German sometimes reg. p.p.* **bespeit**) to spit *or* vomit on.

Bespie'geln, *v.r.* to look at oneself in the glass; to take an example (**an**, from, by); to be mirrored (*in a glass, river, lake*).

Bespin'nen, *ir.v.a.* to spin over; **besponnene Saiten**, covered strings, silver strings (*music*).

Bespit'zen, *v.a.* to thin; **sich —**, to get tipsy (*sl.*).

Bespi'tzt, *p.p. & adj.* tipsy (*sl.*).

Bespöt'teln, Bespot'ten, *v.a.* to jeer at, ridicule.

Bespre'ch—en, *ir.v.a.* to discuss (*a subject*), talk over, arrange, agree upon; review (*a book*); to bespeak, engage; to order; to conjure, charm in words; **sich mit einem —en**, to confer, parley with one; **sich mit einem —en über eine S.**, to deliberate upon a th. with a p. **—ung**, *f* conversation; discussion; review (*of a book*), settlement; conference, parley; charming, conjuring.

Besprin'gen, *ir.v.a.* to leap upon; to cover.
Besprit'zen, *v.a.* to wet with a squirt; to bespatter; to play upon (*with an engine*); to stain (*with blood*).
Bespü'len, *v.a.* to wash (*a shore*); to ripple over, against; **von der See bespült,** sea-washed.
Bes'ser, *adj. & adv.* (*comparative of* **gut**) better; a little more; **je mehr desto —,** the more the better; **desto —,** so much the better; **sich — in Acht nehmen,** to be more careful; **— werden,** to amend, to get better; to clear up (*of weather*); **jetzt steht es mit ihm —,** his affairs are looking up; **er hat es —,** he is better off; **sich eines —n besinnen,** to think better of it; **eines —n belehren,** to set right; **— hinauf,** a little higher up, more upwards; **— schreien,** to shout louder; **Sie können nichts —es thun als,** you can't do better than.
Bes'ser—n, *v.a.* to better, improve upon; to amend, reform; to repair; to correct (*passages in a book*); **nicht zu —n,** incorrigible; **sich —n,** to improve, gain ground, rally, get well; **—e dich!** improve, mend your ways! **—ung,** *f.* improvement, amendment, amelioration; reformation; convalescence; **gute —ung!** I wish you a speedy recovery! **er ist auf dem Wege der —ung,** he is convalescent, *or* is mending; **es ist —ung eingetreten,** there is a change for the better. *Comp.* **—ungs=anstalt,** *f.* house of correction. **—ungs=fähig,** *adj.* capable of improvement, improvable. **—ungs=mittel,** *n.* corrective. **—ungs=schule,** *f.* reformatory.
Best, *adj. & adv.* (*superlative of* **gut**) best; **der erste —e,** the first that comes; **ich fand es am —en,** I thought it best; **aufs —e,** in the best possible way; **aufs —e benutzen,** to make the most of; **nach —em** *or* **meinem —en Wissen,** to the best of my knowledge; **zu Ihrem —en,** in your interest; **zum —en der Armen,** for the benefit of the poor; **das Beste,** the prize; **das —e thun** *or* **gewinnen,** to win the prize; **etwas zum —en geben,** to give as a treat, to treat a p. to a th., to give, to stand (*a few bottles of wine*), to relate (*a story etc.*); **geben Sie uns ein Lied zum —en,** give us a song; **einen zum —en haben,** to hoax one, to turn one into ridicule; **man hatte ihn zum —en,** they were making fun of him; **etwas zum —en (aufs —e) deuten,** to put the best construction on a matter; **reden Sie zu meinem —en,** speak in my favour, intercede for me; **im —en Arbeiten,** in the midst of (*hard*) work; **seine —e Mannschaft,** the pick of his men; **die Lehre von der —en Welt,** optimism; **in den —en Jahren,** in the prime of life; **er ist auf dem —en Wege,** he is in a fair way to . . .; **der —e Mensch von der Welt,** the best fellow in the world; **mein —er,** my dear sir; my dear fellow (*famil.*); **meine —e,** dear madam; my dear Mrs. X. **—ens,** *adv.* in the best way; **empfehlen Sie mich —ens,** remember me most kindly (*to*); **—ens empfohlen!** farewell, good-bye! (*on leavetaking*); **ich danke —ens,** very many thanks, thanks very much, thank you very much. *Comp.* **—möglich,** I. *adj.* best possible. II. *adv.* as well as possible.
Bestal'l—en, *v.a.* to appoint, to invest with (*an office*). **—ung,** *f.* appointment; installation, investiture; salary; warrant, commission. *Comp.* **—ungs=brief,** *m.* (*letters*) patent, diploma, commission.
Besta'nd, *m.* (—es, *pl.* **Bestände**) permanency, duration, continuance; certitude; stability, firmness; amount, value (*of goods in hand*); balance, remainder (*C. L.*); lease of a farm; **von — sein, — haben,** to be durable, lasting, to endure, last: **Kassen—,** cash-balance; **— eines Waldes,** stock of trees (*in a wood*); **der wirkliche — einer Armee,** the effective state (*muster roll*) of an army; **der eiserne — (eines Lesebuchs, einer Hausbibliothek)** what should of necessity be contained (*in a reading book, in a family library*), the necessary constituents; stock contents; **in — geben,** to let on lease; **mit — Rechtens,** lawfully, legally; **der — des Gutes ist ꝛc.,** the estate comprises *etc.;* **Ausstände und Bestände,** assets and debts; **in — geben,** to let to farm, to farm out, to let by lease, to rent (*to*). *Comp.* **—brief,** *m.* lease of a farm. **—buch,** *n.* inventory. **—geld,** *n.* clear account, balance in cash; rent of a farm. **—gut,** *n.* farm let on lease. **—heit,** *f.* (*obs.*) = **Beständigkeit,** stability, constancy, firmness, steadiness. **—inhaber,** *m.* *see* **Beständer.** **—jagd,** *f.* preserve, shooting let on lease. **—los,** *adj.* inconsistent, unstable, shaky, transitory; of no duration. **—losigkeit,** *f.* instability. **—teil,** *m.* constituent part; ingredient.
Bestän'd—er, *m. see* **Pächter.** **—ig,** *adj. & adv.* continual, continuous, perpetual; constant, steady, unchanging, steadfast; durable, invariable; faithful; firm; fixed, standard, binding; continually, perpetually, constantly, faithfully. **—ige Valuta,** standard of value, fixed price; **wir müssen in der —igen Erwartung leben, daß ꝛc.,** we must live in hourly expectation of, *etc.;* **—ige Größen,** constant quantities (*Math.*); **der Wind wehte —ig aus Westen,** the wind had settled in the west; **—iges Wetter,** settled weather; **—er Wind,** steady wind (*Naut.*); **—e Nachfrage,** steady, brisk demand; **—er Liebhaber,** constant, faithful lover; **ein zu Recht —iger Vertrag,** a legal contract. **—igkeit,** *f.* continuance; permanence; perpetuity; perseverance, constancy, faithfulness; steadfastness.
Bestär'k—en, *v.a.* to confirm, corroborate; to strengthen, fortify. **—ung,** *f.* corroboration, confirmation, strengthening.
Bestä'tig—en, *v.a.* to confirm, establish (*in an office, etc.*); to confirm, corroborate, verify, endorse (*statements, opinions, etc.*); to sanction, authorize, make valid (*laws, etc.*); to ratify (*a treaty*); to acknowledge (*the receipt of a letter*); to ascertain (*the number of stags, etc., in a wood*); **gerichtlich —en,** to legalize by oath; **sich —en,** to be confirmed, hold good; **die Nachricht —te sich,** the news received confirmation, proved to be true. **—ung,** *f.* confirmation, corroboration; ratification; sanction. *Comp.* **—ungs=urteil,** *n.* confirmatory judgment.
Bestat't—en, *v.a.* to convey (*to a place*); to bury. **—ung,** *f.* burial.
Bestau'ben, *v.a.* to cover with dust; to get dusty.
Bestäu'ben, *v.a.* to cover with dust.
Beste'ch—en, *ir.v.a.* to prick repeatedly, to stitch; to bribe, corrupt; **den Bandstreifen, das Kapitälchen —en,** to headband (*Bookb.*); **Leder —en,** to quilt (*Shoem.*). **—er,** *m.* (—ers, *pl.* —er) briber; suborner (*of evidence*). **—bar, —lich,** *adj.* corruptible, bribable. **—barkeit,** *f.*, **—lichkeit,** *f.* corruptibility. **—ung,** *f.* bribery; bribe. *Comp.* **—draht,** *m.* shoemaker's waxed end for boot-heels; stitching thread. **—naht,** *f.* flat seam. **—ort,** *m.* shoemaker's pricking awl.
Beste'ck, *n.* (—s, *pl.* —e) case; case of instruments; box of compasses; knife, fork and spoon; case for these; ship's reckoning; table *or* scheme of the dimensions and scantlings of a ship; **das — machen,** to work the reckoning; **mit dem — voraus (zurück) sein,** to be ahead (astern) of the reckoning.
Beste'cken, *v.a.* to stake, rod (*peas, etc.*); to plant (*hop-poles, a bed with potatoes, etc.*); to prick

out (*on a chart, etc.*); to stick over with, adorn, garnish; **mit Schanzpfählen —**, to palisade.

Beste'der, *m.* (—s, *pl.* —) contractor, ship's husband; **Provision des —s,** husbandage.

Beste'h—en, *ir.v.* I. *a.* to undergo, endure; to stand (*a test*); to pass, get through (*an examination*); **nicht —en,** to fail; to be plucked, to get ploughed (*coll.*); to pass through (*dangers, etc.*); to overcome, stand out against (*opposition, etc.*); to purchase; to rent, hire. II. *n.* (*aux.* **f.** and **h.**); to undergo, stand a test; to stand steadfast, withstand, resist; to hold one's own, to come off (*with honour or dishonour*); to be, to exist; to subsist; to last, continue; **er ist bestanden** *or* **er hat in der Prüfung bestanden,** he has passed his examination; **er wird die Prüfung gewiß nicht —en,** he is sure to fail in the examination; **diese zwei Sachen können nicht neben einander —en,** these two things are incompatible, inconsistent with one another; **sein Reich wird nicht —en,** his kingdom will not last; **zwischen ihm und ihr —t rc.,** there exists between her and him, *etc.;* **—en auf (einer S.),** to insist on, persist in, hold out for; **sie bestanden darauf ihn zu sehen,** they insisted on seeing him; **auf seinem Kopfe —en,** to be obstinate; **—en aus,** to consist of, be composed of; **—en in** (*with dat.*) to consist in; **—en mit,** to be consistent, compatible with. **—end,** *p. & adj.* existent, subsistent; **—ende Preise,** ruling prices (*C.L.*); **für sich —end,** absolute, independent.

Besteh'len, *ir.v.a.* to rob, to steal from; **seine Pflicht —,** to neglect one's duty (*poet.*).

Bestei'gen, *ir.v.a.* to ascend (*a mountain; the pulpit, etc.*); to climb (*a tree*); to mount (*a horse*); to scale (*a wall*); to go on board (*a ship*).

Bestel'l—en, *v.a.* to cover; to order; to bespeak; to dispose, arrange; to appoint, constitute; to execute (*a commission*); to deliver (*a message*); to fill with, stock, store; **sie —ten einander auf neun Uhr,** they appointed to meet at nine; **wir haben ihn zu unserm Agenten —t,** we have asked him to meet us at our agent's; we have made (*or* appointed) him our agent; **man hat ihn zu diesem Amte —t,** he has been appointed to this office; **einen Gruß —en,** to give one's compliments, kind regards to; **haben Sie etwas zu —en,** have you any message, can I take any message from you? **einen Platz —en,** to secure a place; **den Acker —en,** to make a field ready for sowing, to till a field; **sein Haus —en,** to settle one's affairs, to prepare for death; **mit ihm ist es schlecht —t,** he is in a bad way. **—er,** *m.* (**—ers,** *pl.* **—er**) bespeaker, orderer; executor (*of a commission*); cultivator; committor (*C. L.*). **—ung,** *f.* bespeaking; order, commission; appointment; commission; delivery; management; arrangement; rendezvous; cultivation. *Comp.* **—arbeit,** *f.* work done to order. **—bezirk,** *m.* district of delivery. **—buch,** *n.* order book. **—geld,** *n.* commission money; **—geld frei,** no charge (is) made for commission. **—ungs=buch,** *n.* order-book. **—ungs=kunde,** *f.* science of agriculture. **—zeit,** *f.* time for tilling; right time for ordering goods. **—zettel,** *m.* note containing an order, order form.

Beste'rnt, *p.p. & adj.* starry; decorated (*with orders*); marked with an asterisk.

Besteu'er—n, *v.a.* to tax. *f.* **—ung,** taxation, imposition of taxes.

Bestia'l—isch, *adj. & adv.* bestial, beastly, brutal; bestially, brutally. **—itä't,** *f.* (*pl.* **—itä'ten**) beastliness, bestiality.

Besti'cken, *v.a.* to embroider.

Be'stie, *f.* (*pl.* **—n**) beast, brute.

Bestie'lt, *p.p. & adj.* petiolate (*Bot.*); furnished with a handle, with a helve.

Bestimm'bar, *adj. & adv.* definable; ascertainable.

Bestim'm—en, *v.a.* to decide; to determine; to settle; to fix, appoint (*a time*); to allot to; to define; **über eine S. —en,** to dispose of a th.; **—en zu,** to destine, intend for; **wir sind alle dazu —t,** we are all destined to *or* for it; **dieses Schiff ist nach Hamburg —t,** this ship is bound for Hamburg; **es war mir vom Schicksal —t,** it was intended for me by fate; **es ist —t in Gottes Rat,** God has willed it; **ich hatte das Geld für Sie —t,** I had intended the money for you; **vorher —en,** to predestinate; **einen —en etwas zu thun,** to induce one to do a thing; **etwas näher —en,** to define s.th. more closely, to modify; **das Gesetz —t, daß,** the law ordains that; **sich —en zu einer S.,** to determine, resolve on, settle. **—end,** *p. & adj.* determining, deciding; determinative (*word*); **das —ende dabei war,** what decided the matter was. **—t,** *p.p., adj. & adv.* fixed, appointed, settled; finite (*Math.*); determinate, determined; positive, certain; precise; distinct; decided; definite; **der —te Artikel,** the definite article; **—t nach,** bound for; **an dem —ten Tage,** on the day appointed; **eine —te Antwort,** a clear, decided, definite answer; **—tes Gehalt,** fixed stipend *or* salary; **ganz —t?** are you quite certain? **ganz —t!** most decidedly. **—theit,** *f.* exactitude; determination; **mit —theit,** positively, with precision, categorically. **—ung,** *f.* act of fixing *or* determining; destination; destiny; vocation; definition; designation; statement; modification; **dienen lerne bei Zeiten das Weib nach ihrer —ung,** a woman should learn to serve betimes according to her calling. *Comp.* **—ungs=grund,** *m.* motive. **—ungs=ort,** *m.* (*place of*) destination. **—ungs=wort,** *n.* modifying, determinating word, word joined to another to determine its meaning or relations (*adjective, adverb, etc.*); the word in compounds which modifies the meaning of the principal component.

Besto'chen, (*p.p.* of **bestechen**), *adj.* corrupted.

Bestoh'len, *p.p.* of **bestehlen.**

Besto'ß—en, *ir.v.a.* to hit, knock against; to injure (*by a knock, etc.*); to smooth, plane down, rough-file; **die Lettern —en,** to dress the type. *Comp.* **—feile,** *f.* rasp. **—hobel,** *m.* jack-plane; dresser (*Typ.*).

Bestra'f—en, *v.a.* to punish; to visit with (*death, etc.*); **mit Worten —en,** to chide. **—ung,** *f.* punishing; punishment; reprimand.

Bestrah'l—en, *v.a.* to irradiate. **—ung,** *f.* irradiation, illumination.

Bestre'b—en, I. *v.r.* to exert oneself, to strive; **sich —en um,** to try to obtain. II. *subst.n.*, **—ung,** *f.* effort, endeavour, exertion.

Bestrei'chen, *ir.v.a.* to spread over, besmear; to graze, brush against; to sweep (*of artillery; of a telescope*); to rake (*with shot*); to touch upon; **mit Butter —,** to butter; **mit Fett —,** to grease; **mit Pflaster —,** to plaster; **mit einem Magnete(n) —,** to touch with a loadstone; **in gerader Linie —,** to enfilade; **eine Küste —,** to coast along, sail along the coast; **von der Seite —,** to flank; **bestrichene Winkel,** flanked angles.

Bestreit'bar, *adj.* disputable, controvertible.

Bestrei't—en, *ir.v.a.* to attack; to combat; to contest, impugn, oppose; to be equal to; to bear, to defray, pay for; **er kann das nicht —en,** he can't afford that; he cannot deny it; **jemandes Bedürfnisse —en,** to supply a person's wants; **die Kosten der Ausrüstung —en,** to cover the costs of the outfit; **seine Geschäfte nicht —en können,** to be unable to manage one's business; **ich weiß nicht, wie ich alle diese Ausgaben —en soll,** I do not know how to meet all these expenses; **mit dieser Summe**

lassen sich deine Ausgaben leicht —en, this sum will easily cover your expenses; er bestritt mir das Recht, he disputed my right. —er, *m.* (—ers, *pl.* —er) opponent, antagonist; defrayer (*of expense*). —ung, *f.* combating; detrayal (*of cost*).

Bestreu'en, *v.a.* to bestrew, sprinkle over.

Bestri'ck—en, *v.a.* to knit on *or* round; to insnare, charm; eine —ende Stimme, a charming voice. —ung, *f.* entanglement; insnaring.

Bestü'ck—en, *v.a.* to furnish (*a ship*) with guns. —t, *p.p. & adj.* —t mit, mounted with. —ung, *f.* armament (*of a ship*).

Bestür'm—en, *v.a.* to storm, assault, assail; to besiege. —ung, *f.* storming; assault.

Bestür'z—en, *v.a.* (*also* bestürzt machen) to startle, surprise, put out; confound, throw into confusion; to terrify, dismay. —t, *p.p. & adj.* confounded, put out, dismayed; —t sein, to stand aghast, be thunderstruck; ein —tes Gesicht machen, to pull a long face. —ung, *f.* confusion; consternation; dismay.

Besu'ch, *m.* (—es, *pl.* —e) visit, call; company, visitors; attending, attendance; frequenting (*of a place*); kurzer —, flying call; langer —, long stay; visitation; einen — abstatten, to pay a visit, make a call; er hat —, he has company, there is somebody with him; wir haben vielen —, we have many visitors. *Comp.* —s=fuß, *m.*; mit einem auf —sfuß stehen, to be on visiting terms with a person. —s=karte, *f.* (visiting) card. —tag, *m.* (regular) visiting day, reception day, at-home day. —zimmer, *n.*, drawing-room, sitting-room, reception room.

Besu'ch—en, *v.a.* to visit; to resort to, to frequent, to call on *or* upon; er —t die Kirche regelmäßig, he attends church regularly; ich —te ihn auf einen Sprung, I just looked in at his residence; seine Vorlesungen werden sehr —t, his lectures are very well attended; ein stark —ter Ort, a place of public resort, that is much frequented. —er, *m.* (—ers, *pl.* —er) visitor.

Besu'deln, *v.a.* to soil, befoul, sully.

Beta'g—en, *v.a.* (*Law*) to appoint a day; to date; (einen) —en, to summon, cite (*to appear in court*). —t, *p.p. & adj.* aged, stricken in years; due (*of a bill*); wohl —t, hoch —t, well advanced in years. —ung, *f.* date.

Beta'kel—n, *v.a.* to rig (*a ship*). —ung, *f.* rigging (*of a ship*).

Beta'st—en, *v.a.* to handle, touch, finger; ungeschickt —en, to maul, fumble. —ung, *f.* feeling, fingering, touching; contact.

Betäu'b—en, *v.a.* to stun, din, deafen; to stupefy; to bewilder, confuse; to addle (*the brain*); to keep under (*one's body*). —end, *p. & adj.* deafening (*noise*); narcotic (*smell*). —ung, *f.* deafening; bewilderment; state of insensibility, stupefaction. —ungs=mittel, *n.* narcotic.

Betau'en, *v.a.* to bedew.

Be'te, I. *f. & n.* the stake lost at cards; person who loses at cards. II. *adj.*; — machen, to win the game (*coll.*); er ist —, he has lost the game, is beasted *or* looed (*coll.*).

Be'te, *f.* beet (*Bot.*).

Betee'ren, *v.a.* to tar.

Betei'lig—en, *v.a.* to assign a share; to interest; bei *or* an einer S. —t sein, to have a share *or* an interest, to be interested in anything; sich bei einer Sache —en, to take an interest in, be interested in; ich würde mich nicht dabei —t haben, wenn, I should not have engaged in it, should not have had anything to do with it, if; die —ten, *pl.* the parties concerned. —ung, *f.* share, interest in an undertaking; participation in a crime.

Be't—en, *v.* I. *a.* to beseech; to utter in prayer; sie —ete ihren Rosenkranz (her), she told her beads; er —ete das Vaterunser, he said the Lord's prayer. II. *n.* (*aux.* h.) to pray; vor (und nach) Tische —, to say grace; er —ete jeden Abend, he said his prayers every night; —en um eine S., to pray for a thing. —er, *m.* (—ers, *pl.* —er) one who prays. *Comp.* —bruder, *m.* devotee, bigot. —buch, *n.* prayer-book. —fahrt, *f.* pilgrimage. —glocke, *f.* prayer-bell, angelus (*Rom. Cath.*). —kissen, *n.* hassock. —saal, *m.* chapel, oratory. —schemel, *m.* hassock. —schwester, *f.* devotee, bigot. —stuhl, *m.* praying-desk, priedieu chair. —stunde, *f.* prayer-time; prayer-meeting; die —stunde halten, to read *or* say prayers, to hold a prayer meeting; to officiate at prayers. —stunden=buch, *n.* breviary. —tag, *m.* day of prayer *or* thanksgiving, fast-day; Rogation day (*in Lent*); Buß= und —tag, day of humiliation. —woche, *f.* Rogation week.

Beteu'er—n, *v.a.* to assert (*the truth of*), protest, asseverate; to swear (*to*). —ung, *f.* asseveration, protestation.

Betä'tig—en, *v.a.* to give practical proof of, to evince by facts; to practise, manifest, put into practice; seine Lehre —en, to act according to one's teaching; sich —en, to bestir oneself, to take active part in a thing. —ung, *f.* practical proof, application, practice.

Betö'r—en, *v.a.* to befool, delude, dupe; to infatuate. —t=heit, *f.* besottedness. —ung, *f.* befooling; delusion, infatuation.

Beträ'n—en, *v.a.* to bedew with tears; to weep for. —t, *p.p. & adj.* tearful, weeping.

Betu'lich, *adj.* engaging, obliging; active, busily stirring; officious. —keit, *f.* officiousness.

Betu'n, *v.r.* to bestir oneself, to be active.

Beti'tel—n, *v.a.* to give a title to; to entitle, style, call. —ung, *f.* entitling, title.

Betöl'p—eln (Betöl'pen), *v.a.* to dupe, cheat. —ung, *f.* duping.

Beto'n—en, *v.a.* to accent, stress, accentuate; to emphasize, lay stress on; eine —te Silbe, an accented syllable, a stress syllable. —ung, *f.* accentuation; emphasis; stress; schwebende —, level stress, fluctuating accent.

Beto'nie, *f.* betony (*Bot.*).

Betra'cht, *m.* (—s) respect; consideration; account; point of view; in —, considering; in — ziehen, to take into consideration; nicht in — kommen, to be out of the question; to be of no moment; in jedem —, in every respect.

Betrach't—en, *v.a.* to view, consider; to contemplate; to weigh, regard, reflect upon; alles recht —et, altogether, taking everything into consideration; wir —en die Sache von einer ganz anderen Seite, we look at the matter in quite a different light. —er, *m.* (—ers, *pl.* —er) one who considers, beholds, contemplates. —ung, *f.* the act of looking at; meditation; contemplation; consideration; view, opinion, way of thinking; —ungen anstellen, to meditate, reflect; in —ung des &c., in consideration of, *etc.*; out of regard for, *etc.*; —ungen machen *or* anstellen über (eine S.) to reflect on a th., to animadvert upon a th. *Comp.* —ungs=bücher, *pl.* books of meditation.

Beträcht'lich, *adj.* considerable. —keit, *f.* considerableness, importance.

Betra'g, *m.* (—es, *pl.* Beträge) amount; sum total.

Betra'gen, I. *ir.v.a.* to lay on, overlay; to come to, amount to; wieviel beträgt meine Rechnung? what does my bill come to? how much is my bill? II. *ir.v.r.* to deport, conduct oneself, to behave; sich schlecht —, to misbehave, to conduct oneself ill. III. *subst.n.* behaviour, conduct, demeanour, bearing.

Betrau'en, *v.a.*; einen mit einer S. —, to entrust s.th. to s.o., to entrust one with a.th.; mit einem Amte —, to appoint to an office.

Betrau'ern, *v.a.* to mourn for, deplore, bewail.
Beträu'feln, *v.a.* to drop upon, to let fall upon in drops, bedrop; to baste (*meat*).
Betre'ff, *m.* (—s) reference, regard; **in — (einer Sache)**, with regard to, as to, touching, in respect of a matter. **—s**, *adv.*, concerning.
Betref'f—en, *ir.v.a.* to fall upon, surprise; to befall; to have to do with, concern, affect, touch; **was mich betrifft**, as for me, so far as I am concerned; **was das betrifft**, as to that; **es betrifft eine Dame**, there is a lady in the case; **auf frischer That, über der That —en**, to take in the act, surprise; **der Dieb wurde auf frischer That betroffen**, the thief was caught in the act. **—end**, *p.*, *adj. & adv.* concerning; with reference to; respective; **das —ende Wort**, the word in question; **der —ende Roman**, the novel referred to; **er las etwas ihn —endes**, he read something about himself; **ein jeder in seiner —enden Abteilung**, each in his own department; **der —ende Offizier**, the officer in question, the officer concerned.
Betrei'b—en, *ir.v.a.* to drive upon; to urge on, push forward, follow up; to manage, carry on, exercise; to pursue (*studies*); to cultivate. **—ung**, *f.* carrying on, management, pushing forward; exercise (*of a profession*); prosecution, pursuit.
Betre't—en, I. *ir.v.a.* to set foot on *or* in; to enter upon, follow; to enter (*a house*); to mount (*a pulpit, etc.*); to tread (*the boards; of birds*); to find, meet with; to surprise, catch. II. *p.p. & adj.* startled, surprised, embarrassed; trodden, beaten. III. *subst.* **—en**, *n.*, **—ung**, *f.* entering, *etc.*; **das —en dieses Weges ist nicht gestattet**, this way is not open to the public, this is a private road. *Comp.* **—ungs=fall**, *m.*; **im —ungsfalle**, in case of being taken in the act.
Betrie'b, *m.* (—es, *pl.* —e) the driving on, pursuit; exercise (*of one's calling, etc.*); carrying on, management (*of a business*); trade, profession; impulse, instigation; working; **wissenschaftlicher —**, scientific management; **im —e**, at work, in operation, going. **—sam**, *adj.* active, industrious. **—samkeit**, *f.* activity; industry. *Comp.* **—s=direktor**, *m.* working manager. **—s=gebäude**, *n.* works. **—s=gerät**, **—s=material**, *n.* rolling-stock (*Railw.*) **—s=jahr**, *m.* business year. **—s=kapital**, *n.* working capital, stock-in-trade. **—s=mittel**, *pl.* plant. **—s=stockung**, *f. or* **—s=störung**, *f.* interruption of work, obstruction to traffic.
Betrin'ken, *v.r.* to get drunk. **betrunken**, *p.p. & adj.* drunk.
Betrof'fen, *p.p.* (*of* **betreffen**) *& adj.* struck with surprise, taken aback, confounded, perplexed. **—heit**, *f.* perplexity, surprise.
Betro'gen, *p.p. of* **betrügen**.
Beträp'feln, *see* **Beträufeln**.
Betrü'b—en, *v.a.* to make muddy, stir up, trouble (*obsol.*); to grieve, afflict; to cast down, depress; **sich —en**, to mourn, to grieve for *or* at, to fret. **—nis**, *f.* (*pl.* **—nisse**), *n.* (—**nisses**, *pl.* **—nisse**) affliction, sorrow, grief; sadness; lowness of spirits. **—t**, *p.p. & adj.* sad, sorrowful, afflicted, melancholy; **zum Tode —t**, grieved to death; **—te Zeiten**, calamitous times; **—te Gedanken**, gloomy thoughts; **—t sein über eine S.**, to be afflicted on account of a.th.
Betru'g, *m.* (—s, *no plur.*; **Betrügerei'en**) fraud, deception; deceit, trickery, imposture; humbug; delusion (*of the senses*).
Betrü'g—en, *ir.v.a.* to cheat, deceive, defraud; **einen um eine S. —en**, to cheat one out of something. **—er**, *m.* (—ers, *pl.* —er) deceiver; swindler, cheat, impostor. **—erei'**, *f.* cheating; deceit; fraud; deceitfulness. **—erisch**, *adj. & adv.* deceitful; fraudulent, knavish; deceptive. **—lich**, *adj.* fraudulent; false, deceptive; illusory, fallacious; **—lich handeln**, to cheat, to play fast and loose. **—lichkeit**, *f.* falsity, fallaciousness; deceitfulness; fraud.

Be'tt, *n.* (*arch. poet. dial.* **Bette**; *dimin.* **Bettchen**, **Bettlein**) (—es, *pl.* —en) bed; channel, bed; layer; lair (*of beasts*), form; **ein elendes —**, a pallet; **— mit Vorhängen**, a four-poster; bed with curtains; **sich zu — (ins —) legen**, to go to bed; **zu — (ins —) bringen**, to put to bed; **am —e**, at the bedside; **das — hüten**, to keep one's bed; **ein — aufschlagen**, to put up a bed; **im —e**, abed, in bed; **auf dem — der Ehre sterben**, to die on the field of battle; **er ist schon zu —**, he is already in bed; **das — überziehen**, to put clean sheets on a bed; **Scheidung von Tisch und —**, divorce from bed and board, divorce a mensa et thoro; **Kranken—**, sick-bed; **Sterbe—**, death-bed; **Wochen—**, child-bed; **zweischläfriges —**, double bed; **Zimmer mit zwei —en**, a double-bedded room. *Comp.* **—behänge**, *n.* bed-curtains, valance. **—brett**, *n.* bed-lath, bed-board. **—decke**, *f.* counterpane; (**wollene —decke**) blanket; (**gesteppte —decke**) quilt. **—flasche**, *f.* hot-water bottle. **—frau**, *f.* bed-maker (*Univ.*). **—fuß**, *m.* foot of the bed; field basil. **—gang**, *m.* space at the bedside. **—genoß**, *m.*, **—genossin**, *f.* bed-fellow. **—gerät**, *n.* bedding, bed-furniture. **—gestell**, *n.* bedstead. **—himmel**, *m.* tester. **—kasten**, *m.* press-bed. **—kranz**, *m.*, **—krone**, *f.* canopy. **—lade**, *f.* press-bed; bedstead. **—lägerig**, *adj.* bed-ridden; confined to bed. **—laken**, *n.* sheet. **—pfanne**, *f.* warming-pan. **—pfoste**, *f.*, **—pfosten**, *m.* bed-post. **—pfühl**, *m.* bolster. **—säule**, *f.* bed-post. **—schieber**, *m.*, **—schüssel**, *f.* bed-pan. **—schragen**, *m.* stretcher, truckle bed. **—schrank**, *m.* press-bed, wardrobe-bedstead. **—sessel**, *m.* sofa-bed. **—sofa**, *n.* bed couch. **—spinde**, **—stelle**, *f.* bedstead. **—tuch**, *n.* sheet. **—überzug**, *m.* pillow-case; bed-tick. **—vorleger**, *m.* bed-rug. **—wärmer**, *m.* warming pan; hot-water bottle. **—wäsche**, *f.* bed-linen, bed-clothes. **—winkel**, *m.* alcove. **—zeug**, *n.* bedding; bed-clothes. **—zwillich**, *m.* ticking, striped cotton.
Bet't—en, *v.a.* to give (*one*) a bed; to make a bed; to put to bed; **sich —en**, to make one's bed; **wie man sich bettet so schläft man**, do well and have well (*prov.*); **er hat sich warm gebettet**, he has feathered his nest, he has a comfortable position; **er ist nicht auf Rosen gebettet**, he does not lie on a bed of roses; **sie —en sich zusammen (von einander)** they sleep together (apart); **ich —e mir auf ihrem Sarge**, her coffin shall be my bed (*poet.*). **—ung**, *f.* bedding; platform (*Arch.*, *Artil.*); **—ung eines Krahns, bewegliche —ung**, traversing platform; **—ungen der Kanonen**, bulge-ways.
Bet'tel, *m.* (—s) act of begging; beggary; trash, rubbish, trumpery; **der ganze —**, the whole (paltry) show; **ist das der ganze —?** is that all the show? **—ei'**, *f.* begging, mendicancy; importunity; trash; **sich auf die —ei legen**, to go begging; **Verein gegen —**, charity organization society. **—haft**, *adj. & adv.* beggarly.
Bet'tel—n, *v.n.* (*aux.* **h.**) to beg; **—n um eine milde Gabe**, to beg for alms; **sich aufs —n legen**, to live by begging, to go begging; **seine Kunst geht —n**, this artist finds no patronage. *Comp.* **—arm**, *adj.* wholly destitute, very poor. **—brief**, *m.* begging-letter; license to beg. **—brot**, *n.* bread of mendicity, of charity. **—bruder**, *m.* professional beggar; mendicant (*friar*). **—brüderschaft**, *f.* begging fraternity (*R. Cath.*). **—bube**, **—junge**, *m.* begging boy. **—dirne**, *f.*, **—mädchen**, *n.* begging-girl. **—frau**, *f.*, **—weib**, *n.* begging woman, beggar

—geld, *n.* alms. **—kram,** *m.* trumpery, trash. **—mann,** *m.* beggar. **—mönch,** *m.* mendicant friar. **—orden,** *m.* order of mendicant friars. **—pfaffe,** *m.* hedge priest. **—sack,** *m.* beggar's bag. **—staat,** *m.* tawdry finery. **—stab,** *m.* beggar's staff; **an den —stab bringen,** to reduce to extreme poverty; **an den —stab kommen,** to be reduced to extreme poverty, become utterly destitute, to come upon the parish. **—stolz,** *m.* beggarly pride. **—suppe,** *f.* charity soup, weak broth; swash. **—vogt,** *m.* beadle. **—volk,** *n.* gang of beggars; beggars, paupers; ragged crew. **—wesen,** *n.* mendicity, pauperism.

Bett'ler, *m.* (—s, *pl.* —), **—in,** *f.* beggar. **—isch,** *adj. see* **Bettelhaft.** *Comp.* **—gesindel,** *n.* beggarly crew, ragged brigade. **—handwerk,** *n.* begging *or* beggar's trade. **—heilkraut,** *n.* Convolvulus sepium. **—könig,** *m.* beggar king; petty king. **—königin,** *f.* beggar queen. **—kraut,** *n.* Clematis vitalba. **—sprache,** *f.* beggar's slang *or* cant.

Betün'chen, *v.a.* to give a coat of plaster.

Betup'fen, Betüp'feln, *v.a.* to dot, touch here and there; to spot.

Bet'ze, *f.* (*pl.* —n) bitch; she-wolf.

Beu'chen, *v.a.* to wash (*in lye*), to buck.

Beu'g—e, *f.* bow, bend; curve; bender (*Coop.*); **Holz—e,** pile of wood; **Knie—e,** bend *or* bending of the knee.

Beu'g—en, *v.* I. *a.* to bend, bow, curve; to inflect (*Gram.*); to humble, depress; to afflict; to mortify. II. *r.* to bend, bow down; to humble oneself; **sich vor einem . . . —en,** to submit to a p. **—er,** *m.* (—ers, *pl.* —er) flexor (*Anat.*). **—sam,** *adj. & adv.* pliant, flexible. **—samkeit,** *f.* pliability; pliancy. **—ung,** *f.* bending; bend, bow; curve (*of a river*); flexure (*Anat.*); warping (*of justice, etc.*); divergence, diffraction (*of light*); inflexion; declension; **die halbe —ung,** demiflexion (*Surg.*); **Knie—ung,** genuflexion. *Comp.* **—e=fähig, —ungs=fähig,** *adj.* capable of inflexion, declinable (*Gram.*). **—e=muskel,** *m. see* **—er. —e=fall,** *m., or* **—ungs=fall,** *m.* (*oblique*) case (*Gram.*).

Beu'l—e, *f.* (*pl.* —en) bump, tumour, swelling; boil; boss (*Arch.*); bruise; dent; dint, dinge; **Frost—e,** chilblain; **venerische —e,** bubo. **—ig,** *adj. & adv.* full of boils *or* protuberances; bruised; full of bosses *or* dents.

Be=un'ruhig—en, *v.a.* to disquiet, disturb; to harass; to trouble. **—ung,** *f.* disturbance, alarm; disquieting.

Be=ur'bar—en, *v.a.* to render arable, to cultivate, till. **—ung,** *f.* cultivation, tilling.

Be=ur'kund—en, *v.a.* to attest, authenticate (*by documents*); to prove. **—er,** *m.* (—ers, *pl.* —er) notary-public. **—et,** *p.p. & adj.* recorded, registered. **—ung,** *f.* documentary authentication, verification.

Be=ur'laub—en, *v.*I. *a.* to give leave of absence to, to grant a furlough to; to disband (*troops*). II. *r.* to take one's leave; to withdraw; **ein Beurlaubter,** one absent on leave.

Be=ur'teil—en, *v.a.* to judge, form an opinion of; to criticise, review (*a work*); **andere nach sich —en,** to judge others by oneself; **nachteilig —en,** to criticise unfavourably. **—er,** *m.* (—ers, *pl.* —er) judge; critic, reviewer. **—ung,** *f.* act of judging; judgment; critical examination; review. *Comp.* **—ungs=kraft,** *f.* (power of) discernment, judgment.

[1]**Beu't—e,** *f.* (*pl.* —en) kneading-trough; wooden beehive. **—en,** *v.a.* to stock a hive with wild bees. *Comp.* **—en=honig,** *m.* wild honey.

[2]**Beu't—e,** *f.* booty, spoil, loot, plunder; prey; **—e der Angst,** prey to anxiety; **auf —e ausgehen,** to go marauding *or* plundering. *Comp.* **—e=gierig, —e=lustig, —e=süchtig,** *adj.* eager for plunder. **—e=zug,** *m.* plundering expedition.

[1]**Beu't—el,** *m.* (—els, *pl.* —el) bag; pouch; **Geld —,** purse, money-bag; sac, cyst; scrotum; a purse of money (*in Turkey* = 500 piastres); pocket (*Bill.*); bolter (*in mills*); **—el werfen,** to bag, pucker; **seinen —el spicken,** to fill one's purse; **einem den —el fegen** *or* **schaben,** to drain a man's purse. **—elig,** *adj.* baggy, bagged; **—elig sein,** to be puckered. *Comp.* **—el=faul,** *adj.* unwilling to part with money. **—el=förmig,** *adj.* purse-shaped. **—el=gans,** *f.* pelican. **—el=kammer,** *f.* bolting-house (*Mill.*). **—el=kasten,** *m.* bolting-hutch (*Mill.*). **—el=krabbe,** *f.*, **—el=krebs,** *m.* purse-crab. **—el=meise,** *f.* titmouse, penduline titmouse. **—el=perücke,** *f.* bagwig. **—el=ratte,** *f.* opossum. **—el=schloß,** *n.* purse-clasp. **—el=schneider,** *m.* cut-purse; pickpocket. **—schneiderei',** *f.* pilfering, swindling. **—el=schnur,** *f.* purse-string. **—el=sieb,** *n.* bolting sieve. **—el=stolz,** I. *m.* purse-pride. II. *adj.* purse-proud. **—el=tier,** *n.* marsupial. **—el=weh,** *n.;* **das —el=weh haben,** to be in debt, hard up (*Coll.*). **—el=werk,** *n.* bolting-mill (*Mill.*).

[2]**Beu'tel,** *m.* (—s, *pl.* —) flax-beater; beetle. **—n,** *v.a.* to make tender by beating; to beat (*flax*).

[3]**Beu'tel,** *m.* (—s, *pl.* —) ripping-chisel.

Beu't—eln, *v.* I. *a.* to bolt (*meal, etc.*). II. *r. & n.* (*aux.* **h.**) to bag, bulge out; to pucker (*of clothes*). **—ler,** *m.* (—lers, *pl.* —ler) pursemaker; glover; breeches-maker.

Bevöl'ker—n, *v.a.* to people, populate. **—ung,** *f.* population.

Bevoll'mächtig—en, *v.a.* to empower, authorize; to invest with full powers; to license, warrant. **—te(r),** *m.* attorney; authorized agent; plenipotentiary. **—ung,** *f.* act of empowering; warrant, authorization; power of attorney.

Bevo'r, I. *conj.* (= **ehe**) before; **— ich dies thue, muß ich . . .,** before doing this, I must . . . II. *adv. & sep. prefix,* before, beforehand; **wenn etwas Wichtiges geschehen sollte, war ich stets — unterrichtet,** if anything important was going to happen I was always informed beforehand.

Bevor'mund—en, *v.a.* (*insep.*) to put under the care of a guardian; to hold in tutelage; to tutor (*fig.*); **der —ete,** ward. **—ung,** *f.* guardianship, tutelage.

Bevor'recht—(ig)en, *v.a.* (*insep.*) to privilege. **—(ig)ung,** *f.* conferring of privilege; concession, exclusive privilege, monopoly. *Comp.* **—(ig)ungs=brief,** *m.* patent, letters patent.

Bevor'stehen, I. *ir.v.n.* (*aux.* **h.**, *dat.*) (*sep.*) to be at hand; to be near, imminent (*of time*); **es steht ihm ein Unglück bevor,** a misfortune awaits him; **die —de Woche,** the next *or* ensuing week. II. *subst.n.* near approach.

Bevor'worten, *v.a.* (*insep.*) to preface, furnish with an introduction; to premise; to advocate (=**befürworten**).

Bevor'zug—en, *v.a.* (*insep.*) to favour; to privilege. **—t,** *p.p. & adj.* privileged; possessed of advantages, specially favoured; **—t sein vor einem,** to have the advantage of a p., to be favoured above another.

Bewa'chen, *v.a.* to watch, guard, keep in custody.

Bewach'sen, *v.a.* to overgrow.

Bewaff'n—en, *v.a.* to arm, provide with arms; to arm (*a magnet*); **mit —eter Hand,** by force of arms. **—ung,** *f.* arming (*of a regiment, etc.; of a magnet*); armament (*of a vessel*); arms, armour.

Bewah'r—en, *v.a.* to keep, preserve; to preserve (*fruit*); to keep (*a secret*); **—en vor,** to guard against, to save, protect from (*cold*); **Gott —e!** God forbid! not at all! nothing of the kind! **behüte und —e!** O dear, no! certainly not! far from it! not by any means!

—er, *m.* (—ers, *pl.* —er) keeper, caretaker; **der Geheimsiegel—er,** keeper of the privy seal. **—ung,** *f.* keeping; preservation. *Comp.* **—sam,** *adj.* cautious, careful (*rare*). **—ungs=mittel,** *n.* preservative.

Bewahr'heit—en, *v.a.* to verify, prove the truth of. **—ung,** *f.* verification; **zur —ung dessen,** in faith whereof (*Law*).

Bewäh'r—en, *v.* I. *a.* to establish as true; to prove, verify, authenticate, certify; to prove by testing, show by trial, approve; **ein —ter Freund,** a trusty *or* tried friend; **ein —ter Schriftsteller,** a standard author. II. *r.* to prove true; to hold good; to stand a test; **das Gerücht —t sich,** the report turns out to be true; **eine Pflanze, die sich als heilsam gegen das Fieber —t,** a plant that is good (*or* a specific) against fever. **—t=heit,** *f.* proved excellence, authenticity. **—ung,** *f.* proof; verification, confirmation; trial.

Bewal'det, *p.p. & adj.* woody, wooded.

Bewal'lung, *f.* embankment.

Bewäl'tigen, *v.a.* to overcome, to overpower, to get the mastery of.

Bewan'der—n, *v.a.* to wander, travel over. **—t,** *p.p. & adj.* skilled, experienced, versed (**in,** in); well read; conversant (**in,** with).

Bewa'ndt, *p.p. & adj.* circumstanced, conditioned; **bei so —en Umständen,** such being the case, under these circumstances; **so ist die Sache —,** that's how it is, so the matter stands. **—nis,** *f.* condition, state (*of affairs*), case; **nach —nis der Umstände,** according to circumstances, as circumstances may require; **was es auch damit für eine —nis hat,** be the case as it may; **es hat damit eine ganz andere —nis,** the case is quite different; **es hat damit folgende —nis,** the matter is as follows; **damit hat es eine eigene —nis,** the circumstances of the case are peculiar, there is a special reason for that, thereby hangs a tale; **bei solcher —nis,** under such circumstances.

Bewa'rb, *imperf. of* **bewerben.**

Bewa'rf, *imperf. of* **bewerfen.**

Bewäs'ser—n, *v.a.* to water; to irrigate. **—ung,** *f.* irrigation; watering.

Bewe'g—en, I. *v.a.* to stir; to move; to agitate, shake; to move, excite, agitate; **es war ein —ter Augenblick,** it was an exciting moment; **sich —en,** to stir, get in motion; **sich in der freien Luft —en,** to take out-of-doors exercise; **sich auf und nieder —en,** to work up and down (*as a piston*); **sich in gebildeten Kreisen —en,** to move in good society; **sich um etwas —en,** to revolve round something; **sich weiter —en,** to move on; **sich zum Mitleiden —en lassen,** to be moved to pity; **—te Zeiten,** stirring times; **eine —ende Geschichte,** a pathetic, touching story; **—ende Kraft,** motive power; **—te See,** agitated, heavy, rough sea. II. *ir.v.a.* to induce, persuade, prevail upon; **bewogen werden zu,** to be led into, induced to; **bewogen von,** actuated by, urged by, moved by. **—er,** *m.* (—ers, *pl.* —er) mover; motor; (*pl.*) muscles of motion. **—bar, —lich,** *adj. & adv.* moveable; mobile, flexible; versatile; changeable; easily persuaded; moving, affecting; stirring, active; **—liches Gut, —liche Habe,** moveables, goods and chattels; **ein —liches Fest,** a moveable feast; **eine —liche Zunge,** a voluble *or* glib tongue. **—barkeit,** *f.*, **—lichkeit,** *f.* mobility, flexibility; moveableness; nimbleness; **—lichkeit der Zunge,** volubility of the tongue; gift of the gab (*sl.*). **—t=heit,** *f.* agitation. **—ung,** *f.* movement; motion; motive; stir, agitation; stimulus, incitement; fermentation; swell, surge (*sea*); **er that es aus eigener —ung,** he did it of his own accord; **in —ung bringen,** to stir up, to set *or* put in motion; **in —ung setzen,** to set agoing, to actuate; **sich in —ung setzen,** to set out, to move; **alle Hebel in —ung setzen,** to set every spring in motion; **er ist stets in —ung,** he is always stirring; **sich** (*dat.*) **—ung machen,** to take exercise; **—ung des Leibes,** physical exercise; **drehende —ung,** rotation, rotary motion; **rückläufige —ung,** retrogression; **—ung der Hände,** gesticulation. *Comp.* **—grund,** *m.* reason (for action), motive, inducement. **—kraft,** *f.* motive power. **—ungs=axe,** *f.* axis of rotation. **—ungs=grund,** *see* **—grund.** **—ungs=kraft,** *f.* motive power, impetus, force. **—ungs=lehre,** *f.* science of mechanics. **—ungs=los,** *adj.* motionless. **—ungs=maß,** *n.* measure of motion; paces (*of a horse*). **—ungs=mittel,** *n.* motor power. **—ungs=spiele,** *n.pl.* movement-games (*in kindergartens*). **—ungs=trieb,** *m.* momentum, impetus. **—ungs=zirkel,** *m.* deferent (*Astr.*).

Beweh'r—en, *v.a.* to arm. **—t,** *p.p. & adj.* armed; windbound (*Naut.*).

Bewei'b—en, *v.r.* to take a wife, to marry. **—t,** *adj.* wedded, married.

Bewei'den, *v.a.* to let cattle graze, to pasture cattle.

Bewei'nen, *v.a.* to weep for, deplore; to mourn, bewail, lament. *Comp.* **—s=wert,** *adj.* deplorable, lamentable.

Bewei's, *m.* (—(s)es, *pl.* —(s)e) act of proving; proof, evidence, demonstration; **—führen,** to prove, adduce proof, to demonstrate; **zum —e dessen dient,** in support of this is the fact; **— der Unmöglichkeit,** reductio ad absurdum; **der — hinkte,** it was a lame argument. **—bar, —lich,** *adj.* demonstrable. *Comp.* **—artikel,** *m.* point to be established by evidence, factum probandum; proof, voucher. **—auflage,** *f.* judicial injunction to produce proof; count (*of an indictment*); (*point of*) argument (*Log.*). **—aufnahme,** *f.* hearing of witnesses. **—führer,** *m.* one producing proof, demonstrator. **—führung,** *f.* demonstration, showing proof. **—grund,** *m.* argument, reason(s), plea, proof, evidence. **—instanz,** *f.* period when proof has to be adduced. **—kraft,** *f.* power of proving, of demonstrating; **der Zeuge hat hier keine —kraft,** this witness's evidence is inconclusive. **—mittel,** *n.* argument, proof, evidence. **—schrift,** *f.* document containing evidence *or* argument. **—stelle,** *f.* quotation in establishment of proof; proof text (*Theol.*). **—zeuge,** *m.* witness.

Bewei'sen, *ir.v.a.* to prove, to show; to demonstrate; to manifest; to establish, make good (*a claim, etc.*); **sich dankbar —,** to show gratitude, to prove grateful.

Bewei'ßen, *v.a.* to whiten.

Bewen'den, I. *ir.v.n.* (*aux.* **f.**) **es — lassen,** to let (*a thing*) be, let take its course, to rest satisfied with, to acquiesce in (*a matter*); **ich lasse es bei Ihrem Urteile —,** I acquiesce in your decision. II. *subst.n.* **dabei hatte es sein —,** there the matter ended; **es mag dabei sein — haben,** let it be so then; **es hat damit sein eigenes —,** there is a special reason for that, thereby hangs a tale.

Bewe'rb, *m.* (—es) endeavour (*to acquire*); business; suit.

Bewer'b—en, *ir.v.r.* (**um eine S.**) to seek to obtain something, to sue for (*a thing*), to solicit (*votes*), to become a candidate for (*an office*); **sich (um ein Frauenzimmer) —en,** to court *or* woo; **sich mit —en,** to compete with. **—er,** *m.* (—ers, *pl.* —er) suitor, solicitor; candidate (*for*); aspirant (*to*); suitor, wooer. **—ung,** *f.* application, candidature, competition, canvass, solicitation; courtship, wooing.

Bewer'fen, *ir.v.a.* to throw at, to pelt; to plaster; **grob —,** to roughcast.
Bewerk'stellig—en, *v.a.* to effect, accomplish, bring about. **—ung,** *f.* effecting; accomplishment, realization, achievement.
Bewi'ckeln, *v.a.* to wrap up, envelop; to wind round, to lap; to swaddle (*an infant*).
Bewil'lig—en, *v.a.* to grant, concede, agree to; **—t werden,** to be carried, to pass (*of motions*). **—ung,** *f.* concession; grant; permission; sanction.
Bewill'kommn—en, *v.a.* to welcome. **—ung,** *f.* welcoming, welcome; reception.
Bewin'den, *ir.v.a.* to wind about; to lap round.
Bewirk'bar, *adj.* what can be brought about, feasible.
Bewir'ken, *v.a.* to effect; to cause; to bring about.
Bewir't—en, *v.a.* to show hospitality to, to entertain (*guests*). **—er,** *m.* host; entertainer. **—ung,** *f.* entertainment, reception, accommodation (*of guests*).
Bewirt'schaft—en, *v.a.* to manage (*a farm, etc.*); to carry on, conduct (*affairs*). **—ung,** *f.* management (*of a farm*).
Bewit'zeln, *v.a.* to treat with light wit, rally, sneer at.
Bewo'g, *impf.*; **Bewö'ge,** *impf.subj.*; **Bewo'gen,** *p.p. of* **bewegen.**
Bewohn'bar, *adj.* habitable; tenantable (*of a house*); **nicht —,** uninhabitable. **—keit,** *f.* habitable condition (*of a house*).
Bewoh'n—en, *v.a.* to inhabit, to dwell, live in. **—er,** *m.* (**—ers,** *pl.* **—er**) inhabitant; occupant, tenant; resident. **—erschaft,** *f.* inhabitants (*coll.*). **—ung,** *f.* occupation; (in)habitation; residence in.
Bewöl'k—en, *v.a.* to cloud, to darken; **sich —en,** to become cloudy *or* overcast; **der Himmel war —t,** the sky was clouded, the sky was overcast with clouds.
Bewor'ben, *p.p. of* **bewerben.**
Bewun'der—n, *v.a.* to admire; to wonder at. **—er,** *m.* (**—ers,** *pl.* **—er**) admirer. **—ung,** *f.* admiration; wonder. *Comp.* **—ns=wert, —würdig, —ungs=wert, —ungs=würdig,** *adj.* worthy of admiration, admirable; wonderful.
Bewu'rf, *m.* (**—s**) plastering; mortar.
Bewür'fe, *imperf.subj. of* **bewerfen.**
Bewur'zeln, *v.n.* (*aux.* **f.**) to strike *or* take root; **ein stark bewurzelter Baum,** a strongly-rooted tree.
Bewu'ßt, *adj.* known; conscious; **die —e Sache,** the matter in question; **sich** (*dat.*) **einer Sache — sein,** to be conscious of a th., to recollect a th.; **ich bin mir keiner Schuld —,** I am not conscious of any guilt; **ich bin mir —, es redlich zu meinen,** I am conscious of meaning well. **—heit,** *f.* knowledge; consciousness. *Comp.* **—los,** *adj.* unconscious, senseless. **—losigkeit,** *f.* unconsciousness; insensibility. **—sein,** *n.* (**—seins**) consciousness; conviction; apperception; sense, sensibility; **er ist nicht bei —sein,** he is unconscious.
Bezahl'bar, *adj.* payable, to be paid.
Bezah'l—en, *v.a.* to pay; to discharge (*a debt*); to repay; to defray (*expenses*); to cash (*a bill, etc.*); **man —t für diesen Artikel,** this article is sold at; **er kann nicht mehr —en,** he is insolvent; **ich will mich schon —t machen,** I will no doubt pay myself, get paid; **im voraus —en,** to pay in advance; **bar —en,** to pay cash *or* ready money; **bei Heller und Pfennig —en,** to pay in full; **abschlägig —en,** to pay in part; **—t werden,** to be duly honoured (*of bills*). **—er,** *m.* (**—ers,** *pl.* **—er**) payer; defrayer. **—ung,** *f.*) payment; pay; **gegen —ung von,** on payment of. *Comp.* **—ungs=schein,** *m. see* **Quittung.**

Bezäh'men, *v.a.* to tame; to curb, subdue; **sich —,** to restrain *or* control oneself.
Bezau'ber—n, *v.a.* to bewitch, enchant; to charm, fascinate. **—ung,** *f.* fascination, charm; enchantment; spell.
Bezeich'n—en, *v.a.* to mark, denote; to designate; to define; to show, characterize; to express; to cover (*a wall, etc.*) with drawings; **Waaren —en,** to mark, label goods; **genau —en,** to give exact directions, to show clearly; **mit Accenten —en,** to accentuate. **—end,** *p. & adj.* characteristic; significant, expressive; **ein —endes Merkmal,** a distinctive mark. **—ung,** *f.* marking; designation, specification; mark, accentuation; notation, numeration; **phonetische —ung,** phonetic notation, phonetic script. *Comp.* **—ungs=zettel,** *n.* label.
Bezei'g—en, *v.a.* (**einem etwas**) to show, give signs of, mark; to express by deed; to manifest; **sich —en,** to show oneself (*kind, etc.*). **—ung,** *f.* manifestation, display; evidence.
Bezet'teln, *v.a.* to label, to ticket.
Bezeu'g—en, *v.a.* to attest, certify, testify; to declare; **seine Achtung —en,** to pay one's respects to. **—ung,** *f.* attestation; testimony.
Bezich't—igen, —ung, *see* **Beschuldigen 2c.**
Bezie'h—en, *ir.v.* I. *a.* to draw over, cover; to string (*a violin, etc.*); to put clean linen (*on a bed*); to hang (*a bed, etc.*); to resort to a place, to frequent (*fairs, etc.*); to take up (*a position*); to enter upon, move into, occupy (*a lodging, etc.*); to get, gain possession of; to draw (*a salary*), receive (*payment*); to draw (*a bill*); to procure, import, get (*goods*); to visit, inspect; to enter (*college*); to bring into relation; to appeal, refer (**auf einen,** to a person); **etwas auf sich** (*acc.*) **—en,** to apply (*a quotation, a remark, a rule, etc.*) to oneself; **ein Lager —,** to encamp; **die Wache —en,** to mount guard; **—ende Fürwörter,** relative pronouns; **im Wege des Buchhandels —en,** to order through a bookseller; **der Bezogene,** drawee, acceptor (*of a bill*). II. *r.* to refer, relate, to make allusion, appeal (**auf,** to); **das —t sich nicht auf den Gegenstand,** that has no bearing on the subject, that is irrelevant, not to the point. **—(ent)lich,** *see* **Bezüglich.** **—er,** *m.* (**—ers,** *pl.* **—er**) drawer (*of a bill*); importer (*of goods*). **—ung,** *f.* act of covering, stringing, taking possession of, entering on, drawing, *etc., see* **—en**; reference (*to a subject*); relation, connection; bearing; **in —ung auf dies,** with reference to this; **in dieser —ung,** in this respect; **in keiner —ung mit,** not pertinent to, irrelevant, having no concern with; **unsere —ungen zum Auslande,** our foreign relations; **in —ung stellen,** to bring to bear (**auf,** upon). *Comp.* **—ungs=begriffe,** *pl.* correlative ideas. **—ungs=fürwort,** *n.* relative pronoun. **—ungs=weise** (*abbrev.* **bezw. bzw.**) *adv.* relatively, making allowance for circumstances.
Bezif'fern, *v.* I. *a.* to mark with figures; **der bezifferte Baß,** figured bass (*Mus.*). II. *n.* to amount to.
Bezi'rk, *m.* (**—s,** *pl.* **—e**) compass; inclosure; circuit; precinct; district; range, sphere; department. **—e,** *pl.* confines; frontiers. *Comp.* **—s=amt,** *n.* jurisdiction of a district. **—s=anwalt,** *m.* district attorney. **—s=feldwebel,** *m.* district-sergeant. **—s=gefängnis,** *n.* county gaol. **—s=gericht,** *n.* county-court. **—s=kommando,** *n.* district command (*Mil.*). **—s=vorsteher,** *m.* poor-law guardian, governor of a ward. **—s=weise,** *adv.* by districts.
Bezoa'r, *m.* bezoar. *Comp.* **—gazelle,** *f.* common gazelle. **—horn,** *n.* trumpeter's shell (*Mollusc.*).
Bezo'g, *impf.*; **Bezö'ge,** *impf.subj.*; **Bezo'gen,**

p.p. of **beziehen.** **Bezogene(r),** *m.* drawee (*C. L.*).
Bezol'len, *v.a.* to levy a toll *or* duty on.
Bezu'ckern, *v.a.* to sugar (*a cake, etc.*).
Bezu'g, *m.* (—**es,** *pl.* **Bezüge**) covering; case; a set (*of strings*); relation, reference; **in — auf (eine S.),** with regard to, in relation to, as to; **— nehmen auf (eine S.),** to refer to; *see* **Beziehen.** *Comp.* **—bedingungen,** *pl.* conditions of delivery, trade-terms. **—nahme,** *f.* reference; **mit (unter) —nahme auf (eine Sache),** respecting. **—s=anweisung,** *f.* order (*for goods, etc.*). **—s=ort,** *m.*, **—s=quelle,** *f.* market for, *or* source of, supply. **—s=spesen,** *pl.* charges of importation; petty charges.
Bezüg'lich, I. *adj. & adv.* relative (**auf eine S.,** to a th.); **dahin —,** apposite, suitable to. II. *prep.* (*with gen.*) respecting, as to.
Bezwe'cken, *v.a.* to aim at, have in view, purpose; to set with tacks; to peg (*a boot*).
Bezwei'feln, *v.a.* to doubt; to call in question; **nicht zu —,** not to be doubted, indubitable, unquestionable.
Bezwin'g—en, *ir.v.a.* to overcome, conquer, subdue; to master; **sich —en,** to restrain, control oneself. **—er,** *m.* (—**ers,** *pl.* —**er**) subduer. **—bar, —lich,** *adj.* conquerable, domitable. **—ung,** *f.* subduing, reduction.
Bi'bel, *f.* (*pl.* —**n**) Bible; Holy Scriptures; **vielsprachige —,** Polyglot Bible. **—tum,** *n.* Biblical studies, Biblical science. *Comp.* **—anstalt,** *f.* Bible-society. **—ausleger,** *m.* commentator, expounder of Scripture; exegete. **—auslegung,** *f.* exposition, *or* interpretation, of the Bible; exegesis. **—buch,** *n.* Bible. **—fest,** *adj.* versed in the Scriptures; true as gospel. **—gemäß,** *adj.* conformable to Scripture, scriptural. **—gesellschaft,** *f.* Bible-society. **—gläubig,** *adj.* strictly adhering to (*the letter of*) the Bible. **—husar,** *m.; er ist ein —husar,* the Bible is his chief weapon (*coll.*). **—kenner,** *m.* one conversant with the Scriptures; Biblical critic. **—kunde,** *f.* Biblical knowledge. **—lehre,** *f.* Bible teaching, scriptural doctrine. **—leser,** *m.* (zealous) reader of the Bible. **—mäßig,** *adj.* scriptural. **—sprache,** *f.* scriptural language. **—spruch,** *m.* Biblical phrase. **—stelle,** *f.* scriptural passage *or* sentence; text; lesson (*read in church*). **—stunde,** *f.* Bible class; instruction in the Bible; Sunday school. **—übersetzung,** *f.* translation of the Bible. **—verein,** *m.* Bible-society. **—werk,** *n.* reference Bible (*with notes and illustrations*); Polyglot Bible. **—wort,** *n.* passage *or* quotation from the Bible, Biblical phrase. **—wort=weiser,** *m.* concordance to the Bible.
Bi'ber, *m.* (—**s,** *pl.* —) beaver, castor. **—in,** *f.* she-beaver, female of the beaver. *Comp.* **—bau,** *m.* beaver's hole *or* lodge. **—baum,** *m.* magnolia. **—ente,** *f.* goosander. **—fänger,** *m.* beaver-trapper. **—fell,** *n.* fur, *or* skin, of the beaver. **—geil,** *n.* beaver's cod, castor(eum). **—hut,** *m.* beaver(-hat). **—klee,** *m.* marsh-trefoil. **—ratte,** *f.* musk-rat. **—schwanz,** *m.* beaver's tail; tile shaped like a beaver's tail. **—schwarz,** *adj. & n.* brownish black. **—taucher, —vogel,** *m. see* **—ente.** **—zahn,** *m.* projecting tooth.
Bi'bi, *m. hum. for* **Biberhut** (*sl.*), hat; belltopper, castor.
Biblio— (*in comp. unaccented*). **—gnosie',** *f.* knowledge of books. **—gra'ph,** *m.* bibliographer. **—graphie',** *f.* bibliography. **—gra'phisch,** *adj.* bibliographic. **—logie',** *f.* book-craft. **—ma'ne,** *m.* (—**ma'nen,** *pl.* —**ma'nen**) bibliomaniac. **—manie',** *f.* bibliomania. **—the'k,** *f.* (*pl.* —**the'ken**) library. **—theka'r,** *m.* (—**theka'rs,** *pl.* —**theka're**) librarian.
Bi'blisch, *adj.* Biblical, scriptural; **—e Geschichte,** Scripture (*or* sacred) history; **—e Theologie,** Biblical Theology.
Bick'beere, *f.* bilberry, blueberry, whortleberry.
Bi'cke, Bi'ckel, *see* **Picke, Pickel.**
Bi'derb, *archaic form of* **Bieder.**
Bie'der, *adj.* upright, honest; staunch, loyal; trusty; ingenuous; honourable. **—keit,** *f.* loyalty, true-heartedness; probity. *Comp.* **—herz,** *n.* loyal heart, true-hearted, honourable fellow. **—mann,** *m.* man of worth, of integrity; man of honour; gentleman; worthy. **—männer,** *pl. of* **—mann**; sometimes used ironically: worthies, philistines. **—meier,** *m.* a would-be man of honour. **—meierei',** *f., or* **—meiertum,** *n.* behaviour of a would-be man of honour. **—sinn,** *m. see* **—keit.** **—ton,** *m.* hearty voice (*rare*).
Bie'g—bar, *adj.* pliable; flexible; declinable. **—e,** *f.* (*pl.* —**en**) curve, bend, bow.
Bie'g—en, *ir.v.* I. *a.* to bend, curve; to bow; to decline, inflect; to refract (*light*). II. *r.* to bend; to warp; to turn, to incline; **sich schmiegen und —en,** to be yielding, to cringe. III. *n.* (*aux.* **s.**) to bend; (*aux.* **h.**) to turn; **um die Ecke —en,** to turn a corner; **—sam,** *adj. & adv.* flexible; yielding; supple; lithe. **—samkeit,** *f.* pliancy; suppleness, flexibility. **—ung,** *f.* bent, curve; bend; declension. *Comp.* **—e=fall,** *m.* case (*Gram.*). **—(e)=muskel,** *m.* flexor. **—ungs=fall,** *m. see* **—e=fall.** **—zange,** *f.* pliers.
Bie'ne, *f.* (*pl.* —**n**) bee; a southern constellation, Apis, the Bee; **Honig—,** honey-bee, hive-bee; **Arbeits—,** working bee, worker; **die faule** *or* **männliche —,** drone; **die —n betreffend,** concerning bees, apiarian; **die —n eines Stockes,** the hive; **die — summt,** the bee hums, buzzes; **sieh die —, wie zornig sie ist,** behold the bee, how angry he is; **der Bien muß,** it cannot be helped, necessity has no law (*coll.*). *Comp.* **—n=bär,** *m.* common bear. **—n=bau,** *m. see* **—n=zucht.** **—n=baum,** *m.* water-elder. **—n=behandlung,** *f.* management of bees. **—n=brut,** *f.* embryo bees, **—n=falk,** *m.* honey buzzard. **—n=fänger, —n=fresser,** *m.* bee-eater (*Orn.*). **—n=fasser,** *m.* a bag to take bees in. **—n=flug,** *m.* stock of bees, of hives. **—n=harz,** *n.*, **—n=kitt,** *m.* bee-bread, bee-glue. **—n=haus,** *n.*, **—n=hütte,** *f.* bee-house, shed for bees, apiary. **—n=heide,** *f.* wild rosemary. **—n=klee,** *m.* creeping white trefoil. **—n=königin,** *f.* queen-bee. **—n=korb,** *m.* bee-hive; garden thyme. **—n=männchen,** *n.* drone. **—n=schwarm,** *m.*, **—n=stock,** *m.* bee-hive. **—n=vater,** *m.* bee-master; hive-owner. **—n=wabe,** *f.* honeycomb. **—n=wachs,** *n.* bee's-wax. **—n=weisel, —n=weiser,** *m.* queen-bee. **—n=wolf,** *m.* bee-eater. **—n=zelle,** *f.* cell (*in honey-comb*). **—n=zellig,** *adj.* honey-combed. **—n=zucht,** *f.* bee-keeping. **—n=züchter,** *m.* bee-master, bee-keeper, apiarian.
Bi'er, *n.* (—**es,** *pl.* —**e**) beer; **Eier—,** egg-flip; **Lager—,** lager (beer), bottled beer, beer for keeping; **dünnes —, halbes —,** small beer; **leichtes —,** bitter ale, pale ale; **dunkles —,** porter; stout; **besonders feines und sehr starkes —,** audit ale (*Univ.*); **zu —e gehen,** to go to the ale-house; **beim —e sitzen,** to sit over one's ale; **etwas wie saures — ausbieten,** to offer s. th. for a trifle, for a mere nothing; **das — ist sauer,** the beer is pricked; **das — hat einen Stich,** the beer has a touch; **Flaschen—,** bottled beer; **— vom Faß, — frisch vom Faß,** draught-ale. *Comp.* **—bank,** *f.* ale-house-bench. **—baß,** *m.* coarse bass voice (*stud. sl.*). **—bauch,** *m.* paunch; corporation (*hum.*). **—bottich,** *m.* beer-vat. **—brauer,** *m.* brewer. **—brauerei',** *f.* brewery; art of brewing.

—bruder, m. pot-companion. —comment, m. students' rules for drinking (stud.). —eifer, m. very great zeal; excessive activity (coll.). —eifrig, adj. extremely zealous, most studious (coll.). —essig, m. vinegar made of beer. —faß, n. beer-cask. —fiedel, f. bad fiddle. —fiedler, m. scraper on a fiddle. —fisch, m. fish cooked in beer; piece of pitch or cork found in one's beer (hum.). —gäscht, m. yeast, beer-froth. —gast, m. beer-house customer. —geld, n. beer-money; gratuity; ale-tax. —hahn, m. tap. —halle, f. beer saloon. —haus, n. ale-house, public house, pot house (vulg.). —heber, m. beer-machine, beer pull, pump. —hefe, f. barm. —kaltschale, f. cold beverage or soup made of beer, lemon, currants and bread-crumbs. —kanne, f. beer-can, ale-pot, tankard. —karren, m. brewer's dray. —kneipe, f. ale-house, pot-house (vulg.). —krug, m. jug, mug, pot. —lachs, m. stated amount of beer played for at cards (stud. sl.). —molken, pl. beer-posset. —p(l)an(t)scher, m. adulterator of beer (fam.). —prober, m. beer-taster. —rede, f. (humor.) speech made at a students' meeting at an ale-house. —reise, f. visiting (in one day) the ale-houses of a town or quarter (fam.). —schank, m. right of retailing beer, place for retailing beer, public house. —schaum, m. beer-froth. —schenk, m. publican, ale-house keeper. —schenke, f. beer-house, pot-house. —schröter, m. cellarman; brewer's drayman. —schwengel, m. see —hebel. —seidel, n. beer-glass, pint, beer-mug. —skat, m. game of cards (Skat) played over one's beer. —stube, f. tap-room. —tanne, f. Canadian spruce. —tonne, f. vat; big-bellied fellow (hum.). —trichter, m. funnel. —wirt, m. publican. —wirtschaft, f. ale-house, public-house. —wisch, m. bush as sign of a public-house. —würze, f. wort, sweet-wort. —zapfer, m. tapster. —zeitung, f. humorous gazette got up to be read at a convivial meeting of (German) students (stud.). —zipfel, m. ribbon attached to the watch (stud.) —zwang, m. monopoly of beer-selling in a district.

Bie'ster, I. m. bistre (Paint.). II. adj. dark, uncertain, astray (prov.).

Biest'milch, f. biestings.

Bie'ten, ir.v.a. to bid, to wish (good morning, etc.); to make a bid (at a sale); to offer, proffer, present (the hand; aid, etc.); weniger — als ein anderer, to underbid s.o.; feil —, to expose, or offer, for sale; Trotz —, to bid defiance to, to face, to defy; einem die Spitze —, to resist, oppose a p.; einem die Stirn —, to face s.o.; Schach —, to check, to give check (to); den Rücken —, to turn one's back on; das dürfte mir niemand —, I would suffer that from no one; ich lasse mir das nicht, I won't stand that, put up with this; ein Unglück bietet dem andern die Hand, misfortunes never come singly. —de(r), Bieter, m. bidder; der Meist—de, the highest bidder.

Bigam—ie', f. bigamy. —isch, adj. bigamous.

Bigno'nie, f. trumpet-flower, bignonia.

Bigo'tt, adj. bigoted. —erie', f. bigotry.

Bijouterie', f. jewellery, trinkets.

Bila'nz, f. (pl. —en) balance; die — ziehen, to strike the balance; reine —, net-balance; rohe —, rough balance, trial-balance. Comp. —bogen, m. balance-sheet. —conto, n., —rechnung, f. balance-account.

Bilanzie'ren, v.a. to balance (an account).

Bild, n. (—es, pl. —er) image, figure, picture; portrait; effigy; idea, image, representation; counterfeit; figure-head; illustration (of a book); metaphor, trope; emblem, symbol; (pl.) court-cards; das gegossene —, the cast, graven image; das schöne —, the beautiful woman (Bild often = Frau, Mädchen in older popular poetry); Frauen—, woman; Gips—, plaster cast; Lebens—, life-picture, biographical description; Manns—, man; Sinn—, emblem, symbol; Stein—, statue; negatives —, negative (Phot.); er wurde im —e verbrannt, he was burnt in effigy; (es bietet sich) ein anderes —, the scene changes; machen Sie sich einmal ein — davon! just picture it to yourself! just fancy!

Bil'd—en, v.a. to form, to fashion, to shape; to constitute, form, compose; to train, discipline; to cultivate; to improve; to organize; ein sehr gebildeter Mann, a highly cultivated man; den Nachzug —en, to form the rear (Mil.), Jupiter —et den Genetiv Jovis, Jupiter becomes Jovis in the genitive. —end, p. & adj. plastic; composing, constituting; educational, instructive; —ende Künste, formative, plastic arts (in a wider sense including architecture, sculpture, painting); —ender Künstler, sculptor; (also) painter, architect. —er, m. (usually —ner) maker, artist. —lich, adj. & adv. figurative, metaphorical; typical. —ner, m. (—ners, pl. —ner) modeller, image-maker, sculptor, statuary; artist; moulder, organizer. —nerei', f. plastic art, sculpture. —nerisch, adj. relating to sculpture; creative. —nis, n. (—nisses, pl. —nisse) portrait; likeness; effigy; parable. —sam, adj. plastic, ductile; cultivable. —samkeit, f. flexibility, adaptiveness, plasticity. —ung, f. formation; form, fashion, shape; organization, constitution; education, cultivation, culture; civilization; gelehrte —ung, f. classical education; liberal education; scholarship; ein Mann von gelehrter —ung, a scholar; ein Mann von feiner —ung, an accomplished gentleman; a man who has had a liberal education; ohne —ung, illiterate, rude, uncultivated. Comp. —e=kraft, f. plastic power. —e=kunst, f. plastic art. —er=achat, m. figurate agate. —er=anbetung, f. image-worship. —er=ausstellung, f. exhibition of pictures. —er=bibel, f. pictorial Bible. —er=blende, f. niche. —er=bogen, m. picture-sheet. —er=buch, n. picture book. —er=deutung, f. iconology. —er=dienst, m. image-worship. —er=fibel, f. illustrated primer. —er=flügel, m. painted moth. —er=form, f. pattern. —er=gallerie, f., picture gallery. —er=gedicht, n. rebus. —handel, m. trade in pictures (paintings, prints). —er=händler, m. picture-dealer. —er=handschrift, f. illuminated manuscript; manuscript containing miniatures. —er=kabinett, n. (small or private) collection of paintings. —er=kenner, m. connoisseur of pictures. —laden, m. picture-dealer's shop. —er=lehre, f. iconology; teaching by allegory. —er=reich, adj. copiously illustrated; figurative, abounding in metaphors. —er=schrift, f. hieroglyphics. —er=sprache, f. metaphorical language. —er=stürmend, adj. iconoclastic. —er=stürmer, m. image-breaker; iconoclast. —former, m. image-maker. —former=kunst, f. plastic art. —gestell, n. pedestal. —gießer, m. bronze-founder. —gießerei', f. art of casting statues, bronze-foundry. —hauer, m. sculptor. —hauerei', f. sculptor's art, sculpture, statuary. —hauer=kitt, m. badigeon. —hauer=kunst, f. art of sculpture. —hauer=schule, f. academy for sculptors. —hauer=werkstatt, f. sculptor's studio. —hübsch, adj. extremely pretty; ein —hübsches Mädchen, a real beauty. —los, adj. void of images or figures. —nis=maler, m. portrait-painter. —sauber, adj. extremely neat, extremely pretty (dial.). —säule, f. statue; —säule zu Pferde, equestrian statue. —säulen=marmor, m. statuary marble. —schnitzer, m. wood-carver. —schnit=

zerei′, *f.* wood-carving. —schön, *adj.* most beautiful, very lovely. —seite, *f.* face, obverse (*of a coin*), head (*as opposed to* "*tail*"). —stecher, *m.* engraver. —stein, *m.* figured stone; chinesischer —stein, Chinese soap-stone. —stöcklein, *n.* statuette on the wayside (*of a saint*). —ungs=anstalt, *f.* educational establishment, school. —ungs=gang, *m.* course of instruction *or* education. —ungs=trieb, *m.* creative principle, forming principle in generation; desire for artistic production, artistic instinct. —weber, *m.* damask-weaver. —weise, *adv.* figuratively. —werk, *n.* sculpture; imagery. —zeug, *n.* diaper.

Bil′lard, *n.* (—s, *pl.* —s) billiards; billiard table; — spielen, to play at billiards. *Comp.* —ball, *m.*, —kugel, *f.* billiard ball. —beutel, *m.*, —loch, *n.* pocket (*of billiard table*). —kellner, *m.* marker. —spiel, *n.* game at billiards. —stock, *m.* cue.

Bil′le, *f.* (*pl.* —n) pickaxe for sharpening millstones; (*pl.*) buttocks (*of a ship*).

Bil′len, *v.a.* to edge (*a millstone*).

Bille′t, *n.* (—s & —tes; *pl.* —te & —s) ticket; note. —ie′ren, *v.a.* to ticket, to label. *Comp.* —abgabe, *f.* giving up *or* returning of tickets. —ausgabe, *f.* distribution of tickets; ticket-office, booking-office. —bureau, *n.*, —schalter, *m.* ticket-office, booking-office. —verkauf, *m.*; der —verkauf beginnt um, the ticket-office opens at, tickets will be sold at.

Bil′lig, *adj.* & *adv.* reasonable, fair, just; moderate, cheap; wenn wir — sein wollen, so habt ihr beide Unrecht gehabt, to be just, you were both in the wrong. —ermaßen, fairly, in justice; das ist nicht mehr als —, that is but fair; es ist —, it stands to reason; ziemlich —, rather cheap, pretty cheap; ein —er Überschlag, a moderate computation. —keit, *f.* reasonableness; fairness; cheapness; der —keit gemäß, in equity. *Comp.* —keits=gericht, *n.* court of equity.

Bil′lig—en, *v.a.* to sanction; to grant; to approve of. —ung, *f.* approval, sanction.

Billio′n, *f.* billion.

Bil′se, *f.*, **Bil′senkraut,** *n.* hen-bane.

Bim′—bam, *int.* ding-dong; heiliger —bam! dear me! (*colloquial expression of great astonishment*). —bambum, *int.* ding-dong. —mel, *f.* shrill-sounding little bell.

Bim′meln, *v.a.* to tinkle; to ring a small bell (*coll.*).

Bim′—sen, *v.a.* to rub with pumice-stone. *Comp.* —s=stein, *m.* pumice-stone.

Bin, *1 ps. sing. pres. ind. of* sein.

Bin′d—chen, *n.* wrist-band. —e, *f.* bandage; band; string, tie; bar, stripe (*Ent.*); tie, bind (*Mus.*); sling; band, plinth (*Arch.*); fillet (*Bookb.*); fesse (*Her.*); eine —e vor die Augen thun, to blindfold; Hals—e, *f.* necktie, cravat; Leib—e, *f.* sash, cummerbund; Stirn—e, bandeau; hinter die —e gießen, to drink (*coll.*); einen *or* eins hinter die —e gießen, to take a glass (*coll.*); die —e fällt mir von den Augen, the scales fall from my eyes. *Comp.* —e=balken, *m.* girder architrave. —e=band, *n.* (*bonnet, etc.*) string. —e=glied, *n.* connecting link. —e=haut, *f.* conjunctiva tunica (*Anat.*). —e=kalk, *m.* Roman cement. —e=mauer, *f.* partition-wall. —e=mittel, *n.* cement. —e=schlüssel, *m.* St. Peter's key. —e=sohle, *f.* sandal. —e=strich, *m.*, —e=zeichen, *n.* hyphen; tie, legato sign (*Mus.*). —e=wort, *n.* conjunction; copula. —e=zeug, *n.* surgeon's case. —faden, *m.* string, twine, packthread. —pfennig, *m.* earnest money. —riemen, *m.* strap, latchet. —ungs=zeichen, *n.* hyphen; legato-sign. —werk, *n.* arbour-work, lattice-work.

Bin′d—en, *ir.v.* I. *a.* to bind, tie; to hoop (*a cask*); to tie up; to restrain; to constrain; to oblige; to measure (*swords in a duel*); —et die Klingen! lock swords (*or* rapiers)! Garben —en, to make up in sheaves; Besen —en, to make brooms; einem etwas auf die Nase —en, to hoax one, tell one a fib; ich werde ihm nicht alles auf die Nase —en, I shall not tell him all my secrets; einem etwas auf die Seele —en, to solemnly enjoin upon one (*to do something*); gebundene Rede, rhythmical speech, metrical language, metre. II. *r.* to bind oneself (*to one*); to make oneself dependent upon; to thicken (*Cook.*). —end, *p.* & *adj.* binding, obligatory (*on*). —er, *m.* (—ers, *pl.* —er) binder; Faß—er, cooper. —er=lohn, *m.* binderage; cooperage. —sel, *n.* (—sels, *pl.* —sel) lashing, seizing (*Naut.*). —ung, *f.* tying, binding, *etc.*; slur, bind, tie; agglutination (*Med.*); cement (*Arch.*); ligature, bind (*Mus.*); connection.

Bin′gelkraut, *n.* mercury (*Bot.*).

Bin′nen, I. *prep. with gen.* & *dat.* within; — eines Monats, within a month; — acht Tagen, in the course of a week; — kurzem, ere long, within a short time, shortly. II. *adv.* within, in the interior; (*in comp.* =) inner, internal, inland. *Comp.* —afrika, *n.* Central Africa. —deich, *m.* inner dam *or* dyke. —geschäft, *n.* firm doing overland trade. —gewässer, *n.* inland water, waters of a continent. —hafen, *m.* basin of a port, wet dock. —handel, *m.* inland trade; home trade. —kolonie, *f.* back settlement. —land, *n.* interior (*of a country*). —ländisch, I. *adj.* internal. II. *adv.* inwards. —stadt, *f.* inland town. —verkehr, *m.* overland trade, inland trade. —vorsteven, *m.* apron (*Naut.*).

Bino′misch, (**Binomia′l,**) *adj.* binomial; der —e Lehrsatz, the binomial theorem.

Bin′s—e, *f.* (*pl.* —en) rush (*Bot.*); sedge; bent-grass; die glatte —e, bulrush. —icht, *adj.* (*obs.*) rush-like. —ig, *adj.* sedgy, rush-grown. *Comp.* —en=blume, *f.* flowering rush. —en=busch, *m.* bed of rushes. —en=decke, *f.* rush-mat. —en=gras, *n.* club-rush; sedge. —en=korb, *m.* frail, rush basket. —en=mark, *n.* pith of rushes. —en=narzisse, *f.* jonquil. —en=reich, *adj.* rushy, juncous, sedgy. —en=wolle, *f.* silky wool of some species of cotton grass.

Bio— (*in comp., with chief accent on the following word*). —gra′ph, *m.* biographer. —graphie′, *f.* biography. —logie′, *f.* biology. —lo′gisch, *adj.* biological. —magnetis′mus, *m.* animal magnetism.

Bi′quadrat, *n.* (—(e)s, *pl.* —e) biquadratic.

Biquadra′tisch, *adj.* biquadratic.

Birg, Birgst, Birgt, *imperative, 2 and 3 pers. sing. indic. of* bergen.

Bir′k—e, *f.* (*pl.* —en) birch-tree. —en, *adj.* birchen. *Comp.* —en=baum, *m. see* —e. —en=besen, *m.* birch-broom. —(en)=häher, *m.* roller (*Orn.*). —en=kork, *m.* a fungus (*Boletus suberosus*). —en=marder, *m.* pine-marten. —en=saft, *m.* lime-juice. —en=schwamm, *m.* birch-agaric. —en=spanner, *m.* birch-moth. —falk, *m.* stone falcon. —hahn, *m.* heath-cock, black cock. —henne, *f.* moor-hen. —huhn, *n. see* —henne. —wild, *n.* black game. —wild=jagd, *f.* grouse-shooting.

Bir′n—e, *f.* (*pl.* —en) pear; reed-piece (*of a clarionet, etc.*); gag. *Comp.* —apfel, *m.* pearmain. —baum, *m. or* —en=baum, *m.* pear-tree. —en=förmig, *adj.* pear-shaped; pyriform (*Anat.*). —en=most, *m.* perry. —kraut, *n.* winter-green (*Tyrola*). —motte, *f.* codling-moth. —mundstück, *n.* pear-bit (*for a horse*). —saft, *m.*, *or* —en=saft, *m.* pear-juice. —wein, *m.* perry.

Birsch, (**Bürsch**), *f.* hunting, deer-stalking.

Bir'sch—en, (Bür'sch—en,) *v.a.* to hunt, to stalk deer. *Comp.* **—rohr,** *n.* sporting rifle. **—er,** *m.* (**—ers,** *pl.* **—er**) hunter; deer-stalker. **—ge=wand,** *n.* hunting suit.

Birst, *3 pers. sing. ind. of* **bersten.**

Bis, I. *prep. or particle joined with a preposition to give it a special or additional force;* as far as to; up to; down to; to; till, until; even to; **— an,** up to, even to; **— an den Hals in Schulden stecken,** to be over head and ears in debt; **sie wurde rot — an die Ohren,** she blushed up to her ears; **— an** *or* **in den Tod, — zum Tode,** till death; **— auf,** to, up to, down to, even to, with the exception of, all but; **sie starben alle — auf drei,** they all died but three; **seine Freundlichkeit erstreckte sich — auf die Bedienten,** his kindness extended down to the very servants; **— auf eine Kleinigkeit,** to within an ace; **er kam — auf eine Meile von der Stadt,** he came to within a mile of the town; **— auf den heutigen Tag,** till to-day; **— aufs** *or* **auf ein Haar,** to a shade, exactly; **alles ist bezahlt — auf einige Mark,** all is paid except a few shillings; **— dahin,** till then, by that time, so far; to that place; **— dato,** hitherto; **— zur Verfallzeit,** till due; **— hierher,** thus far; **— um neun Uhr,** till nine o'clock; **— nach Paris,** as far as Paris; **— über den Kopf ins Wasser gehen,** to go beyond one's depth; **— zu dem Betrage von,** to the amount of, amounting to, to the value of; **er wurde — zu Thränen gerührt,** he was moved even to tears; **von sechs — sieben,** from six to seven; **— jetzt,** till now, hitherto, as yet; **— jetzt noch nicht,** not as yet. II. *conj.* till; **wartet — ich komme,** wait till I come. *Comp.* (*no stress on* **bis**). **—her,** *adv.* as far as here, till the present time, hitherto, up to now, till now. **—herig,** *adj.* of the time until now; hitherto existing. **—lang,** *adv.* so far, as yet. **—weilen,** *adv.* sometimes, now and then, occasionally.

Bi'sam, *m.* musk; **nach — riechend,** musky. *Comp.* **—bock,** *m.* musk-beetle. **—blume,** *f.* sweet centaury, sultan-flower. **—ente,** *f.* muscovy duck. **—hirsch,** *m.* musk-deer. **—katze,** *f.* civet cat. **—knabenkraut,** *n.* Orchis bifolia. **—körner,** *pl.* musk-seed. **—nieren,** *pl.* bag-musk. **—reh,** *n.*, **—tier,** *n.* musk-deer. **—schwein,** *n.* peccary.

Bis'chen, *n.* (**—s,** *pl.* **—**) a little bit, a morsel; a little, a moment (*gen'lly used adverbially*); **kein — Brod,** not a bit (*a morsel*) of bread; **sein — Vermögen,** his little fortune; **ein — früh,** rather early; **ein — bange,** somewhat uneasy *or* frightened.

Bi'schof, *m.* (**—s,** *pl.* **Bi'schöfe**) bishop; bishop (*hot punch of spiced claret*); bishop (*Orn.*). *Comp.* **—s=amt,** *n.* episcopate. **—s=hof,** *m.* episcopal palace. **—s=hut,** *m.* mitre; Alpine-barren-wort. **—s=mütze,** *f. see* **—s=hut. —s=ornat',** *m.* bishop's robes. **—s=sitz,** *m.* (bishop's) see. **—s=stab,** *m.* crosier. **—s=würde,** *f.* episcopal dignity; episcopate.

Bi'schöflich, *adj. & adv.* bishoplike; episcopal, episcopalian; pontific, pontifical (*Rom. Cath.*); **ein —gesinnter,** an episcopalian; **Seine —e Gnaden,** His Grace the Bishop.

Bi'se, *f.* cutting northeasterly wind (*esp'lly in Switzerland*).

Biskui't, Bisqui't, *m.* biscuit; **Savoyer —,** Savoy cake. *Comp.* **—porzellan,** *n.* biscuit *or* bisque ware.

Biß, Bisse, *imperf. ind. & subj. of* **beißen.**

Bis'mut, *m. & n.* (*pl.* **—e**) bismuth; **—enthaltend,** bismuthal. *Comp.* **—säure,** *f.* bismuthic acid.

Bi'son, *m.* (**—s,** *pl.* **—s**) bison.

Biß, *m.* (**—(ss)es,** *pl.* **—(ss)e**) bite; sting. **—chen,** *n. see* **Bischen. —(ss)el** (*famil. & dial.*) *see* **—chen; —(ss)en,** *m.* (**—(ss)ens,** *pl.* **—(ss)en**) morsel, bit; a mouthful; **ein fetter** *or* **ein guter —en,** a toothsome morsel; **keinen —en,** not a bit; **süßer —en,** custard apple. **—(ss)ig,** *adj.* given to biting; biting; rabid; sharp, snappish, cutting. *Comp.* **—(ss)en=weise,** *adv.* in mouthfuls, bit by bit. **—wunde,** *f.* bite, snap.

Bist, *2d pers. sing. pres. ind. of* **sein.**

Bis'ter, *f.* (*pl.* **—n**) bistre, bister.

Bis'tum, *n.* (**—s,** *pl.* **Bistümer**) bishopric; episcopate; diocese, see.

Bit't—e, *f.* (*pl.* **—en**) request, petition, entreaty, supplication, suit, prayer; **demütige —,** supplication; **dringende —e,** solicitation; **ich habe eine —e an Sie,** I have a favour to ask of you; **die sieben —en des Vaterunsers,** the seven petitions of the Lord's Prayer; **die siebente —e,** the seventh petition (*humor. designation of a shrew*); **ich hätte noch eine —e an Sie,** I have one more favour to beg of you; **auf seine —e,** at his request; **eine —e bei einem einlegen,** to make a request of one. **—lich,** I. *adj.* precarious (*Law*). II. *adv.* by way of petition, beggingly. *Comp.* **—brief,** *m.*, **—schreiben,** *n.*, **—schrift,** *f.* written petition; begging letter; **eine —schrift einreichen (bei),** to petition. **—fahrt,** *f.* pilgrimage. **—gang,** *m.* procession. **—gesang,** *m.* rogation, litany. **—gesuch,** *n.* petition, suit, request. **—steller,** *m.*, **—stellerin,** *f.* petitioner, supplicant. **—weise,** *adv.* as a petition, beggingly. **—wort,** *n.* entreaty.

Bit't—en, *ir. v.a.* to ask, request; to entreat; to invite; **da möchte ich doch sehr —en,** mind, please, what you are saying; **für einen —en,** to intercede for one; **einen um Verzeihung —en,** to beg one's pardon; **(einen) zu sich —en,** to invite to one's house; **einen um Erlaubnis —en,** to ask leave of a p.; **darf ich Sie um Ihren (werten) Namen —en?** may I ask your name? **ein Zeichen bat ich,** I asked for a sign (*poet.*); **—e,** don't mention it (*in answer to thanks*); I beg your pardon (= what did you say? *or as a polite contradiction*); **—e, geben Sie mir ein Glas Wasser,** give me a glass of water, please; **darf ich Ihnen helfen? Bitte schön,** may I help you? Please (*do*); **—e, sagen Sie mir,** pray, tell me; **wünschen Sie noch ein Stück Fleisch? Bitte!** do you like another piece of meat? Thank you; **ich —e Sie!** you don't say so! **ich danke Ihnen für Ihre Freundlichkeit. O, —e, es ist gern geschehen,** many thanks for your kindness. Oh, pray don't mention it, you are very welcome. **—er, (der —ende,)** *m.* (**—ers,** *pl.* **—er**) requester, asker, inviter.

Bit'ter, *adj. & adv.* bitter; severe; sharp, stinging; acrimonious; rancorous; **—e Klage,** bitter complaint; **—e Thränen weinen,** to weep bitterly; **—er Ernst,** sad earnest; **—kalt,** bitterly cold. **—keit,** *f.* bitterness; acrimony; (*pl.*) bitter words. **—lich,** I. *adj.* bitterish. II. *adv.* bitterly. **—ling,** *m.* bitter mineral spring; small species of carp; water-pepper. *Comp.* **—apfel,** *m.* colocynth. **—böse,** *adj.*, extremely angry; very wicked. **—distel,** *f.* holy *or* blessed thistle. **—erde,** *f.* magnesia. **—feind,** *adj.* very hostile. **—kalk,** *m.* magnesian limestone. **—klee,** *m.* buck-bean, marsh-trefoil. **—kraut,** *n.* ox-tongue. **—kresse,** *f.* scurvy-grass. **—mandelöl,** *n.* oil of bitter almonds. **—salz,** *n.* Epsom salts; sulphate of magnesia. **—spat,** *m. see* **—kalk. —stein,** *m.* jade. **—stoff,** *m.* bitter principle (*Chem.*). **—süß,** I. *adj.* bitter-sweet. II. *n.* bitter-sweet, woody night-shade (*Bot.*). **—tropfen,** *pl.* bitters. **—wasser,** *n.* water impregnated with sulphate of magnesia. **—weide,** *f.* white willow. **—wurz,** *f.* gentian.

Bitu'm—en, *n.* (*no pl.*) bitumen. **—inö's**, *adj.* bituminous.

Bi'wak (*older* **Bi'vouak**), *n.* (**—s**, *pl.* **—s**) bivouac. **—ie'ren**, *v.n.* (*aux.* **h.**) to bivouac, to be encamped, to camp out.

Biza'rr, *adj. & adv.* strange, odd. **—erie'**, *f.* (*pl.* **—erie'en**) strangeness, oddity.

Bla'ch, *adj.* (*in cpds.*) level. **—e**, *f.* open field (*obs.*). *Comp.* **—feld**, *n.* open field; level land; battle field.

Black=fisch, *m.* cuttle-fish, ink-fish, sepia.

Blaff, *interj.* bang, pop (*the bark of a dog*).

Blaf'fen, *v.n.* (*aux.* **h.**) to bark, to yelp.

Blä'h—en, *v.* I. *a.* to inflate, swell. II. *n.* (*aux.* **h.**) to generate flatulence; to puff, distend; **sich mit etwas —en**, to brag of a thing, to be puffed up *or* elated about a th. **—end**, *p. & adj.* flatulent; windy. **—ung**, *f.* inflation; flatulence. *Comp.* **—sucht**, *f.* flatulency.

Blak, *m.* (**—s**) fume from a charred lamp-wick: stuff, nonsense, rot (*sl.*). **—ig**, *adj.* smoky (*of a lamp*).

Bla'k—en, *v.n.* (*aux.* **h.**) to smoke (*of a lamp*).

Blam—a'ge, *f.* exposure to ridicule, shame, disgrace, failure. **—ie'ren**, *v.a.* to expose to ridicule, stultify; bring into disrepute; **sich —ieren**, to make oneself ridiculous, to make a fool of oneself, to disgrace oneself; **blamiert!** (**blamoren**, *slang*) ha! sold! **er hat sich furchtbar blamiert**, he made a great fool of himself; **da hast du dich wieder einmal schön blamiert**, there you are sold again (*coll.*).

Blank, *adj. & adv.* blank; bright, polished; clean; spruce; naked, bare; **—e Worte**, mere words; **mit einem — stehen**, to be at open enmity with a p.; **—e Lüge**, flat lie; **— ziehen**, to draw (*one's sword*). **—e'tt**, *n.* blank bond, blank letter; carte-blanche. **—o**, *adj. & adv.* blank-, in blank; **in —o trassieren**, to draw in blank. *Comp.* **—leder**, *n.* sleek leather. **—o=accept**, *n.* acceptance in blank. **—o=kredit**, *m.* credit in blank, uncovered credit; unlimited credit. **—scheit**, *n.* (*stay-*)busk.

Blä's'chen, *n.* (**—s**, *pl.* **—**) pustule, pimple, vesicle, small blister; utricle (*Bot.*); **— werfen**, to sparkle, send up little bubbles; **voll —** pustulous.

Bla's—e, *f.* (*pl.* **—en**) bubble; blister; cyst; bladder; pimple; vesicle; flaw (*in metal, glass, etc.*); boiler, copper; alembic; bombast; **—en ziehen**, to blister, raise blisters; **die ganze —e**, the whole lot, the entire crew, one and all (*slang*). *Comp.* **—en=ähnlich**, **—en=artig**, *adj.* vesicular. **—en=bruch**, *m.* rupture of the bladder. **—en=entzündung**, *f.* cystitis, inflammation of the bladder. **—en=gallengang**, *m.* cystic duct. **—en=gries**, *m.* gravel (*Med.*). **—en=grün**, *n.* sapgreen (*for water-colour painting*). **—en=grün=beere**, *f.* buckthorn. **—en=käfer**, *m.* cantharis (*pl.* cantharides), Spanish fly. **—en=kalk**, *m.* magnesian limestone. **—en=katarrh**, *m.* cystic catarrh, blennorrhœa. **—en=kraut**, *n.* bladderwort. **—en=oxyd**, *n.* cystic oxide. **—en=perle**, *f.* pearl-bubble (*Mollusc.*). **—en=pflaster**, *n.* blister. **—en=räumer**, *m.* scoop (*Surg.*). **—en=schlagader**, *f.* cystic artery. **—en=schnecke**, *f.* Bulla. **—en=schnitt**, *m.* lithotomy, cystotomy. **—en=schnur**, *f.* urine-string (*Anat.*). **—en=sonde**, *f.* catheter. **—en=stein**, *m.* calculus. **—en=stein=säure**, *f.* lithic acid. **—en=stein=schnitt**, *m.* lithotomy. **—en=tang**, *m.* sea-wrack, sea-wave. **—en=ziehend**, *adj.* drawing, having a tendency to blister; blistering, epispastic.

Bla's—en, *ir.v.a. & n.* (*aux.* **h.**) to blow; to sound (*trumpets, etc.*); to smelt (*iron, etc.*); to blow (*glass*); **die Flöte —en**, to play the flute; **Lärm —en**, to sound an alarm; **zum Angriffe, zum Rückzuge —en**, to sound the charge, the retreat; **zum Aufsitzen —en**, to sound to horse; **einen Stein —en**, to huff (*at draughts*); **das läßt sich nicht —en**, that cannot be done in a twinkling; **einem in die Ohren —en**, to whisper in one's ear; **sie —en in ei'n Horn**, there is an understanding between them, they play into one another's hands; **was dich nicht brennt, das —e nicht**, let well alone (*prov.*). **—er**, *m.* (**—ers**, *pl.* **—er**) blower; grampus. **—icht**, *adj.* like blisters. **—ig**, *adj.* blistered; bladdery; vesicular. *Comp.* **—e=balg**, *m.* (*pair of*) bellows. **—e=balg=treter**, *m.* organ blower. **—e=balken**, *pl.* washboards (*Naut.*). **—e=baß**, *m.* bassoon. **—e=fisch**, *m.* bottle-nosed whale. **—e=instrument**, *n.* wind-instrument; **Kapelle von —einstrumenten**, brass-band. **—e=loch**, *n.* spout-hole (*of a whale*); blow-hole (*of a flute*). **—e=rohr**, *n.* blow-pipe; peashooter; (*bellows*) pipe. **—e=werk**, *n.* bellows of an organ. **—(s)=instrument**, *n. see* **—e=instrument**. **—(s)=kapelle**, *f.* brass-band. **—(s)=musik**, *f.* music for wind-instruments.

Blä'ser, *m.* (**—s**, *pl.* **—**) player (*on a wind-instrument*); machine for blowing; repelling magnet; tourmaline. **—ei'**, *f.* blowing.

Blasonie'ren, *v.a.* to emblazon.

Blasphem—ie', *f.* blasphemy. **—ie'ren**, *v.a. & n.* (*aux.* **h.**) to blaspheme.

Bla'ß (*compar.* **blasser** & **blässer**; *superl.* **blassest** & **blässest**) *adj. & adv.* pale, pallid; faint in colour; **keine —e Ahnung**, not the faintest idea (*coll.*); **toten—**, pale as death. *Comp.* **—blau**, *n.* pale blue. **—rot**, *n.* pink.

Blä's'—e, *f.* paleness, pallor; star, white spot (*on the face of a horse, etc.*); blaze (*on a cow, etc.*). **—(ß)=chen**, *n.* animal (*cow, horse*) with a blaze (*pet name*).

Bla'tt, *n.* (**—es**, *pl.* **Blätter**) leaf (*of a plant; of a book; of a screen; of a table*); blade (*of the shoulder; of grass; of an oar; of a sword; of scissors, etc.*); newspaper; sheet (*of paper*); breadth (*of stuff*); flap, skirt (*of a coat, etc.*); weaver's reed; written *or* printed music; membrane; **fliegende Blätter**, pamphlets, fly-leaves, occasional papers; name of an illustrated comical Munich paper; **die öffentlichen Blätter**, the (news)papers, the press; **vom —e (weg) spielen**, to play at sight; **Singen vom —**, sight-singing; **Wein von vier Blättern**, wine four years old; **kein — vor den Mund nehmen**, to be plain spoken; **er nimmt kein — vor den Mund**, he does not mince matters; **das steht auf einem andern —e**, that is another thing; **das — hat sich gewendet**, the tables are turned; **das — fiel ihm**, he grew afraid; **mir schießt das —**, I begin to see clearly; I am surprised; **ein neues — (im Lebensbuch) beginnen**, to turn over a new leaf; **ein — einschlagen**, to turn down a leaf (*in a book*). *Comp.* **—ähnlich**, *adj.* leaf-like. **—ansatz**, *m.* stipula. **—auge**, *n.* leaf-bud. **—beil**, *n.* broad axe. **—bezeichnung**, *f.* signature, printer's name (*affixed to a sheet*). **—blei**, *n.* lead in thin sheets. **—blume**, *f.* phyllanthus. **—breite**, *f.* breadth (*of cloth*). **—eisen**, *n.* sheet-iron. **—fleisch**, *n.* pith, *or* pulp, of plants. **—förmig**, *adj.* leaf-shaped. **—gewächs**, *n.* foliage plant. **—gold**, *n.* gold-leaf. **—hüter**, *m.* catch-word (*Typ.*). **—knospe**, *f.* leaf-bud. **—lahm**, *adj.* shoulder-shot, strained in the shoulder. **—laus**, *f.* plant-louse. **—los**, *adj.* leafless. **—reich**, *adj.* leafy, with rich *or* luxuriant foliage. **—=rippe**, *f.* fibre (*of a leaf*). **—scheide**, *f.* sheath (*Bot.*). **—schild**, *n.* a species of grasshopper. **—seite**, *f.* leaf, folio. **—silber**, *n.* silver-leaf. **—stiel**, *m.* leaf-stalk. **—vergoldung**, *f.* gilding with gold-leaf. **—weise**, *adv.* leaf by leaf. **—weiser**, **—zeiger**, *m.* index. **—zeichen**, *n.* book-mark. **—zinn**, *n.* tin-foil.

Blätt'—chen, *n.* (**—chens**, *pl.* **—chen**) leaflet;

blade (*of grass*); small sheet of paper; membrane (*of the brain*); fontanel; (*metallic*) foil; (*pl.*) lamina. —**er**, *see* **Blatt**; (*in comp.*) *see below.* —**erig**, *adj. & adv.* leafy; laminated; flaky; foliated; (*in comp.* =) leaved; foliate. *Comp.* —**er=(ab)fall**, *m.* fall of the leaf, leaves fallen from a tree; defoliation. —**er=erde**, *f.* acetate of potash. —**er=erz**, *n.* black *or* foliated tellurium. —**er=fülle**, *f.* leafiness. —**er=gebackenes**, *n.* puff paste. —**er=gelb**, *adj.* feuillemort. —**er=kohle**, *f.* slaty coal. —**er=los**, *adj.* leafless. —**er=magen**, *m.* third stomach of ruminants, tripe. —**er=schnäbler**, *pl.* lamellirostrals (*Orn.*). —**er=schwamm**, *m.* agaric; (**eßbarer —erschwamm**) mushroom. —**er=spat**, *m.* foliaceous spar. —**er=stand**, *m.* foliation. —**er=tabak**, *m.* leaf-tobacco. —**er=teig**, *m.* puff paste. —**er=werk**, *n.* foliage (*also Paint., Arch.*). —**er=wuchs**, *m.* foliation.

Blat'ten, *v.a.* I. to strip *or* clear of leaves. II. to decoy (*a buck by whistling on a leaf*) (*Hunt.*).

Blat'ter, *f.* (*pl.* —**n**) pustule, pimple, pock; **die —n**, small-pox; **zusammen fließende —n**, confluent small-pox; **—n der Schweine**, measles; **—n der Schafe**, rot. —**ig**, *adj.* papulous, pustular. *Comp.* —**gift**, *n.* virus of small-pox. —**grube**, —**narbe**, *f.* pock-mark. —**kraut**, *n.* a species of ranunculus. —**masig**, —**narbig**, *adj.* marked with small-pox. —**n=impfung**, *f.* vaccination. —**stein**, *m.* variolite.

Blät'tern, *v.* I. *n.* (*aux.* **h.**) to turn over the leaves (*of a book*, **in einem Buche**). II. *a.* to strip of leaves; **sich —**, to exfoliate, to rise in flakes (*Cook.*).

Blau, I. *adj.* blue; azure (*Her.*); **der —e Montag**, Saint Monday, Saint Crispin's day, black Monday; **— machen**, to take a holiday; **die Woche — machen**, to be idle all the week; to take a week's holiday; **einem einen —en Dunst vormachen**, to humbug one, throw dust in one's eyes; **sein —es Wunder sehen**, to be struck with wonder at seeing a thing; **—e Märchen erzählen**, to tell incredible stories, to tell lies; **—es Auge**, black eye; **mit einem —en Auge davonkommen**, to have a narrow escape; to come off cheaply; **es ward mir — und rot um die Augen**, I turned giddy. II. *n.* (—**es**), **das —(e)**, blue (*colour*), blueness; azure; the sky; **ins —e hinein**, hap-hazard, thoughtlessly, at random; **Berliner —**, Prussian blue; **Königs—**, royal blue; **das —e vom Himmel schwatzen**, to talk off a donkey's hind-legs (*coll.*); **—er Brief**, military letter (*in the official blue envelope*); **—es Blut**, blue blood, aristocracy; **—e Bohne**, blue-pill, bullet; **—e Jungen**, German infantry (*fam.*). *Comp.* —**aderig**, *adj.* blue-veined. —**äugig**, *adj.* blue-eyed. —**bart**, *m.* Blue-beard. —**beere**, *f.* bilberry. —**ente**, *f.* the wild duck. —**falke**, *m.* Falco caesius. —**farben=erz**, *n.* cobalt. —**fleckig**, *adj.* blue-spotted. —**fuchs**, *m.* arctic fox. —**fuß**, *m.* blue-hawk. —**gesäuert**, *adj.* impregnated with prussic acid. —**glas**, *n.* smalt. —**grau**, *adj.* livid. —**holz**, *n.* logwood. —**kehlchen**, *n.* blue-throated warbler (*Sylvia suecica*). —**kohl**, *m.* red cabbage. —**krähe**, *f.* the roller (*Orn.*). —**meise**, *f.* blue titmouse. —**säure**, *f.* prussic acid; —**säure=Verbindungen**, cyanides; —**säure=Salze**, prussiates. —**schimmel**, *m.* dapple-grey horse. —**specht**, *m.* nut-hatch; nut-pecker. —**stein**, *m.* azure stone. —**stift**, *m.* blue pencil. —**strumpf**, *m.* blue-stocking; informer (*obsol.*). —**taube**, *f.* wood-pigeon. —**vogel**, *m.* song-thrush.

Bläu—e, *f.* blueness; blue (*for linen, etc.*); azure (*of sky*); blue starch. —**el**, *m.* (—**els**, *pl.* —**el**) beetle, beater; rolling pin, blue starch. —**lich**, *adj.* bluish. —**ling**, *m.* bluecap (*fish*).

Bläu'en, *v.* I. *a.* to cause to be blue, to dye blue (*linen, etc.*). II. *r. & n.* (*aux.* **h.**) to grow *or* appear blue. *See* **Bleuen**.

Blau'en, *v.n.* to be blue; **der Himmel blaut**, the sky is blue; **soweit die Berge —**, so far as the blue peaks are seen.

Blech, *n.* (—**es**, *pl.* —**e**) thin plate of metal; tin; girdle, griddle; stuff, nonsense (*sl.*); **gewalztes—**, rolled metal; **schwarzes (Eisen)—**, sheet-iron; **weißes —**, tin; **starkes —**, double-plate; **reines —**, bosh (*coll.*); **rede doch kein —**, do not talk nonsense (*coll.*).

Ble'ch—en, *v.a. & n.* (*aux.* **h.**) to pay, to fork out; to have to pay, to bleed (*coll.*). —**e(r)n**, *adj.* of sheet-metal *or* tin; **eine —erne Büchse**, a tin canister. —**ner**, *m.* tinman, tinker. *Comp.* —**geschirr**, *n.* tin (*mug, etc.*). —**händler**, *m.* tinman. —**handschuh**, *m.* gauntlet. —**haube**, —**mütze**, *f.* helmet. —**kuchen**, *m.* griddle cake. —**musik**, *f.* brass band; music of a brass band. —**schere**, *f.* shears for cutting tin. —**schläger**, —**schmied**, *m.* whitesmith, tinker. —**zinn**, *n.* tinfoil.

Ble'cken, *v.a.*; **die Zähne —**, to show the teeth (**auf** *or* **gegen einen**, at one).

Blei, *n.* (—**es**) lead; plummet; pencil (= **Bleistift**); **bunte —e**, (*many-*)coloured pencils; **zu Pulver und — verurteilt**, condemned to be shot; **gehacktes —**, slugs; **gerolltes —**, sheet-lead; **— in Blöcken**, pig-lead; **aus —**, **von —**, leaden; **Fenster—**, window leading. —**ern**, *adj.* leaden; **er schwimmt wie ein —erner Fisch (eine —erne Ente)**, he cannot swim. —**ig**, *adj.* lead-like, leaden, plumbiferous. *Comp.* —**ader**, *f.* lode *or* vein of lead. —**arbeit**, *f.* plumber's work. —**arbeiter**, *m.* plumber. —**baryt**, *m.* lead-spar. —**bergwerk**, *n.* lead-mine. —**blüte**, *f.* arseniate of lead. —**dach**, *n.*, —**dächer**, *pl.* the leads. —**decker**, *m.* plumber. —**draht**, *m.* spun lead. —**druse**, *f.* lead-crystals. —**erz**, *n.* lead ore. —**essig**, *m.* lead vinegar. —**farbig**, *adj.* livid, lead-coloured. —**feder**, *f.* lead pencil. —**gelb**, *n* yellow monoxide of lead; chromate of lead. —**gießer**, *m.* plumber. —**gießerei**, *f.* lead works. —**glanz**, *m.* galena, lead sulphide. —**glätte**, *f.* litharge. —**grau**, *adj.* steel grey. —**grube**, *f.* lead-mine. —**hornerz**, *n.* chloride of lead; muriate of lead. —**hütte**, *f.* lead works. —**kalk**, *m. see* —**weiß**. —**kessel**, *m.* vessel lined with lead. —**klumpen**, *m.* pig of lead. —**kolik**, *f.* painter's colic. —**kugel**, *f.* bullet. —**lot**, *n.* plumbline; lead, plummet; **mit dem —lot untersuchen (ergründen)**, to take soundings; **mit dem —lot abmessen**, to plumb. —**mulde**, *f.* pig of lead. —**oxyd**, *n.* lead monoxide. —**recht**, *n.* perpendicular. —**rohr**, *n.* pencil case. —**röhre**, *f.* lead-piping. —**rot**, *n. see* **Mennige**. —**schlage**, *f.* dross of lead. —**schnur**, *f.* sounding line. —**stift**, *m.* lead-pencil. —**stift=hülse**, *f.*, —**stift=rohr**, *n.* pencil case. —**stift=schneider**, —**stift=spitzer**, *m.* pencil-sharper. —**tafeln**, *pl.* sheet-lead. —**vergiftung**, *f.* lead poisoning, plumbism. —**verschluß**, *m.* leading (*at custom houses*). —**wage**, *f.* plumb line, level. —**wasser**, *n.* Goulard water. —**weiß**, *n.* white lead. —**weiß=farbe**, *f.* white paint. —**wurf**, *m.* plummet; heave of the lead (*Naut.*). —**zucker**, *m.* lead acetate, sugar of lead. —**zug**, *m.* act of drawing window-leading; window-leading; glazier's vice.

Blei'ben, I. *ir.v.n.* (*aux.* **s.**) to be, continue, remain, stay; to last, stand, endure; to stay away, tarry; to be left, remain; **wird sie lange —**, will she stay long? **stehen —**, to stop, stand still; **wo sind wir stehen geblieben?** where did we leave off? **dabei muß es —**, there the matter must rest; **wo ist er geblieben?** what has become of him? **Mutter**

bleibt so lange, mother is very long in coming; lassen Sie das —, let that alone; das werde ich wohl — lassen, I shall take good care not to do this; das soll er wohl — lassen, he had better let that alone; I should like to see him attempt that; bleib mir vom Leibe! stand off! davon —, to keep clear of; es bleibt dabei! agreed! es bleibt beim Alten, things go on just as they were; er bleibt bei seiner Meinung, he persists in his opinion; es bleibt unter uns, this is confidential, we will keep it to ourselves; sie sind auf dem Schlachtfelde geblieben, they fell on the battle field; auf dem Platze —, to be slain; sie — mit der Zahlung zurück, they are in arrears; es bleibt uns nichts übrig als, nothing is left us but to; Sie können mit Ihrem Rate zu Hause —, spare me your advice, I don't want it; gelassen —, to keep one's temper; stecken —, to stick fast. II. *subst.n.* abode, stay; hier ist meines — s nicht, here is no abiding-place for me, I cannot stay here. —d, *p. & adj.* permanent, abiding; —de Eindrücke, lasting impressions; —de Farbe, fast colour; wo bleibt . . ? where is?

Bleich, *adj.* pale, wan, pallid; faint; faded. —e, *f.* pallor, paleness; bleaching; bleach-green. —ert, *m.* (—erts, *pl.* —erte) pale red wine. *Comp.* —er=salz, *n.* chloride of lime. —farbig, *adj.* livid. —kalk, *m. see* —er=salz. —platz, *m.* bleaching ground. —pulver, *n.* bleaching-powder. —sucht, *f.* chlorosis, green-sickness. —süchtig, *adj.* maid-pale; chlorotic. —wasser, *n.* chlorine water.

Blei'ch—en, I. *v.a.* to bleach; to blanch; der Ernst, den keine Mühe bleichet, that earnestness (of purpose) which is not afraid of any toil. II. *ir.v.n.* (*aux.* h. & s.) to grow, turn pale; to fade. III. *subst.n.* bleaching. —er, *m.* (—ers, *pl.* —er) bleacher. —erin, *f.* laundress.

Blei'he, *f.* (*pl.* —n) bream (*fish*).

Blen'd—e, *f.* (*pl.* —en) blind; blind window *or* door; niche (*in a wall*); blinker, winker; dark-lantern; blend (*Min.*); sight (*of a gun*); blinds (*Fort.*); diaphragm (*Opt.*); mantlet (*Fort.*); (*folding*) screen; (*pl.*) dead-lights (*Naut.*). *Comp.* —fenster, *n.* blind window; engraver's window screen. —kugel, *f.* smoke-ball. —laterne, *f.* dark lantern, bull's eye. —leder, *n.* blinkers. —leuchter, *m.* chandelier (*Fort.*). —stein, *m.* gutter-tile; brick used with wooden framework, facing stone, slat. —werk, *n.* delusion, optical illusion; fascination; lie, falsehood; jugglery, farce; phantasmagoria; das ist lauter —werk, that 's all a farce, it is all hocus-pocus. —ziegel, *m.* facing brick.

Blen'd—en, *v.a.* to blind, to put out a p.'s eyes; to dazzle; to deceive, hoodwink; to blindfold; to hood (*a falcon*); to deaden (*gold*); to blind (*Fort.*). —end, *p. & adj.* dazzling; brilliant; delusive. —ling, *m.* (—lings, *pl.* —linge) bastard; mongrel. —ung, *f.* blinding; dazzling; deception; diaphragm (*Opt.*); blinds (*Fort.*).

Bleff—ie'ren, *v.a.* to wound. —u'r, *f.* (*pl.* —u'ren) wound.

Blich, Bli'che, *imperf. indic. & subj.* of bleichen (*under II.; only in compounds*).

Blick, *m.* (—es, *pl.* —e) look; glance; view, prospects; glimpse; look, appearance; flash, gleam, lightning (*obs.*); (*pl.*) touches of light (*Paint.*); einen — thun auf einen, to glance at a person; einen — in eine S. thun, to get an insight into a th.; auf den ersten —, at first sight; ein scharfer —, a penetrating glance, penetration; ein verstohlener —, a furtive glance; der böse —, the evil eye. *Comp.* —feuer, *n.* blue-light, signal fire. —gold, *n.* refined gold.

Bli'cken, *v.* I. *n.* (*aux.* h.) to glance, to look; to appear shining; to shine; — lassen, to show; sich — lassen, to appear, to put in an appearance, let oneself be seen. II. *a.* to look, express by looks.

Blieb, Blie'be, *imperf. indic. & subj.* of bleiben.

Blies, Blie'se, *imperf. indic. & subj.* of blasen.

Blind, *adj. & adv.* blind; false, sham; tarnished, dull; blank; hidden; uninflated (*of sails*); without judgment, blind; dazzled; — an *or* auf einem Auge, blind of one eye; —er Soldat, dummy, man of straw; —er Bogen, blank sheet (*Typ.*); —es Gefecht, sham fight; —e Patrone, blank cartridge; —e Kuh spielen, to play at blind man's buff; —e Versteigerung, sham auction; —e Mauer, dead wall; —e Klippen, sunken rocks; —er Passagier, passenger who avoids paying, deadhead; —er Kauf, fictitious purchase; —es Schloß, deadlock; —es Glück, hazard; —er Eifer schadet nur, zeal without knowledge is frenzy (*prov.*); —es Geld, undecipherable coinage; —er Spiegel, a tarnished mirror; — schießen, to fire in the air; — laden, to load with blank cartridge; der —e (die —e 2c.), blind man (woman); die —e, sprit-sail; der —e, dummy (*cards*). —heit, *f.* blindness. —lings, *adv.* blindly, blindfold. *Comp.* —boden, *m.* false bottom. —darm, *m.* caecum. —geborene(r), *m.* one born blind. —gewölbe, *n.* casemate. —holz, *n.* wood to be veneered. —schleiche, *f.* slow-worm, blindworm; snake in the grass (*fig.*).

Blink, I. *adj.* glittering. II. *m.* gleam; clear spot in a cloudy sky.

Blin'ken, *v.n.* (*aux.* h.) to gleam; to twinkle; to wink; to sparkle.

Blin'z—en, —eln, *v.n.* (*aux.* h.) to blink, wink, twinkle, nictitate (*Med.*). —(l)er, *m.* winker, blinker.

Blitz, *m.* (—es, *pl.* —e) flash (*of lightning*); lightning; vom —e gerührt, struck by lightning; wie vom —e gerührt, thunder-struck; Potz —! *interj.* zounds! thunder and lightning! der — schlage drein! deuce take it! weg wie der —, off like a shot. *Comp.* —ableiter, *m.* lightning conductor. —blank, *adj.* resplendent (*or* very) bright *or* shining. —blau, *adj.* black and blue; thunder-struck. —(es)eile, *f.* lightning-rapidity. —funken, *m.* electric spark. —junge, *m.* devil of a boy, sharp lad; fine boy; capital fellow. —mädel, *f.* smart girl; splendid girl. —photographie, *f.* photograph obtained during a flash of lightning. —sauber, *adj.* spruce, very pretty. —schlag, *m.* thunder-clap. —schnell, *adj. & adv.* swift as lightning. —stoff, *m.* electricity. —stoff=haltig, *adj.* charged with electricity. —stoff=sauger, *m.* condenser. —strahl, *m.* lightning-flash, flash of lightning. —zug, *m.* name given to an especially fast train, *e.g.* flying Scotchman.

Blit'zen, *v.* I. *imp. & n.* to lighten; es blitzt, it is lightning; there is a skirt gaping (*girls' sl.*). II. *a.* to glance, flash, sparkle; einen zu Boden —, to strike a p. down (by a glance) like a flash of lightning (*poet.*).

Block, *m.* (—(e)s, *pl.* Blöcke) block, log; boulder; stocks. (Verbrecher) in den — legen, to put (criminals) in the stocks. *Comp.* —blei, *n.* pig-lead. —dreher, *m.* block-maker. —druck, *m.* block-printing. —haus, *n.* log-house; log-rampart (*Mil.*). —holz, *n.* log-timber. —karren, *m.* timber-truck. —nagel, *m.* wooden peg, pin. —rad, *n.* truck wheel; solid wheel. —scheibe (—rolle), *f.* pulley. —säge, *f.* pit-saw. —schiff, *n.* raft; dismantled ship, hulk. —seife, *f.* bar-soap. —stück, *n.* pig (*of iron, etc.*). —taube, *f.* ring dove. —verband, *m.* English bond (*Mas.*). —wagen, *m.* truck. —zinn, *n.* block-tin.

Blocka'de, *f.* (*pl.* —n) blockade. *Comp.* —bre=

cher, *m.* runner of a blockade. **—geschwader,** *n.* blockading squadron.

Blöck'chen, *n.* little block, small log.

Blo'cken, *v.a.* to stretch (*boots*) over the tree *or* last; to block (*hats*).

Blockie'r—en, *v.a.* to block up, to obstruct; to blockade (*Mil.*); **einen Ball —en,** to send a ball into a corner-pocket, to make a coo (*billiards*). **—ung,** *f.* blocking up, blockade.

Blö'd—e, *adj.* weak-sighted, purblind; imbecile; bashful, shy; stupid. **—igkeit,** *f.* purblindness, weakness of sight; imbecility; bashfulness, coyness, timidity. *Comp.* **—sichtig,** *adj.* weak-sighted, purblind; idiotic. **—sinn,** *m.* imbecility; weakness of mind; nonsense; **blühender —sinn,** great nonsense, fine fun; **—sinn machen,** to make great fun; **—sinn schwatzen,** to talk nonsense. **—sinnig,** *adj.*, silly; idiotic.

Blö'ken, *v.n.* (*aux.* **h.**) to bleat; to low.

Blond, *adj.* blond, fair; blond (*lace*); **der (die) —e,** fair-complexioned person; **eine —e,** blond lace (*Comm.*); **eine kühle —e,** a glass of pale Berlin beer (*Berlin sl.*). **—i'ne,** *f.* (*pl.* **—i'nen**) blonde (*woman*). *Comp.* **—kopf,** *m.* fair-haired person. **—lockig,** *adj.* having fair curly hair.

Bloß, I. *adj.* bare, naked; destitute; pure, mere; drawn (*of a sword*); **mit —em Kopfe,** bareheaded; **auf —er Haut,** next to the skin, on the bare skin; **—er Argwohn,** mere suspicion; **der —e Gedanke,** the mere idea, *or* the very thought; **das —e Auge, Schwert,** the naked eye, sword; **—e Worte,** empty words, mere words; **sich — geben,** to expose oneself, to betray oneself; to lay oneself open (*Fenc.*); **— legen,** to lay bare; **es liegt — am Tage,** it is manifest; **—stellen,** to expose, to compromise; **auf einem —en Pferde reiten,** to ride bare-backed. II. *adv.* barely; merely, only; **— um Ihnen zu gefallen,** simply to please you (*coll.*); **es kostet — eine Mark,** it costs only a shilling (*coll.*). *Comp.* **—gestellt,** *adj.* open, unmasked; unprotected. **—legung,** *f.* denudation. **—stellung,** *f.* exposure.

Blö'ße, *f.* (*pl.* **—n**) bareness; nakedness; indigence; bare place (*in a wood, etc.*); weakness, weak point; blot (*at backgammon*); **eine — lassen** (*or* **geben**), to leave open, unprotected; **scharfen Bissen eine — lassen,** to be unprotected against sharp bites; **sich** (*dat.*) **eine — geben,** to expose oneself (*to attack, ridicule, etc.*), to commit oneself.

Blö'ßen, *v.a.* to uncover, expose (*obs.*).

Blou'se, *f.*, **Blu'se,** *f.* (*pl.* **—n**) blouse; smock-frock; shirt-front.

Blü'h—en, *v.n.* (*aux.* **h.**) to bloom, blossom, blow; to flourish; to effloresce; **vier Söhne —ten mir,** I had four sons in the flower of their youth; **es —t sein Glück,** fortune smiles on him; **sein Weizen —t,** he is in luck('*s way*); **die Segel —en in dem Hauche,** the sails open out in the breeze, the sails are swelling in the wind (*poet.*). **—end,** *p. & adj.* blooming; in blossom; verdant; florid; flowery; **das —ende Alter,** prime of life, flower of one's youth; **—ender Blödsinn,** stuff and nonsense; **—ende Jungfrau,** budding maiden.

Blü'm—chen, —lein, *n.* (**—chens, —leins,** *pl.* **—chen, —lein**) floweret; floscule; scut; virginity, maidenhood (*coll.*). *Comp.* **—chen=artig,** *adj.*, very pale, very weak (*of coffee*). **—chen=kaffee,** *m.* very weak coffee (*coll.*).

Blü'meln, *v.n.* (*aux.* **h.**) to be flowery (*in style*); to gather, seek for flowers; to fly from flower to flower (*as a bee*).

Blu'm—e, *f.* (*pl.* **—en**) flower, blossom; star, white spot; bouquet (*of wine*); yeast; gloss (*on linen, etc.*); tip of the tail, scut (*Sport*); efflorescence (*Chem.*); trope, figure; best of anything, choice, pick, élite, flower; virginity, maidenhood (*rare, coll.*); head (*of a pustule, etc.*); **durch die —e sprechen,** to speak in metaphors, to talk with covert allusion; **die —e von etwas haben,** to have the first of a thing; **ich komme dir meine —,** I pledge you the first draught (*of my glass of beer, students' sl.*). **—icht** (*obs.*), **—ig,** *adj.* flowery. **—i'st,** *m.* (**—is'ten,** *pl.* **—is'ten**) florist. *Comp.* **—en=artig,** *adj.* flosculous; flowerlike. **—en=bau,** *m.* floriculture. **—en=becher,** *m.* calyx. **—en=beet,** *n.* flower-bed. **—en=binde,** *f.* festoon. **—en=binse,** *f.* flowering rush. **—en=blatt,** *n.* floral leaf, petal. **—en=blattlos,** *adj.* apetalous. **—en=büschel,** *m.* cluster of flowers; corymb. **—en=decke,** *f.* perianth. **—en=erde,** *f.* garden-mould. **—en=esche,** *f.* flowering ash. **—en=flor,** *m.* show of bloom; show of flowers; flowering time. **—en=gärtner,** *m.* florist. **—en=gehänge, —en=gewinde,** *n.*, **—en=schnur,** *f.* festoon, garland. **—en=gestell,** *n.* flower-stand. **—en=gewächs,** *n.* flowering plant. **—en=göttin,** *f.* Flora, goddess of flowers. **—en=griffel,** *m.* style; pistil (*Bot.*). **—en=händler,** *m.* florist, nurseryman. **—en=hülle,** *f.* involucre. **—en=kelch,** *m.* calyx. **—en=kohl,** *m.* cauliflower. **—en=korb,** *m.* flower-basket; corbel (*Arch.*). **—en=korso,** *m.* battle of flowers. **—en=kranz,** *m.* chaplet of flowers. **—en=krone,** *f.* corolla. **—en=leiste,** *f.* initial *or* final flourish (*Typ.*). **—en=lese,** *f.* flower gathering; anthology. **—en=mädchen,** *n.* girl who binds and sells flowers. **—en=maler,** *m.* flower-painter. **—en=mehl,** *n.* pollen. **—en=pfad,** *m.* flower-strewn path. **—en=reich,** I. *adj.* abounding in flowers; florid. II. *n.* floral kingdom. **—en=scheibe,** *f.* discus. **—en=scheide,** *f.* sheath. **—en=scherbe,** *f.* flower-pot. **—en=schirm,** *m.* umbel. **—en=schrift, —en=sprache,** *f.* language of flowers. **—en=seite,** *f.* hairy side (*of a skin*). **—en=stengel,** *m.* stalk. **—en=stiel,** *m.* peduncle. **—en=stielständig,** *adj.* pedunculate, peduncular. **—en=stock,** *m.* flowering pot-plant; flowers. **—en=strauß,** *m.* nosegay. **—en=stück,** *n.* bed of flowers; flower-painting. **—en=thee,** *m.* imperial tea. **—en=topf,** *m.* flower-pot. **—en=werk,** *n.* festoons, *etc.* **—en=zeit,** *f.* flowering season. **—en=zucht,** *f. see* **—en=bau.** **—en=züchter,** *m.* florist. **—en=zwiebel,** *f.* flower-bulb.

Blü'men, *v.a.* to adorn with flowers (*obs.*); to figure (*silk, etc.*).

Blümera'nt, *adj.* pale-blue (*bleu mourant*); **mir wird ganz —,** I feel quite dizzy *or* giddy (*coll.*).

Blu'se, *f.* blouse, smock-frock; tunic. **—n=mann,** *m.* workman.

Blü'se, *f.* beacon, light-house.

Blut, *n.* (**—es**) blood; race, lineage; sap; juice (*of plants, etc.*); **ein junges —,** a young thing *or* creature; **geronnenes —,** clotted blood, gore; **einem — lassen,** to bleed a person; **— stillen,** to staunch blood; **— auswerfen,** to spit blood; **bis aufs —,** to the quick; **bis aufs — schlagen,** to beat till the blood comes; **von gutem —e,** thorough-bred; **es liegt im —e,** it runs in the blood; **ein Gesicht wie Milch und —,** a complexion like lilies and roses; **böses — machen,** to arouse angry feelings; **mit kaltem —e,** in cold blood; **sein — geriet** *or* **war in Wallung,** his blood was up. **—ig,** *adj. & adv.* bloody, cruel; **—ige Thränen weinen,** to shed tears of blood; **—ige Schlacht,** sanguinary battle; **—ig beißen,** to draw blood by biting. *Comp. Before some adjectives (e.g.* **arm** *and* **jung***) it is used as a mere intensive and does not take the principal accent.* **—abgang,** *m.* loss of blood, hemorrhage. **—ader,** *f.* blood-vessel. **—andrang,** *m.* congestion (*of blood*). **—arm,** *adj.* poor as a church-mouse; deficient in red blood, anæmic. **—auge,** *n.* blood-shot eye. **—aus=**

leerend, *adj.* depletive. —auswurf, *m.* expectoration of blood. —bad, *n.* massacre, carnage, butchery. —bann, *m.* penal judicature. —befleckt, *adj.* blood-stained. —bildung, *f.* sanguification, hematosis. —blatter, *f.* a species of beetle. —brechen, *n.* vomiting of blood. —buche, *f.* copper beech. —durst, *m.* bloodthirstiness. —dürstig, *adj.* bloodthirsty. —egel, *m.* (—igel) leech. —farbig, *adj.* crimson. —fink, *m.* bullfinch. —flagge, *f.* red flag. —flügel, *m.* glory of Kent (*Endromis versicolor*). —fluß, *m.* hemorrhage; monthly courses, menses. —fremd, *adj.* utterly strange. —fülle, *f.* full-bloodedness; plethora. —gang, *m.* flow of blood. —gefäß=lehre, *f.* angiology. —geld, *n.* blood-money, price of blood (*Bibl.*); fine for homicide, weregeld. —gericht, *n.* criminal court. —gerüst, *n.* scaffold for execution. —geschwür, *n.* bloody tumour. —gier, *f.* bloodthirstiness. —gierig, *adj.* sanguinary, bloodthirsty. —hänfling, *m.* red-linnet, red-poll. —harnen, *n.* haematuria (*Med.*); red murrain. —hochzeit, *f.*; die Pariser —, massacre of St. Bartholomew (*Aug. 24, 1572*). —holz, *n.* logwood; Campeachy wood. —hund, *m.* bloodhound; myrmidon; tyrant. —jung, *adj.* very young. —klumpen, *m.* clot of blood. —kraut, *n.* sanguinary, love-lies-bleeding. —kuchen, *m.* blood-residue. —kügelchen, *n.* blood-globule. —lassen, *n.* bleeding. —lauf, *m.* bloody flux; circulation of the blood. —leer, *adj.* bloodless. —mal, *n.* red mole, birthmark. —pfirsch, *m.* nectarine. —rache, *f.* vendetta. —rächer, *m.* avenger of bloodshed. —reich, *adj.* plethoric. —reinigung, *f.* blood-purification. —richter, *m.* criminal judge. —ruhr, *f.* bloody flux. —rünstig, *adj.* bloody, bleeding. —sauer, *adj.* very hard; es sich —sauer werden lassen, to toil hard, to slave. —sauger, *m.* vampire; bloodsucker, extortioner. —schande, *f.* incest. —schänder, *m.* incestuous person. —schreier, *m.* officer who proclaimed a criminal's guilt (*obs.*). —schuld, *f.* blood-guiltiness; capital crime; murder; incest. —schwelle, *f. see* —spat. —serum, *n.* serum of blood. —s=freund, *m.*, —s=freundin, *f.* blood-relation, kinsman, kinswoman. —sieb, *n.* parenchyma (*Anat.*). —spat, *m.* blood-spavin. —stallen, *n. see* —harnen. —stein, *m.* hematite. —stillend, *adj.* styptic. —strieme, *f.* blood-shot stripe; livid weal. —sturz, *m.* violent hemorrhage; bursting of a blood-vessel. —s=verwandt, (mit) *adj.*, related by blood (*to*). —s=verwandtschaft, *f.* consanguinity. —taufe, *f.* baptism of blood. —tausch, *m.* transfusion of blood. —that, *f.* bloody deed, murder. —umlauf, *m.* circulation of the blood. —unterlaufen, *adj.* blood-shot. —vergießen, *n.* bloodshed, slaughter. —urteil, *n.* sentence of death. —warm, *adj.* at blood-heat. —wasser, *n.* lymph; ichor; serum. —wenig, *adv.* very little, next to nothing. —wolle, *f.* fell-wool. —wurst, *f.* black-pudding. —zehnt, *m.* tithe of *or* on live stock. —zeuge, *m.* martyr. —zwang, *m.* dysenteric spasm.

Blü'te, *f.* (*pl.* —n) blossom, flower; bud; bloom; prime (*of life*); blossoming time. *Comp.* —n=auge, *n.* germ. —n=decke, *f.* perianth (*Bot.*). —n=knospe, *f.* bud. —n=stand, *m.* inflorescence. —n=staub, *m.* pollen. —n=stengel, *m.* peduncle. —n=traube, *f.* raceme, bunch. —periode, —zeit, *f.* time of greatest perfection, golden age, classical period. —zeit, *f.* flowering time, prime; *see* —periode.

=blütig *in compounds* (*fr.* Blüte), -flowered, -blossomed.

Bö, *f.* (*pl.* —en) gust, sudden squall of wind; leichte —, white squall; schwere —, black squall.

Blu't—en, *v.n.* (*aux.* h.) to bleed; to shed one's blood, die; to suffer; mir —et das Herz, my heart bleeds; er soll dafür —en, he shall pay for that (*coll.*).

Bock, *m.* (—s, *pl.* Böcke) buck; ram; he-goat; battering-ram; blunder, bull; jack; horse (*for clothes, etc.*); andiron; block; beam; stocks; rack; machine for lifting *or* supporting weights; coach-box; trestle; stool; buttress (*of a bridge*); bridge (*Bill.*); debauched fellow; ein steifer —, a clumsy fellow, clumsy Dick; einem den — stehen (treten), — springen, to play at leap-frog; — springen, to leap the buck (*Gym.*); den — zum Gärtner machen *or* setzen, to set the fox to keep the geese; einen — schießen *or* machen, to make a bull, (commit a) blunder; der — stößt ihn, he mopes, sulks (*vulg.*); weinen, daß einen der — stößt, to sob convulsively (*vulg.*); [*as suffix in comp.* = **1.** male, *as* Reh—, roebuck; Ziegen—, he-goat; **2.** stand, jack, horse, rack, machine, *etc.*, *as* Brand—, Feuer—, fire-dogs; Kutsch—, coach-box; Säge—, machine for sawing wood]. —icht (*obs.*), —ig, *adj.* rutting, in heat; smelling as a goat; lewd; obstinate, sulky. *Comp.* —beinig, *adj.* goat-footed; wayward, stubborn. —decke, *f.* hammer-cloth. —fell, *n.* goat's hide. —gestell, *n.* body of a coach. —käfer, *m.* capricorn-beetle. —kasten, *m.* boot (*of a coach*). —lafette, *f.* sledge-carriage (*for mountain artillery*). —leder, *n.* buckskin. —messer, *n.* comb-maker's knife. —mühle, *f.* timber windmill built on trestles. —pfeife, *f.* bagpipe. —s=bart, *m.* goat's beard. —s=beutel, *m.* flask for Würzburg 'Stein' wine; this wine itself; lady's pouch to carry prayer-book; old-fashioned usage, stupid old custom, the old jog-trot. —s=beutelei, *f.* (attachment to) antiquated customs. —s=beutler, *m.* old pedant. —schemel, *m.* foot-board. —s=füßig, *adj.* goat-footed. —s=horn, *n.* hartshorn; bucks-horn; goats-horn (*Mus.*); einen ins —shorn jagen, to intimidate s.o., to frighten one out of his wits; to bully one. —s=hörner, *pl.* eye-bolts *Naut.*). —spiel, *n.* leap-frog. —sprung, *m.* caper, gambol; capriole; —sprünge machen, to caper, to gambol; to frisk.

Bock, *m.* (—es) (—bier, *n.*) strong Bavarian beer; bock beer; double beer.

Bock'—chen, Böckchen, *n.* (—chens, *pl.* —chen) kid. —eln, *see* Bocken. —isch, *adv.* lecherous.

Bo'cken, *v.n.* (*aux.* h.) to be in heat; to plunge and throw out the hind legs, as a horse; to have a goat-like smell; to be refractory; to sulk.

Bod'den, *m.* (—s, *pl.* —) bay (*on the Baltic*) *e.g.* Greifswalder —, Jasmunder —.

Bo'den, *m.* (—s, *pl.* — *or* Böden) ground; soil; landed property; bottom; floor; footing; loft, garret; barn; crown (*of a hat; of an artichoke*); back (*of a violin, etc.*); ground (*of a texture*); cake (*of wax*); bed (*of a billiard table*); basis (*Anat., Bot., etc.*); eine Dose mit doppeltem —, a box with a false bottom; — fassen, to get a footing; einem — abgewinnen, to gain ground upon one; einen unter den — bringen, to bring a p. to his grave; einen — in ein Faß setzen, to head a cask; auf dem — schlafen, to sleep on the floor (= Fußboden); to sleep in the garret; Zimmer auf ebenem —, room on the ground-floor; zu — schlagen, to knock down; Fecht—, fencing-room; Fuß—, flooring, floor. *Comp.* —balken, *m.* joist. —beschaffenheit, *f.* condition of the soil, nature *or* quality of the soil. —blatt, *n.* outside leaf of tobacco. —blech, *n.* sheathing. —bohne, *f.* dwarf kidney bean. —bretter, *pl.* bottom boards; heading (*of casks*); laths (*of bedsteads*). —eule, *f.* barn-owl. —fenster, *n.* garret window. —fries, *m.* breech-moulding (*of a* cannon). —**geschoß**, *n.* ground-floor. —**has=pel**, *f.* windlass. —**hefe**, *f.* dregs, grounds. —**kammer**, *f.* garret. —**kredit**, *m.* loan on landed security. —**kunde**, *f.* science of soils. —**los**, *adj.* bottomless; enormous; baseless; **das —lose**, *n.* the bottomless deep; **er ist ein —loses Faß**, he is insatiable; he is a spendthrift. —**pumpe**, *f.* bilge-pump. —**rad**, *n.* main wheel (*Hor.*). —**satz**, *m.* dregs, grounds, sediment, residuum. —**ständig**, *adj.* receptacular, hypogynous; original. —**stein**, *m.* nether millstone. —**stück**, *n.* breech (*of a gun*); heading (*of a cask*). —**teig**, *m.* under-crust. —**thür**, *f.* garret-door. —**treppe**, *f.* garret-stairs. —**zins**, *m.* ground-rent; storage.

Bod'me—n, *v.a.* to head (*a cask*); to insure (*vessels*); to reseat (*trousers*); to floor, plank (*a room*). —**rei'**, *f.* bottomry; **Geld auf —rei austhun (aufnehmen)**, to advance (raise) money on bottomry. *Comp.* —**rei'=brief**, *m.* bottomry-bond. —**rei'=geber**, (—**rei'=nehmer**,) *m.* advancer (raiser) of money on bottomry bonds.

Bo'fist, *m.* (—**es**, *pl.* —**e**) puff-ball (*Bot.*).

Bog, Bö'ge, *imperf. indic. & subj. of* **biegen**.

Bo'gen, *m.* (—**s**, *pl.* —, [**Bögen**]) bow; bend; curve; arc; arch, vault; bow (*of a fiddle; of a saddle; of a window, etc.*); port (*Bill.*); bind, tie (*Mus.*); sheet (*of paper*); **ein bedruckter —**, a printed sheet; **ein gedrückter —**, an elliptical arch; **schiefer —**, sloping arch; **fliegender —**, flying buttress; **einen — spannen**, to bend, draw a bow; **innerer —**, intrados; **äußerer —**, extrados; **einen — schlagen**, to describe a curve; **in Bausch und —**, in the lump; **der Fluß macht einen —**, the river makes a bend; **der — zwischen den Mittelpunkten**, amplitude (*Astr.*); **Flitz —**, boy's bow; **Friedens—**, **Regen—**, rainbow. —**er**, **Bogner**, *m.* bow-maker, bowyer (*obs.*). *Comp.* —**bezeichnung**, *f.* signature, sheetmark (*Typ.*). —**bohrer**, *m.* bow-drill. —**dach**, *n.* vaulted roof. —**fläche**, *f.* convexity. —**förmig**, *adj.* arched. —**form**, *f.* folio. —**führung**, *f.* way of bowing, style of bowing (*Mus.*). —**gang**, *m.* arcade. —**gerüst**, *n.* centre timber of an arch. —**größe**, *f. see* —**form**. —**halle**, *f.* portico. —**instrumente**, *pl.* all instruments played with a bow (*Mus.*). —**linie**, *f.* curve. —**rolle**, *f.* lintel of the door-post. —**säge**, *f.* bow-saw. —**schießen**, *n.* archery; —**schieß=gesellschaft**, toxophilite association, archery club. —**schluß**, *m.* key-stone. —**schreiber**, *m.* writer by the sheet; penny-a-liner. —**schuß**, *m.* shot from a bow; curved fire, indirect shot (*Art.*); distance *or* range of a bow shot. —**schütze**, *m.* archer. —**schützin**, *f.* archeress. —**sehne**, *f.* bow-string; chord of a segment. —**seite**, *f.* folio-page. —**sprung**, *m.* curvet (*of a horse*). —**strich**, *m.* stroke of the bow (*Mus.*); style of bowing (*Mus.*). —**thür**, *f.* vaulted door. —**weise**, *adv.* in sheets, by the sheet; archwise. —**zahl**, *f.* number of sheets (*of a book*). —**zirkel**, *m.* bow-compasses, callipers.

Bö'g—en, *see* **Bogen**. —**ig**, *adj.* curved; sinuous.

Boh'le, *f.* (*pl.* —**n**) plank, thick board; madrier (*Fort.*); bowl. *Comp.* —**n=decke**, *f.* raftered ceiling. —**n=säge**, *f.* pit-saw.

Boh'len, *v.a.* to plank, to cover with thick planks.

Böhn'chen, *n.* (—**s**, *pl.* —) little bean.

Boh'ne, *f.* (*pl.* —**n**) bean; mark in a horse's teeth; **Feld—**, horse-bean, field-bean; **Sau—**, broad bean; **türkische —**, French bean, scarlet runner; **weiße —n**, haricot beans; **blaue —**, blue pill, bullet; **keine — wert**, not worth a straw. *Comp.* —**n=baum**, *m.* cytisus. —**n=erz**, *n.* pea ore, granular iron ore. —**n=kaper**, *f.* wild caper. —**n=klee**, *m.* stinking bean-trefoil. —**n=könig**, *m.* Twelfth Night's king. —**n=kuchen**, *m.* Twelfth-Night cake. —**n=schuß**, *m.* mark on a horse's teeth by which its age can be known. —**n=stange**, *f.*, —**n=stecken**, *m.* bean-stick; **lange —nstange**, a person as long as a lamp-post. —**n=stroh**, *n.* bean straw; **grob wie —nstroh**, extremely rude, coarse.

Boh'n—e(r)n, *v.a.* to wax (*a floor, etc.*); to rub, polish (*furniture, etc.*). —**er**, *m.* (—**ers**, *pl.* —**er**), —**erin**, *f.* polisher. *Comp.* —**axt**, *f.* smoothing axe. —**bürste**, *f.* scrubbing-brush. —**lappen**, *m.* cloth for polishing. —**zeug**, *n.* polishing-utensils.

Böhn'hase, *m.* (—**n**, *pl.* —**n**) bungler, botcher; interloper; unlicensed broker.

Bohr, *m.* (—**es**, *pl.* —**e**) auger. *Comp.* —**ahle**, *f.* bradawl. —**egge**, *f.* drill-harrow. —**eisen**, *n.* bit (*of bits and brace*). —**käfer**, *m.* death-watch (*Ent.*). —**kratze**, *f.* the metal taken out of a cannon by boring. —**krätzer**, *m.* scoop (*Min.*). —**loch**, *n.* bored hole, gimlet-hole. —**löffel**, *m.* scouring-bit. —**maschine**, *f.* boring machine. —**muschel**, *f.* Pholas. —**pflug**, *m.* drill-plough. —**pfriem**, *m.* priming-spike (*Artil.*). —**platte**, —**scheibe**, *f.* breast-plate (*of a drill*). —**spitze**, *f.* bit. —**stange**, *f.* boring rod, sinker. —**winde**, *f.* jack (*Art.*). —**wurm**, *m.* ship's borer (*Teredo*). —**zeug**, *n.* boring tools.

Boh'r—en, *v.* I. *a.* to pierce, bore, drill; **ein Schiff in den Grund —en**, to sink a vessel; **das Brett —en, wo es am dünnsten ist**, to pick out the easiest work, to shun trouble; **er mag keine harten Bretter bohren**, he likes to take the easiest work (*prov.*). II. *n.* (*aux.* **h.**) to burrow, bore; to harass. —**er**, *m.* (—**ers**, *pl.* —**er**) borer; bore, gimlet, piercer; **großer —er**, auger; **halbrunder —er**, cylinder-bit; **Drill—er**, drill; **Dreh—er**, hand-brace; **Meißel—er**, auger; **Nagel—er**, gimlet; **Schädel—er**, trephine, perforator (*Surg.*); **Zwick—er**, gimlet, bradawl.

Boi, Boj, Boy, *m.* (—**es**, *pl.* —**e**) baize. —**en**, *adj.* baize.

Boi'salz, *n.* bay-salt.

Bo'je, *f.* (*pl.* —**n**) buoy; **die — steht blind**, the buoy is not visible; **die — wacht**, the buoy is floating. —**r**, *m.* (—**rs**, *pl.* —**r**) vessel for laying buoys; small single-masted Dutch vessel. *Comp.* —**n=kasten**, *m.* caisson. —(**n**)=**reep**, *n.*, —(**n**)=**leine**, *f.*, —(**n**)=**seil**, *n.* buoy-rope.

=**bold** (*a suffix forming nouns, cp. Engl.* -ard, *e.g.* **Trunken—**, drunkard; **Rauf—**, brawler).

Bo'leine, *f.* (*pl.* —**n**) bowline (*Naut.*).

Bol'l—e, *f.* (*pl.* —**en**) ball; bulb; round capsule; onion. —**ig**, *adj.* swollen; bulbous. *Comp.* —**en=gewächs**, *n.* bulbaceous plant.

Böl'ler, *m.* (—**s**, *pl.* —) small mortar *or* cannon.

Boll'werk, *n.* (—(**e**)**s**, *pl.* —**e**) bulwark; bastion, rampart. *Comp.* —**s=wehre**, *f.* counter-guard (*Fort.*). —**s=turm**, *m.* tower bastion.

Bologne'ser, *m.* (—**s**, *pl.* —) (— **Hündchen**) lap-dog; **der kurzhaarige —**, King Charles' dog.

Bo'lus, *m.* bole, coarse red pigment; bolus.

Bolz, *m.* (—**es**, *pl.* —**e**), —**en**, *m.* (—**ens**, *pl.* —**en**) bolt; crossbow bolt *or* arrow; rivet; pin, peg (*of wood, iron, etc.*); heater of an iron; quarrying wedge; **einem alles zu —en drehen**, to misinterpret all one says; **die —en verschießen, die ein anderer gedreht hat**, to be another's cat's-paw. *Comp.* —**en=blech**, *n.* washer; rosette (*Artil.*). —**en=büchse**, *f.* air-gun. —**en=ring**, *m.* shackle. —**en=schloß**, *n.* bar-lock, cylindrical padlock. —(**en**)=**gerade**, *adj. & adv.* bolt upright.

Bombar'd—e, *f.* (*pl.* —**en**) (*obsol.*) great gun, bombard; bombardoon, ancient musical wind-instrument. —**e=me'nt**, *n.* (—**eme'nts**, *pl.* —**eme'nts**) bombardment, shelling. —**ie'r**, *m.* (—**ie'rs**, *pl.* —**ie're**) bombardier.

Bombardie'r—en, *v.a.* to bombard, to shell. —**ung**, *f.* bombardment, shelling. *Comp.* —**schiff**, *n.* gunboat, floating battery. —**käfer**, *m.* brachinus, bombardier-beetle (*Ent.*).

Bombasi'n, *m.* (—**es**) bombazin(e) (*Comm.*).

Bom'bast, *m.* (*also pr.* **Bomba'st**) bombast, fustian; big talk; high-flown language. —**isch**, *adj.* bombastic(al), fustian, inflated, highflown; —**e Rede**, pompous speech, high words.

Bom'be, *f.* (*pl.* —**n**) bomb-shell; bomb; **mit —n beschießen**, to bombard, to shell. *Comp.* —**n=fest**, *adj.* bomb-proof, quite safe; quite certain (*coll.*); **das steht —nfest**, that is quite certain (*fam.*) —**n=kessel**, *m.* mortar. —**n=kiste**, *f.* caisson. —**n=sicher**, *see* —**n=fest**. —**n=werfen**, *n.* shelling; shell-practice. —**n=zünder**, *m.* fuse.

Bom'mel, *f.* (*pl.* —**n**) tassel.

Bon, *m.* (*pl.* —**s**) check, draft, order.

Bonbo'n, *n.* (*pl.* —**s**) bonbon, sweetmeat, sugar-plum.

Bonifizie'ren, *v.a.* to make good, indemnify (*Comm.*).

Bonitä't, *f.* good quality (*of an article*); solvency. credit, reliability (*of a firm*).

Bonitie'ren, *v.a.* to value, to rate, to tax.

Bon'ne, *f.* (dry) nurse; nursery governess.

Bon'ze, *m.* bonze; black-coat, shaveling (*fam.*); bigwig (*hum.*).

Boot, *n.* (—**es**, *pl.* —**e** & **Böte**) boat; **das große** —, the long boat; **Fähr**—, ferry boat; **Rettungs**—, life boat; **mit einem — fahren**, to ride in a boat; **das — aussetzen**, to lower the boat; **das —fahren**, boating. *Comp.* —**s=führer**, —**s=knecht**, *m.* boatman, sailor. —**s=haken**, *m.* boat-hook; species of silurus. —**s=klampen**, *pl.* chocks (*Naut.*). —**s=leute**, *pl.* sailors, crew. —**s=mann**, *m.* boatman; **Hoch—smann**, boatswain. —**s=seil**, —**s=tau**, *n.* painter (*Naut.*).

Bor, **Bo'rax**, *m.* (—**es**) borax. *Comp.* —**sauer**, *adj.* boracic; —**saures Salz**, borate. —**säure**, *f.* boracic acid.

Bord, *m.* (—**es**, *pl.* —**e**) board, ship-board; edge, border, rim; edge (*of a coin*); shore (*of the sea*); **an** —, aboard of, on board; — **an** —, alongside, yardarm and yardarm; **über** —, overboard, above board; **frei an** —, put on board; **ein Schiff von niedrigem —e**, a vessel deep in the water; **Back** —, larboard; **Steuer** —, starboard; **Luv** —, weatherside. *Comp.* —**leiste**, *f.* (gun)wale. —**linie**, *f.* floating-line, water-line.

Bör'de, *f.* fertile plain (*bordering on a river*) (*dial.*).

Borde'll, *n.* (—**s**, *pl.* —**e**) brothel, bawdy house.

Bor'd—en, *v.a.* to board (*a ship*); *see* **Entern**; to edge, border. —**ie'ren**, *v.a.* to trim, edge, border. —**ie'rung**, *f.* border, edging.

Borea'lisch, *adj.* & *adv.* boreal, northern.

Borg, *m.* (—**es**, *pl.* —**e**) borrowing; credit, trust; preventer, spare (*Naut.*); **auf** —, on credit, on tick (*fam.*). *Comp.* —**brassen**, *pl.* preventer-braces (*Naut.*). —**rahe**, *f.* spare-yard (*Naut.*). —(**s**)=**weise**, *adv.* on credit.

Bor'g—en, *v.a.* to borrow; to take on credit; to lend; to give on trust; —**en macht Sorgen**, he who goes borrowing, goes sorrowing (*prov.*). **geborgt**, *p.p.* & *adj.* borrowed; fictitious, false. —**er**, *m.* (—**ers**, *pl.* —**er**) borrower.

Bor'k—e, *f.* (*pl.* —**en**) bark, rind; scab. —**ig**, *adj.* barky; scabby.

Born, *m.* (—**es**, *pl.* —**e**) spring, well, fountain (*high style*); salt-pit. —**haft**, —**ig**, *adj.* watery.

Bornie'rt, *adj.* narrow-minded, ignorant, stupid. —**heit**, *f.* narrow-mindedness.

Borra'go, **Bor'retsch**, *m.* borago (*Bot.*).

Bör'se, *f.* (*pl.* —**n**) purse; exchange; **auf der** —, on 'change; **die tonangebende** —, the standard market. *Comp.* —**n=behörde**, *f.* exchange-committee. —**n=bericht**, *m.* marked report, list of exchange, stock-list. —**n=blatt**, *n.* exchange list; commercial newspaper. —**n=fähig**, *adj.* negotiable; —**nfähige Papiere**, marketable stocks. —**n=gericht**, *f.* commercial board. —**n=gerücht**, *n.* stock-jobbing rumour; hoax. —**n=geschäfte**, *pl.* operations in the stocks. —**n=halle**, *f.* exchange. —**n=kurs**, *m.* rate of exchange. —**n=makler**, *m.* stock-broker. —**n=mäßig**, *adj.* in conformity with the exchange regulations. —**n=ordnung**, *f.* exchange regulation. —**n=papiere**, *pl.* stocks. —**n=schacher**, *m.*, —**n=spiel**, *n.* stock-jobbing. —**n=schwindler**, *m.* stock-adventurer. —**n=spieler**, *m.* stock-jobber. —**n=sprache**, *f.* stock-exchange slang. —**n=zettel**, *m.* stock-list.

Borst, *impf. indic. of* **bersten**.

Borst, *m.* (—**es**, *pl.* —**e**) crack, cleft, chink, burst; **einen — bekommen**, to crack.

Bör'ste, (**Bär'ste**,) *impf. subj. of* **bersten**.

Bor'st—e, *f.* (*pl.* —**en**) bristles; seta (*Bot.*). —**ig**, *adj.* bristly; curly; setaceous (*Bot.*). *Comp.* —**en=artig**, *adj.* bristly; setaceous. —**en=binse**, *f.* bent. —**en=füßler**, *m.* cirripede. —**en=gras**, *n.* sea-reed, bent. —(**en**)=**pinsel**, *m.* bristle paint-brush. —**wisch**, *m.* hearth-brush.

Bor'sten, *v.r.* to bristle up; to stand on end.

Bort, *n.* (**Bört**, *n. dial.*) (—**es**, *pl.* —**e**) shelf, board; **Bücher**—, book-shelf. —**stein**, *m.* edge-stone, border-stone.

Bor'te, *f.* (*pl.* —**n**) edge, border; galloon; trimming; selvage; **goldene** —, gold lace. *Comp.* —**n=arbeit**, *f.* fringe-making, lace-making. —**n=macher**, *m.* lace-make, fringe-maker; ribbon-weaver.

Bor'ten, *v.a.* to trim, to braid (*a dress, etc.*).

Bös, **Bö's—e**, *adj.* & *adv.* bad; ill; evil; wicked; angry; sore; cross, ill-tempered; malicious; **einen —en Ruf haben**, to have a bad reputation; —**e Geister**, evil spirits; **ein —es Weib**, a shrew; **er war sehr —e auf mich** (**über etwas**), he was very angry with me (at *or* about a thing); **sich —e stellen**, to feign anger; —**e Augen**, sore eyes, evil eyes; —**er Blick**, evil eye; **er meinte es nicht —e**, he meant no harm; —**e Zeiten**, bad times, hard times; **das —e Wesen**, epilepsy; **der —e Hund**, the snappish dog; **das —e Ding**, whitlow; **der —e**, the evil one, the foul fiend, the Devil; **das —e**, evil, a sore, mischief; **Gutes mit —em vergelten**, to return evil for good; **damit sieht es — aus**, the look-out for it is bad, it is in a bad way. —**lich**, *adj.* & *adv.* malicious; —**liche Verlassung**, wilful desertion (*Law*). *Comp.* —**artig**, *adj.* malicious, malevolent; virulent (*fevers, etc.*); infectious; wild, vicious; bad, wicked. —**e=wicht**, *m.* (—**ewichts**, *pl.* —**ewichte**, —**ewichter**) scamp, miscreant, scoundrel. —**willig**, *adj.* malevolent.

Bö'sch—en, *v.a.* to slope; to escarp (*Fort.*). —**ung**, *f.* slope; scarp (*Fort.*).

Bos'—haft, *adj.* & *adv.* malicious, ill-intentioned; malignant; mischievous; angry. —**haftigkeit**, *f.* malice, malignity. —**heit**, *f.* malice, spite; malignity; ill-nature; naughtiness (*of a child*); ill-temper; crossness.

Bo'ßel, **Bos'sel** (**Boß=kugel**), *f.* bowl (*at nine pins*). —**n**, *v.n.* (*aux.* **h.**) to play at nine pins.

Bos's—eln, —(**el**)**ie'ren**, *v.a.* & *n.* (*aux.* **h.**) to emboss (*in wax*). *Comp.* —**el=arbeit**, *f.* manufacture of toys, *etc.*; nick-nack. —**ie'r=arbeit**,

f. embossing. —**ie'r=bein,** *n.* embossing stick. —**ie'r=wachs,** *n.* modelling-wax.
Bot, *impf. indic. of* **bieten.**
Bota'n—ik, *f.* botany. —**iker,** *m.* botanist, student *or* teacher of botany. —**isch,** *adj. & adv.* botanical. —**isie'ren,** *v.n.* (*aux.* **h.**) to botanize. *Comp.* —**isie'r=trommel,** *f.* plant-box.
Bo't—e, *m.* (—**en,** *pl.* —**en**) messenger; postman, carrier; **ein eigener —e,** express messenger; **der hinkende —e,** the lame post, the invalid newsmonger; **ein reitender —e,** an estafette, courier; —**en laufen,** to go on messages, to run on errands. —**in,** *f.* female messenger *or* carrier. —**schaft,** *f.* (*pl.* —**schaften**) message, errand; news, intelligence, embassy; **frohe —schaft,** joyful tidings; evangelium, gospel; **eine —schaft besorgen,** to take a message; **eine —schaft ausrichten,** to deliver a message. —**schafter,** *m.* (—**schafters,** *pl.* —**schafter**) ambassador; **der päpstliche —schafter,** nuncio, legate. —**schafterin,** *f.* ambassadress. —**schaftlich,** *adj. & adv.* in the form of a message. —**schafts=sekretär,** *m.* secretary to the ambassador, at the embassy *or* legation. *Comp.* —**en=amt,** *n.* despatch office; office for commissionnaires. —**en=frau,** *f.* female messenger. —**en=gang,** *m.* errand; the distance a messenger goes. —**en=läufer,** *m.* errand-boy; carrier. —**en=lohn,** *m. & n.* messenger's fee. —**en=meister,** *m.* overseer of the messengers (*in German post-offices*); tip-staff. —**en=schiff,** *n.* packet boat; despatch boat. —**en=schild,** *n.* porter's badge.
Bö'te, *impf. subj. of* **bieten.**
Bot'mäßig, *adj.* subject (*as a country*), subordinate, obedient. —**keit,** *f.* dominion, sway.
Bött'cher (Böt'ticher), *m.* (—**s,** *pl.* —) cooper. —**ei',** *f.* trade *or* workshop of a cooper. *Comp.* —**beil,** *n.* cooper's adze. —**holz,** *n.* staves. —**woche,** *f.* first week of the Leipsic fair.
Bot'tich, *m.* (—**es,** *pl.* —**e**) coop, tub, vat, barrel.
Bouillo'n, *f.* clear soup *or* broth; beef-tea. *Comp.* —**tafel,** *f.* portable soup; beef-tea tablet. —**topf,** *m.* pot-au-feu.
Bouque't, *n.* (—**s,** *pl.* —**e,** —**s**) bouquet.
Bousso'le, *f.* (*pl.* —**n**) box-compass.
Bow'le, *f.* (*pl.* —**n**) bowl; spiced wine, cup; **Punsch—,** bowl of punch; **Rotwein—,** claret-cup; **eine — brauen,** to make a bowl.
Bo'xen, *v.n. & r.* to box.
Boy, *see* **Boi.**
Boycottie'r—en, *v.a.* to boycott. —**ung,** *f.* boycotting.
Brach (*pron.* **Brach**), *impf. ind. of* **brechen.**
Brach (*pron.* **Bräch**), *adj. & adv.* fallow, unploughed, untilled. —**e,** *f.* fallow ground, fallowness; state *or* time of rest (*agric.*). *Comp.* —**acker,** *m.* fallow-land. —**distel,** *f.* field-eryngo. —**drossel,** *f.* wryneck (*Orn.*). —**flur,** *f.* tract of fallow-land. —**henne,** *f.* golden plover. —**huhn,** *n. see* —**vogel.** —**jahr,** *n.* year of rest; year of jubilee (*B.*). —**käfer,** *m.* fern beetle, dung beetle. —**läufer,** *m.,* —**lerche,** *f.* field lark. —**männchen,** *n.* mushroom. —**monat,** *m.* June. —**schnepfe,** *f.* curlew. —**vogel,** *m.* curlew; **der kleine —vogel,** dotterel; **der große —vogel,** plover, stone curlew. —**zeit,** *f.* fallowing time.
Brä'che, *impf. subj. of* **brechen.**
Bra'chen, *v.a.* to plough up fallow land; to clear (*a vineyard*) of weeds; to dress (*flax*); to plough and seed (*a pond from which the water has been drawn*).
Brack, *n. & m.* (—**es,** *pl.* —**e**) refuse. —**en,** *v.a.* to sort out (*refuse*); to beat (*flax*). —**er,** *m.* (—**ers,** *pl.* —**er**) sorter. —**ig,** *adj.* brackish. *Comp.* —**wasser,** *n.* brackish water.
Bra'cke, *m.* (—**n,** *pl.* —**n**), hound, setter, pointer.
Brä'gen, *n.* brains. *Comp.* —**wurst,** *f.* pig's-brain sausage.
Brah'me, Brah'ne, *f.* (*pl.* —**n**) border, brim.
Bräh'nen, *v.n.* (*aux.* **h.**) to brim (*of the sow*).
Bram, *m.* (—**es,** *pl.* —**e**) awl, punch; broom, gorse.
Bram— (*in comp.*); —**segel,** *n.* (**das große**) maintop-gallant sail. —**stenge,** *f.* top-gallant mast.
Bramar'bas, *m.* (—(**s**)**es,** *pl.* —(**s**)**e**) braggart. —(**s**)**ie'ren,** *v.n.* to bluster, swagger, hector, draw the long bow.
Brä'me, *f.* brim, edge, border; (*fur*) trimming; hedge, shrubs, *etc.*, as inclosure of a field.
Bran'che, *f.* (*pl.* —**n**), branch, line, department.
Brand, *m.* (—**es,** *pl.* **Brände**) burning; fire, conflagration; fire-brand; gangrene, mortification, sphacelation; mildew; blight; brand (*on cattle*); burn; scald; batch, burning; baking (*of bricks, etc.*); cauterization; mark *or* name burned into a box, *etc.*; particles of burnt powder, *etc.* left in a gun after firing; fuse (*Artil.*); ardour; metal-refining; intoxication (*sl.*); **in — geraten** *or* **kommen,** to take *or* catch fire, to kindle; **in — setzen** *or* **stecken,** to set on fire; **in — stehen,** to be on fire; **der kalte —,** mortification (*of the flesh*); sphacelus; **der heiße —,** gangrene; **mit — und Mord,** with fire and sword; **einen — haben,** to be tipsy (*sl.*); — **im Getreide,** heating of grain; *as the first part of compounds often:* fire-, *sometimes:* brown-. —**er,** *m.* (—**ers,** *pl.* —**er**) (= —**fuchs**) fire-ship; fuse. —**icht,** *adj.* tasting, smelling as if burnt. —**ig,** *adj.* blasted, blighted, gangrenous. —**riechen** *or* —**schmecken,** to have a smell *or* taste of burning. *Comp.* —**ader,** *f.* crural vein. —**beule,** *f.* carbuncle (*Med.*). —**blase,** *f.* blister. —**blatter,** *f.* scar. —**brief,** *m.* official attestation of loss by fire; threatening (*incendiary*) letter. —**direktor,** *m.* commander of the fire-brigade. —**eimer,** *m.* fire-bucket. —**eisen,** *n.* branding-iron. —**ente,** *f.* sheldrake. —**erz,** *n.* bituminous marl. —**eule,** *f.* screech owl. —**fackel,** *f.* incendiary torch, fire brand; —**fackel des Krieges,** torch of war. —**fest,** *adj.* fire-proof. —**fieber,** *n.* inflammatory fever. —**fleck,** *m.* barren piece of land; *see* —**flecken.** —**flecken,** *m.* mark of a burn. —**fluß,** *m.* lava. —**fuchs,** *m.* brant-fox; sorrel horse; freshman in the second semester *or* half. —**gans,** *f.* brent-goose. —**gasse,** *f.* space between houses. —**glocke,** *f.* fire-bell. —**gold,** *n.* refined gold. —**haken,** *m.* chimney-hook. —**kasse,** *f.* fire-insurance-office. —**korb,** *m.* fire-guard. —**korn,** *n.* mildewed corn. —**kugel,** *f.* fire-ball, bomb. —**läden,** *pl.* iron window shutters. —**leger,** *m.* incendiary. —**legung,** *f.* arson. —**leiter,** *f.* fire-ladder. —**loch,** *n.* touch-hole. —**mal,** —**mark,** *n.* scar from burning; brand (*on a criminal, on a box, etc.*); stigma. —**malen,** —**marken,** *v.a.* to brand, stigmatize. —**maschine,** *f.* infernal machine. —**mauer,** *f.* fire-proof wall, party-wall. —**maus,** *f.* field-mouse. —**mehl,** *n.* flour of blighted corn. —**meise,** *f.* coal-titmouse. —**mittel,** *n.* remedy for burns. —**öl,** *n.* empyreumatic oil. —**opfer,** *n.* burnt-offering. —**pfahl,** *m.* stake. —**pfeil,** *m.* fire-bolt. —**probe,** *m.* assay. —**rakete,** *f.* congreve rocket, fire-rocket. —**rohr,** *n.* hose (*of fire engine*). —**röhre,** *f.* train, fuse. —**säure,** *f.* pyroligneous acid. —**schaden,** *m.* damage caused by fire. —**schatzen,** *v.a.* to lay under contribution (*in time of war*); to ravage. —**schatzung,** *f.* extortion, ravages. —**schiefer,** *m.* bituminous schist. —**schiff,** *n.* fire-ship. —**schimmel,** *m.* flea-bitten gray horse. —**silber,** *n.* refined silver. —**sohle,** *f.* first *or* inner sole. —**stätte,** —**stelle,** *f.* scene of a conflagration. —**stein,** *m.* brick. —**stifter,** *m.* incendiary. —**stiftung,** *f.* arson. —**thür,** *f.* fire-proof door. —**versicherung,** *f.* fire-insurance. —

wache, *f.* fire-watch; guard-ship. **—wunde**, *f.* burn; scald. **—zeichen**, *n.* brand, mark of burning; beacon fire; sign of fire. **—zeug**, *n.* the composition of which bombs, shells, *etc.*, are made; tinder. **—ziegel**, *m.* fire-brick.

Bran'd—en, *v.a.* to break, to surge (*of waves*). **—ung**, *f.* seething of waves, breakers; surf.

Brann'te, *impf.* of **brennen**.

Brannt'wein, *m.* (—s, *pl.* —e) brandy, gin, spirits. *Comp.* **—blase**, *f.* still. **—brenner**, *m.* distiller. **—brennerei'**, *f.* distillery. **—geist**, *m.* spirits of wine, alcohol. **—nase**, *f.* bottle-nose (*coll.*). **—schenke**, *f.* gin shop. **—wage**, *f.* alcohol(o)meter.

Braß, *m.* (—(ss)es) heap, lot, rubbish.

[1]**Bras'se**, *m.* (—n, *pl.* —n); **Bras'sen**, *m.* (—s, *pl.* —) carp, bream.

[2]**Bras'se**, *f.* (*pl.* —n) brace; **die großen —n**, the main braces.

Bras'sen, *v.a.* to brace; to trim (*the sails*); **dicht beim Winde gebraßt**, close-hauled.

Brät, Brätst, *3 & 2 ps. sing. pres. ind. of* **braten**.

Bra't—en, I. *reg. & ir.v.a. & n.* (*aux.* **h.**) to roast; (**im Ofen**) to bake; (**auf dem Roste**) to grill, broil; (**in der Pfanne**) to fry; (**am Spieße**) to roast on a spit; (**an der Sonne, in der Sonne**) to bake, to be scorched; **stark gebraten, durchgebraten**, well done; **wenig** (*or* **zu wenig**) **gebraten**, underdone; **zu sehr gebraten**, overdone. II. *subst.n.* roasting, *etc.* III. *m.* (—ens, *pl.* —en) roast meat, joint; **ein fetter —en**, a godsend, a windfall (*colloq.*); **den —en begießen**, to baste the meat; **den —en anstecken**, to spit the roast; **den —en riechen**, to get wind of a thing, to smell a rat (*colloq.*). *Comp.* **—apfel**, *m.* baked apple. **—bock**, *m.* meat-rack (*for an oven*). **—en=brühe**, *f.* juice of a roast, gravy. **—en=fett**, *n.* dripping. **—en=kleid**, *n.* best attire, dress suit (*coll.*). **—en=löffel**, *m.* basting ladle. **—en=meister**, *m.* ruler of the roast. **—en=rock**, *m.* festal garment, evening dress, dress coat (*coll.*). **—en=spicker**, *m.* larder; skewer. **—en=wender**, *m.* turn-spit; roasting-jack. **—fisch**, *m.* fried fish. **—häring**, *m.* red herring. **—kartoffeln**, *pl.* fried potatoes. **—pfanne**, *f.* frying-pan. **—röhre**, *f.* hot-hearth. **—rost**, *m.* gridiron, grill. **—schaufel**, *f.* basting-ladle. **—spieß**, *m.* spit. **—spille**, *f.* windlass (*Naut.*). **—wurst**, *f.* small (German) sausage (*fried or to be fried*).

Brät'ling, *m.* (—s, *pl.* —e) sprat; agaric.

Brat'sche, *f.* viola, tenor violin, alto-viola. *Comp.* **—n=stimme**, *f.* tenor part (*in string music*). **—n=spieler**, (**Bratschi'st**,) *m.* viola player, violist, player of the tenor violin.

Bra'tze, (**Pra'tze, Pra'tsche**,) *f.* paw (*dial.*).

Brau, *m. & n.* (—es, *pl.* —e) (*as the second part of compounds often* **Bräu**, *e. g.* **Löwenbräu, Spatenbräu**), brew. *Comp.* **—berechtigt**, *adj.* licensed to brew. **—bottich**, *m.* brewing-vat. **—gerechtigkeit**, *f.*, **—recht**, *n.* right of brewing. **—haus**, *n.* brewery. **—kessel**, *m.* brewing copper. **—knecht**, *m.* brewer's man. **—wesen**, *n.* brewing business, brewing concerns. **—wirt**, *m.* brewer.

Brauch, *m.* (—es, *pl.* **Bräuche**) use; usage, custom. **—bar**, *adj. & adv.* of use, useful; serviceable, available. **—barkeit**, *f.* utility, usefulness, serviceability; availability.

Brau'ch—en, *v.* I. *c.* to use, make use of; to want, require; to need; to wear; **Sie —en es nur zu sagen**, you only need to mention it; **es —t nur wenig Zeit**, it requires but a short time; **man —te es nicht**, it was not needed; **ich —e ihn nicht weiter**, I have no further occasion for him; **was —en Sie sich zu kümmern?** what need you care? **das könnt' ich grade —en**, that's just my luck; **er —t Chinin**, he uses, employs, takes, quinine; **der Arzt —te Opium**, the doctor administered opium; **man —t sich nicht zu wundern**, it is not to be wondered at; **er —t eine Brunnenkur**, he is taking the waters. II. *v. imp.* (*gen.*); **es —t keines Beweises**, no proof is required.

Bräuch'lich, *see* **Gebräuchlich**.

Brau'e, *f.* (*pl.* —n) brow, eyebrow.

Brau'—en, *v.a.* to brew. **—er**, *m.* (—ers, *pl.* —er) brewer. **—er=gilde**, *f.*, **—er=zunft**, *f.* brewers' guild. **—erei'**, *f.* (*pl.* —erei'en) brewery; brewer's trade.

Braun, *adj.* brown; tawny; **—es Pferd**, dun horse, bay horse; **die —e**, a girl of a dark complexion, brunette; **der —e**, bay horse. **—elle**, *f.* species of warbler. *Comp.* **—bleierz**, *n.* brown phosphate of lead. **—brennen**, *v.a.* to tan, sunburn. **—eisenstein**, *m.* brown iron-ore. **—gelb**, *adj.* bistre; **—gelbes Pferd**, sorrel horse. **—kalk**, *m.* brown spar. **—kehlchen**, *n.* whin-chat. **—kohl**, *m.* borecole. **—kohle**, *f.* brown coal; lignite. **—kohlen=haltig**, *adj.* lignitic. **—rot**, *n.* red ochre; *adj.* russy. **—schecke**, *m.* a piebald horse. **—scheckig**, *adj.* piebald. **—stein**, *m.* manganese. **—streifig**, *adj.* brown-streaked. **—wurz**, *f.* brown-wort; yellow fig-wort.

Brau'ne, *f. incorrectly for* **Braue**.

Bräu'n—e, *f.* brownness; quinsy; **entzündliche —e**, quinsy; **häutige —e**, croup. **—en**, *v.* I. *a.* to tan; to brown (*meat, etc.*). II. *r.* (*aux.* **h.**) to grow *or* become brown. **—lich**, *adj.* brownish.

Braus, *m.* (—(s)es) tumult; **in Saus und — leben**, to live riotously, in revelry, to lead a gay life, a life of enjoyment. **—(s)e**, *see* **Brause**.

Brau'se, *f.* effervescence; fermentation; (**—aufsatz**) rose (*of a watering-pot*); **in der — sein**, to be fermenting. *Comp.* **—bad**, *n.* douche. **—erde**, *f.* bituminous red clay. **—jahre**, *pl.* years of hot-headed youth. **—kopf, —wind**, *m.* blusterer, hot-headed fellow. **—pulver**, *n.* effervescent powder, Seidlitz powder. **—stein**, *m.* zeolite. **—wein**, *m.* sparkling wine.

Brau'sche, *f.* (*pl.* —n) bump (*from a bruise*).

Brau'sen, *v.n.* (*aux.* **h.**) to storm, rage (*as wind*); to bluster; to hum, buzz; to snort; to ferment; to effervesce; to roar, bellow; to be impetuous; to be furious; to water, to sprinkle; **die Ohren — mir**, I have a singing in my ears; **vor Zorn —d**, boiling with rage; **die —de Jugend**, impetuous, passionate youth.

Braut, *f.* (*pl.* **Bräute**) betrothed, affianced bride; intended, fiancée; bride (*only on the wedding day*); **sie ist —**, she is engaged, betrothed; **sie ist meines Freundes —**, she is engaged to my friend, she is the intended of my friend; **bitte grüßen Sie Ihr Fräulein —**, please remember me to your intended *or* to Miss X.; **des Himmels —**, bride of Jesus Christ; nun; **wer das Glück hat, führt die — heim**, fortune gains the bride, *or* the lucky man gains the fair lady (*prov.*); **— in Haaren**, small fennel-flower. **—schaft**, *f.* engagement. *Comp.* **—ausstattung**, *f.* trousseau. **—band**, *n.* wedding favour. **—bett**, *n.* bridal bed. **—führer**, *m.* best man. **—führerin**, *f.* bride's-maid. **—gemach**, *n.* bridal chamber, bride-chamber; nuptial apartment. **—geschenk**, *n.* nuptial present, wedding present. **—geschmeide**, *n.* bridal jewels. **—jungfer**, *f.* bridesmaid; species of butterfly. **—kammer**, *f.* bride-chamber, bridal chamber. **—kleid**, *n.* wedding-dress. **—kranz**, *m.* bridal garland. **—lauf**, *m.* running for the bride, wedding feast (*obs.*). **—leute**, *pl.* bride and bridegroom, betrothed pair, the betrothed. **—lied**, *n.* nuptial song. **—messe**, *f.* mass before the nuptial ceremony. **—nacht**, *f.* wedding-night. **—paar**, *n.* betrothed couple. **—ring**, *m.* ring exchanged on betrothal; wedding-ring. **—schatz**, *m.* dowry. **—schau**, *f.* lookout for a wife; **auf der —schau sein**, *or* **auf die —schau gehen**, to go a-wooing. **—schmuck**, *m.* nuptial ornaments; bridal attire. **—stand**, *m.* state of being betrothed, brideship. **—vater**, *m.* bride's father; **den —vater machen**, to give the bride away. **—werber**, *m.* one who asks a woman in marriage on behalf of another, match-maker. **—werbung**, *f.* match-making. **—zug**, *m.* bridal procession.

Bräu'tchen, *n.* little bride, beloved bride. **—igam**, *m.* (**—igams**, *pl.* **—igame**) affianced, husband elect; fiancé, intended; bridegroom (*on the wedding day only*); **bitte empfehlen Sie mich Ihrem Herrn —igam**, please give my kind regards to your intended, *or* to Mr. X. **—lich**, *adj. & adv.* bridal; bride-like.

Brav, *adj. & adv.* excellent; gallant; honest, upright; worthy; fine; clever; brave; good; **es ist sehr — von Ihnen, daß Sie**, it is very good of you to; **— gemacht!** well done! **er ist ein —er Kerl**, he is a right good fellow, he is a good sort (*coll.*); **ein —es Kind**, a good child. **—heit**, *f.* honesty, uprightness; excellence; bravery. **—o**, I. *m.* (**—os**, *pl.* **—os**) bravo. II. *int.* bravo! *Comp.* **—o=rufen**, *n.* shouts of bravo, cheers, loud acclamation. **—ou'r**, *f.* bravery. **—ou'r=arie**, *f.* bravura (*Mus.*).

Brech'bar, *adj. & adv.* fragile; brittle. **—keit**, *f.* fragility; brittleness; refrangibility.

Bre'che, *f.* brake (*techn.*).

Bre'ch—en, I. *ir.v.a.* to break; to break up *or* asunder; to pluck off, gather; to fracture (*a bone*); to quarry (*stones*); to break through, violate (*a promise, etc.*); to infringe (*an agreement*); to fold (*letters*); to refract, intercept (*a ray*); to crush (*malt, oats, etc.*); to blend, mix (*wine with water; colours, etc.*); to card (*wool*); to hackle (*flax, etc.*); to shed (*teeth*); to force (*a passage*); to break (*a fall, etc.*); to soften (*leather*); to neutralize (*acids*); **eine Treppe —en**, to make a landing-place in a staircase; **eine Sache der Länge nach —en**, to split a thing up; **nichts zu —en und zu beißen haben**, to be sadly pinched; to be starving; **etwas kurz und klein —en**, to break a th. into atoms; **einer Flasche den Hals —en**, to crack a bottle; **Bahn —en**, to force a passage, make a way; **die Ehe —en**, to commit adultery; **den Stab über einen Verbrecher —en**, to sentence a criminal to death; to put on the black cap; to condemn; **Not bricht Eisen**, necessity knows no law (*prov.*); **etwas übers Knie —en**, to do a th. abruptly; **einen Streit vom Zaune —en**, to pick a quarrel; **eine gebrochene Schreibart**, an abrupt style; **gebrochene Schrift**, old English type; **gebrochene Thür**, folding door; **gebrochener Accord**, arpeggio; **gebrochenes Dach**, curved roof; **gebrochene Zahl**, fraction (*Arith.*); **gebrochene Treppe**, staircase with a landing-place. II. *ir.v.r.* to break (*as waves*); to be interrupted; to be refracted; to change; to vomit, become sick; to change colour (*of wine*); to come to a crisis; **die Kälte bricht sich**, the cold is abating, *or* getting less severe; **das ist zum —en**, that is enough to make one sick. III. *ir.v.n.* (*aux.* **f.**) to break, snap off, come asunder; to break forth; to dawn (*as the day*); to become raptured; to become bankrupt; to cut through (*as teeth through the gums*); to appear, occur (*as ore in mines*); to scrape, scratch off; **in Flötzen —en**, to be found in strata; **das Herz bricht mir**, my heart is breaking; **gebrochenen Herzens**, broken-hearted; **die Augen brachen ihm**, his eyes grew dim, he died; **Thränen brachen ihr aus den Augen**, tears flowed from her eyes. IV. *subst.n.* violation; breach; breaking; beating, dressing (*of flax, etc.*). **—erlich, —erisch**, *adj. & adv.* sick, inclined to vomit (*coll.*). **—ung**, *f.* breaking; refraction; arpeggio (*Mus.*); breaking, *viz.*, certain changes of the radical vowel, owing to the influence of vowels in final syllables (*different from ord.* **Umlaut**; *Gramm.*). *Comp.* **—arznei**, *f.* emetic. **—betel**, *m.* ripping chisel. **—bohne**, *f.* common kidney-bean. **—eisen**, *n.* crowbar; lever. **—fieber**, *n.* fever attended with vomiting. **—fliege**, *f.* blue-bottle fly. **—hammer**, *m.* hammer used in copper mills, *or* for pulling down buildings, *etc.* **—kamm**, *m.* hackle; card (*for wool*). **—meißel**, *m.* ripping chisel. **—mittel**, *n.* emetic. **—mühle**, *f.* crushing mill. **—nuß**, *f.* vomit-nut. **—pulver**, *n.* emetic powder. **—punkt**, *m.* point of refraction, diffraction, *etc.* (*Opt.*). **—ruhr**, *f.* cholera. **—stange**, *f.* crowbar. **—ungs=ebene**, *f.* plan of refraction. **—wein**, *m.* antimonial wine. **—weinstein**, *m.* tartar emetic. **—wurz, —wurzel**, *f.* ipecacuanha. **—zeug**, *n.* implements for breaking open doors *or* pulling down houses.

Bredouil'le, *f.* mess, pickle, perplexity (*sl.*); **einem aus der — helfen**, to get one out of a scrape *or* out of a fine mess (*sl.*).

Brei, *m.* (**—es**) pap; pulp, mush; puree; **wie die Katze um den heißen — herumgehen**, to beat about the bush; **den — verschütten**, to spoil an affair; **viele Köche verderben den —**, (too) many cooks spoil the broth (*prov.*). **—icht**, *adj. & adv.* pappy, pulpy. *Comp.* **—artig**, *adj.* paplike. **—geschwulst**, *f.* atheroma (*Med.*). **—napf**, *m.* pap-boat. **—umschlag**, *m.* poultice. **—weich**, *adj.* pulpy.

Breit, *adj. & adv.* broad; wide; flat; **es ist so — als lang**, it is as broad as it is long, it is tantamount to; **weit und —**, far and wide; **4 Zoll —**, four inches wide; **8 Fuß lang und 5 —**, eight feet by five; **eine —gedrückte Nase**, a flattened nose; **sich — machen**, to give oneself airs, to swagger, to boast; **etwas — treten**, to dilate upon a th.; **einen zu einer Sache — schlagen**, to persuade, *or* bully, one to (do) a th.; **einen —en Pinsel führen**, to have a bold touch (*Paint.*); **—e Segel**, square sails; **sie erzählte mir ein Langes und —es darüber**, she spun a long yarn about it. **—e**, *f.* (*pl.* **—en**) breadth, width; gauge (*of a railway line*); measure (*of a column, Typ.*); flat of a sword; latitude; an open plain; **—e (der Darstellung)**, verbosity, prolixity; **der Flachs liegt auf der —e**, the flax is spread (*for drying*); **in die —e gehen**, to grow broader; to get stout. *Comp.* **—axt**, *f.*, **—beil**, *n.* broad-axe. **—beinig**, *adj. & adv.* straddle-legged; with outstretched legs. **—brüstig**, *adj.* broad-chested. **—eisen**, *n.* sculptor's chisel. **—en=grad**, *m.* degree of latitude. **—en=kreis**, *m.* circle of latitude; *pl.* **—en=kreise**, parallels of latitude. **—füßig**, *adj.* broad-footed. **—gestirnt**, *adj.* having a broad forehead, broad-fronted (*of oxen, etc.*). **—gold**, *n.* leaf-gold. **—hammer**, *m.* flattening hammer. **—köpfig**, *adj.* broad-headed; platicephalous. **—laub**, *n.* maple. **—nasig**, *adj.* flat-nosed, broad-nosed. **—randig**, *adj.* having a wide margin; broad-brimmed. **—schnabel**, *m.* broad-bill; wide-mouth; shoveller (*Orn.*). **—schnäbler**, *pl.* latirostrals. **—schulterig**, *adj.* broad-shouldered. **—spur**, *f.* wide gauge (*railw.*). **—spurig**, *adj.* having broad tracks, a wide gauge; (*fig.*) haughty, imperious; bombastic, fustian; **—spurig sein**, to give oneself airs, to be affected. **—spurig=keit,** *f.* haughtiness, importance. **—spur=maschine,** *f.* broad gauge engine (*Railw.*). **—würfig,** *adj.*; **—würfig säen,** to sow broadcast.

Brei'ten, *v.a.* to make broad; to spread out, widen; to flatten out; to square (*sails*).

Brem'mer=schacht, *m.* shaft the depth of one miner.

Brems—, *as the first part of compounds,* = **zum Bremsen,** serving as a brake, brake-. **—klotz,** *m.* brake-block. **—löffel,** *m.* brake-spoon (*Cycl.*). **—rad,** *n.* brake-wheel. **—schwengel,** *m.* handle of a brake. **—stange,** *f.* plunger-rod (*Cycl.*). **—vorrichtung,** *f.*, **—werk,** *n.* breaking gear, brake. **—wagen,** *m.* brake-van (*Railw.*)

[1]**Brem'se,** *f.* (*pl.* **—n**) horse-fly, gadfly.

[2]**Brem'se,** *f.* barnacle; brake, drag-wheel; carriage-lock.

Brem's—en, *v.a.* to put the twitch on (*a horse*); to put on the brake. **—er,** *m.* brakesman.

Brenn'bar, *adj.* that may be burnt; combustible; inflammable. **—keit,** *f.* inflammability; combustibility.

Bren'n—en, *ir.v.* I. *a.* to burn; to brand; to cauterize; to char (*wood*); to distil (*spirits*); to bake (*bricks*); to fire (*pottery*); to anneal; to sting (*as a nettle*); to roast (*coffee*); to bite (*the tongue, as pepper, etc.*); to bream (*a ship*); to fire (*a horse*); **der Sod —t mich,** I have heart-burn; **sich rein (weiß) —en wollen,** to try to exculpate oneself. II. *n.* (*aux.* **h.**) to burn; to be stinging; to smart; **mir —en die Augen,** my eyes smart; **vor Ungeduld —en,** to burn with impatience; **warten Sie, es —t doch nicht,** do wait, there is surely no such hurry; **es —t mir auf den Nägeln,** I am terribly pressed with work; **das Dorf —t lichterloh,** the village is ablaze *or* in flames; **es —t in der Stadt,** there is a fire in the town; **es —t!** fire! **sich —en,** to make a mistake, burn one's fingers. **—end,** *p. & adj.* burning; caustic; smarting; pungent; ardent; eager; fiery; **eine —ende Frage,** a burning (*or* important, vital, urgent) question. **—er,** *m.* (**—ers,** *pl.* **—er**) distiller; brickmaker; burner (*of a gas-lamp*); incendiary. **—erei',** *f.* distillery. *Comp.* **—blase,** *f.* alembic. **—bündel,** *pl.* faggots. **—docht,** *m.* (lamp)-wick. **—eisen,** *n.* curling iron; searing iron. **—glas,** *n.* burning-glass. **—haus,** *n.* distillery; bakehouse; foundry. **—holz,** *n.* firewood. **—kolben,** *m.* alembic, still. **—linie,** *f.* parabola; (cata)caustic curve. **—linse,** *f.* double convex lens. **—material,** *n.* (*pl.* **—materia'lien**) fuel. **—messer,** *n.* firing-iron (*Vet.*). **—mittel,** *n.* corrosive, caustic. **—nessel,** *f.* stinging nettle. **—ofen,** *m.* kiln. **—öl,** *n.* lamp oil. **—pfanne,** *f.* crucible, melting-pot. **—punkt,** *m.* focus. **—punkts=abstand,** *m.* focal distance. **—stoff,** *m.* inflammable matter; phlogiston. **—weite,** *f.* focal distance. **—ziegel,** *m.* kiln (*or* fire) brick.

Bren'z—eln, *v.n.* (*aux.* **h.**) to smell *or* taste of burning. **—lich, —lig,** *adj. & adv.* smelling *or* tasting of burning; empyreumatic; **eine —e Geschichte,** a suspicious matter (*coll.*).

Bre'sch—e, *f.* (*pl.* **—en**) (**gangbare —e,** practicable) breach; **—e schießen in,** to make a breach in; **sich in die —e stellen,** to stand in the gap. *Comp.* **—batterie,** *f.* battering-train.

Brest'haft, *adj.* invalid, infirm, broken (*obs.*).

Brett, *n.* (**—es,** *pl.* **—er**) board; plank; table; shelf; the stage; tray; salver; **schwarzes —,** blackboard, notice board (*Univ.*); **bei einem einen Stein im —e haben,** to have influence with a person, be in favour with him; **er kann durch ein — sehen,** he can see through a brick wall; **ein — vor dem Kopfe haben,** to be stupid, a blockhead; **sechs —er und zwei —chen,** the coffin; **er ist hoch am —e,** he is at the top of the tree; **an das — kommen,** to succeed; **vors — kommen,** to be brought to justice; **da ist die Welt mit —ern vernagelt,** there is the end of it, there nobody can get any further (*coll.*); **die —r,** the stage (*theatr.*); **ein Stück geht über die —er,** a play is acted; **mit —ern belegen,** to floor (*a room, etc.*); **mit —ern täfeln,** to panel. **—chen,** *n.* (**—chens,** *pl.* **—chen**) a little board. **—ern,** *adj.* made of boards, boarded. *Comp.* **—er=bude,** *f.* booth, slab hut; stall. **—er=dach,** *n.* shingle roof. **—er=verschlag,** *m.*, **—er=wand,** *f.* plank partition. **—er=werk,** *n.* planking. **—er=zaun,** *m.* palisade. **—mühle,** *f.* sawmill. **—nagel,** *m.* floor- *or* plank-nail. **—säge,** *f.* pit-saw, plank-saw. **—schneider,** *m.* sawyer. **—spiel,** *n.* any game played on a board, back-gammon, draughts, *etc.* **—stein,** *m.* man at draughts.

Bre've, *n.* (**—(e)s,** *pl.* **—s**) (*papal*) brief.

Brevia'rium, *n.*, **Brevie'r,** *n.* (**—s,** *pl.* **—e**) breviary.

Bre'zel, *f.* (*also spelt* **Bret'zel**) (*pl.* **—n**) cracknel, bun, cake twisted into the form of a double ring.

Brich, *imperat. of* **brechen; Brichst, Bricht,** *2 & 3 p. sing. pres. ind. of* **brechen.**

Bri'cke, *f.* (*pl.* **—n**) lamprey (*Icht.*).

Brief, *m.* (**—es,** *pl.* **—e**) letter; epistle; written document; charter; paper (*of pins*); bills, sellers, offers (*Comm.*); **— fürs Inland,** inland letter; **— fürs Ausland,** foreign letter; **unter — und Siegel,** under hand and seal; **ich gebe es dir mit — und Siegel,** I warrant you, I'll be bound for it; **— und Siegel über etwas haben,** to have in writing, to have a sure pledge; **— und Geld,** bills and money, asked and bid (*Comm.*); **Ihr werter —,** your favour (*Comm.*); **Wechsel—,** draft (*Comm.*); **eingeschriebener —,** registered letter. **—chen,** *n.* (**—chens,** *pl.* **—chen**) note, billet; a hasty line. **—lich,** *adj. & adv.* epistolary, written, by letter; **—licher Verkehr,** correspondence. **—schaften,** *pl.* letters, documents. *Comp.* **—abgabe,** *f.* delivery of letters. **—adel,** *m.* nobility obtained by letters patent. **—annahme,** *f.* reception of letters. **—aufgabe,** *f.* posting *or* mailing (*of*) a letter. **—aufgabe=stempel,** *m.* postmark. **—aufschrift,** *f.* address of a letter. **—ausgabe,** *f.* delivery (*of letters*) at the counter. **—beschwerer,** *m.* letter-weight. **—beutel,** *m.* letter-bag. **—bogen,** *m.* sheet of note paper. **—buch,** *n.* letter-book, copy-book (*C. L.*). **—concept,** *n.* rough copy *or* sketch of a letter. **—couvert,** *n.* envelope. **—einwurf,** *m.* letter-box. **—entwurf,** *m.* first draft of a letter. **—fach,** *n.* 'pigeon-hole,' letter rack. **—felleisen,** *n.* mail; despatch box. **—form,** *f.* form of a letter; epistolary style; **in —form brechen,** to fold as a letter. **—fracht,** *f.*, **—geld, —porto,** *n.* postage. **—geheimnis,** *n.* privacy of letters; **dies ist ein —geheimnis,** this is private and confidential; **das —geheimnis bewahren,** to keep the confidential communication private; **das —geheimnis verletzen,** to disclose the contents of a private letter. **—gewölbe,** *n.* archives. **—gut,** *n.* goods accompanying a bill of lading. **—inhaber,** *m.* holder of a bill of exchange. **—karte,** *f.* letter card; letter bill (*C. L.*). **—kasten,** *m.* letter box; pillar box; post box (*Americ.*). **—klammer,** *m.* letter-clip. **—kouvert,** *n.* envelope. **—mappe,** *f.* portfolio, writing-case. **—marke,** *f.* postage-stamp. **—marken=album,** *n.* postage-stamp album. **—marken=ausstellung,** *f.* philatelic exhibition. **—marken=kunde,** *f.* philately; **zur —markenkunde**

gehörig, philatelic. —marken=liebhaber, *m.* philatelist, stamp-collector. —marken=sammlung, *f.* collection of postage-stamps. —nadeln, *pl.* pins in a sheet. —oblate, *f.* letter-wafer. —papier, *n.* post paper, note paper. —post, *f.* mail, post. —post=tari'f, *m.* rate of postage, table of postage. —presse, *f.* copying press, letter press. —probe, *f.* sample inclosed in a letter. —sack, *m.* letter bag. —schalter, *m.* letter-box (*in a window or wall*). —schreibe=kunst, *f.* art of letter writing, epistolography. —schulden, *pl.* arrears of correspondence. —stecher, *m.* file. —steller, *m.* letter-writer; drawer of a bill; guide for letter writing, polite letter writer; —steller für Liebende, the love-letter writer's manual. —stil, *m.* epistolary style. —streicher, *m.* paper-knife. —tasche, *f.* pocket-book, portfolio. —taube, *f.* carrier pigeon. —taxe, *f.* (*rate of*) postage. —träger, *m.* postman. —umschlag, *m.* envelope. —wage, *f.* letter balance *or* scales. —wechsel, *m.* correspondence; sie steht mit ihnen in —wechsel, she keeps up a correspondence *or* corresponds with them; mit einem einen —wechsel anfangen (unterhalten), to open (carry on) a correspondence with a p.

Brie'fen, *v.a.* to (*transmit by*) mail.

Briet, Brie'te, *ind. & subj. imperf. of* **braten.**

Briga'd—e, *f.* (*pl.* —en) brigade. —ie'r, *m.* (—ie'rs, *pl.* —ie're) brigadier-general. *Comp.* —e=adjutant, *m.* aide-de-camp to a general of brigade.

Brigg, *f.* (—, *pl.* —s) brig.

Brike'tt, *n.* (*pl.* —s) briquette, pulverized coal baked in brickshaped blocks.

Brico'l—e, *f.* rebound of a ball (*Bill.*, *Artil.*). —ie'ren, *v.* I. *a.* to cross a ball into a pocket. II. *n.* (*aux.* h.) to play off the cushion (*Bill.*).

Brilla'nt, I. *adj.* brilliant. II. *m.* (—en, *pl.* —en), brilliant, diamond. —ie'ren, *v.a.* to cut facets on a diamond.

Bril'l—e, *f.* (*pl.* —en) (pair of) spectacles; glasses, goggles (*against dust, glaring sun*); lunette (*Fort.*); hole (*in a closet*); einem eine —e aufsetzen *or* —en verkaufen, to colour any one's spectacles, to influence a person; to hoax, deceive one; durch die schwarze —e sehen, to take a gloomy view of everything; durch eine fremde —e sehen, to see with another p.'s eyes. *Comp.* —en=bogen, *m.* bow of spectacles. —en=futteral, *n.* spectacle-case. —en=macher, *m.* optician. —en=ringe, *pl.* spectacle-frames. —en=schlange, *f.* hooded snake, cobra (*de capello*). —en=schleifer, *m.* spectacle-glass cutter, lens-grinder. —en=tragend, *adj.* spectacled. —en=werk, *n.* lunette. —en=zirkel, *m.* callipers.

Brillie'ren, *v.n.* to shine; to excel.

Brimbo'rium, *n.* trash, nonsense.

Brin'gen, *ir.v.a.* to bring, fetch; to convey; to conduct; to lead, induce, cause; to produce; to bring forth, to bear (*poet.*); Bescheid —, to bring word; eine Sache fertig —, to accomplish a thing; etwas zustande *or* zu Wege —, to accomplish a th., to bring about s.th.; es hoch *or* weit —, to succeed in a high degree; to get on in the world; er hat es mit der Musik sehr hoch hinaus gebracht, he has attained great proficiency in music; einem ein Ständchen —, to serenade a person; ein Opfer —, to make a sacrifice; er bringt es nicht weiter, he does not get on, can get no further; einem eine Gesundheit —, to drink to one's health; an den Bettelstab —, to reduce to beggary; an den Tag —, to bring to light; an sich —, to acquire, take possession of; an den Mann —, to dispose of; to find a husband for, marry; auf die Seite —, to put aside, out of the way, save; achieve (*obs.*); conceal; einen aufs äußerste —, to provoke s.o. greatly; einen auf etwas —, to put one in mind of, suggest something; (etwas) auf einen —, to lay to one's charge; auf die Beine —, to set up, to raise (*an army, etc.*); auf neue Rechnung —, to place to a new account; einen außer sich —, to enrage s.o.; einen dahin —, to induce, prevail upon, persuade one; es dahin —, to bring matters to such a pass; ich bringe es dir, I drink to you, I pledge you! (*obs. stud. sl.*); in Ordnung —, to arrange; in ein System —, to reduce to a system; ins Reine —, to bring to a conclusion; in Erfüllung —, to accomplish; eine Sache ins Gleiche —, to settle a thing; es brachte ihn von Sinnen, it drove him out of his senses; in Rechnung —, to take into account; in Gang —, to set a-going; in Verse —, to versify; in Verdacht —, to throw suspicion on; in schlechten Ruf —, to bring into bad repute; mit sich —, to bring along with; das bringt vielen Aufwand mit, this involves great expenditure; nach Hause —, to see *or* escort home; übers Herz —, to find in one's heart; ich kann es nicht über die Lippen —, I cannot bear to say it; Unglück über seine Familie —, to entail misery upon one's family; einen um etwas —, to cause one to lose something; ums Leben —, to murder. *refl.* to commit suicide; um die Ehre —, to dishonour; unter die Erde —, to bring down to the grave; unter die Leute —, to make known, circulate; unter Regeln —, to reduce to rules; vom Fuße —, to get off (*a boot, etc.*); etwas vor sich (*acc.*) —, to lay by, to save; einen zu sich —, to bring s.o. to one's senses; einen zu etwas —, to induce a p. to do a thing; es *or* sich zu etwas —, to bring oneself to, to contrive; einen zum Singen —, to induce one to sing; zum Schweigen —, to put to silence; zu Papier —, to put (down) on paper, reduce to writing; zu Fall —, to ruin; zur Vollkommenheit —, to bring to perfection; zur Sprache —, to start *or* to broach (*a subject*); wieder zusammen —, to rally (*troops*); meine Stellung bringt es mit sich, my position involves, renders it necessary.

Brin'ger, *m.* (—s, *pl.* —) causer; bearer, carrier.

Bri'se, *f.* (*pl.* —n) breeze, light wind.

Brit'sche, *see* **Pritsche.**

Brö'ckel—n, *v.a.r. & n.* (*aux.* h.) to crumble. —ig, (**Brö'cklig,**) *adj.* crumbly, friable; fragile; crisp.

Bro'cken, *m.* (—s, *pl.* —) crumb, fragment; (*pl.*) scraps. *See the Index of Names.*

Brod, *n.* *See* **Brot.**

Bro'deln, *v.n.* (*aux.* h.) to bubble, to boil up.

Broka't, *m.* (—es, *pl.* —e) brocade. —en, *adj.* brocade(d).

Bro'dem, Bro'den, *m.* (—s) steam, vapour, exhalation; foul air (*Min.*). *Comp.* —fang, *m.* ventilator-pipe.

Brodie'r—en, *v.a. & n.* to embroider. —ung, *f.* embroidery.

Brohk, Brook, *m.* breeching (*of a gun*).

Broi'hahn, *m.* (—s) light, pale and sweet beer made of wheat (*northwest of Germany*).

Brom, *n.* (—s) bromine. —kalium, *n.* bromide of potassium. —wasserstoff=säure, *f.* hydrobromic acid.

Brom'beer—e (*short* **o**), *f.* (*pl.* —en) blackberry; so gemein wie —en, as plentiful as blackberries; —en suchen, to go blackberrying. *Comp.* —falter, *m.* green butterfly. —strauch, *m.* bramble, blackberry bush.

Bromi'd, *n.* (—s) bromide.

Bronch—ia'l, (—als) *adj.* bronchial. —ien, *pl.* (*pron.* Bron'chien) bronchia. —i'tis, *f.* bronchitis.

Bronn, *m.* (—(e)s, *pl.* —en); —en, *m.* (—ens, *pl.* —en) spring, well, fountain (*high style*).

Bron'z—e, *f.* bronze, brass. —**en**, *adj.* made of bronze. —**ie'ren**, *v.a.* to bronze.

Bro'sam, *m.* & *n.* (—(e)s, *pl.* —e); —**e**, *f.* (—e, *pl.* —en) (*dimin.* Bro'sämchen, Bro'sämlein) crumb.

Bro'sche, *f.* (*pl.* —n) brooch.

Brös'chen, *n.* (—s, *pl.* —) (*calf's*) sweetbread.

Brosch—ie'ren, *v.a.* to stitch together (*as a pamphlet*); to weave, embroider (*Manuf.*). —**ie'rt**, *p.p.* & *adj.* in paper cover, in pamphlet form, in boards, stitched. —**ü're**, *f.* (*pl.* —ü'ren) pamphlet. —**ü'ren=schreiber**, *m.* pamphleteer.

Brö'sel, *n.* (*also* Brö'selein) small morsel, crumb. —**n**, *v.a.* & *n.* to crumble.

Brot, *n.* (—es, *pl.* —e) bread; loaf; support, livelihood; ein — Zucker, a loaf of sugar, sugar-loaf; vorgegessenes —, anything enjoyed before it has been paid for; sein — verdienen, to earn one's living; sein eignes — essen, to be one's own master; in jemandes — stehen, to be in a p.'s service; die Kunst geht nach —, art goes a-begging *or* looks for what pays; sein — haben, to have a competency; sein gutes — haben, to be well off; das Weiche vom —e, the crumb of bread; das liebe —, the daily bread; das liebe — nicht haben, to be in great straits; Kampf ums liebe —, struggle for life; er kann mehr als — essen, he is up to a trick or two; sie spart sich das — vom Munde ab, she is stinting herself. *Comp.* —**baum**, *m.* bread-fruit tree. —**beutel**, *m.* food-bag, haversack. —**brei**, *m.* pap, panada. —**erwerb**, *m.* breadwinning. —**gelehrte(r)**, *m.* one who makes learning merely a means of gaining his livelihood, professional scholar. —**herr**, *m.* master; employer; head. —**kammer**, *f.* pantry. —**korb**, *m.* bread-basket; einem den —korb höher hängen, to keep one on short allowance, to reduce a p.'s supplies. —**los**, *adj.* without bread; unprofitable; out of employment; —lose Künste, arts that do not pay. —**mangel**, *m.* dearth. —**neid**, *m.* commercial jealousy, trade rivalry. —**pflaster**, *n.* bread-poultice. —**raspel**, *f.* rasp. —**rinde**, *f.* crust of bread. —**röster**, *m.* toasting fork. —**schau**, *f.* inspection of bread. —**schaufel**, *f.* oven-peel. —**schnitte**, *f.* slice of bread. —**schrank**, —**schragen**, *m.* pantry; bread-cupboard. —**studium**, *n.* study for the purpose of gaining a livelihood, professional study, special line. —**verwandlung**, *f.* transubstantiation. —**wagen**, *m.* provision-waggon (*Mil.*). —**wissenschaft**, *f.* science acquired for the sake of a livelihood, profession.

Brötchen, *n.* (—s, *pl.* —) small roll of bread; French *or* Vienna roll; Milch —, milk roll; Schinken —, ham-sandwich.

Brr! *interj.* ugh! whoa! (*to horses*).

Bruch, I. *m.* (—es, *pl.* Brüche) breach; breaking, breakage; fracture; rupture; hernia; fraction; infringement, violation; crack, flaw; joint (*of a ruler, etc.*); fold, crease; failure, crash; gewöhnlicher —, vulgar fraction; echter —, proper fraction; Decima'l—, decimal fraction; in die Brüche gehen, to break, to be spoilt (*coll.*); in die Brüche kommen, to come to naught, to fail (*coll.*); das geht in die Brüche, that is incalculable, not worth noticing, of no consequence; einen — einrichten, to set a fracture; Ader —, bursting of a blood-vessel; —, der sich nicht aufheben läßt, fraction that cannot be reduced; Ehe—, adultery; Neu—, tillage of fallow land; Knochen—, fracture; Eingeweide—, hernia; Schenkel—, femoral fracture; Stein—, stone quarry. II. *m.* & *n.* (*pron.* Brūch, *gen.* —es, *pl.* Brüche, Brücher), bog, fen, swamp, marsh. —**ig**, *adj.* foggy, marshy. *Comp.* —**artig**, *adj.* swampy, boggy. —**band**, *n.* truss. —**binde**, *f.* sling. —**dach**, *n.* curved roof. —**dorf**, *n.* village near a swamp. —**eisen**, *n.* scrap iron. —**fällig**, *adj.* decaying. —**glas**, *n.* broken glass. —**rechnung**, *f.* fractions (*Arith.*). —**schiene**, —**schindel**, *f.* splint. —**stein**, *m.* quarry stone; ashlar. —**stück**, *n.* fragment. —**stück=weise**, *adv.* fragmentarily, in fragments. —**teil**, *m.* fraction. —**wasser**, *m.* bogwater. —**zahl**, *f.* fractional number.

Brü'chig, *adj.* full of breaks *or* flaws; brittle; fragile; ruptured.

Brü'ck—e, *f.* (*pl.* —en) bridge; viaduct; pontoon; shelf (*Typ.*); bar (*of a buckle*); scaffolding; eine —e über einen Fluß schlagen, to throw a bridge across a river; hängende —e, suspension bridge; einem die —e treten, to give a p. a helping hand, to aid him, to take his part; fliehendem Feind bau' goldene —en, build golden bridges for the fleeing foe (*prov.*); alle —en hinter sich abbrechen, to leave oneself no means of altering one's course of action, to burn one's ships. —**ung**, *f.* wooden floor of a stable. *Comp.* —**en=bahn**, *f.* way across a bridge. —**en=bau**, *m.* bridge-building. —**en=bogen**, *m.* arch of a bridge. —**en=boot**, *n.* pontoon boat. —**en=geld**, *n.* bridge-toll. —**en=joch**, *n.* wooden pier. —**en=kopf**, *m.* tête-de-pont (*Fort.*). —**en=lehne**, *f.* balustrade along a bridge. —**en=pfeiler**, *m.* pier, pile (*of a bridge*). —**en=schreiber**, *m.* receiver of the bridge toll. —**en=wage**, *f.* weigh-bridge, patent weighing machine. —**en=zoll**, *m.* bridge-toll.

Bru'der, *m.* (—s, *pl.* Brüder) brother; friar; — in Apollo, brother-poet; — Studio, student; — Straubinger, travelling artisan (*from* Straubing *in Bavaria*); ein lustiger —, a jolly fellow; gleiche Brüder, gleiche Kappen, share and share alike (*prov.*); das ist es unter Brüdern wert, that's a reasonable price. —**schaft**, *see* Brüderschaft. *Comp.* —(s)=**kind**, *n.* brother's child, cousin. —**kuß**, *m.* fraternal kiss; kiss of peace. —**liebe**, *f.* fraternal love. —**los**, *adj.* brotherless. —**mord**, *m.* fratricide. —**mörderisch**, *adj.* fratricidal.

Brü'der, *pl. see* Bruder; die barmherzigen —, fratelli di misericordia, monk-hospitallers; die niederen —, Minorites; die grauen —, Cistercians; — der heiligen Jungfrau, Carmelites; die mährischen —, Moravian brethren; die böhmischen —, — vom Gesetz Christi, Hussites. —**chen**, *n.* (—chens, *pl.* —chen), —**lein**, *n.* (—leins, *pl.* —lein) little brother; dear old boy. —**lich**, *adj.* & *adv.* fraternal; meine —liche Liebe, my brother (*coll.*). —**lichkeit**, *f.* brotherliness, fraternity. —**schaft**, *f.* brotherhood, fellowship; —schaft trinken, to drink the pledge of brotherhood; to drink to thee and thou. *Comp.* —**gemeinde**, *f.* (*fraternity of*) the Moravians.

Bru'dern, *v.n.* (*aux.* f.); hier ist nichts zu —, nothing to eat here (*coll.*); mit ihm ist nicht gut —, it is better not to joke with him (*coll.*).

Brü'he, *f.* (*pl.* —n) soup, broth; sauce; gravy; infusion; juice; dye; eine lange —, a tirade; long yarn; in der — stecken, to be in a fine mess.

Brü'h—en, *v.a.* to scald. *Comp.* —**faß**, *n.* scalding tub. —**heiß**, *adj.* scalding hot. —**näpfchen**, *n.* sauce-boat. —**pfännchen**, *n.* sauce-pan. —**siedendheiß**, *adj.*; mir ist —siedendheiß, I am dreadfully hot. —**warm**, *adj.* & *adv.* scalding hot, boiling hot; quite fresh; straightway; einem eine S. —warm widererzählen, to retail news to a p. immediately after receiving it.

Brühl, *m.* (—es, *pl.* —e) thicket; marshy ground.

Brül'l—en, *v.a.* & *n.* (*aux.* h.) to roar, bellow; to low. *Comp.* —**affe**, *m.* howler. —**frosch**, *m.* bull-frog. —**ochs**, *m.* roaring bull.

Brum'meln, (**Brüm'meln,**) *v.a.* & *n.* (*aux.* **h.**) to grumble; to mutter.

Brum'm—en, *v.* I. *n.* (*aux.* **h.**) to make a low, continuous, snarling, rolling *or* buzzing noise; to growl; to snarl; to low; to buzz; to grumble; to rumble; **in den Bart —en,** to mutter to oneself; to grumble to oneself. II. *a.;* **ein Lied —en,** to hum an air; **etwas —en,** to mutter something; **er muß —en,** he must go to prison; he sits in jail, he is obliged to be in prison (*coll.*). **—er,** *m.* (**—ers,** *pl.* **—er**) grumbler, growler; blue-bottle fly; great gun; *see* **—baß. —ig, —isch,** *adj.* & *adv.* grumbling, peevish. *Comp.* **—bär, —bart,** *m.* grumbler, growler. **—baß,** *m.* bourdon (*of an organ*); double-bass (*viol*). **—eisen,** *n.* jew's-harp. **—fliege,** *f.* blue-bottle fly. **—käfer,** *m.* dung-beetle. **—kreisel,** *m.,* **—küsel,** *m.* humming-top; musical top. **—schädel,** *m.* head-ache caused by drinking; **einen —schädel haben,** to be seedy.

Brüne'tt, *adj.* brownish; **die —e,** brunette.

Brunft, *f.* rut, heat (*of animals*). **—en,** *v.n.* (*aux.* **h.**) to rut. *Comp.* **—zeit,** *f.* rutting-time.

Brunie'r—en, *v.a.* to burnish. **—er,** *m.* (**—ers,** *pl.* **—er**) burnisher. *Comp.* **—eisen,** *n.,* **—stahl,** *m.* burnisher.

Brun'nen, *m.* (**—s,** *pl.* **—**) spring; well; fountain; well of mineral waters; mineral *or* spring-water; shaft (*Min.*); **meine Pläne sind in den — gefallen,** my plans have miscarried, come to nothing, have ended in smoke: **den — zudecken, wenn das Kind hinein gefallen ist,** to shut the stable-door when the horse is stolen (*prov.*); **— trinken,** to drink the waters. *Comp.* **—arzt,** *m.* physician at a watering-place. **—becken,** *n.* basin of a fountain. **—behälter,** *m.* reservoir. **—bohrer,** *m.* sinking auger. **—eimer,** *m.* well-bucket. **—einfassung,** *f.* well-inclosure. **—gast,** *m.* visitor at a watering place. **—geist,** *m.* spirit (*or* nymph) of a well. **—gräber,** *m.* well-sinker. **—kresse,** *f.* water-cress. **—kur,** *f.* course of mineral waters. **—liste,** *f.* list of visitors at a spa. **—meister,** *m.* inspector of wells; master of a water-cure establishment. **—röhre,** *f.* water-pipe. **—schwengel,** *m.* beam, lift (*for the well bucket*). **—seil,** *n.* well-rope. **—versand,** *m.* sending (*or* transmission) of mineral waters. **—wasser,** *n.* spring water. **—zeit,** *f.* season (*for taking the waters*).

Brunst, *f.* (*pl.* **Brün'ste**) ardour, passion; lust; rut; conflagration, fire (*obsol.*).

Brün'stig, *adj.* & *adv.* burning; ardent; in heat; lustful; sensual. **—keit,** *f.* ardour; heat.

Brust, *f.* (*pl.* **Brüste**) breast; bosom; chest; breast piece (*of a dress*); **von der — entwöhnen,** to wean; **sich in die — werfen,** to bridle up, give oneself airs; **in seine — greifen,** to examine one's conscience; **er hat es auf der —,** he suffers from asthma; he has a cold; **komm an meine —,** come to my heart; **Kind an der —,** suckling baby. *Comp.* **—ader,** *f.* thoracic vein; mammary vein. **—arznei,** *f.* pectoral medicine. **—baum,** *m.* weaver's beam, yarn beam. **—bein,** *n.* breastbone, sternum; merry-thought (*of a fowl*). **—beklemmung,** *f.* sense of oppression. **—beschwerde,** *f.* chest complaint. **—bild,** *n.* half-length portrait; bust. **—blatt,** *n.* breast-bone; breast-piece (*Saddl.*). **—bonbons,** *n.pl.* chest lozenges, cough lozenges. **—bräune,** *f.* angina pectoris (*Med.*). **—drüse,** *f.* pectoral gland; sweet-bread. **—eisen,** *n.* busk of stays. **—entzündung,** *f.* inflammation of the chest. **—fell,** *n.* pleura, diaphragm. **—fell=entzündung,** *f.* pleurisy. **—fleck,** *m.* stomacher; breast-piece of leather apron. **—fleisch,** *n.* breast (*of fowls*). **—flosser,** *pl.* thoracics (*Icht.*). **—gang,** *m.* thoracic duct. **—gefäße,** *pl.* mammary glands. **—glieder,** *pl.* wings (*of birds*); fore-feet (*of mammals*). **—getäfel,** *n.* wainscot. **—glas,** *n.* breast-pump; nipple-glass. **—harnisch,** *m.* breast-armour, cuirass. **—haut,** *f.* pleura. **—höhle,** *f.* cavity of the chest. **—kasten,** *m.* chest (*cavity*). **—kette,** *f.* breast-plate strap (*Saddl.*). **—knochen,** *m.* breast-bone. **—koppeln,** *pl.* pole-pieces (*Saddl.*). **—krank,** *adj.* affected with chest disease; consumptive. **—krankheit,** *f.* disease of the chest. **—krause,** *f.* frill, ruffle. **—latz,** *m.* stomacher, doublet; bib. **—leder,** *n.* leather apron. **—lehne, —mauer,** *f.* breastwork, parapet railing. **—mittel,** *n.* pectoral, expectorant. **—reinigend,** *adj.* expectorant. **—reinigung,** *f.* expectoration. **—schild,** *m.* & *n.* breast-plate; thorax (*Ent.*). **—stimme,** *f.* chest-voice. **—streifen,** *m.* shirt-frill. **—stück,** *n.* breast, brisket (*of meat*). **—tuch,** *n.* neck-cloth. **—warze,** *f.* nipple. **—warzen=deckel,** *m.* nipple-shield. **—wassersucht,** *f.* dropsy of the chest. **—wehr,** *f.* breastwork, rampart. **—werk,** *n.* fore-part of an organ. **—winde,** *f.* wheel and axle (*Min.*).

Brüst'—chen, *n.* little breast. **—ig,** *adj.* (*suffix in comp.* =) -breasted, -chested. **—ung,** *f.* breastwork, rampart; (*window*) sill.

Brüs'ten, *v.r.* to give o.s. airs, to plume oneself (on a th., **über eine S.**), to brag about a th.

Bru't, *f.* (*pl.* **—en**) brood; fry, spawn; brats; act of brooding *or* hatching; **die Henne ist in der —,** the hen is sitting; **— setzen,** to spawn, to stock with spawn; **die ganze — taugt nichts,** they are a worthless set. *Comp.* **—biene,** *f.* drone. **—ei,** *n.* egg for hatching. **—henne,** *f.* sitting hen. **—ofen,** *m.* hatching oven. **—scheibe,** *f.* comb containing the embryo bees.

Bruta'l, *adj.* & *adv.* brutal. **—itä't,** *f.* brutality.

Brü't—en, *v.a.* & *n.* (*aux.* **h.**) to sit (*on eggs*); to brood over, to hatch. **—ig,** *adj.* addled.

Brut'to, *adv.* gross, in gross (*weight, etc.*).

Bu'be (*South German:* **Bub**), *m.* (**—n,** *pl.* **—n**) boy, lad; boy-child; servant; vassal; knave, scamp; knave (*at cards*). *Comp.* **—n=streich,** *m.,* **—n=stück,** *n.* knavish trick.

Büb'—chen, *n.* (**—chens,** *pl.* **—chen**) baby-boy. **—erei',** *f.* (*pl.* **—erei'en**) roguery, villainy, knavish trick. **—in,** *f.* worthless woman. **—isch,** *adj.* knavish, villainous, mischievous. **—lein,** *n. see* **—chen.**

Buch, *n.* (**—es,** *pl.* **Bücher**) book; quire (*of paper*); a full suit (*of cards*); six tricks (*at whist*); **ein rohes —,** a book in sheets *or* quires; **zu —e bringen, ins — eintragen,** to book; **—halten, die Bücher führen,** to keep accounts, to keep the books. *Comp.* **—adel,** *m.* patent nobility. **—binder,** *m.* book-binder. **—binder=gold,** *n.* leaf-gold. **—druck,** *m.* printing of books; typographed (*postage stamps*). **—drucker,** *m.* printer. **—druckerei',** *f.* printing; printing-office. **—drucker=farbe,** *f.* printer's ink. **—drucker=presse,** *f.* printing-press. **—drucker=stock,** *m.* vignette, tail-piece (*Typ.*). **—führer,** *m.* book-keeper. **—gelehrsamkeit,** *f.* book-learning. **—haltung,** *f.* book-keeping; **einfache (—haltung),** by single entry; **doppelte (—haltung),** by double entry. **—handel,** *m.* bookselling-trade; **im Wege des —handels beziehen,** to order through a bookseller. **—händler,** *m.* bookseller. **—handlung,** *f.* bookseller's shop, book shop. **—zeichen,** *n.* bookmark.

Bu'ch—e, *f.* (*pl.* **—en**) beech-tree. **—en, Büchen,** *adj.* beechen, beech. *Comp.* **—eichel,** *f.* beech-nut. **—esche,** *f.* silver beech, white beech. **—fink,** *m.* chaffinch. **—marder,** *m.* pine-marten. **—mast,** *f.* beech-mast. **—weizen,** *m.* buckwheat. **—weizen=grütze,** *f.* Emden grits.

Bu'ch—en, *v.a.* to book, enter, put down (*to*); to charge. **—ung,** *f.* booking, entry.

Bü'cher, *pl. see* **Buch**. **—ei'**, *f.* library. *Comp.* **—aufseher**, **—bewahrer**, *m.* librarian. **—brett**, *n.* bookshelf. **—freund**, *m.* bibliophile. **—gestell**, *n.* bookshelves, book-case. **—halle**, *f.* public library, free library. **—kunde**, *f.* bibliography. **—kundiger**, *m.* bibliographer. **—macher**, *m.* book-wright, literary hack. **—narr**, *m.* bibliomaniac. **—saal**, *m.* library. **—sammlung**, *f.* (*books of a*) library, collection of books. **—schau**, *f.* critical review of books. **—schrank**, *m.* bookcase. **—sprache**, *f.* written *or* literary language. **—ständer**, *m.*; **drehbarer —ständer**, revolving book-case. **—sucht**, *f.* bibliomania. **—tasche**, *f.* satchel. **—trödler**, *m.* second-hand bookseller. **—verleiher**, *m.* owner of a lending library. **—verzeichnis**, *n.* catalogue of books. **—wesen**, *n.* literary concerns, literature. **—wurm**, *m.* bookworm; plodding boy (*in schools*). **—wut**, *f.* bookishness, bibliomania.

Buchs, *m.* see **—baum**. *Comp.* **—baum**, *m.* box-tree.

Büch'se, *f.* (*pl.* —n) box; case; pot, jar; cylindrical vessel; tube; pipe; barrel (*of a rifle*); rifle, carbine; box (*of a wheel*); socket. *Comp.* **—n-kugel**, *f.* rifle-bullet. **—n-lauf**, *m.*, **—n-rohr**, *n.* rifle-barrel. **—n-macher**, *m.* gunmaker. **—n-meister**, *m.* master-gunner. **—n-schaft**, *m.* gun-stock. **—n-schütze**, *m.* rifleman. **—en-schmied**, *m.* armourer. **—n-spanner**, *m.* rifle-charger. **—n-wettschießen**, *n.* rifle-competition.

Buch'stab, *m.* (—en, *pl.* —en), **—e**, *m.* (—ens, *pl.* —en) letter, written character; type; **großer —e**, capital letter. **— für —**, letter by letter, literally. **—ie'ren**, *v.a.* to spell; **falsch —ieren**, to misspell. **—ie'r-buch**, *n.* spelling book, horn book. **—ie'r-methode**, *f.* alphabetic method. **—ie'r-spiel**, *n.* spelling bee. **—ie'rung**, *f.* spelling. **—ig**, *adj.* (*in compds.*) -lettered, consisting of letters. *Comp.* **—en-folge**, *f.* sequence of letters, alphabet. **—en-gleichung**, *f.* algebraic equation. **—en-rätsel**, *n.* logogram. **—en-rechnung**, **—en-rechenkunst**, *f.* algebra. **—en-spielerei**, *f.* composition of anagrams. **—en-tafel**, *f.* alphabet. **—en-versetzung**, *f.* transposition of letters; metathesis (*Gramm.*); anagram. **—en-wechsel**, *m.* interchange of letters.

Buch'stäb—eln, *v.n.* (*aux.* h.) to be literal, to stick to the letter. **—ler**, *m.* (—lers, *pl.* —ler) pedant, precisian. **—lich**, *adj.* & *adv.* literal; verbal; exact; **—liche Bedeutung**, literal import, literal meaning, literalness; **er nimmt alles gleich —lich**, he sticks very much to the letter, he is very matter-of-fact.

Bucht, *f.* (*pl.* —en) inlet; bay; creek. **—en-land**, *n.* indented coast. **—ig**, *adj.* sinuate (*Bot.*).

Bu'ckel, I. *m.* (—s, *pl.* —) hump; hump-back; bump (*Phren.*); bulge; back. II. *f.* (*pl.* —n) boss, stud, knob; umbo (*of a shield*); buckle; (*pl.*) curls. **—ig**, (**Bu'cklicht**; *obsol.*,) *adj.* & *adv.* hump-backed, humpy.

Bück'—en, *v.r.* to bow, make a bow, an obeisance; to stoop, bend; **halte dich nicht so gebückt**, don't stoop so much! **—ling**, *m.* (—lings, *pl.* —linge) bow, obeisance; scrape.

Bück'ling, **Bü'cking**, *m.* (—s, *pl.* —e) kipper, bloater, smoked herring (not cooked).

Bu'de, *f.* (*pl.* —n) stall, booth; lodgings, room, den (*students' slang*); **einem auf die — rücken** *or* **steigen**, to visit one, to come down on one (*coll.*); **Leben in die — bringen**, to make things lively, interesting (*coll.*); **es wird ihm in die — regnen**, things will turn out badly for him (*coll.*). *Comp.* **—n-geld**, *n.*, **—n-zins**, *m.* standing-rent (*for a stall*).

Bud'deln, *v.a.* to dig out; to dig (*dial.* & *coll.*).

Büf'fel, *m.* (—s, *pl.* —) buffalo; coarse thick coat; lout; buff (*leather*). *Comp.* **—haut**, *f.* buffalo hide. **—kopf**, *m.* white-headed duck; blockhead. **—leder**, *n.* buff leather. **—wamms**, *n.* buff-jerkin.

Büf'f—eln, *v.n.* (*aux.* h.) to drudge, to toil hard, to slave (*sl.*). **—elei'**, *f.* hard work (*sl.*). **—ler**, *m.* plodder, smug; one who crams (*sl.*).

Büffe'tt (*sometimes:* **Buffet**, *pron. in the French way*) *n.* (—s, *pl.* —s, **Büffette**) sideboard; bar. **—fräulein**, *n.* bar-maid. **—kellner**, *m.* barman. **—zimmer**, *n.* refreshment room.

Bug, *m.* (—(e)s, *pl.* **Büge**) bend, bow; flexure; shoulder, point of a horse's shoulder; joint, hock, hough; bow (*of a ship*); **das Pferd ist am —e wund**, the horse is collar-galled; **Knie—**, bend of the knee; **Vorder—**, shoulder (*of quadrupeds*). *Comp.* **—anker**, *m.* bower. **—banden**, *pl.* fore *or* breast-hooks. **—lahm**, *adj.* shoulder-strained. **—lähme**, *f.* shoulder-slip, strain. **—spriet**, *n.* bowsprit. **—stange**, *f.* fore-mast. **—stück**, *n.* breast-piece, brisket (*of beef*); hawse-piece (*Naut.*); bow-chase (*Artil.*).

Bü'gel, *m.* (—s, *pl.* —) bent (*or* curved) piece of wood (*or* metal); ring; hoop; guard of a sword-hilt; trigger-guard; gimbals (*Naut.*); (**Steig—**) stirrup. *Comp.* **—brett**, *n.* ironing-board. **—eisen**, *n.* box-iron, flat-iron; tailor's goose. **—eisen-held**, *m.* tailor (*hum.*). **—fest**, *adj.* firm in the stirrups. **—los**, *adj.* without stirrups. **—riemen**, *m.* stirrup leather. **—säge**, *f.* bow-saw. **—tuch**, *n.* ironing blanket.

Bü'g—eln, *v.a.* to smooth (*with a flat-iron*), to iron. **—lerin**, *f.* ironing woman.

Bug—sie'ren, *v.a.* to tow. **—sie'r-boot**, **—dam'pf-boot**, *n.* tug, steam-tug. **—sie'r-tau**, *n.* tow-rope.

Bü'hel, *m.* (—s, *pl.* —) (*dial.*) hill; humpback.

Buh'l—e, *m.* (—en, *pl.* —en) & *f.* (*pl.* —en). **—in**, *f.* (*in a good sense now only in high style and poetry*) lover; lady love, sweetheart; gallant; mistress; paramour.

Buh'l—en, *v.n.* (*aux.* h.) to woo, to make love to; to have illicit intercourse (**mit**, with); to strive (**um**, for); to vie (**mit**, with). **—er**, *m.* (—ers, *pl.* —er) lover, paramour. **—erei'**, *f.* coquetry; wooing; illicit intercourse. **—erin**, *f.* courtesan, kept mistress. **—erisch**, *adj.* amorous; unchaste. **—schaft**, *f.* (*pl.* —schaften) amour; love-affair; object of love, mistress, paramour (*obs.*). *Comp.* **—dirne**, **—schwester**, *f.* paramour; prostitute; wanton; bawd.

Buh'ne, *f.* dam to turn the course of a river; quay, wharf; fish-weil; crawl (*for fish*). *Comp.* **—n-meister**, *m.* quay-keeper, wharfinger.

Büh'n—e, *f.* (*pl.* —en) scaffolding; stage, boards (*of a theatre*); gallery; orchestra (*for musicians*); scene of action. **—en-anweisung**, *f.* stage direction. **—en-behör**, *n.* stage properties. **—en-bekleidung**, *f.* stage-decoration, scenery. **—en-fieber**, *n.* stage-fright. **—en-gerecht**, *adj.* fit for the stage, theatrical. **—en-gott**, *m.* deus ex machina. **—en-kundig**, *adj.* having theatrical experience. **—en-maler**, *m.* scene-painter. **—en-manuskript**, *n.* acting copy. **—en-mäßig**, *adj.* scenic, theatrical. **—en-streich**, *m.* dramatic touch. **—en-stück**, *m.* play for the stage, acting play. **—en-wand**, *f.* side-scene. **—en-tanz**, *m.* ballet. **—en-werk**, *n.* machinery of a theatre. **—en-werkmeister**, *m.* machinist. **—en-wirksam**, *adj.* theatrical, full of scenic effects.

Büh'nen, *v.a.* to board, to provide with a scaffolding.

Buk, **Bü'ke**, *imperf. ind.* & *subj.* of **backen**.

Buko'l—iker, *m.* writer of a bucolic *or* pastoral poem. **—isch**, *adj.* bucolic, pastoral.

Bul'ge, *f.* (*pl.* —n) leather bag, leather bucket.

[1]**Bul'l—e**, *m.* (—en, *pl.* —en) bull, bullock. *Comp.* **—dogge**, *f.*, **—en-beißer**, *m.* bull-dog. **—en-hetze**, *f.* bull-baiting.

[2]**Bul'le**, *f.* (*pl.* —n) seal (*on a deed*); papal bull;

public document; die goldene — (Karls IV.) the Golden Bull (1356). *Comp.* —n=schreiber, *m.* bullist.

Bul'len, *m.* hulk; pontoon (*Naut.*).

Bul'ler—n, *v.n.* to bubble. —ig, *adj.* bubbling, noisy.

Bü'low, *m.*; Vogel—, yellow thrush, oriole, witwal.

Bum, *interj.* see Bums; bim, bam —, ding-dong (*bell*).

Bum'm—el, *m.*; einen —el machen, to go for a stroll, to take a comfortable walk (*coll.*). —elei', *f.* dawdling, loitering; laziness; negligence; das ist ja eine tolle —elei, that is indeed gross carelessness (*coll.*). —elig, *adj.* unpunctual, careless, slow. —eln, *v.n.* (*aux.* h.) to waste one's time, to loaf about; to dangle, to dawdle, to take it easy, to work slowly and carelessly. —ler, *m.* (—lers, *pl.* —ler) idler, loafer, dawdler, slow-coach; tramp. *Comp.* —el=leben, *n.*; er führt ein —elleben, he does not do a stroke of work. —el=zug, *m.* slow train, Parliamentary train.

Bums, *int.* bounce! bang! —(s)en, *v.n.* (*aux.* h.) to bang against something.

Bund, I. *n.* (—es, *pl.* usually —e) bundle; bunch (*of keys, etc.*); truss (*of hay*); knot (*of silk*); hank (*of flax*); bottle (*of straw*); vier — Stroh, four bottles of straw. II. *m.* (—es, *pl.* Bünde) band, tie; bandage; waistband; band of iron; lead in which window-panes are set; point (*at backgammon*); fret (*on guitars, etc.*); league, union, alliance, confederacy; covenant, dispensation; der türkische —, turban; der deutsche —, the German Confederation; der alte und der neue —, the (*covenant of the*) Old and New Testament; zum —e gehörig *or* Bundes=, federal; einen — schwingen, to solder the leadings of a window. *Comp.* —axt, *f.* adze. —band, *n.* shoemaker's thread. —bruch, *m.* violation of a treaty. —brüchig, *adj.* faithless, covenant-breaking. —es=feldherr, *m.* the highest commander of the united military forces of Germany (*i.e., the German emperor*). —es=genoß, *m.* confederate. —es=kanzler, *m.* Chancellor of the (*North German*) Confederation (*title of Count v. Bismarck between 1866 and 1871*). —es=lade, *f.* ark of the covenant (*B.*). —es=mäßig, *adj. & adv.* federal, in accordance with the confederation, as stipulated; —es=mäßige Hülfe leisten, to furnish one's contingent as a federal. —es=rat, *m.* Federal Council (*representatives of all the German states*). —es=schießen, *n.* general *or* national shooting competition. —es=tag, *m.* (*day of the meeting of*) a federal diet. —es=verwandt, *adj.* allied by treaty. —frei, *adj.* bichord (*Mus.*). —holz, *n.* faggots. —schuh, *m.* shoe consisting of a sole strapped to the foot; sandal; clog; symbol and name of the Peasants' Confederation during the German Peasants' War (1525). —seide, *f.* silk in knots. —stege, *pl.* gutter sticks (*Typ.*). —weise, *adv.* in bundles.

Bün'd—chen, *n. dim. of* Bund. —el, *n.* (—els, *pl.* —el) bundle; sein —el schnüren, to pack up one's traps, to prepare to go, to be off (*coll.*). —ig, *adj.* binding; valid; obligatory; convincing, conclusive; terse, laconic, to the point. —igkeit, *f.* conciseness; validity. —nis, *n.* (—nisses, *pl.* —nisse) covenant, alliance, union.

Bun'gel, *m.* (—s) goose-wing (*Naut.*).

Bunt, *adj. & adv.* gay-coloured, motley; stained (*glass*); mixed; spotted; mottled; bright, glaring; coloured (*not in black or white*); variegated; disorderly, topsy-turvy; er macht es (mir) zu —, he goes too far, he is really too bad; es ging — zu, there were fine goings-on; they were all at sixes and sevens; es wurde immer —er, the confusion was ever growing; sie kleidet sich wieder —, she is out of mourning; eine —e Karte, a court-card; —e Waaren, children's toys; —e Reihe machen, to pair off ladies and gentlemen; —e Bleistifte, many-coloured pencils. —heit, *f.* gayness (*of colours*). *Comp.* —druck, *m.* coloured impression, printing in colours; lithographischer —druck, chromolithograph(y). —fleckig, *adj.* variegated, spotted, speckled. —gewürfelt, *adj.* tartan, chequered. —scheckig, *adj.* mixed; parti-coloured, chequered. —schillernd, *adj.* opalescent. —werk, *n.* furriery.

Bun'zen, *m.* see Punzen.

Bür'de, *f.* (*pl.* —n) burden; charge, load; von ihrer — entbunden, delivered.

Bureau', *n.* (—s, *pl.* —s) bureau, escritoire; office. —krat, *m.* (—kra'ten, *pl.* —kra'ten) red-tapist. —kratie', *f.* red-tapism, officialdom. *Comp.* —justiz, *f.* backstairs-justice.

Burg, *f.* (*pl.* —en) fortified place *or* town (*obs.*); castle; citadel; stronghold; (place of) refuge. *Comp.* —bann, *m.* castle precincts; jurisdiction of a castle. —dienst, *m.* service rendered to the lord of the castle. —flecken, *m.* borough. —frau, *f.* lady of the castle. —fräulein, *n.* young lady of the castle; baron's daughter, high-born damsel. —friede, *m.* jurisdiction, precincts of a (baronial) castle; public peace. —gerechtigkeit, *f.* seigniorial rights *or* security. —gericht, *n.* baronial court. —graben, *m.* castle-moat. —graf, *m.* bur(g)grave, lord of a (feudal) castle. —grafschaft, *f.* bur(g)graviate. —knappe, *m.* page at a castle. —lehen, *n.* tenure of a baronial castle. —saß, *m.* subject of the jurisdiction of a feudal castle. —theater, *n.* principal theatre of Vienna (*a model stage*). —verließ, *n.* castle dungeon, keep. —vogt, *m.* steward of a castle, castellan, bailiff. —vogtei', *f.* stewardship of a castle, castellany. —wache, *f.* castle-ward. —warte, *f.* watch-tower.

Bür'g—e, *m.* (—en, *pl.* —en) surety, bail, guarantee, warranter; —en stellen, to find bail. —schaft, *f.* security, bail. —schaft leisten, to give security; —schaft übernehmen, to go bail *or* security; sichere —schaft, good security; *Comp.* —schafts=schein, *m.* bail-bond.

Burge=mei'ster, (*also* Bürge=mei'ster,) *m.* head of a town, master of the borough, burgomaster, mayor (*obs., now replaced by* Bürgermeister).

Bür'ge—n, *v.n.* (*aux.* h.) to go bail (for, für); to give bail; to warrant; das —t mir für seine Treue, that assures me of his fidelity; ich —e für die Güte dieses Artikels, I warrant this article to be good.

Bür'ger, *m.* (—s, *pl.* —) citizen, townsman, burgher, inhabitant of a town; freeman of a city; one of the middle class, commoner; (*in comp. often* =) civic; — und Studenten, town and gown. —lich, *adj. & adv.* citizen-like; characteristic of civil life, civil; simple, homely; sie kann —lich kochen, she understands plain cooking; der —liche Tod, outlawry, civil death (*Law*). —schaft, *f.* citizens (*coll.*); townspeople, corporation. *Comp.* —ausschuß, *m.* common council. —eid, *m.* freeman's oath. —frau, *f.* woman of the middle class. —garde, *f.* national guard; militia; city volunteers. —gardist, *m.* militiaman, volunteer. —krieg, *m.* civil war. —krone, *f.* civic crown. —kunde, *f.* information concerning a man's rights and duties as a citizen; primer of rights and duties of citizenship. —s=mann, *m.* townsman; one belonging to the lower middle classes. —mädchen, *n.* daughter of a citizen; girl of the middle classes. —meister, *m.* mayor, burgomaster. —recht, *n.* civic rights; freedom of a city.

—schule, *f.* middle-class school, higher grade (elementary) school; **höhere —schule,** higher middle-class school (*in wh. no classics are taught*). **—sinn,** *m.* public spirit (*in a citizen*). **—stand,** *m.* citizen class. **—steig,** *m.* pavement, sidewalk. **—tugend,** *f.* public spirit; civic virtue. **—wache, —wehr,** *f.* city-militia; (city) volunteer force. **—wehr=mann,** *m.* militia-man, (city) volunteer.

Bursch, *m.* (**—en,** *pl.* **—en**); **—e,** *m.* (**—en,** *pl.* **—en**) young man, youth, boy, lad; swain (*poet.*); fellow, comrade; student (*usually a German student after the first year*); apprentice; officer's man *or* servant; fellow (*in familiar expressions such as* **alter —, gerie=bener, —,** *etc.*). **—en=schaft,** *f.* (*German*) Students' Association (*formed in 1815 for political purposes*); association of students professing political and liberal principles. **—en=schaft(l)er,** *m.* member of a **Burschen=schaft. —iko's,** *adj.* & *adv.* student-like; jolly, jovial; unceremonious, free and easy; wild. *Comp.* **—en=brauch,** *m.* custom among students, college ways. **—en=bund,** *m.* confederacy of (*German*) students. **—en=komment,** *m.* convivial customs prevailing among students. **—en=sprache,** *f.* students' slang. **—en=leben,** *n.* college life, students' life. **—en=lieder,** *pl.* students' songs.

Bürsch, Bür'schen, *see* **Birsch, Birschen.**

Bürsch'chen, *n.*, **Bürsch'lein,** *n.* little boy, lad; stripling; whipper-snapper (*contempt.*).

Bür'st—e, *f.* (*pl.* **—en**) brush, whisk. *Comp.* **—en=abzug,** *m.* brush-proof. **—en=binder,** *m.* brush-maker. **—en=rad,** *n.* knife-cleaner.

Bür'sten, *v.a.* to brush; **gieb mir eins zu —,** give me a drink (*coll.*); **wir haben was gebür=stet,** we have quaffed our fill (*coll.*).

-bürtig, *adj.* (*especially in compounds*) born, of birth, native of; **ritter—,** of noble descent.

Bur'zel—n, *also* **Pur'zeln,** *v.n.* (*aux.* **f.**) to tumble (*head over heels*). *Comp.* **—baum,** *m.* somersault.

Bür'zel, *m.* (**—s,** *pl.* **—**) croup, rump; hind part of a beast *or* bird.

Busch, *m.* (**—es,** *pl.* **Büsche**) bush; small wood, underwood, brushwood, thicket, copse; covert; tuft; bunch; **auf den — klopfen,** to beat about the bush. **—icht** (*obs.*), **—ig,** *adj.* bushy; shaggy. *Comp.* **—holz,** *n.* underwood. **—klepper,** *m.* highwayman; bushranger. **—spinne,** *f.* bird-catching spider. **—werk,** *n.* brushwood; (*palisade of*) bushes.

Bü'schel, *m.* (**—s,** *pl.* **—**) tuft, bunch; wisp; cluster; bundle; sheaf; fascicle (*Bot.*); pencil (*of rays*). **—ig,** *adj.* & *adv.* tufted. *Comp.* **—artig,** *adj.* tufty, bunchy, bundled; fascicular. **—entladung,** *f.* brush discharge. **—förmig,** *adj.* tufty, bunchy. **—kohl,** *m.* curly kale. **—weise,** *adv.* in tufts, in bunches.

Bu'schen, *v.r.* to grow in bushes *or* tufts.

Bü'se, *f.* (*pl.* **—n**) small boat.

Bu'sen, *m.* (**—s,** *pl.* **—**) breast, bosom; heart; (**Meer**)**—** gulf, bay; **— von Biscaya,** Bay of Biscay; **sich** (*dat.*) **in den** *or* **in seinen — greifen,** to commune with oneself, to examine one's conscience. *Comp.* **—freund,** *m.* bosom friend, intimate friend. **—krause,** *f.* frill, ruffle. **—nadel,** *f.* breast-pin; brooch.

Bus'sard, *m.* (**—(e)s,** *pl.* **—e**) buzzard.

Bu'ß—e, *f.* compensation for injury, amends; fine; penance; atonement; repentance; remedy, help (*obs.*); **—= und Bet=tag,** day of humiliation. *Comp.* **—bank,** *f.*, **—schemel,** *m.* stool of repentance. **—fällig,** *adj.* liable to punishment. **—fertig,** *adj.* penitent. **—fertigkeit,** *f.* contrition. **—psalmen,** *pl.* penitential psalms. **—prediger,** *m.* preacher of penitence; Lent reacher. **—predigt,** *f.* penitential sermon. **—tag,** *m.* penitentiary day, day of (*public*) repentance. **—text,** *m.* text for the sermon on a day of fasting and prayer. **—übung,** *f.* exercise of penance. **—zeit,** *f.* time of repentance and penance; Lent. **—zelle,** *f.* penitentiary cell. **—zucht,** *f.* penitential discipline.

Bü'ß—en, *v.*I. *a.* to make amends for, to atone; to repair, mend; to fill up (*a gap*); to compensate; to expiate; **einen —en,** to make a p. atone, to punish a p. (*obs.* & *poet.*); **seine Lust —en,** to satisfy one's desire; **seinen Durst —en,** to quench one's thirst (*arch.* & *poet.*). II. *n.* (*aux.* **h.**) to suffer for, do penance, atone for (**für**). **—er,** *m.* (**—ers,** *pl.* **—er**) penitent; one under penance; **Lücken —er,** stop-gap. **—ung,** *f.* penance, atonement, expiation.

Büs'te, *f.* (*pl.* **—n**) bust.

Bu'ten, *adv.* (*Low Gm.*, *in cpds.* =) out, outer (*Naut.*).

Butt, *adj.* & *adv.* short and thick, stumpy; blunt; obtuse. **—e,** *f.* (*pl.* **—en**) flounder.

Bütt—e, (**But't—e,**) *f.* (*pl.* **—en**) tub, coop; wooden vessel; basket for carrying on the back, dosser. **—ner,** *m.* (*pl.* **—ner**) cooper.

Büt'tel, *m.* (**—es,** *pl.* **—**) beadle; bailiff; jailer. **—ei',** *f.* jail, jailer's house.

But'ter, *f.* butter; **— schlagen,** to churn; **sich** (*dat.*) **nicht die — vom Brot nehmen lassen,** to look well after one's own interests, to be wide awake (*coll.*); **sich** (*dat.*) **die — vom Brot nehmen lassen,** to suffer o.s. to be fleeced (*coll.*); **Hand von der —!** hands off! let well alone! **wie — an der Sonne dastehn,** to be overcome by one's emotions, to be moved to tears; **gesalzene —,** salt butter. **—ig,** *adj.* buttery. *Comp.* **—bämme, —bemme, —schnitte,** *f.* slice of bread and butter; **—bemmen werfen,** to make ducks and drakes. **—baum,** *m.* butter-tree; oil-palm. **—blume,** *f.* buttercup; ranunculus, marigold. **—brot,** *n.* (*slice of*) bread and butter; **belegtes —brot,** sandwich; **—brot mit Schinken,** ham-sandwich. **—brühe,** *f.* melted butter, butter-sauce. **—büchse,** *f.* butter-cooler. **—faß,** *n.* butter-tub; churn. **—form,** *f.* butter-print. **—säure,** *f.* butyric acid (*Chem.*). **—schäfchen,** *n.*; **ein —schäfchen sein,** to be fastidious. **—stempel, —stößel,** *m.* churn-staff. **—stulle,** *f.* = **—brot**; **—stullen werfen,** to make ducks and drakes (*coll.*). **—teig,** *m.* rich crust, flaky paste. **—vogel,** *m.* butterfly (*dial.*). **—weck,** *m.* butter-roll.

Butt'jer, *m.* (**—s,** *pl.* **—**) awkward fellow; rowdy.

Butz, But'z—en, *m.* core (*of fruit; of a tumour*); sore in the eyes *or* nose; snuff (*of a candle*); **da steckt der —en,** there 's the rub! (*coll.*).

Butz, *m.* blow (*or* stroke), fall (*accompanied by a dull noise*); bogy, bugbear.

Butz'emann, *m.* bogyman, bugbear.

But'zenscheibe, *f.* bull's-eye glass, glass-roundel. *Comp.* **—n=lyrik,** *f.* mock old German lyrics.

Butz'kopf, *m.* grampus, bottle-nosed whale.

C

Words beginning with **Ca...., Ch...., Cl...., Co...., Cu....,** and not given under **C** should be looked for under **K**; those beginning with **Ch,** also under **Sch**; those beginning with **Ce...., Ci....,** or **Cy....,** under **Z** or **K.** Foreign words of the same form and meaning in both languages have, as a rule, been omitted.

C, c, C, c; **C** = Do (*Mus.*); **C=Dur** (**Moll**), (the key of) C major (minor); **Kontra C.,** contra double C; **C. Schlüssel,** C clef, bass key.

Ca'dre, *m.* & *n.* (**—s,** *pl.* **—s**) the frame (*or* skeleton) of a regiment; body (*or* list) of regimental officers, cadre, skeleton.

Ca'fé, *n.* (—s, *pl.* —s) café; coffee-house (*less elegant than a café*); — **chantant,** (small) music hall, sing-song shop.
Ca'lomel, *n.* (—s) calomel, mercurous chloride.
Camb—ie'ren, *v.a.* to deal in bills, to do exchange business. **—i'st,** *m.* (—**is'ten,** *pl.* —**is'ten**) financier.
Campe'scheholz, *n.* Campeachy wood, logwood.
Carambol—a'ge, *f.* cannon (*at billiards*). —**ie'ren,** *v.a.* to cannon (*at billiards*), to collide.
Car'cer, Kar'zer, *m.* & *n.* place of detention, lock-up (*at schools and universities*); **drei Stunden** —, three hours of detention *or* keeping in.
Carré', *n.* (—s, *pl.* —s) square. *See* **Karree.**
Carrie're, *f.* (*pl.* —**n**) career; course; gallop; **eine gute — machen,** to get on in the world, to be quickly promoted.
Cartonn—a'ge, *f.* (*pl.* —**a'gen**) pasteboard work, binding in boards. —**ie'ren,** *v.a.* to put in boards. —**ie'rt,** *adj.* (bound) in boards.
Cäsu'r, *f.* (*pl.* —**en**) cæsura, break in the metrical line; **klingende** —, feminine cæsura; **stumpfe** —, masculine cæsura. *Comp.* —**reim,** *m.* cæsura of one line rhyming with that of a consecutive line.
Ced—e'nt, *m.* (—**en'ten,** *pl.* —**en'ten**) assigner, transferrer. —**ier'bar,** *adj.* transferable, negotiable. —**ie'ren,** *v.a.* to cede, surrender, assign.
Ce'der, *f.* (*pl.* —**n**) cedar. —**n,** *adj.* of cedar. *Comp.* —(**n**)=**holz,** *n.* cedar wood.
Celebr—a'nt, *m.* (—**an'ten,** *pl.* —**an'ten**) officiating priest (*at mass*); celebrant. —**ie'ren,** *v.a.* to celebrate; **das Hochamt —ieren,** to celebrate high mass. —**itä't,** *f.* (*pl.*—**itä'ten**) celebrity, shining light, star.
Cel'l—o, *n.* (—**os,** *pl.* —**os** *or* —**i**) violoncello. —**i'st,** *m.* (—**is'ten,** *pl.* —**is'ten**) violoncello player, (violon)cellist.
Cellula'r, *adj.* (*in compounds* =) cellular. —**Pathologie,** *f.* cellular pathology.
Cellulo'se, *f.* (*pl.* —**n**) cellulose, celluloid, wood-fibre.
Cel'te, *see* **Kelte.**
Ceme'nt, *m.* & *n.* (—(e)s) cement. —**ie'ren,** *v.a.* to cement; to convert into steel. —**ie'rung,** *f.* cementation; converting; **auf die —ierung bezüglich,** cementatory, cementitious, cementing.
Cens—ie'ren, *v.a.* to examine books, *etc.*, before publication; to review, criticise; to censure; to certificate (*school work*). —**or,** *m.* (*pron.* **Cen'sor,** *pl.* —**o'ren**) censor (*of the press*). —**or=amt,** *n.* censorship. —**u'r,** *f.* (*pl.* —**u'ren**) censorship of the press; report (*monthly or at end of school term*), statement of conduct and of marks obtained, school certificate.
[1]**Cent,** *n.*; **pro** —, per cent.
[2]**Cent,** *m.* (—s, *pl.* —s) cent (*a coin in America and Holland*).
[3]**Cent,** *f.* criminal jurisdiction. *Comp.* —**gericht,** *n.* court of penal judicature, hundred-court. —**klage,** *f.* criminal charge.
Centesima'l, *adj.* centesimal, hundredth.
Centifo'lie, *f.* (*pl.* —**n**) centifolious rose, cabbage rose.
Cen'tigramm, *n.* (—(e)s, *pl.* —**e**) centigram, the hundredth part of a gramme.
Cen'timeter, (*m.* &) *n.* (—s, *pl.* —) centimeter, centimetre, the hundredth part of a metre.
Cent'ner, Zent'ner, *m.* (—s, *pl.* —) hundred weight (*abbr.* cwt.). *Comp.* —**last,** *f.* heavy burden. —**schwer,** *adj.* extremely heavy.
Centra'l, *adj.* central. —**e,** *f.* line joining two (*or* more) centres. —**isch,** *adj.* central (*obs.*). —**isie'ren,** *v.a.* to centralize. —**isie'rung,** *f.* centralization.
Cen'trum, *n.* (—s, *pl.* **Cen'tren**) centre; **ins — treffen,** to hit the bull's-eye, to make a bull (*coll.*). *Comp.* —**bohrer,** *m.* centre-bit. —**s=partei,** *f.* the Roman Catholic (ultramontane) party in the German parliament.
Cerea'lien, *pl.* cereals.
Ceremon—ie', *f.* (*pl.* —**ie'en**) ceremony, formality. —**ie'll,** I. *n.* ceremonial. II. *adj.* formal, ceremonious; precise. —**iö's,** *adj.* ceremonious, formal, punctilious; **peinlich —iös sein,** to stand upon ceremonies. *Comp.* —**ien=meister** (*pron.* **Ceremo'nienmeister**), *m.* master of the ceremonies.
Cerevi's, *n.* (—es) beer; (cerevisial) word of honour (*stud. sl.*); **auf** —, upon my (student's) honour! (*stud. sl.*). *Comp.* —**kappe,** *f.*, —**mütze,** *f.* round little brimless drinking *or* beer cap, students' cap.
Cernie'r—en, *v.a.* to invest, besiege, blockade. —**ung,** *f.* investment, siege, blockade. —**ungs=Heer,** *n.* investing army, besieging forces.
Cervela'twurst, *f.* Bologna sausage, Brunswick sausage, best kind of smoked sausage; saveloy (*inferior kind of sausage*).
Ces, *n.* C flat (*Mus.*).
Cessio'n, *f.* (*pl.* —**en**) cession, assignment. —**a'r,** *m.* (—**a'rs,** *pl.* —**a're**) assignee.
Chama'de, *f.* parley, shamade; — **schlagen** *or* **blasen,** to beat *or* sound a parley (*for agreeing on terms of surrender*); to give in (*fig.*).
Chamä'leon, *n.* (—s, *pl.* —s) chameleon. *Comp.* —**artig,** *adj.* chameleonic.
Champag'ner, *m.* (—s) champagne (wine), fizz (*coll.*); **deutscher** —, sparkling hock *or* moselle; **herber** —, dry champagne; **nicht schäumender** *or* **mussierender** —, still champagne; **stark mussierender** —, sparkling champagne; **eine Flasche** —, a bottle of champagne; — **in Eis,** iced champagne. *Comp.* —**bowle,** *f.* champagne-cup. —**pfropfen,** *m.* champagne cork; **die —pfropfen knallten,** the champagne corks popped.
Champag'nern, *v.a.* to drink champagne; to go in for fizz (*coll.*).
Cham'pignon, *m.* (—s, *pl.* —s) champignon, field agaric, eatable mushroom. *Comp.* —**sauce,** *f.* mushroom catsup, ketchup.
Chan, *m.* (—s, *pl.* —**e**) khan; caravanserai.
Chana't, *n.* (—s, *pl.* —**e**) dignity of a khan.
Cha'—os, *n.* (*gen.* —**os**) chaos. —**o'tisch,** *adj.* & *adv.* chaotic.
Chara'de, *f.* (*pl.* —**n**) charade; —**n aufführen,** to act charades.
Charak'ter, *m.* (—s, *pl.* —**e,** *pron.* **Charakte're**) character, mental constitution, disposition; title, dignity; type, print; part (*theat.*). *Comp.* —**bild,** *n.* portrait of a p. drawn from life. —**buchstabe,** *m.* characteristic letter. —**fest,** *adj.*, —**voll,** *adj.* having a firm character, steadfast, reliable. —**kopf,** *m.* face full of expression. —**los,** *adj.* having no firm character, unprincipled, fickle; —**loses Gesicht,** countenance destitute of character, dull *or* lifeless face. —**maske,** *f.* character *or* fancy dress. —**schilderung,** *f.* characterization. —**zug,** *m.* characteristic, trait.
Charakter—isie'ren, *v.a.* to describe a character, to characterize; to style, to give a title to. —**is'tik,** *f.* sketch of a character, characterization. —**is'tisch,** *adj.* characteristic.
Char—frei'tag, —woche, *see* **Kar—freitag, —woche.**
[1]**Char'ge,** *f.* appointment, rank, post, position; **die —n,** officers and non-commissioned officers; **die höchsten Hof—n,** the highest court officials, the principal members of the royal household.
[2]**Char'ge,** *f.* charge, attack, onset (*Mil.*, *obs.*).
Chargie'r—en, *v.a.* to charge, attack (*Mil.*). —**te(r),** *m.* (non-commissioned) officer; **die —ten,** the officers of (students') clubs. —**ung,** *f.* charge, charging (*of a firearm, etc.*).
Chariva'ri, *n.* (—s, *pl.* —s) din, mock-music.

Char'latan, *m.* (—s, *pl.* —s & —e) charlatan, quack (doctor), mountebank; **in der Art eines —s**, quackish. **—erie'**, *f.*, **—is'mus**, *m.* charlatanism, quackery.

Charmie'ren, *v.a.*; mit einem Mädchen —, to carry on a flirtation with a girl.

Charnie'r, *n.*, **Scharnie'r** (—s, *pl.* —e) hinge, joint.

Charpie', *f.* (*pl.* —(e)n) lint; — **zupfen** *or* **schaben**, to pull linen-rags, to shred lint.

Chaussee', *f.* (*pl.* —en) high road. *Comp.* **—bau**, *m.* road making. **—geld**, *n.* turnpike money, toll. **—geld=einnehmer**, *m.* toll-collector, turnpike-keeper. **—haus**, *n.* toll-house. **—inspektor**, *m.* surveyor of roads.

Chaussie'ren, *v.a.* to make a public road.

Check, Scheck, *m.* (—s, *pl.* —s) cheque. *Comp.* **—system**, *n.* system of paying by cheque.

Che'f, *m.* (—s, *pl.* —s) chief, chief commander; principal, head (*of a firm*); **Geschwader —**, admiral in command; **Bataillons —**, commander of a battalion, major; **Kompanie —**, captain.

Chem -ie', *f.* chemistry; **—ie lebender Wesen**, biochemistry. **—ika'lien**, *pl.* chemicals. **—ika'lisch**, *adj.* chemical.

Che'm—iker, *m. also* **—ikus** (*coll.*) scientific *or* analytical chemist; student *or* teacher of chemistry. **—isch**, *adj.* chemical; **—ische Präparate**, chemicals. **—i'st**, *m.* analytical chemist.

Chemise'tt, *n.* (—s), **—e**, *f.* (false) shirt front.

Che'rub, *m.* (—s, *pl.* —s & **Che'rubim**) cherub. **—i'nisch**, *adj.* cherubic.

Chevalere'sk, *adj.* chivalrous, gallant, polite (*to ladies*).

Chica'ne, Schika'ne, *f.* (*pl.* —en) trick, artifice; annoyance.

Chif'fre, *f.* (*pl.* —n) cipher, in ciphers; cryptography.

Chimä'r—e, *f.* (*pl.* —en) chimera, fancy. **—isch**, *adj.* chimerical, fanciful, Utopian; **—ische Hoffnungen**, vain hopes, empty dreams.

Chi'n—a, *f.* & *n.* China, *see the Index of Names;* chinchona, quinquina; Peruvian bark. **—i'n**, *n.* (—i'ns) quinine; **—in und Ammonia**, ammoniated quinine. *Comp.* **—a=rinde**, *f.* quinine, Peruvian bark.

Chir— (*in compds.*). **—omantie'**, *f.* chiromancy. **—u'rg**, *m.* (—ur'gen, *pl.* —ur'gen) surgeon. **—urgie'**, *f.* surgery. **—ur'gisch**, *adj.* surgical.

Chi'ragra, *n.* gout in the hand(s), chiragra.

Chlor, *n.* (—s) chlorine; (*in compounds* =) chloride of. **—a'l**, *n.* chloral. **—a'l=vergiftung**, *f.* chloralism. **—ig**, *adj.* chlorous; **—ig=saures Salz**, chlorite. **—imetrie'**, *f.* chlorometry. **—ofo'rm**, *n.* chloroform. **—o=formie'ren**, *v.a.* to chloroform(ise). *Comp.* **—cal'cium**, *n.* calcium chloride.

Chokola'de, Schokola'de, *f.* (*pl.* —n) chocolate.

Cho'lera, *f.* cholera. *Comp.* **—anfall**, *m.* attack of cholera. **—kommission**, *f.* sanitary commission for the study of cholera-cases and for watching and preventing the spread of the disease. **—mittel**, *n.* remedy for cholera. **—tropfen**, *pl.* cholera-drops.

Chole'risch, *adj.* & *adv.* choleric, bilious; irascible, hot-tempered.

Chor, *m.* & (less frequently) *n.* (—(e)s, *pl.* **Chö're**) choir; chorus, burden; cathedral choir, choristers; multitude, crowd, host (*in this sense often used as a neuter*); (raised seats for a) choir, quire, (church) gallery (*in this sense usually a neuter*); **Gemischter —**, chorus of men and women; **im — singen**, to sing in chorus; to chime in together; **zum — gehörig**, choral; **der dichte —**, the dense crowd (*poet.*); **das — der Vögel**, the feathered tribe (*poet.*). *Comp.* **—altar**, *m.* high altar. **—amt**, *n.* cathedral service. **—artig**, *adj.* choral. **—bischof**, *m.* suffragan *or* local bishop. **—direktor**, *m.* chorus-master, conductor of the chorus; choir-master. **—frau**, *f.* canoness. **—führer**, *m.* first chorister (*Eccl.*); choragus (*Anc. Theat.*). **—gang**, *m.* aisle. **—gehilfe**, *m.* acolyte. **—gesang**, *m.* singing in chorus; choral song; anthem (*Eccl.*); **einstimmiger —gesang**, plain chant, Gregorian chant, canto fermo. **—hemd**, *n.* surplice. **—herr**, *m.* canon, prebendary. **—knabe**, *m.* chorister, choir-boy; *pl.* cherubs (*fam.*). **—leiter**, *m.* master over the choristers. **—nische**, *f.* apse. **—nonne**, officiating nun. **—pult**, *n.* lectern, reading desk. **—rock**, *m.* clergyman's gown; cope; stole. **—sänger**, *m.* chorister, choir man. **—schüler**, *m.* chorister, choir boy. **—stuhl**, *m.* choir stall. **—weise**, *adv.* in chorus, tutti.

Chora'l, *m.* (—s, *pl.* **Chorä'le**) hymn, anthem, sacred song; psalm tune. *Comp.* **—buch**, *m.* hymn book, anthem book. **—mäßig**, *adj.* & *adv.* hymn-like. **—melodie'**, *f.* chorale, tune of a hymn.

Choriam'b—(us), *m.* (—en, *pl.* —en) choriambus (- ◡ ◡ -).

Chrestomathie', *f.* (*pl.* —en) anthology, selection of poems *or* gems of prose, reading book, Reader.

Chri'e, *f.* (*pl.* —(e)n) theme; dissertation *or* essay on chosen topics composed according to definite rules (*Rhetor.*).

Christ, I. *m.* Christ (*the usual form is now* **Christus**, *but the older German shortened form,* **Christ**, *survives in popular hymns and also in some compounds*); — **ist erstanden**, Christ has arisen; **der heilige —**, Christmas; Christmas box *or* gift; **ein wunderlicher —**, a curious sort of fellow, a queer fish (*coll.*). II. *m.* (—en, *pl.* —en) Christian. **—in**, *f.* female Christian. **—en=heit**, *f.* Christendom. **—en=tum**, *n.* Christianity; Christendom. **—=lich**, *adj.* Christian; *adv.* Christian-like; kindly; **—liche Liebe**, charity; **mit dem Mantel —licher Liebe bedecken**, to draw a veil over (a person's failings); **—liche Zeitrechnung**, Christian era; **—lich soziale Partei**, Christian Socialist party. **—lichkeit**, *f.* Christianity; Christian nature. **—us**, *m.* (—i, *Dat.* —o, *Acc.* —um, *Voc.* —e) Christ; **vor —o** *or* **vor —i Geburt**, B. C., before Christ; **nach —i Geburt**, A. C., after Christ, in the year of our Lord, A. D. (= *anno domini*). *Comp.* **—abend**, *m.* Christmas-eve. **—baum**, *m.* Christmas-tree. **—bescherung**, *f.* giving of the presents *or* presents given on Christmas eve. **—dorn**, *m.* prickly-leaved holly. **—en=gemeine** *or* **—en=gemeinde**, *f.* community of Christians. **—en=kind**, *n.* Christian child. **—en=mensch**, *m.*, **—en=seele**, *f.* (good) Christian. **—fest**, *n.* Christmas; **ein fröhliches** *or* **vergnügtes —fest**, a merry Christmas. **—geschenk**, *n.* Christmas present; Christmas box (*to errand-boys, postmen, railway-men, etc.*). **—kindlein**, *n.* infant Jesus. **—mette**, *f.* Christmas matins. **—monat**, *m.* December. **—nacht**, *f.* night of Christmas eve. **—tag**, *m.* Christmas day. **—us=bild**, *n.* image of Christ, image of our Lord; crucifix. **—us=kopf**, *m.* Christ's head; divine countenance. **—zeit**, *f.* Christmas *or* Yule time.

Chri'stel—n, *v.a.* to affect a Christian bearing, to be a bigoted Christian. **—ei'**, *f.* affecting a Christian bearing, bigotry.

Christolo'g—(e), *m.* (—en, *pl.* —en) christologist. **—ie'**, *f.* christology, general doctrines regarding Christ.

Chrom, *n.* (—(e)s) chromium, chrome. **—a'=tisch**, *adj.* chromatic; **—atische Tonleiter**, chromatic scale; **—atische Töne**, chromatics. **—a'tik**, *f.* chromatics, science of colours. *Comp.* **—gelb**, *adj.* chrome-yellow, chromate

of lead. —**sauer**, *adj.* chromic; —**saures Salz**, chromate.
Chro'n—ik, *f.* (*pl.* —**iken**) chronicle; **in eine —ik eintragen**, to chronicle. —**ika**, *f.*; **Bücher der —ika**, Chronicles (*B.*); —**ika eines fahrenden Schülers**, diary of a travelling scholar. —**isch**, *adj. & adv.* chronic. —**olo'g**, *m.* (—**olo'gen**, *pl.* —**olo'gen**) chronologist. —**ologie'**, *f.* chronology. —**olo'gisch**, *adj.* chronological. —**ome'ter**, *m.* (*v.n.*) chronometer, time-piece; metronome (*Mus.*). *Comp.* —**iken=schreiber**, *m.* chronicler, annalist.
Chur, *f. see* **Kur**, *and also the Index of Names.*
Chymie', *f. see* **Chemie**.
Ci'cero=schrift, *f.* pica (*Typ.*).
Cicho'rie, *f.* (*pl.* —**n**) chicory, succory. *Comp.* —**n=kaffee**, *m.* chicory-coffee, roasted chicory.
Ci'der, *m.* (—**s**) cider; **herber**—, tart cider.
Cigar're, *f.* (*pl.* —**n**) cigar; **schwere** —, strong cigar; **abgelagerte** —, matured *or* well-seasoned cigar; **eine — anzünden**, to light a cigar; **die — hat keine Luft**, the cigar does not draw. *Comp.* —**n=arbeiter**, *m.* cigar-maker. —**n=deckblatt**, *n.* wrapper. —**n=einlage**, *f.* filling(s). —**n=etui**, *n.*, —**n=tasche**, *f.* cigar-case. —**n=fabrikant**, *m.* manufacturer of cigars. —**n=spitze**, *f.* cigar-holder, mouth-piece; cigar tip (*last bit of a cigar*). —**n=stummel**, *m.* cigar end.
Cika'de, Cica'de, *f.* (*pl.*—**n**) cicada; grasshopper.
Cin'gulum, *n.* (—**s**, *pl.* —**s** & **Cingula**) cingulum, a sort of belt put over the stole of a Roman Catholic priest.
Cir'ca, Cir'ka, *adv.* about, nearly.
Cirkula'r, *n.* (—**s**, *pl.* —**e**) circular, pamphlet, fly sheet. *Comp.* —**schreiben**, *n.*, —**schrift**, *f.* circular note; round-robin.
Cirkulie'ren, *v.a.* to circulate, to pass *or* send round.
Cis, *n.* C sharp; —, —, C double sharp.
Ciselie'r—en, *v.a.* to engrave with a chisel, to (en)chase. *Comp.* —**arbeit**, *f.* chased work. —**hammer**, *m.* chasing hammer.
Cister'ne, *f.* (*pl.* —**n**) cistern, (water-)tank.
Citadel'le, *f.* (*pl.* —**n**) citadel.
Cit—a't, *n.* (—**a't(e)s**, *pl.* —**a'te**) quotation. —**atio'n**, *f.* citation, summons. —**ie'ren**, *v.a.* to call up, summon; to quote; **aus dem Gedächtnis —ieren**, to quote from memory. *Comp.* —**a'ten=schatz**, *m.* collection of familiar quotations. —**ie'r=zettel**, *m.* summons.
Ci'to, *adv.* immediately, at once.
Citrona't, *n.* (—**s**, *pl.* —**e**) candied lemon.
Citro'ne, *f.* (*pl.* —**n**) lemon. *Comp.* —**n=gelb**, *adj.* lemon-coloured. —**n=holz**, *n.* candle wood. —**n=presse**, *f.* lemon-squeezer. —**n=saft**, *m.* lemon juice; lemon squash (*made of lemon-juice with addition of soda-water and ice*). —**n=sauer**, *adj.*; —**n=saures Salz**, citrate; —**n=saures Eisenoxyd**, citrate of iron. —**n=schale**, *f.* lemon peel. —**n=scheibe**, *f.* slice of lemon. —**n=vogel**, *m.* brimstone butterfly. —**n=trank**, *m.*, —**n=wasser**, *n.* lemonade.
Civi'l, I. *adj. & adv.* civil; courteous; moderate, reasonable (*prices*). II. *n.* civil body, civilians (*opp. to military men*). —**i'st**, *m.* civilian. *Comp.* —**anwärter**, *m.* person (*often an old soldier*) who has a claim to a governmeut appointment; candidate for employment in the civil service. —**anzug**, *m.* plain clothes. —**beamte(r)**, *m.* civil officer, civil servant, government official. —**ehe**, *f.* civil marriage, ceremony before a registrar. —**gericht**, *n.* civil tribunal. —**gerichtsbarkeit**, *f.* civil jurisdiction. —**gesetzbuch**, *n.* code of civil law. —**kammer**, *f.* court for civil law cases; record court. —**klage**, *f.* civil action, lawsuit. —**kleidung**, *f.* plain clothes. —**prozeß**, *m.* civil suit. —**prozeß=ordnung**, *f.* civil code. —**stand**, *m.* citizenship; legal status of a citizen with regard to rights and duties. —**stands=beamter**, *m.* civil official, registrar. —**stands=register**, *n.* registrar's list; parish register. —**trauung**, *f.* (ceremony of) marriage before a registrar. —**versorgung**, *f.* claim to a post in the civil service, a (small) government post. —**verwaltung**, *f.* civil government *or* service.
Civilisat—io'n, *f.* (*pl.* —**io'nen**) civilization, culture; **die —ion betreffend**, civilizational. *Comp.* —**o'risch**, *adj.* promoting (the cause) of civilization. —**ions=bestrebungen**, *pl.* civilizing efforts.
Civilisie'r—en, *v a.* to civilize, to humanize, to refine and enlighten; to polish (*fig.*). —**bar**, *adj.* amenable to civilization.
Close't, *n.* (—**s**, *pl.*—**te** & —**s**) water-closet, W. C.
Coak, Kok, Ko'ke, *m.* (*as a rule used in the plural*: **Koks**) coke.
Cochenil'le, *f.* cochineal.
Co'dex, *m.* (—, *pl.* **Co'dices**) codex, manuscript; code.
Cog'nac, Kog'nak, *m.* (—**s**, *pl.* —**s**) cognac, (French) brandy.
Cölesti'n, *m.* (—**s**) celestine (*Min.*)
Cöliba't, *m. & n.* (—(**e**)**s**) celibacy; bachelor's life, bachelordom.
Colport—a'ge, *f.* sale *or* hawking of books, *etc.*, by itinerant booksellers; colportage (*especially of religious tracts*). —**a'ge=Roman**, *m.* cheap sensational novel, penny dreadful. —**a'ge=Verlag**, *m.* publishing office of cheap, sensational literature. —**eu'r**, *m.* itinerant bookseller, tract vendor, hawker; newsmonger (*fig.*). —**ie'ren**, *v.a.* to hawk about, to sell in the streets; to spread, disseminate (*news*).
Comme'nt, *m.* (—**s**) students' way of living, convivial code among German students; —**reiten**, to make a hobby of the strict observance of the convivial code (*sl.*). *Comp.* —**mäßig**, *adj.* in conformity with students' rules. —**widrig**, *adj.* contrary to students' customs.
Commi's, *m.* (—, *pl.* —) merchant's clerk; counting-house clerk; — **voyageur**, commercial traveller.
Compagno'n, *m.*, **Kompagno'n** (—**s**, —**s**) partner; **stiller** —, sleeping partner.
Cöna'kel, *n.* (—**s**, *pl.* —) dining hall (*in monasteries*).
Conce'pt, Konze'pt, *n.* (—**es**, *pl.* —**e**) rough copy, first draft; **einen aus dem —e bringen**, to confuse a p., to put a p. out; **aus dem —e kommen**, to become confused (*in a speech, etc.*). *Comp.* —**buch**, *n.* note book, scribbling-book. —**papier**, *n.* scribbling paper.
Conch—oi'de, *f.* (*pl.* —**oi'den**) conchoid. —**y'lien**, *pl.* shell fish. —**yliologie'**, *f.* conchology.
Concip—ie'ren, *v.a.* to draw up, to pen (down). —**ie'nt**, *m.* (—**ien'ten**) drawer up (*of a document*), draughtsman.
Conci's, Konzi's, *adj.*, concise, brief, curt.
Consiliie'ren, *v.a.* to give to a student the "consilium abeundi" (*i.e. warning to leave the university*), to rusticate, send down (*Univ. sl.*).
Con'tre, Kon'tre, Kon'ter (*in compounds* =) counter, contra. —**admiral**, *m.* rear-admiral. —**band**, *adj.* contraband. —**bande**, *f.* smuggling; smuggled goods; goods not allowed to be imported, forbidden goods. —**mandie'ren**, *v.a.* to countermand. —**marke**, *f.* check, countermark. —**mine**, *f.* counter mine. —**minen=system**, *n.* araignee (*Fort.*). —**tanz**, *m.* counter-dance, quadrille.
Coquet'te, *see* **Kokett'te**.
Coro'na, *f.* circle of listeners, audience (*Univ. sl.*).
Corrigen'da, *pl.* corrections to be made.
Cö'tus, *m.* (*pl.* **Cö'ten**) division (*of a school form*), (parallel) set.

Coula'n—t, Kula'n—t, *adj.* fluent, easy (*style*); accommodating, complaisant, liberal; fair (*price*). **—z,** *f.* readiness, complaisance; fair-dealing.

Couleu'r, *f.* (shade of) colour; a students' club (*wearing distinctive coloured badges and caps*); **das ist dieselbe — in Grün,** that is the same thing over again with very little difference (*coll.*). *Comp.* **—student,** *m.* student belonging to a club wearing distinctive coloured badges. *See* **Korpsstudent.**

Coulif'se, *f.* (*pl.* **—n**) wing, movable scene; side-scene (*of a theatre*); coulisse, space in a stock-exchange set apart for unofficial business; connecting link (of a railway engine); **in die — sprechen,** (to speak) aside, to speak to a p. behind the scenes; **—n reißen,** to play to the gallery; **hinter den —n stecken,** to know the ins and outs of a thing, to be at the bottom of everything. *Comp.* **—n=fieber,** *n.* stage fright, nervous fear of the footlights. **—n=geschwätz,** *n.* greenroom talk. **—n=intrigue,** *f.* greenroom intrigue. **—n=maler,** *m.* scene-painter. **—n=reißer,** *m.* sensational actor, ranter. **—n=reißerei',** *f.* ranting, playing to the gallery. **—n=rücker,** *m.*, **—n=schieber,** *m.* scene shifter.

Coupé, *n.* (**—s,** *pl.* **—s**) (railway) compartment; carriage.

Couple't, *n.* (**—s,** *pl.* **—s**) comic song (*in operettas*); topical verses *or* lines.

Cour, *f.* court; levee; addresses paid to a lady, courtship; **einem Mädchen die — machen** *or* **schneiden,** to court a girl; **er machte ihr die —,** he paid his addresses to her; **sie läßt sich** (*dat.*) **gern die — machen,** she is a great flirt, she is fond of admiration; **eine — halten,** to hold a levee. *Comp.* **—fähig,** *adj.* being entitled to appear at court. **—macher, —schneider,** *m.* courter, beau, ladies' man; suitor, admirer. **—macherei', —schneiderei',** *f.* flirtation.

Coura'ge, *f.* courage; **das ist doppelte —,** that is twice as much (*coll.*).

Coura'nt, I. *adj.* current; **zu —em Preise,** at the current rate. II. *n.* (**—(e)s**) currency, current money, coin of the realm.

Courbet't—e, Kurbet't—e, *f.* curvet (*of a horse*). **—ie'ren,** *v.n.* to curvet.

Cours, *see* **Kurs.**

Courta'ge, *f.* brokerage, procuration money.

Courti'ne, Kurti'ne, *f.* courtain (*Fort.*).

Cousi'n, *m.* (**—s,** *pl.* **—s**) (male) cousin. **—e,** *f.* (*pl.* **—en**) (female) cousin, (lady) cousin.

Courtisa'n, Kurtisa'n, *m.* (**—s,** *pl.* **—en**) courtier (*obs.*). **—e,** *f.* courtesan.

Couve'rt, *n.* (**—(e)s,** *pl.* **—e** & **—s**) envelope, wrapper; cover (*plate, knife, fork, etc.*); **unter — schicken,** to send under cover. **—ie'ren,** *v.a.* to put in an envelope, to put in a wrapper.

Cujonie'ren, *v.a.*; **einen —,** to harass, vex, torment a person.

Cya'n, *n.* (**—s**) cyanogen (*Chem.*). *Comp.* **—kali(um),** *n.* cyanide of potassium. **—metalle,** *pl.* cyanides. **—wasserstoff=säure,** *f.* hydrocyanic acid.

Cya'ne, *f.* corn flower, blue bottle, blue bonnet.

Cyklo'n, *m.* (**—s,** *pl.* **—e**) cyclone; **auf —e bezüglich,** cyclonic.

Cy'klus, *m.* (**—,** *pl.* **Cyklen**) cycle; **ein — von Vorlesungen über einen Gegenstand,** a course *or* set of lectures on a subject.

Cylin'd—er, *m.* (**—s,** *pl.* **—**) cylinder; chimney (*of a lamp*); top hat. **—risch,** *adj.* cylindrical. **—ro'n,** *n.* high top hat (*sl.*). *Comp.* **—er=bureau,** *n.* roll-top desk, roll-top drop cabinet. **—er=decke,** *f.* cylinder jacket *or* cover. **—er=hemmung,** *f.* cylinder escapement (*Horol.*). **—er=hut,** *m.* top hat. **—er=lampe,** *f.* Argand lamp. **—er=presse,** *f.* roller-press, type revolving press. **—er=scheibe,** *f.* piston. **—er=schreibtisch,** *m.* roll-top drop cabinet. **—er=uhr,** *f.* watch with cylinder (*or* horizontal) escapement, lever watch.

Cym'bel, Zim'bel, *f.* (*pl.* **—n**) cymbal. *Comp.* **—schläger,** *m.*, **—schlägerin,** *f.* cymbalist, cymbal player.

Cy'n—iker, Ky'n—iker, *m.* (**—ikers,** *pl.* **—iker**) cynic (*philosopher*), cynical person. **—isch,** *adj.* cynical, impudent, saucy; grossly sensual; dirty, foul. **—is'mus,** *m.* cynicism; doctrine of the cynics; impudence, shamelessness.

Cy'per, *f.* Cyprus plum. *Comp.* **—wein,** *m.* wine from Cyprus, Cyprian wine.

Cypref'se, *f.* (*pl.* **—n**) cypress. **—n,** *adj.* of cypress, cyprine. *Comp.* **—n=baum,** *m.* cypress (-tree). **—n=hain,** *m.* grove of cypresses.

Cy'ste, *f.* (*pl.* **—n**) cyst (*Med.*).

Cza'ko, *m.* *see* **Tschako.**

Czar, *m.* *see* **Zar.**

Czech, *m.* *see* **Tschech** *in the Index of Names.*

D

D, d, D, d; Re, D (*Mus.*); **D dur,** D major; **D moll,** D minor; *for abbreviations see Index at the end of the German-English part.* *Comp.* **—schieber,** *m.* D-valve (*in steam engines*). **—zug,** *m.* = **Durchgangszug,** through train; corridor train, vestibule train (*Amer.*).

Da, I. *adv.* (*a*) there; here; **hier und —,** here and there; now and then; **— ist sein Zimmer,** there is his room; **— bin ich,** here I am; **wer —?** who goes there? (*Milit.*); **was —?** what is the matter? **wo —?** where? **wo denn —?** where then, pray where? **nichts —!** nothing of the kind, by no means; nonsense; **he —!** halloo! **— draußen,** out there; **— droben (drunten),** up (down) there; **von —,** from there, thence; **— und dort,** here and there; **wieder —,** here again, back once more; **— sein,** to be present, existent, on the spot, at hand, to have arrived; **das —sein,** existence, life; **für mich ist das gar nicht —,** for me it is non-existent; **der Kaiser wird — und — sich aufhalten,** the Emperor will stay at such and such a place; **— bleiben,** to stay. (*b*) where (*obs. & poet.*); **ein Ort, — mich niemand kennt,** a place where I am unknown. (*c*) then, at that time; **wenn ich — noch lebe,** if I am then still alive; **ja, — wird man aber fragen,** true, but then people will ask; **— war es zu spät,** by that time it was too late; **von — an,** thenceforward. (*d*) when (*obs. & poet.*); **zu einer Zeit, — alles sich regte,** at a time when all were stirring. II. *part. generalising,* -ever, -soever, *or merely emphatic;* **es lache, wer — will,** whoever likes may laugh; **als — sind,** such as. III. *part. after* **der, die, das,** *to bring out the relative sense;* **alle, die — kamen,** all who came. IV. *in compds. with preps. for a dat. or acc. sing. & plur. of* **der, die, das,** *or of* **er, sie, es,** *used with regard to things, not persons;* **ich muß Sie —r=an erinnern,** I must remind you of it; **er hat mich — vor gewarnt,** he has warned me of it. V. *interj.*; **—!** there! **—, nun haben wir 's!** there! now we are in for it! VI. *conj.* then, under these circumstances, since, because; inasmuch as; while, whilst; although; **— nun, — doch,** since, since indeed; **—sonst,** whereas; **—hingegen,** on the contrary, whereas; **— sie eine Engländerin ist, so muß sie die englische Sprache verstehen,** as she is an Englishwoman she must understand English; **— der Kaiser einsah, daß,** the Emperor perceiving that.

Dabei', *adv.* thereby, thereat, therewith, by that, by it; at that place, near, close by; with it, with them; at the same time; in doing so; withal, moreover; in view of it, considering; nevertheless; with that; (= *dat. of a dem. or pers. pron. governed by* **bei** *in all its senses*); — **sein**, to be present, to take part, to help, to be of the party; — **stehen**, to stand by; **die —stehenden**, the bystanders; — **bleiben**, to hold out, persist in; — **blieb es**, there the matter ended; **ich bin —**, agreed! I'll make one (*of a party, etc.*), I've no objection; **er ist gescheut und — fleißig**, he is clever and industrious besides; — **sagt' er auch**, moreover he said; **ich bin — nicht gefährdet**, I risk nothing in the matter; — **sah er mich an**, with that he looked at me; **ich habe mir nichts Böses — gedacht**, I did it without meaning any harm, without thinking any evil.

Daca'po, *adv.* da capo; — **rufen**, to encore; — **singen**, to sing a second time.

Dach, *n.* (—**es**, *pl.* **Dächer**) roof; shelter, cover; house; dome (*of an engine boiler*); head; upper stratum (*Min.*); part of a violin; **ohne —**, houseless; — **und Fach**, housing; **weder — noch Fach**, neither house nor home; **einem auf dem —e sitzen**, to watch a person's actions closely (*coll.*); **einem aufs — steigen**, to blow one up, to come down upon one, to give s.o. a good scolding (*coll.*); **es regnet auf sein —**, he is blamed (*coll.*); **bei ihm ist gleich Feuer im —e**, he is very hot-headed, flies into a passion in a moment; **in — und Fach erhalten**, to keep in repair. *Comp.* —**balken**, *m.* roof-tree; girder. —**decker**, *m.* slater, tiler, thatcher. —**fahne**, *f.* weathercock. —**fenster**, *n.* skylight; dormer-window. —**first**, *m.*, —**firste**, *f.*, —**forst**, *m.*, —**förste**, *f.* ridge (*of a roof*); gable-end. —**geschoß**, *n.* garret-story. —**gesperre**, *n.* rafters. —**hase**, *m.* cat (*hum.*). —**kammer**, —**stube**, *f.* garret, attic. —**kehle**, *f.* gutter. —**luke**, *f.* opening in the roof, luthern. —**pappe**, *f.* roofing felt, tar board. —**pfanne**, *f.* pantile, gutter-tile. —**reiter**, *m.* turret on a roof. —**rinne**, *f.* gutter. —**röhre**, *f.* spout of a gutter, gutter-pipe. —**schiefer**, —**stein**, *m.* slate for roofing. —**sparren**, *m.* rafter. —**stroh**, *n.* thatch. —**stuhl**, *see special article.* —**traufe**, *f.* eaves; droppings from the eaves. —**werk**, *n.* roofing. —**ziegel**, *m.* tile.

Da'ch—en, *v.a.* to roof. —**ung**, *f.* roof; roofing.

Dachs, *m.* (—(**s**)**es**, *pl.* —(**s**)**e**) badger; **ein frecher —**, an arrogant fellow (*coll.*). *Comp.* —**bau**, *m.* badger's hole. —**beinig**, *adj.* badger-legged. —**eisen**, *n.*, —**falle**, *f.* badger-gin. —**hund**, *m.* badger-dog. —**jagd**, *f.* badger-baiting.

Däch's—el, *m.* badger-dog; bow-legged person. —**eln**, *v.n.* to go badger-hunting. —**in**, *f.* female badger.

Dach'stuhl, *m.* woodwork of a roof, props and supports of a roof. *Comp.* —**brand**, *m.* burning of the woodwork of a roof.

Dach'te, Däch'te, *indic. & subj. imp.* of **denken**.

Dach'tel, *f.* (*pl.* —**n**) box on the ear.

Da'durch, *adv.* thereby; through that, through it; by this means; in that way; (= *acc. of a dem. or pers. pron. governed by* **durch**).

Dafe'rn, *conj.* if, in case that, provided; — **nicht**, unless.

Dafü'r (*sometimes* **Da'für**, *esp'lly in the meaning* in return for, to make up for) *adv.* for that, for it, for them; on behalf of it; in return for, instead of it; (= *acc. of a dem. or pers. pron. governed by* **für**); **ich kann nichts —**, I can't help it; **ich stehe Ihnen —**, *or* **ich bin dir gut —**, I will be answerable to you for it, I warrant you; **was wird mir —?** what am I to get by it? **teurer, — aber auch besser**, dearer, but better in proportion; — **sein**, to be in favour of, to vote for; — **halten**, to hold as an opinion. *Comp.* —**halten**, *subst n.* opinion, judgment; **nach meinem —halten, meines —haltens**, in my opinion.

Dage'gen (*sometimes* **Da'gegen**), I. *adv.* against it, that, them; in comparison with, over against it; in return, exchange, for it; on the contrary; on the other hand (= *acc. of a dem. or pers. pron. governed by* **gegen**); **ich habe nichts —**, I have no objection. II. *conj.* against that, in objection to that, on the contrary, on the other hand; but then; **das ist wahr, — läßt sich nicht leugnen** 2c., that is true, on the other hand it cannot be denied, *etc.*

Dagg, *n.* (—**s**, *pl.* —**en**), —**e**, *f.* (*pl.* —**en**) rope's end (*Naut.*).

Dahei'm, *adv.* at home; in one's own country.

Dahe'r (*sometimes* **Da'her**), I. *adv.* thence, from that place, from that, (*also conj.*) hence, for that reason, therefore; — **kommt es, daß**, hence it happens that. II. *sep. prefix with verbs of motion* = along; away, as; —**schlendern**, to stroll along, to come up strolling.

Da'herum, *adv.* thereabouts.

Dahie'r, *adv.* here, in this place (*obs.*)

Dahi'n (*sometimes* **Da'hin**), *adv.* thither; to that place, time, state; thitherwards; (*used with verbs as sep. prefix* =) away, along, gone, past; **seine Seele ist —**, his soul has departed; **mein Glück ist —**, my good fortune is all over; **bis —**, up to that time, till then; — **habe ich es nie bringen können**, I could never bring it to that; **er spricht es so —**, he says it lightly, at random; **er äußerte sich —**, he spoke to this effect; **meine Meinung geht —**, my opinion is; **diese Dinge gehören nicht —**, these things have no bearing on the subject; **diese Zeiten sind —**, these times are gone by; **all' seine Sorge ist — gerichtet**, all his care is bent upon that. *Comp.* —**ab**, *adv.* down there. —**aus**, *adv.* out thither; **will er —aus?** is that what he is driving at? —**bringen**, *ir.v.a.* to carry to a place, to bring to a certain point; **es —bringen**, to bring a th. about, to succeed with a th., succeed so far with; (**einen**) —**bringen**, prevail upon, persuade. —**gegen**, *adv.* on the contrary. —**stehen**, *ir.v.n.* to be uncertain. —**stellen**, *v.a.* (**es** *or* **etwas**): —**gestellt sein lassen**, to leave a th. undecided, to offer no opinion on a subject. —**welken**, *v.n.* to wither, fade away.

Dahin'ten, *adv.* behind, behind there.

Dahin'ter, *adv.* behind that *or* it; there behind, *etc.*; **viel Worte und wenig —**, much talk and little in it; **es steckt etwas —**, there is more there than meets the eye; **es ist** *or* **steckt nichts —**, there is nothing in it; — **kommen**, to discover, find out (*coll.*).

Dahl'bord, *m. & n.* gunwale of a ship.

Dahl'en, *v.n.* (*aux.* **h.**) to trifle, dally.

Dakty'l—isch, *adj.* dactylic. —**us**, (*pron.* **Dak'tylus**, *pl.* **Dakty'len**) *m.* dactyl.

Dal'les, *m.* ruin (*Jewish lang.*); **den — haben**, to be short of money (*coll.*).

Dal'li, *interj.* quick! (*dial.*). *f.* ironing machine.

Dam— (*in comp.*). —**bock**, —**hirsch**, *m.* buck, fallow deer. —**geiß**, —**kuh**, *f.* fallow doe. —**kitze**, *f.* fawn. —**wild**, *n.* fallow deer.

Da'mal—ig, *adj. & adv.* then being, of that time; **die —ige Königin**, the then reigning queen. —**s**, *adv.* then; in those days; at that time.

Damasc—e'ner, *indec. adj.* from Damascus, Damascus. —**ie'ren**, *v.a.* to damask; to damaskeen (*steel, etc.*); **ein —ierter Flintenlauf**, a Damascus twist barrel. —**t** (*pron.* **Da'mast**), *m.* (—**tes**, *pl.* —**te**) damask. —**ten** (*pron.* **da'masten**), *adj.* damask, made of damask.

Da'me, *f.* (*pl.* —**n**) lady, gentlewoman; dame; queen (*at cards*); king (*at draughts*); draughts; **wollen wir eine Partie — spielen** *or* **ziehen?** shall we have a game at draughts? **in die —**

kommen, to get a king (*at draughts*). *Comp.* **—n=**, ladies', for ladies. **—n=abteil**, *m.* ladies' compartment, 'for ladies (only)'. **—n=brett** (*also* **Da'mbrett**), *n.* draught-board. **—n=flor**, *m.* show of ladies. **—n=friede**, *m.* treaty of Cambray (1529). **—n=held**, *m.* lady-killer; ladies' man, dangler. **—n=hut**, *m.* lady's hat *or* bonnet. **—n=niederrad**, *n.* ladies' safety (cycle). **—n=pferd**, *n.* ladies' horse, palfrey. **—n=reitkleid**, *n.* riding-habit. **—n=sattel**, *m.* side-saddle. **—n=schneider**, *m.* ladies' tailor. **—(n)=spiel**, *n.* draughts. **—n=ste.r**, *m.* man (*at draughts*). **—n=wahl**, *f.* the ladies' turn (*at a ball when ladies are called upon to select their partners*). **—n=welt**, *f.* ladies, the fair sex. **—n=wetter**, *n.*; **es ist —nwetter**, there is neither dust nor sun.

Däm'chen, *n.* (**—s**, *pl.* **—**) little lady; street walker.

Dä'm—(e)lak, *m.* silly person, fool (*coll.*). **—isch**, *adj. & adv.* silly. **—lich**, *adj. & adv.* dull, silly, stupid. **—lichkeit**, *f.* dulness, silliness, stupidity (*fam.*)

Dami't (*sometimes* **Da'mit**, with this), I. *adv.* therewith, with it, with that; by it *or* this (= *dat. of pers. or dem. pron. governed by* **mit**); **heraus —**, out with it! **was wollte er — sagen?** what did he mean by it? **es ist aus —**, there's an end of it. II. *conj.* (**dami't**) in order to, that, so that, to; **— nicht**, lest; **— ich es kurz mache**, to be brief; **ich sage es dir nochmals, — du es nicht vergißt**, I tell it again to you for fear you should forget it.

Damm, *m.* (**—es**, *pl.* **Däm'me**) dam; dyke; weir; embankment; mole; pier; perinaeum (*Anat.*); sand-bar (*Naut.*); **auf dem — sein**, to be stirring, very well, to feel up to things (*coll.*); **er ist nicht ganz auf dem —e**, he is rather seedy (*coll.*) *Comp.* **—bau**, *m.* building of a dam, dyking. **—bruch**, *m.* bursting of a dyke; crevasse; rupture of the perinaeum. **—grube**, *f.* pit (*for bell-casting*). **—geld**, *n.* quay dues. **—läufer**, *m.* canal boat.

Däm'men, *v.a.* to dam up, off; to restrain, check.

Däm'mer, *m.* (**—s**) dusk, twilight. **—haft**, **—ig**, *adj. & adv.* dusky, dusk. *Comp.* **—licht**, *n.*, **—schein**, *m.* dusk, twilight.

Däm'mer—n, *v.n.* (*aux.* **h.**) to dawn; to grow dusk; **eine —nde Hoffnung**, a gleam of hope. **—ung**, *f.* twilight, dawn. **—ungs=kreis**, *m.* crepuscular zone (*Phys.*).

Dä'mon, *m.* (**—s**, *pl.* **Dämo'nen**) demon. **—isch**, (*pr.* **dämo'nisch**) *adj.* demoniacal, irresistible, overpowering.

Dampf, *m.* (**—es**, *pl.* **Däm'pfe**) vapour, steam; mist; reek, fume, smoke; asthma; **davor hat er —**, he is afraid of that (*coll.*); **das Pferd hat den —**, the horse is broken-winded. *Comp.* **—absperrung**, *f.* shutting off of steam. **—aus=lassungs=röhre**, *f.* escape-pipe (*for steam*). **—bad**, *n.* vapour bath. **—bagger**, *m.* steam dredger. **—brot**, *n.* steam-made bread. **—druck**, *m.* vapour pressure. **—erzeuger**, *m.* steam-generator. **—esse**, *f.* steam-pipe, funnel. **—fähre**, *f.* steam-ferry. **—kessel**, *m.* boiler (*Mech.*); steamer (*Cook.*). **—klappe**, *f.* steam valve. **—kolben**, *m.* piston. **—kolben=stange**, *f.* piston-rod. **—küche**, *f.* steam-kitchen; cooking by steam. **—kur**, *f.* course of vapour baths. **—maschine**, *f.* steam-engine. **—maschinen=gebäude**, *n.* engine-shed. **—messer**, *m.* pressure-gauge. **—nudeln**, *pl.* ribbon vermicelli. **—omnibus**, *m.* steam tramcar. **—schiff**, *n.* steamboat, steamer. **—schiff=fahrt**, *f.* steamboat service. **—schiffahrts=verbindung**, *f.* steam communication. **—spritze**, *f.* steam-engine. **—ventil**, *n.* steam valve. **—webstuhl**, *m.* powerloom. **—weg**, *m.* steam-passage. **—wellenbad**, *n.* steam cataract-bath. **—walze**, *f.* steam-roller.

Dam'pf—en, *v.n.* (*aux.* **h.**) to smoke; to send forth steam; rise as vapour; to reek; to evaporate. **—er**, *m.* (**—ers**, *pl.* **—er**) steamer.

Däm'pf—en, *v.a.* to damp; to suffocate; to quench, to extinguish; to suppress; to quell; to depress; to subdue; to muffle (*drums*); to steam, to stew; to lay (*dust*); to put a mute on (*a violin*); **mit gedämpfter Stimme**, below one's breath, in an undertone. **—er**, *m.* (**—ers**, *pl.* **—er**) extinguisher; damper in steam engines; mute, damper (*on violins, pianos, etc.*). **—ig**, *adj.* short-breathed, asthmatic; short-winded. **—ung**, *f.* quenching, *etc.* *Comp.* **—pfanne**, *f.* stew-pan, stewing pan.

Dana'ch (*sometimes* **Da'nach**), *adv.* after that, afterwards, thereafter; accordingly, according to that; towards, to that; upon that; for that *or* it; (= *dat. of a dem. or pers. pron. governed by* **nach**); **er sieht ganz — aus**, he looks very much like it; **sehen Sie —**, look to it.

Dane'ben, *adv.* near it, next to it, by the side of it; close by, beside; (*also conj.*) moreover, besides, at the same time, also; (= *dat. or acc. of dem. or pers. pron. governed by* **neben**).

Dang, Dä'nge (*rare*) *imperf. ind. & subj. of* **dingen**.

Danie'der (*also* **Darnie'der**) *adv.* on the ground; down; **er liegt krank —**, he is lying ill. *Comp.* **—liegen**, I. *ir.v.n.* to succumb; to be broken; to be ruined *or* subdued; to languish. II. *subst. n.* prostration, depression.

Dank, *m.* (**—es**) thanks; gratitude; reward; prize, palm (*at a tournament*); **— sagen, — abstatten**, to return thanks, to thank; **(einem) seinen verbindlichsten — aussprechen**, to return hearty thanks; **einem für eine Sache — wissen**, to be thankful (grateful, obliged) to s.o. for a th.; **er weiß es** (*gen.*) **mir keinen —**, he is anything but grateful to me for it; **schlechten — mit etw. verdienen**, to be paid with ingratitude for a th.; **mit — annehmen**, to accept with gratitude; **Sie würden mich zu — verpflichten, wenn Sie**, you would much oblige me by; **schönen —!** many thanks! **Gott sei —!** thank God! **der Bettler wünschte mir Gottes —**, the beggar expressed the wish that God might reward me; **es (einem) zu —e machen**, to give satisfaction; **(das Wort sie sollen lassen stahn und) keinen — dazu haben**, much against their will, whether they like it or not (*obs.*) *or* without receiving any special commendation for it. **—bar**, *adj.* grateful, obliged; (**gegen einen**, to a p.); profitable, advantageous; effective. **—barkeit**, *f.* gratitude; **zur —barkeit verpflichtet**, bound in gratitude. *Comp.* **—adresse**, *f.* vote of thanks. **—bezeigung**, *f.* proof *or* mark of gratefulness. **—ens=wert**, *adj.* worthy of thanks. **—fest**, *n.* thanksgiving feast. **—gottesdienst**, *m.* thanksgiving service; Te Deum (*Rom. Cath.*). **—lied**, *n.* hymn of thanksgiving. **—opfer**, *n.* thank-offering. **—predigt**, *f.* thanksgiving sermon. **—rede**, *f.* speech in returning thanks, thanks. **—sagung**, *f.* returning thanks.

Dan'ken, *v.a. & n.* (*aux.* **h.** *dat.*) to thank, return thanks; to owe, be indebted; to return a salute; to decline an offer; **wollen Sie etwas trinken? (ich) danke**, will you drink anything? No, thank you; **dir danke ich mein Leben**, to you I owe my life; **—d erhalten**, received with thanks, paid, settled (*C.L.*).

Dann, *adv.* then, at that time; thereupon; **— und wann**, now and then; **selbst —**, even then. **—en**, *adv.*; **von —en**, (from) thence.

Dara'n (*sometimes* **Da'ran**), **Dran**, *adv.* thereon, thereat, thereby; at *or* on it, that, them; to it *or* that; about, near it *or* that; in regard to it *or* that; (= *dat. or acc. of a dem. or pers. pron. governed by* **an**); **nahe —**, close by, close to; on the eve of; **er war nahe — sein Leben zu verlieren,** he was near losing his life; **jetzt bin ich —,** now it is my turn; **er ist eifrig —,** he is hard at it; **ich weiß nicht wie ich — bin,** I don't know what to think of it; **es war drauf und —, daß er (fortging),** he was nearly (leaving); **— glauben,** to believe in it; **— glauben müssen,** to have to die (*coll.*); **— liegen,** to lie near; to be of importance, to concern; **was liegt —?** what does it matter? **mir ist nichts — gelegen,** it is a matter of indifference to me; **es ist nichts —,** there is nothing in it; it is good for nothing; **einen — nehmen,** to take a p. to task; **— sein,** to be in a certain condition; to be in for a th.; **gut, wohl bei einem — sein,** to be in favour with a person; **übel, schlimm — sein,** to be badly off; **wie ist er mit den Pferden —?** how is he off for horses? **wenn ich recht — bin,** if I am not mistaken; **er will nicht gern —,** he does not like the business; he is unwilling to undertake it; **nicht — wollen,** to decline an undertaking, to keep aloof; **— setzen,** to stake, to hazard; **ich zweifle — ob,** I doubt whether.

Darau'f (*sometimes* **Da'rauf**), **Drauf,** *adv.* thereon, thereupon; upon it, that *or* them; to that; after that; afterwards; then, next; in addition; (= *dat. or acc. of a pers. or dem. pron. governed by* **auf**); **— kommen,** to come to speak of, to call to mind; **wie kommen Sie —?** what put that idea into your head? **— gehen,** to be spent *or* wasted; to be lost, to perish, to die (*coll.*); **gleich —,** directly afterwards; **gerade — zu,** directly towards it; **er will sich nicht — einlassen,** he does not want to go in for it; **— geht er eben aus,** that is just what he aims at; **Sie können sich — verlassen, daß,** you may rest assured that, you may rely on; **er dringt —,** he insists on it; **frisch —! — und dran!** on! at them! **ich wollte — schwören,** I would take my oath on it; **es steht der Kopf —,** it is a capital offence; **etwas — geben,** to give earnest money; to credit, to attach importance to; **den Tag —,** the next day. *Comp.* **—geld** (= **Draufgeld**), *n.* earnest money.

Darau's, Draus, *adv.* thereout, therefrom; thence; from out of it, this, that, them; forth from it; by reason of it *or* that (= *dat. of a pers. or dem. pron. governed by* **aus**); **ich mache mir nichts —,** I do not mind that *or* it; **— folgt,** hence it follows; **was wird am Ende —?** what will be the end of it? **es kann nichts — werden,** nothing can come of it, it cannot be done; **— kann ich nicht klug werden,** I cannot make it out, that beats me.

Dar'ben, *v.n.* (*aux.* **h.**) to starve, famish; to be in want (**an einer S.,** of a th.); **einen — lassen,** to starve a p., to allow a p. to starve.

Dar'biet—en, *ir.v.a.* to offer, to hold out, tender. **—ung,** *f.* offering, tendering; exposition, explanation; **eine künstlerische —ung,** an artistic performance.

Dar'bringen, *ir.v.a.* to bring, to offer; to make (*a sacrifice, etc.*).

Darei'n, Drein, *adv.* thereto, thereinto; into it *or* that; to it *or* that; in addition, over and above; on, along, into *or* against it, that, *etc.*; (= *acc. of a pers. or dem. pron. governed by* **in**); **sich — finden, fügen, schicken,** to accommodate oneself to a thing; **— geben,** to give into the bargain; **oben —,** over and above; **sich — geben,** to submit to; **sich — legen,** to meddle, interpose, interfere; **— reden,** to interrupt; **— willigen,** to consent to: **— schlagen,** to strike at random, to strike in.

Darf; Darfst, *1 & 3; 2 ps. sing. pres. ind. of* **dürfen.**

Dari'n, Drin, *adv.* therein, in there; in, within, at it, that *or* them; (= *dat. of pers. or dem. pron. governed by* **in**); **mit — begriffen,** included. **—nen** (*usually* **drin'nen**), *adv.* there within, inside.

Dar'leg—en, *v.a.* to lay down; to lay open, state, set forth; to demonstrate. **—ung,** *f.* laying down; statement, exposition.

Dar'leh(e)n, *n.* (—**s**, *pl.* — *or* —**e**) loan.

Dar'leih—e, *f.* (*pl.* —**en**) loan. **—en,** *ir.v.a.* to lend (*out*). **—ung,** *f.* lending, loan.

Darm, *m.* (—(**e**)**s**, *pl.* **Där'me**) gut, intestine, bowel; **der dicke —,** the colon. *Comp.* **—bandwurm,** *m.* tape-worm. **—bauchbruch,** *m.* gastrocele. **—bein,** *n.* haunch-bone; *in compounds:* iliac-, ilio-. **—bewegung,** *f.* peristaltic motion. **—bruch,** *m.* enterocele; hernia. **—drüse,** *f.* intestinal gland. **—entzündung,** *f.* enteritis. **—falte,** *f.* ligament of the colon. **—fell,** *n.* peritoneum. **—fieber,** *n.* gastric fever. **—gang,** *m.* intestinal canal. **—grimmen,** *n.* colic. **—haut,** *f.* intestinal membrane, peritoneum. **—kanal,** *m.* intestinal canal. **—lehre,** *f.* enterology. **—netz,** *n.* caul. **—saite,** *f.* catgut string (*Mus.*). **—schleim,** *m.* mucus. **—schnitt,** *m.* enterotomy. **—schwanz,** *m.* appendix to the caecum. **—spritze,** *f.* clyster pipe. **—verschließung,** *f.* stoppage of the bowels. **—verschlingung,** *f.* twisting of the bowels, volvulus. **—würmer,** *pl.* ascarides.

Darna'ch, *see* **Danach; er fragt nichts —,** he does not mind it; **— handeln,** to act accordingly; **— es sich trifft, — es fällt,** as it happens; **es ist billig, aber es ist auch —,** it is cheap, but it is worth no more; **seine Kräfte sind nicht —,** his strength is not equal to it.

Daro'b, *adv.* on account of it, that, them; at it, that, them; (= *dat. of a pers. or dem. pron. governed by* **ob,** *now replaced by* **darüber**).

Dar'r—e, *f.* (*pl.* —**en**) kiln-drying; kiln; phthisis, consumption, atrophy; roup (*in birds*). **—en,** *v.a.* to kiln-dry; to smelt (*copper*). *Comp.* **—fieber,** *n.* hectic fever. **—gekrätz,** *n.* slag. **—haus,** *n.* kiln. **—ofen,** *m.* drying-kiln. **—sucht,** *f.* consumption. **—süchtig,** *adj.* consumptive, hectic.

Dar'reich—en, *v.a.* to reach forth; to proffer, present, administer. **—ung,** *f.* offering.

Dar'stellbar, *adj.* fit to be represented.

Dar'stell—en, *v.a.* to place, bring before; to exhibit, display; to state; to represent; **sich —en,** to present itself (*to the mind, etc.*); **sich —en** (*obs. poet.*) to appear, to come forward, to be seen; **unrichtig —en,** to misrepresent. **—er,** *m.* (—**ers**, *pl.* —**er**) representer, actor. **—ung,** *f.* exhibition; representation; performance; statement; recital; **Christi —ung im Tempel,** presentation of Christ. *Comp.* **—ungs-gabe,** *f.* power of representing *or* describing.

Dar'thun, *ir.v.a.* to prove, demonstrate; to set forth.

Darü'ben, Drü'ben, *adv.* over there, over yonder, beyond, yonder, opposite.

Darü'ber, Drü'ber, *adv.* over that *or* it; thereon, about that; concerning it *or* that; of it *or* that; on that point; over and above; besides; in the mean time, before that; across it *or* that; (= *dat. or acc. of a pers. or dem. pron. governed by* **über**); **eher —,** past it rather; **fünf Mark und —,** five marks and more; **— geht nichts,** nothing surpasses that; **— ist kein Zweifel,** there is no doubt about it; **alles geht drunter und —,** everything is topsy turvy; **sich — (her) machen,** to make for a th., to fall upon a th.; **— ist er gestorben,** he died in the mean time *or* while engaged on it; **wir werden — sterben,** we shall die before that; **— ist er erhaben,** he is above that.

Da'rum (*also* **Daru'm**), **Drum,** *adv.* thereabout, around it *or* that; for it *or* that; respecting it, that, them; therefore; on that account; about that; (= *acc. of pers. or dem. pron. governed by* **um**); — **kommen,** to lose; — **bringen,** to deprive (of); — **weil,** because; — **daß,** (so) that; **er weiß** —, he is aware of it; **es sei** —, let it be so! no matter! for ought I care! **es ist mir sehr — zu thun, nicht 2c.,** it is very important that I should not, *etc.;* **es ist mir nur — zu thun,** all that I ask *or* my only object is to.

Darun'ten, Drun'ten, *adv.* below, down there, beneath.

Darun'ter, Drun'ter, *adv.* under that, it, them, there; beneath it, that, them; among them; less; (= *dat. or acc. of a pers. or dem. pron. governed by* **unter**); **zwei Jahre und** —, two years and under; — **kann ich es nicht geben,** I cannot give it for less; **dies ist das beste** —, this is the best among *or* of them; **was sucht er** —? what is his object in it? **alles ging drüber und** —, all was topsy-turvy. *Comp.* —**liegend,** *adj.* subjacent.

Das, *nom. & acc. of the neut. sing. of* **der.** I. *def. art.* the. II. *rel. pron.* which, that. III. *dem. adj.* that, it. IV. *dem. pron.* that one, it. *Comp.* —**jenige,** *see* **derjenige.** —**mal,** *adv.* this time, this once, for this time. —**selbe,** *see* **derselbe.**

Da'sein, I. *ir.v.n.* (*aux.* **f.**) to be there present, to exist; **das ist noch nicht dagewesen,** that is unprecedented. II. *subst.n.* presence; existence; life; **während meines —s,** whilst I was present; **gleichzeitiges** —, co-existence; **Kampf ums** —, struggle for life, struggle for existence.

Dase'lbst, *adv.* there, in that very place.

Da'sig, *adj.* of that place.

Dä'sig, *adj.* silly, dull (*dial.*).

Daß, *conj.* that; — **nicht,** lest; — **nur nicht,** provided that . . . not; **so** —, so that, so as; **bis** —, till; **nicht — ich wüßte,** not that I know of; — **du kommst, ist mir lieb,** I am glad you have come; **für den Fall — ich sterbe,** in case of my death; **er ist zu stolz als — er es annehmen möchte,** he is too proud to accept it; — **Gott erbarm(e)!** may God have mercy on us! God a mercy!

Datie'r—en, *v.a.* to date; **falsch —en,** to misdate; **zurück —en,** to antedate; **nach —en,** to postdate. —**ung,** *f.* dating (*of a letter*).

Da't—iv, *m.* (—**ivs,** *pl.* —**ive**) dative (*case*). —**o,** *adv.* of the date; **bis —o,** up to date, till now; **de —o,** dated, under date (*of*); from to-day; **a —o,** after *or* from date; of (*the*) date. —**um,** *n.* (—**ums,** *pl.* **Data** *or* **Daten**) date (*of time*); **welches —um haben wir heute?** what day of the month is it? **von welchem —um ist der Brief?** what is the date of the letter? **einige wichtige —a,** a few important facts *or* points.

Datt'el, *f.* (*pl.* —**n**) date (*fruit*). *Comp.* —**baum,** *m.* —**palme,** *f.* date-palm. —**bohne,** *f.* dwarf kidney bean. —**kern,** *m.* date-stone.

Dau'be, *f.* stave (*of a cask*); **in —n schlagen,** to stave (*a cask*).

Däucht (**mir** *and* **mich** —), *irreg. 3. ps. sing. pres. ind. of* **dünken.**

Däuch'te, 3 *ps. sing. imperf. ind. & subj. of* **dünken.**

Däuch'ten, *v.a. &n. imp.* to become likely (*rare*); to appear (*rare & obs.*).

Dau'er, *f.* duration, continuance; length; permanence, durableness; constancy; longevity; **von kurzer** —, short lived; **auf die** —, for long duration; in the long run; **auf die — gemacht,** made to last; **auf die — von 20 Jahren,** for the term of 20 years; **die — eines Geschosses,** time of flight (*of a ball, etc.*). —**haft,** *adj.* durable, permanent; sound; stout. —**haftigkeit,** *f.* durableness, durability; strength. —**lauf,** *m.* running race, long race. —**marsch,** *m.* long march. —**pflanze,** *f.* perennial plant.

[1]**Dau'er—n,** *v.n.* (*aux.* **h.**) to last, continue; to hold out; to keep (*of meat, fruit*); **es —te über eine Stunde ehe,** it was more than an hour before; **das Stück —t mir zu lange,** I find the play too long; **er kann in der Kälte nicht —n,** he cannot stand the cold (*obsol.*); **kurze Zeit —nd,** short lived; **lange —nd,** of long duration.

[2]**Dau'er—n,** *v.a. & imp.* to make sorry, to regret, to grieve; **der arme Kerl —t mich,** I am sorry for the poor fellow; **du —st mich,** I pity you; **es —t mich, es gethan zu haben,** I regret having done it; **mich —t mein Geld nicht,** I do not mind the expenditure; **sich** (*acc.*) **etwas —n lassen,** to grudge, begrudge a th.; **die Ritter ließen sich ihr Blut nicht —n,** the knights did not mind risking their lives, willingly shed their blood.

Dau'men, *m.* (—**s,** *pl.* —) (*arch.* **Daum**) thumb; **einem den — aufdrücken, auf das Auge halten** *or* **setzen,** to keep a tight rein on one; **einem den — halten,** to support, patronize one; to wish a p. well, to accompany s.o. with one's good wishes who undertakes a difficult task. —**Sdick,** *nom. propr.* Tom Thumb. *Comp.* —**beuger,** *m.* flexor. —**dreher,** *m.* flatterer. —**drücker,** *m.* handle, doorlatch; protector, patron (*fam.*). —**klapper,** *f.* castanet. —**kraft,** *f.* handscrew, jack. —**leder,** *n.* thumb-stall. —**schraube,** *f.*, —**stock,** *m.* thumb-screw; **einem —schrauben ansetzen,** to press one hard (*coll.*). —**welle,** *f.* tumbling-shaft.

Däum'ling, *m.* (—**s,** *pl.* —**e**) (*also* **Däumerling**) thumb-stall, cot; **der kleine** —, Tom Thumb.

Dau'n—e, *f.* (*pl.* —**en**) down. —**icht,** —**ig,** *adj.* downy.

[1]**Daus,** *n.* (—(**s**)**es,** *pl.* **Däuser**) deuce (*in dice throwing*); ace (*in card playing*).

[2]**Daus,** *m.;* **wie ein** —, like something remarkably fine; **geputzt wie ein** —, very smart; **ich bin ein — (im Zeichnen),** I can (*sketch*) to perfection; **ei der** —! (*what*) the deuce!

Davo'n, (*sometimes* **Da'von**) *adv.* therefrom, thereof, thereby; of, by, respecting it, that *or* them; thence; hence; away; off (= *dat. of a pers. or dem. pron. governed by* **von**); **was habe ich —?** what do I get by it? **es ist nicht weit** —, it is not far off; **bleibt —!** keep off! — **bringen,** to save; — **kommen,** to make off, escape; **mit genauer Not — kommen,** to have a narrow escape; **sich — machen,** to make off, run away, take to one's heels; — **tragen,** to carry off, get, obtain.

Davo'r (*sometimes* **Da'vor**), *adv.* before it, that *or* them; for, because of, from it, that *or* them; against it, that *or* them; (= *dat. or acc. of pers. or dem. pron. governed by* **vor**); — **fürchte ich mich nicht,** I am not afraid of it; **hüte dich** —, beware of it; — **behüte uns Gott! da sei Gott vor!** God forbid! *see* **Dafür.**

Dawi'der (*sometimes* **Da'wider**), *adv.* against it, that *or* them; to the contrary; (= *acc. of a pers. or dem. pron. governed by* **wider**); **ich habe nichts** —, I have no objection to it; **dafür und** —, the for and against, the pro's and con's; **sich — setzen,** to oppose.

Dazu' (*sometimes* **Da'zu**), *adv.* thereto; to, for, at it, that *or* them; for that purpose, to that end; moreover, besides, in addition; (= *dat. of pers. or dem. pron. governed by* **zu**); — **ist er da,** it is for that purpose that he is there; — **gehört Zeit,** that requires time; — **kommt,** add to this; **noch** —, besides, moreover, to boot; — **kommen,** to arrive (*unexpectedly*), to happen, to supervene; to get by it, obtain; **ich komme nie —, Besuche zu machen,** I can never find time to pay visits; — **thun,** to add to; to make haste, to set about it; — **geben**, to contribute to; **er spricht auch** —, he also has a word to say; **er gehört mit** —, he is one of the party; **sie sang und er blies die Flöte** —, she sang and he accompanied her on the flute. *Comp.* —**mal** (*pron.* **da'zumal**), *adv.* then, at that time.

Dazwi'schen, *adv.* between, amongst them, in between, in the midst of it, that *or* them; there between; (= *dat. or acc. of pers. or dem. pron. governed by* **zwischen**); **es ist der Unterschied** —, (**daß**), there is this difference (that); — **kommen**, to intervene; **wenn nichts — kommt**, if nothing come to prevent (*it*); — **reden**, to interrupt (*a conversation*); **sich — schlagen**, to interpose. *Comp.* —**kunft**, *f.* intervention. —**liegend**, *adj.* intermediate. —**schreiben**, *ir.v.a.* to write between the lines.

Debat't—e, *f.* (*pl.* —**en**) debate. —**ie'ren**, *v.a.* & *n.* to debate.

De'bet, *n.* (—**s**) debit; **im — stehen**, to be on the debit side. *Comp.* —**posten**, *m.* charge; item charged. —**seite**, *f.* left hand side (*of ledger*).

De'bit, *m.* (—**s**) sale. —**a'nt**, *m.* dealer, selling agent; retailer. —**or**, *m.* (—**ors**, *pl.* —**o'ren**) debtor. *Comp.* —**kommission**, *f.* committee appointed to examine a bankrupt's effects. —**masse**, *f.* bankrupt's estate. —**verfahren**, *n.* legal proceedings in case of insolvency.

Debitie'r—en, *v.a.* to debit, charge to one's account; **Waaren —en**, to dispose of, sell goods. —**ung**, *f.* charging, debiting; sale, disposal.

Debütie'ren, *v.n.* (*aux.* **h.**) to make one's first appearance (*on the stage, etc.*).

Deca'n, Deka'n, *m.* (—**s**, *pl.* —**e**) dean. —**a't**, *n.* (—**a'ts**, *pl.* —**a'te**) deanery.

Decem'ber, Dezem'ber, *m.* (—**s**, *pl.* —) December.

Dechan—a't, *n.* (—**a'ts**, *pl.* —**a'te**) office of a dean, deanship. —**ei'**, *f.* deanery. —**t**, (*pron.* **Decha'nt**) *m.* (—**ten**, *pl.* —**ten**) dean.

De'cher, *m.* & *n.* (—**s**, *pl.* —) a quantity *or* number of ten (*especially of hides*).

Decima'l, Dezima'l, *adj.* decimal; **periodischer** —, circulating decimal. *Comp.* —**bruch**, *m.* decimal fraction. —**wage**, *f.* decimal balance.

Deck, *n.* (—**es**, *pl.* —**e**) deck. —**e**, *f.* (*pl.* —**en**) cloth, cover, coverlet, quilt; veil; rug, cover; case; ceiling; roof; skin; integument; coat (*Anat.*); sounding-board (*Mus.*); cover, pretence, pretext; —**e eines Kutscherbockes**, hammer cloth; **geteerte** —, tarpaulin; —**e eines Pferdes**, horse-cover; —**e eines Buches**, book-cover; **unter einer —e stecken**, to conspire together; to be accomplices; **sich nach der —e strecken**, to do as one can, act according to circumstances, to cut one's coat according to one's cloth. —**el**, *m.* (—**els**, *pl.* —**el**) lid, cover (*of a box, etc.*); tympan (*Typ.*); operculum (*Bot.*); cornice (*Arch.*); apron (*Artil.*); hat (*coll.*). *Comp.* —**balken**, *pl.* beams (*of a ship*). —**bett**, *n.* plumeau. —**blatt**, *n.* wrapper (*of cigars*). —**el=becher**, *m.*, **el=kanne**, *f.* tankard with lid. —**el=korb**, *m.* basket with lid. —**en=flechter**, *m.* mat maker. —**en=gemälde**, —**en=stück**, *n.* painted ceiling; sky-scene (*Theat.*). —**farbe**, *f.* body-colour. —**firnis**, *m.* covering varnish for etching. —**gang**, *m.* covert-way (*Fort.*). —**haut**, *f.* integument (*Anat.*). —**mantel**, *m.* cloak (*to a design*). —**netz**, *n.* sweep-net (*Sport*). —**offizier**, *m.* warrant officer, non-commissioned officer; **erster — offizier**, master. —**stroh**, *n.* thatch. —**worpen**, —**wrangen**, *pl.* deck-transoms. —**zeug**, *n.* table-linen.

De'ck—en, *v.a.* to cover (*also Mil.*); to protect, to conceal; to reimburse; to pay for; **den Tisch —en**, to lay the (table)cloth; **es ist gedeckt**, the table is laid; **für sechs Personen —en**, to lay covers for six persons; **einen Wechsel —en**, to meet a bill; **hinlänglich gedeckt sein**, to have sufficient security, be sufficiently assured; **sich —en**, to coincide (*Math.*); **das —en des Zuckers**, claying, bottoming. —**er**, *m.* (—**ers**, *pl.* —**er**) one that covers; slater, thatcher, roofer; layer of a cloth, *etc.*; (*in comp.* =) -decker, *as* **Drei—er**, three-decker (*Naut.*). —**ung**, *f.* covering, protecting, *etc.*; protection; reimbursement, refunding; breastwork, epaulement (*Fort.*); covering (*of a debt, a loss, etc.*); guard (*Fenc.*); congruence, coincidence, equality (*Math.*). *Comp.* —**ungs=truppen**, *pl.* covering party.

Dedicie'ren, Dedizie'ren, *v.a.* to dedicate, inscribe to; to make a present (*of*).

Deducie'ren, Deduzie'ren, *v.a.* to deduct.

Deern, *f.* (*Low Gm. for* **Dirne**) girl (*often said at Bremen, Hamburg, etc.*).

Defe'kt, I. *m.* (—**es**, *pl.* —**e**) defect. II. *adj.* defective; damaged. —**ie'ren**, *v.a.* to purge (*an account*). —**i'v**, *adj.* defective. *Comp.* —**bogen**, *m.* imperfect sheet.

Defens—io'n, *f.* (*pl.* —**io'nen**) defence. —**i'v**, *adj.* defensive; **die —ive ergreifen**, to act on the defensive.

Defilie'r—en, *v.n.* (*aux.* **h.**) to file off; **vorbei —en**, to march past. *Comp.* —**cour**, *f.* levee, drawing-room. —**marsch**, *m.* march past (in parade).

Definiti'v, *adj.* definite; final.

Defraud—a'nt, *m.* (—**an'ten**, *pl.* —**an'ten**) cheat; smuggler. —**ie'ren**, *v.a.* & *n.* (*aux.* **h.**) to cheat; to smuggle.

Def'tig, *adj.* & *adv.* thorough(ly), strong(ly) (*coll. & dial.*).

[1]**De'gen**, *m.* (—**s**, *pl.* —) sword; **zum — greifen**, to draw the sword. *Comp.* —**fläche**, *f.* flat of the sword. —**förmig**, *adj.* ensiform. —**gefäß**, *n.* sword-hilt. —**gehänge**, —**gehenk**, *n.* sword-belt. —**klinge**, *f.* sword-blade. —**knopf**, *m.* pommel; **ein alter deutscher —knopf**, an honest blade, an honest and jolly old fellow, a man of the old stamp. —**koppel**, *f.* sword-belt. —**scheide**, *f.* scabbard. —**stoß**, *m.* sword-thrust. —**stock**, *m.* sword-cane.

[2]**Degen**, *m.* (—**s**, *pl.* —) thane, warrior; vassal; hero; **ein alter Hau—**, a staunch old warrior, an experienced old blade (*usually implying: with little theoretical training*).

Degradie'ren, *v.a.* to degrade; to reduce in rank.

Dehn'—bar, *adj.* extensible, ductile, malleable. —**barkeit**, *f.* extensibility; ductility, malleability. —**holz**, *n.* stretcher (*for gloves, etc.*).

Deh'n—en, *v.* I. *a.* to stretch, extend, lengthen, expand; to drawl (*one's words*); to produce (*a line*); **gedehnte Silbe**, long syllable. II. *r.* to stretch; to last long. —**ung**, *f.* extension; **Ersatz—ung**, *f.* compensatory (vowel-)lengthening (*Gram.*). —**ungs=zeichen**, *n.* mark of lengthening, sign that a vowel sound is sustained; circumflex (*accent*); diastole (*Rhet.*).

Deich, *m.* (—**es**, *pl.* —**e**) dike, dam; embankment. *Comp.* —**anker**, *m.* foundation of a dike. —**graf**, *m.*, —**hauptmann**, *m.* dike-grave *or* reeve. —**kamm**, *m.* ridge, coping of a dike. —**meister**, *m.* dike-master. —**schoß**, *n.* dike-rates. —**vogt**, *m.* dike-inspector. —**wesen**, *n.* diking matters.

Dei'ch—en, *v.a.* to dike. —**er**, *m.* ditcher, diker, navvy.

Deich'sel, *f.* (*pl.* —**n**) pole (*of a carriage*), beam, shaft, thill. *Comp.* —**gabel**, *f.* shafts (*of a cart, etc.*). —**nagel**, *m.* thill-pin. —**pferd**, *n.* shaft-horse, wheeler.

Deich'seln, *v.a.*; **etwas** —, to bring s.th. about, to get a th. done (*coll.*).

Dein, (—, —**e**, —) I. *poss. adj.* thy, thine. II. — (*arch. & poet.*), —**er**, *gen. sing. of* **du**.

of thee, thine; **wir haben — gewartet**, we have waited for thee (*obsol.*). III. *poss. pron.* thine; **dieser Augenblick ist —**, this moment is thine. IV. *n. see* **Mein**, IV. **—er, —e, —es**, *or* **der, die, das —e**, *poss. pron. see* **—ige. —ige**, (**der, die, das —ige**) *poss. pron.* thine; **das —e** *or* **—ige**, thy property, thy part; **thue das —e** *or* **—ige**, do your duty; **die —en** *or* **—igen**, your (thy) family *or* people. *Comp.* **—er=seits**, *adv.* on thy side; for thy part, as concerns thee; in thy turn. **—et=halben, —et=wegen, —et=willen**, *adv.* on thy account, for thy sake, as far as thou art concerned; for aught thou carest. **—es=gleichen**, *indec. adj. & pron.* the like of you, such as thou, of thy kind.

Dei'ning, *f.* swell *or* surge (*of the sea*), surf.

Dein'sen, *v.n.* (*aux.* **h.**) to fall astern (*Naut.*).

Deis'—mus, *m.* deism. **—tisch**, *adj.* deistical.

Deka'd—e, *f.* decade. **—isch**, *adj.* decadal; **—isches Zahlensystem**, decimal system of numbers.

Deka'n, Deca'n, *m.* (—**s**, *pl.* —**e**) dean.

Dekalo'g, *m.* (—**s**) Decalogue.

Dekatie'ren, *v.a.* to hot-press (*cloth*); to lustre.

Deklam—a'tor, *m.* (—**s**, *pl.* **Deklamato'ren**) declaimer. **—atio'n**, *f.* declamation. **—ie'ren**, *v.a.* to declaim.

Deklarie'r—en, *v.a.* to declare; **Waaren am Zollamte —en**, to enter goods at the custom-house; **—ter Wert**, registered value (*of a post packet*).

Deklin—a'bel, *adj.* declinable (*Gram.*). **—a=tio'n**, *f.* declension (*Gram.*); declination. **—ier'bar**, *adj.* declinable. **—ie'ren**, *v.a.* to decline.

Deko'kt, *n.* (—**es**, *pl.* —**e**) decoction.

Dekolletie'r—en, *v.* I. *a.* to cut a dress low, to (leave) bare the neck and shoulders. II. *r.* to wear a low-bodied dress; to go bare-necked; to bare one's neck and shoulders; **sie —t sich zu sehr**, she wears her dresses too low. **—t**, *p.p. & adj.* low (-bodied), open; in a low-cut dress; bare-necked.

Dekor—ie'ren, *v.a.* to decorate. *Comp.* **—a=tio'ns=maler**, *m.* decorator; scene-painter.

Deko'rt, Deco'rt, *n.* (—**es**, *pl.* —**e**) deduction, discount. **—ie'ren**, *v.a.* to discount, abate, deduct.

Dekre't, *n.* (—**es**, *pl.* —**e**) decree. **—a'le**, *f.* (*pl.* **—a'lien**) decretal. **—ie'ren**, *v.a.* to decree.

Delega't, *m.* (—**en**, *pl.* —**en**) delegate. **—ie'=ren**, *v.a.* to delegate.

Delika't, *adj.* delicate, fine, nice, dainty; delicious. **—es'se**, *f.* (*pl.* **—es'sen**) dainty. *Comp.* **—essen=handlung**, *f.* Italian warehouse.

Delinque'nt, *m.* (—**en**, *pl.* —**en**), **—in**, *f.* delinquent.

Delkre'dere, Delcre'dere, *n.* guarantee, security.

Delphi'n, *m.* (—**s**, *pl.* —**e**) dolphin; delphin (*Chem.*). **—isch**, *adj.* delphinic.

Del'ta, *n.* (—**s**, *pl.* —**s**), delta. *Comp.* **—förmig**, *adj.* deltoid, triangular.

Dem, *dat. sing. of* **der, das**; **— sei wie ihm wolle**, be that as it may; **nach —**, according to that; **zu —**, moreover; **bei alle —**, notwithstanding; **es ist an —**, it is so; it is time; **es ist nicht(s) an —**, not so (*i.e.* there is no truth in it). *Comp.* **—gemäß**, *adv.* accordingly, according to that. **—nach**, *conj.* then, since, accordingly, therefore; *see* **Dem. —nächst**, *adv.* thereupon, after this; shortly, soon after. **—ohngeachtet, —ungeachtet**, *conj.* notwithstanding, nevertheless, in spite of that. **—zu=folge**, *conj.* accordingly, according to that.

Demago'g, *m.* (—**en**, *pl.* —**en**) demagogue. **—en=riecher**, *m.* spy on demagogues, demagogue-hunter. **—en=tum**, *n.* demagogism. **—isch**, *adj.* demagogical.

De'mant (*also* **Dema'nt**), *m.* (—**en**, *pl.* —**en**) adamant, diamond (*arch. & poet.*).

Demokra't, *m.* (—**en**, *pl.* —**en**) democrat. **—ie'**, *f.* democracy. **—isch**, *adj.* democratic.

Demonstrie'rstock, *m.* stick for the blackboard.

De'mut, *f.* (—, *no pl.*) humility, lowliness. **—s=voll**, *adj.* humble.

De'mütig, *adj. & adv.* humble, submissive, meek; condescending, gracious (*obs.*).

De'mütig—en, *v.a.* to humble; to humiliate, abase; to subdue; **sich —en**, to submit; to stoop, to eat humble-pie; **gedemütigt werden**, to be humiliated, to have to come down (*a peg*). **—ung**, *f.* humiliation; depression; abjectness.

Den, *acc. sing. of* **der**, *def. art. dem. adj. & rel. pron. & dat. pl. of* **der, die, das**, *def. art. & dem. adj.*

Dena'r, *m.* (—**s**, *pl.* —**e**) denarius.

De'nen, *dat. pl. of* **der, die, das**, *dem. & rel. pron.*; **— welche**, to such as.

Den'gel, *m.* (—**s**, *pl.* —) edge (*of a scythe, etc.*).

Den'geln, *v.a.* to whet a scythe by hammering.

Den'gelfieber, Den'guefieber, *n.* dandy fever, dengue.

Denk'—bar, *adj.* imaginable, conceivable; **das —bar schönste Verhältnis**, the most beautiful (harmonious) relation conceivable. **—barkeit**, *f.* conceivability. **—lich**, (*in compounds*) *adj.* thinkable. *Comp.* **—art**, *f.* way of thinking; mind, disposition; **er hat eine edle —art**, he has noble ideas, is high-minded. **—bild**, *n.* device, image, idea. **—faulheit**, *f.* mental inertness. **—freiheit**, *f.* freedom of thought *or* opinion. **—kraft**, *f.* cogitative faculty; intellectual power. **—lehre**, *f.* logic. **—mal**, *n.* monument, memorial; **zum —mal**, in memory of, in remembrance of. **—münze**, *f.* commemorative medal. **—säule**, *f.* memorial column. **—schrift**, *f.* record; memorial; memoir; memorandum, a formal application; inscription. **—spruch**, *m.* motto, sentence; maxim; devise. **—ungs=art**, *f. see* **—art. —vers**, *m.* commemorative verse. **—würdig**, *adj.* memorable, notable, worthy of thought. **—würdigkeit**, *f.* memorable occurrence; a thing to be remembered; (*pl.*) memoirs; memorabilia, commentaries (*of Cæsar*). **—zei=chen**, *n.* monument; memento. **—zettel**, *m.* memorandum; phylactery; punishment, correction, caution; box on the ear.

Den'k—en, *ir.v.a. & n.* (*aux.* **h.**) to think (**an einen** (*arch. & poet.:* **eines**), of a p.; **an eine Sache** (*arch. & poet.:* **einer S.** *or* **eine S.**), to call to mind, remember; to muse on; to reason, reflect on; to be of opinion, believe, suppose; to hold opinions; (*with* **zu** *& inf.*) to intend, contemplate, design; **sich** (*dat.*) **—en**, to form an idea of, think, imagine, fancy, conceive, realize; **er —t an nichts als**, he only thinks of; **ich —e nicht den Tod**, I am not thinking of death, there is no thought of death in my mind (*poet.*); **so lange ich —en kann**, so long as I can remember; **der Mensch —t, Gott lenkt**, man proposes, God disposes; **auf eine S. —en**, to contrive, plot, plan; **—en Sie sich nur!** only think! imagine! **wo —en Sie hin?** what do you think? what are you thinking of? **ich dächte do'ch** *or* **wo'hl**, I do think so, yes indeed; **bei sich —en**, to think to oneself; **man —e sich**, suppose, imagine; **das habe ich mir wohl gedacht**, I thought as much; **hin und her —en**, to revolve in one's mind; **was —en Sie zu thun?** what do you mean to do? **edel —end**, noble-minded, generous-minded; **ei, ich dächte gar!** why, that is out of the question! **das —en**, thinking, thought, cogitation; **philosophisches —en**, philosophical speculation; **tiefes —en**, deep meditation. **—er**, *m.* (—**ers**, *pl.* —**er**) thinker. *Comp.* **—er=stirn**, *f.* thoughtful brow; intelligent forehead.

Denn, I. *conj.* then; for; than (*after a compar. is now obs. & poet.*); **er ißt nichts, — er ist**

krank, he eats nothing, for he is ill; **wer ist reicher — er?** who is richer than he? II. *adv.* in that case; unless, or else (*obs.*); **er bezahle mich —,** unless he pay me; **ich lasse dich nicht, du segnest mich —,** I will not let thee go, except thou bless me; **es sei —, daß,** unless, provided. III. (*obs.*) but, except; **nichts — Gold,** nothing but gold. IV. *part.;* **wo ist er —?** where can he be? where is he? I wonder where he is? **wieso —?** how so? **was —!** what, indeed!

Den'noch, *conj.* yet, nevertheless, for all that, however.

Denuncia'nt, *m.* (**—en,** *pl.* **—en**) informer.

Depe'sche, *f.* (*pl.* **—n**) despatch; telegram. *Comp.* **—n=reiter,** *m.* mounted telegraph messenger; mounted orderly. **—n=schlüssel,** *m.* telegraph code. **—n=weg,** *m.;* **im —n=wege,** by telegraph.

Deport—atio'n, *f.* transportation. **—ie'ren,** *v.a.* to transport.

Depo'n—ens, *n.* (*pl.* **—en'tia**) deponent (*Gram.*). **—e'nt,** *m.* (**—en'ten,** *pl.* **—en'ten**) depositor (*in savings-banks, etc.*); deponent. **—ie'ren,** *v.a.* to deposit (*valuables*); to depose (*at a law court*).

Depo'sit—or, *m.* (**—ors,** *pl.* **Deposito'ren**) trustee, depositary. **—um,** *n.* (**—ums,** *pl.* **Depo'siten**) deposit. *Comp.* **—en=gelder,** *pl.*, **—en=kasse,** *f.* trustfund. **—en=schein,** *m.* deposit receipt.

Depossedie'ren, *v.a.* to dispossess.

Dep'pen, *v.a.;* **einen —,** to come down on, intimidate a p. (*sl.*)

Deput—a't, *n.* (**—a'ts,** *pl.* **—a'te**) extra allowance, allowances (*to officials*). **—ier'te(r),** *m.* (**—ier'ten,** *pl.* **—ier'te(n)**) deputy, member of a deputation.

Der, (**Die, Das,**) I. *nom. sing. of def. art.* the; **zweimal des Tages,** twice a day. II. *nom. sing. of dem. adj. & pron.* that, this, he, it; that one; **— und —,** such and such a one, so and so; **— Narr —!** fool that he is! **das sind die Männer, welche,** those are the men who; **bei alle dem,** for all that. III. *nom. sing. of rel. pron.* who, which, that; **unser Vater, — Du bist im Himmel,** our Father who art in Heaven; **der Du von dem Himmel bist,** Thou who comest from Heaven; **das wissen wir, die wir die Gemsen jagen,** we who hunt the chamois know that. IV. *Sometimes to be rendered by the Engl. possessive;* **er hat den Arm gebrochen,** he has broken his arm; **sie rief den Sohn,** she called her son; **er hat sich in den Finger geschnitten,** he has cut his finger. V. *gen. & dat. sing. of* **die,** *def. art. & dem. adj. & dat. sing. of* **die,** *dem. & rel. pron.* VI. *gen. of pl.* **die,** *def. art. & dem. adj.* **—en,** *see* **Deren.** **—er,** *gen. pl. of* **der, die, das,** *dem. pron.;* **das Geschlecht —er von Bismarck,** the race of the Bismarcks. **—o,** *gen. pl. of* **der, die,** your; his; **—o Gnaden,** your Grace; **seine Majestät haben —o Ministern befohlen,** His Majesty has directed his ministers; *in compounds:* **—ohalben, —owegen** (*arch.*) = **deshalb, deswegen.** *Comp.* **—ei'nst,** *adv.* at some future time, some day, hereafter. **—einst'tig,** *adj.* that is to be, future. **—gestalt,** *adv.* in such shape *or* manner; to such a degree; **—gestalt, daß,** so that. **—gleichen,** *indec. adj.* of such kind, such like, the like; **—gleichen habe ich nie gesehen,** I never saw the like; **—gleichen Tiere giebt es nicht,** there are no such animals; **und —gleichen,** and so forth. **—jenige,** *see* **Derjenige.** **—lei,** *indec. adj.* of that sort *or* kind. **—maleinst,** *adv. see* **—einst.** **—malen,** *adv.* now, at present. **—malig,** *adj.* actual, of this time. **—maßen,** *adv.* to that degree; in such a manner; so much. **—selbe,** *see* **Derselbe.** **—weile. —weilen,** *adv.* meanwhile. **—zeit,** *adv.* at that time, at present. **—zeitig,** *adj.* for the time being, actual, present.

Derb, *adj. & adv.* compact, firm, solid; powerful, hardy; smart, severe, sharp; hearty; telling, keen; blunt; rough, uncouth. **—heit,** *f.* compactness; firmness; sturdiness; keenness, bluntness; (*pl.*) hard words, home truths.

De'ren, *gen. sing. f. & gen. pl. m. f. & n.* of **der, die, das,** *dem. & rel. pron's;* **kaufe keine Blumen, ich habe — genug,** buy no flowers, I have enough of them; **ich sah zwei Mädchen, — Gesichter sehr schön waren,** I saw two girls, whose faces were very beautiful. *Comp.* **—t=halben, —t=wegen,** (**um**) **—t=willen,** *adv.* for her sake, on her account, on their account, on whose account. (**Deren** *is used for the gen. sing. f. & for the gen. pl. of all genders of* **welcher,** *rel. pron., & occasionally to avoid ambiguity for the poss. adj.* **ihr.**)

Der'jenige, (**Diejenige, Dasjenige,** *pl.* **Diejenigen**) *dem. adj. & pron.* those; such; he, she, it (*before a rel. pron.*).

Deriv—a'tum, *n.* derivative. **—ie'ren,** *v.a.* to derive.

Der'selbe, (**Dieselbe, Dasselbe;** *pl.* **Dieselben**) **Derselbige,** *dem. adj. & pron.* the same, the self-same; **der Wein ist gut, ich kann Ihnen denselben empfehlen,** the wine is good, I can recommend it to you; **er sprach von seinem Sohne und rühmte die Talente desselben,** he spoke of his son and praised his talents; **was befehlen (Höchst) Dieselben?** what is your (*Grace's, Highness's, etc.*) pleasure?

Der'wisch, *m.* (**—(e)s,** *pl.* **—e**) dervish.

[1]**Des,** *n.* D flat (*Mus.*) **—=Dur,** D flat major; **—=Moll,** D flat minor.

[2]**Des,** (*sometimes spelt* **Deß**) *gen. sing.* (*arch. & poet.*) *of def. art.* **der, das; wes Brot ich ess', des Lied ich sing',** whose bread I eat, his opinion I hold (*prov.*). *Comp.* **—falls,** *adv.* in this case; in which case; on that account; therefore. **—fallsig,** *adj.* eventual, pertaining to that case; **—fallsige Bestimmungen,** eventual determinations. **—gleichen,** I. *indec. adj.* similar, such like. II. *adv.* in like manner, after the same fashion, likewise. III. *conj.* as also; **so wohl er als sie, —gleichen sein Vater,** not only he and she, but also his father. **—halb,** *adv. & conj.* on this account, for that reason, therefore. **—wegen, —willen,** *adv. & conj.* on that account, for that reason, therefore; **eben —wegen,** for that very reason.

Desert—eu'r, *m.* (**—eu'rs,** *pl.* **—eu're**) deserter. **—ie'ren,** *v.n.* (*aux.* **s.**) to desert, run away.

Designie'ren, *v.a.* to designate (*for*).

Desinf—ektio'n, *f.* disinfection. **—ektio'ns=mittel,** *n.* disinfectant. **—izie'ren,** *v.a.* to disinfect.

Despektier'lich, *adj.* disrespectful, irreverent.

Despo't, *m.* (**—en,** *pl.* **—en**) despot. **—isch,** *adj.* despotic. **—is'mus,** *m.* despotism, despotic power.

Deß, *see* **Des.**

Des'sen, I. *gen. sing. of the dem. & rel. pron.'s* **der, das,** whose, of whom, of which, of that; whereof. II. *used also occasionally for the poss. adj.* **sein,** *and for the gen. sing. of* **welcher, welches,** *rel. pron.;* **der Herr, — Haus ich kaufte, ist ausgewandert,** the gentleman whose house I bought, has emigrated; **in — Haus ich wohne,** in whose house I live; **Roland ritt hinterm Vater her, mit — Speer und Schilde,** Roland rode behind his father with his (*the father's*) spear and shield. *Comp.* **—t=halben, —t=willen,** (**um —t=halben** & **—t=willen**) *adv. & conj.* therefore, on that account. **—ungeachtet,** *conj.* notwithstanding that, in spite of that.

Destill—ateu'r, *m.* (**—ateu'rs,** *pl.* **—ateu're**) distiller. **—ie'ren,** *v.a.* to distil. **—ie'rung,** *f.*

distillation (*also* —ation). *Comp.* —ier'=blase, *f.*, —ier'=gefäß, *n.* still. —ier'=kolben, *m.* alembic. —ier'=helm, *n.* still-head. —ier'=stube, *f.* laboratory.

Des'to, *adv.* (*used before comparatives*); the, so much; je mehr, — besser, the more, the better; — besser, all the better, so much the better; — eher, all the sooner, with still greater reason; nichts —weniger, nevertheless.

Detai'l, *n.* (—s, *pl.* —s) detail, particular; retail; ins — (ein)gehen, to particularize. —lie'ren, *v.a.* to detail; to retail. *Comp.* —geschäft, *n.*, —handlung, *f.* retail business. —li'st, *m.* retail merchant, shop keeper.

De=Tri'; die Regel —, the rule of three.

Deuch'ten, *see* Däuchten.

Deut, *m.* (—(e)s, *pl.* —e) small coin; trifle; keinen —, not a farthing, not a bit.

Deut—elei', *f.* forced explanation, strained interpretation. —eln, *v.a.* to subtilize; to put a false *or* sophistical explanation on; to explain away; drehn und —eln, turn and twist.

Deu't—en, *v.* I. *a.* to explain, expound, interpret; to apply, give an application to. II. *n.* (*aux.* h.) (auf) to make a sign, to point (*to*); to bode, augur; to signify; —en auf einen, to point to *or* to explain as referring to a person; auf gutes Wetter —en, to be a sign of good weather. —er, *m.* (—ers, *pl.* —er) explainer, interpreter. —ig, *adj. suffix* (*in comp.* =) significant, capable of such *or* so many interpretations, *e. g.* viel —ig, *adj.* capable of many explanations. —lich, *adj. & adv.* distinct, clear; intelligible, articulate. —lichkeit, *f.* distinctness, clearness. —ung, *f.* interpretation; meaning, signification; application; eine falsche —ung, a misconstruction. *Comp.* —ungs=voll, *adj.* susceptible of many interpretations; suggestive; ominous.

Deutsch, *adj. & adv.* German; das —e Reich, the German empire; der —e Bund, the Germanic Confederation (1815–66); der Nord —e Bund, the North German Confederation (1866–1871); der —e Orden, the Teutonic Order (*estab.* 1198); die —herrn, —ritter, *or* Brüder vom —en Hause, the Knights of the Teutonic Order; das —e Ordensland Preußen, the Prussian land governed by the Teutonic Order; das heilige römische Reich —er Nation, the Holy Roman Empire (962–1806); das —e Meer, the German Ocean, the North Sea; die —e Frage, the German question (*strong German Empire with or without Austria, solved in* 1866); der —e Krieg (*war of* 1866); ein —er, a German, a native of Germany; die alten —en, the ancient Germans, the old Teutons; groß —e, men who wished for a political union of German states including Austria (*before* 1866); klein —e, politicians who wished for a united Germany under the leadership of Prussia, to the exclusion of Austria; Ober —, Upper German (*especially South German*); Nieder —, Low German (*North Germ. dialects*); Platt —, Low German; das —e, the German language; übersetze ins —e, put into German; kann er —? does he know German? auf —, in German; *adv.* frankly, honestly, sincerely; — reden, to speak plainly *or* candidly; das heißt auf (gut) —, that is in plain language, that is as much as to say. *Comp.* —herrn, —ritter, *see above.* —herrlich, *adj.* belonging to the Teutonic Order. —land, *n.* Germany. —meister, *m.* Grand Master of the Teutonic Order. —verderber, *m.* corrupter *or* murderer of the German language. —tum, *n.* German nationality; German customs and manners; German patriotism. —tümeln, *v.a.* to play the Teutomane; to affect German manners. —tümelnd, *adj.* posing as a German. —tümelei', *f.* Germanomania; affectation of German manners. —tümlich, *adj.* characteristic of the Germans; thoroughly German.

Devi'se, *f.* (*pl.* —n) device, motto; bill (*of exchange, etc.*).

Deuch'ten, *see* Däuchten.

Dey, *m.* (—s, *pl.* —s) leader of the Janizaries in Algiers; pasha, Oriental despot.

Diagno'se, *f.* (*pl.* —n) diagnosis.

Diako'n, *m.* (—en, *pl.* —en) deacon. —a't, *n.* (—a't(e)s, *pl.* —a'te) diaconate. —is'sin, *f.* deaconess.

Diale'kt, *m.* (—s, *pl.* —e) dialect. —dichtung, *f.* dialect poetry. —forschung, *f.* investigation of dialects. —isch, *adj.* dialectal.

Dialek't—ik, *f.* dialectics. —iker, *m.* (—ikers, *pl.* —iker) dialectician. —isch, *adj.* dialectic.

Dialo'g, *m.* (—s, *pl.* —e) dialogue.

Diama'nt, *m.* (—en, *pl.* —en) diamond. —en, *adj.* of diamonds, set with diamonds, diamond; die —ene Hochzeit, the diamond wedding (the sixtieth anniversary of the wedding day). *Comp.* —en=glanz, *m.* adamantine lustre. —(en)=spitze, *f.* diamond pencil. —(en)=strauß, *m.* spray of diamonds.

[1]**Diät'**, *f.* diet, regimen; knappe —, low diet, short allowance. —e'tik, *f.* dietetics, hygiene.

[2]**Diät'**, *f.* diet, legislative assembly. —en (*pl.*) day's salary, allowance (*esp'lly to deputies*). *Comp.* —en=gelder, *pl.* board wages; allowance for rations; payment of members (of parliament).

Diato'nisch, *adj.* diatonic.

Dich, *acc. of* Du.

Dicht, *adj. & adv.* close (*in texture, etc.*); thick, dense, compact; tight (*as vessels*); — an, — auf, — neben, close by; — beim Winde segeln, to hug the wind; —es Gold, massive gold; ein —er Wald, a thick wood; eine —e Hecke, a thick hedge. —e, *f.* closeness, density (*obs.*). —en, *v.a.* to make close *or* tight; to condense; to caulk (*a ship*). —heit, —igkeit, *f.* closeness (*of texture, etc.*); density; quality of resistance; imperviousness. *Comp.* —hammer, *m.* caulking hammer. —verworren, *adj.* closely entangled.

[1]**Dich'ten**, *v.a.* to make close *or* tight; to condense; to caulk (*a ship*).

[2]**Dich't—en**, I. *v.a. & n.* (*aux.* h.) to compose; to invent; to make verses, write poetry. II. *subst.n.*; meditation, musing; composition of poetry; das —en und Trachten, thoughts, aim, endeavours. —er, *m.* (—ers, *pl.* —er) poet. —erin, *f.* poetess. —erisch, *adj. & adv.* poetic. —erling, *m.* (—erlings, *pl.* —erlinge) would-be poet, poetaster, bardling. —ung, *f.* poetry, poesy; poem; fiction. *Comp.* —er=ader, *f.* poetic vein. —er=freiheit, *f.* poetic license. —er=gott, *m.* Apollo. —er=roß, *n.* Pegasus. —er=wort, *n.* poetical expression; the words of the poet. —kunst, *f.* poetry, poetic art. —ungs=art, *f.* style (*of poetry*). —ungs=kraft, *f.*, —ungs=vermögen, *n.* poetic power, poetic talent, power of imagination.

Dick, *adj. & adv.* big; thick; fat, stout, corpulent; voluminous; ein —er Mensch, a fat, stout man; eine —e Wand, a thick, big wall; —e Milch, curdled milk; das —e Ende, butt-end; —e Freunde sein, to be fast friends, to be very intimate (*coll.*); etwas — haben, to be tired of a th. (*coll.*); sich mit einer Sache — thun, to boast of a thing, to talk big (*coll.*). —e, *f.* thickness, *etc.*; density; body. —icht, *n.* (—ichts, *pl.* —ichte) thicket. *Comp.* —bauch, *m.* paunch. —bäuchig, *adj.* big-bellied. —bein, *n.* thigh. —darm, *m.* great gut. —fellig, *adj.* thick-skinned. —häuter, *pl.* pachydermata. —hülsig, *adj.* thick-shelled. —kopf, *m.* chub (*Icht.*); blockhead, obstinate fellow (*coll.*). —köpfig, *adj.* obstinate (*coll.*). —leibig, *adj.* corpulent. —öhrig, *adj.* dull of hearing.

—**thuer**, *m.* braggart. —**thuerei'**, *f.* bragging, boasting (**mit**, of). —**zirkel**, *m.* callipers.

Dideldu'm, Dideldumdei', *interj.* tweedledum, tweedledee, fiddle-de-dee; heyday (*imitation of fiddling and merry music*).

Die, *f. sing. nom. & acc. of* I. *def. art.* II. *dem. pron.* III. *rel. pron.* IV. *nom. & acc. pl. of* **der, die, das.** *Comp.* —**selbe**, *see* **Derselbe.** —**weil**, *see* **Dieweil.**

Dieb, *m.* (—**es**, *pl.* —**e**) thief; **haltet den —!** stop thief! —**erei'**, *f.* thievery, theft; larceny (*Law*); —**erei verüben**, to pilfer. —**in**, *f.* female thief. —**isch**, I. *adj.* thievish; capital, excellent, jolly (*coll.*). II. *adv.* by theft; splendidly (*coll.*). *Comp.* —(**e**)**s=bande**, *f.* gang of thieves. —(**e**)**s=hehlerei**, *f.* receiving of stolen goods. —**s=helfer**, *m.* thief's accomplice. —**s=gesicht**, *n.* hangdog look. —**s=höhle**, *f.* nest of thieves. —**s=laterne**, *f.* dark lantern. —**s=schlüssel**, *m.* picklock. —**s=sicher**, *adj.* thief- *or* burglar-proof. —**stahl**, *m.* theft, robbery; **kleiner —stahl**, larceny; **der gelehrte —stahl**, plagiarism; **nächtlicher —stahl (mit Einbruch)**, burglary.

Die'le, *f.* (*pl.* —**n**) board, plank, deal; floor (*of a barn*); hall, vestibule; ceiling; loft.

Die'len, *v.a.* to floor; to board, plank.

Die'n—en, *v.n.* (*aux.* **h.**) to serve; to be of service to; to assist; to do service (*as a soldier, a servant, etc.*); to be good for, useful to; **zu etwas —en**, to be fit for something; **bei einem —en**, to be in one's service; **einem —en**, to serve a person; **das —t zu nichts**, that is of no use; **damit ist mir nicht gedient**, I don't like that, that is of no use to, will not do for me; **(Ihnen) zu —en**, at your service; **wozu —t es?** of what avail *or* use is it? **dieses —e zur Antwort**, this may do for an answer; **es soll mir zur Warnung —en**, it will be a warning to me; **kann ich Ihnen mit einem Stück Fleisch —en**, may I help you to a slice of meat? **womit kann ich Ihnen —en?** what can I do for you? —**er**, *m.* (—**ers**, *pl.* —**er**) (man) servant, attendant; official; reverence, bow; **gehorsamer —er!** your obedient servant; no, thank you! **stummer —er**, dumb-waiter, dummy; **wie der Herr, so der —er**, like master like man (*prov.*). —**erin**, *f.* maid servant, maid. —**erschaft**, *f.* the domestics. —**lich**, *adj. & adv.* serviceable. —**lichkeit**, *f.* serviceableness. *Comp.* —**er=tracht**, *f.* livery.

Dienst, *m.* (—**es**, *pl.* —**e**) service; worship; post, employment; office; good turn; **ein guter —**, a kind turn; **gute —e**, kind offices; **im —e**, on duty (*Mil.*), in waiting (*at court*); **in — treten**, to enter service, to go to service; **— nehmen**, to enlist, to go to service; **— bei der Fahne**, active service, service with the colours; **den — aufsagen**, to give notice; **bei einem im —e stehen**, to be in a p.'s service; **in aktivem —e**, in ordinary; with the colours; **einen — suchen**, to look out for a place; **was steht Ihnen zu —en?** what can I do for you? **ein — ist des andern wert**, one good turn deserves another; **es steht Ihnen zu —en**, you are welcome to it, it is at your disposal; **einem auf den — passen**, to watch one closely; **zum —** (*abbr.* **z. D.**), serving with the colours, in active service (*Mil.*); **außer —** (*abbr.* **a. D.**), out of place, off duty, unattached, retired (*Mil.*); **ein Major a. D.**, a major on half pay. —**bar**, *adj.* serviceable; liable to serve; subject; **er macht sich alle Welt —bar**, he makes everybody subservient to him; —**bare Geister**, ministering spirits, servants. —**barkeit**, *f.* servitude, bondage, subjection. —**lich**, *adj. & adv.* connected with the service; official; —**liche Stellung**, official position; — **verhindert**, prevented by duty. *Comp.* —**alter**, *n.* seniority in office. —**anzug**, *m.*, —**kleid**, *n.* uniform, livery. —**beflissen**, *adj.* officious; serviceable; zealous to serve. —**bote**, *m.* domestic servant. —**eifer**, *m.* zeal of office. —**ergeben**, *adj.* devoted. —**fähig**, *adj.* fit for office *or* service. —**fertig**, *adj.* officious; obliging. —**frei**, *adj.* exempt from service *or* military duty; off duty. —**gefällig**, *adj.* complaisant. —**geld**, *n.* money paid in lieu of service. —**grad**, *m.* military rank. —**herr**, *m.* master, lord; employer. —**leistung**, *f.* rendering of service; service. —**lohn**, *m.* servant's wages. —**los**, *adj.* out of service. —**magd**, *f.* maidservant. —**mann**, *m.* vassal, feudatory; out porter, town porter. —**pfennig**, *m.* earnest pledge. —**pflicht**, *f.* liability to service, duty of office; **(allgemeine) —pflicht**, (universal) compulsory military service. —**pflichtig**, —**schuldig**, —**verwandt**, *adj.* liable to do certain services. —**spritze**, *f.* maidservant (*coll.*). —**untauglich**, *adj.* unfit for military service. —**vorschrift**, *f.* rule of the service, instruction. —**willig**, *adj.* ready to serve. —**zeit**, *f.* time spent in service. —**zucht**, *f.* discipline of the service. —**zwang**, *m.* right to another's services; compulsion to serve.

Die'nstag, *m.* (—**s**, *pl.* —**e**) Tuesday.

Dies, *cont. of* **Dieses.** *Comp.* —**bezüglich**, *adj.* referring to this. —**falls**, *adv.* in this case. —**jährig**, *adj.* of this year. —**mal**, *adv.* this time, now. —**malig**, *adj.* this, present. —**seitig**, *adj.* on this side, on our side. —**seits**, *adv. & prep. with gen.* on this side.

Die'ser, *m.*, **Die'se**, *f.*, **Die'ses**, *or* **Dies**, *n.* (*pl.* **diese**) *dem. adj. & pron.* this, that, these, the latter, this one, *etc.*; **dieser ist es, von welchem wir sprachen**, this is the man we spoke of; **am vierten dieses, den vierten dieses**, on the fourth instant; **vor diesem**, ere now; **dieses euer Haus**, this house of yours; **dieser Tage**, (*adverbial gen. pl.*) one of these days; **zur Bewahrheitung dieses**, in faith whereof.

Die'trich, *m.* (—**s**, *pl.* —**e**) pick-lock.

Diewei'l, *adv. & conj.* as long as, during the time that; while; because.

Differenz—ie'ren, *v.a.* to differentiate. *Comp.* —**ia'l=rechnung**, *f.* differential calculus.

Dikt—a't, *n.* (—**a'ts**, *pl.* —**a'te**) dictation. —**atu'r**, *f.* (*pl.* —**atu'ren**) dictatorship. —**ato'risch**, *adj.* dictatorial. —**ie'ren**, *v.a.* to dictate.

Diktionä'r, *n.* (—**s**, *pl.* —**e**) dictionary.

Dilato'r—ium, *n.* writ of respite; postponement. —**isch**, *adj.*; —**ische Behandlung**, dilatory treatment (of affairs).

Dilett—a'nt, *m.* (—**an'ten**, *pl.* —**an'ten**), —**an'tin**, *f.* dilettante, amateur. —**an'tisch**, *adj. & adv.* amateurish.

Dine'r, *n.* (*pl.* —**s**) (*grand*) dinner.

Ding, *n.* (—**es**, *pl.* —**e** *or* —**er**) (**das Dings**, *coll.*) thing; matter; creature; transaction; law court, meeting (*obs.*); cause (*obs.*); **was ist das für ein —?** what is this? **guter —e sein**, to be in good spirits; **gut — will Weile haben**, things take time that are done well; **aller guten —e sind drei**, three is a lucky number (*prov.*); **das böse —**, whitlow; **das geht nicht mit rechten —en zu**, there is something uncanny about it; **vor allen —en**, first of all; above all; **das —s**, (*coll.*) the thing; **der kleine —sda**, the little wight, the little what's his name; —**skirchen**, name given to any place *or* thing, the real name of which one cannot remember; what do you call it? —**bar**, *adj.* that may be bargained for *or* hired. —**elchen**, *n.* little thing. —**lich**, *adj. & adv.* relating to things, not persons; real; judicial (*Law*); —**liche Klage**, real action. *Comp.* —**brief**, —**zettel**, *m.* contract. —**fest**, *adj.* confirmed by law; **einen —fest machen**, to secure *or* arrest a p. —**geld**, *n.* earnest money.

Din'g—en, *reg. & ir.v.a. & n.* to enter into conditions with; to bargain for; to hire; to engage; to bribe; to haggle.
Din'kel, *m.* (—s, *pl.* —) spelt, German wheat.
Din'te, *see* **Tinte.**
Diöce'se, *f.* (*pl.* —n) diocese.
Diphtheri'tis, *f.* diphtheria.
Diphtho'ng, *m.* (—s & —en, *pl.* —e & —en) diphthong. **—ie'ren,** *v.n.* to diphthongize.
Diplo'm, *n.* (—s, *pl.* —e) diploma, patent. **—a't,** *m.* (—a'ten, *pl.* —a'ten) diplomatist. —**a'tiker,** *m.* (—a'tikers, *pl.* —a'tiker) diplomatist, schemer. **—a'tisch,** *adj.* diplomatic; artful; **—atisch getreue Abschrift,** exact copy.
Dir, *dat. sing. of* **Du,** to thee.
Dire'kt, *adj. & adv.* direct; at first-hand; **—e Fahrkarte (nach),** through ticket (for). **—io'n,** *f.* direction; management; directory, board of directors. **—or,** *m.* (—ors, *pl.* —o'ren) director; manager; head-master (*of a school*). — **o'ren=versammlung,** *f.* Headmasters' Conference. **—ora't,** *n.* (—ora'ts, *pl.* —ora'te) headmastership (*of a school*); residence of a governor *or* headmaster. **—o'rium,** *n.* (—o'riums, *pl.* —o'rien) directory; board of directors.
Dirigie'ren, *v.a.* to direct, manage.
Dir'ne, *f.* (*pl.* —n) (*orig., but now arch. & poet.*) maid, girl; (*now*) low woman, bad girl, hussy.
Dis, *n.* (*Mus.*) D sharp. *Comp.* **—dur,** *n.* D-sharp major. **—moll,** *n.* D-sharp minor.
Diska'nt, *m.* (—s, *pl.* —e) treble, soprano. **—i'st,** *m.* (—i'sten, *pl.* —i'sten) treble-singer. *Comp.* **—schlüssel,** *m.* C clef.
Disko'nt, Diskon't—o, *m.* discount; deduction, rebate; **wie viel rechnen Sie —o?** what is the rate of discount? **—ie'ren,** *v.a.* to discount; **—ierter Wechsel,** discounted bill, bill negotiated.
Diskre't, *adj.* separate, distinct; prudent, discreet, modest. **—io'n,** *f.*; **sich auf—ion ergeben,** to surrender at discretion. *Comp.* **—ions=tage,** *pl.* days of grace.
Disku'rs, *m.* (—(s)es, *pl.* —(s)e) discourse.
Dispon—en'da, *pl.* books on sale that may be returned to the publisher. **—e'nt,** *m.* (—e'nten, *pl.* —en'ten) manager; agent. **—i'bel,** *adj.* that may be disposed of; available; unattached (*Mil.*). **—ie'ren,** *v.a. & n.* (*aux.* **h.**) to dispose of; to manage. *Comp.* **—ibilitä'ts=gehalt,** *n.* half-pay (*Mil.*).
Dispositio'n, *f.* (*pl.* —en) disposition, management. *Comp.* **—s=urlauber,** *m.* soldier on prolonged leave of absence, but liable to be called back at any time (*with the first army reserve*).
Disput—atio'n, *f.* (*pl.* —atio'nen) debate; maintenance of a thesis. **—ie'ren,** *v.a. & n.* (*aux.* **h.**) to dispute; to debate.
Dissertatio'n, *f.* (*pl.* —en) dissertation, learned treatise; **Doktor—,** *f.* dissertation written for obtaining the degree of doctor in a university.
Dissiden'ten, *pl.* dissenters, dissidents.
Dissona'nz, *f.* (*pl.* —en) dissonance.
Dis'tel, *f.* (*pl.* —n) thistle. *Comp.* **—fink,** *m.* gold-finch. **—wolle,** *f.* thistle-down.
Diurna'l, *n.* daily-prayer-book; day-book.
Di'van, *m. see* **Diwan.**
Divid—e'nd, Divid—en'dus, *m.* (—e'nds, *pl.* —en'den) dividend (*Arith.*). **—en'de,** *f.* dividend, share. **—ie'ren,** *v.a.* to divide. *Comp.* **—en'den=fonds,** *m.* bonus fund.
Divi's, *n.* (*pl.* —e) hyphen (*Typ.*).
Di'wan, *m.* (—s, *pl.* —s & —e) council; divan, sofa, couch; collection of poems.
Dob'ber, *m.* (—s, *pl.* —) a float, a buoy.
Dö'bel, *m.* peg, plug, pin. **—n,** *v.a.* to peg.
Doce'nt, Doze'nt, *m.* (—en'ten, *pl.* — **en'ten)** University teacher; professor, reader, lecturer; (*often short for* **Privatdocent,** *a distinguished young graduate recognized as teacher at a university, but unsalaried*); **—ent für Germanistik,** university teacher *or* professor of Germanic philology.
Doch, *adv. & conj.; part.* (*accented or unaccented according to the meaning; it is accented if it implies a contradiction or a strong assertion*) yet, still, however, nevertheless; for all that; but; at least; though; surely; **obgleich es verboten ist, geschieht es —,** (*accented*) although it is forbidden, it is done all the same; **o geschähe es —!** (*unacc.*) O how I wish that it would happen! **du willst nicht kommen? —!** (*acc.*) you will not come? O, yes, I will! **wir sind hier nicht allein. —, Lieschen,** we are not alone here. Yes, Lizzie, we are; **leugne nicht, du siehst es —!** (*acc.*) do not deny it, you do see it; **du siehst es —?** (*unacc.*) surely you see it, you can see it, I suppose? **sie ist häßlich, aber er liebt sie —,** (*acc.*) she is ugly, yet he loves her; **hilf mir —!** (*unacc.*) pray (*or* do) help me! **hättest du das — gleich gesagt!** (*unacc.*) if you had but said so at once! **ja —,** yes indeed, yes yes; **nein —,** no, no; **nicht —,** certainly not; **es ist — wohl nichts Böses?** there is nothing wrong, I trust? **laß es —,** please, let it alone! **sei — ruhig!** be quiet, will you! — **Herr Wirt, das haben Sie nicht gut gemacht,** say what you please, Mr. Landlord, you did wrong in this case.
Docht, *m.* (—es, *pl.* —e) wick. *Comp.* **—halter,** *m.* wick-holder; burner (*of a lamp*).
Dock, *m. & n.*; **schwimmendes —,** floating dock. **—e,** *f.* dock (*for vessels*); **—e mit Schleusenthüren,** dry dock. **—en,** *v.a.* to dock (*ships*).
Do'ck—e, *f.* (*pl.* —en) small column, baluster, rail; skein, hank, bundle; doll, smart girl (*obs.*); plug; jack (*of a harpsichord, etc.*). **—en,** *v.a.* to roll together; to wind up into (*a skein*); to stock sheaves. *Comp.* **—en=geländer,** *n.* balustrade.
Dog'ge, *m. & f.* (*pl.* —n) bull-dog, mastiff.
Dog'ma, *n.* (—s, *pl.* —ta, *now usually* **Dog'men**) dogma. **—mengeschichte,** *f.* history of doctrinal theology. **—tik,** *f.* (*pron.* **Dogma'tik**) dogmatics. **—tiker,** *m.* (*pron.* **Dogma'tiker**) (—tikers, *pl.* —tiker) dogmatist. **—tisch,** *adj.* dogmatic.
Doh'le, *f.* (*pl.* —n) jackdaw, daw; prostitute (*sl.*); old hat (*sl.*); **die — krächzt,** the jackdaw caws. *Comp.* **—n=nest,** *n.* jackdaw's nest.
Doh'ne, *f.* (*pl.* —n) bird-snare, gin, springe, noose. *Comp.* **—n=strich,** *m.* springe-line.
Dok'tor, *m.* (—s, *pl.* **Dokto'ren**) doctor; physician, surgeon; **— der Rechte,** doctor of laws (LL.D.); **— der Philosophie,** doctor of philosophy (Ph.D.); **einen zum — machen,** to confer the doctor's degree on a p.; **den — machen,** to obtain the degree of doctor; **er hat seinen — in Berlin gemacht,** he passed his examination for the doctorate at Berlin (*coll.*); **er hat sich den — in München geholt,** he got his doctor at Munich (*coll.*). **—a'nd,** *m.* candidate for a doctor's degree. **—a't,** *n.* (—a't(e)s, *pl.* —a'te), **—grad,** *m.*, **—würde,** *f.* doctorate, doctor's degree. **—in,** *f.* doctor's wife; lady-doctor. **—schaft,** *f.* body of doctors; medical profession. *Comp.* **—arbeit,** *f.* thesis. **—hut,** *m.* doctor's cap; **sich** (*dat.*) **den —hut holen,** to obtain the doctor's degree, to become a doctor. **—ingenieur,** *m.* doctor of engineering (*abbr.* **Dr. Ing.**)
Doktorie'ren, *v.a. & v.n.* to win, *also* to obtain, the degree of doctor, to pass an examination qualifying for the doctor's degree.
Dokumentie'ren, *v.a.* to prove (by documents) to show.
Dolch, *m.* (—es, *pl.* —e) dagger, poniard. *Comp.* **—messer,** *n.* bowie-knife. **—stock,** *m.* swordcane. **—stoß, —stich,** *m.* stab of a dagger.
Dold—e, *f.* (*pl.* —en) umbel; **in —en,** umbellated. **—ig,** *adj.* umbellate, having the form

of an umbel. *Comp.* **—en=tragend**, *adj.* umbelliferous. **—en=traube**, *f.* corymb.

Dol'lar, *m.* (—s, *pl.* —s) dollar.

Dol'man, *m.* dol(i)man.

Dol'metsch, *m.* (*obs.*) = **—er**. **—en**, *v.a.* to interpret. **—er**, *m.* (—ers, *pl.* —er) interpreter. **—erei'**, *f.* stupid *or* confused interpretation. **—ung**, *f.* interpretation.

Dom, *m.* (—(e)s, *pl.* —e) cathedral, cathedral church; dome, cupola (*Arch.*). *Comp.* **—chor**, *m.* choir of a cathedral. **—dechant**, *m.* dean of a cathedral. **—frau**, *f.* canoness. **—freiheit**, *f.* close of a cathedral. **—herr**, *m.* prebendary, canon. **—herrn=schmuck**, *m.* canonicals. **—kapitel**, *n.* (cathedral) chapter; dean and chapter, chapter-house. **—kirche**, *f.* cathedral, minster. **—pfaff**, *m.* canon; bullfinch; **der —pfaff pfeift**, the bullfinch pipes. **—prediger**, *m.* cathedral-preacher; pastor of a cathedral church. **—probst**, *m.* provost of a cathedral. **—sänger**, *m.* cathedral chorister. **—schule**, *f.* cathedral school, grammar school attached to a cathedral. **—stift**, *n.* chapter, cathedral.

Domä'ne, *f.* (*pl.* —n), **Domanial'gut**, *n.* domain, demesne.

Domici'l, **Domizi'l**, *n.* (—s, *pl.* —e) domicile, residence; address for payment (*C. L.*). *Comp.* **—wechsel**, *m.* removal, addressed bill (*comm.*)

Domin—an'te, *f.* (*pl.* —an'ten) dominant (*Mus.*). **—ie'ren**, *v.n.* (*aux.* **h.**) to domineer, to lord it.

Dominika'ner, *m.* (—s, *pl.* —) Dominican friar.

Do'mino, I. *m.* (—s, *pl.* —s) domino (*cloak*). II. *n.* (—s, *pl.* —s) game of dominoes; **—steine**, *pl.* dominoes; **—spielen**, to play at dominoes.

Don'ner, *m.* (—s, *pl.* —) thunder; **vom — gerührt**, thunderstruck. *Comp.* **—büchse**, *f.* blunderbuss. **—keil**, *m.* thunder-bolt. **—schlag**, *m.* thunder-clap. **—strahl**, *m.* flash of lightning. **—s=tag**, *m.* Thursday; **der grüne —stag**, Maundy-Thursday; **der feiste —stag**, Thursday before Lent. **—s=tägig**, *adj.* on Thursday; **—s=täglich**, *adj.* every Thursday, on Thursdays. **—wetter**, I. *n.* thunder storm; scolding, blowing up. II. *int.* zounds! hang it! **—wort**, *n.* terrifying word.

Don'nern, *v.n.* (*aux.* **h.**) to thunder.

Dop'pel—heit, *f.* doubleness, duplicity. *Comp.* **—adler**, *m.* spread eagle (*Her.*); the German Empire; Austria. **—bahn**, *f.* double-track railway. **—becher**, *m.* dice-box. **—bier**, *n.* strong beer. **—bruch**, *m.* compound fracture (*Surg.*); compound fraction. **—deutig**, *adj.* equivocal, ambiguous. **—ehe**, *f.* bigamy. **—fall**, *m.* alternative. **—flinte**, *f.* double-barrelled gun. **—gänger**, *m.* double, fetch, alter ego, wraith. **—gespann**, *n.* four-in-hand. **—griff**, *m.* double fingering, double stop (*mus. inst.*). **—herzig**, *adj.* deceitful. **—kreuz**, *n.* double sharp (*Mus.*). **—läufig**, *adj.* double-barrelled. **—laut(er)**, *m.* diphthong. **—lebig**, *adj.* amphibious. **—leiter**, *f.* pair of steps. **—punkt**, *m.* colon; double-point (*Math.*). **—schein**, *m.* conjunction (*Astrol.*). **—schluß**, *m.* dilemma (*Log.*). **—schritt**, *m.* rapid step, quick march. **—sinn**, *m.* ambiguity. **—spiel**, *n.* duet; double-dealing. **—strom**, *m.* double current. **—stück**, *n.* duplicate. **—telegraph**, *m.* duplex telegraph. **—t=hochrund**, *adj.* double convex. **—thür**, *f.* double door; folding door. **—treppe**, *f.* double flight of steps. **—verhältnis**, *n.* duplicate ratio. **—vers**, *m.* distich. **—währung**, *f.* double standard of currency, bimetallism. **—wesen**, *n.* duality; being with two natures. **—züngig**, *adj.* double-faced, deceitful. **—züngigkeit**, *f.* deceitfulness.

Dop'pel—n, *v.* I. *a.* to double; to sew double; to sole, to line. II. *n.* (*aux.* **h.**) to double one's stakes; to play at dice *or* backgammon; to cheat (*at play*). **—t**, *adj. & adv.* double, two-fold, twice; **drei —t**, three-fold; **in —ter Abschrift**, in duplicate. **—ung**, *f.* sheathing (*Naut.*); cheating (*at play*).

Dorf, *n.* (—es, *pl.* **Dör'fer**) village; **das sind ihm böhmische Dörfer**, that's all Greek to him. **—schaft**, *f.* villagers (*collectively*); village (*community*). *Comp.* **—bengel**, *m.* country bumpkin. **—bewohner**, *m.* villager. **—flur**, *f.* circuit of a village. **—gemeinde**, *f.* rural parish. **—geschichte**, *f.* village story, tale of country life. **—junker**, *m.* country squire. **—krug**, *m.* village inn. **—mäßig**, *adj.* rustic. **—pfarrer**, **—prediger**, *m.* country parson. **—richter**, *m.* village magistrate; chief in a village community. **—schenke**, *f.* village inn. **—schulmeister**, *m.* village schoolmaster. **—schulze**, *m. see* **—richter**.

Dörf—chen (—chens, *pl.* —chen), **—lein**, *n.* (—leins, *pl.* —lein) little village hamlet. **—ler**, *m.* villager. **—lich**, *a.* rustic, peasant-like.

Dorn, *m.* (—es, *pl.* —en; **Dör'ner** (*obs.*)) thorn, prickle; spine; prick-punch; tongue (*of a buckle*); **er ist mir ein — im Auge**, he is a thorn in my side. **—en**, *adj.* thorny (*obs.*). **—icht**, (*obs.*) **—ig**, *adj. & adv.* thorny; spinous. *Comp.* **—besäet**, *adj.* thorny. **—busch**, *m.* bramble. **—fisch**, *m.* stickle-back (*Icht.*). **—fortsatz**, *m.* spinal process. **—gesträuch**, *n.* briers. **—röschen**, *n.* Sleeping Beauty.

Dor'ren, *v.n.* (*aux.* **s.**) to become dry, to dry; to wither, to fade.

Dör'ren, *v.a.* to dry, to bake, to kiln-dry.

Dorsa'l, *adj.* dorsal; **—e Bildungsweise der Konsonanten**, consonants articulated by the action of the ridge (*dorsum*) of the tongue.

Dort, **Dor'ten** (*obs.*) *adv.* there, yonder; **— droben**, up there; **— hinein**, in there; **— herum**, there about; **— hinauf**, up there; **— hinaus**, **— heraus**, out there; **— hinunter**, **— hinab**, down there; **von — aus**, thence. **—ig**, *adj. & adv.* of that place, there. *Comp.* **—her**, *adv.* from yonder, thence. **—hin**, *adv.* to that place, thither.

Dorsch, *m.* (—es, *pl.* —e) cod-fish (*Icht.*).

Do'se, *f.* (*pl.* —n; *dim.* **Dös'chen**) box, snuff-box. *Comp.* **—n=baum**, *m.* mountain pine. **—n=stück**, *n.* painting on a snuff-box.

Do'sis, *f.* (*pl.* **Dosen**) dose; **zu starke —**, overdose.

Dö'sig, *adj.* stupid, dull; **mir ist heute ganz —**; I feel to-day rather stupid (*coll.*).

Dost, *m.* (—s, *pl.* —e), **—en**, *m.* (—ens, *pl.* —en) wild marjoram.

Dot—a'l, *adj.* pertaining to a dower. **—ie'ren**, *v.a.* to endow. *Comp.* **—al=güter**, *pl.* glebe lands.

Dot'ter, *n.* (—s, *pl.* —) yolk of an egg. *Comp.* **—blume**, *f.* marsh-marigold; butter-cup. **—weide**, *f.* yellow willow.

Doublet'te, *f.* duplicate (*postage stamps*).

Doublie'ren, *v.a.* to double (*silk*); to double (*Bill.*).

Douche, *f.* (*pl.* —n) shower-bath.

Doze'nt, see **Docent**.

Dra'che, *m.* (—n, *pl.* —n), (*less good*) **—n**, *m.* (—ns, *pl.* —n) dragon; paper-kite; serpent (*Pyro.*); termagant; **einen —n steigen lassen**, to fly a kite. *Comp.* **—n=artig**, *adj.* dragon-like. **—n=bild**, *n.* likeness of a dragon, image of a dragon. **—n=fliege**, *f.* dragon-fly. **—n=kraut**, *n.*, **—n=wurz**, *f.* dragon's-wort.

Drach'me, *f.* (*pl.* —n) drachm(a), dram.

Dragee', *f. & n.* (—(s), *pl.* —s & —n) sugar-plum.

Drago'ner, *m.* (—s, *pl.* —) dragoon; virago (*coll.*). **—mäßig**, *adj.* like a dragon.

Draht, *m.* (—es, *pl.* **Dräh'te**) thread; wire; file (*for papers*); money (*sl.*); (*pl.*) telegraphic wires. **—en**, *adj.* (made) of wire, wiry. *Comp.*

—antwort, *f.* reply by telegram. —arbeit, *f.* wirework; filigree. —bank, *f.* wire-drawing machine. —bauer, *n.* wire cage. —bericht, *m.* telegraphic information, telegram, wire. —brief, *m.* telegram. —eisen, *n.* draw-plate. —falle, *f.* wire-trap. —fenster, *n.* wire lattice; window with wire blind. —gewebe, *n.* wire-gauze. —gitter, *n.* wire grating; trellis. —hemd, *n.* shirt of chain mail. —kugel, *f.* cross-bar shot. —los, *adj.* wireless; —lose Telegraphie, wireless telegraphy. —panzer, *m.* chain-mail. —puppe, *f.* puppet. —saite, *f.* wire-string. —schere, *f.* wire-shears. —seilbahn, *f.* funicular railway, wire railway. —sieb, *n.* wire-sieve. —spille, —spindel, *f.* head-wire (*for pins*). —spinnen, *n.* wire-drawing. —stift, *m.* wire-tack. —zieher, *m.* wire-drawer. —zieherei, *f.* wire-drawing mill; wire-drawing.

Drah't—en, *v.a.* to wire, send a telegram. —ung, *f.* wire, telegram.

Dräh't—ern, *adj.* of wire, wiry (*obs.*). —ig, *suff.* (*in comp.*) containing such *or* so many threads.

Drainie'ren, *v.a.* to drain.

Draisi'ne, *f.* (*pl.* —n) old-fashioned velocipede; trolly.

Drall, I. *adj. & adv.* tight, close-twisted; strong, firm, plump, robust; smart; sprightly, active; eine —e Dirne, a buxom lass. II. *m.* (—s, *pl.* —e) rifling of a gun.

Dra'ma, *n.* (—s, *pl.* Dramen) drama. —tiker, *m.* (*prom.* Drama'tiker) (—tikers, *pl.* —tiker) dramatist. —tisch, *adj.* (*pron.* drama'tisch) dramatic. —tisie'ren, *v.a.* to dramatize. —tu'rg, *m.* teacher of the dramatic art, writer of critical essays on dramatic poetry and the stage. —turgie', *f.* dramatic theory, dramaturgy. —tur'gisch, *adj.* dramaturgic; —turgische Aufsätze, essays on the theory and practice of the dramatic art.

Dran, see Daran.

Drang, Drän'ge, *impf. ind. & subj.* of dringen.

Drang, *m.* (—(e)s, *no pl.*) throng, crowd; pressure, urgency; hurry; violence; impetus; impulse; distress, oppression; ich habe den — zu, I feel a desire for. —sal, *n.* (—sals, *pl.* —sale), & *f.* (*pl.* —sale) oppression; hardship, misery; labour (*B.*); —sal des Krieges, miseries of war. —salie'ren, *v.a.* to vex, to torment, to harass. *Comp.* —voll, *adj.* crowded; oppressed, miserable; —voll fürchterliche Enge, close and terrible straits.

Dräng'—eln, *v.a.* to press importunately, to harass. —elei', *f.* harassing, crush.

Dräng'—en, *v.* I. *a.* to press, crowd; to urge, hurry; to oppress; to afflict; sich —en, to crowd; sich durch —en, to force one's way through. gedrängt, *p.p. & adj.* crowded, close; gedrängt voll, crammed full. II. *n.* (*aux.* h.) to be in a hurry; to press (*on*); die Zeit —t, time presses. —er, *m.* (—ers, *pl.* —er), —erin, *f.* oppressor; burden, bore.

Drapie'ren, *v.a.* to furnish with drapery.

Drasch, *impf. ind.* of dreschen.

Dras'tisch, *adj.* drastic.

Dräu'en, (*obs. & poet.*) for drohen.

Drauf, *see* Darauf. —geld, *n.* premium, balance, earnest money.

Draus, *see* Daraus.

Drau'ßen, *adv.* outside, out of doors, without; abroad.

Drech'sel—n, *v.a. & n.* (*aux.* h.) to turn (*on a lathe*); Komplimente —, to bandy compliments. gedrechselt, *p.p. & adj.* elaborate; affected. *Comp.* —bank, *f.* turning-lathe.

Drechs'ler, *m.* (—s, *pl.* —) turner; vine-weevil (*Ent.*). —ei', *f.* turner's workshop. *Comp.* —arbeit, *f.* turnery; turning.

Dreck, *m.* (*fam. & dial.*) (—es) mud, dirt, filth; dung; excrement, muck, dregs; im — waten, to walk deep in the mud. —ig, *adj.* muddy, dirty, foul; nasty. *Comp.* —käfer, *m.* dung-beetle. —karren, *m.* scavenger's cart, dung-cart. —loch, *n.* slough.

Dreesch, *also* Driesch, I. *adj.* fallow, uncultivated. II. *m.* (—es, *pl.* —e), fallow land. —ling, *m.* eatable mushroom, champignon.

Dreh'—bar, *adj. & adv.* that may be turned *or* twisted, revolving; —barer Bücherständer, revolving book-case. —ling, *m.* (—lings, *pl.* —linge) spring-wheel, handle of a wheel; sheep suffering from staggers. *Comp.* —achse, *f.* axis of revolution. —bahn, *f.* rope-yard. —bank, *f.* turning-lathe. —baum, *m.* turn-stile; handspike. —brücke, *f.* turn-bridge. —eisen, *n.*, —stahl, *m.* chisel, turning gouge. —krankheit, *f.* giddiness; staggers (*of sheep*). —kreuz, *n.* turnstile. —orgel, *f.* barrel-organ. —punkt, *m.* centre of motion; pivot. —rad, *n.* fly-wheel; cordwheel. —rolle, *f.* mangle. —scheibe, *f.* potter's wheel; turn-plate, turntable; disk. —strom, *m.* rotatory current. —stuhl, *m.* revolving chair; music-stool. —tisch, *m.* dumb-waiter, table turning on a pivot. —turm, *m.* rotatory turret (*Mil.*). —ungsellipsoid, *n.* spheroid. —ungswinkel, *pl.* coordinates (*Math.*). —wage, *f.* torsion-balance. —würfel, *m.* teetotum. —zähler, *m.* turnstile. —zange, *f.* tweezers (*T.*). —zeug, *n.* twisting apparatus, twisters.

Dre'h—en, I. *v.a.* to turn; to twist; to wrest; to distort; sich —en, to turn; die Frage —t sich um, the question hinges on; die Sachen können sich —en, matters may take a (*favourable*) turn; einem eine Nase —en, to hoax one. II. *v.n.* (*aux.* h.) to turn; to veer (*of wind*); an einem Gesetze —en, to twist a law. III. *subst. n.* turning; turn, revolution, rotation; whirling; —en im Kopfe, giddiness, swimming in the head. —end, *p. & adj.* turning; rotary, rotatory; giddy. —er, *m.* (—ers, *pl.* —er) turner; winch; slow waltz. —ung, *f.* turn, rotation; revolution; turning; die halbe —ung der Kurbel, the half stroke of the crank.

Drei, I. *num. adj.* three; ehe man — zählen kann, in a trice. II. *f.* three. —heit, *f.* triad, triplicity. —ling, *m.* (—lings, *pl.* —linge) a number of three, small coin; triplets. —ßig, *num. adj.* thirty; in die —ßig kommen, to get into the thirties. —ßiger, *m.* (—ßigers, *pl.* —ßiger) man of thirty years; wine of 1830; in den —ßiger Jahren, in the thirties. —ßigjährig, *adj.* of thirty years; der —ßigjährige Krieg, the Thirty Years' War (1618-1648). —ßigst, *num. adj.* thirtieth. —ßigstel, *n.* thirtieth part. —ßigstens, *adv.* in the thirtieth place. *Comp.* —achtel, *pl.* three-eighths. —achtel-takt, *m.* time of 3 quavers (*Mus.*). —armig, *adj.* three-armed. —blatt, *n.* trefoil. —blätterig, *adj.* three-leaved. —bund, *m.* Triple Alliance (*Germany, Austria, Italy, since* 1883). —doppelt, *adj. & adv.* triple, three-fold. —eck, *n.* triangle. —eckig, *adj.* triangular, three-cornered; —eckiger Armmuskel, deltoid muscle. —ecks-lehre, —eckmeßkunst, *f.* trigonometry. —ein'heit, *f.* triad; trinity. —ei'nig, *adj. & adv.* triune; der —einige Gott, the Tripersonal God. —ei'nigkeit, *f.* Trinity. —einigkeits-bekenner, *m.* Trinitarian. —einigkeits-lehre, *f.* Trinitarianism. —erlei, *indec. adj.* of three kinds, three-fold. —fach, *adj. & adv.* threefold; triple; treble; (*before comparatives it is sometimes merely a term of amplification*); —fache Größe, trinomial; —fache Krone, triple crown, tiara (*of the pope*); mit —facher Mauer, with triple walls. —faltig, *adj. & adv.* threefold. —faltigkeit, *f.* Trinity. —faltigkeits-blume, *f.* heart's ease, pansy. —farbig, *adj.* tricoloured.

tricolour. —felder=wirtschaft, *f.* three-fallowing, three-fallow system. —firner, *m.* wine three years old. —fuß, *m.* tripod. —gesang, *m.* trio. —gespann, *n.* team of three horses (*in Russia*). —gestirn, *n.* three stars, constellation of three shining lights. —haarig, *adj.* three-haired; der —haarige, Prince Bismarck (*hum.*). —herrschaft, *f.* triumvirate. —hundert, *adj.* three hundred; Zeitraum von —hundert Jahren, tricentenary. —hundertste, *adj.* three-hundredth. —jährig, *adj.* three years old; continuing three years, triennial. —jährlich, I. *adj.* triennial. II. *adv.* every three years. —kaiser=schlacht, *f.* the battle of Austerlitz (1805). —käsehoch, *m.* a tiny little man. —klang, *m.* triad (*Mus.*). —klappig, *adj.* three-keyed (*Mus.*). —könige, *pl.* the wise men of the East. —königs=abend, *m.* the eve of the Epiphany, Twelfth-night (-eve). —königs=fest, *n.* Epiphany. —laut(er), *m.* triphthong. —mal, *adv.* three times, thrice. —malig, *adj.* done three times, repeated three times. —männig, *adj.* triandrian (*Bot.*). —master, *m.* three-master; three-cornered hat. —monatig, *adj.* three months old; lasting three months. —monatlich, *adj. & adv.* quarterly. —namig, *adj.* trinomial. —pfündig, *adj.* weighing three pounds. —prozentig, *adj.* at three per cent. —rad, *n.* tricycle. —reim, *m.* triplet. —ruderige Galeere, —ruderer, *m.* trireme. —schlag, *m.* ambling pace (*of a horse*); triple time (*Mus.*). —schlitz, *m.* triglyph. —schneidig, *adj.* three-edged. —schnitt, *m.* trisection. —schürig, *adj.* mowable three times a year, producing three crops a year. —seitig, *adj.* trilateral. —silbig, *adj.* of three syllables, trisyllabic. —sinnige, *pl.* men who are deaf, dumb, and blind. —sitzer, *m.* tandem (*or* bicycle) for three. —sitzig, *adj.* provided with three seats. —spännig, *adj.* yoked with three horses. —sprachig, *adj.* in three languages. —stimmig, *adj.* in three parts (*Mus.*); —stimmiger Gesang, singing of three voices; trio. —stöckig, *adj.* three-storied. —stündig, *adj.* three hours old; lasting three hours. —stündlich, *adv.* every third hour. —tägig, *adj.* three days old; lasting three days; —tägiges Fieber, tertian fever. —viertel=takt, *m.* time of 3 crotchets. —winkel, *m.* triangle. —zack, *m.* trident. —zackig, *adj.* three-pronged. —zehig, *adj.* tridactylous. —zehn, *adj.* thirteen. —zehnte, *n.* thirteenth. —zehntel, *n.* thirteenth part. —zinkig, *adj.* three-forked, tridented. —zweitel=takt, *m.* time of three minims, three-two time.

Drei'er, I. *gen. of* drei; Tagebuch — Kinder, diary kept by three children. II. *m.* a piece of 3 pfennige (*before 1871, value about a farthing*) (*coll.*).

Dreist, *adj. & adv.* bold; courageous, confident, pert. —igkeit, *f.* boldness; audacity, assurance; confidence; courage; edle —igkeit, wonderful (amount of) cheek (*hum.*); Dumm—igkeit, brazen-facedness; audacity.

Drell, *m.* (—s, *pl.* —e) drill(ing); diaper; strong ticking.

Dre'sch—e, *f.* thrashing. —en, *ir.v.a.* to thrash. —er, *m.* (—ers, *pl.* —er) thrasher. *Comp.* —diele, *f.* thrashing floor. —flegel, *m.* flail. —mühle, *f. see* —werk. —tenne, *f.*, *see* —diele. —walze, *f.* roller. —werk, *n.* thrashing machine.

Dress—ie'ren, *v.a.* to train; to drill; to break in. —ie'rung, —ur', *f.*, breaking in, training.

Driesch, *see* Dreesch.

Driesch'ling, Drüsch'ling, *m.* (—es, *pl.* —e) common mushroom.

Drie'seln, *v.n. imp.* to drizzle.

¹Dril'l—en, *v.a.* to turn round; to drill (*soldiers*). —er, *m.* driller, trainer. —ing, *m.* (—ings, *pl.* —inge) spring wheel. *Comp.* —meister, *m* drill sergeant.

²Dril'l—en, *v.a.* to drill, to bore; to bore, harass, weary, torment; mit dem Ruder —en, to work the steering. *Comp.* —bohrer, *m.* drill. —egge, *f.* drill-harrow. —fisch, *m.* electrical eel. —häuschen, *n.* a kind of pillory. —maschine, *f.* ridge-drill. —säge, *f.* hack-saw.

Dril'lich, Drilch, *m. see* Drell.

Dril'ling, *m.* (—s, *pl.* —e) one of three produced at a birth, triplet.

Drin, *see* Darin.

Drin'g—en, *ir.v.* I. *n.* (*aux.* h. & s.) to press forward; to press, throng, crowd; to penetrate, pierce; durch ... —en, to force one's way through; auf eine S. —en, to be urgent for, insist upon something; in einen —en, to urge strongly upon a person; die Zeit —t, time presses; in den Geist eines Dichters —en, to enter into the spirit of a poet; in die Laufgräben —en, to break into the trenches. II. *a.* (*in Schiller, Goethe, often = the modern* drängen) to urge, force, compel. —end, *p. & adj.* pressing, urgent; cogent; —end ersucht, earnestly *or* urgently requested. —lich, *adj. & adv.* urgent, pressing. —lichkeit, *f.* urgency.

Drin'nen, *adv.* within.

Drisch, *imperative;* **Drischst, Drischt**, *2 & 3 p. sg. pres. ind. of* dreschen.

Drit't—e, *num. adj.* third; durch die —e Hand, indirectly; der —e Mann, the umpire; der Wechsel ist schon in der —en Hand, the bill is already endorsed; zum Ersten, Andern und —en! going, going, gone! den —en abschlagen, to play third (*a game*). —el, *n.* (—els, *pl.* —el) third. —ens, *num. adv.* thirdly. *Comp.* —e=halb, *num. adj.* (*lit.* the third half, *i.e.*) two and a half. —letzt, *adj.* last but two; antepenult. —nächst, *adj.* next but two.

Drob, *see* Darob.

Dro'ben, *adv.* there above, on high.

Droge't(t), *m.* (—s, *pl.* —s) drugget.

Dro'guen, drugs. *Comp.* —erie'waren, *pl.* drugs; groceries. —handlung, *f.* drug-warehouse. —händler, *m.* druggist.

Drogui'st, *m.* (—en, *pl.* —en) druggist.

Dro'h—en, *v.a. & n.* (einem mit etwas *or* einem etwas) to threaten, to menace with. —ung, *f.* threat, menace. *Comp.* —brief, *m.* letter containing threats. —wort, *n.* menace, threat.

Droh'ne, *f.* (*pl.* —n) drone.

Dröh'nen, *v.n.* (*aux.* h.) to utter a low, dull sound; to thud; to roar, boom; to resound.

Dröh'nig, *adj.* slow, sleepy, dawdling (*sl.*).

Drol'licht (*obs.*), **Drol'lig**, *adj. & adv.* droll, amusing, funny, facetious, queer, odd.

Dromeda'r, *m.* (—s, *pl.* —e) dromedary.

Dromme't—e, *f.* (*obs. & poet. for* Trompete) (*pl.* —en), trumpet. —en, *v.n.* (*aux.* h.) to blow the trumpet (*obs.*).

Drosch, Drö'sche, *imperf. ind. & subj. of* dreschen.

Drosch'ke, *f.* (*pl.* —n) cab, hackney carriage, drosky, coach (*Amer.*). —n=gaul, *m.* hackney jade. —n=halteplatz, *m.* cab-stand. —n=kutscher, *m.* cabman, driver; cabby (*hum.*).

¹Dros'sel, *f.* (*pl.* —n) thrush. *Comp.* —bart; König —bart, King Thrushbeard. —beere, *f.* mountain ash.

²Dros'sel, *f.* (*pl.* —n) throttle, throat; Adam's apple. *Comp.* —ader, *f.* jugular vein. —bein, *n.* throttle; collar-bone. —klappe, *f.* throttle valve (*Mach.*).

Dros'seln, *v.a.* to throttle, to strangle.

Drost, *m.* (—es, *pl.* —e) high bailiff (*a noble*). —ei', *f.* bailiffship, bailiwick; residence of a high bailiff; Land—ei', district, shire, province, part of a kingdom (*e.g. of Hanover before 1866*).

Drü'b—en, —er, *see* Darüben, Darüber.

Druck, *m.* (—**es**, *pl.* —**e**) compression, pressure; impulse; squeeze; spring; print; printing; proof, impression; stamp; type; oppression, depression (*of prices; of spirits*); weight; burden; grievance, hardship; — **der Schwer=kraft**, gravitation; **in — geben**, to print, to have printed, to publish; **in — gehen**, to go to be printed, to be printed; **es wird an diesem Buch gedruckt**, this book is in the press. —**bar**, *adj.* that may be pressed *or* printed. *Comp.* —**berichtiger**, *m.* press-corrector, reader for the press. —**berichtigungen**, *pl.* corrigenda, corrections. —**bogen**, *m.* proof-sheet, proof. —**buchstaben**, *pl.* type. —**er=arbeit**, *f.* presswork. —**er=farbe**, —**er=schwärze**, *f.* printer's ink. —**erlaubnis**, *f.* imprimatur. —**fehler**, *m.* misprint, erratum, printer's error. —**fehler=teufel**, *m.* malignant spirit causing misprints. —**fehler=verzeichnis**, *n.* (*list of*) errata. —**fertig**, *adj. & adv.* ready for (the) press. —**festigkeit**, *f.* resistance (*Phys.*). —**form**, *f.* form (*Typ.*); printing-block. —**freiheit**, *f.* liberty of the press. —**höhe**, *f.* head of water, height of fall. —**jahr**, *n.* date of the printing of a book. —**kosten**, *pl.* expenses of printing. —**kraft**, *f.* pressure (*Phys.*). —**läppchen**, *n.* compress (*Surg.*). —**legung**, *f.* (act of) printing. —**messer**, *n.* pressure-gauge. —**modell**, *n.* *n.* printing-block. —**ort**, *m.* place of printing *or* publication; imprint (*of postage stamps*). —**probe**, *f.* proof. —**pumpe**, *f.* forcing pump. —**sache**, *f.* printed matter, printed papers; (by) book post. —**schrift**, *f.* type; publication. —**stange**, *f.* forcing lever. —**stempel**, *m.* piston. —**wage**, *f.* areometer. —**walze**, *f.* pressing roller, cylinder. —**waren**, *pl.* (*cotton*) prints. —**werk**, *n.* forcing-pump.

Dru'ck—en, *v.a.* to press, impress; to stamp; to print. —**er**, *m.* printer. —**erei'**, *f.* press, printing press.

Drü'ck—en, *v.* I. *a.* to press, clasp, squeeze; to pinch; to jam; to oppress, afflict; to vex, depress, weigh down; to annoy, afflict; **den Hut ins Gesicht —en**, to pull one's hat over one's eyes; **sein Siegel auf eine S. —en**, to affix one's seal to a th.; **einen ans Herz —en**, to press a p. to one's heart, to embrace a p.; **einem Geld in die Hand —en**, to slip money in a p.'s hand; **der Alp —t ihn**, he has a nightmare; **der Stiefel —t mich**, the boot pinches me; **wo —t dich der Schuh?** what ails you? what troubles you? (*coll.*); **die (freie) Zeit —t ihn**, time hangs heavy on his hands; **einen im Handel —en**, to drive a hard bargain with one; **den Markt —en**, to overstock the market; **die Preise —en**, to bring down prices; **der Sattel —t das Pferd**, the saddle galls the horse; **gedrückte Stimmung**, depressed mood; depressed tendency, dulness, flatness; **gedrückte Preise**, low prices. II. *n.* (*aux.* **h.**) to gravitate; to draw; to oppress. III. *r.* to get injured by pressure; to shirk work *or* payment; to sneak away, to make oneself scarce, run off (*slang*); **sich um eine Sache —en**, to avoid doing a th., to get out of a th., to shirk (*coll.*). —**eberger**, *m.* poltroon, shy person, shirk (*sl.*). —**end**, *adj.* heavy, oppressive; —**ende Armut**, pinching *or* extreme poverty; —**ende Last**, grievous burden; —**ende Steuer**, heavy taxation; —**ende Verhältnisse**, straitened circumstances; **das —ende benehmen**, to make matters easier. —**er**, *m.* (—**ers**, *pl.* —**er**) handle, latch, latch-key, trigger.

Druck'—sen, *v.a.* to hold back, to hesitate. —**serei'**, *f.* (annoying) hesitation.

Dru'd—e, *f.* witch; nightmare. *Comp.* —**en=baum**, *m.* tree under which witches are supposed to meet, fairy-tree. —**en=beutel**, *m.* puff-ball. —**en=fuß**, *m.* pentagram, pentacle ★, a mystic sign against witches and evil spirits; club-moss (*Bot.*).

Drui'd—e, *m.* (—**en**, *pl.* —**en**) Druid, a Keltic priest. —**en=tum**, *n.* Druidism. —**isch**, *adj.* Druidical. *Comp.* —**en=denkmal**, *n.* cairn, cromlech.

Drum, *short for* **darum**.

Drun't—en, *adv.* below (there). —**er**, *see* **Darunter**; —**er durch sein**, to be lost hopelessly; to be looked down upon (*fam.*).

Dru's—e, *f.* (*pl.* —**en**) decayed ore; glanders. —**icht**, *adj.* decayed, hollowed by weather. —**en=räume**, *pl. m.* cavities in rocks studded with crystals.

Drü's—e, *f.* (*pl.* —**en**) gland; glandular swelling. —**ig**, *adj. & adv.* glandular. *Comp.* —**en=beule**, *f.* bubo (*Med.*). —**en=geschwulst**, *f.* swelling of the glands, struma. —**en=krankheit**, *f.* disease of the glands; strangles.

Dru'sen, *pl.* dregs, lees; husks of grapes.

Dschun'gel, Dschan'gel, *f. & n.* (*pl.* —**n**) jungle.

Du, I. *pers. pron.* thou; **mit einem auf — und — stehen**, to be so intimate with one as to call him 'thou'; to be on intimate terms with a p. —, **der — im Himmel wohnest**, thou who dwellest in heaven. II. *n.* **dein anderes —**, thine other self.

Du'al, *m.* (—**s**, *pl.* —**e**) dual (number). —**is'mus**, *m.* dualism. —**is'tisch**, *adj.* dualistic. —**itä't**, *f.* duality.

Dublet'te, *f.* (*pl.* —**n**) duplicate; doublet

Dublo'ne, *f.* (*pl.* —**n**) doubloon.

Duca'ten, *see* **Dukaten**.

Du'ck—en, *v.* I. *a. & n.* (*aux.* **h.**) to bow; to stoop; to humble (*one*), bring down (*one's*) pride. II. *n. & r.* to duck, dive; to stoop; to knuckle under; to accommodate oneself to circumstances. *Comp.* —**ente**, *f.* diver (*Orn.*).

Duck'mäuser, *m.* (*sometimes spelt* **Tuckmäuser**) (—**s**, *pl.* —) sneak; hypocrite; sly-boots; dissembler, sharper.

Dudel—dei', (*m. &*) *n.* twaddle; verbiage; trifle. —**dumdei'**, interjection imitating the sound of a wooden wind instrument, esp'lly that of a bagpipe (**Dudelsack**); tweedledee; *see* **Dideldum**. —**ei'**, *f.* wretched piping *or* singing.

Du'del—n, *v.n.* (*aux.* **h.**) to play on the bagpipe *or* flute; to play *or* sing badly. *Comp.* —**kasten**, *m.* barrel-organ. —**sack**, *m.* bagpipe.

Dud'ler, *m.* wretched bagpiper *or* flute-player, monotonous singer.

Due'll, *n.* (—**s**, *pl.* —**e**) duel; — **auf Degen, Pistolen**, duel with swords, pistols. —**a'nt**, *m.* (—**an'ten**, *pl.* —**an'ten**) duellist. —**ie'ren**, *v.r.* to fight a duel. —**süchtig**, *adj.* eager to fight duels.

Due'tt, *n.* (—**s**, *pl.* —**e**) duet, duetto.

Duft, *m.* (—**es**, *pl.* **Düf'te**) scent, fragrance, exhalation; vapour. —**ig**, *adj.* misty, charged with vapour; fragrant, odoriferous.

Duf't—en (*obs.* **Düf'ten**) *v.* I. *n.* (*aux.* **h.** & **s.**) to exhale fragrance, to scent, to be odoriferous, to send forth fragrance *or* perfume. II. *a.* to smell; to perfume. —**end**, *adj.* scented.

Duhn(e), *adj.* tipsy (*sl.*)

Duka'ten, *m.* (—**s**, *pl.* —) ducat (*a coin no longer current; value of silver ducat between 3s. and 4s., and of gold ducat about 9s. 4d.*).

Duld'bar, *adj.* endurable, tolerable.

Dul'd—en, I. *v.a.* to suffer, endure; to bear patiently, to put up with; to tolerate (*opinions*); to connive at. II. *subst.n.* sufferance, endurance. —**er**, *m.* (—**ers**, *pl.* —**er**), —**erin**, *f.* sufferer. —**ung**, *f.* endurance; toleration.

Duld'sam, *adj.* enduring, patient, tolerant. —**keit**, *f.* toleration, spirit of toleration.

Dumm, *adj & adv.* dull, stupid; foolish, silly, ridiculous; unpleasant, awkward. —**es Zeug**, (stuff and) nonsense; **eine —e Geschichte**, an awkward affair. —**er Junge**, (*if said to adults*) fool (*the acknowledged word of challenge for a duel*); **das ist** —, that is a nuisance (*coll.*); **na, so** — ! I shall not be such a fool (*coll.*). —**heit**, *f.* stupidity, folly; nonsense; a silly action; (*pl.*) foolish tricks. *Comp.* —**bart**, *m.* dolt. —**dreist**, *adj.* foolhardy; impudent, forward. —**kopf**, —**er=ja(h)n**, *m.* blockhead, simpleton. —**kühn**, *adj.* foolhardy.

Dümm'ler, Dümm'ling, *m.* simpleton.

Dumpf, *adj. & adv.* damp, moist; musty; dull, apathetic; gloomy; stifling, heavy; dull in sound, heavy, hollow, muffled; — **tönen**, to rumble, mutter; to thud; **es macht mir den Kopf ganz** —, it stupefies my brain. —**es Streben**, vague aspirations; striving not clear as to its ultimate goal. —**heit**, *f.* dulness, hollowness; vague aspirations (*obs.*); gloominess; stupor, insensibility, torpor. —**ig**, *adj. & adv.* damp, dank; moist; fusty, musty. —**igkeit**, *f.* dampness, mustiness. *Comp.* —**sinn**, *m.* dull-mindedness, stupefaction.

Du'ne, Dü'ne, *f.* (*pl.* —**n**) sandhill. —**n**, *pl.* dunes.

Dün'g—en, *v.a.* to dung, to manure. —**er**, *m.* (—**ers**) manure, dung; **künstlicher** —**er**, compost. *Comp.* —**e=mittel**, *n.* fertilizer; fertilizing substance. —**jauche**, *f.* liquid manure.

Dun'kel, I. *adj. & adv.* dark, obscure; gloomy, cloudy; dim; mystical; mysterious; faint. II. *subst.n.* (—**s**) obscurity; ambiguity; darkness; **im** —**n**, in the dark. —**heit**, *f.* darkness; obscurity.

Dun'keln, *v.n.* (*aux.* **h.**) to grow dark *or* dim

Dün'kel, *m.* (—**s**) self-conceit; arrogance; — **haben**, to be self-conceited. —**haft**, *adj.* self-conceited; arrogant.

Dün'keln, *imp. v.n.*; **es dünkelt ihm**, he fancies in his conceit (*obs.*).

Dünk—en, *ir.v.* I. *n.* (*aux.* **h.**) *& imp.* to seem, look; appear; **es** —**t mich** (*or* **mir**), **mich** (*or* **mir**) —**t**, methinks, it seems to me, I fancy; **es däuchte ihn**, it seemed to him, he thought; **thue, was dir gut** —**t**, do what you think proper; **es wollte mir** —, it seemed to me, the idea struck me. II. *r.* to imagine oneself, fancy; **sie dünkt sich schön**, she imagines herself beautiful; **sie** —**en sich was**, they think a great deal of themselves; **er dünkt sich was Rechtes**, he has a high opinion of himself; **er dünkt sich was darauf**, he boasts of it, thinks much of himself on account of it, is proud of it, **sich** (*dat.*) —**en lassen**, to conceive an idea, to fancy.

Dünn, *adj.* thin, fine; small, slim; slight (*silk*); weak (*fluids*); serous (*blood*); scarce; rare (*air*); diluted; —**e Ohren haben**, to have a quick ear. —**e**, *f.* slenderness, thinness; sparseness; rarity. —**en**, —**ungen**, *pl.* flanks. *Comp.* —**backig**, *adj.* thin-faced, lantern-jawed. —**bier**, *n.* small beer. —**darm**, *m.* small intestine. —**gesä(e)t**, *adj.* sparsely sown, thinly scattered, scarce. —**leibig**, *adj.* lank. —**schlagen**, *v.a.* to beat out, flatten (*metals*). —**stimmig**, *adj.* shrill. —**tuch**, *n.* lawn.

Dunst, *m.* (—**es**, *pl.* **Dün'ste**) vapour; misty exhalation; fume; steam; **Vogel**—, dust shot; **einem einen blauen** — **vormachen**, to humbug one. —**ig**, *adj. & adv.*, vaporous, misty; foggy; damp. *Comp.* —**bild**, — **gebilde**, *n.* illusive image, phantasm. — **bläschen**, *n.* steam-globule. —**kreis**, *m.* atmosphere. —**loch**, *n.* airhole.

Dun'sten, *v.n.* (*aux.* **h.**) to rise as vapour; to exhale.

Dün'sten, *v.a.* to stew.

Duode'z, *n.* (—**es**) duodecimo.

Dupli'k, *f.* (*pl.* —**en**) rejoinder (*Law*). —**a't**, *n.* (—**a'ts**, *pl.* —**a'te**) duplicate. —**wechsel**, *m.* bill in sets (*Comm.*).

Dur, *adj.* major, sharp (*Mus.*) *Comp.* — **tonart**, *f.* major key, tone major. —**tonleiter**, *f.* major scale.

Durch, I. *prep. with acc.* through; by; by means of; across; throughout, during; owing to; **das ganze Jahr** —, the whole year through; — **den Strom schwimmen**, to swim across the river; — **die Finger sehen**, to be indulgent, not to be particular; — **die Post**, by post; — **Zufall**, by chance; — **Fleiß hat er es erreicht**, he has acquired it by diligence. II. *adv.* throughout; thoroughly; through. III. *sep. & insep. prefix.* (*Verbs, compounded with* **durch**, *when separable, have the principal accent on* **durch**; *when inseparable, on the root of the verb. The meaning of* **durch** *in such compounds is as a rule* through *or* thoroughly (*or* one after another,) *and, in a number of inseparable compounds:* to pass time in.) *Comp.* (*usually not accented on* **durch**). —**au's**, *adv.* throughout, thoroughly, quite; absolutely, positively, by all means; —**aus nicht**, by no means, not at all; **weil Sie es** —**aus wollen**, since you insist upon it; **es ist** —**aus verschieden**, it is altogether different. —**einan'der**, *adv.* in confusion, pell-mell, promiscuously.

Durch'ächzen, *v.a.* (*sep.*) pass in groaning.

Durch'arbeiten, *v.a.* (*sep.*) to work through; **sich** —, to make one's way, get on, get through.

Durch'atmen, *v.a.* (*insep.*) to breathe through; to pervade.

Durch'ätzen, *v.a.* (*sep.*) to corrode completely.

Durchbe'ben, *v.a.* (*insep.*) to thrill through, shake, agitate thoroughly.

Durch'beißen, *ir.v.* (*sep.*) I. *a.* to bite through; to strike home. II. *r.* to fight it out.

Durch'beizen, *v.a.* (*sep.*) to corrode, eat through with a corrosive, macerate.

Durch'be'en, *v.a.* (*sep.*) to go through in praying, to rehearse; (*insep.*) to spend in prayer.

Durchbetteln, *v.* I. *r.* (*sep.*) to beg one's way; to live by begging. II. *a.* (*insep.*) to wander through begging.

Durch'beuteln, *v.a.* (*sep.*) to sift, to bolt (*flour*).

Durch'blasen, *ir.v.a.* (*sep.*) to blow through; to blow to pieces; to blow, play over.

Durchblättern, *v.a.* (*sep. & insep.*) to turn over the leaves (*of a book*); to skim through.

Durch'bleuen, (*sep.*) (*less correctly spelt* **durchbläuen**) *see* **Durchprügeln**.

Durch'blick, *m.* (—**es**, *pl.* —**e**) view, prospect, vista; peep through; penetration.

Durchblicken, *v.* I. *n.* (*aux.* **h.**) (*sep.*) to look, peep, appear through. II. *a.* (*insep. & sep.*) to penetrate, pierce with a look, see through.

Durchbohren, *v.a.* (*sep.*) to bore through; (*insep.*) to penetrate; to pierce; to perforate.

Durch'braten, *ir.v.a.* (*sep.*) to roast well or thoroughly. **durch'gebraten**, *p.p. & adj.* well done.

Durchbrechen, *ir.v.* I. *a. & n.* (*aux.* **f.**) (*sep.*) to break through. II. *a.* (*insep.*) to break or come through, to pierce; **durchbro'chene Arbeit**, open work; filigrane.

Durch'brennen, *ir.v.n.* (*aux.* **h.**) (*sep.*) to burn through; to abscond (*colloq.*).

Durch'bringen, *ir.v.a.* (*sep.*) to bring through; to squander, dissipate; to bring up, rear; **sich** —, to maintain oneself, get on; **sich ehrlich** —, to make shift to gain an honest livelihood; **sich kümmerlich** —, to manage barely to make both ends meet; **er hat sein ganzes Vermögen durchgebracht**, he has squandered all his fortune, he has made ducks and drakes of his fortune; **die Ärzte hoffen ihn durchzubringen**, the doctors hope to pull him through.

Durch'bruch, *m.* (—**es**, *pl.* **Durchbrüche**) breach; rupture; eruption; cutting (of teeth); (religious) awakening.

Durchda'cht, *p.p. & adj.* well weighed; thought over, thought out carefully; studied, planned.
Durchden'ken, *ir.v.a.* (*sep. & insep.*) to think over carefully, reflect on, ponder over.
Durchdauern, *v.a.* (*sep. & insep.*) to last (*over*); **den Winter —**, to winter (*of plants*); to hibernate (*of animals*).
Durch'drängen, *v.a. & r.* (*sep.*) to force through.
Durchdring—en, *ir.v.* I. *n.* (*aux.* f.) (*sep.*) to press, crowd through; to penetrate; to pierce; to permeate; to prevail; to get the mastery; to accomplish; to succeed; **diese Meinung dringt durch**, this opinion prevails. II. *a.* (*insep.*) to penetrate, pierce; to permeate; to pervade. **—end**, *p. & adj.* penetrating; piercing; shrill; acute; keen, sharp. **—lich**, *adj. & adv.* penetrable, permeable. **—lichkeit**, *f.* penetrability. **—ung**, *f.* penetration.
Durch'drücken, *v.a. & n.* (*sep.*) to press through; to straighten (the knees, *in drill*); to gall (*a horse*); **ein Gesetz —**, to carry a bill (through the House) with difficulty (*fam.*).
Durchduf'ten, *v.a.* (*insep.*) to fill with perfume.
Durchdun'sten, *v.n.* (*aux.* h.) (*insep.*) to transpire, be exhaled.
Durcheilen, *v.* I. *n.* (*aux.* f.) (*sep.*) to hurry through. II. *a.* (*insep.*) to hasten through, pass through in haste.
Durcheinan'der. *See* **Durch.**
Durchfahr—en, *ir.v.* I. *n.* (*aux.* f.) (*sep.*) to drive *or* pass through. II. *a.* (*sep.*) to wear out by driving; (*insep.*) to rush through. **—t**, *f.* a passing through; passage; transit; gateway; thoroughfare. **—ts=zoll**, *m.* transit duty.
Durch'fall, *m.* falling through; diarrhœa, looseness of the bowels.
Durch'fallen, *ir.v.n.* (*aux.* f.) (*sep.*) to fall through; to fail, be disappointed *or* unsuccessful; to be ploughed, to be rejected; **durchgefallene Examinanden**, unsuccessful *or* rejected candidates (*for an examination*); **durchgefallene Kandidaten**, black-balled candidates (*for a club*).
Durch'fechten, *ir.v.a.* (*sep.*) to carry one's point; to fight it out; **sich —**, to fight one's way through.
Durch'fegen, *v.a.* (*sep.*) to sweep thoroughly; to chastise, rebuke.
Durch'feilen, *v.a.* (*sep.*) to file through, to give the last polish (to a work of art, a poem).
Durch'feuchten, *v.a.* (*sep.*) to wet thoroughly, to soak, steep.
Durch'feuern, *v.a.* (*sep.*) to heat thoroughly; to pierce (*with shot, etc.*).
Durch'finden, *ir.v.r.* (*sep.*) to find one's way through; to master (*a problem*).
Durchflam'men, *v.a.* (*insep.*) to flash through; to animate, fire.
Durchflattern, *v.a.* (*sep.*) & *n.* (*aux.* f.) (*insep.*) to flutter through.
Durchflech'ten, *ir.v.a.* (*insep.*) to interweave, entwine.
Durchfliegen, *ir.v.* I. *n.* (*aux.* f.) (*sep.*) to fly through (away). II. *a.* (*insep.*) to fly, rush through; to skim through.
Durchfliehen, *ir.v.* I. *n.* (*aux.* f.) (*sep.*) to flee through. II. *a.* (*insep.*) to run through, to flee through.
Durchfließen, *ir.v.* I. *n.* (*aux.* f.) (*sep.*) to flow through. II. *a.* (*insep.*) to run, flow through.
Durch'flößen, *v.a.* (*sep.*) to float through.
Durch'flüchten, *v.* I. *n.* (*aux.* f.) (*sep.*) to flee through. II. *a.* **einen —**, to help a p. to flee through *or* to escape.
Durchfluten, *v.n.* (*aux.* f.) & *a.* (*sep. & insep.*) to flow through, to stream through, to rush through (water).
Durchfor'schen, *v.a.* (*insep.*) to search through, to examine thoroughly, to investigate.
Durchfor'stung, *f.* thinning (*of a forest*).
Durchfressen, *ir.v.a.* (*sep. & insep.*) to eat through; corrode; **sich —**, to get on by living upon others (*vulg.*); to get out of a difficulty, to scrape through (*coll.*).
Durch'fragen, *v.a.* (*sep.*) to ask in turn; to question; **sich —**, to find one's way by asking.
Durchfrieren, *ir.v.* I. *a.* (*insep.*) to freeze completely. II. *n.* (*aux.* f.) (*sep.*) to be chilled through.
Durch'fuhr, *f.* passage, transit. *Comp.* **—zoll**, *m.* transit duty.
Durch'führ—en, *v.a.* (*sep.*) to convey *or* lead through; to bring to an issue; to accomplish, carry out; to modulate (*Mus.*); to support a part (*Theat.*). **—ung**, *f.* the carrying through; carrying out; accomplishment (*of a design*); execution, performance (*of a task*).
Durch'gang, *m.* (—(e)s, *pl.* **Durchgänge**) a passing through; thoroughfare; passage; gateway; channel (*Naut.*); floodgate; transit (*Astr.*). **— verboten!** no thoroughfare! private! *Comp.* **—s=akkord**, *m.* passing *or* transient accord. **—s=fernrohr**, see **—instrument.** **—s=gerechtigkeit**, *f.* right of way; thoroughfare. **—s=handel**, *m.* trade with transit goods. **—s=instrument**, *n.* transit-instrument. **—s=note**, *f.* passing-note (*Mus.*). **—s=schein**, *m.* permit. **—s=wagen**, *m.* through carriage. **—s=zoll**, *m.* transit duty. **—s=zug**, *m.* through train; corridor train, vestibule train (*Amer.*).
Durch'gängig, *adj. & adv.* thorough, radical; general, universal; current, prevailing.
Durchgehen, *ir.v.* I. *n.* (*aux.* f.) (*sep.*) to go, pass through; to pierce; to run away; to escape, elope; to pass, be approved; stampede, bolt; **die Pferde gingen mit uns durch**, we lost all control of the horses, they ran away; **die Maultiere gingen durch**, the mules stampeded; **keine dieser Bills ist noch im Unterhause durchgegangen**, neither of these bills has yet passed the Lower House; **der Antrag ging durch**, the motion was carried; **das geht (mit) durch, das mag so mit —**, that may pass; **er geht grade durch**, he is a very straight man. II. *a.* (*sep.*) to walk, go through *or* over; to look over, to retouch; to peruse; to wear out; **sich** (*dat.*) **die Füße —**, to walk one's feet sore; (*insep.*) to go, walk through. **—d**, *p. & adj.* pervading; **—der Zug**, through-train; **—der Wagen**, through-carriage; **—de Eigenschaft**, general characteristic. **—ds**, *adv.* universally, generally; throughout, in every part.
Durch'gerben, (*sometimes* **Durch'gärben**,) *v.a.* (*sep.*) to dress, to tan (leather) thoroughly; to drub, to beat soundly (*coll.*).
Durch'gießen, *ir.v.a.* (*sep.*) to pour through, filter.
Durchglühen, *v.* I. *n.* (*aux.* h.) (*sep.*) to glow through. II. *a.* (*sep. & insep.*) to make red hot; to inflame, inspire.
Durchgraben, *ir.v.a.* (*sep.*) to dig through; (*insep.*) to pierce by digging.
Durchgrau'en, *v.n.* (*insep.*) to fill with shudder; **die Knechteschar saß kalt durchgraut**, the host of servants sat thrilled with cold horror.
Durch'greifen, *ir.v.* (*sep.*) I. *n.* (*aux.* h.) to pass the hand through; to proceed without ceremony, *or* with vigour; to act decidedly; to prevail. II. *a.* to wear out by handling. **—d**, *p. & adj.* energetic, thorough.
Durchgrübeln, *v.a.* (*sep. & insep.*) to reflect upon, sift thoroughly, examine throughout.
Durch'guß, *m.* (—(ss)es, *pl.* **Durch'güsse**) filtration; strainer, colander; sink.
Durch'hau, *m.* vista (*in a wood*).
Durch'hauen, *ir.v.a.* (*sep. & insep.*) to hew *or* cut through; **sich —**, (*sep.*) to cut one's way through; **einen —**, (*sep.*) to give s.o. a thrashing, to whip a p. soundly (*coll.*).

Durch'hecheln, *v.a.* (*sep.*) to hackle flax thoroughly; to criticize, to censure; to expose a man's weaknesses in detail; to cut up (*a person*).
Durch'helfen, *iv.v.a.* (*sep.*); **einem —,** to help one through *or* out of, to support, assist one; **sich mit etwas —,** to come off with, to get on by; **sich mühsam —,** to work hard to make both ends meet.
Durchhitzen, *v.a.* (*sep. & insep.*) to heat through and through; to heat well *or* thoroughly.
Durchhöhlen, *v.a.* (*sep. & insep.*) to hollow throughout, undermine; to excavate.
Durch'holzen, *v.a.* (*sep.*) to beat thoroughly (*sl.*).
Durchir'ren, *v.a.* (*insep.*) to wander through, to stray.
Durchjagen, *v.* I. *a.* (*sep.*) to hunt through; (*insep.*) to hunt through, gallop over, scour. II. *n.* (*insep.*) (*aux.* **h.**) to pass through in hunting; (*aux.* **s.**) to hasten through.
Durchjam'mern, *v.a.* (*insep.*) to pass in lamentations (*a day, a night*).
Durch'kämpfen, *v.a.* (*sep.*) to fight out; to get by fighting; to maintain (*a point*); **sich —,** to fight one's way through *or* out; **sich durch Schwierigkeiten —,** to overcome difficulties.
Durchkauen, Durchkäuen, *v.a.* (*sep. & insep.*) to chew thoroughly; to repeat over and over again (*coll.*); to ruminate on.
Durchkneten, *v.a.* (*sep. & insep.*) to knead well.
Durch'kommen, *ir.v.n.* (*aux.* **s.**) (*sep.*) to come, get through; to come off; to recover; to pass (*examinations*); **mit seiner Einnahme —,** to make both ends meet; **mit einem —,** to succeed with a person; **so kommt er nicht durch,** in this way he will never succeed; he will not be let off with that; **er wird in der Prüfung schwerlich —,** he will hardly be able to pass his examination.
Durch'können, *ir.v.n.* (*aux.* **h.**) (*sep.*) to be able to get through *or* pass (*coll.*)
Durch'kosten, *v.a.* (*sep.*) to taste (*things*) one after another; to experience fully.
Durchkreu'zen, *v.a.* (*insep.*) to cross (*lit. & fig.*).
Durchla'chen, *v.a.* (*insep.*) to spend (*time*) in laughing.
Durch'lärmen, *v.a.* (*sep.*) to pass, spend (*time*) noisily.
Durch'laß, *m.* (—(ss)es, *pl.* **Durch'lässe**) letting through; what lets through; passage; sieve; filter; opening.
Durch'lass—en, I. *ir.v.a.* (*sep.*) to let through, suffer to pass; to strain; to filter; to transmit (*light, etc.*). **—end,** *p. & adj.* pervious; **nicht —end,** impermeable; **kein Wasser —end,** waterproof; **kein Feuer —end,** fireproof. II. *subst.* **—en,** *n.*, **—ung,** *f.* transmission.
Durch'laucht, *f.* (*pl.* **—en**) Highness, Serene Highness; **Ew.** (= **Euer**) **—,** your Highness; **Se. — haben befohlen** 2c., His Highness gave orders that, *etc.*; **Ew. — wollen geruhen,** may it please your Highness. **—ig,** *adj.* most high, serene; illustrious; august. **—igkeit,** *f.* serene Highness (*obs.*)
Durch'lauf, *m.* running through, passage, flux, diarrhœa.
Durchlaufen, *ir.v.* I. *n.* (*aux.* **s.**) (*sep.*) to run through; to filter. II. *a.* (*insep.*) to run all over; to peruse hastily; to wear out running; **ein Gerücht durchläuft die Stadt,** a report is going about the town; **alle Läden —,** to hunt through all the shops.
Durch'legen, *v.a.* (*sep.*); **eine Straße —,** to cut a street through *or* across.
Durchleuchten, *v.n.* (*sep.*) to shine through. II. *a.* (*insep.*) to fill *or* flood with light, to light (up), illuminate; to send rays through, irradiate.
Durch'liegen, *ir.v.r.* (*sep.*) to make sore by lying; **sich —,** to get bed-sore.

Durchlo'chen, *usually* **Durchlö'chern,** *v.a.* (*insep.*) to perforate, pierce, punch; to violate, infringe (*coll.*).
Durch'lüften, *v.a.* to air.
Durch'lügen, *ir.v.* (*sep.*) I. *a.* to help out by lies. II. *r.* to get off *or* help oneself out by lying.
Durch'machen, *v.a.* (*sep.*) to finish, to accomplish; to experience, suffer; **er hat viel durchgemacht,** he has gone through a good deal.
Durch'marsch, *m.* marching through; getting all the tricks (*at cards*). **—ieren,** *v.n.* (*aux.* **s.**) (*sep.*) to march through.
Durchmessen, *ir.v.a.* (*sep. & insep.*) to measure throughout, to traverse.
Durch'messer, *m.* (—s, *pl.* —) diameter; calibre (*Artil.*).
Durch'müssen, *v.n.* (*aux.* **h.**) (*sep.*) to be obliged to pass, to be forced to get through *or* finish.
Durchmuster—n, *v.a.* (*sep. & insep.*) to pass in review, overhaul; to examine, scrutinize, scan. **—ung,** *f.* examination, inspection, scrutiny.
Durchnähen, *v.* I. *a.* (*sep.*) to sew through; (*insep.*) to quilt. II. *r.* (*sep.*) to work one's fingers sore.
Durchnässen, *ir.v.* I. *n.* (*aux.* **h.**) (*sep.*) to let the wet through. II. *a.* (*insep.*) to wet thoroughly; **wir kamen ganz durchnäßt heim,** we got home wet all over, completely drenched.
Durch'nehmen, *ir.v.a.* (*sep.*) to examine; to analyse; to go through (*something with one*); **einen —,** to censure one.
Durch'paß, *m.* narrow pass, defile. **—(ss)ieren,** *v.a.* (*sep.*) to pass through.
Durch'peitschen, *v.a.* to whip soundly.
Durch'plumpsen, *v.n.* (*aux.* **s.**) (*sep.*) to fail in an examination (*coll.*).
Durch'prügeln, *v.a.* (*sep.*) to beat, cudgel (*soundly*).
Durch'quälen, *v.r.* (*sep.*) to get on with difficulty *or* with great labour.
Durchque'r—en, *v.a.* (*insep.*) to traverse. **—ung,** *f.*; **die —ung des dunkeln Erdteils,** the crossing of the Dark Continent.
Durchrasen, *v.* I. *n.* (*aux.* **s.**) (*sep.*) to run through furiously. II. *a.* (*sep. & insep.*) to rush furiously through *or* over.
Durch'rasseln, *v.a.* (*sl.*) = **durchfallen.**
Durchräuchern, *v.a.* (*sep. & insep.*) to perfume, fumigate; to smoke thoroughly.
Durchrechnen, *v.a.* (*sep. & insep.*) to reckon, count over; to revise; to pass in reckoning (*obs.*).
Durch'regnen, *v.* I. *n. imp.* (*aux.* **s.**) (*sep.*) to rain through. II. *a.* to drench; **wir waren alle völlig durchgeregnet,** we were all completely drenched.
Durch'reiben, *ir.v.a.* (*sep.*) to rub through; to rub sore; **durchgeriebene Kartoffeln,** mashed potatoes.
Durch'reise, *f.* passing through, passage.
Durchreisen, *v.* I. *n.* (*aux.* **s.**) (*sep.*) to travel through; to traverse. II. *a.* (*insep.*) to travel over. **—de(r),** *m.* traveller, passer-through.
Durchreißen, *ir.v.* I. *a.* (*sep. & insep.*) to tear asunder, rend. II. *n.* (*aux.* **s.**) (*sep.*) to break, rend, get torn.
Durchreiten, *ir.v.* I. *n.* (*aux.* **s.**) (*sep.*) to ride through. II. *r.* (*sep.*) to gall by riding. III. *a.* (*insep.*) to ride all over.
Durchrennen, I. *ir.v.n.* (*aux.* **s.**) (*sep.*) to run through, scour. II. *reg.v.a.* (*sep.*) to run through, pierce; (*insep.*) to run all over.
Durchrieseln, *v.* I. *n.* (*aux.* **s.**) (*sep.*) to flow through murmuring. II. *a.* (*insep.*) to flow through.
Durch'riß, *m.* (—(ss)es, *pl.* —(ss)e) breach, rent.
Durch'ritt, *m.* riding through, passage on horseback.
Durch'rühren, *v.a.* (*sep.*) to stir up well; to strain.

Durchrütteln, *v.a.* (*sep. & insep.*) to shake thoroughly.
Durchs = **durch das**.
Durchsägen, *v.a.* (*sep. & insep.*) to saw through.
Durchsalzen, *v.a.* (*sep. & insep.*) to salt well.
Durchsäuern, *v.* (*sep. & insep.*) I. *a.* to leaven thoroughly. II. *n.* (*aux.* **h.**) to become leavened.
Durchschallen, *v.* I. *n.* (*sep.*) to sound through. II. *a.* (*insep.*) to fill with sound.
Durchschauen, *v.* I. *n.* (*aux.* **h.**) (*sep.*) to see through. II. *a.* (*insep.*) to look through, to penetrate; to see into the heart of one; **ich durchschaue seine Kniffe**, I see through his game, I am up to his tricks.
Durchschau'ern, *v.a.* (*insep.*) to chill all over, to fill with shuddering, to fill with awe.
Durch'scheinen, *ir.v.n.* (*aux.* **h.**) (*sep.*) to shine through. **—d**, *p.p. & adj.* transparent; translucent.
Durch'scheuern, *v.a.* (*sep.*) to scour *or* rub through; to wear by rubbing.
Durchschieß—en, *ir.v.* I. *n.* (*sep.*) (*aux.* **h.**) to shoot, fire through; (*aux.* **s.**) to dash, fly through. II. *a.* (*sep.*) to count over, to count by casts; (*insep.*) to shoot through; to interline (*Typ.*); to interleave (*a book*); to cross the shuttle; to partition. **durchschossen**, *p.p. & adj.* interleaved. *Comp.* **—linie**, *f.* space-rule, lead (*Typ.*).
Durchschiffen, *v.* I. *n.* (*aux.* **s.**) (*sep.*) to sail through. II. *a.* (*sep.*) to ship through; (*insep.*) to traverse, to navigate.
Durchschimmern, *v.* I. *n.* (*aux.* **h.**) (*sep.*) to glitter, glimmer through. II. *a.* (*insep.*) to fill with splendour.
Durchschlafen, *ir.v.a.* (*sep. & insep.*) to pass (*in*) sleeping.
Durch'schlag, *m.* opening; strainer, colander; punch, piercer; filter; gun-pick; piercing, punching; straining.
Durch'schlagen, *ir.v.* (*sep.*) I. *a.* to beat through; to make an opening in; to pierce; to open; to strain, filter; to beat soundly. II. *r.* to cut one's way through (*an enemy*); to struggle through life; **sich kümmerlich —**, to live in straitened circumstances, from hand to mouth; **—der Erfolg**, decisive success; complete success. III. *n.* (*aux.* **h.**) to penetrate; to wet through; to operate (*of medicine*); to blot; to have effect; to tell; **Papier, das nicht durchschlägt**, paper on which ink does not run; **man schlägt die Erbsen durch**, one puts the peas through the strainer; **bei seinem geringen Einkommen hat er sich doch durchgeschlagen**, in spite of his small income he yet managed to make both ends meet.
Durch'schlängeln, *v.r.* (*sep.*) to wind through; to meander through.
Durchschleichen, *ir.v.* I. *a.* (*insep.*). II. *r. & n.* (*aux.* **s.**) (*sep.*) to sneak *or* steal through.
[1]**Durch'schleifen**, *ir.v.a.* (*sep.*) to wear out by grinding.
[2]**Durch'schleifen**, *reg.v.a.* (*sep.*) to carry through on a sledge; to drag through.
Durchschlingen, *ir.v.a.* (*sep. & insep.*) to sling through, to interlace, to entwine.
Durchschlüpfen, *v.* I. *a.* (*sep. & insep.*) to slip *or* creep through. II. *n.* (*aux.* **s.**) (*sep.*) to slip through; to escape.
Durchschmettern, *v.* I. *a.* (*sep.*) to dash to pieces; (*insep.*) to fill with the sound of a trumpet. II. *n.* (*aux.* **s.**) (*sep.*) to penetrate with a crashing noise.
Durchschneiden, *ir.v.a.* (*sep. & insep.*) to cut through; to cross one another (*of roads*); to bisect, to intersect; to traverse: to pierce; **das Meer —**, to cross the sea.
Durch'schnitt, *m.* a cutting through; section; profile; cutting (*Railw.*); intersection; average; **— im Kirchenschiffe**, transept; **— eines Gebäudes**, section of a building; **im —**, on the average. **—lich**, *adj. & adv.* average, on an average. *Comp.* **—s=alter**, *n.* average age. **—s=ansicht**, *f.* section (*Arch.*). **—s=bildung**, *f.* average education. **—s=linie**, *f.* line of intersection; diameter. **—s=punkt**, *m.* point of intersection. **—s=riß**, *m.* section (*Arch.*). **—s=sehne**, *f.* secant. **—s=summe**, *f.* average sum. **—s=verhältnis**, *n.* mean proportion. **—s=zahl**, *f.* mean number. **—s=zeichnung**, *f.* section, sectional sketch.
Durchschreien, *ir.v.* I. *n.* (*aux.* **h.**) (*sep.*) to cry through. II. *a.* (*insep.*) to penetrate; to fill with cries.
Durchschreiten, *ir.v.* I. *n.* (*aux.* **s.**) (*sep.*) to stride, stalk, through. II. *a.* (*insep.*) to traverse.
Durch'schuß, *m.* woof, weft; (**—linien**) space-lines (*Typ.*); interleaf.
Durch'schütteln, *v.a.* (*sep.*) to shake thoroughly.
Durchschwär'men, *v.a.* (*insep.*) to spend in revelling (*the night*); to rove, ramble through.
Durchschwei'fen, *v.a. & n.* (*insep.*) to wander through, rove *or* stroll about.
Durchschwel'gen, *v.a.* (*insep.*) to spend in revelry.
Durchschwimmen, *ir.v.* I. *n.* (*aux.* **s.**) (*sep.*) to swim through. II. *a.* (*insep.*) to cross swimming.
Durchschwitz—en, *v.n.* (*aux.* **s.**) (*sep. & insep.*) to sweat through, perspire greatly; **ganz —t**, perspiring at every pore. **—ung**, *f.* diaphoresis.
Durchsegeln, *v.* I. *n.* (*aux.* **s.**) (*sep.*). II. *a.* (*insep.*) to sail, to sail over *or* through.
Durchsehen, *ir.v.* I. *n.* (*aux.* **h.**) (*sep.*) to see *or* look through. II. *a.* (*sep.*) to look over; to review; to revise; (*insep.*) to scrutinize; to penetrate.
Durch'seihen, *v.a.* (*sep.*) to strain, to filter.
Durch'sein, *ir.v.n.* (*sep.*) to have got through a thing; to have finished with a p. *or* a th.
Durch'setzen, *v.* (*sep.*) I. *n.* (*aux.* **h.**) to break, burst through. II. *a.* to sift, size (*ore*); to accomplish, to carry (*anything*) through; to succeed; **sie hat es bei ihm nicht durchgesetzt**, she has not carried her point with him; **er hat es bei den Behörden durchgesetzt**, he has prevailed upon the authorities to do it.
Durchseuf'zen, *v.a.* (*insep.*) to pass in sighing.
Durch'sicht, *f.* perusal; revisal, revision; looking through; vista. **—ig**, *adj.* transparent, pellucid, diaphanous. **—igkeit**, *f.* transparency, diaphaneity; perspicuity. *Comp.* **—s=bild**, *n.* transparency. **—s=lehre**, *f.* dioptics.
Durch'sickern, (**Durch'sintern**,) I. *v.n.* (*aux.* **s.**) (*sep.*) to leak, drip through. II. *subst.n.* leakage; percolation; drippings.
Durch'sieben, *v.a.* (*sep.*) to sift; to garble; to bolt (*flour*).
Durchsitzen, *ir.v.* I. *a.* (*sep.*) to wear out by sitting; (*insep.*) to spend, pass, sit through. II. *n.* (*sep.*) to be in detention.
Durch'sollen, *v.n.* (*aux.* **h.**) (*sep.*) to be forced to pass through.
Durchspä'hen, *v.a.* (*insep.*) to examine, explore.
Durchspielen, *v.a.* (*sep. & insep.*) to play through *or* over; **eine Rolle —**, to support a part.
Durch'sprechen, *v.a.* (*sep.*) to talk over *or* out.
Durchsprengen, *v.* I. *n.* (*aux.* **s.**) (*sep.*) to pass through at full speed. II. *a.* (*sep.*) to burst through; (*insep.*) to gallop through *or* over.
Durchspüren, *v.a.* (*sep. & insep.*) to search through; to beat for game.
Durch'stauben, *v.n.* (*aux.* **h.**) (*sep.*) to penetrate as dust; **es staubt durch**, the dust is coming in (*at the window, etc.*).
Durch'stäuben, *v.a.* (*sep.*) to dust all over; to drive through as dust; to pounce (*a design*).
Durchstech—en, *ir.v.* I. *n.* (*aux.* **s.**) (*sep.*) to pierce

through; to perforate, to stab; to gore. II. *a.* (*sep.*) to cut *or* dig through; **Getreide —en**, to turn corn; **sie stechen mit einander durch**, they play into one another's hands; (*insep.*) to transfix, thrust through; **durchstochen**, rouletted (*of postage stamps*). **—erei'**, *f.* underhand joint practice; **—erei treiben**, to play into each other's hands. **—ung**, *f.* piercing through; perforation; **zusammengesetzte —ung**, compound perforation (*of postage stamps*).

Durchsteigen, *ir.v.* I. *n.* (*aux.* **s.**) (*sep.*) to pass through, to mount through. II. *a.* (*insep.*) to stride, stalk over; to climb up *or* over.

Durch'stich, *m.* cut; aperture; cutting through, cut; intrenchment; roulette (*of postage stamps*).

Durchstöbern, *v.a.* (*sep. & insep.*) to ransack, to rummage all through.

Durchstoßen, *ir.v.a.* (*sep.*) to thrust through; to break *or* injure by thrusting; (*insep.*) to transfix, to thrust through, stab, gore.

Durchstrahlen, *v.* I. *n.* (*aux.* **h.**) (*sep.*) to shine through. II. *a.* (*insep.*) to irradiate.

Durchstreichen, *ir.v.* I. *a.* (*sep.*) to strike out, cross out, erase, cancel; (*insep.*) to roam through. II. *n.* (*aux.* **s.**) (*sep.*) to pass through rapidly; **—de Linie**, trajectory (*of a comet*).

Durchstreifen, *v.a.* (*sep. & insep.*) to roam all over; to make inroads into.

Durch'strich, *m.* erasure; passage (*of birds*).

Durchströmen, *v.a.* (*insep.*) & *n.* (*aux.* **h.**) (*sep.*) to stream, flow rapidly *or* run through.

Durchstür'men, *v.a.* (*insep.*) & *n.* (*aux.* **h.**) to rush through; to agitate.

Durchstürzen, *v.* I. *n.* (*aux.* **s.**) (*sep.*) to fall suddenly through. II. *a.* (*insep.*) to thrust through with vehemence.

Durchsuch—en, *v.a.* (*sep. & insep.*) to search thoroughly, to search all over; **gerichtlich —en**, to search by order of a court. **—ung**, *f.* search.

Durchtanzen, *v.* I. *a.* (*sep.*) to wear through with dancing; to dance through; (*insep.*) to pass in dancing. II. *n.* (*aux.* **s.**) (*sep.*) to dance through.

Durchtoben, *v.* I. *n.* (*aux.* **s.**) (*sep.*). II. *a.* (*insep.*) to rage through, to ravage.

Durchtönen, *v.* I. *n.* (*aux.* **h.**) (*sep.*) to sound through. II. *a.* (*insep.*) to resound, ring with.

Durchtrauern, *v.a.* (*sep. & insep.*) to pass in mourning.

Durch'träufeln, *v.n.* (*aux.* **s.**) (*sep.*) to drop through, to drip.

Durchträumen, *v.a.* (*sep. & insep.*) to pass in dreaming.

Durch'treiben, *ir.v.a.* (*sep.*) to drive through; to carry through, effect; to strain.

Durch'treten, *ir.v.a.* (*sep.*) to tread through, wear out by treading; to tread thoroughly; to work by treading (*earth, etc.*); **die Weintrauben —**, to tread the wine-press.

Durch'trieb, *m.* cattle-path; right of way *or* pasture for cattle.

Durchtrie'ben, *p.p.* (*of insep. v.* **durchtreiben**) & *adj.* sly, artful, cunning; arrant (*knave*); practised, skilled. **—enheit**, *f.* cunning, craftiness, slyness.

Durch'triefen, Durch'tröpfeln, Durch'tropfen, *v.n.* (*aux.* **s.**) (*sep.*) to trickle through.

Durchwachen, *v.a.* (*sep. & insep.*) to watch through, to pass waking.

Durchwachsen, *ir.v.n.* (*aux.* **s.**) (*sep. & insep.*) to grow through; to be streaked (*Bot.*); to be marbled (*of meat*). II. *p.p. & adj.* streaked.

Durchwalken, *v.a.* (*sep. & insep.*) to full *or* mill thoroughly; to give a sound thrashing (*coll.*).

Durchwandern, *v.* I. *n.* (*aux.* **s.**) (*sep.*) to wander through. II. *a.* (*insep.*) to traverse.

Durchwärmen, *v.a.* (*sep. & insep.*) to warm through *or* thoroughly.

Durchwäs'sern, *v.a.* (*insep.*) to irrigate, to soak.

Durchwaten, *v.* I. *n.* (*aux.* **s.**) (*sep.*). II. *a.* (*insep.*) to wade through, to ford.

Durchwe'ben, *v.a.* (*insep.*) to interweave; to intermix.

Durch'weg, *m.* (—es, *pl.* —e) thoroughfare, passage.

Durchwe'g, *adv.* throughout, altogether.

Durchwehen, *v.* I. *n.* (*aux.* **h.**) (*sep.*). II. *a.* (*insep.*) to blow through, breathe through.

Durchweichen, *v.a. & n.* (*aux.* **s.**) (*insep. & sep.*) to soak through; to steep; to become soft.

Durchwei'nen, *v.a.* (*insep.*) to pass in weeping.

Durch'werfen, *ir.v.a.* (*sep.*) to cast through; to riddle, rift.

Durchwinden, *ir.v.* I. *a.* (*sep.*) to wind through. II. *r.* (*sep.*) to struggle (*skilfully*) through; (*insep.*) to entwine.

Durchwintern, *v.* (*sep. & insep.*) I. *a.* to winter. II. *n.* (*aux.* **h.**) to pass the winter; to hibernate.

Durchwirken, *v.a.* (*sep.*) to knead thoroughly; (*insep.*) to interweave (*cloth*).

Durch'wischen, *v.n.* (*aux.* **s.**) (*sep.*) to slip through, escape.

Durchwit'tern, *v.a.* (*insep.*) to intermix with substances dissolved by the action of the air, to intersperse with weathered minerals (*chiefly used in p.p.*).

Durchwühlen, *v.* I. *a.* (*insep.*) to grub, root up; to rummage, ransack. II. *r.* (*sep.*) to work through.

Durchwür'zen, *v.a.* (*insep.*) to fill with spices, to season thoroughly; to scent; to season (*fig.*).

Durch'zählen, *v.a.* (*sep.*) to count over.

Durchzechen, *v.a.* (*sep. & insep.*) to carouse through.

Durch'zeichnen, *v.a.* (*sep.*) to draw through transparent paper, to trace; to counter-draw; **Papier zum —**, tracing paper.

Durchziehen, *ir.v.* I. *a.* (*sep.*) to draw, pull through; to pass through (*threads*); to thread (*needles*); to censure; (*insep.*) to interweave, to interlace, lace; to soak; **ein Land —**, to traverse; **mit Gräben —**, to trench. II. *n.* (*aux.* **s.**) (*sep.*) to go *or* march through.

Durchzit'tern, *v.n.* (*insep.*) (*aux.* **h.**) to thrill (through).

Durch'zoll, *m.* passage-money; transit-duty.

Durchzu'cken, *v.a.* (*insep.*) to give a sudden shock to, to convulse; to flash through.

Durch'zug, *m.* passing through; through-draught; passage; architrave; passage (*of birds; an army, etc.*).

Durch'zwängen, *reg.*, (*rare*) **Durch'zwingen**, *ir.v.a. & r.* (*sep.*) to force (*one's way*) through.

Dür'f—en, *ir.v.n.* (*aux.* **h.**) to be permitted; to need, want; to be able; to feel authorized; (*obsol.*) to dare, venture, trust oneself to; **darf ich fragen?** may I ask? **Sie hätten das nicht thun —en**, you ought not to have done that; **wenn ich bitten darf**, if you please; **jetzt dürfte es zu spät sein**, now it will probably be too late; **darüber —en Sie sich nicht wundern**, you must not be surprised at it; **es darf nur einer . . .**, one has only to . . .; **man darf hoffen**, it is to be hoped; **es dürfte ein Leichtes sein**, it is probably an easy matter; **hier —en keine Zettel angeklebt werden**, stick no bills; **es darf niemand herein**, no one is admitted. **—tig**, *adj.* needy, indigent, poor; sorry, paltry; shabby; insufficient. **—igkeit**, *f.* poverty, neediness; meanness; insufficiency.

Durf'te, Dürf'te, *imperf.ind. & subj. of* **dürfen**.

Dürr, *adj.* dry; arid; lean; meagre; barren, withered; blunt; **—e Worte**, plain language. **—e**, *f.* aridity, dryness, drought; leanness; sterility. *Comp.* **—baum**, *m.* cornelian cherry. **—beinig**, *adj.* spindle-legged. **—leibig**, *adj.* lean. **—maden**, *pl.* maggots, decay.

Durst, *m.* (—es) thirst; — **haben**, to be thirsty; — **stillen**, to quench thirst; **das macht** —, that makes thirsty.

Dur'st—en, (*arch. & poet.*) **Dür'st—en**, *v.n.* (*aux.* **h.**) to be thirsty, to thirst; **nach einer S. —en**, to long for; **es dürstet mich, mich dürstet**, I am thirsty. —**ig**, *adj.* thirsty, athirst; (*rare*) thirst-giving, causing thirst; eager for.

Du'sel, *m.* stupor; giddiness, dizziness, sleepiness; luck, good fortune (*sl.*); **im — sein**, to be half asleep; — **haben**, to have much good luck, to be a lucky fellow (*sl.*). —**ig**, *adj.* giddy, dizzy; sleepy. —**n**, *v.n.* (*aux.* **h.**) to be giddy; to be sleepy; to stagger *or* wander about.

Dust, *m.* (—(e)s) dust (*poet.*).

Dü'ster, *adj. & adv.* dark; gloomy; sad, mournful; dismal. —**heit**, —**keit**, *f.* gloom; gloominess. —**rot**, *adj.* dusky red, lurid.

Dü'stern, *v.n.* (*aux.* **h.**) to be *or* grow dusky, gloomy; to lour.

Düt'—chen, *n.* (—chens, *pl.* —chen), —**e**, **Du't—e**, *f.* (*pl.* —en) paper bag *or* cornet used by grocers. *Comp.* —**chen=dreher**, —**chen=krämer**, *m.* grocer, huckster, petty shopkeeper. —**chen=weise**, *adv.* in retail, in small quantities.

Dutz'end, *n.* (—s, *pl.* —e) dozen. *Comp.* —**weise**, *adv.* by the dozen.

Du'z—en, *also* **Dut'z—en**, *v.a. & r.* to thee and thou; to call one another thou. *Comp.* —**bru=der**, *m.*, —**schwester**, *f.* intimate companion.

Dwars, *adv.* athwart (*Naut.*). *Comp.* —**bal=ken**, *m.* crossbeam. —**schlingen**, *pl.* cross-trees.

Dyna'm—ik, *f.* dynamics. —**isch**, *adj.* dynamic(al).

Dynami't, *n.* (—(e)s) dynamite.

Dyna'st, *m.* (—en, *pl.* —en) feudal lord, ruler, prince. —**ie'**, *f.* (*pl.* —ie'en) dynasty. —**isch**, *adj.* dynastic(al).

Dyspep—sie', *f.* dyspepsia. —**tisch**, *adj.* (*pron.* **dyspep'tisch**) dyspeptic.

E

E, e, E, e; E, mi (*Mus.*); — **dur**, E major; — **moll**, E minor.

Eb'be, *f.* (*pl.* —n) ebb, ebbtide; decline; **die niedrige** —, neap-tide; **die — tritt ein**, the tide is going out; **es ist — in seinem Geld=beutel**, his purse is at a low ebb, he is hard up.

Eb'ben, *v.n.* (*aux.* **h.** & **s.**) to ebb; to fall off, decline; **das Meer ebbt**, the tide goes out.

E'ben, I. *adj.* even, level, plain, smooth; plane (*Mathem.*); open (*country*); suitable, pleasant (*obs.*); exact, particular (*obs.*); **zu —er Erde**, on the ground floor. II. *adv. & part.* evenly, *etc.*; just; precisely; quite; certainly; **es geschieht dir — recht**, it serves you right; — **wollen**, — **thun**, to be about to (*do a thing*); — **deswegen**, for that very reason; — **der=selbe**, the very same; **so—**, even now, just now; **das nun — nicht**, not precisely that, rather the contrary; **ich will mich nicht — rüh=men**, I don't want to boast; — **dich**, even thee; just you; **an — dem Tage**, on that very day; **ich möchte — so gern**, I would just as soon; I would rather; **das wollte ich — sagen**, that is just what I was going to say; **das wäre mir — recht**, that would be just what I should like; — **erst**, but just; — **so viel**, just as much; **das ist eben so viel als . . .**, that is tantamount to . . . . —**heit**, *f.* evenness, smoothness. *Comp.* —**bild**, *n.* image, exact likeness; **das —bild des Schöpfers**, God's image; the human face divine (*poet.*). —**bürtig**, *adj.* of equal birth, equal in rank. —**daselbst**, *adv.* in *or* at the very same place. —**falls**, *adv.* likewise. —**kreisig**, *adj.* concentric. —**maß**, *n.* symmetry, proportion. —**mäßig**, *adj.* symmetrical, proportional; equal, just. —**nächtig**, *adj.* equinoctial. —**sohlig**, *adj.* horizontal (*Min.*). —**zeitig**, *adj.* contemporary.

E'bene, *f.* (*pl.* —n) level tract of country; plain; plane; flatness, levelness; **geneigte —e**, gradient, inclined plane. *Comp.* —**n=büschel**, *m.* sheaf of rays, planes through one line.

E'benen, Eb'nen, I. *v.a.* to make even, level; to roll; to smooth. II. *subst.n.* planishing; facing (*of stones*); —**e Geometrie**, plane geometry; **der —e Weg**, the level road. —**er**, *m.* (—ers, *pl.* —er) leveller.

Eben—i'st, *m.* (—i'sten, *pl.* —i'sten) cabinet-maker (*obsol.*). *Comp.* —**baum**, *m.* ebony tree. —**holz**, *n.* ebony.

E'ber, *m.* (—s, *pl.* —) wild boar; boar. *Comp.* —**esche**, *f.* service tree. —**fleisch**, *n.* brawn, boar's meat. —**hirsch**, *m.* Indian hog. —**schwein**, *n.* wild boar (*obs. & poet.*).

E'cho, *n.* (—s, *pl.* —s) echo; **ein — geben**, to echo, resound. —**en**, *v.n.* (*aux.* **h.**) to echo; to re-echo, resound; to repeat the sound.

Echt, *adj.* genuine; real, pure; authentic; legitimate; fast (*of colours*); staunch; true; lawful; —**er Wein**, pure unadulterated wine; —**es Bier**, Bavarian beer; **ein Schnitt —es**, a small glass of Bavarian beer; —**e Perlen**, real pearls. —**heit**, *f.* genuineness, real *or* pure quality; authenticity; legitimacy. *Comp.* —**gefärbt**, *adj.* ingrained (*colour*).

Eck, *n.* (—s, *pl.* —e) edge; corner; angle; **Drei—**, triangle; **Vier—**, quadrangle; **Acht—**, octagon; **Viel—**, polygon. —**chen**, *n.* (—chens, *pl.* —chen) *dim. of* **Eck**, a small corner; *instead of* **Strecke**: a little bit; **ein —chen gehen**, to go to the next corner, go a short distance; **ich will dich ein —chen auf den Weg bringen**, I will accompany you some little distance. —**e**, *f.* (*pl.* —en) edge; corner; angle, nook; outer angle, coin (*Arch.*); facet; solid angle; distance, space (*coll.*); **geschliffene —e**, facet; **eine ganze** *or* **gute** —, a considerable distance; **um die —e gehen**, to die (*sl.*); **an allen —en und Enden**, everywhere; **von allen —en und Enden (her)**, from all parts. —**ig**, *adj.* angular; cornered; edged. —**igkeit**, *f.* angularity; awkwardness. *Comp.* —**balken**, *m.* corner-post. —**beschläge**, *pl.* corner-clips; head-plates (*of a carriage*). —**brett**, *n.* bracket, corner shelf. —**(en)=steher**, *m.* commissionaire; street-porter; jobbing workman. —**fe=dern**, *pl.* pinions. —**fenster**, *n.* corner *or* projecting window. —**first**, *m.* hip (*Arch.*). —**hölzer**, *pl.* squared timber. —**loch**, *n.* corner-pocket (*Bill.*). —**säule**, *f.* corner pillar; prism (*Opt., Geom.*). —**säulig**, *adj.* prismatic. —**schrank**, *m.* corner cupboard. —**stein**, *m.* corner-stone; curbstone; diamond (*Cards*). —**stütze**, *f.* buttress, stay. —**weise**, *adv.* cornerwise; —**weise schleifen**, to cut into facets (*Jew.*). —**zahn**, *m.* eye-tooth. —**zimmer**, *n.* corner room; room at the corner of a street.

E'cker, *f.* (*pl.* —n) acorn; **Buch—**, beech-nut.

Eclata'nt, *adj. & adv.* brilliant, clear; striking.

E'del, *adj. & adv.* highborn; noble; lofty, exalted; precious; excellent; **der, die —e**, person of noble *or* high birth; the high-minded man *or* woman; **das —e**, nobility (*of mind, etc.*), what is noble; **eine edler Gang**, a rich vein; **edle Teile**, vital parts. —**ing**, *m.* (—ings, *pl.* —inge) nobleman, knight; aristocrat, atheling (*old English*). *Comp.* —**bürger**, *m.* patrician. —**dame**, —**frau**, *f.* gentlewoman, noblewoman. —**gesinnt**, *adj.* noble-minded. —**esche**, *f.* common ash. —**falke**, *f.* falcon. —**fichte**, *f.* silver pine. —**fräulein**, *n.* unmarried lady of noble rank. —**hirsch**, *m.* stag deer. —**hof**, *m.* manor. —**knabe**, *m.* page. —**knecht**, *m.* squire of high degree. page.

—leute, pl. see —mann. —mann, m. nobleman. —männisch, adj. nobleman-like. —metalle, pl. rare metals. —mut, m. highmindedness, generosity, magnanimity. —mütig, adj. noble-minded, magnanimous. —stein, m. precious stone, gem, jewel. —tanne, f. silver fir, abies pectinata; lofty fir. —that, f. noble deed. —weiß, n. edelweiss, lion's foot. —wild, n. deer; high-class game.

Edi'kt, n. (—es, pl. —e) edict. Comp. —al'ladung, letter citatory.

Edie'ren, v.a. to edit; to bring out.

E'dle(r), m. nobleman in rank below a baron; knight; e.g. Gustav, Edler zu Putlitz.

Effe'kt, m. (—es, pl. —e) effect. —en, pl. effects, goods and chattels; securities, stocks (C.L.). —i'v, adj. effective, real, in specie, ready money. Comp. —en-händler, m. stock jobber. —en-handel, m. stock-exchange business (C. L.). —hascherei, f. straining after effect.

Effektuie'ren, v.a. to effect, to execute.

Efflorescie'ren, v.n. to effloresce.

Ega'l, adj. & adv. equal; all one, the same; over and over again, without stopping, always (sl.).

E'gel, m. (—s, pl. —) leech.

Eg'g—e, f. (pl. —en) harrow; listing, selvage; schwere —e, brake. —en, v.a. to harrow.

Ego—is'mus, m. (pl. Egois'men) egotism, selfishness. —i'st, m. (—is'ten, pl. —is'ten) egotist. —is'tisch, adj. selfish, egotistic.

Egrenie'ren, v.a. to gin, clean the cotton.

E'h—e, I. adv. sooner, earlier; before; formerly. II. conj. before, ere; —e er kommt, before he comes. —er, adv. (compar. of ehe) sooner; rather; formerly; earlier; je —er, je lieber, the sooner the better; um so —er, so much the more; nicht —er bis, not until, not unless; ich wollte —er sterben, I would rather die; —er alles andere als, anything but. —est, adj. & adv. (sup. of ehe) earliest; first; next; speediest; soonest; am —esten = am leichtesten, most easily, sooner than anywhere else; mit dem —esten, —ester Tage, very soon, one of these days; aufs —este, by the first opportunity. —estens, adv. as soon as possible, at the earliest opportunity; soon. Comp. —e-dem (—e-dessen), adv. before this time, heretofore; ere now; of old. —e-gestern, adv. the day before yesterday. —e-hin, —e-mals, adv. formerly, of old; —e-mals Professor an, late professor at. —e-malig, adj. of a former time, former, late, old.

E'he, f. (pl. —n) marriage; matrimony; wedlock; zweifache —, bigamy; vielfache —, polygamy; wilde —, concubinage; eine —stiften, to bring about a marriage; eine — vollziehen, to consummate a marriage; eine — schließen, to contract a marriage; —n werden im Himmel geschlossen, marriages are made in heaven (prov.); eine — besiegeln, to consummate a marriage; außer der — geboren, illegitimate. —lich, adj. & adv. matrimonial, conjugal; legitimate; —liche Kinder, legitimate children; —lich machen, to legitimatize. —lichen, v.a. to marry. Comp. —band, n. marriage bond, conjugal tie. —bett, n. nuptial bed. —brechen, ir.v.n. to commit adultery. —brecher, m. adulterer. —brecherin, f. adulteress. —bruch, m. adultery. —bund, m., —bündnis, n. matrimony. —fähig, adj. nubile. —feind, m. marriage-hater, misogamist. —frau, —gattin, f. lawful spouse, wife. —gatte, m. lawful spouse, husband. —gemahl, m., —gemahlin, f. lawful husband, lawful spouse. —gericht, n. divorce court. —gesetz, n. marriage law. —hälfte, f. consort, better-half. —herr, m. wedded lord, husband. —hindernis, n. obstacle or impediment to marriage. —leben, n. wedded or married life. —leiblich, adj. legitimate, lawful. —leute, pl. married people; the married couple. —liebste, f. see —frau. —los, adj. unmarried, single. —losigkeit, f. single life or state; single-blessedness (iron.); celibacy. —mann, m. (pl. —männer) husband, married man. —paar, n. married couple. —pacten, pl. marriage articles. —pflicht, f. conjugal duty. —prokurator, m. matrimonial agent. —recht, n. marriage law; marriage right. —sache, f. matrimonial affair; matrimonial suit. —schänder, m. adulterer. —schatz, m. dowry. —scheidend, adj. divorcive. —scheidung, f. divorce. —scheidungs-proceß, m., —scheidungs-klage, f. divorce suit. —scheidungs-spruch, m. decree absolute (divorce). —scheu, I. subst.f. aversion to marriage. II. adj. adverse to marriage; misogamist. —segen, m. nuptial blessing; issue, children. —stand, m. married state, wedlock. —steuer, f. dowry. —stifter, m., —stifterin, f. matchmaker. —trennung, f. separation a mensa et thoro; judicial separation. —verbindung, f. matrimonial alliance. —vergleich, m. marriage contract. —verlöbnis, n., —verspruch, m. affiance. —vertrag, m. marriage settlement. —weib, n. wedded wife. —werber, m. suitor.

E'hern, adj. brazen, of brass, of bronze.

Eh'ni, m. grandfather, grandsire (Swiss dial.).

Ehr'bar, adj. & adv. honourable, of good repute; respectable; honest; decorous. —keit, f. honesty; respectability; propriety; reputableness; honourableness.

Eh'r—e, f. (pl. —en) honour; reputation; rank; glory; praise; credit; einem —e bezeigen, —e erweisen, to do, show honour to a person; göttliche —e erweisen, to pay divine honours; zur —e gereichen, to redound to one's honour; auf (meine) —e, upon my honour; sich (dat.) eine —e daraus machen, to deem it an honour; in —en halten, to honour; zu —en des Tages, in honour of the day; bei —en bleiben, to preserve one's honour, one's reputation; in —en, in all honour; Ihr Wort in —en, with due deference to you; mit —en zu melden, with all respect; die Prüfung mit —en bestehen, to acquit oneself creditably in an examination, to do well in an examination; einen bei der —e angreifen, to insult, to wound a p.'s honour; um die —e bringen, to dishonour, seduce; einem Wechsel alle —e widerfahren lassen, to honour, meet, a bill (C. L.); mit wem habe ich die —? whom have I the honour to address? —enhaft, adj. honourable. —enhaftigkeit, f. honour, uprightness. —lich, adj. & adv. just, honest; honourable; fair, true-hearted, faithful; ein —liches Begräbnis, a decent burial; ein —licher Narr, a harmless fellow; —lich währt am längsten, honesty is the best policy (prov.); er meint es —lich (mit ihr), his intentions are honourable; mit einem —lich zu Werke gehen, to deal fairly with a p. —lichkeit, f. honesty; honourable dealing. —sam, adj. & adv. honourable, respectable (obs.). Comp. —begierde, f. ambition. —begierig, adj. & adv. ambitious. —beraubung, f. calumniation. —durst, m. thirst for honour or glory. —en-amt, n. post of honour; honorary office; preferment. —en-bahn, f. career of honour; road to honour. —en-besuch, m. visit of ceremony, formal visit. —en-bezeigung, f. mark of esteem, (military) salute. —en-bürgerrecht, n. (honorary) freedom of a city. —en-dame, f. lady or maid of honour. —en-erklärung, f. (full) apology. —en-fall, m. point of honour. —en-fest, adj. honourable (obs.). —en-gedächtnis, n. pious memory. —en-gefolge, n. retinue, escort (of honour). —en-gehalt, m. pension. —en-gelag, —enmahl, *n.* banquet in a person's honour. —en=gericht, *n.* court of honour. —en=geschenk, *n.* presentation, donation. —en=grad, *m.* honorary degree. —en=halber, for honour's sake. —en=hold, *m. old spelling for* Herold herald (*obsol.*). —en=klage, *f.* action for libel. —en=kleid, *n.* state dress. —en=kompanie, *f.* guard of honour; die Front der —en=kompanie abschreiten, to inspect the guard of honour. —en=kränkung, *f.* insult to one's honour, slander, libel. —en=kreuz, *n.* medal (*in shape of a cross*). —en=legion, *f.* Legion of Honour. —en=lüge, *f.* conventional *or* official lie. —en=mann, *m.* man of honour, gentleman; worthy. —en=münze, *f.*, —en=pfennig, *m.* medal. —en=pflicht, *f.*; eine nationale —en=pflicht, a duty imposed by the national honour. —en=pforte, *f.* triumphal arch. —en=platz, *m.*, —posten, *m.* post of honour; place of honour. —en=preis, *m.* price of honour; veronica, speedwell (*Bot.*). —en=punkt, *m.* point of honour. —en=rat, *m.* court of honour (*especially in the case of officers, deciding whether a duel should be fought or not*). —en=raub, *m.* slander; rape. —en=recht, *n.* code of honour; honorary right; Verlust der bürgerlichen —enrechte, civic degradation. —en=rede, *f.* panegyric. —en=rettung, *f.* vindication of honour; apology. —en=rührig, *adj.* slanderous; defamatory; —enrührige Beschuldigung, (in einem Brief oder einer Druckschrift) libel. —en=sache, *f.* affair of honour; duel. —en=säule, *f.* monument. —en=schänder, *m.* libeller; ravisher. —en=sold, *m.* honorarium. —en=stand, *m.* honourable condition, dignity. —en=stelle, *f.* dignity, preferment, post of honour. —en=titel, *m.* honorary title; title of honour. —en=trunk, *m.* banquet in a p.'s honour; toast. —en=voll, *adj. & adv.* honourable, creditable; er wurde —envoll erwähnt, he received honourable mention. —en=wache, *f.* guard of honour; sentry of honour. —en=wächterin, *f.* chaperon, duenna, governess; mit ihrer Erzieherin als —enwächterin, chaperoned by her governess. —en=wert, *adj.* honourable; sehr —enwert, right honourable. —en=wort, *n.* parole; word of honour. —en=zeichen, *n.* badge of honour; augmentation (*Her.*). —erbietig, *adj. & adv.* reverential, respectful; er war sehr —erbietig gegen sie, he showed them great respect. —erbietigkeit, *f.* reverence. —erbietung, *f.* deference, respect, veneration. —erbietungs=bezeugung, *f.* homage. —furcht, *f.* respect, awe. —furchts=los, *adj.* disrespectful, irreverent. —furchts=voll, *adj.* respectful, reverential. —gefühl, *n.* sense of honour. —geiz, *m.* ambition. —geizig, *adj.* ambitious. —gier, *f.* inordinate ambition. —gierig, *adj.* very desirous of honour. —licher=weise, *adv.* in fairness. —los, *adj.* dishonourable. —losigkeit, *f.* infamy, dishonourableness, dishonesty. —pußlich, *adj.* decorous, proper, well-behaved (*coll.*). —sucht, *f.* thirst for honour. —süchtig, *adj.* greedy of honour. —trieb, *m.* honourable impulse; desire for honour. —vergessen, *adj.* unprincipled, regardless of honour, despicable, vile. —vergessenheit, *f.* meanness, vileness. —widrig, *adj.* discreditable, despicable, disgraceful. —würden, *f.* Reverence; Ew. (= Euer) —würden, your Reverence, Reverend Sir. —würdig, *adj.* venerable; respectable, sacred, reverend, worshipful. —würdigkeit, *f.* venerableness.

Eh'r—en, *v.a.* to honour, esteem, revere; (hoch) geehrter Herr, Sir; dear Sir; my dear Sir. —ung, *f.* mark of honour; present.

Ehren— *before proper names, e.g.* Ehren Loth, *is not really connected with* Ehre *but with* Herr, *but can in most cases be rendered by* the worthy —. (*See* Ehrenhold.)

Ei, *int.* indeed! ay! why! *etc.*; — warum nicht gar! you don't say so! you don't mean it! — was! oh, nonsense!

Ei, *n.* (—(e)s, *pl.* —er) egg; hart (weich) gesottenes —, hard (soft) boiled egg; frisches —, new laid egg; faules —, bad *or* addled egg; verlorene —er, poached eggs; ein — zu schälen haben mit, to have a crow to pluck with; sie gleichen sich wie ein — dem andern, they are as like as two peas; er ist eben erst aus dem — gekrochen, he is just out of his shell, he is a greenhorn; kümmre dich nicht um ungelegte —er, don't meddle with things that do not concern you! man muß ihn anfassen, wie ein rohes —, he is extremely touchy; das — will klüger sein als die Henne, don't teach your grandmother to suck eggs; aussehen wie aus dem — gepellt, to look as if one had just stepped out of a band-box. —chen, *n.* little egg. *Comp.* —dotter, *m.* (*& n.*) yolk of egg. —er=becher, *m.* egg-cup. —er=bier, *n.* egg-flip. —er=grütze, *f.* pearl groats. —er=käse, *f.* custard. —er=kuchen, —er=fladen, *m.* omelet, pancake. —er=krebs, *m.* female crawfish. —er=legend, *adj.* oviparous. —er=leger, *pl.* ovipara; diese Hühner sind gute —leger, these hens are good layers. —linie, *f.* ellipse. —er=löffel, *m.* egg-spoon. —er=pflaume, *f.* victoria plum. —er=rahm, *m.* custard. —er=sack, *m.* ovary (*Anat.*). —er=schale, *f.* egg-shell. —er=schnee, *m.* whisked eggs. —er=stock, *m.* ovary (*Bot. & Anat.*). —er=stock=wassersucht, *f.* ovarian dropsy. —er=suppe, *f.* soup made with eggs. —förmig, *adj.* oval, oblong. —gelb, *n.* yolk. —rund, *adj.*, —ründe, *f.* oval, egg-shaped. —weiß, *n.* albumen; white of an egg. —weiß=stoff, *m.* albumen.

Ei'a, *interj.* hey! heyday! —popeia, *interj. & n.* by-by, lullaby, hush-a-by.

Ei'be, *f.* (*pl.* —n) yew tree. —n, *adj.* yew.

Ei'bisch, *m.* (—(e)s, *pl.* —e) marsh-mallow.

Eich, *f.*, —e, *f.*, Aich, *f.*, —e, *f.* (*Arch.*) (*pl.* —en) gauge, standard. —en, *v.a.* to gauge. —er, Ai'cher, *m.* (—ers, *pl.* —er) gauger. *Comp.* —amt, *n.* gauging-office, testing place of weights and measures. —maß, *n.* standard. —meister, *m.* gauger, standard-officer, sealer of weights and measures. —stab, *m.* gauging-rule.

Ei'ch—e, *f.* (*pl.* —en) oak. —el, *f.* (*pl.* —eln) acorn; gland; glans (*Anat.*); club (*Cards*). —en, *adj. & adv.* oaken, of oak. *Comp.* —el=förmig, *adj.* glandiform. —el=häher, *m.* jay. —el=mehl, *n.* ground oak-bark. —el=öl, *n.* nut-oil. —el=schwein, *n.* pig fed on acorns. —en=blatt, *n.* oak-leaf. —en=bruch, *m.* branch of oak-leaves. —en=fest, *adj.* firm *or* hard as an oak. —grund, *m.* vale of oaks. —horn, *see* Eichhorn. —kätzchen, *n.*, —katze, *f.* squirrel. —mast, *f.* oak-mast.

Eich'horn, *n.* (—s, *pl.* Eichhörner) (*dim.* Eichhörnchen) squirrel; sibirisches —, miniver.

Eid, *m.* (—es, *pl.* —e) oath; adjuration; execration; einen — ablegen, leisten, schwören, to take an oath, swear; (einem) einen — abnehmen (lassen), to put (one) on his oath; to swear in; (einem) den — zuschieben, to tender an oath; ich kann einen — darauf ablegen, I can swear to it; — der Treue, oath of allegiance. —lich, *adj. & adv.* sworn, by *or* upon oath; er hat sich —lich verpflichtet, he is under an oath; —lich erhärten, to depose on oath; —liche Aussage, affidavit, sworn deposition. *Comp.* —bruch, *m.* perjury. —brüchig, *adj. & adv.* perjured, forsworn; —brüchig werden, to perjure oneself. —es=formel, *f.* form of oath.

—es-kräftig, *adj.* upon oath, attested. **—es-leistung,** *f.* affidavit; taking an oath, act of swearing. **—genoß,** *m.* confederate. **—genossenschaft,** *f.* league, confederacy. **—schwur,** *m.* oath. **—vergessen,** *adj.* forsworn. **—verweigernd,** *adj.* non-juring.

Ei'dam, *m.* (—s, *pl.* —e) son-in-law.

Ei'dechse, *f.* (*pl.*—n) lizard. *Comp.* **—n-artig,** *adj. & adv.* lizard-like, lacertine.

Ei'der, *m.* (—s, *pl.* —) (**—ente, —gans,** *f.*, **—vogel,** *m.*) eider-duck, eider-goose. *Comp.* **—daunen, —dunen,** *pl.* eider-down.

Ei'fer, *m.* (—s) zeal; ardour, fervour; passion; emulation; **Blinder — schadet nur,** the more haste, the less speed (*prov.*). *Comp.* **—sucht,** *f.* jealousy. **—süchtelei',** *f.* petty jealousy. **—süchtig,** *adj. & adv.* jealous, envious.

Ei'fer—n, *v.n.* (*aux.* **h.**) to be zealous; to act *or* advocate with zeal; to vie, emulate, rival; to declaim passionately against (**gegen**), to be envious; to grow angry at (**über eine S.**). **—er,** *m.* (—ers, *pl.* —er) zealot.

Ei'frig, *adj. & adv.* zealous; eager; passionate; emulous; **sich jemandes — annehmen,** to interest oneself warmly for one. **—keit,** *f.* zeal; zealousness; officiousness.

Ei'gen, *adj. & adv.* proper, own; peculiar, special; nice, delicate; odd, strange, curious; exact; difficult, delicate, ticklish; specific; real; **ein —es Gut,** a freehold; **—e Leute,** serfs; **aus —em Antriebe,** spontaneously; **eine —e Aussprache,** a peculiar pronunciation; **—e Mundart,** idiom; **das ist ihm —,** that is peculiar to him; **—e Wechsel,** bills of exchange drawn upon oneself; **für —e Rechnung,** on *or* for one's own account; **—er Bote,** special messenger. **—heit,** *f.* peculiarity; oddity; idiosyncrasy; (**in der Sprache**) idiom, idiomatic turn. **—s,** *adv.* expressly; on purpose, peculiarly. **—schaft,** *f.* attribute; characteristic quality; nature; character; condition; peculiarity; property; **Farbe ist eine —schaft des Lichtes,** colour is a property of light; **eine göttliche —schaft,** a divine attribute; **in seiner —schaft als,** in his character of. **—tum,** *n.* (**—tums,** *pl.* **—tümer**) property; ownership; **bewegliches —tum,** movable possessions, goods and chattels; **unbewegliches —tum,** real property. **—tums-recht,** *n.* right of possession; law of property; copyright; ownership. **—tums-steuer,** *f.* property tax; **wessen —tum ist dies?** whose property is this? to whom does this belong? **—tümer,** *m.* (**—tümers,** *pl.* **—tümer**) proprietor. **—tümlich,** *adj. & adv.* belonging exclusively to, proper; (*pron.* **eigentüm'lich**) peculiar; original; characteristic; specific; queer, odd. **—tümlichkeit,** *f.* peculiarity; singularity; characteristic. **—tlich,** I. *adj.* proper; true, real; intrinsic; **die —tlichen Umstände,** the real circumstances, the particulars. II. *adv.* properly speaking; in actuality; **was soll das —tlich bedeuten?** what does that really mean? **—tlich habe ich es nicht erwartet,** to tell the truth I did not expect it; **was willst du —tlich?** what do you want, pray? *Comp.* **—art,** *f.* originality, individuality. **—artig,** *adj.* of a peculiar kind, peculiar. **—dünkel,** *m.* self-sufficiency, conceitedness. **—gewicht,** *n.* specific weight. **—gut,** *n.* freehold. **—händig,** *adj. & adv.* with one's own hand; autographic; **—händiger Brief,** autograph letter. **—hilfe,** *f.*, **—hülfe,** *f.* self-help, self-redress. **—liebe,** *f.* self-love. **—lob,** *n.* self-praise, blowing one's own trumpet; **—lob stinkt,** self-praise is no recommendation (*prov.*). **—mächtig,** *adj. & adv.* arbitrary, despotic; **sich** (*dat.*) **—mächtig Recht verschaffen,** to take the law into one's own hands. **—mittel,** *n.* specific remedy. **—name,** *m.* proper name. **—nutz,** *m.* self-interest. **—nützig,** *adj.* selfish. **—nützigkeit,** *f.* selfishness. **—schafts-wort,** *n.* adjective. **—sinn,** *m.* self-will; positiveness, caprice. **—sinnig,** *adj. & adv.* self-willed; capricious; headstrong, obstinate. **—sucht,** *f.* egotism; selfishness. **—süchtig,** *adj.* selfish. **—ton,** *m.*; **—ton eines Vokals,** characteristic sound (*pitch*) of a vowel. **—wille,** *m.* wilfulness.

Eig'n—en, *v.* I. *r.* to be adapted *or* suited (**zu** *for*). II. *n.* (*aux.* **h.**) to be one's own; to suit; befit, behove; **geeignet für, zu,** qualified, suitable for, adapted to; **es —et ihm,** it is his property; it is characteristic of him (*obs.*). **—er,** *m.* (**—ers,** *pl.* **—er**) owner, proprietor.

Ei'—land, *n.* (**—lands,** *pl.* **—lande**) island. **—länder,** *m.* (**—länders,** *pl.* **—länder**) islander. **—ländisch,** *adj. & adv.* insular.

Ei'l—e, *f.* haste, speed, despatch; **große —e,** hurry; **in (der) —e,** in haste; **es hat keine —e,** there is no hurry about it. **—ig,** *adj. & adv.* hasty, quick, speedy, hurried; **die Sache ist nicht so —ig,** the matter is not so urgent; **nicht so —ig!** don't be in such a hurry! **man brachte ihn —ig in ein Boot,** he was hurried into a boat; **sie hatte nichts —igeres zu thun, als die ganze Geschichte in der Nachbarschaft herumzutragen,** she could not rest until she had told the story to the whole neighbourhood. **—igkeit,** *f.* precipitation. *Comp.* **—bote,** *m.* express messenger, courier. **—fertig,** *adj.* hasty, precipitate. **—fertigkeit,** *f.* overhaste; hastiness. **—fuhre,** *f.* quick conveyance. **—gut,** *n.* goods forwarded by passenger *or* mail train, 'with speed,' 'with despatch.' **—marsch,** *m.* forced march. **—post,** *f.* mail-coach. **—sendung,** *f.* parcel (sent) by fast train. **—wagen,** *m.* mail-coach, stage. **—zug,** *m.* express *or* fast train; forced march.

Ei'l—en, *v.* I. *a.* to hasten. II. *r.* to make haste. III. *n.* (*aux.* **s.** *&* **h.**) to hurry, make haste; **eilt,** immediate (*on letters*); **was —en Sie so?** why are you in such a hurry? **sie —en nicht sehr damit,** they take their time over it; **—e mit Weile,** slow and steady wins the race (*prov.*). **—end,** *p.adj. & adv.* speedy; in haste. **—ends,** *adv.* hastily.

Eilf (*obs. & poet.* for **Elf**), *num.* eleven. **—er,** *m.* wine of 1811 (*exceptionally fine*).

Ei'mer, *m.* (—s, *pl.* —) pail, bucket; liquid measure. *Comp.* **—kette,** *f.* bucket-chain. **—weise,** *adv.* by buckets, by pailfuls.

Ein, *adv. & sep. prefix* in, into; **querfeld —,** across the fields; **Jahr aus, Jahr —,** every year, all the year round.

Ein. I. (**Eine, Ein**), *ind.art.* a, an; **was für —,** what sort of, what (*used as an adj.*). II. *num. adj.* one; the same; **noch —mal,** once more; **— für alle Mal,** once for all; **in —em fort, in —em Stücke fort,** incessantly; **sie sind von —er Größe,** they are the same size; **es ist —s,** it is one o'clock; **es ist halb —s,** it is half past twelve. III. *pron.* (**—er, —e, —(e)s**) one, a person, they, people; the one, the (*obs.*); the one for us, our; a certain portion, some (*poet.*); **—s ums andere,** alternately; **noch —s,** another word with you; further; **—er nach dem andern,** one by one; **so —er,** such a one; **—s ist Not,** one thing is needful; **—s schickt sich nicht für alle,** the same thing is not suitable for everybody; **—er für alle und alle für —en,** jointly and severally; **unser —er,** one of us; one such as I; **—s ins andere gerechnet,** taking one with the other; **ich bin — guter Hirte,** I am the good shepherd; **er ist meines Herzen — Geselle,** he is the (chosen) friend of my heart (*obs.*); **an —en hochlöblichen Magistrat,** to the mayor and aldermen of our town; **es ist — Schnee gefallen,** there has been a shower of snow, some snow has fallen. **—er,** I. (**—e, —es**) *see*

Ein III. II. *m.* (—**s**, *pl.* —) unit; number below ten. —**heit**, *f.* oneness; unity; unit; **die —heit der Handlung**, the unity of action; —**heiten von Zeit und Ort**, unities of time and place. —**heitlich**, *adj. & adv.* uniform, unitary; —**heitliche Regierung**, centralized government. —**ig**, I. *adj. & adv.* one, united, accordant, living in concord, agreed, peaceful; single, sole, only (*obs.; see* **Einzig**); **Handels —ig werden**, to agree about price, conclude a bargain; —**ig sein** *or* **werden über (eine S.)**, to agree in *or* upon; **er ist mit sich selbst nicht darüber —ig**, he has not made up his mind about it. II. *adj. & adv.* any, some; (*pl.*) some, sundry, a few; —**ige zehn Jahre**, some ten years; —**ige**, some people. —**igkeit**, *f.* unity; harmony, agreement, union; unanimity; concord; —**igkeit macht stark**, union is strength (*prov.*). —**s**, I. *adv.* of one mind, at one; once, only; **wir sind —s**, we are at one; **mit —s**, all at once, suddenly. II. *f.* (*the number*) one; ace. III. *indec. adj.* one; immaterial; indifferent. IV. *pron.* **laßt uns —s rauchen, singen**, let us have a cigar, a song. —**sam**, *adj. & adv.* lonely, lonesome; solitary, alone; retired. —**samkeit**, *f.* loneliness, solitude. —**st**, *adv.* one time, once, one day; some (*future*) day, some time. —**stens**, *see* —**st**. —**stig**, *adj.* future, to come at some time. —**zelheit**, *f.* singleness, individuality. —**zelheiten**, *pl.* details, particulars. —**zeln**, *adj. & adv.* single, sole, individual; isolated, detached; —**zelnes hat mir gefallen**, some things did please me; **die Bände sind —zeln zu haben**, the volumes are to be had separately; **ins —zelne gehen**, to enter into particulars; —**zeln angeben**, to specify; —**zeln betrachten**, to individualize; **im allgemeinen und im —zelnen**, in general and in particular; —**zeln verkaufen**, to sell at retail. —**zig**, *adj. & adv.* only, single, sole, unique; —**zig in seiner Art**, unique. —**zig=artig**, *adj.* unique. —**zigkeit**, *f.* oneness. *Comp.* —**ander**, *indec. pron.* one another, each other; **an —ander**, in succession; **aus —ander**, asunder, apart, from each other; **bei —ander**, together; **durch —ander**, promiscuously, confusedly, pell-mell; **mit —ander**, one with another, on an average, together; **nach —ander**, successively; **drei Tage nach—ander**, three days running; **neben —ander**, side by side; **von—ander**, *see* **aus—ander**. —**armig**, *adj.* one-armed. —**artig**, *adj.* of one sort. —**äugig**, *adj.* one-eyed. —**back**, *m.* bread *or* cake not turned in baking. —**basisch**, *adj.* monobasic. —**blätterig**, *adj.* monophyllous. —**blumig**, *adj.* uniflorous. —**brüderig**, *adj.* monadelphian. —**deutig**, *adj. & adv.* having but one meaning, unequivocal. —**erlei'**, I. *indec. adj.* of one sort; one and the same; immaterial; all the same. II. *n.* (—**s**) monotony, sameness; **das ewige —erlei**, the unvarying monotony. —**erlei'heit**, *f.* identity, identicalness. —**er=seits**, *adv.* on the one hand *or* side. —**fach**, *adj. & adv.* simple, single; not complex *or* mixed; indivisible; plain, homely, frugal; —**fache Farbe**, primitive colour; —**fach wirkend**, single-actioned. —**fach=heit**, *f.* simplicity; plainness; singleness. —**falt**, *f.* artlessness, simplicity; silliness. —**fältig**, *adj. & adv.* simple, plain; artless; weakminded, silly. —**fältigkeit**, *f.* simplicity; silliness. —**faltspinsel**, *m.* simpleton. —**farbig**, —**färbig**, *adj. & adv.* of one colour; plain (*stuff*); —**farbiges Gemälde**, monochrome. —**förmig**, *adj. & adv.* uniform, unvaried, monotonous. —**förmigkeit**, *f.* uniformity; monotony. —**geboren**, *adj.* only-begotten. —**geschlechtig**, *adj.* unisexual. —**glas**, *n.* monocle. —**händig**, *adj.* one-handed. —**heits=gläubige(r)**, *m.* unitarian. —**heits=lehre**, *f.* monotheism. —**heitsschule**, *f.* (**höhere—heitsschule**) uniform type of secondary school of the highest grade with classical and modern sides in which all pupils receive the same instruction in the lower forms. —**heits=trieb**, *m.* concentrativeness. —**hellig**, *adj. & adv.* with one voice, unanimous; harmonious. —**helligkeit**, *f.* unanimity. —**horn**, *n.* unicorn, one-horned animal. —**iger=ma'ßen**, *adv.* in some measure *or* degree, somewhat, rather. —**jährig**, *adj. & adv.* lasting a year; one year old; —**jährige Pflanze**, annual. —**jährige(r)**, *m.*, *also* —**jährig=Freiwilliger**, *m.* German soldier who serves only one year with the colours (*at his own expense*), German one year volunteer; —**jähriger Freiwilligendienst**, one year's military service. —**klang**, *m* unison; accord, harmony; **in —klang bringen**, to make agree, to tune; **im —klang stehen**, to agree. —**klappig**, *adj.* univalve. —**lappig**, *adj.* monocotyledonous (*Bot.*). —**läufig**, *adj.* one-barrelled. —**mal**, *adv. & part.* once, one time; once upon a time; some (*future*) time; once for all; just, only, for once; **auf —mal**, all at once, suddenly; **noch —mal**, once more; **noch —mal so schön**, twice as beautiful; **nicht —mal**, not even; **auch jetzt nicht —mal?** what, not even yet? **irgend —mal**, some time *or* other; **da es nun —mal so ist**, things being so, as matters stand; **ich bin nun —mal so**, that is my way, my nature (I can't change it); **du wirst nicht —mal rot?** you don't even blush?; (*after imperatives:*) **komm —mal her**, just come here (*for a moment*); **das ist mir —mal unbegreiflich**, well, I must say I can't conceive it; —**mal ist keinmal**, once is no custom (*prov.*); **stellen Sie sich —mal vor**, only think; **es war —mal**, once upon a time there was. —**mal=eins**, *n.* once one; multiplication-table. —**malig**, *adj. & adv.* happening but once, solitary. —**männig**, *adj.* monandrian (*Bot.*). —**master**, *m.* one-masted vessel. —**mut**, *m.* unanimity, concord, agreement. —**mütig**, *adj. & adv.* unanimous, of one mind; with one consent, nem. con. —**mütigkeit**, *f.* unanimity. —**öde**, *f.* (*pl.* —**öden**) solitude, desert, desolate place, wilderness. —**öhrig**, *adj.* one-eared. —**pfünder**, *m.* one-pounder (*Artil.*). —**reihig**, *adj.* of one row; single-breasted (*Tail.*); unilateral (*Bot.*). —**saitig**, *adj.* one-stringed. —**schläferig**, *adj.* single (*of a bed*). —**schürig**, *adj.* single-shear (*as wool*). —**seitig**, *adj. & adv.* one-sided; partial, biassed. —**seitigkeit**, *f.* one-sidedness, partiality, narrow-mindedness. —**silbig**, *adj. & adv.* monosyllabic, taciturn, laconic; —**silbiges Wort**, monosyllable. —**silbigkeit**, *f.* taciturnity. —**sitzig**, *adj.* having but one seat. —**spänner**, *m.* one-horse vehicle. —**spännig**, *adj. & adv.* drawn by one horse. —**spurig**, *adj.* single-railed. —**stimmig**, *adj. & adv.* for *or* of one voice; unanimous. —**stimmigkeit**, *f.* unanimity harmony. —**stöckig**, *adj.* one-storied (*house*). —**st=weilen**, *adv.* in the mean time; for the present, just now; for a while; temporarily, provisionally. —**st=weilig**, *adj. & adv.* temporary, provisional. —**tags=fliege**, *f.* ephemera. —**tägig**, *adj. & adv.* ephemeral. —**tönig**, *adj. & adv.* monotonous. —**tönigkeit**, *f.* monotony. —**tracht**, *f.* concord, union; harmony, agreement. —**trächtig**, *adj. & adv.* harmonious, united, accordant. —**trächtigkeit**, *f.* unanimity; harmony. —**weibig**, *adj.* monogynous (*Bot.*). —**zahl**, *f.* singular number (*Gram.*). —**zehig**, *adj.* one-toed, monodactylous. —**zel(n)**, single, separate, detached, odd. —**zel=aufzählung**, *f.* detailed enumeration. —**zel=ding**, *n.* individual thing; unique thing. **—zel=fall,** *m.* individual case. **—zel=haft,** *f.* solitary confinement. **—zel=kampf,** *m.* single combat, hand-to-hand fight. **—zel=lader,** *m.* single-loader *or* shooting gun. **—zel=leben,** *n.* isolated life. **—zel=verkäufer,** *m.* retailer. **—zel=wesen,** *n.* individual; unique creature (*obs.*). **—zöllig,** *adj.* of one inch, one inch long *or* thick.

Ein'ackern, *v.a.* to plough in.

Ein'arbeiten, *v.r.* to make oneself thoroughly acquainted with.

Ein'äscher—n, *v.a.* to burn to ashes; to calcine; to reduce to ashes, to burn down. **—ung,** *f.* incineration, burning down.

Ein'atmen, *v.a.* to inhale.

Ein'ätzen, *v.a.* to etch in.

Ein'ballen, Ein'ballieren, *v.a.* to pack.

Ein'balsam—(ier)en, *v.a.* to embalm. **—ierung,** *f.* embalmment.

Ein'band, *m.* (—s, *pl.* **Einbände**) binding, cover of a book; **— in Pappe,** in boards; **— in Leinen,** bound in cloth; **halbfranz —,** half bound; **Kalbleder —,** bound in calf; **biegsamer —,** limp cover; **— mit Goldschnitt,** with gilt edges.

Ein'bauen, *v.* I. *a.* to build one thing in another. II. *r.* to build (*a home*) in a place.

Ein'bedingen, *ir.v.a.* to include in the bargain.

Ein'begreifen, *ir.v.a.* to comprehend; to include, contain; **mit einbegriffen,** included, implied.

Ein'behalten, *ir.v.a.;* **einem etwas —,** to keep back s.th. from s.o.; to withhold, save.

Ein'beizen, *v.a.* to etch in; to pickle (*meat*); to soak; to vein (*wood or leather*); to mortify.

Ein'bekommen, *ir.v.a.* to get in (*cash, etc.*).

Ein'beruf—en, *ir.v.a.* to convene; to call in (*currency, etc.*); to call in *or* out (*troops*). **—ung,** *f.;* **—ung der Reserven,** calling in the men of the army reserve for active service.

Ein'betteln, *v.a.* to collect *or* obtain by begging; **sich —,** to get admission by begging.

Ein'betten, *v.a.* to put up a bed in; to imbed; **sich —,** to procure a lodging in.

Ein'bezieh—en, *v.a.* to include. **—ung,** *f.* inclusion.

Ein'bieg—en, *ir.v.* I. *a.* to bend inwards, downwards *or* back; to inflect. **ein'gebogen,** *p.p.* & *adj.* inflected; sinuous. II. *n.* (*aux.* **f.**) **—en in,** to turn into. **—ung,** *f.* the bending inwards; inflection; recess.

Ein'bild—en, *v.a.* (*with dat. of refl. pron.*) to fancy, imagine; to think, believe; to flatter oneself; to take into one's head; to be conceited; **sich** (*dat.*) **etwas auf eine S. —en,** to pique oneself on s.th., to presume upon; **eingebildet,** conceited; imaginary; **du bildest dir ein, du seist von allem unterrichtet,** you imagine yourself informed about all; **er bildet sich viel ein,** he is full of conceit; **sie bildet sich viel auf ihre vornehmen Verbindungen ein,** she piques herself much on her fashionable connections. **—ung,** *f.* imagination; conceit, fancy; **in der —ung vorhanden,** imaginary, fancied. *Comp.* **—ungs=kraft,** *f.* (power of) imagination; **seiner —ungskraft freien Lauf lassen,** to give free range to one's imagination.

Ein'bind—en, *ir.v.a.* to bind (*a book*); to tie up *or* on; to furl (*sails*); to take in (*a reef*); **einem etwas —en,** to enjoin upon, charge with; **einem Patchen etwas —en,** to make a present to one's god-child. *Comp.* **—e=geld,** *n.* god-parent's christening gift. **—e=nadel,** *f.* bookbinder's needle; flat awl.

Ein'blas—en, *ir.v.a.* to blow, breathe into; to whisper, suggest, prompt, insinuate; to blow down (*walls*), blow in (*windows, etc.*). **—ung,** *f.* blowing in; suggestion; insinuation.

Ein'bläser, *m.* (—s, *pl.* —) prompter; suggester; insinuator. **—erei,** *f.* insinuation.

Ein'bleuen, (*less correctly*) **Ein'bläuen,** *v.a.* to knock into one, inculcate.

Ein'blick, *m.* (—es, *pl.* —e) glance into; in sight.

Ein'bohren, *v.a.* to bore a hole in.

Ein'braten, *ir.v.n.* (*aux.* **f.**) to shrink in roasting.

Ein'brech—en, *ir.v.* I. *a.* to break down; to pull down; to break open; to commit burglary, to break into a house. II. *n.* (*aux.* **f.**) to break in, give way; to begin, draw on, approach; to set in (*as winter, etc.*); **die Nacht bricht ein,** night is coming on; **bei —ender Nacht,** at nightfall. **—er,** *m.* (—ers, *pl.* —er) burglar.

Ein'brennen, *ir.v.a.* to burn in, brand; to anneal; **Mehl —,** to stir in flour to soup, *etc.*

Ein'bringen, *ir.v.a.* to bring in; to house; to bring in as profit, yield; to fetch a price; to bring with; to introduce; **etwas wieder —,** to make up for, make good something; **was bringt der Posten ein?** what is the post worth? **sie verlangt ihr Eingebrachtes,** she claims her dowry.

Ein'brocken, *v.a.* to crumble, to break bread, *etc.*, into small pieces; **etwas einzubrocken haben,** to be well off, to have wealth; **sich** (*dat.*) **etwas —,** to get into trouble; to get into a fine mess (*coll.*); **er muß nun ausessen, was er sich eingebrockt hat,** he now reaps what he has sown.

Ein'bruch, *m.* (—s, *pl.* **Einbrüche**) house-breaking, burglary; invasion, inroad; trespass; **— der Nacht,** nightfall. **—s=versicherung,** *f.* insurance against burglary.

Ein'bürger—n, *v.a.* to naturalize; to enfranchise; **Wörter —n,** to adopt foreign words into a language; **sich —n,** to settle as a citizen; **eingebürgerte Lehnwörter,** words borrowed from foreign languages which have become quite German; naturalized loan-words. **—ung,** *f.* naturalization.

Ein'buße, *f.* loss, damage.

Ein'büßen, *v.a.* to suffer loss from, to lose by.

Ein'dämmen, *v.a.* to dam in; to embank; **eingedämmtes Land,** reclaimed land.

Ein'dampfen, *v.n.* (*aux.* **f.**) to dry by evaporation.

Ein'dämpfen, *v.a.* to stew down; to smoke.

Ein'deutschen, *v.a.;* **ein Fremdwort —,** to give to a foreign word a German appearance (*e.g.*, **Bresche, Gruppe, Leutnant, Möbel**).

Ein'drängen, *v.* I. *a.* to squeeze into, to force into. II. *r.* to crowd in; to intrude o.s. into.

Ein'dring—en, *ir.v.n.* (*aux.* **f.**) (**in etwas**) to enter (into) by force; to break in; to press upon; to penetrate, to pierce; to soak; to enforce (*an argument*); to search into (*a matter*). **—lich,** *adj.* penetrating; affecting, impressive, forcible; intrusive, forward; urgent. **—lich=keit,** *f.* impressiveness. **—ling,** *m.* (—lings, *pl.* —linge) intruder.

Ein'druck, *m.* (—es, *pl.* **Eindrücke**) impression, mark, stamp; **— machen,** to produce an impression, a sensation. **—en,** *v.a.* to imprint. *Comp.* **—s=los,** *adj.* unimpressive. **—s=voll,** *adj.* & *adv.* impressive.

Ein'drück—en, *v.a.* to press in; to break; to squeeze together; to crush in; to shut, close. **—lich,** *adj.* & *adv.* impressive.

Ei'nen, *v.a.* to unite, to form into one; **das geeinte Deutschland,** united Germany.

Ein'engen, *v.a.* to narrow, compress, confine; to limit, define closely; to concentrate.

Ei'ner, see **Ein; — nach dem andern,** one by one, by turns; **so —,** such a one.

Ein'ernten, *v.a.* to reap, harvest, gather in; to win, gain, acquire.

Ein'exerzieren, *v.a.* to accustom to drill, to drill thoroughly.

Ein'fädeln, *v.a.* to thread (*a needle*); to devise, manage, contrive (*artfully*); **soll ich Ihnen — ?** shall I thread the needle for you?

Ein'fahr—en, *ir.v.* I. *a.* to bring, carry in (*on wheels*); to run, drive into; to break in (*horses to harness*); to injure by driving over. II. *n.* (*aux.* **f.**) to drive in, enter. **—t,** *f.* (*pl.* **—ten**) entry, entrance; gateway; inlet; mouth (*of a harbour*); descent (*of a mine*).

Ein'fall, *m.* (**—es,** *pl.* **Einfälle**) falling in; inroad, invasion; irruption; incidence (*of light*); downfall; ruin; sudden idea; conceit, fancy, notion; sally; catch (*of a latch, etc.*); detent (*of a watch*); **ein witziger —,** a flash of wit; **ein wunderlicher —,** a whim, freak; **ich geriet auf den —,** it struck me, the thought occurred to me. *Comp.* **—s=haken,** *m.* detent (*of a watch*). **—s=winkel,** *m.* angle of incidence.

Ein'fallen, *ir.v.n.* (*aux.* **f.**) to fall in; to invade, make an inroad, attack; to break in, come in suddenly; to chime in (*Mus.*); to interrupt; to catch (*of a latch, etc.*); to fall to ruin; to occur (*to one's mind*); to alight; to roost; to fall (*as light*); to set in, come on; **es ist mir niemals eingefallen,** it never once entered my head; **sich** (*dat.*) **— lassen,** to take into one's head; **das hätte ich mir nie — lassen,** I should never have dreamt of such a thing; **wie es ihm gerade einfiel,** as the humour seized him; **es will mir nicht —,** I cannot remember it; **was fällt dir ein?** what are you thinking of?; **es fällt mir nicht ein, das zu thun,** I have not the least intention of doing so; **eingefallene Augen,** sunken eyes; **Winkel, unter dem ein Lichtstrahl einfällt,** angle of incidence; **das Licht fällt durch das Fenster ein,** the light shines *or* penetrates through the window. II. *ir.v.a.* **sich** (*dat.*) **den Schädel —,** to split one's skull by a fall. III. *subst. n.* falling in, collapse; incidence (*of light*); striking in (*Mus.*). **—d,** *p.* & *adj.* incident; **—des Fenster,** skylight.

Ein'fällig, *adj.* & *adv.* tottering, ruinous.

Ein'fangen, *ir.v.* I. *a.* to take and shut in; to seize, apprehend, catch; to imprison; to enclose, separate by a fence; **der eingefangene Fuchs,** the bag-fox. II. *n.* (*aux.* **h.**) to catch.

Ein'faff—en, *v.a.* to barrel (*beer*); to sack (*corn*); to enchase; to set (*jewels*); to frame; to border, edge; to bind (*carpets*); to enclose; to trim (*with lace, etc.*). **—er,** *m.* (**—ers,** *pl.* **—er**) stone-setter. **—ung,** *f.* barrelling; enclosing; enclosure; setting; border; trimming; framing; curb (*of a well*); embankment, fencing. *Comp.* **—ungs=band, (Einfaß=band,)** *n.* binding *or* bordering ribbon. **—ungs=gallerie,** *f.* envelope-gallery (*Fort.*).

Ein'fetten, *v.a.* to grease, to lubricate.

Ein'feuchten, *v.a.* to steep; to wet, moisten through.

Ein'feuern, *v.n.* (*aux.* **h.**) to light a fire in, heat the stove; to inflame.

Ein'finden, *ir.v.r.* to appear, make one's appearance; to come and be present, arrive; **ich werde mich dort —,** I shall come to that place.

Ein'flechten, *ir.v.a.* to plait, braid; to interlace, interweave; to put in, mention by the way.

Ein'flicken, *v.a.* to patch in; to sew on a patch; to insert; to foist in.

Ein'fließen, *ir.v.n.* (*aux.* **f.**) to flow in, into; to come in (*of money*); **— auf,** to influence (*obs.*); **mit — lassen,** to drop in a word, throw in a remark, mention casually; **er ließ ein Wort darüber in die Rede mit —,** he let fall a remark concerning it in his speech.

Ein'flößbar, *adj.* infusible.

Ein'flöß—en, *v.a.* (**einem etwas**) to cause to flow in; to instil, imbue, infuse, inspire with, to suggest; **einem Mut —en,** to inspire s.o. with courage; **einem Mitleid —en,** to touch one with pity; **einem ein Verlangen —en,** to excite a desire in a p. **—ung,** *f.* infusion.

Ein'fluß, *m.* (**—(ss)es,** *pl.* **Einflüsse**) flowing in, influx; influence, power, sway, credit; interest (*at court, etc.*); **das Vergnügen hat — auf die Menschen,** men are influenced by pleasure. *Comp.* **—reich,** *adj.* influential. **—röhre,** *f.* ingress-pipe, feed-pipe.

Ein'flüster—n, *v.a.* to whisper to; to insinuate. **—ung,** *f.* whispering to; insinuation, innuendo.

Ein'fordern, *v.a.* to call in (*debts*); to demand (*payment*).

Ein'fressen, *ir. v.* I. *a.* to eat up; to swallow. II. *r.* & *n.* (*aux.* **h.**) to eat into, to corrode.

Ein'fried—(ig)en, *v.a.* to enclose, fence in. **—igung,** *f.* enclosure; **lebendige —igung,** quickset hedge.

Ein'frieren, *ir.v.n.* (*aux.* **f.**) to freeze in; to be ice-bound. **ein'gefroren,** *p.p.* & *adj.* frost-bound.

Ein'fuchsen, *v.a.*; **einen für eine Prüfung —,** to cram a p. for an examination (*sl.*).

Ein'füg—en, *v.a.* to fit in, insert; to join together; to splice; to dovetail; **sich —en,** to become a part *or* a member of. **—ung,** *f.* fitting in; insertion; dovetailing.

Ein'fuhr, *f.* (*pl.* **—en**) import, importation; bringing in, housing (*corn, etc.*); **—= und Ausfuhr=verbot,** prohibitive system. *Comp.* **—handel,** *m.* import trade. **—liste,** *f.*, **—register,** *n.*, **—tabelle,** *f.* bill of lading; import tariff. **—prämie,** *f.* bounty on importation. **—waren,** *pl.* imports, articles of importation. **—zoll,** *m.* import-duty, entrance-duty.

Ein'führbar, *adj.* importable.

Ein'führ—en, *v.a.* to bring in; to import; to introduce (*customs; people; young ladies into society, etc.*); to usher in; to set up, establish; to induct (*to a living, etc.*); **in ein Amt —en,** to invest with an office, install; **einen redend —en,** to quote *or* cite a person's words. **—er,** *m.* (**—ers,** *pl.* **—er**) introducer; importer; inductor. **—ung,** *f.* introduction; importation; installation. **—ungs=schreiben,** *n.* letter of introduction.

Ein'füllen, *v.a.* to fill in, fill up; **in Flaschen —,** to bottle.

Ein'gabe, *f.* petition, presentation (*of a request, etc.*), memorial.

Ein'gang, *m.* (**—(e)s,** *pl.* **Eingänge**) entering, entry; arrival; place of entrance, inlet; doorway, hall; passage (*Anat.*); mouth (*of a river*); adit (*of a mine*); introduction; importation; access; preface, preamble; exordium; prelude, overture; prologue; **— von Geld,** getting in of payment; **nach —,** on receipt *or* payment; **verbotener —,** no admission; **— der Messe,** introit; **keinen — finden,** not to be received, to make no way, have no effect. **—s,** *adv.* on entering; at the beginning. *Comp.* **—s=buch,** *n.* book of entries; entrance book. **—s=deklaration,** *f.* bill of entry. **—s=preis,** *m.* entrance money. **—s=rede,** *f.* inaugural speech *or* lecture; prologue. **—s=stück,** *n.* overture. **—s=zoll,** *m.* entrance duty, import duty.

Ein'gattern, *v.a.* to enclose with hedges *or* fences.

Ein'geb—en, *ir.v.a.* to give in; to insert; to suggest, prompt, inspire; to hand in, deliver, present; to give (*medicine*). **—er,** *m.* (**—ers,** *pl.* **—er**) suggester, prompter. **—ung,** *f.* administration; presentation; inspiration, suggestion.

Ein'geboren, *p.p.* & *adj.* native, indigenous; innate; **es ist jedem (Menschen) —,** it is the inborn tendency of our being; **das Recht der**

— **verleihen**, to naturalize. —**e(r)**, *m.* native; **er ist kein —er**, he is an alien.

Ein'gebrachte(s), *n.* the capital advanced; the dowry of a wife.

Ein'gedenk, *adj.* mindful of, remembering

Ein'gefleischt, *adj.* incarnate; inveterate (*fig.*).

Ein'gehackte(s), *n.* hash, mince.

Ein'gehen, *ir.v.* I. *n.* (*aux.* **ſ.**) to go in, enter; to come in, arrive; to make search, penetrate; to fall into ruin, decay; to cease, come to an end; to understand, conceive; to enter into (*particulars*); to shrink; to come to hand; **auf eine S. —**, to acquiesce in, agree to a thing; **in eine S. —**, to dive, search into a thing, to familiarize oneself with; **auf den Scherz —**, to enter into the spirit of the joke; **er ging eifrig auf** (*sometimes* **in**) **die Sache ein**, he took up the matter warmly; **aus- und —**, to frequent (*a house*); — **lassen**, to give up, leave off, let drop; **er ließ das Geschäft —**, he gave up business; **die Pflanze ist eingegangen**, the plant has withered, is gone; **das geht ihm glatt ein**, he likes to hear such things, he can readily believe that; he learns it with ease; **das will ihm nicht —**, that will not go down with him. II. *a.* **einen Vergleich —**, to come to terms; **eine Wette —**, to make a bet. **ein'gegangen**, *p.p. & adj.* paid, received in cash; **eingegangene Gelder**, receipts. —**d**, *adj. & adv.* searching, exhaustive, in detail.

Ein'gemacht, *p.p. & adj.* preserved, *etc.*; —**e Sachen**, *pl.* sweetmeats, *etc.* —**e(s)**, *n.* preserves; pickles.

Ein'gemeind—en, *v.a.* to incorporate. —**ung**, *f.* incorporation.

Ein'gemummt, *p.p. & adj.* muffled up.

Ein'genommen, *p.p. & adj. see* **Einnehmen**; **von einem —**, prepossessed in favour of; **er ist sehr von ihr —**, he is infatuated with her; **von sich —**, conceited, full of one's own importance; **gegen einen —**, prejudiced against one; **mir ist der Kopf ganz —**, my head is quite stupid. —**heit**, *f.* predilection; prejudice; prepossession.

Ein'gepfarrte(r), *m.* parishioner.

Ein'gericht(e), *n.* guard *or* ward (*of a lock*).

Ein'geschlossenheit, *f.* confinement; sequestration.

Ein'geschnitten, *p.p. & adj. see* **Einschneiden**; incised (*Bot.*); **das —e**, fricassee; hash.

Ein'geschränktheit, *f.* narrowness; frugality; narrow-mindedness.

Ein'geschrieben, *p.p. & adj.* registered; —**er Brief**, registered letter.

Ein'gesessen, *p.p. & adj.* settled, established, residentiary; **der —e**, settler, inhabitant.

Ein'geständnis, *n.* (—(ss)es, *pl.* —(ss)e) avowal, confession, admission.

Ein'gestehen, *ir.v.a.* to confess; to grant; to allow; **eingestandenermaßen**, avowedly.

Ein'geweide, *n.* (—s, *pl.* —) bowels, entrails, intestines. *Comp.* —**schlag=ader**, *f.* cœliac artery.

Ein'geweihte(r), *m.* initiated man, adept.

Ein'gewöhnen, *v.* I. *a.* to accustom to. II. *r.* to get used to; to settle down.

Ein'gewurzelt, *p.p. & adj.* deep-rooted; inveterate.

Ein'gezogen, *p.p. & adj.* retired, secluded, solitary; confiscated. —**heit**, *f.* retirement; solitary life.

Ein'gießen, *ir.v.a.* to pour in; **ein Glas Wein —**, to pour out a glass of wine; to infuse (*into*); to cast in; **mit Blei —**, to fill in with lead.

Ein'gittern, *v.a.* to enclose with bars *or* a railing, to grate.

Ein'graben, I. *ir.v.a.* to dig in; to engrave, chase, cut into; to hide; to bury; **sich —**, to burrow, to intrench oneself.

Ein'greifen, *ir.v.a.* (*aux.* **h.**) to catch, bite, take hold (*of a latch, an anchor, etc.*); to gear together; to interfere with, intrench upon; to strike, touch (*a lyre, etc.*); to set to work, set about; to mark the track (*of deer*); **in einander —**, to interlock (*as cogwheels*), to be interdependent, to coincide; **einem in seine Rede —**, to interrupt one; **in jemandes Rechte —**, to encroach on another's privileges; **einem in sein Amt —**, to intrench upon another's office; **in einander —de Wissenschaften**, cognate sciences; —**de Maßregeln**, energetic measures; **der Hund greift ein**, the dog catches the scent.

Ein'griff, *m.* (—s, *pl.* —e) catching, seizure; encroachment, infringement, interference (with); trespass (*on, in*); invasion; usurpation; catch (*of a lock, etc.*).

Ein'guß, *m.* (—(ss)es, *pl.* **Eingüsse**) pouring in; potion; drench (*Vet.*); cast; mould; infusion. *Comp.* —**röhre**, *f.* feed-pipe; furnace pipe (*Found.*). —**tierchen**, *pl.* infusoria.

Ein'hacken, *v.a.* to cut into, down *or* up.

Ein'häkeln, *v.a.* to hook in, to clasp.

Ein'haken, *v.a.* to fasten with a hook; to hook in, to bite, catch, hold.

Ein'halt, *m.* (—s) stop, check; prohibition; impediment; — **thun**, to stop, check; — **gebieten**, to order to stop, to bring to a standstill.

Ein'halt—en, *ir.v.* I. *a.* to check, restrain; to hold back; to gather, to pucker (*a seam, etc.*); to follow, observe; **die Zeit —en**, to be punctual. II. *n.* (*aux.* **h.**) to stop, leave off; to pause; to desist; **halt ein!** stop! leave off! **mit der Bezahlung —en**, to stop payment. —**ung**, *f.* observance (*of feasts, etc.*).

Ein'handeln, *v.a.* to purchase; **etwas mit —**, to include s.th. in a bargain.

Ein'händig—en, *v.a.*; **einem etwas —en**, to hand s.th. over to s.o.; to deliver; to serve on one (*a writ*). —**ung**, *f.* delivery, consignation. *Comp.* —**ungs=schein**, *m.* bill of delivery.

Ein'hängen, *v.a.* to hang up; to put in; to put on its hinges (*a door*); to ship (*a rudder*); to skid (*a wheel*).

Ein'hauchen, *v.a.* to inhale; to inspire, breathe into; to inculcate, instil.

Ein'hauen, *ir.v.* I. *a.* to hew, cut into *or* open; to cut up; to break open. II. *n.* (*aux.* **h.**) to charge (*Mil.*); **in** *or* **auf den Feind —**, to break in upon the enemy.

Ein'heb—en, I. *ir.v.a.* to lift into; to put a form into the press; to collect. II. *subst.n.* imposing (*Typ.*). —**ung**, *f.* collection (*of taxes*).

Ein'heften, *v.a.* to sew in, to stitch in; to file (*papers, etc.*); to tack together.

Ein'hegen, *v.a.* to fence in, to enclose.

Ein'heimisch, *adj.* native; indigenous; domestic; home-bred; home-made; endemic; vernacular; —**e Produkte**, home produce; —**e Dichtung**, national poetry; —**er Krieg**, civil war; —**e Pflanzen**, indigenous plants; — **machen**, to naturalize, to domesticate, to acclimatize; — **werden**, to settle, to feel at home; **die —en**, the natives.

Ein'heimsen, *v.a.* to get in; to bring home.

Ein'heiraten, *v.r.* to marry into a family.

Ein'heiz—en, *v.a. & n.* (*aux.* **h.**) to light a fire; **wir haben tüchtig eingeheizt**, we have heated our room well; **einem —en**, to make it warm for a person, to frighten one. —**er**, *m.* fireman, stoker. —**ung**, *f.* heating.

Ein'helf—en, *ir.v.n.* (*aux.* **h.**) to prompt, jog the memory; **einem —en**, to assist one. —**er**, *m.* (—**ers**, *pl.* —**er**) prompter.

Ein'hellig, *adj. & adv.* unanimous(ly).

Ein'hemmen, *v.a.* to lock (*a wheel*), put on the drag.

Einhe'r, *adv. & sep. prefix*, along, forth. *Comp.* (*with verbs of motion, often implying stateliness*). —**gehen**, *ir.v.n.* to move along; to pace; to

wander about. —stolzieren, *v.a.* to strut, stalk along.
Ein'hetzen, *v.a.* to break in, to train (*Sport*).
Ein'hol—en, *v.a.* to bring in; to haul home (*the guns, a rope, etc.*); to go to meet; to go and fetch in great state; to obtain; to collect (*votes*); to take in (*sails*); to overtake; to make up for (*lost time, etc.*); retrieve; **jemandes Einwilligung —en,** to get a p.'s consent. **—er,** *m.* (—ers, *pl.* —er) halyard (*naut.*). *Comp.* **—talje,** *f.* (**einer Kanone**), train-tackle (*Artil.*).
Ein'hotzeln, *v.n.* to shrivel.
Ein'hüllen, *v.a.* to wrap *or* muffle up *or* in; to envelop.
Ei'nig—en, *v.a.* to make one, unite, cause to agree; **sich —en,** to agree. **—keit,** *f.* unity, harmony. **—ung,** *f.* union, unification.
Ein'impf—en, *v.a.* to inoculate, vaccinate; to implant. **—ung,** *f.* inoculation; vaccination.
Ein'jagen, *v.* I. *a.* to drive, chase into; to instil; **einem Schrecken —,** to frighten a person, strike terror into one; **einen Hund —,** to train a dog (*for sport*). II. *n.* (*aux.* **s.**) to rush, to gallop in.
Ein'kacheln, *v.a.* to heat very much (*coll.*).
Ein'kalken, *v.a.* to lay in lime; to join with lime; to soak in lime-water.
Ein'kassieren, *v.a.* to cash, to collect (*money, debts*).
Ein'kauf, *m.* purchase, marketing. *Comp.* **—s=geld,** *n.* purchase-money. **—s=rechnung,** *f.* account, bill of costs. **—s=preis,** *m.* cost-price; first cost, prime cost; purchase money.
Ein'kaufen, *v.* I. *a.* to buy in; to purchase; to purvey. II. *r.* **sich** (*dat.*) **etwas —,** to acquire by purchase.
Ein'käufer, *m.* (—s, *pl.* —) purchaser; purveyor.
Ein'kehl—e, *f.* (*pl.* —en) hollow fluting, groove. *Comp.* **—stein,** *m.* gutter-tile.
Ein'kehlen, *v.a.* to groove; to provide with a gutter.
Ein'kehr, *f.* putting up at an inn; inn; lodging; (**bei sich selbst**), contemplation.
Ein'kehren, *v.n.* (*aux.* **s.**) to turn in, to enter; to put up at; to stop at, alight; to make a call (**bei**, upon); **bei** *or* **in sich —,** to examine oneself, turn in on oneself.
Ein'keilen, *v.a.* to wedge in; to fasten with wedges, plug; to inculcate, drive in.
Ein'kellern, *v.a.* to lay in, to cellar.
Ein'kerben, *v.a.* to notch, indent; to crimp (*Fish*); to engrail (*Her.*).
Ein'kerker—n, *v.a.* to imprison, incarcerate. **—ung,** *f.* incarceration, imprisonment.
Ein'ketten, *v.a.* to hook in, to chain.
Ein'kindschaft, *f.* legal adoption; equalization of property amongst children of different marriages.
Ein'klagen, *v.a.* to sue (*at law for a debt*).
Ein'klammer—n, *v.a.* to fasten with cramp-irons; to bracket; to insert in brackets *or* parentheses. **—ung,** *f.* (**das Eingeklammerte**), bracket; parenthesis; the words enclosed in brackets.
Ein'klebebuch, *n.* (—(e)s, *pl.* **Einklebebücher**) book for pasting (scraps, cuttings) in, scrap book.
Ein'kleid—en, *v.a.* to clothe; to invest with (*a uniform, a religious garb, etc.*); to lay out (*a corpse*); **etwas gut —en,** to give a pleasing turn to a thing; **sich —en lassen,** to don a uniform; to become a soldier; to take the veil; to enter a monastery. **—ung,** *f.* clothing; investiture; taking of the veil; wording, form.
Ein'klinken, *v.a.* & *n.* (*aux.* **s.**) to latch; **eingeklinkt,** on the latch.
Ein'knebeln, *v.a.* to gag, fasten by a gag.
Ein'kneipen, *v.* I. *a.* to pinch in. II. *n.* (*aux.* **s.**) to stop at an inn (*slang*).

Ein'knicken, *v.* I. *a.* to break, to bend in (*as the knees*); to fold up (*as a carpenter's rule*). II. *n.* (*aux.* **s.**) to break down; **mit eingeknickten Knieen** *or* **Beinen,** with bent-in knees.
Ein'knüpfen, *v.a.* to tie up, tie in; to add.
Ein'kochen, *v.* I. *n.* (*aux.* **s.**) to decrease and become thick by boiling. II. *a.* to thicken by boiling; to boil down; to preserve; to pot.
Ein'kommen, I. *ir.v.n.* (*aux.* **s.**) to come in; to come forward, appear; to get in; to arrive to become bankrupt; to petition, to apply to, to interpose, intervene; **es kam ihm ein,** it occurred to him; **— gegen,** to protest against; **mit einer Klage, einem Bittschreiben —,** to bring an action (against), to memorialize; **er ist um seinen Abschied eingekommen,** he has sent in his resignation; **die eingekommenen Zinsen,** the interest paid. II. *subst.n.* income, revenue; interest; rent; proceeds; temporalities (*Eccl.*); **ein jährliches —,** (yearly) income, annuity. *Comp.* **—steuer,** *f.* income-tax.
Ein'koppeln, *v.a.* to enclose, fence in.
Ein'kramen, *v.* I. *a.* to put, pack up; to purchase; to arrange, to get into order; **sich —,** to get one's things into order, to arrange one's room. II. *n.* (*aux.* **h.**) to shut up shop, to fail.
Ein'kreisen, *v.a.* to encircle, to isolate.
Ein'kriechen, *ir.v.n.* (*aux.* **s.**) to creep in *or* into to shrink, shrivel up; to veer (*Naut.*).
Ein'kriegen, *v.a.* to get on (*boots, etc.*); to have to swallow (*medicine*) (*coll.*); to overtake (*coll.*).
Ein'krimpen, *v.n.* to slacken (*of the wind*); **gegen den Wind —,** to sail close to the wind.
Ein'kritzeln, *v.a.* to scrawl in *or* on.
Ein'kunft, *f.* (*pl.* **Einkünfte**) coming in, arrival; (*pl.*) rents, income, revenues.
Ein'kürzen, *v.a.* to reduce, to shorten; to warp (*a ship*); to foreshorten (*Art*).
[1]**Ein'lad—en,** *ir.v.a.* to invite; to summon, to cite. **—end,** *p.* & *adj.* inviting, attractive. **—er,** *m.* (—ers, *pl.* —er) host; inviter. **—ung,** *f.* invitation, summons. *Comp.* **—ungs=karte,** *f.* invitation-card. **—ungs=schrift,** *f.* invitation; learned treatise, dissertation, essay; summons
[2]**Ein'lad—en,** *ir.v.a.* to load in, to lade, to freight **—er,** *m.* one who loads. **—ung,** *f.* lading.
Ein'lag—e, *f.* a laying in; enclosure (*in a letter, etc.*); stake (*at play*); deposit; money paid up (*on shares*); share; filler, insides (*of cigars*); stiffening (*in shirts, etc.*); **durch —e,** under cover. *Comp.* **—e=holz,** *n.* wood for inlaying. **—er=recht,** *n.* permission to lodge.
Ein'lagern, *v.a.* to lodge; to billet, quarter; to store; to imbed, stratify.
Ein'laß, *m.* (—(ss)es, *pl.* **Einlässe**) letting in; admission; inlet; wicket-gate. *Comp.* **—geld,** *n.* entrance money. **—karte,** *f.* card of admission, ticket; voucher. **—klappe,** *f.* valve. **—ofen,** *m.* smelting furnace. **—preis,** *m.* *see* **—geld.** **—thür,** *f.* small gate; wicket. **—ventil,** *n.* suction valve.
Ein'lass—en, *ir.v.* I. *a.* to let in, admit; to let in, fix in; to countersink; to immit (*Med.*); **nicht —en wollen,** to refuse admittance. II. *r.* (*with* **auf eine S.** *or* **in eine S.** *or* **mit einer S.**) to engage in; to venture on; to meddle with; **ich lasse mich darauf nicht ein,** I will not have anything to do with it; **auf solche Fragen lasse ich mich nicht ein,** I shall not discuss such questions; **sich ins Gespräch —en,** to enter into conversation; **sich auf eine Klage —en,** to answer an accusation. **—ung,** *f.* trimming; immission (*Med.*); answer (*Law*); *see* **Einlaß.**
Ein'läßlich, *adj.* detailed, particular, special.
Ein'lauf, *m.* (—s) entering; arrival.
Ein'laufen, *ir.v.* I. *n.* (*aux.* **s.**) to come in, arrive; to enter (*a harbour*); to come to hand (*of despatches*); to pour in (*of orders*); to shrink (*of cloth*). II. *a.*; **einem die Thür —,** to assail a p., to bore, trouble, pester a p.

Ein'läuten, *v.a.* to announce by ringing, to ring in (*the New Year, church time, etc.*).

Ein'leben, *v.r.* to grow *or* get accustomed to, to familiarize o.s.; **sich in eine S. —**, to get familiar with, enter into the spirit of a thing; **ein tief eingelebter Zustand**, a state of things long existing and familiar to the people.

Ein'leg—en, *v.a.* to lay, put in; to enclose; to fold up, turn inwards; to store up; to deposit; to gain, earn; to pickle, preserve; to lay in, buy (*for future use*); to couch (*a spear*); to inlay; to quarter, billet (*soldiers*); to set (*vines*); to enter (*a protest*); to put away (*goods*), pack up; to shut up shop; **ein (gutes) Wort für einen —en**, to intercede for one, speak on his behalf; **Ehre —en mit**, to gain honour by; **eingelegte Arbeit**, inlaid work, mosaic work. **—er**, *m.* (**—ers**, *pl.* **—er**) one who lays in, *etc.*; layer, shoot; inlayer; depositor; one who pickles, *etc.*; packer (*of fish, etc.*). **—ung**, *f.* laying; enclosing; preservation. *Comp.* **—e=brettchen**, *n.* veneer. **—e=deckel**, *m.* inner tympan (*Typ.*). **—e=gabel**, *f.* folding fork. **—e=holz**, *n.* veneer. **—e=kapital**, *n.* deposit; capital. **—e=stäbchen**, *n.* fitter (*Weav.*). **—e=stuhl**, *m.* folding-chair.

Ein'leit—en, *v.a.* to introduce; to prelude; to institute (*a lawsuit*); to bring about, manage; to usher in. **—end**, *p.* & *adj.* introductory, preliminary. **—ung**, *f.* introduction, preamble; exordium; (*pl.*) preliminary arrangements. *Comp.* **—ungs=wissenschaften**, *pl.* introductory sciences.

Ein'lenken, *v.* I. *a.* to reduce, to set (*a limb*); to lead into a certain channel (*of conversation, etc.*); to turn right; to restore. II. *n.* (*aux.* **h.**) to bend, turn in; to turn back, come round; to return to; to resume; to amend, reform.

Ein'lernen, *v.a.*; **sich** (*dat.*) **etwas —**, to learn by heart; **einem etwas —**, to make s.o. learn s.th., to hammer s.th. into s.o.

Ein'lesen, *ir.v.a.* to gather, to collect; **im Lateinischen eingelesen sein**, to be well read in Latin, to read Latin with great ease.

Ein'leucht—en, *v.n.* (*aux.* **h.**) to be clear, to be evident; **das will mir nicht —en**, I cannot see that, I am not quite clear (*or* satisfied) about it. **—end**, *part.* & *adj.* evident, obvious.

Ein'liefern, *v.a.* to deliver in *or* up, hand over.

Ein'liegen, *ir.v.n.* (*aux.* **s.**) to be quartered, to lodge in; to be enclosed in.

Ein'lochen, *v.a.* to put into prison (*sl.*).

Ein'löffeln, *v.a.* to give by spoonfuls; (**einem etwas**) —, to administer with a spoon.

Ein'logieren, *v.a.* to lodge with (**bei einem**).

Ein'lösbar, *adj.* redeemable.

Ein'lös—en, *v.a.* to ransom, redeem; to take up (*a bill*); to recover, to discharge (*an account*). **—ung**, *f.* redemption; ransom; taking up of a bill.

Ein'löten, *v.a.* to solder in.

Ein'ludeln, *v.a.* to prime (*a cannon*).

Ein'lullen, *v.a.* to lull asleep.

Ein'machen, *v.a.* to put into; to store up; to wrap, put up; to preserve, to pickle; to slake (*lime*); **den Teig —**, to knead into a dough with water, milk, *etc.* **ein'gemacht**, *p.p.* & *adj.* preserved, pickled. **Ein'gemachtes**, *n.* preserves.

Ein'mahlen, *ir.v.a.* to grind (*for future use*).

Ein'marsch, *m.* (**—es**, *pl.* **Einmärsche**) marching in, entry. **—ieren**, *v.n.* (*aux.* **s.**) to march in, enter.

Ein'mauern, *v.a.* to fix in a wall, to wall up; to immure, imprison.

Ein'meißeln, *v.a.* to work on *or* into with the chisel.

Ein'mengen, *see* **Einmischen**.

Ein'mieten, *v.a.* & *r.* to hire, to rent; to take rooms, to engage lodgings.

Ein'mischen, *v.a.* to intermix, to mingle; **sich —**, to meddle with, interfere; **Nebensachen in einen Prozeß —**, to raise collateral issues.

Ein'mummeln, *v.a.* & *r.* to muffle *or* wrap up.

Ein'münd—en, *v.n.* (*aux.* **h.**) to discharge (waters) into (*a river*); to run into, to join; to inosculate with (*Anat.*). **—ung**, *f.* junction.

Ein'münzen, *v.a.* to coin; to recoin.

Ein'nähen, *v.a.* to sew in; to sew up in; to embale; to take in; to shorten; to embroider.

Ein'nahme, *f.* (*pl.* **—n**) receiving; receipt; revenue; taking (*possession of*); capture; **— und Ausgabe**, receipts and expenditure.

Ein'nehmbar, *adj.* that may be taken; untenable.

Ein'nehm—en, *ir.v.a.* to take in; to gather in; to take (*possession of*), to capture; to accept, receive (*money, etc.*); to engage (*a place*); to take (*medicine*); to occupy (*room*); to charm, bewitch, fascinate; to take in (*sails, ballast, etc.*); to receive (*a person into one's house*); to collect (*taxes*); to include (*in a calculation*); **—en für**, to interest for, prejudice in favour of; **—en gegen**, to prejudice against; **das Herz —en**, to touch the heart; **den Kopf —en**, to take one's head, to make giddy; **das Mittagsmahl —en**, to lunch, to dine (early); **das Nachtessen** *or* **Abendbrot —en**, to sup, to dine (late); **wenig —en**, to have a small income; **eines Andern Stelle —en**, to succeed to another's place; **dieser Geruch nimmt mir den Kopf ein**, this smell makes me faint; **sich von seiner Leidenschaft —en lassen**, to be carried away by one's passion. **ein'genommen**, *p.p.* & *adj.* partial (**für**, to); bigoted; infatuated (**von**, with); prejudiced (**gegen**, against); **er ist für Sie sehr eingenommen**, he is much prepossessed in your favour. **—end**, *p.* & *adj.* captivating, taking, charming, engaging. **—er**, *m.* (**—ers**, *pl.* **—er**) receiver, collector (*of taxes, tolls, etc.*). **—erei'**, *f.* collectorship. **—ung**, *f.* taking in, occupation; capture.

Ein'netzen, *v.a.* to wet, moisten; to sponge (*cloth*).

Ein'nicken, *v.n.* (*aux.* **s.**) to fall asleep.

Ein'niste(l)n, *v.r.* to build one's nest; to settle in a place; to nestle; to creep into; to insinuate (oneself). **ein'genistet**, *p.p.* & *adj.* firmly established, inveterate.

Ein'nötigen, *v.a.* to urge, force to take; **einem etwas —**, to press a thing on one.

Ein'ölen, *v.a.* to oil, to grease.

Ein'ordnen, *v.a.* to dispose in proper order; to arrange; to classify.

Ein'pack—en, *v.* I. *a.* to pack up in; **Waren —en**, to put up goods. II. *n.* (*aux.* **h.**) to pack up; to shut up (*shop*); to stop, to become silent; to give way (*coll.*); to become less good-looking (*coll.*). **—ung**, *f.* packing up.

Ein'pappen, *v.a.* to paste in.

Ein'paschen, *v.a.* to smuggle in.

Ein'passen, *v.a.* & *n.* to fit (*in*).

Ein'passieren, *v.n.* (*aux.* **s.**) to pass in.

Ein'pauk—en, *v.a.* to beat into; to train; to cram. **—er**, *m.* (**—ers**, *pl.* **—er**) crammer. **—erei'**, *f.* cramming.

Ein'pfählen, *v.a.* to enclose with pales; to stockade.

Ein'pfarren, *v.a.* to annex to a parish.

Ein'pfeffern, *v.a.* to season with pepper.

Ein'pferchen, *v.a.* to pen in, crowd; to coop up.

Ein'pflanzen, *v.a.* to plant; to implant. **ein'gepflanzt**, *p.p.* & *adj.* inveterate, innate, implanted.

Ein'pflastern, *v.a.* to fix in a pavement; to enclose with a pavement; to put a plaster on.

Ein'pflöcken, *v.a.* to peg in, plug; to fence in.

Ein'pfropfen, *v.a.* to cork in *or* up; to stuff in, to cram in; to engraft; to implant.

Ein'pichen, *v.a.* to fasten with pitch; to pitch.

Ein'pökeln, *v.a.* to salt, to pickle; **eingepökeltes Fleisch**, corned meat.

Ein'prägen, *v.a.* to imprint; (einem etwas) —, to inculcate, to impress upon, to imbue with; sich (*dat.*) etwas —, to impress something upon one's memory.

Ein'predigen, *v.a.* to inculcate, to preach into; sich —, to practise oneself in preaching, to become a good preacher.

Ein'pressen, *v.a.* to press, to put into the press; to squeeze in, to shut up in the furnace.

Ein'prob(ier)en, *v.a.* to try; to rehearse.

Ein'prügeln, *v.a.* (einem etwas) to beat into.

Ein'puppen, *v.r.* to change into a chrysalis.

Ein'quartier—en, *v.a.* to quarter, to billet; sich bei einem —en, to take up one's quarters at s.one's house. **—ung,** *f.* quartering; (*pl.*) soldiers billeted.

Ein'quellen, *v.a.* to soak, to steep.

Ein'querlen, *v.a.* to twirl in, beat up.

Ein'raffen, *v.a.* to grasp at, to snatch up.

Ein'rahmen, *v.a.* to frame; to tenter (*cloth*).

Ein'ramme(l)n, *v.a.* to ram, drive in *or* down.

Ein'rangieren, *v.a.* to enrol (*Mil.*).

Ein'räuchern, *v.a.* to smoke, to fumigate.

Ein'räum—en, *v.a.* to give up (*a room, a house*); to clear, put away; to house, store; (einem etwas) —en, to concede, allow, grant; (einem) seinen Platz —en, to give up one's place to; einem ein Zimmer —en, to accommodate s.o. with a room. **—ung,** *f.* concession, granting; housing; allowance (*in weighing*).

Ein'raunen, *v.a.* to whisper to, to suggest.

Ein'rechnen, *v.a.* to reckon in *or* add, to comprise *or* include in the account; to allow for.

Ein'rede, *f.* (*pl.* —n) objection, exception; opposition, remonstrance; plea; — thun, to protest against; keine —! no replying! don't gainsay!

Ein'reden, *v.* I. *a.* to persuade one to; to talk one over; to convince one of; einem Mut —, to encourage one. II. *n.* (*aux.* h.) to interrupt; to contradict; to object, oppose; to protest; rede mir nicht ein! don't interrupt me! er läßt sich nicht gern —, he does not like interfering *or* contradicting; lassen Sie sich so etwas nicht —, do not allow yourself to be talked into that.

Ein'reib—en, *ir.v.a.* to rub in; to rub down into, grate; sich —en, to rub oneself, to use embrocation; sich (*dat.*) den Fuß mit Salbe —en, to rub salve on *or* into one's foot; sich (*dat.*) den Arm mit Kampferöl —en, to rub one's arm with camphor-oil. **—ung,** *f.* embrocation, rubbing.

Ein'reichen, *v.* I. *a.* to deliver, hand in, present; to memorialize. II. *n.* to overreach (*of a horse*).

Ein'reihen, *v.a.* to place in a line, row, *or* series; to enrol (*Mil.*); to string; to arrange in due order; to insert; to lay in little pleats; to gather and baste.

Ein'reißen, *ir.v.* I. *a.* to tear down; to demolish; to tumble. II. *n.* (*aux.* s.) to rend, cleave, tear, burst; to spread, prevail, gain ground.

Ein'reiten, *ir.v.* I. *n.* (*aux.* s.) to ride in, to enter on horseback. II. *a.* to break down by riding against, to overturn; to break in.

Ein'renken, *v.a.* to reduce *or* set (*a limb*); to set right again (*fig.*).

Ein'rennen, *ir.v.* I. *a.* to force open by running against. II. *n.* (*aux.* s.) to run in, down, *or* against; offne Thüren —, to force an open door, to beat the air; er ist so dumm, daß man Wände mit ihm — kann, he is a hopeless blockhead, he is very thick-skulled.

Ein'richt—en, *v.a.* to set right; to arrange, order; to adapt; to adjust; to set (*a limb*); to contrive; to organize; to furnish (*a house*); to prepare, to dispose; to reduce to a common denominator, to an improper fraction; sich —en, to settle, establish oneself; sich auf eine S. —en, to prepare for s.th.; sich —en nach, to adapt oneself to; sich darnach —en, to take measures accordingly; gut eingerichtet, well regulated, comfortable. **—ung,** *f.* adjustment; arrangement; contrivance; setting (*Surg.*); accommodation, fittings; furnishing; household establishment; justification (*Typ.*).

Ein'riegeln, *v.a.* to bolt in, shut up.

Ein'ritt, *m.* (—es, *pl.* —e) entry on horseback.

Ein'rollen, *v.a.* to roll up; to enrol.

Ein'rosten, *v.n.* (*aux.* s.) to grow rusty; to get fixed by rust; to become stupid *or* dull by inaction, to be impaired by inactivity; to become clownish; ein eingerostetes Übel, a deeply-rooted, inveterate evil; eingerostete Kehlen, throats unfit for singing for want of drink.

Ein'rück—en, *v.* I. *n.* (*aux.* s.) to march into, to enter; to step into (*another's office*); to succeed s.o. II. *a.* to enter, insert, put in; to advertise; Ein- und Ausrückezeug, machinery that can be joined and disjoined, coupling. **—ung,** *f.* marching in; inserting; insertion; advertisement. *Comp.* **—ungs=gebühren,** *pl.* cost of advertisement *or* insertion (*in a paper*).

Ein'rufen, *ir.v.a.* to call in; to recall.

Ein'rühren, *v.a.* to mix up; to mix and stir; to beat up (*eggs, etc.*); to mix in (*mortar, etc.*).

Ein'sacken, Ein'säckeln, *v.a.* to pocket; to bag; to put into sacks.

Ein'salben, *v.a.* to anoint; to embalm.

Ein'salz—en, *ir.v.a.* to salt, to pickle; Eingesalzene(s), salt provisions. **—er,** *m.* (—ers, *pl.* —er) curer; drysalter.

Ein'samkeit, *v. sub* Ein.

Ein'samm—eln, *v.a.* to collect; to lay up. **—ler,** *m.* (—lers, *pl.* —ler) gatherer, collector; gleaner. **—elung,** *f.* collection.

Ein'sargen, *v.a.* to put in a coffin.

Ein'satz, *m.* (—es, *pl.* Einsätze) putting in; anything inserted; deposit; share, stock; stake; pool (*at cards*); reservoir; pledge; set; nest (*of boxes, etc.*); vice; insertion; paragraph; chiming in (*of a voice, Mus.*); Hemd—, shirt-front. *Comp.* **—becher,** *m.* cup fitting in to another. **—gewicht,** *n.* cup-weight; (*pl.*) set of weights. **—kessel,** *pl.* nest, set of kettles. **—streifen,** *m.* insertion. **—teich,** *m.* fishpond.

Ein'säuern, *v.a.* to leaven; to pickle (*in vinegar*).

Ein'saug—en, *ir.v.a.* to suck in; to imbibe, absorb. **—ung,** *f.* absorption, imbibition. *Comp.* **—e=mittel,** *n.* absorbent.

Ein'schachteln, *ir.v.a.* to put in a box; to fit one box into another; to insert; to mix up.

Ein'schalt—en, *v.a.* to insert, put in, intercalate; eine eingeschaltete Stelle, an interpolation; ein eingeschalteter Tag, an intercalary day. **—ung,** *f.* insertion; interpolation; intercalation. *Comp.* **—ungs=zeichen,** *n.* caret (∧).

Ein'schanzen, *v.a.* & *r.* to intrench, fortify.

Ein'schärfen, *v.a.* (einem etwas) to impress on; to inculcate, enjoin.

Ein'scharren, *v.a.* to scratch, scrape in; to bury (*a beast*); to hide by scraping; sich —, to burrow.

Ein'schätzen, *v.a. refl.;* sich selbst (hoch, niedrig) to assess, to estimate oneself (highly, at a low rate).

Ein'schaukeln, *v.a.* to rock to sleep.

Ein'schenken, *v.a.* to pour in; to pour out, to fill; einem reinen Wein —, to tell one plain (*unwelcome*) truths; schenkt ein! fill your glasses! einem —, to help one to (*wine, etc.*).

Ein'schichten, *v.a.* to stratify, put into a layer *or* stratum. **ein'geschichtet,** *p.p.* & *adj.* interstratified.

Ein'schicken, *v.a.* to send in, present.

Ein'schieb—en, *ir.v.a.* to shove in, to put in; to insert, introduce; to interpolate; eingeschobene Gerichte (—e=gerichte, *pl.*), side-dishes, entremets. —**sel**, *n.* (—**sels**, *pl.* —**sel**) insertion; interpolation; epenthesis. —**ung**, *f.* insertion, shoving in; interpolation. *Comp.* —**e=zeichen**, *n.* parenthesis.

Ein'schießen, *ir.v.* I. *a.* to shoot in *or* down; to batter down, to deposit, to pay in, to contribute (*money*); to put in; **eine Flinte** —, to try *or* season a gun. II. *r.* to practise shooting; to become a good shot.

Ein'schiff—en, *v.* I. *a.* to embark, to ship; to entrain (troops in railway carriages). II. *r.* to go on board, to embark. III. *n.* (*aux.* **f.**) to sail in. —**ung**, *f.* embarkation; shipping; —**ung von Soldaten in Eisenbahnzügen**, entraining of troops.

Ein'schirren, *v.a.* to harness.

Ein'schlachten, *v.a.* to kill for household use.

Ein'schlafen, *ir.v.n.* (*aux.* **f.**) to fall asleep; to die away; to be dropped (*of a subject*); to get benumbed; **der Fuß ist mir eingeschlafen**, my foot is asleep *or* has gone to sleep.

Ein'schläfer—n, *v.a.* to lull to sleep; to lull into security. —**nd**, *p. & adj.* narcotic, soporific; —**nde Mittel**, opiates, soporifics. —**ung**, *f.* the lulling to sleep; soporification.

Ein'schlag, *m.* (—**s**, *pl.* **Einschläge**) act of driving, beating, striking in; thing beaten in; hand shaking (*over a bargain*); wrapping up; wrapper; woof, weft; cooperage; porterage; housing, storing; part turned down *or* in (*as a leaf of a book*); enclosure; tuck, fold, plait; hasp; counsel, advice; **Zettel und** —, warp and woof. *Comp.* —**e=garn**, *n.* weft-yarn. —**e=hut**, *m.* spring hat, folding hat. —**e=messer**, *n.* clasp knife. —**e=seide**, *f.* shot silk.

Ein'schlagen, *ir.v.a.* to drive, knock in; to break, burst in; to break (*in pieces*); to turn down (*a tuck; a page, etc.*); to wrap up (*in paper*), envelop; to sulphur (*wine*); to enter upon (*a course*); to take (*a road*); to bandage (*a hoof*); to enclose; **die Arme** —, to cross one's arms; **Bäume** —, to earth the roots of trees; **Eier** —, to beat eggs; **Getreide** —, to sack corn; **man hat ihm den Hirnschädel eingeschlagen**, they have knocked out his brains. II. *n.* (*aux.* **h.**) to shake hands (*as token of agreement*); to strike (*of lightning*); to dig for; to succeed; to yield a good crop; to have reference to; to concern; (*aux.* **f.**) to sink in (*of colours*); to be checked (*of diseases*); to prosper; **nicht** —, to fail, to miscarry; **dieser Knabe ist gut eingeschlagen**, this boy has turned out well; **schlag ein!** give me your hand on it! agree *or* consent to it! say 'yes'!

Ein'schlägig, *adj. & adv.* belonging to; pertinent; competent; **die —e Litteratur**, the literature (books and articles) on the subject.

Ein'schleichen, *ir.v.r.* (*aux.* **h.**) & *n.* (*aux.* **f.**) to creep in, steal in; to insinuate oneself into.

Ein'schleifen, *ir.v.a.* to grind in; to cut in *or* on.

Ein'schleifen, *v.a. usually* **Ein'schleppen**, *v.a.* to drag in; to bring in; to smuggle in.

Ein'schließ—en, *ir.v.* I. *a.* to lock in *or* up; to close up; to enclose; to comprise, include; to invest (*a tower, etc.*). II. *n.* (*aux.* **h.**) to catch (*of a lock*); to fit close. —**er**, *m.* (—**ers**, *pl.* —**er**) one who shuts up; bucket-valve (*of a pump*). —**lich**, *adj. & adv.* included, inclusive. —**ung**, *f.* locking in, up; inclusion, comprisal; enclosure; blockade; confinement. *Comp.* —**ungs=zeichen**, *n.* bracket; parenthesis.

Ein'schlingen, *ir.v.a.* to swallow (*down*); to interlace.

Ein'schlucken, *v.a.* to swallow, gulp down.

Ein'schlummern, *v.* I. *n.* (*aux.* **f.**) to fall into a slumber, to fall asleep; to die an easy death.

Ein'schlürfen, *v.a.* to sip in, sup up.

Ein'schluß, *m.* (—(**ss**)**es**, *pl.* **Einschlüsse**) enclosure; enclosed letter; parenthesis; **nach** —, after the doors are locked up; **mit** — **der Kinder**, including the children; **Brief mit** —, letter with enclosure; **als** —, under cover. *Comp.* —**zeichen**, *n.* bracket, parenthesis.

Ein'schmeichel—n, *v.r.* to insinuate oneself, creep into favour (**bei einem**, with one). —**nd**, *p. & adj.* insinuating. —**ung**, *f.* ingratiation, insinuation.

Ein'schmeißen, *ir.v.a.* to break, dash in (*vulg.*).

[1]**Ein'schmelzen**, *reg. & ir.v.a.* to cause to melt down; **in einem Schmelztiegel** —, to cast.

[2]**Ein'schmelzen**, *ir.v.n.* (*aux.* **f.**) to melt (down *or* away; (**sich**) —, to melt away, to diminish by melting.

Ein'schmieren, *v.a.* to smear, grease; to oil.

Ein'schnapp—en, *v.n.* (*aux.* **f.**) to catch, snap in. *Comp.* —**feder**, *f.* spring-bolt.

Ein'schneid—en, *ir.v.* I. *a.* to cut into; to cut up; to notch; to make loop-holes. II. *n.* (*aux.* **h.**) to cut. —**end**, *adj.* incisive, decisive, peremptory; thorough, important. —**ung**, *f.* incision. *Comp.* —**e=maschine**, *f.*, —**e=zeug**, *n.* screw *or* wheel-cutting engine. —**e=säge**, *f.* book-binder's handsaw.

Ein'schneien, *v.imp.* to snow into; to snow up.

Ein'schnitt, *m.* (—(**e**)**s**, *pl.* —**e**) cutting in *or* out; incision; cut; notch, indentation; segment (*Math.*); cæsura (*Pros.*); porthole, embrasure, loophole; cutting (*Railw.*); harvest. *Comp.* —**s=tier**, *n.* insect.

Ein'schnüren, *v.a.* to cord; to lace up, to tie; **sich** —, to lace one's stays; **sich eng** —, to lace oneself tightly.

Ein'schöpfen, *v.a.* to fill in; to ladle into.

Ein'schränk—en, *v.a.* to limit, bound; to circumscribe; to narrow; to check, curb; to reduce, *or* cut down, curtail, retrench (*expenses*); to restrict (*rights, etc.*); **sich auf eine S. —en**, to restrict oneself to a th.; **im eingeschränkten Sinne**, in a limited sense; strictly speaking; **eingeschränkte Monarchie**, limited monarchy; **eingeschränkte Ansichten**, narrow views. —**end**, *p. & adj.* restrictive. —**ung**, *f.* restriction; retrenchment; restraint; reservation; **mit —ung**, in a qualified sense, with due allowance.

Ein'schrecken, *v.a.* to frighten into; to silence by terror.

Ein'schreib—en, *ir.v.a.* to write in *or* down; to inscribe; to enter; to book; to register; to enrol; to note; **er ließ sich —en**, he had his name entered; he booked his place; **in die Matrikel —en**, to matriculate; **er schrieb sich ein**, he entered his name; **Gepäck —en lassen**, to book *or* register luggage. —**er**, *m.* (—**ers**, *pl.* —**er**) registrar(y). —**ung**, *f.* inscription; enrolment; registration; entry (*of a name*). *Comp.* —**e=amt**, *n.* registry (*office*). —**e=brief**, *m.* registered letter. —**e=bureau**, *n.* booking-office. —**e=geld**, *n.*, —**e=gebühr**, *f.* entrance money; booking fee; fee for registration. —**e=stube**, *f.* registry-office. —**e=sendung**, *f.* registered letter *or* packet.

Ein'schreit—en, *ir.v.n.* (*aux.* **f.**) to step in; to interfere, interpose. —**ung**, *f.* interposition.

Ein'schrumpfen, **Ein'schrumpeln** (*coll.*) *v.n.* (*aux.* **f.**) to shrink, to shrivel up.

Ein'schub, *m.* (—**s**, *pl.* **Einschübe**) putting in; thing put in addition; leaf of a dining-table; insertion; interpolation (*in a text*).

Ein'schüchter—n, *v.a.* to abash; to intimidate; to overawe. —**ung**, *f.* intimidation.

Ein'schulen, *v.a.* to school; to break in (*a horse*).

Ein'schuß, *m.* (—(**ss**)**es**, *pl.* **Einschüsse**) capital advanced; deposit; share; contribution; payment on account; weft, woof; — **leisten**, to lodge a deposit, advance (*a sum of money*).

Ein'schütten, *v.a.* to pour in (*something dry*); to sack.

Ein'schwärzen, *v.a.* to blacken; to soil; to introduce secretly, to smuggle in.

Ein'schwatzen, *v.* I. *a.* (**einem etwas**) to persuade into by talking, to blarney into. II. *r.* to ingratiate oneself (**bei einem,** with one).

Ein'segn—en, *v.a.* to consecrate; to bless solemnly; to confirm; to ordain. **—ung,** *f.* consecration; benediction; confirmation; ordination.

Ein'sehen, I. *ir.v.a.* to see into; to see, perceive, comprehend; to have skill in; to look over, examine; **das sehe ich ein,** I quite see that; **ich sehe gar nicht ein, warum,** I don't at all see why. II. *ir.v.n.* (*aux.* **h.**) to look into. III. *subst. n.* inspection; consideration; **ein — nehmen,** to see, have regard (to, **auf**); **er sollte ein — haben,** he should have some consideration; **der Himmel hatte ein —,** the sky favoured our wishes (*coll.*).

Ein'seifen, *v.a.* to soap in, to soap, lather; to take in (*sl.*).

Ein'send—en, *ir.v.a.* to transmit; to send in; to remit; **eingesandte Rechnung,** account rendered; **ein kleines ‚Eingesandt,'** a little 'letter to the Editor.' **—er,** *m.* (**—ers,** *pl.* **—er**) remitter; conveyer; contributor; author of a communication; **—er dieses,** our informant *or* correspondent (*Newsp.*). **—ung,** *f.* sending in, transmitting.

Ein'senk—en, *v.a.* to sink in; to bury, lower into a grave; to set (*plants, etc.*), plant. **—er,** *m.* (**—ers,** *pl.* **—er**) slip, layer. **—ung,** *f.* sinking into; depression.

Ein'setz—en, *v.a.* to put, set in; to fix, to place; to set up; to set, plant; to imprison; to coop up; to institute; to nominate, appoint, install; to stake; to pledge; to deposit; to insert (*an advertisement, etc.*); to step *or* set (*masts*); to install, inaugurate; **seinen ganzen Einfluß —en,** to use all one's influence; **einen zum Erben —en,** to declare s.o. one's heir. **—er,** *m.* (**—ers,** *pl.* **—er**) one who puts in, inserts, *etc.*; institutor. **—ling,** *m.* (**—lings,** *pl.* **—linge**) slip. **—ung,** *f.* setting *or* putting in; staking, pledging; investiture, installation; constitution; institution; nomination; appointment; imprisonment. *Comp.* **—gläser,** *pl.* glass jars for preserves. **—rose,** *f.* rosette (*Arch.*). **—stücke,** *pl.* joints of compasses; bits, crooks (*of cornets, etc.*) **—ungs=worte,** *pl.* sacramental words. **—zirkel,** *m.* draught-compasses.

Ein'sicht, *f.* (*pl.* **—en**) insight; intelligence, judgment, discernment; (*pl.*) views; **meiner — nach,** from my point of view; **mit —,** judiciously; **— nehmen in eine S.** *or* **von einer S.,** to examine a thing; **von beschränkten —en,** of narrow views, narrow-minded. **—ig,** *adj.* intelligent, sensible, prudent. *Comp.* **—nahme,** *f.;* **gegen** *or* **nach —nahme,** on sight.

Ein'sickern, *v.n.* (*aux.* **s.**) to soak into; to infiltrate.

Ein'sied—el, *m.* hermit, recluse (*obs.*). **—elei',** *f.* hermitage. **—ler,** *m.* (**—lers,** *pl.* **—ler**) hermit, recluse, anchorite; hermit-crab. **—lerisch,** I. *adj.* hermit-like, secluded, anchoretical, solitary. II. *adv.* in hermit-fashion.

Ein'sieden; *ir.v.a.* & *n.* (*aux.* **s.**) to boil down; to thicken by boiling.

Ein'siegeln, *v.a.* to seal (in *or* up).

Ein'singen, *ir.v.a.* to sing to sleep; **sich —,** to acquire perfection in singing by practice.

Ein'sinken, *ir.v.n.* (*aux.* **s.**) to sink in; give way

Ein'sitzen, *ir.v.* I. *n.* (*aux.* **h.**) to stay at home; (*aux.* **s.**) to get into a coach. II. *a.* to press down by sitting on. **ein'gesessen,** *p.p.* & *adj.* settled, residing, resident, domiciled.

Ein'spannen, *v.a.* to stretch (*in a frame*); to put horses to, to yoke; **die Nasen eingespannt!** do not carry your noses high, show respect (*poet.*).

Ein'sperr—en, *v.a.* to shut *or* lock up; to confine; to coop, pound, cage, fold, *etc.* **—ung,** *f.* confining, imprisonment.

Ein'spielen, *v.* I. *a.* to lull asleep (*by music*). II. *r.* to practise (*music*); **eingespielt,** well practised; **das Quartett ist gut eingespielt,** the ensemble of the quartette is admirable.

Ein'spinnen, *ir.v.* I. *a.* to insert by spinning; to spin round; **einen —,** to put s.o. into prison, to lock up (*sl.*). II. *r.* to spin something round oneself (*as a silk-worm*); to entangle oneself.

Ein'sprache, *f.* (*pl.* **—n**) objection; protest; **— thun** *or* **erheben,** to protest, to take exception.

Ein'sprechen, *ir.v.* I. *a.* (**einem etwas**) to inculcate, instil; to inspire with; to influence, persuade to; **Mut —,** to encourage; **Trost —,** to comfort. II. *n.* (*aux.* **h.**) to protest (against, **gegen**); to traverse (*a plea*); to oppose; to interrupt (*conversation, etc.*); **bei einem —,** to call on one, to pay a short visit to one.

Ein'sprengen, *v.* I. *a.* to sprinkle; to burst open; to split, cleave; to marble (*a book*). II. *n.* (*aux.* **s.**) to gallop into.

Ein'springen, *ir.v.n.* (*aux.* **s.**) to leap in; to catch with the spring (*of locks*); to bend *or* turn in; **—der Winkel,** re-entering angle (*Fort.*); **— für einen anderen,** to take (*at short notice*) the place of some one; **zur Aushilfe —,** to help by taking another person's work; **bei einer Verbindung —,** to join a society, an association, a club (*a students' term*).

Ein'spritz—en, *v.a.* to inject, to syringe. **—er,** *m.* (**—ers,** *pl.* **—er**) syringe. **—ung,** *f.* injection.

Ein'spruch, *m.* (**—s,** *pl.* **Einsprüche**) prohibition, protestation, opposition; **— thun** *or* **erheben,** to enter a protest; to non-placet (*Univ.*); **— thun gegen eine Heirat,** to forbid the banns. *Comp.* **—s=recht,** *n.* (right of) veto; non placet (*Univ.*).

Ein'spunden, *v.a.* to bung (*a cask*).

Ein'stand, *m.* (**—es,** *pl.* **Einstände**) entrance upon an office *or* privilege; **— geben,** to pay one's footing. *Comp.* **—s=geld,** *n.* entrance fee (*to a club, etc.*); bounty (*Mil.*).

Ein'stechen, *ir.v.* I. *a.* to prick, to puncture; to stitch in, to trump. II. *n.* (*aux.* **s.**) to stand out to sea.

Ein'stecken, *v.a.* to stick, put in; to put up; to pocket; to sheathe, to hide away; to imprison.

Ein'steh—en, *ir.v.n.* (*aux.* **s.**) to enter (*a service*); to partake of; to enter into rights; **in die Miete —en,** to take possession of a house; (*aux.* **h.**) **—en für einen,** to be a substitute for s.o.; **—en für (einen** *or* **etwas),** to answer for. **—er,** *m.* (**—ers,** *pl.* **—er**) substitute (*Mil.*); surety, bail.

Ein'stehlen, *ir.v.r.* to introduce oneself stealthily, to steal into.

Ein'steig—en, *ir.v.n.* (*aux.* **s.**) to mount, step into; to get in, to take one's seat (*in a coach, railway-compartment*); to embark. **—er,** *m.* (**—ers,** *pl.* **—er**) passenger (*about to start*). *Comp.* **—e=stelle,** *f.* departure platform.

Ein'stell—en, *v.* I. *a.* to put in; to put into the ranks, to recruit, enlist; to discontinue; to do away with; to put off; to suspend (*payment*); to focus (*Phot.*); to strike (*work*); to abolish (*abuses, etc.*); **das Feuer —en,** to cease firing; **die Arbeit —en,** to suspend work, to (go on) strike. II. *r.* to appear; to set in (*of winter etc.*); **sich wieder —en,** to return. **—ung,** *f.* recruiting, enlistment; cessation; suspension; strike (*from work*); discontinuance; **zeitweilige —ung,** temporary suspension, intermission.

Ein'stemmen, *v.a.* to panel (*a door*); to set akimbo (*the arms*).

Ein'stimmen, *v.n.* to agree, to consent; to join in (*with the voice*), chime in.

Ein'stippen, *v.a.* to dip in, immerse (*coll.*).

Ein'stopfen, *v.a.* to stuff in; to fill (*a pipe*).

Ein'stoßen, *ir.v.a.* to push, drive, knock *or* run in; to ram (*a charge*); to stave (*a cask*).

Ein'streichen, *ir.v.a.* to rub into; to put into, draw in, sweep in, pocket; to fill up (*crevices*); **Alles** —, to clear the board.

Ein'streuen, *v.* I. *a.* to strew into; to intersperse; to disseminate; **eingestreute Bemerkungen,** occasional remarks. II. *n.* **dem Vieh** —, to litter down cattle.

Ein'strich, *m.* (—s, *pl.* —e) act of pocketing *or* clearing (*stakes*); slit, nick; (*pl.*) traverses (*in a mine*); — **an einem Schlüsselbart,** ward in a keybit. *Comp.* —**bohlen,** *pl.* boarding planks (*Min.*).

Ein'stricken, *v.a.* to knit into.

Ein'ström—en, I. *v.n.* (*aux.* s.) to flow *or* stream in. II. *subst.n.* —**ung,** *f.* influx.

Ein'stücken, *v.a.* to piece; to patch.

Ein'studieren, *v.a.* to con; to practise, study, get up; to rehearse; **einstudiert werden,** to be rehearsed, to be in rehearsal.

Ein'stürmen, *v.* I. *n.* (*aux.* s.) to rush in (**auf einen,** upon s.o.); **auf seine Gesundheit** —, to ruin one's health by excesses. II. to overthrow, dash in.

Ein'sturz, *m.* (—es, *pl.* **Einstürze**) fall, downfall, crash; — **von Erdmassen,** landslip, land slide; — **eines Schachtes,** caving in; — **von Erdbauten,** slipping of earthwork; **den** — **drohen,** to threaten to fall.

Ein'stürzen, *v.* I. *n.* (*aux.* s.) to fall in; — **auf einen** *or* **etwas,** to fall upon s.o. *or* s.th. II. *a.* to dash in, demolish.

Ein'tagsfliege, *f.* ephemeral (*or* day *or* May) fly. *Comp.* —**lärm,** *m.* passing noise, noise of short duration.

Ein'tauchen, *v.* I. *a.* to dip in; to immerse; to imbue. II. *n.* (*aux.* s.) to dive, duck, plunge.

Ein'tausch, *m.* (—es, *pl.* —e) exchange.

Ein'tausch—en, *v.a.* to exchange, to barter, to receive in exchange. —**ung,** *f.* exchange.

Ein'teil—en, *v.a.* to divide; to distribute; to classify; to graduate (*a thermometer, etc.*). —**ung,** *f.* distribution; division; economy; arrangement, classification. *Comp.* —**ungs=grund,** *m.* principle of a classification. —**ungs=grad,** *m.* degree.

Ein'tonnen, *v.a.* to barrel (*beer, herrings, etc.*).

Ein'trag, *m.* (—es, *pl.* **Einträge**) woof, weft; prejudice, damage, detriment; (**einem**) — **thun,** to prejudice, injure; **einem Gesetze** — **thun,** to infringe a law; **es thut Ihrer Ehre keinen** —, it is no disparagement to your honour. *Comp.* —**thuend,** *adj.* derogatory.

Ein'trag—en, I. *ir.v.a.* to carry in; to gather in; to work in the woof; to enter, to post (*in a ledger*); to book (*a debt*); to yield, bring in; to register; **auf Landkarten** —**en,** to map; **rein** —**en,** to clear, to net; **ein Geschäft, welches wenig einträgt,** an unprofitable business. II. *subst. n.* —**ung,** *f.* carrying in; entering, registering.

Ein'träg—er, *m.* (—ers, *pl.* —er) registrar; bookkeeper, entering-clerk. —**lich,** *adj.* & *adv.* lucrative; profitable, productive; —**liche Pfründe,** fat living. —**lichkeit,** *f.* profitableness.

Ein'tränken, *v.a.* to steep, soak (*in*), impregnate; to come true, be realized; **ich werde es ihm** —, I'll make him suffer *or* pay for it.

Ein'träufeln, *v.a.* to drop in, instil.

Ein'treffen, *ir.v.n.* (*aux.* s.) to fit in, coincide, agree; to happen, to be fulfilled; to arrive; **nicht zur Zeit** —, to come late, to be over-due; **Ihre Prophezeihung ist eingetroffen,** your prophecy has come true.

Ein'treib—en, *ir.v.a.* to drive in (*into*); to drive home; to collect (*debts*); to exact (*payment*); to embarrass, nonplus. —**er,** *m.* (—ers, *pl.* —er) collector; whipper-in; driver-in. —**ung,** *f.* exaction; collection (*of debts, etc.*); driving in (*stakes*).

Ein'treten, *ir.v.* I. *n.* (*aux.* s.) to enter, step in; to begin; to enter on (*an office*); to set in (*of weather, etc.*); to take place, occur; to set inwards (*of the tide*); to make one's appearance; **für einen** —, to intercede in favour of s.o.; to act as s.o.'s substitute, to take the place of s.o.; **eingetretener Hindernisse halber,** on account of unforeseen obstacles; **der Fluß tritt aus den Bergen aus und in die Ebene ein,** the river issues from the mountains and enters the plain. II. *a.* to stamp; to trample down; to kick open; to tread down (*shoes*).

Ein'trichtern, *v.a.* to pour into with a funnel; **einem etwas** —, to drum into a p.'s head.

Ein'tritt, *m.* (—s, *pl.* —e) entering on (*an office, etc.*); entry, entrance, admission; commencement; setting in (*of winter, etc.*); ingress; — **ins Heer,** enlisting; — **ins Leben,** outset in life. *Comp.* —**s=fähig,** *adj.* admissible. —**s=geld,** *n.* charge for admission, entrance money. —**s=karte,** *f.*, —**s=schein,** *m.* ticket of admission. —**s=zimmer,** *n.* parlour; ante-chamber.

Ein'trocknen, *v.n.* (*aux.* s.) to dry in, to dry up.

Ein'tunken, *v.a.* to dip in; to sop.

Ein'üben, *v.a.* to practise, to exercise; to drill; **sie hat sich** (*dat.*) **das Stück sorgfältig eingeübt,** she has practised the piece carefully.

Ein'verleib—en, *v.a.* to incorporate, to embody; to annex. —**ung,** *f.* incorporation, annexation.

Ein'verständ—igen, *v.a.* to bring to an understanding. —**nis,** *n.* (—nisses, *pl.* —nisse) intelligence, understanding; agreement; **in gutem** —**nisse mit . . . leben,** to be on good terms with; **heimliches** —**nis,** secret understanding, secret intercourse; collusion.

Ein'verstehen, *ir.v.r.* to agree with; to understand one another; **einverstanden sein,** to agree, be agreed (**über eine S.,** upon s.th.); **einverstanden!** agreed!

Ein'wachsen, *ir.v.n.* (*aux.* s.) to grow into *or* in.

Ein'wage, *f.* loss in weight by selling retail.

Ein'wägen, *v.* I. *a.* to weigh and put in; to weigh down. II. *r.* to diminish by being weighed.

Ein'walken, *v.a.* to full close (*cloth*); to oil (*leather*).

Ein'walzen, *v.a.* to roll in (*seeds, etc.*).

Ein'wand, *m.* (—es, *pl.* **Einwände**) objection; pretext. *Comp.* —**frei,** *adj.* & *adv.* without objection; read(il)y.

Ein'wanderer, *m.* (—s, *pl.* —) immigrant.

Ein'wander—n, *v.n.* (*aux.* s.) to immigrate. —**ung,** *f.* immigration.

Ein'wärts, *adv.* inward(s); — **gehen,** to turn in the toes in walking. *Comp.* —**zieher,** *m.* adductor (*muscle*).

Ein'wässern, *v.a.* to soak, steep in water.

Ein'weben, *reg.* & *ir.v.a.* to weave in, interweave; to damask; to intersperse; **eine eingewebte (eingewobene) Erzählung,** an episode.

Ein'wechseln, *v.a.* to change; to acquire by exchange.

Ein'wehen, *v.a.* to blow down (*a hut*).

Ein'weichen, *v.a.* to soak, to steep.

Ein'weih—en, *v.a.* to initiate; to receive (*nuns, etc.*); to ordain; to consecrate; to inaugurate; to handsel; **ein Eingeweihter,** one initiated, adept. —**ung,** *f.* consecration; initiation. *Comp.* —**ungs=feier,** *f.* inaugural ceremony.

Ein'wend—en, *reg.* & *ir.v.a.* to object, take exception to; to oppose; to demur; to challenge (*Law*); **dagegen läßt sich nichts** —**en,** there can be no objection to that; **einzuwenden,** objectionable; **der** —**ende,** the opponent. —**ung,** *f.* objection, exception; reply; plea, *etc.*; —**ungen vorbringen (machen) gegen,** to make objections to *or* against, to demur.

Ein'werfen, *ir.v.a.* to throw in; to break by throwing; to rejoin; to object; to baste.

Ein'wickeln, *v.a.* to envelop, wrap up; to curl (*the hair*); to swaddle; **einen — in,** to entangle a p. in.

Ein'wiegen, *v.a.* to rock asleep; **ſie wiegen und tanzen und ſingen dich ein,** they shall rock, dance, and sing thee to sleep.

Ein'willig—en, *v.n.* (*aux.* **h.**) to consent to, acquiesce in; to subscribe to; to permit. **—ung,** *f.* consent, assent; permission; **ſchriftliche —ung,** acceptance (*Law*).

Ein'wintern, *v.* I. *a.* to preserve till winter. II. *n.* (*aux.* **ſ.**) to be overtaken by winter.

Ein'wirk—en, *v.* I. *a.* to interweave; to work in (*patterns*). II. *n.* (*aux.* **h.**) to influence; to operate. **—end,** *p. & adj.* influential, effective. **—ung,** *f.* influence; interweaving.

Ein'wohn—en, *v.n.* to inhabit; **wir ſind ganz eingewohnt,** we are quite settled; **ſich —en,** to make oneself at home. **—end,** *p. & adj.* inhabiting; inherent. **—er,** *m.* (**—ers,** *pl.* **—er**) inhabitant. **—er=ſchaft,** *f.* inhabitants, population. *Comp.* **—er=zahl,** *f.* amount of population. **—er=zählung,** *f.* census.

Ein'wollen, *ir.v.n.* to wish to get in; **das will mir nicht ein,** I cannot swallow (*or* understand) that.

Ein'wurf, *m.* (**—s,** *pl.* **Ein'würfe**), objection; opening for letters in a pillar-box, *etc.*; **einen — machen,** to make *or* raise an objection, to take exception (*to*).

Ein'wurzeln, *v.n.* (*aux.* **ſ.**) to take root, to root; to become inveterate; **tief eingewurzelte Überzeugungen,** deeply rooted beliefs.

Ein'zacken, *v.a.* to indent; to notch.

Ein'zahl—en, *v.a.* to pay in. **—ung,** *f.* payment, deposit.

Ein'zählen, *v.a.* to deposit; to count in; to include.

Ein'zahnen, *v.a.* to indent; to dovetail.

Ein'zäun—en, *v.a.* to hedge in, to fence in. **—ung,** *f.* fencing in; fence.

Ein'zehren, *v.n.* (*aux.* **h.**) to diminish, lose, waste; **der Wein auf Fäſſern zehrt ein,** wine in wood diminishes by evaporation.

Ein'zeichn—en, *v.a.* to mark in, to note; to draw in; **ſich —en,** to enter one's name; to subscribe. **—ung,** *f.* entering, writing down; subscription.

Ein'ziehbar, *adj. & adv.* retractible; recoverable; liable to confiscation.

Ein'zieh—en, *ir.v.* I. *a.* to draw, pull in; to remove; to get in, take in, collect; to absorb; to inhale; to seize, arrest; to confiscate; to buy in (*at auctions*); to suppress (*an office*); to furl (*sails*); to reduce (*expenses*); to take in, make smaller (*clothes, etc.*); **den Faden —en,** to thread (*a needle*); **die Pfeife —en,** to lower one's tone; **Erkundigungen —en,** to get information. II. *r.* to shrink; to retire from the world; to retrench, reduce expenses. III. *n.* (*aux.* **ſ.**) to enter, march in, to move into, take possession (*of a house, lodgings, etc.*). **ein'ge=zogen,** *p.p. & adj.* retired, solitary, economical; **eingezogen!** draw in, be reserved, be on your guard! **—ung,** *f.* drawing in; inhaling; imbibing; collection; confiscation; arresting; suppression (*of an office*); infiltration; tapering (*of a wall*); trochilus (*Arch.*); **—ung der Reſerve** *or* **Reſerviſten,** calling in of the army reserve.

Ein'zuckern, *v.a.* to sugar (over); to preserve.

Ein'zug, *m.* (**—s,** *pl.* **Einzüge**) entry, (solemn) entrance; moving in (*into a new house, etc.*); **— halten,** to enter. *Comp.* **—s=ſchmaus,** *m.* banquet after a state-entry; house-warming.

Ein'zwängen, *v.a.* to force in, squeeze in, wedge in; to pinch; to confine, constrain.

Ein'zwingen, *ir.v.a.* to force into; **einem etwas —,** to force one to take s.th.

E'=is, *n.* E-sharp (*Mus.*).

Eis, *n.* (**—(ſ)es**) ice; ice-cream; apathy; heartlessness; **— eſſen,** to take an ice; **in — gekühlt,** iced; **auf dem —e laufen,** to skate; **zu — werden,** to congeal, freeze; **vom —e beſetzt,** ice-bound; **gehendes —,** floating ice; **mürbes —,** unsound ice. **—(ſ)ig,** *adj.* icy. *Comp.* **—achat,** *m.* translucent agate. **—apparat,** *m.* refrigerator. **—artig,** *adj.* icy, like ice. **—bahn,** *f.* ice, slide; skating place; opportunity for skating. **—bär,** *m.* polar bear. **—beere,** *f.* snow-berry. **—berg,** *m.* iceberg; snowy-mountain. **—bein,** *n.* pig's foot salted; *see* **Eisbein.** **—blume,** *f.* ice plant. **—bock,** *m.* ice-breaker. **—brecher, —pfahl,** *m.* starling (*of a bridge*). **—bruch,** *m.* breaking up of ice. **—eimer,** *m.* ice-pail. **—fahrt,** *f.* skating. **—fiſcherei,** *f.* fishing under the ice. **—flacken, —flöße,** *pl.* floating icebergs. **—frei,** *adj.* free from ice. **—gang,** *m.* breaking up (and floating) of ice; drift of ice; ice bow (*of a whaler*). **—grau,** *adj.* hoary. **—hufeiſen,** *n.* calkin, ice-shoe. **—keller,** *m.* ice-house. **—kühler,** *m.* cooler. **—lauf,** *m.* skating. **—meer,** *n.* polar sea; **Nördliches —meer,** Arctic ocean; **Südliches —meer,** Antarctic ocean. **—nagel,** *n.* frost-nail; **mit —nägeln beſchlagen,** rough-shod. **—punkt,** *m.* freezing-point. **—ſcholle,** *f.* floe, lump, block of ice. **—ſchrank,** *m.* ice-safe. **—ſchuh,** *m.* snow-shoe. **—ſpat,** *m.* crystalline felspar. **—ſproſſen,** *pl.* brow-antlers. **—ſtein,** *m.* cryolite. **—ſtollen,** *pl.* calkins. **—vogel,** *m.* kingfisher. **—zacken, —zapfen,** *m.* icicle. **—zone,** *f.* frozen zone.

Ei'ſen, *v.* I. *a.* to cause to freeze, to make into ice, to ice; to break the ice from; **los —,** to break loose, free (*coll.*). II. *n.* (*aux.* **ſ.**) to turn to ice.

Eis'bein, *n.* hip-bone (*Anat.*) (*not connected with* **Eis**).

Ei'ſen, *n.* (**—s,** *pl.* **—**) iron; horse-shoe; sword, weapon; iron instrument *or* tool; (*pl.*) irons, fetters; **er ſchlägt über die —,** he kicks over the traces; **an kaltem — ſterben,** to die by the sword; **Not bricht —,** necessity knows *or* has no law; **einen in — legen,** to put one in irons; **Herzen von —,** hearts of steel; **— in Gänſen,** pig-iron; **Guß —,** cast iron; **Roh —,** pig iron; **kohlenſaures —,** carbonate of iron; **man muß das — ſchmieden, ſo lange es heiß iſt,** you must strike the iron while it is hot; **etwas zum alten — werfen,** to consign s.th. to the rubbish heap, to give up as useless *or* superseded (*said of old-fashioned people or ideas*). *Comp.* **—abgang,** *m.* iron-refuse. **—artig,** *adj.* ferruginous. **—bahn,** *f.* railway; railroad (*Amer.*); **mit der —bahn geſchickt werden,** to be railed (of troops); **auf die —bahn gebracht werden,** to be entrained (of troops); **es iſt die höchſte —,** it is high time, no moment is to be lost (*sl.*). **—bahn=aktie,** *f.* railway-share. **—bahn=bremſe,** *f.* brake. **—bahn=damm,** *m.* embankment. **—bahner,** *m.* soldier belonging to the German railway brigade. **—bahn=fahrt,** *f.* railway-journey. **—bahn=geſellſchaft,** *f.* railway company. **—bahn=hof,** *m.* (railway) station; depot (*Amer.*). **—bahn=netz,** *n.* net of railways. **—bahn=(quer)ſchwelle,** *f.* sleeper. **—bahn=ſchienen,** *pl.* rails. **—bahn=ſchmöker,** *m.* book for reading in the railway compartment. **—bahn=ſtrecke,** *f.* line of railway. **—bahn=verbindung,** *f.* communication by rail. **—bahn=wagen,** *m.* railway carriage *or* car. **—bahn=zug,** *m.* railway train. **—baum,** *m.* iron-wood tree. **—bart,** *m.* kingfisher (*Orn.*). **—beißer,** *m.* braggart, bully. **—blau,** *n.* Prussian blue. **—blech,** *n.* sheet-iron. **—blüte,** *f.* arragonite. **—brand,** *m.* loadstone. **—braun=kalk, —**

braun=spat, *m.* dolomite. **—draht**, *m.* iron-wire. **—draht=bandseil**, *n.* flat-rope of iron. **—draht=seil**, *n.* cable of iron-wire. **—druse**, *f.* crystallized iron-ore. **—erde**, *f.* ferruginous earth. **—erz**, *n.* iron-ore. **—farbe**, *f.* iron-grey. **—feilicht**, *n.* iron-filings. **—fest**, *adj.* firm *or* hard as iron; inflexible. **—fleck**, *m.* iron-strain, iron-mould. **—fresser**, *m.* braggart, bully. **—gießerei'**, *f.* iron-foundry. **—guß**, *m.* iron casting, iron founding; cast-iron. **—guß=waren**, *pl.* foundry goods, hardware. **—haltig**, *adj.* containing iron; ferruginous, chalybeate. **—hammer**, *m.* forge(-hammer), iron-works. **—handel**, *m.* iron-trade. **—händler**, *m.* iron-monger. **—hart**, I. *adj.* hard as iron. II. *n.* (—s) vervain (*Bot.*). **—hut**, *m.* steel cap, helmet. **—hütchen**, *n.* aconite (*Bot.*). **—hütte**, *f.* iron-works, forge. **—kalk**, *m.* calcined iron. **—kies**, *m.* iron-pyrites. **—kiesel**, *m.* ferruginous quartz; silicate of iron. **—klumpen**, *m.* pig of iron. **—knecht**, *m.* anvil-plate (*T.*). **—kram**, *m.* iron trade; iron-mongery. **—kraut**, *n.* verbena (*Bot.*). **—krystall**, *m.* crystal of mars. **—mohr**, *m.* black oxide of iron. **—oxyd**, *n.* ferric oxide. **—oxydul**, *n.* ferrous oxide. **—oxydul=oxyd**, *n.* magnetic iron. **—oxydul=salz**, *n.* ferrous salt. **—panzer**, *m.*, **—platte**, *f.* armour-plate, iron-plate. **—quelle**, *f.* ferruginous spring. **—rahm**, *m.* hematite. **—salz**, *n.* sulphate of iron. **—sau**, *f.* pig of iron. **—scheibe**, *f.* miner's compass. **—schimmel**, *m.* iron grey (*horse*). **—schlacke**, *f.* iron-dross. **—schmied**, *m.* blacksmith. **—schüssig**, *adj.* ferruginous. **—schwärze**, *f.* dyer's iron-liquor; ground black-lead. **—stange**, *f.* iron rod. **—tinktur**, *f.* tincture of iron. **—vitriol**, *m.* sulphate of iron, ferrous sulphate. **—waren**, *pl.* iron-mongery, hardware. **—wasser**, *n.* chalybeate water. **—werk**, *n.* iron-work(s). **—zeug**, *n.* iron tools.

Ei'sern, *adj. & adv.* iron, of iron; hard, strong; inflexible; unfeeling; steady, indefatigable; unredeemable; inalienable (*Law*); **—es Kapital**, money sunk of which only the interest is paid; **—es Kreuz**, iron cross (*Prussian war medal*, 1813–15; 1870–71); **—er Bestand**, unchangeable *or* standing stock; indispensable amount; **der —e Landgraf**, Ludwig II. of Thuringia (†1172); **der —e Herzog**, the Iron Duke (*Lord Wellington*); **der —e Kanzler**, the Iron Chancellor (*Prince Bismarck*); **das —e Thor**, the Iron Gates (*of the Danube*).

Ei'tel, *adj. & adv.* vain; frivolous; empty; perishable; nothing but, mere; **— sein auf eine S.**, to be vain of a th.; **—es Geschwätz**, idle *or* silly talk. **—keit**, *f.* vanity; nothingness.

Ei'ter, *m. & n.* (—s) matter, pus; **dünner —**, gleet; **bösartiger —**, purulent discharge. **—ig**, *adj. & adv.* purulent. *Comp.* **—abfluß**, *m.* (*purulent*) discharge. **—befördernd**, *adj.* suppurative. **—beule**, *f.* abscess. **—bläschen**, *n.* pustule, pimple. **—blase**, *f.* carbuncle. **—brust**, *f.* empyema. **—erzeugend**, *adj.* suppurative. **—fluß**, *m.* running (*from a sore*). **—fraß**, *m.* corrosive ulcer. **—gelenk**, *n.* arthritic abscess. **—geschwulst**, *f.* abscess. **—jauche**, *f.* ichor. **—sack**, *m.* cyst (*of a tumour*). **—stock**, *m.* core. **—triefen**, *n.* blennorrhœa (*Med.*) **—ziehen**, *n.* suppurating.

Ei'ter—n, *v.n.* (*aux.* **h.**) to suppurate, fester; to discharge matter. **—nd**, *p. & adj.* suppurative. **—ung**, *f.* suppuration, festering.

E'kel, I. *m.* (—s, *pl.* —) nauseousness, nausea; loathsomeness; disgust, aversion; **es ist mir zum —**, I am sick of it; I am disgusted with it; **dieser —** *or* **dieses —**, that nasty fellow (*coll.*). II. *adj.* (*obs., replaced by* **ekelig**) nauseous; loathsome; disgusting; squeamish; particular (*obs.*), dainty (*obs.*); delicate (*in colour*). **—haft**, *adj. & adv.* nauseous; loathsome, disgusting; fulsome. **—haftigkeit**, *f.* loathsomeness. **—ig** (**Eklig**), *adj. & adv. see* **Ekel**, II.; disagreeable, rude (*coll.*). *Comp.* **—name**, *m.* nickname (*rare, obs.*).

E'kel—n, *v.n.* (*aux.* **h.**) to disgust, sicken, excite loathing; **mir —t davor, es —t mich**, I loathe it, am disgusted with it; it disgusts me; **sich —n vor einer S.**, to loathe a th.

Eklek't—iker, *m.* eclectic philosopher. **—isch**, *adj.* eclectic.

Eklep'sis, *f.* desquamation.

Eklip'—se, *f.* (*pl.* **—sen**) eclipse. **—tik**, *f.* ecliptic. **—tisch**, *adj.* ecliptic.

Eklo'ge, *f.* (*pl.*—**n**) eclogue.

Eksta'se, *f.* (*pl.* **—n**) ecstasy.

Eksta't—iker, *m.* (—**s**, *pl.* —) one in an ecstasy. **—isch**, *adj.* ecstatic.

Elast—izitä't, *f.* elasticity. **—isch**, (*pron.* **elas'=tisch**) *adj.* elastic; **—isches Harz**, india-rubber.

Elb'linger, *m.* sweetwater grape.

El'bogen, *m. see* **Ellbogen**.

Elch, *m.* (—(e)**s**, *pl.* —**e**) elk, moose(-deer).

Elefa'nt, *m.* (**—en**, *pl.* **—en**) elephant; castle (*at chess*); **der — trompetet**, the elephant trumpets. *Comp.* **—en=ansatz**, *m.* elephantiasis (*Med.*). **—en=küken**, *n.* a very tall and fat child (*coll.*). **—en=laus**, *f.* cashew-nut. **—en=papier**, *n.* elephant folio. **—en=rüssel**, *m.* elephant's trunk; Sphinx's elpenor (*Ent.*).

Elega'n—t, I. *adj. & adv.* elegant. II. *m.* (gentle)man of fashion; beau, dandy, coxcomb, masher. **—z**, *f.* elegance, refinement, polish; fashionableness.

Elegie', *f.* elegy, poem written on any subject in elegiac metre (*hexameters & pentameters*) (*such as Goethe's* '*Elegien*'); mournful poem written in any metre (*such as Matthisson's and Hölty's* '*Elegien*').

Ele'gisch, *adj.* elegiac; **—e Verse**, elegiacs mournful verses, melancholy lines.

Elektr—izitä't, *f.* electricity. **—isch**, *adj. & adv.* electric. **—isie'rbar**, *adj. & adv.* electrifiable. **—isie'ren**, *v.a.* to electrify. **—o**, (*in comp.* =) electro. **—on**, *m.* amber; electron. *Comp.* **—izitä'ts=erreger**, *m.* electromotor. **—izitä'ts=leiter**, *m.* conductor. **—izitä'ts=messer**, *m.* electrometer. **—izitä'ts=strom**, *m.* electric current. **—isie'r=maschine**, *f.* electrical machine. **—o=tech'nik**, *f.* electrical engineering. **—o=tech'niker**, *m* electrical engineer. **—o=tech'nisch**, *adj.* electrotechnical (pertaining to electrical engineering). **—o=typ**, *n.* electrotype.

Eleme'nt, *n.* (—**s**, *pl.* —**e**) element; principle. **—a'r**, (*in comp.*) elementary; rudimentary; preparatory. *Comp.* **—a'r=buch**, *n.* primer; first book. **—a'r=lehrer**, *m.* primary teacher, teacher of the elements. **—a'r=schule**, *f.* primary school. **—a'r=stein**, *m.* opal. **—a'r=unterricht**, *m.* primary education.

[1]**E'lend**, *n.* elk (*obs. for* **Elen**). *Comp.* **—s=haut**, *f.* elk skin.

[2]**E'lend** (—**s**) misery, distress; want, penury; foreign country, exile (*obsol.*). II. *adj. & adv.* miserable; wretched, pitiful; **Elender!** wretch! **—ig**, *see* **Elend** **—iglich**, *adv.* miserably, wretchedly.

E'lentier, *n.* (—**s**, *pl.* —**e**) elk, moose(-deer).

Elevatio'ns=winkel, *m.* elevation (*of a gun*).

[1]**Elf**, *m.* (**—en**, *pl.* **—en**), **—e**, *f.* (*pl.* **—en**) elf; fairy; goblin. **—en=haft**, *adj.* fairy-like. *Comp.* **—en=höhe**, *f.* hill where fairies dance. **—en=königin**, *f.* fairy queen. **—en=reigen**, *m.* dance of fairies. **—en=schuß**, *m.* elf-arrow.

[2]**Elf** (*obs.* **Eilf**), *num. adj.* eleven. **—er**, *m.* (—**ers**, *pl.* **—er**) the number eleven; soldier of the eleventh regiment; wine of the year 1811 (**Eilfer**); corpration of eleven. **—te**, *num. adj.* eleventh; **selb —t**, with ten others.

—tel, n. (—tels, pl. —tel) the eleventh part. —tens, adv. in the eleventh place. Comp. —eck, n. hendecagon. —er=lei', indec. adj. of eleven kinds. —fach, adj. elevenfold. —mal, adv. eleven times. —silbig, adj. hendecasyllabic. —te=halb, num. adj. ten and a half.

El'fenbein, n. (—s) ivory. —ern, adj. made of ivory.

Elidie'ren, v.a. to elide, to cut off or suppress (a vowel).

Eliminie'ren, v.a. to eliminate.

Eljen, interj. long live! (Hungar.).

El'le, f. (pl. —n) yard, ell. Comp. —n=breit, adj. an ell broad. —n=handel, m. draper's trade. —n=lang, adj. an ell long. —n=maß, n. ell, yard-measure. —n=reiter or —n=ritter, m. counter-jumper. —n=waaren, pl. drapery, dry-goods (Amer.). —n=weise, adv. by the ell, by the yard.

El'l(en)bogen, m. (—s, pl. —) elbow; mit den — stoßen, to elbow; die — frei haben, to have elbow room.

El'ler, f. (pl. —n) see Erle.

Elli'p—se, f. ellipse; ellipsis. —tisch, adj. elliptical.

Elms'feuer, n.; Sankt —, (Saint) Elmo's fire; Jack o' Lantern.

El'se, f. (pl. —n) alder (tree); shad (fish); sailmaker's awl.

El'se— (in comp.). —baum, m. black alder tree.

El'ster, f. (pl. —n) magpie. Comp. —auge, n. (now usually Hühnerauge) corn on the toe.

El'ter—lich, adj. & adv. parental. —n, pl. parents; nicht von schlechten —n sein, to be first rate, excellent (coll.). Comp. —n=los, adj. orphan, orphaned. —n=mörder, —n=mord, m. parricide, crime of parricide.

Emai'l, m. & n. (—s) enamel. —lie'ren, v.a. to enamel. Comp. —bild, n. painting on enamel.

Emanzipie'ren, v.a. to emancipate; ein emanzipiertes Frauenzimmer, a strong-minded woman; a new woman.

Emballie'ren, v.a. to pack; sich —, to fill out.

Em'ber— (in comp.). —gans, f. ember goose.

Emblema't—isch, adj. & adv. emblematic. —isie'ren, v.a. to symbolize.

Emigrie'ren, v.n. (aux. s.) to emigrate.

Emine'nz, f. (pl. —en) eminence (title).

Em'merling, m. (—s, pl. —e) yellow-hammer (Orn.); cockchafer-grub; (wilder) morello cherry.

Em'mersegel, n. sprit-sail.

Empfa'h(e)n, (arch., poet.) for empfangen.

Empfa'hl, imperf. ind. of empfehlen.

Empfa'nd, Empfän'de, imperf. ind. & subj. of empfinden.

Empfa'ng, m. (—s, pl. Empfän'ge) reception, receipt (of a letter, etc.); den — bescheinigen, to give a receipt for; in — nehmen, to receive. Comp. —nahme, f. receipt. —nehmung, f. reception. —s=anzeige, f. acknowledgment (of receipt). —s=schein, m. receipt. —s=zimmer, n. reception room; drawing-room.

Empfan'gen, ir.v. I. a. to take, to receive; to welcome. II. n. (aux. h.) to conceive, become pregnant.

Empfän'g—er, m. (—ers, pl. —er) receiver; consignee (C.L.); accepter (of a bill). —lich, adj. susceptible; willing to receive. —lichkeit, f. susceptibility. —nis, f. (pl. —nisse) conception; die unbefleckte —nis, Immaculate Conception.

Empfe'hl, m. (—s, pl. —e) see —ung. —bar, adj. recommendable.

Empfeh'l—en, ir. v. I. a. to commend, entrust, to recommend, commend; —en Sie mich ihm bestens, give my compliments or kind regards to him, remember me to him most kindly; sich (dat.) etwas empfohlen sein lassen, to take good care of a th. II. r. to bid farewell; to present one's compliments; —e mich (Ihnen), I wish you good-day; sich heimlich —en, to abscond; sich auf französisch —en, to take French leave, to abscond. —er, m. (—ers, pl. —er) recommender. —ung, f. pl. (recommendation); introduction; compliments; mit schöner —ung an Sie, with best compliments to you. Comp. —ens=wert, —ens=würdig, adj. worthy of recommendation, commendable. —ungs=karte, f. business-card (of commercial travellers); card of introduction (to gentlemen). —ungs=brief, m. letter of introduction.

Empfin'd—bar, adj. sensitive; sensible; perceptible. —elei', f. (pl. —elei'en) sentimentality. —eln, v.n. (aux. h.) to affect sensibility. —ler, m. (—lers, pl. —ler) sentimentalist. —lich, adj. & adv. sensible; sharp; grievous; sensitive; tender; sore; irritable, touchy; nice; fugitive; —liche Farbe, fugitive colour; das ist seine —liche Stelle, that is his sore point; jemand —lich verletzen, to wound a person deeply, to hurt a man's feelings grievously. —lichkeit, f. sensibility; sensitiveness; irritability. —ling, see —ler. —nis, f. sentiment, feeling (rare). —sam, adj. & adv. sensible; feeling; susceptible, sentimental; delicate; touchy. —samkeit, f. susceptibility; sentimentality.

Empfin'd—en, ir.v.a. to feel; to perceive; to be sensible of; to experience; übel —, to take as an offence. —end, p. & adj. sensible, sensitive, sentient; perceptive. —ung, f. sensation; feeling; perception. Comp. —ungs=eigenheit, f. idiosyncrasy, peculiarity of sensation. —ungs=fähig, adj. capable of feeling, susceptible. —ungs=fähigkeit, f. perceptivity. —ungs=kraft, f. power of perception. —ungs=laut, m. interjection; exclamation (obs.). —ungs=los, adj. unfeeling; apathetic; callous. —ungs=sitz, m. sensorium. —ungs=vermögen, n. perceptive faculty. —ungs=wort, n. interjection (obs.).

Empfi'ng (older Empfieng), imp. of empfangen.

Empföh'le, 1 & 3 pers. sing. imperf. subj. of empfehlen.

Empfoh'len, p.p. of empfehlen.

Empfun'den, p.p. of empfinden.

Empha'—se, f. emphasis. —tisch, adj. emphatic; emphatically.

Empi'r—ik, f. empiricism. —iker, m. (—ikers, pl. —iker) empiric. —isch, adj. & adv. empirical.

Empo'r, I. adv. & sep. prefix, up, upwards, on high, aloft. Comp. —arbeiten, v.r. to work one's way up. —bringen, v.a. to raise, to promote. —helfen, ir.v.a. to help up; to assist. —dringen, ir.v.n. (aux. s.) to work up; tiefe Seufzer drangen aus ihrer Brust —, she heaved deep sighs. —heben, ir.v.a. to exalt, raise up; to elevate (the host). —hebung, f. elevation (of the host). —kommen, ir.v.n. (aux. s.) to rise in the world, to thrive. —kömmling, m. (—kömmlings, pl. —kömmlinge) upstart. —ragen, v.a. to tower (über, above). —scheune, f. loft of a barn. —schwingen, ir.v.r. to rise, soar up. —steigen, v.n. to rise, to ascend. —streben, v.n. (aux. h.) to aspire. —strebend, p. & adj. aspiring. —treiben, ir. v.a. to force upwards; to sublimate (Chem.).

Empo'r—e, f. (pl. —en) choir seats, gallery (in churches). —kirche, f. choir, raised gallery.

Empö'r—en, v. I. a. to rouse to anger or indignation; to excite; to enrage. —t, p.p. & adj. indignant. II. r. to revolt, rebel; to grow furious. —end, p. & adj. revolting, shocking. —er, m. (—ers, pl. —er) insurgent. —erisch, adj. & adv. mutinous. —ung, f. rebellion, revolt;

indignation. *Comp.* —**ungs=geist,** *m.* mutinous spirit.

Em'se, *f.* (*pl.* —**n**) ant (*dial. for* **Ameise**).

Em'sig, *adj. & adv.* busy, active; industrious, assiduous; eager, earnest. —**keit,** *f.* industry, assiduity; diligence.

Encyklopädie', *f.* (*pl.* —**en**) encyclopedia.

End'—bar, *adj.* terminable. —**chen,** *n.* (—**chens,** *pl.* —**chen**) fag-end, remnant, bit; **kommen Sie doch noch ein —chen mit,** do accompany me a little further (*coll.*). —**e,** *n.* (—**es,** *pl.* —**en**) end; conclusion, issue; limit; close; termination (*of a lease*); goal, aim, object, purpose; (*point of an*) antler; **ein Hirsch von 10 —en (ein Zehn—er),** a stag with 10 antlers; **der Tag geht zu —e,** the day is declining; **an allen Orten und —en,** everywhere; **von allen —en,** from all quarters; **bis ans** *or* **zum —e,** to the last; **das äußerste —,** the extremity; **das traurige —e,** the catastrophe; **zu dem —e,** for that purpose; **zu dem —e, daß,** in order that; **zu —e,** at an end, over, towards the end; **am —e,** in the end, after all, upon the whole; finally, at last; perhaps, possibly; **das —e vom Liede ist,** the upshot is; **er griff es am rechten —e an,** he set about it the right way; **einer Sache** (*dat.*) **ein —e machen,** to put an end to a thing; **zu —e gehen,** to draw near ethe nd, to expire; **zu —e bringen,** to bring to an end, to finish; **—e gut, alles gut,** all's well that ends well. —**lich,** I. *adj.* final, concluding, last; finite; ultimate. II. *adv.* at last; in short; after all, quickly (*obs.*). —**lichkeit,** *f.* finiteness. —**schaft,** *f.* end, issue. *Comp.* —**absicht,** *f.* final purpose, ultimate intention. —**bescheid,** *m.* ultimatum; definitive sentence *or* judgment. —**buchstabe,** *m.* final letter. —**ergebnis,** *n.* ultimate *or* final result, upshot. —**erklärung,** *f.* ultimatum. —**es=genannte(r),** —**es=unterzeichnete(r),** *m.* undersigned. —**geschwindigkeit,** *f.* terminal *or* remaining velocity. —**giltig,** —**gültig,** *adj. & adv.* final, definitive, conclusive. —**je,** *n.* a rope's end (*Naut.*). —**knospe,** *f.* terminal bud. —**kürzung,** *f.* apocope (*Gram.*). —**los,** *adj.* endless, boundless, infinite. —**losigkeit,** *f.* endlessness, infinity. —**punkt,** *m.* end; terminus, extremity, farthest point. —**reim,** *m.* rhyme at the end of a verse *or* a metrical line; **vorgeschriebene —reime,** bouts-rimés. —**silbe,** *f.* final syllable. —**spruch,** *m.* final judgment *or* sentence. —**station,** *f.* terminus (*Railw.*). —**stehend,** standing at the end; **—stehende Rechnung,** below-given account. —**ursache,** *f.* final cause. —**urteil,** *n.* final decree. —**ziel,** *n.* final aim. —**zweck,** *m.* main design, ultimate purpose, final object.

End'christ, Ent'christ = **Antichrist** (*obs.*).

Ende'misch, *adj. & adv.* endemic.

En'd—(ig)en, *v.* I. *a.* to put an end to, terminate, conclude; to accomplish; to finish; **sein Leben —en,** to die. II. *r.* to end, conclude; to close; **Wortet, die (sich) auf o —igen,** words ending in o. III. *n.* (*aux.* **h.**) to come to a conclusion, stop, cease; to be over; to die. —**ung,** *f.* ending, termination, end.

Endi'vie, *f.* (*pl.* —**n**) endive (*succory*).

Energ—ie', *f.* energy. —**isch,** (*pron.* **ener'gisch**) *adj. & adv.* energetic, with vigour.

En'g, —e, *adj. & adv.* narrow; tight; close; strict; confined; select; **im —eren Sinne,** strictly speaking; **—er Atem,** asthma; **in —er Verwahrung sein,** to be a close prisoner; **—e machen,** to narrow, tighten; **—erer Ausschuß,** select committee; **— gebunden,** confined within narrow limits. —**e,** *f.* (*pl.* —**en**) narrowness; tightness; narrow place; strait; difficulty, dilemma; **einen in die —e treiben,** to drive one into a corner. —**heit,** *f.* narrowness; closeness; tightness; crowded *or* confined state. *Comp.* —**brüstig,** *adj.* narrow-chested; asthmatic. —**brüstige(r),** *m.* asthmatic person. —**herzig,** *adj.* narrow-minded; illiberal. —**paß,** *m.* narrow pass, defile.

En'gel, *m.* (—**s,** *pl.* —) angel; **ein — flog durch das Zimmer,** there was a general silence in the room (*idiom.*). —**chen, (Eng(e)=lein),** *n.* (—**chens,** *pl.* —**chen**) little angel, cherub; siskin (*Orn.*). —**haft,** *adj. & adv.* angelic; angelically. *Comp. In numerous compounds the first part of which is* **engel—** *it means* like an angel, angelic, *e.g.* —**fromm,** —**rein,** —**schön,** *etc.* —**bett,** *n.* open bed without posts —**blümchen,** *n.* mountain everlasting (*Bot.*) —**brot,** *n.* angelic food, manna. —**gleich,** *adj.* angelic. —**hai,** *m.* angel fish. —**haar,** *n.* angels' hair, lametta (*decoration of the Christmas tree*). —**köpfchen,** *n.* cherub's head; sycamore. —**kraut,** *n.* mountain arnica. —**macher,** *m.,* —**macherin,** *f.* baby killer. —**schar,** *f.* angelic host. —**s=gruß,** *m.* annunciation; Ave Maria. —**s=schatz,** *m.* sweetheart, dear love.

En'g—en, *v.* I. *a.* to narrow, to contract; to oppress; to pinch (*as a shoe*). II. *r.* to contract, grow narrow. —**ern,** *v.a.* to make narrower; **verflucht sei, wer seines Nächsten Grenze —ert,** cursed be he that removeth his neighbour's landmark (*B.*).

En'gerling, *m.* (—**s,** *pl.* —**e**) grub of cockchafer.

Engländerei', *f.* (*pl.* —**en**) Anglomania.

[1]**Eng'lisch,** I. *adj.* English; **—es Blau,** royal blue; **—e Haut,** gold-beater's skin; **—e Krankheit,** rickets; **—es Leder,** satinet; **—es Pflaster,** court-plaster; **—er Schweiß,** sweating sickness. II. *adv.* in the English fashion.

[2]**Eng'lisch,** *adj. & adv.* angelic, like angels (*obs.*); **der —e Gruß,** the annunciation; Ave Maria.

Engro's, *indec. adj. & adv.* wholesale.

Enharmo'nisch, *adj.* enharmonic.

Enjambeme'nt, *n.* (—**s**) overflow (*metre*).

En'ke, *m.* (—**n,** *pl.* —**n**) ploughboy (*obs. dial.*).

[1]**En'kel,** *m.* (—**s,** *pl.* —) ankle.

[2]**En'kel,** *m.* (—**s,** *pl.* —) grandson, grandchild; descendant. —**in,** *f.* grand-daughter.

Enkla've, *f.* enclave, a place *or* territory which is entirely surrounded by the territories of another power.

Enkli'ti—ka, *f.* enclitic (*Gram.*). —**sch,** *adj.* enclitic.

Enkomia'st, *m.* (—**en,** *pl.* —**en**) panegyrist.

Eno'rm, *adj. & adv.* enormous, excessive. —**itä't,** *f.* (*pl.* —**itä'ten**) enormity.

Ent, *insep. and unaccented prefix; in composition with other words gen'lly* = forth, from, out, away, dis —; *also has a sense of deprivation, negation or separation; in one or two cases* **ent** *stands for* **an.** *The prefix* **emp—** *is a doublet of* **ent—.** *Notice the glottal stop in compounds beginning with a vowel sound.*

Enta'deln, *v.a.* to degrade in rank; to dishonour.

Entar'ten, *v.n.* (*aux.* **s.**) to degenerate. —**ung,** *f.* degeneration; deterioration.

Entäu'ßer—n, *v.r.* (**einer Sache**) to dispose of; to deprive oneself of; to separate oneself from, divest oneself of; to abstain from; to resign, renounce; **er —te sich seiner Vorrechte,** he gave up his privileges. —**ung,** *f.* renunciation; parting with; alienation (*of property*).

Entbe'hr—en, *v.a.* (*gen.* (*now obs.*) & *acc.,* to do without; to dispense with; to miss, want; **ich kann noch etwas —en,** I have still some to spare; **das Gerücht —t jeden Grundes,** the report is without any foundation; **ich kann dich nicht —en,** I cannot do without you, I cannot spare you; **du sollst —en,** thou shalt renounce! —**lich,** *adj.* dispensable, unnecessary; **—lich machen,** to render superfluous; to supersede —**lichkeit,** *f.* superfluousness. —**ung,**

f. abstinence, want, privation; the doing without; renunciation; self-denial.

Entbie'ten, *ir.v.a.* to bid, command; to announce; to present, offer; **einem seinen Gruß —,** to present one's compliments to a person; **zu sich —,** to send for, summon to one's presence.

Entbin'd—en, *ir.v.a.* to unbind, untie, loosen; to set free, release (*gen. or* **von,** from), disengage; to absolve; to exonerate; to evolve (*gas*); **entbunden werden,** to be delivered, to be confined, to give birth (*of child*). **—ung,** *f.* releasing, absolving; unbinding; release; delivery, confinement, birth. *Comp.* **—ungs=anstalt,** *f.*, **—ungs=haus,** *n.* lying-in hospital, maternity hospital. **—ungs=kunst,** *f.* obstetrics, midwifery. **—ungs=urteil,** *n.* final acquittal, absolution. **—ungs=zange,** *f.* obstetric(al) forceps.

Entblät'tern, *v.a.* to deprive of leaves; **sich —,** to shed its leaves.

Entblö'den, *v.r.* to dare, to venture; to divest oneself of shame; to be ashamed; **er entblödete sich nicht zu behaupten,** he did not blush to affirm, he had the impudence to maintain.

Entblö'ß—en, *v.a.* to denude; to strip; to expose; to uncover (*the head*); to dismantle (*a fortress*); to unsheath. **—t,** *p.p. & adj.* bare; destitute, denuded (**von,** of). **—ung,** *f.* denudation; baring; dismantling; deprivation.

Entblü'hen, *v.n.* (*aux.* **s.**) to blossom up *or* out of, spring up in blossom (*poet.*).

Entbre'chen, *ir.v.r.* to forbear; to abstain from; to break loose from; **sich nicht — können,** not to be able to restrain oneself (*from*).

Entbren'nen, *ir.v.n.* (*aux.* **s.**) to be lighted, to take fire, to become inflamed *or* fired; to break out; to fly into a passion; **in Liebe —,** to fall violently in love.

Entbun'den, *p.p. of* **entbinden.**

Entdeck'bar, Entdeck'lich, *adj.* discoverable.

Entdeck'—en, *v.a.* to discover; to uncover; to disclose; to detect, find out; **sich —en,** to make oneself known, to rise to view; **sein Herz —en,** to unbosom oneself. **—er,** *m.* (**—ers,** *pl.* **—er**) discoverer; discloser; detective. **—ung,** *f.* discovery; detection; disclosure. *Comp.* **—ungs=reise,** *f.* voyage of discovery, expedition.

En't—e, *f.* (*pl.* **—en**) duck; canard; lying newspaper report; **türkische —e,** Indian *or* Guinea duck; **die —e quakt,** the duck quacks. **—erich,** *m.* (**—erichs,** *pl.* **—eriche**) drake; **wilder —erich,** mallard. *Dim.* **—chen,** *n.* (**—chen,** *pl.* **chen**), **—lein,** *n.* (**—leins,** *pl.* **—lein**) duckling. *Comp.* **—en=braten,** *m.* roast duck. **—en=jagd,** *f.* duck shooting. **—en=pfuhl,** *m.* duck pond.

Enteh'r—en, *v.a.* to dishonour; to ravish. **—end,** *adj.* dishonourable, disgraceful. **—er,** *m.* (**—ers,** *pl.* **—er**) dishonourer. **—ung,** *f.* dishonouring; defamation; degradation; ravishing; defloration.

Enteig'n—en, *v.a.* to expropriate. **—ung,** *f.* expropriation.

Entei'len, *v.n.* (*aux.* **s.**) to hasten away from.

Enter'b—en, *v.a.* to disinherit. **—ung,** *f.* disinheriting.

En'ter—er, *m.* (**—ers,** *pl.* **—er**) boarder (*of a ship*). **—n,** *v.a.* to grapple, to board (*a ship*). **—ung,** *f.* boarding (*a ship*). *Comp.* **—beil,** *n.* boarding axe. **—haken,** *m.* grappling hook *or* iron. **—pike,** *f.* boarding-pike.

Entfah'ren, *ir. v.n.* (*aux.* **s.**) to escape; to slip out from; **tiefe Seufzer entfuhren seiner Brust,** deep sighs escaped him.

Entfal'len, *ir.v.n.* (*aux.* **s.**) to fall out of; to escape (*the memory*); to fall from; **die Sache war mir ganz —,** the affair had quite slipped from my memory.

Entfal'ten, *v.a.* to unfold; to deploy; to develop; to grow smooth; **sich —,** to expand.

Entfär'ben, *v.* I. *a.* to deprive of colour; to discolour. II. *r.* to change colour, grow pale.

Entfa'sern, *v.a.* to shred (*beans, etc.*); to take off the fibres.

Entfer'n—en, *v.* I. *a* to remove, put away; to dismiss; to alienate. II. *r.* to absent oneself; to get away; to disappear; to withdraw, retire; to turn off, deviate, wander from, stray from. **—t,** *p.p. & adj.* far off; distant, remote; **—testen Anlaß,** slightest occasion; **weit —t, das zu thun,** far from doing so. **—ung,** *f.* going away, removal; separation; distance, range; eccentricity (*Astr.*); **in gewissen —ungen,** at set distances; **in der —ung sieht man,** far away one sees; **Gewehrfeuer auf eine —ung von,** rifle-fire at a range of. *Comp.* **—ter=weise,** *adv.*; **nicht —terweise,** not in the least. **—ungs=kraft,** *f.* centrifugal force. **—ungs=punkt,** *m.* apsis.

Entfes'seln, *v.a.* to unchain; to release from; **entfesselte Elemente,** raging elements.

Entflam'men, *v.* I. *a.* to inflame, to kindle. II. *n.* (*aux.* **s.**) to be inflamed.

Entflei'scht, *p.p. & adj.* fleshless; lean; **—te Knochen,** skeleton bones; **—te Hände,** hands devoid of flesh.

Entflie'gen, *ir.v.n.* (*aux.* **s.**, *dat.*) to fly away from.

Entflie'hen, *ir.v.n.* (*aux.* **s.**, *dat.*) to run away; to escape, to flee from.

Entflie'ßen, *ir.v.n.* (*aux.* **s.**, *dat.*) to flow from, issue from, emanate from.

Entfrem'd—en, *v.a.* (**einem etwas, etwas von einem**) to estrange; to alienate; to pilfer. **—ung,** *f.* estrangement, alienation.

Entfüh'r—en, *v.a.* to carry off; to abduct; to elope with; to kidnap; **sie hat sich von ihm —en lassen,** she has eloped with him; **er —te sie,** he ran away with her; **ein Mädchen —en und heiraten,** to make a runaway match with a girl. **—er,** *m.* (**—ers,** *pl.* **—er**) abductor; ravisher; kidnapper. **—ung,** *f.* abduction; elopement; kidnapping, rape.

Entge'gen, I. *prep.* (*with preceding dat.*) against, in face of; opposed to; towards. II. *adv. & sep. prefix*, counter; in opposition, towards, in face of, to meet; **der Wind ist uns —,** the wind is ahead of us; **auf, ihm —!** up, let us meet him! *Comp.* **—arbeiten,** *v.a. & n.* (*aux.* **h.**, *dat.*) to work against, to counteract. **—blicken,** *v.n.* (*dat.*) to look forth upon, to look forward to; to meet the looks of. **—eilen,** *v.n.* (*aux.* **s.**, *dat.*) to hasten to meet. **—gehen,** *ir.v.n.* (*aux.* **s.**, *dat.*) to go to meet; to face (*a danger, etc.*). **—gesetzt,** *p.p. & adj.* contrary, opposite. **—gestellt,** *p.p. & adj.* objected; antithetical (*Rhet.*). **—halten,** *ir.v.a.* to hold towards *or* against; to oppose, object; to contrast, compare (*with*). **—kommen,** *ir.v.n.* (*aux.* **s.**, *dat.*) to advance to meet; to meet (*advances; a person, etc.*); to obviate, prevent. **—laufen,** *ir.v.n.* (*aux.* **s.**, *dat.*) to run to meet; to run counter to, oppose. **—nehmen,** *ir.v.a.* to accept, receive. **—sehen,** *ir.v.n.* (*aux.* **h.**, *dat.*) to look forward to; to await, expect. **—setzen,** *v.a.* (*dat. & acc.*) to set over against; to oppose; to contrast, put in competition with; to object, oppose. **—setzung,** *f.* opposing; comparison; antithesis. **—stehen,** *ir.v.n.* (*aux.* **s.**, *dat.*) to stand opposite to; to oppose; to confront, face (*a foe, etc.*). **—stellen,** *v.a.* to oppose; to contrast; **sich —stellen,** to obstruct, stand in the way of. **—wirken,** *v.n.* (*aux.* **h.**, *dat.*) to counteract; to check; to repel (*Med.*). **—ziehen,** *ir.v.n.* (*aux.* **s.**, *dat.*) to advance towards.

Entgeg'n—en, *v.a.* (**einem etwas**) to rejoin, reply; to object; to retort. **—ung,** *f.* reply.

Entge'hen, *ir.v.n.* (*aux.* f., *dat.*) to get away from; to escape, elude; to avoid; to fail; **es kann Ihnen nicht —,** you cannot fail to observe it; **der Atem entging ihm,** he lost his breath.
Entgei'stern, *v.a.* to deprive of the vital principle, of the soul, of life; to startle, shock.
Entge'lt, *m.* & *n.* (—es) requital; retribution; recompense; remuneration. **—lich,** *adj.* to be paid, to be recompensed; **un—lich,** free of charge.
Entgel't—en, *ir.v.a.* (**einem etwas**) to pay, atone for, suffer for; **einen etwas —en lassen,** to make one suffer *or* pay for a thing; **laß mich das nicht—en,** do not let me suffer for that! **er soll mir das —en,** he shall pay for this. **—ung,** *f.* recompense, atonement; **ohne —ung** gratis, free of charge, no charge.
Entgi'ng, *imperf. of* **entgehen.**
Entglei'ſ—en, *v.n.* (*aux.* f.) to run *or* get off the rails; **—en lassen,** to derail (*a train*), to throw a train off the rails. **—ung,** *f.* running off the rails, derailment.
Entglei'ten, *ir.v.n.* (*aux.* f., *dat.*) to slip, slide, escape from.
Entglie'dern, *v.a.* to deprive of members; to dismember; to disorganize.
Entglim'men, *reg.* & *ir.v.n.* (*aux.* f., *dat.*) to become kindled, to blaze up, to shine forth.
Entglü'hen, *ir.v.n.* (*aux.* f.) to kindle; to be kindled.
Entgöt'tern, *v.a.* to deprive of divine attributes, to rob of gods.
Entgrä'ten, *v.a.* to bone (*a fish*).
Entgür't—eln, —en, *v.a.* to ungird.
Enthaa'r—en, *v.a.* to deprive of hair, unhair. **—t,** *p.p.* & *adj.* hairless. *Comp.* **—ungs=mittel,** *n.* depilatory.
Enthal't—en, *ir. v.* I. *a.* to hold, contain; to comprise, comprehend. II. *r.* to keep oneself away; to abstain, forbear; **ich konnte mich des Lachens nicht —en,** I could not help laughing; **sie konnte sich des Weinens nicht —en,** she could not refrain from weeping. **—sam,** *adj.* & *adv.* abstinent, abstemious; temperate; continent, chaste. **—samkeit,** *f.* abstemiousness, abstinence; continence, chastity; temperance. **—ung,** *f.* abstemiousness; keeping away from.
Enthaup't—en, *v.a.* to behead, to decapitate. **—ung,** *f.* beheading, decapitation.
Enthäu'ten, *v.a.* to flay, to skin.
Enthe'ben, *ir.v.a.* to lift off from, take away; (**einen einer Sache**) —, to relieve of, to exempt from; **sich der Verantwortlichkeit — lassen,** to get rid of responsibility; **einen seines Amtes —,** to dismiss a p., to remove a p. from his office.
Enthei'lig—en, *v.a.* to profane, desecrate. **—er,** *m.* (—ers, *pl.* —er) profaner. **—ung,** *f.* desecration, profanation.
Enthül'l—en, *v.a.* to unveil; to reveal. **—ung,** *f.* unveiling; revealing; disclosure.
Enthül'ſ—en, *v.a.* to shell, husk (*peas, etc.*). *Comp.* **—ungs=maschine,** *f.* pulping-machine.
Enthusiasmie'ren, *v.a.* to fill with enthusiasm.
Enthusia's—mus, *m.* enthusiasm. **—t,** *m.* (—ten, *pl.* —ten) enthusiast. **—tisch,** *adj.* enthusiastic.
Entjo'chen, *v.a.* to unyoke, uncouple; to liberate.
Entjung'fern, *v.a.* to deprive of virginity, to deflower, deflour.
Entkei'men, *v.n.* (*aux.* f.) to germinate, to spring out of, to spring up, to sprout.
Entker'nen, *v.a.* to stone, take the kernels out of.
Entklei'den, *v.a.* & *r.* to divest; to unclothe, undress; to strip.
Entknos'pen, *ir.v.n.* (*aux.* f.) to burst forth from the bud, to bud forth.
Entkom'men, *ir.v.n.* (*aux.* f., *dat.*) to get off *or* away, to escape (from).
Entkop'peln, *v.a.* to slip, to uncouple (*dogs*).
Entkor'ken, *v.a.* to uncork.
Entkör'pern, *v.a.* to disembody.
Entkräf't(ig)—en, *v.a.* to debilitate, fatigue, enfeeble, enervate; to exhaust (*land*); to disarm (*passions*); to invalidate (*Log.*). **—et,** *p.p.* & *adj.* effete, exhausted; invalidated (*Log.*). **—ung,** *f.* enervation; exhaustion; inanition (*Med.*); invalidation. *Comp.* **—ungs=fieber,** *n.* low fever.
Entla'd—en, *ir.v.a.* to unlade, unload; to free from, exonerate; to relieve (*of a burden, etc.*); to discharge (*of electricity, etc.*); **die Wolke entlud sich,** the cloud burst. **—er,** *m.* (—ers, *pl.* —er) discharger (*Phys.*). **—ung,** *f.* unloading; discharge; exoneration; eruption.
Entla'ng, *adv.* & *prep.* (*usually with* **an** *and foll. dat.; often with preceding acc.*) along; **an dem Flusse —** *or* **den Fluß —,** along the river.
Entlar'ven, *v.a.* to unmask.
Entlaſ'ſ—en, *ir.v.a.* to let go, permit to leave; to dismiss, discharge; to disband; to prorogue; to absolve, release; to dissolve (*a meeting*); to set free; **mit Pension —en,** to pension off. **—end,** *p.* & *adj.* dismissive. **—ung,** *f.* dismissal; discharge; release; **er bat um** *or* **nahm seine —ung, er ist um seine —ung eingekommen,** he has tendered *or* sent in his resignation. *Comp.* **—ungs=antrag,** *m.*, **—ungs=schein,** *m.*, **—ungs=zeugnis,** *n.* discharge-paper (*Mil.*); ticket-of-leave. **—ungs=schreiben,** *n.* letters of recall; letters dismissary.
Entlaſ't—en, *v.a.* to unburden; to ease; relieve of; **einen für etwas —en,** to credit one with (*C.L.*). **—ung,** *f.* discharge. *Comp.* **—ungs=zeuge,** *m.* witness for the defendant.
Entlau'ben, *v.a.* to strip of foliage.
Entlau'fen, *ir.v.n.* (*aux.* f.) to run away; to escape (from, *dat.*); to desert.
Entle'dig—en, *v.* I. *a.* to set free; to exempt (from, *gen.*); **sein Herz —en,** to make a clean breast of it. II. *r.* to acquit oneself of, rid oneself of; **sich seines Versprechens —en,** to keep one's word *or* engagement; **sich einer Botschaft —en,** to execute one's commission. **—ung,** *f.* discharge, acquittance; release.
Entlee'ren, *v.a.* to empty out.
Entle'gen, *adj.* remote, distant. **—heit,** *f.* remoteness, distance.
Entleh'n—en, *v.a.* (**einem etwas, etwas von einem**) to borrow; **entlehnte Wörter,** loan words. **—er,** *m.* borrower. **—ung,** *f.* borrowing; loan; **uneingestandene —ung,** plagiarism.
Entlei'b—en, *v.* I. *a.* to kill. II. *r.* to commit suicide. **—ung,** *f.* suicide.
Entlei'hen, *ir.v.a.* (**einem etwas**) to borrow (s.th. from a p.).
Entlo'ben, *v.r.* to break off an engagement (*coll.*).
Entlo'cken, *v.a.* (*dat.*) to draw from, to elicit.
Entman'n—en, *v.a.* to castrate; to emasculate; to unnerve, unman. **—ung,** *f.* castration; unmanning; enervation; emasculation.
Entmaſ'ten, *v.a.* to dismast.
Entme'nſcht, *adj.* inhuman, barbarous; brutish.
Entmün'digen, *v.a.* to put (an adult) under tutelage.
Entmu'tig—en, *v.a.* to discourage, dishearten, daunt; **einen durch Blicke —en,** to stare one out of countenance. **—ung,** *f.* discouragement.
Entnah'me, *f.* taking out, ordering; **bei — von 6 Schürzen,** by taking (or ordering) six aprons.
Entneh'm—en, *ir.v.a.* to take away; to free from; to borrow from; to understand from; to learn; to gather; (**Geld**) **auf einen —en,** to draw upon one; **aus einem Buche etwas —en,** to quote from a book; **aus jemandes Worten etwas —en,** to gather from what a p. has said. **—er,** *m.* drawer (*C.L.*).

Entner'v—en, *v.a.* to enervate, to unnerve. **—ung,** *f.* unnerving, enervation.

Entomolo'g, *m.* (**—en,** *pl.* **—en**) entomologist. **—iſch,** *adj.* entomological.

Entpan'zern, *v.r.* to take off one's coat of mail.

Entpfrop'fen, *v.a.* to uncork.

Entpreſ'ſen, *v.a.* to press, squeeze out; **einem etwas —,** to extort something from a person.

Entpup'pen, *v.r.* to burst from the cocoon; **ſich —,** to reveal oneself; to turn out.

Entqual'men, *v.n.* (*aux.* **ſ.**) to rise in vapour.

Entquel'len, *ir.v.n.* (*aux.* **ſ.**, *dat. or* **aus**) to flow forth, issue from.

Entraf'fen, *v.a.* to snatch away; **ſich —,** to disengage oneself from.

Entra'ten, *ir.v.a. & n.* (*aux.* **h.**, *gen.*) to dispense with; to do without.

Enträt'ſeln, *v.a.* to unriddle; to make out; to guess.

Entree', *f. or n.* (**—s,** *pl.* **—s**) entrance; admission; entrée; entrance-money; ante-room.

Entrei'ßen, *ir.v.a.* to tear away; (**einem etwas**) to snatch away, to rescue (*from*).

Entrei'ten, *v.a.* to escape by riding.

Entrich't—en, *v.a.* to pay what is due. **—ung,** *f.* payment, due discharge (*of debts, etc.*).

Entrin'gen, *ir.v.a.* to wrest from, wrench away; to break forth (from); **ein Seufzer entrang ſich ihrer Bruſt,** a sigh escaped her, she heaved a sigh.

Entrin'nen, *ir.v.n.* (*aux.* **ſ.**, *dat.*) to run away, to get away, to escape (*from*).

Entrol'len, *v.* I. *n.* (*aux.* **ſ.**) to roll away *or* down. II. *a.* to unroll. III. *r.* to unfold itself.

Entrü'cken, *v.a.* to snatch away, carry off, remove.

Entrün'd—en, *v.a.* to unround (the lips). **—ung,** *f.* unrounding (*e.g. pronouncing* **eu** *like* **ei,** *or* **ü** *like* **i, ö** *like* **e**).

Entrüſ't—en, *v.* I. *a.* to provoke, make angry, irritate, enrage. II. *r.* to become angry *or* indignant; to fly into a passion. **—ung,** *f.* indignation, anger, wrath.

Entſa'g—en, *v.r. & n.* (*aux.* **h.**, *dat.*) to renounce, resign, disclaim; to waive (*claims*); to relinquish, to abdicate; **der —ende,** disclaimer, renouncer; **geiſtigen Getränken —ende,** teetotallers. **—ung,** *f.* (**auf** *& acc.*) abandonment, renouncement, renunciation, resignation; abdication, abjuration; **bei ſeiner Thron—ung,** on his abdicating the throne.

Entſa'tz, *m.* (**—es**) relief, succour. **—truppen,** *pl.* troops sent to effect the raising of a siege.

Entſchä'dig—en, *v.a.* to indemnify, to compensate. **—ung,** *f.* indemnity, compensation. **—ungs=forderung,** *f.* claim for damages.

Entſcha'len, *v.a.* to wash, take the gum out of (*silk, etc.*), to scour; to shell.

Entſchäu'men, *v.n.* (*aux.* **ſ.**) to gush forth foaming.

Entſcheid'bar, *adj.* determinable.

Entſchei'd—en, *ir.v.* I. *a.* to decide; to decree; to resolve; to arbitrate; to pass sentence, give judgment. II. *r.* to decide; **er entſchied ſich für mich,** he decided in my favour; **das entſchied,** that clinched matters. **—end,** *p. & adj.* deciding; decisive, casting (*vote*); peremptory; critical; definite, final. **—ung,** *f.* decision; crisis. *Comp.* **—ungs=grund,** *m.* motive; ground of judgment. **—ungs=punkt,** *m.* crisis. **—ungs=ſchlacht,** *f.* decisive battle. **—ungs=ſtimme,** *f.* casting vote. **—ungs=voll,** *adj.* decisive; critical. **—ungs=zuſtand,** *m.* crisis.

Entſchie'd, *1 & 3 pers. sing. imperf. ind. of* **Entſcheiden.**

Entſchie'den, *p.p. & adj. or adv. see* **Entſcheiden;** decided. **—heit,** *f.* resoluteness; firmness; determination; decision of character; firmness; energy; **mit —heit,** decidedly, categorically.

Entſchla'fen, *ir.v.n.* (*aux.* **ſ.**) to fall asleep (*obs. poet.*); to die, to pass away; **der (die) Entſchlafene,** the deceased.

Entſchla'gen, *ir.v.r.* (*gen.*) to divest oneself of, get rid of; to part with; to dismiss from one's mind; to decline; to cast off; **ſich der Sorgen —,** to banish care; **ſich eines Wunſches —,** to renounce a wish.

Entſchlei'chen, *ir.v.n.* (*aux.* **ſ.**, *dat.*) to slip off; to sneak away; to escape.

Entſchlei'ern, *v.a. & r.* to unveil; to reveal.

Entſchlie'ß—en, *v.a.ir.* to unlock; **ſich —en,** to determine (**zu,** upon); to decide (**für,** on *or* in favour of), to make up one's mind. **—ung,** *f.* resolution; resolving (*on*); fixed purpose.

Entſchloſ'ſen, *p.p. & adj.* resolved; resolute; determined. **—heit,** *f.* decision; determination, resolution; fixity of purpose.

Entſchlum'mern, *v.n.* (*aux.* **ſ.**) to fall asleep *or* into a slumber; to pass away, to die (gently).

Entſchlüp'fen, *v.n.* (*aux.* **ſ.**) to slip from, to escape; **eine Gelegenheit — laſſen,** to let an opportunity slip; **dem Gedächtnis —,** to escape one's memory; **das Wort entſchlüpfte mir,** the word slipped out *or* slipped from my tongue.

Entſchlu'ß, *m.* (**—(ſſ)es,** *pl.* **Entſchlüſ'ſe**) resolve, resolution; **einen — faſſen,** to form a resolution, to resolve; **zu einem — kommen,** to make up one's mind.

Entſchuld'bar, *adj. & adv.* excusable.

Entſchul'dig—en, *v.a.* to excuse, exculpate; to justify, defend; **ſich —en,** to apologize (**bei, gegen,** to; **wegen,** for); **es läßt ſich nicht —en,** it admits of no excuse; **ich bitte mich zu —en,** pray, excuse me; I would rather be excused; **ich muß mich bei ihm —en, daß ich ꝛc.,** I must apologize to him for, *etc.*; **ſie läßt ſich wegen Unpäßlichkeit —en,** she begs to be excused on account of indisposition; **—en Sie,** I beg your pardon; **zu —en,** excusable. **—ung,** *f.* exculpation; excuse, apology; **ich bitte (Sie) um —ung,** I beg your pardon. *Comp.* **—ungs=ſchreiben,** *n.* written apology.

Entſchwe'ben, *v.n.* (*aux.* **ſ.**) to soar up *or* away.

Entſchwe'feln, *v.a.* to desulphurate.

Entſchwim'men, *ir.v.n.* (*aux.* **ſ.**) to swim off, to escape by swimming.

Entſchwin'den, *ir.v.n.* (*aux.* **ſ.**, *dat.*) to disappear; to vanish.

Entſee'lt, *p.p. & adj.* dead, lifeless.

Entſen'den, *ir.v.a.* to send off; to let fly; to hurl.

Entſetz'bar, *adj.* removable (*from office*); relievable.

Entſet'z—en, I. *v.a.* to displace; (**einen einer Stelle**) to dismiss (*from office*); to suspend; to cashier; to depose (*a king, etc.*); to relieve (*a garrison, etc.*). II. *v.r.* to shudder at, be terrified, amazed, shocked, startled by (**vor**). III. *subst.n.* terror, dread, fright, horror. **—lich,** *adj.* terrific, frightful, horrible, shocking. **—lichkeit,** *f.* (*pl.* **—lichkeiten**) frightfulness, terribleness; atrocity. **—ung,** *f.* dismissal; deposition; suspension; deprivation (*of a clergyman*); relief (*of a garrison*).

Entſin'ken, *ir.v.n.* (*aux.* **ſ.**) to sink down *or* away from, to drop, to fail; **es entſank uns der Mut,** our courage failed us.

Entſin'nen, *ir.v.r.* (**ſich einer Sache**) to recollect, to remember (something).

Entſinn'lichen, *v.a.* to spiritualize.

Entſitt'lichung, *f.* demoralization, depravation.

Entſit'zen, *v.a.* (**einem Pferde**) to dismount (from a horse) (*rare, poet.*).

Entſpin'nen, *ir.v.* I. *a.* to plot, devise (*rare*). II. *r.* to arise, originate in; to ensue; to develop; **es entſpann ſich ein Streit, (ein Gefecht,)** a quarrel arose, (a skirmish began).

Entſpre'ch—en, *ir.v.n.* (*aux.* **ſ.**, *dat.*) to answer, suit; to respond to; to meet (*a demand*); to be adequate to; to correspond to (*expectations*); **es entsprach meinen Erwartungen nicht**, it fell short of *or* did not come up to my expectations. **—end**, *adj.* suitable; corresponding.

Entsprie'ßen, *ir.v.n.* (*aux.* **s.**) to arise, to spring, to sprout; to result (*from*).

Entsprin'gen, *ir.v.n.* (*aux.* **s.**) to spring away, escape; to spring from; to arise, originate in.

Entspru'deln, *v.n.* (*aux.* **s.**) to bubble, gush forth.

Entsprü'hen, *v.n.* to fly forth in sparks *or* drops.

Entstam'men, *v.n.* (*aux.* **s.**, *dat.*) to descend (*from*); **dem Himmel —d**, heaven descended, heaven born.

Entste'h—en, I. *ir.v.n.* (*aux.* **s.**) to begin, originate (**aus**, in); to arise (**aus**, from); to be formed by, to grow out of; to break out (*as fire*); **was ist daraus entstanden?** what has come of it, what has been the upshot of it? **entstehe was da wolle**, come what may; (*aux.* **h.**, *dat.*) to fail, be wanting (*obs.*). II. *subst.n.* beginning, arising, origin. **—ung**, *f. see* **—en** II.; genesis; formation (*of metals*). *Comp.* **—ungs=art**, **—ungs=weise**, *f.* nature, manner of beginning *or* origin.

Entstei'gen, *ir.v.n.* (*aux.* **s.**, *dat.*) to arise from *or* out of, to emerge, to descend from.

Entstel'l—en, *v.a.* to deform, to disfigure, deface, mar, to distort (*a meaning, etc.*); to garble (*an account*); to misrepresent (*facts*). **—t**, *p.p. & adj.* disfigured, deformed. **—ung**, *f.* distortion, misrepresentation; disfigurement; defacement.

Entströ'men, *v.n.* (*aux.* **s.**, *dat.*) to flow forth, to gush down from.

Entstür'zen, *v.n.* (*aux.* **s.**, *dat.*) to fall down from, to tumble away; to burst forth (*from*).

Entsüh'nen, *v.a.* to expiate, atone for.

Entsün'dig—en, *v.a.* to free from sin, to purify; to absolve. **—ung**, *f.* purification; absolution.

Enttäu'sch—en, *v.a.* to undeceive, to disabuse; to disenchant; to disillusion; to disappoint. **—ung**, *f.* disabusing; disillusion; disappointment.

Entthro'n—en, *v.a.* to dethrone. **—ung**, *f.* deposition.

Entvöl'ker—n, *v.a.* to depopulate. **—t**, *adj. & p.p.* depopulated. **—ung**, *f.* depopulation.

Entwach'sen, *ir.v.n.* (*aux.* **s.**, *dat.*) to outgrow.

Entwaff'nen, *v.a.* to disarm.

Entwal'den, *v.a.* to cut down the forests of.

Entwäs'ser—n, *v.a.* to drain; to distil. **—ung**, *f.* draining, drainage.

Ent'weder, *conj.* either; **— dies oder das**, either this or that; **das — oder**, the alternative.

Entwei'ch—en, *ir.v.n.* (*aux.* **s.**) to give way; to escape (*as gas, etc.*); to abscond; to evade (*pursuit, etc.*); to vanish, dissipate (*as darkness, etc.*). **—ung**, *f.* escape; elopement; absconding; disappearance. *Comp.* **—ungs=klappe**, *f.* escape-valve.

Entwei'h—en, *v.a.* to profane, to violate. **—ung**, *f.* profanation; defilement; sacrilege.

Entwen'd—en, *reg.& ir.v.a.* to pilfer, to purloin, to steal; to embezzle. **—ung**, *f.* purloining, theft, embezzlement.

Entwer'f—en, *ir.v.a.* to sketch, trace, rough, draw; to project, draw up (*a document*); to plan, design; to invent (*a plot*); to draught (*a statement*); to frame (*a bill*); **Pläne —en**, to make plans. **—er**, *m.* (**—ers**, *pl.* **—er**) designer; inventor; projector, framer (*of a bill*). *Comp.* **—ungs=ebene**, *f.* projection (*Math.*).

Entwer't—en, *v.a.* to depreciate, reduce in value. **—ung**, *f.* depreciation; cancellation (*of postage stamps*); **Federzug —ung**, penmarked (*stamps*).

Entwi'ckel—n, *v.* I. *a.* to unroll, unfold, untwist; to unwrap; to evolve; to develop; to deploy (*Mil.*); to solve, explain; to display. II. *r.* to expand; to evolve; to develop itself; **es wird sich —n**, it will be cleared up; **es —t sich gut**, things (will) turn out well. **—ung**, *f.* development; evolution; denouement (*Theat.*); formation (*Phys.*); evolution (*Math., Mil.*). *Comp.* **—ungs=lehre**, *f.* doctrine of evolution. **—ungs=periode**, *f.* period of development; (age of) puberty *or* pubescence.

Entwin'den, *ir.v.* I. *a.* (**einem etwas**) to wrest from; to extort. II. *r.* (*dat.*) to extricate oneself; to burst away (*from*).

Entwir'ken, *v.r.* to unfold, to develop itself.

Entwir'ren, *v.a.* to disentangle, unravel; to extricate (*from confusion*).

Entwi'schen, *v.n.* (*aux.* **s.**, *dat.*) to slip away from, give the slip to, steal away.

Entwöh'n—en, *v.a.* (**einen einer Sache, einen von einer Sache**) to disaccustom; to wean (*an infant*). **—ung**, *f.* weaning; disuse.

Entwöl'ken, *v.a.* to uncloud; **sich —**, to clear up.

Entwür'dig—en, *v.a.* to degrade; to dishonour; to profane. **—ung**, *f.* degradation.

Entwu'rf, *m.* (—(e)s, *pl.* **Entwür'fe**) draught (*of a document*); sketch, outline, design; project, plan, sceme; **der erste —**, the first sketch rough draft; **einen — machen**, to make *or* draw up a plan; **einen Gesetz — vorbringen**, to introduce a bill (*in parliament*). *Comp.* **—macher**, *m.* schemer, projector; speculator.

Entwur'zel—n, *v.a.* to root out, to uproot. **—ung**, *f.* rooting out, uprooting, eradication.

Entzau'bern, *v.a.* to disenchant.

Entzie'h—en, *ir.v.* I. *a.* (**einem etwas**) to take away, remove; to withdraw; to deprive of. II. *r.* to avoid; to forsake; to evade, shun; **sich der Gerechtigkeit —en**, to fly from justice; **sich dem Gehorsam —en**, to throw off obedience; **sich seiner Schuldigkeit —en**, to withdraw from *or* shun one's duty. **—end**, *p. & adj.* privative. **—ung**, *f.* withdrawal; removal; deprivation; abstraction (*Chem.*); **—ung des Gebrauchs des Vermögens**, sequestration of property. *Comp.* **—ungs=kur**, *f.* lowering system (*Med.*).

Entziffer—bar, *adj.* explicable; decipherable. **—er**, *m.* (**—ers**, *pl.* **—er**) decipherer. **—n**, *v.a.* to decipher, to make out (*bad writing*); **ein Ziffertelegramm —n**, to decode (*a despatch in cipher*). **—ung**, *f.* deciphering.

Entzü'ck—en, I. *v.a.* to enchant, charm, delight, overjoy. II. **—en**, *subst.n.*, **—ung**, *f.* rapture, delight; **zum —en**, ravishing, charming. **—end**, *p. & adj.* delightful, rapturous, charming. **—t**, *p.p. & adj.* charmed, enraptured, overjoyed; **ich bin —t von ihm**, I am charmed *or* delighted with him.

Entzü'gel—n, *v.a.* to unbridle. **—t**, *p.p. & adj.* unbridled; licentious.

Entzünd'—bar, *adj.* inflammable. **—barkeit**, *f.* inflammability. **—lich**, *adj.* inflammatory.

Entzün'd—en, *v.* I. *a.* to kindle; to inflame; to irritate (*Med.*). II. *r.* to catch fire; to become inflamed; to break out (*as war*). **—et**, *p.p. & adj.* inflamed. **—ung**, *f.* ignition; inflammation. *Comp.* **—ungs=fieber**, *n.* inflammatory fever. **—ungs=widrig**, *adj.* antiphlogistic.

Entzwei', *adv. & sep. prefix*, in two; asunder, apart. *Comp.* **—brechen**, *ir.v.a. & n.* (*aux.* **s.**) to break in two, asunder. **—gehen**, *ir.v.n.* (*aux.* **s.**) to go to pieces, to break. **—sein**, *ir. v.n.* to be torn *or* broken.

Entzwei'—en, *v.* I. *a.* to disunite, to separate; to set at variance. II. *r.* to quarrel; **sie sucht die beiden Menschen zu —en**, she is trying to make mischief between the two people. **—t**, *p.p. & adj.* at variance; **sie hatten sich —t**, they had fallen out. **—ung**, *f.* dissension; variance; estrangement.

En'zian, *m.* (—**s**, *pl.* **—e**) gentian (*Bot.*).

Epaulet'te, *f.* (*pl.* —n) epaulet.

Epheme'r—isch, *adj.* ephemeral; perishable; —ische Waaren, perishable goods (*fruit, etc.*). —e, *f.* ephemera; one-day fever. —i'den, *pl.* ephemerides (*Astr.*); pamphlets, newspapers; diary.

E'pheu, *m.* (—s) ivy; mit — bewachsen, ivy-clad. *Comp.* —artig, *adj.* hederaceous. —ranke, *f.* branch of ivy.

Epidem—ie', *f.* (*pl.* —ie'en) epidemic. —isch, *adj.* (*pron.* epide'misch) epidemic.

Epigo'ne, *m.* (*pl.* —n) epigone, descendant (*of great men*). —n=tum, *n.* decadence *or* decay in literature *or* art.

Epigra'mm, *n.* (—s, *pl.*—e) epigram. —a'tisch, *adj.* epigrammatic, pithy, terse.

E'p—ik, *f.* epic poetry, narrative poetry. —iker, *m.* (—ikers, *pl.* —iker) epic poet. —isch, *adj.* & *adv.* epic. —os, *n.* (*pl.* E'pen) epic poem.

Epikurä'—er, *m.* (—ers, *pl.* —er) epicurean. —i'smus, *m.* epicureanism.

Epi— (*in comp.*); —lepsie', *f.* (*pl.* —lepsie'en) epilepsy. —le'ptisch, *adj.* epileptic. —lo'g, *m.* (—lo'gs, *pl.* —lo'ge) epilogue. —pha'nias=fest, *n.* Epiphany. —so'disch, *adj.* episodical.

Epi'thet—on, *f.* (—ons, *pl.* —a) epithet.

Epi'stel, *f.* (*pl.* —n) epistle.

Epo'che, *f.* (*pl.* —n) epoch; era.

Ep'pich, *m.* (—(e)s, *pl.* —e) ivy; celery, marsh-parsley.

Equilibri'st, *m.* (—en, *pl.* —en) rope-dancer.

Equip—a'ge, *f.* (*pl.* —agen) equipage; equipment; suit *or* set of things; er hat —age, he keeps a carriage. —ie'ren, *v.a.* to fit out, equip; to man (*a ship*).

[1]**Er,** *pers. pron.* he; you (*to inferiors or rudely, spelt with a capital letter, obs.*); — ist es, it is he; — selbst, he himself; wie heißt —? what is your name? (*obs., to inferiors*).

[2]**Er,** *compounded with verbs is insep. and unaccented; the p.p. loses the* ge, *as* erachtet, deemed; *it usually gives to verbs the idea of beginning, or of attainment by the action of the verb; it often equals* auf, *e.g.* erstehen, *etc.; notice the glottal stop in compounds beginning with a vowel sound.*

Erach'ten, I. *v.a.* to think, deem, consider, opine, be of opinion; to imagine, to presume. II. *subst.n.* opinion, judgment; meinem — nach, meines —s, (*abbr.* m. E.) as I think, for aught I know, in my opinion.

Erar'beiten, *v.a.* & *r.* to gain by working.

Erat'men, *v.a.* to draw a deep breath. —d, *p.* & *adj.* breathing heavily, panting, gasping (*poet.*).

Erban'gen, *v.n.* (*aux.* s.) to grow anxious; to fear; er erbangte, his heart misgave him.

Erbar'm—en, I. *v.a.* to move to pity; daß Gott —e! God help us! *used impers'lly* (*with acc.* & *gen.*) to move to pity; mich —et des Armen, I pity the poor man. II. *v.r.* (*with gen. or* über *with acc.*) to pity, commiserate, show mercy to; Herr, —e dich unser! Lord, have mercy upon us! III. *subst.n.* pity, compassion; zum —en, pitiful; er sieht zum —en aus, he looks most wretched. —end, *p.* & *adj.* compassionate. —ung, *f.* pity. *Comp.* —ens=wert, —ens=würdig, —ungs=wert, —ungs=würdig, *adj.* & *adv.* pitiable. —ungs=los, *adj.* pitiless, merciless. —ungs=voll, *adj.* compassionate.

Erbärm'lich, *adj.* & *adv.* pitiable, miserable, wretched; contemptible. —keit, *f.* misery, wretchedness; pitiableness; lowness, meanness.

Erbau'—en, *v.a.* to build up, raise, erect; to cultivate; to edify; sich —en an (*dat.*), to find edification in, to be edified. —er, *m.* (—ers, *pl.* —er) builder; founder; edifier. —lich, *adj.* & *adv.* edifying; improving, tending to edification; instinct with devotion. —lichkeit, *f.* quality of edifying, devotional character *or* frame of mind. —ung, *f.* building up; construction; edification. *Comp.* —ungs=schrift, *f.* devotional publication, religious tract. —ungs=rede, *f.* edifying (*religious*) discourse. —ungs=stunde, *f.* hour of devotion.

Erb'—, *in compounds usually* = hereditary. —bar, *adj.* inheritable.

Erb—e, I. *m.* (—n, *pl.* —n) heir; successor; mutmaßlicher —e, heir presumptive; lachende —en, rejoicing heirs; ohne leibliche —en, issueless, destitute of children. II. *n.* (—es, *pl.* —schaften *or* —güter) heritage, inheritance —in, *f.* female heir, heiress. —lich, *adj.* & *adv.* hereditary, inheritable; —lich besitzen, to possess by inheritance; —lich belastet, affected with a hereditary taint; full of ancestral features; —liche Belastung, hereditary taint, hereditary habit *or* proclivity. —lichkeit, *f.* devolvability of property. —schaft, *f.* heritage, inheritance. *Comp.* —adel, *m.* hereditary nobility. —amt, *n.* hereditary office. —anfall, *m.* heritage. —anspruch, *m.* claim to an inheritance. —begräbnis, *n.* family vault *or* burying-place. —berechtigt, *adj.* qualified to inherit. —besitz, *m.* hereditary possession. —eid, *m.* vassal's oath of fealty. —eigen, *adj.* possessed by inheritance. —einsetzung, —ernennung, *f.* institution of an heir. —fähig, *adj.* capable of inheriting. —fall, *m.* heritage, succession; fortune in reversion. —fällig, *adj.* hereditary, entailed. —fälligkeit, *f.* entail; die —fälligkeit aufheben, to cut off the entail. —fehler, *m.* hereditary defect; family failing. —feind, *m.* hereditary enemy, sworn enemy, old enemy; nation hostile through generations. —folge, *f.* succession by inheritance; heritage; bestimmte —folge, next of kin; die —folge bestimmen, to entail. —folge=krieg, *m.* war of succession. —folger, *m.* heir, successor. —förster, *m.* hereditary gamekeeper. —frau, *f.*, —herrin, *f.* lady of the manor. —genoß, *m.* joint heir. —gericht, *n.* court-baron. —gerichts=herr, *m.* lord of the manor. —gesessen, *adj.* possessed of real property. —grind, *m.* scald-head. —großherzog, *m.* heir of the grand duke. —grund, *m.* heirloom, landed property. —gut, *n.* patrimonial estate; heirloom. —herr, *m.* feudal lord, liege lord, lord of the manor. —herrlich, *adj.* manorial. —kaisertum, *n.* hereditary empire. —kauf, *m.* purchase in perpetuity. —land, *n.* hereditary land; patrimonial acres; die kaiserlichen —lande, the Emperor's patrimonial dominions. —lasser, *m.* testator. —lasserin, *f.* testatrix. —lehre, *f.* tradition. —lehen, *n.* hereditary fief. —los, *adj.* disinherited, without inheritance; without an heir. —nehmer, *m.* inheritor. —onkel, *m.* wealthy uncle whose property a p. hopes to inherit. —pacht, *f.* fee-farm, copyhold. —pächter, *m.* tenant of a long lease, copyholder. —prinz, *m.* heir to a reigning prince. —recht, *n.* right of succession. —register, *n.* rent-roll, terrier. —saß *or* —sasse, *m.* = —herr. —schafts=anteil, *m.* share of inheritance. —schafts=masse, *f.* bulk (*of an inheritance*). —schafts=steuer, *f.* legacy duty, probate duty. —schafts=verfüger, *m.* testator. —schafts=verfügerin, *f.* testatrix. —schafts=verfügung, *f.* disposition of property by will, testament. —schicht, —schichtung, *f.* division of an inheritance. —schichter, —schafts=richter, *m.* judge of probate court. —schleicher, *m.* legacy-hunter. —schoß, *m.* ground rent. —schuld, *f.* charge (*on an estate*), encumbrance. —setzer, *m.* testator. —stände, *pl.* hereditary corporation. —steuer, *f.* legacy duty, probate duty. —steuer=gesetz, *n.* law concerning legacy duty. —stück, *n.*

heirloom. —**süchtig**, *adj.* greedy of inheritance. —**sünde**, *f.* original sin. —**tante**, *f.* wealthy aunt whose property a p. hopes to inherit. —**teil**, *n.* portion, inheritance. —**tochter**, *f.* (*rich*) heiress. —**vertrag**, *m.* settlement of succession. —**vermögen**, *n.* patrimony. —**zins**, *m.* fee-farm rent, ground-rent; quit-rent. —**zins=gut**, *n.* fee-farm. —**zins=mann**, *m.* lease-holder.

Er'ben, *v.* I. *a.* to inherit; **von seinem Vater** —, to succeed to one's father's property; **dies hatte er von seiner Mutter geerbt**, he inherited this from his mother. II. *n.* (*aux.* **s.**) — **auf**, to descend to, to devolve on; **die Krone erbt auf ihn**, he is heir to the crown.

Erbe'ben, *v.n.* (*aux.* **h.** & **s.**) to tremble, to shudder at (**vor**); to vibrate (*of sounds*).

Erbe'ten, *v.a.* to obtain by prayer; to solicit, request.

Erbet'teln, *v.a.* to obtain by begging, to beg.

Erbeu'ten, *v.a.* to gain *or* take as booty, to capture.

Erbie't—en, I. *ir.v.r.* to offer; to volunteer. II. *subst. n.* offer. —**ung**, *f.* offer, proffer.

Erbit't—en, *ir.v.a.* to beg, request, ask for; to obtain by entreaty; to prevail upon; **er läßt sich —en**, he is moved by entreaties; **er läßt sich nicht —en**, he is inexorable. —**lich**, *adj.* & *adv.* exorable, yielding to entreaty.

Erbit'ter—n, *v.a.* to provoke, incense, irritate, embitter; to make uneasy (*poet.*). —**ung**, *f.* exasperation; bitter anger, animosity.

Erblas's—en, *v.n.* (*aux.* **s.**) to grow pale; to fade; to die (*in poetry*). —**ung**, *f.* pallor; growing pale.

Erblei'chen, *ir.v.n.* see **Erblassen**; to turn white.

Erbli'cken, *v.a.* to catch sight of; to descry; to perceive, see, discover; **das Licht der Welt** —, to come into the world; to be born.

Erblin'den, *v.n.* (*aux.* **s.**) to grow blind.

Erbor'gen, *v.a.* to obtain by borrowing, to get on credit, to borrow.

Erbo'sen, **Erbo'ßen**, *v.* I. *a.* to make angry, provoke. II. *r.* to grow angry; to fume, fret. **erbo'st**, *p.p.* & *adj.* vexed, angry.

Erbö'tig, *adj.* ready *or* willing to do a thing.

Erbrau'sen, *v.a.* to (begin to) roar, to send up a roar.

Erbre'chen, I. *ir.v.a.* to break open; to break **sich** —, to vomit, to be sick. II. *subst.n.* breaking open, forcing; opening (*a letter, etc.*); vomiting; **Neigung zum** —, squeamishness.

Comp. —**befördernd**, —**erregend**, *adj.* emetic. —**stillend**, *adj.* ant(i)-emetic.

Erb'se, *f.* (*pl.* —**n**), pea; **die große englische** —, marrow-fat pea; **auf seinen Händen kann man —n säen**, you can sow a peck of peas upon his hands. *Comp.* —**n=brei**, *m.* pease-pudding. —**n=gericht**, *n.* dish of peas. —**n=prinzessin**, *f.* princess on the pea, very delicate and particular girl. —**n=schote**, *f.* pea-pod. —**n=suppe**, *f.* pea-soup.

Erbs'wurst, *f.* pea sausage, condensed pea soup (*in form of a hard sausage, for cooking; used by the Germans in the Franco-German war*).

Erbuh'len, *v.a.* to gain by coquetry *or* by vicious love; to obtain by courting.

Er'd—e, *f.* (*old gen. & dat. sing.* —**en**, *now* —**e**; —**en** *survives in many compounds; pl.* —**en**) earth, ground; soil, clay, dust, dirt; the earth, the world; **auf die —e werfen**, to throw upon the ground; **die —e kauen**, to bite the dust; **auf —en**, on earth, alive, in this world; **zu ebener —e**, on the ground floor; **gelbe —e**, yellow ochre; **gebrannte —e**, terra cotta; **wieder zur —e werden**, to return to dust; **der —e gleich machen**, to level to the ground; **die Küche ist über der —e**, the kitchen is above ground; **über die ganze —e**, all the world over. —**en**, (*first part of comp.*=) earthly, terrestrial, of this world. —**icht**, (*obs.*) —**ig**, *adj.* earthy.

Comp. —**achse**, *f.* axis of the earth. —**amsel**, *f.* ring-ouzel. —**apfel**, *m.* potato. —**arbeiten**, *pl.* earth-works, digging. —**arbeiter**, *m.* digger; navvy (*Railw.*) —**art**, *f.* kind of earth *or* soil, species of clay. —**artig**, *adj.* earthy. —**bahn**, *f.* orbit (*of the earth*). —**ball**, *m.* globe, world. —**bank**, *f.* banquette (*Fort.*); terrace. —**bau**, *m.* earth-work, embankment; underground work, crypt, cave, vault. —**beben**, *n.* earthquake. —**beben=messer**, *m.* seismometer. —**beere**, *f.* strawberry. —**beschreibend**, *adj.* geographical. —**beschreiber**, *m.* geographer. —**beschreibung**, *f.* geography. —**boden**, *m.* the earth, ground, soil; **dem —boden gleich machen**, to raze. —**bohrer**, *m.* ground auger. —**brand**, *m.* subterraneous fire. —**brett**, *n.* mould-board (*of a plough*). —**bürger**, *m.* inhabitant of the earth, mortal. —**bruch**, *m.* a sinking of the ground. —**durchmesser**, *m.* diameter of the earth. —**en=bewohner**, *m.*, —**en=bürger**, *m.*, —**en=geschöpf**, *n.* mortal, human being. —**en=freude**, *f.* earthly joy. —**enge**, *f.* isthmus. —**en=kind**, *n.*, —**en=sohn**, *m.* child of this world, mortal. —**en=kloß**, *m.* clod of earth; **Gott schuf den Menschen aus einem —enkloß**, God formed man of the dust of the ground. —**en=leben**, *n.* life in this world. —**en=not**, *f.* troubles of this life. —**en=ruhm**, *m.* earthly glory. —**en=rund**, *n.* the earth. —**en=schooß**, *m.* the interior of the earth. —**en=wärts**, *adv.* earthwards. —**en=wallen**, *n.* pilgrimage on earth. —**en=wurm**, *m.* earthworm; mortal. —**epheu**, *m.* ground-ivy. —**fahl**, *adj.* clay-coloured, livid, ashy-gray. —**fall**, *m.* sinking of the earth, landslip. —**farben**, —**farbig**, *see* —**fahl**. —**ferne**, *f.* apogee. —**fernrohr**, *n.* terrestrial telescope. —**finsternis**, *f.* solar eclipse. —**fläche**, *f.* surface of the earth. —**floh**, *m.* spring-tail. —**forscher**, *m.* geologist. —**forschung**, *f.* geology. —**galle**, *f.* lesser centaury; vine disease. —**gang**, *m.* vein (*Min.*); tunnel. —**geboren**, *adj.* earth-born. —**geist**, *m.* gnome; Spirit of the Earth. —**geruch**, *m.* earthly smell. —**geschoß**, *n.* ground-floor. —**gewächs**, *n.* land plant *or* vegetable. —**gleicher**, *m.* equator. —**grün**, *n.* sap-green. —**gürtel**, *m.* zone. —**haltig**, *adj.* containing earth. —**halbmesser**, *m.* semidiameter of the earth. —**harz**, *n.* bitumen, asphalt; **gelbes —harz**, amber; **elastisches —harz**, elaterite. —**hase**, *m.* jerboa. —**haue**, *f.* pickaxe. —**höhle**, *f.* cavern. —**kalk**, *m.* limestone marl. —**karte**, *f.* map of the world. —**kloß**, *m.* clod, *see* —**en=kloß**. —**körper**, *m.* terrestrial body. —**kreis**, *m.* globe; orb, sphere of the earth. —**kreis=linie**, *f.* horizon (*line*). —**kresse**, *f.* hedge-mustard. —**kugel**, *f.* terrestrial globe. —**kunde**, *f.* general knowledge of the earth, geography, geology, geognosy. —**kundig**, *adj.* versed in geography, *etc.* —**lage**, *f.*, —**lager**, *n. see* —**schicht**. —**lehre**, *f.* geology. —**linie**, *f.* ground-line (*Paint.*) —**magnetismus**, *m.* terrestrial magnetism. —**männchen**, *n.* gnome, dwarf. —**maus**, *f.* field mouse. —**messer**, *m.* geometrician; mining instrument (*Fort.*). —**meß=kunst**, —**messung**, *f.* geometry; geodesy. —**mittelpunktig**, *adj.* geocentric. —**moos**, *n.* club moss; **purgierendes —moos**, Iceland moss. —**möve**, *f.* puffin. —**morchel**, *f.* truffle. —**nähe**, *f.* perigee. —**naturbeschreibung**, *f.* physical geography. —**oberfläche**, *f.* surface of the earth. —**öl**, *n.* petroleum. —**pech**, *n.* bitumen. —**pfriem**, *m.*, —**pfrieme**, *f.* broom. —**pol**, *m.* pole (*of the earth*). —**reich**, *n.* earth, soil, ground; the world at large. —**rinde**, *f.* crust (*of the earth*). —**röhre**, *f.* drain-pipe. —**rose**, *f.* dwarf white rose. —**rücken**, *m.* ridge of hills, elevation of land. —rund, *n.* the earth. —ſack, *m.* sandbag (*Mil.*). —ſaft, *m.* mineral oil. —ſalz, *n.* rock-salt; saltpetre. —ſcheibe, *f.* disk of the earth. —ſchicht, *f.* layer, stratum; untere —ſchicht, subsoil. —ſchierling, *m.* hemlock. —ſchildkröte, *f.* land-tortoise. ſchlägel, *m.* clod-crusher. —ſchnecke, *f.* shell-snail. —ſchocke, *f.* artichoke. —ſcholle, *f.* clod, glebe. —ſchwamm, *m.* mushroom. —ſchwarz, *n.* coal for fresco painting. —ſpinne, *f.* field-spider. —ſtein, *m.* aetites. —ſtoß, *m.* shock of earthquake. —ſtrich, *m.* zone; der heiße —ſtrich, the torrid zone; die gemäßigten, die kalten —ſtriche, the temperate, frigid zones. —ſtufe, *f.* terrace; brow of a hill. —ſturz, *m.* landslip. —teil, *m.* part of the world; continent. —umſchiffer, —umſegler, *m.* circumnavigator. —umſchiffung, —umſegelung, *f.* circumnavigation. —viertel, *n.* quarter of the globe. —wachs, *n.* ozokerite. —wärme, *f.* the temperature of the earth. —wärts, *adv.* earthwards. —wahrſagerei, *f.* geomancy. —weite, *f.* medium distance of the earth from the sun. —werk, *n.* earthwork. —winkel, *m.* corner, nook of the earth. —zirkel, *m.* circle on the terrestrial globe. —zunge, *f.* neck of land; isthmus; promontory, cape, headland.

Erdar'ben, *v.a.* to save by pinching *or* privation.

Erden'k—en, *ir.v.a.* to excogitate; to invent; to fabricate, coin; to imagine. —bar, —lich, *adj.* imaginable, conceivable; ſich alle —liche Mühe geben, to take all sorts of pains. —ung, *f.* invention; fabrication; excogitation.

Erdich't—en, *v.a.* to invent, devise; to coin, fabricate; to feign; to imagine. —et, *p.p. & adj.* feigned; fictitious. —ung, *f.* fabrication; fiction; feigning. *Comp.* —ungs=gabe, *f.* inventiveness, imaginativeness.

Erdol'chen, *v.a.* to stab with a dagger, to poniard.

Erdrei'ſten, *v.r.* to dare, to presume; darf ich mich —? may I be so bold? ſie erdreiſtete ſich, mir zu ſagen ꝛc., she had the audacity to tell me. (Erdreu'ſten is *dialectic.*)

Erdrin'gen, *v.a.* to obtain by pressing, to obtain by putting pressure on a p.; to press for a th.

Erdröh'nen, *v.n.* (*aux.* h.) to begin to rumble; to vibrate with deep sounds; to sound loudly; to quake.

Erdroſ'ſel—n, I. *v.a.* to throttle, strangle. II. *subst. n.* —ung, *f.* strangulation.

Erdrü'cken, *v.a.* to press to death; to choke, stifle; to crush (*rebellion, etc.*).

Erdul'd—en, *v.a.* to endure, suffer; to put up with. —ung, *f.* endurance; submission (*to*); toleration (*of*).

Erei'fern, *v.r.* to be overzealous; to grow warm, fly into a passion; — Sie ſich nicht! keep your temper! do not get excited!

Ereig'—nen, (Eräug'nen *is an obs. form, occurring in Lessing, etc.,*) *v.r. imp.* to come to pass; to happen, to fall out, to chance; es —nete ſich, daß wir, we happened to. —nis, *n.* (—(ſſ)es, *pl.* —(ſſ)e) event, occurrence; auf alle —niſſe gefaßt, prepared for whatever may (*or* might) happen.

Erei'len, *v.a.* to hasten up to; to overtake.

Eremi't, *m.* (—en, *pl.* —en) hermit. —a'ge, *f.* hermitage.

Erer'ben, *v.a.* to inherit.

Erfah'r—en, I. *ir.v.a.* to come to know, to learn, to be told; to experience; to suffer, undergo; ich —e als gewiß, I hear for certain. II. *p.p. & adj.* experienced, expert, skilful, skilled; ein —ener Soldat, a veteran; ein —ener Arbeiter, a skilled *or* expert workman. —enheit, *f.* experience, practice, skill. —ung, *f.* experience, practice, practical knowledge; auf —ung gegründet, aus —ung entſprungen, geſchöpft, experimental; in —ung bringen, to learn; aus —ung, by, from experience. *Comp.* —ungs=arzt, *m.* empiric (doctor). —ungs=beweis, *m.* practical proof. —ungs=kreis, *m.* circle of experience, sphere of knowledge. —ungs=los, *adj.* inexperienced. —ungs=mäßig, *adj. & adv.* empirical; —ungs=mäßig wiſſen wir, daß, we know from experience that. —ungs=reich, *adj.* experienced. —ungs=ſatz, *m.* principle derived from experience.

Erfaſ'ſen, *v.a.* to lay hold of, to seize; to comprehend; recht —, to realize.

Erfech'ten, *ir.v.a.* to obtain by fighting, to gain; den Sieg —, to win the victory.

Erfind'—bar, *adj.* discoverable, devisable. —ſam, *adj.* inventive. —ſamkeit, *f.* inventiveness, ingenuity.

Erfin'd—en, *ir.v.a.* to find (*out*); to contrive, invent; to fabricate (*a story*); er hat das Pulver nicht erfunden, he will never set the Thames on fire (*prov.*); es wird erfunden werden, daß, it will be found that (*obs.*). —er, *m.* (—ers, *pl.* —er) designer, inventor. —eriſch, *adj. & adv.* inventive. —ung, *f.* invention; device. *Comp.* —ungs=gabe, —ungs=kraft, *f.* power of invention, inventive faculty. —ungs=patent, *n.* inventor's patent. —ungs=reich, —ungs=voll, *adj.* inventive, ingenious. —ungs=wahn, *m.* inventive mania.

Erfi'ſchen, *v.a.* to fish out; to pick up (by artifice).

Erfle'hen, *v.a.* to obtain by entreaty; laß dich —! be moved by my entreaties!

Erfo'lg, *m.* (—es, *pl.* —e) success, successful issue; result; alle Bemühungen blieben ohne —, all efforts proved unavailing. —los, I. *adj.* unsuccessful, unavailing. II. *adv.* vainly, in vain. *Comp.* —reich, *adj.* successful; pregnant in results.

Erfol'gen, *v.n.* (*aux.* ſ.) to ensue, result, come of, follow from; to take place; was wird daraus —? what will be the result? die Antwort iſt noch nicht erfolgt, the answer has not come yet, no answer has been received.

Erfor'der—lich, *adj.* requisite, necessary; —lichen Falls, in case of need, if necessary. —nis, *n.* (—(ſſ)es, *pl.* —(ſſ)e) requisite, exigency; (*pl.*) necessaries (*of life*); —nis zu einem Amte, qualification for an office; nach —nis der Umſtände, according to circumstances.

Erfor'der—n, *v.a.* to require; render necessary; to demand; handle wie es die Sache —t, act as you see fit, according to circumstances.

Erfor'ſch—en, *v.a.* to search into, investigate, explore; to fathom; to discover. —er, *m.* (—ers, *pl.* —er) investigator; discoverer. —lich, *adj.* investigable, *etc.* —ung, *f.* investigation; exploration.

Erfra'gen, *reg. & ir.v.a.* to find out by asking; er iſt nirgends zu —, no one can tell where he is; zu — bei . . ., enquire at . . .

Erfre'chen, *v.r.* to dare, have the impudence to.

Erfreu'—en, *v.* I. *a.* to rejoice, gladden, delight; to cheer, comfort. II. *r.* to rejoice, be rejoiced (über eine S., at, over a th.); to take pleasure (an einer S., in a th.); to enjoy (*gen.*). —lich, *adj.* delightful, gratifying; —liche Nachrichten, gratifying, satisfactory news; das —lichſte für mich iſt, what pleases me most is.

Erfrie'ren, *ir.v.n.* (*aux.* ſ.) to freeze; to suffer cold; to die from cold, perish with cold. erfro'ren, *p.p. & adj.* frozen, benumbed with cold.

Erfri'ſch—en, *v.a.* to freshen, refresh; to recreate; to cool, refrigerate; ſich —en, to take refreshment. —end, *p. & adj.* refreshing, cooling. —ung, *f.* recreation, refreshment; —ungen zu ſich nehmen, to take refreshments.

Erfül'l—en, *v.a.* to fill (*up*); to fulfil, perform, make good; to accomplish; to realize (*expectations*); **eine Bitte —en,** to comply with a request; **sein Versprechen —en,** to keep one's promise; **sich —en,** to be fulfilled. **—ung,** *f.* fulfilment, accomplishment, realization; **in —ung bringen,** to fulfil; **in —ung gehen,** to be in course of fulfilment, be fulfilled.

Ergän'z—en, *v.a.* to complete, perfect; to restore; to supply (*one's place*); to make up (*a deficiency*); to recruit (*an army; one's strength, etc.*); to supplement. **—end,** *p. & adj.* supplementary; completing, complemental. **—ung,** *f.* completion; supplement; complement; reparation; recruiting; redintegration. *Comp.* **—ungs=band,** *m.* supplementary volume. **—ungs=blatt,** *n.* supplement (*sheet*). **—ungs=bogen,** *m.* imperfect sheet, cancel (*Typ.*) **—ungs=farben,** *pl.* complementary colours. **—ungs=heft,** *n.* supplementary number. **—ungs=mannschaft,** *f.* complement (*of soldiers, etc.*). **—ungs=strich,** *m.* bar, ellipsis (*Typ.*). **—ungs=stück,** *n.* complement. **—ungs=wahl,** *f.* bye-election; supplementary election. **—ungs=winkel,** *m.* complement of an angle; supplementary angle (*Math.*). **—ungs=wörterbuch,** *n.* supplement to a dictionary.

Ergat'tern, *v.a.* to pick up, hunt up, obtain (*by trouble and often by stratagem. Coll.*).

Erge'b—en, I. *v.a.* to deliver up, yield to; to give as a result, show, prove; to yield; **angestellte Untersuchungen haben —en,** the examinations instituted have shown. II. *v.r.* to submit, yield, surrender; to acquiesce (*in*); to devote oneself to; to become addicted, give way to; to come to pass, happen; to result, follow; **hieraus ergiebt sich,** hence it follows; **sich in den göttlichen Willen —en,** to resign oneself to the will of God; **sich auf Gnade und Ungnade —en,** to surrender at discretion *or* unconditionally. III. *p.p. & adj.* devoted, attached; resigned; submissive, humble; **unser —en(st)es,** our letter (*C.L.*). **—enst,** (*sup.*) *adj. & adv.* most devoted; most humble; **Ihr —enster Diener,** your obedient servant, yours respectfully; **ich bitte —enst,** I beg respectfully, may I beg . . . ? **ich danke —enst,** I am very much obliged. **—enheit,** *f.* fidelity, loyalty, devotion, resignation; submissiveness; addictedness; **versichern Sie sie meiner —enheit,** present my humble respects to her. **—nis,** *n.* (—ni(ss)es, *pl.* —ni(ss)e) result, consequence; sequel; sum, product (*Math.*). **—ung,** *f.* submission, resignation; surrender (*Mil.*); **mit—ung,** resignedly. *Comp.* **—nis=los,** *adj.* without result, ineffectual, vain.

Erge'hen, *ir.v.* I. *a.* to walk to the end of; **er kann das nicht in einem Tage —,** he cannot go so far in one day (*obs.*). II. *r.* to walk, exercise oneself; **sich im Garten —,** to walk about in the garden; **sich — in,** to indulge in, launch forth into; **sich in Scheltreden —,** to indulge in words of rebuke. III. *n.* (*aux.* **s.**) to go forth; to come out, be issued; to be passed; (**über einen**) to befall, happen, betide; **— lassen,** to issue; **ein Urteil — lassen,** to pass sentence; **Recht — lassen,** to let justice take her course; **etwas über sich — lassen,** to bear patiently; (*used impers'lly with dat.*) to go, fare with; to become of; **es erging ihm schlecht,** things went badly with him; **wie würde es dir — ?** what would become of you? **möge es ihm wohl — !** may he prosper!

Ergei'gen, *v.a. & r.* to gain by fiddling.

Erge'tzen, see **Ergötzen.**

Ergie'big, *adj.* productive. **—keit,** *f.* productiveness; lucrativeness; fertility.

Ergie'ß—en, *ir.v.* I. *a.* to pour out *or* forth. II. *r.* to overflow, gush forth; to empty, discharge itself. fall into; to break forth; **sich in Thränen —en,** to burst into tears. **—ung,** *f.* effusion; efflux; discharge; overflow.

Erglän'zen, *v.n.* (*aux.* **h.**) to sparkle, shine forth; to burst forth in splendour.

Erglim'men, *ir.v.n.* (*aux.* **s.**) to begin to glow; to glimmer, gleam up.

Erglü'hen, *v.n.* (*aux.* **s.**) to (begin to) glow.

Ergöt'z—en, (**Erget'zen** *is an older form,*) *v.a.* to delight, please; **sich an einer S. —en,** to take delight in a th., be amused with s.th. **—end,** *p. & adj.* amusing. **—lich,** *adj.* amusing; delightful. **—lichkeit,** *f.* amusement; delightfulness; (*pl.*) entertainments, enjoyments. **—ung,** *f.* delight; pleasure.

Ergrau'en, *v.n.* (*aux.* **s.**) to grow gray; to dawn; **ergraut ist schon die Welt,** the daylight has died away (*poet.*).

Ergrei'f—en, *ir.v.a.* to lay hold of, seize; to apprehend; to affect, touch; to make use of, avail oneself of; to assume (*the offensive*); to enter on, apply oneself to (*a trade, etc.*); to have recourse to (*means*); **die Waffen —en,** to take up arms; **die Flucht —en,** to take to flight; **eine Partei —en,** to espouse a cause; **auf frischer That —en,** to take in the act; **das Hasenpanier —en,** to take to one's heels; **die Gelegenheit beim Schopfe —en,** to take time by the forelock. **—end,** *p. & adj.* touching, affecting; impressive; prehensile. **—ung,** *f.* seizure, apprehension; taking in hand, taking to.

Ergrim'men, *v.n.* (*aux.* **s.**) to get angry *or* furious; **ergrimmt aussehen,** to look fierce.

Ergrün'd—en, *v.a.* to fathom, investigate, explore thoroughly; to penetrate (*a mystery*); to get to the bottom of; **nicht zu —en,** unfathomable, inexplicable. **—er,** *m.* (—ers, *pl.* —er) investigator. **—lich,** *adj. & adv.* fathomable, penetrable. **—ung,** *f.* fathoming; research; exploration.

Ergrü'nen, *v.n.* (*aux.* **s.**) to grow green.

Erguß', *m.* (*pl.* **Ergüs'se**) effusion; overflow.

Erha'ben, *adj. & adv.* raised, elevated; exalted, noble; lofty, sublime; stately; **—e Arbeit,** relief, embossed work; **halb —e Arbeit,** demi-relief; **ganz —e Arbeit,** high-relief; **—e Arbeit machen,** to emboss; **über sein Schicksal —,** superior to one's fate; **ich bin darüber —, so etwas zu thun,** I am above doing such a thing; **das —e,** the sublime. **—heit,** *f.* sublimity; nobleness, grandeur; relief (*Sculp.*); eminence, illustriousness; protuberance (*Med.*); stateliness.

Erhalt'bar, Erhält'lich, *adj.* obtainable; preservable; sustainable.

Erhal't—en, I. *ir.v.a.* to keep up, to keep from falling; to preserve, uphold in life; to maintain, support; to get, to receive; to obtain; to save, preserve; to maintain (*order; one's place or rank; reputation, etc.*); **einen höhern Preis —en,** to fetch a higher price; **wenn Sie dieses —en,** when this reaches you; **Gott —e den König!** God save the king! **sich —en,** to keep on one's legs, to maintain one's position, to continue (*current, etc.*); **sich —en von,** to subsist on; **sich selbst —en,** to support oneself; **sich in Gunst —en bei,** to keep in favour with; **sich gut —en,** to wear *or* keep well; **sich fest —en auf,** to continue at (*a certain price*); **wir wollen uns in Kleidung selbst —en,** we will find our own clothes. II. *p.p. & adj.* preserved; received; paid (*C. L.*); **gut —en,** in good repair *or* condition. **—er,** *m.* (—ers, *pl.* —er) preserver; supporter; upholder. **—ung,** *f.* obtaining; receipt; maintenance, *etc.* *Comp.* **—ungs=brille,** *f.* sight-preservers. **—ungs=mittel,** *n.* means of subsistence; antiseptic.

Erhan'deln, *v.a.* to buy; to acquire by trade.

Erhän'gen, *v.a. & r.* (**sich**) to hang (*oneself*).

Erhar'ren, *v.a.* to expect; to wait for

Erhar'ten, *v.n.* (*aux.* **s.**) to grow hard, to harden.
Erhär'ten, *v.a.* to harden; to confirm, corroborate; **eidlich —,** to affirm upon oath.
Erha'schen, *v.a.* to snatch (*at*); to seize, catch up; to overtake.
Erhe'b—en, *ir.v.* I. *a.* to heave, lift, raise up; to exalt, elevate; to extol; to set up (*a cry, a shout*); to raise, start (*doubts, etc.*); to promote, advance; to raise in rank; to extol; to collect, gather; to raise (*money*); to levy (*taxes*); to enter (*a protest against*); to bring (*an action against*); to raise to a higher power (*Math.*); to relieve, set off (*by contrast, Paint.*); **Geld —en,** to raise money; to cash money; **eine Erbschaft —en,** to take possession of an inheritance; **eine Zahl ins Quadrat —en,** to square a number; **in den Adelstand —en,** to raise to the peerage. II. *r.* to raise oneself; to rise, start up; to rise up (**gegen,** against); to arise (*as a question*); to spring up; to assume superiority (**über einen,** over a p.); to set up for; to arise and spread abroad; **plötzlich erhob sich ein Gemurmel,** a murmur suddenly arose; **ein Gerücht hat sich erhoben,** a rumour is afloat; **es erhob sich ein heftiger Wind,** a strong breeze sprang up; **sich stolz —en,** to ride the high horse. **—end,** *p. & adj.* elevating; **sich —end,** acclivitous. **—er,** *m.* (**—ers,** *pl.* **—er**) raiser; promoter; collector. **—lich,** *adj. & adv.* important; considerable; cogent, weighty. **—lichkeit,** *f.* importance, consequence; weight. **—ung,** *f.* elevation; promotion; exaltation; levy, collecting; involution (*Math.*); rising ground. *Comp.* **—ungs=art,** *f.* mode of collection (*of taxes*). **—ungs=kosten,** *pl.* expenses of collection. **—ungs=linie,** *f.* line of elevation. **—ungs=winkel,** *m.* angle of elevation; rake (*of a bowsprit*).
Erhei'raten, *v.a.* to obtain by marriage.
Erhei'schen, *v.n.* to require, to claim.
Erhei'ter—n, *v.a.* to cheer, to brighten; to enliven, to exhilarate; **sich —n,** to clear up; to become cheerful. **—ung,** *f.* amusement, fun, cheering up.
Erhel'l—en, *v.* I. *a.* to clear up, to brighten, to illuminate; to clarify. II. *n.* (*aux.* **h.**) to become clear *or* evident, to appear; **daraus —t, daß,** from this it is evident that. **—ung,** *f.* lighting up; illumination. *Comp.* **—ungs=kessel,** *m.* clarifying pan.
Erhen'ken, *obsolete for* **Erhängen.**
Erheu'cheln, *v.a.* to sham, put on, feign.
Erhit'z—en, *v.* I. *a.* to heat; to warm; to inflame. II. *r.* to grow hot *or* warm; to become heated; to get *or* fly into a passion. **—end,** *p. & adj.* inflammatory. **—t,** *p.p. & adj.* heated; flushed; warm; **ganz —t,** all in a heat, all in a glow. **—ung,** *f.* heating.
Erhof'fen, *v.a.* to hope for, expect.
Erhö'h—en, *v.a.* to elevate, raise aloft; to erect; to heighten; to raise, increase; to heighten (*colour; a pleasure, etc.*); to extol, exalt; to enhance (*the value, etc.*). **—t,** *p.p. & adj.* elevated; additional (*of taxes*). **—ung,** *f.* raising; exaltation; elevation; rise, advance; increase; laudation; enhancement; rake (*of a bowsprit*); swelling, protuberance; rising ground; raising of a note (*Mus.*). *Comp.* **—ungs=zeichen,** *n.* sharp, sign in music of the raising of a note.
Erho'l—en, *v.r.* to recover (*consciousness; from emotion; one's breath; one's health*); to rest; to unbend, recreate; **sich** (*dat.*) **Rats —en bei,** to consult s.o., to ask advice of a p.; **sich (wegen) seines Schadens,** *or* **von seinem Schaden —en an,** to retrieve, repair a loss by, with; **sich etwas —en bei,** to reimburse oneself at the expense of. **—ung,** *f.* recovery; recreation; refreshment; reparation; **—ung gewährend,** recreative; **zur —ung der Reisenden,** for the relief of travellers. *Comp.* **—ungs=bedürftig,** *adj.* wanting reaction *or* rest, in need of a change. **—ungs=stunde,** *f.* recreation time, play-hour; leisure-hour.
Erhor'chen, *v.a.* to learn by listening.
Erhö'r—en, *v.a.* to give a favourable hearing; to grant; to hear; (*obs.*); **das ist ganz unerhört,** it is quite unheard of, that is shocking. **—ung,** *f.* favourable hearing (*of a request*).
Erin'ner—lich, *adj. & adv.* present to the memory; **es ist mir —lich,** I remember; **so viel mir —lich ist,** so far as I remember.
Erin'ner—n, *v.* I. *a.* (**einen an eine S.**) to remind, put in remembrance of, call to mind; to draw attention to; to mention; to admonish; (*dial. North Germ.*) to recall, to remember. II. *r.* (*with gen. or* **an** *& acc.*) to recall, remember, call to mind; **haben Sie etwas dagegen zu —n?** have you any objections to it? **haben Sie noch etwas zu —n?** have you any further remark to make? **—end,** *p. & adj.;* **sich —end,** commemorative. **—ung,** *f.* reminiscence; recollection; reminder; remonstrance; **etwas in —ung bringen,** to remind of, call to mind; **ohne vorläufige —ung,** without previous notice; **zur —ung an** (*acc.*), in remembrance of, in memory of. *Comp.* **—ungs=buch,** *n.* memorandum-book. **—ungs=kraft,** *f.,* **—ungs=vermögen,** *n.* memory, recollecting power. **—ungs=kunst,** *f.* mnemonics. **—ungs=schrift,** *f.* memorial, in memoriam. **—ungs=zeichen,** *n.* keepsake.
Erja'gen, *v.a.* to get by great exertion *or* by hot pursuit; to overtake; to hunt down.
Erkal'ten, *v.n.* (*aux.* **s.**) to grow cold; to cool.
Erkäl't—en, *v.* I. *a.* to cool. II. *r.* to catch cold. **—ung,** *f.* catching cold; cold; **eine starke —ung,** a bad cold.
Erkämp'fen, *v.a.* to gain by fighting *or* a struggle.
Erkau'fen, *v.a.* to buy, purchase; to bribe, corrupt; **sich** (*acc.*) **— lassen,** to be corruptible.
Erke'cken, *v.r.* to make bold, to dare.
Erkenn'bar, *adj.* recognizable, capable of being known; perceptible, discernible.
Erken'n—en, *ir.v.a.* to know, perceive, apprehend; to understand; to recognize (**an,** by); to take cognizance of; to grant, permit; to know (*carnally*); to credit (*C. L.*); to judge, decide, pass sentence on; to diagnose (*Med.*); **er gab sein Mißfallen über diese Störung zu —en,** he showed his displeasure at this interruption, intrusion; **sich zu —en geben,** to make oneself known; **der Verbrecher erkannte sich nicht für schuldig,** the criminal pleaded not guilty; **eine Klage für gegründet —en,** to find a true bill; **erkannt sein für,** to be credited with; **für das Seinige —en,** to own to, recognize as one's own. **—tlich,** *adj.* grateful; discernible. **—tlichkeit,** *f.* readiness to acknowledge (*a favour*); gratitude. **—tnis,** I. *f.* (*pl.* **—tnisse**) knowledge, cognition; perception; acknowledgement; recognizance; **zur —tnis kommen,** to repent; **der Baum der —tnis,** the tree of the knowledge of good and evil. II. *n.* (**—tnisses,** *pl.* **—tnisse**) verdict, sentence, judgment. **—ung,** *f.* recognition; perception; diagnosis (*Med.*); (*carnal*) knowledge. *Comp.* **—tnis=grund,** *m.* criterion by which something is known. **—tnis=vermögen,** *n.* faculty of perception, intellectual power. **—ungs=marke,** *f.* distinctive mark. **—ungs=wort,** *n.* watchword; shibboleth. **—ungs=zeichen,** *n.* countersign, badge (*Mil.*).
Er'ker, *m.* (**—s,** *pl.* **—**) bow (*round*), bay (*angular*); jutting; projection. *Comp.* **—fenster,** *n.* jut(ty)-window, oriel, bow *or* bay-window. **—stube,** *f.,* **—stübchen,** *n.,* **—zimmer,** *n.* projecting room, bow *or* bay-windowed room.
Erkie'sen, *ir.v.a.* to choose, elect, select (*obs.*)

Erklär'—bar, —lich, *adj.* explicable. **—bar=keit,** *f.* explicability.

Erklä'r—en, *v.* I. *a.* to explain; to expound; to define; to account for; to declare; to announce, pronounce; **ich kann mir das nicht —en,** I cannot account for it; **—en für,** to pronounce to be; **in die Acht —en,** to outlaw. II. *r.* to explain oneself; to declare oneself for (*a party*); to make an offer of marriage, to propose; **—e dich deutlicher,** explain yourself more clearly; **daraus —t sich sein Benehmen,** that accounts for his conduct. **—er,** *m.* (**—ers,** *pl.* **—er**) commentator; expounder. **—t,** *p.p.* & *adj.* professed, declared; **deutlich —t,** clearly set forth; **ein —ter Feind,** a open *or* sworn enemy. **—ung,** *f.* declaration; explanation; elucidation; definition; avowal; solution (*Math.*); manifesto; **die letzte —ung eines Gesandten,** ultimatum; **letzwillige —ung,** will. *Comp.* **—ungs=art,** *f.* mode of explanation. **—ungs=schrift,** *f.* commentary. **—ungs=versuch,** *m.* attempted explanation. **—ungs=wissenschaft,** *f.* hermeneutics.

Erkleck'lich, *adj.* & *adv.* sufficient; advantageous, profitable; large, considerable.

Erklet'tern, *v.a.* to attain by climbing; to climb up.

Erklim'mbar, *adj.* climbable, attainable.

Erklim'men, *ir.v.a.* to attain by climbing, to climb up.

Erklin'gen, *ir.v.n.* (*aux.* **ſ.**) to sound; to resound.

Erklü'geln, *v.a.* to invent by subtlety; to ascertain by minute *or* subtle investigation.

Erknal'len, *v.n.* to give a report, to crack forth.

Erko'ren, *adj.* select, chosen. **Die —en,** *pl.* the elect.

Erkra'chen, *v.n.* (*aux.* **h.**) to crash, begin to crash.

Erkran'ken, *v.n.* (*aux.* **ſ.**) to fall sick *or* ill.

Erküh'nen, *v.r.* to make bold, to venture, dare.

Erkun'den, *v.a.* to gain information about; to reconnoitre; to explore.

Erkun'dig—en, *v.r.* to enquire, make enquiries (**bei einem nach einer S.,** of a p., for a th.; **wegen einer S.,** about *or* concerning a th.); **sich —en lassen,** to cause enquiry to be made, to send for information. **—ung,** *f.* enquiry, search; **—ungen einziehen über eine S.,** to collect information on, about a th.

Erkün'stel—n, *v.a.* to pretend, to feign, to affect. **—t,** *p.p.* & *adj.* sham; affected; forced (*of style*); artificial; **das —te** affectation. **—ung,** *f.* pretence, sham; affectation.

Erkü'ren, *ir.v.a.* to choose, elect (*obs.* & *poet.*).

Erla'ben, *v.a.* & *r.* to refresh.

Erlah'men, *v n.* (*aux.* **ſ.**) to become lame, to grow weak, to be worn out.

Erlang'bar, *adj.* & *adv.* attainable.

Erlan'g—en, *v.a.* to reach after and obtain; to attain, acquire; **seinen Zweck —en,** to compass one's ends; **man konnte es von ihm nicht —en, daß,** he could not be induced to; **mit Mühe —t,** hard-earned; **wieder —en,** to rescue, retrieve. **—ung,** *f.* attainment (*of a purpose, etc.*); recovery (*law*).

Erla'ß, *m.* (**—(ſſ)es,** *pl.* **—(ſſ)e**) deduction, abatement; allowance (*C. L.*) remission, pardon; indulgence (*R. C.*); dispensation, exemption; order, edict, decree; **allerhöchster —,** imperial *or* royal decree. *Comp.* **—geld,** *n.* dispensation-money. **—jahr,** *n.* year of jubilee. **—urteil,** *n.* sentence of acquittal.

Erlaſ'ſ—en, *ir.v.a.* to let go, release; to remit; to exempt from; to let off from; to dispense with, from; to publish, issue, proclaim; to abate (*in price*); **eine Schuld —en,** to pardon a debt; (**einem**) **die Strafe —en,** to remit a punishment, pardon an offence; **einen Befehl —,** to give an order; **ein Manifest wurde —en,** a proclamation was issued; **—en Sie mir die Antwort auf diese Frage,** excuse my answering this question; **ich —e sie Ihnen,** I dispense you from it; **das —en,** remission. **—ung,** *f.* remission; dispensation; release; issue, issuing.

Erläß'lich, *adj.* & *adv.* pardonable, remissible, venial; **un—,** indispensable.

Erlau'b—en, *v.a.* (**einem etwas**) to allow, permit; to grant, give permission for; to license; **man —e mir,** let me be permitted, I beg leave; **sich** (*dat.*) **—en,** to indulg oneself (*with*); **ich —e mir,** (permit me to drink) your health! (*coll.*) **wenn Sie —en,** by your leave; **er —t sich Frechheiten,** he takes liberties. **—nis,** *f.* (*pl.* **—ni(ſſ)e**) leave, permission; dispensation; **obrigkeitliche —nis,** license; **mit Ihrer —nis,** with your permission; **mit höherer —nis gedruckt,** printed by authority. **—t,** *p.p.* & *adj.* allowed, *etc.*; allowable; lawful. *Comp.* **—nis=brief,** *m.* license, letters patent. **—nis=schein,** *m.* permit.

Erlau'cht, I. *adj.* illustrious, noble. II. *f.* **Ew.** *or* **Eure —,** Your Highness, Your Lordship, Your Grace.

Erlau'ern, *v.a.* to gain by lying in wait; to watch for; to waylay.

Erlau'schen, *v.a.* to get *or* learn by listening, watching *or* stealthy search; to overhear.

Erläu'ter—n, *v.a.* to explain, to illustrate; **durch Beispiele —n,** to exemplify. **—er,** *m.* commentator. **—ung,** *f.* explanation, illustration, elucidation, comment; **zur —ung,** in illustration of.

Er'le, *f.* (*pl.* **—n**) alder. **—n,** *adj.* (made of) alder.

Erle'b—en, *v.a.* to live to see; to experience; **wir werden nie den Tag —en,** we shall never see the day; **ich habe einen glücklichen Tag —t,** I have had a happy day; **hat einer so etwas je —t?** did any one ever see the like? **viele Auflagen —en,** to go through many editions. **—nis,** *n.* (**—ni(ſſ)es,** *pl.* **—ni(ſſ)e**) experience; occurrence, event; adventure; **widrige —niſſe,** adversities.

Erle'dig—en, *v.a.* to set free, to release, to acquit, discharge (*from, gen. or* **von**); to exempt (*from duty*); to execute (*a commission*); to despatch (*business*); to vacate (*an office*); to decide (*affairs*); to remove (*doubts*); to settle (*differences*). **—t,** *p.p.* & *adj.* settled; despatched; in abeyance (*of a fief*); vacant; **eine —te Stelle,** a vacancy; **die —te Pfründe,** the vacant living. **—ung,** *f.* release; discharge; vacancy; expedition, despatch; settlement; voidance, avoidance (*of benefices*); vacation. *Comp.* **—ungs=schein,** *m.* receipt.

Erle'gen, *v.a.* to defeat; to kill (*in single combat*); to pay, pay down.

Erleich'ter—n, *v.* I. *a.* to ease, lighten; to alleviate, lighten, assuage (*grief, etc.*); to relieve (*breathing, etc.*); to facilitate. II. *r.* to relieve nature; to make oneself easy. **—ung,** *f.* lightening; relief; mitigation; alleviation; facilitation.

Erlei'den, *ir.v.a.* to suffer, endure, undergo.

Er'lenkönig, Erl'könig, *m.* (**—es,** *pl.* **—e**) King of elves, fairy king, erl-king. (**Erlen-** *is a mistake for* **Elfen-** *in translating the word from the original Danish poem.*)

Erlern'bar, *adj.* learnable, that can be learned.

Erler'n—en, *v.a.* to acquire, learn (*by experience, study, etc.*). **—ung,** *f.* acquisition (*of knowledge* or *a language*).

Erle'sen, I. *ir.v.a.* to select, elect, choose. II. *p.p.* & *adj.* select; selected. **—e Mannschaft,** picked men.

Erleuch't—en, *v.a.* to light, illuminate, light up; to enlighten; **die —eten,** the illuminati. **—ung,** *f.* enlightenment; illumination.

Erlie'gen, *ir.v.n.* (*aux.* **h.** & **ſ.,** *dat. or* **unter**) to

succumb, to sink under; **dem Gram —**, to die of grief.
Erli′ſcht (**die Lampe —**), *3 p. sing. pres. ind. of* [1]**erlöſchen.**
Erliſ′ten, *v.a.* to obtain by artifice.
Erl′könig, *m., see* **Erlenkönig.**
Erlo′gen, *p.p.* (*of* **Erlügen**) *& adj.* invented by lying, false.
Erlö′s, *m.* (—(ſ)es) proceeds (*of a sale*).
Erlö′ſ—en, *v.a.* to ransom, free, deliver; to rescue; to redeem; to get (*as proceeds from a sale*). **—er,** *m.* (**—ers,** *pl.* **—er**) redeemer, deliverer; Saviour. **—ung,** *f.* release; redemption; deliverance, salvation, redemption.
[1]**Erlö′ſch—en,** *ir.v.n.* (*aux.* **ſ.**) to become effaced *or* obliterated; to be extinguished, go out; to die out; to expire (*of a lease*); to go out of use (*of a custom*). **—ung,** *f.* expiration.
[2]**Erlö′ſch—en,** *v.a.* (*aux.* **h.**) to cause to be extinguished, to extinguish, to put out. **—ung,** *f.* extinction.
Erlo′ſchen, (**das Licht iſt—**) *p.p.* (*of* [1]**erlöſchen**) *& adj.* extinguished; extinct, dead; obliterated (*handwriting*), dull, lifeless, dim (*eyes*); **bei ihm iſt alle Scham —,** he is dead to all sense of shame.
Erlo′ſen, *v.a.* to get *or* obtain by lot.
Erlü′gen, *ir.v.a.* to invent (*a lie*); to fabricate.
Erluſ′tig—en, *v.r.* to amuse oneself. **—ung,** *f.* diversion, amusement.
Ermäch′tig—en, *v.* I. *a.* to empower, authorize. II. *r.* **ſich einer Sache —en,** to seize, usurp a th. (*obs.*). **—ung,** *f.* authorization, warrant.
Ermah′n—en, *v.a.* to admonish, exhort, warn, remind. **—end,** *p. & adj.* hortatory. **—ung,** *f.* admonition, exhortation.
Erman′gel—n, *v.n.* (*aux.* **h.**) to fail, want, be deficient *or* wanting (**an einer S.,** in a th.) to lack, be in want of; **es an nichts —n laſſen,** to do one's utmost, spare no pains; **wir alle —n der** (*gen.*) **Pflichterfüllung,** we all fall short in doing our duty (*obs.*); **ich werde nicht —n zu,** I shall not fail to. **—ung,** *f.* want, deficiency, default, failure; **in —ung der Zahlung,** in default of payment; **in —ung eines Beſſeren,** faute de mieux; **in —ung deſſen,** in default whereof, for want of which. *Comp.* **—ungs=klage,** *f.* cessavit (*Law*).
Erman′nen, *v.r.* to take courage.
Ermä′ßig—en, *v.a.* to limit, abate, lessen; to moderate; to reduce (*prices*). **—ung,** *f.* limitation; moderation; reduction.
Ermat′t—en, *v.* I. *a.* to weary, to weaken. II. *n.* (*aux.* **ſ.**) to faint, grow weary; to fade (*of colours*). **—ung,** *f.* exhaustion, lassitude.
Er′mel, *m.* (**—s,** *pl.* **—**) sleeve (*usually* **Ärmel**).
Ermeſ′ſ—en, I. *ir.v.a.* to measure; to weigh, consider, judge, examine; to estimate; to imagine; to infer, conclude. II. *subst.n.* judgment, estimation, opinion; **meines —ens, nach meinem —en,** in my opinion; **nach beſtem —en,** to the best of my knowledge. **—(ß)lich,** *adj. & adv.* measurable; conceivable.
Ermit′tel—n, *v.a.* to ascertain, to find out; **zu —n,** ascertainable. **—ung,** *f.* inquiry, research.
Ermög′lichen, *v.a.* to render possible *or* feasible.
Ermor′d—en, *v.a.* to murder; to assassinate. **—ung,** *f.* murder, assassination.
Ermü′d—en, *v.* I. *a.* to fatigue, tire out, weary; to wear out, jade, knock up; **leicht zu —en,** easily tired; **um Sie nicht zu —en,** not to be irksome to you. II. *n.* (*aux.* **ſ.**) to be tired, grow weary. **—end,** *p. & adj.* tiring, wearisome, irksome. **—lich,** *adj.* liable to grow weary. **—ung,** *f.* fatigue, weariness.
Ermun′ter—n, *v.a.* to awake, rouse (*from sleep*); to stir up, incite, encourage: to exhort; to cheer up, enliven. **—ung,** *f.* encouragement, enlivenment.
Ermu′tig—en, *v.* I. *a.* to animate, encourage; to inspirit; incite. II. *r.* to take courage. **—igung,** *f.* encouragement.
Ernäh′r—en, *v.* I. *a.* to nourish, feed; to support, maintain. II. *r.* to earn one's livelihood; to subsist on; **ſich von einem —en laſſen,** to depend on some one for support. **—end,** *p. & adj.* nutritive. **—er,** *m.* (**—ers,** *pl.* **—er**) nourisher, fosterer, bread-winner, supporter. **—ung,** *f.* nourishing, sustaining; support, maintenance, nutrition; **ſchlechte —ung,** malnutrition. *Comp.* **—ungs=kunde,** *f.* dietetics.
Erna′nnt, *p.p. see* **Ernennen**; **der —e,** the nominee, the person appointed.
Ernen′n—en, *ir.v.a.* to nominate, appoint; to designate; **einen zum Herzog** 2c. **—en,** to create one a duke *etc.*; **Geſchworene —en,** to impanel a jury; **der —ende,** nominator; **der Ernannte,** nominee. **—er,** *m.* (**—ers,** *pl.* **—er**) nominator. **—ung,** *f.* nomination, appointment; designation. *Comp.* **—ungs=brief,** *m.*, **—ungs=urkunde,** *f.* commission. **—ungs=recht,** *n.* patronage (*of a living*), nomination.
Erneu′—en, *usually* **Erneu′—ern,** *v.* I. *a.* to renew, renovate, repair; to restore; to revive; to recommence; **die Societät —e(r)n,** to renew the partnership; **zu —e(r)n,** renewable. II. *r.* to recommence; to be re-enacted, revived. **—(e)rer,** *m.* (**—erers,** *pl.* **—erer**) renewer. **—(er)ung,** *f.* renewal; renovation; revival.
Ernie′drig—en, (**Ernie′dern** *obs. & poet.*,) *v.a.* to lower, bring low; to humble, degrade, humiliate. **—ung,** *f.* lowering; humiliation, degradation, abasement. *Comp.* **—ungs=zeichen,** *n.* flat (♭), sign of depression (*Mus.*).
Ernſt, I. *m.* (**—es**) earnest, earnestness, seriousness, gravity; assiduity; severity, sternness; **iſt es Ihr —? iſt es Ihnen — damit?** are you in earnest? **in allem —e,** in downright earnest; **das iſt nicht Ihr —?** you don't mean that? surely you are joking? **aus einem Spaß — machen,** to take a joke in earnest; **jetzt wird es —,** this means work, now matters are getting serious. II. *adj. & adv.* earnest; serious, grave, sober; stern. **—haft,** *a. see* **Ernſt** II. **—haftigkeit,** *f.* earnestness; gravity; severity, sternness. **—lich,** *adj. & adv.* earnest; in earnest; fervent, ardent; eager, intent; forcible; **einem etwas —lich verbieten,** to forbid positively. **—lichkeit,** *f. see* **—haftigkeit.**
Ern′te, (*obs. spelling:* **Ernd′te,**) *f.* (*pl.* **—n**) harvest, crops. *Comp.* **—dankfeſt,** *n.* harvest thanksgiving (festival). **—dienſt,** *m.*, **—frohne,** *f.* harvest-labour rendered to the lord of the manor. **—feſt,** *n.* harvest-home; harvest-thanksgiving. **—göttin,** *f.* Ceres. **—monat,** *m.* harvest-month, August. **—reif,** *adj.* fit for the sickle. **—wetter,** *n.* good harvest-weather. **—zeit,** *f.* harvest-time.
Ern′t—en, *v.a.* to harvest, gather in; to reap. **—er,** *m.* (**—ers,** *pl.* **—er**) harvester, reaper.
Ernüch′tern, *v.* I. *a.* to sober; to disenchant. II. *r.* to become sober; to be disenchanted.
Ero′berer, *m.* (**—s,** *pl.* **—**) conqueror.
Ero′ber—n, *v.a.* to conquer; to overcome, gain by force of arms; to win, captivate (*hearts, etc.*); **nicht zu —n,** impregnable. **—ung,** *f.* conquest, acquisition (*by conquest*). *Comp.* **—ungs=ſüchtig,** *adj.* desirous of conquest; **ein —ungsſüchtiges Mädchen,** a coquettish girl, a flirt.
Eröff′n—en, *v.* I. *a.* to open, unclose; to inaugurate; to disclose, reveal; to declare; to notify; to publish (*a sentence*); to open (*a ball; a campaign; an account, etc.*); **ſie —eten ein heftiges Feuer,** they opened a heavy fire. II. *r.* to open; to open (*one's mind, etc.*); to offer,

present itself (*as an opportunity*). **—end,** *p. & adj.* opening, aperient. **—ung,** *f.* opening; disclosure, communication; beginning; overture. *Comp.* **—ungs=rede,** *f.* prologue; opening speech. **—ungs=stück,** *n.* overture (*Mus.*).

Erör'ter—n, *v.a.* to take point by point, to discuss fully *or* in detail; to debate; to settle (*by discussion*); **die Sache läßt sich —n,** the subject is open to discussion. **—ung,** *f.* discussion, debate; **auf eine —ung eingehen,** to enter into a (minute) discussion.

Ero'tisch, *adj.* erotic; **—es Gedicht,** amorous poem.

Erpaſ'ſen, *v.a.* to watch for a favourable opportunity and to take it.

Er'pel, *m.* (**—s,** *pl.* **—**) drake (*obs. & dial.*)

Erpi'cht, *adj.* (**auf eine S.**) intent, bent (*on*); eager (*for*); passionately attached (*to*); greedy (*after*).

Erpo'chen, *v.n.* to rouse by knocking; to get by force *or* obstinacy.

Erpreſ'ſ—en, *v.a.* to press out; to extort, exact; to distrain (*Law*). **—er,** *m.* (**—ers,** *pl.* **—er**) extortioner. **—eriſch,** *adj.* extortionate. **—ung,** *f.* extortion; exaction; **—ungen aus üben,** to practise extortion. *Comp.* **—ungs=verſuch,** *m.* attempt at extortion, blackmailing

Erpro'b—en, *v.a.* to try, prove. **—t,** *p.p. & adj* tried, approved.

Erqui'ck—en, *v.a.* to revive, refresh; to give vigour, strength to; to regale. **—end,** *p. & adj.* refreshing. **—lich,** *adj.* refreshing, reviving. **—ung,** *f.* refreshment, comfort; **zur —ung dienend,** recreative. *Comp.* **—ungs=stunde,** *f.* recreation hour.

Erraf'fen, *v.a.* to obtain (*riches*) by snatching, to amass.

Errat'bar, *adj. & adv.* conjecturable, guessable.

Erra't—en, *ir.v.a.* to guess, divine, find out by conjecture; to solve (*a riddle*); **ich —e es nicht, auf das —en verzichte ich,** I give it up. **—ung,** *f.* divining, guessing.

Erra'tiſch, *adj.* erratic.

Erreg'bar, *adj.* excitable; sensitive; irritable. **—keit,** *f.* excitability; irritability.

Erre'g—en, *v.a.* to excite, stir up, agitate; to provoke; to promote, cause; to inspire (*fear, etc.*). **—end,** *p. & adj.* exciting; **—endes Moment,** starting point of the plot *or* dramatic action. **—er,** *m.* (**—ers,** *pl.* **—er**) agitator. **—t,** *p.p. & adj.* excited; **leicht —t,** irritable, touchy. **—theit,** *f.* agitation; irritability; animation. **—ung,** *f.* stirring up; excitement. *Comp.* **—ungs=mittel,** *n.* stimulant.

Erreich'bar, *adj.* attainable, get-at-able, within reach.

Errei'ch—en, *v.a.* to reach; to attain, arrive at (*a purpose, an end, etc.*); to obtain, gain; to fetch (*a price*). **—ung,** *f.* reaching, arriving at; attainment.

Errei'ten, *ir.v.a.* to overtake riding; to gain *or* reach by riding.

Errett'bar, *adj.* saveable.

Erret't—en, *v.a.* to save, deliver, rescue. **—er,** *m.* (**—ers,** *pl.* **—er**) deliverer; saviour. **—ung,** *f.* rescue, deliverance.

Errich't—en, *v.a.* to set upright; to erect, raise (*a perpendicular, a house, etc.*); to throw up (*barricades*); to establish, set up (*a government*); to found (*an institution*); **einen Bund —en,** to make an alliance *or* a confederation; **ein Testament —en,** to draw up a will. **—ung,** *f.* erection; establishment; drawing up (*of a will*).

Errin'gen, *ir.v.a.* to win, obtain by struggling, wrestling *or* exertion.

Errö't—en, I. *v.n.* (*aux.* **ſ.**) to redden; to colour up, blush; **—en machen,** to put to the blush. II. *n.subst.* **—ung,** *f.* reddening, colouring up; blush.

Erru'fen, *ir.v.a.* to reach by calling; to evoke, call up (*obs.*); **man kann ihn —,** he is within call.

Errun'genſchaft, *f.* (*pl.* **—en**) acquisition, gain; **die großartigen —en der Neuzeit,** the grand achievements of modern times.

Erſät't—igen, *v.a.* to sate, satiate; to satisfy. **—igung,** *f.* sating, satiating; satisfying. **—lich,** *adj. & adv.* satiable, that can be satisfied.

Erſa'tz, *m.* (**—es**) amends, compensation, damages, reparation; set off, equivalent; substitution; **zum — für,** by way of amends for, in exchange for; **einem — geben,** to indemnify one; **— leiſten,** to make amends. *Comp.* **—dehnung,** *f., or* **—länge,** *f.* compensatory vowel-lengthening. **—erbe,** *m.* substitute. **—kommiſſion,** *f.* recruiting commission, commission managing the reserve. **—leiſtung,** *f.* indemnification, reimbursement. **—mann,** *m.* substitute; deputy. **—mannſchaft,** *f.* reserve(s); recruits. **—mittel,** *n.* surrogate; supply, substitute, makeshift. **—pflicht,** *f.* liability to repair, responsibility. **—pflichtig,** *adj.* liable to repair *or* to pay damages, responsible. **—reſerve,** *f.* army reserve. **—reſerviſt,** *m.* a man of the army reserve. **—ſchauſpieler,** *m.* double, understudy. **—ſtück,** *n.* spare thing, duplicate. **—truppen,** *pl.* reserve forces. **—wahl,** *f.* election of a substitute; complementary election; by-election (*Parl.*).

Erſau'fen, *ir.v.n.* (*aux.* **ſ.**) to be drowned.

Erſäu'fen, *v.a.* to drown.

Erſcha'chern, *v.a.* to gain by haggling.

Erſchaf'f—en, *ir.v.a.* to produce, create; **der —ene,** created being. **—er,** *m.* (**—ers,** *pl.* **—er**) creator. **—ung,** *f.* creation.

Erſchal'len, *reg. & ir.v.n.* (*aux.* **ſ.**) to resound, ring; **— laſſen,** to sound *or* spread abroad; to sound, let hear; **es erſcholl ein Gerücht,** a report spread.

Erſchau'dern, Erſchau'ern, *v.n.* (*aux.* **ſ.**) to shudder, be seized *or* thrilled with horror.

Erſchau'en, *v.a.* to see, behold (*obs. & poet.*)

Erſchei'n—en, I. *ir.v.n.* (*aux.* **ſ.**) to shine forth; to appear; to come out (*as a book*); to be clear *or* evident; **—en laſſen,** to show; **ſoeben erſchienen,** just published. II. *subst.n.* appearance; presentation (*at court*). **—ung,** *f.* appearance; apparition, vision (*of spirits*); phenomenon; show; **äußere —ung,** outward appearance, aspect, look, physiognomy, mien; bearing; presence; **das Feſt der —ung Chriſti,** Epiphany; **eine glänzende —ung ſein,** to make a splendid appearance, to cut a fine figure. *Comp.* **—ungs=form,** *f.* outward shape *or* form; species. **—ungs=tag,** *m.* day of issue *or* emission (*C.L.*). **—ungs=welt,** *f.* physical world. **—ungs=zauberei,** *f.* phantasmagoria.

Erſchie'ßen, *ir.v.a.* to shoot; to kill by shooting, to shoot dead; **er hat ſich erſchoſſen,** he has shot himself, he has blown out his brains.

Erſchlaf'f—en, *v.* I. *n.* (*aux.* **ſ.**) to grow slack, slacken; to relax, languish, flag; **die Kräfte —en machen,** to prostrate the strength. II. *a.* to enervate, relax; **—ende Mittel,** *pl.* emollients. **—ung,** *f.* slackening, relaxation; flagging; atony; debility, enervation; effeminacy; **bis zur —ung,** to the uttermost (*sl.*).

Erſchla'gen, *ir.v.a.* to slay, to strike dead.

Erſchlei'chen, *ir.v.a.* to obtain by sneaking *or* surreptitiously; to creep into; to steal upon; **erſchlichen,** surreptitious, gained by sneaking; **erſchlichener Weiſe, erſchlichenerweiſe,** surreptitiously, by tricks, in an underhand way.

Erſchlie'ßbar, *adj. & adv.* that may be opened, disclosed *or* inferred.

Erſchlie'ß—en, *ir.v.a.* to open, unlock, disclose; to conclude, infer. **—ung,** *f.* opening out.

Erſchlu'g, Erſchlü'ge, *impf. ind. & subj.* of **erſchlagen.**

Erschmei'cheln, *v.a.* to obtain by flattery, to wheedle out of.
Erschnap'pen, *v.a.* to catch, snap up.
Erscho'll, Erschöl'le; Erschol'len, *impf. indic. & subj.; p.p. of* **erschallen.**
Erschöpf'bar, *adj.* exhaustible.
Erschöp'f—en, *v.a.* to drain; to exhaust. **—end,** *p. & adj.* exhaustive; exhausting. **—lich,** *see* **Erschöpfbar. —t,** *p.p.& adj.* spent, exhausted, done up; **(ein) —tes Stück Land,** worked-out land. **—theit,** *f.* state of exhaustion, collapse. **—ung,** *f.* exhaustion.
Erschra'k, Erschrä'ke, *impf. ind. & subj. of* [1]**erschrecken.**
[1]**Erschre'ck—en,** *ir.v.n.* (*aux.* **s.**) to be alarmed *or* startled (**über eine S.,** at, by a th.); to start (**vor,** at); **—en Sie nicht!** don't be frightened! **—lich,** *adj. & adv.* terrific, terrible, dreadful.
[2]**Erschre'ck—en,** *v.a.* to cause to be alarmed, to terrify, startle, frighten; **sich —en,** to start, to take fright. **—end,** *p. & adj.* alarming.
Erschrei'ben, *ir.v.a.* to acquire *or* get by writing.
Erschri'ckst, Erschri'ckt, *2d & 3d ps. sing. pres. ind. of* [1]**erschrecken.**
Erschro'cken, *p.p. & adj. see* [1]**erschrecken. —heit,** *f.* fright, fear, terror.
Erschüt'ter—n, *v.* I. *a.* to shake vehemently, convulse; to stagger, cause to waver; to move, affect deeply *or* strongly. II. *n.* (*aux.* **s.**) to shake, quake. **—ung,** *f.* shaking, shock, concussion; convulsion; strong emotion.
Erschwel'len, *ir.v.a.* (*aux.* **s.**) to swell up, be inflated; to expand, be expanded; to protrude, bulge out.
Erschwe'ren, *v.a.* to render more difficult; to aggravate (*guilt, etc.*); to increase (*a burden*).
Erschwim'men, *ir.v.a.* to reach by swimming.
Erschwin'g—en, *ir.v.a.* to reach by soaring; to attain with difficulty *or* the utmost exertion; to manage, to afford, to raise, procure; to pay. **—lich,** *adj.* attainable.
Erse'hen, *ir.v.a.* to descry; to see, perceive; to observe; to learn; to distinguish; to watch for, avail oneself of; **sich** (*dat.*) **etwas —,** to choose, select something for oneself; **hieraus ist zu —,** from this it appears.
Erseh'nen, *v.a.* to long for, desire greatly.
Ersetz'bar, *adj.* reparable; **nicht —,** irreparable.
Erset'z—en, *v.a.* to repair, compensate, make amends for; to retrieve, make good; to reimburse, repay; to indemnify; to restore, re-establish, recruit (*one's forces*); to supply (*one's place*); **sich —en lassen,** to be (able to be) replaced; to find a substitute; **er —t ihn nicht,** he does not fill his place, is not equal to him (*his predecessor*); **etwas —t erhalten,** to recover damages. **—lich,** *adj. & adv.* reparable, retrievable; replaceable. **—ung,** *f.* indemnification, reimbursement; *see* **Ersatz.**
Erseuf'zen, *v.* I. *a.* to obtain by sighing; to sigh after. II. *n.* (*aux.* **h.**) to heave a sigh, to sigh.
Ersicht'lich, *adj.* evident, perceptible, manifest; **hieraus ist —,** by this it appears.
Ersin'gen, *ir.v.a.* to get by singing.
Ersin'n—en, *ir.v.a.* to think out, to excogitate; to devise, to invent; to imagine; to strike out (*a plan*). **ersonnen,** *p.p. & adj.* devised, invented, fabricated. **—lich,** *adj.* imaginable; **auf alle —liche Weise,** in every imaginable *or* possible way.
Ersit'z—en, *ir.v.a.* to acquire by prescription; to gain (*a certificate, etc.*) by passing a certain time in a class without really qualifying by the work done; **sich** (*dat.*) **etwas —en,** to get (*a disease, etc.*) by sedentary habits. **—ung,** *f.* acquirement of property by having possessed and enjoyed it for a term of years.
Erspä'hen, *v.a.* to espy, descry.
Erspa'r—en, *v.a.* to save; to spare. **—nis,** *f.* (*pl.* **—ni(ss)e**), *n.* (**—ni(ss)es,** *pl.* **—ni(ss)e**) savings.
Erspie'len, *v.a.* (**sich** (*dat.*) **etwas**) to gain by playing.
Erspin'nen, *ir.v.a.* (**sich** (*dat.*) **etwas**) to earn, gain by spinning.
Ersprie'ß—en, *ir.v.n.* (*aux.* **s.**) to shoot up, to rise from; to profit, be of use. **—lich,** I. *adj.* useful, profitable; salutary. II. *adv.* advantageously. **—lichkeit,** *f.* usefulness, profit.
E'rst, I. *adj.* (*sup. of* **eher,** *for* **eherst, ehrest,** first (*in number*); first, foremost, prime, leading, superior; **der, die, das —e beste,** the first that comes; **zum —en, fürs —e,** in the first place; at first, during the first time, for some time; **das —e Buch Moses,** Genesis; **das ist das —e, was ich höre,** this is the first I have heard of the story; **mit —er Gelegenheit,** by the first opportunity; **—e Hand,** first hand (*C. L.*); **die —e Kirche,** the primitive church; **zum —en! zweiten! dritten!** going! going! gone! **—er Commis,** head clerk; **die —e Klasse,** the top form (*of a school*), the sixth form; **—e Qualität,** prime quality. II. *adv.* firstly; at first; for the first time; not till; only; but just; **es wurde — heute fertig,** it was only ready to-day; **— als,** only when; **dann —,** not till then; **es muß sich — noch zeigen,** it remains to be seen; **das macht's — recht schlimm,** that makes it all the worse; **nun — recht,** now more than ever; **— recht nicht,** much less still; **wenn so etwas verboten ist, geschieht es — recht,** if such a thing is forbidden, it is done all the more; **er wird es — morgen erfahren,** he will not hear of it till to-morrow; **wer — kommt, mahlt —,** first come, first served; **wäre ich nur — da!** if I were only (*or* but) there. **—ens,** *adv.* firstly, in the first place. **—er, (der, die, das —e,) —erer, —ere, —eres,** *adj. & adv* former; **mit —er Post,** by return of post; **er ist der —e seiner Klasse,** he is the top boy of his form; **er ist der —e der ganzen Schule,** he is the head boy of the school. **—lich,** *adv.* firstly, first. **—ling,** *m.* (**—lings,** *pl.* **—linge**) first-born; (*pl.*) first fruits. *Comp.* **—geboren,** *adj.* first-born. **—geburt,** *f.* primogeniture. **—geburts=recht,** *n.* the right of the first-born; **Esau verkaufte sein —geburtsrecht,** Esau sold his birthright. **—genannt,** *adj.* first named. **—malig,** *adj.* occurring for the first time.
Erstar'ken, *v.n.* (*aux.* **s.**) to grow strong *or* stronger.
Erstar'r—en, *v.* I. *n.* (*aux.* **s.**) to be benumbed; to grow stiff (*with cold*); to become torpid; to become motionless (*with fright*). II. *a.* to stiffen; to freeze, chill. III. *subst. n.* torpidity. **—t,** *p.p. & adj.* benumbed, torpid. **—ung,** *f.* torpidity, numbness, stiffness; chill.
Erstat't—en, *v.a.* to compensate, restore, make good; replace; **Bericht —en,** to report, render an account; **wieder —en,** to restore, to reimburse. **—lich,** *adj.* retrievable. **—ung,** *f.* refunding; compensation, restitution; delivery (*of a report*).
Erstau'n—en, I. *v.n.* (*aux.* **s.**) to be astonished (**über eine S.,** at a th.). II. *subst.n.* astonishment, amazement, surprise; **höchstes —en,** stupefaction; **in —en setzen,** to astonish, amaze; **zum —en,** astonishing(ly). **—end,** *p. & adj.* astonishing. **—lich,** *adj. & adv.* astonishing, amazing, marvellous; **das —liche bei der Sache,** the marvel of the matter. **—lichkeit,** *f.* wonderfulness; stupendousness. *Comp.* **—ens=wert, —ens=würdig,** *adj. see* **—lich.**
Erste'chen, *ir.v.a.* to stab, to run through, pierce.
Erste'h—en, *ir.v.* I. *n.* (*aux.* **s.**) to arise, rise; to originate; to be renewed. II. *a.* to buy, to purchase (*usually, at an auction*); to go through; suffer, endure; **wieder —en,** to buy in. **—ung,** *f.* resurrection; buying; renewal.

Ersteig'—bar, —lich, *adj. & adv.* accessible; that may be scaled.

Erstei'g—en, *ir.v.a.* to ascend, climb, mount; **mit Leitern —en,** to scale. **—ung,** *f.* scaling, climbing; escalade (*Mil.*).

Erster'ben, *ir.v.n.* (*aux.* **s.**) to die, die away; to become extinct; to fade; **erstorbene Glieder,** benumbed limbs; **ich ersterbe Ihr . . . ,** I remain ever your most devoted . . . (*obs.*).

Ersti'ck—en, I. *v.a.* to stifle, suffocate, smother; to suppress; **im Keime —t,** nipped in the bud. II. *v.n.* (*aux.* **s.**) to choke, be choked. III. *subst. n.*, **—ung,** *f.* suffocation, stifling; **heiß zum —en,** stifling hot; **zum —en voll,** crammed to suffocation. *Comp.* **-ungs=tod,** *m.* death from suffocation.

Erstin'ken, *ir.v.n.* (*aux.* **s.**) to become bad, stink-ing; **es ist erstunken und erlogen,** it is a shameless lie (*vulg.*).

Erstor'benheit, *f.* deadness, benumbedness (*of limbs*).

Erstre'b—en, *v.a.* to strive for *or* after; to obtain by endeavour. **—ung,** *f.* pursuit (*of an object*); the act of aspiring.

Erstre'ck—en, *v.* I. *a.* to extend (**auf, bis auf** *with acc.*, **bis zu ꝛc.**). II. *r.* to extend, stretch, run, reach; **die Summe —t sich auf,** the sum amounts to; **sich gleichweit —en,** to co-extend. **—ung,** *f.* prolongation (*of a term*); extension; extent.

Erstrei'ten, *ir.v.a.* to obtain by fighting.

Erstür'men, *v.a.* to take by storm *or* assault.

Ersu'ch—en, I. *v.a.* to beseech, implore, entreat, supplicate (**um,** for); to request, beg. II. *subst. n.* entreaty, solicitation; suit; **auf das —en des Bruders,** at the request of the brother; **auf sein wiederholtes —en,** on his repeated entreaties. **—ung,** *f.* petition. *Comp.* **—ungs=schreiben,** *n.* (written) petition.

Ertan'zen, *v.a. & r.* to gain by dancing.

Ertap'pen, *v.a.* to catch, seize; to detect; to surprise; **auf frischer That —,** to take in the very act; **(einen) auf einer Lüge —,** to detect in a lie.

Ertau'schen, *v.a.* to get by exchange.

Ertei'l—en, *v.a.* (**einem etwas**) to impart, give; to confer, bestow; **Nachricht —en,** to send word, to inform; **ein Amt —en,** to bestow an office; **Rat —en,** to give advice; **Unterricht —en,** to teach, give instruction. **—er,** *m.* (**—ers,** *pl.* **—er**) bestower; **—er der priesterlichen Weihe,** ordaining priest, bishop *or* minister. **—ung,** *f.* bestowal; publication (*of an order*).

Ertö'ten, *v.a.* to kill; to deaden; to mortify (*the flesh*).

Ertö'nen, *v.n.* (*aux.* **s.**) to resound; **— lassen,** to cause to resound; to sound; to raise (*the voice*).

Erto'sen, *v.n.* to roar; to begin to roar.

Ertra'g, *m.* (**—es,** *pl.* **Erträ'ge**) produce; proceeds; profit; revenue; **reiner —** *or* **Rein—,** net profit. *Comp.* **—los,** *adj.* unproductive. **—(s)=fähigkeit,** *f.* productiveness.

Ertra'g—en, *ir.v.a.* to bear, suffer, tolerate, endure; to put up with; **dies will ich nicht länger —en,** I'll stand *or* bear this no longer. **—ung,** *f.* bearing; endurance; forbearance.

Erträg'lich, *adj.* supportable; tolerable; endurable; middling. **—keit,** *f.* bearableness, tolerableness; mediocrity.

Erträn'k—en, *v.a.* to drown. **—ung,** *f.* drowning.

Erträu'men, *v.a.* to dream. **erträumt,** *p.p. & adj.* imaginary, chimerical.

Ertrin'ken, *ir.v.n.* (*aux.* **s.**) to drown, be drowned; **der, die Ertrunkene,** one drowned.

Ertro'tzen, *v.a.* (**von einem etwas**) to obtain by insolence, obstinacy *or* defiance.

Erü'brig—en, *v.* I. *a.* to save, lay by. II. *n.* (*aux.* **h.**) to remain over, be left; **es —t mir nur noch die Bemerkung,** I have only to add. **—t,** *p.p. & adj.* saved; **sein —tes,** his savings. **—ung,** *f.* saving.

Er've, *f.* (*pl.* **—n**) bitter vetch.

Erwa'chen, I. *v.n.* (*aux.* **s.**) to awake; to dawn. II. *subst. n.* awakening.

Erwach'sen, I. *ir.v.n.* (*aux.* **s.**) to grow (**aus,** out of, from); to grow up; to spring, proceed (**aus,** from); to accrue; **der daraus —de Vorteil,** the profit accruing therefrom. II. *p.p. & adj.* grown up; **der, die —e,** adult.

Erwä'g—en, *ir.v.a.* to weigh, ponder; to consider; to discuss; **ich will es —en,** I will think it over; **alles wohl erwogen,** on mature consideration. **—ung,** *f.* consideration; deliberation; **in —ung ziehen,** to take into consideration; **in —ung dessen,** with regard to this.

Erwäh'len, *v.a.* to choose, to elect; **ins Parlament —,** to return to parliament.

Erwäh'n—en, *v.a.* (*& n.* (*aux.* **h.**; *with acc. &* (*obsol.*) *gen.*) to mention, make mention of; to call to notice; **es möge hinreichen zu —en,** suffice it to say; **noch ist zu —en,** it remains to be noticed; **oben —t,** above-mentioned. **—ung,** *f.* mention; **einer Sache —ung thun,** to mention a thing; **bei —ung,** at the mention (*of*).

Erwar'men, *v.n.* (*aux.* **s.**) to become warm, to warm up.

Erwär'm—en, *v.a.* to make warm, to heat. **—ung,** *f.* warming, heating.

Erwar't—en, *v.a.* to look for, expect; to await; **das läßt sich kaum —en,** that is scarcely to be expected. **—et,** *p.p. & adj.* expected. **—ung,** *f.* expectation; anticipation. *Comp.* **—ungs=voll,** *adj.* expectant, full of expectation.

Erwe'ck—en, *v.a.* to rouse, awaken; to stir up; **vom Tode —en,** to resuscitate, to raise (from the dead); **vom Schlafe —en,** to rouse (from sleep); **er —te bei ihnen den Glauben,** he caused them to believe. **—lich,** *adj. & adv.* awakening; enlivening; edifying; exciting devotion. **—ung,** *f.* awaking; resuscitation; incitation; rousing, revival (*religious*). *Comp.* **—(ungs)=mittel,** *n.* incentive. **—ungs=prediger,** *m.* revivalist. **—ungs=wort,** *n.* word of revival.

Erweh'ren, *v.r.* (*gen.*) to guard, defend oneself from; to resist, to forbear; **ich konnte mich des Lachens nicht —,** I could not help laughing; **sie konnte sich der Thränen kaum —,** she could scarcely restrain her tears.

Erweich'bar, *adj. & adv.* that may be softened.

Erwei'ch—en, *v.a.* to soften, to soak; to mollify; to remove, touch. **—end,** *p. & adj.* softening, emollient. **—ung,** *f.* softening, mollification. *Comp.* **—ungs=mittel,** *n.* emollient (*Med.*).

Erwei's, *m.* (**—(s)es,** *pl.* **—(s)e**) proof, demonstration. **—(s)en,** *ir.v.a.* to prove; **einem —(s)en,** to show, pay, render (*mercy, honour, favour, etc.*) to one; **er erwies sich als einen tüchtigen** (*also:* **als ein tüchtiger**) **Geschäftsmann,** he proved himself to be an excellent man of business; **es ist nichts erwiesen,** nothing is proved, not proven (*Scotch law*); **—(s)en Sie mir diesen Dienst,** do me this service; **das Gerücht erwies sich als falsch,** the report turned out to be false. **erwiesen,** *p.p. & adj.* proved, certain; **erwiesenermaßen,** as has been proved. **—lich,** *adj. & adv.* demonstrable, provable. **—lichermaßen,** *adv.* evidently. **—(s)ung,** *f.* showing, proving.

Erwei'terer, *m.* (**—s,** *pl.* **—**) extender, enlarger.

Erwei'ter—n, *v.a.* to make wider; to expand, enlarge, extend; to dilate; to amplify; **sich —n,** to grow larger, to widen, expand, be extended, enlarged. **—ung,** *f.* enlargement, extension; amplification; aggrandizement; dilatation (*Med.*); **die —ung der Adern,** aneurism.

Erwe'rb, *m.* (—es) acquisition, gain; earnings; industry, business (*by which a livelihood is gained*).

Erwer'b—en, *ir.v.a.* to gain, obtain, acquire; to earn; to win. **—er**, *m.*(—ers, *pl.* —er) acquirer. **—nis**, *n.* (—ni(ss)es, *pl.* —ni(ss)e) acquisition, gain; earnings. **—sam**, *adj. & adv.* industrious. **—samkeit**, *f.* diligence (*in earning*), industry. **—ung**, *f.* acquisition, gain; acquiring. *Comp.* **—los**, *adj.* unprofitable; hard (*times*). **—s=fähig**, *adj.* capable of earning one's living. **—s=mittel**, *n.*, **—s=quelle**, *f.* means of living, source of industry. **—(s)=schule**, *f.* industrial school. **—(s)=sinn**, *m.* acquisitiveness, disposition for business. **—s=stand**, *m.* productive class. **—s=zweig**, *m.* branch of industry, line of business.

Erwi'der—n, *v.a.* to return, render in return; to requite; to repay; to retaliate; to reply; **gegenseitig —n**, to give back in return; **—n auf eine S.**, to rejoin, reply, retort in answer to. **—ung**, *f.* return; retaliation; reply, answer. *Comp.* **—ungs=schrift**, *f.* rejoinder (*Law*).

Erwir'ken, *v.a.* to bring about, effect, work out; **einem etwas —**, to procure s.th. for s.o.

Erwi'schen, *v.a.* to catch; to surprise.

Erwit'tern, *v.a.* to scent out; to spy out.

Erwo'g, Erwö'ge; Erwo'gen, *impf. ind. & subj.; p.p.* of **erwägen**.

Erwor'ben, *p.p. & adj. see* **Erwerben; sauer —**, hard got, hard earned; **mit Unrecht —**, ill-gotten; **das —e**, acquisition, perquisite (*Law*).

Erwüh'len, *v.r.* to burst open, burst forth, to be heaving up (*poet.*).

Erwün'sch—en, *v.a.* to wish for, desire. **—t**, *p.p. adj. & adv.* desired; desirable; apropos; **das ist mir sehr —t**, that suits me capitally; **die —te Wirkung**, the desired effect.

Erwür'feln, *v.a.* to win at dice.

Erwür'g—en, *v.* I. *a.* to strangle, choke, throttle; to slaughter; (*poet.*) to kill, to put to death. II. *n.* (*aux.* **s.**) to choke, be suffocated. **—er**, *m.* (—ers, *pl.* —er) strangler. **—ung**, *f.* strangling; strangulation; slaughter.

Erz, *n.* (—es, *pl.* —e) ore; metal; brass, bronze. **—en**, *adj.* brazen. *Comp.* **—abgabe**, *f.* lot, claim (*Min.*). **—ader**, *f.* vein of ore. **—ähnlich**, *adj.* metallic, metalline. **—anbruch**, *m.* native ore. **—arbeiter**, *m.* worker in metal. **—art**, *f.* species of ore. **—artig**, *adj.* metallic. **—aufbereitung**, *f.* cleansing of ore. **—aus=schläger**, *m.* breaker (*Min.*). **—beschickung**, *f.* dressing of ore for fusion. **—beschlagen**, *adj.* brass-bound (*as a desk, etc.*). **—bild**, *n.* bronze statue. **—bruch**, *m.* mine. **—druse**, *f.* crystallized ore. **—fäustel**, *m.* miner's hammer. **—farben**, **—farbig**, *adj.* brassy (*in appearance*). **—gang**, *m.* lode, metallic vein. **—gebirge**, *n.* mountain containing ore; the 'Erzgebirge' in the kingdom of Saxony. **—gießer**, *m.* brass-founder. **—gießerei**, *f.* brass-foundry, bronze casting. **—gräber**, *m.* miner. **—grube**, *f.* pit, mine. **—haltig**, **—haltend**, *adj.* containing ore. **—hütte**, *f.* smelting house. **—klauber**, *m.* ore-picker. **—kunde**, *f.* metallurgy; mineralogy. **—kundige(r)**, *m.* mineralogist. **—lager**, *n.* stratum, metallic deposit. **—messer**, *m.* surveyor of mines. **—probe**, *f.* assay. **—reich**, *adj.* abounding in ore. **—scheidekunst**, *f.* act of ascertaining the nature of ores *or* metals. **—scheider**, *m.* sorter (*of ores*). **—schicht**, *f.* miner's turn of work, shift; mass of ore for smelting within 24 hours. **—stufe**, *f.* piece of ore. **—wäsche**, *f.* place where ore is washed; washing of ore; cradle (*for washing ore*).

Erz— (*in comp.* =) principal; arch-, cardinal, chief, arrant; excellent; very; extremely; high-. **—amt**, *n.* high imperial office (*filled by an elector in the old German empire*). **—bannerherr**, *m.* imperial standard-bearer. **—bischof**, *m.* archbishop. **—bischöflich**, *adj.* archiepiscopal. **—bistum**, *n.* archbishopric. **—bösewicht**, *m.* arrant rogue. **—dekan**, *m.* archdeacon. **—diakonei'**, *f.* archdeaconry. **—dumm**, *adj.* extremely stupid. **—engel**, *m.* archangel. **—feind**, *m.* arch-enemy. **—grobian**, *m.* big bully. **—herzog**, *m.* archduke. **—herzogin**, *f.* archduchess. **—herzogtum**, *n.* archduchy. **—heuchler**, *m.* arch-hypocrite. **—kämmerer**, *m.* lord high chamberlain. **—kanzler**, *m.* lord high chancellor. **—katholisch**, *adj.* ultra-Catholic. **—ketzer**, *m.* arch-heretic, heresiarch. **—kokette**, *f.* out and out flirt, desperate coquette. **—marschall**, *m.* lord high marshal of the empire. **—narr**, *m.* arrant fool. **—pfalzgraf**, *m.* (*old title*) elector palatine. **—schatzmeister**, *m.* lord high treasurer. **—schelm**, *m.* arrant knave. **—schenk**, *m.* lord high cupbearer. **—spieler**, *m.* professed gambler. **—stift**, *n.* archbishopric; archiepiscopal foundation. **—stutzer**, *m.* thorough dandy. **—truchseß**, *m.* lord high steward. **—tugend**, *f.* cardinal virtue. **—vater**, *m.* patriarch. **—väterlich**, *adj.* patriarchal. **—verräter**, *m.* arch-traitor.

Erzähl'bar, *adj.* fit for recital.

Erzäh'l—en, *v.a.* to tell, to relate; **man —t**, people say. **—end**, *p. & adj.* narrative; epic (*poem*). **—er**, *m.* (—ers, *pl.* —er) narrator; reporter; story-teller *or* writer. **—ung**, *f.* narration; account, report; narrative, tale, story *Comp.* **—ungs=weise**, *adv.* in narrative form.

Erzau'bern, *v.a.* to effect by witchcraft.

Erzei'gen, *v.* I. *a.* (**einem etwas**) to show, render, do (*kindness*); to manifest, display (*feeling, etc.*). II. *r.* to prove oneself to be.

Er'zen (*long* **e**), *v.a.* to address a p. as **Er** (*obs.*).

Erzeug'bar, *adj.* that may be generated; producible.

Erzeu'g—en, *v.a.* to procreate, beget (*offspring*); to engender (*disease*); to raise, produce, breed; **Dampf —en**, to generate steam; **Verdacht —en**, to create suspicion; **Verachtung —en**, to breed contempt. **—er**, *m.* (—ers, *pl.* —er) begetter, genitor, father; raiser, grower. **—erin**, *f.* parent, mother. **—nis**, *n.* (—ni(ss)es, *pl.* —ni(ss)e) offspring, product; production. **—ung**, *f.* begetting; procreation; production; generation (*of gas, etc.*).

Erzieh'—bar, *adj.* capable of education; rearable; teachable. **—lich**, *adj.* pertaining to education, educational.

Erzie'h—en, *ir.v.a.* to bring up; to train; to educate; to rear; **wohl erzogen**, well-bred, well-educated. **—er**, *m.*(—ers, *pl.* —er) educator; teacher; (private) tutor. **—erin**, *f.* lady teacher, governess. **—ung**, *f.* rearing, bringing up; education; **schlechte —ung**, bad *or* poor education, ill breeding. *Comp.* **—ungs=anstalt**, *f.* educational establishment; boarding-school; school, academy. **—ungs=art**, *f.* system, mode *or* method of education. **—ungs=buch**, *n.* book on education. **—ungs=fähig**, *adj.* teachable, docile. **—ungs=rat**, *m.* board of education, educational council. **—ungs=fach**, *n.*, **—ungs=kunst**, *f.* education (*as a profession*). **—ungs=kunde**, **—ungs=lehre**, *f.* pedagogy (*as a science*); pedagogics, theory (and practice) of education. **—ungs=los**, *adj.* uneducated. **—ungs=wesen**, *n.* educational matters, pedagogics, public instruction.

Erzie'len, *v.a.* to strive after; to aim at; to get by effort, to obtain; to beget, produce.

Erzit'tern, *v.n.* (*aux.* **s.**) to tremble violently; to shiver.

Erzür'nen, *v.* I. *a.* to irritate; to provoke to anger. II. *r. & n.* (*aux.* **s.**) to grow angry.

Erzwin'gen, *ir.v.a.* to force, enforce; to extort from; **den Sinn —,** to wrest the meaning; **ich kann es nicht —,** I can't master it, I can't accomplish it; **ein erzwungenes Lächeln,** a forced smile.

Es, *pers. pron.* I. (*nom. acc. of 3rd sing. neut.*; *also the archaic genitive of the neuter, surviving only in certain phrases; often shortened to* 's) it; of it; **ich bin — müde** *or* **satt,** I am tired of it; **ich bin — zufrieden,** I am satisfied with it, I have no objection, all right; **er ist — wert,** he is worthy of it, he deserves it; **— nimmt mich wunder,** I am astonished, I wonder. II. *used as a subject of imp. verbs sometimes* = there; **— schneit,** it is snowing, there is snow; **— wird getanzt,** there is dancing, they are dancing; **— wallet und siedet und brauset und zischt,** it bubbles and seethes and hisses and roars; **— giebt Leute,** there are people; **— sagt sich schwer,** it is said with difficulty, it is difficult to say; **von eurer Fahrt kehrt sich 's nicht immer wieder,** from such journeys as yours one does not always return. III. *used demonstratively* = he, she, it, they; **— ist sein erster Versuch,** it *or* this is his first attempt; **— sind Männer von Ansehen,** they are men of position, of consequence; **wer ist dieser Mann? — ist ein Bauer,** who is this man? He is a peasant; **— ist eine Freundin von mir,** she is a friend of mine; **— sind Geschwister,** they are brothers *or* brother and sister. IV. *used as dummy subject, the true subject following the verb, sometimes* = it, there, *etc.*; *sometimes untranslatable*; **— klopft jemand,** somebody is knocking; **— donnern die Höhen,** the heights are thundering; **— friert mich,** I feel cold; **— fröstelt mich,** I am shivering; **— lebe der König,** long live the king! **— sperren die Riesen den Weg,** the giants bar the way; **— ist nicht alles Gold was glänzt,** all is not gold that glitters; **— ist nichts so gut,** there is nothing so good; **— ist ein Gott,** there is a God; **— spiele wer da will,** let them play that like; **— läßt sich auf Deutsch nicht sagen,** you cannot say in German; **— fragt sich, ob,** the question is whether, it is a question if; **— war einmal ein Mann,** there was once a man; **— sei denn,** unless, provided. V. *often used to denote that the subject of the action is vague, mysterious, dreadful*; **— ruft aus den Tiefen,** something calls, a voice is heard from the deep; **und schaudernd dacht ich 's, da kroch 's heran,** and I thought of it shuddering, then something came crawling up to me; **unter mir lag 's bergetief,** beneath me the water was lying as deep as mountains; **— trieb mich um,** the eddy spun me round; **— riß mich hinunter blitzesschnell,** I was carried down (into the abyss) as quick as lightning (by the mysterious and dreadful current). VI. *used as completion of predicate* = so, it; **ich bin —,** it is I; **sie sind —,** it is they; **ich selber bin — nicht mehr,** I myself am no longer so; **wir sind — die es gethan haben,** it is we who did it; **er ist reich, ich bin — auch,** he is rich, I am so too; **er sagt —,** he says so; **ich bat dich, — ihm zu sagen; hast du — gethan?** I asked you to tell him; have you done so? **— gut haben,** to be well off.

Es, *n.* E flat (*Mus.*); **— —,** E double flat; **—-Dur,** E flat major; **—-Moll,** E flat minor.

E'sche, *f.* (*pl.* **—n**) (**—n-baum,** *m.*) ash, ash-tree. **—n,** *adj.* of ash, ashen. *Comp.* **—n-wäldchen,** *n.* ashwood.

E'sel, *m.* (**—s,** *pl.* **—**) ass, donkey; frame with legs, horse; dunce, jackass; **der hölzerne —,** easel; **wilder, gestreifter —,** zebra; **den — (einen) — nennen,** to call a spade a spade; **ein — schilt den andern Langohr,** the kettle calls the pot black; **den — zu Grabe läuten,** to dangle one's feet; **einem einen — bohren,** to make game of one; **vom Pferde auf den — kommen,** to come down in the world; **den Sack schlagen und den — meinen,** to say (*or* do) one thing and mean another; **wenn dem — zu wohl wird, geht er aufs Eis,** pride will have a fall; **er ist ein alter —,** he is an old fool; **der — iaht,** the ass brays, heehaws. **—ei',** *f.* (*pl.* **—ei'en**) asinine behaviour; doltishness; stupid blunder, great folly, stupidity. **—haft,** *adj. & adv.* stupid, donkeyish. **—in,** *f.* she-ass. *Comp.* **—s-arbeit,** *f.* drudgery. **—s-bohne,** *f.* horse-bean. **—s-brücke,** *f.* pons asinorum, crib. **—s-geschrei,** *n.* braying of an ass. **—s-kopf,** *m.* dolt. **—s-ohr,** *n.* ass's ear; dog's ear (*in a book*). **—s-tracht,** *f.* ass's load. **—s-tritt,** *m.* kick of an ass; cowardly revenge.

E'seln, *v.n.* (*aux.* **h.**) to labour hard, to toil; to commit great blunders.

Eskadro'n, *f.* (*pl.* **—en**) squadron.

Eskamotie'ren, *v.a.* to juggle away; to filch.

Eskomptie'ren, Eskontie'ren, *v.a.* to discount; to cash.

Eskor't—e, *f.* (*pl.* **—en**) escort, convoy. **—ie'ren,** *v.a.* to escort, convoy.

Esote'risch, *adj. & adv.* esoteric.

Es'pe, *f.* (*pl.* **—n**) aspen-tree. **—n,** *adj.* aspen. *Comp.* **—n-laub,** *n.* foliage of the aspen; **er zittert wie (ein) —nlaub,** he trembles like an aspen leaf.

Eß'—bar, *adj. & adv.* eatable. **—barkeit,** *f.* (*pl.* **—barkeiten**) eatableness; (*pl.*) eatables. *Comp.* **—gelage,** *n.* feast, banquet. **—gier, —begier,** *f.* craving for food, appetite; gluttony. **—gierig,** *adj. & adv.* ravenous. **—glocke,** *f.* dinner bell. **—korb,** *m.* provision basket. **—löffel,** *m.* tablespoon. **—lust,** *f.* appetite. **—stäbchen,** *pl.* chopsticks. **—stunde,** *f.* meal time, dinner *or* supper hour. **—tisch,** *m.* dining table. **—waren,** *pl.* eatables, victuals, provisions. **—zeit** *or* **—ens-zeit,** *f. see* **—stunde.** **—zimmer,** *n.* dining-room.

Essä'er, Esse'ner, *m.* (**—s,** *pl.* **—**) Essene.

Es'say, *m.* (**—s,** *pl.* **—s**) essay.

Es'se, *f.* (*pl.* **—n**) forge; funnel; chimney. *Comp.* **—n-aufsatz,** *m.* chimney-pot. **—n-feger, —n-kehrer,** *m.* chimney-sweep.

Es's—en, I. *ir.v.a. & n.* (*aux.* **h.**) to eat; to feed (*on*); to take one's meals; **zu Mittag —en,** to lunch, dine (*early*); **zu Abend —en,** to dine (*late*), sup; **was werden wir heut —en?** what shall we have for dinner to-day? **an einem gemeinschaftlichen Tische zusammen —en,** to mess (*Mil. & Naut.*); **sich satt —en,** to eat one's fill; **im Speisehause —en,** to take one's meals at an ordinary; **gern Austern —en,** to be fond of oysters; **er ißt täglich dreimal —,** he takes three meals a day; **ich —e regelmäßig bei ihm,** I board with him. II. *subst. n.* eating; feeding; food, victuals; meal, repast; diet; **ich kann das fette —en nicht vertragen,** fat *or* rich food does not agree with me; **das —en abtragen,** to clear the table. **—er,** *m.* eater; **er ist ein starker —er,** he has a good appetite, he eats much.

Esse'nz, *f.* (*pl.* **—en**) essence.

Es'sig, *m.* (**—s,** *pl.* **—e**) vinegar; (*in comp.* =) vinegar, of vinegar; acetous, acetate of; **damit ist es —!** the matter has turned out a failure, it's all up with it! (*coll.*). *Comp.* **—artig,** *adj.* acetic. **—äther,** *m.* acetic ether. **—bildung,** *f.* acetification. **—brauerei,** *f.* vinegar manufactory. **—fläschchen,** *n.* vinaigrette; vinegar cruet; **—fläschchen- und Ölfläschchen-Gestell,** cruet stand. **—gährung,** *f.* acetous fermentation. **—gurke,** *f.* pickled cucumber. **—messer,** *m.* oxymeter. **—sauer,** *adj.* sour as vinegar; acetous; (*in comp.* =) acetate of. **—säure,** *f.* acetic acid.

Estra'de, *f.* a dais *or* raised portion of a room.
Estimie'ren, *v.a.* to esteem; to estimate.
E'strich, *m.* (—s, *pl.* —e) flooring; unboarded floor; stone floor; plaster floor; pavement.
Etablie'ren, *v.a.* to establish, set up; **sich** —, to settle, to set up in business.
Eta'ge, *f.* (*pl.* —n) floor, story, flat. *Comp.* **—n=ofen,** *m.* oven with shelves *or* stories. **—n=schlüssel,** *m.* latch-key.
Etage're, *f.* (*pl.* —n) whatnot.
Etap'pe, *f.* provisioned halting-place for soldiers; **die — übergehen,** to pass by such a place without stopping. *Comp.* **—n=straße,** *f.* military road.
Eta't, *m.* (—s, *pl.* —s) establishment; list (*of officers, etc.*); budget. **—isie'ren,** *v.a.* to make a statement of; to open the budget; to balance (*C. L.*). *Comp.* **—s=beratung,** *f.* debate on the budget. **—s=buch,** *n.* ledger. **—s=rat,** *m. see* Staatsrat. **—s=summe,** *f.* total of a statement.
E'tepetete, *adj.;* **darin ist er sehr —,** in that respect he is very particular (*dial. & colloq.*).
E'th—ik, *f.* ethics. **—iker,** *m.* (—ikers, *pl.* —iker) moralist; writer on ethics; moral philosopher. **—isch,** *adj.* ethical.
Ethno— (*unaccented, in comp.*). **—gra'ph,** *m.* (—gra'phen, *pl.* —gra'phen) ethnographer. **—graphie',** *f.* ethnography. **—lo'g,** *m.* (—lo'gen, *pl.* —lo'gen) ethnologist. **—logie',** *f.* ethnology. **—lo'gisch,** *adj.* ethnological.
Etiket't—e, *f.* (*pl.* —en) etiquette; label, ticket. **—ie'ren,** *v.a.* to (provide with a) label.
Et'lich, *pron. & adj.* **—e,** *pl. of* **etlich,** some, several; a few; any; **—e Mal** *or* **Male,** now and then; **—e und achtzig Jahre,** four score years and odd (*rare*); **—e Worte,** a few words (*obs.*).
Et'mal, *n.* (—s, *pl.* —e) time from midday to midday, day's reckoning (*Naut.*)
Et'ter, *m.* (—s, *pl.* —) hedge, fence (*dial.*).
Etui', *n.* (—s, *pl.* —s) case, box.
Et'wa, I. *adv.* perhaps, perchance; possible; indeed, forsooth; nearly, about; somewhere; at any time; in some way; **ist 's Ihnen — um 5 Uhr gefällig?** shall we say five o'clock? **was — vorkommen mag,** whatever may happen; **wenn Sie — hören,** if you should hear by any chance. II. *part.;* **er wird doch nicht — glauben,** he will not believe, I hope. **—ig,** *adj. & adv.* possible, eventual; **—ige Schwierigkeiten,** possible contingent difficulties, whatever difficulties may arise.
Et'wan, *adv.* at some time or other (*obs.*); perhaps, possibly (*obs.*). **—ig,** *adj. & adv.* eventual, possible.
Et'was, I. *ind. pron.* (*indec.*) something, somewhat, some (*gen'lly used in apposition to an adj. or noun following it*); **— Neues,** something new, news; **— Neues?** any news? **— Geld,** some money; **— anderes,** something else; **das ist — anderes,** that is a different thing; **irgend —,** anything; **in —, um —,** in some measure, some respects; **ein gewisses —,** a certain what shall I call it; **das will — sagen,** that is saying a great deal; **er gilt — bei ihm,** he is in high favour with him; **er bildet sich — ein,** he is somewhat *or* rather conceited. II. *adj.* some, any; **so —,** such a thing; **so — bedarf Zeit,** such things require time; **nein, so —!** now, what do you say to that! III. *adv.* somewhat; a little; rather; **— weitschweifig,** rather prolix. IV. *n.* entity, a real being.
Et'welch, *ind. pron.* some (*obs.*).
Etymolo'g, *m.* (—en, *pl.* —en) etymologist. **—ie',** *f.* etymology. **—isch,** *adj. & adv.* etymological.
Euch, *pers. pron.* (*acc. & dat. pl. of* **du**) you, to you, yourselves, one another, each other.
Eu'er (*abbrev.* **Ew.**). I. *gen. pl. of* **du,** of you, your. II. *poss. adj.* your, your own. III. *poss. pron.* (**der, die, das —e,** *or* **—er, —e, —es**) yours, your own. *Comp.* **—(er)seits,** *adv.* on your side; for your part; as concerns you; in your turn. **—s=gleichen,** *indec. adj. or pron* of your kind; like you. **(um) —t=halben, —t=wegen, —t=willen,** *adv.* on your account; for your sake; as far as you are concerned; for aught you care.
Eu'le, *f.* (*pl.* —n) owl; dust-brush. **—n nach Athen bringen,** to carry coals to Newcastle; **des einen — ist des andern Nachtigall,** the goose of the one is the swan of the other; **eine — fangen,** to chapel (*a ship*); **großköpfige —,** brown owl; **die — schreit,** the owl hoots (screeches). *Comp.* **—n=flucht,** *f.* dusk **—n=flug,** *m.* secret flight. **—n=spiegel,** *m.* name of a sixteenth-century jester and of a book written about him; Owlglass, Ulenspiegel; jester, wag. **—n=spiegelei',** *f.* buffoonery, mad prank, foolish trick; practical joke.
Eunu'ch, *m.* (—en, *pl.* —en) eunuch.
Euphemis'tisch, *adj. & adv.* euphemistic.
Eupho'nisch, *adj. & adv.* euphonic.
Eur, *contraction of* **Euer.** **—ig,** (**der, die, das —ige**) *poss. pron.* yours; **die —igen,** your family, yours; **ganz der —ige,** yours very truly, ever yours. *Comp.* **—es=, —et=,** (*in comp.*) *see* **Euer.**
Eusta'chisch, *adj.* Eustachian (*Anat.*).
Eu'ter, *n.* (—s, *pl.* —) udder.
Evange'l—isch, *adj. & adv.* evangelical; Protestant. **—ium,** *n.* (—iums, *pl.* **Evange'lien**) gospel.
Evas—, *or* **Evens—,** (*in compds.*). **—kind,** *n.* mortal. **—kostüm,** *n.* nakedness, nudity. **—tochter,** *f.* daughter of Eve.
E'venbaum, *m.* yew tree.
Ew., *abbr.* (*in titles*) *for* **Euer; — Majestät,** Your Majesty.
E'wer, *m.* (—s, *pl.* —) wherry, lighter. *Comp.* **—führer,** *m.* lighterman, waterman.
E'wig, *adj. & adv.* everlasting; eternal; perpetual, for ever; **der —e Jude,** Ahasuerus, the wandering Jew; **das ist — schade,** that is a great pity; **der Rock ist — gut,** the coat is still good; **auf —,** in perpetuity. **—keit,** *f.* eternity; perpetuity; **von —keit zu —keit, in alle —keit,** world without end, from everlasting to everlasting, to all eternity; **in —keit nicht,** never. **—lich,** *adv.* see **Ewig.** *Comp.* **—geld,** *n.* annuity from sunk capital.
Ex, *adv.* finished, over; **die Sache ist —,** the matter is done with, settled (*sl.*); ex, quondam, former, late.
Exa'kt, *adj.* exact, accurate; **—e Wissenschaften,** mathematical sciences.
Exaltie'rt, *adj. & p.p.* over excited.
Exa'm—en, *n.* (—ens, *pl.* **Exa'mina**) examination; **mündliches —en,** oral *or* viva voce examination; **schriftliches —en,** written examination, paper work; **sich einem —en unterziehen,** to go in for an examination; **das —en machen, das —en bestehen** *or* **im —en bestehen,** to pass an examination, to get through, to be passed in an examination; **im —en durchfallen,** to fail in an examination, to be rejected, to be ploughed *or* plucked (*coll.*). **—ina'nd,** *m.* (—inan'den, *pl.* —inan'den) examinee, candidate. **—ina'tor,** *m.* (—ina'tors, *pl.* —inato'ren) examiner. **—inie'ren,** *v.a.* to examine, to test, try.
Exege'—se, *f.* exegesis. **—t,** *m.* (—ten, *pl.* —ten) commentator. **—tik,** *f.* hermeneutics.
Exem'p—el, *n.* (—els, *pl.* —el) example; instance; sum, calculation; **zum —el,** (*abbr.* **z. E.**) for instance. **—la'r,** *n.* (—la'rs, *pl.* —la're) model; copy (*of a book*); specimen. **—la'risch,** *adj. & adv.* exemplary; excellent.

Exe'quien, *pl.* obsequies; masses for the dead.

Exequie'ren, *v.a.* to enforce payment by an execution (*Law*).

Exerzie'r—en, I. *v.a.* to exercise; to drill. II. *subst. n.* drill. *Comp.* **—meister**, *m.* drill-sergeant, drill instructor. **—lager**, *n.* encampment; drilling ground. **—patrone**, *f.* practice cartridge. **—platz**, *m.* parade-ground; drill ground. **—reglement**, *n.* army *or* drill regulations.

Exi'l, *n.* (—(e)s, *pl.* —e) exile, banishment.

Exist—e'nz, *f.* (*pl.* —en'zen) existence; being. **—ie'ren**, *v.n.* (*aux.* **h.**) to exist; to be; to subsist.

Exerzi'tium, *n.*(*pl.* **Exerzi'tien**) exercise; prose.

Exkommunizie'ren, *v.a.* to excommunicate.

Exmatrikulie'ren, *v.a.*; **er läßt sich —**, he ceases to be a student at the University; he takes his name off the University books.

Exo'tisch, *adj.* exotic.

Exped—ie'nt, *m.* (—ien'ten, *pl.* —ien'ten) despatcher; clerk. **—ie'ren**, *v.a.* to despatch, send off (*a parcel, etc.*). **—itio'n**, *f.* despatch, forwarding; expedition (*Mil. etc.*); office (*of a journal, etc.*).

Expekta'nz, *f.* (*pl.* —en) survivorship; expectancy.

Experime'nt, *n.* (—s, *pl.* —e) experiment; **ein — machen** *or* **anstellen**, to make *or* try an experiment. **—ie'ren**, *v.n.* (*aux.* **h.**); **—ie'ren (mit Kaninchen)**, to experiment (upon rabbits).

Explizie'ren, *v.a.* to explain.

Explora'tor, *m.* explorer.

Expo'rt—geschäft, *n.* (*pl.* —e) export house. **—handel**, *m.* export trade, exportation.

Expre'ß, I. *adj.* express. II. *adv.* on purpose; expressly; by express (*train, etc.*).

Exsicca'tor, *m.* (—s, *pl.* —en) dessicator (*chem.*).

Exspiratio'ns=strom, *m.* current of exhaled breath.

Exta'se, *f.* (*pl.* —n) ecstasy.

Extempora'le, *n.* (*pl.* **Extempora'lien**) extempore version, composition done in class, test-paper.

Extemporie'ren, *v.a.* & *n.* to extemporize, improvise.

Exte'rn, *adj.* external, outside. *Comp.* **—=verkehr**, *m.* outside traffic.

Externa't, *n.* (—s, *pl.* —e) day school; day training-college.

Ex'tra, I. *adj.* extra, additional; special. II. *adv.* extra, besides, into the bargain. **—ner**, *m.*(—ners, *pl.* —ner) day boy; oppidan (*Eton*). *Comp.* **—blatt**, *n.* supplement; special edition (*of a newspaper*). **—bote**, *m.* special messenger. **—fein**, *adj.* superfine, of special quality. **—liegezeit**, *f.* (*days of*) demurrage. **—post**, *f.* post-chaise, special mail; **mit — post**, very quickly; **mit —post reisen**, to travel with post-horses, to post. **—stunden**, *pl.* extra lessons; over-time (*in factories*). **—zug**, *m.* special train; excursion train.

Extrahie'r—en, *v.a.* to extract. **—ung**, *f.* evolution (*Math.*).

Extra'kt, *m.* (—(e)s, *pl.* —e) extract, essence.

Extre'm, *n.* (—s, *pl.* —e) extreme; **die —e berühren sich**, the extremes meet. **—itä't**, *f.* (*pl.* —itä'ten) extremity.

Exula'nt, *m.* (—en, *pl.* —en) exile.

Exzelle'nz, **Excelle'nz**, *f.* (*pl.* —en) excellence; Excellency (*title*).

Exzen'tri—sch, *adj.* eccentric. **—zitä't**, *f.* (*pl.* —zitä'ten) eccentricity.

Exzer'pt, *n.* (—es, *pl.* —e) excerpt. *Comp.* **—en=buch**, *n.* commonplace book.

Exze'ß, *m.* (—(ss)es, *pl.* —(ss)e), excess, outrage.

E'y, *now usually* **Ei!** *int.* ah! oh! — **ja doch!** (*accent on the* **ja**) of course, to be sure!

F

F, f, *n.* F, f; F *or* Fa (*Mus.*); (*for abbreviations see the Index at the end of the German-English part*); **etwas aus dem ff verstehen**, to know s.th. thoroughly, to have s.th. at one's fingers' ends.

Fa'bel, *f.* (*pl.* —n) fable, tale, fiction; plot (of a drama); byword (*B.*). **—ei'**, *f.* fabling; fiction. **—haft**, *adj.* fabulous, mythical; incredible. *Comp.* **—dichter**, *m.* fabulist. **—dichtung**, *f.* fable; fable in verse. **—gestalt**, *f.* fabulous creature. **—hans**, *m.* tale-teller. **—land**, *n.* fairy-land. **—lehre**, *f.* theory of fable-writing. **—lese**, *f.* collection of fables. **—schmied**, *m.* fabulist; romancer. **—welt**, **—zeit**, *f.* fabulous *or* mythical age. **—werk**, *n.* fabulous work; work of fiction. **—wesen**, *n.* fabulous creature.

Fa'beln, *v.* I. *a.* to fable, invent and tell stories. II. *n.* (*aux.* **h.**) to tell stories, falsehoods, tales; to talk idly.

Fabri'k, *f.* (*pl.* —en) factory, manufactory. **—a'nt**, *m.* (—an'ten, *pl.* —an'ten) manufacturer. **—a't**, *n.* (—a'tes, *pl.* —a'te) manufacture. **—atio'n** (*pl.* —atio'nen), **—atu'r**, *f.* (*pl.* —atu'ren) fabrication, manufacture. *Comp.* **—arbeit**, *f.* work in a factory; manufactured goods, manufactured article. **—arbeiter**, *m.* factory man, operative. **—arbeiterin**, *f.* factory woman, factory girl. **—besitzer**, *m.* proprietor of a factory *or* works. **—kommissär**, *m.* factory inspector. **—stadt**, *f.* manufacturing town. **—waren**, *pl.* manufactures. **—zeichen**, *n.* trade-mark.

Fabula'nt, **Fabuli'st**, *m.* fabulist; fable writer.

Fabrizie'ren, *v.a.* to fabricate, manufacture.

Facet'te, *f.* (*pl.* —n) facet. *Comp.* **—n=schleifer**, *m.* cutter of facets; diamond cutter.

Fach, I. *n.* (—(e)s, *pl.* **Fä'cher**) compartment, division; department; cell (*Bot.*); shelf, row, pigeon-hole (*of a cupboard, in a library, etc.*); panel (*of a door, etc.*); part, rôle; special subject; special branch (*of a trade or profession*); **ein geheimes —**, a secret drawer; **das Gebäude kommt zu —**, the timber work of the building is raised; **das ist gerade sein —**, that is just his speciality; **vom —**, by profession; **das ist mein — nicht, schlägt nicht in mein —**, that is not within my province; that is not in my line; **er versteht sein — vollkommen**, he is thoroughly master of his subject *or* business; **unter Dach und — bringen**, to house. II. *suff.* (*in comp.* =) -fold; **hundert —**, hundred fold. **—heit**, *f.* -foldness; **Drei—heit**, triplicity. **—lich**, *adj.* professional. *Comp.* **—bildung**, *f.* professional education. **—gelehrte(r)**, *m.* specialist. **—genosse**, *m.* fellow-student, colleague. **—kundig**, *a.* competent. **—lehrer**, *m.* teacher of a special subject, specialist. **—mann**, *m.* expert; **—männisches Urteil**, opinion of an expert; **von — männischer Seite**, from *or* by experts. **—ordnung**, *f.* classification. **—schule**, *f.* school for some special branch of study; technical school. **—simpelei'**, *f.* talking shop (*coll.*). **—simpeln**, *v.a.* to talk shop (*coll.*). **—studium**, *n.* professional study; study of a special subject. **—wand**, *f.* panelled partition. **—weise**, *adv.* by compartments; in compartments; divided into classes. **—werk**, *n.* panelling; framework. **—wissen**, *n.*, **—wissenschaft**, *f.* special *or* professional science. **—zeitschrift**, *f.* periodical of a technical and scientific character.

Fa'che, *f.* breaking of fur *or* wool with the bow.

[1]**Fa'chen**, *v.a.* to bow (*hats, etc.*).

[2]**Fa'chen**, *v.a.* to fan, blow gently, stir.

Fäch—eln, **—ern**, *v.a.* & *n.* (*aux.* **h.**) to fan gently. **—er**, *m.* (—ers, *pl.* —er) fan. *Comp.* **—er=palme**, *f.* fan-palm, palmyra palm

Fä'cherig, *adj.* divided into compartments, cellular.

Fa'cit, *n.* (—s) result, amount, sum (*total*), product.

Fa'ckel, *f.* (*pl.* —n) torch, flambeau. *Comp.* —**ständchen,** *n.* serenade by torchlight. —**träger,** *m.* torch-bearer. —**zug,** *m.* torchlight procession.

Fa'ckeln, *v.* (*aux.* h.) to flare, to blaze; to trifle, fidget; to dally; (*coll.*) = **flunkern, fabeln,** to tarry, to trifle, fib.

Façon, *f.* (—, *pl.* —s) fashion, form, manner.

Fac, 2c. *see* **Fak, 2c.**

Fa'd—e, *adj. & adv.* stale, flat, insipid, dull. —**heit,** *f.* insipidity; staleness; (*pl.*) absurdities.

Fäd'chen, *n.* little thread, *dim. of* **Faden.**

Fä'deln, *v.* I. *a.* to thread (*a needle*); to string. II. *r.* to untwist, ravel out. III. *n.* (*aux.* h.) to be filaceous.

Fa'den, *m.* (—s, *pl.* **Fäden,** *but* (**vier**) **Faden tief**) thread; string, twine, cord; cord (*of wood*); fathom; measure of length (= *6 feet*); rough edge (*of a knife*); file (*for papers*); thread (*of a discourse; of life, etc.*); string (*Anat.*); shred, particle; **zu — schlagen,** to baste; **ein — Seide,** a needleful of silk; **kein trockner —,** not a dry stitch; **er hat keinen trocknen — am Leibe,** he is wet all through; **sie läßt keinen guten — an ihm,** she cries him down; she says that he is good for nothing; **in einem — weg,** uninterruptedly; (**einen**) **am — haben,** to have under one's thumb. *Comp.* —**ähnlich,** —**förmig,** *adj.* thread-like, filamentous, filiform. —**garn,** *n.* linen thread. —**gerade,** —**recht,** *adj. & adv.* perpendicular; dead straight. —**gold,** *n.* gold thread. —**holz,** *n.* cord-wood. —**nackt,** *adj.* stark naked. —**naß,** *adj.* thoroughly wet. —**nudeln,** *pl.* vermicelli. —**scheinig,** *adj.* threadbare. —**weise,** *adv.* by threads, thread by thread. —**werg,** *n.* oakum.

Fago'tt, *n.* (—s, *pl.* —e) bassoon. —**i'st,** *m.* (—**is'ten,** *pl.* —**is'ten**) bassoon-player.

Fa'hen, *ir.v.a.* (*obs. & poetic*) *see* **Fangen.**

Fä'hig, *adj. & adv.* (*with gen.*) able, capable (*of*); clever; fit (*for*); susceptible (*of*); — **zu einem Amte,** qualified for an office; **sich — machen,** to qualify oneself (**zu,** for); **ein —er Kopf,** a man of parts. —**keit,** *f.* capacity, ability; faculty, talent; (*pl.*) abilities; **das geht über meine —keiten,** that is beyond my capacity, that beats me; (*in comp.* =) power, privilege of.

Fahl, *adj. & adv.* fallow; dun, fawn-coloured; faded, pale; **einen auf dem —en Pferd ertappen,** to catch one tripping. *Comp.* —**erz,** *n.* grey copper (*Min.*).

Fähn'—chen, *n.* pennon, lance flag; banner (*Bot.*); **sie trug ein dünnes —chen,** she wore a very threadbare garment. —**drich,** *m. see* —**rich.** —**lein,** *n.* (—**leins,** *pl.* —**lein**) pennon; troop, squad, company (*Mil.*). —**rich,** *m.* (—**richs,** *pl.* —**riche**) cornet, ensign, sub-lieutenant (*Mil.*). *Comp.* —**richs=stelle,** *f.* ensigncy.

Fahn'den, *v.a.*; **auf einen —,** to search for a p.

Fah'ne, *f.* (*pl.* —n) flag, standard, banner; colours (*Mil.*); company; troop; squadron; feather (*of a quill*); vane, weathercock; press-slip (*Typ.*); **Dienst bei der —,** service with the colours, active military service; **die weiße —,** the white flag. *Comp.* —**n=abzug,** *m.* slip *or* galley (*proof*). —**n=eid,** *m.* military oath. —**n=flucht,** *f.* desertion (*of the colours*). —(**n**)**=flüchtig,** *adj.* deserting one's colours. —**n=futter,** *n.* case (*for a flag*). —**n=junker,** *m.* ensign, cornet. —**n=marsch,** *m.* music played whilst the colours are displayed *or* lodged. —**n=schmied,** *m.* farrier to a squadron. —**n=stange,** *f.* flagstaff. —**n=träger,** *m.* ensign, standard bearer. —**n=wache,** —**n=wacht,** *f.* main guard; sentry before the place where the standard is kept. —**n=weihe,** *f.* presentation of colours; benediction of the colours. —**en=weise,** *adv.* by companies; by troops.

Fahr'—bar, *adj. & adv.* practicable; passable; navigable; transportable; —**bares Eis,** open ice. —**barkeit,** *f.* practicableness (*of roads*); navigableness. *Comp.* —**bahn,** *f.* track for vessels, channel; roadway; (rail)way. —**betrieb,** *m.* traffic. —**bogen,** *m.* official report of mining work. —**brücke,** *f.* flying bridge. —**buch,** *n.* mining journal. —**gang,** *m.* carriage-way. —**gast,** *m.* passenger; fare. —**geld,** *n.* fare; carriage; bridge-toll. —**gleis,** *n.* rut (*made by wheels*). —**gut,** *n.* chattels. —**heft,** *m.*; **zusammenstellbares —heft,** tourist's circular ticket. —**karte,** *f.* ticket (*Railw.*); **eine —karte lösen,** to book, take a ticket. —**lässig,** *adj.* negligent; careless; —**lässige Tötung,** homicide *or* manslaughter through negligence. —**lässigkeit,** *f.* negligence, carelessness. —**leder,** *n.* miner's leather apron. —**loch,** *n.* manhole (*in engines*). —**ordnung,** *f.* rule of the road; cycling regulations. —**plan,** *m.* time-table, railway times. —**plan=buch,** *n.* railway-guide. —**plan=mäßig,** *adj.* in accordance with the time-tables, ordinary, regular. —**post,** *f.* stage-coach. —**preis,** *m.* fare. —**rad,** *n.* (bi)cycle, (tri)cycle. —**schacht,** *m.* climbing shaft. —**schein,** *m.* ticket. —**seil,** *n.* driving rein. —**sessel,** *m.*, —**stuhl,** *m.* lift, elevator; bath chair. —**steiger,** *m.* inspector of mines. —**straße,** *f.* high road, carriage road. —**taxe,** *f.* tariff. —**wasser,** *n.* navigable water, channel. —**weg,** *m.* high-road, carriage road. —**weg=gerechtigkeit,** *f.* right of way. —**wind,** *m.* fair wind (*Naut.*). —**zeug,** *n.* vessel.

Fäh'r—e, *f.* (*pl.* —en) ferry; ferry-boat; **fliegende —e,** flying bridge. —**te,** *f.* (*pl.* —**ten**) track, print, mark, trail; **die kalte —te,** cold scent. *Comp.* —**boot,** *n.* ferry-boat. —**geld,** *n.* ferriage, fare. —**gerechtigkeit,** *f.* right of ferrying. —**kahn,** *m.* wherry. —**mann,** *m.* ferryman. —**pacht,** *f.* license to ferry passengers.

Fähr—de, *f.* (*pl.* —**den**), —**lichkeit,** *f.* danger (*obs. & poet.*).

Fah'r—en, *ir.v.* I. *n.* (*aux.* s.) to go (*in any sort of conveyance*); to go towards, make for, go, go on (*obs.*); to travel, pass, proceed; to drive; to go in a boat, row, sail; to depart; to die; to fare, get on, prosper; **darum wollen wir zur Vollkommenheit —en,** let us therefore go on unto perfection (*B.*); **er fährt am besten dabei,** he has the best of the bargain; **er fuhr sehr gut dabei,** it was most profitable to him; **hinauf, herauf —en,** to ascend; **hinab, herab —en,** to descend; **Rad —en,** to cycle; **Zweirad —en,** to ride a bicycle; **auf** *or* **mit der Eisenbahn —en,** to go by rail; **dieser Wagen fährt zweimal wöchentlich,** this coach runs twice a week; **spazieren —en,** to take a drive; **rückwärts —en,** to ride with one's back to the horses *or* engine; **in die Hölle —en,** to go to *or* descend into Hell; **über einen Fluß —en,** to cross a river; **aus dem Hafen —en,** to clear the port; **auf den Grund —en,** to run aground; —**e wohl!** farewell! (*aux.* s. & h.) to deal with, treat; to flash, shoot; to start; **auf einen zu —en,** to rush all of a sudden upon one; **aus der Hand —en,** to slip out of the hand; **aus der Haut —en,** to get very impatient, lose all self-control; **aus dem Bette —en,** to start up out of bed; **es fuhr mir ein plötzlicher Schmerz durch den Kopf,** a sudden pain shot through my head; **einem durch den Kopf —en,** (*impers.*) to strike, occur to one; **einander in die Haare —en,** to fly at one another, come to blows; —**en in,** to rush into; **in die Kleider —en,** to slip on one's clothes; **der Hochmutsteufel ist in ihn**

gefahren, the demon of haughtiness has entered into him; mit der Hand —en, to slip or thrust one's hand (in, into); mit der Hand —en über, to pass one's hand over; —et mir säuberlich mit dem Knaben, deal gently with the young man (*B.*); einem übers Maul —en, to reply rudely, snap one up; es fuhr mir kalt übern Rücken, a cold shudder passed through me; sie fuhr zusammen, she was startled, started back (*from fright, etc.*); gegen den Wind —en, to sail against the wind; —en lassen, to let fly, let go, to abandon, give up, to let slip; die Sorge —en lassen, to banish care; eine Gelegenheit —en lassen, to let an opportunity slip. II. *a.* to drive; to navigate; to convey; to cart; to sail, row (*a boat*); to ride (*a cycle*); to ply (*a ferry*); einen über einen Fluß —en, to ferry one over a river; er fährt sehr gut, he is a good whip. III. *r.*; es fährt sich gut auf dieser Straße, this is a good road for driving; sich müde —en, to tire oneself by driving; in diesem Wagen fährt es sich angenehm, this carriage goes easily, is well hung. —end, *p. & adj.* going, travelling; vagrant; sliding (*Mech.*); —ender Ritter, knight errant; —ende Habe, movables; —ende Artillerie, field artillery; —ende Post, stage coach; —ende Leute, —endes Volk, travelling vagrants; travelling minstrels; —ender Sänger, wandering minstrel; —ender Schüler, travelling student (*in the Middle Ages*). —er, *m.* (—ers, *pl.* —er) driver; cyclist.

Fah'rig, *adj.* unsteady, careless, haphazard, unreliable.

Fahrt, *f.* (*pl.* —en) ride, drive, row, passage, journey, voyage, trip; course (*of a ship*); transit; progress, slowness *or* speed of motion; track; way; burrow; conduit; das Schiff hat harte —, she is a fast sailing ship; hohe —, prosperous journey (*poet.*); — nach Entfernung (Zeit), drive by distance (time); die — verfehlen, to lose way; die — nehmen nach, to stand for (*Naut.*); von der — abweichen, to alter the course; auf der —, immediately, on the spot; auf — etwas zu thun, about to do something (*rare*). *Comp.* —en=liste, *f.* way-bill (*of 'buses, tramcars, etc.*). —flagge, *f.* sailing-signal; blue peter at the mizzen. —haken, *m.*, —haspe, *f.* ladder-hook (*Min.*). —maß, *n.* log (*Naut.*). —messer, *m.* marine surveyor. —stange, *f.* driving bit.

Fak't—isch, *adj. & adv.* actual, proved by facts; de facto; effective. —iti'v, *adj.* causative; factitive (*Gram.*); denoting an effect. —or, *m.* (—ors, *pl.* —o'ren) factor (*C. L., Arith.*); agent; manager, foreman. —orei', *f.* (*pl.* —orei'en) agency (*business*); factory. —um, *n.* (—ums, *pl.* Fak'ta) fact. —u'r(a), *f.* (*pl.* Faktu'ren) invoice; laut —ura, as per invoice. —urie'ren, *v.a.* to invoice. *Comp.* —u'ren=buch, *n.* invoice-book.

Fakul'tas, *f.*; die — für Prima bekommen, to be qualified (by one's examination) to teach a subject in all forms up to the highest.

Fakultä't, *f.* (*pl.* —en) faculty, Board of Studies; die neusprachliche —, the Board of Modern Language Studies, the Modern Language Faculty. *Comp.* —s=studium, *n.* university study.

Falb, *adj.* fallow, pale yellow, pale. —e, *m. & f.*; ein —er, (a) cream *or* dun coloured horse. —icht, —ig, *adj.* inclining to dun; faded; pale yellow.

Fal'bel, *f.* (*pl.* —n) flounce, furbelow.

Fal'ben, *v.n.* to grow fallow; to fade.

Fal'k—e, *m.* (—en, *pl.* —en) falcon, hawk; *see* —aune; einen —en häubeln, enthäubeln, to hood, unhood a hawk; einen —en steigen lassen, to cast a hawk; den —en streichen, to curry favour (bei, with). —au'ne, *f.* (*pl.* —au'nen) falcon (*four or six pounder, Artil.*). —enie'r, *m.* (—enie'rs, *pl.* —enie're), —ner, *m.* (—ners, *pl.* —ner) falconer. —nerei', *f.* falconry; occupation *or* post of falconer; train of servants at hawking. —one'tt, *n.* (—onet'tes, *pl.* —onet'te) falconet (*Artil.*). *Comp.* —en=beize, *f.* falconry. —en=haube, *f.* hood. —en=häuschen, *n.* mew. —en=hof, *m.* place where falcons are kept. —en=jagd, *f.* hawking. —en=schlag, *m.* swoop of the falcon. —en=stange, *f.* perch.

Fall, *m.* (—es, *pl.* Fäl'le) fall; tumble; decay, ruin, decline, downfall; failure; waterfall, cataract; case, event, accident, hap; condition, situation; case (*Gram., Law*); der Wer=—, the nominative case; der Wen—, the accusative case; das ist ganz mein —, that suits me exactly (*coll.*); in dem —e, in that case; Hochmut kommt vor dem —, pride goes before a fall; auf alle Fälle, at all events; ich setze den —, I make the supposition, suppose, take the case; im — der Not, nötigen —s, in case of necessity; im —e (daß), supposing (*that*), if; der vorliegende —, the case in point; auf jeden —, jedenfalls, in any case, by all means; auf keinen —, keinenfalls, on no account; auf alle Fälle, at all events; zu —e kommen, to be ruined; zu —e bringen, to ruin; seduce; einen — thun, to have a fall; das Gut steht auf dem —e, the estate will pass into other hands; ich kam in den —, I had the opportunity of; it so happened that I was obliged to. —s, *adv.* in case, if, supposing that; andern—s, otherwise. —sig, *suff.* (*in comp.* =) happening in such a case as; des—sig, in this case; allen=—sig, happening at all events, eventual. *Comp.* —baum, *m.* toll-bar, turnpike. —beil, *n.* guillotine. —brett, *n.* shutter, sliding board; falling board, wall-shelf, flap. —brücke, *f.* drawbridge; snare, trap. —eisen, *n.* latch-bolt. —endung, *f.* case-ending. —en=leger, —en=steller, *m.* trapper; insidious enemy. —fenster, *n.* sash window. —fertig, *adj.* shaky, about to fall. —gatter, *n.* herse, portcullis. —grube, *f.* pitfall. —hammer, *m.* steam hammer. —holz, *n.* windfallen wood. —hut, *m.* guard to prevent children from falling *or* from being hurt by a fall. —kloben, *m.* knocker. —meister, *m.* flayer. —obst, *n.* windfallen fruit, windfall. —raum, *m.* space through which an object falls. —reep, *n.* ladder-rope, man-board (*Naut.*). —schirm, *m.* parachute. —schloß, *n.* hasp-lock. —strick, *m.* gin, snare; trick, catch. —sucht, *f.* epilepsy. —süchtig, *adj.* epileptic. —tau, *n.* rope-ladder. —thor, *n.* portcullis. —thür, *f.* trap-door. —tisch, *m.* folding table. —treppe, *f.* trap-stairs. —wind, *m.* gust of wind.

Fal'le, *f.* (*pl.* —n) pitfall; trap, snare; catch, latch (*of a door*); valve (*Anat.*); bed (*sl.*).

Fal'len, I. *ir.v.n.* (*aux.* s.) to fall, tumble; to descend; to sink, decline; to subside; to drop; to decrease, diminish, go down (*of prices*); to fall, die; to die away, descend (*Mus.*); to be brought forth; to fail; to be ruined; to be seduced; to fall, flow into; to fall, be spoken; to sound, be heard (*of the report of a gun*); to prove, turn out; to happen; — auf *or* an (*with acc.*), to devolve on, descend to; — auf (*with acc.*), to hit, light on, to occur, to turn upon, to fall upon; — aus, to fall out of, to act out of; — durch, to fall by; — in, to fall into, to meddle with, to interrupt, to incline to, to incur; — über (*with acc.*), to fall, stumble over, to fall upon; — unter, to fall among; to fall under; — lassen, to drop, to let fall, to abate, to put aside; es fällt mir schwer, it is difficult for me; je nachdem es fällt, according as it turns out, happens; der Artikel falle wie er falle, however the article may turn out; es fiel die Bemerkung, the observation was made, it was observed; es fiel ein Schuß, a shot was fired *or* heard; der Würfel ist gefallen, the die is cast; es fielen heftige Reden, strong language was used; das Gespräch fiel auf, the conversation turned upon; er ist nicht auf den Kopf gefallen, he 's no fool; es fällt in die Augen, it catches the eye; es fällt mir schwer aufs Herz, it weighs upon my mind; die Wahl fiel auf mich, I was elected; aus den Wolken —, to be thunderstruck; aus allen Himmeln —, to become thoroughly disillusioned; aus der Rolle —, to act out of part, be inconsistent; es fiel mir aus der Hand, it dropped out of my hand; einem in die Arme —, to fall into one's arms; einem ins Amt —, to interfere with another's duties *or* office; ins Boot —! man the boat! einem in die Zügel —, to seize the bridle of another's horse, to restrain a person; einem in die Rede —, to interrupt a person; einem in die Hände —, to fall into a person's power; in Ohnmacht —, to faint, swoon; mit der Thür ins Haus —, to blunder cut, to act awkwardly; das fällt nicht ins Gewicht, that is light weight, that is of no importance; in ein Land —, to invade a country; in Schlaf —, to fall asleep; es fällt ins Pöbelhafte, it is rather vulgar; ins Rote —, to incline to red; in Schwermut —, to grow melancholy; über den Haufen —, to fall down; von einer Partei —, to abandon a party; von der Gnade —, to fall away from grace; Einkünfte, die von einem Gute —, the revenues of an estate; zu Grunde —, to sink to the bottom; einem zur Last —, to be a burden, troublesome to a person; im Gespräch (ein Wort) — lassen, to drop a word in a conversation; einen Freund — lassen, to forsake a friend; etwas vom Preise — lassen, to take something off the price; einem zu Füßen —, to throw oneself at a person's feet; gefallenes Obst, dropped fruit, windfall; ein gefallenes Mädchen, a seduced girl. II. *ir.v.a.;* er stürzte vom Dache und fiel dabei ein Kind tot, he fell from the roof and killed a child by falling on it; sich wund —, to wound oneself by falling. III. *subst. n.* subsidence; fall; decay; diminution.

Fall—(isse)me'nt, *n.* (—(isse)me'nts, *pl.* —(isse)me'nte) failure, bankruptcy. —ie'ren, *v.n.* (*aux.* h.) to fail; to become bankrupt. —i't, *m.* (—i'ten, *pl.* —i'ten) bankrupt. *Comp.* —i'ten-gericht, *n.* bankruptcy court. —i'ten-gesetz, *n.* bankruptcy laws. —i'ten-masse, *f.* bankrupt's estate *or* assets; Direktor der —i'tenmasse, official assignee.

Fäll'bar, *adj.* fit for felling; precipitable (*Chem.*).

Fäll'—en, *v.a.* to cause to fall, to fell, to lay low; to shoot, bring down; to let fall (*a perpendicular*); to sink (*a shaft*); to pass (*a sentence*); to pull down (*a wall, etc.*); to precipitate (*Chem.*); to lower (*bayonets*); —t das Gewehr! charge! (*Mil.*); mit gefälltem Bajonett angreifen, to charge with fixed bayonets. —ung, *f.* felling; precipitation (*Chem.*). *Comp.* —ungs-mittel, *n.* precipitant (*Chem.*).

Fäl'lig, *adj.* due, payable; (*in comp.* =) ready to fall; — werden, to fall due.

Falsch, I. *adj. & adv.* false, untrue; base, counterfeit, spurious; adulterated; forged; insincere; perfidious, treacherous; wrong (*as an opinion, a card, a note in music*); blank (*Arch.*); angry, wroth (auf einen, with a p.) (*coll.*); —e Münze, base coin; —er Stein, spurious stone; —e Wechsel, forged bills of exchange; —er Mensch, a deceitful person, a double-dealer; —e Zähne, artificial teeth; —e Rippen, short ribs; meine Uhr geht —, my watch goes wrong; —er Discant, falsetto; — darstellen, to misrepresent; Sie verstehen mich —, you misunderstand me; Sie sind — berichtet, you have been misinformed; — spielen, to play out of tune; to cheat (*at cards*); —es Spiel, foul play; —er Spieler, (card) sharper, cheat; —er König, usurper, pretender; — machen, to irritate, exasperate (*coll.*); — werden, to grow cross *or* angry (*coll.*); to learn bad tricks (*of dogs, horses, etc.*); — anführen, to misquote; — aussprechen, to pronounce incorrectly, mispronounce; — schwören, to perjure o.s. II. *subst. m. & n.* (—es), fault; ohne —, without guile; ohne — wie die Tauben, harmless as doves (*B.*); es ist kein — an ihm, he is quite upright; there is no fault in him. —heit, *f.* falsity, untruth; falseness, deceit, guile, perfidy, duplicity; spuriousness. *Comp.* —gläubig, *adj.* heterodox. —gläubigkeit, *f.* heterodoxy, heresy. —münzer, *m.* forger of base coin, coiner.

Fäl'sch—en, *v.a.* to falsify; to adulterate. —er, *m.* (—ers, *pl.* —er) falsifier, forger. —lich, *adv.* falsely; deceitfully; by mistake. —ung, *f.* falsification, forging, forgery; adulteration.

False't(t), *n.* (—es, *pl.* —e) falsetto.

Fält'—chen, *n.* (—chens, *pl.* —chen) crease, wrinkle. —eln, *v.a.* to lay in small plaits *or* folds; to plait, to gather. —ig, *suff.* (*in comp.* =) -fold, *e.g.* viel—ig, manifold.

Fal't—e, *f.* (*pl.* —en) fold, plait; crease; wrinkle; gather (*in dresses, etc.*); in —en legen, to fold; —en werfen, to pucker, to drag; dieses Kleid wirft keine —en, this dress fits without wrinkling; die Stirn in —en ziehen, to knit the brow; die geheimsten —en des Herzens, the inmost recesses of the heart. —ig, *adj. & adv.* having plaits *or* folds; wrinkled; (*in comp.* =) fold, *as* vier—ig, fourfold. —igkeit, *f.* —foldness, *as* Drei—igkeit, triplicity; Trinity. *Comp.* —en-brüche, *pl.* folds in drapery (*Paint.*). —en-kleid, *n.* plaited *or* gathered dress. —en-los, *adj.* unwrinkled, without folds; plain; smooth; open, without hidden blame. —en-magen, *m.* third stomach of ruminants. —en-näher, *m.* plaiter (*on sewing machines*). —en-reich, —en-voll, *adj.* full of folds *or* wrinkles. —en-schlag, —en-wurf, *m.* drapery (*Paint., Sculp.*). —en-weise, *adv.* in folds *or* plaits. —stuhl, *m.* folding chair.

Fal'te—n, *v.a.* to fold; to plait; to double up; to clasp together; to knit (*the brow*); to wrinkle, pucker; mit gefalteten Händen, with hands clasped (*as in prayer*); sich —n, to overlap (*Anat.*); es läßt sich zusammen —n, it can be folded up. —r, *m.* (—rs, *pl.* —r) butterfly, lepidopter.

Falz, *m.* (—es, *pl.* —e) fold; furrow; groove; notch; fluting; rabbet. —ig, *adj.* folded; grooved, furrowed. *Comp.* —amboß, *m.* coppersmith's anvil. —bein, *n.* paper knife, folder. —brett, *n.* folding board (*Bookb.*). —hammer, *m.* soldering hammer. —hobel, *m.* notching plane. —schiene, *f.* grooved *or* tram-rail. —zange, *f.* pliers.

Fal'ze—n, *v.a.* to fold (*paper*); to groove, flute; to join, rabbet; to solder (*tin, etc.*); to trim (*skins*). —r, *m.* (—rs, *pl.* —r) folder.

Famili—ä'r, *adj. & adv.* familiar. —arisie'ren, *v.a.* to familiarize. —aritä't, *f.* familiarity.

Fami'lie, *f.* (*pl.* —n) family; family, order, class, genus; tribe; es liegt in der —, it runs in the family; — haben, to have children; von guter — sein, to be of good family, to be well-born. —n-haft, *adj. & adv.* family-like. *Comp.* —n-ähnlichkeit, *f.* family likeness. —n-angelegenheiten, *pl.* family affairs. —n-anschluß, *m.*; er wünscht —nanschluß, he wishes to be treated like one of the family. **—n=anzeigen,** *pl.*, **—n=nachrichten,** *pl.* births, marriages, and deaths (*in newspapers*); hatches, matches, and despatches (*hum.*). **—n=begräbnis,** *n.* family vault. **—n=blatt,** *n.* family magazine. **—n=brod,** *n.* household bread, home-made bread. **—n=erbstück,** *n.* heirloom. **—en=glück,** *n.* domestic happiness. **—n=fehler,** *m.* hereditary failing. **—n=kreis,** *m.* domestic circle. **—n=los,** *adj.* without any children. **—n=rat,** *m.* family council. **—n=vater,** *m.* head of a *or* the family, paterfamilias. **—n=verkehr,** *m.* visiting in families, social intercourse among families. **—n=vermächtnis,** *n.* entail. **—n=wappen,** *n.* family coat of arms. **—n=zimmer,** *n.* sitting room. **—n=zwist,** *m.* domestic discord; family discord.

Famo's, (*sometimes* **Famö's**), *adj. & adv.* famous; excellent, splendid, capital; **—(s)er Kerl,** capital fellow, regular brick (*coll.*).

Fa'mul—us, *m.* (*pl.* **—i**) graduate assistant to a University professor; amanuensis.

Fana'l, *m. & n.* ship's lantern; lighthouse; beacon (*Mil.*).

Fana't—iker, *m.* (**—ikers,** *pl.* **—iker**) fanatic. **—is'mus,** *m.* fanaticism. **—isch,** *adj. & adv.* fanatic(al). **—isie'ren,** *v.a.* to fanaticize.

Fand, Fän'de, *imperf. ind.* and *subj. of* **finden.**

Fanfa'r—e, *f.* (*pl.* **—en**) flourish of trumpets; signal for the charge; **—e blasen,** to flourish. **—ona'de,** *f.* (*pl.* **—ona'den**) vain boasting.

Fang, *m.* (**—es,** *pl.* **Fän'ge**) catching, capture; snare, trap; fang; talon, claw; booty, draught, catch; death-stroke (*dealt to deer, etc.*); hilt (*of a sword, etc.*); place where anything is taken *or* caught. *Comp.* **—ball,** *m.* play-ball. **—brief,** *m.* warrant of arrest. **—eisen,** *n.* hunting-spear; iron trap. **—garn,** *n.* snaring net. **—leine,** *f.* leash; painter (*of a boat*). **—messer,** *n.* hunting knife. **—schnur,** *f.* noose, lasso; hanging-cord (*on uniforms*). **—spiel,** *n.* cup and ball. **—vogel,** *m.* decoy-bird. **—zahn,** *m.* fang, tusk.

Fan'gen, *ir.v.* I. *a.* to catch, seize; to capture; to take prisoner; to captivate; **es hat gefangen,** it has caught fire, it took effect; **leicht Feuer —,** to catch fire easily; to be easily irritated; **das Pulver will nicht —,** the powder will not take; **den Anker —,** to fish the anchor; **Felle —,** to soften hides; **mit gefangen, mit gehangen,** rogues of a gang on one gibbet must hang (*prov.*). II. *r.* to be caught, become entangled; to catch, take hold. III. *n.* (*aux.* **h.**) to bite; to take hold, clutch, seize.

Fän'ger, *m.* (**—s,** *pl.* **—**) catcher; catch; captor, weapon for despatching game; (*pl.*) tusks.

Fant, *m.* (**—es,** *pl.* **—e**) childish *or* conceited youth, youngster, stripling, puppy, coxcomb.

Fantasie', *see* **Phantasie.**

Far'b—e, *f.* (*pl.* **—en**) colour, tint, hue; dye; complexion; suit (*Cards.*); ink (*Typ.*); colour, pretext; colours, party; kind, description; manner, method; **echte —e,** fast colour; **sie hat viel —e,** she has a high colour, a bright complexion; **die —e bedienen,** to follow suit (*card playing*); **die —e auftragen,** to ink the form (*Typ.*); **die —en zu stark auftragen,** to exaggerate; **mit der —e herauskommen** *or* **—e bekennen,** to avow one's principles; **einer Sache eine gute —e geben,** to put a thing in a favourable light; **—e halten,** to bear body (*Paint.*), not to fade, to stick to one's colours; **—en betreffend,** chromatic. **—en,** *adj.* (*in compds.*) coloured. **—ig,** *adj.* coloured; stained; **der, die —ige,** coloured person. **—en=auftrag,** *m.* laying on of colour, touch (*Paint.*) **—en=bild,** *n.* coloured spectrum. **—en=blumen,** *pl.* pinks. **—en=bogen,** *m.* rainbow. **—en=brechung,** *f.* refraction of colours; blending of colours (*Paint.*). **—en=brett,** *n.* palette; inkboard. **—en=chemie,** *f.* chromaturgy. **—en=druck,** *m.* colour-printing, colour print. **—(en)=holz,** *n.* dyeing-wood. **—en=kleckser,** *m.* dauber. **—en=lage,** *f.* coating of colour. **—en=lehre,** *f.* theory of colours, chromatics. **—en=leiter,** *f.* scale of colours. **—en=rand,** *m.* iris. **—en=reiber,** *m.* colour-grinder. **—en=reich,** *adj.* richly-coloured. **—en=sinn,** *m.* (*fine*) sense of colour. **—en=skala,** *f.* colour chart. **—en=spektrum,** *n.* chromatic spectrum. **—en=spiel,** *n.* opalescence, play of colours. **—(en)=stift,** *m.* coloured crayon. **—(en)=stoff,** *m.* pigment. **—en=strahl,** *m.* coloured ray of light. **—en=stufe,** *f.* gradation of colour, shade, tinge. **—en=tafel,** *f.* cake of paint. **—en=ton,** *m.* tinge, tone of coloration; **gedämpfter —en=ton,** undertone; **mit satten —entönen,** deep-hued. **—en=tragend,** *adj.* wearing coloured badges; **—entragende Verbindungen,** students' clubs which possess distinct colours. **—en=waren,** *pl.* dye-stuffs. **—los,** *adj.* colourless, achromatic, neutral, indifferent. **—losigkeit,** *f.* pallor.

Fär'be, *f.* dyeing; dye house.

Fär'b—en, *v.* I. *a.* to colour, to dye, to stain (*glass, etc.*); to tinge; to give a certain colour to; **in der Wolle —en,** to engrain; **ein in der Wolle gefärbter Aristokrat,** an out and out (a thorough) aristocrat; **mit Blut gefärbt,** blood-stained. II. *r.* to blush. **—er,** *m.* (**—ers,** *pl.* **—er**) dyer. **—erei',** *f.* dyer's trade; dyeing; dye-house *or* works. **—ung,** *f.* colouring; hue, tinge. *Comp.* **—e=hölzer,** *pl.* dye-woods. **—e=kunst,** *f.* art of dyeing. **—er=beere,** *f.* purging buckthorn. **—er=meister,** *m.* master-dyer. **—er=röte,** *f.* madder. **—er=waid,** *m.* woad. **—er=weide,** *f.* sweet-willow. **—e(r)=stoff,** *m.* colouring matter; dye-stuff.

Far'c—e, *f.* (*pl.* **—en**) farce; force-meat; stuffing (*Cook.*). **—ie'ren,** *v.a.* to stuff.

Fari'nzucker, *m.* moist sugar.

Farn, *m.* (**—es,** *pl.* **—e**) fern. *Comp.* **—gebüsch,** *n.* brake. **—kraut,** *n.* fern. **—vorkeim,** *m.* fern-spore, fern-germ.

Fär'se, *f.* (*pl.* **—n**) one-year-old heifer, young cow.

Far'r(e), *m.* (**—(e)n,** *pl.* **—(e)n**) bullock, bull. *Comp.* **—(e)n=auge,** *n.* bull's eye.

Far'renkraut, *n. bad spelling for* **Farnkraut.**

Fasa'n, *m.* (**—s, —en,** *pl.* **—en**) pheasant. **—erie',** *f.* (*pl.* **—erie'en**) pheasantry. *Comp.* **—(en)=garten,** *m.*, **—(en)=gehäge,** *n.*, **—(en)=hof,** *m.* pheasant preserve. **—(en)=hund,** *m.* setter. **—(en)=jagd,** *f.* pheasant-shooting. **—ente,** *f.* pintail duck.

Faschi'ne, *f.* (*pl.* **—n**) fascine (*Fort.*); hurdle. *Comp.* **—n=blendung,** *f.* chanldeier, mantlet. **—n=messer,** *n.* knife to cut fascines *or* to use as a bayonet.

Fa'sching, *m.* (**—s,** *pl.* **—e**) carnival.

Fasci'kel, *m.* (**—s,** *pl.* **—**) file (*of papers*).

Fa'se, *f.* slender thread.

Fa'sel, *m.* (**—s**) hatch, brood, fry; cattle-breeding.

[1]**Fa'sel—n,** *v.n.* (*aux.* **h.**) to breed, to farrow; to prosper. *Comp.* **—hengst,** *m.* stallion. **—vieh,** *n.* breeding cattle.

[2]**Fa'sel—n,** *v.* I. *a.* to separate the threads *or* fibres; **sich —n,** to ravel out. II. *n.* (*aux.* **h.**) to rove, gad about; to act *or* talk foolishly; to dote; to drivel. **—ei',** *f.* (*pl.* **—ei'en**) fickleness, giddiness; drivelling talk; foolishness. **—er,** *m.* (**—ers,** *pl.* **—er**) silly, blundering fellow. **—ig, —haft,** *adj. & adv.* fickle, flighty, silly. *Comp.* **—hans,** *m.* silly fellow, fool; babbler; muddler.

Fä's—eln, —ern, *v.a. see* **Faseln.**

Fa'ser, *f.*, (*pl.* **—n**) thread, fibre, filament, fluff. **—chen,** *n.* (**—chens,** *pl.* **—chen**) fibril. **—icht,**

—**ig**, *adj.* fibre-like; fibrous. —**n**, *v.a. see* —**eln**, I. *Comp.* —**kiesel**, *m.* radiated quartz. —**knorpel**, *m.* fibrous cartilage. —**stoff**, *m.* fibrine.

Fas'nacht, *also* **Faß'nacht**, *f.* night of revel *or* nonsense; Shrove-Tuesday; shrovetide, carnival. *See* **Fastnacht**.

Faß, *n.* (—(ſ'ſ)es, *pl.* **Fäſ'ſer**) vat, tub; cask, barrel; firkin; hogshead; pipe (*of wine, etc.*); vessel; **das große** —, the great (Heidelberg) tun, barrel; **Wein vom** —, wine from the wood; **Bier vom** —, draught-ale; **friſch vom** —, drawn from the wood; **das ſchlägt dem** — **den Boden aus**, that puts an end to it, brings about the catastrophe; that spoils it all. *Comp.* —**band**, *n.* hoop. —**bier**, *n.* draught-beer *or* ale. —**binder**, *m.* cooper. —**boden**, *m.* head of a cask. —**bohrer**, *m.* piercer. —**butter**, *f.* tub butter. —**daube**, *f.* stave. —**faul**, *adj.* tasting of the cask. —**hahn**, *m.* cock, spigot. —**meßkunſt**, *f.* gauging. —**ſpund**, *m.* bung. —**ſchnecke**, *f.* trumpeter's shell. —**waren**, *pl.* merchandise in casks. —**weiſe**, *adv.* by *or* in the cask.

Faſ'ſ—en, *v.* I. *a.* to hold, contain, include; to grasp, seize, lay hold of; to apprehend, comprehend, conceive; to comprise; to fill up, barrel (*beer*); to sack (*corn*); to hive (*bees*); to set, enchase, mount; to clothe, express in a certain form; to take, form (*a resolve, a liking, etc.*); **in einen Rahmen —en**, to frame; **in die Augen —en**, to fix one's eyes upon; **ins Gedächtnis —en**, to keep in memory; **Anſchläge —en**, to form plans; **Abneigung —en**, to take a dislike (**gegen**, for); **Mut —en**, **ſich** (*dat.*) **ein Herz —en**, to take courage; **Wurzel —en**, to take root; **zuſammen —en**, to consider collectively; **kurz —en**, to compress, abridge; to sum up. II. *r.* to collect oneself, recover (*from emotion*); to contain *or* compose oneself; to express oneself; **ſich kurz —en**, to be quick of resolution; to be concise, brief, explicit; to cut it short; **ſich gefaßt machen auf eine S.**, to prepare oneself for a thing; **ſich —en laſſen**, to be frameable, to be comprehended, comprehensible; to allow oneself to be caught (*sl.*); **es läßt ſich nicht in Worte —en**, it is not to be expressed in words; **faſſe dich**, compose yourself. **gefaßt**, *p.p. & adj.* collected, composed, calm; prepared, ready. III. *n.* to be quick (slow) of apprehension; to bite, to catch. —**end**, *p. & adj.*, taking; capable; **in ſich —end**, comprehensive. —(**ß**)**lich**, *adj. & adv.* comprehensible, intelligible, conceivable; **leicht** —(**ß**)**lich**, easily understood. —(**ß**)**lichkeit**, *f.* comprehensibility; easy style. —**ung**, *f.* seizing, grasping; grasp; frame; setting, mounting; comprehension; composure, self-command; style; composition; **in dieſer —ung iſt es kaum verſtändlich**, it is scarcely intelligible as it stands; **aus der —ung bringen**, to disconcert, to overcome a p.'s gravity; **nicht aus der —ung kommen**, to keep one's countenance, to be collected. *Comp.* —**ungs=gabe**, —**ungs=kraft**, *f.*, —**ungs=vermögen**, *n.* power of comprehension, grasp of intellect. —**ungs=los**, *adj.* disconcerted.

Fäß'—chen, *n.* (—**chens**, *pl.* —**chen**) keg. *Comp.* —(**ſſ**)**er=weiſe**, *see* **Faßweiſe**.

Faſt, *adv.* almost, nearly, well nigh; very, strongly, in a high degree (*obs.*); — **nie**, scarcely ever; **ich will dich — ſehr mehren**, I will multiply thee exceedingly (*B.*).

Faſ't—en, I. *v.n.* to fast. II. *subst. n.* fasting. III. *pl.* fast; time of fasting, Lent. *Comp.* —(**en**)**=abend**, (*sometimes* —**el=abend**,) *m.* Shrove-Tuesday. —**en=mäßig**, *adj.* Lenten. —**en=ſonntag**, *m.* Sunday in Lent. —**en=ſpeiſe**, *f.* Lenten food, fish. —**en=zeit**, *f.* Lent, Shrovetide. —**nacht**, *f.* Shrove-Tuesday; shrovetide; carnival; —**nacht halten**, to keep carnival. —**nachts=aufzug**, *m.* masquerade. —**nachts=narr**, *m.* carnival-buffoon. —**nachts=ochſe**, *m.* fattened ox decorated with garlands and ribbons. —**nachts=ſcherz**, *m.* carnival-jest. —**nachts=ſpiel**, *n.* dramatic farce acted, (especially in the sixteenth century), during Lent; carnival play *or* farce. —**tag**, *m.* fast-day; **hoher —tag**, high day; **ſtrenge —tage**, days of obligation.

Fata'l, *adj. & adv.* disagreeable, annoying, odious; calamitous, awkward, unfortunate; **das iſt** —, that's a nuisance; **eine —e Geſchichte**, an awkward business. —**is'mus**, *m.* fatalism. —**itä't**, *f.* fatality; ill-luck, misfortune.

Fa'tum, *n.* (—**s**, *pl.* **Fa'ta**) fate, destiny.

Fat'z—en, *v.* I. *n.* (*aux.* **h.**) to jest, play tricks. II. *a.* to laugh at, make a fool of. *Comp.* —**ke**, *m.* conceited, silly person (*often used in compounds*, e.g. **Patent—ke**, *m.* dandy).

Fau'ch—en, —**zen**, *v.n.* (*aux.* **h.**) to mew and spit (*as cats*).

Fauka'l, *adj.*; —**er Verſchlußlaut**, faucal stop, sound produced by lowering of the velum as breath passes through the nose (*Phonet.*).

Faul, *adj. & adv.* decayed, rotten, putrid; lazy; indolent; sluggish; bad, worthless; brittle; **ſich auf die —e Haut legen**, to indulge, *or* live in idleness; **der —e Fleck**, the sore point, the dirty spot; **eine —e Küſte**, a dangerous coast; —**es Fleiſch**, proud flesh; —**e See**, calm (*Naut.*); —**er Kunde**, bad customer (*C. L.*); —**e Bäuche**, lazy people; —**e Witze**, bad *or* poor jokes; **eine —e Sache, ein —er Zauber**, a difficult matter, a complicated and spoilt affair (*sl.*); —**er Knecht**, ready reckoner; —**e Fiſche**, suspicious actions, subterfuges; —**es Geſchwätz**, idle talk; corrupt communications (*B.*); **er, nicht —, ſtand auf**, suddenly he rose. —**bar**, *adj.* putrescible. —**heit**, *f.* slothfulness; idleness. —**icht**, (*obs.*), —**ig**, *adj. & adv.* appearing *or* tasting rotten; somewhat putrid *or* rotten. *Comp.* —**baum**, *m.* black alder. —**bett**, *n.* couch; bed of ease *or* idleness; couch for lolling; (*fig.*) inactivity, apathy. —**fieber**, *n.* putrid fever; extreme idleness (*sl.*). —**fuß**, *m.* sloth (*Zool.*). —**matte**, *f.* rope mat. —**pelz**, *m.* sluggard. —**pfründe**, *f.* sinecure. —**pfründner**, *m.* one enjoying a sinecure. —**tier**, *n.* sloth.

Fäul'—e, *now usually* —**nis**, *f.* rot, rottenness, corruption, putrefaction, decay; **in —nis übergehen** *or* **geraten**, to putrefy. *Comp.* —**nis=widrig**, *adj.* antiseptic(al); —**niswidriges Mittel**, antiseptic.

Fau'len, *v.n.* (*aux.* **ſ.**) to rot, putrefy, become foul. —**d**, *p. & adj.* putrescent. —**zen**, *v.n.* (*aux.* **h.**) to idle, lounge; to be lazy. —**zer**, *m.* (—**zers**, *pl.* —**zer**) sluggard, idler; easy-chair. —**zerei'**, *f.* sluggishness; idleness.

Faun, *m.* (—**en**, *pl.* —**en**) faun, satyr. —**a**, *f.* fauna. —**en=haft**, *adj. & adv.* faunlike; lascivious. *Comp.* —**en=blick**, *m.* lascivious look.

Fauſt, *f.* (*pl.* **Fäuſ'te**, *dim.* **Fäuſt'chen**) clenched hand, fist; **ſich** (*dat.*) **ins Fäuſtchen lachen**, to laugh in one's sleeve, **die geballte** —, clenched fist; **ſchwer auf der — liegen**, to be hard-mouthed (*of horses*); **auf eigne** —, on one's own responsibility; **Soldat auf eigene** —, a free lance; **mit dem Degen in der** —, sword in hand; **das paßt (geht) wie die — aufs Auge**, it's as like as chalk to cheese, there is neither rhyme nor reason in it; — **kämpfen**, to box. *Comp.* —**dick**, *adj.* thick as a fist; sly; **er hat es —dick hinter den Ohren**, he is a sly rogue, an arrant dissembler. —**gelenk**, *n.*

wrist. —gerecht, *adj.* dexterous. —handschuh, *m.* glove without fingers. —kampf, *m.* boxing-match. —kämpfer, *m.* pugilist, boxer. —pfand, *n.* dead-pledge. —recht, *n.* club-law, law of might. —schlag, *m.* cuff; (*pl.*) fisticuffs. —voll, *adj.* handful.

Fäus't—el, *m.* (—els, *pl.* —el) miner's hammer. —ling, *m.* (—lings, *pl.* —linge) mitten; cudgel; pigmy. —lings, *adv.* with the fist.

Favor—isie'ren, *v.a.* to favour. —i't, *m.* (—i'ten, *pl.* —i'ten), —i'te, —i'tin, *f.* favourite.

Fa'xen, *pl.* fooleries, buffoonery (*coll.*); mach keine —, don't be a fool! do not be fussy! (*coll.*).

Fayen'ce, *f.* (*pl.* —n) fine pottery; delf.

Fe'bruar, *m.* (—s, *pl.* —e) February.

Fech's—en, *v.a.* to gather in the vintage. —er, *m.* (—ers, *pl.* —er) vine stock for transplanting.

Fech't—en, *ir.v.n.* (*aux.* h.) to fight, combat; to fence; —en gehen, to go begging (*coll.*); mit den Händen —en, to gesticulate. —er, *m.* (—ers, *pl.* —er) fighter; fencer; gladiator; swordsman. —erei', *f.* fighting; fencing; dispute. *Comp.* —boden, *m.* fencing school *or* room. —degen, *m.*, —eisen, *n.* foil, rapier. —er=kampf, *m.* sword-fight; gladiatorial combat. —er=spiel, *n.* assault of arms. —er=stellung, *f.* position (*in fencing*); squaring up (*in boxing*). —er=streich, *m.* feint. —handschuh, *m.* fencing-glove. —klub, *m.* fencing club. —kunst, *f.* art of fencing. —übung, *f.* practice with the foils.

Fe'der, *f.* (*pl.* —n), feather; plume; quill, pen; fin (*Icht.*); bristle, prickle, quill (*of beasts*); tail (*of hares*); flaw (*in jewels*); wall-spike (*Fort.*); spring (*of a machine*); style; (*pl.*) feather-bed; in die — diktieren *or* sagen, to dictate; das ist aus meiner —, it is written by me; unter der — haben, to be just writing (*a book*); in —n hängen, to be hung on springs; er ist soeben aus den —n, he is just up. —icht, (*obs.*) —ig, *adj.* & *adv.* feathery; feathered; fleecy. *Comp.* —angel, *f.* spring hinge. —anschuß, *m.* feather-like crystallization. —artig, *adj.* feathery. —ball, *m.* shuttlecock. —ball=schlägel, *m.* racket. —besen, *m.* dusting-brush. —blatt, *n.* spring-plate (*of a lock*). —blech, *n.* steel for watch-springs. —büchse, *f.* pen-case. —busch, *m.* plume; tuft, crest. —erz, *n.* plumose silver-ore. —fechter, *m.* controversialist. —förmig, *adj.* plumiform. —fuchser, *m.* quill-driver, scribbler. —füßig, *adj.* foot-feathered, plumiped. —gehäuse, *n.* spring-case (*for watches*). —haken, *m.* feather-spring (*on triggers*). —halter, *m.* pen-holder. —härte, *f.* elasticity. —hart, *adj.* hard and elastic like a steel spring. —harz, *n.* India rubber. —haspel, *m.* spring-reel (*Angl.*). —haus, *n.* spring-box, barrel. —heber, *m.* spring lever. —hut, *m.* hat, bonnet with feathers. —kasten, *m.* pen-case. —kiel, *m.* quill. —kissen, *n.* feather-stuffed cushion *or* pillow. —klinke, *f.* spring-latch. —kraft, *f.* elasticity. —krieg, *m.* paper war, controversy. —lecker, *m.* penny-a-liner, scribbler. —leicht, *adj.* light as a feather, very light. —leinwand, *f.* swans-down. —lesen, *n.* feather-picking; ceremony, mincing; ohne viel —lesen(s), without much ceremony; nicht viel —lesens machen, to be unceremonious, make short work, to handle roughly. —leser, *m.* stickler for trifles. —los, *adj.* featherless; unfledged. —meißel, *m.* pledget (*Surg.*). —messer, *n.* pen-knife. —nelke, *f.* Sweet William. —pfühl, *m.* bolster. —pose, *f.* quill. —riegel, *m.* spring-bolt. —schloß, *n.* spring-lock. —schmücker, *m.* feather-dresser. —spiel, *n.* spillikins, jack-straws; lure (*of falconers*); falcon (*obsol.*). —spule, *f.* quill. —staub, *m.* down. —strich, —zug, *m.* stroke, dash of the pen. —tüchtigkeit, *f.* penmanship. —vieh, *n.* poultry. —wage, *f.* spring balance. —wechsel, *m.* moulting. —weiß, *n.* stone-alum; asbestus. —werk, *n.* plumage; anything stuffed with feathers; spring of a lock. —wild, *n.* feathered game, wild fowl. —winden, *pl.* spring-tools. —wischer, *m.* pen-wiper. —zeichnung, *f.* pen-and-ink drawing. —zange, *f.* pliers. —zirkel, *m.* spring-dividers.

Fe'dern, *v.* I. *n.* (*aux.* h.) to lose feathers; to be elastic. II. *r.* to moult.

Fee, *f.* (*pl.* —n) fairy; gute —, kind fairy. —erei', *f.* activity of fairies. —n=haft, *adj.* fairy-like, magical. *Comp.* —n=palast, *m.* fairy palace. —n=reigen, *m.* fairy-ring, fairy dance.

Fe'ge, *f.* (act of) sweeping; sweeping-brush.

Fe'g—en, *v.* I. *a.* to cleanse, scour, furbish, sweep; to wipe; to purge (*Med.*); to rub off (*skin or antlers*); to winnow; to rate, scold; to rebuke; einem den Beutel —en, to drain a person's purse. II. *n.* (*aux.* h. & s.) to scamper, scour along; to sweep over, to rush across. —er, *m.* (—ers, *pl.* —er) sweeper; scourer. —sel, *n.* (—sels, *pl.* —sel) sweepings. —ung, *f.* cleansing, sweeping, wiping, scouring. *Comp.* —e=beutel, *m.* purse-drainer. —(e)=feuer, *n.* purgatory. —e=hader, —e=lappen, *m.* dish-clout. —e=sand, *m.* scouring sand. —maschine, *f.* fan, scutcher.

Feh'de, *f.* (*pl.* —n) private warfare, feud; —bieten, to defy. *Comp.* —brief, *m.* (written) challenge, cartel. —handschuh, *m.* glove (*thrown down as a challenge*), gauntlet; den —handschuh aufheben, to accept the challenge. —recht, *n.* feudal law; right of declaring feud.

Fe'h, *f.* (*pl.* —en) Siberian squirrel; minever, skins of Siberian squirrel, calabar skins.

Fehl, I. *m.* (—s, *pl.* —e) fault, failure (*B. for* —er). II. *adv.* & *sep. prefix*, wrong, wrongly, amiss; erroneously; in vain; (*in comp. gen'lly* =) mis-. —bar, *adj.* fallible. —barkeit, *f.* fallibility. *Comp.* —betrag, *m.* missing amount, deficit. —bitte, *f.* vain request; eine —bitte thun, to meet with a refusal. —blatt, *n* missing leaf *or* card. —bogen, *m.* imperfect sheet. —druck, *m.* misprint; foul impression (*Typ.*); error (*stamp*). —gang, *m.* the wrong way; walk to no purpose; einen —gang thun, to miss one's way; not to succeed. —gebären, *v.n.* (*aux.* h.) to miscarry. —geburt, *f.* miscarriage, abortion. —gehen, *ir.v.a.* to go astray; not to succeed; to miss the way. —greifen, *ir.v.a.* to make a mistake, to err. —griff, *m.* blunder, mistake. —jahr, *n.* year of a bad harvest. —kauf, *m.* bad bargain. —ritt, *m.* ride in vain *or* astray. —schießen, *ir.v.a.* to miss one's aim; —geschossen! wrong! mistaken! (*coll.*). —schlag, *m.* wrong stroke, miss (*as at cricket*); disappointment. —schlagen, *ir.v.n.* (*aux.* h. & s.) to miss one's blow; to miscarry, fail, be disappointed; seine Hoffnungen schlugen —, his hopes were disappointed. —schließen, *ir.v.n.* (*aux.* h.) to draw a wrong conclusion. —schluß, *m.* wrong inference. —schritt, *m.* false step; error. —schuß, *m.* miss; shot that has missed its aim. —stoß, *m.* miss (*in thrusting, shoving, etc.*). —treten, *ir.v.n.* (*aux.* h.) to trip, to stumble. —tritt, *m.* stumble, false step; error; failure, fault, lapse; einen —tritt thun, to miss one's footing, to stumble; das Mädchen hat einen —tritt gethan, the girl has gone astray, has lost her honour. —wurf, *m.* false throw, miss. —ziehen, *ir.v.n.* (*aux.* h.) to pull amiss; to draw a blank (*in a lottery*). —zug, *m.* wrong move (*Chess, etc.*); blank (*in lotteries*).

Feh'l—en, *v.* I. *a.* to miss. II. *n.* (*aux.* h.) to miss; to fail, err, be in the wrong; to be absent; to be due; to be wanting, deficient; to offend; to ail; **weit gefehlt!** far from the mark! mistaken, wrong! **ihr —t nichts,** she stands in need of nothing; **es kann nicht —en, daß er . . .,** he cannot fail to . . .; **es konnte ihm nicht —en,** he could not fail (of success); **an mir soll es nicht —en,** I shall not be wanting, it shall not be my fault (*if*); **es —te nur, daß,** all that was wanting was; **das —te noch!** and that too! **das —te nur noch,** that would be the last straw, Heaven forbid! **es —t nicht viel, du überredest mich,** almost thou persuadest me (*B.*); **es —te uns an Lebensmitteln,** we fell short of provisions; **es —t ihm an Mut,** he is wanting in courage; **was —t Ihnen?** what ails you? **es —t ihm immer etwas,** he is always ailing; **ihr —t nichts,** she is quite well; **es —t ihm noch viel,** he is deficient in many things; **es —en lassen an** (*dat.*), to be wanting in, come short in; **er ließ es an nichts —en,** he spared no pains; he provided everything, saw that all was there; **es —en noch 10 Minuten an 12,** it is 10 minutes to 12; **es —en im Ganzen 30,** altogether 30 are missing; **dieser Artikel —t mir,** I am out of this article (*C.L.*). **—end,** *p. & adj.* erring, wanting, deficient; **das —ende,** want.

Feh'ler, *m.* (**—ers,** *pl.* **—er**) fault, defect; want; failing; error, blunder; **einen eines —ers beschuldigen,** to accuse one of, blame one for a fault. **—frei,** *or* **—los,** *adj.* faultless. **—haft,** *adj.* faulty, defective; incorrect. **—haftigkeit,** *f.* faultiness; incorrectness.

Fehm. *m. see* **Feimen.**

Fe[illegible]**—e,** *also* **Fe'me,** (*older spelling* **Veh'me,**) *f.* secret and popular self-appointed criminal tribunal (*in Westphalia of old*); **die heilige —e,** the secret court of justice and its laws. *Comp.* **—ding, —gericht,** *n.* secret court, vehmic court. **—recht,** *n.* rights and customs of the vehmic court. **—richter,** *m.* judge presiding over a vehmic court. **—statt, —stätte,** *f.* place where the secret tribunal met.

Fehn, *n.* (**—s,** *pl.* **—**) moorland, fen.

Fei, *f.* (*pl.* **—en**) *poetic for* **Fee,** fairy.

Fei'en, *v.a.* to charm one (**gegen eine S.,** against a th.). **gefeit,** *p.p. & adj.* (**gegen**) charmed, proof (against).

Fei'er, *f.* (*pl.* **—n**) cessation from work, rest; recess; holiday; solemnity; solemnization, celebration; festival. **—lich,** *adj. & adv.* solemn; festive; **—lich begehen,** to solemnize. **—lichkeit,** *f.* (*pl.* **—lichkeiten**) solemnity; pomp, ceremony. *Comp.* **—abend,** *m.* time for leaving off work; evening of rest; eve of a holiday; **—abend machen,** to leave off work; to knock off (*coll.*). **—abend=arbeit,** *f.* extra work. **—abend=glocke,** *f.* vesper-bell, curfew-bell. **—brauch, —gebrauch,** *m.* ceremony. **—gesang,** *m.* solemn hymn. **—gesell,** *m.* workman out of employ. **—gewand, —kleid,** *n.* festive raiment. **—stunde,** *f.* festive hour; hour of rest. **—tag,** *m.* holiday; day of rest, Sunday; festival. **—tags=kleid,** *n.* Sunday clothes, holiday garment. **—täglich,** *adj.* belonging to a holiday, festive.

Fei'er—n, *v.* I. *n.* (*aux.* **h.**) to give up work, be idle, tarry, rest; to make holiday; to lie fallow; **da ist nicht zu —n,** there is no time to be lost; **dann wird das Land —n und ihm seine —gefallen lassen,** then shall the land rest and enjoy her sabbaths (*B.*). II. *a.* to celebrate, solemnize; to observe; to extol, to honour.

[1]**Fei'g—e,** *adj.* cowardly, dastardly, faint-hearted; crumbling, rotten (*Min.*); **eine —e Memme,** poltroon. **—heit,** *f.* cowardice. **—ling,** *m.* (**—lings,** *pl.* **—linge**) coward, dastard. *Comp.* **—herzig,** *adj.* cowardly, fainthearted.

[2]**Fei'g—e,** *f.* (*pl.* **—en**) fig; box on the ear; eruption on the eyelids; figshell (*Mollusc.*); **einem die —e weisen,** to snap one's fingers at a person, defy him; to fig a p. (*vulg.*). *Comp.* **—blatter, —warze,** *f.* pimple; boil, tumour. **—bohne,** *f.* horse-bean. **—en=baum,** *m.* fig-tree. **—en=blatt,** fig-leaf; (*pl.*) subterfuges.

Feil, *adj. & adv.* to be sold; venal; bribable; mercenary; **— bieten,** to offer for sale; **— haben,** to have for sale, to be ready to sell; **dieses Pferd ist mir um keinen Preis —,** I should not sell this horse for any money; **— tragen,** to hawk; **—er Mensch,** hireling; **—e Dirne,** prostitute. **—heit,** *f.* venality; prostitution.

Feil'—bar, *adj.* that may be filed. **—e,** *f.* (*pl.* **—en**) file. **—icht,** *n.* (**—ichtes,** *pl.* **—ichte**), **—sel,** *n.* (**—sels,** *pl.* **—sel**) file dust. *Comp.* **—bogen,** *m.* steel-saw. **—en=hauer,** *m.* file-cutter. **—kloben, —stock,** *m.* hand-vice. **—späne,** *pl.*, **—staub,** *m.* filings.

Fei'len, *v.a.* to file, to polish. **gefeilt,** *p.p. & adj.* filed, polished, elaborate.

Feil'sch—en, *v.a. & n.* (*aux.* **h.**) to haggle about the price, to bargain; to cheapen. **—er,** *m.* (**—ers,** *pl.* **—er**) haggler, bargainer.

Feim, *m.* (**—es,** *pl.* **—e**) froth, foam (*obs.*).

Fei'men, *m.* (**—s,** *pl.* **—**) hay-stack.

Fein, *adj. & adv.* fine, not coarse; delicate; nice; goodly (*B.*); beautiful; polite; cultivated, refined; elegant; fashionable; acute, quick; sly, artful; beautiful, excellent, capital (*coll.*); **er ist — heraus,** he is a lucky fellow (*coll.*); **—er Mann,** well-bred man; **—e Welt,** fashionable *or* polite society, people of fashion; **—er Ton,** good form; **—er Kopf,** clever person; **—e Sitten,** good manners; **—er Verstand,** cultivated understanding; **—es Gefühl,** fine feeling; **—er Fuchs,** sly fellow; **—er Regen,** drizzling rain; **sei mir — klug,** mind, be wise! **es ist — warm hier,** it 's nice and warm here! **er spricht kein —es Englisch,** he does not speak the King's English. **—e** (*obs.*), **—heit,** *f.* fineness; refinement; sharpness (*of the senses*); delicacy (*of feeling*); politeness; elegance; cunning; purity (*of gold, etc.*); rarity (*of the air*); (*pl.*) niceties (*of language, etc.*). *Comp.* **—bäckerei,** *f.* fancy bakery. **—brenner,** *m.* refiner of metals. **—fühlend,** *adj.* sensitive. **—fühlig,** *adj.* of delicate feeling, thin-skinned. **—fühligkeit,** *f.* **—gefühl,** *n.* delicacy *or* refinement of feeling, tact. **—gehalt,** *m.* proportion of fine metal (*in coins or bullion*), standard. **—gespitzt,** *adj.* sharp-pointed. **—gezeichnet,** *adj.* finely drawn, minutely detailed. **—hörend, —hörig,** *adj.* quick of hearing. **—macher,** *m.* refiner; finisher (*of paper*). **—malerei',** *f.* miniature painting. **—sichtig,** *adj.* sharp-sighted, quick of sight. **—s=liebchen,** *n.* darling, sweetheart (*obs. & poet.*). **—schmecker,** *m.* gourmet, fine-feeder, gastronomist. **—spindel=bank, —spulmaschine,** *f.* jack-frame. **—spinnmaschine,** *f.* spinning jenny. **—zinn,** *n.* grain tin.

Feind, I. *adj.* hostile. II. *m.* (**—es,** *pl.* **—e**) enemy, foe; **der böse —,** the very adversary; the evil one; **abgesagter —,** mortal *or* sworn enemy. **—in,** *f.* foe, enemy. **—lich,** *adj. & adv.* hostile, inimical; **das —liche Heer,** the enemy. **—lichkeit,** *f.* hostility. **—schaft,** *f.* enmity, hatred, hostility. **—schaftlich,** *adj. & adv.* hostile. **—selig,** *adj. & adv.* hostile; malignant. **—seligkeit,** *f.* malignity; hostility, war.

Feist, I. *adj.* fat; **—er Sonntag,** the last Sunday before Lent. II. *m. see* **—e,** I. **—e,** I. *n.* (**—es**) fat, suet (*of deer, etc.*). II. *f.*, **—igkeit,** *f.* obesity. *Comp.* **—zeit,** *f.* season for venison (*when deer are fat*).

Fei'xen, *v.n.* to grin (*dial. & coll.*).

Fel'b—e, *f.*, **—er** *or* **—inger,** *m.* white willow.

Fel'bel, *m.* (**—s**) velveteen; long-poil.

Fel'chen, *m.* (—s, *pl.* —) a kind of salmon (*plentiful in the Bodensee and other Swiss lakes*).

Feld, *n.* (—es, *pl.* —er) field, open land, plain; ground; field (*Mil.*); area; field of action, sphere; department (*of a science, etc.*); square (*of a chessboard*); panel; pane; compartment; shield; **das freie** —, plain; **das — bebauen**, to till the ground; **das — bebauend**, agricultural; **über — gehen**, to go across country; to go a journey; **ins — rücken, zu —e ziehen**, to take the field; **das — behalten, behaupten**, to win the day; **ein Heer ins — stellen**, to take the field with an army; **im freien — liegen**, to bivouac; **— gewinnen**, to gain ground; **noch im weiten —e**, still very uncertain, unsettled; **die Sache steht noch im weiten —**, that 's still a long way off, very remote. **—ig**, *adj. & adv.* (*in compounds*) having fields *or* squares. *Comp.* **—anger**, *m.* ridge between two fields. **—apotheke**, *f.* dispensary tent (*Mil.*). **—apotheker**, *m.* field-apothecary. **—arbeit**, *f.* agricultural labour. **—artillerie**, *f.* field *or* light artillery, field guns. **—arzt**, *m.* military *or* army surgeon. **—bäcker**, *m.* army-baker. **—bahn**, *f.* military railway. **—bau**, *m.* agriculture, tillage. **—bett**, *n.* camp-bed. **—binde**, *f.* scarf, sash (*Mil.*). **—blume**, *f.* wild-flower. **—binse**, *f.* field-rush. **—brustwehr**, *f.* glacis. **—chirurg**, *m.* army surgeon. **—dieb**, *m.* thief that robs the fields. **— dienst**, *m.* rural statute-labour; active service. **—dienst=übung**, *f.* field-practice, petty manœuvre in time of peace; **eine —dienstübung abhalten**, to hold a field day. **—flasche**, *f.* soldier's flask, canteen. **—ei'n, —ei'nwärts**, *adv.* across country; across the fields. **—flucht**, *f.* desertion. **—flüchtig**, *adj.* runaway. **—frucht**, *f.* produce of the fields; *pl.* **—früchte**, crops. **—fuß**, *m.* war-footing. **—geflügel**, *n.* birds that harbour in the field. **—gehäge**, *n.* warren; covert, preserve. **—geist**, *m.* sylvan spirit; satyr, faun. **—geistlicher**, *m.* army chaplain, acting chaplain (to His Majesty's forces). **—gepäck**, *n.* baggage (*of an army*). **—gerecht**, *adj.* broken, well-trained to sport. **—gerät**, *n.* baggage of an army; implements of husbandry. **—gericht**, *n.* court-martial. **—geschirr**, *n.* implements of agriculture; harness of farm-horses. **—geschrei**, *n.* warcry; war-whoop. **—gottesdienst**, *m.* camp service. **—hauptmann**, *m.* commander-in-chief; general (*obs.*). **—herr**, *m.* commander-in-chief; general. **—herrn=kunst**, *f.* generalship; strategy. **—herrn=stab**, *m.* baton. **—herrn=würde**, *f.* supreme command. **—hospital**, *n.* field hospital, ambulance. **—huhn**, *n.* partridge. **—hüter**, *m.* field watch, field guard. **—hütte**, *f.* soldier's hut. **—jäger**, *m.* game-keeper for the smaller game; a soldier (*or* officer) employed in carrying orders, king's *or* minister's messenger; orderly. **—kanzlei**, *f.* army office. **—kasse**, *f.* military chest. **—kessel**, *m.* camp kettle. **—koch**, *m.* army cook, sutler. **—kochgerät**, *n.* camp kettles. **—koffer**, *m.* portmanteau used in a campaign. **—lager**, *n.* camp. **—läufer**, *m.* golden plover (*Orn.*). **—lazarett**, *n.* ambulance. **—lerche**, *f.* skylark. **—mark**, *f.* landmark; boundary; fields of a village. **—marschall**, *m.* field-marshal. **—marschalls=stab**, *m.* marshal's baton. **—meister**, *m.* flayer. **—messer**, *m.* geometrician, land surveyor. **—meßkunst**, *f.* art of surveying. **—mohn**, *m.* common poppy. **—musik**, *f.* military music. **—mütze**, *f.* foraging cap. **—post**, *f.* military post, army post. **—posten**, *m.* outpost of an army. **—prediger**, *m.* army chaplain, acting chaplain (to His *or* Her Majesty's forces). **—probst**, *m.* principal chaplain (*Mil.*). **—rose**, *f.* wild rose; **wohlriechende —rose**, sweetbriar. **—rute**, *f.* pole for surveying. **—schaden**, *m.* damage done to the fields. **—schanze**, *f.* redoubt, field-work. **—scher, —scherer**, *m.* army surgeon. **—schlacht**, *f.* battle. **—schlange**, *f.* culverin (*old-fashioned long gun*). **—schmiede**, *f.* forge of an army blacksmith. **—schnecke**, *f.* slug. **—schöppe**, *m.* land commissioner. **—schreiber**, *m.* military clerk. **—schule**, *f.* field school (*for the children of the soldiers*). **—schwamm**, *m.* mushroom. **—soldat**, *m.* soldier in the field, soldier on active service. **—spat**, *m.* felspar. **—sperling**, *m.* hedge sparrow. **—stecher**, *m.* field glass. **—stein**, *m.* landmark. **—stück**, *n.* field-piece (*Artil.*); landscape. **—stuhl**, *m.* camp-stool, folding chair. **—verpflegung**, *f.* purveyance of an army. **—wache, —wacht**, *f.* advanced post, outpost; **—wachen ausstellen**, to post pickets. **—webel**, *m.* colour-sergeant, sergeant-major. **—weg**, *m.* lane, field-path; furlong. **—wehre**, *f.* precinct, boundary; outer intrenchment. **—werk**, *n.* field-work (*Fort.*). **—wirtschaft**, *f.* agriculture. **—winde**, *f.* wild convolvulus. **—zeichen**, *n.* military sign, for recognition, field badge; sash; banner. **—zeug**, *n.* munition; ordnance. **—zeugmeister**, *m.* master of the ordnance; **General —zeugmeister**, master-general of the ordnance. **—zug**, *m.* campaign, expedition.

[1]**Fel'ge**, *f.* (*pl.* —n) felly (*of a wheel*); rim (*cycl.*). *Comp.* **—n=hauer**, *m.* wheelwright.

[2]**Fel'ge**, *f.* fallow (*Agr.*).

[1]**Fel'gen**, *v.a.* to provide (*a wheel*) with fellies.

[2]**Fel'gen**, *v.a.* to turn the ground; to plough for the second *or* third time.

Fell, *n.* (—es, *pl.* —e) skin, hide; fur; film; **einem das — über die Ohren ziehen**, to flay, fleece one; **er hat ein sehr dickes —**, he is very thick-skinned; **— auf dem Auge**, film of the eye. *Comp.* **—bereiter**, *m.* currier; furrier. **—gar**, *adj.* duly-dressed (*of skins*). **—händler**, *m.* dealer in hides, furrier, fellmonger. **—werk**, *n.* skins, furs.

Fel'lah, *m.* (—s, *pl.* —s) fellah.

Fell'eisen, *n.* (—s, *pl.* —) knapsack, portmanteau, wallet, valise.

Fels, *m.* (—(s)en, *pl.* —(s)en) (*poet. and high style*), **—(s)en**, *m.* (—(s)ens, *pl.* —(s)en) rock, cliff. **—icht**, (*obs.*) **—ig**, *adj.* rock-like; rocky. *Comp.* **—abhang**, *m.* slope of a rock. **—absturz**, *m.* fall of rocks and remains thereof. **—artig**, *adj.* rocky. **—blöcke**, *pl.* boulders.

Fel'sen (*in comp.*) **—bock**, *m.* wild goat. **—fest**, *adj.* firm as a rock, unshakable; **das steht — fest**, that is quite sure. **—geröll e**, *n.* particles rubbed off from rocks, scree. **—gras**, *n.* Iceland moss. **—harnisch**, *m.* rocky armour; scales hard as rock. **—hart**, *adj.* hard as rock; stony. **—insel**, *f.* rocky island. **—keller**, *m.* cellar cut in the rock; name of inns in mountainous districts. **—klippe**, *f.* cliff. **—kluft**, *f.* chasm; cleft in rocks. **—rebe**, *f.* clematis. **—riff**, *n.* ledge of rocks, reef. **—riß**, *m.* reef of rocks. **—ritze**, *f.* crevice in a rock. **—schlucht**, *f.* rocky gorge. **—schicht**, *f.* layer of rock. **—schwalbe**, *f.* mountain swallow. **—steg**, *m.* rocky path, path through rocks. **—spitze**, *f.* peak, crag. **—ufer**, *n.* bluff. **—wand**, *f.* face of a cliff, steep side of a rock, precipitous rock, precipice. **—verließ**, *n.* rocky keep, dungeon hewn in a rock. **—ziege**, *f.* wild she-goat.

Fen'chel, *m.* (—s) fennel. *Comp.* **—holz**, *n.* sassafras. **—öl**, *n.* oil of fennel, anathol.

Fenn, *n.* (—s, *pl.* —e) fen, swamp, marsh, bog.

Fen'ster, *n.* (—s, *pl.* —) window; glass-frame of a hotbed; **ein blindes —**, mock-window; **gewölbtes —**, bow-window; **gemalte, bunte —**, stained windows; **zum — hinaus sehen**, to look out of the window; **zum — hinein,** in at the window; **einem die — einwerfen,** to break a p.'s windows. **—ig, fenstrig,** *suff.* (*in comp.* =) windowed, with windows. *Comp.* — **angel,** *f.* casement-hinge. **—austritt,** *m.* balcony. **—band,** *n.* glass-holder; window cramp-iron. **—bank,** *f.* sill. **—beschläge,** *pl.* casement, iron work of a window. **—blei,** *n.* lead for windows. **—bogen,** *m.* arch of a window. — **brett,** *n.*, sill, elbow-board. **—brüstung,** *f.* elbow-place, sill of a window, breast-wall. **—fach,** *n.* pane, square of a window. — **flügel,** *m.* wing of a window; half casement. **—futter,** *n.* sash, frame of a window. **—gardine,** *f.* window-curtain. **—geld,** *n.*, **—steuer,** *f.* window-tax. **—giebel,** *m.* frontal, pediment. **—gitter,** *n.* window-grate, lattice. **—höhle,** *f.* side piece of a window, aperture in which a window may be fitted. **—jalousie,** *f.* Venetian blind. **—kitt,** *m.* putty. **—kreuz,** *n.* cross-work of a window, cross-bars. **—laden,** *m.* window-shutter. — **nische,** *f.* embrasure. **—parade,** *f.*; **einem Mädchen —parade machen,** to court by walking up and down before the house of a beloved girl. **—pfeiler,** *m.* pier. **—pfosten,** *m.*, — **säule,** *f.* window-post. **—polster,** *n.* window-cushion. **—rahmen,** *m.* window-frame. — **raute,** *f.* pane of glass. **—riegel,** *m.* sash-bolt; window fastener. **—rollen,** *pl.* sash-pulleys. **—roll=jalousie,** *f.* Venetian blind. — **scheibe,** *f.* pane of glass. **—schieber,** *m.* sash. **—spiegel,** *m.* spy-mirror in a window; pier-glass. **—stock,** *m.* mullion, pediment. **—thür,** *f.* glass door. **—vertiefung,** *f.* recess of a window, embrasure. **—zelt,** *n.* awning.

Fen'stern, *v.* I. *a.* to furnish with windows; to scold. II. *n.* (*aux.* **h.**) to make love beneath the sweetheart's window (*dial. also* **fensteln**).

Ferch, *m.* (**—es,** *pl.* **—e**) noxious damps in mines.

Fer'ge, *m.* (**—n,** *pl.* **—n**) ferry-man (*obs. & poetic*); mariner (*B.*).

Fe'rien, *pl.* vacation, holidays; **die großen —,** the long vacation, the summer holidays. — **kursus,** *m.* (*pl.* **—kurse**) holiday course (*of lectures*) (*comp. the Engl. University extension courses*). **—reise,** *f.* holiday excursion, trip.

Fer'kel, *n.* (**—s,** *pl.* **—**) young pig, sucking pig; dirty person; blot; **eine Tracht —,** a litter of pigs; **— werfen,** to litter, farrow; **das — quiekt,** the little pig squeaks. **—n,** *v.n.* to farrow. *Comp.* **—kaninchen,** *n.* guinea-pig.

Ferme'nt, *n.* (**—s,** *pl.* **—e**) ferment.

Fermentie'ren, *v.n.* (*aux.* **h.**) to ferment.

Fernambuk'holz, *n.* (**—es**) Brazil-wood.

Fern, *adj. & adv.* far, distant, far off, remote; **von —,** afar, at a distance; covertly, secretly; **so—, in so—,** so far as, if, in case; **das sei mir —,** far be it from me; **das sei — !** God forbid! (*B.*); **in wie—,** how far, in what measure *or* degree; **sich — halten,** to keep *or* stand aloof (*from*); **er steht mir —,** he has no close connection with me; **er steht — von mir,** he is far from me; **einen von sich — halten,** to keep a p. at a distance; **diese ist nicht von —e mit jener zu vergleichen,** this girl is not in the least to be compared with that. **—e,** *f.* (*pl.* **—en**) remoteness, distance, distant place *or* time; **aus der —e,** from afar; **in der —e,** in the distance, at a distance, far off; **in die —e,** to a distance; **sich in der —e halten,** to keep away *or* out of reach; **in der —e liegend,** remote, in the far future, uncertain; **das liegt noch in weiter —e,** that is still looming in the distant future. **—er,** *adj. & adv.* farther; furthermore, moreover; **und so —er,** and so on, et cetera; **—er im Amte bleiben,** to continue in office. **—ig,** *adj.* of last year, old (*B.*). **—ung,** *f.* distance (*Paint.*). *Comp.* **—abdonnernd,** *adj.* the thunder gradually dying away in the distance. **—ansicht,** *f.* distant view; perspective. **—darstellung,** *f.* perspective representation. **—er=hin,** *adv.* for the future, henceforward. **—er=weit,** *adj. & adv.* further, furthermore; additional; henceforth. **—gefühl,** *n.* presentiment. **—glas,** *n.* telescope. **—haltung,** *f.* keeping off. **—hintreffend,** *adj.* hitting far away; darter (*Apollo*); long range. **—hörer,** *m.* receiver (*of a telephone*). **—rohr,** *n.* telescope. **—schaulich,** *adj.* seen distantly *or* perspectively. **—schaulichkeit,** *f.*, **—schein,** *m.* perspective. **—schreiber,** *m.* telegraph. — **schrift,** *f.* writing seen at a distance; telegraphic *or* heliographic signal. **—sicht,** *f.* prospect, perspective view. **—sichtig,** *adj.* far- *or* long-sighted. **—sprech=amt,** *n.* telephone office. **—sprech=betrieb,** *m.* telephony. — **sprecher,** *m.* telephone; **einen durch den —sprecher anrufen,** to ring a p. up. **—sprech=stelle,** *f.* telephone office; public telephone. **—sprech=wesen,** *n.* telephone service. **—ste=hende(r),** *m.* outsider. **—treffend,** *adj.* long-range. **—verkehr,** *m.* foreign traffic *or* service; long-distance traffic. **—wirkung,** *f.* telekinesis; **seelische —wirkung,** telepathy. **—zeich=nung,** *f.* perspective drawing. **—zug,** *m.* long-distance train.

Fer'ner, *m.* (**—s,** *pl.* **—**) snow mountain, glacier.

Fer'newein, Fir'newein, *m.* (**—s, —e**) wine of last year; fine old wine (*dial. & poet.*).

Fer'se, *f.* (*pl.* **—n**) heel; track, footsteps; hind part of a horse's hoof; **die —n zeigen,** to take to one's heels; **einem auf den —n sein** *or* **folgen,** to pursue one closely. *Comp.* **—n=bein,** *n.* heel-bone. **—n=eng,** *adj.* with narrow hoofs. **—n=flechte,** *f.* tendo Achillis. **—n=geld,** *n.*; **—ngeld geben,** to give leg-bail. **—n=punkt,** *m.* nadir (*Astr.*). **—n=schlag,** *m.* kick (*of a horse*).

Fer'tig, *adj. & adv.* ready to start, ready, prepared; complete, finished, perfect; skilful, dexterous; accomplished (*as a musician*); ready-made; fluent; perfect (*B.*); **ich bin —,** I have done; **er ist —,** he is ruined, it is all over with him; he is drunk (*coll.*); **er spricht — Deutsch,** he speaks German fluently, with perfect ease; **sich — machen,** to get ready; **sich — halten,** to be in readiness; to be prepared; **sehen Sie zu, wie Sie — werden,** see what you can do, how you can manage; **mit etwas — sein,** to have done with s.th.; to have finished s.th.; **man konnte ohne ihn nicht — werden,** there was no getting on *or* doing without him; **— werden,** to finish with a thing; **mit einem — werden,** to manage, settle a person, bring him to reason; **mit ihm ist kein — werden,** there is no dealing with him; **wir sind — mit einander,** it is all over between us; **—!** make ready! prepare! — **keit,** *f.* skill, dexterity; fluency; completeness; **—keit im Spielen,** execution (*Mus.*). *Comp.* **—machen,** *n.* adjustment (*Typ.*). — **macher,** *m.* finisher; adjuster (*Typ.*); foreman. **—stellung,** *f.* completion.

Fer'tig—en, *v.* I. *a.* to make, get ready, finish, prepare; to despatch. II. *r.* to prepare; to flee, hasten over (*B.*). **—er,** *m.* (**—ers,** *pl.* **—er**) maker; performer; consigner. **—ung,** *f.* making, fabrication.

Fes, *n.* F flat (*Mus.*).

Fesch, *adj.* fashionable, stylish; smart; dashing (*sl.*); **sie ist ein —es Mädel,** she is an up-to-date girl (*coll.*).

Fes'sel, *f.* (*pl.* **—n**) fetter, chain; fetlock joint (*of a horse*); (*pl.*) irons, handcuffs; **einem —n anlegen,** to put one in irons, handcuff one. *Comp.* **—ballon,** *m.* captive balloon. **—bein,** *n.* pastern. **—bein=gelenk,** *n.* pastern joint. **—frei, —los,** *adj.* unfettered.

Fes'seln, *v.a.* to fetter, chain; to fasten, attach; to captivate; to arrest (*attention*); to put in irons; **—de Unterhaltung,** interesting conversation.

[1]**Fest,** I. *adj. adv. & sep. prefix,* fast, firm, stable; solid, hard; fixed, immovable; close (*of texture*); permanent, constant; certain (*of an income*); invulnerable; strong, solid; well-versed; fortified; thoroughly (*coll.*); **—es Auge,** steady eye; strict eye (*fig.*); **—er Eimer,** water-tight pail; **—er Entschluß,** firm resolve; **—e Farben,** fixed colours; **—en Fuß fassen,** to gain a (firm) footing; **— sein gegen,** to be proof against; **—es Gehalt,** fixed salary; **—e Gesundheit,** robust health; **—e Grundsätze,** fixed principles; **—er Glaube,** steady faith; **—er Handel,** fast bargain; **in —en Händen,** in the hands of people who may be relied on *or* who will keep a thing; not to be sold; **—er Knoten,** tight knot; **—e Körper,** solid bodies; **—er Kunde,** regular customer; **das —e Land,** terra firma, continent, mainland; **eine —e Masse,** compact mass; **—er Ort,** fortress; **—e Preise,** fixed prices; **—er Schlaf,** sound sleep; **— umschlossen,** closely surrounded; **einen Handel — machen,** to close a bargain; **so viel steht —,** this (*at least*) is evident *or* certain; **einen —(e) durchprügeln,** to give one a thorough thrashing (*coll.*); **nur — drauf los!** go at it with might and main! (*coll.*); **(etwas) — behaupten,** to maintain positively. II. *suff.* (*in comp.* =) versed in, *as* **bibel—,** versed in Scripture; **sattel —,** firm in the saddle; well versed in. **—e,** *f.* (*pl.* **—en**) firmness, solidity, confirmation; stronghold; prison; **—e des Himmels,** firmament of heaven (*B.*). *Comp.* **—binden,** *ir.v.a.* to tie, bind fast. **—gebannt,** *adj.* spell-bound. **—halten,** *ir.v.* **I.** *a.* to hold fast; to arrest. II. *n.* (*aux.* **h.**) to hold on, cling, adhere to. **—land,** *n.* continent. **—machen,** *v.a.* to fasten, fix; to steady; to fortify (*towns, etc.*); to consolidate (*liquids, etc.*); to house (*guns*); to bind (*servants, etc.*); to make secure; to belay (*ropes*). **—nehmen,** *ir.v.a.* to seize, take hold of, arrest; to apprehend. **—setzen,** *v.a.* to fix (*a day, etc.*); to settle; to stipulate; to lay down as a rule; to effect a lodgment (*Mil.*); to arrest; **sich —setzen,** to settle; to gain a footing (**an,** in). **—setzung,** *f.* establishment; appointment. **—stellen,** *v.a.* to fix, settle, establish, confirm. **—stehend,** *adj.* stationary, well established; old (*custom*).

[2]**Fest,** *n.* (**—es,** *pl.* **—e**) festival; holiday; feast; fête; banquet; **bewegliches —,** movable feast; **man muß die —e feiern wie sie fallen,** Christmas comes but once a year, enough is as good as a feast (*prov.*); **ein — geben,** to give a (great) banquet *or* treat. **—lich,** *adj. & adv.* festive, solemn, splendid. **—lichkeit,** *f.* festivity, solemnity. *Comp.* **—abend,** *m.* festival evening; eve of a holiday. **—essen,** *n.* banquet. **—geber,** *m.* host, entertainer, giver of a feast. **—gebrauch,** *m.* feast-rite, ritual. **—geläute,** *n.* festive peal ofbells, chime. **—halle,** *f.* banqueting hall. **—kleid,** *n.* holiday attire; evening dress. **—mahl,** *n.,* **—schmaus,** *m.* banquet, feast. **—opfer,** *n.* oblation. **—ordner,** *m.* the person responsible for all the arrangements for a festival; master of ceremonies. **—ordnung,** *f.* order of proceedings at a festival. **—rede,** *f.* speech of the day *or* evening. **—redner,** *m.* official speaker. **—schmuck,** *m.* festive attire. **—spiel,** festival play. **—tag,** *m.* holiday, festival day. **—täglich,** *adj.* festival, holiday. **—trommeten=schall,** *m.* the sound of festive (*or* joyous) trumpets.

Fes't—en (*obs. & poet.*), **—igen,** *v.a.* to make fast *or* firm; to make, render solid, compact; to settle, establish, confirm. **—igkeit,** *f.* firmness, fixedness; solidity; soundness; steadiness; constancy; closeness; decision. **—ung,** *f.* fastness; fortress; stronghold; citadel. *Comp.* **—ungs=arrest,** *m.* imprisonment in a fortress. **—ungs=bau,** *m.* fortification; government works (*for convicts*). **—ungs=baukunst,** *f.* science of fortification. **—ungs=gefangene(r),** *m.* criminal condemned to work in a fortress. **—ungs=pfahl,** *m.* palisade. **—ungs=strafe,** *f.* confinement in a fortress. **—ungs=viereck,** *n.* four fortresses (in North Italy). **—ungs=wall,** *m.* rampart. **—ungs=werk,** *n.* fortification.

Festo'n, *m.* (**—s,** *pl.* **—s**) festoon.

Fe'tisch, *m.* (**—(e)s,** *pl.* **—e**) fetish. *Comp.* **—anbetung,** *f.,* **—dienst,** *m.* fetishism, worshipping of idols.

Fett, I. *n.* (**—es**) fat; grease; the cream, essence; tallow; **Nieren—,** suet; **Schweine —,** lard; **Braten—,** dripping; **er hat sein — weg,** he has got his punishment (*coll.*); **— ansetzen,** to grow fat. II. *adj. & adv.* fat; plump; greasy; adipose; rich; lucrative; **das macht den Kohl nicht —,** that won't make much difference, be of much use; **eine —e Pfründe,** a fat living; **—er Druck,** large-faced type, clarendon (*Typ.*); **—e Seide,** raw silk. **—e** (*obs.*) *f.,* **—heit,** *f.* fatness, greasiness; richness. **—ig,** *adj. & adv.* fatty, greasy; **sich** (*dat.*) **die Finger —ig machen,** to grease one's fingers. *Comp.* **—ader,** *f.* adipose vein. **—auge,** *n.* drop of grease floating on broth, scum. **—bäuchig,** *adj.* paunchy. **—darm,** *m.* fat *or* straight gut. **—fleck(en),** *m.* grease-spot. **—gänge,** *pl.* adipose ducts. **—gans,** *f.* penguin. **—glanz,** *m.* resinous lustre. **—glänzend,** *adj.* shiny. **—haut,** *f.* adipose tissue. **—kelle,** *f.* basting-ladle. **—körper,** *pl. m.* fatty bodies. **—kram,** *m.* chandlery. **—krämer,** *m.* chandler. **—leibig,** *adj.* obese. **—magen,** *m.* fourth stomach of ruminants. **—pflanzen,** *pl.* succulent plants. **—reihe,** *f.* (*chem.*) fatty series, aliphatic series. **—stein,** *m.* elaolite. **—sucht,** *f.* obesity. **—thon,** *m.* fuller's earth. **—wachs,** *m.* adipocere (*Chem.*). **—wanstig,** *adj.* big-bellied, paunchy. **—zellen,** *pl.* adipose cells.

Fet'ten, *v.a.* to make fat *or* greasy; to grease.

Fet'z—en, I. *m.* (**—ens,** *pl.* **—en**) rag, tatter, shred. II. *v.a.* to shred. **—er,** *m.* shoddy-machine.

Feucht, *adj.* moist, damp; muggy; **von —er Natur,** phlegmatic; **—er Brand,** gangrene; **ein —es Weib,** a mermaid; a woman of bad reputation (*sl.*). **—e** (*obs. & poet.*), **—heit,** *f.* humidity, damp. **—igkeit,** *f.* moisture; dampness, humours (*of the body*). *Comp.* **—fröhlich,** *adj.* merry with a moistened throat, jovial in one's cups (*stud. sl.*). **—igkeits=messer,** *m.* hygrometer. **—kalt,** *adj.* moist and cold. **—kammer,** *f.* wetting-room (*Typ.*). **—verklärt,** *adj.* humid (and) bright; **das —verklärte Blau,** the bright humid blue. **—zieher,** *m.* hygroscope.

Feuch'ten, *v.a. & n.* (*aux.* **h.**; *usually in compounds* **an—** *or* **be—**), to wet, moisten, damp. **gefeuchtet,** *p.p. & adj.* washed.

Feuda'l, *adj. & adv.* feudal; capital (*sl.*). *Comp.* **—recht,** *n.* feudal law.

Feu'er, *n.* (**—s,** *pl.* **—**) fire; ardour, passion; spirit; mettle; brilliancy (*jewel*); **— anmachen, — anzünden,** to light a fire; **— anlegen,** to put on fuel; to set on fire; **Öl ins — gießen,** to add fuel to the fire (*prov.*); **das — eröffnen,** to open fire; **das — einstellen,** to cease firing; **im — sein,** to be under fire, to be fired upon; **— geben,** to fire (*Milit.*); **— eines (edeln) Weines,** raciness, body of wine; **leicht — fangen,** to be easily set on fire, easily thrown into a passion; **— speien,** to vomit fire; in — und Flamme geraten über eine S., to fire up at a th.; darf ich Sie um — bitten? may I ask you for a light for my cigar? —ig, feurig, *adj.* fiery; ardent, passionate, fervid; der —ige Busch, the burning bush. —ig=flüssig, *adj.* molten, volcanic. *Comp.* —anbeter, *m.* fire-worshipper. —ar=tig, *adj.* igneous. —bake, *f.* beacon. —ball, *m.* fire-ball. —becken, *n.* chafing-dish. —berg, *m.* volcano. —beständig, *adj.* fire-proof (*Chem.*). —blond, *adj.* auburn (of hair). —bock, *m.* andiron, fire-dog. —bohne, *f.* scarlet runner. —braun, *adj.* made brown by heat, red-hot. —büchse, *f.* tinder-box; fire-box. —dienst, *m.* fire-worship. —eifer, *m.* ardent zeal, ardour. —eimer, *m.* fire-bucket. —esse, *f.* chimney; furnace, forge. —fangend, *adj.* inflammable. —fest, *adj.* fire-proof. —flaschen, *pl.* powder-flasks. —flüssig, *adj.* molten. —gatter, *n.* fender; fire-guard. —gefährlich, *adj.* liable to take fire, combustible. —glocke, *f.* alarm-bell. —gradmesser, *m.* pyrometer. —haken, *m.* pot-hook; poker. —herd, *m.* hearth, fire-side, fireplace. —holz, *n.* fuel. —hüter, *m.* fire watch (*in mining*); stoker. —io! —jo! *int.* (*cry of*) fire, ho! —kasse, *f.* fire-insurance-office. —kieke, *f.* foot-warmer, foot-stove. —kraut, *n.* scarlet lichen. —kugel, *f.* bomb. —kreuz, *n.* fiery cross. —kunst, *f.* pyrotechnics. —lärm, *m.* cry of fire. —leute, *pl.* firemen, fire brigade. —linie, *f.* fighting-line, front line in battle. —lösch=anstalt, *f.* engine house; (*pl.*) arrangements for extinguishing fires. —lösch=apparat, *m.* fire-extinguisher. —lösch=wesen, *n.* organization of fire-brigades. —los, *adj.* cloudy (*of jewels*). —luft, *f.* inflammable air, hydrogen. —mal, *n.* mole; scar (*from a burn*). —malerei, *f.* encaustic painting. —mann, *m.* fireman; stoker. — —männchen, *n.* will-o-the-wisp. —mauer, *f.* shaft of a chimney; party-wall. —melde=stelle, *f.* office where notice of a fire should be given. —nelke, *f.* scarlet lychnis. —ofen, *m.* furnace, stove. —ordnung, *f.* fire regulations. —pfanne, *f.* chafing-dish; censer. —platte, *f.* back of a chimney. —probe, *f.* fire ordeal, trial by fire; crucial test. —punkt, *m.* focus. —rad, *n.* Catherine wheel. —regen, *m.* rain of fire. —reiter, *m.* a rider who summons help at a fire. —rettungs=apparat, *m.* fire-escape. —rohr, *n.* fire-lock; rifle; *pl.* fire-arms. —rost, *m.* fire-grate. —rot, *adj.* red as fire. —säule, *f.* fiery column. —s=brunst, *f.* fire, conflagration. —schaden, *m.* damage caused by fire. —schau, *f.* official inspection to guard against fire. —schein, *m.* glare of fire, fire-light. —schiff, *n.* fire-ship. —schirm, *m.* fire-screen. —schlange, *f.* fire-snake, cannon. —schlund, *m.* fiery abyss; crater; cannon, gun. —schür=eisen, *n.* poker. —schwaden, *m.* fire-damp (*Min.*). —schwamm, *m.* German tinder. —schwärmer, *m.* squib. —s=gefahr, *f.* danger of fire. —s=not, *f.* conflagration; calamity resulting from fire. —speiend, *adj.* spitting fire, volcanic; —speiender Berg, volcano. —spritze, *f.* fire-engine. —stahl, *m.* steel for striking fire. —stätte, *f.* place of a conflagration; fireplace. —stein, *m.* flint. —stelle, *f.* hearth; house. —stoff, *m.* caloric. —strafe, *f.* punishment of death by fire. —strahl, *m.* flash of fire. —taufe, *f.* baptism of fire; die —taufe erhalten, to be under fire for the first time. —thon, *m.* fire-clay. —turm, *m.* beacon, light-house. —vergoldung, *f.* hot gilding. —versicherung, *f.* fire-insurance. —versicherungs=police, *f.* fire-policy. —wache, *f.* fire-watch; fireman on watch. —warte, *f.* lighthouse; beacon. —waffe, *f.* gun; *pl.* fire-arms. —wehr, *f.* fire-brigade. —werk, *n.* fireworks; heute abend ist großes —werk, to-night there will be a grand display of fireworks. —werk=künstler, *m.* pyrotechnist. —werker, *m.* firework maker; gunner, artilleryman. —werkerei', *f.* pyrotechnics. —zange, *f.* tongs. —zauber, *m.* enchanted fire, miraculous blaze of fire surrounding a place, fire-magic. —zeichen, *n.* signal by a lighted fire; flash; fiery meteor. —zeug, *n.* materials for striking fire; tinder-box; match-box. —zunder, *m.* touchwood; materials for excitement (*poet.*).

Feu'er—n, *v.* I. *a.* to fire; to kindle. II. *n.* to burn, glow. —ung, *f.* firing; fuel. —ungs=material, *n.* fuel.

Fex, *m.* (—es, *pl.* —e) weak person; fool, crazy (*in compounds: e.g.* Bergfex, an enthusiastic climber, a man madly fond of climbing).

Fia'ker, *m.* (—s, *pl.* —) hackney-coach, cab (*Austrian*). *Comp.* —kutscher, *m.* hackney-coachman.

Fias'ko, *n.* (—s, *pl.* —s) failure; — machen, to break down, fail utterly.

Fi'bel, *f.* (*pl.* —n) primer, hornbook, spelling book.

Fi'b—er, *f.* (*pl.* —ern) fibre. —ri'n, *n.* (—ri'ns) fibrine. —rö's, *adj.* fibrous.

Ficht, Fichtst, *3 & 2 pres. sing. pres. indic. of* fechten.

Fich't—e, *f.* (*pl.* —en) common spruce, picea excelsa. —en, *adj.* of pine-wood, pine. *Comp.* —en=apfel, *m.* pine-apple; pine-cone. —en=baum, *m. see* Fichte. —en=harz, *n.* common resin. —en=holz, *n.* pine-wood. —en=stamm, *m.* trunk of a pine-tree. —en=zapfen, *m.* pine-cone.

Fi'cken, *v.a. & n.* to make quick movements to and fro; to flick. —facke(r)n, *v.n.* to intrigue; to shuffle (*obs.*). —facker, *m.* (—fackers, *pl.* —facker) intriguer; cheat (*obs.*).

Fideikommi'ß, *m.* (—(ss)es, *pl.* —(ss)e) feoffment in trust; entail; ein — aufheben, to cut off the entail. —(ss)ä'r, *m.* (—(ss)ä'rs, *pl.* —(ss)ä're), (—besitzer, *m.*,) trustee. *Comp.* —gut, *n.* entailed property; property vested in trustees.

Fide'l, *adj. & adv.* merry, jolly; kreuz —, very merry, very jolly. —itä't, (*also* Fidulitä't,) *f.* jollity (*coll.*).

Fi'dibus, *m.* (—(ss)es, *pl.* —(ss)e) paper match for a long pipe, spill.

Fie'ber, *n.* (—s, *pl.* —) fever; hitziges —, inflammatory fever; kaltes —, ague, intermittent fever; auszehrendes —, hectic fever. —haft, *adj. & adv.* feverish. —haftigkeit, *f.* feverishness. —isch, *adj. & adv.* feverish. *Comp.* —anfall, *m.* attack of fever. —artig, *adj.* febrile. —frost, *m.*, —kälte, *f.* shivering fit (*as in ague*); chill. —hitze, *f.* feverish heat, heat of the fever; cauma (*Med.*); bis zur —hitze, up to fever point. —krank, *adj.* feverish. —mittel, *n.* medicine that makes the fever go down, febrifuge. —rinde, *f.* Peruvian bark. —schauder, *m.* ague-fit, shivering-fit. —tag, *m.* day on which a fever comes on. —traum, *m.* feverish dream; hallucination. —wechsel, *m.* intermission of fever. —zufall, *m.* attack of fever.

Fie'bern, *v.n.* (*aux.* h.) to be in *or* have a fever; to be feverish; to rave.

Fie'del, *f.* (*pl.* —n) fiddle. —er, (Fied'ler,) *m.* (—ers, *pl.* —er) fiddler. —n, *v.a.* (*aux.* h.) to fiddle, scrape on the fiddle. *Comp.* —bogen, *m.* fiddle-stick, fiddle-bow, bow.

Fie'derig, *adj. & adv.* feathered, plumed; pinnate (*Bot.*).

Fie'dern, *v.a.* to furnish, adorn with feathers (*rare, mostly used in the p.p.* gefiedert).

Fiel, Fie'le, *imperf. ind. & subj. of* fallen.

Fieng (*now usually spelt* Fing) *sing. imperf. of* fangen (*obs.* fahen).

Figu'r, *f.* (*pl.* —en) figure; diagram; trope.

figure of speech; piece (*Chess*); figure-head (*of a ship*); court-card. **—a'bel**, *adj.* capable of being brought to a certain, fixed form. **—abilitä't**, *f.* figurability (*Phys.*). **—a'l**, *adj.* figurate. **—a'nt**, *m.* (**—an'ten**, *pl.* **—an'ten**), **—an'tin**, *f.* stage-walker, dummy, ballet-dancer. **—en=tanz**, *m.* square dance, figure dance. **—ie'ren**, *v.a. & n.* (*aux.* **h.**) to figure; to cut a figure; **—ier'te Zeuge**, figured, fancy clothes. **—is'mus**, *m.* typical teaching. **—i'st**, *m.* (**—i'sten**, *pl.* **—i'sten**) sculptor, carver. *Comp.* **—al'=baß**, *m.* figured bass (*Mus.*). **—al'=gesang**, *m.* prick song, figurate descant. **—al'musik**, *f.* figurate counterpoint. **—ier'=bank**, *f.* figuring *or* eccentric lathe.

Figür'lich, *adj. & adv.* figurative, metaphorical.

File't, *n.* (—s, *pl.* —s, —en) netting, net-work; filet (*of meat*); book-binder's tool. *Comp.* **—nadel**, *f.* netting-needle. **—schraube**, *f.* netting-vice.

Filia'l, *n.* (—s, *pl.* —e), **—e**, *f.* (*pl.* —en) affiliated institution; branch establishment *or* office. *Comp.* **—geschäft**, *n.* branch establishment. **—kirche**, *f.* chapel of ease, under-parochial church. **—schule**, *f.* school annexed to another.

Filigra'n, *n.* (—s) filigrane, filigree.

Film, *m.* (—s, *pl.* —e) film (*Phot.*).

Filtrie'r—en, *v.a.* to filter, to strain. **—ung**, *f.* filtration. *Comp.* **—apparat**, *m.* filter. **—kanne**, *f.* decanter; coffee-biggin. **—papier**, *n.* filter-paper. **—schicht**, *f.* filter-bed. **—trichter**, *m.* strainer. **—tuch**, *n.* straining cloth.

Filz, *m.* (—es, *pl.* —e) felt; blanket (*Typ.*); tomentum (*Bot.*); rebuke, snubbing (*obs.*); (*also* **—er**, *m.*) curmudgeon, miser, niggard; rude fellow (*obs.*). **—ig**, *adj.* of felt; like felt; fluffy, nappy; stingy; sordid. *Comp.* **—ballen**, *pl.* engraver's balls for cleaning. **—deckel**, *m.* blanket, damper (*Typ.*). **—hut**, *m.* felt hat. **—unterlage**, *f.* blanket (*Typ.*)

Fil'zen, I. *adj.* of felt. II. *v.a.* to felt; to snub; III. *v.n.* (*aux.* **h.**) to be niggardly.

[1]**Fim'mel**, *m.* (—s, *pl.* —) iron wedge; sledge hammer.

[2]**Fim'mel**, *m.* (—s, *pl.* —) fimble hemp (*Bot.*).

Final'stock, *m.* (—s, *pl.* **Final'stöcke**) tail-piece (*Typ.*).

Fina'nz, *f.* (*usually in the pl.* **Finan'zen**) finances; cash; **die —en betreffend**, financial; **die hohe —**, the great financiers. **—ie'll**, *adj. & adv.* financial. *Comp.* **—amt**, *n.* treasury-board. **—ausschuß**, *m.* committee of ways and means, finance-committee. **—gericht**, *n.* court of exchequer. **—kammer**, *f.* treasury board, board of revenue. **—kunde**, *f.* science of finance. **—mann**, *m.* financier; money-maker. **—minister**, *m.* minister of finances, (*in England*) Chancellor of the Exchequer, (*in America*) Secretary of the Treasury. **—ministerium**, *n.* ministry of finances, (*in England*) Treasury. **—plan**, *m.* budget. **—rat**, *m.* councillor on the board of revenue. **—welt**, *f.* moneyed class; the great financiers *or* bankers. **—wesen**, *n.* finance(s). **—wirtschaft**, *f.* budget.

Find'bar, *adj.* findable, to be met with.

Fin'del, *pref.* (*in comp.* =) foundling. *Comp.* **—haus**, *n.* foundling hospital. **—kind**, *n.* foundling, hedge-born child. **—mutter**, *f.*, **—vater**, *m.* adoptive parent; guardian of a foundling.

Fin'd—en, *ir.v.* I. *a.* to find; to meet with; to light upon, discover; to think, deem, consider; **für gut —en**, to think proper; **statt—en**, to take place; **statt—en lassen**, to suffer to take place; **große Freude —en an einer S.**, to take great delight in a th.; **Geschmack an einer S. —en**, to relish a th.; **wie —en Sie diesen Wein?** how do you like this wine?; **ich will ihn schon —en**, he shall not go unpunished. II. *r.* to find oneself; to be found; to be (*in health, condition, or place*); to present itself, offer, occur; (*with* **zu**) to find one's way to, to submit to, comply with; **er läßt sich zu allem willig —en**, he complies with, agrees to anything; **sich zurecht —en**, to see one's way clearly; **fanden Sie sich zurecht?** did you find your way?; **ich weiß mich nicht zurecht zu —**, I am quite at sea; **ich kann mich dar(e)in nicht —en**, I cannot reconcile myself to it, I don't know what to make of it; **es wird sich —en**, it will be seen, we shall see; **es fand sich oft**, it often happened; **das Wort —et sich bei Shakespeare**, the word occurs in Shakespere; **sich geschmeichelt —en**, to feel flattered; **sich in einen —en**, to get on with a p., to accommodate oneself to a p., to understand a p. **—er**, *m.* (**—ers**, *pl.* **—er**) finder, discoverer. **—ig**, *adj.* resourceful; sharp, ingenious. **—igkeit**, *f.* resourcefulness; sharpness, shrewdness, ingenuity. **—ling**, *m.* (**—lings**, *pl.* **—linge**) foundling. **—ung**, *f.* finding; discovery. *Comp.* **—e=buch**, *n.* reference book; inventory. **—e=lohn**, **—er=lohn**, *m.* reward for returning things found. **—e=ort**, *m.* place where anything is found. **—lings=block**, *m.* erratic block, drift block.

Fines'se, *f.* (*pl.* —n) finesse, stratagem.

Fing, **Fin'ge**, *imperf. indic. & subj. of* **fangen**.

Fin'ger, *m.* (—s, *pl.* —) finger; talon, toe, division of claws; **mit —n weisen auf (einen)**, to point at; **einem auf die — klopfen**, to rap one over the knuckles, check, rebuke one; **einem auf die — sehen**, to have a strict eye upon one; **sich** (*dat.*) **die — verbrennen**, to get into a mess; **an den —n hersagen**, to have at one's finger ends; **durch die — sehen**, not to look at too strictly, to connive *or* wink at; **mir sagt's mein kleiner —**, a little bird told me; **aus den —n saugen**, to invent; **er hat lange —, macht krumme —**, he is light-fingered, is given to pilfering; **das Heer der langen —**, light-fingered gentry; **bei geraden —n verhungern**, to starve on honesty; **die — gehörig setzen**, to finger (*Mus.*). **—ig**, *adj. & adv.* having fingers, fingered. **—ling**, *m.* (**—lings**, *pl.* **—linge**) finger-stall. *Comp.* **—beine**, *pl.* phalanges (*Anat.*). **—breit**, *adj.* a finger broad. **—brett**, *n.* keys (*of a piano*). **—entzündung**, *f.* whitlow. **—fertigkeit**, *f.* manual skill, dexterity; execution (*Mus.*). **—förmig**, *adj.* digitate. **—fuß**, *m.* dactyl. **—gang**, *m.* fingering (*Mus.*). **—gelenk**, *n.* finger-joint. **—glied**, *n.* phalanx (*Anat.*). **—hut**, *m.* thimble; foxglove (*Bot.*). **—hut=futteral**, *n.* thimble-case. **—kraut**, *n.* cinquefoil. **—leiter**, *m.* finger-guide (*Mus.*). **—nerven**, *pl.* digital nerves. **—platte**, *f.* door-guard, finger-plate. **—satz**, *m.*, **—setzen**, *n.* fingering (*Mus.*). **—spitze**, *f.* tip of the finger, finger-end; **es juckt ihn in den —spitzen**, his fingers are itching. **—sprache**, *f.* finger talk, hand-language, dactylology, chirology; **Kenner der —sprache**, chirologist. **—stock**, *m.* glove-stretcher. **—übung**, *f.* fingering, finger-exercises (*Mus.*). **—zahl**, *f.* digit (*Arith.*). **—zeig**, *m.* sign with the finger; indication, hint.

Fin'gern, *v.* I. *a. & n.* (*aux.* **h.**) to finger, to play with the fingers. II. *a.* to furnish with fingers.

Fingie'r—en, *v.a.* to feign, forge, invent. **—t**, *p.p. & adj.* assumed, put on, fictitious, imaginary.

Fink, **—e**, *m.* (—en, *pl.* —en) finch; rake; student belonging to no (colour wearing) corporation (*stud.sl.*); **ein lustiger —**, a jolly fellow (*sl.*); **der — schlägt**, the finch sings. *Comp.* **—en=falk**, **—en=habicht**, *m.* sparrow-hawk. **—en=ritter**, *m.* knight-errant. **—en=schaft**, *f.* students who are not members of any organized students' club (*stud.sl.*). **—en=schlag**, *m.* singing of the finch.

Fin'k–eln, –en, *v.n.* (*aux.* **h.**) to go fowling, to catch birds. **–ler,** *m.* (**–lers,** *pl.* **–ler**) bird-catcher, fowler.

Fin'n–e, *f.* (*pl.* **–en**) fin; claw (*of a hammer*); blotch, pimple; stud (*of a lathe*). **–ig,** *adj.* & *adv.* pimpled, blotchy; measled (*of pigs*). *Comp.* **–fisch, –wal,** *m.* fin-back (*whale*).

Fin'ster, *adj.* & *adv.* dark, obscure; gloomy; dim; morose; sad; **im –n,** in the dark; **– blicken, aussehen,** to frown, to look black. **–e,** *f.* darkness, gloominess (*obs.*). **–ling,** *m.* (**–lings,** *pl.* **–linge**) enemy to progress *or* enlightenment; obscurantist, bigot; ignoramus. **–nis,** *f.* darkness; obscurity; gloom; eclipse. *Comp.* **–kammer,** *f.*, **–kasten,** *m.* dark room, camera obscura.

Fin'te, *f.* (*pl.* **–n**) feint (*in fencing*); false attack; trick, artifice, wile; fib.

Fip(p)s, *m.* (**–(s)es,** *pl.* **–(s)e**) fillip; thin, agile little man; nickname for a tailor. **–(s)en,** *v.a.* to fillip.

Fir'lefanz, *m.* (**–es**) nonsense, foolery, hocus-pocus; flourish; frippery. **–er,** *m.* (**–ers,** *pl.* **–er**) trifler, buffoon, talker *or* writer of nonsense. **–erei',** *f.* nonsense, foolery, trifling.

Fir'm–a, *f.* (*pl.* **Fir'men**) firm, (commercial) house, establishment, business; power of attorney. *Comp.* **–en=buch,** *n.* commercial *or* trade directory. **–en=schreiber,** *m.* sign-painter.

Firmamen't, *n.* (**–(e)s,** *pl.* **–e**) firmament, vault of heaven.

Fir'm–eln, –en, *v.a.* to confirm (a Rom. Cath. term). **–elung,** *f.* confirmation. **–ling,** *m.* (**–lings,** *pl.* **–linge**) candidate for confirmation, confirmee.

Firn, I. *adj.* & *adv.* (*obs.*) of last year; old (*obs.*). II. *m.* (**–(e)s,** *pl.* **–en**), **–er,** *m.* (**–ers,** *pl.* **–er**) (*orig.*) snow on the mountains from the preceding year *or* years; mountain top covered with everlasting snow, snow-covered mountain; glacier. **–e=wein,** *m.* old wine, excellent wine. *Comp.* **–feld,** *n.* glacier.

Fir'nis, *m.* (**–(ss)es,** *pl.* **–(ss)e**) varnish, gloss. **–(ss)en,** *v.a.* to varnish. **–(ss)er,** *m.* varnisher. *Comp.* **–baum,** *m.*, **–spille,** *f.* lacquer-tree, stagmaria.

First, *m.* (**–es,** *pl.* **–e**), **–e,** *f.* (*pl.* **–en**) ridge (*of a house or hill*); coping (*of a wall*); summit, top; roof (*of a pit*); **– wo die Glocken hangen,** belfry where the bells are hanging. *Comp.* **–en=balken,** *m.* ridge-piece. **–en=nagel,** *m.* roofing-pin. **–en=stempel,** *pl.* props in a mine. **–en=weise,** *adv.* towards the surface (*Min.*). **–en=ziegel,** *m.* ridge-tile.

Fir'sten, *v.n.* to be provided with high towers and battlements (*rare, poet.*).

Fis, *n.* F-sharp; **– –,** F double sharp.

Fisch, *m.* (**–es,** *pl.* **–e**) fish; marker (*at cards*); (*pl.*) Pisces (*Astr.*); **gesund wie ein –,** as sound as a roach; **das sind faule –e,** these are paltry excuses; those fish won't fry; **wie ein – auf trocknem Sand,** like a fish out of water; **stumm wie ein –,** mute as a fish, silent as the grave; **nicht Fleisch, nicht –,** neither fish nor flesh. **–bar,** *adj.* & *adv.* that may be fished. **–icht** (*obs.*), **–ig,** *adj.* & *adv.* fishy. *Comp.* **–aar, –adler,** *m.* osprey. **–abdruck,** *m.* ichthyolite. **–angel,** *f.* fishing-hook. **–artig,** *adj.* fishlike. **–band,** *n.* hinge-hook. **–bärn,** *m.* little fishing net. **–bauch=schiene,** *f.* fish-bellied rail (*Railw.*). **–behälter,** *m.* fish-tub. **–bein,** *n.* fishbone; whalebone; **weißes –bein,** bone of cuttle fish. **–beinern,** *adj.* of whalebone. **–beschreibung,** *f.* ichthyology. **–blech,** *n.*, **–boden,** *m.* fish-drainer. **–blase,** *f.* swimming bladder of fishes. **–blut,** *n.* fish-blood; **–blut in den Adern haben,** to be cold-blooded *or* unfeeling. **–blütig,** *adj.* unfeeling. **–brut,** *f.* fry. **–eidechse,** *f.* ichthyosaurus. **–er=barke,** *f.*, **–er=boot,** *n.* fishing boat. **–er=dorf,** *n.* fishing village. **–(er)=gerät,** *n.* fishing tackle. **–(er)=gerechtsame,** *f.* privilege of fishing. **–er=hütte,** *f.* fisherman's hut. **–er=innung, –er=gilde,** *f.* fishmongers' company. **–er=kahn,** *m.* fishing boat. **–(er)=korb,** *m.*, **–(er)=reuse,** *f.* creel *or* pot for catching eels, lobsters, *etc.* **–er=ring,** *m.* papal ring (*with representation of St. Peter as fisherman*); fisherman's ring. **–(er)=zeug,** *n.* fishing tackle. **–fang,** *m.* catching fish, fishing; fishery. **–flosse,** *f.* fin. **–gabel,** *f.* harpoon. **–gericht,** *n.* dish of fish. **–geruch,** *m.* fishy smell. **–gräte,** *f.* bone of a fish. **–häher,** *m.* heron. **–hälter,** *m.* fish-pond, place for keeping fishes. **–hamen,** *m.* hand-net. **–handel,** *m.* fish-trade. **–händler,** *m.* fishmonger. **–haut,** *f.* fish-skin; eel-skin; shagreen. **–kasten,** *m.* cauf, live box. **–kelle,** *f.* fish-slice. **–kreser,** *m.*, **–kieme,** *f.* gill. **–köder,** *m.* bait for fishes. **–kundige(r),** *m.* ichthyologist. **–laich,** *m.* spawn. **–lehre, –kunde,** *f.* ichthyology. **–leim,** *m.* isinglass. **–milch,** *f.* soft roe, milt. **–möve,** *f.* little tern (*Orn.*). **–netz,** *n.* fishing net. **–otter,** *f.* otter. **–recht,** *n.* right of fishing. **–reich,** *adj.* abounding in fish. **–reiher,** *m.* heron. **–rogen,** *m.* roe, spawn. **– rost,** *m.* double (*hanging*) gridiron. **–satz,** *m.* fry. **–schuppe,** *f.* scale of fishes. **–schuppen=ausschlag,** *m.* ichthyosis (*Med.*). **–speise,** *f.* fish-diet. **–strich,** *m.* spawning; spawn (*of fish*). **–teufel,** *m.* sea-devil. **–teich,** *m.* fish pond. **–thran,** *m.* fish-oil, train oil. **–versteinerung,** *f.* ichthyolite. **–wate,** *f.* drag-net. **–weib,** *n.* fish-wife. **–weiher,** *m.* fish-pond. **–wirtschaft,** *f.* management of fisheries; trawlers' association. **–zeug,** *n.* fishing tackle. **–zucht,** *f.* pisciculture. **–zug,** *m.* haul, draught (*of fish*).

Fi'sche–n, *v.a.* & *n.* (*aux.* **h.**) to fish; **im Trüben –n,** to fish in troubled waters, to benefit by the difficulties of others. **–r,** *m.* (**–rs,** *pl.* **–r**) fisher; fisherman; angler, hooker; fishing gull. **–rei',** *f.* fishery; fishing. **–rin,** *f.* fisherwoman, fisherman's wife *or* daughter.

Fisematen'ten, *pl.* fuss, humbug, excuses, subterfuges; shuffling (*dial. sl.*).

Fisk–a'l, *m.* (**–a'ls,** *pl.* **–a'le**) deputy of the exchequer; attorney-general, crown solicitor. **–a'lisch,** *adj.* & *adv.* fiscal; **–alisches Eigentum,** government property. **–us** (*pron.* **Fis'kus**), *m.* exchequer, treasury; **was nicht nimmt –us, das nimmt Christus,** what is not taken by the State is taken by the Church (*prov.*).

Fis't–el, *f.* (*pl.* **–eln**) fistula (*Surg.*); reed, tube; pipe; falsetto (*voice*). **–eln, –ulie'ren,** *v.n.* (*aux.* **h.**) to sing falsetto. **–ulö's,** *adj.* & *adv.* fistulous. *Comp.* **–el=artig,** *adj.* fistulous. **–el=schnitt,** *m.* syringotomy (*Surg.*). **–el=stimme,** *f.* falsetto, feigned voice.

Fit't–ich, (**–ichs,** *pl.* **–iche**), **–ig,** *m* (**–igs,** *pl.* **–ige**) wing, pinion.

Fitz'bohne, *f.* (*pl.* **–n**) French bean.

Fitz'chen, *n.* (**–s,** *pl.* **–**) a little thread; a little bit.

Fit'ze, *f.* (*pl.* **–n**) skein; fold; wrinkle; **einem eine – reißen,** to blow one up, frown on a p.

Fit'zen, *v.a.* to tie up into skeins; to fold, wrinkle; to knit the brow; to tease (*hair, etc.*); to whip, chastise.

[1]**Fix,** *adj.* & *adv.* quick, nimble, active; ready, smart; adroit; **– und fertig,** quite ready; **mach –!** be quick! **außen –, innen nix,** great show, but no substance (*prov.*); **ein –es Kerlchen,** a smart (little) fellow.

[2]**Fix,** *adj.* & *adv.* firm, fixed; settled, stated (*of wages, etc.*). **–ati'v,** *n.* fixing agent, fixative (*Chem.*). **–ie'ren,** *v.a.* to fix, settle, establish; to fix the eyes on; **eine Zeichnung –ie'ren,** to fix *or* bind a sketch by a fixative; **einen**

—ie'ren, to look at one fixedly, to stare at one. **—um**, *n.* (—ums, *pl.* —a) fixed *or* stated sum, fixed stipend. *Comp.* **—stern**, *m.* fixed star.

Flach, *adj.* & *adv.* flat, plain, level; shallow, superficial; **da kennst du ihn —**, in that respect you do not know him at all (*coll.*); **die —e Hand**, palm (*of the hand*); **das liegt auf der —en Hand**, that 's quite plain, evident (*coll.*); **ein —er Säbelhieb**, blow with the flat of the sabre. **—heit**, *f.* flatness; shallowness; insipidity. *Comp.* **—feld**, *n.* open field, plain. **—gänge**, *pl.* planks of a ship's bottom. **—gedrückt**, *adj.* depressed. **—gegraben**, *adj.* dug out so as to form a shallow basin. **—geschliffen**, *adj.* tabulated (*of jewels*). **—hohleisen**, *n.* sculptor's gouge. **—kopf**, *m.* shallow pate, blockhead. **—land**, *n.* flat country, low country, plain. **—maler**, *m.* lacquerer. **—relief**, *n.* bas relief. **—schnäbler**, *pl.* fly-catchers (*Orn.*). **—teller**, *m.* salver, flat plate. **—vertieft**, *adj.* concave. **—werk**, *n.* flat-tile roofing.

Fla'ch—en, *v.a.* to flatten, level (down) plain. **—ung**, *f.* levelling.

Flä'ch—e, *f.* (*pl.* —en) flatness; level plain; plane surface; superficies; **geneigte —e**, inclined plane. **—lich**, *adj.* & *adv.* inclining to flatness. *Comp.* **—en=größe**, *f.* extent of surface, area. **—en=inhalt**, *m.* superficial contents, area. **—en=maß**, *n.* superficial measure, square measure. **—en=meßkunst, —en=messung**, *f.* measuring of surfaces, planimetry. **—en=raum**, *m.* extent of surface, area. **—en=reich**, *adj.* rich in squares, polyhedral. **—en=zahl**, *f.* square number. **—en=zoll**, *m.* square inch.

Flachs, *m.* (—(s)es, *pl.* —(s)e) flax; (*pl.*) varieties of flax; **wilder —**, dodder; **lebendiger —**, asbestos. **—(s)en, —(s)icht**, *adj.* flaxen. *Comp.* **—acker**, *m.* flax-land. **—ähnlich**, *adj.* flaxen. **—artig**, *adj.* of flax kind. **—bart**, *m.* first down on the chin. **—bau**, *m.* flax-growing. **—bläuel**, *m.* swingle-staff. **—brecher**, *m.* flax-scutcher. **—brech=maschine**, *f.* scutching machine. **—darre**, *f.* flax-drying house. **—haar**, *n.* flaxen hair. **—haarig**, *adj.* flaxen haired, tow haired. **—hechel**, *f.* hatchel. **—hede**, *f.* flax-tow. **—kopf**, *m.* flaxen hair; flaxen-haired person. **—raufe**, *f.* ripple. **—röste**, *f.* flax-hole; flax-steeping, retting tank. **—samen**, *m.* linseed. **—seide**, *f.* dodder. **—stein**, *m.* asbestos. **—zurichtung**, *f.* flax-dressing.

Fla'ck—en, *v.a.* to clean by beating with sticks. *Comp.* **—maschine**, *f.* scutching machine.

Fla'ckerig, *adj.* & *adv.* flickering.

Fla'ckern, *v.n.* (*aux.* **h.**) to flare, flicker.

Flaco'n, *n.* (—s, *pl.* —s) phial; scent-bottle.

Fla'den, *m.* (—s, *pl.* —) flat cake; cow dung.

1Fla'der, *m.* (—s, *pl.* —n) maple-tree.

2Fla'der, *f.* (*pl.* —n) irregular vein (*in metals or wood*), streak, knot. **—ig**, *adj.* & *adv.* veined, streaked; with cracks *or* flaws.

Flageole'tt, *n.* (—s, *pl.* —e) flageolet. *Comp.* **—ton**, *m.* flute-like tone.

Flag'g—e, *f.* (*pl.* —en) flag, colours, ensign, standard; **National —e**, colours; **brittische —e**, Union Jack; **amerikanische —e**, stars and stripes; **die —e hissen**, to hoist the flag; **seine —e gehißt haben**, to show one's colours; **die —e streichen**, to strike *or* haul down the colours; to give in (*fig.*). *Comp.* **—(en)=schiff**, *n.* flag-ship. **—en=stock**, *m.* flag-staff. **—en=führer**, *m.*, **—en=offizier**, *m.* flag-officer. **—en=knopf**, *m.* (masthead) truck. **—en=leine**, *f.* flag-line, signal-halyard. **—en=tuch**, *n.* bunting.

Flag'gen, *v.a.* & *n.* (*aux.* **h.**) to display the flag; to signal with flags; to salute by striking colours; to dress with flags; **auf halber Stange —en**, to hoist the flag at half mast.

Flam'berg, *m.* (—es, *pl.* —e) broadsword (*of a knight*); sword, brand (*poet.*).

Flam'm—e, *f.* (*pl.* —en) flame, blaze, flash; love, sweetheart; **Feuer und —e für eine Sache sein**, to be quite enthusiastic about a thing; **—en schlagen**, to flame, to be blazing. **—icht** (*obs.*), **—ig**, *adj.* & *adv.* flame-like; watered; grained. *Comp.* **—en=bach**, *m.* blazing stream, fiery rivulet (*stream of heated metal*). **—en=meer**, *n.* ocean of flames. **—en=ofen**, *m.* puddling furnace. **—en=pein, —en=qual**, *f.* torment of flames. **—en=säule**, *f.* fiery column. **—en=schrift**, *f.*, **—en=züge**, *pl.* letters, writing of fire; indelible characters. **—en=tod**, *m.* death by fire.

Flam'men, *v.* I. *n.* (*aux.* **h.**) to flame, to blaze; to glow. II. *a.* to singe; to water (*silks, etc.*).

Flam'meri, (—s, *pl.* —s), flummery, blanc-mange(r).

Flane'll, *m.* (—s, *pl.* —e) flannel.

Flan—eu'r, *m.* (—s, *pl.* —s) saunterer. **—ie'ren**, *v.a.* to saunter.

Flan'k—e, *f.* (*pl.* —n) flank, side; **in die —e fallen**, to attack (*the enemy*) in the flank. **—ie'ren**, *v.* I. *a.* to flank; to protect the flanks of (*Mil.*). II. *n.* (*aux.* **h.**) to roam about, rove.

Flap'p—en, *pl.* clamps (*of a gun-carriage*). **—ig**, *adj.* flapping.

Flaps, *m.* (—(s)es, *pl.* —(s)e) awkward, boorish person (*coll.*).

Fla'sch—e, *f.* (*pl.* —n; *dim.* **Fläsch'chen**, *n.*) flask, phial, bottle; scent bottle; **Nachbarin! euer Fläschchen!** neighbour! your smelling bottle! **die geschliffene —e**, the decanter; **Leidener —e**, electrical *or* Leyden jar; **auf —en ziehen**, to bottle. **—ner**, *m.* (—ners, *pl.* —ner) tinman (*dial.*). *Comp.* **—en=adresse**, *f.* bottle label. **—en=bier**, *n.* bottled beer. **—en=büchse**, *f.* air-gun. **—en=held**, *m.* toper. **—en=kühler**, *m.* ice-pail (*for wine*). **—en=kürbis**, *m.* bottle-gourd. **—en=schanze**, *f.* electric battery. **—en=schild**, *n.* bottle-label. **—en=ständer, —en=teller, —en=untersetzer**, *m.* bottle-stand. **—en=zieher**, *m.* bottle-jack. **—en=zug**, *m.* tackle of pulleys, compound pulley; **doppelter —enzug**, double purchase.

Fla'ser, *f.* (*dial.*) see **2Flader.**

Flat'ter—er, *m.* (—ers, *pl.* —er) inconstant person, weather-cock; cheiropter (*Zoöl.*). **—haft**, *adj.* & *adv.* fickle, inconstant, wavering; volatile; **—haft sein**, to be infirm of purpose. **—haftigkeit**, *f.* inconstancy, fickleness, vacillation. **—ig**, *see* **—haft.** *Comp.* **—aspe, —pappel**, *f.* trembling poplar, aspen. **—geist, —sinn**, *m.* inconstancy, fickleness; fickle person. **—mine**, *f.* fougade.

Flat'tern, *v.n.* (*aux.* **h.** & **s.**) to flutter, to hang loose, float in the wind; to dangle; to roam about, ramble; to be unsteady, flighty; to flirt.

Flau, *adj.* & *adv.* feeble, weak, faint; insipid; dull, flat; slack (*of trade*); stagnant; indifferent, lukewarm; **mir wird — zu mute**, I feel faint; **der Wind wird —er**, it is growing calm; **— machen**, to depress (*the exchange*). **—heit, —igkeit**, *f.* flatness; dulness, deadness (*of trade*).

Flaum, *m.* (—es, *pl.* —e, —en) down; bristle; catkin. **—ig**, *adj.* & *adv.* downy. *Comp.* **—bart**, *m.* downy beard; stripling. **—feder**, *f.* down.

Flaus, (**Flausch**,) *m.* (—(s)es, *pl.* —(s)e) tuft of wool *or* hair; pilot cloth, coarse coating. *Comp.* **—rock**, *m.* coat made of coarse cloth, pea jacket (*esp'lly a warm winter coat*).

Flau'se, *f.* (*pl.* —n) trick, juggle, shuffling, shift, evasion, false pretence. *Comp.* **—n=macher**, *m.* shuffler.

Fläz, *m.* (—es, *pl.* —e) coarse, lubberly fellow.

Flech's—e, *f.* (*pl.* —en) tendon, sinew. **—ig**, *adj.* & *adv.* sinewy. *Comp.* **—en=artig**, *adj.* sinewy. **—en=haube**, *f.* caul.

Flech't—e, *f.* (*pl.* —en) twist, braid; plait; tress

(*of hair*); basket-work; hurdle; hamper; dry scab; tetter, herpes (*Med.*); lichen (*Bot.*); tetter; lichen. *Comp.* —**band**, *n.* ribbon plaited *or* twisted into the hair. —**binse**, *f.* plaiting rush. —**en=artig**, *adj.* herpetic (*Med.*); of the nature of lichens. —**en=ausschlag**, *m.* herpetic eruption. —**korb**, *m.* wicker-basket. —**rohr**, *n.* cane-plaiting. —**stroh**, *n.* plaiting (*for hats, etc.*). —**werk**, *n.* wicker-work; wattling. —**zaun**, *m.* plashing, fence made of plashing, quickset hedge.

Flech't—en, *ir.v.* I. *a.* to plait, braid, twist; to wreathe, twine together; to bind, fasten; to interlard; **durch** *or* **in einander —en**, to entwine, interlace; **einen Korb —en**, to plait, make a basket; **ein geflochtener Zaun**, hurdle, plashing fence; **aus Weidenzweigen geflochten**, wicker; **geflochtener Korb (Stuhl)**, wicker (chair). II. *r.* to plait; **Binsen —en sich leicht**, rushes plait easily. —**er**, *m.* (—**ers**, *pl.* —**er**), —**erin**, *f.* one who braids *or* plaits. —**ing**, *n.* (—**ings**) shrouds and other rigging at the masthead.

Fleck, *m.* (—(e)s, *pl.* —e) piece (*of ground*); place, spot, plot; blemish, flaw; blot, stain, spot; patch, shred; tripe; **auf dem —e**, upon the spot; **gehe nicht vom —e**, don't stir! **wir kommen nicht vom —**, we do not get on *or* along; **es ist noch ein guter — hin**, it is still at some distance; **— im Auge**, speck in the eye; **den rechten — treffen**, to hit the right nail on the head, to strike home. —**chen**, *n.* (—**chens**, *pl.* —**chen**) speckle; little piece. —**en**, *m.* (—**ens**, *pl.* —**en**) *see* **Fleck**; borough, market-town, country-town. —**icht**, (*obs.*) —**ig**, *adj.* & *adv.* like spots; spotted, stained, speckled. *Comp.* —**ausmacher**, *m.* cleaner (*of clothes*). —**en=los**, *adj.* spotless. —**fieber**, *n.* spotted fever. —**seife**, *f.* scouring soap. —**stein**, *m.* scouring stone. —**wasser**, *n.* benzine, scouring water.

Fle'cken, *v.* I. *a.* to spot, stain, speckle; to patch; to flatten (*wire*). II. *n.* (*aux.* **h.**) to blot; to spot, stain, to soil; to make progress (*coll.*); **es will nicht —**, the work does not get on, is unsuccessful; **es fleckt mir nicht**, I cannot get on with my work; **heute hat es gefleckt**, to-day I have done a good deal.

Fle'der—n, *v.n.* (*aux.* **h.**) to flutter. II. *a.* to dust with a feather-brush. *Comp.* —**fisch**, *m.* flying-fish. —**maus**, *f.* bat. —**tier**, *n.* cheiropter. —**wisch**, *m.* feather broom, duster, goose wing; rapier (*coll.*).

Fleet, *n.* flowing water, canal, water-way between rows of houses (*in Hamburg*); whaler's outfit.

Fle'gel, *m.* (—**s**, *pl.* —) flail; clown, lout; churl. —**ei'**, *f.* boorish behaviour, rudeness, coarseness; insolence; churlishness. —**haft**, *adj.* & *adv.* clownish, rude; churlish; unmannerly, ungentlemanly; impertinent, insolent. —**haftigkeit**, *f.* clownishness; churlishness; rudeness; ungentlemanly behaviour. *Comp.* —**jahre**, *pl.* years of indiscretion, hobbledehoyhood; **noch in den —jahren**, still in one's teens, unfledged, unpolished, without manners. —**klappe**, *f.* flail-thong. —**wischer**, *m.* sponge (*Artil.*).

Fle'geln, *v.* I. *a.* to beat with a flail, thresh. II. *n.* (*aux.* **h.**) to behave clownishly; **sich in einen Stuhl (hin) —**, to place o.s. boorishly in a chair; to loll inelegantly in a chair.

Fle'hen, I. *v.a.* & *n.* (*aux.* **h.**) to implore, beseech, supplicate; **zu einem um eine S. —**, to pray to s.o. for s.th. II. *subst.n.* prayers; supplication. —**d**, *p.* & *adj.* suppliant, imploring. —**tlich**, *adj.* & *adv.* suppliant, imploring; —**tlich bitten**, to beseech; —**tliche Bitte**, earnest prayer, supplication, entreaty.

Fleisch, *n.* (—**es**) flesh; meat; pulp (*of fruit*); cellular tissues (*in leaves*); (*pl.*) fleshy parts; **gehacktes —**, mince-meat; **wildes —**, proud flesh; **ins —**, to the quick; **das ist weder — noch Fisch**, that is neither fish, flesh, fowl nor good red herring. —**ern**, *adj.* fleshy; flesh; fleshly, carnal (*obs.*). —**icht** (*obs. & poet.*), —**ig**, *adj.* & *adv.* like flesh; fleshy; plump, fat; pulpy. —**igkeit**, *f.* fleshiness. —**lich**, *adj.* & *adv.* fleshly, carnal, sensual. —**lichkeit**, *f.* sensuality, carnal-mindedness. *Comp.* —**abfall**, *m.* refuse of meat. —**auswuchs**, *m.* fleshy excrescence; proud flesh. —**bank**, *f.* butcher's stall, shambles. —**bruch**, *m.* sarcocele (*Surg.*). —**brühe**, *f.* beef tea, mutton broth; broth, meat soup; gravy. —**es=lust**, *f.* fleshly, carnal lust. —**es=vergehen**, *n.* carnal crime. —**extrakt**, *m.* extract of meat; bovril. —**farbe**, *f.* flesh-colour. —**farben**, *adj.* flesh-coloured. —**faß**, *n.* salting tub. —**fressend**, *adj.* carnivorous. —**fresser**, *m.* carnivorous animal. —**gewächs**, *n.* fleshy tumour *or* excrescence; sarcoma. —**hacker**, —**hauer**, *m.* butcher. —**haken**, *m.* flesh-hook. —**halle**, *f.* meat-market. —**horn**, *n.*, —**kamm**, *m.* fleshy comb on a fowl's head. —**kammer**, *f.* larder. —**kloß**, *m.* carbonade of chopped meat, meat ball. —**klößchen**, *n.* meat ball. —**kost**, *f.* meat diet. —**krone**, *f.* coronet of a horse's hoof. —**kuchen**, *m.* meat-pie; pastry. —**lake**, *f.* brine, pickle (*of meat*). —**lappen**, *m.* wattles (*of a cock*). —**los**, *adj.* fleshless. —**made**, *f.* maggot. —**markt**, *m.* shambles; meat-market. —**pastete**, *f.* meat-pie. —**schätzer**, *m.* inspector of meat markets. —**schau**, *f.* inspection of shambles. —**schnitte**, *f.* slice of meat; cutlet, steak. —**speise**, *f.* animal food; dish of meat. —**suppe**, *f.* broth. —**steuer**, *f.* tax on meat. —**ton**, *m.* carnation (*Paint.*). —**topf**, *m.* flesh-pot. —**ware**, *f.* meat; —**waren=handlung**, *f.* provision warehouse, ham-and-beef shop. —**werdung**, *f.* incarnation (*Theol.*).

Flei'sch—en, *v.* I. *a.* to flesh; to clear of flesh. II. *n.* (*aux.* **h.**) to touch the flesh. —**er**, *m.* (—**ers**, *pl.* —**er**) butcher. *Comp.* —**er=gang**, *m.* bootless errand, useless trouble. —**er=handwerk**, *n.* butcher's trade. —**er=hund**, *m.* butcher's dog. —**er=talg**, *m.* unmelted tallow.

Fleiß, *m.* (—**es**) diligence, industry, application, assiduity; **mit —**, industriously; intentionally; **— anwenden**, to take pains, exert oneself; **er hat es mit — gethan**, he has done it on purpose. —**ig**, I. *adj.* & *adv.* industrious, diligent, assiduous; **ein —iger Besucher**, a frequent *or* regular visitor; **—ig beten**, to pray constantly. —**iglich**, *adv.* diligently, assiduously (*obs.*).

Flei'ßen, *ir.v.r.* to be industrious *or* diligent; to be zealous for; to delight in. **geflissen**, *p.p.* & *adj.* assiduous, busy.

Flektie'ren, *v.a.* to inflect (*Gram.*).

Flen'nen, *v.n.* (*aux.* **h.**) to make wry faces, grin; to whine; to weep (*used contemptuously*).

Flens— (*in comp.*) —**stücke**, *pl.* slices of whale-meat. —**gat**, *n.* blubber port-hole.

Flet(h), *n.* *see* **Fleet**.

Flet'sch—en, *v.a.*; **die Zähne —en**, to grin, show the teeth. *Comp.* —**zahn**, *m.* projecting tooth.

Fleuch, *imper. of* **fliehen** (*obs.*); **Fleuchst, Fleucht**, *2 & 3 pers. sing. pres. ind.* of **fliehen** (*obs.*).

Fleug, *imper. of* **fliegen** (*obs.*); **Fleugst, Fleugt**, *2 & 3 pers. sing. pres. ind. of* **fliegen** (*obs.*).

Fleuß, *imper. of* **fließen** (*obs.*); **Fleußest, Fleußt**. *2 & 3 pers. sing. pres. ind.* of **fließen** (*obs.*).

Flexio'n, *f.* (*pl.* —**en**), inflection (*Gram.*); **Nominal—**, inflection of nouns; **Verbal—**, inflection of verbs. —**s=lehre**, *f.* accidence (*Gram.*).

Fle'zen, *v.r.* to sit *or* lie down in a boorish and impolite manner (*coll.*).

Flibustie'r, *m.* (—**s**, *pl.* —) filibuster, buccaneer, freebooter, pirate.

Flicht, *imper. of* **flechten; Flichtst, Flicht,** *2 & 3 pers. sing. pres. ind. of* **flechten.**

Fli'ck—en, I. *v.a.* to patch, mend, repair; to bungle; **zusammen —en,** to patch up; **einem etwas am Zeuge —en,** to pick holes in a person's coat; to find fault with a person. II. *m.* (—**ens,** *pl.* —**en**) patch; botch. —**er,** *m.* (—**ers,** *pl.* —**er**) patcher; cobbler. —**erei',** *f.* patchwork; mending; bungling. *Comp.* —**arbeit,** *f.* patchwork; bungling work. —**fleck,** —**lappen,** *m.* patch. —**messer,** *n.* glazier's knife. —**reim,** *m.* make-shift rhyme. —**schneider,** *m.* jobbing tailor, botcher. —**schuster,** *m.* job bootmaker. —**werk,** *n.* patch-work; botched work. —**wort,** *n.* expletive.

Flie'der, *m.* (—**s**) elder; **spanischer** —, lilac, syringa vulgaris. *Comp.* —**beere,** *f.* elderberry. —**blau,** *adj.* lilac. —**thee,** *m.* infusion of elder blossoms.

Flie'ge, *f.* (*pl.* —**n**) fly; sight (*of a gun*); fluke (*of an anchor*); light-minded *or* lightly-conducted person; **die — summt,** the fly buzzes; **eine leichte** —, a loose fish; **spanische —n,** cantharides; **von —n beschmissen,** fly-blown; **zwei —n mit einer Klappe** *or* **einem Schlage treffen,** to kill two birds with one stone. *Comp.* —**n=baum,** *m.* elm. —**n=dreck,** *m.* fly-blow. —**n=falle,** *f.* fly-trap (*also Bot.*). —**n=fänger,** *m.* fly-catcher (*Orn.*). —**n=fürst,** —**n=gott,** *m.* Beelzebub (*as spreader of plague and infectious diseases by means of flies*). —**n=garn,** —**n=netz,** *n.* fly-net. —**n=gift,** *n.* fly-poison *or* paper. —**n=holz,** *n.* quassia-wood. —**n=klappe,** —**n=klatsche,** *f.* fly-flap. —**n=kopf,** *m.* turned letter (*Typ.*). —**n=pilz,** *m.* toadstool. —**n=schrank,** *m.* meat-safe. —**n=wedel,** *m.* fan for flies, fly-brush.

Flie'g—en, I. *ir.v.n.* (*aux.* **s.** & **h.**) to fly; to rush; **ein Wort —en lassen,** to let slip a word; **Gebäude in die Luft —en lassen,** to blow up buildings. II. *subst. n.* flight; —**en der Glieder,** shivering fit. III. *pl.* flies. —**end,** *p. & adj.* flying; flowing; **ein —endes Lager,** a flying camp; —**ende Haare,** loose, flowing hair; **ein —endes Blatt,** a flysheet, a pamphlet; —**ende Fahnen,** flying colours; —**ende Kolonne,** movable column; —**ende Hitze,** intermittent fit; —**ender Fuchs,** vampire bat. —**er,** *m.* (—**ers,** *pl.* —**er**) flyer; middle stay-sail (*Naut.*).

Flie'h—en, *ir.v.* I. *n.* (*aux.* **s.**) to flee, hasten away, escape; to rush (*rare*); —**et, ihr Sorgen!** begone cares! **zu einem —en,** to take refuge with one. II. *a.* to shun, avoid, get out of the way of; **der —ende,** fugitive. *Comp.* —**kraft,** *f.* centrifugal force.

Flie'se, *f.* (*pl.* —**n**) flag, floorstone; paving tile.

[1]**Fließ,** *also* **Vlies,** *n.* (—**es,** *pl.* —**e**) fleece, tuft of wool; **das goldene** —, the golden fleece. —**ritter,** *m.* Knight of the Order of the Golden Fleece.

[2]**Fließ,** *n.* (—**es,** *pl.* —**e**) flowing water, rivulet, brooklet, rill (*obs.*). *Comp.* —**gold,** *n.* gold found in streams.

Flie'ß—en, *ir.v.n.* (*aux.* **h.** & **s.**) to flow, run; to melt; to gutter; to trickle down; to pass away, elapse (*of time*); to be smooth (*of words*); to blot; —**en aus,** to proceed from, result; **sanft —en,** to glide smoothly; **strömend heraus —en,** to gush out; **hieraus —t,** hence it follows; **meine Ader —t,** I am in the mood *or* vein; **meine Adern —en geöffnet,** the blood gushes out of my opened veins. —**end,** *p., adj. & adv.* flowing; running; drifting; fluid; fluent; smooth, easy; **eine Sprache —end sprechen,** to speak a language fluently. *Comp.* —**blattern,** —**pocken,** *pl.* confluent smallpox. —**harz,** *n.* turpentine. —**papier,** *n.* blotting-paper; unsized paper. —**wasser,** *n.* flowing water; lymph.

Flie'te, *f.* (*pl.* —**n**) fleam, lancet; spool (*Weav.*).

Flim'mer, *m.* (—**s**) glimmer, glitter; tinsel; gold sand.

Flim'mern, *v.n.* (*aux.* **h.**) to glitter, glisten, sparkle; to twinkle (*star*); to vibrate (*air*); **die Augen — mir,** my eyes are swimming.

Flin'der, *m.* (—**s**) tinsel, spangle.

Flink, *adj. & adv.* bright; brisk, agile, quick, nimble, alert; lively. —**heit,** *f.* nimbleness, quickness; liveliness.

Flin't—e, *f.* (*pl.* —**en**) gun, musket, rifle; **die —e ins Korn werfen,** to throw up the game *or* the sponge (*coll.*); **die —e abdrücken,** to fire off a rifle. *Comp.* —**en=kolben,** *m.* butt-end of a gun. —**en=kugel,** *f.* musket ball. —**en=lauf,** *m.* gun-barrel. —**en=schaft,** *m.* gunstock. —**en=schuh,** *m.* carabine case. —**en=stein,** *m.* gun-flint. —**sand,** *m.* pebble sand.

Flir'ren, *v.n.* (*aux.* **h.**) to flit about; *see* **Flimmern.**

Flis'pern, Flis'tern, (*obs.*); *see* **Flüstern.**

Flit'ter, *m.* (—**s,** *pl.* —) tinsel, spangle, mock-gold. —**haft,** —**ig,** *adj. & adv.* tinsel; showy. *Comp.* —**gelehrsamkeit,** *f.* sham learning. —**glanz,** *m.* false lustre; lustre of spangles. —**gold,** *n.* tinsel; leaf gold. —**haube,** *f.* cap with spangles. —**wochen,** *pl.* honeymoon. —**sand,** *m.* sparkling sand. —**schein,** *m.* lustre of spangles; false lustre. —**staat,** *m.* tinsel finery, tawdry finery. —**werk,** *n.* gewgaw.

Flit'tern, *v.n.* (*aux.* **h.**) to flit about; to glitter.

Flitz— (*in comp.*) —**bogen,** *m.* boy's bow; cross-bow. —**pfeil,** *m.* small arrow.

Flit'zen, *v.a.* to move rapidly, to flit (*of bats*).

Flocht, Flöch'te, *imperf. ind. & subj. of* **flechten.**

Flo'ck—e, *f.* (*pl.* —**en**) flake (*of snow*); flock (*of wool, hair, etc.*); waste of wool, hemp, *etc.*; flaky stone. —**ig,** *adj. & adv.* flaky; filamentous, flocculent; —**iges Blei,** arseniate of lead. *Comp.* —**en=artig,** *adj.* flaky. —**en=bett,** *n.* flock bed. —**en=lesen,** *n.* picking at the bed-clothes (*in illness*). —(**en**)**=seide,** *f.* waste silk, floss silk. —**en=tuch,** *n.* coarse cloth. —**feder,** *f.* down. —**feuer,** *n.* flame, flashing fire. —**wolle,** *f.* waste wool.

Flo'cken, I. *v.n.* (*aux.* **h.**) to flake, come down in flakes. II. *v.a.* to beat into flocks, to form into flakes.

Flog, Flö'ge, *imperf. ind. & subj. of* **fliegen.**

Floh, *m.* (—**s,** *pl.* **Flö'he**) flea; **einem einen — ins Ohr setzen,** to send a p. away with a flea in his ear, to make a p. uneasy and suspicious (*prov.*); **er hört die Flöhe husten,** he hears the grass grow (*prov.*). *Comp.* —**biß,** —**stich,** *m.* flea-bite. —**farbe,** *f.* puce-colour.

Flö'hen, *v.a. & r.* to catch fleas; to rid of fleas.

Flor, I. *m.* (—(**e**)**s,** *pl.* **Flö're**) gauze; crape; veil. II. *m.* (—**es**) & *f.* blossoming; bloom; blossom, blossoming time; flourishing state, prosperity. —**a,** *f.* Flora; the goddess of flowers; the vegetable kingdom, the plants and trees, flora (*Bot.*). —**en,** *adj. & adv.* of gauze *or* crape. —**e'tt,** *n.* (—**et'tes,** *pl.* —**et'te**) coarse silk; silk refuse; foil. —**ie'ren,** *v.n.* (*aux.* **h.**) to flourish, prosper. *Comp.* —**artig,** —**ähnlich,** *adj.* gauzy. —**band,** *n.* crape (*for a hat*). —**binde,** *f.* crape-band. —**e'tt=band,** *n.* sarsanet ribbon. —**e'tt=seide,** *f.* sarsanet. —**stuhl,** *m.* gauze loom. —**tuch,** *n.* gauze. —**weber,** *m.* gauze weaver.

Flos'kel, *f.* (*pl.* —**n**) flourish, showy phrase; *pl.* fine writing, rhetorical phrases.

Flos'keln, *v.n.* (*aux.* **h.**) to use flowery language.

Flos's—e, *f.* (*pl.* —**en**) fin; float (*on a fishing net*). —**ig,** *adj.* finned, finny; provided with floats. *Comp.* —(ß)=feder, *f.* fin. —(ß)=füßig, *adj.* having finned feet.

[1]Floß (*short* o), Flöſ'ſe, *imperf. ind. & subj. of* fließen.

[2]Floß (*long* o), *n.* (*& m.*) (—(ß)es, *pl.* Flö'ße) float, raft; float, buoy; pig of iron; flowing water. *Comp.* —beamte(r), *m.* inspector of rafts. —bett, *n.* scaffolding erected in water; mould for metal castings. —brücke, *f.* floating bridge. —führer, *m.* raftsman. —garn, *n.* floating fishing-net. —graben, *m.* canal. —holz, *n.* floated timber. —loch, *n.* lock (*of canals*). —netz, *n. see* garn. —platz, *m.* timber-yard (*for floated wood*).

Flö'ße, *f.* (*pl.* —n) floating of timber; float; raft; washing trough (*for ore*).

Flö'ße—n, *v.a.* to cause to flow; to rinse; to float, cause to float; to skim (*milk*); to fish with a floating net; to instil, infuse. —r, *m.* (—rs, *pl.* —r) one who floats (*timber*); raftsman.

Flö'te, *f.* (*pl.* —n) flute; die — blaſen, to play (on) the flute. *Comp.* —n=artig, *adj.* flute-like. —n=bläſer, *m.* flute-player. —n=bohrer, *m.* flute-maker. —n=pfeife, *f.* open pipe (*in organs*). —n=regiſter, *n.*, —n=zug, *m.* flute-stop (*in organs*).

Flö't—en, *v.a. & n.* (*aux.* h.) to play on the flute; to sing (*as a nightingale*); to whistle (*dial.*); —en gehen, to be lost (*sl.*); einer Sache nach —en, to give a thing up as lost (*sl.*). —i'ſt, *m.* (—iſ'ten, *pl.* —iſ'ten) flute-player, flutist.

Flott, I. *adj. & adv.* buoyant; luxuriant, abundant; gay, fast, jolly; ein —er Student, (Bruder Studio) a jolly student; es ging — her, there were fine doings, they lived in fine style; —leben, to live fast, to live in clover, to lead a jolly life. II. *adv.* afloat. III. *m. & n.* cream (*dial.*); grease (*dial.*). *Comp.* —we'g, *adv.* smartly, promptly; unhesitatingly.

Flot't—e, *f.* (*pl.* —en) fleet, navy; floating stage (*Shipb.*); dye; Heer und —e, army and navy. —il'le, *f.* (*pl.* —il'len) flotilla, squadron. *Comp.* —en=abteilung, *f.* detachment of a fleet, squadron. —en=demonſtration, *f.* naval demonstration. —en=dienſt, *m.* naval service, service in the navy. —en=führer, *m.* admiral. —en=ſchau, *f.* naval review. —en=verein, *m.* naval league.

Flottie'ren, *v.n.* to fluctuate; to be uncertain.

Flöz, *n.* (*rarely* Flötz, *m.*) (—es, *pl.* —e) layer, stratum, deposit; Kohlen—, seam of coal; in —en, stratified. *Comp.* —aſche, *f.* clay-marl. —bau, *m.* working of a stratum. —gebirge, *n.* mountain formed in strata; secondary rocks, sedimentary rocks (*Geol.*). —gebirgs=arten, *pl.* secondary rocks (*Geol.*). —klüfte, *pl.* faults (*Min.*). —lage, —ſchicht, *f.* stratum, bed, layer. —ſandſtein, *m.* new red sandstone. —ſchwarte, *f.* upper stratum. —treppe, *f.* stairs with broad steps.

Fluch, *m.* (—es, *pl.* Flü'che) curse, malediction; execration; oath; cause of evil, curse. *Comp.* —beladen, *adj.* under a curse, accursed. —ens=wert, —(ens)=würdig, *adj.* accursed, execrable. —gebäude, *n.* villainous piece of work. —geſchick, *n.* accursed fate. —maul, *n.* blasphemer; bad swearer.

Flu'ch—en, *v.* I. *n.* (*aux.* h.) to curse, swear; to damn, imprecate; to blaspheme; to use bad language, to use strong language; einem —en, to curse one; auf einen —en, to imprecate evil upon a p., to swear at one. II. *a.* to utter curses, curse, execrate; einem Böſes an den Hals —en, to curse one, wish one evil. —er, *m.* (—ers, *pl.* —er) curser; swearer.

Flucht, *f.* (*pl.* —en) flight, escape; flight (*of birds*); covey (*of pigeons*); place of refuge; play, swing (*of a door-hammer, etc.*); row, straight line; floor, story; fünf Zimmer in einer —, five rooms on one flat opening into one another; ſechs Fenſter in einer —, six windows in a row; eine — Treppen, a flight of steps; eine — Zimmer, a suite of rooms; die — ergreifen, ſich auf die — begeben *or* machen, to run away; in die — ſchlagen, to put to flight. *Comp.* —bau, *m.*, —röhre, *f.* refuge, retreat (*Sport*). —ebene, *f.* vanishing plane. —linie, *f.* base-line; vanishing line.

Flüch't—en, *v.* I. *a.* to save by flight, rescue, secure. II. *r. & n.* (*aux.* ſ.) to flee, take to flight, escape; ſich —en auf, in, to take to (*a tree, etc.*), to betake oneself to, take refuge in; er —ete (ſich) nach England, he fled to England. —er, *m.* (—ers, *pl.* —er) fugitive. —ig, *adj. & adv.* flying, fugitive, runaway; transient, fleeting; volatile (*Chem.*); fleet; hasty, inconsiderate; cursory, slight, desultory; casual; fickle, changeable; vagabond; —iges Geſtein, brittle stone *or* rock; —ig werden, to run away, abscond; —iges Salz, sal volatile; —ige Gewänder, flowing robes; —ige Hand, running hand; ich habe das Buch nur —ig durchgeblättert, I have only just glanced at the book. —igkeit, *f.* fleetness, transitoriness; nimbleness; volatility; inconstancy; hastiness, carelessness. —igkeits=fehler, *m.* mistake owing to inadvertence, slip; slip of the pen. —ling, *m.* (—lings, *pl.* —linge) fugitive refugee; deserter. *Comp.* —ig=machung, *f.* volatilization (*Chem.*).

Flu'der, *n.* (—s, *pl.* —) waste weir; channel (*Mill.*).

Flug, *m.* (—es, *pl.* Flü'ge) flying; flight, soaring; flock; swarm; covey; im —e, flying, in haste; quickly, forthwith; einen Vogel im —e ſchießen, to shoot a bird on the wing. —s, *adv.* hastily, speedily, quickly, at once. *Comp.* —bahn, *f.* trajectory. —beulen, *pl.* shingles (*Med.*). —biene, *f.* working bee. —blatt, *n.* pamphlet, fly-sheet, broadsheet; fugitive piece, handbill. —fertig, *adj.* ready to fly; very hurried. —feuer, *n.* erysipelas. —fiſch, *m.* flying fish. —hafer, *m.* wild oats. —haut, *f.* wing-membrane. —hörnchen, *n.* flying squirrel. —kraft, *f.* power of flight. —loch, *n.* pigeon-hole; entrance to a hive. —maſchine, *f.* flying-machine. —mehl, *n.* mill-dust. —ſand, *m.* quicksand, moving sand. —ſchießen, *n.* shooting (when the bird) is on the wing. —ſchiff, *n.* cutter. —ſchnell, *adj.* very swift. —ſchrift, *f.* pamphlet. —waſſer, *n.* spray. —werk, *n.* flies (*Theat.*).

Flü'gel, *m.* (—s, *pl.* —) wing; sail (*of a windmill*); one side of a folding door *or* double window; flap (*of a coat*); wing (*of a house; of an army*); flank; aisle (*of a church*); casement (*of a window*); leaf (*of a folding door*); fluke (*of an anchor*); lappet (*of a cap*); wing, lobe (*Anat.*); grand piano; die — hängen laſſen, to be crestfallen, to despond. —ig, *adj. & adv.* having wings, winged. *Comp.* —adjutant, *m.* aide-de-camp (*military attendant of a sovereign*). —bauer, *m.* maker of grand pianos. —decke, *f.* wing-sheath; mit —decken verſehen, coleopterous. —fenſter, *n.* casement window. —förmig, *adj.* wing-shaped. —füßler, *pl.* fin-footed molluscs. —haube, *f.* cap with lappets. —horn, *n.* buglehorn. —lahm, *adj.* broken-winged; winged (*Hunt.*). —los, *adj.* wingless. —mann, *m.* file-leader, fugleman; tall, stately man. —mantel, *m.* mantle with loose hanging sleeves. —offen, *adj.* wide open. —paar, *n.* pair of wings. —pferd, *n.* Pegasus. —ſchlag, *m.* flapping of wings. —ſchlag=ader, *f.* pterygoid artery. —ſpitze, *f.* tip of the wing. —ſtange, *f.* vane-spindle. —thür, *f.* folding door. —tuch, *n.* sails (*of a wind-

mill). —welle, *f.* axle of a windmill. —werk, *n.* poultry, fowls.
Flü'geln, *v.a.* to furnish with wings, to wing; to hit in the wing.
Flüg'ge, *adj.* fledged.
Flu'h(e), Flü'h(e), (*dial.*) *f.* (*pl.* —(e)n) mass of rock; precipice; stratum, layer.
Flu'id—um, *n.* (—ums, *pl.* —a) fluid, liquid.
Flun'der, *m.* (—s, *pl.* —) flounder.
Flunk, *m.* (—es, *pl.* —en), —e, *f.* (*pl.* —en) fluke (*of an anchor*).
Flunkerei', *f.* sham; bragging; story-telling (*coll.*).
Flun'kern, *v.n.* (*aux.* h.) to tell fibs; to brag, boast (*coll.*).
Flu'or, *m.* fluor-spar; (*in comp.* =) fluorine. —metalle, *pl. n.* fluorides. —wasserstoff=säure, *f.* hydrofluoric acid.
Flur, I. *f.* (*pl.* —en) fields, meadows; plain; common. II. *m.* (—es, *pl.* —e, Flü're) flag, paving-stone; paved floor; floor; entrance-hall; corridor; die —en begehen, beziehen, to perambulate *or* beat the bounds of a parish. *Comp.* —brief, *m.* terrier (*Law*). —gang, *m.* corridor; beating the bounds of a parish. —grenze, —scheidung, *f.* bounds of a parish. —hüter, *m.* field-guard; ranger. —schütz, *m.* rural guard, ranger. —stein, *m.* boundary-stone.
Fluß, *m.* (—(ss)es, *pl.* Flüs'se) flow, flux; river; kleiner —, stream; state of melting *or* fusion, melted metal; paste (*diamonds*); catarrh; (*course of*) humours; rheumatism; issue, running; flush (*at cards*); fluency, flow (*of speech*); — im Nacken, crick in the neck; weißer —, whites (*Med.*); (den) — abwärts, down stream; (den) — aufwärts, up stream. *Comp.* —artig, *adj.* catarrhal; rheumatic; river-like. —äther, *m.* fluoric ether. —bad, *n.* river bath *or* bathing. —bett, *n.* channel, bed of a river. —eisen, *n.* iron in fusion. —erde, *f.* earthy fluor-spar. —fall, *m.* waterfall. —fieber, *n.* influenza. —krebs, *m.* river crawfish. —mittel, *n.* flux. —nixe, *f.* water nymph, naiad. —ochs, *m.*, —pferd, *n.* hippopotamus. —pricke, *f.* lamprey. —reich, *adj.* abounding in rivers, well watered. —sauer, *adj.* fluorated. —säure, *f.* hydrofluoric acid. —scheide, *f.* fork in a river. —schiffe, *pl.* river boats *or* craft. —schiffer, *m.* waterman, master of a river boat. —schiff=fahrt, *f.* river navigation *or* traffic. —spat, *m.* fluor spar; spavin (*Vet.*). —stoff, *m.* humour (*Med.*). —trüsche, *f.* eel-pout. —wage, *f.* T level. —wasser, *n.* running water. —welt, *f.* river world *or* region.
Flüs'sig, *adj.* & *adv.* fluid, liquid; fusible; melted; rheumatic; — machen, to melt, to liquefy; to convert into ready money. —keit, *f.* fluidity, liquidity; fluid, liquid; humour (*Vet.*).
Flüs'ter—er, *m.* (—ers, *pl.* —er) whisperer. —n, *v.a.* & *n.* (*aux.* h.) to whisper.
Flüß'chen, *m.* (—s, *pl.* —) rivulet, stream(let).
Flü'te, *f.* (*pl.* —n) fly-boat (*dial.*).
Flut, *f.* (*pl.* —en) flood; inundation, deluge; billows, waves; water, liquid; torrent, stream, volley; high-water, flood-tide; die Sünd —, the Flood; die volle —, spring tide; die kleine —, neap tide; die Hoch —, flood tide, high water; zur —zeit, at high water; die — kommt, the tide is rising; die — geht, the tide is ebbing; mit Hilfe der — hinüber fahren, to tide over; eine — von Worten, a torrent of words. *Comp.* —bett, *n.* channel; mill-race. —brecher, *m.* breakwater. —gang, *m.*, —ge=rinne, *n.* channel; trough (*in mills*), mill-race. —hafen, *m.* tidal harbour. —rad, *n.* hydraulic wheel. —tabellen, *pl.* tide tables. —thor, *n.* flood-gate. —wasser, *n.* tidal water; mill-race. —zeichen, *n.* high-water mark. —zeit, *f.* flood tide, high water.

Flu't—en, *v.n.* (*aux.* h.) to flood; to rise, flow, be at high water, swell; to stream, crowd; es —et, the tide is coming up *or* in.
Focht, Föch'te, *imperf. ind. & subj. of* fechten.
Fo'ck—e, *f.* (*pl.* —en) fore-sail. *Comp.* —mast, *m.* fore-mast. —segel, *n.* fore-sail. —stag, *m.* fore-stay. —wand, *f.* fore-shrouds.
Fo'cus, Fo'kus, *m.* focus. *Comp.* —länge, *f.* focal length.
Föder—alis'mus, *m.* federalism. —ati'v, *adj.* & *adv.* federative, confederate.
Fo'dern, *dial. & poet. for* fordern.
Foh'l—e, *f.* (*pl.* —en) mare, filly. —en, I. *n.* (—ens, *pl.* —en) foal, filly, colt. II. *v.a.* & *n.* (*aux.* h.) to foal.
Föhn, Fön, *m.* (—es, *pl.* —e) (wet) south wind in Switzerland; thaw-wind; storm; der — ist los, the storm is raging. —ig, *adj.* blown by the south wind; stormy, tempestuous.
Foh're, *f.* (*pl.* —n) trout. *See* Forelle.
Föh're, *f.* (*pl.* —n) pine, Scots fir.
Fol'g—e, *f.* (*pl.* —en) succession, series, order; consequence; sequel; continuation; line; train, attendance; set, suit; event, result, issue, effect; conclusion, inference; futurity, future time; die —e war, the result was; üble —en, bad consequences; —e leisten, to obey, to comply with; zu —e, in pursuance of, in consequence of; in der —e, subsequently, hereafter, in the future; in —e dessen, dem zu —e, according to, in pursuance of which; daraus läßt sich die —e ziehen, from that we may infer; einem Gesuche —e geben, to grant a petition; —e von Karten, sequence. —lich, I. *adv. & conj.* consequently, therefore, accordingly, then. II. *adj.* future, subsequent. III. *adv.* afterwards, subsequently. —sam, *adj.* & *adv.* obedient, tractable, docile. —samkeit, *f.* obedience. *Comp.* —e=alter, *n.* after times. —e=leistung, *f.* obedience. —en=los, *adj.* of no consequence; without effect. —en=reich, *adj.* pregnant with results, of great consequence. —e(n)=reihe, *f.* order of succession, series. —e=recht, —e=richtig, *adj.* logical, logically correct; consistent; conclusive. —e=richtigkeit, *f.* logical consequence. —e=satz, *m.* corollary, deduction. —e=schluß, *m.* logical result. —e=stern, *m.* satellite. —e=welt, *f.* posterity. —e=widrig, *adj.* inconsequent; incoherent. —e=zeiger, *m.* catch-word (*Typ.*). —e=zeit, *f.* time to come; posterity.
Fol'g—en, *v.n.* (*aux.* s., *dat.*) to follow, attend, wait on; to keep pace with; to follow (*in time, rank, etc.*); to succeed (auf, to); to obey, attend to, conform to; ich —te ihm, I followed him; —en aus, to result from, ensue, be the consequence of; seinen Lüsten —en, to follow one's desires; dem Strom —en, to swim with the stream; seinem Kopfe —en, to act wilfully, to act according to one's lights; to persist in one's whim; —en lassen, to cause to follow, to deliver up; —en Sie mir, take my advice. —end, *p.* & *adj.* subsequent, next; auf einander —end, consecutive; —ende Woche, next week; —endes, the following (words). —ender=gestalt, —ender=maßen, *adv.* as follows, in the following manner. —er, *m.* (—ers, *pl.* —er), —erin, *f.* follower; successor (*obs. & poet.*). —erei', *f.* false deduction. —ern, *v.a.* to infer, conclude, reason out; falsch —ern, to draw wrong inferences; hieraus läßt sich —ern, hence we may infer. —erung, *f.* inference, deduction. —erungs=weise, *adj.* by inference.
Folia'nt, *m.* (—en, *pl.* —en) folio volume.
Fo'li—e, *f.* (*pl.* —en) thin leaf of metal; silvering of mirrors; foil; mit —e belegte Oberfläche, silvered surface; zur —e dienen, to be a foil, to set off; einer Sache eine —e geben, to set a thing off. —ie'ren, *v.a.* to page (*a book*); to

silver (*a mirror*). **—ie'rung**, *f.* paging, foliation, silvering. **—o**, *n.* (—os) folio; page; **groß —o**, atlas. *Comp.* **—en=schläger**, *m.* leaf-beater. **—o=format**, *n.* folio size.

Fol'ter, *f.* (*pl.* —n) rack; torture; **auf die — legen** *or* **spannen**, to put to the rack. **—er**, *m.* (—ers, *pl.* —er) torturer, tormentor. *Comp.* **—bank**, *f.* rack. **—gerät**, *n.*, **—werkzeuge**, *pl.* implements of torture. **—kammer**, *f.* torture chamber. **—knecht**, *m.* torturer. **—pein**, *f.* anguish. **—qual**, *f.* torture, torment.

Fol'ter—n, *v.a.* to put to the rack, torture, torment. **—ung**, *f.* act of torturing, torture.

Fond, *m.* (—s, *pl.* —s) ground, foundation; back of a carriage; **— im Handel**, stock in trade; *see* **—s**. **—s**, *m.* & *pl.* fund; landed property; stock, capital, public funds, stocks. *Comp.* **—s=besitzer**, *m.* fund-holder. **—s=börse**, *f.* stock-exchange.

Font—ä'ne, (*pl.* —ä'nen), **—ai'ne**, *f.* (*pl.* —ai'nen) fountain. **—ane'll**, *n.* (—ane'lls, *pl.* —anel'le), **—anel'le**, *f.* (*pl.* —anel'len) issue, fontanel. *Comp.* **—ane'll=erbse**, *f.* issue-pea.

Fop'p—en, *v.a.* to quiz, fool, hoax, mystify. **—er**, *m.* (—ers, *pl.* —er) jeerer, quiz. **—erei'**, *f.* quizzing, mystification, hoaxing.

For'c—e, *f.* strong point; the highest card of a suit. **—ie'ren**, *v.a.* to take by assault; to force, overurge. **—iert'heit**, *f.* roughness, rudeness.

For'derer, *m.* (—s, *pl.* —) demander; dun.

For'der—n, *v.a.* to demand, ask; to claim, require, exact; to summon; to challenge; **wie viel —n Sie dafür?** how much do you want for it? **vor Gericht —n**, to summon before a court; **Rechenschaft von einem —n**, to call one to account; **heraus—n**, to call out, challenge; **zu viel —n**, to overcharge; **wer an mich zu —n hat**, whoever has claims on me; **gefordert**, demanded, exacted. **—ung**, *f.* demand; claim; requisition; summons; challenge. **—ungs=satz**, *m.* postulate. *Comp.* **—gebühr**, *f.* fee for a summons.

För'der—er, *m.* (—ers, *pl.* —er), **—erin**, *f.* furtherer, promoter; patron, patroness. **—lich**, *adj.* & *adv.* furthering; promotive (*of*); conducive (*to*); beneficial, useful; **auf das —lichste**, in the speediest manner possible; in the most helpful way. **—lichkeit**, *f.* conduciveness (*to*).

För'der—n, *v.a.* to further, promote, advance; to benefit; to despatch, expedite; **die Schritte munter —n**, to walk on (briskly); **zu Tage —n**, to bring to light. **—nis**, *n.* (—ni(ss)es, *pl.* —ni(ss)e) furtherance, help. **—sam**, *adj.* & *adv.* furthering; useful; expeditious. **—samst**, *adv.* first of all; most expeditiously. **—ung**, *f.* furtherance, help; advancement; despatch; hauling (*Min.*). *Comp.* **—schacht**, *m.* engine shaft. **—seil**, *n.* rope used in mines. **—strecke**, *f.* mine tramway. **—wagen**, *m.* mine-tram.

Forel'le, *f.* (*pl.* —n) trout. *Comp.* **—n=fang**, *m.* trout-fishing. **—n=kirsche**, *f.* species of morello cherry. **—n=salat**, *m.* spotted coss-lettuce.

For'ke, *f.* (*pl.* —n) pitchfork, large fork.

Form, *f.* (*pl.* —en) form; figure; make, fashion; mode, fixed form *or* habit; method of procedure; model, pattern; block; last (*for shoes*); mould; form (*Typ.*); form, voice (*Gram.*); **in gehöriger —**, in due form; **in (aller) — Rechtens**, legally; **in aller —**, in due form; **gegen die —**, informal; **der — wegen**, for form's sake; **leidende —**, passive voice; **über die — schlagen**, to block (*hats*), to put on the last (*shoes*); **das Reich der —en**, the realm of (artistic) forms, art (*Schiller*). **—a'l**, *adj.* & *adv.* formal; **die —ale Bildung**, instruction intended to develop the mental faculties, mental gymnastics; grammatical, philosophical and literary training (*instruction to be obtained chiefly by means of the study of the writings of the ancient classics*). **—a'lien**, *pl.* formalities. **—alis'mus**, *m.* formalism. **—ali'st**, *m.* (—alis'ten, *pl.* —alis'ten) formalist. **—alitä't**, *f.* (*pl.* —alitä'ten) formality; (*pl.*) forms (*of courts, etc.*). **—at'**, *n.* (—a'ts, *pl.* —a'te) form, size (*of a book*). **—bar**, *adj.* & *adv.* that may be formed, plastic. **—el**, *f.* (*pl.* —eln) form; formula; **Zauber —el**, charm. **—e'll**, *adj.* & *adv.* formal. *Comp.* **—al=bildend**, *adj.* developing the mental faculties. **—arbeit**, *f.* casting, mould-making; cast-work. **—at=buch**, *n.* size-book (*Typ.*). **—atio'ns=silbe**, *f.* formative syllable. **—bekleidung**, *f.*, **—mantel**, *m.* mould-case (*Typ.*). **—brett**, *n.* mould. **—drähte**, *pl.* mould wires (*in paper making*). **—einrichtung**, *f.* imposing (*Typ.*). **—el=buch**, *n.* formulary. **—en=ausgleich**, *m.* form-association, levelling (*Gram.*). **—en=bildung**, *f.* morphology, accidence. **—en=gießer**, *m.* moulder in brass. **—en=krämer**, *m.* formalist. **—en=lehre**, *f.* accidence (*Gram.*). **—en=macher**, **—en=schneider**, *m.* pattern-maker; moulder; fashioner. **—en=wesen**, *n.* formality; ceremoniousness; ceremonies. **—erde**, *f.* modelling clay. **—erz**, *n.* rich silver ore. **—gebung**, *f.* fashioning. **—kopf**, *m.* wig-block. **—los**, *adj.* shapeless; formless; informal; impolite. **—losigkeit**, *f.* shapelessness; unceremoniousness; want of manners. **—presse**, *f.* gold-beater's press. **—rahmen**, *m.* chase (*Typ.*); frame (*Pap.*). **—scheibe**, *f.* smallest pane of glass; turning top of a potter's wheel. **—schrot**, *n.* mould-shot. **—stück**, *n.*, **—stein**, *m.* mould-work (*Arch.*). **—trieb**, *m.* formal impulsion, law-giving instinct, philosophical instinct (*Schiller*). **—übertragung**, *f.* form-association, levelling (*Gram.*). **—ula'r=buch**, *n.* precedent-book (*Law*). **—waren**, *pl.* fancy articles. **—wechsel**, *m.* change of form; accommodation-bill (*C. L.*).

For'm—en, *v.a.* to form, mould, model, shape, fashion; to put on the block (*hats*); to model. **—er**, *m.* (—ers, *pl.* —er) fashioner, former, shaper, moulder. **—erei'**, *f.* modelling, moulding. **—ie'ren**, *v.a.* to form; to mould; to arrange; **sich —**, to attain to the age of puberty (*of girls*); to fall in (*Mil.*); **Glieder —ieren**, to fall in (*Mil.*); **in Seiten —ieren**, to make up into pages. **—ula'r**, *n.* (—ula'rs, *pl.* —ula're, —ula'rien) form; formula, schedule; **unausgefülltes —ular**, blank; precedent (*Law*). **—ulie'ren**, *v.a.* to formulate. **—ulie'rung**, *f.* formulation, precise wording.

För'm—ig, *suff.* (*in comp.* =) -formed, -shaped. **—lich**, *adj.* & *adv.* formal, ceremonious; well-shaped; downright, express, unmistakable; as it were; **eine —liche Schlacht**, a pitched battle; **er hat es —lich darauf abgesehen**, it is clearly his intention; **es ist —lich lächerlich**, it is really ridiculous. **—lichkeit**, *f.* formality.

Forsch, *adj.* active, quick, strong, doughty (*dial.*).

For'sch—en, I. *v.a.* & *n.* (*aux.* **h.**) to search out, search; to enquire; to investigate, scrutinize; **einer der nach Wahrheit —t**, a seeker after truth; **bei einem —en**, to examine, pump one; **—ender Blick**, scrutinizing glance. II. *subst.* *n.* investigation. **—er**, *m.* (—ers, *pl.* —er) searcher; investigator; researcher; speculator; scholar. **—ung**, *f.* investigation, enquiry; research. *Comp.* **—begier(de)**, *f.* inquisitiveness; love of investigating. **—begierig**, *adj.* inquisitive. **—er=blick**, *m.* searching glance. **—er=geist**, **—er=sinn**, *m.* spirit of enquiry, enquiring mind, mind of a scholar. **—kraft**, *f.* penetration, sagacity. **—ungs=gebiet**, *n.* field of research. **—ungs=reise**, *f.* voyage of discovery. **—ungs=reisende(r)**, *m.* explorer.

Forst, *m.* (—es, *pl.* —e) forest, wood. **—lich**, *adj.* & *adv.* relating to a forest. *Comp.* **—aka=**

demie, *f.* school of forestry. —akademiker, *m.* student of forestry. —amt, *n.* commission *or* board of woods and forests. —aufseher, *m.* ranger. —beamte(r), *m.* forest officer, verderer. —bereiter, *m.* mounted inspector of woods. —direktion, *f.* woods-and-forests commission. —eleve, *m. see* —akademiker. —frevler, *m.* trespasser in a forest. —gefälle, *n.* revenue arising from forests. —geräume, *n.* clearing. —gerecht, *adj.* skilled in forest matters; in good condition. —gerechtigkeit, *f.* forest rights *or* laws. —gesetz, *n.* forest law. —haus, *n.* ranger's *or* forester's house. —hut, *f.* forest inspection. —hüter, *m.* forester's assistant, woodman. —kunde, *f.* science of forestry. —mäßig, *adj. & adv.* according to forest laws. —mann, *m.* forester, verderer, ranger. —meister, *m.* ranger. —ordnung, *f.* forest laws. —rat, *m.* commissioner *or* commission of woods. —recht, *n.* forest laws. —schreiber, *m.* clerk in a woods-and-forests-office. —revier, *n.* forest district. —ung, *f.* forest. —verwaltung, *f.* management of woods. —wesen, *n.* forestry, everything relating to woods. —wissenschaft, *f.* wood-craft. —zögling, *m.* student in a school of forestry.

For'st—en, *v.a.*; einen Wald —en, to afforest a wood. —ung, *f.* afforesting; forest, wood.

För'ster, *m.* (—s, *pl.* —) forest-keeper, ranger, verderer. —ei', *f.* ranger's house.

[1]**Fort**, *n.* (—s, *pl.* —s) fort, small fortress, fortication; Außen—, detached fort.

[2]**Fort**, *adv. & sep. prefix*, on; away, off, gone; forth, forward, onward; quickly; continuously; er ist schon —, he is off, away; es will mit ihm nicht recht —, he does not get on; ich muß —, I must be off; mein Mantel ist —, my cloak is lost; all' mein Geld ist —, all my money is gone *or* spent; — ist —, gone is gone; — mit dir! begone! leave the room! so —, immediately; und so —, and so forth, and so on; in einem —, — und —, continually, uninterruptedly; er schrieb in einem —, he continued to write; immer —, always. *Comp. If the second part of the compound is a verb, the accent falls on* Fort *and the verb is separable.* —a'n, *adv.* onward, from this time, henceforth; continuously. —ackern, *v.a.* to continue ploughing. —arbeiten, *v.* I. *n.* (*aux.* h.) to continue to work. II. *a.* to work away, remove. III. *r.* to get on. —bau, *m.* continuation of building. —bauen, *v.n.* to keep on building. —begeben, *ir.v.r.* to withdraw, retire; to depart. —bestand, *m.* continuation, permanence, duration. —bestehen, *ir.v.n.* (*aux.* h.) to continue to stand firm; to last, endure; to persist; to continue to subsist. —bewegen, *v.a. & r.* to continue moving, to move on. —bewegung, *f.* locomotion (*of animals*). —bilden, *v.r.* to continue one's studies —bildungs-anstalt, *f.* finishing school; adult school; selecta (*an advanced class added to the highest form of several high schools for girls and intended to train future mistresses; the course lasts two or three years*); institution for higher education. —bildungs-schule, *f.* evening school for apprentices; *see also* —bildungs-anstalt. —bleiben, *ir.v.n.* to stay away. —bringen, I. *ir.v.a.* to bring onwards, to get away; to help on, support; to remove, transport; to rear; er ist nicht — zu bringen, you can't get rid of him; sich —bringen, to make one's way, get on in life. II. *subst. n.*, —bringung, *f.* conveyance, transport; rearing; promotion, advance. —dauer, *f.* continuance, permanence, duration; —dauer nach dem Tode, immortality, existence after death. —dauern, *v.n.* (*aux.* h.) to continue, last on, endure. —dauernd, *p. & adj.* lasting, permanent; incessant. —eilen, *v.n.* (*aux.* s.) to hasten away; to press forward. —erben, *v.* I. *n.* (*aux.* s.) to descend from generation to generation. II. *r.* to be inherited. —fahren, *ir.v.* I. *n.* (*aux.* s.) to drive off *or* away, depart; (*aux.* h.) (mit *or* in einer S. —) to continue, proceed, go on. II. *a.* to carry away; to remove (*in a vehicle*); drive off (*in a carriage*). —führen, *v.a.* (eine S.) to lead forth; to carry *or* lead on, extend; to keep on, continue; to pursue; to proceed; to carry on. —führung, *f.* continuation; conveyance; persecution, pursuit. —gang, *m.* progression; progress, advance; departure; continuation; success; —gang haben, to get on, to proceed; die Sache wird ihren —gang haben, the affair (matter) will take its course, take place. —gehen, *ir.v.n.* (*aux.* s.) to go away, go forth; to go on *or* forward; to progress; to continue; wenn das so —geht, if this continues, in time; es geht —, we are on the move. —haben, *ir.v.a.*; sie möchte ihn —haben, she would like to see him gone, to be rid of him. —heben, *ir.v.a.* to carry away, remove; (*B.*) hebe dich fort! begone! —helfen, *ir.v.a.* to help one to escape; einem *or* einer —helfen, to help one on; sich kümmerlich —helfen, to make shift to live. —hi'n, *see* —an. —jagen, *v.* I. *a.* to chase, drive off *or* away; to drum out (*of the army*). II. *n.* (*aux.* h.) to continue to hunt; (*aux.* s.) to gallop, ride off. —kommen, I. *ir. v.n.* (*aux.* s.) to get away, escape; to get lost; to get on, thrive; to succeed; damit kommt man nicht fort, that will never do; mach, daß du —kommst, get away with you, make haste and get off. II. *subst.n.* advancement, progress; prosperity. —können, *ir.v.n.* (*ellipt.; a verb of motion to be supplied*) to be able to proceed, go on *or* get away. —lassen, *ir.v.a.* (*ellipt.; a verb of motion to be supplied*) to suffer to go; nicht —lassen, to detain, keep. —lauf, *m.* progress, advancement; continuation. —laufen, *ir.v.n.* (*aux.* s.) to run away, escape; to run on; to continue on. —laufend, *p. & adj.* running, continuous; continued. —machen, *ir.v.* I. *n.* (*aux.* h.) to make haste. II. *r.* to get away, take oneself off. —mögen, *ir.v.n.* (*ellipt.; a verb of motion to be understood*) to wish to go. —müssen, *ir.v.n.* (*ellipt.; a verb of motion to be supplied*) to be obliged to go; to have to clear out; to die (*fig.*). —packen, *v.r.* to withdraw, retire; packe dich —! be off! —pflanzen, *v.a.* to transplant; to propagate; to communicate (*disease*); to transmit. —pflanzung, *f.* propagation; transmission. —pflanzungs-fähig, *adj.* capable of engendering, having attained puberty, generative, reproductive; transmissible (*Phys.*). —pflanzungs-organe, *pl.* sexual organs. —pflanzungs-trieb, *m.* instinct of propagation, generative instinct. —reise, *f.* departure; progress. —reisen, *v.n.* (*aux.* s.) to travel on; to depart; (*aux.* h.) to continue a journey. —reißen, *ir.v.a.* to carry away (*by passion, etc.*), to sweep away. —rücken, I. *v.a. & n.* (*aux.* s.) to move away *or* on; to advance. II. *subst. n.* advancement. —rückend, *p. & adj.* progressive. —satz, *m.* continuation; process, apophysis (*Anat.*). —schaffen, I. *v.a.* to get out of the way; to transport, remove; to dismiss, discard, discharge; to get rid of. II. *ir.v.n.* to continue to create. —schaffung, *f.* removal; transportation; dismissal, discharge. —schaffungs-mittel, *n.* means of conveyance *or* transportation. —scheren, *v.r.* to be gone (*vulg.*). —schießen, *ir.v.n.* (*aux.* s.) to shoot forward, to rush along *or* away; (*aux.* h.) to continue shooting. —schiffen, *v.* I. *n.* (*aux.* s.) to sail away, set sail. II. *a.* to ship, transport, convey by water. —schnellen, *v.a.* to

jerk off, send off with a jerk *or* filip. **—schlagen,** *ir.v.a.* to beat, strike off. II. *n.* (*aux.* **h.**) to continue striking. **—schleichen,** *ir.v.a.* & *r.* to sneak off, steal away. **—schreiten,** *ir.v.n.* (*aux.* **s.**) to move forward, go on, proceed; to make progress, improve; —**schreiten mit,** to keep pace with. **—schreitend,** *p.* & *adj.* progressive. **—schreitung,** *f.* progression, consecutive chords (*Mus.*). **—schritt,** *m.* progress; advance, development, improvement; —**schritte machen,** to advance. **—schritts-partei,** *f.* Progressists, radical party (*Polit.*). **—schwemmen,** *v.a.* to wash away (*of floods*). **—sehnen,** *v.r.* to wish oneself away. — **—setzen,** *v.a.* to put, set forward; to put away; to carry on; to continue; to pursue; to transplant (*a tree*); **wieder —setzen,** to resume; **nicht —setzen,** to discontinue. **—setzer,** *m.* continuer. **—setzung,** *f.* continuation; carrying on, pursuit, prosecution; **—setzung folgt,** (**Forts. f.**) to be continued (*in our next*). — **spinnen,** *ir. v.* I. *n.* (*aux.* **h.**) to keep on spinning. II. *a.* to spin out, prolong. **—sprengen,** *v.n.* (*aux.* **s.**) to ride off at full speed. **—springen,** *ir.v.n.* (*aux.* **s.**) to jump away; (*aux.* **h.**) to continue leaping, jumping. **—stehlen,** *ir.v.a.* to steal away secretly; **sich —stehlen,** to abscond, sneak off. **—stoßen,** *ir.v.* I. *a.* to push on *or* away; to propel, press out; to force along. II. *n.* (*aux.* **h.**) to continue pushing. **—stoßung,** *f.* pushing on *or* away; propulsion; protrusion; expulsion. **—strömen,** *v.n.* (*aux.* **s.**) to flow on with, be carried away by; (*aux.* **h.**) to continue flowing. **—stürmen,** *v.n.* (*aux.* **s.**) to rush furiously on *or* away; (*aux.* **h.**) to continue to storm *or* roar. **—treiben,** *ir.v.a.* to drive away *or* onward; to force out, to propel; to carry on; to maintain; to pursue, prosecute, continue; **sie treiben es noch immer so —,** they go on just in the old way. **—treibung,** *f.* driving away; expulsion; continuation. — **währen,** *v.n.* (*aux.* **h.**) to last on, continue to be, endure. **—während,** *p. adj.* & *adv.* lasting, continuous, perpetual, incessant, permanent. **—wälzen,** *v.a.* to roll forward *or* away; **sich —wälzen,** to roll on. **—wandern,** *v.n.* (*aux.* **h.**) to wander on *or* outward; to emigrate. **—weisen,** *ir.v.a.* to show the way; to send, turn away. **—wollen,** *ir.v.n.* (*aux.* **h.**) (*ellipt.; a verb of motion to be understood*) to wish to go away; to intend to leave *or* go on; **es will mit ihm nicht mehr —,** his affairs do not thrive any longer, are in a bad way. **—ziehen,** *ir.v.* I. *a.* to draw *or* drag along, away. II. *n.* (*aux.* **s.**) to move on, proceed, march on; to march off, depart; to leave (*a house*); to emigrate; to migrate. **—zucht,** *f.* propagation. **—zug,** *m.* onward march, advance; departure; leaving (*a house*); migration.

For'te, *adv.* forte (*Mus.*). *Comp.* **—pia'no,** *n.* (**—pia'nos,** *pl.* **—pia'nos**) piano-(forte).

Fossi'l, *n.* (**—s,** *pl.* **—ien**) fossil. *Comp.* **—ien-bildung,** *f.*, **—werden,** *n.* fossilization. **—ien-haltig,** *adj.* fossiliferous. **—lehre,** *f.* science of fossils.

Foura'g—e, *f.* forage. **—ie'ren,** *v.n.* (*aux.* **h.**) to go foraging. **—eu'r,** *m.* (**—eu'rs,** *pl.* **—eu'r**) forager. *Comp.* **—ier'-mütze,** *f.* foraging cap. **—ie'rungs-kommando,** *n.* foraging party. **—ier'zug,** *m.* foraging expedition.

Fourie'r, Furie'r, *m.* (**—s,** *pl.* **—e**) quartermaster (*Mil.*); forerunner; petty officer.

Fournier', *n.* (**—s,** *pl.* **—e**) veneer. **—en,** *v.a.* to inlay, veneer. *Comp.* **—holz,** *n.* wood for inlaying, veneer.

Fracht, *f.* (*pl.* **—en**) freight, cargo, load; freightage, carriage (*by land*), freight (*by sea*); **in gewöhnlicher —,** at the usual freight; **ein Schiff in — nehmen,** to charter a vessel; **in — geben,** to freight. **—bar,** *adj.* & *adv.* transportable, that may be freighted. *Comp.* **—aufseher,** *m.* supercargo. **—bedingungen,** *pl.* terms of freight. **—besorger,** *m.* shipping agent. **—brief, —zettel,** *m.* bill of lading; way-bill. **—frei,** *adj.* & *adv.* carriage free. **—fuhre,** *f.* land-carriage. **—fuhrmann,** *m.* carrier. **—gebühr, —geld,** *n.*, **—lohn,** *m.* freightage, carriage. **—gut,** *n.* lading, cargo; goods sent by goods train. **—handel,** *m.* carrying trade. **—kontrakt,** *m.* charter-party. **—mäkler,** *m.* shipping *or* forwarding agent. **—post,** *f.* stage-waggon. **—schiff,** *n.* merchantman, trading vessel. **—stück,** *n.* package. **—versender,** *m.* consigner. **—wagen,** *m.* waggon; **mit dem größten —wagen,** with the greatest pleasure (*sl.*). **—zulage,** *f.*, **—zusatz, —zuschlag,** *m.* extra freight.

Frach't—en, *v.a.* & *n.* (*aux.* **h.**) to freight, load; to carry (*freight*); to ship; **wohin habt Ihr gefrachtet?** where are you bound for? **—er,** *m.* (**—ers,** *pl.* **—er**) freighter. **—ung,** *f.* shipping.

Frack, *m.* (**—es,** *pl.* **—s** and **Frä'cke**) dress-coat; tail-coat (*coll.*); **— und weiße Binde,** evening dress. *Comp.* **—schoß,** *m.* flap *or* tail of a dress-coat. **—zwang,** *m.* obligation to wear evening dress, to appear in full dress.

Fra'ge, *f.* (*pl.* **—n**) question, interrogation, enquiry; questionable *or* uncertain thing; **eine — thun** *or* **stellen (an einen),** to ask a p. a question; **eine — bejahen,** to answer in the affirmative; **das ist eben die —,** that is just the point *or* question; **ohne —,** no doubt; **gerichtliche —,** interrogatory, enquiry; **eine — enthaltend,** interrogatory; **stark in — sein,** to be in great demand; **peinliche —,** examination by torture; **in — ziehen, stellen,** to call in question; **es ist sehr die —,** it is very doubtful *or* questionable; **davon ist jetzt nicht die —,** that is out of the question now; **na, die —!** I think so, rather! (*coll.*).

Fra'g—en, *reg.* & (*less good*) *irreg. v.a.* & *n.* (*aux.* **h.**) to ask, enquire, interrogate, question; to ask for (**nach**); to ask for advice, consult (**um**); to care about, mind; **der —te mich,** he asked me; **darf ich Sie —en,** may I ask you? **ich —te gar nichts darnach,** I did not care a rush about it; **niemand —t nach mir,** nobody cares for me, troubles himself about me; **hat jemand nach mir gefragt?** has anyone asked for me? **um Erlaubnis —en,** to ask permission; **wegen einer Sache —en,** to ask concerning a matter; **sich nach einem Orte hin —en,** to ask one's way to a place; **es —te sich, ob,** the question was whether; **wer viel —t, erhält viel Antwort,** many questions many answers (*prov.*). **—end,** *p.adj.* & *adv.* interrogative; interrogatory; **er sah sie —end an,** he looked at her enquiringly. **—er,** *m.* (**—ers,** *pl.* **—er**) questioner; examiner. **—lich,** *adj.* & *adv.* questionable; doubtful; **die —liche Sache,** the matter in question. **—lichkeit,** *f.* questionableness. *Comp.* **—e-amt,** *n.* intelligence-office, enquiry office. **—e-buch,** *n.* catechism. **—e-lehre,** *f.*; **zur —elehre gehörig,** catechetical. **—e-lehrer,** *m.* catechist. **—e-liste,** *f.* list of questions. **—(e)-selig,** *adj.* fond of asking questions; inquisitive. **—ens-wert,** *adj.* & *adv.* worth enquiring about. **—(e)-punkt,** *m.* point in question. **—(e)-satz,** *m.* interrogative sentence. **—(e)-schüler,** *m.* catechumen. **—(e)-spiel,** *n.* game of cross-questions. **—e-steller,** *m.* interrogator. **—e-stellung,** *f.* formulation of a question. **—(e)-weise,** I. *f.* catechetical method. II. *adv.* interrogatively, in the form of a question. **—(e)-wort,** *n.* interrogative. **—würdig,** *adj.*, questionable, doubtful. **—(e)-zeichen,** *n.* mark *or* note of interrogation. **—e-zeichenlied,** *n.*; **das liebe, alte —ezeichenlied,** the dear old song with the many signs of interrogation (*viz. Arndt's poem:* ‚Was ist des Deutschen Vaterland?'). **Fragme'nt,** *n.* (—**s**, *pl.* —**e**) fragment. —**a'risch,** *adj. & adv.* fragmentary.

Frakt—io'n, *f.* (*pl.*—**tio'nen**) fraction. —**u'r,** *f.* (*pl.* —**u'ren**) black letter, Gothic character, Old English type; fracture (*Surg.*). *Comp.* —**u'r=schrift,** *f.* engrossing hand; (*a kind of*) large German characters.

Frank, I. *adj. & adv.* free; frank, open; — **und frei,** quite frankly, without any restraint. II. *m.* (—**en**, *pl.* —**en**) franc (*a coin*). —**atu'r,** *f.* prepayment. —**ie'ren,** *v.a.* to post-pay, to stamp, to send post-paid; —**ier'ter Brief=umschlag,** stamped envelope. —**o,** *adv.* post-paid; carriage-paid; —**o München,** delivered free at M.; —**o ab London;** to be delivered in L.; —**o bis London,** post-paid to L. *Comp.* —**ie'rungs=vermerk,** *m.* mark of being post-paid. —**ie'rungs=zwang,** *m.* obligation to prepay letters. —**o=brief,** *m.* post-paid letter. —**o=fracht,** *f.* free carriage. —**o=gebühr,** *f.* carriage, postage. —**o=spesen,** *pl.* free of cost, no charges. —**o=vermerk,** *m.* notice of prepayment. —**o=zettel,** *m.* advice of postage due. —**o=zinsen,** *pl.* no interest charged.

Fran's—e, *f.* (*pl.*—**en**; *dim.* **Fräns'chen**) fringe; valance. —**en,** *v.a.* to fringe. —**icht,** *adj. & adv.* like fringe. —**ig,** *adj. & adv.* fringed.

Fran'z—e, *m.* (—**en**, *pl.* —**en**) Frenchman (*obs. & poet.*). —**o'se,** *m.* (—**o'sen**, *pl.* —**o'sen**) Frenchman. —**ö'seln,** *v.n.* (*aux.* **h.**) to ape the French. —**o'sen,** *pl.* syphilis (*Med.*). —**o'sentum,** *n.* French nationality. —**ö'sin,** *f.* Frenchwoman. —**ösie'ren,** *v.a.* to Frenchify. —**ö'sisch,** *adj.* French. *Comp.* —**apfel,** *m.* rennet apple. —**band,** I. *m.* calf binding; calf-bound book. II. *n.* fancy silk ribbon. —**bohne,** *f.* French bean. —**brannt'wein,** *m.* cognac. —**brot,** *n.* French roll. —**gold,** *n.* French gold leaf. —**mann,** *m.* (*pl.* —**männer**) Frenchman. —**obst,** *n.* fruit of wall *or* dwarf trees; French fruits. —**o'sen=harz,** *n.* guaiacum (*Med.*). —**o'sen=holz,** *n.* guaiacum (*Bot.*). —**o'sen=sucht,** *f.* Gallomania. —**perlen,** *pl.* false pearls.

Franziska'ner, *m.* (—**s**, *pl.* —), —**in,** *f.* Franciscan friar, grey friar; Franciscan nun.

Frapp—a'nt, *adj. & adv.* striking, surprising. —**ie'ren,** *v.a.* to strike, to astound.

[1]**Fraß, Frä'ße,** *imperf. ind. & subj. of* **fressen.**

[2]**Fraß** (*long* **a**), *m.* (—**es**, *pl.* **Frä'ße**) feeding; food (*for beasts*); repast; pasture; immoderate appetite, voracity; glutton; caries (*Med.*); **voll Raub und** —, full of extortion and excess (*B.*). *Comp.* —**trog,** —**zuber,** *m.* feeding-trough.

Fratz, *m.* (—**en**, *pl.* —**en**) ugly *or* silly person (*obs.*). —**e,** *f.* (*pl.* —**en**) grimace; odd *or* ridiculous thing; caricature; whim; phiz; mask (*Arch.*); —**en schneiden,** to make faces. —**en=haft,** *adj. & adv.* distorted, ridiculous, whimsical, grotesque. —**en=haftigkeit,** *f.* buffoonery; apishness; grotesqueness. *Comp.* —**en=bild,** *n.* caricature. —**en=gesicht,** *n.* apish face; fright; mask (*Arch.*). —**en=maler,** *m.* caricaturist. —**en=schneider,** *m.* grinner, silly boy.

Frau, *f.* (*pl.* —**en**) woman; wife; lady; dame; madam; mistress; **meine** —, my wife; **Herr und** —, master and mistress; **Herr und** — **Professor Scherer,** Professor and Mrs. Scherer; **alte** —, crone; **junge** *or* **jung verheiratete** —, bride; **eine vornehme** —, a gentlewoman, lady; **adlige** —, lady, gentlewoman; **liebe** —, my dear, my love; **gnädige** —, my lady, your ladyship; **Unsre (liebe)** —, Our Lady, the Holy Virgin; — **Fiedler,** Mrs. Fiedler; — **Dr. Fiedler,** Mrs. Fiedler; **die** — **Doktor** (*less good:* **Doktorin**), the doctor's wife; **die** — **Rat** (*less good:* **Rätin**) the counsellor's lady; **die** — **Gräfin,** the countess, her ladyship; **wie geht's Ihrer** — **Gemahlin, Herr Gerrans?** how is Mrs. Gerrans? **Ihre** — **Schwester,** your (*married*) sister; **Ihre** — **Mutter,** your mother; — **Nachtigall,** Dame Nightingale (*in old popular songs*); **Für** —**en,** Ladies; ladies' cloak-room (*at railway station*); **wie die** —, **so die Magd,** hackney-mistress, hackney-maid (*prov.*). —**chen,** *n.* (—**chens**, *pl.* —**chen**) little woman, good woman; dear little wife, wifey; my dear (wife). —**en=haft,** *adj. & adv.* woman like, womanly. *Comp.* —**base,** *f.* (Mrs.) gossip. —**basen=geschwätz,** *n.* idle talk, gossip. —**en=abteil,** *m.* ladies' compartment (*Railw.*). —**en=anwalt,** *m.* advocate of the emancipation of women. —**en=anzug,** *m.* female dress. —**en=arzt,** *m.* ladies' doctor, specialist for women's diseases, gynæcologist. —**en=bewegung,** *f.* movements and questions affecting the position of women. —**en=bild,** *n.* female figure, woman (*obs.*). —**en=bildungs=verein,** *m.* women's educational association. —**en=college,** *n.* college for women students. —**en=coupé,** *n.* compartment for ladies (*Railw.*). —**en=erwerb,** *m.* employment of women; **Gesellschaft zur Hebung des** —**enerwerbes,** society for promoting the employment of women. —**en=faden,** *m.* gossamer. —**en=feind,** *m.* woman-hater. —**en=fest,** *n.* Lady-day. —**en=frage,** *f.* question of woman's rights; the emancipation of the female sex. —**en=glas,** *n.* mica, Muscovy glass (*Min.*). —**en=gut,** *n.* property brought *or* possessed by the wife. —**en=gymnasium,** *n.* classical (secondary) school for women. —**en=haar,** *n.* women's hair; maiden-hair (*Bot.*). —**en=haß,** *m.* misogyny. —**en=hasser,** *m.* misogynist. —**en=handschuh,** *m.* lady's glove; columbine (*Bot.*). —**en=haus,** *n.* brothel. —**en=heilkunde,** *f.* gynæcology. —**en=heim,** *n.* home *or* refuge for women. —**en=held,** *m.* Don Juan, ladies' man. —**en=hemd,** *n.* chemise. —**en=herrschaft,** *f.* petticoat government. —**en=hochschule,** *f.* University College for women. —**en=hut,** *m.* bonnet, lady's hat. —**en=jäger,** *m.* gay Lothario. —**en=käfer,** *m.* lady-bird. —**en=kirche,** *f.* Church of Our Lady, St. Mary's Church. —**en=kleid,** *n.* gown, robe, dress. —**en=kleidung,** *f.* women's dress; **Verein für Verbesserung der** —**enkleidung,** society for the improvement of women's dress, Rational Dress Association. —**en=kloster,** *n.* nunnery. —**en=knecht,** *m.* devotee to women, women's slave. —**en=liebe,** *f.* woman's love; love for women. —**en=milch,** *f.* women's milk; **Lieb=**—**enmilch,** a famous Rhenish wine. —**en=münster,** *n.* Cathedral of Our Lady, St. Mary's, Notre Dame. —**en=putz,** *m.* female finery, women's ornaments. —**en=rock,** *m.* woman's gown, skirt. —**en=sattel,** *m.* side-saddle. —**en=schuh,** *m.* woman's shoe; lady's slipper (*Bot.*). —**en=sommer,** *m.* gossamer. —**ens=leute,** *pl.* women, womankind, womenfolk. —**ens=person,** *f.* female. —**en=staat,** *m.* female community; see —**enputz.** —**en=stand,** *m.* wifehood; womanhood; coverture (*Law*). —**en=stift,** *n.* (religious) foundation for women; nunnery. —**en=stimme,** *f.* female voice. —**en stimmrecht,** *n.* women's suffrage. —**en=stühle,** *pl.* places in churches *or* pews assigned to women. —**en=sucht,** *f.* immoderate fondness for women. —**en=tag,** *m.* Lady-day. —**en=teil,** *m.* wife's portion, dowry. —**en=tracht,** *f.* female dress. —**en=verein,** *m.* ladies' (*benevolent*) association. —**en=volk,** *n.*, —**en=welt,** *f.* womankind; ladies' realm. —**en=zimmer,** *n.* women's apartment (*obs.*); women, womankind (*obs.*); female, woman; womankind; **das ledige** —**enzimmer,** spinster. —**en=**

zimmerchen, *n.* little woman, young lady. —en=zimmerlich, *adj.* womanlike, womanly. —en=zopf, *m.* lady's (long) plait of hair. —en=zwinger, *m.* harem.

Fräu'lein, *n.* (—s, *pl.* —) girl (*of the better classes*); young lady; unmarried lady; Miss; das älteste — Siepmann, Miss Siepmann (*as distinguished from her younger sisters* e.g. Miss Dolly Siepmann); meine —! young ladies! das gnädige —, Miss —; her ladyship; jawohl, gnädiges —, quite so, Miss . . .; quite right, your ladyship; ein adliges —, a nobleman's daughter; Ihre (*and* Ihr) — Braut, your intended, Miss . . .; ich habe mit Ihrer (*and* Ihrem) — Tochter getanzt, I have danced with your daughter; Liebes — Lieschen, dear Miss Lizzie; ein Männlein und ein —, a male and a female (*B.*). —chen, *n.* Missy (*as an address*). *Comp.* —steuer, *f.* tax levied for the dowry of a princess. —stift, *n.* foundation, establishment for single ladies of rank, *or* daughters of officers *or* civil servants.

Frech, *adj. & adv.* shameless, bold, insolent, impudent; mit —er Stirn, brazen-faced. —heit, *f.* insolence, impudence, shamelessness, audacity, cheek (*coll.*).

Fregat'te, *f.* (*pl.* —n) frigate.

Frei, *adj. & adv.* free (von, of); unconfined, uncontrolled; at liberty; frank, outspoken; bold; loose; voluntary; vacant; disengaged; exempt, clear; independent; acquitted; exonerated; exempted; post-paid, carriage-free; — ausgehen, to come off scot free; Briefe — machen, to postpay letters; Güter — machen, to clear goods; Passagiere haben 60 Pfund Gepäck —, passengers are allowed 60 lbs. of luggage; —er Anstand, easy deportment; —es Feld, open country; full scope; —es Geleit, safe conduct; —e Hand, steady hand, liberty, full authority; aus —er Hand, without a model, voluntarily, at first hand, offhand; —er Handel, free trade; —er Handwerker, artisan belonging to no guild; unter —em Himmel, in the open (air); —en Lauf lassen (einer Sache, *dat.*), to let a matter take its own course; —e Stelle, vacancy; aus —en Stücken, voluntarily, of one's own accord; darf ich so — sein? may I take the liberty? ist dieser Platz —? is this seat disengaged? — heraus, frankly; ich sagte es ihm — heraus, I told him plainly; ins —e gehen, to take the air; —er Teil, commercial partnership free of all expense or loss; —er Tag, holiday; —e Zeit, leisure; die —en Künste, the liberal arts; —e Liebe, the living together of a man and a woman without sanction either of the state or the church; —e Bühne, private theatre kept by an association of authors, critics and lovers of theatricals, not subjected to stage censorship and not conducted for the sake of profits, where certain plays of the very latest type are being acted; —e Gemeinde, independent religious association of very rationalistic views; —es deutsches Hochstift, society for the promotion of arts and sciences at Frankfort on the Main; —e Stätte, place of refuge; der, die —, free person, independent person. —e, *n.* the open air; open space. —heit, *m. & f.* tramp, vagabond (*obs.*); gipsy (*obs.*). *f.* freedom, liberty, privilege, immunity; franchise; license; charter; place of refuge, sanctuary (*obs.*); in —heit, at liberty; ich nehme mir die —heit, Sie darum zu bitten, I take the liberty of asking you for it. —lich, *adv.* to be sure, certainly, truly, by all means; I confess, admit. *Comp.* —acker, *m.* free ground (*i.e. exempt from taxes or socage*). —altar, *m.* portable altar; altar with special privileges. —bauer, *m.* peasant exempt from socage service. —beuter, *m.* freebooter, pirate. —beuterei', *f.* freebooting, piracy. —billet, *n.* complimentary *or* free-admission ticket. —brief, *m.* charter; privilege, license; patent. —bürger, *m.* free citizen; citizen of a free city *or* republic; burgess. —bürgerlich, *adj.* republican. —bürgersinn, *m.* republicanism. —corps, *see* —korps. —denker, —geist, *m.* freethinker. —denkerei', *f.* freethinking, latitudinarianism. —eigen, *adj.* freehold. —erdi'ngs, *adv.* spontaneously, voluntarily. —frau, —in, *f.* baroness. —geben, to set free, emancipate; to release; to give a holiday. —gebig, *adj.* liberal, generous. —gebigkeit, *f.* liberality, generosity. —gebung, *f.* emancipation; release. —geboren, *adj.* free-born. —geding, *n.* miner's (*piece or job*) wages. —gelassen, *adj.* freed; enfranchised. —gelassene(r), *m. f.* freedman, freedwoman; libertine. —gepäck, *n.* allowed luggage, luggage conveyed free. —gesinnt, *adj.* liberal. —gläubig, *adj.* independent in faith. —gläubigkeit, *f.* independence in belief. —graben, *m.* canal (*destined to receive and take away superfluous water, Mill.*). —gut, *n.* freehold; goods that are duty-free. —guts=besitzer, *m.* freeholder. —hafen, *m.* free port. —häusler, *m.* owner of houses enjoying special civic privileges. —halten, *ir.v.a.*; einen —halten, to treat, pay a man's expenses. —halter, *m.* defrayer of expenses. —hand=schießen, *n.* free-hand shooting. —hand=zeichnen, *n.* free-hand drawing. —handel, *m.* free trade. —händler, *m.* free-trader; believer in principles of free trade. —hart, *m.* tramp. —heits=brief, *m.* charter. —heits=kampf, —heits=krieg, *m.* war of independence; die (deutschen) —heits-kriege, the wars of liberation (against Napoleon I. 1813–15). —heits=mann, *m.* a man desiring (national) independence; patriot. —heits=urkunde, *f.* charter. —herr, *m.* baron. —herrin, —in, *f. see* —frau. —herrschaft, *f.* barony. —herr=schend, *adj.* sovereign. —herrscher, *m.* sovereign. —herzig, *adj.* open-hearted, frank. —herzigkeit, *f.* frankness. —korps, *n.* volunteer corps. —kugel, *f.* charmed bullet which will always hit its aim. —lager, *n.* bivouac. —lassen, *ir.v.a.* to let out on bail; to set free. —lassung, *f.* emancipation. —lauf=fahrrad, *n.* free wheel (bicycle). —lehen, *n.* freehold, fee-simple. —licht=malerei, *f.* plain-air painting. —machen, *n.*, —machung, *f.* freeing; emancipation. —mann, *m.* freeman; freeholder. —marke, *f.* (adhesive) postage stamp. —markt, *m.* (famous autumn) fair (*at Bremen*). —maurer, *m.* free-mason. —maurerisch, *adj.* masonic. —maurerei, *f.* freemasonry. —maurer=loge, *f.* freemasons' lodge. —meister, *m.* master (*of a guild or trade*). —meisterschaft, *f.* freedom of a guild. —messe, *f.* free, privileged fair *or* market. —mündig, *adj.* free-spoken. —mut, *m.* frankness. —mütig, *adj. & adv.* candid, frank. —mütigkeit, *f.* ingenuousness. —paß, *m.* passport. —saß, *m.* (—sassen, *pl.* —sassen) yeoman. —scharen, *pl.* volunteer corps. —schärler, *m.* volunteer; armed insurgent. —schein, *m.* license. —schule, *f.* free school. —schüler, *m.* scholar of a free school. —schulzen=gericht, *n.* freehold farm. —schütz(e), *m.* free-archer; rifleman; marksman who uses charmed bullets. II. *n.* floodgate. —sinn, *m.* liberality of mind. —sinnig, *adj.* freeminded, enlightened; strongly liberal; radical (*Pol.*); —sinnige Ansichten, broad views. —sitz, *m.* freehold. —sprechen, I. *ir.v.a.* (*sep.*) to acquit, absolve. II. *subst.n.*, —sprechung, *f.* acquittal; absolution; emancipation. —staat, *m.* republic. —staats=bürger, *m.*

republican. —**statt**, *f.*, —**stätte**, *f.* sanctuary, place of refuge. —**stehen**, *ir.v.n.* to be free; **es steht dir —**, you are at liberty, you may. —**stellen**, *v.a.*; —**stellen einem etwas**, to leave s.th. to one's option, to give a choice, permit. —**stunde**, *f.* leisure-hour, play-hour. —**tisch**, *m.* free table, free board (*often given to poor University students in German families*). —**treppe**, *f.* outside staircase. —**truppe**, *f.* volunteer corps. —**übungen**, *fem. plur.* calisthenics. —**wasser**, *n.* right of fishing, common of piscary; superfluous water. —**willig**, *adj.* voluntary; spontaneous. —**willige(r)**, *m.* volunteer; **einjährig —williger**, volunteer in the German army who serves one year only with the colours. —**willigen=schein**, *m.*, —**willigen=zeugnis**, *n.* certificate qualifying for one year's military service as a volunteer. —**willigkeit**, *f.* spontaneity; goodwill. —**zettel**, *m.* passport; warrant; permit. —**zügig**, *adj.* having a right to emigrate without being taxed. —**zügigkeit**, *f.* right of choosing one's domicile, ability of free movement, self-location.

[1]**Frei'en**, *v.a.*, to free, set free, relieve (*obs.*); **der Gefreite**, the lance corporal (*a man relieved from mounting guard*).

[2]**Frei'—en**, I. *v.a.* to woo, court; **nach Geld —en**, to look out for a fortune in wooing; **jung gefreit hat niemand gereut**, happy the wooing that's not long in doing (*prov.*); **schnell gefreit, lange bereut**, marry in haste and repent at leisure (*prov.*). II. *v.a.* to give in marriage to a p. (*rare*). III. *subst. n.* (*act of*) wooing. —**er**, *m.* (—**ers**, *pl.* —**er**) wooer, suitor; **auf —ers Füßen gehen**, to be on the lookout for a wife. —**erei'**, *f.* courting. —**te**, *f.* courtship; **auf der —te sein**, to be wooing, to be on the lookout for a wife. *Comp.* —**werber**, *m.* matrimonial agent; matchmaker. —**werbung**, *f.* match-making.

Frei'dig, *adj.* bold, courageous; gamesome, wanton (*obs. dial.*). —**keit**, *f.* boldness.

Frei'tag, *m.* (—**s**, *pl.* —**e**) Friday (*lit. day of* **Freia**, *the wife of Wodan*); **der stille —**, Good Friday.

Freithof, *m.* (*obs.*) see **Friedhof**.

Fremd, *adj. & adv.* strange, foreign; not one's own; unfamiliar; unknown; unusual, peculiar; unaccustomed; **ich bin hier —**, I am a stranger in this place (country); —**e Pflanzen**, exotic plants; **dies kommt mir sehr — vor**, this seems very strange to me; **es war mir —**, I was not aware of it; —**es Gut**, other people's property; **gegen einen — thun**, to cut one. —**e**, *f.* foreign country; place away from home; **in der —e**, abroad. —**e(r)**, *m.* foreigner; stranger; guest; —**e haben**, to have guests *or* company. —**heit**, *f.* foreignness, strangeness. —**ling**, *m.* (—**linges**, *pl.* —**linge**) stranger, foreigner, alien; (*pl.*) erratic blocks (*Geol.*). *Comp.* —**artig**, *adj.* strange; heterogeneous; extraneous (*Chem.*). —**artigkeit**, *f.* heterogeneousness; oddness. —**en=amt**, *n.* alien office. —**en=buch**, *n.* visitors' book. —**en=führer**, *m.* guide, cicerone; **ein —enführer durch Berlin**, a Berlin guide. —**en=recht**, *n.* alien laws; right over *or* of aliens. —**en=zimmer**, *n.* spare-room; reception-room; coffee-room (*in a hotel*). —**herrschaft**, *f.* foreign rule. —**ländisch**, *adj.* foreign. —**süchtig**, *adj.* fond of foreign ways. —**werden**, *n.* estrangement. —**wörterbuch**, *n.* dictionary of foreign (*adopted*) words.

Frequent—ati'v, *adj.* frequentative. —**ie'ren**, *v.a.* to frequent.

Fres'ko— (*in comp.*) —**gemälde**, *n.* (*pl.* **Fres'ken**) fresco painting. —**malerei'**, *f.* painting in fresco.

Fres'se, *f.* (*pl.* —**n**) mouth (*vulg.*).

Fres's—en, I. *ir.v.a. & n.* (*aux.* **h.**) to eat (*of beasts*); to devour greedily, cram; to consume, destroy; to eat into (*as ulcers*); to corrode; to fret (*as moths*); to spread, diffuse itself (*as fire*); **Vogel friß oder stirb**, it is neck or nothing, there is no alternative; **seinen Verdruß in sich —en**, to swallow one's vexation; **sie hat einen Narren daran gefressen**, she is infatuated with it, dotes upon it; **pflanzen—ende Tiere**, herbivorous animals; **fleisch—ende Tiere**, carnivorous animals. II. *subst. n.* act of feeding; feed, food (*for beasts*); **ein gefundenes —en**, the very thing (desired). —**a'lien**, *pl.* eatables (*vulg.*). —**er**, *m.* (—**ers**, *pl.* —**er**) glutton; voracious eater. —**erei'**, *f.* gluttony; feast. *Comp.* —**(ß)=bauch**, *m.* glutton. —**(ß)=begierde**, —**(ß)=gier**, *f.* voracity, greediness, gluttony. —**(ß)=fieber**, *n.* abnormal appetite. —**(ß)=lust**, *f.* excessive appetite. —**(ß)=sack**, *m.* provender-bag; voracious person. —**(ß)=süchtig**, *adj.* voracious. —**(ß)=trog**, *m.* manger, feeding-trough. —**(ß)=zange**, *f.*, —**(ß)=zängelchen**, *n.* feeler (*of insects*).

Frett, *n.* (—**es**, *pl.* —**e**) ferret (*rare*). —**chen**, *n.* (—**chens**, *pl.* —**chen**) (little) ferret. *Comp.* —**wiesel**, *n.* ferret.

Freu'd—e, *f.* (*pl.* —**en**) joy, gladness; delight, pleasure; satisfaction; **plötzlicher Ausbruch der —e**, transport (of joy); **mit —e**, *or* —**en**, gladly, joyfully, with pleasure; **vor —e außer sich sein**, to be beside oneself with joy; **seine —e haben an einer S.**, to take delight in a th.; **es macht mir große —e**, it gives me great pleasure; —**e an seinen Kindern erleben**, to live to find one's children a source of happiness; **geteilte —e ist doppelte —e**, shared joys are doubled (*prov.*). —**ig**, *adj. & adv.* joyful, joyous, cheerful. —**igkeit**, *f.* joyousness. *Comp.* —**e=glänzend**, *adj.* beaming with joy. —**en=arm**, *adj.* joyless. —**en=becher**, *m.* cup of joy. —**en=botschaft**, *f.* glad tidings. —**en=fest**, *n.*, —**feier**, *f* festival, feast. —**en=feuer**, *n.* bonfire. —**en=geschrei**, *n.* shout of joy; cheers. —**en=leer**, —**en=los**, *adj.* joyless. —**en=leben**, *n.* merry life. —**en=mädchen**, *n.* prostitute. —**en=reich**, *adj.* joyful; overjoyed. —**en=schießen**, *n.* firing of guns for joy; festive shooitng-match. —**en=störer**, *m.* mischief maker; killjoy. —**en=tag**, *m.* day of rejoicing. —**en=taumel**, *m.* transport of joy.

Freu'—en, I. *v.a.* & (*usually*) *imp.* to make glad *or* give pleasure to; **es —t mich (daß)**, I am glad (that). II. *v.r.* to rejoice, be glad (**über eine S.** *or* **einer S.**, at a thing; *the gen. is now less usual*); to find pleasure in; **ich —e mich darüber**, I am glad of it; **er —t sich über sein neues Buch**, he is pleased with his new book; **sie —t sich am Glück ihrer Kinder**, she takes delight in the happiness of her children; **sich auf eine S. —en**, to rejoice in anticipation of, at the idea of a thing; **wir —en uns zu erfahren**, we are pleased to learn. III. *subst.n.* **das war ein —en**, there were great rejoicings.

Freund, *m.* (—**es**, *pl.* —**e**) friend; kinsman, relative; love (*obs. & poet.*); (*pl.*) Quakers; — **der Wahrheit**, lover of truth; —**e im Glücke**, fair weather friends; —**e erkennt man in der Not**, a friend in need is a friend indeed (*prov.*); **ein — von mir**, a friend of mine; — **Hain**, Death (*personified*); **ich bin kein — von (vielen Worten)**; I do not like (making many words). —**in**, *f.* female friend, lady friend; lady-love (*poet.*). —**lich**, *adj.* friendly, kind; affable; cheerful; **das ist sehr —lich von Ihnen**, that is very kind of you; —**liches Wesen**, affable *or* kindly manners; —**liches Wetter**, fair weather; —**liches Zimmer**, cheerful room. —**lichkeit**, *f.* kindness; pleasing demeanour; pleasantness; affability (*of* *persons of rank*). **—schaft**, *f.* friendship; intimacy; relationship (*obs.*). **—schaftlich**, *adj.* friendly. **—schaftlichkeit**, *f.* friendly disposition. *Comp.* **—dienstlich**, *adj.* friendly in helping. **—los**, *adj.* friendless. **—recht**, *n.* right arising from kinship. **—willig**, *adj.* ready to help (*as a friend*). **—schafts=bund**, *m.* friendly alliance; bond of friendship. **—schafts=dienst**, *m.* good offices, friendly turn. **—schafts=versicherung**, *f.* protestation of friendship. **—schafts=wechsel**, *m.* accommodation-bill (*C. L.*). **—schafts=zeichen**, *n.* token of friendship.

Fre'vel. I. *adj. & adv.* (*obs. & poet.*) *see* **—haft.** II. *m.* (**—s**, *pl.* **—thaten**) misdeed, wanton offence, mischief; outrage; sacrilege; light-mindedness, wantonness; wickedness; **voll —s**, filled with violence (*B.*). **—haft, Fre'=ventlich, Frev'lerisch**, *adj. & adv.* wicked; wantonly offensive; mischievous; malicious; outrageous; insolent. **—haftigkeit**, *f.* wickedness; wantonness; outrageousness; blasphemy. *Comp.* **—gericht**, *n.* criminal court. **—lust**, *f.*, **—mut, —sinn**, *m.* malicious *or* mischievous disposition; wantonness. **—that**, *f.* outrage. **—wort**, *n.* wicked word; insult; blasphemy.

Fre'v—eln, *v.n.* (*aux.* **h.**) to commit a crime, offence *or* outrage (**gegen, wider einen; an einem**, against one) to trespass; to insult; to outrage; to blaspheme. **—eler, —ler**, *m.* (**—(e)lers**, *pl.* **—(e)ler**) wicked person; criminal; transgressor; outrager; blasphemer.

Fricassie'ren, Frikassie'ren, *v.a.* to fricassee.

Fridericia'nisch, *adj.* belonging to the age of King Frederick II. of Prussia.

Frie'd—e, (*less good:* **Frie'd—en**,) *m.* (**—ens**, *pl.* **—ens=schlüsse**) peace; tranquillity; **—e(n) machen** *or* **schließen**, to make peace; **in —en lassen**, to let alone; **—en halten**, to keep quiet; **dem —en traue ich nicht**, I smell a rat (*coll.*); **—e ernährt, Un—e verzehrt**, by wisdom peace, by peace plenty (*prov.*); **ein fauler —e**, a hollow truce; **der westfälische —e**, the Peace of Westphalia (*1648, ending the Thirty Years' War*). **—lich**, *adj. & adv.* peaceable, peaceful, pacific. **—lichkeit**, *f.* peacefulness, peaceableness. **—sam**, (*obs. & poet.*) *see* **—lich.** **—selig**, *adj. & adv.* most peaceful. *Comp.* **—brüchig**, *adj.* violating the peace. **—e=fürst**, *see* **—ens=fürst.** **—e=gebot**, *n.* order to keep the peace. **—e=machend**, *adj.* pacifying, pacific. **—ens=absicht**, *f.* pacific intention. **—ens=bruch**, *m.* breach of the peace. **—ens=brüchig**, *adj.* guilty of a breach of the peace. **—ens=einleitungen**, (*pl.*) preliminaries of peace. **—ens=fest**, *n.* festival on the conclusion *or* anniversary of peace. **—ens=fahne, —ens=flagge**, *f.* flag of truce. **—ens=fürst**, *m.* Prince of Peace; Christ. **—ens=fuß**, *m.* peace-footing (*Mil.*). **—ens=gericht**, *n.* court held by justices of the peace. **—ens=pfeife**, *f.* calumet (of peace). **—ens=präsenzstärke**, *f.* (legal) peace strength (*of an army*). **—ens=richter**, *m.* justice of the peace. **—ens=schluß**, *m.* conclusion of peace. **—ens=stifter**, *m.* peacemaker. **—ens=störer**, *m.* disturber of the peace; rioter. **—ens=störung**, *f.* disturbance. **—ens=tag**, *m.* day (*anniversary*) of peace. **—ens=unterhandlung**, *f.* negotiation for peace. **—ens=vertrag**, *m.* treaty of peace. **—ens=vermittler**, *m.* mediator. **—e=voll**, *adj.* peaceful. **—fertig**, *adj.* peaceable; **selig sind die —fertigen**, blessed are the peacemakers (*B.*). **—fertigkeit**, *f.* peaceableness. **—(e)=los**, *adj.* not peaceable, quarrelsome.

Fried=hag, —zaun, *m.* fence. **—hof**, *m.* churchyard, cemetery, (*orig.*) walled-in yard.

Frie'r—en, I. *ir.v.n.* (*aux.* **h.** & **s.**) to freeze; **der Fluß ist gefroren**, the river is frozen over. II. *ir.v.a. & imp.* to freeze, to chill; **hat es gefroren?** did it freeze? **es —t**, there is a frost; **mich —t**, I am cold; **ich habe mir die Finger steif gefroren**, my fingers are stiff with cold. III. *subst. n.* freezing, congelation; shivering (*with cold*). *Comp.* **—punkt**, *m.* freezing-point.

[1]**Fries**, *m.* (**—(s)es**, *pl.* **—(s)e**) frieze, baize, friezed cloth. *Comp.* **—rock**, *m.* dreadnaught Kilkenny; (double) flannel petticoat.

[2]**Fries**, *m.* (*& n.*), **Frie'se**, *f.* frieze (*Arch.*) **mit einem —e versehen**, to frieze.

Frie'sel—, *n.pl.* purples (*Med.*) (*in comp.*). **—fieber**, *n.* miliary fever. **—flechten**, *f.* miliary herpes.

Frikandel'le, *f.* (*pl.* **—n**), meat ball, rissole.

Friktio'n, *f.* friction. *Comp.* **—s=fidibus**, *m.*, **—s=zündhölzchen**, *n.* lucifer-match. **—s=scheibe**, *f.* friction-plate.

Frisch, *adj. & adv.* fresh; cool; new; unused, recent; raw; green; ruddy (*complexion*); sharp, brisk, fresh (*wind*); gay, lively, blithe; sprightly, alert, vigorous; **—, fromm, frei, froh**, brisk, pious, free, joyous (*is the motto of the German gymnastic clubs*). **—!** *adv.* cheerly on! bravely on! **— und froh**, happily, joyfully; **etwas — wagen**, to venture boldly on a th.; **— auf!** look alive! cheer up! be quick! **— darauf los!** courage! on then! at them! **von —em**, afresh, anew; **—e Wäsche anziehen**, to change one's linen; **auf —er That**, in the (very) act; **—e Milch**, new milk; **—e Eier**, new-laid eggs; **—e Wäsche**, clean linen; **—e Spur**, hot scent (*Sport.*); **— und gesund**, well and hearty; **—e Fische, gute Fische**, never put off till to-morrow (*prov.*); **es geht ihm — von der Hand**, he is a quick worker; **— gewagt ist halb gewonnen**, a good beginning is half the battle (*prov.*). **—e**, *f.*, **—heit**, *f.* freshness; coolness; liveliness; vigour; cool spot. **—ling**, *m.* (**—lings**, *pl.* **—linge**) young wild boar. **—ung**, *f.* metal-refining. *Comp.* **—backen**, *adj.* newly-baked. **—eisen**, *n.* refined iron; brittle iron. **—er=dings**, *adv.* afresh, anew. **—esse**, *f.* puddling furnace. **—feuer**, *n.* refining fire. **—gestein**, *n.* compact, solid rocks. **—herd, —ofen**, *m.* puddling furnace. **—malerei**, *f.* fresco painting. **—pfanne**, *f.* smelting kettle; kettle used for parting silver from copper. **—schlacke**, *f.* metal dross.

Fri'sch—en, *v.a.* to cool, refresh; to revive; to encourage; to refine, to polish. **—er**, *m.* (**—ers**, *pl.* **—er**) refiner of metals.

Fris—eu'r, *m.* (**—eu'rs**, *pl.* **—eu're**) hair-dresser. **—ie'ren**, *v.a.* to curl *or* dress the hair; to nap (*cloth*); to trim. **—u'r**, *f.* (*pl.* **—u'ren**) hair-dressing; mode of dressing the hair; head-dress; head of hair; trimming. *Comp.* **—ier'=bohrer**, *m.* sinking-auger. **—ier'=eisen**, *n.* curling-tongs. **—ier'=holz**, *n.* hair-dresser's block. **—ier'=mantel**, *m.* dressing-jacket, peignoir. **—ier'=mühle**, *f.* cloth-dressing mill.

Frist, *f.* (*pl.* **—en**) space of time; period; appointed time, set term; respite; delay, days of grace. *Comp.* **—brief**, *m.* letter of respite. **—(en)=weise**, *adv.* at certain times; by intervals; by instalments. **—erstreckung**, *f.* extension of a term. **—gesuch**, *n.* motion in arrest of judgment (*Law*). **—mittel**, *n.* palliative. **—tag**, *m.* day of grace *or* respite.

Fris't—en, *v.a.* to fix a term for; to grant delay, postpone; to respite; to reprieve; **einem das Leben —en**, to prolong *or* spare one's life; **so viel haben, um das Leben zu —en**, to have *or* earn enough to keep body and soul together. **—ung**, *f.* fixing a term; prolongation.

Friß; Frißt, *imperative; 2 & 3 pers. sing. pres. ind. of* **fressen.**

Frivo'l, *adj. & adv.* frivolous. **—ität'**, *f.* frivolity.

Froh, *adj. & adv.* glad, joyous, joyful; gay, mirthful; happy; **— sein über (eine S.)**, to be rejoiced at, pleased with, glad of (a thing); **einer Sache — werden**, to enjoy a thing, take pleasure in it; **—en Mutes**, cheerful; **—en Herzens**, glad of heart; **—e Nachricht**, glad tidings; **—e Botschaft**, gospel; good tidings. *Comp.* **—lo'cken**. I. *v.n.* (*aux.* **h.**) to exult, triumph, shout for joy; **—locket dem Herrn!** rejoice in the Lord! II. *subst. n.* exultation, triumph. **—mut**, *m.*, **—sinn**, *m.* cheerfulness, happy disposition. **—mütig**, **—sinnig**, *adj. & adv.* cheerful, joyful, happy.

Fröh'lich, *adj. & adv.* joyous, joyful; gay, blithesome; jovial; merry, frolicsome; gladsome; **ein —es Neujahr**, a happy New Year; **—machen**, to gladden, cheer, exhilarate. **—keit**, *f.* joyfulness; joyousness; gaiety; gladness.

Frohn, **Fröhn**, *see* **Fronen**, **Frönen**.

Fromm (**—er**, **—st**, *also* **frömmer**, **frömmst**), *adj. & adv.* useful, doughty (*obs.*); honest, excellent, worthy; pious, godly, devout; innocent, harmless; artless; just, upright (*B.*); quiet (*of horses, etc.*); **—es Schaf**, poor simpleton; **—es Pferd**, quiet horse; **—er Wunsch**, vain wish; **—er Eifer** *or* **—e Wut**, religious fanaticism; **—e Landsknechte**, staunch troopers (*obs.*); **—er Knecht**, goodly servant; **der —e Gott**, the good, helpful Lord. **—e**, *m.* I. pious person. II. use, advantage, benefit (*obs.*); **es dient dir zum —en**, it is for your good; **zu Nutz und —en**, for the advantage of.

Frömmelei', *f.* affected piety, pietism, hypocrisy; bigotry.

Fröm'm—eln, *v.n.* (*aux.* **h.**) to affect piety. **—elnd**, *p. & adj.* canting, hypocritical; **—elnde Sprache**, cant. **—igkeit**, *f.* piety, devoutness; innocence; meekness; kindness. **—ler**, *m.* (**—lers**, *pl.* **—ler**), **—ling**, *m.* (**—lings**, *pl.* **—linge**) hypocrite, canting person; devotee; Tartuffe.

From'm—en, *v.n.* (*aux.* **h.**, *dat.*) to advance the interest of, advantage, avail, profit, benefit; **was, wozu —t es dir?** what does it profit you, what good is it to you?

Fron. I. *adj.* pertaining to the lord (Lord); lordly; sacred, holy. II. *m.* (**—es**, *pl.* **—e**) sergeant to a lord, beadle, bailiff (*obs.*). III. *f.* (*pl.* **—en**) service due to the lord of a manor; enforced *or* statute labour; drudgery. **—bar**, *adj.* liable to statute labour *or* socage service. **—de**, *f.* public jail; *see* **—dienst**. **—e**, *f.* (*pl.* **—en**) *see* **Fron** III. **—en**, *v.n.* (*aux.* **h.**) *see* **Frönen**. *Comp.* **—acker**, *m.* land held in socage, by servile tenure. **—altar**, *m.* high (*or* holy) altar (*Rom. Cath.*). **—amt**, *n.* high mass (*Rom. Cath.*); public office. **—arbeit**, *f.* socage, statute-labour; drudgery. **—bauer**, *m.* bondman, tenant in villainage. **—bote**, *m.* beadle. **—dienst**, *m.* compulsory service, statute labour. **—fasten**, *pl.* the four ember-weeks; quarter-fastings (*Rom. Cath.*). **—feste**, *f.* public *or* common jail. **—fuhre**, *f.* compulsory furnishing of teams in performing statute labour. **—geld**, *n.* money paid in lieu of statute labour. **—herr**, *m.* lord entitled to exact socage-service. **—hof**, *m.* socage-farm. **—knecht**, *m.* socager. **—lehen**, *n.* socage-tenure. **—leichnam**, *m.* Christ's holy body (*lit.* body of our Lord). **—leichnams=fest**, *n.* Corpus Christi Day. **—los**, *adj.* exempt from compulsory service. **—pflichtig**, *adj.* obliged to do statute labour. **—vogt**, *m.* overseer of compulsory labour, taskmaster. **—weise**, *adv.* in socage.

Fron'de, *f.* Fronde; **Mitglied der —**, frondeur.

Frö'n—en, *v.n.* (*aux.* **h.**) to do socage-service, labour as a vassal; to toil, drudge; to be a slave to, to pander to; **jemandes Launen —en**, to humour a person's whims; **der Trunkenheit —en**, to be addicted to liquor. **—er**, *m.* (**—ers**, *pl.* **—er**) serf, vassal; drudge.

Fron't—(e), *f.* (*pl.* **—en**) front, face, forepart; front, head (*of an army*); **— machen gegen**, to face *or* front. **—a'l**, *adj.* in *or* to the front, direct. *Comp.* **—a'l=feuer**, *n.* direct fire. **—angriff**, *m.* attack in front. **—linie**, *f.*; **in —linie**, drawn up abreast (*Nav.*).

Fror; **Frö're**, *imperf. ind.; subj. of* **frieren**.

Frosch, *m.* (**—es**, *pl.* **Frö'sche**) frog; inhabitant of fen, silly person (*sl.*); very young student, silly school-boy (*dial.*); species of whelk; lampas (*Vet.*); bracket; cracker (*Firew.*); nut, frog, handle of the fiddle-bow (*Viol.*); ranula (*Med.*); **der — quakt**, the frog croaks; **sei kein —**, don't (you) be a fool; don't make a fuss (*coll.*); **einen — haben**, to be cracked *or* crazy (*sl.*). *Comp.* **—arten**, *pl.* batrachians, ranidæ. **—braten**, *m.* roasted hind legs of a frog. **—eisen**, *n.* farrier's lancet. **—gequake**, *n.* croaking of frogs. **—hecht**, *m.* pike. **—keule**, *f.* hind-leg of a frog. **—laich**, *m.* frog-spawn. **—löffel**, *m.* water-plantain. **—mäuseler** *or* **—mäuse=krieg**, *m.* battle of the frogs and mice. **—quappe**, *f.*, **—wurm**, *m.* tadpole. **—schenkel**, *m.* hind-leg of a frog.

Frösch—e, *pl.* crotches in an organ. **—lein**, *n.* (**—leins**, *pl.* **—lein**) little frog. *Comp.* **—lein=geschwulst**, *f. & m.* ranula (*Med.*).

Frost, *m.* (**—es**, *pl.* **Frös'te**) frost; chill, coldness; apathy; feverish shivering; **vom —e beschädigt**, frost-bitten; **der — läßt nach**, the frost is less keen; **— in den Füßen**, chilblains; **vor — beben**, to shiver with cold. **—ig**, *adj. & adv.* frosty; chilly, cold; frigid. **—igkeit**, *f.* frigidity. *Comp.* **—beule**, *f.* chilblain. **—fieber**, *n.* fever and ague. **—mittel**, *n.* remedy for frostbites. **—punkt**, *m.* freezing point. **—salbe**, *f.* ointment against chilblains. **—wetter**, *n.* frosty weather.

Frös't—eln, I. *v.a. & imp.* to make chilly, cause to shiver; to freeze a little; **mich —elt**, I feel chilly, I am shivering. II. *v.n. & imp.* to shiver (with cold), to feel chilly; **es —elt**, it freezes a little; **ich —le**, I feel chilly. III. *subst. n.* shiver, chill; **ein —eln haben**, to be shivering, to shiver with cold.

Frottie'r—en, *v.a. & n.* to rub (*the skin*). *Comp.* **—bürste**, *f.* flesh-brush.

Frucht, *f.* (*pl.* **Früch'te**) fruit; crop; corn, grain; result, effect; product; profit; (*pl.*) produce, harvest; **eingemachte Früchte**, preserves. **—bar**, *adj. & adv.* fruitful, fertile; prolific. **—barkeit**, *f.* fruitfulness, fertility; fecundity. *Comp.* **—abgabe**, *f.* tax on produce. **—ansetzen**, *n.* germination (*of the fruit in the blossom*). **—acker**, *m.* corn-field. **—ast**, *m.* fruit-bearing branch. **—auge**, *n.* bud, germ. **—ausfuhr**, *f.* exportation of grain. **—bar=machung**, *f.* fertilization. **—bau**, *m.* cultivation of crops. **—beet**, *n.* hot-bed (*of manure*). **—behältnis**, *n.*, **—behälter**, *m.* pericarp. **—bildung**, *f.* fructification. **—boden**, *m.* granary; receptacle (*Bot.*). **—brand**, *m.* ergot. **—bringend**, *adj.* fructiferous; productive; profitable; **die —bringende Gesellschaft**, name of an important linguistic and literary association of the 17th century. **—folge**, *f. see* **—wechsel**. **—garten**, *m.* orchard; kitchen-garden. **—geländer**, *n.* espalier. **—genuß**, *m.*, **—nutzung**, *f.* usufruct. **—göttin**, *f.* Pomona (*of trees*), Ceres (*of crops*). **—handel**, *m.* fruit-trade, corn-trade. **—haus**, *n.* corn-magazine; granary; hot-house. **—halter**, *m.* matrix. **—häutchen**, *n.* epicarp. **—gülte**, *f.* rent to be paid in corn. **—hülse**, *f.* husk, shell. **—hülle**, *f.* pericarp. **—keim**, *m.* germ, embryo. **—kern**, *m.* kernel. **—knospe**, *f. see* **—auge**.

—knoten, *m.* seed-bud, germ. **—korb,** *m.* fruit-basket. **—korn,** *n.* seed-corn. **—los,** *adj.* fruitless; barren; useless. **—losigkeit,** *f.* fruitlessness. **—makler,** *m.* corn-broker. **—mark,** *n.* pulp. **—messer,** I. *m.* corn-measure. II. *n.* fruit-knife. **—mus,** *n.* stewed fruit. **—röhre,** *f.* pistil (*Bot.*). **—schauer, —scheuer,** *f.* barn, granary. **—schrumpf,** *m.* waste of corn in warehousing. **—speicher,** *m.* corn-loft *or* magazine. **—sperre,** *f.* prohibition of corn exportation. **—stiel,** *m.* peduncle (*Bot.*). **—versteinerung,** *f.* carpolite. **—wechsel,** *m.* rotation of crops. **—zehnte,** *m.* tithe in corn. **—zins,** *m.* rent paid in corn.

Früch't'chen, *n. dim. of* **Frucht; ein sauberes —,** a young scamp *or* scapegrace.

Fruch'ten, *v.n.* (*aux.* **h.**) to be of use *or* profit; to avail; to have effect, bear fruit.

Frug; Frü'ge, *imperf. indic.; subj.* of **fragen.**

Fruga'l, *adj. & adv.* frugal.

Früh, —e, *adj. & adv.* early; in the morning; speedy; forward; premature; **heute —,** (early) this morning; **morgen —,** to-morrow morning; **übermorgen —,** in the morning of the day after to-morrow; **—morgens, am —en Morgen,** early in the morning; **—e Morgenstunden,** small hours of the day; **—er oder später,** sooner or later; **ein —er Tod,** an early *or* untimely death; **— genug ankommen,** to arrive in (good) time; **von — bis spät,** from morning till evening, all day long. **—e,** *f.* early hour, early morning; **in aller —e,** very early, the first thing in the morning. **—er,** *adj. & adv.* (*comp. of* **früh**) earlier, sooner; prior; former; formerly; **in —er als acht Tagen,** in less than eight days. **—estens,** *adv.* as early as possible; at the earliest, not before, not earlier than. **—ling,** *m.* (**—lings,** *pl.* **—linge**) spring; animal born in spring; child born too soon; **zum —ling gehörig,** vernal. *Comp.* **—apfel,** *m.* summer apple. **—gebet,** *n.* morning prayer. **—geburt,** *f.* premature birth; abortion. **—gottesdienst,** *m.* morning service. **—jahr,** *n.* spring. **—klug,** *adj.* precocious. **—lings=fliege,** *f.* caseworm. **—lings=jahre,** *pl.* youth. **—lings=mäßig,** *adj.* spring-like. **—lings=nachtgleiche,** *f.* vernal equinox. **—lings=sonate,** *f.* a famous sonata of Beethoven for violin and piano (*opus 24*). **—messe,** *f.* early mass, first mass. **—mette,** *f.* matins. **—prediger,** *m.* morning preacher. **—reif,** I. *adj.* precocious, forward; **—reife Früchte,** forced fruit. II. *m.* morning frost. **—reife,** *f.* precocity, forwardness. **—rot,** *n.* morning-red. **—schoppen,** *m.* beer drunk in a restaurant before lunch (*esp'lly after a great feast*) (*stud. sl.*). **—stück,** *n.* breakfast. **—stücken,** *v.a. & n.* to breakfast; to breakfast on. **—trunk,** *m.* morning-draught. **—winter,** *m.* beginning of winter. **—zeit,** *f.* morning-time. **—zeitig,** *adj. & adv.* early; in good time; forward; premature, untimely. **—zeitigkeit,** *f.* precocity; untimeliness. **—zug,** *m.* early train, morning train.

Fuchs, *m.* (**—(s)es,** *pl.* **Füch'se**) fox; fox's fur; chestnut *or* light bay horse; a species of butterfly; red-haired person; cunning, false *or* sly person; freshman, fresher (*Univ.*); fluke (*Bill.*); **goldner —** *or* **Gold—,** gold piece, gold coin (*coll.*); **ein alter —,** an old sly-boots, a cunning person; **der — bellt,** the fox barks; **ein jeder — verwahre seinen Balg,** every man for himself; **stirbt der — so gilt der Balg,** Jack's a-light (words of a certain game of forfeit). **—(s)en,** I. *v.n.* (*aux.* **h.**) to hunt foxes; to make a chance hit, to fluke (*Bill.*). II. *v.a.* to play a trick on; to quiz; to cheat, to vex; **es —(s)t mich,** I am very angry (*coll.*). III. *v.r.* to be *or* get angry, to feel vexed (*coll.*). **—(s)erei',** *f.* acting the fox. **—(s)er,** *m.* (**—(s)ers,** *pl.* **—(s)er**) stock-jobber; fluker. **—(s)icht, —(s)ig,** *adj.* fox-like; red, carrotty; furious (*sl.*). **—jes,** *pl.* foxes (*Naut.*). *Comp.* **—angeln,** *pl.* fox-traps. **—balg,** *m.* fox-skin. **—bart,** *m.* red beard. **—bau,** *m.* fox-hole, kennel. **—eisen,** *n.*, **—falle,** *f.* fox-trap. **—grube, —höhle,** *f.* hole *or* kennel of a fox. **—jagd,** *f.* fox-hunt. **—jäger,** *m.* fox-hunter. **—pelz,** *m.* fur of a fox; **den —pelz anziehen,** to use a dodge. **—rot,** *adj.* fox-coloured, red. **—schwanz,** *m.* fox's tail, brush; **den —schwanz streichen,** to flatter; to toady; **den —schwanz abgeben,** to backbite. **—schwänzer,** *m.* toad-eater; fawner; backbiter. **—schwänzerei',** *f.* sycophancy; backbiting. **—teufels=wild,** *adj.* exceedingly angry (*coll.*). **—wild,** *adj.* very angry (*coll.*).

Füchs'—chen (**—chens,** *pl.* **—chen**), **—lein** (**—leins,** *pl.* **—lein**), *n.* little fox. **—(s)en, —(s)eln,** *see* **Fuchsen.** **—(s)er,** *see* **Fuchser.** **—(s)in,** *f.* she-fox, vixen.

Fuch'sia, Fuch'sie, *f.* fuchsia (*Bot.*).

Fuch'tel, *f.* (*pl.* **—n**) broadsword; rod, ferule; blow *or* punishment inflicted by these, whipping; **einen unter der — haben,** to keep a tight hand over one. *Comp.* **—klinge,** *f.* flexible unedged sword.

Fuch'teln, *v.* I. *a.* to strike with the flat of the sword; to beat, whip. II. *n.* (*aux.* **h.**) to brandish a sword *or* switch; to fidget with.

Fuch'tig, *adj.* angry, annoyed (*sl.*).

Fu'der, *n.* (**—s,** *pl.* **—**) load, cart-load; large measure (*for wine, grain, etc.*). **—ig,** *adj. & adv.* containing a 'fuder.' *Comp.* **—weise,** *adv.* by cartloads.

Fug, *m.* (**—es**) suitableness, convenience; reason; right; due authority; **mit —,** fittingly, justly; **mit — und Recht,** with full right; **mit gutem —,** justly, with good reason. **—e,** *f.* (*pl.* **—en**) joint, seam; joining, rabbet, rabbeting; suture, seam (*Anat., Bot.*); **aus den —en bringen,** to put out of joint, to unhinge; **die Zeit ist aus den —en,** the time is out of joint. *Comp.* **—en=gelenk,** *n.* articulation (*Anat.*). **—en=leim,** *m.* bee-glue, bee-bread. **—los,** *adj.* without good reason; unjust, unreasonable; incompetent. **—losigkeit,** *f.* incompetence; unreasonableness, injustice.

Fuga'to, *n.* fugue-passage (*Mus.*).

Fu'g—e, *f.* fugue (*Mus.*). **—en=haft, —ie'rt,** *adj.* in the style of a fugue.

Fu'gen, *v.* I. *a.* to join, to unite by rabbeting; to groove. II. *n.* (*aux.* **h.**) to fit, to join.

Fü'g—en, *v.* I. *a.* to fit together, join, unite; to join, to rabbet; to ordain, direct, dispose; to add; **wie Gott es —t,** as God ordains. II. *r.* to accommodate oneself to; to be fitted, be suitable *or* proper; **sich in eine S. —en,** to accommodate oneself to, to submit to a thing. III. *r. & imp.* to come to pass, happen; coincide; **wie es sich —t,** as occasion demands. **—ig,** *adj. & adv.* fit, suitable. **—lich,** *adj. & adv.* fit, suitable, convenient, proper, reasonable, pertinent; **er hätte —lich schweigen können,** he might very well have held his tongue; **er konnte es nicht —lich vermeiden,** he could not well avoid it. **—lichkeit,** *f.* suitableness, fitness; pertinence; justice. **—sam,** *adj. & adv.* adaptive; pliant, yielding; submissive, agreeable; supple; **ein —sames Kind,** an obedient child. **—samkeit,** *f.* pliancy; submission. **—ung,** *f.* fitting together, joining; joint; articulation; arrangement; disposition (*of God*), dispensation, decree; juncture; submission, resignation; **durch eine —ung Gottes,** providentially. *Comp.* **—e=bank,** *f.* joiner's bench; grooving plane. **—e=wort,** *n.* conjunction, connecting word.

Fühl'bar, *adj. & adv.* sensible; perceptible; palpable; susceptible. **—keit,** *f.* sensibility, susceptibility· perceptibility; tangibility.

Füh'l—en, *v.a. & n.* (*aux.* **h.**) to feel, to perceive by the organs of sensation; to have a sense of, be convinced of; to be sensitive to, impressed by; to experience, know; to touch; **einem den Puls —en,** to feel a person's pulse; **einem auf den Zahn —en,** to sound a p.'s opinion; **alles was lebt, —t,** every living creature has perceptions; **Lust —en,** to be inclined; **vorher —en,** to have a presentiment of; **sich —en,** to feel, feel oneself, to be felt, to have a feeling; **sich müde —en,** to feel tired; **der Blinde fühlt sich nach dem Bette,** the blind man gropes about for the bed. **—end,** *p. & adj.* sensitive; feeling; susceptible. **—er,** *m.* (**—ers,** *pl.* **—er**) feeler. **—ung,** *f.* feeling; touch (*Mil.*); **—ung mit dem Feinde bekommen,** to come into touch with the enemy. *Comp.* **—eisen,** *n.* probe (*Surg.*). **—faden,** *m.*, **—horn,** *n.* feeler (*of insects*). **—kraft,** *f.* faculty of perception, susceptibility. **—kraut,** *n.* sensitive plant. **—los,** *adj.* unfeeling, cold, hard, insensible (**gegen,** to). **—losigkeit,** *f.* apathy; want of feeling, hardheartedness.

Fuhr; Füh're, *imperf. indic.; subj.* of **fahren.**

Führ'bar, *adj.& adv.* transportable; manageable.

Fuh'r—e, *f.* carrying, conveyance; conveyance, cart, vehicle; cart-load, waggon-load; carriage-fare. *Comp.* **—frohne,** *f.* socage-service with team and waggon. **—gelegenheit,** *f.* means, opportunity of transport *or* conveyance. **—herr,** *m.* coach proprietor, job-master. **—knecht,** *m.* carter's man. **—lohn,** *n.* driver's wages; carriage, freight, fare. **—mann,** *m.* carrier; driver, coachman; waggoner. **—manns=pferd,** *n.* cart-horse. **—schlitten,** *m.* sledge for conveying goods. **—straße,** *f.*, **—weg,** *m.* highway, carriage-road. **—wagen,** *m.* freight-waggon. **—werk,** *n.* vehicle, carriage; cart, waggon. **—wesen,** *n.* carrying-trade (*in carts, waggons, etc.*); carriages (*coll.*); **das —wesen bei einem Heere,** baggage, waggon train of an army.

Füh'r—en, *v.a.* to carry, convey, bring; to bear (*a name, title, etc.*); to lead, conduct, guide; to manage; to carry on; to keep (*books*); to hold, contain; to drive; to deal (*a blow, etc.*); to handle (*an oar*); to wear (*a sword*); **sich —en,** to conduct oneself, to behave; **mit sich —en,** to carry along with, to have about one, to contain, to run (*gold, etc.*); to cause, demand; **Klage —en,** to complain (**über,** of); **das große Wort —en,** to brag, boast; to lay down the law; **Krieg —en,** to wage war; **das Wort —en,** to be spokesman; **die Feder —en,** to write; **zu Gemüte —en,** to impress on the mind; **zum Munde —en,** to raise to one's lips; **im Schilde —en,** to have an intention, to plan; **in Versuchung —en,** to lead into temptation; **einen hinters Licht —en,** to impose on a person; **einen Prozeß —en,** to carry on a lawsuit, to plead a cause; **aus dem Lande —en,** to export; **ins Land —en,** to import; **das Schwert —en,** to wear, wield, *or* handle the sword; **das Ruder, das Regiment, die Regierung —en,** to sit at the helm, to govern, to rule; **die Haushaltung —en,** to keep the house; **ein Wappen —en,** to bear, have a coat of arms; **ein Leben —en,** to lead a life; **die Aufsicht —en,** to superintend; to invigilate (*at examinations*); **auf das Eis** *or* **Glatteis —en,** to lead into danger; **bei sich —en,** to carry about one; **er —te ihn gefangen mit sich,** he led him captive; **er —te seine Truppen über die Brücke,** he marched his troops across the bridge; **eine Mauer —en um einen Ort,** to enclose a place with a wall; **sonderbare Reden —en,** to hold strange language; **eine stolze Sprache —en,** to speak authoritatively; **den Beweis —en,** to prove; **Waren —en,** to deal in; **wohin soll das —en?** what are we coming to? **—er,** *m.* (**—ers,** *pl.* **—er**) leader; guide, conductor; director; driver; pilot; tutor; fugue-theme (*Mus.*); manager. **—erin,** *f.* conductress, directrice. **—erschaft,** *f.* guidance, direction; guides (*coll.*). **—ung,** *f.* leading, conducting, guiding; conduct, behaviour; guidance; management; direction; command; keeping (*of books*). *Comp.* **—band,** *n.* leading string.

Füll'—bar, *adj. & adv.* that may be filled. **—e,** *f.* fulness, abundance, plenty; fulfilment (*rare*); stuffing (*Cook.*); contents; **die Hülle und —e haben,** to have abundance, live in ease; **in Hülle und —e,** plentifully, plenty of.

Fül'l—en, *v.a.* to fill, fill up; to stuff; to put in; to bottle (*off*); **wieder —en,** to replenish. **—er,** *m.* (**—ers,** *pl.* **—er**) filler. **—sel,** *n.* (**—sels,** *pl.* **—sel**) stuffing (*Cook.*); stop-gap. **—ung,** *f.* filling (*up*), stuffing; thing filled, contents; stuffing (*Cook.*); first-fruits (*B.*). *Comp.* **—apparat,** *m.* feeding-apparatus (*Steam*). **—brett,** *n.* panel. **—erde,** *f.* fuller's earth. **—feder,** *f.* self-feeding pen, fountain pen, reservoir pen. **—haar,** *n.* hair used for stuffing. **—horn,** *n.* horn of abundance, cornucopia. **—kelle,** *f.* filling-trowel; ladle. **—kraut,** *n.* cabbages stuffed with forced meat. **—mund,** *m.* foundation of a building. **—öff=nung,** *f.* charging-hole (*Artil.*). **—röhre,** *f.* feed-pipe. **—wort,** *n.* expletive.

Fül'len, I. *n.* (**—s,** *pl.* **—**) foal, filly; colt. II. *v.n.* (*aux.* **h.**) to foal. *Comp.* **—stute,** *f.* brood-mare. **—zucht,** *f.* foal-breeding.

Fum'mel, *m.* projecting rim on strong shoes.

Fum'meln, *v.a.;* **an etwas herum —,** to handle a thing awkwardly and shyly (*coll.*).

Fund, *m.* (**—es,** *pl.* **—e**) finding; thing found; discovery, invention; **einen — thun,** to find something, to make a find *or* a discovery. *Comp.* **—buch,** *n.* inventory. **—geld,** *n.* reward for restoring something found. **—grube,** *f.* mine, shaft (*where ore is found*); mine (*of information*); source (*of wealth or knowledge*). **—ort,** *m.* place where a thing is found. **—recht,** *n.* claim *or* right from discovery. **—schein,** *m.* doctor's certificate as to cause of death; certificate of discovery.

Fund—ame'nt, *n.* (**—ame'nts,** *pl.* **—amen'te**) foundation, basis, base. **—amentie'ren,** *v.a.* to lay the foundation. **—atio'n,** *f.* foundation. **—ie'ren,** *v.a.* to found; to endow; to consolidate. **—ie'rt,** *p.p. & adj.* funded, consolidated. **—ie'rung,** *f.* founding; foundation; funding. *Comp.* **—amenta'l=stimme,** *f.* fundamental note (*Mus.*). **—amenta'l=satz,** *m.* fundamental principle. **—ame'nt=stein** *m.* foundation stone. **—atio'ns=system, -ie'rungs=system,** *n.* funding system.

Fün'de, *obs. for* **Fände.**

Fünf, —e, (*obs.*) *num. adj.* five; **— vom Hundert,** five in the hundred, five per cent; **— gerade sein lassen,** to wink at a thing, to be not over-rigorous; **das —te Rad am Wagen sein,** to be the fifth wheel to the cart, to be superfluous. **—(e),** *f.* (*pl.* **—en**), **—er,** *m.* (**—ers,** *pl.* **—er**) the number five; cinque (*at dice*); fives (*a game*); a soldier of the fifth infantry regiment; wine of the year 1805; a piece *or* note of five (*marks, florins, francs*), fiver. **—er=ausschuß,** *m.* committee of five. **—erlei',** *indec. adj. & adv.* of five (*sorts, ways, etc.*); **das Wort kann —erlei bedeuten,** the word can have five meanings. **—t,** *num. adj.* fifth; **eine —te,** a fifth (*Mus.*). **—tel,** *n.* (**—tels,** *pl.* **—tel**) fifth part. **—teln,** *v.a.* to divide into fifths. **—tens,** *adv.* fifthly, in the fifth place. **—zig,** (*also* **funfzig**) *num. adj.* fifty; **er ist in den**

zigen, he is in the fifties, between fifty and sixty. —ziger, m. (—zigers, pl. —ziger, a man of fifty years; wine of the year '50; ein vorgerückter —ziger, a man well up in the fifties, —zigjähriger Mann, a man of fifty; —jährige Jubelfeier, celebration of an event that happened 50 years ago. —zigst, *num. adj.* fiftieth. —zigstel, *n.* (—zigstels, *pl.* —zigstel) fiftieth part. *Comp.* —blatt, *n.* creeping cinquefoil. —blätt(e)rig, *adj.* five-leaved. —doppelt, *adj.* quintuple. —eck, *n.* pentagon. —eckig, *adj.* pentagonal. —fuß, —füßler, *m.* pentapodic, a verse of five feet. —gesang, *m.* quintet. —hebig, *adj.* of five accents. —jährig, *adj.* five years old. —jährlich, *adj.* every five years. —kantig, *adj.* pentagonal. —klang, *m.* fifth (*Mus.*). —mann, *m.* quinquevir. —prozentig, *adj.* of (at *or* giving) five per cent. —schiffig, *adj.*; —schiffige Kirche, a five-aisled cathedral. —seitig, *adj.* pentahedral. —silbig, *adj.* pentasyllabic. —sprachig, *adj.* pentaglot. —spiel, *n.* quintet. —stimmig, *adj.* (*arranged*) for five voices. —tägig, *adj.* of five days. —täglich, *adj.* recurring every fifth day. —te=halb, *num. adj.* four and a half. —zack, *m.* five-pronged fork. —zehn (*also* funfzehn), *num. adj.* fifteen. —zehntel, —zehn=teil, *n.* fifteenth (*part*). —zöllig, *adj.* five inches long.

Fungie'ren, *v.n.* (*aux.* h.) to discharge (*an office*); to officiate.

Fungö's, *adj. & adv.* fungous, spongy.

Fun'k—e, *m.* (—en, *pl.* —en), —en, *m.* (—ens, *pl.* —en, *dim.* Fünk'chen, Fünk'lein, *n.* sparklet) spark, sparkle, scintillation; flash; glimpse; ray; particle, jot, bit (*fig.*); die letzten —en seiner Liebe, the last remnants of his love. *Comp.* —el=neu, *adj.* bran(d)-new. —el=nagelneu, *adj.* bran(d)-new, spick and span. —en=fänger, *m.* spark-catcher (*on locomotives, etc.*). —en=holz, *n.* touch-wood. —en=sehen, *n.* twinkling of the eyes, photopsy (*Med.*). —en=wurm, *m.* glow-worm.

Fun'keln, I. *v.n.* (*aux.* h.) to emit sparks; to sparkle, glitter, glisten, twinkle. II. *subst.n.* sparkling; coruscation (*Phys.*).

Funktio'n, *f.* (*pl.* —en) office, function; religious service. —ie'ren, *v.n.* (*aux.* h.) to officiate, to perform the duties of an office.

Fun'zel, *f.* old lamp that is burning badly (*sl.*).

Für, I. *adv. It stands often in poetical or archaic German instead of the mod.* vor: *e.g.* sich herfür drängen, fürtrefflich; Stück — Stück, apiece, each, piece by piece; Schritt — Schritt, step after step; Mann — Mann, man by man; — und —, for ever and ever. II. *prep.* (*with acc.*) for; instead of; in favour of; for the sake of; against; on behalf of; in return for; as; — Bezahlung annehmen, to take in payment; es — einen Schimpf achten, to consider it as an affront; ich lebe wöchentlich — zwanzig Mark, I live at the rate of twenty marks a week; ich — meine Person, as for me; — sich, for oneself alone; in an undertone; single, on his own authority; an und — sich, in itself, taken by itself, in the abstract; — sich leben, to live alone *or* privately; er hat Vermögen — sich, he has property of his own; — Ernst halten, to take in earnest; ich habe es — mein Leben gern, I like it above all things; — und wider, pro and con; was —? what sort of? was waren das — Fragen? what kind of questions were those? was — Leute auch da sein mögen, whatever kind of people may be there; es — gut halten, to deem it advisable, to think it well. *Comp.* —baß, *adv.* further, forward, on (*obs.*). —bitte, *f.* intercession; eine —bitte einlegen, to intercede; öffentliche —bitte, public prayers. —bitter, *m.* intercessor. —e'rst, *adv.* first of all, at first. —lie'b, *adv.*; —lieb nehmen, to be content with, put up with; er nimmt mit allem —lieb, he puts up with anything. —nehm. *adj.* distinguished, high, aristocratic (*obs.; now* Vornehm). —sehung, *f.* providence (*of God; obs.; now* Vorsehung). —sorge, *f.* precaution; care; provision. —sorge=erziehung, *f.* trustee education. —sorger, *m.* guardian, provider. —sprech, *m.* (*obs.*) *see* —sprecher. —sprache, *f.* intercession; defence (*Law*). —sprechen, *ir.v.a.* to speak in favour of, to intercede. —sprecher, *m.* intercessor; advocate. —treff'lich, *adj.* excellent (*obs.; now* Vortrefflich). —wa'hr, *adv.* verily, indeed, forsooth. —witz, *m.* meddling, pertness (*see* Vorwitz). —wort, *n.* pronoun; good word; intercession.

Fur'ch—e, *f.* (*pl.* —en) furrow; wrinkle. —ig, *adj. & adv.* furrowed. *Comp.* —en=egge, *f.* drill-harrow. —en=rain, *m.* ridge. —en=weise, *adv.* in furrows. —en=zieher, *m.* a kind of drill-plough.

Fur'ch—en, *v.a.* to plough up in furrows; to wrinkle, knit (*the brow, etc.*).

Furcht, *f.* (*no pl.*) fear, terror, dread, fright, awe; in — setzen, to terrify; — haben, to be afraid; außer sich vor —, frightened out of one's senses; aus — vor einem Unfalle, for fear of an accident; einem — einflößen, to strike a p. with fear. —bar, *adj. & adv.* frightful, dreadful; formidable; fearful; er ist —bar klug, freundlich, he is awfully clever, kind (*coll.*) —barkeit, *f.* terribleness; frightful thing. —sam, *adj. & adv.* timid, timorous, fearful, faint-hearted; —sam machen, to dishearten, intimidate, to abash. —samkeit, *f.* timidity, faint-heartedness; cowardice. *Comp.* —los, *adj.* fearless. —losigkeit, *f.* fearlessness.

Fürch't—en, *v.* I. *a. & n.* (*obsol. and dial. impf.* er forchte, *instead of the usual* er fürchtete; *aux.* h.) to fear, be afraid of; to dread; to stand in awe of; Gott —en, to fear God; es ist *or* steht zu —en, it is to be feared. II. *r.* to be afraid, to stand in fear (vor, of). —erlich, *adj. & adv.* fearful, frightful, horrible. —erlichkeit, *f.* awfulness, frightfulness.

Für'der, I. *adj.* further, onwards. II. *adv.* henceforward; further.

Fu'rie, *f.* (*pl.* —n) fury. *Comp.* —n=ähnlich, —n=artig, *adj.* like a fury.

Furie'r, *see* Fourier. *Comp.* —schütz, *m.* orderly.

Furnie'r, *see* Fournier.

Furo're, *n.*; der Künstler hat — gemacht, the artist has created quite a sensation.

Fürst, *m.* (—en, *pl.* —en) prince, sovereign; paladin (*poet.*); chief; der — dieser Welt, the Devil. —enschaft, *f.* princely dignity; principality. —en=tum, *n.* (—entums, *pl.* —Fürstentümer) principality, kingdom, princely dominion; princely estate *or* character (*B.*). —in, *f.* princess. —lich, *adj. & adv.* princely; —liche Durchlaucht, Serene Highness. —lichkeit, *f.* princeliness; magnificence; (*pl.*) princely personages. *Comp.* —bischof, *m.* bishop of princely rank. —en=bank, *f.* princes' seat in the old German diet. —en=birn, *f.* bergamot. —en=brief, *m.* princes' patent. —en=diener, *m.* a server of princes; courtier. —en=geschlecht, *n.* race of princes. —en=gunst, *f.* princely favour. —en=gut, *n.* crown lands. —en=haus, *n.* court, house *or* family of a prince. —en=hut, *m.* prince's coronet *or* crown. —en=mäßig, *adj.* princely, princelike. —en=stamm, *m.* race of princes, princely house; dynasty. —en=stand, *m.* princely rank *or* dignity, princes (*coll.*). —en=tag, *m.* diet *or* assembly of princes.

Für'sten, *v.a.* to exalt to the rank of a prince *or* of a principality.

Furt, *f.* (*pl.* **—en**) ford.
Furun'kel, *m.* furuncle, boil (*Med.*).
Furz, *m.* (**—es**, *pl.* **Für'ze**), fart. **—en**, *v.a.* to fart.
Fuschelei', *f.* fraudulent dealing, trickery.
Fu'sch—eln, **—en**, *v.n.* (*aux.* **h.**) to perform hastily *or* carelessly; to pass lightly (*over*); to cheat. **—erei'**, *f.* cheating.
Fu'sel, *m.* (**—s**) bad brandy, gin. **—ig**, *adj.* adulterated with fusel oil; intoxicated from bad liquor. *Comp.* **—politiker**, *m.* pot-house politician.
Füselie'r, Füsilie'r, *m.* (**—s**, *pl.* **—e**) light-infantry soldier, fusileer. **—en**, *v.a.; einen* **—en**, to shoot a p. (*Mil.*). *Comp.* **—bataillon**, *n.* third battalion in a German infantry regiment.
Fus'sel, *m. & f.* fuzz, fluff (*coll.*). **—ig**, *adj.* fuzzy, fluffy; **sich den Mund —ig reden**, to talk oneself out of breath (*sl.*).
Fuß, *m.* (**—es**, *pl.* **Fü'ße**) foot; footing; base, pedestal, foot; stem (*of a glass*); bottom, lowest part; foot (*measure*); standard; scale (*of living*); terms (*of acquaintance*); **trockenen —es**, dry-shod; **stehenden —es**, immediately; **mehrere — hoch**, several feet high; **die Sache hat Hand und —**, the thing is to the purpose, is pertinent, is capital; **weder Hand noch —**, neither rhyme nor reason; **festen —es**, without stirring, unflinchingly, resolutely; **festen — fassen**, to gain a firm footing, establish *or* plant oneself, **die Füße in die Hände nehmen**, to make great haste; **er wehrte sich mit Händen und Füßen**, he defended himself tooth and nail; **ich werde ihm Füße machen**, I'll make him find his legs; **er ist (heute) mit dem linken —e zuerst aufgestanden**, he is in a temper (*coll.*); **auf den Füßen**, up, not in bed, on one's legs, out (*Mil.*); **auf einem großen —e leben**, to live in grand style; **auf gleichem —e**, upon the same level, on equal terms, alike; **auf gutem —e**, upon good terms; **auf vertrautem —e**, on intimate terms; **auf freiem —e**, at liberty, at large, independent; **auf eignen Füßen stehen**, to be self-supporting, independent; **auf schwachen Füßen stehen**, to rest on a weak foundation, to be shaky, shallow; **auf freien — setzen**, to set at liberty; **auf preußischen — setzen**, to organize on the Prussian system; **fest auf den Füßen**, sure-footed; **sich auf die Füße machen**, to take to one's heels; **auf die Füße helfen**, to help (up), assist; **sich** (*dat.*) **den — verstauchen**, to sprain one's ankle; **auf die Füße bringen**, to raise (*troops, etc.*); **mit dem —e stoßen**, to kick; **mit Füßen (unter die Füße) treten**, to trample upon; to spurn; **über den — gespannt sein**, *or* **auf gespanntem —e mit einem leben**, to be on bad terms with a p.; at daggers drawn with a p.; **unter den — geben**, to hint, to suggest; **vor die Füße werfen**, to reject with disdain; **zu —**, on foot; **Soldat zu —**, foot-soldier; **zu —e gehen**, to go on foot, walk; **schlecht zu —e sein**, to be a poor walker; **sich einem zu Füßen werfen**, to throw oneself at a person's feet. *Comp.* **—angel**, *f.* man-trap. **—anmunden**, *n.* raising the foot to the mouth (*Gymn.*). **—ball**, *m.* football. **—ballen**, *m.* ball of the foot. **—bänder**, *pl.* ligaments of the foot-bones; jesses (*Falc.*). **—bank**, *f.* foot-stool. **—bedienter**, *m.* foot-man. **—bekleidung**, *f.* foot-covering. **—breit**, *m.*; **ein —breit Landes**, a foot of ground. **—beuge**, **—biege**, *f.* instep. **—blatt**, *n.* flat *or* sole of the foot. **—boden**, *m.* floor; ground; flooring. **—decke**, *f.* carpet; coverlet for the feet; travelling-rug; bed-side rug. **—eisen**, *n.* trap; fetters; calkin (*on shoes, etc.*). **—fall**, *m.* prostration; **einen —fall thun vor**, to fall prostrate at the feet of. **—fällig**, *adj.* prostrate, on one's knees. **—fest**, *adj.* sure-footed. **—flasche**, *f.* hot-water bottle, foot-warmer. **—frei**, *adj.*; **—freies Kostüm**, dress (*of ladies*) that does not quite reach down to the feet. **—gänger**, *m.* pedestrian; foot-soldier. **—garde**, *f.* foot guards. **—gesimse**, *n.* ornaments about a pedestal in the form of a cornice; socle. **—gestell**, *n.* pedestal, basis. **—getäfel**, *n.* parquet. **—getast**, *n.* (*obs.*), **—klaviatur**, *f.* pedals of an organ. **—krank**, *adj.* suffering from the feet, footsore. **—gicht**, *f.* podagra. **—kalt**, *adj.* cold for *or* at the feet. **—knöchel**, *m.* anklebone. **—kranz**, *m.* base (*of a column*). **—lecker**, *m.* toady. **—muskelbinden**, *pl.* fascia. **—punkt**, *m.* nadir. **—register**, *n.* pedal-stop. **—reiniger**, *m.* scraper, door-mat. **—reise**, *f.* walking tour. **—rücken**, *m.* instep. **—sack**, *m.* foot-muff. **—schemel**, *m.* footstool; treadle. **—sicher**, *adj.* sure-footed. **—sohle**, *f.* sole of the foot. **—spur**, *f.* track, foot-mark. **—standbild**, *n.* pedestrian statue. **—stapfe**, *f.* foot-step, trace. **—steig**, *m.* foot-way, footpath. **—taste**, *f.* organ-pedal. **—tritt**, *m.* kick; footstep; step, foot-board (*of carriages*); treadle; pedal. **—unterlage**, *f.* plinth (*Arch.*). **—volk**, *n.* foot-soldiers, infantry. **—wanne**, *f.* foot-tub. **—wurzel**, *f.* tarsus.
Fu'ßen, *v.n.* (*aux.* **h.**) (**auf**, *with dat.*) to have *or* place one's foot on; to get a footing; to perch, to light; to build, depend, rely, rest (**auf**, on). II. *a.* **etwas — auf** (*acc.*), to build, found something on.
Fü'ß—eln, *v.n.* (*aux.* **h.**) to play with the feet; to move one's feet quickly about, to shuffle; **mit einander —eln**, to touch each other's feet. **—er**, *m.* one having feet. **—ig**, *suff.* (*in comp.* =) having feet, -footed. **—ler**, *m.* (*in comp.*) one having feet; **Drei-, Vier-, Fünf-, Sechs-, —ler**, verse containing 3, 4, 5, 6 feet; **Vier—ler**, quadruped. **—ling**, *m.* (**—lings**, *pl.* **—linge**) foot of a stocking; sock. **—lings**, *adv.* on, by *or* at the feet; **—lings fallen**, to fall (*or* light) on one's feet.
Futsch, *int.* off! lost! ruined; **er ist —**, he is gone (*coll.*); **—ika'to!** gone! (*sl.*).
[1]**Fut'ter**, *n.* (**—s**) fodder, provender, forage; food; feed; **er steht in gutem —**, he is well fed; **das — sticht ihn**, he grows insolent from high living; **— fassen**, to be foraging (*Mil.*). *Comp.* **—bau**, *m.* culture of forage. **—beutel**, **—sack**, *m.* nose-bag, provender bag. **—boden**, *m.* hayloft. **—bohne**, *f.* horse-bean. **—geld**, *n.* money paid for the food of animals. **—gerste**, *f.*, **—hafer**, *m.* barley, oats used as provender. **—holer**, *m.* forager. **—kammer**, *f.* hayloft. **—kasten**, *m.* corn-bin. **—klee**, *m.* meadow-clover. **—knecht**, *m.* hostler, servant to attend to the feeding of cattle. **—korn**, *n.* corn for cattle. **—kraut**, *n.* herbs for fodder. **—mütze**, *f.* foraging cap. **—schwinge**, *f.* winnowing-fan. **—trog**, *m.* trough.
[2]**Fut'ter**, *n.* (**—s**, *pl.* **—**) case; sheath; lining, inner covering; lining (*of dresses, etc.*); **— von Fenstern, Thüren, 2c.**, window-case, door-case. **—a'l**, *n.* (**—a'ls**, *pl.* **—a'le**) case, covering; box; bandbox; sheath. *Comp.* **—a'l=macher**, *m.* case *or* sheath-maker. **—a'l=messer**, *n.* case *or* sheath knife. **—hemd**, *n.* under-vest. **—mauer**, *f.* lining-wall. **—tuch**, **—zeug**, *n.* stuff for lining.
[1]**Füt'ter—n**, *v.* I. *a.* to feed; to give fodder to. II. *n.* (*aux.* **h.**) to be good food for; to feed. **—ung**, *f.* foddering, feeding; food, forage, provender.
[2]**Füt'ter—n**, *v.a.* to line; to cover; to case; to stuff; to fur. **—ung**, *f.* lining; casing; doubling (*Naut.*); chemise (*Fort.*).
Futu'r—isch, *adj.* future. **—um**, *n.* (**—ums**, *pl.* **Futu'ra**) future tense.

G

G, g, G, g; G, sol (*Mus.*); **der — Schlüssel,** the treble clef; **— dur,** G major; **— moll,** G minor.

Gab, Gä'be, *imperf. ind. & subj. of* **geben.**

Ga'be, *f.* (*pl.* **—n**) gift, donation; yield; alms; offering; dose (*Med.*); endowment, talent; **Steuern und —n,** taxes and imposts; **ein Mensch von herrlichen —n,** a man of splendid endowments, of wonderful gifts *or* talents; **milde —,** alms, charity. *Comp.* **—n=bringer, —spender,** *m.* dispenser of gifts, giver of good gifts; almsgiver. **—n=fresser,** *m.* one that takes bribes; corrupt judge. **—n=sammlung,** *f.* collection of charities. **—n=tanz,** *m.* cotillon.

Ga'bel, *f.* (*pl.* **—n**) fork; prong; trigger (*of a cross-bow*); tendril (*Bot.*); merry-thought (*of a fowl*); frog (*of a horse's hoof*); (*pl.*) shafts (*of a cart, etc.*); **eine — mit zwei Zinken,** a two-pronged fork; **in die — ziehen** (*obs.*), **die — geben,** to fork, to make a move which threatens two pieces (*Chess*). **—er,** *see* **Gabler.** **—icht** (*obs.*), **—ig,** *adj. & adv.* forked, fork-like. *Comp.* **—anker,** *m.* small bow-anchor; cramp-iron. **—bäume,** *pl.*, **—deichsel,** *f.* pair of shafts (*of a cart, etc.*). **—förmig,** *adj.* forked; bifurcated; **sich —förmig teilen,** to fork off. **—frühstück,** *n.* luncheon; meat breakfast. **—fuhrwerk,** *n.*, **—wagen,** *m.* waggon with shafts. **—gehörn,** *n.* forked antlers. **—holz,** *n.* forked wood; (*pl.*) futtocks (*Naut.*). **—klinge,** *f.* forked blade. **—kopf,** *m.* crown (*Cycl.*). **—nadel,** *f.* hair-pin. **—pferd,** *n.* shaft-horse, wheeler. **—scheiden,** *pl.f.* fork blades (*Cycl.*). **—schnäpper,** *m.* fly-catcher. **—spaltung, —teilung,** *f.* bifurcation. **—stange,** *f.* forked pole. **—stich,** *m.* thrust; prod. **—stiel,** *m.* fork-handle. **—stück,** *n.* swivel-gun; connecting-rod. **—stütze,** *f.* thill-prop. **—zacke, —zinke,** *f.* prong (*of a fork*).

Ga'bel—n, *v.* I. *a.* to fork; to pitchfork; to pierce; to gore. II. *r.* to run out, branch off like a fork. III. *n.* **er —t tüchtig,** he eats heartily (*coll.*). **—ung,** *f.* forking, furcation, bifurcation (of a way).

Gä'be, *adj. in the alliterative phrase* **es ist gang** (*or* **gäng**) **und gäbe,** it is in vogue, customary, it is the usual thing to do.

Gab'ler, *m.* (**—s,** *pl.* **—**) fork-fish; stag two years old, brocket.

Ga'ck—eln, —ern, (**—sen.**) I. *v.n.* (*aux.* **h.**) to cackle; to chatter, prattle, tattle; **Hühner, die viel —eln, legen wenig Eier,** great boast, small roast (*prov.*). II. *subst. n.* cackling; chatter. **—elei',** *f.* cackling.

Ga'den, *m.* (**—s,** *pl.* **—**) room; small house containing but one room; story, floor (*obs.*).

Gaf'fel, *f.* (*pl.* **—n**) fork. *Comp.* **—baum,** *m.* gaff (*Naut.*). **—fall,** *m.* throat-halliards (*Naut.*). **—segel,** *n.* gaff-sail (*Naut.*).

Gaf'f—en, *v.n.* (*aux.* **h.**) to gape, stare; **sich blind —en,** to stare one's eyes out. **—er,** *m.* (**—ers,** *pl.* **—er**), **—erin,** *f.* starer, gaper, idle looker on. **—erei',** *f.* gaping.

Gaga't, *m. & n.* (**—s,** *pl.* **—e**) jet, black amber. **—en,** *adj.* jet, jetty. **—kohle,** *f.* pitch-coal.

Ga'ge, *f.* (*pl.* **—n**) wages, salary, pay.

Gäh, *adj. & adv. see* **Jäh.**

Gahn (*obs. & poet.*) = **gehen.**

Gäh'n—en, I. *v.n.* (*aux.* **h.**) to yawn; to gape; **—en steckt an,** yawning is catching (*prov.*). II. *subst. n.* yawning. **—er,** *m.* (**—ers,** *pl.* **—er**) yawner. *Comp.* **—affe,** *m.* gaping fool, gaper. **—krampf,** *m.* yawning fit, convulsive yawning. **—laut,** *m.* hiatus. **—sucht,** *f.* yawning disease.

Gäh'stotzig, *adj. & adv.* precipitous(ly) (*dial.*).

Gais, *see* **Geiß.**

Ga'la, *f.* gala; pomp, show; drawing room (at court); **in —,** in court, gala *or* full dress; **in großer —,** in court dress; in full fig (*coll.*). *Comp.* **—anzug,** *m.* court dress, presentation suit, gala dress. **—ball,** *m.* dress ball. **—cour,** *f.* drawing room. **—degen,** *m.* dress sword. **—hut,** *m.* court hat. **—kleid,** *n.* court dress, full dress; *pl.* state robes. **—uniform,** *f.* dress uniform. **—vorstellung,** *f.* dress performance (*Theat.*). **—wagen,** *m.* state carriage, glass coach. **—zimmer,** *n.* state room.

Galakto—me'ter, *m.*, **—sko'p,** *n.* lactometer, lactoscope, milk-gauge.

Gala'n, *m.* (**—s,** *pl.* **—e**) gallant, lover; sweetheart, suitor, paramour. **—t,** *adj.* gallant; coquettish; amorous; dissolute; courteous, polite (*to ladies*); elegant, smart, fashionable, spruce (*obs.*); **—te Krankheit,** syphilis.

Galanterie', *f.* gallantry, courtesy. *Comp.* **—arbeit,** *f.*, **—ware,** *f.* jewellery; fancy-goods. **—degen,** *m.* dress-sword. **—händler,** *m.* dealer in fancy goods. **—waren,** *pl.f.* (the finer and more ornamental kinds of **Kurzwaren**), fancy wares, fancy goods.

Gal'ban, *m.* (**—harz,** *n.*) galbanum.

Galeas'se, *f.* galeas, galleass.

Galee're, *f.* (*pl.* **—n**) galley. *Comp.* **—n=anker,** *m.* grapnel. **—n=sklave,** *m.* galley-slave. **—n=volk,** *n.* crew of a galley.

Galeo'ne, *f.* (*pl.* **—n**) galleon.

[1]**Galeo't,** *m.* (**—en,** *pl.* **—en**) galley-slave.

[2]**Galeo't,** *f.*, **Galeo't—e,** *f.* (*pl.* **—en**) galiot, small galley, trading vessel of two masts.

Gal'gant, *m.* (**—es,** *pl.* **—e**) galangal (*Bot.*).

Gal'gen, *m.* (**—s,** *pl.* **—**) cross-beam; gallows; **geh an den —!** go and be hanged!; **sein Bild ist an den — geschlagen,** he was executed in effigy; **der lichte—,** the gallows shone upon by the early morning sun (*criminals were hung in the early morning*); **es steht — und Rad darauf,** it is a capital crime. *Comp.* **—art,** *f.* rogues. **—bube, —schelm, —schwengel,** *m.* gallows-bird. **—förmig,** *adj.* formed like gallows; **ein —förmiges Kreuz,** potence (*Her.*). **—frist,** *f.* short delay, respite, reprieve. **—gesicht,** *n.* hang-dog look. **—humor,** *n.* grim humour. **—presse,** *f.* lithographic lever-press. **—strick,** *m.* scoundrel, one who ought to be hung. **—vogel,** *m.* gallows-bird, criminal; raven.

Galio'n, *n.* (**—s,** *pl.* **—s** *and* **—e**) figure-head (of a ship).

Galit'zenstein, *m.;* **weißer —,** sulphate of zinc; **blauer —,** sulphate of copper.

Galja'ß, *f.* (*pl.* **—(ss)en**) galiot.

Galjo't, *f.* (*pl.* **—en**) galiot. *See* **Galeot.**

Gal'l—e, *f.* (*pl.* **—en**) gall, bile; rancour, spite; choler; gall-nut; flaw (*in casting, etc.*); imperfection, defect; pool, quagmire; moisture; kidney-shaped ore; stony place (*in fields*); swelling under the tongue (*of horses*); **seine —e ausschütten,** to vent one's spleen; **Gift und —e speien,** to give vent to one's rage; **die —e läuft ihm über,** his wrath is excited, his blood is up; **einem die —e rege machen,** to provoke one. **—icht,** *adj. & adv.* (*obs.*) gall-like. **—ig,** *adj. & adv.* gall-like; biliary; bilious; easily excitable; choleric; bitter. *Comp.* **—apfel,** *m.* gall-nut. **—apfel=aufguß,** *m.*, **—apfel=extrakt,** *m.* infusion, extract of gall-nut. **—apfel=fliege, —en=fliege,** *f.* gall-fly. **—e=führend,** *adj.* bilious, venomous. **—en=artig,** *adj.* bilious. **—en=behältnis,** *n.*, **—en=blase,** *f.* gall-bladder. **—en=bitter,** *adj.* bitter as gall. **—en=blasen=schlagadern,** *pl.* the cystic arteries. **—en=brechen,** *n.* bilious vomiting. **—en=ergießung,** *f.* overflow of bile. **—en=fieber,** *n.* bilious fever. **—en=**

fluß, *m.* discharge of bile. **—en=gang**, *m.* biliary duct. **—en=kolik**, *f.*, **—en=krampf**, *m.* cholera, bilious colic. **—en=krankheit**, *f.* bilious complaint. **—en=ſtein**, *m.* gall-stone. **—(en)=ſucht**, *f.* jaundice. **—(en)=ſüchtig**, *adj.* choleric; melancholic; bilious. **—glas**, *n.* bull's eye (*in glass*). **—us=ſäure**, *f.* gallic acid.

Gal'len, *v.a.* to take the gall out of fishes; to prepare with gall-nuts.

Gäl'len, *v.n.* to get bitter, to become embittered (*rare*); to turn into gall, to make bitter; to spoil (*poet.*).

Gal(l)erie', *f.* (*pl.* **—en**) gallery; lobby; alley; foot-board (*Locom.*).

Gal'lert, (*m.* &) *n.* (**—s**, *pl.* **—e**), **—e**, *f.* (*pl.* **—en**) gelatine; jelly; gluten. *Comp.* **—artig**, *adj.* gelatinous. **—ſäure**, *f.* pectic acid.

Gäl'lig, *adj.* hard (*Min.*).

Gallomanie', *f.* Gallomania.

Gallo'ne, *f.* (*pl.* **—n**) gallon.

Gal'mei, *m.* (—(e)**s**) cadmia, calamine.

Galo'n, *m.* (**—s**, *pl.* **—s**) galloon; gold *or* silver lace.

Galo(n)nie'ren, *v.a.* to bind with galloon; to trim with lace; **galonnierte Diener**, livery-servants, flunkeys in livery.

Galo'pp, *m.* gallop; **kurzer —**, hand-gallop; canter; **in — ſetzen**, to put to a gallop; **im —**, at a gallop, galloping, **in geſtrecktem —**, at full gallop; **in vollem —**, at full speed; **es geht mit ihm im — (zu Ende)**, he is sinking fast; **einen kurzen — reiten**, to be cantering. **—a'de**, *f.* (*pl.* **—a'den**) gallopade. **—ie'ren**, *v.n.* (*aux.* **h.**) to gallop; **—ierende Schwindſucht**, rapid consumption; phthisis florida.

Galo'ſche, *f.* (*pl.* **—n**) galosh, golosh, overshoe.

Gal'ſterig, *adj.* rancid (*dial.*).

Galt, Gäl'te, *imp. ind.* & *subj.* of **gelten.**

Galt, *adj.* barren, giving no milk (*dial.*); *see* **gelt.**

Galva'n—iſch, *adj.* galvanic. **—iſie'ren**, *v.a.* to galvanize. **—iſie'rung**, *f.* galvanization. **—i'smus**, *m.* galvanism. *Comp.* **—ogra'ph**, *m.* electrotypist. **—ogra'phiſch**, *adj.*; **—ographiſche Abbildung**, electrotype. **—olo'g**, *m.* lecturer on galvanism. **—oplaſ'tiſch**, *adj.* galvanoplastic, electrotypic, metalloplastic; **—oplaſtiſcher Abdruck**, electrotype. **—o=plaſ'tik**, *f.* galvanoplastic process, electro-metallurgy.

Gaman'der, *m.* (**—s**, *pl.* **—**) germander, heart-clover.

Gama'ſchen, *pl.* gaiters; **— über der Hoſe zu tragen**, leggings; **ich hatte hölliſche — vor dem General**, I was in mortal terror of the general (*coll.*). **—tum**, *n.* military pedantry. *Comp.* **—dienſt**, *m.* pedantry (*as to uniform, etc.*) in military matters; pipe-clay (service). **—held, —menſch, —ritter**, *m.* born soldier, martinet, pipe-clay (*hero*).

Gam'be, *f.* (*pl.* **—n**) bass-viol.

Gams'wurz, *f.* auricula.

Gan'erb—e, *m.* (**—en**, *pl.* **—en**) joint-heir; co-proprietor. **—ſchaft**, *f.* alliance of noble families *or* joint heirs to protect their lives and property; joint heirs *or* proprietors.

Gang, *m.* (**—es**, *pl.* **Gän'ge**) going; motion, movement; progress; carriage, gait; pace; step; stroll, walk; walk, alley, avenue; message, pursuit, errand; way; gangway; ball-alley; passage, corridor; lode, mineral-vein; duct (*Anat.*); place of resort, haunt; passage (*of music; of arms*); pass, lunge (*Fenc.*); round (*in boxing*); course (*of a disease; of the planets; of a lawsuit; at dinner; of a river; of the seasons, etc.*); way (*of acting*); action (*of a drama*); flow, cadence (*of verse*); board (*of a deck, Naut.*); worm (*of a screw*); **man bezahlt ihm eine Guinee für jeden —**, he is paid a guinea for every visit; **einen — thun**, to go, run on an errand; **das Pferd hat einen guten —**, the horse has good action; **man lauert auf alle ſeine Gänge**, all his movements are watched; **ich habe einige Gänge zu machen**, I have several places to call at; **der — des menſchlichen Geiſtes**, the march of human intellect; **eine Mühle mit fünf Gängen**, a mill with five stones; **in — bringen, ſetzen** &c., to set a-going, to start, to bring into fashion; **im —e**, at work, in operation, current; **einmal im —e**, once set agoing; **in vollem —e**, in full activity; **der — der Gerechtigkeit**, the course of justice; **der — der Dinge**, the way of the world; **der bedeckte —**, sap, mine (*Fort.*), covered way, portico (*Arch.*); **offener —** porch; **unterirdiſcher —**, underground passage. **—bar**, *adj.* customary; current; marketable; frequented; practicable, passable; **—bare Münze**, current coin; **—bare Erklärung**, usual explanation; **—bare Artikel**, staple commodities; **Waſſerröhren —bar erhalten**, to keep water-pipes in order. **—barkeit**, *f.* currency; practicable condition (of a road); saleableness. **—haft**, *adj.* & *adv.* in veins *or* streaks. *Comp.* **—bar=machung**, *f.*; **man beſchloß die —barmachung des Weges**, it was decided to make the road practicable. **—bord**, *m.* gangway. **—gebirge**, *n.* mountain containing veins of ore. **—häuer**, *m.* lodesman. **—meiſter**, *m.* gangmaster. **—pfoſten**, *m.* baluster. **—rad**, *n.* tread wheel. **—ſäule**, *f.* column of a portico. **—ſpill**, *n.* capstan; **loſes —ſpill**, crab. **—vögel**, *pl.* Ambulatores (*Orn.*). **—weiſe**, *adv.* in veins; so much a visit. **—woche**, *f.* Rogation week (*Rom. Cath.*).

Gäng, *adj.* & *adv.* current, passing; in fashion; customary; swift; **— und gebe** (*also* **gang und gäbe**), customary, traditional; **was nicht mehr — und gebe iſt**, what is no longer in use, fashionable *or* customary; **Geld, das im Kauf — und gebe iſt**, current money.

Gän'gel—n, *v.* I. *n.* (*aux.* **ſ.**) to toddle, walk like a little child. II. *a.* to teach a child to walk; to lead a child in walking; to lead like a child, to lead by the nose; to manage, control; to rock (*a cradle*); to chop up (*meat*). **—ei'**, *f.* leading in strings. *Comp.* **—band**, *n.* leading string. **—wagen**, *m.* go-cart.

Gan'gen, (*obsol.* & *poet.*) *p.p. of* **gangen** (*obs.*) = **gehen**; *hence* **gangen** (*obs.* & *dial.*) = **gegangen.**

Gän'ger, *m.* (**—s**, *pl.* **—**) (*usually in cpds.*) goer, walker.

Gän'gig, *adj.* & *adv. see* **Gäng**; containing veins; in veins; quick, fleet; (*as suff. in comp. also* =) going; having passages *or* walks.

Gan'ner, *m.* (**—s**, *pl.* **—**) merganser, goosander (*Orn.*).

Gans, *f.* (*pl.* **Gän'ſe**) goose (*pl.* geese); pig of iron; **die — ſchnattert**, the goose cackles (gaggles); **Gänſe nudeln**, to cram geese; **dumme —**, queen goose, ninny, silly, foolish girl; **die weißwängige —**, common barnacle; **die goldne —**, a silly young heiress; **die Gänſe gehen überall barfuß**, human nature is always the same; **er iſt ſo dumm, daß ihn die Gänſe beißen**, he can't say bo to a goose; **ausſehen wie eine — wenn es blitzt**, to look like a dying duck (in a thunderstorm). **—(ſ)ern**, *v.a.* (*aux.* **h.**) to tread the goose.

Gäns'chen, *n.* (**—s**, *pl.* **—**) gosling; goosey; goosey, goosey gander (*Nurs. r.*); a silly young girl; **es flog ein — über den Rhein und kam als Gickgack wieder heim**, send a fool to the market, and a fool he will return; how much an ass that has been sent to Rome excels an ass that has been kept at home (*prov.*). *Comp.* **—ampfer**, *m.* snakeweed (*Bot.*). **—artig**, *adj.* resembling a goose, goose-like; anserine

(*Zoöl.*). —**baum**, *m.* plane-tree. —**blümchen**, *n.* daisy. —**blume**, *f.* daisy; dog daisy. —**braten**, *m.* roast-goose. —**brust**, *f.* (**geräucherte**) (smoked) breast of a (Pomeranian) goose. —**dumm**, *adj.* as green as duckweed (*coll.*). —**feder**, *f.* goose-feather, goose-quill. —**flieder**, *m.* guelder-rose. —**e=fuß**, *m.* goose's foot; Chenopodium (*Bot.*). —**füßchen**, *pl.* inverted commas, quotation marks. —**gang**, *m.* goose-step; a game. —**gekröse**, *n.* goose-giblets. —**haut**, *f.* goose-skin; goose-flesh; **es überläuft mich eine —haut**, my flesh creeps *or* is all turned to goose-flesh. —**kiel**, *m.* goose-quill. —**klein**, *n.* giblets. —**küchlein**, —**küken**, *n.* gosling. —**leber=pastete**, *f.* potted goose liver, pâté de foie gras. —**löffel**, *m.* goose-bill (*Surg.*). —**marsch**, *m.* goose-step; Indian file, follow-my-leader; **im —marsch gehen**, to walk in single file. —**pfeffer**, *m.* giblets. —**schmalz**, *n.* goose-dripping. —**schwarzsauer**, *n.* giblets dressed in goose-blood (*Cook.*). —**spiel**, *n.* game of fox and geese. —**stall**, *m.*, —**stiege**, *f.* goose coop *or* pen. —**trift**, *f.* goose-green; right of pasturing geese. —**wein**, *m.* Adam's ale, water. —**weiß**, *n.* goose in jelly (*Cook.*). —**zucht**, *f.* breeding of geese.

Gän'se— (*in compounds*) —**haft**, *adj.* & *adv.* goose-like; simple, stupid. —**rich**, *m.* (—**richs**, *pl.* —**riche**) gander.

Gant, *f.* (*pl.* —**en**) auction; failure, bankruptcy. *Comp.* —**anwalt**, *m.* trustee in bankruptcy. —**buch**, *n.* inventory of a (bankrupt) sale. —**haus**, *n.* auction-mart. —**mann**, —**schuldner**, *m.* bankrupt. —**mäßig**, *adj.* insolvent. —**masse**, *f.* bankrupt's estate. —**recht**, *n.* law of bankruptcy; auction laws.

Gan'ten, *v.n.* (*aux.* **h.**) to institute a legal execution; **um eine S. —**, to bid for something at an auction.

Ganz, I. *adj.* whole, entire; all; complete; excellent; **das —e Haus**, the whole house; **die —e Welt**, all the world; **von —em Herzen**, with all my heart; **es ist mein —er Ernst**, I am quite in earnest; **ein —er Mann**, a true man, a downright good fellow; **die —e Nacht hindurch**, all through the night, all night long; **eine —e Zahl**, an integer; **die —e Summe, der —e Betrag**, the full amount, the total; — **machen**, to complete, to mend; **eine —e Note**, a semibreve (*Mus.*); **in —er Figur**, full length. II. *adv.* quite; wholly, altogether; perfectly; **ich bin — Ohr**, I am all attention; **sie war — Freude**, she was full of joy; — **anders**, altogether different; — **und gar**, totally; — **und gar nicht**, not at all, by no means; — **und gar nichts**, nothing at all; — **wohl**, — **gut**, very well; — **gleich**, all the same; —**fremd**, an utter stranger; — **der Ihrige**, yours truly, yours very truly. —**e(s)**, *n.* whole, entirety; integer (*Arith.*); gross; **im —en**, upon the whole, generally; **im Großen und —en**, on the whole, generally speaking, altogether; **im —en genommen**, in general, taken by the lump, taken in the gross; **im —en handeln**, to sell wholesale. —**heit**, *f.* totality, entireness. *Comp.* —**hufig**, *adj.* whole-hoofed. —**hüfner**, *m.* peasant keeping a team of four horses. —**randig**, *adj.* entire (*of leaves*). —**sache**, *f.* entire (*postage stamps*). —**sachen**, *pl.* entires (*envelopes, post-cards, wrappers*). —**seide**, *f.* pure silk, all silk. —**wolle**, *f.* pure wool, all wool.

Gänz'lich, *adj.* & *adv.* complete, full, entire, total.

Gar, I. *adj.* (*indec.*) finished, complete, ready; prepared; cooked; in good cultivation; refined (*of metals*); dressed (*of skins*); **Fleisch das nicht — ist**, underdone meat; **Leder — machen**, to dress leather. II. *adv.* & *part.* quite, entirely, fully, absolutely; very, even; at all; perhaps; I hope; — **nicht**, not at all, by no means; — **nichts**, nothing at all; — **oft**, very often; — **selten**, very rarely; — **zu**, much too, far too; — **keiner**, not a single one, none whatever; — **zu neugierig**, over-inquisitive; — **kein Zweifel**, not the least doubt; **es ist mit ihm — aus**, it is all over with him (*dial.*); **warum nicht —!** you don't say so! never! **ist er krank oder — tot?** he is ill? not dead, I trust? **so— der Gedanke!** the very thought! **das ist — wohl möglich**, that is quite possible; **vielleicht gefällt er mir —**, perhaps I may even like him. —**e**, *f.* condition of anything dressed *or* made ready, readiness; mellowness (*of land*); batch of hides (*obs.*). —**en**, *v.a.* to refine; to dress; to cook thoroughly. *Comp.* —**arbeit**, *f.* metal-refining. —**aus**, I. *adj.* completely finished. II. *m.* (& *n.*) (*indec.*) (*usual pron.* **Gar'aus**) utter ruin; finishing stroke; end; death; **einem den —aus machen**, to complete one's ruin, to undo *or* kill one, to finish a person off. —**eisen**, *n.* refined iron; smelter's iron probe. —**koch**, *m.* master of a cook-shop. —**könig**, *m.* regulus of copper. —**küche**, *f.* cook-shop, eating-house. —**leder**, *n.* tanned leather. —**machen**, *n.* tanning; refining. —**ofen**, *m.* refining furnace. —**probe**, *f.* assay. —**salz**, *n.* well-boiled salt. —**stück**, *n.* piece of purified salt. —**wage**, *f.* brine-gauge.

Garantie', *f.* (*pl.* —**en**) guarantee, security.

Garantie'ren (für eine S.), *v.a.* to guarantee (a th.); to find security (for a th.).

Gärb, *see* **Gerb**.

Gar'be, *f.* (*pl.* —**n**) sheaf; neck of beef; milfoil, yarrow (*Bot.*). *Comp.* —**n=binder**, *m.* sheaf-binder. —**n=feuer**, *n.* Chinese fire (*Pyr.*). —**n=schichter**, *m.* labourer who piles the sheaves. —**n=zehnte**, *m.* tithe on sheaves.

Gar'd—e, *f.* (*pl.* —**en**) guard; guards; —**e zu Fuß** *or* —**e=Infanterie**, foot-guards; —**e=Kavallerie**, horse-guards; **bei der —e**, in the guards; **die preußische —e**, the Prussian guards. *Comp.* —**dragoner**, *pl.* dragoon guards. —**grenadiere**, *pl.* grenadiers of the guards. —**i'st**, *m.* (*pl.* —**i'sten**) soldier of the guards, guardsman. —**regiment**, *n.* regiment of the guards; crack regiment (*coll.*).

Gardero'b—e, *f.* wardrobe; stock of clothes; cloak-room, closet; **wo ist die —e?** where is the cloak-room? where can we leave our things? —**ie'r**, *m.* keeper of the wardrobe, attendant at a cloak-room; property-man (*Theat.*).

Gar'dian, *m.* (—**s**); **Pater —**, father guardian.

Gardi'ne, *f.* (*pl.* —**n**) curtain. *Comp.* —**n=arm**, —**n=haken**, *m.* curtain-hook. —**n=predigt**, *f.* curtain-lecture, wife's lecture.

Gä'r—e, *f.* (*pl.* —**en**) fermentation; fermenting point; leaven; yeast; bouquet of wine. *Comp.* —**bottich**, *m.* fermenting-vat. —**dauer**, *f.* duration of fermentation. —**kammer**, *f.* fermenting room. —**mittel**, *n.*, —**stoff**, *m.* leavening stuff, yeast. —**teig**, *m.* leaven. —**ungs=fähig**, *adj.* fermentable. —**ungs=küche**, *f.* dyer's fermenting-vat. —**ungs=lehre**, *f.* zymology. —**ungs=mittel**, *n.*, —**ungs=stoff**, *m.* yeast, barm, *etc.* —**ungs=prozeß**, *m.* process of fermentation.

Gä'r—en, *ir.v.* I. *n.* (*aux.* **h.** & **s.**) to ferment, work; to bubble up, effervesce; **es —t in den Köpfen**, their (people's) minds are in a state of fermentation, are full of discontent, of projects, *etc.*; **der Wein ist (hat sich) zu Essig gegoren**, the wine has turned to vinegar. II. *subst.n.* fermentation. —**ung**, *f.* fermentation, ferment; **der Teig kommt in —ung**, the dough begins to rise.

Ga'ren, *v.a.* to dress, to refine (*Techn.*).

Garibal'di— (*in comp.*)—**bluse**, —**jacke**, *f.* garibaldi. —**jäckchen**, *n.* loose bodice.

Gar'mond (—**schrift**), *f.* long primer (*Typ.*).

Garn, *n.* (—**s**, *pl.* —**e**) yarn; thread; net; snare, decoy; twine; **wollenes** —, worsted, wool; **ins — locken**, to decoy. —**en**, *adj.* of thread. *Comp.* —**enden**, *pl.* thrums. —**falle**, *f.* net for catching birds. —**handel**, *m.* trade in yarn, cotton, *or* twine. —**knäuel**, *m.* ball of thread. —**sack**, —**schlauch**, *m.* sweep-net. —**spule**, *f.* weaver's spool. —**strähn**, *m.*, —**strähne**, *f.* hank *or* skein of yarn. —**stricker**, *m.* netter. —**wage**, *f.* instrument for ascertaining the quality of yarn. —**wickel**, *m.* thread paper. —**winde**, *f.* reel, hasp. —**zug**, *m.* drawing of the nets.

Garna'le, Garne'le, *f.* prawn (*large*); shrimp (*small*).

Garn—ie'ren, *v.a.* to trim; to garnish. —**ie'rung**, *f.* trimming; garnish. —**itu'r**, *f.* trimming; border; set; mountings, fittings; **zweite —itur**, second uniform; uniform which is no longer very good.

Garniso'n, *f.* (*pl.* —**en**) garrison; **mit einer — versehen**, to garrison (*a town*); **von — entblößen**, to disgarrison; **in — liegen**, to be quartered (at *or* in). —**ie'ren**, *v.n.* to be in garrison. *Comp.* —**dienst**, *m.* garrison duty. —**lazarett**, *n.* military hospital. —**prediger**, *m.* military chaplain.

Garrot't—e, *f.* garroting; throttling-instrument. —**ie'ren**, *v.a.* to garrote; to compress a man's windpipe, strangle a person.

Gar'stig, *adj.* & *adv.* filthy, foul; obscene; detestable; nasty; ugly; horrid; spoiled, rusty. —**keit**, *f.* filthiness; nastiness; vileness; ugliness; obscenity.

Gärt'chen, *n.* (—**s**, *pl.* —) little garden.

Gar'ten, *v.a.* to go begging (*obs.*).

Gar'ten, *m.* (—**s**, *pl.* **Gär'ten**) garden. *Comp.* —**ammer**, *f.* ortolan (*Orn.*). —**anlage**, *f.* garden-parterre. —**arbeit**, *f.* gardening. —**bau**, *m.* horticulture. —**bau=ausstellung**, *f.* horticultural show. —**bau=verein**, *m.* horticultural society. —**beet**, *n.* garden-bed. —**buch**, *n.* book on gardening. —**butterblume**, *f.* ranunculus. —**distel**, *f.* artichoke. —**erde**, *f.* garden-mould; **feinste —erde**, pure mould. —**geländer**, *n.* espalier. —**gerät**, *n.* gardening-tools. —**gewächs**, *n.* pot-herb. —**haus**, *n.* summer-house. —**kalender**, *m.* gardener's calendar. —**knecht**, *m.* garden-labourer. —**kräuter**, *pl.* pot-herbs, vegetables. —**kunst**, *f.* horticulture. —**künstler**, *m.* horticulturist. —**laube**, *f.* arbour; title of a widely-read German family magazine. —**lauben=roman**, *m.* novel of the kind to be met with in the 'Gartenlaube'; family novel. —**leiter**, *f.* garden-ladder. —**lokal**, *n.* tea *or* beer garden. —**saal**, *m.* saloon with a door opening into the garden. —**säge**, *f.* grafting saw. —**schere**, *f.* garden-shears, pruning shears. —**schwamm**, *m.* mushroom. —**spritze**, *f.* garden hose *or* engine, lawn-sprinkler. —**stuhl**, *m.* garden chair. —**walze**, *f.* garden roller. —**wesen**, *n.* gardening, horticulture. —**wirtschaft**, *f.* horticulture; restaurant in a (*public*) garden, tea *or* beer garden.

Gahre, —**n**, *see* **Gäre**, —**n**.

Gärt'ner, *m.* (—**s**, *pl.* —) gardener. —**ei'**, *f.* gardening, horticulture. —**in**, *f.* gardener's wife; female gardener. —**isch**, *adj.* & *adv.* horticultural. —**n**, *v.n.* (*aux.* **h.**) to garden. *Comp.* —**bursche**, *m.* gardener's man, under-gardener. —**kunst**, *f.* gardening, horticulture. —**messer**, *n.* garden-knife, pruning knife.

Gas, *n.* (—(**s**)**es**, *pl.* —(**s**)**e**) gas; **das — abdrehen** (**andrehen**), to turn off (on) the gas. *Comp.* —**artig**, *adj.* gaseous. —**behälter**, *m.* gasometer, gas-holder. —**beleuchtung**, *f.* lighting by gas; **bei —beleuchtung**, by gaslight. —**beleuchtungs=anstalt**, *f.* gas-works. —**beleuchtungs=gesellschaft**, *f.* gas company. —**brenner**, *m.* burner. —**entbindung** *or* —**entwickelung**, *f.* evolution of gas. —**leitungs=röhre**, —**röhre**, *f.* gas-pipe. —**messer**, *m.* (gas) meter. —**ofen**, *m.* gas-stove. —**strumpf**, *m.* mantle. —**uhr**, *f.* (gas) meter.

Gä'sch—en, *v.n.* (*aux.* **h.**) to ferment; to froth, foam. —**end**, *p.* & *adj.* effervescing; yeasty. —**t**, *m.* (—**tes**) beading (*of wine*); yeast; *see* **Gischt**.

Gascona'de, *f.* (*pl.* —**n**) brag.

Gäß'chen, *n.* (—**s**, *pl.* —) (*narrow*) lane, alley.

Gas'se, *f.* (*pl.* —**n**) street; lane; alley, path, row; **auf der** —, in the street; **eine — ohne Ausgang**, a blind alley; **Hans in allen —n**, busy-body. *Comp.* —**n=bettler**, *m.* tramp. —**n=bube**, —**n=junge**, *m.* street-arab, young loafer; **sich wie ein —n=bube benehmen**, to behave like a blackguard. —**n=dieb**, *m.* pickpocket. —**n=dirne**, *f.* woman of the town, prostitute. —**n=hauer**, *m.* street song, vulgar song. —**n=kehrer**, —**n=kot=führer**, *m.* scavenger, street sweeper. —**kot**, *m.* dirt. —**n=laterne**, *f.* street lamp. —**n=laufen**, *n.* running the gauntlet (*Mil.*). —**n=pöbel**, *m.* mob, tag-rag. —**n=rinne**, —**n=schleuse**, *f.* gutter. —**n=treter**, *m.* vagabond; lounger. —**n=troß**, —**n=volk**, *n.* street-mob, rabble. —**n=vogt**, *m.*, beadle. —**n=wirt**, *m.* tavern-keeper, publican. —**n=witz**, *m.* vulgar wit, low jest.

Gast, *m.* (—**es**, *pl.* **Gä'ste**) guest, visitor; stranger; customer; fellow, person; stranger, star (*Theat.*); (*pl.* —**en**) sailor; **Gäste haben**, to have company; **Gäste empfangen**, to receive company, do the honours; **ungebetener** —, intruder; **ein — auf Erden**, a stranger on the earth; **einen zu —e bitten**, to invite s.o.; **sich selbst zu —e bitten**, to be an uninvited guest; to come and take pot-luck with a p.; **ein grober** —, a clown, a rude fellow; **ein saubrer** —, a fine sort of chap; **ein schlauer** —, a knowing fellow; **zu —e sein**, to be a guest, a visitor. —**erei'**, *f.* (*pl.* —**erei'en**) entertainment, feast, banquet. —**ie'ren**, *v.* I. *a.* to entertain. II. *n.* (*aux.* **h.**) to to be a guest; to act for a short time at a strange theatre, to star, *etc.*; to perform duty for another. —**lich**, *adj.* hospitable; convivial. *adv.* as guests, in the quality of guests. —**lichkeit**, *f.* hospitality. —**ie'rung**, *f.* entertainment of guests; hotel-keeping. *Comp.* —**becher**, *m.* goblet for pledging guests. —**bett**, *n.* spare bed. —**bitter**, *m.* inviter of guests. —**frei**, *adj.* & *adv.* hospitable. —**freiheit**, *f.* hospitality. —**freund**, *m.* intimate friend; guest; host. —**freund=(schaft)lich**, *adj.* hospitable. —**freundlichkeit**, *f.* hospitality. —**freundschaft**, *f.* hospitality. —**geber**, —**halter**, *m.* host, landlord. —**gebot**, *n.* feast, banquet, treat. —**gebrauch**, *m.* guest-rite. —**haus**, *n.* restaurant; inn; tavern. —**herr**, *m.* host. —**hof**, *m.* hotel; inn; —**hof=besitzer**, proprietor of a hotel; innkeeper. —**kleid**, *n.* dress-suit. —**mahl**, *n.* entertainment, banquet. —**mutter**, *f.* matron (*in hospitals*); sister who receives the poor and strangers in convents. —**ordnung**, *f.* regulation for inn-keepers. —**predigt**, *f.* sermon preached in a strange church; trial sermon. —**recht**, *n.* right of demanding hospitality; usages of hospitality; bond of hospitality; the right of entertaining *or* keeping a hotel. —**rolle**, *f.* part played by a stranger, starring part (*Theat.*); —**rollen geben**, to go on a starring tour, to star it. —**spiel**, *n.* starring. —**stube**, *f.*, —**zimmer**, *n.* stranger's room; spare (bed-)room; coffee-room in a tavern *or* hotel; travellers' room. —**tafel**, *f.*, —**tisch**, *m.* table-d'hôte. —**verwandt**, *adj.* allied by hospitality (*through* belonging to a —freundschaft *or league made amongst friends for the purpose of exercising hospitality to one another*). **—weise,** *adv.* as a guest *or* stranger. **—wirt,** *m.* landlord, innkeeper. **—wirtin,** *f.* hostess; landlady. **—wirtschaft,** *f.* inn-keeping; inn; **—wirtschaft treiben,** to keep an inn; **eine —wirtschaft errichten,** to open an inn. **—zimmer,** *n. see* ~stube.

Gas'ten, *v.a.* to entertain (*rare*); **Zehren und ~ leert Küche, Keller und Kasten,** spending your money with many a guest, empties the kitchen, the cellar, the chest (*prov.*).

Gas'tr—isch, *adj.* gastric. **—ono'm,** *m.* (—ono'ms *or* —ono'men, *pl.* —ono'men) gourmet, epicure. **—onomie',** *f.* gastronomy. **—ono'=misch,** *adj.* epicurean; pertaining to the art *or* science of good eating, gastronomic.

Gat, Gatt, *n.* (—s, *pl.* —s & —en) hole; stern (*Naut.*).

Gä't—en, Jä't—en, *v.a.* to weed. **—er,** *m.* (—ers, *pl.* —er) weeder. *Comp.* **—hacke, —haue,** *f.* hoe.

Gät'lich, *adj. & adv.* (*dial.*) tolerable, middling; convenient; middle sized.

Gat't—e, *m.* (—en, *pl.* —en) spouse, husband; consort; mate. **—en,** *pl.* married people. **—in,** *f.* consort, spouse, wife; lady (*fam.*); mate (*of animals*). *Comp.* **—en=glück,** *n.* conjugal happiness. **—en=rechte,** *pl.* marital rights.

Gat't—en, *v.a.* to match, pair, couple, unite; to sort; **sich —en,** to pair, to unite. **—ung,** *f.* kind, class, sort; species, genus; race, breed; family (*of plants*); gender; style. **—ungs=begriff,** *m.* conception of a species; generic notion. **—ungs=charakter,** *m.* generic character. **—ungs=maler,** *m.* genre-painter. **—ungs=name,** *m.*, **—ungs=wort,** *n.* generic name, class name; noun appellative, common noun.

Gat'ter, *n.* (—s, *pl.* —) railing, grating, lattice; trellis; frame (*Paint.*). *Comp.* **—stäbe,** *pl.* bars of a grating. **—ständer,** *m.*, **—säule,** *f.* frame in which the saw is fixed (*in sawmills*). **—thor,** *m.*, **—thür,** *f.* swing gate, grated door; spar-gate (*Fort.*). **—werk,** *n.* lattice work.

Gattie'ren, *v.a.* to classify, sort; to mix.

Gau, *m.* (*& n.*) (—es, *pl.* —e) district; province; country (*as opp. to city*); tract, stretch (*of country*). *Comp.* **—dieb,** *m.* thievish vagabond; cunning thief. **—ding** (*obs.*), **—gericht,** *n.* petty sessions. **—genossenschaft,** *f.* all the inhabitants of the district; association of men of the district. **—graf,** *m.* lieutenant of a county. **—grafschaft,** *f.* shire, county.

Gauch, *m.* (—es, *pl.* —e & Gäu'che) cuckoo (*obs.*); fool, simpleton, gawk; cuckold; oddity, odd fish. *Comp.* **—bart,** *m.*, **—haar,** *n.* first down of a beard. **—hafer,** *m.* wild oats (*Bot.*).

Gaudie'ren, *v.n.* to rejoice (*dial.*).

Gau'kel, *m.* (*pl.* —en), **—ei',** *f.* (*pl.* —ei'en) legerdemain, juggling; quick movement; trick, illusion, imposture. **—er,** *m. see* Gaukler. **—haft, —icht** (*obs.*), **—ig,** *adj. & adv.* buffoon-like; juggling; delusive. *Comp.* **—becher,** *m.* juggler's cup. **—bild,** *n.* illusion, phantasm. **—licht,** *n.* will-o'-the-wisp. **—mann,** *m.*, **—männchen,** *n.* puppet. **—possen,** *pl.* juggling tricks. **—spiegel,** *m.* magic mirror, mirror for practising optical deceptions. **—spiel, —werk,** *n.* juggling, trick; illusion. **—spielerei,** *f.* juggling; optical deception. **—sprung,** *m.* caper, antic. **—tasche,** *f.* juggler's bag.

Gau'keln, *v.* I. *n.* (*aux.* h.) to flutter about; to produce illusions; to juggle, play tricks. II. *a.* to deceive; to get by juggling; **sich in Illusionen —,** to delude oneself with foolish hopes.

Gauk'ler, *m.* (—s, *pl.* —) buffoon; juggler, conjurer; dancer, tumbler: charlatan; impostor; African eagle; dungbeetle. **—ei',** *f.* jugglery. **—haft, —isch,** *see* Gaukelhaft. **—in,** *f.* female conjurer. *Comp.* **—blume,** *f.* maiden-wort.

Gaul, *m.* (—(e)s, *pl.* Gäu'le) horse, nag; **elender —,** (miserable) jade; **tüchtiger —,** strong saddle-horse; **einem geschenkten — sieht man nicht ins Maul,** never look a gift horse in the mouth; a gift must not be examined too minutely; beggars must not be choosers (*prov.*).

Gaum, *m.* (—es, *pl.* —e) (*obs. & poet.*), **—en,** *m.* (—ens, *pl.* —en) palate, roof of the mouth; taste; **der harte —en,** the hard palate; **der weiche —en,** the soft palate, the velum. *Comp.* **—en=laut,** *m.* palatal (sound); **vorderer —enlaut,** palatal (*Phonet.*); **hinterer —enlaut,** guttural (*Phonet.*). **—en=reiz,** *m.* tickling of the palate. **—en=segel,** *n.* velum, soft palate.

Gau'ner, *m.* (—s, *pl.* —) rogue, sharper, swindler; cheat. **—ei',** *f.* swindling, knavery, imposture. **—isch,** *adj. & adv.* swindling, cheating; thievish. **—tum,** *n.* body of sharpers, blackguardism. *Comp.* **—bande,** *f.* gang of swindlers, set of sharpers. **—herberge,** *f.* rookery of thieves. **—sprache,** *f.* thieves' Latin *or* slang, cant. **—streich,** *m.* rascally trick, sharper's trick. **—welt,** *f.* criminal world, race *or* crew of sharpers.

Gau'nern, *v.n.* (*aux.* h.) to swindle, cheat, trick, sharp; to lead a sharper's life.

Gau'p—e, *f.* (*pl.* —en), (**—loch,** *n.*), dormer-window.

Gaut'sche, *f.* (*pl.* —n) swing. **—n,** *v.a.* to couch (*Pap.*); to receive into the corps of printers by a kind of baptism, to initiate. **—r,** *m.* (—rs, *pl.* —r) workman who lays the sheets on the pressing-board (*Pap.*).

Ga'ze, *f.* (*pl.* —n) gauze; **feine —,** gossamer.

Gazel'le, *f.* (*pl.* —n) gazelle.

Ge—, *an unaccented prefix, is used especially to form:* (1) Collective nouns *derived from substantives, nearly all of the neuter gender, the root vowel of the substantives being, if possible, modified*; *e.g.* **Gestein, Gefild(e), Gewässer, Gewölk, Gebüsch, Gesträuch.** (2) Verbal nouns *denoting repetition or continuation of the action of the verb, all of the neuter gender and without plural; e.g.* **Gebalge, Geheul, Gerede, Gewirrsel, Geseufze, Gestöhne.** (3) Past participles; *e.g.* **geachtet,** (esteemed) *fr.* **achten, geächtet,** (outlawed) *fr.* **ächten, geboren** (born) *fr.* **gebären.** *In words beginning with a vowel the glottal stop should be made after the* **ge—.** *In older German a number of past participles were formed without the prefix* **ge—,** *and some of these forms survive in poetry or popular and dialectic phrases:* **kommen, gangen, bissen.** *See also* **worden.** *For any words not given in the following lists see the simple words.*

Gea'cht, *adj.*; **der —e Schein,** octile (*Astr.*).

Geäch'tete(r), *m.* outlaw, proscript.

Geäch'ze, *n.* (—s) continual groaning.

Geä'der, *n.* (—s) veins, the venous system; vein-like ornaments; marbling. **—t, Gea'dert,** *adj.* veined, veiny; grained.

Geäf'ter, *n.* (—s) deer's track, dew claws; hind claw.

Geai'cht, *p.p. & adj. see* **Eichen** (*formerly spelt* **Aichen**); **auf eine S. — sein,** to understand a matter thoroughly; **darauf bin ich —,** in this matter I am an expert (*coll.*).

Gear'tet, *suff.* (*in comp.* =) natured, disposed, formed, conditioned.

Geä'se, Geä'ß, *n.* deer's mouth; food, feeding of deer; grazing, pasture; lure for a hawk.

Geb., *short for* **geboren, geborene, Geborener; Frau Anna Müller, geb.** (= **geborene**) **Schulze,** Mrs. Müller, née Schulze; *see* **Geboren.**

Gebä'ck, *n.* (—es, *pl.* —e) baking; batch; pastr

Geba'ckene(s), *n.* anything baked; pastry: fritters.
Gebal'ge, *n.* (—s) tussle, scuffle.
Gebä'lk, *n.* (—es) beams of a building, timber-work; entablature of a column. *Comp.* —**träger,** *m.* atlas, telamon (*Arch.*).
Geba'r, Gebä're, *impf. ind. & subj. of* **gebären.**
Gebär'den, *see* **Geberden.**
Geba'ren, Gebah'ren, I. *v.r.* to seem, appear; to conduct oneself. II. *subst. n.* conduct.
Gebä'r—en, I. *ir.v.a.* to bring forth, produce; to give birth to; **geboren haben (ein Kind),** to be delivered (of a child); **geboren werden,** to be born; **zur Unzeit —en,** to miscarry. II. *subst. n.* parturition; child-bearing. —**end,** *p. & adj.* procreative; **eine —ende Frau,** a woman in labour *or* travail; **lebendige Junge —end,** viviparous. —**erin,** *f.* woman in labour, mother. *Comp.* —**anstalt,** *f.,* —**haus,** *n.* lying-in-hospital. —**mutter,** *f.* womb, uterus. —**mutter=schnitt,** *m.* hysterotomy, Cæsarian section. —**zeit,** *f.* time of delivery.
Gebäu'de, *n.* (—s, *pl.* —) building, edifice; **Lehr —,** system. —**steuer,** *f.* inhabited house duty. (*Also, poetic,* **Gebäu.**)
Ge'be, Gä'be, *adj. & adv.* acceptable; in vogue, customary; current, *see* **Gäbe.**
Ge'ben, I. *v.* I. *ir.a.* to give; to present; to confer, bestow; to yield, furnish, produce; to render; to translate; to grant; to deal; to play, act; to show, express; to prove; to lead to; **Acht —,** to pay attention, give heed; **sich** (*dat.*) **ein Ansehen —,** to give oneself airs; **sich** (*dat.*) **das Ansehen —,** to assume the appearance of; **Befehl —,** to order; **Beifall —,** to approve (of), to applaud; **ein Beispiel —,** to set an example; **Bescheid —,** to (tell in) answer; **von etwas Bescheid —,** to inform, bring word of; **Bewegung —,** to impart motion to; **sich** (*dat.*) **die Ehre —,** to do oneself the honour; **Fersengeld —,** to run away (*coll.*); **frei —,** to set at liberty; to give a holiday to; **der Direktor will uns den Nachmittag frei —,** the head-master is going to give us a half holiday; **Gewinn —,** to yield profit, turn out well; **ein Spiel verloren —,** to own that a game is lost, throw up the game; **sich verloren —,** to give o.s. up as lost; **Hitze —,** to throw out heat; **einem das Jawort —,** to accept a man's offer of marriage, to consent to marry a man; **einem vierzig Jahre —,** to take one to be 40 years old; **Karten —,** to deal; **wer muß —, an wem ist das —?** whose deal is it? **falsch —,** to mis-deal; **kund —,** to announce, notify; **es kurz —,** to express in few words, to cut it short; **einem Zimmer Luft —,** to air a room; **sich** (*dat.*) **Mühe —,** to take pains, to endeavour; **Nachricht —,** to send word; **einem Recht —,** to own that a p. is right; **einem das Recht zu einer S. —,** to empower s.o.; **einem gewonnen Spiel —,** to acknowledge that another person has won the game, to throw up one's hand; **dem Pferde die Sporen —,** to set spurs to one's horse; **einem Schuld —,** to impute blame to, accuse; **verloren —,** to look upon as lost; **das gibt die gesunde Vernunft,** common sense teaches that; **sein Wort (auf eine S.) —,** to pledge one's word; **gute Worte —,** to beg, entreat, ask for pardon; to speak (**einem,** one) fair; **die Zeit wird es —,** time will show; **Zeugnis —,** to bear witness; **ans Licht, an den Tag —,** to bring to light, to publish; **etwas an die Hand —,** to give the right of preëmption; **einem etwas an die Hand —,** to suggest s.th. to s.o.; **sein Leben an etwas —,** to stake one's life on something; **auf die Post —,** to post; **auf Zinsen —,** to put out at interest; **sich zufrieden — (mit),** to acquiesce **(in); auf eine Sache etwas —,** to set value on a thing; **nichts auf eine S. —,** to think nothing of a th.; **wenig — auf,** to set little value on; **darauf ist nichts zu —,** that is of no importance whatever; **in Pension —,** to place at a boarding school; to put to board; **ich habe mich bei Herrn Doktor Schultz in Pension gegeben,** I have arranged to have board and lodging with Dr. Schultz; **in die Lehre —,** to apprentice; **von sich —,** to emit (*a smell, a sound, etc.*), to vomit, to utter; **Gott gebe!** God grant; **gegeben zu London,** given, written at London (*at foot of documents*); **er gab den Faust,** he performed the part of Faust; **was wird heute abend gegeben?** what play will be acted to-night? **gegebener Fall,** case put; **gegebenen Falls,** in the case of emergency, if occasion should arise; **das Gegebene,** known quantity (*Math.*), given fact. II. *r.* to yield, give in; to surrender; to prove oneself to be; to abate; to relent; **Mädchen und Burgen müssen sich —,** maidens and towns (castles) must surrender; **sich gefangen —,** to surrender; **sich zufrieden —,** to put up with, submit to, be content with, to be quiet, compose oneself; **sich** (*acc.*) **bloß** *or* **preis —,** to lay oneself open, expose oneself to; **einen** *or* **eine S. preis —,** to give up, sacrifice a p. *or* a th.; **sich kund —,** to make oneself known; **Erstaunen gab sich in aller Mienen kund,** surprise was expressed on every countenance; **das gibt sich** that will pass by, that will get better, that will not last long; **der Schmerz hat sich gegeben,** the pain has abated; **der Eifer wird sich —.** the zeal will cool; **das Tuch gibt sich,** the cloth stretches. III. *a. imp.;* **es gibt,** there is, there are; **was gibt's?** what is the matter? **was gibt's Neues?** what's the news? **gibt's etwas Schöneres?** what is more beautiful? **es wird sich schon —,** it will follow in due course; **der größte Prahler, den es gibt,** the greatest braggart living; **es gibt einen guten Grund dafür,** there is a good reason for that; **es gibt sich von selbst,** it is a matter of course; **es gibt nichts Derartiges,** there is nothing of the kind; **es gibt Fälle,** there are cases; **es gab einen Zank,** a quarrel arose; **es gibt heute noch Regen,** there will be rain to-day. II. *subst.n.* giving; **das — hat kein Ende bei ihr,** she is never done giving; **am — sein,** to have the deal (*Cards*); **— ist seliger denn Nehmen,** it is more blessed to give than to receive (*prov.*). **Geber,** *m.* (—ers, *pl.* —er), **Geberin,** *f.* giver, dispenser, donor. *Comp.* **Gebe=fall,** *m.* dative case.
Gebei'n, *n.* (—s, *pl.* —e) bones (*coll.*); frame, skeleton; *pl.* corpse, remains; limbs.
Gebel'fer, *n.* (—s) continual yelping *or* barking.
Gebe'll, *n.* (—s) continual barking, baying; clamour, bawling, howling.
Geber'de, *f.* (*pl.* —n) air, bearing; gesture; gesticulation; mien; countenance; **Christus ward an —n als ein Mensch erfunden,** Christ was made in the likeness of man, was found in fashion like a man (*B.*). *Comp.* —**n=kunde,** *f.* mimicry. —**n=spiel,** *n.* pantomime, dumb show; play of features *or* of countenance, action (*Theat.*); gesticulation, dumb action. —**n=spieler,** *m.* mimic; actor in a pantomime. —**n=sprache,** *f.* language of gesture, conversation by gestures.
Geber'd—en, *v.r.* to deport oneself; to behave; **sich —en als ob,** to do as if. —**ig,** *adj. & adv.* of a good bearing *or* countenance, mannerly. —**ung,** *f.* bearing; behaviour; gesticulation.
Gebe't, *n.* (—es, *pl.* —e) prayer; **das — des Herrn,** the Lord's prayer; **sein — verrichten,** to say one's prayers; **sein Tisch— sprechen,** to say grace; **ein — sprechen,** to offer prayers

ins — nehmen, to examine, question closely (*coll.*). *Comp.* **—buch,** *n.* prayer-book, Book of Common Prayer; breviary, mass-book (*R. C.*). **—formel,** *f.* form of prayer. **—riemen,** *m.*, **—schnur,** *f.* phylactery.
Gebe'ten, *p.p. of* **bitten.**
Gebet'tel, *n.* (—s) importunity, continual begging.
Gebie'rst, Gebie'rt; Gebie'r, *2. & 3. ps. sing. pres. ind.; imperative of* **gebären.**
Gebie't, *n.* (—(e)s, *pl.* —e) jurisdiction; district; province; sphere; department; **das — der Beredsamkeit,** the province of eloquence; **das — der Gelehrsamkeit,** the domain of learning; **auf deutschem —,** on German ground.
Gebie't—en, *ir.v.a.* (**einem etwas**) to command, order, bid; to lay down the law; to govern, to rule; **Stillschweigen —en,** to impose silence; **die Freundschaft —et,** friendship demands. **—end,** *p. & adj.* commanding; imperious; **die —ende Art,** the imperative mood; **die —ende Stunde,** the impulse of the hour. **—er,** *m.* (—ers, *pl.* —er) lord; master, commander. **—erin,** *f.* mistress. **—erisch,** *adj.* domineering; dictatorial; peremptory, imperative, imperious; **—erisch sein,** to domineer, to have imperious ways, to play the master.
Gebil'de, *n.* (—s, *pl.* —) thing formed *or* built; creation; creature; structure; image; pattern (*Weav.*); form.
Gebil'det, *p.p. & adj.* shaped; educated, accomplished; well-bred; refined; **die —en,** the cultured *or* educated classes; **—er Mann,** a gentleman, a well-brought-up man, a man of education *or* culture.
Gebim'mel, *n.* ringing *or* tinkling of the bells (*coll.*).
Gebin'de, *n.* (—s, *pl.* —) bundle; bond, joining; a row of tiles; skein; cask.
Gebi'rg, *n.* (—es, *pl.* —e), **—e,** *n.* (—es, *pl.* —e) mountain; mountain-chain; highland; rock, species of soil. **—ig,** *adj. & adv.* mountainous. **—isch,** *adj. & adv.* living *or* situated in the mountains (*rare*). *Comp.* **—s=art,** *f.* species of stone *or* rock. **—s=äste, —s=arme,** *pl.* spurs of a mountain. **—s=bewohner,** *m.* mountaineer, highlander. **—s=ebene,** *f.* highland plain. **—s=kamm, —s=rücken,** *m.* mountain ridge. **—s=land,** *n.* hilly country. **—s=stock,** *m.* centre and highest part of a mountain-chain. **—s=volk,** *n.* mountain tribe, highlanders. **—s=zug,** *m.* mountain chain.
Gebis'sen, *p.p. of* **beißen.**
Gebi'ß, *n.* (—(ss)es, *pl.* —(ss)e) set of teeth; bridle-bit; **ein künstliches —,** a set of artificial teeth; **einem Pferde ein — anlegen,** to put a bit on a horse. *Comp.* **—kette,** *f.* curb.
Gebla'se, *n.* trumpeting, blowing.
Geblä'se, *n.* blast-engine; forge bellows; blowpipe (*Chem.*); **das — anlassen,** to set the bellows going. *Comp.* **—luft,** *f.* blast from the bellows. **—werk,** *n.* blast-apparatus.
Gebli'chen, *p.p. of* **bleichen.**
Geblie'ben, *p.p. of* **bleiben.**
Geblie'bene(n), *pl.* the killed (*in battle*).
Geblö'k, *n.* (—es, *pl.* —e) bleating, bellowing.
Geblü'mt, *adj.* flowered; figured; flowery.
Geblu'te, *n.* (—s) continued bleeding.
Geblü't, *n.* (—es) blood, mass of blood; line, race, family; consanguinity; **es steckt im —,** it runs in the family; **Prinz von —,** prince of the blood.
Gebo'gen, *p.p. of* **biegen;** *adj.* bent, curved; hooked; arched; vaulted; **eine —e Nase,** an aquiline nose, a Roman nose.
Gebo'ren, *p.p. of* **gebären;** *adj.* (*abbreviated* **geb.**) born; by birth, naive; **unehelich —,** base-born; **tot —,** still-born, illegitimate; **ein —er Deutscher,** a native of Germany, a German by birth; **ein —er Dichter, Maler, etc.,** a born poet, artist, *etc.;* **sie ist eine —e N.,** she was a Miss N.; **was für eine —e ist sie?** what was her maiden name? **Frau Professor Schiller, geb. v. Lengefeld,** Mrs. Schiller, late *or* née Fräulein von Lengefeld.
Gebor'gen, *p.p. of* **bergen; — sein,** to be in safety, out of danger. **—heit,** *f.* (*place of*) security.
Gebor'sten, *p.p. of* **bersten.**
Gebo't, *n.* (—es, *pl.* —e) command; commandment, precept; order; bid, offer; **einem zu —e stehen,** to be at one's disposal; **die zehn —e,** the ten commandments; **das vierte —** the fourth commandment (*the German fourth corresponds to the English fifth, the German ninth and tenth together to the English tenth*); **diese Mittel stehen mir nicht zu —e,** these means are not within my reach; **Not kennt kein —,** necessity has no law (*Prov.*); **ein — thun,** to make an offer; **das erste — thun,** to start a price, give the first bid.
Gebo'ten, *p.p. of* **bieten** and **gebieten.**
Gebra'cht, *p.p. of* **bringen.**
Gebrä'me, *n.* (—s) border, edging; skirts (*B.*).
Gebra'nnt, *p.p. of* **brennen; —es Kind scheut das Feuer,** a burnt child dreads the fire; once bit, twice shy (*Prov.*).
Gebräu', *n.* (—s, *pl.* —e) brewing; what is brewed; mixture (*fig.*).
Gebrau'ch, *m.* (—s, *pl.* **Gebräu'che**) employment, use; disposal; usage, custom; way, manner; practice, fashion; wear; rite, ceremony; **von einer S. — machen,** to make use of a th.; **ein alter —,** an ancient (well established) custom; **wie es der — mit sich bringt,** according to custom; **es ist nicht mehr der —, daß,** it is no longer customary to: **falscher —,** improper use *or* application, abuse (*of words, etc.*); **zum —e,** for the use (*of*); **zum eigenen —,** for my personal use; **erster —,** handsel; **außer — kommen,** to go out of use, to fall into disuse. *Comp.* **—s=anweisung,** *f.* directions for use. **—s=zettel,** *m.* label with directions for use.
Gebrau'ch—en, *v.a.* to use, make use of; to need, want; **dies ist zu nichts zu —en,** this is of no use (whatever); **sich —en lassen zu,** to lend oneself to, be instrumental *or* subservient to; **—en Sie mein Wörterbuch noch?** do you still require my dictionary? **Arznei —en,** to take medicine; **ich —e dazu mehrere Tage,** I (shall) want several days for this; **—t der Zeit!** make (good) use of the time! (*the use of the gen. is obs. & poet.*); **—te Sachen,** second-hand articles; worn garments.
Gebräuch'lich, *adj. & adv.* usual, customary; current; **die —e Orthographie,** the current spelling; **nicht mehr —,** no longer used, obsolete; **— sein,** to be in use. **—keit,** *f.* usualness, customariness, commonness, frequency.
Gebrau's, —(s)e, *n.* (—(s)es) roaring; singing, ringing.
Gebre'che, *n.* (—s) continued vomiting; continued breaking; pig's snout; rooting place of wild boars; rotten-stone.
Gebre'chen, I. *ir.v.n.imp.* (*dat.*) to lack, be wanting, fail; **es soll Ihnen an nichts —,** you shall want for nothing; **es gebricht ihm an (ihm gebricht) Geld,** he is short of money. II. *subst.n.* infirmity; want, need; defect; frailty.
Gebrech'lich, *adj.* defective; invalided: infirm; crazy; frail; sickly. **—lichkeit,** *f.* infirmity; frailty.
Gebrei'te, *n.* (—s) plain; open field.
Gebres'te, *n.* (—s, *pl.* —n) defect, infirmity; disease, illness.
Gebres'ten, I. *v.n.* to be wanting, defective (*obs.*). II. *subst. n.* **das —,** the want, bodily defect, disease, malady, illness.

Gebro'chen, *p.p.* of **brechen.** **—heit,** *f.* broken condition; exhaustion; **die —heit seiner Stimme ist . . .,** his broken voice is . . .

Gebrö'ckel, *n.* (—s) gratings; constant crumbling; **Fels—,** scree.

Gebro'del, *n.* (—s) bubbling up, boiling.

Gebrü'der (*abbr.* **Gbr.**) *pl.* brothers; **— Mappin,** Mappin Brothers (*abbrev. Bros.*); **die — Grimm,** the brothers Grimm.

Gebrü'll, *n.* (—es) roaring.

Gebrum'me, *n.* (—s) murmuring, growling, humming; grumbling, growls.

Gebü'hr, *f.* (*pl.* —en) duty; propriety, seemliness; due; office; fee, money due; moderation; (*pl.*) fees, wages, salary, taxes, expenses, payment, emolument; tax; **seine — leisten,** to do one's duty; **nach —,** according to merit; **nach Standes—,** according to rank; **über —,** to excess, more than one's due, immoderately; **—en (an die Obrigkeit),** dues, rates and taxes. *Comp.* **—en=frei,** *adj.* free of charge, free of taxes.

Gebü'hr—en, *v.* I. *n.* (*aux.* **h.**) to be due, belong of right to; to appertain to; **Ehre, dem Ehre —(e)t,** honour to whom honour is due; **Dir —(e)t die Majestät und Gewalt,** thine is the majesty and the power; **es —t dir,** it is due to you; it is your duty. II. *r. & imp.* to be fit, proper, becoming; **wie sich's —t,** as it ought to be, in a becoming manner, properly. **—end,** *p. & adj.* due, fit, meet, befitting; **Ihre Tratte soll —enden Schutz finden,** your draft shall be duly honoured; **—endermaßen,** duly, in a fitting manner. **—lich,** *adj. & adv.* fitting, suitable, proper; decent; becoming. **—lichkeit,** *f.* fitness, propriety.

Gebu'nd, *n.* (—es, *pl.* **Gebün'de**) truss, bundle, bunch, hank, skein, *etc.*

Gebun'den, *p.p. of* **binden**; *adj.* bound, obliged; metrical; *see* **Binden**; **—e Wärme,** latent heat; **—e Noten,** sustained notes (*Mus.*); **—e Rede,** language bound (*or* regulated) by a certain rhythm; metre, versification, poetry. **—heit,** *f.* constraint; subjection; **—heit der Auffassung,** narrowness of conception.

Gebür'tig, *adj. & adv.* native (of, **aus**), born in.

Gebu'rt, *f.* (*pl.* —en) labour; delivery; birth; production; thing born; origin; family; extraction; **unzeitige —,** abortion; **von —,** by birth; of good birth; **vor Christi —,** before Christ, B.C.; **in der — sterben,** to die in child-bed; **in der — bleiben,** to die immediately after birth; **die — abtreiben,** to bring about a miscarriage; **von (seiner) — an,** from his birth. *Comp.* **—s=anzeige,** *f.* notification of a birth. **—s=arbeit,** *f.* labour. **—s=brief, —s=schein,** *m.* certificate of birth. **—s=fehler,** *m.* natural defect. **—s=feier,** *f.*, **—s=fest,** *n.* celebration of a birthday. **—s=haus,** *n.* house where a p. was born. **—s=helfer,** *m.* accoucheur. **—s=helferin,** *f.* midwife. **—s=hülfe,** *f.* midwifery. **—s=jahr,** *n.* year of birth. **—s=land,** *n.* native land. **—s=lehre,** *f.* obstetrics. **—s=liste,** *f.*, **—s=register,** *n.* register of births. **—s=mal,** *n.* mole. **—s=ort,** *m.* native place. **—s=recht,** *n.* birthright. **—s=schmerzen, —s=wehen,** *pl.* labour-pains. **—s=stadt,** *f.* native town. **—s=stolz,** *m.* pride of birth. **—s=tag,** *m.* birthday; **einem zum —stag Glück wünschen,** to wish a p. many happy returns of the day; **zu deinem —stage, lieber Fritz, wünsche ich dir von Herzen Glück,** my dear Fred, on the occasion of your birthday I heartily wish you many happy returns of the day. **—s=tags=kind,** *n.* person whose birthday is celebrated. **—s=zange,** *f.* forceps.

Gebü'sch, *n.* (—es, *pl.* —e) cluster of bushes, bush, shrubs, thicket, underwood; copse; **mit — bewachsen,** bushy.

Gebü'schelt, *adj. & adv.* tufted; bushy, fascicled.

Geck, *m.* (—en, *pl.* —en) silly person, fool, fop, coxcomb; **einem den —en stechen,** to sneer, scoff, laugh at a p.; **den —(en) mit etwas treiben,** to ridicule a th. **—enhaft,** *adj.* foolish, foppish. **—enhaftigkeit,** *f.* folly; foppery, foppishness. *Comp.* **—stock,** *m.* (pump) handle.

Ge'cken, *v.* I. *a.* to banter; to make a fool of. II. *n.* to play the fool *or* fop.

Geda'cht, (*p.p.* of **denken, gedenken; der —e Herr,** the aforesaid gentleman; **die —e Zahl,** the number imagined and borne in mind.

Gedächt'nis, *n.* (—(ss)es, *pl.* —(ss)e) memory; remembrance; memorial, monument; **ein starkes, treues —,** a retentive memory; **ein schlechtes, kurzes —,** a bad, short memory; **aus dem — hersagen,** to recite by heart; **ein — stiften,** to erect a monument; **zum — an,** (*acc.*) in remembrance *or* commemoration of; **es ist meinem — entfallen,** it escaped my memory; **ins — zurückrufen,** to call to mind. *Comp.* **—buch,** *n.* memorandum book. **—fehler,** *m.* slip of the memory. **—feier,** *f.* commemoration; **(kirchliche)** memorial service. **—kunst,** *f.* mnemonics. **—mal,** *n.* monument; souvenir; token of remembrance. **—münze,** *f.* commemorative medal. **—rede,** *f.* speech in memory of a p. **—säule,** *f.* monument. **—tafel,** *f.* monumental tablet. **—tag,** *m.* anniversary, commemoration day. **—übung,** *f.* exercise for strengthening the memory. **—zeichen,** *n.* keepsake, souvenir.

Gedan'ke, *m.* (—ns, *pl.* —n) thought, idea; opinion; design, purpose; care, concern; sketch (*Draw.*); meditation; **willst du es thun? Kein —!** will you do it? I do not think of it! (*coll.*); **da fällt mir ein — ein,** a thought occurs to my mind; **seine —n nicht beisammen haben,** to be absent-minded, inattentive; **seine —n zusammen nehmen,** to collect one's thoughts; **das bringt mich fast auf den —n,** that makes me almost suppose; **sich** (*dat.*) **etwas aus den —n schlagen,** to banish a thing from one's mind; **mit dem —n umgehen zu reisen, zu heiraten,** to be thinking of travelling, of marrying; **in —n vertieft,** absorbed in thought; **—en sind zollfrei,** opinions are free; **in —n sah sie sich,** in fancy she saw herself (*a queen, etc.*); **in —n beiwohnen,** to be present in spirit; **sich** (*dat.*) **—n über eine S. machen,** to be uneasy about a th.; **sich** (*dat.*) **—n auf eine S. machen,** to nurse the idea of obtaining something; **einen auf andere —n bringen,** to divert a man's thoughts; to make a p. alter his mind; **seinen —n nachhängen,** to muse; **sich in die —n geben über eine S.,** to meditate, reflect on a subject. *Comp.* **—n=austausch,** *m.* exchange of thoughts, interchange of ideas, communication. **—n=dieb,** *m.* plagiarist. **—n=folge,** *f.* train of thought. **—n=kreis,** *m.* range of ideas. **—n=gang, —n=lauf,** *m.* train, order of thoughts. **—n=leer,** *adj.* void of ideas. **—n=lesen,** *n.* thought-reading. **—n=los,** *adj.* thoughtless. **—n=losigkeit,** *f.* thoughtlessness. **—n=raub,** *m.* plagiarism. **—n=reich,** *adj.* fertile in ideas. **—n=reichtum,** *m.* fertility of the mind. **—n=schnell,** *adj. & adv.* quick as thought. **—n=späne,** *pl.* detached thoughts; aphorisms. **—n=splitter,** *pl. m.* flashes of thought, aphorisms, aperçus. **—n=stille,** *f.* pensiveness. **—n=strich,** *m.* dash. **—n=voll,** *adj.* thoughtful, pensive; deep in thought. **—n=vorbehalt,** *m.* mental reservation. **—n=welt,** *f.* ideal world; range of ideas.

Gedä'rm, *n.* (—(e)s, *pl.* —e) entrails, bowels. *Comp.* **—vorfall,** *m.* prolapsus (*of the intestines*).

Gedäu'cht, *p.p. of* **dünken.**
Gede'ck, *n.* (—**es,** *pl.* —**e**) covering; cover; set of table linen; knife and fork (*coll.*); set of covered pipes in an organ; roof; — **für zwanzig Personen,** table-cloth linen to dine twenty persons; **Hoftafel zu achtzig —en,** dinner table at court spread for eighty persons.
Gedei'h—en, I. *ir.v.n.* (*aux.* **s.**) to increase; to thrive, get on well; to grow; to prosper, succeed; to redound to; to tend, turn out to; to do good to; **er ißt viel, aber es —t ihm nicht,** he eats a great deal, but it does him no good; **schwere Speisen —en mir nicht,** heavy food does not agree with me; **Unrecht Gut —t nicht,** ill-got, ill-spent (*prov.*); **die Sache ist nun dahin gediehen, daß,** the affair is now come to such a point that. II. *subst.n.* thriving, prosperity, success; growth; advantage; **Gott gebe sein —en dazu!** may God grant his blessing on it! may God give it success. **—lich,** *adj. & adv.* prosperous; salutary, beneficial; favourable; nutritive.
Gede'nk, *adj. & adv.* thoughtful, mindful. **—bar,** *adj. & adv.* conceivable, imaginable.
Geden'k—en, *ir.v.* I. *n.* (*aux.* **h.**) (*with gen.* (*obs.*, and *in some popular phrases*) *and* (*ordinarily*) **an** *& accus.*), to bear in mind, remember; (*with gen.*) to make mention of; to mention; to intend, design, propose, plan; **—e mein, meiner!** remember me! think of me!; **ich habe oft an mein fernes Lieb gedacht,** I have often thought of my love who is so far away; **einer Sache nicht —en,** to pass over a thing in silence; **dessen nicht zu —en, daß . . . ,** not to mention that . . . ; **jemandes in Ehren —en,** to make honourable mention of someone; **ich habe seiner immer nur im Guten gedacht,** I have always spoken well of him. II. *a.* (**einem etwas**), to remember to the advantage (*or usually*) disadvantage of; **ich will es ihm schon —en,** I'll make him pay for it yet; **gedacht,** borne in mind, thought, mentioned, stated. III. *impers.* **es gedenkt mir, daß,** methinks *or* it seems to me that (*obs.*); **mich denkt des Ausdrucks noch,** I still remember the expression (*obs. & poet.*); **das —en,** memory; **zu Ihrem —en,** in memory of you; **seit Menschen —en,** within the memory of man, from time immemorial. *Comp.* **—buch,** *n.* memorandum-book; journal, album, day-book. **—spruch,** *m.* motto. **—tag,** *m.* commemoration day; anniversary. **—zettel,** *m.* memorandum; phylactery.
Gedi'cht, *n.* (—**es,** *pl.* —**e**) poem; fiction, fable. *Comp.* **—album,** *n.* lyrical album. **—form,** *f.*; **in —form,** in verse. **—(e)=sammlung,** *f.* a collection of poems, anthology (of lyrics).
Gedie'gen, *p.p., adj. & adv.* solid, massy; unmixed, pure; genuine, true; pithy; sterling; superior; splendid, funny (*coll.*); **—e Kenntnisse,** profound erudition; **—es Gold,** pure gold; **—er Witz,** a capital joke; **das ist —,** that's excellent, capital, that's funny (*coll.*). **—heit,** *f.* solidity; genuineness; sterling quality; purity; pithiness.
Gedie'h, Gedie'he; Gedie'hen, *3 p. sing. ind. & subj. imperf.; and p.p. of* **gedeihen.**
Gedin'ge, *n.* (—**s,** *pl.* —) love of bargaining; bargain, contract: **in — arbeiten,** to do job-work, to work by the job, to work by contract. *Comp.* **—arbeit,** *f.* job-work, contract-work. **—geld,** *n.*, **—preis,** *m.* contract price *or* wages. **—träger,** *m.* taker.
Gedon'ner, *n.* (—**s**) protracted thundering.
Gedop'pelt, *p.p. & adj. & adv.* double.
Gedra'ng, *adj.* narrow, (*rare*) strait.
Gedrän'g—e, *n.* (—**es**) crowding; crowd, press, throng; need, distress; difficulty; dilemma; **ins —e geraten,** to get into a scrape *or* embarrassment: to get into a crowd; **es ist viel —e danach,** it is greatly run after. **—t,** *adj. & adv.* crowded, thronged; serried; compact; terse, concise. **—theit,** *f.* terseness.
Gedrei'(e)t, *adj.* ternate; trifoliate (*Bot.*).
Gedri'tt, *adj. & adv.* ternary, trinal; trine (*Astrol.*); formed of three; **—er Schein,** aspect of planets distant from one another 120°, trigon, trine (*Astrol.*).
Gedro'schen, *p.p.* of **dreschen.**
Gedruck'te(s), *n.* printed matter, printed papers, print.
Gedrun'gen, *p.p. of* **dringen;** *adj.* thickset: solid. **—heit,** *f.* compactness, closeness terseness.
Gedu'del, *n.* (—**s**) continual tooting *or* piping bad music (*on a wind instrument*).
Gedu'ld, *f.* patience, forbearance, endurance; **einen Augenblick —, wenn ich bitten darf,** just wait a moment, please; **jemandes — ermüden,** to wear out a p.'s patience; **endlich war meine — erschöpft, ging mir die — aus,** at last I lost all patience; **fasse dich in —!** possess your soul in patience! **er hat nirgends lange —,** he never stays long anywhere; **das Haus steht in der —,** the house is sheltered from the wind. **—ig,** *adj. & adv.* patient, forbearing.
Gedul'den, *v.r.* to have patience, wait patiently; (*with gen.*) to bear with (*obs.*).
Gedun'gen, *p.p. of* **dingen.**
Gedun'sen, *p.p. of obs.* **dinsen,** *adj.* bloated, puffed up; turgid.
Gedu'rft, *p.p. of* **dürfen.**
Gee'ckt, *adj. & adv.* angular, cornered.
Gee'hrt, *p.p. of* **ehren; —er Herr,** Sir; **Ihr —es vom 16 April,** your favour of April 16 (*C.L.*).
Geeig'net, *p.p. of* **eignen;** *adj. & adv.* fit, meet, suitable, appropriate; susceptible; capable (*of*)
Geest, *f.* **—land,** *n.* high, dry land.
Gefä'chel, *n.* (—**s**) continued fanning.
Gefa'hr, *f.* (*pl.* —**en**) danger, peril, risk; **große — laufen,** to run great risk; **der — trotzen,** to brave the danger; **auf die — hin ihn zu beleidigen,** at the risk of hurting his feelings; **in — bringen,** to endanger; **mit — seines Lebens,** at the risk of his life; **es hat keine —,** there is no danger; **es ist — im Verzuge,** delay is dangerous; **für Rechnung und — von,** for account and risk of. *Comp.* **—bringend,** *adj.* dangerous (**für,** for). **—los,** *adj.* safe, secure, without risk. **—losigkeit,** *f.* safety, security. **—voll,** *adj.* perilous, dangerous.
Gefähr'—de, *f.* (*pl.* —**den**) risk, danger; fraud, deceit; **ohne —de,** without any intention to cheat. **—den,** *v.a.* to endanger, imperil; to risk; to compromise; **ich bin dabei nicht —det,** I run no risk in the matter. **—lich,** *adj. & adv.* dangerous; hazardous; considerable; enormous; **etwas sehr —lich machen,** to represent s.th. as extremely dangerous; to exaggerate; **thun Sie doch nicht so —lich!** don't make such a fuss! (*coll.*). **—lichkeit,** *f.* dangerousness, danger; insecurity; perilous situation *Comp.* **—de=eid,** *m.* oath of integrity.
Gefah're, *n.* (—**es**) continual driving.
Gefä'hrt, *n.* (—**es,** *pl.* —**e**) vehicle, cart; **vierspänniges —,** coach and four (*in hand*).
Gefähr't—e, *m.* (—**en,** *pl.* —**en**), **—in,** *f.* travelling companion, comrade, fellow; consort, mate.
Gefä'll, *n.* (—**es,** *pl.* —**e**), **—e,** *n.* (—**es,** *pl.* —**e**) fall, drop (*of a river*); slope, descent; incline fallen trees; (*pl.*) income, revenue; taxes, dues, profit; **ein gutes — haben,** to drink like a fish (*coll.*); **die Mühle hat ein gutes —e,** the mill has a good head of water. *Comp.* **—holz,** *n.* felled wood; fallen trees. **—wechsel,** *m.* point where the gradient changes (*Railw.*). **—wesen,** *n.* (*state of the*) revenues.

Gefal'l—e, *m.* (—ens) *see* **—en. —en,** *m.* (—ens, *pl.* —en) pleasure; preference, choice; favour; kindness; **einem zu —en sprechen,** to seek to please one by flattery; **thun Sie es mir zu —en,** do it to please *or* oblige me, do it for my sake. *Comp.* **—sucht,** *f.* excessive desire to please; coquetry. **—süchtig,** *adj.* desirous to please; coquettish; **die —süchtige,** the coquette, flirt.

[1]**Gefal'len,** *ir.v.n.* (*aux.* **h.**, *dat.*) to suit, please; **wie es euch gefällt,** as you like it; **wie es Ihnen gefällt,** as you please; **es gefällt ihm,** he is pleased with it; **sich** (*dat.*) **etwas — lassen,** to put up with a thing; to be pleased with something; **das kann man sich noch allenfalls — lassen,** well, we 'll let that pass; that may do; **er läßt sich alles —,** he puts up with anything; **das lasse ich mir nicht —,** I will not stand that; **das lasse ich mir —,** that 's nice; **sich** (*dat.*) **einen Vorschlag — lassen,** to consent to a proposal; **sich** (*dat.*) **— in,** to flatter oneself with; to take pleasure in; **er gefiel sich in der Idee, daß . . .;** he hugged himself in the belief that. . . .

[2]**Gefal'len,** *p.p. of* **fallen; das Los ist —,** the die is cast, there is no going back. **—e(r),** *m.*, **—e,** *f.* fallen person; **die —en,** the dead (*Mil.*).

Gefäl'lig, *adj. & adv.* pleasing, agreeable; courteous, obliging; kind; complaisant; due, payable; **ist es Ihnen — zu?** would you like to? **was ist Ihnen —?** what would you like to have? what can I get you? I beg your pardon, did you speak? **Ihr —es Schreiben,** your favour; **Ihrer —en Antwort entgegensehend,** awaiting (the favour of) your reply. **—keit,** *f.* (*pl.* —keiten) pleasingness; complaisance, courtesy; obligingness; favour; (*pl.*) good offices; **bloß aus —keit für Sie,** only to oblige you, as a favour. **—st,** *adv.* if you please, I beg; **nehmen Sie —st Platz,** pray, be seated.

Gefä'llst, Gefä'llt, *2 & 3 p. sing. pres. ind. of* **gefallen.**

Gefäl't—el, *n.* (—els) gather, fold, pleats. **—et,** *p.p. & adj.* folded, pleated.

Gefan'gen, *p.p. & adj.* captured, caught; captive; imprisoned; **— nehmen,** to take prisoner, to captivate; **sich — geben,** to surrender as prisoner; **— halten,** to detain; **— setzen,** to imprison; **— sitzen,** to be in prison. **—e(r),** *m.* captive, prisoner. **—schaft,** *f.* captivity, imprisonment. *Comp.* **—haltung,** *f.* detention in custody, confinement. **—nehmung,** *f.* arrestation, seizure, imprisonment. **—wärter,** *m.* jailer.

Gefäng'—lich, *adj. & adv.* imprisoned, captive; **—lich einziehen,** to imprison; **—liche Haft,** imprisonment. **—nis,** *n.* (—ni(ss)es, *pl.* —ni(ss)e) prison, jail; **zu zweijährigem —nisse verurteilen,** to sentence to two years' imprisonment. *Comp.* **—nis=beschließer, —nis=wärter,** *m.* turnkey, jailer. **—nis=strafe,** *f.* (pain of) imprisonment. **—nis=wesen,** *n.* prison matters. **—nis=zucht,** *f.* prison discipline.

Gefa'sert, *p.p. & adj.* fibrous; **—es Papier,** granite paper.

Gefä'ß, *n.* (—es, *pl.* —e) vessel; handle; hilt; vase; receptacle; vessels (*coll.*). **—ig,** *adj. & adv.* vascular. *Comp.* **—bildung,** *f.* vascular structure. **—haut,** *f.* retina. **—lehre,** *f.* angiology. **—system,** *n.* vascular system.

Gefa'ßt, *p.p. & adj.* ready, prepared; composed, calm; written; **sich** (*acc.*) **auf eine S. — machen,** to be prepared for a th. **—heit,** *f.* composure, presence of mind.

Gefe'cht, *n.* (—es, *pl.* —e) fight, battle, combat; engagement, encounter; **das — abbrechen,** to cease firing. **—e,** *n.* (—es) constant fighting. *Comp.* **—s=bereitschaft,** *f.* readiness for a fight, fighting trim. **—s=formation.** *f.* order of battle, formation for an engagement. **—s=klar,** *adj.* clear for action (*nav.*). **—s=lehre,** *f.* tactics. **—s=schießen,** *n.* field firing-exercise. **—s=übung,** *f.* manœuvre, sham fight, field day.

Gefe'ge, *n.* (—s) continued sweeping *or* brushing; velvet, rub, fraying (*from stag's horns*).

Gefei't, *adj.* (**gegen**) charmed, proof against.

Gefes'selt, *p.p. & adj. see* **Fesseln;** (*in comp.* =) with fetlocks.

Gefie'del, *n.* (—s) continual fiddling, scraping.

Gefie'der, *n.* (—s) feathers, plumage; fowl; feathered tribe; springs of a lock *or* clock; **erstes flaumiges —,** down; **seltenes —,** odd fish, rara avis. **—t,** *p.p. & adj.* feathered; pinnate (*Bot.*).

Gefie'l, Gefie'le, *1 & 3 p. sg. impf. ind. & subj. of* **gefallen.**

Gefil'de, *n.* (—s) fields, open country; plain, region.

Gefla'cker, *n.* (—s), continual flickering.

Geflat'ter, *n.* (—s) continued fluttering.

Gefle'cht, *n.* (—es, *pl.* —e) braided work, wicker work; network; braids, tresses; plexus (*Anat.*).

Gefle'ckt, *p.p. & adj.* spotted, speckled, freckled maculose.

Geflen'ne, *n.* (—s) continued whining.

Gefli'cke, *n.* (—s) patchwork, botchery.

Geflie'ß, *n.* (—es) run, water-course, gully.

Geflim'mer, *n.* (—s) glittering; scintillation.

Geflis'sen, *adj. & adv.* diligent, industrious, assiduous; **— sein,** to take pains; **er ist — alles zu entdecken, was in der Familie vorgeht,** he makes it his business to discover whatever passes in the family. **—heit,** *f.* diligence, assiduity; endeavour. **—tlich,** I. *adj. & adv.* wilful, intentional, premeditated; on purpose. II. *adv.* with malice aforethought (*Law*).

Gefloch'ten, *p.p. of* **flechten.**

Geflo'gen, *p.p. of* **fliegen.**

Geflo'hen, *p.p. of* **fliehen.**

Geflos'sen, *p.p. of* **fließen.**

Geflü'gel, *n.* (—s) winged creatures; birds, poultry. **—t,** *p.p. & adj.* winged; **—tes Wort,** familiar quotation, household word. *Comp.* **—händler,** *m.*, poulterer. **—mäster,** *m.* poultry-feeder *or* crammer.

Geflun'ker, *n.* (—s) glittering; *see* **Aufschneiderei.**

Geflüs'ter, *n.* (—s) whisper, continued whispering.

Gefoch'ten, *p.p. of* **fechten.**

Gefol'g—e, *n.* (—es) train, attendance, suite, retinue; consequences; **im —e haben,** to be attended with. **—schaft,** *f.* followers, adherents; comitatus; clientship. **—s=mann,** *m.* follower, vassal, thane.

Gefra'ge, *n.* (—s) (*continual*) questioning; cross-questioning.

Gefra'gt, *p.p. of* **fragen;** in demand, sought after (*C.L.*); **wenig —,** easy (*C.L.*).

Gefran's(e)t, *p.p. & adj.* fringed.

Gefrä'ßig, *adj. & adv.* voracious, greedy. **—keit,** *f.* voracity, gluttony, greediness.

Gefrei'te(r), *m.* soldier between the ordinary private and the lowest non-commissioned officer, lance corporal (*exempt from mounting guard*).

Gefrier'—bar, *adj.* congealable. **—en,** *ir.v.n.* (*aux.* **s.**) to freeze, congeal. **Gefrorene(s),** *n.* ice, ices, ice cream. *Comp.* **—punkt,** *m.* freezing-point; **das Thermometer steht auf dem — punkt,** the thermometer is down to zero.

Gefro'ren, *p.p. of* **frie'ren.**

Gefü'g—e, I. *n.* (—es) joining, fitting together; structure; layer, stratum; grooves, joints; texture. II. **—ig,** *adj. & adv.* pliant; adaptable, tractable, docile; accommodating. **—igkeit,** *f.* pliancy, yielding disposition.

Gefü'hl, *n.* (—s, *pl.* —e) feeling, touch, sense of feeling; sensation; state of mind: sentiment, apprehension; consciousness. *Comp.* **—los,** *adj. & adv.* unfeeling, hard; apathetic; **—los gegen,** insensible to. **—losigkeit,** *f.* heartlessness, unfeelingness; apathy. **—s=art,** *f.* disposition. **—s=mensch,** *m.* emotional character; sentimentalist. **—voll,** *adj. & adv.* feeling; full of expression; tender; affectionate; sentimental; sensitive.

Gefü'llt, *p.p.& adj.* filled; double (*Bot.*).

Gefun'den, *p.p. of* **finden.**

Gefü'nft, *adj. & adv.* quinary, formed of five; **—er Schein,** quintile.

Gefun'kel, *n.* (**—s**) glittering.

Gefu'rcht, *adj.* sulcate.

Gega'cker, *n.* (**—s**) cackle, cackling (*of geese*).

Gegan'gen, *p.p. of* **gehen.**

Gegei'ge, *n.* (**—s**) fiddling.

Ge'gen, I. *prep.* (*with acc.; in older German with dat.*) towards, to, in the direction of; about, somewhere near; against, opposed to; over against; opposite to; compared with; in presence of; before; in exchange, in return for; for, to; **— den Strom,** against the current; **— die Vernunft,** contrary to reason; **— das Abkommen,** contrary to the agreement; **— einander,** opposite; mutually, reciprocally; **— einander stellen,** to compare (*people, things*), to confront (*one person with another*); **—bare Bezahlung,** for ready money, for cash; **— doppelten Schein,** on double receipt; **hundert — eins, es gelingt ihm,** a hundred to one he will succeed; **— Quittung,** on giving *or* receiving a receipt; **— Empfang,** on receipt; **Geld leihen — einen Wechsel,** to lend money on a bill; **ein Heilmittel —,** a remedy for; **— hundert Mann,** about a hundred men; **— dreißig Jahre alt,** about thirty years old, nearly thirty; **es geht — Morgen,** morning will soon break; **— diese Zeit,** by this time, about this time; **wie ein Tropfen Wasser — das Meer,** as a drop of water to the ocean; **Sie sind jung — mich,** you are young in comparison with me; **eins — das andere halten,** to compare one thing with another; **die Liebe Gottes — die Menschen,** God's love to man; **er hat was davon — mich erwähnt,** he told me something of it; **lassen Sie sich nichts — ihn merken,** don't mention a word of it to him; **die Mode ist so verschieden — früher,** fashion is so different from what it was; **sich — einen neigen,** to bow to a person; **— Osten,** eastward, towards the east; **sich verstellen —,** to dissemble towards, with; **— (einen *or* etwas) angehen,** to oppose. II. *adv. & in comp.* = contrary, opposing, counter, *etc.* *Comp.* **—abdruck, —abzug,** *m.* counter-impression, counter-proof. **—abweichen,** *v.n.* to counter-disengage (*Fenc.*). **—absicht,** *f.* opposite intention. **—anklage,** *f.* counter-charge. **—anschlag,** *m.* counterplot. **—anstalt,** *f.* counter-preparation. **—antwort,** *f.* rejoinder. **—bedingung,** *f.*; **wir haben zur —bedingung gemacht, daß . . .,** in return, we have stipulated that . . . **—befehl,** *m.* counter-order; **—befehl geben,** to countermand. **—beleidigung,** *f.* retaliation, reprisals. **—bericht,** *m.* counter-statement. **—bescheinigung,** *f.* counter-attestation. **—beschuldigung,** *f.* recrimination. **—besuch,** *m.* return of a visit; **einen —besuch machen,** to return a visit. **—beweis,** *m.* counter-evidence. **—bewegung,** *f.* reaction. **—beziehung,** *f.*, **—bezug,** *m.* reciprocal relation, correlation. **—bild,** *n.* antitype, contrast; counterpart. **—billet,** *n.* check (*at theatres, etc.*). **—bitte,** *f.* counter-petition. **—böschung,** *f.* counterscarp (*Fort.*). **—dienst,** *m.* service rendered in return; **einen —dienst leisten,** to reciprocate a service. **—druck,** *m.* reaction; counter-pressure; counter-proof (*Typ.*). **—einander,** *adv.*; **—einander geneigt,** converging (*Math.*). **—einander=haltung, —einander=stellung,** *f.* comparison; confronting. **—einander=stoßen,** *n.* shock, collision. **—erstattung,** *f.* return-payment, indemnification. **—farben,** *pl.* complementary colours. **—forderung,** *f.* counter-claim, set-off. **—füßler,** *m.* dweller in the antipodes, antipode. **—gang,** *m.* counter-approach (*Mil.*). **—gefühl,** *n.* opposite feeling; aversion. **—gesang,** *m.* antiphony. **—gewalt,** *f.* retaliation, reprisals. **—gewicht,** *n.* counterpoise; **das —gewicht halten,** to counterpoise; **einem das —gewicht halten,** to neutralize a man's influence. **—gift,** *n.* antidote. **—gruß,** *m.* reciprocal greeting; return-salute. **—hall,** *m.* resonance, echo. **—halt,** *m.* counter-pressure; resistance; holdfast, prop. **—halten,** (*sep.*) *v.* I. *a. see* **Halten;** to bet on a card. II. *n.* (*aux.* **h.**) to resist; to keep out; to endure. **—hölzer,** *pl.* cross-trees (*Naut.*). **—klage,** *f.* recrimination; cross-bill (*Law*). **—laufgraben,** *m.* counter-approach (*Mil.*). **—liebe,** *f.* mutual love, return of love; **er fand mit diesem Vorschlag keine —liebe,** his proposal met with no support, was not accepted (*coll.*). **—licht,** *n.* false light (*Paint.*). **—macht,** *f.* opposing power, adversary. **—marke,** *f.* check. **—marsch,** *m.* countermarch. **—mine,** *f.* countermine. **—mittel,** *n.* remedy, antidote. **—papst,** *m.* anti-pope. **—part,** I. *n. see* **—teil.** II. *m.* adversary, antagonist; partner; **den —part halten,** to maintain the contrary. **—partei,** *f.* opposite party. **—rechner,** *m.* controller. **—rechnung,** *f.* check-account, control; discount; counter-reckoning; **Rechnung und —rechnung,** debit and credit; **durch —rechnung beglichen *or* saldiert,** counterbalanced by. **—rede,** *f.* contradiction; reply, counter-plea, replication. **—reformation,** *f.* Anti-Reformation (*in Germany-Austria in the 16th and 17th centuries*); **—reiz=mittel,** *n.* counter-irritant. **—rimesse,** *f.* counter-remittance. **—revolution,** *f.* counter-revolution. **—revolutionär,** *m.* anti-revolutionist. **—richtung,** *f.* contrary direction. **—sang,** *m.* antiphony. **—satz,** *m.* something opposed; antithesis; contrast; opposition; rejoinder; **als —satz für,** in payment *or* return for; **im —satze zu,** in opposition to. **—sätzlich,** *adj.* contrary, adverse, opposite. **—schein,** *m.* reflection (*Phys.*); opposition (*Astr.*); counter-deed *or* bond. **—schläger,** *m.* a horse that kicks. **—schrift,** *f.* reply in writing, refutation; rejoinder. **—schritt,** *m.* counter-step; **—schritte thun,** to take counter-measures. **—seite,** *f.* opposite side; reverse. **—seitig,** *adj.* reciprocal, mutual; opposite; **der —seitige Teil,** the opposing party; **—seitige Freundschaft,** mutual friendship; **sich —seitig beziehend,** correlative. **—seitigkeit,** *f.* reciprocity; **das beruht ganz auf —seitigkeit,** it is cordially reciprocated, I feel just the same (*coll.*). **—sicherheit,** *f.* counter-security, counter-pledge. **—sinn,** *m.* contrary sense; **im —sinne nehmen,** to misinterpret. **—sonne,** *f.* parhelion. **—spiel,** *n.* counterpart, reverse; opposition, opponent (*Dram.*); playing against another. **—spieler,** *m.* opponent, antagonist (*Dram.*). **—spruch,** *m.* contradiction. **—stand,** *m.* subject; object; affair; **das ist kein —stand,** that is nothing, that is not the difficulty; **so ein —stand von 6 Flaschen,** a matter of some 6 bottles or so; **er ist der —stand des Gelächters der Gesellschaft,** he is the laughing-stock of the company. **—stands=glas,** *n.* object-glass. **—ständlich,** *adj. & adv.* objective. **—ständlichkeit,** *f.* objectivity. **—steigerung,** *f.* anticlimax. **—stich,** *m.* counter-thrust. **—stimme,** *f.* counterpart (*Mus.*); dissentient voice. **—stoß,** *m.* counter-thrust; reaction (*Phys.*). —

strich, *m.* stroke against the grain. **—strom**, *m.*, **—strömung**, *f.* eddy, counter-current. **—strophe**, *f.* antistrophe. **—stück**, *n.* counterpart; companion picture; antithesis. **—sub=jekt**, *n.* counter-subject of a fugue. **—tausch**, *m.* exchange; interchange. **—thätlichkeit**, *f.* reprisals. **—teil**, I. *m.* adversary (*obs.*). II. *n.* contrary, reverse; **er thut gerade das —teil**, he does just the reverse; **das —teil behaupten**, to maintain the contrary; **im —teil, —teils**, on the contrary. **—teilig**, *adj.* relating to the adverse party; contrary. **—treten**, *v.a.* to back-pedal (*Cycl.*). **—ü'ber**, I. *adv.* opposite, face to face; abreast; **einander —über**, facing one another. II. *prep.* (*with preceding dat.*) opposite (*to*), over against; opposed to; in presence of; in relation to, as concerns. **—ü'ber=liegend, —ü'berstehend**, *adj.* opposite; — **überliegende Winkel**, alternate angles. — **ü'bersetzen**, *v.r.*; **setzen Sie sich mir —über**, sit opposite to me. **—ü'berstellung**, *f.* opposition; comparison; antithesis; confrontation. **—unterschrift, unterzeichnung**, *f.* countersignature. **—untersuchung**, *m.* an inqury made by the adverse *or* opposite party. **—ver=hör**, *n.* cross-examination. **—verpflichtung**, *f.* counter-obligation. **—verschanzung**, *f.* contravallation. **—verschreibung**, *f.* collateral deed; counter-bond. **—versicherung**, *f.* counter-security; reinsurance. **—vorstellung**, *f.* remonstrance. **—vorwurf**, *m.* recrimination. **—wall**, *m.* counterscarp. **—wart**, *f.* presence, present time; **in —wart vieler Zeugen**, in the presence of many witnesses. **—wärtig**, *adj.* & *adv.* present, actual, extant; at present, just now; **—wärtige Preise**, current prices; **einem —wärtig sein**, to be present to one's mind; **immer war seiner Einbildung der Gedanke —wärtig**, his imagination was haunted by the thought; **—wärtiges Schreiben**, these presents, the present. **—wechsel**, *m.* counter bill of exchange. **—wehr**, *f.* resistance, defence. **—wert**, *adj.* equivalent. **—wind**, *m.* adverse wind. **—winkel**, *m.* alternate angle. **—wir=kung**, *f.* reaction; counter-action. **—zauber**, *m.* amulet. **—zeugnis**, *n.* counter-evidence. **—zeichnen**, *v.a.* to countersign. **—zeichnung**, *f.* countersignature. **—zug**, *m.* adversary's move (*in chess, etc.*), counter-move. — **zwangs=mittel**, *n.* reprisals.

Ge'gend, *f.* (*pl.* **—en**) region; tract of country; neighbourhood; **in unserer —**, in our parts; **die — um Potsdam**, the environs of Potsdam; **in welcher —?** whereabouts?

Gegess'en, *p.p. of* **essen**.

Gegir're, *n.* (**—s**) cooing (*of doves*).

Gegli'chen, *p.p. of* **gleichen**.

Geglie'dert, *adj.* having members; jointed; articulate; constructed organically, organized.

Geglit'ten, *p.p. of* **gleiten**.

Geglom'men, *p.p. of* **glimmen**.

Geg'ner, *m.* (**—s**, *pl.* **—**), **—in**, *f.* opponent; adversary. **—isch**, *adj.* & *adv.* antagonistic. **—schaft**, *f.* opponents (*coll.*); antagonism.

Gegol'ten, *p.p. of* **gelten**.

Gego'ren, (*less good:* **Gegohren**,) *p.p. of* **gären**.

Gegoss'en, *p.p. of* **gießen**.

Gegriff'en, *p.p. of* **greifen**.

Gegrö(h)'le, *n.* bad singing and clamouring (*coll.*).

Geha'ben, *ir.v.r.* to fare; to conduct oneself, to behave; **gehabt euch wohl**, farewell.

Gehä'big, *adj.* & *adv.* well off, wealthy; comfortable.

Geha'cke, *n.* (**—s**) hacking, chopping, mincing.

Geha'der, *n.* (**—s**) brawling.

Gehä'ge, *see* **Gehe'ge**.

Geha'lt, I. *m.* (**—s**, *pl.* **—e**) constituent parts; contents; capacity; cubature; hold (*of a ship*); room, extent; proportion of gold *or* silver in a mass; intrinsic value; merit; import. II. *n.* (**—s**, *pl.* **Gehäl'ter**) salary, stipend, emoluments (*professors, judges*); pay (*soldiers*); wages (*servants*); pay; allowance; **bei einem im —e stehen**, to be in a person's pay; **in — stehend**, commissioned; **auskömmliches —**, sufficient income, living wage. *Comp.* **—los**, *adj.* worthless; shallow, superficial. **—losigkeit**, *f.* worthlessness; superficiality. **—reich**, *adj.* of great value; racy (*of wine*); solid. **—s=aufbesserung, —s=erhöhung, —s=ver=mehrung, —s=zulage**, *f.* increase of salary.

Gehal'ten, *p.p.* & *adj.*, *see* **Halten**; bound, obliged; sober, steady; **gut —**, well kept; well treated; **— werden für**, to be taken for.

Gehän'ge, *n.* (**—s**, *pl.* **—**) hanging; declivity; pendants, anything that hangs; festoons, ears (*of a dog*).

Gehäs'sig, *adj.* hating; spiteful; odious; **einem — sein**, to hate one (*obs.*); **das —e**, odium. **—keit**, *f.* hatefulness, odiousness; spitefulness; animosity.

Gehau', *n.* (**—es**, *pl.* **—e**) the part of a forest where wood is being cut *or* felled, clearing; copse; continual striking; felling of wood.

Gehäu'f—e, *n.* congeries. **—t**, *p.p.* & *adj.* heaped. **—t=blütig**, *adj.* aggregate.

Gehäu'se, *n.* (**—s**, *pl.* **—**) box, case; binnacle; core (*of fruit*); shell; hilt; **— einer Reliquie**, shrine.

Gehe'ck, *n.* (**—s**) hatch, brood; covey.

Gehe'ge, Gehä'ge, *n.* (**—s**, *pl.* **—**) hedge, fence, enclosure, enclosed place, precinct; preserve; woodland; **einem ins — kommen**, to encroach on a person's property *or* rights, to cross a person's path, to disturb a p., to intrude.

Gehei'm, *adj.* secret; clandestine, concealed, private; mysterious (*rare*); **ins —**, secretly; **—e Tinte**, sympathetic ink; **der —e Sinn**, mystical sense; **—es Siegel**, privy seal; **—e Wissenschaft**, occult science; **mit einer S. — thun**, to conceal what one is doing; **—er Rat**, privy council; *see* **—rat**. **—nis**, *n.* (**—ni(ss)es**, *pl.* **—ni(ss)e**) secret; mystery; secrecy; arcanum. *Comp.* **—bote**, *m.* confidential messenger. **—buch**, *n.* secret journal (*of a commercial house*). **—bund**, *m.* secret society; secret league *or* alliance. **—haltung**, *f.* keeping secret; secrecy. **—konto**, *n.* private account. **—kräftig**, *adj.* sympathetic, of a mysterious power. **—lehre**, *f.* secret *or* mysterious doctrine; **jüdische —lehre**, cab(b)ala. **—mittel**, *n.* secret remedy, arcanum, nostrum, quack-medicine. **—nis=krämer**, *m.*, **—nis=krä=merin**, *f.* secret-monger; mystagogue. **—nis=krämerei**, *f* (affectation of) mysteriousness. **—polizei**, *f.* detective police (service). — **polizist**, *m.* detective. **—(e)=rat**, *m.* privy councillor. **—rats=viertel**, *n.* quarter where all the Privy Councillors live, fashionable part of a town (*especially with reference to Berlin*), West End. **—schloß**, *n.* letter-lock, alphabetic-lock. **—schreibekunst**, *f.* cryptography. — **schreiber**, *m.* private secretary, confidential clerk; notary (*of a prince*). **—schrift**, *f.* cipher-writing, secret characters; steganographic writing, cryptography; **Telegramm in —schrift**, code-telegram; **in —schrift abgefaßt**, ciphered; **in —schrift Geschriebenes**, cryptogram, writing in cipher. **—sein**, *n.* secrecy. **—siegel**, *n.* privy seal. **—siegel=bewahrer**, *m.* Keeper of the Privy Seal, Lord Privy Seal. **—sprache**, *f.* secret language; cant; cipher language. **—thuerei**, *f.* mysteriousness; secretiveness (*Phrenol.*). **—thuerisch**, *adj.* affecting mysteriousness, mysterious. **—thür**, *f.* private door, jib door. **—treppe**, *f.* private staircase, back-stairs. **—wirkend**, *adj.* sympathetic; of mystical influence. **—zimmer**, *n.* private cabinet, closet (*of a prince*).

Gehei'ß, *n.* (—es) command, order, injunction.

Ge'hbar, *adj.* practicable, passable.

Ge'h—en, I. *ir.v.n.* (*aux.* s.) to go, move, walk, proceed; to walk (*not run or ride*); to leave, go away; to extend to; to rise (*of dough*); to run (*high, as waves*); to blow (*as wind*); to go, to work (*of machinery*); to succeed, go on well; to circulate, be current; to go off, sell well; to apply to, be aimed at; (*used impers'lly, with dat.*) to go *or* fare with, to be (*in health, etc.*); er kam gegangen, he came on foot; lassen Sie ihn —en, let him alone; — doch! — schon! ach —n's! oh come! nonsense! — deiner Wege! get you gone! wo —t es hier hin? where does this lead to? die Sache —t gut, the affair is in a good way; wann —t der Zug nach Hannover? when does the train for Hanover leave? das Buch —t gut, the book sells well; 20 Buch —en auf ein Ries, 20 quires make a ream; das —t nicht, that will not *or* won't do, that is not possible, impossible; es wird schon —en, no doubt it will do, that will all come right, it can easily be done; es —t ein heftiger Wind, a violent gale is blowing; die Thür —t, the door is opened; als erster Versuch —t es, as a first attempt it may pass; seine Absicht ging dahin, his intention was, he purposed; sich —en lassen, to take it easy; to indulge one's inclinations; to speak freely; los —en, to go *or* fly off, to break loose *or* out; to begin; to fight a duel; einem nahe —en, to affect one closely; schief —en, to turn out badly; schwarz —en, to wear mourning; verlustig —en (einer S.), to lose (a th.); verloren —en, to get lost; schlafen —en, to go to bed; spazieren —en, to go for a walk, to take a walk; das Pferd —t einen ruhigen Gang, the horse has an easy pace; wie —t's (Ihnen)? how do you do? how are you? wie —t's deinem Bruder? O, es —t, how is your brother? Oh, pretty well; wie wird mir's —en? what will become of me? das —t mir durch Mark und Bein, that goes through and through me; das —t über alles, that beats everything; das —t mir über alles, that goes for everything with me; I like it better than anything; es ist mir gerade so gegangen, it was just the same with me, the same happened in my case; das —t mir nahe *or* zu Herzen, that touches me nearly, that hurts me, I am very sorry for it; es läßt sich hier gut —en, it is good walking here; er läßt es sich dort ganz wohl —en, he enjoys himself very much there; schwanger —en, to be pregnant, with child; mit großen Entwürfen schwanger —en, to be full of great projects; —en an, to reach to, to begin, to go to, to go on; — nicht an meine Briefe! do not go near my letters, do not touch my letters! es —t ans Leben, it is a matter of life and death; einem an die Hand —en, to assist one; schwer an etwas —en, to set about a thing reluctantly *or* with difficulty; an einer S. vorbei—en, to pass a th.; da ging es an ein, then there began a; —en auf, to concern, to be directed to; to face, overlook; die Worte gingen auf mich, the words were aimed at me; darauf —en, to be spoiled, spent, wasted, consumed; sein ganzes Geld wird darauf —en, it will cost him his whole fortune; in diesem Hause —t viel darauf, the expenses in this house are very great; bei diesem Ritt sind viele Pferde darauf gegangen, in this ride many horses were ruined; er wird darauf —en, it will be his death (*coll.*); aufs Land —en, to go into the country; auf Leib und Leben —en, to be a matter of life and death; es —t auf Mittag, it is getting on to noon; einer S. auf den Grund —en, to go to the bottom of a th.; auf die Jagd —en, to go a hunting; auf das Land —en, to go into the country; auf die Neige —en, to draw to a close; wie viel Pfennige —en auf eine Mark? how many pfennigs are in a mark? auf Reisen, *or* auf die Reise, —en, to travel; auf bösen Wegen —en, to lead a bad life; es —t aus G=dur, the piece is in G major; — mir aus den Augen, get out of my sight; auseinander —en, to part, separate; to open; aus den Fugen —en, to get out of joint; aus dem Wege —en, to step aside, stand out of the way; durch —en, to pervade; to run away; durch den Kopf *or* Sinn —en, to pass through the head, to cross one's mind, to strike, occur; durchs Herz —en, to cut to the heart; entgegen —en, to go to meet; es —t gegen Morgen, it is getting on towards morning; in die Welt hinein —en, to launch into the world; die Wirtschaft —t hinter sich, the business is going down, affairs are growing worse; hinzu —en, to approach; in sich —en, to retire into oneself, to repent; die Thür —t in den Angeln, the door turns on its hinges; in Erfüllung —en, to come true, be realized, come to pass; in Federn —en, to be hung on springs; in die Höhe —en, to rise; ins vierte Jahr —end, approaching four years; das —t mit in den Kauf, that is into the bargain; in Seide —en, to wear silk; in Stücke —en, to go to pieces; der Strom —t mit Eis, the river is full of drift ice; er —t mit der Jahreszahl, he is as old as the century; —en nach, to go in search of, to lead to; die Zimmer —en alle nach der Straße, all the rooms face the street; Alles —t nach Wunsch, everything is going on as well as we could wish; nach Brod —en, to go a begging; to seek a livelihood; Kunst —t nach Brot, art requires employment (*prov.*); das —t über die Bäume, *or* über alle Pappelbäume, that is beyond belief (*coll.*); über Land —en, to go across country; einem über sein Geld —en, to take a p.'s money; darüber —t nichts, nothing is better than that; es —t um Geld, money is at stake, it is a matter of pounds, shillings and pence; es —t um nichts, we are playing for love; einem um den Bart —en, to wheedle, coax, flatter one; unter die Leute —en, to go into society; unter die Soldaten —en, to enlist; von statten —en, to go on well, to proceed, to succeed; es —t ihm von der Hand, he is a quick and successful worker; es —t etwas vor, something is going on; was —t hier vor? what is taking place here? vor Anker —en, to cast anchor; mein Wunsch —t vor, my wish must be considered first; vor sich —en, to proceed; to take place; voran —en, to go before; —en Sie voran, you go first! after you; vorbei —en, to pass by; zu einem —en, to go to see one; zum Abendmahl —en, to take the communion; zu Fuß —en, to walk; zu Grunde —en, to break down, to be ruined, to be wrecked; einem zur Hand —en, to help one; mit sich zu rate —en, to deliberate, consider; behutsam zu werke —en, to set about cautiously. II. *subst.n.* going; walking; das —en wird ihm sauer, he has difficulty in walking; des —ens müde sein, to be tired of walking; das —en und Kommen, the going and returning. *Comp.* —entfernung, *f.* (*an hour's, etc.*) walk (*distant*); die —entfernung beträgt drei Stunden, it is a three hours' walk. —geschwindigkeit, *f.* speed at which one walks. —rock, *m.* frock-coat. —versuch, *m.* attempt to walk, attempt at walking. —werk, *n.* wheel-work, movement (*of a clock, etc.*).

Gehe'nk, *n.* (—es, *pl.* —e) belt, sword-belt; handle; hook; strap (*for hanging something up by*).

Geheu'er, *adj. & adv.* secure against anything ghostly, safe; **nicht —,** uncanny, haunted.
Geheu'l, *n.* (—s) howling, yelling.
Gehil'fe, *see* Gehülfe.
Gehil'ze, *n.* (—s, *pl.* —e) hilt (*obs.*).
Gehi'rn, *n.* (—s, *pl.* —e) brain, brains; sense; **das kleine —,** cerebellum; **einem das — einschlagen,** to knock out a man's brains. *Comp.* **—behälter,** *m.* brain-pan. **—eiterung,** *f.* abscess of the dura mater (*Med.*) **—entzündung,** *f.* inflammation of the brain, brain-fever. **—erschütterung,** *f.* concussion of the brain. **—erweichung,** *f.* softening of the brain. **—häutchen,** *n.* the membrane covering the brain. **—krankheit,** *f.* cerebral affection, disorder of the mind. **—lehre,** *f.* craniology. **—los,** *adj.* brainless; senseless. **—wassersucht,** *f.* hydrocephalus. **—wölbung,** *f.* fornix.
Geho'ben, *adj.* (*fr.* **heben,** *v.a.*); **—e Sprache,** elevated speech, high style; **fünfmal —e Verse,** verses of five beats *or* accents; **—e Stimmung,** high spirits, joyful frame of mind.
Gehö'ft, *n.* (—es, *pl.* —e) farm premises, farm.
Gehö'hn, —e, *n.* (—s) continual scoffing.
Gehol'fen, *p.p.* of **helfen.**
Gehö'lz, *n.* (—es, *pl.* —e) wood, copse. *Comp.* **—sämereien,** *pl.* seed of a tree.
Gehö'r, *n.* (—s) hearing; audience; musical ear; **ein gutes —,** a quick ear; **zu — kommen,** to be heard; to be performed; **sich — verschaffen,** to make oneself heard; **der Vernunft — geben,** to listen to reason; **— schenken,** to lend an ear, to give a hearing to; to grant. **—en,** *see* **Gehören.** *Comp.* **—fehler,** *m.* defect in hearing. **—gang,** *m.* acoustic duct, auditory passage. **—lehre,** *f.* acoustics. **—los,** *adj. & adv.* deaf. **—mangel,** *m.* defective hearing, deafness. **—nerv,** *m.* auditory nerve. **—organ,** *n.* organ of hearing. **—rohr,** *n.*, **—trichter,** *m.* ear-trumpet. **—trommel,** *f.* tympanum.
Gehor'chen, *v.n.* (*aux.* **h.**, *dat.*) to obey; **der Vernunft —,** to listen to reason.
Gehö'r—en, *v.* I. *n.* (*aux.* **h.**, *dat.*) to belong to, appertain to; to be due to; **das —t nicht hierher,** (*less good, but coll.:* **hier nicht her,**) that is nothing to the purpose, is beside the question; **—t das Ihnen?** is it yours? **wo —t dies hin?** where does this go? **er —t mit dazu,** he is one of them; **dazu —t Geld und Zeit,** that requires time and money; **diese Handschuhe —en zusammen,** these gloves are fellows; **—en unter** (*acc.*), to pertain to, to be subject to, to fall under; **vor einen —en,** to fall under the cognizance of one; **das —t nicht auf den Tisch,** that does not go on the table; **dazu —t doch eine Unverschämtheit;** well, that is impudence! II. *r. & imp.* to be suitable *or* proper; **wie sich's —t,** as is right; as is beseeming; properly, suitably, duly; **ich verlange nur, was sich —t,** I only ask for what is fair. **—ig,** *adj. & adv.* belonging, appertaining; fitting, suitable, requisite, proper, fit, due; **nicht zur Sache —ig,** irrelevant; **—iger Lügner,** thorough liar; **er hat es —ig bekommen,** he got it in fine style; **ich hab's ihm —ig gegeben,** I have given him a bit of my mind; **ich habe ihn —ig heimgeschickt,** I have sent him about his business; **das —ige,** what is necessary. **—igkeit,** *f.* suitableness, fitness, propriety; competence, competency.
Gehör'n, *n.* (—s) horns, antlers.
Gehö'rnt, *p.p. & adj.* horned; **der —e Siegfried,** Horny Siegfried, Siegfried the invulnerable (*whose skin was as hard as horn*).
Gehor'sam, I. *adj. & adv.* obedient, dutiful; submissive; obsequious; **Ihr —er Diener,** your obedient servant (*at the end of letters to newspapers, etc.*); **—er Diener!** catch me! no, thank you (*coll.*). II. *m.* (—s) (**—keit,** *f. obs.*) obedience, dutifulness; **der dem Landesfürsten schuldige —,** the allegiance due to one's sovereign; **aus — gegen,** in obedience to; **— leisten,** to obey; **einem den — aufkündigen,** to announce to one that he will no longer be obeyed, to renounce allegiance to one; **ich verlange —,** I will be obeyed. **—st,** *adj. & adv.* (*sup.*) most obedient, most humble; yours obediently (*at the end of letters*).
Geh'r—e, *f.* (*pl.* —en), **—en,** *m.* (—ens) wedge; gusset; gore; bevel; anything wedge-shaped; oblique direction. **—en,** *v.a.* to bevel. **—ig,** *adj. & adv.* oblique; bevelled. **—ung,** *f.* diagonal direction; bevel; **Stoß auf —ung,** mitre-joint. *Comp.* **—hobel,** *m.* bevel-plane. **—holz, —maß,** *n.* bevel. **—ungs-kolben,** *m.* soldering iron.
Gehu'del, *n.* (—s) bungling; rabble.
Gehül'f—e, *m.* (—en, *pl.* —en), **—in,** *f.* helpmate; assistant. *Comp.* **—en-prüfung,** *f.* examination of an apothecary's assistant.
Gei'er, *m.* (—s, *pl.* —) vulture, hawk; **hol' dich** *or* **daß dich der —!** deuce take you! confound you! **der braune —, (Bastard—,)** griffon-vulture. *Comp.* **—adler,** *m.* bearded vulture. **—falke,** *m.* gerfalcon.
Gei'fer, *m.* (—s) slaver, drivel; venom; wrath; **seinen — auslassen,** to vent one's spleen. **—ig,** *adj. & adv.* slavering; drivelling. *Comp.* **—läppchen, —tuch,** *n.* slobbering-bib.
Gei'fer—n, *v.n.* (*aux.* **h.**) to slaver, drivel, foam at the mouth to vent one's anger. **—er,** *m.* (**—ers,** *pl.* **—er**), slaverer, venomous person, slanderer.
Gei'ge, *f.* (*pl.* —n) violin; fiddle (*coll.*); whipping post *or* block; **der Himmel hängt ihm voller —n,** he sees the bright side of things, he is full of pleasant anticipations, perfectly hopeful and happy. *Comp.* **—n-artig,** *adj.* fiddle-shaped. **—n-bogen,** *m.* (violin) bow, fiddle-stick (*coll.*). **—n-bohrer,** *m.* drill. **—n-futteral,** *n.*, **—n-kasten,** *m.* violin-case. **—n-harz,** *n.* clarified resin, colophony. **—n-sattel, —n-steg,** *m.* fiddle-bridge. **—n-stimme,** *f.* violin part.
Gei'g—en, *v.a. & n.* (*aux.* **h.**) to play (on) the violin, to fiddle; **er —te als ich zu ihm kam,** when I came to him he was playing on the violin; **er —t ebenso gut wie ich,** he plays the violin as well as I; **ich werde dir etwas —en,** I'll take care to do nothing of the kind (*coll.*). **—er,** *m.* (**—ers,** *pl.* **—er**), **—erin,** *f.* violinist, violin player, fiddler. **—erei',** *f.* continued fiddling.
Geil, *adj.* fat; luxuriant, rank; lascivious; insolent, proud; voluptuous, lewd; obscene; **—es Fleisch,** proud flesh; **—er Blick,** wanton glance. **—e,** *f.* (*pl.* **—en**) *see* **—heit;** manure; richness of soil; (*pl.*) testicles. **—heit,** *f.* rankness, luxuriance; lewdness; rut.
Gei'len, I. *v.a.* to manure; to castrate; to prune. II. *v.n.* (*aux.* **h.**) to be lascivious; to satisfy lascivious desires; to ask for presents (in an importunate way); to leap over impetuously. III. *subst. n.* lasciviousness; importunity (*B.*).
Gei'sel, (*less correctly:* **Gei'ßel,**) *m.* (—s, *pl.* — *and* —n) hostage.
Gei'ser, *m.* (—s, *pl.* —) geyser, hot water fountain.
Geist, *m.* (—es, *pl.* —er) spirit; soul, mind, intellect; genius; courage; ghost, spirit; spirit, volatile liquid; **der schöne —, der Schön—,** bel-esprit, wit; **ich weiß, wes —es Kind er ist,** I know his disposition, his way of thinking, his intellectual power; **den — aufgeben,** to give up the ghost, to breathe one's last; **der heilige —,** the Holy Ghost, the Holy Spirit, the Spirit; **die Ausgießung des heiligen —es** the outpouring of the Holy

Ghost; **ich glaube an den heiligen —**, I believe in the Holy Ghost; **ein frommer Sinn läßt sich von heiligen — lenken**, a devout mind is guided by the Holy Spirit; **— einer Sprache**, genius of a language; **voll — und Leben**, sprightly, vivacious; **dieser Wein hat —**, this wine has body. **—erhaft**, *adj.* & *adv.* supernatural; ghostly; ghostlike. **—ig**, *adj.* & *adv.* spiritual, mental, intellectual; witty; spiritual, immaterial; **—ige Getränke**, spirituous drinks; **—ige Liebe**, platonic love. **—igkeit**, *f.* spirituality; spirituousness. **—lich**, *adj.* & *adv.* spiritual, religious; clerical, ecclesiastic; **selig sind, die da —lich arm sind**, blessed are the poor in spirit (*B.*); **in den —lichen Stand treten**, to take orders, enter the church; **—liches Recht**, canon law; **—liche Güter**, church lands. **—liche(r)**, *m.* clergyman, minister, divine, priest. **—lichkeit**, *f.* spirituality; priesthood, clergy, the church. *Comp.* **—begabt**, *adj.* gifted, talented. **—er=ähnlich**, *adj.* spectral. **—er=bann**, *m.*, **—er=bannung**, **—er=beschwörung**, *f.* exorcism. **—er=banner**, **—er=beschwörer**, *m.* necromancer; exorcist. **—er=bild**, *n.* phantom. **—er=bleich**, *adj.* pale as a ghost. **—er=erscheinung**, *f.* apparition. **—er=geschichte**, *f.*, **—er=märchen**, *n.* ghost-story. **—er=glaube**, *m.* belief in ghosts. **—er=mäßig**, *adj.* ghostly. **—er=müdend**, *adj.* fatiguing to the mind. **—er=quickend**, *adj.* refreshing to the mind. **—er=reich**, *n.*, **—er=welt**, *f.* spirit-world, the realm of spirits; spiritual, intellectual world. **—er=seher**, *m.* visionary, ghost-seer. **—er=seherei**, *f.* ghost-seeing; visions. **—er=stunde**, *f.* the hour when spirits walk the earth, midnight; witching hour. **—es=abwesend**, *adj.* absent-minded, absent in mind. **—es=arbeit**, *f.* head-work. **—es=arm**, *adj.* poor in the spirit, unintellectual, dull, stupid. **—es=bildung**, *f.* mental culture. **—es=erstarrung**, *f.* mental torpidity. **—es=fähigkeiten**, *pl.* intellectual powers. **—es=funke**, *m.* flash of wit. **—es=gabe**, *f.* talent. **—es=gegenwart**, *f.* presence of mind. **—es=genuß**, *m.* intellectual enjoyment. **—es=größe**, *f.* intellectual greatness; magnanimity. **—es=gymnastik**, *f.* training of the mind. **—es=kraft**, *f.* mental vigour. **—es=krank**, *adj.* diseased in mind, insane. **—es=krankheit**, *f.* mental disorder, insanity. **—es=schwäche**, *f.* imbecility. **—es=schwung**, *m.* enthusiasm; flight of fancy. **—es=(ver)störung**, *f.* mental derangement; mental disorder; bewilderment. **—es=stumpf**, *adj.* torpid, imbecile. **—es=träge**, *adj.* intellectually lazy *or* dull. **—es=verwandt**, *adj.* congenial. **—es=verwirrung**, *f.* mental disturbance, delirium. **—es=zerrüttung**, *f.* derangement of the mind. **—los**, *adj.* unintellectual. **—losigkeit**, *f.* mental dulness; spiritlessness. **—reich**, *adj.*, **—voll**, *adj.* gifted, ingenious, clever, witty.

Geiß, *f.* (*pl.* **—en**) (*less correct:* **Gais, Geis**, *f.*, *pl.* **Geisen**) goat, wild-goat; roe. **—lein**, *n.* (**—leins**, *pl.* **—lein**) kid. *Comp.* **—bart**, *m.* common meadow-sweet. **—baum**, white mountain maple. **—blatt**, *n.* honeysuckle, woodbine. **—bock**, *m.* he-goat, roe-buck. **—bub**, *m.* boy who keeps the goats, goatherd. **—fuß**, *m.* goat-weed; meadow-sweet; punch (*Carp.*). **—herde**, *f.* herd of goats. **—hirt**, *m.* goat-herd. **—melker**, *m.* goat-sucker (*Orni.*).

Gei'ßel, *f.* (*pl.* **—n**) scourge, lash, whip; chastisement; cutting reproach *or* sarcasm; **Gottes —**, the scourge of God, Attila. *Comp.* **—brüder**, *pl.* flagellants. **—hieb**, *m.* lash *or* cut with a scourge. **—mönch**, *m.* flagellant. **—rute**, *f.* scourge.

Gei'ß—eln, *v.a.* to scourge, lash, whip; to criticize severely; to torment. **—(e)ler**, *m.* scourger, flagellant. **—elung**, *f.* scourging, flagellation.

8*

Gei'tau, *n.* (*pl.* **—e**) brail, clew-line (*Naut.*).

Geiz, *m.* (**—es**) avarice; greediness; covetousness; stinginess; inordinate desire; small side shoots on tobacco, the vine, *etc.* **—haft, —ig**, *adj.* & *adv.* avaricious, covetous; niggardly; sordid; eager; **—ig nach**, covetous of. *Comp.* **—hals, —hammel, —kragen**, *m.* miser, niggard, skinflint, curmudgeon, save-all, pinch-penny.

Gei'zen, *v.n.* (*aux.* **h.**) to covet, to be covetous; to desire greatly; to be stingy; **mit etwas —**, to be economical of a thing; **— mit der Gegenwart**, to make the most of the present day; **— nach einer S.**, to covet a th., aspire to a th.

Gejam'mer, *n.* (**—s**) continued wailing *or* lamentation.

Gejauch'ze, (*less elegant:* **Gejuch'ze**, *with long* **u**,) *n.* (**—s**) repeated huzzaing; rejoicing.

Geju'bel, *n.* (**—s**) jubilation, great rejoicing.

Geka'nnt, *p.p. of* **kennen**.

Gekei'fe, *n.* (**—s**) nagging, continual scolding *or* quarrelling.

Geke'lcht, *adj.* calycled, calyculate (*Bot.*).

Gekel'ter, *n.* (**—s**) repeated pressing; quantity of wine pressed at one time.

Geke'rbt, *adj.* crenate.

Geki'cher, *n.* (**—s**) continued tittering.

Gekie'lt, *adj.* carinate.

Gekitz'el, *n.* (**—s**) continual tickling.

Gekläf'f(e), *n.* (**—s**) continual yelping.

Gekla'ge, *n.* (**—s**) continued wailing, plaint.

Geklap'per, *n.* (**—s**) continued rattling, clatter.

Geklat'sche, *n.* (**—s**) continued cracking; clapping of hands; pattering; prattling, gossipping, tittle-tattle.

Geklim'per, *n.* (**—s**) constant tinkling; bad playing, strumming (*on a piano*).

Geklin'gel, *n.* (**—s**) tinkling; ringing of a bell.

Geklir'r(e), *n.* (**—s**) clanking, clashing.

Geklo'ben, *p.p.* (*rare*) *of* **klieben** (*obs.*).

Geklom'men, *p.p. of* **klimmen**.

Geklö'ne, *n.* silly talk, bosh (*coll.*).

Geklop'fe, *n.* (**—s**) continued knocking.

Geklü'ft, *n.* (**—es**) row of clefts, series of chasms.

Geklun'gen, *p.p. of* **klingen**.

Geknat'ter, *n.* (**—s**) continual crackling.

Geknäu'lt, *adj.* gathered into a round head, glomerate.

Gekni'ckt, *p.p.* & *adj.* bent down, subdued, disheartened, morose.

Gekniff'en, *p.p. of* **kneifen**.

Geknip'pen, *for* **gekneipt** (*sl.*).

Gekni'rsch, *n.* (**—es**) grinding, gnashing (*of teeth*).

Gekni'ster, *n.* (**—s**) continual crackling (*of fire, etc.*); rustling.

Gekol'ler, *n.* (**—s**) continual rumbling; continual gobbling (*of turkeys, etc.*); rage.

Geko'nnt, *p.p. of* **können**.

Gekö'pert, *p.p.* & *adj.* twilled.

Geko'ren, *p.p. of* **kiesen**.

Geko'se, *n.* (**—s**) continual caressing, billing and cooing (*fam.*); sweet prattling, loving talk.

Gekrab'bel, *n.* crawling, sprawling (*coll.*).

Gekra'ch(e), *n.* (**—s**) continual cracking; crash; **— der Geschütze, des Donners**, peal of artillery, of thunder.

Gekrä'chz, *n.* (**—es**) croaking.

Gekrä'tz, *n.* (**—es**) waste, refuse, sweeps (*Min.*)

Gekräu'sel, *n.* (**—s**) curling; curl; ruffle, frill.

Gekrei'sch, *n.* (**—es**) continual shrieking, shrieks.

Gekrit'zel, *n.* (**—s**) scrawling, scrawl.

Gekro'chen, *p.p. of* **kriechen**.

Gekrö'nt, *adj.* crowned; coronate.

Gekrö's, —(s)e, *n.* (**—(s)es**) mesentery (*Anat.*) pluck (*of a calf*), intestines, bowels, entrails; frill, ruff; calf's pluck; giblets (*of a goose*).

Gekün'stelt, *p.p.* & *adj.* artificial, affected.

Gel, *adj.* (*dial.*) = **gelb**.

Gela'ch(e), *n.* (**—s**) continual laughing.

Gelä̈ch'ter, *n.* (—s) laughter, laugh; laughing-stock; in ein schallendes — ausbrechen, to burst into a peal of laughter, a loud laugh; wieherndes —, horse-laugh; einen zum — machen, to make a p. a laughing stock, to make sport of a p.; sich dem — aussetzen, to expose oneself to ridicule, to make an exhibition of oneself.

Gela'den, *p.p. of* laden; —! load! (*Mil.*); schwer — haben, to be tipsy (*coll.*).

Gela'g(e), *n.* (—s) things laid together; layer; feast, banquet; revel; ein — halten, to revel; ins — (hinein), at random, heedlessly.

Gelä'hmt, *p.p. & adj.* paralyzed.

Gela'hrt, *obs. for* gelehrt.

Gelal'le, *n.* (—s) lisping, stammering (*like a child*).

Gelän'de, *n.* (—s) arable land; (tract of) country, ground; region.

Gelän'der, *n.* (—s, *pl.* —) railing, rails; balustrade; parapet; trellis; espalier. —t, *adj.* railed. *Comp.* —baum, *m.* espalier. —fenster, *n.* window with balcony. —säule, *f.* baluster.

Gela'ng, Gelän'ge, *3p. sing. impf. ind. & subj. of* gelingen.

Gelän'ge, *n.* (—s) great stretch of land; large field.

Gelan'g—en, *v.n.* (*aux.* s.) to reach, arrive at, attain to; to get; to get admitted to; ans Ziel, zu seinem Zwecke —en, to attain one's end, accomplish one's purpose; etwas an einen —en lassen, to get something delivered, to transmit, address something to one; auf die Nachwelt —en, to be handed down to posterity. —ung, *f.* attainment.

Gelär'm(e), *n.* (—es) (*continual*) bustle, noise.

Gela'ß, *m. & n.* (—(ss)es, *pl.* —(ss)e) relics, heritage; room; space.

Gelas'sen, *p.p. of* lassen; *adj. & adv.* calm; cool, composed, collected; passive; patient; deliberate; — bleiben, to keep one's temper, to remain calm; scheinbar —, betraying no emotion. —heit, *f.* self-possession; moderation; calmness; patience, resignation; deliberateness.

Gelati'n—e, *f.* gelatine. —ö's, *adj.* gelatinous.

Gelau'fe, *n.* (—s) running to and fro.

Geläu'fig, *adj. & adv.* fluent, ready; familiar; current; voluble; eine —e Hand, a current hand; —e Zunge, voluble tongue; er spricht Deutsch —, he speaks German fluently; das ist ihm —, that is easy to him, he is conversant with *or* understands that. —keit, *f.* easiness; facility; skill; fluency.

Gelau'nt, *adj.* disposed; humoured; wie ist er heute —? in what humour is he to-day? gut —, in good humour; schlecht *or* übel —, cross, peevish, out of temper; nicht —, out of spirits *or* temper.

Gelau't, *n.* (—s) crying of dogs on the scent.

Geläu't(e), *n.* (—s) ringing, pealing of bells; chime, peal of bells; tinkling of bells.

Gelb, I. *adj. & adv.* yellow; —e Rübe, carrot. II. *n. see* —e. —e, I. *n.* yellow colour; yellow colouring matter; das —e im Ei, yolk. II. *f.* yellowness; plant colouring yellow; ochre; jaundice. —heit, *f.* yellowness. —lich, *adj. & adv.* yellowish. —ling, *m.* (—lings, *pl.* —linge) yellow-hammer (*Orn.*). *Comp.* —ammer, *see* —ling. —brüstchen, —kehlchen, *n.* pettichaps (*Motacilla*). —bunt, *adj.* variegated with yellow. —erde, *f.* yellow ochre. —fink, *see* —ling. —fuchs, *m.* sorrel horse. —gießer, *m.* brass-founder. —gießer=waren, *pl.* brass-ware. —holz, *n.* yellow wood, fustic. —kupfer, *n.* bronze, brass. —lich=braun, *adj.* yellowish brown. —schecke, *f.* yellow and white piebald horse. —schnabel, *m.* kingfisher (*Orn.*); callow bird; saucy brat; pert young jackanapes, greenhorn. —specht, *m.* yellow woodpecker. —sucht, *f.* jaundice. —veigelein, *n.* wall-flower (*dial.*). —weiß, *n.* cream-white. —vogel, *m.* golden oriole.

Gel'ben, *v.* I. *a.* to make yellow. II. *r. & n.* (*aux.* h.) to turn yellow.

Geld, *n.* (—es, *pl.* —er) coin; money; cash; bares — *or* bar —, ready money, cash, money in hand; kleines —, change; gangbares —, good, current money; gemünztes —, coin; totes —, dead capital; öffentliche —er, public funds; von seinem — leben, to live on one's income; nicht bei —e sein, to be short of money; für — und gute Worte, for love or money; — und Gut, wealth; er hat — wie Heu, he is rolling in wealth. *Comp.* —adel, *m.* purchased nobility; aristocracy of wealth. —angelegenheit, *f.* money-matter. —anlage, *f.* investment. —anleihe, *f.* loan (of money). —anweisung, *f.* postal-order, cheque. —aristokratie, *f.* aristocracy of wealth. —ausleiher, *m.* money-lender. —begierde, *f.* greediness for money; avarice. —beschneidung, *f.* coin-clipping. —beutel, *m.* money-bag, purse. —brief, *m.* letter containing money; registered letter. —büchse, *f.* till, money-box. —buße, *f.* fine, penalty. —einnehmer, *m.* cashier, receiver of money. —entschädigung, *f.* indemnity. —ersatz, *m.* reimbursement. —erwerb, *m.* money-making. —es=wert, *m.* what is equivalent to money; — und —eswert, the wherewithal (*coll.*). —feilscher, *m.* money-grubber. —forderung, *f.* pecuniary claim *or* demand. —freier, *m.* fortune-hunter. —fressend, *adj.* extravagant. —gefälle, *pl.* money-dues. —gehalt, *m.* intrinsic value of a coin, money-value. —geizig, *adj.* avaricious. —geschäfte, *pl.* money transactions. —gier, *see* —begierde. —gierig, *adj.* greedy after money, avaricious. —handel, *m.* money-dealing, banking; stockjobbing. —hülfe, *f.* pecuniary aid; subsidy. —kasse, *f.* till. —kasten, *m.* money-box, strong box, cash-box. —katze, *f.* money-belt, pouch. —klemme, *f.* scarcity of money, money-pressure. —krisis, *f.* financial crisis. —kurs, *m.* course of exchange. —kurszettel, *m.* exchange-list. —lade, *f.* till. —leute, *pl.* moneyed men, financiers, bankers, brokers. —los, *adj.* impecunious, poor, badly off. —losigkeit, *f.* impecuniosity. —macher, *m.* coiner. —makler, *m.* money-broker. —männchen, *n.* mandrake. —mangel, *m.* scarcity of money. —männer, *see* —leute. —mittel, *pl.* funds, resources. —posten, *m.* sum of money; item (*in an account-book*). —prägen, *n.* coining. —preis, *m.* rate of exchange; cash price. —rücksicht, *f.* mercenary point of view. —schneider, *m.* sharper, shark; coin-clipper. —schneiderei, *f.* overcharging, swindling. —sache, *f.* money-matter; in —sachen hört die Gemütlichkeit auf, business is business (*prov.*). —schrank, *m.* chest; feuerfester —schrank, fire-proof safe. —sendung, *f.* remittance. —stand, *m.* state of the money-market. —stock, *m.* money-safe. —stolz, I. *adj.* purse-proud. II. *m.* purse-pride. —strafe, *f.* fine. —stück, *n.* coin. —sucht, *f.* avarice. —süchtig, *adj.* avaricious. —tisch, *m.* counter. —umlauf, *m.* circulation of money. —umsatz, *m.* exchange of money. —verlegenheit, *f.* pecuniary embarrassment. —vorschuß, *m.* advance of money. —währung, *f.* currency. —wechsel, *m.* exchange of money. —wechsler, *m.* money-changer. —wert, *m.* value in money; value of currency. —wesen, *n.* monetary matters, finance. —wucher, *m.* usury. —wucherer, *m.* usurer.

Gele'ckt, *p.p. & adj.* very neat; er sah aus wie —, he looked spick-and-span. —heit, *f.* great

neatness; prettiness of style, tea-tray style (*Paint.*).
Gelee', *n.* (—s, *pl.* —s,) jelly.
Gele'ge, *n.* laying (*of eggs*); eggs laid.
Gele'gen, *p.p. of* **liegen**; situated; convenient; fit, proper, opportune; **es ist mir jetzt nicht — hinzugehen**, it does not suit me, I do not feel inclined to go there just now; **zu —er Zeit**, opportunely, in due time; **es kommt mir gerade —**, it just suits me; **es ist mir wenig daran —**, it is of little consequence to me; I do not care much for it; **es ist nichts daran —**, it is of no importance, it does not matter; **Sie kommen mir sehr —**, you come very opportunely. **—heit**, *f.* occasion; opportunity; convenience; favourable moment; **ich werde es ihm bei —heit zurückgeben**, I shall return it to him when I have an opportunity; **bei dieser —heit**, on this occasion; **gute —heiten**, facilities; **—heit machen**, to act as a (good-natured) go-between; **eine —heit vom Zaune brechen**, to hunt for a pretext; **alle —heit(en) eines Hauses kennen**, to know every nook and corner of a house; **die —heit des Hauses**, the privy, W.C. (*coll.*); **—heit macht Diebe**, opportunity makes the thief, an open door may tempt a saint (*prov.*). **—lich**, I. *adj.* occasional, incidental; opportune. II. *adv.* on an occasion, incidentally; at times; at one's convenience; at one's leisure; opportunely, as occasion offers; **wenn Sie ihn —lich sehen**, if you should chance to see him; **ich erfuhr —lich**, I heard accidentally. *Comp.* **—heits=dichter**, *m.* one that composes poems for particular occasions. **—heits=kauf**, *m.* bargain. **—heit(s)=macher**, *m.* go-between; assignation maker; procurer. **—heits=schrift**, *f.* pamphlet, composition written for a particular occasion.
Geleh'r—ig, *adj.* docile, teachable; intelligent. **—igkeit**, *f.* docility; intelligence. **—sam**, *adj. & adv. see* **—ig**. **—samkeit**, *f.* learning, erudition. **—t**, *adj.* learned; instructed, well-informed. **—te(r)**, *m.*, **—te**, *f.* learned person, man of learning, scholar; **es ist noch kein —ter vom Himmel gefallen**, one is not born learned; **den —ten ist gut predigen**, a word to the wise is enough. **—theit**, *f. see* **—samkeit**. *Comp.* **—ten=beruf**, *m.* profession of a scholar. **—ten=kreise**, *pl.* scholars, the learned. **—ten=leben**, *n.* life of a scholar. **—ten=republik**, *f.* republic of letters. **—ten=schule**, *f.* grammar school, high school, college. **—ten=stand**, *m.* learned profession; literati. **—ten=verein**, *m.* literary society *or* club. **—ten=wesen**, *n.* all that concerns letters and science, arts and science. **—ten=zeitung**, *f.* literary *or* scientific magazine *or* periodical.
Gelei'er, *n.* (—s) continued grinding of a barrel-organ; drawling; monotonous talking.
Gelei'se, *n.* (—s, *pl.* —) *usually* **Gleis**, *n.* (—(s)es, *pl.* —(s)e) track (*of a wheel*); rut; line of rails; gauge; **einfaches, doppeltes —**, single, double way; **— für abfahrende, ankommende Züge**, down line, up line; **die Maschine ist aus dem — gekommen**, the engine ran off the rails; **auf ein falsches — geraten**, to get on the wrong track; to be put out (*fig.*); **das — halten**, to follow the track; **im (alten) — bleiben**, to go on in the old way.
Gelei't, *n.* (—(e)s, *pl.* —e) conducting, accompanying; retinue; guard, escort; **— bei Leichen**, funeral train; **einem das — geben**, to accompany *or* escort one; to see a p. off; **freies —**, safe conduct. *Comp.* **—(s)=amt**, *n.* office of convoys; custom-house, toll-office (*C.L.*). **—(s)=brief**, *m.* advice-note; custom-house receipt; letter of safe conduct. **—(s)=bediente(r)**, *m.* excise-man. **—(s)=schein**, *m.* permit; passport. **—s=schiff**, *n.* convoy. **—(s)=einnahme**, *f.* custom-receipts; custom-house; excise office. **—(s)=einnehmer**, *m.* excise officer; toll-keeper. **—(s)=kammer**, *f.* board of convoy. **—(s)=reiter**, *m.* mounted escort. **—(s)=stern**, *m.* satellite. **—(s)=tafel**, *f.*, **—(s)=tari'f**, *m.* toll table; table of convoy-duties.
Gelei'te—n, *v.a.* to accompany, to escort; **Gott — dich!** God speed thee; God be with you! **—r**, *m.* (—rs, *pl.* —r) guide, conductor.
Gele'nk, I. *adj. & adv.* pliant, supple; limber; nimble. II. *n.* (—(e)s, *pl.* —e) joint, articulation; knuckle; wrist; vertebra; link; hinge; knot (*Bot.*); **keine —e haben**, to be stiff in the joints, awkward in movement; **sich den Arm aus dem —e fallen**, to dislocate one's arm by a fall. **—ig**, *adj. & adv.* pliable, pliant, supple; nimble; jointed, articulated, having links; geniculate (*Bot.*). **—igkeit**, *f.* flexibility; suppleness; nimbleness. *Comp.* **—band**, *n.* ligament of a joint. **—ende**, *n.* head (*of a bone*). **—geschwulst**, *f.* white swelling. **—hügelchen**, *n.* tubercle. **—kuppelung**, *f.* joint-coupling. **—ring**, *m.* hinge, turning-joint. **—schalig**, *adj.* crustaceous. **—schlüssel**, *m.* folding-key. **—schmerz**, *m.* gout. **—verbindung**, *f.* articulation. **—verrenkung**, *f.* dislocation of the joint. **—wirbel**, *m.* turning-joint.
Geler'ne, *n.* (—s) continual learning.
Gele'se, *n.* (—s) continual reading.
Geleuch't(e), *n.* (—s) lights; illumination; miner's lamp.
Gelich'ter, *n.* (—s) gang, set, lot, crew, riffraff; **das sind Leute eines —s**, they are all of the same stamp.
Gelieb't—e(r), *m.* lover; sweetheart, love, darling; **meine —en!** my brethren! (*Eccl.*). **—e**, *f.* sweetheart, lady-love, mistress.
Gelie'hen, *p.p. of* **leihen**.
Geli'nd, —e, *adj. & adv.* smooth, soft; gentle; lenient; mild, tender; **bei —em Feuer**, at a slow fire; **eine —e Strafe**, a lenient *or* slight punishment; **—estens gesagt**, to put it as mildly as possible. **—igkeit, —heit**, *f.* mildness, lenity, indulgence; sleekness.
Gelin'gen, I. *ir.v.n.* (*aux.* **s.**) (**einem**) to succeed, to prosper; **sein Plan ist ihm nicht gelungen**, his plan did not succeed; **es gelang mir nicht, meinen Plan auszuführen**, I was not able to carry out my plan, I did not succeed in carrying out my scheme; **es gelingt mir**, I succeed, prosper in; **es ist ihm vorbei gelungen**, he has failed (*coll.*). II. *subst. n.* success.
Gelis'pel, *n.* (—s) whispering; lisping.
Gelit'ten, *p.p. of* **leiden**.
Gel'len, *v.n.* (*aux.* **h.**) to sound loud and shrill, to yell; to tingle (*of ears*). **—d**, *p. & adj.* shrill, piercing.
Gelo'b—en, *v.a.* to promise solemnly, vow; **mit Hand und Mund —en**, to swear, to take a solemn oath; **das —te Land**, the land of promise, the Holy Land. **—ung**, *f.* solemn promise, vow. **—ungs=** (*in comp.* =) votive.
Gelöb'nis, *n.* (—(ss)es, *pl.* —(ss)e) solemn promise, vow.
Gelo'ck, *n.* (—es) curls, ringlets, locks (*coll.*).
Gelof'fen, (*dial.*) *p.p.* of **laufen**.
Gelo'gen, *p.p.* of **lügen**.
[1]**Gelt**, *adj.* & *adv.* not giving milk; barren, farrow. *Comp.* **—ling**, *m.* gelding; eunuch; one year old calf *or* deer.
[2]**Gelt**, (*supposed to be the pres. subj. of* **—en** *used as int.*, shall that be so? =) is it not so? do you not think so? truly!
Gel't—en, *ir.v.n.* (*aux.* **h.**) to be worth, have value (*for*); to be valid *or* of force; to have influence, be in favour (*with*); to prove effectual, prevail; to pass current; to be esteemed; to pass for; to be admitted, to be permitted; to

be real *or* true; to concern, apply to, be aimed at; to be the question; to rest upon, to have at stake, to have to do with; *often used as imp. with acc. of the amount of value, the thing at stake, etc. and a dat. of the person or the thing for which anything has value or whom it concerns;* **—end machen,** to make good, to urge, assert, vindicate; to set off, show to advantage; to plead (*as excuse*); **sich —end machen,** to maintain one's dignity, one's rights, to put oneself forward; **seine Rechte —end machen,** to maintain one's rights; **—en lassen,** to let pass, not to dispute, admit; **das will ich —en lassen,** granted! **wie viel gilt dies?** what is the price *or* value of this? **jetzt gilt's!** now's the time! now for it! **was gilt's** *or* **was gilt die Wette?** what do you bet? **es gilt einen Schilling,** I bet you a shilling; **es gilt!** done! **diese Münze gilt bei uns nicht,** this coin will not pass with us, is not current here; **bei Gott gilt kein Ansehen der Personen,** with God there is no respect of persons (*B.*); **laß meine Bitte vor dir —en,** let my supplication be accepted before thee (*B.*); **die meisten Stimmen —en,** most votes carry; **diese Note gilt einen Takt,** this note is equal to one bar; **ein Dukaten gilt fünf und einen halben Gulden,** a ducat is worth five guldens and a half (*about 9s. 2d.*); **es gilt mir gleich viel,** it is all the same to me; **sein Wort gilt viel bei,** his word has great weight with; **das gilt nicht,** that is not allowed, is not fair play, does not count; **was von dir gilt, gilt eben nicht gerade auch von mir,** what is true of you, is not necessarily true of me; **der gute Wille gilt für die That,** the will is taken for the deed; **es gilt für ausgemacht,** it is taken for granted; **er gilt für einen redlichen Mann,** he passes for an honest man, he is supposed to be honest; **diese Bemerkung (Kugel) galt mir,** this remark (bullet) was aimed at, intended for, me; **es gilt Ihnen!** good health! I drink to you! **es gilt Sieg oder Tod!** victory or death! **es gilt mir die Ehre,** my honour is at stake; **es galt unser Leben,** our life was at stake; **und wenn es mein Leben gilt!** though it cost me my life! **es gilt Kampf, es gilt zu kämpfen,** combat's the word, now for a fight; **es gilt einen Versuch,** it depends on a trial; **das laß' ich —en,** hear! hear! well done! **hier gilt's!** now for a struggle! **es gilt,** done, be it so (*B.*); **was gilt's,** of a surety, forsooth; **was gilt's, ob,** surely . . . not (*B.*); **jetzt gilt's die Begeisterung zu entflammen,** the main point now is to fire the enthusiasm. **—er,** *m.* he who pays; debtor; creditor. **—ung,** *f.* value, worth; currency; duration (*of a note*); quantity (*Pros.*); acceptation (*of a word*); **sich** (*dat.*) **—ung verschaffen,** to make oneself felt *or* respected, to bring one's influence to bear; **ohne —ung,** of no account. *Comp.* **—ungs=bereich,** *m.*, **—ungs=gebiet,** *n.* (**einer Verordnung**) district where a law is in force.

Gel'te, *f.* (*pl.* **—n**) pail, bucket; wine measure.

Gelüb'de, *n.* (—s, *pl.* —) vow. *Comp.* **—opfer,** *n.* sacrifice offered in fulfilment of a vow.

Gelun'gen, *p.p. of* **gelingen,** well done. *adj.* capital, funny, rare (*coll.*).

Gelü'st, *n.* (—s, *pl.* —e) desire, longing, appetite; lust.

Gelüs'te—n, *v.a. & n.* (*aux.* **h.**) *& usually imp.* to desire, long for, hanker after; to lust after; **mich —t da(r)nach,** I long for it; **sich** (*acc.*) **seines Gegenstandes** (*obs.*) *o.* **nach einem Gegenstande) —n lassen,** to covet; **ich bin gewiß, das** (*older:* **des**) **läßt er sich nicht —n.** I am certain he never thinks of it.

Gel'ze, *f.* (*pl.* —n) spayed *or* gelded sow; young sow not yet capable of generation.

Gel'zen, *v.a.* to geld, spay, castrate.

Gema'ch, I. *adj.* comfortable, convenient, easy. II. *adv.* softly, gently; gradually, by degrees, slowly; **—!** stop! gently, don't be in (such) a hurry; hold there! **— geht auch weit,** slow and steady wins the race (*prov.*). III *n.* (—(e)s, *pl.* **Gemä'cher**) chamber, room; closet (*high style*); **heimliches —,** privy, W.C.

Gemäch'lich, *adj. & adv. see* **Gemach**; **—er Mensch,** one who loves his ease; **— leben,** to live at ease, comfortably. **—keit,** *f.* convenience, comfort, ease.

Gemäch't(e), *n.* (—(e)s, *pl.* —e) handiwork, thing framed; workmanship; creature; (*pl.*) genitals; **denn er kennt, was für ein — wir sind,** for He knoweth our frame (*B.*).

Gema'cht, *p.p. & adj. see* **Machen**; **—e Wechselbriefe,** bills ready for endorsement; **ein —er Mann,** one whose fortune is made *or* assured. **—heit,** *f.* affectation.

Gema'hl, I. *m.* (—s, *pl.* —e), consort, husband. II. *n.* (—s) consort, queen, spouse (*obs. & poet.*); **der König und sein —,** the king and his queen. **—in,** *f.* consort, wife; spouse; **wie geht's Ihrer Frau Gemahlin, Herr Bolz?** how is Mrs. Bolz?

Gemah'nen, *v.a.* to remind (**einen an eine S.** one of a th.) *used as imp.*; **es gemahnt mich,** it strikes me, it seems to me.

Gemä'kel, *n.* (—s) continual nagging, fault-finding.

Gemäl'de, *n.* (—s, *pl.* —) picture, painting. *Comp.* **—ausstellung,** *f.* exhibition of pictures. **—händler,** *m.* picture-dealer. **—saal,** *m.* picture-gallery.

Gema'rk, *n.* (—es, *pl.* —e) (*rare; usually*) **—ung,** *f.* landmark, boundary; district; precincts.

Gemä'ß, I. *n.* (—es, *pl.* —e) measure. II. *adj. & adv.* conformable, suitable, commensurable, proportionable; **eine mir —e Anschauung,** a view suitable to my own. III. *prep.* (*with preceding or following dat.*) conformably to, in conformity with, agreeably to, according to; **dem Zwecke nicht —,** unsuitable; **der Natur —,** according to nature. **—heit,** *f.* conformity, suitableness. **—igt,** *adj.* temperate; moderate.

Gemaß'regelte(r), *m.* victim of over-discipline.

Gemäu'er, *n.* (—s, *pl.* —) masonry, connected walls; **ein altes —,** ruins, decayed walls.

Geme'cker, *n.* (—s) (*continued*) bleating.

Gemei'n, *adj. & adv.* common, plentiful; public, general; familiar; low, vulgar; ordinary, common; profane; servile, (*with dat.*) common, belonging in common to; **der —e Menschenverstand,** common sense; **—e Weide,** common of pasture; **—es Benehmen,** mean, low conduct; **—er Tag,** week day, ordinary day; **—e Geschichte,** profane history; vulgar, low, indecent story; **der —e Mann,** the man in the street, common people; **mit dem —en Manne zu reden,** to speak the language of common life; **das —e Recht,** common law; **das —e Wesen** (*usually* **das —wesen**) the commonwealth; **die —e Meinung,** the general view, public opinion; **—er Soldat,** private; **die —en,** the privates, the rank and file, the Tommies (*fam.*); **das Haus der —en,** the House of Commons (*Parl.*); **—e Brüche,** vulgar fractions; **— thun,** to behave familiarly, make oneself familiar; **— machen,** to make common, to popularize, spread, promulgate, diffuse; **sich — machen,** to demean oneself; **sich nicht — machen mit,** to keep (*one*) at a distance, to hold aloof from, not to be too familiar with; **der Tod ist allen Menschen —,** death is common to all; **auf —e Kosten die Reise machen,** to make the journey at joint expense; **mit**

einem —e Sache machen, to make common cause with a p., to join a p. in an undertaking; es war ihnen alles —, they had all things in common: ins — (in — *is obs.*), in common, common. —e, *obs. & poet. for* —de. —e(r), *m.* commoner; layman; private (*Mil.*), Tommy Atkins (*Mil. sl.*); die —en, the rank and file (*Mil.*). —heit, *f.* community; vileness; meanness, lowness, vulgarity; coarseness; commonness. —iglich, *adv.* usually, generally. —sam, *adj. & adv.* common; held in common, joint, combined, mutual; familiar. —samkeit, *f.* community, common possession; mutuality. —schaft, *f.* community; mutual participation, common possession *or* interest; communion; union; partnership; intercourse, society, familiarity. —schaft der Güter *or* Güter —, community of goods; —schaft zwischen Seele und Leib, the union of soul and body; —schaft haben mit, to be connected, consort, have intercourse with; was hat das Licht für —schaft mit der Finsternis? what is there in common between light and darkness? etwas in —schaft haben, to hold *or* have s.th. in common. —schaftlich, *adj. & adv.* common, mutual; joint; es geht auf —schaftliche Kosten, the expenses are borne in common; —schaftliche Sache machen, to make common cause; sich —schaftlich teilen in eine S., to be joint partakers of *or* in a th.; —schaftlich speisen, to dine together; —schaftlicher Nenner, common denominator; —schaftliche Note, collective note (*Pol.*); die Folgen —schaftlich tragen, to share the consequences. —schäftlichkeit, *f.* community of possession; concert, mission; solidarity, joint responsibility. *Comp.* —acker, —anger, *m.* common. —faßlich, *adj. & adv.* intelligible to an ordinary mind, popular, generally comprehensible, elementary. —gefährlich, *adj.* dangerous to the commonwealth, publicly dangerous. —geist, *m.* public spirit, esprit de corps. —gläubiger, *pl.* bankrupt's creditors. —gültig, *adj.* generally admitted *or* received. —gut, *n.* common *or* public property; die Hauptgrundsätze einer Wissenschaft zum —gut machen, to popularise the main theories of a science. —herrschaft, *f.* joint estate; common jurisdiction. —hin, *adv.* commonly. —holz, *n.* wood *or* fuel possessed in common. —hut, *f.* common pasture. —kapitalien, *pl.* joint stocks. —name, *m.* collective noun. —nützig, —nützlich, *adj.* of general *or* public utility, generally useful. —nützigkeit, *f.* public utility. —ort, *m.* common. —platz, *m.* common; commonplace, platitude. —recht, *n.* common law. —schaden, *m.* common nuisance; universal offender. —schädlich, *adj.* harmful to the commonwealth. —schafts-ehe, *f.* community of wives *or* husbands. —schuldner, *m.* bankrupt. —sinn, *m.* common impulse, public spirit. —sinnig, *adj.* public spirited. —spruch, *m.* common saying. —trift, —weide, *f.* common. —verständlich, *see* —faßlich. —wesen, *n.* public affairs; community; commonwealth.

Gemein'de, *f.* (*pl.* —n) municipality; corporate body; community; parish; congregation, parishioners; die christliche —, the Christian communion, the church; zur — gehörig, public, municipal; von der — ausschließen, to excommunicate. *Comp.* —anger, *m.* common. —auflagen, *pl.* local rates. —ausschuß, *m.* common council; vestry. —bezirk, *m.* municipality. —boden, —grund, *m.* parish plot. —gesang, *m.* congregational singing. —glied, *n.* member of a community, parishioner. —haus, *n.* town-hall. —kind, *n.* child on the parish *or* the village community. —land, *n.* common. —rat, *m. see* —ausschuß; alderman, town-councillor, vestry councillor. —rats-präsident, *m.* mayor; chairman of town council. —schule, *f.* parish school; board school. —vorstand, *m.* local board. —weide, *f.* common.

Gemen'g—e, *n.* (—s) mingling; mixture; medley; mélée, fray (*Mil.*); Hand—e, hand to hand fight. —sel, *n.* (—sels) medley, compound, hodge-podge. *Comp.* —stoffe, *pl.* constituent parts of a mixture. —teile, *pl.* ingredients of a mixture.

Geme'rk, *n.* (—es, *pl.* —e) mark, token; trace of the stag.

Gemes'sen, *p.p. of* messen, *& adj.* measured; limited; precise, formal; sedate; positive; —er Befehl, express *or* strict order. —heit, *f.* precision, strictness; measured demeanour.

Gemet'zel, *n.* (—s, *pl.* —) slaughter, carnage, massacre.

Gemie'den, *p.p. of* meiden.

Gemi'sch, *n.* (—es, *pl.* —e) mixture; medley.

Gem'me, *f.* (*pl.* —n) gem, cameo. *Comp.* —n-abdruck, *m.*, —n-abguß, *m.* paste. —n-kundige(r), *m.* lapidary.

Gemo'cht, *p.p. of* mögen.

Gemor'de, *n.* (—s) massacre, murdering.

Gems, *f.* (*pl.* —(s)en), *usually* **Gem's—e**, *f.* (*pl.* —en) chamois, Alpine goat. *Comp.* —bock, *m.* chamois-buck. —(s)en-freche, *f.* boldness of chamois. —(s)en-fuß, *m.* pelican (*Surg.*). —(s)en-geier, *m.* vulture of the Alps. —(s)en-leder, *n.* chamois leather. —tier, *n.*, —ziege, *f.* doe of the chamois.

Gemün'd(e), *n.* (—s) opening of a river into another *or* into a lake.

Gemun'kel, *n.* (—s) low muttering sounds, mutterings; secret talk *or* gossip.

Gemur'mel, *n.* (—s) murmuring, murmur; es geht ein —, it is whispered about.

Gemur're, *n.* (—s) grumbling, murmuring.

Gemü'se, *n.* (—s, *pl.* —) (**Gemüs**, *n. dial.*) vegetables, greens. *Comp.* —bau, *m.* cultivation of vegetables. —garten, *m.* kitchen garden. —händler, *m.* green-grocer. —schüssel, *f.* vegetable dish; dish of vegetables.

Gemu'ßt, *p.p. of* müssen.

Gemü't, *n.* (—es, *pl.* —er) mind; soul; heart; disposition; spirit; temper; (*pl.*) people; er ist ganz —, he is full of feeling *or* cordiality, he is all heart; er hat kein —, he has no feeling; sich (*dat.*) etwas zu —e ziehen, to take a thing to heart, to appropriate a th.; einem eine S. zu —e führen, to remind one of a thing, remonstrate with s.o. concerning a th., bring s.th. home to a p.'s heart and conscience. —lich, *adj. & adv.* goodnatured; kindly; agreeable; cheerful, hearty; simple; affectionate; full of good feeling, comfortable, cosy, snug; nur immer —lich! don't get angry! don't let us disturb ourselves! ein —liches Volk, a good-natured people; es ist (wir sind *or* befinden uns) hier recht —lich, it is (we feel) very comfortable here; —liche Dichtung, poetry of sentiment. —lichkeit, *f.* (the quality of the) good-natured, sanguine, easy-going disposition; good nature; kindliness; cheerfulness; pleasantness; cordiality; sentiment, tenderness of feeling; freedom from pecuniary cares; comfortableness; da hört (sich) denn doch die —lichkeit auf! this is too much! (*coll.*); in Geldsachen hört die —lichkeit auf, business is business (*prov.*). *Comp.* —los, *adj & adv.* devoid of feeling, unfeeling, wanting in fine feeling; morose; cheerless. —s-art, —s-anlage, —s-beschaffenheit, *f.* character, disposition, turn of mind, temper. —s-bewegung, *f.* emotion, affective process (*Phil.*). —s-eigenheit, *f.* peculiarity of mind *or* temper. —s-erholung, *f.* mental recreation. —s-fähigkeit, *f.* faculty of the mind. —s-fassung, *f.* temper. —s-gabe, *f.* mental faculty. —krank, *adj.* diseased in mind. —s-krankheit, *f.* mental disorder, melancholy. **—s=lage,** *f.* affective state (*Phil.*). **—s=neigung,** *f.* mental bias. **—s=regung,** *f.* emotion. **—s=richtung,** *f.* turn of mind. **—ruhe,** *f.* composure, calmness, unconcernedness. **—s=stimmung,** *f.*, **—s=zustand,** *m.* frame of mind, humour; affective state (*Phil.*). **—voll,** *adj.* cheerful, kindly, affectionate; agreeable.

Gen, (*with short* e) *prep.* (*with acc.; older: dat.*) *abbrev'd from* **gegen,** towards, to; **—Himmel,** heavenwards; **— Rom,** towards Rome (*obs.*).

Gena'belt, *adj.* umbilicate (*Bot.*).

Genä'he, *n.* (—s) continual sewing; needle work.

Gena'nnt, *p.p. of* **nennen,** called, surnamed.

Gena's, Genä'se, *imperf. indic. & subj. of* **genesen.**

Genä'schig, *adj.* dainty, lickerish; given to eating *or* getting dainties by stealth.

Genä'sel, *n.* (—s) speaking through the nose.

Genau', *adj. & adv.* close-fitting; tight; close, strict; intimate; particular, accurate, minute, exact, precise, rigid; sparing, close-fisted, parsimonious; **der —este Preis,** the lowest price; **— um drei Uhr,** at three precisely; **— zur Zeit,** in the very nick of time; **erzählen Sie uns die Sache —,** give us all the particulars; **mit —er Not,** hardly, with great difficulty; **mit —er Not entkommen,** to have a narrow escape; **—er Kostenanschlag,** bill of items, exact estimate; **in —em Verstande,** in a limited sense; **—es Gewissen,** scrupulous conscience; **—er Anschluß,** tight fit; **ich weiß —, daß,** I know for certain that; **ich kenne ihn —,** I know him well; **es nicht — nehmen,** to make allowance for, look indulgently on, not be too particular; **er nimmt es mit der Wahrheit nicht so —,** he is not very exact *or* scrupulous in his statements; **— genommen,** strictly speaking; **nachdem ich es mir — überlegt habe,** after careful reflection. **—igkeit,** *f.* accuracy, precision, exactness, closeness; parsimony.

Gendar'm, *m.* (—s, —en, *pl.* —en) military policeman, police-soldier; gendarme.

Genealo'g, *m.* (—en, *pl.* —en) genealogist. **—ie',** *f.* (*pl.* —ie'en) genealogy. **—isch,** *adj.* genealogical.

Genehm', *adj.* acceptable, approved of, agreeable; **wenn es mir — sein wird,** when it will suit me; **— halten,** to approve of, agree to, to grant. **—igen,** *v.a.* to approve, sanction; to accept of; to accept (*a bill*); to admit; to grant; to ratify (*a treaty*). **—igung,** *f.* acceptance; approbation; consent; ratification; license, permission. *Comp.* **—halten,** *subst. n.*, **—haltung,** *f.* approval, assent; ratification.

Genei'gt, *p.p. of* **neigen,** & *adj.*; **—zu,** inclined, disposed to; having a propensity for; **der —te Leser,** the kind reader; **einem ein —es Gehör geben,** to give one a favourable hearing. **—heit,** *f.* inclination; propensity; affection.

Genera'l, I. *adj. & adv.* general. II. *m.* (—s, *pl.* —e (*less good* Generä'le, *obs.* Genera'ls)) general, (supreme) commander; **Kommandierender —,** general commanding a German army corps. **—a't,** *n.* (—ates, *pl.* —ate) generalship; superintendence; district under the inspection of a general. **—in,** *f.* general's wife. **—isie'ren,** *v.a.* to generalize. **—issi'mus,** *m.* generalissimo. **—itä't,** *f.* (*pl.* —itäten) body of generals, the generals. **—schaft,** *f.* generalship; general officers. *Comp.* **—adjutant,** *m.* aide-de-camp; adjutant-general. **—advokat,** *m.*, **—anwalt,** *m.* attorney-general. **—archivar,** *m.* registrar-general. **—arzt,** *m.* (surgeon-) general; **—arzt W. D. Wilson,** Surgeon-General W. D. Wilson. **—baß,** *m.* thorough-bass. **—befahrung,** *f.* inspection of a mine. **—beichte,** *f.* universal confession. **—feld'marschall,** *m.* general field-marshal, generalissimo. **—feld'wachtmeister,** *m.* major-general (*obs.*). **—feld'zeugmeister,** *m.* master-general of the ordnance; commander-in-chief, generalissimo (*Aust.*). **—fiskal,** *m.* attorney *or* solicitor-general. **—gouverneur,** *m.* governor-general. **—intendant,** *m.* storekeeper-general, chief of the commissariat (*Mil.*); general manager (*Theat.*). **—kasse,** *f.* treasury. **—kommando,** *n.* command in chief, office of the commanding-general. **—konsul,** *m.* consul-general. **—leut'nant,** *m.* lieutenant-general. **—majo'r,** *m.* major-general. **—marsch,** *m.* general (*beat of the drum*); **den —marsch schlagen,** to beat the general, to beat to arms. **—nenner,** *m.* common denominator; **Brüche unter den —nenner bringen,** to reduce fractions to a common denominator. **—o'berst,** *m.* colonel-general. **—pächter,** *m.* farmer-general (of taxes, *obs.*). **—pardon,** *m.* general amnesty. **—plan,** *m.* principal plan. **—post'direktor,** *m.* postmaster-general. **—probe,** *f.* dress-rehearsal; final rehearsal. **—profoß,** *m.* provost-marshal. **—quartier'meister,** *m.* head of the general staff (*obs.*). **—quittung,** *f.* receipt in full. **—staaten,** *pl.* States-General (of Holland). **—staats'anwalt,** *m.* advocate-general. **—stab,** *m.* staff (*Mil.: each army corps in Germany has its own* **—stab**); **der große —stab,** the Great General Staff (*consisting only of military men*). **—stäbler,** *m.* staff-officer. **—sta'bs=arzt,** *m.* surgeon-general, director-general of the army medical department. **—stabs=karte,** *f.* topographical map, ordnance map. **—stabs=offizier,** *m.* staff-officer. **—stabs=reise,** *f.* (*annual*) journey of the chief of the Great General Staff with the staff officers for the study of tactical and strategic problems. **—statthalter,** *m.* Stadtholder-General (*of the United Netherlands*). **—stelle,** *f.* generalship. **—superintendent,** *m.* superintendent-general (*of the clergy; highest clergyman in some states*). **—synode,** *f.* general synod *or* convention. **—umschalter,** *m.* general commutator. **—versammlung,** *f.* general meeting *or* assembly. **—vikar,** *m.* vicar-general; chancellor of a diocese (*Rom. Cath.*). **—vollmacht,** *f.* general power of attorney. **—zahlmeister,** *m.* paymaster-general; controller of the navy.

Gen—eratio'n, *f.* generation; procreation. **—ere'll,** *adj.* general; universal. **—e'risch,** *adj. & adv.* generic. **—erö's,** *adj.* generous, liberal; ready to give; noble-minded. **—e'tisch,** *adj.* genetical. **—ita'lien,** *pl.* genital organs.

Ge'nitiv, *m.* (—s, *pl.* —e) genitive case.

Ge'n—us, *n.* (*pl.* —era) genus; gender.

Gene's—en, *ir.v.n.* (*aux.* s.) to grow well; to be getting on well, to be mending; to recover; **eines Kindes —en,** to be delivered of a child. **—ende(r),** *m.*, **—ende,** *f.* convalescent. **—ung,** *f.* recovery; convalescence; **auf dem Wege der —ung,** in a fair way of recovery.

Geneu'ß, (*obs. & poet.*) *imperat. of* **genießen; Geneu'ßest, Geneu'ßt,** *obs. & poet.* 2 & 3 *p. sing. pres. indic. of* **genießen.**

Geni'ck, *n.* (—(e)s, *pl.* —e) back of the neck, nape, neck; **zum — gehörig,** cervical; **sich** (*dat.*) **das — brechen,** to break one's neck. *Comp.* **—drüse,** *f.* cervical gland. **—fang,** *m.* stab in the neck. **—fänger,** *m.* hanger, couteau de chasse. **—krampf,** *m.* cerebro-spinal fever (*Anat.*). **—schmerz,** *m.* pain in the nape of the neck, crick in the neck.

Genia'l, *adj. & adv.* highly gifted, ingenious, gifted with genius. **—isch** (*obs.*) = **genial.** **—itä't,** *f.* (*pl.* —itäten) powers *or* gifts of a genius; geniality; originality.

Genie', *n.* (—s) genius, talent, capacity; man of genius; engineering; engineer corps. *Comp.* **—korps,** *n.* Royal engineers. **—streich,** *m.*

stroke of genius; ingenious trick. **—wesen,** *n.* military engineering.

Genie'ren, *v.a.* to embarrass, trouble, to be in one's way, make uneasy, inconvenience; to bore; **sich —,** to feel awkward; **— Sie sich nicht,** don't disturb yourself; make yourself at home; **geniert Sie mein Rauchen,** do you mind my smoking?

Genieß'bar, *adj. & adv.* eatable, edible; palatable, relishable; enjoyable; **er ist heute gar nicht —,** he is unbearable to-day, he is very cross (*or* dull) to-day. **—keit,** *f.* quality of being fit for food, relishable *or* enjoyable.

Genie'ßen, *ir.v.a.* (*n.* (*aux.* **h.**) *with acc.; obs. & poet. with gen.*), to eat *or* drink; use as food; to enjoy; to have the pleasure, benefit *or* use of; to catch the scent (*of dogs*); **dieser Wein ist nicht zu —,** this wine is not drinkable; **— Sie doch ein wenig davon,** pray, taste a little of it; **etwas —,** to take some food, some refreshments; **das Abendmahl —,** to partake of the Lord's supper; **er hat das Seinige** *or* **sein Gutes genossen,** he has had his day, has had his share of the good things of life; **laß mich der neuen Freiheit —,** let me enjoy my new freedom (*poet.*); **nicht zu —,** detestable; **einem etwas für genossen hingehen lassen,** to let one off, to excuse a p. doing a th.; to let one go unpunished for a th.; **etwas für genossen annehmen,** to do without a th., not to insist on getting a thing.

[1]**Geni'ste,** *n.* (**—s**) fragments of twigs, straws; nidification; nest; eggs, young birds.

[2]**Geni'ste,** *f.* (*pl.* **—n**) broom.

Ge'nius, *m.* (man of) genius (*pl.* **Genie's,** men of genius); guardian angel (*pl.* **Ge'nien,** genii); **— einer Sprache,** genius of a language; **dem — einer Sprache entsprechend,** idiomatic.

Geno'mmen, *p.p. of* **nehmen.**

Genör'gel, *n.* (**—s**) continual grumbling, nagging.

Genoss'—e, Geno'ß, *m.* (**—(ss)en,** *pl.* **—(ss)en**), **—in,** *f.* (*pl.* **—innen**) comrade, companion, colleague; partner; chum; mate; confederate; accomplice. **—enschaft,** *f.* company, fellowship, association; partnership; confederacy; **wirtschaftliche —enschaften,** industrial and provident societies, co-operative societies. *Comp.* **—enschafts=gesetz,** *n.* law relating to societies. **—enschafts=tag,** *m.* day of meeting of co-operative societies. **—same** [illegible]. district, village community.

Geno'ß, Genös'se, *imperf. indic. & subj. of* **genießen.**

Gen're, *m. & n.* style, kind, genre. *Comp.* **—bild,** *n.* genre picture. **—maler,** *m.* painter of scenes from every-day life.

Gentia'ne, *f.* (*pl.* **—n**) gentian, bitter-wort.

Genu'g, Genu'ng (*obs. & poet.* = **genug**), *indec. adj.* (*with gen.*) & *adv.* enough, sufficient, sufficiently; **es ist über und über —,** there is enough and to spare; **— zu leben haben,** to have a competency; **— der Thränen!** no more crying! have done with crying! **Glückes —,** plenty of happiness; **— des Streites,** a truce to quarrelling! **— davon!** let us have no more of this! **er ist Mannes —,** he is man enough; (*but usually now with nomin.*) **ich bin nicht Kenner, Künstler, — um zu,** I am not a sufficiently good judge, not enough of an artist to; **einem — thun,** to satisfy one, give one satisfaction; **es ist an einem —,** one will do; **—, mein Kind!** very well, my dear! **—sam,** *adj. & adv.* enough; sufficient. **—samkeit,** *f.* sufficiency. *Comp.* **—thuend,** *adj.* giving satisfaction, satisfying, satisfactory; atoning. **—thuung,** *f.* satisfaction, compensation; amends; atonement; **sich** (*dat.*) **selbst —thuung verschaffen,** to right oneself, do oneself justice, to take the law into one's own hands; **einem — geben,** to give s.o. satisfaction, to make amends; to fight a duel; to apologize.

Genü'g—e, *f. & n.* sufficiency, competency; satisfaction; discharge (*of a duty*); **volle —e,** full satisfaction; **zur —e,** enough, sufficiently; **an alledem habe ich kein —e** (*or* **—en**), all that does not satisfy me; **um Ihnen —e zu thun** (*or* **zu leisten**), to satisfy you. **—lich,** *adj. & adv.* sufficient; satisfactory; pleasant; frugal. **—sam,** *adj. & adv.* easily satisfied; contented; moderate; frugal. **—samkeit,** *f.* moderation; contentedness.

Genü'g—en, *v.* I. *a.* (*aux.* **h.**) to be enough, to suffice; (*with dat.*) to satisfy; **einem Wechsel —en,** to meet a bill; **sich** (*dat.*) **—en lassen** (**an**), to be satisfied with; **laß es dir —en, daß,** be content that; **das —t,** that will do. II. **—en,** *subst.n.* satisfaction; competency; sufficiency; **seiner Schuldigkeit ein —en leisten,** to acquit o.s. of a duty. **—end,** *p. & adj.* sufficient; satisfying; satisfactory; fair, fairly well.

Genu'ng, *adv.* (*instead of* **genug,** *the correct and usual, often rhyming with* **jung,** *is obs. and especially occurs in poetry*) enough.

Genüs'sel, *n.* brood; **Schlangen—,** brood of vipers.

Genu'ß, *m.* (**—(ss)es,** *pl.* **Genüs'se**) enjoyment, pleasure, gratification; profit, use; usufruct; taking (*of food, etc.*); partaking (*of the communion*); **lebenslänglicher —,** life interest. *Comp.* **—mensch,** *m.* man of pleasure. **—mittel,** *n.* (*usually pl.*) luxury; **Nahrungs= und —mittel,** necessaries and luxuries. **—reich,** *adj.* enjoyable. **—sucht,** *f.* inordinate desire for enjoyment, epicureanism, sensuality. **—süchtig,** *adj.* pleasure-seeking, epicurean.

Geo— (*unaccented, in comp.*) **—däsie',** *f.* geodesy, surveying. **—gnos'tisch,** *adj. & adv.* relating to geognosy, geological. **—gra'ph,** *m.* (**—graphen,** *pl.* **—graphen**), geographer. **—gra'phisch,** *adj. & adv.* geographical. **—lo'g,** *m.* (**—logen,** *pl.* **—logen**) geologist. **—lo'gisch,** *adj. & adv.* geological. **—me'ter,** *m.* (**—meters,** *pl.* **—meter**) geometrician. **—metrie',** *f.* geometry; Euclid. **—me'trisch,** *adj. & adv.* geometrical.

Geö'hrt, Geo'hrt, *adj.* with ears; auriculate (*Bot.*)

Geor'gel, *n.* (**—s**) continual organ playing.

Georg—i'ne, *f.* (*pl.* **—inen**) dahlia. *Comp.* **—en=planet, —s=stern,** *m.* Uranus, Georgium Sidus.

Gepaa'rt, *adj.* conjugate, germinate (*Bot.*).

Gepä'ck, *n.* (**—(e)s,** *pl.* **—e**) luggage, baggage; **sein — bekleben lassen,** to have one's luggage labelled; **einem ins — fallen,** to surprise a man, to come upon him unawares; **sein — einschreiben lassen,** to book one's luggage, to have one's baggage registered (*Amer.*). *Comp.* **—annahme, —ausnahme,** *f.* cloak-room (*for all small luggage*). **—aufgabe,** *f.* luggage office. **—ausgabe,** *f.* cloak-room; luggage (*delivery*) office. **—beklebezettel,** *m.* label. **—droschke,** *f.* cab (*with rails on the top*) for luggage, luggage cab. **—expedition,** *f.* luggage office. **—netz,** *n.* luggage rack. **—schein,** *m.* luggage ticket; receipt (*for luggage registered for abroad*). **—träger,** *m.* (*railway*) porter. **—wagen,** *m.* luggage van.

Ge'pard, *m.* (**—katze,** *f.*) Indian leopard.

Gepfef'fert, *p.p. of* **pfeffern.**

Gepfei'fe, *n.* (**—s**) continual whistling, piping.

Gepfif'fen, *p.p. of* **pfeifen.**

Gepflo'gen, *p.p. of* **pflegen. —heit,** *f.* custom, habit.

Gepfro'pft, *p.p. of* **pfropfen; — voll (von),** crammed full of, filled to the last place.

Gepfu'sch(e), *n.* (**—s**) bungling work.

Gepin'sel, *n.* (**—s**) daubing, daub.

Gepla'cke, *n.* (**—s**) drudgery, misery.

Geplä'nkel, *n.* (—s) skirmishing (*Mil.*).

Geplap'per, *n.* (—s) continual babbling, chatter.

Geplä'rr, *n.* (—(e)s) monotonous singing *or* reciting.

Geplät'scher, *n.* (—s) splashing, downpour.

Geplau'der, *n.* (—s) small talk; chat; babbling.

Gepo'che, *n.* (—s) knocking; beating; bravado.

Gepol'ter, *n.* (—s) rumbling noise, din.

Geprä'ge, *n.* (—s) stamp, impression; coinage; stamp, character; **einer S.** (*dat.*) **ihr — aufdrücken**, to put a stamp on a thing, to give a th. its (*peculiar*) character.

Gepra'hle, *n.* (—s) bragging.

Geprän'ge, *n.* (—s) pageantry, pomp, ostentatious display.

Gepras'sel, *n.* (—s) crackling; clatter.

Geprei'st, (*obs.*) *p.p. of* **preisen.**

Geprie'sen, *p.p. of* **preisen.**

Gequa'ckel, *n.* (—s) idle, foolish talk (*coll.*).

Gequa'sel, *n.* (—s) silly talk, twaddle (*coll.*).

Gequat'sch(e), *n.* (—(e)s) empty twaddle (*coll.*).

Gequol'len, *p.p. of* **quellen.**

Ger, *m.* (—s, *pl.* —e) spear; javelin. *Comp.* **—werfen**, *n.* hurling of the spear (*part of German gymnastics*).

G(e)ra'd—e, I. *adj.* straight, direct; erect; upright; straightforward, honest; even; **—er Lichtstrahl**, direct ray of light; **—er Gang**, erect gait; **—e Linie**, straight line; **—er Mann**, plain man, upright man; **—e Zahl**, even number; **—e oder un—e**, odd or even; **—er Takt**, binary measure (*Mus.*); **fünf —e sein lassen**, not to be too punctilious, to stretch a point in favour; **der —e Weg ist der beste**, honesty is the best policy (*prov.*); **—eswegs**, straightway, directly, at once; **seine —en Glieder haben**, to have one's shape and features, to have no deformity. II. *adv. see* —e I. quite; just; **sie stehen einander —e gegenüber**, they are diametrically opposed; **—e heraus**, frankly, bluntly; **sagen wir es —e heraus!** let us speak plainly! **nach —e**, by degrees, ultimately; **ich war —e dort**, I happened to be there; **er kam —e als ich fortging**, he came just as I was going away; **ich bin —e dabei den Brief fertig zu schreiben**, I am just about to finish the letter; **—e das (das —e) Gegenteil**, the very opposite, quite the contrary; **er ist nicht —e mein Freund**, I do not regard him exactly as a friend; **diese Stelle war ihm —e recht**, this place was the very thing for him; **—e recht**, just right, in the nick of time; **da schrie er —e recht**, at that he cried more than ever; **—e darum weil**, just for that very reason; **nun —e**, now especially, now more than ever; **nun —e nicht**, now certainly not! (*coll.*); **—e so viel wie**, just as much as; **—e so . . . wie**, just as if . . . III. **—e**, *f.* straightness; straight line; **in die —e bringen**, to straighten. **—heit**, *f.* straightness; uprightness (*of character*); evenness (*of a number*); rectitude. *Comp.* **—e=an's**, *adv.* straight on *or* ahead, right ahead. **—bohrer**, *m.* auger. **—führung**, *f.* slide-bar, slide; guides. **—führungs=stangen**, *pl.* guide bars, motion bars. **—(e)=halter**, *m.* orthopædic apparatus; apparatus for keeping the head straight (*Phot.*). **—e=hi'n**, *adv.* straight in, rashly, inconsiderately; unceremoniously. **—läufig**, *adj.* having a straight course, direct; orthotropone. **—linig**, *adj.* rectilineal, rectilinear. **—sinn**, *m.* upright disposition, integrity, straightforwardness, honesty. **—sinnig**, *adj.* straightforward, upright, honest. **—(e)=stehend**, *adj.* perpendicular. **—(e)=we'g**, *adv.* plainly, frankly, freely. **—(e)=zu'**, *adv.* straight on; directly; point blank, flatly; candidly; actually; **das ist —ezu Wahnsinn**, that is sheer madness; **mit einem —ezu sein**, to deal plainly with a person.

Gerä'ms, *n.* (—(s)es, *pl.* —(s)e) kind of frame, bowerlike enclosure (*dial.*).

Gera'nnt, *p.p. of* **rennen.**

Gera'se, *n.* (—s) fury, raging.

Geras'sel, *n.* (—s) clatter, clanking, clash.

Gera'te—n, I. *ir.v.n.* (*aux.* **s.**) to get, fall *or* come into, to *or* upon; to hit (*upon*); to turn out (*well*); to prove; to prosper, succeed, thrive; **in Zorn, in Entzücken —n**, to fly into a passion, to go into raptures; **in Unruhe —n**, to become alarmed; **in schlechte Gesellschaft —n**, to get into bad company, to fall in with bad people; **in Armut, an den Bettelstab —n**, to come to poverty, to beggary; **in Vergessenheit —n**, to fall into oblivion; **in Brand —n**, to catch fire; **an den Unrechten —n**, to catch a Tartar; **an den rechten Mann —n**, to fall in with the right person, to fall into good hands; **unter Räuber —n**, to fall in with robbers; **einander in die Haare, an einander —n**, to fall out; to come to blows; **an eine falsche Adresse —n**, to be delivered at the wrong house *or* to the wrong person; **aus der Bahn —n**, to go off the line *or* path; **ich bin auf den Gedanken —n**, I hit upon the idea, the thought, *or* it, struck me; **auf den Sand —n**, to run aground; **ins Stocken —n**, to come to a standstill; **in große Gefahr —n**, to (come to) run a great risk; **das Schiff geriet durch den Sturm nach . . .**, the ship was cast by the storm on the coast of . . .; **Alles gerät ihm**, everything succeeds with him, he succeeds in everything; **die Torte ist vorzüglich geraten**, the tart is a great success; **es — oder verderbe**, hit or miss; **wohl —ne Kinder**, well brought-up, well bred children. II. **—n**, *p.p.* & *adj.* successful; advisable; **nicht —n**, failed, unsuccessful; **das —nste wäre**, the best course would be. *Comp.* **—wohl**, *n.* (*sometimes misspelt* **geradewohl**) haphazard, chance; **aufs —wohl**, at random, in a happy-go-lucky manner.

Gerä't, *n.* (—es, *pl.* —e) implements, tools; utensils, vessels; effects, chattels; furniture; luggage; tackle; household stuff. **—schaft**, *f.* (*us. in the pl.*) *see* **Gerät.** *Comp.* **—kammer**, *f.* lumber-room. **—kasten**, *m.*, **—schafts=kasten**, *m.* tool-box; implement-box (*of sewing-machines*). **—turnen**, *n.*, **—übungen**, *pl.* gymnastic exercises with poles, *etc.*, *or* on cross-bar, double-bar, *etc.*

Gerä'tst, Gerä't, *2 and 3 p. pres. ind. of* **geraten.**

Gerau'fe, *n.* (—s) coming to blows, scuffle.

Gerau'm, *adj.* & *adv.* roomy, spacious, ample; **—e Zeit**, long time; **vor —er Zeit**, long ago.

Gerä'um—ig, *adj.* & *adv.* roomy, spacious. **—igkeit**, *f.* roominess, spaciousness. **—te** (—tes), **—de** (—des), *n.* clearing in a wood fresh land.

Gerau'ne, *n.* (—s) whisperings.

Gerä'usch, *n.* (—es, *pl.* —e) noise; bustle, stir *Comp.* **—laut**, *m.* consonant. **—los**, *adj* noiseless. **—voll**, *adj.* noisy.

Geräus'per, *n.* (—s) clearing of the throat.

Ger'b—en, *v.a.* to tan, dress; **weiß —en**, to taw; to refine (*steel, etc.*); to polish; to thrash; to vomit (*sl.*). **—er**, *m.* (—ers, *pl.* —er) tanner. **—erei'**, *f.* tannery, tan-yard; tanner's trade. *Comp.* **—e=brühe**, *f.* dyeing-liquor. **—erei'=abfälle**, *pl.* tanneries. **—er=grube**, *f.* tan-pit. **—er=hof**, *m.* tanyard. **—er=lohe**, *f.* tanner's spent bark. **—er=messer**, *n.* fleshing knife. **—(e)=stoff**, *m.* tannine, tannic acid. **—säure**, *f.* tannic acid. **—stahl**, *m.* hammered *or* refined steel.

Gere'cht, *adj.* & *adv.* just, righteous; upright; lawful, just; fit, right, suitable; skilled; **die —en**, the just; **der —e**, the Allrighteous; **der —e erbarmt sich seines Viehes**, a righteous man regardeth the life of his beast; in allen Sätteln —, fit for anything; einem — werden, to do justice to, to compensate one; einer Sache — werden, to do justice to, to take into account. —igkeit, *f.* righteousness, justness; justification; justice; right; privilege, license; (einem, einer Sache) —igkeit widerfahren lassen, to do justice to; die —igkeit, Justice; eine alte —igkeit, an old privilege, claim. —sam, *adj. & adv.* rightful, lawful, legitimate. —same, *f.* title; privilege; right; prerogative. *Comp.* —igkeits=pflege, *f.* administration of justice. —machung, *f.* justification.

Gere′(e)d, *adj. & int.* ready, all clear (*Naut.*).

Gere′de, *n.* (—s) talk, report; rumour; ins — kommen, to get talked about; ins — bringen, to cause to be talked about; to gossip about; to slander; es geht das —, the rumour is.

Gere′den, *v.a.* to promise (*obs.*).

Gerei′chen, *v.n.* (*aux.* h.) to bring out, cause, contribute to; to turn out, redound to, conduce to; dies gereichte ihm zum Verderben, this brought about his ruin; es gereicht ihm zur Ehre, it does him credit, redounds to his honour.

Gerei′me, *n.* (—s) making of (bad) verses.

Gerei′zt, *p.p. of* reizen, *& adj.* irritated; vexed. —heit, *f.* irritation.

Gerenn′ne, *n.* (—s) running to and fro.

Gereu′en, *v.a.imp.* to cause repentance; es gereut mich, I repent (of); I am sorry (for); es wird (soll) Sie —, you will (shall) repent it; sich (*acc.*) etwas — lassen, to regret something; diese That wird mich niemals —, I shall never repent of this deed; er läßt sich keine Mühe —, he grudges *or* spares no trouble.

Ger′gel, *m.* (—s) groove, notch, croze. —n, *v.a.* to groove, croze (*staves of a cask*).

Geri′cht, *n.* (—s, *pl.* —e) court of justice; judgment; jurisdiction; justice; tribunal; place of execution; dish, course; heute Mittag gab es drei —e, to-day we had three dishes for lunch; das jüngste —, the last judgment, doomsday; vor —, in(to) court; vor — fordern, to summon; vor — stellen, to arraign; — halten, zu — sitzen, to sit in judgment on, to try; einen beim —e verklagen, to prosecute a person; mit einem ins — gehen, to enter into judgment with one. —lich, I. *adj.* judicial; legal; forensic; —liche Medizin, forensic medicine; —liche Schritte, legal measures; —liche Tierarzneikunde, veterinary jurisprudence. II. *adv.* judicially; in legal form; einen —lich belangen, to sue a p. at law, go to law with s.o. —lichkeit, *f.* legal qualification; legal proceedings. —s=barkeit, *f.* jurisdiction. *Comp.* —s=akten, *pl.* records. —s=aktuar, *m.* clerk of the court. —amt, *n.* court of justice. —s=amtmann, *m.* president of a court of justice. —s=bank, *f.* tribunal. —s=beamte(r), *m.* magistrate, justiciary. —s=befehl, *m.* writ. —s=beisitzer, *m.* judge-lateral, assessor. —bescheid, *m.* sentence. —s=bezirk, *m.* circuit, jurisdiction. —s=buch, *n.* register. —s=diener, *m.* beadle; usher of the court; summoner. —direktor, *m.* president of a court of justice. —s=folge, *f.* posse comitatus. —s=gang, *m.* legal procedure. —s=gebühren, —s=gefälle, *pl.* court-fees, law-charges. —s=halter, *m.* justiciary. —s=handel, *m.* law-suit. —s=hof, *m.* court of justice, tribunal. —s=hörigkeit, *f.* competence of a court. —s=kanzlei, *f.* record-office. —s=kosten, *pl.* law expenses; einen zu den —skosten verurteilen, to condemn one to pay the costs. —s=person, *f.* magistrate, gentleman of the long robe, judge. —s=pflege, *f.* administration of justice. —s=platz, *m. see* —s=stätte. —s=posaune, *f.* last trumpet (*B.*). —s=rat, *m.* justice; counsellor. —s=schöppe, *m.* assistant judge. —s=schreiber, *m.* clerk of the court. —s=schulze, *m.* magistrate. —s=sprengel, *m.* jurisdiction. —s=stadt, *f.* town that has a court of justice, assize-town. —s=statt, —s=stätte, *f.* session-house, court; place of execution. —s=stube, *f.* court-room. —s=stuhl, *m.* tribunal; judge's chair. —s=tag, *m.* court-day. —s=unterthan, *m.* one under the jurisdiction of a court. —s=verbesserung, *f.* law-reform. —s=verfahren, *n.* proceedings at law, rules of court. —s=verhandlungen, *pl.* pleadings, law proceedings; records. —s=verwalter, —s=verweser, *m.* administrator of justice, justiciary. —s=verwaltung, —s=verwesung, *f.* administration of justice. —s=vogt, *m.* magistrate, justiciary. —s=wegen, *adv.;* von —swegen, on account of the law, by warrant. —s=zimmer, *n.* justice-room. —s=zwang, *m.* jurisdiction.

Gerie′ben, *p.p. of* reiben, *& adj.* cunning, sly.

Gerie′sel, *n.* (—s) rippling, purling.

Gerie′t, Gerie′te, *imperf. indic. & subj. of* geraten.

Geri′ng, *adj. & adv.* small, little, trifling, petty; unimportant; mean, low; humble; scanty; limited, circumscribed; slender; deficient in weight; inferior in quality; indifferent; —er Preis, low price; mein —es Verdienst, my humble merit; er giebt es nicht —er, he does not sell it for less; —er machen, to lessen, diminish; (etwas) — schätzen, halten, achten, to esteem lightly, disregard, despise; nicht im —sten, not in the least; nicht das —ste, not the least bit, nothing at all; —e Kenntnisse, limited knowledge, poor information; —e Kost, poor fare; mit —en Ausnahmen, with but few exceptions; wir kamen in nicht —e Verlegenheit, we were not a little embarrassed; —er Wein, inferior, bad wine; —e Leute, people in humble circumstances; ein —es, a trifle, nearly, almost; sich (*dat.*) nichts —es einbilden, to think no little of oneself; die —en wie die Großen, the lowly and the great, rich and poor; ich bin nicht —er als er, I am as good as he; nichts —eres als . . ., nothing short of . . .; ein —erer, an inferior person. —heit, *f.* smallness; meanness, humbleness (*of birth, etc.*); lowness (*of price, etc.*). *Comp.* —achtung, *f.* disregard; contempt, disdain. —fügig, *adj.* insignificant; trifling, trivial; light; mean. —fügigkeit, *f.* insignificance; paltriness; trifle. —haltig, *adj.* of base alloy; of little worth; below the standard; weak, futile. —haltung, *see* —achtung. —schätzig, *adj.* depreciatory; disdainful, disrespectful; derogatory; contemptuous; mean, contemptible. —schätzung, *f. see* —achtung; mit —schätzung behandeln, to treat with contempt.

Gerinn′—bar, *adj.* coagulable. —e, *n.* (—es, *pl.* —e) continual running, flowing; running water; gutter; trough (*of a mill*); mill-race; channel. *Comp.* —haue, *f.* gutter-hook.

Gerin′n—en, *ir.v.n.* (*aux.* f.) to curdle; to coagulate; to congeal; to clot. —sel, *n.* coagulated matter. —t, *adj.* channelled (*Bot.*). —ung, *f.* coagulation.

Gerip′pe, *n.* (—s, *pl.* —) skeleton; framework.

Geri′ppt, *p.p. of* rippen, *adj.* ribbed; groined; fluted; —es Papier, laid paper.

Geris′sen, *p.p. of* reißen; *adj.* sly, cunning (*coll.*).

Gerit′ten, *p.p. of* reiten.

German—is′mus, *m.* (*pl.* —ismen) Germanism, German idiom. —i′st, *m.* (—is′ten, *pl.* —is′ten) student *or* teacher of German and Germanic philology; student *or* teacher of old

German law. **—is'tik,** *f.* German and Germanic philology. **—is'tisch,** *adj.* pertaining to German and Germanic philology, Germanic (*the older term* Teutonic *should not be used*); **—is'tische Studien,** studies in the domain of the Germanic languages and literatures. *Comp.* **—is'ten=kneipe,** *f.* convivial meeting of professors and students of German philology. **—is'ten=verein,** *m.* association of students of German and Germanic philology.

Ger'n(e), *adv.* (*comp.* **lieber; gerner** *is obs. & dial.: sup.* **am liebsten**) with pleasure, willingly, readily; fain; often (*dial.*); **nicht —,** reluctantly; **etwas — haben,** to like a thing; **ein Mädchen — haben,** to be fond of a girl; **so habe ich es —,** that is what I like; **er hört sich — reden,** he likes to hear himself talk; **herzlich —, von Herzen —,** with all my (one's) heart; **er tanzt, spielt, reitet —,** he likes, loves, is fond of, dancing, playing, riding; **ich esse es —,** I like it (*to eat*); **er ist überall — gesehen,** he is everywhere welcome; **ich würde es sehr — sehen, wenn Sie . . .,** I should very much like you to, should be delighted if you . . .; **ich möchte — wissen, ob . . .,** I should like to know if . . .; **das ist — möglich,** that is quite possible, very likely; **das glaube ich —,** that I can readily believe; **es ist — geschehen,** you are very welcome (to it), do not mention it; **er sagte —,** (*dial.*) he often said, he used to say; **Lessing warf die persönliche Würde — weg,** Lessing was apt to throw away his personal dignity, L. easily *or* often threw away his p. d.; **dieses Holz verfault —,** this wood is apt to rot (*dial.*); **dafür kannst du gut und — fünf Mark geben,** you need not fear to give five marks for it, it is well worth five marks; **die meisten Leute trinken lieber roten Wein als weißen,** most people prefer red wine to white. *Comp.* **—e=groß,** *m.* would-be-great. **—gese=hen,** *adj.* welcome. **—witz,** *m.* would-be-wit.

Gerö'chel, *n.* (—s) rattling in the throat.

Gero'chen, *p.p. of* (*1*) **riechen;** (*2*) **rächen** (*usually poetic*).

Geröh'rich(t), *n.* (—s, *pl.* —e) reeds; reedy place.

Gerol'l(e), *n.* (—(e)s) continual rumbling, rolling.

Geröl'l(e), *n.* (—(e)s) rubble, boulders, scree; mass of water-worn material.

Geron'nen, *p.p. of* (*1*) **rinnen;** (*2*) **gerinnen.**

Gerös'tete(s), *n.* what has been grilled; broil.

Ger'ste, *f.* (*pl.* —n) barley. **—n,** *adj.* (of) barley. *Comp.* **—n=acker,** *m.* field of barley. **—n=brot,** *n.* barley-bread, barley-loaf. **—n=brühe,** *f.* barley-water, barley-broth. **—n=graupen,** *pl.* peeled barley, Scotch barley; (**feine**) pearl barley. **—n=grütze,** *f.* pearl barley. **—n=korn,** *n.* barley-corn; sty (*in the eye*). **—n=mehl=brei,** *m.* barley-flour gruel. **—n=milch,** *f.* orgeat. **—n=saft,** *m.;* **der edle—saft,** beer (*students' sl.*). **—n=schleim,** *m.* (barley) gruel. **—n=trank,** *m.,* **—n=wasser,** *n.* barley water. **—n=zucker,** *m.* barley-sugar.

Ger'te, *f.* (*pl.* —n) twig, switch; whip; measure (= *a rood*).

Geru'ch, *m.* (—(e)s, *pl.* **Gerü'che**) smell, sense of smell; odour; scent; savour; reputation; **im —e der Heiligkeit,** in the odour of sanctity. *Comp.* **—los,** *adj.* without the sense of smell; scentless, odourless; not scented. **—losma=chung,** *f.* deodorizing; disinfecting. **—s=nerv,** *m.* olfactory nerve. **—s=sinn,** *m.* sense of smell. **—s=werkzeug,** *n.* organ of smell.

Gerü'cht, *n.* (—es, *pl.* —e) rumour, report; Fame; **es geht das —,** it is rumoured, reported; **das — ist im Umlauf,** the report is afloat; **es ist ein bloßes —,** it is a mere rumour. **—lich,** *adj. & adv.* according to report. *Comp.* **—(s)=weise,** *adv. see* **—lich; —(s)=weise verlautet,** the story goes.

Geru'fe, *n.* (—s) repeated calling, continual shouts.

Geru'hen, *v.n.* (*aux.* **h.**) to condescend, to deign, to be pleased; **Eure Majestät wollen allergnädigst —,** may it please your Majesty; **Seine Majestät haben geruht,** his Majesty has been pleased, has signified his pleasure.

Geru'hig, *adj.* perfectly calm (*poet.*).

Gerum'pel, *n.* (—s) continual rumbling, rattling.

Gerüm'pel, *n.* (—s) lumber, rubbish. *Comp.* **—kammer,** *f.* lumber room.

Gerun'd—ium, *n.* (—iums, *pl.* —ien *or* — ia) gerund. **—i'visch,** *adj.* gerundial.

Gerun'gen, *p.p. of* **ringen.**

Gerun'zel, *n.* (—s) wrinkles (*coll.*); constant frowning.

Gerü'st, *n.* (—es, *pl.* —e) scaffold(ing); stage; frame, stand; trestle, rack; cradle; **das — abreißen,** to take down the scaffolding. *Comp.* **—kammer,** *f.* room for tools. **—künstler,** *m.* machinist, stage carpenter (*Theat.*). **—stange,** *f.* scaffolding-pole.

Gerüt'tel, *n.* (—s) continual shaking *or* jolting.

Ges, *n.* G-flat.

Gesä'g—e, *n.* (—s) continual sawing. **—t,** *adj.* serrate.

Gesa'gt, *p.p. of* **sagen; —, getan,** no sooner said than done (*prov.*).

Gesal'bader, *n.* (—s) balderdash, silly talk.

Gesal'zen, *p.p. of* **salzen,** *adj.* exorbitant (*price*) (*coll.*).

Gesä'me, *n.* (—s) seeds.

Gesa'mt, (*older spelling:* **Gesa'mmt,**) *adj. & adv.* whole, entire, all; united, joint, common; total, collective; **der —e Adel,** the whole body of the nobility; **das —e Volk,** the whole nation, all the people; **alle ins —,** collectively, one and all. **—e(s),** *n.* the whole, the (sum) total. **—heit,** *f.* totality; the whole; all; **in der —heit genommen,** taken collectively. **—schaft,** *f.* corporate body; *see* **—heit.** *Comp.* **—aben=teuer,** *n.* collection of romantic stories (*rare*); book of mediæval fiction. **—ausgabe,** *f.* edition of the complete works (*of an author*). **—belehnung,** *f.* joint investiture. **—betrag,** *m.* sum-total. **—bewußtsein,** *n.* collective consciousness. **—erbe,** *m.,* **—erbin,** *f.* sole heir, heiress. **—ertrag,** *m.* entire proceeds, total produce. **—forderung,** *f.* total charges *or* claim. **—gebrauch,** *m.* exclusive use. **—le=hen,** *n.* fief held by several men in common (*obs.*). **—macht,** *f.* joint forces; whole power. **—masse,** *f.* total estate (*Comm.*). **—ministe=rium,** *n.* body of ministers, the whole cabinet. **—regierung,** *f.* central power; joint government. **—staat,** *m.* united state *or* country; **der deutsche —staat,** United Germany. **—tonnengehalt,** *m.* total tonnage. **—übersicht,** *f.* general survey. **—wille(n),** m. collective will, joint desire. **—wohl,** *n.* public *or* common weal. **—zahl,** *f.* total number, sum total.

Gesa'ndt, *p.p. of* **senden. —e(r),** *m.* one who has been sent, messenger, envoy; ambassador; **der päpstliche —e,** the nuncio; **er ist ein —er, aber kein geschickter,** he is an ambassador, but not a skilful one. **—in,** *f.* ambassador's wife, ambassadress. **—schaft,** *f.* embassy, legation. **—schaftlich,** *adj. & adv.* ambassadorial, diplomatic, belonging to an embassy; **—schaftlicher Auftrag,** diplomatic mission. *Comp.* **—schafts=hotel,** *n.* embassy, legation. **—schafts=personal,** *n.* members of an embassy, legation. **—schafts=posten,** *m.* ambassador's post, ambassadorial position. **—schafts=wesen,** *n.* diplomacy. **—sekretär,** *m.* secretary to an embassy.

Gesa'ng, *m.* (—es, *pl.* **Gesän'ge**) singing; lay, song, melody; poem, poetry; canto; warbling (*of birds*); **Lob—,** hymn, psalm; **dieses Mu-**

sikstück hat keinen —, there is no melody in this piece of music; **zweistimmiger —**, duet; **mehrstimmiger —**, part-song, glee. *Comp.* **—buch**, *n.* book of songs; hymn-book. **—lehrer**, *m.* singing master. **—stimme**, *f.* voice-part. **—stunde**, *f.* singing lesson. **—verein**, *m.* choral union, glee club, choral society, philharmonic society. **—weise**, I. *f.* melody, tune. II. *adv.* in the manner of a song.

Gesä'ß, *n.* (**—es**, *pl.* **—e**) seat; bottom; breech.

Gesa'tz, *n.* (**—es**, *pl.* **Gesät'ze**) set, nest; couplet.

Gesä'tz, Gese'tz, *n.* stanza (*obs. metre*).

Gesau'fe, Gesäuf'te, *n.* (*poet.*) (**—s**) carousing, hard drinking.

Gesäu'mt, *adj.* bordered, fimbriate.

Gesau'se, *n.* (**—s**) rushing, whistling; buzzing.

Gesäu'sel, *n.* (**—s**) murmuring, gentle rustling.

Geschä'ft, *n.* (**—es**, *pl.* **—e**) employment, occupation; calling; affair; speculation; business; transaction; commercial establishment; **engros —**, wholesale business; **Detail —**, retail business; **ein solides —**, a substantial house; **ein — anfangen, aufgeben**, to begin, to give up business; **gute —e machen**, to do well in a business, to prosper; **ein natürliches — verrichten**, to relieve o.s., to go somewhere (*coll.*); **große —e machen**, to do extensive business; **in —en stehen mit**, to be connected in business with; **welches — betreiben Sie?** what is your trade *or* occupation? what line of business are you in? **sich** (*dat.*) **ein — daraus machen**, to make it one's business; **erst das — und dann das Vergnügen**, business before pleasure (*prov.*). **—ig**, *adj. & adv.* busy, active; industrious; energetic; zealous; officious. **—igkeit**, *f.* activity; zeal; industry, officiousness. **—lich**, *adj. & adv.* relating to business, commercial, business-like; on business. *Comp.* **—s=adreßkarte**, *f.* business-card. **—s=anteil**, *m.* share in a business. **—s=fach**, *n.* line of business. **—auftrag**, *m.* commission. **—s=fertig**, *adj.* smart in business. **—s=frei**, *adj.* unoccupied, unemployed. **—s=freund**, *m.* connection, (commercial) correspondent; customer. **—s=führer**, *m.* manager. **—s=gang**, *m.* daily routine of a business. **—s=gegend**, *f.* business *or* commercial quarter of a town; the city (*London*). **—s=geheimnis**, *n.* secret of the trade; secret of the firm, patent. **—s=gehülfe**, *m.* clerk in an office; assistant. **—s=geist**, *m.* turn for business. **—s=genoß**, *m.* partner. **—s=haus**, *n.* commercial firm. **—s=inhaber**, *m.* owner of a firm, principal. **—s=kreis**, *m.* line of business; province; practice (*of doctors*). **—s=lokal**, *n.* place of business; counting-house; office; shop; stores; warehouse. **—s=losigkeit**, *f.* inactivity; leisure; dulness of trade. **—s=mann**, *m.* (*pl.* **—s=leute**, tradesmen, tradespeople) man of business, tradesman, trader. **—s=mäßig**, *adj. & adv.* businesslike. **—s=personal**, *n.* staff *or* employees of a house. **—s=reisender**, *m.* commercial traveller. **—s=schwung**, *m.* briskness of trade. **—s=sprache**, *f.* commercial language, mercantile terms. **—s=stil**, *m.* commercial style. **—s=stille**, *f.* dulness of trade. **—s=stube**, *f.* office. **—s=stunden**, *pl.* business hours, office hours. **—s=teilhaber**, *m.* partner; **stiller —steilhaber**, sleeping partner, silent partner. **—s=träger**, *m.* representative, agent (*of a firm*); chargé d'affaires, (*diplomatic*) consul. **—s=verbindung**, *f.* business connection. **—s=verhältnisse**, *pl.* condition of trade. **—s=verkehr**, *m.* commercial intercourse. **—s=verlegung**, *f.* removal (of a business). **—s=verwalter**, *m.* manager. **—s=zeit**, *f.* office hours. **—s=zimmer**, *n.* office. **—s=zweig**, *m.* branch of business; **besonderer —s=zweig**, specialty.

Gescha'h, (*obs.* **Gescha'ch**,) **Geschä'he**, *imperf. ind. & subj. of* **geschehen**.

Geschä'ker, *n.* (**—s**) joking, dallying, playfulness.

Geschau'kel, *n.* (**—s**) swinging up and down, see-saw, rolling (*of a ship*), rocking (*of a cradle*).

Gesche'ckt, *adj.* piebald; variegated.

Gesche'hen, *ir.v.n.* (*aux.* **s.**) to come to pass; to happen; to happen to; to be done; **es ist ein Unglück —**, a misfortune, an accident, has happened; **es geschehe was da wolle**, whatever may happen; **es kann —, daß**, it may chance that; **es geschieht ihm recht**, it serves him right; **es geschieht ihm unrecht**, he is wronged; **das kann nicht ohne große Kosten —**, that cannot be executed without great expense; **es geschieht viel für die Armen**, a great deal is done for the poor, the poor are well cared for; **es geschicht mir ein Dienst damit**, it is doing me a kindness; **ich weiß nicht, wie mir geschieht**, I don't know what is wrong with me; **es ist so gut wie —**, it is as good as done; **es ist um ihn —**, he is undone, done for; it is all over with him, he is lost; **es geschehe!** be it so! **Dein Wille geschehe**, Thy will be done (*B.*). II. *p.p. & adj.*; **—e Dinge sind nicht zu ändern**, what is done cannot be undone; **nach —er Arbeit**, after one's work is finished; **— zu Hannover, den 5 Januar**, given at Hanover, the fifth of January. **—e(s)**, *n.* what is done. *Comp.* **—lassen**, *n.* letting alone, letting things go, non-interference; conniving (*at things*).

Gescheh'nis, *n.* (**—(ss)es**, *pl.* **—(ss)e**) event.

Geschei't, (*sometimes spelt* **Gescheid**, *also* **Gescheidt**; *sometimes also* **Gescheut**,) *adj.* shrewd, sensible, judicious, clever, wise; **ich kann nicht — daraus werden**, I do not comprehend it; **nicht recht —**, a little cracked, only half-witted; **du bist wohl nicht recht —**, you are, I suppose, not right in your mind; **sei doch —!** don't be a fool, be reasonable! **sei — und komm' mit uns**, be a good boy and come along with us; **daraus kann nichts —es werden**, nothing good can come of it. **—heit**, *f.* prudence, discretion; cleverness.

Geschel'te, *n.* (**—s**) continual scolding.

Geschen'k, *n.* (**—es**, *pl.* **—e**) present, gift, donation; **einem ein — machen mit**, to make one a present of. *Comp.* **—fuß**, *m.*; **(mit einem) auf dem —fuße stehen**, to be upon such terms as admits of the exchange of presents. **—geber**, *m.* donor *or* giver of presents. **—nehmer**, *m.* recipient of presents.

Gescheu't, *see* **Gescheit**.

Geschi'cht, *obs. 3 pers. sing. pres. ind. of* **geschehen**.

Geschicht'chen, *n.* (**—s**, *pl.* **—**) anecdote.

Geschi'cht—e, *f.* (*pl.* **—en**) history; story; event; affair, business, concern; **alte, mittlere, neuere —e**, ancient, mediæval, modern history; **biblische —e**, Scripture (history); **Heiligen —en**, legends of saints; **eine schöne —e!** a nice affair, a pretty business; **eine schwierige —e**, a difficult task (*coll.*); **eine dumme —e**, a nuisance; **die ganze —e**, the whole concern; **das wäre eine schöne —e!** that would be a nice thing, indeed! **die alte —e!** the old story over again! **eine fatale** *or* **verflixte —e**, a desperate business, a pretty mess (*coll.*); **mache doch keine —en!** don't make a fuss! (*coll.*). **—lich**, *adj. & adv.* historical, historically true; **er hat —lich denken gelernt**, he has learned to see things in the light of history. *Comp.* **—en=buch**, *n.* story-book. **—s=buch**, *n.* history book. **—s=erzählung**, *f.* historical narrative; statement of facts. **—s=forscher**, *m.* historian. **—s=forschung**, *f.* historical research. **—s=freund**, *m.* lover of history. **—s=gemälde**, *n.* historical painting. **—s=mäßig**, *adj.* historical. —(s)=schreiber, *m.* historian. —s=wissenschaft, *f.* science of history. —s=zug, *m.* historical trait, anecdote.

Geschi'ck, *n.* (—es, *pl.* —e) fitness, knack, aptness, skill, aptitude; fate, destiny; dieser Rock hat kein —, this coat is badly cut; kurz und dick hat kein —, short and big looks like a pig (*prov.*); etwas ins — bringen, to put s.th. to rights, to set a th. right. —lichkeit, *f.* skill, cleverness, dexterity, adroitness; art; ability. —t, *p.p. & adj.* adapted, fit; able, dexterous; —t zu, clever at, qualified for.

Geschi'cke, *n.* (—s) continual sending on errands, coming and going of messengers.

Geschie'be, *n.* erratic blocks. —blöcke, *pl.* boulders. —formation, *f.* unstratified deposit.

Geschie'den, *p.p. of* scheiden. —heit, *f.* state of separation.

Geschie'ht, *3 pers. sing. pres. ind. of* geschehen.

Geschie'nen, *p.p. of* scheinen.

Geschi'lf, *n.* (—es) spot overgrown with weeds.

Geschim'pf(e), *n.* (—(e)s) abusive language.

Geschi'rr, *n.* (—es, *pl.* —e) vessel; table utensils; crockery; implements; harness (*of horses*); equipage; apparatus; connecting gear, gearing; die Pferde legen sich ins —, the horses pull hard, step out bravely; ins — gehen, to exert o.s.; aus dem — kommen, to rest; to become embarrassed (*coll.*). *Comp.* —brett, *n.* cupboard. —kammer, *f.* harness-room; pantry, china-closet; plate-closet; tool-house. —meister, *m.* one who has the charge of tools, officer in charge of the baggage (*Mil.*); boatswain (*Naut.*). —schnalle, *f.* harness-buckle.

Geschis'sen, *p.p. of* scheißen.

Geschle'cht, *n.* (—es, *pl.* —er) genus; kind, species; sex; race, family; generation; gender; männliches —, male sex; masculine gender (*Gram.*); das schöne —, the fair sex; das sächliche —, the neuter gender (*Gram.*); die —er, the two sexes; the old wealthy patrician families (*of old German towns; obs.*). —lich, *adj.* sexual, generic. *Comp.* —er=kunde, *f.* genealogy. —los, *adj.* without sexual distinction, neuter. —s=adel, *m.* hereditary nobility. —s=alter, *n.* generation. —s=art, *f.* genus, kind; generic character. —s=baum, *m.* pedigree. —s=beschreiber, *m.* genealogist. —s=folge, *f.* generation. —s=glied, *n.* one of a family *or* generation; *pl.* genitals (*Anat.*). —s=krankheit, *f.* disease of the genital organs. —s=kunde, —s=lehre, *f.* genealogy. —s=lehen, *n.* hereditary fief. —s=linie, *f.* lineage, pedigree. —s=los, *see* —los. —s=lust, *f.* sexual enjoyment. —s=name, *m.* family name, surname. —s=register, *n.* genealogical table, pedigree. —s=reif, *adj.* having attained the age of puberty, fully developed. —s=reife, *f.* puberty. —s=system, *n.* Linnæan system. —s=tafel, *f.* genealogical table, table of descent. —s=teile, *pl.* sexual *or* genital organs, genitals, privates. —s=trieb, *m.* sexual instinct. —s=unterschied, *m.* difference of the sexes; difference of sex. —s=verbindung, *f.* sexual intercourse. —s=wahl, *f.* sexual selection. —s=wappen, *n.* family arms. —s=wort, *n.* generic word; article.

Geschle'ck—(e), *n.* (—s) licking, smacking, continual kissing.

Geschlep'p(e), *n.* (—(e)s, *pl.* —(e)) dragging; trail; train; drag (*Sport.*); heavy luggage.

Geschli'chen, *p.p. of* schleichen. *adj.* suitable, welcome (*coll.*); das kommt mir gerade —, that 's the very thing I want (*coll.*).

Geschlif'fen, *p.p. of* schleifen. *adj.* polished, polite. —heit, *f.* polish, refinement.

Geschlin'ge, *n.* (—s, *pl.* —) gluttony; pluck (*of slaughtered beasts*); festoon, garland.

Geschlis'sen, *p.p. of* schleißen.

Geschlof'fen, *p.p. of* schliefen (*obs.*).

Geschlos'sen, *p.p. of* schließen; —e Kette, endless chain; —e Gesellschaft, club, private party.

Geschluch'ze, *n.* (—s) continual sobbing.

Geschlun'gen, *p.p. of* schlingen.

Geschma'ck, *m.* (—es, *pl.* Geschmä'cke) taste, flavour; savour; relish, fancy; good taste; dies hat einen guten —, this tastes good; — an einer S. finden, to relish *or* take a fancy to a thing; über den — läßt sich nicht streiten, there is no disputing about *or* accounting for tastes (*prov.*); der — ist verschieden, tastes differ (*prov.*). *Comp.* —los, *adj.* tasteless, insipid; without taste, in bad taste. —losigkeit, *f.* want of taste, bad taste; das ist eine —losigkeit, that is bad taste. —s=empfindung, —s=kunde, —s=lehre, *f.* æsthetics. —s=nerv, *m.* gustative nerve. —s=sache, *f.*; das ist —s=sache, that is a matter of taste. —s=sinn, *m.* sense of taste; taste for the beautiful. —voll, *adj.* tasteful; having good taste, stylish, elegant. —widrig, *adj.* contrary to good taste, in bad taste, tasteless, inelegant.

Geschmäck'ler, *m.* (—s) pretender to taste.

Geschmat'ze, *n.* (—s) smacking, noisy kissing.

Geschmau'se, *n.* (—s) banqueting, feasting.

Geschmei'd—e, *n.* (—es, *pl.* —e) anything wrought in metal; set of jewellery, jewels, trinkets. —ig, *adj. & adv.* malleable; ductile; pliant, yielding; supple, flexible; smooth, soft. —igkeit, *f.* malleability; tractability; suppleness, flexibility. *Comp.* —e=händler, *m.* jeweller. —e=kästchen, *n.* jewel-case.

Geschmei'ß, *n.* (—es, *pl.* —e) dung, dirt; fly-blow, eggs (*of insects*); vermin; rabble, dregs of society.

Geschmet'ter, *n.* (—s) braying, flourish (*of trumpets*); warbling (*of a canary*).

Geschmie're, *n.* (—s) smearing, greasing; scrawl(ing), daub(ing); adulteration (*of wine*).

Geschmie'rt, *p.p. of* schmieren. *adj.* well-oiled, smooth; das geht wie —, that comes off very well (*coll.*).

Geschmis'sen, *p.p. of* schmeißen.

Geschmol'zen, *p.p. of* schmelzen.

Geschmor'te—(s), *n.* (—n) stew.

Geschmun'zel, *n.* (—s) smirking.

Geschnä'belt, *adj.* beaked; rostrate.

Geschnar'che, *n.* (—s) snoring.

Geschnat'ter, *n.* (—s) cackling, chatter.

Geschnie'gelt, *p.p. of* schniegeln. *adj.* spruce, trim, smart; — und gebügelt, spick-and-span.

Geschnit'ten, *p.p. of* schneiden.

Geschno'ben, *p.p. of* schnauben.

Geschnur're, *n.* (—s) purring; humming.

Gescho'ben, *p.p. of* schieben.

Geschol'ten, *p.p. of* schelten.

Geschöpf, *n.* (—es, *pl.* —e) creature; production.

Gescho'ren, *p.p. of* scheren.

Geschos'sen, *p.p. of* schießen.

Gescho'ß, *n.* (*with short* o) (—(ss)es, *pl.* —(ss)e) dart, missile, projectile, arrow; shoot, sprout; fire-arm; story, floor. —spiegel, *m.* wooden-bottom (*Artil.*).

Geschrä'ge, *n.* (—s, *pl.* —) paling; hurdle.

Geschrau'bt, *p.p. & adj.* screwed, twisted; affected. —heit, *f.* affectation in style.

Geschrei', *n.* (—s, *pl.* —e) screams, cries; cry; clamour, shouting, outcry; discredit, disrepute; noises of animals (*as braying, crowing, etc.*); ins — kommen, to get talked about, get a bad name; ins — bringen, to bring into disrepute; das — hinter einem her, hooting, hoot; es geht ein —, there is a rumour, it is rumoured; viel — um nichts, much ado about nothing; viel — und wenig Wolle, great cry and little wool; great boast, small roast (*prov.*).

Geschrei'b—e, *n.* (—es) continual writing. —

sel, *n.* (—sel(e)s) scribble, writing deficient in form and contents.

Geschrie'ben, *p.p. of* schreiben.

Geschrie'en, *p.p. of* schreien.

Geschrit'ten, *p.p. of* schreiten.

Geschro'ben, *p.p. of* schrauben.

Geschun'den, *p.p. of* schinden.

Geschü'r, *n.* (—es) dross.

Geschüt'te, *n.* (—s) repeated pouring; mixed layers, heaps. **—l,** *n.* (—l(e)s) quaking, shaking.

Geschü'tz, *n.* (—es, *pl.* —e) gun, cannon, piece of ordnance; **das grobe** *or* **schwere —,** the big guns, heavy artillery; weighty reasons (*fig.*); **leichtes —,** light artillery; **gezogenes —,** rifled gun; **das — aufpflanzen,** to mount the guns; **das — spielen lassen,** to play the cannon. *Comp.* **—aufstellung,** *f.* planting of guns. **—bank,** *f.* barbette. **—bedienung,** *f.* working of the guns. **—bedienungs-mannschaft,** *f.* artillerymen serving a piece. **—donner,** *m.* roar *or* booming of the guns. **—feuer,** *n.* heavy firing, cannonade; artillery practice. **—kampf,** *m.* artillery duel. **—kugel,** *f.* cannonball. **—kunst,** *f.* gunnery. **—park,** *m.* park *or* train of artillery. **—pforte,** *f.* port-hole (*Nav.*). **—probe,** *f.* trial of guns. **—protze,** *f.* carriage of a gun. **—rohr,** *m.* barrel of a gun. **—salve,** *f.* discharge *or* volley of artillery. **—weite,** *f.* bore (*of a cannon*). **—wesen,** *n.* gunnery. **—zug,** *m.* train, park of artillery.

Geschwa'der, *n.* (—s, *pl.* —) squadron (*Mil.*, *Nav.*). *Comp.* **—verband,** *m.* all the battleships forming one squadron. **—weise,** *adv.* in squadrons.

Geschwä'tz, *n.* (—es, *pl.* —e) idle *or* continual talking, babble; tittle-tattle, gossiping; rigmarole; **was soll dies —?** what is the meaning of this babble? **—ig,** *adj. & adv.* talkative, gossiping, garrulous. **—igkeit,** *f.* talkativeness.

Geschwei'ft, *p.p. of* schweifen. *adj.* arched (*postage stamps*).

Geschwei'ge, *adv. lit.* (I) am silent (about); not to mention, let alone; much less; far from; to say nothing of; **ich habe ihn nicht gesehen, — denn angesprochen,** I have not seen, much less spoken to him; **ich fürchte seine Freundschaft, — denn seine Feindschaft,** I fear his friendship, still more (not to speak of) his enmity.

Geschwei'gen, *ir.v.* I. *n.* (*aux.* h.) (*gen.*) to pass by in silence, say nothing of, not to mention (*obs.*). II. *a.* to silence, appease (*obs.*).

Geschwel'ge, *n.* (—s) revelry, rioting.

Geschwie'gen, *p.p. of* schweigen.

Geschwi'nd, *adj. & adv.* quick, swift, fast; prompt; **sie wußte nicht, was sie — sagen sollte,** she did not know at the moment what to say; **mach' —!** be quick! **—igkeit,** *f.* quickness; velocity; **in der —igkeit,** hurriedly, on the spur of the moment; **die —igkeit vermindern,** to slow down, to slacken the movement; **Anfangs—igkeit,** initial velocity; **volle —igkeit,** full speed; **—igkeit (eines Schiffes),** rate (of sailing *or* steaming); **—igkeit ist keine Hexerei,** velocity is no sorcery, sleight of hand is no magic (*prov.*). *Comp.* **—igkeits-messer,** *m.* tachometer. **—marsch,** *m.* quick march; quick time. **—presse,** *f.* fly-press (*Typ.*). **—schreibekunst,** *f.*, **—schrift,** *f.* stenography.

Geschwi'rr, *n.* (—es) whirring, whizzing; buzz.

Geschwis'ter, *n.* (*obs.*), *now usually pl.* sisters, brothers, brother and sister, brothers and sisters; **sie sind —,** they are brother and sister; **meine —,** my brothers and sisters. **—lich,** *adj.* brotherly, sisterly. *Comp.* **—kind,** *n.* nephew *or* niece; first cousin.

Geschwol'len, *p.p. of* schwellen.

Geschwom'men, *p.p. of* schwimmen.

[1]**Geschwo'r—en,** *p.p. of* schwören. **—(e)ne(r),** *m.* juror; sworn official; master of a guild. **—(e)nen,** *pl.* jury; **einen vor die —(e)nen stellen,** to send a p.'s case to the assizes. *Comp.* **—(e)nen-ausspruch,** *m.* verdict of the jury. **—(e)nen-gericht,** *n.* jury. **—(e)nen-liste,** *f.* jury-list; panel; **auf die —(e)nenliste setzen,** to empanel. **—(e)nen-obmann,** *m.* foreman of the jury.

[2]**Geschwo'ren,** *p.p. of* schwären.

Geschwu'lst, *f.* (*pl.* Geschwül'ste) swelling; tumour; **— in der Kehle,** quinsy.

Geschwun'den, *p.p. of* schwinden.

Geschwun'gen, *p.p. of* schwingen.

Geschwü'r, *n.* (—(e)s, *pl.* —e) ulcer, sore, abscess; **künstliches —,** seton; **in ein — verwandeln,** to ulcerate, form into an abscess. **—ig,** *adj.* ulcerous. *Comp.* **—bildung,** *f.* ulceration. **—öffnung,** *f.*, **—schnitt,** *m.* lancing of an abscess.

Gesech'st, *adj. & adv.* of six parts; **—er Schein** *or* **—schein,** sextile aspect.

Geseg'nen, *v.a.* (**einem etwas**) to bless.

Gesei'n = sein *or* **= gewesen** (*obs. & dial.*).

Gesel'l—(e), *m.* (—en, *pl.* —en) companion; comrade; partner; fellow; brother, member (*of a society*); journeyman; **ein lustiger —,** a jolly fellow; **ein lockerer —,** a loose fish; **drei —,** three chums (*coll.*). **—enschaft,** *f.* journeymanship; body of journeymen. **—ig,** *adj. & adv.* social; sociable; companionable; chummy (*coll.*); gregarious; **—iger Verein,** club, society; **—ige Zusammenkunft,** social gathering; **man lebte —ig,** there was much social life. **—igkeit,** *f.* sociableness; good fellowship; **sie haben viel —igkeit,** they see many people, they give many parties. **—schaft,** *f.* society; association; company, party, social gathering; company; troop; partnership; fellowship; club; **geschlossene —schaft,** club; **feine** *or* **bessere —schaft,** good society; **einem —schaft leisten,** to keep one company; **mit einem in —schaft treten, stehen,** to enter into partnership, be in partnership with a person; **schlechte —schaften verderben gute Sitten,** evil communications corrupt good manners. **—schafter,** *m.* (—schafters, *pl.* —schafter) companion; associate; partner; member of a society *or* company; **er ist ein guter —schafter,** he is good company; **stiller —schafter,** sleeping partner. **—schafterin,** *f.* lady companion. **—schaftlich,** *adj. & adv.* social, sociable; companionable; gregarious; co-operative; **—schaftliche Produktion,** co-operative *or* joint production; **—schaftliche Bildung,** culture given by moving in good society. **—schaftlichkeit,** *f.* sociable disposition, sociability; social life. **—ung,** *f.* associating, joining with; matching, association. *Comp.* **—en-bildungs-verein,** *m.* workingmen's institute. **—en-grad,** *m.* second grade among freemasons. **—en-herberge,** *f.* workingmen's boarding-house. **—en-jahre,** *pl. see* **—enzeit.** **—en-lohn,** *m.* journeyman's wages. **—en-stand,** *m.* service *or* state of a journeyman. **—en-verein,** *m.* mechanics' club. **—en-zeit,** *f.* time of service as journeyman. **—igkeits-trieb,** *m.* social instinct. **—schafts-anzug,** *m.* frock coat; evening dress. **—schafts-bank,** *f.* joint-stock bank. **—schafts-dame,** *f.* lady companion; lady in waiting; chaperone. **—schafts-geist,** *m.* esprit de corps; social disposition. **—schafts-glied,** *n.* member of a society. **—schafts-handlung,** *f.* trading company. **—schafts-haus,** *n.* clubhouse; casino. **—schafts-kreis,** *m.* circle of acquaintances. **—schafts-lied,** *n.* social song, glee; drawing-room song. **—schafts-name,** *m.* firm (*C. L.*).

—**schafts=reise**, *f.* co-operative travel(ling), co-operative tour; Cook's tour (*London*); Stangen's tour (*Berlin*). —**schafts=spiel**, *n.* social game, round game. —**schafts=theater**, *n.* private *or* amateur theatre. —**schafts=verderber**, *m.* kill-joy. —**schafts=vertrag**, *m.* social contract; deed of partnership. —**schafts=wappen**, *n.* company's coat of arms. —**schafts=widrig**, *adj. & adv.* contrary to the rules of society; anti-social. —**schafts=zimmer**, *n.* reception room, drawing-room; club room.

Gesel'l—en, *v.* I. *a.* to join, associate. II. *r.* to join, ally, associate oneself with; to keep company with; **Gleich und Gleich —t sich gern**, birds of a feather flock together (*prov.*).

Gesen'k—(e), *n.* (—(e)s, *pl.* —(e)), declivity; hollow; bottom (*of a pit, Min.*); layer; weight, lead; socket; stamp, form; **im —e schmieden**, to swage; **das Mährische —e**, the Moravian chain (*of mountains*). *Comp.* —**amboß**, *m.* swage-anvil; rifle-maker's anvil. —**tiefe**, *f.* depth of a subterranean shaft (*Min.*).

Gesef'sen, *p.p. of* **sitzen**.

Gese'tz, *n.* (—es, *pl.* —e) law, statute, commandment, decree; rule; precept; strophe; **das natürliche, göttliche, bürgerliche —**, the natural, divine, civil law; **ein — geben, bekannt machen, umgehen, aufheben, halten, brechen**, to give, to promulgate, to elude, to repeal, to keep, to violate a law; **zum —e werden**, to become law, to pass into law; **einem das — schärfen**, to read one a lecture. —**lich**, *adj. & adv.* lawful, legitimate, legal; statutory. —**lichkeit**, *f.* legality, lawfulness. —**t**, *see* **Gesetzt**. *Comp.* —**buch**, *n.* lawbook; code. —**entwurf**, *m.* draught of a bill (*Parl.*). —**es=kraft**, *f.* force of law, legal power *or* sanction; —**eskraft erhalten (erlangen)**, to be enacted. —**es=schärfe**, *f.* rigour of the law. —**gebend**, *adj.* legislative; —**gebender Körper**, legislative body, legislature. —**geber**, *m.* legislator, lawgiver. —**gebung**, *f.* legislation. —**gebungs=gewalt**, *f.* legislative power. —**gültig**, —**kräftig**, *adj.* legally sanctioned, having the force of law. —**kundig**, *adj.* versed in law; —**kundiger Lord**, law-lord. —**los**, *adj. & adv.* lawless; anarchical. —**losigkeit**, *f.* lawlessness illegality; anarchy. —**mäßig**, *adj. & adv.* lawful, legitimate, legal. —**sammlung**, *f.* code *or* body of laws. —**tafel**, *f.* table of laws; **die (mosaischen) —tafeln**, decalogue. —**vorschlag**, *m.* bill (*Parl.*). —**vollzieher**, *m.* sheriff, executor of the laws. —**widrig**, *adj. & adv.* illegal, contrary to law.

Gese'tzt, *p.p. & adj.* fixed, established, appointed; steady, sedate, demure; in type, set up; *used with a case absolute or as conj.* granted, supposing, in case; **von —en Jahren**, arrived at years of discretion, of a certain age; —**en Alters**, of mature age; —**en Benehmens**, of sedate behaviour; —**en Falles**, take the case, let us suppose; — **es sei wahr**, supposing it to be true. —**heit**, *f.* steadiness, sedateness.

Geseuf'ze, *n.* (—s) continual sighing.

Gesi'cht, *n.* (—(e)s) sight; eyesight; eye; (*pl.* —er) visage, countenance; look; mien, face; grimace; (*pl.* —e) sight; vision, apparition; **das steht gut zu —e**, that is becoming, looks well; **ein freundliches — machen**, to look kindly; **ein saures — machen**, to look surly; **ein langes — machen**, to pull a long face; **er machte ein langes —**, he looked disappointed, his countenance fell; —**er schneiden**, to make faces; —**e sehen**, to see visions; **kurzes — haben**, to be shortsighted; **aus dem —e verlieren**, to lose sight of; **einem ins —**, to a person's face; **aller guten Sitte ins — schlagen**, to make light of *or* act contrary to good manners; **ins — fassen**, to face. *Comp.* —**s=achse**, *f.* visual axis. —**s=ausdruck**, *m.* features, physiognomy; **sein —s=ausdruck**, the expression of his countenance. —**s=bildung**, *f.* physiognomy. —**s=deuter**, *m.* physiognomist. —**s=deuterei**, —**s=deutung**, *f.* (*science of*) physiognomy. —**s=eindruck**, *m.* sight impression. —**s=farbe**, *f.* complexion. —**s=feld**, *n.*, —**s=kreis**, *m.* field of vision, horizon; **seinen —skreis erweitern**, to enlarge one's mental horizon *or* the range of one's ideas; **das liegt außer seinem —s=kreis**, that is beyond him, out of the range of his ideas. —**s=kunde**, *f.* physiognomy. —**s=linie**, *f.* facial line, lineament; visual line; level; outer line of a work (*Fort.*). —**s=punkt**, *m.* point of view, aspect. —**s=rose**, *f.* erysipelas. —**s=schmerz**, *m.* face-ache. —**s=schwäche**, *f.* weakness of sight. —**s=sinn**, *m.* sense of sight. —**s=strahl**, *m.* visual ray. —**s=täuschung**, *f.* optical illusion. —**s=veränderung**, *f.* change of countenance. —**s=verzerrung**, *f.* grimace. —**s=wahrnehmung**, *f.* sight, perception. —**s=weite**, *f.* range of the eye, eye-shot. —**s=winkel**, *m.* facial angle; angle of vision. —**s=zug**, *m.* feature, lineament.

Gesie'bent, *adj. & adv.* septenary, proceeding by sevens.

Gesi'ms, *n.* (—(s)es, *pl.* —(s)e) cornice; moulding; shelf; case; — **an einer Thür**, door-case; — **an Fenstern**, window-sill; — **an einer Mauer**, entablature, pediment; **Kamin—**, chimney-piece. *Comp.* —**hobel**, *m.* moulding-plane. —**kachel**, *f.* cornice-tile. —**stein**, *m.* mould-brick. —**uhr**, *f.* time-piece, clock.

Gesin'd—e, *n.* (—es) followers, retainers (*obs.*); domestic servants, menials (*coll.*). —**el**, *n.* (—els), —**lein**, *n.* (*obs.*) rabble; vagabonds. *Comp.* —**e=amt**, *n.* registry-office for servants. —**e=bier**, *n.* small beer. —**e=buch**, *n.* register for servants and workpeople. —**e=lohn**, *m.* servants' wages. —**e=brot**, *n.* household bread. —**e=posten**, *m.* menial office. —**e=stube**, *f.* servants' room. —**e=vermittlungs=stelle**, *f.* agency *or* registry office for domestic servants.

Gesi'nn—t, *adj.* minded, disposed, affected; **für die Regierung gut oder übel —t**, well *or* ill disposed to the government; **sie sind alle gleich —t**, they are all of the same mind; **französisch, österreichisch —t**, affecting the French, the Austrian party; **Gustav Adolf war protestantisch —t und daher gesonnen, den deutschen Protestanten zu helfen**, Gustavus Adolphus was a Protestant, and for this reason he intended to help the German Protestants; **ein königlich —ter**, a royalist; **feindlich —t**, ill-disposed, bearing ill-will towards; **wie ist er —t?** what are his views? to what party does he belong? —**ung**, *f.* disposition; sentiment; conviction; intention; **politische, religiöse —ung**, political, religious, views *or* opinions. *Comp.* —**ungs=genosse**, *m.* one having the same views; political friend. —**ungs=los**, *adj.* characterless. —**ungs=treu**, *adj.* staunch, loyal. —**ungs=tüchtig**, *adj.* loyal, true-hearted, constant, staunch; well affected to the government (*iron.*). —**ungs=tüchtigkeit**, *f.* loyalty, true-heartedness, constancy, staunchness of character.

Gesip'p—e, *n.* (—(e)s) kindred, kin (*obs.*). —**t**, *adj.* related (*obs.*).

Gesit't—et, *adj.* mannered; well-bred; polished; polite; civilized; moral. —**ung**, *f.* civilization; good breeding; morality.

Gesit'ze, *n.* (—s); **das ewige — bekommt einem nicht**, a mere sedentary life is not healthy.

Gesö'ff, *n.* (—(e)s) hard drinking; swipes, bad liquor.

Gesof'fen, *p.p. of* **saufen**.

Geso'gen, *p.p. of* **saugen.**
Geson'nen, *p.p. of* **sinnen; — sein,** to intend; **was sind Sie — zu thun?** what have you resolved upon? **ich bin — abzureisen,** it is my intention to depart; **ich bin nicht —,** I do not feel disposed to, I do not intend *or* propose.
Gesot'ten, *p.p. of* **sieden.**
Gespal'ten, *adj.* cleft; (*in comp.*) —fid (*e.g.* **acht—,** octofid).
[1]**Gespa'n,** *m.* (—**en** & —**es**; *pl.* —**en** & —**e**) mate, fellow, comrade (*obs.*); husband (*obs.*).
[2]**Gespa'n,** *m.* (—(**e**)**s**, *pl.* —**e**) count, head of the district (*in Hungary*). **—schaft,** *f.* district, county.
Gespa'nn, I. *n.* (—(**e**)**s**, *pl.* —**e**) team; couple. II. *see* [1]**Gespan.**
Gespa'nnt, *pp. of* **spannen,** *adj. & adv.* intent, eager; intense; stretched, tight; **mit —er Aufmerksamkeit,** with close attention; **in der —esten Erwartung,** in the most anxious expectation; **ich bin sehr auf den Ausgang —,** I await the result with the greatest anxiety; **—e Verhältnisse,** strained relations; **mit —en Blicken,** with eager looks; **— mit einem,** on bad terms with s.o.; **auf —em Fuße mit einem stehen** *or* **mit einem über den Fuß — sein,** to be on bad terms with s.o. **—heit,** *f.* tension; intentness; anxiety; disagreement; estrangement; bad terms.
Gespar'r(e), *n.* (—(**e**)**s**) rafters (*of a roof*).
Gespe'nst, *n.* (—**es**, *pl.* —**er**) spectre, apparition; ghost; Sirex spectrum (*Mollusc.*); **es geht ein — in diesem Hause um,** this house is haunted. **—erhaft, —ig, —isch,** *adj. & adv.* ghostly; ghostlike. *Comp.* **—er=artig,** *adj.* spectral. **—er=erscheinung,** *f.* apparition of a ghost; hallucination. **—er=geschichte,** *f.* ghost story. **—er=glauben,** *m.* belief in ghosts. **—er=schiff,** *n.* phantom ship, Flying Dutchman. **—er=spuk,** *m.* witchery. **—er=stunde,** *f.* hour when spectres walk the earth, midnight hour. **—er=sucht,** *f.* mania of seeing apparitions.
Gesper're, *n.* (—**s**) rafters; safety catch, click and ratchet-wheel (*of a watch*); clasps (*of a book*); carriage head; encumbrance; resistance; block (*in a street*); hiatus (*Metre*); fuss (*fig.*).
Gespi'ckt, *p.p. of* **spicken,** *adj.*; **ein wohl —er Geldbeutel,** a well-lined purse.
Gespie'en, *p.p. of* **speien.**
Gespie'le, I. *m.* (—**n**, *pl.* —**n**), **—in,** *f.* playmate. II. *n.* (—**s**) playfellow, intimate friend (*obs.*); continual playing.
Gespin'n—e, *n.* (—**es**) continual spinning. **—st,** *n.* (—**stes**, *pl.* —**ste**) what is spun, web, spun yarn; unsubstantial fabrication; **von feinem —ste,** fine-spun; **wie das —st, so der Gewinnst,** no pains, no gains (*prov.*).
Gesplis'sen, *p.p. of* **spleißen** (*obs.*).
Gesponn'nen, *p.p. of* **spinnen.**
Gespo'ns, *m. & n.* (—(**s**)**en**, *pl.* —(**s**)**e**) bridegroom, bride; husband, wife (*poet.*).
Gespö'tt, *n.* (—**es**) mockery, derision; laughing-stock. **—el,** *n.* (—**els**) mockery, quizzing.
Gespot'te, *n.* (—**s**) continual jeering, derision.
Gesprä'ch, *n.* (—**es**, *pl.* —**e**) conversation, talk; discourse; colloquy; parley; dialogue; **sich** (*acc.*) **mit einem in ein — einlassen, ein — mit einem anknüpfen,** to enter into conversation with one; **es ist das — der ganzen Stadt,** it is the talk of the town, it is all over the town; **das — auf (einen Gegenstand) bringen,** to introduce (*a subject*). **—ig,** *adj. & adv.* talkative, communicative; affable; sociable. **—igkeit,** *f.* conversational gift; talkativeness; affability. *Comp.* **—buch,** *n.* book of dialogues. **—s=gegenstand,** *m.* topic (*of conversation*). **—s=weise,** *adv.* colloquially; by way of conversation. **—s=zimmer,** *n.* parlour.
Gesprei'zt, *p.p. of* **spreizen.** *adj.* spread out; **—e Lippen,** lips drawn back at the corners; **—er Stil,** affected style; **mit —en Beinen,** with legs wide apart.
Gespren'ge, *n.* (—**s**) sprinkling; blasting; fragment blasted; pent-roof.
Gespre'ngt, *p.p. of* **sprengen.** *adj.* bipartite, split.
Gesprit'ze, *n.* (—**s**) spouting, spirting; playing (*of fire-engines, etc.*).
Gespro'chen, *p.p. of* **sprechen.**
Gespros'sen, *p.p. of* **sprießen.**
Gespru'del, *n.* (—**s**) sputtering, bubbling; bubbling noise; bubbling spring.
Gesprun'gen, *p.p. of* **springen.**
Gespu'ke, *n.* (—**s**) ghost-walking, haunting.
Ges'sen = Gegef'sen, *p.p. of* **essen** (*obs.*).
Gesta'de, *n.* (—**s**) bank, shore, beach.
Gesta'lt, I. *f.* (*pl.* —**en**) form, shape, figure; stature; mien, air; aspect, manner; vision; **Arznei in — von Pulver,** medicine in a powder; **folgender —,** in the following manner; **solcher —, daß,** in such a way as to; **welcher —?** how? **das Abendmahl unter beiden —en** *or* **unter beiderlei —,** communion in both kinds; **sich in seiner wahren — zeigen,** to show oneself in one's true character; **nach — der Sachen,** according to circumstances. II. *p.p. of* **stellen,** placed, fashioned. *adj. & adv.* shaped; **bei so —en Sachen,** such being the case. *Comp.* **—en=bildung,** *f.* formation of figures, modelling. **—en=reich,** *adj.* rich in forms. **—los,** *adj. & adv.* shapeless; immaterial; misshapen. **—ungs=fähig,** *adj.* capable of shaping *or* of being formed; plastic. **—ungs=talent,** *n.* talent for organization. **—verwandlung,** *f.* transfiguration.
Gestal't—en, *v.* I. *a.* to form, fashion. II. *r.* to take shape, to appear; to turn out; **es —ete sich zu seinem Besten,** it turned out to his advantage. **—end,** *p. & adj.* formative. **—et,** *p.p. & adj.*; **wohl —eter Mensch,** well-made man. **—ung,** *f.* formation, forming; modelling; form, figure, shape; thing modelled *or* formed; condition, state; phase.
Gestam'mel, *n.* (—**s**) stammering, stuttering.
Gestan'd, Gestän'de, *imperf. indic. & subj. of* **gestehen.**
Gestan'den, *p.p. of* [1]**stehen;** [2]**gestehen.**
Gestän'd—ig, *adj.* confessing; **—ig sein,** to confess, to have made a confession; **er ist es** (*gen.*) **—ig,** he acknowledges it; **ein —iger Verbrecher,** an approver (*Law*). **—nis,** *n.* (—(**ss**)**es**, *pl.* —(**ss**)**e**) confession, avowal.
Gestän'ge, *n.* (—**s**) poles, spears, stakes; enclosure of stakes; poles of a hydraulic engine; antlers; sweep, rod (*Min.*); wooden tramway for a truck (*Min.*).
Gesta'nk, *m.* (—**es**, *pl.* **Gestän'ke**) bad smell, stench; stink (*vulg.*); **die Luft mit — erfüllen,** to poison the air.
Gestat't—bar, *adj.* allowable. **—en,** *v.a.* to permit, allow, grant. **—ung,** *f.* permission, consent.
Ges'te, *f.* (*with hard* **g**) (*pl.* —**n**) gesture.
Geste'hen, *ir.v.a.* to own, confess, acknowledge; to admit, grant; **offen gestanden,** to speak frankly; to tell the plain truth; **das muß ich —!** I say! well, I never! is it possible!
Gestei'n, *n.* (—**s**, *pl.* —**e**) stone, rock; minera[l] precious stones. *Comp.* **—gang,** *m.* vein, streak, lode. **—kunde, —lehre,** *f.* mineralogy; geognosy. **—kundige(r),** *m.* mineralogist; geognost.
Geste'll, *n.* (—(**e**)**s**, *pl.* —**e**) stand; frame; bookcase; jack; trestle; clothes-horse; towel-horse; pedestal; frame and wheels (*of a vehicle*); stretcher, skeleton (*of an umbrella*); rims (*of spectacles*); head-stall (*of a bridle*); foot-stalk (*Bot.*); curbstone (*of a well*). **—ung,** *f.* presentation of a commission (*Mil.*). *Comp.* **—macher,** *m.* wheelwright. **—ungs=aufschub** *m.* delay of a trial.

Gestem'me, *n.* (—s) joints (*Carp.*).

Ge'ster—ig, Ge'strig, *adj. & adv.* of yesterday; **wir beziehen uns auf unser ergebenes Gestriges,** we refer to our letter of yesterday. **—n,** I. *adv.* yesterday; **—n vor** (*or* **in**) **vierzehn Tagen,** yesterday fortnight; **—n abend,** last night, yesterday evening; **—n früh,** yesterday morning; **ich bin nicht von —n,** I am no fool, not without experience (*coll.*). II. *n.* yesterday; the past; **das ewige —n** *or* **ewig gestrige,** that which eternally belongs to yesterday, that which has prescription on its side, established custom, everyday routine.

Geste'rnt, *adj. & adv.* starry; covered with stars.

Gesti'chel, *n.* (—s) continual pricking; sneering.

Gestie'felt, *p.p. & adj.* booted; **—er Kater,** puss in boots; **— und gespornt,** booted and spurred, fully equipped; **— kommen, an — kommen,** to come up (*coll.*).

Gestie'gen, *p.p. of* **steigen.**

Gestie'lt, *adj.* helved; stalked (*Zoöl.*); stemmed (*Bot.*).

Gestikulie'ren, *v.n.* (*aux.* **h.**) to gesticulate.

Gesti'rn, *n.* (—es, *pl.* —e) star; stars; constellation. **—t,** *adj.* starred, starry. *Comp.* **—forscher,** *m.* astronomer. **—kunst,** *f.* astronomy; astrology. **—stand,** *m.* constellation of the stars.

Gesti'rnt, *suff.* (*in comp.* =) -fronted, -browed.

Gesto'ben, *p.p. of* **stieben.**

Gestö'ber, *n.* (—s) drift (*of dust or snow*); storm.

Gesto'chen, *p.p. of* **stechen.**

Gestobt (*long* **o**), *adj.* stewed; **—e Kartoffeln,** stewed potatoes.

Gestoh'len, *p.p. of* **stehlen; der** *or* **das kann mir — werden,** he *or* that does not interest me t all, I do not care for him *or* it in the slightest (*coll.*).

Gestöh'ne, *n.* (—s) moaning, groaning.

Gestol'per, *n.* (—s) tottering, stumbling.

Gestor'ben, *p.p. of* **sterben.**

Gesto'ßen, *p.p. of* **stoßen.** *adj.* pounded (*sugar*).

Gestot'ter, *n.* (—s) stammering.

Gesto'vt, *adj.*; **—e Muscheln,** stewed shells.

Gestra'hlt, *p.p. of* **strahlen.** *adj.* stellate, radiate.

Gestram'pel, *n.* (—s) stamping.

Gesträu'ch, *n.* (—(e)s, *pl.* —e) shrubs, bushes; shrubbery.

Gestre'ckt, *adj.* procumbent, trailing.

Gestren'g(e), *adj. & adv.* severe, strict, rigorous; (*obs. formerly used in addressing members of the gentry*) **Ew. —en,** Your Honour; **—er Herr,** Gracious Sir, Your Worship; **—e Frau,** Gracious Madam, Your Ladyship; **—er Ritter,** Gracious Knight, dread knight; **die drei —en Herren,** the three severe days in May (*May 13, 14, 15*).

Gestreu', *n.* flowers *or* boughs strewn about.

Gestri'chen, *p.p. of* **streichen; frisch —,** newly painted; **—es Maß,** stricken measure.

Gestru'del, *n.* (—s) boiling (*of a whirlpool*); bubbling up.

Gestrüp'p(e), *n.* (—(e)s) briers, brushes, underwood.

Gestüb'(b)e, *n.* dust; coal-dust; cement (*Smeltw.*).

Gestüm'per, *n.* (—s) bungling; bungling work.

Gestun'ken, *p.p. of* **stinken** (*vulg.*).

Gestü't, *n.* (—es, *pl.* —e), stud; breed of horses. *Comp.* **—garten,** *m.* stud. **—hengst,** *m.* stallion; stud-horse. **—stute,** *f.* brood-mare.

Gesu'ch, *n.* (—(e)s, *pl.* —e) petition, request, suit, supplication. **—e,** *n.* (—es) continual seeking. **—t,** *adj.* choice; in demand; farfetched; affected. **—theit,** *f.* choiceness; exquisiteness; fashionableness; ffectation.

Gesu'del, *n.* (—s) dirty work; daub, scrawl.

Gesum'me, *n.* (—s) humming, buzzing.

Gesu'nd, *adj. & adv.* sound, healthy; well; not ailing; wholesome; salutary; salubrious; **—er Menschenverstand,** common sense; **wieder — werden,** to get well again, to be restored to health; **das ist mir nicht —,** that does not agree with me; **das ist ihm — !** that serves him right! **—heit,** *f.* soundness of health, health; wholesomeness; salubrity; soundness (*of wood, etc.; of one's views, etc.*); **bei guter —heit sein,** to be in good health; **wie steht es um Ihre —heit?** how is your health? **eine —heit ausbringen,** to propose *or* give a toast; **auf Ihre —heit!** your (very good) health! (**zur**) **—heit!** God bless you! (*to a person sneezing*). **—heitlich,** *adj.* sanitary. *Comp.* **—brunnen,** *m.* mineral well; watering-place. **—heitsamt,** *n.*, **—heits-kommission,** *f.* sanitary board. **—heits-halber,** *adv.* for the sake of health. **—heits-kordon,** *m.* sanitary cordon. **—heits-kunde, —heits-lehre,** *f.* hygiene. **heits-pflege,** *f.* regimen. **—heits-polizei,** *f.* sanitary police *or* inspectors. **—heits-probe,** *f.* quarantine. **—heits-rat,** *m.* board of health; member of such board. **—heits-regel,** *f.* regimen. **—heits-schein,** *m.* certificate of (good) health. **—heits-widrig,** *adj.* unhealthy; unwholesome. **—heits-zustand,** *m.* state of health (*of a p.*); sanitary conditions (*of a place*).

Gesun'den, *v.n.* (*aux.* **s.**) to recover one's health.

Gesun'gen, *p.p. of* **singen.**

Gesun'ken, *p.p. of* **sinken.**

Getä'fel, *n.* (—s) wainscot; inlaying, panelling, wainscotting; **— eines Fußbodens,** inlaid wooden floor.

Getän'del, *n.* (—s) trifling, dallying, toying, play.

Getha'l, *n.* dales and valleys (*poet.*).

Getha'n, *p.p. of* **thun; gesagt, —,** no sooner said than done (*prov.*).

Geteilt'heit, *f.* state of separation, fact of being separated.

Getie'r, *n.* (—es) animals; animal.

Gethu'e, *n.* (—s) doings; goings on; pretence; **was soll nur das —?** what 's all the good of all that fuss *or* of that affectation? (*coll.*).

Geti'gert, *adj.* striped, marked.

Geto'be, *n.* (—s) din, roaring.

Getö'tet, *see* **Töten; —e Briefe,** dead letters, annulled documents (*Law*).

Getö'n(e) *n.* (—(e)s) continual sounding, clang.

Getö'nt, *p.p. of* **tönen.** *adj.*; **—es Papier,** tinted paper.

Getö's, *n.* (—(s)es), **Geto'se, Getö'se,** *n.* (—s) deafening noise, din, uproar, clashing.

Getra'b(e), *n.* (—(e)s) trotting.

Getram'pel, *n.* (—s) stamping, trampling.

Geträ'nk, *n.* (—es, *pl.* —e) drink, beverage; potion; **geistiges —,** (spirituous) liquor; *pl.* spirits; **abgezogene —e,** distilled waters.

Getra'tsch, Geträ'tsch, *n.* (—es) useless talk, tittle-tattle, twaddle, babbling, gossip (*coll.*).

Getrau'—en, *v.r.* to dare, venture; to trust; **ich —e mich** (*not* **mir**) **nicht dahin,** I dare not go there; **ich —e mich nicht, dieses zu thun** (*obs.* **ich —e mich dessen nicht**), I dare not do that.

Getrei'be, *n.* (—s) constant urging *or* driving; — (*or* **Getriebe**) **der Parteien,** the working tactics of the parties.

Getrei'de, *n.* (—s) corn, grain. *Comp.* **—arten,** *pl.* cereals. **—bau,** *m.* corn-growing, agriculture. **—boden,** *m.* corn land; granary. **—börse,** *f.* corn exchange. **—brand,** *m.* blast *or* blight in corn, uredo. **—fege,** *f.* winnowing machine. **—fuhre,** *f.* waggon-load of corn. **—gülte,** *f.* rent paid in corn. **—händler,** *m.* corn merchant. **—kümmel,** *m.* cumin-brandy made of rye. **—land,** *n.* corn-growing country; corn-land. **—mangel,** *m.* dearth of corn. **—mähmaschine,** *f.* corn-cutter. **—wucher,** *m.* usurious trade in corn. **—wurm,** *m.* corn-weevil.

Getre'nnt, *p.p. of* **trennen. —heit,** *f.*, **—sein,** *n.* separation. *Comp.* **—blumig,** *adj.* diœcious (*Bot.*).

Getreu', *adj. & adv.* faithful, true, trusty, loyal; **ein —es Gedächtnis,** a retentive memory; **unsern lieben —en,** to our trusty and well-beloved (subjects). **—lich,** *adv.* faithfully, truly, loyally.

Getrie'be, *n.* (—s) driving, drift; motion, agitation; motive power, machine; spring; works; machinery; pinion; driving-gear; lantern-wheel; **— des Lebens,** bustle of life; **— der Menschen,** busy life of men; **— einer Uhr,** works, spring of a watch; **— zum Abstoßen,** disconnecting gear. *Comp.* **—maß,** *n.*, **—zirkel,** *m.* watchmaker's spring-dividers. **—scheibe,** *f.* pinion-plate.

Getrie'ben, *p.p. of* **treiben.** *adj.;* **—e Arbeit,** chased work.

Getrip'pel, *n.* (—s) constant tripping to and fro.

Getrof'fen, *p.p. of* **treffen.**

Getro'gen, *p.p. of* **trügen.**

Getrom'mel, *n.* (—s) beating of drums.

Getröp'fel, *n.* (—s) constant dripping.

Getro'st, I. (*orig. a p.p. of* **trösten**) *adj. & adv.* comforted, of good cheer, confident, trustful, of good hope; **—en Mutes,** of good courage; **er bildet sich — ein,** he fondly imagines. II. *int.* cheer up! **nur —!** courage! never mind!

Getrö'sten, *v.r.* to hope with confidence, hope for, be confident, wait patiently; to trust; to be solaced (**mit,** by); **sich einer Sache —,** to expect something with confidence (*obs.*).

Getrun'ken, *p.p. of* **trinken.**

Getum'mel, *n.* (—s) continuous exercising *or* movement.

Getüm'mel, *n.* (—s) tumult; bustle, turmoil.

Getüp'felt, *adj.* dotted, spotted (*Bot.*).

Geü'bt, *p.p. of* **üben. —heit,** *f.* skill, dexterity, practice.

Geu'ßest, Geußt; Geuß, *2 & 3 pers. sing. pres. indic.; imperat. of* **gießen.**

Gevat'ter, *m.* (—s, *pl.* —n), **—in,** *f.* godfather, godmother, sponsor; gaffer; gossip; intimate friend; **— Schneider und Handschuhmacher,** small trades-people; **— stehen,** to stand godfather *or* sponsor; **einen zu — bitten,** to ask one to stand sponsor (to); **er steht bei einem meiner Kinder —,** he is godfather to one of my children; **sie ist meine —in,** she is my godmother; **meine Uhr steht —,** my watch is in pawn (*coll.*). **—schaft,** *f.* sponsorship; sponsors. *Comp.* **—brief,** *m.* written invitation to stand sponsor. **—schmaus,** *m.* christening feast. **—s=leute,** *pl.* sponsors. **—s=mann,** *m.* godfather. **—geschenk,** *n.*, **—stück,** *n.* present sent to a sponsor (*by a co-sponsor*) before the christening.

Gevie'r—e, *n.* (—s) quadripartition; bratticing. **—t,** I. *adj.* quartered; squared; quaternary. II. *n.* (—es, *pl.* —e), **—te,** *n.* (—s) square; quadrature; M-quadrat (*Typ.*); **ins —te bringen,** to square; **es mißt drei Zentimeter ins —t,** it is 3 centimetres square. *Comp.* **—t=fuß,** square foot. **—teilt,** *adj.* quartered; dragged asunder. **—t=maß,** *n.* square measure. **—t=schein,** *m.* quartile aspect (*Astr.*). **—t=wurzel,** *f.* square root.

Gewä'chs, *n.* (—(s)es, *pl.* —(s)e) anything growing; plant, vegetable, herb; growth; sprout, offshoot; excrescence; **ein Rohr von einem —e,** a cane with but one joint; **ausländisches —,** exotic. *Comp.* **—haus,** *n.* greenhouse; conservatory. **—kunde, —lehre,** *f.* botany. **—reich,** I. *adj.* rich in plants, etc. II. *n.* vegetable kingdom.

Gewach'sen, *see* **Wachsen; einem, einer Sache — sein,** to be a match for a p., equal to a th.

Gewa'hr, *adj.;* **etwas** *or* **einer Sache** (*becoming obs.*) **— werden,** to perceive, become aware of; to see; **ich wurde meines Irrtums** *or* (*now usually*) **meinen Irrtum bald —,** I soon became aware of my mistake. **—en,** *v.a.* (*& n. with gen. obs. & poet.*) *see* **—werden. —sam,** I. *m. & n.* (*rarely f.*) (—es, *pl.* —e) surety, safety; custody; prison; proviso. II. *adj.* wary (*rare*). *Comp.* **—haber,** *m.* trustee.

Gewä'hr, *f.* (*pl.* —en) custody, safe-keeping; security, warrant, guarantee; testimony; **— leisten (für eine S.)** to go bail (for a th.), to guarantee (a th.). *Comp.* **—leistung,** *f.* granting, *etc.;* guarantee; giving bail. **—schaft,** *f.* warrant, security, bail. **—schein,** *m.* warrant, bond. **—s=mangel,** *m.* default of bail. **—s=mann,** *m.* voucher, guarantee; guarantor, surety, authority; **Elisabeth ist mein —s=mann dafür,** I have it on Elizabeth's authority; **mein —smann sagt mir,** my informant tells me.

Gewä'hr—en, *v.* I. *a.* to be surety for, warrant, guarantee; to grant, accord, vouchsafe; to give, impart, afford; **Vergnügen —en,** to afford pleasure. II. *n.* (*aux.* **h.**) to last, continue; **—en lassen,** to let alone, leave to go on as it will, indulge; **für etwas —en,** to go security for; **einen —en lassen,** to let a p. do as he pleases; **laß ihn —!** let him alone! **laß mich —!** let me alone, don't interfere, leave it to me! **—ung,** *f.* granting, warranting, *etc.*, grant (*Law*); **er hat die —ung seiner Bitte erlangt,** his request has been granted.

Gewäl'de, *n.* (—s) forest, wood, woodland.

Gewa'lt, *f.* (*pl.* —en) might, power; force, violence; authority; dominion; **höhere —,** main act, act of God *or* Providence; **mit (aus) aller —,** with all one's might; **sie wollen mit aller — neue Länder entdecken,** they are determined to discover new countries; **einem — anthun,** to do one violence; **einem Mädchen — anthun,** to violate *or* ravish a maiden; **sich** (*dat.*) **selbst — anthun,** to commit suicide; to put a restraint upon, constrain oneself; **einer Stelle — anthun,** to wrest the sense of a passage; **mit —,** by force, forcibly, perforce; **eine Sprache in der — haben,** to be master of a language, to have command of a language; **die ausübende —,** the executive power. **—ig,** *adj. & adv.* powerful, potent, mighty; strong, intense; violent; valiant; big, vast, prodigious; **—iges Verbrechen,** atrocious crime; **sich —ig irren,** to be egregiously mistaken; **—ig reich,** enormously rich; **—ig lieb haben,** to be excessively fond of; **der —ige,** mighty man; **—iger beim Heere,** provost marshal (*obs.*); **die —igen der Erde,** the rulers of the earth. **—sam,** *adj. & adv.* forcible, violent; **—sam verfahren,** to use violence. **—same,** *f.* judicial authority. **—samkeit,** *f.* violence. *Comp.* **—brief,** *m.* power of attorney; warrant. **—geber,** *m.* client, constituent, person authorizing. **—haber,** *m.* holder of power; autocrat, dictator. **—haberei',** *f.* despotism. **—herrschaft,** *f.* despotism. **—herrscher,** *m* despot. **—lüstern,** *adj.* ambitious of power. **—marsch,** *m.* forced march. **—raub,** *m.* usurpation. **—schein,** *m.* warrant. **—streich,** *m.* arbitrary act, illegal measure. **—sucht,** *f.* thirst for power. **—that,** *f.* deed of violence, outrage; atrocity; foul play. **—thätig,** *adj. & adv.* violent, outrageous; **—thätiger Angriff,** assault; **—thätiger Mensch,** brutal man. **—träger,** *m.* attorney; plenipotentiary. **—zug,** *m.* forced march.

Gewa'lzt, *p.p. of* **walzen;** rolled, milled.

Gewa'nd, *n.* (—(e)s, *pl.* —e, *high style & poet.; usually* **Gewän'der**) garment, dress, raiment, garb; drapery; vestment; cloth. *Comp.* **—händler,** *m.* woollen-draper. **—haus,** *n.* clothworker's hall; drapery shop; (*at Leipzig*) great hall for exquisite world-famed concerts (**Gewandhauskonzerte**).

Gewa'ndt, *p.p. of* **wenden.** *adj.* active, nimble; adroit; skilled; **— in (einer S.),** good at *or* at home in (a th.). **—heit,** *f.* adroitness, dexterity; versatility; knack; cleverness.

Gewan'dung, *f.* (*pl.* —en) drapery.

Gewa'nn, Gewän'ne, (*see* Gewönne) *imperf. indic. & (recent) subj. of* **gewinnen.**
Gewar'ten, *v.a. & n.* (*aux.* h.) (*gen.*) to look, hope, wait for, expect (*obs.*).
Gewär'tig, *adj. & adv.* awaiting, expectant; attentive; **einer Sache — sein,** to expect *or* hope for something; **ich bin von ihm jeder Unfreundlichkeit —,** I expect every unpleasantness at his hands; **ich bleibe Ihrer Befehle —,** I shall attend to your orders; **einem — sein,** to be ready to help *a p.* **—en,** *v.a., r. & n.* to be prepared for, to expect.
Gewä'sch, *n.* (—es) idle talk, twaddle.
Gewa'sche, *n.* (—s) continual washing.
Gewa'schen, *p.p. of* **waschen; sich — haben,** to be excellent, capital, first rate (*coll.*).
Gewäs'ser, *n.* (—s, *pl.* —) waters (*coll.*); water; flood; **die — fallen,** the floods subside.
Gewe'be, *n.* (—s) weaving, web, weft; texture; tissue, fabric; cells (*of bees*); **das — der Adern,** plexus. *Comp.* **—lehre,** *f.* histology.
Gewe'ckt, *p.p. of* **wecken.** *adj.* lively, bright, sprightly, clever, wide-awake. **—heit,** *f.* sprightliness, liveliness, vivacity.
Gewe'hr, *n.* (—es, *pl.* —e) weapon; gun, musket, rifle, firelock; **Seiten—,** sword; **an die —e!** stand to your arms! fall in! **setzt die —e zusammen!** pile arms! **die Mannschaft trat unters —,** the men stood to their arms; **das — strecken,** to lay down arms; **— auf!** shoulder arms! draw swords! **faßt das — an!** shoulder arms! **— ab** *or* **— beim Fuß!** order arms! **ins — rufen,** to call to arms; **zum — greifen,** to take up arms; **— über!** *or* **schultert's —!** slope arms! **— in Ruh'!** cease fire! **das Seiten— pflanzt auf!** fix swords! fix bayonets! **präsentiert das —!** present arms! *Comp.* **—fabrik,** *f.* manufactory of rifles. **—feuer,** *n.* firing; discharge of musketry. **—kammer,** *f.* armoury. **—handlung,** *f.* gunsmith's shop. **—kreuz,** *n.* gunrack. **—lauf,** *m.* gun-barrel. **—pyramide,** *f.* pile of arms. **—rick,** *n.* gun-case. **—riemen,** *m.* sling. **—schein,** *m.* gun license.
Gewei'h, *n.* (—es, *pl.* —e) horns, antlers. *Comp.* **—kronleuchter,** *m.* branching lustre, chandelier.
Gewei'ne, *n.* (—s) crying; whining.
Ge'weling, *f.* (*pl.* —en) bulkhead (*Naut.*).
Gewe'llt, *p.p. of* **wellen;** corrugated (*iron*).
Gewen'de, *n.* (—s) turning; change of clothes; suit; the length of the furrow; team; acre, field; **ein — machen,** to turn the plough.
Gewer'b—e, *n.* (—(e)s) trade, business; craft, industrial pursuit; profession, calling; message; vertebra, joint; **sich** (*dat.*) **ein —e aus . . . machen,** to make a trade of; **er war seines —es ein Tischler,** he was a joiner by profession. **—lich,** *adj. & adv.* industrial; professional. **—sam,** *adj.* engaged in industrial pursuits, industrious. **—samkeit,** *f.* industry. *Comp.* **—e=ausstellung,** *f.* industrial exhibition. **—e=bank,** *f.* tradesmen's bank, industrial bank. **—e=steuer,** *f.* tax paid for carrying on a trade, tax on patents. **—e=steuer=pflichtig,** *adj.* bound to take out a license. **—fleiß,** *m.* industry (*in trade*). **—fleißig,** *adj.* industrious, manufacturing. **—(e)=freiheit,** *f.* liberty to exercise a trade, freedom of trade. **—kunde,** *f.* technology. **—kundige(r),** *m.* technologist. **—(e)=museum,** *n.* industrial *or* technological museum. **—(e)=ordnung,** *f.* trade regulations. **—schein,** *m.* patent; license. **—(e)=schule,** *f.* industrial school, technical school, mechanics' institute. **—(e)=schüler,** *m.* pupil of an industrial *or* a technical school. **—(e)=schulwesen,** *n.* system of *or* matters connected with industrial *or* technical schools. **—s=erzeugnisse,** *pl.n.* manufactures. **—s=lauben,** *pl.* arcades. **—s=leute,** *f.* tradespeople, tradesmen. **—s=mäßig,** *adj.* professional. **—s=zweig,** *m.* branch of industry, line of business. **—thätig,** *adj.* industrial. **—treibend,** *adj.* carrying on a trade, exercising a profession; manufacturing. **—(e)=verein,** *m.* tradesmen's union *or* club, trade union; technological society.
Gewer'k, *n.* (—s, *pl.* —e) machine; works; machinery; manufacture; guild, corporation. **—schaft,** *f.* guild, corporation; mining company. *Comp.* **—en=kux,** *m.* share in a mine. **—en=probierer,** *m.* assayer to a mine. **—haus,** *n.* factory. **—s=meister,** *m.* master of a trade; manufacturer. **—s=mäßig,** *adv.* in factory fashion. **—verein,** *m.* trade-union.
Gewe'sen, *see* Sein; **mein —er Freund,** my friend that was, my former friend; **eine —e Schönheit,** a ci-devant beauty, a faded beauty.
Gewi'chen, *p.p. of* **weichen.**
Gewi'cht, *n.* (—es, *pl.* —e) weight, heaviness; gravity, importance, moment; stress; **das — halten,** to be full weight; **volles — geben,** to give full weight; **ein stehendes —,** equipoise; **das — nicht haben,** to be short in weight; **an — haben,** to weigh; **schwer ins — fallen,** to be very heavy; to carry great weight, to be of great importance (*fig.*); **an — verlieren,** to lose in weight. **—ig,** *adj. & adv.* of full weight; weighty; heavy; important, momentous; forcible; impressive. **—igkeit,** *f.* weightiness, weight; full weight; importance. *Comp.* **—aicher,** *m.* assizer of weights. **—kunst, —lehre,** *f.* statics. **—los,** *adj.* of no weight; unimportant. **—s=abgang,** *m.* deficiency in weight. **—s=abnahme,** *f.* loss in weight. **—voll,** *adj. & adv.* weighty, ponderous; full of importance.
Gewi'ckelt, *p.p. of* **wickeln; schief — sein,** to be completely mistaken, to be altogether on the wrong track (*coll.*).
Gewie'gt, *adj.* experienced; skilled, clever; shrewd.
Gewie'her, *n.* (—s) neighing; horse-laugh (fig.).
Gewie'sen, *p.p. of* **weisen.**
Gewi'ld, *n.* (—es) game (*obs.*).
Gewi'llt, *adj. & adv.* willing, disposed; **— sein,** to be determined, to intend.
Gewim'mel, *n.* (—s) swarming, crawling; crowd, swarm, busy throng.
Gewim'mer, *n.* (—s) whining, wailing, moaning.
Gewin'de, *n.* (—s, *pl.* —) contortions; sinuosity, winding; anything wound; skein (*of thread*); hilt (*of a sword*); festoon; wreath; worm (*of a screw*); joints, hinges; labyrinth (*of the ear*); whirl (*of shells*). *Comp.* **—bohrer,** *m.* wimble.
Gewi'nn, *m.* (—es, *pl.* —e) gaining, winning; earnings, gain, profit; produce; prize; winnings; proceeds; advantage; **der reine —** *or* **Rein—,** net profits; **— und Verlust-konto,** profit and loss account; **mit — verkaufen,** to sell to advantage; **— abwerfen,** to yield a profit; **das ist schon (ein) —,** that is something gained. **—bar,** *adj. & adv.* obtainable, gainable. *Comp.* **—anteil,** *m.* share in the profits, dividend. **—bringend,** *adj.* profitable, lucrative. **—liste,** *f.* list of the winning numbers. **—los,** *adj. & adv.* profitless, unprofitable. **—nummer,** *f.* winning number. **—rechnung,** *f.* profit account. **—reich,** *adj.* profitable. **—sucht,** *f.* eagerness for gain, greediness, avarice. **—süchtig,** *adj.* avaricious, greedy of gain. **—voll,** *adj.* lucrative, profitable.
Gewin'n—en, *ir.v.* I. *a.* to win, gain, obtain, acquire; to earn; to gain over, prevail on; to conquer; to take, assume; **den Vorsprung —en,** to get the start (*of one*); **das Freie —en,** to gain the open (field); **eine Strecke Weges —en,** to travel, go a certain distance; **die**

Oberhand —en, to get the mastery of; ich konnte es nicht über mich —en, I could not bring myself to (do it); das große Los —en, to win *or* draw the first prize; einen für (eine S.) —en, to interest one in, gain one over to; es —t das Ansehen, als wenn, it seems as if; einen zum Freunde —en, to make one a friend; ich habe Ehrfurcht vor ihm gewonnen, he has inspired me with respect; einen lieb —en, to become fond of a person; wie gewonnen, so zerronnen, easy come, easy go (*prov.*). II. *n.* (*aux.* h.) to gain, improve; er —t bei näherer Bekanntschaft, he improves on acquaintance; an Klarheit —en, to gain in clearness. —er, *m.* (—ers, *pl.* —er) winner, gainer. —st, *see* Gewinn. —ung, *f.* gaining; gain, produce; extraction (*Chem.*).

Gewin'sel, *n.* (—s) whining, moaning.

Gewir'bel, *n.* (—s) whirling; roll (*of drums*); roulade (*Mus.*); warbling.

Gewi'rk, *n.* (—es) weaving; web, texture; — der Bienen, honeycomb.

Gewir'r(e), *n.* (—(e)s) confusion, complication, entanglement; maze; wards (*of a lock*); whirl (*of ideas*).

Gewi'ß, I. *adj. & adv.* sure, certain; assured; positive, true; undoubting; undoubted; stable, steady, fixed; sure, certain; ich bin dessen —, I am sure of it; seiner Sache — sein, to be sure of what one says; to be sure of one's facts *or* one's ground, to know a th. thoroughly; —(ss)er Preis, fixed price; von —(ss)er Hand, on good authority; er behauptete es als —, he asserted it as a fact; ein —(ss)er, a certain person, some one; sein —(ss)es haben, to have a fixed income; ich bin —, I know for a certainty; das —(ss)e, certainty; seine Stimme ist mir —, I am sure of his vote. II. *adv.* certainly, surely, no doubt; of a surety; probably; apparently; das ist — ein Streich von ihm, that is a trick of his, I'll be bound; du hast — kein Geld? you have probably no money? Sie wollten uns — überraschen? you wanted to surprise us, did you not? wußten Sie, daß er fort war? —! did you know he had gone? Of course I did, most certainly! —heit, *f.* certainty; surety; certitude; firmness (*of a resolution*); ich werde mir —heit darüber verschaffen, I shall obtain reliable information as to that, I shall put an end to all doubt about it. —lich, *adv.* certainly, surely, assuredly (*obs.*). *Comp.* —(ss)er=maßen, *adv.* in a certain measure *or* manner, in some sort, to some extent, so to speak, as it were.

Gewis'sen, *n.* (—s) consciousness; conscience; sich (*dat.*) ein — über eine S. machen, to make a thing a matter of conscience, to have scruples about a thing; er macht sich kein — daraus, zu betrügen, he does not scruple to cheat; einem etwas ins — schieben, to make one morally responsible for a thing; Sie haben das Unglück meines Freundes auf dem —, you are morally responsible for the misfortune of my friend; ein enges —, a delicate conscience; ein weites — haben, to be not overscrupulous; das habe ich nicht auf dem —, my conscience is free on that point; er hat es gethan, um sich mit seinem — abzufinden, he did it to soothe his conscience; einem (schwer) aufs — fallen, to come home to one's conscience; ein gut — ist ein sanftes Ruhekissen, a good conscience sleeps through thunder (*prov.*). —haft, —haftig, (*obs.*) *adj. & adv.* conscientious; scrupulous. —haftigkeit, *f.* conscientiousness. *Comp.* —los, *adj.* unconscientious; unprincipled, unscrupulous. —losigkeit, *f.* want of principle, unscrupulousness. —s=angst, *f.* anguish, qualms of conscience. —s=bisse, *pl.* pangs of conscience; remorse. —s=ehe, *f.* marriage (*or* union) not sanctioned by either the State or the Church, not sanctioned by law. —s=frage, *f.* case of conscience; difficult case; —sfragen thun, to ask home questions. —s=freiheit, *f.* freedom of conscience. —s=freund, *m.* father confessor. —s=lehre, *f.* casuistry. —s=pflicht, *f.* bounden duty. —s=rüge, *f.* remorse. —s=prüfung, *f.* self-examination. —s=zwang, *m.* restraint of conscience; intolerance. —s=zweifel, *m.* doubt, scruple.

Gewit'ter, *n.* (—s, *pl.* —) thunder-storm, tempest, storm; es steigt ein — auf, ein — ist im Anzuge, a thunder-storm is gathering; das — hat in dieses Haus eingeschlagen, the lightning has struck this house. —haft, *adj. & adv.* stormy; charged with electricity. *Comp.* —gewölk, *n.* storm-clouds. —luft, *f.* heavy *or* sultry air before a thunder-storm. —regen, *m.* thunder-shower. —schlag, *m.* thunderclap. —schwanger, —schwer, —schwül, *adj.* sultry (*air*). —schwüle, *f.* sultriness. —stange, *f.* lightning-rod. —vogel, *m.* petrel *or* stormbird. —wolke, *f.* thunder-cloud.

Gewit'tern, *v.n. imp.;* es gewittert, it thunders, there is thunder and lightning.

Gewit'zel, *n.* (—s) affected witticism; raillery.

Gewit'z—igt, —t, *adj.* taught wisdom by experience; shrewd.

Gewo'ben, *p.p. of* weben.

Gewo'ge, *n.* waving; fluctuation; rocking; waves (*poet.*).

Gewo'gen, *p.p. of* (1) wiegen; (2) wägen. *adj.* (einem) kind, favourable; friendly; affectionate; sich (*dat.*) einen — machen, to secure *or* gain one's affection *or* favour; bleib mir —! be off with you! (*coll.*); Ihr wohl—er König, your well-affectioned king. —heit, *f.* attachment, affection; kindness; good will.

Gewo'hn, *adj.* used to, accustomed (*obs.*).

Gewoh'n—t, *p.p. & adj.* being in the habit of, accustomed, used to; jung —t, alt gethan, what one learns in youth is remembered in old age, what is bred in the bone will not out of the flesh (*prov.*); —t sein, to be used to, to be wont; ich bin es nicht —t, I am not used to it; er ist —t Berge zu steigen, he is in the habit of climbing; —t werden, to get used to. —heit, *f.* (*pl.* —heiten) habit; custom; practice; usage; wont; zur —heit werden, to grow into a habit; aus —heit, from habit; nach seiner —heit, according to his custom; —heit wird zur zweiten Natur, long custom grows into habit, custom is a second nature (*prov.*). *Comp.* —heits=mäßig, *adj. & adv.* customary, routine; —heitsmäßiger Bummler, professional loafer. —heits=mensch, *m.* creature *or* slave of habit. —heits=recht, *n.* prescriptive law *or* right. —heits=sünde, *f.* habitual *or* besetting sin. —heits=tier, *n.;* der Mensch ist ein —heitstier, man is a creature of habit (*prov.*). —heits=trinker, *m.* habitual *or* confirmed drunkard.

Gewöh'n—en, *v.a. & r.* to accustom, habituate; to inure; to train, break in; sich —en, to get into the habit of; sich an eine S. —en, to get accustomed to a th. —t, *p.p. & adj.* habituated, trained; man hat ihn —t Berge zu steigen, he has been trained to climb mountains. —lich, *adj. & adv.* usual, ordinary, customary; trite, commonplace; inferior, common, vulgar; familiar (*example*); das —liche, the usual thing; eine —liche Frau, an everyday woman; a vulgar woman; —liche Leute, ordinary people; etwas über das —liche hinaus, something out of the common. —ung, *f.* custom, habitude; accustoming; die —ung an das Klima, acclimatization; —ung der Haustiere, domestication of animals.

Gewöl'be, *n.* (—s, *pl.* —) vault, arch; cellar;

shop, warehouse; depot, store; **Kauf —**, store, warehouse; **Kreuz —**, groined vault. *Comp.* **—ähnlich, —artig,** *adj.* arch-like, vault-like. **—bogen,** *m.* arch of a vault. **—bock,** *m.* wooden arch, centring of a vault. **—fenster,** *n.* skylight; bow-window. **—pfeiler,** *m.* buttress; shaft of an arch. **—schlußstein,** *m.* keystone. **—stein,** *m.* vaulting stone, voussoir. **—stütze,** *f.* flying buttress. **—winkel,** *m.* flank, haunch of an arch. **—zins,** *m.* shop-rent.

Gewö'lk, *n.* (—es) clouds, mass of clouds.

Gewönne, *imperf. subj. of* **gewinnen.**

Gewon'nen, *p.p. of* **gewinnen; wie —, so zerronnen,** easily won, easily run; lightly come, lightly go (*prov.*).

Gewor'ben, *p.p. of* **werben.** *adj.* raised, levied; **—e Truppen,** hired soldiers, levies.

Gewor'den, *p.p. of* **werden.**

Gewor'fen, *p.p. of* **werfen.** *adj.*; **— Gut,** jetsam.

Gewü'hl, *n.* (—es) rooting up; tumult, bustle; bustling throng.

Gewun'den, *p.p. of* **winden.** *adj.* spiral; tortuous; twisted; flexuous; sinuous. **—heit,** *f.* sinuosity.

Gewun'ken, *p.p. of* **winken** (*hum., coll.*).

Gewü'rm, *n.* (—es) worms; reptiles; vermin.

Gewü'rz, *n.* (—es, *pl.* —e) spice; aromatics; seasoning; groceries. **—haft, —ig,** *adj. & adv.* spicy, aromatic. *Comp.* **—artig,** *adj.* spicy. **—büchse,** *f.* spice-box. **—fleisch,** *n.* curry, ragout. **—händler, —krämer,** *m.* grocer, spicer. **—kram,** *m.* groceries, spices (*for retail*). **—kuchen,** *m.* gingerbread. **—nägelein,** *n.* (*obs.*), **—nelke,** *f.* clove. **—reich,** *adj.* rich in spices; spicy, aromatic. **—ware,** *f.* groceries. **—wein,** *m.* spiced wine.

Gewu'ßt, *p.p. of* **wissen.**

Geza'ckt, *adj.* notched, pectinate, serrated.

Gezä'h, *n.* (—es) set of tools (*of miners*). *Comp.* **—kasten,** *m.* tool-box (*of miners*).

Gezä'hnt, Geza'hnt, *adj.* notched, cogged, toothed; indented, dentate; perforated (*of postage stamps*).

Gezän'k(e), *n.* (—(e)s) quarrel; squabble; continual quarrelling, wrangling.

Gezap'pel, *n.* (—s) struggling, kicking; floundering.

Geze'hnt, *adj.* decimated.

Gezei't, *f.* term; flood-tide, tide. **—en,** *pl.* hours (*R. C.*). *Comp.* **—en=buch,** *n.* breviary.

Geze'lt, *n.* (—es, *pl.* —e) tent, canopy.

Gezer're, *n.* (—s) pulling about, tussle.

Gezeter, *n.* (—s) screaming, screams, outcry.

Gezie'fer, *n.* (—s) vermin, insects.

Gezie'hen, *p.p. of* **zeihen.**

Gezie'm—en, *v.r. & n.* (*aux.* **h.**) *imp.* to be suitable, to be fit, to become; **es —t sich nicht für ihn,** it is not the proper thing for him to do; **wie es sich —t,** as is fit *or* becoming; **leben wie seinem Stande —t,** to live up to, *or* in accordance with, one's rank. **—end, —lich,** *adj.* proper, becoming; seemly; due; suitable; **mit —ender Ehrfurcht,** with due reverence; **sich —end aufführen,** to behave properly.

Gezie'r—e, *n.* (—s) affectation; prudery. **—t,** *adj. & adv.* affected · prim; studied. **—theit,** *f.* affectation; studied mannerism.

Gezir'p(e), *n.* (—(e)s) chirping.

Gezi'sch, *n.* (—es) hissing; whizzing. **—el,** *n.* (—s) whispering.

Gezo'gen, *p.p. of* **ziehen,** rifled, twisted; **—e Geschütze,** rifled cannons; **—er Lauf, —es Rohr,** rifled barrel; **—es Licht,** dipped candle; **—e Wechsel,** *m.pl.* drawn bills, drafts; **in die Länge —,** wire-drawn; spun out.

Gezü'cht, *n.* (—es) brood, breed; race, set, crew (*contempt*).

Gezwei'g, *n.* (—es, *pl.* —e) branches (*of a tree*).

Gezwei't, *adj.* binary; bipartite, binate.

Gezwe'rg, *n.* (—es) dwarf; brownies (*obs.*).

Gezwit'scher, *n.* (—s) chirping, twitter, warbling.

Gezwun'gen, *p.p. of* **zwingen.** *adj. & adv.* forced, overstrained, unnatural, affected; **—es Wesen,** affected manners; **— lachen,** to affect a laugh. **—heit,** *f.* constraint; affectation; stiffness.

Gib, Gibst, Gibt, *see* **Gieb, Giebst, Giebt.**

Gib'berig, *adj.*; **nach einer Sache — sein,** to be desirous for, to hanker after a thing (*coll.*).

Gi'cht, *f.* gout; convulsive fits; furnace-mouth. **—isch,** *adj. & adv.* gouty. *Comp.* **—bruch,** *m.*, **—brüchigkeit,** *f.* palsy. **—brüchig,** *adj.* gouty; paralytic, palsied; **der —brüchige,** the man sick of the palsy (*B.*).

Gick'gack, Gig'gack, *m.* (—s, *pl.* —s) gabble of geese; stupid goose. *See* **Gänschen.**

Gib; Gibst, Gibt, *imperat.; 2 & 3 pers. sing. pres. indic. of* **geben.**

Gie'bel, *m.* (—s, *pl.* —) gable, gable end; pediment; house-top; summit; nose (*coll.*). **—ig,** *adj. & adv.* gabled. *Comp.* **—balken,** *m.* roof-tree. **—dach,** *n.* gabled roof. **—feld,** *n.* pediment. **—fenster,** *n.* dormer-window; gable window; **halbrundes —fenster,** fanlight. **—haus,** *n.* house with a gable end. **—säule,** *f.* king-post; crown-post. **—saum,** *m.* border of the gable. **—schwalbe,** *f.* house-swallow.

Gie'beln, *v.a.* to put on a gable, to gable.

Gie'k— (*Naut.*) **—baum,** *m.* main-boom. **—segel,** *n.* main-sail. **—tau,** *n.* topping-lift.

Gie'ke, *f.* (*pl.* —n) foot-stove.

Gien, *f.* winding tackle (*Naut.*).

Gieng, Gien'ge, *see* **Ging, Ginge.**

Gier (*obs.:* **—de**), *f.* eagerness, inordinate desire, greediness.

Gie'r—en, *v.n.* (*aux.* **h.**) to long (**nach einer S.,** for a th.); to lurch; to deviate from the course, to sheer, yaw (*Naut.*); **laß das Schiff nicht —en!** steady! **—ig,** *adj. & adv.* eager, greedy, covetous (**nach,** for, of). **—igkeit,** *f.* eagerness, greediness. *Comp.* **—brücke, —fähre,** *f.* trail-flying-bridge. **—laps,** *m.* greedy person (*coll.*). **—tau,** *n.* trail.

Gie'ßel, *m.* (—s) hole through which fused metal is poured; spout.

Gie'ß—en, *ir.* I. *v.a.* to pour forth, pour; to shed; to spill; to cast; to mould (*candles*); to sprinkle, to water; **Öl ins Feuer —en,** to pour oil on the flame, add fuel to the flame; **ist heute schon gegossen?** have the flowers been watered today? **gegossene Arbeit,** cast-work. I. *n. imp.* **es —t,** it is pouring, raining fast; **es —t mit Mollen,** it is raining cats and dogs (*coll.*). **—er,** *m.* (—ers, *pl.* —er) founder; ewer. **—erei',** *f.* watering; foundry; casting, founding. **—ung,** *f.* fusion (*rare*). *Comp.* **—bach,** *m.* mountain torrent. **—bad,** *n.* shower-bath, douche. **—becken,** *n.* basin, ewer. **—erde,** *f.* earth for moulds. **—erz,** *n.* bronze. **—faß,** *n.* ewer. **—form,** *f.* mould. **—haus,** *n.*, **—hütte,** *f.* foundry. **—kanne,** *f.* ewer; watering can, watering-pot. **—kannen=aufsatz, —kopf,** *m.* rose of a watering can. **—loch,** *n.* spout; hole of a mould; funnel of a furnace. **—mutter,** *f.* mould, matrix. **—ofen,** *m.* founding furnace. **—opfer,** *n.* libation. **—rinne,** *f.* gutter, sink. **—röhre,** *f.* pipe of a watering-pot. **—stein,** *m.* porous granite; sink. **—tafel,** *f.* frame for casting mirrors on. **—tiegel,** *m.* melting-pot. **—tisch,** *m.* chandler's mould-frame. **—trichter,** *m.* funnel. **—waren,** *pl.* cast-metal goods.

Gift, I. *f.* gift (*obs.*); **— und Gabe,** present(s) (*obs.*). II. *n.* (—s, *pl.* —e) poison, virus, venom; virulence, malice; **darauf kannst du — nehmen,** you may be quite sure of that, you may take your oath on that (*coll.*); **voll — und Galle,**

full of rage and malice; — **und Galle speien**, to give vent to one's spite and malice; **schleichendes** —, slow poison. **—ig**, *adj. & adv.* poisonous, venomous; pernicious; malignant, spiteful; angry, waxy (*coll.*). **—igkeit**, *f.* venom; anger, wrath (*coll.*). *Comp.* **—arznei**, *f.* poisonous drug; antidote. **—baum**, *m.* poison tree *or* oak; upas tree. **—becher**, *m.* poisoned cup. **—bissen**, *m.* bait, poisoned bit. **—fang**, **—gang**, *m.* chimney of arsenic works. **—geschwollen**, *adj.* swelled *or* filled with poison. **—haltig**, *adj.* poisonous, venomous. **—hauch**, *m.* blight. **—hütte**, *f.* arsenic works. **—kies**, *m.* arsenical pyrites. **—kobalt**, *m.* native arsenic. **—lehre**, *f.* toxicology. **—los**, *adj.* harmless; poisonless. **—mehl**, *n.* flowers of arsenic; poisoned flour. **—mischer**, *m.*, **—mischerin**, *f.* poisoner. **—mischerei**, *f.* poisoning. **—mittel**, *n.* antidote. **—mord**, *m.* poisoning. **—regen**, *m.* blight. **—schlange**, *f.* venomous serpent, poisonous snake. **—stein**, *m.* white arsenic ore. **—trank**, *m.* poisonous draught. **—voll**, **—reich**, *adj.* venomous, full of poison. **—zahn**, *m.* venomous fang. **—zunge**, *f.* envenomed tongue.

Giga'nt, *m.* (**—en**, *pl.* **—en**) giant (*Myth.*). **—enhaft**, **—e'sk**, **—isch**, *adj.* gigantic.

Gi'gerl, (**—s**, *pl.* **—n**) fop, dandy, masher (*coll.*).

Gil'b—e, *f.* yellow colour; yellow ochre. **—icht** (*obs.*), **—ig** (*rare*), *adj. & adv.* yellowish.

Gil'de, *f.* (*pl.* **—n**) guild, corporation; guild-meeting; guild-banquet. *Comp.* **—brief**, *m.* charter of a corporation.

Gil'tig, *see* **Gültig**.

Giltst, **Gilt**, *2 & 3 pers. sing. pres. ind. of* **gelten**.

Gim'pel, *m.* (**—s**, *pl.* **—**) bullfinch; dunce, ninny, simpleton. **—ei'**, *f.* coxcombry; silliness. *Comp.* **—haft**, *adj.* silly, foolish.

Ging, **Gin'ge**, *imperf. indic. & subj. of* **gehen**.

Gin'gang, *m.* gingham (*kind of striped cloth*).

Gin'ster, *m.* (**—s**, *pl.* **—**) broom.

Gip'fel, *m.* (**—s**, *pl.* **—**) summit, top; pinnacle; climax, height. *Comp.* **—ständig**, *adj.* terminal (*Bot.*). **—stein**, *m.* top-stone.

Gip'fel—n, *v.r. & n.* (*aux.* **h.**) to reach the zenith, climax; to culminate; to rise to a peak; **seine Behauptungen —ten darin**, his assertions culminated in this.

Gips (*less good* **Gyps**), *m.* (**—(s)es**, *pl.* **—(s)e**) gypsum; plaster of Paris, stucco. *Comp.* **—abdruck**, **—abguß**, *m.* plaster cast. **—anwurf**, *m.* plastering. **—arbeit**, *f.* stucco work. **—bild**, *n.* stucco figure, figure in plaster. **—brennen**, calcination of plaster. **—decke**, *f.* stucco ceiling. **—figuren-händler**, *m.* dealer in plaster images. **—guß**, *m.* plaster casting. **—malerei**, *f.* painting in fresco. **—steinartig**, *adj.* gypseous.

Gip's—en, *v.a.* to plaster. **—er**, *m.* plasterer.

Giraf'fe, *f.* (*pl.* **—n**) giraffe.

Gir—a'nt, *m.* (**—an'ten**, *pl.* **—an'ten**) endorser. **—a't**, *m.* (**—aten**, **—ats**, *pl.* **—aten**) endorsee. **—ie'ren**, *v.a.* to circulate; **einen Wechsel —ieren**, to endorse a bill (**auf**, **an**, in favour of). **—o**, *n.* (**—os**, *pl.* **—os**, **Gi'ri**) endorsement; **sein —o geben**, to endorse; **unausgefülltes —o**, blank endorsement. *Comp.* **—o-bank**, *f.* transfer *or* deposit bank, bank of circulation. **—geschäft**, *n.* clearing-house business. **—konto**, *n.* drawing-account, banking account; **ich habe mein —konto bei . . .**, my bankers are . . ., I am banking with . . .

Gir'ren, *v.n.* (*aux.* **h.**) to coo.

Gis, G-sharp (*Mus.*).

Gisch—en, *v.n.* to foam, froth, boil; to ferment (= **gähren**). **—t**, *m.* foam, froth, ebullition, spray; yeast; fermentation (= **Gährung**).

Giß'—en, *v.a.* to estimate by guess; **gegißter Kurs**, course found by dead reckoning (*Naut.*). **—ung**, *f.* dead reckoning.

Git'ter, *n.* (**—s**, *pl.* **—**) trellis; grating, lattice. railing; fire-guard; fence; fret (*Her.*); **durch das — verkleinern**, to reduce by squares (*Paint.*). *Comp.* **—bett**, *n.* cot (with rails). **—blech**, *n.* grating of iron wire (*used in roasting*); gridiron. **—erker**, *m.* balcony. **—fenster**, *n.* lattice window; window with cross-bars. **—flechter**, *m.* lattice-maker. **—laube**, *f.* trellis-work arbour. **—thor**, *n.* trellised gate. **—thür**, *f.* grated door. **—werk**, *n.* trellis-work; grating. **—zaun**, *m.* fence of trellis-work.

Git'tern, *v.a.* to lattice; to grate; to rail; **das gegitterte B**, A-sharp (*Mus.*); **gegitterte Leinen**, Arabias (*C.L.*).

Glac—é', *see* **—e'-handschuhe**. **—ie'ren**, *v.a.* to glaze; to freeze. *Comp.* **—é'-handschuhe**, *pl.* kid gloves. **—is'-abhang**, *m.*, **—is'-böschung**, slope of the glacis (*Fort.*).

Gladiato'risch, *adj. & adv.* gladiatorial.

Glan'der, *f.* (*pl.* **—n**) slide; flake of ice; tail of a comet; species of corn-weevil.

Glanz, *m.* (**—es**, *no pl.*) lustre; gleam; gloss, glossiness; polish; brightness; splendour, magnificence; illustriousness; glory; glance; glare; — **der Gesundheit**, bloom of health; — **eines Stoffes**, gloss of a stuff. *Comp.* **—blatt**, *n.* jeweller's foil. **—bürste**, *f.* polishing-brush. **—erz**, *n.* plumbago. **—farbe**, *f.* brilliant colour. **—gold**, *n.* gold foil. **—kattun**, *m.* glazed calico. **—leder**, *n.* patent leather. — **—leinwand**, *f.* glazed linen. **—los**, *adj.* lustreless; not shiny. **—papier**, *n.* glazed paper. **—periode**, *f.* days of glory, palmy days; most brilliant period. **—presse**, *f.* glazing calender (*for cloth*). **—punkt**, *m.* brightest point, climax; **der —punkt des Tages (Abends)**, the culminating point, the great attraction of the day (evening). **—reich**, *adj.* resplendent. — **ruß**, *m.* lamp-black. **—seite**, *f.* bright side of anything. **—spat**, *m.* feldspar. **—stein**, *m.* brilliant; opal. **—stelle**, *f.* brilliant passage. **—taffet**, *m.* silk lustring. **—umleuchtet**, *adj.* radiant. **—wichse**, *f.* varnish (*for boots*).

Glän'ze, *f.* gloss; glossing-machine, polisher.

Glän'z—en, *v.* I. *n.* (*aux.* **h.**) to shine, glitter, gleam, sparkle; **es ist nicht alles Gold was —t**, all is not gold that glitters (*prov.*); **er will gern —en**, he wishes to show off, he loves display; **durch Abwesenheit —en**, to be conspicuous by absence. II. *a.* to gloss; to polish; to burnish; to glaze. **—end**, *p.*, *adj. & adv.* brilliant; splendid; **—ende That**, glorious deed; **—endes Elend**, splendid pauperism. **—er**, *m.* (**—ers**, *pl.* **—er**) glosser, finisher, burnisher. *Comp.* **hammer**, *m.* planishing hammer.

Glas, *n.* (**—(s)es**, *pl.* **Glä'ser**) glass; drinking-glass; tumbler; **ein — Wein**, a glass of wine; **ein Wein—**, a wine-glass; **er trank drei — Bier**, he emptied three glasses of beer; **er kaufte drei Gläser**, he bought three glasses; **die Gläser des Hirsches**, the eyes of the stag; **unter — und Rahmen bringen**, to frame; **Glück und — wie bald bricht das**, happiness is fragile as glass (*prov.*); **zu tief ins — gucken**, to drink too much. **—(s)er**, *m.* (**—(s)ers**, *pl.* **—(s)er**) glazier. **—(s)icht**, (*obs.*) *adj. & adv.* glassy, vitreous, glass-like. **—(s)ig**, *adj.* glassy. **—(s)ie'ren**, *v.a.* to glaze; to ice; to varnish; to frost (*Cook.*). **—(s)u'r**, *f.* glazing, glaze; icing; varnish; **—ur der Zähne**, enamel of the teeth. *Comp.* **—ähnlich**, **—artig**, *adj.* glassy, vitreous. **—asche**, *f.* alkali. **—blase-röhre**, *f.* blow-pipe. **—brennen**, *n.* annealing. **—brocken**, *m.* cullet, broken glass (*for re-melting*). **—cylinder**, *m.* lamp-chimney. **—einziehen**, *n.* glazing. **—elektricität**, *f.* vitreous electricity. **—(s)er-kitt**, *m.* putty. **—(s)er-meister**, *m.* master-glazier. **—erz**, *n.* silver-glance. **—fabrik**, *f.* glass-works. **—feuchtigkeit**, *f.* vitreous humour (*of the eye*).

flasche, *f.* glass bottle; decanter. —fluß, *m.* paste (*for diamonds*). —geschirr, *n.* glass, table-glass. —glanz, *m.* vitreous lustre. —glocke, *f.* bell-glass, glass-shade. —grün, *adj.* bottle-green. —hafen, *m.* crucible. —harmonika, *f.* musical glasses. —händler, *m.* dealer in glass. —haus, *n.* hot-house, green-house, conservatory. —haut, *f.*, —häutchen, *n.* choroid coat (*Anat.*). —hell, *adj.* diaphanous. —hütte, *f.* glass-works. —kasten, *m.* glass-case; show-case. —kitt, *m.* diamond cement. —kolben, *m.* flask (*Chem.*). —koralle, —perle, *f.* glass bead. —linse, *f.* lens. —malerei, *f.* glass-painting; picture on glass. —messer, *m.* vitrometer; glass-cutter. —ofen, *m.* glass-furnace. —perle, *f.* bead. —porzellan, *n.* transparent porcelain. —röhre, *f.* glass-tube. —satz, *m.* frit. —scheibe, *f.* pane of glass. —scherbe, *f.* piece of broken glass; (*pl.*) cullet. —schirm, *m.* glass shade. —schleifen, *n.* grinding of glass. —schrank, *m.* cupboard with glass doors *or* for glass. —splitter, *m.* shiver of glass. —stock, *m.* glass bee-hive. —tafel, *f.* glass-plate; a square *or* pane of glass. —tiegel, —topf, *m.* crucible, glass-melting pot.

Glä'schen, *n.* (—s, *pl.* —) little glass; ein — zu viel *or* über den Durst, a drop too much.

Gläser— *in comp.* —abkühler, *m.* cooling-vessel for glasses. —klang, *m.* jingling (sound) of glasses. —serviette, *f.* doily.

Glä'sern, *adj.* of glass; vitreous; glassy; crystalline.

Glast, *m.* (—es, *pl.* Gläs'te) radiance (*dial. & poet.*).

Glatt, (*comp.* —er, *sup.* —est, *better than* glät'ter, glät'test, *which also occur*). I. *adj.* smooth, even; polished; slippery; bland, flattering, sweet; fresh, blooming; bare; sleek; — zu machen, to smooth, polish; es ist sehr — zu gehen, it is very slippery walking; —er Sammet, plain velvet; —e Worte, sweet *or* flattering words; —e Zunge, a smooth tongue; —es Gesicht, smooth *or* sleek face; —es Kinn, smooth *or* beardless chin; —e Stirn, fair, unfurrowed forehead; —er Satz, letter-type; ein —es Geschäft, good and easily disposed-of business. II. *adv.* smoothly; quite, entirely; plainly; die Sache ging ganz —, the affair came off very smoothly, without the slightest hitch; er hat alles — abgemacht, he has settled the whole business; ein Geschäft — abwickeln, to settle a business easily; — abschlagen, to give a flat denial; — heraus sagen, to tell bluntly, plainly, frankly; — weg, plainly, openly; — rasieren, to shave close; — streichen, to smooth down; — anliegen, — sitzen, to fit close. —heit, *f. see* Glätte. *Comp.* —eis, *n.* slippery ice, glazed frost; aufs —eis führen, to mislead, bring into a dilemma. —eisen, *v.n. imp.*; es glatteist, there is a glazed frost, it is very slippery. —eisen, *n.* curling-tongs; smoothing-iron. —köpfig, *adj.* sleek-headed, bald. —züngig, *adj.* smooth-tongued.

Glät't—e, *f.* smoothness; polish, gloss; sleekness; plainness; slipperiness; politeness; litharge. *Comp.* —eisen, *n.* smoothing-iron. —werkzeug, *n.*, —zahn, *m.* smoothing, polishing, *or* burnishing, tool.

Glät't—en, *v.a.* to smooth; to glaze; to plane; to polish. —er, *m.* (—ers, *pl.* —er) burnisher; polisher; polishing tool.

Glat'z—e, *f.* bald spot; bald part of the head; tonsure; bald head. —ig, *adj. & adv.* bald-pated, bald. *Comp.* —kopf, *m.* bald-pate, bald-headed person.

Glau, *adj.* bright, lively, quick (*dial.*). *Comp.* —äugig, *adj.* bright-eyed; sharp-sighted (*poet.*).

Glau'b—e, *m.* (—ens) faith; belief; credence; credit (*obs.*); religious faith; creed; (einem *or* einer Behauptung) —en schenken, to give credence to; etwas auf Treu' und —en annehmen, to believe a th. implicitly, accept it on trust *or* on the good faith of a p.; einen —en bekennen, to profess a religion; seinen —en verleugnen, von seinem —en abgehen, sich seines —ens abthun, to abjure one's faith, become an apostate (*poet.*); der —e macht selig, faith alone makes happy (*prov.*). —haft, —haftig, *adj. & adv.* credible; authentic; faithful, true. —haftigkeit, *f.* credibility; authenticity. —ig, *adj.* (*dial. for* gläubig) believing, religious; credulous. —lich, *adj. & adv.* credible, likely. —lichkeit, *f.* credibility, probability. *Comp.* —en-fest, *adj.* firm, strong in one's faith. —ens-artikel, *m.* article of faith. —ens-bekenntnis, *n.* confession of faith, creed; apostolisches —ensbekenntnis, the Apostles' creed; Nicänisches —bekenntnis, Nicene creed. —ens-bruder, *m.* brother in the faith, co-religionist. —ens-eifer, *m.* religious zeal. —ens-formel, *f.* confession of faith. —ens-freiheit, *f.* religious liberty. —ens-genoß, *m.* co-religionist; fellow-believer. —ens-gericht, *n.* inquisition. —ens-lehre, *f.* dogmatics, dogmatic *or* doctrinal theology. —ens-lehrer, *m.* dogmatist. —ens-meinung, *f.* religious opinion. —partei, *f.* denomination. —ens-punkt, *m.* article of faith. —ens-reiniger, *m.* religious reformer. —ens-richter, *m.* inquisitor. —ens-satz, *m.* dogma. —ens-schwärmer, *m.* fanatic. —ens-streit, *m.*, —ens-streitigkeit, *f.* religious controversy. —ens-streiter, *m.* champion of the faith. —ens-verbesserung, *f.* reformation (*of religious beliefs*). —ens-verleugner, *m.* renegade. —ens-wissenschaft, *f.* theology. —ens-wut, *f.* fanaticism. —ens-zeuge, *m.* martyr. —ens-zwang, *m.* constraint *or* restraint in matters of religion *or* worship; intolerance, persecution. —ens-zweifel, *m.* scruple in matters of faith, scepticism. —würdig, *adj. & adv.* worthy of belief, credible, authentic. —würdigkeit, *f.* credibility; authenticity.

Glau'be—n, *v.a. & n.* (*aux.* h.) to believe, trust, have faith in, give credence to; to believe; to think, suppose; to imagine; wenn man es ihm —n soll, if he is to be believed; an eine S. —n, to believe in a thing; einem (etwas) —n, to believe one; er wollte mich —n machen, he wished to make me believe; ich — Ihnen aufs Wort, I take your word for it; einen Gott —n, to believe in a God (*obs. & poet.*); es — jeder seinen Ring den echten, let every one consider his ring to be the true one (*obs. & poet.*); an Gott —n, to believe *or* trust in God; das ist nicht zu —n, that is incredible; ich — wohl, I dare say, I should think so, indeed!

Glau'bersalz, *n.* (—es) Glauber's salt, sulphate of soda.

Gläu'big, *adj.* believing; faithful, full of faith; devout; credulous. —e(r), *m.*, —e, *f.* believer; *pl.* die —en, the (true) believers, the faithful. —er, *m.* (—ers, *pl.* —er) creditor; *pl.* die —er, the creditors.

Gleich, I. *adj. & adv.* even, level; straight; equal, equivalent; like, resembling; proportionate, adequate; in —em Maße, in the same measure; in —er Weise, likewise; zu —; also, at the same moment; zu —er Zeit, at the same time; ein —er Boden, a level *or* even ground; — machen, to level; dem Boden — machen, to make even with the ground, to raze; von —em Alter, of the same age; von —em Werte, equivalent; das ist *or* gilt mir —, that is all the same, *or* all one, to me; einem — kommen, — sein, to become *or* be equal to a p., to equal one; sich (*dat.*) — bleiben, to be always oneself, the same; sich einem — stellen, to put oneself on a par with another; es einem — thun, to equal, match one; es einem — thun wollen, to vie with one; meines —en, the like of me, my equal; er sucht seines —en, er hat seines —en nicht, he has not his equal; ohne —en, sonder —en, matchless, peerless; ich achte mich ihm —, I think myself his equal; von seines —en gerichtet werden, to be tried by one's peers; die Tochter ist *or* sieht ihrer Mutter —; the daughter resembles her mother; das sieht ihm —, that is just like him; in —em Werte stehen, to be at par; ins —e bringen, to arrange; ich werde ein —es für dich thun, I will do as much for you; einem —es mit —em vergelten, mit —er Münze bezahlen einem *or* einen, to pay one off in the same coin; — und — gesellt sich gern, birds of a feather flock together (*prov.*); —e Brüder, —e Kappen, like pot, like cover (*prov.*). II. *adv.* alike, equally, exactly; immediately, instantly, directly, presently; — alt, of the same age; — ewig, co-eternal; —viel, all the same, just as much; —viel, ob es wahr ist, even if it be true; — anfangs, at the very beginning; — nachher, immediately after; ich bin — wieder zurück, I shall return immediately; Kellner! —, mein Herr! waiter! Coming, sir! — bei der Hand, prompt, ready, at hand; — jetzt, at once; just now; das ist — geschehen, that is easily (soon) done; es schlägt — drei, it is on the stroke of three; ich dachte es —, I thought as much; — als ich ihn sah, as soon as I saw him; — als ob, just as if; — als, as, as much as. III. *part.* in großen Städten ist doch — alles anders, in large towns, you see, everything is different; wie ist doch — der Name? what is the name now (I can't remember)? IV. *conj.* although; ist er — nicht reich, so thut er doch . . ., although he is not rich, yet he acts (does) . . .; wären Sie — mein Vater, even though you were my father. —bar, *adj.* & *adv.* comparable. —e, *f.* evenness, equality (*rare*); etwas in die —e (*usually* ins —e) bringen, to settle a thing; Tag- und Nacht—e, equinox. —heit, *f.* equality, identity; par; likeness, similarity; evenness. —nis, *n.* (—ni(ss)es, *pl.* —ni(ss)e) image; similitude; simile, comparison; allegory; parable; Christi —nisse, the parables of Christ. —sam, *adv.*, as if, as it were, as though; almost. —ung, *f.* equation; —ung des ersten, zweiten, dritten Grades, simple, quadratic, cubic equation. *Comp.* —altrig, *adj.* of the same age. —artig, *adj.* homogeneous; similar; analogous. —bedeutend, *adj.* synonymous; —bedeutende Wörter, synonyms. —berechtigt, *adj.* having equal right, equally entitled. —bürtigkeit, *f.* equality of birth. —deutig, *adj.* synonymous. —empfindung, *f.* sympathy. —entfernt, *adj.*, equidistant. —er=gestalt, —er=maßen, —er=weise, *adv.* in like manner, likewise. —falls, *adv.* & *conj.* likewise, also, even, in like case. —farbig, *adj.* of the same colour. —förmigkeit, *f.* uniformity. —fühlend, *adj.* sympathetic. —gefühl, *n.* sympathy. —geltend, (*dat.*) *adj.* equivalent (*to*), tantamount (*to*). —gesinnt, *adj.* likeminded. —gestaltet, *adj.*, of the same shape. —gestimmt, *adj.* tuned to the same pitch; congenial. —gewicht, *n.* equilibrium, equipoise; (proper) balance; politisches —gewicht, balance of power, relative strength of great states; das europäische —gewicht, the balance of power of Europe, the balance of power of the great European states; einem das —gewicht halten, to counterbalance a p.'s influence, to cope with one; das —gewicht eines Schiffes, the balancing of a ship. ins —gewicht bringen, to equilibrate, equipoise; im —gewicht erhalten, to balance (equally), to keep in equal balance; das —gewicht verlieren, to lose one's balance; das —gewicht wiederherstellen, to redress the balance; das —gewicht aufheben, to turn the scales, upset the balance; im —gewicht ruhend, well poised. —gewichts=lehre, *f.* statics. —gewichts=punkt, *m.* centre of gravity. —gewichts=stange, *f.* balancing-pole. —giltig, *see* —gültig. —gradig, *adj.* on the same scale. —gültig, *adj.* indifferent (gegen, to); mir ist es —gültig, it is all the same to me, I am quite indifferent on the subject. —gültigkeit, *f.* equivalence (*rare*), unconcern; indifference. —heits=association, *f.* association by identity. —heits=zeichen, *n.* sign of equation (=). —jährig, *adj.* of the same age, coeval. —klang, *m.* unison; consonance. —kommend, *adj.* equivalent to. —läufig, —laufend, *adj.* parallel. —lautend, —lautig, I. *adj.* consonant; of the same tenor *or* contents; —lautende Abschrift, duplicate, counterpart. II. *adv.* in conformity; consonantly. —machung, *f.* levelling; equalization. —mäßig, *adj.* & *adv.* uniform; similar; symmetrical; equal. —maß, *n.* symmetry; proportion; commensurateness, uniformity. —meßbar, *adj.* commensurable. —messer, *see* —er. —mut, *m.* equanimity. —mütig, *adj.* even-tempered, calm. —mütigkeit, *f. see* Gleichmut. —namig, *adj.* of the same name; homonymous; correspondent (*Math.*). —nis=rede, *f.* parable, allegory. —nis=weise, *adv.* in the form of a parable *or* an allegory; by way of simile. —nis=wort, *n.* figurative expression. —sam, *adv.* as it were. —schenkelig, *adj.* isosceles. —schritt, *m.* equal step (*Mil.*). —seitig, *adj.* equilateral; reciprocal. —silbig, *adj.* parasyllabic, of the same number of syllables. —sinn, *m.* synonymy; equability. —sinnig, *adj.* equable; synonymous. —stellung, *f.* equalization; comparison. —stimmig, *adj.* in unison; unanimous; congenial. —strom, *m.* continuous current. —teilig, *adj.* equally divided; divisible into equal parts. —ungs=linie, *f.* line of the equator. —viel, *adv.* no matter, all the same; all one. —weit, *adj.* & *adv.* equidistant; parallel; er ist —weit davon entfernt, Unrecht zu thun, als, he is as far from doing wrong as. —wert, *m.* equivalent. —wie, *conj.* & *adv.* as, just as, even as. —winkelig, *adj.*, equiangular. —wohl, *conj.* & *adv.* nevertheless, notwithstanding, yet, for all that, however. —zeitig, I. *adj.* contemporary; simultaneous. II. *adv.* together, at the same time; —zeitig geschehend, coincident. —zeitigkeit, *f.* contemporary existence; simultaneousness; synchronism. —zu, *adv.* straightway; without ceremony.

Glei'ch—en, *ir.v.* I. *n.* (*aux.* h., *dat.*) to equal; to match, be equal to; to resemble; er —t sich immer noch, he is still the same, unchanged. II. *reg. v.a.* to cause to be equal, to equalize, to adjust; to make alike; to smooth, level; to liken, compare (*obs.*); ich gleich' sie einem Rosenstock, I liken her to a rosebush (*obs.* & *poet.*); ihr sollt euch ihnen nicht —en, ye shall not do as they (*B.*); Tage und Nächte —en, to make days and nights of equal length. —er, *m.* (—ers, *pl.* —er) one who makes even *or* equal; equator; equalizer, leveller. —ung, *f.* equation (*Math. Astr.*); equalization; adjusting, sizing; levelling.

Gleis, Glei'se, *n.*, *see* Geleise.

Gleis'ner (*less correct:* Gleiß'ner), *m.* (—s, *pl.* —). —in, *f.* hypocrite; dissembler, double-dealer, pharisee. —ei', f. hypocrisy; shamming; simulation. —isch, adj. hypocritical.

Glei'ße—n, (reg. & ir., v.n. (aux. h.) to shine, to glitter; to dissemble, play the hypocrite; —d, deceitful, hypocritical.

Gleit, n. (pl. —e) timber-slide, shoot.

Glei't—en, (reg. & ir.v.n. (aux. s. & h.) to glide, slide; to slip; —ende Reime, gliding rhymes, i.e. rhymes in which the rhyming vowels stand in the last syllable but two (e.g. unmerited: inherited; reisende: preisende). Comp. —bahn, f. slide, slideway; launching way (Naut.). —lineal, n., —stange, f. guide, slide-bar.

Glet'scher, m. (—s, pl. —) glacier. Comp. —bildung, f. glacial formation. —schliff, n. rock polished by glaciers. —spalte, f. crevasse.

Glich, Gli'che, imperf. ind. & subj. of gleichen.

Glied, n. (—es, pl. —er) limb, member; member (of a club, etc.); rank, file (Mil.); term (Math. & Log.); article (Bot.); generation; link (of chains); joint (Anat.); das männliche —, penis; —er formieren, to fall in; aus dem —e treten, to quit the ranks; in Reih' und —, in the ranks; in order of battle; die —er strecken or recken, to stretch oneself; die äußeren —er eines Verhältnisses, extremes; Vettern im dritten —e, third cousins; doppelte —er, rickets; in —ern links! left file (Mil.); schließt die —er! double the file! (Mil.). —erig, adj. & adv. limbed, jointed; groß—erig, large-limbed. Comp. —abnehmung, f. amputation of a limb. —buße, f. indemnification for bodily injury (Law). —er=ablösung, f. amputation. —er=abstand, m. space between the ranks (Mil.). —er=band, m. ligament. —er=bau, m. formation, structure, organization; articulation; frame. —er=feuer, n. file-firing, volley. —er=fluß, m. rheumatism. —er=fuge, f. articulation. —er=hülse, f. loment. —er=krankheit, f. disease of the joints, gout. —er=lahm, adj. paralytic, palsied. —er=lähmung, f. paralysis. —er=mann, m. lay-figure, manikin. —er=puppe, f. puppet, jointed doll. —er=reißen, n., —er=schmerz, m. pain in the limbs, gout, rheumatism. —er=satz, m. period (Rhet. etc.). —er=schwamm, m. white swelling. —er=tiere, pl. articulated animals (Zoöl.). —er=weise, adv. by joints, by links; in files. —er=zucken, n., —er=zuckung, f. convulsive movement, convulsion. —los, adj. without limbs or members. —maßen, pl. limbs, members (of the body); gesunde —maßen haben, to be sound of limb; ein Mann von starken —maßen, a strong-limbed, powerfully built man. —weise, adv. limb by limb; in files.

Glie'der—n, v.a. to provide with limbs or members; to joint; to organize; to form into ranks or files. —ung, f. organization; articulation; scansion; forming into files; structure.

Glim'm—en, (reg. & ir.v.n. (aux. h.) to glimmer, glow; —ende Asche, embers; das Feuer —t unter der Asche, the fire slumbers, glows under the ashes. —er, m. (—ers) faint glow, glimmering; mica, glimmer. —erig, adj. glimmering; micaceous. —ern, v.n. to glimmer, shine dimly. Comp. —käfer, m. fire-fly, glowworm. —licht, n. glimmering. —stengel, m. cigar, weed (coll.).

Glimpf, m. (—es) indulgence, mildness, forbearance, gentleness; mit —, kindly, gently; mit Fug und —, with right and justice; sich mit — aus der Sache ziehen, to extricate oneself from a matter without injury to one's reputation. —lich, adj. forbearing, indulgent, gentle, kind, moderate.

Glitsch, adv. & int. hu[illegible] up! —e, f. (pl. —en) slide. —en, v.n. (aux. h. & s.) to slide; to glide; to slip. —erig, —ig, adj. slippery.

Glitt, Glit'te, imperf. ind. & subj. of gleiten.

Glit'zern, v.n. (aux. h.) to glitter, glisten.

Glo'b—us, m. (pl. —en; rarely —usse) globe.

Glöck—chen (—chens, pl. —chen), **—lein,** n. (—leins, pl. —lein) small bell; kleine —lein klingen auch, little bells often have a loud sound (prov.). —ner, m. (—ners, pl. —ner) bell-ringer; sexton.

Glo'cke, f. (pl. —n) bell; clock; glass shade; Italian iron; bell-like excrescence; anything in the form of a bell; receiver (Chem.); basket of a foil; cup (of a flower); lamp-shade, globe; was ist die — (usually Uhr)? what o'clock is it? — zehn werde ich da sein, I shall be there at ten; etwas an die große — hängen, to blaze a thing abroad, make a great fuss about a th.; die —en läuten, to ring the bells; er hat die —n läuten hören, weiß aber nicht, wo sie hängen, he hears but does not understand; einem sagen was die — geschlagen hat, to give one a good set down or scolding (coll.); da war die — gegossen, there was an end of the matter (coll.). Comp. —n=blume, f. Canterbury-bell, blue-bell. —n=blumig, adj. campaniform (Bot.). —n=deckel, m. dish-cover. —n=förmig, adj. bell-shaped. —n=geläute, n. peal of bells; bell-ringing; chime; er hielt unter —ngeläute seinen Einzug, he made his entry amidst a peal of bells. —n=gerüst, n. bell-frame. —n=gewicht, n. weight (of a clock). —n=gießer, m. bell-founder. —n=gut, n. bell-metal. —n=hammer, —n=klöppel, m. clapper of a bell. —n=klang, m. sound of a bell, chime. —n=läuter, m. bell-ringer. —n=magnet, m. bell-shaped magnet. —n=schlag, m. stroke of the clock, stroke of the hour; mit dem —nschlag, as the clock strikes. —n=schwengel, m. lever to a bell; bell-clapper. —n=seil, n. bell-rope. —n=speise, f. see —ngut. —n=spiel, n chime(s). —n=stube, f. bell-loft. —n=stunde, f. an hour by the clock; er saß hier eine geschlagene —nstunde, he was sitting here a whole hour; alles mit der —nstunde machen, to be as punctual as the clock. —n=telegraph, m. bell-telegraph, sounder. —n=tiere, pl. verticella. —n=turm, m. steeple, belfry, campanile. —n=weihe, —n=taufe, f. benediction of a bell. —n=zieher, m. bell-ringer; bell-pull. —n=zug, m. bell-rope; bell-sto[p] (in organs).

Glomm, Glöm'me, imperf. ind. & subj. of glimmen.

Glo'r—ie, f. (pl. —ien) glory; halo. —ifizie'ren, v.a. to glorify. —io'le, f. halo, glory. —iö's, adj. glorious; excellent, capital (coll.). Comp. —reich, —würdig, adj. glorious; — würdigen Andenkens, of glorious memory.

Gloss—a'r, n. (—ars, pl. —are or —arien) glossary. —a'tor, m. (—ators, pl. —ato'ren) commentator; glossologist. —e, f. (pron. Glos'se) (pl. —en) gloss, comment; a certain kind of a poem; über alles (zu allem) —en machen, to carp, sneer at everything. —ie'ren, v.a. to gloss, comment on, to supply with marginal notes; to write stanzas or poems on single lines of other poems (e.g. four lines would be glossed in four stanzas), to discuss some given subject in a number of stanzas. Comp. —en=macher, m. severe critic, faultfinder. —en=sammlung, f. collection of glosses or marginal notes. —ogra'ph, m. glossographer.

Glot'z—en, v.n. (aux. h.) to gape; to stare. Comp. —auge, n. staring eye, goggle-eye.

Gluch'zen, v.n. (aux. h.) to gobble (of t[ur]keys); to cluck (of hens); to sob.

Glück, n. (—es, no pl.) luck, hap; fortun[e], good luck; success; happiness; fate, lot, condition; (einem) — wünschen, to congratulate (a p.); — auf! (miner's greeting) good luck! jeder ist seines —es Schmied, every one is the architect of his own fortune (*prov.*); — und Glas, wie bald bricht das, fortune and glass soon break, alas! glass and luck, brittle muck (*prov.*); mancher hat mehr — als Verstand, Fortune favours fools (*prov.*); wer das — hat, führt die Braut heim, Fortune gains the bride (*prov.*); das — hilft dem Tapfern *or* ist dem Kühnen hold, Fortune favours the brave (*prov.*); — hat Neider, he who prospers is envied (*prov.*); ich wünsche Ihnen — zum neuen Jahre, I wish you a happy New Year; ich wünsche Ihnen viel — zum Geburtstage, I wish you many happy returns of the day; viel — auf den Weg! I wish you God speed! a pleasant journey to you! — auf! — zu! viel —! good luck! God speed you! Gott gebe — dazu, may God grant his blessing to it; es war ein —, it was lucky; zum —e, by good fortune; alles auf das — ankommen lassen, to commit everything to chance; etwas auf gut — hin wagen, to let a thing take its chance; auf gut —, at random, at a venture, taking my chance; auf — oder Unglück, for better, for worse; Jagd nach dem —, fortune-hunting; — haben, to be lucky, to succeed; — machen, to succeed; sein — machen, to make one's fortune; zu meinem —e, luckily for me; es war ein großes —, daß, it was most fortunate that; er kann von — sagen, daß es ihm gelungen ist, it was a piece of good luck, a lucky chance that he succeeded; da können Sie von — sagen, you may call, *or* count, yourself lucky *or* a lucky person; Hans im —, Hans in luck; dem —e im Schoße sitzen, to be a favourite of fortune. —lich, *adj. & adv.* fortunate, lucky; happy; prosperous, successful; auspicious; —liche Reise! farewell! a safe journey! God speed you! —licherweise, by good fortune, fortunately; sich —lich schätzen, to count oneself happy, congratulate oneself; ich war so —lich, ihn zu sehen, I had the pleasure of seeing him, I was fortunate enough to see him; wenn ich —lich zurückkomme, if I am spared to return; —lich von statten gehen, to go, *or* come, off well; —lich ist, wer vergißt, was nicht mehr zu ändern ist, he is lucky who forgets what cannot be mended, we must endure what we can't cure (*prov.*); dem —lichen schlägt keine Stunde, to the happy time is swift (*prov.*). *Comp.* —bringend, *adj.* fortunate; bringing good luck. —s=bahn, *f.* high road to fortune. —s=bote, *m.* bearer of good tidings. —s=botschaft, *f.* glad tidings. —selig, *adj.* blissful, very happy, highly blessed. —seligkeit, *f.* blissfulness, rapture. —s=fall, *m.* (—s=fälle, *pl. is often used as pl. of* Glück *q. v.*) lucky incident, chance, a piece of good luck. —s=göttin, *f.* goddess of fortune, Fortune. —s=güter, *pl.* gifts of fortune, good things of this world, wealth; mit —s=gütern reich gesegnet, very rich. —s=hafen, *m.* safe port. —s=jägerei, *f.* fortune-hunting. —s=kind, *n.* spoiled child *or* favourite of fortune, lucky person; upstart. —s=pilz, *m.* lucky fellow, lucky chap (*coll.*); upstart. —s=ritter, *m.* adventurer. —s=spiel, *n.* game of hazard. —s=spinne, *f.* money-spinner. —s=stand, *m.* prosperity; state of happiness. —s=stern, *m.* lucky star. —s=stunde, *f.* propitious hour *or* moment. —s=topf, *m.* Fortune's urn; in den —stopf greifen, to meet with luck (*coll.*). —s=umstände, *pl.* (*often used as pl. of* Glück) fortune; circumstances. —s=wahn, *m.* imaginary happiness. —s=wechsel, *m.* reverse of fortune. —verheißend, —weissagend, *adj.* auspicious, of good augury. —wünschend, *p. & adj.* congratulating, congratulatory. —wünschung, *f.*, —wunsch, *m.* congratulation, compliments (of the season); einem seinen —wunsch abstatten, einem seine (besten) —wünsche aussprechen, to congratulate one; herzlichste *or* beste —wünsche, heartiest congratulations. —wunsch=schreiben, *n.* congratulatory letter. —s=wurf, *m.* lucky throw.

Glu'ck—e, *f.* (*pl.* —en) (—henne, *f.*) clucking hen. *Comp.* —flasche, *f.* travelling flask (*coll.*). —e(r)n, gluck'sen, *v.n.* (*aux.* h.) to cluck (*as hens*); to gurgle (*like water*).

Glü'ck—en, *v.n.* (*aux.* h. & s.) *imp.* (einem) to prosper, to succeed, to turn out well; es —t ihm alles, everything succeeds with him; es —te nicht, it failed, miscarried; es wollte mir nirgends —en, I failed everywhere; es ist ihm geglückt, he has been successful.

Glü'h—e, —ung, *f.* state of being red hot; ignition; incandescence. *Comp.* —feuer, *n.* glowing fire. —hitze, *f.* red heat. —lampe, *f.* incandescent lamp. —licht, *n.* incandescent light. —ofen, *m.* fiery furnace. —schale, *f.*, —täßchen, *n.* cupel. —span, *m.* iron scale. —stoffe, *pl.m.* smokeless fuel. —strumpf, *m.* mantle (*of an incandescent gas burner*). —wein, *m.* mulled wine; hot claret cup, negus. —wind, *m.* sirocco. —wurm, *m.* glow-worm.

Glü'hen, *v.* I. *a.* to make red hot; to mull (*wine*); Rache —, to breathe (forth) vengeance. II. *n.* (*aux.* h.) to glow; to burn; vor Wonne —, to be in a rapture of joy. —d, *p. & adj.* glowing, ardent; —de Kohle, live coal; wie auf — den Kohlen sitzen, to feel on hot irons, to be on thorns (*coll.*).

Glu'p—en, —schen, *v.n.* (*aux.* h.) to look sullen; to look with an evil eye (*dial. & coll.*). —isch, *adj.* sullen; insidious; malicious.

Glut, *f.* (*pl.* —en) fire; heat; glow; ardour; passion; curlew (*Orn.*). *Comp.* —asche, *f.* embers. —auge, *n.* fiery eye. —esse, *f.* blast-forge. —hauch, *m.* scorching breath. —meer, *n.* ocean of fire. —messer, *m.* pyrometer. —pfanne, *f.* chafing-dish; coal-pan. —rot, *adj.* fiery red, red hot. —zange, *f.* fire-tongs.

Glyp't—ik, *f.* gem-engraving. —othe'k, *f.* collection of works of sculpture (*e.g. at Munich*).

Glyzeri'n, *n.* (—s) glycerine.

Gna'd—e, *f.*, (*pl.* —n) favour; goodwill, kindness; grace; clemency, mercy, pardon; quarter (*Mil.*); durch Gottes —e, by the grace of God; Wir, von Gottes —en, König von, We, by the grace of God, king of; Gottes —e, divine grace; Königtum von Gottes —en, divine right of kings; eine —e erweisen, to show, *or* grant, a favour; —e angedeihen, widerfahren lassen, to pardon; um —e rufen, to cry out for mercy; —e für Recht ergehen lassen, to show mercy; Ew. (Euer), *or* Eure, —en, your Honour, your Grace; zu —en annehmen, to take into favour; zu —en halten, to excuse, to pardon (*graciously*); halten zu —n! if it please your Lordship! (*obs.*); sich auf —e und Un—e ergeben, to surrender at discretion, unconditionally; die Sonne geht zu —en, the sun is setting (*dial.*). *Comp.* —en=akt, *m.* act of grace. —en=bezeigung, *f.* favour conferred upon an inferior, grace. —en=beruf, *m.* calling of grace; vocation. —en=bild, *n.* wonder-working (*or* miraculous) image, image of the Holy Virgin, shrine. —en=brief, *m.* letter of pardon; warrant, diploma. —en=brot, *n.* maintenance derived from the favour and compassion of another; bread of charity, pittance; —enbrot essen, to live on sufferance; von —enbrot leben, to live on charity; (*of old servants*) to be boarded at the master's charge. —en=bund, *m.* covenant of grace. —en=frist, *f.* respite. —en=gehalt, *m. & n.*, —

en=geld, *n.* allowance, pension. —**en=geschenk**, *n.* dole, gratification, donation. —**en=jahr**, *n.* year of grace; year's revenue granted to the family of an official at his death. —**en=kette**, *f.* chain of honour. —**en=mittel**, *n.* means of grace (*offered by the Church*). —**en=ordnung**, *f.* divine ordinance. —**en=ort**, —**en=platz**, *m.* place of pilgrimage. —**en=reich**, I. *n.* kingdom of mercy. II. *adj.* merciful, gracious. —**en=sold**, *m.* pension. —**en=stoß**, *m.* finishing stroke, deathblow. —**en=stuhl**, *m.* mercy-seat. —**en=wahl**, *f.* (particular) election (of grace), predestination. —**en=weg**, *m.* way of mercy *or* grace; **eine Strafe im —enwege erlassen**, to remit a punishment by way of grace. —**en=wirkung**, *f.* effect of divine grace. —**en=zeichen**, *n.* token of favour. —**en=zeit**, *f.* time of grace.

Gna'den, *v.n.* to be gracious, to show grace *or* mercy; **gnade uns Gott!** God have mercy upon us! God be merciful unto us and help us!

Gnä'dig, *adj. & adv.* merciful, kind; favourable, gracious; benevolent, propitious; **Gott sei uns —!** God have mercy upon us! **er ist noch — davon gekommen**, he has, after all, got off easily *or* cheaply; he has had a narrow escape; —**er Herr**, Sir, my Lord; —**e Frau**, Madam, my Lady; **aller —st**, most gracious. —**lich**, (*obs.*) *see* **Gnädig**.

Gnar'ren, *v.n.* (*aux.* **h.**) to snarl.

Gnei'ßig, *adj.* containing gneiss.

Gno'm, *m.* (—**en**, *pl.* —**en**) gnome. —**e**, *f.* (*pl.* —**en**) maxim, apophthegm. —**iker**, *m.* (—**ikers**, *pl.* —**iker**) writer of sententious poetry. —**isch**, *adj.* sententious. —**o'nik**, *f.* gnomonics.

Gnost—ici'smus, *m.* gnosticism. —**iker**, *m.* (*pron.* **Gnos'tiker**) (—**ikers**, *pl.* —**iker**) gnostic.

Gnu, *n.* (—**s**, *pl.* —**s**) horned horse, gnu.

Gnub'bern, *n.* itch, scab (*in sheep*).

Gnug, **Gnüge**, *see* **Genug**, **Genüge**.

Go'belin, *m.* (—**s**, *pl.* —**s**) (high warped) tapestry, gobelin.

Go'ckel, **Gö'ckel=hahn**, *m.* rooster, cock.

Gohr, **Gö'hre**, *imperf. ind. & subj. of* **gähren**.

Göhr, **Gör**, **Jör**, *n.* (—**s**, *pl.* —**en**) small (unmannered) child (*coll.*); **ein niedliches —**, a pretty little thing (*coll.*); **so'n —**, what a brat! (*sl.*).

Go'jim, *pl.* strangers, Christians (*Jew.sl.*).

Golat'schen, *pl.* fritters filled with marmalade. *Comp.*—**gesicht**, *n.* stupid, broad moon-face.

Gold, *n.* (—**es**) gold; money; wealth; **nicht mit — zu bezahlen**, above price; **weg, du Traum, so — du bist**, away with thee, dream, however golden thou art! **es ist nicht alles —, was glänzt**, all is not gold, that glitters (*prov.*). —**chen**, *n.* darling, love; *see* —**kind**. —**en**, *adj.* gold (*made of gold*), golden (*like gold*); gilt; precious; happy; —**ene Hochzeit**, golden wedding, fiftieth wedding-day; —**ene Regel**, rule of three, golden rule; —**ener Schlüssel**, (*i.e.* **Kammerherrnschlüssel**), golden key, viz., sign of the dignity of an Imperial chamberlain (*poet.*); —**ene Schlüssel austeilen**, to appoint to the office of chamberlain; —**ene Berge versprechen**, to make extravagant (and rash) promises, to promise a p. heaps of money (*prov.*); **sich** (*dat.*) —**ene Berge versprechen**, to cherish exaggerated hopes, to expect to find Tom Tiddler's grounds; **dem fliehenden Feinde —ene Brücken bauen**, to make a bridge of silver for the flying foe (*prov.*); **der —ene Mittelweg**, **die —ene Mittelstraße**, the golden mean; **der —ene Schnitt**, sectio aurea; **die —ene Zeit**, the golden age, the idyllic age, the early years of the world, the primeval time of innocence, peace, and happiness; —**ene Füchse**, gold pieces, yellow-boys (*sl.*); **die —ene Legende**, the Golden Legend (*by Jacobus de Voragine*); **ein Buch mit —enem Schnitte**, a gilt-edged book; **er ist noch —en gegen seinen Bruder**, he is an angel as compared with his brother; **die —ene Aue**, district between the Thuringian Forest and the Harz Mountains; —**ene Ader**, piles (*Med.*). —**ig**, *adj.* golden. *Comp. often — corresponds to* golden *or* yellow; —**ader**, *f.* vein of gold; hemorrhoidal vein. —**ammer**, *m.* yellow-hammer (*Orn.*). —**anstrich**, *m.* gilding. —**apfel**, *m.* tomato; golden pippin. —**arbeiter**, *m.* goldsmith; jeweller. —**artig**, *adj.* golden. —**barren**, *m.* ingot of gold. —**bergwerk**, *n.* gold-mine. —**blatt**, —**blättchen**, *n.* leaf-gold. —**blech**, *n.* plate of gold. —**borte**, *f.* gold lace. —**braun**, *adj.* chestnut, auburn. —**blume**, *f.* marigold. —**butte**, *f.* plaice. —**draht**, *m.* gold-wire. —**durchwirkt**, *adj.* interwoven with gold. —**erde**, *f.* auriferous earth. —**erz**, *n.* gold ore. —**faden**, *m.* spun gold. —**farbe**, *f.* gold-colour; orpiment. —**finger**, *m.* ring-finger. —**fisch**, *m.* gold fish; rich heiress (*coll.*). —**fuchs**, *m.* yellow-dun horse; gold coin, yellow-boy (*sl.*). —**führend**, —**haltig**, *adj.* auriferous. —**gefäße**, *pl.*, —**geschirr**, *n.* gold-plate. —**gehalt**, *m.* proportion of gold. —**gelb**, I. *adj.* golden. II. *n.* orpiment. —**gespinnst**, *n.* spun gold. —**gewicht**, *n.* troy-weight. —**glimmer**, *m.* yellow mica. —**götze**, *m.* golden image; mammon. —**gräber**, *m.* digger for gold. —**gries**, *m.* gold dust. —**grube**, *f.* gold mine. —**gulden**, (—**gülden**, *obs.*,) *m.* gold florin (*worth about 10 shillings* (*first coined*) *in Florence 1252*). —**haar**, *n.* golden hair; goldylocks (*Bot.*). —**hähnchen**, —**hähnlein**, *n.* golden-crested wren (*Orn.*); yellow anemone (*Bot.*). —**junge**, *m.* darling boy. —**käfer**, *m.* rose-bug. —**käfer=schuhe**, *pl.* bronze-coloured (ladies') shoes. —**kies**, *m.* auriferous pyrites. —**kind**, *n.* darling, love, pet. —**klumpen**, *m.* lump of gold, nugget; ingot of gold. —**korn**, *n.* grain of gold. —**lack**, *m.* gold-varnish; wall-flower. —**lahn**, *m.* flattened gold-wire, plate-gold. —**lauter**, *adj. & adv.* pure as gold. —**legierung**, *f.* gold alloy. —**leiste**, *f.* gilt cornice. —**macher**, *m.* alchemist. —**macherei**, —**macherkunst**, *f.* alchemy. —**münze**, *f.* gold coin; gold medal. —**münz=system**, *n.* monetary system based on a gold currency. —**nieder=schlag**, *m.* precipitate of gold. —**plattierung**, *f.* gold-plating. —**regen**, *m.* laburnum; gold(en) rain (*Myth.*, *Firew.*). —**reich**, *adj.* rich in gold. —**sachen**, *pl.* jewellery. —**salpeter**, *m.* nitrate of gold. —**säure**, *f.* auric acid. —**schale**, *f.* cupel (*Chem.*). —**schaum**, *m.* gold leaf. —**scheider**, *m.* gold-refiner. —**scheide=wasser**, *n.* aqua regia. —**schlag**, *m.* gold-leaf, gold-foil. —**schläger**, *m.* gold-beater. —**schläger=häutchen**, *n.* gold-beater's skin. —**schmied**, *m.* goldsmith. —**schnitt**, *m.* gilt edges of a book; **mit —schnitt**, with gilt edges. —**stange**, *f.* ingot of gold. —**stein**, *m.* chrysolite. —**stickerei**, *f.* embroidery in gold. —**stoff**, *m.* gold brocade; tinsel. —**stück**, *n.* piece of unwrought gold; gold coin. —**stufe**, *f.* piece of gold ore. —**tresse**, *f.* gold lace. —**überzug**, *m.* gold wash; coating of gold. —**wage**, *f.* scales for weighing gold, gold-balance; **er legt jedes Wort auf die —wage**, he weighs his words well; **alles auf die —wage legen**, to be very, *or* most, particular. —**währung**, *f.* gold standard. —**waren**, *pl.* jewellery. —**wasser**, *n.* choice Dantzic brandy, gold cordial. —**wirker**, *m.* gold-weaver. —**wirker=kunst**, *f.* gold-weaving. —**wolf**, *m.* jackal. —**zieher**, *m.* gold-wire drawer.

Golf, I. *m.* (—(e)**s**, *pl.* —**e**) gulf; **der —strom**, the Gulf Stream. II. *n.* golf (*a game*). —**spielen**, *n.* golfing. —**spieler**, *m.* golfer.

Goliar'den, *pl.* goliards, mediæval students, travelling scholars of the Middle Ages. *Comp*

—lyrik, *f.*, **—poesie**, *f.* songs in rhymed Latin verses composed in a popular style by the travelling students (*especially in the 12th and 13th centuries*).

Go'lias, *m.* mediæval travelling student.

Gol'ler, *m. see* **Koller**.

Golm, *m.* (**—es**, *pl.* **—e**) hill (*dial.*).

[1]**Göl'te**, *impf.subj. of* **gelten** (*to be preferred to the more recent* **gälte**).

[2]**Göl'te**, *f.* (*pl.* **—n**) wooden tub, pail, bucket (*dial.*).

Gon'del, *f.* (*pl.* **—n**) gondola; vessel; car of a balloon. *Comp.* **—fahrer**, **—schiffer**, *m.* gondolier.

Gon'deln, *v.a.* to go in a gondola; to be, *or* row, in a boat (*coll.*); to walk leisurely (*coll.*).

Gön'n—en, *v.a.* not to envy, not to grudge; to favour; to wish well to; to bestow, to grant; to permit; **ich —e es ihm**, I do not begrudge it him, he has well deserved it; **ich —e ihm sein Glück**, I am glad that he has been so fortunate; **ich —e es ihm nicht**, I grudge it him; **einem alles Gute —en**, to wish any one all happiness; **sie —t sich das liebe Brot nicht**, she grudges herself the very bread she eats; **er —t sich nie einen Augenblick Ruhe**, he never allows himself a moment of rest; **ich will mir jetzt Ferien —en**, I shall now take a holiday; **—en Sie mir die Ehre Ihres Besuches**, favour me with a visit. **—er**, *m.* (**—ers**, *pl.* **—er**) well-wisher; patron, protector. **—erhaft**, *adj.* favouring; patronizing. **—erin**, *f.* patroness; favourer. **—erschaft**, *f.* patrons; patronage.

Gö'pel, *m.* (**—s**) winch, coal-gin; lever; capstan. *Comp.* **—hund**, *m.* whim-beam. **—knecht**, *m.* whim-stopper. **—rad**, *n.* pulley. **—seil**, *n.* rope of a gin *or* lever.

Gor, *sing. imperf. ind. of* **gären**.

Gösch, *m.* (*& f.*), **—e**, *f.* jack (*small flag*) (*Naut.*). *Comp.* **—gast**, *m.* signal-man. **—stock**, *m.* jack-staff.

Go'sche, *f.* mouth (*coll., dial.*). **—rl**, *n.* little mouth; kiss, buss (*dial., coll.*).

Go'se, *f.* Goslar-beer, pale and light ale.

Gos'se, *f.* (*pl.* **—n**) gutter; sink; a drain, sewer, kennel; mill-hopper. *Comp.* **—n=stein**, *m.* sink.

Goß, Gös'se, *imperf. indic. & subj. of* **gießen**.

Gott, *m.* (**—es**, *pl.* **Göt'ter**) God; god; **lieber —**, O Lord! (*in prayers*); **O mein —!** O God! **mein —!** Good Heavens! dear me! **daß sich — erbarme! — steh' uns bei!** the Lord have mercy upon us! God help us! **— grüße dich, grüß' (dich) —!** good day! **— befohlen! gehen Sie mit —!** good-bye! adieu! God be with you! **wollte —!** would to God! **— gebe!** God grant! **bei —! — weiß es! — ist mein Zeuge!** God knows! I swear to God! **vergelt es —! lohn' es —!** God reward, *or* bless, you for it! **will's —, so — will!** please God! **bewahre, behüte —! — bewahre, behüte! — behüte und bewahre! da sei — vor!** God forbid! by no means; I do not think of it (*coll.*); **— sei Dank, — Lob!** thank God! **um —es willen!** for God's sake! **leider —es!** alas! sad to say; **so wahr mir — helfe!** so help me God; **—es Wege sind wunderbar**, the decrees of Providence are unfathomable (*prov.*); **— hilft denen, die sich selbst helfen**, aid yourself and God will aid you (*prov.*); **leben wie — in Frankreich**, to live a life free from cares (*coll.*); **den lieben — einen guten Mann sein lassen**, not to care for anything; to let matters slide (*coll.*). **—heit**, *f.* deity; divinity; God-head. *Comp.* **—ähnlich**, *adj.* godlike, divine. **—ergeben**, *adj.* resigned to God's will, devout. **—es=acker**, *m.* God's acre, graveyard, church-yard. **—es=dienst**, *m.* divine service, public worship; **dem —es=dienste beiwohnen.** to attend divine service; **der —esdienst ist aus**, the service is over; **den —esdienst verrichten**, to officiate. **—es=dienstlich**, *adj.* relating to divine service, religious. **—es=erde**, *f.* the earth; consecrated ground. **—es=fahrt**, *f.* pilgrimage. **—es=friede**, *m.* peace of God; the truce of God, Treuga Dei (*first observed in 1031*). **—es=furcht**, *f.* fear of God, piety. **—es=fürchtig**, *adj.* pious; God-fearing. **—es=geißel**, *f.* scourge of God (*surname of Attila, King of the Huns*, † *453*). **—es=gelehrtheit**, **—es=gelehrsamkeit**, *f.* divinity, theology. **—es=gelehrt**, *adj.* versed in divinity. **—es=gelehrte(r)**, *m.* divine, theologian. **—es=gericht**, **—es=urteil**, *n.* divine judgment; ordeal. **—es=gnadentum**, *n.* theory of the divine right of kings, legitimism. **—es=haus**, *n.* place of worship, church, chapel. **—es=käfer**, *m.* lady-bird. **—es=kasten**, *m.*, **—es=lade**, *f.* collecting boxes (in churches), poor-box. **—es=lästerer**, *m.* blasphemer. **—es=lästerlich**, *adj.* blasphemous. **—es=leugner**, *m.* atheist. **—es=leugnerisch**, *adj.* atheistical. **—es=leugnung**, **—es=leugnerei**, *f.* atheism. **—es=lohn**, *m.* God's reward; **um einen —es=lohn**, for the love of God, for no reward. **—es=mann**, *m.* pious man; divine, minister, theologian. **—es=pfennig**, *m.*, **—es=geld**, *n.* God's penny, earnest-money. **—es=reich**, *n.* Kingdom of God; theocracy. **—es=tisch**, *m.* the Lord's table, communion-table. **—es=tischrock**, *m.* Sunday clothes. **—es=verächter**, *m.* impious person. **—(es)=vergessen**, *see* **vergessen**. **—es=weisheit**, *f.* theosophy. **—es=welt**, *f.* God's wide world. **—es=wort**, *n.* the Bible, God's word. **—gefällig**, *adj.* pleasing to God. **—gefälligkeit**, *f.* piety. **—gesandte(r)**, *m.* one sent by God, the Messiah. **—lo'b**, *int.* thank God! God be praised! **—los**, *adj.* irreligious, ungodly, godless; wicked, impious; **die —losen kriegen die Neige**, the wicked get the dregs of the cup (*coll.*). **—losigkeit**, *f.* ungodliness. **—mensch**, *m.* God incarnate, God made flesh, God and man. **—=sei=beiuns**, *m.* (*euphemism for*) the devil. **—selig**, *adj.* godly, pious; blessed. **—seligkeit**, *f.* godliness, piety, devotion. **—s=jämmerlich**, *adj. & adv.* very wretched (*coll.*). **—vergessen**, *see* **—los**. **—verhaßt**, *adj.* hated by God; abominable, odious. **—voll**, *adj.* godly; splendid, capital, funny (*coll.*); **eine —volle Geschichte**, a capital story (*coll.*).

Gott'chen, *interj.*; **ach —**, dear, dear! (*coll.*).

Göt't—erhaft, *adj.* godlike. **—erschaft**, *f.*, **—ertum**, *n.* the gods (*coll.*); essence of a god, divine nature. **—in**, *f.* goddess. **—lich**, *adj.* godlike, divine; godly; most excellent, capital; **das —liche**, that which is characteristic of a god, the divine nature, godliness. **—lichkeit**, *f.* divinity; godliness. *Comp.* **—er** *as the first part of many compounds:* divine, heavenly. **—er=abend**, *m.* heavenly evening. **—er=ausspruch**, *m.* oracle. **—er=bild**, *n.* image of a god, beautiful form; beautiful woman *or* man. **—er=bote**, *m.* messenger of the gods, Mercury, Hermes. **—er=brücke**, *f.* rainbow, bow of Iris. **—er=dämmerung**, *f.* twilight of the gods, last fight and end of the (old Germanic) gods, end of the world. **—er=dichtung**, **—er=lehre**, *f.* mythology. **—er=dienst**, *m.* polytheism. **—er=gestalt**, *f.* divine form. **—er=gleich**, *adj.* godlike, godly. **—er=glück**, *n.* highest happiness. **—er=haus**, *n.* temple. **—er=lust**, *f.* pleasure of the gods; exquisite pleasure. **—er=sage**, *f.* myth. **—er=sitz**, *m.* Olympus. **—er=speise**, *f.* ambrosia. **—er=spruch**, *m.* oracle. **—er=trank**, *m.* nectar. **—er=welt**, *f.* Olympus; paganism. **—er=wesen**, *n.* everything relating to the gods, mythology; divine being. **—er=wonne**, god-like beatitude *or* bliss. **—er=wort,** *n.* oracle. **—er=zeichen,** *n.* omen, augury. **—er=zeit,** *f* mythological age.

Göt'ze, *m.* (—n, *pl.* —n) idol, false deity. **—ntum,** *n.* idolatry. *Comp.* **—n=bild,** *n.* idol. **—n=dienst,** *m.* idolatry. **—n=opfer,** *n.* an idolatrous sacrifice. **—n=tempel,** *m.* temple of an idol, heathenish temple.

Gouvern—an'te, *f.* (*pl.* —anten) governess. **—eme'nt,** *n.* (—ements, *pl.* —ements) government. **—eu'r,** *m.* (—eurs, *pl.* —eure) governor; private tutor (*obs.*).

Grab, *n.* (—es, *pl.* Grä'ber) grave, tomb, sepulchre; ruin, utter misery, destruction; **einen zu —e geleiten,** to attend a p.'s funeral; **einen ins — bringen,** to cause a p.'s death. *Comp.* **—ähnlich, —artig,** *adj.* sepulchral. **—denkmal,** *n.* tomb. **—einfassung,** *f.* enclosure of a grave. **—es=rand,** *m.* brink of the grave. **—es=schlummer,** *m.* sleep of death. **—es=stimme,** *f.* sepulchral voice. **—geläute,** *n.* knell. **—gerüst,** *n.* catafalque. **—gesang,** *m.* funeral song, dirge. **—gewölbe,** *n.* vault, tomb. **—hügel,** *m.* cairn, barrow. **—krug,** *m.* funeral urn. **—legung,** *f.* sepulture, interment, burial. **—lied,** *n.* funeral song, dirge. **—mal,** *n.* (sepulchral) monument, tomb. **—rede,** *f.* funeral sermon. **—schrift,** *f.* epitaph. **—stätte,** *f.* burying-place; sepulchre, tomb; family vault; (*pl.*) catacombs. **—stein,** *m.* tombstone, gravestone. **—tuch,** *n.* winding-sheet, shroud.

Gra'b—en, *ir.v.a.* to dig; to ditch, trench; to engrave; to impress; **einem eine Grube —en,** to lay a snare for one; **wer andern eine Grube gräbt, fällt selbst hinein,** the biter bit (*prov.*). *Comp.* **—eisen,** *n.* graving tool, digging instrument. **—e=kelle,** *f.* spud; trowel. **—meißel, —stichel,** *m.* graving tool. **—scheit,** *n.* spade.

Gra'ben, *m.* (—s, *pl.* Grä'ben) ditch; trench; moat; canal; sewer; ravine; **über den — sein,** to be out of danger (*coll.*). *Comp.* **—böschung,** *f.* counterscarp. **—pflug,** *m.* draining-plough. **—schere,** *f.* tenaille (*Fort.*). **—zieher,** *m.* ditcher. **—zug,** *m.* line of ditches *or* trenches.

Grab'beln, *v.n.* (*aux.* h.) to grope; to tickle, to scratch.

Grä'ber, *m.* (—s, *pl.* —) digger; graving tool, spade; **Toten —,** grave-digger.

Gräbst, Gräbt, *2 & 3 p. s. pres. ind. of* **graben.**

Grad, *m.* (—es, *pl.* —e) step; degree; rate; grade, stage, rank; power (*Math.*); **in hohem —e,** highly; **im höchsten —e,** exceedingly; **im höchsten —e zerstreut,** absent-minded to a degree. **—atio'n,** *f.* gradation; comparison (*Gram.*). **—ie'ren,** *v.a.* to refine (*gold*); to graduate (*salt*). **—ig,** *adj.* (*in cps.* =) of so many degrees. **—ua'l,** *n.* (—s, *pl.* —e) gradual, grail (*R.C.*). **—ue'll,** *adj. & adv.* gradual. **—uie'ren,** *v.a. & n.* (*aux.* h.) to graduate, to take a *or* one's degree. **—uier'te(r),** *m.* graduate (*of a University*). *Comp.* **—abteilung, —einteilung,** *f.* graduation. **—bogen,** *m.* graduated arc; sextant. **—buch,** *n.* nautical almanac. **—ier'=eisen,** *n.* sculptor's chisel. **—ier'=faß,** *n.* refining cask. **—ier'=wage,** *f.* water-balance. **—leiter,** *f.* scale. **—linig,** *adj. see* **Gerade.** **—messer,** *m.* graduator. **—meßkunst,** *f.* gradimetry. **—messung,** *f.* measuring of degrees.

Graf, *m.* (—en, *pl.* —en) earl (*in England*), count (*foreign*). **—schaft,** *f.* dignity of a count *or* earl; shire, county (*abroad*), earldom (*in England*). **—entum,** *n. see* **—schaft.** *Comp.* **—en=bank,** *f.* bench of the counts of the German empire; peer's bench. **—en=tag,** *m.* assembly of the counts of the German empire. **—en=würde,** *f.* earldom. **—schafts=gericht,** *n.* county-court.

Grä'f—eln, *v.n. & imp.* (*aux.* h.) to play the lord. **—in,** *f.* countess. **—lich,** *adj.* belonging to an earl *or* count; like a count *or* earl.

Gram, I. *m.* (—(e)s) grief, sorrow, affliction; aversion. II. *adj.* averse; **einem — sein,** to dislike a p., to bear one a grudge; **einem — werden,** to become angry with a person. *Comp.* **—gefurcht,** *adj.* woe-worn. **—voll,** *adj.* melancholy, gloomy, sad.

Grämelei', *f.* moroseness; peevishness.

Grä'm—eln, *v.n.* (*aux.* h.) to be fretful, irritable, *or* morose. **—en,** I. *v.a.* to grieve. II. *v.r.* to grieve (for), fret (**über eine S.,** at a th.); **sich zu Tode —en,** to die of grief *or* of a broken heart. III. *subst.n.* sorrow, grief. **—lich,** *adj.* peevish, morose, sullen.

Gramm, *n.* (—s) gramme (15.438 *grains troy*); *abbr.* **G.**

Gramma't—ik, *f.* (*pl.* —iken) grammar; **vergleichende —ik,** comparative grammar; **elementare —ik des Deutschen,** German primer. **—isch, —ika'lisch,** *adj.* grammatical; **—ischer Fehler,** grammatical mistake; **grober —ischer Fehler,** bad grammatical mistake, howler (*sl.*); **er kann nicht —ikalisch (richtig) schreiben,** he is unable to write with grammatical correctness, to write in accordance with the rules of grammar; **—ischer Wechsel,** grammatical change (*change between consonants of the same kind according to fixed grammatical laws, e.g.* h-g, f-b, *etc.*). **—iker,** *m.* (—ikers, *pl.* —iker) grammarian.

Gran, *n. & m.* (—es, *pl.* —e) grain (*Pharm.*). **—ie'ren, —ulie'ren,** *v.a. & n.* to granulate.

Grana't, *m.* (—(e)s, *pl.* —e) garnet; pomegranate; **edler —,** carbuncle. *Comp.* **—apfel,** *m.* pomegranate. **—blüte,** *f.* pomegranate blossom. **—kern,** *m.* pomegranate seed. **—schnur,** *f.* garnet necklace. **—stein,** *m.* garnet.

Grana't—e, *f.* (*pl.* —en) grenade, (bomb) shell; shrimp (*dial.*). *Comp.* **—en=hagel,** *m.* shower *or* storm of shell. **—en=splitter,** *pl.*, **—en=stücke,** *pl.* splinters of shell. **—kartätschen,** *pl.* shrapnel-shells. **—kugel,** *f.* shell.

Grand, *m.* (—es) gravel (*dial.*). **—icht, —ig,** *adj.* gravelly. *Comp.* **—mehl,** *n.* whole meal.

Gran'd—e, *m.* (—en, *pl.* —en) grandee. **—ez'za,** *f.* grandeeship; solemn gravity.

Granie'ren, *v.a.* to pulverize.

Grani't, *m.* (—(e)s, *pl.* —e), granite. **—en,** *adj.* granitic. *Comp.* **—artig, —förmig,** *adj.* granitic.

Gran'n—e, *f.* (*pl.* —en) beard (*of corn*), whiskers (*of a cat*); needle (*Bot.*); bristle. **—ig,** *adj.* bearded. *Comp.* **—en=los,** *adj.* beardless.

Grans, *m.* (—(s)es, *pl.* —(s)e), **Gran'sen,** *m.* (—s, *pl.* —) fore-part of a ship (*dial.*).

Grän'ze, *see* **Grenze.**

Gra'phisch, *adj. & adv.* graphic.

Graphi't, *m.* (—s, *pl.* —e) graphite, plumbago, black lead. *Comp.* **—tiegel,** *m.* black-lead crucible.

Grap'pe, *f.* (*pl.* —n) grape-stalk.

Grap'sch—en (*also* **Grap's—en**), *v.a.* to seize upon hastily, to snatch; to take away secretly (*coll.*). **—ig,** *adj.* given to snatching away greedily (*coll.*).

Gras, *n.* (—(s)es, *pl.* Grä'ser) grass; **ins — beißen,** to bite the dust, to be killed (*coll.*); **er hört das — wachsen,** he fancies himself exceedingly wise, he fancies he can see through a brick wall (*prov.*); **darüber ist — gewachsen,** that is all forgotten; **ins — thun,** to put out to grass; **sich mit — bedecken,** to bring forth grass. **—(s)icht** (*obs.*), **—(s)ig,** *adj.* grassy. **—(s)ung,** *f.* grazing. *Comp.* **—affe,** *m.* young fool, young boy *or* (*usually*) girl, apish young person frolicking on the lawn (*obs.*). **—anger,** *m.* grass-plot, green. **—artig,** *adj.* gramineous. **—bank,** *f.* seat of grass. **—ebene,** *f.* grassy plain; prairie. —faser, *f.* grassy fibre. —fleck, *m.* grass-plot; grass-stain. —fressend, *adj.* herbivorous, graminivorous. —fütterung, *f.* feeding on grass. —halm, *m.* blade of grass. —hüpfer, *m.*, —pferd, *n.* grasshopper. —land, *n.* meadow-land. —lilie, *f.* asphodel. —loch, *n.* horizontally bored hole for blasting. —mäher, *m.* grass-cutter. —mücke, *f.* hedge-sparrow. —platz, *m.* grass-plot, lawn, green. —reich, *adj.* rich in grass. —rost, *m.* mildew. —schnecke, *f.* slug. —stück, *n.* grass-plot. —teppich, *m.* velvety lawn. —weide, *f.* pasture. —wuchs, *m.* growth of grass.

Gräs'—chen, —lein, *n.* blade of grass. —ling, *m.* gudgeon; grayling; vine-sprig.

Gra'se—n, *v.n.* (*aux.* h.) to graze (*of animals*); to cut grass; nach einer S. —n, to aspire to a th.; in einer S. —n, to satisfy oneself on a th. —r, *m.*, —rin, *f.* grass-cutter. —r=liedlein, *pl.* songs of the peasant lads and lasses.

Grassie'ren, *v.n.* (*aux.* h.) to prevail, rage (*of diseases*).

Gräß'lich, (Graß,) *adj.* terrible, shocking, horrible, monstrous. —keit, *f.* horribleness; atrocity.

Grat, *m.* (—es, *pl.* —e) point; edge, ridge; roof tree; hip, slope; rabbet; groin (*Arch.*). *Comp.* —bogen, *m.* hip-roof, cross-springer. —hobel, *m.* rabbet-plane. —säge, *f.* groove-saw. —tier, *n.* chamois (*dial. & poet.*).

Grät'—e, *f.* (*pl.* —en) fishbone. —en, *v.n.* (*aux.* h.) to pick fishbones. —ig, *adj. & adv.* full of fish-bones, bony. *Comp.* —en=stich, *m.* feather stitch.

Grat—ia'l, *n.* (—ials, *pl.* —iale) donation; gratuity. —ias, *n.* (*pron.* Gra'tias) grace, thanks; das —ias sprechen, to return thanks. —ifikatio'n, *f.* gratification; supplement. —is (*pron.* Gra'tis), *adv.* free of charge. —ulie'ren, *v.a.* (einem) to congratulate (a person). *Comp.* —is=beilage, *f.* free supplement. —is=exemplar, *n.* presentation copy, specimen copy. —ulatio'ns=schreiben, *n.* congratulatory letter.

Grät'schen, *v.a.* to straddle one's legs (*Gym.*).

Grau, I. *adj.* gray, grizzled; hoary; venerable, ancient; colourless; vague; sombre; —es Altertum, remote antiquity; —er Bär, grizzly bear; —e Zeiten, olden time(s), times of yore; —e Vorzeit, times of antiquity, the dim, hazy past; seit —er Vorzeit, from times immemorial; das —e Elend, splitting headache on the morning after a carousal; das —e Männchen, the little man in a gray coat (*the devil*); das —e Kloster, monastery of the Gray friars; a famous Berlin grammar school; darüber lasse ich mir keine —en Haare wachsen, I do not trouble my head about that, I do not take that to heart. II. *subst. n.* gray colour; dawn. —chen, *n.* Neddy (*pet name for a donkey*). —heit, *f.* grayness. —lich, *adj. & adv.* grizzly, grayish. *Comp.* —blau, *adj.* grayish blue. —brot, *n.* brown bread. —haarig, *adj.* grizzled, gray-haired. —kehlchen, *n.* warbler. —kopf, *m.* grayheaded person. —pappel, *f.* white poplar. —rock, *m.* (one wearing a) gray coat; Bruder —rock, gray friar, friar of orders gray. —rötlich, *adj.* sorrel (*horse*). —scheckig, *adj.* gray spotted. —schimmel, *m.* gray horse. —tier, *n.* ass, donkey. —werk, *n.* calabar *or* squirrel skins; minever.

[1]**Grau'en,** *v.n.* (*aux.* h.) to grow gray; to dawn; das — des Morgens, the dawn of day.

[2]**Grau'—en,** I. *v.n. & imp.* (einem) to have a horror of; to have an aversion to; to be afraid of; es —t mir vor, I shudder at; mir —t's vor dir, I shudder to look upon thee; mir —t vor Gespenstern, I have a fear of ghosts; es —t mir wenn ich daran denke, I shudder to think of it. II. *subst. n.* horror, dread, terror; es wandelte ihn ein —en an, he was seized with fear. —enhaft, *adj. & adv.* horrible; uncanny; dreadful. —en=voll, *adj.* awful, horrible. —lich, *adj.* horrible, horrifying; timorous. —s, *m.* (—(s)es), horror, dread; dreadful thing. —sam, *adj. & adv.* cruel, inhuman, fierce; horrible, terrible; gruesome. —samkeit, *f.* cruelty, ferocity. —s=lich, *adj.* gruesome, horrible (*coll.*).

Grau'l—en, *v.* I. *r.* to be afraid, to fear, to shudder (*especially of ghosts, spectres in the dark*); du —st dich doch nicht vor Gespenstern, you are not afraid of any spectres, I hope? einen weg —en, to frighten a p. away (*coll.*). II. *imp.; es* —t mir davor, I am afraid of it, I shudder at the thought of it (*coll.*).

Gräu'el, *see* Greuel.

Grau'pe, *f.* (*pl.* —n) peeled grain, pearl peeled barley, groat; grain (*Min.*). —ln, I. *v.n.imp.* to sleet *or* hail; to drizzle. II. *pl.* sleet. *Comp.* —l=erz, *n.* granular ore. —l=wetter, *n.* sleety weather. —n=grütze, *f.* barley-groats. —n=schleim, *m.* barley water. —n=suppe, *f.* barley broth.

Graus, Grauß, (*dial.* Grus, Gruß,) *m.* (—es) coarse sand, gravel; rubbish; bad, dirty coal (*dial.*); in — zerfallen, to fall into decay.

Grau's—en, I. *v.n. & imp.* to feel horror; mir —et, I shudder. II. *subst. n.* horror, terror, awe, dismay. —en=haft, —ig, *adj.* horrible, gruesome, dreadful. —en=erregend, *adj.* terror-striking, horrid, awful.

Grav—eu'r, *m.* (—eurs, *pl.* —eure) engraver. —ie'ren, *v.a.* to engrave, to aggravate. —ie'=rend, *p.& adj.* suspicious. —ie'rer, *m.* engraver. —ü're, *f.* engraving. *Comp.* —ie'r=meißel, *m.* graver. —ie'r=kunst, *f.* act of engraving. —ie'r=zeug, *n.* engraving tools.

Gra'v—is, *m.* grave accent. —itä't, *f.* gravity. —itä'tisch, *adj. & adv.* grave, serious. —itie'=ren, *v.n.* (*aux.* h.) to gravitate. *Comp.* —ita=tio'ns=kraft, *f.* force of gravitation.

Gra'zi—e, *f.* (*pl.* —en) Grace; grace, gracefulness. —ö's, *adj.* graceful.

Greep, *n.* (—es, *pl.* —e) cutwater (*Naut.*).

Greif, *m.* (—(e)s, *pl.* —e) griffin, griffon; a kind of vulture. *Comp.* —klaue, *f.* claw, talon. —pferd, —roß, *n.* hippogriff, hippogryph. —schnabel, *m.* pelican (*Surg.*). —stein, *m.* gryphite.

Grei'fbar, *adj. & adv.* seizable; palpable.

Grei'f—en, *ir.v.* I. *a. & n.* (*aux.* h.) to grasp; to snatch at; to comprehend; to touch; to take root; to stand one's ground; man kann es mit Händen —en, it is as clear as noonday, easily comprehended; so finster, daß man es —en kann, darkness that may be felt; die Zahl ist zu hoch gegriffen, it has been reckoned too high, the number is not so great; es ist völlig aus der Luft gegriffen, that is pure invention. II. *n.* (*aux.* h.) to have effect, to prevail; to feel; to handle; to bite (of an anchor); auf dem Klavier falsch —en, to strike a false note on the piano; einem ans Leben —en, to attempt a p.'s life; einem an den Puls —en, to feel a p.'s pulse; in jemands Tasche —en, to put one's hand into another's pocket, make him pay for; in einander —en, to work on each other (*as cog-wheels*); (einem) in die Seele —en, to touch a p. to the quick; —en nach, to snatch at; um sich —en, to gain ground, spread; einem unter die Arme —en, to help a p. (*fig.*); einem unter das Kinn —en, to chuck one under the chin; —en zu, to have recourse to, to employ; zu den Waffen —en, to take up arms. *Comp.* —holz, *n.* wooden handle.

Grei'n—en, *v.n.* (*aux.* h.) to cry; to whine; to growl, quarrel; to grin. —er, *m.* (—ers, *pl.* —er) grumbler; quarreller (*dial.*); Eberhard der —er, Eberhard the Quarrelsome (*Count of Würtemberg*, †1392).

Greis, I. *adj.* hoary. II. *m.* (—(ſ)es, *pl.* —(ſ)e) old man. —(ſ)enhaft, *adj.* senile, oldish. —(ſ)enheit, *f.* senility. —(ſ)in, *f.* old woman. *Comp.* —(ſ)en=alter, *n.* old age, senility.

Gre'ling, *n.* (—s) hawser (*Naut.*).

Grell, *adj.* dazzling; glaring (*of colours*); hard; shrill (*sounds*); — gegen eine S. abſtechen, to contrast strongly with. —e, —heit, *f.* harshness; vividness; glaringness.

Grem'p—el, *m.* rubbish. —eln, *v.n.* (*aux.* h.) to sell old things (*dial.*). —ler, *m.* second-hand dealer. *Comp.* —el=werk, *n.* old goods, old clothes, lumber.

Grenadie'r, *m.* (—s, *pl.* —e) grenadier; mountain salmon. *Comp.* —block, *m.* monkey-block.

Gren'z—e, *f.* (*pl.* —en) frontier; boundary, limit, border; term; extreme point. —lich, *adj.* bordering. *Comp.* —acker, *m.* boundary-field. —bereiter, *m.* (mounted) boundary *or* frontier inspector. —bewohner, *m.* borderer. —en=los, *adj.* boundless, unlimited. —en=losigkeit, *f.* boundlessness; infinitude. —festung, *f.* frontier-fortress. —gegend, *f.* frontier district, border land. —gemeinſchaft, *f.* contiguity. —gott, *m.* Terminus. —jäger, *m.* excise-officer. —linie, *f.* boundary line, line of demarcation. —kette, *f.*, —ſchnur, *f.* cordon (*Mil.*). —mal, *n.* landmark. —nachbar, *m.* neighbour. —ſcheide, *f.* boundary. —ſoldat, *m.* border soldier. —ſtein, *m.* landmark; boundary-stone. —wache, *f.* military cordon. —wächter, *m.* frontier-guard. —wall, *m.* rampart marking the boundary; der alte römiſche —wall, limes. —wehr, *f.* barrier; troops protecting a boundary district. —wert, *m.* limit, maximum *or* minimum value. —zeichen, *n.* landmark. —zoll, *m.* transit duty, customs. —zoll=behörde, *f.* custom-house authorities, customs officers.

Gren'zen, *v.* I. *n.* (*aux.* h.) to border (on, an *with acc.*); to adjoin; to be bounded by. II. *a.* to border; to limit. —er, *m.* (—ers, *pl.* —er) person living on the frontier, borderer; soldier of the Austrian military border.

Greu'—el, *m.* (—els, *pl.* —el) horror; abomination; outrage; es iſt mir ein —el, I abominate it, I loathe it. —lich, *adj.* & *adv.* frightful; atrocious; heinous; dreadful. *Comp.* —el=that, *f.* atrocity, deed of horror.

Grey'erzerkäſe, Grei'erzerkäſe, *m.* Gruyèr cheese (*usually* Schweizerkäſe).

Grie'be, *f.* (*pl.* —n) residuum of lard, tallow.

Griebs, *m.* (—(ſ)es, *pl.* —(ſ)e) core (*of fruit*); refuse.

Grie'nen, *v.n.* to grin, to smile continually in a silly way (*coll.* & *dial.*).

Gries, *m.* (—(ſ)es) gravel; coarse sand; groats; Embden grits, semolina. —(ſ)eln, *v.a.* & *n.* (*aux.* h.) to break into small pieces, to grind, to crumble. —(ſ)icht, (*obs.*) —(ſ)ig, *adj.* & *adv.* gritty, gravelly; calculous (*Med.*). *Comp.* —brei, *m.* thick gruel. —flechte, *f.* herpes. —gerſte, *f.* French barley. —gram, *m.* ill-humour; grumbler, morose person. —grämig, —grämiſch, —grämlich, *adj.* morose, surly, sullen, peevish. —kolik, *f.* nephritic colic. —mehl, *n.* pollard. —mittel, *n.* anti-nephritic. —pudding, *m.* semolina pudding. —ſuppe, *f.* semolina soup, gruel. —trank, *m.* thin water-gruel.

Griff, Griffe, *imperf. ind.* & *subj. of* greifen.

Griff, *m.* (—es, *pl.* —e) grip, grasp; hold, catch; pinch; hand-hold *or* foot-hold (mountain); handle (*of an umbrella*); hilt (*of a sword*), haft; ear (*of a cup, etc.*); fret (*of guitars*); touch (*Mus.*); rounce (*Typ.*); handful; talons, claws, clutch; art, trick, artifice; einen falſchen — thun, to touch a wrong note to make a mistake; etwas im —e haben, to know a thing by the touch; to be good at a thing. —el, *m.* (—els, *pl.* —el) style; graver; slate-pencil; style, pistil (*Bot.*). —ig, *adj.* (*in comp.* =) -handed. *Comp.* —brett, *n.* fret-board, neck (*of a violin, guitar, etc.*); finger-board (*of a piano*). —el=artig, *adj.* styloid. —el=förmig, *adj.*; —elförmiger Fortſatz, styloid process (*Anat.*). —el=los, *adj.* without styles *or* pistils. —loch, *n.* key-hole of wind instruments.

Gril'l—e, *f.* (*pl.* —en) cricket (*Ent.*); whim, freak, caprice, vagary, crotchet; melancholy thought; die —e zirpt, the cricket chirps; ſich (*acc.*) mit —en plagen, —en fangen, to be full of fancied cares, to be low-spirited, to have a bee in one's bonnet, to worry. —enhaft, —ig, *adj.* & *adj.* whimsical, capricious. —enhaftigkeit, *f.* fancifulness, capriciousness. *Comp.* —en=fänger, *m.* capricious person, whimsical *or* odd fellow. —en=fängerei, *f.* fancifulness; whims; hypochondria.

Grimaſ'ſe, *f.* (*pl.* —n) grimace.

Grimm, I. *m.* (—(e)s) fury, rage. II. *adj.* (*obs.* & *poet.*) *see* —ig; die —e Königin, the fierce queen (*obs.* & *poet.*). —ig, *adj.* & *adv.* enraged, furious, wrathful; fierce, grim; violent. —igkeit, *f.* fury, ferocity, grimness. *Comp.* —darm, *m.* colon (*Anat.*). —ſchnaubend, *adj.* breathing wrath, full of rage, furious.

Grim'm—en, I. *v.n.* (*aux.* h.) to be in a fury, rage, fume; es —t mich im Bauche, I have the colic (*obs.*). II. *subst.* gripes; colic.

Grind, *m.* (—(e)s, *pl.* —e) scab; scurf; mange; stag's head; groats; filth. —icht (*obs.*), —ig, *adj.* & *adv.* scabbed, scabby, scurfy. *Comp.* —kopf, *m.* scald-head. —kraut, —wurzkraut, *n.* scabious; grounsel.

Grin'ſen, I. *v.n.* (*aux.* h.) to grin; to simper; to sneer. II. *subst.n.* grin, sneer.

Grip'pe, *f.* (*pl.* —n) influenza.

Grips, *m.* (—(ſ)es) brains, ability (*coll.*); neck (*coll.*).; einen beim — kriegen, to collar a p.

Grob, *adj.* & *adv.* (gröber, gröbſt) large, big; thick; coarse; rude, uncivil; clownish; clumsy, uncouth; rough; gross; —er Scherz, broad joke; —er Fehler, bad mistake, howler (*Gram. coll.*); —e Schrift, large-sized type; —es Geſchütz, big *or* great guns; —e Waren, heavy articles of proportionately little value; —e Stimme, deep, rough voice; —e Münze, large pieces of money; —es Gewicht, gross weight; einen — anfahren, to handle one roughly, address one rudely; aus dem —en arbeiten, to roughhew; to surmount the first difficulties; aus dem Gröbſten heraus ſein, to be out of the worst, to have achieved the most difficult part of one's task. —heit, *f.* coarseness; grossness; rudeness; insolence; —heiten ſagen, to say rude things. —ian, *m.* (—ians, *pl.* —iane) rude fellow, clown, boor, brute; large-limbed man. —ianis'mus, *m.* Grobianism (*a certain kind of popular German coarse literature of the 16th century*). *Comp.* —eiſen, *n.* merchant-iron. —fleiſchig, *adj.* brawny. —körnig, *adj.* coarse-grained. —ſchmied, *m.* blacksmith. —ſinnig, *adj.* having blunted, coarse senses. —ſinnlich, *adj.* gross-minded; very sensuous, voluptuous.

Gröb'lich, *adj.* & *adv.* somewhat coarse *or* gross; — beleidigen, to insult grossly.

Gröbs, *see* Griebs.

Gro'den, *m.* (—s) land gained from the sea; alluvium.

Grog, *m.* (—s, *pl.* —s) grog.

Grö'hlen, Grö'len, *v.a.* (*aux.* h.) to bawl, squall.

Groll, *m.* (—(e)s) ill-will, hatred, enmity; resentment; — hegen, to bear a grudge.

Grol'len, *v.n.* (*aux.* h.) (*usually dat. but also with* auf (*acc.*), gegen, *or* mit) to bear ill-will, to be angry with; to roar; to rumble (*of thunder*).

Gro(o)t, *m.* groat (*old Bremen money*).
Grop'pe, *f.* (*pl.* **—n**) bullhead, miller's thumb.
[1]**Gros** (*with long* **o** & **s** *not sounded*), *n.* gross; **en —**, wholesale; **das — der Armee**, the main body. *Comp.* **—gewicht**, *n.* brutto weight.
[2]**Gros** (*short* **o**, & **s** *pron.*), **Groß** (*short* **o**), *n.* (—(ss)es, *pl.* —(ss)e) gross, twelve dozen.
Gro'schen, *m.* (*short* **o**) (**—s**, *pl.* **—**) small silver coin now no longer in use, worth a little more than a penny; money. *Comp.* **—schreiber**, *m.* penny-a-liner, quill-driver.
Groß (*with long* **o**), (**grö'ßer, grö'ß(es)t**), I. *adj.* & *adv.* tall (*of size*); high; large; big, vast; huge, great; large in number; important; eminent; grand; **— werden**, to grow big *or* tall; **— ziehen**, to bring up; **— sprechen**, to talk big, to brag, to draw the long bow (*coll.*); **— thun**, to swagger, to give oneself airs; **sich** (*acc.*) **mit etwas — thun**, to boast *or* brag of a thing; **im —en handeln**, to carry on wholesale trade; **—enteils**, for the most part, generally, chiefly; **—e Augen machen**, to stare (*in surprise*); **—e Bohnen**, broad beans; **—e Ferien**, long vacation; **—er Ozean**, Pacific; **—er Buchstabe**, capital letter; **Klein und —**, rich and poor; **—e Havarie**, general average; **das —e Loos**, first (lottery) prize; **—e Quarte**, major fourth (*Min.*); **—er Rat**, full council; **—e Kleinigkeit**, mere trifle; **ein —es Tausend**, twelve hundred (*obs.*); **— denken**, to think nobly; **— auftreten**, to lord it, assume airs; **nicht — nötig haben**, to have no great need of; **das —e an**, what is great in; **im —en**, on a large scale, wholesale; **im ganzen und —en**, on the whole, generally speaking; **ins —e treiben**, to exaggerate. II. *n.* (**—es**) gross, *see* **Gros**. **—e(r)**, *m.* grandee; **der —e Kurfürst**, Friedrich Wilhelm, Elector of Brandenburg (*1640-88*); **der —e Schweiger**, Field-Marshal Count H. v. Moltke; **die — deutschen**, German politicians (*before 1866*) who wished for a united Germany including Austria. **—heit**, *f.* greatness; largeness (*of mind or views*); nobleness. *Comp.* **—artig**, *adj.* & *adv.* grand, grandiose, noble, magnificent; egregious. **—artigkeit**, *f.* grandeur. **—avantur**, *f.* general adventure (*C. L.*). **—backig**, *adj.* chubby. **—bauer**, *m.* yeoman. **—binder**, *m.* cooper. **—brüstig**, *adj.* & *adv.* deep *or* broad-chested. **—elterlich**, *adj.* concerning, belonging to, *or* coming from grandparents. **—eltern**, *pl.* grandparents. **—enkel**, *m.* great grandson. **—enkelin**, *f.* great granddaughter. **—en=teils**, *adv.* mainly, in a great measure, to a large extent. **—fürst**, *m.* grand-duke. **—fürstentum**, *n.* grandduchy. **—garn**, *n.* sweep-net. **—gliederig**, *adj.* large-limbed. **—handel**, *m.* wholesale trade. **—händler**, *m.* wholesale dealer *or* merchant. **—handlung**, *f.* wholesale warehouse *or* firm. **—herr**, *m.* grand seignior; Sultan (of Turkey). **—herrisch**, *adj.* & *adv.* lordly. **—herrlich**, *adj.* belonging to the Sultan; seigniorial; most excellent. **—herzig**, *adj.* magnanimous. **—herzigkeit**, *f.* magnanimity. **—herzog**, *m.* grand-duke. **—herzogin**, *f.* grand-duchess. **—herzoglich**, *adj.* grand-ducal. **—herzogtum**, *n.* grand-duchy. **—hundert**, *n.* the long hundred (*120*) (*obs.*). **—industrie**, *f.* manufacture. **—industrielle(r)**, *m.* wholesale manufacturer. **—jährig**, *adj.* of age; **—jährig werden**, to come of age. **—jährigkeit**, *f.* majority, coming of age, full age. **—kammer=herr**, **—kämmerer**, *m.* lord-chamberlain. **—kanzler**, *m.* lord-high-chancellor. **—kaufmann**, *m.* wholesale merchant. **—knecht**, *m.* head man-servant on a farm, foreman; main knight (*Naut.*). **—knochig**, *adj.* large-boned. **—kopf=fliege**, *f.* gad-fly. **—kreuz**, *n.* grand cross (*of Europe*). **—leibig**, *adj.* big-bellied. **—lippig**, *adj.* thick-lipped. **—mächte**, *pl.* the great powers (*of Europe*). **—mächtig**, I. *adj.* high and mighty. II. *adv.* enormously. **—mannssucht**, *f.* megalomania. **—maschig**, *adj.* wide-meshed. **—maul**, *n.* braggart. **—mäulig**, *adj.* wide-mouthed; bragging. **—meister**, *m.* grand master. **—mögend**, *adj.* high and mighty; worshipful. **—mut**, *f.* magnanimity; generosity. **—mütig**, *adj.* magnanimous; generous. **—mutter**, *f.* grandmother. **—mütterlich**, *adj.* of, by, pertaining to a grandmother. **—nasig**, *adj.* bottle-nosed; arrogant (*coll.*). **—neffe**, *m.* grand-nephew. **—nichte**, *f.* grandniece. **—oktav**, *m.* large octavo; full organ. **—oheim**, **—onkel**, *m.* great-uncle, grandfather's (grandmother's) brother. **—prahler**, *m.* boaster, braggart. **—prahlerei**, *f.* brag. **—pratschig**, *adj.* arrogant. **—quart**, *m.* large quarto. **—schatzmeister**, *m.* grand-treasurer; First Lord of the Treasury. **—schnäbler**, *pl.* gross-beaks (*Orn.*). **—schnauzig**, **—schnäuzig**, *adj.* broad-mouthed, big-talking, boasting, swaggering, tongue-valiant. **—seite**, *f.* hypotenuse. **—siegel=bewahrer**, *m.* Keeper of the Privy Seal, Lord Privy Seal. **—sprecher**, *m.* boaster, swaggerer. **—sprecherei'**, *f.* boasting; boast, brag, drawing the long bow. **—sprecherisch**, *adj.* boastful; swaggering; grandiloquent. **—spurig**, *adj.* arrogant, conceited. **—staaten**, *pl.* the great powers (*of Europe*). **—stadt**, *f.* large town. **—städter**, *m.* inhabitant of a large town. **—städtisch**, *adj.* fashionable; of a large town; **—städtischer Arbeiter**, metropolitan workman, workman in a large town. **—tante**, *f.* great aunt. **—that**, *f.* great deed, noble exploit, feat, bravery. **—thuer**, *m.* braggart. **—ur=enkel**, *m.* great-great-grandson. **—vater**, *m.* grandfather. **—vater=stuhl**, *m.* armchair, easy-chair. **—väterlich**, *adj.* of, by, pertaining, to a grandfather. **—vikar**, *m.* vicar apostolic. **—wanstig**, *adj.* big-bellied. **—würdenträger**, *m.* high dignitary. **—zügig**, *adj.* on a grand scale.
Größ—e, *f.* (*pl.* **—en**) tallness, height; size, largeness; bulk; greatness; quantity; power; magnitude; enormity; great person; degree; length; **von mittlerer —e**, of medium size; **in natürlicher —e**, life-size; **bekannte, gegebene —e**, known quantity. **—er**, *comp. of* **Groß**; elder. *Comp.* **—en=lehre**, *f.* mathematics. **—en=reihe**, *f.* series. **—en=vergleichung**, *f.* conversion of ratios. **—en=wahn**, *m.* megalomania. **—ten=teils**, *adv.* for the most part, chiefly.
Gros'sel, *f.* (*pl.* **—n**) whortleberry. *Comp.* **—beere**, *f.* gooseberry.
Grossi'st, *m.* (**—en**, *pl.* **—en**) wholesale merchant.
Grossula'r, *m.* (**—s**, *pl.* **—e**) green garnet.
Grot, *m.* (**—es**, *pl.* **—e**) groat (*old Bremen coin*).
Grote'sk, *adj.* & *adv.* grotesque. **—e**, *f.* (*pl.* **—en**) grotesque(ness).
Grot'te, *f.* (*pl.* **—n**) grotto. *Comp.* **—n=arbeit**, *f.* rock-work.
Grub, Grü'be, *imperf. ind.* & *subj. of* **graben**.
Gru'b—e, *f.* (*pl.* **—en**) pit; hole, cavity; mine; ditch; quarry; grave, scar, mark; (**einem**) **eine —e graben**, to lay a snare for; **wer andern eine —e gräbt fällt selbst hinein**, the biter will be bit (*prov.*); **in die —e fahren**, to go down to the grave. *Comp.* **—en=arbeiter**, *m.* miner. **—en=aufstand**, *m.* report of a mine. **—en=axt**, *f.* pickaxe. **—en=bau**, *m.* mining. **—en=blende**, *f.*, **—en=licht**, *n.* miner's lantern. **—en=ende**, *n.* vine-layer. **—en=gas**, *n.* fire-damp, gas in mines. **—en=gericht**, *n.* bergmote. **—en=gezäh**, *n.* miner's tools. **—en=gut**, *n.* mineral. **—en=köhler**, *m.* pit-miner. **—en=lampe**, *f.* (safety) lamp. **—en=pulver**, *n.* blasting powder. **—en=schlacke**, *f.* slag. **—en=steiger**, *m.* overseer of a mine. **—en=**

wetter, *n.* damps, fire-damp. **—ig,** *adj.* lacunose.

Grüb'chen, *n.* (—s, *pl.* —) little cavity; dimple (*in the face*); chuck-farthing.

Grübelei', *f.* (*pl.* —en), musing, meditation, brooding; needless subtlety, hypercriticism.

Grü'bel—haft, *adj. & adv.* hypercritical; over-subtle; brooding, melancholy. *Comp.* **—kopf,** *see* Grübler. **—krank,** *adj.* splenetic. **—krankheit,** *f.* spleen.

Grü'b—eln, *v.n.* (*aux.* h.) to rake, stir, rummage; to refine, be hypercritical, rack one's brains; to brood, indulge in melancholy meditation. **—elnde Vernunft,** pondering reason, carping criticism. **—ler,** *m.* (—lers, *pl.* —ler) hypercritic, refiner, over-subtle reasoner, gloomy meditator, speculator.

Gruft, *f.* (*pl.* Grüf'te) grave; vault; cavity; cave. *Comp.* **—gewölbe,** *f.* vault. **—kirche,** *f.* crypt.

Grum'mel, *m.* (—s) distant thunder. **—n,** *v.n.* (*aux.* h.) to rumble; **es —t,** there is a noise of distant thunder.

Grum'met, *n.* (—s) after-math, second crop.

Grün, *adj. & adv.* green, verdant; fresh, vigorous; raw; unripe; inexperienced; favourable; **—e Ware, —es,** greens; **bei Mutter — schlafen,** to camp out, to sleep in the open, under a tree (*sl.*); **das —e Gewölbe,** famous art museum at Dresden; **meine —e Seite,** the side of me where the heart is, my heart; **—e Hochzeit,** first wedding; **—er Junge,** a young man without experience, greenhorn, jackanapes; **— bleiben,** to continue flourishing (*viz. the remembrance of a p.*); **es wird mir — und gelb vor den Augen,** I have a giddiness in my head; **auf keinen —en Zweig kommen,** not to get on in the world; **einem nicht — sein,** to bear a grudge against one; **viel —es,** young people; **—e Häute,** undressed skins; **—er Verstand,** sound understanding; **—e Bekanntschaft,** short acquaintance; **der —e König,** king of spades (*rare*); **—er Tisch,** official table, red tape, officialism; gaming-table. II. *n.* green colour, verdure. **—e,** *f.* greenness, verdure; green; nature; verdigris. **—lich,** *adj. & adv.* greenish; **ins —liche fallend,** of a greenish hue. **—ling,** *m.* green-finch; wood-lark; green agaric (*Bot.*); Mr. Verdant Green, freshman (*Univ. sl.*). *Comp.* **—baum,** *m.* privet. **—donnerstag,** *m.* Maundy Thursday. **—holz,** *n.* mountain pine; dyer's green-weed. **—kohl,** *m.* (green) kale, pot herbs. **—kram,** *m.*, **—kraut,** *n.* greens, greengrocery. **—rock,** *m.* hunter, huntsman; gamekeeper; chasseur. **—schnabel,** *m.* any bird with a green beak; saucy young person, greenhorn. **—span,** *m.* verdigris. **—specht,** *m.* green woodpecker.

Grund, *m.* (—es, *pl.* Grün'de) ground, earth, soil; land, estate; ground; bottom; base; valley, dale; dregs, lees; foundation, basis, groundwork; rudiments, elements, first principles; reason, cause, motive; argument; ground (*of a fabric*); background, ground, priming (*Paint.*); **aus welchem —e ?** for what reason? **wir sitzen auf dem —e,** we are aground; **auf den — fahren,** to run aground; **zu —e gehen,** to sink, founder; to go to ruin, to be ruined; **einer Sache zu —e liegen,** to underlie, be at the bottom of a th.; **zu —e richten,** to undo, to ruin; **des Meeres tiefe Gründe,** the bosom, the unfathomable depths of the ocean; **ich habe hier keinen — mehr,** I am out of my depth here; **im —e,** at the bottom; after all, really; **auf — meiner Vollmacht,** in virtue of my authority; **aus dem —e** *or* **von — aus,** fundamentally, thoroughly, radically; **liegende Gründe,** landed property; **die ersten Gründe einer Wissenschaft,** the rudiments of a science; **die Nachricht entbehrt jedes —es,** the news is without any foundation. **—el,** *f.* (*pl.* —eln) groundling (*Icht.*). **—ie'ren,** I. *v.a. see* Gründen. II. *subst. n.* grounding; priming (*Paint.*). *Comp.* **—angeln,** *n.* bottom-fishing. **—anstrich,** *m.* first coat. **—artikel,** *m.* fundamental article. **—balken, —baum,** *m.* foundation-beam; keel (*of a ship*). **—baß,** *m.* thorough-bass (*Mus.*). **—bau,** *m.* foundation; substructure; underpinning. **—bedeutung,** *f.* original meaning. **—bedingung,** *f.* main condition. **—begriff,** *m.* fundamental principle. **—beschaffenheit,** *f.* fundamental quality. **—besitz,** *m.* landed property. **—besitzer,** *m.* landed proprietor. **—besitztum,** *n.* (höheres, freies) free tenure. **—bestandteil,** *m.* primary *or* essential component. **—blei,** *n.* sounding-lead, plummet. **—böse,** *adj.* radically bad. **—brühe,** *f.* bilge-water; dregs. **—buch,** *n.* register of landed property; Doomsday-book (*in England*). **—ebene,** *f.* ground-plan. **—ehrlich,** *adj.* thoroughly honest. **—eigenschaften,** *pl.* fundamental properties. **—eigentum,** *n.* landed real property. **—einheit,** *f.* absolute unit. **—einkommen,** *n.* land-revenue. **—eis,** *n.* ground-ice. **—eisen,** *n.* probe. **—entwurf,** *m.* first draught, rough sketch. **—faden,** *m.* thread of the warp. **—falsch,** *adj.* fundamentally wrong; thoroughly false. **—farbe,** *f.* ground colour, priming; primitive colour. **—fehler,** *m.* radical fault. **—feld,** *n.* dead colour; ground. **—fest,** *adj.* solid; real, landed. **—feste,** *f.* basis. **—firnis,** *m.* priming-varnish. **—fläche,** *f.* base, basis; area (*Geom.*). **—gelehrt,** *adj.* thoroughly erudite, most scholarly, of profound erudition. **—gerechtigkeit,** *f.* territorial jurisdiction. **—gesetz,** *n.* statute, fundamental law. **—hefe,** *f.* lees, sediment. **—herr,** *m.* lord of the manor. **—herrlichkeit, —herrschaft,** *f.* manor; seigniorial right; lord *or* lady of the manor. **—ier'=bällchen,** *n.* ground-dabber (*etching*). **—irrtum,** *m.* fundamental mistake *or* error. **—kapital,** *n.* stock. **—kette,** *f.* ground warp (*Weav.*). **—kraft,** *f.* main strength. **—lage,** *f.* foundation, basis; rudiments; base. **—legend,** *adj.* laying a foundation; **die —legende wissenschaftliche Ausgabe,** the first really scientific edition, standard (critical) edition. **—leger,** *m.* founder. **—legung,** *f.* laying the foundation. **—lehre,** *f.* fundamental doctrine; (*pl.*) principles. **—linie,** *f.* outline; ground-line, base-line; (*pl.*) sketch. **—los,** *adj. & adv.* bottomless; unfathomable; boundless; unfounded, causeless. **—losigkeit,** *f.* unfathomableness; groundlessness. **—mauer,** *f.* foundation wall. **—mörtel,** *m.* concrete. **—neigung,** *f.* nature propensity. **—pfahl,** *m.* pile. **—pfeiler,** *m.* main support; basis; foundation-pillar. **—recht,** *n.* landlord's privilege *or* right, fundamental law. **—rechte,** *pl.* rights of man. **—regel,** *f.* fundamental rule; axiom; first principle. **—register,** *n. see* **—buch.** **—rente,** *f.* ground-rent. **—riß,** *m.* first sketch; ground-plan (*of a building*); epitome, compendium, outlines; syllabus (*of a course of lectures*); brief encyclopædia. **—satz,** *m.* principle; rule of conduct; axiom. **—sätzlich,** *adj.* (based) on principle; **ich thue das —sätzlich niemals,** I have made it a point never to do this. **—satzlos,** *adj.* unprincipled. **—säule,** *f.* pedestal, foot, basis, supporter. **—schelm,** *m.* arrant rogue. **—schlag,** *m.* model (*of stairs, of a roof, etc.*). **—schlecht,** *adj.* radically bad, thoroughly bad *or* wicked. **—schnitt,** *m.* projection. **—schoß,** *m.* land-tax, cess. **—schuld,** *f.* mortgage on land. **—schwelle,** *f.* ground-sill (*Arch.*); railway-sleeper. **—see,** *f.* ground-swell. **—sprache,** *f.* original language. **—stein,** *m.* foundation *or* corner-stone. —steuer, *f.* land-tax. —stimme, *f.* bass voice. —stoff, *m.* element; base, radical (*Chem.*). —strich, *m.* down-stroke (*opp. to hair-stroke*). —stück, *n.* real estate; essential part; piece of ground, premises. —stürzend, *adj.* destructive, revolutionary; —stürzende Änderungen, radical changes. —stütze, *f.* main support, basis. —teilchen, *n.* atom. —text, *m.* original text. —ton, *m.* key-note. —übel, *n.* fundamental evil, the root of all evil. —vermögen, *n.* primitive force; landed property; capital, fund. —verschieden, *adj.* entirely different. —verschiedenheit, *f.* radical difference. —wachs, *n.* beebread. —wägekunst, *f.* hydrostatics. —wahrheit, *f.* fundamental truth. —wasser, *n.* underground water. —werk, *n.* ground-work. —wesen, *n.* primary essence (*of a thing*); being of beings. —wort, *n.* radical word; determinative word (*of a compound*). —zahl, *f.* cardinal number; unit. —zehnte, *m.* land tithe. —zins, *m.* ground-rent. —zug, *m.* principal feature of a thing; outline; characteristic.

Grün'd—en, *v.* I. *a.* to ground; to establish; to found; to sound, to fathom; to lay the ground-colour, to prime; to hatch (*Engr.*); to size (*Bookb.*); to ground (*a pupil*); to base (*an argument*); ge—ete Ansprüche, established claims. II. *r.* to rest, to be based, to rely (on, auf *with acc.*). III. *n.* (*aux.* h.) to sound, to feel the bottom. —er, *m.* (—ers) founder; establisher; speculator in *or* promoter of risky financial enterprises, promoter, jobber. —erschwindel, *m.* swindling by speculative founders of bubble-companies. —ertum, *n.* mania for wild speculative enterprises, mania for founding bogus companies. —lich, *adj. & adv.* thorough; profound; radical; fundamental; solid, well-founded; —liche Kenntnisse in einem Fache haben, to be thoroughly well-grounded *or* versed in, be master of a subject. —lichkeit, *f.* thoroughness, profundity; solidity; ein Buch von großer —lichkeit, a book of deep research, a book containing full and thorough information. —ling *m.* (—lings, *pl.* —linge) gudgeon, groundling. —ung, *f.* foundation, establishment; commercial *or* financial enterprise; priming; founding. *Comp.* —ungseisen, *n.* engraver's burnisher *or* scratching knife. —ungs-schwindel, *see* —erschwindel.

Grü'n—en, *v.n.* to grow *or* be green; to flourish, thrive; to be well disposed to, to be devoted to (*obs.*); mein Herze soll dir —en, my heart shall love thee, be devoted to thee (*obs. & poet.*). —eln, (grüneln, *rare*,) to (begin to) grow green. —end, *p. & adj.* verdant.

Grun'z—en, I. *v.n.* (*aux.* h.) to grunt. II. *subst. n.* grunt. —er, *m.* (—ers, *pl.* —er) grunter.

Grup'p—e, *f.* (*pl.* —en) group; cluster. —ie'ren, *v.a.* to group. —ie'rung, *f.* grouping, arrangement; organization. *Comp.* —enweise, *adv.* in groups *or* clusters.

Grus, *m.* rubbish; slack. —sand, *m.* coarse sand; gravel. —thee, *m.* tea-dust.

Gru'sel, *m.* (—s) cold shuddering; fright. —ig, *adj.* causing fright, awful, uncanny. —n, *v.n.* (*aux.* h.) *imp.* to cause shuddering, to make shudder; es —t mir, I shudder.

Gruß, *m.* (—es, *pl.* Grü'ße) salute; salutation, greeting; mit bestem Gruß Ihr, yours very truly; einen — ausrichten, to convey one's kind regards. *Comp.* —formel, *f.* form of salutation.

Grü'ßen, I. *v.a.* to greet; to salute; to bow to; to present compliments to; — lassen, to send respects, compliments, kind regards to; bitte —Sie ihn von mir, please remember me to him, give him my kind regards; meine Mutter läßt deine Schwester herzlich —, my mother sends her love to your sister; er läßt euch alle —, he desires to be remembered to you all. II. *subst. n.* greeting.

Grüß'fuß, *m.*; mit einem auf dem — stehen, to be on bowing terms with a p.

Grüt'z—e, *f.* peeled grain, groats; —e im Kopfe haben, to be clever, to be a man of brains (*colloq.*); rote —e, groats cooked with preserved juice of fruits and eaten with milk *or* cream-sauce. *Comp.* —brei, *m.* gruel. —händler, *m.* dealer in groats. —kopf, *m.* blockhead.

Guar'dian, *m.* (—s, *pl.* —e) (*convent*) prior; Pater —, father superior.

Gub'el, *m.* (—s) mouldy, muddy earth, clay soil

Guck, *m.* (—s) look, peep. —en, *v.n.* (*aux.* h.) to look, to peep; to peer; der Schelm —t ihm aus den Augen, his looks bespeak the rogue he is. —er, *m.* (—ers, *pl.* —er) peeper; eyeglass, spy-glass; Opern —er, opera glass. *Comp.* —auge, *n.* peeper. —kasten, *m.* peep show, raree-show. —loch, *n.* loop-hole.

Guck'guck, *see* Kuckuck.

Guhr, *f.* guhr (*Min.*); fermentation.

Guillotinie'ren, *v.a.* to guillotine.

Guinee', *f.* (*pl.* —n) guinea.

Guirlan'de, *f.* (*pl.* —n) garland; scallop (*stamps*).

Guitar're, *f.* (*pl.* —n) guitar.

Gul'den, *m.* (—s, *pl.* —) florin, guilder (*Dutch*) (*gen'lly = about 1s. 8d.*) *Comp.* —zettel, *m.* banknote of one florin.

Gül'den, *adj.* golden (*obs. & poet.*)

Gült'—bar, *adj.* subject to rent (*rare*). —e, *f.* ground rent; revenues of an estate; import, tribute, charges *or* payment (in kind). —ig, *adj. & adv.* valid, legal; authentic; done in due form; binding; current; admissible; applicable; available; —ig nach, good to go to (*on passports*); eine Anklage für —ig erklären, to bring in a true bill; —ig machen, to render valid, to ratify. —igkeit, *f.*, validity, lawfulness; currency (*of coins*); Fahrkarten mit dreißigtägiger —igkeit, tickets available for thirty days; Behauptung von allgemeiner —igkeit, universal proposition. *Comp.* —brief, *m.* lease. —buch, —register, *n.* rent-roll. —herr, *m.* lord of the manor.

Gum'mi, *n.* (—s) gum; elastisches — *or* — elasticum, India-rubber; — arabicum, gum (Arabic). —g, *adj.* gummy, gummous. *Comp.* —artig, *adj.* gummy. —artikel, *pl.* India rubber goods *or* articles. —band, *n.* elastic. —baum, *m.* India-rubber tree. —fichte, *f.* balsam-bearing pine. —gutt, —gutta, *n.* gamboge. —harz, *n.* gum-resin. —lack, *m.* gum-lac. —mantel, *m.* mackintosh. —schlauch, *m.* India rubber tube. —schleim, *m.* mucilage. —schuhe, *pl.* galoshes. —zug, *m.* elastic (*on boots*).

Gummie'r—en, *v.a.* to gum; —te Briefumschläge, adhesive envelopes. —ung, *f.* gumming, gum.

Gun'd—el (—els), —ling, *m.* (—lings), (—elkraut, *n.*,) wild thyme, creeping thyme. *Comp.* —el-beere, —el-rebe, *f.*, —er-mann, *m.* ground-ivy; rock-rose.

Gün'sel, *m.* (—s, *pl.* —) bugle (*Bot.*).

Gunst, *f.* (*pl.* —bezeugungen) favour, grace, goodwill; kindness; affection; partiality; leave, permission; zu —en, in favour of, on behalf of; zu meinen —en, in my favour, to my credit; es geht hier alles nach —, everything goes by favour here; mit —, with permission; sich um jemandes — bewerben, to court a person's favour. *Comp.* —bezeugung, *f.* favour, kindness.

Gün'st—ig, *adj. & adv.* favourable, gracious; propitious; kind; well-affected, friendly; advantageous; einen —ig für jemand stimmen, to move a person in favour of another. —ling, *m.* (—lings, *pl.* —linge) favourite, minion-

Comp. —lings=wesen, *n.*, —lings=wirt=schaft, *f.* favouritism.

Gur'gel, *f.* (*pl.* —n) gullet, throat; einem die — zuschnüren, to strangle a person; durch die — jagen, to squander in drinking, to gulp down (*vulg.*). —ei', *f.* gargling; bad singing. *Comp.* —wasser, *n.* gargle. —n, *v.* I. *n.* (*aux.* h.) to utter a gurgling *or* guttural sound; —e mir das Brautlied vor, sing our spousals in deep groans (*poet.*). II. *a.* (*& r.*) to gargle.

Gur'ke, *f.* (*pl.* —n) cucumber, gherkin; nose (*vulg.*); sich —n herausnehmen, to take liberties (*sl.*). *Comp.* —n=gut, *n.* Turkish porcelain. —n=hobel, *m.* cucumber-slicer. —n=maler, *m.* dauber. —n=salat, *m.* cucumber salad; was versteht der Bauer von —nsalat? what does a peasant know about cucumber salad? this is quite beyond him (*prov.*). —n=zeit, *f.* (saure —nzeit *or* Zeit der sauren —) dull season (*for journalists,* viz. *the latter part of the summer*) (*coll.*).

Gur're, *f.* (*pl.* —n) bad horse, screw; shad (*Icht.*).

Gur'ren, *v.n.* (*aux.* h.) to coo.

Gurt, *m.* (—es, *pl.* —e), —e, *f.* (*pl.* —en) girth; girdle, belt; strap; webbing. *Comp.* —bett, *n.* stretcher-bed. —gehenk, *n.* belt; something hanging from a belt. —haken, *m.* girth-hook. —riemen, *m.* girth-leather *or* strap. —sims, *m.*, —werk, *n.* plinth (*of a pillar*).

Gür'tel, *m.* (—s, *pl.* —) girdle; belt, sash; waistband; girth; zone; shingles (*Med.*); fascia, belt (*Astr.*); virgin-zone, virginity, maidenhood (*fig.*). *Comp.* —bahn, *f.* circular railway (*in large towns*). —band, *n. see* —. —kette, *f.* chatelaine. —schleiche, *f.* hair-worm. —tier, *n.* armadillo.

Gür't—en, *v.a.* to gird, to girdle; sich —en, to put on one's belt, to make (oneself) ready, prepare (oneself) for. —ler, *m.* (—lers, *pl.* —ler) girdler, belt-maker.

Guß, *m.* (—(ss)es, *pl.* Güs'se) pouring out, gush; downpour, torrent of rain; spout; gutter; casting, founding; cast; fount (*Typ.*); schmiedbarer —, malleable cast iron. *Comp.* —abdruck, *m.* plate, stereotype plate (*Typ.*); cast. —eisen, *n.* cast iron. —eisern, *adj.* made of cast iron. —form, *f.* casting mould. —mutter, *f.* matrix (*Typ.*). —regen, *m.* (*also* Regen—) sudden shower (*of rain*). —rohr, *n.* cast-iron pipe. —schale, *f.* shot-mould. —stahl, *m.* cast steel. —stein, *m.* sink, gutter. —waren, *pl.* castings. —werk, *n.* work of cast metal.

Gut, (besser, best) I. *adj. & adv.* good, desirable, excellent; pleasant; kind virtuous; friendly; clever; well; respectable, solid (*C.L.*); für — finden, to think proper; es — haben, to be well off; —e Tage haben, to have an easy life; — haben, to have to one's credit; fügen Sie dies zu meinem — haben bei Ihnen hinzu, add this to my credit with you; ich habe fünf Pfund bei ihm —, he owes me £5; zu —e halten, to excuse; — heißen, to approve of, sanction; es mag für diesmal — sein, I will pass it over this time, I will for this once take no notice of it; lassen wir es — sein, well, let it pass, never mind that; es wird schon noch alles gut werden, it will, no doubt, all turn out well; lassen Sie es — sein, never mind, do not mention it, no more of it; sich (*dat.*) einen —en Tag machen, to make a day of it, take a holiday, take it easy, enjoy oneself thoroughly; (etwas) wieder — machen, to make amends for; Sie haben — reden, it is easy for you to talk; den Gelehrten ist — predigen, a word is enough to the wise; einem — sein, to be favourably disposed to, to care for one, to love one: sie sind wieder —, they have made it up, are friendly again; — sein, — sagen, — stehen für, to be answerable for, warrant, be security for; es ist (schon) —, that will do, enough; einem etwas — *or* zu —e schreiben, to place s.th. to one's credit; — thun, to behave well, to do good; sich (*dat.*) etwas zu —e thun, to give oneself up to enjoyment; einem etwas zu —e halten, to make allowance for some one; er thut sich viel darauf zu —, he prides himself very much on it; sich (*dat.*) auf eine Sache etwas zu —e thun, to pique oneself upon, to be proud of, a thing; er wird bald wieder —, his anger is soon over; er hat das —e, he has this good quality; —er Absatz, ready sale; —es Wetter, fine weather; die —e Stube, the room to look at, the (rarely used) drawing room, reception room; die —en Taktteile, the strong accents (*Mus.*); ein —es Mädchen, a good-natured girl; —es, good things, good; im —en, in a friendly manner, amicably, gently, willingly; Ende —, Alles —, all 's well that ends well; ein —es Wort findet eine —e Statt, a good word always tells, *or* goes a long way (*prov.*); —en Mutes, —er Dinge sein, to be of good cheer, in good spirits; —er Hoffnung sein, to live in hope(s); to be with child, to be in the family way; eine —e Stunde, a full hour; — 25 Mark, quite 25 marks; — eine Viertelstunde, quite a quarter of an hour; eine —e Viertelstunde, a full quarter of an hour; das hat —e Wege, we need not trouble about that yet, that is (still) a long way off, that is of no importance; —er Rechner, quick at figures; in —em Glauben, in good faith, bona fide; das hat —e Weile, there is no hurry about that; (einem) zu —e kommen, to be beneficial to; mein Geigenspiel kam mir hier sehr zu —e, my violin playing was here of great use to me; sie ist so — Schuld daran wie ich, she is as much to blame in this as I am; es ist so — als hätte er sie geheiratet, he has as good as married her; der —e Ort, Jewish cemetery; es ist sein —er Wille, it is his own free will; uns zu —e, for our benefit; — gemeint, well meant; kurz und —, in short; —e Worte, fair words; einem —e Worte geben, to speak one fair; zu —er Letz (*obs.*), zu — erletzt, finally; stehst du (dich) — mit ihm? are you on friendly terms with him? das —e an der Geschichte, the best of the joke, the fun of it; — sein zu, to be good, proper for. — und gern, *adv.* quite willingly, easily; — und gern zehn Tausend, at least ten thousand. II. *n.* (—es, *pl.* Gü'ter) good thing, blessing; property; goods, possession; country-seat, estate; farm; gift, endowment; metal, ware, commodity; unrecht — gedeihet nicht, ill-gotten gain never prospers (*prov.*); ein erworbenes —, an acquisition; ein heimgefallenes —, escheat (*Law*); Hab und —, all one's property, goods and chattels; das hochwürdige —, the consecrated bread, the Host; — und Blut, life and property; — und Geld, Geld und —, wealth. —heit, *f.* goodness, kindness. *Comp.* —achten, *n.* judgment; (legal) advice; opinion; nach Ihrem —achten, as you think proper; nach —achten, at discretion. —achtlich, *adj. & adv.* by way of an opinion. —artig, *adj.* good-natured; not malignant, mild (*of fevers*). —aufgelegt, *adj.* well disposed, in good humour. —befinden, *n.* pleasure, discretion; approval; nach Ihrem —befinden, upon your own terms. —denkend, *adj.* well-meaning. —dünken, *n.* opinion. —edel, *m.* chasselas. —eingerichtet, *adj.* well-arranged; well-furnished. —erz, *n.* good *or* rich ore. —gebahnt, *adj.* well-beaten (*of roads*). —gelaunt, *adj.* in a good temper, good-humoured. —gewicht, *n.* allowance, boot. —haben, *n.*

outstanding debt; credit, balance in one's favour; ich habe noch ein kleines —haben bei Ihnen, a small sum still stands to my credit with you. —heißung, *f.* approbation, consent. —herzig, *adj.* good-hearted; kind. —mütig, *adj.* good-natured. —ſager, *m.* surety, bondsman. —ſagung, *f.*, —ſagen, *n.* security. —s=beſitzer, —s=herr, *m.* lord of a manor; gentleman farmer, landowner. —s=herrlich, *adj.*; —sherrliche Privilegien, rights exercised by the lord of the manor, manorial rights. —s=pflichtig, *adj.* liable to socage-service. —ſteuer, *f.* property-tax. —s=zwang, *m.* lord-of-the-manor's authority over his tenants. —thäter, *m.* benefactor (*usually* Wohlthäter). —that, *f.* charitable act (*usually* Wohlthat). —willig, *adj.* voluntary; obliging. —willigkeit, *f.* willingness.

Güt'chen, *n.* (—s, *pl.* —) small estate.

Gü't—e, *f.* kindness; goodness; excellence; purity; favour; haben Sie die —e, be so kind as; in (der) —e, auf dem Wege der —e, by fair means, by private agreement, in a kind *or* friendly way; durch (die) —e des Herrn Dr. W., by (the) favour of Dr. W.; erſter —e, of the first rank, first-rate (*coll.*); erſter —e fahren, to travel first-class (*Railw. coll.*); meine —! good gracious! I du meine —, I say! (*exclamation denoting astonishment, coll.*). —ig, *adj. & adv.* good, kind; gracious; benevolent, charitable; indulgent; —ig gegen einen, good to one; ſeien Sie ſo —ig und geben es ihm, kindly give it to him; der Brief, den Sie mir —igſt geſchrieben haben, the letter which you were kind enough to write me. —igkeit, *f.* goodness, kindness, graciousness; benevolence. —lich, *adj. & adv.* amicable, friendly; —licher Vergleich, amicable settlement; ſich (*dat.*) —lich thun, to enjoy oneself; —lich beilegen, to settle amicably. *Comp.* —er=abtretung, *f.* surrender of a bankrupt's estate. —er=anſchlag, *m.* valuation of goods. —er=bahnhof, *m.* goods station. —er=ballen, *m.* bale of goods. —er=beſtätiger, —er=beſtätter, —er=beſchaffner, *m.* consignor. —er=brief, *m.* bill of lading. —er=expedition, *f.* goods department, forwarding office, receiving office. —er=gemeinſchaft, *f.* joint property (*of husband and wife*). —er=handel, *m.* estate-agency, real-estate business. —er=mäkler, *m.* land jobber. —er=maſſe, *f.* bankrupt's assets. —er=ſchuppen, *m.* goods depot. —er=verſicherung, *f.* insurance on goods. —er=vertreter, *m.* trustee. —er=wagen, *m.* luggage-van, truck. —er=zug, *m.* goods-train; freight-train; mit —erzug, by goods-train.

Guttaper'cha, gutta-percha, India rubber. *Comp.* —ſchlauch, *m.* gutta-percha hose.

Guttura'l, *adj.*; —Vokal, (Konſonant,) *m.* guttural *or* back vowel, (consonant).

Gutz'gauch, *m.* cuckoo (*obs.*).

Gymnaſ—ia'ſt, *m.* (—iaſ'ten, *pl.* —iaſ'ten) grammar-school boy, boy on the classical side of a first-grade school. —ium (*pron.* Gymna'ſium), *n.* (—iums, *pl.* Gymna'ſien) grammar-school, classical school of the first grade; Mädchen—ium, grammar-school for girls. —tik (*pron.* Gymnaſ'tik), *f.* gymnastics. —tiſch (*pron.* gymnaſ'tiſch), *adj.* gymnastic. *Comp.* —ia'l=abiturient, *m.* sixth form boy of a first-grade classical school who is going to take (*or* who has taken) his leaving-certificate examination; young man who has been trained at a classical school. —ia'l=bildung, *f.* classical education. —ia'l=direktor, *m.* head-master of a first-grade classical school, head-master of a grammar-school. —ia'l=lehrer, *m.* teacher *or* assistant master at a first grade classical school.

Gynan'driſch, *adj.* gynandrian.

H

H, h, *n.* H, h; B, si (*Mus.*); *for abbr. see Index. Note that in German this letter is always fully sounded at the beginning of words or syllables, while in the middle or at the end of words or syllables it only serves to mark the length of the preceding vowel.*

Haar, *n.* (—es, *pl.* —e) hair; filament; nap, pile; wool; hairy *or* woolly side of skins; trifle; die —e ſtanden mir zu Berge, my hair stood on end; mit Haut und —(en), completely, entirely, altogether; —e auf den Zähnen haben, to have plenty of spirit, to be plucky; to be not easily frightened, to show fight; —e laſſen müſſen, to be fleeced, to be cheated; es iſt kein gutes — an ihm, he is a good-for-nothing fellow; there is no redeeming feature about him; ſie läßt ihm kein gutes —, she won't admit that he has a single good quality, she cuts him up mercilessly; bei den —en herbeiziehen, to drag in by the head and shoulders; das iſt bei den —en herbeigezogen, that is far-fetched; ein — in einer S. finden, to be disgusted with a thing, to find a flaw in a thing; einem gern in die —e wollen, to wish to pick a quarrel with one; auf ein —, aufs —, to a T, exactly; um ein —, bei einem —, within an ace; bei einem —e wäre er umgekommen, he escaped with his life by a hair's breadth; ſie wäre ums — ertrunken, she had a narrow escape from drowning; ſich (*dat.*) die —e machen, to dress one's hair; das — aufwickeln, to curl one's hair; nicht (um) ein —, kein —, not a jot, not in the least; es fehlte kein —, ſo wurde ſie getötet, she was within an ace of being killed; ſie hat kein — von ihrer Mutter, she is not in the least like her mother; graue —e bekommen, to grow gray; darüber laſſe ich mir keine grauen —e wachſen, that won't affect me much, I do not take that much to heart; ſie liegen ſich fortwährend in den —en, they are always at loggerheads. —icht, (*obs.*) *adj.* like hair. —ig, *adj.* hairy, haired; of hair; pilose (*Bot.*); hazy (*horizon*); strange, queer, funny (*coll.*). —igkeit, *f.* hairiness. *Comp.* —ader, *f.* capillary vein. —angel, *f.* horsehair fishing line. —aufſatz, *m.* false hair. —aufwickler, *m.* curling-pin; curl-paper; curling tongs. —band, *n.* hair lace; fillet. —beize, *f.* depilatory. —beutel, *m.* hair-bag; einen —beutel haben, to be tipsy (*coll.*). —breite, *f.* hair's breadth. —buche, *f.* yoke-elm. —bürſte, *f.* hair-brush. —buſchel, *m.* tuft of hair. —dick, *adj.* fine as a hair. —draht, *m.* finest gold wire. —farbe, *f.* colour of the hair. —färbeſtoff, *m.* hair-dye. —farn, *m.* maiden-hair fern. —faſer, *f.* filament. —faſerig, *adj.* capillary. —feder, *f.* down (*on birds*); hair-spring. —fein, *adj.* fine as a hair; delicate; capillary; subtile. —flechte, *f.* braid of hair. —flechter, *m.* worker in hair. —förmig, *adj.* capilliform. —gefäß, *n.* capillary vessel. —geſtirn, *see* —ſtern. —hammer, *m.* hammer for sharpening a scythe. —haube, *f.* hair-cap; periwig. —klauberei, *f.* hair-splitting. —klein, *adj. & adv.* to a hair, to a nicety; —klein alles erzählen, to tell with every detail. —komet, *m.* tailed *or* bearded comet. —kopf, *m.* head of hair. —kranz, *m.* tonsure. —krauſe, *f.* toupee; tonsure. —kräusler, —künſtler, *m.* hair-dresser. —locke, *f.* ringlet; lock of hair. —los, *adj.* hairless, bald; napless (*of cloth*). —nadel, *f.* hair-pin; ornamental pin for the hair. —nerven, *pl.* ciliary nerves (*Anat.*). —pflanze, *f.* capillary plant. —putz, *m.* head-dress, coiffure; hair ornament. —röhrchen, *n.* capillary tube. —ſalbe, *f.* pomatum. —ſchaber, *m.* tanner's scraping knife. —schaf, *m.* Guinea sheep. —scharf, *adj. & adv.* very fine, very sharp *or* subtile. —scheitel, *m.* crown of the head; parting of the hair. —schleife, *f.* ribbon, bow for the hair; braid of hair. —schmuck, *m.* ornament for the hair. —schneide=kabinet, *n.* hair-dresser's room, toilet saloon. —schopf, *m.* tuft of hair. —schuppen, *pl.* scurf. —schwarte, *f.* pericranium. —schwefel, *m.* native sulphur in filaments. —schweif, *m.* tail of a comet. —seide, *f.* the single threads of the cocoons. —seil, *n.* hair cord; seton (*Surg.*). —silber, *n.* virgin silver in filaments. —stern, *m.* comet. —strang, *m. see* —seil. —sträu=bend, *adj.* bristling the hair, atrocious, shocking. —strich, *m.* hair-stroke, up stroke (*in writing*). —tour, *f.* false hair. —tragend, *adj.* capillary (*Bot.*). —tuch, *n.* mohair; hair-cloth; canvas (*for wool-work, etc.*); coarse stuff for straining, *etc.*; peignoir. —weide, *f.* osier. —wickel, *m.* curl-paper. —wulst, *f.* hair-pad; rolled hair. —wurzel, *f.* root of the hair. —zange, *f.* tweezers. —zitz, *m.* half-chintz (*Manuf.*). —zopf, *m.* cue, pigtail. —zottig, *adj.* shaggy.

Haa'ren, *v.* I. *r. & n.* (*aux.* h.) to lose hair; to shed hair. II. *a.* to scrape off the hair (*obs.*).

Hab—e, *f.* property, goods, possessions, fortune; handle, hold; —' und Gut, goods and chattels, all one's property; fahrende —e, movables; liegende—e, immovable property, immovables.

Ha'ben, I. *ir.v.a.* to have; to possess; to hold (*a sentiment, etc.*); to bear (*a name*); to ail; to be obliged, to feel the necessity of; to contain; an sich (*dat.*) —, to have (*faults; a disease, etc.*), to smack of; er hat das so an sich, that is just his manner; wo — Sie das her? where have you picked that up? where did you get that from? etwas am Griff —, to know by the touch *or* by constant practice; am Schnürchen —, to have at one's finger-ends; auf sich —, zu sagen —, zu bedeuten, to be of consequence, to signify; es hat sich was! yes, indeed! true indeed! (*coll.*); sie dankte ihm. Es hat sich nichts zu danken! she thanked him. No reason for giving thanks! (*coll.*); es hat nichts auf sich! never mind! no matter! it does not signify! — Sie etwas dawider? have you anything to say against? wenn Sie nichts dagegen —, so komme ich auch, if you do not object, I will come too; er hat viel von seinem Vater, he resembles his father in many points; jetzt habe ich Sie! now I have caught you! auf diesen Menschen hat er's, it is to this man he objects, for this man he has a dislike; bei sich —, to have about *or* with one; zu — in allen Buchhandlungen, to be had at all booksellers; hinter sich —, to have done with, be past *or* through; to be backed up by, to have at one's disposal; was habe ich davon? what do I get by it? vor sich —, to have still to do, to be in sight of; wen meinst du vor dir zu —? whom do you think you are speaking to? Geld zu gut —, to have a balance in one's favour; zum besten —, to make a fool of, mock; zum Freunde —, to have for a friend; es ist nicht zu —, it is not to be had; Aussicht — auf, to command a view of; to have expectations of; Anwendung — auf, to bear application to, to apply to; hab Acht! take care! ich habe nichts dagegen, I have no objection to it; habt Dank! thanks! I thank you! wir — nichts als Undank davon, we get nothing but ingratitude for our pains; ein Datum —, to bear a date; Durst —, to be thirsty; Eile —, to be in a hurry; to admit of no delay; es hat keine Eile, Gefahr oder Not, there is no hurry, danger, or need; fertig —, to have finished; gern —, to like, to be fond of; er hat es gut, he has a fine time, a pleasant life of it; lieb —, to love; habe Mut! take courage! pluck up courage! Nachsicht —, to be indulgent, to make allowance for; nötig —, to need; es hat seine Richtigkeit, it is all right, quite correct; Recht (Unrecht) —, to be right (wrong); ein hab' ich ist besser als zehn hätt' ich, a bird in the hand is worth two in the bush (*prov.*); den Schaden —, to bear the cost, sustain damage; wer hat (die) Schuld? who is to blame? statt —, to take place; es nicht für ungut —, not to take amiss; Sie — die Wahl, take your choice, you have the right to choose: es hat gute Wege, there is no hurry about it, no need to be anxious, it is all right; er will es (*old gen.*) nicht Wort —, he will not own it; es (*old gen.*) hat mich Wunder, I wonder at it (*obs.*); was hat er? what ails him? what is the matter with him? den Mann hat's, he is deeply in love (*coll.*); — wollen, to wish for; was will er —? what does he want (order)? ich will ihn damit nicht geschimpft —, I don't wish to insult him by saying so; ausdrücklich — wollen, to be positive about. *Used as aux.* = to have; er hätte es thun können, he might have done it; er konnte es nicht umgangen —, he could not have avoided it. II. *ir.v.r.* to behave; sich darum —, to grieve for a th.; habe dich doch nicht so! do not make such a fuss! do not be so foolish (*coll.*). III. *subst. n.* credit; creditors (C.L.); having; Soll und —, debit and credit.

Ha'ber, *m.* (*dial.*) = Hafer, *m.* —feld=trei=ben, *n.* (kind of) popular lynch justice practised at night by Bavarian peasants. —feld=treiber, *m.* one taking part in this popular justice. —mus, *n.* oatmeal mush. —stroh, *n.* oat-straw.

Hab—haft, *adj.* possessed; einer Sache —haft werden, to get hold of, to take possession of, to seize, take a thing. —schaft, *f.*, —seligkeit, *f.* all that a person has, property, fortune, effects; kit (*Mil.*). —selig, *adj.* wealthy (*prov.*). *Comp.* —e=dank, *m.* thanks (*obs.*). —e=nichts, *m.* a penniless fellow (*colloq.*); Herr von —enichts, Sir Lackland, Mr. Penniless. —e=recht, *m.* arguer, dogmatist, dogmatical person. —gier, *f.*, —sucht, *f.* covetousness, avarice, greediness. —gierig, —süchtig, *adj.* avaricious, covetous, greedy.

Ha'bicht, *m.* (—s, *pl.* —e) hawk. *Comp.* —s=fang, *m.* hawk-catching; claw *or* pounce of a hawk. —s=inseln, *pl.* the Azores. —s=nase, *f.* hooked aquiline nose, Roman nose.

Habilit—atio'n, *f.* formal admission of an academical lecturer into the faculty to which he desires to attach himself (*after he has obtained the 'venia legendi'*). —ations=schrift, *f.* probationary treatise embodying the results of original research that is submitted by a candidate for a University teachership to the faculty with which he wishes to attach himself in order to obtain the 'venia legendi' and to give lectures as a recognized Privatdozent at the University. —ie'ren, *v.r.* to acquire the right of giving lectures at universities; er hat sich an der Universität Berlin *or* in Berlin —iert, he has been recognized as a teacher *or* lecturer at Berlin University.

Ha'chel, *f.* (*pl.* —n) awn; short cloak (*obs.*).

Hack, *m.* (—es, *pl.* —e) hack, stroke (*with an axe or any cutting instrument*); — und Mack, tag, rag and bob-tail. —e, *f.* (*pl.* —en) hatchet; pickaxe; mattock, hoe.

Ha'cke, *f.* (*pl.* —n) heel (*of a shoe*); afterpiece, shoulder, heel (*Naut.*). —n, *m.* (—ns, *pl.* —n) heel (*of a shoe*); sich (*dat.*) die —n nach einer Sache ablaufen, to run to many places for a thing (*coll.*). *Comp.* —n=leder, *n.* heel-piece.

Ha'ck—en, *v.a.* to chop, hash, mince, hack;

to hoe, grub up; to cleave (*wood*); to pick, peck up. —er, *m.* (—ers, *pl.* —er) chopper. *Comp.* —axt, *f.* chopping-axe. —balken, *m.* taffrail; transom (*Naut.*). —bank, *f.*, —block, *m.* chopping-block. —beil, *n.* chopper. —bord, *n.* taffrail (*Naut.*). —(e)=brett, *n.* chopping-board; dulcimer; piano (*sl.*). —fleisch, *n.* mince meat.

Hä'ck—erling, *m.* (—erlings) chopped straw. —se, *f.* (*pl.* —sen) hock, hamstring. —sel, *n.* (—sels) chopped straw; anything chopped fine. *Comp.* —erlings=maschine, *f.* chaff-cutting engine *or* machine. —erlings=schneider, *m.* straw *or* chaff cutter.

Hack'schen, *v.a.* to talk indecently, use foul language (*coll.*).

Häck'sen, *v.a.* to hamstring.

Ha'del, *f.* (*pl.* —n) bunch of ears of corn. *Comp.* —gras, *n.* panic grass (*Bot.*).

[1]**Ha'der**, *m.* (—s, *pl.* —n) rag, tatter (*dial.*). *Comp.* —lade, *f.* rag-chest. —lump, *m.* rag-man; tatterdemalion. —lumpen, *pl.* rags. —schneider, *m.* rag-cutting machine.

[2]**Ha'der**, *m.* (—s) quarrel, brawl, dispute, strife. —ei', *f.* constant wrangling. —er (—ers, *pl.* —er) wrangler, brawler. *Comp.* —geist, *m.* spirit of contention. —sucht, *f.* quarrelsome disposition. —süchtig, *adj.* quarrelsome.

Ha'dern, *v.n.* (*aux.* h.) to wrangle, strive, quarrel, squabble, dispute.

Ha'fen, *m.* (—s, *pl.* Häfen) haven, port, harbour; refuge; earthen vessel, pot (*dial.*); einen — anthun, to make a port (*Naut.*); jeder — findet seinen Deckel, no pot is so ugly as not to find a cover (*prov.*). *Comp.* —abgabe, *f.* harbour dues. —anker, *m.* moorings. —arbeiter, *m.* longshoreman. —baum, *m.* harbour-bar. —brücke, *f.* pier, mole. —damm, *m.* pier, jetty, breakwater. —gäste, *pl.* foreign vessels in a port. —gatt, *n.* harbour-mouth. —gebühr, *f.*, —geld, *n.* port-dues. —kette, *f.* boom chain. —lotse, *m.* harbour-pilot. —räumer, *m.* dredging machine. —sperre, *f.* blockade, closing of a harbour, embargo. —stadt, *f.* sea-port town. —spesen, *pl.*, —zoll, *m.* port-dues.

Ha'fer, *m.* (—s) oats; der — sticht ihn, he grows saucy, good luck has spoilt him. *Comp.* —artig, *adj.* avenaceous. —bau, *m.* growing of oats. —brei, *m.* oatmeal porridge. —brot, *n.* oat-cake. —grütze, *f.* groats; englische —grütze, Quaker oats. —kasten, *m.*, —kiste, *f.* oat-bin. —mus, *n.* oatmeal mush. —saat, *f.* oats-sowing; oat-crop. —sack, *m.* sack for oats; nose-bag. —schleim, *m.* water-gruel. —spreu, *f.* oat-chaff. —stroh, *n.* oat-straw; grob wie —stroh, very rude. —suppe, *f.* oatmeal soup. —zins, *m.* avenage, rent paid in oats.

Haff, *n.* (—(e)s, *pl.* —s *and* —e) gulf, bay, inland sea. *Comp.* —deich, *m.* dike on the sea-shore.

Haf'ner, *m.* (—s, *pl.* —) potter (*dial.*).

Haft, I. *m.* (—es, *pl.* —e) hold, keeping hold, firmness; rivet, clasp, brace; crotchet. II. *f.* (*pl.* —en) custody; prison; arrest; imprisonment; zur — bringen, to put under arrest; (aus) der — entlassen, to discharge from custody; in enger —, in close custody. III. *m.* & *n.* (—es, *pl.* —e) day-fly. IV. *suff.* (*second part of comp.* =) possessing; causing; giving; like. —bar, *adj.* & *adv.* responsible, bound. *Comp.* —befehl, —brief, *m.* warrant of arrest. —dauer, *f.* term of imprisonment. —geld, *n.* earnest; retaining-fee. —pflicht, *f.* liability, responsibility; solidare —pflicht, solidarity; mit beschränkter —pflicht, limited (liability). —pflicht=gesetz, *n.* employers' liability act.

Haf't—en, *v.r.* (*aux.* h.) to cling to; to cleave, adhere to; to remain; to be fixed; —en für, to go bail for, to bear the blame *or* loss; to be responsible for; Schulden —en auf dem Gute, the estate is encumbered *or* mortgaged; es —et ein Verdacht auf ihm, suspicion rests on him; es —et nichts an ihm, bei ihm, nothing affects him, he retains, remembers nothing. —ung, *f.* security, bail; mit beschränkter —ung, limited (liability) (*C.L.*).

Hag, *m.* (—es, *pl.* —e) hedge, fence; place fenced in; bush; coppice, grove; grass-plot; meadow. *Comp.* —apfel, *m.* crab-apple. —e=buche, *f.* hornbeam, yoke-elm. —e=butte, *f.* hip, haw. —e=dorn, *m.* hawthorn. —e=drüsen, *pl.* king's evil. —eiche, *f.* holm-oak. —e=rose, *f.* dog-rose. —e=stolz, *m.* (—estolzes *and* —estolzen, *pl.* —estolzen) (old) bachelor. —messer, *n.* hedge-bill, bill-hook.

Ha'gard, Ha'gart, *m.* (—s, *pl.* —e), **Ha'ger=falk**, *m.* haggard, harrower.

Ha'gel, *m.* (—s) hail; small shot; grape *or* case shot; shower (*of stones, etc.*); Jan—, the mob. *Comp.* —dicht, *adj.*, thick as hail. —gans, *f.* snowgoose. —gießerei, *f.* shot-foundry. —korn, *n.* hail-stone; stye (*in the eye*). —kugel, *f.* grape shot. —schaden, *m.* damage done by hail. —sicher, *adj.* hail proof. —versicherung, *f.* insurance against loss by hail, insurance against damage done by hail. —wetter, *n.* hail storm.

Ha'geln, *v.n. imp.* to hail.

Ha'ger, *adj.* haggard; thin, lean, slender, lank, meagre. —keit, *f.* leanness, meagreness, slenderness. —n, *v.n.* (*aux.* h.) to grow lean.

Haha', I. *interj.* ha-ha! aha! II. *n.* ha ha!

Hahaha', *interj.* tehee!

Hahe', *interj.* ware there! ware chase! (*to hounds*).

Hä'her, *m.* (—s, *pl.* —) jay.

Hahn, *m.* (—(e)s, *pl.* Häh'ne, *obs.* Hah'nen; *dim.* Hähn'chen, cockerel) cock; stop-cock; cock (*on a gun, etc.*); der — kräht, the cock crows; es wird kein — danach krähen, nobody will care anything about it *or* a brass farthing for it, nobody will take any notice of it; der — im Korbe sein, to be cock of the walk; ein tüchtiger —, ein Haupt —, a jolly student (*coll.*); junge Hähne, young madcaps (*coll.*); einem den roten — aufs Dach setzen, to set fire to a man's house; den — am Gewehr spannen, to cock a gun. —rei, *m.* (—reis, *pl.* —reie) cuckold. *Comp.* —en=balken, *m.* roost; collar-beam, beam at the gable end of the house. —en=bart, *m.* wattles. —en=fuß, *m.* ranunculus (*Bot.*). —en=geschrei, *n.* cock-crowing; cock-crow. —en=kamm, *m.* cock's comb; yellow rattle (*Bot.*); great scallop (*Mollusc.*). —en=krat, —en=ruf, —en=schrei, *m.* cock-crowing. —en=plan, *m.* cock-pit. —en=schlagen, *n.* Aunt Sally (*game*), cock-shy (*coll.*). —en=tritt, *m.* cock's tread; treadle; string-halt (*Vet.*); cock-pimpernel. —schlüssel, *m.* key of a stop-cock.

Hai, (—fisch,) *m.* (—s, *pl.* —e) shark; Scharen von —fischen, shoals of sharks. *Comp.* —roche, *m.* Mediterranean ray.

Hai'de, *f.* (*pl.* —n) heath, *see* Heide.

[1]**Hain**, *m.* (—es, *pl.* —e) grove, wood, thicket. *Comp.* —ampfer, *m.* woodsorrel. —buche, *f.* hornbeam. —bund, *m.* society of young poets at the University of Göttingen in the seventies of the eighteenth century who wrote in a patriotic and popular style.

[2]**Hain**, *see* Hein.

Häk'—chen, *n.* (—chens, *pl.* —chen) little hook, crochet; apostrophe; was ein —chen werden will krümmt sich beizeiten, a thorn comes into the world point foremost (*see under* Haken). —elei', *f.* crochet-work; chaffing, teasing, taunting, fault-finding, quarrel(ling). —(e)lig, *adj.* & *adv.* like a hook; hooked; deli cate; captious, critical. *Comp.* **—el=arbeit,** *f.* crochet-work. **—el=haken,** *m.* **—el=nadel,** *f.* crochet-needle; tambour-needle. **—el=kasten,** *m.* crochet case. **—el=stahl,** *m.* turner's chisel.

Hä'keln, *v.* I. *a.* to catch with a hook; to crochet. II. *r.* to attach oneself to, cling, stick to; to tease, to chaff; to censure.

Ha'k—en, I. *m.* (**—ens,** *pl.* **—en**) hook, clasp, clamp; grappling-iron; clasper; difficulty; **die Sache hat einen —en,** there is a but in the matter, there is a hitch in the business; **was ein —en werden will, krümmt sich beizeiten,** as the twig is bent the tree is inclined (*see under* **Häkchen**); **—en schlagen,** to double (*as hares*). II. *v.a.* to hook; to grapple; **sich —en an,** to catch in. III. *v.n. & imp.;* **da —t es,** there 's the rub. **—icht,** *adj. & adv.* like a hook (*obs.*). **—ig,** *adj. & adv.* hooked. **—lig,** *see* **Häkelig.** *Comp.* **—en=band,** *n.* hinge-plate. **—en=blatt, —en=blech,** *n.* staple, clasp. **—en=bohrer,** *m.* wimble. **—en=büchse,** *f.* arquebuse. **—en=förmig,** *adj.* hooked, hook-like, uncinate. **—en=haue,** *f.* mattock. **—en=nagel,** *m.* tenter-hook. **—en=rad,** *n.* swing wheel. **—en=schlüssel,** *m.* picklock. **—en=schütze,** *m.* arquebusier. **—en=spieß,** *m.* harpoon. **—en=zahn,** *m.* tusk; corner-tooth. **—en=zapfen,** *m.* tenon.

Hala'li, *int. & n.* harkee, mort, kill, death (*fox hunting*) (*Sport.*). **—blasen,** to sound a mort.

Halb, I. *adj.* half; **der —e Ton,** semitone; **— so viel,** half as much; **— französisch,** *n.* mongrel French; **eine —e Stunde,** half an hour; **— zehn,** half past nine; **um — elf Uhr, um zehn (und) ein — Uhr,** at half past ten; **es schlägt —,** the half hour strikes; **die Uhr schlägt voll und —,** the clock strikes the (full) hours and half hours; **fünfte — Ellen,** four ells and a half; **mit —em Ohre zuhören,** to listen with one ear, to listen inattentively; **zum —en Preise,** at half the price, (at) half-price; **mit —er Stimme,** in an undertone; mezza voce (*Mus.*). II. *adv.* by halves, half; **— und —,** so so, middling; almost, tolerably; **— so viel,** half as much; **noch — mal so viel,** half as much again; **noch — (ein)mal so groß,** half as big again; **weder — noch ganz,** neither one thing nor another. III. *n.* half; *as a suffix* = account, reason, because [*as* **deshalb,** on this, that account] *or* = side [*as* **außer—,** outside]. IV. *pref.* (*in comp.*) *gen'lly* = semi, demi, half. **—e(s),** *n.* half, moiety. **—en,** I. *v.a.* to halve, bisect (*obs.*). II. (**—er**), *prep.* (*with preceding gen.*) for, on account of, on behalf of, because of, for the sake of. **—heit,** *f.* incompleteness; lukewarmness; supineness; superficiality. **—ling,** *m.* (**—lings,** *pl.* **—linge**) half-breed, hybrid, mongrel. *Comp.* **—amtlich,** *adj.* semi-official. **—art,** *f.* sub-species. **—atlas,** *m.* satinet. **—baß,** *m.* barytone. **—befahren; —befahrenes Volk,** *n.* common (*i.e. not able*) seamen. **—bier,** *n.* small beer. **—bild,** *n.* half length portrait, bust. **—bildung,** *f.* superficial culture; semi-civilization, smattering of civilization. **—bruder,** *m.* half-brother. **—bürtig,** *adj.* of the half blood. **—dach,** *n.* shed-roof. **—decker, —deckflügler,** *pl.* hemiptera (*Ent.*). **—dunkel,** *n.* dusk, twilight. **—erhaben,** *adj.* in basso-relievo. **—franzband,** *m.* half-leather binding. **—gamaschen,** *pl.* short gaiters. **—gar,** *adj.* underdone. **—gelehrte(r),** *m.* smatterer, superficial scholar. **—geschoß,** *n.* entresol. **—gesicht,** *n.* profile. **—getrennt,** *adj.* androgynous. **—gott,** *m.* demigod. **—gut,** *n.* alloy of equal parts of tin and lead. **—hemd,** *n.* front. **—hose,** *f.* knickerbockers; bloomers (*of women*). **—insel,** *f.* peninsula. **—insel=förmig,** *adj.* peninsular. **—jährig,** *adj.*, lasting six months; six months old. **—jährlich,** *adj.* occurring every six months, half-yearly. **—kreis,** *m.* semi-circle **—kreis=förmig,** *adj.*, semicircular. **—kugel,** *f.* hemisphere. **—laut,** *adj. & adv.* in an undertone. **—leder,** *n.;* **—leder mit Goldschnitt,** half calf with gilt edges. **—leinen=band,** *m.* (bound in) half cloth. **—mann,** *n.* demi-man; eunuch; small farmer. **—maske,** *f.* half-mask, low mask; loup. **—mensch,** *m.* demi-man; centaur; brute. **—messer,** *m.* radius. **—monatsschrift,** *f.* fortnightly (review *or* magazine). **—mond,** *m.* crescent, half-moon. **—mond=förmig,** *adj.* crescent-shaped. **—mond=meißel,** *m.* gouge. **—mutter,** *f.* stepmother. **—nächtig,** *adj.;* **—nächtige Lampen,** lamps that burn till about midnight. **—pacht,** *f.* renting of a farm for half of the produce. **—part,** *m.* halves; **auf —part eintreten,** to go halves. **—pferd,** *n.* centaur; meadow-sorrel. **—rund,** *adj.* semi-circular. **—säure,** *f.* oxide. **—schatten,** *m.* mezzo-tinto. **—scheid,** *f.* moiety. **—schlag,** *m.* mongrel, mixed breed. **—schreitig,** *adj.* chromatic (*Mus.*). **—schuh,** *m.* slipper. **—schürig,** *adj.* of second shearing; premature, imperfect; inferior; **—schüriges Lob,** half-hearted praise. **—schürigkeit,** *f.* inferiority; half-heartedness. **—seite,** *f.* column (*Typ.*). **—silber,** *n.* platina. **—sopran,** *m.* mezzo-soprano. **—stämmig,** *adj.* half grown. **—stiefel,** *m.* laced boot; short boot. **—strumpf,** *m.* sock. **—täglich,** *adj.* occurring twice a day; lasting twelve hours. **—tinte,** *f.* mezzo-tinto. **—trauer,** *f.* half-mourning. **—uniform,** *f.* undress-uniform. **—verdeck,** *n.* quarter-deck. **—vers,** *m.* half-line, hemistich. **—vokal,** *m.* semi-vowel. **—weg** (*poet.*), **—wegs,** *adv.* half way; tolerably (*coll.*). **—welt,** *f.* demi-monde. **—wisserei,** *f.* superficial knowledge. **—zirkel,** *m.* semi-circle.

Halbie'r—en, *v.a.* to cut in halves, to halve, bisect. **—t,** bisected (*of postage stamps*). **—ung,** *f.* bisection.

Hal'de, *f.* (*pl.* **—n**), slope, declivity; hill-side; hillock; dead heap, pit heap, cinder tip.

Half, *imperf. ind. of* **helfen.**

Häl'fte, *f.* (*pl.* **—n**) half, moiety; middle; **bessere —,** better half, wife; **um die — teurer,** half as dear again.

Half'ter, *f.* (*pl.* **—n**), *sometimes m. & n.* (**—s,** *pl.* **—**) halter; frontlet; T bandage; gallows (*vulg.*); holster. *Comp.* **—band,** *n.*, **—leine,** *f.* halter rope. **—geld,** *n.*, groom's gratuity at the purchase of a horse.

Half'tern, *v.a.* to put on the halter.

Hall, *m.* (**—s,** *pl.* **—e**) sound, resonance.

Hal'l—e, *f.* (*pl.* **—en**) hall, great room; public room; common hall; gallery; portico, vestibule, porch; saltwork-buildings; market; bazaar; large shop; **Trink —e,** pump-room. *Comp.* **—leute** (*called* **Hallo'ren,** *in Halle on the Saale*), *pl.* workmen in saltworks.

Hal'len, *v.n.* (*aux.* **h.**) to sound, resound, clang.

Hal'lig, *f.* (*pl.* **—en**) small island not protected by dikes (*especially in the North Sea*).

Halm, *m.* (**—(e)s,** *pl.* **—e**) blade; stalk; **Getreide auf dem —,** green corn; standing corn, crop. **—en,** *v.n.* (*aux.* **h.**) to get stalks. **—ig,** *adj.* stalky. *Comp.* **—früchte,** *pl.* cerealia. **—knoten,** *m.* joint of a stalk. **—lese,** *f.* gleaning. **—pfeife,** *f.* oaten-pipe.

Hälm'chen, *n.* (**—s,** *pl.* **—**) a little stalk; **das — ziehen,** to draw lots with (long and short) stalks (*children's play*).

Hals, *m.* (**—(s)es,** *pl.* **Häl'se**) neck; throat; **etwas auf dem —e haben,** to be troubled, encumbered, plagued with a thing; **sich** (*dat.*) **auf den — laden,** to bring upon oneself; **auf**

dem —e sitzen, to importune; to be a burden to one; das wächst mir aus dem —e, I am sick of that; aus vollem —e, heartily, with all one's might; aus vollem —e schreien, to scream at the top of one's voice; bleiben Sie mir damit vom —, leave me alone with that; einem um den — fallen, to fall on a person's neck, to embrace and kiss a person; sich (*dat.*) vom —e schaffen, to get rid of; er muß — geben, he must give an account *or* answer; einem über den — kommen, to surprise one; über — und Kopf, headlong; — über Kopf, head over heels; precipitately; bis an den —, over head and ears, up to the eyes; das geht ihm an den —, that may cost him his head; einen langen — machen, to crane the neck; den — brechen, to break one's neck; einem den — brechen, to ruin a p.; to undo a man; einer Flasche den — brechen, to crack a bottle; sich (*dat.*) etwas an den — reden, to bring s.th. upon oneself by inconsiderate talk; sich (*dat.*) die Schwindsucht an den — ärgern, to vex oneself into consumption; böser —, sore throat; Geiz—, miser; Schwarten—, tramp (*obs.*). —(s)ig, *suff.* (*in comp.* =) having a neck. *Comp.* —abschneider, *m.* cutthroat, usurer. —ader, *f.* jugular vein. —band, *n.* collar; necklace. —bein, *n.* collarbone. —binde, *f.* cravat; neck-tie, scarf. —bräune, *f.* quinsy. —brechen, *n.* break-neck (exploit). —brechend, *adj.* break-neck, dangerous, perilous. —brüchig, capital (*crime*). —dreher, *m.* wry-neck. —eisen, *n.* iron collar, pillory. —entzündung, *f.* inflammation of the throat. —gehänge, *n.* neck-chain *or* ornament. —gericht, *n.* criminal court; gallows. —gerichts=ordnung, *f.* criminal constitution *or* code (*Law*). —geschmeide, *n.* neck-ornaments. —geschwür, *n.* abscess in the neck *or* throat; sore throat. —haar, *n.* mane. —harnisch, *m.* gorget. —joch, *n.* neck-yoke. —kappe, *f.* cowl. —kette, *f.* chain for the neck. —kragen, *m.* cape, collar. —krause, *f.* frill, ruff (*for the neck*). —pulsader, *f.* carotid artery. —recht, *n.* power over life and death. —ring, *m.* scarf ring; collar; eccentric ring, eccentric hoop. —röhre, *f.* wind-pipe. —sache, *f.* matter of life and death; hanging matter. —schild, *n.* prothorax (*Ent.*). —schleife, *f.* bow of a necktie. —schlinge, *f.* noose. —schloß, *n.*, —schnalle, *f.* stock-buckle. —schmuck, *m.* necklace. —schwindsucht, *f.* laryngophthisis. —starrig, *adj.* stiff-necked, stubborn, obstinate, headstrong. —starrigkeit, *f.* obstinacy, stubbornness. —starrkrampf, *m.* tetanus. —stimme, *f.* falsetto. —strafe, *f.* capital punishment. —sucht, *f.* bronchitis. —tuch, *n.* neck-cloth, neckerchief, wrap for the neck, comforter, muffler. —verbrechen, *n.* capital crime. —weh, *n.* sore throat. —wirbel, *m.* cervical vertebra.

Hal'se, *f.* (*pl.* —n) dog-collar (*hunt.*); tack (*of a sail*); hawser; die —n aufstechen, to ease the tacks; die —n umholen, to tack about, to jib.

Hal'sen, *v.a.* to fall on a p.'s neck, embrace (*obs.*).

Halt, I. *m.* (—(e)s, *pl.* —e) hold, holding, footing; support; purchase; holdfast; stop, halt; firmness; Mensch ohne inneren —, person wanting in steadiness of character *or* purpose. II. *int.* halt! hold! stop! III. *adv. & part.* (= ich halte) (I) hold, (I) think, in (my) opinion (*dial.*); in my opinion, I think; er wird — nicht kommen, I don't think he will come. —bar, *adj. & adv.* tenable, defensible; strong; durable; valid. —barkeit, *f.* tenableness, defensibility; durability, firmness, strength; last, wear; validity. *Comp.* —los, *adj.* without support, unsteady, straggling; rootless; vain; unprincipled. —losigkeit, *f.* instability, unsteadiness; emptiness; want of principle(s).

Hal't—en, *ir.v.a.* to hold; to keep; to retain; to support, maintain; to detain, keep back; to constrain; to contain, include; to observe, perform, celebrate; to deliver, perform; to give; to endure, hold out against; to think; to deem, consider; to treat, use; to value; rechts (links) —en! keep to the right (left); Frieden —en, to keep peace; Freundschaft —en, to live on friendly terms; einen frei —en, to pay a p.'s expenses, to stand s.o. a treat; einen schadlos —en, to indemnify a p.; sich schadlos —en, to pay oneself; einen bei seinem Worte —en, to keep one to his word; Hochzeit —en, to celebrate one's marriage; Mahlzeit —en, to dine, sup, *etc.*; eine Zeitung —en, to take in a newspaper; auf eine S. —en, to insist upon a thing, lay stress upon it; auf (gute) Ordnung —en, to insist on (good) order being kept; to maintain (good) order, to keep up discipline; er hält auf frische Luft, he is particular about good air; große Stücke auf einen —en, to think highly, make much of one; —en für, to look upon as, consider, think, take to be; ich —e dafür, (daß), I hold (that); —en gegen, to hold against, to contrast with; ich —e ihm das zugute, I excuse that in him; das Abendmahl —en, to administer the sacrament; Schule —en, to give a lesson (at a school); Vorlesungen —en, to deliver, *or* give, lectures; eine Rede —en, to make *or* deliver a speech, to speak (*in public*); eine Note —en, to dwell on, sustain a note; Stich —en, to stand the test; es mit einem —en, to side with a p.; ich —e es mit dem Wein! give me the wine! reinen Mund —en, not to divulge; Wasser —en, to be water-tight; ein Kind über die Taufe —en, to stand sponsor to a child; im Zaume —en, to keep a tight hand on; Schritt —en, to keep pace, walk in step; Stimmung —en, to keep in tune (*of pianos*); Inventur —en, to take stock; einem ein Bein —en, to trip one up; so will ich es gehalten wissen, I will have it so; ich pflege es so zu —en, so damit zu —en, such is my way; ich —e mir zwei Hunde, I keep two dogs; —en Sie das, wie Sie wollen, please yourself (about that); sich (*dat.*) Wagen und Pferde —en, to keep one's (own) carriage; Tinte und Papier muß man sich selbst —en, one must supply one's own ink and paper. II. *n.* (*aux.* h.) to stop, halt; to hold out, endure, stand firm; to bear (*of ice*); to insist on; —en an, to stick, *or* cleave, to; an sich —en, to restrain oneself; to hold one's breath; auf Träume —en, to believe in dreams; auf eine S. —en, to watch over, see to a thing; auf seine Ehre —en, to be jealous of one's honour; ich —e nicht viel von ihm, I do not think much of him; er hält viel von Ihnen, he thinks highly of you; es hält schwer, it is difficult; er hält es mit den Liberalen, he sides with the Liberals; dicht —en, to be watertight; —en Sie an! lassen Sie —en! stop (the carriage)! III. *r.* to hold out; to maintain oneself, to keep (*one's position, etc.*); to behave; to last, keep good; to observe a strict diet; to take (*good or bad*) care of one's health; sich im Preise —en, to remain steady; to hold oneself; das Wetter hält sich, the weather continues fair (*or* bad); die Festung hält sich, the fortress holds out; sich —en an (*acc.*), to adhere to, depend upon, betake oneself to; ich werde mich deswegen an Sie —en, I shall look to you for it; sich bereit —en, to hold oneself in readiness; sich reinlich —en, to keep oneself clean; sich krumm —en, to stoop; sich links —en, to keep to the left; sich —en an, zu, to keep near, to attach oneself to; sich zu Hause —en, to stay indoors, to keep at home; gehalten, bound, obliged, reserved, sustained, supported, sober, staid, calm. —er, *m.* (—ers, *pl.* —er) holder; keeper; observer; hold, support; reservoir; receptacle; penholder (*coll.*). —ig, *adj.* yielding, rich (*of ore*); *as a suffix* (*in compounds* =) holding, containing; *e.g.* erz—ig, containing ore. —ung, *f.* holding; keeping; maintenance; support, prop; deportment, carriage; mien; fulfilling; delivery (*of speeches, etc.*); session, holding of a session; harmony (*of colour, etc.*); Charakter ohne sittliche —ung, unstable character; mit —ung, restraining oneself, with reservation, composedly; —ung der Börse, state of 'Change, feeling on 'Change; —ung einer Zeitung, politics *or* principles of a paper. *Comp.* —nagel, *m.* linch-pin. —(e)platz, *m.*, —(e)stelle, *f.* halting-place, resting place; (small) station; —(e)stelle für Droschken, cab-stand. —signal, *n.* block-signal.

Hal'ter, *adv. & part. dial.* = Halt, III.

Häl'ter, *m.* (—s, *pl.* —) holder; receptacle, reservoir.

Hältst, Hält, *2 & 3 ps. sing. pres. ind. of* halten.

Halun'ke, *m.* (—n, *pl.* —n) rascal, scamp.

Hämati't, *m.* (—s, *pl.* —e) bloodstone.

Ha'men, I. *m.* (—s) fishing-hook; draw-net. II. *v.a.* to net.

Hä'misch, *adj.* malicious, mischievous; spiteful; —es Wesen, malice, spitefulness; —es Lachen, sardonic laugh; —e Freude, malignant joy.

Häm'ling, *m.* (—s, —e) eunuch.

Hamm, *m.* forest (*obs.*); bog, marsh (*obs.*).

Ham'mel, *m.* (—s, *pl.* Hämmel) wether; süßer —, duck, pet (*of a child*); um auf besagten — zurück zu kommen, to return to our subject (*coll.*). *Comp.* —bein, *n.*; einem beim —beine *or* bei seinen —beinen kriegen, to get hold of a person, to call a person to account (*sl.*). —braten, *m.* roast mutton. —fleisch, *n.* mutton. —keule, *f.* leg of mutton. —pelz, *m.* sheepskin coat. —rippchen, *pl.* mutton chops. —schlägel, *m.* leg of mutton. —sprung, *m.* division (*Parl.*).

Ham'meln, *v.a.* to geld lambs.

Ham'mer, *m.* (—s, *pl.* Hämmer) hammer; forge; knocker; bully; powerful man; hammer-headed shark; Karl der —, Charles Martel. *Comp.* —bahn, *f.* face of the hammer. —eisen, *n.* hammered iron, wrought iron. —herr, *m.* iron-master; owner of a foundry. —hütte, *f.* forge; iron-works. —schlag, *m.* stroke with a hammer; hammer-scales, scales, *or* chips, which fly from the iron in hammering. —schloß, *n.* percussion-lock. —schmied, *m.* blacksmith, forge-man; hammer-smith. —stiel, *m.* handle of a hammer. —werk, *n.* foundry, iron-works. —zeichen, *n.* blaze (*mark on trees*).

Häm'mer—bar, *adj.* malleable. —er, *m.* (—ers, *pl.* —er) hammerer. —lein, *n.*, —ling, *m.* clown; gnome; demon, devil; merry Andrew; Meister —lein, Meister —ling, Jack Ketch, hangman.

Häm'mern, *v.a. & n.* (*aux.* h.) to hammer.

Hämm'ling, *m.* *See* Hämling.

Hämorrhoi'd—en (—al'knoten), *pl.* hemorrhoids.

Ham'pelmann, *m.* jumping Jack, manikin, Punch; dunce, unreliable fellow.

Ham'ster, *m.* (—s, *pl.* —) hamster (*Zoöl.*).

Hand, *f.* (*pl.* Hän'de; *in some phrases* Han'den, *e.g.* abhanden, vorhanden) hand; paw (*of some beasts*); hand (*as measure of height*); handwriting; side, direction; source, origin; (*pl.*) workmen; die flache —, the palm of the hand; die hohle —, the palm of the hand; die — ballen, to clench the fist; ehrliche — geht durch alle Land', honesty is the best policy (*prov.*); tote —, mortmain; eine — wäscht die andere, one good turn deserves another (*prov.*); er ist stets mit der Antwort bei der —, he is always ready with an answer; ich habe es aus guter —, I have it on good authority; die letzte — an eine Sache legen, to give the finishing touch to a thing; — anlegen, to set to work; obere —, feudal lord; untere —, vassal; freie —, liberty of action, freedom; die — abziehen von, to abandon, withdraw aid from; sich die Hände geben, to shake hands; — und Fuß *or* Hände und Füße haben, to be to the purpose, to be well written *or* done; das hat weder — noch Fuß, that has neither head nor tail, there is neither rhyme nor reason in this (*prov.*); die Hände in den Schoß legen, to do nothing; an die linke —, zur linken — antrauen lassen, to contract a left-handed marriage; Ehe zur linken —, left-handed *or* morganatic(al) marriage; darauf gebe ich (dir) die —, I promise it; einem an die *or* zur — gehen, to give one a helping hand; einem Mittel zu einer Sache an die — geben, to put one in the way of doing a th.; einem auf die — sehen, to watch a p. closely; auf die — geben, to pay into one's hand, give earnest; auf den Händen tragen, to treat with great tenderness; es liegt auf der (flachen) —, it is very plain, obvious; auf eigene —, for oneself, at one's expense; aus der —, quickly, adroitly; aus freier —, spontaneously, voluntarily, by hand; aus (*or* von) der — in den Mund leben, to live from hand to mouth; aus zweiter — kaufen, to buy second hand; bei der —, at hand, in readiness; hinter der —, saved, laid past, subsequently; hinter der — sein, to be youngest player (*Cards*); schwer in der — liegen, to pull hard at the bit; in die — nehmen, to undertake (the direction *or* execution of); mit stürmender —, by storm, by assault; man kann es mit Händen greifen, it is grossly palpable; nach der — erziehen, to train, bring up according to one's own views; nach der — kaufen, to buy in the lump; nach der —, afterwards (*obs.*); über die — mit, on ill terms with; unter der —, privately; unter Händen haben, to have in hand; einem unter die Hände kommen, to get into a p.'s power; von der — gehen, to be easy; die Arbeit geht ihnen von der —, the work is nothing to them, they are quick at their work; vor der —, for the present, just now; meanwhile; vor die — nehmen, to take in hand, set to work; von guter —, on good authority; zur — sein, to be at hand, ready; seid zur —, bear a hand, be ready, make haste! einem etwas in die Hände spielen, to help a person to gain a thing; einem etwas aus den Händen spielen, to make a p. lose a thing. —el, *m. see* Handel, *with its deriv.'s and comp.'s.* —haft, *adj. & adv.* acting, actual, in the act. —lich, *adj. & adv.* easily managed, tractable; handy, wieldy; moderate. —lung, *f.* action, deed; performance, acting; act (*of a play*); transaction; business, trade, commerce; shop, warehouse; firm. *Comp.* —anlegung, *f.* setting to work; seizure (*Law*). —arbeit, *f.* manual labour; needle-work. —arbeiter, *m.* mechanic; workman; labourer. —arbeit-stickerei, *f.* hand-worked embroidery. —arbeits-unterricht, *m.* instruction in needle-work, in manual skill *or* in mechanics. —ärmel, *m.* wristband. —atlas, *m.* school-atlas. —aufheben, *n.* show of hands. —auflegen, *n.* consecration (*by laying on of hands*), imposition of hands. —aufzug, *m.* elevator by hand. **—ausgabe**, *f.* pocket-edition. **—ballen**, *m.* ball of the thumb. **—baum**, *m.* lever. **—becken**, *n.* wash-hand basin. **—beil**, *n.* hatchet. **—besatz**, *m.* wristband. **—blatt**, *n.* wristband; cuff; ruffle. **—bohrer**, *m.* gimlet. **—bibliothek**, *f.* select reference library. **—buch**, *n.* handbook, manual; compendium, vademecum; **—buch für Reisende**, travellers' guide; **—buch für Eisenbahnen**, Railway ABC.; **—buch für London**, London Guide; **—buch des feinen Tons**, code of etiquette; Don't; **—buch für stilistische Übungen**, manual of composition. **—decke**, *f.* small cover; saddle-cloth. **—eimer**, *m.* pail. **—eisen**, *n.* manacle, hand-cuff. **—exemplar**, *n.* copy in regular use, (*usually, in the case of scholars, containing manuscript additions*). **—fackel**, *f.* link, torch. **—fäustel**, *m.* miner's hammer. **—faß**, *n.* basin; pail. **—fertig**, *adj.* skilful with one's hands. **—fertigkeit**, *f.* manual skill; **Lehrer für —fertigkeit**, manual teacher. **—fertigkeits-unterricht**, *m.* instruction in manual practice. **—fesseln**, *pl.* hand-cuffs. **—fest**, *adj. & adv.* strong, sturdy, firm; binding; **einen —fest machen**, to take a p. into custody; **ein —festes Pferd**, a manageable horse; a horse well broken in. **—feste**, *f.* bond (*Law*). **—feuerwaffe**, *f.* portable fire-arm, gun, musket; **—feuerwaffen**, *pl.* hand-arms, small arms, musketry. **—flügler**, *pl.* Cheiroptera. **—förmig**, *adj.* hand-shaped. **—gebrauch**, *m.* daily use. **—geld**, *n.* earnest; bounty (*Mil.*); pocket-money; advance (*C. L.*). **—gelenk**, *n.* wrist. **—gemein**, *adv.* hand to hand; in close combat; at fisticuffs; **—gemein werden**, to come to close quarters. **—gemenge**, *n.* hand to hand fight, close fight; scrimmage, scuffle, affray. **—gepäck**, *n.* small *or* portable luggage. **—gewehr**, *n.* hand-gun, small gun; side-arm. **—greiflich**, *adj.* palpable, obvious. **—griff**, *m.* handle; grip, grasp; sleight of hand; knack; handrail. **—habe**, *f.* handle. **—haben**, *ir.v.a.* (*insep.*) to handle; to manage; to administer; to maintain; **gut zu —haben**, handy. **—habung**, *f.* handling; management; administration. **—karren**, *m.* hand-barrow, truck. **—käse**, *m.* small German cheese. **—kauf**, *m.* purchase in the lump; retail; **den —kauf lösen**, to take handsel. **—klapper**, *f.* castanet. **—korb**, *m.* work-basket; hand-basket. **—krause**, *f.* wrist-ruffle. **—künstig**, **—künstlich**, *adj. & adv.* mechanical. **—kurbel**, *f.* cranked handle. **—kuß**, *m.* kissing of the hand. **—langer**, *m.* handy-man, underworker, drudger, hack; helper, jobber. **—langer-dienst**, *m.* work of an understrapper; work of a literary hack; drudgery. **—lehen**, *n.* free, *or* hereditary, fief. **—leiter**, I. *m.* wrist-guide. II. *f.* small ladder, steps. **—leuchter**, *m.* (flat) bedroom, candle-stick. **—lexikon**, *n.* pocket *or* school-dictionary. **—lohn**, *m.* wages of manual labour. **—lungs-beflissene(r)**, **—lungs-diener**, *m.* (merchant's) clerk. **—lungs-genoß**, *m.* business-partner. **—lungs-gesetz**, *n.* mercantile law. **—lungs-grundsatz**, *m.* trade-principle. **—lungs-inhaber**, *m.* merchant. **—lungs-reisende(r)**, *m.* commercial traveller. **—lungs-spesen**, **—lungs-unkosten**, *pl.* business expenses. **—lungs-weise**, *f.* mode of dealing; way of acting. **—lungs-zeichen**, *n.* trade-mark. **—mehr**, *n.* majority (*ascertained by a show of hands*); **durch offnes —mehr gewählt**, elected by show of hands. **—münze**, *f.* small coin. **—nähmaschine**, *f.* sewing-machine worked by hand. **—papier**, *n.* hand-made paper. **—pauke**, *f.* tympan. **—pferd**, *n.* near horse in a team; led horse. **—quehle**, *f.* towel (*dial.*). **—ramme**, *f.* paving-ram. **—reichung**, *f.* charity; help, aid. **—schlag**, *m.* shaking hands (*as a pledge*); blow with the hand. **—schraube**, *f.* handscrew; handvice. **—schreiben**, *n.* autograph-letter; autograph. **—schrift**, *f.* (*abbrev.* **Hs.** manuscript, **Hss.** manuscripts); handwriting; signature; manuscript; bond. **—schriften-deutung**, *f.* graphology. **—schriften-kunde**, *f.* palæography. **—schriftlich**, *adj. & adv.* in manuscript; in (*one's own*) writing; in virtue of a note of hand. **—schuh**, *m.* glove. **—schuh-macher**, *m.* glover. **—schuldschein**, *m.* promissory note. **—seite**, *f.* near side (*in driving, etc.*). **—siegel**, *n.* signet. **—spake**, *f.* hand-spike (*Naut.*). **—spiel**, *n.* keys in an organ; hot-cockles (*game*). **—steuerung**, *f.* hand gear. **—streich**, *m.* coup de main, sudden attack, surprise; **der —streich auf die kleine Festung glückte**, the sudden attack on the small fortress was successful. **—stuhl**, *m.* hand-loom. **—tasten**, *pl.* finger-board (*Mus.*). **—trommel**, *f.* tambourine. **—tuch**, *n.* towel. **—tuch-drell**, *m.* towelling. **—umdrehen**, *n.*; **im —umdrehen**, in a moment. **—verkäufer**, *m.* retailer. **—veste**, *f.* signature (*obs.*). **—voll**, *f.* handful. **—vollweise**, *adv.* by, *or* in, handfuls. **—waffen**, *pl.* small arms. **—wagen**, *m.* hand-barrow. **—wahrsager**, *m.* chiromancer. **—wahrsagerei**, *f.* chiromancy. **—werk**, *n.* handicraft; trade; calling; employers' association; guild; **er ist seines —werks ein Schneider**, he is a tailor by trade; **ein —werk betreiben**, to follow a trade; **einem das —werk legen**, to forbid one to exercise his trade, to put a stop to a p.'s proceedings; to put a p. down; **einem ins —werk pfuschen**, to encroach upon a p.'s business, to compete with a p.; **sein —werk verstehen**, to understand one's business, to be up to one's work; **das —werk grüßen**, to visit the masters of one's trade, to seek work *or* relief (*said of travelling journeymen*); **das —werk halten**, to meet (*of a guild*); **—werk hat goldenen Boden**, trade is the mother of money (*prov.*). **—werker**, *m.* artisan; workman. **—werker-stand**, *m.* manual labouring class, artisans. **—werker-verein**, *m.* working men's club *or* association; trade-union. **—werks-älteste(r)**, *m.* president of a corporation, master of a guild. **—werks-bursche**, *m.* travelling artisan. **—werks-genoß**, *m.* fellow tradesman. **—werks-innung**, *f.* guild. **—werks-junge**, *m.* apprentice. **—werks-kunde**, **—werks-lehre**, *f.* technology. **—werks-leute**, *pl.* artisans, craftsmen, mechanics. **—werks-mäßig**, *adj. & adv.* mechanically, by rote, without thinking; according to trade rules; professionally. **—werks-meister**, *m.* master-mechanic. **—werks-zunft**, *f.* guild. **—wörterbuch**, *n.* school *or* pocket-dictionary. **—wurzel**, *f.* wrist. **—zeichen**, *n.* monogram; sign-manual. **—zeichnung**, *f.* drawing; (**frei —zeichen,**) **freie —zeichnung**, free-hand-drawing. **—zug**, *m.* check (*upon bank-bills*).

Händ'—chen, *n.* (**—chens**, *pl.* **—chen**) little hand. **—e**, *pl. of* **Hand**; (*in comp.* =) of hands. **—ig**, *suff.* (*in comp.* =) -handed. **—ler**, *m.* (**—lers**, *pl.* **—ler**) dealer. *Comp.* **—e-auflegung**, *f.* laying on of hands. **—e-druck**, *m.* shake of the hand, hand-shaking. **—e-klatschen**, *n.* clapping of hands, applause. **—e-spiel**, *n.* gesticulation; game of hot cockles. **—e-werk**, *n.* handiwork; handwork.

Han'del, *m.* (**—s**, *pl.* **Händel**) transaction, business; affair; trade, traffic, commerce; law-suit, action; bargain (*pl.*); difference, quarrel, fray; dispute; **—s eins** (*usually* **—s einig**) **werden**, to conclude the bargain, come to an agreement; **— treiben**, to trade; **— im Großen**, wholesale; **— im Kleinen**, retail; **einen — schließen, machen**, to make, conclude a bargain; **— und Wandel**, trade in general, general behaviour:

ein abgekarteter —, a got-up *or* preconcerted affair; ein böser —, a bad business; Händel mit einem suchen, to pick a quarrel with one; den — aufkündigen, aufsagen, to break a bargain; den — an sich reißen, to engross the trade; — mit dem Auslande, foreign commerce *or* trade. —schaft, *f.* trade, commerce, mercantile knowledge; mercantile community. —schaftlich, *adj. & adv.* mercantile. *Comp.* —s, *as the first part of numerous compounds* = commercial, mercantile, trade-; of commerce *or* trade, business. —s=abgabe, *f.* duty (*C.L.*). —s=adreßbuch, *n.* commercial directory. —s=amt, *n.* board of trade. —s=angelegenheit, *f.* trade matter. —s=artikel, *pl.* articles of commerce, merchandise, goods. —s=ausschuß, *m.* committee of merchants. —s=beflissene(r), *m.* (merchant's *or* commercial) clerk, young man occupied in trade. —s=bericht, *m.* commercial report. —s=betrieb, *m.* business; mercantile pursuits. —s=bilanz, *f.* balance of trade. —s=billet, *n.* note (*C.L.*). —s=brauch, *m.* trade-custom. —s=brief, *m.* mercantile letter. —s=buch, *n.* ledger; record (*in law-courts*). —s=bündnis, *n.* commercial treaty. —s=diener, *m.* (merchant's *or* commercial) clerk; office boy, errand boy. —s=einig, *a.*; —seinig werden, to come to an agreement, to come to terms, to agree about buying or selling at a certain price. —s=fach, *n.* mercantile line. —s=faktorei, *f.* trade settlement in foreign towns (*as distinct from* Kolonie). —s=firma, *f.* firm. —s=flotte, *f.* fleet of merchantmen, merchant ships, merchant marine, mercantile marine. —s=frau, *f.* tradeswoman; merchant's wife. —s=freiheit, *f.* free trade; liberty of trade. —s=freund, *m.* business-friend, correspondent. —s=gärtner, *m.* market gardener, florist. —s=geist, *m.* commercial spirit. —s=genoß, *m.* partner. —s=genossenschaft, *f.* partnership; trading company. —s=gericht, *n.* tribunal of commerce, commercial board *or* tribunal. —s=geschäft, *n.* commercial transaction *or* business. —s=gesellschaft, *f.* trading company; partnership in trade. —s=gesetz, *n.* commercial law. —s=gesetz=gebung, *f.* commercial legislation. —s=gewicht, *n.* avoirdupois weight. —s=haus, *n.* mercantile house, trading firm. —s=herr, *m.* (great) merchant, head of a commercial house. —s=hochschule, *f.* highest kind of commercial school *or* college, commercial academy. —s=kammer, *f.* chamber of commerce. —s=kapital, *n.* stock in trade; trading capital. —s=kollegium, *n.* board of trade. —s=konjunktur, *f.* course of the market. —s=korrespondenz, *f.* commercial correspondence. —s=kreise, *pl.m.* the merchants. —s=krise, *f.* commercial crisis, period of disturbance of *or* depression in trade. —s=lage, *f.* state of commerce. —s=leute, *pl.* tradespeople; merchants. —s=mann, *m.* merchant; man of business, tradesman. —s=ministerium, *n.* Board of Trade. —s=minister, *m.* president of the Board of Trade; Minister of Commerce. —s=platz, *m.* emporium, mart. —s=politik, *f.* mercantile policy. —s=rat, *m.* board of trade; member of such board. —s=recht, *n.* privilege of trade; license of trading; commercial law. —s=reise, *f.* business tour, round of business. —s=reisende(r), *m.* commercial traveller; Gasthof für —sreisende, commercial hotel. —s=sache, *f.* commercial affair; a lawsuit relating to commerce. —s=schiedsgericht, *n.* commercial court of arbitration. —s=schiff, *n.* merchantman, trading-vessel. —s=schule, *f.* commercial school, (higher) commercial college. —s=schüler, *m.* student at a commercial college. —s=sperre, *f.* prohibition of commerce, check on commerce. —s=stadt, *f.* commercial town. —s=stand, *m.* trading class; the merchants; the commercial world; mercantile interest. —s=umsatz, *m.* trade returns. —s=verbindung, *f.*, —s=verein, *m.* commercial league *or* union. —s=verbindungen, *pl.* connections in business. —s=verbot, *n.* interdiction of commerce. —s=verkehr, *m.* commercial intercourse. —s=verordnung, *f.* trade-regulation. —s=vertrag, *m.* commercial treaty. —s=volk, *n.* commercial people *or* nation. —s=vorrat, *m.* stock in trade. —s=wesen, *n.* anything relating to commerce *or* trade, business. —s=zeichen, *n.* trade-mark. —s=zettel, *m.* promissory note. —s=zweig, *m.* branch of trade. —treibend, *adj.* trading, commercial.

Hän'del, *pl. of* Handel; — anfangen *or* suchen, to pick a quarrel. *Comp.* —sucher, *m.* quarreller. —sucht, *f.* quarrelsomeness, pugnacity. —süchtig, *adj.* quarrelsome, pugnacious.

Han'deln, *v.* I. *a.* to manage, treat (*obs.*). II. *n.* (*aux.* h.) to behave, act; to treat of (*in writing or speaking*); to bargain, haggle, cheapen; to deal, trade, traffic; mit sich — lassen, to be easy to deal with; to lower the price; er hat als Vater an mir gehandelt, he has been a father to me; ich werde gegen Sie so —, wie Sie gegen mich —, I will treat you as you treat me; als es zu — galt, when it came to the scratch, came to the moment of acting; nichts zu —? old clo'? (*street-cry*). III. *r. & imp.*; es —t sich um, the question is, it is at stake, it concerns; um was handelt es sich? what is the point in question? wovon — die Aufsätze? what is the subject of the essay?

Ha'nebüchen, *adj.* strong, great (*coll.*).

Hanf, *m.* (—es) hemp. —en, *adj.* hempen *Comp.* —bau, *m.* hemp-culture. —breche, *f.* hemp-brake. —hechel, *f.*, —kamm, *m.* hatchel. —öl, *n.*, hemp-seed oil. —samen, *m.* hemp-seed. —wurzel, *f.* strangle-weed.

Hän'f—en, *adj.*, hempen. —in, *f.* fimbrel hemp. —ling, *m.* (—lings, *pl.* —linge) linnet.

Hang, *m.* (—es) slope, declivity; (*sometimes pl.* Hän'ge) inclination, bias, propensity; projection, jut, *n.*; einen — zu etwas haben, to be prone *or* inclined to a th. *or* to do a th.

Hän'ge, *f.* (*pl.* —n) hinge; loft; drying-loft; (*in comp. gen'lly* =) hanging.

Han'gel— (*in cpds.*) —leiter, *f.* horizontal ladder (*gymn.*). —tau, *n.* rope horizontally suspended (*gymn.*).

Han'geln, *v.n.* to travel along a horizontal bar hanging (*gymn.*).

Han'g—en, *ir.v.n.* (*aux.* h. & s.) to hang, be suspended, dangle; to slope; to cleave to, cling, adhere; to be attached to; to be given to; to tend; to catch, to clog; to turn upon, depend on; bis zu *or* auf etwas —en, to hang down to. *Comp.* —end=flötz, *n.*, —end=schicht, *f.* layer on the top of another. —pflicht, *f.* steerage (*Naut.*). —zirkel, *m.* callipers.

Hän'g—en, *v.* I. *a.* to cause to hang, hang, suspend, attach, fasten; den Mantel nach dem Winde —en, to sail with the tide, be a time-server; sich —en, to hang oneself; man —t (*or* die Nürnberger —en) keinen, man hätte (*or* sie hätten) ihn denn, no catch, no have (*prov.*); sein Herz an einen (eine S.) —en, to set one's heart on a person (a thing), to depend on a person (a thing). II. *n.* (*aux.* h.); *see* Hangen; an einander —en, to cleave together, to be firmly attached to one another; sehr am Gelde —en, to be very fond of money; mit allem, was drum und dran —t, with all that pertains to it; —en bleiben, to catch, be caught on; not to advance, to remain pending; to remain a spinster; die Sache bleibt —en, there's a hitch in the matter, the affair does not go on; —en lassen, to give up, discontinue; mit einem —en, to have a quarrel with s.o. (*sl.*). —end, *p. & adj.* hanging, pendulous. —er, *m.* (—ers, *pl.* —er) pendant (*in comp.* =) hanger. —ig, *adj. & adv.* hanging, pendant, sloping; declivitous. —sel, *n.* (—sels, *pl.* —sel) anything by which a thing can be hung up; clothes-loop. *Comp.* —e=balken, *pl.* trussing-pieces (*Arch.*). —e=bauch, *m.* paunch-belly. —e=boden, *m.* drying-loft. —e=brücke, *f.* suspension-bridge. —e=bügel, *m.* stirrup. —e=dach, *n.* pent-house. —e=gerüst, *n.* hanging scaffold. —e=kette, *f.* drag-chain. —e=lampe, *f.* hanging lamp. —e=leuchter, *m.* lustre, chandelier. —e=matte, *f.* hammock. —e=muskel, *m.* suspensory muscle. —ens=wert, *adj.* deserving to be hanged. —e=ohren, *pl.* drooping ears. —e=riemen, *m.* brace; (*pl.*) brace-springs. —esche, *f.* weeping-ash. —e=schloß, *n.* padlock. —e=seil, *n.* leash. —e=wage, *f.* level. —e=weide, *f.* weeping willow. —e=werks=brücke, *f.* suspension-bridge with iron-braces. —e=zirkel, *m.* (wing)-callipers.

Han'ke, *f.* (*pl.* —n) haunch (*of a horse*). *Comp.* —n=knochen, *m.* haunchbone (*of a horse*). —n=tief, *adj.* low in the hind-quarters.

Hän'sel—n, *v.a.* to receive, *or* initiate, into a society with ridiculous ceremonies; to make a fool of. *See the Index of Names under* Hans. *Comp.* —becher, *m.* cup offered to a novice on initiation. —geld, *n.* novice's fees; entrance-money; footing.

Hantel, *f.* (—, *pl.* —n) dumb-bell. —n, *v.n.* (*aux.* h.) to exercise with dumb-bells.

Hantie'r—en, *v.* I. *a.* to handle, wield; to manage. II. *n.* (*aux.* h.) to work with the hands; to do business, carry on a trade; to bustle about. —er, *m.* (—ers, *pl.* —er) tradesman. —ung, *f.* business, employment; trade; management.

Ha'perig, *adj. & adv.* rugged; embarrassed.

Ha'per—n, *v.n. & imp.* to stop, stick fast, hitch; es —t am Gelde, the money is wanting; da —t es, there's the rub; es —t mit der Sache, there is a hitch in the matter, there is something wrong about the matter; the affair is at a standstill.

Happ, *m.* (—es, *pl.* —e), —en, I. *m.* (—ens, *pl.* —en) mouthful, morsel; mit einem einen —en essen, to eat something with a p. (*coll.*). II. *v.n.* (*aux.* h.) to snap, bite. —ig, *adj.* greedy, great, large, excessive; ein —iges Stück Geld, a large sum of money (*sl.*). —s, Haps, *m.* bite (*coll.*); mit einem *or* auf einen Haps, at a bite, quickly; keinen —s, not a bit.

Här'—chen, *n.* (—chens, *pl.* —chen) little hair. —en, *adj.* made of hair; hairy.

Häresie', *f.* (*pl.* —en) heresy.

Häre'—tiker, *m.* (—tikers, *pl.* —tiker) heretic. —tisch, *adj.* heretical.

Har'fe, *f.* (*pl.* —n) harp; corn-screen; die — schlagen, to play the harp. *Comp.* —n=saite, *f.* harp-string. —n=schläger, *m.* harpist. —n=spiel, *n.* harp-playing. —n=zug, *m.* set of harp-strings.

Har'f—en, I. *n.* (*aux.* h.) to play the harp. II. *a.* to screen corn. —eni'st, *m.* (—eni'sten, *pl.* —eni'sten), —ner, *m.* (—ners, *pl.* —ner) harper, harpist.

Hä'ring, *m.* (—s, *pl.* —e) herring; geräucherter —, smoked herring, bloater; gesalzener —, pickled herring; gedörrter —, kipper(ed herring). *Comp.* —s=bändiger, *m.* grocer's apprentice (*coll.*). —s=fang, *m.* herring-fishery. —s=jäger, *m.* herring-smack. —s=lake, *f.* herring-pickle. —s=milch, *f.* soft roe of herrings. —s=zeit, *f.* herring season.

Har'ke, *f.* (*pl.* —n) rake; einem zeigen, was eine —e ist, to give a p. a good set down, to give one a good piece of one's mind (*coll.*). —n, *v.a. & n.* to rake.

Harl'ekin, *m.* (—s, *pl.* —e) Harlequin. —a'de, *f.* harlequinade, buffoonery. —et'te, *f.* Columbine.

Harm, *m.* (—s) grief, sorrow, affliction. —los, *adj.* harmless; inoffensive; without sorrow. —voll, *adj.*, sorrowful.

Här'men, *v.* I. *a.* to afflict, grieve. II. *r.* to feel wretched, to grieve, pine, fret, worry.

Harmonie', *f.* (*pl.* —en) harmony; concord; union. —ren, *v.n.* (*aux.* h.) to agree; to harmonize; to be in unison; to live in concord; to sympathize. *Comp.* —gesetz, *n.* tonal law; *pl.* laws of harmony. —lehre, *f.* harmonics. —musik, *f.* music of wind-instruments; brass-band.

Harmo'nik, *f.* harmonics. —a, *f.* (*pl.* —as) harmonica. —a=zug, *m.* corridor train (*coll.*). —er, *m.* harmonizer, harmonist.

Harmo'ni—sch, *adj.* harmonious. —um, *n.* (—ums, *pl.* —ums *or* Harmonien) harmonium, parlour organ.

Harmoto'm, *m.* harmotome, cross-stone, staurolite.

Harn, *m.* (—s) urine; den — lassen *or* —en, *v.n.* (*aux.* h.) to urinate, to make water. *Comp.* —absätze, *pl.* urinary excretions. —beschwerden, *pl.* urinary disorder, difficulty in passing urine. —blase, *f.* (urinary) bladder. —blasen=bruch, *m.* rupture of the bladder. —blasen=gries, *m.* gravel. —blasen=stein=schnitt, *m.* lithotomy. —brennen, *n.*,—drang, *m.* scalding in the bladder. —fluß, *m.* discharge of urine; unwillkürlicher —fluß, incontinence of urine. —gang, *m.* urethra. —leiter, *m.* urethra; catheter. —plätze, *pl.* urinals. —röhre, *f.* urinary passage, urethra. —röhren=verengerung, *f.* stricture of the urethra. —ruhr, *f.* diabetes. —stein, *m.* stone in the bladder. —stoff, *m.* urea (*Chem.*). —strenge, *f.* strangury. —treibend, *adj.*; —treibendes Mittel, diuretic. —zapfer, *m.* catheter. —zwang, *m.* strangury.

Har'nisch, *m.* (—(e)s, *pl.* —e) harness, armour; in — jagen, bringen, to enrage, to provoke; in — geraten, to fly into a passion, to talk with great warmth and emotion.

Har'nischen, *v.a.* to put on armour (*obs.*); geharnischt, armour-clad; angry, violent; geharnischte Sonnette, aggressive (political) sonnets written by Fr. Rückert against Napoleon I. and the French oppression of Germany.

Harpegg—iatu'r, *f.* succession of arpeggios. —ie'ren, *v.a. & n.* (*aux.* h.) to play arpeggio.

Harpu'ne, *f.* (*pl.* —n) harpoon; — der Walfischfänger, whale-lance; abschießbare —, gun-harpoon. *Comp.* —n=geschütz, *n.* harpoon-gun, whaling-gun. —n=haken, *m.* lance-hook.

Harpunie'r, *m.* (—s, *pl.* —e) harpooner. —en, *v.a.* to harpoon, to strike.

Harpy'e, *f.* (*pl.* —n) harpy. —n=artig, *adj.* harpy-like.

Har'ren, *v.n,* (*aux.* h.) to wait in expectation, wait, tarry, delay; — auf, (*acc.*) to wait for, hope for, trust in.

Harsch (*short* a), *adj. & adv.* harsh, rough, raw; hard. —en, *v.n.* (*aux.* h. & s.) to harden; to cicatrize.

Hart (*short* a), *adj. & adv.* (härter, härtest) hard; harsh, rough, severe; stern, austere; cruel; obstinate; difficult; stiff, solid; tough; crude (*Paint.*); high (*fever*); major (*Mus.*); —e Laute, harsh sounds; surd consonants —er Dreiklang, major accord; —es Futter, corn, oats, *etc.*, as fodder; —e Kälte, severe cold; —e Not, dire necessity; —er Schlaf, sound sleep; —es Mittel, severe measure, rough remedy; —es Geld, specie; —e Stirn, brazen face; einen —en Leib haben, to be strong and hardy; to be costive *or* constipated; — **gewöhnt sein,** to be accustomed to rough it; — **an,** close by; **es wird — halten,** it will be attended with difficulties; **das Fieber hat ihn — mitgenommen,** the fever has shaken him severely; **es fällt mir —,** it is hard for me. *Comp.* **—fleischig,** *adj.* brawny; muscular. **—flügler,** *pl.* coleoptera. **—gesinnt,** *adj.* hard-hearted. **—gesotten,** *adj.*; **—gesottener Sünder,** a hardened sinner, a confirmed sinner. **—gläubig,** *adj.* sceptical. **—gummi,** (*m.* &) *n.* vulcanized india-rubber, hardened caoutchouc, hard rubber, vulcanite. **—guß,** *m.* chilled work, case-hardened castings. **—häuter,** *pl.* scleroderms (*Icht.*). **—häutig,** *adj.* thick-skinned; callous, unfeeling. **—häutigkeit,** *f.* callosity. **—herzig,** *adj.* hard-hearted. **—holz,** *n.* hornbeam. **—hörig,** *adj.* deafish. **—leibig,** *adj.* costive, constipated. **—mäulig,** *adj.* hard-mouthed; unruly. **—näckig,** *adj.* headstrong, obstinate. **—nagel,** *m.* clout-nail. **—schalig,** *adj.* testaceous. **—schnaufen,** *n.* roaring (*Vet.*). **—sehnig,** *adj.* sinewy.

Här't—e, *f.* (*pl.* **—en**) harshness; severity, rigour; hardiness; roughness, crudeness, harshness. **—en,** *v.a.* to harden; to temper. **—er,** *m.* (**—ers,** *pl.* **—er**) hardener. **—igkeit,** *f.* hardness. **—lich,** *adj.* hardish. **—ung,** *f.* hardening; tempering. *Comp.* **—pulver,** *n.* tempering powder.

Hartschie'r, *m.* (**—s,** *pl.* **—e**) guard, sentry; soldier of the (Austrian imperial) body-guard (*orig.:* archer). *See* **Hatschier.**

Harz, *n.* (**—es,** *pl.* **—e**) resin, rosin. **—icht,** (*obs.*) **—ig,** *adj.* resinous. *Comp.* **—baum,** *m.* pine-tree; pitch-tree. **—förmig,** *adj.* resiniform. **—galle,** *f.* collection of resin in the wood of the pine. **—gebend,** *adj.* yielding resin, resiniferous. **—gummi,** (*m.* &) *n.* resinous gum. **—haltig,** *adj.* resinoid. **—kohle,** *f.* resinous coal. **—reißen, —scharren,** *n.* tapping to extract resin from trees. **—stoffe,** *pl.* resinoids. **—tanne,** *f.* pitch-fir. **—tragend,** *adj.* resiniferous.

Har'ze—n, *v.* I. *n.* (*aux.* **h.**) to collect, *or* scrape off, the resin from pines; to stick like resin. II. *a.* to rub with resin. **—r,** *m.* resin-gatherer; curmudgeon, skinflint.

Hasard'spiel, *n.* game of chance, game of hazard, betting game, gambling.

Ha'sche—n, I. *v.a.* to catch, to seize. II. *v.n.* (*aux.* **h.**) **—n nach,** to snatch at, strain after, to aim at. III. *subst. n.* catching; tig (*game*). **—rei',** *f.* a snatching at, running after.

Hä'scher, *m.* (**—s,** *pl.* **—**) bailiff, catchpole; policeman, myrmidon, a tyrant's bodyguard. **—ei',** *f.* police-practices; the police. *Comp.* **—er=knechte,** *pl.*, **—er=schaar,** *f.* sheriff's officers; police, band of body-snatchers (*coll.*).

Häs'—chen (**—chens,** *pl.* **—chen**), **—lein,** *n.* (**—leins,** *pl.* **—lein**) young hare, leveret. **—(s)in,** *f.* female hare, doe hare.

Haschie'ren, *v.a.* to hatch (*in engraving*); to hash, mince (*in cooking*).

Ha'se, *m.* (**—n,** *pl.* **—n**) hare; coward; coxcomb; **drei —n,** a leash of hares; **einen —n aufjagen,** to start a hare; **einem —n das Fell abziehn,** to skin a hare; **da liegt der — im Pfeffer,** that's the difficulty; **viele Hunde sind des —n Tod,** there is no fighting against fearful odds (*prov.*); **mein Name ist —,** I do not know, I have not the faintest notion (*coll.*). **—n=haft,** *adj.* & *adv.* faint-hearted, timid, cowardly; leporine. *Comp.* **—n=aar, —n=adler,** *m.* erne. **—n=ampfer,** *m.* wood-sorrel. **—n=artig,** *adj.* leporine. **—n=balg,** *m.*, **—n=fell,** *n.* hareskin. **—n=braten,** *m.* roast hare. **—n=fuß,** *m.* foot of a hare; poltroon, coward. **—n=füßig,** *adj.* cowardly. **—n=hatz, —n=hetze,** *f.* coursing. **—n=herz,** *n.* coward. **—n=jagd,** *see* **—n=hatz**; **das ist ja keine —n=jagd,** there is no hurry about that. **—n=hund,** *m.* harrier. **—n=klee,** *m.* trefoil. **—n=klein,** *n.* jugged hare (*Cook.*). **—n=kopf,** *m.* hare's head; hair-brained fellow, coxcomb. **—n=lager,** *n.* hare's form. **—n=maul,** *n.* brill (*Icht.*). **—n=mund,** *m.*, **—n=scharte,** *f.* hare-lip. **—n=öhrchen,** *pl.* inverted commas. **—n=panier,** *n.* flight; **das —n=panier ergreifen,** to take to one's heels. **—n=schrot,** *m.* small shot (*for hares*). **—n=zwirn,** *m.* thick thread, *or* twine, for hare nets.

Ha'sel, *f.* (*pl.* **—en**) hazel-bush. *Comp.* **—huhn,** *n.* blackcock, wood-grouse. **—maus,** *f.* dormouse. **—nuß,** *f.* hazel-nut. **—nußfarbig,** *adj.* nut-brown. **—staude,** *f.* hazel, hazel-bush.

Hasel—a'nt, *m.* coxcomb; buffoon (*vulg.*). **—ie'ren,** *v.a.* to frisk about, to play the fool.

Hä'seln, *adj.* hazel.

Has'pe, (**Häs'pe,**) *f.* (*pl.* **—en**) hasp, hinge; hook; clamp; holdfast, staple. **—l,** *m.* (**—ls**) reel; whim, windlass; capstan; winding-engine; electric fly, electric reaction-mill (*electr.*); hook (*for the hinge of a door*); staple; turnstile. **—ln,** *v.a.* & *n.* (*aux.* **h.**) to wind on a reel; to draw up with a windlass; to move quickly; to do mechanically; to chatter. *Comp.* **—l=knecht,** *m.* man working a windlass. **—l=welle,** *f.* windlass-roller. **—l=winde,** *f.* capstan-bar.

Haß, *m.* (**—(ss)es**) hate, hatred, enmity. *Comp.* **—erregend,** *adj.* odious, hateful.

Has'se—n, *v.a.* to hate, detest. **—r,** *m.* (**—rs,** *pl.* **—r**) hater; enemy. *Comp.* **—ns=wert,** *adj.* hateful, odious.

Häß'lich, *adj.* odious; base; wicked, vicious; unpleasant; loathsome; ugly; repulsive; offensive; ill-favoured; deformed; **ein —es Gesicht,** an ugly face; **eine —e Antwort,** a nasty answer; **eine —e Geschichte,** a bad business, an unpleasant affair; **ein —er Geruch,** an offensive smell; **eine —e Sitte,** an objectionable custom; **— gegen einen,** disagreeable to a p. **—keit,** *f.* ugliness, unsightliness; wickedness, badness; loathsomeness.

Hast, *f.* haste, hurry; precipitation. **—en,** *v.* I. *a.* to hasten, to rush along. II. *n.* (*aux.* **h.**) & *imp.* to haste. **—ig,** *adj.* & *adv.* hasty, rash; precipitate; irritable, passionate; **sie fiel ihm —ig in die Rede,** she interrupted him abruptly. **—igkeit,** *f.* hastiness; rashness; passionateness; irritability.

Hät'schel—n (*ä pronounced either short or long*), *v.a.* to coax, caress, fondle; to pamper. *Comp.* **—hans,** *m.* person caressed *or* petted, pet (*name given to Goethe by his mother; see* **Hans** *in the Index of names*).

Hat'schen, *v.n.* (*aux.* **h.**) to be limp, hang loose.

Hatschie'r, *m.* (**—s,** *pl.* **—e**) archer, halberdier; imperial horseguard (*at Vienna*).

Hat'te, Hät'te, *imperf. ind.* & *subj. of* **haben.**

Hät'te, *imperf. indic. of* **haben** (*obs.* & *poetic*); **wo Roland jüngst gestritten hätt',** where Roland had but recently fought (*poet.*); **einen goldenen Becher er hätt' empfangen von seiner Buhle,** he had received from his lady-love a golden goblet (*poet.*).

Hat'z(e), *f.* (*pl.* **—en**) hunt, place of a hunt, coursing; racecourse, arena, pack of hounds; **Bären—,** bear hunting.

Hau, *m.* (**—es,** *pl.* **—e**) cutting, felling, stroke; blow, place where wood is felled. **—bar,** *adj.* & *adv.* fit for felling. **—e,** *f.* (*pl.* **—en**) hoe mattock, pickaxe.

Hau'b—e, *f.* (*pl.* **—en**) cap, coif; hood; tuft, crest; top; cupola; dome; crown (*of a bell*) ferule; cap-sheaf (*of a stack*); coping (*of a wall*); second stomach of ruminants (*Zoöl.*); **unter die —e bringen,** to provide a husband for, marry (*a girl*); **unter die —e kommen,** to get a husband, to get married. *Comp.* —**en=ente**, *f.* tufted duck. —**en=flor**, *m.* crape for caps. —**en=kram**, *m.* millinery. —**en=lerche**, *f.* crested lark. —**en=meise**, —**en=merle**, *f.* crested titmouse. —**en=schachtel**, *f.* cap-box, bandbox. —**en=schleife**, *f.* cap-ribbon. —**en=stock**, —**en=kopf**, *m.* milliner's block.

Haubit'z—e, *f.* howitzer. *Comp.* —**en=feuer**, *n.* discharge of howitzers, shell fire. —**granate**, *f.* howitzer-grenade *or* shell.

Hauch, *m.* (—**es**) breath; breeze; puff; whiff; aspiration (*Gram.*); inspiration; touch (*of antiquity*). —**en**, *v.* I. *n.* (*aux.* **h.**) to breathe, respire. II. *a.* to breathe out, exhale; to blow; to aspirate. *Comp.* —**blatt**, *n.* uvula. —**laut**, *m.* spirantic sound, spirant. —**zeichen**, *n.* mark of aspiration.

Hau'der—er, *m.* (—**ers**, *pl.* —**er**) hackney coach; hackney coachman; carriage-jobber (*dial.*).

Hau'dern, *v.n.* (*aux.* **h.**) to keep hackney coaches; to go in a hackney coach (*dial.*).

Hau'—en, *ir.v.* I. *a.* to hew, cut, chop; to fell; to carve, chisel; to lash; to mow; to break (*stones*); to engrave; to strike, beat; **einen hinter die Ohren —en**, to box a p.'s ears; **einer übers Ohr —en**, to cheat a p. II. *r.* to cut, *or* hurt, oneself; to cut one's way through *or* out. III. *n.* (*aux.* **h.**) to cut; to strike; **um sich —en**, to lay about one; **über die Schnur —en**, to overshoot the mark, to exaggerate; **nach etwas —en**, to strike at a thing; —**en und stechen**, to cut and to thrust; **das ist weder gehauen noch gestochen**, that is neither the one nor the other, there is neither rhyme nor reason in that; **in die Pfanne —en**, to put to the sword, to cut to pieces; **in die Eisen —en**, to overreach (*of a horse*). —**e**, *pl.* = **Hiebe, Prügel, Schläge** (*sl.*); —**e kriegen**, to be thoroughly beaten *or* whipped (*sl.*). —**er**, *m.* (—**ers**, *pl.* —**er**) hewer, miner; wild boar; cutting instrument; (*pl.*) tusks, fangs; **Stein=—er**, stone-cutter; **Bild—er**, sculptor. *Comp.* —**bajonnett**, *n.* sword-bayonet. —**degen**, *m.* broadsword; swordsman; undaunted warrior, brave soldier (*often without much knowledge of tactics and strategy*); **alter —degen**, old blade. —**hammer**, *m.* miner's pick. —**klinge**, *f.* blade of a broadsword. —**land**, *n.* clearing. —**meißel**, *m.* cutting chisel. —**zahn**, *m.* boar's tusk.

Hauf, *m.* (—**es**, (*obs.*) *pl.* —**en**), —**e**, *m.* ((*dial.*) (*obs.*) —**es**, *pl.* —**en**), —**en**, *m.* (—**ens**, *pl.* —**en**) heap, pile, hoard; large sum; great number; crowd; troop; company; body; swarm; mass of the people, the multitude, populace, vulgar; **über den —en stoßen**, to overthrow; **alle Bedenken über den —en werfen**, to throw aside, *or* overboard, all scruples; **über den —en fallen**, to tumble down, to perish; **in —en**, in heaps, by heaps; **wer wird auf das Geschrei des großen —ens hören?** who would pay attention to the clamour of the multitude? **dort kommen sie in hellen —en**, there they are advancing in large bodies; **in —en legen, schichten**, to heap up; **zu —(en)**, together; **Heu—en**, hay-cock. *Comp.* —**en=weise**, *adv.* in heaps; in crowds. —**en=wolke**, *f.* cumulus.

Häu'fel—n, *v.* I. *a.* to earth (*potatoes*); to form into little heaps. II. *n.* to play blind-hookey. —**blütler**, *pl.* aggregate flowers.

Häuf—en, *v.a.* to accumulate; to heap up; to earth up; **sich —en**, to accumulate, to increase. —**ung**, *f.* heaping.

Häu'fig, I. *adj.* copious, abundant; frequent; repeated. II. *adv.* often; abundantly. —**keit**, *f.* frequency; quickness (*of the pulse*).

Häuf'lein, *n.* (—**s**, *pl.* —) little heap; small body of men, troop *or* company.

Haupt, *n.* (—**es**, *pl.* **Häup'ter**; *with numbers often* —; *dat. pl.* **Häup'ten** *in the obs. phrase* **zu Häupten** *as opposed to* **zu Füßen**) head; leader, chief; chief town *or* place; **aufs —schlagen**, to defeat totally; **einem das —abschlagen**, to behead a person; **einen um —es=länge überragen**, to tower head and shoulders above a person; **bemoostes —**, student of many terms, old student (*sl.*); (*in comp.* =) main, principal. *Comp.* —**absicht**, *f.* chief design. —**ader**, *f.* cephalic vein. —**agentur**, *f.* principal agency. —**altar**, *m.* high altar. —**artikel**, *m.* principal article; leader. —**aufgebot**, *n.* general levy of the people. —**augenmerk**, *n.*; **sein —augenmerk auf (eine S.) richten**, to direct one's chief attention to. —**balken**, *m.* architrave; (*pl.*) principals. —**baß**, *m.* thorough-bass. —**befahrung**, *f.* general inspection (of mines). —**begriff**, *m.* leading idea. —**betrag**, *m.* sum total. —**beweis**, *m.* main proof. —**binde**, *f.* head-band, fillet. —**bischof**, *m.* metropolitan bishop. —**brett**, *n.* head-piece of a bedstead. —**buch**, *n.* ledger. —**buchstabe**, *m.* capital letter. —**draht**, *m.* primary wire. —**ein=fahrt**, *f.*, —**eingang**, *m.* main entrance. —**fach**, *n.* principal subject, chief subject. —**fatzke**, *m.* thoroughly conceited fellow (*sl.*). —**feder**, *f.* main-spring. —**fehler**, *m.* main defect; capital fault. —**flügel**, *m.* main wing (*Arch.*). —**form**, *f.* chief form. —**frage**, *f.* leading question. —**gasse**, *f.* chief lane. —**gebälke**, *n.* entablature. —**geld**, *n.* poll-tax; capital; capitation fee. —**geschoß**, *n.* first floor, principal story. —**gesims**, *n.* cornice (*of columns*); entablature (*Arch.*). —**gestell**, *n.* head-stall; chief frame *or* stand. —**gläubiger**, *m.* chief creditor. —**grind**, *m.* scald (*Med.*). —**grund**, *m.* main motive *or* reason; foundation, basis. —**grundsatz**, *m.* fundamental *or* leading principle. —**hahn**, *m.* a jolly fellow; a true fighting cock (*stud. sl.*). —**handlung**, *f.* principal action; main plot; chief commercial establishment. —**inhalt**, *m.* general, *or* principal, contents. —**jagd**, *f.* battue. —**kerl**, *m.*; **er ist ein —kerl**, he is a trump (*coll.*). —**kessel**, *m.* main boiler. —**kirche**, *f.* cathedral, parish church. —**kissen**, *n.* pillow. —**knoten**, *m.* main plot. —**lager**, *n.* principal camp; headquarters. —**land**, *n.* mainland; mother-country. —**lehens=herr**, *m.* lord-paramount. —**lehre**, *f.* main doctrine, fundamental doctrine. —**lehrer**, *m.* chief master. —**leidenschaft**, *f.* ruling passion. —**leid=tragende(r)**, *m.* chief mourner. —**leiter**, *m.*, —**leitung**, *f.* principal conductor. —**los**, *adj.* headless; without a leader. —**mahlzeit**, *f.* chief meal. —**mann**, *m.* (—**mannes**, *pl.* —**leute**) captain; **der —mann von Kapernaum**, the centurion. —**mann=schaft**, —**manns=stelle**, *f.* captaincy. —**mast**, *m.* main mast. —**mime**, *m.* principal leader (*sl.*). —**mucker**, *m.* thorough pietist; out and out bigot (*sl.*). —**narr**, *m.* arrant fool. —**nenner**, *m.* common denominator. —**nieder=lage**, *f.* general defeat; principal magazine *or* warehouse; emporium. —**pastor**, *m.* chief clergyman, pastor primarius. —**person**, *f.* principal person; chief character. —**pfosten**, *m.* crown-post (*Arch.*). —**post**, *f.*, —**postamt**, *n.* general post-office; **zahlbar am —postamt in London**, payable at the General Post Office (G. P. O.), London. —**prämie**, *f.* first prize. —**punkt**, *m.* main point; cardinal point; chief feature. —**quartier**, *n.* headquarters. —**quelle**, *f.* main source; fountain-head. —**quer=balken**, *m.* architrave. —**register**, *n.* index; main stop (*Org.*). —**religion**, *f.* prevailing religion. —**reparatur**, *f.* thorough repair. —**rolle**, *f.* leading character *or* part. —**ruder**, *n.* stroke-oar. —**sache**, *f.* chief matter, main point; (*pl.*) essentials. —ſächlich, I. *adj.* essential, principal, main, of chief importance. II. *adv.* essentially, chiefly, particularly, above all; darauf kommt es —ſächlich an, that's the main point. —ſächlichſt, I. *sup. adj.* capital. II. *adv.* above all things. —ſatz, *m.* main point; leading theme (*Mus.*); axiom; principal clause, principal sentence (*Gram.*). —ſängerin, *f.* primadonna. —ſchelm, *m.* arrant rogue. —ſchiff, *n.* flagship. —ſchlacht, *f.* pitched battle; great, *or* decisive, battle. —ſchlüſſel, *m.* master-key. —ſchluß=maſchine, *f.* series-dynamo. —ſchmuck, *m.* ornament for the head; principal ornament. —ſchuldner, *m.* principal debtor. —ſchule, *f.* principal school. —ſegel, *n.* main sail. —ſeite, *f.* principal side, front (*of a building*); face (*of a coin*). —ſpaß, *m.* capital joke. —ſprache, *f.* principal language, chief tongue; literary language (*obs.*); Lehrbuch der deutſchen —ſprache, grammar of literary German. —ſtadt, *f.* metropolis, capital. —ſtädtiſch, *adj.* metropolitan. —ſtag=ſegel, *n.* main-stay sail. —ſtamm, *m.* main stem *or* trunk; leading, *or* elder, branch (*of a race*); chief tribe. —ſtände, *pl.* states-general. —ſteuer, *f.* poll-tax; principal tax. —ſtimme, *f.* leading voice; solo. —ſtraße, *f.* principal street, high street; highway, main road. —ſtrom, *m.* main stream, inducing current, primary current. —ſtück, *n.* principal piece; head-piece; head; chapter, section; chief article; important point. —ſtütze, *f.* main support, mainstay. —ſünde, *f.* cardinal sin; besetting sin. —ſumme, *f.* sum total. —ton, *m.* key-note; principal accent. —treffen, *n.* *see* —ſchlacht. —trumpf, *m.* best trump. —tugend, *f.* cardinal virtue. —urſache, *f.* main cause. —verbrechen, *n.* capital crime, high misdemeanour. —verzeichnis, *n.* general catalogue. —wache, *f.* main-guard; main-guard house. —werk, *n.* principal work; chief matter; masterpiece. —witz, *m.* capital joke (*coll.*). —wort, *n.* noun-substantive; chief word. —wunde, *f.* wound in the head; dangerous wound. —zahl, *f.*, —zahlwort, *n.* cardinal number. —zeichen, *n.* cardinal sign. —zeuge, *m.* principal witness. —zug, *m.* leading feature; principal train; principal direction of a lode. —zweck, *m.* chief object.

Häupt'—ling, *m.* (—s, *pl.* —e) chief, leader. —lings, *adv.* head-foremost, head over heels, headlong. *Comp.* —el=kohl, *m.* hearted cabbage, hearts. —el=ſalat, *m.* cabbage-lettuce.

Haus, *n.* (—ſes, *pl.* Häu'ſer) house; residence; housing, casing, frame; household; family; race; home; firm; shell; fellow (*coll.*); zu —(ſ)e, at home; er iſt überall zu —(ſ)e, he is well up in everything; he is very widely read; nach —(ſ)e, homeward, home; von —(ſ)e, from home; auf ihn kannſt du Häuſer bauen, you may pin your faith on him, you may trust him implicitly; von —(ſ)e aus, from the very beginning, fundamentally, originally; von —(ſ)e aus Vermögen haben, to have property of one's own; der Herr vom —(ſ)e, the master of the house; mit der Thür ins — fallen, to do (*a thing*) awkwardly, to blunder something out; mit herzlichen Grüßen von — zu —, with our united kind regards to all of you; von gutem —(ſ)e, of a good family; ein großes — machen, to live in great style; wo ſind Sie zu —(ſ)e? what countryman are you? where do you come from? ein neues — beziehen, to remove to a new house; das — hüten, to stay at home; nirgends zu —(ſ)e ſein, to have no fixed home; to know no subject thoroughly; ſein — beſtellen, to prepare for death; — und Hof, one's all, house and home; ſie trieben ihn von — und Hof, they drove him from hearth and home; gut — halten, to be a good housekeeper; thut als ob ihr zu —(ſ)e wäret, make yourself at home; mit ſeinen Gedanken nicht zu —(ſ)e ſein, to be absent-minded *or* inattentive; bleibt mir damit zu —(ſ)e! don't bother me about that, keep that to yourself! altes —, old boy, old chap, old man (*coll.*); altes —, was machſt du? well, old boy, how are you? nicht wohl zu —(ſ)e, not in one's right mind (*vulg.*). *Comp.* —andacht, *f.* family prayers, private devotion. —angelegenheiten, *pl.* family affairs. —arbeit, *f.* in-door work; domestic work; home work (*of school children*). —apotheke, *f.* family medicine chest. —arreſt, *m.* confinement in one's own house *or* indoors. —arznei, *f.* domestic medicine. —arzt, *m.* family-doctor; unſer —arzt, our medical man, our doctor. —backen, *adj.* home-baked; homely, plain; —backnes Brot, home-made bread. —bedarf, *m.* household necessaries; für den —bedarf, for the house, for family use. —bediente(r), *m.* indoor-servant. —be(ſ)itzer, *m.* proprietor of a house. —bettelei, *f.* begging at the door; Verein gegen —bettelei, association against mendicancy, charity organization society. —brauch, *m.* family custom; domestic use. —brief, *m.* conveyance, purchase-contract of a house. —brot, *n.* household bread. —buch, *n.* housekeeping-book. —burſch, *m.* foot-boy; fellow-lodger. —dieb, *m.* a thievish person who is a member of the household; burglar. —diener, *m.* household domestic, man-servant. —drache, *m.* scold, vixen. —durch=ſuchung, *f.* domiciliary visit (*by the police*). —ehre, *f.* family honour; housewife (*coll.*). —eigentümer, *m.* *see* —beſitzer. —einbrecher, *m.* burglar. —einrichtung, *f.* domestic arrangement. —flur, *f.* entrance-hall of a house; vestibule. —frau, *f.* mistress of a house *or* family; housewife; landlady. —freund, *m.* family friend. —friede, *m.* domestic peace, domestic security. —friedens=bruch, *m.* disturbance of domestic peace and security. —geflügel, *n.* poultry. —geld, *n.* rent. —genoß, *m.*, —genoſſin, *f.* dweller in the same house, fellow lodger; inmate of the same family. —genoſſen, *pl.*, —genoſſenſchaft, *f.* family, household, inmates (*coll.*); domestic servants. —gerät, *n.* utensils for the house, household furniture. —geſinde, *n.* domestic servants. —glück, *n.* domestic happiness. —gott, *m.* household god. —gottes=dienſt, *m.* (family) prayers, family worship, private service. —hahn, *m.* domestic cock. —halt, *m.* housekeeping; house, household. —halten, I. *ir.v.a.* to keep house; to husband, economize; ſie hält ihm —, she keeps house for him. II. *subst. n.* housekeeping; management. —hälter, —halter, *m.* householder, housekeeper; good manager, economist. —hälterin, *f.* housekeeper. —hälteriſch, *adj.* economical, housewifely, thrifty. —haltung, *f.* *see* —halt; economy, housewifery. —haltungs=kunſt, *f.* domestic economy. —hammel, *m.* stay-at-home. —herr, *m.* master of the house; landlord. —hoch, *adj. & adv.* as high as a house. —hofmeiſter, *m.* steward, major-domo. —jungfer, *f.* unmarried daughter of the house; housemaid. —kapelle, *f.* private chapel; private band. —kleid, *n.* house-dress; deshabille. —knecht, *m.* porter; boots (*at an inn*). —knochen, *m.* house-key, latch-key (*sl.*). —koſt, *f.* household fare. —kreuz, *n.* domestic affliction; wife (*sl.*). —krieg, *m.* domestic dissension. —leben, *n.* domestic *or* home life. —lehrer, *m.* private tutor. —lehrerin, *f.* governess. —lehrer=ſtelle, *f.* (private) tutorship. **—leinwand,** *f.* home-spun linen. **—mädchen,** *n.* housemaid; **einziges —mädchen,** house-parlour-maid; general servant. **—magd,** *f.* housemaid, servant of all work. **—leute,** *pl.* people of the house *or* family; lodgers; domestic servants; tenants. **—mann,** *m.* I. (*pl.* **—leute**) fellow-lodger; tenant, lodger; (*pl.*) domestics. II. (*pl.* **—männer**) house-porter. **—manns-kost,** *f.* plain food, homely fare. **—mast, —mästung,** *f.* stall-feeding of swine. **—meier,** *m.* groom of the chambers; major-domo. **—meister,** *m.* house-steward. **—miete,** *f.* (house-)rent. **—mittel,** *n.* household medicine *or* remedy. **—mutter,** *f.* mother of a family; matron. **—mütterlich,** *adj. & adv.* matronly. **—mütze,** *f.* skull-cap. **—ordnung,** *f.* household regulation(s), daily routine. **—pflanze,** *f.* greenhouse-plant. **—postille,** *f.* book of family devotions. **—prediger,** *m.* domestic chaplain. **—rat,** *m.* household furniture. **—recht,** *n.* domestic right; domestic authority. **—regiment,** *n.* household government. **—riegel,** *m.* bolt of the street door. **—schabe,** *f.* black beetle. **—schatz,** *m.* privy purse (*of a prince*); treasury, anthology, family book (*of poetry, etc.*). **—schlüssel,** *m.* key of the street-door. **—schuh,** *m.* slipper. **—schwamm,** *m.* dry rot. **—segen,** *m.* domestic blessing, children. **—sorge,** *f.* domestic care. **—stand,** *m.* domestic state; household. **—suchung,** *f.* domiciliary visit (*by the police*). **—suchungs-befehl,** *m.* search-warrant. **—tafel,** *f.* table of duties to one's neighbour. **—taufe,** *f.* private baptism. **—teufel,** *m.* termagant, shrew. **—thür,** *f.* street-door, front-door. **—tier,** *n.* domestic animal. **—trauung,** *f.* wedding in a house. **—truppen,** *pl.* household troops. **—tuch,** *n.* homespun. **—unke,** *f.* earth-toad; home-bird. **—tyrann,** *m.* domestic tyrant. **—unkosten,** *pl.* household expenses. **—unterstützung,** *f.* outdoor relief. **—übel,** *n.* family affliction. **—vater,** *m.* father of a family. **—verstand,** *m.*; **—verstand haben,** to have common sense, to be sensible. **—vertrag,** *m.* family compact; *see* **—brief.** **—verwalter,** *m.* steward. **—vogt,** *m.* prison-overseer; jailer. **—vogtei,** *f.* prison. **—wappen,** *pl.* family arms. **—wäsche,** *f.* home-washing; house-linen. **—wesen,** *n.* domestic concerns, household. **—wirt,** *m.* master of a house; landlord; host. **—wirtin,** *f.* housewife; mistress of a house; landlady; hostess. **—wirtschaft,** *f.* housekeeping; domestic economy. **—zins,** *m.* house-rent. **—zucht,** *f.* home discipline.

Häus'—chen, *n.* (**—chens,** *pl.* **—chen**) small house, cottage; **aus dem —chen,** beside oneself, confused, overcome; **sie ist vor Freude ganz aus dem —chen,** she is beside herself with delight. **—(e)ln,** *v.n.* (*aux.* **h.**) to live in a small way; to do servant's work; to build houses with cards. **—ler,** *m.* (**—lers,** *pl.* **—ler**) cottager; occupant of a house. **—lerschaft,** *f.* cottagers (*coll.*). **—lich,** *adj.* domestic; thrifty; plain; household; **—liche Aufgaben,** home work, home lessons (*of school children*); **—licher Kreis,** domestic circle; **im —lichen Kreise,** by the fireside; **—licher Unterricht,** private teaching, private tuition; **sich —lich niederlassen an einem Orte,** to settle at, *or* in, a place. **—lichkeit,** *f.* domesticity; simplicity; frugality.

[1]**Hau'sen,** *v.n.* (*aux.* **h.**) to house, lodge, reside; to dwell; to keep house; to live economically; to manage; to riot; to rage; to act, go on, proceed; to haunt; to infest. **—ie'ren,** *v.n.* (*aux.* **h.**) to hawk about; to go about peddling. **—ie'rer,** *m.* (**—ierers,** *pl.* **—ierer**) pedlar. *Comp.* **—ier-handel,** *m.* hawking, peddling, pedlary, colportage (*of books, pamphlets*).

[2]**Hau'sen,** *m.* (**—s,** *pl.* **—**) sturgeon. *Comp.* **—blase,** *f.* isinglass, fish glue. **—rogen,** *m.* spawn of sturgeon, caviare.

Haus'se—e, *f.* rise, advance (*C. L.*). **—en,** *v.n.* (*aux.* **h.**) to speculate on a rise.

Hau'ßen, *adv.* (= **hie außen**) *lit.* out here, here outside; out of doors; abroad (*obs. & poet.*).

Haut, *f.* (*pl.* **Häu'te**) hide; skin; tunic, coat; cuticle, membrane; film; outside planking (*of a ship*); **sich seiner — wehren,** to defend one's own life; **seine — (selbst) zu Markte tragen,** to do at one's own risk, to risk one's life; **seine — teuer verkaufen,** to sell one's life dearly; **einem die — über die Ohren ziehen,** to flay a p., to fleece, *or* cheat, a p.; **bis auf die —,** to the skin; **naß bis auf die —,** wet to the skin, sopping wet (*coll.*); **auf der faulen — liegen,** to be idle, to take it easy; **treue alte —,** good old soul, true penny; **ehrliche, lustige —,** honest fellow, jolly dog; **er steckt in keiner guten —,** he is a sickly fellow; **ich möchte nicht in seiner — stecken,** I should not like to be in his place; **es steckt ihm in der —,** it is in his nature; **mit — und Haar,** altogether; thoroughly, out and out; **er ist nichts als — und Knochen,** he is a mere bag of bones; **es ist um aus der — zu fahren,** it's enough to drive one mad; **mit ganzer —,** safe, unharmed; **die — ist allweg näher als das Hemd,** charity begins at home (*prov.*). *Comp.* **—absonderung,** *f.* cutaneous secretion. **—artig,** *adj.* skin-like. **—ausdünstung,** *f.* perspiration. **—ausschlag,** *m.* cutaneous eruption. **—beschuppung,** *f.* desquamation. **—bräune,** *f.* croup. **—drüsen-krankheit,** *f.* scrofula. **—falten,** *pl.* wrinkles. **—farbe,** *f.* complexion. **—geschwulst,** *f.* edema. **—lehre,** *f.* dermatology. **—moos,** *n.* nettle-rash. **—pflege,** *f.* sanitary *or* cosmetic care of the skin, cosmetics. **—planken,** *pl.* outer planking of a ship. **—reinigend,** *adj.*; **—reinigende Mittel,** cosmetics, medicines for improving the complexion.

Hautboi'st (*three syllables*), *m.* (**—en,** *pl.* **—en**) hautboy player.

Häut'—chen, *n.* membrane; pellicle, film. **—en,** *v.* I. *a.* to skin. II. *r.* to cast the skin. **—eln,** *v.a.* to peel, skin. **—ig,** *adj. & adv.* membranous, cuticular; (*in comp.* =)-skinned. **—ung,** *f.* skinning; casting of the skin.

Hautelis'se, *f.* high-warp tapestry. *Comp.* **—n-stuhl,** *m.* upright loom.

Havarie', Haverei', *f.* damage by sea; average; **große —,** gross average; **kleine —,** particular average.

Havarie'ren, *v.* I. *a.* to injure. II. *n.* to make average.

Ha'velock, *m.* (**—s,** *pl.* **—s**); **Herren-—,** ulster.

He! *int.* ha! **—da!** ho there!

He'be, *f.* (*pl.* **—n**) lever, pulley, instrument for heaving *or* lifting; *see* **—opfer.** **—l,** *m.* (**—ls,** *pl.* **—l**) instrument for heaving *or* lifting; lever, jack; pry; leaven (*Bak.*). **—ln,** *v.a. & n.* (*aux.* **h.**) to move with a lever.

He'b—en, *ir.v.* I. *a.* to lift, raise, heave; to draw up; to elevate; to exalt; to levy; to make prominent, relieve, set off (*Paint., etc.*); to remove, put an end to; to settle (*disputes*); to cure (*disorders*); to reduce (*fractions*); to clear (*an equation*); to patronize (*art, etc.*); to receive (*money*); **eine Dame aus dem Wagen —en,** to help a lady out of a carriage; **aus dem Sattel —en,** to unhorse; **aus der Taufe —en,** to stand sponsor to; **ein fünfmal gehobener Vers,** a verse of five beats *or* accents; **—e dich weg,** begone! get away! **Wein aus dem Fasse —en,** to draw wine from the cask with a siphon; **einen —en,** to drink a glass of beer (*sl.*). II. *r.* to rise; **der Teig —t sich,** the dough is rising; **ihr Busen hob sich,** her bosom was heaving; **die Preise —en sich,** prices are looking up; der Handel —t sich wieder, commerce is reviving; vier zugezählt, vier abgezogen —t sich, four added and four subtracted leaves the same whole; das —t sich, that balances the matter, that makes us quits; unsere Forderungen —en sich, our demands balance each other; in gehobener Stimmung sein, to be in an exalted frame of mind, to be in high spirits. III. r. (= sich halten) to hold o.s. by, to hold on to (*dial.*); es —t sich nicht, it does not hold (*dial.*). **—er**, *m.* (—ers, *pl.* —er) lifter, raiser, heaver; lever; crane; elevator (*Anat.*); siphon. **—ig**, *adj.*; ein fünf—iger Vers, a verse of five accents. **—lich**, *adj. & adv.* that may be raised *or* heaved. **—ung**, *f.* raising; lifting; heaving; patronage, encouragement; receiving; levy; solution; revenue; tax; elevation, rising ground; arsis (*Mus.*); accented syllable, accent, beat (*Metre*). *Comp.* **—amme**, *f.* midwife. **—arzt**, *m.* accoucheur. **—arzneikunst**, *f.* obstetrics. **—e=arm**, *m.* lever, piston. **—e=balken**, *m.* lever, crowbar. **—e=band**, *n.* truss. **—e=baum**, *m.* lever. **—e=bock**, *m.* machine for lifting, crane. **—e=daumen**, *m.* lever, lift. **—e=eisen**, *n.* crow-bar; elevatory (*Surg.*). **—e=griff**, *m.* lifting handle. **—e=krahn**, *m.* hoisting, *or* elevating, crane. **—e=kunde**, *f.* obstetrics. **—e=lade**, *f.* crane. **—el=arm**, *m.* arm of a lever. **—el=führung**, *f.* lever-guide. **el=kraft**, *f.* leverage (-power). **—el=punkt**, *m.* bearing. **—el=übersetzungsverhältnis**, *n.* proportion of the lever-arms. **—el=verhältnis**, *n.* leverage. **—e=muskel**, *m.* elevator (*Anat.*). **—e=opfer**, *n.* heave-offering. **—e=punkt**, *m.* fulcrum. **—er=förmig**, *adj.* siphon-shaped. **—e=rolle**, *f.* register of dues and taxes (*Law; obs.*). **—e=schraube**, *f.* lifting screw. **—e=stange**, *f.* handspike. **—e=walze**, *f.* lifting roller. **—e=werk**, **—e=zeug**, *n.* tools for lifting weights. **—e=winde**, *f.* windlass. **—e=zänglein**, *n.* elevatory (*Surg.*). **—ungs=beamte(r)**, *m.* receiver of public money, excise-officer. **—ungs=kammer**, *f.* inland-revenue office.

Hebrä'—er, *m.* (—ers, *pl.* —er) Hebrew. **—isch**, *adj. & adv.* Hebrew.

Hebra—is'mus, *m.* Hebraism. **—i'st**, *m.* (—is'ten, *pl.* —is'ten) Hebrew scholar, Hebraist.

He'ch—el, *f.* (*pl.* —eln) hatchel, hackle, flax-comb; censurer; durch die —el ziehen, to censure severely. **—elei'**, *f.* continuous hackling; continuous censuring. **—eln**, *v.a.* to hackle; to satirize, censure severely, criticize, lash. **—elung**, *f.* hackling, hatchelling; censuring *or* satirizing, slashing criticism. **—ler**, *m.* (—lers, *pl.* —ler) hackler; censurer; satirist. *Comp.* **—el=bank**, *f.* hackling-bank. **—el=scherz**, *m.* sarcasm, biting jest. **—el=schrift**, *f.* satirical writing. **—el=werg**, *n.* tow.

Hech'se, *f.* (*pl.* —n) hamstring, gambrel.

Hecht, *m.* (—es, *pl.* —e) pike (*Icht.*). *Comp.* **—bars**, **—barsch**, *m.* light spotted perch. **—grau**, *adj.* light gray. **—kraut**, *n.* water-milfoil.

Heck, *n.* (—(e)s, *pl.* —e) lattice-work fence; gate in such fence; afterdeck, stern. **—e**, *f.* (*pl.* —en) hedge; inclosure; brush-wood; lebendige —e, quickset hedge; dichte —e, thick-set (hedge); tote —e, paling. **—icht**, *adj. & adv.* (*obs.*) hedge-like. **—ig**, *adj.* covered with hedges *or* copse. *Comp.* **—balken**, *m.* wing-transom (*Naut.*). **—en=baum**, *m.* hedge-tree; dogwood. **—en=beschneider**, **—en=binder**, *m.* hedger. **—en=buche**, *f.* hornbeam. **—en=gang**, *m.* lane between hedges. **—en=hopfen**, *m.* wild hop. **—en=rose**, *f.* dog-rose. **—en=schere**, *f.* hedge-clipper. **—en=schlehe**, *f.* sloe. **—en=sichel**, *f.* hedge-bill. **—en=zaun**, *m.* quickset hedge. **—geschütz**, *n.* stern-chaser **—jagd**, *f.* stern-chase; shooting over hedges· poaching. **—jäger**, *m.* poacher.

He'ck—e, *f.* (*pl.* —en) hatch, brood, breed; breeding-time; breeding-cage. **—en**, *v.a. & n.* (*aux.* h.) to hatch, to breed, to produce. *Comp.* **—groschen**, *m.* lucky money, by vulgar superstition believed to multiply itself. **—lauge**, *f.* mother water (*Chem.*). **—männchen**, *n.* money-spinner. **—münze**, *f.* **—pfennig**, *m.* luck(y) penny, nest-egg. **—zeit**, *f.* pairing time.

He'de, *f.* tow, oakum. **—n**, *adj.* of tow *or* oakum.

He'derich, *m.* (—es, *pl.* —e) hedge-mustard.

Heer, *n.* (—es, *pl* —e) army; host; multitude; das wilde, wütende —, Wodan's (Arthur's) chase; the host of the wild huntsman, the wild hunt; stehendes —, standing army; Dienst im aktiven —e, service in the ranks, service with the colours. *Comp.* **—bann**, *m.* ban, summons to arms; general levy, militia. **—es=abteilung**, *f.* division of an army. **—es=einrichtung**, *f.* army-organization. **—es=flucht**, *f.* desertion. **—es=flüchtig**, *adj.*; —esflüchtig werden, to desert. **—(es)=flüchtige(r)**, **—es=flüchtling**, *m.* deserter. **—es=folge**, *f.* (compulsory) military service; —esfolge leisten, to join the army. **—es=haufen**, *m.* host, army. **—es=macht**, *f.* military forces, armed intervention; troops. **—es=schar**, *f.* (*see* —schar) army, host, legion; die himmlischen —es=scharen, the heavenly host. **—fahrt**, *f.* campaign. **—flucht**, *f.* desertion. **—flügel**, *m.* wing of an army, flank. **—führer**, *m.* leader of an army, general, commander-in-chief. **—gerät**, *n.* baggage, military train. **—haufe**, *m.* corps, division, squadron, column of an army; little army. **—holz**, *n.* jay (*Orn.*). **—meister**, *m.* commander-in-chief; grand master (*of an order*). **—pauke**, *f.* kettle-drum. **—säule**, *f.* column of an army. **—schar**, *f.* legion, host, army; der Herr der —scharen, the Lord of Hosts. **—schau**, *f.* review (of troops), military review. **—spitze**, *f.* vanguard. **—steuer**, *f.* war-tax. **—straße**, *f.* military road; highway. **—strom**, *m.* principal river, main waterway (*poet.*). **—ver=pflegungsamt**, *n.* commissariat-department. **—wagen**, *m.* baggage-waggon; Charles' Wain. **—wesen**, *n.* army affairs. **—wurm**, *m.* army-worm, grass worm, snake worm (*migrating host of larvæ of Sciara militaris*). **—zug**, *m.* train, *or* march, of an army; army on the march; campaign. **—zwang**, *m.* forced military service.

Heer'de, *f.* (*pl.* —n) *see* **Herde.**

He'f—e, *f.* (*pl.* —en) yeast, barm; dregs, sediment; auf die —e, bis zur —e, to the very dregs. **—icht**, (*obs.*) *adj. & adv.* yeast-like. **—ig**, *adj. & adv.* barmy, yeasty; full of lees. *Comp.* **—en=brot**, **—en=gebäck**, *n.* bread, *or* pastry, baked with yeast. **—en=teig**, *m.* leavened dough.

Heft, *n.* (—es, *pl.* —e) haft, handle, hilt, fastening, pin, hook; number, *or* part, of a work; stitched, *or* paper-covered, book; copy-book; einem das — in die Hand geben, to allow a p. to have all his own way; einem das — entwinden, to wrest the power from s.o.; das — in der Hand haben, to govern, be at the helm of affairs; eine Sache beim —e fassen, to set the right way to work; die Zeitschrift erscheint in zwanglosen —en, the periodical appears in occasional numbers. **—e**, *f.* act of tying up (*vine-tendrils*). **—el**, *m. & n.* (—els, *pl.* —el) pin, peg, hook, clasp; —el und Schlingen, hooks and eyes. **—eln**, *v.a.* to fasten (*with hooks and eyes*), clasp, pin. *Comp.* **—weise**, *adv.* in numbers, in parts.

Hef't—en, *v.a.* to fasten; to stitch, sew; to pin; to hook, to fix. **—ung**, *f.* fastening, attaching, stitching. *Comp.* **—faden**, *m.* basting thread

—lade, *f.* bookbinder's sewing frame *or* press. **—maschine,** *f.* sewing machine; sewing book. **—nadel,** *f.* stitching needle. **—pflaster,** *n.* sticking plaster. **—schnur,** *f.* pack-thread.

Hef't—ig, *adj. & adv.* forcible, violent; vehement, furious, impetuous; passionate; fervent. **—igkeit,** *f.* vehemence, violence, impetuosity.

He'g—e, *f.* preserving; care; preserve.

He'g—en, *v.a.* to hedge *or* fence about, to inclose; to protect, preserve; to comprise, contain; to shelter; to cherish, take care of; to have, entertain (*doubt, dislike, etc.*); **—en und pflegen,** to cherish and protect, to foster with great care. **—er,** *m.* (**—ers,** *pl.* **—er**) keeper; hoarder; socager; forester. *Comp.* **—e=holz,** *n. see* **—e=wald.** **—e=reiter,** *m.* gamekeeper. **—e=säule,** *f.* landmark. **—e=tiere,** *pl.* preserved game. **—e=wald,** *m.* forest fenced in. **—e=wasser,** *n.* fish-preserve. **—e=weide, —e=wiese,** *f.* inclosure (*of a common*). **—e=zeit,** *f.* close time (*for game*).

He'her, *see* **Häher.**

Hehl, *n.* (—(e)s) concealment; **er hat der Sache** (*gen.*) **kein** *or* **nicht —, er hat es** (*old gen.*) **kein —, er macht kein — daraus,** he makes no secret of it. **—en,** *v.a.* to conceal. **—er,** *m.* (**—ers,** *pl.* **—er**) concealer, receiver (of stolen goods); **der —er ist so schlimm wie der Stehler,** the receiver is as bad as the thief (*prov.*). **—erei',** *f.* act of concealing stolen property.

Hehr, *adj. & adv.* exalted, majestic, sublime; august, sacred; **hoch und —,** high and commanding.

Hei'da, Hei'sa, *int.* huzza!

[1]**Heid—e,** *f.* (*pl.* **—en**), heath; uncultivated land; heather, broom, heath (*Bot.*); brushwood; thicket. **—el,** *see the comp's.* **—ig,** *adj. & adv.* heathy. *Comp.* **—e=bienenkraut,** *n.* wild rosemary. **—e=blüte,** *f.* heath blossom. **—e=boden,** *m.* heathy soil. **—e=busch,** *m.* furze, gorse. **—e=drossel,** *f.* red-wing. **—e=flachs,** *m.* flaxweed. **—e=geflügel,** *n.* moorgame. **—e=gewächse,** *pl.* heaths. **—e=ginster,** *m.* gorse, furze. **—e=hahn,** *m.* heathcock. **—e=kraut,** *n.* heather. **—e=land,** *n.* heath, a tract of barren country. **—el=beere,** *f.* bilberry; whortleberry. **—el=hahn,** *see* **—e=hahn.** **—e=lerche,** *f.* wood-lark; meadowlark. **—en=geld,** *n.* money paid for pasturage. **—en=röslein,** *n.* wild rose (*title of a well known allegorical poem of Goethe*). **—e=rauch,** *m.* fog on a heath *or* in a forest. **—(e=)schnucke,** *f.* sheep of the (Lüneburg) heath. **—e=schwamm,** *m.* species of mushroom.

[2]**Heid—e,** *m.* (**—en,** *pl.* **—en**), **—in,** *f.* heathen, Gentile, pagan; **Juden und —en,** Jews and Gentiles; **stark wie ein —e,** very strong; **zu —en machen,** to heathenize. **—en=schaft,** *f.*, **—en=tum,** *n.* heathendom; paganism; pagans. **—nisch,** *adj. & adv.* heathenish, pagan. *Comp.* **—e=korn,** *n.* buckwheat (*introduced by Saracens*). **—en=angst,** *f.* a mortal fright (*coll.*). **—en=apostel,** *m.* apostle to the Gentiles. **—en=bekehrer,** *m.* missionary. **—en=bekehrung,** *f.* conversion of heathens, mission to heathens, missionary work among heathens. **—en=bild,** *n.* idol. **—en=christ,** *m.* heathen proselyte. **—en=geld,** *n.* enormous sum of money. **—en=lärm,** *m.* very great noise. **—en=mäßig,** *adj. & adv.* very large; **—enmäßig viel Geld,** an enormous sum of money. **—en=sitte,** *f.* heathenish custom.

Heidi', *int.* away! **— gehen,** to get lost (*sl.*).

Heidu'ck, *m.* (**—en,** *pl.* **—en**) Hungarian footsoldier; footman (in Hungarian costume).

Hei'kel(ig), *see* **Häkel(ig)**; ticklish; difficult; dainty.

Heil, I. *adj. & adv.* unhurt, sound, whole; healed, well; **seine Wunde ist —,** his wound is healed up. II. *n.* (**—(e)s,** prosperity, happiness, welfare; salvation, redemption; **das ewige —,** the eternal welfare *or* salvation; **im Jahre des —s,** in the year of grace, in the year of our Lord; **sein — versuchen,** to try one's luck, take one's chance; **es war mir zum —,** it was lucky for me, fortunately; **gut —!** (*call of members of athletic and gymnastic clubs, perhaps to be rendered by*) good cheer! good luck! **all —!** (*call of members of cycling clubs*) good luck! **— dem König!** long live the king! **— dir im Siegerkranz,** *or* **— unserm König, —,** God save the king! **— dir!** hail! **— dem Volke, welches, &c.,** happy the people that, *etc.*; **— dem Manne, der . . .,** blessed be the man who . . **—and,** *m.* (**—ands,** *pl.* **—ande**) Saviour. **—bar,** *adj. & adv.* that can be cured, curable; that will heal, healable. **—barkeit,** *f.* curableness. **—froh,** *adj.* wholly glad, very happy (*dial.*); extremely pleased.

Hei'l—en, *v.* I. *a.* to heal, cure, make well. II. *n.* (*aux.* **s.**) to grow well, to heal; **—end,** healing, curative, remedial. **—er,** *m.* (**—ers,** *pl.* **—er**) healer. **—sam,** *adj. & adv.* healing; wholesome; salutary, beneficial; **die Lektion wird ihm sehr —sam sein,** the lesson will do him a great deal of good. **—samkeit,** *f.* wholesomeness, salutariness; salutary effect. **—ung,** *f.* curing, healing; cure. *Comp.* **—anstalt,** *f.* medical establishment, sanatorium, hospital. **—art,** *f.* method of cure *or* curing. **—bad,** *n.* mineral bath. **—bringend,** *adj.* salutary, blessing. **—bringer,** *m.* bringer of blessings; Saviour. **—brunnen,** *m.* mineral springs, spa. **—butte,** *f.* halibut (*Icht.*). **—gehülfe,** *m.* barber-surgeon. **—gymnastik,** *f.* hygienic gymnastics; kinesipathy; **schwedische —gymnastik,** movement cure, lingism. **—holder, —holunder,** *m.* dwarf-elder (*Bot.*). **—kraft,** *f.* healing power. **—kräftig,** *adj.* having sanative power, possessing medicinal virtue, curative; **—kräftige Eigenschaft,** medical property. **—kraut,** *n.* medicinal herb. **—kunst, —kunde,** *f.* medicinal science, healing art, therapeutics. **—kundig,** *adj.* skilled in medicine. **—künstler,** *m.* empiric, medical quack; physician (*rarely in this sense*). **—los,** *adj. & adv.* wicked, profligate, abandoned, godless; heinous; disastrous; dreadful; wretched; very large, enormous (*coll.*); **eine —lose Angst,** a terrible fright; **—los viel Geld,** no end of money (*coll.*). **—losigkeit,** *f.* reprobate condition; wickedness; wretchedness. **—mittel,** *n.* remedy; medical drug. **—mittel=lehre,** *f.* pharmacology, materia medica; **zur —mittel=lehre gehörig,** pharmacological. **—pflaster,** *n.* healing plaster; **(das englische)** sticking plaster. **—plan,** *m.* mode of treatment. **—quelle,** *f.* mineral springs, medicinal waters, wells. **—prozeß,** *m.* healing process, cure, recovery. **—s=armee,** *f.* Salvation army. **—serum,** *n.* antitoxic serum, antitoxin; **—serum gegen Diphtheritis,** diphtheria antitoxin. **—s=mittel,** *n.* means of salvation. **—s=monat,** *m.* December. **—s=ordnung,** *f.* way of salvation; **göttliche —sordnung,** divine dispensation, economy of salvation. **—stätte,** *f.* place of cure. **—stoff,** *m.* anything curative. **—stoffkunde, —stoff=kunst,** *f.* materia medica. **—s=wahrheiten,** *f.pl.* ground principles of Christianity, cardinal truths of Christianity. **—wasser,** *n.* medicinal *or* mineral water. **—wurz,** *f.* medicinal herb.

Hei'lig, *adj. & adv.* holy, godly; sacred; inviolable; solemn; venerable, august; **der —e Abend** *or* **—abend,** Christmas eve; **ein —er Mann,** a holy man; **eine —e Pflicht,** a sacred duty; **ein —er Ort,** a sacred place; **des Herrn —er Tempel,** the Lord's holy temple (*obs.*); **das —e Abendmahl,** the Lord's supper, communion; —es Bein, os sacrum; —e Woche, Passion week; der —e Christ, Jesus Christ; Christmas; —e Jungfrau, the holy virgin, the blessed virgin (Mary; *abbr.* B. V. M.); — sprechen, to canonize; — versprechen, to promise solemnly. —e(r), *m.*, —e, *f.* saint; ein wunderlicher —er, a queer fellow, an odd fish (*coll.*). —e(s), *n.* holy thing, sacred thing. —keit, *f.* holiness, sanctity, sacredness; Seine —keit, His Holiness. —lich, *adv.* in a holy manner. —tum, *n.* (—tums, *pl.* —tümer) holy place, sanctuary; relic; sacred thing. *Comp.* —abend, *m.* Christmas Eve. —en=bein, *n.* bone of a saint. —en=bild, *n.* image, *or* picture, of a saint. —en=blende, *f.* niche for image of a saint. —en=buch, *n.* book of legends of saints. —en=dienst, *m.* worship of saints. —en=glanz, *m.* halo. —en=haus, *n.*, —en=kapelle, *f.* chapel of a saint; shrine. —en=kalender, *m.* menology, menologium. —en=schein, *m.* halo (*of glory*), glory, gloriole; (*in painting*) aureola; nimbus. —halten, *n.*, —haltung, *f.* religious observance, the keeping holy. —machend, *adj.* sanctifying. —spre=chung, *f.* canonization. —tums=schändung, *f.* sacrilege.

Hei'lig—en, *v.a.* to hallow, sanctify; to consecrate; to keep holy; to sanction, justify; der Zweck —t die Mittel, the end justifies the means. —ung, *f.* hallowing, sanctification; consecration. *Comp.* —ungs=kraft, *f.* sanctifying power.

Heim, I. *adv.* home, homeward; — fallen, to devolve, revert to; einem — leuchten, to light one home; to send one about his business, to give a p. a piece of one's mind; der wurde — geschickt, he caught it. II. *n.* (—s, *pl.* —e) home; domicile, dwelling, abode; hamlet; township; (*obs. m. & n.*) inclosure; — für Genesende, convalescent home. —at, *f.* (*pl.* —aten) home, native place *or* country. —at=lich, *adj. & adv.* native, belonging to one's home. —at=wärts, *adv.* homewards, home. —chen, *n.* (—chens) cricket. —isch, *adj. & adv.* home-bred; domestic, home-like; native, national; indigenous; sich —isch machen, to make oneself at home, to settle down. —lich, *adj. & adv.* private, secluded, secret; stealthy, underhand; secretive, close; domesticated; homely; comfortable, snug; *see* Geheim; —lich lachen, to laugh secretly, to laugh in one's sleeve; —lich thun, to affect a mysterious and knowing air. —lichkeit, *f.* secrecy; secret; privacy; place of retirement. *Comp.* —at=los, *adj.* without a country *or* home, homeless. —at=recht, *n.* right of a native *or* naturalized person. —ats=gesetz, *n.* law of settlement. —ats=kunde, *f.* study of actual, *or* local, surroundings; acquaintance with, *or* instruction in, home surroundings. —ats=schein, *m.* certificate of being a native *or* naturalized. —fahrt, *f.* return *or* journey home. —fall, *m.* devolution, reversion, escheat. —fällig, *adj.* revertible, devolving. —führen, *v.a.* to lead home; die Braut — führen, to bring home one's bride, to carry off the bride. *See* Braut. —führung, *f.* (einer Braut) bringing home a bride. —gang, *m.* way home; departure home; death. —kehr, —kunft, *f.* return home. —kommen, *ir.v.n.* (*aux.* s.) to return home. —lich=haltung, *f.* concealment. —lich=thuerei, *f.*, —lich=thun, *n.* affectation of secrecy. —rechts=brief, *m.* certificate of naturalization. —reise, *f.* homeward voyage; return. —ritt, *m.* ride home. —ruf, *m.*, —rufung, *f.* call *or* summons home, recall. —stätte, *f.* home(stead); toft (*Law*); —stätte für arme Greise, home for the aged poor; —stätte für Irrsinnige, lunatic asylum. —stellen, *v.a.* (einem etwas) to refer to, to leave to. —steuer, *f.* marriage portion, dowry. —suchen, *v.a.* to visit, frequent; to punish, requite. —suchung, *f.* visitation; affliction. —tücke, *f.* malice, secret malice, underhand trick. —tückisch, *adj.* malicious, mischievous, crafty, treacherous. —weg, *m.* way home, return home; auf dem —wege, coming home, on the way home. —wärts, *adv.* homeward, home. —weh, *n.* home-sickness, nostalgia. —zahlen, *v.a.* to repay, refund, return.

Hein, *m.*; Freund —, Death (*coll.*).

Heint, Hint, *adv.* this night, to-night (*obs. & dial.*); last night (*obs. & dial.*); to-day (*dial.*).

Heinz, *m.* (—en, *pl.* —en) machine for drawing water from a great depth; der faule —, athanor (*Chem.*). *Comp.* —en=kunst, *f.* art of drawing up water; chain-pump. —en=seil, *n.* chain of a pump.

Hein'zel— (*in comp.*) —bank, *f.* board to cut *or* carve upon. —männchen, *n.* brownie.

Hei'rat, *f.* (*pl.* —en) marriage; nuptials, wedding; — aus Liebe, love-match; die — ist rückgängig gemacht, the match is broken off; auf — ausgehen, to look out for a wife. *Comp.* —s=antrag, *m.* offer of marriage, proposal; einer Dame einen —santrag machen, to propose to a lady. —s=bureau, *n.* matrimonial agency *or* office. —s=fähig, *adj.* marriageable. —s=gesuch, *n.* demand in marriage, offer of marriage. —s=gut, *n.* marriage portion, dowry; ohne —s=gut, portionless. —s=kandidat, *m.* marrying man, suitor; match (*coll.*). —s=kandidatin, *f.* marrying woman; match (*coll.*). —s=konsens, *m.* (marriage) license. —s=kontrakt, *m.* marriage-contract, marriage-settlement. —s=lust, *f.* desire to marry, inclination for marrying. —s=lustig, *adj.* desirous of marrying. —s=macher, —s=stifter, *m.* match-maker. —s=schein, *m.* marriage certificate. —s=schwindel, *m.* dabbling in match-making. —s=vermittler(in), *m.* (*f.*) go-between, match-maker, matrimonial agent.

Hei'raten, *v.a. & n.* (*aux.* h.) to marry; to wed (*high style*); to take in marriage, to take for a wife *or* husband; zum zweiten Male —, to marry again, to take a second wife *or* husband; Schiller heiratete Frl. Charlotte von Lengefeld, Schiller married Miss Charlotte von Lengefeld; sie hat ihren Jugendgeliebten endlich geheiratet, she has at last become married to the friend of her youth.

Hei'sch—en, *v.a.* to ask, demand; to postulate (*obs. & poet.*). *Comp.* —e=satz, *m.* postulate.

Hei'ser, *adj. & adv.* hoarse. —keit, *f.* hoarseness.

Heiß, *adj. & adv.* hot; burning; boiling, torrid; ardent; passionate; fervid; vehement; mir ist —, I feel warm; einem die Hölle — machen, to terrify one, aggravate a p.'s alarm; einem den Kopf — machen, to make one's blood boil, trouble *or* worry one; —e Gebete, fervent prayers; —e Kastanien, baked chestnuts; —er Kampf, hot combat; —e Liebe, ardent love. *Comp.* —blütig, *adj.* warm-blooded. —hunger, *m.* ravenous hunger, voracious appetite. —hungrig, *adj.*, ravenously hungry, voracious. —sporn, *m.* hot-spur, fire-brand.

Hei'ß—en, *ir. v.* I. *a.* to command, enjoin, bid, direct; to name, call, denominate; einen gehen —en, to bid one go; er hieß ihn herein kommen, he bade him come in; thue, wie dir geheißen, do as you are bid; gut —en, to approve of; einen willkommen —en, to bid one welcome; wer hieß mich auch alles wagen? how could I have taken it into my head to risk everything? wer hat Sie das geheißen? who bade you do that? who told you to do that? II. *n.* (*aux.* h.) to be called, to bear a name; to mean, signify; das —t, that is to say, that is (really), that is equal to; wie —en Sie? what is your name? wie —t dieses Dorf? what is the name of this village? wie —t das auf Deutsch, what is that in German? what is the German for this? er lachte geradezu, was so viel —en sollte als, he laughed outright, as much as to say; das —e ich lügen, that 's what I call a lie; das —t gelaufen, that 's good running; I call that good running; was soll das —en? what is the meaning of this? what do you mean? das will wenig —en, that is of little consequence; das will etwas —en, that is saying a good deal. III. *n. imp.* es —t, it is said, reported; damit es nicht —e, that it may not be said; wie es im Liede —t, as the song says; hier —t es mit Recht, one may well say here; jetzt —t es Mut! now for courage!

Hei'ster, *m.* (—s, *pl.* —) *also f.* (*pl.* —n) young tree, young beech tree.

Hei'ter, *adj. & adv.* serene, clear, bright; happy, cheerful, glad; calm, unruffled; — werden, to grow bright, to clear up; to become interesting (*coll.*); to get slightly tipsy (*coll.*). —keit, *f.* serenity, brightness; cheerfulness.

Hei'zbar, *adj. & adv.* that may be heated; —e Zimmer, rooms with stoves *or* fireplaces.

Hei'z—en, *v.a.* to heat; to make a fire; mit Holz, Steinkohlen —en, to burn wood, coals; dieses Zimmer —t sich gut, this room is easily heated. —er, *m.* (—ers, *pl.* —er) stoker, maker of a fire; heating-apparatus. —ung, *f.* heating; fuel. *Comp.* —apparat, *m.* heating-apparatus, heater. —effekt, *m.* calorific effect, temperature. —kraft, *f.* heating power. —loch, *n.* stoke-hole. —material, *n.* fuel. —ort, *m.* fire-place. —röhre, *f.* heating pipe. —wert, *m.* heating power (*of coal*).

Hekatom'be, *f.* (*pl.* —n) hecatomb.

Hekta'r, *m. & n.* (—s, *pl.* —e) hectare.

Hek'tisch, *adj. & adv.* hectic.

Hek'to— (*in comp.*) —gramm, *n.* hectogramme. —gra'ph, *m.* hectograph. —liter, *n. & m.* hectolitre.

Held, *m.* (—en, *pl.* —en) hero; champion; famous person; principal person; — eines Romans, the hero, the principal person of a novel. —enhaft, *adj. & adv.* heroic. —enschaft, *f.* heroism; heroes. —entum, *n.* heroism; heroic age. —entümlich, *adj. & adv.* heroic. —in, *f.* heroine. *Comp.* —enalter, *n.* heroic age. —enbahn, *f.* heroic career. —enbild, *n.* hero (*poet.*). —enbuch, *n.* book of heroes (*a collection of mediæval popular metrical romances*); das deutsche —enbuch, collection of mediæval German heroic poems. —endichter, *m.* epic poet. —endichtung, *f.* heroic, *or* epic, poetry. —engedicht, *n.* epic. —engeist, *m.* heroic spirit. —enkühn, *adj. & adv.* brave as a hero. —enmäßig, —enmütig, *adj. & adv.* heroic, of heroic valour. —enmut, *m.* heroism, heroic valour *or* spirit. —enrolle, *f.* part of the, *or* a, hero. —ensage, *f.* heroic saga *or* legend. —enschar, *f.* band of heroes. —ensinn, *m.* heroism, heroic spirit. —enthat, *f.* heroic deed, bold exploit. —entod, *m.* heroic death. —enweib, *n.* heroic woman, heroine.

Hel'f—en, *ir.v.n.* (*aux.* h., *dat.*) to help, aid, assist; to succour; to avail, profit, do good to; to remedy; to deliver; einem auf die Spur —en, to put one on the track; was hülfe es dem Menschen, wenn, what is a man profited if (*B.*); einem zu seinem Rechte —en, to see that one gets his rights; was hilft's, wozu hilft's? of what use is it? what 's the good of it? es hilft (zu) nichts, it is of no use, it is no good; hilf Gott! hilf Himmel! Heaven preserve me! Good Heavens! bless you! (*to one sneezing*); so wahr mir Gott —e! so help me God! es hilft Ihnen nichts zu . . ., it is of no use for you to . . .; dem ist nicht (mehr) zu —en, he is past help; that is irremediable; ich kann mir nicht —en, I cannot help it; I don't know what to do; ich kann mir nicht —en, ich muß sagen, I cannot help saying; er weiß sich zu —en, he can manage, can take care of himself; er weiß sich immer zu —en, he is fruitful in resources. —er, *m.* (—ers, *pl.* —er) helper, assistant. *Comp.* —ershelfer, *m.* accomplice, abettor. —recht, *n.* right of seizing and selling a defendant's property. —rede, *f.* evasion, excuse. —willig, *adj.* ready to help.

Helio— (*in comp. does not take the principal accent.*) —graphie', *f.* heliography. —tro'p, *m.* heliotrope. —zen'trisch, *adj.* heliocentric.

Hell, *adj. & adv.* clear, bright, luminous; brilliant; clear, distinct, ringing; plain, evident; fair (*hair*); wir Sachsen sind —e, we Saxons are enlightened, wide awake (*coll.*); —er Mittag, broad noonday; am —en lichten Tage, in broad daylight; ein —er Tag, a fine day; —es Gelächter, loud laugh, ringing laughter, a hearty laugh; —e Thränen, big, round tears; —e Augenblicke, lucid intervals; in —en Haufen, in full force, in large numbers; —er Neid, pure jealousy; seine —e Freude an einer Sache haben, to evince an evident pleasure in a thing; —e Farben, light colours; um einen —en Spott bekommen, to get a dead bargain; die —e Wahrheit, the plain truth. —e, —heit (*rare*), *f.* clearness, distinctness; light, brightness, brilliancy, transparency. —en, *pl.* glades, clearings (*in woods*). —en, *v.a.* to make clear *or* bright, to clarify. —igkeit, *f.* clearness; brightness, splendour; loudness. —ung, *f.* act of clearing, of making clear *or* bright; clearing up; clearness, brightness. *Comp.* —äugig, *adj.* bright-eyed; clear-sighted. —braun, *adj.* light brown. —denkend, *adj.* clear-headed. —dunkel, I. *adj.* dusky. II. *n.* twilight, dusk; chiaroscuro. —hörig, *adj.*; —hörig werden, to begin to listen intently, to begin to pay much attention. —kopf, *m.* clear-headed person. —leuchtend, *adj.* luminous. —rot, *adj.* light, *or* bright, red. —sehen, *n.* clairvoyance. —sehend, *adj.* clear-sighted, keen-sighted, wide awake. —seher, *m.*, —seherin, *f.* clairvoyant, somnambulist. —sichtig, *adj.* clear-sighted, shrewd. —violett, *adj.* mauve.

Hellebar'd—e, (Hellebar't—e,) *f.* (*pl.* —en) halberd, halbert. —ier', *m.* (—iers, *pl.* —iere) halberdier. *Comp.* —eneisen, *n.* head of a halberd. —enförmig, *adj.* auriculate (*Bot.*). —enträger, *see* —ier.

Helle'n—isch, *adj. & adv.* Hellenic, Greek. —is'mus, *m.* (*pl.* —ismen) Hellenism.

Hel'ler, *m.* (—s, *pl.* —) small copper coin once current in several German states, still current in Austria (*less than a farthing*), farthing, mite (*B.*); kein roter —, not a farthing; bei — und Pfennig, to the last farthing, the whole sum; der letzte —, the last farthing. *Comp.* —arm, *adj.* excessively poor.

Hel'ling, *f.* (*pl.* —en) stocks, slip (*Shipb.*).

[1]**Helm,** *m.* (—es, *pl.* —e) helmet; dome, cupola; helm (*of an alembic*); caul; — ab zum Gebet! helmets off for prayers! (*Mil.*); gut unterm — verwahrt sein, to have good brains. —artig, *adj.* helmet-like; galeate(d) (*Bot.*). —en, *v.a.* to crest a coat of arms. *Comp.* —busch, *m.* crest, plume of a helmet. —dach, *n.* dome, cupola. —fenster, —gitter, —visi(e)r, *n.* visor of a helmet. —förmig, *adj.* galeate (*Bot.*). —gewölbe, *n.* vaulted roof. —kamm, *m.* crest. —kappe, *f.* casque. —kraut, *n.*

scutellaria. —lehen, *n.* fief entailed on heirs male. —röhre, *f.* helmet-nozzle. —rost, *m.* bars. —schieber, *m.* beaver, visor. —schlange, *f.* hooded snake. —schmuck, *m.*, —zier, *f.*, —zierat, *m.* ornament of a helmet, crest; badge. —strauß, —stutz, *m.* crest, plume. —sturz, *m.* visor.

²**Helm**, *m.* & *n.* (—es, *pl.* —e) (*usually in cpds.*) handle, helve. —en, *v.a.* to furnish with a handle. *Comp.* —stock, *m.* tiller (*Naut.*).

Helo't, *m.* (—en, *pl.* —en) helot. —en=tum, *n.* helotry, helotism. —isch, *adj.* helotic, slave-like, slavish.

Hem'd—(e), *n.* (—(e)s, *pl.* —(e)n, *dial.* —er) shirt; Frauen—(e), chemise; im bloßen —e, in one's shirt; bis aufs —, to the skin; das —(e) wechseln, to put on a clean shirt; das — ist mir näher als der Rock, blood is thicker than water; charity begins at home (*prov.*). —chen, *n.* (—chens, *pl.* —chen) little shirt; chemisette. *Comp.* —ärmel, *m.* shirt-sleeve. —en=hals, *m.* shirt-collar. —en=matz, *m.* little child with nothing but a shirt on (*coll.*). —hose, *f.* combination. —kragen, *m.* shirt-collar; hohe —kragen, stick-ups. —krause, *f.* frill. —leinwand, *f.* shirting. —nadel, *f.* shirt-pin. —schlitz, *m.* shirt-opening.

Hemisphä'r—e, *f.* (*pl.* —en) hemisphere. —isch, *adj.* & *adv.* hemispherical.

Hemm'bar, *adj.* & *adv.* that may be stopped *or* checked, impedible.

Hem'm—en, *v.a.* to hem in, to check, stop; to hinder, retard; to prohibit; to put on the drag *or* brake; to stop, deaden (*Naut.*); to curb, restrain (*passions, etc.*). —nis, *n.* (—ni(ss)es, *pl.* —ni(ss)e) check, obstruction, clog. —ung, *f.* arrest, restraint; checking, stopping; catch (*of a gun*); escapement (*of a watch*); prohibition. *Comp.* —feder, *f.* stopper (*Horol.*). —kette, *f.*, —schuh, *m.* drag-chain, brake. —ungs=spruch, *m.*, —ungs=urteil, *n.* arrest of judgment.

Hengst, *m.* (—es, *pl.* —e) stallion; male of the zebra, camel, *or* ass; bucket-pole in a draw-well. *Comp.* —füllen, *n.* colt. —geld, *n.* covering-fee, money paid for covering.

Hen'k—el, *m.* (—els, *pl.* —el) handle (*of a basket, of a pot, etc.*); ring, ear; hook; shank (*of a button*). —elig, *adj.* & *adv.* with a handle, handled. —eln, *v.a.* to furnish with a handle, ring, ear *or* hook (*by which to hang, etc.*). —en, *v.a.* to hang a p. on the gallows, to make a p. swing (*obs.* now replaced by hängen, aufhängen). —er, *m.* (—ers, *pl.* —er) hangman, executioner, Jack Ketch; tormentor; tyrant; the devil; was zum —er! what the deuce! geh zum —er! scher dich zum —er, go to the devil, go to Jericho! (*vulg.*); hol' euch der —er! deuce take you! (*vulg.*); ich frage den —er darnach, I don't care a straw, *or* a fig, about it (*vulg.*); das taugt den —er nichts! that 's not worth a button, that 's rot; daraus werde der —er klug, I cannot make head or tail of it, that would puzzle Old Nick himself (*coll.*); sein eigener —er sein, to be a self-tormentor. —erei', *f.* hangman's trade *or* house; hangman and assistants. *Comp.* —el=korb, *m.* basket with handles. —el=krug, *m.* jug, mug. —el=napf, *m.* porringer with an ear. —el=topf, *m.* pot with a handle. —ens=wert, *adj.* deserving to be hanged. —er=beil, *n.* executioner's axe. —er=frist, *see* Galgenfrist. —er=geld, *n.* hangman's wages. —ers=knecht, *m.* hangman's assistant; tormentor, torturer. —er=mäßig, *adj.* & *adv.* hangman-like, barbarous. —er(s)=mahl, *n.* last meal before execution; farewell dinner. —ers=strick, *m.* halter, rope for hanging.

Hen'ne, *f.* (*pl.* —n) hen; die — gluckt, the hen clucks; eine blinde — findet auch einmal ein Korn, a blind hen can sometimes find her corn, a blind man may perchance hit the mark (*prov.*); die — für das Ei geben, to make a stupid exchange; fette —, stone-crop (*Bot.*).

Hep, Hep Geschrei, *n.* the rabble's cry against the Jews, fanatic clamoring of the Antisemites.

Hepat—algie', *f.* pain in the liver; liver-complaint. —i'tis, *f.* inflammation of the liver.

Her, *adv.* hither, here, this way; near (*of place*); since, ago (*of time*); hin und —, to and fro, hither and thither; up and down, on all sides, there and back; ich dachte lange hin und —, I turned the matter over in my mind for a long time; hin und — sprechen, to debate, argue; das hin und —, indecision; rings um uns —, round about us; wo sind Sie —? where do you come from? what countryman are you? vom Anfange —, from the very beginning; wie lange ist es —? Fünf Jahre —, how long ago is it? Five years; das ist schon lange —, that is long ago; es ist etwa zwei bis drei Jahre —, daß wir uns trafen, it is between two and three years since we met; noch keine Viertelstunde —, not a quarter of an hour ago; die ganze Zeit —, all this time, all along; von oben (unten) —, from above (below); hinter einem — sein, to follow close on one, to press, *or* urge, one; die Hand —, give me your hand! geben Sie —, give it, let us have it! — damit, out with it! kommen Sie —, come here! wo hat er das —? where did he get that? hinter einer S. — sein, to be about, to be earnest in pursuit of, take pains to acquire something; von Süden —, from the south; weit —, from afar; nicht weit — sein, to be of low extraction; to be of little value; es ist nicht weit — mit ihm, he is not up to much; sein Unwohlsein ist nicht weit —, his indisposition is of no great importance. [**Her**, *as prefix to prepositions (used adverbially), is unaccented; as prefix to verbs it takes the accent and is separable; it sometimes signifies*, down, downwards; *sometimes*, out, off; *gen'lly its signification in all comp.'s is* motion hitherward, up, upwards.] *Comp.* —ab, —an, —auf, —aus, *see* Herab, Heran, Herauf, Heraus. —bei, *see* Herbei. —bemühen, *v.a.* to trouble one to come (up); sich —bemühen, to take the trouble of coming. —bestellen, *v.a.* to order hither, bid come; to appoint a meeting. —beten, *v.a.* to pray *or* say off mechanically. —bewegen, *v.a.* to move towards, to advance. —bringen, *ir.v.a.* to bring hither, in *or* up; to establish; to transmit (*from ancestors*); —gebracht, handed down (to our own times), customary, established (*by traditional usage*); —gebrachter Ton, —gebrachtes Wesen, conventionalism; —gebrachte Gewohnheit, ancient *or* established custom. —ein, *see* Herein. —erzählen, *v.a.* to tell over, rehearse; to relate, recite, narrate. —erzählung, *f.* detailed recital, narration (*rare*). —fahren, *ir.v.* I. *n* (*aux.* s.) to come hither, approach, arrive in a carriage *or* vessel; to move hastily along; über einen —fahren, to pounce upon, attack, inveigh against one. II. *a.* to bring, drive. —fallen, *ir.v.n.* (*aux.* s.) to fall hither *or* towards (*one*); über einen —fallen, to assail one (*with blows, angry words, etc.*). —finden, *ir.v.r.* to find one's way to a place. —fließen, *ir.v.n.* (*aux.* s.) to flow on, up, hither; to issue *or* proceed (*from*), originate (*in*). —für, *see* —vor. —gang, *m.* way hither; course of events *or* of a story, circumstances, proceedings; occurrence; der ganze —gang der Sache, the details of the story, the whole story. —geben, *ir.v.a.* to give here *or* up, to deliver; to give away, hand over; geben Sie mir gefälligst das Brot —, I'll trouble you for the bread, please pass me the bread; **ich will mich gar nicht dazu —geben,** I will not lend myself, *or* be a party, to that, I will have nothing to do with it; **Waren —geben für,** to sell goods at. **—gehen,** *ir.v.n.* (*aux.* **s.**) to go, walk, come hither, to approach; (*gen'lly used as v. imp.*) to come to pass, happen; to go on, be carried on; **vor etwas —gehen,** to go before; **über etwas —gehen,** to set to, set about something; **es geht über ihn —,** it is his turn now, he is attacked, cut up; **da geht es heiß —,** there is hot work going on there; **es geht lustig —,** things are going on merrily; **es geht armselig bei ihm —,** he lives in a poor way, is badly off; **so geht es (in der Welt) —,** that 's the way of the world, such is life; **wir wollen gleich darüber —gehen,** we shall set about it immediately, presently; **geh —,** come along (*dial*). **—gehören,** *v.n.* (*aux.* **h.**) to belong to (*this place, the matter in question*); to be to the purpose; **diese Bemerkungen gehören nicht (hier) —,** these remarks are out of place (here). **—gehörig,** *adj. & adv.* apposite, pertinent. **—halten,** *ir.v.* I. *a.* to hold forth *or* out, offer, tender. II. *n.* (*aux.* **h.**) to pay, suffer (*for*), bear the brunt (*of*); **sein Beutel muß —halten,** he has to pay. **—holen,** *v.a.* to fetch; **weit —geholt,** far-fetched. **—kommen,** I. *ir.v.n.* (*aux.* **s.**) to come hither *or* near, approach, advance; to be caused by; to be derived *or* descended (from); to be transmitted; to be established as a custom; to be the consequence (*of*), originate (*in*), arise (*from*); **wo kommt dies Wort —?** what is the derivation of this word? **wo soll die Zeit —kommen?** how shall we find the time? II. *subst. n.* origin, extraction, descent; traditional custom, usage; **es ist ein altes —kommen,** *or* **eine —gebrachte Sache,** it is an old custom. **—kömmlich,** *adj. & adv.* traditional, customary, usual. **—können,** *ir.v.n.* (*aux.* **h.**) to be able to come *or* go (*hither, near, etc.*). **—kunft,** *f.* coming hither, arrival; origin, descent, extraction. **—laden,** *ir.v.a.* to summon *or* invite hither. **—lallen,** *v.n.* (*aux.* **h.**) to say in a faltering, *or* lisping, manner. **—lassen,** *ir.v.a.* to let, permit to come (*hither, etc.*). **—laufen,** *ir.v.n.* (*aux.* **s.**) to run hither *or* near; **ein —gelaufener Kerl,** a vagabond *or* adventurer. **—legen,** *v.a.* to lay down (*here, etc.*); **Waren —legen,** to import goods. **—leiern,** *v.a.* to recite, *or* deliver, in a monotonous manner. **—leiten,** *v.a.* to lead, conduct hither; to derive (**von,** from); to draw from, deduce; to refer to (*cause or origin*); **sich —leiten,** to be derived from, to date from. **—leitung,** *f.* derivation; deduction. **—lesen,** *ir.v.a.* to read off, recite. **—locken,** *v.a.* to entice (*hither, on*), allure, decoy. **—machen,** *v.r.* (**über etwas**) to set about; (**über einen**) to fall upon, fall foul of. **—marsch,** *m.* march hither; approach. **—müssen,** *v.n.* (*aux.* **h.**) to be obliged to come (*hither*) *or* appear. **—murmeln,** *v.a.* to murmur forth. **—nach,** *adv.* (*pron.* **herna'ch**) afterwards, hereafter, after this *or* that; **—nach?** what next? then? (*with preced'g acc.*); **den Tag —nach,** the day after. **—nehmen,** *ir.v.a.* to take, *or* get, from (*somewhere*); to deduce, derive; **wo nimmt er die Geduld —?** how has he the patience? **einen —nehmen,** to take one to task (*coll.*). **—nehmung,** *f.* deduction. **—nehmungslohn,** *m.* salvage upon recapture (*C. L.*). **—nennen,** *ir.v.a.* to name in succession, call over, recite. **—nie'der,** *adv. & sep. prefix* down (*hither*). **—peitschen,** *v.a.* to whip up. **—plappern,** *v.a.* to prattle out *or* off. **—rechnen,** *v.a.* to reckon up, enumerate. **—rechnung,** *f.* enumeration, specification. **—recken,** *v.a.* to stretch forth. **—reichen,** *v.a.* to reach, hand (*to*). **—reise,** *f.* journey hither, homeward journey. **—richten,** *v.a.* to fit up; to arrange; to prepare. **—rücken,** *v.n.* (*aux.* **s.**) to approach *or* draw near; to push on. **—rühren,** *v.n.* (*aux.* **h.**) (**von**) to originate (*in*), proceed, flow (*from*). **—sagen,** *v.a.* to recite, repeat, rehearse; to tell (*one's beads*); **das Tischgebet —sagen,** to say grace **—schaffen,** *reg.* to bring hither, to move near, to produce, procure. **—schießen,** *ir.v.* I. *n.* (*aux.* **s.**) to rush along, run, *or* fly, hither. II. *a.* to shoot hither; to advance (*money*). **—schlagen,** *ir.v.a.* to strike without hesitation; **schlag —!** strike, if you dare! **schlag mir den Ball —!** send me the ball. **—schreiben,** *ir.v.* I. *a.* to write hither, to this place. II. *r.* (**von**) to come, arise (*from*); to date (*from*); to originate (*in*). **—singen,** *ir.v.a.* to sing off. **—stammen,** *v.n.* (*aux.* **s.**) to descend, come, be derived (**von,** from). **—stammung,** *f.* descent, extraction, origin; derivation. **—stellbar,** *adj. & adv.* reparable, that may be restored. **—stellen,** *v.a.* to place here; to set up, establish, raise; to produce; **das läßt sich leicht —stellen,** that can be easily effected, produced; (**wieder**) to re-establish, repair, restore; to restore (*to health*); to reduce (*Chem.*); **er ist wieder ganz —gestellt,** he is quite restored to health again; **stellt euch —!** as you were (*Austrian Mil.*). **—steller,** *m.* restorer. **—stellung,** *f.* re-establishment, restoration; recovery. **—stellungs-mittel,** *n.* restorative. **—stottern,** *v.a.* to stammer out. **—strecken,** *v.a.* to stretch out, forth, extend; to advance (*money*). **—strich,** *m.* down-bow (*Mus.*); return of migratory birds. **—sturz,** *m.* rushing *or* crowding on, crowd, rush on. **—stürzen,** *v.n.* (*aux.* **s.**) to rush, plunge in (**über** *with acc.* upon). **—träger,** *m.* tell-tale (*vulg.*). **—über,** *adv. & sep. prefix* (*pron.* **herü'ber**) over hither, to this side, across. **—um, —unter, —vor,** *see* **Herum, Herunter, Hervor.** **—wagen,** *v.r.* to venture near, to venture to come to a place. **—wärts,** *adv.* in this direction, hitherwards. **—weg,** *m.* way hither. **—wieder,** *adv.* (*pron.* **herwie'der**) again, back again. **—winken,** *v.a.* to beckon to approach. **—zahlen,** *v.a.* to pay down. **—zählen,** *v.a.* to reckon up, enumerate. **—zaubern,** *v.a.* to conjure up. **—ziehen,** *ir.v.* I. *a.* to draw, pull near *or* hither. II. *n.* (*aux.* **h.**) to draw, move, march hither; to remove to a place; **—ziehen über einen,** to attack a p. sharply, to cut a p. up. **—zu,** *adv. & sep. prefix* (*pron.* **herzu'**) hither, to here, near. **—zug,** *m.* up-train.

Hera'b, *adv. & sep. prefix,* down (*hither*), down here; down from; downward; (*with preced'g acc.*) **den Berg —,** down (*from*) the mountain; **die Treppe —,** down (*the*) stairs; **von oben —,** from above; in a superior way *or* tone. *Comp.* **—bemühen,** *v.* I. *a.* to give a person (**einen**) the trouble of coming down. II. *r.* to take the trouble of coming down. **—hängend,** *adj. & adv.* pendulous; flowing. **—kommen,** *ir.v.n.* (*aux.* **s.**) to come down; to be reduced in circumstances, to be brought low. **—lassen,** *ir.v.* I. *a.* to lower, to let down. II. *r.* to condescend, deign; to stoop; **—lassend,** condescending, affable. **—lassung,** *f.* condescension, courtesy, affability. **—sehen,** *ir.v.n.* (*aux.* **h.**) to look down (**auf einen** *or* **etwas,** upon a p. *or* a th.), to despise. **—setzen,** *v.a.* to put lower down; to lower, degrade; to undervalue; to disparage; to reduce (*in price*); to depress; **—gesetzte Preise,** reduced prices. **—setzung,** *f.* degradation; abatement, reduction; disparagement, depreciation. **—sinken,** *ir.v.n.* (*aux.* **s.**) to sink down; to debase, *or* degrade, oneself. **—steigen,** *ir.v.n.* (*aux.* **s.**)

to descend, step down; to dismount. —**stim=men,** v.a. to lower; to tune lower; to deject, depress; to moderate (one's pretensions, etc.); **er muß die Saiten etwas —stimmen,** he must come down a peg or two. —**stimmung,** f. lowering; lowering of the pitch (Mus.); dejection; depression. —**wärts,** adv. downwards. —**wollen,** ir.v.n. to wish to come down. —**wünschen,** v.a. to imprecate, call down upon. —**würdigen,** v.a. to degrade, abase; to depreciate. —**würdigung,** f. degradation, abasement; disparagement.

Heral'd—ik, f. heraldry. —**isch,** adj. heraldic.

Hera'n, adv. & sep. prefix, on (hither), near, along; up along, upwards, from away; (with preced'g acc. signifies motion towards the speaker); **er ging an sie —,** he went up to them; **nur —!** come on! advance! Comp. —**bilden,** v.a. to bring up, educate. —**kom=men,** ir.v.n. (aux. s.) to come on, near or nigh; to approach; to come alongside (Naut.); to set-in. —**kunft,** f. approach. —**nahen,** v.n. (aux. s.) to draw near, approach. —**rücken,** v.n. (aux. s.) to push onward, advance; to draw near. —**wachen,** v.n. to sit up for. —**wachsen,** ir.v.n. (aux. s.) to grow up; **das —wachsende Geschlecht,** the rising generation. —**ziehen,** ir.v. I. a. & n. (aux. s.) to draw near. II. a. to draw on or along with; to draw into. interest in; to tow.

He'rauch, m. (—s) haze; peat-smoke.

Herau'f, adv. & sep. prefix, up (hither); upwards, from below (towards the speaker). Comp. —**beschwören,** v.a. to conjure up; to bring on, occasion. —**blicken,** v.n. (aux. h.) to glance up or upwards. —**kommen,** ir.v.n. (aux. s.) to come up; —**kommen in der Welt,** to get on or rise in the world; —**kommen lassen,** to order up. —**müssen,** v.n. to be obliged to come up. —**steigen,** ir.v.n. to come up (as a storm).

Herau's, adv. & sep. prefix, out (hither); from within, forth, from among (towards the speaker); —! turn out! (Mil.); — **damit! — mit der Sprache!** out with it! speak out! **er ist fein** (or **schön**) **heraus,** he is a lucky fellow (coll.); **von innen —,** from within; **er hat es —,** he has found it out; he understands it (coll.); **rund, frei —,** flatly, bluntly, fearlessly; **(nach) vorn —,** in the front (of the house); **da —,** this way out. Comp. —**arbeiten,** v. I. a. to work out. II. r. to extricate oneself. —**bekommen,** ir.v.a. to get out; to make out, guess; to remove; to get back in exchange; **ich bekomme eine Mark —,** I get a shilling change; **er kann die Aufgabe nicht —bekommen,** he is unable to solve the problem. —**bringen,** ir.v.a. to bring out; to get out; to find out; to understand; to force out; **seine Kosten —bringen,** to cover one's expenses. —**fahren,** ir.v.n. (aux. s.) to drive or sail out; to rush, fly or burst out; to slip out or drop a word. —**finden,** ir. v. I. a. to find out, discover. II. r. to find one's way out; to see one's way clearly. —**fordern,** v.a. to challenge; to provoke; to defy; to demand positively; **einen zum Zweikampf —fordern,** to challenge s.o. (to a duel); —**forderndes Benehmen,** defiant conduct. —**forderung,** f. challenge; provocation. —**fühlen,** v.a. to discover or select by touch or feeling. —**gabe,** f. giving back, delivering up; editing (of a book); edition; publication. —**geben,** ir.v.a. to give forth, hand out, deliver up; to publish; to edit; **können Sie mir —geben?** can you give me change? —**geber,** m. editor (man of letters); publisher (bookseller). —**heben,** ir.v.a. to lift or take out; to render prominent, make conspicuous, lay stress on; to throw into relief, set off; to pick out (Typ.). —**klauben,** v.a. to get out (with difficulty). —**kommen,** ir.v.n. (aux. s.) to come out or forth; to appear, issue; to become known; to be published; to prove correct; to amount to; to be of use, yield profit; **was wird dabei —kommen?** what will be the use of it? what will be the upshot? **es muß ganz natürlich —kommen,** it must appear quite natural; **so —kommen als ob,** to seem as if; **aus etwas —kommen,** to recover from; **das kommt dabei —, wenn man lügt,** that's the result of telling lies; **es kommt auf eins —,** it is all the same in the end. —**locken,** v.a. to entice out, to elicit. —**machen,** v. I. a. to get, take out (stains, etc.); to shell (nuts, etc.). II. r. to go out or abroad. —**müssen,** ir.v.n. to be obliged to come or go out. —**nehmen,** ir.v.a. to take out, draw forth; **sich** (dat.) **etwas —nehmen,** to presume, to make or be so bold, venture; **sich** (dat.) —**nehmen,** to choose, take for oneself, to draw (a moral, etc.). —**platzen,** v.n. (aux. s.) to blurt out. —**pres=sung,** f. extortion. —**putzen,** v.a. to dress up, decorate, set off. —**ragen,** v.n. to jut out. —**reden,** v.n. (aux. h.) to speak, speak freely. —**reißen,** ir.v.a. to pull out; to tear out; to free, deliver, extricate. —**rücken,** v. I. a. to move out. II. n. (aux. s.) to march out, come forth; **mit der Sprache —rücken,** to speak out freely. —**rufen,** v.a. to call before the curtain (theat.); to turn out the guard (mil.). —**schälen,** v.a. to obtain by peeling, to sift, to pick out; **aus verworrenen Überlieferungen den geschichtlichen Kern —schälen,** to sift or pick out what is historically true from a mass of confusing traditions. —**schlagen,** v.a.; **möglichst viel —schlagen aus einer Sache,** to make the most of a thing. —**setzen,** v.a. to set out, expose; to eject. —**stehen,** ir.v.n. (aux. h.) to stand out, project. —**stellen,** v. I. a. to put out, expose. II. r. to turn out, to prove (**als wahr oder falsch,** true or false); **im Laufe der Untersuchung stellte sich —, daß . . .,** in the course of the inquiry it appeared that . . . —**streichen,** ir.v.a. to extol, praise, puff. —**thun,** ir.v.a. to put forth, take out. —**treten,** I. ir.v.a. to step out; to retire (from a firm); to protrude. II. subst. n. protuberance; extravasation; withdrawal. —**wachsen,** ir.v.n. (aux. s.) to grow out, to develop; **das wächst mir zum Halse —,** that begins to bore me, I have had enough of that. —**wickeln,** v.r. to extricate o.s. —**ziehen,** ir.v. I. a. to extract. II. n. (aux. s.) to march out.

Herb, adj. & adv. acid, sharp; astringent; harsh; tart; unpleasant; bitter; sullen; austere; —**e Not,** dire necessity; —**er Tod,** grim death. —**e,** f. acidity; harshness; austerity, severity. —**heit,** —**igkeit,** f. bitterness, acerbity, harshness. —**lich,** adj. & adv. somewhat bitter, rather harsh.

Herbei', adv. & sep. prefix, hither, near, on, this way, into the vicinity of (the speaker or point contemplated). Comp. —**bringen,** ir.v.a. to bring on or up, to produce. —**führen,** v.a. to bring about, up or near; to induce; to cause, give occasion for, give rise to. —**schaffen,** reg. & ir.v.a. to collect; to produce, procure, provide; to raise (money). —**ziehen,** ir.v. I. a. to draw or pull near, towards. II. n. (aux. s.) to draw, march near, approach.

Her'berg—e, f. (pl. —en) shelter, quarters, inn, public house; —**e zur Heimat,** meeting-house, house of call, home, family inn (for journeymen-mechanics, etc.); **einem —e geben,** to lodge a p. —**en,** v.a. & n. (aux. h.) to shelter, harbour, lodge, to shelter, entertain (wishes, views, etc.). Comp. —**s=mutter,** f., —**s=vater,** m. hostess, host of an inn.

Herbori'st, m. (—en, pl. —en) herbalist.

Herbst, m. (—es, pl. —e) autumn; fall (Amer.), harvest-season; harvest, crop, vintage. —**en,**

v. 1. *a.* to harvest, to gather in. II. *n. imp.*; **so oft es —et,** always, when autumn comes. **—lich,** *adj. & adv.* autumnal; in autumn. **—lichkeit,** *f.* autumnal season; autumnal look. **—ling,** *m.* (**—lings,** *pl.* **—linge**) autumnal fruit; animal born in autumn. *Comp.* **—anfang,** *m.* beginning of autumn. **—flocken,** *pl.* gossamer. **—leute,** *pl.* harvesters. **—mäßig,** *adj.* autumnal. **—rose,** *f.* hollyhock. **—zeit,** *f.* autumn; harvest *or* vintage time. **—zeitlose,** *f.* common meadow saffron.

Herd, *m.* (**—es,** *pl.* **—e**) hearth, fire-place, fire-side; house, home; place where fowlers catch birds; central seat (*of rebellion, etc.*); seat (*of disease*); crater; focus; source; bottom, saddle (*of a block, Naut.*); **eigner — ist Goldes wert,** there's no place like home (*prov.*). *Comp.* **—besen,** *m.* hearth-brush. **—eisen,** *n.* poker. **—geld,** *n.* hearth *or* house tax. **—löffel,** *m.* assaying ladle. **—probe,** *f.* assay of silver. **—steuer,** *f.*, **—zins,** *m. see* **—geld. —vogel,** *m.* decoy-bird.

Her'de, *f.* (*pl.* **—n**) drove, flock, herd; crowd, multitude. *Comp.* **—hammel,** *m.* ram, bell-wether. **—n=weise,** *adv.* in flocks *or* herds.

Herei'n, *adv. & sep. prefix,* in hither, in here; inward; **hier —,** this way, in here; **von (dr)außen —,** from without; **—!** come in! **— ohne anzuklopfen,** come in without knocking; turn the handle (*notice on a door*). *Comp.* **—bestellen,** *v.a.* to order to come *or* be brought in. **—bitten,** *ir.v.a.* to invite (*one*) to come in. **—dürfen,** *ir.v.n.* to be allowed to come in. **—fall,** *m.* bad business; **das war ein großartiger —fall,** we (*or* they) have been thoroughly disappointed in this (*coll.*). **—fallen,** *ir.v.n.* (*aux.* **s.**) to fall into; to come to grief, to be badly off, to get the worse, to be disappointed (*coll.*); **mit der Thür ins Haus —fallen,** to blurt out what one has to say, to say s.th. abruptly. **—lassen,** *ir.v.a.* to admit; **laß ihn —!** let him come in! bid him come in! **—müssen,** *ir.v.n.* (*aux.* **h.**) to be obliged to come in; **die Stühle müssen —,** the chairs must be brought in. **—regnen,** *v.n.* (*aux.* **h.**) to rain into. **—wollen,** *ir.v.n.* to wish to come in.

Herfür', *see* **Hervor** *and* **Für.**

He'ribann, *obs. & poet.* for **Heerbann.**

He'ring, *see* **Häring.**

Herku'lisch, *adj.* Herculean.

Her'ling, *m.* (**—s,** *pl.* **—e**) unripe grape, wild grape, sour grape (*B.*).

Hermanda'd, *f.* fraternity; **die heilige —,** the Inquisition.

Hermaphrodi't, *m.* (**—en,** *pl.* **—en**) hermaphrodite.

Her'me, *f.* statue of Mercury. *pl.* **—n=säulen,** hermæ.

Hermeli'n, *n. & m.* (**—s,** *pl.* **—e**) ermine; ermine-fur; cream-coloured horse.

Hermeneu't, *m.* (**—en,** *pl.* **—en**) interpreter; commentator. **—ik,** *f.* hermeneutics.

Herme'tisch, *adj. & adv.* air-proof, hermetical; **— verschlossen,** closed hermetically.

Hero'—en, *see* **Heros. —i'ne,** *f.* (*pl.* **—i'nen**) heroine. **—isch,** *adj. & adv.* heroic. **—i'smus,** *m.* heroism. **—s,** *m.* (*pron.* **He'ros,** *pl.* **Hero'en**) hero, demi-god. *Comp.* **—en=alter,** *n.* heroic age. **—en=kultus,** *m.* hero-worship. **—en=sage,** *f.* heroic legend.

He'rold, *m.* (**—(e)s,** *pl.* **—e**) herald; proclaimer; harbinger. *Comp.* **—s=figuren,** *pl.* heraldic figures. **—s=kunst, —s=wissenschaft,** *f.* heraldry, heraldic art. **—s=mantel, —s=rock,** *m.* tabard.

Herr, *m.* (**—(e)n,** *pl.* **—en**) master; lord; gentleman; sir (*in address*); Mr. (*before proper names*); principal; **Ihr — Vater,** your father; **meine —en,** gentlemen; **einer Sache, von einer Sache, über eine Sache — sein,** to be master of a thing, to have at one's disposal *or* in subjection; **— über eine Sache werden, einer Sache — werden,** to master, subdue a thing; **der seines Mutes — ist,** he that ruleth his spirit (*B.*); **— zur See sein,** to rule the waves; **den großen —n spielen,** to play the grand gentleman, to lord it; **der — Gott,** God, the Lord; **unser — Gott,** our Lord, Lord God; **wie der — so der Knecht,** like master like man (*prov.*); **gestrenge —en regieren nicht lange,** a heavy shower is soon over; too great severity is of no long durance (*prov.*). **—chen,** *n.* (**—chens,** *pl.* **—chen**) young master; lordling; fop. **—ig,** *adj. & adv.* having a lord. **—in,** *f.* lady; mistress. **—isch,** *adj. & adv.* domineering; imperious; magistral; masterful. **—lich,** *adj. & adv.* lordly; grand, magnificent; glorious; capital; excellent. **—lichkeit,** *f.* lordliness; excellence; splendour, grandeur, glory; great joy; **die —lichkeit Gottes,** the majesty of God. **—schaft,** *f.* lordship; dominion; mastery, control; government; sovereign authority; power, command; manor, estate, domain; master and mistress, employers (*of servants*); person *or* persons of rank; **meine —schaften,** ladies and gentlemen! **hohe —schaften,** people of high rank, illustrious persons; **ist die —schaft zu Hause?** are your master and mistress (is your master *or* mistress) at home? **die junge —schaft,** the children of the master *or* lord; **(etwas) unter seine —schaft bringen,** to bring under one's rule *or* dominion, to subdue; **die —schaft gebende Binde,** (power bestowing) diadem (*poet.*). **—schafteln,** *v.n.* (*aux.* **h.**) to lord it (*rare*). **—schaftler,** *m.* petty lord *or* master, petty tyrant (*rare*). **—schaftlich,** *adj. & adv.* belonging to *or* referring to a lord *or* master; seigniorial, manorial; proceeding from a lord; fit for a lord; lordly; **—schaftliche Gefälle,** seigniorial revenues; **—schaftlicher Befehl,** lord's command; **—schaftliche Wohnung,** elegant *or* high class family residence, mansion; **—schaftlicher Wagen,** (gentleman's *or* lady's) private carriage. **—schen, ɩc.,** *see* **Herrschen.** *Comp.* **—en=arbeit,** *f.* compulsory service; **dieser Schneider macht nur —enarbeit,** this tailor works for gentlemen only. **—en=bank,** *f.* peers' bench, bench of lords. **—en=bier,** *n.* strong beer. **—en=brot,** *n.* master's bread; **—enbrot essen,** to be in service, be dependent. **—en=diener,** *m.* gentleman's servant. **—en=dienst,** *m.* lord's service; forced service; service (*in a family*). **—en=fahrer,** *m.* gentleman rider (*cycl.*). **—en=gerechtsame,** *f.* rights of a manorial lord. **—en=gülte,** *f.* tax paid to the lord of the manor. **—en=haus,** *n.* manor (house); mansion; House of Lords. **—en=huter,** *m.* Moravian, *see* **—nhuter. —en=leben,** *n.* high life; **ein —enleben führen,** to live like a lord, to live in grand style. **—en=leute,** *pl.* rich land-owners, peasant nobility (*dial.*). **—en=los,** *adj.* out of service *or* employment; masterless; ownerless; **—enlose Güter,** derelicts, unclaimed goods. **—en=losigkeit,** *f.* state of being without a master; state of being unclaimed. **—en=meister,** *m.* Grand Master. **—en=moral,** *f.* (selfish) code of morality made by men and applying to men only (as opposed to women); special code of morality applying to gentlemen (as opposed to the lower classes), upper class morality. **—en=pfarre,** *f.* benefice in the gift of a patron. **—en=recht,** *n.* seigniorial right. **—en=reiten,** *n.* owners up, gentlemen's race (*sport*). **—en=reiter,** *m.* gentleman rider. **—en=schneider,** *m.* tailor (who works for gentlemen only). **—en=sonntag,** *m.* Shrove Tuesday (*obs.*). **—en=stand,** *m.* rank of a lord *or* gentleman; gentry. **—en=vogel,** *m.* jay. **—gott,** *m.* Lord God; (image of Christ on the) crucifix; **(ach)**

—gott! Lord! Good God! good heavens! good gracious! **den —gott einen guten Mann sein lassen,** to let matters take their course; **er lebt wie der —gott in Frankreich,** he lives like a fighting-cock. **—gotts=händler,** *m.* dealer in crucifixes. **—gotts=schäfchen,** *n.* lady-bird. **—gott(s)=schnitzer,** *m.* carver of crucifixes. **—je', ach —!** (**je** = **Jesus**), *also* **Herrje'=mineh!** good heavens! goodness me! **—n=huter,** *pl.* the Moravian brethren. **—n=huter(in,** *f.*) *m.* Moravian. **—n=hutertum,** *n.* Moravianism. **—schafts=haus,** *n.* manor house; mansion. **—schafts=recht,** *n.* sovereign authority, jurisdiction.

Herr'sch—en, *v.n.* (*aux.* **h.**) to rule, govern, be lord *or* master of; to domineer; to prevail; to rage, be prevalent; to be in vogue; **„komm her", —te er,** "approach," he ordered haughtily. **—end,** *p. & adj.* ruling; predominant, prevailing. **—er,** *m.* (**—ers,** *pl.* **—er**) ruler, lord, sovereign; commander; **willkürlicher —er,** despot; **unumschränkter —er,** autocrat; **Selbst —er,** autocrat. **—erisch,** *adj. & adv.* in the manner of, pertaining to a ruler. *Comp.* **—begier, —begierde,** *f.* lust of power. **—begierig,** *adj.* greedy of power, ambitious, imperious. **—er=binde,** *f.* diadem. **—er=blick,** *m.* commanding look *or* aspect. **—er=familie,** *f.* reigning family, dynasty. **—er=geist,** *m.* commanding spirit. **—er=stab,** *m.* sceptre. **—er=stuhl,** *m.* throne. **—er=wille,** *m.* sovereign will. **—er=willkür,** *f* despotism. **—er=wort,** *n.* word of command. **—gier, —lust, —sucht,** *f. see* **—begier. —wut,** *f.* tyranny, lust of power.

Herum', *adv. & sep. prefix,* round about, around, right round, about; (**umher** = about, up and down.); **überall —,** everywhere; **rings, rund —,** all round; **hier —,** hereabouts; **in der ganzen Stadt —,** all over the town; **um . . . —** round . . . about; **er wohnt gleich um die Ecke —,** he lives in the first house *or* just round the corner; **um die Zeit —,** about the time; **ich ging erst um den Dom —, darauf ging ich in ihm umher,** I first went right round the cathedral, afterwards I paced up and down in its interior. *Comp.* **—balgen,** *v.r.* to strike out right and left; to have a scuffle, to go fighting about. **—betteln,** *v.n.* (*aux.* **h.**) to go about begging. **—bringen,** *ir.v.a.* to bring *or* get round; to bring over, induce, persuade; to circulate. **—drehen,** *v.a.* to turn round; to misconstrue; **sich —drehen (um),** to hinge, turn *or* depend (*on*). **—fahren,** *ir.v.n.* (*aux.* **s.**) to take a drive *or* sail around; to dart, fly, rush about. **—fragen,** *reg. & ir.v.n.* (*aux.* **h.**) to ask round *or* one after the other. **—geben,** *ir.v.a.* to hand *or* pass round. **—gehen,** *ir.v.n.* (*aux.* **s.**) to go round; to make the round (*Mil.*); to surround; to wander *or* walk about; to be current (*of reports*); to be prevalent; **die Mauer ging einst um die ganze Stadt —,** the wall once enclosed the whole town; **es geht mir im Kopfe —,** it runs in my head *or* mind; **—gehen lassen,** to send *or* pass round; **ich lasse mir die Sache im Kopfe —gehen,** I am carefully considering the matter. **—holen,** *v.a.* to bring over *or* round. **—kommen,** *ir.v.n.* (*aux.* **s.**) to come round (*a corner, etc.*); to go *or* travel about; to become known; **Leute, die viel in der Welt —gekommen sind,** people who have seen much of the world; **mit etwas —kommen,** to finish a thing, to get a thing done. **—laufen,** *ir.v.n.* (*aux.* **s.**) to run about, rove. **—läufer,** *m.* rover; vagabond, tramp. **—naschen,** *v.a.;* (**an einer S.**) **überall —naschen,** to nibble everywhere (at a th.). **—nehmen,** *ir.v.a.* to take to task. **—reichen,** *v.a. & n.* to hand about, to pass round. **—schiffen,** *v.n.* (*aux.* **s.**) to sail about; **um . . . —schiffen,** to sail round, to double (*a cape*). **—schlagen,** *v.r.* to struggle, to fight with. **—schweifend,** *p. & adj.* wandering; vagrant. **—schwenken,** *v.n.* (*aux.* **s.**) to wheel (*Mil.*). **—streichen,** *ir.v.n.* (*aux.* **s.**) to rove about. **—streicher,** *m.* rover; vagabond. **—treiben,** *ir.v.* I. *a.* to drive round. II. *r.* to dawdle, loiter about; to gad about. **—tummeln,** *v.* I. *a.* to put *or* keep in motion, to work, exercise. II. *r.* to bustle about. **—watscheln,** *v.n.* to dawdle about, along. **—werfen,** *ir.v.a.* to cast around, to turn with a sudden movement, cast in another direction. **—wühlen,** *v.n.* (*aux.* **h.**) to root about (*in*); to rummage (*in*). **—ziehen,** *ir.v.* I. *a.* to draw, pull about. II. *r.* to surround; to run along; **sich mit etwas —ziehen,** to have something on one's mind. III. *n.* (*aux.* **s.**) to rove, wander about; to change one's dwelling. **—ziehend,** *p. & adj.* itinerant, strolling; nomadic.

Herun'ter, *adv. & sep. prefix,* down; downward (*toward the speaker or point contemplated*); off; **— mit ihm!** down with him! **den Hut —!** off with your hat! hats off! *Comp.* **—bringen,** *ir.v.a.* to get down; to lower, reduce. **—kommen,** *ir.v.n.* (*aux.* **s.**) to come down; to alight; to be reduced (*in circumstances*); to decline, decay. **—kriegen,** *v.a.* to get down; to lower, reduce (*coll.*). **—machen,** *v.a.* to take down, lower; to abuse, upbraid, cut up, give a thorough scolding. **—setzen,** *v.a.* to reduce, lower; to degrade. **—wärts,** *adv.* downwards. **—werfen,** *ir.v.a.* to throw down *or* off; to throw (*a rider*). **—ziehen,** *ir.v.* I. *a.* to pull down. II. *n.* (*aux.* **s.**) to march down, descend.

Hervor', (*archaic* **Herfür',**) *adv. & sep. prefix,* forth; forward, out; **— mit euch!** come out! advance! *Comp.* **—bringen,** *ir.v.a.* to bring forth, produce; to generate, beget; to utter; to elicit. **—bringung,** *f.* bringing forth, production; procreation; utterance. **—gehen,** *ir.v.n.* (*aux.* **s.**) to go *or* come forth; to result, arise, follow (*as a consequence*); to come off (*victorious, etc.*). **—heben,** *ir.v.a.* to bring into prominence; to raise above the surface; to set off, relieve; to call special attention to. **—leuchten,** *v.n.* (*aux.* **h.**) to shine forth; to become clear *or* evident; to be conspicuous *or* distinguished. **—machen,** *v.r* to appear, make one's appearance. **—ragen,** *v.n.* (*aux.* **h.**) to project, stand out, jut forth; to rise above, overtop, tower up; to exceed, surpass. **—ragend,** *p. & adj.* prominent; distinguished, salient. **—ragung,** *f.* projection, prominence. **—rufen,** *ir.v.a.* to evoke, call forth; to call before the curtain, to encore (*of actors*). **—stechen,** *ir.v.n.* (*aux.* **h.**) to stand out, jut out; to be conspicuous; **—stechend,** glaring, conspicuous, striking. **—stehen,** *ir.v.n.* (*aux.* **s.**) to project; **—stehende Backenknochen,** high cheek-bones. **—suchen,** *v.a.* to seek out, search for. **—tauchen,** *v.n.* (*aux.* **s.**) to emerge (*as from under water*); to come forth, appear suddenly. **—thun,** *ir.v.r.* to put oneself forward; to distinguish oneself, excel; to come into view *or* prominence. **—treten,** *ir.v.n.* (*aux.* **s.**) to step forth *or* forward; to come forward; to stand out; **—treten lassen,** to throw into bold relief.

Herz, *n.* (**—ens,** *pl.* **—en**) heart; breast; bosom; feeling, sympathy; will; courage, spirit; mind; centre, inner part (*of a thing*); vital part; marrow, pith (*Bot.*); core; hearts (*cards*); darling, love, dearest; **der — und Nieren prüft,** he who trieth the hearts and reins (*B.*); **das innre —,** the innermost heart; **ein — und eine Seele,** two hearts that beat as one, bosom friends; **das — zu einer Sache haben,** to find it in one's heart to do a thing, to dare to do a thing; **es liegt mir am —en,** I have it at heart; **einem etwas ans — legen,** to urge a th. on one; **einem ans — gewachsen**

sein, to be very dear to one; auf dem —en haben, to have at heart; aufs —fallen, to weigh on one; schwer aufs—fallen, to oppress *or* worry a p.; sein — an eine S. hängen, to set one's heart on a thing; das — auf der Zunge tragen, to be frank, speak one's mind freely; Hand aufs —! speak openly! aus dem —en, sincerely, earnestly; einem einen Stich ins — geben, to cut one to the quick, grieve a p. deeply; mit — und Mund, sincerely, earnestly; etwas übers — bringen, to bring oneself to do something, to reconcile oneself to a thing; ich kann es nicht übers — bringen, I can't find it in my heart to do it; ein Kind unter dem —en tragen, to be with child; ich weiß, wie es ihm ums — ist, I know how he feels; von —en, heartily, cordially; von ganzen —en, with all my heart; von —en kommen, to come from the heart, to be heartfelt, sincere; von —en gehen, to be genuine; einem von —en gut sein, to love one dearly; frisch vom —en weg reden, to speak one's mind freely; ich will es vom —en haben, I wish to have it off my mind; sein — ausschütten, to open one's heart, to unbosom oneself; sein — in die Hände nehmen, to take heart *or* courage; sich (*dat.*) ein — fassen, to take courage; to take heart; ein — zu einem fassen, to repose confidence in one; einem ein — einsprechen, to encourage one; es will ihm das — abstoßen, it will break his heart; wes das — voll ist, des geht der Mund über, out of the abundance of the heart the mouth speaketh (*B.*). —chen, *n.* (—chens, *pl.* —chen) little heart; darling, sweetie, pet; corcule (*Bot.*). —haft, *adj. & adv.* courageous, stout-hearted, brave. —haftigkeit, *f.* courage, bravery, manliness. —ig, *adj. & adv.* charming, sweet; dear, beloved; (*in comp.* =) -hearted. —igkeit, *f.* heartiness; loveliness; (*in comp.* =) -heartedness. —lich, *adj. & adv.* hearty, cordial, affectionate; —lich gern, most willingly, with all one's heart; wir haben es —lich satt, we are heartily sick of it. —lichkeit, *f.* heartiness, cordiality, sincere affection and kindness. *Comp.* —ader, f. aorta (*Anat.*). —allerliebst, *adj.* best beloved; charming; dearest. —allerliebste(r), *f.* (*m.*) dearest love. —arterie, *f.* aorta. —arznei, *f.* cordial. —beben, *n.* palpitation of the heart. —beklommen, *adj.* anxious; oppressed at heart. —bethörend, *adj.* stupefying the heart, alluring the heart. —beutel, *m.* pericardium. —beutel=entzündung, *f.* pericarditis. —beutel=wassersucht, *f.* dropsy of the pericardium. —bewegend, *adj.* pathetic; stirring. —blatt, *n.* diaphragm; inmost leaf (*Bot.*); darling; hearts (*cards*). —blume, *f.* liverwort. —bube, *m.* knave of hearts. —dame, *f.* queen of hearts (*cards*). —e=leid, *n.* deep sorrow *or* affliction. —en=bändiger, *m.* subduer of hearts. —en=bube, —en=dame, &c. *see* —bube, —dame &c. —ens=angelegenheit, *f.* love affair. —ens=angst, *f.* anguish of mind, deep anxiety. —ens=einfalt, *f.* single-heartedness. —ens=freude, *f.* joy of one's heart, great joy. —ens=freund, *m.* bosom-friend. —ens=fülle, *f.* depth of feeling. —ens=gedanke, *m.* innermost thought. —ens=güte, *f.* kindness of heart. —ens=kind, *n.* darling. —ens=königin, *f.* queen of one's heart, lady-love. —ens=kundige(r), *m.* one who knows the human heart. —ens=kündiger, *m.* searcher of the hearts, prover of hearts, (God) which knoweth the heart (*B.*). —ens=lust, *f.* great joy; nach —enslust, to one's heart's content. —ens=reue, *f.* heartfelt contrition. —ergießung, *f.*, —erguß, *m.* outpouring of the heart, unbosoming. —ergreifend, *adj.* affecting. —erhebend, *adj.* raising the heart *or* mind, heart-stirring. —erschütternd, *adj.* appalling. —erweiterung, *f.* dilatation of the heart. —fell, *n.* pericardium. —fibern, *pl.* heart-strings. —finger, *m.* ring-finger. —förmig, *adj.* heart-shaped. —gegend, *f.* cardiac region. —gespann, —gesperr, *n.* cardialgy. —grube, *f.* pit of the stomach, cardiac region. —haut, *f. see* —fell. —innig, *adj. & adv.* hearty, heart-felt. —kammer, *f.* ventricle of the heart. —klappe, *f.* valve (of the heart) —klopfen, *n.* palpitation of the heart. —kolbe, *f.* tendril. —(en)=könig, *m.* king of hearts. —krampf, *m.* spasm of the heart. —kränkend, *adj.* mortifying. —lieb, *adj. & adv.* very dear, dearly beloved. —lieb'chen, *n.* sweetheart. —lieb'ster, *m.* my own dear love; —liebster Jesu, gentle Jesus (*often in hymns*). —los, *adj. & adv.* heartless; faint-hearted. —muschel, *f.* cockle (*Mollusc.*). —nervengeflecht, *n.* cardiacal plexus. —ohr, *n.* auricle of the heart. —röhre, *f.* aorta. —schlächtig, *adj.* broken-winded. —schlag, *m.* throb *or* beating of the heart; apoplexy of the heart, paralysis of the heart; bis zum letzten —schlage, to the last day of my life. —stärkend, *adj.* cordial; cardiac. —stoß, *m.* finishing blow; quietus. —verknöcherung, *f.* ossification of the heart. —weh, *n.* heartache; grief. —zerreißend, *adj.* heart-rending.

Her'zen, *v.a.* to press to one's heart, to caress, to fondle, to embrace.

Her'zog, *m.* (—s, *pl.* Herzöge) duke. —in, *f.* duchess. —lich, *adj. & adv.* ducal. —tum, *n.* (—tums, *pl.* —tümer) duchy, dukedom.

Herzu', *adv. & sep. prefix*, up, towards a place. —laufen, *v.a.* to run up, to come up running.

Hes, *n.* B-flat (*obs.*).

Hetä're, *f.* (*pl.* —n) (*Greek*) courtesan.

Hetero—do'x, *adj.* heterodox. —doxie', *f.* heterodoxy. —ge'n, *adj.* heterogeneous.

Het'ze, *f.* (*pl.* —n) baiting; chase, hunt, course; baiting-place; pack, troop; pack of hounds; hot pursuit; wild *or* mad race; hurry; strait, dilemma, multitude, swarm (*coll.*).

Het'z—en, *v.* I. *a.* to hunt, to run after, pursue; to provoke; to incite, set on; fast zu Tode gehetzt, almost worried to death; mit allen Hunden gehetzt sein, to be full of craft, to be up to every trick. II. *n.* (*aux.* h.) to hunt. —er, *m.* (—ers, *pl.* —er) baiter; instigator, inciter. —erei', *f.* baiting; harassing; setting on, inciting; —erei der Prüfungen, worry of examinations. *Comp.* —bahn, *f.*, —garten, *m.* bull-ring, place for baiting wild beasts. —en=reiter, *m.* whipper-in. —haus, *n.* animal's house *or* cage; *see* —bahn. —hund, *m.* stag hound, sporting dog. —jagd, *f.* hunt, chase (*of wild beasts*); great hurry; wir leben in der reinen —jagd, we are almost driven to death (*coll.*). —los, *adj.*; —los machen, to uncouple (*dogs*). —zeit, *f.* hunting season.

Heu, *n.* (—es) hay; Geld wie —, money in abundance; man muß — machen weil die Sonne scheint, make your hay while the sun shines, make use of the sun while it shines (*prov.*), strike while the iron is hot (*prov.*). —bar, *adj.* yielding hay (meadow). *Comp.* —baum, *m.* hay-pole. —boden, *m.*, —bühne, *f.* hay-loft. —bund, —bündel, *n.* bottle, truss of hay. —feim(en), —fein(en), *m.*, —feme, *f.*, —fimme, *f.* hay-stack, (hay-)rick. —gabel, *f.* pitchfork. —gewinn, *m.* hay-crop. —mäher, *m.* mower; bee-eater (*Orn.*). —miete, *f.* (hay) rick, hay-stack. —monat, *m.* July (*dial.*). —ochse, *m.* blockhead, stupid fellow (*sl.*). —pferd, *n.* green grasshopper. —scheibe, *f.*

lap-cock. —**schober**, *m.* hay-rick, haystack. —**schrecke**, *f.* great green grasshopper; locust (*B.*). —**schrecken=artig**, *adj. & adv.* locust-like. —**schrecken=baum**, *m.* locust-tree. —**sense**, *f.* scythe. —**zehnte**, *m.* tithe paid in hay.

Heuch—elei', *f.* hypocrisy, dissimulation; cant.

Heu'ch—eln, *v.* I. *a.* to feign, affect, simulate. II. *n.* (*aux.* **h.**) to dissemble, sham, to play the hypocrite; to put on (an air of righteousness *or* piety). —**ler**, *m.* (—**lers**, *pl.* —**ler**), —**lerin**, *f.* hypocrite, dissembler. —**lerisch**, *adj. & adv.* hypocritical; false; dissembling. *Comp.* —**el=bube**, *m.* hypocritical villain. —**el=rede**, *f.* hypocritical *or* dissembling speech. —**el=schein**, *m.*, —**el=werk**, *n.* hypocrisy, sham appearance, false pretence; **mit falschem —el=schein**, with a dissembling voice *or* mien (*poet.*). —**el=thräne**, *f.* crocodile tear.

Heu'—en, I. *v.a.* to make hay. II. *s.* haymaking. —**er**, *m.* (—**ers**, *pl.* —**er**), —**erin**, *f.* haymaker.

Heu'er, *f.* hire; rent, lease (*dial.*). —**er**, *m.* (—**ers**, *pl.* —**er**) one who hires. —**ling**, *m.* (—**lings**, *pl.* —**linge**) tenant, lodger; hireling; day-labourer (*dial.*). —**n**, *v.a.* to hire; rent; charter (*a ship*), engage, hire (*sailors*) (*dial.*); marry (*rare*). *Comp.* —**brief**, —**kontrakt**, *m.* charter, charter-party. —**ling**, *m.* hired rural labourer.

Heu'er, *adv.* (in) this year (*dial.*).

Heu'l—en, *v.n.* (*aux.* **h.**) to howl, yell, scream; **der Wind —t**, the wind roars, wails, moans; —**en und Zähneklappen**, weeping and gnashing of teeth (*B.*); **mit den Wölfen —en**, to do at Rome as the Romans do. —**er**, *m.* (—**ers**, *pl.* —**er**), —**erin**, *f.* howler; croaker; reactionary. *Comp.* —**kreisel**, *m.* humming-top. —(**e**)=**meier**, —(**e**)**michel**, *m.* a person (*child*) given to crying, a sulky person, blubberer, whimperer, Peter grievous. —(**e**)=**meierei'**, *f.* whimpering.

Heu'rig, *adj. & adv.* of this year; present (*dial.*). —**e(r)**, *m.* wine of this year, new wine.

Heu't—e, *adv.* to-day, this day; **von —e an**, from this day forward; —**e vor acht Tagen**, this day week, a week ago; —**e über vierzehn Tage**, this day fortnight; —**e über vier Wochen**, a month from to-day; —**e über ein Jahr**, a year hence; —**zutage**, now-a-days; —**e früh**, this morning; —**e abend**, to-night; —**e nacht**, this night, to-night; —**e morgen**, this morning; —**e rot, morgen tot**, here to-day, gone to-morrow (*prov.*); — **mir, morgen dir**, every one in his turn; to-day mine, to-morrow yours (*prov.*). —**ig**, *adj. & adv.* of to-day, of the present time; modern; **mit der —igen Post**, by to-day's mail; —**igestags**, now-a-days; **am Heutigen**, to-day, at this day; **Ihr Heutiges**, your favour of to-day (*C. L.*); **unterm Heutigen**, under this day's date; **die —ige Nummer der Times**, to-day's Times.

Hexa—e'der, —**e'dron**, *n.* hexahedron. —**meter**, *m.* (*pron.* **Hexa'meter**) (dactylic) hexameter (verse). —**me'trisch**, *adj.* hexametrical.

He'x—e, *f.* (*pl.* —**en**) witch, sorceress; hag. —**en**, *v.* I. *a.* to conjure up; to gain by witchcraft; to bewitch. II. *n.* (*aux.* **h.**) to conjure, to practise sorcery. —**er**, *m.* (—**ers**, *pl.* —**er**) wizard, sorcerer. —**erei'**, *f.* witchcraft, sorcery; jugglery; **Geschwindigkeit ist keine —erei**, conjuring requires no magic; **das ist keine —erei**, that is no extraordinary performance; —**erei treiben**, to practise witchcraft. —**erich**, *m.* (*coll.*) = —**er**. *Comp.* —**en=bann**, *m.* spell, charm. —**en=brut**, *f.* crew of witches. —**en=buch**, *n.* conjuring book. —**en=glaube**, *m.* belief in witchcraft. —**en=hammer**, *m.* malleus maleficarum (a book used in trying women who were supposed to be witches). —**en=kessel**, *m.* witches'-kettle; hurly-burly, hubbub (*fig.*). —**en=kraut**, *n.* enchanter's nightshade (*Bot.*); mandrake. —**en=kreis**, *m.* magic circle; fairy ring. —**en=kunst**, *f.* witchcraft. —**en=meister**, *see* —**er**. —**en=probe**, *f.* witches' ordeal. —**en=prozeß**, *m.* trial for witchcraft. —**en=sabbath**, *m.* witches' vigil. —**en=schuß**, *m.* lumbago. —**en=stich**, *m.* herring-boning (*Semp.*). —**en=wesen**, *n.* witchcraft, witchery. —**en=zunft**, *f.* band of witches.

Hibri'disch, Hybri'disch, *adj.* hybrid, mongrel.

Hi'cken, *v.n.* (*aux.* **h.**) to hiccough (*dial.*).

Hid'delich, *adj.* confused, fussy, rash (*coll.*).

Hie, *adv. see* **Hier**; — **und da**, here and there, now and then; — **Welf**, — **Waibling!** a Guelph, a Ghibelline! —**sig**, *adj. & adv.* of this place *or* country. *Comp. see* **Hier** *in comp.* —**bevo'r**, *adv.* before this, heretofore. —**nie'den**, *adv.* here below, in this world.

Hieb, Hie'be, *imperf. ind. & subj.* of **hauen**.

Hieb, *m.* (—**es**, *pl.* —**e**) blow (*with a stick*), cut (*with a sword or an axe*); cut, gash; scar; sarcasm, cutting remark; **einen — haben**, to be a little tipsy *or* cracked; **der — sitzt**, that's a good hit; **auf den ersten — fällt kein Baum**, Rome was not built in one day (*prov.*); **auf — und Stich gehen**, to cut and thrust (*Fenc.*); **freien — haben**, to have the right of felling timber. —**er**, *m.* rapier. *Comp.* —**fechten**, *n.* broadsword exercise; — **und Stoß=fechten**, cut and thrust. —**waffe**, *f.* weapon for cutting, broadsword, rapier. —**wunde**, *f.* wound from a cut, sword wound *or* cut.

Hief, *m.* (—**es**, *pl.* —**e**) sound given by the hunting-horn, bugle-call. *Comp.* —**horn**, *n.* hunting-horn. —**riemen**, *m.* bugle-strap. —**stoß**, *m.* mort.

Hielt, Hiel'te, *imperf. ind. & subj. of* **halten**.

Hieng, *obs. for* **Hing**.

Hier, *adv.* here; present; in this place; in this point *or* matter; at these words; as to this; *in comp. with a prep.* = *the prep. with a case of the dem. pron.* **dies**; — **herum**, hereabouts; — **zu Lande**, in this country; **Herrn M.** — *or* **hie(r)selbst**, Mr. M. of this place, *Mr. M., Local*, (*as address*). *Comp.* (**hier** *usually remains unaccented; it takes the accent if* **hier** *is to be emphasized*). —**ab**, *adv.* herefrom, from this, *etc.* —**an**, *adv.* hereon, on, at *or* by this. —**auf**, *adv.* hereupon, upon this, at this; up here; after that, afterwards, then. —**aus**, *adv.* out of this, from here, from this, hence, hereby, by this. —**außen**, *adv.* out here. —**bei**, *adv.* hereby, by, at, in *or* with this; inclosed. —**bevor**, *adv.*, heretofore. —**durch**, *adv.* through this place, through here; by this means; by this, hereby. —**ein**, *adv.* in(to) this place, in(to) this. —**für**, *adv.* for this, for it, instead of this. —**gegen**, (**Hie=gegen**,) *adv.* against this *or* it; in return for this. —**her**, *adv.* to this place, this way, hither; **bis —her**, hitherto, till now, so far; **nicht —her gehörend**, not to the purpose, off the mark. —**herum**, *adv.* hereabouts, in this neighbourhood. —**hin**, *adv.* in this direction, this way. —**in**, *adv.* herein; in this. —**ländisch**, *adj.* of this country. —**lands**, *adv.* in this country. —**mit**, *adv.* herewith, (along) with this; saying, doing this. —**nach**, *adv.* after this; hereupon; according to this. —**nächst**, *adv.* next to this, after this; close by. —**neben**, *adv.* close by; besides. —**orts**, *adv.* here, in *or* of this place. —**sein**, *n.* being here, sojourn here; presence. —**selbst**, *adv.* here, in this very place; local (*in addresses*). —**über**, *adv.* over here; concerning this; hereat; on this account. —**um**, *adv.* about *or* round this place; about *or* concerning this. —**unten**, *adv.* down here, here below. —**unter**, *adv.* hereunder; under this *or* it; in, by this; among these. —von, *adv.* hereof, of *or* from this. —wider, *adv.* against this. —zu, *adv.* to this; add to this; moreover; to it, for it. —zwischen, *adv.* between; between these things.

Hier—ar'chisch, *adj. & adv.* hierarchical. —a'tisch, *adj. & adv.* sacerdotal. —o=gly'phe, *f.* hieroglyph. —ogly'phen=schrift, *f.* hieroglyphic writing. —o=gly'phik, *f.* hieroglyphics. —o=mantie', *f.* hieromancy.

Hie'sig, *adj. & adv.* of this place *or* country.

Hieß, Hie'ße, *imperf. ind. & subj. of* heißen.

Hift'horn, *see* Hiefhorn.

Hihi', *interj.* ha-ha-ha (*imitation of laughter*).

Hilf, Hilfst, Hilft, *imperat.; and 2 & 3 pers. sing. pres. ind. of* helfen.

Hil'fe, Hilf'lich, ꝛc. *see* Hülfe, Hülflich, ꝛc.

Him'beer—e, *f.* (*pl.* —en) raspberry. *Comp.* —gelee, *n.* raspberry jam. —saft, *m.* raspberry juice. —strauch, *m.* raspberry bush.

Him'mel, *m.* (—s, *pl.* —) heaven; heavens, sky, firmament; tester, canopy, roof; zone, clime; unter freiem —, in the open air; wie vom — gefallen sein, to be astounded; gerechter —! good heavens! dem — sei Dank, daß wir . . .! thank heaven, we . . .! in den, bis in den, — erheben, to extol to the skies; to praise up to the skies; so weit der — blau ist, everywhere; das Blaue vom — herunter lügen, schwören, to lie audaciously, swear black is white; aus allen —n fallen, to be bitterly disappointed *or* utterly disillusioned; um —s Willen! for heaven's sake! —ei', *f.* affected piety, canting manner. —n, *v.n.* (*aux.* h.) to turn up the eyes, to affect piety (*prov.*). *Comp.* —ab, *adv.* from heaven, from on high. —an, —auf, *adv.* heavenwards. —an=strebend, *adj.* heaven-aspiring, stretching up to heaven. —bett, *n.* four-post bed, four-poster. —blau, *adj.* sky-blue. —brot, —s=brot, *n.* manna; red clover. —empor, *adv.* heavenwards. —entfernt, *adj. & adv.* diametrically opposite, very distant. —faden, *m.* gossamer. —fahrt, *f.* ascension; —fahrt Christi, Ascension day; —fahrt Mariä, assumption of the blessed Virgin. —fahrts=fest, *n.*, —fahrts=tag, *m.* Ascension day. —hoch, *adj.* high as heaven, very high; —hoch jauchzend, shouting up to heaven with delight. —reich, *n.* kingdom of heaven; bliss; des Menschen Wille ist sein —reich, my mind to me a kingdom is; a man's will is his heaven; a burden which one chooses is not felt (*prov.*). —s=achse, *f.* celestial axis. —s=angel, *f.* pole of the heavens, celestial pole. —s=beschreiber, *m.* astronomer. —s=beschreibung, *f.* astronomy, uranography. —s=bild, *n.* heavenly image; constellation. —s=blau, *n.* the blue sky. —s=bogen, *m.* vault of heaven; rainbow. —s=braut, *f.* nun. —s=breite, —s=höhe, *f.* solar altitude, distance (*of a star*) from the equator. —schlüssel, *n.* primrose. —schön, *adj. & adv.* divinely beautiful. —schreiend, *adj.* crying to heaven, most atrocious *or* revolting. —s=enge, *f.* heavenly nook. —s=erscheinung, *f.* phenomenon *or* portent in the skies. —s=feste, *f.* firmament. —s=feuer, *n.*, —s=glut, *f.* fire of heaven; divine inspiration; stars; lightning. —s=gabe, *f.* heavenly gift, blessing. —s=gegend, *f.* quarter of the heavens; climate; die vier —sgegenden, the four points of the compass. —s=gewalt, *f.* heavenly power; supernatural, irresistible power. —s=gewölbe, *f.* firmament. —s=gleicher, *m.* equator. —s=globus, *m.* celestial globe. —s=gürtel, *m.* zone. —s=haus, *n.* firmament; house (*Astrol.*). —s=heer, *n.* heavenly host. —s=karte, *f.* celestial chart *or* map. —s=kerze, *f.* sun, moon, and stars. —s=körper, *m.* celestial body. —s=kost, *f.* ambrosia; heavenly food = the sacrament. —s=kugel, *f.* celestial globe. —s=kunde, *f.* astronomy. —s=länge, *f.* astronomical longitude. —s=lauf, *m.* motion of the heavenly bodies. —s=lehre, *f.* uranology. —s=leiter, *f.* Jacob's ladder. —s=lerche, *f.* sky-lark. —s=licht, *n.* celestial light; sun, moon; (*pl.*) luminaries; das große —slicht, the sun. —s=luft, *f.* ether, air of heaven. —s=lust, *f.* heavenly delight. —s=mächte, *pl.* heavenly powers. —s=manna, *f.* heavenly manna; Persian manna. —s=meß=kunst, *f.* uranometry. —s=pol, *m.* pole of the heavens. —s=punkt, *m.* zenith. —s=rand, *m.* the horizon. —s=raum, *m.* the heavens. —s=speise, *f.* heavenly food, sacramental bread, food for celestials, ambrosia. —stein, *m.* sapphire. —(s)=strich, *m.* climate; latitude, zone. —s=tau, *m.* dew from heaven; manna. —s=trank, *m.* nectar. —stürmend, —stürmerisch, *adj.* Titanic. —stürmer, *m.* Titan. —s=wächter, *m.* St. Peter. —s=wagen, *m.* the Great Bear, Charles' Wain. —s=zeichen, *n.* sign of the zodiac. —s=zelt, *n.* canopy of heaven. —s=zirkel, *m.* celestial sphere. —träger, *m.* sky, *or* canopy, bearer; atlas. —wärts, *adv.* heavenwards. —weit, *adj. & adv.* as distant as heaven from earth, very distant; unsere Ansichten sind —weit von einander verschieden, our views are diametrically opposed, very widely different.

Himm'lisch, *adj. & adv.* heavenly, celestial; ethereal; divine; beatific; splendid, beautiful, lovely, capital (*coll.*); —e Fügung, divine ordinance, decree of Providence; die —en Mächte, the powers above; das —e Reich, the Celestial Empire, China; die —en, the Celestials; —e Sehnsucht, longing for heaven, spiritual longing; ein —er Abend, a lovely evening (*coll.*); —er Vater, our Father in Heaven; good God.

Hin, *adv. & sep. prefix expressing motion from the speaker or point contemplated*, hence, that way, thither, towards that place; *used in regard to time to come or expressing duration of time*, towards, on, along; *sometimes implying simply motion with no distinct reference to direction*, along; gone, lost; spent; undone; nach . . . —, to, towards; — und her, there and back, forwards and backwards; — oder her, this way or that way, more or less; nicht — nicht her, neither one thing nor another; er weiß weder — noch her, he is at his wits' end, he does not know what to do; — und her überlegen, denken, to rack one's brains about, turn over in one's mind; — wie her, six of one and half a dozen of the other; — und wieder, to and fro, away and home again; now and then; Fahrschein für — und zurück, return ticket; nach vielem —=und=her=Schreiben, after many letters had passed on both sides; Mode —, Mode her, ich werde . . ., whatever the fashion is (in spite of fashion), I shall . . .; so —, tolerably, so so; er ist —, he is lost, undone, ruined, dead; he has arrived there; — ist —, gone is gone, lost is lost, no good in crying over spilt milk; oben —, von oben —, along the upper part, on the surface; sich nur so — behelfen, to drag on a painful existence; es ist noch weit —, it is still a long way off; auf Ihr Wort —, on your word; ich wage es darauf —, then *or* with regard to that I shall risk it. —nen, *adv.*; von —nen, hence, from here; von —nen scheiden, to die. —ten, —ter, *see* Hint, Hinter. *Comp.* (*in comp. with verbs* hin *is sep. and has the accent; with preps. & advs. is insep. and the accent is on the prep. or adv.*). —ab, —an, *see* Hinab, Hinan. —altern, *v.n.* (*aux.* s.) to grow old, to age. —arbeiten, *v.* I. *n.* (*aux.* h.) (auf eine

S.) to aim at, struggle towards. II. *r.* to work one's way towards, attain with difficulty. —**auf, —aus,** *see* **Hinauf, Hinaus.** —**bannen,** *v.a.* to conjure (*to a place*); —**gebannt,** spell-bound (*to*). —**begeben,** *ir.v.r.* to betake oneself, repair (**zu,** to). —**bestellen,** *v.a.* to order *or* appoint to a place (*away from the speaker*). —**blick,** *m.* look at *or* towards a thing; prospect; **im —blick auf,** with regard to. —**blicken,** *v.n.* (*aux.* **h.**) to look towards. —**blühen,** *v.n.* (*aux.* **s.**) to fade away. —**bluten,** *v.n.* (*aux.* **h.**) to bleed to death, die. —**bringen,** *ir.v.a.* to bring *or* carry away; to spend, pass; to spend, squander; **sich kümmerlich —bringen,** to make shift to live, to eke out a miserable existence. —**brüten,** *v.n.* (*aux.* **h.**) to be in a state of lethargy, to pass in brooding. —**denken,** *ir.v.n.* (*aux.* **h.**) to think of *or* away; **wo denken Sie —?** what are you thinking of? —**deuten,** *v.n.* (*aux.* **h.**) to point, aim, show the way; **auf eine S. —deuten,** to intimate a thing, to point to *or* to hint at a thing. —**deutung,** *f.* (**auf eine S.**) hint, hinting (at a th.), intimation (of a th.). —**drang,** *m.* crowding, thronging on, onset. —**durch,** *adv. & sep. prefix,* through, away through; throughout; thither away; **den ganzen Tag —durch,** all day long. —**durchlassen,** *ir.v.a.* to let through, to let pass; to transmit. —**eilen,** *v.n.* (*aux.* **s.**) to hasten (*away*) to. —**ein,** *see* **Hinein.** —**fahren,** *ir.v.* I. *n.* (*aux.* **s.**) to drive on; to go away, depart; to cease; to sail by, near, along; to cycle past; to die; to pass over lightly; **fahre —, Mitleid!** farewell, pity! **mit der Hand über eine S. —fahren,** to pass one's hand over anything. II. *a.* to convey to. —**fahrt,** *f.* journey thither, passage out, passage to a place; drive there; decease; **auf der —fahrt,** on the outward journey; on the way there; driving thither. —**fall,** *m.* falling down; fall; decay. —**fallen,** *ir.v.n.* (*aux.* **s.**) to fall down, to decay. —**fällig,** *adj.* falling down; frail, weak, perishable; ready to fall, decaying untenable (*of reasons*). —**fälligkeit,** *f.* decrepitude, frailty, feebleness; weakness (*of arguments*). —**finden,** *ir.v.r.* to find one's way to a place. —**fort,** *adv.* henceforth, in future. —**fracht,** *f.* freight outwards. —**führung,** *f.* guiding, leading to *or* on. —**für, —füro,** (*obs.*) *see* —**fort.** —**gabe,** *f.* giving away; surrender; resignation; devotedness. —**gang,** *m.* going away; passage to; departure; decease. —**geben,** *ir.v.* I. *a.* to give to *or* away; to give up, surrender, resign; to sacrifice. II. *r.* to resign oneself to, to give oneself up to; to indulge in. —**gebung,** *f.* giving away; surrender; resignation; addiction, devotion. —**gegen,** *adv. & conj.* on the contrary, on the other hand; but; whereas. —**gehen,** *ir.v.n.* (*aux.* **s.**) to go to that place: to go (*anywhere*); to pass; to elapse; **es geht —,** it is passable; **es mag —gehen,** it may pass; **etwas —gehen lassen,** to pass over, to let pass, not to mind a th. —**geraten,** *ir.v.n.* (*aux.* **s.**) to fall, light come *or* get to a place by chance *or* accident; **wo ist er —geraten?** what has become of him? —**gerissen** (*p.p. of* —**reißen**) carried away, enthusiastic, entranced. —**gestreckt,** *p.p. & adj.* prostrate. —**gleiten,** *ir.v.n.* (*aux.* **s.**) to slip away. —**halten,** *ir.v.a.* to hold towards any one, stretch out, proffer; to put off, delay; to keep at bay; to keep, preserve; **einen —halten,** to keep a p. in suspense, put one off, amuse, divert one. —**haltung,** *f.* holding forth, putting off; delay. —**hängen,** *v.* I. *n.* (*aux.* **h.**) to hang down, incline. II. *a.* to hang up; to defer, put off. —**helfen,** *ir.v.* I. *n.* (*aux.* **h.**) to help *or* assist a person in getting to (*a place, etc.*). II. *r.* to support oneself with difficulty, to struggle on. —**knieen,** *v.n.* (*aux.* **s.**) to kneel down. —**kommen,** *ir.v.n.* (*aux.* **s.**) to come *or* get to, to arrive at; **nirgends —kommen,** not to go anywhere, never to go out, to see no company; **wo ist er —gekommen?** what has become of him? —**kränkeln,** *v.n.* (*aux.* **h.**) to languish under disease. —**kunft,** *f.* coming thither, arrival there. —**langen,** *v.* I. *a.* (**einem etwas**) to hand, reach over. II. *n.* (*aux.* **h.**) to reach to a place; to be adequate, to suffice. —**länglich,** *adj.* sufficient, adequate; —**längliches Auskommen,** sufficient means, a competence, living wage. —**länglichkeit,** *f.* sufficiency; competency. —**lassen,** *ir.v.a.* to suffer to go to; to let pass, admit. —**laufen,** *ir.v.n.* (*aux.* **s.**) to run thither *or* away; **er mag —laufen,** let him run *or* go his way. —**legen,** *v.* I. *a.* to lay down; to put away. II. *r.* to lie down. —**machen,** *v.* I. *a.* to put, fasten, fix to. II. *r.* to betake oneself, to go to a place. —**marsch,** *m.* march thither *or* to a place. —**nahme,** *f.* taking to, with *or* away; receiving, reception. —**nehmen,** *ir.v.a.* to take away *or* from one; to carry away, transport, ravish; to take with *or* along; to bear, suffer. put up with; **ich werde es nicht so —nehmen,** I shall not put up with it. —**neigen,** *v.r. & n.* (*aux.* **h.**) to incline to; to bend *or* lean towards. —**opfern,** *v.a.* to sacrifice, despatch. —**passen,** *v.n.* (*aux.* **h.**) to fit, suit (**in,** for), to be fit for. —**pflanzen,** *v.a.* to plant out, plant there. —**quälen,** *v.r.* to drag on a painful existence. —**raffen,** *v.a.* to take, snatch, sweep away. —**reichen,** *v.* I. *a. see* —**langen** I. II. *n.* (*aux.* **h.**) to reach to the desired point; to suffice, be sufficient. —**reichend,** *p. & adj.,* —**reichlich,** *adj.* sufficient, adequate, enough. —**reise,** *f.* out journey, journey *or* voyage thither; **—-und-Rück-Reise,** the double journey, out and return journey. —**reißen,** *ir.v.a.* to carry along with violence; to overpower, overcome; to delight, charm, transport; **sich —reißen lassen,** to allow oneself to be carried away, to give way to. —**richten,** *v.a.* to direct *or* turn to *or* towards (*a place*); to execute (*a malefactor*); to spoil, ruin; (*dial.* = **herrichten**) to prepare, arrange, to set right. —**richtung,** *f.* execution. —**ritt,** *m.* ride thither. —**rücken,** *v.a. & n.* to move to *or* towards; to march on, move away. —**schaffen,** *v.a.* to transport to (*a place*). —**scheiden,** *ir.v.n.* (*aux.* **s.**) to depart, to die; **der —geschiedene,** the deceased. —**schießen,** *ir.v.n.* (*aux.* **s.**) to shoot to *or* towards; to rush, hasten along, fly away. —**schiffen,** *v.* I. *n.* (*aux.* **s.**) to sail to a place; to sail along. II. *a.* to convey *or* transport to (*in a ship*). —**schlachten,** *v.a.* to kill, murder, butcher. —**schlagen,** *ir.v.* I. *a.* to knock down, in, to *or* towards. II. *n.* (*aux.* **s.**) to fall down heavily; **lang —schlagen,** to fall down at full length (*coll.*). —**schlängeln,** *v.r.* to wind, meander along. —**schleichen,** *v.n.* to creep along. —**schleppen,** *v.a.* to drag to, on *or* along. —**schmachten,** *v.n.* (*aux.* **s.**) to languish; to lead a languishing, lingering life. —**schmeißen,** *ir.v.a.* to throw *or* fling down. —**schwinden,** *ir.v.n.* (*aux.* **s.**) to pass away, vanish: —**schwindend,** evanescent. —**sehen,** *ir.v.n.* (*aux.* **h.**) to look (*away*) towards *or* at. —**sehnen,** *v.r.* to long to be there, to be away. —**setzen,** *v.* I. *a.* to set *or* put to, down *or* away; to confine (*in prison. vulg.*). II. *r.* to sit down. —**sicht,** *f.* view, consideration, respect, regard; **in —sicht auf,** with regard to, concerning; **in mancher —sicht,** in many respects; **Sie haben in dieser —sicht recht,** you are right in this respect *or* on this point. —**sichtlich**, —**sichts**, *prep.* (*with gen.*) with regard to, as to, touching. —**siechen**, *v.n.* to pine away (*from disease*). —**sinken**, *ir.v.n.* (*aux.* s.) to sink down, swoon, faint away. —**stellen**, *v.a.* to put in a place; to put down; to represent; **etwas schroff —stellen**, to represent a thing as quite certain; **das wollen wir doch nicht so schroff —stellen**, let us not be too positive about this. —**streben**, *v.n.* (*aux.* h.) (**nach etwas**) to tend towards; to strive after. —**strecken**, *v.* I. *a.* to stretch along *or* out; to knock down, lay low. II. *r.* to lie down at full length. —**streichen**, *ir.v.* I. *n.* (*aux.* s.) to move, pass along; to pass away; to depart. II. *a.* to rub, stroke towards; to spread (*butter, etc.*). —**strich**, *m.* gliding *or* passing away, departure. —**sturz**, *m.* falling headlong; precipitation. —**stürzen**, *v.n.* (*aux.* s.) to fall headlong, tumble down; to rush forward, to hasten to. —**taumeln**, *v.n.* to reel along. —**thun**, *ir.v.a.* to put *or* place (*coll.*); **wo soll ich es —thun?** where shall I put it, what shall I do with it? **ich weiß nicht, wo ich diesen Menschen —thun soll**, I can't think where I have seen this man. —**trauern**, *v.a.* to pass in sorrow *or* mourning. —**träumen**, *v.a.* to dream away. —**treten**, *ir.v.n.* (*aux.* s.) to step along, to tread; to step up (**vor, zu**, to). —**tritt**, *m.* departure, death (*high style*). —**über**, *adv. & sep. prefix*, over there *or* thither, across, **da —über**, over there, that way; **er ist —über**, he has passed away, he is dead. —**überbringen**, *ir.v.a.* (*sep.*) to bring across; to transpose (*Math.*). —**um**, *adv.* about, that way about; **dort —um**, round that way. —**unter**, *adv. & sep. prefix*, down (*hence*), downward, from up here. —**unter=klaffen**, *v.n.* to yawn in a downward direction, yawn down. —**unter=schlucken**, *v.a.* to swallow, gulp down; to ingurgitate. —**unterwärts**, *adv.* downwards. —**wagen**, *v.r.* to venture to (*a place*). —**wärts**, *adv.* in that direction, thitherward. —**weg**, *m.* way to a place, way thither. —**weisen**, *ir.v.a.* to show (*the way*) to; **auf eine S. —weisen**, to point to, towards *or* at, to refer, allude to; —**weisend**, pointing to, alluding to, demonstrative (*Gram.*). —**weisung**, *f.* direction; hint, allusion; **unter —weisung auf** (*acc.*), with reference to. —**welken**, *v.n.* to wither away, to droop. —**werfen**, *ir.v.a.* to throw, fling to *or* down; to write down *or* sketch hastily; to drop (*a word*); —**geworfene Worte**, dropped words, occasional utterances. —**wieder**, —**wiederum**, *adv.* again, once more; on the other hand; in return. —**wollen**, *ir.v.n.* (*aux.* h.) to want to go to; to aim at, tend to; **ich merke, wo er —will**, I see what he is driving at. —**wurf**, *m.* throwing to *or* away; hasty sketch. —**zahlen**, *v.a.* to pay down (*cash*). —**zählen**, *v.a.* to count out *or* down. —**zaubern**, *v.a.* to produce as by magic; to conjure away. —**zeichnen**, *v.a.* to sketch down, sketch hastily; **er hat das nur so —gezeichnet**, he has only made a rough sketch of it. —**ziehen**, *ir.v.* I. *a.* to draw along, extend, protract; to draw to, attract. II. *n.* (*aux.* s.) to move off *or* along; to remove to; to pass away, depart. —**zielen**, *v.n.* (*aux.* h.) **auf eine S. —zielen**, to aim at a thing. —**zu**, *see* **Hinzu**. —**zug**, *m.* marching along; removal to (*a place*).

Hina'b, *adv. & sep. prefix*, down (*thither*), downwards; — **mit ihm!** throw him down! down with him! **den Strom —**, down the river, down stream. *Comp.* —**lassen**, *ir.v.a.* to let down, lower. —**steigen**, *ir.v.n.* (*aux.* s.) to descend. —**stürzen**, *v.* I. *n.* (*aux.* s.) to fall down (*from a precipice*). II. *a.* to throw down, precipitate.

Hina'n, *adv. & sep. prefix*, up to (*a place*), towards, up (*away from the speaker or point contemplated*). *Comp.* —**steigen**, *ir.v.n.* (*aux.* s.) to mount, ascend, climb up. —**ziehen**, *ir.v.* I. *n.* (*aux.* s.) to move, march up, ascend. II. *a.* to draw upward.

Hinau'f, *adv. & sep. prefix*, up (*thither*), up (*thence*), upwards, up to; **da —, dort —**, up there; **den Fluß —**, up the river; **sich — arbeiten**, to work one's way up. *Comp.* —**schwingen**, *ir.v.n.* to leap *or* spring up, swing oneself up, to rise by hard work, to mount. —**steigen**, *ir.v.n.* (*aux.* s.) to mount, ascend. —**stimmen**, *v.a.* to raise the pitch of (*Mus.*)· to raise, increase (*one's pretensions, etc.*). —**wagen**, *v.r.* to venture up.

Hinau's, *adv. & sep. prefix*, out (*hence*), out (*thither*), forth, away out; beyond; **vorn —**, in the front; **hinten —**, at the back part *or* in the back (*of a house, etc.*); — **mit ihm!** turn him out! **dort —**, out there; **über —**, beyond; **ich weiß nicht wo —**, I don't know the way to get out; I don't know what to do; **zum Fenster —**, out of the window; **zum Fenster — sehen**, to look out at the window; **über den Termin —**, beyond rent-day *or* the term. *Comp.* —**gehen**, *ir.v.n.* (*aux.* s.) to go *or* walk out of; **über eine S. —gehen**, to surpass, exceed, go beyond, to project, to transcend something; **auf etwas** (*acc.*) —**gehen**, to aim at; to look on; to end in; **das Zimmer geht auf den Garten —**, the room looks on *or* into the garden; **die Rede ging darauf —**, the discourse turned on; the principal aim of the speech was. —**hängen**, *v.n.* to put out, to project. —**kommen**, —**laufen**, *ir.v.n.* (*aux.* s.) to come *or* run out of (*a place, etc.*), to terminate in a certain way; **auf eins (dasselbe) —laufen**, to come; to amount to the same thing; **die Rede lief darauf —**, *see* —**gehen**. —**machen**, *v.r.* to go *or* get out. —**reichen**, *v.n.* (*aux.* h.) to stretch out (**über**, beyond). —**rücken**, *v.a.* to postpone. —**schieben**, *ir.v.a.* to defer, postpone. —**sein**, *ir.v.n.* to have gone out; **über eine S. —sein**, to be above a thing, not to care for *or* mind a thing; **darüber bin ich —**, I am past that, I do not mind it. —**setzen**, *v.a.* to put off, postpone, defer; to put out (*of doors*); **sich über eine S. —setzen**, to pass over, set at naught, disregard a thing. —**sollen**, *v.n.* to have to go out; to have a certain aim; **wo soll das —?** where is this to end? —**wärts**, *adv.* outwards. —**weisen**, *ir.v.a.* to turn out. —**werfen**, *ir.v.a.* to expel, eject. —**wollen**, *ir.v.n.* to wish to go out; to aim at; to end in; **wo wollte er —?** what was he driving at? **wo will das —?** what will be the end *or* upshot of it? **hoch —wollen**, to aim at great things, to have lofty aspirations. —**ziehen**, *ir.v.* I. *a.* to pull out to; prolong, protract. II. *n.* (*aux.* s.) to march out, go out.

Hind, —**e**, (*pl.* —**en**), —**in**, *f.* hind.

Hin'der-bar, *adj. & adv.*, preventable, that may be hindered. —**lich**, *adj.* (*with dat.*) & *adv.* hindering, obstructive, embarrassing.

Hin'der-n, *v.a.* to hinder, impede, obstruct, embarrass; to cross, thwart; **was —t mich, es zu thun?** what prevents me from doing it? **sie —t mich am Schreiben**, she prevents me from writing. —**nis**, *n.* (—**ni(ss)es**, *pl.* —**ni(ss)e**) hindrance, impediment, obstacle. —**ung**, *f.* hindering; impediment. *Comp.* —**nis=rennen**, *n.* steeple-chase, hurdle-race.

Hinei'n, *adv. & sep. prefix*, in (*thither*), into, from out here; **in den Tag —**, thoughtlessly, at random; —! nur —! step in! go in! mitten —, (*right*) in the middle; bis in die Stadt —, right into the town, into the very town; da —, nicht hier —, into that place, not into this. *Comp.* —arbeiten, *v.r.* to work one's way into; sich in eine Sache —arbeiten, to make oneself perfectly acquainted, to familiarize oneself with a matter. —denken, *ir.v.r.* (in eine S.) to fancy oneself in; to go deeply into. —finden, *ir.v.r.* to see one's way, understand, become familiar with. —gehen, *ir.v.n.* (*aux.* s.) to go into, to be contained. —legen, *v.a.* (einen) to get a p. into a mess, to get the better of a p. (*coll.*). —lesen, *ir.v.r.* to read deeply, go deeply into (*an author, etc.*). —reden, *v.* I. *n.* (*aux.* h.) (in einen) to lecture (*one*); ins Blaue —reden, to talk without thinking, to talk nonsense. II. *r.* sich in Zorn —reden, to talk oneself into a passion; sich in Unsinn —reden, to end by talking folly. —reiten, *ir.v.n.* (*aux.* s.) to ride into; Sie haben mich schön —geritten, you have got me into a nice mess (*coll.*). —thun, *ir.v.a.* to put into; to add to; to mix with; einen Blick —thun, to glance into. —wollen, *ir.v.n.* (*aux.* h.) to wish *or* be willing to go in; das will mir nicht in den Kopf —, I cannot conceive *or* understand that.

Hing, Hin'ge, (*obs.* Hieng, Hien'ge,) *imperf. ind. & subj. of 1.* hangen; *2.* hängen.

Hin'k—en, *v.n.* (*aux.* h. & s.) to go lame, halt, hobble, limp; es hinkt mit ihm, things are going ill with him; die Sache —t, there is a hitch in the matter; auf beiden Seiten —en, to halt between two opinions; (der) —ende Bote, lame messenger; bad news; title of a popular almanac; der —ende Teufel, the Devil on two sticks.

Hin'nen, *adv.* from hence; von —, away from here, from hence; von — scheiden, to depart from hence, to depart this life, to die.

Hin't—en, *adv.* behind; in the rear; at the end, aft; von —en, from behind; von·—en angreifen, to attack in the rear; —en anfügen, to add, annex; (nach)·—en hinaus wohnen, to live at the back of a house; es hieß immer Herr B. —en und vorn, it was always Mr. B. here, Mr. B. there, Mr. B. everywhere. *Comp.* —an, *adv.* aside; behind, after. —ansetzen, *v.a.* to treat slightingly, neglect. —ansetzung, *f.* neglecting; disregard; slighting; postponing. —en=drein, —en=nach, *adv* after, afterwards, after the event; last. —en=über, *adv.* upside down, backwards. —en=vorn, I. *adv.* in an inverted state. II. *subst. n.* inversion.

Hin'ter, I. *adj. & insep. prefix*, hind, hinder, back; der, die, das —e, he, she, that which is behind *or* follows; der —e, the posterior, backside. II. *adv. & sep. prefix*, behind, back; backwards; down (*as* —bringen, to get down, swallow). III. *prep.* behind; after; back of, in rear of; (*with acc. when implying motion to a place; with dat. when implying rest or limitea or circular motion in a place*); er stand erst — mir, dann trat er — meinen Bruder, first he stood behind me and then he stepped behind my brother; — her, after, behind; immer — einem her sein, to be always at a p.'s heels, to be constantly urging *or* worrying one; —(da)s Licht führen, to dupe, deceive, take in; sich — die Arbeit her machen, to set to work; — einander, one after another, in succession, together; — einander weg, without drawing breath, uninterruptedly; fünfmal — einander, five times running; er hat es (dick *or* faustdick) — den Ohren, he is a very cunning fellow; ich werde es mir — die Ohren schreiben, I shall take good care to remember it, I shall certainly not forget it; der Haushalt ist — sich gegangen, the household has grown worse; die Heirat ist — sich gegangen, the match is broken off; — dem Berge halten, to keep one's thoughts secret, to dissemble; mit seiner Absicht — dem Berge halten, to conceal one's designs; das hätte ich nicht — ihm gesucht, I should not have thought him capable of that; — sich sehen, to look back; — eine S. kommen, to find a th. out, to discover a th.; er steckt — der Sache, he is the secret mover in the matter; es steckt etwas — der Sache, there is something in the matter, more is meant than meets the eye. —e, *m.* posterior. —ste, *adj.* hindmost, last; sternmost (*Naut.*); —st=zuvörderst, the last first. *Comp.* —ansicht, *f.* back-view, back-elevation (*Arch.*). —backe, *f.* buttock. —bein, *n.* hindleg; sich auf die —beine setzen *or* stellen, to stand on one's hindlegs; to resist to the utmost, to object altogether, to show fight. —bleiben, I. *ir.v.n.* (*aux.* s.) (*insep.*) to remain behind, survive. II. *subst. n.* remains, rest. —bliebene(r), *m.*, —bliebene, *f.* he *or* she that has remained behind, relict, survivor. —boden, *m.* back-loft *or* garret. —bringen, *ir.v.a.* (*insep.*) (einem etwas) to inform (*a p. of a th.*) (*usually said of secret information*). —bringer, *m.* informer; spy; tell-tale. —bringung, *f.* (secret) information. —bug, *m.* hough; knuckle (*of veal*). —deck, *n.* poop. —drein, *adv.* after; afterwards; too late. —fuß, *m.* hind-foot. —gäßchen, *n.* back-street. —gebäude, *n.* back-building; out-house. —gehen, *ir.v.a.* (*insep.*) to deceive, cheat, impose on. —geschirr, *n.* crupper, breechings. —gestell, *n.* back of a carriage; back-part (*of a chair*); horse's hind-quarters; backside (*vulg.*). —glied, *n.* rear rank (*Mil.*); minor proposition (*Log.*); consequent (*Math.*). —grund, *m.* background. —halb, *adv. & prep.* (*with gen.*) behind. —halt, *m.* ambush; reserve. —halten, *ir.v.a.* (*insep.*) to hold back, to practise reserve; to conceal, deceive. —haltig, —hältig, —hältisch, *adj.* reserved, close. —hand, *f.* back of the hand; hind-quarter (*of a horse*); youngest hand (*at cards*). —haupt, *n.* back part of the head, hind head; occiput. —her, *adv.* behind; afterwards; wer —her kommt, den beißen die Hunde, the dogs bite the hindermost (*prov.*). —hof, *m.* backyard. —kastell, *n.* quarter-deck (*Naut.*). —lader, *m.* breechloader. —lage, *f.* deposit, pledge. —land, *n.* inland province, hinterland. —laß, *m. see* —lassenschaft. —lassen, I. *ir.v.a.* (*insep.*) to leave behind; to leave an order; to bequeath; die —lassenen, the survivors *or* heirs. II. *p.p. & adj.* posthumous. —lassenschaft, *f.* testator's estate. —lauf, *m.* hindleg (*sport*). —leder, *n.* hind-quarter (*of a shoe*). —legen, *v.a.* (*insep.*) to deposit; to consign. —leger, *m.* depositor. —legte(s), *n.* deposit. —legung, *f.* deposition. —list, *f.* fraud; cunning, artifice, wile. —listig, *adj. & adv.* cunning, insidious, artful, wily. —mann, *m.* rear-rank man; subsequent endorser (*of cheques*); wer ist mein —mann? who plays after me? —mast, *m.* mizzen-mast. —perron, *m.* back platform (*on tram cars*). —pferd, *n.* shaft-horse. —pforte, *f.* back-gate; (*pl.*) stern-ports (*Naut.*). —riegel, *m.* crossbar. —rücks, *adv.* backwards; from behind; secretly, insidiously. —s = — das. —saß, *m.* (—sa(ss)en, *pl.* —sa(ss)en) copy-holder; small farmer *or* tenant. —sattel, *m.* pillion. —satz, *m.* apodosis. —schiff, *n.* hind part of a ship. —sitz, *m.* back seat. —stich, *m.* back stitch. —strich, *m.* apostrophe (*sign of*). —stube, *f.* back-room. —stück, *n.* hind, back piece. —tau, *n.* stern-fast (rope). —teil, *n.* hind-part, back-part; stern. —thür, *f.* backdoor; loophole, escape, outlet (*fig.*). —**treffen**, *n.* reserve; rearguard. —**treiben**, *ir.v.a.* (*insep.*) to hinder, baffle, thwart. —**treibung**, *f.* frustration, thwarting. —**verdeck**, *n.* quarter-deck. —**wäldler**, —**walds=mann**, *m.* backwoodsman, squatter. —**wand**, *f.* back-wall; back scenery (*Theat.*). —**wärts**, *adv.* backwards, behind.

Hinwe'g. I. *m.* journey *or* way thither, there. II. *adv. & sep. prefix*, away forth from here, off; let us go! *Comp.* —**gehen**, *ir.v.a.* (*aux.* **f.**) to go away; (**über eine S.**) to pass lightly over. —**nahme**, *f.* taking way. —**raffen**, *v.a.* to snatch away; to shatter. —**sehen**, *ir.v.n.* (*aux.* **h.**) to look away; (**über eine S.**) to take no notice of, overlook. —**setzen**, *v.r.* (**über eine S.**) to disregard, treat with contempt *or* indifference.

Hinzu', *adv. & sep. prefix*, to, toward; near; to it, in addition. *Comp.* —**fügen**, *v.a.* to add to, annex; to pay in addition. —**fügung**, *f.* addition; apposition (*Gram.*). —**gehören**, *v.n.* (*aux.* **h.**) to be one of; to belong to. —**kommen**, *ir.v.n.* (*aux.* **f.**) to approach, arrive at; to be added to; **es kommt noch** —, **daß** **2c.**, add to this, that, *etc.* —**setzen**, *v.a.* to add (to). —**thun**, I. *ir.v.a.* to add. II. *subst.n.* addition; **ohne jemands** —**thun**, without any one's aid *or* coöperation. —**treten**, *ir.v.n.* (*aux.* **f.**) to step up to; to join in. —**ziehen**, *ir.v.a.* to draw to; to take in addition; to take into consultation; **mit** —**ziehung der Speisen**, including all expenses, all charges included.

Hip'pe, *f.* (*pl.* —**n**) sickle, scythe; hedging *or* pruning-bill; wafer.

Hippur'säure, *f.* hippuric acid.

Hirn, *n.* (—(**e**)**s**, *pl.* —**e**) brain, brains; **zum** — **gehörig**, cerebral. —**lein**, *n.* (—**leins**, *pl.* —**lein**) cerebellum. *Comp.* —**arm**, *adj.* brainless; weakminded. —**brüten**, *n.* melancholy madness. —**deckel**, *m. see* —**schädel**. —**erschütterung**, *f.* concussion of the brain. —**geburt**, *f.*, —**gespinnst**, *n.* chimera, phantom; whim. —**haut**, *f.* meninges; **die obere**, (**untere**) —**haut**, the dura (pia) mater. —**holz**, *n.* cross-cut timber. —**kammer**, *f.* brain-cell. —**krank**, *adj.* brain-sick; feeble in intellect; crazy. —**krankheit**, *f.* brain-disease; insanity. —**lehre**, *f.* craniology. —**los**, *adj.* brainless, silly. —**mark**, *n.* medullary substance of the brain. —**schädel**, *m.*, —**schale**, *f.* skull, cranium. —**schädel=fuge**, —**schädel=naht**, *f.* suture. —**schädel=haut**, *f.* pericranium. —**spinnengewebe**, *n.* arachnoid tunic. —**süchtig**, *adj.* brain-sick. —**teil**, *n.* brain substance. —**wut**, *f.* frenzy. —**wütig**, *adj.* mad.

Hirsch, *m.* (—**es**, *pl.* —**e**) stag, hart; (red) deer; hard wood; **wie der** — **schreit nach frischem Wasser**, as the hart panteth after the water brooks (*B.*); **der** — **schreit** *or* **röhrt**, the stag bellows; **der** — (**wenn angeschossen**) **klagt**, the stag (when wounded) sobs. *Comp.* —**artig**, *adj.* cervine. —**beer=dorn**, *m.* common buckthorn. —**bock**, *m.* stag, buck. —**braten**, *m.* venison. —**bremse**, *f.* stag-fly. —**brunst**, *f.* rutting season of deer. —**dorn**, *m.* buckthorn. —**fährte**, *f.* track of a deer. —**fänger**, *m.* hanger, couteau de chasse. —**fleisch**, *n.* venison. —**geweih**, *n.* head, horns of a stag, antlers. —**halsig**, *adj.* ewe-necked. —**holunder**, *m.* guelder-rose. —**horn**, *n.* horn of a stag; hartshorn. —**horn=flechte**, *f.* Iceland moss. —**jagd**, *f.* stag-hunt *or* hunting. —**käfer**, *m.* stag-beetle. —**kalb**, *n.* fawn, young deer. —**keule**, *f.* haunch of a deer. —**kuh**, *f.* hind. —**lattig**, *m.* colt's foot. —**lauf**, *m.* foot of a deer. —**leder**, *n.* buckskin. —**ledern**, *adj.* made of buckskin; —**lederne Handschuhe**, buff-gloves. —**petersilie**, —**wurz**, *f.* mountain parsley. —**talg**, *m.* suet of deer. —**ziege**, *f.* Indian gazelle. —**ziemer**, *m.* haunch of venison. —**zunge**, *f.* hart's tongue (*Bot.*).

Hir'se, *f.* millet. *Comp.* —**brei**, *m.* millet-pap. —**drüse**, *f.* sebaceous gland. —(**n**)=**fieber**, *n.* miliary fever. —(**n**)=**flechte**, *f.* scurf. —(**n**)=**fink**, *m.* green finch. —**n=förmig**, *adj.* miliary.

Hirt, *m.* (—**en**, *pl.* —**en**), —**e**, *m.* (—**en**, *pl.* —**en**) herdsman, shepherd; pastor; keeper. —**en**, *adj.* (*in comp. gen'lly* =) shepherd's, pastoral. —**en=schaft**, *f.* life *or* occupation of a shepherd; shepherds (*coll.*); pastoral government. —**in**, *f.* shepherdess. —**lich**, *adj.* pastoral. *Comp.* —**en=amt**, *n.* pastor's office *or* duties. —**en=brief**, *m.* pastoral letter (*Rom. Cath.*). —**en=dichter**, *m.* pastoral poet, bucolic. —**en=dichtung**, *f.* pastoral poetry, bucolic poetry. —**en=flöte**, —**en=pfeife**, *f.*, —**en=rohr**, *n.* rural, oaten pipe; Pan's pipe. —**en=gedicht**, *n.* pastoral poem, bucolic, eclogue. —**en=gott**, *m.* Pan. —**en=mäßig**, *adj.* pastoral. —**en=hund**, *m.* shepherd's dog. —**en=leben**, *n.* pastoral life. —**en=lied**, *n.* pastoral song. —**en=los**, *adj.* without a shepherd *or* guardian. —**en=mädchen**, *n.* shepherdess. —**en=spiel**, —**en=stück**, *n.* pastoral (play). —**en=stab**, *m.* shepherd's staff, crook; bishop's crozier. —**en=stamm**, *m.* pastoral race. —**en=stand**, *m.* pastoral condition. —**en=tasche**, *f.* shepherd's pouch. —**en=volk**, *n.* pastoral people, nation of shepherds.

His, *n.* B-sharp.

His's—e, *f.* (*pl.* —**n**) pulley, tackle. —**en**, *v.a.* to hoist. *Comp.* —**e=tau**, (**Hiß'tau**), *n.* halliard.

Hist, *int.* hush! hoi! (= to the left!); **der eine will** —, **der andere hott**, one pulls one way, the other another.

Histo'r—ie, *f.* (*pl.* —**ien**) history; story; narrative. —**iker**, *m.* (—**ikers**, *pl.* —**iker**) historian, student of history. —**ik**, *f.* art of history-writing. —**isch**, *adj. & adv.* historical. *Comp.* —**ien=maler**, *m.* historical painter.

Histör'chen, *n.* (—**s**, *pl.* —) little story, anecdote.

Hit'z—e, *f.* heat; hotness; ardour; passion; rut; batch (*of bread*); height (*of fever*); **in** —**e geraten**, to fly into a passion; **in der** —**e trinken**, to drink when one is hot; **in die** —**e bringen**, to put into a great heat *or* passion; **in der ersten** —**e**, in the first transport. —**ig**, *adj. & adv.* hot; ardent, passionate; inflammatory, burning; hot-headed, hasty; heady; spirited; rutting; —**ige Krankheit**, acute malady *or* disease; —**iges Fieber**, high fever, burning fever. —**igkeit**, *f.* heat; ardour, passion; choleric temper; vehemence. *Comp.* —**blase**, —**blatter**, *f.* pustule, blister. —**blütig**, *adj.* choleric. —**köpfig**, *adj.* hot-headed. —**kopf**, *m.* hotheaded person. —(**e**)=**messer**, *m.* pyrometer.

Hit'zen, *v.a. & n.* (*aux.* **h.**) to heat.

Hob, **Hö'be**, *imperf. ind. & subj. of* **heben**.

Ho'bel, *m.* (—**s**, *pl.* —) plane. —**n**, *v.a.* to plane to polish, take the rough off. *Comp.* —**bank**, *f.* joiner's bench. —**diamant**, *m.* glazier's diamond. —**späne**, *pl.* shavings.

Ho'ben, *abbr. of* **hie oben** (*obs. & rare*).

Hobo'—e, *f.* (*pl.* —**en**) hautboy. —**i'st**, *m.* (—**is'ten**, *pl.* —**is'ten**) hautboy player.

Hoch, I. (*long* **o**) *adj. & adv.* (*when followed by* **e** *of the inflected cases* **ch** *becomes* **h**, *as:* **hoher**, **hohe**, **hohes**, *or* **der**, **die**, **das hohe**; *comp.* **höher**; *sup.* **höchst**) high; tall, lofty; noble, sublime; proud; expensive, dear; deep; great; **das Hohe**, the sublime; **der Hohe**, great man; **die Hohen**, the great; — **und Niedrig**, rich and poor; **drei Mann** —, three men deep; **ein hoher Sinn**, a lofty mind; **ein hoher Genuß**, a great enjoyment; **er trug hohen Sinn**, he had a noble mind; **hohe Worte machen,** to make fine phrases; **eine hohe Farbe,** a bright colour; **der hohe Adel,** the peerage, the nobility; **hohe Blüte,** full bloom; **hoher Gewinn,** big prize (*in a lottery*); **hohe Herrschaften,** people of high rank; **bei hoher Strafe,** under a heavy penalty; **ein hoher Fünfziger,** a man well, *or* high, up in the fifties; **ein hoher Eid,** a solemn oath; **hoher Baß,** barytone; **hohe Jagd,** deer *or* boar hunting; **das hohe Lied,** the Song of Solomon, the Song of Songs; **die hohe Woche,** Lent; **hohes Neujahr,** feast of Epiphany; **die hohe Pforte,** the Sublime Porte; **die hohe Obrigkeit,** the government; **mit Erlaubnis der hohen Obrigkeit,** by permission of the authorities; **hohe See,** open sea, main sea; **hohe Flut, —flut,** high tide *or* water, flood-tide; **— am Tage** *or* **hoher Tag,** broad day, broad daylight; **hohes Alter,** old age; decline of life; **in hohem Ansehn stehen,** to enjoy great authority; **in hoher Blüte stehen,** to be very prosperous; **die Dichtung stand in hoher Blüte,** it was a golden age of poetry; **auf hohem Fuße,** in great style; **die hohe Schule, die —schule,** University; academy; **höhere Knabenschule,** secondary school for boys, grammar school; **höhere Töchterschule,** high school for girls; **höhere Tochter,** girl attending a high school for girls (*coll.*); **der König in höchst eigener Person,** the king himself; **das Leben ist der Güter Höchstes nicht,** life is not the most valuable of man's possessions; **einen — leben lassen** *or* **einem ein — bringen,** to toast, to drink a person's (very good) health; **— lebe der König!** long live the king! **— gehen,** to run, to run high; **es geht bei ihnen — her,** they live in great style; **der Rhein geht hoch,** the waters of the Rhine run high *or* are swollen; **er steht beim Direktor — angeschrieben,** he is in the headmaster's good books; **— halten,** to think highly of; **— aufnehmen,** to take (*kindly or ill*), attach great importance to; **— aufhorchen,** to prick up one's ears, listen attentively; **es zu — anfangen,** to undertake above one's abilities; **es in einer S. aufs höchste bringen,** to bring anything to the highest degree of perfection; **— achten, — schätzen,** to esteem highly; **— zu stehen kommen,** to cost dear; **höhere Berufe,** learned professions; **höherer Blödsinn,** great nonsense; **höhere Bildung,** liberal education; **höherer Offizier,** superior officer; **die höchst Besteuerten,** those who pay the heaviest rates and taxes; **aufs höchste, zum höchsten,** at best, at the most; **wenn es aufs höchste kommt,** when the worst comes to the worst; **der Geldkurs steht —,** cash is at a high premium; **— fallen,** to fall from a great height. II. *n.* (**—s**) cheer; toast. *Comp.* **—achtung,** *f.* esteem, regard; **in** *or* **mit vorzüglicher.—achtung,** yours respectfully, yours very faithfully (*at the end of a letter*). **—achtungs=voll,** *adj. & adv.* most respectful. **—adelig,** *adj.* most noble, belonging to the highest aristocracy. **—alpen,** *pl.* the greater Alps. **—altar,** *m.* high altar. **—amt,** *n.* high-mass. **—bahn,** *f.* overhead railway. **—bau,** *m.* building above ground. **—bejahrt, —betagt,** *adj.* very aged, well advanced in years. **—bewegt,** *adj.* deeply agitated; highly wrought. **—bootsmann,** *m.* boatswain. **—brüstig,** *adj.* high-breasted, high-chested. **—deutsch,** *adj. & adv.* high-German. **—dieselben,** *pron.* Your Highness (*in addressing princes*). **—druck,** *m.* high pressure; relief-printing. **—ebene,** *f.* elevated plain, table-land. **—edel,** *adj.* right noble. **—edelgeboren,** *adj.* high-born; honourable (*title*). **—ehrwürdig,** *adj.* right reverend. **—ehrwürden,** (**Ew.**) your Reverence. **—entzückt,** *adj.* in ecstasy. **—eigen,** *adj.* his, her highness's own. **—erfreut,** *adj.* highly rejoiced. **—erhaben,** *adj.* sublime; in high relief. **—fahrend,** *adj.* haughty. **—fein,** *adj.* superfine. **—fliegend,** *adj.* soaring high, lofty, ambitious. **—flöte,** *f.* flageolet. **—fürstlich,** *adj.* serene, illustrious; **Ew. —fürstliche Gnaden,** Your Serene Highness. **—gebietend,** *adj.* invested with high command; high and mighty; dread (*in titles*). **—gebirge,** *n.* high mountain-chain. **—geboren,** *adj.* right honourable. **—geehrt,** *adj.* highly honoured, highly respected; **— geehrter Herr,** (Dear) Sir (*in letters*); **—geehrter Herr Doktor,** Dear Doctor X., (Dear) Sir. **—gefühl,** *n.* high feeling; delight, enthusiasm; **im —gefühl des Sieges,** exulting in one's *or* his victory. **—gelag,** *n.* banquet. **—gelahrt** (*obs.*), **—gelehrt,** *adj.* very learned. **—gelobt,** *adj.* highly praised; magnified, blessed. **—geneigt,** *adj.* most gracious. **—genuß,** *m.* delight. **—gericht,** *n.* supreme penal court; gallows. **—gesinnt,** *adj.* high-minded, noble-minded. **—gespannt,** *adj.* exaggerated; arrogant; high-wrought. **—gestimmt,** *adj.* high-pitched; lofty-minded. **—gewässer, —wasser,** *n.* high water; freshet. **—gradig,** *adj.* of a high degree, intense; **—gradige Nervosität,** very great nervosity; **—gradige Erregung,** extreme excitement. **—halsig,** *adj.* long-necked. **—herzig,** *adj.* noble-minded, high-spirited; proud. **—holz,** *n.* tree-top. **—kettig,** *adj.* of the high warp. **—kraut,** *n.* dill. **—land,** *n.* highland, upland. **—länder,** *m.* highlander. **—meister,** *m.* grand master. **—meistertum,** *n.* grand-mastership. **—mögend,** *adj.* high and mighty, most powerful. **—mut,** *m.* haughtiness, pride, arrogance; **—mut kommt vor dem Fall!** pride goeth before destruction (*prov.*). **—mutig,** *adj.* of great courage. **—mütig,** *adj.* haughty, proud, arrogant. **—nasig,** *adj.* haughty, supercilious, arrogant, insolent. **—notpeinlich,** *adj.* penal; **—notpeinliche Halsgerichtsordnung,** criminal jurisdiction, penal code. **—ofen,** *m.* smelting furnace. **—priester,** *m.* high priest. **—rad,** *n.* high(-wheeled) bicycle, high wheel; **übersetztes —rad,** front driver (*Cycl.*). **—rot,** *adj.* bright-red, crimson. **—rund,** *adj.* convex, oval. **—schätzung,** *f.* esteem. **—schollig,** *adj.* fruitful, rich (*of soil*). **—schule,** *f.* university; **technische —schule,** polytechnic academy; **—schule für Musik,** academy for music. **—schüler,** *m.* university student. **—schul=lehrer,** *m.* university professor. **—schul=wesen,** *n.* university affairs. **—schuß,** *m.* shot in the air. **—schwanger,** *adj.* far advanced in pregnancy; very near her confinement. **—see=flotte,** *f.* deep-sea fleet, battle fleet. **—selig,** *adj.* late (*of the dead*), deceased; **der —selige König,** His late Majesty (the King); **mein —seliger Herr Großvater,** my late (*lamented*) grandfather (*of royal personages*). **—sinn,** *m.* high-mindedness. **—stämmig,** *adj.* tall, lofty, high grown (*of trees*); standard (*of roses*). **—stapler,** *m.* swindler. **—stift,** *n.* chapter of a cathedral; archbishopric. **—straße,** *f.* highway. **—strebend,** *adj.* aspiring, aiming at great things, ambitious. **—ton,** *m.* principal accent. **—tönend,** *adj.* high-sounding, high flown, grandiloquent. **—tonig,** *adj.* having the principal accent. **—trabend,** *adj.* bombastic. **—traber,** *m.* high-stepping horse. **—trächtig, —tragend,** *adj.* great with young (*of animals*). **—verbrechen,** *n.* capital crime. **—verdient,** *adj.* highly meritorious, very worthy. **—verrat,** *m.* high treason. **—verräter.** *m.* person guilty of high treason. —

wald, *m.* high forest. **—wassermarke**, *f.* **—wasserstands-messer**, *m.* high-water mark. **—weg**, *m.* high-road, causeway. **—weide**, *f.* alp. **—weise**, *adj.* very wise, enlightened. **—wichtig**, *adj.* highly important. **—wild**, *n.* venison, red deer, higher sort of game. **—wohlgeboren**, *adj.* nobly born; high and noble; right honourable; **Ew. —wohlgeboren**, right honourable Sir, your Honour. **—würde**, *f.* prelacy; **Ew. —würden**, your Reverence, reverend Sir; **—würden Gnaden**, Your Grace (*title of an abbot*). **—würdig**, *adj.* right reverend; highly venerable; holy, sacred; **das —würdige Gut, das —würdigste**, the host. **—zeit**, *see* **Hochzeit**. **—zu(ver)eh'rend**, *adj.* highly esteemed.

Hoch'heimer, *m.* (**—s**) hock.

Höch'—lich, *adv.* highly, greatly, mightily; grievously. **—st**, I. *adj.* (*see* **Hoch**) highest, uppermost, utmost, extreme; **die —ste Not**, the direst need, last extremity; **aufs —ste**, at most; **es ist mit ihnen aufs —ste gekommen**, they are reduced to the last extremity. II. *adv.* most, at the most, very, in the highest degree; (*in comp. gen'lly* =) all, most; **das ist das —ste, was ich geben kann**, that is the very outside I can give; **—st schädlich**, highly injurious; **—st gemein**, grossly vulgar. **—stens**, *adv.* at the most, utmost *or* outside; at the best. *Comp.* **—st-leistung**, *f.* best performance; record; **die bisherige —stleistung noch übertreffen**, to beat the record.

Hoch'zeit, *f.* (*pl.* **—en**) festivity; nuptials, wedding, marriage; **— machen** *or* **halten**, to get married, celebrate one's wedding; **— zu Kana**, wedding at Cana. **—er**, *m.* bridegroom (*dial.*). **—erin**, *f.* bride (*dial*). **—lich**, *adj. & adv.* nuptial, bridal. *Comp.* **—(s)band**, *n.* wedding-favour. **—(s)bett**, *n.* bridal bed. **—bitter**, *m.* person employed to invite guests to a rural wedding. **—(s)feier**, *f.*, **—(s)fest**, *n.* wedding-feast *or* festival. **—(s)gebräuche**, *pl.* nuptial rites. **—(s)gedicht**, *n.* epithalamium. **—(s)gewand**, *n.* bridal dress, wedding-garment. **—(s)gott**, *m.* Hymen. **—(s)kranz**, *m.* bridal wreath. **—(s)kuchen**, *m.* bridal-cake. **—(s)-leute**, *pl.* wedding-guests. **—(s)mahl**, *n.*, **—(s)schmaus**, *m.* wedding-banquet. **—(s)mutter**, *f.* bride's mother. **—(s)schmuck**, *m.* bridal ornaments. **—s-vater**, *m.* bride's father.

Ho'cke, *f.* (*pl.* **—n**) shock, heap of sheaves. **—ln**, *v.n.* to carry on one's back.

Ho'ck—en, *v.* I. *n.* (*aux.* **h.**) to get on another's back; to crouch, cower; to squat; **immer hinter dem Ofen** *or* **zu Hause —en**, never to stir out, to be a stay-at-home. II. *a.* to set up (*sheaves*) in heaps *or* stooks; *see* **—eln**. **—er**, *m.* (**—ers**, *pl.* **—er**) one who puts up sheaves; stay-at-home, recluse. *Comp.* **—(e-)spiel**, *n.* game at cards; leap-frog.

Hö'cker, *m.* (**—s**, *pl.* **—**) any protuberance; hump, bunch, knob; **einen — haben**, to be hunchbacked; **ich will die — eben machen**, I will make the crooked places straight (*B.*). **—chen**, *n.* little hump; tubercle (*Bot.*). **—icht** (*obs.*), **—ig**, *adj. & adv.* humpy, gibbose; rugged; uneven; tuberous, tuberculous; hunchbacked. *Comp.* **—flügel**, *m.* hump-backed beetle (*Ent.*). **—tier**, *n.* animal with a hump.

Ho'de, *f.* (*pl.* **—n**), **—(n)**, *m.* (**—n(s)**, *pl.* **—n**) testicle. *Comp.* **—n-bruch**, *m.* scrotal hernia. **—n-sack**, *m.* purse, scrotum.

Hof, *m.* (**—es**, *pl.* **Hö'fe**) yard, court-yard; farm; country-house; manor; palace; court; household (*of a sovereign*); circle (*round the eyes*); halo; corona (*Opt.*); inn, hotel; (*in comp. gen'lly* =) court, royal; **am, bei —e**, at court; **einem den — machen**, to pay court to one; **einer Dame den — machen**, to pay one's addresses to a lady, to dance attendance on a lady; **der Bairische —**, Bavarian hotel. *Comp.* **—acker**, *m.* field belonging to a farm *or* estate. **—amt**, *n.* employment at court; office in the royal household. **—arzt**, *m.* court-physician. **—bauer**, *m.* proprietor of a farm, peasant proprietor, farmer; serf (*rare*). **—beamte(r)**, *m.* court-official. **—buchhändler**, *m.* bookseller to the court, bookseller in ordinary to His (*or* Her) Majesty. **—burg**, *f.* royal residence, imperial palace (*in Vienna*). **—dame**, *f.* lady (*or* maid) of honour, lady in waiting; lady of the court; **oberste —dame**, mistress of the robes. **—dichter**, *m.* court poet, poet laureate. **—dienst**, *m.* office at court; socage. **—fähig**, *adj.* having the right to appear at court; admissible *or* presentable at court. **—fähigkeit**, *f.* right of admission *or* presentation at court. **—farbe**, *f.* royal livery. **—fräulein**, *n.* maid of honour. **—freiheit**, *f.* privileges of *or* granted by a court; district enjoying privileges from the court. **—freundschaft**, *f.* friends at court; false friendship. **—futtermeister**, *m.* purveyor to the royal stables. **—fütterung**, *f.* stall-feeding. **—gebrauch**, **—brauch**, *m.* court-etiquette. **—gefolge**, *n.* retinue of a court. **—gerät**, *n.* farming implements; kitchen-utensils of a court. **—gericht**, *n.* high court of justice. **—gesinde**, *n.* household of a prince; courtiers, court; servants on a farm *or* estate. **—günstling**, *m.* court-favourite. **—gut**, *n.* domain, demesne. **—haltung**, *f.* household of a prince; court. **—herr**, *m.* lord of the manor. **—hörig**, *adj.* manorial, belonging to the lord of the manor. **—hund**, *m.* watch-dog. **—jäger**, *m.* ranger, royal game keeper. **—jägerei**, *f.* ranger's house; court rangers (*coll.*). **—junker**, *m.* page; equerry. **—kammer**, *f.* exchequer. **—kanzlei**, *f.* chancery of a court. **—kapelle**, *f.* court-chapel; a prince's private singers and band. **—kapell-meister**, *m.* director of the royal orchestra. **—kaplan**, *m.* chaplain in ordinary to the king (*or* queen). **—kasse**, *f.* prince's private purse *or* income, civil list. **—kavalier**, *m.* gentleman in waiting; courtier. **—kirche**, *f.* court-church. **—kreise**, *pl.* courtly (*or* court) circles. **—kriegsrat**, *m.* imperial council of war (*at Vienna*); a member of this council. **—künste**, **—ränke**, *pl.* court-intrigues, court-tricks. **—lager**, *n.* residence of the court. **—lecker**, *m.* court-toady. **—leute**, *pl.* courtiers; bondsmen, socagers. **—lieferant**, *m.* purveyor to the court, to his Majesty the King. **—manier**, *f.* court-manner. **—mann**, *m.* courtier; farm-steward. **—männisch**, *adj.* courtier-like. **—marschall**, *m.* court-marshal, marshal of the King's household; Lord Chamberlain (*in England*). **—mäßig**, *adj.* court-like, courtly. **—meier**, *m.* farm-steward; farmer. **—meister**, *m.* private tutor (*obs.*); steward. **—meisterei**, *f.* steward's house; tutorship (*obs.*); pedagogism, pedantry. **—meisterin**, *f.* governess in a private family (*obs.*); wife of a farm-steward; housekeeper. **—meistern**, *v.* I. *n.* to act as private tutor; to play the pedant. II. *a.* to censure, find fault with, criticize. **—meister-stelle**, *f.* tutorship. **—narr**, *m.* prince's jester. **—platz**, *m.* court-yard. **—prediger**, *m.* court-chaplain; **ordentlicher —prediger**, chaplain in ordinary. **—rat**, *m.* aulic council; aulic councillor; a title of honour. **—raum**, *m.* courtyard; yard. **—schatzmeister**, *m.* treasurer to the royal household. **—schau-spieler**, *m.* actor at the theatre royal. **—schranz(e)**, *m.* mean flatterer *or* courtier. **—schulze**, *m.* justice of the farm; wealthy (Westphalian) farmer. **—sitte**, *f.* court-etiquette. **—sitz**, *m.* prince's residence. **—staat**, *m.* court-state; household of a court *or* prince;

court-dress. —**tag**, *m.* drawing-room day; day of a levee; day of forced labour for the lord of the manor. —**theater**, *n.* theatre-royal; court-theatre. —**thor**, *n.* yard-gate. —**thür**, *f.* yard-door. —**wagen**, *m.* royal carriage. —**wehr**, —**gewehrung**, *f.* farm-stock. —**welt**, *f.* the court; fashionable life. —**wesen**, *n.* court-ways; court-affairs. —**zeitung**, *f.* court-gazette. —**zirkel**, *m.* circle at court. —**zug**, *m.* princely *or* royal train.

Höf—elei', —**erei'**, *f.* flattery; courtly attention.

Höf'—isch, *adj. & adv.* courtly; courteous; fawning; **die —ische Lyrik**, courtly lyrics (*especially betw. 1170 and 1250*); **das —ische Epos**, court epic (*especially betw. 1170 and 1250*); **die —ische Dichtung**, poetry of the Knights (*twelfth and thirteenth centuries in Germany*). —**ler**, *m.* (—**lers**, *pl.* —**ler**) courtier; adherent of the court-party. —**lich**, *adj. & adv.* polite, courteous. —**lichkeit**, *f.* politeness, courtesy. —**ling**, *m.* (—**lings**, *pl.* —**linge**) courtier. *Comp.* —**lichkeits=bezeigung**, *f.* mark of attention, of politeness.

Hof'—fart (*short* **o**), *f.* arrogance, pride, haughtiness; pomp. —**färtig**, *adj. & adv.* haughty, insolent, arrogant.

Hof'f—en, I. *v.a. & n.* (*aux.* **h.**) to hope; to expect, look for; **auf eine S. —en**, to hope for a thing; **das —e ich**, I hope so, I hope I shall; **es ist** (*or* **steht**) **zu —en**, it is to be hoped; **ich will nicht —en, daß**, I hope it is not the case that. II. *subst.n.* hoping, expecting; —**en und Harren macht manchen zum Narren**, he who lives on hope dies of hunger (*prov.*). —**entlich**, *adv.* it is to be hoped, let us hope so, I hope. —**nung**, *f.* hope; **guter —nung sein**, to be of good cheer; to be confident; to be with child, pregnant; **Vorgebirge** *or* **Kap der guten —nung**, Cape of Good Hope; **einem —nung auf eine S. machen**, to give one reason to hope for *or* expect; —**nung geben auf eine S.**, to hold out hopes for; to bid fair to; **zu den schönsten —nungen berechtigen**, to justify the fondest hopes; **ein zu den schönsten —nungen berechtigender junger Mann**, a young man of great promise. *Comp.* —**nungs=los**, *adj.* hopeless; past all hope. —**nungs=losigkeit**, *f.* despair. —**nungs=schimmer**, *m.* ray of hope. —**nungs=reich**, —**nungs=voll**, *adj. & adv.* promising, hopeful, bidding fair.

Hofie'ren, *v.n.* (*in most meanings now obs.; aux.* **h.**) to live like a lord, to banquet; to play, have *or* make music; to obey the call of nature (*vulg.*); (*with dat.*) to court, to flatter.

Höft, *n.* (—**es**) foreland; headland; mole.

Ho'h—e, —**er**, **2c.**, *see* **Hoch**. —**eit**, *see* **Hoheit**. *Comp.* —**e=lied**, *n.* (**Salomonis**) Song of Solomon, the Song of songs. —**e=priester**, *m.* (**ein —erpriester, des —enpriesters, die —enpriester, zwei —epriester**) high priest. —**e=priesterlich**, *adj.* pontifical, pertaining to the high priest *or* his office; **die —enpriesterlichen Gewänder**, the pontifical robes.

Hö'he, *f.* (*pl.* —**n**) height, altitude; loftiness; summit, top; high place; elevation, hill, mountain; high rank; depth; dearness (*of price*); intensity, brilliancy; **in die —**, aloft, upward, up; **in die — fahren**, to start up, to jump up *or* to one's feet; **in der —**, aloft, above; **von der —**, from above; **auf der — von Dover**, off Dover; **— des Meeres**, offing; **die — der Sonne nehmen**, to take an observation (of the sun's altitude); **die — von einem Kap nehmen**, to weather a cape; **auf gleicher —**, on a level; **die — gewinnen**, to reach the summit; **in die — richten**, to raise; **alle Artikel gehen in die —**, everything is going up (*in price*); **die — eines in Reih' und Glied aufgestellten Bataillons**, the depth of a battalion; **sie hat** (**beim Singen**) **eine schöne —**, the upper notes of her voice are good; **das ist** (**mir**) **die rechte —**, that's surely the right way of doing things (*iron.*). —**r**, *see* **Hoch**. *Comp.* —**n=kreise**, *pl.* parallels of altitude. —**n=linie**, *f.* contour (line). —**n=messer**, —**n=zirkel**, *m.* altimeter; astrolabe; theodolite. —**n=meßkunst**, *f.* altimetry. —**n=rauch**, *see* **Herauch**. —**n=richtung**, *f.* elevation (*Artil.*); **dem Geschütz die —nrichtung geben**, to elevate a gun. —**n=verhältnis**, *n.* proportion of altitude; interval (*Mus.*). —**n=zug**, *m.* chain *or* ridge of hills. —**punkt**, *m.* culminating point, height, zenith, climax.

Ho'heit, *f.* highness, elevation, loftiness; majesty; supreme power; sovereignty; sublimity; nobleness; high rank; Highness (*title*). —**lich**, *adj.* sovereign; —**liche Rechte**, sovereign rights, regalia. *Comp.* —**blickend**, *adj.* august. —**s=rechte**, *pl.* rights of a sovereign; regalia.

Hohl, I. *adj. & adv.* empty; hollow, dull (*of sound*); concave, hollow; vain, shallow, empty; fistulous (*Med.*); **die —e Hand**, the hollow of the hand; palm; —**e Seite**, weak side. II. *n.* (—**es**, *pl.* —**e**) depth (*of a ship*). *Comp.* —**äugig**, *adj.* hollow-eyed. —**backig**, *adj.* hollow-cheeked, lantern-jawed. —**beil**, *n.*, —**deichsel**, (*m. &*) *f.* grooving adze. —**bohrer**, *m.* wimble. —**docke**, *f.* mandrel. —**driller**, *m.* chamfering-drill. —**eisen**, *n.* gouge. —**erhaben**, *adj.* concavo-convex. —**fenster**, *n.* bow-window. —**fläche**, *f.* concave surface, concavity. —**gang**, *m.* casemate. —**gerinne**, *n.* tree-watercourse. —**geschliffen**, *adj.* concave. —**geschoß**, *n.* shell, hollow. —**geschwür**, *n.* fistula. —**hand**, *f.* hollow of the hand; palm. —**hobel**, *m.* chamfering plane. —**kehle**, *f.* hollow, furrow; groove; gutter. —**kirsche**, *f.* black alder-tree. —**köpfig**, *adj.* empty-headed. —**kreisel**, *m.* humming-top. —**kugel**, *f.* shell (*Artil.*); hollow ball. —**linse**, *f.* concave lens. —**maß**, *n.* dry measure. —**meißel**, *m.* hollow chisel. —**muschel**, *f.* conch. —**raum**, *m.* hollow space, cavity, well; lacuna. —**ring**, *m.* hollow dish-stand. —**rinne**, *f.* chamfer. —**rückig**, *adj.* hollow in the back. —**rund**, *adj.* concave. —**rundung**, —**ründe**, *f.* concavity. —**schiene**, *f.* U-shaped rail. —**sonde**, *f.* hollow probe. —**spiegel**, *m.* concave mirror. —**stab**, *m.* catheter. —**treppe**, *f.* winding stairs. —**wasser**, *n.* a high sea. —**weg**, *m.* defile; excavated passage. —**werk**, *n.* gutter-tile roof. —**zahn**, *m.* hemp-nettle; one of the middle teeth (*Vet.*). —**ziegel**, *m.* gutter tile. —**zirkel**, *m.* spherical compasses.

Höh'l—e, *f.* (*pl.* —**en**) cavity, hollow; hole; cave, cavern; grotto; den; burrow. —**en**, *v.a.* to hollow out, excavate. —**er**, *m.* (—**ers**, *pl.* —**er**) excavator. —**ig**, *adj.* cavernous. —**ung**, *f.* excavation, cavity; hollow; concavity; socket. *Comp.* —**en=artig**, *adj.* cave-like. —**en=bewohner**, *m.* cave-dweller, troglodyte. —**en=tiere**, *pl.* troglodytic animals, fossil animals found in caverns.

Hohn, *m.* (—(**e**)**s**) scorn, disdain, derision; (**einem** *or* **einer S.**) —**sprechen**, to scoff, to insult, to defy, to hold in contumely; bid defiance; **einem zum —e**, in defiance of one, for the purpose of insulting one; **das spricht der Wahrheit —**, that flies in the face of truth. *Comp.* —**epiepeln**, *v.a.*, —**igeln**, *v.a.* to scoff a p., to make sport of a p. (*sl.*). —**gelächter**, *n.* scornful laughter; laughing-stock. —**lächeln**, I. *v.n.* (*aux.* **h.**) (*sep.*) to sneer; **er lächelte —**, he laughed disdainfully (*coll.*). II. *subst. n.* sneer. —**lachen**, I. *v.n.* (*aux.* **h.**) (*insep.*) to scoff, mock, sneer, laugh at. II.

subst. n. —**lache,** *f.* scornful laughter, loud sneer. —**rede,** *f.* scornful language *or* speech.

Höh'n—en, *v. a.* to scoff, jeer, laugh at; to treat with scorn. —**er,** *m.* (—**ers,** *pl.* —**er**) mocker, scorner. —**erei',** *f.* mockery, derision, scorn. —**isch,** *adj.* scornful, sneering.

Hoho', *int.* (*expressing doubt*) hum! ah!

Ho'jah(n)en, Hu'jahnen, *v.n.* (*aux.* **h.**) to bray; to yawn outrageously (*dial.*).

Hök—e, *m.* (—**en,** *pl.* —**en**), —**er,** *m.* (—**ers,** *pl.* —**er**), —**erin,** *f.* huckster, hawker. —**ern,** *v.n.* (*aux.* **h.**) to retail (*small provisions*); to hawk, to huckster. —**erei',** *f.* huckstering, retailing; huckster's shop. *Comp.* —**er=frau,** *f.*, —**er=weib,** *n.* huckstress, market-woman, fruit-woman, basket woman; **schimpfen wie ein —erweib,** to use Billingsgate language. —**er=laden,** *m.* huckster's shop. —**er=mäßig,** *adj.* huckster-like.

Hokuspo'kus, *m.* & *n.* jugglery; thimble-rigging; hocus-pocus; — **machen,** to play off some hocus-pocus, to make mysterious movements whilst saying words the meaning of which the spectator does not know.

Hold, *adj.* & *adv.* favourable; propitious; gracious; kind, friendly; pleasing, charming, lovely; —**er Friede,** gentle peace; **mein —es Mädchen,** my sweet girl; **einem — sein,** to favour one; to love one; **meine —e!** sweetheart! —**chen,** *n.* love, darling, sweetheart. —**e(r),** *m.*, —**e,** *f.* well-wisher, friend; vassal. —**in,** *f.* (*sometimes* **Hul'din**) female friend; darling, sweetheart (*obs.*). *Comp.* —**(an)lächelnd,** *adj.* sweetly smiling. —**selig,** *adj.* most gracious, most lovely, most charming, sweet (*intensified form of* **hold**); **gegrüßet seiest du —selige,** hail thou that art highly favoured (*B.*). —**seligkeit,** *f.* sweetness, gracefulness, loveliness; graciousness.

Hol'der, *see* **Holunder.** —**n,** *adj.* of elder-wood. *Comp.* —**blut,** —**blüte,** *f.* elder-blossom (*dial.*). —**wasen,** *m.* meadow, grass plot with elder trees (*dial.*).

Ho'len, *v.a.* to draw to *or* towards oneself to haul; to (go and) fetch; to take; to fetch (*a price*); to get, to catch; **Atem —,** to draw breath; — **lassen,** to send for; **sich** (*dat.*) **bei einem Rat(s) —,** to consult a person; **sich** (*dat.*) **bei einem Trost —,** to seek comfort from a p.; **sich** (*dat.*) **einen Korb —,** to have one's offer of marriage refused; **sich** (*dat.*) **eine Nase —,** to come in for a rebuke; to get snubbed (*coll.*); **sich** (*dat.*) **ein Fieber —,** to catch a fever; **der Teufel hol' es!** deuce take it! confound it!

Hol'ster, *f.* (*pl.* —**n**) holster.

Holk, Hulk, *m.* (—**es,** *pl.* —**e**) hulk, boat, barge.

Hol'la, *int.* halloo! holla! **und damit —!** and there's an end of it!

Hol'länder, *m.* dairy-farmer; cylindrical paper-mill. —**ei',** *f.* dairy-farm, Dutch farm; cattle run. —**n,** *v.a.* to grind rags into a pulp by means of a 'Holländer;' to skate in the Dutch way. *Comp.* —**kasten,** *m.* vat (of rag-engine).

[1]**Hol'le,** *f.* comb, wattle, crest.

[2]**Hol'le,** *f. see the Index of names.*

Höl'l—e, *f.* (*pl.* —**en**) hell, the infernal regions; chimney-corner; hot place in a furnace; **zur —e gehörig,** infernal; **Himmel und —e aufbieten,** to move heaven and earth; **einem die —e heiß machen,** to terrify one; **in die —e kommen, zur —e fahren,** to go to hell. —**isch,** *adj.* & *adv.* hellish, infernal; terrific, abominable; very strong (*coll.*); dreadfully, awfully (*coll.*); **ein —ischer Kerl,** a devil of a fellow (*coll.*); —**ische Angst,** mortal fear (*coll.*). *Comp.* —**en=angst,** *f.* mortal terror, fright *or* anxiety. —**en=bund,** *m.*, —**en=bündnis,** *n.* infernal alliance. —**en=brand,** *m.* hell-flames; infernal heat; hell-rake, scoundrel. —**en=brodem,** *m.* infernal exhalation. —**en=brut,** *f.* hellish crew. —**en=drache,** *m.* devil; termagant (*vulg.*). —**en=fahrt,** *f.* (*Christ's*) descent into hell. —**en=fluß,** *m.* infernal river. —**en=fürst,** *m.* prince of hell, Satan. —**en=gegend,** *f.* infernal regions. —**en=kunst,** *f.* hellish art. —**en=loch,** *n.* dreadful abyss. —**en=mächte,** *pl.* powers of darkness. —**en=maschine,** *f.* infernal machine. —**en=pein,** *f.* hell-torments; excruciating pain, agony. —**en=richter,** *m.* Minos. —**en=schlund,** *m.* infernal gulf, bottomless pit. —**en=stein,** *m.* caustic stone —**en=wächter,** *m.* Cerberus. —**en=wut,** *f.* fury, devilish rage. —**en=zwang,** *m.* influence of evil spirits over men; means of influencing the powers of darkness; **Fausts —enzwang,** Doctor Faustus' conjuring book.

[1]**Holm,** *m.* (—**es,** *pl.* —**e**) holm, islet; hill, hillock; dockyard.

[2]**Holm,** *m.* (—**es,** *pl.* —**e**) crossbeam, rail.

Hol'per, *m.* (—**s,** *pl.* —, —**n**) small hillock; unevenness (*of a road*); jolt, shock (*in driving*). —**icht,** (*obs.*), —**ig,** *adj.* rugged, rough, uneven, bumpy; clumsy, unpolished; stammering. —**n,** *v.n.* (*aux.* **h.**) to jolt; to stick fast.

Holst, Hulst, *m.* (—**es,** *pl.* —**e**) common holly.

Hol'terpolter, Hol'terdipolter, *adv.* helter-skelter; slap-dash; **das ging —,** it was done in the greatest hurry and with much noise.

Holun'der, (**Hollun'der,**) *m.* (—**s,** *pl.* —) elder; **spanischer —,** lilac. *Comp.* —**beere,** *f.* elderberry. —**blüte,** *f.* elder-flower. —**büchse,** *f.* popgun (*of elderwood*). —**strauch,** *m.* elder bush.

Holz, *n.* (—**es,** *pl.* —**e, Höl'zer**) wood; piece of wood; firewood; timber; grove, copse; wooden stick; idol; gunstock; **wo man — haut, da fallen Späne,** from chipping come chips (*prov.*). —**bar,** *adj.* that may be felled. *Comp.* —**abfall,** *m.* waste wood. —**acker,** *m.* wooded piece of land. —**alkohol,** *m.* wood alcohol. —**apfel,** *m.* crab, wild apple. —**anbau,** *m.* forest-culture. —**arbeiter,** *m.* worker in wood. —**arm,** *adj.* destitute of wood. —**artig,** *adj.* ligniform; ligneous; woody. —**asche,** *f.* wood-ashes. —**aufseher,** *m.* overseer of the wood. —**axt,** *f.* axe for cutting wood. —**bau,** *m.* cultivation of wood; timber-work. —**bauer,** *m.* peasant who carries firewood to market; timber-grower. —**beize,** *f.* wood-stain. —**beizen,** *n.* wood staining. —**bild,** *n.* wooden figure. —**bildner,** *m.* wood-carver *or* engraver. —**binder,** *m.* fagot-maker. —**birne,** *f.* wild pear. —**bock,** *m.* sawing-jack; capricorn-beetle; tick. —**boden,** *m.* wood-loft; soil for growing wood. —**bohrer,** *m.* auger; wood-beetle. —**bohrmuschel,** *f.* shipworm. —**bräme,** *f.* underwood. —**brand=malerei,** *f.* xylography, poker-work. —**bund,** —**bündel,** *n.* faggot. —**druck,** *m.* xylographic impression, block-print (*Typ.*). —**druck(er)kunst,** *f.* block-printing. —**essig,** *m.* pyroxylic acid. —**fäule,** —**fäulnis,** *f.* dry rot. —**farren,** *pl.* tree-ferns. —**faser,** *f.* woody fibre. —**feile,** *f.* rasp. —**feurung,** *f.* fire-wood; combustion of wood. —**flöße,** *f.* a raft for floating wood. —**flößer,** *m.* raftsman. —**frei,** *adj.* having free fuel; —**freies Papier,** paper free from cellulose. —**frevel,** *m.* mischief done to wood; stealing of wood; infringement of forest-law. —**frevler,** *m.* offender against forest-laws. —**fuhre,** *f.* carrying *or* conveying wood; cart-load of wood. —**geist,** *m.* pyroxylic spirit. —**gefälle,** *pl.* proceeds of a wood *or* forest. —**geld,** *n.* wood-money. —**gerecht,** *adj.* versed in forestry. —**gerechtigkeit,** *f.* right over a wood; free supply of wood; firebote (*Law*). —**glitsche,** *f.* timber slide. —**gründung,** *f.* first coating of wood, priming. —**hacker,** *m.* wood-cutter, wood-cleaver; wood(s)man; lumberman (*Amer.*).

—häher, *m.* jay. **—handel**, *m.* timber-trade. **—händler**, *m.* timber-merchant. **—hau**, *m.* place in a forest where trees are felled. **—hauer**, *m.* wood-cutter. **—hof**, *m.* wood-yard, timber-yard; lumber-yard (*Amer.*). **—imprägnierung**, *f.* wood-preserving. **—kammer**, *f.* wood-chamber; wood-house; **ein Engel aus der —kammer**, no beauty. **—kitt**, *m.* glue. **—kohle**, *f.* charcoal. **—komment**, *m.*; **mit einem auf dem —komment stehen**, to be on cudgelling terms with s.o. (instead of giving satisfaction, *student's sl.*). **—lager**, *n.* wood-yard. **—lege**, *f.* wood-loft. **—macher**, *see* **—hauer**. **—malerei**, *f.* panel-painting. **—mosaik**, *f.* wood-inlaying. **—nagel**, *m.* tre(e)nail. **—nager**, *m.* wood-worm. **—obst**, *n.* wild fruits. **—ofen**, *m.* stove for burning wood. **—pantine**, *f.* = **—pantoffel**, *m.* clog. **—pflaster**, *n.* wooden pavement. **—pflock**, *m.* peg. **—raspel**, *f.* rasp. **—raum**, *m.* wood-house. **—rechen**, *m.* wooden grate of a lock to let water through. **—recht**, *n.* firebote (*Law.*). **—reißer**, *m.* tree-marking instrument. **—säger**, *m.* sawyer. **—sauer**, *adj.* pyroligneous. **—säure**, *f.* ligneous acid; vinegar of wood. **—schieber**, *m.* oven-rake. **—schiene**, *f.* tram-rail. **—schlag**, *m.* felling wood; right of felling wood; place where trees are felled. **—schlägel**, *m.* mallet. **—schläger**, *m.* wood-cutter; woodman; lumberman (*Amer.*). **—schneider**, *m.* sawyer; wood-carver *or* engraver. **—schnepfe**, *f.* woodcock. **—schnitt**, *m.* wood-cut, engraving in wood. **—schnitzer**, *m.* carver in wood. **—schober**, *m.* wood-stack. **—schraube**, *f.* wooden screw. **—schuh**, *m.* clog. **—späne**, *pl.* shavings. **—splitter**, *m.* splinter. **—stall**, *m.* wood-house. **—stamm**, *m.* tree-trunk. **—stein**, *m.* lithoxyle. **—stich**, *see* **—schnitt**. **—stoß**, *m.* pile (*of wood*). **—taube**, *f.* wood-pigeon; **die —taube girrt**, the wood pigeon coos, mourns. **—taxe**, *f.* fixed price of wood. **—teer**, *m.* vegetable tar. **—trage**, *f.* hand-barrow. **—trift**, *f.* forest pasture; raft. **—ungs=recht**, *n.* right of cutting wood. **—verband**, *m.* truss-work. **—verbindung**, *f.* joint. **—verwalter**, *m.* wood-factor. **—wagen**, *m.* wood-cart. **—wand**, *f.* wooden wall. **—ware**, *f.* wooden article. **—weg**, *m.* way in a wood that leads only to a place where trees are felled and does not go any further; glade; dilemma; (**sehr** *or* **stark**) **auf dem —wege sein**, to be quite on the wrong track. **—werk**, *n.* woodwork; framework; wainscotting. **—wesen**, *n.* forest-affairs. **—wurm**, *m.* bore-worm. **—zeit**, *f.* time for cutting wood. **—zucht**, *f.* forest-culture. **—zunder**, *m.* touchwood.

Hol'z—en, *v.* I. *n.* (*aux.* **h.**) to cut *or* gather wood. II. *a.* to provide *or* cover with wood; to cudgel (*obs.*); to fight clumsily (*students' sl.*); **den Ofen —en**, to heat the oven. **—erei'**, *f.* (*obs.*) clumsy fight; thrashing. **—icht**, (*obs.*) **—ig**, *adj.* woody; ligneous; well-wooded. **—ung**, *f.* cutting *or* gathering of wood; wood, forest; cudgelling (*S.*).

Höl'zern, *adj.* wooden; awkward.

Hölz'lein, *n.* little stick, castanet; **die — schlagen**, to sound the castanets.

Homilie'enschreiber, *m.* homily writer, homilist.

Homo—ge'n, *adj.* homogeneous. **—genitä't**, *f.* homogeneity. **—lo'g**, *adj.* homologous. **—ny'm**, I. *adj.* homonymous. II. *n.* homonym.

Homöopa'th, *m.* (—en, *pl.* —en) homœopathist; homœopathic doctor. **—ie'**, *f.* homœopathy. **—isch**, *adj.* homœopathic.

Hone'tt, *adj.* & *adv.* honest; genteel; respectable.

Ho'nicht, *adj.* like honey; honeyed (*rare* & *obs.*).

Ho'nig, *m.* (—s) honey; **geseimter —**, liquid honey; **Scheiben —**, honey in combs; **einem — ums Maul schmieren**, to wheedle round a p.; **— im Munde, Galle im Herzen**, soft of speech, hard of heart (*prov.*). *Comp.* **—bau**, *m.* culture of honey. **—bär**, *m.* common bear. **—behälter**, *m.*, **—behältnis**, *n.* nectary. **—bereitung**, *f.* mellification. **—blume**, *f.* honey-flower; balm. **—erzeugend**, *adj.* honey-producing. **—essig**, *m.* oxymel. **—fladen**, *m.* honey-cake. **—gefäß**, *n.* honey-jar; nectary. **—kelch**, *m.* nectary. **—klee**, *m.* white trefoil. **—kuchen**, *m.* gingerbread. **—magen**, *m.* honey-bag (*of bees*). **—monat**, **—mond**, *m.* honeymoon. **—organ**, *n.* nectary. **—rede**, *f.* honied language. **—säure**, *f.* oxymel. **—saft**, *m.*, nectar. **—scheibe**, *f.* honeycomb. **—seim**, *m.* virgin honey. **—stein=säure**, *f.* mellitic acid. **—stimme**, *f.* honied voice. **—trank**, *m.* mead. **—wabe**, *f.* honeycomb. **—wasser**, *n.* hydromel. **—wicke**, *f.* meadow-vetch. **—zelle**, *f.* honey-cell; alveolus.

Honneu'r, *n.* (—s, *pl.* —s) honour; **die —s machen**, to salute (*Mil.*); to do the honours.

Honor—a'r, *n.* (—a'rs, *pl.* —a're) fee; **—ar für Vorlesungen**, lecture fee; **—ar für ärztlichen Rat**, fee for professional medical attendance; **—ar für ein Buch**, publisher's compliment, fee for the copyright. **—a'nt**, *m.* (—an'ten, *pl.* —an'ten) acceptor of a bill. **—atio'ren**, *pl.* people of rank. **—ie'ren**, *v.a. see* **Ehren**; to honour (*a bill*); to pay a fee; to clear, sail round (*a rock, etc.*). **—ie'rung**, *f.* fee; payment of an honorarium; acceptance (*of a bill*). **—ig**, *adj.* of honour, honourable.

Hoofd, *n.* (—es, *pl.* —e) pier; headland, foreland.

Hop, *see* **Hopp**.

Hop'fen, I. *m.* (—s, *pl.* —) hop; hops; **an ihm ist — und Malz verloren**, he is past amending, trouble is thrown away on him. II. *v.a.* to mix with, impregnate with hops. *Comp.* **—bau**, *m.* culture of hops. **—bauer**, *m.* hop-grower. **—keim**, hop-sprig *or* bud. **—klee**, *m.* yellow clover. **—schimmel**, *m.* hop-blight. **—stange**, *f.* hop-pole; lanky person, May pole, long Meg. **—stengel**, *m.* hop-bind, hop-vine. **—stichel**, *m.* dibble. **—zapfen**, *pl.* hop-cones *or* flower-buds. **—zupfer**, *m.* hop-picker.

Höpf'ner, *m.* (—s, *pl.* —) hop-grower.

Hopp, *int.* hop! **—lala!** away! now be off! there he (it) goes!

Hop'pelpoppel, *n.* (—s, *pl.* —) beaten-up egg with rum.

Hop—s, I. *m.* (—(s)es, *pl.* —(s)e) hop, skip, jump. II. *int. see* **Hopp**. **—sen**, *v.n.* (*aux.* **h.**) to hop, jump; to dance (*coll.*). **—ser**, *m.* hop, hop-waltz. *Comp.* **—la**, **—sa**, *int.* hey-day! hallo! (*if something is dropped, if a person jumps*). **—s=tanz**, *see* **—ser**.

Ho'ra, *f.* (*pl.* —s) hour; horary prayer.

Hör'bar, *adj.* & *adv.* audible; **nicht —**, inaudible.

Horch, *imperat. of* **—en**, *used as int.* hark! **—e**, *f.*; **sich auf die —e stellen**, to set o.s. to listen (*rare*).

Hor'ch—en, *v. n.* (*aux.* **h**). (*with dat. or* **auf** & *acc.*) to hearken, listen, give ear to; to obey to be an eavesdropper. **—er**, *m.* (—ers, *pl.* —er) listener; eavesdropper; **—er an der Wand hört seine eigne Schand'**, listen at a hole, and you 'll hear news of yourself; he that looks through a keyhole may see what will vex him (*prov.*). **—sam**, *adj.* & *adv.* attentive, heedful. *Comp.* **—gang**, *m.* mine for listening, casemate (*Fort.*). **—rohr**, *n.* ear-trumpet; stethoscope. **—winkel**, *m.* secret corner where one can overhear a conversation.

Hor'de, *f.* (*pl.* —n) horde, troop; nomadic tribe; gang. *Comp.* **—en=weise**, *adv.* in hordes.

Hö'r—en, *v.a.* & *n.* (*aux.* **h.**) to hear; to hearken, listen; **ich —te bei ihm, „Faust,"** I attended his lectures on "Faust." **—en auf einen** *or* eine S. to give heed to, to obey; to learn; schwer —en, to be hard of hearing; fein —en, to have a good ear *or* hearing; einen kommen —en, to hear one coming; ich habe sagen —en, I have been told, I have heard it said; auf diesem Ohre —e ich nicht, I am deaf of this ear; an einer S. —en, to recognize by *or* in; ein Kolleg —en, to attend lectures *or* a course of lectures; —en Sie mal, I say! (*coll.*); na, —en Sie, well, I confess! (*coll.*); er will nicht —en, he will not listen; gehört werden, to be sounded (*of a letter, etc.*); er hört sich gern, he likes to hear himself talk; sich —en lassen, to let oneself be heard, to sing, speak, *etc.*, before company; das läßt sich —en, that sounds all right, there's something in that, that is worth considering; der Hund —t auf den Namen . . ., the dog answers to the name of . . .; von sich —en lassen, to write; laß dann und wann von dir —en, let us hear from you now and then; wer nicht — will muß fühlen, he that won't listen must feel (*prov.*). —er, *m.* (—ers, *pl.* —er) hearer, auditor, University student attending lectures. —erschaft, *f.* hearers, students, audience (*coll.*). —ig, *adj.* belonging to; (*in comp.*) = -hearing; -eared. —ige(n), *pl.* bondsmen. *Comp.* —en=sagen, *n.* hearsay, rumour. —mittel, *n.* medium *or* means of hearing. —nerv, *m.* auditory nerve. —rohr, *n.*, —trichter, *m.* ear-trumpet; stethoscope. —saal, *m.* auditory, lecture-room. —weite, *f.* reach of hearing; in —weite, within earshot, within hearing. —werkzeug, *n.* acoustic instrument. —zeuge, *m.* ear-witness.

Ho'rizont, *m.* (—(e)s, *pl.* —e) horizon; der scheinbare *or* terrestrische —, the sensible horizon; das geht über meinen —, that's beyond me. —a'l, *adj.* & *adv.* horizontal. —a'le, *f.* horizontal line, level. *Comp.* —al'=schuß, *m.* point-blank shot.

Horn, *n.* (—es, *pl.* Hör'ner) horn; bugle, horn; feeler (*of insects*); top, projecting peak; hard *or* horny skin; hoof (*of horses*); beak (*of birds*); cape, headland, point; crescent-shaped bay; das — wird geblasen, *or* erschallt, the horn is sounded; Hörner schmetterten, bugles were sounded; — des Überflusses, cornucopia; einem die Hörner bieten, to oppose, offer resistance to a person; sich (*dat.*) die Hörner ablaufen, to sow one's wild oats; etwas auf seine eignen Hörner nehmen, to take upon oneself the responsibility of a thing; Hörner tragen, to be a cuckold; mit einem in ein — blasen, to agree with one in opinion, to conspire with one; Klappen —, cornet-à-piston; Wald —, French horn; Jagd —, bugle horn. —icht (*obs.*), —ig, *adj.* & *adv.* horny; callous. —i'st, *m.* (—is'ten, *pl.* —is'ten) bugler, bugleman, performer on the horn. —ung, *m.* February (*obs.*). *Comp.* —amboß, *m.* bickern, bick-iron. —arbeit, *f.* work in horn. —artig, *adj.* horny, like horn. —auswuchs, *m.* horny excrescence. —baß, *m.* horn-stop (*in organs*). —baum, *m.* hornbeam. —becher, *m.* drinking horn. —beule, *f.* corn (*Vet.*). —bläser, *m.* horn-blower, bugle-player. —bock, *m.* horned ram. —drechsler, —dreher, *m.* turner in horn. —eule, *f.* horned owl. —feile, *f.* hoof-file. —förmig, *adj.* corniform. —füßig, *adj.* hoofed. —haut, *f.* horny skin; horny coat (of the eye), cornea (*Anat.*). —häutigkeit, *f.* callosity. —haut=schnitt, *m.* couching a cataract. —hecht, *m.* garfish (*Icht.*). —kirsche, *f.* cornelian cherry. —klüftig, *adj.* cloven-hoofed. —knopf, *m.* horn-button. —ochs, *m.* blockhead, duffer. —quecksilber, *n.* protochloride of mercury. —rose, *f.* wild rose. —schröter, *m.* horn-beetle. —signal, *n.* bugle-call. —silber, *n.* chloride of silver. —spaltig, *adj.* hoof-cleft. —spitze, *f.* mouthpiece of a horn. —strauch, *m.* cornel-tree; dogwood. —ungs=blume, *f.* daffodil. —vieh, *n.* horned cattle; duffer (*vulg.*). —wände, *pl.* hoof-quarters (*Vet.*).

Hor'ni—s, *f.* (*pl.* —(ss)e), —sse, *f.* (*pl.* —ssen) hornet.

Hörn—chen, *n.* cornicle, little horn; French roll; er bläst mit ihm in ein —chen, they are in the same boat (*coll.*). —en, I. *v.a.* to furnish horns; to change into horn; to cuckold; der gehörnte Siegfried, horny Siegfried, Siegfried whose skin was as hard as horn. II. *v.n.* (*aux.* h.) to butt; to blow the horn. III. —er, *see* Horn. —ern, *adj.* horny, of horn. —ig, *adj.* (*in comp.* =) -horned. *Comp.* —er=baum, *m.* dogwood; cornelian cherry-tree. —er=schall, *m.* bugle-sound, sound of horns. —er=schluß, *m.* dilemma. —er=sporn, *m.* knob for cows' horns. —er=träger, *m.* cuckold. —er=tragend, *adj.* horned.

Horo—graphie', *f.* dialling. —sko'p, *n.* (—skops, *pl.* —skope) horoscope; einem das —skop stellen, to draw up some one's horoscope, to cast a p.'s nativity.

Horst, *m.* (—es, *pl.* —e) eyrie; tuft (*of trees, grass, or corn*); shrubbery; thicket; top of a rock; sand-bank. —en, *v.n.* (*aux.* h.) to build an eyrie, to nest; to roost; to perch.

Hort, *m.* (—es, *pl.* —e) hoard, treasure; safe retreat; refuge, shield (*B.*).; protection, talisman, protector; mein höchster —, my highest protector; my highest treasure, my love.

Horten'si—a, *f.* (*pl.* —en) hydrangea (*Bot.*).

Hös'chen, *n.* (—s, *pl.* —) small-clothes; pollen (*on the legs of bees*).

Ho'se—e, *f.* (*pl.* —en) (pair of) trousers (*mostly* —en, *pl.*); thigh (*of horses and poultry*); hollow cylinder, spout; tub, pail; firkin; Knie—en, breeches (for riding): knickerbockers; kurze —en, knickerbockers; lederne —en, leather breeches; —en bekommen, to go into knicker(boeker)s; sich auf die —e setzen, to work hard (*sl.*); einem die —en stramm ziehen, to give a boy a sound beating (*coll.*); das Herz fiel ihm in die —en, he lost courage (*coll.*); sie hat die —en an, the wife wears the breeches, is master of the house. *Comp.* —en=band, *n.* trousers-belt *or* string, knee-band, garter. —en=band=orden, *m.* order of the Garter. —en=gurt, —en=gürtel, *m.* waist-band. —en=klappe, *f.*, —en=latz, *m.* breeches-flap. —en=los, *adj.* unbreeched. —en=lose(r), *m.* sansculotte. —en=naht, *f.*; Hand an der —ennaht, middle finger touching the seam of the trousers (*Mil.*). —en=schlitz, *m.* trousers-opening, cod-piece. —en=schützer, *m.* knee-cap, spatter-dashes. —en=strecker, *m.* stretcher (for trousers). —en=träger, *m.* braces. —en=zeug, *n.* trousering (material).

Hosp—ita'l, *n.* (—itals, *pl.* —itäler) hospital. —ita'liter, (—ita'l=ritter,) *m.* knight-hospitaller. —itali't, *m.* (—italiten, *pl.* —italiten) inmate of a hospital. —italitä't, *f.* hospitality. —ita'nt, *m.* (—itan'ten, *pl.* —itan'ten) occasional *or* temporary auditor at school lessons *or* university lectures. —itie'ren, *v.n.* (*aux.* h.) to be present at lessons, to do school visiting, to be an occasional visitor at lessons *or* lectures for the sake of study and criticism. —i'z, *n.* (—izes, *pl.* —ize) hospice.

Ho'stie, *f.* (*pl.* —n) the consecrated wafer, the host. *Comp.* —n=gefäß, *n.* pyx. —n=häus=lein, *n.* tabernacle. —n=teller, *m.* paten.

Hote'l, *n.* (—s, *pl.* —s) hotel. *Comp.* —wagen, *m.* carriage belonging to a hotel, hotel omnibus. —waggon, *m.* hotel car (*Americ.*); dining car; Pullman car (*Railw.*).

Hott! *int.* ho! gee ho! (= to the right!). **—en,** *v.n.* (*aux.* h.) to drive (*coll.*). *Comp.* **—o=gaul,** *m.* child's rocking-horse.

Hot'te, *f.* (*pl.* —n) vintager's dosser, fruit-measure.

Hottehü'h! I. *int.* ho! gee ho! hoy! (*a term used by drivers*). II. *subst.* gee-gee (*children's word for horse*).

Hot'zel, —n, *see* Hutzel, *ꝛc.*

Hu! *int.* (*expressing horror*) ugh! hugh!

Hub, Hü'be, *obs. for* Hob, Hö'be.

Hub, *m.* (—es, *pl.* Hü'be) lifting, raising, heaving; lift; impetus; stroke, travel (*of a piston, etc.*); what is raised by a piston-stroke; selection, picking out; thing *or* person picked out, the best of a thing. *Comp.* **—höhe,** *f.* height to which anything is to be raised. **—länge,** *f.* length of stroke. **—wechsel,** *m.* change of stroke. **—zähler,** *m.* indicator (*of an engine*).

Hu'be, *f.* (*pl.* —n) hide (*of land*) (*obs.*).

Hü'bel, *m.* (—s, *pl.* —) hillock; tubercle, pimple. **—icht,** *adj.* knob-like; tuberculous.

Hü'ben, *adv.* on this side; — **und drüben,** on this side and on the other side, on either side.

Hübsch, *adj. & adv.* handsome, pretty; fine; nice; good, proper; fair; **eine —e runde Summe,** a good round sum; **ein —es Vermögen,** a considerable *or* large fortune; **einem — thun,** to flatter one; **sei — artig!** be nice and good; **das will ich — bleiben lassen,** I will take good care not to do that; **es ist nicht —,** it is not fair, not nice. **—heit,** *f.* prettiness, beauty; fairness.

Huch, *m.,* **—e,** *f.* huck, salmon, river-trout.

Hu'cke, *f.* (*pl.* —n) back; stack of hay. **—n,** *see* Hocken. *Comp.* **—pack,** *adv.* pick-a-back.

Hu'del, *m.* (—s, *pl.* —) rag, tatter; trash; ragamuffin; tramp (*obs.*). **—ei',** *f.* badly-done work; bungling; vexation; bad treatment. **—icht,** (*obs.*) **—ig,** *adj. & adv.* ragged; paltry; badly *or* carelessly done, bungling; huddled together.

Hu'del—n, *v.* I. *a.* to do negligently, to bungle; to huddle up; to vex, tease; to worry; to juggle. II. *n.* (*aux.* h.) to lead an idle life. **—er,** *m.* (—ers, *pl.* —er) bungler, teaser, vexer; juggler.

Huf, *m.* (—es, *pl.* —e) hoof. **—er,** *m.* (—ers, *pl.* —er) hoofed animal. **—ig,** *adj. & adv.* (*suffix in comp.* =) -hoofed. *Comp.* **—bein,** *n.* coffin-bone (*Vet.*). **—beschlag,** *m.* horse-shoeing; horse-shoes. **—eisen,** *n.* horse-shoe. **—eisen=dorn,** *m.* punch. **—eisen=förmig,** *adj.* horse-shoe (shaped). **—eisen=sack,** *m.* shoeing-apron, farrier's pouch. **—eisen=tisch,** *m.* table shaped like a horseshoe. **—haar,** *n.* fetlock. **—hammer,** *m.* shoeing hammer. **—kratze,** *f.* hoof-picker. **—kraut,** *n.* rose of Jericho. **—lattich,** *m.* colt's foot (*Bot.*). **—nagel,** *m.* hob-nail. **—schlag,** *m.* horse-shoeing; kick from a (horse's) hoof, horse's kick; hoof mark; tramp of a horse's feet. **—schmied,** *m.* farrier. **—schmiede=handwerk,** *n.* farriery. **—tiere,** *pl.* Ungulata (*Zoöl.*). **—zeug,** *n.* shoeing tools. **—zwängig,** *adj.* hoof-bound, narrow-heeled.

Hu'fe, *f.* (*pl.* —n) hide (of land), *see* Hube. *Comp.* **—n=geld,** *n.* land-tax. **—n=hafer,** *m.* avenage. **—n=meister,** *m.* collector of land-rents. **—n=richter,** *m.* country magistrate, county-court judge. **—n=schlag,** *m.* field divided into hides.

Hüf'ner, *m.* (—s, *pl.* —) owner of a hide of land.

Hüf't—e, *f.* (*pl.* —en) hip, haunch; quarter (*of a ship*). **—ig,** *adj.* haunched. *Comp.* **—ader,** *f.* sciatic vein. **—bein, —blatt,** *n.* hip-bone. **—bruch,** *m.* fracture of the hip. **—en=lahm,** *adj.* hip-shot. **—gelenk,** *n.* hip-joint. **—pfanne,** *f.* socket of the hip-bone. **—schmerz,** *m.* sciatica. **—stück,** *n.* haunch (*of meat*). **—verrenkung,** *f.* dislocation of the hip. **—weh,** *n.* sciatic gout, sciatic pains, sciatica.

Hü'gel, *m.* (—s, *pl.* —) hillock, knoll, hill; projection; knob; **sie führten ihn auf einen — des Berges,** they led him unto the brow of the hill (*B.*). **—icht,** *adj.* hill-like (*obs.*). **—ig,** *adj.* hilly; hill-like. *Comp.* **—a'b,** *adv.* down hill. **—ameise,** *f.* red ant. **—a'n, —au'f,** *adv.* up hill. **—kette,** *f.* chain of hills.

Hü'geln, *v.* I. *a.* to form into hills, to heap up, raise. II. *r.* to rise like a hill.

Huhn, *n.* (—es, *pl.* Hüh'ner) (*dim.* Hühn'chen, *n.*) hen; partridge, bird; chap, fellow (*coll.*); **das — gluckt, gackert,** the hen clucks, cackles; **ein junges —,** chicken, pullet; **kalekutisches, türkisches —,** turkey; **ich habe ein Hühnchen mit dir zu pflücken** *or* **zu rupfen,** I have a bone to pick with you, I have a crow to pluck with you; **er ist ein verrücktes —,** he is a mad chap (*sl.*); **ein unsolides —,** a loose fish; a man too fond of drinking; **zwei Völker Hühner,** two covies of partridges.

Hüh'ner, *see* Huhn (*in comp. gen'lly* = chicken, hen); **vor die — gehen,** to go to the dogs (*sl.*). *Comp.* **—aar,** *m.* kite; griffon-vulture. **—artig,** *adj.* gallinaceous. **—auge,** *n.* corn (*on the foot*). **—blindheit,** *f.* night-blindness. **—braten,** *m.* roast fowl, roast chicken. **—brühe,** *f.* chicken broth. **—darre,** *f.* roup. **—dieb,** *m.* poultry-stealer; kite. **—ei,** *n.* hen's egg. **—falke,** *m.* goshawk; falcon. **—garn,** *n.* partridge-net. **—geier, —habicht,** *m.* goshawk. **—händler,** *m.* poulterer. **—haus,** *n.* hen-house, fowl-house. **—hof,** *m.* poultry-yard. **—hund,** *m.* pointer; setter. **—jagd,** *f.* partridge-shooting. **—korb,** *m.* hen-coop. **—korn,** *n.* Indian corn. **—leiter, —stiege,** *f.* hen-roost; very steep and narrow staircase, break-neck stairs (*coll.*). **—markt,** *m.* poultry market. **—pastete,** *f.* chicken-pie. **—ruf,** *m.* bird-call. **—schrot,** *n.* partridge shot. **—schwanz,** *m.* fan-tailed pigeon. **—seuche,** *f.* pip. **—stall,** *m.* fowl-house, chicken's place. **—stange,** *f.* hen-roost, perch for fowls. **—vieh,** *n.* poultry. **—vögel,** *pl.* gallinaceous birds. **—weihe,** *f.* kite. **—zucht,** *f.* poultry rearing, keeping of poultry.

Hu'i! I. *int.* (*expressing pleasure; disgust; rapid motion, etc.*) quick! on! ha! pshaw! II. *m.*; **in einem —,** in a twinkling, in a trice.

Huld, *f.* grace, favour, affection, kindness; graciousness; clemency. *Comp.* **—göttin,** *f.*; **die drei —göttinnen,** the three Graces. **—reich, —voll,** *adj. & adv.* gracious, benevolent, favourable. **—reiz,** *m.* irresistible charm.

Hul'de, (**Hul'da,**) *f.* goodly spirit; uncanny female mountain sprite (*euphem. appellation*).

Hul'dig—en, *v.n.* (*aux.* h.) (**einem**) to do homage, to swear allegiance; to pay homage, *or* one's respects, to; to embrace, subscribe to (*an opinion, etc.*); **gehuldigte Herrschaft,** feudal lord; **dem Fortschritte —en,** to be a friend of progress; **sich** (*dat.*) **von einem —en lassen,** to receive the oath of allegiance *or* homage from a p.; **einer Dame —en,** to pay one's attentions, *or* (marked) respects, to a lady. **—ung,** *f.* homage, oath of allegiance; admiration, respect, attention; favour; **—ung leisten,** to do homage; **Reise zur —ung,** journey to receive *or* do homage. *Comp.* **—ungs=eid,** *m.* oath of allegiance *or* fealty. **—ungs=pflichtig,** *adj.* subject to homage.

Hul'din, *f. see* **Huldgöttin** *and* **Hold.**

Hül'fe, *imperf. subj. of* **helfen.**

Hül'f—e, *f.* (*pl.* —en), **Hil'f—e,** help, aid, succour; relief; redress; remedy; **—e leisten,** to aid; **zur —e dienend,** auxiliary; **wo keine —e mehr ist,** past remedy; **mit —e der Nacht,** under cover of night *or* darkness; **einen um —e bitten,** to ask a p. for help, to call in a p.'s assistance; **etwas zu —e nehmen,** to make use of a th.; **—e finden in einer S.,** to be helped by a th.; **einem zu —e kommen,** to come to one's aid; **er kam mir schnell zu —e,** he rushed to my assistance. **—lich,** *adj. & adv.* helpful; helping, auxiliary, adjutory. *Comp.* **—begierig,** *adj.* eager to help. **—(e)=ruf,** *m.* cry for help. **—e=leister,** *m.* one who brings help *or* relief. **—e=leistung,** *f.* aid, help, relief. **—los,** *adj. & adv.* helpless, destitute. **—losigkeit,** *f.* helplessness. **—reich,** *adj.* helpful, benevolent. **—s=armee,** *f.* auxiliary army. **—s=bedürftig,** *adj.* requiring help; needy, indigent. **—s=begriff,** *m.* supplementary concept. **—s=bischof,** *m.* suffragan, bishop. **—s=buch,** *n.* elementary text-book, manual; book of reference. **—s=frist,** *f.* days of grace. **—s=geld,** *n.* subsidy, pecuniary aid; **—sgelder zahlen,** to subsidize. **—s=genoß,** *m.* ally, confederate. **—s=grund,** *m.* subsidiary reason. **—s=heer,** *n.* auxiliary troops *or* forces; relief column *or* forces. **—s=kasse,** *f.* relief fund, provident *or* charitable fund. **—s=kirche,** *f.* chapel of ease. **—s=lehrer,** *m.* young assistant master before he is definitely appointed (*after which time he is no longer called* **Hülfslehrer** *but* **ordentlicher Lehrer**); substitute teacher, stop-gap. **—s=leistung,** *f.* aid, assistance. **—s=linie,** *f.* auxiliary *or* artificial line (*Math.*). **—s=macht,** *f.* auxiliary power. **—s=maschine,** *f.* pilot-engine. **—s=mittel,** *n.* remedy; expedient, auxiliary means; **letztes —smittel,** last resort. **—s=prediger,** *m.* curate. **—s=priester,** *m.* assistant priest. **—s=quelle,** *f.* resource, expedient. **—s=recht,** *n.* right of execution (*Law*). **—s=satz,** *m.* lemma (*Math.*). **—s=steuer,** *f.* subsidy, subsidizing rate. **—s=truppen,** *pl.* auxiliaries. **—s=verein,** *m.* relief society, benevolent *or* charitable society. **—s=vertrag,** *m.* subsidiary treaty. **—s=wissenschaft,** *f.* auxiliary science. **—s=wort,** *n.* auxiliary word, expletive. **—s=wörterbuch,** *n.* dictionary to a particular work, vocabulary *or* glossary (*appended to a work*). **—s=wurz,** *f.* hollyhock. **—s=zeitwort,** *n.* auxiliary verb. **—s=zwang,** *m.*, **—s=vollstreckung,** *f.* execution of a judicial sentence.

Hüll'bar, *adj. & adv.* that may be covered.

Hül'l—e, *f.* (*pl.* **—en**) cover, covering, envelope; wrapping; integument; raiment, garments; pod, husk, sheath; veil; cloak; mask; hood *or* cap; second stomach of ruminants; **die irdische —e,** the mortal frame, the body; **—e der Nacht,** shades *or* cover of night; **die —e und die Fülle,** clothing and food, all that is wanted; abundance; **in —e und Fülle,** in plenty; **die Übersendung und —e einer Ware,** the transport and packing of an article; **die —e fiel mir schmerzlich von den Augen,** I was cruelly disabused. *Comp.* **—blatt,** *n.* involucral leaf. **—en=los,** *adj. & adv.* unveiled, uncovered, naked, open; clear.

Hül'len, *v.a.* to wrap up, muffle, cover, envelope; to hide; **in Dunkel —,** to veil in obscurity, to make obscure; **die Sonne war in dichte Nebel gehüllt,** the sun was veiled by thick clouds *or* hidden in mist; **sich in Schweigen —,** to be wrapped up in silence.

Hül's—e, *f.* (*pl.* **—en**) hull, shell, husk. **—icht,** *adj. & adv.* (*obs.*) leguminous; pod-like. **—ig,** *adj. & adv.* husked, shelly, leguminous. *Comp.* **—en=artig,** *adj.* leguminous. **—en=baum,** *m.* locust-tree. **—en=frucht,** *f.* pod, legume. **—en=früchte,** *pl.* podded grains, podders, pulse, legumes, leguminous plants. **—en=frucht=händler,** *m.* greengrocer. **—en=wurm,** *m.* case-worm.

Hül'sen, *v.* I. *a.* to hull, shell, husk. II. *r.* to come off, shell; to pod.

Hulst, *m.* (**—es,** *pl.* **—e**) common holly (*tree*).

Huma'n, *adj. & adv.* humane; affable. **—io'ra,** (**—itä'ts=studien**), *pl.* humanities (*usually classics and poetry*). **—i'st,** *m.* (**—is'ten,** *pl.* **—is'ten**) humanist, classical student and scholar at the time of the Renaissance. **—is'mus,** *m.* humanism, revival of learning; classical education. **—isie'ren,** *v.a.* to humanize. **—itä't,** *f.* humanity.

Hum'bug, *m.* (**—s**) humbug, swindle; **der reine —,** a regular humbug, a downright swindle.

Humera'le, *n.* (**—s,** *pl.* **—s**) shoulder cape, humeral, amice (*of priests*).

Humin'säure, *f.* ulmic acid, humic acid.

Hum'm—el, *f.* (*pl.* **—n**) humble bee; drone; bag-pipe; romp, hoyden. **—elchen,** *n.* (**—elchens,** *pl.* **—elchen**) Italian bagpipe; thorough-bass drone (*organs*). **—en,** *v.a. & n.* (*aux.* **h.**) to hum, to buzz, to drone. *Comp.* **—el=baß,** *m.* thorough-bass (*Mus.*). **—el=fänger,** *m.* drone-catcher (*at beehive entrance-holes*).

Hum'mer, *m.* (**—s,** *pl.* **—**) lobster. *Comp.* **—fang,** *m.* lobstering. **—schere,** *f.* claw of a lobster.

Humo'r, *m.* (**—s**) humour; frame of mind, mood; humorous vein; **feiner —, versteckter —,** sly humour; **derber —,** broad humour; **heiterer —,** sportive humour; **ausgelassener —,** wanton *or* fantastic humour. **—es'ke,** *f.* (*pl.* **—es'ken**) humorous sketch, funny story, squib (*coll.*). **—i'st,** *m.* (**—is'ten,** *pl.* **—is'ten**) humorist, humorous person *or* writer. **—is'tika,** *pl.* facetious *or* humorous writings. **—is'tisch,** *adj. & adv.* humorous, facetious.

Hum'pen, *m.* (**—s,** *pl.* **—**) bumper, tumbler, tankard, bowl.

Hum'p—eln, *v.* I. *a.* to do awkwardly, bungle (*rare*). II. *n.* (*aux.* **h.**) to hobble, limp along. **—ler,** *m.* (**—lers,** *pl.* **—ler**) hobbler, bungler.

Hu'mus, *m.* mould, vegetable earth, ulmous substance, humus. *Comp.* **—boden,** *m.* vegetable soil. **—sauer,** *adj.* humic, ulmic.

Hund, *m.* (**—(e)s,** *pl.* **—e**) dog; hound; dog-star; stove in front of another, Prussian stove; **der — bellt, heult, winselt,** the dog barks, howls, whines; **auf dem —e,** miserable, ruined, reduced in circumstances, down (*vulg.*); **auf den — kommen,** to be reduced to misery, to go to the dogs; **das ist unterm —,** that is very bad, quite worthless (*coll.*); **damit lockt man keinen — vom Ofen,** that is of no use, that will answer no purpose; **da liegt der — begraben,** there's the rub! that's the sore point! (*coll.*); **vor die —e gehen,** to go to the dogs; **wie ein begossener —** (*or* **Pudel**), with his tail between his legs, crestfallen; **blöder — wird selten fett,** faint heart ne'er won fair lady (*prov.*); **bellende —e beißen nicht,** great barkers are never great biters (*prov.*); **viele —e sind des Hasen Tod,** there is no fighting against fearful odds (*prov.*); **der Knüppel liegt beim —e,** we must get along as best we may; **kein — nimmt ein Stück Brot von ihm,** no one will have anything to do with him; **kommt man über den —, so kommt man auch über den Schwanz,** after the main part is done the rest will cause no trouble (*prov.*); **ein — Landes,** the sixth part of an acre. **—e,** (*in* (*comp. often* =) low, miserable, wretched, contemptible (*vulg.*). *Comp.* **—e=arbeit,** *f.* very hard work (*vulg.*). **—e=artig,** *adj.* canine. **—e=bellen,** *n.* barking of dogs. **—e=blume,** *f.* dandelion. **—e=elend,** *adj.* very miserable, wretched. **—e=ende,** *n.* cable-eye, rope-maker's end. **—e=fleisch,** *n.* dog's meat. **—e=fressen,** *n.* dog's food; bad food. **—e=futter,** *n.* food for dogs; dog biscuits; miserable fare. **—e=geifer,** *m.* slaver of a dog. **—e=halsband,** *n.* dog-collar. **—e=hütte,** *f.* dog-kennel. **—e=junge,** *m.* boy who has the care of dogs; young rascal, blackguard (*vulg.*). **—e=kälte,** *f.*; **eine wahre —kälte,** a very severe cold. **—e=kerl,** *m.* scamp, scoundrel. **—e=koppel,** *f.* leash (for a hound); leash or pack (of hounds). —e=krankheit, *f.* distemper. —e=läufer, *m.* truck-boy. —e=leben, *n.* wretched life. —e=loch, *n.* wretched hole; dog-kennel. —e=müde, *adj.* dead tired. —e=scheu, *adj.* afraid of dogs. —e=seuche, *f.* distemper. —e=trab, *m.* jog-trot. —e=wache, *f.* second watch (*Naut.*). —e=wärter, *m.* kennel-man. —e=wetter, *n.* wretched weather, beastly weather (*coll.*), not fit to turn a dog out. —e=zucht, *f.* breeding, training of dogs. —e=züchter, *m.* breeder of dogs, dog fancier. —s=affe, *f.* baboon. —s=auge, *n.* dog's eye; species of plantain; impudent or envious person. —s=blume, *f.* dandelion. —s=dorn, *m.* hawthorn. —s=fott, *m.* cowardly rascal (*vulg.*); ein —s=fott giebt mehr *or* besser als er kann, you cannot expect a man to give more than he has (*prov.*). —s=fötterei', *f.* scoundrelism (*vulg.*). —s=gerecht, *adj.* understanding dogs. —s=hai, *m.* spotted dog-fish. —s=kirsche, *f.* white bryony. —s=kopf, *m.* dog's head; dog-fish; wild flax. —s=krampf, *m.* cynic spasm. —s=ledern, *adj.* of dogskin. —s=loden, *pl.* dog's hair; abuse. —s=recht, *n.* dog's share of spoil. —s=stern, *m.* Sirius. —s=tage, *pl.* dog-days, canicular days. —s=tags=ferien, *pl.* long vacation, (long) summer holidays. —s=tod, *m.* dog's bane. —s=wurzel, *f.* yam. —s=wut, *f.* canine madness, rabies, hydrophobia. —s=zähne, *pl.* canine teeth.

Hün'd—eln, *v.n.* (*aux.* h.) to pup, whelp; to act in a sneaking *or* fawning manner. —in, *f.* she-dog, bitch. —isch, *adj.* doggish, canine; fawning; cynical; impudent, shameless.

Hun'dert, I. *num. adj.* hundred; (*in comp.* =) having *or* with a hundred. II. *subst. n.* (—s, *pl.* —e) hundred; cent; zu —en, by hundreds; —e von Pferden, hundreds of horses; zehn vom — *or* zehn Prozent, ten per cent; — vom —, cent per cent; groß *or* das große —, the long hundred, sixscore, hundred and twenty; alle — Jahre wiederkehrend, centenary, secular; — Jahre alt, centenarian; — gegen eins zu wetten, to bet *or* lay a hundred to one. —er, *m.* (—ers, *pl.* —er) hundred; figure indicating the hundreds. —st, *adj.* hundredth; das —ste ins Tausendste werfen, to talk nonsense, muddle up things; vom —sten ins Tausendste kommen, to talk on and on, to discuss no end of subjects; das weiß der —ste nicht, not one in a hundred knows that. —stel, *n.* hundredth part. —stens, *adv.* in the hundredth place. *Comp.* —er=lei, *indec. adj. & adv.* of a hundred different kinds; of all kinds (*coll.*). —fach, —fältig, *adj.* hundredfold, centuple. —fuß, —füßler, *m.* centipede. —gradig, *adj.* centigrade. —herr, *m.* centumvir. —jährig, *adj.* of a hundred years; centenary, centenarian; der —jährige Krieg, the hundred years' war (*between England and France in the XIV–XV cent.*); die —jährige Feier von Schillers Geburt, the centenary of Schiller's birth, the hundredth anniversary of Schiller's birthday. —jährlich, *adj.* centennial. —mal, *adv.* a hundred times. —mark=schein, *m.* bank-note of one hundred marks (*about £5*). —malig, *adj.* done a hundred times. —pfünder, *m.* hundred-pounder (*Artil.*). —pfündig, *adj.* weighing one hundred pounds. —schaft, *f.* a hundred men belonging together. —tausend, a *or* one hundred thousand; —tausende von Exemplaren, hundreds of thousands of copies. —teilig, *adj.* centigrade. —weise, *adv.* by hundreds.

Hü'ne, *m.* (—n, *pl.* —n) giant. —n=haft, *adj. & adv.* gigantic. *Comp.* —n=bett, —n=grab, *n.* barrow, cairn, sepulchral mound. —n=gestalt, *f.* mighty figure. —n=mäßig, *adj.* gigantic, colossal (*of size*); athletic, Herculean (*of strength*). —n=schwert, *n.* enormous sword, mighty sword. —n=weib, *n.* woman of gigantic stature.

Hun'ger, *m.* (—s) hunger, appetite; famine; low diet (*Med.*); violent desire; vor —, —s sterben, to die of hunger; — haben, to be hungry; — ist der beste Koch, hunger is the best sauce (*prov.*). —ig, hungrig, *adj. & adv.* hungry, starving; poor (*of soil*). *Comp.* —folter, *f.* torture of starvation. —harke, *f.* large rake. —jahr, *n.* year of famine. —kandidat, *m.* candidate without an appointment, waiting for an appointment. —kur, *f.* lowering diet. —leider, *m.* starveling; needy wretch; miser. —leiderei, *f.* pinching poverty, starvation. —quelle, *f.* spring which often dries up. —pfote, *f.*; an den —pfoten saugen, to be extremely hard up, to have nothing to eat (*orig. said of bears*). —rechen, *m.* large rake *or* harrow. —s=not, *f.* dearth, famine. —stelle, *f.* poor appointment *or* place. —tod, *m.* death from starvation. —tuch, *n.* black cloth covering the altar in Lent; am —tuche nagen, to live in extreme misery.

Hun'ger—n, *v.* I. *n.* (*aux.* h.) to hunger, be hungry; to fast, starve; ich —e, I am starving myself, I am lowering my diet; —n nach einer S., to long for a th. II. *a. imp.*; mich —t, es —t mich, I am hungry.

Hun'grig, see Hungerig. —keit, *f.* hunger, appetite; starvation.

Hun'ten (hie unten), *adv* below here (*obs. rare*).

Hupf, *m.* (—es, *pl.* —e) hop, jump. —en, *v.n.* to spring, jump (*dial.*).

Hüp'f—en, *v.n.* (*aux.* h. & s.) to hop; to frisk about; to leap, skip, dance; ihr Herz —te vor Freude, her heart leapt with joy. —er, *m.* (—ers, *pl.* —er) hopper; skipper; hop, jump; flea; jerboa. *Comp.* —spiel, *n.* hop-scotch. —stein=spiel, *n.* throwing ducks and drakes.

Hür'de, *f.* (*pl.* —n) hurdle; fold, pen. *Comp.* —n=aufseher, *m.* pound-keeper. —n=draht, *m.* coarse iron-wire. —n=geflecht, *n.* basketwork. —n=gerte, *f.* twig used for hurdles. —n=lager, *n.* sheepfold, pen. —n=schlag, *m.* penning of sheep, folding.

Hür'd—en, *v.a. & n.* (*aux.* h.) to hurdle; to fold, pen (*sheep*). —ung, *f.* hurdle-work; sheep-folding.

Hu're, *f.* (*pl.* —n) whore, prostitute, harlot; bad woman, wench. —n, *v.n.* (*aux.* h.) to prostitute oneself; to fornicate. —r, *m.* (—rs, *pl.* —r) fornicator. —rei', *f.* fornication, harlotry. —risch, *adj. & adv.* whorish, lecherous, lewd. *Comp.* —n=handwerk, *n.* trade of prostitution. —n=haus, *n.* brothel. —n=weib, *n.* profligate woman, prostitute.

Hür'nen, *adj.* of horn, impenetrable, invulnerable (*obs.*); — Seyfried, horny Siegfried.

Hurr, —e, *int.* whirr! —e, —e, hurry-skurry!

Hurra', *int.* hurra(h)! —schreien, to shout hurrah, to cheer. *Comp.* —patriotismus, *m.* jingoism.

Hur'tig, *adj. & adv.* quick, swift, agile, nimble, alert, active; prompt; presto (*Mus.*); mach' —, be quick! —keit, *f.* swiftness, agility, promptness; dash.

Husa'r, *m.* (—en, *pl.* —en) hussar. *Comp.* —en=jacke, *f.* dolman. —en=mäßig, *adj.* hussar-like. —en=(pelz)mütze, *f.* busby. —en=tasche, *f.* sabre-tache.

Husch, I. *int.* (*enjoining silence, or speed, or expressing a shudder*) hush! quick! er macht alles immer —, —, he does everything in the greatest hurry, most superficially (*coll.*); seinen — nehmen, to take a run *or* start (*coll. & poet.*). II. *m.* (—es, *pl.* —e) sudden movement; sudden shower. —(el)ig, *adj.* hastily done, superficial. —eln, *v.n.* (*aux.* s.) to move about rustling.

Hu'schen, *v.* I. *n.* (*aux.* s.) to slip away, vanish; to slip (*over*). II. *a.* to box one's ears (*rare*); to thrash (*rare*); to steal, snatch away.

Hü'sing, *n.* (—s, *pl.* —e) housing (*Naut.*).

Hus'sa(h), *int.* huzza! — rufen, to huzza.

Hu'sten, I. *v.n.* (*aux.* h.) to cough, to have a cough. II. *v.a.* to cough (*up*); ich werde dir etwas —, you may whistle for it. III. *m.* (—s) cough; Keuch—, Stick—, hooping cough. *Comp.* —anfall, *m.* fit of coughing. —fieber, *n.* catarrhal fever. —kuchen, *m.* cough-lozenge. —mittel, *pl.* pectorals. —stillend, *adj.* pectoral.

Hü'steln, *v.n.* (*aux.* h.) to cough a little and frequently.

[1]Hut, *m.* (—es, *pl.* Hü'te) hat; bonnet (*for ladies*); sugar-loaf; cover, lid; top of a mushroom; coping; — mit hohem Kopfe, high-crowned hat; schlaffer —, slouched hat; ein weicher —, a soft felt hat; ein — Seesalz, 172 pounds of sea-salt; den — aufs Ohr setzen, to put one's hat wrong on, to assume a threatening air; viele Köpfe unter einen — bringen, to reconcile many conflicting opinions; unter einem —e stecken, to row in the same boat; etwas *or* einen unterm —e haben, to have s.th. *or* a p. in one's power; den — vor einem abnehmen, to take off one's hat to a person. *Comp.* —band, *n.* hat-band. —besatz, *m.* trimming of a hat *or* bonnet. —boden, *m.* crown of hat. —feder, *f.* plume *or* feather for a hat *or* bonnet. —form, *f.* hat-block. —futter, *n.* hat-lining. —futteral, *n.* hat-case *or* box. —krämpe, *f.* brim of a hat. —los, *adj.* without a hat. —macher, *m.* hatter. —masche, *f.* loop to a hat. —schachtel, *f.* hat-box. —schleife, *f.* cockade. —schnur, *f.* hat band *or* string; das geht denn doch über die —schnur, that is past all joke, that cannot be tolerated (*coll.*). —schraube, *f.* hat-stretcher. —schwenken, *n.* waving of hats. —tresse, *f.* hat-lace. —zucker, *m.* loaf-sugar.

[2]Hut, *f.* (*pl.* —en) keeping, guarding; protection, shelter; guard, charge, care; ward; tending (*of cattle*); pasture, pasturage; right of pasture; flock, herd; auf der —, auf seiner —, on one's guard; sei auf deiner —, be on your guard, look out! *Comp.* —geld, *n.* herd's wages. —mann, *m.* herdsman.

Hüt'chen, *n.* (—s, *pl.* —) little hat; extinguisher; (Zünd)—, percussion-cap.

Hü't—en, *v.* I. *a.* to watch, to guard; to tend, keep; einen vor einer S. —en, to defend, preserve one from; das Bett —en, to be confined to one's bed. II. *r.* to be on one's guard, take care; to shun; er —ete ihn wie seinen Augapfel, he kept him as the apple of his eye; —en Sie sich vor ihm! be on your guard with him! ehe ich mich —en konnte, before I was aware; ich —e mich vor seiner Gesellschaft, I shun his society, I keep away from him. —er, *m.* (—ers, *pl.* —er) keeper; guardian; herdsman. —erei', *f.* surveillance. —ung, *f.* guarding (*against*), preserving; pasture; cattle-tending. *Comp.* —ungs=recht, *n.* right of common.

Hut'sche, (**Hiet'sche,** *dial.*) *f.* (*pl.* —n) footstool; *see* Schaukel. —n, *v.n.* (*aux.* h.) to slip, slide.

Hüt'te, *f.* (*pl.* —n) cot, cottage, hut; tent, tabernacle; forge, smelting-house, foundry; kiln, furnace; shed; poop; Ober—, top-gallant-poop (*Naut.*). *Comp.* —n=after, *m.* slag, waste matter. —n=amt, *n.* board superintending furnaces, *etc.* —n=arbeiter, *m.* workman in a foundry. —n=bau, *m.* smelting business attached to a mine. —n=bewohner, *m.* cottager. —n=gericht, *n.* court of mines. —n=herr, *m.* proprietor of a foundry. —n=hundert, *n.* twenty-five (pieces). —n=industrie, *f.* metal foundries. —n=knappschaft, *f.* body of smelters and founders. —n=kunde, *f.* metallurgy. —n=leute, *pl.* smelters, founders, foundrymen, *etc.* —n=meister, *m.* overseer of a foundry. —n=rauch, *m.* flowers of arsenic, arsenical fume; substance given off from metals, when melting, in the form of smoke. —n=werk, *n.* foundry, smelting-house, stamping-mill. —n=wesen, *n.* smelting business, everything relating to smelting, metallurgy.

Hut'zel, *f.* (*pl.* —n) dried apple *or* pear; wild pear; old shrivelled person. —ig, *adj.* shrivelled. —n, *v.n.* (*aux.* s.) to shrivel, shrink; to become wrinkled.

Hyä'ne, *f.* (*pl.* —n) hyena; gestreifte —, striped hyena, laughing hyena; gefleckte —, spotted hyena, tiger-wolf; — des Schlachtfeldes, death-hunter; die — lacht, the hyena laughs.

Hyazin'the, *f.* (*pl.* —n) hyacinth. —n, *adj.* hyacinthine.

Hydra'nt, *m.* (—en, *pl.* —en) hydrant, water-post, fire-plug, stand-pipe.

Hydra't, *n.* (—es, *pl.* —e) hydrate.

Hydrau'l—ik, *f.* hydraulics. —isch, *adj.* hydraulic.

Hydria'tik, *f.* water-course, water-cure.

Hydro—chlor'säure, *f.* hydrochloric acid. —cipe'd, *n.* (—cipeds, *pl.* —cipede) water-bicycle. —genie'rt, *adj.* hydrogenated. —gen'=metalle, *pl.* hydrurets. —gen'=pol, *m.* negative pole. —me'ter, *m.* & *n.* hydrometer. —me'trisch, *adj.*; —metrische Wage, aerometer. —pa'thisch, *adj.* hydropathic. —phobie', *f.* hydrophobia. —sta'tik, *f.* hydrostatics.

Hyetome'ter, *m.* & *n.* rain-gauge, pluviometer.

Hym'ne, *f.* (*pl.* —n) hymn. —n=haft, *adj.* hymnic, hymnal. *Comp.* —n=buch, *n.* hymn-book. —n=dichter, *m.* hymn-writer, composer of hymns. —n=dichtung, *f.* hymnology.

Hyper'—bel, *f.* (*pl.* —beln) hyperbola (*Math.*); hyperbole. —borä'er, *m.*, —borä'isch, *adj.* Hyperborean. —kritik, *f.* (*pron.* Hy'perkritik) hypercriticism. —kritisch, *adj.* (*pron.* hy'perkritisch) overcritical, exceptionally critical.

Hypno'se, *f.* (*pl.* —n) hypnosis; für — empfänglich, hypnotizable; durch —, hypnotically.

Hypno't—isch, *adj.* hypnotic, soporific; psychic(al); —ische Mittel, hypnotics, soporifics; —ischer Zustand, sleep-waking. —iseu'r, *m.* hypnotizer. —isier'bar, *adj.* hypnotizable; leicht —isierbar, sensitive. —isie'ren, *v.a.* to hypnotize, psychologize. —isie'rung, *f.* hypnotization. —is'mus, *m.* hypnotism; Anhänger des —ismus, hypnotist.

Hypochon'd—er, —ri'st, *m.* hypochondriac. —rie', *f.* hypochondria. —risch, *adj.* hypochondriac(al), splenetic; —rische Launen, vapours.

Hypokri't, *m.* hypocrite. —isch, *adj.* hypocritical.

Hypotenu'se, *f.* (*pl.* —n) hypothenuse.

Hypothe'k, *f.* (*pl.* —en) mortgage; eine — aufnehmen, to raise money on *or* by mortgage; mit —en belastet, encumbered with mortgages. —a'risch, *adj.* mortgage; —arischer Gläubiger, mortgagee.

Hypo—the'se, *f.* (*pl.* —thesen) hypothesis. —the'tisch, *adj.* hypothetical.

Hyste'risch, *adj.* & *adv.* hysterical; einen —en Anfall bekommen, to go off into hysterics.

I

I, i, I, i; *as abbr.* J. = Ihre, your; their. *For other abbreviations see the Index of abbreviations at the end of the German-English part.*

I, Je, Ih, *int.* ah! ha! — freilich! to be sure! of course! — nun! well! well then! — was!

(= was denken Sie wohl?) nothing of the kind! — wo! (= wo denken Sie hin?) certainly not! by no means!

J'a(h), *n.* bray of an ass. **—en**, *v.n.* to bray, to heehaw (*like an ass*).

J'bisch, *m.* marshmallow (*Bot.*).

Ich, I. *pers. pron.* I; — **selbst**, I myself; — **bin es**, it is I. — **Elender!** miserable wretch that I am! II. *n.* self; ego; **mein zweites —**, my second self; **sein eigenes — suchen**, to be self-seeking. **—e(l)n**, *v.n.* to be egotistic, always to speak *or* think of self. **—heit**, *f.* the notion I, individuality; self; selfishness. **—ler**, **—ling**, *m.* egotist. *Comp.* **—sucht**, *f.* selfishness.

Ichthyo—logie', *f.* ichthyology. **—pha'g**, *m.* (**—phagen**, *pl.* **—phagen**) ichthyophagist.

Idea'l, I. *n.* (**—s**, *pl.* **—e**) ideal; image, pattern; **er ist das — eines Redners**, he is the model of an orator, he is a born orator. II. *adj. & adv.* ideal; notional; intellectual; imaginary, Utopian; abstract; perfect, incomparably beautiful; **—er Mensch**, **—angelegter Mensch**, man of ideals; **—er Ratschlag**, counsel of perfection; **—er Schauspieler**, perfect actor. **—isch**, *adj. & adv.* ideal (*obs.*). **—isie'ren**, *v.a.* to idealize. **—is'mus**, *m.* idealism. **—is'tisch**, *adj.* idealistic. **—itä't**, *f.* ideality.

Idee', *f.* (*pl.* **—en**) idea; notion, conception; thought, imagination, fancy; intention, purpose; **keine —!** by no means, certainly not! (*coll.*); **keine (blasse) — von einer S. haben**, to be altogether in the dark about a th.; **kommen Sie eine — näher heran**, advance just a tiny bit! (*coll.*). **—ll**, *adj.* existing in idea, ideal, imagined, imaginary. **—(e)n-haft**, *adj.* in idea. *Comp.* **—(e)n-lehre**, *f.* ideology. **—(e)n-tausch**, *m.* exchange of ideas. **—(e)n-verbindung**, *f.* association of ideas. **—(e)n-welt**, *f.* imaginary *or* ideal world, world of ideas.

J'den, *pl.* Ides (*in ancient Rome, the 15th day of March, May, July, October, and the 13th of the other months*).

Ident—ifizie'ren, *v.a.* to identify. **—isch** (*pron.* **iden'tisch**), *adj. & adv.* identical. **—itä't**, *f.* identity.

Idio—ma'tisch, *adj.* idiomatic. **—pa'thisch**, *adj.* idiopathic.

Idio't, *m.* (**—en**, *pl.* **—en**) idiot. **—ikon**, *n.* (**—ikons**, *pl.* **—iken**) dictionary of provincial and idiomatic words and phrases). **—isch**, *adj.* idiotic. **—is'mus**, *m.* idiom; idiocy.

Idolatrie', *f.* idolatry.

Idy'l—e, *f.* (*pl.* **—en**) idyl. **—enhaft**, **—isch**, *adj. & adv.* idyllic, pastoral.

J'gel, *m.* (**—s**, *pl.* **—**) hedgehog, urchin. **—icht** (*obs.*), **—ig**, *adj. & adv.* urchin-like; prickly. **—n**, *v.a. & imp.* to vex, annoy (*obs.*). *Comp.* **—fisch**, *m.* sea-urchin. **—käfer**, *m.* prickly-beetle. **—klee**, *m.* snail trefoil. **—stein**, *m.* echinite. **—weizen**, *m.* bearded wheat.

Igit'te, *interj.* (*of abhorrence*); **—fi!** how nasty, how disgusting (*dial.*).

Ignor—a'nt, *m.* (**—an'ten**, *pl.* **—an'ten**) ignoramus. **—a'nz**, *f.* ignorance. **—ie'ren**, *v.a.* to take no notice of; **einen —ieren**, to cut a person, ignore a p.'s presence.

Ihm, *pers. pron.* (*dat. sing. of* **er, es**) (to) him, (to) it; (to) you (*when addressing inferiors, now obs.*).

Ihn, *pers. pron.* (*acc. sing. of* **er**) him; it; you (*when addressing inferiors, now obs.*). **—en**, (*dat. of* **sie**, *pl.*) (to) them; (*and with cap., dat. of* **Sie**) (to) you.

Ihr, I. *pers. pron.* **1.** (*nom. pl. of* **du**) ye, you; **2.** (*dat. of* **sie**, *f. sing.*) to her, to it; to you (*when addressing a woman of inferior rank; now obs.*). II. *poss. adj.* (*orig. gen. of pers. pron.*; **ihr, ihre, ihr**) her; its; their; (*with cap.*) your. III. *poss. pr.* (*orig. gen. of pers. pron.*) hers, its, theirs; (*with cap.*) yours. **—e**, (**der, die, das —e**) *see* **—ige**. **—er**, I. *pers. pron.* **1.** (*gen. of* **sie**, *3 pers. f.*) of her, of it; **2.** (*gen. of* **sie**, *3 pers. pl.*) of them; (*with cap.*) of you; **mich jammert —er**, I pity them (*obs.*); **es waren —er viele**, there were many of them; **Gott wird sich —er erbarmen**, God will have compassion on them. II. *poss. adj.* (*gen. & dat. sing. & gen. pl. of* **ihr**) of her, to her; of their; (*with cap.*) of your. **—ige**, (**der, die, das —ige**; *pl.* **die —igen**) *poss. pron.* hers, its, theirs; (*with cap.*) yours; **das —ige**, your property; your duty, *etc.*; **die —igen**, your family; **der, die —ige**, yours (*very truly, sincerely, etc., at the end of a letter*). **—o**, *old gen. pl. of* **ihr**, *artificially revived in chancery lang. and only used as adj. in addressing persons of rank*, her, his, your; **— Gnaden**, Your (*or* His) Lordship, Your (*or* Her) Ladyship. *Comp.* **—er-lei**, *indec. adj.* of her, of its, of their kind; (*with cap.*) of your kind (*rare*). **—er-seits**, *adv.* in her, its, their turn; for her, its, their part; as far as she, it, they are concerned; (*with cap.*) for your part, in your turn. **—es-gleichen**, *indec. adj. & adv.* of her, its, their kind; like her, it, them (*with cap.*) of your kind; like you; *see* **Gleich**. **—et-halben**, **—et-wegen**, **—et-willen**, *adv.* on her, its, their account *or* behalf; for her, its, their sake; so far as she, it, they are concerned; (*with cap.*) on your account, *etc.*

Ihr'zen, *v.a.* to address a p. with the pronoun **Ihr** (ye *or* you). *See* **Duzen**.

Ikono—klas'tisch, *adj.* iconoclastic. **—stro'ph**, *m.* (**—strophen**, *pl.* **—strophen**) engraver's mirror.

Il'ge, *f.* (*pl.* **—n**) yellow iris, water-flag.

Ilia'de, **J'lias**, *f.* Iliad.

Ilk, *m.* (**—s**, *pl.* **—e**) polecat, fitchet (*dial.*).

Illat—io'n, *f.* inference. **—i'v**, *adj.* illative.

Illegiti'm, *adj.* illegitimate. **—itä't**, *f.* illegitimacy.

Il'literat, *m.* (**—en**, *pl.* **—en**) illiterate person.

Illumin—atio'n, *f.* (*pl.* **—ationen**) illumination. **—ie'ren**, *v.a.* to illuminate (*a town; books*). **—ie'rt**, *adj.* illuminated; tipsy (*coll.*).

Illuso'risch, *adj.* illusory.

Illustrie'rt, *adj.* illustrated.

Il'tis, *m.* (**—(ss)es**, *pl.* **—(ss)e**) polecat, fitchet.

Im, *contr. for* **in dem**, in the, within the; **— Augenblick**, at once, in a moment.

Imaginä'r, *adj.* imaginary; floating (*capital*); **—e Größe**, unreal value; imaginary quantity (*Math.*).

Im'biß, *m.* (**—(ss)es**, *pl.* **—(ss)e**) light meal; **ein bescheidener —**, a little something, some light refreshments. *Comp.* **—halle**, *f.* refreshment-bar.

Im'—ker, *m.* (**—kers**) beemaster. **—kerei'**, *f.* beekeeping. **—me**, *f.* (*pl.* **—men**) bee.

Immatrikul—atio'n, *f.* matriculation. **—ie'ren**, *v.a.* to matriculate; to enter; **sich —ieren lassen**, to matriculate.

Immedia't, *adj. & adv.* immediate. **—isie'ren**, *v.a.* to make free *or* directly dependent on the empire. *Comp.* **—bericht**, *m.*, **—eingabe**, *f.*; **—bericht, —eingabe, an S. M. den Kaiser**, petition, memorial presented to the sovereign. **—stände**, *pl.* immediate (*or* free) state.

Im'mer, I. *adv.* perpetually, continually; always; ever; every time; more and more; nevertheless; yet, still; **auf —**, for ever; **noch —**, still; **— und ewig**, for ever and ever, eternally; **— schlimmer**, worse and worse; **— weiter!** on and on; **— fort! — zu!** further! forward! go on! **— besser**, better and better; **sage es ihm —**, by all means tell him; **— zu!** keep on! **— gerade aus**, keep straight ahead; **wo nur —**, wheresoever; **wer —**, whoever; wie —, however, how in the world; er bittet — um Hülfe, aber ich wüßte nicht, daß er je andern geholfen hätte, he is always asking for help, but I do not know that he ever helped others. II. *part.* er mag es — thun, he is welcome to do it; er ist doch — dein Vater, remember that after all he is your father; er scheint nicht zu kommen, wir wollen uns nur — setzen, it seems as if he were not coming, let us take our seats; was er nur — haben mag! I wonder what can be (again) the matter with him! *Comp.* —dar, *adv.* always, ever. —fort, *adv.* continually, perpetually, evermore. —grün, *adj.* evergreen. —hin (*pron.* immerhi'n), I. *adv. & part.* always, all the time; in spite of everything; no matter; after all; I care not; still, yet; thue es — hin, well, you may do it, I do not object; —hin mag die Welt wissen, the world is welcome to know. II. *int.* well and good! — mehr, *adv.* more and more; ever more. — während, *adj.* endless, eternal, perpetual. —zu, *adv. & int.* always; continually forward, go on; never mind; es regnet —zu, it rains without stopping.

Immobi'l, *adj.* immovable; not ready for war. —ien, *pl.* real estate, immovables; dead stock.

Immortel'le, *f.* (*pl.* —n) everlasting. —n=kranz, *m.* wreath of everlasting flowers.

Immuni—sie'ren, *v.a.* to immunize, immunify (*Med.*). —tä't, *f.* immunity, exemption.

Imparochie'rt, *adj.* annexed to a parish.

Im'perat—iv, *m.* (—ivs, *pl.* —ive) imperative mood. —o'risch, *adj. & adv.* imperious.

Imperial'fraktur, *f.* great-primer (*Typ.*).

Impertine'nt, *adj.* impertinent, insolent; — blond, sandy-haired. —ien, *pl.* irrelevant points in a suit; insolent behaviour, impertinent words *or* actions.

Impetr—a'nt, *m.* petitioner. —a't, *m.* defendant.

Im'pf—en, *v.a.* to ingraft, inoculate; to vaccinate. —er, *m.* grafter; vaccinator. —ling, *m.* child that has been *or* is about to be vaccinated. —ung, *f.* inoculation, vaccination. *Comp.* —anstalt, *f.* institution for vaccination. —arzt, *m.* vaccinator; inoculator. —reis, *n.* graft-twig (*Hort.*). —schein, *m.* certificate of vaccination. —stoff, *m.* vaccine matter *or* lymph.

Implizie'ren, *v.n.* to imply.

Imponie'ren, *v.n.* (*aux.* h.) (einem) to impress forcibly, strike (*one*). —d, *part.adj.* imposing, impressive.

Impor't—en, *pl.* imports. —ie'ren, *v.a.* to import.

Im'post, *m.* (—s, *pl.* —en) impost; (*pl.*) taxes, duties, customs.

Imprägnie'r—en, *v.a.* to impregnate. —ung, *f.* impregnation, preparation of timber.

Imprima'tur, *n.* Press! einem Druckbogen das — erteilen, to mark a sheet for Press.

Improvis—a'tor, *m.* improvisator, extemporizer. —ie'ren, *v.a.* to improvise.

Impulsi'v, *adj.* impulsive.

In, *prep. expressing rest or* (*limited or circular*) *motion in a place* (*with dat.*); *implying motion to or towards* (*with acc.*), in, at, into, to, within; — kurzem, shortly, soon, in a short time; — Schutz nehmen, to take under protection; — der Schule, at school; — Musik setzen, to set to music; — (die) See stechen, to put to sea; — die Nacht hinein, late into the night; — der besten Absicht, with the best intentions; — die Kirche gehen, to go to church; — etwas, a little, somewhat; — aller Frühe, very early, at daybreak; zehn Fuß — die Länge, 10 feet long; — Geschäften ausgehen, to go out on business; — Kupfer stechen, to engrave on copper. *Comp.* —begriff, —dem, &c., *see* Inbegriff, Indem &c.

Inan'griffnahme, *f.* start, beginning made with a thing, setting about a thing.

Inan'spruchnahme, *f.* laying claim to; requisition (*Mil.*); zur — des Kredits, for using credit.

In'begriff, *m.* (—es, *pl.* —e) contents, tenor, purport; summary, abstract, epitome; sum total; circuit, compass; essence; mit —, including; mit — der Spesen, including charges. —en, *adv.*, inclusively, including.

Inbetrieb'setzung, *f.* beginning of the work starting.

In'brunst, *f.* ardour, fervour.

In'brünstig, *adj. & adv.* ardent, fervent.

Incestuö's, *adj. & adv.* incestuous.

Incid—e'nt, *adj.* casual. —en'tien, *pl.* incidents, incidentals. —e'nz, *f.* incidence. *Comp.* —e'nz=fall, *m.* incident. —e'nz=punkt, *m.* secondary point. —e'nz=winkel, *m.* angle of incidence.

Incidie'ren (mit), *v.n.* to be incident (on a line) (*Math.*); eine Linie incidiert mit einer andern, one line is incident on another (*Math.*).

Indeklina'bel, *adj.* indeclinable.

Indelikates'se, *f.* (*pl.* —n) indelicacy.

Inde'm, I. *adj.* just now, this moment. II. *conj.* during the time that, whilst, while, as; in that; since, because, as; ich gewähre es, — ich hoffe, I grant it in the hope that.

Indemni—sie'ren, —fizie'ren, *v.a.* to indemnify. —tä't, *f.* indemnity.

Independ—entis'mus, *m.*, —en'tentum, *n.* independence (*Theol.*). —e'nz, *f.* independence.

Inde's, Inde'ß, Indes'sen, I. *adv.* meantime, meanwhile; lesen Sie —, read in the meantime. II. *conj.* whilst, while; however, nevertheless.

In'dex, *m.*; auf den — setzen, to proscribe (a book).

In'dienststellung, *f.*; eines Schiffes —, commissioning of a (war)ship.

Indigena't, *n.* (—s, *pl.* —e) right of a native.

In'dig,—o, *m.* (—(o)s) indigo; (das —blau) indigo-blue. *Comp.* —oti'n=säure, *f.* anilic acid.

Indign—ie'ren, *v.a.* to offend, make indignant. —itä't, *f.* (*pl.* —itäten) indignity; affront, disgrace.

In'dikativ, *m.* (—s, *pl.* —e) indicative (*mood*).

Indisponi'bel, *adj.* not to be disposed of, not available.

Individu—alitä't, *f.* (*pl.* —alitäten) individuality. —e'll, *adj.* individual.

Indivi'du—um, *n.* (*pl.* —en) individual.

Indi'zienbeweis, *m.* circumstantial proof

Indoss—ame'nt, *n.* (—amen'tes, *pl.* —amen'te) indorsement. —a'nt (—an'ten, *pl.* —an'ten), —e'nt (—en'ten, *pl.* —en'ten), *m.* indorser. —ie'ren, *v.a.* to indorse.

Induktio'n, *f.* (*pl.* —en) induction. *Comp.* —s=apparat, *m.* (static) inductor. —s=elektrizität, *f.* electricity by induction. —s=strom, *m.* induction current, induced current. —s=vermögen, *n.* inductive capacity.

Industri'—e, *f.* (*pl.* —en) industry. —e'll, *adj.* industrial, manufacturing. —el'le, *pl. m.* manufacturers and tradesmen. —ö's, *adj.* industrious. *Comp.* —e=ausstellung, *f.* industrial exhibition, exhibition of products of industry. —e=gesellschaft, *f.* trade-union. —e=ritter, *m.* sharper, swindler.

Induzie'rt, *p.p. & adj.* induced, secondary.

In'egal, *adj. & adv.* inequal; uneven.

Ineinan'der, *adv. & sep. prefix*, into one another; confusedly. *Comp.* —flechten, *ir.v.a.* to interlace. —fügen, *v.a.* to join. —greifen, *ir.v.a.* (*aux.* h.) to grasp one into the other, to gear; to co-operate.

Inempfang'nahme, *f.* reception, receiving.
Infa'm, *adj. & adv.* infamous. **—ie'**, *f.* infamy.
Infa'nt, *m.* infante. **—in**, *f.* infanta.
In'fanter—ie, *f.* infantry. **—ist**, *m.* (**—isten**, *pl.* **—isten**) foot-soldier.
In'fel, *see* **Inful**.
Infe'rien, *pl.* funeral sacrifices.
Inferie'ren, *v.a.* to carry into; to deduce, infer.
In'finit, *adj.* infinite. **—ä't**, *f.* infinity. **—iv**, *m.* (**—ivs**, *pl.* **—ive**) infinitive (*mood*). *Comp.* **—esima'l=rechnung**, *f.* differential calculus.
Infizie'ren, **Infektie'ren**, *v.a.* to infect.
Inflektie'ren, *v.a.* to inflect.
Inflexio'n, *f.* (*pl.* **—en**) inflection.
Influe'nz, *f.* condensation, statical induction. *Comp.* **—maschine**, *f.* inductive machine.
Influe'nza, *f.* influenza.
Inform—atio'n, *f.* legal investigation; testimony, report; information. **—a'tor**, *m.* (**—ators**, *pl.* **—ato'ren**) private tutor. **—ie'ren**, *v.a.* to inform, to give information.
In'ful, *f.* (*pl.* **—n**) bishop's mitre. **—ie'ren**, *v.a.* to invest, adorn with a mitre.
Infus—io'n, *f.* (*pl.* **—ionen**) infusion. **—o'risch**, *adj. & adv.* infusorial. **—o'rien**, *pl.* infusoria. *Comp.* **—io'ns=tierchen**, *pl. see* **—orien**.
Ingang'setzung, *f.* starting (*of a machine*).
In'gebäude, *n.* building within an inclosure *or* wall; interior of a building.
Ingenieu'r, *m.* (**—s**, *pl.* **—e**) engineer. *Comp.* **—kunst**, *f.* engineering; art of fortification.
Inglei'chen, *adv. & conj.* likewise, also; moreover (*obs.*).
In'grimm, *m.* (**—s**) concealed *or* sullen rage, anger, wrath; violent anger. **—ig**, *adj. & adv.* furious, fiercely angry; spiteful.
Ingross—atio'n, *f.* entering in books; registration. **—a'tor**, **—i'st**, *m.* registrar (*of mortgages*).
Ing'wer, *m.* (**—s**) ginger. *Comp.* **—bier**, *m.* ginger-beer. **—kraut**, *n.* poor-man's-pepper (*Bot.*).
In'hab—en, *ir.v.a.* to have in one's possession, to possess. **—er**, *m.* (**—ers**, *pl.* **—er**) possessor, holder, bearer (*of a bill*); proprietor; occupant; commander; **—er einer Pfründe**, incumbent.
In'hafen, *m.* (**—s**, *pl.* **Inhäfen**) inner harbour.
In'halt, *m.* (**—s**) contents; what is held in a thing; tenor, purport, substance; capacity; extent, area; sense, meaning; **nach — der von Ihnen erhaltenen Nachrichten**, from the tenor of your advices; **dessen Haupt— ist**, the principal contents of which are. *Comp.* **—leer**, **—los**, *adj.* empty, unmeaning, of no *or* trifling contents. **—reich**, **—schwer**, **—voll**, *adj.* rich in, weighty with, full of contents, full of meaning, significant. **—s=angabe**, **—s=anzeige**, *f.*, **—s=verzeichnis**, *n.* table of contents, index. **—s=maß**, *n.* measure of capacity, cubic measure.
Inhäre'nt, *adj.* inherent.
Inhibito'ri—um, *n.* (**—ums**, *pl.* **—en**) inhibition (*Law*).
Injizie'ren, *v.a.* to inject.
Inju'rie, *f.* (*pl.* **—n**) insult; slander; abuse. *Comp.* **—n=klage**, *f.* action for insult *or* libel.
Inkarna't, I. *adj.* incarnate. II. *n.* **—i'n**, *n.* flesh-colour, carnation.
Inkas'so, *n.* cashing, encashment; **das — besorgen**, to get cashed, to get paid. *Comp.* **—spesen**, *pl.* charges for collecting *or* recovering (*C.L.*).
Inklinatio'nsnadel, *f.* dipping-needle.
In'konsequen—t, *adj.* inconsistent. **—z**, *f.* (*pl.* **—zen**) inconsistency.
Inkulp—a'nt, *m.* prosecutor. **—a't**, *m.* accused, defendant. **—ie'ren**, *v.a.* to accuse, incriminate.
Inkuna'bel, *f.* (*pl.* **—n**) book printed during the early period of the art of printing, fifteenth century print (*1440–1500*). **—n**, incunabula.
In'lage, *f.* (*pl.* **—n**) inclosure, enclosure.
In'land, *n.* inland; native country, home.
In'länd—er, *m.* (**—ers**, *pl.* **—er**), **—erin**, *f.* inlander; native. **—isch**, *adj. & adv.* inland; indigenous; native; home-made; internal; **—isches Fabrikat**, home-produce; **—ischer Verbrauch**, home-consumption.
In'laut, *m.* (**—es**, *pl.* **—e**) sound (letter *or* letters) in the interior of a word *or* syllable; **in mir steht i im — des Wortes**, in the word MIR the I is the medial sound; **im —**, medially.
In'leute, *pl.* inmates, lodgers.
In'lieg—end, *p. & adj.* enclosed, inclosed. **—er**, *m.* lodger, inmate.
Inmit'ten, *adv. & prep.* (*with gen.*) in the midst.
In'n—e, *adv. & sep. prefix*, within; **mitten —e**, right in the midst; **zwischen beiden —e**, between the two, intermediate. **—en**, *adv.* within. **—er**, *see* **Inner**. **—ig**, I. *adj. & adv.* intimate, internal; heartfelt, sincere, cordial, hearty; fervent, ardent; **—ige Freundschaft**, close friendship; **—ig lieben**, to love deeply *or* sincerely; **—iger Fleiß**, intense application. **—igkeit**, *f.* cordiality, heartiness; sincerity; fervour, ardour; intimacy. **—iglich**, *adv.* intimately, heartily, cordially, fervently. **—ung**, *f.* guild, corporation, society. *Comp.* **—e=behalten**, *ir.v.a.* to keep back, to detain. **—e=haben**, *ir.v.a.* to occupy, to possess, to be master of; to know, understand, be thoroughly acquainted with, to have at one's fingers' ends. **—e=habung**, *f.* possession. **—e=halten**, *ir.v.* I. *a.* to hold, keep in. II. *r.* to stay within doors. III. *n.* to stop, pause, leave off; **ganz —ehalten**, to come to, make a full stop. **—en=haut**, *f.* endocarp (*Bot.*). **—en=pol=maschine**, *f.* radial coils dynamo. **—en=welt**, *f.* the world within us; inner life; conceptions, ideas. **—e=stehen**, *ir.v.n.* to be in equilibrium, to balance. **—e=werden**, I. *ir.v.n.* to perceive, become conscious *or* aware of. II. *subst. n.* perception. **—ungs=brief**, *m.* charter of a guild. **—ungs=glied**, *n.* member of a corporation.
In'ner, *adj.* interior; internal; intestine, domestic; intrinsic; spiritual; **—e Angelegenheiten eines Staates**, internal affairs of a state, affairs connected with the home department; **—e Schiffsladung**, inboard cargo; **der —e Teil einer Stadt**, the interior of a town; the city; **das —e Auge**, the spiritual eye; **das —e Herz**, the innermost heart, the heart's core (*poet.*); **—e Mission**, home-mission; **der —e Verbrauch**, home-consumption; **der —e Wert**, intrinsic value. **—e(s)**, *n.* interior; inner self, heart, soul; **das —e der Erde**, the bowels of the earth; **Ministerium des —en**, Home Office (*Engl.*); Ministry of the Interior *or* of the Home Department; **Minister des —en**, Home Secretary (*Engl.*); **im tiefsten —en**, in the inmost recesses of the heart. **—lich**, *adj. & adv.* interior, inner, inward; internal, intestine; hearty; intrinsic; mental; **—lich anzuwenden**, to be taken (*internally*). **—lichkeit**, *f.* inwardness; subjectivity; subjectiveness, intrinsicalness; cordiality. **—st**, *adj. & adv.* (*sup. of* **inner**) inmost; **das —ste**, inner man *or* self; bottom of the heart *or* soul; **im —sten**, in one's heart, at heart. *Comp.* **—halb**, *adv. & prep.* (*with gen.*) within; on the inside.
Inrotulie'ren, *v.a.* to file (*writs*).
In'saß, *m.* (**—(s)sen**, *pl.* **—(s)sen**) inmate; inhabitant; member of a parish.
Ins— (*in comp.*) **—beson'dere**, *adv.* especially, in particular. **—gehei'm**, *adv.* secretly, privily. **—gemei'n**, *adv.* in common; usually. **—gesa'mmt**, *adv.* all together, in a body. **—künf'tige**, *adv.* in the time to come, henceforth. **—le'bentreten**, *n.* birth, first appearance. **—werk'setzen**, *n.* organization, working.

In'schrift, *f.* (*pl.* **—en**) inscription; legend. *Comp.* **—en=kunde,** *f.* art of deciphering inscriptions.

Insek't, *n.* (**—s,** *pl.* **—en**) insect; **—en summen,** insects buzz. *Comp.* **—en=artig,** *adj.* of the insect kind. **—en=fressend,** *adj.* insectivorous. **—en=kenner,** *m.* entomologist. **—en=kunde, —en=lehre, —ologie',** *f.* entomology.

In'sel, *f.* (*pl.* **—n**) island. **—chen,** *n.* islet, little island. *Comp.* **—bewohner,** *m.* islander. **—gruppe,** *f.* group of islands. **—land,** *n.* island. **—meer,** *n.* archipelago. **—reich,** I. *n.* island-realm. II. *adj.* abounding with isles, full of isles. **—stadt,** *f.* town built on an isle, insular town. **—volk,** *n.* islanders. **—welt,** *f.* archipelago.

Inser—a'nt, *m.* (**—an'ten,** *pl.* **—an'ten**) advertiser. **—a't,** *n.* (**—ates,** *pl.* **—ate**) advertisement in a paper. **—ie'ren,** *v.a.* to insert. **—tio'n,** *f.* advertising; advertisement.

In'siegel, *n.* (**—s,** *pl.* **—**) seal (*obs. & poet.*).

Insig'nien, *pl.* insignia; paraphernalia, badge *or* mark of office *or* dignity.

Inso'—fern, —weit, *adv. & conj.* in as far as, inasmuch as; according as.

Insolubilitä't, *f.* insolubility.

Insolve'nz, *f.* insolvency. *Comp.* **—erklärung,** *f.* declaration of insolvency.

Inson'derheit, Inson'ders, *adv.* separately, apart; especially, in particular.

Inspizie'ren, *v.a.* to inspect; to superintend.

Instandhal'tung, *f.* keeping in good repair, maintenance.

In'ständig, *adj. & adv.* instant, urgent, earnest; **auf das —ste,** most particularly.

Instand'setzung, *f.* getting ready; reparation, reinstatement, restoration.

Insta'nz, *f.* instance; instigation; court of judicature; **höhere —,** superior court; **in letzter —,** in the last resort, without further appeal; **von der — abgewiesen,** out of court; **von der — entbunden,** discharged (*not acquitted*). *Comp.* **—en=zug,** *m.* successive appeal.

In'stehend, *adj.* instant, impending.

In'ster, *n.* (**—s**) calf's pluck; tripe, entrails.

Insti'nkt, *m.* (**—es,** *pl.* **—e**) instinct. **—lich,** *adj. & adv.* instinctive. *Comp.* **—artig, —mäßig,** *see* **—lich.**

Insti—tuie'ren, *v.a.* to institute. **—tu't,** *n.* (**—tuts,** *pl.* **—tute**) institution; academy.

Instruie'ren, *v.a.* to instruct; **einen Prozeß —,** to draw up, prepare a case (*Law*).

Insul—a'ner, *m.* (**—aners,** *pl.* **—aner**), **—a'nerin,** *f.* islander. **—a'risch,** *adj.* insular.

Insurgie'ren, *v.n.* to raise an insurrection, to revolt.

Intabulie'ren, *v.a.* to register.

Integra'l, *n.*, **—e,** *f.* integral. *Comp.* **—rechnung,** *f.* integral calculus. **—zahl,** *f.* integer.

Intellige'nz, *f.* intelligence, cleverness; sharpness. *Comp.* **—blatt,** *n.* advertiser (*newspaper*). **—bureau,** *n.* intelligence department; inquiry and information office. **—komptoir,** *n.* advertising office, inquiry office.

Intend—a'nt, *m.* (**—an'ten,** *pl.* **—an'ten**) steward, manager, director; superintendent (*esp'lly with regard to theatres*). **—a'nz,** *f.* board of management; superintendence; **das Stück ist durch die —anz,** the play has been accepted. *Comp.* **—antur'sekretär,** *m.* officer of the commissariat department.

Intensitä't, *f.* (*pl.* **—en**) intensity.

Intensi'v, *adj.* thorough, thoroughly; **—e Landwirthschaft,** high farming.

In'terdikt, *n.*; **mit dem — belegen,** to place under an interdict.

Interess—a'nt, *adj.* interesting. **—e,** *n.* (*pron.* **Interes'se**) (**—es,** *pl.* **—en**) interest; advantage; (*pl.*) interest (*on money*); **—e an einer S. nehmen,** to take an interest in a th., to be interested in a th. **—e'nt,** *m.* (**—en'ten,** *pl.* **—en'ten**) party interested *or* concerned; partaker, sharer. **—ie'ren,** *v.a. & r.* to interest; to take an interest. **—ie'rt,** *p.p. & adj.* interested; selfish, self-interested.

In'terim, *n.* (**—s**) interim, mean-time. **—is'tisch,** *adj. & adv.* provisional, ad interim. *Comp.* **—s=anleiheschein,** *m.* scrip (*C. L.*). **—s=quittung,** *f.* provisional receipt. **—s=regierung,** *f.* provisional government, interregnum. **—s=schein,** *m.* sight-entry. **—s=uniform,** *f.* undress (uniform). **—s=verwalter,** *m.* (**einer Pfründe**) commendatory. **—s=wechsel,** *m.* bill ad interim, provisional bill of exchange.

Inte'rn, *adj. & adv.* internal. **—a't,** *n.* (**—ats,** *pl.* **—ate**) boarding school. **—e(r),** *m.* native.

Interpolie'ren, *v.a.* to interpolate (*a text*).

Interpun—gie'ren, *v.a.* to punctuate, to put in the stops and commas. **—ktio'n,** *f.* (*pl.* **—ktionen**) punctuation, putting in the stops.

Interversio'n, *f.* embezzlement.

Inti'm, *adj. & adv* intimate; **—e Bekanntschaft,** close connection; **—e Freunde,** fast friends. **—itä't,** *f.* intimacy.

In'timus, *m.* intimate friend, chum.

Intra'de, *f.* (*pl.* **—n**) prelude (*Mus.*); (*trumpet-*)flourish; (*pl.*) revenues.

In'transitiv, *adj.* intransitive. **—um,** *n.* intransitive verb.

Intrig—a'nt, I. *adj.* intriguing. II. *m.* (**—an'ten,** *pl.* **—an'ten**) intriguer. **—ie'ren,** *v.a.* to (form an) intrigue, to plot and scheme.

Invali'd, *adj.* weak, invalid. **—e,** *m.* (**—en,** *pl.* **—en**) invalid; disabled soldier. **—itä't,** *f.* disability (*of a workman, soldier*). **—ie'ren,** *v.a.* to invalidate. *Comp.* **—en=haus, —en=heim,** *n.* hospital for disabled soldiers. **—en=liste,** *f.* retired *or* superannuated list. **—en=pension,** *f.* old age pension. **—en=versicherung,** *f.* old age insurance.

Invent—a'r, *n.* (**—ars,** *pl.* **—are, —arien**) inventory; **ein —ar aufnehmen von einer S.,** to take, make, *or* draw up an inventory of a th. **—ie'ren,** *v.a.* to inventory, to schedule. **—u'r,** *f.* (*pl.* **—uren**) taking an inventory; inventory; **—ur halten,** to take stock (*C. L.*). *Comp.* **—ar=stück,** *n.* fixture.

Invoka'vit, *m.* the first Sunday in Lent.

In'volucrum, *n.* involucre.

Involvie'ren, *v.n.* to involve.

In'wärt—ig, *adj. & adv.* internal, inward. **—s,** *adv.* inwards, internally.

In'wendig, *adj. & adv.* interior, inside, inward.

In'wohn—en, *v.n.* (*aux.* **h.**) to dwell in; to be inherent. **—end,** *p. & adj.* inherent. **—er,** *m.* (**—ers,** *pl.* **—er**) lodger, inhabitant.

In'zicht, *f.* accusation, charge; internal evidence of crime, proof.

In'zucht, *f.* breeding in and in, inbreeding; **durch — erzeugte Tiere,** inbred animals.

Inzwi'schen, *adv. & conj.* in the mean time, meanwhile; however; **— daß,** while (*obs.*).

I'per, *f.* (*pl.* **—n**) common elm.

I'pelig, *adj.* over-particular (*coll.*).

Ir'd—en, *adj.* earthen, made of earth *or* clay; **—enes Geschirr,** earthenware, crockery; **—ene Pfeife,** clay-pipe. **—isch,** *adj. & adv.* earthly, terrestrial; earthy; **—ische Dinge,** earthly things, temporal affairs; **—isch gesinnt,** worldly-minded; **—ische Überreste** mortal remains.

Ir'gend, *adv.* any; some; perhaps; ever, at any time; about, nearly; in any way, anywhere; *before a pron., adj. or pronominal adverb often* = soever, at all, ever, *etc.*; **— einer, — jemand,** any body, some one; **auf — eine Art,** in some way or other, somehow; **— ein anderer,** some one else; **um — einer Ursache willen,** for some reason or other; **—**

etwas, anything at all; — wie, anyhow; wo —, wherever; wer — anständig ist, a person with any pretensions to respectability; wenn ich — kann, if I possibly can; ist — eine Hoffnung vorhanden? is there any hope (*at all*)? *Comp.* —einmal, *adv.* at any time, ever. —wie, *adv.* anyhow, in any way. —wo, *adv.* anywhere, at any place whatever; somewhere. —woher, *adv.* from some place or another. —wohin, *adv.* to some place or another. —womit, *adv.* with whatsoever.

Iri'diumspitze, *f.;* mit —, iridium-pointed.

Ironie', *f.* irony.

Iro'nisch, *adj. & adv.* ironical.

Ir'r—e, I. *adj. & adv.* in error, astray, out of the right track; in perplexity, confused, puzzled; disconcerted; in a state of alarm; wandering, delirious, insane, wavering; doubtful, suspecting; —e gehen, to go astray; ich bin —e an euch, I stand in doubt of you (*B.*); er redet —e, he is raving; es geht —e im Schlosse, the castle is haunted; an einem ganz —e werden, not to know what to make of one; sie entsetzten sich aber alle und wurden —e, and they were all amazed and were in doubt (*B.*); laß dich nicht —e machen, do not allow yourself to be put out, do not get bewildered. II. *f.* wandering; mistaken course; place of wandering, labyrinth; in der —e gehen, to wander about without direction, to go astray. —e(r), *m.* madman. *Comp.* —block, *m.* erratic block. —e=laufen, *n.* miscarriage (*of letters, etc.*). —en=anstalt, *f.*, —en=haus, *n.* lunatic asylum. —en=häusler, *m.* inmate of a madhouse, madman. —fahrt, *f.* going astray; wandering about. —führer, *m.* misleader. —gang, *m.* intricate way, labyrinth, bootless errand. —gängig, *adj.* labyrinthine; intricate. —garten, *m.* maze. —gebäude, *n.* labyrinth. —geist, *m.* erring spirit, rover, gadder. —glaube, *m.* heresy. —gläubig, *adj.* heterodox, heretical. —kopf, *m.* madman. —köpfig, *adj.* crack-brained, crazed. —lauf, *m.* wandering; ramble; erring course. —läufer, *m.* vagrant, rover. —lehre, *f.* false doctrine, heresy. —lehrer, *m.* teacher of false doctrines, heretic. —lehrig, *adj.* heterodox. —licht, *n.* Will o' the Wisp. —lichteln, —lichtern, —lichterie'ren, *v.n.* (*aux.* h.) to hop about like a Will o' the Wisp. —pfad, *m.* intricate way, labyrinth; wrong path, path of error. —rede, *f.* wild *or* irrational talk, delirious talk. —sinn, *m.* insanity; delirium. —stern, *m.* comet; wandering star. —wahn, *m.* delusion; erroneous opinion. —weg, *m.* wrong way. —wisch, *m. see* —licht.

Ir'r—en, *v.* I. *n.* (*aux.* h. *&* s.) to go astray, err, wander; to lose one's way; to rove, ramble; to be mistaken *or* deceived. II. *a.* to mislead, lead astray, deceive; to disturb, puzzle; to vex; to make wavering; sich —en lassen, to let oneself be misled *or* disconcerted; laß dich das nicht —en, do not allow that to disturb you, don't trouble yourself about that. III. *r.* to be mistaken; to commit an error; sich in einem —en, to mistake one for another; to be mistaken in one's expectations of a person, to be disappointed in a p. —ig, *adj. & adv.* erroneous, false; wrong; —igerweise, by mistake, erroneously, falsely. —igkeit, *f.* error, erroneousness, incorrectness. —sal, *n.* (—sals, *pl.* —sale) erring; sin; error; labyrinth, maze. —tum, *m.* (—tums, *pl.* —tümer) error, mistake; deception: false step, fault; erroneous idea; einem seinen —tum benehmen, to undeceive one, disabuse a p.'s mind; —tum vorbehalten, errors excepted. —tümlich, *adj. & adv.* erroneous. —ung, *f.* error, mistake; misunderstanding; difference.

Irritie'ren, *v.a.* to irritate.

Isabel'le, *f.* (*pl.* —n) light bay *or* cream-coloured horse. *Comp.* —n=pferd, *see* Isabelle. —n=farbe, *f.* yellow-dun, cream-colour.

Isochrom'firnis, *m.* print-varnish (*made of oil of turpentine, mastic, and glass*).

Isogo'n, *n.* (—s, *pl.* —e) equiangular figure.

Isol—atio'n, *f.* insulation. —atio'ns=vermögen, *n.* insulating property. —a'tor, —ie'r=schemel, *m.* insulator, insulating chair. —ie'ren, *v.a.* to isolate; to insulate. —ie'rung, *f.* insulation, isolation. *Comp.* —ie'r=glocke, *f.* bell-shaped insulator, cup-insulator.

Isother'misch, *adj.* isothermal.

Ist, *3 p. sg. pres. ind. of* sein.

Ist— (*in comp.*) —einnahmen, *pl.* net receipts. —bestand, *m.*, —stärke, *f.* actual *or* effective force.

Isth'misch, *adj. & adv.* pertaining to an isthmus; —e Spiele, Isthmian games (*famous Greek games which took place near Corinth*).

Iß, Issest, Ißt, *imp. 2 & 3 sg. pres. ind. of* essen.

I'tzo, Itzt, Itzun'der, *adv.* now, at present (*obs.*).

J

J, j, J, j; *for abbreviations see the Index of abbreviations at the end of the German-English part.*

Ja. I. *adv. & part.* yea, yes; ay (*used to add force to another particle or to the verb, usually pronounced very lightly but sometimes with a long and emphatically accented* a, *especially in phrases denoting command or insistence*; *e.g.* nimm dich — in Acht, be sure to take care; geh — nicht dahin, do not go there on any account; er soll — nicht zu früh ausgehen, let him be careful not to go out too soon; ist es auch wirklich so wie Sie sagen? — doch! is it really as you tell me? Indeed it is; — mit seinen Kenntnissen, yes, indeed, with all his knowledge; truly; indeed, certainly, forsooth, surely; even; well; you know; of course; —wohl, — freilich, — wahrhaftig, — wahrlich, yes, indeed, to be sure, of course, certainly; — doch, yes, yes; to be sure; er ist — mein Freund, why, he is my friend; ich gebe mir — Mühe, I do take pains; er ist — mein Sohn, he is my son, you see; da ist er —! well, there he is; Sie sehen — ganz blaß aus, dear me, you look quite pale; wenn es — sein muß, if it must needs be; wenn er — kommt, if indeed he come at all; ich sagte es —, I told you so; ich wünsche, daß du es thust, — ich bitte darum, I wish, nay I beg, that you will do it; warum schreibst du nicht? Ich schreibe —, why do you not write? Don't you see I am writing? da steht er —! there he stands, don't you see him? du hörst —, but you hear; ich habe es dir — schon gesagt, but I have told you before; — was ich sagen wollte, oh! by the way, I was going to tell you. II. *n.* (—s, *pl.* —s) yes; aye; assent; affirmation; — sagen, to consent; mit einem — beantworten, to answer in the affirmative; die —s überwiegen, *or* die meisten Stimmen sind für das --ausgefallen, the ayes have it; —wohl (*used as a reluctant admission*); ich will es ihm —wohl sagen, well! I will not say that I shall not tell him (*some time or other*). *Comp.* —bruder, —herr, *m.* compliant person, one unable to say no, ninny; toady. —wort, *n.* yes; affirmation; consent; (einem sein *or*) das —wort geben, to accept a suitor.

Jach, *adj. & adv.* precipitate, hasty; at once.

Ja'chern, Jach'tern, *v.n.* (*aux.* h.) to act boisterously, to romp.

Jacht, *f.* (*pl.* —en) yacht.

Jäck'chen, *n.* (—s, *pl.* —) vest, jacket *or* short coat for children.

Ja'cke, *f.* (*pl.* —n) jacket; jerkin, waistcoat; vest. —n, *v.a.* to provide with a jacket.

Ja'ckeln, Jä'ckeln, *v.n.* (*aux.* h.) to hurry *or* ride about aimlessly; to hunt.

Jagd, *f.* (*pl.* —en) chase, hunt; hunting, shooting; pursuing, pursuit; huntsmanship; right of hunting *or* shooting; anything taken in hunting, game, venison; the huntsmen, hounds, *etc.*; hunting-ground; auf die Löwen— gehen, to go lion-hunting; — machen auf, (*acc.*) to give chase to, to hunt *or* run after anything; die wilde —, Wodan's chase, Arthur's chase; Lützows wilde —, Lützow's wild chase, *i.e.* the (*volunteer*) chasseurs of the Prussian Major von Lützow in the Wars of Liberation (1813). —bar, *adj.* fit for the chase, fair game. —barkeit, *f.* quality of being chasable; right of hunting *or* shooting. *Comp.* —anzug, *m.* hunting-suit. —berechtigt, *adj.* licensed to shoot. —berechtigung, *f.* shooting-license. —beute, *f.* (huntsman's) bag (*fig.*). —bezirk, *m.* hunting-ground, preserve. —flinte, *f.* fowling-piece. —folge, *f.* right of following one's game. —freund, *m.* sportsman. —frevel, *m.* poaching. —gerät, —zeug, *n.* hunting-equipage. —gerecht, *adj.* skilled in the chase; broken in (*of dogs*). —gerechtigkeit, *f.* shooting-license. —gesellschaft, *f.* shooting-party. —gesetz, *n.* game-law. —grenze, *f.* boundary of a hunting-district. —haus, *n.* hunting-box, shooting-box. —horn, *n.* hunting-horn. —hund, *m.* sporting-dog, hound. —kleid, *n.*, —kleidung, *f.* hunting-suit. —klepper, *m.* cover-hack. —kundig, *adj. see* —gerecht. —kunst, *f.* sportsmanship. —leute, *pl.* huntsmen, hunters. —liebhaber, *m.* sportsman. —literatur, *f.* sporting literature. —lust, *f.* fondness for the chase; amusement *or* pleasure of the chase. —partie, *f.* hunting party, hunting expedition. —pferd, *n.* hunter. —recht, *n.* right of the chase; game laws; shooting license. —rohr, *n.* fowling piece. —schiff, *n.* yacht. —schloß, *n.*, —sitz, *m.* hunting-seat. —spieß, *m.* boar-spear; hunter's spear *or* pole. —stück, *n.* picture of a hunt, *etc.*; hunting-piece (*Mus.*). —stücke, *pl.* bow-chasers (*Naut.*). —tasche, *f.* game-bag. —uhr, *f.* hunting-watch. —wesen, *n.* everything relating to sport *or* woodcraft, hunting concerns. —zug, *m.* hunting expedition; express train; four-in-hand.

Ja'gen, *v.* I. *n.* (*aux.* h. & s.) to hunt, chase; to go, drive at full speed, to race, gallop; to follow, pursue; nach einer S. —, to pursue with all one's might, endeavour earnestly to obtain; davon —, to scamper away; vorbei —, to gallop past, sweep by; (auf) Hasen —, to go out coursing hares, to go hare-shooting; (auf) Füchse —, to go fox-hunting; (auf) Rotwild —, to go deer-stalking; gut gejagt haben, to have had good sport. II. *a.* to hunt, chase; to chase away, drive off; to force to depart; to drive, force; to follow *or* succeed rapidly; ein Witz jagte den andern, one witty remark followed the other without ceasing; einen auf die Straße —, to turn a p. into the street; aus dem Hause —, to turn out of doors; einem eine Kugel durch den Kopf —, to blow a person's brains out; in die Flucht —, to put to flight; in Harnisch —, to exasperate; ein Pferd zu Tode —, to ride a horse to death. III. *subst.n.* running with great speed; galloping; hunting, chasing, shooting; hot pursuit.

Jä'ger, *m.* (—s, *pl.* —) hunter, huntsman, sportsman; game-keeper; herring-smack; marksman, chasseur (*Mil.*); rifleman; der wilde —, the wild *or* weird huntsman; ein gewaltiger — vor dem Herrn, a mighty hunter before the Lord. —ei', *f.* huntsmanship, venery; woodcraft; huntsmen, gamekeepers (*coll.*); ranger's house; eager desire *or* effort to obtain something; berittene —ei, mounted riflemen, yeomanry cavalry. —isch, *adj. & adv.* sportsmanlike. —ling, *m.* (—lings, *pl.* —linge) cockney sportsman. *Comp.* —chor, *m.* huntsman's chorus (*Mus.*). —gehege, *n.* hunting district, hunting ground. —haus, *n.* ranger's *or* huntsman's house. —horn, *see* Jagdhorn. —kleid, *n.* shooting-suit. —kunst, *f.* science of the chase, woodcraft. —künste, *pl.* sportsmen's tricks. —latein, *n.* huntsman's slang. —mäßig, *adj. see* —isch. —meister, *m.* head-keeper; master of hounds. —rüstung, *f.*, —zeug, *n.* hunter's equipage. —s=mann, *m.* hunter, huntsmann (*poet.*) —sprache, *f.* sportsman's language *or* slang. —stange, *f.* hunting spear. —stock, *m.* jib-boom. —troß, *m.* crowd of huntsmen.

Jäh, *adj.* rapid, sudden; hasty, rash, precipitate; steep, precipitous; ein —es Ende, a sudden *or* violent end; —e Flucht, headlong flight; —er Schrecken, panic; —er Tod, sudden death; —e Höhe, steep height. —e, —igkeit, *f.*, haste, precipitation; suddenness; steepness, declivity, precipitousness; precipice. —lings, *adv.* precipitously; abruptly; suddenly, in violent haste. *Comp.* —zorn, *m.* sudden anger; passionateness; irritability. —zornig, *adj.* hasty; irritable, passionate.

Jahn, *m.* strip of land cut out for agricultural labour; swath; felled timber laid up in rows. *Comp.* —hauer, *m.* wood-cutter.

Jah'nen, *v.a.* to keep in the line (*dial.*).

Jahr, *n.* (—(e)s, *pl.* —e) year; die —e, age, years; ein — ins andere, one year with another; ein — ums *or* übers andere, every other year; übers —, a year hence *or* next year; um ein — auf oder ab, a year more or less; — für —, alle —e, year by year, every year; es geht ins vierte — daß, it is more than three years since; vor — und Tag, a year and a day since, quite a year ago; a long time ago; er ist schon bei —en, he is already advanced in years; in den besten —en, in the prime of life; zu —en kommen, to begin to grow old; seit einigen —en, of late years, for some years; vor einem —e, a year ago; fette —e, prosperous years (*B.*); seit undenklichen —en, time out of mind; — aus, — ein, all the year round. *Comp.* —anleihe, *f.* annuity. —begängnis, *n.* anniversary (*rare*). —buch, *n.* annual register, annual chronicle. —e=lang, lasting for years. —es=beitrag, *m.* annual *adj.* subscription. —es=bericht, *m.* annual report. —(es)=feier, *f.*, —(es)=fest, *n.* annual celebration, anniversary. —es=folge, *f.* (nach, in) chronological order. —es=frist, *f.* space of a year; innerhalb —esfrist, within a year. —es=hälfte, *f.* half year. —es=kursus, —es=kurs, *m.* the year's work (*of a school*). —es=lauf, *m.* course of the year. —(es)=lohn, *m.* annual wages. —(es)=rechnung, *f.* yearly account; calculation of the years, era. —(es)=rente, *f.* annual income. —es=tag, *m.* anniversary. —es=versammlung, *f.* anniversary meeting. —es=viertel, *n.* quarter of a year. —es=viertel=tag, *m.* quarter-day. —es=wechsel, *m.* new year; beste Glückwünsche zum —es=wechsel, with all good wishes for a bright and prosperous new year. —es=zahl, *f.* date of the year. —es=zeit, *f.* season. —fünf(t), *n.* lustrum. —gang, *m.* annual course; annual set (*of publications, etc.*); year's growth (*of wine, corn, etc.*); Wein von einem guten —gange, wine of a good year *or* growth; ein —gang Predigten, sermons for every Sunday of the year. —gebung, *f.* judicial declaration of a p.'s majority. —**gedächtnis**, *n.* yearly commemoration. —**gehalt**, *m.* annual salary, yearly stipend. —**geld**, *n.* yearly allowance; pension. —**gewächs**, *n.* annual. —**hun'dert**, *n.* century, age. —**hun'dert=wende**, *f.* (the close of the old and the) beginning of a new century. —**markt**, *m.* annual fair. —**pacht**, *f.* yearly tenure, leasehold. —**pächter**, *m.* leaseholder; yearly tenant. —**ring**, *m.* yearly circle in a tree. —**schluß=bilanz**, *f.* annual balance. —**schuß**, *m.* growth of a year. —**tau'send**, *n.* millennium. —**weise**, *adv.* annually. —**woche**, *f.* prophetic week (= *a year*). —**wuchs**, *m.* year's growth. —**ze'hend**, —**ze'hnt**, *n.* decennium, decade.

Jäh'r—en, *v.r.*; es —t sich heute, der Tag —t sich heute, daß . . ., it is a year to-day since. —**ig**, *adj. & adv.* a year old; lasting a year; a year ago; (*in comp.* =) years old; of every (*2nd*, *3rd*, *etc.*) year; zwei—ig, biennial. happening every second year, lasting two years. —**lich**, *adj. & adv.* yearly, annual. —**ling**, *m.* yearling.

Ja'kobs— (*in comp.*) —**brüder**, *m.pl.* pilgrims (*obs.*). —**leiter**, *f.* Jacob's ladder. —**mantel**, *m.* scallop (*Mollusc.*). —**stab**, *m.* quadrant (*Naut.*); Orion's belt; hollyhock (*Bot.*). —**straße**, *f.* Milky Way; way to the shrine of St. Jacob (*of Compostella*); auf St. —straße gehen, to be a pilgrim (*obs.*).

Jalo'n, *m.* jalon, directing staff, directing mark (*Mil.*). —**nie'ren**, *v.a.* to mark out (*ground*).

Jalousi'en, *pl.* Venetian blinds. —**zug**, *m.* blind lift *or* pull.

Jama'ikapfeffer, *m.* Jamaica pepper, pimento, allspice.

Jam'b—e, —**us**, *m.* (—en, —us, *pl.* —en) iambus. —**isch**, *adj.* iambic; —ischer Vers, iambic.

Jam'mer, *m.* (—s) lamentation; misery; distress, wretchedness; epilepsy (*prov.*); pity, compassion; es ist — und Schade *or* —schade, daß ꝛc., it is a great pity, a thousand pities, that, *etc.*; es ist ein —, it is a pity, it is sad.

Jam'mer—n, *v.* I. *n.* (*aux.* h.) to lament, mourn, grieve; to moan, cry, wail. II. *a. & imp.* to move to pity; to grieve; to pity, deplore; meine Seele —te der Armen, my soul was grieved for the poor (*B.*); mich —t seine (*& obs. poet.:* seiner) Not, I pity his misery; ihn —te des Volks, he was moved with compassion toward the people (*B.*); es —te den Hirten des alten hohen Herrn, the shepherd took pity on the aged noble lord (*poet.*); der Zustand des Kranken —te den Arzt, the doctor beheld the state of the patient with pity; meine Freunde —n mich, I pity my friends. *Comp.* —**anblick**, *m.* pitiable sight. —**blick**, *m.* piteous look. —**geschrei**, *n.* cry of lamentation. —**gesicht**, *n.* rueful countenance. —**gestalt**, *f.* pitiable figure *or* object. —**knechtschaft**, *f.* wretched slavery. —**lappen**, *m.* weakling, man without courage and energy (*coll.*). —**leben**, *n.* miserable, wretched life. —**lied**, *n.* song of lamentation; dirge. —**mann**, *m.* man of woe. —**ns=würdig**, *adj.* lamentable. —**prinz**, *m. see* —lappen. —**ruf**, *m.* wail. —**thal**, *n.* valley of sorrows, vale of tears. —**ton**, *m.* doleful accent. —**voll**, *adj.* lamentable, woful, pitiable, miserable. —**welt**, *f.* world of woe. —**zustand**, *m.* piteous condition.

Jäm'mer—lich, *adj. & adv.* deplorable, pitiable, wretched. —**lichkeit**, *f.* wretchedness; pitiableness. —**ling**, *m.* pitiable wretch.

Jan'hagel, *m.* (—s) rabble, mob.

Janitscha'r, *m.* (—en, *pl.* —en) janizary.

Jan'ken, *v.n.* (nach einer S.) to whine (for a th.), to hanker (after a th.) (*dial.*).

Ja'nuar, *m.* (—s, *pl.* —e), **Jän'ner**, *m.* (—s, *pl.* —) (*dial. & poet.*) (month of) January.

Japanie'ren, *v.a.* to japan.

Jap'pen, **Jap'sen**, *v.n.* (*aux.* h.) to gape; to pant; to yawn (*dial.*).

Jasmi'n, *m.* (—s, *pl.* —e) jasmine, jessamine.

Jas'pis, *m.* (—(s)ses, *pl.* —(s)se) jasper. *Comp* —**anstrich**, *m.* marbling.

Jast, *m.* (—es) hot temper; vehemence (*dial.*).

Jä'ten, *v.a.* to weed; Werkzeug zum —, weeding-tool, weeder; hoe.

Jau'che, *f.* (*pl.* —n) any filthy fluid; suds, swipes; ichor.

Jauch'zen, *v.n.* (*aux.* h.) to shout with joy; to huzza; to exult, triumph, rejoice.

Jau'eln, **Jau'len**, *v.a.* to whine, to howl (*of dogs*) (*coll.*).

[1]**Je**, I. *adv.* ever, at any time, at every time; in any case; at a time; each, apiece; (*before comparatives* =) the; von — her, always, all along, at all times, from the beginning; — zuweilen, just now and then, sometimes, at times; — zwei, two at a time, in pairs; er gab den drei Knaben — zwei Äpfel, he gave the three boys two apples each; — und —, now and then, at times; constantly, always, forever; — einer um den andern, one after another, by turns, alternately; — nachdem, — nach Umständen, according as; that depends; — eher, — lieber, the sooner the better; — mehr, — besser, the more the better, the more the merrier; — länger hier, — später dort, the longer we delay here, the later we shall be there; — länger desto schlimmer, the longer the worse; ich habe sie — länger — lieber, the longer I know her the better I love her; die Blume — länger — lieber, honeysuckle; — im siebenten Jahr, every seventh year. II. *int.* well! ah! why! — nun! well now! well then! well really! *Comp.* —**dennoch**, *adv. & conj.* nevertheless, notwithstanding, yet (*obs.*). —**doch**, *adv.* however, notwithstanding, nevertheless, yet. —**glich**, *see* Jeglich. —**=länger=je=lieber**, *n.* honeysuckle, woodbine. —**mals**, *adv.* ever, at any time. —**mand**, *indef. pron.* (*gen.* —mandes; *dat.* —mand, *better than* —mandem, —manden; *acc.* —mand, *better than* —manden) somebody, some one, anybody anyone; sonst —mand = (—mand anders), somebody, anybody else; irgend —mand, any one; (*used as adj. with adj. used as subst.*) —mand Fremdes, some stranger. —**weilen**, *adv.* (*Swiss for* bis *or* zuweilen), at times, sometimes. —**weilig**, *adv.* actual, momentary; der —weilige Direktor, the headmaster for the time being.

[2]**Je** (*abbr. of* Jesus), *int.* heavens! gracious! —mine! Herr —mine (= *Je(su‿do)mine*), good gracious!

Je'd—er, —e, —es, I. *adj.* each, every, either; an —em Orte, in every place, everywhere; —e leiseste Berührung, the least *or* slightest touch. II. *pron.* (ein —er, eine —e, ein —es) each, every, either; every one, everybody; Alle und —e, one and all, all and every one; —em das Seine, to every man his due; —er fege vor seiner Thür, every one should sweep before his own door; —er ist seines Glückes Schmied, every man is the architect of his own fortune; —er ist sich selbst der Nächste, charity begins at home, every man is dearest to himself. *Comp.* —**en=falls**, *adv.* at all events, in any case, however. —**er=hand**, —**er=lei**, *indec. adj.* of every *or* any kind. —**er=mann**, *pron.* every man, every one, everybody. —**er=männiglich**, *pron.* all together, everybody. —**er=manns=bürger**, *m.* cosmopolitan. —**er=zeit**, *adv.* at any time, always, ever. —**es=mal**, *adv.* each time, always; —esmal wenn, whenever. —**es=malig**, *adj.* existing, actual, then being;

wie es die —esmaligen Zustände erheischen, according to circumstances. —weder, —wede, —wedes, *pron.* every, each, every one.

Jeg'lich—er, —e, —es, *adj. & pron.* every, each; ein —es hat seine Zeit, to everything there is a season (*B.*).

Je'n—er, —e, —es, I. *dem. adj.* yon, that, yonder; auf —er Seite des Flusses, on the other side of the river; in —em Leben, in —er Welt, in the life to come, in the other world. II. *dem. pron.* that one, that person; the former (*opp. to* dieser, &c.); —e, welche, those who; bald dieses, bald —es, now one thing, now another. —ig, *pron.* (*suff. in comp. as,* derjenige, &c.) that. *Comp.* —seit, *prep.* (*with gen.*) beyond, on the other side. —seitig, *adj. & adv.* opposite; ulterior. —seits, I. *adv.* on the other side, on yonder side; in the world to come. II. *n.* the next world, the life to come.

Jeremia'de, *f.* (*pl.* —n) jeremiad, tale of grief, complaint.

Jeru'salemsblume, *f.* scarlet lychnis.

Jesui't, *m.* (—en, *pl.* —en) Jesuit. —in, *f.* female Jesuit. —isch, *adj.* Jesuitical. —is'=mus, *m.*, —en=tum, *n.* Jesuitism. *Comp.* —en=kloster, *n.* convent of Jesuits. —en=orden, *m.* order of the Jesuits. —en=pulver, *n.* Peruvian bark.

Jet'z—ig, *adj.* present, now existing, actual, modern; —iger Zeit, now-a-days; der —ige König, the reigning *or* present king; zum —igen Kurs, at the current rate of exchange. —o (*obs.*), —t, *adv.* at the present time, now; gleich —t, gerade —t, instantly, this very moment; für —t, for the present; von —t an, from this time, henceforth; bis —t, till now, up to now, as yet, hitherto; nur —t erst, eben —t, but just now; das —t, the present, the present time. —und, (*obs.*), —un'der (*obs.*), now. *Comp.* —t=malig, *adj.* present. —t=mals, *adv.* now, at present. —t=welt, *f.* present, actual world.

Joch, *n.* (—es, *pl.* —, —e; Jö'cher (*obs.*)) yoke; cross-beams, transom, arch; chain *or* ridge of mountains; mountain pass; trellis work for vines; measure of land; ins — spannen, to yoke; sich ins — spannen, to work hard, to slave; zwei — Ochsen, two pair of oxen. —en, *v.a.* to yoke. —ig, *adj.* (*mostly in comp.* =) coupled, yoked. *Comp.* —baum, *m.* hornbeam. —bein, *n.* process of the cheek bone. —brücke, *f.* bridge resting on piles. —hölzer, *pl.* crossbars. —pfahl, *m.* buttress pile. —spannung, *f.* space between the supports of a wooden bridge. —träger, *m.* crossbeams of a bridge.

Jo'ckei, Jo'ckey, *m.* (—s, *pl.* —s) jockey.

Jo'ckeln, *v.a.* to move, go, drive (*coll.*).

Jod, *n.*, —i'ne, *f.* iodine; mit — behandeln, to iodate (*Chem.*); to iodize (*Med. Phot.*). —i't, *n.* iodide of silver. —ofo'rm, *n.* iodoform.

Jo'del—er, Jod'ler, *m.* peculiar kind of Tyrolese *or* Swiss herdsmen's *or* peasant girls' song; singer of such song. —n, *v.n.* (*aux.* h.) to yodel *or* utter the cry of the Tyrolese herdsmen.

Johan'n—is, *see* Johannis. —i'ter, *m.* (—iters, *pl.* —iter) St. John (of Jerusalem) knight; White Cross knight; knight hospitaller; member of an ambulance society for the nursing of the sick and wounded in modern wars. —i'terin, *f.* nun of the order of St. John. *Comp.* —i'termeister, *m.* grand master of the order of St. John. —i'terorden, *m.* order of the Knights of St. John, order of Malta.

Johan'nis (*in comp. for* Johannes, *gen'lly in names of plants, etc., ripening about St. John's day*). —beere, *f.* currant. —beer=saft, *m.* currant-juice. —beer=strauch, *m.* currant-bush. —blut. —kraut, *n.* St. John's wort. —brot, *n.* carob-bean, locust-bean. —fest, *n.* *see* —tag. —feuer, *n.* St. John's fire. —fliege, *f.* Spanish fly. —käfer, —wurm, *m.* glow-worm. —nacht, *f.* St. John's eve (*night of June 24*). —tag, *m.* midsummer day. —traube, *f.* bunch of currants. —trieb, *m.* after sprig, second bloom; love affair of an elderly person, second love, late love.

Joh'len, Jo'len, *v.n.* (*aux.* h.) to howl, to hoot, to hoop, to bawl, to shout "Io".

Jol'le, Jöl'le, *f.* (*pl.* —n) yawl, jolly-boat, wherry. *Comp.* —n=führer, *m.* wherry-man.

Jon'ke, Jun'ke, *f.* (*pl.* —n) Chinese junk.

Jo'p—e, —pe, *f.* (*pl.* —n) cutaway coat, (shooting) jacket.

Jot, *n.* (*short* o) (—s, *pl.* —s) letter J. —a, *n.* (*long* o) (—as) iota; jot, whit.

Journa'l, *n.* (—s, *pl.* —e) journal, newspaper; daybook (*C. L.*). —i'st, *m.* (—is'ten, *pl.* —is'ten) journalist. —is'tik, *f.* journalism.

Jovia'l—isch, *adj. & adv.* jovial. —itä't, *f.* joviality.

Ju'bel, *m.* shout of joy, loud rejoicing, exultation, jubilation; public joy *or* festivity. —ei', *f.* public rejoicing, merrymaking. *Comp.* —feier, *f.*, —fest, *n.* jubilee. —gesang, *m.* song of rejoicing. —geschrei, *n.* shout of exultation. —greis, *m.* old man celebrating his jubilee. —jahr, *n.* year of jubilee; jubilee (*in the R. C. church*); alle —jahre einmal, rarely, sparingly (*coll.*); das kommt nur alle —jahr(e) vor, this is of very rare occurrence (*coll.*). —ouverture, *f.* a famous overture by C. M. v. Weber. —paar, *n.* married pair celebrating their silver *or* golden wedding. —predigt, *f.* jubilee sermon. —ruf, *m.* acclamation, shout of joy. —schmaus, *m.* banquet of rejoicing. —sonntag, *m.* second Sunday after Easter. —tag, *m.* day of rejoicing *or* jubilee. —ton, *m.* joyous sound *or* tone. —voll, *adj.* joyful, rejoicing.

Ju'beln, *v.n.* (*aux.* h.) to rejoice, shout with joy, exult, triumph, be triumphant.

Jubil—a'r, *m.* (—ars, *pl.* —are), —a'rin, *f.* celebrator of a jubilee. —a'te, *m.* third Sunday after Easter. —ä'um, *n.* (—äums, *pl.* —äen) jubilee. —ie'ren, *v.n.* (*aux.* h.) to exult.

Juch, —he', —hei'(sa), —hei'rasa(sa), *int.* hurrah! huzza!

Juchhei'en, Juch'zen, *v.n.* to huzza.

Juch'zer, *m.* shout of joy.

Ju'chert, Ju'chart, *m.* (*a Swiss field measure*) acre.

Juch't, *m. & n.* (—es); —en, I. *m.* (—ens) Russia leather, Muscovy hides. *Comp.* —band, —ein=band, *m.* bound in Russia. II. *adj.* in *or* made of Russia leather.

Juck, *m.* (—es, *pl.* —e) start; im —(e), in a twinkling.

Ju'ck—en, Jü'ck—en, *v.* I. *n.* (*aux.* h.) to itch; die Ohren —en ihm, his ears itch; he is inquisitive; die Finger —en mir nach ihm, my fingers itch to be at him; sein Fell —t ihn, his skin is itching (in anticipation of blows), he wishes for a fight (*vulg.*). II. *a. & imp.* to itch; to rub, scratch; sich —en, to scratch oneself; wen's —t, der kratze sich, let those whom the cap fits wear it (*prov.*).

Ju'cker, *m.* quick half-bred coach-horse. *Comp.* —gespann, *n.* team of juckers. —zug, *m.* four small quick-running coach-horses.

Jucks, *m.* (—(s)es, *pl.* —(s)e), *see* Jux.

Juda—isie'ren, *v.a.* to judaize. —is'mus, *m.* Judaism.

Ju'de, *m.* (—n, *pl.* —n) Jew; usurer; miser; der ewige —, the wandering Jew; haust du meinen —n, hau' ich deinen —n, tit for tat (*coll.*). —nheit, —nschaft, *f.* Jews (*coll.*). —ntum, *n.* Judaism. —ntümlich, *adj. & adv.* Jewish, according to Judaism. *Comp.*

—n=apfel, *m.* Adam's apple (*Anat.*); tomato. —n=art, *f.* Jewish manner *or* custom. —n=baum, Christ's thorn (*Bot.*). —n=christ, *m.* Jewish proselyte. —n=gasse, —n=straße, *f.* street inhabited by Jews. —n=genoß, *m.* convert to Judaism. —n=hetze, *f.* Jew baiting, prosecution of Jews (by the Antisemites). —n=land, *n.* Judea; Palestine. —n=schaft, *f.* body of Jews; Jewish population. —n=schule, *f.* Jewish school; synagogue; es geht hier her wie in einer —nschule, what an uproar, it is Bedlam broke loose.

Jüdelei', *f.* Jewish way of acting; usury; Jewish dialect; Yiddish.

Jü'd—eln, *v.n.* (*aux.* h.) to act *or* speak like a Jew; to practise usury. —in, *f.* Jewess. —isch, *adj. & adv.* Jewish.

Ju'gend, *f.* youth; adolescence, period of youth; young people; — hat keine Tugend, you cannot put an old head on young shoulders; boys are boys (*prov.*). —lich, *adj. & adv.* youthful, juvenile. —lichkeit, *f.* youthfulness. *Comp.* —alter, *n.* (*days of*) youth. —blüte, *f.* bloom of youth. —eselei, *f.* silly deed of a young fellow. —fehler, *m.* youthful fault. —feuer, *n.* ardour of youth. —freuden, *pl.* pleasures of youth. —freund, *m.* friend of one's youth; early friend, schoolday friend, chum; lover of young people; the boys' (*or* girls') own paper. —fülle, *f.* exuberance of youth; fulness of youth, *i.e.*, fulness of youthful beauty. —gefährte, —genoß, *m.* companion of one's youth; play-fellow. —jahre, *pl.* early days. —kräftig, *adj.* fresh, vigorous. —land, *n.* land of one's youth, where one's youth is spent. —liebe, *f.* early love, first love. —schöne, —schönheit, *f.* bloom of youth. —schriften, *pl.* books for the young. —schriftsteller, *m.* writer of books for the young, writer of juvenile literature. —spiel, *m.* juvenile game. —spiele, *pl.* games, sports. —streich, *m.*, —stück, *n.* youthful prank *or* frolic; —streiche machen, to sow one's wild oats. —sünde, *f.* sin of young men *or* women, youthful offence. —trotz, *m.* youthful perversity. —wehr, *f.* school volunteers. —welt, *f.* young people; the world in its prime. —zeit, *f.* time of youth, youth.

Jul—, Yule. *Comp.* —block, *m.* big log of wood for a bright and warm Christmas fire. —feuer, *n.* fire lit at Yuletide on hills *or* on public places. —klapp, *n.* Christmas present (tied up in a parcel and thrown in at the door with the shout of —klapp) (*dial.*).

Ju'lap, Ju'lepp, *m.* (—es, *pl.* —e) julep.

Jul'i, *m.* (—s), **Ju'lius**, *m.* July; Mitte —, in the middle of July.

Jung, *adj. & adv.* (jün'ger, jüngst) young, youthful; new, fresh; recent; early; green; na, was da wohl — wird, well, what is that going to be (*coll.*); —e Erbsen, green peas; ein —es Blut, a young person; youngster; die —en, the young; the boys; —er Boden, land but recently drained; der —e Morgen, early morning; —er Wein, new wine; die —e Frau, newly-married woman, bride, young wife. —e, *m.* (—en, *pl.* —en *or* —ens (*dial. & coll.*)) boy (der —e, the boy; ein —e, a boy) lad; stripling, youth; apprentice. —e(s), *n.* young, offspring; ein —es, a young one; das —e eines Löwen, lion's whelp; cub; —e werfen, *see* —en; — gewohnt, alt gethan, what is bred in the bone will never come out of the flesh (*prov.*). —enhaft, *adj. & adv.* boyish. —enschaft, *f.* boys; young folk (*coll.*). —fer, *see* Jungfer. —heit, *f.* quality of being young, new *or* fresh. *Comp.* —brunnen, *m.* well of rejuvenescence. —e=magd, *f.* chambermaid (*prov.*). —en=arbeit, *f.* work for the young *or* for apprentices. —en=jahre, *pl.* years of boyhood *or* apprenticeship. —en=mäßig, *adj.* boyish. —frau, *f.* young woman, maid, maiden, virgin; Virgo (*Ast.*); heilige —frau, Holy *or* Blessed Virgin; aufblühende —frau, budding virgin; —frau von Orleans, maid of Orleans; zu einer —frau herangewachsen, grown up to maidenhood; von der —frau Maria geboren, born of the Virgin Mary; die klugen (thörichten) —en, the wise (foolish) virgins. —frauen=kloster, *n.* nunnery. —frauen=schänder, *m.* debaucher of virgins. —fräulich, *adj. & adv.* maidenly, coy, becoming a virgin. —fräulichkeit, *f.* maidenliness, virginal modesty *or* purity; coyness. —frauschaft, *f.* maidenhood; virginity. —gesell, *m.* bachelor; youngest journeyman. —gesellen=leben, *n.* life of a bachelor. —gesellen=stand, *m.* bachelorhood. —herr, *m.* young sir, young gentleman. —mann, *m.* ordinary *or* unpractised seaman. —meister, *m.* junior master of a guild. —tier, *n.* fawn.

Jun'gen, *v.a.* to bring forth young (*of animals*).

Jün'g—er, I. *adj.* (*comp. of* jung) younger; later; junior; puisné. II. *m.* (—ers, *pl.* —er), —erin, *f.* disciple; follower, adherent. —erhaft, *adj. & adv.* in the manner of a disciple. —erschaft, *f.* discipleship; disciples (*coll.*). —ferchen, *n.* little miss. —ferlich, *adj. & adv.* maidenlike, virginal; coy, timid. —ferlichkeit, *f.* girlishness; maidenliness; coyness. —ling, *m.* (—lings, *pl.* —linge) young man, youth; stripling. —st, I. *adj.* (*sup. of* jung) youngest; latest, last; das —ste Gericht, der —ste Tag, day of judgment, the last day, doomsday; Ihr —stes Schreiben, your last letter; sie ist die —ste nicht mehr, she is no longer very young. II. *adv.* lately, recently, the other day aus dem —st Gesagten, from what has just been said. —stens (—st=hin), *see* —st II. *Comp.* —er=recht, *n.* right of juniority (*opp. to primogeniture*). —lings=bund, —lings=verein, *m.* (christlicher) young men's (Christian) association, Y. M. (C.) A.

Jung'fer, *f.* (*pl.* —n) virgin, maid, young girl; Miss; spinster; chambermaid; lady's maid; unmarried housekeeper; instrument for beheading criminals; block to which prisoners were chained *or* locked; maiden fortress; paving-beetle, rammer; Venus's shell (*Conch.*); dragon-fly; dead-eye (*Naut.*); alte —, old maid; nackte —, meadow-saffron; — im Grünen, — im Busch, fennel flower; die — küssen, to be (*secretly*) executed, to be killed by a machine; —n werfen, to throw ducks and drakes. —schaft, *f.* virginity, maidenhood. *Comp.* —blüte, *f.* sundew (*flower*). —n=finger, *m.* ring-finger. —n=gold, *n.* virgin gold. —n=häutchen, *n.* hymen (*Anat.*). —n=honig, *m.* virgin honey. —n=käfer, *m.* lady-bird. —n=kamm, *m.* Venus's comb. —n=kind, *n.* bastard, natural child; first-born. —n=knecht, *m.* ladies' man; beau, fop. —n=krankheit, *f.* green-sickness. —n=kranz, *m.* bridal wreath; periwinkle. —n=nelke, *f.* maiden-pink. —n=raub, *m.* rape. —n=räuber, *m.* ravisher. —n=rede, *f.* maiden speech. —n=schänder, *m.* ravisher. —n=schwarm, *m.* swarm of young bees. —n=stand, *m.* virginity; spinster-condition, life of a spinster. —n=wachs, *n.* virgin wax.

Ju'ni (—s), **Ju'nius**, *m.* June; gegen Ende —, towards the end of June.

Jun'ker, *m.* (—s, *pl.* —) young nobleman *or* aristocrat; squire; youngster. —ei', *f.* behaviour of young aristocrats; aristocratic arrogance; — Voland, name given to Mephistopheles in Goethe's 'Faust.' —haft, —isch, —lich, *adj. & adv.* cavalier; like a young nobleman. —ie'ren, —n, *v.n.* (*aux.* h.) to assume aristocratic airs *or* ways. —schaft, *f.* body of young noblemen *or* squires. —schaftlich, *adj.*

& *adv.* pertaining to a young nobleman. —**tum**, *n.* aristocratic manners; petty feudal nobles; haughtiness of the petty feudal nobility.
Juno'nisch, *adj.* Juno-like, majestic.
Ju'pe, Jup'pe, *see* **Jope, Joppe.**
Ju'piters— (*in comp.*) —**mond**, —**trabant**, *m.* satellite of Jupiter. —**vogel**, *m.* eagle.
Ju'r—a, *pl.* law; —**a studieren**, to study law. —**a't**, *m.* (—**aten**, *pl.* —**aten**) deponent (*on oath*); church-warden. —**a'to**, *adv.* upon oath. —**i'disch**, *adj.* juridical; —**idisches Kunstwort**, law-term. —**i'st**, *m.* (—**is'ten**, *pl.* —**is'ten**) lawyer; law-student. —**isterei'**, *f.* jurisprudence; lawyer's tricks, quibbling. —**is'tisch**, *adj.* & *adv.* relating to the law, legal, in law; **die —istische Fakultät**, the faculty of law, the board of legal studies. *Comp.* —**is=konsu'lt**, *m. see* **Rechtsgelehrte(r).** —**is=prude'nz**, *f.* jurisprudence.
Just, *adv.* just, exactly; just now, but just; **das ist — nicht nötig**, that is not altogether necessary. —**ifizie'ren**, *v.a.* to justify; *see* **Hinrichten.** —**ie'ren**, *v.a.* to adjust; to justify (*Typ.*). —**ie'rer**, *m.* (—**ierers**, *pl.* —**ierer**) adjuster; justifier. —**i'z**, *f.* justice; administration of the law. —**izia'r**, *m.* justiciary. *Comp.* —**ie'r=gewicht**, *n.* standard. —**ie'r=wage**, *f.* adjusting balance. —**i'z=amt**, *n.* court of law. —**i'z=beamte(r)**, *m.* officer of justice. —**i'z=kollegium**, *n.*, —**i'z=hof**, *m.*, —**i'z=kammer**, —**i'z=stelle**, *f.* court *or* chamber of justice. —**i'z=kommissär**, *m.* (*in North Germany*) attorney-at-law. —**i'z=minister**, *m.* minister of justice (*similar to Lord Chancellor*). —**i'z=mord**, *m.* judicial *or* legal murder. —**i'z=pflege**, *f.* administration of justice. —**i'z=rat**, *m.* counsellor of justice; King's *or* Queen's Counsel (*Eng.*). —**i'z=wesen**, *n.* justiciary system, anything connected with the administration of justice.
Ju'te, *f.* (*pl.* —**n**) jute, jute, pat.
Juwe'l, *m.* (& *n.*) (—**s**, *pl.* —**e** & —**en**) jewel, gem, precious stone, bijou. —**ie'r**, *m.* (—**iers**, *pl.* —**iere**) jeweller, goldsmith. *Comp.* —**en=handel**, *m.* jeweller's business. —**en=händler**, *m.* jeweller. —**en=kästchen**, *n.* jewel-case *or* casket. —**en=schmuck**, *m.* set of jewels. —**en=uhr**, *f.* watch set with jewels.
Jux, *m.* (—**es**, *pl.* —**e**) joke, jest, fun, frolic, lark (*coll.*). —**ig**, *adj.* full of jest *or* fun, frolicsome, funny (*coll.*); dirty, filthy, obscene (*sl.*).
Ju'xen, *v.a.* to joke, jest, make sport; **einen —**, to make sport of a person.

K

Words not given under **K** should be looked for under **C.** Foreign words of the same form and meaning in both languages have, as a rule, been omitted.

K, k, *n.* K, k, *as abbr.* **K.** *or* **k.** = **kaiserlich, königlich**, imperial, royal; *for other abbreviations see the Index of abbreviations at the end of the German-English part.*
Kaa'ba, *f.* caaba.
Kaak, *m.* (—**es**, *pl.* —**e**) heavy squall (*of wind*) gust; pillory (*prov.*).
Kaba'l—e, *f.* (*pl.* —**en**) cabal, intrigue. —**is'tisch**, *adj.* cabalistic. *Comp.* —**en=macher**, *m.* caballer. —**ie'ren**, *v.n.* (*aux.* **h.**) *or* —**en schmieden**, to cabal, intrigue, unite secretly for the purpose of intrigue. —**i'st**, *m.* (—**is'ten**, *pl.* —**is'ten**) cabalist.
Kaba'ne, *f.* (*pl.* —**n**) hut, cot, cabin.
Kaba'sche, Kaba'cke, *f.* (*pl.* —**n**) pot-house (*coll.*); hole, wretched dwelling (*coll.*).
Kab'bala, *f.* cabala (*Hebr.*).
Kabbelei', *f.* (*pl.* —**en**) squabble, quarrel (*coll.*).
Kab'bel—n, *v.n.* (*aux.* **h.**) & *r.* to bandy words, to squabble, quarrel (*coll.*); **die See —t, geht —n**, the sea leaps against the wind. —**ung**, *f.* washing away of the shore by the sea.
Ka'bel, *f.* (*pl.* —**n**) cable; lot; **unterirdisches —**, underground cable; **unterseeisches —**, submarine cable. —**n**, *v.a.* & *n.* (*aux.* **h.**) to allot; to draw lots; to cable, to send a cablegram. —**ung**, *f.* allotment, lot (*dial.*); cablegram. *Comp.* —**gar**, —**aring**, *f.* messenger, voyol (*Naut.*). —**dampfer**, *m.* steamer for laying cables. —**depesche**, *f.* cable(gram); **eine —depesche senden**, to cable. —**garn**, *n.* rope yarn. —**länge**, *f.* cable's length (*120 fathoms*). —**legung**, *f.* laying of a (telegraphic) cable. —**seil**, —**tau**, *n.* cable. —**tanz**, *m.* sailor's hornpipe. —**weise**, *adv.* by lots (*dial.*).
Ka'beljau, *m.* (—**s**, *pl.* —**s** & —**e**) codfish. *Comp.* —**leberthran**, *m.* cod-liver oil.
Ka'bestan, *m.* (—**s**, *pl.* —**e**) capstan, capstern.
Kabine'tt, *n.* (—**s**, *pl.* —**e**) cabinet; collection (*of coins, gems, etc.*); private room; water-closet; small room, closet; business room of a prince; select council of a prince, body of ministers, members of the cabinet council. *Comp.* —**photographie**, *f.* cabinet photograph. —**stück**, *n.* cabinet specimen. —**s=auslese**, *f.* choice wine. —**s=befehl**, *m.* royal (*or* imperial) order, order of the sovereign, order given in council. —**s=frage**, *f.* cabinet question; question of vital importance; **die —sfrage stellen**, to threaten to resign (*of a prime minister*); **aus einer S. eine —sfrage machen**, to declare a question to be of vital importance. —**s=justiz**, *f.* high-handed *or* warped justice. —**s=krisis**, *f.* ministerial crisis. —**s=minister**, *m.* cabinet minister; secretary of state. —**s=ordre**, *f. see* —**befehl.** —**s=rat**, *m.* cabinet council. —**s=sekretär**, *m.* private secretary. —**s=siegel**, *n.* privy seal. —**s=sitzung**, *f.* cabinet council, meeting of His (*or* Her) Majesty's ministers.
Kabriole'tt, *n.* (—(**e**)**s**, *pl.* —**e**) cab; fore-part of a stage-coach, coupé.
Kabu'se, *f.* (*pl.* —**n**) hut; caboose.
Ka'chel, *f.* (*pl.* —**n**) hollow earthen vessel, Dutch tile, tile for stoves, *etc.* *Comp.* —**form**, *f.* mould for Dutch tiles. —**ofen**, *m.* earthenware *or* tile stove.
Kack, *n.*, —**e**, *f.* excrement, stool (*vulg.*). —**en**, *v.n.* (*aux.* **h.**) to go to stool (*vulg.*).
Kackerlack'e, *see* **Kakerlak.**
Kada'ver, *m.* (—**s**, *pl.* —) corpse. *Comp.* —**fliege**, *f.* carrion fly.
Kad'dich, Kad'dig, *m.* (—**s**, *pl.* —**e**) juniper.
Kade'nz, *f.* (*pl.* —**en**) cadence.
Ka'der, *m.* (—**s**) double-chin (*dial.*).
Kade'tt, *m.* (—**en**, *pl.* —**en**) cadet; midshipman; younger son (*rare*). *Comp.* —**en=anstalt**, *f.* military training school. —**en=corps**, *n.* cadet corps, corps of cadets. —**en=haus**, *n.*, —**en=schule**, *f.* military academy. —**en=schulschiff**, *n.* training-ship (*for the navy*).
Kä'fer, *m.* (—**s**, *pl.* —) beetle, chafer; young girl (*sl.*); **sie ist ein niedlicher** *or* **netter —**, she is a pretty creature (*sl.*). *Comp.* —**artig**, *adj.* coleopterous. —**sammlung**, *f.* collection of beetles. —**schnecke**, *f.* scarabee snail.
Kaff, *n.* (—(**e**)**s**) chaff; nonsense, bosh (*sl.*).
Kaf'fee, *m.* (—**s**) coffee; coffee-party; — **brennen, rösten**, to roast coffee; — **muß sich setzen**, coffee must settle; **eine Tasse — trinken**, to take a cup of coffee; **wollen Sie morgen nachmittag zum — zu uns kommen?** will you come to coffee to-morrow afternoon? *Comp.* —**base**, *f.*, —**schwester**, *f.* coffee-lover. —**bohne**, *f.* coffee bean; —**bohnen**, unground coffee. —**brenner**, *m.* coffee-roaster. —**brett**, *n.* coffee-tray. —**brötchen**, *n.* rusk, bun.

—geschirr, *n.* coffee-service, coffee-things. —kanne, *f.* coffee-pot. —klatsch, *m.* ladies' (afternoon) coffee-party (*coll.*). —löffel, *m.* coffee-spoon. —maschine, *f.* machine for making coffee. —pauke, —trommel, *f.*, —schütter, *m.* coffee-roaster. —schale, *f.*, —schälchen, *n.* coffee-cup. —wirt, *m.* keeper of a coffee-house. —schwester, *f.* great lover of coffee (*also said of men*) (*coll.*). —seihe, *f.*, —trichter, *m.* coffee-strainer. —sorten, *pl.* coffees.

Kaf'fer, *m.* (—s, *pl.* —n) Kaffir; duffer, boor (*sl.*).

Kä'fig, (Kä'fich, Kä'ficht, (*obs.*)) *m.* (*& n.*) (—s, *pl.* —e) cage; bird-cage; prison.

Kaf'tan, *m.* (—s, *pl.* —e) caftan.

Kahl, *adj. & adv.* bare, bald, naked; callow, unfledged (*of birds*); threadbare; dismantled; sterile, barren; leafless; paltry, poor, sorry; cold, dry; dull; destitute of money; empty; —e Ausflucht, paltry *or* poor excuse; — bestehen, to come off but poorly; ein —er Mensch, a dull, heavy man, one without energy; —es Geschwätz, empty, idle talk; — abgeschoren, close-cropped. —heit, *f.* baldness (*of the head, of a mountain, etc.*), bleakness; barrenness; poverty; misery. *Comp.* —bäuche, *pl.* apodes (*Icht.*). —fleckig, *adj.* having threadbare spots. —fuß, *m.* francolin (*Orn.*). —köpfig, *adj.* baldheaded.

Kahm, (Kahn,) *m.* (—s) mould (*on liquids*). —en, *v.n.* (*aux.* h. & s.) to grow mouldy. —ig, *adj. & adv.* mouldy, stale; ropy (*of wine*).

Kahn, *m.* (—s, *pl.* Käh'ne, *dim.* Kähn'chen) boat, wherry, skiff; scapha (*Surg.*). —bar, *adj. & adv.* navigable for small boats. —en, *v.n.* (*aux.* h.) to go in a boat. *Comp.* —bein, *n.* scaphoid bone, navicular bone. —führer, *m.* master of a boat; waterman. —geld, *n.* ferriage; boat-money. —schnabel, —schnäbler, *pl.* boat-bill (*Orn.*).

Kai, *m.* (—s, *pl.* —e) quay, wharf; pier. —en, *v.a.* (die Raaen) to set (*the yards*) apeak (*Naut.*). *Comp.* —gebühr, *f.*, —geld, *n.* wharfage, pier-money.

Kai'man, *m.*, (—s, *pl.* —s) cayman, alligator.

Ka'ins=zeichen, *n.* mark of Cain.

Kai'ser, *m.* (—s, *pl.* —) emperor; (*in comp. gen'lly* =) imperial, emperor's; der deutsche —, the German Emperor, the Kaiser; — und Reich, Emperor and Empire; den — einen guten Mann sein lassen, to let matters take their course *or* remain as they are; über (*or* um) des —s Bart streiten, to quarrel about trifles; auf den alten — borgen, to contract debts without thinking of paying them; auf den alten — hinein leben, to lead a wild life; dem — geben was des —s ist, to render unto Cæsar the things which are Cæsar's (*B.*); wo nichts ist hat der — sein Recht verloren, where nought's to be got, kings lose their scot; you cannot get blood out of a stone (*prov.*). —in, *f.* empress; die —in und Königin, the Queen-Empress; die —in Wittwe, Mutter, the Empress Dowager. —lich, *adj. & adv.* imperial; die —lichen, the imperial troops; the Austrian troops (*in older German, especially in the 30 and in the 7 years' wars*); the Imperialists; (gut) —lich gesinnt, siding with the Emperor; on the side of the imperial party. —ling, *m.* (—lings, *pl.* —linge) would-be emperor; golden agaric; bird's eye (*Bot.*). —los, *adj.*; die —lose Zeit, time of Interregnum (*1150-73*); (*also 1806-71*), time of anarchy. —tum, *n.* (—tums, *pl.* —tümer) empire; imperial dignity; reign (*B.*); —tum von Gottes Gnaden, emperorship by divine right. *Comp.* —burg, *f.* imperial castle. —haus, *n.* imperial family *or* house. —krone, *f.* imperial crown; crown-imperial (*Bot.*). —manöver, *n.* grand military manœuvre of one or several army-corps at which the Emperor is present and in which he sometimes assumes command himself. —mantel, *m.* large (gentleman's) cloak, ulster; mother-of-pearl-butterfly; species of voluta. —papier, *n.* foolscap. —pracht, *f.* imperial state *or* splendour. —reich, *n.*, —staat, *m.* empire. —schlange, *f.* boa constrictor. —schnitt, *m.* Cæsarean section. —stadt, *f.* imperial town; —stadt an der Spree, (Donau,) Berlin, (Vienna). —wahl, *f.* election of an emperor (*in the old German empire*). —wetter, *n.* glorious weather. —wort, *n.* word *or* promise of an emperor; ein —wort soll man nicht drehn und deuteln, the word of an Emperor should not be turned and twisted (*prov.*). —würde, *f.* imperial dignity.

Kajü'te, *f.* (*pl.* —n) cabin; erste —, saloon.

Ka'kadu, *m.* (—s, *pl.* —s & —e) cockatoo.

Kaka'o, *m.* (—s) cocoa; cacao (*Med.*).

Ka'keln, *v.a.* to talk bosh, talk in a silly way (*dial.*).

Ka'kerlak, *m.* (—s, *pl.* —en) albino; cockroach.

Kako— (*short* a) (*in comp.*) —kratie', *f.* bad government. —phonie', *f.* cacophony. —phrasie', *f.* bad pronunciation.

Kak'tus, *m.* (— *or* —(ss)es, *pl.* — *or* —(ss)e) cactus, hedgehog-thistle.

Kalabas'se, *f.* (*pl.* —n) calabash.

Kalan'der, *m.* (—s) calendering machine.

Ka'lauer, *m.* pun (*coll.*). —n, *v.a.* to make puns (*coll.*).

Kalb, *n.* (—es, *pl.* Käl'ber) calf; fawn; tomfool, blockhead; bolster (*Naut.*); transom (*of a gun-carriage*); ein — abbinden, to wean a calf; das — ins Auge schlagen, to tread on some one's toes (*fig.*); das goldene — anbeten, to worship the golden calf; mit fremdem —e pflügen, to plough with another person's heifer (*B.*), to profit by another's work *or* invention, to plagiarize. —e, *f.* (*pl.* —en) heifer; (*pl.*) the chocks (*Naut.*). —en, *v.n.* (*aux.* h.) to calve. —ern, to behave in a silly way, to be wanton *or* frolicsome, to dally, romp. *Comp.* —fell, *n.* calf's skin; drum. —fleisch, *n.* veal. —fleisch=pastete, *f.* veal-pie. —leder, *n.* calf (*leather*); in —leder gebunden, bound in calf. —s=braten, *m.* roast veal. —s=bröschen, *n.*, —s=drüse, —s=milch, *f.* calf's sweetbread. —s=hirn, *n.* calf's brains. —s=kotelett, *n.* veal cutlet. —s=keule, *f.*, —s=schlägel, *m.* leg of veal. —s=kopf, *m.* calf's head; blockhead. —s=nierenbraten, *m.* loin of veal. —s=pergament, *n.* vellum. —s=schnitten, *pl.* veal-cutlets. —s=ysopkraut, *n.* summer savory (*Bot.*).

Käl'ber, *pl. of* Kalb. —ei', *f.* (*pl.* —ei'en) foolish wantonness. —n, I. *v.n.* (*aux.* h.) to calve; to vomit; to be wanton *or* frolicsome. II. *adj.* of veal. *Comp.* —drüse, *f.* calf's sweetbread. —lab, *n.* rennet. —magen, *m.* rennet of a calf. —stoß, *m.* leg of veal. —zahn, *m.* calf's tooth; dentil (*Arch.*).

Kalcinie'r—en, *v.a.* to calcine. —ung, *f.* calcination.

Kaldau'nen, *f.pl.* intestines, tripe.

Kalefak'tor, *m.* (—s, *pl.* Kalefakto'ren) fire-maker, furnace-man.

Kaleidosko'p, *n.* (—s, *pl.* —e) kaleidoscope.

Kalekut'tischer Hahn, *m.* turkey-cock.

Kalen'der, *m.* (—s, *pl.* —) calendar, almanac; das steht nicht in meinem —, that is nothing to me, I know nothing of that. *Comp.* —rechnung, *f.* style; Russische —rechnung, old style.

Kale'sche, *f.* (*pl.* —n) light carriage; calash (*obs.*).

Kalfak'ter, *m. see* Kalefaktor. —n, *v.* I. *a.* to inform against, accuse, denounce. II. *n.* (*aux.* h.) to be a toady, fawn on.

Kalfa'ter—n, *v.n.* (*aux.* h.) to calk, repair (*a ship*). —(er), *m.* (—(er)s, *pl.* —(er)) calker.
Ka'li, *n.* (—s) potash, potassium; ätzendes —, caustic potash; blausaures —, cyanide of potassium; chlorsaures —, chlorate of potassium. *Comp.* —bicarbonat, *n.* bicarbonate of potash. —hydrat, *n.* potassium hydrate. —lauge, *f.* potash-lye. —nitrat, *n.* saltpetre. —pflanze, *f.* glasswort, alkaline plant. —salpeter, *n.* nitre.
Kali'ber, *n.* (—s, *pl.* —) calibre, bore of a gun; kind, quality, power (*of intellect, etc.*); diameter. *Comp.* —mäßig, *adj.* true to gauge. —zirkel, *m.* callipers.
Kalibrie'ren, *v.a.* to take the size, to gauge.
Kali'f, *m.* (—en, *pl.* —en) caliph, khalifa. —a't, *n.* (—es, *pl.* —e) caliphate.
Kalk, *m.* (—(e)s, *pl.* —e) lime; ungelöschter —, quicklime; gelöschter —, slaked lime; kohlensaurer —, carbonate of lime; verwitterter —, lime slaked in the air; zu — brennen, to calcine lime; mit — bewerfen, to rough-cast; mit — beweißen, to whitewash, to plaster. —en, *v.a.* to mix, dress or cover with lime. —icht, *adj.* & *adv.* limelike (*obs.*). —ie'ren, *v.a.* to copy by rubbing with chalk and tracing. —ig, *adj.* & *adv.* chalky. *Comp.* —ablagerungen, *pl.* calcareous deposits. —anwurf, *m.* plaster, parget of lime. —artig, *adj.* calcareous. —boden, *m.* calcareous soil. —brennen, *n.* lime-burning. —brennerei, *f.* lime-kiln. —bruch, *m.* limestone quarry. —brühe, *f.* lime-water. —erde, *f.* calcareous earth. —fels, *m.* limestone, calcareous rock. —gebirge, *n.* calcareous mountain-chain, calcareous formation. —hütte, *f.* lime-kiln. —kelle, *f.* trowel. —licht, *n.* lime-light. —malerei, *f.* fresco-painting. —milch, *f.* lime-water. —mulde, *f.* mortar-trough. —ofen, *m.* lime-kiln. —stein, *m.* limestone. —wand, *f.* plaster-wall.
Kal'kul, *m.* (—s, *pl.* —e) calculation. —ie'ren, *v.a.* to calculate.
Kalligra'ph, *m.* (—en, *pl.* —en) calligraphist. —ie', *f.* calligraphy.
Kal'mäuser, *m.* (—s, *pl.* —) misanthrope; anchoret; dotard; miser. —ei', *f.* misanthropy; affectation of piety; niggardliness. —n, *v.n.* (*aux.* h.) to live a retired life; to muse; to dote, to be niggardly.
Kal'mus, *m.* (—) calamus.
Ka'lomel, *n.* (—s) mercurious chloride, calomel.
Kalo'ri—e, *f.* (*pl.* —en) caloric unit, heat unit, calory. —me'ter, *m.* (& *n.*) calorimeter. —metrie', *f.* measurement of heat.
Kalot'te, *f.* priest's skull-cap; the clergy.
Kalt, *adj.* & *adv.* (käl'ter, käl'test) cold, chill; frigid, gelid; indifferent; passionless; reserved; calm; dull, senseless: —e Zone, frigid zone; —es Fieber, ague; —er Schl[ag], flash of lightning that strikes but does not set on fire; —er Brand, gangrene; — keilen, to quarry without blasting; —e Schale, *see* Kaltschale; mir ist —, I am cold; einen — machen, to kill a p. (*vulg.*); einen — stellen, to dispose of a p., to make a p. innocuous, to render a p. incapable of interfering (*coll.*); — bleiben, to keep cool, keep one's temper; —e Angst, chill of terror. *Comp.* —blütig, *adj.* calm, composed; cold-blooded; deliberate. —blütigkeit, *f.* cold-bloodedness; composure. —brüchig, *adj.* brittle from cold; cold short. —grundig, —gründig, *adj.* cold (*of land*). —guß, *m.* casting with interruption. —scha'le, *f.* cup; *e.g.* Wein—schale, claret cup. —schmied, *m.* brazier. —sinn, *m.* coldness; indifference, insensibility. —sinnig, *adj.* cold; indifferent. —wasser=heilanstalt, *f.* hydropathic establishment. —was'ser=kur, *f.* cold-water treatment, hydropath[y].

Käl'te, *f.* cold, coldness, chilliness; frigidity; indifference; vor — zittern, to shiver with cold; die — läßt nach, the cold is breaking up. —n, *v.a.* to make cold, to cool; mit Eis —n, to ice. *Comp.* —erzeugend, *adj.* frigorific. —erzeugungs=maschine, *f.* freezing apparatus, ice-machine. —grad, *m.* degree of cold. —mischung, *f.* freezing mixture.
Kam, Ka'mest; Kä'me, 1 (& 3), 2 *p. sing. imperf. indic.*; 1 (& 3), *sing. imperf. subj. of* kommen.
Kamaril'la, *f.* court-party (*Pol.*).
Kama'sche, *see* Gamasche.
Kamee', Kame'o, *m.* (—s, *pl.* Kame'en) cameo.
Kame'l, *n.* (—s, *pl.* —e) camel; blockhead, stupid fellow (*coll.*); Mücken zu —en machen, to make mountains of mole-hills. *Comp.* —abteilung, *f.* camel corps. —bock, *m.* Indian antelope. —führer, —treiber, *m.* camel-driver. —garn, *n.* mohair. —haar, *n.* camel's hair. —hären, *adj.* camel-hair. —hengst, *m.* male camel. —kuh, —stute, *f.* female camel.
Kame'lie, *f.* (*pl.* —n) camellia.
Kamelopa'rd, *m.* (—en, *pl.* —en) camelopard.
Kamelo'tt, *m.* (—(e)s) camelot; camel's hair stuff; camlet.
Kamera'd, *m.* (—en, *pl.* —en) comrade, mate, companion, fellow; chum (*fam.*). —lich, *adj.* & *adv.* comrade-like, companionable. —schaft, *f.* comradeship, fellowship. —schaftlich, *see* —lich.
Kamera'l, *adj.* & *adv.* financial. —ia, —ien, *pl.* science of finance. —i'st, *m.* (—i'sten, *pl.* —i'sten) student *or* teacher of the science of finance; financier. *Comp.* —sache, *f.* matter of finance. —wesen, *n.* finances. —wissenschaft, *f. see* —ia.
Kamil'le, *f.* (*pl.* —n) camomile.
Kami'n, *m.* (& *n.*) (—s, *pl.* —e) chimney; fire-place, fireside. *Comp.* —aufsatz, *m.* overmantel, upper part of a fireplace, chimney-ornament. —besen, *m.* hearth-brush. —ecke, *f.*, —winkel, *m.* chimney-corner. —feger, *m.* (chimney) sweep. —feuer, *n.* fire in an open fireplace; open fire; open fireplace. —gerät, *n.* fire irons. —gesims, *n.*, —sims, *m.* mantel-piece. —gestell, *n.* fire-dogs. —gitter, *n.* fender; fire-guard. —haken, *m.* chimney-hook. —klappe, *f.* chimney valve *or* trap; damper. —platte, *f.* the back of a chimney. —röhre, *f.* the flue of a chimney. —rost, *m.* grate. —schirm, *m.* fire-screen. —teppich, *m.* hearth-rug. —vorsetzer, *m.* fender.
Kamiso'l, *n.* (—s, *pl.* —e, Kamisö'ler) waistcoat; jacket, short dressing-gown; doublet.
Kamm, *m.* (—es, *pl.* Käm'me) comb; carding-machine; ridge (*of hills*); bit (*of a key*); edge, rim (*of casks*); button (*of a violin*); cog-tooth (*of a wheel*); beard (*of an oyster*); mane (*of a horse*); upper part of the neck (*of oxen*); tuft; crest (*of birds; of a helmet; of a rampart*); comb (*of a cock*); weaver's reed; stalk (*of grapes*); dovetailed wood; trappings; enger —, small-tooth comb; der — schwillt ihm, he bristles up; he gives himself airs, grows arrogant; he is beginning to assert himself; den — aufsetzen, to carry a high head; alle über einen — scheren, to treat *or* judge all alike; man muß nicht alles über einen — scheren, all feet tread not in one shoe (*prov.*). *Comp.* —artig, *adj.* pectinate. —balken, —baum, *m.* cog-beam. —bürste, *f.* comb-cleaning brush. —flossen, *pl.* pectinals. —flosser, *m.* pectinal (*Icht.*). —förmig, *adj.* comb-like; —förmiger Staubbeutel, anther (*Bot.*). —garn, *n.* combed wool-yarn, worsted (yarn). —garn=stoffe, *pl.m.* fine fabrics made of worsted yarn. —haar, *n.* mane. —macherei, *f.* comb-making. —maschine, *f.* comb-cutting machine; carding

machine. **—muschel,** *f.* scallop. **—rad,** *n.* cog-wheel. **—stück,** *n.* neck-piece (*of beef, etc.*). **—wellen,** *pl.* white caps *or* horses. **—wolle,** *f.* carded, worsted *or* long wool. **—wollen=ware,** *f.* worsted goods. **—zahn,** *m.* tooth of a comb; tooth *or* cog of a wheel; species of bat.

Käm'mel—n, *v. a.* to card (*wool*). **—ung,** *f.* wool-carding.

Käm'm—en, *v.a.* to comb; to gear; to card; to dovetail, to splice; **sich —en,** to comb one's hair. **—er,** *m.* (**—ers,** *pl.* **—er**) comber, carder. **—erei',** *f.* wool-combing. **—(er)ling,** *m.* waste wool. **—ung,** *f.* combing.

Kam'mer, *f.* (*pl.* **—n**) small room; bedroom; room; chamber (*of a gun, mine, etc.*); cavity, hollow; ventricle (*of the heart*); chamber (*of deputies, etc.*); board, office, chamber; board of finances, exchequer; district; shooting-ground; **die dunkele —,** camera obscura; **die erste —,** the Upper House, House of Lords; **die zweite —,** Lower House, House of Commons. *Comp.* **—amt,** *n.* office of the exchequer. **—anwalt, —advokat,** *m.* chamber counsel. **—archiv,** *n.* the rolls. **—band,** *n.* fillets (*Artil.*). **—beamte(r),** *m.* clerk to the exchequer *or* board of finance. **—bediente(r),** *m.* valet-de-chambre; official of the exchequer. **—dame,** *f.* lady of the bedchamber. **—degen,** *m.* dress-sword (*worn at court*). **—diener,** *m.* valet; (**des Königs**) groom of the chambers. **—direktor,** *m.* director of the board of finances *or* domains. **—frau,** *f.* waiting woman. **—fräulein,** *n.* maid of honour. **—gefälle,** *pl.* revenues of a prince's domains *or* of the exchequer. **—gericht,** *n.* supreme court of judicature; court of appeal; exchequer. **—gut,** *n.* crown land; public revenue. **—herr,** *m.* chamberlain; gentleman of the bed-chamber. **—herrn=schlüssel,** *m.* gold key of a chamberlain. **—jäger,** *m.* prince's huntsman; rat-killer. **—jungfer,** *f.* chambermaid, lady's maid. **—kätzchen,** *n.* chambermaid (*coll.*). **—kapelle,** *f.* private chapel; prince's private singers and band. **—knabe,** *m.* page. **—kollegium,** *n.* board of revenues, board of finance. **—konsulent,** *m.* chamber-counsel. **—konzert,** *n.* concert given in a prince's rooms; concert without orchestra. **—lehen,** *n.* fief of the crown; fief of the exchequer. **—musik,** *f.* chamber music; musicians of a prince's chapel or band. **—musiker,** *m.* chamber musician, musician of the chapel. **—präsident,** *m.* chancellor of the exchequer; president of the chamber of deputies; speaker (*of the House of Commons*). **—pächter,** *m.* farmer, holder of crown lands. **—prokurator,** *m.* attorney to the exchequer. **—rat,** *m.* member of the board of finance, counsellor of the exchequer; chamber counsel. **—richter,** *m.* (*anal. to*) baron of the exchequer; president. **—sänger,** *m.*, **—sängerin,** *f.* private singer to a prince. **—säule,** *f.* cellular voltaic pile (*Physics*). **—schlüssel,** *m.* chamber-key; chamberlain's key; forelock (*of guns, Naut.*). **—schreiber,** *m.* clerk to the exchequer. **—thürsteher,** *m.* gentleman-usher. **—verhandlungen,** *pl.* debates in the chamber. **—wesen,** *n.* finance. **—wissenschaft,** *f.* science of finance, cameralia. **—zahlmeister,** *m.* keeper of the privy purse. **—zofe,** *see* **—jungfer.**

Käm'mer—chen (**—chens,** *pl.* **—chen**), **—lein,** *n.* (**—leins,** *pl.* **—lein**) closet, small chamber. **—ei',** *f.* chamberlain's office; clerks of the treasury; exchequer; board of domains *or* finances. **—er,** *m.* (**—ers,** *pl.* **—er**) chamberlain; treasurer. *Comp.* **—chen=spiel,** *n.* prison-bars.

Kam'mer—tuch, *n.* (**—tuches,** *pl.* **—tücher**) cambric.

Kampan'je, *f.* poop (*Naut.*). *Comp.* **—flagge,** *f.* national flag.

Käm'pe, (**—n,** *pl.* **—n**) champion.

Kampe'sche=holz, *n.* Campeachy wood, logwood.

Kampf, *m.* (**—es,** *pl.* **Käm'pfe**) combat, fight, contest; struggle, effort; **— ums Dasein,** struggle for life; **— bis aufs Messer,** war to the knife; **wo der — am heißesten tobt,** the thick of the fight *or* battle; **— der Anschauungen,** conflict of opinions. *Comp.* **—begier(de),** *f.* eager desire for combat, pugnacity. **—begierig,** *adj.* eager for combat. **—erprobt,** *adj.* veteran, tried in battle. **—fähig,** *adj.* effective (*Mil.*); **ein Schiff —fähig machen,** to clear a ship for action. **—fertig,** *adj.* ready for action, for combat. **—gefährte, —genoß,** *m.* companion in arms, fellow-combatant. **—geschrei,** *n.* war-cry, battle-cry. **—gier,** *see* **—begier.** **—hahn,** *m.* game cock, fighting cock; (*fig.*) wrangling disputant. **—kunst,** *f.* pugilism. **—lust,** *see* **—begier.** **—ordnung,** *f.* order of battle. **—platz,** *m.* place of combat, field of battle; arena; lists; cockpit; **den —platz betreten,** to enter the lists. **—preis,** *m.* prize. **—richter,** *m.* umpire. **—spiel,** *n.* tilting, tournament; prize-fighting; gymnastic game. **—übung,** *f.* gymnastic exercise; tilting practice; drilling (*Mil.*). **—unfähig,** *adj.* disabled. **—versucht,** *adj. see* **—erprobt.**

Käm'pf—en, *v.* I. *n.* (*aux.* **h.**) to fight, to combat; to strive, struggle; **um eine S. —en,** to fight for (*or* in order to obtain *or* keep) a thing; **für eine S. —en,** to fight for (*or* in order to protect) a thing. II. *a.* to fight (*a battle*). **—er,** *m.* (**—ers,** *pl.* **—er**) combatant, fighter; champion; prize-fighter, pugilist; impost, coussinet (*Arch.*).

Kam'pfer, Kam'pher, *m.* (**—s**) camphor. **—n,** *v.a.* to camphorate. *Comp.* **—milch,** *f.* camphorated emulsion. **—sauer,** *adj.* camphorated.

Kampie'ren, *v.a.* to camp, to be encamped; **unter freiem Himmel —,** to camp out.

Kana'l, *m.* (**—s,** *pl.* **Kanä'le**) canal (*artificial*); channel (*natural*); pipe, drain, sewer; cutting; **über den — hinüber,** across channel. *Comp.* **—arbeiter,** *m.* navvy, banker. **—brücke,** *f.* drawbridge; aqueduct. **—schifffahrt,** *f.* canal navigation. **—schloß,** *n.* canal-lock.

Ka'nape(e), *n.* (**—s,** *pl.* **—s**) sofa, settee.

Kana'rien—, (*in comp.* =) canary. **—bastard,** *m.* mule canary. **—hahn,** *m.* cock canary. **—hecke,** *f.* aviary, inclosure for canaries. **—vogel,** *m.* canary-bird. **—weibchen,** *n.* hen canary.

Kana'ster, Kna'ster, *m.* (**—s**) canister-tobacco.

Kanda're, *f.* (*pl.* **—n**) curb-bit (*of a bridle*). **—n,** *v.a.* to put on the curb *or* bridle-bit.

Kandela'ber, *m.* (**—s,** *pl.* **—**) candelabrum, chandelier; **Straßen —,** street lamp.

Kan'delzucker, Kan'diszucker, *m.* sugar-candy.

Kandid—a't, Candid—a't, *m.* (**—aten,** *pl.* **—aten**) *abbr.* **Kand., Cand.,** candidate; probationer; divinity student reading for holy orders **Cand. phil.** = **Kandidat der Philosophie,** student (of philosophy, history *or* languages) near his examination; **aufgestellter —,** nominee; **als —aten aufstellen,** to nominate; **als —at (für eine Stelle) auftreten,** to stand (for a post), to send in one's name (for a post), to come forward as a candidate, to become a candidate. **—ie'ren,** *v.a.* to stand (*for a post*).

Kandie'r—en, *v.a.* to candy. **—t,** *p.p.* & *adj.* candied.

Kanee'l, *m.* (**—s**) cinnamon.

Kän'guruh, *n.* (**—s,** *pl.* **—s**) kangaroo.

Kanin'chen, *n.* (**—s,** *pl.* **—**) rabbit, cony; **ein Satz —,** a nest of rabbits. *Comp.* **—bau,** *m.* rabbit-burrow. **—berg,** *m.*, **—gehäge,** *n.* rabbit-warren. **—höhle,** *f. see* **—bau.** **—kasten,** *m.* rabbit-hutch. **—wärter,** *m.* warrener.

Kan'ker, *m.* (**—s,** *pl.* **—**) spider; canker (*on trees*).

Kann, Kannst, *1 (& 3), 2 p. sing. pres. indic. of* **können.**

Kan'ne, *f.* (*pl.* **—n,** *dim.* **Känn'chen**) can, tankard, mug; jug; quart *or* pot (*liquid measure*); **in die — steigen,** to drink (*by order of the president at a students' feast*) (*stud. sl.*). *Comp.* **—n=bürste,** *f.* bottle-brush. **—n=deckel,** *m.* pot-lid. **—n=gießer,** *m.* pewterer; **politischer —n=gießer,** would-be politician (*title of a Danish comedy by Holberg*). **—n=gießerei,** *f.* political twaddle. **—(n)=gießern,** *v.* to talk in a silly and narrow-minded way about politics. **—n=weise,** *adv.* by quarts *or* pots. **—n=zinn,** *m.* pewter.

Kannelie'r—en, *v.a.* to chamfer, groove, flute, channel. **—t,** *adj.* fluted. **—ung,** *f.* channelling.

Kan'(n)evas, *m.* (—(s)ses, *pl.* —(s)se) canvas.

Kanniba'lisch, *adj.* cannibal, ferocious; enormous, extraordinary (*sl.*); **uns ist — wohl,** we feel awfully jolly (*sl.*); **—e Hitze,** tremendous heat (*sl.*).

Kann'te; Kann'test, *1 & 3; 2 p. sing. imperf. indic. of* **kennen.**

Ka'non, *m.* (—s, *pl.* —s) canon (*Mus., Eccl.*); **— der Schullektüre,** general agreement and authoritative syllabus of authors to be read in school. **—ika't,** *n.* (—ikates) prebend, canonry. **—ikus,** *m.* (*pron.* **Kano'nikus,** *pl.* **Kano'niker, Cano'nici**) prebendary, canon. **—isch,** *adj. & adv.* (*pron.* **Kano'nisch**) canonical; **—isches Ansehn,** canonicity. **—isie'ren,** *v.a.* to canonize. **—is'sin,** *f.* canoness, woman enjoying a prebend.

Kanon—a'de, *f.* cannonade. **—e,** *f.* (*pron.* **Kano'ne;** *pl.* **—en**) cannon, gun, piece of ordnance; tube (*of a watch or clock-key*); high boot; (*older stud. sl.*) jack-boot; **ein Paar —en,** a pair of riding boots (*sl.*); **die Traube der —e,** the button; **der Kopf der —e,** the muzzle; **der Stoß der —e,** the breech; **die Seele, der Lauf der —e,** the bore, calibre of a gun; **gezogene —e,** rifled gun; **die —en fest machen,** to house the guns; **eine —e auffahren,** to mount a gun; **eine —e abnehmen,** to dismount a gun; **eine —e richten,** to point a gun; **eine —e vernageln,** to spike a gun; **die —en einholen,** to haul the guns home, run in the guns; **unter aller —e,** beneath contempt, quite worthless (*sl.*). **—ie'r,** *m.* (—iers, *pl.* —iere) gunner. **—ie'ren,** *v.a. & n.* to cannonade. *Comp.* **—en=bereich,** *m.* cannon-range. **—en=boot,** *n.* gun-boat. **—en=donner,** *m.* boom, peal, roar, of cannon; cannonade. **—en=fest,** *adj.* cannon-proof. **—en=feuer,** *n.* artillery fire, cannonade. **—en=fieber,** *n.* dread of powder and shot; **das —enfieber haben,** to funk before a battle (*coll.*). **—en=futter,** *n.* food for powder. **—en=gebrüll,** *n.* roar of cannon. **—en=gut,** *n.* gun-metal. **—en=keller,** *m.* casemate. **—en=kugel,** *f.* cannon-ball. **—en=lauf,** *m.* barrel of a piece of ordnance. **—en=park,** *m.* park of artillery. **—en=schlag,** *m.* maroon. **—en=schuß,** *m.* cannon shot, gunshot; **mit —enschüssen begrüßen,** to honour with a salute. **—en=schuß=weite,** *f.* cannonshot range. **—en=stiefel,** *pl.* jack-boots. **—en=wall,** *m.* battery. **—en=wischer,** *m.* sponge. **—ier'=kammer,** *f.* gun-room (*Naut.*).

Kanta'te, *f.* (*pl.* —n) cantata.

Kan't—e, *f.* (*pl.* —en) edge, sharp corner; brim; border; margin; ledge; list, border, selvage (*of cloth*); fine lace; **spitze —e,** corner; **scharfe —e,** edge; **flache —e,** face, side; **Geld auf die hohe —e legen,** to put money by, to save money; **es steht auf der —e,** it is rather shaky, is unsafe; **an allen —en** *or* **an allen Ecken und —en,** on all sides, everywhere; **mit —en besetzen,** to trim with lace. **—ig,** *adj. & adv.* edged, cornered, angular. *Comp.* **—en=brett,** *n.* shelf for pots, mugs, *etc.* **—en=kleid,** *n.* dress trimmed with lace. **—en=schienen,** *pl.* edge-rails (*Railw.*). **—en=tuch,** *n.* lace-bordered handkerchief. **—en=zwirn,** *m.* thread for lace.

[1]**Kan'ten,** *v.a.* to furnish with edges; to turn on edge, to tilt; to square (*a stone*); **nicht —!** this side up (*on boxes*).

[2]**Kan'ten,** *m.* top *or* bottom crust, first cut of a loaf.

Kanti'ne, *f.* (*pl.* —n) canteen.

Kanto'n, *m.* (—s, *pl.* —e) canton. **—ie'ren,** *v.n.* to be quartered, to be in cantonment. **—ie'rung,** *f.* cantonment. **—i'st,** *m.*; **ein unsicherer —ist,** a man that cannot be depended upon, an unreliable *or* shifty fellow (*sl.*).

Kan'tor, *m.* (—s, *pl.* **Kanto'ren**) precentor; leader of a church choir; organist; village schoolmaster. **—a't,** *n.* (—ates, *pl.* —ate) precentorship; precentor's, organist's, *or* schoolmaster's house. **—ei',** *f. see* **—at;** class of choristers.

Kan'zel, *f.* (*pl.* —n) pulpit; **sich von der — ablesen lassen,** to have one's banns (of marriage) published. **—ei',** *see* **Kanzlei.** **—i'st,** *m.* (—is'ten, *pl.* —is'ten) chancery-clerk. **—n,** *v.a. & n.* (*aux.* **h.**) to chide (*vulg.*). **—ie'ren,** *v.a.* to crossbar, to cross out, to cancel. *Comp.* **—deckel, —himmel,** *m.* canopy over a pulpit. **—lied,** *n.* hymn before the sermon. **—mäßig,** *adj.* suited to the pulpit. **—redner,** *m.* (eloquent) clergyman. **—vortrag,** *m.* sermon; elocution of a preacher.

Kanz—lei', *f.* (*pl.* **—leien**) chancery (*different from English chancery*), office, government-office; (*in some countries*) seal-office; personnel of the chancery; court of justice; **die —lei der auswärtigen Angelegenheiten,** foreign office. **—ler,** *m.* (—lers, *pl.* —ler) chancellor; **Reichs—ler,** Imperial Chancellor, Ch. of the Empire. *Comp.* **—lei=archiv,** *n.* the rolls, archives of chancery *or* of any public office. **—lei=beamte(r),** *m.* chancery clerk, government official. **—lei=dekret,** *n.* order in chancery. **—lei=deutsch,** *n.*, **—lei=sprache,** *f.* chancery language (*esp'lly important for the development of the German lit. lang. 14th–16th cent.*). **—lei=diener,** *m.* official *or* messenger of a government office, tip-staff. **—lei=gerichts=hof,** *m.* court of chancery. **—lei=mäßig,** *adj.* lawyer-fashion, in legal style. **—lei=papier,** *n.* foolscap paper. **—lei=personal,** *n.* staff (*of a public office*). **—lei=schreiben,** *n.* writ of chancery. **—lei=schrift,** *f.* engrossing-hand. **—lei=siegel,** *n.* seal of chancery. **—ler=stelle, —ler=würde,** *f.* chancellorship.

Kanzo'ne, *f.* (*pl.* —n) canzonet (*Mus.*).

Kaoli'n, *n.*, (—s) china clay, porcelain clay.

Kap, *n.* (—s, *pl.* —s) cape (*Geog.*).

Kapau'n, *m.* (—s, *pl.* —e) capon; eunuch. **—en,** *v.a.* to castrate.

Kapazitä't, *f.* (*pl.* —en) capacity; authority; **Professor Z. war eine — ersten Ranges auf dem Gebiete der englischen Sprachwissenschaft,** Professor Z. was one of the first authorities in the field of English philology.

Kapella'n, *see* **Kaplan.**

Kapel'l—e, *f.* (*pl.* —en) chapel; private band *or* choir. *Comp.* **—direktor, —meister,** *m.* bandmaster, conductor of a choir *or* orchestra.

[1]**Ka'per,** *m.* (—s, *pl.* —) captor, taker of a ship; freebooter, corsair, pirate; privateer. **—ei',** *f.* (*pl.* —eien) privateering. **—n,** *v.* I. *n.* (*aux.* **h.**) to cruise as a privateer. II. *a.* to capture, to catch. *Comp.* **—brief,** *m.* letter of marque (and reprisal). **—schiff,** *n.* privateer, corsair, pirate-ship.

[2]**Ka'per,** *f.* (*pl.* —n) caper (*Bot.*).

Kapilla'r, *adj.* capillary. **—itä't,** *f.* capillary attraction. *Comp.* **—gefäß,** *n.* capillary (vessel).

Kapita'l, I. *n.* (—s, *pl.*—ien) capital, principal, stock; **das eingeschossene —,** the deposit; **das imaginäre —,** floating capital; **das tote —,** unemployed capital; **— und Zinsen,** principal and interest. II. *n.* (*pl.* **Kapitä'ler**) capital (*Arch.*). III. *adj.* capital. **—isie'ren,** *v.a.* to convert into capital. **—i'st,** *m.* (—is'ten, *pl.* —is'ten) capitalist; stockholder. *Comp.* **—konto,** *n.*, **—rechnung,** *f.* stock-account. **—kräftig,** *adj.* well provided with capital, wealthy, substantial. **—steuer,** *f.* property tax. **—verbrechen,** *n.* capital crime. **—wirtschaft,** *f.* management of capital.

Kapitäl'chen=schrift, *f.* small capitals (*Typ.*)

Kapitä'n, *m.* (—s, *pl.* —e) captain (*of a ship*). *Comp.*—**s=posten,** *m.*,—**s=stelle,** *f.* captaincy, captainship.

Kapi'tel, *n.* (—s, *pl.*—) head, chapter; chapter (*Eccl.*); topic; **einem ein — lesen,** to read s. o. a lecture; **ein — halten,** to hold a chapter, to convene the canons. **—n,** *v.a.* to divide into chapters; to lecture, to reprimand. *Comp.* **—fest,** *adj.* well-versed (*in scripture*). **—haus,** *n.* chapter house. **—weise,** *adv.* by chapters.

Kapitul—atio'n, *f.* capitulation; (re)enlistment; **meine —ation lautet auf 6 Jahre,** I am enlisted for 6 years. **—ie'ren,** *v.n.* (*aux.* **h.**) to capitulate; to (re-)enlist.

Kapla'n, *m.* (—(e)s, *pl.* **Kaplä'ne**) chaplain. *Comp.* **—stelle,** *f.* chaplaincy.

Kapo'res, *adj.* spoilt, broken (*sl.*). *See* **Kaput.**

Käp'p—chen, *n.* (—chens, *pl.* —chen) little cap; cowl. **—i,** *n.* (—is, *pl.* —is) military cap.

Kap'p—e, *f.* (*pl.* —en) cap; hood; cowl, capuchin; hooded mantle, cape; upper part *of various things, as* ridge, coping, top, dome, toe-piece, *etc.*; bonnet (*Fort.*); cap (*of a gun*); heelplate; caplike cover; cowl, cloak of invisibility, sheath (*Bot.*); **Tarn —e,** hiding cape (*obs.*); **jedem Narren gefällt seine —e,** every one has his hobby; **etwas auf seine eigne —e nehmen,** to make oneself responsible for a th.; to answer for a th. (*coll.*); **gleiche Brüder gleiche —en,** birds of a feather flock together (*prov.*). *Comp.*—**en=förmig,** *adj.* hood-shaped, cowled. **—en=macher,** *m.* cap maker. **—en=mantel,** *m.* cloak with cape *or* hood. **—en=stiefel(n),** *pl.* top-boots. **—fenster,** *n.* dormer-window. **—kragen,** *m.* cowl, hood. **—naht,** *f.* hem; flat-seam. **—zaum,** *m.* cavesson; curb, restraint.

Kap'p—en, *v.a.* to provide with a hood; to piece; to chop; to lop, top; to castrate. **—er,** *m.* (—ers, *pl.* —er) lopper; one who cuts up the whale (*on board whalers*). *Comp.* **—hahn,** *m.* capon. **—messer,** *n.* cleaver.

Kapriciö's, *adj.* & *adv.* capricious.

Kaprio'le, *f.* (*pl.* —n) caper.

Kap'sel, *f.* (*pl.* —n) cover, case; box; capsule; cap (*of fire-arms*). **—ig,** *adj.* capsular. **—n,** *v.a.* to inclose in a case *or* capsule. *Comp.* **—artig,** *adj.* resembling a case *or* cover; capsular. **—band,** *n.* capsular ligament (*Anat.*). **—tragend,** *adj.* capsular.

Kapu't, *adj.* done; lost; spoilt, broken; **— gehen,** to get broken, to come to pieces (*coll.*).

Kapu'z—e, *f.* (*pl.* —en) cowl; cape, hood. **—i'ner,** *m.* (—iners, *pl.* —iner) capuchin monk. *Comp.* **—kresse,** *f.* tropæolum. **—predigt,** *f.* capuchin's sermon (*the funny address of the capuchin in "Wallenstein's Lager"*).

Kar— (*in comp.; older spelling* **Char—**, *originally meaning 'sorrow,' 'care'*) **—freitag,** *m.* Good Friday. **—woche,** *f.* week before Easter, Passion week.

Karabi'n—er, *m.* (—ers, *pl.* —er) carbine, rifle. **—ie'r,** *m.* (—iers, *pl.* —iere) carbineer.

Karaf'fe, Karaffi'ne, *f.* (*pl.* —n) carafe, decanter, glass water-bottle.

Kara'kter, *m.*; *see* **Charakter.**

Karambol—a'ge, *f.* (*pl.* —n) cannon (*Bill.*). **—ie'ren,** *v.n.* to cannon, to collide.

Kara't, *n.* (—(e)s, *pl.* —e) carat. **—ig,** *adj.* (*in comp.* =) containing so many carats. **—ie'ren,** *v.a.* to alloy. *Comp.* **—gewicht,** *n.* troy-weight.

Karau'sche, *f.* (*pl.* —en) crucian (*Icht.*).

Karava'nen=thee, *m.* caravan-borne tea.

Karawa'n—e, *f.* (*pl.* —en) caravan. **—serei',** *f.* (*pl.* —sereien) inn for caravans, caravanserai.

Karbat'sche, *f.* (*pl.* —n) leather scourge. **—n,** *v.a.* to whip, to flog soundly.

Karbol'säure, *f.* carbolic acid.

Karbona'de, *f.* (*pl.* —n) chop, cutlet.

Karbon'säure, *f.* carbonic acid.

Karbun'kel, *m.*(—s, *pl.*—) car(b)uncle; furuncle.

Kär'cher, *m.* (—s, *pl.* —) carter (*dial.*).

Kardät'sche, *f.* (*pl.* —n) carding-comb; curry-comb. **—n,** *v.a.* to card wool; to curry. **—r,** *m.* carder; one who curries (*a horse*).

Kar'de, *f.* (*pl.* —n) card, carding instrument. **—n,** *v.a.* to card, to comb wool.

Kardee'l, *n.* (—s, pl. —e) strand of a cable.

Kardina'l, I. *m.* (—s, *pl.* **Kardinä'le**) cardinal; a special cup of hock, lemon, and sugar. II. *adj.* cardinal. **—a't,** *n.* cardinalate. *Comp.* **—käfer,** *m.* glowworm. **—tugenden,** *pl.* cardinal virtues. **—würde,** *f. see* **—at. —zahlen,** *pl.* cardinal numbers.

Kardu'se, *f.* (*pl.* —n) cartridge, cartouche.

Karei'en, *v.a.* to singe, to dress (*woollen stuff*).

Kare'nz(zeit), *f.* time during which a man who has been employed at some manufactory is pledged not to enter any rival establishment in the district.

Karessie'ren, *v.a.* to caress, to fondle, to hug.

Karfun'kel, *m.* (—s, *pl.* —) carbuncle (*gem*). **—n,** *v.n.* (*aux.* **h.**) to sparkle like a carbuncle.

Karg, *adj.* & *adv.* (**kär'ger, kär'g(e)st**), miserly, niggardly, stingy; scanty; sterile (*soil*); **eine —e Antwort,** a short answer. **—heit,** *f.* parsimony, stinginess; poverty (*of soil*); scantiness.

Kar'ge—n, *v.n.* (*aux.* **h.**) to be stingy *or* penurious; **mit etwas —n,** to be sparing of; **ein anderer —t, da er nicht soll,** another withholdeth more than is meet. **—r,** *m.* (—rs, *pl* —r) miser; penurious person.

Kärg'lich, *adj.* & *adv.* somewhat penurious; scanty, poor; **—e Kost,** short commons, poor food. **—keit,** *f.* penuriousness, scantiness.

Karie'ren, *v.n.* (*aux.* **h.**) to suffer a want of anything; to fast (*as a school punishment*).

Karikatu'r, *see* **Karrikatur.**

Kario'l, *n.* (—s, *pl.* —e), **—e,** *f.* (*pl.* —en) gig.

Karkas'se, *f.* (*pl.* —n) carcass.

Karmeli'ter, *m.* (—s, *pl.* —) & *adj.* Carmelite. **—in,** *f.* Carmelite nun.

Karmesi'n, *adj.* crimson.

Karmi'n, *m.* (—s) carmine.

Karneo'l, Karnio'l, *m.* (—s, *pl.* —e) cornelian.

Kar'neval, *m.* (& *obs. n.*) (—s, *pl.* —s & —e) carnival.

Karni'ckel, *n.* little rabbit (*coll.*); **das — hat angefangen,** the kettle began it (*coll.*); **er ist ein —,** he is an artful dodger *or* a sly rogue.

Karnie's, *n.*(—(s)es, *pl.*—(s)e) cornice, moulding.

Ka'ro, *n.* (—s, *pl.* —s) square; diamonds (*cards*).

Karos'se, *f.* (*pl.* —n) state coach.

Karot'te, *f.* (*pl.* —n) carrot; roll *or* stalk tobacco

Kar'pfen, *m.* (—s, *pl.* —) carp.

Karpoli'then, *pl.* carpolites, petrified fruits.

Kar'r—e, *f.* (*pl.* —en) cart, wheelbarrow, barrow; **zur** *or* **in die —e verurteilen,** to condemn to hard labour.

Kar'ren, I. *m.* (—s, *pl.* —) vehicle with one *or* two wheels; car; dray; *see* **Karre**; carriage (*Typ.*); **den — gründlich fest** *or* **in den Kot fahren,** to come to a deadlock in s. th., to get stuck in the mud (*fig.*); **an demselben — ziehen,** to row in the same boat. II. *v.a.* to carry transport in a cart, to cart. III. *v.n.* (*aux.* h.) to drive a cart; to wheel a barrow. *Comp.* —baum, *m.* shaft of a cart. —führer, *m.* drayman, carter. —gabel, *f.* cart-shafts. —gaul, *m.* cart-horse. —schieber, *m.* worker with a wheelbarrow.

Karre'te, *f.* old lumbering carriage, rickety and bumpy carriage (*sl.*).

Kar(r)ik—atu'r, *f.* (*pl.* —aturen) caricature. —aturi'st, *m.* (—aturi'sten, *pl.* —aturi'sten) caricaturist. —ie'ren, *v.a.* to caricature.

Karrio'le, *f.* (*pl.* —n) gig.

Kar(r)io'len, *v.n.* to move along quickly, to drive (*sl.*).

Kärr'ner, *m.* (—s, *pl.* —) carter; drayman.

Karst, *m.* (—es, *pl.* —e) mattock, two-pronged fork. —en, *v.a.* to hoe, work with a mattock.

Kartät'sche, *f.* (*pl.* —n) canister-shot; case-shot; grape-shot. *Comp.* —n=büchse, *f.* canister filled with case-shot. —n=feuer, *n.* fire of grape-shot. —n=granaten, *pl.* shrapnel-shells. —n=kugel, *f.* ball in a cartouche. —n=schuß, *m.* case-shot.

Kartau'ne, *f.* (*pl.* —n) cannon-royal; halbe —, demi-cannon.

Kart—au'se, *f.*, *older* **Karth—au'se,** (*pl.* —ausen), Carthusian convent *or* monastery. —äu'ser, *m.* (—äusers, *pl.* —äuser) Carthusian friar. —au'sisch, *adj.* Carthusian. *Comp.* —äu'ser=likör, *m.* Chartreuse.

Kar'te, *f.* (*pl.* —n) card, visiting *or* playing card; map, chart; paper of patterns, charter; calendar; bill, waybill; list, register; bill of fare; programme; certificate (*from a teacher*); die große —, Magna Charta; ein Spiel —n kaufen, to buy a pack of cards; ein Spiel —n spielen, to play a game of cards; —n schlagen, to tell fortunes by cards; einem in die —n sehen, to spy out, discover a p.'s designs; die —n durchschauen, to be in the secret, in the plot; aus einer — spielen, both to play the same game; eine angelegte —, a concerted plan; —n abheben, to cut (*cards*); an wem ist das —ngeben? whose turn is it to deal? *Comp.* —n=besuch, *m.* leaving (visiting) cards upon (*a person*). —n=blatt, *n.* a single card. —n=brief, *m.* letter-card. —n=etui, *n.* card-case. —n=folge, *f.* sequence; —nfolge von 5 —n, quint. —n=haus, *n.* house of cards; chimerical project. —n=kunde, *f.* familiarity with maps, map reading. —n=kunst, *f.*, —n=kunststück, *n.* card-trick. —n=künstler, *m.* one who plays tricks with cards. —n=papier, *n.* cardboard. —n=sammlung, *f.* collection of maps; atlas. —n=schläger, *m.*, —n=schlägerin, *f.* fortune-teller (*with cards*). —n=schlag, *m.* trick with cards; gambler's trick. —n=spiel, *n.* card-playing; game at cards; pack of cards. —n=stecher, *m.* engraver of maps and charts. —n=werk, *n.* atlas. —n=zeichner, *m.* designer of maps.

Karte'll, *n.* (—s, *pl.* —e) challenge (*to single combat*); cartel (*communication or agreement, between enemies in time of war*); im — stehen (mit einem), to be allies (with s.o.). *Comp.* —schiff, *n.* ship with flag of truce. —träger, *m.* second, bearer of a challenge (*for a duel*).

Kar'ten, *v.* I. *n.* (*aux.* h.) to play at cards. II. *a.* to concert, plot, contrive, bring about.

Kartof'fel, *f.* (*pl.* —n) potato; —n in der Schale *or* Pell—n, potatoes in their jackets; junge —, new potato; gebratene —, fried potato; gestampfte, gequetschte —, mashed potato; abgekochte —, boiled potato; —n legen, pflanzen, to plant potatoes. *Comp.* —bau, *m.* potato-culture. —kloß, *m.* potato-dumpling. —knollen, *m.* tuber. —krankheit, —pest, *f.* potato-rot. —kraut, *n.* potato-tops, stalks of potatoes. —mus, *n.* mashed potatoes.

Kartogra'phisch, *adj.*; —e Verlagsanstalt, publishing house for maps.

Kartomanti'e, *f.* art of fortune-telling by cards.

Karto'n, *m.* (—s, *pl.* —s) cardboard; cartoon; pasteboard box; portfolio; boards (*Bookb.*). —ie'ren, *v.a.* to bind in boards. —ie'rt, *p.p.* & *adj.* in boards.

Kartu'sche, *f.* (*pl.* —n) cartouche, cartridge.

Karusse'll, *n.* (—s, *pl.* —s *or* —e) roundabout, merry-go-round; carousel (*Amer.*).

Karyati'den, *pl.* Caryatides (*figures of women in long robes supporting entablatures*).

Kar'zer, *m.* & *n.* (—s, *pl.* —) lock up (*in schools*), students' prison; 4 Stunden —, four hours of detention *or* being kept in.

Ka'sch(e)mir, *m.* (—s) cashmere.

Kä'scher, *m.* (—s, *pl.* —) hoop-net; gauze-net. —n, *v.a.* to catch with a hoop-net; to catch.

Kä's—e, (*South German:* Käs,) *m.* (—es, *pl.* —e) cheese; curds; flower (*of cauliflower*); seed (*of poplars*); crown (*of artichokes*); Schweizer —e, Gruyère. —icht (*obs.*), —ig, *adj.* caseous, cheesy, pale (*of the complexion*) (*coll.*). *Comp.* —e=blättchen, *n.* local newspaper of no importance. —e=bohrer, *m.* cheese-scoop. —e=brett, *n.* cheese-stand. —e=butter, *f.* curds; cream-cheese. —e=form, *f.* cheese-mould. —e=händler, —e=krämer, *m.* cheese-monger. —e=horde, —e=hürde, *f.* crate on which cheeses are dried. —e=kammer, *f.* cheese-room, dairy. —e=laib, *m.* whole cheese. —e=made, —e=milbe, *f.* maggot. —e=messer, *n.* very large pocket knife (*sl.*); sword of a foot soldier (*sl.*). —e=stoff, *m.* caseine. —e=wasser, *n.* whey.

Ka'sel, *f.* (*pl.* —n) chasuble (*R. Cath.*).

Kasemat'te, *f.* (*pl.* —n) casemate.

Kä's—en, *v.* I. *a.* to turn into cheese. II. *r.* & *n.* (*aux.* h. & s.) to curdle. —erei', *f.* dairy where cheese is made.

Kaser'ne, *f.* (*pl.* —n) barracks. *Comp.* —n=arrest, *m.* detention in barracks. —n=hof=blüten, *pl.* Tommy Atkins' choice expressions sergeants' bulls.

Ka'simir, *m.* (—s) kersey, thin woollen cloth.

Kas'perle, *m.* Punch. *Comp.* —theater, *n.* Punch (and Judy) show.

Kas's—a, —e, *f.* (*pl.* —(e)n) money-chest; till; safe; pay-office; ticket-office, booking office (*at a theatre, railway, etc.*); office-counter (*in a bank*); ready money, cash; schlecht bei —e sein, to be hard up; gut bei —e sein, to be in cash; to be flush (of money) (*sl.*); —e machen, to make up the cash account; die —e führen, to keep the cash, to manage *or* look after the money matters, to act as cashier. —ie'r, (—iers, *pl.* —iere) —ie'rer, *m.* (—ierers, *pl.* —ierer) cashier, treasurer. —ie'ren, *v.a.* to collect in cash; *see below*. *Comp.* —a=depot, *n.* cash deposit. —en=anweisung, *f.* treasury bill; paper money. —en=beamter, *m.* revenue official *or* clerk. —en=bestand, —en=betrag, *m.* balance in hand. —en=betrug, *m.* embezzlement (*of public money*). —en=buch, —a=buch, *n.* cash-book. —en=dieb, *m.* embezzler. —en=führer, *m.* cashier. —en=gehülfe, *m.* teller. —en=schein, *m.* treasury note; bank-note. —en=schrank, *m.* fire-proof safe. —en=stück, *n.* play drawing full houses, stock piece. —en=sturz, *m.* audit. —en=tisch, *m.* counter. —en=übersicht, *f.* balance-sheet. —en=verwalter, —en=wart, *m.* treasurer.

Kassatio'n, *f.* cashiering, quashing; cashierment, military degradation. —s=urteil, *n.* reversal of judgment.

Kasserol'le, *f.* (*pl.* —n) stewpan.

Kas'si—a, *f.* cassia. *Comp.* —en=öl, *n.* oil of cassia.

Kassie'r—en, *v.a.* to cashier, dismiss; to annul;

to quash (*a judgment*); *see under* **Kassa**. —**ung**, *f.* quashing; cashiering; cassation.

Kassona'de, *f.* cask sugar.

Kasta'nie, *f.* (*pl.* —n) chestnut; **für andere die —n aus dem Feuer holen**, to be made a catspaw of (*prov.*). *Comp.* —**n=baum**, *m.* chestnut tree; **bitterer (wilder) —nbaum**, horse-chestnut tree. —**n=braun**, *adj.* chestnut (*brown*), maroon. —**n=gehölz**, *n.* chestnut grove.

Käst'chen, *n.* (—s, *pl.* —) *see* **Kasten**; little box, casket; trumpeter's shell; alveole (*Anat.*).

Kas'te, *f.* (*pl.* —n) caste; corporation. —**n=tum**, *n.* existence of castes. *Comp.* —**n=geist**, *m.* spirit of caste. —**n=mäßig**, *adj.* caste-like. —**n=wesen**, *n.* caste-system.

Kastei'—en, *v.a.* to chastise, chasten, mortify. —**ung**, *f.* chastisement, mortification (*of the flesh*), chastening; penance, castigation.

Kaste'll, *n.* (—(e)s, *pl.* —e) small fort *or* castle.

Kas'ten, *m.* (—s, *pl.* —) box, chest, coffer; press; hutch; boot (*of a coach*); setting (*of jewels, etc.*); case (*Typ.; of pianos, etc.*); body; frame (*of coaches, etc.*); cornloft (*B.*); chamber (*B.*); cupboard; bucket; wind-chest, sounding-board (*Org.*); caisson; fund, treasure, public fund; military prison (*sl.*); — **bekommen**, to be sent to the military prison (*sl.*); **der — Noahs**, Noah's ark; **Bau —**, box of bricks; **einem hinter den — gehen**, to steal a p.'s money; — **der Zähne**, socket-hole of teeth. *Comp.* —**herr**, —**pfleger**, —**meister**, —**vogt**, *m.* treasurer, vestry-man; overseer of a public granary. —**schloß**, *n.* box-lock. —**vogtei**, *f.* administration of ecclesiastical property.

Kas'tor, *m.* (—s, *pl.* —s) beaver, castor.

Kastr—a't, *m.* (—aten, *pl.* —aten) eunuch. —**ie'ren**, *v.a.* to castrate; —**ierte Bücher**, *pl.* expurgated texts *or* editions of books.

Kasua'lien, *pl.* casualties; incidental fees.

Ka'suar, *m.* (—s, *pl.* —e) cassowary.

Kasuis'tik, *f.* casuistry.

Ka'sus, *m.* (—, *pl.* —) case; condition.

Kat, I. *n.* cat, cat-ship (*Naut.*). II. *f.* cat-o'-nine-tails; **vor eine — legen**, to moor (*boats*).

Katafa'lk, *m.* (—s, *pl.* —e) tomb of state; catafalque.

Kata—kom'be, *f.* (*pl.* —**komben**) catacomb. —**lepsie'**, *f.* catalepsy. —**lo'g**, *m.* (—**logs**, *pl.* —**loge**) catalogue, list. —**logisie'ren**, *v.a.* to catalogue. —**ra'kt**, *m.* waterfall, cataract; cataract (of the eye). —**stro'phe**, *f.* catastrophe.

Kata'rrh, *m.* (—s, *pl.* —) catarrh, cold in the head. *Comp.* —**a'l=fieber**, *n.* rheumatic fever; influenza.

Katas'ter, *m.* & *n.* (—s, *pl.* —) land-register. *Comp.* —**amt**, *n.* land-registry office.

Katech—e't, *m.* (—eten, *pl.* —eten) catechist, lecturer. —**e'tik**, *f.* Socratic method; catechizing. —**e'tisch**, *adj.* & *adv.* catechetical. —**isie'ren**, *v.a.* to catechize. —**is'mus**, *m.* (*pl.* —**ismen**) catechism.

Kategor—ie', *f.* (*pl.* —**ieen**) category. —**isch**, (*pron.* **katego'risch**) *adj.* & *adv.* categorical; positive; **der —ische Imperativ**, the categorical imperative (of Kant).

Ka'ter, *m.* (—s, *pl.* —) tom-cat; indisposition after a (students') carouse (*sl.*); cold (*fam. for* **Katarrh**); **der gestiefelte —**, Puss in boots; **moralischer —**, displeasure with oneself, dejection, self-reproach. —**ig**, *adj.* (*or* **verkatert**) seedy, crapulous (*coll.*). *Comp.* —**frühstück**, *n.* late breakfast on stimulants after a great feast *or* ball. —**idee**, *f.* rum *or* foolish idea, absurdity, nonsense, bosh (*sl.*).

Kathar'tisch, *adj.* & *adv.* cathartic, purgative.

Kathe'd—er, *m.* & *n.* (—ers, *pl.* —er) professor's lecturing desk. —**ra'le**, *f.* (*pl.* —**ralen**) cathedral. *Comp.* —**er=blüte**, *f.* pulpit flower of rhetoric; professor's unintentional joke. —**er=held**, *m.* controversialist. —**er=sozialismus**, *m.* professional *or* academic socialism. —**er=sozialist**, *m.* socialist professor. —**er=weisheit**, *f.* professional wisdom; pedants' advice.

Kathe'ter, *m.* (—s, *pl.* —) catheter, bougie (*surg.*).

Kathol—i'k, *m.* (—iken, *pl.* —iken) (Roman) Catholic. —**isch** (*pron.* **katho'lisch**), *adj.* catholic; —**isch werden**, to turn (Roman) Catholic. —**izis'mus**, *m.* Roman Catholicism.

Kattu'n, *m.* (—s, *pl.* —e) cotton, calico; **ostindischer —**, chintz. —**en**, *adj.* made of calico *or* cotton. —**e'ts**, *pl.* checker, checked cottons. *Comp.* —**druckerei**, *f.* cotton-printing, calico-printing. —**fabrik**, *f.* manufactory of calico. —**leinwand**, *f.* union, linen with a cotton weft. —**papier**, *n.* chintz paper. —**wolle**, *f.* cotton.

Kätz'chen, *n.* (—s, *pl.* —) kitten; catkin (*Bot.*).

Katz—e, *f.* (*pl.* —en) cat, puss, she-cat; species of cowry (*Mollusc.*); cavalier (*Fort.*); battering-ram; skin pouch *or* moneybag; pulmonary complaint (*of miners*); catkin (*Bot.*); hook; **die —e miaut**, the cat mews; **die —e schnurrt**, the cat purrs; *see* **Kat**; **eine falsche —e**, a deceitful person; **neunschwänzige —e**, cat-o'-nine-tails; **die —e läuft ihm den Rücken hinauf**, he shudders at it; **die —e im Sack kaufen**, to buy a pig in a poke (*prov.*); **er macht ein Gesicht wie die —e wenn's donnert**, he looks like a dying duck in a thunderstorm, he looks queer *or* displeased (*sl.*); **in der Nacht sind alle —en grau**, all cats are grey in the dark (*prov.*); **wenn die —e nicht zu Hause ist, tanzen die Mäuse**, when the cat's away the mice will play (*prov.*); **die —e läßt das Mausen nicht**, what is bred in the bone will out in the flesh; **sieht doch die —(e) den Kaiser an**, a cat may look at a king; **sie vertragen sich wie —e und Hund**, they led a cat and dog life; **der —e die Schelle anhängen** *or* **umhängen**, to bell the cat; **das ist für die —e**, that is too little; that's not worth anything (*coll.*); **naß wie eine —e**, sopping wet, wet all through; **das trägt die —e auf dem Schwanze fort**, that's a mere trifle; **wie die —e um den heißen Brei gehen**, to beat about the bush. —**en=haft**, *adj. see* —**en=artig**. —**en=schaft**, *f.* cat tribe, feline family. *Comp.* —**balgen**, *v.r.* to scuffle noisily, to brawl. —**balger**, *m.* brawler. —**en=artig**, *adj.* catlike, feline. —**en=auge**, *n.* cat's eye. —**en=balg**, *m.*, —**en=fell**, *n.* cat's skin *or* fur. —**en=buckel**, *m.* humped back (*like a cat's*); **einen —enbuckel machen** *or* —**enbuckeln (vor einem)**, to make a profound reverence; to crouch, to cringe. —**en=eule**, *f.* horned owl. —**en=geschlecht**, *n.* cat tribe, feline family. —**en=geschrei**, *n.* caterwauling; mewing. —**en=glimmer**, *m.*, —**en=gold**, *n.* mica. —**en=jammer**, *m.* indisposition occasioned by intoxication; seediness, crapulence (*sl.*); **einen moralischen —jammer haben**, to have a touch of compunction, to resolve to mend one's ways; to be down in the dumps (*coll.*); *see* **Kater**. —**en=jämmerlich**, *adj.* & *adv.* headachy, seedy, miserable, low-spirited (*after a carouse*). —**en=kopf**, *m.* box on the ear (*coll.*). —**en=leben**, *n.* the nine lives of a cat (*vulg.*). —**en=musik**, *f.* caterwauling; charivari, tin-kettle music, mock music; **einem eine —enmusik bringen**, to hoot and howl before a p.'s house. —**en=pfötchen**, *n.* mountain everlasting; crow's feet, wrinkles; —**enpfötchen machen** *or* **geben**, to pretend to be friendly. —**en=pfote**, *f.* cat's paw. —**en=rücken**, *m.* cambering of a ship's keel. —**en=silber**, *n.* mica. —**en=sprung**, *m.* cat's leap; **es ist nur ein —ensprung dahin**, it is but a stone's throw distant. —**en=steg**, —**en=steig**, *m.* narrow path; **den —en**

steig gehen, to take a crooked course, go astray. —en=tisch, *m.* cat's table, side-table; am —entische essen, to eat at the little folks' table, to dine at a side-table; to eat alone in a corner (*punishment for children*). —en=wäsche, *f.* a cat's lick, superficial, poor washing.

Kät'zin, *f.* she-cat (*rare*).

Kauder—ei', *f.* usury in trifles. —er, (*pron.* Kau'derer) *m.* usurer.

Kau'der—n, *v.n.* (*aux.* h.) to gobble (*as a turkey*); to talk gibberish. *Comp.* —wälsch, —welsch, *adj. & n.* broken language; gibberish, jargon. —wälschen, —welschen, *v.n.* to talk gibberish, jabber; to speak cant.

Kau'—en, (Käu'—en, *rare, dial.*) I. *v.a.* to chew, to masticate; an den Nägeln —en, to bite the nails. II. *subst.n.* mastication, chewing; das —en auf dem Gebiß, champing the bit. *Comp.* —gebiß, *n.* mouthing bit. —muskel, *m.* masticatory muscle. —tabak, *m.* tobacco for chewing; feiner —tabak, lady-twist; quid. —werkzeuge, *pl.* masticators. —zahn, *m.* grinder, molar tooth.

Kau'ern, *v.n.* (*aux.* f.) & *r.* to squat, to cower; sich zusammen —, to crouch. —d, *p. & adj.* squat; couchant (*Her.*).

Kauf, *m.* (—es, *pl.* Käu'fe) buying, purchase; bargain; wohlfeilen, guten —es, cheap; leichten —es weg= *or* davonkommen, to get off easily, with little loss; einem in den — treten, to outbid another; zu —, for sale; in den —, over and above, into the bargain; durch —, by purchase; durch — an sich (*acc.*) bringen, to buy; — ist —, a bargain 's a bargain; (einem) etwas auf den — geben, to give earnest; in den — geben, to throw into the bargain. —bar, *adj. & adv.* purchasable, that may be bought *or* sold. *Comp.* —anschlag, *m.* estimate of a thing which is to be sold; bill posted up to advertise the sale of anything. —brief, *m.* bill of sale. —buch, *n.* book of accounts, journal (*C.L.*). —fahrer, *m.* merchantman. —fahrtei', *f.* navigation for the purpose of commerce. —fahrtei'flotte, *f.* fleet of merchantmen. —fahrtei'=schiff, *n.* merchantman. —geld, *n.* purchase-money; earnest-money. —gut, *n.* merchandise. —handel, *m.* commerce, traffic (*opposed to* Tauschhandel). —haus, *n.* warehouse, stores; market-house; merchant's house. —herr, *m.* merchant. —kontrakt, —vertrag, *m.* bill of sale. —kraft, *f.* purchasing power. —laden, *m.* (merchant's) shop; store. —leute, *pl.* merchants; tradespeople, shopkeepers. —lustig, *adj.* inclined to buy; die —lustigen, *pl.* buyers. —mann, *see* Kaufmann. —männisch, *adj. & adv.* mercantile, commercial; —männische Regel, rule of business; in —männischer Hinsicht, commercially, from a business point of view. —platz, *m.* market-place, market. —preis, *m.* purchase-money; prime cost. —recht, *n.* right of purchase. —schilling, *m.* earnest-money. —steuer, *f.* stamp duty on conveyance. —weise, *adv.* by purchase. —wert, *m.* marketable value. —würdig, *adj.* marketable. —zwang, *m.* obligation to buy; ohne —zwang, on approval, without obligation as to purchase; inspection invited.

Kau'fen, *v.a. & n.* (*aux.* h.) to buy, purchase; to get by purchase; bei wem — Sie gewöhnlich? with whom do you deal as a rule? auf Borg —, to buy on credit; wieder an sich —, to re-purchase; sich (*dat.*) einen —, to call a p. to account, to blow a p. up (*coll.*); sich (*dat.*) einen Affen —, to get tipsy (*sl.*); das — geistlicher Ämter, simony; Karten —, to take in cards.

Käu'f—er, *m.* (—ers, *pl.* —er) purchaser, buyer; chapman. —lich, I. *adj.* marketable; saleable; venal, corruptible. II. *adv.* by purchase; —lich an sich (*acc.*) bringen, to buy; —lich überlassen, to sell. —lichkeit, *f.* being for sale; venality, corruptibility.

Kauf'mann, *m.* (—s, *pl.* Kaufleute; Kaufmänner (*obs.*)) merchant; tradesman, shopkeeper; — im Großen, wholesale dealer *or* merchant; — im Kleinen, retailer, shopkeeper. —schaft, *f.* body of merchants *or* tradesmen; mercantile class; commerce. *Comp.* —s=ballen, *m.* bale of goods. —s=buch, *n.* book of accounts, journal. —s=diener, *m.* merchant's clerk; shopman. —s=frau, *f.* tradesman's or merchant's wife. —s=geist, *m.* mercantile spirit. —s=gut, *n.* merchandise. —s=hand, *f.* mercantile handwriting. —s=innung, *f.* trading company, guild. —s=junge, *m.* merchant's *or* shopkeeper's apprentice. —s=laden, *m.*, —s=gewölbe, *n.* shop; store (*Am.*). —s=stand, *m.* mercantile class, merchants; rank *or* condition of the trading classes.

Kau'l—e, *f.* (*pl.* —en) bullet. *Comp.* —bars, —barsch, *m.* ruff, species of perch. —frosch, *m.*, —kröte, *f.* tadpole. —huhn, *n.* hen without a tail. —quappe, *f.* tadpole, polliwig (*coll.*).

Kaum, *adv.* with difficulty, hardly, scarcely, almost not; but just, just now; — noch, but a moment ago; — (der Gefahr) noch entgehen, — entwischen, to have a very narrow escape; — war er da als, he was no sooner there than; — daß er nicht überlaut rief, he could scarcely keep from shouting out.

Kau'peln, *v.n.* (*aux.* h.) to chaffer, to barter.

Kau'ri, *m.* (—s, *pl.* —s) cowry-shell.

Kausa'l, *adj.* causal, causative. *Comp.* —nexus connection between cause and effect, causality. —partikel, *f.* causative (particle).

Kau'scher, *see* Koscher.

Kaus't—ik, *f.* art of etching. —ika, *pl.* corrosive substances. —isch, *adj. & adv.* caustic.

Kaute'l, *f.* caution; precaution; reservation.

Kautio'n, *f.* security, bail; unter —, under bonds; gegen gute —, on good security; — legen, stellen, to give bail.

Kaut'schuk, *m.* (—s) caoutchouc, India rubber. —dichtung, *f.* india-rubber packing. —rohr, *n.* india-rubber pipe.

Kauz, *m.* (—es, *pl.* Käu'ze) screech-owl; odd fellow; fellow, chap; ein lustiger —, a jolly dog.

Kau'zen, *v.n.* (*aux.* h. & f.) & *r.* to stoop; to cower; to cringe.

Kavalie'r, *m.* (—s, *pl.* —e) cavalier; courtier; knight; gentleman.

Ka'valler—ie, *f.* cavalry, horsemen, horse (*collect.*). —i'st, *m.* (—is'ten, *pl.* —is'ten) mounted trooper, horseman. *Comp.* —ie=kaserne, *f.* horse-barracks. —ie=offizier, officer of cavalry *or* of horse. —ie=stiefel, *m.* jack-boot, top-boot.

Kave'nt, *m.* (—en'ten, *pl.* —en'ten) guarantee, guarantor. —ie'ren, *v.n.* (*aux.* h.) to give security for, guarantee.

Ka'viar, *m.* (—s) caviare; — fürs Volk, caviare to the general (*prov.*). *Comp.* —brötchen, *n.* sandwich with caviare.

Kavie'ren, *v.a.* to answer for, to warrant.

Keb'f—e, *f.* (*pl.* —en) concubine. —en, *v.n.* (*aux.* h.) to take as a concubine; to live in concubinage. —in, *f. see* —e. *Comp.* —(s)=ehe, *f.* concubinage. —(s)=kind, *n.* illegitimate child, bastard. —(s)=weib, *n.* concubine, mistress.

Keck, *adj. & adv.* quick, alert; sprightly, lively; fearless, daring; pert, saucy, forward, impudent; bold (*in painting*); bright (*of colour*). —heit, *f.* boldness, audacity; pertness; impudence; vigour; dash. —lich, *adv.* pertly, boldly.

Ke'gel, *m.* (—s, *pl.* —) cone; skittle; nine-pin; shoulder-bone (*of a horse*); sight, aim (*Artil.*); detent (*of a gun*); depth of a letter (*Typ.*); illegitimate child (*obs.*); dumpy person; boor;

sign of an ale-house with skittle-ground; ein Spiel —, a set of nine-pins; — schieben, to play at [illegible]ine-pins *or* skittles; er hat weder Kind noch —, he has neither kith nor kin; mit Kind und —, with all one's belongings. —er, Kegl—er, *m.* (—ers, *pl.* —er) nine-pins *or* skittles player. —icht, —ig, *adj. & adv.* conical. —n, *v.* I. *n.* (*aux.* h.) to play at nine-pins *or* skittles. II. *a.* to throw; to roll; to form into a cone. *Comp.* —ähnlich, *adj.* conical, conoidal. —aufsetzer, *m.* marker (*at nine-pins*). —bahn, *f.* ninepin *or* skittle alley. —förmig, *adj.* coniform, cone-shaped. —junge, *m.* marker (*at nine-pins*). —kugel, *f.* (heavy) ball (*to knock down the nine-pins*); bowl. —linie, *f.* parabola. —linig, *adj. & adv.* parabolical. —schieber, —spieler, *m.* skittle-player. —schnitt, *m.* conic section; Lehre von den —schnitten, conic sections, conics. —schnitt=linie, *f.* ellipse; parabola; hyperbola. —schieber, *m.* skittle-player; conical valve. —schub, *m.* (*see* —bahn). —spiel, *n.* playing at nine-pins. —stumpf, *m.* obtuse cone.

Keh'l—e, *f.* (*pl.* —en) throat; throttle; swallow; voice; chamfer, fluting; channel, gutter; gorge (*Fort.*); breast of a bastion; aus voller —e lachen, to laugh heartily; etwas ist in die unrechte —e gekommen, a crumb has gone the wrong way. —ig, *adj.* grooved, fluted; tausend —ig, of a thousand voices. *Comp.* —ader, *f.* jugular vein. —band, *n.* stay (*Arch.*). —bräune, *f.* quinsy. —buchstabe, *m.* guttural letter. —deckel, *m.* epiglottis (*Anat.*). —gebälk, *n.* collar-beam (*Arch.*). —hobel, *m.* fluting plane. —holz, *n.* privet. —knorpel, —knochen, —kopf, *m.* larynx. —kopf=spiegel, *n.* laryngoscope. —kopf=verschluß, *m.* temporary closing of the larynx, glottal catch. —kopf=verschluß=laut, *m.* glottal stop, glottal catch. —laut, *m.* guttural sound. —lauter, *m.* guttural. —leiste, *f.* moulding (*Arch.*). —rinne, *f.* gutter. —stimme, *f.* guttural voice. —stück, *n.* gorget. —ziegel, *m.* gutter-tile.

Keh'len, *v.a.* to chamfer, flute, hollow, groove, channel; to cut (*out*) the throat (*of a fish*).

Keh're, *f.* (*pl.* —n) turning; turn; return; tour; way, direction; ganz aus der —, quite wrong, in the contrary direction.

[1]**Keh'r—en**, *v.* I. *a.* to turn; das Schwert in die Scheide —en, to put up the sword into the sheath; eine Sache zum Besten —en, to make the best of a th.; die rauhe Seite heraus —en, to show one's worst side; das Oberste zu unterst —en, to turn everything upside down. II. *r.* to turn; sich an einen (etwas) —en, to regard, heed, follow, stick to a p. (*a thing*); sich zur Buße —en, to become penitent. III. *n.* (*aux.* s.) to turn, return; to wheel round; rechts um —t (euch)! right about turn! —t! turn about! wheel! in sich (*acc.*) —en, to retire into oneself; repent. —t, *n.*; —t machen, to wheel (*Mil.*). *Comp.* —aus, *m.* concluding dance; clearance, turn out; flogging; end. —reim, *m.* refrain. —seite, *f.* reverse side, tail(s) (*coll.*); draw-back, disadvantage, the reverse of the medal. —wie'der, *n.* blind alley. —zeile, *f.* refrain, line recurring at the end of every stanza *or* part of a stanza.

[2]**Keh'r—en**, *v.a.* to sweep, brush, cleanse by sweeping; turn out (*a room*); neue Besen —en gut, new brooms sweep clean (*prov.*); —e vor deiner eignen Thür, mind your own business! —er, *m.* (—ers, *pl.* —er) sweeper, sweep. —icht, *n.* (—ichts) sweepings. *Comp.* —aus, *m.* Sir Roger (*dance*). —besen, *m.* broom, besom. —bürste, *f.* brush; whisk. —icht=faß, *n.*, —icht=kasten, *m.* dust bin, rubbish box. —icht=kärrner, *m.* dustman. —kleid, *n.* dress with train. —wisch, *m.* duster.

Kei'chen, *see* Keuchen.

Kei'f—en, *ir.v.n.* (*aux.* h.) to bark, yelp; to scold, upbraid, chide. —er, *m.* (—ers, *pl.* —er) scolder; brawler. —erin, *f.* shrew, scold. —isch, *adj.* scolding, quarrelsome.

Keil, *m.* (—es, *pl.* —e) wedge; wedge-shaped piece; coin (*Artil.*); keystone (*of an arch*); clock (*of a stocking*); bolt, thunderbolt; key, wedge, pin; quoin (*Typ.*); das spitze Ende eines —s, the thin end of the wedge; es giebt —e! they are coming to blows! there's a row! (*coll.*); —e kriegen, to get thrashed (*coll.*); auf einen groben Klotz gehört ein grober —, he will give tit for tat (*prov.*); ein — treibt den andern, one nail drives out another. *Comp.* —ähnlich, —artig, —förmig, *adj.* wedge-shaped, cuneiform. —hacke, *f.* pickaxe. —halter, *m.* jib. —inschrift, *f.* cuneiform inscription. —nute, *f.* groove, key-bed. —schrift, *f.* cuneiform characters. —schrift=kunde, *f.* sphenography.

Kei'len, *v.* I. *a.* to wedge, fasten with a wedge; to cleave, split with a wedge; to drub, thrash (*sl.*); to drive (*Typ.*); to induce a person (by strong persuasion) to do a thing; to win a p. over to a cause, to make a p. join an association (*coll.*). II. *r.* to be cuneiform.

Kei'ler, *m.* (—s, *pl.* —) wild boar (*2 years old*).

Keim, *m.* (—(e)s, *pl.* —e) germ; bud, shoot; embryo; origin; im —e ersticken, to nip in the bud. *Comp.* —blatt, *n.* cotyledon (*Bot.*). —es=anlage, *f.* germinal purpose, germ-organism. —frei, *adj.* sterile, free from bacilli; —frei machen, to sterilize (*Med.*). —frucht, *f.* sporangium. —hülle, *f.* perisperm. —kraft, *f.* vitality. —würzelchen, *n.* radicle (*Bot.*).

Kei'men, *v.n.* (*aux.* h. & s.) to germinate, sprout, shoot forth; to arise, spring up; to begin to show itself; im —, in embryo.

Kein, *adj.* not any, no, not a, not one; — Gedanke! no such thing! that is not to be thought of! nonsense! (*coll.*); — Mensch, no one; es ist —e so wichtige Sache, it is not so important a matter; er ist — Student mehr, he is no longer a student, his undergraduate days are over; —e halbe Stunde vor dem Anfang der Prüfung, within half an hour of the examination; es sind noch —e acht Tage, it is not a week yet. —er, —e, —es, *pron.* no one, not any one, none; er ist —er der Stärksten, he is none of the strongest; —er von beiden, neither of them, neither the one nor the other; er giebt —em etwas nach, he is inferior to none; —es dieser Bücher gefällt ihm, he does not like any of these books. *Comp.* —er=lei, *indec. adj.* of no sort, not any; auf —erlei Weise, by no means, in no way. —er=seits, *adv.* on neither side. —es=weg(e)s, *adv.* in no wise, by no means, not at all. —mal, *adv.* not once, never; einmal ist —mal, once does not count, the exception proves the rule (*prov.*). —seitig, *adj.* taking neither side, neutral. —seitigkeit, *f.* neutrality.

Kelch, *m.* (—es, *pl.* —e) chalice; calyx, flower-cup; cup, goblet; zwischen Lipp' und —es Rand schwebt der finstern Mächte Hand, there's many a slip 'twixt cup and lip (*prov.*). *Comp.* —artig, *adj.* cup-like. —blatt, *n.* sepal. —deckelchen, *n.* chalice-lid. —glas, *n.* cup-like glass, crystal goblet. —narbe, *f.* umbril, eye (*Bot.*). —röhrchen, *n.* tube (*Bot.*). —schleier, *m.* cloth to cover the chalice (*R. C.*). —weihe, *f.* consecration of the communion-cup.

Kel'le, *f.* (*pl.* —n) trowel; scoop, ladle; boot, basket (*of a waggon*); fish-slice; er läßt die — nicht an der Pfanne kleben, he does not let the grass grow under his feet; essen was die — giebt, to take pot-luck.

Kel'l—er, *m.* (—ers, *pl.* —er) cellar. —erei',

f. cellarage; cellarers (*coll.*). **—erer,** *m.* keeper of a cellar *or* tavern. **—ner,** *m.* (—ners, *pl.* —ner) *see* —erer; servant at an inn; waiter; barkeeper, tapster. **—nerin,** *f.* female servant at an inn; waitress; barmaid. **—nern,** *v.a.* to act as a waiter *or* waitress (*coll.*). *Comp.* **—er=geschoß,** *n.* basement. **—er=gewölbe,** *n.* vault. **—er=knecht,** *m.* cellarman. **—er=lager,** *n.* stand for casks. **—er=meister,** *m.* butler. **—er=schnecke,** *f.* slug. **—er=wechsel,** *m.* fictitious bill of exchange, proforma bill, accommodation-bill (*C. L.*). **—er=wirt,** *m.* keeper of a wine cellar *or* of an underground beer shop. **—er=wohnung,** *f.* underground lodgings. **—er=wurm,** *m.* woodlouse; regular customer at an underground beer-shop (*coll.*). **—er=zins,** *m.* cellarage.

Kel'ter, *f.* (*pl.* —n) wine-press; **die — treten,** to work the wine-press, to tread the grapes. **—er,** *m.* (—ers, *pl.* —er) wine-presser *or* treader. **—n,** *v.a.* to tread *or* press (*grapes*). *Comp.* **—faß,** *n.*, **—zuber,** *m.* tub which receives the pressed juice, wine-dosser. **—haus,** *n.* presshouse. **—treter,** *see* —er.

Kem(e)na'te, *f.* (*pl.* —n) ladies' room with a stove *or* fireplace in a mediæval castle (*obs.*).

Kenn'bar, *adj. & adv.* knowable, distinguishable, recognizable; distinct, conspicuous. **—keit,** *f.* cognoscibility; conspicuousness.

Ken'n—en, *ir.v.a.* to know; to have cognizance of; to be acquainted with; **von Ansehen —en,** to know by sight; **—en lernen,** to get to know, to become acquainted (with). **—tlich,** *adj. & adv.* knowable, discernible, distinguishable (**an einer S.,** by a th.). **—tlichkeit,** *f.* discernibleness, quality of being distinguishable. **—tnis,** *see* **Kenntnis.** **—ung,** *f.* mark on a horse's tooth by which its age can be known; **—ung des Landes,** landmark, beacon (*Naut.*). *Comp.* **—ens=wert,** *adj.* worth knowing. **—wort,** *n.* motto, device (*on a closed letter, etc.*). **—zahl, —ziffer,** *f.* index of a logarithm. **—zeichen,** *n.* distinguishing mark, characteristic; sign, token; symptom; symbol; criterion. **—zeichnen,** *v.a.* to mark, characterize. **—zug,** *m.* characteristic, distinctive trait.

Ken'ner, *m.* (—s, *pl.* —) knower; judge, connoisseur. **—haft,** *adj. & adv.* as a connoisseur. **—schaft,** *f.* connoisseurs (*coll.*); connoisseurship. *Comp.* **—auge,** *n.*, **—blick,** *m.* eye *or* glance of a connoisseur.

Kennt'nis, *f.* (*pl.* —(ss)e) knowledge, information; acquirements; skill; science; notice, information; cognizance; **— nehmen von,** to take cognizance of; **ein Mann von vielen —(ss)en,** a man of wide information *or* of much knowledge (learning); **er hat schöne philologische —(ss)e,** he knows a great deal about philology; **sie hat seltene —(ss)e,** she is particularly well informed; **einen in — setzen von,** to apprize a p. of, inform of; **sich von etwas in — setzen,** to gain intelligence of *or* inform o.s. about something. *Comp.* **—arm, —los,** *adj.* ignorant. **—nahme,** *f.* getting information, taking cognizance of; information. **—reich, —voll,** *adj.* well informed, learned.

Ken'ter—n, *v.a.* to capsize, cant, overturn. *Comp.* **—haken,** *m.* grappling-iron.

Ker'b—e, *f.* (*pl.* —en) notch, jag, indent, nick; groove; **den Pfeil in die —e legen,** to fit the arrow to the bow; **in die —e pfropfen,** to graft in the cheek (*Hort.*). **—ig,** *adj.* notched, jagged. **—ling,** *m. see* —tier. *Comp.* **—eisen,** *n.* wire-gauge. **—holz,** *n.* notched stick; tally; **aufs —holz schneiden,** to tally; **etwas bei einem auf dem —holz haben,** to have s.th. on s. one's score, to be on a p.'s books, to be in debt to a p.; **das kommt nicht aufs —holz,** there will be no charge for this. **—maschine,** *f.* crimping iron. **—schnitzerei',** *f.* chip-carving. **—tier,** *n.* insect. **—tier=kunde, —tier=lehre,** *f.* entomology. **—zähnig,** *adj.* notched, crenate, indented.

Ker'bel, *m.* (—s) chervil.

Ker'ben, *v.a.* to notch, jag, indent; to mill (*the edge of coins*).

Ker'ker, *m.* (—s, *pl.* —) prison, jail, dungeon. **—haft, —lich,** *adj.* prison-like. *Comp.* **—artig, —mäßig,** *adj.* prison-like. **—fieber,** *n.* jail-fever. **—haft,** *f.* imprisonment. **—meister,** *m.* jailer. **—schmach,** *f.* disgrace of imprisonment. **—turm,** *m.* donjon, keep.

Kerl, *m.* (—s, *pl.* —e) fellow; manly fellow; varlet, worthless fellow; manservant; **ein ganzer —,** a man indeed, a fine fellow; **ein lustiger —,** a jolly chap; **sie ist ein netter —,** she is a nice one (*sl.*); **du bist ein lieber —,** you are a dear (*coll.*). **—chen,** *n.* (—chens, *pl.* —chen) little fellow, little chap; jolly fellow.

Ker'mes, *m.* kermes, a scarlet dye (*obtained from certain insects*).

Kern, *m.* (—s, *pl.* —e) kernel, pip, stone (*of fruit*); pith (*of wood*); heart (*of a tree, etc.*); bore, calibre (*of a gun*); grain (*of corn; of leather*); nucleus (*of comets*); marrow, essence; best part; brisket (*of beef*); élite, flower, picked men (*of an army*); root (*of a matter*); stopper (*of wind-instruments*); quick (*of a hoof*). **—haft,** *adj. & adv.* pithy; substantial, solid; vigourous, energetic, robust; pregnant. **—haftigkeit,** *f.* pithiness, raciness; solidity. **—icht,** (*obs.*) *adj.* kernel-like. **—ig,** *adj.* full of kernels; *see* —haft. *In cpds.* **Kern—** *often means* choice, very, thoroughly. **—artig,** *adj.* kernel-like. **—branntwein,** *m.* noyau. **—deutsch,** *adj. & adv.* pure German, thoroughly German, German to the core. **—eis,** *n.* firm ice. **—faul,** *adj.* rotten at the core. **—fest,** *adj.* very firm *or* solid. **—fleisch,** *n.* choice meat; pulp, pith. **—frucht,** *f.* stone fruit. **—gehäuse,** *n.* core. **—gestalt,** *f.* fundamental form. **—gesund,** *adj.* thoroughly sound *or* healthy. **—haus,** *n.* core. **—holz,** *n.* heart of a tree. **—kammer,** *f.* cell (*Bot.*). **—maß,** *n.* calibre. **—recht,** *adj.* well-bored (*Artil.*); level, horizontal. **—schuß,** *m.* horizontal shot, point-blank shot **—schuß=batterie,** *f.* direct-gun battery. **—schwarz,** *adj.* peach-black. **—seife,** *f.* grained soap; first-rate soap. **—spruch,** *m.* pithy saying. **—substanz,** *f.* perisperm, albumen (*Bot.*). **—truppen,** *pl.* choice troops, picked men. **—wort,** *n.* pithy word, word of deep meaning.

Ker'nen, *v.a.* to take the kernel out, to stone (*fruit*); to pick, select; to provide with kernels *or* seeds, to granulate; to churn; **sich —,** to curdle, to turn to butter.

Ker'ze, *f.* (*pl.* —n) candle, waxlight, taper; **gegossene —,** mould candle. *Comp.* **—n=gerade,** *adj.* straight as a dart, bolt upright. **—n=gießer, —n=zieher,** *m.* chandler. **—en=hell,** *adj.* lit up with candles. **—n=licht,** *n.* candle-light. **—n=träger,** *m.* taper-bearer.

Kes'sel, *m.* (—s, *pl.* —) kettle; caldron, boiler; valley, basin-like hollow; basin (*of a fountain, etc.*); bell (*Arch.*); bore (*Artil.*); bell-like muzzle; mouth-piece (*of wind instruments*); excavation; cover; burrow, den; crater; battery of sunk mortars. **—er,** *see* **Keßler.** *Comp.* **—asche,** *f.* potash. **—batterie,** *f.* mortar battery. **—bier,** *n.* home-brewed beer. **—braun,** *adj.* copper-coloured. **—flicker,** *m.* tinker; would-be politician. **—förmig,** *adj.* caldron-shaped. **—gestell,** *n.* kettle-stand. **—gewölbe,** *n.* cupola-like roof. **—haken,** *m.* pot-hook. **—jagen,** *n.* battue-shooting. **—kamin,** *m.* boiler-chimney. **—loch,** *n.* basin-shaped hole. **—macher,** *m.* coppersmith, brazier. **—pauke,** *f.* kettle-drum. **—platte,** *f.* boiler-plate. **—probe,** *f.* testing of a boiler. **—schläger, —schmied,** *see* —macher. **—stein,**

m. deposit, incrustation, sediment, fur (*on the inside of kettles*). **—thal,** *n.* basin-like dale; valley surrounded by mountains. **—treiben,** *n.* circular beat, battue shooting.

Kes'sel—n, *v.* I. *r.* to dip; become hollow. II. *n.* (*aux.* **h.**) to make kettles; to root up the ground; **der Wind —t,** the wind chops about.

Keß'ler, *m.* (—**s**, *pl.*—) brazier; tinker.

Ket'te, *f.* (*pl.* —**n**) chain; fetter, bond; connected series, train, concatenation; chain, range; chain (*Danc.*); cordon (*Mil.*); measure (= 10 metres); (*pl.*) bondage, slavery; **an die — legen,** to chain up; **galvanische —,** galvanic battery; **— und Einschlag,** warp and woof. *Comp.* **—n=anker,** *m.* moorings. **—n=baum,** *m.* weaver's beam. **—n=blume,** *f.* dandelion. **—n=brüche,** *pl.* continued fractions (*Arith.*). **—n=brücke,** *f.* suspension-bridge. **—n=gebirge,** *n.* mountain-chain. **—n=geklirr, —n=gerassel,** *n.* clanking of chains. **—n=gesang,** *m.* catch (*Mus.*). **—n=glied,** *n.* link of a chain. **—n=hund,** *m.* tie dog, watch-dog. **—n=kasten,** *m.* gear case (*cycl.*). **—n=kugel,** *f.* chain-shot. **—n=kunst,** *f.* chain-pump. **—n=los,** *adj.* unchained. **—n=panzer,** *m.* coat of mail. **—n=rad,** *n.* sprocket *or* chain wheel. **—n=rahmen,** *m.* tambour-frame; embroidery-frame. **—n=rechnung, —n=regel,** *f.* chain-rule, double rule of three. **—n=ring,** *m.* chain-loop, link of a chain. **—n=schluß,** *m.* sorites (*Log.*). **—n=schützer,** *m.* chain-guard (*of a watch*). **—n=schutzgehäuse,** *n.* gear-case (*cycl.*). **—n=stich,** *m.* chain-stitch. **—n=strebe,** *f.* chain stay. **—n=triller,** *m.* sustained shake (*Mus.*). **—n=tanz,** *m.* ladies' chain; chain-dance, linked *or* interlaced dance. **—n=zug,** *m.* ornaments in the shape of a chain.

Ket'tel—n, *v.a.* to fasten with a little chain; to embroider with chain work; to link. *Comp.* **—haken,** *m.*, **—nadel,** *f.* tambour needle.

Ket'ten, *v.a.* to chain, to fetter; to connect with; to link *or* tie to.

Ket'zer, *m.* (—**s**, *pl.*—), **—in,** *f.* heretic; **ästhetischer —,** a man who has his own views about art which do not agree with those that are generally accepted. **—ei',** *f.* heresy. **—haft, —isch,** *adj.* & *adv.* heretical, heterodox. **—schaft,** *f.*, **—tum,** *n.* heresy; body of heretics. *Comp.* **—buch,** *n.* heretical book. **—gericht,** *n.* (*court of*) inquisition. **—haupt,** *n.* heresiarch. **—macherei,** *f.* mania of branding dissentients as heretics. **—meister,** *m.* grand inquisitor. **—mütze,** *f.* painted cap worn by heretics condemned to be burnt. **—richter,** *m.* inquisitor. **—riecher,** *m.* heretic-hunter. **—schrift,** *f.* heretical writing. **—verbrennung,** *f.* burning of heretics, auto-da-fé. **—zunft,** *f.* heretical sect.

Keu'ch—en, (**Kei'ch—en,**) *v.n.* (*aux.* **h.**) to pant, gasp; to cough. *Comp.* **—husten,** *m.* (—**s**) hooping cough.

Keu'le, *f.* (*pl.* —**n**) club; pestle; anything club-shaped; hind leg (*of a beast*); leg (*of meat*). *Comp.* **—n=förmig,** club-shaped. **—n=lahm,** *adj.* lame in the thigh *or* hind leg. **—n=schlag,** *m.* blow of a club.

Keu'ler, *m. see* **Keiler.**

Keu'per, *m.* red marl, keuper (*Geol.*).

Keusch, *adj.* & *adv.* chaste, maidenly, pure; modest; **das —este Mädchen,** the most innocent girl. **—heit,** *f.* chastity, purity; modesty; continence; incorruptibility (fig.); **Priesterin der —heit,** vestal. *Comp.* **—heits=gelübde,** *n.* vow of chastity. **—heits=gürtel,** *m.* girdle of virginity; virgin knot (*poet.*). **—heits=wächterin,** *f.* duenna.

Ki'cher, (**—erbse,**) *f.* (*pl.* —**n**) chick-pea (*Bot.*).

Ki'chern, *v.n.* (*aux.* **h.**) to giggle, titter; to chuckle.

Kicks, *m.* (—(**s**)**es**, *pl.* —(**s**)**e**) miss (*Bill.*). **—(s)en,** to miss the ball (*Bill.*).

Kie'bitz, Ki'bitz, *m.* (—**es**, *pl.* —**e**) peewit; green plover; **—e hüten,** to die an old maid.

[1]**Kie'fer,** *m.* (—**s**, *pl.* —) jaw; jaw-bone; gill; shell (*of peas*). *adj.* (*in comp.* =) maxillary. **—ig,** *adj.* & *suff.* with jaws; **groß—ig,** large-jawed. *Comp.* **—muskel,** *m.* muscle of the lower jaw. **—winkel,** *m.* angle of the jaws, distance between the rows of teeth.

[2]**Kie'fer,** *f.* (*pl.* —**n**) (Scots) pine, common pine, Scots fir, pinus sylvestris. **—icht,** (*obs.*) *adj.* fir; resinous. **—n,** *adj.* made of fir, fir. *Comp.* **—gehölz,** *n.* pine-grove. **—holz,** *n.* pine wood, red deal. **—zapfen,** *m.* fir-cone.

Kie'ke, *f.* (*pl.* —**n**) foot-warmer, foot-stove.

Kie'k—en, *v.a.* to peep (*dial.* & *coll.*); **ein junger —indiewelt,** a young jackanapes, verdant green (*coll.*). **—er,** *m.*; **etwas auf dem —er haben,** to desire to get s.th. (*dial. sl.*).

[1]**Kiel,** *m.* (—**s**, *pl.* —**e**) quill; halm, straw. **—en,** *v.* I. *a.* to feather (*an arrow*); to quill (*a harpsichord*). II. *n.* (*aux.* **h.**) to become fledged. *Comp.* **—bett,** *n.* coarse feather-bed. **—federn,** *pl.* quills.

[2]**Kiel,** *m.* (—**s**, *pl.* —**e**) keel; vessel; carina, keel (*Bot.*); **falscher** *or* **loser —,** false keel; **den — legen,** to set the keel; **— oben,** bottom up; **mit breitem —,** broad-bottomed. **—en,** *v.a.* to furnish with a keel. *Comp.* **—bank,** *f.* careening wharf. **—förmig,** *adj.* keel-shaped; carinate (*Bot.*). **—geld,** *n.* keelage. **—herr,** *m.* captain. **—holen,** *v.a.* to careen (*a vessel*); to keelhaul (*a sailor*). **—kropf,** *m.* (person afflicted with the) goitre. **—kröpfig,** *adj.* goitrous. **—raum,** *m.* (ship's) hold (*Naut.*). **—recht,** *n.* keelage. **—richtung,** *f.* head. **—schwein,** *n.*, keelson. **—wasser,** *n.* bilge-water, steerage way; wake (*of a ship*).

Kie'me, *f.* (*pl.* —**n**) gill of a fish; **durch die —n atmend,** gill-breathing.

Kien, *m.* (—(**e**)**s**, *pl.* —**e**) resinous wood; pine-wood; pine-resin. **—en,** *adj.* & *adv.* of fir. **—ig,** *adj.* & *adv.* resinous. *Comp.* **—apfel,** *m.* pine-cone. **—baum,** *m.* Scotch fir. **—fackel,** *f.* pine-torch. **—harz,** *n.* resin of pine trees. **—holz,** *n.* resinous wood. **—öl,** *n.* oil of turpentine. **—ruß,** *m.* lamp-black.

Kie'pe, *f.* (*pl.* —**n**) wicker basket for the back, back-basket, dosser; large bonnet.

Kies, *m.* (—(**s**)**es**, *pl.* —(**s**)**e**) gravel; river sand-bank; pyrites; quartz; money (*sl.*). **—(s)ig,** *adj.* gravelly; gritty. *Comp.* **—artig,** *adj.* gravelly; pyritous. **—gang,** *m.* gravel-walk. **—haltig,** *adj.* gravelly, containing gravel. **—sand,** *m.* gravelly *or* pebbly sand. **—weg,** *m.* gravel *or* gravelled walk.

Kie'sel, *m.* (—**s**, *pl.* —) pebble, flint-stone; silex, silica. **—ig,** *adj.* flinty, pebbly; silicious. *Comp.* **—artig,** *adj.* silicious. **—erde,** *f.* silica, silicious earth. **—glas,** *n.* flint-glass. **—grund,** *m.* pebbly ground *or* bottom. **—hart,** *adj.* hard as a flint. **—herz,** *n.* flinty *or* hard heart. **—klumpen,** *m.* pudding-stone. **—sand,** *m.* coarse gravel. **—sandstein,** *m.* silicious sandstone. **—sauer,** *adj.* silicated. **—säure,** *f.* silicic acid. **—stoff,** *m.* silicon. **—stein,** *m.* pebble, flint stone; pebbly boulder.

[1]**Kie'sen,** *ir.v.a.* to select, choose, elect (*obs.* & *high style*).

[2]**Kie'sen,** *v.a.* to cover with gravel.

Ki'kel=kakel, *n.*, tittle-tattle (*coll.*).

Kikeriki', *int.* cock-a-doodle-doo.

Kil'le=kil'le, *int.* kitcher-kitcher.

Kilo—gra'mm, *n.* (—**gramms**, *pl.* **gram'me**) kilogram. **—me'ter,** *n.* (—**meters**, *pl.* — **meter**) kilometre (about $\frac{5}{8}$ of an English statute mile) = 1093·6 yards (one Engl. mile = 1760 yards). **—meter=karte,** *f.* railway ticket available for a distance of 1000 kilometres to be gone over at any time during the year (*issued in Baden*).

Kimm, *m.* (—s) dip of the horizon (*Naut.*). **—e**, *f.* (*pl.* **—en**) edge, border, brim, chime; notch (*for staves and in the sight of rifles and guns*).

Kim'm—en, *v.a.* to provide with a brim *or* chime; to notch. **—ung**, *f.* mirage; floor-heads (*of a ship*). *Comp.* **—hobel**, *m.* chime plane. **—wasser**, *n.* bilge water.

Kind, *n.* (—es, *pl.* —er; *obs. & poet:* —) child; **ein kleines —**, a small child, a baby; **— im Mutterleibe**, embryo, fœtus, child unborn; **unmündiges —**, infant (child); **nachgeborenes —**, posthumous child; **totgeborenes —**, still-born child; **— der Liebe**, natural *or* illegitimate child; **ein — bekommen**, to get a child; **ein — abtreiben**, to procure abortion; **sie wird kein — mehr haben**, she is past child-bearing; **ein echtes Berliner —**, a native of Berlin; **ein echtes Londoner —**, a regular cockney; **das — beim rechten** *or* **bei seinem Namen nennen**, to call a spade a spade; **ein — aus der Taufe heben**, to stand sponsor to a child; **— des Todes**, one doomed to death; **—er Gottes**, the pious; all mankind; **—er der Welt**, children of this world; the worldly wise; worldlings; **— des Glückes**, a lucky person; **eines —es genesen**, to be delivered of a child; **an —es Statt annehmen**, to adopt; **wes Geistes — ist er?** what sort of a person is he? **mein —!** my dear, my dear child! **— und Kindes —**, children and grandchildren; **drei kleine —**, three little children (*poet.*); **er hat weder — noch Kegel**, he has neither kith nor kin; **ich komme mit — und Kegel**, I am coming, bag and baggage; **(wieder) zum — werden**, to grow childish; **das — mit dem Bade ausschütten**, to go much too far, to reject the good together with the bad (*prov.*); **wenn das — ertrunken ist, wird der Brunnen zugedeckt**, after death the doctor; lock the stable-door when the steed is stolen (*prov.*). **—chen** (—chens, *pl.* —chen) (*also* **—erchen**), **—lein**, *n.* (—leins, *pl.* —lein) (*also* **—erlein**) baby, infant, little child; **sich liebes —chen** *or* **lieb Kind bei einem machen**, to curry favour with a p. **—erei'**, *f.* childish trick; childishness; trifle, childish matter; **eine reine —erei**, pure childishness. **—eln**, *v.n.* (*aux.* **s.**) to trifle, act childishly. **—haft**, *adj. & adv.* childlike, childish. **—heit**, *f.* childhood, infancy; **von —heit an**, from infancy *or* childhood. **—isch**, *adj. & adv.* childish. **—lich**, *adj. & adv.* childlike; filial. **—lichkeit**, *f.* childlike disposition *or* manners. **—schaft**, *f.* relation of a child to its parents; filiation; adoption (*B.*). *Comp.* **—bett**, *n.* childbed; **ins —bett kommen**, to be brought to bed. **—betterin**, *f.* lying-in woman, woman that has just been delivered. **—bett=fieber**, *n.* puerperal fever. **—s=kopf**, *m.* child's head; childish person, fool; child; **sei kein —skopf**, don't be (so) childish! **—taufe**, *f.* christening.

Kin'delbier, *n.* (—s) christening feast (*dial.*).

Kin'der, *pl. see* **Kind**. *Comp.* **—amme**, *f.* wet-nurse. **—austhun**, *n.* baby-farming. **—brei**, *m.* pap. **—dieb**, *m.* kidnapper of children. **—feind**, *m.* child-hater. **—frau**, **—wärterin**, *f.* nurse. **—fräulein**, *n.* nursery governess. **—freund**, *m.* child-lover; child's own book. **—garten**, *m.* kindergarten; infant-school. **—glaube**, *m.* credulity, faith of a child. **—heilanstalt**, *f.* hospital for children. **—jahre**, *pl.* (years of) childhood. **—lehre**, *f.* instruction in the catechism; Sunday-school; **—lehre halten**, to catechize. **—liebe**, *f.* love of children; filial love. **—los**, *adj.* childless. **—mädchen**, *n.*, **—magd**, *f.* nurse, nursemaid. **—märchen**, *n.* nursery tale. **—mord**, *m.* infanticide; **der bethlehemitische —mord**, the massacre of the Innocents. **—mörder**, *m.*, **—mörderin**, *f.* infanticide. **—mutter**, *f.* mother; midwife. **—narr**, *m.* person who dotes on children. **—pferd**, *n.* hobby-horse. **—plage**, *f.* nuisance of children. **—pocken**, *pl.* small-pox. **—posse**, *f.* childish trick, foolery. **—pulver**, *n.*, **—puder**, *m.* soothing powder for infants. **—raub**, *m.* kidnapping. **—reime**, *pl.* nursery rhymes. **—schlafstube**, *f.* night nursery. **—schuhe**, *pl.* children's shoes; **die —schuhe ausgetreten, ausgezogen, abgelegt haben**, to be no longer a child, to have put away childish things, to be past the spoon, out of the leading-strings, to have put off childish ways; to be a young gentleman *or* a young lady. **—sinn**, *m.* child-like mind. **—spiel**, *n.* children's game; child's play, easy matter; trifle; **es ist kein —spiel**, it is not easy, not a trifle, no joke. **—spielstube**, *f.*, **—spielzimmer**, *n.* (day) nursery. **—spielwaren**, *pl.*, **—spielzeug**, *n.* toys, playthings. **—spott**, *m.* laughing-stock *or* sport for children. **—stube**, *f.* (day) nursery. **—tag**, *m.* Innocents' day. **—taufe**, *f.* infant baptism. **—verse**, *pl.* nursery rhymes. **—wagen**, *m.* perambulator, go-cart. **—wäsche**, *f.* baby-linen. **—welt**, *f.* children; life *or* doings of children. **—wiege**, *f.* cradle. **—wurm**, *m.* ascaris. **—zähne**, *pl.* milk-teeth. **—zeug**, *n.* playthings, trifles; baby-linen. **—zucht**, *f.* education of children, pedagogy.

Kin'der—n, *v.a.* to play the child, to behave childishly; to get children (*vulg.*). **—ei'**, *f.* childishness, childish trick.

Kin'des (*gen. of* **Kind**, *q.v.*). *Comp.* **—alter**, *n.* infancy, childhood; child's age. **—beine**, *pl.*; **von —beinen an**, from infancy *or* childhood. **—kind**, *n.* grandchild. **—kinder**, *pl.* grandchildren, posterity. **—liebe**, *f.* filial love; philoprogenitiveness. **—mörderin**, *f.* woman who has killed her newborn babe. **—not**, *f.* labour, travail; **in —nöten sterben**, to die in childbed. **—pflicht**, *f.* filial duty. **—recht**, **—teil**, *n.* portion of inheritance due to a child. **—statt**, *f.*; **Annahme an —statt**, adoption.

Kin'kerlitzchen, *pl.* trifles, useless things (*coll.*).

Kink'horn, *n.* cornet (*Mus.*); whelk (*Mollusc.*).

Kinn, *n.* (—es, *pl.* —e) chin; lower jaw; spout of a gutter. *Comp.* **—backe(n)**, *m.* jaw, jawbone, mandible. **—backen=drüsen**, *pl.* maxillary glands. **—backen=krampf**, *m.* tetanus. **—bart**, *m.* beard on the chin; imperial. **—grube**, *f.*, **—grüblein**, *n.* dimple in the chin. **—kette**, *f.*, **—reif**, *m.* curb. **—ketten=stange**, *f.* curb-bit. **—lade**, *f.* jawbone. **—riemen**, *m.* cheek-strap (*of caps*).

Kip'pe, *f.* (*pl.* —n) edge, brink; dangerous situation; see-saw; assay-balance; **auf der — stehen**, to be on the point of losing one's balance, in a dangerous situation. **—lig**, *adj.* doubtful, undecided; dangerous (*coll.*).

Kip'peln, *v.* I. *a.* to clip (*money*); **sich —**, to wrangle. II. *n.* (*aux.* **h.** & **s.**) to see-saw.

Kip'pen, *v.* I. *a.* to tilt, tip over, to upset, to cut the edges off, clip; to lop; **den Anker —**, to fish the anchor; **— und wippen**, to clip money. II. *n.* (*aux.* **h.** & **s.**) to topple over, lose one's balance; to upset, overturn; to weigh; **mit dem Stuhle —**, to balance oneself on a chair.

Kip'per, *m.* (—s, *pl.* —) money-clipper. **—ei'**, *f.* money-clipping; usury. **—n**, *v.n.* (*aux.* **h.**) to clip money; to carry on usury. *Comp.* **—geld**, *n.* base coin, clipped money.

Kir'ch—e, *f.* (*pl.* —en) church; building, service *or* members of a church; **die streitende —e**, the church militant; **die herrschende —e**, the established church; **anglikanische —e**, church of England. **—lich**, *adj. & adv.* ecclesiastical; church; spiritual; ritual; churchy (*coll.*); **—liches Begräbnis**, Christian burial.

—**lichkeit**, *f.* attachment to *or* accordance with the church; religiosity. —**ner**, *m.* (—**ners**, *pl.* —**ner**) sexton, sacristan; church-clerk. *Comp.* —**abtrünnige(r)**, *m.* schismatic. —**dorf**, *n.* village with a church. —**fahne**, *f.* vane on a church. —**gang**, *m.* going to church; aisle; —**gang halten**, to be churched. —**genoß**, *m.*, —**genossin**, *f.* parishioner. —**halle**, *f.* church-porch. —**herr**, *m.* church-patron; vicar. —**hof**, *m.* churchyard, graveyard. —**messe**, *f.* fair; *see* —**weihe**. —**spiel**, *n.* parish; **nicht zu einem —spiele gehörig**, extra-parochial; **dem —spiele zur Last fallen**, to come upon the parish. —**spiel=leute**, *pl.* parishioners. —**spiel=vorsteher**, *m.* church-warden. —**sprengel**, *m.* diocese. —**turm**, *m.* (church) steeple. —**turm=spitze**, *f.* spire. —**weihe**, *f.* consecration *or* dedication of a church; church-festival. —**weih=fest**, *n.* church-festival.

Kir'chen, *pl. see* **Kirche**. —**haft**, *adj. & adv.* church-like. —**tum**, *n.* the church; everything connected with the church; churchdom. *Comp.* —**ablaß**, *m.* indulgence (*R. C.*). —**älteste(r)**, *m.* church-warden, elder, vestryman. —**amt**, *n.* church-office, ecclesiastical function; eldership; consistory, church-wardens (*coll.*). —**bann**, *m.* excommunication; interdict; **in den —bann thun**, to excommunicate *or* interdict. —**bau**, (**Kirch'bau**,) *m.* erection of a church. —**bekleidung**, *f.* pulpit-hangings. —**besuch**, *m.* attendance at church. —**besucher**, *pl.* congregation. —**buch**, *n.* ritual, liturgy; parochial register; service-book. —**buße**, *f.* penance imposed by *or* done in the church. —**chor**, *m.* choir of the church. —**diebstahl**, —**raub**, *m.* sacrilege. —**diener**, *m.* church-officer; sexton; sacristan. —**dienst**, *m.* church-service; ecclesiastical office. —**dienstlich**, *adj.* relating to the church service *or* office; —**dienstliche Handlungen**, religious observances *or* ceremonies. —**einkünfte**, *pl.* church revenues. —**fahne**, *f.* standard *or* banner used in church ceremonies. —**fest**, *n.* church festival. —**fluch**, *m.* anathema. —**flüchtige(r)**, *m.* seeker of sanctuary. —**freiheit**, *f.* immunity of the church; ecclesiastical liberty. —**frevel**, *m.* sacrilege. —**friede**, *m.* union of the members of the church; security of church property. —**fürst**, *m.* ecclesiastical prince, high dignitary of the church; prelate. —**gänger**, (**Kirch'gänger**,) *m.* churchgoer. —**gebet**, *n.* common prayer. —**gebet=buch**, *n.* book of common prayer, prayer-book. —**gebiet**, *n.* diocese. —**gebrauch**, *m.* church-rite *or* observance; **ein Buch, das die —gebräuche enthält**, ritual. —**gefäß**, *n.* church-vessel; (*pl.*) church-plate. —**geld**, *n.* fund belonging to a church. —**gelder**, *pl.* church property. —**gemein(d)e**, *f.* parish; congregation. —**gemeinschaft**, *f.* church-membership. —**gerät**, *n.* sacred vessels *or* garments. —**gericht**, *n.* ecclesiastical court, consistory. —**gesang**, *m.* church-singing; hymn, anthem, psalm. —**gesangbuch**, *n.* hymn-book. —**geschichte**, *f.* ecclesiastical history. —**gesetz**, *n.* canon; (*pl.*) decretals. —**gesetzlich**, —**gesetzmäßig**, *adj.* canonical. —**glaube**, *m.* creed, dogma of a church. —**grund**, *m.* glebe (*land*). —**gut**, *n.* church property, glebe. —**jahr**, *n.* ecclesiastical year. —**konvent**, *m.* convocation; meeting (*of the parishioners*) in connection with church affairs. —**lehen**, *n.* ecclesiastical fief. —**lehre**, *f.* church doctrine. —**lehrer**, *m.* father of the church; teacher of church *or* religious doctrine. —**lied**, *n.* church hymn. —**lieder=buch**, *n.* hymn-book. —**maus**, *f.*; **arm wie eine —maus** *or* **die reine —maus sein**, to be as poor as a church mouse, to be extremely poor. —**musik**, *f.* sacred music. —**oberhaupt**, *n.* head of the church. —**oblate**, *f.* sacramental wafer —**ordnung**, *f.* church discipline; ritual. —**ornat**, *n.* canonicals. —**pfleger**, *m.* church-warden. —**probst**, *m.* provost of an ecclesiastical establishment. —**rat**, *m.* consistory, ecclesiastical court; member of a consistory; church-committee. —**rätlich**, *adj.* consistorial. —**räuberisch**, *adj.* sacrilegious. —**recht**, *n.* privilege *or* right of the church; church-law, canon-law. —**rechtlich**, *adj. & adv.* canonical. —**rechts=gelehrte(r)**, —**rechts=kundige(r)**, *m.* canonist. —**regiment**, *n.*, —**regierung**, *f.* church government *or* polity; hierarchy. —**register**, *n.* church *or* parochial register. —**rock**, *m.* cassock. —**sache**, *f.* ecclesiastical affair. —**sänger**, *m.* chorister, choir-boy. —**satz**, *m.* ecclesiastical tenet; patronage; advowson. —**schiff**, *n.* nave. —**schänder**, *m.* sacrilegious person. —**sitz**, *m.* seat in a church; pew. —**spaltung**, *f.* schism. —**staat**, *m.* Papal territory, Ecclesiastical States. —**stand**, *m.* seat, place in a church. —**steuer**, *f.* church-rate. —**streit**, *m.*, —**streitigkeit**, *f.* religious controversy; dissension in the church. —**stück**, *n.* sacred music (*Mus.*). —**stuhl**, *m.* pew; seat in church. —**trennung**, *f.* schism. —**vater**, *m.* father of the church; **die —väter**, the holy fathers, the early fathers. —**verband**, *m.* church membership. —**verbesserer**, *m.* reformer. —**verbesserung**, *f.* church reform, reformation of the church. —**versammlung**, *f.* synod; convocation; vestry. —**vogt**, *m.* church-warden; beadle. —**vorschrift**, *f.* church-law; ordinance of the church; liturgy. —**vorsteher**, *m.* church-warden; **Versammlung der —vorsteher**, vestry-meeting. —**weise**, *f.* sacred melody. —**wesen**, *n.* church matters. —**zettel**, *m.* list of services for each Sunday, services on each Sunday. —**zucht**, *f.* church discipline, ecclesiastical discipline.

Kir'mes, **Kirm'se**, *f.* church fair; *see* **Kirchmesse**.

Kirr, —**e**, *adj. & adv.* tame, familiar; tractable, submissive.

Kir'r—en, *v.* I. *a.* to tame, make tractable; to bait; to allure; to call (*of hens*). II. *n.* (*aux.* **h.**) to coo. —**ung**, *f.* taming; baiting, alluring; bait; baiting-place.

Kirsch, *m.* short for **Kirschbranntwein**.

Kir'sch—e, *f.* (*pl.* —**en**) cherry; **mit großen Herren ist nicht gut —en essen**, the weak always go to the wall *or* come off worst (*prov.*); **mit ihm ist nicht gut —en essen**, he is not an easy man to deal with. —**en**, *adj.* cherry, of cherry-wood. *Comp.* —**baum**, *m.* cherry-tree. —**baum=holz**, *n.* cherry-wood. —**branntwein**, —**geist**, *m.* cherry brandy. —**en=stiel**, *m.* cherry stalk. —**kern**, *m.* cherry stone. —**kuchen**, *m.* cherry-tart. —**wasser**, *n.* cordial made from cherries, cherry brandy.

Kir'sei, *m.* kersey (*C. L.*).

Kis'sen, *n.* (—**s**, *pl.* —, *dim.* **Kiß'chen**, **Kiß'lein**, *n.*) cushion, pillow; pad (*Engr.*); bolster (*Naut.*). *Comp.* —**bezug**, —**überzug**, *m.*, —**ziehe**, —**züge**, *f.* pillow-slip *or* case.

Kis't—e, *f.* (*pl.* —**en**) box, chest, coffer, trunk; thing, matter, affair (*sl.*); **eine —e Fensterglas**, a crate of glass; **das ist ja eine nette —e**, that's a pretty mess (*sl.*). —**ler** (—**lers**, *pl.* —**ler**), —**ner** (—**ners**, *pl.* —**ner**), *m.* chest *or* trunk-maker. *Comp.* —**en=bau**, *m.* embankment of piles and brushwood. —**en=pfand**, *n.* daughter's portion (*Law*).

Kitt, *m.* (—**es**, *pl.* —**e**) cement; putty; lute, luting (*Chem.*); solder.

Kit'tel, *m.* (—**s**, *pl.* —) smock-frock; blouse.

Kit'ten, *v.a.* to cement; to (fasten with) putty; to lute; to cement (*fig.*).

Kit'z—e, *f.* (*pl.* —**en**) cat, kitten; (—**lein**, *n.*) kid, fawn. —**eln**, *v. n.* (*aux.* **h.**) to lamb, kid (*coll.*).

Kit'zel, *m.* (—s) itching; tickling, titillation; inordinate desire, appetite; der — sticht ihn danach, he has a longing for it. —ig, *adj. & adv.* ticklish; touchy; nice, delicate, difficult; critical. *Comp.* —litteratur, *f.* sensational literature; pornographic literature.

Kit'zel—n, *v.a.* to tickle, titillate; to gratify, tickle; es —t mich, I have a longing, something tickles me, it pleases me; I feel nettled at it; I feel tempted.

Kitz'—ler, *m.* (—lers, *pl.* —ler) tickler; clitoris (*Anat.*). —lich, —lig, *see* —elig. —lichkeit, *f.* ticklishness.

Kix, *see* Kicks. —en, *v.n.* (*aux.* h.) to miss a ball.

Klabas'tern, *v.a.* to rummage noisily.

Klabau'termann, *m.* (—s) hobgoblin, bogyman (*as seen on ships doomed to be wrecked*).

Klack, *m.* (—es, *pl.* Klä'cke) cleft; fissure, chink.

Klack, —s, *int.* slap-bang!

Klad'de, *f.* (*pl.* —n) rough draft, rough copy; day-book (*C. L.*).

Kladderadat'sch, *int.* (*if a thing falls down with a bang*) slap-bang! bounce! name of a satirical illustrated weekly (Berlin) paper.

Klaff, *m.* bark, yelp; small lid. —en, *v.n.* (*aux.* h. & s.) to bark, yelp; to clatter; to chatter, prate; to gape, yawn; to split open; to be ajar. —end, *p. & adj.* gaping, yawning; ajar. —er, *m.* (—ers, *pl.* —er) barking dog; slanderer, gossip.

Kläf'f—en, *v.n.* (*aux.* h.) to bark, yelp; to be quarrelsome, brawl. —er, *m.* hound that opens false (*Sport*); chatterer; brawler; slanderer, gossip.

Klaf'ter, *f.* (*pl.* —n) fathom (= *6 feet*); cord (*of wood*). —ig, *adj.* containing a cord. *Comp.* —holz, *n.* cord-wood. —maß, *n.* wood-measure. —schläger, *m.* wood-cleaver. —weise, *adv.* by the cord *or* fathom.

Klaf'tern, *v.n. & a.* to measure with outspread arms; to fathom; to cord up.

Klag'—bar, *adj. & adv.* liable to complaint, actionable; —bar machen, to bring before a court of law; —bar werden, to sue at law, to go to law. —e, *f.* (*pl.* —en) complaint, lament; grievance, ground of complaint; accusation, impeachment; action, indictment; eine —e eingeben, anhängig machen, anstellen, to bring an action (wider *or* gegen, against); eine —e auf Schadenersatz, an action for damages; mit einer —e abgewiesen werden, to be non-suited; —e über, gegen *or* wider einen führen, to complain of a p.; to bring an action against a person.

Kla'g—en, *v.* I. *a.* bewail; einem eine Sache *or* sein Leid —en, to complain to one of a th. . . .; (um) einen Toten —en, to mourn for s.o. who is dead. II. *r.* to be indisposed; to complain (*obs.*). III. *n.* (*aux.* h.) to complain, lament (über, um, for); to complain (über, of); to sue (*at law*). —end, *p. & adj.* complaining; plaintive; der —ende, the plaintiff. *Comp.* —e-dichter, *m.* elegiac poet. —e-fall, *m.* accusative case (*obs.*). —(e)-gesang, *m.* threnody; *see* —elied. —e-haus, *n.* house of mourning. —e-lied, *n.* lamentation, mournful song; elegy; dirge. —e-lustig, *adj.* litigious; querulous. —ens-wert, *adj. & adv.* lamentable, deplorable. —e-ruf, *m.* lamentation. —e-stimme, *f.* plaintive voice. —eule, *f.* screech-owl. —e-weib, *n.* (hired) female mourner. —los, *adj. & adv.* uncomplaining; indemnified; —los stellen, to satisfy, indemnify. —(e)-punkte, *pl.* heads of a charge, counts of an indictment; grievances. —(e)-ruf, *m.* lamentation. —sache, *f.* suit, action. —(e)-schrift, *f.* accusatory writing, bill of complaint, writ. —(e)-sucht, *f.* disposition to complain, querulousness. —(e)-süchtig, *adj. & adv.* litigious; querulous. —(e)-ton, *m.* plaintive *or* doleful tone. —weise, *adv.* by way of complaint. —würdig, *adj.* lamentable, pitiful, woeful.

Klä'g—er, *m.* (—ers, *pl.* —er) plaintiff, complainant. —erei', *f.* litigiousness; constant complaining. —erisch, *adj. & adv.* relating to the plaintiff; litigious; der —erische Advokat, plaintiff's counsel. —lich, *adj. & adv.* lamentable, deplorable; doleful; miserable, wretched, pitiful. —lichkeit, *f.* deplorableness; misery.

Klamm, I. *adj. & adv.* tight, close, narrow; hard; stiff; compact; scarce; clammy; oppressed in breathing. II. *n.* (—es) spasm, cramp. III. *f.* (*pl.* —en) ravine, mountain cleft, glen; cañon, canyon. —er, *f.* (*pl.* —ern) clamp, clasp; brace; rivet; clamp, holdfast; bracket; parenthesis; in —ern, in brackets, as a *or* in parenthesis, parenthetical. —ern, *v.* I. *a.* to clasp, clamp, rivet; sich an eine S. —ern, to cling to a th. II. *n.* (*aux.* h.) to clasp. *Comp.* —er-satz, *m.* sentence in a parenthesis. —gällig, *adj.* very hard; massive, pure. —gold, *n.* massive gold. —lötig, *adj.* weighing scarcely half an ounce.

Klam'pe, *f.* (*pl.* —n) clamp; holdfast; (*pl.*) cleats (*Naut.*).

Klang, Klan'gest; Klän'ge, *1 (& 3), 2 p. sing. imperf. indic.; 1 (& 3) p. sing. imperf. subj. of* klingen.

Klang, *m.* (—es, *pl.* Klän'ge) sound; ringing (*of bells*); clang; ring (*of money*); timbre (*Mus. & Phonet.*); tone; keinen guten — haben, to be held in ill repute; ohne Sang und —, privately, clandestinely; Dauer und —, quantity and quality (*of vowel sounds*). *Comp.* —boden, *m.* sounding-board. —gebend, *adj.* sonorous. —gedicht, *n.* sonnet (*rare*). —lehre, *f.* theory of sound, acoustics. —los, *adj.* soundless, mute, unaccented; unceremonious; secret; without (a word of) praise. —malerei, *f.* imitative music, onomatopœia. —messer, *m.* phonometer (*Phys.*). —nachahmend, *adj.* imitative of sound, onomatopoetic. —reich, *adj.*, —voll, *adj.* sonorous, full-sounding. —stufe, *f.* interval (*Mus.*). —wort, *n.* onomatopoetic word.

Klapp, I. *m.* (—es, *pl.* —e) clap, slap, blow; ein — ins Gesicht, a slap in the face. II. *int.* bang! clack! —e, *f.* (*pl.* —en) flap; lid; valve; damper; falling-board; key, stop (*of a musical instrument*); flap, cuff (*of a dress*); bed (*sl.*); mouth (*sl.*); eine Flöte mit elf —en, an eleven-keyed flute; zwei Fliegen mit einer —e treffen, to kill two birds with one stone; in die —e gehen *or* steigen, to go to bed; halt deine —e, shut up! (*sl.*). —ig, provided with a valve, valvular. —s, *see* Klapp. —sen, *v.a.* to slap, smack; to flap. *Comp.* —bank, *f.* folding bench. —bord, *m.* washboard (*Naut.*). —en-loch, *n.* vent (*Mech.*). —en-trompete, *f.* chromatic trumpet. —fenster, *n.* trap *or* sky-light window. —(en)-horn, *n.* key bugle, cornet à piston. —horn-verse, *pl.* ludicrous verses (*of 4 lines after a given pattern in which the* Klappenhorn *played a prominent part*). —hut, *m.* opera-hat. —kragen, *m.* turn-down collar. —mütze, *f.* cap with flaps. —pult, *n.* folding desk. —reime, *pl.* capped verses; verse in which the last word of the second line rhymes with the initial word of the first. —sitz, *m.* bracket; flap-seat. —(en)-stiefel, *m.* top-boot. —stoß, *m.* stroke downwards (*Bill.*). —stuhl, *m.* camp-stool, folding-chair. —tisch, *m.* folding-table. —thür, *f.* trap-door.

Klap'p—en, *v.* I. *a.* to flap, strike together rapidly. II. *n.* (*aux.* h.) to clap, flap; to clatter, rattle; to fit, suit, go well together; to sound well; es —t nicht, it does not come work out right, it goes badly, there is no sense in it; it will not do, it won't wash (*sl.*); **wenn es zum —en kommt,** if things come to a head, if the matter gets serious (*sl.*).

Klap'per, *f.* (*pl.* —n, rattle; clapper (*of a mill*), flier (*Weav.*).

Klap'per—n, I. *v.n.* (*aux.* h.) to clatter, rattle; to click; to chatter (*with the teeth*); to sound the gong (*hum.*); **der Storch —t,** the stork clatters; **die (Klapper=)Schlange —t,** the (rattle)snake rattles. II. *subst.n.*; **—n gehört zum Handwerk,** puff is part of the trade; **Heulen und Zähne—n,** weeping and gnashing of teeth (*B.*). **—ig,** *adj.* weak, deficient (*coll.*). *Comp.* **—bein,** *n.* skeleton; loose bone; Death. **—blech,** *n.* cithern. **—dürr,** *adj.* very thin and dry, thin as a rake. **—kasten,** *m.* bad piano. **—mann,** *m.* man with a rattle; Death (*vulg.*). **—mühle,** *f.* mill with a clapper; chatterbox (*vulg.*). **—schlange,** *f.* rattlesnake. **—storch,** *m.* (common white) stork.

Klar, I. *adj. & adv.* clear; limpid; bright; serene; distinct; plain; easy to be understood; evident; pure; light-coloured; ready (*Naut.*); **— zum Gefecht,** ready for the fight; **eine —e Stimme,** a clear voice; **die Riemen — machen,** to ship the oars; **an sich —,** self-evident; **etwas ins —e setzen,** to clear up a point; **noch nicht im —en sein,** not yet to see one's way, to be not yet clear about a th.; **ins —e kommen mit einem,** to come to a clear understanding with s.o.; **einen ins —e setzen,** to set one right; **ich will ihn darüber gleich ins —e setzen** *or* **kommen lassen,** I will soon clear him up about that point *or* make him see how the land lies; **er muß sich darüber — werden,** he must make up his mind concerning it; **einem —en Wein einschenken,** to tell one the plain truth; **das —e vom Ei,** the white of the egg. II. *m.* (—es) fine linen *or* batiste. **—e,** *f.* (*pl.* —en) thin sauce *or* broth; thin paste. **—heit,** *f.* clearness; brightness; transparency; lucidity; purity; fineness; plainness. **—ifizie'ren,** *v.a.* to clarify. *Comp.* **—äugig,** *adj.* clear-eyed; clear-sighted. **—düster,** *adj.* chiaroscuro. **—stellen,** *v.a.*; **eine Sache —stellen,** to clear up a matter.

Klä'r—e, *f.* clearness, purity, brightness; delicacy of texture; stuff for clearing *or* refining; starch (*prov.*). **—en,** *v.a.* to clear, clarify, purify; to brighten, polish; **sich —en,** to settle, become clear. **—lich,** *adv.* clearly. **—sel,** *n.* (—sels) clarified sugar. *Comp.* **—kessel,** *m.* clarifier. **—maschine,** *f.* distilling machine.

Klarinet't—e, *f.* (*pl.*—en) clarinet, clarionet. **—i'st,** *m.* (—is'ten, *pl.* —is'ten) clarionet-player.

Klarie'ren, *v.a.* to clear a ship (at the custom-house).

Klas's—e, *f.* (*pl.* —n) class, rank. **—ifizie'ren,** *v.a.* to classify. **—iker,** *m.* (—ikers, *pl.* —iker) classic, first-rate writer, classical author. **—isch,** *adj. & adv.* classic, classical; **das ist —isch!** that 's first rate, that beats everything! **eine —ische Entschuldigung,** a remarkable *or* wonderful excuse. *Comp.* **—n=ältester,** *m.* top boy of a form; **—enältester der Prima,** head boy *or* captain of the school. **—n=eintei=lung,** *f.* classification. **—n=geist,** *m.* spirit of caste. **—n=lehrer,** *m.* form master. **—n=mütze,** *f.* form cap (*in German schools as a rule each form has its distinct cap*). **—n=steuer,** *f.* graduated rate. **—n=stolz,** *m.* caste feeling, pride of caste. **—n=zimmer,** *n.* school room.

Klatsch, I. *m.* (—es, *pl.* —e) slap, smack, pop; crack (*of a whip*); gossip. II. *int.* pop! crack! smack! **—e,** *f.* (*pl.* —en) fly-flap; babbler, gossip.

Klat'sch—en, *v.* I. *a.* to clap; to divulge by gossiping, blab, tell tales; **Beifall —en,** to applaud. I. *n.* (*aux.* h.) to smack; to clap; to crack; to babble (*vulg.*); **in die Hände —en,** to clap the hands. **—er,** *m.* (—ers, *pl.* —er) clapper, applauder. **—erei',** *f.* babble; tattle; backbiting, scandal. **—haft,** *adj.* gossiping, tattling. **—haftigkeit,** *f.* babbling *or* gossiping disposition. *Comp.* **—base,** *f.* gossip, tell-tale. **—büchse,** *f.* popgun; chatterbox. **—geschichte,** *f.* scandal, piece of gossip. **—gevatter,** *m.* gossip. **—maul,** *n.* babbler (*vulg.*). **—naß,** *adj.* wet all through, sopping wet. **—rose,** *f.* corn-poppy. **—tante,** *f.*, **—weib,** *n. see* **—base.**

Klät'scher, *m.* (—s, *pl.* —), **—in,** *f.* prating gossip. **—ei',** *f.* gossip, scandal.

Klat'te, *f.* (*pl.* —n) tangle, tangled mass.

Klau'be—n, *v.* I. *a.* to pick, pick out, cull. II. *n.* (*aux.* h.); **an einem Knochen —n,** to pick a bone; **über einer S. —n,** to ponder over, hammer at a thing. **—r,** *m.* (—rs, *pl.* —r) picker, culler; caviller. **—rei',** *f.* picking, culling; (*pl.*) minutiæ; **Wort—rei,** catching at words, hair-splitting, cavilling. **—richt,** *n.* (—richts) refuse (*Min.*).

Klau'—e, *f.* (*pl.* —en) claw, talon, fang; fluke (*of an anchor*); hoof; paw; clutch. **—en,** *v.a.* to claw, to clutch. **—ig,** *adj.* having claws, *etc.* *Comp.* **—en=fett,** *n.* neat's-foot oil. **—en=förmig,** *adj.* ungulate. **—en=hieb,** *m.* stroke, blow (*of a paw* or *talon*). **—en=seuche,** *f.* disease in the feet of cattle. **—en=steuer,** *f.* tax on cattle.

Klau's—e, *f.* (*pl.* —en) closet; cell, hermitage; mountain-pass, defile; pit, hole; den (*coll.*). **—el,** *f.* (*pl.* —eln) clause; appendix; stipulation, condition; section of a musical strain *or* movement, musical period. **(—ener,)** **—(s)=ner,** *m.* (—(e)ners, *pl.* —(e)ner), **—(s)nerin,** *f.* hermit, recluse. **—u'r,** *f.* (*pl.* —uren) confinement, seclusion; clasp (*of a book*). **—u'r=arbeit,** *f.* class exercise (to be written in a given time), examination paper, test paper.

Klaviatu'r, *f.* (*pl.* —en) key-board (of a piano).

Klavie'r, *n.* (—s, *pl.* —e) piano-forte; square *or* grand piano. *Comp.* **—auszug,** *m.* piano-forte arrangement. **—kasten,** *m.* case of a piano-forte. **—lehrer,** *m.* piano-forte teacher, music master. **—schlüssel,** *m.* tuning key; C-clef. **—schule,** *f.* manual of exercises for the piano. **—stimmer,** *m.* piano-forte tuner. **—stuhl,** *m.* music stool. **—stunde,** *f.* lesson on the piano(-forte), piano-lesson. **—unterricht,** *m.* lessons on the piano(-forte); music lessons.

Klavizim'bel, (**Klavezim'bel,**) *n.*=**Klavier** (*sl.*).

Kle'b—en, *v.* I. *a.* to fasten with paste, *etc.*, to paste, glue. II. *n.* (*aux.* h.) to cleave, stick, adhere (**an,** to); **es bleibt nichts bei ihm —en,** he is very forgetful; **er läßt die Kelle nicht an der Pfanne —en,** he does not let the grass grow under his feet; **er läßt nichts an der Haue —en,** he gives tit for tat; **es —t wie Wachs,** it sticks like wax; **am Irdischen —en,** to be worldly minded; **an der Scholle —en,** to be bound to the soil; to be unwilling to travel. **—er,** *m.* (—ers, *pl.* —er) one who pastes on; blll poster; adhesive substance; gum; gluten. **—richt,** (*obs.*) *adj. & adv.* sticky, gluelike. **—(e)rig,** *adj. & adv.* adhesive; sticky, viscous, glutinous; clammy; **—erige Hände haben,** to be light-fingered (*coll.*); **—erige Stimme,** thick, harsh voice. **—(e)rigkeit,** *f.* stickiness. *Comp.* **—e=blatt,** *n.* poster. **—(e)=garn,** *n.* net for catching larks. **—e=gesetz,** *n.* law that enjoins the pasting of stamps in a clerk's, workman's, *or* servant's book (*coll.*). **—e=gummi,** *m.* gum, stickfast. **—e=gut,** *n.* entailed property, entail. **—e=marke,** *f.* stamp stating the time of service to be pasted in the service-register (*coll.*). **—e=rute,** *f.* lime-twig. **—(e)=pflaster,** *n.* sticking-plaster; (**englisches**) court-plaster. **—(e)=stoff,** *m.* gum, gluten. **—(e)=werk,** *n.* lute, paste-work. **—e=zettel,** *m.* poster.

Kle'ckern, *v.n.* to slobber (*while eating or drinking*).
Kleck—s, *m.* (—(s)es, *pl.* —(s)e) blot, (ink)stain, blur; **voller —se,** blotty. **—(s)en,** *v.* I. *n.* (*aux.* **h.**) to blot, blur; to trickle down; to splutter (*of pens*). II. *a.* to daub, stain; to scrawl. **—(s)er,** *m.* (—(s)ers, *pl.* —(s)er) scrawler, scribbler, paper blotter (*of a bad writer*); dauber (*of a bad painter*). **—(s)erei',** *f.* constant blotting; scrawl (*bad writing*); daubing, daub (*bad painting*). **—(s)ig,** *adj. & adv.* blotty, blotchy, blurred.
Kleda'ge, *f.* = Kleidung (*sl.*).
Klee, *m.* (—s) clover, trefoil; clubs (*cards*); **wenn es nur erst über den grünen — ist,** when the first start has been made. *Comp.* **—blatt,** *n.* (leaf of) trefoil, clover-leaf; trio, triplet. **—blatt-bogen,** *m.* trefoil arch. **—dame,** *f.* queen of clubs. **—salz,** *n.* sorrel-salt. **—salz-kraut,** *n.* wood-sorrel. **—säure,** *f.* oxalic acid.
Klei, *m.* (—(e)s, *pl.* —e) clay, loam, marl. **—icht,** (*obs.*) **—ig,** *adj.* clayey. *Comp.* **—acker,** *m.* clay-land. **—boden,** *m.* clay-soil.
Klei'b—en, *ir.v.* I. *a.* to stick, glue, paste, to build with mud. II. *n.* (*aux.* **h.**) to cleave, adhere. **—er,** *m.* (—ers, *pl.* —er) botcher; builder with mud; nut-hatch (*Orn.*). **—ig,** *adj.* adhesive, sticky. *Comp.* **—er-lehm,** *m.* clay mixed with straw. **—(er)-werk,** *n.* mud-walling.
Kleid, *n.* (—es, *pl.* —er) article of clothing, garment; garb; dress; coat; cover, case; cloth (*of a sail*); (*pl.*) garments; **—er machen Leute,** clothes make the man (*prov.*); **Reit—,** habit. **—chen,** *n.* (—chens, *pl.* —chen) little dress *or* garment. *Comp.* **—er-behälter,** *m.* wardrobe. **—er-bürste,** *f.* clothes-brush. **—er-geld,** *n.* allowance for clothes. **—er-geschäft, —er-magazin,** *n.* ready-made clothes shop. **—er-gestell,** *n.* clothes stand *or* rack. **—er-handel,** *m.* old-clothes trade. **—er-krämer,** *m.* old-clothes man. **—er-kämmerer,** *m.* master of the wardrobe. **—er-leinwand,** *f.* linen, lining for dresses. **—er-macher,** *m.* tailor. **—er-macherin,** *f.* dressmaker. **—er-narr,** *m.* over-dressed fop, dandy. **—er-ordnung,** *f.* sumptuary law. **—er-pflock,** *m.* clothes-peg. **—er-rock,** *m.* skirt. **—er-schoner,** *m.* caoutchouc border. **—er-schrank,** *m.* wardrobe. **—er-schützer,** *m.* dress-guard (*Cycl.*). **—er-spind,** *n.* cupboard for clothes, wardrobe. **—er-tracht,** *f.* costume. **—er-trödel,** *see* **—erhandel.** **—er-trödler,** *m.* old-clothes man. **—er-verleiher,** *m.* costumer. **—er-verwahrer,** *m.* keeper of the wardrobe. **—er-zimmer,** *n.* dressing-room.
Klei'd—en, *v.* I. *a.* to clothe, dress, provide with clothing; to deck, adorn; to fit, suit, become; to mount (*a gun*); to cover. II. *r.* to dress oneself; to find oneself in clothes; **sich gut —en,** to dress well. III. *n.* (*aux.* **h.**, *dat.*) to fit, suit, *or* be becoming to. **—sam,** *adj. & adv.* fitting well, becoming; **nicht —sam,** unbecoming. **—samkeit,** *f.* becomingness. **—ung,** *f.* clothing, dress; costume; drapery; mounting (*of guns*). *Comp.* **—ungs-stück,** *n.* article of clothing *or* dress; garment; (*pl.*) clothes.
Klei'—e, *f.* (*pl.* —en) bran, pollard. **—icht,** (*obs.*) **—ig,** *adj.* branny. *Comp.* **—en-artig,** *adj.* branny. **—en-brod,** *n.* bran-bread. **—en-—mehl,** *n.* pollard.
Klein, I. *n.* (—s) giblets (*Cul.*); broken fragments. II. *adj. & adv.* little, small; insignificant; petty; mean; minute, exact; scanty; neat, nice; minor; **der —e Mann, die —en Leute,** the lower classes, the artisans, workmen and labourers; **—e Geister,** small wits; narrow-minded people; **—e Leiden,** petty annoyances; **ein —er Puls,** a feeble pulse; **die —e Terz,** the minor third; **eine —e Stunde,** less than an hour; **ein —es Verbrechen,** a petty crime, minor offence; **—e Propheten,** minor prophets; **—(e)s Geld,** small money, change; **im —en,** on a small scale, minutely, in miniature, in retail; **— bringen, — kriegen,** to make out, to understand (*coll.*); **ins —e bringen,** to abridge; **ins —e gehen,** to enter into details; **um ein —es,** by a hair's breadth, very nearly; **es ist noch um ein —es, so ist der Gottlose nimmer,** for yet a little while and the wicked shall not be (*B.*); **über ein —es,** in a short time; **das ist ihm ein —es,** that's a trifle to him; **bei —em,** by degrees; **von — ab, an, auf,** from infancy *or* childhood; **sich — machen,** to humble oneself; **— bleiben,** to be stunted; **— werden,** to grow small, diminish, decrease, to subside; **Leute, bei denen es — hergeht,** people badly off; **der, die, das —e,** the little one, child, boy, *or* girl; **wer das —e nicht ehrt, ist des Großen nicht wert,** who will not keep a penny shall never have many (*prov.*); **die —en,** the young; **keiner soll mich — bringen,** no one shall get the better of me, outdo *or* surpass me; **er läßt sich nicht — kriegen,** he will not let himself be beaten, he does not give in (*coll.*); **ein — Bischen, ein — wenig,** a very little, a tiny bit. **—er,** *adj. comp. of* **klein**; lesser, younger; **—ere Brüder,** Minorites, Franciscan friars. **—heit,** *f.* littleness, smallness; pettiness, insignificance; trifle; **—heit des Geistes** *or* **der Gesinnungen,** narrow-mindedness. **—igkeit,** *f.* trifle. **—lich,** *adj.* rather small; mean, paltry, petty, trivial. **—lichkeit,** *f.* meanness, littleness, paltriness. *Comp.* **—bänker,** *pl.* costermongers. **—baß,** *m.*, **—baßgeige,** *f.* violoncello. **—bauer,** *m.* small farmer *or* freeholder. **—bild,** *n.* miniature. **—bogen-form,** *f.* small folio. **—denkend,** *adj.* small *or* narrow minded, of a mean disposition. **—deutsch,** *adj.*; **die —deutschen,** politicians (before 1866) who wished for a united Germany under the leadership of Prussia to the exclusion of Austria. **—drucker,** *m.* job-printer. **—fügig,** *adj.* paltry, insignificant, mean. **—geist,** *m.* narrow *or* small-minded person; mean soul; frivolity. **—geistig, —geisterisch,** *adj.* trifling, frivolous, small-minded, of a narrow mind, of a mean spirit. **—geld,** *n.* small change, change; **ihm fehlt dazu das nötige —geld,** he cannot afford it, he is not rich enough for that (*coll.*). **—gewehrfeuer,** *n.* musketry fire. **—gewerbe,** *n.* management of business on a small scale, small industry. **—gläubig,** *adj.* of little faith, faint-hearted. **—gut,** *n.* petty wares. **—handel,** *m.* retail trade. **—händler,** *m.* shopkeeper, retailer. **—herzig,** *adj.* faint-hearted; narrow-minded. **—hundert,** *n.* exact hundred (*as opposed to the* (*obs.*) **Großhundert** = *120*). **—kinder-bewahranstalt, —kinder-schule,** *f.* infant school; public nursery, crèche. **—kinder-bücher,** *pl.* books for the bairns. **—kinder-schule,** *f.* infant school. **—kohle,** *f.* druss, small coal. **—krämerei,** *f.* pettifogging, pedantry. **—krieg,** *m.* petty *or* guerilla warfare. **—laut,** *adj. & adv.* low-spirited, dejected, meek, quiet; **—laut werden,** to despond, to become despondent. **—maler,** *m.* miniature-painter. **—maschig,** *adj.* with fine meshes. **—meister,** *m.* coxcomb; prig; would-be artist; master in a very limited sphere. **—meisterei,** *f.* coxcombry; pedantry. **—messer,** *m.* micrometer. **—mut,** *m.* pusillanimity; despondency. **—mütig,** *adj.* fainthearted; dejected, desponding; **die —mütigen,** the feeble-minded. **—mütigkeit,** *see* **—mut.** **—russe,** *m.* inhabitant of Russia Minor (*Southwestern Russia*). **—schmied,** *m.* toolmaker. **—schmieds-ware,** *f.* hardware. **—siedlung,** *f.* small holding. **—sinn,** *m.* narrow-mindedness. **—sinnig,** *adj.* petty, small-minded. **—staaten,**

pl.; deutsche —staaten, Hesse, Saxe-Weimar, other Saxon duchies, Oldenburg, Brunswick, Hamburg, Bremen. —städter, m. inhabitant of a small provincial town, Gothamist; die deutschen —städter, the inhabitants of the (small) provincial towns of Germany. —städterei', f. provincial manners, habits, or way of thinking. —städtisch, adj. provincial, countrified. —steller, m. by-pass. —stoßen, v.a. to pound (in a mortar). —süchtig, adj. paltry, mean. —verkehr, m. retail trade. —vieh, n. small cattle, viz., sheep, goats, pigs. —ware, f. hardware; trinkets. —ziemer, m. red-wing.

Klei'nigkeit, f. (pl. —en) trifle, bagatelle, small matter; (pl.) toys, small trinkets; sich mit —en abgeben, to fritter one's time away; to go in for or to busy o.s. with trifles; es kommt mir auf eine — nicht an, I shan't stand out for or mind a trifle. Comp. —s=geist, —s=sinn, m. trifling or petty disposition. —s=krämer, m. punctilious, pedantic person; trifler; pettifogger.

Klei'nod, n. (—s, pl. —e or Kleino'dien) jewel, gem; treasure; (pl.) insignia of royalty, crown-jewels. Comp. —ien=händler, m. jeweller. —ien=kästchen, n. casket, jewel-case.

Klei'ster, m. (—s) paste, stickfast. —ig, adj. pasty, sticky. —n, v.a. to paste. Comp. —tiegel, m. paste-pot.

Klemm, adj. & adv. see Klamm; —e Zeiten, hard times (prov.). —e, f. (pl. —en) instrument for squeezing or holding fast, clip, holdfast; defile, narrow pass; straits; distress, difficulty, dilemma, pinch; in der —e sein, to be in a fix. —en, reg. & ir.v. I. a. to squeeze, pinch, cramp; to press close; to take away secretly, to pilfer (sl.). II. r. to press oneself (into, between); to get jammed or locked (as wheels); to get (one's finger, etc.) pinched. —er, m. (—ers, pl. —er) griping person, miser; pince-nez; clip (cycl.). Comp. —haken, m. cramp-iron, hold-fast.

Klem'p—ern, v.n. (aux. h.) to work in tin; to clink, tinkle. —ner, m. (—ners, pl. —ner) tinman, tinker. —nerei', f. tinman's trade or workshop.

Klep'per, m. (—s, pl. —) nag, hack.

Kle'r—iker, m. (—ikers, pl. —iker) cleric, priest, clergyman. —isei', f. clerical set. —us, m. clergy.

Klet'te, f. (pl. —n) bur, burdock; sich wie eine — an einen anhängen, to stick to one like a bur.

Klet't—en, v. I. a. to card wool. II. r. to stick to, adhere. —er, m. (—ers, pl. —er) wool-carder.

Klet'ter—n, v.n. (aux. h. & s.) to climb, clamber; to scramble up (mountain peaks); —nde Pflanze or Kletterpflanze, climber. —er, m. climber. Comp. —fuß, m. scansorial foot. —füßig, adj. zygodactylous, yoke-footed (Orni.). —rose, f. climbing rose, rose creeper. —stange, f. climbing pole; greasy pole. —vögel, pl. scansorials.

Kli'cker, m. (—s, pl. —) marble, taw.

Klie'b—en, reg. & ir.v.a. to cleave, split. —ig, adj. cleavable. Comp. —eisen, n. cleaver. —holz, n. sawed timber.

Klie'ren, v.a. to write very badly (coll.).

Kliet'schig, adj. not fully baked, sodden (of bread) (coll.).

Kli'ma, n. (—s, pl. —ta or —te) climate. —kte'risch, —tisch (pron. klima'tisch), adj. climacteric; —tischer Kurort, health resort. Comp. (das hitzige) —fieber, n. calenture.

Klimbi'm, m. musical entertainment; party; festival; arrangement (sl.).

Klim'me, f. (pl. —n) wild grape.

Klim'men, reg. & (usually) ir.v.n. (aux. h. & s.) to climb (auf eine S.); to aspire to (nach einer S.); er ist bis zum Gipfel des Ruhms geklommen, he reached or raised himself to the pinnacle of fame. Comp. —ziehen, n. mounting a ladder hand over hand without using the legs (Gymn.); rising from straight-arm to bent-arm hang on the horizontal bar (Gymn.). —zug, m. see —ziehen.

Klim'per—n, v.n. (aux. h.) to jingle, tinkle; to chink; to play badly (on the piano, etc.); to strum. —ei', f. jingling, strumming. —er, m. (—ers, pl. —er), —kasten, m. a poor piano (coll.). —ling, m. (—lings, pl. —linge) strummer, thrummer; bungler.

Klin'ge, f. (pl. —n) blade; sword; defile (prov.); vor die — fordern, to challenge; mit der — ausmachen, to decide by the sword; über die — springen, to be put to death; einen über die — springen lassen, (orig. einem den Kopf or den Kopf eines Menschen über die — springen lassen), to put s.o. to the sword; eine gute — führen (or schlagen), to be a good swordsman. Comp. —n=probe, f. assay of sword-blades. —n=stahl, m. steel for sword-blades.

Klin'gel, f. (pl. —n) small bell, handbell. —n, v.n. (aux. h.) to tinkle, ring the bell; es —t, there is a ring at the door, some one is ringing; es wurde nach dem Diener geklingelt, the bell was rung for the servant, the servant was rung for; die Telephonglocke wurde nach dem Kaufmann geklingelt, the merchant was rung up. Comp. —bahn, f. (small and slow) branch line; (where a bell is fixed to the engine) loop line; huckleberry road (Amer.). —beutel, m. purse with a bell for collecting in churches; collection bag; alms dish (Engl.). —draht, m. bell-wire. —schnur, f. bell-rope. —zieher, m. bell-pull.

Klin'g—en, I. ir.v.n. (aux. h.) to sound, emit a sound; to tinkle, clink, ring; to chime; diese Frage —t sonderbar, this is or seems to be a strange question; die Gläser —en lassen, to touch glasses (in drinking); die Ohren —en mir, my ears are singing or tingling. II. reg.v.a. to ring, tinkle; weiter —en, to propagate (or spread) a sound; gewiß haben Ihnen die Ohren geklungen, your ears must have burned, there was much friendly talk about you; —en einer Glocke, ding-dong of a bell; —en der Glocken, ringing of bells; —en der Ohren, singing in or of the ears; —en der Gläser, touching of glasses. —end, p. & adj. resonant, sonorous; tönendes Erz oder —ende Schelle, sounding brass or a tinkling cymbal (B.); —ende Worte, high sounding words, mere words; —ende Münze, (hard) cash, ready money; mit —endem Spiele, drums beating, with full band, triumphantly; —ender Ausgang, feminine ending; sonorous termination (metre); —ender Reim, feminine rhyme. Comp. —gedicht, n. sonnet. —klang, m., —ling, n. ding-dong, jangle. —lingling! int. ding-dong! —stein, m. phonolite.

Kli'n—ik, f. (pl. —iken) clinics; clinical hospital. —iker, m. (—ikers, pl. —iker) clinical physician. —ikum, n. (—ikums, pl. —iken) clinical hospital; clinical lecture or demonstration. —isch, adj. clinical.

Klin'k—e, f. (pl. —en) latch; clinched end of a bolt. —en, v.a. & n. (aux. h. & s.) to press the latch, to open or shut a door. Comp. —bolzen, m. rivet. —en=schloß, n. latch-lock. —haken, m. staple or hook to receive the latch.

[1]Klin'ker, m. (—s, pl. —) (Dutch) clinker, klinker(-brick).

[2]Klin'ker, m. (—s, pl. —), Klin'kart, m. flat bottomed ship, clincher (obs.).

Klin'se, f. (pl. —n) cleft, crack, chink, gap.

Klipp, m. (—(e)s, pl. —e) snapping noise; snap with the fingers; — klapp! click-clack! —

und klar, quite clear; obvious (*coll.*). *Comp.* **—kanne**, *f.* wooden jug with a lid. **—kram**, *m.* paltry trinkets, toys, small wares. **—krämer**, *m.* seller of small wares, toyseller. **—schenke**, *f.* small beer-house. **—schuld**, *f.* paltry debt. **—schule**, *f.* infant school; hedge-school; bad school.

Klip'p—e, *f.* (*pl.* **—en**) cliff, crag, steep rock; danger; obstacle; bird-trap; **blinde —e**, sunken rock. **—er**, *m.* (**—ers**, *pl.* **—er**) sculptor's mallet. **—ig**, *adj.* rocky, craggy. *Comp.* **—en=bock**, *m.* wild goat. **—en=fisch**, *m.* lub-fish, wolf-fish. **—en=hase**, *m.* Alpine hare. **—en=kalk**, *m.* upper strata of the Carpathian sandstone (*Geol.*). **—en=reihe**, *f.* ledge, reef of rocks. **—en=vogel**, *m.* white mew *or* gull. **—en=wand**, *f.* rocky wall.

Klir'ren, *v.n.* (*aux.* **h.** & **s.**) to clink, clank, clash, jingle, clatter.

[1]**Klitsch**, *interj.* flap! clash! slap! **—klatsch!** click-clack! splish-splash! **—en**, *v.n.* to clash.

[2]**Klitsch**, *m.* (**—es**, *pl.* **—e**) soft mass (*as dough*). **—e**, *f.* estate (*dial.*, *coll.*). **—e=naß**, *adj.* sopping wet (*coll.*) **—ig**, *adj.* not properly baked, sodden; **—iges Brot**, doughy bread.

Klit'ter, *m.* (**—s**, *pl.* **—**) blot, blur. **—ig**, *adj.* blotted, blurred. **—n**, *v.a.* & *n.* (*aux.* **h.**) to blot; to scrawl; to enter into details. *Comp.* **—buch**, *n.* waste-book. **—schuld**, *f.* petty debt.

Klit'zeklein, *adj.* & *adv.* quite small, tiny (*coll.*).

Kloa'ke, (*pl.* **—n**) sewer, cloaca; sink.

Klob, Klo'best; Klö'be, *1* (& *3*), *2 p. sing. imperf. ind.; and 1* (& *3*) *p. sing. imperf. subj. of* **klieben**.

Klo'b—en, *m.* (**—ens**, *pl.* **—en**) slit piece of wood; block, pulley; hand-vice; cramp; staple; bird-gin; log of wood; bundle (*of flax*); cheek (*of a balance*); pivot; potence (*Heral.*). **—er**, *m.* (**—ers**, *pl.* **—er**) cleaver. **—ig**, *adj.* log-like; that may be cleft; rude, awkward, boorish, stiff (*of persons*) (*sl.*). *Comp.* **—en=arbeit**, *f.* work by the pulley. **—en=fang**, *m.* bird-catching. **—en=holz**, *n.* logwood. **—en=säge**, *f.* pit-saw. **—en=seil**, *n.* pulley rope.

Klö(h)'nen, *v.a.* to talk and talk, to talk at great length (*coll.*).

Klomm, Klom'mest; Klöm'me, *1* (& *3*), *2 p. sing. imperf. ind.; and 1* (& *3*) *p. sing. imperf. subj. of* **klimmen**.

Klop'se, *pl.* (*of an obs.* **Klopf**), blows (*coll.*); **es setzt —**, it will, *or* has, come to blows (*coll.*).

Klöp'fel, *m.* (**—s**, *pl.* **—**) club, cudgel; clapper; knocker; clog (*for a dog*); mallet; drumstick; *see* **Klöppel**. **—n**, *v.a.* & *n.* to tap gently (*at a door*); to clog.

Klop'f—en, *v.* I. *a.* to beat, pound; to knock. II. *n.* (*aux.* **h.**) to beat, knock; to clap, pulsate violently, throb; **in die Hände —en**, to clap the hands; **sanft —en**, to tap, pat; **die Form —en**, to plane down (*Typ.*); **Steine —en**, to break stones; **Wäsche —en**, to bat linen; **auf den Busch —en**, to beat (*for game*); to beat about the bush, to sound a person (*fig.*). **—er**, *m.* (**—ers**, *pl.* **—er**) beetle; beater; knocker. *Comp.* **—fechter**, *m.* pugilist; bully; polemic. **—fechterei'**, *f.* pugilism; polemics. **—hengst**, *m.* castrated stallion. **—holz**, *n.* beetle; planer (*Typ.*). **—jagd**, *f.* beat. **—keule**, *f.* driving-mallet. **—maschine**, *f.* batting machine; willow. **—see**, *f.* heavy, chopping sea.

Klöp'pel, *m.* (**—s**, *pl.* **—**) bobbin, bone (*for lace*). **—ei'**, *f.* lace making.

Klöp'pel—n, *v.a.* & *n.* to make lace; **geklöppelte Spitzen**, bobbin-lace. *Comp.* **—arbeit**, *f.* bobbin-work, cushion-lace. **—arbeiter**, (**Klöpp'ler**,) *m.*, **—arbeiterin**, (**Klöpp'lerin**,) *f.* lace-maker. **—garn**, *n.* yarn *or* thread used in making lace. **—holz**, *n.* bobbin; uncleaved wood. **—kissen**, *n.* cushion for lace-making. **—lade**, *f.* box *or* desk for lacemaking. **—maschine**, *f.* bobbin-machine. **—nadel**, *f.* needle for making lace. **—seide**, *f.* lace-silk. **—spitze**, *f.* pillow-lace, bone-lace. **—zwirn**, *m.* lace-thread.

Klops, *m.* (**—(s)es**, *pl.* **—(s)e**) cooked (*or* fried) meat-ball, mince-meat ball, force-meat ball.

Klose'tt, *n.* (**—s**, *pl.* **—s** *or* **—e**) cabinet; water-closet (*W.C.*). *Comp.* **—papier**, *n.* toilet paper.

Kloß (*long* **o**), *m.* (**—es**, *pl.* **Klö'ße**) clod, lump; meat-ball; dumpling; blockhead. **—ig**, *adj.* & *adv.* clod-like; doughy.

Klo'ßen, *v.a.* to break the clods of earth.

Klo'ster (*long* **o**), *n.* (**—s**, *pl.* **Klöster**) monastery, nunnery, convent, cloister, abbey; **ins — gehen**, to take the veil (*of women*), to turn monk. **—tum**, *n.* (**—tums**) monastic state. *Comp.* **—bau**, *m.*; **der alte —bau**, the ancient monastic pile. **—bogen**, *m.* Gothic arch. **—brauch**, *m.* monastic usage *or* rule. **—bruder**, *m.* friar. **—frau**, *f.*, **—fräulein**, *n.* nun. **—gang**, *m.* cloister(s). **—geistliche(r)**, *m.* monk. **—gelübde**, *n.* monastic vow. **—gemeinde**, *f.* fraternity, sisterhood; parish belonging to a convent. **—gewand**, *n.* monastic dress. **—gut**, *n.* estate belonging to a convent. **—jungfer**, *f.* nun. **—leben**, *n.* monastic life; single life. **—leute**, *pl.* conventuals, monks, nuns. **—ordnung**, *f.* discipline of a convent. **—pforte**, *f.* convent-gate. **—schule**, *f.* monastery school; monastic school; school kept by monks; convent school; school established in a former convent. **—schwester**, *f.* lay-sister. **—vorsteher**, *m.* superior of a monastery. **—wesen**, *n.* monastic affairs. **—zwirn**, *m.* thread for making nun's lace.

Klö'sterlich, *adj.* & *adv.* monastic, conventual.

Klotz, *m.* (**—es**, *pl.* **Klöt'ze**) block; log, lump (*of wood*); stump; bed (*of a mortar*); sledge-hammer; blockhead; lout; **auf groben — gehört ein grober Keil**, rudeness must be met by rudeness; the biter must be bit (*prov.*). **—en**, *v.a.* to pay (*sl.*); **er hat viel —en müssen**, he has had to pay a pretty penny (*sl.*). **—ig**, *adj.* blockish; lumpish; cloddy; log-like; rude, boorish (*sl.*); big, enormous (*sl.*); **eine —ige Summe Geld kosten**, to cost no end of money (*sl.*). *Comp.* **—holz**, *n.* wood in blocks. **—kopf**, *m.* blockhead. **—köpfig**, *adj.* stupid.

Klub, *m.* (**—s**, *pl.* **—s**) club. **—(b)i'st**, *m.* (**—bi'sten**, *pl.* **—bi'sten**) member of a club (*obs.*).

Klu'cke, *f.* hen. **—n**, *v.a.* to cluck.

Klu'ckern, *v.n.* to gurgle.

Kluft, *f.* (*pl.* **Klüf'te**) cleft, gap; chasm, gulf; ravine, abyss; cavern, cave, grotto, den; log of wood; anything cleft; pincers, tongs; stratum, layer; scarf (*Naut.*); joint-rule (*Carp.*).

Klüf't—en, *v.a.* to cleave, split. **—ig**, *adj.* cleft, split; cracked.

Klug, *adj.* & *adv.* (*comp.* **klü'ger**; *sup.* **klügst**) intelligent, subtle; wise, sagacious; prudent; skilful; shrewd, clearsighted; clever; cunning; **er ist nicht recht —**, he is half crazy, he is half-witted; **Sie sind nicht —**, you don't mean to say so! (*coll.*); **aus etwas — werden**, to see through *or* understand a thing; **daraus kann ich nicht — werden**, I can make neither head nor tail of it; **ein —er Mann**, a clever man; a sensible man; **eine —e Antwort**, an ingenious *or* witty reply; **ein —er Einfall**, a good idea; **—e Hunde**, sagacious dogs; **nun bin ich so — wie vorher**, I'm just as wise as I was; **ich bin dadurch um nichts klüger**, I am not a whit the wiser for it; **sich — dünkend**, self-conceited; **durch Schaden wird man —**, a burnt child dreads the fire (*prov.*); **das Klügste wäre nun wohl**, it would probably be best, **der Klügste giebt nach**, the wiser head gives in, better bend than break (*prov.*); **auch der Klügste kann (sich) irren**, to err is human (*prov.*). —

heit, *f.* prudence, good sense; sagacity; wit; shrewdness; discretion; policy. *Comp.* —gewandt, *adj.* circumspect, ingenious. —heits=lehren, —heits=regeln, *pl.* practical wisdom, rules of prudence; rules of worldly wisdom, prudentials. —heits=rücksicht, *f.* prudential consideration.

Klügelei', *f.* cavilling, sophistry, subtilizing.

Klü'g—(e)ler, *m.* (—lers, *pl.* —ler) pretender to wisdom, would-be-wit; sophist, quibbler, caviller, critic; wiseacre. —eln, *v.n.* (*aux.* h.) to subtilize, refine, criticize; to affect wisdom. —lich, *adv.* prudently, wisely, discreetly, shrewdly. —ling, *see* —(e)ler.

Klump, *m.* (—s, *pl.* —en) *and* (*usually*) —en, *m.* (—ens, *pl.* —en) mass, clod, lump; cluster; heap; ball; —en Blut, clot of blood; —en Gold, ingot; auf einen —en, all of a heap. —icht, (*obs.*) —ig, *adj.* cloddy, clotted, in lumps. *Comp.* —en=weise, *adv.* in lumps *or* clusters. —fuß, *m.* club-foot. —füßig, *adj.* club-footed.

Klümp'—chen, *n.* (—chens, *pl.* —chen) little lump *or* clod; small particle, globule; —chen Gold, nugget; (wie) ein —chen Unglück, (like) a picture of misery (*coll.*). —erig, *adj.* lumpy, cloddy; —erig werden, to clot.

Klüm'pern, *v.r.* & *n.* (*aux.* h.) to clot; to form clumps, clusters *or* clods; to agglomerate.

Klun'ker, *f.* (*pl.* —n) & *m.* (—s, *pl.* —) a thing which hangs *or* dangles; tassel; clot, clod (*of dirt*). —ig, *adj.* clotted, dirty, bedraggled. —n, *v.n.* (*aux.* h.) to hang down like tassels, to hang and draggle. *Comp.* —milch, *f.* clotted milk, sour milk. —wolle, *f.* dag-wool.

Klup'p—e, *f.* (*pl.* —en) pincers; barnacles; screw-stock; trap, gin; straits; dilemma. —en, *v.a.* to squeeze into a slit *or* fissure, to pinch. —ig, *adj.*; —iges Gehörn, branched horn (*of a deer*).

Klü'se, *f.* (*pl.* —n) hawse, hawse-hole (*Naut.*).

Klut'ter, *f.* (*pl.* —n) decoy-whistle, bird-call.

Klü'ver, *n.* (—s, *pl.* —) jib (*Naut.*); Außen —, Buten —, flying jib. *Comp.* —baum, *m.* jib-boom. —fall, *m.* jib-halliards. —fock, *n.* foretop-stay-sail.

Klystie'r, *n.* (—s, *pl.* —e) enema, injection, clyster. —en, *v.a.* to administer an enema (to). *Comp.* —schlauch, *m.* India rubber tube of an enema, clyster pipe. —spritze, *f.* syringe, squirt; selbstthätige —spritze, irrigator.

Knab'bern, *v.a.* & *n.* (*aux.* h.) to gnaw, nibble.

Kna'be, *m.* (—n, *pl.* —n; *dim.* Knäb'chen, Knäb'lein) boy; youth, lad; male child; alter —, old boy, old fellow; braver —, gallant youth, fine lad; nasser —, drunkard (*obs.*). —nhaft, *adj.* & *adv.* boyish. —nhaftigkeit, *f.* boyishness. —nschaft, *f.* boyhood; boys (*coll.*). *Comp.* —n=alter, *n.* boyhood. —n=lehrer, *m.* teacher of boys, teacher at a boys' school. —n=mäßig, *adj.* boyish. —n=schule, *f.* boys' school, school for boys. —n=streich, *m.* boyish trick. —n=zeit, *f.* youth, boyhood.

Knack, I. *m.* (—es, *pl.* —e) cracking noise; crack, split, snap; underwood; broken stones. II. *int.* crack! snap! —en, *v.a.* & *n.* (*aux* h.) to crack. —er, *m.* (—ers, *pl.* —er) cracker. —ern, *v.n.* (*aux.* h.) to crackle. —erig, *adj.* & *adv.* crackling, crisp. —s, *see* Knack; er hat einen —s weg *or* seine Gesundheit hat einen —s bekommen, his health has been injured for life (*coll.*). *Comp.* —mandel, *f.* soft-shelled almond, almond in the shell. —stiefel, *m.*; alter —stiefel, old grumbler, old fogey. —wurst, *f.* saveloy, hard *or* smoked sausage.

Knall, *m.* (—es, *pl.* —e) sharp report, crack, clap; detonation; — und Fall, all at once, immediately (*coll.*); — und Fall war eins, no sooner was the gun fired than the game fell. —ig, *adj.* & *adv.* glaring, striking, very, extremely (*sl.*).

Knal'l—en, *v.* I. *n.* (*aux.* h.) to burst, explode, detonate; to snap, crack, pop; mit einem Gewehre —en, to fire a gun; (*aux.* s.) der Pulverturm —te in die Luft, the powder-magazine blew up with a loud report. II. *a.* to crack, lash, smack; to explode; to fire. *Comp.* (before adjectives denoting a colour — intensifies, *e. g.* —rot, extremely red; —gelb, glaring yellow). —bonbon, *m.* cracker. —büchse, *f.* pop-gun. —effekt, *m.* stage effect; clap trap (*contempt*); the chief, supreme effect (*coll.*). —erbsen, *pl.* detonating balls. —gas, *n.* inflammable gas, oxy-hydrogen gas. —gebläse, *n.* oxy-hydrogen blow-pipe. —gelb, *adj.* extremely yellow. —glas, *n.* Prince Rupert's drops, anaclastic glass. —gold, *n.* fulminating gold. —luft, *f.* explosive air. —pulver, *n.* fulminating powder. —queck=silber, *n.* fulminate of mercury. —rot, *adj.* of a glaring red. —signal, *n.* detonating (fog) signal (*Railw.*).

Knapp, *adj.* & *adv.* close-fitting; neat; narrow, tight; scanty; scarce, barely sufficient; accurate, exact; concise; reserved; paltry, mean; sein —es Auskommen *or* — sein Auskommen haben, to have barely enough to live on; —e Kost, little food, scant food; short commons (*coll.*); —e Zeiten, hard times; es geht — zu in diesem Hause, they live very poorly, they are economizing as much as possible, they are in straitened circumstances in this house; — hal'ten, to keep on short allowance, to keep a tight rein (on a p.); —e Diät, low diet; das Geld ist — bei ihm, money is scarce with him; die Börse ist —, money is scarce on 'change; mit —er Not, barely, only just, with difficulty. —heit, *f.* scantiness, scarcity; narrowness, tightness; meanness, poorness; hardness. *Comp.* —sack, *m.* knapsack.

Knap'p—e, *m.* (—en, *pl.* —en) boy, youth, esquire, shield-bearer; candidate for knighthood; adherent, attendant; workman, apprentice; Berg—e, miner. —enhaft, *adj.* & *adv.* esquire-like; apprentice-like. —schaft, *f.* novitiate of a knight; body *or* society of workmen (*as miners*). *Comp.* —schafts=kasse, *f.* fund for the benefit of poor miners. —schafts=schule, *f.* corporation-school.

Knap'pen, *v.a.* & *n.* (*aux.* h.) to crack; to pinch off; to nibble; to pinch, be stingy; to halt.

Knaps, *int. see* Knack. —(s)en, *v.n.* to pinch.

Knar'pelig, *adj.* & *adv.* crisp.

Knar're, *f.* creaking noise; rattle; military rifle (*sl.*).

Knar'r—en, *v.a.* & *n.* (*aux.* h.) to creak, squeak; to groan; to rattle; der Nachtwächter —t, the watchman springs his rattle. —ig, *adj.* & *adv.* creaking.

Knast, *m.* (—es, *pl.* —e) knot (*in wood*); log of oak; stiff person; dried up, morose fellow; alter —, dry old stick; einen — sägen, to snore (*vulg.*). —er, *m.* (—ers, *pl.* —er); alter —er, old, worm-eaten book; old bookworm, old fogey. —ern, *v.n.* (*aux.* h.) to crackle. *Comp.* —er=bart, *m.* old greybeard, old fogey *or* grumbler.

Knas'ter, *m.* (—s, *pl.* —) canaster tobacco.

Knat'tern, *v.n.* (*aux.* h.) to rattle, crackle; das — des Gewehrfeuers *or* der Gewehre, the rattle of musketry.

Knau'el, Knaul, Knäu'el, *m.* & (*usually*) *n.* (—s, *pl.* —) clue, ball, hank, skein; knot, crowd, throng; Scleranthus (*Bot.*); zum — geballt, coiled up. —n, *v.a.* & *r.* to form into a ball, coil up. *Comp.* —wickelmaschine, *f.* winder.

Knauf, *m.* (—es, *pl.* Knäu'fe) button; capital (*Arch.*); knob; pommel (of a sword's hilt).

Knaul, *see* **Knauel.**
Knau'peln, *v.n.* (*aux.* **h.**) to nibble; to crunch.
Knau'ser, *m.* (—**s**, *pl.* —) niggard. —**ei',** *f.* niggardliness. —**ig,** *adj. & adv.* niggardly. —**n,** *v.n.* (*aux.* **h.**) to be stingy *or* sordid.
Knaut'sch—en, *v.a.* to crumple, rumple. —**ig,** *adj. & adv.* crumpled.
Kne'bel, *m.* (—**s**, *pl.* —) branch, slip; club, stick; short piece of wood used in fastening *or* for drawing ropes, *etc.*, together; gag (*of the mouth*); cross-bar; clapper of a bell; twisted moustache; (*pl.*) the prominent knuckles of the clenched fingers.
Kne'bel—n, *v.a.* to fasten *or* tighten with a short stick; to bind (*sheaves*); to gag (*the mouth*); **die Presse —n,** to muzzle the press. *Comp.* —**bart,** *m.* (*twisted*) moustache; —**bart an der Unterlippe,** imperial. —**gebiß,** *n.* snaffle-bit. —**trense,** *f.* snaffle.
Knecht, *m.* (—**es**, *pl.* —**e**) servant, farm-servant; thrall; slave, bondman; vassal; squire, man-at-arms, soldier; page; journeyman; trestle; jack; **fauler —,** ready-reckoner; —**Ruprecht,** Santa Claus, St. Nicholas. *Comp.* —**s=arbeit,** *f.*, —**s=dienst,** *m.* menial work, drudgery. —**s=blöße,** *f.* destitution, lowliness of a servant. —**s=gestalt,** *f.* form of a servant (*B.*). —**s=sinn,** *m.* servile spirit. —**s=stand,** *m.* menial station.
Knech'teln, *v.n.* (*aux.* **h.**) to fawn, flatter, act a servile part.
Knech't—en, *v.a.* to reduce to servitude, to enslave. —**isch,** *adj. & adv.* as a servant; servile, crawling. —**schaft,** *f.* servitude, slavery. —**ung,** *f.* enthralment, subjugation; servitude.
Kneif, *m.* (—**s**, *pl.* —**e**) crooked knife; clasp-knife; hedge-bill.
Kneif—en, *ir.v.a.* to pinch, squeeze, nip; to cog (*dice*); to retire parrying (*Fenc.*); to withdraw from an engagement, to shirk a duel (*sl.*); **den Wind —en,** to hug the wind. —**er,** *m.* (—**ers**, *pl.* —**er**) person *or* thing that pinches; a person who withdraws from fulfilling an engagement *or* an obligation; eye-glass, pince-nez; goosander (*Orn.*). *Comp.* —**kuß,** *m.* pinching of a person's cheek in kissing. —**küßchen,** *n.* baby's kiss. —**mal,** *n.* mark left by a pinch. —**zange,** *f.* large tongs *or* pincers; (*small tongs*) tweezers.
Knei'pe, *f.* (*pl.* —**n**) instrument for pinching; pinch, straits, beer house, public house; students' clubhouse; **auf der —,** in the beer-house; **den ganzen Tag in der — liegen,** to spend the whole day in the public house *or* at the students' club.
Knei'p—en, I. *reg. & ir.v.a.* to pinch, nip; to gripe; **mit glühenden Zangen —en,** to torture with red-hot tongs. II. *reg. v.n.* (*aux.* **h.**) to frequent a beer-house; to tipple. III. *subst. n.* colic, gripes. —**er,** *m.* (—**ers**, *pl.* —**er**) tippler; frequenter of a beer-house. —**erei',** *f.* hard drinking; frequenting of public houses. *Comp.* —**abend,** *m.* evening given over to revelry by students. —**bruder,** *m.* toper, tippler. —**en=leben,** *n.* life spent in ale-houses. —**genie,** *n.* a p. who passes all his time in the ale-house; a p. who can stand a great amount of beer (*coll.*). —**gesellschaft,** *f.* party of students who spend the evening together singing and drinking. —**lied,** *n.* drinking-song. —**name,** *m.* name by which a student is known at his club, student's nickname. —**wart,** *m.* student charged with the care of the beer at drinking-parties. —**wirt,** *m.* ale-house keeper, publican.
Kneipie'r, *m.* (*pron.* **Kneipje'**) (—**s**) toper, tippler; ale-house keeper, publican (*coll.*).
Knel'ler, *m.* (—**s**) very bad tobacco.
Knet'bar, *adj.* that can be kneaded, plastic; mouldable.
Kne't—en, I. *v.a.* to knead. II. *subst. n.* kneading, moulding; massage; shampooing. *Comp.* —**trog,** *m.* kneading-trough.
Knick, I. *int.* crack! II. *m.* (—**es**, *pl.* —**e**) crack, flaw; angle in a curve; quickset hedge; **einen — bekommen,** to receive an injury to one's health (*coll.*).
Kni'ck—en, *v.* I. *a.* to bend and crack; to crack; to break; to collect by pinching; **einen Hasen —en,** to break the neck of a hare. II. *n.* (*aux.* **h.** & **s.**) to crack; to break; to be weak in the knees; to be niggardly; **ein geknicktes Dasein,** a blighted life; **ein geknickter Mann,** a broken-down man. —**er,** *m.* (—**ers**, *pl* —**er**) niggard, screw; parasol with jointed stick; marble, taw (*dial.*); instrument for breaking *or* cracking. —**erei',** *f.* niggardliness. —**(e)rig,** *adj. & adv.* stingy, sordid, niggardly. —**ern,** *v.n.* (*aux.* **h.**) to be sordid *or* stingy; to chaffer, higgle; to crackle. —**s,** *m.* (—**(s)es**, *pl.* —**(s)e**) crack; bow, courtesy, reverence. —**sen,** *v.* I. *a. see* —**en.** II. *n.* (*aux.* **h.**) to bow, courtesy; (*aux.* **s.**) **sie —sten von dannen,** they retired bowing. *Comp.* —**e=bein,** I. *n.* weak legged *or* kneed person (*sl.*). II. *m.* a glass of liquor (*usually maraschino*) with the yolk of an egg. —**holz,** *n.* brushwood.
Knie, *n.* (—**(e)s**, *pl.* —**e**) knee; anything knee-like; knee (*Naut.*); bent, angle; joint; **euch lege ich's auf die —e,** I leave my fate in your hands, I leave the decision with you (*poet.*); **in die —e sinken,** to totter; **etwas übers — brechen,** to hurry a matter, to make short work of a th.; **auf die —e fallen,** to go down on one's knees. *Comp.* —**band,** *n.* garter; ligament of the knee; kneeband (*Mech.*). —**beuge,** *f.* bend *or* hollow of the knee. —**beugung,** *f.* genuflexion. —**binde,** *f.* knee-cap (*Surg.*). —**bug,** *m. see* —**kehle**; joint of the upper part of a horse's hind-leg; knuckle (*of veal, etc.*). —**bügel,** *m.* leather cover for the knee (*Min.*). —**decke,** *f.* coachman's apron. —**fall,** *m.* falling on one's knees; genuflexion. —**fällig,** *adv.* upon one's knees. —**flechse,** *f.* hamstring; **die —flechse durchschneiden,** to hamstring. —**förmig,** *adj.* geniculate. —**galgen,** *m.* gibbet, gallows with cross-beam. —**geige,** *f.* violoncello. —**gelenk,** *n.* knee-joint. —**hoch,** *adj. & adv.* up to the knees; knee-high. —**hose,** *f.* breeches; knickerbockers. —**kappe,** *f.* knee-cap, cover for the knee (*of a horse*). —**kehle,** *f.* hollow *or* bend of the knee; fetlock joint. —**kissen,** *n.* hassock. —**scheibe,** *f.* knee-cap. —**schiene,** *f.* piece of armour protecting the knee. —**schwamm,** *m.* white swelling (*Med.*). —**stück,** *n.* knee, knee-piece; knee-harness; half-length portrait.
Knie'en, *v.* I. *n.* (*aux.* **h.**) to be on one's knees, to be kneeling, to kneel; (*aux.* **s.**) to go down on one's knees. II. *a.* to bend into the form of a knee. III. *r.* **sich wund —,** to kneel until one's knees are sore. —**d,** *p. adj. & adv.* kneeling, on one's knees; with bended knee.
Kniff, Kniff'fest; Kniff'se, *1 (& 3), 2 p. sing. imperf. indic.; 1 (& 3) p. sing. imperf. subj. of* **kneifen.**
Kniff, *m.* (—**(e)s**, *pl.* —**e**) pinch; twitch; crease; fold; trick, stratagem, dodge; **geheime —e,** underhand dealings. —**eln,** *v.n.* (*aux.* **h.**) to finesse, act artfully. —**en,** *v.a.* to fold, to crease. —**ig,** *adj. & adv.* tricking, intriguing. —**lig,** *adj.* difficult, intricate (*coll.*). *Comp.* —**maschine,** *f.* crimping machine.
Knipp, *m.* (—**es**, *pl.* —**e**), —**s,** *m.* (—**(s)es**, *pl.* —**(s)e**) snap of the fingers; **einem einen — schlagen,** to snap one's fingers at a person. —**en,** *see* **Knipsen.** *Comp.* —**kugel,** *f.* marble. —**schere,** *f.* small-pointed scissors.
Knips, *see* **Knipp.** —**(s)en,** *v.n.* (*aux.* **h.**) to click; to snap one's fingers.

Knirps, *m.* (—(s)es, *pl.* —(s)e) pigmy, dwarf; little man. —**(s)ig**, *adj.* stunted, dwarfish; of small stature.

Knir'ren, *v.n.* (*aux.* h.) to creak; *see* Knirschen.

Knir'schen, *v.a.* & *n.* (*aux.* h.) to gnash; to crunch, grind; to grate, creak.

Kni'ster—ig, *adj.* crackling, crisp. —**n**, *v.n.* (*aux.* h.) to crackle; to flicker, blaze; to crepitate (*Chem.*); to crumple. *Comp.* —**gold**, *n.* tinsel. —**röcheln**, *n.* rattling in the throat.

Knit'tel, *see* Knüttel.

Knit'ter, *m.* (—s, *pl.* —) crease, fold, rumple. —**ig**, *adj.* creased, wrinkled, rumpled; highly irritable. —**n**, *v.* I. *a.* (*aux.* h.) *see* Knistern. II. *a.* to rumple, crease. III. *r.* to become crumpled; to be irritated *or* vexed (*vulg.*). *Comp.* —**gold**, *n.* tinsel.

Kni'xen, *see* Knicks, Knicksen.

Kno'bel, *pl.* dice. —**n**, *v.n.* to throw dice (um eine S., for a th.).

Knob'lauch, *m.* (—s) garlic.

Knö'chel, *m.* (—s, *pl.* —) knuckle; joint; ankle-bone; dice; vertebra of the spine. —**chen**, *n.* (—chens, *pl.* —chen) ossicle; small joint.

Knö'chel—n, I. *v.n.* (*aux.* h.) to play with dice; to play with knuckle-bones. II. *subst.n.* *see* —**spiel**. *Comp.* —**gelenk**, *n.* ankle-joint. —**spiel**, *n.* game with dice.

Kno'ch—en, *see* Knochen. —**icht**, (*obs.*) —**ig**, *adj.* & *suffix*, bony; -boned.

Kno'chen, *m.* (—s, *pl.* —) bone; in — verwandeln, zu — werden, to ossify; stark von —, bony, strong-limbed; seine — schonen, to take good care of oneself; naß bis auf die —, wet to the skin; er ist nichts als Haut und —, he is a mere bag of bones. *Comp.* —**ansatz**, *m.* epiphysis (*Anat.*). —**arbeiter**, *m.* bone-turner. —**artig**, *adj.* bony. —**auswuchs**, *m.* protuberance of a bone. —**beschreibung**, *f.* osteology, osteography. —**brand**, *m.* necrosis. —**bruch**, *m.* fracture of a bone. —**dürr**, *adj.* nothing but skin and bone. —**erde**, *f.* phosphate of lime. —**fäule**, —**fäulnis**, *f.* caries. —**fett**, *n.* fat of bones, bone-grease. —**fortsatz**, *m.* apophysis. —**fraß**, *m.* caries. —**fügung**, *f.* articulation of the bones. —**gelenk**, *n.* joint. —**gebäude**, —**gerippe**, —**gerüst**, *n.* skeleton. —**haus**, *n.* charnel-house. —**haut**, *f.* periosteum. —**haut=entzündung**, *f.* periostitis. —**lager**, *n.* bone deposit, bone bed. —**lehre**, *f.* osteology. —**mann**, *m.* skeleton; Death. —**mark**, *n.* marrow of the bones. —**mehl**, *n.* bone-dust. —**naht**, *f.* suture (*Anat.*). —**öl**, *n.* neat's-foot oil. —**pfanne**, *f.* cavity of a bone in which another turns *or* moves. —**rüttler**, *m.* bone-shaker (*cycl.*). —**schwund**, *m.* atrophy of the bones. —**splitter**, *m.* splinter of a bone. —**system**, *m.* osteological *or* osseous system. —**verbindung**, *see* —**fügung**. —**ware**, *f.* bone-turner's goods. —**werk**, *n.* mass of bones. —**wuchs**, *m.* ossification, condition of bones. —**zange**, *f.* bone nippers. —**zerlegung**, *f.* osteotomy.

Knö'cher—icht (*obs.*), —**ig**, *adj.* very thin and bony, fleshless. —**n**, *adj.* bony, osseous.

Knö'del, *m.* (—s, *pl.* —) & *f.* (*pl.* —n) dumpling.

Knol'l—e, *f.* (*pl.* —en), —**en**, *m.* (—ens, *pl.* —en; *dim.* Knöll'chen) clod, lump; protuberance, knot, lump, knob; bulb; tuber; tumour; tubercle. —**ig**, *adj.* knotty, knobby; tuberous; bulbous. *Comp.* —**bein**, *n.* elephantiasis. —**en=artig**, *adj.* globular. —**en=gewächs**, *n.* bulbous *or* tuberous plant. —**fuß**, *m.* club-foot. —**gras**, *n.*, —**hafer**, *m.* tall oat-grass. —**sucht**, *f.* knotty gout.

Knopf, *m.* (—es, *pl.* Knöp'fe) button; button-like thing; knob *or* ball on some other body; head; top, pommel; knot, bud; stud; boss; acorn; condyl; dumpling; fellow (*coll.*); mit zwei Reihen Knöpfe, double-buttoned, double-breasted; Knöpfe haben, to have money (*vulg.*); Taljereeps —, Matthew Walker's knot (*Naut.*); alter Weiber—, false knot (*Naut.*); den — auf dem Beutel halten, to be parsimonious, to be stingy; ein gemütlicher —, a jolly fellow (*coll.*); ein alter Degen—, an old soldier *or* officer (*coll.*); die —e bekommen, to be made lance-corporal (Gefreiter); mit den Knöpfen herausrücken, to pay up (*coll.*). *Comp.* —**draht**, *m.* button-wire; head-wire (*for pins*). —**form**, *f.* button-mould. —**gießer**, *m.* button-founder. —**holz**, *n.* uncovered button (*to be covered*); block on which pin-heads are formed. —**loch**, *n.* button-hole. —**nadel**, *f.* pin. —**naht**, *f.* suture (*Surg.*). —**öse**, *f.* button-shank. —**seide**, *f.* silk-twist; button-silk.

Knöpf'—chen, *n.* *dim.* *of* Knopf, *q. v.* —**eln**, *v.a.* to knot. —**en**, *v.a.* to button. —**er**, *m.* button-hook. —**ig**, *adj.* provided with buttons.

Knor'pel, *m.* (—s, *pl.* —) cartilage, gristle. —**haft**, —**ig**, *adj.* gristly, cartilaginous. *Comp.* —**artig**, *see* —**ig**. —**band**, *n.* cartilaginous fibre uniting bones. —**fische**, *pl.* cartilaginous fishes. —**haut**, *f.* membrane investing the cartilage. —**ring**, *m.* annular cartilage.

Knor'r—en, *m.* (—ens, *pl.* —en) knotty excrescence; knot, knag; bunch, hunch; ankle; knuckle. —**icht** (*obs.*), —**ig**, *adj.* knotty, bunchy, knobbed, gnarled.

Knos'p—e, *f.* (*pl.* —en, *dim.* Knösp'chen) bud; leaf-knot, gem, eye. —**ig**, *adj.* budlike; covered with buds, budding. *Comp.* —**en=artig**, *adj.* bud-like. —**en=behälter**, *m.* conceptacle (*Bot.*). —**en=bildung**, *f.* gemmation. —**en=decke**, *f.* tegument. —**en=häutchen**, *n.* hymen (*Bot.*). —**en=kern**, *m.* nucellus. —**en=stand**, *m.* gemmation. —**en=tragend**, *adj.* gemmiferous. —**en=treiben**, *n.* budding (forth), gemmation.

Knos'pen, *v.n.* (*aux.* h.) to bud (forth).

Kno't—e, *m.* boor, workman; cad (*vulg.*). —**en**, I. *m.* (—ens, *pl.* —en) knot; knot (*Naut.*); node (*Bot.*, *Surg.*, *Astr.*); capsule; knob, joint; tangle; tie, bow of ribbon; ganglion; growth, tubercle (*Med.*); plot; difficulty; zehn —en in einer Stunde laufen, to make ten knots an hour; einen —en schlagen *or* schürzen, to tie a knot; einen —en lösen, to undo a knot; to solve a difficulty, to unravel a plot; das Ding hat einen —en (an sich), there's a hitch in the affair; da steckt der —en, there's the rub; der gordische —en, the Gordian knot. II. *v.a.* & *n.* (*aux.* h.) to knot. —**enhaft**, —**ig**, *adj.* & *adv.* knotty, knaggy; articulate, tuberous, jointed (*Bot.*); tubercular (*Med.*); brutish, boorish, ungentlemanly, rude. —**igkeit**, *f.* knottiness; nodosity (*Med.*); loutishness, ungentlemanliness (*coll.*). *Comp.* —**en=ader**, *f.* sciatic vein. —**en=arbeit**, *f.* knotted work, netting. —**en=bildung**, *f.* formation and growth of tubercles. —**en=lösung**, *f.* winding up of the plot, development; dénoument, catastrophe (*Dram.*). —**en=punkt**, *m.* knot; point of junction; junction (*Railw.*). —**en=schnur**, *f.* knotted string. —**en=schürzung**, *f.* working up of the plot, complication, epitasis (*Dram.*). —**en=stock**, *m.* knotty stick. —**en=strick**, *m.* Franciscan's girdle.

Knöt'—chen, *n.* (—chens, *pl.* —chen) little knot; tubercle. —**erich**, *m.* (—erichs) knot grass. *Comp.* —**erich=artig**, *adj.*; —**erich=artige** Gewächse, *pl.* polygonaceous plants (*Bot.*).

Knub'b—e, —**en**, *m.* knot. —**ig**, *adj.* huge.

Knuff, *m.* (—s, *pl.* Knüf'fe) knock, cuff, thump. —**en**, **Knüf'feln**, *v.a.* to cuff, buffet; to push: to beat. —**ig**, *adj.* & *adv.* thoroughly, thorough, very (*coll.*).

Knüll, *adj.* tipsy (*vulg.*).

Knül'le, *f.* (*pl.* —**n**) crumple, pucker. —**n**, *v.a.* to crumple.

Knüp'f—en, I. *v.a.* to fasten together, join; to tie, knot; to suspend; **sich —en an** (*acc.*), to be connected with; **ein Bündnis —en**, to form an alliance; **den Knoten auseinander —en**, to undo the knot. II. *subst.* —**en**, *n.*, —**ung**, *f.* uniting, tying, knitting.

Knüp'pel, *m.* (—**s**, *pl.* —) stick, cudgel; clog; small roll (*Bak.*); winch *or* lever (*Ropem.*); boor; **der — liegt beim Hunde**, there is the difficulty, there is no choice, do or die. *Before adjectives it intensifies; e.g.* —**satt**, quite satisfied. —**haft**, —**icht** (*obs.*), —**ig**, *adj.* & *adv.* club-like; rude, loutish. —**n**, *v.a.* to cudgel; to clog. *Comp.* —**brücke**, *f.* pole-bridge, rustic bridge. —**dick**, *adj.* very thick; **er hat es —dick hinter den Ohren**, he is a very sly rogue (*coll.*); —**dick voll**, crammed full. —**damm**, *m.* road made of round logs of wood, lumpy road. —**holz**, *n.* wood in logs, faggots. —**steig**, —**weg**, *m.* bad, rugged path. —**stock**, *m.* knotted stick.

Knup'pern, *see* **Knabbern**.

Knur'r—en, I. *v.n.* (*aux.* **h.**) to growl, snarl; to grumble, snarl; to purr. II. *subst. n.* purring, snarling; rumbling. —**ig**, *adj* & *adv.* growling, snarling. *Comp* —**kater**, —**kopf**, *m.* growler.

Knus'per—ig, *adj.* crisp, crackling. —**n**, *v.a.* to nibble, to crunch.

Knu'te, *f.* (*pl.* —**n**) knout; **die — bekommen**, to be knouted. —**n**, *v.a.* to lash with the knout.

Knut'schen (*long* **u**), *v.a.* to crumple; to caress, to smother with caresses.

Knüt'tel, **Knit'tel**, *m.* (—**s**, *pl.* —) cudgel, club; mallet; clog; line for hammocks. *Comp.* —**gedicht**, *n.* poem in doggerel. —**reim**, *m.* doggerel rhyme. —**vers**, *or* **Knit'telvers**, *m.* metrical line containing four accented syllables with an indefinite number of unaccented syllables, the rhymes being either in couplets or intermittent, the rhythm usually ascending, (a verse that is rather better than the English) doggerel.

Knüt'ten, *v.a.* & *n.* (*aux.* **h.**) to knit (*dial.*).

Koalisie'ren, *v.r.* to form a coalition, combine.

Koa'xen, *v.n.* (*aux.* **h.**) to croak (*as frogs*).

Ko'balt, *m.* (—**s**) cobalt. *Comp* —**beschlag**, *m.* efflorescence of cobalt. —**graupen**, *pl.* amorphous grey cobalt. —**oxidul**, *n.* protoxide of cobalt. —**spiegel**, *m.* transparent cobalt ore. —**stufe**, *f.* piece of cobalt ore.

Ko'bel, *m.* (—**s**, *pl.* —) dove-cot; small cabin. *Comp.* —**lerche**, *f.* crested lark.

Ko'be—n, *m.* (—**ns**, *pl.* —**n**) cabin, hut; pig-sty. —**r**, *m.* (—**rs**, *pl.* —**r**) shallow two-handled basket, hamper, dosser; fishing-net with poles.

Ko'bold, *m.* (—(**e**)**s**, *pl.* —**e**) goblin, hobgoblin, familiar spirit, elf, sprite; —**schießen**, to turn a somersault. *Comp.* —**spuk**, *m.* apparition of hobgoblins. —**streich**, *m.* impish trick.

Kobolz'=schießen, **Kobol'zen**, *v.n.*(*aux.* **h.**) to go head over heels, to make *or* turn a somersault.

Koch, *m.* (—**es**, *pl.* **Kö'che**) cook; **viele Köche verderben den Brei**, many cooks spoil the broth (*prov.*); **Hunger ist der beste —**, hunger is the best sauce (*prov.*); **man weiß hier nicht, wer — oder Kellner ist**, one cannot tell the man from the master here (*prov.*).

Ko'ch—en, *v.* I. *n.* (*aux.* **h.**) to cook; to boil; to ripen (*of grapes*); **er —t vor Zorn**, he is boiling with rage; **die See —t**, the sea is stormy. II. *a.* to cook; to boil; to make; to look after the cooking; to digest; **Seife —en**, to make *or* boil soap; **sie —t schlecht**, she is a bad cook; **gekochtes Obst**, stewed fruit; **sich —en**, to soften by boiling, to boil; **dies Fleisch —t sich gut**, this meat boils well; **das Wasser —t**, the water boils; **es wird überall mit Wasser gekocht**, people are the same everywhere (*prov.*). —**er**, *m.* (—**ers**, *pl.* —**er**) person who cooks *or* prepares; cooking machine. *Comp.* —**birne**, *f.* cooking pear. —**buch**, *n.* cookery-book. —**frau**, *f.* cook who comes by the day, cook hired for a special occasion. —**gefäß**, —**gerät**, —**geschirr**, *n.* cooking vessel *or* utensil. —**herd**, *m.* kitchen-range, cooking stove. —**holz**, *n.* fire-wood. —**kelle**, *f.*, —**löffel**, *m.* ladle. —**kessel**, *m.* caldron, copper. —**kraut**, *n.* pot-herbs. —**kunst**, *f.* culinary art. —**künstler(in)**, *m.*(*f.*) clever cook. —**maschine**, cooking-apparatus. —**obst**, *n.* fruit for stewing, cooking (apples, etc.). —**ofen**, *m.* oven, cooking-stove. —**pfanne**, *f.* saucepan; stew-pan. —**punkt**, *m.* boiling point. —**salz**, *n.* kitchen-salt. —**salz=geist**, *m.*, —**salz=säure**, *f.* muriatic acid. —**studentin**, *f.* young lady going to a school of cookery, cookery student (*coll.*). —**topf**, *m.* kitchen-pot; seething-pot; porridge-pot. —**wein**, *m.* wine for use in cooking. —**zeug**, *n.* kitchen utensils *or* furniture. —**zucker**, *m.* brown *or* moist sugar.

Kö'cher, *m.* (—**s**, *pl.* —) quiver; pen-case (*sl.*).

Kö'chin, *f.* (*pl.* —**nen**) female cook.

Ko'dak, *m.* (—**s**, *pl.* —**e**) kodak.

Kö'der, *m.* (—**s**, *pl.* —) bait, lure; heel-leather. —**n**, *v.a.* to bait, lure, decoy. *Comp.* —**fisch**, *m.* fish as bait.

Ko'dex, *m.* (—**es**, *pl.* —**e** *or* **Co'dices**) codex, manuscript; code. *Comp.* —**telegramm**, *n.* code telegraph *or* wire.

Kodi—fizie'ren, *v.a.* to codify. —**zi'll**, *n.* codicil.

Ko'fen, *m.* (—**s**, *pl.* —) *see* **Koben**.

Kofe'nt, *m.* (—**s**, *pl.* —**e**) small *or* thin beer.

Kof'fer, *m.* (—**s**, *pl.* —) trunk, portmanteau box; **Hand—**, bag. —**chen**, **Köf'ferchen**, *n.* (—**chens**, *pl.* —**chen**) little trunk. *Comp.* —**deckel**, *m.* box-lid. —**riemen**, *m.* trunk-strap. —**träger**, *m.* porter.

Kog'nak, *m.* (—**s**, *pl.* —**s**) cognac.

Kohä—re'nz, *f.* coherence. —**sio'n**, *f.* cohesion. —**sio'ns=kraft**, *f.* cohesive power.

Kohl, *m.* (—**s**, *pl.* —**e**) cabbage; cole; rigmarole; stuff and nonsense, twaddle, bosh (*coll.*); **Blumen—**, cauliflower; **Braun—**, **Grün—**, greens; **Rot—**, red cabbage; **Weiß—**, cabbage; **Sprossen—**, sprouts; **Brüsseler—**, Brussels sprouts; **aufgewärmter —**, an old story, cold kale warmed up; **— machen**, (*fam.*) to blunder; **das macht den — nicht fett**, that does not help us much; **schöne Worte machen den — nicht fett**, fair words will not feed the cat *or* fill the sack (*prov.*). —**en**, *v.n.* (*aux.* **h.**) to chatter nonsense, to prose (*coll.*). *Comp.* —**bauer**, *m.* cabbage-grower. —**hase**, *m.* (common) hare. —**kopf**, *m.* head of cabbage; blockhead. —**ra'bi**, *m.* cabbage-turnip. —**rübe**, *f.* rape; cabbage-turnip. —**saat**, *f.*, —**same**, *m.* rape, cole-seed. —**stengel**, —**strunk**, *m.* cabbage-stalk. —**weiß'ling**, *m.* common white butterfly.

Koh'l—e, *f.* (*pl.* —**en**) charcoal; (**Stein=**) coal; carbon; **abgeschwefelte —e**, coke; **glühende —en**, red hot *or* live coals; **ausgebrannte —en**, cinders; **glimmende —en**, embers; —**en einnehmen**, to coal (*of ships*); **zu —e werden**, to turn to coal; **in —e verwandeln**, to char, to carbonize; **zu —e verbrennen**, to be reduced to cinders; **auf glühenden —en sein** *or* **sitzen**, to be on thorns; **mit der Hand in die —en schlagen**, to burn one's fingers (by a foolish undertaking); **feurige —en auf jemandes Haupt sammeln**, to heap coals of fire on a p.'s head (*B.*).

Koh'l—en, *v.a.* & *n.* (*aux.* **h.**) to burn with charcoal; to char; to draw with charcoal; to carbonize. *Comp.* —**en=abbau**, *m.* coal-mining, working of coal. **—en=arbeiter,** *m.* coal-miner, pitman, collier. **—en=artig,** *adj.* coaly; carbonic. **—en=bank,** *f.* coal-bed. **—en=becken,** *n.* coal-field; coal-pan. **—en=blende,** *f.* anthracite. **—en=bergwerk,** *n.* coal-mine, colliery. **—en=brenner,** *m.* charcoal-burner. **—en=brennerei,** *f.* charcoal-burning; charcoal-kiln. **—en=dämpfer,** *m.* coal-extinguisher. **—en=dampf, —en=dunst,** *m.* vapour, smoke of burning coals. **—en=gestübe,** *n.* coal-dust; slack. **—en=glut,** *f.* live coals. **—en=gruppe,** *f.* carboniferous group. **—en=grus,** *m.* slack. **—en=händler,** *m.* coal-merchant. **—en=haltig,** *adj.* carboniferous, containing coal. **—en=holz,** *n.* wood for charcoal. **—en=hornblende,** *f.* anthracite. **—en=hütte,** *f.* charcoal-kiln. **—en=kalk,** *m.* carboniferous limestone. **—en=kasten,** *m.* coal-box, coal-scuttle. **—en=kläre,** *f.* coal-dust. **—en=klein,** *n.* small coal, slack. **—en=lager,** *n.* colliery. **—en=lösche,** *f.* refuse of coal-pits. **—en=ofen,** *m.* charcoal-kiln; coal-stove. **—en=platz,** *m.* coal-hole; place where charcoal is made. **—en=riß,** *m.* charcoal sketch. **—en=sauer; —ensaures Soda,** carbonate of soda; **—ensaure Jungfrau,** seller of mineral waters in public places (*coll.*); **—ensaure Salze,** carbonates; **—ensaurer Kalk,** calcium carbonate. **—en=säure,** *f.* carbonic acid. **—en=schiff,** *n.* collier. **—en=schlacke,** *f.* coal-cinder. **—en=schuppen,** *m.* coal-shed. **—en=schütte,** *f.* coal-scuttle. **—en=schwarz,** *n.* charcoal black. **—en=station,** *f.* coaling station. **—en=stift,** *m.* charcoal-pencil. **—en=stoff,** *m.* carbon. **—en=wasserstoff=gas,** *n.* hydrocarbon. **—en=werk,** *n.* colliery. **—en=zeichnung,** *f.* charcoal-drawing. **—holz,** *n.* wood for charcoal, common privet. **—rabe,** *m.* raven. **—(pech)=rabenschwarz,** *adj.* quite black, jet black. **—schwarz,** *adj.* coal-black.

Köh'ler, *m.* (—s, *pl.* —) charcoal-burner; collier. **—ei',** *f.* charcoal-burning; charcoal-kiln. *Comp.* **—glaube,** *m.* implicit faith.

Kohor'te, *f.* (*pl.* **—n**) cohort.

Ko'je, *f.* (*pl.* **—n**) cabin; berth (*rare*); **eine — mit zwei Betten,** a cabin with two berths.

Kokar'de, *f.* (*pl.* **—n**) cockade.

Kok, *m.* (*pl.* **—es, Koaks**), **—e,** *f.* **—s,** *pl.* coke.

Koke'tt, *adj.* coquettish. **—e,** *f.* (*pl.* **—en**) flirt, coquette. **—ie'ren,** *v.n.* (*aux.* **h.**) to flirt, coquet.

Koko'n, *m.* (—s, *pl.* —s) cocoon.

Ko'kos— (*in comp.*) **—baum,** *m.*, **—palme,** *f.* cocoa-nut palm. **—nuß,** *f.* cocoa-nut.

¹**Kol'b—en,** *m.* (—ens, *pl.* **—en**) club, mace; club-like thing; butt-end; knob, knot; mallet; round smoothing-iron; burnisher; soldering-iron; piston, sucker; alembic; spadix (*Bot.*); feeler (*Ent.*); stag's horn; large bottle; tip of a cannon-sponge. **—icht,** (*obs.*) **—ig,** *adj.* club-like; knotty. *Comp.* **—en=aufgang,** *m.* up-stroke of a piston. **—en=bürste,** *f.* bottle-brush. **—en=förmig,** *adj.* club-shaped. **—en=glas, —en=gefäß,** *n.* alembic. **—en=hirsch,** *m.* stag with knags for horns. **—en=hub,** *m.* stroke of the piston. **—en=lauf,** *see* **—en=hub. —en=niedergang,** *m.* down-stroke of the piston. **—en=recht,** *n.* club-law. **—en=röhre,** *f.* chamber of a pump. **—en=spiel,** *n.* motion of the piston. **—en=stange,** *f.* piston-rod. **—en=streich,** *m.* blow with a club *or* butt-end. **—en=träger,** *m.* mace-bearer. **—en=tragend,** *adj.* spadiceous (*Bot.*). **—en=ventil,** *n.* piston-valve.

Kol'ben, *v.* I. *a.* to provide with a thick end; to work *or* clean with a thick-ended instrument; to bore guns; to lop. II. *n.* (*aux.* **h.**) to get horns *or* spikes; to bat.

Ko'libri, *m.* (—s, *pl.* —) humming-bird.

Koli'k, *f.* (*pl.* **—en**) colic.

Kolk, *m.* (—es, *pl.* **Köl'ke**) gully, pool, pond. *Comp.* **—rabe,** *m.* common raven.

Kol'ken, Kolk'sen, *v.n.* to speak badly, indistinctly; to vomit.

Kollabor—a'tor, *m.* (—ators, *pl.* **—ato'ren**) collaborator, fellow worker; assistant master (*obs.*). **—atu'r,** *f.* collaborator's post, assistant mastership (*obs.*). **—ie'ren,** *v.n.* to collaborate, to work together.

Kollationie'ren, *v.a.* to collate; to check off (*Typ.*).

Kolle'g, *n.* (—s, *pl.* **—ien** & **—ia**) administrative assembly; board, council; University (*or* College) lecture; **— halten** *or* **lesen,** to give (*or* deliver) a course of lectures, to lecture (**über eine S.** on a th.); **— hören,** to hear (*or* attend) a course of lectures *or* a lecture; **— belegen,** to put one's name down (*or* enter one's name) as a student attending a course of lectures; **— schinden,** to attend lectures without paying the lecture fees; **— schwänzen,** to cut lectures; **— testieren,** to testify to a student's attendance at lectures; **— nachschreiben,** to take (down) lecture notes. **—e,** *m.* (**—en,** *pl.* **—en**) comrade; colleague; **Herr —e** *or* **Lieber —e** *is a usual form of address among German university and school teachers.* **—ia'l, —ia'lisch,** *adj. & adv.* collegiate; colleague-like. **—ium,** *n.* (**—iums,** *pl.* **—ien** *or* **—ia**) lecture; commission, society, board, staff. *Comp.* **—geld,** *n.* lecture fee. **—heft,** *n.* lecture notes. **—mappe,** *f.* portfolio for lecture notes.

Kollekt—a'neen, *pl.* literary gleanings. **—a'nt,** *m.* (**—an'ten,** *pl.* **—an'ten**) collector of alms. **—e,** *f.* (*pl.* **—en**) collection; collect, short prayer; hymn sung during collection. **—ie'ren,** *v.a.* to collect. **—i'v, —i'visch,** *adj.* collective. **—a'nea, —a'neen=buch,** *n.* commonplace book.

¹**Kol'ler, Gol'ler,** *n. & m.* (—s, *pl.* —) cape of a coat, collar; neck-armour; jerkin, doublet; buff-waistcoat; bodice.

²**Kol'ler,** *m.* (—s) frenzy, rage; staggers (*Vet.*); leather trousers of German students in full 'Wichs'; **den — bekommen,** to go mad; **in — und Kanonen,** in full fig (*stud. sl.*). **—ig, —isch,** *adj.* afflicted with the staggers; crazy.

¹**Kol'lern,** *v.n.* (*aux.* **h.**) to have the staggers; to be crazy.

²**Kol'lern,** *v.n.* (*aux.* **h.**) to roll about; to rumble; to coo (of pigeons); to gobble (of turkeys); **Steine vom Berge herunter —,** to roll boulders down the mountain. *Comp.* **—gang,** *m.* crushing mill with vertical runners. **—stein,** *m.* mill-stone, roller.

Kollett', *n.* (—s, *pl.* **—e** *or* (*dial.*) **—er**) cape; collar; jerkin; riding-jacket (*obs.*).

Kollidie'ren, *v.n.* (*aux.* **h.**) to come into collision, collide.

Kollie'ren, *v.a.* to lay (a ball) under the cushion (*Bill.*).

Kol'lo, *m. & n.* (—s, *pl.* —s, **Kolli**) bale (*of goods*) package.

Kolludie'ren, I. *v.n.* (*aux.* **h.**) to act in collusion with. II. *n.* collusion.

Ko'lon, *n.* (—s) colon.

Kolon—ia'l, *adj.* colonial. **—ie',** *f.* (*pl.* **—ieen**) colony. **—isie'ren,** *v.a.* to colonize. **—i'st,** *m.* colonist, settler, planter. *Comp.* **—ia'l=mensch,** *m.* enthusiast for colonization. **—ia'l=minister,** *m.* Secretary of State for the Colonies, Colonial Secretary (*Engl.*). **—ia'l=ministerium,** *n.* Colonial Office. **—ia'l=politik,** *f.* policy with regard to colonization. **—ia'l=schwärmer,** *m.* enthusiast for colonization. **—ia'l=waren,** *pl.* colonial produce, groceries. **—ia'l=waren=händler,** *m.* dealer in colonial produce, provision merchant, grocer.

Kolon'ne, *f.* (*pl.* **—n**) column.

Kolopho'nium, *n.* (—s) colophony, rosin.

Koloquin'te, *f.* (*pl.* **—n**) colocynth, bitter-apple.

Koloratu'ren, *pl.* grace notes (*Mus.*). *Comp.* **—sängerin**, *f.* florid singer, prima donna.

Kolor—ie'ren, *v.a.* to colour; to illuminate. **—i't**, *n.* (**—its**) colouring, hue, shade.

Kolo'ß, *m.* (**—(ss)es**, *pl.* **—(ss)e**) colossus. **—(ss)a'l**, *adj. & adv.* colossal, gigantic, huge; very, extremely, immensely (*coll.*); **er hat —(ss)ales Schwein**, he is a most lucky chap (*coll.*); **freut mich —(ss)al**, extremely pleased.

Kolportie'ren, *v.a.* to hawk, distribute (tracts).

¹Kol'ter, *m.* (**—s**, *pl.* **—**) thick cloth, coverlet.

²Kol'ter, *n.* (**—s**, *pl.* **—**) ploughshare.

Kolum'ne, *f.* (*pl.* **—n**) column; page. *Comp.* **—n=maß**, *n.* scale, ruler (*Typ.*). **—n=schnur**, *f.* page-cord. **—n=titel**, *m.* running title, heading. **—n=weise**, *adj.* in columns. **—n=ziffer**, *f.* folio.

Kombinie'ren, *v.a.* to combine.

Kombü'se, *f.* caboose, cook's room, galley.

Kome't, *m.* (**—en**, *pl.* **—en**) comet. *Comp.* **—en=bahn**, *f.* orbit of a comet. **—en=schweif**, *m.* tail of a comet. **—en=system**, *n.* cometary system.

Ko'mi—k, *f.* comicality; fun, comic deportment; **unfreiwillige —**, unintentional comicality. **—ker**, *m.* (**—kers**, *pl.* **—ker**) comic writer; comedian. **—sch**, *adj.* comical, funny, droll, humorous; peculiar; strange; **ich finde das etwas —sch von ihm**, I think it rather strange of him (*coll.*); **ein —scher Kauz**, a queer fish.

Komit—a't, *n.* (**—ats**, *pl.* **—ate**) suite; attendance; county (*in Hungary*). **—i'v**, *n.* (**—ivs**) legal authority.

Komi'tien, *pl.* comitia.

Kom'ma, *n.* (**—s**, *pl.* **—s**, **—ta**) comma.

Kommand—a'nt, *m.* (**—an'ten**, *pl.* **—an'ten**) commander. **—itä'r**, *m.* (**—itärs**, *pl.* **—itäre**) sleeping partner, limited partner (*C.L.*). **—i'te**, *f.* (*pl.* **—iten**) sleeping partnership; branch establishment; command (*Mil.*). **—o**, *n.* (*pron.* **Komman'do**; **—os**, *pl.* **—os**) command; **ein —o Soldaten**, a detachment of soldiers. *Comp.* **—i't=gesellschaft**, *f.* joint stock company, limited liability company. **—o=pfeife**, *f.* boatswain's whistle. **—o=stab**, *m.* baton. **—o=wort**, *n.* word of command.

Kommandie'r—en, *v.a.* to command, to order; **wer —t hier?** who is the officer in command? **das Regiment ist schon —t**, the regiment has been detailed; **der höchst —ende**, the (senior) officer in command.

Kom'men, I. *ir.v.n.* (*aux.* **f.**) to come, approach; to get to *or* at, arrive; to shoot, spring up; to arise, proceed from; to come about, fall out, happen; to cost; **wie viel kommt das Pfund? Das Pfund kommt 3 Mark**, how much is the pound? The pound costs 3 shillings; **gegangen, geritten —**, to come on foot, on horseback; **gelaufen —, gesprungen —**, to come running, jumping; **— Sie hierher**, come this way; **— Sie doch**, do come; **wie gerufen —**, to come opportunely; **einem etwas —**, to drink to a p.'s health, to pledge s.o. (*students' sl.*); **(etwas) — sehen**, to foresee; **kommt mir nicht so**, don't speak to me in that way, don't bother me; **mir darf er so nicht —**, he must not treat me so; **einen — lassen**, to send for a p.; **etwas — lassen**, to order a thing; **dahin dürfen sie es nicht — lassen**, they must not let it come to that point; **es ist weit mit ihm ge—**, he has fallen very low; **es mag — was will, es komme wie es will**, whatever may happen; **mir kam der Gedanke**, the thought occurred to me *or* crossed my mind; **er soll mir schon —**, he shall make the first move; **der soll mir nur wieder —!** just let him show his face here again! **wenn Sie mir so —**, oh! if you take it in that way; **nun warte! du kommst mir auch schon einmal wieder**, very good! I shall pay you for that before I have finished with you; **sie sind mir abhanden gekommen**, I have lost, mislaid them; **die —de Woche**, next week; **die —de Fracht**, freight home *or* inwards; **frei —**, to get off free; **einem gleich —**, to be equal to s.o.; **einem zu nahe —**, to injure one; **diese Ware kommt der andern bei Weitem nicht nach** *or* **gleich**, this article is not nearly so good as the other; **weit —**, to make great progress; **zu kurz —**, to come off a loser, to fall short of; **einem hoch zu stehen —**, to cost a p. dear; **wenn es hoch kommt**, at the most; **so wie es gerade kommt**, just as it turns out; **es kann — daß**, it is possible that; **es kann nicht anders —, als daß er**, he cannot but; **zu spät —**, to be late; **an eine S. —**, to attain, reach to; **an das Licht —**, to be brought to light, **nun kommt es** (*or* **die Reihe**) **an mich**, now it is my turn; **etwas an sich (heran) — lassen**, to await a thing quietly; **(hart) an einander —**, to quarrel, to come to blows; **einem ans Leben —**, to attempt a p.'s life, to cut s. o. to the quick; **an jemandes Stelle —**, to succeed to one's post; **er kann nicht an sie —**, he can get no hold on, find nothing against them; **an den Tag —**, to come to light, to be discovered; **ans Land —**, to land; **wie kamen Sie darauf?** how did you (come to) think of that? what suggested that thought to you? **auf eine S. —**, to think of, come to mention a th.; **auf die Welt —**, to be born; **wieder auf sein Vorhaben —**, to return to one's purpose; **im Fallen wieder auf die Füße —**, to fall on one's feet; **auf seine Kosten —**, to recover one's expenses; **ich kam auf die Schule**, I was sent to school; **es auf das Äußerste — lassen**, to let matters come to the worst; **auf eins heraus —**, to come *or* amount to the same (thing); **auf einen Namen —**, to remember a name; **er ist mir aus den Augen ge—**, I have lost sight of him, I have not seen *or* met him again; **es kam mir aus dem Sinn**, I forgot; **aus einander —**, to fall out; to lose sight of one another; **außer** *or* **aus der Fassung, außer sich —**, to lose one's self-control; **aus der Mode —**, to go out of fashion; **hinter eine S. —**, to discover a th.; **in der Leute Mund —**, to be talked of, get a bad name; **in Verlegenheit —**, to be embarrassed, to get into trouble; **in Verfall —**, to decay; **es kam mir in den Sinn**, it occurred to me; I remembered; **in Gang —**, to be set going; **in den Himmel —**, to go to Heaven; **in das Fleisch —**, to come in the flesh (*B.*); **einem in den Weg** *or* **Wurf —**, to come across, to thwart a p.; **in Richtigkeit —**, to come to a settlement; **in die unrechte Kehle —**, to go down the wrong way; **über etwas ins Reine** *or* **Klare —**, to get to understand a thing; to arrive at a clear understanding about it; **es kommt nichts darnach**, nothing will come of it; **— Sie gut nach Hause!** get home safely! **wir kamen glücklich nach Hause**, we got home all right; **über eine S. —**, to come upon a th.; to get over a th.; **Furcht kam über mich**, I was seized with fear; **ich kann nicht darüber kommen**, I cannot get over that, I shall not (*or* never) forget it; **um eine S. —**, to lose a thing; **unter die Leute —**, to be spread abroad, made known; **viel unter die Leute —**, to go much into society; **von Kräften —**, to lose one's strength; **von Sinnen —**, to lose consciousness; to go mad; **nicht vom Fleck —**, not to get any further, to be at a standstill; **davon —**, to get off, to escape; **sie — mir nicht von der Seite**, they never leave me; **das kommt davon**, that comes of it, that is the result of it; **vor einen —**, to come into a p.'s presence; **zu etwas —**, to attain to, to come to, to get, obtain, to find time for; **er wird**

schon zu etwas —, he will no doubt make his way in the world; wie kamen Sie dazu? how did you come to (do) that? how did you come by that? how did you get this? dazu kommt noch, besides, add to that; zu Falle —, to be ruined; zu statten —, to be of use, serviceable; zu stande —, to be arranged, to take place; mit etwas zu stande —, to accomplish something; einen zur Rede, zum Worte — lassen, to allow a p. to speak; zu Kräften —, to recover strength; zu Atem —, to get breath; zur Besinnung, zu sich —, to come to oneself *or* one's senses; zu Vermögen —, to come into a fortune; es ist mir zu Ohren gekommen, I have been told; zu Tage —, to come to light, to be discovered, to become known; wenn es zum Treffen kommt, when it comes to the scratch; sich (*dat.*) etwas zu Schulden — lassen, to become guilty of, to incur the blame of; er kam mit dem Finger zwischen die Thüre, his finger was squeezed *or* pinched in the door. *The p.p. was in older Gm. formed without the prefix* ge—, *and* — *survives as a past part. in poetry, e.g. in the hymn* es ist das Heil uns — her, salvation has come to us. II. *subst. n.* coming, arrival. —d, *p. & adj.* der, die, das —de, the coming; the comer; —de und Gehende, comers and goers; —de Woche, next week, the coming *or* ensuing week.

Kommend—a'tor, *m.* (—ators, *pl.* —ato'ren) one who holds a benefice in commendam. —a'nt, *see* Kommandant. —e (*pron.* Kommen'de), *f.* (*pl.* —) prebend.

Komme'nt, *m.* (—s) students' customs; student law *or* code.

Komment—a'r, *m.* (—ars, *pl.* —are) commentary, comment. —ie'ren, *v.a.* to comment on *or* upon; to furnish with notes, to annotate. —a'tor, *m.* commentator, expositor.

Komme'rs, *m.* (*stud. slang*) drinking-bout, student's convivial gathering on a large scale. —(s)ie'ren, *v.n.* to hold a drinking-bout. *Comp.* —buch, *n.* book containing a collection of students' (patriotic, popular, comic, drinking) songs (usually with their melodies, to be sung at students' convivial gatherings).

Kommer'zienrat, *m.* councillor of commerce (*a title conferred on distinguished financiers and men of business*).

Kommi'ß, *n.* (*m.*) (—, *pl.* —) uniform (*sl.*); er ist beim —, he is a soldier (*coll.*). *Comp.* —brot, *n.* regimental bread. —kopf, *m.* military pedant, regular Tommy Atkins (*coll.*). —mütze, *f.* regulation cap, service cap. —schuhe, —stiefel, *pl.* regulation shoes, regulation boots. —tuch, *n.* army-cloth, regulation cloth for uniforms.

Kommiss—ä'r, *m.* (—ärs, *pl.* —äre) commissary, commissioner. —io'n, *f.* (*pl.* —ionen) commission, committee. —ionä'r, *m.* (—ionärs, *pl.* —ionäre) commissionaire; agent; commissioner. *Comp.* —io'ns=bericht, *m.* report of a commission *or* committee. —ions=buch, *n.* order-book. —io'ns=gebühr, *f.* commission (charges). —io'ns=geschäft, *n.* commission business, commission trade.

Kommittee', Komite', *n.* (—s, *pl.* —s) committee.

Komm'lich, *adj.* convenient, comfortable (*dial.*). —keit, *f.* comfort, convenience (*dial.*).

Kommo'de, I. *adj. & adv.* commodious. II. *subst.f.* (*pl.* —n) chest of drawers.

Kömmst, Kömmt, *2 & 3 p. sing. pres. indic. of* kommen (*obs. in literary Gm.; still used coll.*).

Kommun—is'mus, *m.* communism. —i'st, *m.* (—is'ten, *pl.* —is'ten) communist. *Comp.* —a'l=garde, *f.* town-militia. —a'l=gardist, *m.* militia-man. —a'l=schule, *f.* parish board-school. —a'l=steuer, *f.* (local) rate.

Kommuta'tor, *m.* (—s, *pl.* —en) circuit-changer, switch.

Komöd—ia'nt, *m.* (—ian'ten, *pl.* —ian'ten) comedian; actor. —ie (*pron.* Komö'die), *f.* (*pl.* —ien) comedy; play. *Comp.* —ien=haus, *n.* play-house, theatre.

Kompagnie', *f.* (*pl.* —en) company (*Mil.*). *Comp.* —chef, *m.* captain. —front(e), *f.*; in —fronten vorbei marschieren, to defile in companies. —geschäft, *n.* joint business, copartnership; ein —geschäft gründen (auflösen), to go into (dissolve) partnership.

Kompagno'n, *m.* (—s, *pl.* —s) partner, associate; stiller —, sleeping partner.

Kompa'n, Kumpa'n, *m.* (—es, *pl.* —e) companion, mate (*obs.*).

Komparie'ren, *v.n.* to appear in answer to a summons.

Kom'paß, *m.* (—(ss)es, *pl.* —(ss)e) compass. *Comp.* —häuschen, *n.* binnacle. —rose, *f.* rhumb card (*Naut.*).

Kompet—e'nt, I. *adj.* competent. II. *subst.m.* (—en'ten, *pl.* —en'ten) competitor. —e'nz, *f.* competence, competition; —enz eines Falliten, bankrupt's allowance. *Comp.* —e'nz=streit, *m.* question of jurisdiction.

Kompil—a'tor, *m.* (—s, *pl.* —en) compiler. —ie'ren, *v.a.* to compile.

Komplime'nt, *n.* (—s, *pl.* —e) compliment; greeting; bow; obeisance; keine —e! no ceremony! ohne viel —e! please do not stand on ceremony! —ie'ren, *v.a.* to compliment; eine Dame —ieren, to bow to a lady (*obs.*).

Komplizie'ren, *v.a.* to complicate.

Komplo't(t), *n.* (—(e)s, *pl.* —e) plot.

Komponie'ren, *v.a. & n.* to compose (*Mus.*). —i'st, *m.* (—is'ten, *pl.* —is'ten), —is'tin, *f.*, composer.

Kompo'st, *m.* (—s) compost (*agric.*).

Kompo't(t), *n.* (—s, *pl.* —e) stewed fruit; jam.

Kompressio'ns=maschine, *f.* condensing engine.

Komprimie'ren, *v.a.* to compress air.

Kompromittie'ren, *v.a.* to compromise; sich —, to commit oneself.

Komtu'r, *m.* (—s, *pl.* —e) commander of an order. —ei', *f.* commandery.

Konchy'li—en, *pl.* shell-fish. —ologie', *f.* conchology.

Kondens—atio'n, *f.* condensation. —a'tor, *m.* condenser (*Mach.*). —ie'ren, *v.a.* to condense.

Konditio'n, *f.* (*pl.* —en) condition, stipulation; situation; in — gehen, to enter service. —ie'ren, *v.n.* (*aux.* h.); bei einem —ieren, to be in one's employment. —ie'rt, *p. & adj.* conditioned.

Kondi'tor, *m.* (—s, *pl.* Kondito'ren) pastry-cook, confectioner. —ei', *f.* confectioner's shop.

Kondu'kt, *m.* (—es, *pl.* —e) funeral train.

Konfe'kt, *n.* (—es, *pl.* —e) comfits, sweetmeats.

Konfektio'n, *f.* confection; manufacture of *or* trade in ready-made articles of dress. —eu'se, *f.* dress *or* mantle-maker; girl who sells at a mantle-maker's shop (*coll.*). *Comp.* —s=artikel, *pl.* ready-made articles (of dress). —s=dame, *f.*, —s=fräulein, *n. see* —euse. —s=geschäft, *n.* ready-made clothes shop, outfitting business.

Konfer—e'nz, *f.* (*pl.* —en'zen) conference. —ie'ren, *v.n.* (*aux.* h.) to confer. *Comp.* —e'nz=zimmer, *n.* meeting-room; masters' room.

Konfessio'n, *f.* (*pl.* —en) confession; creed. —e'll, *adj.* confessional. *Comp.* —s=wechsel, *m.* change of creed *or* communion.

Konfirm—a'nd, *m.* (—an'den, *pl.* —an'den), —an'din, *f.* candidate for confirmation, catechumen. —atio'n, *f.* confirmation. —ie'ren, *v.a.* to confirm. *Comp.* —an'den=unterricht, *m.* instruction preparatory to confirmation.

Konfiszie'ren, *v.a.* to confiscate.

Konföderie'r—en, *v.r.* to unite in a league. —t, *p.p. & adj.* confederate.

Konfu's, *adj.* puzzled, confused.
Konglomera't, *n.* (—s, *pl.* —e) conglomerate.
Kongre'ß=mitglied, *n.* member of Congress.
Kongruie'ren, *v.n.* (*aux.* h.) to agree; to coincide (*Math.*).
Kö'nig, *m.* (—s, *pl.* —e) king; regulus (*Chem.*); **der drei —e Tag**, Twelfth-day; **der — Pharao**, Pharaoh; **die heiligen drei —e**, the three Magi; **das erste Buch der —e**, the first book of Kings (*B.*); **zum — machen, — einsetzen**, to make, create, king; **er wurde zum —e gewählt**, he was elected king; **Herz —**, king of hearts (*cards*); **mein Herzens —**, the king of my heart. **—in**, *f.* queen; **—in Mutter**, queen mother; **—in Wittwe**, queen dowager. **—lich**, *adj.* royal, sovereign (dignity), kingly *or* queenly (demeanour), regal (insignia); **ein —lich Gesinnter**, a royalist; **sich —lich freuen**, to be as happy as a king (*coll.*); **sich —lich unterhalten**, to enjoy oneself immensely (*coll.*). **—tum**, *n.* (—tums, *pl.* —tümer) kingship, royalty; monarchical principle; **—tum von Gottes Gnaden**, kingship by divine right *or* by divine grace. *Comp.* **—reich**, *n.* kingdom, realm. **—s=adler**, *m.* golden eagle. **—s=binde**, *f.* diadem. **—s=brief**, *m.* royal charter. **—s=freund**, *m.* royalist. **—s=hof**, *m.* royal palace *or* court. **—s=krone**, *f.* crown of a king; crown-flower. **—s=leutnant**, *m.* Count Thoranc (*lieutenant du roi de France*) who played an important part in Goethe's early life. **—s=mann**, *m.* royalist. **—s=mord, —s=mörder**, *m.* regicide. **—s=schießen**, *n.* rifle-match (*winner being named 'king'*). **—s=schuß**, *m.* best shot. **—s=sitz**, *m.* throne; royal residence. **—s=stab**, *m.* sceptre. **—s=straße**, *f.* King's parade; highway. **—s=treu**, *adj.* royalistic. **—s=urlaub**, *m.* conditional leave after two years' service (*Mil. obs.*). **—s=würde**, *f.* royal dignity; kingship.
Ko'nisch, *adj. & adv.* conical.
Konjugie'ren, *v.a.* to conjugate (*a verb*).
Kon'junktiv, *m.* (—s, *pl.* —e) subjunctive.
Konka'v, *adj.* concave. **—itä't**, *f.* concavity.
Konkla've, *n.* (—s) conclave; assembly of cardinals for the election of a pope.
Konkord—a't, *n.* (—ats, *pl.* —ate) concordat, treaty on ecclesiastical matters with the pope. **—a'nz**, *f.* concordance; agreement.
Konkubina't, *n.* (—(e)s, *pl.* —e) concubinage; **im — lebend**, concubinary.
Konkurr—e'nt, *m.* (—en'ten, *pl.* —en'ten) competitor; rival (shop). **—e'nz**, *f.* (*pl.* —en'zen) competition; opposition; concurrence. **—ie'ren**, *v.n.* (*aux.* h.) to compete; to concur. **—ie'rend**, *p. & adj.* competitive.
Konku'rs, *m.* (—(s)es, *pl.* —(s)e) meeting of creditors; bankruptcy, failure; **es ist ein — eröffnet worden**, a fiat of bankruptcy has been issued; **Erkennung des —es**, judicial assignment of an insolvent's property; **— machen, in — geraten**, to call one's creditors together, to fail. *Comp.* **—behörde**, *f.* commission of bankruptcy. **—erklärung**, *f.* declaration of insolvency. **—eröffnung**, *f.* opening of bankruptcy proceedings. **—gericht**, *n.* court of bankruptcy. **—masse**, *f.* estate of a bankrupt, mass. **—ordnung**, *f.* regulations concerning insolvency. **—verfahren**, *n.* proceedings in insolvency.
Kön'nen, *ir.v.* I. *a.* to know, understand (*how to do a thing*); to have skill in; to have power, be able to; **er kann nichts**, he knows nothing, he can do nothing; **laufe was du kannst**, run as fast as you can; **solche Leute — bei Hofe viel**, such people have great influence at court; **das Gekonnte wieder vergessen**, to forget what one has once known. [**Können** *is used for* **gekonnt** *when accompanying an inf. in compound tenses; as,* **er hätte es thun —**, he might have done it.] II. *n.* (*aux.* h.) to be able; to be permitted; **es kann sein**, it may be; **ich kann mich irren**, I may be mistaken; **ich konnte nichts als**, I could do nothing but; **ich konnte nicht anders als**, I could not but, I could not help; **was kann ich dafür?** how can I help it? **er kann nichts dafür**, it is not his fault; **ich kann nicht umhin zu bemerken**, I cannot help remarking; **ich kann nicht mehr**, I can do no more, I am quite knocked up; **sie kann ganz vorzüglich Deutsch**, she knows German extremely well; **sie kann gut deklamieren**, she recites well, is a clever reciter; **sie kann viele Gedichte auswendig**, she knows many poems by heart; **ich kann nicht anders**, I cannot act otherwise; **nicht weiter —**, to be at a standstill; **er kann auf keinem Fuße stehen**, he has not a leg to stand on; **man kann hoffen**, it is to be hoped; **er kann gut reiten**, he rides well, he knows how to ride.
Konnossemе'nt, *n.* (—s) bill of lading.
Konn'te, Konn'test, *1 (& 3), 2 p. sing. imperf. indic. of* **können**.
Konrek'tor, *m.* (—s, *pl.* **Konrekto'ren**) senior assistant master of a grammar school (*obs.*).
Konseque'nt, I. *adj.* consistent; consequential. II. *adv.* by natural sequence; consequently.
Konserv—a'tor, *m.* (—ators, *pl.* **Konservato'ren**) keeper, curator; taxidermist. **—ati'v**, *adj.* conservative; **die —ativen**, the Conservatives, the Tories (*Engl.*). **—ie'ren**, *v.a.* to preserve, conserve.
Konsign—atio'n, *f.* consignment, lodgment. **—ie'ren**, *v.a.* to consign.
Konsilie'ren, *v.a.* to rusticate (*Univ.*).
Konsisto'r—ium, *m.* (—iums, *pl.* —ien, —ia) consistory; ecclesiastical court for provinces *or* districts appointed by the crown. *Comp.* **—ia'l=rat**, *m.* consistorial council; member of a consistorial court.
Konskribie'r—en, *v.a.* to levy (troops). **—te(r)**, *m.* conscript.
Konso'le, *f.* (*pl.* —n) console; console-table; bracket.
Konsolidie'ren, *v.a.* to consolidate; **konsolidierte Staatspapiere**, stocks, consols.
Konson—a'nt, I. *adj.* consonant, agreeing. II. *m.* (—an'ten, *pl.* —an'ten) consonant; sound caused by narrowing *or* closure of the oral passages while the current of exhaled breath passes through the mouth cavity, voice check. **—a'nz**, *f.* agreement, concord (*Mus.*). **—ie'ren**, *v.n.* to be consonant.
Konsor'ten, *pl.* associates; accomplices; parties (*Law*); **Z. und —** (= Z and his accomplices), men like Z. (*contemptuous*).
Konsta'bler, *m.* (—s, *pl.* —) gunner (*Naut.; Mil. obs.*). *Comp.* **—kammer**, *f.* gun-room.
Konstatie'ren, *v.a.* to prove well-founded, to substantiate.
Konstitutione'll, *adj. & adv.* constitutional.
Konstruie'ren, *v.a.* to construe; to construct.
Konstruktio'nsfehler, *m.* mistake in the drawing.
Kon'sul, *m.* (—s, *pl.* —n) consul. **—a'risch**, *adj. & adv.* consular. **—a't**, *m.* (—ats, *pl.* —ate) consulate. **—e'nt**, *m.* (—en'ten, *pl.* —en'ten) counsel, counsellor, advocate.
Konsultie'ren, *v.a.* to consult.
Konsu'm, *m.* (—s) consumption. **—e'nt**, *m.* user, consumer. *Comp.* **—verein**, *m.* coöperative society *or* stores; **Beamten—verein**, civil service stores.
Konsumie'ren, *v.a.* to consume, use.
Konta'nt, *adj. & adv.* ready, ready money. **—en, Konten'ten**, *pl.* cash; ready money. *Comp.* **—geschäft**, *n.* ready-money business.
Kon'terfei, *n.* (—(e)s, *pl.* —e) portrait, likeness; counterfeit.

Kontinenta'l=sperre, *f.* Continental system of Napoleon I. (*1806*), Berlin decree.
Kon'to, *n.* (—s, *pl.* —s, **Konti**) account, credit; — **geben**, — **nehmen**, to give, to take credit; **ein** — **saldieren**, to balance an account; **a** — **Zahlung**, payment on account; **wollen Sie mir hundert Pfund a — geben?** will you give me a hundred pounds on account? *Comp.* —**korrent**, *m.* & *n.* current account. —**saldo**, *n.* balance account.
Konto'r, *n.* (—s, *pl.* —e) counting-house; office.
Kon'tra, (*in comp.* =) counter; contra; **per** —, against which. —**alt**, *m.* contralto (*Mus.*). —**baß**, *m.* double-bass, bass-viol. —**buch**, *n.* pass-book, customer's book. —**fuge**, *f.* counterfugue. —**punkt**, *m.* counterpoint; **den** —**punkt betreffend**, contrapuntal (*Mus.*). —**signie'ren**, *v.a.* to countersign.
Kontraha'ge, *f.* challenge for a duel (*sl.*).
Kontrah—e'nt, *m.* (—**en'ten**, *pl.* —**en'ten**) contractor. —**ie'ren**, *v.a.* & *n.* (*aux.* **h.**) to contract; to stipulate, bargain for.
Kontra'kt, I. *adj.* contracted; crippled. II. *m.* (—(e)s, *pl.* —) contract, bargain.
Konträ'r, *adj.* adverse.
Kontrol'l—e, *f.* (*pl.* —**en**) control; counter-register; army-list. —**eu'r**, *m.* (—**eurs**, *pl.* —**eure**) controller, comptroller. —**ie'ren**, *v.a.* to control. *Comp.* —**amt**, *n.* board of control. —**ie'r=amt**, *n.* clearing-office at a railway station. —**ie'r=blatt**, *n.* counterfoil (*of exchequer bills*). —**versammlung**, *f.* roll-call *or* muster of reserve men.
Kontuma'z, *f.* contempt of court; quarantine.
Kontu'r, *f.* (*pl.* —**en**) contour, outline.
Konven—ie'nz, *f.* (*pl.* —**ien'zen**) suitableness, propriety; convenience. —**ie'ren**, *v.n.* to be proper *or* convenient.
Konve'nt, *m.* (—s, *pl.* —e) convention; the Convention (*French Revolution*). —**ione'll**, *adj.* & *adv.* conventional. *Comp.* —**iona'l=strafe**, *f.* doomage, penalty for retarded delivery (*C. L.*). —**io'ns=münze**, *f.* assimilated coinage.
Konversatio'ns=lexikon, *n.* encyclopædia (of general information).
Konvertie'rung, *f.* (*pl.* —**en**) conversion.
Konvolu't, *n.* (—s, *pl.* —e) a bundle of papers.
Konzedie'ren, *v.a.* to concede, to make a concession.
Konzentr—ie'ren, *v.a.* to concentrate; **sich rückwärts** —**ieren**, to fall back; to flee, run away (*hum.*). —**ie'rung**, *f.* concentration. —**isch**, *adj.* (*pron.* **konzen'trisch**) concentric.
Konze'rt, *n.* (—s, *pl.* —e) concert; concerto. *Comp.* —**besucher**, *m.* concert-goer. —**flügel**, *m.* grand piano. —**haus**, *n.* concert-hall. —**meister**, *m.* leader *or* conductor of an orchestra. —**saal**, *m.* concert hall, music room; symphony hall. —**stück**, concerted piece; concerto.
Konzertie'ren, *v.n.* to give, *or* play in, a concert.
Konzessio'n, *f.* (*pl.* —**en**) concession, grant, patent, license; **eine** — **haben**, to be licensed. *Comp.* —**s=abgabe**, —**s=steuer**, *f.* license tax.
Kö'per, *m.* (—s) twill, tweel. —**n**, *v.a.* to twill, tweel. *Comp.* —**tuch**, *n.* twilled cloth.
Kopf, *m.* (—**es**, *pl.* **Köp'fe**) head (*of men and beasts*); jowl (*of fishes*); top (*of pins, trees, nails, mountains, etc.*); crown (*of hats*); head (*of plants*); root (*of hair*); muzzle (*of a gun*); bowl (*of a pipe*); that part of the binding of a book which bears the title; pommel; person, individual; brains; abilities; disposition; — **oder Schrift?** heads or tails? **ein fähiger** —, a clever fellow; **ein fauler** —, a shiftless fellow; **ein leerer** —, empty-headed fellow, blockhead; **einen eigensinnigen** — **haben**, to be obstinate; — **haben**, to have sense, judgment; **einem den** — **bieten**, to resist; **einer Gefahr den** — **bieten**, to brave a danger; **seinem** —**e folgen**, to go one's own way; **es gilt ihm den** *or* **seinen** —, his life is at stake; **den** — **hängen lassen**, to despond; **einem den** — **einnehmen**, (*of smells*) to get into a person's head; **einem den** — **vor die Füßen legen**, to behead a p.; **der** — **steht darauf**, it is a capital offence; **mir steht der** — **nicht danach**, I have no inclination for it; **den** — **aufsetzen**, to be obstinate; **einem den** — **zurecht setzen**, to bring a p. to reason; **einem den** — **waschen**, to reprimand a p. sharply, to give a p. a piece of one's mind; **sich einem an den** — **werfen**, to throw oneself at a p.'s head; **seinen** — **an** (**eine S.**) **setzen**, to set one's heart on, strain every nerve to obtain; **einem auf den** — **kommen** *or* **steigen**, to take a p. to task (*coll.*); **er ist nicht auf den** — **gefallen**, he is no fool, he is clever, sharp, wide awake; **sich auf den** — **stellen**, to do one's utmost; **und wenn du dich auf den** — **stellst, er wird nicht kommen**, he will not come, whatever you do; **mit dem** —**e durch die Wand wollen**, to run full tilt at everything (*coll.*); **einem auf den** — **Schuld geben**, to accuse a p. to his face; **den** — **aus der Schlinge ziehen**, to get out of the scrape; **aus dem** —**e**, by heart, from memory; **sich** (*dat.*) **etwas aus dem** —**e schlagen**, to banish s.th. from one's thoughts; **einem beim** —**e nehmen**, to get hold of a p., to arrest a p.; **es geht ihm zu viel durch den** —, he has too much to think of; — **für eine Sache haben**, to have a turn for a th.; **etwas im** —**e haben**, to be intelligent; to be preoccupied, out of humour, a little tipsy; **er hat Grütze im** —**e**, he is clever; **es geht mir im** —**e herum**, it weighs on (runs in) my mind; **er hat weiter nichts im** —**e als das**, his mind runs perpetually on that matter; **die Leute steckten die Köpfe zusammen**, the people were agitated; **sich** (*dat.*) **den** — **zerbrechen**, to rack one's brains; **das will mir nicht in den** —, I cannot understand that *or* take that in; **sich** (*dat.*) **in den** — **setzen**, to fancy, take into one's head; **in den** — **steigen**, to go to one's head; **mit dem** —**e voran**, head foremost; **der Gottlose fährt mit dem** —**e hindurch**, the wicked man hardeneth his face (*B.*); **nach dem eignen** —**e leben**, to live and do just as one pleases; **nach Köpfen stimmen**, to (vote by) poll; **um einen** — **größer**, a head taller; **einem über den Kopf wachsen**, to grow too much for s.o., outgrow a p.; **bis über den** —, over head and ears; **bis über den** — **in Schulden**, up to the eyes in debt; **über Hals und** —, precipitately; **Hals über** —, head over heels; — **unter sich**, head over heels (*rare*); **ein Brett vor dem** —**e haben**, to be very stupid; **einen vor den** — **stoßen**, to offend s.o., to give offence *or* umbrage to a p.; **einem zu** —**e steigen**, to go *or* fly to a p.'s head (*of wine*); **von** — **zu Fuß**, from top to toe; **viel Köpfe, viel Sinne; so viel(e) Köpfe, so viel(e) Sinne**, many heads, many minds; every man has his own opinion (*prov.*); **was man nicht im** —**e hat, muß man in den Beinen** *or* **Füßen haben**, use your head to save your heels; who falls short in the head must be long in the heels (*prov.*). *Comp.* —**arbeit**, *f.* study. —**band**, *n.* head-band, fillet. —**besteuerung**, *f.* capitation tax. —**bohrer**, *m.* trephine (*Surg.*). —**brechend**, *adj.* very puzzling *or* difficult. —**drüse**, *f.* cephalic gland. —**ende**, *f.* bed-head. —**fest**, *adj.* constant, steady, persevering. —**fieber**, *n.* brain-fever. —**fluß**, *m.* rheumatic affection of the head. —**geld**, *n.* poll-tax. —**gewand**, *n.* amice (*Eccl.*). —**grind**, *m.* scald-head (*Med.*). —**hänger**, *m.* low-spirited person; hypocrite, hypocritical devotee. —**haut**, *f.* scalp. —**kissen**, *n.* pillow. —**längs**, *adv.* headlong. —**los**, *adj.* headless; silly, stupid. —**nicken**,

n. nod. —**nuß**, *f.* cuff, box on the ear (*vulg.*). —**pfühl**, *m.* bolster; pillow. —**putz**, *m.* coiffure. —**quote**, *f.* so and so much per head. —**rechnen**, *n.* mental arithmetic. —**salat**, *m.* cabbage-lettuce. —**scheu**, *adj.* skittish; shy. —**schmerz**, *m.*, —**schmerzen**, *pl.* headache. —**schüttelnd**, *adj. & adv.* shaking the head. —**schur**, *f.* hair-cutting. —**sprung**, *m.* plunge into the water head first, header. —**stehend**, *adj.* inverted (*of postage stamps*). —**stimme**, *f.* falsetto. —**stück**, *n.* head-piece; mouthpiece. —**ü'ber**, *adv.* head foremost. —**un'ter**, *adv.* head down, headlong. —**wassersucht**, *f.* hydrocephalus. —**weh**, *n.* headache. —**werfend**, *adj.* tossing the head; haughty. —**wunde**, *f.* wound in the head. —**zahl**, *f.* number of persons. —**zange**, *f.* forceps. —**zerbrechen**, *n.*; **ohne viel —zerbrechen**, without much pondering. —**zeug**, *n.* head-gear, head-dress.

Kop—ie', *f.* (*pl.* —**ieen**) copy. —**ie'ren**, *v.a.* to copy. —**i'st**, *m.* (—**i'sten**, *pl.* —**i'sten**) copyist, transcriber. *Comp.* —**ie'r=buch**, *n.* copy-book. —**ie'r=maschine**, *f.* copying-press.

Köp'f—en, *v.* I. *a.* to behead; to poll, lop; to cup. II. *n.* (*aux.* **h.**) to form a head (*of plants*). —**ig**, *adj.* headstrong; (*in comp.* =) -headed. —**lings**, *adv.* headlong. *Comp.* —**maschine**, *f.* guillotine.

Kop'pel, *f.* (*pl.* —**n**) strap *or* chain for linking, sword-strap; leash; leash *or* couple of dogs; string (*of horses*); number of people; double-main (*Org.*); district *or* pasture possessed in common by two *or* more persons *or* over which they have certain common rights; enclosure.

Kop'pel—n, Kup'pel—n, *v.a.* to couple, leash, tie together, unite; to fence, enclose; to join; to bring together. —**ung**, *f.* coupling; leashing. *Comp.* —**balken**, *m.* tie-beam. —**band**, *n.* leash. —**genoß**, *m.* sharer in rights. —**gerechtigkeit**, *f. see* —**recht**. —**jagd**, *f.* joint shooting. —**kette**, *f.* drag-chain. —**recht**, *n.* right enjoyed in common with others. —**seil**, *n.* leash. —**wirtschaft**, *f.* distribution *or* rotation of crops (*Agr.*).

Kop'pen, *v.n.* (*aux.* **h.**) to eructate, hiccough; to bite the crib (*of horses*).

Kopul—atio'n, *f.* (*pl.* —**ationen**) (*now usually* **Trauung**) marriage service. —**ati'v**, *adj.* copulative; —**ative Bindewörter**, copulative conjunctions. —**ie'ren**, *v.a.* to unite in marriage, to marry; to couple, to pair.

Kor, Ko'rest; Kö're, *1 (& 3), 2 p. sing. imperf. indic.; imperf. subj. of* **kiesen**.

Koral'l—e, *f.* (*pl.* —**en**) coral. —**en**, *adj.* coralline. —**i'ne**, *f.* coralline. *Comp.* —**en=artig**, *adj.* coral, coralline. —**en=fischer**, *m.* coral-diver *or* fisher. —**en=riff**, *n.* coral-reef. —**en=schnur**, *f.* string of coral beads, coral necklace. —**en=schwarz**, *n.* black coral. —**en=tier**, *n.* coral zoöphyte, coralline. —**en=wurzel**, *f.* common polypody.

Koramie'ren, Ko'ram nehmen, *v.a.* to take to task, to blow (a p.) up (*sl.*).

Korb, *m.* (—**es**, *pl.* **Kör'be**, *dim.* **Körb'chen**) basket; hamper; crate; (*of a coach*); pannier; rejection; **einen — bekommen**, to receive a refusal; **einem einen — geben**, o refuse s.o.'s offer of marriage; **Hahn im —e sein**, to be cock of the walk. *Comp.* —**bett**, *n.* wickerwork-bedstead. —**flasche**, *f.* bottle, flask enclosed in wickerwork. —**gitter**, *n.* hurdle-work. —**handel**, *m.* basket-trade. —**pfennig**, *m.* market-penny (*saved by a dishonest messenger for himself whilst marketing for another*); unlawful gain. —**rapier**, *n.*, —**schläger**, *m.* basket-hilted rapier. —**schanze**, *f.* gabionade (*of hurdles filled with earth*). —**wagen**, *m.* basket-carriage.

Kor'de, *f.* (*pl.* —**n**) string; (*pl.*) cords of the Jacquard machine. —**l**, *f.* (*pl.* —**ln**) cord; strong thread. —**lie'ren**, *v.a.* to cord; to pipe.

Kordia'l, *adj.* hearty; jolly, merry (*obs.*).

Kordo'n, *m.* (—**s**, *pl.* —**s**) cord, line; cordon, line of soldiers *or* military posts.

Kor'duan, *m.* (—**s**, *pl.* —**e**) cordovan, Spanish leather.

Kö'ren, *v.a.* to talk (*dial.*); to talk as small babies do (*dial.*).

Korin'the, *f.* (*pl.* —**n**) dried currant.

Kork, *m.* (—**es**, *pl.* —**e** *and* **Kör'ke**) cork. —**en**, I. *adj.* of cork, corky. II. *v.a.* to cork. *Comp.* —**artig**, *adj.* suberose. —**baum**, *m.* cork (*tree*). —**form**, *f.* model in cork. —**frucht**, *f.* caryopsis. —**geld**, *n.* corkage. —**gürtel**, *m.* cork (saving) belt. —**maschine**, *f.* corking machine. —**pfropf**, *m.* cork. —**sauer**, *adj.* suberic. —**scheibe**, *f.* sheet-cork. —**stoff**, *m.* suberine. —**zieher**, *m.* cork-screw.

Kork'se—n, *v.a.* to work badly, to proceed awkwardly (*coll.*). —**rei'**, *f.* bad work, patch-work (*coll.*).

Korn, *n.* (—**s**, *pl.* **Kör'ner**) grain (*of sand, gold, wheat, etc.; in leather, etc. . . .*); corn (*in general*); rye; component part of stones and metals; standard of metal, alloy; sight (*upon a gun*); **türkisches** *or* **welsches —**, maize; **der Acker trägt das zehnte —**, the field gives a ten-fold increase on the sowing; **auf dem —e haben**, to have one's eye on, have a design upon; **aufs — nehmen**, to take aim at; **von gutem Schrot und —**, of full weight and due value; **ein Mann von altem Schrot und —**, a man of the good old stamp, of the right sort. *Comp.* —**abbruch**, *m.* refuse of corn. —**ähre**, *f.* ear of corn; spica (*Astr.*). —**artig**, *adj.* frumentaceous. —**bau**, *m.* cultivation of cereals. —**bauer**, *m.* husbandman. —**blau**, *adj.* blue like the corn-flower. —**blume**, *f.* corn-flower. —**boden**, *m.* granary. —**börse**, *f.* corn-exchange. —**brand**, *m.* blight in corn. —**fege**, *f.* winnowing machine. —**flur**, *f.* corn-fields. —**förmig**, *adj.* granular, granulated. —**fraß**, *m.* blight in corn. —**garbe**, *f.* sheaf of corn. —**gesetz**, *n.* corn-law. —**gülte**, *f.* tax paid in corn. —**händler**, *m.* corn-merchant. —**kammer**, *f.* granary. —**kasten**, *m. see* —**lade**; —**kasten einer Mühle**, hopper. —**lade**, *f.* corn-bin. —**rade**, *f.* corn-cockle. —**rose**, *f.* corn-cockle; red poppy; burnet-rose. —**schwinge**, *f.* fan. —**sperre**, *f.* prohibition to export *or* import corn, corn laws. —**umstecher**, *m.* man employed to turn stored corn.

Körn'—chen, *n.* (—**chens**, *pl.* —**chen**) grain, granule. —**el=ung**, *f.* granulation. —**en**, *v.* I. *a.* to form into grains, to granulate; to grain (*leather*); to bait, allure, decoy. II. *r.* to form into grains, granulate. III. *n.* (*aux.* **h.**) to granulate; to run to seed. —**er**, *pl.* granulations (*Med.*); *see* **Korn**. —**icht**, (*obs.*) —**ig**, *adj.* granular, granulated, corny, seedy; pithy, nervous; **das —ige Eisen**, crystalline iron. —**ung**, *f.* granulation; alluring. *Comp.* —**er=fressend**, *adj.* graminivorous.

Kornel'le, *f.* (*pl.* —**n**) cornel, dogwood.

Korne'tt, I. *m.* (—**s**, *pl.* —**s**) cornet (*Mil.*). II. *n.* (—**s**, *pl.* —**e**) cornet (*Mus.*). *Comp.* —**bläser**, *m.* cornet-player.

Kör'per, *m.* (—**s**, *pl.* —) body; bulk, substance; carcass; **toter —**, corpse. —**chen**, *n.* (—**chens**, *pl.* —**chen**) little body; corpuscle; particle, molecule. —**haft**, *adj.* corporeal. —**lich**, *adj. & adv.* bodily; corporeal; material; corpuscular; —**liche Anlage**, (bodily) constitution, temperament; —**licher Winkel**, solid angle; —**licher Eid**, oath taken in person; —**liche Strafe**, corporal punishment; **das —liche**, materiality. —**lichkeit**, *f.* corporeality, materialness, concreteness. —**schaft**, *f.* corporate body, corporation. —**schaftlich**, *adj.* of a corporation. *Comp.* **—all**, *n.* material world. **—anlage**, *f.* constitution; temperament. **—bau**, *m.* bodily structure, frame; build, make; **von kräftigem —bau**, strong bodied, of robust build; **von schönem —bau**, finely shaped, of fine physique. **—beschaffenheit**, *f.* constitution (of body). **—bildung**, *f.* bodily structure, physique; formation of the body. **—fülle**, *f.* corpulence, plumpness. **—größe**, *f.* stature; tallness. **—kraft**, *f.* physical power. **—lehre**, *f.* somatology; solid geometry, stereometry (*Math.*). **—los**, *adj.* immaterial, incorporeal. **—losigkeit**, *f.* bodiless state, immateriality. **—maß**, *n.* cubic measure; cubature; (*pl.*) measures of capacity. **—masse**, *f.* bulk. **—messung**, *f.* stereometry. **—reich**, *n.* material world. **—schwäche**, *f.* debility, bodily weakness. **—stärke**, *f.* physical strength. **—stellung**, *f.* attitude. **—stimmung**, *f.* temperament, constitution. **—stoff**, *m.* matter. **—strafe**, *f.* corporal punishment. **—teilchen**, *n.* particle, molecule. **—übung**, *f.* bodily exercise, athletics, gymnastics. **—verletzung**, *f.* bodily injury; (*pl.*) deeds done in the body (*Law*). **—welt**, *f. see* **—reich**. **—winkel**, *m* solid angle. **—zahl**, *f.* cubic number. **—zerrüttung**, *f.* break-up of the constitution.

Korpora'l, *m.* (**—s**, *pl.* **—e**) corporal. **—schaft**, *f.* half section, squad.

Korporatio'n, *f.* (*pl.* **—en**) guild, body.

Korps, *n.* (—, *pl.* —) army corps (*consisting of 2 divisions or 4 brigades*); a special kind of expensive and somewhat exclusive students' club with distinctive colours and emblems where duelling is much encouraged; **fliegendes —**, flying column. **—bruder**, **—bursch**, *m.* member of a 'Korps,' fast student. **—kommandeur**, *m.* commander of an army-corps (a **Kommandierender General**). **—manöver**, *n.* large manœuvres (*in which at least one whole army corps takes part*). **—student**, *m.* member of a 'Korps'; fast student. **—geist**, *m.* esprit de corps; party spirit (*polit.*).

Kor'pus, I. *m. see* **Körper**. II. *f.* long primer (*Typ.*).

Korre'kt, *adj.* correct. **—heit**, *f.* correctness. **—or**, *m.* (**—ors**, *pl.* **Korrekto'ren**) press-corrector. **—u'r**, *f.* (*pl.* **—uren**) correction (*Typ.*); proof for correction; **zweite —ur**, revise: **—uren lesen, besorgen**, to read *or* correct proofs. *Comp.* **—io'ns=haus**, *n.* house of correction. **—u'r=bogen**, *m.* printer's proof. **—u'r=zeichen**, *n.* (*mark of*) correction.

Korrespond—e'nt, *m.* correspondent. **—e'nz**, *f.* correspondence, epistolary intercourse. **—e'nz=karte**, *f.* post-card. **—ie'ren**, *v.n.* to correspond.

Korrido'r, *m.* (**—s**, *pl.* **—e**). *Comp.* **—zug**, *m.* corridor-train, vestibule-train.

Korrigie'ren, *v.a.* to correct; to read (*proofs*).

Korse'tt, *n.* (**—(e)s**, *pl.* **—e**) (pair of) stays; corset (*rare*). *Comp.* **—macherin**, *f.* corset-maker. **—schoner**, *m.* vest. **—stange**, *f.* corset busk.

Koryphä'e, *m.* (**—n**, *pl.* **—n**) corypheus; leader of a choir *or* company.

Ko'scher, *adj. & adv.* pure (*according to Jewish law*); **nicht ganz —**, not very proper *or* respectable, shady (*coll.*).

Ko'sen, *v.* I. *a.* to caress. II. *n.* (*aux.* **h.**) to talk fondly *or* intimately, to chat; to make love.

Ko'sinus, *m.* cosine (*Math.*).

Kossa't, Kossä't, *m.* (**—en**, *pl.* **—en**) cottager.

Kost, *f.* food, fare, victuals; entertainment, board; **in (der) — sein**, to board; **in (die) — geben, thun**, to put out to board; **einen in (die) — nehmen, einem die — geben**, to board one; **wir waren in der — bei . . .**, we boarded at *or* with . . .; **kräftige —**, substantial *or* rich food; **schmale —**, slender fare, poor living; low diet; **— und Wohnung (Logis)**, board and lodging. *Comp.* **—gänger**, *m.*, **—gängerin**, *f.* boarder. **—geber**, *m.* keeper of a boarding-house. **—geld**, *n.* board-expenses; apprentice's allowance; alimony (*Law.*); **—geld bekommen**, to be on board-wages (*of servants*). **—halter**, *m.* keeper of a boarding-establishment. **—häppchen**, *n.* tit-bit. **—haus**, *n.* boarding-house. **—regel**, *f.* diet. **—verächter**, *m.* dainty person; **kein —verächter sein**, to eat anything and everything; to fall to heartily.

Kost'bar, *adj. & adv.* costly, expensive; precious; valuable; **ein —er Witz**, an excellent *or* capital joke. **—keit**, *f.* (*pl.* **—keiten**) costliness; preciousness; jewel, valuable.

[1]**Kos't—en**, *pl.* cost(s), expense(s), expenditure, charge(s); sacrifice, cost; **es geht auf meine —en**, it is at my expense, I shall pay for it, I will be answerable for the expenses, charge it to me, put it down to my account; **die —en bestreiten** *or* **tragen**, to defray the expenses; **einem —en machen**, to put a p. to expense; **in die, zu den —en verurteilen**, to condemn a p. to pay all costs; **die —en herausschlagen, auf die —en kommen**, to recover expenses; **sich in —en stürzen**, to incur (great) expense; **ich habe es auf meine —en erfahren**, I have learned it to my cost; **auf —en seiner Ehre**, at the expense of his honour. *Comp.* **—en=anschlag**, *m.* estimate (of cost). **—en=aufwand**, *m.* expenditure. **—en=ausgleichung**, *f.* balance of expenses. **—en=betrag; der veranschlagte —enbetrag beläuft sich auf**, the expenditure has been estimated at. **—en=ersatz**, *m.* compensation for outlay. **—en=frei, —en=los**, *adj.* free of charge *or* expense. **—en=preis**, *m.* cost-price, prime-cost; **unter —enpreis verkaufen**, to sell at a loss. **—en=punkt**, *m.* (matter of) expense(s). **—en=rechnung**, *f.* bill of costs. **—en=scheu**, *adj.* afraid of expenses, parsimonious. **—en=verzeichnis**, *n.* list of expenses. **—spielig**, *adj.* expensive, costly. **—spieligkeit**, *f.* costliness, expensiveness.

[2]**Kos'ten**, I. *v.a.* to taste; to try, make trial of. II. *subst. n.* tasting.

[3]**Kos't—en**, *v.a.* (**einem** (*obs.*) *or* **einen** (*now more usual*) **etwas**) to cost; to require; **sich** (*acc.*) **etwas viel —en lassen**, to go to great expense for a th.; **es —et Zeit**, it requires time; **es —e was es wolle**, whatever the cost may be, at any cost *or* price, at any sacrifice.

Köst'lich, *adj. & adv.* costly; precious; exquisite; excellent; delicious; **das ist —!** that's capital! that's a good joke! **—keit**, *f.* delicacy; preciousness; costliness; excellence.

Kostü'm, *n.* (**—s**, *pl.* **—e**) costume. **—fest**, *n.* fancy-dress-ball. **—kunde**, *f.* historical study of costumes. **—ie'ren**, *v.a.* to dress; to drape.

Kotele'tt, *n.* (**—en**, *pl.* **—en**) cutlet, chop; **Kalbs—en**, veal cutlets; **Hammel—en**, mutton chops.

[1]**Kot**, *n.* (**—es**, *pl.* **—e**) cot, shed; (*also* **—e**, *f. pl.* **—en**) saltwork. *Comp.* **—knecht**, *m.* salt-boiler. **—saß, —sasse, Köt'ner**, *m.* cottager.

[2]**Kot**, *m.* (**—(e)s**) dirt, filth; mire, mud; dung; excrement; **aus dem —e ziehen**, to take out of the gutter, raise from misery. **—ig**, *adj. & adv.* dirty, muddy, mucky, filthy. *Comp* **—abzucht**, *f.* sewer, sink. **—blech**, *n.* mudguard (*Cycl.*). **—grube**, *f.* sewer; cess-pool. **—kärrner**, *m.* scavenger. **—lache**, *f.* slough, miry place, puddle. **—schützer**, *m.* mudguard (*Cycl.*).

Kö'ter, *m.* (**—s**, *pl.* —) big dog, cur; watchdog.

Kothu'rn, *m.* (**—s**, *pl.* **—e**) cothurnus, buskin.

Kot'ze, *f. also m.* (**—ns** *and* —, *pl.* **—n**) coarse great coat (*dial.*); shaggy coverlet (*dial.*).

Köt'ze, *f.* (*pl.* —n) basket (for the back).
Kot'zen, *v.r. & n.* (*aux.* h.) to vomit (*vulg.*).
Koulis'se, *f.* (*pl.* —n) *see* Coulisse.
Krab'be, *f.* (*pl.* —n) crab; little child (*coll.*).
Krab'belig, *adj. & adv.* crawling; groping.
Krab'bel—n, *v.* I. *n.* (*aux.* h. & s.) to grope, crawl (about), grabble. II. *a. & n.* (*aux.* h.) & *imp.* to itch; es —t mir am Halse, my neck itches; something is crawling on my neck.
Krach, *m.* (—es, *pl.* —e) crack, crash; quarrel; commercial crisis; mit einem einen — bekommen, to come to quarrel with a p.; der große —, the great (financial) crash (*in 1873*).
Kra'chen, I. *v.n.* (*aux.* h. & s.) to crack; to crash; to roar; to crackle; to fail, be ruined. II. *v.a.* to crack (*nuts, etc.*). III. *subst.n.* crack, crash, roar.
Kräch'z—en, *v.* I. *a.* to croak out, say croakingly. II. *n.* (*aux.* h.) to croak; to caw; die Krähe —t, the crow caws; der Rabe —t, the raven croaks.
Kra'cke, *f.* (*pl.* —n) jade; screw.
Kraft, I. *f.* (*pl.* Kräf'te) strength; vigour; power, force; energy; efficiency; validity; virtue, efficacy (*of medicines, etc.*); essence, substance; fire, spirit; lebendige —, vis viva; bewegende —, moving force, motive power; in voller —, in full force and vigour; mit voller (Dampf) —, at full steam; in — setzen, to enforce (*a law, etc.*), to execute (*judgment, etc.*); außer — setzen, to annul, abrogate; in — treten, to come into force; das geht über meine Kräfte, that is beyond me, too much for me; was in meinen Kräften liegt, as far as in me lies, as far as I can; aus allen Kräften, with all one's might; von Kräften kommen, to decay in strength; in —, *see* Kraft II.; absolute Größe einer —, intensity. II. *prep.* (*with gen.*) in virtue of, on the strength of, by authority of; — meines Amtes, by virtue of my office. *Comp.* —anstrengung, *f.* effort. —aufwand, *m.* effort, expenditure of force *or* energy. —ausdruck, *m.* pithy expression. —äußerung, *f.* manifestation of strength *or* vigour. —bedarf, *m.* (*of a machine*) force required. —brühe, *f.* strong broth. —dichter, *m.* force-condenser (*Mech.*). —einheit, *f.* unit of force. —fülle, *f.* great vigour. —(kunst)stücke, *pl.* feats of strength, athletic feats. —lehre, *f.* dynamics. —los, *adj.* impotent, powerless; ineffectual; null; invalid. —maschine, *f.* receiver, motor. —mehl, *n.* wheaten starch. —messer, *m.* dynamometer. —mittel, *n.* energetic means; powerful remedy. —probe, *f.* trial of strength. —sammler, *m.* accumulator. —sprache, *f.* powerful, energetic, pithy language. —übertragung, *f.* transmission *or* transport of force. —verlust, *m.* loss of power. —voll, *adj.* full of strength, vigorous, powerful; pithy.
Kräf'tig, *adj. & adv.* strong, powerful; robust; pithy, forcible; efficacious; valid; strengthening, nourishing. —keit, *f.* robustness; energy; efficaciousness; validity, full force.
Kräf'tig—en, *v.a.* to strengthen; to invigorate; to enforce; to corroborate; to stablish (*B.*). —ung, *f.* strengthening, invigoration.
Kra'gen, *m.* (—s, *pl.* — *better than:* Krä'gen) throat (*obs.*); collar; cape; neck (*of a bottle; of a lute, etc.*); band; frill; beim — nehmen, fassen, to collar; es geht ihm an Kopf und — *or* an den —, it will cost his life; Geiz—, miser; Klapp—, turn-down collar; Steh—, stand-up collar; und sollte es mir auch den — kosten, though I should have to die for it. *Comp.* —mantel, *m.* mantle with cape.
Krag'stein, *m.* corbel, console, bracket.
Krä'h—e, *f.* (*pl.* —en) crow; Saat—e, rook; die —e krächzt, the crow caws; eine —e hackt der andern die Augen nicht aus, there's honour among thieves (*prov.*). —en, *v.n.* (*aux.* h.) to crow; to speak with a shrill voice, to screech; darnach —t kein Hahn, nobody troubles about it; der Kranich —t, the crane clangs. *Comp.* —en=auge, *n.* crow's eye; corn on the foot. —en=feder, *f.* crow-quill. —en=fuß, *m.* crow's-foot; crow-bar; (*pl.*) bad writing, scrawl. —en=pfoten, *pl.* crow's feet, wrinkles.
Kra(h)n, Krahn, *see* Kran.
Kräh'wink—el, *m.* name of an imaginary town of Philistines, Gotham. —el=landsturm, *n.* militia of Gotham, wretched soldiery. —ler, *m.* (—lers, *pl.* —ler) inhabitant of Krähwinkel, Gothamist, stupid person, narrow-minded man; rustic.
Krake'el, Krake'hl, *m.* (—s, *pl.* —e) row, violent quarrel. —en, *v.n.* (*aux.* h.) to brawl.
Kra'kelfüße, Krak'selfüße, *pl.* illegible characters, illegible handwriting, scrawl (*coll.*).
Kral, *m.* (—s, *pl.* —e) kraal (*of the Zulus, etc.*).
Kral'l—e, *f.* (*pl.* —en) claw, clutch, talon. —en, *v.a. & n.* (*aux.* h.) to claw; to clutch. —icht, *adj.* claw-like (*obs.*). —ig, *adj.* clawed. *Comp.* —en=förmig, *adj.* claw-shaped. —en=hieb, *m.* stroke with a claw.
Kram, *m.* (—es, *pl.* Krä'me) retail trade; shop; small wares; stuff, rubbish, trumpery; affair, business (*vulg.*); das taugt nicht in meinen —, that will not do for me; es paßte nicht in seinen —, it did not suit his purpose; das verdirbt mir den ganzen —, that spoils all my plans, the whole affair; sein ganzer —, one's all; den — zumachen, to shut up one's shop. *Comp.* —handel, *m.* retail trade. —laden, *m. also* —bude, *f.* small shop, retail shop, stall. —kammer, *f.* lumber room. —knecht, *m.* packer. —waren, *pl.* retail articles.
Kra'me—n, *v.n.* (*aux.* h.) to retail (*goods*), to keep a small shop; to rummage, move, stir; to arrange; man hat immer etwas zu —n, there is always something to be done *or* to be put in order; mit etwas —n, to display, make a show of something. —rei', *f.* rummaging; fumbling; arranging.
Krä'mer, *m.* (—s, *pl.* —) shopkeeper, tradesman, grocer, haberdasher. —ei', *f.* shopkeeping, retailing; trading; commercial, mercenary. —haft, —isch, *adj. & adv.* shopkeeper-like; shoppy (*coll.*). *Comp.* —bude, *f.*, —laden, *m.* shop. —latein, *n.* dog-latin. —mäßig, *adj.* like a shopkeeper. —meister, *m.* master of a tradesman's guild. —pfund, *n.* pound avoirdupois. —seele, *f.* narrow *or* mercenary mind. —stand, *m.* shopkeepers; stall. —volk, *n.* nation of shopkeepers.
Kram'men, *v.a.* to strike with the claws, clutch.
Kram'(me)t(s)— (*in comp.*) —vogel, *m.* fieldfare.
Kram'pe, *f.* (*pl.* —n) cramp-iron; staple; clasp. —n, *v.a.* to cramp, to fasten.
Kräm'p—e, *f.* (*pl.* —en) brim, flap (*of a hat*). —el, I. *m.* (*coll.*) lumber, trash, stuff, rubbish; lot. II. *f.* (*pl.* —en) card, carding-comb. —(e)ler, *m.* (—(e)lers, *pl.* —(e)ler) wool-carder. —eln, *v.a.* to card. —en, *v.a.* to turn up, to put a brim to (*a hat*). *Comp.* —el=haken, *m.* teeth of a carding-comb.
Krampf, *m.* (—es, *pl.* Kräm'pfe) cramp, spasm; convulsion; fit; den — bekommen, to be in convulsions; in Krämpfen, in (spasmodic) fits. —en, *v.a. & r.* to contract convulsively; to clasp convulsively. —haft, I. *adj. & adv.* convulsive; spasmodic; —haft schluchzen, to sob convulsively, to be seized with a sobbing fit; —haftes Lachen, convulsions of laughter, convulsive laughter; —es Lächeln, sardonic grin; —e Zuckung, convulsion. II. *adv.* enormously, strongly (*sl.*). —haftigkeit, *f.* convulsiveness.

Comp. **—ader,** *f.* varicose vein; varix. **—artig,** *see* **—haft. —husten,** *m.* convulsive cough. **—lindernd. —stillend,** *adj.* antispasmodic.

Kran, *m.* (—(e)s, *pl.* Krä'ne; *dimin.* Krän'chen) crane; **mit einem —e aufwinden** *or* **heben,** to crane (up). *Comp.* **—(en)=arm,** *m.* crane-beam. **—balken,** *m.* horizontal beam of a crane, jib; cat-head. **—baum, —ständer,** *m.* upright post of a crane. **—geld,** *n.* cranage.

Kränchen=brunnen, *m.* (mineral) waters (of Ems).

Kranich, *m.* (—s, *pl.* —e) crane; **der — schreit, trompetet, (kräht,)** the crane cries, trumpets, (clangs). *Comp.* **—beere,** *f.* cranberry. **—hals,** *m.* geranium. **—schnabel,** *m.* Pelargonium. **—schnabel=zange,** *f.* crane's-bill (*Surg.*).

Krank, *adj.* & *adv.* (**krän'ker, krän'k(e)st**) out of health, ill, sick, diseased; **— an einer S.,** ill of; **— werden,** to fall ill; **sich — stellen,** to feign illness; **sich — lachen (über eine S.), — lachen wollen,** to shriek with laughter (at a th.), to split one's sides with laughter; **es war zum — lachen,** it was absurdly funny, it made us shriek with laughter; **— am Beutel,** short of money. **—e(r),** *m.*, **—e,** *f.* invalid. **—haft,** *adj.* & *adv.* diseased, morbid. **—haftigkeit,** *f.* diseased state, morbidity. *Comp.* **—en=anstalt,** *f.* hospital. **—en=attest,** *n.* certificate of illness. **—en=bericht,** *m.* bulletin; hospital report. **—en=besuch,** *m.* visitation of the sick; doctor's visit. **—en=bett,** *n.* sick-bed; **vom —en=bette aufstehen,** to recover from an illness. **—en=buch, —en=diarium,** *n.* doctor's visiting-book. **—en=haus,** *n.* infirmary, hospital. **—en=kasse,** *f.* workmen's sick-fund. **—en=korb,** *m.* litter *or* stretcher for the sick *or* wounded. **—en=kost,** *f.* diet, regimen. **—en=lager,** *see* **—enbett. —en=liste,** *f.* sick-list. **—en=mutter,** *f.* sick-nurse. **—en=pflege,** *f.* sick-nursing. **—en=sänfte,** *f.* *see* **—en=korb. —en=schiff,** *n.* hospital ship. **—en=stuhl,** *m.* invalid chair. **—en=träger,** *m.* stretcher-bearer. **—en=verschlag,** *m.* cockpit (*Naut.*). **—en=wagen,** *m.* ambulance-waggon *or* carriage. **—en=wärter,** *m.*, **—en=wärterin,** *f.* sick-attendant, sick-nurse. **—en=wesen,** *n.* hospital and nursing arrangements. **en=zettel,** *m.* bulletin; sick-list.

Kränk'—bar, *adj.* liable to be hurt *or* aggrieved. **—elei',** *f.* sickliness. **—eln,** *v.n.* (*aux.* h.) to be sickly *or* in bad health; not to flourish. **—lich,** *adj.* & *adv.* sickly, unhealthy, infirm. **—lichkeit,** *f.* sickliness, morbid state. **—ling,** *m.* (—lings, *pl.* —linge) sickly person.

Krän'ke, *f.* epilepsy, falling sickness (*rare*); **die —e kriegen,** to fall ill, to get the falling sickness (*coll.*).

Kran'ken, *v.n.* (*aux.* h.); **an einer S. —,** to suffer from (*a disease*), to be lacking in.

Kränk'—en, *v.a.* to make ill (*obs.*); to vex, grieve; to insult, offend; to injure, wrong; impair, detract from; **das —t,** that hurts; **jemandes Rechte —en, einen an seinen Rechten —en,** to encroach upon a p.'s rights; **es —te mich tief,** it cut me to the heart; **einen um etwas —en,** to do a p. out of, take a thing from s.o. (*coll.*); **auf eine —ende Art,** insultingly, cuttingly. **—ung,** *f.* grieving, humbling, offending; wrong, insult, outrage; mortification, grief.

Krank'heit, *f.* (*pl.* —en) illness, sickness; disease, malady, complaint; **sich** (*dat.*) **eine — zuziehen,** to contract a disease; **eine — bekommen, in eine — (ver)fallen,** to fall ill; **an einer —heit sterben,** to die of an illness. *Comp.* **—s=bericht,** *m.* bulletin; medical report. **—s=entscheidung,** *f.* crisis. **—s=erreger,** *m.* morbific agent. **—s=erscheinung,** *f.* symptom of a disease. **—s=lehre,** *f.* pathology. **—s=stoff,** *m.* morbid matter. **—s=träger,** *m.* disease bearer, morbific agent. **—s=verlauf,** *m.* progress of a disease. **—s=zeichen,** *n.* symptom. **—s=zufall,** *m.* attack of illness. **—s=zustand,** *m.* state of disease, morbid state, case.

Kranz, *m.* (—es, *pl.* **Krän'ze**) garland, wreath, crown; bridal wreath; virginity, innocence (*fig.*); cushion for the head (*when carrying weights on it*); cornice; festoon, cincture (*Arch.*); brim; rim; edge, crest, ridge; valance; society, circle; **ein — von schönen Frauen,** a circle of beautiful women, a galaxy of beauty. *Comp.* **—ader,** *f.* coronal vein. **—binden,** *n.* making of the bridal (myrtle) wreath by all the bridesmaids on the day before the wedding. **—förmig,** *adj.* wreath-like; coronoid. **—gesims,** *n.* cornice. **—jungfer,** *f.* bridesmaid. **—los,** *adj.* uncrowned; no longer a virgin.

Kränz'—chen, *n.* (—chens, *pl.* —chen) little garland; small circle, society, club (*esp'lly of young ladies*) girls' club, young ladies' (weekly) club. **—en,** *v.a.* to crown, to wreath. **—lein,** *see* **—chen; sie hat ihr Kränzlein verloren,** she has lost her innocence; she has got into trouble (*coll.* & *euphem.*).

Krapf, *m.* (—es, *pl.* —en). **—en,** *m.* (**—ens,** *pl.* **—en**) fritter; doughnut; tartlet.

Krapp, *m.* (—es) madder (a red dye).

Kraß, *adj.* & *adv.* crass, coarse; gross; uncultivated; **—(ss)e Unwissenheit,** gross ignorance; **—er Fuchs,** freshman, fresher, student just come up, undergraduate in his first term (*sl.*); **—er Philister,** downright Philistine.

Kra'ter, *m.* (—s, *pl.* —) crater.

Kratz, *m.* (—es, *pl.* —e) scratch; scar. **—e,** *f.* (*pl.* —en) scraper; carding-comb. **—ig,** *adj.* easily offended, irritable, gruff.

Krät'z—e, *f.* (*pl.* —en) itch, scab; mange; waste of metal, scrapings, clippings. **—er,** *m.* (—ers, *pl.* —er) *see* **Kratzer;** scraper; bad wine; wadhook; worm (*of a gun*). **—ig,** *adj.* & *adv.* itchy, scabious, psoric (*Med.*); scabby; rough. *Comp.* **—artig,** *adj.* itch-like, scabious. **—kupfer,** *n.* copper obtained from copper-refuse. **—messing,** *m.* brass clippings; pin and needle maker's refuse. **—salbe,** *f.* ointment against the itch.

Krat'z—en, *v.* I. *a.* & *n.* (*aux.* h.) to scratch, scrape; to card, tease; to grate; to be harsh to the taste; to scrawl, scribble; to itch, tickle; **sich hinter den Ohren —en,** to scratch one's head; to show signs of embarrassment; **der Rauch —t mich im Halse,** the smoke affects my throat; **es —t mich,** I have a tickling, an itching; **auf einen Haufen —en,** to scrape together and heap up. II. *n.* (*aux.* s., **aus —en** *or*) **von der Stelle —en,** to decamp (*vulg.*). **—er,** *m.* (—ers, *pl.* —er) person *or* thing that scrapes. *Comp.* **—bürste,** *f.* scrubbing-brush; irritable person, cross-patch, quick-tempered person (fig.). **—bürstig,** *adj.* easily excited *or* ruffled, irritable, quick-tempered (*esp'lly said of girls and women*). **—eisen,** *n.* scraping-iron; scraper; scratcher (*Eng.*); **(des Schornsteinfegers)** chimney-sweep's brush. **—fuß,** *m.* awkward bow, scrape; dame Partlet. **—füßler,** *m.* a p. given to bowing and scraping, overpolite person. **—maschine,** *f.* carding machine.

Krau'chen, *used in jest for* **kriechen.**

Kraus, *adj.* & *adv.* crisp, curly; crisped, plaited, crinkled; irregular, intricate; nappy; **ein —(s)es Gesicht, eine —(s)e Stirn machen,** to knit one's brows, frown; **er macht (treibt) es zu —,** he carries things too far, he is too bad. **—(s)e,** *f.* (*pl.* —(e)n) crispness; frill, ruffle. **—(s)en,** *v.n.* (*aux.* h.) *see* **Kräusen; sich —(s)en,** to be curly; to become curled *or* crisp. **—heit,**

f. crispness, curliness. *Comp.* —**bart**, *m.* curly beard; curly-bearded man. —(s)e=**minze**, *f.* curled mint. —**flor**, *m.* (crisped) crape. —**kopf**, *m.* curly-head; curly-headed person. —**salat**, *m.* endive. —**taback**, *m.* shag.

Kräu'f—e, *see* **Krause**. —**el**, *m.* (—**els**, *pl.* —**el**) ruffle, frill. —**eln**, *v.* I. *a.* to curl, crisp; to crimp, goffer; to nap, frieze; to mill (*coin*); to fold, plait. II. *r.* & *n.* (*aux.* **h.**) to curl, crisp, be ruffled; **gekräuselt**, curly, crimped; **der Menschheit Schnitzel —eln**, to dress up the chips of human life and thought, to trim up man's poorest shreds; to serve up to men the most miserable trifles. —**en**, *v.a.* to curl, crisp. —**ler**, *m.* (—**lers**, *pl.* —**ler**) one who curls *or* frizzles; **haar—ler**, hair-dresser. *Comp.* —**el=eisen**, *n.* curling-tongs. —**el=kamm**, *m.* dressing-comb.

Kraut, *n.* (—**es**, *pl.* **Kräu'ter**) herb; plant, vegetable; cabbage; weed; leaves of a plant, sumac; scamp, fellow; **für den Tod ist kein — gewachsen**, there is no cure for death; **das ist ein böses —**, that is bad *or* unpleasant; **Muß ist ein bitter —**, necessity is painful, unpleasant; **durch einander wie — und Rüben**, higgledy-piggledy; **ins — schießen**, to grow rankly *or* apace, to spread rapidly; **rheinisches —, Rheinisch—**, a kind of fruit jelly. —**en**, I. *v.a.* & *n.* (*aux.* **h.**) to hoe, to weed. II. *subst. n.* weeding. *Comp.* —**acker**, *m.* cabbage field *or* garden. —**artig**, *adj.* herbaceous. —**beet**, *n.* cabbage-bed. —**för=mig**, *adj.* herb-like; dendroid (*Min.*). —**fressend**, *adj.* herbivorous. —**garten**, *m.* kitchen-garden. —**hacke**, *f.* hoe. —**händler**, *m.* market-gardener. —**junker**, *m.* country-bumpkin, ignorant young squire. —**kammer**, *f.* powder-room (*Naut.*). —**löffel**, *m.* gunner's ladle. —**salat**, *m.* cabbage-lettuce.

Kräu'ter—er, *m.* (—**ers**, *pl.* —**er**) herbalist. —**ich, Kräu'tich**, *n.* (—**ichs**, *pl.* —**iche**) leaves and stalk of plants —**n**, *v.n.* (*aux.* **h.**) to gather herbs; to botanize. *Comp.* —**artig**, *adj.* herbaceous. —**auszug**, *m.* tincture. —**bier**, *n.* medicated ale. —**boden**, *m.* loft for drying herbs. —**brühe**, *f.* vegetable soup. —**buch**, *n.* herbal, herbalist's book; botanical treatise. —**fressend**, *adj.* herbivorous. —**gewölbe**, *n.* druggist's shop. —**käse**, *m.* green cheese. —**kenner**, *m.* herbalist, botanist. —**kenntnis**, *f.* botanical knowledge. —**kissen**, *n.* medicated pillow *or* cushion. —**kunde, —lehre**, *f.* botany. —**reich**, I. *adj.* abounding in herbs. II. *n.* vegetable kingdom. —**sammler**, *m.* herbalist. —**suppe**, *f.* Julienne soup, vegetable soup. —**thee**, *m.* infusion of herbs. —**trank**, *m.* decoction of herbs. —**wein**, *m.* medicated wine. —**zucker**, *m.* conserve.

Krawat'te, *f.* (*pl.* —**n**) cravat; tie, scarf.

Krawa'll, *m.* (—**s**, *pl.* —**e**) uproar, riot. —**en**, *v.n.* (*aux.* **h.**) to riot.

Kra'xeln, *v.a. for* **Krabbeln = Klettern; auf die Berge —**, to climb up mountains (*coll.*).

Kreatu'r, *f.* (*pl.* —**en**) creature; all living creatures (*poet.*); tool, vassal, dependent, client (*contempt*); **feile —**, hireling.

Krebs, *m.* (—(s)**es**, *pl.* —(s)**e**) crayfish; Cancer (*Ast.*); ulcer, cancer (*Med.*); canker (*Bot.*); return book, remainder; breast-plate (*B.*); — **der Gerechtigkeit**, breastplate of righteousness; **rot wie ein —**, as red as a lobster; **eine andere Art von —en**, something very different (*prov.*). —(s)**en**, *v.n.* (*aux.* **h.**) to catch crayfish; to crawl about; to secure an advantage by sacrificing s.th. that should be reverenced (*sl.*). *Comp.* —**artig**, *adj.* like a crustacean; cancerous; —**artige Tiere**, crustacea(ns). —**bil=dung**, *f.* cancerous growth. —**fäule**, *f.* cancer. —**gang**, *m.* crab's walk; retrograde movement, decline. —**gängig**, *adj.* retrograde. —**kreis**, *m.*, —**linie**, *f.*, —**wendekreis**, *m.* Tropic of Cancer. —**schaden**, *m.* cancerous sore; inveterate vice. —**schere**, *f.* crayfish's *or* crab's claw. —**suppe**, *f.* crayfish-soup. —**zucht**, *f.* crab-farming.

Kreden'z—en, *v.a.* to taste (*wine before presenting it to a prince*); to present after tasting. —**er**, *m.* (—**ers**, *pl.* —**er**), —**erin**, *f.* foretaster, cup-bearer. *Comp.* —**teller**, *m.* salver. —**tisch**, *m.* side-board; (table of) prothesis (*eccl.*).

Kredi't, *m.* (—**es**) credit; **der laufende —**, open credit; **den — übertreiben**, to overdraw one's account. —**ie'ren**, *v.* I. *a.* to give on trust. II. *n.* (*aux.* **h.**) to give credit. —**i'v**, *n.* (—**ivs**, *pl.* —**ive**) credentials; letter of credit. *Comp.* —**anstalt**, *f.* banking institution. —**brief**, *m.* letter of credit. —**eröffnung**, *f.* opening of an account, lodging a credit (**bei**, with). —**fähig**, *adj.* solvent, sound, solid. —**losigkeit**, *f.* discredit, absence of credit.

Kre'do, *n.* (—**s**, *pl.* —) creed.

Kre'gel, *adj.* sound, hale; lively, brisk (*dial.*).

Kreid—e, *f.* (*pl.* —**en**) chalk; crayon; **bei einem in die —e geraten**, to get into a person's debt; **mit zwölf Mark bei einem in der —e stehen**, to owe a p. twelve marks; **tief in der —e sitzen**, to be cribbled with debts; **mit doppelter —e anschreiben**, to overcharge; **geschlämmte —e**, whiting. —**en**, *v.a.* to chalk; to cover with chalk. —**icht**, (*obs.*) —**ig**, *adj.* chalky, cretaceous; covered with chalk. *Comp.* —**e(n)=artig**, *adj.* chalky. —**e=formation**, *f.*, —**e=gebilde**, *n.* chalk formation; cretaceous group. —**e=grube**, *f.* chalk-pit. —**e=stift**, *m.* chalk-pencil, chalk, crayon. —**e=weiß**, *adj.* deadly pale; **er wurde —eweiß**, he turned as white as a sheet. —**e=zeichnung**, *f.* chalk-drawing.

Krei'er, *m.* (—**s**, *pl.* —) Baltic three-master.

Kreie'ren, *v.a.* to create, to make.

Kreis, *m.* (—(s)**es**, *pl.* —(s)**e**) circle, ring; circle (*Geom.*); sphere (*of action, etc.*); orbit; circuit, district; **Deutschlands —(s)e**, districts of the (old) German Empire; **mehrere —(s)e bilden in Preußen einen Regierungsbezirk**, in Prussia several circuits make a government district; **städtischer (ländlicher) —**, urban (rural) circuit; **im —(s)e**, round about; **einen — beschreiben**, to describe a circle; **die —(s)e einer Himmelskugel**, the circles of a celestial globe; **das liegt außer meinem —(s)e**, that is not within my province; **im —(s)e seiner Familie**, in the bosom of his family; **alles geht mit mir im —(s)e herum**, my head is swimming; **in allen —(s)en des Lebens**, in every walk of life; **die höchsten —(s)e**, the upper ten (thousand), the aristocracy; **sich im —(s)e drehend**, rotatory; **im —(s)e um etwas herumgehen**, to turn, revolve round something; **im —(s)e herum schicken**, to circulate; **sich im —(s)e bewegen**, to revolve, to turn round and round; not to get on, not to get nearer one's aim. *Comp.* —**abschnitt**, *m.* segment of a circle. —**amtmann**, *m.* bailiff *or* chief civil officer of a circuit. —**arzt**, *m.* doctor of the district. —**ausschnitt**, *m.* sector (*Math.*). —**bahn**, *f.* orb, orbit. —**beamte(r)**, *m.* district civil officer. —**be=hörde**, *f.* jurisdiction, government of a district. —**beitrag**, *m.* contingent furnished by a district. —**bewegung**, *f.* circular motion. —**blatt**, *n.*; — **und Amts=blatt** (semi-official) district newspaper. —**bogen**, *m.* circular arch; arc. —**brief**, *m.* circular letter; proclamation. —**direktion**, *f.* government of a district. —**drehung**, *f.* rotation. —**eintei=lung**, *f.* division into circuits *or* districts. —**fläche**, *f.* circular surface. —**förmig**, *adj.* circular, rotund. —**fuge**, *f.* catch, canon

(*Mus.*). —**gang,** *m.* circular movement *or* walk; labyrinth; revolution. —**geometrie,** *f.* electoral division of a country. —**gericht,** *n.* district-court; county-court (*Engl.*). —**hauptmann,** *m.* prefect of a district; Lord Lieutenant of a county (*Engl.*). —**lauf,** *m.* movement in an orbit, rotation, revolution; circulation; course; period; orbit, trajectory; series of recurrent changes; succession (*of the seasons, etc.*). —**linie,** *f.* circumference. —**messung,** *f.* cyclometry. —**ordnung,** *f.* district-regulations. —**physikus,** *m.* doctor of the district. —**richter,** *m.* district-judge. —**rund,** *adj.* circular. —**säge,** *f.* circular saw. —**schattig,** *adj.* periscian. —**schreiben,** *n.* circular (*letter*). —**schule,** *f.* district *or* county school. —**sprung,** *m.* pirouette. —**stadt,** *f.* district *or* county town. —**stände,** *pl.* general council; (*in Germ.*) representatives of the districts. —**strom,** *m.* circuit. —**tag,** *m.* diet of a circuit (presided over by the **Landrat**). —**truppen,** *f.pl.* troops of the district, militia. —**umfang,** *m.* circumference. —**viertel,** *n.* quadrant. —**vierung,** *f.* quadrature of the circle.

Krei'sen, *v.* I. *n.* (*aux.* **h.**) to move in a circle; to form a circle; to revolve; to whirl round; to circulate; **die Flasche — lassen,** to pass the bottle round. II. *a.* to surround, walk round; to make round. *See* **Kreißen.**

Krei'schen, *ir.v.n.* (*aux.* **h.**) to shriek, screech, scream; to crackle, hiss (*as fat when cooking*); to be glaring; —**de Stimme,** shrill voice.

Krei'sel, *m.* (—**s,** *pl.* —) top; staggers (*Vet.*); **den — treiben,** to spin a top. —**n,** *v.r.* & *n.* (*aux.* **h.**) to turn round, revolve; to whirl round as a top; to spin a top. *Comp.* —**bohrer,** *m.* drill. —**wind,** *m.* whirlwind.

Krei'ß—en, (**Krei'sen,**) I. *v.n.* (*aux.* **h.**) to cry out in labour; to be in labour. II. *subst. n.* labour. —**ende,** *f.* parturient, woman in labour.

Kremortar'tari, *m.* cream of tartar.

Krem'pe, *see* **Krämpe.**

Krem'pel, *m.* worthless things, rubbish; **der ganze —,** the whole concern, the lot (*coll.*).

Kreoso't, *n.* (—**s**) creosote. —**haltig,** *adj.* creosotic. —**ie'ren,** *v.a.* to creosote.

Kre'peln, Krö'peln, *v. n.* to trudge on (*dial. coll.*). *Comp.* —**stuhl,** *m.* easy chair (*dial.*).

Krepie'ren, *v.* I. *n.* (*aux.* **s.**) to die, fall (*of beasts*); to burst, splinter (*of shells*).

Krepp, *m.* (—**s,** *pl.* —**e**) crape. —**en,** *v.a.* to crape, crisp; to nap, frieze (*cloth*); to wave the hair. *Comp.* —**eisen,** *n.* waving-iron. —**flor,** *m.* crisped crape. —**macher,** *m.* crape-weaver. —**maschine,** *f.* craping machine.

Krep'pe, *f.* (*pl.* —**n**) hair-pad.

Kres'se, *f.* (*pl.* —**n**) cress; gudgeon.

Kre'thi; — und Plethi, all the world and his wife, tag-rag and bob-tail.

Kreti'n, *m.* (—**s,** *pl.* —**s**), —**e** (—**en,** *pl.* —**en**) cretin. —**en-haft,** *adj.* idiotic, cretin-like.

Kret'ten, *v.a.* to vex, tease, annoy (*dial. & coll.*).

Kreuch; Kreuchst, Kreucht, *imperat.; 2 & 3 p. sing. pres. ind.* (*now obs.*) *of* **kriechen.**

Kreuz, *n.* (—**es,** *pl.* —**e**) cross, crucifix; cross (*of a sword, an anchor, etc.*); cross-bar; small of the back, loins; backbone; croup, crupper; club (*Cards*); sharp (*Mus.*); dagger, obelus (*Typ.*); peel (*Typ.*); crosier; affliction; **Verein vom Roten —,** Red Cross Society; **Haus —,** domestic cross, shrew; trouble at home; *used as intensive before oaths, as:* —**donnerwetter!** —**sackerlot!** hell and blazes! *and before adjectives, as:* —**fidel,** very happy; —**brav,** extremely good, most worthy, thoroughly honest; (in) **die — und Quer, — und quer,** zigzag, in all directions; — **und quer fragen,** to cross-question, cross-examine; **zu —e kriechen,** to humble oneself, to repent; **das — machen, ein — schlagen,** to cross oneself; **ans — schlagen,** to fix *or* nail to the cross; **das — vor einem machen,** to hold a p. in horror; **sein — über (eine S.) machen,** to relinquish, give up; **übers —,** across, crosswise; **ins — segeln,** to tack; **ins — legen,** to lay crossways; **sich ins — legen,** to lie down with outstretched arms in the shape of a cross; (**sich**) **das — brechen,** to break one's back; **am —e stehen,** to be in a dilemma; **das — nehmen,** to take the cross and go on a crusade. *Comp.* —**abnahme,** —**abnehmung,** *f.* descent from the cross. —**arm,** *m.* cross-bar. —**band,** *n.* cross-beam; cross-ligament; postal *or* newspaper wrapper; **unter —band,** under wrapper, in bands, as a newspaper *or* by bookpost. —**bein,** *n.* os sacrum. —**beinig,** *adj.* cross-legged. —**berg,** *m.* Calvary. —**bild,** *n.* crucifix. —**blütler,** *pl.* cruciferous plants. —**brav,** *adj.* thoroughly honest *or* good. —**bube,** *m.* knave of clubs. —**dame,** *f.* queen of clubs. —**erhöhung,** *f.* elevation of the cross; holy-rood day. —**es-tod,** *m.* death on the cross, crucifixion. —**fahne,** *f.* banner of the cross. —**fahrer,** *m.* crusader; cruiser, privateer. —**fahrt,** *f.* cruise; crusade; pilgrimage. —**feuer,** *n.* cross-fire (*Mil.*). —**fidel,** *adj.* as pleased as Punch, as happy as a lark. —**flügel,** *m.* transept. —**gang,** *m.* procession with the cross; cross-aisle; cross-walk; archway; cloisters (*in a convent*); cross-lode. —**gebälke,** *pl.* cross-beams. —**gewebe,** *n.* crossing (*Weav.*). —**gewölbe,** *n.* cross-shaped vault. —**haspel,** *f.* windlass. —**heer,** *n.* army of the cross, host of crusaders. —**holz,** *n.* piece of wood crossing another at right angles; buckthorn; mistletoe. —**kirche,** *f.* church in the form of a cross; church of the Holy Cross. —**knoten,** *m.* double knot, sailor's knot. —**lahm,** *adj.* lame in the hip; broken-backed; **ein Pferd —lahm reiten,** to break a horse's back. —**lied,** *n.* crusaders' song. —**mars,** *m.* mizzen-top (*Naut.*). —**maß,** *n.* T-square; gauge (*Typ.*). —**messer,** *n.* poniard. —**naht,** *f.* cross-stitched seam. —**orden,** *m.* order of the cross. —**otter,** *f.* common viper. —**predigt,** *f.* crusading sermon. —**punkt,** *m.* point of intersection of two *or* more lines (*Math.*), junction (*Railw.*). —**ritter,** *m.* crusader. —**schiff,** *n.* cruiser. —**schmerz,** *m.* lumbago. —**schnitt,** *m.* crucial incision. —**schraffierung,** *f.* cross-hatching. —**segel,** *n.* mizzen-top-sail. —**spinne,** *f.* cross *or* diadem spider, garden-spider. —**sprung,** *m.* caper; —**sprünge machen,** to double. —**stab,** *m.* crosier. —**ständig,** *adj.* decussate. —**steif,** *adj.* stiff in the loins. —**stellung,** *f.* cross-like position; pas croisé (*Danc.*). —**stenge,** *f.* mizzen-top-mast. —**stock,** *m.* cross-bars (*of a window*); window. —**tag,** *m.* rogation-day. —**unglücklich,** *adj.* thoroughly wretched, altogether miserable. —**verband,** *n.* cross-band (*Surg.*); bond (*Mas.*). —**verhör,** *n.* cross-examination. —**weg,** *m.* crossing (of roads) cross-way. —**weh,** *n. see* —**schmerz.** —**weise,** *adv.* cross-wise, crossways; across. —**woche,** *f.* rogation-week. —**zeichen,** *n.* sign of the cross. —**zeitungs-männer,** *pl.* blind followers of the (highly conservative) Kreuzzeitung, very conservative politicians. —**zug,** *m.* crusade. —**zügel,** *pl.* coupling reins.

Kreu'z—en, *v.* I. *a.* to mark with a cross; to thwart, cross; to cross, intercross, interbreed races. II. *r.* to make the sign of the cross; to intersect; to cross one another; to meet; to clash. III. *n.* (*aux.* **h.**) to cross; to cruise; to tack about. —**er,** *m.* (—**ers,** *pl.* —**er**) kreuzer, farthing, groat (*a small coin, current in Austria till* 1900); cruiser; privateer; **dieser Regierung keinen —er für einen —er,** we shall not vote a single farthing to this government for (the construction of) a(nother) cruiser. —er=flotte, *f.*, —er=geschwader, *n.* squadron of cruisers. —igen, *v.a.* to crucify. —igung, *f.* crucifixion. —ung, *f.* crossing; cruising; cross-breeding, interbreeding; *see* —punkt. —ungs=punkt, *m.* railway crossing; junction; meeting (*of two roads*).

Krib'bel—n, *v.* I. *n.* (*aux.* h.) to crawl about, swarm; to itch, tickle, prick. II. *a.* to irritate; das —t ihn im Kopfe, that annoys him. —ig, *adj.* irritable. *Comp.* —kopf, *m.* irritable person.

Krib(b)s'=krab(b)s, *m.* hotch-potch, medley; — der Imagination, crotchets of imagination, odd fancies.

Krickelei', *f.* scrawl; provocations, annoyances; fretfulness; cavilling, wrangling (*vulg.*).

Kri'ck—eln, *v.a.* & *n.* (*aux.* h.) to be fretful *or* captious; to scrawl. —lich, *adj.* fretful, captious; fussy.

Krie'ch—en, *ir.v.n.* (*aux.* h. & s.) to creep, crawl; to cringe, sneak, crouch, fawn; aus dem Ei —en, to be hatched. —er, *m.* (—ers, *pl.* —er) sneak, cringing person. —erei', *f.* servility, fawning, cringing. —erisch, *adj.* fawning, cringing. *Comp.* —bohne, *f.* dwarf kidney-bean. —pflanzen, *pl.* creepers. —tiere, *pl.* reptiles.

Krieg, *m.* (—(e)s, *pl.* —e) war; strife, quarrel; hostility; — bis aufs Messer *or* — auf Tod und Leben, war to the knife; — im Frieden, great manœuvres; sham war; (mit einem *or* gegen einen) — führen, to wage war, to make war (upon *or* against); ein Land mit — überziehen, to invade, carry war into a country; der innerliche *or* innere —, civil war; im —e, at war, in time of war; in den — ziehen, to go to war, to take the field; — beginnen, to go to war, to commence hostilities; einem Lande den — erklären, to declare war against a country; den — wieder anfangen, to resume hostilities. *Comp.* —erschöpft, *adj.* war-worn, worn out by war. —fertig, *adj.* ready for war. —führend, *adj.* belligerent. —führung, *f.* conduct of war, strategy; warfare. —gerüstet, *adj.* fully equipped *or* armed, ready for war. —geübt, *adj.* inured to war.

Krie'g—en, *v.* I. *n.* (*aux.* h.) to wage war, war; to dispute. II. *a.* to get, catch (*coll.*); to obtain, gain, get (*coll.*); etwas klein —en, to understand, master something (*vulg.*); ich will dich schon —en, I shall get hold of you and make you do it; I'll pay you off yet; das werden wir schon —en, I shall manage that all right; we shall get it before long (*coll.*). —er, *m.* (—ers, *pl.* —er) warrior, soldier. —erin, *f.* female warrior, warlike woman, Amazon. —erisch, *adj.* & *adv.* warlike, martial; soldier-like. *Comp.* —er=mäßig, *adj.* & *adv.* warrior-like. —er=stand, *m.* profession of arms; soldiers, military men. —er=verband, *m.* association of military clubs. —er=verein, *m.* association of veterans *or* disbanded soldiers.

Kriegs— (*in comp.*) —adel, *m.* military nobility. —akademie, *f.* staff-college. —amt, *n.* war-office. —artikel, *m.* article of war. —aufgebot, —aufruf, *m.* call to arms. —baukunst, *f.* fortification, military engineering. —bedarf, *m.* military stores, ammunition. —behörde, *f.* war office, war department. —budget, *n.* army budget. —bühne, *f.* theatre of war, seat of war. —denkmünze, *f.* war medal. —dienst, *m.* active military service; duty. —dienstpflichtige(r), *m.* one bound to serve, conscript. —drangsal, *n.* (*f.*) horror(s) of war. —drommete, *f.* war trumpet (*poet.*). —eid, *m.* military oath. —erklärung, *f.* declaration of war. —eröffnung, *f.* commencement of hostilities. —etat, *m.* war footing; war budget. —fahr=zeug, *n.* man-of-war. —fall, *m.* case of war. —flotte, *f.* navy. —freiwillige(r), *m.* volunteer (for active service). —fuhre, *f.* conveyance required in war. —fuß, *m.* war footing *or* establishment; auf —fuß, on a war footing, if mobilized; auf den —fuß setzen, to mobilize, to put (*a ship*) in commission. —gefährte, —genosse, *m.* fellow-soldier. —gefangene(r), *m.* prisoner of war. —geleit, *n.* military escort. —gerät, *n.*, —gerätschaften, *pl.* baggage; implements of war; equipage. —gericht, *n.* court martial; er wird vor ein —gericht gestellt werden, he will have to appear before a court martial, he will be court-martialled. —gerichtlich, *adv.* by court martial. —geschichte, *f.* military history; war story, anecdote from the war. —geschick, *n.* vicissitudes of war. —geschrei, *n.* rumour of war; watchword *or* rallying word; battle-cry. —geschwader, *n.* squadron. —gesetz, *n.* martial law. —glück, *n.* fortune of war; military success. —gott, *m.* god of war, Mars. —göttin, *f.* goddess of war, Bellona. —hafen, *m.* naval port *or* station. —händel, *pl.* military affairs. —handwerk, *n.* profession of arms, military profession. —haufe(n), *m.* body of troops. —heer, *n.* army, host. —held, *m.* warrior-hero, great warrior. —herr, *m.* commander-in-chief, generalissimo. —hospital, *n.* military hospital. —hülfe, *f.* subsidies; auxiliaries. —kamerad, *see* —gefährte. —kammer, —kanzlei, *f.* war-office. —kasse, *f.* military chest. —kassierer, *m.* paymaster. —knecht, *m.* soldier (*B.*). —kontrebande, *f.* contraband of war. —kunde, *f.* military science; tactics, strategy. —kundig, I. *adj.* skilled in war. II. *n.* great tactician and strategist. —kunst, *f.* art of war. —läufte, *pl.* course of the war, occurrences of the war. —leben, *n.* warfare; military life. —list, *f.* stratagem. —losung, *f.* watchword. —macht, *f.* belligerent power; forces, troops. —minister, *m.* minister of war; Secretary of State for War (*Engl.*). —ministerium, *n.* war office, war department. —müde, *adj.* tired *or* weary of war. —musik, *f.* martial music. —not, *f.* stress of war. —pferd, *n.* war-horse; charger. —panier, *n.* standard of war. —pflicht, *f. see* —dienst. —pflichtig, *adj.* subject to military service. —rat, *m.* council of war, war-council; (head-)clerk in the War-office. —recht, *n.* martial law; court martial (*obs.*); articles of war; sword-law; —recht über einen halten *or* ergehen lassen, to try one by court-martial (*obs.*). —regierung, *f.* military government. —ruf, *m.* war-cry; summons to arms. —rüstung, *f.* preparation for war; armour; accoutrements. —satt, *adj.* tired of war. —schaden, *m.* damage *or* loss inflicted by war. —schar, *f.* body of troops. —schauplatz, *m.* seat of war, theatre of war (*Amer.*). —schiff, *n.* man-of-war, battle-ship (*Naut.*). —schuld, *f.* debt occasioned by war. —schule, *f.* military academy *or* college. —schüler, *m.* cadet, military pupil. —seerecht, *n.* maritime law (as applicable in time of war. —spiel, *n.* game of war; prisoner's base (game). —sprache, *f.* military language. —steuer, *f.* war-tax; contribution levied upon the enemy. —straße, *f.* military road. —that, *f.* warlike deed; military exploit. —übung, *f.* military practice; manœuvres. —verfassung, *f.* military constitution. —verpflegungs=amt, *n.* commissariat department. —volk, *n.*, —völker, *pl.* forces; military nation. —vorrat, *m.* military stores; ammunition. —wagen, *m.* war chariot; ammunition waggon. —wesen, *n.* military affairs; war department; war. —zahlamt, *n.* army pay-office. —zahlmeister, *m.* paymaster to the army. —zeug, *n.* ordnance. —zögling, *see* —schüler. —zucht, *f.* military discipline. —zug, *m.* military expedition. —

zustand, —stand, *m.* state of war. **—zwang,** *m.* military execution. **—zweck,** *m.*; **für —zwecke,** for purposes of war, for military purposes.

Krimina'l, *adj.* criminal. **—i'st,** *m.* (**—i'sten,** *pl.* **—i'sten**) professor of *or* authority on criminal law. *Comp.* **—abteilung,** *f.* criminal court. **—gerichtsbarkeit,** *f.* criminal jurisdiction. **—gesetzbuch,** *n.* penal code. **—gesetzgebung,** *f.* penal legislation. **—sache,** *f.* criminal case. **—verfahren,** *n.* criminal prosecution. **—vergehen,** *n.* indictable offence.

Krim'meln, *v.n.* (*aux.* **h.**); **— und wimmeln,** to crawl about in great numbers (*coll.*).

Krim'mer, *m.* (**—s,** *pl.* **—**) crim-lambskin, Crimean lambskin.

Krim'p—e, *f.* shrinking (*of cloth, etc.*); **in die —e gehen,** to shrink. **—en,** *v.* I. *a.* to damp *or* shrink cloth. II. *r.* & *n.* (*aux.* **s.**) to shrink; to crumple. *Comp.* **—frei,** *adj.* that does not shrink, well shrunk.

Krims'krams, *m.* medley of old useless things (*coll.*); nonsense, trash.

Krim'stecher, *m.* (**—s,** *pl.* **—**) field glass.

Krin'gel, *m.* (**—s,** *pl.* **—**) twisted bun, cracknel; ring, circle.

Krinoli'ne, *f.* (*pl.* **—n**) crinoline, hoop-petticoat.

Krip'p—e, *f.* (*pl.* **—en**) crib, manger; hurdle-work; fence; caisson; infant asylum, foster-home. **—en,** *v.a.* to fence with hurdle-work; to strengthen (*a dike*) with hurdle-work. *Comp.* **—en=beißer, —en=setzer,** *m.* crib-biter, miserable jade. **—en=reiter,** *m.* parasite, poor farmer. **—en=verein,** *m.* (ladies') association for supporting an infant asylum. **—en=wehr,** *n.* wattled dike.

Kri'se, Kri'sis, *f.* (*pl.* **Kri'sen**) crisis.

Kris'peln, *v.a.* to crisp, grain (*leather, etc.*).

Krit—e'rium, *n.* (**—eriums,** *pl.* **—erien**) criterion. **—i'k,** *see* **Kritik.** **—isch** (*pron.* **kri'tisch**), *adj.* & *adv.* critical. **—isie'ren,** *v.a.* to criticize; to review; to censure.

Kriti'k, *f.* (*pl.* **—en**) criticism; review, critique; **einer — unterziehen,** to criticize; to review (*a book*); **wohlwollende —,** favourable criticism; **ungünstige —,** adverse criticism, stricture; **unter aller —,** beneath contempt, wretchedly bad. **—as'ter,** *m.* carping *or* foolish critic. **—er,** (*pron.* **Kri'tiker**) *m.* (**—ers,** *pl.* **—er**) (**—en=schreiber,** *m.*) critic, reviewer. **—los,** *adj.* uncritical, undiscriminating.

Krit't—el, *m.* (**—els,** *pl.* **—el**) captiousness, carping criticism, doubt; **eigensinniger —el,** wayward captiousness. **—elei',** *f.* (*pl.* **—eleien**) frivolous *or* carping criticism. **—(e)ler,** *m.* (**—(e)lers,** *pl.* **—(e)ler**) fault-finder, petty-minded critic. **—(e)lig, —lich,** *adj.* fault-finding, captious, punctilious; nice, difficult.

Krit'teln, *v.n.* (*aux.* **h.**) to criticize eagerly and frivolously; **an einem Kunstwerke (herum) —,** to carp at a work of art.

Kritz, *m.* (**—es,** *pl.* **—e**) scratch, scrawl; dash of the pen. **—elei',** *f.* scratch; scrawl, scrawling. **—eln,** *v.* I. *a.* to scratch. II. *n.* (*aux.* **h.**) to splutter (*as pens*). **—ler,** *m.* (**—lers,** *pl.* **—ler**) scribbler. **—lich,** *adj.* badly written, scrawly, illegible; **—liche Handschrift,** scrawl, illegible handwriting.

Kroch, Kro'ch(e)st; Krö'che, *1* (& *3*), *2 p. sing. imp. ind.*; *1* (& *3*) *p. sing. subj. of* **kriechen.**

Krokodi'l, *n.* (**—s,** *pl.* **—e**) crocodile. *Comp.* **—schluß,** *m.* sophistical argument, trap (*Log.*).

Kroko'n=säure, *f.* croconic acid.

Kro'kos, Kro'kus, *m.* crocus, saffron (*B.*).

Krol'len, *v.a.* & *r.* to crisp, to curl (*up*).

Kro'n—e, *f.* (*pl.* **—en**) crown; coronet; diadem, king; kingdom; tonsure; crown, top; halo; florin (*Austria*); corona (*Anat., Arch., Bot.*); crest (*Fort.*); highest point; head; crowning work, paragon, pattern, glory; brim (*Bell found.*); **sie ist die —e aller Frauen,** she is a pearl amongst women; **das setzt seiner Treulosigkeit die —e auf,** that puts the finishing touch to his perfidy; **das setzt seinen Verdiensten die —e auf,** that is his crowning merit; **dem Verdienste seine —en,** honour to whom honour is due; **was ist ihm in die —e gefahren,** what is the matter with him? (*coll.*). **—en,** *see* **Kronen** *in comp.* *Comp.* **—anwalt,** *m.* counsel for the crown, public prosecutor; attorney-general. **—band,** *n.* coronary ligament (*Anat.*). **—beamte(r),** *m.* officer of the crown. **—bewerber,** *m.* aspirant to the crown. **—erbe,** *m.* heir to the crown. **—feldherr,** *m.* field-marshal-general. **—gut,** *n.* crown-lands, royal domain. **—hirsch,** *m.* stag with crown-antlers. **—lehen,** *n.* fief of the crown. **—leuchter,** *m.* chandelier. **—prinz,** *m.* crown-prince, heir apparent, heir to the throne. **—prinzessin,** *f.* crown-princess, princess-royal. **—prinzlich,** *adj.* relating *or* belonging to the crown-prince; **das —prinzliche Paar,** the crown-prince and the crown-princess. **—rat,** *m.* Privy Council. **—räuber,** *m.* usurper. **—rede,** *f.* speech from the throne. **—zeuge,** *m.* witness of the crown.

Krön'—chen, *n.* (**—chens,** *pl.* **—chen**) little crown; little crest (*of waves*); coronet (*Bot.*). **—en,** I. *v.a.* to crown; **gekrönter Dichter,** poet-laureate. II. *subst.* **—chen,** *n.* little crown, coronet; coronule (*Bot.*); crest (*of waves*). **—ung,** *f.* coronation. *Comp.* **—ungs=eid,** *m.* coronation oath. **—ungs=feier(lichkeit),** *f.* coronation ceremony. **—ungs=gesang,** *m.* coronation anthem. **—ungs=mahl,** *n.* coronation banquet. **—ungs=münze,** *f.* medal struck to commemorate a coronation.

Kro'nen— (*in comp.*) **—artig,** *adj.* coronal; coronary. **—bein,** *n.* coronal bone (*Vet.*). **—blatt,** *n.* petal. **—gold,** *n.* eighteen-carat gold. **—los,** *adj.* uncrowned; apetalous (*Bot.*). **—orden,** *m.* (Prussian) order of the Crown. **—steuer,** *f.* coronation-tax *or* gift to the sovereign. **—träger,** *m.* crowned head, sovereign.

Krons'beere, *f.* (*pl.* **—n**) cranberry.

Kropf, *m.* (**—es,** *pl.* **Kröp'fe**) crop, craw, maw (*of birds*); wen, goitre (*Med.*); excrescence (*Bot.*); bunches, glanders (*Vet.*); bow (*of ships*); projecting part, top of a wall. **—icht,** (*obs.*) **—ig,** *adj.* strumous, affected with goitre. *Comp.* **—ader,** *f.* varicose vein. **—artig,** *adj.* wen-like, goitrous. **—eisen,** *n.* crow-bar. **—gans,** *f.* common pelican. **—mittel,** *n.* antistrumatic. **—rad,** *n.* middle shot-wheel. **—stein,** *m.* corner-stone.

Kröp'f—en, *v.* I. *a.* to bend at right angles, to form a knee; to cram (*poultry*); to lop. II. *n.* (*aux.* **h.**) to gorge; to feed. **—er,** *m.* pouter pigeon. **—ig,** *adj. see* **Kropficht.** **—ung,** *f.* corner-moulding; cramming.

Krop'(p)zeug, *n.* tag-rag and bobtail; small children (*dial.* & *coll.*); **das kleine —,** little ones; pack of young brats (*dial.*).

Kroquie'ren, *v.a.* to make a sketch of (*Mil.*).

Krö'schen, *v.a.* to fry in butter *or* lard.

Krö'sel, *m.* & *n.* crow iron, glazier's iron. **—n,** *v.a.* to groove.

Krö't—e, *f.* (*pl.* **—en**) toad, paddock; malicious person; little creature; child; ugly wretch; **ein paar —en in der Tasche haben,** to be well off (*sl.*); **ich habe nur noch ein paar erbärmliche —en in der Tasche,** I have only a few miserable coins in my pocket (*sl.*); **eine niedliche kleine —e,** a pretty little thing (girl) (*vulg.*). **—ig, —isch,** *adj.* toad-like; malicious; obstinate. *Comp.* **—en=auge,** *n.* toad-stone. **—en=stecher,** *m.* blunt penknife. **—en=weibchen,** *n.* female toad.

Kroto'n— (*in comp.*) **—säure,** *f.* crotonic acid.

Kroup, Krupp, *m.*, (—s) croup.
Krü'ck—e, *f.* (*pl.* —en) crutch; crook-like *or* T-shaped stick *or* tool; scraper, rake; bridge (*Bill.*); beater; pick-lock; head of a cork-screw; **an —en gehen,** to walk with crutches. *Comp.* **—en=förmig,** *adj.* in the form of a crutch. **—(en)=stock,** *m.* crutch; walking-stick with a crook.
Krug, *m.* (—es, *pl.* **Krü'ge**) pitcher, jug; mug, tankard; pot; public-house; **der — geht so lange zum Wasser bis er bricht,** the pitcher goes so often to the well that it comes home broken at last; let well alone; the grey goose will be caught at last (*prov.*). *Comp.* **—bier,** *n.* beer in stone bottles. **—förmig,** *adj.* pitcher-shaped.
Krü'ger, *m.* (—s, *pl.* —) publican (*obs.*).
Kru'ke, *f.* (*pl.* —n) stone jar.
Krul'l— (*in comp.*) **—farn,** *m.* maiden-hair fern. **—haar,** *n.* curled (*horse-*)hair.
Krüm'—chen, —elchen, *n.* (—(el)chens, *pl.* —(el)chen) little crumb; little bit. **—(e)lig,** *adj.* crumbly, crumby. **—eln,** *v.r.* & *n.* (*aux.* **h.**) to crumble; **sich —eln,** to crumble away.
Kru'me, *f.* (*pl.* —n) the crumb (*of bread*); young blade of corn; vegetable mould.
Krumm, *adj.* & *adv.* (—er, —st; *less good:* **krüm'mer, krümmst**), crooked, bent, curved, wry; circuitous; bow, bandy; twisted; bowed, arched; halting, spavined; indirect, artful, dishonest; **der —e,** the hare (*Hunt.*); **—e Linie,** curve; **—e Kniee,** knock-knees; **—es Maul,** wry mouth; **ein —es Roß,** a halting *or* spavined horse; **ein —er Kerl,** a boorish, ungentlemanly fellow (*coll.*); **—e Finger machen,** to be light-fingered; **die Hand — machen,** to beg; **— sitzen,** to cower; **eine —e Haltung haben,** to stoop; **— werden,** to grow crooked, to warp; **— liegen,** to suffer want (*coll.*); **sich — legen,** *also* (**— liegen**), to cut down one's expenses (*coll.*); **—e Wege,** crooked, underhand ways; **einen — ansehen,** to look askance at one; **einem etwas — nehmen,** to be offended with a p. on account of s.th. he has done *or* said; **nimm's nicht —,** don't take it amiss! (*coll.*); **es geht — mit ihm,** things are not going well with him; **sich — lachen,** to split one's sides with laughing; **(einen) — und lahm schlagen,** to beat unmercifully; **sich — sitzen,** to grow crooked with constant sitting. *Comp.* **—achse,** *f.* cranked axle. **—ästig,** *adj.* gnarled. **—beinig,** *adj.* bandy-legged, crooked-legged. **—buckel,** *m.* hunchback. **—halsig,** *adj.* wry-necked. **—holz,** *n.* crooked timber; knee-timber. (*Shipb.*); dwarf mountain pine; underwood. **—horn,** *n.* animal with crumpled horns; cornet (*Mus.*); trumpet-shaped organ pipe. **—linig,** *adj.* curvilinear. **—nasig,** *adj.* hook-nosed. **—schnabel,** *m.* crooked bill; curlew (*Orn.*). **—stab,** *m.* crook; crosier; episcopal dignity *or* rule; **unterm —stab ist gut wohnen,** subjects of ecclesiastical rulers have a pleasant life. **—stroh,** *n.* litter. **—zapfen,** *m.* crank. **—zirkel,** *m.* bow-compasses.
Krümm'—bar, *adj.* that may be bent *or* curved, curvable. **—e,** *f.* (*pl.* —en) crookedness; winding, intricacy; curvature; circuitous way.
Krüm'm—en, *v.* I. *a.* to bend, curve, crook, crumple; **niemand soll dir ein Haar —en,** no one shall hurt a hair of your head. II. *r.* to grow crooked; to wriggle; to writhe; to wind; to curve; to cringe, fawn; **auch ein Wurm —t sich,** even a worm will turn. **—ung,** *f.* bend, curve; curvature; stoop; turn, winding; contortion. *Comp.* **—ungs=halbmesser,** *m.* radius of curvature.
Krup'pe, *f.* (*pl.* —n) crupper (*of a horse*).
Krüp'pel, *m.* (—s, *pl.* —) cripple; **zum — machen,** to cripple. **—haft, —ig,** *adj.* & *adv.* crippled, imperfect, stunted. *Comp.* **—baum,** *m.* dwarf tree.
Krup'pisch, *adj.*; **—e Kanonen,** Krupp guns.
Krustace'en, *pl.* crustacea.
Krus't—e, *f.* (*pl.* —en, *dim.* **Krüst'chen**) crust; scurf (*on the skin*); fur (*on a boiler, etc.*); **anstoßende —e,** kissing crust; **sich mit —e überziehen,** to (in)crust. **—ig,** *adj.* crusty. *Comp.* **—en=artig,** *adj.* crust-like; crustaceous. **—en=tiere,** *pl.* crustacea.
Kryp't—a, *f.* (*pl.* —en), **—e,** *f.* (*pl.* —en) crypt. **—oga'misch,** *adj.* cryptogamous (*Bot.*). **—ony'm,** *adj.* anonymous; pseudonymous.
Krysta'll, Krista'll, *m.* (—s, *pl.* —e) crystal. **—en,** *adj.* of crystal; crystalline. **—ig,** *adj.* crystal-like. **—i'nisch,** *adj.* crystalline. **—isier'bar,** *adj.* crystallizable. **—isie'ren,** *v.a.* to crystallize. **—isie'rung, —isatio'n,** *f.* crystallization. *Comp.* **—bildung,** *f.* crystallization. **—fläche,** *f.* facet. **—flasche,** *f.* water-bottle, carafe. **—fluß,** *m.* composition used in manufacturing artificial crystals. **—form,** *f.* crystalline form. **—glas,** *n.* artificial crystal. **—hell,** *adj.* clear as crystal; crystalline; transparent, translucent. **—kunde, —lehre,** *f.* crystallography. **—stein,** *m.* transparent quartz. **—wasser,** *n.* water of crystallization.
Kube'be, *f.* (*pl.* —n) cubeb. *Comp.* **—n=öl,** *n.* essence of cubebs.
Kü'bel, *m.* (—s, *pl.* —) bucket, pail, tub; coal-measure. *Comp.* **—system,** *n.* bucket-system (*in mines*). **—träger,** *m.* hodman.
Kub—ie'ren, *v.a.* to take the cubic measure of; to cube. **—isch,** *adj.* (*pron.* **ku'bisch**) cubic.
Kubi'k—, *pref.* (*in comp.* =) cube, cubic. *Comp.* **—berechnung,** *f.* cubature. **—fuß,** *m.* cubic foot. **—inhalt,** *m.*, **—maß,** *n.* cubic contents. **—wurzel,** *f.* cube-root. **—zahl,** *f.* cube, cubic number; **auf die —zahl erheben,** to cube, to raise to the third power.
Ku'bus, *m.* (*pl.* **Kuben**) cube.
Kü'che, *f.* (*pl.* —n) kitchen; cooking, culinary art; servants in the kitchen; **eine gute — führen,** to keep a good table; **die schwarze —,** laboratory (*Alchym.*); **kalte —,** cold victuals, cold meat; **die — betreffend,** culinary; **es raucht in der —,** the mistress is scolding; **in des Teufels — kommen,** to get into a scrape. *Comp.* **—n=abfall,** *m.* kitchen-stuff, refuse. **—n=amt,** *n.* office of cook; kitchen. **—n=anrichte,** *f.* dresser. **—n=einrichtung,** *f.* kitchen-furniture. **—n=dragoner,** *m.* (female) cook; strong kitchen wench (*coll.*). **—n=fee,** *f.* cook (*coll.*). **—n=gerät, —n=geschirr,** *n.* kitchen utensils. **—n=herd,** *m.* (kitchen-) range, kitchener. **—n=latein,** *n.* apothecary's *or* dog Latin. **—n=meister,** *m.* head-cook, chef; steward; **bei ihnen ist Schmalhans —nmeister,** they live in a very frugal (*or* poor) way (*coll.*). **—n=personal,** *n.* persons employed in the kitchen. **—n=rolle,** *f.* rolling-pin. **—n=rost,** *m.* kitchen-grate; gridiron. **—n=schrank,** *m.* kitchen-cupboard. **—n=schreiber,** *m.* clerk of the kitchen. **—n=tisch,** *m.* kitchen table. **—n=verschlag,** *m.* caboose (*Naut.*). **—en=wagen,** *m.* luncheon car, dining car (*Railw.*); carriage for conveying kitchen utensils and provisions. **—n=zettel,** *m.* bill of fare; menu.
Ku'chen (*long* **u**), *m.* (—s, *pl.* —) (*dim.* **Küchelchen**) cake; tart; clot (*of blood*); what is left after pressing; **ja —!** don't you wish you may get it! nonsense! you may whistle for it! *Comp.* **—bäcker,** *m.* pastry-cook. **—form,** *f.* cake-mould. **—förmig,** *adj.* in the form of a cake; placentiform. **—pfanne,** *f.* cake-tin. **—rädchen,** *n.* jagging wheel. **—teig,** *m.* dough for cakes.
Küch'lein (*long* **ü**), *n.* (—s, *pl.* —) chicken.
Küch'ler (*long* **ü**), *m.* (—s, *pl.* —) pastry-cook.

Ku'ckuck, *m.* (—s, *pl.* —e) cuckoo; deuce, devil; **der — ruft** *or* **schreit**, the cuckoo calls; **der — und sein Küster**, the deuce (*coll.*); **hol's der —!** deuce take it! **hol' ihn der —**, let him go to Jericho! (**beim**) —, (**zum**) —! confound it! the deuce! **wie zum — soll ich das anfangen**, how in the world am I to set about it? **das mag der — wissen**, the devil knows it; **des —s werden**, to go mad. *Comp.* **—s=blume**, *f.* cuckoo-flower; meadow-lychnis. **—s=ruf**, *m.* cuckoo's note. **—s=weibchen**, *n.* hen of a cuckoo.

Kud'delmuddel, *m.* motley crowd, medley, omniumgatherum (*coll.*).

Ku'fe, *f.* (*pl.* **—n**) vat, tub; runner of a sledge.

Kü'fer, (**Küf'ner**,) *m.* (—s, *pl.* —) cooper; cellarman. **—ei'**, *f.* cooperage; cooper's workshop. **—n**, *v.n.* (*aux.* **h.**) to work as a cooper.

Ku'gel, *f.* (*pl.* **—n**) ball; globe, sphere; molecule; ball, bullet, projectile; ball (*of a thermometer*); head (*of a bone*); bullet (*Her.*); rounded *or* flattened summit of a mountain; **man hat ihm eine schwarze — geworfen**, he was black-balled; **matte —**, spent bullet; **—n und Granaten**, shot and shell; **die — (eines Beines) einrenken**, to reduce a dislocation; **—n wechseln**, to fight a duel with pistols; **sich** (*dat.*) **eine — durch den Kopf jagen**, to blow one's brains out; **eine jede — hat ihren Zweck**, every bullet has its billet (*prov.*); **eine jede — trifft ja nicht**, not every bullet hits home (*prov.*). **—icht**, (*obs.*) **—ig**, *adj.* spherical, globular. *Comp.* **—abschnitt**, *m.* segment of a sphere. **—ähnlich**, *adj.* spherical; spheroidal. **—artig**, *adj.* globular. **—ausschnitt**, *m.* cone with spherical base. **—bahn**, *f.* trajectory; way of the bullet; bowling-green. **—bohrer**, *m.* ball-extractor (*Surg.*). **—büchse**, *f.* rifle. **—dicke**, *f.* ball-calibre. **—dreieck**, *n.* spherical triangle. **—dreieck=lehre**, *f.* spherical trigonometry. **—fang**, *m.* rifle-butt; butts (*Artil.*). **—fest**, *adj.* shot-proof. **—fläche**, *f.* spherical surface. **—form**, *f.* spherical form; bullet-mould. **—förmig**, *see* **—icht**. **—futter**, *n.* leather, *etc.*, in which bullets are wrapped. **—garten**, *m.* park of artillery. **—gelenk**, *n.* socket (*Anat.*); ball and socket (*Mech.*). **—gerade**, **—gleich**, *adj.* straight-bored. **—gewinde**, *see* **—gelenk**. **—gewölbe**, *n.* cupola. **—gießer**, *m.* bullet-caster, bullet-mould. **—helm**, *m.* thole, cupola (*Arch.*). **—kästchen**, *n.* ballot-box. **—kreisel**, *m.* humming-top. **—lager**, *n.* ball bearing. **—laterne**, *f.* globe-lantern. **—lehre**, *f.* spherics. **—loch**, *n.* pocket (*Bill.*). **—löffel**, *m. see* **—zieher**. **—los**, *m.* decision by ballot. **—maß**, *n.* shot-gauge, ball-calibre. **—messer**, *m.* spherometer. **—patrone**, *f.* ball-cartridge. **—probe**, *f.* shot-gauge. **—rakete**, *f.* shot-racket. **—rund**, *adj.* spherical; quite round, round as a ball. **—schnitt**, *m.* spherical section. **—spiel**, *n.* bowling. **—spritze**, *f.* machine-gun; mitrailleuse (*in the Franco-German War, 1870-71*). **—thee**, *m.* gunpowder tea. **—tresse**, *f.* string of balls. **—wagen**, *m.* caisson; ammunition-waggon. **—wahl**, *f.* election by ballot; ballot. **—wand**, *f.* target. **—wechsel**, *m.* exchange of shots; **dreimaliger —wechsel**, three shots to be fired on each side. **—winkel**, *m.* spherical angle. **—zähl=apparat**, *n.* abacus. **—zange**, *f.* ball-extractor, bullet-forceps; tongs for red-hot shot (*Artil.*). **—zapfen**, *m. see* **—gelenk** (*Mech.*). **—zieher**, *m.* worm, wadhook; ball-extractor, bullet-drawer. **—zirkel**, *m.* bullet-dividers.

Kü'gelchen, *n.* (—s, *pl.* —) globule.

Ku'gel—n, *v.* I. *n.* (*aux.* **s.**) to roll; (*aux.* **h.**) to bowl; to ballot. II. *a.* to roll; to make globular; **sich —n**, to roll, to assume a globular form; **sich —n vor Lachen**, to split one's sides with laughing (*coll.*); **das ist zum —n**, that is extremely funny (*coll.*). **—ung**, *f.* rounding; rolling, bowling; balloting; ballot.

Ku'guar, *m.* (—s, *pl.* —) puma (*Zool.*).

Kuh, *f.* (*pl.* **Kü'he**) cow; female of deer, *etc.*; stupid person; **die — muht**, the cow moos; **er sieht es an wie die — das neue Thor**, he stares at it like a fool; **blinde — spielen**, to play at blind man's buff; **dumme —**, silly goose! **junge —**, heifer; **milchende —**, milk cow; anything lucrative. *Comp.* **—blume**, *f.* marsh-marigold. **—brücke**, *f.* orlop deck (*Naut.*). **—euter**, *n.* cow's udder. **—fladen**, *m.* cow-dung. **—fuß**, *m.* crow-bar; cow's foot; old gun; military rifle (*sl.*). **—haut**, *f.* cowhide; **das läßt sich auf keine —haut schreiben**, that cannot be put very briefly *or* in a nutshell (*coll.*). **—hessig**, *adj.* knock-kneed (*Vet.*); awkward. **—horn**, *n.* cow's horn; cowherd's horn. **—hürde**, *f.* cow-stall. **—krätze**, *f.* cow-itch. **—lymphe**, *f.* vaccine. **—magd**, *f.* dairy-maid, farm servant attending to the cows. **—mist**, *m.* cow-dung; cow-blakes, casings (*dry*). **—molken**, *pl.* whey. **—pocken**, *pl.* cow-pox. **—pocken=stoff**, *m.* vaccine matter. **—pocken=impfung**, *f.* vaccination. **—reigen**, **—reihen**, *m.* call of the Alpine cowherds, cowherd-melody, ranz des vaches. **—schelle**, *f.* cow-bell; pulsatilla (*Bot.*). **—weide**, *f.* pasturage for cattle.

Kühl, *adj.* & *adv.* cool; fresh; **eine —e Blonde**, a pint of white beer (*Berl.*). **—e**, I. *n.* **des Morgens —e**, the morning freshness; the cool hours of the morning; **im —en sitzen**, to sit in the shade. II. *f.* coolness; coldness; freshness; cool; cool spot *or* place; breeze. *Comp.* **—apparat**, *m.* refrigerator. **—bottich**, **—eimer**, *m.*, **—faß**, *n.* cooler. **—gefäß**, *n.* cooler, refrigerator. **—mittel**, *n.* cooling draught, refrigerant. **—ofen**, *m.* cooling furnace; annealing oven. **—raum**, *m.* refrigerating chamber. **—rohr**, *n.*, **—schlange**, *f.* worm (*of a still*). **—segel**, *n.* wind-sail. **—trank**, *m.* cooling drink.

Küh'l—en, *v.* I. *a.* to cool; to refresh; to ice (*wine, etc.*); **seinen Mut** *or* **sein Mütchen an einem —en**, to vent one's rage on one. II. *r.* & *n.* (*aux.* **h.**) to grow cool; **das Wetter —t sich**, the weather grows cool; **der Wind —t**, the wind freshens. **—end**, *p.* & *adj.* cooling; refrigerant. **—er**, *m.* (—ers, *pl.* —er) cooler; refrigerator. **—ung**, *f.* cooling, freshness; breeze.

Kühl'te, *f.* (—n) fresh gale; **heftige —**, squall.

Ku(h)le, *f.* (*pl.* **—n**) pit (*dial.*).

Kühn, *adj.* & *adv.* bold, daring; audacious; **— machen**, to embolden; **dem —en gehört die Welt**, Fortune favours the brave (*prov.*). **—heit**, *f.* courage, boldness, daring, intrepidity; audacity. **—lich**, *adv.* boldly.

Kujo'n, *m.* (—s, *pl.* —e) scoundrel. **—ie'ren**, *v.a.* to torment, vex, annoy.

Kula'n—t, *adj.* accommodating, obliging, liberal, fair, easy to deal with (*C.L.*). **—z**, *f.* accommodating character, fair dealing, liberality, readiness to oblige.

Ku'li, *m.* (—s, *pl.* —s) cooly, coolie.

Kulis'se, *see* **Coulisse**.

Kulm, *m.* (—s, *pl.* —e) top of a mountain, summit. **—inie'ren**, *v.n.* (*aux* **h.**) to culminate; to attain the zenith. *Comp.* **—inatio'ns=punkt**, *m.* culminating point.

Kult, *m.* (—(e)s, *pl.* —e), **Kul'tus**, *m.* (—) public (religious) worship; form of worship; church ceremonies. **—ivie'ren**, *v.a.* to cultivate. **—u'r**, *f.* cultivation; culture; civilization. *Comp.* **—u'r=kampf**, *m.* struggle with Rome (*inaugurated by the Prussian May Laws of 1873*) (*coll.*). **—u'r=stufe**, *f.* grade of civilization. **—us=minister**, *m.* minister of public worship and instruction, minister of ecclesiastical affairs and public instruction.

Kum'me, *f.* (*pl.* —**n**) basin, bowl; basin (*Naut.*).

Küm'mel, *m.* (—**s**, *pl.* —) caraway-seeds; **echter** —, cumin; — **und Dill** *or* **Salz**, pepper-and-salt (*colour*). —**n**, *v.* I. *a.* to flavour with caraway. II. *n.* (*aux.* **h.**) to drink cumin-brandy; to drink hard. *Comp.* —**brot**, *n.* bread made with caraway-seeds. —**bruder**, *m.* toper. —**käse**, *m.* cheese with caraway-seeds. —**spalter**, *m.* skin-flint. —**traube**, *f.* muscatel grape. —**türke**, *m.* tippler, toper (*coll.*). —**wasser**, *n.* caraway brandy, cumin brandy.

Küm'melblättchen, *n.* cardsharper's (three-card) trick.

Kum'mer, *m.* (—**s**) grief, sorrow; trouble; care; arrest, seizure; heap of ruins, rubbish; dirt, mud; **mit** — **behaftet**, care-worn; — **haben für**, to be anxious about (*dial.*); **sie hatte** —, **es könnte ihm ein Schaden zustoßen**, she feared some accident might happen to him (*dial.*); **Hunger und** — **leiden**, to be in great distress, in penury; **sich** (*dat.*) — **machen über eine S.**, to fret at, grieve about a th.; **das ist mein geringster** —, that is the least of my troubles. *Comp.* —**frei**, —**los**, *adj.* untroubled, without care, careless. —**stunden**, *pl.* hours of sorrow. —**voll**, *adj.* sorrowful, painful, doleful.

Küm'merlich, I. *adj.* & *adv.* sorrowful; needy, miserable; hard; wretched; pitiful, despicable; — **leben**, to live in penury *or* misery. II. *adv.* scarcely, barely, with great trouble. —**keit**, *f.* misery; grief.

Küm'mer—**n**, *v.* I. *a.* to grieve, afflict, trouble; to concern; **was** —**t mich das?** what is that to me? what do I care? II. *r.* to care about (**um einen** *or* **eine S.**); to grieve for (**über eine S.**). III. *n.* (*aux.* **h.** & **f.**) to fret; to be in grief; to get along badly, not to thrive; **ich** —**e mich nicht darum**, I do not trouble my head about it; —**n Sie sich nicht um ihn**, don't take any notice of him; —**n Sie sich um Ihre eigenen Angelegenheiten**, mind your own business. —**nis**, *f.* (*pl.* —**ni(ss)e**) annoyance; affliction; anxiety, care.

Kum'(me)t, *n.* (—**es**, *pl.* —**e**) horse-collar, hame. *Comp.* —**decke**, *f.* hame-cover. —**holz**, *n.* hame. —**kette**, *f.* fastening-chain (*of hames*). —**macher**, *m.* harness-maker. —**pferd**, *n.* draught-horse.

Kumm'karre, *f.* (*pl.* —**n**), —**n**, *m.* (—**ns**, *pl.* —**n**) dust-cart.

Kumpa'n, *m.* (—**s**, *pl.* —**e**) companion, fellow.

Kumpf, *m.* (—**es**, *pl.* **Küm'pfe**) deep basin, bowl (*dial.*); trough (*dial.*); pond; nut.

Kund, *indec. adj.* (*only used predic'ly*) known; **die Sache ist** —, it is generally known; — **machen**, — **thun**, to show, set forth, make known, notify, inform; **sich** — **geben**, to manifest, prove o.s. *or* itself; — **werden**, to become known, to come to light, to transpire; **sich** — **thun**, to declare; **laßt eure Bitten vor Gott** — **werden**, let your requests be made known unto God (*B.*); — **und zu wissen sei hiemit**, know all men by these presents. —**bar**, *adj.* notorious, well-known. —**barkeit**, *f.* notoriety, publicity. —**e**, *f.* (*pl.* —**en**) *see* **Kenntnis**; information, notice; news, intelligence, tale; (*as the second part of comp'ds.*) science; —**e von etwas nehmen**, to take cognizance of. —**e**, *m.* (—**en**, *pl.* —**en**), —**in**, *f.* customer; client; fellow; **ein schlauer** *or* **geriebener** —**e**, a sharp *or* sly customer; **ein fester** —**e**, a regular customer; **du bist mir ja ein netter** —**e**, well, you are a nice fellow (*mild form of rebuke*). —**ig**, *adj.* & *adv.* knowing, skilful, versed, experienced, learned; informed, aware; familiar (*with*), knowing thoroughly, expert; known; **einer Sache** —**ig**, thoroughly acquainted with a thing; **ein des Weges** —**iger**, one who knows the way; **die** —**igen**, people who know, the initiated. —**schaft**, *f.* custom; customers; goodwill (*C.L.*); practice; intelligence, notice, information; **auf** —**schaft ausgehen**, to go out to reconnoitre, to go scouting; —**schaft einziehen**, to collect information; **die** —**schaft schenken**, to patronize, give one's custom. —**schaften**, *v.* I. *n.* (*aux.* **h.**) to scout, spy, reconnoitre. II. *a.* to find out. —**schafter**, *m.* (—**schafters**, *pl.* —**schafter**) spy, emissary, scout. —**schafterei'**, *f.* spying, espionage. *Comp.* —**enfänger**, *m.* tout, drummer (*Amer.*). —**enwechsel**, *m.* bill of exchange received from a customer. —**enzahl**, *f.* number of customers, connection, custom. —**gebung**, *f.* demonstration (*of joy, etc.*). —**machung**, *f.* proclamation, publication, declaration.

Künd'bar, *adj.* that may be called in *or* reclaimed at notice.

Kün'd—**en**, *v.a.* *see* **Kund thun**; to publish (*banns*). —**igen**, *v.a.* to give notice *or* warning; to recall; to publish, make known; **ich habe meinem Diener gekündigt**, I have given my servant notice (to leave). —**igung**, *f.* notice, warning; **halbjährliche** —**igung**, six months' notice.

Künf'tig, I. *adj.* future; coming, to come, next; —**e Zeiten**, time(s) to come; —**e Woche**, next week; **das** —**e Leben**, the future life; **das** —**e**, futurity; **ins** —**e**, in future, for the future; **seine** —**e Frau**, his wife that is to be; his intended, the future Mrs. X. II. *adv.* for the future, henceforth, hereafter. *Comp.* —**hi'n**, *see* — II.

Kun'kel, *f.* (*pl.* —**n**) distaff; spinning room; women (*coll.*). *Comp.* —**adel**, *m.* nobility on the mother's side. —**lehen**, *n.* petticoat-hold (*Law*). —**magen**, *pl.* maternal relations (*Law*).

Kunnte, *obs.* & *poet. for* **konnte**.

Kunst, *f.* (*pl.* **Kün'ste**) art; skill, dexterity, address; trade, profession; trick, artifice; sleight of hand; machine, engine; water-work; **die freien Künste**, the liberal arts; **Magister der freien Künste**, Master of Arts, M.A.; **die schwarze** —, black art, magic, necromancy; mezzotint (*Engr.*); **die handwerksmäßigen Künste**, the mechanical arts; **die schönen Künste**, the fine arts; **die bildenden Künste**, the pictorial arts, painting, architecture, and sculpture; **die redenden Künste**, the rhetorical arts, poetry and music; **mit** —, artfully, artificially; **durch** — **hergestellt** *or* **bereitet**, artificial; **brotlose** —, profitless business, thankless task; **das ist keine** —, that is easy enough; **er ist mit seinen Künsten zu Ende**, he is at his wits' end; **seine** — **an einer Sache versuchen**, to try one's skill *or* one's hand at a th.; — **geht nach Brot**, art requires support *or* a protector, the artist must live (*prov.*). *Comp.* —**adel**, *m.* nobility of *or* conferred by art. —**akademie**, *f.* academy of fine arts. —**anlage**, *f.* artistic talent; pleasure grounds. —**arbeit**, *f.* work of art; artificial work. —**ausdruck**, *m.* technical term. —**ausstellung**, *f.* exhibition of works of art, art-gallery. —**bäcker**, *m.* fancy baker, confectioner. —**ballade**, *f.* literary ballad (*as opposed to the popular or national ballad*). —**bau**, *m.* construction, constructive work. —**beflissen**, *adj.* devoted to *or* zealous in studying an art. —**beflissene(r)**, *m.* art-student. —**begabt**, *adj.* talented. —**beilage**, *f.* pictorial supplement. —**beruf**, *m.* talent for art, artistic calling. —**bildung**, *f.* artistic training. —**butter**, *f.* artificial butter, margarine. —**dichter**, *m.* literary (*as opp. to popular*) poet, poet of a literary age. —**dichtung**, *f.* poetry of a literary age, *see* —**poesie**. —**drechsler**, *m.* turner in ivory. —**(und Buch)=druckerei**, *f.* artistic printing (*office*). —**dünger**, *m.* artificial manure (*guano, etc.*); fertilizer. —**epos**, *n.* literary epic; romantic epic (*both opposed to the national heroic epic*). —**erfahren**, *adj.* experienced *or* skilled in an art. —**erfahrene(n)**, *pl.* connoisseurs. —**erfindung**, *f.* ingenious invention. —**fertig**, *see* —**erfahren**. —**feuerwerker**, *m.* pyrotechnist. —**feuerwerkerei′**, *f.* pyrotechnics. —**fleiß**, *m.* industry. —**freund**, *m.* lover *or* patron of the fine arts. —**gärtner**, *m.* florist, nursery gardener. —**gärtnerei**, *f.* horticulture. —**gebäude**, *n.* artistic building; museum; art-repository. —**gebiet**, *n.* province of art. —**gebilde**, *n.* work of art. —**gefäß**, *n.* artistic vase. —**gefühl**, *n.* artistic feeling, feeling *or* taste for art, feeling of a true artist. —**gemäß**, *adj.* artistically *or* technically correct. —**genoß**, —**genosse**, *m.*, —**genossin**, *f.* fellow-artist. —**genossenschaft**, *f.* fellowship of artists. —**genuß**, *m.* (artistic) treat; **es war ein musikalischer —genuß**, it was a (musical) treat. —**gerecht**, *see* —**gemäß**. —**geschichte**, *f.* history of art. —**geschwür**, *n.* fontanel (*Surg.*). —**gestänge**, *pl.* poles of a hydraulic engine. —**getriebe**, *n.* machine; machinery. —**geübt**, *adj.* practically acquainted with art, skilled in art. —**gewebe**, *n.* web made with skill *or* art; intrigue. —**gewerbe**, *n.* handicraft; —**gewerbe-ausstellung**, *f.* exhibition of arts and crafts, industrial exhibition. —**gewerbe=museum**, *n.* industrial exhibition, museum of (*local, provincial*) industries. —**gewerbe=schule**, *f.* industrial school of art, polytechnic. —**graben**, *m.* canal; conduit; aqueduct. —**griff**, *m.* dexterity, skill in exercising an art, knack; craft; trick, artifice. —**guß**, *m.* cast works of art. —**halle**, *f.* art-museum. —**händler**, *m.* dealer in works of art; print-seller. —**handlung**, *f.* print-shop; fine-art repository; trade in works of art. —**höhle**, *f.* artificial cavern *or* grotto. —**jünger**, *m.* art-student. —**kabinett**, *n.*, —**kammer**, *f.* cabinet of curiosities *or* works of art. —**kenner**, *m.* art-connoisseur. —**kniff**, *m.* artifice, trick, dodge. —**lehre**, *f.* technology. —**liebhaber**, *m.* amateur, dilettante; lover of art. —**liebhaberei′**, *f.* taste *or* love for art. —**los**, *adj.* artless, naive, simple, natural; unsophisticated; destitute of art. —**losigkeit**, *f.* artlessness; want of art. —**mäßig**, *adj.* artistically correct; technical. —**meister**, *m.* surveyor of water-works, engineer. —**mittel**, *n.* artificial means *or* remedy. —**neid**, *m.* jealousy *or* envy of artists. —**pause**, *f.* pause for effect. —**periode**, *f.* flourishing *or* golden period of art. —**poesie**, *f.* poetry of a literary age, literary poetry, romantic poetry (*as opposed to the naive, national and popular poetry*). —**rad**, *n.* wheel of a water-work. —**rede**, *f.* oration. —**redner**, *m.* rhetorician. —**rednerisch**, *adj.* rhetorical. —**reich**, *adj.* full of art, ingenious; artistic; artificial. —**reise**, *f.* journey to study art; professional *or* starring tour. —**reiter**, *m.*, —**reiterin**, *f.* equestrian performer; circus rider, circus girl. —**reiterei′**, *f.* circus-riding, equestrianism. —**richter**, *m.* fine-art critic. —**richtern**, *v.n.* to criticize, play the critic. —**sache**, *f.* artistic concern; work of art. —**sammlung**, *f.* collection of works of art *or* articles of virtu. —**schacht**, *m.* draining shaft, engine-shaft (*Min.*). —**schreiner**, *m.* cabinet-maker. —**schule**, *f.* academy *or* school of arts; artistic school (*e.g.* Lake School). —**sinn**, *m.* taste *or* talent for art. —**sprache**, *f.* technical language, technical terminology. —**springer**, *m.* acrobat. —**sprung**, *m.* acrobatic feat. —**stecher**, *m.* engraver. —**steiger**, *m.* surveyor of waterworks (*Min.*). —**stickerei**, *f.* fine-art needlework. —**straße**, *f.* causeway, high-road. —**stück**, *n.* work of art; trick, cunning device, a clever thing. —**tischler**, *m.* cabinet-maker. —**tischlern**, *v.a.* to do cabinet work. —**trieb**, *m.* mechanical instinct (*of animals*); artistic instinct. —**verein**, *m.* art-union. —**verfahren**, *n.* artistic process. —**verlag**, *m.* firm of print-publishers; picture dealer's rooms, print-seller's shop. —**verleger**, *m.* fine-art publisher. —**verständige(r)**, *m.* expert (in matters of art); connoisseur; artist. —**verwandte(r)**, *m.* follower of the same art *or* trade. —**voll**, *adj.* ingenious, artistic. —**weise**, —**manier**, *f.* style *or* manner of an artist. —**werk**, *m.* work of art, artistic production; machine, engine; water-work; **das alte —werk**, antiquity. —**widrig**, *adj.* against the rules of art. —**wissenschaft**, *f.* æsthetics. —**wissenschaftlich**, *adj.* æsthetic. —**wolle**, *f.* artificial wool, shoddy wool, mungo wool. —**wort**, *n.* technical term. —**zeug**, *n.* machinery of water-works. —**zweig**, *m.* branch of art.

Künstelei′, *f.* (*pl.* —**en**) elaboration, artificiality; affected ways; artfulness; affectation (of nicety *or* subtlety); mannerism (*in literature*); artificial work.

Kün′st—eln, *v.* I. *a.* to elaborate; to over-refine, produce with much art; **gekünstelt**, artificial, elaborate, affected. II. *n.* (*aux.* **h.**) —**eln an einer S.** to bestow great pains on a th. —**ler**, *m.* (—**lers**, *pl.* —**ler**), —**lerin**, *f.* artist; virtuoso; artiste, performer (*Theat.*); artificer. —**lerei′**, *f.* life and manner of an artist. —**lerisch**, *adj.* artistic, artist-like. —**lerschaft**, *f.* body *or* society of artists, artists (*coll.*); artistic power, artistic greatness. —**lich**, *adj.* artificial; artful; ingenious; artificial, imitated false; —**liche Blumen**, artificial flowers; —**liche Haare**, false hair; —**liche Zähne**, artificial teeth; —**licher Diamant**, paste diamond. —**tum**, *n.* artistic power, artistic greatness, capacity *or* importance of an artist. *Comp.* —**ler=druck**, *m.* artist's proof. —**ler=laufbahn**, *f.* artistic career, career of an artist. —**ler=verein**, *m.* society of artists, artists' club.

Kun′terbunt, *adj. & adv.* pell-mell, higgledy-piggledy; gaudy, parti-coloured; **er redet —es Zeug**, he talks quite incoherently (*coll.*); **bei X. geht es — her**, at X.'s things are in a pretty mess (*coll.*).

Kü′p—e, *f.* (*pl.* —**en**) large tub, vat (*of dyers*). —**er**, *m.* (—**ers**, *pl.* —**er**) cooper, cellarman.

Kupellie′ren, *n.* cupellation.

Kup′fer, *n.* (—**s**, *pl.* —) copper, copper vessels; copper coin; copper-plate print; **in — stechen**, to engrave on copper. —**icht** (*obs.*), —**ig**, *adj.* coppery, like copper; blotched. —**n**, I. *adj.* of copper; —**ner Kessel**, copper kettle. II. *v.a.* to copper, line *or* mount with copper. III. *subst. n.*, —**ung**, *f.* copper-sheathing (*Naut.*). *Comp.* —**beschlag**, *m.* copper-sheathing. —**blatt**, *n.* copper-plate print. —**blech**, *n.* sheet-copper. —**blüte**, *f.* capillary red copper-ore. —**brand**, *m.*, —**brand=erz**, *n.* cupreous coal. —**draht**, *m.* copper-wire. —**druck**, *m.* copper-plate printing; copper-plate print. —**druckerei**, *f.* trade *or* office of a copper-plate printer. —**druck=papier**, *n.* plate-paper. —**feil**, —**feilicht**, *n.* copper-filings. —**fest**, *adj.* copper-fastened; coppered. —**folie**, *f.* copper-foil. —**frischen**, *n.* copper-refining. —**frisch=ofen**, *m.* copper finery. —**gehalt**, *m.* copper alloy. —**geld**, *n.* copper money. —**grün**, I. *adj.* eruginous. II. *n.* mountain green, chrysocolla. —**händler**, *m.* copper-merchant; print seller. —**haltig**, *adj.* containing copper. —**hammer**, *m.* hammer for copper; copper mill. —**hütte**, *f.* copper works. —**kalk**, *m.* oxide of copper. —**kies**, *m.* copper pyrites.

—könig, *m.* regulus of copper. —laſur, *f.* lazulite. —legierung, *f.* alloying with copper —münze, *f.* copper-coin; ein paar —münzen a few coppers (*coll.*). —niederſchlag, *m.* precipitated copper. —oxyd, *n.* black oxide of copper, cupric oxide. —oxidul, *n.* red oxide of copper, cuprous oxide; ſalzſaures —oxidul, cuprous chloride. —platte, *f.* copper-plate; (*pl.*) copper sheathing. —pol, *m.* negative pole. —preſſe, *f.* rolling press. —probe *f.* assay of copper-ore. —rot, I. *adj.* copper-coloured. II. *n.* vitriol. —röte, *f.* virgin copper; copper-colour. —roſt, *m.* verdigris. —ſammlung, *f.* collection of engravings. —ſchlag, *m.* copper-dross. —ſchmied, *m.* brazier; coppersmith. —ſpäne, *pl.* copper-filings. —ſtechen, *n.* engraving on copper. —ſtecher, *m.* copper-plate engraver. —ſtich, *m.* copper-plate engraving *or* print. —ſtich=laden, *m.* print-shop. —ſtich=platte, *f.* copper plate for engraving. —tiegel, *m.* copper crucible. —verkleidung, *f.* copper sheathing. —vitriol, *m.* & *n.* blue vitriol; sulphate of copper. —ware, *f.* brazier's ware. —werk, *n.* copper-works; set of copper-plates.

Kup'p—e, *f.* (*pl.* —en) top, summit; vaulted arch; head (*of a nail*). —el, *f.* (*pl.* —eln) cupola, dome, spire; lamp-shade. —ig, *adj.* peaked, topped. *Comp.* —el=dach, *n.* dome-shaped roof. —el=gewölbe, *n.* cupola, dome, round arch. —el=raum, *m.* cupola. —nagel, *m.* thickheaded nail.

Kup'pel, *see* Koppel. —ei', *f.* match-making; pandering. *Comp.* —bolzen, *m.* coupling *or* drag bolt. —gelenk, *n.* coupling-link. —pelz, *m.* match-maker's reward *or* brokerage. —ſtange, *f.* connecting-rod.

Kup'p—eln, *v.a.* to make a match; to pander, procure. —elung, *f.* joint; coupling, match-making. —ler, *m.* (—lers, *pl.* —ler), —lerin, *f.* match-maker, procurer. —lerhaft, —leriſch, *adj.* procuring, match-making.

[1]**Kur**, (*older* Cur,) *f.* (*pl.* —en) cure; medical *or* hygienic treatment; course of treatment; course of baths, taking the waters; health resort; er war in Karlsbad in der —, he was drinking the waters at Karlsbad; in der — haben, to treat; ſich in die — eines Arztes begeben, to consult a doctor, to undergo medical treatment; er iſt in der —, he is under medical treatment; he is taking the waters, the baths; mein Freund ging zur — nach Reichenhall, my friend went to Reichenhall for his health *or* to be treated; die — ſchlägt an, the cure is taking effect; Waſſer —, hydropathy. —ie'ren, *v.a.* to cure; er iſt —iert, he is cured, his health is restored; ſich —ieren laſſen, to go to be treated medically, to get cured. *Comp.* —arzt, *m.* physician at a health resort. —gaſt, *m.* patient at a health resort. —haus, *n.* pump-room, casino (*at watering-places*). —liſte, *f.* list of visitors at a watering-place, *etc.* —methode, *f.* method of treatment. —ort, *m.* health resort. —pfuſcher, *m.* quack. —pfuſcherei', *f.* quack practices. —ſaal, *m.* pump-room, casino.

[2]**Kur, Kür** (*obs.*), *f.* election; right of electing; electoral dignity; electorate. *Comp. usually:* electoral *or* of the electorate of . . . *e.g.* —bairiſch, *adj.* of the electorate of Bavaria. —brandenburg, *n.* electorate of Brandenburg. —erbe, *m.* hereditary prince of an electorate. —fürſt, *m.* elector (*in the old German empire*); der große —fürſt, the Great Elector, Frederick William of Brandenburg (*1640–88*). —fürſten=bank, *f.* electors' bench in the old German diet. —fürſten=tag, *m.* diet *or* meeting of German electors. —fürſtentum, *n.* electorate. —fürſtlich, *adj.* electoral. —haus, *n.* electoral house *or* family. —heſſiſch, *adj.* of the electorate of Hesse. —hut, *m.* electoral cap *or* crown. —länder, *pl.* electoral dominions. —mede, *f.* landlord's right to (*choose*) the best cattle. —pfalz, *f.* the Palatinate; der —fürſt von der Pfalz *or* von —pfalz, the Elector Palatine. —recht, *n.* right of electing (*an emperor*). —ſchwert, *n.* sword of the elector of Saxony. —würde, *f.* electoral dignity, electorship.

Kur—a'nd, *m.* (—an'den, *pl.* —an'den), —an'din, *f.* minor, ward. —ate'l, *f.* guardianship, trusteeship, curatorship.

Kuran'zen, (Koran'zen,) *v.a.* to give a p. a severe scolding, to blow a p. up.

Kü'raß, *m.* (—(ſ)ſes, *pl.* —(ſ)ſe) cuirass. —(ſſ)ie'r, *m.* (—(ſſ)iers, *pl.* —(ſſ)iere) cuirassier.

Kura'tor, *m.* (—s, *pl.* Kurato'ren) curator, guardian, trustee.

Kur'b—e, —el, *f.* (*pl.* —en, —eln) winch, crooked handle; crank; spit (*Typ.*); horns (*Artil.*); die —el am Fernſprecher drehen, to turn the handle of a telephone. —e(l)n, *v.n.* (*aux.* h.) to turn the winch. *Comp.* —el=achſe, *f.* cranked axle. —el=arm, *m.* crank-lever. —el=lager, *n.* crank bracket. —el=ſpieß, *m.* boar-spear. —el=ſtange, *f.* connecting-rod (*in locomotives*). —el=welle, *f.* crank-shaft. —el=zapfen, *m.* crank-pin.

Kür'bis, *m.* (—(ſ)ſes, *pl.* —(ſ)ſe) pumpkin, gourd. *Comp.* —baum, *m.* calabash tree. —flaſche, *f.* gourd-bottle. —förmig, *adj.* formed like a gourd. —gewächſe, *pl.* cucurbitaceous plants.

Kü'r—en, *v.a.* to choose, elect (*obs.*). *Comp.* —turnen, *n.* voluntary gymnastic exercises (*after the ordinary drill has been gone through*).

Kuria'l=ſtil, *m.* legal style.

Ku'rie, *f.* (*pl.* —n) curia; papal court; legislative assembly; Herren—, assembly of nobles.

Kurie'r, *m.* (—s, *pl.* —e) courier; express —reiten, to ride express. *Comp.* —ſtiefel, *m.* jackboot. —zug, *m.* express train.

Kurio's, *adj.* singular; curious; mir iſt ganz — zu Mute, I feel queer. —(ſ)itä't, *f.* (*pl.* —ſitäten) curiosity; rarity.

Kur'kum—a, *f.* turmeric. —i'n, *n.* root of turmeric plant, curcumine.

Kur'r—e, *f.* (*pl.* —en) turkey-hen; heath-hen; gurnet (*Icht.*). —en, *v.a.* & *n.* (*aux.* h.) *see* Knurren; to coo. —ig, *adj.* (*obs.*) fiery, untamed; strange; irritable. *Comp.* —hahn, *m.* turkey-cock.

Kurr—en'de, *f.* (*pl.* —n) procession and singing of poor schoolboys in the streets (*obs.*). these schoolboys collectively (*obs.*). —enda'ner, —en'den=ſchüler, *m.* poor schoolboy singing in the streets for bread (*e.g. Martin Luther*).

Kurre'nt, *adj.* current. *Comp.* —buchſtaben, *pl.* italics. —ſchrift, *f.* running hand. —ſchuld, *f.* running score.

Kurs, *m.* (—(ſ)es, *pl.* —(ſ)e) (rate of) exchange course (*of a ship or current*); exchange, rate of exchange; welchen — geben Sie für dieſen Wechſel? what rate of exchange do you give for this bill? die —(ſ)e ſind gefallen, the exchange has fallen; der — iſt pari, exchange is at par. *Comp.* —buch, *n.* time-table, railway guide, railway ABC, Bradshaw (*Eng.*), Appleton (*Amer.*). —zettel, *m.* exchange list.

Kürſch'ner, *m.* (—s, *pl.* —) furrier. —ei', *f.* furrier's trade, furriery. *Comp.* —gare, *f.* skin-dressing. —ware, *f.* furs and skins.

Kurſie'ren, *v.n.* (*aux.* h.) to circulate, to be current.

Kurſi'v, *m.adj.* cursive; — gedruckt, italicized, printed in italics. *Comp.* —druck, *m.* italics, printing in italics. —ſchrift, *f.* italics.

Kur'sus, *m.* (—, *pl.* Kur'se) course (*of lectures or lessons*).

Kurz (kür'zer, kür'z(e)st), I. *adj.* short, brief; abrupt; summary; concise, compendious; **—en Atem haben,** to be asthmatic *or* short of breath; **—er Auszug,** abstract, epitome; **ein —es Ende,** a hurried end; a little bit *or* way; **—e Seeen,** chopping sea; **—es Futter,** corn, oats, *etc.* (*opp. to* **langes Futter,** hay, straw, *etc.*); **—er Galopp,** canter; **ein —es Gesicht haben,** to be short-sighted; **—e Sicht,** short sight, short-date (*C.L.*); **ein —es Verfahren,** a summary proceeding; **—e Waren,** *pl.* hardware, petty wares; **—e Wechsel, —es Papier,** short (*dated*) bills; **— abbrechen,** to end abruptly; **— abfertigen,** to be short with, dismiss abruptly; **— abgestoßen,** staccato; **— abweisen,** to cut (*a p.*) short; **— angebunden sein,** to be short *or* sharp (*of speech*); **— erzählen,** to relate in few words; **sich — fassen,** to be brief; **einen — halten,** to keep a p. short (*of money, etc.*), to keep under; **— und klein hauen, schlagen,** to cut to pieces, beat to a jelly; **um es — zu machen,** to sum up, to be short, to cut a long story short; **den Kürzern ziehen, zu — kommen,** to be the loser; to get the worst of it; **in —em,** ere long, shortly; **— vorher,** a little while before; **— nachher, hernach, da(r)nach, darauf,** a little while afterwards; **über — oder lang,** sooner or later; **vor —em, seit —em,** only just, not long ago; **— und bündig,** concise, succinct; **— und gut,** in a word, briefly, plainly; **einen —weg Fritz nennen,** to call a p. simply Freddy; **einen um einen Kopf kürzer machen,** to behead a p.; **der langen Rede —er Sinn,** the pith of the matter; **etwas — kriegen,** to understand, get the knack of a thing; **—er Hand,** without a moment's hesitation. II. *adv.* in short, in a word. *Comp.* **—a'b,** *adv.* briefly, in a few words, abruptly. **—atmig,** *adj.* short-winded, asthmatic; broken-winded. **—dauernd,** *adj.* transient. **—flügelig,** *adj.* short-winged, brachypterous. **—gefaßt,** *adj.* concise; compact; succinct. **—gefesselt,** *adj.* short in the pasterns. **—haarig,** *adj.* short-haired; short in the nap. **—hörnig,** *adj.* short-horned. **—lebig,** *adj.* short-lived. **—leibig,** *adj.* short-waisted. **—messerschmied,** *m.* cutler. **—schluß,** *m.* short circuit (*electr.*). **—schreibekunst,** *f.* stenography, shorthand writing. **—schreiber,** *m.* short-hand writer. **—schrift,** *f.* short-hand writing, stenography. **—sichtig,** *adj.* near-sighted; short-sighted; of short date (*as bills*). **—silbig,** *adj.* short-syllabled; **—silbiger Mann,** man of few words. **—u'm,** *adv.* in short, to sum up. **—waren,** *f.pl.* smallwares made of metal, *etc.*; hardware. **—warenhändler,** *m.* hardware dealer. **—we'g,** *adv.* simply, plainly; offhand; curtly; only. **—weil,** *f.* pastime; **seine —weil mit einem haben,** to make sport of a p. **—weilen,** *v.r. & n.* (*aux.* **h.**) to divert, amuse (*oneself*). **—weilig,** *adj.* amusing, pleasant; facetious, merry.

Kür'ze, *f.* shortness, brevity; conciseness; short space of time; short syllable; **in (der) —,** shortly, soon, briefly, concisely; **in aller —,** with all possible despatch; **in (die) — bringen,** to abridge; **sich der — befleißigen,** to be brief; **—e ist der Rede** (*or* **des Witzes**) **Würze,** brevity is the soul of wit (*prov.*).

Kür'z—en, *v.a.* to shorten; to abbreviate, curtail; to dock (*accounts*); to beguile, while away (*time*); **einen um etwas —en,** to defraud, cheat a p. out of something. **—lich,** *adv.* lately, not long ago; shortly, soon; briefly, in few words. **—ung,** *f.* shortening; abbreviation.

Ku'schen, *v.r. & n.* (*aux.* **h.**) to crouch, to lie down; to submit, be quiet; **kusch (dich)!** lie down! (*to dogs*).

Kuß, *m.* (—(s)ses, *pl.* Küs'se) kiss; **einem einen — (or eine — Hand) zuwerfen,** to kiss one's hand to a person. **—lich,** *adj.* = küßlich. *Comp.* **—hand,** *f.* kissing the hand; **mit — Hand thun,** to do with pleasure; **einem —hände (or eine —hand) zuwerfen,** to kiss one's hand to a person.

Küs's—en, *v.a.* to kiss, salute with a kiss; to touch lightly; **einen wach —en,** to awake with a kiss *or* kisses. **—er,** *m.* (—ers, *pl.* —er), **—erin,** *f.* kisser. **—erei',** *f.* frequent kissing. **—(er)=ig, —(ß)=lich,** *adj.* kissable, made for kissing. **—(ß)lein,** *n.* little kiss; **ein —(ß)lein in Ehren kann niemand verwehren,** a chaste kiss need not be refused (*prov.*).

Küs'te, *f.* (*pl.* —n) coast, shore; strand, beach; **das Land längs der —,** the littoral; **an der — hinfahren,** to coast, sail along a coast; **angesichts der walliser —,** off the Welsh coast. *Comp.* **—n=aufnahme,** *m.* survey of the coast; surveyor's sketch of the coast. **—n=batterie,** *f.* shore-battery. **—n=befestigungen,** *pl.* maritime fortifications, shore defences. **—n=fahrer,** *m.* coaster. **—n=fahrt,** *f.* coasting. **—n=fluß,** *m.* small river rising near the coast. **—n=geschwader,** *n.* home squadron, channel-fleet. **—n=handel,** *m.* coasting trade. **—n=land,** *n.* land along the shore, maritime country. **—n=provinz,** *f.* maritime province. **—n=vertiefung,** *f.* indentation in the coast. **—n=wache,** *f.* coast-guard (*station*). **—n=wächter,** *m.* coast-guardsman. **—n=wachtschiff,** *n.* guard-ship; revenue cutter.

Küs'ter, *m.* (—s, *pl.* —) sacristan, sexton. **—ei',** *f.* office *or* dwelling of a sexton. **—in,** *f.* sacristan's wife; sextoness, female sacristan.

Ku'stos, *m.* (*pl.* Kusto'den) keeper, custodian; curator; catchword (*Typ.*); direction (*Mus.*).

Ku'te, *f.* small hole in the ground (*dial.*).

Kut'sch—e, *f.* (*pl.* —en) carriage; coach; **sich** (*dat.*) **—e und Pferde halten,** to keep one's carriage; **zweisitzige leichte —e,** victoria. **—er,** *m.* (—ers, *pl.* —er) coachman, driver; sour wine (*coll.*). **—ie'ren,** *v.n.* (*aux.* **h.** & **f.**) to drive in a carriage; to drive a coach. *Comp.* **—bock,** *m.* (*coach*) box. **—bock=decke,** *f.* hammer-cloth. **—en=bauer, —en=fabrikant,** *m.* coach-builder. **—en=geschirr,** *n.* carriage-harness. **—(en)=gestell,** *n.* frame of a carriage. **—(en)=himmel,** *m.* roof of a carriage. **—(en)=kasten,** *m.* body of a carriage; boot, box under the seat of a coach. **—en=leder,** *n.* apron. **—en=raum,** *m.* (**innerer**) inside of a carriage. **—en=reihe,** *f.* row of carriages. **—(en)=schlag,** *m.* carriage-door. **—en=thor,** *n.* porte cochère. **—en=tritt,** *m.* foot-board; carriage steps. **—er=bock,** *m.* box. **—er=handschuh,** *m.* driving-glove. **—er=sitz,** *m.* driving seat. **—er=spiel,** *n.* very good game of cards (for the one side) (*coll.*). **—er=stube,** *f.* servants' hall. **—er(=wein),** *m.* inferior wine.

Kut'te, *f.* (*pl.* —n) cowl; **die — anlegen,** to don the cowl, to turn monk. *Comp.* **—n=träger,** *m.* monk.

Kut'tel, *f.* (*pl.* —n) tripe; entrails. *Comp.* **—hof,** *m.* slaughter-house.

Kut'ter, *m.* (—s, *pl.* —) cutter (*Naut.*).

Kuve'rt, *n.* (—s, *pl.* —e) cover; envelope. **trocknes —,** dinner exclusive of wine.

Kux, *m.* (—es, *pl.* —e) share in a mine; claim. *Comp.* **—inhaber,** *m.* holder of a mining share, adventurer.

L

L, l, *n.* L, l; *as abbr.* **L.** = **Länge,** length, longitude; **l.** = **lies,** read; *for other abbreviations see Index of abbreviations at the end of the German-English part.*

Laat'sche, *f. see* **Latsche.**

Lab, *n.* (—es) rennet. —en, *v.a.* to coagulate with rennet. *Comp.* —kraut, *n.* Galium. —magen, *m.* rennet-bag.

Lab'be, *f.* (*pl.* —n) hanging lip; mullet (*Icht.*); long-tailed gull (*Orn.*). —rig, *adj.* insipid, soft (*of food*). —rn, *v.a. & n.* (*aux.* h.) to lap, lick up; to make a lapping sound; to twaddle, blab; to chat.

Lab'berdan, *m.* (—es, *pl.* —e) salt-cod.

La'be, *f.* (*pl.* —n) refreshment; comfort.

La'b—en, *v.a.* to refresh, recruit, revive; to comfort; to delight; sich mit Speisen —en, to take some refreshment; sich an einer Speise —en, to enjoy a dish thoroughly, to eat of a dish to one's heart's content; sich an Speise und Trank —en, to partake of refreshments. —sal, *n.* (—sals, *pl.* —sale) refreshment; cordial; comfort. —ung, *f.* refreshing; refreshment, cordial; recreation. *Comp.* —e=becher, —e=kelch, *m.*, —e=schale, *f.*, —e=trunk, *m.* refreshing cup *or* draught, cordial. —e=wein, *m.* generous wine, cordial.

Labe't, *n.*; — machen, to loo, to beast (*Cards*).

Labi—a'l, *m.*; (—als, *pl.* —ale) labial sound *or* letter. —um, *n.* (*pron.* La'bium) (—ums, *pl.* —ia, —ien) languet (*in organs*).

Labor—a'nt, *m.* (—an'ten, *pl.* —an'ten) chemical student, student in a laboratory (*obs.*). —ato'rium, *n.* (—atoriums, *pl.* —atorien) laboratory. —ie'ren, *v.n.* (*aux.* h.) (an einer Krankheit *or* unter einer Schwierigkeit) to labour under (*a disease; a difficulty, etc.*).

Labyrin'thisch, *adj.*, labyrinthian, mazy.

Lach'bar, *adj.* that may be tapped (*for resin*).

¹**La'ch—e**, *f.* (*pl.* —en) cut in a tree, mark; tree marked; path cut through a thicket. —en, *v.a.* to cut *or* blaze trees; to cut a path through a thicket. *Comp.* —baum, *m.* tree marked; boundary-tree.

²**La'che**, *f.* (*pl.* —n) laugh, laughter; eine — aufschlagen, to burst out laughing; eine große — aufschlagen, to burst into a tremendous laugh.

³**La'ch—e**, *f.* (*pl.* —en) pool, puddle, stagnant water. —ig, *adj.* marshy, sloughy.

Lä'ch—eln, I. *v.n.* (*aux.* h.) to smile (über einen *or* eine S., at a p. *or* a th.); einem —eln, to smile upon *or* at a p.; albern —eln, to simper, sniggle; geziert —eln, to smirk; höhnisch, spöttisch —eln, to sneer. II. *v.a.* to smile (*applause, etc.*); sein Auge —elte Freude, joy beamed in his eyes; wir beide —elten „ja", we both assented by a smile; durch —eln bringen zu . . ., to smile into . . . III. *v. imp.*; es —elt mich, it makes me smile (*obs.*). IV. *subst. n.* smile; simper; sneer. —erbar, (*sl.*) *see* —erlich. —erlich, *adj. & adv.* inclined to laugh; laughable; ridiculous; droll, comical; sich —erlich machen, to make a fool of oneself; etwas ins —erliche ziehen, to turn s.th. into ridicule; einen —erlich machen, to make fun of s.o., to turn a person into ridicule; mir ist gar nicht —erlich zu Mute, I am in no laughing mood; I am very serious; I feel depressed. —erlichkeit, *f.* absurdity. —ern, *v.a.*; es —ert mich, it makes me laugh, I can't help laughing (*obs.*). —ler, *m.* (—lers, *pl.* —ler), —lerin, *f.* smiler; empty head, flatterer.

La'ch—en, I. *v.n.* (*aux.* h.) to laugh; über (einen *or* eine S.) —en, to laugh at; der Thoren —en, to laugh at fools (*high style*); einem —en, to smile on a p.; ihm —t das Herz im Leibe, his heart leaps for joy; his heart rejoices; aus vollem Halse —en, to laugh heartily, uproariously; —en, daß einem die Augen übergehen, to laugh until the tears come; in die Faust —en *or* sich (*dat.*) ins Fäustchen —en, to laugh in one's sleeve; das Glück —t ihm, Fortune smiles upon him *or* is favourable to him; dem Tapferen —t das Glück, Fortune favours the brave (*prov.*); wer zuletzt —t, —t am besten, those laugh best who laugh last (*prov.*); wer gewinnt hat gut —en, let him laugh that wins; du kannst wohl —en, you may consider yourself lucky indeed; hier ist nichts zu —en, there is nothing to laugh at; das ist nicht zum —en, that is no laughing matter, no joke. II. *v.a.* sich tot, sich (*dat.*, einen Buckel *or* den Buckel voll —en, to die *or* split one's sides with laughing; einen aus dem Schlafe —en, to awake a p. with laughter; ha, —te der König! ha! cried the king, laughing. III. *subst. n.* laughter, laugh; sich (*dat.*) das —en verbeißen, to choke one's laughter; unter —en, laughingly. —end, *p. & adj.* laughing, smiling; pleasant; glad. —er, *m.* (—ers, *pl.* —er) laugher; er hat die —er auf seiner Seite, he has the laugh on his side. *Comp.* —anfall, *m.* fit of laughter, laughing fit. —ens=wert, *adj.* laughable, ridiculous. —gas, *n.* laughing gas. —krampf, *m.* convulsive *or* hysterical laughter. —lust, *f.* inclination to laugh. —lustig, *adj.* fond of laughing *or* mirth, merry. —maul, *n.* giggler. —muskel, *m.* muscle of risibility. —taube, *f.* turtle dove; merry girl (*sl.*). —zahn, *m.* front tooth.

Lachs, *m.* (—(s)es, *pl.* —(s)e) salmon; einen — (im Skat) fangen, to win the game, the loser standing the treat; echter doppelter —, real Dantzig brandy twice distilled (*of the 'Salmon' distillery*). *Comp.* —brut, *f.* salmon fry. —fang, *m.* salmon catching; salmon leap; salmon-season. —farbig, *adj.* salmon-coloured. —reuse, *f.* salmon weir. —schinken, *m.* fillet of smoked ham.

Lach'ter, *n.* (—s, *pl.* —) & *f.* (*pl.* —n) fathom.

Lack, *m.* (—(e)s, *pl.* —e) lac, gumlac; varnish, lacker; wall flower (*Bot.*). —ie'ren, *v.a.* to lacker, varnish; to cheat, take in (*coll.*); da war mein Freund der —ierte, there my friend was thoroughly taken in (*coll.*); —ierte Waren, japanned wares. —ie'rer, *m.* (—ierers, *pl.* —ierer) varnisher, japanner. *Comp.* —arbeit, *f.* Japan ware; lacquered work. —farbe, *f.* wall-flower colour; lac dye, lake. —firnis, *m.* lacquer, varnish. —leder, *n.* patent leather. —stiefel, *pl.* patent-leather boots, dress boots.

Lackei', *see* Lakai.

Lack'mus, *m.* (—(s)es) litmus. *Comp.* —kraut, *n.*, —pflanze, *f.* turnsole.

La'dan; —gummi, —harz, *n.* ladanum.

La'de, *f.* (*pl.* —n) box, chest, case; trunk; press; frame (*Weav.*); sounding-board (*of organs*); meeting of a guild *or* society; place of meeting; toothless part of a horse's jaws; Bundes —, ark of the covenant (*B.*).

¹**La'd—en**, I. *ir.v.a.* to load, lade; to freight; to load (*a gun*); to charge (*Phys.*); blind —en, to load with blank cartridge; scharf —en, to load with ball; ins Schiff —en, to ship; er hat schwer *or* schief geladen, he is half seas over; auf sich (*acc.*) —en, to draw upon oneself, to incur; ein Verbrechen auf sich —en, to commit a crime. II. *m. see* Laden. —er, *m.* (—ers, *pl.* —er) loader; longshoreman (*in shipping trade*). —ung, *f.* loading, lading; freight; cargo; burden (*Naut.*); charge, load; volley; full quantity; ein in —ung liegendes Schiff, a vessel taking in cargo; in —ung liegen nach, to be loading for; die —ung anbrechen, to break bulk; —ung einnehmen, to take in cargo *or* freight; ohne —ung, empty, in ballast; volle —ung, full freight. *Comp.* —e=baum, *m.* boom. —e=brief, *m.* bill of lading. —e=bühne, *f.* platform for loading goods. —e=frist, *f.* time allowed for loading. —e=geld, *n.* charge for lading. —e=maß, *n.*, gun-charge measure. —e=pforte.

f. ballast-port (*Naut.*). **—e=pfropf,** *m.* wad. **—e=schaufel,** *f.* gun-ladle, charger (*Artil.*). **—e=schein,** *see* **—ebrief.** **—e=stock,** *m.* ramrod. **—e=stopfer,** *m.* rammer. **—e=tasche,** *f.* cartridge-box. **—e=wasserlinie,** *f.* load-line. **—e=zeug,** *n.* implements for loading guns. **—ungs=fähigkeit,** *f.* tonnage of a ship. **—ungs=flasche,** *f.* Leyden jar. **—ungs=hafen,** *m.* lading-port. **—ungs=interessent,** *m.* person interested in a cargo, part-owner of a cargo. **—ungs=strom,** *m.* current of charge (*Electr.*). **—ungs=verzeichnis,** *n.* ship's manifest.

²La'd—en, *ir.* (*& obs. reg.*) *v.a.* to invite; to cite, summon. **—ung,** *f.* invitation; summons. *Comp.* **—e=brief,** *m.* note of invitation; summons. **—e=geld,** *n.* fee paid for a summons (*Law*).

La'den, *m.* (—s), I. (*pl.* —) shutter, window-shutter; sash; **die — der Läden waren geschlossen,** the shutters of the shops were down. II. (*pl.* **Läden**) shop, stall, store; portlid (*Naut.*); **einen — anlegen,** to set up a shop; **einen — halten,** to keep a shop. *Comp.* **—bank,** *f.* counter. **—besitzer,** *m.* shopkeeper. **—bursch,** *m.* shop-boy. **—dieb,** *m.* shop-lifter. **—diener,** *m.* shopkeeper's clerk, shopman. **—fenster,** *n.* sky-light; shop-front, shop-window; show-window. **—flügel,** *m.* movable half of a window shutter. **—gehülfe,** *m.* shop-man, assistant. **—hüter,** *m.* commodity that will not go off, drug in the market; shopkeeper (*coll.*). **—kasse,** *f.* till. **—jungfer,** *f.*, **—mädchen,** *n.* shop-woman, shop-girl. **—meister,** *m.* master-tradesman of a company. **—preis,** *m.* selling-price, retail price; published price (*of books*). **—riegel,** *m.* sash-bolt. **—schwengel,** **—schwung,** *m.* counter-jumper (*coll.*). **—tisch,** *m.* counter. **—zins,** *m.* shop-rent.

Lädst, Lädt, *2 & 3 p. sing. pres. ind. of* **laden.**

Lafet'te, *f.* (*pl.* —n) gun-carriage; **auf die — bringen, heben,** to mount a gun (*upon its carriage*); **von der — abheben,** to dismount a gun. *Comp.* **—n=halter,** *m.* wedge put under a gun-carriage at sea. **—n=schwanz,** *m.* trail of a gun-carriage. **—n=stange,** *f.* bolt pin of a gun-carriage. **—n=wand,** *f.* cheek of a gun-carriage; bed of a great gun.

Laf'fe, *m.* (—n, *pl.* —n, *dim.* **Läff'chen**) fop, puppy. *Comp.* **—n=mäßig,** *adj.* puppyish.

Läffelei', *f.* (*pl.* **—en**) courting, toying, caressing.

Läff'eln, *v.a. & n.* (*aux.* **h.**) to toy, dally, fondle.

Lag, Lä'ge, *1 (& 3) p. sing. imperf. ind. & subj. of* **liegen.**

La'ge, *f.* (*pl.* —n) situation, aspect, site, position; attitude, posture; bearing (*of a coast*); guard (*Fenc.*); state, condition; circumstances; incident; fate; layer, stratum, bed; couch, coat (*of paint*); tier (*of guns*); gathering (*Typ.*); course (*Arch.*); **in —,** on one's guard; **außer —,** off one's guard; **bei dieser — der Dinge** *or* **dieser Sach—,** under these circumstances; **eine schlimme —,** a hard case; **ein Schiff mit drei —n,** a three-decker; **volle —,** broadside. **—r,** *n.* (—rs, *pl.* —r *or* (*dial.*) **Läger**) place for lying down, couch, bed; sick-bed; sickness, illness; lair, den, hole, cover, *etc.* (*of beasts*); camp, encampment bed, stratum, layer; stock, supply; storehouse, warehouse; guard (*Fenc.*); stand (*for casks*); dregs, sediment; stocking-weaver's frame; groove for the band in the stock (*of a gun*); **das —r aufnehmen,** to take an inventory of stock in hand; **ein —r aufschlagen (abstecken),** to pitch (*mark out*) a camp; **sein —r machen,** to pitch one's tent *or* tents; **auf —r haben,** to stock, have *or* keep in stock; **ein —r beziehen,** to move into a camp; **aufs —r bringen,** to warehouse, store (up); **ein unruhiges —r haben,** not to sleep, to be a restless sleeper; **ein langes —r haben,** to have a long illness; **vom —r aufstehen,** to rise from a bed of sickness; **nach halbjährigem —r** after being confined to bed for six month *Comp.* **—n=weise,** *adv.* in layers; in tiers in strata; **—nweise übereinander legen,** to stratify.

Lä'gel, *n.* (—s, *pl.* —) barrel, keg (*of wine*); cruise (*of oil*); cask (*of steel*); cringle (*Naut.*).

La'ger— (*in comp.*) **—apfel,** *m.* storing-apple. **—aufseher,** *m.* store-keeper. **—balken,** *m.* beam laid over piers of a bridge; windbeam. **—bestand,** *m.* inventory of goods. **—bier,** *n.* beer brewed for keeping, lager (beer); **ein Glas —bier,** a glass of lager. **—buch,** *n.* merchant's stock-book; register. **—diener,** *m.* warehouse clerk. **—faß,** *n.* pipe, vat, tun kept in the cellar. **—fieber,** *n.* camp-fever. **—geld,** *n.*, **—zins,** *m.*, **—miete,** *f.*, **—gebühren,** *pl.* charge for warehousing; storage, warehouse rent. **—gerät,** *n.* camp-furniture. **—gewicht,** *n.* standard weight. **—haus,** *n.* warehouse, storehouse; stock, bonded stores. **—holz,** *n.* fallen timber; sleeper (*of wooden bridges*); stand for casks. **—hütte,** *f.* camp-hut; barrack. **—konto,** *n.* warehouse account. **—meister,** *m.* quarter-master; overseer of a warehouse. **—obst,** *n.* fruit for keeping. **—platz,** *m.* place of encampment; place for storing; bed (*Geol.*). **—punkt,** *m.* place of the trunnions (*Artil.*). **—raum,** *m.* storeroom. **—ruhr,** *f.* dysentery in a camp. **—seuche,** *f.* infectious camp disorder. **—statt, —stätte,** *f.* resting-place; couch, bed, lodging; encampment. **—wache,** *f.* camp-watch. **—wall,** *m.* rampart; shoal (*Naut.*). **—wand,** *f.* solid rock wall. **—wein,** *m.* wine for keeping.

Lä'gerig, *suff.* (*in comp.* =) -lying; *e.g.* **bett—,** lying in bed, confined to one's bed.

La'ger—n, I. *v.n.* (*aux.* **h.** *&* **s.**) *& r.* to lie down, rest; to encamp, be encamped; to couch, harbour; to lie spread out, to be stored; to be beaten down; to be in layers; **die Schatten hatten sich über die Ebene gelagert,** the shadows lay upon the plain; **er ließ die Kameele sich —n,** he made his camels to kneel down (*B.*). II. *v.a.* to lay down; to place, post; to encamp (*troops*), pitch (*tents*); to store; to beat down; **ich will selbst meine Schafe weiden und ich will sie —n,** I will feed my flock and will cause them to lie down (*B.*). III. *subst.n.* **—ung,** *f.* lying down; recumbent position; encampment; storing; stratification.

Lagu'ne, *f.* (*pl.* —n) lagoon.

Lahm, *adj. & adv.* lame; halt; crippled; impotent; paralyzed; languid; paltry; loose, shaky; **ein —er, eine —e,** a lame person, a cripple; **— an Gliedern,** paralyzed; **— gehen,** to limp. **—en,** *v.n.* (*aux.* **h.** *&* **s.**) to be lame, to be limping. **—heit,** *f.* lameness.

Läh'm—e, *see* **—ung**; spring-halt (*Vet.*).

Läh'm—en, *v.a.* to lame, disable, cripple; to paralyze; to enervate, paralyze, blunt; **gelähmt,** paralyzed. **—ung,** *f.* laming, maiming; lameness; paralysis; palsy.

Lahn, *m.* (—es, *pl.* —e) thin metal plate; tinsel; **schraubenförmiger —,** ribbon-wire. *Comp.* **—gold,** *n.* tinsel gold. **—tresse,** *f.* gold *or* silver lace.

Laib, *m.* (—es, *pl.* —e) loaf (*of bread*); **ein — Käse,** a cheese. **—le,** *n.* small loaf (*dial.*).

Laich, *m. & n.* (—es) spawn. **—e,** *f.* spawning time. **—en,** *v.n.* (*aux.* **h.**) to spawn. *Comp.* **—teich,** *m.* breeding-pond. **—zeit,** *see* **—e.**

Lai'e, *m.* (—n, *pl.* —n) layman; person not learned, uninitiated; **die —n,** the laity; **— in einer Kunst,** one who knows nothing of an art, uninitiated. **—n=haft,** *adj.* belonging to the laity; uninitiated, unprofessional. **—n=schaft,** *f.* laity; state of a layman. *Comp.* **—n=bruder,** *m.* lay-brother. **—n=güter,** *pl.* temporalities.

—n=priester, *m.* lay-priest. —n=stand, *m.* laity. —n=unterricht, *m.* instruction by laymen. —n=welt, *f.* laity, laymen.
Lai'lich, Lai'lach, *see* Leilach.
Lakai', *m.* (—s *and* —en, *pl.* —en) lackey, flunkey, footman. *Comp.* —en=haft, *adj.* flunkey-like, cringing. —en=sitz, *m.* dickey, rumble.
La'ke, *f.* (*pl.* —n) brine, pickle.
La'ken, *n.* (—s, *pl.* —) cloth for covering; sheet; tablecloth; shroud; sail.
Lako'nisch, *adj. & adv.* laconic.
Lakrit'ze, *f.* (*pl.* —n) (Spanish) licorice; eine Stange —, a stick of licorice.
Lal'len, *v.a. & n.* (*aux.* h.) to speak thick; to stammer; to lisp; to babble, speak imperfectly.
La'ma, *n.* (—s, *pl.* —s) lama.
Lamais'mus, *m.* the Buddhist religion in Thibet and Mongolia.
Lam'bertsnuß, *f.* filbert.
Lamel'le, *f.* lamina. —n, *pl.* leaflets.
Lamentie'ren, *v.a.* to lament.
Lamen'to, *n.* (—s, *pl.* —s) lamentation, wail.
Lamet'ta, *n.* lametta, angels' hair (*decoration on Christmas trees*).
Laminie'ren, to flatten (*metal*).
Lamm, *n.* (—s, *pl.* Läm'mer) lamb. *Comp.* —artig, *adj.* lamb-like. —braten, *m.* roast lamb. —fell, *n.* lamb's skin. —fleisch, *n.* lamb. —fromm, —herzig, *adj.* gentle as a lamb. —s=viertel, *n.* quarter of lamb. —zeit, *f.* lambing-time.
Lämm'—chen, (—chens, *pl.* —chens), —lein, (—leins, *pl.* —lein) *n.* lambkin.
Lam'men, *v.a.* (*aux.* h.) to bring forth lambs.
Läm'mer, *pl. see* Lamm. —chen, *n.* (—chens, *pl.* —chen) lambkin; (*pl.*) fleecy clouds; catkins. *Comp.* —geier, *m.* lammergeir; large vulture. —hirt, *m.* shepherd. —hüpfen, *n.* dancing of young girls among themselves without any gentlemen (*coll.*). —schwänzchen, *n.* tail of a lamb; yarrow (*Bot.*); lustig wie ein —schwänzchen, as merry as a lark. —wolke, *f.* cirrus. —wolle, *f.* lamb's-wool.
Lam'pe, *f.* (*pl.* —n) lamp; (*pl.*) footlights; auf die — gießen, to wet one's whistle (*vulg.*); er hat keinen Docht in seiner —, he has no brains (*coll.*). *Comp.* —n=anzünder, *m.* lamp-lighter. —n=boden, *m.* base of a lamp; bracket. —n=brenner, *m.* burner —n=cylinder, *m.* (lamp-)chimney. —n=docht, *m.* (lamp-)wick. —n=fieber, *n.* stage-fever, stage-fright; das —n-fieber haben, to be suffering from stage-fever; to be afraid of appearing before the public. —n=gestell, *n.* lamp-post; candlestick (*in theatres*). —n=glocke, *f.* lamp-shade *or* globe. —n=hell, *adj.* lit up *or* lighted by lamps. —n=licht, *n.*, —n=schein, *m.* lamp-light. —n=putzer, *m.* lamp-lighter; candle-snuffer. —n=schimmer, *m.* subdued light of a lamp. —n=schirm, *m.* lamp-shade. —n=untersatz, *m.* lamp-stand.
Lampio'n, *m.* (—s, *pl.* —s) Chinese lantern.
Lampre'te, *f.* (*pl.* —n) lamprey.
Land, *n.* (—es) land (*as opp to water*); country (*as opp. to town*); land, soil, ground; plain, arable land; (*pl.* Län'der) piece of ground, bed, plot; (*pl.* —e (*poet.*) & Län'der) country, region, territory, state; inhabitants of a country: über —, by land, overland; das feste —, terra firma, continent, mainland; Platt—, plattes —, low country, plain; Hoch —, highlands, mountainous country; an das — steigen, to land, to go ashore; vom —e stoßen, to put to sea; auf das — gehen, to go ashore; to go into the country; auf dem —e, in the country; über — gehen, to go across country; to go for a journey; zu Wasser und zu —e, by sea and by land; hier zu —e, in this country: das ist des —es nicht der Brauch, that is not customary here; Einfalt (Unschuld *or* Gänschen) vom —e, silly goose, country cousin; außer —es, abroad; — und Leute regieren, to govern a country; des —es verweisen, to exile; woher des —es? from what country? seitdem sind viele Tage ins — gegangen, many a day has passed since then; aus aller Herrn Ländern, from all countries, from all over the world; alle —e sind seiner Ehre voll, the whole earth is full of his glory (*B.*); das heilige —, the Holy Land; das — der Phantasie, the realm of fancy; das — der Träume, dreamland; das — der Elfen, fairyland; das gelobte —, the land of promise, Canaan; bleibe im —e und nähre dich redlich, dwell in the land, and thou shalt be fed (*prov.*). —bar, *adj.* fit for landing; accessible. —en, *v.a. & n.* (*aux.* h. & s.) to land, disembark; to invade. —ung, *f.* landing, debarcation. *Comp.* —adel, *m.* provincial nobility; landed gentry. —am=mann, *m.* Swiss magistrate. —amt, *n.* office in the country; provincial court of justice; land-office; land-court. —anker, *m.* shore anchor. —anwachs, *m.* alluvium. —arbeit, *f.* agricultural labour. —armee, *f.* land-forces. —arzt, *m.* country doctor. —auf=enthalt, *m.* sojourn in the country. —auf=nahme, *f.* survey of the country, topography. —ausschuß, *m.* provincial militia; national committee. —bank, *f.* provincial bank. —bär, *m* common brown bear. —bau, *m.* agriculture. —bauer, *m.* farmer; peasant. —baumeister, *m.* inspector of public buildings; country architect *or* surveyor. —besitzer, *m.* landed proprietor. —bettler, *m.* tramp. —bewohner, *m.* dweller in the country. —bote, *m.* country messenger *or* carrier. —brief=bestellgebühr, *f.* rural tax to defray the cost of a letter-carrier. —buch, *n.* public register of landed property; provincial code; das alte englische —buch, Doomsday-book. —drost, *m.* chief magistrate of a district (*in the former kingdom of Hanover*). —drostei', *f.* High Bailiwick, district or province (*in the former kingdom of Hanover until 1866*). —edel=mann, *m.* country-nobleman; country-squire. —eigentum, *n.* landed property. —eigen=tümer, —eig(e)ner, *m.* landed proprietor. —ein'wärts, *adv.* up the country, inland. —enge, *f.* isthmus. —erbe, *m.* heir to landed property. —fahrer, *m.* rambler; vagrant. —feste, *f.* embankment. —festung, *f.* inland fortress. —flagge, *f.* flag hoisted when land is descried. —flüchtig, *adj.* fugitive; —flüchtig werden, to fly one's country. —flüchtigkeit, *f.* voluntary exile. —fracht, *f.* carriage. —fracht=wesen, *n.* carrying trade by land. —fräulein, *n.*, —jungfer, *f.* country-girl, young lady from the country. —fremd, *adj.* foreign; strange to *or* stranger in a country; quite strange *or* new. —friede(n), *m.* public peace; treaty relating to public peace; dem —frieden nicht trauen, to suspect, be upon one's guard. —friedens=bruch, *m.* breach *or* violation of the public peace. —fuhre, *f.* land-carriage; conveyance by land. —gängig, *adj.* current; epidemic. —geistliche(r), *m.* country clergyman. —gemeinde, *f.* village community; country parish. —gericht, *n.* county court; assize; petty sessions. —gerichts=rat, *m.* counsellor of a provincial court. —gerichts=tag, *m.* court-day. —graf, *m.* landgrave. —gräfin, *f.* landgravine. —gräflich, *adj.* belonging to a landgrave. —grenze, *f.* landmark; boundary. —gültig, *adj.* valid, current, legal; —gültiges Gesetz, common law, law of the land. —gut, *n.* estate, manor, country-seat. —han=del, *m.* inland trade, trade in the country, overland trade. —haus, *n.* country-house; house

where the states of a country meet. **—jäger,** *m.* gendarme; mounted policeman. **—jäger=meister,** *m.* grand master of the chase, *etc.;* master of the hounds. **—jugend,** *f.* young people of a village. **—junker,** *m.* country squire; rustic. **—kammer,** *f.* provincial board of finance. **—karte,** *f.* map. **—karten=druck,** *m.* map-printing. **—karten=kunde,** *f.* map-reading. **—karten=stich,** *m.* map engraving. **—karten=sammlung,** *f.* atlas. **—kennung,** *f.* land *or* sea marks. **—kirche,** *f.* country *or* village church. **—krämer,** *m.* country-shop-keeper; pedlar. **—krieg,** *m.* war on land. **—kundig,** *adj.* knowing the country well; well known, notorious. **—kutsche,** *f.* stage-coach. **—läufer,** *m.*, **—läuferin,** *f.* vagabond, tramp. **—läufig,** *adj.* strolling, vagrant; customary, ordinary, current; idiomatic. **—leben,** *n.* country-life. **—leute,** *pl.* country people. **—luft,** *f.* country air. **—lust,** *f.* country sport. **—macht,** *f.* land-forces, the army; continental power. **—mädchen,** *n.* country-girl, girl from the country. **—mann,** *m.* countryman; farmer, peasant. **—mark,** *f.* boundary of a country; country, territory. **—marschall,** *m.* marshal of a province. **—maß,** *n.* standard measure. **—messer,** *m.* land-surveyor. **—messerei',** **—meßkunst,** **—messung,** *f.* land-surveying; practical geometry. **—miliz,** *f.* yeomanry, provincial militia. **—nähe,** *f.* land-fall (*Naut.*). **—partie,** *f.* picnic, excursion in(to) the country. **—pfarre,** *f.* country living. **—pfarrer,** **—prediger,** *m.* country parson; **—prediger von Wakefield,** Vicar of Wakefield. **—pfleger,** *m.* governor *or* prefect of a province. **—plage,** *f.* natural scourge *or* calamity, public nuisance. **—polizei,** *f.* rural police, gendarmery. **—pomeranze,** *f.* unsophisticated country girl; country miss (*coll.*). **—ralle,** *f.* corncrake, landrail. **—rat,** *m.* sub-prefect, the head of the administration of a Prussian district (*Kreis*); cantonal council (*in Switzerland*). **—ratte,** *f.* land-rat; landsman, landlubber. **—recht,** *n.* civil code, statute law; common law. **—rechtlich,** *adj.* according to common law. **—regen,** *m.* general rain thoughout the country. **—reise,** *f.* overland journey; journey into the country. **—reiter,** *m.* mounted gendarme *or* police officer. **—reiterei',** *f.* mounted police; office *or* district of the 'Landreiter.' **—rentmeister,** *m.* receiver of the revenues of a country *or* district; land-steward. **—richter,** *m.* junior judge in a county-court; sheriff of a county. **—rücken,** *m.* ridge (of land). **—saß,** *m.* resident in a country; freeholder; feudal lord. **—sässig,** *adj.* having the rights of a freeholder *or* feudatory. **—scheide,** *f.* boundary. **—schmarotzer,** *m.* stack parasite. **—schnecke,** *f.* common snail, slug. **—schreiber,** *m.* (*anal. to*) clerk to the petty sessions. **—schule,** *f.* village *or* country school. **—see,** *m.* lake. **—ser = Landsmann,** (*coll.*). **—seuche,** *f.* epidemic. **—sitz,** *m.* country-seat. **—s=knecht,** (**Lanzknecht** *is a bad spelling,*) *m.* common foot soldier, hired trooper, mercenary, (XVI. cent.) lansquenet. **—s=leute,** *pl.* countrymen, compatriots; **er und sie sind —sleute,** both he and she come from the same country. **—s=mann,** *m.*, **—s=männin,** *f.* compatriot, countryman; **was für ein —s=mann sind Sie?** from what country do you come *or* hail? what is your native country? **er ist ein —smann von Ihnen,** he is a countryman of yours. **—s=männisch,** *adj.* like a countryman. **—s=mannschaft,** *f.* state of belonging to the same country; fellow-countrymen; association of students from the same country. **—soldat,** *m.* private, soldier of the land-forces; (*pl.*) militia, yeomanry. **—spitze,** *f.* cape, promontory, headland. **—stadt,** *f.* country town; inland town. **—stand,** *m.* one of the states of a country; deputy, representative, member; **die —stände,** the states (*coll.*). **—ständisch,** *adj.* relating to the states of a country; **—ständische Verfassung,** representative government. **—stand=schaft,** *f.* members of the states, deputies (*coll.*); dignity of deputy *or* representative **—standsrecht,** *n.* right of imperial representation. **—steuer,** *f.* land-tax. **—straße,** *f.* highroad, highway. **—streicher,** *m.*, **—streicherin,** *f.* tramp. **—streicherei',** *f.* vagrancy. **—strich,** *m.*, **—strecke,** *f.* tract of land, district; climate. **—sturm,** *m.* storm on land; general summons and levy of the people; last reserve (*comprising all men capable of bearing arms that are not included in the* '*Linie,*' *the* '*Reserve,*' *and the* '*Landwehr*'); local militia; **Krähwinkler —sturm,** militia of Gotham. **—sturz,** *m.* land-slip. **—tafel,** *f.* map; register office; public register of landed property. **—tag,** *m.* diet; meeting of the chambers *or* legislative assembly. **—tagen,** *v.n.* to hold a diet (*insep.*). **—tags=abgeordnete(r),** *m.* deputy to the diet. **—tags=abschied,** *m.* final resolution of the government laid before the assembled states; prorogation. **—tags=fähig,** *adj.*, having the right of assisting and voting at a diet. **—tags=verhandlungen,** *pl.* transactions of the diet. **—transport,** *m.* land-carriage, over-land-conveyance. **—truppen,** *pl.* land-forces. **—üblich,** *adj.* usual, customary in a country. **—ungs=boot,** *n.* shore-boat. **—ungs=ort,** **—ungs=platz,** *m.* landing-place. **—ungs=truppen,** *pl.* troops *or* forces ready for landing. **—vogt,** *m.* governor of a province, high bailiff. **—vogtei',** *f.* dignity, office, district *or* dwelling of a governor of a province. **—volk,** *n.* country-people; peasantry. **—wärts,** *adv.* landward; **tief —wärts,** far inland. **—wehr,** *f.* any work for the protection of the country; second reserve (*between the* '*Reserve*' *and the* '*Landsturm*'); militia, yeomanry. **—wehrmann,** *m.* militia-man. **—wein,** *m.* wine of the country. **—wind,** *m.* land breeze. **—wirt,** *m.* husbandman, farmer; **Bund der —wirte,** farmers' alliance. **—wirtschaft,** *f.* farming, husbandry. **—wirtschaftlich,** *adj.* agriculture; **—wirtschaftlicher Arbeiter,** agricultural labourer; **—wirtschaftliche Ausstellung,** agricultural show; **—wirtschaftliche Geräte,** farming implements. **—wohnung,** *f.* country-house. **—wort,** *n.* provincialism. **—zeichen,** *n.* land-mark. **—zins,** *m.* field-rent. **—zunge,** *f.* neck *or* tongue of land, point.

Lan'dauer, *m.* (**—s,** *pl.* **—**) landau.

Länd'—chen, *n.* (**—chens,** *pl.* **—chen**) little country. **—e,** (*pl.* **—en**) landing-place (*obs.*). **—erei',** *f.* landed property; domain, territory. **—ler,** *m.* (**—lers,** *pl.* **—ler**) slow country waltz. **—lich,** *adj.* rural, country-like; customary in a country; **—lich, sittlich,** other countries, other customs (*prov.*); **—lich, schändlich,** rural and bad. **—lichkeit,** *f.* rusticity, ruralness. *Comp.* **—er=kenntnis,** **—er=kunde,** *f.* knowledge of (foreign) countries; geographical knowledge; geography. **—er=los,** *adj.* without lands; bereft of country. **—er=reich,** **—er=gewaltig,** *adj.* possessed of many lands *or* provinces. **—er=sucht,** *f.* thirst for territory *or* conquest, land grabbing. **—er=teilung,** *f.* distribution of *or* into provinces.

Lan'des— (*in comp.*) **—adel,** *m.* nobility of a country. **—älteste(r),** *m.* president *or* deputy of the nobility of a country. **—anleihe,** *f.* domestic loan. **—anwalt,** *m.* president of a provincial court. **—archiv,** *n.* national archives. **—art,** *f.* soil and climate of a country;

national character and customs. —aufnahme, *f.* survey of the country, topography. —ausschuß, *m.* committee of the states *or* chambers; permanent committee, commission. —bank, *f.* national bank. —beschaffenheit, *see* —art. —beschreibung, *f.* topography. —erzeugnis, *n.* home-produce; product of a country. —flagge, *f.* national flag. —fürst, *m.* reigning prince, sovereign. —fürstin, *f.* sovereign princess of a country. —gebiet, *n.* territory. —gebrauch, —brauch, *m.* custom of a country. —gericht, *n.* supreme court. —geschichte, *f.* history of a country. —gesetz, *n.* law of the land; die geschriebenen —gesetze, statute law. —gestüt(e), *n.* national stock-stud. —gewächs, *n.* home-produce. —grenze, *f.* boundary, frontier. —herr, *m.* lord of a country, ruler, sovereign. —herrlich, *adj.* sovereign. —herrschaft, *f.* sovereignty; the crown; reigning prince and princess. —hoheit, *f.* sovereignty. —hoheits-recht, *n.* royal prerogative. —huldigung, *f.* oath of fealty. —kammer, *f.* board of finance. —kasse, *f.* public treasury. —kenntnis, —kunde, *f.* knowledge of a country. —kind, *n.* native; preußisches —kind, native of Prussia, born in Prussia. —kirche, *f.* established church. —kollegium, *n.* board of government, provincial council. —münze, *f.* legal coin of the country. —mutter, *f.* sovereign princess. —obrigkeit, *f.* supreme power, magistracy *or* government. —ordnung, *f.* custom, regulation of a country; standing order. —pflicht, *f.* oath of fealty. —polizei, *f.* national police. —regierung, *f.* government of the country; the regency. —sache, *f.* national affair. —schatz, *m.* public treasure. —schuld, *f.* national debt. —schule, *f.* national school. —sitte, *f.* custom, manner of a country. —sperre, *f.* prohibition of foreign commerce. —sprache, *f.* language of a country. —stelle, *f.* constituted authority. —tracht, *f* national costume. —üblich, *adj.* customary in a country. —valuta, *f.* lawful currency. —vater, *m.* sovereign; father of his people; a special German students' song. —verfassung, *f.* constitution of a country. —verrat, *m.* high treason. —verräter, *m.* traitor to his country. —verwalter, —verweser, *m.* viceroy *or* prefect. —verwaltung, *f.* administration of the country. —verweisung, *f.* banishment; exile. —verwiesen, *adj.* banished, exiled. —verwiesene(r), *m.* exile. —währung, *f.* money *or* standard currency of a country. —wohl, *n.* national welfare. —zeitung, *f.* official gazette.

Land'schaft, *f.* (*pl.* —en) province, district; provincial states (= *representatives*) of a country; *see* —s-ausschuß; suburbs; environs; landscape, scenery. —er, *m.* (—ers, *pl.* —ers) landscape-painter. —erei', *f.* landscape-painting. —lich, *adj.* provincial; *see* Landständisch; relating to landscape-painting; ein —liches Wort, provincialism. *Comp.* —s-ausschuß, *m.* committee of the states. —s-fach, *n.* (profession of) landscape painting. —s-gärtnerei, *f.* landscape-gardening. —s-haus, *n.* house of assembly (*of the states*). —s-maler, *m.* landscape-painter. —s-malerei', *f.* landscape painting. —s-recht, *n.* provincial law.

Lang, I. *adj. & adv.* (länger, längst) long; tall; high, lofty; protracted, lengthy; am längsten *or* aufs längste, at farthest, at the latest; zehn Zoll — und vier Zoll breit, ten inches (*long*) by four (*wide*); vor —en Jahren, vor —er Zeit, long ago; ein —es und Breites schwatzen, to talk at great length *or* a great deal; über kurz oder —, sooner or later; —e Briefe (Wechsel), bills drawn at a long date; —e Brühe, thin broth, clear soup; —e Hände haben, to have wide influence; er machte ein —es Gesicht, he looked very black, much disappointed; —e Finger machen, to be given to pilfering; auf die —e Bank schieben, to put off, protract, delay; aus —er Weile thun, to do by way of killing time; ihm wird die Zeit —, time hangs heavy on his hands *or* goes slowly with him; etwas des —en und Breiten erzählen, to tell something in great detail; er kommt auf längere Zeit, he is going to stay some time; so seid Ihr die längste Zeit Abt hier gewesen, then you will not be abbot here very much longer *or* any longer. II. *adv. & prep. preceded by acc.*, long; for, during; Jahre —, for years; Tage —, for days together; tag—, nacht—, for many days and nights; meilen—, for miles; den Fluß — gehen (*dial. for* entlang) to walk along the river. III. —e, *adv.* (länger; am längsten, längst) a long while, long; by far; von —e her, of long standing, of old; auf —e, for a long time; bis wie —e sind Sie zu Hause? up to what hour are you at home? schon —e bereit, ready long ago; sie konnten —e kein Wort sprechen, for a long time they were unable to utter a word, it was a long time before they could speak; es ist für mich —e gut, it is quite good enough for me; er ist —e nicht so gelehrt, he is not nearly so learned; nicht —e darauf, shortly after; je länger je lieber, the longer the better; das hat nicht —e gedauert, that did not last long; ich habe es schon länger bemerkt, I noticed it some time since; es hat am längsten gedauert, it shall not last any longer; it must not go on any longer; was machen Sie so —e! how slow (*long*) you are! länger machen, to lengthen; to prolong, extend; wenn er es noch länger so macht, if he goes on in this way; —e machen, to be long about *or* in doing; er kann —e zurück denken, he can recollect far back; ohne sich —e zu besinnen, without any hesitation; den muß man nicht erst —e fragen, one need not wait to consult him; wer wird erst —e fragen? who would hesitate? er wird es nicht mehr —e machen, he has not long to live (*coll.*); er kommt noch —e nicht, he will not be here for a long time yet; es ist noch —e nicht fertig, it is not nearly ready; —e nicht so gut, not nearly so good; er ist noch —e kein Goethe, he is far from being a Goethe; so —e bis, until; schon —e vorbei, long since past. —en, *v.* I. *n.* (*aux.* h.) (*arch. poet.*) to long; to stretch, reach, extend; to proceed, go; to be sufficient; to reach after; —en und bangen in schwebender Pein, longing and fearing in pain and suspense; in die Tasche —en, to put one's hand in one's pocket; nach (einer S.) —en, to reach after, stretch out the hand for; es —t so weit es kann, it will go as far as it can; das Geld wird nicht —en, that money will not suffice; ich kann damit nicht —en, I cannot live on that, I cannot make it do; wenn der Tag beginnt zu —en, kommt der Winter erst gegangen, as the day lengthens, the cold strengthens; ich werde ihn mir schon —en, I shall certainly get hold of him and speak seriously to him (*coll.*). II. *a.* to reach and give; to fetch; to seize; to take. —sam, *adj. & adv.* slow; tardy, backward; heavy, dull; not so fast! gently! —sam backen, to bake at a slow fire; —sam begreifend, dull of comprehension. —samkeit, *f.* slowness, tardiness, dulness. *Comp.* —atmig, *adj.* long-winded. —baum, *m.* perch (*of an ammunition waggon*). —blätterig, *adj.* long-leaved. —bleigeschoß, *n.* oblong shot *or* ball. —erwünscht, *adj.* long wished for. —e-weile, —weile, *f.* (*gen. & dat. if preceded by the article* —en-weile, *if not preceded by the article* —er-weile), weariness of mind, tediousness, boredom, ennui; aus —e(r)=weile, from ennui, by way of pastime, to pass the time; from sheer tedium; —e=weile empfinden, to feel bored *or* dull; nicht für die —eweile, not idly, not without good reason, in earnest; thoroughly; Seine Drohung ist nicht für die —e=weile, when he threatens he means it. —(e)=feld, *n.* (einer Kanone) chase. —finger, *m.* thief, pick-pocket (*coll.*). —fingerig, *adj.* long-fingered; light-fingered. —gefesselt, *adj.* long in the pastern. —haarig, *adj.* long-haired; shaggy. —hals, *m.* long-necked person; kind of barnacle. —hin, *adv.* long, far. —holz, *n.* beams and planks (*Naut.*). —jährig, *adj.* of long standing, of many years; —jähriger Freund, old friend; —jährige Erfahrung, experience of many years. —kreis, *m.* oval, ellipse. —lebig, *adj.* tenacious of life; long-lived. —mut, —mütigkeit, *f.* forbearance, patience, long-suffering disposition. —mütig, *adj.* forbearing, patient. —ohr, *n.* long-eared person *or* beast; ass; ein Esel nennt den andern —ohr, the pot calls the kettle black. —rund, *adj.* oval. —schattig, *adj.* casting a long shadow. —schiff, *n.* nave (*of a church*) (*Arch.*). —schläfer, *m.* lie-a-bed. —schnä=bler, *pl.* longirosters (*Orn.*). —schwanz, *m.* long-tailed animal; tomtit (*Orn.*). —schwelle, *f.* ground-plate (*Railw.*); capping-piece (*Hydr.*). —sichtig, *adj.* long-sighted; of long date; —sichtige Wechsel, bills (*of exchange*) drawn at long sight. —stielig, —stietzig, *adj.* tiresome, tedious, circumstantial (*coll.*). —viereck, *n.* parallelogram. —weile, *see* —e=weile. —weilen, *v.r.* (einen) to bore. —weiler, *m.* tedious person, bore. —weilig, *adj.* tedious, irksome; —weilige Person, bore. —wierig, *adj.* lasting, protracted, lingering; lengthy; tedious; chronic. —zeher, *pl.* Macrodactyles (*Orn.*). —zeile, *f.* long line; stabreimende —zeile, alliterative (long) line. —ziehen, *n.* lengthening; drawing out (*Mus.*).

Län'g—e, *f.* (*pl.* —en) length; tallness, size; quantity; longitude; length of time; sling (*Naut.*); der —e nach, lengthwise; according to length; der —e nach gehend, laufend, longitudinal; auf, in die —e, in the end, in the long run; in die —e ziehen, to protract, spin out; der —e lang hinfallen, to fall at full length; zwanzig Fuß in der —e, twenty feet long. —lich, *adj.* longish, elliptical; oblong; —lich rund, oval. —s, *adv. & prep.* (*with gen. or dat.*) along; —s des Flusses *or* dem Flusse, along the river's bank. —st, *adv.* long ago, long since; ich weiß es schon —st, I have known it for a long time. —stens, *adv.* at the furthest *or* at the most; at the latest. *Comp.* —e=feld, *n.* chase (*Artil.*). —e=lang, *adv.* in his (her, its) full length. —en=abweichung, *f.* falling short (*Artil.*). —en=bruch, *m.* longitudinal fracture (*Surg.*). —en=(durch)schnitt, *m.* longitudinal section. —en=faser, *f.* grain (*in wood*). —en=grad, —en=kreis, *m.* degree (*circle*) of longitude. —en=maß, *n.* linear measure; instrument for measuring lengths. —en=schwingung, *f.* longitudinal oscillation. —en=unterschied, *m.* difference of length *or* longitude. —en=wachstum, *n.* growth in length. —e=zeichen, *n.* mark of length; —ezeichen über Vokalen, sign marking vowel-length, macron. —st=lebende(r), *m.* survivor.

Län'gen, *v.a.* to lengthen, extend, stretch; to roll out (*dough*); to thin (*soup*); to slacken; to divide lengthways.

Languſ'te, *f.* (*pl.* —n) spiny lobster, crawfish.

Lan'tan, *n.* (—s) lanthanium (*metallic substance*).

Lan'ze, *f.* (*pl.* —n) lance, spear; lancer; whalespear; die — einlegen, to couch the spear; eine Schwadron von 100 —n, a squadron of 100 lancers; — in 'n Schuh! lance in rest! (*Mil.*). *Comp.*—n=blatt, *n.* head *or* blade of a lance. —n=brechen, *n.* joust, tilt. —n=förmig, *adj.* lance-shaped; lanceolate. —n=reiter, *m.* lancer, uhlan. —n=schaft, —n=stock, *m.* spear-staff. —n=schuh, *m.* rest for a lance. —n=spitze, *f.* spear-head. —n=stechen, *n.* joust, tournament. —n=träger, *m.* spearman, pike-man; lancer; uhlan.

Lanzet'te, *f.* (—n) lancet.

Lapida'r, *adj.* lapidary; concise, pithy.

Lappa'lie, *f.* (*pl.* —n) bagatelle, trifle; bauble.

Lap'p—en, I. *m.* (—ens, *pl.* —en) flap (*of the ear*); lobe (*Anat.*, *Bot.*); patch; rag, shred; duster, clout; (*pl.*) rags tied to a stick *or* line and used to scare birds, *etc.*; flank-meat (*Butch.*); (*pl.*) ears (*of hounds*); (*pl.*) wattles; durch die —en gehen, to abscond (*sl.*). II. *v.a.* to patch, mend; gelappt, with lobes. —erei', *f.* patch-work; trifle, bagatelle. —ern, *see* Läppern. —icht, *adj. & adv.* flabby, flaccid (*obs.*). —ig, *adj.* ragged, tattered; lobate, lobulated. *Comp.* —en=los, *adj* acotyledonous (*Bot.*). —en=mann, —en=sammler, *m.* rag-man. —en=schuld, *f.* petty debt. —ohrig, *adj.* lap-eared.

Läpp'—chen, *n.* (—chens, *pl.* —chen) small patch; lobe. —erei', *f.* trifle, bauble.

Läp'p—ern, *v.a. & n.* (*aux.* h.) to lap, sip. II. *r.*; sich zusammen —ern, to mount up, accumulate. —isch, *adj.* silly, trifling, childish; effeminate. *Comp.* —er=schulden, *pl.* petty debts. —er=weise, *adv.* little by little.

Lär'che, *f.* (*pl.* —n), —n=tanne, *f.* larch.

La'ren, *pl.* household gods, Lares.

Larifa'ri, *n.* prattle, nonsensical talk; stuff! fiddle-faddle! no matter!

Lärm, *m.* (—(e)s), —en, *m.* (*obs.*) (—s) noise, bustle; alarm; uproar; row; fuss; blinder —, false alarm; — blasen, to sound an alarm; — machen, to make a noise, to cause an uproar; make a fuss; viel — um nichts, much ado about nothing. *Comp.* —bläser, *m.* alarmist. —glocke, *f.* tocsin. —kanone, *f.* alarm-gun. —knarre, *f.* watchman's rattle. —pfeife, *f.* alarm whistle, policeman's whistle. —platz, *m.* alarm-post.

Lär'm—en, *v.n.* (*aux.* h.) to make a noise, an uproar; to be noisy; to bluster. —er, *m.* (—ers, *pl.* —er) noisy person; blusterer.

Lar've, *f.* (*pl.* —n, *dim.* Lärv'chen) mask; face; larva, grub; spectre, ghoul; masked person; einem die — abziehen, to unmask a p.; jedes hübsche Lärvchen, every pretty face; das niedliche Lärvchen, that pretty wench (*vulg.*). *Comp.* —n=gesicht, *n.* masked *or* hypocritical face; ugly person, fright. —n=mantel, *m.* domino. —n=zustand, *m.* chrysalis state.

Las, Lä'se, *1* (*& 3*) *pers. sing. imperf. indic. & subj. of* lesen.

Lasch, *adj.* lax, loose, flabby.

La'sche, *f.* (*pl.* —n) stripe sewed on; flap, lappet; gore, gusset; shoe-latchet; groove.

La'schen, *v.a.* to furnish with flaps; to put in a gore *or* gusset; to sew in a piece; to lash (*vulg.*); to join wood by a groove.

La'se, *f.* (*pl.* —n) pitcher, can (*with spout*).

Laſ—ie'ren, *v.a.* to paint, to glaze. —u'r, *f.* glazing, transparent coating.

Laß, *adj.* weary; lazy; loath; slack; spiritless; wer — ist in seiner Arbeit, he that is slothful in his work (*B.*); — der Arbeit, sick of work. —heit, *f.* laziness; weariness. *Comp.* —band, *n.*, —binde, *f.* bandage for tying up a vein after bleeding. —becken, *n.* bleeding-basin. —baum, *m.* boundary-tree. —besitzer, *m.* copy-holder, lease-holder. —brief, *m.* deed of enfranchisement. —eisen, *n.* lancet, fleam; tapping-bar (*Found.*). —gut, *n.* leasehold. —pflichtig, *adj.* subject to ground-rent.

—sünde, *f.* venial sin. **—zins,** *m.* ground-rent.

Las'sen, I. *ir.v.n.* (*aux.* **h.**) to let appear, to look, appear; to become, suit; **es läßt ihr nicht übel,** it is rather becoming to her; **er läßt jünger als vorher,** he looks younger than he did (*obs.*); **nun läßt der Hut erst schön,** now the hat looks really well (*obs.*); **das würde mir übel —,** it would ill become me (*obs.*). II. *ir.v.a.* to let, leave alone, refrain from doing; to omit; to forbear; to leave (*open, closed, etc.*); to leave, let, keep; to relinquish, let go; to sell; to abandon, desert; to let run; to grant, allow; to part with; **dies sollte man thun und jenes nicht —,** this ought ye to have done and not to leave the other undone (*B.*); **laß mich zufrieden!** let me alone! don't bother me! **laß das!** don't! **laß das Spaßen!** no more nonsense! a truce to joking! **um den Preis kann ich es nicht —,** I can't sell it at that price; **ich lasse dich nicht, du segnest mich dann,** I will not let thee go except thou bless me (*B.*); **laß!** don't! **einen bei seiner Meinung —,** to let a p. keep his opinion; **mit sich reden —,** to listen to reason; **das muß ihm sein ärgster Feind —,** his worst enemy must allow that; **laß (es) gut sein,** never mind; **zur Ader, Blut —,** to bleed; **Wein vom Fasse —,** to draw off wine from a cask; **von etwas —,** to renounce, abandon, relinquish a thing; **von seiner Meinung —,** to change one's opinion; **wie man einen Knaben gewöhnt, so läßt er nicht davon,** train up a child in the way he should go and when he is old he will not depart from it (*B.*); **ich kann von ihm nicht —,** I cannot give him up *or* part from him; **laß die Hände davon!** hands off! don't meddle with that! **sein Wasser —,** to make water; **einem Zeit —,** to give a p. time; **einem den Vortritt —, den Vorzug —,** to yield the precedence to a p.; **das muß man ihm —,** we must grant him that point; **sein Leben — für,** to lay down one's life for; **sie kann ihre Bücher nicht alle —,** she has not room for all her books; **sie weiß ihre Reichtümer nicht zu —,** she does not know what to do with all her money; **sich vor Freude nicht zu — wissen,** not to know what to do for joy; **sich aufs Knie nieder —,** to kneel down; **aus dem Spiele —,** to leave out of the question; **aus der Hand —,** to drop; **aus den Händen —,** to let go *or* slip; **Alles beim Alten —,** to leave matters as they were; **sie ließ ihren Thränen freien Lauf,** she gave vent to her tears; **vom Stapel —,** to launch; **unerwähnt —,** to pass over in silence *or* without mention; **vor sich** (*acc.*) *or* **zu sich —,** to admit to one's presence; **ich ließ ihn in die Stube,** I let him enter the room, I showed him into the room; **ich ließ ihn in der Stube,** I left him in the room; **einen beim Amte —,** to retain a p. in his office; **einen nicht von sich —,** to keep a p., not to allow him to leave; **Haar** *or* **Haare —,** to pay for; to be fleeced; **thun, was man nicht — kann,** to do what one cannot help doing; **laß das Weinen!** stop crying! *When governing another verb in the inf.* (*to which it frequently gives a passive sense*) *often* = to cause, make, effect, get done; to order, command; to permit, suffer; to let; **der Richter ließ die Zeugen abhören,** the judge caused the witnesses to be examined; **er hat sich einen Zahn ausziehen —,** he has had a tooth drawn; **(etwas) bleiben** *or* **sein —,** to leave alone, not to do; **das wird er wohl bleiben —,** he will take good care not to do that; **sich sehen** *or* **blicken —,** to show oneself, to put in an appearance; **sich bitten, nötigen —,** to wait to be pressed; **laß dich belehren,** be advised; **sich** (*dat.*) **etwas einfallen —,** to take s.th. into one's head; **das läßt sich denken,** that may easily be imagined, that is very natural; **das läßt sich hören,** that sounds plausible; **Holz läßt sich nicht dehnen,** wood is not ductile; **ich lasse mir nichts einreden,** I am not to be talked over, I won't be convinced; **davon ließe sich viel sagen,** much might be said on that subject; **es läßt sich nicht leugnen,** there is no denying; **wenn es sich thun läßt,** if it can be done; **hier läßt's sich gut sitzen,** this is a pleasant place to sit; **der Wein läßt sich trinken,** the wine is not bad, is drinkable; **ich lasse mich danach verlangen,** I have a great wish for it; **sich keine Mühe verdrießen —,** to make every effort, take great pains; **er läßt mir keine Ruhe,** he gives me no peace; **er läßt sich nicht aus der Fassung bringen,** there is no putting him out of countenance; **ich werde mir das gesagt sein —,** I shall remember that, take due notice of it; **fahren —, los —,** to let slip, let go; **fallen —,** to drop; **fragen —,** to have enquiries made, to enquire, ask; **geschehen —,** to let pass, allow to happen; **grüßen —,** to send greetings, kind regards to; **sich hören —,** to speak, sing, play, *etc.*, in company; **er hat sich lange nicht auf der Geige hören —,** he has not played the fiddle anywhere for a long time; **— Sie von sich hören,** let us hear from you; **kommen —,** to send for, to order; **gehen —,** to let go; **gut sein —,** to let pass, to approve; **laß (es) gut sein,** never mind; **liegen —,** to let lie, leave behind; **gelten —,** to allow, admit as valid; **ich werde mir nichts merken —,** I shall seem to know nothing of it; **sich rühren —,** to allow oneself to be moved; **ich lasse mich nicht leicht rühren,** I am not easily moved; **der Dichter läßt ihn sagen,** the poet makes him say; **einem sagen —,** to send a p. word; **sich** (*dat.*) **nichts sagen —,** to be deaf to entreaty *or* argument; to take no advice; **ich habe mir sagen —,** I have been told; **— Sie sich sagen,** let me tell you; **den Zügel schießen —,** to let the reins loose; **einen Brief schreiben —,** to have a letter written; **ins Reine schreiben —,** to have a fair copy made; **laß dich nicht wieder sehen,** don't show your face (here) again; **— Sie sich trösten,** be comforted; **es läßt sich übersetzen,** it admits of translation; **es läßt sich nicht übersetzen,** it cannot be translated, it defies translation; **diese Blumen — sich nicht verpflanzen,** these flowers won't bear transplanting; **warten —,** to keep waiting; **einen wissen —,** to inform a p., to let one know; **das läßt sich thun,** that may easily be done; **— Sie das sein,** let well alone, leave it alone, don't meddle with that; **der Dichter läßt die Helden schon in ihre Heimat zurückgekehrt sein,** the poet represents the heroes as again in their homes; **er ließ das Heer vorrücken,** he ordered the army to advance. *As forming the Imper.* = let; **laßt uns gehen,** let us go. III. *subst. n.* letting, leaving, permitting; **sein Thun und —,** his actions, conduct.

Läs'sest, Läßt, 2 & 3 *p. sing. pres. ind. of* **lassen.**

Läs'[s]—ig, *adj. & adv.* inactive, sluggish, lazy. **—igkeit,** *f.* laziness, *etc.* **—(ß)=lich,** *adj. & adv.* pardonable, venial; mild, indulgent. **—(ß)=lichkeit,** *f.* veniality; indulgence.

Last, *f.* (*pl.* **—en**) load, charge, burden, weight; tonnage; cargo, freight; waist (*Naut.*); charge, encumbrance; tax, impost; weight (*of care; of age, etc.*); measure (*varying in different countries*); **das Schiff ist bei seiner —,** the ship is freighted; **die — brechen,** to break bulk; **zur — sein, fallen,** to be a burden to, a charge on, to trouble; **der Gemeinde zur — fallen,** to come upon the parish; **einem eine S. zur — legen,** to charge *or* tax a p. with a th. to impute s.th. to s.o.; zu —en von, to the debit of (*C. L.*); nach Abzug der —en, deducting all charges; einem zur — schreiben, to charge to a p.'s account; viele — machen, to cause much trouble; die halbe —, ton; ein Schiff von 200 —en, a ship of 400 tons burden. —a'die, *f.* (*pl.* —adien) wharf, quay. —bar, *adj.* capable of bearing a burden; oppressive; —bare Tiere, beasts of burden. —ig, *adj.* freighted, having a certain load; weighty, heavy; ein zwei —iges Schiff, a vessel of 4 tons burden; ein gleich —iges Schiff, a ship upon an even keel. —igkeit, *f.* burden, tonnage. *Comp.* —en=frei, *adj.* unburdened; free from taxes *or* charges. —geld, *n.* tonnage; ransom. —kahn, *m.* lighter. —pferd, *n.* pack-horse. —sand, *m.* ballast-sand. —schiff, *n.* transport-ship. —tier, *n.* beast of burden; wie ein —tier arbeiten, to drudge; to work like a nigger, to slave (*coll.*). —träger, *m.* porter.

Las'ten, *v.* I. *n.* (*aux.* h.) to weigh on, press heavy upon; to oppress; es — Schulden auf dem Gute, the estate is encumbered with debts. II. *a.* to burden, load, lade.

Las'ter, *n.* (—s, *pl.* —) vice; depravity; degraded person. —haft, *adj.* vicious, wicked, abandoned. —haftigkeit, *f.* viciousness, wickedness. *Comp.* —frei, *adj.* free from vice. —knecht, *m.* slave to vice. —leben, *n.* vicious life. —sinn, *m.* vicious propensity. —that, *f.* heinous deed, crime. —voll, *adj.* profligate.

Läs'ter—er, *m.* (—ers, *pl.* —er) slanderer, calumniator; Gottes—er, blasphemer. —haft, *adj.* vicious, wicked. —lich, *adj.* & *adv.* shameful, disgraceful, shocking; dreadful, excessive (*vulg.*); scandalous; slanderous, abusive; sacrilegious, blasphemous; wicked. —n, *v.a.* to revile, rail at; to slander, defame; to outrage; to blaspheme. —ung, *f.* reviling; abuse, slander; blasphemy. *Comp.* —geschichte, *f.* piece of scandal. —maul, *n.* slanderer; backbiter; blasphemer; einem das —maul stopfen, to stop a man's abusive mouth. —rede, *f.* slander, calumny. —schrift, *f.* lampoon, libel. —schule, *f.* school for scandal. —süchtig, *adj.* slanderous, given to scandal. —wort, *n.* invective; blasphemy. —zunge, *f.* termagant-tongue.

Läs'tig, *adj.* burdensome, troublesome, annoying; tedious; einem — fallen, to bore a p., to hinder *or* inconvenience one. —keit, *f.* burdensomeness, troublesomeness.

Lasu'r, *m.* (—s) lapis lazuli; azure, ultramarine; *see* Lasieren. *Comp.* —blau, *adj.* sky-blue. —grün, *n.* green bice. —stein, *m.* lapis lazuli.

Latei'n, *n.* (—s) Latin language; schlechtes —, Krämer —, dog Latin; hier geht mein — zu Ende, here I am at the end of my resources, now I am out of it. —er, *m.* (—ers, *pl.* —er) Latin scholar; bad shot, cockney sportsman (*Hunt.*). —isch, *adj.* Latin; auf —isch, in Latin; —ische Brocken, scraps of Latin, a smattering of Latin; —ische Buchstaben, Roman characters, ordinary (Roman) type. *Comp.* —schule, *f.* grammar school. —los, *adj.*; —lose schule, school in which no Latin is taught; commercial school; primary school.

Later'ne, *f.* (*pl.* —n) lantern, lamp; lantern (*tower*); shaft, turret; chimney-cowl; lantern (*in mills*); head (*vulg.*); etwas in der — haben, to be half-seas over; die große —, the poop lantern; die magische —, the magic lantern. *Comp.* —n=anzünder, *m.* lamp-lighter. —n=gabeln, *pl.* lamp-stays. —n=pfahl, *m.* lamp-post; mit dem —npfahl winken, to give a broad hint (*coll.*). —n=träger, *m.* lantern-bearer; lamp-post.

Latinitä't, *f.* Latinity.

Latitudina'rier, *m.* (—s, *pl.* —) latitudinarian, a man of broad and liberal views, especially with regard to religious belief.

Latri'ne, *f.* (*pl.* —n); cesspool; (water-)closet.

Lat'sch—e, *f.* (*pl.* —en) down-trodden shoe *or* slipper; sloven, slut; shaggy *or* downy foot; spiritless person, slovenly woman. —ig, *adj.* shuffling, negligent, slovenly; insipid. *Comp.* —bein, *n.*, —fuß, *m.* slovenly, shuffling walker; bear's paw. —beinig, —füßig, *adj.* heavy-footed, clumsy-footed. —gang, *m.* shuffling, clumsy gait.

Lat'sche—n, *v.n.* (*aux.* h.) to shuffle along; to waddle. —r, *m.* (—rs, *pl.* —r) shuffler, waddler.

Lat'te, *f.* (*pl.* —n) lath; young slender tree; rod; diagonal brace (*Fort.*); eine (lange) —, a may-pole, lanky person. *Comp.* —n=arrest, *m.* close arrest (*Mil.*). —n=brett, *n.* board of a window-sill. —en=verschlag, *m.* latticed partition. —n=werk, *n.* lattice-work. —n=zaun, *m.* paling.

Lat't—en, *v.a.* to lath; to batten. —ung, *f.* lattice-work, lathing.

Lat'tich, *m.* (—(e)s, *pl.* —e) lettuce.

Latwer'ge, *f.* (*pl.* —n) electuary.

Latz, *m.* (—es, *pl.* Lä'tze; *dim.* Lätz'chen) bib; flap; pinafore. *Comp.* —en=schnur, *f.* gut-cord. —mütze, *f.* cap with flaps. —schürze, *f.* apron with bib.

Lau, *adj.* & *adv.* lukewarm, tepid; indifferent, half-hearted. —heit, —igkeit, *f.* lukewarmness, tepidity; indifference. *Comp.* —warm, *adj.* lukewarm, tepid; indifferent.

Laub, *n.* (—es, *pl.* —e *and* Läu'ber; *dim.* Läub'chen) foliage, leaves; foliage (*Arch.*) · spades (*Cards*). —e, *f.* (*pl.* —en) bower, arbour; covered way; piazza; porch; arcade; vaulted place. —icht, (*obs.*) —ig, *adj.* foliaceous, leafy, leaflike. *Comp.* —band, *n.* scroll-work (*of a door*). —dach, *n.* roof of foliage. —daus, *n.* ace of spades. —en=dach, *n.* roof of an arbour. —en=gang, *m.* arcade, covered way; arboured walk. —er=hütte, *f.* tabernacle; *see* —hütte. —er=hüttenfest, *n.* feast of Tabernacles. —erde, *f.* vegetable mould. —fall, *m.* fall of the leaf, defoliation. —farbe, *f.* vegetable colour. —förmig, *adj.* leaf-shaped, foliage-like. —frosch, *m.* tree-frog. —gang, *see* —engang. —gehänge, —gewinde, *n* festoon, garland. —gitter, *n.* lattice work, trellis. —holz, *n.* wood bearing leaves (*opp. to firs, etc.*). —hütte, *f.* bower, hut made of branches; cottage overgrown with foliage; tabernacle. —könig, *m.* king of spades. —los, *adj.* leafless. —pflanzen, *pl.* a class of plants (*seaweeds, mushrooms, lichens*). —rost, *m.* mildew on vines. —säge, *f.* fret-saw; cock-saw; compass-saw. —säge=arbeit, *f.* fretwork. —streu, *f.* litter of leaves. —thaler, *m.* a six-franc piece (*obs.*). —verzierung, *f.* foliage (*Art.*). —werk, *n.* foliage; leaves, trees (*Paint., etc.*); crocket (*Arch.*).

Lauch, *m.* (—(e)s, *pl.* —e) leek. *Comp.* —knob=lauch, *m.* Spanish garlic. —suppe, *f.* leek-broth.

Lau'er, *f.* ambush, lurking-place; lurking, lying-in-wait; auf der — sein *or* liegen, to lie in wait, to be on the lookout, to lurk. —er, *m.* (—ers, *pl.* —er) spy, lurker. *Comp.* —grube, *f.* pit to lie in wait in (*for game*).

Lau'ern, *v.n.* (*aux.* h.) to watch, observe keenly; to lurk, lie in wait for; (auf einen *or* etwas) to await with impatience (*coll.*).

Lau'er, *m.* (—s) wine of the second press; sour wine.

Lauf, *m.* (—es), (*pl.* Läu'fe) course, career, run; current; currency; track, path (*of a comet, etc.*); progress; course (*of ships; of time; of the sun, etc.*); spinning-wheel; barrel (*of a gun*); hoop (*of a sieve*); drum (*in mills*); ankle-bone; bed (*of a river*); (*pl. also* **Läu'fer**) run (*Mus.*); rutting-season; (*pl.* **Läuf'te**) leg, foot (*of quadrupeds*); **freien — lassen,** to give full scope to, to give vent *or* free play to, to indulge; **seinen Gefühlen freien — lassen,** to give vent to one's feelings; **— der Begebenheiten,** course of events; **am Ende seines —es,** at the close of his career; **in vollem —e,** at full speed; **das ist (einmal) der — der Welt,** that's the way of the world; such is life; **der Gerechtigkeit ihren** *or* **freien — lassen,** to let justice take its course; **ein Gewehr mit zwei Läufen,** a double-barrelled gun; **Schafe nach dem —e verkaufen,** to sell sheep as they pass; **einen einzelnen — machen,** to run a heat. **—erei',** *f.* running about. *Comp.* **—bahn,** *f.* career; race-course; course. **—band,** *n.* leading-string, leading-rein. **—bank,** *f.* go-cart. **—bohne,** *f.* scarlet runner. **—bohrer,** *m.* gun-barrel bore. **—brett,** *n.* plank, carriage of a press (*Typ.*). **—brief,** *m.* circular. **—brücke,** *f.* plank-bridge; pontoon; gangway. **—bursche,** *m.* errand-boy, messenger-boy; printer's devil. **—feuer,** *n.* train of gunpowder; running fire (*Mil.*); wild-fire; **sich wie ein —feuer verbreiten,** to spread like wildfire. **—fuß,** *m.* foot adapted for running. **—gang,** *m.* gallery. **—geld,** *n.* money for travelling expenses; earnest. **—gerüst,** *n.* plank-bridge for mounting a scaffolding. **—gewicht,** *n.* sliding weight. **—graben,** *m.* trench. **—hund,** *m.* greyhound, beagle. **—jagen,** *n.* coursing. **—junge,** *see* **—bursche.** **—käfer,** *m.* carabus, ground-beetle. **—karren,** *m.* truck. **—kran,** *m.* travelling crane. **—kugel,** *f.* rifle-ball. **—maschine,** *f.* velocipede (*obs.*). **—paß,** *m.* passport; dismissal; **einem den —paß geben,** to dismiss a person. **—planke,** *f.* gangway. **—pfanne,** *f.* cooler (*Sugar.*). **—rad,** *n.* working wheel, tread-wheel. **—schiene,** *f.* main-line rail. **—schranken,** *pl.* barriers. **—schritt,** *m.* double; **im —schritt!** (advance) at the double! double the pace! **—seil,** *n.* running loop. **—spiel,** *n.* race. **—treppe,** *f.* back staircase. **—wagen,** *m.* go-cart. **—walzen,** *pl.* cylinders, runners. **—werk,** *n.* wheel-work (*of a clock*). **—zaum,** *m.* leading string. **—zeit,** *f.* rutting-time. **—zettel,** *m. see* **—paß;** circular; official order sent on by the post-office to recover mis-sent letters *or* to have post-horses ready in advance. **—ziel,** *n.* goal. **—zirkel,** *m.* calliper-compasses.

Lau'fen, I. *ir.v.n.* (*aux.* **h.** & **s.**) to run; to go; to flow; to ooze; to move (*as trains, planets, etc.*); to walk (*dial.*); to trend, to extend *or* stretch; to leak; to curdle; to be in circulation; to run down, gutter; to rut; to rise (*of dough*); to frequent, haunt; to sue for, run after; to pass (*of time*); **es läuft ein Gerücht, daß,** it is rumoured that; **von Pontius zu Pilatus —,** to leave no stone untouched (*coll.*); **aus allen Kräften —, über Hals und Kopf —,** to run at full speed; **gelaufen kommen,** to come running; **die Augen — ihm voll Wasser,** his eyes fill with tears; **der Teig läuft,** the dough is rising **die Uhr läuft,** the watch gains; **das Blut läuft in den Adern,** the blood circulates in the veins; **die Milch läuft,** the milk curdles; **der Wechsel läuft noch,** the bill has still some time to run; **(schließlich) auf eins hinaus —,** to come to the same thing in the end; **auf alle Bälle —,** to frequent balls; **aufs Blatt —,** to come at call (*of deer*); **er weiß darauf zu —,** he is a man of inexhaustible resources (*coll.*); **hinter die Schule —,** to play truant; **einem in die Arme —,** to throw oneself into a person's arms; to come across a p. quite unexpectedly; **das läuft ins Geld,** that runs into money; **nach dem Arzt —,** to run for the doctor; **nach einem Amte —,** to sue for an office; **um die Wette —,** to run for a wager, to race; **vor einem —,** to run away from one; **wider, zuwider —,** to run counter to; **das läuft wider die gesunde Vernunft,** that is opposed to common-sense; **mir läuft das Wasser im Munde zusammen,** my mouth waters; **zu Ende —,** to run out, to expire; **alle Welt läuft in seine Vorlesungen,** every one attends his lectures; **—de Gicht,** flying gout; **das —de Jahr, der —de Monat,** the present *or* current year, month; **vom 3ten —den Monats,** from the 3rd inst.; **—de Wechsel,** bills in circulation; **zum —den Preise,** at the current rate; **der —de Geldpreis,** the rate of exchange; **—de Rechnung,** current account; **der —de Termin,** the present quarters; **die —den Geschäfte,** the course of affairs, the daily business; **auf dem — den bleiben,** to keep well posted up; **auf dem — den sein,** to be well acquainted with, to have the latest news in a matter, to be down to date; **einen über eine Sache auf dem —den halten,** to keep a p. well informed about *or* well posted up in a th. II. *ir.v.a.* to contract by running; to run; **sich wund —,** to run until the feet are sore; **in den Boden —,** to run aground; **der Wind läuft Schulen,** there is a dead calm; **Gassen, Spießruten —,** to run the gauntlet; **sich müde —,** to tire oneself with running; **Sturm —,** to charge with the bayonet, to assault, to storm; **Gefahr —,** to run a risk; **wir liefen dabei Gefahr, vom Winde von den Felsen gefegt zu werden,** in doing this we ran the risk of being swept off the rocks by the wind; **Schlittschuh —,** to skate; **es läuft sich hier schlecht,** this is not a good place for running. III. *subst.n.* running, run; **da ging es an ein —,** everybody made off, there was a general stampede; **ins — bringen,** to set a-going.

Läu'f—er, *m.* (**—ers,** *pl.* **—er**) runner; courser; racer; sand-glass; running footman; messenger; bishop (*Chess*); shoot, sucker; stair-linen, stair-cover; strip of crumb-cloth; *etc.*; decoy-bird; upper millstone; runner (*of sledges*); slider (*of mathematical instruments*); muller (*for colours*); running passages (*Mus.*); ground-beetle (*Ent.*); hunting-spider; willow-wren; (*pl.*) a genus of birds of the order of Cursores. **—ig, —isch,** *adj.* running; current, in heat; lecherous. **—te,** *see* **Lauf.** *Comp.* **—er=zug,** *m.* move with the bishop.

Läuffst, Läuft, *2 & 3 p. sing. pres. ind. of* **laufen.**

Läug'—bar, —nen, ꝛc. *see* **Leugnen.**

Laug'—e, (*pl.* **—en**) lye, buck; **einem den Kopf mit scharfer —e waschen,** to give a p. a sound rating; **die —e seines Spottes,** his biting sarcasm, his caustic wit. **—enhaft, —ig, —icht,** *see* **—enartig.** *Comp.* **—en=artig,** *adj.* like lye; alkaline. **—en=asche,** *f.* alkaline ashes, potash. **—en=kasten,** *m.* alum-chest. **—en=salz,** *n.* alkaline salt; **Pflanzen —ensalze,** vegetable alkalies; **feuerbeständige —ensalze,** fixed alkalies. **—en=ständer,** *m.* soap maker's lye-jar. **—en=tuch,** *n.* bucking-cloth (*Soapb.*). **—en=wäsche,** *f.* bucking of clothes; clothes-steep. **—en=wasser,** *n.* lye.

Lau'g—en, *v.* I. *a.* to soak in lye, to buck; to soak out. II. *n.* (*aux.* **h.**) **das Faß —t,** the cask causes the wine to taste of the cask.

Laun—e, *f.* (*pl.* **—en**) humour, temper, mood, vein; whim, caprice, fancy, freak; **gleiche —e,** even temper; **bei (guter) —e,** in a good humour, in good spirits; **nicht bei —e,** out of humour, low spirited; disinclined; **übler —e sein,** to be in a bad humour, to be in a sulk, sulky; **er hat heute seine —e,** he is in one of his cross moods to-day; **er war gerade bei —e,**

he just happened to be in a good mood; **eine —e des Glückes**, a freak of fortune; **in gute —e versetzen**, to put into a good temper. **—en**, *v.n.* (*aux.* **h.**) to have whims, be in a certain mood (*only used in the past part.*); **gelaunt**, disposed; **gut gelaunt**, in good humour. **—enhaft**, *adj.* fanciful, whimsical, capricious; peevish; **ein —enhafter Einfall**, a quaint conceit, an odd fancy. **—enhaftigkeit**, *f.* capriciousness; whimsicality; waywardness. **—ig**, *adj. & adv.* humourous, witty, droll; amusing; playful; (*in comp.* =) -humoured, -tempered. **—igkeit**, *f.* playfulness, *etc.* **—isch**, *adj.* ill-humoured, peevish, splenetic.

Lau'rer ꝛc., *see* **Lauerer ꝛc.** **—ei'**, *f.* (continual) espionage; (constant) lurking, spying.

Laus, *f.* (*pl.* **Läu'se**) louse; **einem eine — in den Pelz setzen**, to cut out work for s.o., give a p. trouble (*vulg.*); **die — läuft ihm über die Leber**, he flies into a passion; **eine — im Ohr haben**, to have a bad conscience (*vulg.*). **—(s)en**, (*vulg.*) *v.a.* to rid of lice; to fleece; to thrash. **—(s)erei'**, *f.* ridding of lice; trumpery thing; stinginess. **—(s)ig**, *adj. & adv.* (*vulg.*) lousy; mean, sordid; miserable; enormous, terrible. *Comp.* **—bub(e)**, *m.* miserable fellow (*vulg.*).

Lau'sch—e, *f.* lurking, eavesdropping, lying in wait; hiding-place; *see* **—platz**; **auf der —e stehen**, to lie in wait. **—ig**, *adj.* given to prying *or* listening; snug, comfortable; peaceful, pleasant. *Comp.* **—platz**, *m.* snug, quiet corner.

Lau'sch—en, *v.n.* (*aux.* **h.**) to listen to, to hearken (*elev.*); to watch; to lie in wait, to eavesdrop; to flicker up, to peep up; to glimmer; to half-slumber, lounge. **—er**, *m.* (**—ers**, *pl.* **—er**) ears (*of the wolf, fox, deer, etc.*); (**—erin**, *f.*) eavesdropper, listener.

Lau'se— (*in comp.*) **—bube**, *m.* wretched urchin, low fellow, miserable knave (*vulg.*). **—ding**, *n.* trumpery thing (*vulg.*). **—geld**, *n.* trifle; bad metal (*vulg.*). **—kerl**, *m.* low fellow (*vulg.*).

Läu'se, *pl. see* **Laus**; little knots in wool (*C.L.*). *Comp.* **—pulver**, *n.* insect-destroyer. **—sucht**, *f.* herodian *or* pedicular disease; lice disease (*of plants*).

Laut, I. *adj. & adv.* loud; noisy; audible; aloud; sonorous; open, public; forte (*Mus.*); **mit —er Stimme**, in a loud voice; **— lachen**, to laugh aloud *or* outright; **— werden**, to become known, get abroad, to become noisy *or* clamorous; **— werden lassen**, **— machen**, to divulge, to betray, discover; **die Hunde sind —**, the dogs give tongue; **ich sage es —**, I say it openly; **seine Gefühle — werden lassen**, to show, give utterance to one's feelings; **der Schnee ist —**, the snow crackles under the feet. II. *m.* (**—es**, *pl.* **—e**) sound, tone; speech, sound; audible noise *or* utterance; purport, tenor; **die —e betreffend**, phonological, phonetic; **keinen — von sich geben**, not to utter a sound; not to write; **Briefe eines —es**, letters of the same tenor; **— geben**, to bay, to give tongue. III. *prep.* (*usually with gen.* [*rarely with dat., which should be avoided*]) according to, by the tenor *or* terms of; in consequence of; in virtue of; **— Bericht**, as per advice, as advised (*C. L.*); **— Faktura**, as per invoice; **— Verfügung**, as directed; **— habender Macht**, by virtue of the authority invested in one. **—bar**, *adj. & adv.* audible; notorious, public. **—heit**, *f.* sonorousness; loudness. **—ie'ren**, *v.a. & n.* (*aux.* **h.**) to read according to the phonetic system, to read phonetically. **—ier'=methode**, *f.*, **—ier'=system**, *n.* phonetic method, phonetic system (*especially with regard to elementary reading*). **—lich**, *adj.* regarding the sound, in sound; phonetic. *Comp.* **—angleichung**, *f.* assimilation of sounds. **—bezeichnung**, *f.* marking *or* designation of sounds, sound notation; designation of the sounds. **—differenzierung**, *f.* dissimilation of sounds. **—eigenheiten**, *pl.* phonetic peculiarities, peculiarities of sound. **—gesetz**, *n.* phonetic law. **—gymnastik**, *f.* phonetic exercises. **—gymnastiker**, *m.* advocate of phonetic exercises; phonetician (*coll.*). **—lehre**, *f.* science of sound; phonology; phonetics. **—los**, *adj.* silent, mute; without uttering a sound, speechless, astounded; **es herrschte —lose Stille**, all was hushed. **—nachahmung**, **—nachbildung**, *f.* imitation of sound; onomatopœia. **—physiologie**, *f.* physiology of sounds. **—schrift**, *f.* phonetic spelling, phonetic transcription *or* script; phonography. **—spaltung**, *f.* differentiation of sounds. **—system**, *n.* phonetic system, system of sounds. **—tafel**, *f.* sound-chart. **—unterschied**, *m.* difference in sound, phonetic difference. **—verhältnis**, *n.* relation *or* interrelation of sounds. **—verschiebung**, *f.* sound-shifting, Grimm's law (and modern extensions of it); **erste —verschiebung**, first *or* Germanic sound-shifting; **zweite —verschiebung**, second *or* High German sound-shifting. **—vertauschung**, *f.* permutation *or* substitution of sounds. **—wandel**, *m.* change of sounds, phonetic change. **—zeichen**, *n.* phonetic symbol.

Lau'te, *f.* (*pl.* **—n**) lute. **—ni'st**, *m.* (**—ni'sten**, *pl.* **—ni'sten**) lute-player. *Comp.* **—n=schlagen**, *n.* lute-playing. **—n=schläger**, *m.* lute-player.

Lau't—en, *v.n.* (*aux.* **h.**) to sound; to utter a sound; to purport, run, read; **das —et seltsam**, that sounds *or* seems strange; **die Worte —en so**, the words run thus *or* as follows; **wie —et sein Name?** what is his name? **wie —et das dritte Gebot?** what is the third commandment? **die Antwort —ete günstig**, the answer was favourable; **sein Urteil —et dahin**, his opinion is, that, *etc.*; **der Brief —et also**, the letter is to this effect; **das Urteil —et auf Tod**, the criminal is condemned to death. **—er**, *m.* (**—ers**, *pl.* **—er**) sound.

Läu't—en, *v.a. & n.* (*aux.* **h.**) to ring, peal, toll; **zur Kirche —en**, to ring the bells for church; **er hat —en hören, weiß aber nicht, wo die Glocken hängen**, he heard bells chiming, but he does not know whence the sound came. II. *subst.n.* ringing, tolling. **—er**, *m.* (**—ers**, *pl.* **—er**) bell-ringer.

Lau'ter, I. *adj.* clear, pure; unmixed; genuine; undefiled; **—e Absichten**, disinterested motives; **—bin ich vor deinen Augen**, I am clean in thine eyes (*B.*). II. *adv.* (*used as indec. adj.*) downright, mere, nothing but, pure and simple; **er trinkt — Wein**, he drinks nothing but wine; **es sind — Lügen**, it is all lies; **es sind nicht — Gelehrte auf der Welt**, not everybody is a scholar; **aus — Neid**, out of sheer envy; **sie ist — Leben**, she is all animation. **—keit**, *f.* purity, clearness; uprightness, sincerity.

Läu'terer, *m.* (**—s**, *pl.* **—**) purifier, refiner.

Läu'ter—n, *v.* I. *a.* to purify, refine, clear; to rectify (*spirits*); to purge; to refine (*metals, sugar, etc.*); to thin (*a wood*). II. *n.* (*aux.* **h.**) to enter an appeal for revision of a sentence (*Law*). **—ung**, *f.* purification; refining. *Comp.* **—bottich**, *m.* clearing-vat. **—feuer**, *n.* purifying fire; purgatory fire. **—haus**, *n.* refining house (*Sugar.*). **—kessel**, *m.* copper for sugar refining. **—kunst**, *f.* art of refining. **—tuch**, *n.* filter. **—vorrichtung**, *f.* clearing apparatus.

La'va, *f.* (*pl.* **Laven**) lava.

Laven'del, *m.* (**—s**) lavender. *Comp.* **—geist**, *m.* essence of lavender. **—wasser**, *n.* lavender water.

Lavi'ne, *see* **Lawine**.

Lavie'ren, *v.n.* (*aux.* **h.**) to tack (*Naut.*).

Lawi'ne, *f.* (*pl.* **—n**) avalanche.

Lax, *adj. & adv.* lax, loose; **—e Moral**, easy morals; **—e Sitten**, licentious manners *or* habits. **—a'nz**, *f.* (*pl.* **—an'zen**) aperient. —

heit, —itä't, *f.* laxity, looseness. **—ie'ren,** *v.* I. *n.* to take aperient medicine, to purge oneself. II. *a.* to purge. *Comp.* **—ie'r=mittel,** *n.* aperient, purge.

Lazare't(t), *n.* (—s, *pl.* —e) hospital; military hospital. *Comp.* **—fieber,** *n.* hospital fever. **—gehülfe,** *m.* hospital nurse; orderly. — **(kranken)wagen,** *m.* (field) ambulance, hospital waggon. **—wesen,** *n.* hospital service *or* arrangements.

Laz(z)aro'ne, *m.* (Neapolitan) beggar, lazzarone.

Le'b—en, I. *v.n.* (*aux.* h.) to live, be alive; to pass one's life; to dwell, live; to feed (**von,** on); **—en von,** to feed on, subsist on, to support oneself by; **von seinen Renten —en,** to live on one's means, have a fixed income; **es —e der König!** long live the King; **es —e England!** England forever! **mein (dein, sein) —e lang —en lang,** all my (your, his) life; **es —e die Freiheit!** liberty for ever! **hoch —en lassen,** to cheer, to drink (to) the health of; **so wahr ich —e,** as sure as I am alive; **so wahr Gott —t,** as sure as there is a God; **er ist es, wie er leibt und —t,** it is his very self; **er ist sein Vater wie er leibt und —t,** he is the very image of his father; **in den Tag hinein —en,** to live from hand to mouth, for the moment, in a happy-go-lucky way; **—(e) wohl! —en Sie wohl!** farewell! **er hat zu —en,** he has enough to live on, he has a competency; **nein, so etwas lebt nicht!** well, I never! you do not mean it! (*coll.*); **es —t alles an ihm,** he is full of life; **für sich —en,** to live alone, to live for oneself; **für eine Sache** *or* **einer Sache** (*dat.*) **—en,** to devote o.s. to a th.; **der Gerechtigkeit —en,** to live unto righteousness (*B.*); **er weiß zu —en,** he is a man of the world, he is well bred; **der Gerechte wird seines Glaubens —en,** the just shall live by faith (*B.*); **der Hoffnung —en,** to live in hope of; **man hat Ihren Vater —en lassen,** your father's health was drunk. II. *v.a.* to live (a life); **sich satt —en** *or* **sich satt gelebt haben,** to be weary of life; **hier lebt es sich gut,** it is pleasant living here. III. *subst.n.* (—ens, *pl.* —en) life; activity; vivacity; noise, ado, stir; living, subsistence; conduct; vital principle; the quick; darling; biography; way of life; **am —en, bei —en sein,** to be alive; **das geht ihm ans —en,** that will cost his life; his life is in danger; **es gilt sein —en,** his life is at stake; **bei Leib und —en,** upon pain of death; **bei meinem —en,** as I live, as long as I live; **bis aufs —en,** to the quick; **einem Pferde einen Nagel ins —en schlagen,** to drive a nail into the quick of a horse; **aus dem —en gegriffen,** taken from real life; **auf —en und Tod,** at the risk of one's life; lasting, fast; **Kampf auf —en und Tod,** mortal combat; **für sein —en gern thun,** to be very fond of doing; **ich darf es für mein —en nicht thun,** I dare not do it for the life of me; **ins —en setzen,** to give birth to; **ins — rufen,** to call into existence, to originate, start, establish; **ins —en treten,** to be born; to be started, established, to set up; **nach dem —en,** from life; **ums —en,** for (*my, thy, his, etc.*) life; **ums —en kommen,** to perish; **ums —en bringen,** to make away with, kill; **sein —en lassen,** to lay down one's life, to die; **sich** (*dat.*) **das —en nehmen,** to commit suicide, to kill oneself; **das war ein —en, als er kam,** there was a fine stir on his arrival; **Zeit meines —ens,** all my life long; **Ausdruck des gemeinen —ens,** every-day expression; **ein neues —en beginnen,** to turn over a new leaf (*coll.*); **— in die Bude bringen,** to make things lively, interesting (*coll.*). **—end,** *p. & adj.* living, alive; lively; **die —enden und die Toten,** the quick and the dead (*B.*); **—endes Wasser,** running water; **—ende Bilder,** tableaux vivants; **—ende Sprachen,** living tongues, modern languages; **—ende Hecken,** quickset hedges; **—ender Kalk,** unslacked lime; **der Tote bietet dem —enden die Hand,** the heir-at-law inherits as a matter of course; **ein hier —ender Freund,** a friend who lives here; **unter den noch —enden,** amongst the survivors; **lange —end,** long lived. **—endig,** *see* **Lebendig. —ens,** *see* **Lebens** *in comp.* **—haft,** *adj. & adv.* lively, vivacious, sprightly; gay, bright; smart, brisk; vivid; brilliant; strong, vigorous, forcible. — **haftigkeit,** *f.* liveliness, vivacity, sprightliness, gaiety, *etc.* **—ig,** *suff.* (*in comp.* =) -lived. *Comp.* **—e=hoch,** *n.* cheering, cheer; toast; **auf einen ein —ehoch ausbringen,** to drink to *or* propose a person's health. **—e=mann,** *m.* man of the world, worldling; epicurean; person enjoying life. **—e(n)=lang,** *n.* whole life, life-time. **—kuchen,** *m.* gingerbread. **—los,** *adj.* lifeless; inanimate. — **losigkeit,** *f.* lifelessness; impassiveness, dulness. **—tag,** *m.*; **das habe ich mein —tag nicht gesehen,** I never saw that in all my life; **meine —tage,** all the days of my life. **—zeit,** *f.* life-time; **bei meinen —zeiten,** during my life; **zu —zeiten meines Vaters,** in my father's lifetime. *See* **—ens=zeit.**

Leben'dig, *adj. & adv.* living, alive; active; lively; vivacious; vivid; strong, convincing; quick; vivifying; **—es Fleisch,** quick; **—e Hecke,** quickset hedge; **—es Silber,** quicksilver; **—es Wasser,** running *or* spring water; **—er Quell,** a running brook; **—machende Gnade,** quickening grace (*Theol.*); **der —e Gott,** the living God; **—es Geleit,** personal escort; **fünf —e Kinder,** five children living; **der —e Odem,** the breath of life (*B.*); **—e Unterhaltung,** animated conversation; **—e Anteilnahme,** warm interest; **—e Blumen,** natural flowers; **—er Schwefel,** natural brimstone; **bei —em Leibe,** alive; **tot oder —,** dead or alive; **es wird schon — auf der Straße,** people are already astir in the street. **—keit,** *f.* being alive; liveliness, vivacity. *Comp.* **—gebärend,** *adj.* viviparous. — **machend,** *adj.* vivifying, reviving; enlivening. **—machung,** *f.* vivification, quickening. — **werden,** *n.* animation (of conversation); commencement of life.

Le'bens— (*in comp.*) **—abend,** *m.* evening *or* decline of life. **—abriß,** *m.* biographical sketch. **—alter,** *n.* age. **—art,** *f.* way, mode of living, life; profession, trade; manners, breeding; **—art haben,** to be well-bred, to know what to do; **ohne —art,** ill-bred, ungentlemanly. **—assekuranz,** *f.* life-insurance. **—aufgabe,** *f.* life-work. **—bahn,** *f.* course, career. **—balsam,** *m.* restorative balsam. **—baum,** *m.* tree of life; arbor vitae. **—be=dingung,** *f.* condition essential to life; condition of vital importance. **—bedürfnisse,** *pl.* necessaries of life. **—beschreiber,** *m.* biographer. **—beschreibung,** *f.* biography. — **besserung,** *f.* reformation. **—bild,** *n.* sketch of a p.'s life, biography. **—blut,** *n.* life-blood. **—blüte,** *f.* prime of life. **—dauer,** *f.* duration of life; **lange —dauer,** longevity; **auf —dauer,** for life. **—eiche,** *f.* evergreen oak. **—elixir,** *n.* restorative, life-giving balsam. **—erhalter,** *m.* life-preserver. **—er=haltungs=trieb,** *m.* instinct of self-preservation. **—fähig,** *adj.* vital. **—fähigkeit,** *f.* vitality. **—flamme,** *f.*, **—feuer,** *n.* vital spark; vital energy. **—frage,** *f.* vital question. **—fratze,** *f.* ugly reality. **—freude, —freudigkeit,** *f.* enjoyment of life, pleasure of living. **—froh,** *adj.* happy. **—führung,** *f.* conduct of life. **—fülle,** *f.* fulness *or* plenitude of life; vigour. —gang, *m.* animal economy, vital functions; career, fate, life. —gefahr, *f.* danger of one's life; mit —gefahr, at the risk *or* peril of one's life. —gefährlich, *adj.* perilous, fraught with danger to life. —gefährte, —genoß, *m.*, —gefährtin, —genossin, *f.* companion through life, life-partner, husband, wife. —geist, *m.* principle *or* spirit of life; cordial, brandy, *etc.*; (*pl.*) animal spirits. —genuß, *m.* enjoyment of life. —geschichte, *f.* biography. —gestalt, *f.* the form one has in life; ein Bild in —gestalt, a full length picture. —glück, *n.* happiness of life. —glut, *f.* vital flame. —groß, *adj.* life-size. —größe, *f.* life-size. —güter, *pl.*, —habe, *f.* good things of this life, earthly possessions. —haltung, *f.* standard of life. —hauch, *m.* breath of life; life. —jahr, *n.* year of one's life; im dreißigsten —jahre, at the age of thirty. —klugheit, *f.* worldly wisdom. —kraft, *f.* vigour, vital power; vitality (*Med.*). —kreis, *m.* surroundings. —länglich, *adj. & adv.* perpetual; (—lang), life-long; for, through, during life; auf —lang, for life; —länglicher Gnadengehalt, pension for life; —längliches Mitglied, life member; —längliche Zwangsarbeit, penal servitude for life; —längliche Rente, life annuity, annuity for life. —länge, *f.* length *or* duration of life. —lauf, *m.* course, line, career of life. —lehre, *f.* biology; precept, rule of life. —licht, *n.* lamp of life; einem das —licht ausblasen, to take away a person's life. —luft, *f.* vital *or* life-sustaining air; atmosphere necessary for a p.'s life; oxygen. —lust, *f.* pleasure in life; love of life. —lustig, *adj.* enjoying life; cheerful, jovial, jolly. —magnetismus, *m.* animal magnetism. —mittel, *n.* food; provisions. —müde, *adj.* weary, tired of life. —mut, *m.* lively disposition; vital energy. —notdurft, *f.* bare necessaries of life. —ordnung, *f.* regulation of life; diet, regimen. —pfad, *m.* path of *or* through life. —pflicht, *f.* practical duty. —prozeß, *m.* animal economy, vital functions. —quell, *m.*, —quelle, *f.* source, spring of life. —regel, *f.* rule of conduct, maxim, precept. —reise, *f.* journey through life. —reiz, *m.* charm of life; pleasurable excitement. —rente, *f.* life-annuity. —rettungs-apparat, *m.* life-saving apparatus, life-belt. —satt, *see* —müde. —stellung, *f.* social position. —strafe, *f.* capital punishment; bei —ensstrafe, on pain of death. —tag, *m.* day of one's life, life. —thätigkeit, *f.* vitality; activity. —teile, *pl.* vitals, vital parts. —trieb, *m.* vitality. —trunken, *adj.* in exuberant vitality, full of vitality. —umstand, *m.* circumstances of one's life; anecdote. —unterhalt, *m.* livelihood, subsistence. —verrichtungen, *pl.* vital functions. —versicherungs-anstalt, —versicherungs-gesellschaft, *f.* life-insurance office, life assurance company. —voll, *adj.* full of life *or* vigour. —vorgang, *m.* phenomenon of life, event of life. —wandel, *m.* life, conduct. —wärme, *f.* vital warmth. —wasser, *n.* aqua vitae; cordial; spirits. —weg, *m.* path of life; leading conduit *or* passage (*Anat.*). —weise, *f.* mode of life, habits; diet. —weisheit, *f.* worldly wisdom. —zeit, *f.* time of life, age; lifetime; auf —zeit, for life; Mitglied auf —zeit, life-member; bei —zeit, during life, in life; auf —zeit zweier Personen, for the term of two lives; zur —zeit meines Vaters, in my father's lifetime, as long as my father was alive.

Le'ber, *f.* (*pl.* —n) liver; (*in comp. often* =) liver-coloured; frei von der — weg sprechen, to speak one's mind frankly, plainly. *Comp.* —anschwellung, *f.* enlargement of the liver. —beschwerde, *f.* liver-complaint. —blume, *f.* (anemone) hepatica (*Bot.*). —braun, *adj.* liver-coloured. —entzündung, *f.* hepatitis (*Med.*). —fleck(en), *m.* freckle. —gang, *m.* hepatic duct. —klee, *m.* liverwort; common clover. —krank, *adj.* having a liver-complaint. —reime, *pl.* humorous extempore verses originally made at dinner by persons eating a pike's liver, and invariably beginning with die Leber ist von einem Hecht; doggerel rhymes (*obs.*). —thran, *m.* cod-liver oil. —wurst, *f.* liver-sausage; white sausage.

Leb'kuchen, *m.* (—s, *pl.* —) gingerbread, spice-cake. *Comp.* —bäcker, (Leb'küchler,) *m.* baker of gingerbread.

Lech'zen, *v.n.* (*aux.* h.) to gape *or* split from drought; to be parched with thirst; nach einer S. —, to languish, long for, pant for a thing; nach Blut —, to thirst for blood.

Leck, I. *adj.* leaky, leaking; das Schiff ist —, the ship leaks, lets in water. II. *m. & n.* (—es, *pl.* —e) leak; einen — bekommen, to spring a leak. —a'ge, *f.* leakage.

[1]**Le'cken**, *v.n.* (*aux.* h.) to let in water, to leak; (*aux.* s.) to run, trickle out.

[2]**Le'cken, Lö'cken**, *v.n.* (*aux.* h.) (*obs.*) to spring; to strike *or* run against; to resist; *see* Läcken.

[3]**Le'ck—en**, *v.a.* to lick; to touch lightly; an den Fingern, sich (*dat.*) die Finger —en, to lick one's fingers; sich (*dat.*) die Finger nach etwas —en, to desire something greedily; das ist wie geleckt, that's as neat *or* nice as hands could make it; am Dache —en, to flame, flare up (*of a flame*). —er, *m.* (—ers, *pl.* —er) licker; dainty person; sweet-tooth; kisser, slobberer; fawner, toady; scamp; green-horn; tongue. II. *adj.* delicate, dainty, very nice; lickerish, dainty-mouthed, nice. —erei', *f.* daintiness; lickerishness; dainty, tit-bit. —erhaft, *adj.* dainty, lickerish. —erhaftigkeit, *f.* daintiness, lickerishness. —erheit, *f.* delicacy. —erli, *pl*; Basler —li, famous little ginger-cakes made at Basel. —ern, *v.n.* (*aux.* h.) to be dainty *or* lickerish. nach einer S. —ern, to long for a thing. *Comp.* —er-bissen, *m.* dainty, tit-bit. —er-gericht, *n.* dainty dish, luxurious repast. —er-maul, —er-mäulchen, *n.* dainty person, person fond of tit-bits, sweets, etc. —er-werk, *n.* dainties, sweets.

Le'der, *n.* (—s, *pl.* —) leather; skin; anything made of leather; ungegerbtes —, undressed leather; lohgares —, tanned leather; weiches —, kid; zugerichtetes —, dressed *or* curried leather; vom — ziehen, to draw one's sword; einem das — gerben, to thrash a p. —ei', *f.* leather-work. —n, I. *adj.* leathern, of leather; dull, tedious, heavy; Philistine; eine —ne Seele, a bore, duffer (*coll.*). II. *v.a.* to curry, dress (*as leather*); to garnish, furnish with leather, to thrash. *Comp.* —arbeiter, *m.* worker in leather. —artig, *adj.* leathery, tough. —band, I. *m.* binding in calf. II. *n.* leather strap *or* thong. —bereiter, *m.* leather-dresser, currier. —bereitung, *f.* leather-dressing. —beutel, *m.* leather bag. —braun, *adj.* tawny. —handel, *m.* leather trade. —händler, *m.* dealer in leather. —haut, *f.* thick skin; cutis vera (*Anat.*). —hosen, *pl.* leather breeches. —kalk, *m.* quick-lime. —koffer, *m.* trunk. —leim, *m.* size. —leinwand, *f.* dowlas. —pappe, *f.* leather board. —riemen, *m.* leather strap; strop (*for shaving*). —schwärze, *f.* currier's black. —sitz, *m.* leather bottom. —streifen, *m.* leather thong. —werk, *n.* leather articles. —zeug, *n.* shoulder belt, leather articles of a soldier's accoutrements. —zucker, *m.* marsh-mallow paste; schwarzer —zucker, liquorice lozenges.

Le'dig, *adj. & adv.* empty; free, unencumbered, untrammelled; idle, unoccupied; vacant; unmarried, single; exempt (*from*); **—es Frauenzimmer,** spinster; **—er Mann,** bachelor; **—er Stand,** single-blessedness (*coll.*), celibacy; **aller Pflichten los und —,** exempt from all duties; **los und — sprechen,** to absolve, to acquit; **eine —e Stelle,** a vacancy; **eine —e Stunde,** a leisure hour; **— gehen,** to be unemployed, to idle about; **— bleiben,** to remain a spinster, to be left on the shelf (*of girls*); to remain a bachelor; **ich bleibe —,** I shall not marry; **— sein,** to be single; to live in single-blessedness (*coll.*). **—en,** *v.a.* to acquit, set free (*rare, poet.*). **—keit,** *f.* celibacy. **—lich,** *adv.* only, quite, entirely, purely, solely, merely. *Comp.* **—lassung,** *f.* release. **—sprechung,** *f.* acquittal; granting the freedom of a company.

Lee, *n.* lee, lee-side (*Naut.*); **das Ruder in —!** ease the helm! **in — fallen,** to drive to leeward. *Comp.* **—segel,** *n.* studding-sail.

Leer, *adj. & adv.* empty; void, vacant; blank; inane; hollow, vain; **—es Blatt,** clean sheet of paper; **mit —en Händen,** empty-handed; **—er Raum,** empty space, vacuum, blank space; **—es Stroh** thrashed straw; **—es Stroh dreschen,** to beat the air, to pour water into a sieve; **ein —es Gerücht,** an unfounded report, a report devoid of truth; **ein —es Papier,** a blank; **es wird nicht so — abgehen,** something will be gained, something will come of it yet; they will come to blows. **—e,** *f.* (*pl.* **—en**) void, emptiness, vacancy; blank; vacuum; emptiness, nothingness. **—heit,** *f.* emptiness; futility; inanition (*Med.*). *Comp.* **—darm,** *m.* jejunum. **—faß,** *n.* emptying vat. **—gebrannt,** *adj.* burnt-out.

Lee'ren, *v.a.* to empty, void, clear out, pour out; **der Saal leerte sich in fünf Minuten,** the room was cleared in five minutes.

Lef'ze, *f.* (*pl.* **—n**) lip; languet (*of an organ-pipe*).

Lega'l, *adj. & adv.* legal, lawful. **—isie'ren,** *v.a.* to legalize, to validate. **—isie'rung,** *f.* legalization. **—itä't,** *f.* legality.

Lega't, I. *m.* (**—en,** *pl.* **—en**) legate. II. *n.* (**—s,** *pl.* **—e**) legacy; **bedingtes —,** contingent bequest. **—a'r,** *m.* (**—ars,** *pl.* **—are**) legate. **—io'n,** *f.* (*pl.* **—ionen**) legation, embassy. *Comp.* **—ions'=rat,** *m.* counsellor to a legation. **—ions'=sekretär,** *m.* secretary of legation.

Le'gel, *m. see* **Lägel.**

Le'g—en, *v.* I. *a.* to lay, put, place; to deposit; to lay (*snares; dust; corn, etc.*); to set, plant (*potatoes, etc.*); **Eier —en,** to lay eggs; **einen Fußboden —en,** to lay down a floor; **einen Teppich —en,** to put down a carpet; **einem das Handwerk —en,** to put a stop to a p.'s proceedings, to throw a spoke into a p.'s wheel; **einem die Karten —en,** to tell a p.'s fortune from cards; **einem etwas nahe —en,** to give a p. a hint, to make a strong suggestion; **kreuzweise, quer —en,** to lay across, to cross; **in die Nesseln —en,** to put into the wrong place, to make a mistake; **ein kluges Huhn —t auch einmal vorbei,** even a clever person may make a mistake; **an die Kette —en,** to chain up; **an den Tag —en,** to make known; show; **Hand an (eine S.) —en,** to turn one's hand to, take in hand; **einem (etwas) ans Herz —en,** to bring home to a p.; **Hand an sich selbst —en,** to commit suicide; **sich auf die Bärenhaut, auf die faule Seite, aufs Ohr, auf den Rücken —en,** to be lazy, to take it easy, to play the sluggard; **sich aufs Bitten —en,** to have recourse to entreaty; **Geld auf Zinsen —en,** to invest capital; **großen Wert auf eine S. —en,** to attach great importance to a th., to esteem a th. very highly; **aus einander —en,** to put asunder, to unfold, explain, analyze; **die Sachen durch einander —en,** to put things higgledy-piggledy; **einem Einquartierung ins Haus —en,** to quarter soldiers on a p.; **die Hände in den Schoß —en,** to sit with one's hands in one's lap, to fold one's hands, to be idle; **einem Worte in den Mund —en, auf die Zunge —en,** to prompt a p., to ascribe words to a p. falsely; **ein Feld in den Grund —en,** to map a field; **sich ins Mittel —en,** to interpose; **in Asche —en,** to reduce to ashes; **Bresche in etwas** (*acc.*) **—en,** to batter in (*Mil.*); **eine Decke über den Tisch —en,** to spread a cloth on the table; **sich** (*acc.*) *or* **ein Schiff vor Anker —en,** to cast anchor; **sich vor eine Stadt —en,** to encamp before, to besiege a town; **einem den Kopf vor die Füße —en,** to cut off a p.'s head; **zur Schau —en,** to expose to view; **zur Schuld —en,** to charge with. II. *r.* to lie down; to go to bed; to cease, fall, subside, abate; to settle; to be quiet; **sich auf eine S. —en,** to apply oneself to, give oneself up to, devote oneself to. III. *n.* (*aux.* **h.**) to steer, keep (towards, **nach**; off, **von**). **—er,** *m.* (**—ers,** *pl.* **—er**) layer, placer; lifter, layer (*in paper-mills*); setter (*of plants*); water-barrel. *Comp.* **—e=brett,** *n.* gangway. **—e=geld,** *n.* entrance-money. **—e=henne,** *f.,* **—e=huhn,** *n.* laying-hen. **—e=schuß,** *m.* shot from a spring-gun. **—e=stachel,** *m.* ovipositor (*Ent.*). **—e=stein,** *m.* coping-stone. **—e=zeit,** *f.* laying-season. **—föhre,** *f.* dwarf-pine.

Legen'de, *f.* (*pl.* **—n**) legend. **—n=haft,** *adj.* legendary. *Comp.* **—n=buch,** *n.,* **—n=sammlung,** *f.* book *or* collection of legends, legendary.

Le'ger=wall, *m.* lee-shore (*Naut.*).

Legio'n, *f.* (*pl.* **—en**) legion. **—ä'r,** *m.* (**—ärs,** *pl.* **—äre**) legionary; member of the Legion of Honour. *Comp.* **—s=kreuz,** *n.* cross of the Legion of Honour. **—s=soldat,** *m.* legionary.

[1]**Legie'ren,** *v.a.* to bequeath (*obs.*).

[2]**Legie'r—en,** *v.a.* to thicken (*soup*); to alloy **—ung,** *f.* alloy.

Legislat—io'n, *f.* legislation; legislative power. **—u'r,** *f.* legislature.

Legiti'm, *adj.* legitimate. **—ie'ren,** *v.a.* to legitimize; to make lawful. **—itä't,** *f.* legitimacy. *Comp.* **—atio'ns=marke,** *f.* mark *or* badge of genuineness, trade-mark.

Leh'd—e, *f.* waste *or* fallow land. **—ling,** *m.* (**—lings,** *pl.* **—linge**) mushroom.

Le'h(e)n, *n.* (**—(e)s,** *pl.* **—**) fief, fee, feudal tenure; loan (*obs.*) (*pl.*) investiture, enfeoffment; **als — besitzen** *or* **zu — tragen,** to hold in fee; **zu — geben,** to invest with; **unbedingtes, freies —,** fee simple. **—bar,** *adj.* feudal; capable of holding a fief. **—barkeit,** *f.* feudality. *Comp.* **—(s)=adel,** *m.* feudal nobility. **—bauer,** *m.* peasant holding land on feudal tenure. **—besitz,** *m.* copy-hold. **—(s)=brief,** *m.* bill of enfeoffment; title-deed. **—dienst,** *m.* feudal service, vassalage. **—(s)=entsetzung, —s=einziehung,** *f.* seizure of *or* distraint upon a fief, dispossession. **—(s)=eid,** *m.* oath of allegiance. **—erbe,** I. *m.* successor to a fief. II. *n.* hereditary fief. **—(s)=fähig,** *see* **—bar.** **—(s)=fall,** *m.* vacancy *or* escheat of a feudal tenure. **—(s)=frau,** *f.* lady-paramount; female vassal. **—(s)=frei,** *adj.* allodial; **ein Gut —frei machen,** to alienate an estate in mortmain. **—geld,** *n.* (renewal) fine. **—gut,** *n.* estate in fee; **freies —gut,** freehold. **—(s=)herr,** *m.* liege lord. **—hof,** *m.* court-leet. **—(s=)leute,** *pl.* lieges, vassals, tenantry. **—(s)=mann,** *m.* vassal. **—recht,** *n.* feudal right; right of investiture; feudal law. **—s=folge,** *f.* succession to a fief; feudal obligation to serve in war; —**sfolge leisten**, to follow one's liege-lord to war. —**s=herrlichkeit**, *f.* feudality; dignity of a feudal lord. —**s=pflicht**, *f.* vassalage; homage; fealty. —**s=system**, *n.*, —**s=verfassung**, *f.* feudal system. —**s=treue**, *f.* allegiance. —**s=verhältnis**, *n.* vassalage. —**s=wesen**, *n.* feudalism.

Lehm, *m.* (—**es**, *pl.* —**e**) loam, clay; mud. —**e(r)n**, *adj* loamy; of mud. —**icht**, (*obs.*) —**ig**, *adj.* loamlike, loamy. *Comp.* —**arbeit**, *f.*, —**bau**, *m.* mud-walling, building with mud. —**artig**, *adj.* loamy. —**boden**, *m.* loamy, clayey soil; clay-floor. —**formerei**, *f.* moulding in clay; clay-modeller's studio *or* work-shop. —**grube**, *f.* loam-pit. —**hütte**, *f.* mud-hut. —**kleber**, —**klicker**, *m.* worker in clay. —**stein**, *m.* clay-brick.

Leh'ne, *f.* (*pl.* —**n**) support for leaning against *or* on, prop; hand-rail; balustrade; battlement; arm *or* back of a chair; gallows (*Typ.*); slope, inclined plane; linch-pin.

Leh'n—en, *v.a. & n.* (*aux.* **h.** & **s.**) to lean, incline, recline; to rest; to lay, put; **das Heer —te sich an einen Wald**, the army was drawn up with a wood in its flank *or* rear; **der eine Gang —t sich mit dem andern**, one lode runs into another. *Comp.* —**bank**, *f.* flank *or* bench with a back. —**beet**, *n.* garden-bed sloping from a sunny wall. —**brett**, *n.* back-board (*Naut.*); reclining-board. —**fenster**, *n.* window with embrasure *or* breastwork. —**sessel**, —**stuhl**, *m.* easy chair, arm-chair.

Leh'n—en, *v.* I. *a.* to lend, to borrow (*obs.*). II. *n.* (*aux.* **h.**) to hold from (*obs.*). *Comp.* —**satz**, *m.* lemma (*Mathem.*). —**wort**, *n.* loan-word, word borrowed from another language.

Lehr'—bar, *adj.* teachable. —**barkeit**, *f.* capability of being taught, teachableness. —**e**, *f.* (*pl.* —**en**) doctrine, dogma, tenet, theory; science; rule, precept; moral; system of instruction; apprenticeship, time of learning; model, mould, pattern; gauge; centre (*Arch.*); measure, rule; calibre; equilibrium; **in die —e geben** *or* **thun**, to bind apprentice; **er ist bei Herrn N. in der —e**, he is serving his time with Mr. N.; **laßt euch dies zur —e dienen!** let this be a warning to you! **die —e von der besten Welt**, the theory of the best world, optimism.

Leh'r—en, *v.a.* (**einen** *or* (*obs.*) **einem etwas**) to teach, instruct; to inform; to show, prove; to take the calibre of; **einen lesen —en**, to teach a p. to read; **er —et meine Hände streiten**, he teacheth my hands to war (*B.*); **die Zeit wird es —en**, time will show *or* tell; **öffentlich —en**, to give public lectures, to be a professor. —**end**, *p. & adj.* didactic; instructive, *etc.* —**er**, *m.* (—**ers**, *pl.* —**er**) teacher, master; instructor; **öffentlicher —er**, public teacher, professor; **Haus—** *or* **Privat —**, private tutor; **Klassen —er**, form master; —**er des Deutschen**, German master. —**erin**, *f.* woman teacher, mistress; governess; **Klassen —erin**, form-mistress; **Haus —erin**, governess (*either* resident *or* daily); **Privat —erin**, visiting governess; **Musik —erin**, music mistress; —**erin der französischen Sprache**, French mistress. —**erschaft**, *f.* body of teachers; condition of a teacher. —**haft**, *adj.* instructive; fond of teaching; —**hafter Natur sein**, to be naturally fond of teaching —**ling**, *m.* (—**lings**, *pl.* —**linge**) pupil, disciple, scholar; apprentice; novice, tyro. —**samkeit**, *f.* docility. *Comp.* —**amt**, *n.* office of a teacher; **wissenschaftliches —amt**, professorship; **geistliches —amt**, ministry, ecclesiastical function. —**amts=kandidat**, *m.* candidate for a mastership, probationer, probationary teacher, assistant master not yet duly appointed. —**anstalt**, *f.* school, academy; **höhere —anstalt**, secondary school; **städtische —anstalt**, municipal school. —**art**, *f.* method of teaching. —**aufgabe**, *f.* programme of work; —**aufgabe der Obersecunda**, work to be done in the Upper V. —**auftrag**, *m.* professorship; **einen —auftrag erhalten**, to be appointed (university) professor. —**basis**, *f.* doctrinal basis. —**bataillon**, *n.* school battalion. —**begier**, *f.*, —**begierde**, *f.* desire of teaching *or* instructing. —**befähigung**, *f.* certificate of qualification to teach; —**befähigung für alle Klassen**, qualification to teach in all forms. —**begierig**, *adj.* eager to teach. —**begriff**, *m.* system; outline, manual of a science. —**beruf**, *m.* scholastic profession; teaching line (*coll.*). —**bogen**, *m.* centre, centering (*wooden framework on which an arch, etc., is constructed*). —**bote**, *m.* apostle, missionary. —**brief**, *m.* indenture of an apprentice; didactic epistle. —**brett**, *n.* templet (*Arch.*); mould, pattern; bottom (*Fort.*). —**buch**, *n.* manual (*of instruction*); compendium, text-book. —**bursche**, *m.* apprentice. —**dichter**, *m.* didactic poet. —**er=bildungsanstalt**, *f.*, —**er=seminar**, *n.* training-college for teachers. —**erinnen=seminar**, *n.* training college for women teachers (*in Germany often attached to a large high school for girls*). —**er=kollegium**, *n.* staff of teachers of the same school. —**er=prüfung**, *f.* examination for teachers. —**er=stand**, *m.* status of teachers, body of teachers, members of the teaching profession. —**er=stelle**, *f.* place of teacher; tutorship (*in a family*); mastership (*at a school*); professorship (*at a University*). —**er=stellung**, *f.* status of teachers. —**er=welt**, *f.* scholastic world. —**er=zeitung**, *f.* scholastic *or* educational journal. —**er=zeugnis**, *n.* teacher's certificate *or* diploma. —**fach**, *n.* teaching profession. —**fähig**, *adj.* capable of teaching. —**form**, *f.* didactic form; method of teaching. —**freiheit**, *f.* freedom of teaching; freedom of the teacher. —**gabe**, *f.* talent for teaching. —**gang**, *m.* course (*of instruction, lectures, etc.*). —**gebäude**, *n.* system (*of a science, etc.*). —**gedicht**, *n.* didactic poem. —**gegenstand**, *m.* subject taught, branch of study. —**gehülfe**, *m.* junior assistant teacher, teacher of the elements, usher. —**geld**, *n.* money paid for instruction; apprentice's premium; bought experience; —**geld geben**, to pay dear for one's wisdom. —**grund**, *m.* principle, basis (*of a science, etc.*). —**herr**, *m.* master, employer. —**jahre**, *pl.* years of apprenticeship; **seine —jahre ausstehen** *or* **durchmachen**, to serve out one's time. —**junge**, *m.* apprentice. —**jünger**, *m.* disciple. —**kanzel**, *f.* (professor's) lecturing desk (*Austrian*). —**körper**, *m.* (body of) teachers, (body of) professors, (teaching) staff. —**kraft**, *f.*; **ausgezeichnete —kräfte**, distinguished teachers. —**kunst**, *f.* didactics; art of teaching. —**lings=stand**, *m.* apprenticeship; novitiate —**mädchen**, *n.* apprentice-girl. —**mäßig**, *adj. & adv.* dogmatic. —**meinung**, *f.* dogma; hypothesis. —**meister**, *m.* teacher, instructor; master of a trade. —**meisterin**, *f.* preceptress, master's wife. —**meisterlich**, *adj. & adv.* preceptorial; pedantic. —**mittel**, *n.* means of instruction, apparatus (*for instruction*). —**plan**, *n.* course of instruction, programme of work, school-curriculum. —**probe**, *f.* (*time of*) probation, novitiate, trial lesson. —**punkt**, *m.* point of doctrine, tenet. —**reich**, *adj.* instructive. —**saal**, *m.* lecture-room; class-room. —**satz**, *m.* thesis; dogma; theorem; aphorism; precept. —**spruch**, *m.* maxim, adage. —**stand**, *m.* body of teachers, scholastic profession (*as opposed to* **Nährstand** *and* **Wehrstand**, men of business and soldiers). **—stelle**, *see* **—erstelle**. **—stil**, *m.* didactic style; dogmatic style. **—stoff**, *m.* matter of instruction. **—stube**, *f.* schoolroom. **—stuhl**, *m.* professorial chair; professor's *or* teacher's seat. **—stunde**, *f.* (*teacher's*) lesson, (*professor's*) lecture. **—thätigkeit**, *f.* teacher's work, professorial work, educational work. **—verbesserung**, *f.* reformation of doctrine; improvement in methods of instruction. **—vertrag**, *see* **—brief**. **—weg**, *m.*, **—weise**, *f.* method of teaching. **—widrig**, *adj.* contrary to an accepted doctrine *or* dogma, heterodox. **—zeit**, *f.* apprenticeship. **—ziel**, *n.* aim to be attained (by the instruction). **—zwang**, *m.* compulsory subjection to a certain teaching *or* doctrine.

Lei *as the second part of compounds* = of . . . kind, of . . . sorts, *e.g.* **fünfer—**, of five sorts; **aller—**, of all kinds; **keiner—**, of no kind.

Leib, *m.* (—(e)s, *pl.* —er) body; waist; belly; womb; bodice; trunk, body; life (*obs.*); **toter —**, corpse (*of a man*); carcass (*of an animal*); **gut bei —e sein**, to be plump, fat; **— an —**, hand to hand (*combat*); **— und Magen-Gericht**, favourite dish (*fam.*); **auf — und Leben**, for one's life, for a capital crime; **mit — und Leben**, with heart and soul; **es ging ihm an — und Leben**, his life was at stake; his life was forfeit(ed); **bei —e nicht!** not for your life! not on any account! **einem auf den — rücken**, **(scharf) zu —e gehen**, to attack a p. sharply, to close in on s.o.; **bei —es Leben**, during life, in the body; **bei lebendigem —e**, (all) alive; **bleib mir vom —e! drei Schritt vom —e!** keep off! **bleib mir damit vom —e**, don't bother me about that; **am —e strafen**, to inflict corporal punishment; **am ganzen —e zittern**, to tremble all over; **einem eine Rolle auf den — schreiben**, to write a part expressly for an actor; **einer Sache geradezu auf den — gehen**, to go straight to the point; **sich** (*dat.*) **den — voll schlagen**, to eat one's fill (*vulg.*); **kein Hemd auf dem —e haben**, not to have a shirt to one's back; **kein Herz im —e haben**, to have no heart, to have no courage; **verstopften — haben**, to be constipated; **gesegneten —es**, pregnant; **gesegneten —es sein**, to be with child, to be in the family way; **der — des Herrn**, the body of the Lord, the Eucharist, the consecrated wafer; **unser irdischer —**, our mortal clay; **ist der — glatt oder gereiht?** is the body (bodice) plain *or* full? **—chen**, *n.* (—chens, *pl.* —chen) bodice; corset. **—en**, *v.n.* (*aux.* **h.**) *in the phrase:* **wie er —t und lebt**, just as he is, just himself, his very self. **—haft**, **—haftig** (*often pron.* **leibhaf'tig**), *adj. & adv.* corporal, bodily, in one's own person *or* body; living; real, true; incarnate; **—haftig erscheinen**, to appear in person *or* visibly; **es ist sein —haftiges Ebenbild**, **er ist es —haftig**, it is his very image; **der —haftige Teufel**, the devil incarnate. **—ig**, *only used as a suffix;* having such and such a body; **dickleibig**, corpulent. **—lich**, *adj.* bodily, corporal; natural, one's own; temporal; **mit —lichen Augen sehen**, to see with one's own eyes; **der sein —liches Angesicht im Spiegel beschaut**, a man beholding his natural face in the glass (*B.*); **—licher Bruder**, full brother; **—licher Vetter**, cousin german; **ihr —licher Sohn**, her own son; **—liche Güter**, carnal things (*B.*); earthly goods; **—licher Tod**, natural death. **—lichkeit**, *f.* corporeality. *Comp.* **—arzt**, *m.* physician in ordinary (*to the king, etc.*). **—binde**, *f.* scarf; girdle, waistband; bandage; (*hygienic*) belt. **—buch**, *n.* favourite book (*coll.*). **—bürge**, *m.* hostage. **—diener**, *m.* page; valet de chambre. **—ei'gen**, *adj.* bond, in thraldom *or* villanage; **ein —eigener**, serf, bondman; **eine —eigene**, bondwoman. **—ei'genschaft**, *f.* bondage, serfdom; vassalage. **—ei'gentum**, *n.* proprietary right over the person of another. **—essen**, *n.* favourite dish (*coll.*). **—farbe**, *f.* favourite colour (*coll.*). **—frone**, *f.* soccage, personal statute service. **—fuchs**, *m.* freshman who acts as a sort of fag to an older student (**Korpsstudent**); favourite chestnut horse. **—garde**, *f.* bodyguard, life-guards. **—gardist**, *m.* life-guardsman. **—gedinge**, (**Libding**,) *n.* transference of a holding from father to son; jointure, settlement; life annuity; dower; appanage; stipulation of a landlord selling his property in addition to the purchase-money. **—geleit**, *n.* safe-conduct. **—gericht**, *n.* favourite dish (*coll.*). **—gurt**, **—gürtel**, *m.* waist-belt. **—gut**, *n.* estate for life. **—jäger**, *m.* prince's own huntsman *or* gamekeeper; chasseur (*Mil.*); rifleman of the guard *or* of the royal rifles. **—knecht**, *m.* groom of the royal stables. **—kompagnie**, *f.* colonel's own company, first company of a regiment. **—kutscher**, *m.* one's own coachman; royal coachman. **—lakai**, *m.* prince's own valet. **—los**, *adj.* incorporeal. **—pacht**, *f.* lease for life. **—page**, *m.* page in ordinary. **—pferd**, *n.* one's own riding-horse; favourite horse. **—regiment**, *n.* life-guards; prince's own regiment. **—rente**, *f.* life-annuity; **Geld auf —rente anlegen**, to sink money in an annuity. **—rentner**, *m.* annuitant. **—rock**, *m.* close-fitting coat; dress-coat. **—schaden**, *m.* bodily defect; rupture. **—schmerz**, *m.* (*us. pl.*), **—schneiden**, *n.* stomachache, colic. **—schneider**, *m.* tailor to a prince. **—schwadron**, *f.* first squadron of a cavalry regiment. **—spruch**, *m.* favourite saying *or* maxim. **—stück**, *n.* favourite piece, favourite tune *or* air (*Mus.*). **—wache**, *f.* body-guard, life-guards. **—wächter**, *m.* soldier of the body-guard, satellite. **—wäsche**, *f.* body-linen. **—zahnarzt**, *m.* court dentist, his majesty's own dentist. **—zeichen**, *n.* signs of murder on a dead body. **—züchter**, *m.*, **—züchterin**, *f.* life-annuitant. **—zwang**, *m.* constipation.

Lei'bes— (*in comp.*) **—bau**, *m.* build of body, form. **—beschaffenheit**, *f.* physical constitution; temperament. **—beschwerde**, **—beschwerung**, *f.* bodily infirmity; constipation. **—bürde**, *f.* fruit of the womb, fetus. **—dicke**, *f.* corpulence; thickness. **—erbe**, *m.* legitimate heir; offspring; (*pl.*) issue. **—frucht**, *f.* offspring; fetus, embryo; **Tötung der —frucht**, feticide. **—gebrechen**, *n.*, **—fehler**, *m.* bodily infirmity *or* deformity. **—gefahr**, *f.* bodily peril. **—gestalt**, *f.* figure, shape. **—größe**, *f.* stature. **—haft**, *f.* arrest. **—kraft**, *f.* physical strength; **aus —kräften**, with might and main; **er schrie aus —kräften**, he shouted at the top of his voice. **—leben**, *n.* bodily life; **bei —leben**, while alive; **bei —leben nicht!** not for your life! **—nahrung**, *f.* food; **—nahrung und -Notdurft**, bodily needs. **—öffnung**, *f.* opening of the bowels, motion. **—pflege**, **—sorge**, *f.* care of the body. **—stärke**, *see* **—kraft**. **—stellung**, *f.* posture, attitude. **—strafe**, *f.* corporal punishment. **—übung**, *f.* bodily exercise; **sich** (*dat.*) **—übung machen**, to take exercise, to go in for gymnastics *or* games. **—übungs-kunst**, *f.* gymnastics.

[1]**Leich**, *m.* (—es, *pl.* —e) song consisting of a number of stanzas of unequal length; **die Lieder und Leiche der Minnesinger**, the songs and lays of the minnesingers (songs consisting of stanzas of equal length and songs consisting of stanzas of unequal length); lay.

[2]**Leich**, *see* **Laich**.

Lei'ch—e, *f.* (*pl.* —en) dead body, corpse; funeral; omitted word(s) (*Typ.*); **zur —e gehen,** to attend a funeral (*dial.*). **—enhaft,** *adj.* corpse-like, cadaverous; funereal. **—nam,** *m.* (—nams, *pl.* —name) body; dead body, remains; **seines —nams pflegen,** to eat and drink well (*coll.*). *Comp.* **—dorn,** *m.* corn. **—dorn=schneider,** *m.* chiropodist.

Lei'chen, *pl. see* **Leiche.** *Comp.* **—acker,** *m.* church-yard, burying-ground. **—artig,** *adj.* cadaverous. **—begängnis,** *n.* funeral obsequies. **—begleiter,** *m.* mourner; follower at a funeral; **bezahlter —begleiter,** mute. **—begleitung,** *f.*, **—geleit,** *n.* funeral procession. **—besorger,** *m.* undertaker. **—beschauer,** *m.* coroner. **—bestattung,** *see* **—begängnis.** **—bitter,** *m.* he who invites to a funeral. **—bitter=gesicht,** *n.* woeful *or* woebegone countenance. **—blaß,** *adj.* pale as death. **—blässe,** *f.* ghastliness. **—buch,** *n.* register of deaths and burials. **—chor,** *m.* funeral dirge. **—dieb,** *m.* body-snatcher. **—dienst,** *m.* burial-service. **—duft,** *m.* cadaverous smell. **—essen, —mahl,** *n.*, **—schmaus,** *m.* funeral repast. **—eule,** *f.* screech-owl. **—fackel,** *f.* funeral torch. **—farbe,** *f.* pallor of death. **—feld,** *n.* field strewed with dead bodies, battle field. **—feier,** *f.*, **—fest,** *n.* obsequies. **—frau,** *f.* woman who lays out corpses. **—gebräuche,** *pl.* funeral rites. **—gebühr,** *f.* burial-fee. **—gedicht,** *n.* funeral poem. **—gepränge,** *n.* funeral pomp. **—geruch,** *see* **—duft.** **—gerüst,** *n.* catafalque. **—gesang,** *m.* dirge. **—gewand, —hemd,** *n.* winding sheet, shroud. **—gruft,** *f.*, **—gewölbe,** *n.* burial vault; catacomb. **—haus,** *n.* house of mourning. **—kammer,** *f.* room where corpses are deposited, mortuary; dissecting room. **—kasse,** *f.* funds of a burying-club. **—kommissar(ius),** *m.* undertaker. **—musik,** *f.* dead march, funeral music. **—öffnung,** *f.* dissection; post-mortem examination. **—phantasie,** *f.* Elegiac Phantasy (*by Schiller*). **—predigt, —rede,** *f.* funeral oration. **—schau,** *f.* inquest on a dead body. **—schauer,** *m.* coroner. **—schau=stätte,** *f.* morgue. **—schleier,** *m.* shroud. **—stein,** *m.* tombstone. **—still,** *adj.* quite still. **—träger,** *m.* bearer. **—tuch,** *n.* shroud; pall; face-cloth. **—untersuchung,** *f.* post mortem examination, inquest. **—vogel,** *m.* screech owl. **—verbrennung,** *f.* cremation. **—wache, —weihe,** *f.* watching by the dead, wake. **—wagen,** *m.* hearse. **—zug,** *m.* funeral procession; look of death.

Leicht, *adj. & adv.* light, not heavy; easy, not difficult, facile; nimble; mild (*of tobacco*); light (*of wine*); slight; trifling; superficial; fickle, flighty; feeble, faint; easy, free; **eine —e Fliege,** a loose fish; **—en Absatz finden,** to be disposed of easily, to go off rapidly, to sell readily; **etwas auf die —e Achsel nehmen,** to take, treat a th. lightly, to take it easy; **—e Bewegung,** easy, graceful movement; **mit —er Bewegung des Kopfes,** with a slight nod; **—en Fußes,** light of foot; **—es Gewebe,** light, flimsy texture; **es ward mir —er ums Herz,** I felt relieved; **—en Kaufs,** at a cheap rate, easily; **den Kopf — machen,** to open one's mind; **—e Naht,** basting; **—e Reiterei,** light horse; **—er Sinn,** cheerful temper; **das kann — sein,** that is very possible; **nicht —,** not easily, seldom, scarcely; **wie — ist ein Unglück geschehen!** how easily an accident may happen! **— nehmen,** to treat lightly, take coolly; **es ist — gesagt,** it is easy to say; **— über eine Sache hin gehen,** to treat a th. superficially, to pass over a th. lightly; **ich kann es nicht — thun,** I cannot well do it; **es ist nicht — zu befürchten,** it is but little to be feared; **außer ihm wird es nicht — jemand thun,** I see no one except himself who is likely to do it; **die Arbeit geht ihr — von der Hand,** she is quick at work; **es kann — anders kommen,** it may easily turn out otherwise; **es zieht — den Sinn ab,** it tends to draw away the mind. **—er,** *m.* (—ers, *pl.* —er), (**—er=schiff,** *n.*,) lighter (*Naut.*). **—heit, —igkeit,** *f.* lightness; agility; facility; ease, readiness. **—lich,** *adj. & adv.* lightly, easily. *Comp.* **—bedeckt,** *adj.* lightly covered. **—beschwingt,** *adj.* rapid-flying. **—beweglich,** *adj.* quick; changeable, mobile. **—blütig,** *adj.* sanguine; lively, playful. **—faßlich,** *adj.* easily understood, popular. **—fertig,** *adj.* light, frivolous; volatile; wanton; loose; inconsiderate, unscrupulous. **—fertigkeit,** *f.* frivolity; light-mindedness; wantonness; libertinism; mischievousness. **—fuß,** *m.* light-minded (giddy *or* frivolous) person; giddy head; **er ist ein —fuß,** he is a happy-go-lucky fellow. **—flüssig,** *adj.* very fusible, easily dissolved. **—füßig,** *adj.* nimble, light of foot. **—gläubig,** *adj.* credulous. **—hi'n,** *adv.* lightly, superficially. **—lebigkeit,** *f.* lightheartedness, easy-going disposition. **—sinn,** *m.*, **—sinnigkeit,** *f.* levity, frivolity; indiscretion; thoughtlessness; **das sagen Sie in Ihrem jugendlichen —sinn,** surely you have not considered what you have just said (*coll.*). **—sinnig,** *adj.* frivolous, light-minded; thoughtless. **—verderblich,** *adj.* perishable (*of goods*).

Leid, I. *adj.* painful, disagreeable (*old noun used only predicatively with* **sein, thun, werden,** *and dat.*); **es ist mir —,** I am sorry, I regret; **es that mir — um Sie,** I pitied you, I was sorry for you; **einem etwas — machen,** to make one repent of, to put a p. out of conceit with a thing; **sein Vergehen ist ihm —,** he is sorry for his fault; **es wird dir einmal — werden,** you will one day be sorry for it *or* repent it; **laß dir das nicht — sein,** don't trouble about that; do not feel sorry about it, do not regret having done it! **ein —(e)s,** hurt, harm, injury, ill; **einem ein —es thun** *or* **zufügen,** to harm, injure s.o.; **sich** (*dat.*) **ein —(e)s anthun,** to make away with oneself. II. *n.* (—es) harm, hurt, injury, wrong; pain; sorrow, grief; mourning; **in Lieb und —,** in pleasure and grief, in good and bad days, in good fortune and ill fortune, for better (and) for worse; **einem sein — klagen,** to pour out one's troubles to a p.; **vor — vergehen,** to die of a broken heart; **— tragen über eine S.,** to repent of a th.; **um einen — tragen,** to mourn, to be in mourning for a p.; **das — führen,** to be chief mourner; **einem etwas zu —e thun,** to wrong, injure, hurt a p.; **habe ich Ihnen etwas zu —e gethan?** have I done anything to offend (*or* vex) you? **was ist Ihnen zu —e geschehen?** what has happened to you? what has put you out? what is wrong? **er that es mir zu —e,** he did it to vex me; **keinem zu —e und keinem zu Liebe,** impartially.

Lei'd—en, I. *ir.v.a.* to suffer, bear, endure; to put up with, tolerate, permit; to admit; to wink at; **—en mögen,** to like; **ich kann ihn nicht —en,** I can't stand him; **ich mag ihn wohl —en,** I rather like him; **Schaden —en,** to sustain loss *or* injury; **—e und meide,** bear and forbear; **diese Stelle —et eine zweifache Erklärung,** this passage admits of a two-fold interpretation; **der Tag des Herrn ist groß und sehr erschrecklich, wer kann ihn —en?** the day of the Lord is great and very terrible, and who can abide it? (*B.*); **das wird hier nicht gelitten,** that is not permitted here; **es litt mich dort nicht länger,** I could not bear staying there any longer; **er ist bei uns sehr wohl gelitten,** he is very popular with us. II. *ir.v.n.* (*aux.* **h.**) to suffer; to be in pain; **seins**

Gesundheit wird darunter —en, his health will suffer from it; sie ist sehr —end, she is very ailing, is a great sufferer; sie —et an den Nerven, she has a nervous complaint; er —et am Herzen, he suffers from a weak heart; sie —et an Schlaflosigkeit, she suffers from insomnia; er —et an den Augen, his eyes are weak. III. *subst.n.* suffering; passive condition; (*with pl.* —en) affliction; calamity; malady; disease, pain; misery, distress; endurance; das —en Christi, the passion of our Lord; Werthers —en, the sorrows of Werther; der Mensch ist zum —en geboren, man is born to trouble; ein altes —en, a complaint of long standing; er ist mondsüchtig und hat ein schweres —en, he is lunatic and sore vexed (*B.*). —end, *p. & adj.* suffering; passive; das —ende Zeitwort, the passive verb; —ender Gehorsam, passive obedience; der, die —ende, the patient. —enschaft, *see* Leidenschaft. —er, *adv. & int.* unfortunately, to my regret; I am sorry to say; alas! —er Gottes! most unfortunately! —er sehen wir, daß . . ., we are sorry to see that . . ., we see that unfortunately . . .; —er müssen wir zugeben, we must reluctantly admit. —ig, *adj. & adv.* disagreeable; abominable, loathsome; grievous, distressing; nasty; pitiful, poor, miserable; shocking; accursed; —ige Lehre, damnable doctrine; —iger Trost, poor comfort; der —ige Teufel, Satan himself. —lich, *adj. & adv.* sufferable, tolerable; middling, passable; so —lich, tolerably well; ich bin noch so —lich weggekommen, I have got off rather easily. —lichkeit, *f.* mediocrity; tolerableness. *Comp.* —ens=becher, —ens=kelch, *m.* cup of sorrow. —ens=bruder, *m.* fellow-sufferer; constant sufferer. —ens=gefährte, —ens=genosse, *m.* fellow-sufferer, companion in misfortune. —ens=geschichte, *f.* history of one's sufferings; history of Christ's passion. —ens=matt, *adj.* grief-worn. —ens=probe, *f.* ordeal. —ens=stationen, *pl.* (die zwölf) the stations of Christ's passion. —ens=unfähigkeit, *f.* impassibility. —en(s)=voll, *adj.* full of sorrow *or* suffering. —ens=woche, *f.* Passion-week. —tragend, *adj.* mourning; der —tragende, mourner. —voll, *adj.* full of grief, painful, sorrowful, mournful. —wesen, *n.* lamentation; sorrow; sorrowing; zu unserm großen —wesen, to our great regret.

Lei'denschaft, *f.* (*pl.* —en) violent emotion *or* desire; passion; rage. —lich, *adj.* passionate, vehement, impassioned, warm. —lichkeit, *f.* passionateness. *Comp.* —s=frei, *adj.* dispassionate. —s=los, *adj.* apathetic, calm. —s=losigkeit, *f.* apathy.

Lei'er, *f.* (*pl.* —n) lyre; hurdy-gurdy; barrel-organ; humdrum tune; old story; lyric poetry *or* song; Lyra (*Astr.*); barrel-churn; part of a plough, pomelion (*of a plough*); roasting-jack; winch; immer die alte —, always the old story; immer bei der alten — bleiben, to be always harping on the same string. —ei', *f. see* Geleier. —er, *m.* (—ers, *pl.* —er) organ-grinder. *Comp.* —förmig, *adj.* lyre-shaped; lyrate (*Bot.*). —gang, *m.* humdrum course of business, routine. —kasten, *m.* barrel-organ (*coll.*). —mädchen, *n.* girl grinding an organ. —mann, *m.* organ-grinder; lantern-fly (*Ent.*); der alte —mann, the old organ grinder, the old singer (*coll.*).

Lei'ern, *v.a. & n.* (*aux.* h.) to play on the lyre; to harp on the one string, to strum off monotonously; to grind a barrel-organ; to drawl; to dawdle; to trifle; to turn (with) a winch; besser geleiert als gefeiert, better to do something than nothing; einem die Ohren voll —, to din into a p.'s ears.

Lei'h—en, *ir.v.a.* to lend; to borrow; to hire, let; to take on credit *or* conditionally; to bestow, attribute, confer; Bücher aus einer Leihbibliothek —en, to get books from a circulating library. —er, *m.* (—ers, *pl.* —er) lender; borrower; hirer. *Comp.* —bibliothek, *f.* circulating library. —haus, *n.* loan-office, pawnbroker's shop. —kasse, *f.* loan-office.

Lei'kauf, Leit'kauf, *m.* (—(e)s, *pl.* Lei'käufe) drink on concluding and in confirmation of a bargain, earnest.

Lei'lach, *n.* (—s, *pl.* —e), **Lei'laken**, *n.* (—s, *pl.* —), **Lei'lich**, *n.* (—s, *pl.* —e), shroud, linen cloth, bed cloth.

Leim, *m.* (—es) adhesive substance; glue; size; bird-lime; gelatine; — sieden, to boil glue; to do unprofitable work; auf den — gehen, to fall into the trap; auf de'n — krieche (*or* gehe) ich nicht, I shall not let myself in for that, you will not catch me there (*coll.*); aus dem —e gehen, to get out of joint (*coll.*). —ig, *adj.* gluey, viscous. *Comp.* —farbe, *f.* water-colour, distemper (*Paint.*). —fuge, *f.* glued joint. —grund, *m.* (*gilder's*) sizing. —kessel, *m.* size-copper. —kitt, *m.* joiner's cement *or* putty. —pinsel, *m.* glue-brush. —rute, *f.* lime-twig. —sieder, *m.* glue-maker; bore; plodding student. —stoff, *m.* gluten. —tiegel, —topf, *m.* glue-pot. —vergoldung, *f.* water-gilding, gilding in water-size. —wasser, *n.* size; glue-water; lime-water. —zucker, *m.* gelatine sugar. —zwinge, *f.* glueing cramp *or* press.

Lei'm—en, *v.a.* to glue; to lime; to size; to dress (*hats*); to entrap, cheat. —er, *m.* (—ers, *pl.* —er) gluer; sizer. —ung, *f.* sizing.

Lein, *m.* (—(e)s, *pl.* —e) flax; linseed; linen (*poet. and in comp.*). —e, *f.* (*pl.* —en) cord, line, rope; leash; pole (*Typ.*); measuring-line; vein; an der —e haben, to hold by a string, to have in one's power; von einem an der —e gehalten werden, to be in a p.'s leading-strings. —en, I. *adj.* linen. II. *n.* (—ens, *pl.* —en) linen; linen goods. *Comp.* —bau, *m.* cultivation of flax. —blüte, *f.* flax-flower. —boden, *m.* linen warp. —bödig, *adj.* with a linen warp. —drucker, *m.* linen-printer. —en=nadel, *f.* embroidery needle. —en=probe, *f.* sample of linen. —en=zeug, *n.* linen. —en=zwirn, *m.* thread. —fasern, *f.pl.* lint. —feld, *n.* flax-field. —fink, *m.* linnet. —firnis, *m.* printer's varnish. —knoten, *m.* husk of linseed. —kraut, *n.* wild flax. —kuchen, *m.* oil-cake. —same(n), *m.* flax-seed, linseed. —strumpf, *m.* thread stocking. —tuch, *n.* linen-cloth; sheet. —wand, *see* Leinwand. —weber, *m.* linen-weaver. —weberei, *f.* manufacture of linen; factory. —weberstuhl, *m.* weaver's loom. —zeug, *n.* linen.

Lein'wand, *f.* (*pl.* —e = —arten) linen, linen cloth; canvas (*Paint.*); gebleichte —, bleached *or* white linen; ungebleichte —, brown linen; grobe —, sack-cloth, bale-cloth; gezupfte —, lint; geblümte —, diaper; gesteifte —, buckram; — zu Betttüchern, sheeting; auf — ziehen, to mount on canvas. —en, *adj.* linen. *Comp.* —band, *m.* cloth-binding, volume bound in cloth. —handel, *m.* linen-drapery; linen-trade. —kittel, *m.* linen smock. —krämer, *m.* linen-draper. —malerei, *f.* painting on canvas. —schabsel, *n.* lint.

Lei'se, *adj. & adv.* low, soft, not loud; gentle; slight, imperceptible; fine, delicate; mit —r Stimme, in a low voice, in an undertone; nicht der —ste Laut, not the least sound; nicht die —ste Ahnung, not the faintest idea *or* suspicion; — hören, ein —s Gehör haben, to have a good hearing, to be quick of hearing; — schlafen, to sleep lightly, to be a light sleeper; — **auftreten,** to tread noiselessly, to proceed cautiously, to act humbly; — **berühren,** to touch lightly upon, to treat superficially; **etwas — nehmen,** not to trouble much about a th.; **mir wird —r ums Herz,** I feel greatly relieved. *Comp.* **—gänger, —treter,** *m.* sneak, spy. **—hörig,** (**Leis'hörig,**) *adj.* quick of hearing.

Leist'bar, *adj.* practicable, performable.

[1]**Lei'ste,** *f.* (*pl.* —n) groin; spavin. *Comp.* **—n=band,** *n.* inguinal ligament. **—n=bruch,** *m.* rupture in the groin.

[2]**Lei'ste,** *f.* (*pl.* —n, *dim.* **Leist'chen,** *n.* bandelet) long strip serving as edge; what is enclosed by it; beading, moulding; fillet, reglet (*Arch.*); ledge, border; selvage; bracket, clamp; plinth; edge (*of books*); tail-piece (*Typ.*); channel, flute; slope, incline; rut. *Comp.* **—n=hobel,** *m.* rabbet-plane. **—n=thür,** *f.* battened door. **—n=werk,** *n.* entablature coping; beading, mouldings.

[1]**Leis't—en,** *v.a.* to perform, accomplish; to afford, give; to do; to fulfil; to produce; **den Eid der Treue —en,** to take the oath of allegiance; **einem hülfreiche Hand —en,** to give a p. a helping hand, help s.o.; **Bürgschaft —en,** to give bail; **einer gerichtlichen Aufforderung Folge —en,** to answer a summons; **Buße —en,** to do penance; **Widerstand —en,** to offer resistance; **Zahlung —en,** to make payment, pay a debt; **Verzicht auf eine S. —en,** to renounce, resign, give up, to do without a thing; **dieser Knabe —et Tüchtiges im Lateinischen,** this boy is good at Latin; **er wird nie etwas —en,** he will never do any good; **ich kann mir das —en,** I can afford it, I can afford to get *or* have *or* do this (*coll.*); **er hat sich einen neuen Hut geleistet,** he has treated himself to a new hat (*coll.*). **—ung,** *f.* act of doing, rendering *or* performing; performance, execution; payment; production; result, effect (*of a force*); **eine tüchtige —ung,** a creditable performance, an excellent piece of work; **—ung der Bürgschaft,** going bail. *Comp.* **—ungs=fähigkeit,** *f.* capacity for work; mechanical power (*of a machine*).

[2]**Lei'sten,** *m.* (—s, *pl.* —) shoemaker's last; **auf** *or* **über den — schlagen,** to put on the last; **Alles über einen — schlagen,** to treat all alike, value all alike; **sie sind alle über einen — geschlagen,** they are all of the same stamp. *Comp.* **—arbeit,** *f.* routine work.

Leit'bar, *adj.* manageable, that may be led.

Lei't—en, *v.a.* to lead, guide, conduct; to train, to direct; to convey; to manage, oversee; to govern; **einen irre —en,** to mislead a p.; **anderswohin —en,** to turn aside; **sich —en lassen,** to allow oneself to be led, to be tractable, docile; to be actuated (**von,** by); **nicht —end,** non-conducting; **die —enden Kreise,** influential persons, the governing classes, those in authority. **—er,** *m.* (—ers, *pl.* —er) leader, guide, conductor; conductor (*Phys.*); manager; governor; stay (*Naut.*). **—ung,** *f.* leading, guidance, direction; management; charge, care; government; conduit; conduction, transmission (*Phys.*); guide for directing the motion of a machine; (*pl.*) points, switches (*Railw.*); **die —ung der öffentlichen Angelegenheiten,** the conduct of public affairs; **die —ung haben,** to lead, to have the lead of; **die oberste —ung einer S. haben,** to superintend a th.; to be manager of a th.; to be the officer in command; **die —ung in die Hand nehmen,** to take the lead, to undertake the management, to take the reins. *Comp.* **—arm,** *m.* crank. **—artikel,** *m.* leader. **—band,** *n.* leading-string. **—faden,** *m.* clue; guide, key (*to an art or science*); manual; primer. —**fähig,** *adj.* that may be led *or* conducted; capable of conducting (*Phys.*). **—feuer,** *n.* train of gunpowder. **—gerade,** *f.* director, generator (*Mathem.*). **—graben,** *m.* conduit-ditch, drain. **—gesang,** *m.* catch, canon. **—hammel,** *m.* bell-wether; leader. **—linie,** *f.* directrix. **—mittel,** *n.* vehicle, means of conveyance. **—motiv,** *n.* motif recurring throughout a whole composition. **—muschel,** *f.* characteristic shell. **—riemen,** *m.* driving-rein; leash. **—röhre,** *f.* conduit-pipe; hose; feeder. **—satz,** *m.* (*pl.* **—sätze**) thesis. **—schiene,** *f.* switch (*Railw.*). **—seil,** *n.* rein; leash. **—stange,** *f.* conducting-rod. **—stern,** *m.* guiding star; pole-star. **—tau,** *n.* manrope (*Naut.*). **—ton,** *m.* leading note. **—ungs=behörde,** *f.* committee of directors. **—ungs=draht,** *m.* telegraph-wire. **—ungs=fähigkeit,** *f.*, **—ungs=vermögen,** *n.* capability of being led; conductibility. **—ungs=regel,** *f.* prescription. **—ungs=rohr,** *n.* pipe; main (*for gas*). **—zaum,** *m.* bridle, rein. **—zungen,** *pl.* points (*Railw.*).

Lei'te, *f.* (*pl.* —n) declivity, slope (*of a hill*).

Lei'ter, *f.* (*pl.* —n) ladder; rack (*of a waggon*); scale, gamut (*Mus.*). *Comp.* **—baum,** *m.* side of a ladder in which the rungs are inserted; peg-ladder. **—ersteigung,** *f.* escalade (*Mil.*). **—gang,** *m.*, **—gerüst,** *n.* mason's or bricklayer's ladder. **—sprosse,** *f.* rung of a ladder. **—stange,** *f.* see **—baum.** **—wagen,** *m.* waggon with rails *or* racks.

Lekt—io'n, *f.* (*pl.* **—ionen**) lesson; rebuke; **einem eine —ion lesen,** to give one a lecture *or* scolding. *Comp.* **—io'ns=buch,** *n.* lectionary.

Lek'tor, *m.* (—s, *pl.* **Lekto'ren**) foreign teacher of his mother tongue appointed for a time by German Universities; (*the German* **Lektoren** *have not the status and duties of the English University Lecturers*). **—a't,** *n.* (**—ats,** *pl.* **—ate**) office of a lector, lectorship.

Lektü're, *f.* (*pl.* —n) reading.

Lemu'r, *m.* (—s, *pl.* —en) maki, lemur (*Zool.*); (*pl.*) lemures, evil spirits.

Len'de, *f.* (*pl.* —n) loin, loins; thigh; haunch, hip. *Comp.* **—n=braten,** *m.* roast loin *or* sirloin; rump of beef. **—n=gegend,** *f.* lumbar region. **—n=gicht,** *f.* sciatica. **—n=knochen,** *m.* hip-bone. **—n=krankheit,** *f.* sciatica. **—n=lahm,** *adj.* hip-shot; weak in the loins; lazy. **—n=stück,** *n.* loin; fillet. **—n=weh,** *n.* lumbago. **—n=wirbel,** *m.* lumbar vertebra

Len'k—bar, *see* **—sam.**

Len'k—en, *v.a.* to bend, turn; to guide, direct; to manage; to steer; to rule; to order; to govern (*a horse*); **—en (in),** to turn (into); **einen Wagen —en,** to drive a carriage; **ein Zweirad —en,** to steer a bicycle; **das Gespräch auf einen Gegenstand —en,** to turn the conversation upon a subject; **der Mensch denkt, Gott —t,** man proposes, God disposes (*prov.*); **die Aufmerksamkeit auf sich —en,** to attract attention; **die Schritte —en,** to turn, to go; **sich —en,** to turn. **—bar,** *adj.* that can be directed, that may be guided; **—bares Luftschiff,** steerable air-ship, navigable balloon. **—er,** *m.* (**—ers,** *pl.* **—er**) ruler, disposer; guide; rod (*Mech.*). **—sam,** *adj.* tractable, manageable, docile; flexible. **—samkeit,** *f.* manageableness, docility. **—ung,** *f.* directing, governing, ruling; management; steering. *Comp.* **—achse,** *f.* movable axle-tree (*of carriages*). **—rad,** *m.* caster-wheel; front wheel (*Cycl.*). **—riemen,** *m.* rein. **—schemel,** *m.* transom-bed (*Artil.*). **—seil,** *n.* guiding-rope. **—stange,** *f.* connecting rod; handle-bar (*Cycl.*). **—steuer,** *n.* helm, rudder. **—zaum,** *m.* bridle, rein.

Lens, *adj.* empty, free, clear; exhausted (*dial.*).

Lenz, *m.* (—es, *pl.* —e) spring; prime, bloom (*of life*). **—lich,** *adj.* vernal.

Leopa'rd, *m.* (—en, *pl.* —en) leopard.

[1]**Ler'che, Lär'che**, *f.* (*pl.* —n) larch. *Comp.* **—n=baum**, *m.*, **—n=tanne**, *f.* larch-tree. **—n=harz**, *n.* larch-tree resin.

[2]**Ler'che**, *f.* (*pl.* —n) lark; **die — singt, tiriliert, wirbelt, schmettert**, the lark sings, trills, warbles, carols; **—n streichen**, to catch larks with a net. *Comp.* **—n=garn**, *n.* net for catching larks. **—n=gesang**, *m.* singing *or* song of the lark. **—n=herd**, *m.* decoy for larks. **—n=stößer**, *m.* sparrow-hawk. **—n=streichen**, *n.* netting of larks. **—n=strich**, *m.* migration of larks. **—n=wirbel**, *m.* warbling of larks.

Lern'bar, *adj.* that may be learnt, learnable.

Ler'n—en, I. *v. a.* to learn; to study; **lesen —en**, to learn to read; **er wird sie lieben —en**, he will come to love her; **die bösen Leute wollen nicht sich schämen —en**, the unjust knoweth no shame (*B.*); **ich habe ihn kennen —en**, I have got to know him, I have become acquainted with him; **ich habe Vieles entbehren —en**, I have learnt to do without many things. II. *v.n.* (*aux.* **h.**) **er hat noch ein Jahr zu —en**, he is within a year of his time; **gelernt**, learned by serving an apprenticeship, trained, expert; **ein gelernter Schuster**, a shoemaker by trade. III. *subst. n.* learning; **das —en wird ihm schwer**, he learns with difficulty. *Comp.* **—begier(de)**, *f.* desire of learning. **—begierig**, *adj.* desirous of learning. **—eifer**, *m.*, **—lust**, *f.* zeal for learning. **—fähig**, *adj.* capable of learning, teachable; intelligent. **—fleiß**, *m.* application, diligence in studying. **—fleißig**, *adj.* studious, assiduous. **—freiheit**, *f.* freedom of the student. **—zeit**, *f.* time for study; apprenticeship.

Les'—bar, *adj.* legible; readable, worth reading. **—barkeit**, *f.* legibility; readableness. *Comp.* **—art**, *f.* manner of reading; reading; **nach der gewöhnlichen —art**, according to the ordinary version; **kritischer Text mit allen abweichenden —arten**, critical text with all the various readings.

Le'se, *f.* (*pl.* —n) gleaning; gathering, collecting; harvest; vintage; gleanings; trick (*Cards*); **die — machen**, to win the odd trick.

Le's—en, I. *ir.v.a.* to gather, collect, glean; to pick; to pick out *or* up; (*also used intrans'ly with aux.* **h.**) to read; to lecture (**über einen Gegenstand**, on a subject); **er hat viel gelesen**, he has read much, he is well read; **Ähren —en**, to glean; **Wein —en**, to gather ripe grapes; **einem den Text** *or* **die Leviten —en**, to lecture, reprimand a p. severely; **die Messe —en**, to say mass; **lies laut**, read out; **für sich —en**, to read to o.s.; **was liest du aus diesem Briefe?** what do you understand from, make out of this letter? **sich leicht —en lassen**, to be easily read; to be very readable; **es liest sich wie . . .**, it reads like . . .; **er liest über Goethes schwierigere Gedichte**, he lectures on Goethe's more difficult poems; **heute wird nicht gelesen**, there are no lectures to-day (*Univ.*). II. *subst. n.* gathering; reading; course; lecture; **Ähren—en**, gleaning; **Wein—en**, vintage. **—er**, *m.* (—ers, *pl.* —er), **—erin**, *f.* gatherer; gleaner; reader. **—erei'**, *f.* desultory *or* thoughtless reading; **eine solche —erei!** what twaddle! what trash! **—erlich**, *adj. & adv.* legible. **—erlichkeit**, *f.* legibility. **—erschaft**, *f.* readers (*collect.*). **—ung**, *f.* reading; **der Gesetzentwurf kam zur (ersten, zweiten) —ung**, the bill was read (for the first, second time). *Comp.* **—e=bibliothek**, *f.* lending library (*obs.*). **—e=buch**, *n.* reader, reading-book. **—e=dachs**, *m.* book-worm (*coll.*). **—e=gesellschaft**, *f.* reading-party; literary society; book club. **—e=halle**, *f.*; **öffentliche —ehalle**, free library; **akademische —ehalle**, Union Society (*Oxf. Camb.*). **—e=holz**, *n.* wind-fallen wood. **—e=kabinett**, *n.* reading-room. **—e=kränzchen**, *n.* reading society, reading club. **—e=kreis**, *m.* reading society. **—e=lampe**, *f.* reading-lamp. **—e=(lehr)methode**, *f.* method of teaching to read. **—e=lust**, *f.* love of reading. **—ens=wert, —ens=würdig**, *adj.* worth reading. **—e=probe**, *f.* first rehearsal, reading (*of a drama*). **—e=pult**, *n.* reading-desk; **stellbares —e=pult**, adjustable reading-desk. **—e=ratte**, *f.* hard reader, book-worm (*coll.*). **—er=kreis**, *m.* circle of readers, the reading public. **—er=lohn**, *m.* vintager's wages. **—e=saal**, *m.* reading-room; lecture-room. **—e=schule**, *f.* elementary school. **—e=schüler**, *m.* pupil learning to read, abecedarian. **—e=stoff**, *m.* subject of reading. **—e=stücke**, *pl.* selections for reading. **—e=stunde**, *f.* reading lesson; hour for reading. **—e=süchtig**, *adj.* passionately fond of reading. **—e=welt**, *f.* reading public. **—e=wut**, *f.* mania for reading. **—e=zeichen**, *n.* stop; book-mark, book-marker. **—e=zeit**, *f.* time for reading; vintage-time. **—e=zimmer**, *n.* reading-room; study.

Lethar'gisch, *adj. & adv.* lethargic.

Let't—en, I. *m.* (—ens, *pl.* —en) potter's clay, loam. II. *adj.* of clay. **—icht**, (*obs.*) **—ig**, *adj.* clayey, loamy. *Comp.* **—en=boden**, *m.* clay-soil.

Let'ter, *f.* (*pl.* —n) letter, character; type; **Lateinische, Deutsche —n**, Roman, Gothic type; **kursive lateinische —n**, Italics. *Comp.* **—n=druck**, *m.* printing, letterpress.

Lett'ner, *m.* (—s, *pl.* —) rood-loft, gallery between the nave and choir.

[1]**Let'ze**, *f.* (*pl.* —n) defence, rampart; round-way.

[2]**Let'ze**, *f.* (*pl.* —n) leave-taking, farewell; parting-gift; parting-cup; **zu guter —**, at parting, to finish well, for a last farewell (*obs.*). **—n**, *v.a.* to rejoice, gratify, refresh, comfort; **sich —n (an einer S.)** to enjoy *or* relish (a th.).

Letzt, I. *adj. & adv.* last; latest; extreme; ultimate; final; **eine —e Erklärung**, an ultimatum; **die —e Ölung**, extreme unction; **es ist mit ihm aufs —e gekommen**, he is ruined, undone, put to his last shifts; **in der —en Zeit**, of late, lately; **mein —es**, my death-blow, my end; **er ist der —e, dem ich mich anvertrauen würde**, he is the last man I would trust; **das —e**, the last thing, the end, the last extremity; **er gäbe das —e hin**, he would shed his last drop of blood; **das wird mich aufs —e bringen**, that will finish me, this will be the death of me; **der —ere**, the latter; **der —verstorbene**, the late, the deceased; **Alle, bis auf den —en Mann**, all to a man. II. *adv.* lately, of late, in the last place. III. *f.* **—e**, *f.* (*for* **Letze**) end, conclusion (*obs.*); **auf die —e**, at the end, at last (*obs.*); **zu guter —(e)**, finally, to sum up, as a fitting conclusion. **—ens**, *adv.* lastly; in the last place; lately, of late, recently; finally. **—erer**, *m.*, **—ere**, *f.*, **—eres**, *n.* (**der, die, das —ere**) the latter. **—lich**, *adv.* lastly, at last; finally; to conclude; lately, the other day. *Comp.* **—erwähnt, —genannt**, *adj.* last-named. **—hi'n**, *see* **—lich**. **—jährig**, *adj.* last-year's, of last year. **—lebende(r)**, *m.* survivor. **—verstorben**, *adj.* late. **—willig**, I. *adj.* testamentary; **—willige Verfügung**, testament, will; **ohne —willige Verfügung gestorben**, died intestate. II. *adv.* by will.

Leu, *m.* (—en, *pl.* —en) lion (*Poet.*).

Leuch'te, *f.* (*pl.* —n) any object giving light, *as* sun, lamp, lantern, beacon, signal, *etc.*; shining light, star (*in science, art*); **blinde —**, dark lantern.

Leucht'—en, I. *v.n.* (*aux.* **h.**) to shine, emit light; to beam, gleam, burn, glare, glimmer; to phosphoresce (*of the sea*); to lighten; **einem die Treppe hinunter —en,** to light a p. down stairs; **einem heim —en,** to send s.o. about his business, to give a p. a rough welcome, to give a sharp answer; **das —et in die Augen,** that is evident; **sein Auge —ete vor Zorn,** his eye flashed with rage; **—en wie die Sonne,** to shine forth as the sun (*B.*); **das Wetter —et,** there is sheet-lightning. II. *subst.n.* shining, burning; glare; coruscation; **Meer —en,** phosphorescence (of the sea); **Wetter —en,** sheet lightning. **—end,** *p. & adj.* shining, bright; lucid. **—er,** *m.* (**—ers,** *pl.* **—er**) candlestick. *Comp.* **—er=arm,** *m.* branch of a chandelier. **—er=dille,** *f.* socket, hollow cylinder of a candlestick. **—er=säule,** *f.* stand of a candlestick. **—feuer,** *n.* beacon-fire. **—gas,** *n.* illuminating gas. **—käfer,** *m.* glow-worm, firefly. **—kugel,** *f.* fire-ball; (*pl.*) Roman candles (*Firew.*). **—rakete,** *f.* rocket, light-ball. **—schiff,** *n.* light-ship. **—späne,** *pl.* pine-chips used as torches. **—stein,** *m.* Bologna-stone; phosphor. **—stoff,** *m.* luminous matter. **—turm,** *m.* lighthouse. **—wurm,** *m.* glow-worm.

Leug'bar, *adj.* deniable.

Leug'n—en, I. *v.a.* to deny; to disown, disavow, gainsay, recant; **nicht zu —en,** undeniable, unquestionable; **das Gesagte —en,** to retract, take back one's own words. II. *subst.n. see* **—ung.** **—er,** *m.* (**—ers,** *pl.* **—er**) denier, disclaimer. **—ung,** *f.* disavowal.

Leu'mund, *m.* (**—es**) rumour, report; reputation; **ein guter —,** a good name; **gut beleumundet,** of good fame. *Comp.* **—s=zeugnis,** *n.* certificate of good conduct.

Leut'chen, *pl.* people of humble rank; nice people; **—!** (my) dear people!

Leu't—e, *pl.* people, persons; men; the world; servants; guests; grown-up people; men (*Mil., opp. to officers*); **eigne —e,** serfs; **—e von Stand,** gentlefolk, persons of position; **vor allen —en,** openly, before all the world; **unter die —e kommen,** to go into society; **aus Kindern werden —e,** children grow into men and women; **er kennt seine —e,** he knows whom he has to deal with; **wir sind geschiedene —e,** it is all over between us, we are no longer friends; **es giebt gewisse —e,** there are some people. **—selig,** *adj.* affable, pleasant, courteous; popular; humane, gentle. **—seligkeit,** *f.* kindness; affability; geniality, good nature; popularity. *Comp.* **—e=placker, —e=plager, —e=schinder,** *m.* extortioner, blood-sucker. **—e=scheu,** *adj.* unsociable, shy, misanthropic. **—priester,** *m.* secular priest.

Leut'nant, (*till recently* **Lieu'tenant,**) *m.* (**—s,** *pl.* **—s**) lieutenant; **Herr — Z.,** lieutenant Z.; **Frau — Z.,** Mrs. Z., the wife of Lieutenant Z.; **zu Befehl, Herr —,** very well, sir; **Ober —,** first lieutenant; **General —,** lieutenant general. *Comp.* **—s=stelle,** *f.* lieutenant's commission, lieutenancy.

Levi't, *m.* (**—en,** *pl.* **—en**) Levite; **einem die —en lesen,** to lecture a person. **—isch,** *adj.* Levitical.

Levko'je, *f.* (*pl.* **—n**) stock, stock-gilliflower.

Lexika'li—en, *pl.* things connected with a dictionary. **—sch,** *adj.* dictionary-like; from a lexicographic standpoint.

Le'xik—on, *n.* (**—ons,** *pl.* **—a**) dictionary; **Konversations —on,** dictionary of universal knowledge, encyclopædia. **—ogra'ph,** *m.* (**—ographen,** *pl.* **—ographen**) compiler of a dictionary, lexicographer.

Lia'ne, *f.* (*pl.* **—n**) liana (*tropic climbing plant*).

Li'as=formation, *f.* Lias(sic) formation *or* system.

Libe'll, *n.* (**—s,** *pl.* **—e**) libel. **—i'st,** *m.* (**—is'ten,** *pl.* **—is'ten**) libeller, lampooner.

Libel'le, *f.* (*pl.* **—n**) dragon-fly; (water-) level.

Libera'l, *adj.* liberal; **die —en,** the Liberals, the liberal party. **—is'mus,** *m.* Liberalism. **—itä't,** *f.* (*pl.* **—itäten**) liberality; generosity.

Licen—tia't, *m.* (**—tiaten,** *pl.* **—tiaten**) licenciate. **—z** (*pron.* **Lice'nz**), *f.* (*pl.* **Licen'zen**) license. **—zie'ren,** *v.a.* to license.

Licht, I. *adj. & adv.* light; luminous, bright; lucid; clear; light; thin, open; **—er Tag,** broad daylight, high noon; **(so) wird dein ganzer Leib — sein,** thy whole body shall be full of light (*B.*); **—e Maschen,** wide meshes; **eine —e Zukunft,** a bright future; **das —e im Walde,** a clearing, an open space in a wood; **im —en,** in diameter, in width *or* breadth; **Juwelen — fassen,** to set jewels wide apart; **— werden,** to grow clear. II. *n.* (**—es,** *pl., with difference of meaning,* **—er** *&* **—e**) light; luminary; sun, moon; candle; candlestick; opening; window; eye (*of game*); touch-hole; **es werde —!** let there be light! (*B.*); **— geben,** to give light, to enlighten; **das — der Welt erblicken,** to be born; **er ist ein großes —,** he is a shining light, a star, a great man; **jetzt geht mir ein — auf,** now I begin to see my way; **wo viel — ist, da ist auch viel Schatten,** every light has its shadow; the brighter the light, the deeper the shadow (*prov.*); **einem ein — aufstecken über eine S.,** to open a p.'s eyes to a fact; **einem das — halten,** to assist a p.; **— machen,** to strike a light, light (*a candle, etc.*); **ans — bringen,** to bring forth, to divulge; **ans — kommen,** to come to light; **ans — treten,** to become known, to be published; **am, bei(m) —e besehen,** to examine closely; **bei —e,** by day, in daylight; **bei —e betrachtet,** looked at closely, taking everything into account; **einem aus dem —e gehen,** to stand out of s.o.'s light; **einen hinters — führen,** to take a p. in, to humbug a p.; **einem, sich** (*dat.*) **selbst im —e stehen,** to stand in a p.'s *or* one's own light; **gegossenes —,** mould candle; **gezogenes —,** dip; **Wachs— waxlight,** taper. **—chen, —lein,** (**—leins,** *pl.* **—lein**) small light *or* taper. *Comp.* **—arbeit,** *f.* work done by candle-light. **—auge,** *n.* glass-eye. **—bad,** *n.* solar bath, insolation (*Med.*). **—bild,** *n.* photograph; lime-light view. **—blau,** *adj.* light-blue. **—blick,** *m.* flash of light; ray (*of hope, etc.*); clear spot (*in the sky*). **—bogen,** *m.* voltaic arc. **—brechend,** *adj.* light-refracting. **—brechung,** *f.* refraction of light. **—büschel,** *m.* pencil of rays. **—dämpfer,** *m.* extinguisher. **—druck,** *m.* phototype, photographic printing. **—er=büchse,** *f.* case for keeping the matches dry (*Artil.*). **—er=fabrik,** *f.* candle-manufactory. **—er=loh,** I. *adj.* blazing. II. *adv.* ablaze. **—farb(en), —farbig,** *adj.* light-coloured. **—form,** *f.* mould for candles. **—gestalt,** *f.* phase, phasis; bright *or* beautiful figure. **—gießer,** *m.* tallow-chandler. **—glanz,** *m.* lustre, brightness. **—gürtel,** *m.* Milky Way. **—halter, —knecht, —stecker,** *m.* save-all; sconce. **—hell,** *adj.* lighted up; very bright. **—hütchen,** *n.* extinguisher. **—kegel,** *m.* cone of rays. **—kerze,** *f.* taper; wax-light. **—körper,** *m.* luminary. **—kreis,** *m.* luminous circle, halo. **—leer, —los,** *adj.* dark; obscure; rayless. **—lehre,** *f.* optics; photology. **—manschetten,** *pl.* candlestick ornaments on which the wax falls. **—maschine,** *f.* electric engine. **—messe, —meß,** *f.* Candlemas. **—messer,** *m.* photometer. **—nelke,** *f.* lychnis **—papier,** *n.* photogenic paper. **—punkt,** *m.* luminous point; ray. **—putze, —schere,** *f.* pair of snuffers. —schein, *m.* lustre of a candle *or* light. —scheu, *adj.* shunning the light; anti-educational. —schirm, *m.* lamp shade, eye-protector. —schwingung, *f.* light-wave. —sehen, *n.* photopsy (*Med.*). —seite, *f.* bright side. —spalter, *m.* prism. —spur, *f.* luminous trail. —stärke, *f.* intensity of the light. —stock, *m.* candlestick. —stoff, *m.* luminous matter, light. —strahl, *m.* ray, beam; streamer (*of the Aurora Borealis*). —stumpf, *m.* candle end. —träger, *m.* save-all; candleholder, candlestick; phosphorus (*Phys.*); light-bearer. —voll, *adj.* resplendent, luminous; clear, lucid (*of a speech*). —wolke, *f.* luminous cloud. —ziehen, *n.* making candles. —zieher, *m.* tallow-chandler. —zug, *m.* candle mould.

1Lich't—en, *v.a.* to light, light up; to clear (*a wood*), to thin (*the ranks*); die Reihen —eten sich, the ranks grew thinner. —er, I. *m.* (—ers, *pl.* —er) match (*Artil.*); (*pl.*) lights, candles; lights (*Paint.*). —ung, *f.* clearing; thinning; glade.

2Lich'ten, *v.a.* to lift up, raise, heave up; den *or* die Anker —, to weigh anchor, to cast off the moorings.

3Lich'te—n, *v.a.* to lighten, unload. —r, *m.* (—rs, *pl.* —r) lighter, barge. *Comp.* —r=geld, *n.* lighterage.

Lid, *n.* (—es, *pl.* —er) lid, eye-lid; die —er schließen, to close one's eyes.

Li'dern, *v.a.* to garnish, furnish with leather, to line *or* pack with leather.

Lieb, *adj.* & *adv.* dear, beloved; valued, esteemed; attractive, charming, delightful; good; favourite; unsere —e Frau, our Lady, the virgin Mary; — haben, to love, like, be fond of; — gewinnen, to grow *or* become fond of; am —sten haben, to love *or* like best; meine —ste Beschäftigung, my favourite employment; es ist mir —, daß, I am glad that; so ist es mir —, so habe ich es am —sten, that is how I like it best; es wäre mir —, I should like, I should be glad; es ist mir nicht —, I am sorry, I regret; das wäre Ihnen gewiß nicht —, you will be sure not to like it; das ist aber — von Ihnen, that is indeed most kind of you; das Kind ist gar zu —, the child is really too pretty; wenn Ihnen Ihr Leben — ist, as you value your life; wenn es Ihnen — ist, if it is agreeable to you, if you like; sich (*dat.*) etwas — sein lassen, to be content *or* pleased with a thing; es mag ihm — oder leid sein, whether he like it or not; in — und Leid, in joy and grief, in good and evil fortune; for better, for worse; etwas —es, anything pleasing, the beloved one; etwas —es haben, to have a sweetheart; einem —es und Gutes thun, erzeigen, to be very kind to, bestow favours upon a p.; ich weiß nur —es und Gutes von ihm, I can only speak well of him; sie thut ihm —es, she will do him good (*B.*); (*used in familiar phrases somewhat pleonastically*, *cp.* for dear life; *occasionally as a mere particle, often untranslatable*) um das —e Brod arbeiten, to work for one's bare subsistence; sie hat nicht das —e Brot im Hause, she has not even a crust of bread; den —en, langen Tag, the live-long day; ich habe meine —e Not mit ihm, I have no end of trouble with him; die —e Zeit, time; ach, du —e Zeit! good gracious! dear me! der —e Gott, God (almighty); das weiß der —e Himmel, heaven only knows; —er, laß nicht Zank sein, let there be no strife, I pray thee (*B.*). —chen, *n.* (—chens, *pl.* —chen) love, darling, pet, sweetheart. —den, *f.* (*word of address used amongst sovereigns; exclusively in the form* Ew. Liebden = Euer Liebden); Ew. —den, my dear prince. —elei', *f.* billing and cooing; flirtation. —eln, *v.n.* (*aux.* h.) to bill and coo, to flirt, to dally, trifle with; to caress. —er, I. *adj. comp. of* lieb, *q.v.* II. *adv. comp. of* gern & lieb; rather, sooner, more willingly; ich thäte es —er selbst, I would rather do it myself; es ist mir —er, I prefer; —er sterben als leiden, better die than suffer; um so —er, weil, so much the more so since; es ist mir nur um so —er, I only like it all the better; warum nicht —er gar vierzig? why not rather forty (*at once and have done with it, etc.*)? je eher, je —er, the sooner the better. III. *m.* mein —er, my dear fellow. —es, (*in comp.*) *see* Liebes. —ler, *m.* (—lers, *pl.* —ler) (*male*) flirt. —lich, *adj.* & *adv.* lovely; charming, delightful; enjoyable; pleasing, sweet. —lichkeit, *f.* charm, loveliness, sweetness, pleasantness. —ling, *m.* (—lings, *pl.* —linge) darling, favourite, pet. —lings, *in comp.* = favourite. —schaft, *f.* love; love-affair; predilection; eine —schaft haben, to be in love; flüchtige —schaft, flirtation; ernste —schaft, attachment, engagement. —st, *sup.* of lieb *and* gern; der, die —ste, dearest, love, sweetheart; das esse ich am —sten, I like that best, this is my favourite dish. *Comp.* —äugeln, *v.n.* (*aux.* h.) to ogle, cast amorous looks at. —frauen=kirche, *f.* church of our Lady. —frauen=milch, *f.* a choice Rhenish wine. —haber, *m.* lover; gallant, paramour; amateur; fancier. —haberei', *f.* inclination, fondness; partiality; hobby; favourite amusement; aus —haberei malen, to paint for amusement, as an amateur. —haberisch, *adj.* lover-like; amateur-like. —haber=konzert, *n.* amateur concert. —haber=rolle, *f.* lover's part (*Theat.*). —haber=theater, *n.* private theatre; amateur theatricals, dramatic club. —herzen, (*rare*) —kosen, (*sep. & insep.*) *v.a.* to pet, caress, fondle, hug. —kosung, *f.* caressing, blandishment. —kosungs=wort, *n.* word of endearment, pet word. —lings=idee, *f.* favourite idea *or* scheme, pet idea. —lings=sohn, *m.* favourite son. —los, *adj.* loveless; unloving, unkind, hardhearted. —thätig, *adj.* charitable, beneficent. —wert, *adj.* highly esteemed, beloved.

Lie'be, *f.* love; affection; kindness; passion; joy, pleasure, inclination (*obs.*), charity; beloved one, love, dear; Lieb und Leid, joy and sorrow; Lieb und Lust, pleasure and delight, heart's delight; es wohnet Lieb bei —, joy is bound up with love, love gives joy (*obs.* & *poet.*); kindliche —, filial love *or* piety; christliche —, Nächsten—, Christian charity; meine brüderliche —, my brother (*sl.*); — zur Sache, love of the subject *or* of the cause; — zum Vaterlande, love of country; ein Lied der —, von —, a love-song; mit — thun, to do willingly; mit Lust und — thun, to do with all one's heart; eine heftige — einflößen, to inspire a passion; thun Sie mir die —, have the kindness to, oblige me by; abgöttische —, idolatry; mir zu —, from affection for me, for my sake; eine — ist der andern wert, one good turn deserves another (*prov.*); alte — rostet nicht, old love is never forgotten (*prov.*); — macht erfinderisch, love makes inventive (*prov.*); von der — kann man nicht leben, the flames of love won't boil the pot (*prov.*). *Comp.* —bang, *adj.* anxious with love. —blind, *adj.* blinded by love. —diener, *m.* slave to love; wheedler; adulator. —dienerei', *f.* toadyism, adulation. —leer, —los, *adj.* loveless; unloving. —trunken, *adj.* intoxicated with love. —wund, *adj.* love-striken.

Lie'ben, *v.* I. *a.* to love, be fond of; to like; to fancy; to cherish (*an idea, etc.*). II. *n.* (*aux.* h.) to be in love; to be dear (*obs.*); sie liebet mir, I love her (*obs.*). —d, *p.* & *adj.* loving; deine dich —de Schwester, your loving or affectionate sister; **dein dich —der Wilhelm B.**, yours affectionately, William B.; **der, die —de**, the lover, friend.

Lie'bes, *n. see under* **Lieb**; **nicht wissen, was man einem (alles) — anthun soll**, to be full of tender attentions towards a p. *Comp.* (*of* **Liebe** *with inorganic* **s**) **—abenteuer**, *n.* love-adventure. **—andenken**, *n.* love-token. **—angelegenheiten**, *pl.* love-affairs. **—antrag**, *m.* love-suit, proposal. **—apfel**, *m.* tomato. **—bewerbung**, *f.* courtship. **—blick**, *m.* loving glance. **—bote**, *m.* harbinger of love. **—brief**, *m.* love-letter. **—brunst**, *f.* amorous transports, love-fit. **—dichter**, *m.* erotic poet, writer of love-poems. **—dienst**, *m.* kind act; labour of love; **einem einen —dienst erweisen**, to do one a kindness. **—erklärung**, *f.* declaration of love. **—frühling**, *m.* dawn of love. **—gaben**, *pl. f.* **(im Kriege)** presents to soldiers in the field, comforts for the soldiers. **—gedicht**, *n.* love-poem. **—genuß**, *m.* enjoyment of love. **—geschichte**, *f.* love-story, romance, novel. **—glück**, *n.* happiness of love; good luck in love. **—glut**, *f.* amorous flame *or* rapture. **—gott**, *m.* Cupid. **—götter**, *pl.* Amoretti, Loves. **—göttin**, *f.* Venus. **—gunst**, **(eines Weibes)** *f.* favours. **—gürtel**, *m.* girdle of Venus. **—handel**, *m.* love intrigue. **—heirat**, *f.* love-match. **—kampf**, *m.* amorous combat; combat against love. **—kind**, *n.* natural, illegitimate child. **—klage**, *f.* amorous complaint. **—knoten**, *m.* true lovers' knot. **—krank**, *adj.* love-sick. **—kühn**, *adj.* emboldened by love. **—künste**, *pl.* artifices of love. **—lied**, *n.* love-song. **—liedchen**, *n.* love-ditty. **—lust**, *f.* pleasure of love. **—mahl**, *n.* love-feast; agape, banquet; **jährliches —mahl der Offiziere**, great annual dinner of the military officers (*of a garrison or a regiment*). **—mühe**, *f.*; **Verlorene —müh**, Love's Labour 's Lost. **—not**, **—pein**, **—qual**, *f.* pains of love. **—paar**, *n.*, **—leute**, *pl.* a pair of lovers. **—pfand**, *n.* love-token; pledge of love; child. **—pfeil**, *m.* love-shaft. **—pflicht**, *f.* charitable duty. **—raserei**, *f.* amorous frenzy. **—rausch**, *m.* transport of love. **—ritter**, *m.* knight-errant; gay Lothario, Don Juan. **—roman**, *m.* love-romance, novel. **—sache**, *f.* love-affair. **—sänger**, *m.* erotic poet. **—spiel**, *n.* amorous play; dalliance, flirtation. **—sprache**, *f.* language of love *or* lovers. **—stern**, *m.* star propitious to love. **—that**, *f.*, **—werk**, *n.* labour of love; charity, alms-deed. **—trank**, *m.* love-potion, philtre. **—treue**, *f.* constancy. **—trunken**, *adj.* intoxicated with love, in ecstasies of love. **—verständnis**, *n.* amour, love-intrigue; love-secret. **—werben**, *n.* love-suit, courtship. **—wonne**, *f.* bliss of love. **—worte**, *pl.* words of love, loving words. **—zauber**, *m.* love-spell. **—zeichen**, *n.* love-token.

Lied, *n.* (**—es**, *pl.* **—er**) song, ditty, lay; ballad; air, tune; **geistliches —**, hymn, psalm; **(das hohe) — Salomonis**, Song of Solomon; **das Hohe —**, the Song of Songs; **immer das alte —**, always the old story; **das Ende vom —e**, the end of the affair; **davon kann ich auch ein — singen**, I can tell the same tale; **wes Brot ich ess', des — ich sing'**, I stand up for those that employ me; never quarrel with your bread and butter (*prov.*); **ein anderes — anstimmen**, to sing another tune; to change one's tone. **—chen**, *n.* (**—chens**, *pl.* **—chen**) little air *or* song, ditty. *Comp.* **—er=absatz**, **—er=abschnitt**, *m.* strophe, couplet. **—er=buch**, *n.* book of songs; **—er=buch geistlicher Gesänge**, hymn-book. **—er=dichter**, *m.* lyric poet; song-writer. **—er=kranz**, *m.* choral society; collection of songs. **—er=reich**, *adj.* tuneful. **—er=sammlung**, *f.*, *see* **—erbuch**. **—er=sänger**, *m.* ballad-singer, singer. **—er=tafel**, *f.* singing-club; glee-club; choral society. **—er=vater**, *m.* president of a glee-club *or* musical society. **—er=vers**, *m.* stanza. **—form**, *f.* ballad *or* song form.

Lie'derlich, *adj. & adv.* (= **lüderlich**) loose, careless; slovenly, disorderly; lewd, dissolute; **—es Frauenzimmer**, a sloven; fast, abandoned woman; **ein —er Mensch, Bruder —, Hans —**, rake, debauchee; **eine —e Person**, a sloven; a loose fish. **—keit**, *f.* negligence; slovenliness, disorderliness; debauchery, dissoluteness.

Lief, Lie'fe, *1 (& 3) p. sing. imperf. ind. & subj. of* **laufen**.

Liefer—a'nt, *m.* (**—an'ten**, *pl.* **—an'ten**), **—er**, *m.* (**—ers**, *pl.* **—er**) contractor, purveyor; furnisher. **—bar**, *adj.* deliverable; to be delivered.

Lie'fer—n, *v.a.* to deliver, hand over, give; to furnish, supply; to yield; **einen —n**, to ruin s. o. (*coll.*); **er ist geliefert**, he is lost, ruined, done for (*coll.*); **eine Schlacht —n**, to give battle; **ein Werk in Heften —n**, to publish a work in numbers; **einen Beweis —n**, to furnish proof; **zu —n in acht Tagen**, deliverable in 8 days; **zu —n an Herrn . . .**, to be delivered to Mr. . . . **—ung**, *f.* delivering, delivery; supplying, purveying; supply; number (*of a work*); **auf —ung**, on delivery; **dritte —ung**, third part *or* number; **zahlbar bei —ung**, to be paid on delivery; **sofortige —ung**, for immediate delivery; **—ungen ausschreiben**, to make requisitions (*Mil.*); **—ung in Naturalien**, payment in kind. *Comp.* **—ungs=bedingungen**, *pl.* conditions on which a work is contracted for, specifications. **—ungs=frist**, *f.* term for delivery. **—ungs=geschäft**, *n.* business undertaken on contract; time bargain. **—ungs=preis**, *m.* price agreed on. **—ungs=schein**, *m.* bill of delivery, receipt. **—ungs=vertrag**, *m.* contract (*for supplying*). **—ungs=weise**, *adv.* in numbers *or* parts. **—ungs=zahl**, *f.* number to be supplied. **—ungs=zeit**, *f.* time of *or* term for delivery.

Lie'g—en, *ir.v.n.* (*aux.* **h.** & **s.**) to lie, be recumbent; to lie (*ill, dead, etc.*); to be situated; to be; to consist in; to lodge, be quartered; to lie, cover; **—en bleiben**, to keep (*one's bed*), to remain, lie over, to be, to be left *or* forgotten, not to go off; **unter der Last —en bleiben**, to sink under the burden; **—en haben**, to have in store, have ready, possess; **—en lassen**, to let lie, to leave, to let alone, to discontinue; **—en und stehen lassen**, to leave in disorder, to neglect; **einen links —en lassen**, to neglect, disregard a p.; **laß das —en!** let that alone! **für tot —en lassen**, to leave for dead; **müßig —en lassen**, not to use (*one's money*); **gefangen —en**, to be in prison; **krank —en**, to lie in bed ill; **nahe —en**, to lie *or* be near; to be natural, obvious; **die Sache —t nahe**, the thing is easily imagined, that is obvious; **da —t der Knoten** *or* **der Hase im Pfeffer, da —t's**, there 's the rub; **wie —t die Sache?** how does the matter stand? **der Handel und Wandel —t**, trade is dull, there is no business to be transacted; **—en an** (*dat.*), to lie (*on*), to adjoin; **Berlin —t an der Spree**, Berlin is situated on the Spree; **das —t mir am Herzen**, I am deeply interested in that; **der Hund —t an der Kette**, the dog is on the chain; **es —t viel, wenig, nichts daran**, it matters much, little, nothing, *or* it does not matter; **daran —t mir nichts**, that does not concern me, I don't care; **was —t Ihnen daran**, what does that matter to you? **wem —t daran?** who cares about it? **—t etwas daran?** does it matter, is it of any consequence? **daran —t alles**, that's the main point; **es —t mir viel daran**, it matters much to me, it is of importance to me; **es lag in meiner Absicht**, it was my intention; **wenn es nur daran —t**, if that is all; **es —t uns sehr daran zu wissen**. we are very anxious to know; **so viel an mir —t**, as far as I am concerned *or* can; **woran liegt es, daß . . .?** how does it come that . . .? **an wem —t die Schuld?** whose fault is it? **es —t an Ihnen**, it depends on you; **es —t am hellen Tage, vor Augen**, it is obvious, as clear as day; **auf dem Halse —en**, to bother, trouble a p.; **es —t mir auf dem Herzen**, my heart is oppressed; **auf Flaschen —en**, to be in bottles; **der Ton —t auf der letzten Silbe**, the accent is on the last syllable; **einem auf der Zunge —en**, to be at the tip of a p.'s tongue; **es —t außer meinem Plane**, that goes beyond my plan; **—en bei**, to be near, close to, with; **—en in**, to lie in, be in, be comprised in; **es —t schon darin**, it is implied, comprised in (*what has been said, etc.*); **das Pferd —t schwer in der Faust**, the horse is hard-mouthed; **einander in den Haaren —en**, to be at loggerheads; **im Vorteil —en**, to have the advantage (*Fenc.*); **im Streite —en**, to dispute, fight with; **einem in den Ohren —en**, to din into s. o.'s ears, pester s. o. about; **es —t mir in allen Gliedern**, I have a trembling, heaviness, *etc.*, in all my limbs; **es —t im Blute**, it runs in the blood; **in Garnison —en**, to be quartered (**in**, at); **das —t mir noch immer im Sinne**, I cannot get that out of my mind; **nach Osten —en**, to look towards the east, to face east; **immer über den Büchern —en**, to be always poring over books; **das Schiff —t vor Anker**, the ship is lying *or* riding at anchor; **vor einer Festung —en**, to besiege a fortress; **(mit einander) vor Gericht —en**, to go to, be at law; **zu Bett —en**, to keep one's bed; to be in bed; **einem zur Last —en**, to bore a person, to importune some one. **—end**, *p. & adj.* recumbent; horizontal; situated; **—ende Gründe** *or* **Güter**, landed estates, real property, immovables; **—ende Schrift**, italics; **—endes Geld**, money producing no interest. **—enschaft**, *f.* real estate; (*pl.*) immovables. **—er**, *m.* (**—ers**, *pl.* **—er**) one lying; ship lying at a place; floor-timbers (*Naut.*); lower blade (*of shears*). *Comp.* **—e=geld**, *n.* demurrage. **—en=lassen**, *n.* discontinuance. **—e=tag**, *m.* day of rest; (*pl.*) lay-days (*Naut.*). **—e=zeit**, *f.* time of lying (*for wine, etc.*); lay-days; quarantine; **extra —ezeit**, days of demurrage.

Lieh, Lie'he, *1 (& 3) p. sing. imperf. ind. & subj. of* **leihen**.

Lies; Lie'sest (Liest), Liest, *imperat; 2 & 3 pers. sing. pres. ind. of* **lesen**.

Lies'pfund, *n.* lis-pound ($\frac{1}{20}$ of a ship's pound).

Ließ, Lie'ße, *1 (& 3) p. sing. imperf. ind. & subj of* **lassen**.

Lieut'enant, *see* **Leutnant**.

Ligatu'r, *f.* (*pl.* **—en**) ligature (*Mus., Typ., Surg.*)

Ligus'ter, *m.* (**—s**) privet (*Bot.*).

Likö'r, *m.* (**—s**, *pl.* **—e**) liqueur, cordial. *Comp.* **—gestell, —service**, *n.* liqueur-stand.

Li'la, I. *adj.* lilac (*coloured*). II. **—k**, *m.* (**—ks**) lilac (*Bot.*). *Comp.* **—rot**, solferino.

Lil'ie, *f.* (*pl.* **—n**) lily; fleur-de-lis. *Comp.* **—n=artig**, *adj.* liliaceous. **—n=blaß**, *adj.* pale as a lily. **—n=hand**, *f.* lily-white hand. **—n=haut**, *f.* lily-white skin. **—n=stengel**, *m.*; **einem mit dem —n=stengel winken**, to give a person a delicate hint (*coll.*).

Li'mes=kommission, *f.* commission appointed to investigate the traces of the old Roman boundary (*limes*) in the west and south of Germany.

Lim—et'te, *f.* (*pl.* **—etten**) lime. **—ona'de**, *f.* lemonade. **—o'ne**, *f.* (*pl.* **—onen**) lemon; citron. *Comp.* **—o'nen=saft**, *m.* lemon-juice.

Limit—ati'v, *adj.* restrictive, limiting.

Li'mit—o, *n. & m.* (**—os**, *pl.* **—os**, **—i**), **—um**, *n.* (**—ums**, *pl.* **—a**) fixed price.

[1]**Lin'de**, *f.* (*pl.* **—n**) linden, lime-tree; **unter den —n**, chief street of Berlin. **—n**, *adj.* made of linden-wood. *Comp.* **—n=allee**, *f.*, **—n=gang**, *m.* avenue of lime-trees. **—n=bast**, *m.* inner bark of lime-trees. **—n=saft**, *m.* lime-juice. **—n=stadt**, *f.* = **Leipzig**. **—n=straße**, *f.* street *or* road planted with lime-trees.

[2]**Lin'de**, *adj. & adv.* soft, gentle.

Lin'derer, *m.* (**—s**, *pl.* **—**) soother; alleviator.

Linder—n, *v.* I. *a.* to mitigate, alleviate, soften; to soothe, allay; to mitigate; to tranquillize; to temper. II. *r.* to be soothed; to abate. **—nd**, *p. & adj.* lenitive, soothing; **ein —erndes Mittel**, a lenitive, an anodyne. **—ung**, *f.* alleviation, mitigation; palliation; commutation; comfort; **einem —ung verschaffen**, to afford s. o. relief. **—ungs=mittel**, *n.* lenitive.

Lin'digkeit, *f.* (*pl.* **—en**) mildness, gentleness (*obs.*); **eure — lasset kund sein allen Menschen**, let your moderation be known unto all men (*B.*).

Lind'wurm, (*rarely:* **Lin'denwurm**,) *m.* winged serpent *or* dragon (*obs. poet.*).

Linea'—l, I. *n.* (**—ls**, *pl.* **—le**) ruler; hemmer, guide (*on sewing-machines*). II. *adj.* lineal. **—r, —risch**, *adj.* linear. *Comp.* **—r=zeichnung**, *f.* outline, sketch.

Li'nie, *f.* (*pl.* **—n**) line (*Math., Mil., Fort., Mus.*); line, equator; lineage; row; bounds (*of decorum, etc.*); **krumme —**, curve; **dicke, breite —n**, full strokes; **— einer Kriegsflotte**, line of battle; **—n ziehen**, to rule (*paper, etc.*); **gerade —**, direct line; **in der ersten —**, in the first rank; **sich in —n stellen**, to draw up, to dress (*Mil.*); **— machen**, to make face, front (*Mil.*); **auf gleicher — mit**, equal with *or* to; **— halten**, to keep in line; to write straight. *Comp.* **—n=blatt**, *n.* sheet with ink *or* transparent lines (*as a guide in writing*). **—n=feuer**, *n.* file-firing. **—n=förmig**, *adj.* linear. **—n=offizier**, *m.* officer of the line. **—n=papier**, *n.* ruled paper. **—n=perspektive**, *f.* linear perspective. **—n=regiment**, *n.* regiment of the line. **—n=schiff**, *n* ship of the line, man-of-war. **—n=system**, *n.* diatonic scale (*Mus.*). **—n=truppen**, *pl.* troops of the line, regulars. **—n=zieher**, *m.* ruler; ruling-pen.

Liniie'r—en, *v.a.* to rule. *Comp.* **—feder**, *f.* drawing-pen. **—maschine**, *f.* ruling machine.

Lingui'st, *m.* (**—en**, *pl.* **—en**) linguist. **—ik**, *f.* science of language. **—isch**, *adj.* linguistic.

Link, *adj. & adv.* left, left-handed; clumsy, awkward; sinister (*Her.*); **— sein**, to be left-handed; **die —e Seite**, the wrong side (*of cloth, etc.*), the reverse (*of coins*), the near side (*of a horse*), larboard; **zur —en**, to the left; **sich an der** *or* **zur —en Hand trauen lassen**, to contract a morganatic marriage. **—e**, *f.* left hand, left; Left, Liberal (*Pol.*); **zur —en**, on *or* to the left. **—heit**, *f.* awkwardness; awkward action, blunder. **—isch**, *adj. & adv.* awkward; wrong. **—s**, *adv.* to the left; on the left; wrong-side-out; left-handed; awkwardly; wrongly; **—s um!** left turn! left about! **—s um kehrt!** left about turn! **alles —s anfangen**, to do everything the wrong way; **—s sein**, to be left-handed; **Sie sind weit —s**, you are far out *or* very much mistaken; **—s essen**, to eat with the left hand; **—s nehmen**, to miscontrue; **—s hin, —s her**, along on the left. *Comp.* **—hand**. *f.* left-handed person.

—s=gewinde, *n.* left-handed screw. **—s=macher,** *m.* one who will prove that wrong is right. **—rheinisch,** *adj.* on the left bank of the Rhine.

Lin'nen, *see* **Leinen.**

Lino'n, *m.* (**—s,** *pl.* **—s**) French lawn, cambric.

Lin'se, *f* (*pl.* **—n**) lentil; lentil-like mole *or* freckle; lens; ball, pendulum-bob; **welsche —n,** laburnum. **—n=haft,** *adj.* lenticular; lens-shaped. *Comp.* **—n=entzündung,** *f.* inflammation of the crystalline lens. **—n=erz,** *n.* pea-ore. **—n=förmig,** *adj.* lentiform, lenticular. **—n=gericht,** *n.* dish of lentils. **—n=glas,** *n.* lens. **—n=kapsel,** *f.* capsule of the crystalline lens.

Lip'p—e, *f.* (*pl.* **—en**) lip; notch (*Naut.*); mortise, groove; sinking of the metal, spewing (*Artil.*); **sich** (*dat.*) **die —en ablecken,** to smack one's lips; **es soll nicht über meine —en kommen,** it shall not pass my lips, I shall not speak of it; **sich** (*dat.*) **die —en beißen, sich** (*acc.*) **auf die —en beißen,** to bite one's lips; **die —en hängen lassen,** to mope *or* sulk; **die —en aufwerfen,** to curl one's lip, to purse up one's mouth; to pout; to sneer; **zwischen —' und Kelches Rand schwebt der finstern Mächte Hand,** many a slip 'twixt cup and lip. **—ig,** *adj.* lipped, *as* **dünn—ig,** thin-lipped. *Comp.* **—en=buchstabe, —en=laut,** *m.* labial. **—en=förmig,** *adj.* labiate.

Liqui'd, *adj.* liquid; payable; **—e Forderungen,** debts actually owing; **—erkannte Schuld,** judgment debt.

Li'quid—a, *f.* (*pl.* **—ae** *or* **Liqui'den**) liquid sound (*m, n, l, r*) (*Gram.*). **—a'tor,** *m.* (**—ators,** *pl.* **—ato'ren**) liquidator, administrator (*of an estate*). **—ie'ren,** *v.a.* to liquidate. *Comp.* **—atio'ns=verfahren,** *n.* verification of the debts.

Lis'pel, Lis'pel, *m. in compds.* **—laut, —ton,** *m.* lisped *or* whispered sound. **—er** (**—ers,** *pl.* **—er**), **Lisp'ler** (**Lisp'lers,** *pl.* **Lisp'ler**), *m.* lisper. **—n,** *v.a. & n.* (*aux.* **h.**) to lisp; to whisper; to rustle, murmur softly.

List, *f.* (*pl.* **—en**) cunning, craft, artfulness; stratagem, trick, finesse, ruse; **arge —,** arrant cunning; **mit eiteln —en umgehen,** to imagine deceits (*B.*); **— gegen —, — über —,** diamond cuts diamond (*prov.*). **—ig,** *adj. & adv.* crafty, cunning, deceitful, sly; astute; **—ige Anläufe,** wiles (*B.*). **—igkeit,** *f.* craftiness.

Lis'te, *f.* (*pl.* **—n**) list, roll, catalogue; inventory; panel (*of jurors*); **in eine — eintragen,** to enrol, to register.

Litanei', *f.* (*pl.* **—en**) litany; jeremiad.

Li'ter, *m. & n.* (**—s,** *pl.* **—**) litre (*rather less than a quart*).

Litew'k—a, *f.* (*pl.* **—en**) litevka (*Mil.*).

Lit'faßsäule, *f.* (*pl.* **—n**) (street) pillar on which bills are posted.

Lit'(t)er—a, *f.* (*pl.* **—ä**) letter. **—ä'r, —a'risch,** *adj.* literary; **—är=geschichte,** literary history. **—a't,** *m.* (**—aten,** *pl.* **—aten**), **—a'tor,** *m.* (**—ators,** *pl.* **—ato'ren**) man of letters; writer; (*pl.*) literati. **—a'tentum,** *n.* condition of a litterateur; literary world. **—atu'r,** *f.* literature; bibliographical guide; **die alte —atur,** the classics, classic lore. *Comp.* **—atu'r=blatt,** *n.*, **—atu'r=zeitung,** *f.* literary gazette, (literary and critical) review. **—atu'r=geschichte,** *f.* history of literature. **—atu'r=geschichtlich,** *adj.* with regard to literary history, on literature. **—atu'r=verein,** *m.* literary society.

Lithogra'ph, *m.* (**—en,** *pl.* **—en**) lithographer. **—ie',** *f.* lithography; lithographic drawing. **—ie'ren,** *v.a.* to lithograph, draw *or* etch on stone. **—isch,** *adj. & adv.* lithographic; **—ische Anstalt,** lithographic printing-office. *Comp.* **—ie'r=papier,** *n.* transfer-paper.

Litt, Lit'te, *1* (*& 3*) *p. sing. imperf. ind. & subj. of* **leiden.**

Liturgie', *f.* (*pl.* **—en**) liturgy.

Litur'gisch, *adj.* liturgical.

Lit'z—e, *f.* (*pl.* **—en**) cord, string; strand; braid; piping (*on dresses, etc.*); gold *or* silver cord *or* thread; galloon; heddle (*Weav.*). **—ung,** *f.* lacing (*Naut.*); lace-trimming. *Comp.* **—en=besatz,** *m.* braiding.

Livree', Livrei', (*poet.*) *f.* (*pl.* **—en**) livery; servants. *Comp.* **—bediente(r),** *m.* livery-servant, footman in livery, boy in buttons. **—borte,** *f.* livery-lace.

Lob, *n.* (**—(e)s**) praise; commendation; eulogy; fame, reputation; **einem — erteilen,** to give praise to s. o., to praise a p.; **zum —e von,** in praise of; **einem zum —e nachsagen,** to tell, say to a p.'s credit, in s.o.'s praise; **einem ein gutes — geben,** to give a p. a good character; **Gott (sei) —!** thank God! **Gott sei — und Dank,** Heaven be praised! **einem ein — einschreiben,** to give one a good mark.

[1]**Lo'b—en,** *v.a.* to praise, commend, laud; to do credit to, honour; to approve; to value, estimate; **sich —end über einen aussprechen,** to speak highly of some one; **ich —e mir den Frieden!** give me peace! **da —e ich mir ein gutes, warmes Bett!** commend me to *or* give me a good warm bed! **das Werk —t den Meister,** the work shows the master, the work reflects honour upon its maker; **das ist an ihm zu —en,** that is praiseworthy in him; **gelobt sei Gott!** God be praised! **—er,** *m.* (**—ers,** *pl.* **—er**) praiser, extoller. **—esam, —esan,** honourable, worthy; laudable (*obs.*); **Kaiser Rotbart —esam,** the noble emperor Frederic Barbarossa; **mein Herr Magister —esan,** my honourable pedagogue, Sir Moralizer (*poet.*). *Comp.* **—ens=wert, —ens=würdig,** *adj.* praiseworthy. **—es=erhebung,** *f.* high praise, encomium. **—gedicht,** *n.* panegyric in verse. **—gesang,** *m.* song of praise, hymn. **—hudelei',** *f.* fulsome praise, base flattery. **—hudeln,** *v.a.* (*insep.*) to flatter, praise fulsomely *or* extravagantly. **—hudler,** *m.* toady, mean flatterer. **—lied,** *n. see* **—gesang. —preisen,** *insep. v.a.* to praise, extol; **—preiset den Herrn!** praise the Lord. **—preisung,** *f.* praise, glorification. **—rede,** *f.* panegyric, eulogy; **einem** *or* **auf einen eine —rede halten,** to eulogize s. o. **—redner,** *m.* panegyrist. **—singen,** *ir.v.n.* (*aux.* **h.**) (*sep.*) (**einem**) to sing praises to. **—spruch,** *m.* eulogy.

[2]**Lobe—n,** *v.a.* to promise, assure (*obs., now replaced by* **geloben**); **das gelobte Land,** the land of promise. *Comp.* **—tanz,** *m.* public dance in certain villages (*dial.*).

Löb'lich, *adj.* laudable, commendable; honourable, worthy. **—keit,** *f.* praiseworthiness.

[1]**Loch,** *m.* brush-wood, wood (*obs.; in compound names reduced to* **—lo, —loo, —lohe, —lohn**). *Comp.* **—taube,** *f.* wood-pigeon.

[2]**Loch,** *n.* (**—es,** *pl.* **Lö'cher**) hole; opening, cavity; gap, breach; pore (*of the skin; of stones, etc.*); eye, hole (*in bread, cheese, needles, etc.*); pocket (*Bill.*); blind alley; prison; den; lurking-place; rent, tear; foramen (*Anat.*); **einem ein — in den Kopf werfen,** to break a person's head by throwing (*a stone, etc.*); **einem ein — in den Leib reden** *or* **fragen,** to pester a p. with chatting *or* with questions (*coll.*); **Löcher im Strumpfe haben,** to be out at heels; **einen ins — stecken** *or* **setzen,** to send a p. to prison (*coll.*); **aus dem —e jagen,** to draw, unearth (*foxes, etc.*); **ein — machen,** to miss; **ins — spielen,** to pocket (*Bill.*); **einen vors (Ofen) — schieben,** to make a cat's paw of a p.; **einem zeigen, wo der Zimmermann das — gemacht (gelassen) hat,** to show s.o. the

door; ein — bekommen, to fail, miscarry (*coll.*); die Pauke hat ein —, the affair has been broken off abruptly; ein — zumachen, to stop a hole, to pay a debt; ein — zu und das andere aufmachen, to rob Peter to pay Paul, to pay one debt by contracting another; auf (aus) dem letzten —e pfeifen, to be in great straits; to be at the last gasp; er pfeift aus dem letzten —, it will soon be all up with him; der Wind bläst aus einem kalten —e, the wind blows from a cold quarter; wie ein — saufen, to drink like a fish; ein — in den Mond bohren, to run away from one's creditors; und sie ließen ihn eilend aus dem —e, and they brought him hastily out of the dungeon (*B.*). *Comp.* —bohrer, *m.* borer; auger, piercer. —eisen, *n.* punch. —feile, *f.* rifler. —maschine, *f.* punching-machine. —säge, *f.* fret-saw, key-hole *or* compass-saw. —scheibe, *f.*, —stempel, *m.*, —zange, *f.* punch. —tiefe, *f.* depth of a hole.

Lö'ch—elchen, *n.* (—elchens, *pl.* —elchen) small hole; eyelet; foramen (*Anat.*); dimple. —eln, *v.a.* to make little holes in. —er, *pl. see* Loch. —ericht, (*obs.*) —erig, *adj.* full of holes; porous; perforated; —erichte Brunnen, broken cisterns (*B.*). —erigkeit, *f.* porosity. —ern, *v.a.* to perforate, to punch.

Lo'chen, *v.a.* to perforate; to punch; to blaze (*a tree*).

1**Lo'ck—e,** *f.* (*pl.* —en) lock (*of hair, etc.*); curl, ringlet; flock (*of wool, etc.*); sich (*dat.*) —en brennen lassen, to have one's hair curled (*with irons*); in —en legen, to curl. —en, *v.a. & r.* to curl. —icht, (*obs.*) —ig, *adj.* curly. *Comp.* —en=bau, *m.*, —en=gebäude, *n.* mass of artificial curls; coiffure of curls. —en=haar, *n.* curly hair. —en=kopf, *m.* curly-haired *or* curly-headed person. —en=wulst, *m.* mass of thick curly hair.

2**Lo'cke,** *f.* decoying (*obs.*); lure, bait, bird-call (*obs.*); decoy bird (*obs.*).

Lo'ck—en, *v.a. & n.* (*aux.* h.) to decoy; to allure, bait; to call; to cluck; to attract, entice, tempt; einem Thränen aus den Augen —en, to draw tears from s. o.'s eyes; aus einem —en, to draw *or* wrest from a p.; einen Hund —en, to call *or* whistle to a dog; damit kann man keinen Hund vom Ofen —en, that's of no use whatever, that won't draw, that's no good. —er, *m.* (—ers, *pl.* —er) enticer, seducer; call of the Swiss herds (*prov.*) —ung, *f.* enticing; allurement. *Comp.* —aas, *n.* lure, bait. —ente, *f.* decoy-duck. —flöte, *f.* bird-call. —gesang, *m.* alluring song. —herd, *m.* decoy-floor. —mittel, *n.* bait, inducement. —ruf, *m.* call-note (of a bird). —speise, *f.* bait. —stimme, *f.* alluring voice; call. —vogel, *m.* decoy-bird; allurer.

Lö'cken, *v.n.* to kick, run (*against*) (*obs.*); wider den Stachel —, to kick against the pricks (*B.*); to be obstinate, to resist.

Lo'cker, *adj. & adv.* loose, slack; light, spongy; not dense *or* compact, not firm; lax; wild, disorderly; dissolute; — Boden, light soil; — werden, to grow loose (*of teeth from which the gum has shrunk*); er läßt nicht —, he will not abate (relax) an inch, he does not let go, he holds fast; — machen, to loosen, to relax; — leben, to lead an extravagant *or* disorderly life; da geht es — her! things are going on at a fine rate there! ein —er Gesell, Zeisig, loose living fellow, reckless fellow, loose fish. —heit, *f.* looseness; lightness; sponginess; extravagance; libertinism; laxity.

Lo'ckern, *v.a.* to make loose *or* spongy; to break up (*soil*); das Blumenbeet lockert sich in die Höhe, the flowers push up and loosen the soil (*poet.*). II. *n.* (*aux.* s.) to become loose *or* spongy; to lead a wild *or* extravagant life.

Lo'de, *f.* (*pl.* —n) young shoot; young tree.

Lo'den, *m.* (—s, *pl.* —) coarse woollen waterproof cloth. *Comp.* —stoffe, *pl.* waterproof cloths.

Lo'der—n, *v.n.* (*aux.* h.) to blaze, flame up, flare; to glow, burn.

Löf'fel, *m.* (—s, *pl.* —) spoon; ear of a hare *or* rabbit; großer —, ladle; kommen Sie zu einem — Suppe zu uns, come and take potluck with us; thun als hätte man die Weisheit mit —n gegessen, to play the wiseacre; to make a great show of wisdom *or* learning; einen über den — barbieren, to cheat s. o.; einen — aufheben und eine Schüssel zertreten, to be penny wise and pound foolish. —chen, *n.* (—chens, *pl.* —chen) small spoon. —ei', *f.* love-making, spooning; eating with a spoon. —er, (Löff'l—er,) *m.* (—ers, *pl.* —er) one who eats with a spoon; gallant, spoon (*vulg.*). *Comp.* —blech, *n.* spoon-rack; spoon-metal. —förmig, *adj.* spoon-shaped; cochleariform (*Bot.*). —gans, *f.* pelican. —garde, *f.* ill-trained soldiers, the awkward squad. —haken, *m.* scoop. —schale, *f.* bowl of a spoon. —schmied, *m.* spoon-maker. —stiel, *m.* spoon-handle. —weise, *adv.* by spoonfuls.

Löf'feln, *v.a. & n.* (*aux.* h.) to eat (*eagerly*) with a spoon; to ladle out; to be given to spooning (*vulg.*); sich —, to drink in response to a p.'s having drunk one's health (*sl.*), to show oneself grateful (*sl.*).

Log, Lö'ge, *1 p. sing. imperf. ind. & subj. of* lügen.

Log(g), *m. & n.* (—s, *pl.* —e) log (*Naut.*). —en, *v.n.* (*aux.* h.) to heave the log. —er, *m.* logheaver; lugger. *Comp.* —buch, *n.* the log (*Naut.*). —gat, *n.* limber-hole.

Logarith'm, —us, *m.* (*pl.* —en) logarithm. —isch, *adj.* logarithmic. *Comp.* —en=tafel, *f.* table of logarithms.

Lo'g—e, *f.* (*pl.* —en) box (*in a theatre*); Freemasons' lodge. —eme'nt, *n.* (—ements, *pl.* —ements) lodgment, lodgings. —ie'ren, *v.n.* (*aux.* h.) to lodge, dwell. —i's, *n.* lodging(s); Kost und —is, board and lodgings. *Comp.* —en=meister, *m.* master of a lodge (*Freem.*). —en=schließer, —en=wärter, *m.* box-keeper. —ie'r=besuch, *m.*; —ierbesuch haben, to have a guest *or* friends staying in the house. —ie'r=haus, *n.* lodging-house, boarding-house.

Lo'gi—k, *f.* (*pl.* —ken) logic. —ker, *m.* (—kers, *pl.* —ker) logician. —sch, *adj.* logical.

1**Loh,** *f.* (*pl.* —en) bog, morass, peat-moor (*obs.*). *Comp.* —boden, *m.* peaty ground.

2**Loh,** *m. & n.* (—es, *pl.* —e, Lö'her) (*obs.*) wood; bushes; grove. *Comp.* (*in names;* Hohenlohe, *etc. and in*) —eiche, *f.* oak.

3**Loh,** *adj.* blazing, flaming, flaring, burning.

1**Lo'h—e,** *f.* (*pl.* —en) blaze, flame, ardour, fire; mildew (*Agr.*); lichter — brennen (*for* in lichter —e) to be all in a blaze; Waber—e, Web—e, blazing fire (*round the castle of the sleeping battle-maiden*). *Comp.* —feuer, *n.* blazing fire.

2**Lo'h—e,** *f.* (*pl.* —en) tanning-bark, tan. *Comp.* —beize, *f.* tanning; tan-pit. —brühe, *f.* ooze, tannin. —farben, —braun, *adj.* tawny, auburn. —faß, *n.* tan-vat. —gar, *adj. & adv.* tanned. —gerber, *m.* tanner. —gerberei, *f.* tanner's trade; tan-yard. —grube, *f.* tanpit. —mühle, *f.* tanning-mill. —rinde, *f.* oak-bark (for tanning).

1**Lo'hen,** *v.n.* to blaze *or* flare (up), to flame.

2**Lo'hen, Lö'hen,** *v.a.* to (steep in *or* prepare with) tan.

Lö'her, *m.* (—s, *pl.* —) tanner.

Lohn, *m.* (—es, *pl.* Löh'ne) reward, recompense; requital; (*also n.*) payment; salary; wages; pay (*Mil.*); Undank ist der Welt —, one meets with nothing but ingratitude in this world (*prov.*); **der Arbeiter ist seines —es wert,** the labourer is worthy of his hire (*B.*); **bei einem in — stehen,** to be in a p.'s pay *or* service; **Dienstbotenlöhne,** wages.

Loh'n—en, *v.a. & n.* (*aux.* **h.**) (**einem für eine Sache** *or* (*obs.*) **einer S.**), to reward, recompense; to requite; to pay; to repay; **einen —en,** to pay a p. (*for work*); **einem etwas —en,** to reward, requite one for something; **thue ich es gerne, so wird mir gelohnet,** if I do this thing willingly I have a reward (*B.*); **Gott —' es dir!** God reward you for it! **einem mit Undank —en,** to repay s.o. with ingratitude; **in Amerika —t man die Arbeit besser als in England,** work is better paid in America than in England; **es —t sich der Mühe,** it is worth while; **das —te (sich) auch grade die** *or* **der Mühe,** it was well worth the trouble (*generally conditional and ironical*). **—end,** *p. & adj.* remunerative. *Comp.* **—arbeit,** *f.* hired labour. **—arbeiter,** *m.* labourer, hireling. **—bediente(r), —diener,** *m.* valet de place, servant engaged by the day *or* temporarily. **—erhöhung,** *f.* raising of wages; rise in wages. **—handwerk,** *n.* piece-work. **—junge,** *m.* salaried apprentice. **—kutsche,** *f.* hackney-coach. **—kutscher,** *m.* hackney coachman; keeper of livery stables. **—lakai,** *m. see* **—bediente(r).** **—schreiber,** *m.* literary hack. **—süchtig,** *adj.* venal, mercenary. **—tag,** *m.* pay-day. **—zuschlag,** *m.* additional *or* extra payment; raising of wages; rise in wages.

Löh'n—en, *v.a.* to pay (*wages, etc.*). **—ung,** *f.* pay. *Comp.* **—ungs-tag,** *m.* pay-day.

Loka'l, I. *adj.* local, stationary; **—es,** local concerns; (*chronicle of*) local events. II. *n.* (—(e)s, *pl.* —e) locality, place; hall; appointed place; shop. **—isie'ren,** *v.a.* to localize. **—itä't,** *f.* locality; **—itäten eines Hauses,** ins and outs of a house. *Comp.* **—behörde,** *f.* local authority. **—blatt,** *n.* local (news)paper. **—kenntnis,** *f.* knowledge of a place. **—miete,** *f.* rent for a place of business. **—patriotismus,** *m.* local *or* parish patriotism; narrow patriotism, particularism. **—sage,** *f.* local tradition, local legend. **—verhältnisse,** *pl.* local concerns. **—vermieter,** *m.* house-agent.

Lo'kativ, *m.* (**—s**) locative case.

Lokomobi'l—e, *f.* portable engine. **—itä't,** *f.* having the power of locomotion.

Lokomoti've, *f.* (*pl.* **—n**) locomotive, engine; **einem Zuge vorangeschickte —,** pilot-engine. *Comp.* **—n-bahn,** *f.* railway, railroad. **—n-bauer,** *m.* locomotive engineer. **—(n)-führer,** *m.* engine-driver. **—n-pfeife,** *f.* steam whistle.

Lo'ko-verkehr, *m.* local trade; local intercourse.

Lolch, *m.* (**—es,** *pl.* **—e**) darnel, ray (*Bot.*).

Lom'bard, *m.* (**—s**) lombard, pawnshop; pawn-ticket; deposit-bank, bank of deposits. *Comp.* **—bestände,** *pl.* advances of money on security or pledges. **—geschäft,** *n.* loan business. **—verkehr,** *m.* loan-business on securities. **—zettel,** *m.* pawn- *or* lombard-ticket. **—zinsfuß,** *m.* rate of interest for lombarding.

Lombardie'ren, *v.a.* to lombard; to pawn; to lend; to advance.

Lom'ber, *n.* (**—s,** *pl.* **—**) ombre. **—n,** *v.n.* (*aux.* **h.**) to play at ombre.

Loos, Loos'en, Loot'se, *see under* **Los, Lotse.**

Lor'beer, *m.* (**—s,** *pl.* **—(e)n**) laurel, bay. **—e,** *f.* (*pl.* **—en**) laurel-berry, bay-berry. *Comp.* **—baum,** *m.* laurel *or* bay-tree. **—blatt,** *n.* laurel *or* bay-leaf. **—hain,** *m.* laurel-grove. **—kranz,** *m.* laurel-wreath.

Lorch, Lork, *m.* (**—es,** *pl.* **—e**) toad; spiteful person, rascal (*dial. sl.*).

Lorgnet'te, *f.* (*pl.* **—n**) eye-glasses; eye-glass, monocle.

Lor'ke, *f.* poor, bad beverage, thin and nasty broth; weak coffee; slops (*prov.*).

[1]**Los,** *n.* (—(ſ)es, *pl.* —(ſ)e) lot, lottery ticket *or* prize; share, allotment; fate, destiny, chance, fortune; **das große — gewinnen,** to win the first prize; **das — ist geworfen,** the die is cast; **das — ziehen,** to draw lots; **durchs — entscheiden,** to decide by lot; **ihm wurde ein glückliches —,** his lot was a happy one. **—(ſ)en,** I. *v.n.* (*aux.* **h.**) to draw lots (**um,** for). II. *subst. n.* **—(ſ)ung,** *f.* drawing lots. *Comp.* **—(ſ)es-kugel,** *f.* ballot, little ball. **—topf,** *m.* urn for lots *or* tickets; urn of fate.

[2]**Los,** I. *adj. & adv.* (*not often used attributively*); loose; slack; free; flowing, dishevelled; disengaged, released; **— sein, — werden,** (*with gen.* (*obs.*), *acc. or* **von**) to get loose from, rid of, free from; **einer** (*obs.*) *or* **eine Person — werden,** to get rid of a person; **sei — von deiner Krankheit,** thou art loosed from thine infirmity (*B.*); **der Gefangene ist —,** the prisoner is free, at large, has escaped; **der Anker ist —,** the anchor drags; **überall —!** let go everywhere! **nur —! — davor!** very well, begin, fire away! (*coll.*); **was ist hier —?** what 's the matter? what is wrong? **was ist denn —?** what's up? (*coll.*); **Verrat ist —,** treason is abroad; **der Teufel ist —,** hell is broke loose; **es muß etwas — sein,** something must have happened, there is something in the wind; **mit seinem Wissen ist nicht viel —,** his knowledge is nothing to boast of; **mit seiner Begabung ist nicht viel —,** he is not particularly clever (*coll.*); **etwas — haben,** to know something thoroughly (*coll.*); **er hat es —,** he is a clever fellow (*coll.*); **mein Geld bin ich —,** I have lost my money (*coll.*). II. *suffix* = less; **hoffnungs—,** without hope. III. *adv. & sep. prefix,* on, forward, up to, off; away; *giving to verbs with which it is compounded the idea:* **1.** *of* loose, free, **2.** *of unrestrained, violent action or motion; and* **3.** *of commencement,* **darauf — leben,** to live from hand to mouth to live carelessly; **wacker darauf — lügen, trinken,** to lie shamelessly, to drink stoutly; **es geht —,** it commences, it breaks out; hostilities commence, war begins; **frisch drauf —!** courage! at him! go on! (let us) go at it with a will! **—! schießt —!** fire away! **nun geht das Weinen —,** now (*or* then) they fall a-crying, begin to cry. **—(ſ)e,** *adj. & adv.* loose; not firm *or* fixed; unsteady; vagrant; wanton; dissolute, vicious; base, spurious; sportive, mischievous; wily; roguish, naughty useless; abusive; **—(ſ)es Band,** loose string, slight bond of connection; **—(ſ)es Gesindel,** vagabonds, blackguards; **—(ſ)es Gut,** spare stores (*on ships*); **—(ſ)es Haar,** loose, flowing *or* dishevelled hair; **—(ſ)er Kalk,** untempered mortar; **ein —(ſ)es Maul haben,** to have a bad tongue; **—(ſ)er Kiel,** false keel; **—(ſ)es Kind,** young urchin; **—(ſ)e Lehre,** vain, foolish doctrine, vanity (*B.*); **ein —(ſ)er Mast,** a jury mast; **ein —(ſ)er Vogel,** a roguish person; a loose fish; **einem —(ſ)e Worte geben,** to abuse s.o.

Los— (*in comp.*) **—ankern,** *v.a.* to unanchor, to weigh the anchor of. **—arbeiten,** *v.* I. *a.* to loosen, work off; to disengage. II. *r.* to extricate oneself, get free. III. *n.* (*aux.* **h.**) to work on *or* away. **—bekommen,** *ir.v.a.* to loosen; to get *or* set free; to get to understand (*coll.*). **—binden,** *ir.v.a.* to untie, detach, undo, unstring; to unfurl; to set free. **—bitten,** *ir.v.a.*; **einen —bitten,** to beg a p. off, to obtain a p.'s release by entreaty. **—brechen,** *ir.v.* I. *a.* to break off *or* loose. II. *n.* (*aux.* **s.**) to break loose, forth *or* out; to burst forth *or* out, to break away, rush off; **der Sturm bricht —,** the storm is bursting.

—brennen, *ir.v.* I. *a.* to discharge, to fire (off) (*a gun*); to let off (*fireworks*). II. *n.* (*aux.* **s.**) to go off (*as a gun*). **—bringen**, *ir.v.a.* to get loose *or* off; to disengage; to loosen. **—bröckeln**, *v.a.*, *r.* & *n.* (*aux.* **s.**) to crumble off. **—bürgen**, *v.a.* to bail (*out of prison*). **—donnern**, *v.n.* (*aux.* **h.**) to burst forth like thunder; to storm at. **—drehen**, *v.a.* to untwist, twist off. **—drücken**, *v.* I. *a.* to loosen, detach. II. *a.* & *n.* (*aux.* **h.**) to fire off (*a gun*); **—gedrückt!** fire! (*Mil.*); **er legte an und drückte —**, he took aim and fired. **—eisen**, *v. a.* to clear of ice; **(einen) —eisen**, to get (a p.) away with much difficulty, to free from an embarrassing situation (*coll.*). **—fahren**, *ir.v.n.* (*aux.* **s.**) to come off, become loose suddenly; **auf einen —fahren**, to fly (out) at a p. **—feuern**, *v.a.* to discharge, shoot. **—geben**, *ir.v.a.* to set free; to emancipate. **—gebung**, *f.* release; discharge; emancipation. **—gehen**, *ir.v.n.* (*aux.* **s.**) to come *or* go off; to become loose; **(auf einen)** to fly at, attack; to charge (*the enemy*); to undertake *or* set about anything; to begin (*suddenly*); to explode; to fight a students' duel; **da ging das Zanken —**, then they fell a-quarrelling; **frisch auf etwas —gehen**, to set about anything with a will; **nicht —gehen**, to miss fire, flash in the pan; **es geht bald —**, war will soon break out; **es geht bald wieder —**, hostilities will soon be resumed; **dieses Gewehr geht schwer —**, the trigger of this gun is stiff; **es geht auf den Winter —**, winter is drawing near; **das Eis geht —**, the ice is breaking up; **sie sind —gegangen**, they have fought a duel (*Univ.*). **—gürteln**, **—gurten**, *v.a.* to ungird; to ungirth (*a horse*). **—haben**, *v.a.*; **er hat die Sache unheimlich —**, he understands the thing uncommonly well (*coll.*); **viel —haben**, to be very clever. **—hacken**, *v.a.* to loosen by hoeing. **—häkeln**, **—haken**, *v.a.* to unclasp, unhook. **—hauen**, *v.a.* to cut loose, off *or* away. **—helfen**, *ir.v.n.* **(einem)** to help (a p.) to get free. **—hetzen**, *v.a.* to set on (*a dog*). **—holz**, *n.* cross-bar, transom. **—kaufen**, *v.a.* to redeem, ransom; **sich —kaufen**, to buy oneself off (*Mil.*). **—käuflich**, *adj.* redeemable. **—ketten**, *v.* I. *a.* to unchain. II. *r.* to break loose. **—kitten**, *v.a.* to undo what is fastened with cement. **—knallen**, *v.a.* & *n.* (*aux.* **s.**) to explode; to let off. **—knüpfen**, *v.a.* to untie. **—kommen**, *ir.v.n.* (*aux.* **s.**) to get loose *or* off; to get rid of; to get free, to be set free, to escape. **—lassen**, *ir.v.* I. *a.* to let loose, let go; to release, set free; to let off (*a gun*); to utter, break out into; **einen Brief —lassen**, to write a letter (*coll.*); **einen Witz —lassen**, to say something witty, make a joke (*coll.*); **laß mich —!** leave go! let me go! **Hunde —lassen**, to set dogs on, to unchain dogs. II. *n.* (*aux.* **h.**) to become detached. **—lassung**, *f.* setting free, *etc.*; release. **—legen**, *v.* I. *a.* to loosen. II. *n.* (*aux.* **h.**) to begin (*coll.*); to set about. **—lösen**, *v.a.* to loosen, detach. **—löten**, *v.a.* to unsolder. **—machen**, *v.* I. *a.* to loosen, make loose; to undo; to disengage; to detach; to separate; to set at liberty. II. *r.* to get away; to disengage *or* extricate oneself (*from*); to get rid (*of*); to get free (*from*); **ich kann mich nicht von ihm —machen**, I cannot get away from him. **—platzen**, *v.n.* (*aux.* **s.**) to burst (*out*); to burst off. **—reden**, *v.* I. *r.* to exculpate oneself, clear oneself by talking. II. *n.* (*aux.* **h.**) to talk at random, wildly; to begin talking. **—reißen**, *ir. v.* I. *a.* to pull *or* tear off *or* away; to separate by violence. II. *r.* to break loose; to tear oneself away (**von**, from; **aus**, out of). III. *n.* (*aux.* **s.**) to snap; to break off *or* loose. **—sagen**, *v.* I. *a.* see **—sprechen**. II. *r.* to refuse; **sich —sagen von**, to resign, to retract, to renounce; **ich sage mich von der Sache —**, I'll have nothing more to do with the matter. **—sagung**, *f.* renunciation, withdrawal. **—schießen**, *ir. v.* I. *a.* to fire off, discharge; to begin (*a speech, a story*) (*coll.*). II. *n.* (*aux.* **s.**) **auf einen —schießen**, to fly at, rush upon a p. **—schlagen**, *ir.v.* I. *a.* to knock off, loosen by striking; to sell (*cheap*), to undersell, to get off (*one's wares*). II. *n.* (*aux.* **h.**) to attack (**auf einen**); to belabour. **—schnallen**, *v.a.* to unbuckle. **—schneiden**, *ir. v.* I. *a.* to cut off, *or* loose. II. *n.* (*aux.* **h.**) to begin to cut. **—schnüren**, *v.a.* to unlace, undo. **—schrauben**, *v.a.* to unscrew, to screw off. **—schütteln**, *v.a.* to shake off, shake loose. **—schwören**, *ir.v.a.* to clear, set free by taking an oath, by bearing testimony on oath. **—spannen**, *v.a.* to unbend, relax; to unyoke, unharness. **—sprechen**, I. *ir.v.a.* to declare free, release; to acquit, absolve; to free (*an apprentice, etc.*); **einen von einer Verbindlichkeit —sprechen**, to release a p. from an engagement; **die Kirche hat das Recht —zusprechen**, the church has power to absolve from sin. II. *subst. n.* absolution; acquittal; discharge. **—sprengen**, *v.* I. *a.* to spring, to burst off. II. *n.* (*aux.* **s.**) **(auf einen)** to gallop (against *or* at a person); **ein Roß —sprengen**, to make a horse gallop. **—springen**, *ir.v.n.* (*aux.* **s.**) to fly off, burst loose, crack; **—springen auf** (*acc.*); to fly at, rush upon. **—spülen**, *v.a.* to wash away. **—stecken**, *v.a.* to unpin, take down (*a tucked-up dress, etc.*). **—stürmen**, *v.n.* (*aux.* **s.**) **(auf eine S.)** to rush upon a th.; **auf seine Gesundheit —stürmen**, to take no care of, to injure one's health. **—trennen**, *v.a.* to rip, unsew, to separate. **—weichen**, *v.* I. *a.* to loosen by soaking. II. *n.* (*aux.* **s.**) to soften and come off. **—wickeln**, *v.* I. *a.* to unwind, untwist; to uncurl; to unravel. II. *r.* to shake off; to extricate oneself (*from*). **—winden**, *ir.v.a.* to untwist; to wrench loose. **—zetern**, *v.n.* (*aux.* **h.**) to commence to cry, to cry out. **—ziehen**, *ir.v.* I. *a.* to draw off *or* awry; to set out, to march away. II. *n.* (*aux.* **h.**) **auf, über, gegen einen —ziehen**, to rail at, inveigh against s.o.; (*aux.* **s.**). **—zupfen**, *v.a.* to pull, pluck off.

Lös'—bar, *adj.* soluble; resolvable. **—lich**, *adj.* & *adv.* soluble; pardonable. **—lichkeit**, *f.* solubility; pardonableness.

[1]**Lösch'—en**, *ir.v.* I. *n.* (*aux.* **s.**) to go out, be extinguished; **das Papier —t**, the paper absorbs the ink. II. *a.* to extinguish, quench; to cancel (*a debt*); to blot out; to slake (*lime*); to lay (*dust*); to quench (*thirst*); to liquidate, discharge, cancel (*a debt*); to obliterate (*something written, etc.*; *a recollection*); **ein nicht zu —ender Durst**, an unquenchable thirst. **—er**, *m.* (**—ers**, *pl.* **—er**) extinguisher, *etc.* **—ung**, *f.* quenching; extinguishing; slaking; cancelling. *Comp.* **—anstalt**, *f.* fire-brigade premises. **—apparat**, *m.* appliances for putting out fires. **—blatt**, *n.* (sheet of) blotting-paper. **—brand**, *m.* quenched firebrand. **—eimer**, *m.* fire-bucket. **—gerät**, *n.* fireman's apparatus. **—kalk**, *m.* quicklime. **—mannschaft**, *f.* fire-brigade. **—papier**, *n.* blotting paper, blotter; **angeführt mit —papier**, you are taken in, I have caught you (*coll.*).

[2]**Lö'sch—en**, *v.a.* to unlade, discharge, lighten (*a ship*). **—er**, *m.* (**—ers**, *pl.* **—er**) unloader, longshoreman. **—ung**, *f.* unlading, discharge disembarkation (*Naut.*). *Comp.* **—geld**, *n.* wharfage; unlading charges. **—platz**, *m.* discharging wharf; port of delivery. **—ungsspesen**, *pl.* landing charges (*C. L.*).

[1]**Lo's—en**, I. *v.n.* (*aux.* **h.**) to draw lots (**um**, for).

II. *s.f.* drawing lots. —**ung**, *f.* drawing lots. *Comp.* —**kugel**, *f.* ballot.

²Lo'ſ—en, *v.n.* to listen, to hearken (*dial.*). —**ung**, *f.* watchword, word of command, rallying word; sign, signal; **Geld ist die —ung**, money is the thing. *Comp.* —**ungs=schuß**, *m.* signal shot. —**ungs=wort**, *n.* watchword.

Lö'ſ—en, *v.a.* to loosen; to untie, unbind, relax; to detach; to break off, give up; to absolve; to dissolve; to solve; to answer (*a riddle, etc.*); to redeem, ransom; to discharge (*a gun*); to take (*a ticket*); to resolve (*Math.*); to get by purchase *or* in exchange; **die Seele —en**, to unbind the soul; **die Zunge —en**, to make a p. speak; **ein Siegel —en**, to break a seal; **sein Versprechen —en**, to fulfil one's promise; **Geld aus etwas —en**, to make money by the sale of a thing; **ein Pfand —en**, to redeem a pledge; **sein Verhältnis zu einem —en**, to give up all connection with a p.; **Gefangene —en**, to set free prisoners; to ransom prisoners; **Rätsel —en**, to solve *or* guess riddles; **eine Schwierigkeit —en**, to explain a difficulty; **Zweifel —en**, to clear away doubts; **den Knoten eines Schauspiels —en**, to unravel the plot of a play; **diese Arznei —t den Schleim von der Brust**, this medicine loosens the phlegm; **einen Kontrakt —en**, to annul a contract; **Wasser —en**, to carry off water by a sewer; **eine Kanone —en**, to fire off a gun. —**end**, *p. & adj.* solvent (*C. L.*); expectorant; solvent (*Chem.*). —**ung**, *f.* loosening; firing (*of guns*); solution, explanation; denouement; unravelling (*of a plot*); setting free; redemption (*of a pledge*); remission, absolution; solution (*Math., Med., Chem.*); resolution (*of an equation*); money receipts. *Comp.* —**e=geld**, *n.* ransom. —**e=mittel**, —**ungs=mittel**, *n.* expectorant; solvent; means of redemption. —**e=schlüssel**, *m.* power of forgiving sins, St. Peter's key. —**ungs=buch**, *n.* cash-book for daily sales.

Lot, *n.* (—(e)s, *pl.* —e) lead; solder; perpendicular; plummet, sounding-lead; half an ounce; **Kraut und —**, powder and shot. —**en**, *v.a. & n.* (*aux.* **h.**) to sound, take soundings; to plumb; to try (*Carp.*); **das Erz —et**, the ore yields but a few ounces per cwt. *Comp.* —**leine**, *f.* plumb-line. —**recht**, *adj.* perpendicular. —**wage**, *f.* half-ounce scale.

Lö't—e, *f.* soldering; solder. —**en**, *v.a.* to solder. —**er**, *m.* (—**ers**, *pl.* —**er**) solderer. —**ig**, *adj.* weighing half an ounce, of due alloy; pure; **das feinste Silber ist 16—ig**, the finest silver is of 12 dwts.; —**iges Erz**, ore of which the cwt. contains but ½ oz. of silver. —**igkeit**, *f.* fineness. *Comp.* —**asche**, *f.* soda; ashes used in manufacturing glass. —**eisen**, *n.* soldering-iron. —**form**, *f.* mould of about 1000 leaves (*Goldb.*). —**kolben**, —**hammer**, *m. see* —**eisen**. —**korn**, —**kupfer**, *n.* link for soldering. —**rohr**, *n.* blow-pipe. —**salz**, *n.* soda, potash. —**schlosser**, *m.* padlock-maker. —**zinn**, *n.* pewter for soldering.

Lo'tos, *m.* (—, *pl.* —) lotus.

Lot'se, *m.* (—n, *pl.* —n), (**Lots'mann**, *m.*) pilot. —**n**, *v.a.* to pilot; to get a p. to a place (*coll.*). *Comp.* —**n=barke**, *f.* pilot-boat. —**n=geld**, *n.*, —**n=gebühr**, *f.* pilotage, pilot's fee. —**n=wasser**, *n.* tract of water through which a vessel must be piloted.

Lot'ter, I. *adj.* loose, slack (*prov.*); slovenly; vagrant; licentious. II. *m.* (—s, *pl.* —) *see* —**bube**. —**ei'**, *f.* laziness; vagabondage; negligence; disorderly life. —**ig**, *adj.* loose; slovenly, sluttish. —**n**, *v.n.* to lead a lazy life, to loaf about. *Comp.* —**bett**, *n.* couch for lolling on (*dial.*). —**bube**, *m.* vagabond, rascal; idle, lazy fellow.

Lotterie', *f.* (*pl.* —**en**) lottery; **in die — setzen**, to take a lottery-ticket. *Comp.* —**einnehmer**, —**kollekteur**, *m.* lottery-office keeper. —**gewinn(st)**, *m.* winning number; prize in a lottery. —**los**, *n.* lottery-ticket. —**plan**, *m.* scheme for a lottery. —**spieler**, *m.* person who puts into a lottery. —**zettel**, *m.* lottery-ticket.

Lot'to, *n.* (—s), (—**spiel**, *n.*) loto.

Lö'w—e, *m.* (—en, *pl.* —en) lion; Leo (*Astr.*); **der —e brüllt**, the lion roars; **Silber —e**, puma. —**enhaft**, *adj.* lion-like, leonine. —**in**, *f.* lioness; avalanche (*dial.*). *Comp.* —**en=äffchen**, *n.* little lion-monkey; silky tamarin. —**en=anteil**, *m.* lion's share. —**en=art**, *f.* lion-nature; lion species. —**en=artig**, *adj.* lion-like. —**en=bändiger**, *m.* lion-tamer. —**en=garten**, *m.* a park in which lions (and other wild animals) are kept. —**en=gebrüll**, —**en=geschrei**, *n.* roaring, roar of a lion. —**en=grimm**, *m.* fury of a lion. —**en=grube**, —**en=höhle**, *f.* lions' den. —**en=herz**, *n.* lion's heart; Cœur-de-lion; Regulus (*Astr.*). —**en=herzig**, *adj.* lion-hearted, brave. —**en=jagd**, *f.* lion-hunt(ing). —**en=maul**, *n.* lion's mouth; snap-dragon (*Bot.*). —**en=stark**, *adj.* strong as a lion. —**en=stärke**, *f.* gravy fresh from the meat (*coll.*). —**en=zahn**, *m.* lion's tooth; dandelion (*Bot.*).

Loyalitä't, *f.* loyalty.

Luchs, *m.* (—(s)es, *pl.* —(s)e) lynx; sly, cunning person. —(**s**)**en**, *v.a. & n.* (*aux.* **h.**) to be wide awake to, look sharply after (*one's own interests*); **etwas —(s)en, einem etwas ab —(s)en**, to steal, pilfer, to swindle a p. out of a th. (*coll.*). *Comp.* —**äugig**, *adj.* lynx-eyed. —**fell**, *n.* lynx-fur *or* skin. —**katze**, *f.* bay lynx, wild-cat; caracal.

Lü'cke, *f.* (*pl.* —n) gap, chasm; break; breach; hole (*in teeth*); blank; deficiency; deficit; hiatus; omission. —**n=haft**, *adj.* having gaps; defective, incomplete. —**n=haftigkeit**, *f.* incompleteness, want of connection. *Comp.* —**n=büßer**, *m.* stop-gap, locum-tenens; make-shift; expletive. —**n=büßerei**, *f.* filling-up (*of a gap or void*), make-shift. —**n=los**, *adj.* uninterrupted, successive.

Lud, Lü'de, *1 (& 3) p. sing. imperf. indic. and subj. of* **laden**.

Lu'del, *f.* (*pl.* —n) feeding-bottle; (*nickname for*) tobacco-pipe; priming-powder (*Firew.*). *Comp.* —**birne**, *f.* powder-horn (*Artil.*). —**faden**, *m.* quick *or* priming-match.

Lu'der, *n.* (—s, *pl.* —) bait, lure, decoy; carrion; (*horse-*)flesh; anything rousing disgust *or* indignation; low scoundrel (*vulg.*); hussy, low jade (*vulg.*); debauchery; **ein geriebenes kleines —**, a very sly rogue (*vulg.*); **das ist unter allem —**, that is unspeakably abominable (*vulg.*); — **ansetzen**, to put on flesh (*vulg.*). —**n**, *v.* I. *a.* to lure, bait, decoy. II. *n.* (*aux* **h.**) to lead a dissolute life. *Comp.* —**kerl**, *m.* low blackguard. —**krähe**, *f.* carrion-crow. —**leben**, *n.* lewd debauched life. —**mäßig**, *adj.* execrable; lewd.

Lü'derlich, **2c.**, *see* **Liederlich**, **2c.**

Luft, *f.* (*pl.* **Lüf'te**) air; atmosphere, breeze, zephyr, light wind; breath; relief, vent; gas; **umgebende —**, ambient (air); **in die — sprengen**, to blow up; **in die — sprechen**, to talk to no purpose; **in freier —**, in the open air; (**frische**) — **schöpfen**, to draw breath, to go into the air; **an die — gehen**, to go out, take an airing; — **machen**, to give air (*to*), to loosen, undo, unbutton, to lop *or* prune, to set free, to relieve, to disengage, to ease (*the chest etc.*), to open (*one's heart*), to give vent to (*anger, etc.*), to break through; **er machte seinen Gefühlen —**, he gave vent to his feelings; **sich** (*dat.*) **im Gedränge — machen**, to break through the crowd; **einer Wurzel — machen**, to loosen the earth round roots; — **lassen**, to leave at large, not to restrain; — genug haben (anderwärts *or* in der Welt), to have sufficient elbow-room; to have a good opening in the world, to have the world before one; einem — schaffen, to procure a p. breathing time, to give (*or* gain for) a p. time; die — anhalten, to keep one's mouth shut, to keep quiet *or* silent (*coll.*); in die — springen wollen, to be ready to jump out of one's skin (*for joy, etc.*); in die — fahren, to be blown up; in die — werfen, to throw up; gute — haben, to draw well (*of a chimney, etc.*); aus der — greifen, to fabricate, invent; es liegt in der —, it is in the air; das hängt in der —, that has no foundation; that is still undecided; einen an die — setzen, to turn a p. out of doors; nach — schnappen, to pant for breath; der — aussetzen, to expose to the air; die — erneuern, to air (*a room, etc.*); die — ist rein, the coast is clear; nun ist die — rein; heraus mit der Sprache! speak out now, as no one is listening! —ig, *adj. & adv.* airy, breezy; aerial; transparent; vaporous; lofty; flighty, unsteady; light, thin; gaseous; es sieht bei ihm —ig aus, his affairs are in a bad way (*coll.*). —ikus, *m.* a happy-go-lucky fellow (*sl.*). *Comp.* —artig, *adj.* aeriform; gaseous. —ballon, *m.* balloon. —behälter, *m.* air-reservoir. —beschaffenheit, *f.* state *or* quality of the atmosphere; climate. —beschreibung, *f.* meteorology, aerography. —beständig, *adj.* resisting the action of the atmosphere. —bild, *n.* vision; fancy. —bildung, *f.* aerification. —bläse, *f.* bubble; vesicle (*Bot.*); air-bladder (*Icht.*). —dicht, *adj.* air-tight, air-proof, hermetical. —druck, *m.* atmospheric pressure. —druck=maschine, *f.* pneumatic engine. —elektrizitäts=messer, *m.* electrometer. —erscheinung, *f.* meteor, atmospheric phenomenon. —fahrer, *m.* aeronaut. —fahrt, aeronautic excursion, ascent in a balloon. —fang, *m.* ventilator. —farbe, *f.* azure. —fenster, *n.* window to admit air. —feuchtigkeits=messer, *m.* hydrometer. —förmig, *adj.* aeriform. —gebäude, *n.* castle in the air. —gebilde, *n.*, —gestalt, *f.* aerial form; vision, phantom. —gefäß, *n.* air-vessel (*Bot., Orn., Ent.*); (*pl.*) the lungs. —gefilde, *pl.* aerial fields. —geist, *m.* spirit of the air. —gleichgewichts=lehre, *f.* aerostatics. —güte, *f.* salubrity of the air. —hahn, *m.* cock to admit air. —hauch, *m.* breath of air. —heizung, *f.* heating by hot-air pipes. —kalk, *m.* gypsum. —kanal, *m.* (air) flue, air passage. —kissen, *n.* air-cushion. —klappe, *f.* ventilator, air-valve. —kompressor, *m.* hydraulic compressor. —kreis, *m.* atmosphere. —kunde, *f.* aerology. —leer, *adj.* exhausted (*of air*); —leerer Raum, vacuum. —linie, *f.*; in der —linie, as the crow flies. —loch, *n.* air-hole, vent, breathing-hole; ventilator; register (*of a chimney*); stigma (*Ent.*). —mantel, *m.* casing (*of a chimney*). —messer, *m.* aerometer. —meßkunst, *f.* pneumatics. —perspektive, *f.* aerial perspective. —post, *f.* pneumatic post (*see* Rohrpost). —pumpe, *f.* air-pump, pneumatic pump; forcing-pump (*Artil.*). —pumpen=glas, *n.*, —pumpen=glocke, *f.* receiver of an air-pump. —raum, *m.* air-filled space; atmosphere. —reifen, *m.* pneumatic tire (*cycl.*). —reinigung, *f.* ventilation. —reise, *f.* ascent in a balloon. —röhre, *f.* air-tube; trachea, windpipe (*Anat.*); air-vessel (*Bot.*); zur —röhre gehörig, bronchial. —röhren=äste, *pl.* bronchiæ, bronchial tubes. —röhren=deckel, *m.* epiglottis. —röhren=entzündung, *f.* bronchitis; laryngitis; croup; inflammation of the windpipe. —röhren=kopf, *m.* larynx. —röhren=schnitt, *m.* tracheotomy. —röhren=schwindsucht, *f.* bronchial phthisis. —röhren=spalt, *m.* glottis (*Anat.*). —sauger, *m.* aspirator, exhauster. —säule, *f.* column of air; blast. —säure, *f.* carbonic acid. —schacht, *f.* air-shaft (*in tunnels, etc.*). —scheibe, *f.* ventilator (*in a window*). —scheu, *adj.* afraid of fresh air. —schicht, *f.* stratum of air. —schiff, *n.* balloon. —schiffer, *m.* aeronaut. —schiffer=abteilung, *f.* aeronautic department. —schiff=fahrt, *f.* aerial locomotion, navigation of the air. —schiff(fahrts)=kunde, *or* —kunst, *f.* aeronautics. —schlauch, *m.* air tube, pneumatic tire (*cycl.*). —schloß, *n.* castle in the air. —schöpfen, *n.* respiration, drawing breath. —schwärmer, *m.* serpent (*Firew.*). —schwere, *f.* specific gravity of the air. —segel, *n.* wind-sail (*Naut.*); sail of a windmill. —spiegelung, *f.* mirage. —springer, *m.* vaulter, tumbler. —sprung, *m.* leap, caper, spring. —stäubchen, *n.* atom. —stein, *m.* aerolite. —stoff, *m.* gas. —stöpsel, *m.* valve. —stoß, *m.* blast. —strich, *m.* climate, zone. —strom, *m.* current of air. —teilchen, *n.* particle of air. —ton, *m.* air-tone (*Paint.*). —verdichter, *m.* air-condenser. —verdünnung, *f.* rarefaction of the air. —wage, *f.* air-poise, aerometer. —wägekunst, *f.* aerostatics. —warze, *f.* stigma (*Ent.*). —werk, *n.* air-pump, forcing pump. —zeiger, *m.* air-dried brick. —zieher, *m.* ventilator. —zug, *m.* draught of air; shaft; windage (*Artil.*). —zug=erzeuger, *m.* fan; ventilator.

Lüft'chen, *n.* (—s, *pl.* —) breath of wind, gentle breeze.

Lüf't—en, *v.a.* to lift up, raise; to air (*a room*); to ventilate; to expose to the air; to relieve (*one's heart, etc.*); to bare (*roots*); to lop, prune (*trees*); sich —en, to take the air; to loosen (*one's dress*); den Hut —en, to raise one's hat. —ung, *f.* airing, ventilation (*of rooms*).

1**Lug**, *m.* lie (*obs.*); *in the phrase* — und Trug, falsehood and deceit.

2**Lug**, *n.* (—es, *pl.* —e) opening; lurking-place; den, cave; watch-tower; — ins Land, look-out; a name given to hills and watch-towers.

Lü'ge, *f.* (*pl.* —n) lie, falsehood, untruth; sham; kleine —, white lie; einen —n strafen, einen der — bezichtigen, to accuse s. o. of telling a lie, to give the lie to a p.

Lu'gen, *v.n.* (*aux.* h.) to look or peep out; to gaze; to watch; to spy.

Lü'g—en, I. *ir.v.a. & n.* (*aux.* h.) to lie, tell a lie (*to*); to fib; to invent; to romance; to deceive, be false; to sham; in seinen Beutel —en, to lie to one's own advantage; daß ich nicht —e, to tell the truth, really; einem die Haut, die Jacke *or* die Ohren voll —en, to cram a p. with lies; wer —t, der stiehlt auch, lying and thieving go together; er —t wie gedruckt, he lies like a jockey; wer einmal —t, dem glaubt man nicht, a liar is not believed even when he speaks the truth (*prov.*). II. *subst. n.* lying, *etc.* —enhaft(ig), *adj. & adv.* lying, false; untrue; deceitful. —enhaftigkeit, *f.* lying disposition, mendacity; falseness. —ner, *m.* (—ners, *pl.* —ner), —nerin, *f.* liar; hypocrite; er wurde zum —ner an mir, he deceived me, did not keep his word to me; einen zum —ner machen, to call s. o. a liar, to make a p. a liar. —nerisch, *see* —enhaft. *Comp.* —en=fürst, —en=vater, *m.* Satan. —en=geist, *m.* Satan; consummate liar. —en=lehre, *f.* false doctrine; sophism. —en=prophet, *m.* false prophet —en=zunge, *f.* lying tongue; liar.

Lu'ke, *f.* (*pl.* —n) dormer-window; hatch, hatchway (*Naut.*); *see* Loch, Lücke. *Comp.* —n=deckel, *m.*, —n=klappe, *f.* door *or* lid of a hatchway.

Lul'l—en, *v.a. & n.* (*aux.* h.) to sing, lull (*to*

sleep); to lull. —**er**, *m.* (—**ers**, *pl.* —**er**) luller; baby's bottle; doze. *Comp.* —**gesang**, *m.* lullaby.

Lüm'mel, *m.* (—**s**, *pl.* —) lout, ruffian. —**ei'**, *f.* ruffianism, clownishness. —**haft**, *adj.* ruffian-like, ungentlemanly; awkward, boorish.

Lump, *m.* (—**s**, —**en**, *pl.* —**e**) rag (*obs.*), ragged fellow, ragamuffin; scamp, scoundrel; low fellow; miserly person, skinflint; lump-fish, sea-owl (*Icht.*). —**en**, *m.* (—**ens**, *pl.* —**en**) rag, tatter; clout; trumpery thing; ragged dress; lump-sugar; species of blenny. II. *v.a.* to treat like a ragamuffin; **sich —en lassen**, to require much entreaty; **ich will mich nicht —en lassen**, I don't intend to act shabbily; I will do the thing properly and well. —**erei'**, *f.* (*pl.* —**ereien**) rascality; paltry thing; shabbiness, meanness; trash, rubbish. —**icht**, (*obs.*) —**ig**, *adj.* ragged, tattered; shabby; mean, stingy; **die —igen paar Mark**, those few miserable shillings (*coll.*). —**igkeit**, *f.* raggedness; shabbiness. *Comp.* —**en=baron**, *m.* trumpery baron. —**en=brei**, *m.* first stuff (*Paperm.*). —**en=ding**, *n.*, —**en=sache**, *f.* trifle; trashy thing. —**en=geld**, *n.* paltry sum, trifling expense; **um ein —engeld**, dirt-cheap. —**en=hülle**, *f.* covering of rags. —**en=gesindel**, —**en=pack**, —**en=volk**, *n.* riff-raff, rabble. —**en=handel**, *m.* rag-trade; pitiful trade. —**en=händler**, *m.* dealer in rags. —**en=hund**, —**en=kerl**, *m.* scamp; mean, contemptible fellow. —**en=kammer**, *f.* sorting-room (*Paperm.*). —**en=kram**, *m.* rag-trade; trumpery trade; trash. —**en=papier**, *n.* rag paper. —**en=sold**, *m.* paltry pay. —**en=streit**, *m.* trifling dispute; quarrel between ragamuffins. —**en=trog**, *m.*, —**en=stampfe**, *f.* stamping trough (*Paperm.*). —**en=zeug**, *n.* trash, stuff.

Lumpacivagabun'dus, *m.* name given to a scamp, vagabond.

Luna'risch, *adj.* lunar; **sub—**, terrestrial, sublunary; **sub—e Existenz**, life on earth.

Lunet'te, *f.* lunette (*Fort.*); collar-plate (*Mach.*)

Lun'ge, *f.* (*pl.* —**n**) lung(s); lights; **aus voller — schreien**, to cry as loud as one can. *Comp.* —**n=blase**, *f.*, —**n=bläschen**, *n.* vesicle of the lungs. —**n=drüse**, *f.* bronchial gland. —**n=entzündung**, *f.* inflammation of the lungs. —**n=faul**, *adj.* consumptive; broken-winded. —**n=fäule**, *f.* consumption, phthisis; dry-rot. —**n=fieber**, *n.* pulmonary fever. —**n=flügel**, *m.*, —**n=blatt**, *n.*, —**n=lappen**, *m.* lobe of the lungs. —**n=hieb**, *m.* cut at the lungs; taunt, rub; **das war ein —nhieb**, that was a home-thrust. —**n=kammer**, *f.* pulmonary ventricle. —**n=krankheit**, *f.* pulmonary disease. —**n=mittel**, *n.* a pulmonic. —**n=probe**, *f* experiment with *or* test of the lungs. —**n=schlag**, *m.* apoplexy of the lungs. —**n=schützer**, *m.* respirator. —**n=seuche**, *see* —**n=fäule**. —**n=sucht**, —**n=schwindsucht**, *f.* phthisis. —**n=süchtig**, *adj.* phthisical. —**n=tuberkulose**, *f. see* —**n=schwindsucht**.

Lun'ger—er, *m.* (—**ers**, *pl.* —**er**) loafer, idler. —**ig**, *adj.* idle. —**n**, *v.n.* (*aux.* **h.** & **s.**) to idle, loll about.

Lün'se, *f.* (*pl.* —**n**) linch-pin, axle-pin.

Lun'te, *f.* (*pl.* —**n**) match, slow-match (*Artil.*); fox's brush; — **riechen**, to smell a rat (*coll.*). *Comp.* —**n=gewehr**, *n.* musket. —**n=kiste**, *f.* match-box.

Lu'pe, *f.* (*pl.* —**n**) magnifying glass; **unter die — nehmen**, to examine minutely.

Lüp'fen, **Lup'fen**, *v.a.* to lift (*dial.*).

Lupi'ne, *f.* (*pl.* —**n**) lupine (*Bot.*).

Lup'pe, *f.* (*pl.* —**n**) loop, ball, bloom (*Ironw.*). *Comp.* —**n=feuer**, *n.* smelting furnace.

Lust, *f.* (*pl.* **Lüs'te**) pleasure, joy, delight; fancy, inclination, desire, wish, longing; lust, carnal pleasure; mirth, fun; **nach aller —**, **nach Herzens —**, to one's heart's content; — **haben (zu)**, to be inclined, to wish, to like, to be in a mood, to have a mind (*for a th. or to do a th.*); **seine — an einer S. haben**, to take pleasure in a th.; **einem — zu etwas machen**, to excite a p.'s desire for something, to give s.o. a taste for a thing; **jeder, der — hat**, any one who likes; **einem die — benehmen**, to put a p. out of conceit (*with a th.*), **die — dazu ist ihm vergangen**, his wish for it is gone; **er zeigte wenig —**, he evinced little disposition to; **ich hatte nicht übel —** *or* **große — ihn durchzubleuen**, I had a great mind to give him a thrashing; **die — kommt** *or* **wandelt mich an, ich bekomme —**, I have taken a fancy (*to*), I am in the mood (*for*), I feel inclined (*to*); **ich habe heute rechte — zu lernen**, I am in a studious mood to-day; **seine — büßen**, to gratify one's desire; **sie ist meine ganze —**, all my delight is bound up in her; **er arbeitet, daß es eine — ist**, it is a pleasure to see how he works; **es ist eine wahre —**, it is a real treat. —**bar**, *adj.* agreeable, amusing. —**barkeit**, *f.* amusement, diversion, pleasure; sport; (*pl.*) revels. —**ig**, *adj. & adv.* merry, gay; sportive; jolly, jovial; amusing, droll, comical; **ein —iger Bruder**, a jolly fellow; **die —ige Person**, clown, fool; merry Andrew; **eine —ige Geschichte**, a funny story, a lark, piece of fun; **sich —ig machen**, to make merry; **sich über einen —ig machen**, to make fun of (a p.), to laugh at a p.; —**iger Baum**, tree pleasant to the eyes (*B.*); **da geht es —ig her!** fine doings there! —**ig an die Arbeit!** on with the work! get on! —**ig! immer —ig!** come on! courage! work away! merry's the word! —**igkeit**, *f.* gaiety; mirth, jollity; drollness. *Comp.* —**dirne**, *f.* prostitute. —**fahrt**, *f.* pleasure-excursion. —**feuer**, *n.* bonfire. —**garten**, *m.* pleasure-grounds *or* garden. —**gehölz**, *n.* shrubbery; grove. —**gefühl**, *n.* pleasurable sensation. —**gewächs**, *n.* ornamental plant. —**häuschen**, *n.* summer-house; shooting-box. —**ig=macher**, *m.* buffoon, wag, clown, jester, merry Andrew. —**ort**, *m.* place of amusement; pleasure grounds. —**partie**, *f.* pleasure-party. —**sam**, *adj.* (*obs. poet.*) pleasurable; **ein Schloß —sam = ein Lustschloß**. —**schiff**, *n.* yacht, pleasure-boat. —**schloß**, *n.*, —**sitz**, *m.* country-seat, villa. —**seuche**, *f.* syphilis. —**spiel**, *n.* comedy. —**spiel=dichter**, *m.* writer of comedies. —**störer**, —**verderber**, *m.* kill-joy. —**wäldchen**, *n.* shrubbery; grove. —**wandeln**, *v.n.* (*aux.* **h.** & **s.**) *insep.* to promenade, to walk for one's pleasure.

Lüstelei', *f.* fondness for dainties.

Lüs't—eln, *v.n.* (*aux.* **h.**) (**nach**) to long for, desire. —**en**, *v.* I. *a. imp.*; **es —et mich (nach einer S.**, for a th.), I desire, long for; **es —et mich sehr danach**, I have a great desire for it, I long to do it. II. *n.* (*aux.* **h.**) to wish, long (**nach**, for). —**ern**, I. *adj.* (**nach einer S.** *or* **auf eine S.**) greedy (for); desirous, covetous (of); lascivious; —**erne Erzählungen**, lascivious, indecent stories; **mit —ernen Augen**, with longing eyes. II. *v.n. & a.imp.* to lust, hanker after; **das Schiff —ert gut aufs Ruder**, the vessel answers readily to her helm. —**ernheit**, *f.* concupiscence. —**ling**, *m.* (—**lings**, *pl.* —**linge**) voluptuary, sensualist, debauchee.

Lüs't—er, *m.* (—**ers**) lustre. —**rin**, *m.* (—**rins**, *pl.* —**rine**) lustring. *Comp.* —**er=joppe**, *f.* light short coat of lustre.

Lutie'ren, *v.a.* to lute.

Lut'sch—en, *v.n.* (*aux.* **h.**) to suck (*coll.*). —**er**, *m.* (—**ers**, *pl.* —**er**), (—**beutel**, *m.*) baby's sucking bag, titty-bag (*coll.*).

Lütt, Lüttj, *adj.* small, little (*dial.*).
Lut'ter, *m.* (—s) brandy of the first distillation. **—n,** *v.n.* (*aux.* h.) to distil weak brandy.
Luv, *f.* loof, luff, weatherside (*Naut.*); **die — abstechen, gewinnen,** to gain the weather side. **—en,** *v.n.* (*aux.* h.) to ply to windward. *Comp.* **—baum,** *m.* outrigger. **—brassen,** *pl.* weather-braces (*Naut.*). **—gierig,** *adj.* weatherly; **—gierig sein,** to gripe (*Naut.*). **—halter,** *m.* ship plying to windward. **—seite,** *f.* weather-side (*Naut.*). **—ständer,** *m.* wind-pipe (*Hydr.*). **—wall,** *m.* weather-shore. **—wand,** *f.* weather-shrouds. **—wärts,** *adv.* windward, weatherly; **Helm —wärts!** bear away!
Luxuriö's, *adj.* luxurious.
Lu'xus, *m.* (—, *no pl.*) luxury, sumptuousness, extravagance. *Comp.* **—ausgabe,** *f.* expensively got up edition, édition de luxe. **—artikel,** *m.* article of luxury; (*pl.*) luxuries, fancy articles. **—(ein)band,** *m.* superior or fancy binding. **—verbot,** *n.* sumptuary law. **—zug** (*abbrev.* **L. Zug**), *m.* saloon-train.
Lyce—i'st, *m.* (**—is'ten,** *pl.* **—is'ten**) student at a lyceum. **—um** (*pron.* **Lyce'um**), *n.* (**—ums,** *pl.* **Lyce'en**) grammar-school, college.
Lympha'tisch, *adj.* lymphatic.
Lym'phe, *f.* (*pl.* **—n**) lymph. *Comp.* **—drüse,** *f.* lymphatic gland.
Lyn'chen, *v.a.* to lynch.
Ly'r—a, *f.* (*pl.* **—en**) lyre, harp; Lyra (*Ast.*). **—ik,** *f.* lyric poetry. **—iker,** *m.* (**—ikers,** *pl.* **—iker**) lyric poet. **—isch,** *adj.* lyric(al). *Comp.* **—a=spieler,** *m.* lyrist.
Lyso'l, *n.* (—s) lysol(e) (*Chem.*).

M

M, m, *n.* M, m; *in abbr.* **M.** = **1. Mark,** mark; **2. Monat,** month (*C.L.*); **3. Meile,** mile; **4. Modell,** model, pattern; **5. Mittelsorte,** medium kind; *for other abbreviations see the Index at the end of the German-English part.*
Maal, *see* **Mahl, Mal.**
¹**Maar,** *f.* (*pl.* **—en**) lake-crater (*in the Eifel*).
²**Maar,** *m. see* **Mahr.**
Maaß, *see* **Maß.**
Maat, *m.* (**—s,** *pl.* **—e**) mate (*Naut.*); comrade, pal (*dial.*). **—schaft,** *f.* the mates; ship's crew.
Maat'jes=hering, *m.* (**—s,** *pl.* **—e**) mat(t)ie, matty, white herring.
Maccaro'nisch, *adj.* macaronic; **—es Gedicht,** macaronic poem (*consisting of verses written in a mixture of two or more languages, usually the vernacular and Latin*).
Mäce'n, *m.* (**—s,** *pl.* **—e**) Mæcenas, patron (*of fine art and letters*). **—a't,** *n.* (**—ats**), **—a'tentum,** *n.* (**—atentums**) patronage of art and letters. **—isch,** *adj.*; **kein —isch Alter blühte der deutschen Kunst,** no age of patrons fostered German art.
Machan'delbaum, *m.* juniper (*dial.*), *see* **Wachholder.**
Mach'—bar, *adj.* feasible, practicable. **—e,** *f.* making; production; **noch in der —e,** still in hand; **in die —e nehmen,** to take in hand, set about, **in der —e sein,** to be in hand; **in der —e haben,** to have in hand; **einen in der —e haben,** to treat a p. roughly, thrash s.o. (*vulg.*); **er versteht sich auf die —e,** he knows how to puff his goods, how to beat the big drum (*coll.*).
Ma'ch—en, *v.a.* to make; to do, to manufacture, fabricate, to create; to cause; to effect, produce; to give as product; to constitute, amount to; to prepare; to represent (*as*); to play, act; to signify; to pocket (*a billiard-ball*); to bring to, reduce; to arrange, get ready, dress; to write (*a composition*); to gain (*an experience, etc.*); to commit (*faults, etc.*); to secure (*the trick, etc.*); to walk out; to travel, perform (*a journey*); **große Augen —en,** to stare; **ärger —en,** to make worse, to exaggerate; **Ernst —en (mit einer S.),** to set about (a th.) seriously; **Epoche —en,** to make a sensation; **Epoche —end,** epoch-making; sensational; **fertig —en,** to finish; **Feuer, ein Licht —en,** to light a fire, a candle; **—en Sie ein anständiges Gebot,** make a fair offer, name a reasonable sum; **ein Haus —en,** to keep up a house, keep open house, **den großen Herrn —en,** to play the fine gentleman; **Holz —en,** to cleave *or* chop wood (*for fuel*); **kehrt —en,** to turn; **ein Komma —en,** to put a comma; **einem den Kopf warm —en,** to cause a p. anxiety, give s.o. trouble; **etwas —en lassen,** to cause a thing to be done, have it made, to order a th., to bespeak a th., bespeak; **was —t die Rechnung,** how much does the account come to? **drei mal drei —t neun,** three times three are nine; **Spaß —en,** to joke, jest; **gemeinschaftliche Sache —en,** to make common cause, to act in concert; **einem Schmerz —en,** to give some one pain, grieve one; **er —te den Tell,** he played the part of Tell; **einen weiten Weg —en,** to come a long way, take a long walk; **ohne viel Wesens zu —en,** without much ado, without great ceremony; **so —t es jeder,** every one does the same; **—e es mir nicht noch einmal so,** don't let me catch you doing it a second time; **was —en Sie?** how are you? what are you doing? **was —t das?** what does that matter? **das —t nichts,** that is of no consequence· **er macht es zu bunt,** he goes too far; **er —t es mir zu lange,** he bores me; **das —t, daß,** *or* **weil, ꝛc.,** that comes from, that is because, *etc.*; **das —t sein veränderter Bart,** that is owing to the change in his beard; **das —t mir nichts,** that is nothing to me; **—e, daß du fortkommst,** make haste to get away; **—(e) doch, —(e) fort, —(e) zu,** go on! do make haste! **so —e doch!** do be quick, pray make haste! **—e, sonst gehe ich,** be quick or I shall go; **sagen Sie mir, was er —t,** tell me about him, what is he doing, *etc.*; **sich** (*dat.*) **einen Begriff —en,** to form an idea; **sich** (*dat.*) **allerlei Gedanken —en,** to take all kinds of (*queer*) ideas into one's head; **lassen Sie mich nur —en,** just let me have my own way; **sich** (*dat.*) **die Haare —en lassen,** to have one's hair dressed; **sich** (*dat.*) **viel Bewegung —en,** to take plenty of exercise; **sich** (*dat.*) **ein Vermögen —en,** to acquire a fortune, to make a *or* one's fortune; **einem Beine —en,** to cause a p. to get away quickly, drive s. o. off; **sich beliebt —en (bei einem),** to make oneself beloved, ingratiate oneself with a p.; **es —t sich nicht, läßt sich nicht gut —en,** it is not practicable, it cannot be (done); **es —t nicht viel aus,** it does not make much difference; **das —t sich gut,** that looks well; **sie —t sich gut in diesem Kleide,** she looks well in this dress; **es —t sich schlecht, wenn Sie,** it does not look well for you to; **es —te sich, daß,** it happened *or* it so happened that; **wenn es sich nicht —t,** if there is no opportunity; **die Sache hat sich schon gemacht,** the affair is already settled; **der Knabe —t sich jetzt,** the boy is now getting on *or* doing well; **es wird sich —en,** it is likely to be done, it is likely to happen; **wird ge—t, —en wir,** I (*or* we) shall do it (*coll.*); **wie geht's? Es —t sich (ja);** how are you? Oh, pretty well, not bad, so, so; **er —te sich krank,** he pretended to be ill; **sich naß —en,** to get wet; **er** *or* **sein Befinden —t sich wieder,** he is getting better; **sich** (*dat.*) **viel zu schaffen —en,** to give oneself great trouble; **sich an einen —en,** to approach, accost a p.; to attack a p.; **sich an** *or* **über eine S. —en, sich**

darüber her —en, to set about, begin, take in hand; **sich auf die Seite —en,** to abscond; **sich auf den Weg —en.** to set out, depart; **wir wollen uns auf die Beine —en,** now let us start; **sich** (*dat.*) **viel (wenig) aus etwas —en,** to care for, to make much of (not to care, to care little, to make little of); **ich —e mir ein Vergnügen daraus,** it is a pleasure to me; **daraus ist nichts zu —en,** nothing can be done in the matter; **ich —e mir nichts daraus,** I don't care, don't mind it; **dabei ist nichts zu —en,** there is nothing to be done for it, **was ist damit (dabei) zu —en,** what is to be done with *or* about it? what can I do? **ich —e alles mit,** I will join in anything; **sich davon, fort, aus dem Staube —en,** to make o. s. scarce, to run away; **einen zum König, zum Doktor, 2c., —en,** to make a p. a king, a doctor, *etc.;* **sich** (*dat.*) **etwas zum Gesetze —en,** to make it a rule *or* law for oneself; **etwas zu Gelde —en,** to turn something into money, to sell; **gemachte Blumen,** artificial flowers. **—er,** *m.* (**—ers,** *pl.* **—er**), **—erin,** *f.* maker. **—erei',** *f.* making, make; workmanship; bungling work; **Gleich—erei,** levelling (system). *Comp.* **—e(r)=lohn,** *m.* (*& n.*) cost of making. **—werk,** *n.; elendes* **—werk,** wretched, bungling piece of work.

Macht, *f.* (*pl.* **Mä'chte**) might, strength, force; power, potency; forces, army; power, powerful state; authority; **aus, mit aller —,** with all one's might, with might and main; **über —,** beyond measure; **er schlug mit aller —,** he struck with all his strength *or* as hard as he could; **aus eigner —,** on one's own responsibility, by one's own authority; **es steht nicht in meiner —,** it is not in my power; **sich in der — haben,** to be master of oneself; **zu etwas (Fug und) — haben,** to be able to do a th.; **eine — auf die Beine bringen,** to levy forces; to raise an army; **die vollziehende —,** the executive power; **gesetzgebende —,** legislative power; **einem — zu etwas geben,** to authorize *or* to empower a p. to do a th., **nach —,** according to one's ability; **der Herr ist meine —,** the Lord is my strength (*B.*); **die Mächte,** the powers; **die europäischen Großmächte,** the great European powers. *Comp.* **—befugnis,** *f.* competency. **—bereich,** *m.* sphere of power *or* influence. **—blick,** *m.* commanding aspect. **—fülle,** *f.* fulness *or* plenitude of power, authority. **—gebot,** *n.* authoritative order, strict order. **—haber,** *m.* lord, ruler. **—haberisch,** *adj.* dictatorial, despotic. **—herr, —herrscher,** *m.* despot. **—los,** *adj.* powerless; weak. **—losigkeit,** *f.* impotence; powerlessness, weakness. **—ruf,** *m.* powerful *or* impressive summons. **—spruch,** *m.* authoritative sentence, decision *or* decree; positive determination; **einen —spruch thun,** to give a peremptory decision *or* order. **—stellung,** *f.* powerful *or* strong position, political power, authority. **—voll,** *adj.* mighty. **—vollkommenheit,** *f.* plenitude of power, authority, absolute power; **aus eigner —vollkommenheit,** on one's own authority. **—wort,** emphatic word; **ein —wort sprechen,** to interpose *or* assert one's authority. **—zeichen,** *n.* emblem of power.

Mäch'tig, I. *adj. & adv.* mighty, powerful; vast, huge; immense; intense; **einer Sache — sein,** to be master of, have the mastery of, to possess; **sie ist des Deutschen vollkommen —,** she is thoroughly conversant with German, she has a thorough mastery of the German language. II. *adv.* much, in a great degree, enormously. **—keit,** *f.* power; powerfulness; substance; richness; depth.

Mack, *n.;* **Hack und —,** rag-rag and bob-tail.

Madam'chen, *n.* (*coll.*) dear madam.

Mäd'chen, *n.* (**—s,** *pl.* **—**) girl; maiden; maid; sweetheart; **gefallenes —,** a fallen, lost, seduced *or* ruined girl; **— für Alles,** maid-of-all-work, general servant; **das — aus der Fremde,** the Fair Stranger (*poem by Schiller*); **das — von Orleans,** the Maid of Orleans (*Joan of Arc*); **mein einzig geliebtes —,** my own dear love. **—haft,** *adj. & adv.* girlish; maidenly. **—haftigkeit,** *f.* girlishness; maidenliness. **—schaft,** *f.* maidenhood; maidens (*coll.*). *Comp.* **—bett,** *n.* servant(-girl)'s bed. **—gymnasium,** *n.* secondary school for girls in which Latin and Greek are taught. **—heim,** *n.*, **—herberge,** *f.* home *or* refuge for young girls; (maid-)servants' home. **—held,** *m.*, **—jäger,** *m.* one who runs after girls; libertine, Don Juan. **—kammer,** *f.* (maid-) servants' bedroom, attic. **—name,** *m.* girl's name; maiden name (*of a married lady*). **—raub,** *m.* rape. **—sommer,** *m.* end of summer, Indian summer. **—schule,** *f.* girls' school, school for girls, young ladies' boarding establishment; **höhere —schule,** high school for girls, (young) ladies' college.

Ma'de—e, *f.* (*pl.* **—en**; *dim.* **Mad'chen,** *n.*) maggot, mite; worm. **—ig,** *adj.* worm-eaten; maggoty. *Comp.* **—en=kraut,** *n.* soap-wort. **—en=sack,** *m.* worm-bag, the human body. **—en=wurm,** *m.* ascaris.

Mä'del, *n.* (**—s,** *pl.* **—,** *less good* **—s**) *see* **Mädchen** (*coll.*).

Madon'nen— (*in comp.*) **—bild,** *n.* image *or* picture of the Virgin Mary.

Mael'strom, Mahl'strom, *m.* (**—s**) vortex, whirlpool.

Mag, Magst, *1* (*& 3*), *2 pers. sing. pres. indic. of* **mögen.**

Magazi'n, *n.* (**—s,** *pl.* **—e**) magazine (*C.L., Mil., Lit.*); warehouse; storehouse; repository; foot-board; boot (*of a coach*). **—ie'ren,** *v.a.* to warehouse. *Comp.* **—aufseher, —verwalter,** *m.* manager of goods-department (*Railw.*); warehouse-keeper. **—gewehr,** *n.* magazine-rifle. **—schiff,** *n.* store-ship.

Magd, *f.* (*pl.* **Mäg'de**) maid, virgin; maidservant; kitchen-maid; general servant; **siehe, ich bin des Herren —,** behold the handmaid of the Lord (*B.*). **—tum,** *n.* (**—tums**) maidenhood; virginity (*obs.*).

Mäg'd—chaft, *adj. & adv.* servant-like; maidlike. **—lein,** *n.* (**—leins,** *pl.* **—lein**) maiden. *Comp.* **—e=herberge,** *f.* (maid-)servants' home. **—e=stube,** *f.* servant(-maid)'s room; (maid-)servants' hall.

Ma'g(e), *m.* (**—n,** *pl.* **—n**) relation (*obs.*).

Ma'gen, *m.* (**—s,** *pl.* **—** *& less good:* **Mä'gen**) stomach; maw, craw, gizzard; **sich** (*dat.*) **den — verderben,** to get *or* have indigestion; **einen guten — haben,** to have a good digestion; to brook an affront (*coll.*); **etwas** *or* **einen im — haben,** to hate the mention of a p. *or* of a th. (*coll.*); **seine Augen sind größer als sein —,** he wishes for more than he can eat: his bark is worse than his bite. *Comp.* **—arznei,** *f.*, **—mittel,** *n.* stomachic. **—beschwerden,** *pl.* indigestion. **—bitter,** *m.* stomachic bitter(s), bitter cordial (for the stomach). **—brennen,** *n.* heart-burn. **—drücken,** *n.* pressure on the stomach. **—erkältung,** *f.* chill on the stomach. **—fieber,** *n.* gastric fever. **—haut,** *f.* lining membrane of the stomach. **—katarrh,** *m.* catarrh of the stomach, gastric catarrh. **—krampf,** *m.* spasm in the stomach. **—krebs,** *m.* cancer in the stomach. **—leiden,** *n.* gastric complaint. **—mund,** *m.* upper orifice of the stomach. **—pflaster,** *n.* plaster for the stomach; satisfying dish, substantial meal. **—saft,** *m.* gastric juice. **—säure,** *f.* acidity (*of the* stomach). —schmerz, m. (us. pl.) pains in the stomach, stomach-ache. —schwäche, f. dyspepsia. —spritze, f. stomach-pump. —stärkung, f. stomachic, tonic. —tropfen, pl. cordial, drops.

Ma'ger, *adj. & adv.* meagre, lean; thin, spare; poor; pitiful; sterile; das —e, the lean (*of meat*). —keit, f. leanness; poorness, *etc.* —n, *v.n.* (*aux.* h. & s.) to grow thin *or* lean (*rare*).

Magi'e, *f.* magic.

Ma'gi—er, *m.* (—ers, *pl.* —er) magician; (*pl.*) magi. —ca, *f.*; Laterna —ca, magic lantern. —ker, *m.* (—kers, *pl.* —ker) magician. —sch, *adj.* magic(al).

Magis't—er, *m.* (—ers, *pl.* —er) schoolmaster; —er der freien Künste, master of arts (*M.A.*). —er=haft, *adj.* pedantic, didactic. —ra'nd, *m.* (—ran'den, *pl.* —ran'den) one about to become a magister, candidate for the degree of M. A. —ra't, *m.* (—rats, *pl.* —rate) magistrate; municipal council. —ratu'r, *f.* magistracy. *Comp.* —ra'ts=mitglied, *n.* member of a municipal council. —ra'ts=person, *f.* magistrate.

Magna't, *m.* (—en, *pl.* —en) magnate, grandee (*Hungarian noble*). —enschaft, *f.* body of nobles. *Comp.* —en=tafel, *f.* chamber of magnates.

Magne'sia, *f.* magnesia; doppeltkohlensaure —, bicarbonate of magnesia, soluble magnesia.

Magne'sium, *n.* (—(s)) magnesium.

Magne't, *m.* (—s, —en, *pl.* —e) magnet, load-stone. —isch, *adj.* magnetic. —iseu'r, *m.* (—iseurs, *pl.* —iseure) magnetizer, mesmerizer. —isie'ren, I. *v.a.* to magnetize. II. *subst. n.* magnetization. —is'mus, *m.* magnetism; mesmerism; tierischer —ismus, animal magnetism. *Comp.* —eisen, *n.* magnetic iron. —elektrisch, *adj.* magneto-electric. —nadel, *f.* magnetic needle.

Magni'f—ikus, *adj.*; Rektor —ikus, rector (*title of the heads of German universities corresponding to the English* principal *or* (vice-) chancellor). —ize'nz, *f.* (*pl.* —izen'zen) magnificence (*also used as title*). —i'k, *adj. & adv.* magnificent.

Mahago'ni, *n.* (—s) mahogany.

Mäh'—bar, *adj.* mowable. —der, —derin (*dial.*), *see* —er, —erin (*dial.*).

Mä'h—en, *v.a. & n.* (*aux.* h.) to mow, cut, reap; to mow down; das ist ihm eine gemähte Wiese, that is nuts to him (*coll.*). —er, *m.* (—ers, *pl.* —er), —erin, *f.* mower, reaper. —ig, *adj.* mowable, requiring to be mowed. *Comp.* —er=lohn, *m.* mower's, reaper's wages. —(e)=zeit, *f.* mowing time. —maschine, *f.* reaping machine, mower.

Mahd, *f.* (*pl.* —en) mowing; swath; mowing time; mower's day's work.

Mah'di, *m.* (—s, *pl.* —s) Mahdi.

[1]**Mahl**, *n.* (—s, *pl.* —e) assembly (*obs.*). *Comp.* —schatz, *m.* dowry (*poet.*). —statt, —stätte, *f.* place of meeting; court (*obs.*).

[2]**Mahl**, *n.* (—es, *pl.* —e, Mäh'ler) meal, repast; banquet. *Comp.* —zeit, *f.* meal-time, meal; (ich wünsche Ihnen eine gesegnete) —zeit! (may your meal be blessed), I hope you have made a good dinner (*expression used in certain parts of Germany at the conclusion of a meal; unknown in England*); Prost —zeit! don't you wish you may get it! no idea of it! you are much mistaken! you may whistle for it! (*coll.*).

[3]**Mahl**, *n. see* Mal.

Mah'l—en, *reg. & ir.v.a. & n.* (*aux.* h.) to grind; to mill; to pound, bray; zu Pulver —en, to pulverize; wer zuerst kommt, (der) —t zuerst, first come, first served (*prov.*). *Comp.* —gang, *m.* set of mill-stones. —gast, *m.* miller's customer. —geld, *n.* miller's fee. —ge=rinne, *n.* channel conveying the water to the wheels of a mill. —groschen, *m. see* —geld. —korn, *n.* grist. —metze, *f.* multure. —mühle, *f.* grinding-mill. —stein, *m.* millstone. —steuer, *f.*; Schlacht=und=—steuer, tax on meat and bread, cattle and corn. —zahn, *m.* grinder, molar. —zwang, *m.* obligation to have one's corn ground at a certain mill.

Mäh'lich, *obs. adj. & adv. see* Allmählich.

Mahn'bar, *adj.* demandable.

Mäh'n—e, *f.* (*pl.* —en) mane. —ig, *adj.* with a mane, maned. *Comp.* —en=busch, *m.* helmet plume. —en=decke, *f.* mane-sheet.

Mah'n—en, *v.a.* to remind; to admonish, exhort; to warn; to urge on (*to a duty, etc.*); to incite; to remind to pay, to dun; einen wegen einer Schuld —en, to press a p. for payment, to demand payment (*of a debt*) of a p. —er, *m.* (—ers, *pl.* —er) admonisher; dun. —ung, *f.* admonition, exhortation; dunning. *Comp.* —brief, *m.*, —schreiben, *n.* dunning letter monitory epistle. —ruf, *m.* warning cry. —wort, *n.* word of exhortation. —zettel, *m* reminder; demand note.

Mahr, *m.* (—(e)s, *pl.* —e) nightmare (*dial.*).

Mähr'chen, *see* Märchen.

Mäh're, *f.* (*pl.* —n) mare; jade, hack.

Mai, *m.* (—s [*rarely* — *or* (*obs. & poet.*) —en], *pl.* —e) May; des Lebens —, the springtime of life. *Comp.* —blume, *f.* lily of the valley. —bowle, *f.* drink made of different kinds of wine with addition of woodruff, sugar, *etc.* —forelle, *f.* salmon trout. —gesetze, *n.pl.* the May Laws (*in Prussia, 1871, against the Roman Catholic clergy*). —käfer, *m.* cockchafer; soldier of the third Garde-Grenadier regiment (*Berlin; coll.*). —käfern, *v.a.* to be going to make a speech (*sl.*). —regen, *m.* rain in May; —regen bringt Segen, rain in May is lucky (*prov.*). —schein, *m.* new moon in May; saxifrage. —trank, *m.* wine flavoured with woodruff. —vogel, *m.* cuckoo; butterfly (*dial.*).

Maid, *f. see* Magd, Mädchen (*poet. & dial.*).

Mai'e, Mei'e, *m. obs. for* Mai.

Mai'—e, *f.* (*& m.*) (*pl.* —n) green bough, birch branches (*for decoration*); young birch-tree; may-pole; etliche hieben —en von den Bäumen, others cut down branches off the trees (*B.*); wenn alle Hüte sich und Helme schmücken mit grünen Maien, when the caps and helmets are all garlanded with green branches. *Comp.* —baum, *m.* young birch-tree; maypole. —feier, *f.*, —fest, *n.*; Teilnahme am —fest, maying.

Mai'—en, I. *v.n.* to be May; es —t, it is May, May begins. II. *old gen. of* Mai *occurring in compds.* —en=glück, *n.* bliss of May. —en=haft, *adj.* Maylike. —en=licht, *n.* light of a May day (*poet.*).

Mais, *m.* Indian corn, maize.

Maisch, Meisch, *m.* (—es, *pl.* —e), —e, *f.* mash; mashing. —en, *v.a.* to mash. *Comp.* —bottich, *m.*, —kufe, *f.* mash tun, mashing tub, fermenting-vat. —holz, *n.*, —krücke, *f.* scoop.

Maitres'se, *f.* (*pl.* —n) (kept) mistress.

Majestä't, *f.* (*pl.* —en) majesty; Majesty. —isch, *adj.* majestic. *Comp.* —s=beleidigung, *f.* offence against the sovereign, crime of leze-majesty; high treason. —s=brief, *m.* charter. —s=plural, *m.* the "we" of a sovereign. —s=recht, *n.* (*royal, etc.*) prerogative. —s=rechte, *n.* regalia. —s=schänder, —s=verbrecher, *m.* one guilty of high treason. —s=verbrechen, *n.* high treason.

Majo'r, *m.* (—s, *pl.* —e, *obs.* —s) major (*Log., Mil.*); major proposition (*Log.*). —a't, *n.* (—ats, *pl.* —ate) right of primogeniture; inheritance attached to seniority. —e'nn, *adj.* of (full) age. —ennitä't, *f.* majority. —in, *f.* major's wife; der Herr — und die Frau —in, the major and his lady. —itä't, *f.* (*pl.* —itäten) majority. *Comp.* —a'ts=erbe, I.

m. heir in right of primogeniture. II. *n.* inheritance attached to primogeniture. **—a'ts=gut,** *n.* property entailed on the eldest child. **—a'ts=herr,** *m.* he who has the right of primogeniture; eldest of the family. **—domus,** *m.* major-domo. **—s=ecke,** *f.* critical period in an officer's career (*when it is doubtful if a 'Hauptmann' will be promoted 'Major'*); **er ist glücklich um die —s=ecke gekommen,** he has managed to get his majorship (*coll.*). **—s=rang, —s=stelle,** *f.* majorship, rank of a major (*Mil.*).

Majorisie'r—en, *v.n.* to beat by a majority of votes; **bei der Abstimmung wurden wir —t,** when the votes were taken we were outvoted.

Majus'kel, *f.* capital (*letter*); small capital (*Typ.*).

Makadamisie'r—en, *v.a.* to macadamize (*roads, etc.*). **—t,** *p.p. & adj.* macadamized.

Makaro'n—e, *f.* (*pl.* **—en**) chestnut; macaroon. **—i,** *pl.* macaroni.

Ma'kel, *m.* (**—s,** *pl.* **—**) stain, spot; defect, fault. **—ig,** *adj.* spotted, stained. *Comp.* **—los,** *adj.* spotless, immaculate. **—losigkeit,** *f.* spotlessness.

Mäkelei', *f.* (*pl.* **—en**) broking, brokerage; censoriousness, criticism.

Mä'k—elig, *adj.* censorious; fastidious. **—eln,** *v.* I. *n.* (*aux.* **h.**) to act as a broker, to be a broker. II. *a. & n.* (*aux.* **h.**) to carp at; to haggle (*in buying*); **—le nicht!** don't criticize too nicely, don't be too dainty! **mit seinem Gewissen —eln,** to compound with one's conscience. **—eler, Ma'k—ler,**) *m.* (**—(e)lers,** *pl.* **—(e)ler**) broker; officially authorized middle-man: usurer; agent, negotiator; meddler; fault-finder; censorious person; **der ehrliche Makler,** the honest broker. *Comp.* **—ler=geschäft,** *n.* broker's business. **—ler=lohn,** *m.* brokerage.

Makre'le, *f.* (*pl.* **—n**) mackerel.

Makro'ne, *f.* (*pl.* **—n**) macaroon.

Makulatu'r, *f.* (*pl.* **—en**) waste paper; bad book. *Comp.* **—bogen,** *m.* waste sheet (*Typ.*).

[1]**Mal,** *n. see* [2]**Mahl.**

[2]**Mal,** I. *n.* (**—es,** *pl.* **—e** *and* **Mä'ler**) sign, mark, token; stain, spot, mark, mole; boundary-mark; goal; starting-point; point of time, time, bout, turn (*in this latter sense frequently used as suffix in comp.*); **Mutter —,** mole; **das erste —,** the first time; **sie gefällt aufs erste —,** she pleases at first (*sight*); **ein —,** once; **dieses eine —,** this once; **auf ein —, mit einem —,** all at once, suddenly; **ein für alle —,** once for all; **noch ein—,** once more; **noch ein— so groß,** as large again, double; **ein— ist kein—,** once does not count (*prov.*); **für kein—,** not even for once; **zu verschiedenen —en,** at different times; **wie viel —?** how many times? **alle—,** every time, always; **alle— wenn,** whenever; **ein— ums andere,** by turns, alternately; **es ist halb— so breit,** it is half the breadth, half as broad; **zwei— fünf ist zehn,** twice five *or* two fives are ten. II. *adv. & part.* (*shortened from* **einmal** *and always unaccented*) = once, *etc.*; **es war — ein König,** once upon a time there was *or* there was once a king; **es ist — nicht anders in der Welt,** that is the way of the world, you see; **schön? sie ist nicht — hübsch,** handsome? she is not even pretty; **hör' —!** just listen! **sag' — an,** but tell me; **kommen Sie — her!** just come here! (*coll.*); **sieh —** *or* **da seh' — einer!** well, I say! (*coll.*). **—ig,** *adj. & adv.* of so many times (*as* **dreimalig,** happening *or* repeated three times). *Comp.* **—baum,** *m.* boundary-tree. **—graben,** *m.*, **—grube,** *f.* boundary ditch. **—pfahl,** *m.*, **—säule,** *f.* boundary pillar. **—stein,** *m.* boundary stone; monumental stone. **—zeichen,** *n.* mark, sign; memorial; aim, butt.

Ma'l—en, *v.a.* to paint; to portray, delineate; **nach der Natur —en,** to paint from nature; **sich —en lassen,** to sit for one's picture, to have one's portrait taken; **mit trockenen Farben —en,** to draw in crayons; **auf nassen Kalk —en,** to paint in fresco; **mit** *or* **in Wasser —en,** to paint in water-colours; **man muß den Teufel nicht an die Wand —en,** talk of the devil and he'll appear (*prov.*); **er kann sich** (*dat.*) **'was —en lassen,** don't he wish he may get it; **sie ist zum —en,** she is very beautiful; **sich —en,** to be reflected; to represent oneself (*itself*). *Comp.* **—kasten,** *m.* paint-box.

Ma'ler, *m.* (**—s,** *pl.* **—**), **—in,** *f.* painter, artist. **—ei',** *f.* painting; manner of painting; bad painting, daub; picture; **schlechter —,** dauber. **—isch,** *adj. & adv.* picturesque, graphic. **—schaft,** *f.* painters (*coll.*). *Comp.* **—akademie,** *f.* academy of painting. **—atelier,** *n.* painter's *or* artist's studio. **—esel,** *m.* easel. **—firnis,** *m.* varnish for pictures. **—gold,** *n.* painter's gold; ormolu. **—kunst,** *f.* art of painting. **—pinsel,** *m.* paint-brush. **—scheibe,** *f.* palette. **—schule,** *f.* school of painting; school of painters; school for painters, school of art. **—silber,** *n.* silver powder. **—staffelei,** *f.* easel. **—stock,** *m.* maul-stick. **—stuhl,** *m.* sketching-stool. **—tuch,** *n.* (*painter's*) canvas.

[1]**Mall,** *f.* model, mould (*Naut.*). *Comp.* **—brief,** *m.* building contract.

[2]**Mall,** *adj.* silly (*dial.*); **—e Hexe,** silly witch.

Mal'ter, *m. & n.* (**—s,** *pl.* **—**) corn-measure; wood-measure; **englischer —,** quarter. **—n,** *v.a.* to cord (*wood*); to take the multure.

Malte'ser— (*in comp.*) **—hund,** *m.* Maltese lap-dog. **—kreuz,** *n.* Maltese cross. **—orden,** *m.* order of Malta *or* of St. John. **—ritter,** *m.* knight of Malta.

Malvasi'er, *m.* (**—s**) malmsey (*grape or wine*).

Mal've, *f.* (*pl.* **—n**) mallow. *Comp.* **—n=artig** *adj.* malvaceous (*Bot.*).

Malz, *n.* (**—es,** *pl.* **—e**) malt; **an ihm ist Hopfen und — verloren,** he is (quite) hopeless (*prov.*). **—en,** *v.a. & n.* (*aux.* **h.**) to malt. *Comp.* **—bereitung,** *f.* maltage, malting. **—bier,** *n.* ale. **—boden,** *m.* malt-loft. **—bottich,** *m.* steeping-trough. **—darre, —dörre,** *f.* malt-kiln. **—schrot,** *n.* bruised malt, grist. **—tenne,** *f.* malt-floor *or* barn. **—trank,** *m.* malt-liquor.

Mäl'z—en, *see* **Malzen.** **—er,** *m.* (**—ers,** *pl.* **—er**) malster. **—erei',** *f.* malting, malt-house.

Mama', *f.* (**—,** *pl.* **—s**) mamma. *Comp.* **—kind,** *see* **Muttersöhnchen.**

Mamelu'ck, *m.* (**—en,** *pl.* **—en**) soldier of the (old) light Egyptian horse, Mameluke; apostate; hypocrite.

Mam'mon, *m.* (**—s**) pelf, mammon, worldly riches. *Comp.* **—s=diener, —s=knecht,** *m.* mammon-worshipper, worldling.

Mam'mut, *n.* (**—(e)s,** *pl.* **—s & —e**) mammoth. *Comp.* **—geschäft,** *n.* large stores (*hum.*).

Mamse'll, *f.* (*pl.* **—en,** *or* **—s**) miss. damsel; shop-girl; stewardess (*on a farm*).

[1]**Man,** *indef. pron.* (*only used in the nom. sing.; in other cases of the singular an oblique case of* **einer** *is used*) people, one, they, we, you, a person; **— sagt,** it is said, they say; **— lasse mich in Frieden,** let me alone; **— pocht,** somebody is knocking; **heutzutage reist — von London nach Hannover in zwanzig Stunden,** it is now (*only*) a twenty hours' journey from London to Hanover; **— hat mir gesagt,** I was *or* have been told; **— erlaube mir,** I beg leave (*to*); **— muß es thun,** it must be done; **das kann — nicht wissen,** there is no knowing; (*referring to a known subject*) **— willige ein oder nicht,** whether they will or no; (*as stage direction:*) **— sieht N. an einem Tische lesend,** N. is discovered at a table reading; **— schneide A. D. im Punkte B.,** bisect A D in B.

[2]**Man,** *adv.* only, but (*dial.*); **das ist — wenig,** that is but little; **geh — ja nicht hin,** mind you do not go! **es waren — wenige Leute da,** there were only a few people present (*coll.*).

Manch, (**—er, —e, —es**), *indef adj. & pron.* many a, many a one; **das habe ich — liebes Mal gehört,** I have heard that many a time; **das wird —em leid sein,** that will grieve many a one; **ich habe Ihnen gar —es zu erzählen,** I have much to tell you; **—es hält man mit Unrecht für ein Glück,** many things are wrongly counted a happiness. **—e,** *pl see* **Manch,** many; some, several **—es,** *see* **Manch,** many a thing; many things. *Comp* **—einer,** many a man, many a one. **—erlei,** *indec. adj.* of several sorts, various, sundry, divers; **auf —erlei Art,** in various ways; **er sagte mir —erlei,** he told me many things. **—mal,** *adv.* sometimes; often.

Manches'ter, *m.* (**—s,** *pl.* **—**), (**—sammt,** *m.*) velveteen; corduroy. **—tum,** *n.* Manchester school (*of free-traders*) *See Index of names.*

Manchet'te, *see* **Manschette.**

Mandari'nen=thee, *m.* mandarin tea.

Manda't, *n.* (**—(e)s,** *pl.* **—e**) mandate; authorization; brief. **—a'r,** *m.* (**—ars,** *pl.* **—are**) attorney, proxy, mandatory.

[1]**Man'del,** *f.* (*pl* **—n**) almond (*Bot.*); tonsil (*Anat.*); **gebrannte —,** burnt almond. *Comp.* **—bräune,** *f.* tonsilitis. **—brei,** *m.* almond-pap. **—entzündung,** *f.* inflammation of the tonsils, tonsilitis. **—kleie,** *f.* bran of almonds, almond powder. **—krähe,** *f.* roller.

[2]**Man'del,** *f* (*pl.* **—n**) number of fifteen; fifteen sheaves **—n,** *v.* I. *n.* (*aux.* **h.**) to yield many sheaves. II *a.* to put up in heaps *or* shocks of ten to fifteen sheaves; to count by fifteens. *Comp.* **—weise,** *adv.* by fifteens.

Mandoli'ne, Mando're, *f.* (*pl.* **—n**) mandolin.

Mandrago'ra, *f* mandrake (*Bot.*).

Ma'nen, *pl.* manes.

[1]**Mang,** *adv.* among, between (*dial. & coll.*).

[2]**Mang—** (*in comp.*) **—futter, —korn,** *n.* mixed fodder. **—sprache,** *f.* mixture of languages.

Manga'n, *n.* (**—s**) manganese. **—sauer,** *adj.*; **—saure Salze,** manganates. **—säure,** *f.* manganic acid.

Man'g—e, —el, *f.* (*pl* **—en, —eln**) mangle, calender, rolling-press. **—eln, —en,** *v.a.* to mangle, calender.

Man'gel, *m.* (**—s,** *pl.* **Mängel**) want, lack, deficiency; defect, blemish; dearth; distress, penury; **an einer S. — haben** *or* **leiden,** to be in want of a th.; **aus — an,** for want of, in default of; **—s Bericht,** for want of advice (*C.L.*); **—s Annahme,** for non-acceptance; **in —geraten,** to be reduced to want. **—haft,** *adj.* defective (*also Gram.*); imperfect; faulty. **—haftigkeit,** *f.* defectiveness; imperfection; faultiness.

Man'geln, *v.* I. *n.* (*aux.* **h.**) *& imp.* to want, lack, fail; **an mir soll es nicht —,** I shall do my part, shall not fail; **mir wird nichts —,** I shall not want (*B.*); **er läßt es sich** (*dat.*) **an nichts —,** he denies himself nothing; **es mangelt mir an barem Gelde,** I am in want of ready money, I am short of cash.

Manichä'er, *m.* (**—s,** *pl.* **—**) Manichee; usurer; creditor, dun (*students' slang*).

Manie', *f.* (*pl.* **—en**) mania; madness.

Manie'r, *f.* (*pl.* **—en**) manner, way; deportment; fashion, habit; style; mannerism; grace notes (*Mus.*); (*pl.*) manners; **mit guter —,** with a good grace; **das ist keine —,** that is not the proper way, that is not the way to act. **—lich,** *adj.* mannerly, civil, polite. **—lichkeit,** *f.* politeness. **—t,** *adj.* affected; mannered (*Paint.*). **—theit,** *f.* mannerism.

Ma'nifest, *n.* (**—es,** *pl.* **—e**) manifesto. *Comp.* **—atio'ns=eid,** *m.* sworn declaration of insolvency. **—ie'ren,** *v.a.* to manifest, to swear an affidavit to one's insolvency (*Law*).

Mani'p—el, I. *m.* (**—els,** *pl.* **—el**) maniple, company of foot-soldiers in the Roman army (*Mil.*). II. *n.* a narrow strip worn on the left arm, maniple (*R. Cath. Eccl.*). **—ulie'ren,** *v.a.* to manipulate.

Man'ko, *m.* (**—s**) deficit: defect, deficiency.

Mann, *m.* (**—es,** *pl.* **Män'ner**) man; male; husband; (*pl.* **—en**) retainer, liege, vassal; (*pl.* **—**) soldier, man; **der gemeine —,** common people, the lower classes; the man in the street; **der wilde —,** the wild man of the woods; **den lieben Gott einen guten — sein lassen,** to let things take their course; **die Soldaten standen drei — hoch,** the soldiers were drawn up three deep; **der General mit dreitausend —,** the general with three thousand men; **seinen — finden,** to find one's match; **an den — bringen,** to get rid of, find a purchaser for; **seine Tochter an den — bringen,** to dispose of one's daughter in marriage; **einen — nehmen,** to marry; **einen — suchen (finden),** to seek (find) a husband; **Bitte (Frau Doctor B.) grüßen Sie Ihren —,** please remember me to Dr. B. *or* to the doctor; **du bist ein — des Todes, wenn ...,** you are a dead man if ...; **— der Freiheit,** a free man; **seinen — stehen, stellen,** to be a man of courage, not to flinch; **einen — stellen,** to find a man; **wenn die Not an den — kommt** *or* **geht,** in case of necessity; **Selbst ist der —,** every one must depend on himself; if you want a thing well done, do it yourself (*prov.*); **ein Wort ein —** *or* **ein — ein Wort,** an honest man's word is as good as his bond, an honest man is as good as his word (*prov.*); **der dritte —,** the third party, agent, middleman; **wollen Sie den vierten — machen?** will you take a hand and make the fourth? **er ist nicht —(e)s genug es zu thun,** he is not man enough *or* sufficiently brave to do it; **so viel auf (für) den —,** so much a *or* per head; **wir stehen alle für einen —,** we are as one man, we share the responsibility; **— für —,** one and all; **das Volk erhob sich wie ein —,** the nation rose as one man; **— gegen —,** hand to hand (*fight*); **du wärst mir mein —,** you would be the last person I should apply to (*iron.*); **du wärst nie mein —,** you would be the last person I should apply to, you would never do for me; **alle — hoch!** all hands aloft! (*Naut.*); **tausend — zu Fuß,** a thousand foot; **mit — und Maus,** every living soul; **mit — und Maus untergehen,** to go down with all on board. **—bar,** *adj.* marriageable, fit to marry, having attained to (wo)manhood. **—barkeit,** *f.* marriageable age, (wo)manhood, (wo)man's estate; puberty. **—haft,** *adj. & adv.* manly; brave, valiant; strenuous. **—haftigkeit,** *f.* manliness; bravery. **—heit,** *f.* manhood, virility; manliness, courage, valour. **—schaft,** *f.* body of picked men; troops, forces, crew *Comp.* **—es=alter,** *n.* manhood. **—es=kraft,** *f.* manly vigour *or* strength. **—es=würde,** *f.* dignity of a man. **—gut,** *n.* male fief. **—loch,** *n.* man-hole. **—s=bild,** *n.* man, male person (*coll.*). **—s=dick, —s=hoch,** *adj.* stout, tall as a full-grown man. **—schafts=rolle,** *f.* muster-roll. **—s=hemd,** *n.* shirt. **—s=kerl,** *m.* (*thorough*) man. **—s=kloster,** *n.* monastery. **—s=leute,** *pl.* men-folk, men. **—s=person,** *f.* man. **—(e)s=stamm,** *m.* male line. **—s=stimme,** *f.* male voice. **—s=tief,** *adj.* a fathom deep. **—s=toll,** *adj.* mad after men. **—s=tollheit,** *f.*, **—s=wut,** *f.* passion for men, andromania, nymphomania, furor uterinus (*Med.*). **—s=zucht,** *f.* discipline (*Mil.*). **—weib,** *n.* virago; hermaphrodite.

Männ'—chen, *n.* (—chens, *pl.* —chen) little man; male (*of beasts, birds, etc.*); **mein —chen**, my dear husband; **—chen machen**, to frisk, to squat, to beg (*as a dog*). **—in**, *f.* woman (*B.*); virago. **—isch**, *adj.* masculine, mannish, unwomanly. **—lein**, *n. see* **—chen**; **ein —lein und ein Fräulein**, a male and a female (*B.*). **—lich**, *adj.* male; masculine; manly; bold, valiant; male (*Bot.*); **—liche Reime**, masculine rimes (*the last syllable of the metrical line having a stress*); **—liche Kleidung**, man's clothes; **—liches Alter**, man's estate. **—lichkeit**, *f.* manhood, virility; masculinity; manliness, bravery, manfulness. *Comp.* **—er=chor**, *m.* men's choir; chorus of men (*Theat.*). **—er=freundschaft**, *f.* friendship between men, firm *or* reliable friendship. **—er=gesangverein**, *m.* men's choral society, glee club. **—er=mordend**, *adj.* homicidal. **—er=süchtig**, *adj.* longing after men, mad after men. **—er=treu(e)**, *f.* eryngo (*Bot.*). **—er=würde**, *see* **Manneswürde**. **—er=volk**, *n.* men.

Man'nig, (**Man'nich**,) *adj.* many (*obs.*). *Comp.* **—fach**, **—faltig**, *adj.* various, manifold, diverse, multifarious; **—faltig machen**, to diversify, to vary. **—faltigkeit**, *f.* multiplicity, variety, diversity.

Män'niglich, *indec. adj.* every man, everybody, one and all; individually and collectively.

Manome'ter, *m.* (—s, *pl.* —) manometer; steam gauge, pressure-gauge.

Manö'v—er, *n.* (—ers, *pl.* —er) manœuvre; review, manœuvres. **—rie'ren**. I. *v.n.* (*aux.* **h.**) to manœuvre; to hold a review. II. *subst. n.* manœuvring, manœuvres. *Comp.* **—er=krieg**, *m.* sham campaign (*for practice*).

Mansar'de, *f.* (*pl.* —n) attic. *Comp.* **—n=dach**, *n.* curved *or* broken roof. **—n=fenster**, *n.* attic window, dormer window. **—n=wohnung**, *f.* lodgings in a garret *or* on the top-floor. **—n=zimmer**, **—n=stübchen**, *n.* attic.

Mansch, **Mantsch**, *m.* (—(e)s, *pl.* —e) paddling, dabbling; squash.

Man'sche—n, **Mant'sche—n**, *v.a. & n.* (*aux.* **h.**) to paddle, dabble, splash; to mix up; to meddle. **—rei'**, *f.* dabbling; squash.

Manschet'te, *f.* (*pl.* —n) cuff; wrist-frill; **—n haben (vor einer S.)**, to be afraid, to be in fear (of a th.) (*coll.*); **die —n zittern ihm**, he is in a great funk (*coll.*). *Comp.* **—n=fieber**, *n.* abject fear. **—n=knopf**, *m.* stud; **doppelte —n=knöpfe**, links.

Man'tel, *m.* (—s, *pl.* **Män'tel**; *dim.* **Män'telchen**) cloak, mantle; gown, robe, cloak of state; pall; envelope, sheathing; mantel, mantelpiece; jacket, casing (*of a cylinder, etc.*); convex surface (*of a ball, etc.*); roof (*Min.*); runner (*Naut.*); canvas-bag (*of a fire-ball, Artil.*); top; crown (*of a bell*); coping (*of a wall*); cage, well (*of a staircase*); mantle, cloak, pretence; **der dänische —**, maiden (*instrument of torture*): **den — nach dem Winde hängen**, to temporize, to trim one's sails according to the wind, to set one's sail to every wind; **einer Sache ein Mäntelchen umhängen**, to cloak *or* palliate a thing. *Comp.* **—kragen**, *m.* cape (of a cloak). **—riemen**, *m.* cloak-strap. **—sack**, *m.* portmanteau, valise. **—stoff**, *m.*, **—tuch**, *n.* mantling. **—träger**, *m.* pall-bearer (*obs.*); time-server; trimmer. **—weit**, *adj.* voluminous. **—zeug**, *n.* mantling.

Mantil'le, *f.* (*pl.* —n) mantilla.

Manua'l, *n.* (—s, *pl.* —e) note-book; journal, wastebook (*C.L.*); key-board (*Mus.*).

Manufaktu'r, *f.* (*pl.* —en) manufacture; manufactory. **—i'st**, *m.* (—i'ten, *pl.* —i'ten) manufacturer; maker; dealer in manufactured articles. *Comp.* **—arbeiter**, *m.* factory-hand. **—industrie**, *f.* manufacturing industry; **—industrie und ihre Erzeugnisse**, manufactures. **—waren**, *pl.* manufactured goods; articles of manufacture; dry goods. **—waren=händler**, *m.* dealer in manufactured goods; linen-draper; mercer.

Manuskrip't, *n.* (—(e)s, *pl.* —e) handwriting; manuscript (*of an author*); copy (*Typ.*); **Bühnen —**, acting copy; **als — gedruckt**, printed (*or* type-written) for private circulation only; **den Bühnen gegenüber als — gedruckt**, right of acting reserved.

Map'pe, *f.* (*pl.* —n) portfolio, case; map.

Mar, *see* **Mahr**.

Maras'mus, *m.* (—, *pl.* **Marasmen**) marasmus, decay of the body.

Mär'chen, *n.* (—s, *pl.* —) tale, story; fairy-tale, fable, legend; rumour; **— von tausend und einer Nacht**, the Thousand and One Nights', the Arabian Nights (entertainment). **—haft**, *adj.* in the form of a tale; fabulous, fictitious. **—haftigkeit**, *f.* fabulousness. *Comp.* **—buch**, *n.* book of fairy tales. **—erzähler**, *m.* storyteller. **—welt**, *f.* fabulous world, world of romance.

Mar'der, *m.* (—s, *pl.* —) marten; marten-fur. *Comp.* **—falle**, *f.* trap for catching martens.

Mä're, *f.* (*obs. & poet.*) news, tidings; rumour; tradition; *see* **Märchen**.

Marel'le, *f.* (*pl.* —n) morel (*cherry*); small yellow apricot, Turkey apricot.

Margari'n, *n.* (—ins) margarine. *Comp.* **—butter**, *f.*, **—fett**, *n.* margarine, margerine. **—sauer**, *adj.* margaric.

Mari'en— (*in comp.*) **—bild**, *n.* image of the virgin Mary. **—blume**, *f.* daisy. **—dienst**, *m.* worship of the Holy Virgin. **—dorn**, *m.* Scotch thistle; sweet brier. **—fäden**, *pl.* gossamer. **—fest**, *n.* Lady-day. **—glas**, *n.* Muscovy glass, isinglass-stone. **—glöckchen**, *n.* Canterbury bells. **—gras**, *n.* feather-grass. **—käfer**, *m.* lady-bird. **—kapelle**, *f.* Lady-chapel. **—würmchen**, *n.* lady-bird.

Mari'ne, *f.* (*pl.* —n) marine, navy; **bei der — dienen**, to serve in the navy; **in — kreisen**, among naval experts. *Comp.* **—akademie**, *f.* Royal Naval College. **—amt**, *n.* navy-board *or* office, Admiralty. **—arsenal**, *n.* navy-yard. **—artillerie**, *f.* naval artillery, naval guns, naval gunners. **—minister**, *m.* minister of naval affairs; First Lord of the Admiralty (*Engl.*), Secretary of the Navy (*U. S. A.*). **—maler**, *n.* marine *or* sea-painter. **—ministerium**, *n.* ministry of naval affairs, Admiralty (*England*), Navy Department (*U. S. A.*). **—offizier**, *m.* naval officer. **—reserve**, *f.* naval reserve. **—schule**, *f.* naval school *or* college. **—soldat**, *m.* marine. **—truppen**, *pl.* marines. **—werft**, *f.* navy-yard, government dock-yard. **—wesen**, *n.* naval affairs.

Marinie'ren, *v.a.* to pickle.

Marionet'te, *f.* (*pl.* —n) puppet. *Comp.* **—n=spiel**, *n.* puppet-show.

Marje'll, *f.*, **—chen**, *n.* (*dial.*) girl; maid-servant; silly girl, wench, goose.

[1]**Mark**, *f.* (*pl.* —en) mark, boundary, limit; borders, border-country, march; district; wood, pasture held in common; **die — = die — Brandenburg**, March (*or, formerly*, Electorate) of Brandenburg. *Comp.* **—baum**, *m.* boundary tree. **—genoß**, *m.* joint-proprietor of land. **—gericht**, *n.* district court. **—graf** *m.* margrave, count of the marches. **—gräfin**, *f.* margravine. **—scheide**, *f.* boundary. **—scheidekunst**, *f.* art of surveying; subterraneous geometry. **—scheider**, *m.* (*mine*) surveyor. **—scheideriß**, *m.* plot of a mine. **—scheidezug**, *m.* line of demarcation. **—scheidung**, *f.* determination of a boundary. **—stein**, *m.* landmark, boundary stone.

[2]Mark, f. (pl. —) (abbrev. M. Mk.) silver weight; mark (a modern German coin worth about one shilling or twenty-four cents). —gewicht, n. troy-weight. —rechnung, f. calculation in marks. —schein, m.; 100 —schein, 100 mark note (nearly £5). —stück, n. mark (or shilling) piece, bob (coll.); 20 —stück, 20 mark piece (nearly a sovereign). —währung, f. currency of the German empire.

[3]Mark, n. (—es) marrow; pith; pulp; core; essence; mettle; strength, vigour; — in den Knochen haben, to be of great strength; durch — und Bein dringen, to penetrate to the very marrow, to cut to the quick. —icht, (obs.) —ig, adj. marrowy; pithy. Comp. —gefäß, n. medullary vessel. —holz, n. pithy wood. —los, adj. marrowless; pithless.

Mar'ke, f. (pl. —n) mark, token; countermark; signature (C. L.); label; check (Theat.); ticket (for lectures, dinners); brand; certificate (from a teacher); marker, counter, fish; pole (used in surveying); postage-stamp; stamp. Comp. —n-album, album for postage-stamps.

Mar'k—en, v.a. to settle a boundary. —ung, f. demarcation; boundary; district; fields common to a village.

Mär'k—er, m. (—ers, pl. —er) inhabitant of a boundary district, of the marches; native of the march of Brandenburg, Brandenburger. —isch, adj.; —ische Konfession, Brandenburg Confession.

Marketen'der, m. (—s, pl. —) sutler. —in, f. sutler-woman, canteen-woman. —n, v.n. (aux. h.) to carry on the trade of sutler.

Markie'r—en, v.a. to mark; to make prominent, to indicate; to raise; den Feind —en, to point out (Mil.). —t, p.p. & adj. marked, distinguished, prominent.

Markt, m. (—es, pl. Märk'te) market, mart; market-place; market-town; emporium; bargain, business; Jahr—, (yearly-)fair; Märkte beziehen, to frequent fairs; es ist zweimal wöchentlich —, the market is held twice a week; seine Haut zu —e tragen, to risk one's life; zu —e bringen, to take to the market, to offer for sale; eine Anleihe auf den — bringen, to issue a loan; mit etwas — halten, to trade, deal in something. Comp. —amt, n. board for regulating market affairs. —bericht, m. report or statement of the market. —bude, f. stall, booth. —fähig, adj. marketable. —flecken, m. small market-town, borough. —freiheit, f. right of holding a market; market-privilege. —gängig, adj. current; —gängiger Preis, market price. —geld, n., —geschenk, n. money to be spent in a market or at a fair, fairing. —gemeinde, f. borough, market-town. —gerechtigkeit, see —freiheit. —geschäft, n. business done on the market. —gut, n. market wares. —halle, f. covered market; stalls in a large building. —helfer, m. porter, packer (at fairs). —leute, pl. keepers of stalls; frequenters of a fair or market, people who wish to sell their goods in a market. —meister, —schreiber, m. clerk of the market; inspector. —ordnung, f. market-regulation(s). —platz, m. market-place. —recht, n. see —freiheit; market regulations; market-toll. —schiff, n. market-boat. —schreier, m. quack, mountebank. —schreierei, f. quackery, charlatanry. —zettel, m. register of market-prices, averages. —zoll, m. duty on goods brought to market.

Mark'ten, v.n. (aux. h.) to higgle, bargain (um eine S., for a th.); to sell in the market.

Mar'lien, Mar'ling, f. marline (Naut.).

Marmela'de, f. (pl. —n) marmelade.

Mar'melstein, m. marble (poet.). —en, adj. made of marble (poet.).

Mar'mor, m. (—s, pl. —e) marble. —ie'ren, v.a. to marble, grain. —ie'rt, p.p. & adj. marbled, mottled; mit —ie'rtem Schnitt, marble-edged (Bookb.). —n, adj. marble, marble-like, made of marble. Comp. —arbeiter, m. marble-cutter. —band, m. marbled binding. —bild, n. marble-statue or bust. —bruch, m., —grube, f. marble quarry. —glatt, adj. as smooth as marble. —glätter, n. marble-rubber. —kalt, adj. cold as marble. —platte, f. marble slab. —schleifer, m. marble-polisher. —schnitt, m. marbled edges.

Maro'd—e, adj. weary, tired out, knocked-up. —eu'r, m. (—eurs, pl. —eure & —eurs) marauder, pillager. —ie'ren, v.n. (aux. h.) to maraud, to pillage; to rove as a freebooter or soldier in quest of plunder.

Maro'ne, f. (pl. —n) edible or sweet chestnut.

Maroqui'n, m. (—s), (Marok'ko-leder, n.) Morocco-leather, morocco.

Marot'te, f. (pl. —n) freak, whim, piece of folly.

Marqueu'r, m. (—s, pl. —s) billiard-marker, marker; waiter.

Marqui'se, f. (pl. —n) marchioness; marquee (tent).

Mars, m. & f. (—, pl. —(s)en) top (Naut.); der große —, main-top. Comp. —laterne, f. top-lantern. —schoten, pl. top-sail sheets.

[1]Marsch, f. (pl. —en) marsh, fen, bog; — am Meere, salt-marsh. —ig, adj. marshy. Comp. —krankheit, f. marsh-fever, ague. —land, n., —en-land, n. fenland, bogland, marshy country. —länder, —en-bewohner, m. inhabitant of a marshy district.

[2]Marsch, I. m. (—es, pl. Mär'sche) march; marching; march (Mus.); verdeckte Märsche, stolen marches; den — schließen, to bring up the rear; sich auf den — begeben, to march out, to set out; den — schlagen, blasen, to strike up a march; einem den — blasen, to send a p. about his business (coll.). II. int. march! forward! be off! —! —! double (the pace)! —ie'ren, v.n. (aux. h. & s.) to march; Mann für Mann —ieren, to file (off); Mann für Mann vorbei —ieren, to file past; du kannst —ieren! be off! (coll.). Comp. —anzug, m. marching kit. —bataillon, n. battalion on the march. —befehl, m. marching-orders. —diätetik, f. hygienic rules to be observed on a march. —fähig, adj. fit for marching. —fertig, adj. ready to march or to start, in marching order. —geschwindigkeit, f. (marching-)pace. —kolonne, f. marching column (of an army). —lager, n. bivouac; (pl.) travelling (trunnion) holes (Artil.). —ordnung, f. order of march or of sailing. —quartier, n. quarters for moving troops. —route, f. line of march. —säule, f. column of an army on the march.

Mar'schall, (obs. Mar'schalk,) m. (—s, pl. Mar'schälle) marshal. —in, f. marshal's wife. Comp. —amt, n. marshalship. —s-stab, m. marshal's baton. —s-würde, f. marshalship.

Mar'stall, m. (—s, pl. Marställe) royal stables; royal or princely stud.

Mar'ter, f. (pl. —n) rack, torture; torment, pang; martyrdom. —er, m. (—ers, pl. —er) torturer, tormenter. —n, v.a. to torture; to inflict martyrdom on; to torment; sich (dat.) den Kopf (zer)—n, to rack one's brains. —tum, n. (—tums) martyrdom; martyrs. Comp. —bank, f. rack. —gerät, n. instruments of torture. —geschichte, f. martyrology; Christ's passion. —holz, n. cross (of torture). —kammer, f. torture chamber. —pfahl, m. stake (of torture). —tod, m. martyrdom, cruel death. —voll, adj. full of torture, excruciating. —woche, f. Passion week.

Mär'ter—er, —in, see Märtyrer, ꝛc.

Marti'ni, *see* **Martin** *in Index of names.*
Mär'tyrer, *m.* (—s, *pl.* —), **—in**, *f.* martyr. **—tum**, (**Mär'tyrtum**,) *n.* (—s) martyrdom. *Comp.* **—geschichte**, *f.* martyrology. **—krone**, *f.* crown of martyrdom. **—tod**, *m.* martyrdom; **den —tod sterben**, to suffer martyrdom.
Marty'ri—um, *n.* (—ums, *pl.*—ien) martyrdom.
Marun'ke, *f.* (*pl.* —n) red egg-plum.
März, *m.* (—es, *older and in some comps.*: —en) March. **—lich**, *adj.* March-like, of March; **vor —lich**, existing before the great revolution of 1848 and swept away by it; *see* **—tage**. *Comp.* **—(en)=bier**, *n.* beer brewed in March. **—(en)=wind**, *m.* March wind, cutting wind. **—feld**, *n.* national assembly of the Franks. **—monat**, *m.* month of March. **—nägelein**, *n.* mezereon (*Bot.*). **—schein**, *m.* new moon in March. **—tage**, *pl.* days of the revolution of 1848 in Berlin and Vienna. **—veilchen**, *n.* sweet violet. **—wasser**, *n.* water from March snow.
Marzipa'n, *m.* (—s) marchpane (*a compound of almonds, rose-water, and sugar*).
Ma'sch—e, *f.* (*pl.* —en) mesh, stitch; eyelet-hole; link (*of mail*); **eine —e fallen lassen (aufnehmen)**, to drop (pick up) a stitch (*in knitting*); **—e am Hute**, cockade. **—en**, *v.a.* to net. **—ig**, *adj.* meshy, reticulated, netted. *Comp.* **—en=werk**, *n.* net-work.
Maschi'n—e, *f.* (*pl.* —en) machine; steam engine; machinery, apparatus; **eine —e aufstellen**, to adjust an engine; **eine —e anlassen**, to start an engine; **eine —e abstellen**, to stop an engine. **—erie'**, *f.* machinery. **—ie'ren**, *v.a.* to produce *or* work by machinery; to clean (*corn*) by a machine. **—i'st**, *m.* (—is'ten, *pl.* —is'ten) machinist; engine-driver; engineer; scene-shifter; stage-carpenter. *Comp.* **—en=bau**, *m.* machine-making. **—en=bauer**, *m.* machine-maker, engine-builder, engineer. **—en=baumeister**, *m.* mechanical, practical engineer. **—en=druck**, *m.* machine impression. **—en=führer**, *m.* engine-driver, engine-man. **—en=garn**, *n.* machine-spun yarn (mule-) twist. **—en=gebäude**, *n.* engine-room; engine-shed. **—en=geschütz**, *n.* machine gun. **—en=gestell**, *n.* frame. **—en=gewehr**, *n.* machine rifle. **—en=kraft**, *f.* mill-power. **—en=lehre**, *f.* science of engineering, mechanics. **—en=mäßig**, *adj.* mechanical, automatic. **—en=meister**, *m.* mechanical engineer; traffic manager (*Railw.*); stage-carpenter; conductor (*Typ.*). **—en=ofen**, *m.* engine furnace. **—en=raum**, *m.* engine-room; engine-shed. **—en=schacht**, *m.* engine-shaft. **—en=schlosser**, *m.* blacksmith for machinery. **—en=schmierer**, *m.* lubricator, greaser. **—en=schreiber**, *m.* typewriter, typist. **—en=spitzen**, *pl.* machine-made lace. **—en=(web=)stuhl**, *m.* power-loom. **—en=techniker**, *n.* mechanical engineer. **—en=werk**, *n.* machinery. **—en=zeichnen**, *n.* engineering drawing.
Ma'ſ—e, *f.* (*pl.* —en) mark, spot, scar (*obs.*). **—er**, *f.* (*pl.* —ern), *also m.* (—ers, *pl.* —er) vein, streak (*of wood*), veined wood; speck, spot. **—ericht**, (*obs.*) **—erig**, *adj.* mottled, streaky, speckled; measled. **—ern**, *pl.* measles. **—ern**, *v.a.* to grain; **sich —ern**, to get streaky *or* knotty. **—ig**, *adj.* scarred; spotted. *Comp.* **—er=fleck**, *m.* speckle, vein. **—er=holz**, *n.* veined wood. **—ern=krank**, *adj.* ill with measles.
Mas'holder, *m.* (—s, *pl.* —) maple-tree.
Mas'k—e, *f.* (*pl.* —en; *dim.* **Mäsk'chen**,) mask; mask, disguise; mask (*Fort.*); masquerader; ugly hag; **einem die —e abnehmen**, to unmask a p.; **eine —e setzen**, to play for safety (*Bill.*); **die scherzende —e**, the muse of comedy; **die ernste —e**, the muse of tragedy. **—era'de**, *f.* (*pl.* —eraden) masquerade. **—ie'ren**, *v.a.* to mask; to put on a mask, disguise. *Comp.* **—en=anzug**, *m.*, **—en=kleid**, *n.* fancy dress; disguise, masquerading costume. **—en=ball**, *m.* masked ball, fancy-dress ball, masquerade. **—en=blume**, *f.* personate flower. **—en=fest**, *n.* masquerade, carnival, mummery **—en=freiheit**, *f.* license enjoyed at a masquerade. **—en=tänzer**, *m.* masked dancer. **—en=verleiher**, *m.* dealer in fancy costumes, costumier. **—en=zug**, *m.* fancy-dress procession, masquerading procession.
[1]**Maß**, **Mä'ße**, *1 (& 3) pers. sing. imperf. indic. & subj. of* **messen**.
[2]**Maß**, *n.* (—es, *pl.* —e) measure (*for a coat, etc.*); moderation; (*also f.*) quart; measure, gauge, rate; metre, measure; measure, dimension, proportion; limit; degree; time (*Mus.*); *see* **—e**; **in vollem —e**, amply, completely; **— halten**, to observe moderation; **in hohem —e**, in a high degree, very; **einem (das) — zu einem Rock nehmen**, to take a p.'s measure for a coat; **eine — Bier**, a pot of beer; **nach dem —e**, in proportion to, according to; **weder — noch Ziel halten, kennen**, to know no bounds, to exceed all bounds; **das — überschreiten**, to go too far; **alles mit —**, everything in moderation, moderation in all things; **gehäuftes —**, heaped measure; **das — nicht haben**, not to be standard measure; **ein gerüttelt und geschüttelt —**, full measure pressed down and running over. **—e**, *f.* (*pl.* —en) measure; proportion, just measure; mode, manner, way; (*generally used in the plural and in comp. with another word*) **mit —en**, with propriety, in moderation, moderately; **ohne —en**, excessively: **über die —en, über alle —en**, beyond measure, out of all bounds; **bester —en**, in the best way; **beliebiger —en**, as one pleases; **folgender —en**, in the following way, as follows; **gewisser —en**, in some degree, to a certain extent; **bekannter —en**, as is known; **gehöriger —en**, duly; **verabredeter —en**, according to agreement; **hergebrachter —en**, according to custom; **solcher —en**, in such a manner; **was —en**, whereas, in what manner (*Law*); **wenn es sich in der —e verhält**, such being the case (*obs.*); **in der —e wie**, as (*obs.*). **—en**, I. *v.a.* to measure (*rare*). II. *adv.* seeing, as, whereas (*obs.*); (*in comp.* =) in the measure, degree, *or* manner. *Comp.* **—einheit**, *f.* unit of measure. **—gabe**, *f.* measure, proportion; **nach —gabe seiner Kräfte**, according to his powers. **—gebend**, *adj.* authoritative, decisive; standard; **das kann nicht —gebend für uns sein**, that cannot influence us *or* be a standard for us; **die —gebenden Kreise**, the leading circles; those in authority. **—gebung**, *f.* measure, proportion, limitation; **ohne —gebung**, without restriction *or* condition, without disparagement, without presuming to dictate. **—haltung**, *f.* moderation, modesty. **—kanne**, *f.*, **—krug**, *m.* tankard, quart-pot. **—liebe**, *see* **Maßliebe**. **—los**, *adj.* boundless, without measure, exorbitant. **—nahme**, **—nehmung**, *f.* measuring; measure; mode of acting. **—regel**, *f.* measure; **—regeln danach nehmen** *or* **treffen**, to take steps accordingly, take the necessary precautions. **—regeln**, *v.a.* to reprimand, to inflict disciplinary punishments on (*public servants, soldiers, etc.*). **—regelung**, *f.* reprimand, disciplinary punishment. **—stab**, *m.* measure; standard; scale; **in großem —stabe**, on a large scale; **einen —stab an eine S. legen**, to apply a rule *or* standard to a th.; **verjüngter —stab**, reduced scale, graduated scale (*of reduction*); **in verjüngtem —stabe**, on a small *or* reduced scale. **—stock**, *m.* carpenter's rule, gauge. **—topf**, *m.* two-quart pot. **—verhältnis**, *n.* proportion; *pl.* dimensions. **—voll**, *adj.* moderate, sober-minded.

[1]**Mas'se**, *f.* (*pl.* **—n**) cue (*Bill.*); sculptor's mallet.

[2]**Mas's—e**, *f.* (*pl.* **—en**) mass, lump; block · substance, stuff; paste, dough; property, assets; **in —en aufstellen**, to mass (*Mil.*); **die —e der Nation**, the bulk of the nation; **sich zur —e melden**, to lodge a claim (*on a bankrupt's estate*). **—enhaft**, *adj.* in a mass, in large crowds; bulky; enormous. **—ig**, *adj.* large. **—i'v**, *adj.* massive, massy, solid; clumsy; **—ives Haus**, house built of stone. *Comp.* **—en=armut**, *f.* pauperism. **—en=aufgebot**, *f.* levy en masse, general levy (*Mil.*). **—en=bildung**, *f.* massing (*of troops*). **—en=erhebung**, *f.* rising up of the whole people. **—en=feuer**, *n.* general volley. **—en=gebirge**, *n.* mountain mass. **—en=kurator**, *m.* creditor's syndic *or* assignee. **—en=mord**, *m.* general massacre. **—en=produktion**, *f.* production on a large scale. **—en=quartier**, *n.* lodgings for many in one place, under the same roof. **—en=teilchen**, *n.* particule, molecule. **—en=verkauf**, *m.* selling (by) wholesale. **—en=weise**, *adv.* in large numbers, in heaps; in a lump.

Mä'ßig, *adj. & adv.* moderate; frugal; mean; middling; discreet; containing (*one, etc.*) measure; andante (*Mus.*); **helden—**, heroic, heroically; **— genießen**, to enjoy in moderation. **—keit**, *f.* moderation, temperance, frugality; moderateness; mediocrity. *Comp.* **—keits=verein**, *m.* temperance society *or* union; **strenger —keitsverein**, total abstinence society. **—keits=vereinler**, *m.* teetotaller, total abstainer; blue ribbon (*coll.*).

Mä'ßig—en, *v.a.* to moderate; to temper; to mitigate, allay, assuage; to restrain, check; **sich —en**, to restrain oneself, keep one's temper, be moderate; **den Schritt —en**, to slacken one's pace; **die gemäßigte Zone**, the temperate zone. **—ung**, *f.* diminution; moderation; mitigation.

Ma'ßlieb—e, *f.*, **—chen**, *n.* daisy.

[1]**Mast**, *m.* (**—es**, *pl.* **—en**) mast; **einen — absegeln**, to carry away a mast; **einen — einsetzen**, to set up a mast; **der große —**, mainmast; **der vordere —**, foremast; **der hintere —**, mizzen-mast. **—en**, *v.a.* to furnish with a mast *or* masts. **—er**, (**—ers**, *pl.* **—er**) *suffix in comp.* -master, of so many masts; *as*: **Drei—er**, three-master. *Comp.* **—baum**, *m.* mast. **—en=setzer**, *m.* mast-maker. **—korb**, *m.* scuttle, round top, bower, crow's-nest. **—los**, *adj.* without masts. **—wächter**, *m.* lookout (man), top-man (*Naut.*). **—wärts**, *adv.* aback.

[2]**Mast**, I. *f.* mast, acorns, beech-nuts, *etc.*; fattening (*pigs, etc.*); stall-feeding; food; **auf der — haben**, to fatten. II. *adj. & adv.* sleek, fat; well-fed. **—en**, *v.n.* (*aux.* **s.**) to grow fat. **—ig**, *see* **Mast** II.; robust; thick (*of corn, etc.*). **—ung**, *f.* fattening. *Comp.* **—darm**, *m.* rectum. **—freiheit**, *f.* right of feeding pigs, *etc.*, in a wood. **—futter**, *n.* fattening-pasture. **—gans**, *f.* fat goose. **—geld**, *n.* pannage. **—kalb**, *n.* fatted calf. **—kur**, *f.* gavage (*Med.*). **—ochse**, *m.* fattened (*or* stalled, *B.*) ox. **—schwein**, *n.* fat *or* fattened hog *or* pig. **—vieh**, *n.* cattle for fattening; fattened cattle. **—zeit**, *f.* time for fattening cattle.

Mä'st—en, *v.a.* to feed, fatten, cram; **gemästet**, stall-fed, fat; **das gemästete Kalb schlachten**, to kill the fatted calf (*B.*); **sich —en**, to live opulently. **—er**, *m.* (**—ers**, *pl.* **—er**) cattle-fattener *or* feeder. **—ung**, *f.* fattening.

Ma'stix, *m.* (**—(es)**, *pl.* **—e**) (*gum*) mastic.

Masur'ka, *f.* (**—**, *pl.* **—s**) mazurka.

Matado'r, *m.* (**—s**, *pl.* **—e**) matador (*in a bull-fight*); eminent person, great swell, big gun (*coll.*); excellent player of games, crack player, champion.

Materia'l, I. *n.* (**—s**, *pl.* **—ien**) material, substance; stock, equipment, plant; baggage, artillery, materiel (*Mil.*); *pl.* materials, ingredients, products; drugs; groceries; **rollendes —**, rolling stock (*Railw.*); **liegendes —**, railway-plant. II. *adj.* material. **—is'mus**, *m.* materialism. **—i'st, is'm**, *m.* (**—is'ten**, *pl.* **—is'ten**) materialist, sensualist; druggist; grocer. **—is'tisch**, *adj.* materialistic, relating to matter. *Comp.* **—(waren)=geschäft**, *n.*, **(waren)=handlung**, *f.* trade in colonial produce; grocer's business, grocery stores. **—is'tengewölbe**, *n.* grocer's shop, provision merchant's stores. **—waren**, *pl.* groceries.

Mate'ri—e, *f.* (*pl.* **—en**) matter, stuff; subject; cause, matter; pus (*Med.*) **—e'll**, *adj.* material, real; **—elle Ursache**, material (*as opp. to formal*) cause; **—eller Mensch**, matter-of-fact person; man of no higher aspirations.

Mathemati'k, *f.* mathematics.

Mathema'ti—ker, *m.* (**—kers**, *pl.* **—ker**) mathematician. **—sch**, *adj.* mathematical.

Matrat'ze, *f.* (*pl.* **—n**) mattress.

Matri'kel, *f.* (*pl.* **—n**) roll, register; matriculation; **in die — eintragen**, to matriculate. *Comp.* **—schein**, *m.* certificate of matriculation.

Matrikular'—beiträge, *pl.*, **—umlage**, *f.* proportionate payment, quota; contributions from the federal states to the Imperial Exchequer.

Matri'ze, *f.* (*pl.* **—n**) matrix, mould; die; small anvil.

Matro'se, *m.* (**—n**, *pl.* **—n**) sailor. *Comp.* **—n=art**, *f.* sailor-fashion. **—n=jacke**, *f.* sailor's (pea-)jacket. **—n=kleider**, *pl.* sailor's clothes, slops (*coll.*). **—n=tanz**, *m.* sailor's hornpipe. **—n=taufe**, *f.* ceremony on crossing the line.

Matsch, I. *m.* (**—es**, *pl.* **—e**) mash, squash, pulp; mud (*esp'lly after snow has been melting*); slush; loo; **es ist ein —, daß man nicht durch kann**, one can hardly get along for the mud; **— machen**, to make all the tricks; **— werden**, to lose all the tricks (*at cards*). II. *adj. see* **—ig**. **—en**, *v.a.* to squash, mash, bruise; to splash; to capot. **—ig**, *adj.* in pulp, slushy, mashed, muddy, dirty.

Matt, I. *adj.* mate (*at chess*); faint, feeble, languid, exhausted; heavy; flat, insipid, jejune; tasteless; dull, dim, dead; lifeless; spent (*of balls*); **die Eisenbahnaktien waren ziemlich —**, railway shares were rather dull *or* heavy; **—geschliffenes Glas**, frosted glass; **—e Stimme**, inaudible *or* faint voice. II. *n.* (**—s**) mate; **— machen**, to mate, to exhaust; **Schach (und) —**, checkmate. **—heit**, *f.* faintness, weakness, lassitude; dulness, dimness. **—igkeit**, *f.* languor, exhaustion, fatigue. *Comp.* **—äugig**, *adj.* heavy *or* dim eyed. **—blau**, *adj.* pale blue. **—gold**, *n.* dead gold. **—herzig**, *adj.* faint-hearted, spiritless; languid.

[1]**Mat'te**, *f.* (*pl.* **—n**) mat. *Comp.* **—n=binse**, *f.* mat-weed. **—n=flechter**, *m.* mat-maker, straw-platter. **—n=zeug**, *n.* matting.

[2]**Mat'te**, *f.* (*pl.* **—n**) meadow, mead (*dial. poet.*).

Maturitä't, *f.* maturity, ripeness. *Comp.* **—s=examen**, *n.*, **—s=prüfung**, *f.* (*sometimes called* **Matu'rum**, *n.*) leaving examination at the first grade secondary boys' schools (*entitling the successful candidates to proceed to the University*), examination for leaving certificates.

Matz, *m.* (**—es**, *pl.* **—e**), *see p.* 779; simpleton; blockhead; name (*for a starling, canary or monkey*); **das verhält sich so oder ich will — heißen**, if that's not so I'm a fool.

Mätz'chen, *n.* (**—s**, *pl.* **—**) dunce, young fool, little silly; **— machen**, to play the fool.

Mat'ze, *f.* (*pl.* **—n**), **—n**, *m.* (**—ns**, *pl.* **—n**) unleavened bread. *Comp.* **—kuchen**, *m.* unleavened cake.

Mau, *adj.* middling, rather bad, poor, not good (*sl.*); **das Essen war —**, the food was poor; **ich fühle mich heute sehr —**, I feel rather out of sorts *or* seedy to-day (*coll.*).

Mau'en, *v.n.* (*aux.* **h.**) to mew.

Mau'er, *f.* (*pl.* **—n**) wall; battlement. *Comp.* **—absatz,** *m.* redan. **—anker,** *m.* cramp-iron, clamp. **—arbeit,** *f.* masonry. **—befestigung,** *f.* circumvallation. **—blende,** *f.* niche in a wall. **—blume,** *f.* wall-flower. **—blümchen,** *n.* lady without a partner (*at a dance*), wall-flower. **—brecher,** *m.* battering-ram. **—bruch,** *m.* mural breach. **—dach,** *n.* coping of a wall. **—fest,** *adj.* walled; firm as a rock. **—fraß,** *m.* decay of the stones in a wall. **—hut,** *m.*, **—kappe,** *f.* coping, coping-stone. **—kelle,** *f.* trowel. **—kitt,** *m.* mortar. **—klammer,** *f.* cramp-iron. **—krone,** *f.* mural crown. **—leiste,** *f.* moulding of a wall. **—lehm,** *m.* mortar made of clay and straw. **—mantel,** *m.* lining of a wall. **—meister,** *m.* master-mason. **—polie'rer,** *m.* bricklayer's foreman. **—ritze,** *f.* gap, crevice. **—sand,** *m.* sand for mortar. **—schwalbe,** *f.* black martin, swift. **—stein,** *m.* building stone; brick. **—wall,** *m.* rampart lined with stone. **—werk,** *n.* masonry, stone-work; walls (*coll.*). **—ziegel,** *m.* brick. **—zinne,** *f.* pinnacle, battlement.

Mau'—ern, *v.* I. *n.* to build with stone *or* brick, to make a wall. II. *a.* to wall up, *or* in, to immure. **—(e)rer,** *m.* *see* **Maurer.** **—(e)rung,** *f.* walling; bricklaying; **—erung mit Lehm,** daubing.

Mau'ke, *f* (*pl.* **—n**) malanders (*Vet.*).

Maukelei', *f.* *see* **Mogelei.**

[1]**Maul,** *n.* (**—s,** *pl.* **Mäu'ler**) mule. *Comp.* **—esel,** *m.*, **—pferd, —tier,** *n.* mule; boy who has left school and has not yet begun residence *or* has not yet matriculated at the University (*no longer a donkey, not yet a horse. Stud'ts sl.*). **—esel=treiber,** *m.* muleteer. **—tier=artig,** *adj.* mulish.

[2]**Maul,** *n.* (**—s,** *pl.* **Mäu'ler**) mouth (*of beasts and vulgarly of persons*); muzzle, chops; tongue; loquacity, gabble; chops (*of firearms*); peristoma (*Bot.*); **alle bösen Mäuler des Dorfes,** all the scandalmongers (*or* gossips) of the village; (*some of the foll. phrases are colloquial and most are vulgar*) **ein —machen, das — hängen,** *or* **hängen lassen,** to pout; **ein schiefes — ziehen,** to look disappointed, sulky, to pout; **das — voll nehmen, ein großes — haben,** to brag; **ein loses, ungewaschenes — haben,** to have a bad, venomous tongue; **sich** (*dat.*) **das — verbrennen,** to be too ready with one's tongue; **halt(e das) —!** hold your tongue! shut up! **einem das — aufbrechen,** to force a p. to speak; **das — aufsperren,** to gape; **hier hilft kein — spitzen, es muß gepfiffen sein,** there is no use mincing the matter, say it out; **das — zu brauchen wissen,** to have a flippant tongue; **sich** (*dat.*) **etwas am — abbrechen** *or* **absparen,** to stint o.s. in food; **sich selbst aufs — schlagen,** to contradict o.s.; **er ist nicht aufs — gefallen,** he has a nimble tongue, he is always ready with an answer **einem etwas ins — schmieren,** to make a th. very easy for a p., to assist s.o. (with words and advice); **er redet wie es ihm ins — kommt,** he says whatever comes uppermost; **in der Leute Mäuler kommen,** to be much talked of, to become the talk of the town; **einem nach dem —e reden,** to flatter a p. by chiming in with all his views; **das — wässert ihm danach,** that makes his mouth water; **das — ist ihm zugefroren,** he has lost his tongue; **habt Ihr kein —?** have you lost your tongue, can you not speak? *Comp.* **—affe,** *m.* one who stands with his mouth open, silly person; **—affen feil haben** *or* **halten,** *see* **—affen. —affen,** *v.n.* (*aux.* **h.**) (*insep.*) to stand gaping *or* idling about, to lounge about. **—afferei',** *f.* idle lounging, lazy life. **—christ,** *m.* professing Christian, hypocrite. **—drescher,** *m.* chatterbox. **—faul,** *adj.* too lazy to speak, slow of speech, taciturn. **—fertigkeit,** *f.* loquacity. **—freund,** *m.* lip-friend, one who professes to be a friend, flatterer. **—hänger(in,** *f.*), *m.* pouter, moper, sulky person. **—held,** *m.* braggart, big talker; braggadoccio. **—knebel,** *m.* gag. **—korb,** *m.* muzzle. **—schelle,** *f.* slap in the face, box on the ear. **—schellen,** (*insep.*) **—schellie'ren,** *v.a.* (**einen**) to give a p. a slap in the face, box a p.'s ears. **—schloß,** *n.* padlock. **—sperre,** *f.* lock-jaw. **—tapfer,** *adj.* bold of speech. **—tasche,** *f.* *see* **—schelle**; pouting person. **—tot,** *adj.*; **einen —tot machen,** to silence a p. **—trommel,** *f.* jews'-harp. **—werk,** *n.*; **ein gutes —werk haben,** to have the gift of the gab.

Maul'beer—e, *f.* (*pl.* **—en**) mulberry. *Comp.* **—baum,** *m.* mulberry tree. **—feigenbaum,** *m.* sycamore.

Mäul'chen, *n.* (**—s,** *pl.* **—**) little mouth; tender kiss (*obs.*).

Mau'len, *v.n.* to sulk, pout, mope (*coll.*).

Maul'wurf, *m.* (**—s,** *pl.* **Maulwürfe**) mole. *Comp.* **—s=fang,** *m.* mole-catching; mole-trap. **—s=gang,** *m.* mole-track. **—s=haufen, —s=hügel,** *m.* mole-hill.

Maur—e, *m.* (**—en,** *pl.* **—en**), **—in,** *f.* Moor. **—isch,** *adj.*, Moorish, Moresque; **—ischer Bogen,** Moorish, horse-shoe arch; **—ische Sprache,** morisco.

Mau'r—er, *m.* (**—ers,** *pl.* **—er**) mason, bricklayer, builder; (**Frei**)**—er,** freemason. **—erei',** *f.* masonry; (*free-*)masonry. **—erisch,** *adj.* masonic. *Comp.* **—er=arbeit,** *f.* masonry. **—er=gesell,** *m.* journeyman mason. **—er=gesellschaft,** *f.* freemasons' lodge. **—er=handwerk,** *n.* masonry. **—er=kelle,** *f.* mason's trowel. **—er=meister,** *m.* master-mason. **—er=pinsel,** *m.* whitewash brush.

Maus, *f.* (*pl.* **Mäu'se**) mouse; duck, darling; nasal muscle of a horse; thick part of the thumb; hairy mole; **die — pfeift,** the mouse squeaks; **es ist — wie Mutter,** it is six of one and half a dozen of the other, **liebe kleine —,** my dear darling (*coll.*); **wenn die Katze nicht zu Hause ist, tanzen die Mäuse,** when the cat's away the mice will play (*prov.*); **mit Speck fängt man Mäuse,** good bait catches fine fish (*prov.*); **Mäuse im Kopfe,** a bee in your bonnet, crotchets, whims; **Mäuse machen,** to make difficulties; **das ist alles den Mäusen gepfiffen,** that is labour lost; **er soll mir keine Mäuse machen,** he shan't come over me; **da beißt keine** (*or* **die**) **— keinen Faden ab,** nothing of it will be altered, that's settled and done with: **wenn die Mäuse satt sind, dann schmeckt das Mehl bitter,** when the mice have had enough the meal is nasty (*prov.*). **—(s)en,** I. *v.n.* (*aux.* **h.**) to catch mice; (*aux.* **h.** & **s.**) to steal noiselessly about. II. *v.a.* to pilfer, purloin. III. *subst. n.* mousing, mouse-hunting. **—(s)erei',** *f.* pilfering, prigging. **—ig,** *adj.*, mousy, smelling of mice; **wer sich —ig macht, den fressen die Katzen,** he who acts like a mouse will be eaten by the cats (*prov.*) (confused with **—ig** under **Mause**) *Comp.* **—(s)e=falle,** *f.* mouse-trap. **—(s)e=katze,** *f.* mouser; thief. **—(s)e=still,** *adj.* & *adv.* still as a mouse. **—(s)e=tot,** *adj.* as dead as a doornail. **—fahl,** *adj.* mouse-coloured.

Mau'schel, *m.* (**—s,** *pl.* **—**) nickname denoting a Jew (*as term of reproach*). **—n,** *v.n.* (*aux.* **h.**) to act *or* speak like a Jew.

Mäus'chen, Mäus'lein, *n.* little mouse, mousie (*coll.*); **mein —,** little duckie, my darling, my pet, love. **—still,** *adj.* quite hushed; **es ist —still,** one might hear a pin drop.

Mäu'se— (*in comp.*) **—artig,** *adj.* mouselike; murine. **—falk(e),** *m.* buzzard. **—falle,** *f.* mouse-trap. **—fänger,** *m.* mouse-catcher, mouser. **—fraß,** *m.* damage done by mice. — **gift,** *n.* rat's bane, arsenic. **—nester,** *pl.;* **—nester im Kopfe haben,** to be absent-minded. **—ohr,** *n.* small ear (*of a horse*); (**—öhrchen,** *n.*) forget-me-not. **—schwanz,** *m.* mouse's tail; rat's tail (*of hair*). **—turm,** *m.* tower near Bingen in the middle of the Rhine.

Mau'ſ—e, (**Mau'ße,**) **Mau'ſ—er,** (**Mau'ßer,**) *f.* moulting, mewing; moulting season; casting the shell (*of crayfishes*); **in der —er sein,** to be moulting. **—en, —ern,** *v.r.* to cast the skin · to moult; (*of the voice*) to break. **—ig,** *adj.;* **sich —ig machen,** to show off, to give o. s. airs; **mach dich nicht —ig!** none of your airs! *Comp.* **—er=feder,** *f.* shed feather. **—er=kasig,** *m.* mew.

Mau'ser=gewehr, *n.* (—s, *pl.* —e) Mauser rifle (*made by the brothers Mauser*).

Mäu'ſ—erich, *m.* male mouse (*coll.*). **—in,** *f.* female mouse (*coll.*).

Maut, *f.* (*pl.* **—en**) custom, duty; toll; custom-house. **—bar,** *adj.* subject to duty. **—ner,** *m.* (**—ners,** *pl.* **—ner**) customs officer; toll gatherer. *Comp.* **—amt,** *n.* custom-house; board of customs. **—beamte(r),** *m.* customs officer. **—frei,** *adj.* duty-free. **—recht,** *n.* right of toll.

Ma'xim—a, *f.* master-note (*Mus.; obs.*). **—a'l,** *adj.* (*only in compounds*) maximum. **—e,** *f.* (*pron.* **Maxi'me**) (*pl.* **—en**) maxim. *Comp.* **—al'=belastung,** *f.* maximum load. **—al'=gewicht,** *n.* maximum weight. **—al'=thermometer,** *n.* registering-thermometer.

Maxi'm—geschütz, *n.*, **—kanone,** *f.* Maxim (gun); machine gun.

Mayor', *m.* (—s, *pl.* —s) mayor; **Frau des —,** mayoress; **Würde** *or* **Amt des —,** mayorship, mayoralty.

Mecha'n—ik, *f.* (*pl.* **—iken**) mechanics; mechanism. **—iker,** *m.* (**—ikers,** *pl.* **—iker**), **—ikus,** *m.* (*pl.* **—iker**) mechanician. **—isch,** *adj.* & *adv.* mechanical; **—ische(r) Webstuhl,** power-loom; **die —ischte Bewegung,** the most mechanical movement. **—is'mus,** *m.* mechanism.

Me'ckern, *v.n.* (*aux.* **h.**) to bleat; to sing in a trembling *or* tremolo voice.

Medail'l—e, *f.* (*pl.* **—en**) medal; **die Kehrseite der —e,** the dark side of the picture *or* the question; **Inhaber der goldenen —e,** gold medallist. **—o'n,** *n.* (**—ons,** *pl.* **—ons**) medallion; locket. *Comp.* **—en=sammler,** *m.* medallist. **—en=stecher,** *m.* engraver of medals.

Me'di—a, *f.* (*pl.* **—en, —ae**), a voiced stopped consonant, a sonant stop *or* (ex)plosive, (b, d, g); **tonlose —en,** weakly articulated voiced stops.

Media'n— (*in comp.*) **—ader,** *f.* median-vein (*Anat.*). **—folio,** *n.* demi-folio. **—größe,** *f.* median size. **—oktav,** *m.* demi-octavo. **—papier,** *n.* median-paper.

Median'te, *f.* (—n) mediant (*Mus.*).

Mediatisie'ren, *v.a.* to mediatize (*i.e. annex a small state, etc., whilst granting a certain form of home rule to it*).

Medikam—e'nt, *n.* (**—ents,** *pl.* **—en'te**) medicine, medical remedy, drug, physic, medicament.

Me'dikus, *m.* (**—,** *pl.* **Me'dici**) medical man, practitioner, physician; **Doktor —,** medical man, doctor (*coll.*).

Medizi'n, Medici'n, *f.* (*pl.* **—en**) medicine; physic, medicine; **gerichtliche —,** forensic medicine. **—a'l,** *adj.* & *adv.* medicinal. **—er,** *m.* (**—ers,** *pl.* **—er**) medical man; medical student. **—ie'ren,** *v.n.* (*aux.* **h.**) to take medicine; to quack. **—isch,** *adj.* medical; medicinal; **—ische Fakultät,** faculty of medicine. *Comp.* **—al'=behörde,** *f.* board of health. **—al'=gewicht,** *n.* troy-weight. **—al'=rat,** *m. see* **—albehörde;** officer of a board of health; officer of health (*a title given to distinguished German doctors*). **—al'=verordnungen,** *pl.* sanitary regulations. **—al'=waren,** *pl.* medicinal drugs. **—karren,** *m.* medicinal canteen. **—wagen,** *m.* ambulance waggon.

Medull—a'r, —ö's, *adj.* medullary; pithy (*Bot.*).

Medu'ſe, *f.* (*pl.* **—n**) Medusa; jelly-fish.

Meer, *n.* (**—es,** *pl.* **—e**) sea; ocean; **auf dem —e,** (out) at sea, on the sea, on the main; **am —e,** on the seashore; at *or* by the sea-side; **unter dem —e,** submarine; **vom —e bespült,** washed by the sea; **—e zwischen den Wendekreisen,** inter-tropical seas; **das offne —,** the main, the high seas; **auf offenem —e,** on the open sea, on the high seas; **das weite —,** the open sea; **das Schwarze —,** the Black Sea; **das Atlantische —,** the Atlantic (*Ocean*); **das Stille —,** the Pacific. *Comp.* **—artig,** *adj.* sea-like, marine. **—bake,** *f.* buoy, beacon. **—beherrscherin,** *f.* queen of the seas, England. **—beschreibung,** *f.* hydrography. **—boden, —es=boden,** *m.* bottom of the sea. **—busen,** *m.* gulf, bay. **—enge,** *f.* straits, channel. **—es=arm,** *m.* inlet. **—es=brandung,** *f.* surf, breakers. **—es=flut,** *f.* high water; waves of the sea. **—es=küste,** *f.* sea-coast. **—es=schlund,** *m.* abyss of the sea, the deep. **—es=spiegel,** *m.* sea level; **über dem —esspiegel,** above the level of the sea. **—es=stille,** *f.* calm at sea, calmness of the sea; dead calm. **—es=strom,** *m.*, **—es=strömung,** *f.* ocean-current, current of the sea. **—es=woge,** *f.* billow. **—fahrt,** *f.* sea-trip, cruise; sea-voyage. **—farben, —farbig,** *adj.* sea-green. **—ferkel,** *n.* porpoise. **—fräulein,** *n.*, **—frau,** *f.* mermaid, siren. **—gegend,** *f.* maritime region **—gestade,** *n.* sea-coast. **—gott,** *m.* sea-god, water-god, Neptune. **—gras,** *n.* sedge; seaweed. **—greis,** *m.;* **alter —greis,** old fogey, man who has old-fashioned views. **—grün,** *adj.* sea-green. **—hafen,** *m.* sea-port. **—handel,** *m.* maritime trade. **—herrschaft,** *f.* supremacy at sea. **—huhn,** *n.* water-hen. **—igel,** *m.* sea-urchin. **—jungfer,** *f.* mermaid, siren. **—kalb,** *n.* seal. **—kater,** *m.*, **—katze,** *f.* long-tailed monkey. **—kohl,** *m.* sea-kale. **—krähe,** *f.* cormorant. **—leuchten,** *n.* phosphorescence of the sea, phosphoric lights on the sea. **—luft,** *f.* sea-breeze. **—nymphe,** *f.* sea-nymph, nereid. **—pflanze,** *f.* marine plant. **—räuber,** *m.* pirate. **—rettig,** *m.* horse-radish. **—sand,** *m.* sea-sand; (**feiner**) silt. **—schaum,** *m.* sea-froth, sea-foam; meerschaum. **—schaum=kopf,** *m.* meerschaum (-bowl). **—schaum=pfeife,** *f.* meerschaum (-pipe). **—schiff,** *n.* sea-going vessel. **—schildkröte,** *f.* turtle. **—schlund,** *m.* whirlpool, eddy. **—schwalbe,** *f.* tern. **—schwein,** *n.* porpoise. **—schweinchen,** *n.* guinea-pig. **—stadt,** *f.* seaport town. **—straße,** *f.* strait; ship's course *or* track. **—tang,** *m.* sea-weed. **—taufe,** *f.* christening (*of sailors*) on crossing the line. **—umflossen, —umschlossen, —umschlungen,** *adj.* sea-washed, sea-beaten, sea-encircled, sea-girt. **—ungeheuer,** *n.* sea-monster **—wärts,** *adv.* seawards. **—weib,** *n.*, **—weibchen,** *n.* mermaid, siren. **—wunder,** *n.* sea-phenomenon; sea-monster, sea-serpent; wonder, miracle. **—zunge,** *f.* sole (*Icht.*); creek.

Megä're, *f.* (*pl.* **—n**) Megæra; shrew, vixen.

Mehl, *n.* (**—s,** *pl.* **—e**) meal, flour; farina (*Bot.*); dust, powder; **aus — bestehend,** farinaceous. **—icht,** (*obs.*) **—ig,** *adj. see* **—artig.** *Comp.* **—artig,** *adj.* flour-like; mealy; farinaceous. **—beutel,** *m.* bolter, sifter. **—brei,** *m.* meal-pap; flummery. **—faß,** *n.* meal-tub; flour-barrel. **—gebend,** *adj.* farinaceous. **—käfer,** *m.* meal-worm-beetle, tenebris (*Ent.*). —

kasten, *m.* flour-tub. **—kleister,** *m.* paste. —**kloß,** *m.* flour-dumpling. **—loch,** *n.* scuttle (*of a mill*). **—sack,** *m.* flour-sack; **plump wie ein —sack,** lubberly, dumpy person. **—speise,** *f.* farinaceous dish *or* food; **süße —speise (als Nachtisch),** sweets, pudding, pastry. **—staub=artig,** *adj.* farinaceous. **—suppe,** *f.* soup in which flour is mixed; gruel. **—teig,** *m.* dough. **—thau,** *see* **Meltau.** **—wurm,** *m.* meal-worm. **—wurzel,** *f.* yam. **—zucker,** *m.* powdered sugar, ground sugar.

Mehr, I. *ind. num. adj.* (*gen'lly indec. but pl.* **—e,** *now usually* **—ere** = more than one) more; (*pl.*) several, sundry, divers; **— als einer,** more than one; **ich seh' im Busch der kleinen Feuer —,** I see some more little fires in the bushes (*poet.*); **hast du der Freunde —,** have you any more friends? (*poet.*); **—ere schöne Blumen,** several fine flowers; **morgen ein —es,** more of this to-morrow; **—ere Male, zu —eren Malen,** several times; frequently. II. *adv.* more; above, upwards; past; further; besides; longer; rather; **kein Kind —,** no longer a child; **nicht lange —,** not much longer; **kein Wort —!** not another word! **— noch,** what is more, too; **— als zehn Uhr,** past ten; **immer —,** more and more; **er ist es noch —,** he is still more so; **nicht —,** no more, no longer; **um so —,** so much the more; **ja, was noch — ist,** not only so, but in addition; **— groß als klein,** rather tall than short, tallish; **es ist nicht — als billig,** it is only fair; **das thut er nicht — wie gern,** he does not ask better than to do it, he does it gladly; **je — er hat, je — er will, nie schweigen seine Wünsche still,** the more he has the more he wants, he is never satisfied; **je — ich ihm gebe, desto — verlangt er,** the more I give him, the more he asks; **was bringst du —?** what news? **wer noch —?** who else? **was ist's denn nun —?** well? and then? **und dergleichen —,** and more of the same kind, more such, et cetera. III. *n.* (**—es,** *pl.* **—e**) majority; increase; surplus; **es ist ein — von zwanzig gegen zwölf,** there is a majority of eight (*poet.*). *Comp.* **—aufwand,** *m.* additional expenditure; excess of expenditure. **—ausgabe,** *f.* additional *or* increased expenditure; overissue (*Finance*). **—betrag,** *m.* surplus. **—bezahlung,** *f.* surplusage. **—bieter,** *m.* outbidder, higher bidder. **—blätterig,** *adj.* many-leaved, polypetalous. **—blumig,** *adj.* many-flowered. **—deutig,** *adj.* ambiguous. **—deutigkeit,** *f.* ambiguity. **—einnahme,** *f.* increased income, surplus receipts. **—en=teils,** *adv.* for the most part, mostly. **—ere=mal,** *adv.* several times. **—erlei,** *indec. adj.* of more than one kind, various, diverse. **—fach,** *adj.* & *adv.* manifold; several times, more than once. **—fächerig,** *adj.* multilocular. **—forderung,** *f.* increased demand, higher claim. **—gebot,** *n.* outbidding. **—genannt,** *adj.* mentioned *or* named several times, aforesaid. **—gewicht,** *n.* surplus-weight, over-weight, excess-weight. **—gliederig,** *adj.* complex (*Math.*). **—heit,** *f.* majority. **—heits=beschluß,** *m.* decision by a majority; **durch —heitsbeschluß,** by a majority of votes; **wir wurden durch —heitsbeschluß zurückgewiesen,** we were outvoted. **—jährig,** *adj.* several years old. **—lader,** *m.* (*1887*) = **Repetiergewehr.** **—malig,** *adj.* repeated, reiterated. **—mals,** *adv.* again and again; more than once, several times. **—samig,** *adj.* polyspermous. **—seitig,** *adj.* polygonal. **—silbig,** *adj.* polysyllabic; **—silbiges Wort,** polysyllable. **—sitzer,** *m.* multicycle. **—stimmig,** *adj.* for several voices; of several parts; **—stimmige Musik,** music in several parts. **—wert,** *m.* greater value; surplus of value. **—zahl,** *f.* plurality, majority; plural (*Gram.*); **die große —zahl,** the great majority, the bulk; **überwiegende —zahl,** vast majority. **—zahlig,** *adj.* consisting of many numbers; **eine —zahlige Periode,** period of a circulating decimal.

Meh'r—en, *v.* I. *a.* & *r.* to increase, augment; to multiply. II. *a.* & *n.* to decide by majority of votes (*prov.*). **—er,** *m.* (**—ers,** *pl.* **—er**) augmenter, enlarger, increaser; factor (*Arith.*); **allezeit —er des Reichs,** at all times augmenter *or* perpetual enlarger of the Empire (*semper augustus*). **—er, —ere, —eres,** (*obs.*). I. *adj.* (*compar. of* **mehr**) greater; farther; **mit noch —erem Rechte,** with still greater reason. II. *see* **Mehr** I. **—(e)st,** *adj.* & *adv.* (*sup. of* **mehr**) most; **das —ste davon,** the most of it (*obs.* & *vulg.*); **die —sten Stimmen,** majority, most votes (*obs.* & *vulg.*). **—heit,** *f.* majority. **—ung,** *f.* multiplication; augmentation, increase.

Mei'd—en, *ir.v.a.* to avoid, shun, flee from; to reject (*B.*); **einen —en,** to turn away from a p. (*B.*). **—lich,** *adj.* (*in comp.*) avoidable.

Mei'dinger, *m.* stale joke, old and hackneyed story, Joe Miller (*fam.*); chestnut (*sl.*).

Mei'er, *m.* (**—s,** *pl.* **—**) majordomo (*obs.*); steward (*of an estate*); tenant of a (dairy-)farm, (dairy-)farmer. **—ei',** *f.* (dairy-)farm; farmhouse. **—in,** *f.* farmer's *or* steward's wife. *Comp.* **—brief,** *m.* deed of a fee-farm. **—gut,** *n.*, **—hof,** *m. see* **—ei.** **—haus,** *n.* farm-house. **—lehen,** *n.* copyhold. **—zins,** *m.* rent paid for a leasehold farm.

Mei'ern, *v.a.* cheat (*coll.*); **einen —,** to take a person in; to hoax a person (*coll.*).

Mei'le, *f.* (*pl.* **—n**) mile; **englische —,** English mile (*1.609 kilometres*); **deutsche —,** German mile (*7.420 kilometres, about 5 English miles*); **französische —,** league (*4.450 kilometres, about 2.75 English miles*); **geographische —,** geographical *or* nautical mile (*1.816 kilometres* (*Engl.*), *7.420 kilometres* (*Germ.*)). *Comp.* **—n=breit,** *adj.* a mile broad; miles broad. **—n=fern,** *adv.* miles away. **—n=länge,** *f.* length of a mile. **—n=stein,** *m.* mile-stone. **—n=stiefeln,** *pl.* seven-league(d) boots. **—n=weit,** *adv.* for miles. **—n=zeiger,** *m.* mile-stone.

Mei'ler, *m.* (**—s,** *pl.* **—**) charcoal-kiln *or* pile. *Comp.* **—decke,** *f.* turf covering of a charcoal kiln. **—kohle,** *f.* charcoal. **—köhler,** *m.* charcoal-burner.

[1]**Mein,** (**—, —e, —**) I. *poss. adj.* my, mine, **—es teils,** for my part, as for me; **—es Wissens,** so far as I know; **dieser — Sohn,** my son here; **die —en,** my family, friends, people; **das —e,** my duty, my share, my property; **—e vielen Freunde,** my numerous friends. II. *poss. pron.* (*orig. gen.*) mine; **dieses Haus ist —,** this house is mine; **— ist die Schande,** mine is the shame; **steh auf, du Schwester mein,** rise, my sister (*poet.*). III. *old gen. sing. of* **ich; gedenke —,** think of me; **vergiß — nicht,** do not forget me! (*obs.*). IV. *n.* my own, my property; **das — und Dein,** the meum and tuum, what is mine and what is thine. V. *int.* (**ei du — [Gott!]**) oh, pray! really! dear me! good gracious; O my! **—e, (der, die, das —e,) —er, —e, —es, —ige, (der, die, das —ige,)** *poss. pron.* mine; **nicht dein Bruder, sondern —er** *or* **der —ige,** not your brother but mine; **das —ige,** my own, my duty, my share, my property; **die —(ig)en,** my friends, my family; **ich habe das —ige gethan,** I have done my part *or* duty. **—er,** *see* **Mein** III.; **erbarme dich —er,** have pity upon me; **ich war —er nicht mehr mächtig,** I had lost control over myself. *Comp.* **—er=seits,** *adv.* for my part; in my turn. **—es=gleichen,** *indec. adj. or pron.* my equals, such as I. **—et=**

halben, —et=wegen, —et=willen, *adv.* for my sake; so far as I am concerned; for aught I care.

²Mein, (*in comp.* =) false; mean. —eid, *m.* false oath, perjury; einen —eid leisten *or* schwören, to perjure oneself, to commit perjury; fahrlässiger —eid, involuntary perjury caused by gross carelessness. —eidig, *adj.* perjured; —eidig werden, to commit perjury, to perjure o. s.; der —eidige, perjurer. —eidigkeit, *f.* perjury. —friede, *m.* false, hollow peace (*obs.*). —kauf, *m.* fraudulent purchase (*obs.*).

Mei'n—en, *v.a. & n.* (*aux.* h.) to be of opinion, think, suppose; to mean, purpose; to deem fitting; to signify; to love, be fond of (*obs.*); das will ich —en, I should think so indeed, of course, to be sure; ja, —te er, wenn . . ., yes, said he, if . . .; man sollte —en, er wäre närrisch, one would think he was a fool; wenn Sie es so —en, if you look at it in that way, if you put it on that ground; nun, wenn Sie —en, well, if you think proper; wenn Sie es wirklich so —en, if that is really what you mean, if that is truly your opinion; was —en Sie dazu? what do you think of it? was —en Sie damit? what do you mean by that? damit sind Sie gemeint, that is meant for you; ich —e nicht *or* bin nicht gemeint zu . . ., I do not intend to . . .; er —t es gut, he means well; die Sonne —t es gut, the sun is very hot (*coll.*); er —te Wunder, was er thäte, he thought he was doing great things, acting most generously; es böse mit einem —en, to mean no good to a p.; to be not well disposed towards a p.; wohl—end, well disposed, well intentioned; —en Sie? do you say so? do you think so? Freiheit, die ich —e, Freedom that I love (*poet.*); die Holde, die ich —e, the fair one, whom I love (*poet.*). —ung, *f.* thought; opinion, notion; meaning, signification; intention; will; meiner —ung nach, to my thinking; jemandes —ung teilen, to share *or* agree with s. o.'s opinion; einem anderen eine bessere —ung von einem beibringen, to make a p. think better of s. o. else; einem seine —ung sagen, to give a person a bit of one's mind; die öffentliche —ung, public opinion; vorgefaßte —ung, preconceived opinion, prejudice; eine zu gute —ung von sich haben, to have too favourable an opinion of oneself, to be conceited. *Comp.* —ungs=austausch, *m.* interchange of ideas; comparing notes. —ungs=äußerung, *f.* expression of opinion. —ungs=genoß, *m.* partisan; one who holds the same opinions. —ungs=streit, *m.* conflict of opinion. —ungs=verschiedenheit, *f.* diversity of opinion, divergence of views; dissension, disagreement. —ungs=wechsel, *m.* change of opinion *or* mind.

Meira'n, *see* Majoran.

Mei'se, *f.* (*pl.* —n) titmouse, tomtit.

Meist, I. *adj.* (*sup. of* mehr) most; die —en, most people; die —en Schüler lesen gut, most of the pupils read well; die —en Stimmen bejahen, the Ayes have it; seine —e Zeit, most of his time; das —e, the most (*part*). II. *adv.* am —en, most of all, for the most part, mostly; der Tüchtige ist am —en bereit das Verdienst anderer anzuerkennen, those who excel are most ready to acknowledge the merit of others. —ens, —en=teils, *adv.* generally, usually, mostly, as a rule; ich bin —ens um sechs Uhr zu Hause, I am generally in at six o'clock; es waren —ens noch ganz junge Leute, they were for the most part very young people. *Comp.* —begünstigungs=klausel, *f.* most-favoured-nation clause. —begünstigungs=vertrag, *m.* commercial treaty on the basis of the most favoured nation. —betrag, *m.* maximum amount. —bietend, *adj.* bidding highest; —bietend verkaufen, to sell to the highest bidder, to sell by auction. —bietende(r), *m.* highest bidder. —gebot, *n.* best offer, highest bid.

Mei'ster, *m.* (—s, *pl.* —) master, chief, boss (*Amer.*), leader; teacher; freeman; master-workman; master (*as title*); — in einer S. sein, to excel in s. th.; einen zum — machen, to make s. o. free of a company; — vom Stuhl, master of the lodge; seiner Gefühle — werden, to restrain one's feelings; er hat in ihm seinen — gefunden, he has met with his match in him; — Gottfried von Straßburg, Master Gottfried of Strasburg; Ihr seid ein — Steuermann, you are a well tried *or* professional helmsman; — Hämmerlein, Jack Ketch; ein — im Schießen, a crack shot; Übung macht den —, practice makes perfect (*prov.*); kein — fällt vom Himmel, no man is born a master of his craft (*prov.*). —haft, I. *adj.* masterly; skilful. II. *adv.* in a masterly manner. —haftigkeit, *f.* mastery; masterliness. —in, *f.* mistress, master's wife, wife of a master-tradesman; Herr — und Frau —in, my dear master and mistress. —lich, *see* —haft. —schaft, *f.* mastery, eminent skill; freedom (*of a guild, etc.*); body of masters of a lodge *or* of a trade-guild; championship; um die —schaft streiten, to compete for the championship. *Comp.* —arbeit, *f.* masterly performance. —bild, *n.* masterly picture *or* portrait. —dieb, *m.* expert thief. —druck, *m.* masterly touch (*Paint.*). —genossenschaft, *f.* trades union; guild. —gesang, *m.* song of a Meistersinger. —gesell, *m.* foreman; master-journeyman. —grad, *m.* Master's degree, degree of M. A.; grade of Master (*Freem.*); freedom (*of a guild*). —hand, *f.* master's hand. —lauge, *f.* caustic lye. —lied, *n.* song of a mastersinger, composed according to the strict rules of the mastersingers. —recht, *n.* freedom of a company. —sänger, —singer, *m.* mastersinger, German poet belonging to a guild mostly composed of masters of trades (*esp'lly in the XV-XVI centuries*). —spieler, *m.* virtuoso; champion. —streich, *m.* masterly stroke. —stück, *n.* masterpiece. —stuhl, *m.* grand master's chair (*Freem.*). —ton, *m.* melody of a song by a mastersinger. —werk, *n.* masterly work; sein —werk, his greatest work, his highest achievement, his supreme effort, chef d'œuvre. —zug, *m.* master-stroke.

Mei'ster—n, *v.* I. *a.* to master; to rule, control; to censure, find fault with; to excel (in); sie —ten Gott, they spake against God (*B.*). II. *n.* (*aux.* h.) to play the (school)master. —er, *m.* (—ers, *pl.* —er) carping critic, one who sets up for a master; vanquisher.

Mei'ßel, I. *m.* (—s, *pl.* —) chisel. II. *m.* (—s, *pl.* —) & *f.* (*pl.* —n) plug of lint, pledget (*Surg.*). —n, *v.a.* to chisel.

Melancholie', *f.* melancholy.

Melancho'liker, *m.* (*pl.* —) person of a melancholy temperament.

Melancho'lisch, *adj.* melancholy.

Melas'se, *f.* (*pl.* —n) molasses, treacle.

Mel'd—en, *v.* I. *a.* to announce; to inform, apprize of, notify; to report; to send (a p.) word, to recount, tell; to mention; einen —en, to announce a person; to report a p.; den Empfang eines Briefes —en, to acknowledge the receipt of a letter; Sie haben zu —en, it is your turn to say (*how many points, etc. at cards*); mit Ehren zu —en, saving your presence; er bedrohte sie, daß sie ihn nicht —eten, he charged them that they should not make him known (*B.*); ohne Ruhm zu —en, be it said without vanity. II. *r.* to announce oneself; to come forward, make a claim (*of creditors*); to report oneself (*Mil.*); **sich —en lassen,** to send in one's name *or* card, have one's coming announced; **bitte, —en Sie mich dem Herrn Doktor,** please tell the doctor that I am here; **sich —en zu einer S.** *or* **für eine S.,** to apply for a th.; **sich zu einer Prüfung —en,** to have one's name entered for an examination; **man muß sich zeitig —en,** early application is desirable *or* necessary; **der Winter —et sich dies Jahr zeitig,** winter is setting in early this year. **—er,** *m.* (**—ers,** *pl.* **—er**) announcer, informer. **—ung,** *f.* advice, notice, notification; announcement; report; **—ung thun,** to notify, to give information; to make mention of. *Comp.* **—e=amt,** *n.* information office; office for registration. **—e=brief,** *m.* letter of advice. **—ens=wert,** *adj.* & *adv.* worth reporting *or* mentioning. **—e=reiter,** *m.* mounted orderly. **—e=schiff,** *n.* advice *or* despatch boat. **—e=stelle (für Feuersbrünste),** *f.* fire (brigade) station. **—e=zettel,** *m.* registration form.

Melie'r—en, *v.a.* to mix, mingle; to shuffle. **—t,** *p.p.* & *adj.* variegated, mixed; **grau —t,** mixed with gray, pepper and salt (*coll.*).

Melini't, *n.* (**—s**) melinite (*Chem.*).

Meliorie'ren, *v.a.* to ameliorate.

Me'lis, (**—zucker,**) *m.* (*coarse*) loaf-sugar.

Melis'se, *f.* (*pl.* **—n**) balm, balm-mint.

Melk, *adj.* milch. **—en,** *reg.* & *ir.v.* I. *a.* to milk; to drain, impoverish; **frisch gemolkene Milch,** new(-drawn) milk. II. *n.* (*aux.* **h.**) to give milk. **—er,** m. (**—ers,** *pl.* **—er**) milker. **—erei',** *f.* milking, dairy. *Comp.* **—eimer,** *m.*, **—gefäß,** *n.* milk-pail. **—kübel,** *m.* milking-tub. **—schemel,** *m.* milking stool. **—tuch,** *n.* strainer. **—vieh,** *n.* cattle giving milk. **—zeit,** *f.* milking time.

Mel'nicker, Mel'necker, *m.* excellent Bohemian wine (*from Melnik*).

Melod—ie', *f.* (*pl.* **—i'en**) melody, tune, air.

Melo'disch, *adj.* melodious.

Melodra'm—(a), *n.* (**—(a)s,** *pl.* **—en**) melodrama. **—a'tisch,** *adj.* melodramatic.

Melo'ne, *f.* (*pl.* **—n**) melon. *Comp.* **—n=kürbis,** *m.* squash, pumpkin.

Mel'tau, *m.* (**—s**) mildew, blight; rust.

Mem'me, *f.* coward, poltroon. **—rei',** *f.* cowardice.

Memoi'renschreiber, *m.* writer of memoirs.

Memor—abi'lien, *pl. see* **Denkwürdigkeiten.** **—ia'l,** *n.* (**—ials,** *pl.* **—iale**) memorial; day-book (*C. L.*); **(einem) ein —ial einreichen,** to present a memorial to s.o., to petition s.o., to memorialize a p. *or* a body. **—ie'ren,** *v.a.* & *n.* (*aux.* **h.**) to commit to memory, to learn by heart; **haben Sie Ihre Rolle gut —iert?** do you know your part thoroughly? *Comp.* **—an'den=buch,** *n.* note-book. **—ial'=buch,** *n.* day-book, memorandum-book (*C. L.*). **—ier'=stoff,** *m.* matter to be committed to memory (*esp'lly in schools*).

Mena'ge, *f.* (*pl.* **—n**) household; set of dishes; **Platt —,** (set of) casters.

Menagerie', *f.* (*pl.* **—en**) menagerie. **—wagen,** *m.* travelling menagerie.

Menagie'ren, *v.a.* to manage, to treat with consideration; to economize, save; **sich —,** to moderate *or* restrain oneself.

Men'ge, *f.* (*pl.* **—n**) great quantity *or* number; multitude, crowd; mass; **die große —,** the masses, the multitude; the million; **in großer —,** in abundance, abundantly; **eine — Geld, Geld die —** *or* **in —,** plenty of money, lots of money (*coll.*); **eine — Bücher,** a great many books; **Freunde die —,** scores of friends; **eine große — Wasser,** a large body of water; **Wein die schwere —,** no end of wine; **die — muß es bringen,** numbers must do it (*prov.*), **die Kunst ist keine Dienerin der —,** Art is no handmaid to the multitude.

Men'g—en, *v.a.* to mix, mingle, blend (**unter eine S., mit einer S.,** with a th.); to shuffle; **sich —en,** to concern o.s. about, meddle with, interfere in; **sich unter die Zuschauer —en,** to mix with the crowd (*of spectators*); **er —t sich in alles,** he meddles with everything; he is a busy-body. **—er,** *m.* (**—ers,** *pl.* **—er**) mingler, mixer. **—erei',** *f.* mingling, mixing; mixture; confusion. **—sel,** *n.* (**—sels**) medley; mess, hodge-podge. *Comp.* **—futter,** *n.*, **—korn,** *m.* mash; mixed grain *or* food. **—gestein,** *n.* conglomerate (*Geol.*). **—werk,** *n.* medley.

Men'nig, Men'ning, *m.* (**—s**) minium, red lead; **gelber —,** chrome yellow.

Men(n)oni't, *m.* (**—en,** *pl.* **—en**) Mennonite, Mennonitist (*member of a religious sect*).

Mensch, I. *m.* (**—en,** *pl.* **—en**) human being, man, person; (*pl.*) people, the world, mankind; **kein —,** nobody, not a soul; **eine Menge —en,** a crowd of people; **es wohnen 10,000 —en in dieser Stadt,** this town has 10,000 inhabitants; **einzelner —,** individual; **der — gewordene Gott,** God incarnate; **des —en Sohn,** the son of man, Christ; **unter die —en kommen,** to see something of the world, mix in society; **einen neuen —en anziehen,** to change one's ways completely, to turn over a new leaf; **zum ordentlichen —en machen,** to make a respectable person, to humanize, to lead into the paths of respectability; **der — denkt, Gott lenkt,** man proposes, God disposes (*prov.*). II. *n.* (**—es,** *pl.* **—er**) woman; wench; hussy. **—heit,** *f.* human nature, humanity; the world, mankind. **—lein,** *n.* (**—leins,** *pl.* **—lein**) little (bit of a) man. **—lich,** *adj.* & *adv.* human; humane; well-bred; respectable; **irren ist —lich,** to err is human (*prov.*); **—lich gesprochen,** humanly speaking; **—lich machen,** to humanize; **etwas —liches begehen,** to be guilty of a human weakness, to make a slip; **es ist ihm 'was —liches begegnet,** he has erred; he has died, he has gone the way of all flesh. **—lichkeit,** *f.* humanity, human nature; humanity, humaneness. *Comp.* **—en=affen,** *pl.* apes resembling man, anthropomorphous apes. **—en=ähnlich,** *adj.* like man, human, anthropomorphous. **—en=alter,** *n.* generation, age. **—en=antlitz,** *n.* human face *or* countenance. **—en=art,** *f.* race of men, kind *or* species of man; **das ist —enart,** such are men, such is human nature. **—en=bildung,** *f.* civilization; creation of man. **—en=blut,** *n.* human blood. **—en=dieb,** *m.* kidnapper. **—en=familie,** *f.* the human race. **—en=feind,** *m.* enemy to mankind; misanthropist. **—en=feindlich,** *adj.* misanthropic. **—en=fressend,** *adj.* anthropophagous. **—en=fresser,** *m.* man-eater, cannibal. **—fresserei',** *f.* cannibalism, anthropophagy. **—en=freund,** *m.* philanthropist. **—en=freundlichkeit,** *f.* affability, sociability; philanthropy. **—en=gedenken,** *n.* memory of man; **seit —engedenken,** from time immemorial. **—en=geschlecht,** *n.* human race, mankind. **—en=gestalt,** *f.* human shape. **—en=gewühl,** *n.* throng of men, large crowd. **—en=händler,** *m.* slave-dealer; kidnapper. **—en=haß,** *m.* misanthropy. **—en=heil,** *n.* welfare *or* salvation of mankind. **—en=herz,** *n.* human heart. **—en=kenner,** *m.* one who knows mankind, keen observer of human nature, psychologist. **—en=kind,** *n.* human being; **aber —en=kind, besinnen Sie sich doch!** but my dear fellow, please remember! (*coll.*); **ein sonderbares —enkind,** a queer fellow *or* fish. **—en=kraft,** *f.* human strength. **—en=kunde,** *f.* anthronology. **—en=kunst,** *f.* human skill.

—en=leben, *n.* human life; life of man. —en=leer, *adj.* deserted. —en=liebe, *f.* philanthropy, charity; love of men; human love. —en=menge, *f.* crowd. —en=mög'lich, *adj.* within human power (*often used emphatically instead of* möglich). —en=mög'lichkeit, *f.* possibility; es war keine —enmöglichkeit durch die Menge durchzukommen, there was not the slightest chance of getting through that crowd. —en=mörder, *m.* murderer; homicide. —en=opfer, *n.* human sacrifice. —en=pack, *n.* rabble, low people. —en=pflicht, *f.* duty of man. —en=recht, *n.* right of man, right of humanity; human law. —en=reich, *adj.* populous. —en=satzung, *f.* human institution. —en=scheu, *adj.* unsociable; misanthropic. —en=schinder, *m.* extortioner. —en=schlag, *m.* race of men. —en=seele, *f.* soul of men; es war keine —enseele zu erblicken, not a living soul was to be seen. —en=troß, *m.* crowd. —en=verstand, *m.* human understanding; (gesunder) common sense. —en=volk, *n.* mankind, people. —en=witz, *m.* cleverness *or* artfulness of man. —en=wohl, *n.* human weal. —en=würde, *f.* dignity of man *or* of human nature. —en=würdig, *adj.* worthy of a human being.

Menstruie'ren, *v.n.* (*aux.* h. & s.) to menstruate.

Mensu'r, *f.* (*pl.* —en) measure; mensuration; proper distance between two duellists (*Fenc.*); fencing ground; students' duel; measure (*Mus., Danc.*); diapason, standard size and thickness (*of organ-pipes, etc.*); auf die — gehen, *or* auf der — stehen, to fight a student's duel *or* duels. *Comp.* —al'=gesang, *m.* rhythmic chant.

Menue'tt, *n.* (—s, *pl.* —s & —e) & (*obs.*) *f.* (*pl.* —en) minuet.

Mephi'tisch, *adj.* mephitic, pestilential.

Mer'gel, *m.* (—s) marl. —ig, *adj.* marly. —n, *v.a.* to manure with marl. *Comp.* —ablagerung, *f.* bed of marl. —boden, *m.* marly soil.

Merk, *m.* (—es, *pl.* —e) mark (*dial.*).

Merk'bar, *adj. & adv.* noticeable, sensible; evident.

Mer'k—en, *v.a. & n.* (*aux.* h.) to mark, note, observe; to take a note of; to bear in mind; to mark, stamp; to perceive; sich (*dat.*) etwas —en, to remember; sich (*dat.*) etwas —en lassen, to show s. th., betray a feeling of s. th.; dabei sollt ihr —en, daß . . ., hereby ye shall know that . . .; sich (*dat.*) nichts —en lassen, to take no notice, seem to know nothing of a thing; einem etwas —en lassen, to intimate (*obs.*); —e wohl! wohlgemerkt! now mark! observe! take notice! mark me! auf eine S. *or* einen —en, to pay attention to a th. *or* a p.; er wird es nicht —en, he will never be any the wiser; ich —e wohl, daß . . ., I perceive very well, I am quite aware that . . .; ich —te, wo er hinaus wollte. I knew what was coming or what he was driving at. —er, *m.* (—ers, *pl.* —er) marker, noter; observer; critic; judge, censurer (*of the old mastersingers*); faculty of observation; den richtigen —er haben, to be quick in observing. —lich, *see* —bar; ein sehr —licher Unterschied, a very marked difference. *Comp.* —buch, —büchlein, *n.*, notebook, memorandum-book. —eisen, *n.* stamp. —ens=wert, *adj & adv.* remarkable. —e=wohl, *n.* a nota-bene. —mal, *n.* sign, mark; characteristic; symptom. —pfahl, *m.* signpost. —satz, *m* maxim. —wort, *n.* cue. —würdig, *adj. & adv.* remarkable; noticeable, noteworthy; —würdiger Weise hat er . . ., the strange thing is that he has . . . —würdigkeit, *f.* remarkableness; curiosity; lion (*coll.*); salient point. —zeichen, *n.* mark; characteristic; memorandum; stamp.

Merku'r, *m.* (—s) mercury; Mercury.

Mer'le, *f.* (*pl.* —n) blackbird.

Merz, *obs. spelling of* März.

Merz—en, *v.a.* to reject (*obs.*) *see* Ausmerzen. —vieh, *n.* culls, cattle which are rejected.

Meschug'ge, *invar.adj.* not in his right mind, silly, foolish, cracked (*sl.*).

Mesmer—isie'ren, *v.a.* to mesmerize. —is'=mus, *m.* (—ismus) mesmerism.

Mes'ner (*less good:* Meß'ner), *m.* (—s, *pl.* —) sacristan, sexton; priest celebrating mass.

Mes'se, *f.* (*pl.* —n) mass; fair; fairing; hohe —, high *or* grand mass; stille —, low mass; in die — gehen *or* — hören, to go to mass; die — lesen, to say *or* celebrate mass; die — besuchen *or* beziehen, to attend the fair; die — beschicken, to send goods to the fair.

Meß— (*from* Messe *in both senses; in comp.*) — amt, *n.* celebration of mass. —brief, *m.* bill of exchange payable at a fair. —buch, *n.* missal, mass-book; catalogue of books sent to a fair; merchant's ledger for business done at a fair. —bude, *f.* stall at a fair. —diener, *m.* priest's attendant at mass. —freiheit, *f.* privilege of holding a fair. —fremde(r), *m.* visitor at a fair. —geld, *n.* money taken at a fair; stallage. —gerät, *n.* ornaments and utensils used in celebrating mass. —geschenk, *n.* fairing. —gewand, *n.* priest's vestment, stole, chasuble. —glocke, *f.*, —glöcklein, *n.* bell calling to mass, sacring bell. —gut, *n.* goods sent to *or* bought at a fair. —hemd, *n.* alb, alba. —katalog, *m.* list of new publications (*issued at the great Leipzig fair before the beginning of the publishing season*). —opfer, *n.* sacrifice of the mass. —priester, *m.* mass-priest. —pult, *n.* lectern, mass-book desk. —stand, *m.* booth at a fair. —tuch, *n.* corporale, communion cloth. —wein, *m.* wine used at mass. —woche, *f.* fair-week. —zeit, *f* fair-time.

Mes's—en, I. *ir.v.n.* (*aux.* h.) to measure; to hold, contain. II. *ir.v.a.* to measure; to scan; to survey; to compare; mit der Elle —en, to measure by the ell *or* yard; nach der Wasserwage —en, to level; den Körperinhalt —en, to gauge; sich —en mit, to compete with; sich mit einem nicht —en können, to be no match for a p.; er maß mich vom Scheitel bis zur Sohle, he eyed me from top to toe. III. *subst. n.* measuring; admeasurement; mensuration; survey. —er, *m.* (—ers, *pl.* —er) measurer; surveyor; (*suffix in comp.* =) -meter, *e.g.* Gas—er, gasometer, gas meter. —ung, *f. see* III. —en.

Meß'—bar, *adj.* measurable. —barkeit, *f.* measurability. *Comp.* (*connected with* messen) —band, *n.* measuring tape. —brief, *m.* certificate of admeasurement (*of a ship's tonnage*). —fahne, *f.* surveyor's flag. —geld, *n.* money paid for measuring; metage. —geschirr, *n.* any measuring-instrument. —holz, *n.* measuring rod, fathom. —kanne, *f.* liquid-measure. —kette, *f.* surveyor's chain. —kunst, —lehre, *f.* surveying; practical geometry. —leine, *f.* measuring-line. —rute, *f.* mete-yard, surveyor's rod. —scheibe, *f.* sextant, quadrant. —tisch, *m.* surveyor's table.

Mes'ser, *n.* (—s, *pl.* —) knife; das große — führen, to draw the long bow; das — sitzt ihm an der Kehle, he is put to his last shift; Krieg bis aufs —, war to the knife. *Comp.* —bänkchen, *n.*, —bock, *m.*, —böckchen, *n.* knife-rest. —besteck, *n.* knife-case. —heft, *n.* knife handle. —held, *m.* rowdy. —klinge, *f.* blade of a knife. —scheide, *f.* knife-sheath. —schmied, *m.* cutler. —schmiede=ware, *f.* cutlery. —spitze, *f.* point of a knife. —stich, *m.* thrust *or* stab with a knife.

Messi'—as, *m.* Messiah. —a'de, *f.* (*pl.* —aden) epic poem about the Messiah.

Mes'sing, *n.* (—s, *pl.* —e) brass. **—en**, *adj.* brazen, of brass. *Comp.* **—artig**, *adj.* brassy. **—blech**, *n.* sheet-brass. **—draht**, *m.* brass wire. **—geschirr**, *n.* kitchen utensils of brass. **—hütte**, *f.*, **—werk**, *n.* brass foundry. **—schmied**, *m.* brazier. **—ware**, *f.* brass ware.
Mesti'ze, *m.* (—n, *pl.* —n) mestizo, mestino (*child of a white man and a red Indian*).
Met, *m.* (—(e)s, *pl.* —e) mead.
Meta'll, *n.* (—(e)s, *pl.* —e) metal; timbre (*of the voice*); **edle —e**, *pl.* precious metals; **unedle —e**, base metals. **—en**, *adj.* metal; brass. **—isch**, *adj.* metallic; **—ischer Beigeschmack**, money, cash (*accompanying a letter, a request, etc.*) (*coll.*). **—u'rg**, *m.* (—ur'gen, *pl.* —ur'gen) metallurgist. *Comp.* **—arbeiter**, *m.* worker in metals; metallist. **—bildung**, *f.* metallization. **—farbe**, *f.* bronze colour. **—geld**, *n.* specie. **—glanz**, *m.* metallic lustre. **—kunde**, *f.* metallurgy. **—probe**, *f.* assay. **—versetzung**, *f.* alloy, alloying. **—vorrat**, *m.* (**der Bank**), bullion (of the bank) **—waren**, *pl.* hardware.
Meta—morpho'se, *f.* (*pl.* —morphosen) metamorphosis. **—pher**, *f.* (*pron.* **Meta'pher**) metaphor. **—physi'k**, *f.* metaphysics. **—phy'siker**, *m.* (—physikers, *pl.* —physiker) metaphysician.
Meteo'r, *n.* (—s, *pl.* —e) meteor. **—olo'g**, *m.* (—ologen, *pl.* —ologen) meteorologist. *Comp.* **—eisen**, *n.* meteoric iron. **—stein**, *m.* aerolite, meteoric stone. **—stern**, *m.* shooting star.
Me'ter, *n.* (*also m.*) (—s, *pl.* —) metre; **nach —n messen**, to measure by metres. **—kilogramm**, *n.* kilogram-metre. **—system**, *n.* metric system. **—weise**, *adv.* by the metre *or* by the yard.
Metho'd—e, *f.* (*pl.* —en) method; way, manner; mode. **—ik**, *f.* theory of method. **—iker**, *m.* student of method, master of method. **—isch**, *adj.* methodical. **—i'st**, *m.* Methodist. *Comp.* **—en=lehre**, *f.* methodology. **—is'ten=lehre**, *f.* Methodism. **—is'ten=prediger**, *m.* Methodist preacher. **—is'tisch**, *adj.* methodistical.
Me'tr—ik, *f.* versification; prosody; theory of metre. **—isch**, *adj. & adv.* metrical. **—um**, *n.* (—ums, *pl.* —a) metre.
Metrono'm, *n.* (—s, *pl.* —e) metronome.
[1]**Met'te**, *f.* (*pl.* —n) matins; early morning service. *Comp.* **—n=glöcklein**, *n.* matins-bell.
[2]**Met'te**, *f.* (*pl.* —n) gossamer (*prov.*).
Mett'wurst, *f.* (*pl.* **Mettwürste**) Bologna sausage.
[1]**Met'ze**, *f.* (*pl.* —n) Matty, Tilly; prostitute (*vulg.*).
[2]**Met'z—e**, *f.* (*pl.* —en) dry measure (*no longer in use, generally* = .67 *of a Scheffel or 3.44 litre*); peck; miller's fee, multure. **—en**, *v.n.* (*aux.* **h.**) to take the fee for grinding. **—ner**, *m.* (—ners, *pl.* —ner) miller's man who takes the multure. *Comp.* **—en=weise**, *adv.* by pecks. **—korn**, *n.* multure, miller's fee.
Metz—elei', *f.* (*pl.* —eleien) massacre; butchery. **—eln**, *v.a.* to butcher; to massacre. **—ge**, **—ig**, *f.* shambles. **—gen**, *see* **—eln**. **—ger**, *m.* (—gers, *pl.* —ger) butcher (*dial.*). *Comp.* **—el=bank**, *f.* shambles. **—el=suppe**, *f.* pudding broth, sausage soup.
Meuch—elei', *f.* (*pl.* —eleien) plot, conspiracy. **—eln**, *v.a.* to plot, conspire; to assassinate. **—ler**, *m.* (—lers, *pl.* —ler) conspirer; assassin. **—lerisch**, *adj.* treacherous. **—lings**, *adv.* like an assassin, treacherously. *Comp.* **—el=mord**, *m.* assassination. **—el=mörder**, *m.* assassin. **—el=mörderisch**, *adj.* assassin-like; dastardly. **—el=rotte**, *f.* band of assassins.
Meu'te, *f.* (*pl.* —n) pack of hounds.
Meuterei', *f.* (*pl.* —en) mutiny, riot; **— machen**, to mutiny.
Meu'ter—er, *m.* (—ers, *pl.* —er) mutineer. **—isch**, *adj.* mutinous. **—n**, *v.a.* to mutiny.

Miau'en, *v.n.* (*aux.* **h.**) to mew; to caterwaul.
Mich, *acc. of* **ich**, me; **— selbst**, myself.
Michae'lis, *n.* (**—tag**, *m.*) Michaelmas (*day*) **zu** *or* **auf —**, at Michaelmas.
Mied, **Mie'de**, *1 (& 3) p. sing. imperf. indic. & subj. of* **meiden**.
Mie'der, *n.* (—s, *pl.* —) bodice, corset-like bodice; chemisette, vest.
Mie'ne, *f.* (*pl.* —n) mien, look, expression; countenance; air, bearing; **die — haben**, to look, appear; **sich** (*dat.*) **die — geben als ob**, to affect to; **— machen**, to look as if, seem, threaten; **der Feind machte — uns anzugreifen**, the enemy showed signs of attacking us; **eine saure —**, a frown; **eine dreiste —**, an air of assurance; **er verzog keine —**, his countenance remained unaltered, he did not betray the slightest emotion; **sie hat in der Wirklichkeit viel zu leiden, aber äußerlich verzieht sie keine —**, she really suffers a great deal, but she does not show it; **gute — zum bösen Spiele machen**, to make the best of a bad bargain; to make a virtue of necessity; what can't be cured must be endured. *Comp.* **—n=deuter**, **—n=forscher**, *m.* physiognomist. **—n=kunde**, *f.* science of physiognomics. **—n=spiel**, *n.*, **—n=sprache**, *f.* pantomime, dumb show; exchange of looks; play of expression; **—n und Gebärdenspiel**, by-play (*of an actor*).
Mies, *adj.* (*coll.*) weakly; out of sorts; poor; **das Wetter ist sehr —**, the weather is very poor. *Comp.* **—(s)e=peter**, *m.* weakling. **—(s)e=katze**, *f.* puss. **—(s)e=petrig**, *adj.* seedy, not up to much. **—(s)e=petrigkeit**, *f.*; **seine Miesepetrigkeit wird er nicht los**, he cannot shake off *or* get rid of his squeamishness.
Mies'muschel, *f.* (*pl.* —n) edible mussel.
[1]**Mie'te**, *f.* (*pl.* —n) mite.
[2]**Mie'te**, *f.* (*pl.* —n) stack, shock, rick.
[3]**Mie't—e**, *f.* (*pl.* —n) pay; hiring, renting, hire; rent; **fällige —e**, rent payable; **die — ist heute fällig**, the rent falls due to-day; **rückständige —**, arrears of rent; **in der —e haben**, to have on hire, hold on lease; **in die —e geben**, to let out; **in die —e nehmen**, to hire, rent; **die —e aufsagen**, to give notice *or* warning; **zur —e wohnen**, to be a lodger *or* tenant. **—ling**, *m.* (—lings, *pl.* —linge) mercenary, hireling. *Comp.* **—(s)=bedingung**, *f.* terms of hire *or* lease. **—besitz**, *m.* tenancy. **—frei**, *adj.* rent-free. **—fuhre**, *f.* hired vehicle. **—(s)=geld**, *n.* earnest; rent. **—herr**, *m.* landlord; tenant; lodger. **—kaserne**, *f.* large house in which there are many lodgings. **—(s)=kontrakt**, *m.* lease; agreement. **—kutsche**, *f.* hackney-coach; hired carriage. **—(s)=leute**, *pl.* lodgers. **—lings=schar**, *f.* troop of mercenaries. **—(s)=lohn**, *m.* hire; servants' wages. **—(s)=mann**, *m.* lodger. **—pferd**, *n.* job-horse. **—steuer**, *f.* (communal) tax upon rents (*in a few German towns*). **—(s)=truppen**, *pl.* mercenaries. **—(s)=vertrag**, *see* **—kontrakt**. **—zettel**, *m.* bill, card (*of lodgings, etc., 'to let'*). **—zins**, *m.* rent.
Miet—en, *v.a.* to hire; to rent; to engage *or* take (*a cab*); to charter (*a ship*). **—er**, *m.* (—ers, *pl.* —er) hirer; tenant, lodger, lessee. **—ung**, *f.* hiring, renting.
Mie'ze, *f.* (*pl.* —n, *dim.* **Miez'chen**) pussy, puss; *see Index of Proper Names.*
Migrä'ne, *f.* (*pl.* —n) sick headache. *Comp.* **—stift**, *m.* headache pencil.
Mikro'be, *m. & f.* (—n, *pl.* —n) microbe.
Mikro—kos'mus, *m.* microcosm. **—lo'g**, *m.* (—logen, *pl.* —logen) punctilious person; collector of trifles *or* nick-nacks. **—pho'n**, *n.* microphone. **—sko'p**, *n.* (—skops, *pl.* —skope) microscope. **—sko'pisch**, *adj.* microscopic.

—skopisch untersuchen, to examine under the microscope.

Mil'be, f. (pl. —n) mite; voller —n, mity.

Milch, f. milk; milt, soft roe; juice (Bot.); emulsion; saure —, geronnene —, dicke —, curdled milk, sour milk; abgerahmte —, skimmed milk; die — ist sauer geworden, the milk has turned sour; wie — und Blut, like cream and roses. —en, v.n. (aux. h.) to give milk. —er, m. (—ers, pl. —er) milter, soft-roe(d) fish, male fish; soft roe, milt of a fish. —erei', f. dairy. —haft, —icht, (obs.) —ig, adj. milky; in the form of an emulsion. —ner, see —er. Comp. —ader, f. lacteal vein. —ähnlich, —artig, adj. lacteal. —bart, m. downy beard; beardless youth; greenhorn, milk-sop. —brei, m. milk-pap. —brot, —brötchen, n. French roll. —bruder, m. foster-brother. —drüse, f. lacteal gland. —ferkel, n. sucking pig. —fieber, n. lacteal fever. —frau, f. woman who sells milk, dairy-woman. —gebend, adj. lacteal. —gefäß, n. milk vessel; lacteal vessel. —gesicht, n. whey-face, muffin-face. —glas, n. milk-glass, opalescent glass. —haltig, adj. lactiferous. —kaffee, m. coffee with milk. —kammer, f., —keller, m. dairy. —kuh, f. milch cow. —kur, f. milk diet (as cure). —magd, f. dairy-maid, milk-maid. —mann, m. milk-man, dairyman. —rahm, m. cream. —ruhr, f. infantine diarrhœa. —sauer, adj. lactic. —säure, f. lactic acid. —schwester, f. foster-sister; woman fond of milk. —sieb, n. strainer for milk. —speise, f. milk diet. —straße, f. Milky Way, galaxy. —suppe, f. milk porridge; soup made with milk. —wasser, n. whey. —weiß, adj. milky white. —wirtschaft, f. dairy; dairy-farming. —zucker, m. sugar of milk.

Mild, —e, adj. & adv. mild; soft; tender, gentle, kind; liberal, generous (obs.); charitable; pliant, bland (of food); —e Strafe, light punishment; eine —e Gabe, an alms, a charity; —e Stiftungen, benevolent institutions or foundations, charities; —e Früchte, mellow fruit; seine —e Hand aufthun, to show o. s. liberal or charitable. —e, f. mildness, gentleness, etc.; charitableness; generosity; mildness (of weather, etc.); clemency, ductility.

Mil'd—ern, v.a. to soften; to mitigate, alleviate; to modify, qualify, tone down; to extenuate; to humanize; —ernde Umstände, extenuating circumstances. —erer, m. (—erers, pl. —erer) softener, moderator. —erung, f. mitigation, alleviation; modification; moderation; correction (of an acid). Comp. —erungs=ausdruck, m. euphemism. —erungs=gründe, pl. extenuating circumstances. —erungs=mittel, n. lenitive. —herzig, adj. tender, kindhearted, charitable. —herzigkeit, f. tenderness of heart; charitableness. —reich, adj. charitable, benign. —thätig, adj. charitable. —thätigkeit, f. beneficence, liberality.

Militä'r, I. m. (—s, pl. —s) military man, soldier. II. n. (—s) the military, soldiery, army, soldiers. —isch, adj. & adv. like a soldier, soldier-like, military, soldierly; —isches Aussehn, soldierly or martial appearance. Comp. —anwärter, m. soldier (especially a sergeant) who after having served his time may claim a civil employment. —arzt, m. military surgeon. —beamte(r), m. military official. —behörden, pl. military authorities, war department. —bevollmächtigte(r), m. military attaché. —budget, n. army-budget or estimates. —dienst, m. (aktiver) active service. —dienst=pflicht, f. liability to serve in the army. —dienst=zeichen, n. stripe, buckle, etc., showing the period of a soldier's service. —frei, adj. exempt from military service. —fromm, adj. very quiet, trained to stand fire (of horses). —gericht, n. military court; court martial. —gerichtsbarkeit, f. military jurisdiction or court. —grenze, f. military frontier. —herrschaft, f. militarism. —intendant, m. commissary general. —intendantur, f. commissariat. —kabinett, n. military cabinet. —kapelle, f. military band. —maß, n. standard. —medizinalwesen, n. army medical service. —musik, f. martial music; military band. —musiker, m. bandsman. —mütze, f. foraging cap. —pflicht, f. duty to serve in the army, compulsory military service, conscription; seiner —pflicht genügen, to serve one's time. —pflichtig, adj. subject to military duty, bound to serve in the army. —stand, m. profession of arms. —stiefel, pl. regulation boots. —tuch, n. army cloth. —verwaltung, f. military department. —vorlage, f. army-bill. —wesen, n. the army; military affairs; war department. —wirtschaft, f. militarism.

Milita'ria, pl. military affairs; on service, in the army (on letters).

Mili'z, f. (pl. —en) militia; yeomanry. —soldat, m. militia-man; yeoman.

Milkst, Milkt, obs. & dial. for melkst, melkt.

Mill—iar'de, f. milliard. —io'n, f. (pl. —ionen), million. —ionä'r, m. millionaire.

Milz, f. milt, spleen; mich sticht die —, I have a stitch in my side. Comp. —ader, f. splenic vein. —beschwerde, —beschwerung, —krankheit, f. disorder of the spleen; hypochondriasis. —süchtig, adj. splenetic, hypochondriac.

Mi'm—e, m. (—en, pl. —en) mine; mimic-actor, mime. —en, v.a. to act, to do (sl.). —ik, f. mimicry; mimic art; affair, story, thing (sl.). —iker, m. (—ikers, pl. —iker) mimic. —isch, adj. mimic.

Mimo'se, f. (pl. —n) mimosa, sensitive plant.

Min'der, adj. & adv. less; smaller, lesser; inferior; minor; nicht mehr, nicht —, neither more nor less; die —e Anzahl, the lesser number, minority. —heit, f. minority; inferiority. Comp. —bedarf, m. smaller demand or consumption (than was reckoned on, etc.). —einnahme, f. decrease of receipts. —gut, adj. inferior. —jährig, adj. under age; er ist —jährig, he is a minor. —jährige(r), m. a minor. —wertig, adj. inferior, of poor quality. —zahl, f. minority; inferior number.

Min'der—n, v.a. to diminish, abate, lessen; to narrow; sich —n, to grow less. —ung, f. decrease, diminution.

Min'dest, adj. & adv. least, smallest, lowest; nicht das —e, not the least, not a jot; aufs —e, zum —en, at least; nicht im —en, not in the least, not at all, by no means. —ens, adv. at least. Comp. —betrag, m. minimum. —bietende(r), m. lowest bidder.

Mi'ne, f. (pl. —n) mine (Fort., Min.); secret plot; eine — springen lassen, to spring a mine; alle —n springen lassen, to make every effort. Comp. —n=äste, pl. branches of a mine (Fort.). —n=auge, n. shaft of a mine. —n=brunnen, m. well (Fort.). —n=gang, m. entrance to a mine; gallery in a mine. —n=gräber, m. miner. —n=hals, m. entrance to a gallery. —n=kammer, f. chamber of a mine. —n=system, n. araignee (Fort.). —n=zweig, m. side gallery.

Minera'l, n. (—s, pl. —e, —ien) mineral. —isch, adj. mineral. —o'g, m. (—ogen, pl. —ogen) mineralogist. —ogie', f. mineralogy. —o'gisch, adj. mineralogical. Comp. —ien=kabinett, n., —ien=sammlung, f. cabinet, collection of minerals. —moor, n. & m. marsh containing mineral waters. —kunde, —lehre, f. mineralogy. —reich, I. n. mineral kingdom. II. adj. rich in minerals.

Miniatu'r, *f.* (*pl.* **—en**) miniature. *Comp.* **—bild**, *n.* miniature.

Minie'r—en, *v.a.* to mine; to undermine. **—er**, *m.* (**—ers**, *pl.* **—er**) miner, sapper. *Comp.* **—korb**, *m.* earth-barrel. **—kunst**, *f.* art of mining; subterraneous engineering (*Fort.*). **—pflug**, *m.* subsoil plough. **—werkzeug**, *pl.* miner's tools.

Mi'nim—e, *f* (*pl.* **—en**) minim (*Mus.*). *Comp.* **—al'=thermometer**, *m.* registering *or* minimum thermometer.

Minis'ter, *m.* (**—s**, *pl.* **—**) minister; Secretary of State (*Engl.*); **erster —**, prime-minister, premier; **bevollmächtiger —**, plenipotentiary; **— des Äußeren** (*or* **Auswärtigen**), Minister of Foreign Affairs; Secretary of State for Foreign Affairs, Foreign Secretary (*Eng.*); **— des Inneren**, minister for Home Affairs; Home Secretary, Secretary of State for the Home Department (*Eng.*); **— der Finanzen**, minister of Finances; Chancellor of the Exchequer (*Eng.*); **— der Justiz**, Minister of Justice; Lord Chancellor (*Eng.*); **— für die Kolonien**, Colonial Secretary, Secretary of State for the Colonies (*Eng.*). **—ia'l**, *adj.*, **—ie'll**, *adj. & adv.* ministerial. **—ia'len** (mediæval term), *pl.* government officials, knights holding government posts. **—ium** (*pron.* **Ministe'rium**), *n.* (**—iums**, *pl.* **—ien**) ministry; government; government house *or* offices; body of clergy; **—ium des Inneren**, Home Office; **Kriegs—ium**, War Office; **—ium für die Kolonien**, Colonial Office; **im —ium sein**, to be in the cabinet, to be in office, to hold office. *Comp.* **—ial'=gebäude**, *n.* ministry building, Government offices. **—ial'=rat**, *m.* councillor in the ministry. **—krisis**, *f.* ministerial crisis. **—präsident**, *m.* president of cabinet council; prime minister. **—rat**, *m.* cabinet council. **—verantwortlichkeit**, *f.* ministerial responsibility.

Ministr—a'nt, *m.* (**—an'ten**, *pl.* **—an'ten**) sacristan; priest celebrating mass. **—ie'ren**, *v.a.* to minister, to officiate, to assist the priest at the altar.

Min'n—e, *f.* love (*obs. & poet.*). **—en**, *v.a. & n.* (*aux.* **h.**) to love; **sinnen und —en**, musing and loving. **—ig(lich)**, *adj. & adv.* lovely, charming; lovable; loving. *Comp.* **—e=hof**, *m.* court *or* tribunal of love (*the German, made after the* (*fictitious*) *French cour d'amour*). **—e=lied**, *n.* love-song; minnesong. **—e=lieder=handschrift**, *f.* manuscript containing songs of the minnesingers. **—e=lohn**, *m.* reward of love. **—e=sang**, *m.* minnesong; old German lyric poetry; **—esangs Frühling**, the songs composed by minnesingers up to the time of Walther von der Vogelweide. **—e=sänger**, **—e=singer**, *m.* minnesinger (*German lyric poet of the* 12*th or* 13*th century*). **—sold**, *m.* reward of love. **—werben**, *n.* suing for love, wooing.

Minor—e'nn, *adj.* minor. **—ennitä't**, *f.* minority (*of a person*). **—itä't**, *f.* minority.

Mi'nus, I. *adv.* II. *n.* minus. **—kel** (*pron.* **Minus'kel**), *f.* (*pl.* **Minus'keln**) small letter. *Comp.* **—betrag**, *m.* discount by which the amount of exchange is lessened. **—elektrizität**, *f.* negative electricity. **—zeichen**, *n.* minus-sign (—).

Minu'te, *f.* (*pl.* **—n**) minute. *Comp.* **—n=lang**, *adj.* lasting a minute; of a minute's duration; lasting several minutes *or* for minutes. **—n=weise**, *adv.* by minutes, (happening) every minute. **—n=weiser**, **—n=zeiger**, *m.* minute-hand.

Min'ze, *f.* mint (*Bot.*).

Mir, *dat. of* **ich**, me, to me; **ein Buch von —**, a book belonging to me *or* written by me, a book of mine; **jetzt ist es an —**, now it is my turn; **— nichts, dir nichts**, without more ado; quite coolly, unceremoniously; **laßt — das bleiben**, (*ethical dative and not to be translated*) don't do that, let that alone; **wie du —, so ich dir**, scratch me and I'll scratch you; tit for tat; **heute —, morgen dir**, every one in his turn (*prov.*).

Mira'kel, *n.* (**—s**, *pl.* **—**) miracle. *Comp.* **—spiel**, *n.* miracle-play.

Misanthro'p, *m.* (**—en**, *pl.* **—en**) misanthropist. **—isch**, *adj. & adv.* misanthropic.

Misch'bar, *adj.* miscible, mixable, compoundable. **—keit**, *f.* miscibility.

Mi'sch—en, *v.* I. *a.* to mix, mingle; to blend; to compound; to adulterate; to shuffle (*cards*); **die Karten betrügerisch —en**, to pack the cards. II. *r.* to mix, blend, combine; to interfere, meddle with; **sich in fremde Angelegenheiten —en**, to meddle with other people's affairs; **sich ins Gespräch —en**, to join in the conversation; **gemischte Ehe**, marriage of persons of different religions. **—er**, *m.* (**—ers**, *pl.* **—er**) mixer; meddler; shuffler. **—ling**, *m.* (**—lings**, *pl.* **—linge**) mongrel. **—ung**, *f.* mixture; medley; compound; composition; alloy. *Comp.* **—art**, *f.* mongrel-race, cross-breed. **—ehe**, *f.* mixed marriage. **—farbe**, *f.* mixed colour. **—futter**, *n.* mixed fodder *or* provender. **—gefäß**, *n.*, **—krug**, *m.* vessel for mixing, mixing vessel *or* tub. **—gericht**, *n.* ragout. **—masch**, *m. n. & adv.* medley, hotch-potch. **—spiel**, *n.* tragi-comedy. **—teil**, *m.* ingredient. **—ungs=gewicht**, *n.* atomic weight. **—ungs=rechnung**, *f.* rule of alligation. **—ungs=verhältnis**, *n.* ratio of combination *or* of components. **—ungs=verwandtschaft**, *f.* chemical affinity. **—volk**, *n.* mixed race *or* breed.

Mi'sepetrig, *adj. see* **Miesepetrig**.

Misogy'n, *m.* (**—s**, *pl.* **—e**) misogynist.

Mis'pel, *f.* (*pl.* **—n**) medlar; medlar-tree.

Miß, *adv. &* (*properly*) *insep. prefix* (*some verbs in comp. with* **miß** *have the inf. & p.p. sep. as well as insep.; such verbs are marked below sep. & insep.*) = mis-, dis-, amiss; false, *etc.* **—lich**, **Mis'lich**, *adj. & adv.* doubtful, precarious, uncertain; difficult, delicate; critical, dangerous; disagreeable; **es sieht mit ihm —lich aus**, he seems in a bad way. **—lichkeit**, *f.* difficulty; uncertainty; peril, risk; perplexity; critical condition; fatality. *Comp.* **—achten**, *v.a.* (*sep. & insep.*) to disregard, esteem lightly; to neglect, slight. **—achtung**, *f.* disregard, disrespect; neglect. **—arten**, *v.n.* (*aux.* **s.**) (*sep. & insep.*) to degenerate; **—(ge)artet**, degenerate. **—behagen**, I. *v.n.* (*aux.* **h.**, *dat.*) to displease; **es —behagt mir hier**, I am not comfortable here. II. *subst. n.* displeasure, discontent, uncomfortableness, discomfort. **—behaglich**, *adj. & adv.* disagreeable, uncomfortable, unpleasant. **—bilden**, *v.a.* (*p.p.* **—gebildet**, misshapen) to misshape, deform. **—bildung**, *f.* deformity; bad education. **—billigen**, *v.a.* (*sep. & insep.*) to disapprove, disallow, condemn. **—billigung**, *f.* disapprobation, disapproval. **—brauch**, *m.* misuse; abuse. **—brauchen**, *v.a.* (*rarely and obsol. with gen.*) (*sep. & insep.*) to misuse; to abuse; to trespass on; to take in vain (*the Lord's name*). **—bräuchlich**, *adj. & adv.* founded upon abuse, perverted, improper. **—deuten**, *v.a.* (*sep. & insep.*) to misinterpret; to misconstrue, interpret unfavourably. **—erfolg**, *m.* failure, ill success. **—ernte**, *f.* bad harvest. **—fal'len**, I. *ir.v.n.* (*aux.* **h.**, *dat.*) to displease, to be disagreeable to; **es —fällt mir**, I dislike it. II. *subst. n.* displeasure, dissatisfaction. **—fällig**, *adj. & adv.* displeasing, disagreeable, offensive, shocking; **einem —fällig sein**, to be displeasing to a p., to displease s. o.; **sich —**

fällig äußern über, (*acc.*) to find fault with. —gebären, *ir.v.a.* to miscarry; —geboren, abortive. —gebilde, *n.* monster. —geburt, *f.* unnatural birth; abortion; monster. —geschick, *n.* misfortune; mishap; disaster. —gestalt, I. *f.* monster; deformity. II. *adj.* (—gestaltet, —gestaltig), deformed; misshapen. —gestalten, *v.a.* to deform; to misshape. —gestimmt, *p.p. & adj.* in ill-humour. —glück = —geschick (*rare*). —glü'cken, *v.n.* (*aux.* s.) not to succeed, to fail, miscarry; der Plan ist ihm —glückt, his scheme has failed. —gö'nnen, *v.a.* (einem etwas) to begrudge, to grudge, regard with envy; er hat seinem Kameraden diesen Erfolg —gönnt, he has grudged his comrade this success. —greifen, *ir.v.n.* (*aux.* h.) (*sep. & insep.*) to lay hold of the wrong thing; to miss; to mistake. —griff, *m.* touching the wrong note (*Mus.*); blunder, mistake; failure. —gunst, *f.* envy, illwill. —günstig, *adj.* envious, jealous. —handeln, *v.* I. *n.* (*aux.* h.) (*sep.*) to do wrong. II. *a.* (*insep.*) to abuse, ill-treat. —handlung, *f.* abuse, ill usage; misdeed; —handlung der Waren im Schiffe, embezzlement of the cargo. —heirat, *f.* ill-assorted match, misalliance. —hellig, *adj.* dissonant; dissentient, disagreeing. —helligkeit, *f.* dissonance; disagreement, dissension. —hören, *v.n.* to misunderstand, mistake (*poet.*). —jahr, *n.* bad, unproductive year. —kennen, *ir.v.a.* (*sep. & insep.*) to misjudge, mistake. —klang, *m.* dissonance, discord. —klingen, *ir.v.n.* (*aux.* h.) (*sep. & insep.*) to jar, be discordant (*obs.*). —kredit, Mis'kredit, *m.* discredit, disesteem; in —kredit bringen, to discredit, to bring into ill repute. —laut, *m.* ugly sound, cacophony. —liebig, *adj. & adv.* not in favour, displeasing; (etwas) —liebig aufnehmen, to take amiss *or* ill, show displeasure at; sich —liebig machen bei einem, to incur the displeasure of a p., to get into a p.'s bad books. —liebigkeit, *f.* ill favour; disgrace. —lin'gen, I. *ir.v.n.* (*aux.* s.) & *imp* (*with dat.*) to turn out ill, miscarry, prove unsuccessful. II. *subst. n.* failure, miscarriage; disappointment. —mut, *m.* displeasure; discontent; despondency; ill-humour; sadness. —mutig, *adj.* dejected; discouraged; discontented; sullen, cross, peevish. —raten, *ir.v.* I. *n.* (*aux.* s.) to turn out a failure, miscarry; —ratenes Kind, a badly brought up, a misbegotten child; (*aux.* h.) (*sep. & insep.*) to guess wrong. II. *a.* (einem etwas) to dissuade (a p.) from. —stand, *m.* critical *or* embarrassing position *or* condition; impropriety, indecorum; a nuisance; inconvenience. —stimmen, *v.* I. *a.* (*insep. & sep.*) to tune badly, put out of tune; to put out of temper. II. *n.* (*aux.* h.) to be discordant. —stimmung, *f.* discordance, discord; dissension; ill-humour. —ton, *m.* dissonance, false tone *or* sound. —tönen, *v.n.* (*aux.* h.) (*sep.*) to be dissonant *or* out of tune. —trauen, I. *v.n.* (*aux.* h., *dat.*) to mistrust, distrust, suspect. II. *subst. n.* suspicion, mistrust; —trauen in einen setzen, to suspect a p.; —trauen gegen sich selbst, diffidence, modesty. —trauens-votum, *n.* vote of censure; vote of want of confidence. —trauisch, *adj.* distrustful; suspicious. —tritt, *m.* false step. —vergnügen, *n.* displeasure, discontent, dissatisfaction; regret. —vergnügt, *adj. & adv.* dissatisfied, discontented; displeased; malcontent. —verhalten, *n.* misconduct. —verhältnis, *n.* disproportion, wrong proportion; incongruity, disparity, unsuitableness; unfriendly relations. —verständnis, *n.* misunderstanding, misconception; unfriendly relations; error. —verstehen, *ir.v.a.* to misunderstand, mistake. —verwaltung, *f.* maladministration. —wachs, *m.* bad growth; failure of crops, scarcity of crops.

Missa'l, —e, *n.* (—s, *pl.* —en, —ien) missal.

Mis'sen, *v.a.* to be *or* do without, to dispense with; to lack; to feel the want of.

Mis'sest (*or* Mißt,) **Mißt; Miß;** *2 & 3 pers. sing. pres. indic.; imperative of* messen.

Mis'se—that, *f.* (*pl.* —thaten) misdeed, offence, crime. —thäter (—thäters, *pl.* —thäter) *m.* evil-doer, offender; criminal.

Missio'n, *f.* (*pl.* —en) mission. —ä'r, *m.* (—ärs, *pl.* —äre) missionary. *Comp.* —s-anstalt, *f.* mission; mission-house. —s-gesellschaft, *f.* missionary society. —s-haus, *n.* seminary for missionaries.

Mist, *m.* (—es) dung, manure, excrement; dung-heap; dirt; fog (*Naut.*); trash, bosh, rubbish (*sl.*). —en, *v.* I. *n.* (*aux.* h.) to dung; es —et, there is a fog (*coll. & Naut.*). II. *a.* to manure; to clean (*the stable*). —ig, *adj.* dungy; dirty; foggy. *Comp.* —beet, *n.* hotbed. —fink, *m.* bramble-finch; hoopoe; dirty, filthy person (*vulg.*). —fuhre, *f.* carting of manure; a load of manure. —gabel, *f.* pitchfork, dung-fork. —haufen, *m.* dung-hill. —jauche, *f* liquid manure. —lache, —pfütze, *f.* puddle formed by manure drainings.

Mis'tel, *f.* (*pl.* —n) mistletoe, golden bough.

Mis'tig, *adj.* misty, foggy (*Naut.*); dirty.

Miszella'neen, Miszel'len, *f.pl.* miscellanies.

[1]**Mit, Mitt**, *obs. adj.:* (*in* Mit-tag, zu mitter Nacht) mid, middle, central.

[2]**Mit**, *adv. & sep. prefix*, along, along with, together *or* in company with; in unison; likewise, also; simultaneously; (*in comp. with subst.'s and pron.'s gen'lly* =) fellow-, joint-, co-, sym-, *etc.*; (*in comp. with verbs gen'lly* =) along, in common with, with, simultaneously, co-, *etc.;* — dabei sein, to be (one) of the party, to be there too, to make one of a number, to be concerned in a matter; das gehört — dazu, that belongs to it also; that is part of it; komm' —, come along with me (us), come too. II. *prep.* (*with dat.*) with; along with, at the same time with, in company with; by; composed of; possessed of, *etc.;* at; to; — einander, together; alle — einander, all together; — Absicht thun, to do intentionally; — einem gleiches Alter haben, to be of the same age *or* as old as a p.; — einem Schlage, at a blow; — einem Male, suddenly, all at once; — dem Glockenschlage, as the clock struck; — voller Dampfkraft, (at) full steam *or* speed; — dem Abend, in the evening; — Tagesanbruch, at daybreak; — Muße, at leisure; — barem Gelde, for ready money; — Namen, by name, by the name of, called; — der Eisenbahn, by train; — der Post, by post; — Gewalt, by force; — diesem Ausdrucke, by this expression; — nichten, by no means; — goldenen Buchstaben, in golden characters; — der Zeit, in time, by and by; — der ersten Gelegenheit, upon the first occasion, by the first opportunity; — einem Worte, in a word; — Vorsicht, with caution, cautiously; — Protest zurückschicken, to return under protest; ein Topf — Honig, a pot of honey das Buch, — welchem er mir ein Geschenk gemacht hat, the book with which he presented me; — etwas geizig sein, to be niggardly of a th.; was ist — ihm? what has happened to him? was hat er — ihr vor? what plans has he regarding her? sie trennen sich — heute, from to-day they part; — fünfzehn Jahren, at the age of fifteen.

Mit'älteste(r), *m.* one of the oldest; co-elder, coadjutor.

Mit'arbeite—n, *v.a.* to assist; to work together, co-operate. —r, *m.* (—rs, *pl.* —r) fellow

labourer; contributor (*to a journal*), correspondent; collaborator.
Mit'beamte(r), *m.* fellow in office, colleague.
Mit'bedacht, *adj.* having also a legacy; **der —e**, co-legatee.
Mit'begleitung, *f.* concomitancy.
Mit'bekommen, *ir.v.a.* to get with *or* at the same time; to receive when leaving; to get as dowry.
Mit'besitz, *m.* joint possession. **—en**, *ir.v.a.* to possess in common. **—er**, *m.* (—ers, *pl.* —er) joint owner.
Mit'beten, *v.n.* (*aux.* h.) to join in prayer.
Mit'beteiligt, *adj.* taking part in *or* with, having an interest in (*with others*).
Mit'bevollmächtigte(r), *m.* joint commissary.
Mit'bewerb—en, *ir.v.a.* to enter into competition (um, for). **—er**, *m.* (—ers, *pl.* —er) competitor, rival. **—ung**, *f.* competition.
Mit'bringen, *ir.v.a.* to bring along with (*one*); **das Mitgebrachte**, bride's dowry.
Mit'bruder, *m.* colleague, fellow, confrère, brother (*in the faith, etc.*).
Mit'brüderschaft, *f.* (*pl.* —en) confraternity; brotherhood.
Mit'bürger, *m.*, **—in**, *f.* fellow-citizen.
Mit'christ, *m.*, **—in**, *f.* fellow-Christian.
Mit'dasein, *n.* co-existence.
Mit'—diener, —bediente(r), *m.* fellow-servant.
Mit'dürfen, *ir.v.n.* (*aux.* h.) (*ellipt.*) to be allowed to go along with, to have permission to join.
Mit'eigen—tum, *n.* joint property. **—tümer**, *m.* joint-proprietor.
Miteinan'der, *adv.* with one another, together, jointly.
Mit'einfallen, *ir.v.n.* (*aux.* s.) (*sep.*) to coincide.
Mit'empfinden, *ir.v.a.* to sympathize.
Mit'erb—e, *m.* co-heir. **—en**, *v.n.* (*aux.* s.) to inherit conjointly. **—in**, *f.* co-heiress.
Mit'ess—en, *ir.v.n.* & *n.* (*aux.* h.) to eat along with. **—er**, *m.* mess-mate; (*pl.*) skin-maggots, grubs (*Med.*).
Mit'fahren, *ir.v.n.* (*aux.* s.) (**mit einem**) to go in a carriage *or* boat with a p.; (*aux.* h.) (**einem**) to treat, behave to a p. (*B.*).
Mit'fangen, *v.a.* to catch together, to catch at the same time; **mitgefangen, mitgehangen**, caught together, hanged together (*prov.*).
Mit'—fühlend, *adj.* sympathetic. **—gefühl**, *n.* compassion, sympathy.
Mit'führen, *v.a.* to bring along with (*up to, away from*); to carry along with; **unser Reisender führt Proben mit**, our traveller *or* agent will lay patterns *or* samples before you.
Mit'—gabe, *f.* present given on parting; present given with something; dowry. **—geben**, *ir.v.a.* to give to a departing guest; to give with; to give as dowry; **einem einen Führer —geben**, to send a guide with a p.
Mit'geborene(r), *m.* contemporary (*rare*); brother (*poet.*); *pl.* brothers and sisters (*poet.*).
Mit'gefangene(r), *m.* fellow-prisoner.
Mit'gehen, *ir.v.n.* (*aux.* s.) to accompany; **das geht noch mit**, that may be tolerated, that will do (too); **eine S. — heißen**, to steal a thing (*coll.*); **gehen Sie mit?** are you coming with us, are you coming too?
Mit'genoß, *m.* co-partner; consort; companion. **—(ss)enschaft**, *f.* co-partnership, comradeship.
Mit'genuß, *m.* participation in other people's enjoyment; enjoyment in common with other people.
Mit'geschöpf, *n.* fellow-creature.
Mit'gewinnst, *m.* joint profit.
Mit'gift, *f.* (*pl.* —en) dowry.
Mit'glied, *n.* member; **— des Parlament's**, member of Parliament, M.P.; **Kongreß—**, member of Congress, M.C.; **— einer Kirchengemeinde**, parishioner, member of a congregation. **—schaft**, *f.* membership, fellowship.
Mit'halten, *ir.v.a.* to hold conjointly with; to be one of a party; to take in (*a paper*) together with others, to be a subscriber to (*with others*); to side with; **eine Stunde —**, to take a class along with another person; **ich halte mit**, I'll join you; **wollen Sie —?** will you be one of our party?
Mit'helfe—n, *ir.v.a.* & *n.* (*aux.* h.) to co-operate with; to help, assist. **—r**, *m.* (—rs, *pl.* —r) assistant.
Mit'herrsch—aft, *f.* joint dominion. **—er**, *m.* co-regent.
Mithi'n, *adv.* & *conj.* consequently, therefore.
Mit'kämpfe—n, *v.n.* (*aux.* h.) to take part in a fight, fight along with. **—r**, *m.* fellow-combatant, comrade in arms.
Mit'kläger, *m.* co-plaintiff.
Mit'kommen, *ir.v.n.* (*aux.* s.) to come along with; **dieser Schüler kommt mit**, this pupil can follow (*the lecture, etc.*), is getting on well, will be promoted; **ich kann mit dir nicht —**, I cannot keep up with you.
Mit'können, *ir.v.n.* (*aux.* h.) (*ellipt.*) to be able to go *or* to come along, *or* to keep up with.
Mit'laufen, *ir.v.a.* (*aux.* s.) to run along with; to do as others do, take part in (*something*).
Mit'laute—n, *v.a.* to sound along with. **—r**, *m.* (—rs, *pl.* —r) (old term for) consonant.
Mit'leid, *n.* (—s) pity, compassion; sympathy (*Med.*); **— mit einem haben**, to have pity on a p., to be indulgent towards s. o. **—s=bezeugung**, *f.* condolence. **—s=los**, *adj.* pitiless, unfeeling.
Mit'leid—en, I. *ir.v.n.* (*aux.* h.) to suffer at the same time; to feel for, pity, suffer with; to sympathize (*Med.*). II. *subst. n.*, *see* **Mitleid**, **—enschaft**. **—enschaft**, *f.* sympathy (*Med.*): joint suffering *or* bearing; **in —enschaft ziehen**, to affect, involve, implicate; **einen zur —enschaft ziehen**, to make a p. contribute (his share), to involve a p. in a loss. **—ig**, *adj.* compassionate. *Comp.* **—ens=wert, —(en)s=würdig**, *adj.* pitiable, piteous.
Mit'lesen, *ir.v.a.* to read with others *or* at the same time; to take in (*a paper, etc.*) with others.
Mit'machen, *v.a.* to take part in; to do as others do; **er macht alles mit**, he is ready for anything, joins in everything, is a good companion; **alle Moden —**, to follow every fashion; **er hat viel mitgemacht**, he has seen a good deal of life; **er hat viele Feldzüge mitgemacht**, he has seen much active service, he has taken part in many campaigns.
Mit'mehrer, *m.* coefficient (*Arith.*).
Mit'mensch, *m.* (—en, *pl.* —en) fellow-creature; brother, one's neighbour.
Mit'mögen, *ir.v.n.* (*aux.* h.) (*ellipt.*) to wish to go along with, to be anxious to join.
Mit'nehmen, *ir.v.a.* to take with one; to take in addition; to treat harshly; to criticize severely; to weaken, exhaust; to desolate (*a country*); to tolerate, put up with; **auf der Reise einen Ort —**, to call at a place on one's way; **einen Verdienst —**, to take the opportunity of doing a stroke of business *or* of turning an honest penny; **das Spiel hat ihn etwas mitgenommen**, gaming has brought him down somewhat; **eine Stunde —**, *see* **Mithalten**; **das ist immer mitzunehmen**, that is not by any means to be refused; **die Kritiker haben ihn sehr mitgenommen**, the critics have been very hard upon him, have cut him up.
Mit'pächter, *m.* joint holder *or* tenant.
Mitrailleu'se, *f.* (*Mil.*) mitrailleuse.
Mit'rechnen, *v.* I. *a.* to include in the reckoning. II. *n.* (*aux.* h.) **das rechnet nicht mit**, that does not count.

Mit'reden, *v.* I. *n.* (*aux.* **h.**) to join in the conversation; to put in a word; to speak at the same time. II. *a.* **hier habe ich auch ein Wort mitzureden,** I have also a word to say in this; **Sie haben hier nichts mitzureden,** you have no say in this matter, this is not your business, this is out of your province.

Mit'reisen, *v.n.* (*aux.* **h.**) to travel along with; **der —de, ein —der,** the, a, fellow-traveller.

Mit'reißen, *ir.v.a.* to tear *or* drag along with; to involve in one's own violent actions *or* emotions.

Mit'schuld, *f.* complicity, participation in guilt. **—ig,** *adj.* accessory to a crime, participating in guilt. **—ige(r),** *m.* accomplice. **—ner,** *m.* joint-debtor.

Mit'schüler, *m.*, **—in,** *f.* schoolfellow, fellow-pupil; **sie war meine —in,** she and I were at school together.

Mit'sein, *ir.v.n.* (*aux.* **s.**) to co-exist with; to be together with; to have gone with.

Mit'singen, *ir.v.a. & n.* (*aux.* **h.**) to join in singing; to accompany with the voice.

Mit'sollen, *ir.v.n.* (*aux.* **h.**); (*ellipt.*) **er soll mit,** he is to go with (us, him, them).

Mit'spiele—n, *v.a. & n.* (*aux.* **h.**) to join in play with; to take a hand (*at cards*); to accompany (*Mus.*); **einem übel —n,** to use one ill, to play one a trick. **—r,** *m.*, **—rin,** *f.* playfellow; partner; accompanist.

Mit'stimmen, *v.n.* (*aux.* **h.**) to vote with; to give one's vote (*along with others*).

Mit'tag, I. *m.* (**—s,** *pl.* **—e**) mid-day, noon; meridian; south; **gegen —,** towards noon, southerly; **heller —,** broad noon; **zu — essen,** to take one's mid-day meal, to lunch, to dine (early). II. *n.* dinner (*coll.*); **zu — bleiben,** to stay to luncheon *or* (early) dinner; **— machen,** to take dinner; to halt for noon-day rest. **—s,** *adv.* at noon; at dinner. *Comp.* **—s=brod, —s=essen,** *n.* mid-day meal, lunch, (early) dinner; **er gab ihnen ein —sessen,** he entertained them at dinner. **—s=fläche,** *f.* plane of the meridian. **—s=gesellschaft,** *f.* company to luncheon *or* (early) dinner. **—s=hell,** *adj.* bright as noon-day. **—s=höhe,** *f.* meridian altitude; **—shöhe der Sonne,** the sun's altitude. **—s=kreis,** *m.* meridian. **—s=küste,** *f.* southern coast. **—s=länge,** *f.* meridional longitude. **—s=linie,** *f.* line of the meridian. **—s=luft,** *f.* southern breeze; noon-day air. **—s=meer,** *n.* (*poet.*) Mediterranean. **—s=punkt,** *m.* south *or* meridian point. **—s=ruhe,** *f.*, **—s=schlaf,** *m* siesta, mid-day nap. **—s=stunde,** *f.* noon; dinner-hour. **—s=tisch,** *m.* mid-day meal; **der —stisch kostet hier 3 Mark,** dinner is here, *or* you get a dinner at this place, for 3 shillings. **—s=uhr,** *f.* sun-dial. **—s=volk,** *n.* southern people. **—s=zeit,** *f.* noon-tide; lunch *or* (early) dinner-time. **—s=zirkel,** *m.* meridian.

Mit'täg—ig, *adj.* noon-day. **—lich,** *adj. & adv.* mid-day, occurring (regularly) at noon, meridian, meridional, southern.

Mit'tänzer, *m.* **—in,** *f.* (dancing) partner.

Mit't—e, *f.* (*pl.* **—en**; *in poetry gen. & dat. also* **—n**) middle, midst; centre; mean, medium; **von —e zu —e,** from centre to centre; **(gegen) —e Januar,** (*about*) the middle of January; **einer aus unserer —e,** one from our midst, one from amongst us, one of our circle; **das Reich der —e,** the Middle Empire, the Chinese empire; **in die —e nehmen,** to put between two fires, to attack on both sides (*Mil.*); **die (rechte) —e halten,** to observe the happy mean. **—el, —en, —er, —ler,** *see* **Mittel, Mitten, Mitter—, Mittler.** *Comp.* **—e=fünfziger,** *m.* man half-way between fifty and sixty years of age. **—fasten,** *pl.* mid-Lent. **—schiffs,** *adv.* amid-ships. **—sommer,** *m.* midsummer. **—woch,** *m.* (**—s**) Wednesday. **—wöchentlich, —wochlich,** *adj. & adv.* of *or* occurring on every Wednesday. **—wochs,** *adv.* every Wednesday, on a Wednesday.

Mit'teilbar, *adj.* communicable; contagious (*Med.*). **—keit,** *f.* communicability.

Mit'teil—en, *v.* I. *a.* (**einem etwas**) to communicate; to impart, give; apprise; **einer Sache eine Bewegung —en,** to impart a motion to a thing. II. *r.* to communicate one's thoughts, *etc.*; to spread, communicate itself, be contagious **—end,** *p. & adj.*, **—sam,** *adj.* communicative. **—samkeit,** *f.* communicativeness. **—ung,** *f.* communication; intelligence; **vertrauliche —ung,** private and confidential communication, secret information.

Mit'tel, I. *n.* (**—s,** *pl.* **—**) middle, midst; remedy; expedient; means; abilities, wealth, property; ratio; average; medium, mean; medium (*Phys.*); vehicle; **der Zweck heiligt die —,** the aim justifies the means; **ein unfehlbares —,** a specific; **bei —n sein,** to be well off; **sich ins — schlagen, legen, ins — treten,** to interpose, mediate, intercede; **durch gelinde —,** by fair means; **hier giebt's kein —,** there is no help for it, nothing can be done; **alle ersinnlichen — anwenden,** to employ every possible means; **neue — anwenden,** to change one's tactics; **medizinische —,** prescriptions, drugs, nostrums; **das arithmetische —,** the arithmetical mean; **die — besitzen es auszuführen,** to possess the means to carry it out; **meine — erlauben es nicht,** I cannot afford it; **— und Wege,** ways and means; **im —,** on the average, averaging. II. *adj.* (**mittler, mittelst**; *rarely used in the pos. except in comp'ds*) middle, mid, central, inner; mean; **der mittlere Finger,** the middle finger; **mittler Weile, mittlerweile,** meanwhile; **ein mittlerer Vierziger,** a person between forty and fifty years of age. **—bar,** *adj. & adv.* mediate; indirect; collateral. **—barkeit,** *f.* indirectness. **—s, —st,** *adv. & prep.* (*with gen.*) by means of, by the help of, through. **—st,** *adj. sup. of* **Mittel,** midmost, middlemost. *Comp.* **—alter,** *n.* middle age; Middle Ages (*hist.*). **—alterlich,** *adj.* mediæval. **—amerika,** *n.* Central America; **—amerikanische Inseln,** the West Indies. **—arrest,** *m.* solitary confinement with low diet (*as a rule three days*) (*Mil.*). **—art,** *f.* intermediate sort; cross-breed. **—artig,** *adj.* middling; hybrid. **—begriff,** *m.* intermediate idea; middle term (*Log.*). **—darm,** *m.* great gut. **—deutsch,** *adj.* Middle German (*dialects, viz., Rhenish, Thuringian, Saxon, Silesian*). **—deutschland,** *n.* Central Germany. **—ding,** *n.* something intermediate between two other things. **—ernte,** *f.* average harvest. **—farbe,** *f.* intermediate colour; mezzotinto. **—finger,** *m.* middle finger. **—fuß,** *m.* metatarsus, instep; middle-sized foot. **—galopp,** *m.* half-trot, amble. **—gebirge,** *n.* central chain of mountains; secondary chain of mountains; intermediate mountain (*Min.*). **—glied,** *n.* middle limb *or* member; middle term (*Log.*); intermediate stage. **—grad,** *m.* comparative degree. **—größe,** *f.* medium size; **von —größe,** medium-sized. **—gut,** *adj.* middling, of medium quality; second-rate. **—haut,** *f.* mesocarp (*Bot.*). **—heer,** *n.* central army. **—hochdeutsch,** *n.* middle High German (*1100–1500; best period 1170–1250*). **—klassen,** *f.pl.* middle classes in Gm. secondary schools for boys (**Untertertia, Obertertia, Untersekunda,** age 13–16 years). **—kreis,** *m.* equator. **—ländisch,** *adj.* inland; **das —ländische Meer,** the Mediterranean (Sea). **—latein,** *n.* Low *or* Mediæval Latin. **—laut,** *m.* mediant (*Mus.*). **—loch,** *n.* side pocket (*Bill.*). **—los,** *adj.* without means, poor, destitute. **—losigkeit,** *f.* lack of means, destitution. **—maß,** *n.* average; middling size; mediocrity; mean. **—mäßig**, *adj.* middling, indifferent, ordinary. **—mäßigkeit**, *f.* mediocrity. **—mast**, *m.* main-mast (*Naut.*). **—partei**, *f.* moderate party (*Pol.*). **—preis**, *m.* average price. **—punkt**, *m.* centre; central point, focus; **nach dem —punkte der Schwere streben**, to gravitate. **—punkts=kraft**, *f.* central force. **—raum**, *m.* intermediate space, interval. **—ruhe**, *f.* half-cock (*in rifles*). **—satz**, *m.* mean proposition. **—schlag**, *m.*, *see* **—art**. **—schule**, *f.* intermediate school, secondary school (*term used in Austria, Baden, etc. for* **höhere Schule**; *in Prussia* **—schule** *denotes a lower and non-classical kind of secondary school*). **—schul=unterricht**, *m.* secondary education. **—schul=wesen**, *n.* all that concerns secondary schools. **—s=mann**, *m.*, **—s=person**, *f.* mediator; umpire. **—staaten**, *pl.* secondary states; **deutsche —staaten**, Wurtemberg, Baden, Saxony, Hesse, Mecklenburg, Oldenburg. **—stadt**, *f.* middle-sized town. **—stand**, *m.* middle class(es). **—ständig**, *adj.* intermediate (*Bot.*). **—stelle**, *f.* centre, intermediate place, half-way house. **—stimme**, *f.* (**hohe**) tenor; (**tiefe**) baritone; mezzo-soprano; (*pl.*) middle parts (*of a musical composition*). **—straße**, *f.* middle street, central road; mean, medium; **die goldne —straße**, the golden mean; **ich halte mich auf der —straße**, I steer the middle course, I am holding the happy mean. **—stück**, *n.* middle piece; interlude (*Mus.*). **—stufe**, *f.* intermediate step *or* degree. **—ton**, *m.* mediant (*Mus.*). **—treffen**, *n.* centre (*of an army*), main body. **—wall**, *m.* curtain (*Fort.*). **—wand**, *f.* partition wall. **—weg**, *m.*, *see* **—straße**; **einen —weg einschlagen**, to adopt a middle course, to make a compromise. **—zeit**, *f.* mean time; Middle Ages (*rare*). **—zeitig**, *adj.* doubtful *or* common (*of the quantity of syllables in Pros.*).

Mit'ten, *adv.* (*used with a prep. following*) midway; **— in**, **— auf**, in the midst, middle of; **— aus**, from amidst *or* among; **— durch**, through the middle; **— entzwei**, in two, in the middle; **—inne**, right in the middle, midway; **—mang**, right among (*sl.*); **—unter**, amongst, in the midst of; **— in der Nacht**, in the middle of the night; **— in der Luft**, in mid-air.

Mit'ter— (*in comp.*) **—nacht**, *f.* midnight; north. **—nächtig**, *adj. & adv.* nocturnal; midnight; gloomy. **—nächtlich**, *adj. & adv.* happening every midnight; *see* **—nächtig**; northern. **—nachts**, *adv.* at midnight. **—nachts=gegend**, *f.* north. **—nachts=stunde**, *f.* hour of midnight, midnight hour.

Mitt'ler, *comp. of* **mittel** (*for which it is gen'lly used*); **—e Schnelligkeit**, average speed; (**das**) **—e Verhältnis**, mean ratio; **eine Person von —en Jahren**, a middle-aged person.

Mitt'ler, *m.* (**—s**, *pl.* **—**) mediator, intercessor; third party; **unser —**, Christ. **—in**, *f.* mediatrix. *Comp.* **—amt**, *n.* mediatorial office. **—tod**, *m.* expiatory death.

Mittlerwei'le, *adv.* meanwhile, in the meantime.

Mit'tönen, *v.n.* (*aux.* **h.**) to sound with *or* simultaneously.

Mitun'ter, *adv.* among other things; occasionally, now and then.

Mit'unter—schreiben, **—zeichnen**, *v.a. & n.* (*aux.* **h.**) to add one's signature (*to some other person's*), to countersign. **—schrift**, *f.* joint signature.

Mit'verbrecher, *m.*, **—in**, *f.* accomplice.

Mit'verschworene(r), *m.* fellow-conspirator, accomplice.

Mit'verwalt—er, *m.* co-administrator. **—ung**, *f.* joint management *or* administration.

Mitvor'mundschaft, *f.* joint guardianship.

Mit'welt, *f.* the age we live in; our age, our own times; the present generation, our contemporaries.

Mit'wirk—en, *v.n.* (*aux.* **h.**) to co-operate, concur, assist, contribute towards; to collaborate; to take a part (*in a concert, etc.*). **—end**, *p. & adj.* co-operative; assisting; subsidiary; collateral. **—ung**, *f.* co-operation, assistance.

Mit'wisse—n, I. *ir.v.n.* (*aux.* **h.**); **um etwas —n**, to be privy to, know of a thing. II. *subst. n.* cognizance; **ohne mein —n**, without my knowledge, unknown to me. **—nschaft**, *f.* joint knowledge; *see* **—n** II. **—r**, *m.* one cognizant of a secret; confidant, accessory.

Mit'zählen, *v.* I. *a.* to include in an account; to count in. II. *n.* (*aux.* **h.**) to count along with others *or* another.

Mit'zechen, *v.n.* (*aux.* **h.**) to drink *or* to carouse in company.

Mit'ziehen, *ir.v.* I. *a.* to drag along with (*others*). II. *n.* (*aux.* **s.**) to travel along with; to move along with (*from one's house, etc.*).

Mit'zweck, *m.* (**—es**, *pl.* **—e**) secondary aim.

Mixtu'r, *f.* (*pl.* **—en**) *see* **Gemisch**; mixture (*Pharm.*); furniture (*in organs*).

Mnemo'ni—k, *f.* mnemonics. **—sch**, *adj.* mnemonic.

Mnemotech'nik, *f.* mnemotechnics, mnemotechny.

Mö'b—el, *see* **Möbel**. **—lie'ren**, *v.a.* to furnish; **—lierte Zimmer zu vermieten**, furnished apartments (to let). **—lie'rer**, *m.* (**—lierers**, *pl.* **—lierer**) upholsterer, house-furnisher.

Mö'bel, *n.* (**—s**, *pl.* **—**, *better than* **—n**) piece of furniture; (*pl.*) furniture. *Comp.* **—entwürfe**, *pl.* designs for furniture. **—händler**, *m.* upholsterer; furniture-dealer, cabinet-maker. **—kattun**, *m.* chintz. **—lack**, *m.* furniture polish **—tischler**, *m.* cabinet-maker. **—wagen**, *m.* furniture(-removal) van.

Mobi'l, I. *adj.* movable; active, nimble; ready to march, mobile (*Mil.*); **— machen**, to put in motion; to mobilize (*troops*). II. *n.* (**—s**, *pl.* **—e**) motive power. **—e**, *n.*; **perpetuum —e**, perpetual motion. **—ia'r**, *n.* (**—iars**, *pl.* **—iare**) furniture. **—ien**, *pl.* goods and chattels, furniture. **—isie'ren**, *v.a.* to mobilize. *Comp.* **—befehl**, *m.* order of mobilization. **—ia'r=erbe**, *m.* heir to the goods and chattels, personal property. **—ia'r=masse**, *f.* movable property of a bankrupt. **—machung**, *f.* mobilization. **—machungs=geld**, *n.*, **—machungs=zulage**, *f.* bounty, increase of pay at the beginning of a campaign, field allowance.

Moch'te, **Möch'te**, *1* (*& 3*) *pers. sing. imperf. ind. & subj. of* **mögen**.

Modalitä't, *f.* modality.

Mo'd—e, *see* **Mode**. **—isch**, *adj.* fashionable. **—i'st**, *m.*, **—is'tin**, *f.* milliner.

Mo'de, *f.* (*pl.* **—n**) fashion, mode, vogue; custom; **—werden**, to come into fashion; **die — angeben**, to set the fashion; **nach der —**, fashionable, fashionably; **aus der — kommen**, to go out of fashion; **in die — kommen**, to come into fashion, to come up. *Comp.* **—artikel**, *m.* fashionable article, (**neuer**) novelty; fancy article. **—ausdruck**, *m.* fashionable term, expression in vogue. **—dame**, *f.* lady of fashion. **—(n)=journal**, *n. see* **—zeitung**. **—händler(in**, *f.*), *m.* dealer in fancy articles *or* novelties; milliner. **—hans**, **—narr**, *m.* fop, dandy. **—kram**, **—tand**, *m.* nick-nacks, novelties. **—waren**, *pl.* fancy goods. **—welt**, *f.* fashionable world. **—zeitung**, *f.* magazine of fashions.

Mo'del, **Mo'dul**, *m.* (**—s**, *pl.* **—(n)**) module (*Arch.*); pattern; cotton-printing block; mould; matrix

Mo'del—n, *see* **Modellieren**; figure, work in patterns (*on stuffs*); to give an impression (*with an iron*); to embellish; **sich —n nach einem**, to model o.s. on a p., to take a p. for one's model. *Comp.* **—brett,** *n.* founder's mould. **—holz,** *n.* wooden mould *or* form. **—tuch,** *n.* sampler.

Mode'll, *n.* (—s, *pl.* —e) model; mould, form; sculptor's *or* painter's model; pattern; sample; draught. **—ie'ren,** *v.a.* to model, mould, fashion. **—ie'rer,** *also* **Modelleu'r,** *m.* (—ierers, *pl.* —ierer) modeller; pattern cutter *or* maker. *Comp.* **—ier'=klasse,** *f.* class for drawing, *etc.*, from the life *or* from models. **—ier'=zimmer,** *n.* room for modelling in *or* for drawing from the model. **—puppe,** *f.* lay-figure. **—steher,** *m.*, **—steherin,** *f.* sculptor's *or* painter's model, artist's model, posturer. **—zeichnung,** *f.* academy-figure, drawing from the life.

Mo'der, *m.* (—s) mud; mould, mouldering, decay; mother (*on wine, etc.*); damp, close air. **—ig,** *adj.* mouldy, musty; muddy; rotten, decaying. **—n,** *v.n.* (*aux.* s. & h.) to putrefy, rot. *Comp.* **—duft,** *m.* musty smell *or* air. **—erde,** *f.* mould, compost, rotten earth. **—fleckig,** *adj.* mildewed. **—geruch,** *m.*, *see* **—duft.**

Moderateu'r=lampe, *f.* moderator-lamp.

Mo'dern, *v.n.* to putrefy, rot.

Mode'rn, *adj.* modern; fashionable; **die —e,** the very latest German literature, the new realistic school of writers. **—isie'ren,** *v.a.* to modernize.

Modifizie'ren, *v.a.* to modify, qualify.

Modulie'ren, *v.a.* to modulate (*Mus., etc.*).

Mo'dus, *m.* (*pl.* **Modi**) mood (*Gram.*).

Mo'gel—n, *v.a.* to cheat (*at cards*) (*coll.*). **—ei',** *f.* cheating, trickery (*coll.*).

Mö'g—en, *ir.v.a. & n.* (*aux.* h.) to be willing; to like; to desire, have a mind to; to be able; to be permitted *or* at liberty to do; to be possible; (*used as modal auxiliary* = may, might, let;) **ich möchte gern mit Ihnen sprechen,** I should like to speak to you, allow me to speak to you; **ich mag nicht,** I won't, I do not like; **ich mag das nicht,** I do not like that; **ich mag nicht nach Hause,** I don't want to go home; **ich mag nicht ausgehen,** I do not like *or* care to go out; **ich möchte gern,** I should like, I would fain; **ich möchte lieber,** I would *or* had rather; **es mag geschehen,** let it (*come*), very well, I don't care; **man mag eintreten,** walk in; **das Haus mochte noch etwa hundert Ellen weiter entfernt sein,** the house may have been another hundred yards further off; **es mochte wohl schon vier Uhr sein, als wir,** it was perhaps as late as four o'clock when we; **wie dem auch sein mag, dem mag sein wie ihm wolle,** be that as it may; **es mag daraus entstehen, was da wolle,** whatever happens *or* may come of it; **was ich auch (immer) thun mag, es ist dir nicht recht,** no matter what I do, I cannot please you; **ich ließ ihm sagen, er möchte zu mir kommen,** I sent him word to call on me; **das möchte schwer zu beweisen sein,** (*I fear*) it will be difficult to prove that; **Sie möchten sich wohl irren,** I am afraid you are mistaken, you may perhaps be mistaken; **es möchte wohl besser sein, wenn Sie nicht kämen,** it would doubtless be better if you did not come; **man möchte aus der Haut fahren,** it is enough to make one jump out of one's skin; **er mag nun zusehen wie er durchkommt,** let him get out of the scrape as best he can (*I shan't trouble myself*); **das Herz möchte mir zerspringen,** my heart is ready to break; **er möchte wohl, wenn er könnte,** he would like to, if he could; **daraus möchte wohl nichts werden,** very likely nothing will come of it; **möge es ihm wohl bekommen!** much good may it do him! **möchte es doch geschehen!** oh, how I wish it would happen! **ich wünsche (wünschte), daß er kommen möge** (möchte), I wish he would come, I wished him to come; **das möchte ich doch einmal sehen!** well, I should like to see that! I never! well, really! **—en Sie klatschen!** let them gossip! **—e er sich in Acht nehmen!** let him beware *or* look out! **sage ihm, er —e sogleich zu Bette gehen,** tell him to go to bed directly; **leiden —en,** to like (**mögen** *is used for p.p.* **gemocht,** *when immediately preceded by an inf.*); **ich hätte es ihm nicht sagen —en,** I should not have liked to tell him, I could not have told him; **ich habe es nicht thun —en,** I did not like *or* care to do it. **—lich,** *adj. & adv.* possible; practicable, feasible; **—lichen Falls,** if possible; **alles —liche,** all that is (was) possible; **sein —liches, sein —lichstes thun,** to do one's utmost; **das einzige mir —liche Mittel,** the only means in my power; **alles —liche Glück wünschen,** to wish all sorts of happiness; **er gab alle —lichen Versprechungen,** he made all kinds of promises; **der Anblick giebt den Engeln Stärke, da keiner dich ergründen mag,** the aspect gives strength to the angels, though none can fathom thee; **ist es —lich?** is it possible? **—licherweise habe ich ihm mißfallen,** I may possibly have displeased him; **alles —liche,** every conceivable thing; all sorts of things; **wie soll man es —lich machen?** how is it to be done *or* achieved? **so schnell wie —lich, —lichst schnell,** as soon *or* as speedily (quickly) as possible. **—lichkeit,** *f.* possibility; feasibility, practicability; contingency; potentiality; **nach —lichkeit,** as far as possible, as much as one can, as far as lies in one's power; **einem die —lichkeit verschaffen,** to make it possible for a p., to put s. o. in the way of; **es ist keine —lichkeit (vorhanden)** there is no chance. **—lichst,** *adv.*, *see* **—lich;** as much as, *etc.* possible; **—lichst bald** *or* **bald —lichst,** as soon as possible. *Comp.* **—lichen=falls,** *adv.* if possible; possibly. **—licher=weise,** *adv.* as far as possible; possibly; perhaps. **—lichkeits=fälle,** *pl.* possibilities, emergencies, contingencies. **—lich=sein,** *n.*, *see* **—lichkeit.**

Mohn, *m.* (—s, *pl.* —e) poppy. *Comp.* **—saft,** *f.* poppy juice, opium. **—stoff,** *m.* narcotine.

[1]**Mohr,** *m.* (—en, *pl.* —en) Moor; black, negro; darky (*coll.*); chimney-sweep; Ethiop's mineral; **das heißt einen —en bleichen** *or* **(weiß) waschen,** that is attempting the impossible; **einen —en kann man nicht weiß machen,** one cannot wash a blackamoor white; **weißer —,** albino. **—in,** *f.* negress. **—isch,** *adj.* Moorish. *Comp.* **—en=farbig,** *adj.* of a dark colour; pitch-black. **—en=fürst,** *m.* Moorish prince. **—en=knabe,** *m.* negro boy, nigger boy (*coll.*). **—en=land,** *n.* country of the Moors, Ethiopia; nigger-land (*coll.*). **—enländisch,** *adj.* Moorish, moresque, Ethiopian. **—en=trommel,** *f.* tambourine. **—en=wäsche,** *f.* washing of a blackamoor; **—enwäsche vornehmen,** to attempt the impossible. **—en=weib,** *n.* negress, black *or* negro woman.

[2]**Mohr,** *m.* (—s, *pl.* —e) water (*in stuffs*); mohair; moreen; watered stuff. **—en,** *see* **Moirieren; gemohrt,** moiré. *Comp.* **—band,** *n.* watered ribbon. **—kleid,** *n.* dress of watered stuff. **—rübe,** *f.* carrot; *see* **Möhre.**

[3]**Mohr,** *n. see* **Moor.**

Möh're, *f.* (*pl.* —n) carrot; **spanische —,** yellow parsnip.

Moiré', *m.* (—s, *pl.* —s) water, cloud, tabby; watered *or* clouded silk; moreen.

Moirie'ren, *v.a.* to water; cloud (*silk, etc.*).

Molas'se, *f.* (*pl.* —n) molasse (*sandstone belonging to the tertiary stratum*).

Molch, *m.* (—es, *pl.* —e) salamander; monster; spiteful person.

Molek—ü'l, *n.* (—s, *pl.* —e) molecule. **—ula'r,**

adj. molecular. **—ula'r=strom,** *m.* elementary current.

Molk, Möl'ke, *obsol. 1 p. sing. imperf. indic. & subj. of* **melken.**

Mol'k—e, *f.* (*pl.* **—en**) whey. **—erei',** *f.* dairy. **—icht,** (*obs.*) **—ig,** *adj.* whey-like, containing whey. *Comp.* **—en=artig,** *adj.* wheyish. **—en=kur,** *f.* whey-regimen. **—en=faß,** *n.* whey-tub. **—en=säure,** *f.* acid of milk. **—en=trank,** *m.* posset.

Moll, I. *adj. & n.* (**—s**) minor (*Mus.*). II. *m.* (**—s,** *pl.* **—e** *and* **—s**) mull (*muslin*); species of marmot. **—e,** *see* **Mulde.** **—ig,** *adj.* soft; comfortable, pleasant, snug (coll.); **hier ist's recht —ig,** it is very cosy here. **—us'ke,** *f.* (*pl.* **—usken**) mollusk. *Comp.* **—tonart,** *f.* minor key. **—tonleiter,** *f.* minor scale.

Molsch, *adj. & adv.* soft, over-ripe.

Mol'ten, *m.* dirty half-melted snow (*dial.*).

Mome'nt, I. *m.* (**—s,** *pl.* **—e**) moment. II. *n.* momentum; impetus; instance; motive; **das erregende —,** the initial impulse (bringing about the development of the dramatic action), the starting point of the plot. **—a'n,** *adj. & adv.* momentary, for the present, just now.

Mona'd—e, *f.* (*pl.* **—en**) monad, atom; **die Lehre von den —en,** doctrine of monads (*of Leibnitz*). **—isch,** *adj.* monadic. *Comp.* **—en=lehre,** *f.* theory of monads (*Philos.*).

Mona'rch, *m.* (**—en,** *pl.* **—en**) monarch. **—ie',** *f.* (*pl.* **—ieen**) monarchy. **—isch,** *adj.* monarchical.

Mo'nat, *m.* (**—s,** *pl.* **—e**) month; **vor anderthalb —en,** a month and a half ago, six weeks ago; **er hat ein Gehalt von 4800 Mark, macht 400 Mark pro —,** his salary is 4800 marks, that is 400 marks per month *or* monthly. **—ig,** *suff.* (*in comp.* =) of so many months; **nach einer sechs—igen Reise,** after a six months' tour; **ein drei—iges Kind,** a child of three months. **—lich,** *adj.* monthly; menstrual; **eine drei —liche Zeitschrift,** a quarterly magazine. *Comp.* **—(e)lang,** *adj. & adv.* lasting a month *or* months; for months. **—s=bericht,** *m.* monthly report. **—s=buch,** *n.* ledger, monthly book. **—s=fluß,** *m.* menses. **—s=frist,** *f.* space of a month. **—s=geld,** *n.* monthly pay, monthly wages. **—s=rose,** *f.* monthly rose. **—s=schrift,** *f.* monthly publication, monthly magazine; **halb—sschrift,** fortnightly review *or* magazine; **drei—sschrift,** quarterly. **—s=tag,** *m.* day of the month, date. **—s=weise,** *adv.* monthly; **die Zahlung erfolgt —s=weise,** the payment will be made by monthly instalments. **—s=zeiger,** *m.* calendar-hand on a clock. **—s=zeit,** *f.* monthly period (*Med.*).

Mönch, *m.* (**—es,** *pl.* **—e**) monk, friar; spire; spindle (*of spiral staircase*); plant that flowers but bears no fruit; dandelion; friar, monk (*Typ.*); lock, sluice; black-cap (*Orn.*); name given to several birds, butterflies, and mollusks. **—erei',** *f.* monkishness, monkery. **—isch,** *adj.* monastic, monkish. **—lein,** *n.* (**—leins,** *pl.* **—lein**) little monk, my dear monk. **—tum,** *n.* monasticism. *Comp.* **—s=geist,** *m.* monastic spirit. **—s=kappe, —s=kutte,** *f.* cowl, monk's hood; capuche. **—s=kloster,** *n.* monastery. **—s=orden,** *m.* monastic order. **—s=platte, —s=krone,** *f.* (monastic) tonsure. **—s=kutte,** *f.* monk's frock; **ohne —skutte,** unfrocked, uncowled. **—s=schrift,** *f.* monk's letters, monkish handwriting; black letter. **—s=wesen,** *n.* monachism, monasticism, monastic life. **—s=zucht,** *f.* monastic discipline.

Mond (*long* **o**), *m.* (**—es,** (*obs.* **—en** *surviving in compds.*), *pl.* **—e**) moon; satellite; lune (*Geom.*); month; lunette (*Fort.*); **die —e des Jupiter,** the satellites of Jupiter; **der — nimmt ab,** the moon is on the wane; **zunehmender —,** waxing moon; **den — betreffend,** lunar; **unter dem —e,** sublunary; **der halbe —,** crescent, halfmoon (*Astr.*), ravelin, half-moon (*Fort.*). *Comp.* **—bahn,** *f.* moon's orbit. **—beglänzt,** *adj.* lit up by the moon; moon-lit; **—beglänzte Zaubernacht,** moon-lit magic night. **—beschreibung,** *f.* selenography. **—blind, —äugig,** *adj.* moon-blind. **—en=glanz,** *m.* brightness of the moon. **—en=lauf,** *m.* lunar revolution. **—(en)=nacht,** *f.* moon-light night. **—(en)=schein,** *m.* moonshine. **—finsternis,** *f.* eclipse of the moon. **—fläche,** *f.* moon's disc. **—flecken,** *m.* macula. **—gebirge,** *n.* lunar mountain. **—gestalt,** *f.* phase (*of the moon*); form of the moon. **—hell,** *adj.* moon-lit. **—jahr,** *n.* lunar year. **—kalb, Mon'kalb,** *n.* mole, mooncalf, false conception; monster; duffer (*coll.*). **—phasen,** *pl.* phases of the moon. **—scheibe,** *f.* disc of the moon. **—schein,** *m.* moonlight; bald spot on the head. **—schein=sonate,** *f.* moonlight sonata (*for the piano-forte, by Beethoven*). **—sichel,** *f.* crescent. **—stein,** *m.* moonstone, selenite. **—strahl,** *m.* moonbeam. **—sucht,** *f.* lunacy; somnambulism. **—süchtig,** *adj.* lunatic; walking in one's sleep, moonstruck, addicted to somnambulism. **—tafeln,** *pl.* lunar tables. **—umlauf,** *m.* lunar revolution. **—viertel,** *n.* quadrature (*Astr.*); quarter of the moon. **—uhr,** *f.* clock showing the changes of the moon. **—wechsel,** *m.* change of the moon. **—zirkel,** *m.* lunar cycle.

Mone'ten, *pl.* money (*sl.*).

Monie'ren, *v.a.* to warn; to censure.

Mono—die', *f.* (*pl.* **—dieen**) monody. **—gamie',** *f.* monogamy. **—ga'misch,** *adj.* monogamous. **—gra'mm,** *n.* (**—gramms,** *pl.* **—gramme**) monogram. **—lo'g,** *m.* (**—logs,** *pl.* **—loge**) monologue. **—po'l,** *n.* (**—pols,** *pl.* **—pole**) monopoly; **—pol treiben, —polisie'ren,** to monopolize. **—thei'smus,** *m.* monotheism. **—to'n,** *adj.* monotonous. **—tonie',** *f.* monotony.

Monstr—a'nz, *f.* monstrance, pyx (*Eccl.*). **—ö's,** *adj.* monstrous. **—ositä't,** *f.* monstrosity.

Mon'strum, *n.* (**—s,** *pl.* **Monstra**) monster.

Monsu'n, *m.* (**—s,** *pl.* **—e**) monsoon.

Mon'—tag, *m.* Monday; **des —tags,** every Monday; on Mondays; **der blaue —tag,** holiday *or* idle Monday; **—tag wird nicht wochenalt,** Monday does not outlast the week (*prov.*). **—täglich, —tägig,** *adj. & adv.* every Monday; on Mondays. **—tags,** *adv.* on Monday; every Monday. *Comp.* **—tags=blatt,** *n.*, **—tags=zeitung,** *f.* Monday-journal. **—tags=post,** *f.* Monday's post *or* mail.

Monta'n=industrie, *f.* mining-industry.

Mont—eu'r, *m.* (**—eurs,** *pl.* **—eure**) engine-fitter. **—ie'ren,** *v.a.* to erect, set up, fit up, adjust, mount (*machines*); to mount (*jewels*); to clothe, equip (*soldiers*); to supply with a horse; **ein Schiff —ieren,** to man a ship. **—ie'rung,** *f.* mounting, adjusting, erection (*of an engine*); uniform; equipment (*Mil.*). **—u'r,** *f.* uniform, regimentals; livery. *Comp.* **—ie'rungs=kammer,** *f.* magazine, depot *or* stores of army accoutrements. **—ie'rungs=kosten,** *pl.* expenses for erecting. **—ie'rungs=stücke,** *pl.* mountings, soldiers' uniforms, equipment, regimentals.

Moor, *n.* (**—s,** *pl.* **—e**) moor; bog, swamp. **—ig,** *adj.* marshy; fen, bog. *Comp.* **—bad,** *n.* mud-bath. **—eiche,** *f.* bog-oak. **—ente,** *f.* shoveller, fen-duck. **—erde,** *f.* peaty soil. **—gegend,** *f.*, **—land,** *n.* fen-country, marshy land. **—gras,** *n.* sedge. **—hahn,** *m.* moor-fowl, red grouse. **—huhn,** *n.* coot. **—torf,** *m.* turf, peat. **—wasser,** *n.* boggy water.

[1]**Moos,** *n.* (**—(s)es,** *pl.* **—(s)e**) moss; **isländisches —,** Iceland moss; **irländisches —,** Carragheen moss. **—(s)ig,** *adj.* mossy. *Comp.*

—bank, *f.* mossy seat. **—bedeckt, —bewachsen,** *adj.* moss-grown. **—lager,** *n.* mossy couch. **—stein,** *m.* mossy stone.

²**Moos,** *n.* money, cash, the needful (*sl.*).

Mops, *m.* (**—ses,** *pl.* **Möp'se**) pug; blockhead; peevish person. **—(s)ig,** *adj.* pug-nosed; ugly; **sich —(s)ig machen,** to assert oneself (*sl.*). *Comp.* **—gesicht,** *n.* pug-face; ugly person.

Mop'sen, *v.r.* to be vexed (*sl.*); to be bored (*sl.*).

Mora'l, *f.* morals, ethics; moral philosophy; moral (*of fables, etc.*); **einem die — lesen,** to read a p. a lecture. **—isch,** *adj. & adv.* moral; **—ische Betrachtungen anstellen,** to moralize; **—isch schlecht,** wicked; **—isch unmöglich,** morally impossible; **einen —ischen haben,** to have qualms of conscience, to feel the prick of conscience, of self-reproach (*coll.*); **—ische Person,** corporate body (*Law*); **—ischer Roman,** novel with a moral tendency. **—isie'ren,** *v.n.* (*aux.* **h.**) to moralize. **—i'st,** *m.* (**—is'ten,** *pl.* **—is'ten**) moral philosopher, moralist. **—itä't,** *f.* morality. *Comp.* **—philosophie,** *f.* moral philosophy, ethics.

Mora'st, *m.* (**—s,** *pl.* **Moräs'te**) morass, marsh, bog. **—ig,** *adj.* marshy; miry, muddy; dirty. *Comp.* **—loch,** *n.* quagmire.

Morato'ri—um, *n.* (**—ums,** *pl.* **—en**) letter of respite.

Mor'chel, *f.* (*pl.* **—n**) edible fungus, morel.

Mord, *m.* (**—es,** *pl.* **—e**) murder; homicide; sword (*L*[illegible]); **es ist der reine —,** it is a terrible business (*sl.*); **Zeter und —** (*usually* **—io**) **schreien,** to cry murder; **einen — begehen,** *see* **—en** I.; **— und Tod!** zounds! **—io,** *int.* murder! *Comp.* (**—s-** *is emphatic:* great, very, fine, *e.g.* **—s-geschrei,** terrible outcry; **—s-kalt,** fearfully cold). **—acht,** *f.* outlawry for murder. **—anschlag,** *m.* murderous design, attempt on a p.'s life. **—axt,** *f.*, **—beil,** *n.* murderous weapon *or* axe. **—begierde, —gier, —lust, —sucht,** *f.* desire for murder, sanguinary disposition, bloodthirstiness. **—begierig, —süchtig,** *adj.* bloodthirsty. **—brand,** *m.* arson. **—brenner,** *m.* incendiary. **—eisen,** *n.* murderous steel. **—element!** *interj.* my goodness! **—geschichte,** *f.* tale of a murder. **—geschrei,** *n.* cries of murder. **—gesell,** *m.* accomplice in a murder. **—grimmig,** *adj.* cruel, murderous. **—nacht,** *f.* night of a murder. **—rächer,** *m.* avenger of blood. **—raserei,** *f.* sanguinary rage; **einen Anfall von —raserei haben,** to run amuck. **—schlacht,** *f.* bloody battle. **—s-kerl,** *m.* fine, strapping fellow, a tip-topper (*coll.*), a devil of a fellow (*coll.*). **—s-lärm,** *m.*, **—s-spektakel,** *m.* dreadful noise, awful row, hell let loose (*sl.*). **—that,** *f.* murder, murderous deed. **—versuch,** *m.* attempt to murder. **—wut,** *f. see* **—raserei.**

Mor'den, *v.a.* to murder; to slay, kill.

Mör'der, *m.* (**—s,** *pl.* **—**) murderer, destroyer. **—in,** *f.* murderess. **—isch,** *adj.* murderous, bloody. **—lich,** *adj. & adv.* fearful, terrible; cruel; enormous (*sl.*); **—lich groß,** awfully big (*sl.*). *Comp.* **—grube,** *f.* den of assassins, cut-throat den; **aus seinem Herzen keine —grube machen,** to wear one's heart upon one's sleeve, to be very outspoken (*coll.*). **—hand,** *f.* hand of an assassin.

Morel'le, *f.* (*pl.* **—n**) morel (*cherry*).

Mo'res, *pl.* morals; good manners; **einen — lehren,** to teach a p. manners (*coll.*).

Morgana'tisch, *adj.* morganatic, left-handed (*marriage*).

Mor'gen, I. *adv.* to-morrow; **— früh,** to-morrow morning; **über—,** the day after to-morrow; **— über 8 Tage,** to-morrow week; **—, —, nur nicht heute, sagen immer träge Leute,** "to-morrow, to-morrow, not to-day," 'tis thus the idle ever say (*prov.*). II. *n.* (**—s,** *pl.* **—**) the next day. III. *m.* (**—s,** *pl.* **—**) morning; dawn; east; **— ist auch ein Tag,** we may postpone that till to-morrow; **alle —,** every morning; **des —s,** in the morning, of a morning; **früh —s, am frühen —,** early in the morning; **heute —, diesen —,** this morning; **gestern —,** yesterday morning; **vorgestern —,** the morning of the day before yesterday; **guten —,** good morning; **anbrechender —,** dawn; **ja —!** don't you wish you may get it! **eines schönen —s,** one fine morning; **das Antlitz gegen —,** the face turned eastwards; **so fern der — ist vom Abend,** as far as the east is from the west (*B.*). IV. *m.* (**—s,** *pl.* **—**) measure of land, acre; rod, perch. **—d,**

Mor'gig, *adj.* of to-morrow; morning; **der —de Tag,** the next day, to-morrow; **meine —de Abreise,** my departure which is fixed for to-morrow. **—dlich, —haft,** *adj.* in *or* of the morning, matutinal. **—s,** *adv.* in the morning. *Comp.* **—andacht,** *f.* morning devotion, morning prayers; matins (*R.Cath.*). **—anzug,** *m.* morning dress; undress. **—ausgabe,** *f.* morning edition (*of a newspaper*). **—besuch,** *m.* morning call. **—brot,** *n.* breakfast. **—dämmerung,** *f.* day-break, dawn; **in der —dämmerung,** in the early twilight. **—gabe,** *f.* gift of the bridegroom to his bride the day after marriage. **—gang,** *m.* morning walk; easterly lode. **—gegend,** *f.* eastern country. **—göttin,** *f.* Aurora. **—land,** *n.* the east; the Orient, Levant; **die Weisen aus dem —lande,** the three wise men from the East. **—länder,** *pl.* oriental countries. **—ländisch,** *adj.* eastern, oriental; **—ländische Erzählung,** eastern *or* oriental tale; **das —ländische Kaisertum,** the Greek Empire. **—lied,** *n.* morning hymn, morning song. **—luft,** *f.* morning-breeze, morning-air. **—post,** *f.* early mail. **—punkt,** *m.* due east. **—rot,** I. *adj.* rosy like the morn. II. *n.*, **—röte,** *f.* dawn, aurora; bloom, prime. **—schön,** *adj.* as beautiful as the early day. **—segen,** *m.* morning prayer; matins. **—seite,** *f.* eastern side. **—sonne,** *f.* morning sun; rising sun. **—ständchen,** *n.* day-break serenade. **—stern,** *m.* morning-star, day-star; club with iron spikes on it, cudgel. **—stunde,** *f.* morning hour; **—stunde hat Gold im Munde** (*lit.* the morning hour has gold in its hand), early to bed and early to rise, makes a man healthy, wealthy, and wise; the early bird catches the worm (*prov.*). **—tisch,** *m.* dressing-table. **—unterhaltung,** *f.* (**musikalische**) matinée musicale. **—wache,** *f.* morning watch (*Naut.*). **—wecker,** *m.* alarum-clock. **—weite,** *f.* eastern amplitude. **—wind,** *m.* morning breeze; east wind.

Mormo'n—e, *m.* (**—en,** *pl.* **—en**), **—in,** *f.* Mormon. **—entum,** *n.* (**—entums**) Mormonism; the Mormons.

Mor'phium, *n.* (**—s**) morphine.

Morsch, *adj.* decaying, rotten; worm-eaten. **—heit,** *f.* rottenness.

Mör'ser, *m.* (**—s,** *pl.* **—**) mortar (*also Artil.*); compass-box (*Naut.*). *Comp.* **—keule,** *f.* pestle. **—laffette,** *f.* mortar-carriage.

Mortalitä'ts-tabelle, *f.* table(s) of mortality.

Mör'tel, *m.* (**—s,** *pl.* **—**) mortar; plaster, cement; **mit grobem — bewerfen,** rough-cast. *Comp.* **—arbeit,** *f.* stucco-plastering. **—kelle,** *f.* trowel. **—teig,** *m.* impastation. **—träger,** *m.* hodman. **—trog,** *m.* hod.

Mosai'k, *f.* mosaic, mosaic-work. *Comp.* **—arbeit,** *f.* mosaic-work. **—fußboden,** *m.* tessellated pavement.

Mos—a'isch, *adj.*, Mosaic. **—es,** *m.*; **die fünf Bücher —es** *or* **—is,** the Pentateuch; **das erste Buch —is,** Genesis; **das zweite,** Exodus;

das dritte, Leviticus; das vierte, Numbers; das fünfte, Deuteronomy; —es und die Propheten haben, to be very wealthy (*coll.*).

Moschee', *f.* (*pl.* —en) mosque.

Mo'schus, *m.* musk. *Comp.* —**ente**, *f.* muscovy duck. —**rose**, **Mosch'rose**, *f.* musk-rose. —**tier**, *n.* musk deer.

Moski'te, *f.* (*pl.* —n), **Moski'to**, *m.* (—s, *pl.* —s) mosquito.

Moskowi't—er, *m.* (—ers, *pl.* —er), —**erin**, *f.* Muscovite. —**isch**, *adj.* Muscovite.

Most, *m.* (—es, *pl.* —e) new wine; must; cider; juice of fruit. —**eln**, *v.* I. *n.* (*aux.* h.) to smell, taste of must; to taste new (*of wine*); **wissen, wo Barthel — holt**, to be initiated, to know all about a th., to be behind the scenes. II. *a.*, *see* —**en**. —**en**, *v.a.* to make cider *or* most. —**icht** (*obs.*), —**ig**, *adj.* cider-like. *Comp.* —**kelter**, —**presse**, *f.* wine-press; cider-press.

Mo'strich, *m.* (—s), mustard.

Mot—et'te, *f.* motett (*Mus.*). —**io'n**, *f.* movement, exercise; motion (*in parliament, etc.*); **sich** (*dat.*) (**eine kleine**) —**ion machen**, to take some exercise. —**i'v**, *n.* (—iv(e)s, *pl.* —ive) motive; subject, motif (*Mus.*). —**ivie'ren**, *v.a.* to assign *or* show the reason *or* reasons of; to cause, give rise to.

Mo'tor, *m.* (—s, *pl.* **Moto'ren**) motor; **elektromagne'tischer** —, dynamo; **hydrau'lischer** —, water-motor. *Comp.* —**boot**, *n.* motor-boat. —**dreirad**, *n.* motor-tricycle. —**en=haus**, *n.* power-house. —**wagen**, *m.* motor-carriage, motor-car. —**zweirad**, *n.* motor-bicycle.

Mot't—e, *f.* (*pl.* —en) moth; whim. —**ig**, *adj.* full of moths; moth-eaten. *Comp.* —**en=fraß**, *m.* damage done by moths. —**en=pulver**, *n.* insect powder.

Moussie'ren, *v.n.* to effervesce, sparkle, fizz; —**der Champagner**, sparkling champagne, fizz.

Mö've, **Mö'we**, *f.* (*pl.* —n) sea-gull, mew.

Muck, *m.* (—es, *pl.* —e), —**s**, *m.* (—(s)es, *pl.* —(s)e) faint sound; **keinen — thun**, not to utter a sound; **keinen — haben**, to have no spunk (*sl.*); **nicht — sagen**, not to utter a word. —**e**, *f.* (*pl.* —en) whim, freak, caprice; sulks; difficulty; (*pl.*) pranks; **ein Pferd das —en hat**, a vicious horse; **er hat seine —en**, he has his crotchets; **das Ding hat seine —en**, there is a hitch in the matter.

Mü'cke, **Mu'cke**, *f.* (*pl.* —n) gnat, midge; fly; (*beauty-*)patch; extortioner; aim, sight (*of a gun*); fork-like implement; —**n seigen und Kameele verschlucken**, to strain at a gnat and swallow a camel; **aus einer — einen Elefanten machen**, to make a mountain of a molehill (*prov.*); —**n zu Kameelen machen**, to make mountains of molehills (*prov.*); **mit Geduld und Spucke fängt man eine Mucke**, be patient, persevere, and you will arrive (*prov.*). *Comp.* —**n=fängerei**, *f.* fancifulness; fussiness; vain enquiry. —**n=fett**, *n.* something absurd, mare's nest; **eine nnach —nfett schicken**, to send a p. on a fool's errand. —**n=flor**, *m.*, —**n=netz**, *n.* mosquito curtain. —**n=pulver**, *n.* insect-destroyer. —**n=seiger**, *m.* fidgety *or* fussy person. —**n=stachel**, *m.* gnat's sting. —**n=stich**, *m.* sting of a gnat.

Mu'ck—en, *v.n.* (*aux.* h.) to utter a low sound; to grumble, mutter; to budge, move; to twitch; to sulk; to be whimsical; to hold one's tongue; —**e nicht!** not a word! **es —t**, there is a hitch in the matter; **meine Zähne —en**, my teeth are grumbling, I have a dull toothache. —**er**, *m.* (—ers, *pl.* —er), —**erin**, *f.* sulky person; grumbler; secretly malicious person; *see* **Mucker**. —**ern**, *v.n. imp.* to twinge, to ache. —(**i**)**sch**, *adj.* capricious, peevish. —**sen**, *v.r.* to stir; to utter a faint sound; **sich nicht —sen**, to be absolutely silent; **nicht gemuckst**, hush! don't stir!

Mu'cker, *m.* (—s, *pl.* —) bigot, hypocrite; strait-laced clergyman, narrow-minded and puritanical parson. —**ei'**, *f.* cant. —**haft**, —**ig**, *adj.* canting. —**n**, *v.n.* (*aux.* h.) to be a bigot *or* hypocrite. —**tum**, *n.* bigotry; cant.

Mud'delig, *adj.* dirty (*coll.*).

Mü'd—e, *adj.* & *adv.* weary, tired; **ich bin des Wartens —e**, I am tired of waiting; **ich bin es —e, auf ihn zu warten**, I am tired of waiting for him; **zum Umfallen —e**, tired to death; **sich bei einer S.** *or* **durch eine S. —e machen**, to tire oneself with (*doing*) something; **sich —e arbeiten**, to work till one is tired; **des Lebens —e**, weary *or* sick of life. —**igkeit**, *f.* weariness, fatigue; lassitude.

[1]**Muff**, *m.* (—es, *pl.* —e) pouter, sulky person; deep bark, bay; cross, growling dog.

[2]**Muff**, *m.* (—es, *pl.* **Müf'fe**), —**e**, *f.* (*pl.* —en) muff; socket-joint.

[3]**Muff**, *m.* (—es) mouldy smell; mould. —**en**, *v.n.* (*aux.* h.) to smell musty. —**ig**, **Müf'fig**, *adj.* musty; rank; sulky.

Müff'chen, *n.* (—s, *pl.* —) mitten, muffettee.

[1]**Muf'f—el**, *n.* (—els, *pl.* —el) animal with large hanging lips; blubber-faced person; fountain, spout, *etc.*, in the form of a beast's mouth; canting person. —(**e**)**lig**, *adj. see* —**ig**; blubber-faced; not amiable, cross, rough, sulky (*sl.*). —**eln**, *v.a.* & *n.* (*aux.* h.) to mumble; to eat gluttonously; to close the teeth in speaking; to mutter; to pout, mope, sulk, to be in bad spirits (*sl.*). —**en**, *v.n.* (*aux.* h.) to mutter, grumble; to sulk; to bark. —**er**, *m.* (—ers, *pl.* —er) morose fellow, grumbler. —**ig**, *adj.* glum, pouting, sulky. *Comp.* —**el=gesicht**, *n.* blubber face; blubber-faced person; animal's face as ornament (*Arch.*).

[2]**Muf'fel**, *f.* muffle (*Chem.*). *Comp.* —**ofen**, *m.* assay-furnace.

Mü'h—e, *f.* (*pl.* —en) trouble, pains, toil, labour; **nicht der —e wert**, not worth while; **es verlohnt sich der —e**, it is quite worth while; **die** *or* **seine —e umsonst haben**, to lose one's labour; **keine —e scheuen**, to spare no pains; **mit —e**, painfully, with difficulty, hardly, ill; **sich** (*dat.*) —**e geben**, to take pains; **sich** (*acc.*) **keine —e verdrießen lassen**, to spare no pains; **einem —e machen**, to give a p. trouble; **es macht mir —e, ihm das zu sagen**, it pains me *or* it costs me an effort to say that to him. —**en**, *v.a.* & *r.* to trouble; to grieve; **sich —en** (**mit einer S.**), to trouble oneself, to take pains (*about a th.*). —**sal**, *n.* (—sals, *pl.* —sale), *f.* (*pl.* —sale) toil; distress, trouble, affliction; care; difficulty. —**sam**, *adj.* & *adv.* toilsome, laborious; painful, irksome; assiduous, painstaking; **sich —sam ernähren**, to struggle hard to get a living. —**samkeit**, *f.* difficulty; laboriousness; trouble. —**selig**, *adj.* & *adv.* toilsome; wretched; weary. —**seligkeit**, *f.* hardship. *Comp.* —(**e**)=**los**, *adj.* without toil *or* trouble. —(**e**)=**losigkeit**, *f.* ease, easiness, facility. —(**e**)=**voll**, *adj.* laborious, troublesome, irksome. —**waltung**, *f.* care, pains, assiduity; **für seine —waltung**, for his trouble.

Mu'h—en, *v.n.* (*aux.* h.) to low (*of cows*). —**kuh**, *f.* moo-cow.

Müh'l—e, *f.* (*pl.* —en) mill; a game played with draughtsmen; draughts; see-saw, double ruff (*at whist*); a gymnastic exercise; **das ist Wasser auf seine —e**, that is grist to his mill. *Comp.* —**bach**, *m.* mill stream. —**bereiter**, *m.* caretaker of the machinery in a paper-mill. —**beutel**, *m.* bolter. —**bursche**, *m.* miller's man. —**en=bau**, *m.* construction of mills. —**en=bauer**, *m.* millwright. —**en=bremse**, *f.* stop of a windmill. —**en=metze**, *f.* multure. —**en=teich**, *m.* mill pond. —**knappe**, *m.* miller's man. —**lauf**, *m.* box, drum. —**ständer**, *m.* axis of a windmill. —steiger, *m.* head-man *or* inspector of mills. —trichter, *m.* mill-hopper. —wasser, *n.* mill-race. —wehr, *n.* mill-dam. —welle, *f.* revolving shaft of a mill-wheel. —werk, *n.* mill. —zwang, *m.* obligation to have one's corn ground at a certain mill.

Muh'me, *f.* (*pl.* —n, *dim.* Mühm'chen) aunt; female cousin *or* relation.

Mulat't—e, *m.* (—en, *pl.* —en), —in, *f.* mulatto; —innen, female mulattoes, mulattresses.

Mul'd—e, *f.* (*pl.* —en) tray; trough; tub; bowl; hutch (*Bak.*); pannier; hollow, cavity (*Min.*); eine —e Blei, a pig of lead; es gießt wie mit —en (*or* Mollen), it is raining cats and dogs (*coll.*). —ig, *adj.* trough-shaped. *Comp.* —en=blei, *n.* pig-lead.

Mu'le— (*in comp.*) —garn, *n.* mule-twist.

1**Mull, Müll**, *n.* (—s) dust, rubbish; mould. *Comp.* —abfuhr, *f.* carting of dust. —kiste, *f.* dust-bin. —wagen, *m.* dust-cart, dustman's cart.

2**Mull**, *m.* (& *n.*) (—s) mull (*muslin*).

Mül'le, *f.* (*pl.* —n) red mullet.

Mül'ler, *m.* (—s, *pl.* —) miller; species of parrot; meal-worm (*Ent.*); miller's thumb (*Icht.*). —ei', *f.* miller's trade. —in, *f.* miller's wife; miller's daughter. *Comp.* —esel, *m.* miller's donkey; drudge; dunce. —gaze, *f.* (*silk*) bolting-cloth. —gesell, —knappe, *m.* miller's man *or* apprentice; die —gesellen schlagen sich, they are plucking geese in Scotland (*it is snowing*). —lieder, *n.pl.* the miller's songs (*famous songs written by W. Müller and composed by F. Schubert*). —sack, *m.* sack of meal.

Mulm, *m.* (—s, *pl.* —e) rottenness of wood; rotten wood; dust of rotten wood; mould; dust; ore-dust. —en, *v.* I. *a.* to pulverize, reduce to powder. II. *n.* (*aux.* s.) to turn to dust, crumble. —icht, —ig, *adj.* worm-eaten, decayed; mouldy, loose; friable.

Multi—plikan'dus, *m.* (*pl.* —plikanden) multiplicand. —plikatio'n, *f.* multiplication. —plikati'v, *adj.* multiplying; tending to multiply. —plikati'vum, *n.* multiplying numeral (*as once, twice, etc.*). —plika'tor, *m.* (—plikators, *pl.* —plikato'ren) multiplier. —plizie'ren, *v.a.* to multiply.

Mul'tipl—um, *n.* (—ums, *pl.* —a) multiple.

Mul'ton, Mul'tum, *m.* (—s) swan's down.

Mu'lus, *m.* mule; boy who has left school and is to go to the Univ. but has not yet begun residence (*students' sl.*). *See* Maultier.

Mu'mi—e, *f.* (*pl.* —en) mummy. —enhaft, *adj.* mummy-like. —fizie'ren, *v.a.* to mummify, to embalm.

Mumm, *m.*; keinen — haben, to have no pluck (*sl.*); to have no inclination (*sl.*).

1**Mum'me**, *f.* a kind of strong (*Brunswick*) beer.

2**Mum'm—e**, *f.* (*pl.* —en) mask; masker. —el, *n.* (—els, *pl.* —el) bugbear, bogey, frightful apparition. —eln, *v.n.* (*aux.* h.) to speak indistinctly; *see* —en. —en, *v.a.* to muffle up; to mask, disguise. —er, *m.* (—ers, *pl.* —er) masker, mummer. —erei', *f.* mummery; buffoonery. *Comp.* —el=greis, *m.* very old man, old fogey. —en=gesicht, *n.* mask, visor. —en=kleid, *n.* masquerading costume. —en=schanz, *f.* (*obs.*) & *m.*, —en=spiel, *n.* masquerade.

Müm'mel,—chen, *n.* water-lily; mermaid (*dial.*).

Mum'pitz, *m.* (—es), bosh, stuff, nonsense (*sl.*).

1**Mund**, *m.* (—es, *pl.* —e *and* Mün'der) mouth; orifice, opening; reinen — halten, to keep a secret *or* a counsel; kein Blatt vor den — nehmen, to speak out; den — halten, to hold one's tongue; den — voll nehmen, to talk big; den — spitzen, to screw up one's mouth; sich (*dat.*) eine S. am —e absparen, to stint o. s. in food for a thing; die Hand auf den —! keep it dark! not a word! sie redet jedermann nach dem —e, she agrees with everybody; auf den — schlagen, to contradict flatly; er ist wie auf den — geschlagen, he is quite confounded; Sie nehmen mir das Wort aus dem —e, that is just what I was going to say; einem etwas in den — legen, to suggest to a p. what to say; to attribute remarks, *etc.*, to s. o.; in aller Leute — sein, to be much talked of; von der Hand in den — leben, to live from hand to mouth; *see under* Maul. *Comp.* —art, *f.* idiom, dialect. —artig, (*obs.*) —artlich, *adj.* peculiar to a dialect, dialectic. —bäcker, *m.* baker to a royal household. —bedarf, *m.* provisions, victuals. —enge, *f.* narrowing of mouth. —faul, *adj.* tongue-tied; taciturn. —fäulnis, *f.* scurvy of the mouth. —freund, *m.* lip-friend. —gerecht, *adj.* easy to pronounce; easy to eat; suitable, pleasant. —höhle, *f.* cavity of the mouth. —kanal, *m.* mouth-passage. —klemme, *f.* tetanus. —knebel, *m.* gag. —koch, *m.* prince's cook. —loch, *n.* orifice, mouth. —reif, *m.* hoop *or* neck of a cannon's mouth. —schenk, *m.* cup-bearer. —sperre, *f.* lock-jaw. —stück, *n.* mouth-piece; mouth, orifice; mouth, muzzle (*Artil.*); reed (*of a hautboy, etc.*); bridle-bit; mouth, tongue (*vulg.*). —teil, *m.* allowance, ration. —tot, *adj.* & *adv.* dead in law; not allowed to speak; einen —tot machen, not to allow a p. to get a word in. —verschluß, *m.* closure of mouth passage. —voll, *m.* mouthful. —vorrat, *m.* victuals, provisions. —werk, *n.* mouth; glib tongue; er hat ein gutes —werk, he has the gift of the gab (*coll.*).

2**Mund**, *f.* (*obs.*) (*in comp.* = hand; protection); (*with confusion of gender*) Morgenstunde hat Gold im —e, early to bed and early to rise, makes a man healthy, wealthy, and wise; the early bird catches the worm (*prov.*). *Comp.* —tot, *adj.* dead in law. —walt, *m.* guardian (*obs.*).

Münd'—chen, *n.* (—chens, *pl.* —chen) little mouth. —e, (*obs.*) *f.* mouth (*of a river*). —en, *v.n.* (*aux.* h.) to fall into, flow into. —lich, *adj.* & *adv.* oral, verbal, by word of mouth; viva voce; —liche Auskunft, information by word of mouth; —licher Verkehr, personal intercourse; —liche Prüfung, oral examination, viva voce examination *or* test. —lichkeit, *f.* oral proceedings (*Law*); oral character (*of anything*). —ung, *f.* mouth (*of a river*), estuary; mouth, orifice; railway terminus. —ungs=weite, *f.* calibre (*of a gun*).

Münd'—el, *m.* (—els, *pl.* —el) pupil; ward; minor. —ig, *adj.* of age; —ig werden, to come of age; einen für —ig erklären, einen —ig sprechen, to declare a p. of age; der —ige, person of age, major. —igkeit, *f.* majority. *Comp.* —el=geld, —el=gut, *n.* property of a ward *or* minor. —el=sicher, *adj.* absolutely safe; das Geld wurde —elsicher angelegt, the investment made was absolutely safe. —el=stand, *m.* pupilage. —ig=machung, —ig=sprechung, *f.* declaring (*a person*) of age; emancipation.

Mun'd—en, *v.n.* (*aux.* h.) to taste well, to be appetizing; es —et mir, I relish that, I like it; ich lasse es mir —en, I fall to heartily.

Mundie'ren, *v.a.* to cleanse; to make a fair copy of.

Mun'd—um, *n.* (—ums, *pl.* —a) fair copy.

Munitio'n, *f.* (*pl.* —en) ammunition, military *or* naval stores. *Comp.* —s=kasten, *m.* ammunition chest; caisson. —s=wagen, *m.* ammunition waggon, caisson; tender (*Railw.*).

Mun'keln, *v.a.* & *n.* (*aux.* h.) to whisper about; to do secretly; man munkelt, it is rumoured; im Dunkeln ist gut —, night is the friend of lovers.

Mün'ster, (*m.* &) *n.* (—s, *pl.* —) cathedral, minster.

Mun'ter, *adj.* awake; vigilant; lively; gay, blithe, merry; vigorous; bright (*of colours*); allegro (*Mus.*); **du bist wohl nicht ganz —**, are you mad? *adv.*, actively, briskly. **—keit**, *f.* liveliness, sprightliness; vigilance.

Mün'ze, *f.* (*pl.* **—n**) coin, money; coinage; medal; change, small money; the mint; **—n schlagen**, to coin, make coins; **klingende —**, cash; **mit gleicher — bezahlen**, to pay with the same coin; **einen mit barer —e bezahlen**, to give s. o. a Roland for his Oliver; **geben Sie mir für einen Thaler —**, give me (small) change for a three-mark piece; **für bare — nehmen**, to take as gospel, believe.

Mün'z—en, *v.a. & n.* (*aux.* **h.**) to coin; to forge (*new words, etc.*); **auf** (**einen** *or* **etwas**) **—en**, to aim at; **gemünztes Geld**, specie; **es war auf ihn gemünzt**, that was meant for him. **—er**, *m.* (**—ers**, *pl.* **—er**) coiner, minter; forger. *Comp.* **—amt**, *n.* board *or* directory of the mint; mint-office. **—anstalt**, *f.* the mint. **—einheit**, *f.* unit, standard of currency. **—en=kabinett**, *n.* cabinet of coins. **—(en)=kunde**, *f.* numismatics. **—fälscher**, *m.* utterer of base coin, money-clipper. **—fälschung**, *f.* debasing of coin, money clipping; forging of coin. **—freiheit**, *f.* privilege of coining. **—fund**, *m.* discovery of coins. **—fuß**, *m.* standard (of coinage). **—gepräge**, *n.* coin-stamp. **—gehalt**, *m.* standard of the currency, alloy. **—gewicht**, *n.* standard weight. **—haus**, *n.* the mint. **—herr**, *m.* sovereign; master of the mint. **—justie'rer**, *m.* mint-assayer. **—kosten**, *pl.* (cost of) coinage. **—kundig**, *adj.* skilled in numismatics. **—kunst**, *f.* art of coining. **—meister**, *see* **—herr**. **—ordnung**, *f.* mint regulations. **—platte**, *f.* planchet, coin-plate. **—prägung**, *f.* coinage. **—probe**, *f.* assay (*of coin*). **—recht**, *n.* right of coining. **—sammlung**, *f.* collection of coins. **—schlag**, *m.* coinage. **—schrift**, *f.* inscription on a coin. **—sorte**, *f.* kind of coin. **—stadt**, *f.* town where a mint is. **—stempel**, *m.* die. **—stück**, *n.* coin; planchet. **—verfälscher**, *m.* utterer of base coin. **—währung**, *f.* standard (*value*) of coin. **—wert**, *m.* standard (*of the currency*). **—wesen**, *n.* mint matters; monetary system. **—zusatz**, *m.* alloy.

Mür'b—e, I. *adj.* mellow; tender; well-cooked; short, crisp; friable; unsound (*of ice*); decayed, brittle; weary; pliable; **—e machen**, to curb, bend, humble; (**vom Schicksal**) **—e gemacht**, broken, battered. II. *f.*, **—igkeit**, *f.* mellowness; tenderness; dry-rot; friability; suppleness.

Mur'bruch, *m.* landslip (*dial.*).

Murk'sen, *v.n.* to grunt; to grumble (*vulg.*).

Mur'mel, *f.* (*pl.* **—n**) marble (*dial.*). *Comp.* **—spiel**, *n.* game at marbles.

Mur'mel—n, *v.a. & n.* (*aux.* **h.**) to murmur; to mutter; to whisper. *Comp.* **—tier**, *n.* marmot.

Mur'ner, *m.* (**—s**, *pl.* **—**) cat (*in fables, etc.*).

Mur'r—en, *v.a. & n.* (*aux.* **h.**) to murmur, mutter, grumble. *Comp.* **—kopf**, *m.* surly person, grumbler. **—köpfig**, *see* **Mürrisch**.

Mür'risch, *adj.* surly, morose, sullen.

Mus, *n.* (**—(s)es**, *pl.* **—(s)e**) soft boiled vegetable food; pap; marmalade; stewed fruit, *etc.*, jelly; **zu — schlagen**, to beat to a jelly.

Mus'teil, Muß'teil, *m.* (**—s**, *pl.* **—e**) widow's portion.

Mu'schel, *f.* (*pl.* **—n**) mussel, shell-fish; shell; conch (*Anat.*); basket-hilt (*of cutlasses, etc.*); whelk; cam (*Mach.*); thumb (*of a latch*). **—icht**, (*obs.*) **—ig**, *adj.* conchoidal. *Comp.* **—gehäuse**, *n.* shell (*of mussels, etc.*). **—gericht**, *n.* ostracism. **—grus**, *m.* alluvial deposits of shells. **—insekt**, *n.* cochineal. **—kenner**, *m.* conchologist. **—kenntnis, —kunde, —lehre**, *f.* conchology. **—linie**, *f.* conchoid. **—sammlung**, *f.* collection of shells. **—tiere**, *pl.* mollusks.

Mu'schelig, *adj.* soft, comfortable, snug (*coll.*).

Mu's—e, *f.* (*pl.* **—en**) muse. **—e'um**, *n.* (**—eums**, *pl.* **—een**) museum; study (*obs.*); literary club *or* society. **—ici**, *see* **Musikus**. **—ik, —ikalisch, &c.**, *see* **Musik**. **—isch**, *adj.* sacred *or* devoted to the Muses. **—izie'ren**, *v.n.* (*aux.* **h.**) to perform *or* practise music; **des Abends wurde stets —iziert**, we always had music in the evenings. *Comp.* **—en=almanach**, *m.* almanac of the Muses, almanac containing contributions from contemporary lyric poets, poetical annual. **—en=berg**, *m.* Parnassus, Helicon. **—en=freund**, *m.* lover, patron of poetry. **—en=gott**, *m.* Apollo. **—en=kunst**, *f.* poetry. **—en=quell**, *m.* Hippocrene. **—en=roß, —en=tier**, *n.* Pegasus. **—en=sitz**, *m.* seat of the Muses; academy, university. **—en=sohn**, *m.* poet; student. **—en=stadt**, *f.* University town (*e.g.*: **—enstadt an der Pleiße** = Leipzig; **—enstadt an der Leine** = Göttingen; **—enstadt am Neckar** = Tübingen *or* Heidelberg).

Musi'k, *f.* music; band of musicians; **in — setzen**, to set to music; **ohne — abziehen**, to steal away; **da ist — drin**, that is good; there is something in that. **—a'lien**, *pl.* music (books); musical compositions. **—a'lisch**, *adj. & adv.* musical; skilled in music; **ein —alisches Gehör**, a good ear for music; **ich bin nicht —alisch**, I am not musical, I am no musician. **—a'nt**, *m.* (**—an'ten**, *pl.* **—an'ten**) musician (*prov.*); **herumziehende —anten**, (*in England*) German band; **die —anten**, ready money; **hier liegt ein —ant begraben!** I am stumbling over s.th. (*coll.*); **da sitzen die —anten!** there 's the rub! **—an'ten=knochen**, *m.* funny-bone. **—er** (*pron.* **Mu'siker**), *m.* (**—ers**, *pl.* **—er**) musician; composer. **—us** (*pron.* **Mu'sikus**), *m.* (*pl.* **Mu'sici**) musician; member of an orchestra. *Comp.* **—a'lien=handlung**, *f.* music-seller's shop; music shop. **—a'lien=leih=institut**, *n.* lending library of music. **—aufführung**, *f.* musical performance. **—bande**, *f.* brass band; street musicians. **—chor**, *m. & n.* chorus; choir (*also Arch.*). **—corps**, *n.* band. **—direktor, —dirigent, —meister**, *m.* conductor; leader of an orchestra; bandmaster (*Mil.*). **—drama**, *n.* opera. **—fest**, *n.* musical festival. **—kenner**, *m.* connoisseur of music. **—mappe**, *f.* music-case. **—saal**, *m.* concert room. **—stimme**, *f.* part (*in music*). **—stück**, *n.* piece of music. **—stunde**, *f.* music lesson. **—truppe**, *f.* band of musicians. **—verein**, *m.* musical society.

Musi'v, —isch, *adj.* mosaic. *Comp.* **—gold**, *n.* mosaic gold.

Musk, —us, *see* **Moschus**.

Muska't, *m.* (**—s**, *pl.* **—e**), **—e**, *f.* (*pl.* **—en**) nutmeg; **was versteht die Kuh von —en?** what's the good of listening to *or* consulting an ignoramus? **—el'ler**, *m.* (**—ellers**) muscadine (-wine); muscadine (-grape), muscatel. *Comp.* **—el'ler=wein**, *m.* muscadine (-wine); muscatel. **—(en)=baum**, *m.* nutmeg tree.

Mus'k—el, *see* **Muskel**. **—ulö's**, *adj. & adv* muscular, sinewy.

Mus'kel, *m.* (**—s**, *pl.* **—n**), *f.* (*pl.* **—n**) muscle. **—ig, Muskulö's**, *adj.* muscular; with muscles. *Comp.* **—anstrengung**, *f.* muscular exertion. **—band**, *n.* ligament. **—bau**, *m.* muscling (*Paint.*); contexture of muscles. **—faser**, *f.* muscular fibre. **—lehre**, *f.* myology. **—mann**, *m.* lay figure. **—stärke**, *f.* muscular strength. **—zergliederung, —zerlegung**, *f.* myotomy.

Muske't—e, *f.* (*pl.* **—en**) musket, gun; (*pl.*) musketry. **—ie'r**, *m.* (**—iers**, *pl.* **—iere**) musketeer; (*pl.*) musketry. *Comp.* **—en=feuer**, *n.* musketry fire. **—en=salve**, *f.* volley from muskets.

[1]**Muß**, *n. see* **Mus**.

²Muß, Mußt, I. *1 (& 3) & 2 pers. sing. pres. indic. of* müssen. II. *s.* (*indec.*) necessity, compulsion; — ist eine bittre Nuß, necessity is a hard master (*prov.*); es ist ein —, one must, it is necessary. *Comp.* —preuße, *m.* Prussian against his own wishes, subject of a state annexed by Prussia (in 1866) (*obs.*).

Mu'ße, *f.* leisure, spare *or* idle time; bei —, mit —, at leisure, leisurely. *Comp.* —stunde, *f.* leisure hour. —zeit, *f.* spare time.

Musselin', *m.* (—s, *pl.* —e) muslin. —en, *adj.* muslin. *Comp.* —kleid, *n.* muslin dress.

Müs'sen, *ir.v.n. aux. of mood,* to be obliged, have to, must; to be bound by duty, *etc.*; (*preceded by the inf. of another verb,* müssen *is used for p.p.* gemußt); ich muß nicht vergessen (*obs. for* ich darf nicht vergessen), I must not forget, I am bound not to forget, I will not forget; ich muß fort, I must go; es mußte ein Patent genommen werden, a patent had to be taken out; ich muß lachen wenn . . ., I cannot help laughing when . . .; du mußt, du magst wollen oder nicht, you must, whether you will or no; wenn es geschehen muß, if it is inevitable; wenn das Fieber nicht nachläßt — wir zum Doktor schicken, if the fever does not go down we shall have to send for the doctor; er kommt noch, er müßte denn krank sein, he is sure to come still, unless he is ill; das werde ich nie von ihm glauben, er müßte es mir denn sagen, that I will never believe of him, unless I have it from his own lips; wer muß es nur gewesen sein? who can it have been? (*obs.*); es mußte sich gerade so fügen, daß . . ., chance would have it that . . .; es muß gewiß schon spät sein, it is late, no doubt; er muß ein ehrlicher Mann sein, he is certainly an honourable man; eine Frau wie sie sein muß, a true woman, a pattern woman; er hätte fleißiger sein —, he ought to have been more diligent; ich habe es thun —, I had *or* I have been obliged to do it; Sie — mit mir kommen, do come with me!

Mü'ßig, *adj. & adv.* idle, unemployed, at leisure; disengaged; vacant; —e Stunde, —e Zeit, leisure hours, leisure; eine —e Frage, a question not worth discussing, an idle question; — gehen, to idle, be idle; — hinbringen, to idle away; sein Geld — lassen, to let capital lie idle, dead. *Comp.* —gang, *m.* idleness; slothfulness; —gang ist aller Laster Anfang, slothfulness is the parent of all evil, idleness is the root of all evil (*prov.* —gänger, *m.* idler, slothful person; truant.

Muß'te, Müß'te, *1 pers. sing. imperf. indic. & subj. of* müssen.

Mus'ter, *n.* (—s, *pl.* —) model; pattern; sample; standard; example, paragon; — ohne Wert, sample without value, pattern post; sich (*dat.*) zum — nehmen, to take as a model; nach — machen, to make to a pattern; nach —, according to pattern. —er, *m.* (—ers, *pl.* —er) model *or* pattern maker; reviewer; inspector (*of troops*). —haft, *adj. & adv* exemplary; classical, standard. —haftigkeit, *f.* exemplariness. —ig, *suffix* (*in comp.* =) of such and such a design *or* pattern.

Mus'ter—n, *v.a.* to muster; to pass in review; to survey, examine critically; to criticize, find fault with, censure; to enrol (einmustern); to figure, make a design on; gemusterter Stoff, fancy cloth, figured stuff. —ung, *f.* mustering, muster, review; inspection. *Comp.* —anstalt, *f.* model school; normal college. —aussetzen, *n.* designing. —bild, *n.* paragon; model; ideal. —buch, *n.* book of patterns; standard work. —gültig, *adj.* standard, classical. —karte, *f.* pattern-card. —knabe, *m.* model *or* show-boy. —(karten=)reiter, *m.* commercial traveller (*coll.*). —leistung, *f.* splendid achievement, record. —platz, *m.* place of mustering, review-ground. —probe, *f.* pattern. —reisen, *n.* travelling for orders. —schriftsteller, *m.* model writer, standard author. —schule, *f.* model school. —schüler, *m.* model pupil, show-boy. —schutz, *m.* protection of a design, trade-mark protection, patent of a design. —stück, *n.* piece to serve as model *or* pattern; classical extract; specimen; (*pl.*) studies (*Paint., etc.*); deutsche —stücke, extracts from classical German authors, German anthology. —ungs=büchlein, *n.* manual of field exercises, *etc.* —ungs=tag, *m.* muster *or* review-day. —werk, *n.* standard work. —wirtschaft, *f.* model farm. —wort, *n.* paradigm, sample word. —zeichenschule, *f.* school of design. —zeichner, *m.*, —zeichnerin, *f.* designer. —zeichnung, *f.* design.

Mus'tier, *n.* moose-deer.

Mut, *m.* (—es, *dim.* Müt'chen) disposition, mettle, spirit, courage; fortitude, boldness; state of mind, mood, humour; gutes *or* guten —es sein, to be of good cheer; einem — machen, einflößen, to encourage a p.; — fassen, to pluck up heart, to pick up courage; einem guten — machen, to put a p. into good humour; wie ist dir zu —e? how do you feel? es ist mir nicht wohl zu —e, I do not feel well, I feel poorly; Sie wissen nicht, wie mir zu —e ist, you little know what I feel; mir war sonderbar zu —e, I felt queer; Gut giebt —, wealth makes a p. bold; mir fiel der —, my heart failed me; nur nicht den — verloren! don't lose courage, never say die! seinen — *or* sein Mütchen an einem kühlen, to vent one's anger on a person. —e, *f.* (*pl.* —en) request, demand, suit (*obs.*). —ig, *adj. & adv.* courageous, brave, valiant, stout-hearted, spirited; mettlesome; —ig! courage! dem —igen lächelt das Glück, Fortune favours the brave (*prov.*). *Comp.* —beseelt, —erfüllt, —voll, *adj.* full of courage, filled with courage, very courageous, high-spirited. —jahr, *n.* year in which one aspires to the freedom of a company; time which elapses between an artisan's suing to be admitted as a master and his obtaining his suit. —los, *adj.* without vigour; despondent, spiritless; discouraged, dejected. —losigkeit, *f.* despondency, dejection. —maßen, *v.a.* (*insep.*) to have an idea of; to suppose, presume, surmise, guess. —maßer, *m.* conjecturer. —maßlich, *adj. & adv.* conjectural, presumable; probable; colourable. —maßlichkeit, *f.* probability. —maßung, *f.* surmise. —maßungsweise, *adv.* by *or* as a guess. —wille, *m.* wantonness, mischief, mischievousness; petulance; high spirits; sauciness; prank; aus —willen, in wanton sport. —willig, *adj. & adv.* wanton, mischievous, petulant; roguish, naughty; saucy; —willig(er Weise), on purpose; malice prepense; wilfully, lightly; sich —willig in Gefahr begeben, to rush into danger.

Mu'ta, *f.* (*pl.* Mutä) mute, stop, explosive consonant (*either voiced* b, d, g, *or voiceless* p, t, k).

Mu't—en, *v.* I. *n.* (*aux.* s.) to be minded *or* disposed; *only used in the p.p.* gemutet *or* (*more common*) gemut; wohl gemut sein, to be of good cheer, to be cheerful. II. *a.* to demand, sue for, claim; (um) eine Grube —en, to sue for permission to work a mine. —er, *m.* (—ers, *pl.* —er) petitioner. —ung, *f.* demand (*for the freedom of a company, admission to a guild, etc.*); demand for a concession; *see* —e.

Mutie'ren, *v.a.* (*aux.* h.) to change, break (*as the voice*).

Mu'toskop, *n.* (—s, *pl.* —e) mutoscope.

Mut'ter, *f.* (*pl.* Mütter; *used without art. some-*

times gen. —**s**; *dat.* —**n** (*coll.*)) mother; matron, dame; (*pl.* —**n**) nut *or* box of a screw, female screw, screw-nut; matrix (*Found.*); pipe (*of muskets, pistols, etc.*); catch (*to a hook*); **bei — Grün übernachten,** to sleep under a tree *or* a bush, to pass the night in the open (*sl.*). —**schaft,** *f.* maternity, motherhood. *Comp.* —**ast,** *m.* main branch. —**band,** *n.* ligament of the womb. —**beschwerde,** *f.* hysterical affection, hysterics. —**biene,** *f.* queen-bee. —**bruder,** *m.* mother's brother, maternal uncle. —**erde,** *f.* mother earth; garden mould. —**fieber,** *n.* puerperal fever. —**füllen,** *n.* female foal. —**gesellschaft,** *f.* parent society; maternity society. —**gottes=bild,** *n.* image of the Blessed Virgin. —**hals,** *m.* neck of the matrix (*Anat.*). —**haus,** *n.* training-school for nurses. —**herz,** *n.* maternal heart; darling mother. —**kind,** *n.* human being; mother's pet, weakling. —**kirche,** *f.* mother-church; cathedral; parish church. —**korn,** *n.* ergot. —**kuchen,** *m.* placenta. —**lamm,** *n.* ewe-lamb. —**land,** *n.* mother-country. —**lauge,** *f.* mother-lye; mother-water. —**leib,** *m.* womb; **vom —leibe an,** from one's birth. —**liebe,** *f.* motherly love. —**los,** *adj.* motherless. —**mal,** *n.* birth-mark, mole. —**milch,** *f.* mother's milk. —**mord,** *m.* matricide. —**pferd,** *n.* mare. —**pflicht,** *f.* maternal duty. —**schaf,** *n.* ewe. —**scheide,** *f.* vagina. —**schnitt,** *m.* Cæsarian operation. —**schraube,** *f.* female screw, screw-nut. —**schwein,** *n.* sow. —**schwester,** *f.* mother's sister, maternal aunt. —**seele,** *f.* human being; **keine —seele,** not a soul; —**seelen=allein,** quite *or* all alone. —**söhnchen,** *n.* mother's darling, spoilt child, weakling. —**sprache,** *f.* mother-tongue, parent language. —**stadt,** *f.* metropolis; native town. —**stand,** *m.* maternity. —**stelle,** *f.*; —**stelle vertreten an** *or* **bei einem,** to be a mother to a p. —**stock,** *m.* solid mountain mass; stock-beehive. —**teil,** *m.* inheritance from the mother. —**wehen,** *pl.* birth-pains. —**witz,** *m.* mother-wit; **eine Unze —witz ist besser als ein ganzes Pfund Schulwitz,** one ounce of mother-wit is worth a pound of clergy, common sense is worth all the other senses.

Müt'ter—chen, *n.* dear little mother, mamsie, granny. —**lich,** *adj. & adv.* motherly, maternal; on the mother's side. —**lichkeit,** *f.* motherliness.

Mutz, *m.* (—**es,** *pl.* —**e**) stumpy thing *or* person.

Mütz'chen, *n.* (—**s,** *pl.* —) little cap *or* bonnet.

Müt'ze, *f.* (*pl.* —**n**) cap; calyptra (*Bot.*); second stomach of ruminants; **die — vor einem abziehen,** to acknowledge a p.'s superiority; **das war ihm nicht nach der —,** that did not suit him, he did not like that (*coll.*). *Comp.* —**n=blech,** *n.* peak of a cap.

Myria'de, *f.* (*pl.* —**n**) myriad.

Myrmido'ne, *m.* (—**n,** *pl.* —**n**) myrmidon.

Myr'rhe, *f.* (*pl.* —**n**) myrrh.

Myr'te, *f.* (*pl.* —**n**) myrtle.

Myst—e'rium, *n.* (—**eriums,** *pl.* —**erien**) mystery. —**eriö's,** *adj. & adv.* mysterious. —**ifizie'ren,** *v.n.* to mystify.

Mys'ti—k, *f.* mystics. —**ker,** *m.* (—**kers,** *pl.* —**ker**) mystic. —**sch,** *adj.* mystic(al).

My'th—e, *f.* (*pl.* —**en**) myth, fable. —**isch,** *adj.* mythical. —**olo'g,** *m.* (—**ologen,** *pl.* —**ologen**) student of *or* writer on mythology. —**ologie',** *f.* mythology. —**us,** *m.* (*pl.* —**en**) myth.

N

N, n, *n.* N, n, *in abbr.* **N** = **1. Namen,** name; **2. Norden,** north; **3.** (*on railway time-tables, etc.*) **Nacht,** night, *and* **Nachmittag,** afternoon; **n.** = **1. nach,** after; **2. neu.** new. *For other abbreviations see the Index of Abbreviations at the end of the German-English part.*

'n, *shortened fr.* **ein, einen,** a, an; *or fr.* **ihn,** him (it); *or for* **guten** *in* **'n Morgen,** good morning, *or* **'n Abend,** good evening.

Na, *int.* well! come now! — **nach!** now then! come, be quick! — **nur nicht hitzig!** well, well, don't get angry! —, **ich will denn nur weiter gehen,** well then, since I must go on; —, **das wäre!** well, that 's a nice thing! come now! oh, nonsense! —, —! well, well, go gently! —**nu'!** there now! well, I never! — **ob!** should n't I? rather! most certainly!

'nab = **hinab,** down (*dial. & poet.*).

Na'be, *f.* (*pl.* —**n**) nave, hub (*of a wheel*). *Comp.* —**n=band,** *n.* axle-tree hoop. —**n=büchse,** *f.* wheelbox.

Na'bel, *m.* (—**s,** *pl.* **Näbel**) navel; eye, germ, hilum (*Bot.*); key-stone (*Arch.*); nombril (*Her.*); focus, umbilical point (*Math.*); **zum — gehörig,** umbilical. —**ig,** *adj.* bossy; umbilicate. *Comp.* —**binde,** *f.* navel-bandage. —**bruch,** *m.* omphalocele. —**förmig,** *adj.* umbilicate. —**schnur,** *f.*, —**strang,** *m.* umbilical cord.

Na'beln, *v.a.* to provide with a boss *or* nombril; to bind down the navel (*of an infant*).

Nach, I. *adv. & sep. prefix,* after, behind; afterwards; conformably; — **und** —, little by little, by degrees, by and by, gradually; — **wie vor,** now as ever *or* before, as usual; **mir —!** follow me! — **gerade,** gradually, by degrees, at last; **hinten** —, afterwards, behind. II. *prep.* (*with dat.*) after, behind, following; after, later; towards, to; in conformity with, according to, agreeably to; in imitation of, after the manner of; on the authority of; by; at; in; for, considering; like to; — **Süden,** towards the south, southwards; — **Abend zu,** westward; **seinem Alter — ist er groß,** he is tall for his age; — **der Aussage meines Freundes,** according to what my friend says; — **einem ausschauen,** to look (*out*) for a p.; **seinem Aussehen** —, to judge by his appearance *or* countenance; — **der Schweiz reisen,** to go *or* travel to Switzerland; — **Hannover reisen,** to go to H., to set out for H.; **er ist — Österreich gereist,** he has left for Austria; **die Flucht — Ägypten,** the flight into Egypt; — **Deutschland bestimmte Postsendungen,** the mails for Germany; — **Brot schreien,** to cry for bread; — **Diktat schreiben,** to write from dictation; —**einander,** one after another, successively; — **der Elle,** — **dem Gewichte,** by the ell *or* yard, by weight; — **Empfang des Gegenwärtigen,** on receipt of this; — **einer S. fragen,** to enquire for a th.; **im Jahre — von Christi Geburt,** in the year of our Lord; — **dem Gedächtnis,** from memory; — **deutschem Gelde,** in German money; — **österreichischer Währung,** according to Austrian currency; — **französischem Geschmacke,** in French fashion, taste *or* style; — **beendetem Gottesdienst,** after divine service, church being over, after church; — **der rechten Hand zu,** towards the right; — **Hause,** home; **ich gehe — Hause,** I am going home; **das Fenster geht — dem Hofe hin(aus),** the window looks into the court; **das thut ihm keiner** —, no one will match him at that; no man can rival him *or* come up to him in that; **meiner Meinung** —, in my opinion; **nur dem Namen — kennen,** to know only by name; — **oben,** upwards, on high; — **alphabetischer Ordnung,** in alphabetical order; — **der Regel,** according to the rule(s); generally, as a rule, regularly; — **der Reihe, der Reihe** —, in turn, by turns; **schicken** —, to send for; — **meiner Uhr,** by my watch; **sich — einer S. umsehen,** to look round for something; to look out *or* about for a th.; **wenn es — dem Verfasser ginge,** if the author is to be believed; if the wishes of the author were to be carried out; **ein Viertel — fünf,** a quarter past five; **werfen —,** to throw at; **der Wirklichkeit —,** in reality; **— einer Woche,** a week hence; **zeichnen —,** to draw from *or* after; **— sich ziehen,** to bring on, be followed by, to cause; **— Tabak, (Rosen) riechen,** to smell of tobacco (roses). *For compounds with* **nach** = after-, *not given in the following lists, see the simple words.*

Nach'acht—en, *v.n.* (*aux.* **h.**, *dat.*) to act in conformity with, observe, live up to. **—ung,** *f.* observance; rule; **dies diene Ihnen zur —ung,** let this serve for your guidance.

Nach'äffe—n, *v.a. & n.* (*aux.* **h.**, *dat. & acc.*) to ape, mimic. **—r,** *m.* (—rs, *pl.* —r) servile imitator; mimic. **—rei',** *f.* aping, mimicry.

Nach'ahm—bar, —lich, *adj.* imitable.

Nach'ahm—en, *v.a. & n.* (*aux.* **h.**, *dat.*) to imitate, copy; to mimic; to forge, counterfeit; **einen —en,** to imitate *or* mimic s. o.; **einem —en in . . .,** to imitate a p. in . . ., to follow a p.'s example in; **—end,** imitative; **nachgeahmt,** imitated, copied, counterfeit, artificial; **nachgeahmter Diamant,** paste diamond. **—er,** *m.* (—ers, *pl.* —er) imitator, copier; counterfeiter. **—erei',** *f.* love of mimicry; servile imitation. **—ung,** *f.* imitation; counterfeiting. *Comp.* **—ens=wert,** *adj.* worthy of imitation. **—ungs=gabe,** *f.* imitative faculty. **—ungs=trieb,** *m.* imitative instinct.

Nach'arbeit, *f.* subsequent *or* additional work, extra work; copy.

Nach'arbeiten, *v.* I. *n.* (*aux.* **h.**, *dat.*) to work after *or* from; to strive to reach; to follow. II. *a.* to copy; to touch up, retouch; to make good, make up for.

Nach'art—en, *v.n.* (*aux.* **f.**, *dat.*) to resemble, take after. **—ung,** *f.* resemblance.

Nach'bar, *m.* (—s, —n, *pl.* —n), **—in,** *f.* neighbour; **nächster —,** next door neighbour; **Stuben —,** fellow-lodger. **—lich,** *adj.* neighbouring; neighbourly. **—schaft,** *f.* neighbourhood, vicinity; (*people of the*) neighbourhood; **in der nächsten —schaft,** in the immediate neighbourhood. **—schaftlich,** *adj.* relating to the neighbourhood, neighbourly. *Comp.* **—dorf,** *n.* neighbouring village. **—haus,** *n.* adjoining house, next-door house. **—recht,** *n.* right of settling in a village; privileges of a village community. **—s=leute,** *pl.* neighbours. **—staat,** *m.* neighbouring state. **—volk,** *n.* neighbouring nation.

Nach'bau, *m.* additional building. **—en,** *v.a.* to build after a model; to build subsequently; to improve, make alterations in (*a building*).

Nach'bedenken, *ir.v.a.* to think of afterwards, to consider afterwards *or* too late; **nachbedacht,** considered too late.

Nach'besser—er, *m.* (—ers, *pl.* —er) corrector, improver. **—n,** *v.a.* to mend, improve, repair; to touch up. **—ung,** *f.* touching up; repair; correction after revision, later improvements.

Nach'bestellen, *v.a.* to order subsequently; to order a fresh supply; **von diesem Gericht will ich noch etwas —,** I will order some more *or* another help of this dish.

Nach'bet—en, *v.a. & n.* (*aux.* **h.**, *dat.*) to pray after; to pray later; to parrot, echo. **—er,** *m.* (—ers, *pl.* —er) thoughtless repeater of another's sayings, blind adherent *or* follower. **—erei',** *f.* blind adherence.

Nach'bewilligung, *f.* supplementary vote *or* grant.

Nach'bezahl—en, *v.a.* to pay later; to pay the rest. **—ung,** *f.* additional *or* subsequent payment.

Nach'bild, *n.* copy, imitation, counterfeit. **—en,** *v.a.* to copy; to form *or* mould from; to counterfeit; **er muß sich (noch) —en,** he must finish *or* continue his education. **—ner,** *m.* (—ners, *pl.* —ner) imitator, copier. **—ung,** *f.* copy facsimile; copying, counterfeit.

Nach'blättern, *v.a.* to turn over the leaves of a book (*in looking for something*).

Nach'bleibe—n, *ir.v.n.* (*aux.* **f.**) to be left behind; to be left over; to be kept in (*at school*); to survive; to lag behind; **einem weit —n,** to fall far short of another's excellence, *etc.;* **—n lassen,** to detain, keep in (*a school-boy*). **—nd,** *p. & adj.* residuary. **—r,** *m.* (—rs, *pl.* —r) pupil in detention, boy kept in. *Comp.* **—n=lassen,** *n.* detention.

Nach'blicken, *v.n.;* **einem —,** to look *or* gaze after a person.

Nach'blüte, *f.* (*pl.* —n) second blossom; second blossoming.

Nach'bohren, *v.a.* to bore after *or* again, to bore (a hole) larger, to widen.

Nach'brennen, *ir.v.* I. *a.* to burn, roast *or* distil again. II. *n.* (*aux.* **f.**) to hang fire.

Nach'bringen, *ir.v.a.* to bring later *or* after; to fetch up; to bring on.

Nach'bürg—e, —schaft, *f.* collateral security.

Nach'büßen, *v.a.* to atone *or* suffer for afterwards.

Nach'datieren, *v.a.* to post-date (*a letter, etc.*).

Nachde'm, I. *adv.* afterwards; **je —,** accordingly; that depends. II. *conj.* after the time that; according as, according to the way that; **je — es sich trifft,** according to circumstances; **je — es kommt,** just as it comes; **je — er sich benimmt,** according to his conduct, that depends on his conduct.

Nach'denk—en, I. *ir.v.n.* (*aux.* **h.**); **einem —en,** to follow, enter into the thoughts of another; **über eine S. —en,** to think, reflect, consider, ponder *or* muse (on), meditate (on). II. *subst.n.* reflection, meditation, consideration. **—end,** *p. & adj.* reflecting, thoughtful, pensive. **—lich,** *adj. see* **—end;** important, critical (*rare*).

[1]**Nach'dicht—en,** *v.a.* to imitate (*in a poem*). **—ung,** *f.* imitation *or* copy of another's poetry.

[2]**Nach'dichten,** *v.* I. *a.* to tighten again. II. *n.* to become tighter.

Nach'drängen, *v.* I. *a. & n.* (*aux.* **h.**) to press, crowd, push. II. *r.* to press after, to push after, follow eagerly, seek to enter.

Nach'dringen, *ir.v.n.* (*aux.* **f.**) to press after; to pursue hotly.

Nach'druck, *m.* second pressing (*of grapes*); inferior wine; reprint; energy, vigour; stress; weight; expressiveness; piracy, literary theft; piratical edition; **— verboten,** copyright; **mit — handeln,** to act with energy; **mit — sagen,** to say emphatically, with (great) emphasis; **— auf eine S. legen,** to lay stress upon a th. **—en,** *v.a.* to pirate (*a book, etc.*); to counterfeit; to reprint. **—er,** *m.* (—ers, *pl.* —er) piratical printer, *or* publisher; literary pirate. *Comp.* **—s=voll,** *adj.* emphatic(al), forcible.

Nach'drück—en, *v.* I. *a.* to apply after-pressure; to urge forward, push. II. *n.* (*aux.* **h.**) to ruminate. **—lich,** *adj. & adv.* energetic, vigorous, emphatic; expressive; express; **—lich sagen,** to say emphatically; **—lich handeln,** to act energetically. **—lichkeit,** *f.* forcibleness; explicitness; energy.

Nach'dunkeln, *v.n.* to grow darker, to darken (*Paint.*); to deepen (*Paint.*).

Nach'eid, *m.* oath subsequently taken.

Nach'eifer, *m.* (—s) emulation. **—er,** *m.* (—ers, *pl.* —er) rival; emulator.

Nach'eifer—n, *v.n.* (*aux.* **h.**) (*dat.*) to follow eagerly, be emulous of, emulate. **—ung,** *f.* emulation.

Nach'eilen, *v.n.* (*aux.* **f.**) to hasten after, pursue.

Nacheinan'der, *adv.* one after another, by *or*

in turns. *Comp.* **—folgend**, *adj.* successive, subsequent.

Nach'empfind—en, *ir.v.a.* to feel afterwards; to enter into *or* appreciate a th.; **die Schönheit eines Gedichtes —en**, to enter into, feel, the beauty of a poem. **—end**, *adj.* (capable of) entering into the peculiarity *or* beauty of (*a poem, a piece of music, etc.*), sympathetic, receptive (*opposed to* **schöpferisch**, *productive*). **—ung**, *f.* = **—s=vermögen**, *n.* the faculty of appreciating the beauty *or* the qualities of s.th.

Na'chen, *m.* (**—s**, *pl.* **—**) boat, skiff (*poet.*).

Nach'erbe, *m.* residuary legatee.

Nach'ernte, *f.* second *or* after-crop; gleaning.

Nach'erzählen, *v.a.* (**einem etwas**) to repeat what one has heard; **dem Englischen nach=erzählt**, (imitated *or* adapted) from the English.

Nach'essen, I. *ir.v.a. & n.* (*aux.* **h.**) to eat after *or* afterwards. II. *subst. n.* second course; dessert.

Nach'exerzieren, *v.n.*, (*aux.* **h.**) to repeat the manual exercises; to have an extra drill; to do a th. after all the others have finished (*coll.*).

Nach'fahren, *ir.v.n.* (*aux.* **f.** *dat.*) to follow in a carriage *or* boat; to die (*B.*).

Nach'färben, *v.* I. *a.* to imitate a colour; to re-dye. II. *n.* (*aux.* **h.**) to grow darker.

Nach'folge, *f.* succession (*in office, etc.*), reversion; imitation; following; **— Christi**, imitation of Christ; **die —n**, the results, consequences, effects.

Nach'folge—n, *v.n.* (*aux.* **f.**) (**einem**) to follow; to imitate, to succeed. **—nd**, *p. & adj.* subsequent. **—r**, *m.* (**—rs**, *pl.* **—r**) successor, imitator; **S. Hirzel's —r**, successor to S. Hirzel, late S. Hirzel.

Nach'forderung, *f.* (*pl.* **—en**) after-claim.

Nach'forsch—en, *v.n.* (*aux.* **h.**) to enquire *or* search after; to trace; to investigate. **—er**, *m.* (**—ers**, *pl.* **—er**) enquirer, searcher after. **—ung**, *f.* quest, search, investigation.

Nach'frage, *f.* (*pl.* **—n**) enquiry; demand, request, call; **— halten, anstellen**, to enquire after; **Angebot und —**, supply and demand; **die — nach diesem Artikel war wenig be=lebt**, this article was little in demand; **es ist viele — nach dieser Ware**, this article is in great demand.

Nach'fragen, *reg. & ir.v.* (*aux.* **h.**, *dat.*) to enquire about, ask; to care about; **er fragt (nach) allem nichts nach**, he does not care about anything (*coll.*); **er fragt nichts dar=nach**, he cares nothing about it.

Nach'frist, *f.* prolongation of a term, additional respite.

Nach'fühlen, *v.a.* to feel after *or* with (a p.); **ich kann es ihm so recht —**, I know well what he must have felt, I can fully sympathize with him.

Nach'füllen, *v.a.* to fill up, add.

Nach'geben, *ir.v.* I. *a.* to give after, in addition *or* again; to relax; to give up, yield; to grant; **er giebt keinem etwas nach**, he is inferior to none. II. *n.* (*aux.* **h.**) to give way, slacken; to sink; to comply with; to yield, defer to; to give in (to a p.); **einem in einer S. nicht(s) —**, to be in no way inferior to; not to give in to a p. in a matter, to stick to one's point. **—d**, *p. & adj.* compliant, yielding.

Nach'geboren, *p.p. & adj.* younger; posthumous.

Nach'gebot, *n.* subsequent *or* higher bid.

Nach'geburt, *f.* after-birth; placenta (*Med.*).

Nach'gehen, *ir.v.n.* (*aux.* **f.**, *dat.*) to be behind *or* slow; to follow, pursue; to trace; to mind, attend to; to obey; to give oneself up to; to apply oneself to; **meine Uhr geht nach gegen die Bahnhofsuhr**, my watch is slow by the station clock. **—ds**, *adv.* afterwards, hereafter; next to this.

Nachg(e)ra'de, *adv.* by degrees, gradually, at length.

Nach'gesang, *m.* (*pl.* **Nachgesänge**) epode.

Nach'geschwader, *m.* rear of a fleet.

Nach'giebig, *adj.* flexible; yielding; obliging, compliant, indulgent. **—keit**, *f.* yielding *or* weak disposition; complaisance; indulgence; obsequiousness.

Nach'gießen, *ir.v.a.* to pour after; to cast after *or* from, take a cast of.

Nach'glanz, *m.* after splendour; reflection.

Nach'grab—en, *v.a.* (*dat.*) to dig for, excavate. **—ung**, *f.* digging for a th.; excavation.

Nach'grübeln, *v.n.* (*aux.* **h.**, *dat.*) to subtilize, refine upon; to search minutely into; to ponder over.

Nach'grummet, *n.* (**—s**) third crop of grass *or* hay.

Nach'gründen, *v.a.* to give an additional coat to (*Paint.*).

Nach'guß, *m.* copy from a cast.

Nach'hall, *m.* resonance, reverberation, echo. **—en**, *v.* I. *n.* (*aux.* **h.**) to resound, to echo. II. *a.* to repeat.

Nach'halt—en, *ir. v.* I. *a.* to hold *or* celebrate after; **eine Stunde —en**, to give an extra lesson later on, to make up for a lesson missed. II. *n.* (*aux.* **h.**) to last, hold out. **—ig**, *adj.* lasting.

Nach'hangen, *ir.v.n.* (*aux.* **h.**), **Nach'hängen**, *v.n.* (*aux.* **h.**) to track (*Sport.*); (**einer S.**) **—**, to give o. s. up to; to indulge in; **der Schwer=mut —**, to give way to melancholy; **seinen Gedanken —**, to be wool-gathering; to muse.

Nach'hauen, *ir.v.n.* (*aux.* **h.**) to parry and thrust (*Fenc.*); **dem Feinde —**, to pursue the enemy and cut them down (*as cavalry*).

Nach'helfe—n, *ir.v.n.* (*aux.* **h.**, *dat.*) to lend a helping hand, help; to retouch; to prompt; to push forward. **—r**, *m.* (**—rs**, *pl.* **—r**) helper.

Nachhe'r, *adv.* afterwards, after that; later in the day; subsequently. **—ig**, *adj.* subsequent, later, posterior.

Nach'herbst, *m.* end of autumn.

Nach'hieb, *m.* thrust after having parried; pursuit (*of the enemy*) sword in hand (*Mil.*).

Nach'hinken, *v.n.* (*aux.* **f.**); **einem —**, to limp after a p.; to hobble behind s. o.; **nachgehinkt kommen**, to be too late; to imitate clumsily.

Nach'holen, *v.a.* to fetch afterwards; to fetch up, make up for; to retrieve, recover; to overtake.

Nach'hülfe, *f.* aid, help (*to success, progress, etc.*). *Comp.* **—kursus**, *m.* supplementary course. **—stunden**, *pl.* additional lessons, private teaching *or* tuition, (private) coaching.

Nach'hut, *f.* rearguard (*Mil.*); after-feeding.

Nach'jag—d, *f.* pursuit. **—en**, *v.* I. *n.* (*aux.* **f.**, *dat.*) to pursue eagerly, hunt after; **der Gerech=tigkeit —en**, to follow after righteousness (*B.*). II. *a.* to send, discharge after; **einem eine Kugel —en**, to send a ball *or* to fire a shot after a person.

Nach'kauen, *v.a.* to chew after; **einem etwas —**, to repeat mechanically the words and views of another p. (*coll.*).

Nach'—klang, *m.* echo, resonance; reverberation; after-effect; reminiscence. **—klingen**, *ir.v.n.* (*aux.* **h.**) to resound, echo; to continue to sound.

Nach'komme, *m.* (**—n**, *pl.* **—n**) descendant, child; successor; **ohne —n**, without issue.

Nach'kommen, *ir. v.n.* (*aux.* **f.**, *dat.*) to come after, to follow; to come later; to (re)join, overtake; to act up to; to execute, fulfil; to comply with; to observe, obey; **einer Sache —**, to get a thing done, execute it; **seinen Verbindlichkeiten —**, to meet one's engagements; **gehen Sie nur voran, in fünf Minu=**

ten werde ich —, walk on, I will join you in five minutes. —schaft, *f.* posterity, descendants, successors, children; future generations; ohne —schaft, without issue, childless.

Nach'kömmling, *m.* (—s, *pl.* —e), *see* Nachkomme.

Nach'können, *ir.v.n.* (*aux.* h.) to be able to follow.

Nach'laß, *m.* (—(ss)es, *pl.* Nachlässe) anything left, residuum; legacy; left papers; literary remains; estate of one deceased; relaxation; remission; abatement; deduction; discount, allowance, drawback; intermission; ohne — arbeiten, to work incessantly.

Nach'lassen, I. *ir.v.a.* to leave behind; to transmit; to let follow; to slacken, relax; to discontinue, give over; to remit, mitigate; to grant, yield, give up; (einem etwas) —, to remit, to permit; etwas vom (*or* am) Preise —, to take something off the price of a thing, to make a reduction in the price; er ließ ihm etwas an der Strafe nach, he remitted part of his punishment. II. *ir.v.n.* (*aux.* h.) to slacken, give way; to subside, abate; to flag; to diminish; to cease; die Kälte läßt nach, the cold is abating; lassen Sie doch nach! pray, have done! die Frage läßt nach, the demand is no longer so great, is growing less brisk (*C.L.*); im Fleiße —, to become less diligent; er hat im letzten Quartal in der Schule sehr nachgelassen, his school work last term has been much worse than before; die nachgelassenen Werke, the posthumous works. III. *subst. n.* relaxation; abatement, reduction; remission; flagging, *etc.* —d, *p.* & *adj.* intermittent. —schaft, *f.*, *see* Nachlaß.

Nach'lässig, *adj.* & *adv.* negligent, careless; remiss; unaffected; indolent, supine. —keit, *f.* negligence, carelessness; inaccuracy; remissness.

Nach'laufen, *ir.v.n.* (*aux.* s., *dat.*) to run after.

Nach'leben, I. *v.n.* (*aux.* h., *dat.*) to live later; to survive; to conform to, obey, live up to. II. *subst. n.* after-life; conformity of life to.

Nach'legen, *v.a.* to add to, to lay on more.

Nach'lese, *f.* gleaning; gleanings; supplement; — halten, to glean. —n, I. *ir.v.a.* & *n.* (*aux.* h.) to glean; to read after; to re-read, read again; to make up for by subsequent reading. II. *subst. n.*, *see* —; re-reading; beim —n, on reading again. —r, *m.* (—rs, *pl.* —r) gleaner; one who reads after *or* in the manner of.

Nach'liefer—n, *v.a.* to furnish subsequently; to complete. —ung, *f.* subsequent delivery.

Nach'mach—en, *v.a.* to copy, imitate; to mimic; to counterfeit; to do subsequently; das soll mir einer —en! I challenge *or* defy any one to do the same! mach es mir nach, do as I do. —er, *m.* (—ers, *pl.* —er) imitator; counterfeiter, forger. —ung, *f.* imitation; counterfeiting.

Nach'mahd, *f.* after-math.

Nach'malen, *v.a.* to paint after (*a style*); to copy; to counterfeit (*a signature*).

Nach'mal—ig, *adj.* subsequent. —s, *adv.* afterwards.

Nach'mann, *m.*, *see* Hintermann: near kinsman, heir (*B.*); subsequent endorser.

Nach'messe, *f.* low mass; latter part of a fair.

Nach'messen, *ir.v.a.* to measure again; to re-survey.

Nach'milch, *f.* strippings.

Nach'mittag, *m.* afternoon; eines —s, one afternoon, of an afternoon. —s, *adv.* in the afternoon; P. M. (=*post meridiem*) (*Railw.*). *Comp.* —s=schläfchen, *n.* after-dinner nap, siesta.

Nach'mittäg—ig, —lich, *adj.* taking place in *or* during the afternoon, post-meridian.

Nach'—nahme, *f.* reimbursement; unter — nahme Ihrer Spesen, carrying your charges forward, reimbursing yourself for outlay, charges following the goods. —nehmen, *ir. v.a.* to take after *or* besides; to make charges follow (*the goods*), to carry forward one's expenses, to collect charges, to reimburse oneself for charges. *Comp.* —nahme=betrag, *m.* amount to be collected on delivery. —nahme=gebühr, *f.* collection fee, fees of reimbursement by anticipation. —nahme=sendung, *f.* parcel to be paid for on delivery; value-payable article; C. O. D. parcel.

Nach'ordnen, *v.a.* to class next after.

Nach'pfeifen, *ir.v.a.* & *n.* (*aux.* h., *dat.*) to whistle after; to repeat whistling; ich kann meinem Gelde —, I may whistle for my money.

Nach'pfuschen, *v.a.* & *n.* (*aux.* h.) to copy in a bungling manner.

Nach'pinseln, *v.a.* to retouch (*Paint.*); to daub.

Nach'porto, *n.* (—s, *pl.* —s) additional charge for overweight, *etc.* (*on letters or parcels*).

Nach'rechn—en, *v.a.* & *n.* (*aux.* h.) to reckon subsequently; to reckon over again; to check an account; to verify a calculation. —er, *m.* auditor, examiner of accounts.

Nach'rede, *f.* subsequent remark; epilogue; rejoinder; report, rumour; calumny; in üble — bringen, to slander s.o., injure a p.'s reputation.

Nach'red—en, *v.a.* & *n.* (*aux.* h.) to imitate the manner of speaking; to repeat (*what another has said*); einem etwas —en, to talk of s.o., to slander a p.; einem alles auf Treu' und Glauben —en, to swear by a person. —er, *m.* slanderer. —ner, *m.* later speaker.

Nach'reifen, *v.n.* (*aux.* s.) to ripen after being gathered.

Nach'reißen, I. *ir.v.a.* to tear along *or* after; to tear more *or* wider; to copy; einen Witz —, to repeat a joke. II. *subst.n.*; beim —, in copying.

Nach'reiten, *v.a.* to get through *or* up afterwards; ein Kolleg —, to copy another student's lecture-notes if one has missed the lecture (*sl.*).

Nach'richt, *f.* (*pl.* —en) news; account; information; report; advice; notice; ausführliche —, full advices, detailed account; öffentliche —, (public) advertisement; schlechte —, bad news, ill tidings; zur —! Notice! einem — geben, to let s.o. know, advise a p., warn s.o., send a p. word; von einer S. — einziehen, to obtain information regarding; nach allen — en, by all accounts. —lich, *adj.* & *adv.* by way of information.

Nach'richte—n, *v.a.* & *n.* (*aux.* h.) to direct attention to; to re-adjust; to arrange in imitation of; to condemn finally; to execute. —r, *m.* (—rs, *pl.* —r) executioner (*obs.*).

Nach'rücken, *v.* I. *n.* (*aux.* s.) (einem) to move *or* march after (a p.). II. *a.* to advance.

Nach'ruf, *m.* call, shout after (a p.); refrain (*Mus.*); farewell; posthumous fame, memory; poem, notice, *etc.*, in honour of one dead; in memoriam; ein — könnte ihn nicht mehr erreichen, he is beyond call *or* out of hearing.

Nach'rufen, *ir.v.a.* & *n.* (*aux.* h.); einem —, to call after a p.; einen —, to call to one to follow.

Nach'ruhm, *m.* (—s) posthumous fame *or* glory.

Nach'rühmen, *v.a.*; einem etwas —, to praise a p. in his absence *or* after his death.

Nach'sagen, *v.a.* to repeat; to repeat after (a p.); to relate on the faith of; to speak (*well or ill*) of; das muß ich ihm zum Ruhme —, I must say that in his praise.

Nach'satz, *m.* minor term *or* proposition (*Log.*); apodosis (*Gram.*); additional stake.

Nach'schauen, *v.a.*; einem —, to look *or* gaze after a p.

Nach'schicken, *v.a.* to send after; to forward to; to send afterwards.

Nach'schießen, *ir.v.* I. *a.* to shoot later; **einem —,** to shoot, send (*a ball*) after s.o. (*going away*); **Gelder —,** to make a subsequent payment, to supply more money. II. *n.* (*aux.* **s.**) to dart after; to spring up later, bud a second time.

Nach'schiffen, *v.* I. *n.* (*aux.* **s.**) to sail in pursuit of; to sail later. II. *a.* to send by water to.

Nach'schlag, *m.* after-stroke; complementary *or* grace-note (*at the end of a trill, etc.*); base coin.

Nach'schlage—n, I. *ir.v.a. & n.* (*aux.* **h.**) to strike afterwards; to strike (a p.) as he goes away; to counterfeit (*coins*); to syncopate a note that follows another (*Mus.*); to consult (*a book, etc.*), to look up (*a passage*); **der Lernende möge Regel X —n,** the student is referred to rule X. II. *ir.v.n.* (*aux.* **s.**) to take after, resemble. III. *subst. n.* consulting, referring to; **beim —n,** on looking . . . up, on reference to (*the book, etc.*); **Buch zum —n,** book of reference. *Comp.* **—buch,** *n.* memorandum-book; book of reference.

Nach'schleichen, *ir.v.n.* (*aux.* **s.**) (**einem**) to sneak, creep after; to spy.

Nach'schleifen, I. *ir.v.a.* to whet *or* grind again. II. *reg. v.a.* to drag, trail along; to drag on a sledge; to slur (*a note*).

Nach'schleppen, *v.a.* to drag, trail after; to tow (*Naut.*); **sich mühsam dem Heere —,** to crawl with great difficulty after the army.

Nach'schlüssel, *m.* false-key.

Nach'schmecken, *v.n.* (*aux.* **h.**) to leave a taste behind.

Nach'schmieren, *v.a.* to copy badly, to scribble *or* scrawl notes.

Nach'schoß (*short* **o**), *m.* subsequent tax; young sprig, shoot.

Nach—schreiben, *ir.v.a. & n.* (*aux.* **h.**) to imitate the writing of; to write from dictation; to take notes (*of a lecture, etc.*); to write down; to transcribe, write out; to write to a p. after his departure. **—schreiber,** *m.* transcriber; copyist; one who takes notes. **—schrift,** *f.* postscript; transcript, copy; lecture-notes; dictation.

Nach'schub, *m.* new batch; fresh supply, reinforcement.

Nach'schuß, *m.* subsequent shot; supplement; second edition; after-payment, payment in addition; additional stake; new shoot; second batch; **ich habe den —,** I shoot next.

Nach'schwarm, *m.* second swarm (*of bees*).

Nach'schwatzen, *v.a.* (*aux.* **h.**) to repeat(gossip).

Nach'sehen, I. *ir.v.n.* (*aux.* **h.**) to look after (**einem,** a p.); to see, look for; to attend to; **sieh nach, daß es geschieht,** see that it is done. II. *ir.v.a.* to look after *or* into; to revise, examine; to inspect; **einem etwas —,** to overlook, to take no notice of, pardon, to connive at, to grant respite, be indulgent to. III. *subst.n.;* **das (leere) — haben,** to be disappointed, to have one's trouble for naught; **nun haben wir das —,** now we may whistle for it.

Nach'setz—en, *v.* I. *a.* to set *or* place after, behind; to set below in value; to slight; to add to; to renew one's stake. II. *n.* (*aux.* **s.**, *dat.*) to follow, pursue, hunt after. **—ung,** *f.* pursuit; depreciation; lower estimate, disregard.

Nach'sicht, *f.* indulgence; forbearance; clemency; pity; revisal, inspection; **— haben mit,** to be indulgent towards, make allowance for. **—ig,** *adj.* forbearing, indulgent. **—igkeit,** *f.* good nature, indulgence. *Comp.* **—s=brief,** *m.* letter of respite. **—s=tag,** *m.* day of grace. **—s=voll,** *adj.* indulgent, considerate.

Nach'silbe, *f.* added syllable, suffix, (*e. g.* **—chen, —lein**).

Nach'sinnen, I. *ir.v.n.*(*aux.***h.**)(**einer Sache** (*dat.*) *or* (*more usually*) **über eine Sache**) to muse, meditate, reflect on. II. *subst.n.* reflection, contemplation, study.

Nach'sommer, *m.* the end of summer; Indian summer.

Nach'spähen, *v.n.* (*aux.* **h.**, *dat.*) to watch, spy; to look anxiously after; to explore, investigate.

Nach'spiel, *n.* (—**s**, *pl.* —**e**) afterpiece; voluntary (*Mus.*); sorti (*Mus.*); later event, sequel.

Nach'spielen, *v.* I. *n.* (*aux.* **h.**, *dat.*) to imitate, play after (a p.). II. *a.* to return a lead (*at cards*); **eine andere Farbe —,** to lead another suit; **nach dem Gehöre —,** to repeat playing by ear, to play by ear.

Nach'spotten, *v.a. & n.* (*aux.* **h.**) (**einem**) to hoot after s.o.; to laugh at a p. behind his back.

Nach'sprechen, *ir.v.a. & n.* (*aux.* **h.**) (**einem**) to repeat another's words; to mimic a p.

Nach'spür—en, *v.n.* (*aux.* **h.**, *dat.*) to track, trace out; to investigate. **—ung,** *f.* tracking; search, investigation.

Nächst, I. *sup.adj., see* **Nah**; next, nearest, closest; **—en Monats,** proximo; **der —e Beste,** the first that comes; **die —en Beziehungen,** the most intimate relations; **die —en Freunde,** the fastest, closest, most intimate friends; **das —e Mal,** the next time; **—er Nachbar,** next door neighbour; **—er Tage, mit—em,** as soon as possible, very soon; **mit —er Post,** by return of post; **die —e Stadt,** the nearest town; **der —e Tag,** the following day; **—e Vergangenheit,** the immediate past, what has just happened; **das aller —e Mal,** the very next time; **—er Zeit,** very soon; **im —en Augenblick,** the next moment; **der —e Weg,** the nearest way, the shortest cut; **der —e Zweck,** the first *or* immediate object; **Jeder ist sich selbst der —e,** charity begins at home; near is my shirt, but nearer is my skin (*prov.*); **der, die —e,** neighbour, fellow-creature, fellow-man; **das —e,** what is nearest. II. *adv.* next; soon; lately; **am —en,** nearest. III. *prep.* (*with dat.*) next to, after. **—ens,** *adv.* shortly, very soon; by and by. *Comp.* **—best(e),** *m.* second-best. **—de'm,** *adv.* immediately, thereupon. **—en=liebe,** *f.* Christian charity. **—folgend,** *adj.* immediately following; **—folgender Tag,** next day. **—vorhergehend,** *adj.* immediately preceding.

Nach'stehen, *ir.v.n.* (*aux.* **h.**) to stand after, follow; (**einem**) —, to yield, be inferior to; **er steht keinem nach,** he is inferior to none; **—de Worte,** the following words; **die —d verzeichneten Sorten,** the kinds *or* qualities mentioned below; **wie —d bemerkt,** as mentioned below.

Nach'stell—en, *v.* I. *n.* (*aux.* **h.**, *dat.*) to lay traps for; to lie in wait for; to waylay. II. *a.* to place after; to put back (*clocks, etc.*); to consider inferior. **—er,** *m.* (—**ers**, *pl.* —**er**) setter of traps, waylayer. **—ung,** *f.* setting snares; snare; ambush; plot; pursuit.

Nach'steuer, *f.* supplemental tax; additional contribution.

Nach'stich, *m.* (—**s**, *pl.* —**e**) copy of an engraving.

Nach'stimmen, *v.* I. *n.* (*aux.* **h.**) to vote subsequently *or* again; to vote like another. II. *a.* to tune (*an instrument*) to the same key as another.

Nach'stoß, *m.* second thrust, after-thrust (*Fenc.*); **den —stoß haben,** to play after a p. (*Bill.*).

Nach'stoßen, *ir.v.a. & n.* (*aux.* **h.**) to push, thrust after *or* again; to play after; to have a second chance (*Bill.*); to parry and thrust (*Fenc.*).

Nach'streben, *v.n.* (*aux.* **h.**, *dat.*) to strive after, aspire to; to emulate.

Nach'stück, *n.* afterpiece.

Nach'—sturz, *m.* (—(**e**)**s**) rushing after; later

(land-)slip; second *or* complemental verification (*of accounts*). —**stürzen**, *v.* I. *n.* (*aux.* **s.**) (**einem**) to rush after. II. *a.* to throw, precipitate after; to swallow (*more wine*).

Nach'such—en, I. *v.a. & n.* (*aux.* **h.**) to search for; **etwas, um eine S. —en**, to sue for. II. *subst.n.* —**ung**, *f.* search, enquiry; application.

Nach'sündflutlich, *adj.* post-diluvian.

Nach'sylbe, *see* Nachsilbe.

Nacht, *f.* (*pl.* **Näch'te**) night; darkness; **bei —, in der —, des —s**, (*irreg. gen.*) in the night, during the night, at night; **bei — und Nebel davon gehen**, to escape under cover of the night; **über —**, during the night, at night, in one night; **zu — essen**, to sup; **über — kommen**, to come unexpectedly; **in tiefer —**, at dead of night; **mitten in der —**, in the middle of the night; **es wird —**, it grows dark; **gute — sagen**, to bid good-night; to bid farewell, to take leave (*obs.*); **Märchen von 'Tausend und eine —'**, the Arabian Nights' (Entertainments); **in der — sind alle Katzen grau**, all cats are gray in the dark (*prov.*); **die — ist keines Menschen Freund**, night has no friend (*prov.*). —**s**, *adv.* by night, at night. *Comp.* —**arbeit**, *f.* night-work; night-study; lucubration (*of a scholar*). —**blind**, *adj.* blind at night. —**bogen**, nocturnal arch (*Astr.*). —**dienst**, *m.* night duty (*Mil.*). —**essen**, *n.* supper. —**eule**, *f.* screech-owl. —**feier**, *f.* vigil. —**geschirr**, *n.* chamber(-pot), pot (*coll.*). —**gleiche**, *f.* equinox. —**glocke**, *f.* night-bell. —**hemd**, *n.* night-shirt (*men*); night dress (*women*). —**herberge**, *f.* night's lodging; inn. —**kleid**, *n.* night-dress; undress. —**lager**, *n.* night's lodging *or* quarters. —**leuchter**, *n.* bed-room candlestick. —**licht**, *n.* bed-room candle; night light. —**mahl**, *n.* supper; *see* Abendmahl. —**mahr**, *m.* —**männchen**, *n.* nightmare. —**mette**, *f.* nocturn (*Eccl.*). —**musik**, *f.* serenade. —**mütze**, *f.* night-cap; sleepy and stupid fellow. —**pfauenauge**, *n.* emperor-moth; hawk-moth. —**quartier**, *n.* quarters for the night; **einem —quartier geben**, to put a p. up for the night. —**rat**, *m.* night watchman (*sl.*). —**reise**, *f.* night journey, nocturnal travel. —**rock**, *m.* night-dress, night-gown; dressing-gown (*rare*). —**runde**, *f.* night-round, patrol. —**sack**, *m.* travelling-bag. —**schichter**, *m.* night-worker (*Min.*). —**schlafend**, *adj.*; **bei —schlafender Zeit**, when all are at rest (*coll.*). —**schwärmer**, *m.* moth, nocturnal butterfly, sphinx; rake. —**ständchen**, *n.* serenade. —**stück**, *n.* night-piece; gloomy, dismal scene. —**stuhl**, *m.* night-stool, commode, close-stool. —**tisch**, *m.* pedestal, bed-side cupboard. —**tischchen**, *n.* (**vor dem Bette**) pedestal-cupboard. —**topf**, *m.* chamber, pot. —**uhr**, *f.* clock with illuminated dial. —**wache**, *f.* night-watch; vigil; watch (*Naut.*). —**wächter**, *m.* watchman; listless person; **er ist der reine —wächter**, he is a sleepy, indolent fellow; **das ist unter dem (reitenden) —wächter**, that is beneath contempt (*sl.*); **der —wächter tutet**, the watchman tootles. —**wandeln**, I. *v.n.* (*aux.* **h.**) (*insep.*) to walk in one's sleep. II. *subst.n.* somnambulism. —**wandler**, *m.*, —**wandlerin**, *f.* somnambulist. —**zeug**, *n.* clothing for the night, night things.

Nach't—en, *v.n.* (*aux.* **h.**) & *imp.*; **es —et**, it is growing dark, night is coming on.

Näch't—en, *v.* I. *n.* (*aux.* **h.**) *see* übernachten. II. *a.* **einen —en**, to put s. o. up for the night. III. *adv.* last night (*obs.*). —**igen**, *see* —**en** I. —**lich**, I. *adj.* nightly, nocturnal; gloomy, dismal; **bei —licher Weile**, in the night-time. II. *adv.* at night. *Comp.* —**e=lang**, *adv.* for whole nights, for nights together.

Nach'teil, *m.* (—**s**, *pl.* —**e**) disadvantage, prejudice, detriment, damage; **sich im —e befinden**, to be at a disadvantage, to have the worst of it; **das würde mir zum großen —(e) gereichen**, that would be very much to my disadvantage; **er ist dabei sehr im —(e)**, it is greatly to his disadvantage; — **bringen**, to injure. —**ig**, *adj.* disadvantageous, prejudicial; hurtful; derogatory; —**ig sprechen von**, to speak unfavourably *or* disparagingly of.

Nach'thun, *ir.v.a.* (**einem etwas**) to imitate, do the like; to do afterwards; **es einem — wollen**, to try to rival *or* emulate a p.

Nach'tigall, *f.* (*pl.* —**en**) nightingale; **die — schlägt**, the nightingale sings *or* warbles. —**en=schlag**, *m.* warbling *or* song of the nightingale.

Nach'tisch, *m.* (—**es**, *pl.* —**e**) dessert.

Nach'tönen, *v.n.* (*aux.* **h.**) to resound, re-echo, reverberate; to linger (*of musical sounds*).

Nach'trab, *m.* rear, rear-guard (*Mil.*). —**en**, *v.n.* (*aux.* **s.**) (**einem**) to follow at a trot.

Nach'trachten, *v.n.*, *see* Nachstreben, Nachstellen.

Nach'trag, *m.* (—**s**, *pl.* **Nachträge**) supplement; addendum; payment of arrears.

Nach'trag—en, *ir.v.a.* (**einem etwas**) to bear *or* carry after; to add, supply in addition; to bear a grudge, be resentful; to pay up (*arrears*); to post up (*books*); **einen Posten in eine Rechnung —en**, to put an additional item into an account. —**end**, *p. & adj.* resentful. *Comp.* —**s=artikel**, *m.* additional article. —**s=zahlung**, *f.* additional payment.

Nach'träglich, I. *adj.* subsequent; supplementary, additional, supplemental. II. *adv.* by way of appendix *or* supplement; subsequently.

Nach'trete—n, *ir.v.n.* (*aux.* **s.** *dat.*) to follow after; to follow closely. —**r**, *m.* (—**rs**, *pl.* —**r**) follower, imitator, adherent; blind follower, uncritical adherent.

Nach'trieb, *m.* (—**es**, *pl.* —**e**) young shoot, later sprout.

Nach'trillerer, *m.* (—**s**, *pl.* —) songster of no depth and originality; bardling.

Nach'trinken, *ir.v.* I. *n.* (*aux.* **h.**) (**einem**) to drink after; to drink in imitation of; to pledge a p. in return for a pledge (*stud. sl.*). II. *a.* **Wasser auf eine Arznei —**, to drink water after taking medicine.

Nach'üb—en, *v.a. & n.* (*aux.* **h.**) to practise afterwards *or* again; to go again through one's drill *or* one's exercises. —**ung**, *f.* repeated *or* subsequent drill *or* exercises.

Nach'urlaub, *n.* prolongation of leave, extended leave (of absence) *or* furlough (*Mil.*).

Nach'verlangen, *v.a.* to demand in addition, over and above.

Nach'verzollung, *f.* additional payment of duty; post-entry.

Nach'wachsen, *ir.v.n.* (*aux.* **s.**, *dat.*) to grow after; to grow up to; to grow again; **es wachsen ihm andere Zähne nach**, he is cutting new teeth.

Nach'wägen, Nach'wiegen, *v.a.* to weigh again; to verify the weight of.

Nach'wandeln, *v.n.* (*aux.* **s.**); **einem —**, to walk after a p., to follow a p.'s example.

Nach'wehen, *pl.* after-pains; painful consequences.

Nach'weinen, *v.a. & n.* (*aux.* **h.**); **einem —**, to cry after a p., to bewail a p.'s departure *or* death, to lament a p.'s loss *or* death.

Nach'weis, *m.* (—(**s**)**es**, *pl.* —(**s**)**e**), *see* —(**s**)**ung**, information; citation. —**bar**, —**lich**, *adj.* authenticated, demonstrable, assignable (*as a reason*). —(**s**)**en**, I. *ir.v.a.* (**einem etwas**) to point out, show, indicate; to refer to; to prove; to authenticate; to establish (*a claim*). II. *subst. n.*, —(**s**)**ung**, *f.* proof, demonstration; direction; intelligence, information; reference. —(**s**)**e**, (*in comp.*) *see* —(ſ)ung (*in comp.*). —(ſ)er, *m.* (—(ſ)ers, *pl.* —(ſ)er) director; index, pointer. *Comp.* —(ſ)e=zahl, *f.* number of pages in a ledger. —(ſ)ungs=bureau, *n.* enquiry-office; information office; registry-office. —(ſ)ungs=kalender, *m.* directory; almanack. —(ſ)ungs=zeichen, *n.* sign of reference, asterisk (*); direction (*Mus.*).

Nach'welt, *f.* after-times, posterity, future generations; die ſpäteſte —, the remotest ages; der — überliefern, to hand down to posterity.

Nach'wiegen, *see* Nachwägen.

Nach'winken, *v.n.* (*aux.* h.); einem —, to beckon to one who is departing.

Nach'winter, *m.* end of winter; second winter.

Nach'wirk—en, *v.a. & n.* (*aux.* h.) to operate *or* take effect afterwards; to weave again *or* later. —ung, *f.* after-effect; consequences, result.

Nach'wolle, *f.* second wool.

Nach'wollen, *ir.v.n.* (*aux.* h.); einem —, to wish to *or* be about to follow a p.

Nach'wort, *n.* last word; concluding remarks, epilogue.

Nach'wuchs, *m.* after-growth; young wood; recruits; der junge —, the rising generation.

Nach'zahl—en, *v.a.* to pay afterwards; to take an additional *or* higher-priced ticket; to pay the remainder *or* difference. —ung, *f.* after-payment. —ungs=marke, *f.* late stamp, extra-postage stamp.

Nach'zählen, *v.a.* to count over again, to count (*one's change*); to check.

Nach'zeichn—en, *v.a.* to draw after *or* from, to copy. —ung, *f.* copy.

Nach'ziehen, *ir.v.* I. *a.* to draw after *or* along with; to imitate (*lines*). II. *n.* (*aux.* ſ.) (einem) to march *or* go after, to follow; to remove to the same house.

Nach'zins, *m.* quit-rent.

Nach'zotteln, *v.n.* (*aux.* ſ.); einem —, to trot after a person.

Nach'zucht, *f.* breeding (*of cattle*); cattle, breed; late swarm (*of bees*).

Nach'zug, *m.* marching after; next move (*in chess*); train, suite, rear, rearguard (*Mil.*).

Nach'zügler, *m.* straggler; camp-follower.

Nack'—edei, *m.* naked child (*coll.*). —ig, —icht, *adj.* naked (*sl.*).

Nack'en, *m.* (—s, *pl.* —) nape of the neck, neck; scrag (*of mutton, etc.*); long black hair, chignon; einem den — beugen, to curb a p.'s selfwill *or* pride; einem auf dem — ſitzen, liegen, to be at a p.'s heels, to press *or* harass a p. (*Mil.*), to be a burden to a p., to pester a p.; den — aufrecht tragen, to carry a high head; den Schelm im — haben, to be a roguish person, to be fond of teasing. *Comp.* —haar, *n.* back hair. —ſchlag, *m.* blow from behind; abuse (*of one absent*); (*pl.*) reverses.

Nackt, (*less good* Nack'end,) *adj.* naked, bare, nude; callow (*of birds*); mit —en Worten, in plain words, bluntly, openly. —heit, *f.* nakedness. *Comp.* —armig, *adj.* bare-armed.

Na'del, *f.* (*pl.* —n) (Näh—) needle; (Steck—) pin; (Bruſt—) brooch; etching-point; trigger; quill (*of a porcupine*); needle (*of crystals; of the compass; of pines*); hand (*of a clock, etc.*); Stopf—, darning-needle; Näh—, sewing needle; Strick—, knitting-needle; mit —n befeſtigen, to pin; ſich von *or* mit der — nähren, to earn one's living by needlework; wie auf —n ſein *or* gehen, to be on thorns; to be on pins and needles; das iſt mit der heißen — gemacht, that was done in a hurry. —n, *v.a.* to pin; to sew (*boots and gloves*). *Comp.* —arbeit, *f.* needlework. —brief, *m.* paper of pins. —buch, *n.* needle-book. —büchſe, *f.* needle *or* pin-case. —feder, *f.* steel-spring (*of a needle-gun*). —förmig, *adj.* needle-shaped. —futteral, *n.* needle-case. —geld, *n.* pin-money. —halter, *m.* needle-holder (*in sewing-machines*); *see* —ſonde. —holz, *n.* conifers, coniferous trees; conifer forest. —kiſſen, *n.* pin-cushion. —knopf, —kopf, *m.* head of a pin. —öhr, *n.* eye of a needle. —ſonde, *f.* needle-bearer (*Surg.*). —ſtein, *m.* needle-stone; loadstone. —ſtich, *m.* prick of a pin *or* needle; stitch; pin-hole.

Nad'ler, *m.* (—s, *pl.* —) pin *or* needle maker.

Na'gel, *m.* (—s, *pl.* Nägel) nail (*on fingers, toes*); nail, stud, tack; hölzerner —, plug, peg, pin, trunnel; kleiner —, tack; großer —, spike; keinen — breit, not an inch; an den — hängen, to put on the shelf, to shelve, give up, abandon (*coll.*); es brennt mir auf den Nägeln (die Nägel), the matter is urgent, I am hard pressed *or* much driven; an den Nägeln kauen, to bite one's nails, to muse; ſich (*dat.*) die Nägel ſchneiden, to cut one's nails; einen — haben, to be conceited; einen — einſchlagen, to drive in a nail; mit Nägeln beſchlagen, to clout; to stud (*as an ornament*); ein — zu meinem Sarge, a nail in my coffin.

Na'gel—n, *v.a.* to nail, spike; die Bekleidung des Schiffes mit den Enden über einander —n, to sheath *or* plank a ship with clincher-work. *Comp.* —bohrer, *m.* piercer, gimlet. —bürſte, *f.* nail-brush. —eiſen, *n.* nail-iron; heading-tool; nail-mould; cartridge-drawer (*Artil.*). —feſt, *adj.* nailed, immovable; niet- und —feſte Gegenſtände, fixtures. —geſchwür, *n.* whitlow. —neu, *adj.* quite new, brand-new. —probe, *f.* nail test, thumb-nail (*in drinking*); supernaculum; die —probe machen, to thumb one's glass; nicht die —probe iſt im Glaſe geblieben, no heel-taps are left in the glass. —ſchere, *f.* nail-scissors. —ſchmied, *m.* nail-maker, nailer. —zange, *f.* nail-nippers. —zieher, *m.* nail-claw, nail-extractor, claw-hammer.

Näg—elchen (—elchens, *pl.* —elchen), —lein, *n.* (—leins, *pl.* —lein) tack; little nail.

Na'ge—n, *v.a. & n.* (*aux.* h.) to gnaw, nibble; to pick (*bones*); to bite; to sting, rankle; —nde Sorgen, carking cares; —ndes Gewiſſen, remorseful conscience; am Hungertuche —n, to be starving *or* famishing. —r, *m.* (—rs, *pl.* —r) gnawer; rodent. *Comp.* —tiere, *pl.* rodents. —wurm, *m.* remorse; care.

Näg'lein, *n.* (—s, *pl.* —) *see* Nägelchen; clove (*dial. & poet.*); Muskaten und —, (*recipe for a*) love potion (*sweet and bitter ingredients*). *Comp.* —öl, *n.* oil of cloves.

Nag'ler, *m.* (—s, *pl.* —) nailer, nail-maker.

Na'h(e), *adj. & adv.* (näher, nächſt) near, close, neighbouring; near, imminent; near, closely related *or* attached, kindred; almost; —e Gefahr, impending danger; —er Freund, close friend; —e Stadt, neighbouring town; — bei der Kirche, close to the church; wie — ſind Sie verwandt? how nearly are you related? das Weinen war ihr ſehr —, she was very near crying; — liegen, to border upon; es geht mir —, it concerns me closely, grieves me to the heart; das müſſen Sie ſich nicht ſo — gehen laſſen, you must not take that so much to heart; Ihr neulicher Verluſt iſt mir ſehr — gegangen, I was much grieved by your recent loss; (einem) etwas — legen, to explain, make clear a thing; ich werde es ihm — legen, I shall urge it upon him; (einem) — kommen, to approach; einem zu — kommen *or* treten, to injure *or* offend s. o., to interfere with a p., to hurt a p.'s feelings; komm' mir nicht zu —! keep away, keep your distance! Jemandes Anſehen (*dat.*) zu — treten, to dispute *or* question a p.'s authority; to hurt a p.'s dignity; der Wahrheit zu — treten, to violate truth; — **und fern**, far and wide; — **an**, — **bei**, near, close by; — **aneinander**, close to one another, contiguous; — **daran sein**, to be near, to be on the point of. *Comp.* **—e=hin**, **—e=zu**, *adv.* nearly, almost. **—verkehr**, *m.* traffic.

Nä'h—e, *f.* nearness, proximity; neighbourhood; environs; **es ist ganz in der —e**, it is quite close; **in nächster —e**, within call; **in der —e betrachten**, to look at closely. **—er**, *see* **Nah**; **—ere Umstände**, particulars; **—ere Bekanntschaft**, closer acquaintance; greater familiarity, intimacy; **bei —er Betrachtung**, on further consideration; **treten Sie —er, meine Herren**, approach, gentlemen; walk in, gentlemen; please, step this way! **um der Sache —er zu kommen**, to come to the point, to go into *or* to go to the root of a matter; **der Einbildungskraft —er bringen**, to familiarize the imagination with; **dem Horizonte —er bringen**, to depress the pole (*Astr.*); **—ere Auskunft**, further information, more particulars; **—ere Rechte**, prior rights *or* claims; **—eres Objekt**, direct object; **das Hemd ist mir —er als der Rock**, blood is thicker than water (*prov.*). **—ere(s)**, *n.* details; **—eres bei der Expedition dieses Blattes**, for further *or* fuller particulars apply at the office of this paper; **das —ere wollen Sie ersehen aus . . .**, for particulars, please refer to *or* see . . .

Na'h—en, *v.r. & n.* (*aux.* **s.**, *dat.*) to approach, come up, draw near. **—bar**, *adj.* approachable, accessible.

Nä'h—en, I. *v.a. & n.* (*aux.* **h.**) to sew, stitch; to do needlework; **mit weiten Stichen —en**, to baste; **überwendlich —en**, to overcast, whip. II. *subst.* **—en**, *n.*, **—ung**, *f.* sewing. **—erei'**, *f.* sewing; needlework. **—erin**, *f.* needle-woman, seamstress. *Comp.* **—garn**, *n.* sewing-cotton. **—kasten**, *m.*, **—kästchen**, *n.* lady's workbox. **—kissen**, *n.* sewing-cushion; pin-cushion. **—korb**, *m.* lady's work-basket. **—kunst**, *f.* (art of doing) needlework. **—maschine**, *f.* sewing-machine. **—nadel**, *f.* (sewing-)needle. **—rahmen**, *m.* embroidery-frame; work-frame. **—ring**, *m.* tailor's thimble. **—täschen**, *n.* housewife. **—zeug**, *n.* sewing requisites *or* things, work-box.

Nä'her—n, *v.* I. *a. & n.* (*aux.* **h.**) to bring near; to approximate. II. *r.* to approach, draw near. **—ung**, *f.* approach; approximation.

Nahm, Nah'mest; Näh'me, *1 (& 3) and 2 pers. sing. imperf. indic.; 1 & 3 pers. sing. imperf. subj. of* **nehmen**.

Näh'r—en, *v.* I. *a.* to nourish, supply with nourishment; to keep, support; to nourish, cherish; to nurse, suckle; **ein Handwerk, das seinen Mann —t**, a trade by which a man may support himself. II. *r.* to gain a livelihood; to live by; to support oneself by; **sich kümmerlich —en**, to earn a scanty living, to have a great difficulty in making both ends meet; **sich —en von**, to live on. III. *n.* (*aux.* **h.**) to be nourishing. **—end**, *p. & adj.* nutritious. **—er**, *m.* (**—ers**, *pl.* **—er**), **—erin**, *f.* supporter, nourisher. **—ung**, *f.* feeding, nourishment, nutrition; bringing up. *Comp.* **—boden**, *m.* fertile soil. **—geld**, *n.* money allowed for maintenance. **—mittel**, *n.* (*usually pl.*) articles of food; means of subsistence. **—mutter**, *f.* foster-mother, nursing mother, alma mater (*Univ.*). **—stand**, *m.* working-class. **—wert**, *m.* nutrition, nutritive quality.

Nahr'—haft, *adj.* nourishing, nutritive; alimentary, productive; lucrative; substantial, rich (*food*); good (*season*). **—haftigkeit**, *f.* nutritiousness; profitableness; richness. **—ung**, *f.* nourishment, food; livelihood; profession, business, trade; **seiner —ung nachgehen**, to strive to get a livelihood; to attend to one's business. *Comp.* **—ungs=anordnung**, *f.* diet. **—ungs=aufnahme**, *f.* reception of food. **—ungs=brei**, *m.* chyme. **—ungs=flüssigkeit**, *f.* chyle. **—ungs=kanal**, *m.* alimentary canal. **—ungs=los**, *adj.* without food; without resources, poor; unsubstantial; unprofitable. **—ungs=mittel**, *n.* provisions, victuals; means of subsistence. **—ungs=mittel=fälschung**, *f.* adulteration of food. **—ungs=mittel=steuer**, *f.* duty on provisions. **—ungs=saft**, *m.* chyle (*Phys.*). **—ungs=sorgen**, *pl.* cares of life, difficulty in making both ends meet; **—ungssorgen haben**, to make a precarious living, to struggle for (bare) existence. **—ungs=stoff**, *m.* nutriment. **—ungs=vorschrift**, *f.* regimen. **—ungs=wert**, *m.* nutritive value *or* quality, nutritiousness. **—ungs=zweig**, *m.* branch of industry, trade; livelihood.

Naht, *f.* (*pl.* **Näh'te**) seam; suture (*Anat.*, *Bot.*, *Surg.*); juncture fissure (*of planks*); **aufgetrennte —**, rip; **aus der — gegangen**, seam-rent *or* -burst; **die — ist aufgegangen**, the seam has come undone; **einem auf die —** *or* **Nähte fühlen**, to sound a p. *Comp.* **—los**, *adj.* seamless; weldless. jointless.

Näh'terin, *f. see* **Näherin**.

Nai'v, *adj. & adv.* naive, ingenuous; objective. **—ität'**, *f.* naiveté; simplicity; objectivity.

Naja'de, *f.* (*pl.* **—n**) naiad, water nymph.

Na'm—e, *m.* (**—ens**, *pl.* **—en**) name; title; character, reputation; denomination, exponent (*Math.*); **dem —en nach**, nominally; **ich kenne ihn nur dem —en nach**, I know him only by name *or* reputation; **—ens A**, named *or* called A., of the name of A.; **im —en des Königs**, in the king's name, by order of the king; **in Gottes —en**, in the name of God, for God's sake! very well! all right! do as you please! for aught I care; **ich mag den —en nicht haben, daß ich . . .**, I will not have it said of me that I . . .; **unter dem —en**, under the pretext; **unter dem angenommenen —en**, under the assumed name; **Irrtum im —en**, misnomer; **er geht unter dem —en**, he is known by the name of; **das Kind beim rechten —en nennen**, to call a spade a spade, to speak plainly; **sich** (*dat.*) **einen —en machen**, to make oneself a name; **die —en verlesen**, to call over the names; **unter unseren vereinten —en**, under our joint signature. **—ens**, *see* **Namens** (*in comp.*). **—entlich**, I. *adj.* by name, nominal; **—entlicher Aufruf**, calling up by name, roll-call. II. *adv.* particularly, especially. **—haft**, *adj. & adv.* indicated by name, named, specified; especial; renowned; **—haft machen**, to name; **etwas —haftes gewinnen**, to gain something considerable. *Comp.* **—en=buch**, *n.* nomenclature; treatise on proper names. **—en=büchlein**, *n.* first reading-book (*dial.*). **—en=christ**, *m.* nominal Christian. **—en=deutung**, **—en=erklärung**, *f.* explanation of names, definition of terms. **—en=geber**, *m.* namer, denominator. **—en=liste**, *f.* list of names, roll; nomenclature. **—en=los**, *adj. & adv.* nameless; anonymous; unspeakable, dreadful. **—en=tausch**, **—en=wechsel**, *m.* change of name; metonymy. **—en=vertauschung**, *f.* metonymy. **—en=zettel**, *m.* list of names; list of actors, play-bill.

Na'mens— (*in comp.*) **—aufruf**, *m.* calling over of names, (roll-)call. **—fest**, *n.*, **—tag**, *m.* festival of the anniversary of one's saint; birthday (*coll.*). **—vetter**, *m.* namesake. **—unterschrift**, *f.* signature. **—zug**, *m.* flourish with a signature, monogram.

Näm'lich, Nem'lich, I. *adj.*; **der, die, das —e**, the (self-)same; **dieser —e Mensch**, the very man. II. *adv.* namely, to wit, that is to say; you know, of course; (*abbreviated* **i.e.** *or* **viz.**). **—keit**, *f.* sameness, identity.

Nan'kin(g), *m.* (—s) nankeen.
Nä'nie, *f.* (*pl.* —n) nenia, elegy; funeral song.
Nann'te, Nann'test, *1 (& 3) and 2 pers. sing. imperf. indic. of* **nennen.**
Nanu', *interj.* (*denoting astonishment, anger, impatience, disappointment*); —, **was soll denn das?** come, what 's this? (*coll.*).
Napf, *m.* (—es, *pl.* **Näp'fe**) basin, bowl; dish; pan; porringer; drinking-cup. *Comp.* —**kuchen,** *m.* raised cake baked in a basin.
Näpf'chen, *n.* —s, *pl.* —) little bowl *or* basin; cup (*of acorns, etc.*); **in das — treten,** to get into a scrape (*coll.*).
Nar'be, *f.* (*pl.* —n; *dim.* **Närb'chen**) scar; cicatrice, seam; grain (*in leather*); stigma (*Bot.*); sod; bed, layer of vegetable-mould; eye (*of an egg; of seed*); hasp.
Nar'b—en, (När'ben,) *v.* I. *a.* to scar, mark, seam; to grain, pommel (*leather*); to nap, twill (*cloth*); to cut and raise sods; **sich —en,** to cicatrize, form a scar. II. *n.* (*aux.* **h.**) *see* **sich —en.** —**icht,** (*obs.*) —**ig,** *adj.* scarred; cicatricose; grained. *Comp.* —**en=bildung,** *f.* cicatrization. —**en=los,** *adj.* unmarked; unscarred. —**en=seite,** *f.* grain-side (*of leather*).
Narcis'se, Narzis'se, *f.* (*pl.* —n) narcissus; **gelbe —,** (common) daffodil.
Nar'de, *f.* (*pl.* —n) nard, spikenard.
Narko'tisch, *adj.* narcotic; —**e Mittel,** narcotics.
Narr, *m.* (—en, *pl.* —en), **När'rin,** *f.* fool; jester, buffoon; lunatic, madman (mad woman); idiot; **Hans —,** crazy Jack, blockhead, stupid fellow; pawn (*Chess.*); **ein — von Hause aus,** a born fool; **einen — abgeben,** to play the fool; **einen zum —en haben,** to make a fool of a p.; to make game of s. o.; **sich zum —en hergeben, machen,** to make a fool of oneself, to make oneself a laughing-stock; **einen — an einem gefressen haben,** to be dotingly fond of a p., to have taken a great fancy to a p.; **jedem —en gefällt seine Kappe,** everyone likes his own hobby best (*prov.*); **ein — kann mehr fragen, als sieben Weise beantworten können,** a fool may ask more questions in one hour than a wise man can answer in seven years (*prov.*). —**etei',** *f.* (*pl.* —**eteien**) fooling, tomfoolery. —**heit,** *f.* folly; hobby; piece of folly. *Comp.* —**en=doktor,** *m.* mountebank. —**en=fastnacht,** *f.* Shrove-Tuesday. —**en=fest,** *n.* fools' festival, all-fools' day. —**en=gang,** *m.* fool's errand. —**en=geschwätz,** *n.* stuff and nonsense. —**en=hände,** *pl.*; —**enhände beschmieren Tisch und Wände,** a white wall is paper for a fool (*prov.*). —**en=haus,** *n.* madhouse. —**en=jacke,** *f.* harlequin's jacket. —**en=kappe,** *f.* fools' cap, cap and bells, coxcomb. —**en(s)=posse,** *f.* (*usually plur.*) foolery, tomfoolery, trifle, nonsense; —**enspossen treiben,** to fool *or* play the fool, to play mad pranks. —**en=schiff,** *n.* Ship of Fools. —**en=seil,** *n.* line to lead a fool; **einen am —enseil führen,** to make a fool of a p., to lead a p. by the nose. —**en=streich,** *m.* foolish trick. —**en=teiding,** *f.* (*obs.*) *see* —**etei.**
Närr'—chen, *n.* (—**chens,** *pl.* —**chen**) little fool. —**in,** *f.* mad woman, lunatic, fool. —**isch,** *adj. & adv.* foolish; crazy, silly, mad; extravagant, wild; merry; droll; strange; ridiculous; **man möchte —isch werden,** it is enough to drive one mad; **ganz —isch auf eine S. sein,** to be a complete fool about *or* to dote on a th.
Nar'ren, *v.* I. *n.* (*aux.* **h.**) to play the fool. II. *a.* to make a fool of a p.
Narzis'se, *f, see* **Narcisse.**
Nas—a'l, *adj.* nasal; an organ-stop. —**alie'ren,** *v.a.* to nasalize, to pronounce with a nasal sound. —**ig,** *suffix* (*in comp.* =) -nosed. *Comp.* —**al'=laut,** *m.* nasal sound. —**(s)=horn,** *n.* rhinoceros.
Na'sch—en, *v.a. & n.* (*aux.* **h.**) to eat dainties; to nibble (*secretly*); **gern —en,** to have a sweet tooth, be something of a gourmand. —**haft,** —**ig,** *adj.* sweet-toothed, loving dainties. —**haftigkeit,** *f.* love of good eating, daintiness. *Comp.* —**katze,** *f.* nibbler of dainties, sweet-tooth; greedy creature. —**maul,** *n., see* **Näscher.** —**werk,** *n.* dainties, sweetmeats.
Nä'sch—er, *m.* (—**ers,** *pl.* —**er**), —**erin,** *f.* sweet-tooth; greedy creature; one who eats dainties secretly. —**erei',** *f.* eating by stealth, nibbling of dainties on the sly; dainty, titbit. —**ig,** (*dial.*) *see* **Naschig.**
Na'se, *f.* (*pl.* —n) nose, snout; nozzle; spout (*of a pipe*); hook (*of a tile*); beak; heel (*of a gun-stock*); nose-piece (*of a plough*); **eine feine — haben,** to have a good nose, a keen sense of smell; **alle — lang,** every minute *or* moment (*sl.*); **immer der — nach** *or* **lang,** keep straight on! (*coll.*); **einem eine lange — machen,** to take a sight at s.o. (*sign of mockery*); **eine — bekommen** *or* **sich** (*dat.*) **eine — holen,** to be rebuked *or* snubbed (*official and military language*); **seine — in jeden Quart stecken,** to poke one's nose into every corner; **eine gebogene —,** a Roman nose; **die — rümpfen,** to turn up one's nose; **einem eine — drehen,** to make a fool of a p.; **die Sache hat eine —,** there 's a hitch in the matter; **einem (etwas) an der — ansehen,** to see by a p.'s face; **an der — führen** (*or* **herumführen**), to lead by the nose; **zupfe** *or* **fasse dich an deiner (eignen) —,** sweep before your own door; **einem etwas an (auf) die — binden, heften,** to hoax s.o.; **sich** (*dat.*) **einen auf der — sitzen lassen,** to let o.s. be humbugged; **einem auf der — spielen,** to make sport of a p.; **auf der — liegen,** to have fallen down, to have come to grief, to be in bed *or* in trouble (*coll.*); **einem die Würmer aus der — ziehen,** to pump a p.; **es schnupfte ihm in der —,** it annoyed him; **in die — steigen,** to be perceptible (*of smells*); **die — in ein Buch stecken,** to read (quickly, superficially); **das sticht ihm in die —,** he covets that; **mit langer — abziehen,** to go off with a flea in one's ear, to be balked; **mit der — gegen etwas rennen,** to run one's head against; **der — nach gehen,** to follow one's nose; **er hat sich viel Wind um die — gehen lassen,** he has seen many lands; **sich** (*dat.*) **die — begießen,** to tope; to get drunk (*coll.*); **einem etwas unter die — reiben,** to cast s.th. in a p.'s teeth, throw in a p.'s face; **einem die Thür vor der — zumachen,** to shut the door in a p.'s face; **mir vor der —,** under my very nose; **die —n eingespannt!** do not carry your head too high! (*rare*). *Comp.* —**n=bluten,** *n.* bleeding at *or* from the nose. —**n=buchstabe,** *m.* nasal (*letter*). —**n=flügel,** *m.* side *or* wing of the nose. —**n=gewächs,** *n.* polypus in the nose. —**n=höhle,** *f.* cavity of the nose-bone. —**n=klemmer,** —**n=kneifer,** *m.* pince-nez. —**n=länge,** *f.* length of a nose, small amount, trifle (*coll.*); **einem um eine —nlänge voraus sein,** to be just ahead of a p. (*coll.*). —**n=laut,** *m.* nasal sound (*m, n*). —**n=loch,** *n.* nostril. —**n=quetscher,** *m.* shell; simple wooden coffin with a flat lid (*sl.*). —**n=rücken,** *m.* bridge of the nose. —**n=rümpfen,** *n.* turning up one's nose; sneer. —**n=sattel,** *m.* —**n=scheidewand,** *f.* nose-septum. —**n=schleim,** *m.* mucous discharge from the nose. —**n=stüber,** *m.* rap on the nose. —**n=stübern,** *v.a.* to fillip, rap a p. on the nose. —**n=ton,** *m.* nasal sound *or* tone. —**n=tropfen,** *m.* snivel. —**n=wärmer,** *m.* comforter, muffler. —**rümpfer,** *m.* sneerer. one who turns up his

nose (*at*). —**weis**, *adj. & adv.* pert, saucy; impertinent; inquisitive; self-sufficient; **Jungfer —weis**, Miss Pert, Miss Wiseacre; **Musje** (**Mosje**) **—weis**, Master Sauce-box, Master Jackanapes, Jack Sauce. **—weisheit**, *f.* pertness, sauciness; impudence.

Nä'se—ler, *m.* (—**lers**, *pl.* —**ler**) sniffler; one who speaks through the nose. **—ln**, *v.n.* (*aux.* **h.**) to snuffle, snivel; to scent (*of dogs*); to speak through the nose.

Nas'führen, *v.a.* to lead by the nose.

Na'sig, (**Nä'sig**,) *adj. in cpds., e.g.:* **groß—**, having a large nose; **hoch—**, proud; stuck up (*coll.*).

Naß, I. *adj. & adv.* (**nasser**, **nassest**, & **nässer**, **nässest**) wet, humid, moist; liquid; drunk; **nasse Ware**, liquids; **nasser Bruder**, **nasser Knabe** (*obs.*), toper, tippler; **— machen**, to wet; **— werden**, to get soaked *or* drenched; **es wird nasse Augen setzen**, many a tear will be shed about it; **Vergoldung auf nassem Wege**, water-gilding. II. *n.* (—(**ss**)**es**) humidity, wetness; liquid. *Comp.* **—kalt**, *adj.* raw, cold and damp.

Nas'sauern, *v.a.;* **bei einem —**, to get o. s. entertained at another's expense without making any return; to sponge on a p. (*coll.*).

Näs'se, *f.* wet, wetness, humidity. **—n**, *v.* I. *a.* to wet, to moisten. II. *n.* (*aux.* **h.**) to become wet; to emit moisture.

Natio'n, *f.* (*pl.* —**en**) nation. **—a'l**, *adj.* national. **—a'le**, *n.* (**der Mannschaften**) military register giving the names, rank, *etc.* of the officers and men. **—alisie'ren**, *v.a.* to nationalize; to naturalize; **sich —alisieren**, to be naturalized, to adopt the habits and manners of a nation; **er hat sich —alisieren lassen**, he has become naturalized. **—alitä't**, *f.* nationality. *Comp.* **—al'=dank**, *m.* benevolent institution founded by the nation for her invalid soldiers. **—al'=flagge**, *f.* national flag; Union jack (*Brit.*); Stars and Stripes (*Am.*). **—al'=garde**, *f.* national guard. **—al'=gardist**, *m.* soldier of the national guard; volunteer (*Engl.*). **—al'=hymne**, *f.* national anthem; God save the King. **—al'=liberal**, *adj.* National-Liberal; Liberal Unionist (*Engl.*). **—al'=ökonom**, *m.* political economist, sociologist, student *or* teacher of political economy. **—al'=ökonomie**, *f.* political economy. **—al'=sachen**, *pl.* domestic, home concerns. **—al'=schuld**, *f.* national debt. **—al'=verein**, *m.* national league.

Nativitä't, *f.* (*pl.* —**en**) nativity; **einem die — stellen**, to cast a p.'s horoscope. *Comp.* **—s=steller**, *m.* astrologer.

Na'trium, *n.* (—**s**) sodium, natrium; **aus — bestehend**, sodic.

Na'tron, *n.* (—**s**) natron; **kohlensaures —**, sodium carbonate; **zweifach kohlensaures —**, sodium bicarbonate; **salpetersaures —**, sodium nitrate; **salzsaures —**, sodium chloride; **arseniksaures —**, sodium arsenate. *Comp.* **—haltig**, *adj.* sodaic.

Nat'ter, *f.* (*pl.* —**n**) adder, viper, asp.

Natu'r, *f.* (*pl.* —**en**) natuer; nature, disposition, temperament, constitution; creature, person; naturally, to be sure, of course (*sl.*); **es ist seiner — nach kalt**, it is naturally, by its nature cold; **ein von — fester Ort**, a natural stronghold; **es liegt in der — der Sache**, it is in the nature of things; **das ist mir von — zuwider**, I have a natural aversion to that; **nach der — zeichnen**, to draw from the life, from nature; **zur andern — werden**, to become second nature; **Gewohnheit wird zur zweiten —**, use is second nature; **hitzige —en**, fiery natures, hot-tempered people; **solche —en sind selten**, such characters are rare; **er hat eine starke —**, he has a strong constitution; **sie ist etwas bequemer —**, she is of a rather easy disposition; **„kommst du mit'?" —!** "are you coming with us?" Of course I am! (*coll.*). **—a**, *f.;* **in —a bezahlen**, to pay in kind. **—a'l**, **—a'lien**, *see* **Natural**. **—e'll**, *n.* (—**ells**, *pl.* —**el'le**) nature, disposition. *Comp.* **—anlage**, *f.* disposition, temperament. **—begebenheit**, *f.* phenomenon. **—beobachtung**, *f.* study of nature. **—beschreiber**, *m.* naturalist, writer of natural history. **—bursche**, *m.* natural man, child of nature, unceremonious fellow. **—dichter**, *m.* self-taught poet. **—erscheinung**, *f.* natural phenomenon. **—erzeugnis**, *n.* natural production. **—farbig**, *adj.* natural colour; **—farbene Wolle**, natural wool. **—fehler**, *m.* natural defect. **—forscher**, *m.* student of natural science, scientist, naturalist; natural philosopher. **—forscher=versammlung**, *f.* congress of scientists; **britische —forscher-versammlung**, meeting of the British Association for the advancement of science. **—forschung**, *f.* natural science. **—gabe**, *f.* gift of nature; (*pl.*) (natural) talents *or* gifts. **—gemäß**, *adj. & adv.* conformable to nature, natural. **—genuß**, *m.* delight in (the beauties of) nature. **—geschichte**, *f.* natural history. **—gesetz**, *n.* law of nature. **—getreu**, *adj.* true to nature, true to life. **—glaube**, *m.* natural (*as opp. to revealed*) religion. **—hang**, *m.* natural propensity. **—heilung**, *f.* natural cure, self-cure. **—historiker**, *m.* writer of natural history. **—kenner**, **—kundige**(**r**), *m.*, *see* **—forscher**. **—kind**, *n.* child of nature. **—kneipen**, *n.* enjoyment of the beauties of nature (*coll.*). **—kraft**, *f.* power of nature. **—kunde**, **—lehre**, *f.* natural science, natural philosophy, physics, physiology. **—produkte**, *pl.* natural productions. **—recht**, *n.* natural right, law of nature. **—reich**, *n.* kingdom of nature; nature. **—seltenheit**, *f.* natural curiosity. **—simpeln**, *n.* enjoyment of the beauties of nature, roaming about in the fields and forests, out-of-door life (*coll.*). **—spiel**, *n.* freak of nature. **—stand**, *m.* state of nature. **—trieb**, *m.* instinct. **—widrig**, *adj.* unnatural. **—wissenschaft**, *f.* natural science; **beschreibende —wissenschaften**, Mineralogy, Botany, Zoölogy. **—wissenschaftler**, *m.* student of natural science. **—wissenschaftlich**, *adj.;* **—wissenschaftliche Methode**, scientific method; **—wissenschaftlicher Grad**, science degree; **—wissenschaftlicher Doktorgrad**, degree of Sc. D. **—wüchsig**, *adj.* indigenous, natural. **—züchtung**, *f.* natural training. **—zug**, *m.* characteristic.

Natura'l—ien, *pl.* natural productions; natural curiosities, specimens for a natural-history collection. **—isie'ren**, *v.a.* to naturalize; **sich —isieren lassen**, to become naturalized. **—isie'rung**, *f.* naturalization. **—is'mus**, *m.* naturalism; natural religion. **—i'st**, *m.* (—**is'ten**, *pl.* —**is'ten**) naturalist; one taught by nature *or* experience. *Comp.* **—lasten**, *pl.* charges to be paid in kind. **—leistung**, *f.* payment in kind. **—ien=kabinet**(**t**), *n.*, **—ien=sammlung**, *f.* natural-history collection, museum of natural curiosities. **—sammler**, **—verkäufer**, *m.* naturalist. **—zins**, *m.* rent paid in corn *or* flesh.

Natür'lich, I. *adj. & adv.* natural; innate; genuine; unaffected; not artificial; artless; **—er Weise**, of course; **—er Witz**, native, genuine humour *or* wit; **—e Tonleiter**, key of C major; **das geht ganz — zu**, that is quite natural; **das geht nicht — zu**, there is something strange or uncanny in this. II. *adv.* of course, certainly, naturally. **—keit**, *f.* naturalness; genuineness; artlessness.

Nau't—ik, *f.* art of navigation; nautical affairs. **—ilus**, *m.* nautilus. **—isch**, *adj.* nautical.

Ne, *see* **Nee**.

Ne'bel, *m.* (—**s**, *pl.* —) mist; **dichter —**, fog, **leichter —**, haze; nebula; **der — fällt**, the mist comes down. **—haft**, *adj.* foggy; nebulous.

misty; hazy (*notions*). —**icht**, (*obs.*) —**ig**, (**Ne'blicht**, **Ne'blig**,) *adj.* misty, hazy, foggy; cloudy; nebulous. *Comp.* —**bank**, *f.* fog-bank. —**bilder**, *pl.* dissolving views. —**fleck**, *m.* nebula (*Ast.*); nebulous spot on the eye (*Med.*). —**häutchen**, *n.* coating of mist (*Med.*). —**horn**, *n.* fog-horn. —**kappe**, *f.* hood used in a mist; hood of mist, mist-cap (*round the summit of mountains*); magic hood. —**krähe**, *f.* hooded crow. —**land**, *n.* land of mist, England (*hum.*). —**monat**, *m.* month of fogs, November. —**regen**, *m.* drizzle. —**schicht**, *f.* stratus (*of cloud*). —**signal**, *n.* fog-signal. —**stern**, *m.* nebulous star; nebula. —**streif**, *m.* nebula, streak of mist. —**wetter**, *n.* foggy weather.

Ne'beln, *v.n.* (*aux.* **h.**) to be *or* grow misty *or* foggy; **es nebelt**, there is a fog.

Ne'ben, I. *adv.* beside; — **an's**, out to one side, off sideways, by. II. *prep. with acc. when expressing motion absolutely; with dat. when expressing rest or limited motion;* near, next to, by the side of, close to; with; besides; — **mir**, at my side, beside me; **stellen Sie es — mich**, put it beside me; **er stand (ging) — mir**, he stood (walked) by my side; **er trat — mich**, he came up to me; — **einander**, side by side, abreast. — **einander bestehen**, to co-exist; — **einander stellen**, to place side by side, to compare; — **einander gestellt**, in juxtaposition; — **andern Dingen**, amongst other things. *Comp.* (*in comp.* = accessory, secondary, collateral, incidental, *opposed to* **Haupt** —, chief . . .). —**absicht**, *f.* secondary object *or* aim; mental reservation. —**allee**, *f.* parallel walk; sidewalk. —**altar**, *m.* side-altar, by-altar. —**amt**, *n.* sub-office. —**a'n**, *adv.* close by; next door. —**anführer**, *m.* second in command. —**arbeit**, *f.* work of secondary importance; work done along with other work; work done after hours *or* in leisure hours. —**ausgang**, *m.* side-passage; private entrance. —**axe**, *f.* conjugate axis. —**bahn**, *f.* siding; branch-line, secondary line. —**bedeutung**, *f.* secondary signification. —**begriff**, *m.* subordinate idea, accessory notion. —**bei'**, *adv.* close by; along with something else; by the way; incidentally; besides, by the by. —**bericht**, *m.* additional information *or* report. —**betrachtung**, *f.* secondary consideration. —**beweis**, *m.* additional *or* collateral proof. —**blatt**, *n.* supplement; stipula (*Bot.*); floral leaf. —**blick**, *m.* side-glance. —**bruder**, *m.* fellow-man; brother (*B.*). —**buhler**, *m.*, —**buhlerin**, *f.* rival. —**buhlerei'**, *f.* rivalry. —**christ**, *m.* fellow-Christian. —**ding**, *n.* accessory; secondary matter. —**einander-stehen**, *n.*, —**einander-stellung**, *f.* juxtaposition. —**einander-liegen**, *n.* contiguity. —**einander-schaltung**, *f.* parallel arrangement. —**eingang**, *m.* side-entrance. —**einkünfte**, —**einnahmen**, *pl.* perquisites; incidental income *or* emoluments. —**erbe**, *m.* co-heir. —**fach**, *n.* subsidiary subject, additional subject. —**figur**, *f.* accessory, subordinate figure (*Paint.*). —**flügel**, *m.* additional *or* side-wing (*of a house*). —**fluß**, *m.* tributary, feeder. —**folge**, *f.* indirect result. —**forderung**, *f.* accessory claim. —**frage**, *f.* side-question. —**gang**, *m.* by-way, passage; side-aisle; collateral vein (*Min.*). —**gasse**, *f.* side-street, lane. —**gebäude**, *n.* wing of a building; adjoining *or* annexed building; outhouse. —**gebühren**, *pl.* perquisites. —**geschmack**, *m.* flavour. —**gedanke**, *m.* simultaneous idea, secondary thought; simultaneous purpose; subordinate idea; (*Mus.*) secret purpose, mental reservation. —**geschöpf**, *n.* fellow-creature. —**gesetz**, *n.* by-law. —**gewinn**, *m.* extra profit. —**handlung**, *f.* subordinate action; episode; by-play. —**handlungs-haus**, *n.* branch-establishment. —**haus**, *n.* adjoining house. —**he'r**, —**hi'n**, *adv. see* —**bei**. —**interesse**, *f.* subordinate interest; private interest. —**kirche**, *f.* chapel of ease. —**kosten**, *pl.* extras; incidental expenses. —**land**, *n.* dependency. —**leitung**, *f.* secondary conductor. —**linie**, *f.* collateral line (*Geneal.*); branch-line (*Railw.*); parallel line; ledger-line (*Mus.*); **jüngere —linie**, younger branch. —**mann**, *m.* by-stander, man alongside; man right or left of one (*Mil.*). —**mensch**, *m.* fellow-creature. —**mond**, *m.* mock-moon; satellite. —**ordnung**, *f.* co-ordination. —**pfarre**, *f.* living of a chapel of ease. —**pforte**, *f.* side-door. —**planet**, *m.* satellite. —**posten**, *m.* incidental item of expense. —**rolle**, *f.* subordinate part. —**rücksicht**, *f.* secondary *or* private consideration. —**sache**, *f.* matter of secondary importance; accessory; incident; **als —sache**, accidental, non-essential. —**sächlich**, *adj.*; **eine —sächliche Rolle spielen**, to be of secondary importance. —**satz**, *m.* subordinate sentence; incidental proposition; parembole (*Log.*). —**schiff**, *n.* side-aisle. —**schluß**, *m.* shunt, derivation. —**schoß**, —**schößling**, *m.* sucker, shoot. —**schüssel**, *f.* side-dish; entremets. —**sitzer**, *m.* person sitting by the side of another. —**sonne**, *f.* mock-sun, parhelion. —**sproß**, *m.* side-shoot, sucker. —**stehend**, *adj.* & *adv.* proximate, annexed; in the margin; **der —stehende**, by-stander. —**straße**, *f.* side-street. —**strom**, *m.* tributary, feeder; induction current. —**stube**, *f.* adjoining room. —**stunde**, *f.* leisure hour. —**tempus**, *n.* secondary tense. —**thür**, *f.* side-door; next door. —**tisch**, *m.* side-table. —**ton**, *m.* second (*Mus.*); secondary accent. —**tonig**, *adj.* having the secondary accent. —**treppe**, *f.* side- *or* back-stairs. —**umstand**, *m.* accidental *or* accessory circumstance. —**ursache**, *f.* accidental cause; secondary reason. —**verdienst**, *m.* incidental gain; perquisites. —**verordnung**, *f.* by-law. —**versammlung**, *f.* extraordinary meeting; overflow meeting; private meeting. —**versicherung**, *f.* collateral assurance. —**vormund**, *m.* co-guardian. —**weg**, *m.* by-way; (*pl.*) indirect means. —**weib**, *n.* concubine. —**weibig**, *adj.* perigynous. —**werk**, *n.* extra-work. —**wind**, *m.* side-wind. —**winkel**, *m.* adjacent angle. —**wort**, *n.* accessory word, aside. —**zoll**, *m.* extra duty. —**zug**, *m.* additional organ-stop. —**zweck**, *m.* subordinate aim, by-purpose. —**zweig**, *m.* side-branch; collateral branch.

Nebst, *prep.* (*with dat.*) with, together *or* along with, in addition to, besides.

Ne'ck—en, *v.a.* to tease, rally, quiz; to irritate, provoke; to harass (*Mil.*); **was sich liebt, —t sich**, those who love one another are fond of teasing one another. —**er**, *m.* (—**ers**, *pl.* —**er**) quiz, tease, banterer. —**erei'**, *f.* banter, raillery, chaff. —**isch**, *adj.* & *adv.* teasing, fond of teasing; merry; droll; queer, odd.

Nee, *interj.* no (*dial.* & *coll.*).

Nef'fe, *m.* (—**n**, *pl.* —**n**) nephew. *Comp.* —**nschaft**, *f.* relationship of a nephew; nephews (*collect.*).

Ne'g—ativ, I. *adj.* negative (*Math.*, *Phys.*, *Phot.*). II. (—**ativ-bild**,) *n.* negative. —**ie'ren**, *v.a.* to deny; to negative (*a proposal*).

Ne'ger, *m.* (—**s**, *pl.* —) negro, black man, black; blackie, darkie (*coll.*); nigger (*contempt.* & *coll.*). —**in**, *f.* negress, black woman. *Comp.* —**aufseher**, *m.* negro-driver. —**chor**, *m.* negro minstrel troupe, niggers (*at watering places*). —**handel**, *m.* slave-trade. —**knabe**, *m.* negro boy, nigger-boy. —**schiff**, *n.* ship with negro slaves. —**sklave**, *m.* negro; **flüchtiger —sklave**, maroon.

Negligé', *n.* (—**s**, *pl.* —**s**) undress, desnabille.

Nego—cia'nt, *m.* (—**cian'ten**, *pl.* —**cian'ten**)

negotiator, wholesale merchant. **—ciie'ren,** *v.a.* to negotiate, to traffic. **—tiatio'n,** *f.* negotiation, operation, transaction.

Neh'm—en, *ir.v.* I. *a.* to take; to seize, lay hold of; to take, receive; **einem etwas —en,** to take s.th. from a p.; **wie man's nimmt,** according as you take it; **wie man's —en will,** that depends (*on the way you take it*); **einen Anfang —en,** to begin; **Anstand —en,** to pause, hesitate, demur; **Augenschein (von etwas) —en, (etwas) in Augenschein —en,** to take a view of, inspect; **ein Ende —en,** to come *or* to be brought to an end, to terminate; **ein ehrenvolles Ende —en,** to die an honourable death; **—en wir den Fall,** let us take the case, let us suppose *or* assume; **das lasse ich mir nicht —en,** I shall not be dissuaded from that, I shan't allow that (*privilege, etc.*) to be taken from me; **ich lasse es mir nicht —en, Sie zu begleiten,** I insist upon accompanying you; **den Mund voll —en,** to talk big; **sie —en sich beide nichts,** the one is as good as the other; **Partei —en (für einen),** to side (with a p.); **Platz —en,** to take a seat *or* place; **—en Sie, bitte, Platz,** pray be seated; sit down, please; **Reißaus —en,** to decamp (*vulg.*); **sich** (*dat.*) **von seinem Rechte nichts —en lassen,** to suffer no encroachment upon one's rights; **Schaden —en,** to suffer damage; **überhand —en,** to take the upper hand, get the better of; **übel —en,** to take amiss; **das Wort —en,** to begin to speak; **das wird sich nichts —en,** it is the same thing; **—t ein Beispiel daran,** let this be an example to you; **etwas auf sich** (*acc.*) **—en,** to charge o.s. with, undertake a th.; **sich** (*dat.*) **viel heraus —en,** to presume; **auseinander —en,** to undo; to take to pieces; **einen beim Worte —en,** to take a p. at his word; **beim Schopf —en,** to take by the forelock; **—en für,** to take for, to mistake for, to take as; **nicht für ungut —en,** not to take amiss; **einen ins Gebet —en,** to speak seriously to, to take s.o. to task; **in Kost —en,** to board (a p.); **mit in den Kauf —en,** to take into the bargain; **mit Gewalt —en,** to take by force; **mit sich —en,** to take along with, carry away; **über sich** (*acc.*) **—en,** to undertake (*obs.*); **zu sich —en,** to take into one's house; **Nahrung zu sich —en,** to take food; **es nimmt mich Wunder,** (*lit.* wonder of it seizes me) it astonishes me; I am surprised at it; *subseq.*: **das u. m. W.** II. *r.* to conduct o.s., to behave (*obs.*).

Neh'rung, *f.* (*pl.* **—en**) narrow tongue of land separating a small bay (**Haff**) from the (Baltic) sea; **die Kurische —,** a long and narrow tongue of sand-hills between the Baltic and the bay of Courland (**Kurisches Haff**) near Memel.

Neid, *m.* (**—es**) envy; grudge; jealousy; **vor — vergehen,** to die with envy *or* jealousy; **— gegen einen hegen,** to be envious of a p.

Nei'd—en, *v.a. & n.* (*aux.* **h.**) to envy; **einem etwas —en,** to envy *or* begrudge a p. something. **—er,** *m.* (**—ers,** *pl.* **—er**) envier, grudger. **—isch,** *adj.* envious; jealous (**auf einen,** of a p.). *Comp.* **—bau,** *m.* building undertaken to injure another. **—ens=wert,** *adj.* enviable. **—hammel, —hart,** *see* **—er. —los,** *adj.* unenvious.

Nei'ge, *f.* (*pl.* **—n**) inclination of the head, bow, courtesy; brow of a slope; slope, incline; decline, decay; sediment, dregs; **auf die — gehen,** to decline, to draw to an end; **es geht mit ihm auf die —,** he is on the decline; **auf der — sein,** to be coming to an end, to run out; **unser Vorrat geht stark auf die —,** our stock (of this article) is nearly exhausted, we are almost out of this article (*C. L.*); **den Becher bis zur — leeren,** to drain the cup to the dregs.

Nei'g—en, *v.* I. *a.* to tilt, bend over; to incline, bend, bow. II. *r. & n.* (*aux.* **h.**) to make a reverence, bow; to dip; to lean; to slope; to decline, wane; to bend towards; **der Tag —t sich,** the day is far spent, is declining; **der Tag hat sich geneigt,** the day is done; **(sich) zu etwas —en,** to be prone to, inclined for; **sich zu Ende —en,** to draw to a close; **er —t zu Erkältungen,** he is very apt to catch cold, he easily gets a cold. **—ung,** *f.* inclination, disposition, propensity, tendency; taste (*for art, etc.*); affection; gradient, incline; slope; bias; dip; inclination (*Math., Astr.*); **—ung haben** *or* **fassen zu,** to take a fancy to, **geneigt,** inclined, bent (*physically*); inclined, disposed, well-affectioned; **geneigter Leser,** kind reader; **geneigtes Gehör,** ready hearing, willing ear. *Comp.* **—ungs=ebene, —ungs=fläche,** *f.* inclined plane. **—ungs=lot,** *n.* axis of incidence. **—ungs=nadel,** *f.* dipping needle. **—ungs=winkel,** *m.* angle of incidence.

Nein, *adv.* no; **mit — beantworten,** to answer in the negative; **— und abermals —!** no! a thousand times no! **— doch** (*no stress on the* **doch**), no, indeed! no, certainly no!

Nekro—lo'g, *m.* (**—logs,** *pl.* **—loge**) obituary (notice), necrology. **—ma'nt,** *m.* (**—man'ten,** *pl.* **—man'ten**), **—man'tin,** *f.* necromancer. **—mantie',** *f.* necromancy.

Nek'tar, *m.* (**—s**) nectar. *Comp.* **—pfirsche,** *f.* nectarine.

Nel'ke, *f.* (*pl.* **—n**) pink, carnation, gilliflower; **gefüllte —,** double pink; **Gewürz—,** clove. *Comp.* **—n=artig,** *adj.* caryophyllaceous. **—n=baum,** *m.* clove-tree. **—n=öl,** *n.* oil of cloves. **—n=pfeffer,** *n.* allspice, Jamaica pepper. **—n=rinde,** *f.*, **—n=zimmet,** *m.* clove-cinnamon. **—n=stock,** *m.* gilliflower *or* carnation plant.

Nenn'bar, *adj.* nameable; **nicht —,** unmentionable, unspeakable.

Nen'n—en, *ir.v.a.* to name, call, term, style, denominate; to mention by name, speak of; **das —e ich . . .,** that is what I call . . .; **sich —en,** to be called; **wie —t er sich?** what is his name? **ich hörte ihn —en,** I heard his name mentioned; **einer, der nicht genannt sein will,** one who does not wish his name to be known, who wishes to remain anonymous; **Karl genannt der Kühne,** Charles surnamed the Bold; **diese sogenannten Doktoren,** these so-called doctors; **obengenannt,** above-mentioned; **ein Ding beim rechten Namen —en,** to call a spade a spade; **wer darf das Kind beim rechten Namen —en,** who dares call the child by its true name? **—er,** *m.* (**—ers,** *pl.* **—er**) namer; denominator. **—ung,** *f.* naming; nomination; mention; entry (*for a game*); **mit —ung seines Namens,** (in) mentioning his name. *Comp.* **—ens=wert,** *adj. & adv.* especially worth mentioning; notable, important, considerable; **es ist nichts —enswertes,** it is not worth mentioning. **—fall,** *m.* nominative case. **—wert,** *m.* nominal value; **zum —wert,** at par (*C. L.*). **—wort,** *n.* noun, substantive.

Neolo'g, *m.* (**—en,** *pl.* **—en**) neologist, innovator.

Nepo't—e, *m.* (**—en,** *pl.* **—en**) nephew (*rare*); relative (*rare*). **—is'mus,** *m.* nepotism.

Nerei'de, *f.* (*pl.* **—n**) Nereid.

Nergelei', (**Nörgelei',**) *f.* nagging; grumbling, incessant fault-finding.

Ner'gel—er, (**Nör'gel—er,**) *m.* (**—ers,** *pl.* **—er**) grumbler, fault-finder; malcontent. **—ig,** *adj. & adv.* grumbling, fault-finding. **—n,** *v.* I. *n.* (*aux.* **h.**) to grumble. II. *a.* to harass by grumbling.

Nerv, *m.* (**—(e)s** & **—en,** *pl.* **—en**), **—e,** *f.* (*pl.* **—en**) (*obs.*) nerve; sinew; string (*of a bow*); vein (*of a leaf*); filament. **—en,** *see* **Nerven** *in comp.* **—icht** (*obs.*). **—ig,** *adj.* nervous; sinewy;

nerved; vigorous; pithy. **—ö's**, *adj.* nervous; forcible.

Ner'ven— (*in comp.*) **—ähnlich**, *adj.* neuroid. **—anatomie'**, *f.* neurotomy. **—anfall**, *m.* nervous attack. **—anregung**, *f.* nerve impulse. **—aufregung**, *f.* nervous excitement. **—bau**, *m.* texture of the nerves; nervous system. **—beschwerde**, *f.* nervous complaint. **—druck**, *m.* pressure on the nerves. **—durchschneidung**, *f.* neurotomy. **—entzündung**, *f.* neuritis. **—erregung**, *f.* nervimotion. **—erschütterung**, *f.* succussion. **—faser**, *f.* nerve fibre. **—fieber**, *n.* nervous fever; **ansteckendes —fieber**, typhus. **—fieber=artig**, *adj.* typhoid. **—gewebe**, *n.* nervous plexus. **—haut**, *f.* retina. **—knoten**, *m.* ganglion. **—krank**, *adj.* nervous, suffering from the nerves. **—krankheit**, *f.* nervous affection. **—kunde**, **—lehre**, *f.* neurology. **—lähmung**, *f.* palsy. **—leiden**, *n.* nervous complaint *or* affection. **—los**, *adj.* nerveless. **—mittel**, *n.* neurotic. **—reiz**, *m.* nervous irritation. **—saft**, *m.* nervous fluid. **—schlag**, *m.* (nervous) apoplexy. **—schmerz**, *m.* neuralgia. **—schwach**, *adj.* of weak nerves, nervous. **—schwäche**, *f.* nervousness, nervous debility *or* prostration. **—stärkend**, *adj.* strengthening the nerves; neurotic; **—stärkendes Mittel**, tonic, pick-me-up (*coll.*). **—strang**, *m.* nerve-fibre. **—system**, *n.* nervous system. **—thätigkeit**, *f.* nerve function. **—zuckungen**, *pl.* vellications. **—zufall**, *m.* nervous attack.

Nes'sel, *f.* (*pl.* **—n**) nettle; **eine taube —**, a dead nettle. *Comp.* **—ausschlag**, *m.*, **—fieber**, *n.*, **—sucht**, *f.* nettle-rash. **—brand**, *m.* burning of a nettle-sting. **—kraut**, *n.* hemp-nettle; **ein Kränzchen von —kraut tragen**, to have one's love despised (*obs.*). **—tuch**, *n.* nettle-cloth, muslin; stuff made from nettle fibres.

Nest, *n.* (**—es**, *pl.* **—er**) nest; eyrie (*of large birds of prey*); haunt; bed; nidus; paltry place, hole, cluster; **ein — voll**, a brood (*of birds*); **die Polizei fand das — leer**, the police found the bird(s) flown; **Krähwinkel ist ein rechtes —**, K. is a regular hole; **—er ausnehmen**, to bird-nest, to go bird-nesting; **ein — bauen**, to make a nest, to nidificate; **eigen — ist stets das Best'**, home is home, be it never so homely (*prov.*); **jedem Vogel gefällt sein —**, the crow thinks her own bird fairest (*coll.*). **—ling**, *m.* (**—lings**, *pl.* **—linge**) nestling. *Comp.* **—feder**, *f.* down. **—flüchter**, *m.* autophagous bird; *pl.* autophagi (*opp. to* **—hocker**). **—förmig**, *adj.* nidiform. **—häkchen**, *n.* nest-chicken, nestling, youngest child; pin-basket; pet of the family. **—hocker**, *m.* insessorial bird; *pl.* insessores. **—küchlein**, *n.* nestling, youngest chick.

Nes'tel, *f.* (*m.n.*) (*pl.* **—n**) string, (tagged) lace; point (*obs.*); **beschlagene —**, a lace in. *Comp.* **—beschlag**, *m.* tag (*of a lace*). **—knüpfen**, *n.* a charm by which married people (*esp'lly newly married people*) are supposed to be made incapable of begetting children. **—nadel**, *f.* bodkin.

Nes'teln, *v.a.* to lace, fasten with a lace.

Nett, *adj.* & *adv.* neat, spruce, trim; nice; clear, unambiguous; pretty. **—heit**, **—igkeit**, *f.* neatness, spruceness; prettiness. **—o**, *see* **Netto**.

Net'to, *adv.* (*abbr.* n^0) net, clear (*of all charges*); **— Kassa im Voraus**, net cash in advance. *Comp.* **—betrag**, *m.* net amount. **—einnahme**, *f.* net profits. **—ertrag**, *m.* net proceeds, net produce. **—gewicht**, *n.* net weight. **—preis**, *m.* real *or* net price, fixed price; **—preis drei Schillinge**, three shillings net.

Netz, *n.* (**—es**, *pl.* **—e**) net, snare; caul; midriff; retina; plexus; reticle (*Anat.*); network; crease (*in cloth*). **—chen**, *n.* (**—chens**, *pl.* **—chen**) little net. *Comp.* **—aderig**, *adj.* reticulated. **—ball**, *m.*, **—ball=spiel**, *n.* lawn-tennis. **—ball=verein**, *m.* lawn-tennis club. **—flügler**, *pl.* neuroptera (*Ent.*). **—förmig**, *adj.* reticulated, reticular. **—haut**, *f.* retina; omentum (*Anat.*). **—jagen**, *n.* net-snaring. **—nadel**, *f.* netting-needle. **—stricker**, *m.* netter. **—zeichnen**, *n.* drawing on paper divided into squares.

Net'z—en, *v.a.* to wet, moisten; to steep. **—ung**, *f.* wetting, moistening; steeping. *Comp.* **—faß**, *n.* steeping-tub.

Neu, *adj.* & *adv.* new; fresh; recent; modern; novel; **die —(er)e Geschichte**, modern history; **—e Menschen**, upstarts, parvenus (*poet.*); **—en Mut schöpfen**, to gain fresh courage; **— aufgelegt**, reprinted; **was giebt's —es?** what news is there? **das ist mir nichts —es**, I knew that long ago; **aufs —e**, **von —em**, anew, afresh, again, once more; **etwas — machen**, to renovate; **ein Schauspiel — besetzen**, to re-cast a play; **aufs —e zurichten**, to dress anew; **die —eren**, the moderns. **—er**, I. *m. see* **—ling**; new arrival. II. *comp. of* **neu**; newer; modern; **die —eren Sprachen**, modern languages; **in —erer Zeit**, in recent times, of late years; **—ere Richtung**, reform movement (*e.g. in mod. lang. teaching*) modern methods. **—erer**, **—rer**, *m.* (**—(e)rers**, *pl.* **—(e)rer**) innovator; neologist (*in language*). **—erlich**, *adj.* & *adv.* newly, lately. **—ern**, *v.n.* (*aux.* **h.**) to innovate. **—heit**, *f.* (*pl.* **—heiten**) newness; novelty. **—igkeit**, *f.* (*pl.* **—igkeiten**) news, piece of news; new production; novelty; **—igkeit des Tages**, event of the day; *pl.* current events. **—lich**, I. *adj.* late, recent. II. *adv.* the other day, quite recently; **—lich Morgens**, the other morning. **—ling**, *m.* (**—lings**, *pl.* **—linge**) novice, neophyte; freshman; stranger; tyro, new hand. *Comp.* **—anbauer**, *m.* new settler, colonist. **—angekommen**, *adj.* newly arrived. **—auflage**, *f.* new edition, reprint. **—(ge=)backen**, *adj.* fresh; new-fangled (*theories*); **der —(ge)backene**, upstart. **—bau**, *m.* building in course of erection. **—begierde**, *f.* desire for news. **—bekehrte(r)**, *m.* neophyte. **—bruchland**, *n.* ground newly broken and cleared. **—druck**, *m.* reprint. **—er=dings**, *adv.* recently. **—erfunden**, *adj.* newly-invented. **—erungs=sucht**, *f.* desire of innovation. **—er=wählt**, *adj.* recently elected. **—geboren**, *adj.* new-born. **—gestaltung**, *f.* reorganization. **—gier(de)**, *f.* curiosity, inquisitiveness. **—hochdeutsch**, *n.* New *or* Modern High German. **—igkeits=krämer**, *m.* news-monger. **—jahr**, *n.* New Year. **—jahrs=abend**, *m.* New Year's eve. **—jahrs=geschenk**, *n.* New Year's gift. **—jahrs=wunsch**, *m.* New-Year's congratulation, good wishes for the New Year; New Year's card. **—lateinisch**, *adj.* Neo-Latin. **—licht**, *n.*, **—mond**, *m.* new-moon. **—lot**, *n.* decagram. **—modisch**, *adj.* fashionable. **—philolog**, *m.* modern language student *or* teacher, student of modern languages. **—philologen=tag**, *m.* meeting of mod. language teachers and scholars. **—philologen=verein**, *m.* Modern Language Association. **—platoniker**, *m.* Neo-Platonist. **—silber**, *n.* German silver, argentine. **—sprachler**, *m.* modern philologist. **—sprachlich**, *adj.*; **—sprachlicher Verein**, Modern Languages Association. **—sterdings**, quite recently. **—testamentlich**, *adj.* relating to the New Testament. **—verjüngt**, *adj.* restored to youth, rejuvenated. **—vermählt**, *adj.* newly-married; **die —vermählte**, the bride; **die —vermählten**, the newly married couple. **—zeit**, *f.* modern times. **—zeitlich**, *adj.* of *or* in modern times, modern. **—zoll**, *m.* centimetre.

Neu'm—en, *f.pl.* dots (*of various shapes, inmediæval music notations*). **—ie'ren**, *v.a.* **—ierte**

Hff., MSS. (provided) with mediæval music notations.

Neun, I. *num. adj.* nine; **alle —(e) schieben,** to throw down the whole nine (*at nine-pins*); **einer aus —(en),** one (out) of nine. II. *f.* (*pl.* **—en**) nine. **—er,** *m.* (**—ers,** *pl.* **—er**) nine; the number nine; one of nine; soldier of the 9th regiment. **—t,** *num. adj.* ninth; **der —te Januar,** the ninth of January; **heute haben wir den —ten,** to-day is the 9th; **zum —ten,** ninthly. **—tel,** *n.* (**—tels,** *pl.* **—tel**) ninth part. **—tens,** *adv.* ninthly, in the ninth place. **—zig,** *num. adj. & f.* ninety. **—ziger,** *f.* I. *m.* (**—zigers,** *pl.* **—ziger**) man of (over) ninety years; soldier of the 90th regiment; **ein mittlerer —ziger,** a man in the middle of the nineties. II. *indec. adj.;* **in den —ziger Jahren,** in the nineties; between 1890 and 1900. **—zigste,** *num. adj.* (**der, die, das**) ninetieth. **—zigstel,** *n.* (**—zigstels,** *pl.* **—zigstel**) ninetieth part. **—zigstens,** *adv.* in the ninetieth place. *Comp.* **—achteltakt,** *m.* nine-eight time (*Mus.*). **—auge,** *n.* river-lamprey. **—eck,** *n.* nonagon. **—eckig,** *adj.* nonagonal. **—erlei,** *indec. adj.* of nine different sorts. **—fach, —fältig,** *adj.* nine-fold. **—jährig,** *adj.* nine years old, extending over nine years. **—jährlich,** *adj.* recurring every ninth year, novennial. **—mal,** *adv.* nine times. **—männig,** *adj.* enneandrous. **—monatig,** *adj.* nine months old; lasting nine months. **—monatlich,** *adj.* every nine months. **—pfünder,** *m.* nine-pounder. **—stimmig,** *adj.* for nine voices (*M.*). **—stündig,** *adj.* of nine hours. **—tägig,** *adj.* lasting nine days; nine days old; **—tägige Seelenmesse,** novenary (mass). **—täglich,** *adj.* repeated, recurring every nine days. **—tehalb,** *indec. adj.* eight and a half. **—teilig,** *adj.* of nine parts. **—weibig,** *adj.* having nine pistils *or* styles (*Bot.*); enneagynous. **—wöchentlich,** *adj.* recurring every ninth week. **—wöchig,** *adj.* nine weeks old; lasting nine weeks. **—zahl,** *f.* ennead. **—zehn,** *num. adj.* nineteen. **—zehntel,** *n.* nineteenth part. **—zehntens,** *adv.* in the nineteenth place. **—zigerlei,** *indec. adj.* of ninety different sorts. **—zig=jährig,** *adj.* ninety years old. **—zigmal,** *adv.* ninety times.

Neur—algie', *f.* neuralgia. **—al'gisch,** *adj.* neuralgic. **—asthenie',** *f.* neurasthenia. **—asthe'niker,** *m.* person suffering from neurasthenia. **—i'n,** *n.* neurine. **—o'm,** *n.* neuroma. **—o'se,** *f.* neurosis.

Neutr—a'l, *adj.* neutral. **—alisie'ren,** *v.a.* to neutralize. **—alitä't,** *f.* neutrality.

Neu'tr—um, *n.* (**—ums,** *pl.* **—a**) neuter.

Ni'belungen, *pl.* the Nibelungs. **—frage,** *f.* see **—theorie.** **—lied,** *n.* the Lay of the Nibelungs (*great Middle High German popular epic*). **—strophe,** *f.* stanza (*of four long lines*) in which the Lay of the Nibelungs is written. **—theorie,** *f.* theory concerning the origin and composition of the Song of the Nibelungs.

Nicht, I. *adv.* not; no; **ganz und gar —, durchaus —,** not at all, by no means, on no condition, in no way; **— doch!** (*only — is accented,* **doch** *has no stress*) no, but no, don't! certainly not! **noch —,** not (*as*) yet; **— einmal,** not even, not so much as; **— ein Mal,** not once; **es ist keiner, der — wüßte,** every one knows· **so viel ich weiß —, — daß ich wüßte,** not so far as I know; **— daß uns das von ihm wundert,** not that this surprises us in him; **er reist — mehr,** he does not travel any longer, he travels no longer; **— Ehre, — Reichtum,** neither honour nor riches; **und ich auch —,** nor I either; **Sie thun es, — wahr?** you will do it, won't you? **— wahr?** is it not so? **wo — . . .,** if not . . . II. *part.* is it not? **wie schön ist — die Eintracht!** how beautiful is concord! (is it not?) **wie liebte ich ihn —!** how I did love him! (did n't I?) III. *subst.* naught, nothing (*obs.*); **mit —en,** by no means, not at all; **zu —e,** to ruin, to naught; **zu —e machen,** to annihilate, destroy, ruin, bring to naught; **zu —e werden,** to perish, to be ruined, to get spoiled, to fail; **sie wollten meines Rates —,** they wanted none of my advice, they did not wish for my advice; **hier ist meines Bleibens —,** I cannot stay here; **ich kenne deiner —,** I do not know you (*obs.*). IV. *redundant negation; common in older German for the sake of emphasis, and surviving in poetry and in popular speech;* **das disputiert ihm niemand —,** no one questions that about him; **Gott ist niemals — von seinem Volk geschieden,** God is never separated from his people. *Often in older German after verbs implying negation* or *impediment, etc.;* **verhüt' es Gott, daß ich nicht Hülfe brauche,** God forbid that I should need help! V. *prefix* (*in comp.* =) non-, un-, in-, dis-. **—ig,** *adj. & adv.* null, void; invalid; vain, empty; transitory; perishable; **—ig machen,** to annul, abolish; **für —ig erklären,** to quash, declare null and void. **—igkeit,** *f.* nullity; nothingness; futility, vanity; perishableness. **—s,** *see* **Nichts.** *Comp.* **—achtung,** *f.* want of esteem, disrespect. **—anerkennung,** *f.* disavowal; repudiation (*of debts*). **—angabe,** *f.* non-entry (*of goods at the custom-house*); misprision (*of treason, Law*). **—annahme,** *f.* non-acceptance. **—ding,** *n.* nonentity. **—duldung,** *f.* intolerance. **—erscheinung,** *f.* non-appearance; default (*Law*). **—gebrauch,** *m.* disuse. **—gedenken,** *n.* forgetfulness; oblivion. **—haltung,** *f.* non-observance; adjournment (*of a meeting, etc.*). **—leiter,** *m.* non-conductor (*Phys.*). **—militär,** *m.* civilian. **—rauch=coupé,** *n.,* **—raucher=abteil,** *m.* compartment where smoking is not allowed. **—raucher,** *m.* non-smoker; **für —raucher,** not smoking, no smoking allowed (*on railway carriages*). **—sein,** *n.* non-existence, nullity. **—verantwortlichkeit,** *f.* irresponsibility. **—wesentlich,** *adj.* non-essential. **—wirklichkeit,** *f.* unreality. **—wissen,** *n.* ignorance. **—wollen,** *n.* unwillingness. **—zahlung,** *f.* non-payment; **—zahlung eines Wechsels,** dishonouring a bill. **—zulassung,** *f.* non-admission.

Nich'te, *f.* (*pl.* **—n**) niece.

[1]**Nichts,** I. *ind. & indec. pron.* (*orig. genit. of* **Nicht**; *cp.* **dich soll — gelüsten,** you shall not be desirous of anything (*obs.*)) naught, nothing; *adverb'ly:* in nothing, nowise; not at all; **— als, — außer,** nothing but, nothing short of; **— der Art,** nothing of the kind, no such thing; **— dergleichen,** no such thing; **—destoweniger,** nevertheless, notwithstanding, however; **ganz und gar —, durchaus —, schlechterdings, rein, lauter —, — in der Welt,** nothing at all, nothing whatever, not at all; **— mehr,** nothing more, no more; **mir —, dir —,** quite coolly, without more ado; **er that es mir — dir —,** he did it without so much as asking leave; **wissen Sie — Neues?** have you no news? **das hat — zu sagen, schadet —,** that is of no consequence; **so viel wie —,** next to nothing; **— weniger als,** anything but; **— wert,** of no value; **wenn es weiter — ist,** if that is *or* be all; **das ist ihm wie —,** he does not mind that; **sonst —!** nothing more! is that all! **hier ist — zu lachen,** there is nothing to laugh at in this; **es ist — Gutes an ihm,** there is no good in him; **es ist — daran, an der Sache,** there is no truth in it; **aus — wird —,** from nothing nothing comes; **es kann aus**

der Sache — werden, nothing can come of it; **für — achten,** to think little *or* nothing of, to slight; **es ist — damit,** there is nothing in it, nothing of the sort; **um —,** for nothing; **um — spielen,** to play for love; **um — und wieder —,** without any cause whatever; for nothing at all; **— von dem,** no such thing; **— davon!** not a word of that! **zu — werden,** to come to naught, to fall to the ground. II. *n.* (*pl. sometimes* **Nichtse**) nothingness; nonentity; nothing; chaos; nihility; insignificance; **ein bloßes —,** a mere nothing, a trifle; **saget niemand —,** do not tell anybody anything (*obs.*); **ein Habe—,** a penniless fellow; **ein Tauge—,** a worthless fellow. *Comp.* **—nutz,** *m.* good-for-nothing fellow, ne'er-do-weel. **—nutz(ig), —nützig,** *adj.* useless, worthless. **—nutzigkeit,** *f.* futility; worthlessness. **—thuer,** *m.* idler. — **thuerei',** *f.*, **—thun,** *n.* idling, inaction. — **würdig,** I. *adj.* worthless; contemptible; vile; annoying (*coll.*); trifling, unimportant (*obs.*). II. *adv.* of no account. **—würdigkeit,** *f.* futility; worthlessness; baseness; (*pl.*) base actions.

[2]**Nichts,** *n.* flowers of zinc, zinc-flowers.

[1]**Nick,** I. *m.* (**—es,** *pl.* **—e**) nod. II. *n.* neck (*prov.*). **—en,** *v.n.* (*aux.* **h.**) to nod; to wink; to doze.

[2]**Nick,** *m.* (**—s,** *pl.* **—e**) water-sprite, merman. See **Nix.**

[1]**Ni'ckel,** *m.* (**—s,** *pl.* **—**) Nicholas; mannikin; contemptible fellow; nag; *also n. & f.* strumpet; jade. *Comp.* **—mann,** *m.* water-sprite.

[2]**Ni'ckel,** (*in comp.* =) nickel (*metal*), of nickel; **ein paar —,** a few coppers. **—oxyd,** *n.* nickelic oxide. **—oxydul,** *n.* nickelous oxide. — **stahl,** *m.* nickel steel, nickeliferous steel.

Nid (*dial.*) = **unter,** beneath, below, under; **— dem Wald,** below the forest; **— der Enns,** below *or* to the right of the river Enns (Lower Austria).

Nie, *adv.* never (before), at no time; **— und nimmer,** never (*before*) and never (*after*); at no time. *Comp.* **—bewölkt,** *adj.* never-clouded. **—mals,** *adv.* at no time, never. **—mand,** *see* **Niemand.**

Nie'—den, Ni'den, *adv.* down, below; here below. **—der, —drig,** *see* **Nieder, Niedrig.**

Nie'der, I. *adj.* nether, under, beneath; low; subordinate; inferior; primary; low, mean; vulgar; **Hoch und —,** high and low, rich and poor; **der —e Adel,** the gentry; **ein —er,** an obscure person, one of mean birth; **die —n,** inferiors. II. *adv. & sep. prefix,* down; low; **auf und —,** up and down; **— mit den Verrätern!** down with the traitors! **—ung,** *f.* low country *or* ground; lowland; plain, flat country. *Comp.* **—begeben,** *ir.v.r.* to descend. **—beugen,** *v.a.* to bend down; to humiliate; to depress. **—brechen,** *ir.v.a. & n.* (*aux.* **s.**) to break down. **—brennen,** *ir.v.a. & n.* (*aux.* **s.**) to burn down (*to the ground*). **—deutsch,** *adj.* Low German, North German. **—deutschland,** *n.* lower Germany, North Germany. — **druck,** *m.* low pressure. **—drücken,** *v.a.* to press, weigh down; to beat down (*prices*); to depress; to keep down; to overwhelm. — **fahren,** *ir.v.* I. *n.* (*aux.* **s.**) to descend rapidly; **—gefahren zur Hölle,** descended into Hell. II. *a.* to knock over, run down. **—fahrt,** *f.* descent. **—fall,** *m.*, **—fallen,** *n.* downfall; prostration. **—fallen,** *ir.v.n.* (*aux.* **s.**) to fall down; to alight (*of birds*); **vor einem —fallen,** to fall at a p.'s feet. **—fränkisch,** *adj.* Low Franconian. **—gang,** *m.* setting (*of the sun*); descent; down-stroke (*Mech.*). **—gehen,** *ir. v.n.* (*aux.* **s.**) to descend; to sink; to subside; to set (*of the sun*). **—geschlagen,** *p. & adj.* dejected, low-spirited, cast-down. **—geschlagenheit,** *f.* dejection, low spirits. **—halten,** *ir.v.a.* to hold *or* keep down. **—hocken,** *v.n.* (*aux.* **s.**) to cower; to squat. **—holen (eine Fahne),** to haul down *or* lower (a flag). **—holz,** *n.* coppice, underwood. **—jagd,** *f.* coursing. **—knallen,** *v.a.* to shoot down (*coll.*). **—kommen,** *ir.v.n.* (*aux.* **s.**) to be confined, lie in. — **kunft,** *f.* descent; delivery, confinement. — **lage,** *f.* laying down; (*bonded*) warehouse; depot; agency (*C.L.*); emporium; defeat, overthrow; **eine gänzliche —lage erleiden,** to suffer a total or crushing defeat; **in die —lage bringen,** to warehouse. **—land,** *n.* low-lying land; **die —lande,** the Netherlands *or* Low Countries. **—länder,** *m.* dweller in a low-lying country; Low German (*obs.*); Netherlander, Dutchman. **—ländisch,** *adj.* Netherlandish, Dutch. — **lassen,** *ir.v.* I. *a.* to let down. II. *r.* to sit down; to settle, establish oneself; to alight. **—lassung,** *f.* lowering; establishment; settlement, colony. **—lassungs=recht,** *n.* right of settling. **—legen,** *v.* I. *a.* to lay down, deposit; to abdicate; to resign (*an office*); to leave off (*business*); to lay down (*arms*); to store, warehouse; **ein Kind —legen,** to put a child to bed. II. *r.* to lie down, go to bed. — **legung,** *f.* deposition; abdication; resignation. **—machen,** *v.a.* to put down; to cut down; to slay, massacre. **—rad,** *n.* safety bicycle, rear driving machine; **—rad mit Vorderantrieb,** front driving safety (*cycl.*). **—reißen,** *ir.v.a.* to tear down, to demolish. **—reiten,** *ir.v.a.* to ride down, ride over. — **rollen,** *v.n.* (*aux.* **s.**); **der Vorhang rollt —,** the curtain falls. **—sachsen,** *n.* Lower Saxony (*North Germ.*). **—sächsisch,** *adj.* Low Saxon (*North Germ.*). **—schießen,** *ir.v.* I. *a.* to shoot down. II. *n.* (*aux.* **s.**) to shoot, rush down. **—schlag,** *m.* act of striking down; down-stroke; beat, fall (*Mus.*); outcome, upshot; sediment, deposit; result; **der —schlag der ins Stocken geratenen Bewegung,** the result (so far) of the movement which has come to a standstill. — **schlagen,** *ir.v.* I. *a.* to strike down; to cast down; to fell (*oxen; trees*); to let down; to prostrate; to precipitate (*Chem.*); to alloy; to quiet, pacify; to put an end to; to quash; to depress; to refute; **jemandes Hoffnung —schlagen,** to deprive s. o. of all his hopes, to disappoint a p. II. *n.* (*aux.* **s.**) to fall down heavily; **die Wage schlägt —,** the balance turns; (*aux.* **h.**) to beat time (*Mus.*). **—schlagend,** *p. & adj.* disheartening, depressing; quieting. **—schmettern,** *v.a.* to dash to the ground; **—schmetternde Worte,** crushing words. — **schrift,** *f.* what is written down, writing, copy, notes; **—schrift einer Vorlesung,** lecture notes. **—senken,** *v.* I. *a.* to let down. II. *r.* to sink, settle down. **—setzen,** *v.* I. *a.* to set, put down; to deposit; to ground (*arms, Mil.*); to establish, appoint. II. *r.* to sit down; **sich zwischen zwei Stühle —setzen,** to fall between two stools. **—stechen,** *ir.v.a.* to strike down (*with a dagger or bayonet*). **—steigen,** *ir.v.n.* (*aux.* **s.**) to descend, step down. **—strecken,** *v.* I. *n.* to stretch on the ground; to fell. II. *r.* to lie down. **—stürzen,** *v.* I. *a.* to precipitate, throw *or* hurl down. II. *n.* (*aux.* **s.**) to fall down with vehemence. **—strich,** *m.* downstroke; down-bow (*Mus.*). **—treten,** *ir.v.a.* to tread, trample down; to tread down (*shoes*) at the heel; to wear the heels (*of shoes*) crooked. **—trächtig,** *adj.* low, mean, abject; (*dial.*) kind to the lower people, blithe to the people (= **leutselig**). **—trächtigkeit,** *f.* baseness; vile action. **—trinken,** *ir.v.a.* to gulp down; **einen —trinken,** to drink a p. under the table. **—wald,** *m.* coppice. **—wärts,** *adv.* downwards; **—wärts gekehrt,** reversed (*Her.*).

Nied'lich, *adj. & adv.* pretty, nice, dainty, elegant; **das verborgene Brot ist —,** bread eaten in secret is pleasant (*obs.*, *B.*); **das ist ja recht** —, that's a pretty state of things, a nice mess indeed! (*coll.*). **—keit**, *f.* prettiness, niceness.

Nied'nagel, *m.* (**—s**, *pl.* **Niednägel**) agnail, hangnail.

Nie'drig, *adj. & adv.* low; lowly, humble, obscure; base, abject, vile, vulgar; mean; **—e Prämie**, short premium (*C.L.*); **—halten**, to keep down (*prices*); **eine S. —er hängen**, to make a th. more accessible; **— spielen**, to play low; **— stimmen**, to lower (*the pitch*); **ausländische Fonds gingen —er**, foreign stocks fell; **meine —e Hütte**, my humble cottage; **eine —e Meinung von einem haben**, to have a poor opinion of a p.; **von —em Stande**, of low birth *or* standing. **—keit**, *f.* lowness; lowliness.

Nie'mand, *ind. pron.* (**—(e)s**, *dat.* **—** (*better than* **—em** *or* **—en**), *acc.* **—** (*better than* **—en**)) nobody, no one; **— anders**, no one else; **— Fremdes**, no stranger.

Nie're, *f.* (*pl.* **—n**) kidney; nodule; (*pl.*) reins, loins; *see* **—nkartoffel**; **zu den —n gehörig**, renal; **der Herz und —n prüft**, God that trieth the hearts and reins (*B.*); **das geht mir an die —n**, that cuts me to the quick (*rare*). *Comp.* **—n=beschwerde**, *f.* kidney complaint. **—n=braten**, *m.* roast loin. **—n=entzündung**, *f.* nephritis. **—n=fett**, *n.* suet (*round kidneys*). **—n=förmig**, *adj.* reniform, kidney-shaped. **—n=kartoffel**, *f.* kidney-potato. **—n=krankheit**, *f.* disease of the kidneys. **—n=stein**, *m.* stone in the kidneys; jade-stone. **—n=stück**, *n.* loin of veal with the kidney. **—n=weh**, *n.* nephritic pain, nephralgy. **—n=weise**, *adv.* in nodules (*Min.*).

Nie's—eln, *v.n.* to snuffle; to rain gently and continually (*sl.*). **—en**, I. *v.n.* (*aux.* **h.**) to sneeze. II. *subst. n.* sneeze; sneezing. *Comp.* **—e=pulver**, *n.* sneezing-powder; snuff. **—(s)=krampf**, *m.* spasmodic sneezing.

Nieß — (*in comp.*) **—brauch**, *m.* usufruct. **—braucher**, *m.*, **—braucherin**, *f.* usufructuary. **—nutz**, *m.* = **—brauch**.

Niet, *n.* (**—es**, *pl.* **—e**) rivet; **— und nagelfest**, clinched and riveted, nailed fast. **—en**, *v.a.* to rivet, clinch. *Comp.* **—blumig**, *adj.* epigynous. **—nagel**, *m.* riveting nail; rivet.

Nie'te, *f.* (*pl.* **—n**) blank (*in a lottery*).

Nihilis'mus, *m.* Nihilism.

Nikoti'n, *n.* (**—s**) nicotine.

Nimm; Nimmst, Nimmt, *imperat. sing.; 2 & 3 pers. sing. pres. ind. of* **nehmen**; **er ist vom Stamme Nimm**, he is very greedy, grasping, *or* rapacious (*coll.*).

Nim'mer, *adv.* never (more); at no time; no more (*rare*); **nun und —**, (*lit.* now and no more) never, at no time; **nie und —**, never (*before*) and never (*after*); **es ist noch um ein Kleines, so ist der Gottlose —**, for yet a little while and the wicked shall not be (*B.*); **wenn — Holz da ist**, where no wood is (*B.*); **man sieht ihn —**, he is no more to be seen (*poet.*). *Comp.* **—mehr**, *adv.* never more; never; not at all. **—mehrs=tag**, *m.* (day after) doomsday, the Greek Kalends. **—satt**, I. *adj.* insatiable. II. *m.* glutton; wolf (*in the fable*). **—wiedersehen**, *n.*; **auf —wiedersehen**, farewell forever; **er verschwand auf —wiedersehn**, he disappeared and was not seen any more.

[1]**Nipp**, *m.* (**—es**, *pl.* **—e**) nip, sip. **—en**, *v.a. & n.* (*aux.* **h.**) to sip, nip; **er —t zu gern**, he is too fond of tippling. *Comp.* **—flut**, *f.* neap-tide.

[2]**Nipp—** (*in comp.*) **—sachen**, *pl.* nick-nacks, trinkets, mantel-piece ornaments. **—tisch**, *m.* what-not, fancy table.

Nir'gend(—s), (**—wo**), *adv.* nowhere, nowhere at all.

Ni'sche (*long* **i**), *f.* (*pl.* **—n**) niche.

Nis's—e, Niß, *f.* (*pl.* **—(ss)e**) nit. **—ig**, *adj.* lousy, nitty.

Nis't—e(l)n, *v.n.* (*aux.* **h.**) to nestle; to build a nest. *Comp.* **—kasten**, *m.*, breeding-cage.

Nitr—a't, *n.* nitrate. **—ö's**, *adj.* nitrous. *Comp.* **—o=glyceri'n**, *n.* nitro-glycerine.

Nivellie'r—en, *v.a.* to level. **—ung**, *f.* levelling. *Comp.* **—instrument**, *n.* (*water-*, *spirit-*,) level. **—wage**, *f.* spirit-level.

[1]**Nix**, *m.* (**—es**, *pl.* **—e**) water-sprite, merman. **—e**, *f.* (*pl.* **—en**) water-nymph, mermaid.

[2]**Nix**, (*dial. & coll.*) see **Nicht, Nichts**.

No'bel, I. *adj.* (*comp.* **nobler**) noble; highborn; beautiful, grand, stylish (*sl.*); liberal (*coll.*); **sich — machen**, to be very generous *or* liberal (with one's money) (*coll.*). II. *m.* (**—s**, *pl.* **—s**) noble (*a former English coin*); Noble (*name of the Lion in the animal epic of Reynard the Fox*).

[1]**Noch**, *adv. & part.* in addition; besides; further; still, yet, as yet; **— dazu**, moreover; **— einer**, another, one more; **— sechs Meilen**, six miles more; **— einmal**, once more, over again, encore; **— einmal so viel**, as much again; **— etwas**, something more; **— etwas?** anything else? **— nicht**, not yet; **wo —?** where else? **was —?** what else? **er und — einige**, he and some others; **das fehlte nur —**, that was all that was wanting, that is the last straw; **was — mehr ist**, what is more; **er kann — viele Jahre leben**, he may still live many years; **— lieber wollte ich**, still more should I like, I should even prefer; **weil er mein Vetter ist, ist er — nicht mein Freund**, because he is my cousin it does not follow that he is my friend; **wäre er auch — so reich**, if he were as rich again; **wenn er auch — so lange bleibt**, if he stays ever so long; **es sei — so wenig**, be it ever so little; **— vor kurzem**, until recently; **ich habe ihn — gestern gesehen**, I saw him only yesterday; **— heute abend**, this very night; **ehe er — aus dem Zimmer war**, before he was well out of the room. *Comp.* **—mal**, *adv.* once again; twice; *it is often added to exclamations for the sake of emphasis;* **Donnerwetter —mal!** zounds! **—malig**, *adj.* repeated. **—mals**, *adv.* once more, again.

[2]**Noch**, *conj.* nor; **weder M. — N.**, neither M. nor N; **— Sie, — ich**, neither you nor I (*obs.*).

Nock, *n.* (**—es**, *pl.* **—e**), *f.* (*pl.* **—n**) arm (*of a yard, Naut.*). *Comp.* **—takel**, *n.* yard-tackle.

No'cke, *f.* (*pl.* **—n**), **—n**, *m.* (**—ns**, *pl.* **—n**), **—rl**, *n.* (**—rls**, *pl.* **—rl**) dumpling (*dial.*).

Nö'l—en, *v.a.* to dawdle, to be slow (*dial.*). **—er**, *m.* slow-coach. **—ig**, *adj.* slow, squeamish (*dial.*). *Comp.* **—e=meier**, *m.* slow-coach (*coll.*).

Noma'd—e, *m.* (**—en**, *pl.* **—en**), nomad. **—isch**, *adj.* nomadic.

No'men, *n.* (**—s**, *pl.* **Nomina**) noun. **—klatu'r**, *f.* (*pl.* **—klaturen**) nomenclature.

Nomin—alis'mus, *m.* Nominalism. **—ativ** (*pron.* **No'minativ**), *m.* (**—ativs**, *pl.* **—ative**) nominative. **—e'll**, *adj.* nominal. *Comp.* **—al'=betrag**, *m.* nominal value.

No'ne, *f.* (*pl.* **—n**) none; ninth (*Mus.*); (*pl.*) nones.

Non'ne, *f.* (*pl.* **—n**; *dim.* **Nönn'chen, Nönn'lein**) nun, religious sister; humming-top; night-butterfly; white nun (*Orn.*); mould (*Found.*). *Comp.* **—n=kloster**, *n.* nunnery. **—n=weihe**, *f.* taking of the veil.

Nop'pe, *f.* (*pl.* **—n**) nap (*of cloth*). **—n**, *v.a.* to nap.

Nord, *m.* (**—es**) north; north wind (*poet.*); **— zum Westen**, north by west; **dem —en entgegengesetzt**, Antarctic. **—en**, *m.* (**—ens**, *pl.* **—en**) north; northern region. **—isch**, *adj.* northern; Norse; north from the Alps (*obs.*); borean, hyperborean; **alt —isch**, Old Norse,

Scandinavian. *Comp.* —**deutsch**, *adj.* North-German. —**er=breite**, *f.* north latitude. —**er=sonne**, *f.* north sun, midnight-sun. —**kap**, *n.* North Cape. —**länder**, *m.* Northerner; (*pl.*) northern nations. —**ländisch**, *adj.* northern. —**lands=fahrt**, *f.* Arctic voyage *or* expedition. —**licht**, *n.* aurora borealis, northern lights. —**licht=schein**, *m.* glare of the polar *or* northern lights. —**meer**, *n.* northern *or* Arctic ocean. —**pol**, *m.* north pole. —**pol=fahrt**, *f* arctic expedition. —**schein**, *m.* zodiacal light. —**see**, *f.* North Sea, German Ocean. —**stern**, *m.* polar-star. —**wärts**, *adv.* northward. —**weiser**, *m.* compass. —**wind**, *m.* north-wind; Boreas.

Nörd'lich, *adj. & adv.* northern, northerly, Arctic, septentrional; —**e Breite**, north latitude; —**e Abweichung**, northerliness; —**e Lage**, northern aspect; — **liegen von**, to lie (to the) north of; —**st**, **am meisten** —, northernmost; **das** —**e Eismeer**, the Arctic Ocean.

Nör'geln, *v.n.* (*aux.* **h.**) *see* **Nergeln.**

Norm, *f.* (*pl.* —**en**) rule, standard, model, norm, criterion; signature (*Typ.*). —**a'l**, *adj.* normal, regular. —**ie'ren**, *v.a.* to rule. *Comp.* —**al'=arbeitstag**, *m.* ordinary working day, legally fixed maximum. —**al'=bahn**, *f.* main line (*railw.*). —**al'=gas**, *n.* standard gas. —**al'=geschwindigkeit**, *f.* proper speed, allowed speed. —**al'=gesetz**, *n.* general law. —**al'=gewicht**, *n.* standard weight. —**al'=kerze**, *f.* standard candle. —**al'=klasse**, scratch (*Lawn T.*). —**al'=kleidung**, *f.* normal dress. —**al'=maß**, *n.* standard measure. —**al'=nummer**, *f.* average marks (*School*). —**al'=satz**, *m.* limited price (*C.L.*). —**al'=uhr**, *f.* standard clock. —**al'=zeile**, *f.* direction line (*Typ.*).

Nor'ne, *f.* (*pl.* —**en**) old German goddess of Fate (*3 in number*); Norn.

Nö'sel, **Nö'ßel**, *n. & m.* (—**s**, *pl.* —) chopin, pint.

Not, I. *f.* (*pl.* **Nö'te**) need, want; necessity, compulsion; exigency; trouble, difficulty; danger; distress, misery; fight (*obs.*); **wenn die** — **an den Mann kommt**, in case of need, when necessity urges; **aus** —, from necessity; **aus der** — **eine Tugend machen**, to make a virtue of necessity; **mit** —, with difficulty, scarcely; **mit genauer** —, narrowly, with great difficulty, with much ado; **mit knapper**—, with the greatest difficulty; **ohne** —, unnecessarily, without cause; **über** —, more than necessary; **in Nöten sein**, to be in trouble; **von nöten** *or* **vonnöten sein**, to be necessary *or* needful; **vonnöten haben**, to want, to require; **zur** —, at a pinch, at the worst, scarcely (*enough*); **die schwere** —, epilepsy; (**Schock**) **schwer(e)** —! damnation! **was, schwere** —, **soll das bedeuten**? what the devil does that mean? (*vulg.*); — **haben**, to suffer want; **wir hatten unsere liebe** —, **um . . .**, we had much ado to . . .; **Sie werden Ihre liebe** — **mit ihm haben**, he will give you no end of trouble; **er hat seine liebe** — **mit dem Reden**, he has great difficulty in speaking (*coll.*); **die Sache hat** —, the case is urgent (*dial.*); **einen Wechsel** — **leiden lassen**, to dishonour a bill; **in Nöten sein**, to be in distress; **in (Kindes)Nöten sein**, to be with child; to be in travail; **wenn es die** — **erfordert**, if need be; **zur** — **würde es ausreichen**, it would do at a pinch; **es hat keine** — **damit**, no fear; **er macht uns viele** —, he causes us much anxiety; — **bricht Eisen**, necessity knows no law; necessity is the mother of invention (*prov.*); **wenn die** — **am größten, ist Gottes Hilfe am nächsten**, man's extremity is God's opportunity, when need is greatest help is nearest (*prov.*); **in der** — **frißt der Teufel Fliegen**, in default of a soul the devil puts up with a fly (*prov.*); — **kennt kein Gebot**, necessity has no law (*prov.*); — **lehrt beten**, necessity is the mother of invention (*prov.*). II. *adj.* needful, necessary; wanting; — **thun**, to be necessary; **wenn es** — **thut**, in case of necessity; **mir ist** *or* **thut** —, I want; **Friede thut uns** —, we need peace. *Comp.* —**adresse**, *f.* emergency address (in case of need). —**anker**, *m.* sheet-anchor. —**arbeit**, *f.* work of necessity. —**ausgang**, *m.* emergency exit, escape door. —**bau**, *m.* temporary building. —**behelf**, *m.* makeshift; expedient. —**bremse**, *f.* brake for emergency-cases. —**brücke**, *f.* temporary bridge, pontoon bridge. —**damm**, —**deich**, *m.* temporary dike. —**dringend**, *adj.* pressing, urgent. —**durft**, *f.* necessaries of life; necessity; **seine** —**durft verrichten**, to ease nature. —**dürftig**, *adj.* scanty; needy, indigent, hard-up; —**dürftiger Reim**, poor rhyme; **das** —**dürftige**, what is absolutely necessary. —**dürftigkeit**, *f.* indigence; want. —**erbe**, *m.* legal heir. —**fall**, *m.* case of necessity; **im** —**fall**, in case of need, if necessary; at a pinch (*coll.*). —**feuer**, *n.* alarm-fire. —**flagge**, *f.* flag of distress. —**gedrungen**, *adj.* compulsory, by force, by constraint, needs, perforce. —**geschrei**, *n.* cry of distress. —**hafen**, *m.* harbour of refuge. —**helfer**, *m.* helper in need. —**hemd**, *n.* magic shirt (*protecting a warrior*). —**hülfe**, *f.* help in need. —**jahr**, *n.* year of scarcity. —**klausel**, *f.* distress-clause (*C.L.*). —**lage**, *f.* distressed condition, calamity. —**leidend**, *adj.* needy; suffering distress; dishonoured (*of bills*); **die** —**leidenden**, the sufferers. —**leine**, *f.* cord communicating with the engine in emergencies, bell cord *or* pull (*Railw.*). —**lüge**, *f.* official falsehood; (*forced*) shift, fib, white lie. —**mast**, *m.* jury mast. —**mittel**, *n.* shift, expedient. —**nagel**, *m.* make-shift, stop-gap. —**pfeife**, *f.* alarm whistle, danger whistle. —**pfennig**, *m.* savings; **einen** —**pfennig zurücklegen**, to lay by for a rainy day. —**recht**, *n.* right of necessity. —**ruder**, *n.* preventer-rudder (*Naut.*). —**sache**, *f.* case of necessity, urgent case. —**schlange**, *f.* culverin (*obs.*, *Artil.*). —**schuß**, *m.* shot of distress. —**signal**, *n.* distress *or* danger-signal (*Railw. Naut.*). —**stand**, *m.* state of distress, critical state. —**stands=gesetz**, *n.* emergency bill, provisional bill passed in times of distress. —**taufe**, *f.* private baptism (*in fear of the infant's death*). —**thür**, *f.* escape-door, emergency exit. —**wehr**, *f.* self-defence; **aus** —**wehr**, in self-defence; **Totschlag aus** —**wehr**, justificiable homicide. —**wendig**, *adj.* necessary; **schlechterdings** *or* **unumgänglich** —**wendig**, indispensable, inevitable; **das** —**wendige**, necessity, necessaries; —**wendiger Weise**, of necessity. —**wendigkeit**, *f.* urgency; necessity. —**werk**, *n.* work of necessity. —**wörterbuch**, *n.* pocket *or* conversation dictionary, handy dictionary. —**zeichen**, *n.* signal of distress. —**zucht**, —**züchtigung**, *f.*, —**züchtigungs=versuch**, *m.* indecent assault, rape, violation, ravishment. —**züchtigen**, *v.a.* (*insep.*) to ravish, to violate; to assault (*Law*). —**züchtiger**, *m.* ravisher. —**zwang**, *m.* the compulsion of necessity, the force of circumstances.

No'ta, *f.* (*pl.* —**s**) *see* **Note**; **sich** (*dat.*) **etwas ad** —**m nehmen**, *see* **Anmerken.** —**r**, *see* **Notar.**

Notabilitä'ten, *f. pl.* notables, big folk, lions, (*coll.*).

Nota'r, *m.* (—**s**, *pl.* —**e**) notary; **öffentlicher** —, notary public. —**ia't**, *n.* (—**iats**, *pl.* —**iate**) office of a notary; **von** —**iatswegen**, by order of a notary. —**ie'll**, *adj. & adv.* notorial: attested by a notary; —**iell beglaubigt**, signed by a notary public, by a solicitor *or* a commissioner for oaths. *Comp.* **—s=instrument,** *n.*, **—s=urkunde,** *f.* notarial document.

No'te, *f.* (*pl.* **—n**) note; memorandum; banknote; bill, account; diplomatic note; note (*of music*); (*pl.*) music; **gute —, die — ‚gut,'** high marks, a good report (*school*); **erhöhte —,** sharp; **ganze —,** semi-breve, whole note; **halbe —,** minim, half note; **schwarze —,** crotchet, quarter note; **geschwänzte —,** quaver, eighth note; **in —n setzen,** to write down (*an air*); **—n abschreiben,** to copy music; **nach —n,** in a superior way, properly, with a vengeance; **nach** (*or* **von**) **—n spielen, singen,** to play, sing at sight; **es kommt ihm auf eine Hand voll —n nicht an,** he is not over-particular (*in what he says, etc.*). *Comp.* **—n=ausgabe,** *f.* the issue of (bank-)notes. **—n=bank,** *f.* bank of issue, issuing bank. **—n=beilage,** *f.* musical supplement. **—n=bezeichnung,** *f.* musical notation. **—n=blatt,** *n.* sheet of music. **—n=buch,** *n.* music-book. **—n=druck,** *m.* music-printing; printed music. **—n=format,** *n.* oblong quarto (*Typ.*). **—n=gestell,** *n.*, **—halter,** *m.* music-stand. **—n=handlung,** *f.* music shop. **—n=lesen,** *n.* reading of music. **—n=linie,** *f.* line; staff. **—n=mappe,** *f.* music portfolio. **—n=papier,** *n.* music-paper. **—n=schlüssel,** *m.* clef. **—n=stecher,** *m.* engraver of music. **—n=system,** *n.* staff. **—umlauf,** *m.* circulation of (bank-)notes.

Notie'r—en, *v.a.* to note, make a memorandum of; to quote (*prices, etc.*). **—ung,** *f.* quotation (*of prices*).

Notifizie'ren, *v.a.* to notify.

Nö'tig, *adj. & adv.* needful, necessary; **etwas — haben,** to want, stand in need of; **— machen,** to necessitate; **durchaus —,** absolutely necessary; **ein neuer Rock ist** *or* (*coll.*) **thut ihm sehr —,** he is in great need of a new coat; **—en Falls,** in case of necessity; **das —e besorgen,** to provide *or* do all that is necessary; **das zum Leben —,** the necessaries of life.

Nö'tig—en, I. *v.a.* to necessitate; to oblige, force, compel; to press (*a guest*); to invite; **sich —en lassen,** to stand upon ceremony, to need pressing; **lassen Sie sich nicht lange —en,** pray do not wait to be asked, help yourself; **er ließ sich nicht lange —en,** he required little pressing. II. *subst.n.*, **—ung,** *f.* urgency; constraint; entreaty.

Noti'z, *f.* (*pl.* **—en**) notice; cognizance; note, memorandum. *Comp.* **—buch,** *n.*, **—tafel,** *f.* note-book. **—en=krämer,** *m.* pedant, dry-as-dust scholar.

Notorietä't, *f.* notoriety.

Noto'risch, *adj.* notorious; **ein —er Säufer,** a confirmed drunkard; **ein —er Spieler,** an habitual gambler.

No'v—a, —itä'ten, *pl.* novelties; new publications. **—el'le,** *see* **Novelle.** **—i'z,** *m.* (**—izen,** *pl.* **—izen**), **—i'ze,** *f.* (*pl.* **—izen**) & *m.* (**—izen,** *pl.* **—izen**) novice, probationer, acolyte. **—izia't,** *n.* (**—iziates,** *pl.* **—iziate**) noviciate. *Comp.* **—itäten=zettel,** *m.* list of new publications.

Novel'l—e, *f.* (*pl.* **—en**) short tale of fiction, short novel (*usually in prose*); supplementary law; **—e zum Anarchistengesetz,** additional clause to the bill against the anarchists; **Paul Heyses —en in Versen,** P. Heyse's short stories in verse, metrical tales, verse novels; **Romane und —en,** novels and short tales; **die —en des Justinian,** the Novels, the constitutions *or* laws of Justinian. **—et'te,** *f.* (*pl.* **—etten**) very short story, sketch. **—i'st,** *m.* (**—is'ten,** *pl.* **—is'ten**), **—is'tin,** *f.* writer of short stories *or* sketches, novelist. **—is'tisch,** *adj.* novelistic, in the style of a novel. *Comp.* **—en=haft,** *adj.* in the manner of a novel. **—en=schreiber,** *m. see* **—ist.** **—en=kranz,** *m.* cycle *or* collection of short stories.

Novem'ber, *m.* (**—s**) November.

Nu, I. *int.* well! well now! II. *m. & n.* the passing moment, instant; **im —,** in a trice, in no time; **im rechten —,** in the nick of time.

Nüch'tern, *adj. & adv.* fasting; sober; grown sober again; temperate; calm; reasonable; insipid, jejune; prosaic; Philistine; **ich bin noch ganz —,** I have not yet eaten anything, I have not yet broken my fast, I have not had any breakfast; **ein —es Urteil,** a dispassionate judgment. **—heit,** *f.* fasting condition; temperance; sobriety; calmness; prosiness, **in der —heit bereut er, was er in der Trunkenheit gethan,** when he is sober he regrets what he has done when drunk. *Comp.* **—werden,** *n.* sobered condition; disillusion.

Nü'cke, *f.* (*prov.*) whim, fancy; *see* **Tücke.**

Nu'del, *f.* (*pl.* **—n**) little threads of paste: **Faden —n,** vermicelli; **italienische —n,** macaroni; **Gänse—n,** paste balls for cramming geese. **—n,** *v.a.* to cram (*poultry*). *Comp.* **—dick,** *adj.* plump, round as a ball. **—suppe,** *f.* vermicelli soup.

Null, I. *indec. adj.* nil, null; **— und nichtig,** null and void. II. *f.* (*pl.* **—en**) naught, cipher; blank; **er ist eine wahre —,** he is a nobody, a mere cipher. **—itä't,** *f.* (*pl.* **—itäten**) nullity, invalidity. *Comp.* **—grad, —punkt,** *m.* zero. **—linie,** *f.* vacuum line. **—partie,** *f.* love-set (*Lawn T.*). **—spiel,** *n.* love-game (*L.T.*).

Numer—a'le, *n.* (**—ales,** *pl.* **—alien**) numeral adjective. **—ie'ren,** I. *v.a.* to number; to ticket. II. *subst.n.*, **—ie'rung,** *f.* numbering; numeration.

Nu'mer—i, *pl.* Numbers (*B.*). **—o,** *dat. & abl. of* **—us,** number; **—o 3,** number 3. **—us,** *m.* number (*Gram.*).

Nume'risch, *adj. & adv.* numerical.

Num'mer, *f.* (*pl.* **—n**) number; cipher; mark; lottery-ticket; jail; **ein in —n erscheinendes Werk,** a serial; **eine nette** *or* **feine —,** a nice sort *or* specimen (*also used ironically*) (*coll.*); **sich auf — Sicher stellen,** to place oneself in security; **er ist** *or* **sitzt in — Sicher,** he is in prison (*coll.*); **— Eins,** number one, the best place, the post of honour. *Comp.* **—folge,** *f.* numerical order.

Nun, I. *adv.* now, at present; under present circumstances; (*also part.*) now, well; **von — an,** henceforth; **— erst gestand er,** it was only then that he confessed; **— und nimmer (mehr)** never, nevermore; **— traf es sich, daß,** now it happened that; **wenn —,** now if; **er mag — kommen oder nicht,** whether he come or no; **— und?** well, and afterwards? **sei es —, daß er hier oder dort ist,** whether he be here or there; **ich möchte — freilich,** I should wish indeed (*that, etc.*); **— wie steht's?** well, how are you? how are matters going on? **— also,** well then! II. *conj.* indeed, then; now; **wenn —,** supposing; **es ist — einmal (nicht) so,** well, it can't be helped; **— es einmal so ist,** since it is so; **— ich sie dir empfehlen kann, sterb' ich ruhig,** now that I can commend her to you, I die in peace; **— du mich kennst,** now that you know me. III. *int.* well! come on! gently! **— ja!** that's true enough, that is all right (*expresses hesitating or reluctant assent*). *Comp.* **—mehr, —meh'ro** (*obs.*), *adv. & conj.* now, by this time; henceforth. **—mehrig,** *adj.* present, actual, now existing.

Nun'ti—us, *m.* (**—us,** *pl.* **—en** *or* **—i**), (papal) nuncio.

Nur, *adv. & part.* only, merely; scarcely; a little while ago, a moment ago, but just; *after* **wer, was, wie, wo** = ever, soever, possibly, in any way; — weiter, go on, get on; — mehr (*Austrian dial.*) = — noch, still only; wenn —, provided that; wer —, whoever; so viel ich — kann, as much as ever I can; Alles — nicht, anything rather than; geh — ! do go! er mag — gehen! let him go by all means, he is quite at liberty to go! ich will's — gestehen, well, I will confess it; — nicht ängstlich! don't fear! nicht — . . ., sondern auch . . ., not only . . ., but also . . .; sie bekamen alle etwas, — er nicht, they all got something except him; — noch eine Zeile, only one line more; was er — denkt? I wonder what he thinks; hier ist Geld, — schweige! here is money, but don't tell! but not a word! sehen Sie —, was Sie gemacht haben, just look at what you have done; wie kommt er — hierher? but how can he have come here? blast —, ihr Winde, blow on, ye winds; laßt mich — machen! (just) let me do it! let me alone! er ist —(eben) angekommen, he is only just come; ich muß — (*no stress*) bald meinen Herrn aufsuchen, I really must go soon and look for my master; — so *with verbs denotes great ease or great rapidity, thoroughness* (*coll.*); die Federn flogen — so, the feathers were flying fast; es klappte — so, everything fitted in admirably; es ging — so, it went off first-rate *or* rapidly; — so thun, to pretend to do a thing without taking any trouble about it, to do it with a wave of the hand.

Nuß, *f.* (*pl.* Nüs'se) nut (*also Mech.*); walnut; in die Nüsse gehen, to go a-nutting, to be lost; eine taube —, an empty nut; keine taube — wert, not worth a straw; harte —, difficult task; in einer —, in a nutshell; Nüsse auskernen, to shell nuts; ich will ihm eine — zu knacken geben, I will give him a nut to crack (*coll.*); wir haben noch eine — mit einander zu knacken, I have still a crow to pluck with you; welsche —, walnut. *Comp.* —baum, *m.* walnut tree; nut-tree. —braun, *adj.* nut-brown, hazel. —kern, *m.* kernel of a nut. —knacker, *m.* nut-cracker; alter —knacker, old fogey (*coll.*). —schale, *f.* nut-shell; small boat, canoe. —schraube, *f.* feather-screw. —staude, *f.* hazel.

Nü'ster, *f.* (*pl.* —n) (*pl.*) nostrils (*of horses*).

Nut, *f.* (*pl.* —en), **—e**, *f.* (*pl.* —en) groove, key-seat, furrow; gutter; — und Zapfen, mortise and tenon. —en, *v.a.* to groove. *Comp.* —hobel, *m.* grooving plane.

Nut'sch—er, *m.* (—ers, *pl.* —er) suckling. *Comp.* —beutel, *m.* infant's feeding bottle.

Nutz, **—e**, I. *adj.* useful, profitable; das ist zu nichts —, that is good for nothing, useless. II. *m.* (—es) use, profit; advantage; utility; sich (*dat.*) etwas zu —e machen, to turn to advantage, to avail o.s. of, to profit by; zu — und Frommen, for the benefit, to the advantage. —bar, *adj.* useful, profitable; lucrative; fit for use. —barkeit, *f.* usefulness; fitness for use. —en, I. *v.a.* to make use of; er —t sein Gut jährlich auf 4000 Mark, he draws £200 per annum from his property. II. *v.n.* (*aux.* h., *dat.*) to be of use *or* profitable; was —t es, daß . . .? what avails it, that . . .? zu etwas —en, to be good for. III. *m. see* Nutz II.; —en abwerfen, to yield a profit; mit 30% —en verkaufen, to dispose of with a profit of 30 per cent, to make 30 per cent on a sale; von —en, of use, profitable; —en aus einer S. ziehen, to turn a th. to advantage. —ung, *f.* using; usufruct; emolument; produce, yield. *Comp.* —anwendung, *f.* utilization; practical application. —arbeit, *f.* effective work (*of machinery*). —bäume, baumhölzer, *pl.* timber for carpentering. —garten, *m.* kitchen-garden. —holz, *n.* (stove-)timber. —kraft, *f.* effective power. —leistung, *f.* (eines Ofens) efficiency, duty (*of a furnace*). —los, *adj.* useless, unprofitable. —losigkeit, *f.* uselessness. —nießen, *v.a.* (*insep.*) to derive profit from; to have the usufruct of. — nießer, *m.* usufructuary. —nießung, *f.* usufruct. —reich, *adj.* profitable. —ungsanschlag, *m.* estimate of the profits of an estate. —wild, *n.* game kept for shooting.

Nütz, **—e**, *see* Nutz I.; die Gottseligkeit ist zu allen Dingen —e, godliness is profitable unto all things (*B.*). —en, *v.n.* to be of use; to make use of (*poet.*) (*impers.*); wozu —t das? what good is that? what is the good of that? das —t und schadet auch nichts, that does nothing one way or another. —lich, *adj. & adv.* useful; advantageous; conducive. —lichkeit, *f.* utility, usefulness; profitableness. *Comp.* —lichkeits-prinzip, —lichkeits-system, *n.* utilitarianism. —lichkeits-rücksichten, *pl.* considerations of utility, practical considerations.

Nym'phe, *f.* (*pl.* —n) nymph; courtesan; chrysalis, pupa. *Comp.* —n-artig, —n-haft, *adj.* nymph-like. —n-blume, *f.* water-lily.

O

O, **o**, I. *n.* O, o; goldenes —, Colias hyale (*Ent.*); O-Beine, *pl.* bandy legs. *As abbr.* O. = 1. Ordre, Order, order; 2. Osten, east; 3. Oxygen, oxygen. *For other abbreviations see the Index of Abbreviations at the end of the German-English part.* II. *int.* oh! O! — pfui doch! oh, fie! o, daß er doch bald käme! how I wish he would come soon!

Oa'se, *f.* (*pl.* —n) oasis.

¹Ob, *conj.* if, whether; I wonder if; es fragt sich —, I wonder whether; — es wahr ist oder nicht, whether it be true or not; wer weiß, — er nicht krank ist, who knows but he may be ill; — er wohl wieder kommt? will he come back, do you think? willst du gehen? Na —, (*with accent on the* ob) will you go? Well, I should rather think so, not very likely that I won't; thun als —, to pretend, make believe; Sie haben doch getanzt? Und —! (*with strong accent on* ob) you danced, I suppose? Didn't I? — . . . schon, — . . . auch *or* wohl, even though, although; — . . ., — nicht, whether . . . or not; — Ihr es anerkennt, — nicht, whether you acknowledge it or not. *Comp.* —gleich, —schon, —wohl, —zwar, *conj.* (*in older German often separable, e.g.* ob er gleich müde war, although he was tired; und ob ich schon wanderte im finstern Thal, yea, though I walk through the valley of the shadow of death (*B.*); although, albeit, notwithstanding.

²Ob, I. *prep.* (*with dat.*) over; above, on, upon; (*with gen.*) on account of; beyond; — den Gesetzen halten, to uphold the laws; — der Enns, above the (*river*) Enns (*part of Austria*); — dem Wald, above the forest (*part of the Swiss canton Unterwalden*); er zürnte mir — meines Freimuts, he was angry with me on account of my frankness. II. *adv.* —en, *see* Oben. —er, —erst, —ig, —rig, &c., *see* Ober, Oberst, Obig, &c. *Comp.* —acht, *f.* oversight, superintendence; care; etwas in —acht nehmen, to take heed of s.th.; —acht auf einen geben, to keep a watchful eye on s. o. —bemeldet, berührt, —besagt, genannt, &c. *adj.* above-mentioned, aforesaid. —dach, *n.* shelter; lodging; unter —dach bringen, to place under shelter. —dachlos, *adj.* unsheltered; homeless; Asyl für —dachlose, asylum for the homeless, house of refuge; night shelters; casual ward. —losigkeit, *f.*

houselessness, homelessness. —**herrschaft**, *f.* supremacy. —**hut**, *f.* guard, keeping, care, protection; **in —hut nehmen**, to take care of. —**liegen**, *ir.v.n.* (*sep.*) (*aux.* **s.**) to get the upper hand, prevail (*B.*); (*aux.* **h.**, *dat.*) to be incumbent on *or* imposed as a duty; to apply oneself to, to be devoted to, to study; **es liegt mir —**, it is incumbent on me, is my duty. —**liegend**, *p. & adj.* incumbent; **meine —liegende Pflicht**, my bounden duty. —**liegenheit**, *f.* duty. —**longum**, *n.* oblong (*Math.*). —**macht**, *f.* supreme power *or* authority. —**mann**, *m.* overseer; foreman (*of a jury*); umpire. —**mannschaft**, *f.* inspectorship; arbitration. —**siegen**, *v.n.* (*aux.* **h.**, *dat.*) (*sep.*) to conquer, overcome. —**sieger**, *m.* vanquisher. —**sorge**, *see* **Vorsorge**. —**walten**, *v.n.* (*aux.* **h.**) (*sep.*) to prevail; to exist.

Obduktio'n, *f.* judicial post-mortem examination.

Obedie'nz, *f.* obedience (*R.C.*).

O=Bein—e, *pl.* bandy legs (*opp.* **X=Beine**). —**ig**, *adj.* bandy-legged.

O'ben, *adv.* above, aloft, on high; at the top; on the surface; previously; **von — bis unten**, from top to bottom; **von — nach unten**, downward; **— auf sein**, to be joyful, in good health, in high spirits (*coll.*); **— auf der Liste**, at the head, top of the list; **von — herab behandeln**, to treat haughtily; **— etwas abschneiden**, to cut a piece off from the top; **dort —**, up there; **— im Hause**, up-stairs, at the top of the house, **weiter —**, **mehr —**, higher up; **— abschöpfen**, to treat superficially; **den Kopf — behalten**, to remain calm and collected; **mir steht die ganze Wirtschaft bis hier —**, I am heartily sick of the whole concern. *Comp.* —**a'n**, *adv.* at the head; in the first place. —**angegeben**, *adj. & adv.* above-named *or* pointed out. —**au'f**, *adv.* above, atop; on the surface; uppermost. —**drei'n**, —**ei'n**, *adv.* over and above, into the bargain, what's more. —**erwähnt**, —**gesagt**, **2c.**, *adj.* aforesaid, above mentioned. —**hi'n**, *adv.* along the surface; slightly, cursorily, without any deeper feeling; superficially; **etwas —hin abthun**, to half-do, do badly *or* perfunctorily. —**hinaus**, *adv.*; **Hans —hinaus**, ambitious person.

O'ber, I. *prep.* (*with dat.*) over, above, beyond, upon (*obs.*). II. *adj.* situated above, upper, higher, superior; chief, principal; **der —e**, the chief, the superior; **die —n**, one's betters; those in authority; **das —e**, the top. III. *m.* trump knave, highest knave. —**in**, *f.* mother superior. —**schaft**, *f.* supremacy. —**st**, *see* **Oberst**. *Comp. gen'lly* = upper, chief, head. —**acht**, *f.* ban of the empire. —**älteste(r)**, *m.* senior master (*of a guild*); alderman. —**amtmann**, *m.* high bailiff, farmer of crown lands (*in Germany*). —**appellationsgericht**, *n.* high court of appeal. —**arm**, *m.* arm above the elbow. —**aufseher**, *m.* inspector-general. —**aufsicht**, *f.* superintendence. —**bau**, *m.* superstructure, building above ground. —**baudirektor**, *m.* director of public works. —**baumeister**, *m.* chief architect, director of works. —**befehl**, *m.* supreme command. —**bein**, *n.* thigh. —**befehlshaber**, *m.* commander-in-chief. —**berg'amt**, *n.* mining commission, board of mines. —**berg'hauptmann**, —**berg'meister**, —**berg'rat**, *m.* chief officer in a mining-office. —**bett**, *n.* coverlet, plumeau. —**boden**, *m.* garret. —**bramsegel**, *n.* main-royal (*Naut.*). —**bürgermeister**, *m.* chief burgomaster; (**von London**) lord-mayor. —**commando**, *n.* chief command. —**consistorialrat**, *m.* member of the supreme consistorial court. —**deutsch**, *adj.* upper German, South German. —**ei'gentumsherr**, *m.* lord-paramount. —**einnehmer**, *m.* receiver-general (*of taxes, etc.*). —**feldherr**, *m.* commander-in-chief. —**feldzeugmeister**, *m.* master of the ordnance. —**feuerwerker**, *m.* chief gunner (*Artil.*). —**fiskal**, *m.* attorney-general. —**fläche**, *f.* surface; **gekrümmte —fläche**, curved surface. —**flächen=härtung**, *f.* case-hardening (*of steel*). —**flächlich**, *adj. & adv.* superficial. —**forst'amt**, *n.* Board of Woods and Forests. —**förster**, *m.* head-forester; upper ranger. —**fuß**, *m.* instep. —**gärtner**, *m.* head gardener. —**gärung**, *f.* surface-fermentation. —**gericht**, *n.* supreme court. —**gerichts=herr**, *m.* chief magistrate. —**geschoß**, *n.* upper story. —**gewalt**, *f.* supreme power *or* authority; supremacy; the upper hand. —**glied**, *n.* major term (*Log.*); upper part of the principal cornice (*Arch.*). —**halb**, *adv. & prep.* (*with gen.*) above, at the upper part of. —**hand**, *f.* back of the hand; metacarpus, wrist; upperhand, ascendancy; precedence; **die —hand gewinnen**, to get the better (of a p., **über einen**); (**einem**) **die —hand geben**, to yield the precedence. —**haupt**, *n.* upper part of the head; head, chief, master. —**haus**, *n.* upper part of a house; House of Peers; —**haus und Unterhaus**, House of Lords and House of Commons, (both Houses of) Parliament. —**haut**, *f.*, —**häutchen**, *n.* cuticle, epidermis. —**hemd**, *n.* linen shirt, dress shirt. —**herr**, *m.* supreme lord, sovereign. —**herrlich**, *adj.* sovereign. —**herrschaft**, *f.* sovereignty. —**hof'gericht**, *n.* supreme court of judicature. —**hof'meister**, *m.* lord-high-steward; tutor to a prince. —**hof'prediger**, *m.* chief chaplain to a prince. —**ingenieur**, *m.* chief engineer. —**jäger**, *m.* first huntsman; sergeant in a rifle battalion. —**jä'germeister**, *m.* Grand *or* Chief Master of the Hunt; Master of the Buckhounds. —**kämmerei**, *f.* chancellor's office. —**kämmerer**, —**kam'merherr**, *m.* lord-high-chamberlain. —**kanzlei'direktor**, *m.* master of the rolls. —**kellner**, *m.* chief butler; head waiter. —**kir'chenrat**, *m.* high *or* supreme consistory (*Protestant*); member of a high consistory. —**klassen**, *pl.* upper forms, in German higher secondary schools of a nine years' course (**Obersekunda** (II. a), **Unterprima** (I. b), **Oberprima** (I. a), average age of scholars: 16–19). —**kleid**, *n.* upper garment. —**kiefe**, *f.* upper jaw. —**konsistorial'rat**, *m.* member of the supreme consistorial court. —**körper**, *m.* upper part of the body. —**kriminal'gericht**, *n.* court of King's Bench. —**land**, *n.* high country, highland. —**länder**, *m.* mountaineer; South German. —**lan'desgericht**, *n.* Supreme Court of Justice. —**lauf**, *m.* upper course (*of a river*). —**lehnsherr**, *m.* lord-paramount. —**lehrer**, *m.* professor, upper teacher, senior assistant master, a teacher qualified to teach in the highest forms of first grade schools. —**lehrer=prüfung**, *f.* examination for the Upper Teacher's Certificate (qualification to teach his subject in all forms of first grade secondary schools). —**lehrer=zeugnis**, *n.* Upper Teacher's Certificate (of efficiency), U. T.'s Diploma. —**leib**, *m.* upper part of the body *or* of a dress. —**leitung**, *f.* supreme direction, management; open-air and overhead conveyance, aerial line; overland *or* aerial wire (*Tel.*). —**licht**, *n.* sky-light, full sky-light. —**licht(=fenster)**, *n.* fan-light (*over a door*). —**leutnant**, *m.* first lieutenant. —**macht**, *f.* superiority, ascendency; supreme authority. —**pfarre**, *f.* rectory, rectorship. —**pfarrer**, *m.* rector. —**post'amt**, *n.*, —**post'direktion**, *f.* general post-office. —**post'meister**, *m.* postmaster general. —**präsident**, *m.* lord-lieutenant, highest civil official of a (Prussian) province. —**priester**, *m.* high-priest.

—priesterlich, adj. pontifical. —priestertum, n. pontificate. —prima, f. first division of the highest class in a first grade secondary boys' school, Upper VI. (I. a = U. VI.). —primaner, m. pupil of the highest class, sixth form boy. —rabbiner, m. chief rabbi. —realschule, f. higher modern school (mod. langs., mathematics, science; 9 years' course). —rech'nungskammer, f. audit-office. —richter, m. chief justice. —rinde, f. outer bark; upper crust. —rock, m. surtout, great coat. —satz, m. major term (of a syllogism). —schenkel, m. upper part of the thigh. —schiedsrichter, m. referee (Tennis). —schlächtig, adj. overshot (of a mill). —schul'rat, m. board of public instruction, educational council, education department; member of such a board. —schwelle, f. lintel; architrave. —sekundaner, m. Upper V. boy. —staats'anwalt, m. attorney general. —stabs'arzt, m. staff-surgeon-major (Mil.). —stall'meister, m. Lord Grand Master of the Horse. —steiger, m. master miner. —steuermann, m. first mate. —stimme, f. treble, soprano. —stübchen, n. upper garret; bei ihm ist's im —stübchen nicht richtig, he is not quite right in the upper story, he has a screw loose somewhere, is cracked. —tasse, f. cup. —tertia'ner, m. Upper IV. boy. —tribunal, n. supreme court. —trumpf, m. matadore (Cards). —verdeck, n. upper deck. —vor'mundschaft, f. chief guardianship. —vor'mundschaftsgericht, n. Court of Chancery (Eng.). —vor'steher, m. director. —wasser, n. freshet, landfloods; upper water (Hyd.); —wasser haben, to have the upper hand; —wasser bekommen, (fig.) to have or to get the upper hand, to feel self-confident. —wärts, adv. upwards. —welt, f. upper world, this world. —zähne, pl. upper teeth. —zeug, n. upper garments. —zoll'amt, n. general custom-office. —zug, m.; Kessel mit —zug, double-story boiler.

O'berst, I. sup. adj. see Ober; top; supreme; highest; das —e zu unterst kehren, to turn upside down, topsy-turvy; er ist der —e, er sitzt zu — in seiner Klasse, he is head of his class; er ist der —e der ganzen Schule, he is the captain of the school. II. m., (O'brist, obs.) (—en, pl. —en) chief; colonel (Mil.). Comp. —en-stelle, f. colonelcy, colonelship. —inhaber, m. honorary colonel (of a regiment). —leut'nant, m. lieutenant-colonel. —wacht'meister, m. major.

O'big, adj. above, foregoing, above-mentioned.

Obje'kt, n. (—s, pl. —e) object. —iv, I. adj. objective, impartial, dispassionate. II. n. (—s) objective case; object-glass. —i'visch, adj. objective (obs.). —ivitä't, f. objectivity.

Obla'te, f. (pl. —n) wafer (Confect.); (sealing) wafer; consecrated wafer, host. Comp. —n-schachtel, f. pyx (Rom. Cath.). —n-teller, m. wafer-dish, paten.

Oblig—a't, adj. & adv. in duty bound; obligato (Mus.); mit —ater Violinbegleitung, Pianobegleitung, with obligato violin-, piano-accompaniment. —ato'risch, adj. obligatory. —atio'n, f. obligation; obligation, bond, debenture. —o, (pron. Ob'ligo) n. (—os, pl. —os) obligation to pay; liability; engagement; security. Comp. —ations'-inhaber, m. bondholder. —ations'-konto, n. debenture book. —ations'-recht, n. law of obligations. —ations'-schein, n. bond. —ations'-schuldner, m. bond-debtor, obligor.

Obo'e, f. (pl. —n) hautboy, oboe.

O'brigkeit, f. (pl. —en) magistrates (coll.), authorities; sich der — überliefern, to give oneself up to justice. —lich, I. adj. magisterial; —licher Befehl, government order; eine —liche Person, a magistrate. II. adv. by authority; —lich bewilligen, to license.

O'brist, obs. for Oberst (Mil.).

Obscö'n, adj. obscene. —itä't, f. obscenity.

Observ—a'nz, f. (pl. —an'zen) observance. —ato'rium, n. (pl. —atorien) observatory.

Obsku'r, adj. obscure. —a'nt, m. (—an'ten, pl. —an'ten) opponent of knowledge and progress.

Obst, n. (—es; pl. —e, coll. pl. Öb'ster) fruit (coll.); frisches —, green or fresh fruit; trockenes —, dried fruit; gekochtes —, stewed fruit; eingemachtes —, preserved fruit; — in Büchsen, fruit in tins. Comp. —bau, m. fruit-culture. —baum, m. fruit-tree. —boden, m. soil suited to fruit-trees; store-room for fruit. —brecher, m. tool for gathering fruit. —darre, f. fruit kiln. —ernte, f. gathering of fruit; crop of fruit. —garten, m. orchard. —händler, m. fruiterer. —kammer, f. fruit-loft. —kelter, f. fruit-press. —kenner, m. pomologist. —kern, m. pippin. —korb, m. fruit-basket; corbel (Arch.). —kuchen, m. open fruit-tart. —lese, f. fruit-gathering. —mus, n. jam. —reich, adj. abounding in fruit. —satz, m. price of fruit; eingekochter —saft, jelly, syrup. —schale, f. skin of fruit, peel, paring; fruit dish. —wein, m. wine made of fruit; home-made wine; cider, perry. —zeit, f. fruit season.

Och, interj. Oh (dial.).

O'cher, O'cker, m. (—s) ochre. —artig, —haltig, adj. ochraceous.

Ochlokratie', f. (pl. —en) mob-rule; democracy.

Ochs, m. (—(s)en, pl. —(s)en), **Och'se**, m. (—n, pl. —n) ox; lout; stupid fellow, duffer, blockhead; der — brüllt, the ox lows; da stehen die —(s)en am Berge, that's the difficulty, there 's the rub; von einem —en kann man nicht mehr als Rindfleisch verlangen, what can you expect from an ox but beef? —(s)ig, adj. immense, vast, huge (sl.).

Och'sen, I. v.n. (aux. h.) to bull (of cows); to work hard, slave, cram, grind (of students). II. pl. see Ochs. —haft, adj. oxlike; stupid, coarse, rude. Comp. —auge, n. bull's eye, ox-eye; oval or round window (Arch.); small clouds foreboding storms in southern latitudes. —bauer, m. cattle-dealer, grazier; farmer using oxen for horses. —braten, m. roast-beef. —fleisch, n. beef. —galle, f. ox-gall; bull's eye (in glass). —gespann, n. ox-team. —handel, m. cattle trade. —haut, f. ox-hide, bull's hide. —hirt, m. neat-herd. —kopf, m. bull's head; blockhead; person leaning on his elbows. —köpfig, adj. bull-headed. —leder, n. neat's leather. —post, f. slow travelling. —rippe, f. rib of beef. —stall, —stand, m. ox-stall, bullock-shed. —treiber, m. driver of oxen, drover. —wagen, m. ox-waggon. —ziemer, m. bull's pizzle; ox-tail; cow-hide, horsewhip. —züchter, m. grazier. —zunge, f. ox-tongue; neat's tongue.

Octroyie'ren, v.a. to dictate, impose, force upon; to grant (a charter); octroyierte Handelsgesellschaft, licensed trading company.

Od, m. (—s) od (supposed to give rise to the phenomena of mesmerism, magnetism); vom —handelnd, odic. Comp. —licht, n. odic light.

O'de, f. (pl. —n) ode. Comp. —n-dichter, m. ode-maker, writer of odes. —n-dichtung, f. ode poetry, writing of odes.

Ö'd—e, I. adj. waste, desert, desolate, tedious, uninteresting (sl.). II. f. (pl. —en) desert; solitude. Comp. —acker, m. fallow land; 500 Quadratmeilen —acker, 500 square miles of uncultivated land.

O'dem, m. (—s) breath, respiration (poetic).

Ö'den, v.a. to be tiresome, to bore (sl.); sich —, to be or feel bored.

O'der, conj. or; or else, otherwise.

O'dermennig, *m.* agrimony, liverwort.

O'fen, *m.* (—s, *pl.* Öfen) oven; stove; furnace; kiln; mine *or* chamber not yet filled with powder (*Fort.*); hinter dem — hocken, to be a stay-at-home, not to leave the chimney-corner; der feurige —, the fiery furnace (*B.*); den Hund vom — zu locken wissen, to be able to do something, to be clever and energetic. *Comp.* —bank, *f.* bench near the stove *or* fire. —darren, *n.* kiln-drying. —geld, *n.* charge for baking *or* ovening. —hocker, *m.* stay-at-home, molly-coddle. —kachel, *f.* Dutch tile. —loch, *n.* mouth of a stove. —rohr, *n.*, —röhre, *f.* stove-pipe *or* funnel; space in a stove for keeping things warm. —schaufel, —schippe, *f.* fire-shovel. —schirm, *m.* fire-screen. —setzer, *m.* maker *or* setter-up of stoves. —thür, *f.* stove-door; vent-hole of a stove *or* oven. —schwärze, *f.* black lead, stove-polish. —vorsetzer, *m.* fender.

Of'fen, *adj. & adv.* open; not shut; unclosed; frank, outspoken, candid; sincere; public, vacant; overt; clear; —er Wechsel, blank cheque, letter of credit; —e Rechnung, running account; in —er Rechnung stehen mit, to have a running account with; —e Police, floating policy; ein Posten steht in unserm Buche noch —, there is an item owing in our books for which we have no security; —es Eis, loose ice; —er Leib, open bowels; —e Briefe, unsealed letters; letters patent; —es Karree, hollow square (*Mil.*); —e Stelle, vacancy; eine —e Stelle besetzen, to fill up a vacancy; eine Stelle — lassen, to leave a blank; —e Tafel halten, to keep open house; —e Städte, unfortified towns; — gesagt, to speak candidly; frei und — handeln, to act straightforwardly; auf —er Straße, in the open street, in public; — zu Tage liegen, to be evident; auf —er That, in the very act; —e Thüren einrennen, to carry coals to Newcastle (*prov.*). —bar, *adj. & adv.* manifest, evident, obvious; notorious, public; palpable; declared (*enemy*). —ba'ren, *v.a.* to manifest, reveal, discover; to disclose; to publish; sein Herz —baren, to open one's heart, to break one's mind to some one, to unbosom oneself; geoffenbarte Religion, revealed religion. —ba'rt, *adj.* disclosed, revealed. —ba'rung, *f.* manifestation; revealing, disclosure; revelation; —barung St. Johannis, Revelation of St. John, Apocalypse. —heit, *f.* openness; candour, *etc. see* Offen; unzarte —heit, bluntness. *Comp.* —barungs=glaube, *m.* belief in revealed religion. —herzig, *adj.* candid, sincere. —herzigkeit, *f.* frankness, candour, sincerity; sein Rock hat auf dem Rücken einige —herzigkeiten, the back of his coat is rather out of repair *or* is more holy (*having holes*) than righteous (*coll.*). —kundig, *adj.* public, notorious; etwas —kundig werden lassen, to allow a thing to become known *or* to get abroad. —stehend, *adj.* open.

Offensi'v, *adj.* offensive, aggressive. —e, *f.* offensive; die —e ergreifen, to assume the offensive, to act on the offensive.

Öf'f—entlich, *see* Öffentlich. —nen, *v.a. & r.* to open. —nend, *p. & adj.* opening; aperient. —ner, *m.* (—ners, *pl.* —ner) opener; sley, cotton-opener. —nung, *f.* opening; dissection; aperture, gap; mouth; orifice; outlet; evacuation (*Med.*); rechteckige —nung, rectangular notch; für gehörige —nung Sorge tragen, to take care that the bowels are kept open.

Öf'fentlich, *adj. & adv.* public, open; with open doors; —e Schule, public school (*as opposed to a private school; but not* '*public schools*' *in the narrower and especially English sense of the term*); — bekannt machen, to proclaim; auf —er Straße, in the open street. —keit, *f.* publicity, public act.

Offer'te, *f.* (*pl.* —n) offer, tender. *Comp.* —n=brief, *m.* circular; sealed tender.

Offiz—ia'l, *m.* (—ials, *pl.* —iale) official; officiating priest, *etc.* —ia'nt, *m.* (—ian'ten, *pl.* —ian'ten) civil officer; minister, officiating priest. —ie'll, *adj. & adv.* official, on the authority of the state, authoritative; —ieller Bericht, official report. —ie'r, *m.* (—iers, *pl.* —iere) (military) officer; all the chessmen except the king and pawns; zu —ieren haben, to be officered by; mit —ieren versehen, to officer; abgedankter —ier, retired officer; pensionierter —ier, officer on half-pay; zur Disposition gestellter —ier, officer on the retired list; vom Gemeinen zum —ier machen, to raise from the ranks. —i'n, *f.* (*pl.* —inen) workshop; laboratory; chemist's shop; printing-office. —ine'll, *adj.* medicinal. —iö's, *adj.* officious; semi-official. *Comp.* —ier'=deck, *n.* quarter-deck (*Naut.*). —ier'=mäßig, I. *adj.* officer-like. II. *adv.* in an officer-like way. —ier'=kasino, *n.* officers' club. —ier'=korps, *n.* body of officers, the officers. —ier'=patent, *n.* commission. —iers'=aspirant, *m.* military aspirant, gentleman cadet. —iers'=bursche, *m.* orderly. —iers'=examen, *n.* examination passed before attaining officer's rank. —iers'=laufbahn, *f.* profession *or* career of a (military) officer.

Oft, *adv.* (öf'ter, öf'test) oft, often, frequently; so — du kommst, every time you come; wie — ist 3 in 6 enthalten? how many times is 3 contained in 6? *Comp.* —mals, *adv.* oftentimes, often, frequently, repeatedly. —malig, *adj.* frequent, repeated.

Öf'ter, *see* Oft, I. *adv.* more frequently; often; je — ich ihn sehe, desto — &c., the more I see of him, the more, etc. II. *adj.* more frequent; ein —es Kommen, more frequent visits. —s, *adv. for* öfter.

O'heim, Ohm, (**Öhm** (*poet.*),) *m.* (—s, *pl.* —e) uncle.

Ohm, *m. & n.* (—es, *pl.* —e), —e, *f.* (*pl.* —en) aam, liquid measure (= *about 40 gallons*).

Ohn, *obs. for* Ohne. *Comp.* —erachtet, —geachtet, —gefähr, —längst, *see* Unerachtet, Ungeachtet, Ungefähr, Unlängst.

Oh'ne, *prep.* (*with acc.*) without, apart from; but for, not to speak of; except, save; besides; — daß, but that, save that; — Weiteres, without more ado; — Frage, doubtless; — Bericht, for want of advice (*C.L.*); — daß ich es wußte, without my knowledge, unknown to me; sie treffen sich selten — daß sie sich zanken, they seldom meet without quarrelling; das *or* die Sache ist nicht —, there is some truth in it, there is something to be said for that (view); sie ist gewiß schön, ihre Schwester aber ist auch nicht —, she is no doubt beautiful, but her sister is by no means plain either; dieser Wein ist nicht —, this wine is not to be despised, is by no means bad; that's a capital wine. *Comp.* —de'm, —die's, —hi'n, *adv.* apart from this, besides; all the same; moreover; likewise. —glei'chen, *adj.* unequalled. —ho'se(n), *m.* sans-culotte; Frenchman (*obs.*). —ho'sentum, *n.* sans-culottism. —sorge; Hans —sorge, careless fellow.

Ohn'—macht, *f.* fainting fit, faintness, swoon, syncope; impotency, weakness; in —macht fallen, to swoon; es wandelte ihn eine —macht an, he was seized with faintness, he fell down in a swoon, faint. —mächtig, *adj.* swooning, in a swoon; faint, weak, powerless, feeble; —mächtig werden, to faint, swoon.

Ohr, *n.* (—(e)s, *pl.* —en) ear, thing like an ear;

handle; eye (*of a needle*); auricle (*Mollusc.*); ogive (*Arch.*); **geneigtes —**, favourable hearing, ready ear; **ein — in ein Buch einschlagen**, to turn down a leaf in a book; **—en der Fische**, gills; **— des Schlüssels**, handle of a key; **sich aufs — legen**, to lie down, to go to bed (*coll.*); **mir braust es in den —en**, I have a singing in my ears; **es klingt mir in den —en**, my ears ring *or* tingle; **einem in den —en liegen**, to keep dinning (*something*) into s.o.'s ears; **einem sein — leihen**, to lend a p. one's ear, to give s.o. a hearing, to listen to a p., to be (secretly) influenced by a p.; **einem sein — verschließen**, to refuse to listen to a p.; **die —en steif halten**, to keep up one's courage, to keep erect; **einem die —en voll schreien**, to deafen a p. with crying; **dicke —en haben**, to be dull of hearing; **die —en aufknöpfen** *or* **aufsperren**, to listen with close attention *or* attentively; to prick up one's ears; **die —en spitzen**, to prick up one's ears; **die —en hängen lassen**, to look crestfallen; **mit gesenkten —en**, down-hearted; **noch nicht trocken hinter den —en**, but a boy, a greenhorn; **sich** (*dat.*) **etwas hinters — schreiben**, to note a th., store it up in one's mind, to take it to heart; **er hat es** (**dick** *or* **faustdick**) **hinter den —en**, he is pretty (*or* extremely) wide-awake, he is very sharp; **einen übers — hauen**, to cheat a p.; **einem das Fell über die —en ziehen**, to fleece a p.; **bis über die —en**, over head and ears; up to the eyes; **er steckt bis über die —en in Schulden**, he is over head and ears in debt, he is up to the eyes in debt; **sie wurde bis über die —en rot**, she blushed up to the roots of her hair; **den Kopf zwischen die —en nehmen und davon gehen**, to bolt; **vor jemands —en**, in a p.'s hearing; **einem zu —en kommen**, to come to a p.'s ears; **vor meinen —en**, in my hearing; **er hatte kein — dafür**, he would not listen to it; **zu einem — hinein, zum andern hinaus**, in at one ear and out at the other; **so weit ein — trägt**, within ear-shot. **—ig**, *see under* Öhr. *Comp.* **—(en)=brausen**, *n.* singing in the ears. **—bügel**, *pl.* swivels. **—(en)=drüse**, *f.* parotid gland. **—drüsen=bräune**, *f.* mumps. **—en=arzt**, *m.* specialist for diseases of the ear, aural surgeon, aurist. **—en=beichte**, *f.* auricular confession. **—en=beulen**, *pl.* mumps. **—en=bläser**, *m.* prompter, tell-tale; backbiter; toady. **—en=diener**, *m.* sycophant. **—en=(aus)fluß**, *m.* discharge from the ear. **—en=höhle**, *f.* cavity of the ear. **—en=kitzel**, *m.* tickling in one's ears; inquisitiveness. **—en=leiden**, *n.* disease of the ear, auditory disease. **—(en=)nerv**, *m.* acoustic *or* auditory nerve. **—en=reißen**, *n.* ear-ache. **—en=schmalz**, *n.* ear-wax. **—en=schmaus**, *m.* musical treat. **—en=schmerz**, *m.* ear-ache. **—en=spange**, *f.* ear-pendant. **—(en)=trommel**, *f.* drum of the ear. **—en=zeuge**, *m.*; **Augen und —zeuge**, eye and ear-witness. **— eule**, *f.* horned owl. **—feige**, *f.* box on the ear. **—feigen**, *v.a.* (*insep.*) to box a p.'s ears. **— flügel**, *m.* lobe of the ear. **—förmig**, *adj.* auriculate (*Bot.*); auriform. **—gehänge**, **—gehenk**, **—geschmeide**, *n.* ear-ring. **—hänger**, *m.* one dispirited. **—trichter**, *m.* ear-trumpet. **—trompete**, *f.* Eustachian tube (*Anat.*). **—wurm**, *m.* earwig (*Ent.*).

Öhr, *n.* eye (*of a needle*); ear, handle; iron ring, catch. **—chen**, *n.* (**—chens**, *pl.* **—chen**) auricle (*Bot.*); little ear. **—en**, **Öh'ren**, *v.a.* to furnish with ears; **geohrt**, **geöhrt**, eared, with ears. **—ig**, **Oh'rig**, *adj.* (*in comp.* =) -eared; **des Silenus —ig Tier**, the long-eared animal (= the donkey) of Silenus.

Ökono'm, *m.* (**—en**, *pl.* **—en**) economical person; farmer, agriculturist; manager, steward, housekeeper. **—ie'**, *f.* economy; agriculture; domestic economy. **—isch**, *adj.* economical. *Comp.* **—ie=gebäude**, *n.* farm-buildings.

Ok't—aeder, *n.* (**—aeders**, *pl.* **—aeder**) octahedron. **—a'nt**, *m.* (**—an'ten**, *pl.* **—an'ten**) octant, sextile. **—a'v**, **—a've**, **rc.** *see under* **Oktav**. **—o'ber**, *m.* (**—obers**) October.

Okta'v, *n.* (**—s**, *pl.* **—e**) octavo; **breites —**, crown-octavo. **—a**, *f.* eighth class (*in a preparatory school, second lowest form*). **—e**, *f.* (*pl.* **—en**) octave (*Mus.*, *Eccl.*). *Comp.* **—band**, *m.* volume in octavo; 8vo. **—en=gänge**, *pl.* successions of octaves. **—en=register**, *n.* octave-stop. **—flöte**, *f.* flageolet.

Okto—dez'=format, *n.* octo-decimo, 18mo. **—go'n**, *n.* (**—gons**, *pl.* **—gone**) octagon. **—gona'l**, **—go'nisch**, *adj.* octagonal. **—gy'nisch**, *adj.* octogynous (*Bot.*).

Okul—a'r, I. *adj.* ocular. II. *n.* eye-piece. **—ie'ren**, *v.a.* to graft, to inoculate. **—i'st**, *m.* (**—is'ten**, *pl.* **—is'ten**) oculist. *Comp.* **—ar'=glas**, *n.* eye-glass (*in optical instruments*). **—ier'=messer**, *n.* grafting-knife.

Ökume'nisch, *adj.* œcumenical (*council*).

Öl, *n.* (**—s**, *pl.* **—e**) oil; **fette —e**, fat *or* fixed oils; **ätherische —e**, essential oils; **heiliges —**, chrism; **mit — schmieren** *or* **tränken**, to lubricate with oil, to oil; **— ins Feuer gießen**, to throw oil on the fire, to add fuel to the fire; **in — malen**, to paint in oil(s). **—en**, *v.a.* to oil; to anoint. **—icht** (*obs.*), **—ig**, *adj.* oily; unctuous. **—er**, *m.* lubricator (*cycl.*). **—ung**, *f.* oiling; lubrication; anointing, consecration; **letzte —ung**, extreme unction. *Comp.* **—bauer**, *m.* grower of olive-trees, owner of an olive-yard. **—baum**, *m.* olive-tree; **wilder —baum**, oleaster. **—beere**, *f.* olive. **—behälter**, *m.* oil-receptacle (*in a lamp*). **—berg**, *m.* Mount of Olives. **—bild**, *n.* oil-painting. **—bildend**, *adj.*; **— bildendes Gas**, olefiant gas. **—blatt**, *n.* olive-leaf; (symbol of) peace and good will (*fig. opposed to* **Lorbeer**). **—druck=bild**, *n.* chromo-lithograph; chromo-lithography. **—farbe**, *f.* oil-colour; **mit —farben malen**, to paint in oil(s). **—farben=händler**, *m.* oil-man. **—farben=handlung**, *f.* oil-shop. **—firnis**, *m.* oil-varnish, boiled oil. **—flasche**, *f.* oil-flask; holy-vial (*R.C.*). **—garten**, *m.* olive-garden. **—gemälde**, *n.* oil-painting. **—götze**, *m.* phlegmatic, tedious person, bore; blockhead, dunce; **steh doch nicht da wie ein —götze**, don't stand there like a post! **—handel**, *m.* oil-trade. **—händler**, *m.* oil-man, oil-merchant. **—handlung**, *f.* oil-shop. **—kelter**, *f.* oil-press. **—kitt**, *m.* putty. **—kuchen**, *m.* cake baked in oil; oil-cake. **—lese**, *f.* olive-harvest. **—malerei**, *f.* painting in oil. **—mühle**, *f.* oil-mill; **—mühle mit Keilpresse**, Dutch oil-press. **—papier**, *n.* transparent paper; transparent oiled paper. **—ruß**, *m.* lamp-black. **—saat**, *f.* rape-seed. **—same(n)**, *m.* linseed, rape-seed; oily grain. **—sauer**, *adj.*; **—saures Salz**, oleate. **—säure**, *f.* oleic acid. **—schläger**, *m.* oil-miller; oil-presser. **—spritze**, *f.* oil-syringe, lubricator. **—stein**, *m.* grinder's oil-stone; (**türkischer**) Turkey (*oil-*)stone; Jew-stone. **—süß**, *n.* glycerine. **—vergoldung**, *f.* oil gilding. **—werk**, *n.* oil-mill. **—zucker**, *m.* glycerine. **—zweig**, *m.* olive branch (*symbol of peace and goodwill*).

Oliga'rch, *m.* (**—en**, *pl.* **—en**) oligarch. **—ie'**, *f.* oligarchy. **—isch**, *adj.* oligarchical.

O'leum, *n.* (**—s**, *pl.* **—s**) *see* **Schwefelsäure**.

O'lim, I. *adv. see* **Ehemals**. II. *n.*; **zu —s Zeiten**, in former times, in days of yore (*coll.*).

Oli've, *f.* (*pl.* **—n**) olive. *Comp.* **—n=baum**, *m.* olive-tree. **—n=braun**, **—n=farbe**, *f.* olive-colour. **—n=grün**, *adj.* olive-green. **—n=öl**, *n.* olive-oil.

Olm, *m.* (**—s**, *pl.* **—e**) proteus (anguinus) (*Zoöl.*).

O'mama, *f.* (*pl.* —**s**) grannie (*children's lang.*).
Ominö's, *adj.* ominous.
Om'nibus, *m.* (—, —(ss)es, *pl.* —, —(ss)e) omnibus, 'bus (*coll.*); **mit dem — fahren**, to go by omnibus, to take the 'bus.
Onanie', *f.* onanism, self-pollution, masturbation.
On'kel, *m.* (—**s**, *pl.* —) uncle; elderly person, old chap (*sl.*); **er ist ein riesig gemütlicher —**, he is an awfully jolly old chap (*sl.*).
Onomatopöie', *f.* onomatopœia.
Ooli'th, *m.* oölite.
Opa'k, *adj.* opaque.
Opalisie'rend, *adj.* opalescent (*of glass*).
O'papa, *m.* (—**s**, *pl.* —**s**) granddad (*children's lang.*).
O'per, *f.* (*pl.* —**n**) opera; opera-house. —**ateu'r**, *m.* (—**ateurs**, *pl.* —**ateurs**, —**ateure**) operator; operating surgeon. —**ati'v**, *adj.* operative. —**et'te**, *f.* (*pl.* —**etten**) operetta. —**ie'ren**, *v.a.* & *n.* to operate; to perform an operation (*Surg.*); to operate, to manœuvre (*Mil.*); to effect. —**nhaft**, *adj.* in the style of an opera. *Comp.* —**atio'ns=plan**, *m.* plan of campaign (*Mil.*). —**n=buch**, *n.* book of the opera; libretto. —**n=dichter**, *m.* librettowriter. —**n=glas**, *n.*, —**n=gucker**, *m.* opera-glass. —**n=haus**, *n.* opera-house. —**n=komponist**, *m.* composer of an opera. —**n=musik**, *f.* operatic music. —**n=sänger**, *m.*, —**n=sängerin**, *f.* opera-singer. —**n=text**, *m.* *see* —**nbuch**. —**n=zettel**, *m.* play-bill of an opera.
Op'fer, *n.* (—**s**, *pl.* —) offering, sacrifice; victim, martyr; (**einem**) **zum — werden** *or* **fallen**, to fall a victim (to a p.); **ich habe ihm viele — gebracht**, I have made many sacrifices for him, I have sacrificed much for him; — **an Gut und Blut**, sacrifice(s) of life and prosperity. —**er**, *m.* (—**ers**, *pl.* —**er**) sacrificer.
Op'fer—n, *v.a.* & *n.* (*aux.* **h.**) to sacrifice, offer as a sacrifice, immolate; **einem etwas —n**, to sacrifice, give up something for a p. (*or for a cause*). —**ung**, *f.* offering, sacrifice. *Comp.* (*often* = sacrificial) —**altar**, *m.* sacrificial altar. —**becken**, *n.* sacrificial basin *or* cup. —**binde**, *f.* fillet. —**brot**, *n.* consecrated bread *or* wafer. —**dienst**, *m.* worship by sacrifices; office of sacrificer. —**flamme**, *f.* flame consuming the victims. —**freudig**, *adj.* willing *or* ready to make sacrifices, self-sacrificing. —**gabe**, *f.* offering. —**gebet**, *n.* prayers during part of the celebration of Mass; offertory. —**gebrauch**, *m.* sacrificial rite. —**geld**, *n.* money-offering. —**herd**, *m.* altar. —**kasten**, —**stock**, *m.* poor-box. —**lamm**, *n.* sacrificial lamb; the Lamb (Jesus); innocent victim. —**priester**, *m.* sacrificer. —**schale**, *f.* dish for receiving the blood of the victim. —**schmaus**, *m.* sacrificial repast. —**tier**, *n.* victim. —**tod**, *m.* sacrifice of one's life; expiatory death (*of Christ*). —**trank**, —**wein**, *m.* oblation-drink; libation. —**willig**, *adj.* see —**freudig**. —**willigkeit**, *f.* readiness to make sacrifices, ready devotion.
Opia't, *n.* (—**s**, *pl.* —**e**) opiate.
Opponie'ren, *v.a.* to oppose.
Opt—ie'ren, *v.a.* to choose; —**ieren für eine S.**, to choose a th., decide in favour of a th. —**ativ** (*pron.* **Op'tativ**) *m.* (—**ativs**) optative.
Op't—ik, *f.* optics. —**iker**, *m.* (—**ikers**, *pl.* —**iker**), —**ikus**, *m.* optician. —**isch**, *adj.* optic(al).
Optim—a'ten, *pl.* aristocrats. —**is'mus**, *m.* optimism. —**itä't**, *f.* excellence.
Ora'kel, *n.* (—**s**, *pl.* —) oracle. —**haft**, *adj.* oracular. *Comp.* —**befragen**, *n.*, —**einholung**, *f.* consultation of an oracle. —**mäßig**, *adj.* oracular. —**spruch**, *m.* oracle, oracular sentence.
Ora'keln, *v.a.* to speak oracularly, to speak like Sir Oracle.
Oran'ge, *f.* (*pl.* —**n**) orange. —**n**, *adj.* orange-yellow; orange. —**rie'**, *f.* orangery. *Comp.* —**n=blüte**, *f.* orange-blossom. —**n=farbig**, *see* —**n**. —**n=schale**, *f.* orange-peel.
Orangu'tang, *n.* (—**s**, *pl.* —**e**) orang-outang.
Ora'nien— (*in comp.*) —**flagge**, *f.* flag of the prince of Orange. —**männer**, *pl.* Orangemen.
Orato'rium, *n.* (—**s**, *pl.* **Oratorien**) oratorio (*Mus.*); oratory.
Orches'ter, *n.* (—**s**, *pl.* —) orchestra. *Comp.* —**begleitung**, *f.* orchestral accompaniment; orchestration. —**konzert**, *n.* orchestral concert. —**satz**, *m.* concerted piece (*Mus.*).
Orchestrie'r—en, *v.a.* to orchestrate, to score. —**ung**, *f.* orchestration, scoring.
Orda'le, *n.* (—**s**, *pl.* **Ordalien**) ordeal.
Or'den, *m.* (—**s**, *pl.* —) order; decoration, distinction, medal. —**tlich**, *adj.* & *adv.* orderly, regular; proper; usual; downright, out and out; —**tlicher Arzt**, physician in ordinary; **ein —tlicher Lehrer**, a teacher on the staff of a college *or* school; **ein —tlicher Professor**, professor in ordinary; —**tliche Mahlzeit**, proper meal; **ein —tlicher Mann werden**, to become steady *or* a steady character; —**tliches Mädchen**, respectable girl; —**tlicher junger Mann**, steady young fellow, young man of orderly habits; —**tliche Schlacht**, pitched battle; —**tlich stellen, legen**, to arrange; —**tlich schlagen**, to beat regularly (*of the pulse, etc.*); **waschen Sie ihm —tlich den Kopf**, give him a good blowing up; **sie haben ihn —tlich durchgeprügelt**, they thrashed him soundly; **ich bin —tlich froh, daß er nicht bei uns war**, I am truly glad he was not with us; **das ist —tlich nett von dir**, that is really nice of you (*coll.*). —**tlichkeit**, *f.* regularity, orderliness; respectability. *Comp.* —**s=alter**, *n.* necessary age for admission to an order. —**s=band**, *n.* ribbon of an order. —**s=bruder**, *m.* member of an order; friar, monk. —**s=geistliche(r)**, *m.* ecclesiastic, priest who is a member of a religious order. —**s=gelübde**, *n.* vow, profession; **das —s=gelübde ablegen**, to take the (monastic) vows, to profess. —**s=gesellschaft**, *f.* religious fraternity *or* order; chapter. —**s=haus**, *n.* religious house. —**s=kette**, *f.* collar distinguishing an order. —**s=kleid**, *n.* monastic garb *or* habit; cassock of an order. —**s=pfründe**, *f.* commandery. —**s=regel**, *f.* statute(s) of an order. —**s=schwester**, *f.* sister, nun. —**s=verbrüderung**, *f.* confraternity. —**s=verleihung**, *f.* conferring of an order. —**s=zeichen**, *n.* badge of an order.
Or'der, *f.* (—, *pl.* —**n**), **Or'dre** (*pl.* —**s**) order, command; order (*Mil.*, *C.L.*); **bis auf weitere —**, for the present, until further orders; — **parieren**, to obey orders; **Ihrer — gemäß**, in obedience to your orders; **für mich an die — des . . .**, pay to the order of . . . *Comp.* —**buch**, *n.* orderly book; order book. —**geber**, *m.* drawer, giver of a bill.
Ordin—a'le, *n.* (—**ales**, *pl.* —**alia**), (—**al'=zahl**, *f.*) ordinal number. —**ä'r**, *adj.* & *adv.* common, ordinary; low, vulgar; —**ärer Preis**, published price (*of books*); —**äre Havarie**, petty average (*C.L.*); **ein —ärer Mensch**, a vulgar fellow. —**aria't**, *n.* form-mastership, duties of a form-master (*at a school*); (full) professorship (*at a University*). —**a'rium**, *n.* budget. —**a'rius**, *m.* (university) professor in ordinary; form-master, master in charge of a class; bishop of a diocese; **er ist —arius für deutsche Sprache und Litteratur an der Universität B.**, he is professor of German language and literature at the University of B.; **er ist zum —arius der Unterprima gemacht**, he has been appointed form-master of the Lower Sixth. —**a'te**, *f.* (*pl.* —**aten**) ordinate (*Geom.*). —**atio'n**, *f.* ordination, investment. —**ie'ren**, *v.a.* to ordain; **sich —ieren lassen**, to take (holy)

orders. **—ie'rt**, *p.p. & adj.* in (holy) orders. *Comp.* **—är'=schritt**, *m.* ordinary time (*Mil.*).

Ord'n—en, *v.a.* to arrange, set in order, regulate; to organize; to class, to classify; to draw up in regular order; to order; to construe (*a sentence*). **—er**, *m.* (**—ers**, *pl.* **—er**) regulator, arranger; director. **—ung**, *f.* arrangement; order; military array; order (*Arch.*); class, rank; classification; regulation; **aus der —ung**, disarranged; **in —ung**, in order, correct, right; **nicht in der —ung**, not in order, wrong; **das finde ich ganz in der —ung**, I think that quite right; **die Sache ist in —ung**, it is all right; **die Sache ist jetzt in —ung**, the matter is now settled *or* arranged; **etwas in —ung bringen**, to arrange *or* settle a thing, to put a th. straight; **nach der —ung**, in order, in succession; **zur —ung!** Order, Order! Chair! **ehemalige —ung der Dinge**, old régime; **auf —ung halten**, to be orderly, enforce good order. *Comp.* **—ungs=gemäß**, **—ungs=mäßig**, *adj. & adv.* orderly, regular, according to order. **—ungs=los**, *adj.* disorderly. **—ungs=sinn**, *m.* orderliness; sense of order. **—ungs=widrig**, *adj.* irregular. **—ungs=zahl**, *f.* ordinal number.

Ordonna'nz, *f.* (*pl.* **—en**) order, general order; orderly; **auf — sein**, to be on orderly duty. *Comp.* **—mäßig**, *adj.* according to order *or* to the duties of an orderly. **—offizier**, *m.* orderly officer; aide-de-camp. **—reiter**, *m.* mounted orderly.

Orga'n, *n.* (**—s**, *pl.* **—e**) organ; organon; voice. **—isch**, *adj.* organic. **—isie'ren**, *v.a.* to organize. **—is'mus**, *m.* (*pl.* **—ismen**) organism. **—i'st**, *m.* (**—is'ten**, *pl.* **—is'ten**) organist.

Or'gel, *f.* (*pl.* **—n**) organ (*Mus.*). **—ei'**, *f.* continual organ-grinding, wretched (mechanical) music. *Comp* **—artig**, *adj.* like organ-pipes, in gradual succession. **—bälge**, *pl.* organ-bellows. **—bauer**, *m.* organ-builder. **—chor**, *n.* organ-loft. **—gehäuse**, *n.*, **—kasten**, *m.* organ-case. **—harmonium**, *n.* organ harmonium, American organ. **—klang**, *m.* swell of an organ. **—konzert**, *n.* organ-recital. **—pfeife**, *f.* organ-pipe; (*pl.*) steps of stairs, little steps (*said of children*); **die —pfeifen probieren**, to voice the pipes of an organ. **—punkt**, *m.* pedal-note. **—register**, *n.* organ-stop. **—spiel**, *n.* organ-playing. **—spieler**, *m.* organist. **—stimme**, *f.* organ-stop. **—treter**, *m.* bellows-blower. **—zug**, *m.* organ-stop; row of organ-pipes.

Or'geln, *v.a.* (*aux.* **h.**) to grind a barrel-organ, to strum.

Orient—a'lisch, *adj.* oriental, eastern. **—ali'st**, *m.* orientalist; student *or* teacher of oriental languages *or* customs. **—ie'ren**, *v.* I. *a.* to turn towards the east. II. *r.* to find one's way about, to get acquainted with (*a place, a matter*), to learn how the land lies; **sich nicht —ieren können**, to be all at sea; **er —iert sich leicht in jeder Stadt**, he easily finds his way in any town; **darüber muß ich mich noch besser —ieren**, I must get still more information about this matter. **—ie'rung**, *f.* orientation (*of a church*); survey.

O'riflamme, *f.* (*pl.* **—n**) oriflamb, oriflamme.

Origin—a'l, I. *adj.* original, innate, inherent. II. *n.* (**—als**, *pl.* **—ale**) original, oddity. **—alitä't**, *f.* originality. **—e'll**, *adj.* original. *Comp.* **—al'=ausgabe**, *f.* first edition. **—al'=gemälde**, *n.* original (*painting*). **—al'=(hand=)schrift**, *f.* autograph. **—al'=mensch**, *m.* original, oddity, character. **—al'=werk**, *n.* text, original work; work in the vernacular.

Orka'n, *m.* (**—s**, *pl.* **—e**) hurricane.

Or'logschiff, *n.* man-of-war (*obs.*).

Orna't, *m.* (**—(e)s**, *pl.* **—e**) official costume; vestments, robes; full fig (*coll.*).

Ornitho—lo'g, *m.* (*pl.* **—logen**) ornithologist. **—logie'**, *f.* ornithology.

Or'phisch, *adj.* Orphic.

[1]**Ort**, *m.* (**—es**, *pl.* **Ör'ter**, **—e**) place, spot; locality; region; point; miner's pick; termination (*of a mine*); point, corner, end, edge, (*obs.*); **— der Handlung**, scene of action; **an — und Stelle gelangen**, to arrive on the spot, at one's destination; **am unrechten —e**, misplaced, in the wrong place, out of place; **an allen —en, aller—en, aller—s**, everywhere; **recht am —**, in the right place; **das ist hier sehr am —e**, that is very appropriate here, quite suitable to this case; **an welchem —e?** where? **es an seinen — gestellt sein lassen**, to leave alone *or* undecided; **der Plan ist höheren —es genehmigt**, the authorities have approved of the project; **ich werde Sie geeigneten —es empfehlen**, I shall recommend you in the proper quarters *or* to the proper persons; **hiesigen —es**, of this place; **der düstere —**, the dark place, the darkness; **öffentlicher —**, place of public resort; **ich meines —es**, I for my part. **—schaft**, *f.* (inhabited) place; village; market-town; people of a district; **die meisten —schaften**, most of the towns and villages. *Comp.* (*with — meaning 'place' are usually formed with* **—s**; *those with — meaning 'termination' or 'edge' are as a rule formed with —*). **—beschreibend**, *adj.* topographical. **—(s)=beschreibung**, *f.* topography. **—häuer**, *m.* miner who works **vor Ort**, *i.e.* at the termination of a mine, who prolongs a gallery. **—scheit**, *n.* splinter-bar of a waggon. **—stein**, *m.* corner-stone; boundary stone. **—s=adverb**, *n.* adverb of place. **—s=angelegenheit**, *f.* local concern. **—s=anwesend**, *adj.* present. **—s=arme(r)**, *m.* parish poor. **—s=behörde**, *f.* local authorities. **—s=beschaffenheit**, *f.* nature *or* configuration of a place. **—s=gedächtnis**, *n.* memory for places. **—s=geistliche(r)**, *m.* parish priest, local clergyman *or* minister. **—s=geld**, *n.* miner's wages. **—s=geschichte**, *f.* local history. **—s=sinn**, *m.* local sense, bump of locality (*Phren.*). **—s=statut**, *n.* local bylaw. **—s=veränderung**, *f.* change of place, locomotion. **—s=verweisung**, *f.* expulsion from a place. **—s=vorstand**, *m.* village authorities. **—s=vorsteher**, *m.* village magistrate; mayor. **—s=zeit**, local time.

[2]**Ort**, *m.* (*n.*) (**—(e)s**, *pl.* **—e**) shoemaker's awl.

[3]**Ort**, *m.* quarter (*of weights, etc.*).

Ortho—do'x, *adj.* orthodox; straight-laced (*clergyman*). **—doxie'**, *f.* orthodoxy. **—graphie'**, *f.* orthography. **—gra'phisch**, *adj.* concerning the spelling; **—graphische Reform**, spelling reform.

Ört'lich, *adj.* local. **—keit**, *f.* locality.

'e, *f.* (*pl.* **—n**) shank of a button; eye, ear (*of needles, etc.*); **Haken und —n**, hooks and eyes.

Ost, *m.* (**—es**) east, orient; east-wind; **— zu Nord**, east by north. **—en**, *m.* (**—ens**) east the east, orient. **—er**, *see* **Oster**. *Comp.* **—grenze**, *f.* eastern frontier. **—in'dienfahrer**, *m.* East-Indiaman (*Naut.*). **—meer**, *n.* (*poet.*), **—see**, *f.* Baltic (Sea). **—rand**, *m.* eastern horizon. **—see=waren**, *pl.* Baltic goods. **—wärts**, *adv.* eastward.

Osteolo'g, *m.* (**—en**, *pl.* **—en**) osteologist. **—ie'**, *f.* osteology, anatomy of the bones and bone-tissue.

O'ster, **—n**, *n. & f.pl.* Easter; Passover; **zu —n**, at Easter; **—n halten**, to receive the sacrament at Easter. *Comp.* **—abend**, *m.* Easter-eve. **—blume**, *f.* pasque-flower; daisy; daffodil; **(weiße)** wood-anemone. **—ei**, *n.* Easter-egg.

—feiertag, *m.* Easter-day. —ferien, *pl.* Easter vacation. —fest, *n.* Easter; —fest der Juden, Passover. —feuer, *n.* bonfire on Easter-eve. —fladen, —kuchen, *m.* Passover-bread. —lamm, *n.* paschal lamb. —lied, *n.* Easter hymn. —miete, *f.*, —zins, *m.* rent due at Easter. —palme, *f.* Paschal palm *or* bough. —programm, *n.* (*in schools*) prospectus of school issued at Easter, to which is usually prefixed a scientific treatise by one of the teaching staff. —tag, *m.* Easter Sunday; der zweite —tag, Easter Monday. —woche, *f.* Easter week; holy week. —zeit, *f.* Eastertide.

Ö'st—erlich, *adj.* Paschal, Easter. —lich, *adj.* eastern, easterly, oriental.

Oszillie'r—en, *v.n.* (*aux.* h.) to oscillate. —ung, *f.* oscillation.

Ot'ter, *f.* (*pl.* —n) adder; viper (*B.*). II. *f.* (*pl.* —n) otter. *Comp.* —balg, *m.* otter's skin. fang, *m.* otter-hunting. —(n)=gezücht, *n.* generation of vipers (*B.*). —gift, *n.* poison of a viper, viper's sting.

Oval'werk, *n.* oval chuck (*of a lathe*).

Oxal'säure, *f.* oxalic acid.

Ox'hoft, *n.* (—(e)s, *pl.* —e) hogshead.

Oxy'd, *n.* (—(e)s, *pl.* —e) oxide. —ie'ren, *v.a.* & *n.* (*aux.* h. & s.) to oxidize. —hydrat, *n.* hydroxide. —ie'rung, *f.* oxidation. —u'l, *n.* (—uls, *pl.* —ule) protoxide; Eisen —ul, ferrous oxide.

O'zean, *m.* (—s, *pl.* —e) ocean; der große *or* stille —, the Pacific; der atlantische —, the Atlantic; jenseits des atlantischen —s, transatlantic; zum — gehörig, —isch, oceanic. *Comp.* —dampfer, *m.* Atlantic (*etc.*) liner. —fahrt, *f.* ocean sailing.

Ozo'n, *n.* (—s) ozone; in — verwandeln, to ozonify.

P

Words not found under P should be looked for under B.

P, p, *n.* P, p; *for abbr., see the Index of abbreviations at the end of the German-English part.*

Paar, I. *adj.* even; like, matching, correlevant; diese Handschuhe sind kein —, these gloves are not fellows; — oder unpaar, odd or even; *used with* ein *as an ind. & indec. num. adj.*, ein *being also indec.*, some, a few; man trifft dort immer ein — Leute, one always meets a few people there; Herr N. hat ein — mal nach Ihnen gefragt, Mr. N. has asked for you several times; mit ein — Worten, in a few words; in ein — Tagen, in a few days; er schoß ein paar Tauben, he shot a few pigeons. II. *n.* (—s, *pl.* —e) pair, couple; brace; ein Paar Tauben *or* ein Tauben —, a pair of pigeons, 2 doves; ein — Pistolen, a brace of pistols; ein — Strümpfe, a pair of stockings; es ist ein schönes —, they are a handsome couple; — und —, — bei —, two and two, in couples; sie werden wohl ein — werden, it looks like a match; ein glücklich liebend —, a happy couple (of lovers); zu —en treiben, to scatter, to rout completely. —ig, *adj.* *Comp.* —weise, *adv.* by pairs, in couples; —weise gehen, to walk two and two. —zeit, *f.* pairing time.

Paa'r—en, *v.* I. *a.* to pair, sort, match; to pair, couple. II. *r.* to pair, couple (*as birds*); to unite; to join on to; gepaart, conjugate (*Bot.*), paired. —ung, *f.* coupling, copulation.

Pabst, *see* Papst.

Pacht, *m.* (—es, *pl.* —e), (*usually*) *f.* (*pl.* —en) tenure, lease; rent; in — geben, to let on lease; in — nehmen, to take a lease of; in — haben, to have on lease; ein —, der zu jeder Zeit aufgehoben werden kann, a tenancy at will. —bar, *adj.* farmable, tenantable. —en, *v.a.* to take a lease of, to farm, rent. —er, *see* Pächter. —lich, *adj.* & *adv.* on lease. —ung, *f.* taking on lease, farming; leasehold estate. *Comp.* —bauer, *m.* tenant-farmer. —besitz, *m.* tenure on lease. —brief, —kontrakt, —vertrag, *m.* lease; deed of conveyance. —geld, *n.* rent. —grundstück, *n.* tenement. —gut, *n.*, —hof, *m.* farm, leasehold estate. —herr, *m.* landlord. —leute, *pl.* tenants, tenantry. —weise, *adv.* on lease. —zins, *m.* rent.

Päch'ter, *m.* (—s, *pl.* —) farmer, tenant, lessee; — auf willkürlichen Widerruf, tenant at will. —schaft, *f.* tenancy; tenantry.

Pacifizie'ren, *v.a.* to pacify.

Paciß—e'nt, *m.*; die —en, the contracting parties. —ie'ren, *v.n.* to make a contract.

Pack, I. *m.* (—es, *pl.* —e, Pä'cke; *dim.* Päck'chen) packet, parcel; bundle, bale; baggage (*Mil.*); ein — Papiere, a file *or* bundle of papers; mit Sack und —, with bag and baggage. II. *n.* (—es) the common throng, rabble, pack; — schlägt sich, — verträgt sich, the crowd are foes one minute and friends the next. —en, *m.* (—ens, *pl.* —en) bale.

Packa'ge, *f.* mob, rabble (*vulg.*).

Pa'ck—en, *v.* I. *a.* to pack (*up*); to stow away; to lay hold of, seize, grasp; ich kann dir nicht sagen, wie es mich gepackt hat, I cannot tell you what a hold it has taken upon me, how much it affected me. II. *r.*; —' dich! be gone! get away! clear out! —end, *adj.* thrilling. —er, *m.* (—ers, *pl.* —er) packer; seizer; wholesale commission agent (*in the Black Forest*); boar-hound. —erei', *f.* packing up; baggage. *Comp.* —an, *m.* large dog (*coll.*). —bindfaden, *m.* cord, twine. —garn, *n.* pack-thread. —esel, *m.* pack-ass; drudge, fag. —haus, *n.* baggage warehouse; packing-room. —hof, *m.* custom-house; bonded warehouse. —kammer, *f.* parcels-office, cloakroom, goods-office. —kasten, *m.* packing case; boot (*of a carriage*). —korb, *m.* hamper. —kosten, *pl.* charges for packing. —leinwand, *f.* pack-cloth, sacking. —maschine, *f.* bundling press, packing press. —nadel, *f.* packing-needle. —papier, *n.* wrapping paper, (strong) brown paper. —pferd, *n.* pack-horse; baggage-horse. —raum, *m.* packing-room; stowage (*Naut.*). —sattel, *m.* pack-saddle. —träger, *m.* porter. —wagen, *m.* baggage-waggon; goods-van. —wesen, *n.* everything relating to baggage *or* packing. —zeug, *n.* materials used in packing.

Pädago'g, *m.* (—en, *pl.* —en) pedagogue. —ik, *f.* pedagogy. —isch, *adj.* educational. —ium, *n.* (—iums, *pl.* —ien) secondary school (*usually a private educational institution*), academy, cramming establishment.

Pad'de, *f.* (*pl.* —n) (*dial.*) frog; toad.

Pad'deln, *v.n.* (*aux.* h.) to paddle.

Paff, I. *m.* (—s, *pl.* —e) bang, pop; whiff. II. *int.* pop! bang! piff —! pop, bang! ganz — sein, to be utterly astonished *or* amazed (*coll.*). —en, *v.n.* (*aux.* h.) to pop; (*also v.a.*) to puff, whiff; to emit whiffs (*of smoke*); daß es (nur so) —t, with a vengeance (*vulg.*).

Pa'ge, *m.* (—n, *pl.* —n) page; dress-holder (*obs.*).

Pa'gin—a, *f.* (*pl.* —as) page (*of a book*); folio. —ie'ren, *v.a.* to page, to mark *or* number the pages.

Pago'de, *f.* (*pl.* —n) pagoda. *Comp.* —n=baum, *m.* sacred fig of India.

Pah! *int.* pshaw! pooh!

Pair, *m.* (—s, *pl.* —s) peer. —in, *f.* peeress. —ie', (*pl.* —ieen), —schaft, *f.* (*pl.* —schaften) peerage. *Comp.* —s=kammer, *f.* House of Lords. —s=schub, *m.* nomination of new peers (*for political purposes*), creation of peers.

Pa'ken, *v.n.* (*aux.* **h.**) to quack (*as ducks*).
Pake't, *n.* (—s, *pl.* —e) packet; parcel (*not a letter*). *Comp.* **—beförderung**, *f.* parcels-delivery, carrying trade. **—boot**, *n.* packet(-boat). **—post**, *f.* parcel-post.
Pakt, *m.* (—s, *pl.* —e), **—um**, *n.* (—ums, *pl.* —a), **—io'n**, *f.* agreement, compact, covenant. **—ie'ren**, *v.n.* (*aux.* **h.**) to covenant, agree (*on*), to come to terms (*about*).
Pa'lankin, *m.* (—s, *pl.* —s & —e) palanquin.
Paläo—graphie', *f.* palæography. **—ntolo'=gisch**, *adj.* palæontological.
Pala'st, *m.* (—es, *pl.* **Paläs'te**) palace. *Comp.* **—artig**, *adj.* palatial. **—dame**, *f.* lady in waiting, lady of the bed-chamber. **—vorsteher**, *m.* prefect of a palace.
Palati'n, *m.* (—s, *pl.* —), **—us**, *m.* (count) palatine.
Pa'letot, *m.* (—s, *pl.* —s) overcoat, great-coat. *Comp.* **—marder**, *m.* thief who steals overcoats.
Palet'te, *f.* (*pl.* —n) pallet, palet(te).
Palis(s)an'der=holz, *n.* rosewood.
Pal'lasch, *m.* (—es, *pl.* —e) broadsword, cut-and-thrust sword.
Pallisa'd—e, *f.* (*pl.* —en) palisade. **—ie'ren**, *v.a.* to fence in, palisade. *Comp.* **—en=ver=schanzung**, *f.* stockade.
Palliati'v, *adj.* palliative.
Pal'li—um, *n.* (—ums, *pl.* —en) pallium; pall.
1**Pal'm—e**, *f.* (*pl.* —en) palm(-tree); palm-branch; palm-leaf; palm, triumph (*fig.*). **—ig**, *adj.* covered with palms. *Comp.* **—(en)=grau=pen**, *pl.*, **—(en)=mehl**, *n.* sago. **—(en)=gewächse**, *pl.* palms. **—(en)=öl**, *n.* palm-oil. **—i'n=säure**, *f.* palmic acid. **—sonntag**, *m.* Palm Sunday. **—woche**, *f.* Passion week.
2**Pal'me**, *f.* (*pl.* —n) palm (*measure*); hand-breadth (*obs.*).
Pamps, *m.* pap (*coll.*). **—(s)en**, *v.a.* to stuff (*coll.*).
Panacee', *f.* (*pl.* —en) panacea.
Pandek'ten, *pl.* pandects.
Pandu'r, *m.* (—en, *pl.* —en) Pandour (*orig. South Slavonic irregular of the Austrian army noted for marauding and cruelty, now incorporated in the army*).
Panee'l, *n.* (—s, *pl.* —e), **—e**, *f.* (*pl.* —en) panel; wainscot.
Panie'r, *n.* (—s, *pl.* —e) banner, standard.
Pa'n—ik, *f.* (—iken) panic. **—isch**, *adj.*; **—ischer Schrecken**, panic.
Panis'brief, *m.* letter of sustenance (*obs.*).
Panop'tikum, *n.* (—s, *pl.* —s) panopticum; **— in London**, Madame Tussaud's.
Pan'se, *f.* (*pl.* —n), **—n**, **Pan'ze—n**, *m.* (—ns, *pl.* —n) first stomach of ruminants; paunch.
Panthe—is'mus, *m.* Pantheism. **—is'tisch**, *adj.* Pantheistic.
Pan'ther, *m.* (—s, *pl.* —) panther.
Panti'ne, *f.* (*pl.* —n) clog, patten.
Pantof'fel, *m.* (—s, *pl.* —, *better than* —n) slipper; pope's sandal *or* shoe; **in —n**, in slippers; **dem Papste den — küssen**, to kiss the pope's toe; **unter dem — stehen**, to be henpecked, to be under petticoat government, to be too much married (*coll.*). *Comp.* **—baum**, *m.* cork-tree. **—held**, *m.* henpecked husband. **—holz**, *n.* cork. **—regiment**, *n.* petticoat government.
Pantomi'm—e, *m.* (—en, *pl.* —en) pantomime actor; buffoon. **—e**, *f.* (*pl.* —en) pantomime; dumb show. **—isch**, *adj.* pantomimic.
Pant'schen, *v.n.* & *v.a.* to mix up, meddle. *See* **Man(t)schen**.
Pan'zer, *m.* (—s, *pl.* —) cuirass, coat of mail; iron-clad, man-of-war; iron-plates. *Comp.* **—ärmel**, *n.* vambrace. **—drehturm**, *m.* movable iron-clad tower. **—handschuh**, *m.* gauntlet. **—hemd(e)**, *n.* shirt of mail, coat of mail. **—kette**, *f.* carcanet. **—klinge**, *f.* rapier. **—kreuzer**, *m.* armoured cruiser, large cruiser. **—macher**, *m.* armourer. **—masche**, *f.* link of chain-mail. **—reiter**, *m.* cuirassier. **—rock**, *m.* coat of mail. **—schiff**, *n.* armour-plated ship, iron-clad. **—zug**, *m.* armoured train.
Pan'zer—n, *v.* I. *a.* to arm with a coat of mail. II. *r.* to put on mail armour; to arm oneself (*against*); **gepanzert**, mail-clad; **ein gepan=zerter Zug**, an armoured train; **—brechende Stahlgranaten**, steel shells that will pierce the coating of armoured trains *or* ironclads. **—ung**, *f.* armour-plating.
Päo'nie, *f.* (*pl.* —en) peony.
Papagei', *m.* (—s, —en, *pl.* —en) parrot; **kleiner —**, parrakeet; (*fam.*) Polly, Poll, Jacko; **wie ein — schwätzen**, to prate like a parrot. *Comp.* **—taucher**, *m.* puffin. **—weibchen**, *n.* female parrot.
Pap'chen, *n. dim. of* **Papagei**, Polly, Poll.
Papie'r *n.* (—s, *pl.* —e) paper; document; (*pl.*) papers, notes, bills, securities; **zu — bringen**, to write down; **sich nur auf dem —e schlagen**, to fight only with pen and ink; **Staats —e**, government bonds, stocks; **gemachtes —**, bills ready for endorsement; **— ist geduldig**, paper does not blush; **gern zög' ich Gewinn vom —e**, I should like to speculate in shares and securities. **—en**, *adj.* made of paper; papery, paper-like; paper; **—ener Stil**, soulless *or* unnatural, artificial style. *Comp.* **—abgänge**, *pl.* waste-paper. **—adel**, *m.* patent nobility. **—beschwerer**, *m.* paper-weight. **—blatt**, *n.*, **—bogen**, *m.* sheet of paper. **—düte**, *f.* paper bag. **—drache**, *m.* kite. **—fabrikation**, *f.* manufacture of paper. **—geld**, *n.* paper money *or* currency; bank note(s), cheque(s). **—gulden**, *m.* (paper) florin. **—händler**, *m.* stationer; paper-merchant. **—handlung**, *f.*, **—laden**, *m.* stationer's shop. **—korb**, *m.* waste-paper basket. **—maché'**, *n.* papier-maché. **—mäkler**, *m.* bill-broker. **—masse**, *f.* paper pulp; *see* **—maché**. **—schnitzel**, *m.* scrap of paper. **—spekulant**, *m.* stock-jobber. **—staude**, *f.* papyrus. **—stempelpresse**, *f.* embossing press. **—streifen**, *m.* web of paper. **—tapete**, *f.* paper-hanging. **—umlauf**, *m.* paper currency. **—valuta**, *f.* paper value. **—ware**, *f.* stationery; **(feine)** fancy stationery. **—währung**, *f.* value of a bill of exchange, bank-note. **—wäsche**, *f.* paper cuffs and collars.
Papillo'te, *f.* (*pl.* —n) curl-paper.
Papi—s'mus, *m.* popery. **—s'tisch**, *adj.* popish.
Papp, *m.* (—es, *pl.* —e), **—e**, *f.* pap; paste; **(geleimte)** pasteboard; stuff under the sheathing of a ship's bottom; dressing (*of cloth, etc.*); **in —e gebundenes Buch**, book in boards; **gekautschte —e**, mill-board; **nicht von —**, thorough(ly) (*coll.*); **er bekam Prügel, die waren nicht von —**, he got a good thrashing (*coll.*). **—en**, *adj.* pasteboard. **—icht** (*obs.*), **—ig**, *adj.* pappy, sticky, pasty. *Comp.* **—arbeit**, *f.* card-board work. **—band**, *n.* (binding in) boards. **—bogen**, *m.* sheet of cardboard. **—(en)=deckel**, *m.* pasteboard (cover). **—dose**, *f.*, **—kasten**, *m.*, **—schachtel**, *f.* bandbox; pasteboard box. **—en=presse**, *f.* mill-board press. **—en=stiel**, *m.* trifle; **um einen —enstiel**, for a mere song, dirt-cheap (*coll.*). **—er=lapapp!** *int.* (*fam.*) rubbish! nonsense! fiddlesticks! **—schädel**, *m.* blockhead (*coll.*).
Pap'pel, *f.* (*pl.* —n) poplar; marsh-mallow. **—n**, *adj.* of poplar wood. *Comp.* **—allee**, *f.*, **—gang**, *m.* avenue of poplars. **—espe**, *f.* aspen.
Pap'peln, *v.a.* to babble (*coll.*).
Päp'peln, *v.a.* to feed a child with pap, to bring a child up by hand *or* with the bottle.
Pap'pen, *v.a.* to (stick with) paste; to do card-board work.
Papst (*long* **a**), *m.* (—es, *pl.* **Päp'ste**) pope.

pontiff, Holy Father; W. C. (*coll.*). **—tum**, *n.* (**—tums**) papacy; popery; pontificate; papal dignity. *Comp.* **—krone**, *f.* tiara, triple crown. **—wahl**, *f.* election of a pope; conclave (of cardinals); students' drinking game. **—würde**, *f.* papal dignity, papacy, pontificate.

Päp'st—in, *f.* female pope; **—in Johanna**, Pope Joan. **—isch**, *adj.* popish. **—ler**, *m.* (**—lers**, *pl.* **—ler**) papist. **—lerei'**, *f.* popery; popish tendencies. **—lich**, *adj.* papal, papistical, pontifical; **—licher Stuhl**, Holy See.

Para'—bel, *f.* (*pl.* **—beln**) parable; simile; parabola (*Geom.*). **—bo'lisch**, *adj. & adv.* parabolic; figurative, in form of a parable. **—dig'ma**, *n.* (**—digmas**, *pl.* **—digmen**, **—digmata**) paradigm.

Para'd—e, *f.* (*pl.* **—en**) parade; display; military review; parry, ward (*Fenc.*); **—e über ein Regiment abhalten**, to pass a regiment in review; **eine —e abnehmen**, to hold a review. **—ie'ren**, *v.n.* (*aux.* **h.**) to parade, make a show; **mit etwas —ie'ren**, to parade, show off, make a show of s. th. *Comp.* **—e=anzug**, *m.* full dress *or* uniform, review order. **—e=aufzug**, *m.* review. **—e=bett**, *n.* bed of state; **auf dem —ebett liegen**, to lie in state. **—e=marsch**, *m.* march past. **—e=pferd**, *n.* horse for review; object for show; picked scholar, show boy (*in schools*). **—e=platz**, *m.* parade ground. **—e=schritt**, *m.* slow (*or* ordinary) pace. **—e=stellung**, *f.* the drawing up of troops on parade. **—e=stückchen**, *n.*; **das ist sein —estückchen**, that is his show-piece. **—e=zimmer**, *n.* state apartment.

Paradie's, *n.* (**—(s)es**, *pl.* **—(s)e**) paradise; upper gallery, the gods (*sl.*). **—(s)isch**, *adj.* heavenly; delightful. *Comp.* **—feige**, *f.* banana. **—vogel**, *m.* bird of Paradise.

Parado'x, I. *adj.* paradoxical. II. *n.* (**—es**, *pl.* **—en**) paradox.

Paralle'l, *adj.* parallel. **—e**, *f.* parallel (*Math.*, *Fort.*); parallel passage; comparison. *Comp.* **—bibel**, *f.* reference Bible. **—cötus**, *m.* parallel division *or* set. **—kreis**, *m.* parallel (*of latitude*). **—lineal**, *n.* parallel ruler. **—linie**, *f.* parallel (line). **—ogra'mm**, *n.* parallelogram; **—ogramm der Kräfte**, parallelogram of forces; **das Wattsche —ogramm**, Watt's parallel motion. **—stelle**, *f.* parallel passage, literary parallel. **—trapez**, *n.* trapezium.

Paralysie'ren, *v.a.* to paralyze.

Parasi't, *m.* (**—en**, *pl.* **—en**) parasite.

Para't, *adj.* prepared, ready.

Pär'chen, *n.* (**—s**, *pl.* **—**) little pair; loving couple, lovers.

Pardau'tz! *interj.* bang! crash! there goes!

Par'd—el, *m.* (**—els**, *pl.* **—el**) leopard, panther. **—er**, *m.* (**—ers**, *pl.* **—er**) panther, leopard.

Pardo'n, *m.* (**—s**, *pl.* **—s**) pardon; quarter; **um — bitten**, to call for quarter.

Parenthe'se, *f.* (*pl.* **—n**) parenthesis.

Parfor'ce, *adv.* perforce. *Comp.* **—hund**, *m.* species of stag-hound. **—jagd**, *f.* hunting, coursing (*in England*). **—peitsche**, *f.* hunting-whip. **—ritt**, *m.* steeple-chase.

Parfu'm, *n.* (**—s**, *pl.* **—s**); **Parfü'm**, *n.* (**—(e)s**, *pl.* **—e**) perfume, scent. **—ie'ren**, *v.a.* to perfume, scent.

Pa'ri, *n.* (**—s**, *pl.* **—s**) & *adv.* par; **al — stehen**, to be at par.

[1]**Parie'r—en**, *v.a.& n.* (*aux.* **h.**) to parry, ward off (*Fenc.*); to stop (*a horse*), throw him on his haunches. **—ung**, *f.* parrying. *Comp.* **—stange**, *f.* bow *or* cross-bar of a sword-hilt.

[2]**Parie'ren**, *v.a.* (*aux.* **h.**) to obey, follow.

[3]**Parie'r—en**, *v.a.* to set like against like, to bet, wager. **—ung**, *f.* bet, wager (*obs.*).

Paritä't, *f.* parity, equality. **—isch**, *adj.* on a footing of equality; **—ische Schule**, undenominational *or* unsectarian school; **Preußen ist ein —ischer Staat**, in Prussia there is absolute religious equality.

Park, *m.* (**—(e)s**, *pl.* **—e**) park. *Comp.* **—anlagen**, *pl.* pleasure-grounds. **—aufseher**, *m.* park-keeper.

Parke'tt, *n.* (**—(e)s**, *pl.* **—e**) inlaid floor, parquetry (floor); (orchestra) stalls, reserved front seats in the pit; bar. **—ie'ren**, *v.a.* to inlay; **die Fußböden sind —iert**, the floors are inlaid. *Comp.* **—platz**, *m.* (orchestra) stall.

Parlame'nt, *n.* (**—(e)s**, *pl.* **—e**) parliament. **—ä'r**, *m.* (**—ärs**, *pl.* **—ärs**, **—äre**) (*officer with*) flag of truce. **—a'risch**, *adj.* parliamentary. **—ie'ren**, *v.n.* (*aux.* **h.**) to parley (*Mil.*). *Comp.* **—ä'r=schiff**, *n.* cartel-ship. **—s=akte**, *f.* act of parliament. **—s=anhänger**, *m.* parliamentarian. **—s=(mit)glied**, *n.* member of parliament (M.P.). **—s=ordnung**, *f.* parliamentary regulation(s).

Parodie', *f.* (*pl.* **—en**) parody. **—ren**, *v.a.* to parody.

Paro'le, *f.* (*pl.* **—n**) parole; password, watchword; **— d'honneur**, word of honour, parole. *Comp.* **—befehl**, *m.* order (*given at the muster*). **—buch**, *n.* order-book.

Part, *m. & n.* (**—(e)s**, *pl.* **—e**) part; share; **halb —!** I cry halves! **—ici'p**, **—ici'pium**, *n.* *see* **—izip**, **—izipium**. **—ie'll**, *adj. & adv.* partial. **—ie'ren**, *v.* I. *a.* to part, divide, distribute. II. *n.* (*aux.* **h.**) to shuffle; to cheat. **—i'kel**, *f.* (*pl.* **—ikeln**) particle. **—ikula'r**, *see* **Partikular**. **—isa'n**, *m.* (*pl.* **—isans**, **—isanen**) partisan. **—isa'ne**, *f.* (*pl.* **—isanen**) partisan, kind of halberd. **—itiv**, *adj.* (*pron.* **par'titiv**) partitive, distributive. **—itu'r**, *f.* score (*Mus.*). **—izi'p**, *n.* (**—izips**, *pl.* **—izipe**), **—izi'pium**, *n.* (**—izipiums**, *pl.* **—izipien**, **—icipia**) participle; **—icipium Präsentis**, present participle; **—icipium Perfecti Passivi**, past participle. **—izipia'l**, *adj.* participial. **—izipie'ren**, *v.n.* (*aux.* **h.**) to participate, share (**an einer S.**, in a th.). **—nerschaft**, *f.* partnership.

Partei', *f.* (*pl.* **—en**) party, part; party, detachment (*Mil.*); faction, party; side, plaintiff *or* defendant (*Law*); **— ergreifen, sich zu einer — schlagen**, to side with a p., to espouse a side; **außer — bleiben**, to remain neutral; **in einer Sache — sein**, to be an interested party; **in diesem Hause wohnen vier —en**, there are four families *or* households under this roof. **—en**, *v.r.* to split into parties; to side with. **—isch**, **—lich**, *adj.* partial, biassed, one-sided; factious. **—lichkeit**, *f.* partiality, bias. *Comp.* **—anhänglichkeit**, *f.* partisanship. **—führer**, *m.*, **—haupt**, *n.* leader of a party. **—gänger**, *m.* partisan; factionist; military adventurer; captain of freebooters. **—geist**, *m.* party spirit. **—genosse**, *m.* political friend, partisan. **—getriebe**, **—treiben**, *n.* party doings *or* concerns; political machinery *or* motives. **—los**, *adj.* impartial, neutral. **—losigkeit**, *f.* impartiality; neutrality. **—rücksichten**, *pl.* party considerations. **—süchtig**, *adj.* factious. **—wut**, *f.* frenzy of (contending) parties.

Parte'ke, *f.* (*pl.* **—n**) piece of bread (*obs.*)

Parter're, *n.* (**—s**, *pl.* **—s**) ground-floor; parterre, flower-border; pit (*Theat.*); **mein Studierzimmer ist —**, my study is on the ground-floor. *Comp.* **—publikum**, *n.* the pit (*Theat.*).

Partie', *f.* (*pl.* **—en**) parcel, lot; part; company; pleasure excursion; game (*of whist, etc.*); set (*tennis*); (matrimonial) match; parcel, lot (*C. L.*); **in —en von 6 bis 12 Stück**, in lots of from 6 to 12 pieces; **in —en billiger**, in lots *or* larger quantities cheaper; **eine — machen**, to go on an excursion, to make a trip; to play a game; **ich weiß, Sie machen sehr gern eine —**, I know you are fond of a rubber; **eine gute — machen**, to make a good match; **sie hat seinet-**

wegen mehrere —en ausgeschlagen, she has refused several offers for his sake; bei der, mit von der — sein, to be one of the company; — mit Spiel=vor, advantage set (*Tennis*). *Comp.* —geld, *n.* expenses (*for the table, cards, etc.*) at play; wir spielen nur ums —geld, we only play for the table (*Bill.*). —preise, *pl.* wholesale prices.

Partikular—isie'ren, *v.a.* to particularize. —is'mus, *m.* particularism. —i'st, *m.* (—is'ten, *pl.* —is'ten) separatist. *Comp.* —geschichte, *f.* history of a particular state *or* period. —recht, *n.* special law.

Partou't, *adv.* absolutely; by all means. *Comp.* —billet, *n.* ticket admitting to all performances or seats (*Theat.*).

Par'ze, *f.* (*pl.* —n) Fate; destiny, fate; die —n, the Fates, the weird sisters.

Parzel'l—e, *f.* (*pl.* —en) parcel, lot (*of ground*). —ie'ren, *v.a.* to parcel out, divide into lots.

Pasch, *m.* (—es, *pl.* —e) dice; doublets (*at dice*); einen — setzen, to make the numbers at each end the same (*dominoes*); — werfen (*or* paschen), to throw doublets (*at dice*).

Pa'scha, *m.* (—, —s, *pl.* —s) pasha, pacha.

Pa'sch—en, *v.a.* to smuggle. —er, *m.* (—ers, *pl.* —er) smuggler. *Comp.* —handel, *m.* smuggling trade.

Pascho'll! *int.* (*Russian*) get away! away with you! (*coll.*);—machen, to leave, make off (*coll.*).

Pas'pel, *m.* (—s, *pl.* —), *f.* (*pl.* —n) edging (*on a dress, etc.*). —n, *v.a.* to pipe (*a dress*).

Pasqui'll, *n.* (—s, *pl.* —e) lampoon, squib. — a'nt, *m.* (—an'ten, *pl.* —an'ten) lampooner. —ie'ren, *v.a.* & *n.* (*aux.* h.) to lampoon.

Paß, *m.* (—(s)ses, *pl.* Päs'se) pace, amble; pass, defile; passage, thoroughfare; haunt; narrows (*Naut.*); passport, papers, pass; measure; den — gehen, to amble, pace; einem den (Lauf) — geben, to send a p. about his business; *used adv'b'ly* = fitly, suitably, well; der Rock ist ihm (zu) —, the coat fits him; das kommt mir zu —, that is very opportune for me, that suits me downright (*coll.*); ihm sitzt die Mütze nicht recht zu —, he is cross *or* out of humour (*coll.*). —(ss)a'bel, *adj.* & *adv.* passable, tolerable. —(ss)a'ge, —(ss)agie'r, —(ss)en, —(ss)ie'ren, *see* Passage; Passagier, *rc.* — lich, *adj.* & *adv.* fit, suitable, proper. *Comp.* —amt, *n.* passport office. —brief, *m.* passport; permit. —gang, *m.* amble. —gänger, *m.* ambler, ambling nag. —karte, *f.* sea-chart; passport. —zwang, *m.* obligation to have a passport.

Passa'ge, *f.* (*pl.* —n) passage, thoroughfare; arcade, gallery; passage (*Mus., etc.*). *Comp.* —instrument, *n.* transit-instrument (*Astr.*).

Passagie'r, *m.* (—s, *pl.* —e) passenger, traveller; ein blinder —, stray passenger picked up on the way *or* who does not pay. *Comp.* — bureau, *n.* booking-office. —geld, *n.* fare. —gut, *n.* passenger's luggage. —stube, *f.* waiting-room. —zug, *m.* passenger train.

Passa'nt, *m.* (—en, *pl.* —en) passer-by.

Passat'wind, *m.* trade-wind.

Pas'sen, *v.* I. *n.* (*aux.* h.) to watch, wait for; to pass, not be able to play; to fit; to suit, be becoming; to correspond with; to harmonize with; — auf (*acc.*), to notice, to be attentive to, to watch, wait for; der Schlüssel paßt zum Schloß, the key fits the lock; er paßt in jede Gesellschaft, he is fit for any society; er paßt nicht zum Gelehrten, he will not do for a scholar; er paßt gar nicht zum Kaufmann, he will never make a business-man, he is not fitted for trade; das paßt sich nicht, that is not becoming; das paßt mir ausgezeichnet, that suits me admirably; das paßt in seinen Kram, that suits his purpose exactly; dies paßt nicht zur Sache, this is beside the question; es paßt zu seiner Rolle, it suits his part *or* character; das paßt, that will do; sie — zu einander, they are well matched *or* suit each other; wie das paßt! how nicely that suits! II. *r.* to be fit, proper, suitable, convenient. III. *a.* to adapt; to fit on. —d, *p.* & *adj.* fit, fitting, suitable; becoming, appropriate, seemly; opportune; to the purpose; das —de Wort, the right word; das —de Wort sagen, to say the right thing; für —d halten, to think proper.

Passie'rbar, *adj.* passable, traversable.

Passie'r—en, *v.n.* (*aux.* f.) to pass, travel over, through *or* across; to pass muster, be tolerable; to pass, be current; to come to pass, happen; nicht zu —en, impassable; —en für, to pass as; mag —en, it will (just) *or* may do; ich will ihn —en lassen, I won't stop him; was ist ihm —t? what has happened to him? (*coll.*); ist nichts Neues —t? is there no news? (*coll.*). *Comp.* —gewicht, *n.*, mint-allowance, tolerated deficiency. —schein, *m.* permit.

Pass—io'n, *f.* (*pl.* —ionen) passion. —ionie'=ren, *v.r.* to be passionately interested in; —ioniert, impassioned. —iv, *see* Passiv. *Comp.* —ions'=betrachtung, *f.* Lenten meditation. —ions'=brüder, *pl.* Passionists. — ions'=prediger, *m.* preacher in Passion week. —ions'=predigt, *f.* Good Friday sermon.

Pas'siv, I. *adj.* passive. II. *n.* (—s), —um, *n.* (—ums, *pl.* —a) passive voice; passive verb; (*pl.*) liabilities; passive debts (*C. L.*); Aktiva und —a, assets and liabilities (*C.L.*). —isch, *adv.* passively. —itä't, *f.* passivity.

Pas't—a, —e, *f.* (*pl.* —en) paste; paste (*jewels*). —e'l, *see* Paste(l). —et'chen, *n.* patty, little pasty. —e'te, *f.* (*pl.* —eten) pie; pastry; da haben wir die —ete! here's a pretty kettle of fish! *Comp.* —eten=bäcker, *m.* pastry-cook. —eten=bäckerei, *f.* pastry-cook's business. —eten=fleisch, *n.* meat baked in a pie; meat-pie.

Paste'll, *n.* (—s, *pl.* —e) pastel, crayon; in —, in crayon. *Comp.* —farben, *pl.* coloured crayons. —maler, *m.* drawer in crayons. —malerei, *f.* pastel-painting. —stift, *m.* crayon.

Pasti'che, *f.* (*pl.* —n) pasticcio.

Pastil'le, *f.* (*pl.* —n) pastil, lozenge.

Pastina'ke, *f.* (*pl.* —n) parsnip.

Pas'tor, (**Pasto'r,**) *m.* (—s, *pl.* Pasto'ren) pastor, clergyman, vicar, Protestant minister. —a'l, *adj.* pastoral. —a'le, *n.* (—ales, *pl.* ales) idyl; pastoral (*Mus., Eccl.*). —a't, *n.* (—ats, *pl.* —ate) pastorate, charge; incumbency. —in (*pron.* Pasto'rin), *f.* clergyman's wife. *Comp.* —al'=konferenz, *f.* clerical conference. —al'=schreiben, *n.* pastoral (*letter*). — at(s)'=haus, *n.* parsonage, vicarage; manse.

Pat'chen, *n.* (—s, *pl.* —) god-child.

Pa't—e, *m.* (—en, *pl.* —en), —e, —in, *f.* godparent, godfather, godmother; sponsor; godchild. *Comp.* —en=geld, —en=geschenk, *n.*, —en=groschen, —en=pfennig, *m.* sponsor's christening gift. —en=kind, *n.* god-child. —en=stelle, *f.* sponsorship; bei einem Kinde — enstelle vertreten, to stand sponsor (godfather *or* godmother).

Pate'nt, I. *n.* (—s, *pl.* —e) letters patent; patent, charter; commission (*Mil.*); ein — nehmen, to take out a patent. II. *adj.* smart, spruce, elegant (*coll.*). —ier'bar, *adj.* patentable. —ie'ren, *v.a.* to patent; to grant a patent to. *Comp.* —amt, *n.* patent-office. —anmeldung, *f.* application for a patent. —anwalt, *m.* patent solicitor *or* agent. —beschreibung, *f.* specification. —brief, *m.* letters patent; license. —fatzke, *m.* a man dressed with exaggerated elegance; dandy (*coll.*). — listen, *pl.* register or patents. —schutz, m. protection of property in inventions; patent laws. —träger, m. patentee. —verschluß, m. patent stopper, screw stopper, patent cork.

Paternos'ter, n. (—s, pl. —) paternoster; every tenth bead in a rosary; rosary; chaplet (*Arch.*). *Comp.* —**draht**, m. Bologna wire. —**kunst**, f., —**werk**, n. chain-pump, dredger.

Path—e'tisch, adj. & adv. pathetic. —**olo'g**, m. (—ologen, pl. —ologen) pathologist. —**olo'gisch**, adj. pathological.

Patie'nt, m. (—en, pl. —en), —**in**, f. patient; —en in (ärztlicher) Behandlung, patients under (medical) treatment.

Pa'tina, f. patina, verd-antique, ærugo (nobilis); mit — überzogen, æruginous.

Patri—archa'lisch, adj. patriarchal. —**mo'nium**, n. (—monium, pl. —monien) patrimony. —**o't**, m. (—oten, pl. —oten) patriot. —**o'tisch**, adj. & adv. patriotic. —**oti's'mus**, m. patriotism; in —otismus machen, set up for a patriot; Hurrah—otismus, jingoism. *Comp.* —**oten=liga**, f. League of patriots.

Patris'tik, f. patristic learning *or* theology, patristics.

Patri'zier, m. (—s, pl. —) patrician. —**haft**, **Patri'zisch**, adj. patrician. —**tum**, n. (—tums) patricianism; patricians (*coll.*). *Comp.* —**herrschaft**, f. aristocracy, aristocratic government.

Patro'n, m. (—s, pl. —e) fellow; patron; patron saint; patron (*of a living*); fellow (*often in a bad sense*); Schiffs—, master, owner of a ship; ein unzuverlässiger —, a shifty fellow; lustiger —, jolly fellow. —**a't**, n. (—ats, pl. —ate) advowson, patronage. —**e**, *see under* Patrone. —**in**, f. patroness. —**y'mikon**, n. (—ymikons, pl. —ymika, —ymiken) patronymic. —**y'misch**, adj. patronymic. *Comp.* —**ats'=berechtigt**, adj. having the gift of a living, the right of presentation. —**ats'=pfarre**, f. collative living.

Patro'ne, f. (pl. —n) pattern; pasteboard cover; cartridge, cartouch (*Mil.*); stencil; — für jeden, round of ammunition; das —n=malen, stencilling process; mit —n malen, to stencil. *Comp.* —**n=büchse**, f. cartridge-box. —**n=hülse**, f. cartridge-case, empty cartridge. —(**n**)=**tasche**, f. cartridge-box, pouch.

Patrouil'l—e, f. (pl. —en) patrol (*Mil.*). —**ie'ren**, v.n. (*aux.* h. & s.) to patrol.

Patsch! I. *int.* slap! pop! II. m. (—es, pl. —e) smack, clap, smash; dirt, mud (*coll.*). —**e**, f. (pl. —en) loud blow, slap, clap; flap; beater; (*little*) hand; mire, mud; dilemma, difficulty; einen in die —e bringen, to get a p. into a scrape (*coll.*); in der —e sitzen, to be in a fix (*coll.*); einen in der —e sitzen lassen, to leave a p. in the lurch (*coll.*).

Pat'sch—en, v. I. n. (*aux.* h. & s.) to slap, smack; to paddle, splash (*in water, mud, etc.*); to patter down (*of rain*). II. a. to splash; to smack, slap; to pat, tap; er —te ihm das Wasser ins Gesicht, he splashed the water in his face. *Comp.* —**füßig**, adj. web-footed. —**hand**, f., —**händchen**, n. tiny hand (*of babies*). —(**e**)**naß**, adj. wet to the skin.

Pat'schuli, n. (—s) patchouli.

Patt, *indec. adj.*; — machen *or* setzen, to stalemate (*Chess*); — sein, to be stalemated.

Pat'te, f. (pl. —n) flap (*of a coat*).

Pat'zig, adj. & adv. snappish; saucy; insolent, pert (*in answering*); — thun, to behave insolently (*coll.*). —**keit**, f. arrogance.

Pauk—a'nt, m. (—an'ten, pl. —an'ten) duellist. —**e**, f. (pl. —en) kettle-drum (*Mus.*); tympanum (*Anat.*); coffee-roaster; speech, rebuke (*sl.*); einem eine —e halten, to rebuke a p.; türkische —e, big drum; der —e ein Loch machen, to put an end to a th. abruptly, to cut the Gordian knot; die —e hat ein Loch, there is an end to their intimacy; einem eine —e halten, to lecture a p., blow s.o. up (*sl.*).

Pau'k—en, v. I. n. (*aux.* h.) to beat the kettledrums; to speechify; (sich) mit einem —en, to fight a duel with a p., to have a round with the gloves *or* foils, to fence (*Sl.*). II. a. to beat, thrash, drub; er —t die Kanzel, he thumps the pulpit. —**er**, m. (—ers, pl. —er) kettle-drummer; duellist; school-teacher (*sl.*). —**erei'**, f. (pl. —ereien) row; thrashing; duel (*sl.*). —**i'st**, m. (—is'ten, pl. —is'ten) player of the kettle-drum. *Comp.* —**arzt**, m. doctor present at a students' duel. —**boden**, m. fencing-floor. —**en=fell**, n. skin of the kettle-drum; tympanum. —**en=gang**, m. ear-duct. —**en=klang**. —**en=schall**, m. sound of the kettle-drum. —**en=schlägel**, m. kettle-drumstick. —**en=wirbel**, m. roll of the kettle-drum. —**handschuh**, m. fencing-glove. —**zeug**, n. rapiers.

Pauperis'mus, m. pauperism.

Paus'—backe, f. chubby face; chubby-faced person. —**backig**, —**bäckig**, adj. chubby-faced.

Pausch, (**Paus**,) &c. *see* Bausch, (Baus,) &c. —**en**, I. v.a. to beat small; to melt. II. *subst.n.* liquation.

Pau's—e, f. (pl. —en) pause, stop, rest; rest, interval (*Mus.*); ganze —e, semibreve-rest; halbe —e, minim rest; viertel —e, crotchet rest. —**ie'ren**, v.n. (*aux.* h.) to pause.

Pau's—en, v.a. to trace, calk, counter-draw. —**leinwand**, f. tracing cloth. —**papier**, n. tracing paper. —**zeichnung**, f. counter-drawing, calking.

Pa'vian, m. (—s, pl. —e) baboon; blockhead.

Pa'villon, m. (—s, pl. —s) pavilion.

Pech, n. (—es) pitch; cobbler's wax; ill luck (*coll.*); scrape; das ist —! how annoying! horrendes —, shocking bad luck (*coll.*); wer — angreift, besudelt sich, who touches pitch will be defiled (*prov.*). —**ig**, adj. bituminous; pitchy. —**ler**, m. (—lers, pl. —ler) pitch-maker. —**ö's**, adj. unlucky, unfortunate (*sl.*). *Comp.* —**artig**, adj. bituminous. —**draht**, m. cobbler's thread, waxed end. —**fackel**, f. torch. —**finster**, adj. pitch-dark. —**holz**, n. resinous wood. —**kohle**, f. bituminous coal. —**kranz**, m. pitch ring *or* wreath. —**pflaster**, n. pitch-plaster. —**ra'benschwarz**, adj. pitch black. —**steinkohle**, f. jet. —**tanne**, f. common spruce; American pitch-pine. —**tonne**, f. tar-barrel. —**vogel**, m. unlucky person (*coll.*).

Peda'l, n. (—s, pl. —e) pedal; legs, feet. *Comp.* —**harfe**, f. double-actioned harp.

Peda'nt, m. (—en, pl. —en) pedant. —**erie'**, f., —**is'mus**, m. pedantry. —**in**, f. pedantic woman. —**isch**, adj. pedantic; precise, crotchety.

Pede'll, m. (—s, pl. —e) beadle; proctor's man, bull-dog (*Univ. sl.*).

Pe'gel, n. (—s, pl. —) water-gauge, water-mark post; liquid measure. —**stand**, m. water-mark. —**n**, v.a. & n. (*aux.* h.) to take the soundings, sound; to gauge.

Peil, *see* Pegel. —**en**, v.a. to sound; to gauge; to measure; das Land —en, to take the bearings of the coast; die Sonne —en, to take the sun's altitude. *Comp.* —**holz**, n., —**stock**, m. gauge-rod of a pump. —**kompaß**, m. azimuth compass. —**lot**, n. plummet.

Pein, f. pain, agony, torture. —**igen**, v.a. to torture; to rack; to torment, harass, annoy. —**iger**, m. (—igers, pl. —iger) torturer, tormentor; plague. —**igung**, f. tormenting; torment. —**lich**, adj. painful, distressing; tormenting; difficult; minute, over-nice; capital, penal, on pain of death; —liche Frage, awkward question; rack, torture; —liche Klage, action for trespass; —liche Gerichtsbarkeit, criminal jurisdiction; einen in —liche Untersuchung nehmen, to try a p. for his life; —liche Unruhe, anxiety, worry; —lich befragen, to examine by torture; —lich genau, scrupulously exact. —lichkeit, *f.* painfulness; criminal jurisdiction; minute exactness.

Peit'sche, *f.* (*pl.* —n) whip, lash, scourge; cat-o'-nine-tails; mit der — klatschen, knallen, to crack a whip. *Comp.* —n=griff, *m.* whip-handle. —n=hieb, *m.* lash with a whip. —n=riemen, *m.*, —n=schnur, *f.* thong of a whip.

Peit'schen, *v.a.* to (horse)whip, flog, scourge, lash; to sweep *or* drive along.

Peke'sche, *f.* (*pl.* —n) laced *or* frogged coat (*obs.*).

Pelleri'ne, *f.* cape; —n=mantel (für Herren), ulster.

Pe'likan, *m.* (—s, *pl.* —e) pelican.

Pel'l—e, *f.* (*pl.* —en) skin, peel (*coll.*). —en, *v.a.* & *v.n.* to peel, to skin (*coll.*); wie aus dem Ei gepellt, spick and span; — Kartoffeln, potatoes in their jackets *or* skin.

Pelluciditä't, *f.* diaphaneity, pellucidity.

Peloto'n, *n.* (—s, *pl.* —s) file, platoon (*Mil.*). *Comp.* —feuer, *n.* file-firing.

Pelz, *m.* (—es, *pl.* —e) pelt, fur; furred coat; skin (*coll.*); skim (*on milk, etc.*); mit — füttern, to line with fur; einem den — ausklopfen, to give a p. a good thrashing; einem Läuse in den — setzen, to play a p. a dirty trick; einem (dicht) auf den — rücken, to press a p. hard (*coll.*); einem den — waschen, to blow a p. up; einem (eins) auf den — brennen, to fire at a p.; Faul—, lazybones. —en, I. *v.a.* to graft, inoculate. II. *adj.* furred, fur. —ig, *adj.* furry. —icht, *adj.* cottony (*Bot.*). *Comp.* —besetzt, *adj.* trimmed with fur. —futter, *n.* fur-lining. —handel, *m.* fur-trade. —händler, *m.* furrier. —kragen, *m.* fur-lined collar; fur-tippet. —mantel, *m.* fur-lined cloak. —ware, *f.*, —werk, *n.* furriery, furs.

Pen'del, *n.* & *m.* (—s, *pl.* —) pendulum. —n, *v.a.* to oscillate. *Comp.* —länge, *f.* length of pendulum. —schwingung, *f.* oscillation. —stange, *f.* pendulum-rod. —uhr, *f.* pendulum clock.

Penetra'nt, *adj.* penetrating, intense, strong (*especially with regard to smell*).

Penn—a'l, *n.* (—als, *pl.* —ale, —äle) pen-case; (*also m. pl.* —äler) (grammar-)school; grammar-school boy (*stud. sl.*). —ä'ler, *m.* schoolboy (*coll.*). —alis'mus, *m.* fagging(-system) (*coll.*).

Pen'n—e, *f.* (*pl.* —en) tramp lodging-house. —en, *v.n.* to sleep in the open air (*sl.*) *Comp.* —bruder, *m.* homeless tramp who camps out in the open (*coll.*).

Pensio'n, *f.* (*pl.* —en) pension; boarding-house; boarding-school; board and lodging; mit — verabschiedet, pensioned off. —ä'r, *m.* (—ärs, *pl.* —äre) pensioner; boarder. —a't, *n.* (—ats, *pl.* —ate) boarding-school. —ie'ren, *v.a.* to put on half-pay, pension (*off*). —ie'r=te(r), *m.* pensioner. —ie'rung, *f.* pensioning off, superannuation. *Comp.* —s=anstalt, *f.*, *see* —at. —s=beitrag, *m.* sum deducted from pay for the pension fund. —s=berechtigung, *f.* right to a pension. —s=liste, *f.* retired list. —s=stand, *m.*; in den —sstand treten, to be pensioned off, to retire on a pension.

Pen'f—um, *n.* (—ums, *pl.* —a) task, lesson; course; curriculum.

Pen'taeder, *n.* (—s, *pl.* —) pentahedron.

Per, *prep.* by, *etc.*; zweimal — Jahr, twice a year; — Kahn, by boat; — Post, by post; — Achse, by land(-carriage), by waggon; — Adresse des Herrn Professor W. B., care of Professor W. B.

Pe'reat! I. *int.*; — die Traurigkeit! — tristitia! away with sadness! (*stud.'s sl.*); pereant die Pfaffen! down with the priests! II. *n.* (—s, *pl.* —s); einem ein — bringen, to serenade a p. with rough music, to drink confusion to a p.; ein — dem...! groans for...!

Peremptо'risch, *adj.* & *adv.* peremptory.

Perennie'rend, *adj.*; —e Pflanze, perennial.

Perfe'kt, I. *adj.* perfect. II. —um, *n.* (—ums, *pl.* —a) perfect tense. *Comp.* —bildung, *f.* formation of the perfect.

Perfi'd—(e), *adj.* perfidious, insidious. —ie', *f.* (*pl.* —ieen), —itä't, *f.* perfidy, perfidiousness; insidiousness.

Pergame'nt, (**Pergame'n**, *n. rare* (*poet.*),) *n.* (—(e)s, *pl.* —e) parchment; feines —, vellum. —en, *adj.* (of) parchment. *Comp.* —ähnlich, —artig, *adj.* parchment-like; membranous. —band, *m.* parchment cover; book bound in parchment *or* vellum; membranous ligament. —bereiter, *m.* parchment-maker. —handschrift, *f.* vellum manuscript. —papier, *n.* thick vellum. —rolle, *f.* parchment scroll.

Perikar'pi—um, *n.* (*pl.* —en) pericarp.

Perio'd—e, *f.* (*pl.* —en) period; phrase, period (*Mus.*); repetend (*Mus.*); catamenia, menses (*Med.*); eine mehrzahlige —e, a circulating period. —isch, *adj.* & *adv.* periodic(al); —ischer Dezimalbruch, recurring decimal; —ische Zeitschrift, periodical (magazine). *Comp.* —en=bau, *m.* structure of a period, style.

Peri—pate'tiker, *m.* (—patetikers, *pl.* —patetiker) peripatetic. —pate'tisch, *adj.* peripatetic. —petie', *f.* the turning point of the dramatic action. —pherie', *f.* periphery, circumference.

Perkussio'n, *f.* (*pl.* —en) percussion. *Comp.* —s=gewehr, *n.* percussion-gun. —s=satz, *m.* priming *or* detonating composition. —s=zündhütchen, *n.* percussion-cap.

Perl'—chen, *n.* (—chens, *pl.* —chen) little pearl *or* bubble. —e, *f.* (*pl.* —en) pearl; bead; sparkling drop *or* bubble; sie ist eine —e von einem Mädchen, she is a pearl amongst girls; —en vor die Säue werfen, to cast pearls before swine; —en bedeuten Thränen, pearls denote tears (*prov.*). —en, —ig, *adj.* of pearl, pearly. *Comp.* —asche, *f.* pearl-ash. —birne, *f.* honey-pear. —bohne, *f.* dwarf French bean. —en=ähnlich, *adj.* pearly. —en=bank, *f.* bank of pearl-oysters. —en=blase, *f.* pearl bubble (*Mollusc.*). —en=druck, *m.* pearl type (*Typ.*). —en=fischer, *m.* pearl-fisher *or* diver. —en=grau, *adj.* pearl-gray. —en=muschel, *f.* pearl oyster; (indische) mother-of-pearl shell. —en=schnur, *f.* string of pearls. —en=stickerei, *f.* embroidery in pearls; beading. —graupen, *pl.* pearl barley. —henne, *f.* guinea hen. —huhn, *n.* guinea-fowl. —mutter, *f.* mother-of-pearl. —mutter=schnecke, *f.* pearl cowry. —schrift, *f.* pearl (*Typ.*). —thee, *m.* gunpowder tea. —weiß, *n.* pearl powder.

Per'len, *v.n.* (*aux.* h.) to sparkle, glisten; to fall like drops; to rise in bubbles; der Wein perlt im Glase, the wine in the glass sparkles; —der Wein, sparkling wine; —d spielen, to pearl a passage (*Mus.*).

Permutie'r—en, *v.a.* to permute, to exchange. —ung, *f.* permutation.

Perpendi'k—el, *m.* & *n.* (—els, *pl.* —el) pendulum; plummet-line. —ula'r, —ulä'r, *adj.* & *adv.* perpendicular. —ulä're, *f.* perpendicular (line); eine —uläre ziehen, to square, to draw a perpendicular.

Perple'x, *adj.* confused (*sl.*).

Perro'n, *m.* (—s, *pl.* —s) platform.

Perrü'cke, *f.* (*pl.* —n) wig, periwig; alte —n, old fellows *or* fogies. *Comp.* —n=stock, *m.* wig-block.

Perso'n, *f.* (*pl.* —en) person; rôle, character; personal appearance; stumme —, dumb part; hervorragende —, (great) personage, big gun (*coll.*); great swell (*coll.*); klein von —, of short stature; die handelnden —en, the dramatis personæ; in —, personally; von — kennen, to know by sight; ich für meine —, I, for my part; die beteiligten —en, the parties; die — ansehen, to have respect to persons; ohne Ansehn der —, without distinction of persons. —a'l(e), n. (—al(e)s) staff, personnel; members of a household *or* of a company. —a'lien, *pl.* personalities; traits of character *or* incidents in a person's life; personal attacks. —ifikatio'n, *f.* personification. —ifizie'ren, *v.a.* to personify. —ifizie'rung, *f.* personification, impersonation. *Comp.* —al'=abgabe, *f.* poll-tax. —al'=arrest, *m.* attachment of a person. —al'=freiheit, *f.* exemption from statute labour. —en=beförderung, *f.* conveyance of passengers. —en=dampfer, *m.* passenger-boat *or* steamer. —en=frage, *f.* question of personality, personal question. —en=fuhrwerk, *n.* stage-coach. —en=name, *m.* personal noun. —en=post, *f.* stage- *or* mail-coach. —en=stand, *m.* state of population. —en=steuer, *f.* poll-tax. —en=tarif, *m.* passenger-tariff. —en=verkehr, *m.* passenger traffic. —en=verwechselung, *f.* mistake in the person. —en=verzeichnis, *n.* register of persons; dramatis personæ. —en=zug, *m.* passenger train.

Persön'lich, I. *adj.* personal. II. *adv.* in person, personally. —keit, *f.* personality; individuality; er hat *or* ist eine sehr angenehme —keit, he is a very pleasant person *or* man.

Perspekti'v, *n.* (—es, *pl.* —e) telescope; opera-glass. —e, *f.* (*pl.* —en) perspective. —isch, I. *adj.* perspective. II. *adv.* in perspective; in prospect.

Pertinen'z—ien, (—stücke,) *pl.* appurtenances.

Pe'sel, *m.* (—s, *pl.* —) best room in the house (*dial.*); bore; slow, dull fellow (*dial.*, *coll.*).

Pest, *f.* (*pl.* —en) plague, pestilence; pestilential fever; contagion; nuisance; daß dich die —! plague on you! —ile'nz, I. *f.* (*pl.* —ilen'zen) pestilence. II. *int.* damnation! confounded! —ilenzia'lisch, *adj.* pestilential. *Comp.* —artig, *adj.* pestilential. —beule, —blase, *f.*, —flecken, *m.* plague-spot. —geruch, —gestank, —hauch, *m.* pestilential smell *or* stench. —haus, *n.* plague hospital. —krank, *adj.* infested with the plague, plague-stricken. —luft, *f.* pestilential *or* foul air. —ordnung, *f.* regulations for a plague-stricken district. —stoff, *m.* plague-virus. —zeit, *f.* time of plague.

Petar'de, *f.* (*pl.* —n) petard.

Pe'ter, *m.* (—s) Peter; dummer —, simpleton; langweiliger —, slow fellow, bore; schwarzer —, old maid (*game of cards*). *Comp.* —männchen, *n.* a Papal coin of the 17th century. —s=kirche, *f.* St. Peter's (*at Rome*). —s=pfennig, *m.* Peter's pence.

Petersi'lie, *f.* parsley; ihm ist die — verhagelt, he has met with misfortune; er sieht aus, als ob ihm die — verhagelt wäre, he looks crestfallen (*coll.*).

Peti't, *f.*, (—schrift,) brevier (*Typ.*).

Petitionie'ren, *v.a.* to petition (um eine S., for a th.).

Petrefa'kt, *m.* & *n.* (—(e)s, *pl.* —en) petrefact, fossil. *Comp.* —en=kunde, *f.* palæontology.

Petro'leum, *n.* (—s) petroleum. *Comp.* —boot, *n.* petroleum-driven boat. —koch=apparat, —kocher, *m.* petroleum cooking-stove. —selbst=fahrer, *m.* petroleum motor.

Pet'schaft, *n.* (—s, *pl.* —e) seal, signet. *Comp.* —ring, *m.* signet-ring. —stecher, *m.* seal engraver.

Petschie'r, *n.* (—s, *pl.* —e) (*obs.*) *see* Petschaft. —en, *v.a.* to seal (*obs.*).

Pet'to, *m.*; in — haben, to have, to keep to oneself; to have in one's mind, to intend; to have in reserve.

Petz, (**Betz**,) *m.* (—es, *pl.* —e) (*abbrev. of* Bernhard) Bruin (*the bear*) (*obs.*).

Pet'ze, *f.* (*pl.* —n) she-bear; bitch.

Pet'zen, *v.a.* (*aux.* h.) to inform (against) (*sl.*); to sneak (*sl.*).

Pfad, *m.* (—es, *pl.* —e) path. *Comp.* —eisen, *n.* socket, pivot. —gerechtigkeit, *f.* right of way. —los, *adj.* pathless. —sucher, *m.* pioneer.

Pfaff, *m.* (—en, *pl.* —en), —e, *m.* (—en, *pl.* —en) priest; parson (*usually in a contempt. sense*) (*coll.*). —entum, *n.* clericalism, priestly rule, priesthood; priests (*coll.*). *Comp.* —en=bischen, *n.* dainty. —en=feind, *m.* enemy of the priests; Ulrich von Hutten (†1523). —en=geschmeiß, —en=gezücht, *n.* priests (*contempt.*), clerical band *or* gang, black coats, white ties, black brigade. —en=herrschaft, *f.* clerical rule. —en=knecht, *m.* slavish adherent of the clergy. —en=list, *f.* priestcraft. —en=platte, *f.* priest's tonsure. —en=schnitt, *m.*, —en=stück, *n.* Pope's eye, best piece in roast meat. —en=wesen, *n.* priests (*coll.*); clerical doings *or* machinations.

Pfäf'f—isch, *adj.* priest-like; clerical; priest-ridden. —lein, *n.* (little) priest (*hum.*). —ling, *m.* (—lings, *pl.* —linge) priest-ridden person.

Pfahl, *m.* (—s, Pfäh'le) pale; stake, post; pile, prop; picket; pillory; in meinen vier Pfählen, in my own house, within my own four walls; ein — im Fleische, a thorn in the flesh (*B.*); das Eintreiben von Pfählen, pile-driving. *Comp.* —bau, *m.* pile-work. —bauer, *m.* pile-builder; lake-dweller. —bauten, *pl.* lake-dwellings. —brücke, *f.* bridge built on piles. —bürger, *m.* suburban citizen; man behind the times; Philistine. —bürgertum, *n.* Philistinism. —graben, *m.* palisaded ditch. —hecke, *f.* palisade, paling. —ramme, *f.*, —rammler, *m.* pile-driver (*Naut.*). —werk, *n.* paling; pilework; stockade, palisade; timber-work. —zaun, *m.* paling.

Pfäh'l—en, *v.a.* to enclose with a paling; to prop; to tie up, train (*on stakes*); to impale; to drive in piles. —ung, *f.* impalement.

Pfalz, *f.* Palatinate; (imperial) palace (*obs.*); (die bairische) — *or* (Rhein) —, Rheno-Bavaria (*with the capital Speier*); Kurfürst Friedrich V. von der —, Frederick V., Elector Palatine. *Comp.* —graf, *m.* Count-Palatine, Palsgrave. —gräfin, *f.* Countess Palatinate, Palsgravine. —gräflich, *adj.* belonging to a Palsgrave. —grafschaft, *f.* Palatinate.

Pfäl'z—er, *m.* (—ers, *pl.* —er), —erin, *f.* inhabitant of the Palatinate; inhabitant of Rheno-Bavaria (*district on the left bank of the Rhine*). —er, —isch, *adj.* belonging to the Palatinate; —er Weine, wines from the Hardt hills in the Bavarian Palatinate (Rheinpfalz, bairische Pfalz), *e. g.* Deidesheim, Dürkheim wines.

Pfand, *n.* (—es, *pl.* Pfän'der) pledge; pawn; mortgage; security; guarantee, forfeit; Pfänder spielen, to play at forfeits; was soll der thun, dem dies — gehört? what shall be done to the owner of this? zum —e setzen, to pawn, to mortgage; to pledge (*one's honour*, *word*). —bar, *adj.* that can be pledged. *Comp.* —belastung, *f.* mortgage. —brief, *m.* (deed of) mortgage. —buch, *n.* register of mortgages. —gebühr, *f.* interest on mortgage; pledge-money. —gewähr, *f.* mortgage security. —gläubiger, *m.* mortgagee. —gut, *n.* lands given in mortgage. —haus, *n.* pawn-office. —herr, —inhaber, *m.* mortgagee; holder of a pawn-ticket. —kontrakt, *m.* bill of sale. —lehen, *n.* fee mortgaged. —leiher, *m.* pawnbroker. —lösung, *f.* redeeming of a pledge. —recht, *n.* lien; hypothecary law. —rechtlich, *adj.* hypothecary. —saß, *m.* mortgagee. —satz, *m.* mortgage. —schein, *m.* pawn-ticket. —schilling, *m.* money received on a pledge. —schuld, *f.* debt on a mortgage. —stück, *n.* pledge. —verleiher, *m.* pawnbroker.

—vertrag, *m.* mortgage contract. —verschreibung, *f.* mortgage deed.
Pfänd'bar, *adj.* distrainable.
Pfän'd—en, *v.a.;* einen um eine S. —en, to seize, distrain s.th. from s.o.; eine S. —en, to take s.th. away; to take in pledge. —er, *m.* (—ers, *pl.* —er) creditor who distrains, distrainer; field-constable. —lich, *adj. & adv.* as a pledge, hypothecary. —ung, *f.* seizure, execution; distraint. *Comp.* —er=spiel, *n.* game of forfeits. —ungs=befehl, *m.* warrant of distress.
Pfan'n—e, *f.* (*pl.* —en) pan; caldron, copper; socket (*Anat.*); powder-pan (*Gun.*); the part of a sling in which the stone is placed; ingot-mould; den Feind in die —e hauen, to put the enemy to the sword, to cut . . . to pieces, to chop . . . into mince-meat (*coll.*). *Comp.* —en=deckel, *m.* saucepan-lid, lid of a pan; hammer, cap of a gun. —en=flicker, *m.* tinker. —en=geld, *n.* brewing tax. —en=haus, *n.*, —en=herd, *m.* salt-works. —en=ziegel, *m.* pantile. —kuchen, *m.* pancake; fritter; doughnut (*dial.*).
Pfän'ner, *m.* (—s, *pl.* —) proprietor of saltworks; shareholder in saltworks.
Pfar'r—e, *f.* (*pl.* —en) pastorate, pastorship; living; parsonage; vicarage; parish; erst die —e, dann die Quarre, first a living, then wiving (*prov.*). —ei', *f.* (*pl.* —eien) *see* —e. —ei'lich, *adj.* belonging to the vicar *or* priest; parochial. —er, *m.* (—ers, —er) clergyman, parson; minister; priest. —erin, *f.* parson's wife. *Comp.* —acker, *m.* glebe-land. —amt, *n.* incumbency, pastorate. —amts=vertreter, *m.* curate. —besetzungsrecht, *n.* patronage. —bezirk, *m.* parish. —buch, *n.* parish register. —frau, *f.* parson's wife. —gebühren, *pl.* clergyman's fees. —gefälle, *pl.* revenues of a living. —gut, *n.* glebe-land. —haus, *n.* parsonage; rectory, vicarage; manse. —herr, *m.* = —er. —kind, *n.* parishioner. —kirche, *f.* parish-church. —land, *n.* glebe-land. —schule, *f.* parochial school. —stelle, *f.* parsonage, living, curacy. —verleihung, *f.* bestowal of a living. —zehente, *m.* parochial tithe.
Pfau, *m.* (—(e)s, —en, *pl.* —en) peacock; der — schreit, the peacock screams. *Comp.* —en=auge, *n.* peacock's eye; Bombyx pavonius (*Ent.*); spot in a peacock's tail. —en=ei, *n.* peahen's egg. —en=kranich, —en=reiher, *m.* Balearic crane (*Orn.*). —en=schwanz, —en=schweif, *m.* peacock's tail. —en=stolz, *m.* ostentation. —(en)=taube, *f.* fan-tailed pigeon. —en=wedel, *m.* fan of peacock's feathers. —en=weibchen, *n.*, —henne, *f.* peahen. —rad, *n. see* —enschwanz.
Pfef'fer, *m.* (—s, *pl.* —) pepper; da liegt der Hase im —, there's the rub (*prov.*); im — sein, to be in a pickle (*coll.*); wo der — wächst, Jericho, Hongkong (*coll.*).
Pfef'fer—n, *v.a.* to pepper; to season; to thrash; die Preise sind gepfeffert, the prices are exorbitant; sie —ten mit Steinen, they peppered (them) with stones; sie —ten auf die Hasen, they peppered away *or* let fly at the hares (*coll.*). *Comp.* —büchse, *f.* pepper-caster. —fresser, *m.* toucan (*Orn.*). —gurke, *f.* (pickled) gherkin. —korn, *n.* pepper-corn. —kuchen, *m.* gingerbread; spice-cake. —kümmel, *m.* cumin. —land, *n.* Jericho (*coll.*). —minz(e), *f.* peppermint. —minz=küchelchen, *n.* peppermint (lozenge). —münze, *see* —minz(e). —nuß, *f.* gingerbread nut. —sack, *m.* pepper-bag; grocer, shopkeeper (*coll.*). —staude, *f.*, —strauch, *m.* pepper-plant.
Pfeif'chen, *n.* (—s, *pl.* —) little pipe *or* whistle; sein — rauchen, to enjoy one's pipe, to smoke *or* take one's forty whiffs (*coll.*).
Pfei'f—e, *f.* (*pl.* —n) pipe, tube; blow-pipe; (Quer—e) fife; organ-pipe; whistle; tobacco-pipe; hollow bone; cell (*of a honeycomb*); offene (gedeckte) —e, open (stopped) pipe; tönende —e, sounding tube; eine —e stopfen, to fill a pipe; die —e einziehen, to draw in one's horns; man muß sich —en schneiden, während man im Rohr sitzt, make hay while the sun shines (*prov.*). *Comp.* —drossel, *f.* song-thrush. —en=beschlag, *m.*, —en=beschläge, *n.* mounting of a pipe. —en=boden, *m.* sounding-board of an organ. —en=bohrer, *m.* pipe-bore. —en=brett, *n.* rack for pipes; organ-sieve. —en=erde, *f.* pipe-clay. —en=form, *f.* organ-frame; pipe-mould. —en=förmig, *adj.* tubular. —en=gestell, *n. see* enbrett. —en=kopf, *m.* bowl of a pipe. —en=rohr, *n.* reed (*for playing on*); pipe-stem. —en=spitze, *f.*, —en=mundstück, *n.* mouthpiece (*of a pipe*). —en=stiel, *m.* shank *or* tube of a pipe; (*pl.*) spindle-shanks (*vulg.*). —en=strauch, *m.* mock-orange, (white) syringa. —en=stummel, *m.* short pipe. —en=thon, *m.* pipe-clay. —en=werk, *n.* organ-pipes.
Pfei'f—en, *ir.r.a. & n.* (*aux.* h.) to pipe; to whistle; to hiss; to whiz; to wheeze; to make a whistling *or* scratching noise; Mäuse und Ratten —en, mice and rats squeak; tanzen müssen wie jemand —t, to have to dance to another's piping; ich will dir was —en! very likely, indeed! don't you wish you may get it! you will not get it for me! (*coll.*); ich —e auf deine Ermahnungen, I do not care a straw for your fine speeches *or* admonitions; darauf —e ich, I do not care (*coll.*). —er, *m.* (—ers, *pl.* —er) piper, fife-player; whistler.
Pfeil, *m.* (—s, *pl.* —e) arrow, dart; bolt; shaft. —er, *see* Pfeiler. *Comp.* —eisen, *n.* arrow-head. —feder, *f.* feather of an arrow. —förmig, *adj.* arrow-shaped. —gerade, *adj.* straight as a bolt. —geschwind, *adj.* (as) swift as an arrow. *adv.* rapidly. —köcher, *m.* quiver. —naht, *f.* sagittal suture. —regen, *m.* shower of arrows. —schnelle, *f.* swiftness of an arrow. —schuß, *m.* bow-shot. —schütze, *m.* archer. —spitze, *f. see* —eisen.
Pfei'ler, *m.* (—s, *pl.* —) pillar; prop; upright, door-post, jamb; pier. *Comp.* —förmig, *adj.* pillar-shaped. —stein, *m.* basalt. —tisch, *m.* console. —weite, *f.* space between two pillars; interpilaster.
Pfen'nig, (Pfen'ning, *obs.*,) *m.* (—s, *pl.* —e, —) the one hundredth part of a mark; —e zu Rate haltend und Thaler wegwerfend, to be penny-wise and pound-foolish; wer den — nicht ehrt, ist des Thalers nicht wert, take care of the pennies and the pounds will take care of themselves (*prov.*). *Comp.* —ausgabe, *f.* penny-edition. —fuchser, *m.* pinch-penny, miser. —fuchsern, *v.n.* (*aux.* h.) to be stingy *or* close-fisted. —gülte, *f.* interest *or* rent paid in money. —magazin, *n.* penny magazine; penny dreadful (*coll.*); cheap journal. —meister, *m.* purser, treasurer. —schenke, *f.* pot-house, low public house. —weise, *adv.* by pennyworths, in small doles *or* driblets.
Pferch, *m.* (—es, *pl.* —e) fold, pen; sheep-dung. —en, *v.a.* to pen, to fold; to manure. *Comp.* —hütte, *f.*, —karren, *m.* shepherd's hut *or* cot. —lager, *n.* sheepfold; stock of sheep belonging to a fold. —schlag, *m.* sheepfolding.
Pferd, *n.* (—es, *pl.* —e) horse; das — wiehert, the horse neighs; zu —e sitzen, to be on horseback; zu —e! to horse! vom —e auf den Esel kommen, to come down in the world; das — beim Schwanze (auf) zäumen, das — hintern Wagen spannen, to put the cart before the horse; sich aufs hohe — setzen, to get on one's high horse; einem willigen —e muß man nicht die Sporen geben, never spur a willing horse (*prov.*). —chen, *n.* (—chens, *pl.* —chen) pony. *Comp.* —e=arbeit, *f.* horse-labour; drudgery.

—e=arzt, *m.* veterinary surgeon. —e=aus=fuhr=verbot, *n.* law prohibiting the export of horses. —e=ausstellung, *f.* horse-show. —e=bahn, *f.* tramway. —e=bändiger, *m.* horse-breaker. —e=behang, *m.* harness, trappings. —e=beschlag, *m.* horse-shoeing; horse-shoes. —e=bestand, *m.* effective force of horses *or* cavalry. —e=bremse, *f.* horse-fly. —e=decke, *f.* horse-rug, horse-cover; housing. —e=fuß, *m.* horse's foot; club-foot; cloven foot. —e=futter, *n.* fodder, provender. —e=geschirr, *n.* harness. —e=gurt, *m.* horse-girth. —e=haar, *n.*, —e=haaren, *adj.* horse-hair. —e=händler, *m.* horse-dealer. —e=huf, *m.* horse's hoof; colt's foot (*Bot.*). —e=junge, *m.* stable-boy. —e=käfer, *m.* dung-beetle. —e=knecht, *m.* ostler, groom. —e=kraft, *f.* horse-power; Maschine von 20 —ekräften, 20 horse-power machine; indizierte, nominelle —ekraft, indicated, nominal horse-power. —e=krippe, *f.* manger. —e=kum(me)t, *n.* horse-collar. —e=kundige(r), *m.* good judge of horses; hippologist. —e=leine, *f.* rein; towing-rope. —e=mäßig, *adj.* equine. —e=milch, *f.* mare's milk. —e=pille, *f.* horse-ball; *pl.* horse drippings. —e=rennbahn, *f.* race-course. —e=rennen, *n.* horse-race; horse-racing. —e=schau, *f.* horse-show. —e=schwemme, *f.* horse-pond. —e=seuche, *f.* murrain. —e=stall, *m.* stable. —e=stärke, *f.* horse-power. —e=striegel, *m.* curry-comb. —e=tränke, *f.* horse-pond, watering-place. —e=verleiher, *m.* keeper of livery stables. —e=verschlag, —e=wagen, *m.* horse-box (*on a steamboat, railway*). —e=wechsel, *m.* relay of horses. —e=zucht, *f.* breeding of horses.

Pfet'te, *f.* (*pl.* —n) purlin(e), templet (*Archit.*).

[1]**Pfiff, Pfif'fest; Pfif'fe**, *1 (& 3) & 2 pers. sing. imperf. ind.; 1 & 3 pers. sing. imperf. subj. of* pfeifen.

[2]**Pfiff**, *m.* (—es, *pl.* —e) whistle; whiff; moment; mere nothing, trifle; trick; einen — thun, to give a whistle; einem auf den — gehorchen, to come at a p.'s call; den — verstehen, to know the tricks of the trade, to be a knowing fellow; keine —e! no nonsense! —ig, *adj. & adv.* sly, artful, cunning, crafty. —igkeit, *f.* artfulness, craftiness. —ikus, *m.* (—ikus, *pl.* —ikusse) clever fellow, sly dog (*coll.*).

Pfif'ferling, *m.* (—s, *pl.* —e) kind of mushroom; trifle; keinen — wert, not worth a rap *or* a straw.

Pfing'st—en, *n.* (—ens, *pl.* —en) & *pl. indec.* Whitsuntide, Pentecost. —lich, *adj.* Pentecostal; Whitsun-. *Comp.* —abend, *m.* eve of Whitsuntide. —baum, *m.* young birch-tree (*see* Maie). —ferien, *pl.* Whitsun holidays, Whitsuntide recess (*Parliam.*). —fest, *n. see* —en. —montag, *m.* Whitmonday. —ochs, *m.* ox decked out and led through the streets at Whitsuntide; geputzt wie ein —ochs, as gaudy as a peacock, dressed up to date *or* to the nines. —sonntag, *m.* Whitsunday. —tag, *m.* day of the feast of Pentecost; Whitsunday; der zweite —tag, Whitmonday; —tage, Whitsun holidays.

Pfinz'tag, *m.* Thursday (*lit.* fifth day) (*dial.*).

Pfir'sich, *m.* (—s, *pl.* —e) & *f.* (*pl.* —e); —e, **Pfir'sche**, *f.* (*pl.* —en) peach. *Comp.* —blüte, *f.* peach-blossom. —branntwein, *m.* persico. —kern, *m.* peach-stone.

Pflag, *obs. & poet. 1 & 3 pers. sing. imperf. indic. of* pflegen.

Pflanz'—bar, *adj.* plantable. —e, *f.* (*pl.* —en) plant; seedling; du bist mir eine saubere —e! you're a nice person, indeed! —lich, *adj.* vegetable. *Comp.* —eisen, *n.* dibble, setting iron. —en=anatomie, *f.* anatomy of plants. —en=art, *f.* species of plants. —en=asche, *f.* ashes of plants. —en=beet, *n.* bed (*of plants*). —en=beschreibung, *f* description of plants. —en=bildung, *f.* organization of plants. —en=buch, *n.* herbal; flora. —en=butter, *f.* vegetable butter. —en=chemie, *f.* chemistry of plants. —en=diät, *f.* vegetable diet. —en=erde, *f.* vegetable mould. —en=esser, *m.* vegetarian. —en=exemplare, *pl.* botanical specimens. —en=familie, *f.* family of plants. —en=farbe, *f.* vegetable dye. —en=faser, *f.* vegetable fibre. —en=forscher, *m.* botanist (*especially an expert*). —en=fressend, *adj.* graminivorous, herbivorous. —en=garten, *m.* botanical garden. —en=gattung, *f.* genus of plants. —en=geographie, *f.* geographical distribution of plants. —en=gift, *n.* vegetable poison. —en=gewächse, *pl.* plants, vegetable productions. —en=haus, *n.* greenhouse, conservatory. —en=keim, *m.* germ of a plant; *pl.* embryo; Entwickelung des —enkeims, germination. —en=kenner, *m.* botanist. —en=kenntnis, —en=kunde, *f.* botany. —en=kost, *f.* vegetable diet. —en=leben, *n.* vegetable life, vegetation; ein —enleben führen, to vegetate. —en=lehre, *f.* botany; book on botany. —en=organ, *n.* part of plant (*root, stem, leaf, etc.*). —en=physiologie, *f.* physiology of plants. —en=presse, *f.* botanist's press. —en=reich, I. *n.* vegetable kingdom. II. *adj.* rich in plants. —en=reste, *pl.* fossil, (remains of) plants. —en=saft, *m.* sap. —en=sammeln, *n.* gathering of plants, botanizing, herborization. —en=sammler, *m.* collector of plants, herbalist. —en=sammlung, *f.* herbarium. —en=sauger, *m.* parasitic plant. —en=säure, *f.* vegetable acid. —en=stein, *m.* phytolite, fossil plant. —en=stengel, *m.* stalk *or* stem of a plant. —en=stoff, *m.* vegetable matter; *pl.* vegetable remains. —en=stoffwechsel, *m.* vegetable metabolism (*the chemical and other changes which go on during life*). —en=symbolik, *f.* symbolic meaning of plants. —en=system, *n.* classification of plants, taxonomy, botanical system. —en=systematik, *f.* systematic botany. —en=systematisch, *adj.* concerning the taxonomy of plants. —en=tier, *n.* zoophyte. —en=varietät, *f.* variety of plants. —en=wachstum, *n.* vegetation, growth of plants. —en=welt, *f.* vegetable kingdom, flora; —enwelt des Hochgebirges (Meeres), alpine (marine) flora. —en=wuchs, *m.* vegetation. —en=zelle, *f.* vegetable cell. —en=zellen=stoff, *m.* cellulose. —en=zergliederung, *f.* anatomy of plants. —en=zucht, *f.* cultivation of plants; nursery. —en=züchter, *m.* cultivator of plants, nurseryman. —garten, *m.* nursery (*for plants*). —gärtner, *m.* nurseryman. —ort, *m.* settlement. —reis, *m.* scion. —schule, *f.* nursery; seminary, training college. —staat, *m.* colony. —stock, *m.* setting stick, dibble. —zeit, *f.* season for planting.

Pflänz'—chen, *n.* (—chens, *pl.* —chen) little plant, seedling. —ling, *m.* (—lings, *pl.* —linge) young plant, seedling.

Pflan'z—en, *v.a.* to plant, set *or* lay out; to plant (*guns*). —er, *m.* (—ers, *pl.* —er) planter; owner of a plantation; settler, colonist; dibble. —ung, *f.* planting; plant; plantation; settlement, colony.

Pflas'ter, *n.* (—s, *pl.* —) plaster; pavement; flag; greased patch (*for firearms*); beauty-patch; eingelegtes —, tessellated pavement; unregelmäßiges —, pebble *or* rubble pavement; englisches —, court-plaster; das — treten, to loaf about; (in) London ist ein teures —, London is an expensive place; das — aufreißen, to take up the pavement. —er, *m.* (—ers, *pl.* —er) pavior, paver. *Comp.* —bandstein, *m.* curbstone. —einfassung, *f.* border of a pavement. —geld, *n.* road rates; toll. —kasten, *m.* plaster-case; surgeon, saw-bones (*sl.*). —ramme, *f.* paving-beetle

—rücken, *m.* top of a pavement. —setzer, *m.* pavior. —stein, *m.* paving-stone. —stößel, *m.* paving-beetle. —treter, *m.* loafer, idler, lounger. —treterei', *f.* loafing, idling. —ziegel, *m.* paving-tile. —zoll, *m.* excise, octroi.

Pfläs'terchen, *n.* (—s, *pl.* —) patch (*for the face*); Schön—, beauty patch.

Pflas'ter—n, *v.a.* to put a plaster on; to plaster; to pave; der Weg zur Hölle ist mit guten Vorsätzen ge—t, the way to hell is paved with good intentions (*prov.*).

Pflau'me, *f.* (*pl.* —n) plum; gedörrte —n, dried prunes; geschmorte —n, stewed prunes. *Comp.* —n=kern, *m.* plum-stone. —n=kuchen, *m.* plum-cake; open plum tart. —n=mandeln, *pl.* bitter almonds. —n=mus, *n.* stewed plums; plum jam.

Pfle'ge, *f.* care; rearing, bringing up; fostering; nursing; cultivation; encouragement (*of arts, etc.*); superintendence; administration; guardianship; district; Kranken —, sick nursing; in die — geben, to put out to nurse; (*of babies*) to put out to board (bei, with).

Pfle'g—en, *reg. & ir.v.* I. *a.* (pflegte, gepflegt) (*aux.* h.; *gen. & acc.*) to tend, nurse, foster, take care of; er —te seines Amtes, he performed the duties of his office; —e sein! attend to him! (*B.*); —e deines Vaters, take care of your father (*B.*); —e deinen kranken Vater, nurse your invalid father; einen hegen und —en, to cherish and love a p.; jemandes Freundschaft —en, to cultivate a p.'s friendship; sich —en, to take care of o.s., er —te seinen Leib (*or, now more rarely,* seines Leibes), he lived well, he pampered himself; to do, to go in for, undertake, carry on (*often with old gen. and the old strong imperf. and p.part.* pflog, gepflogen); wir pflogen Rats mit einander, we took counsel together; sie pflogen (*also* pflegten) der Ruhe, they rested, they took rest; seiner Bequemlichkeit —en, to take one's ease; der Liebe —en, to enjoy the pleasures of love; [illegible]r Wollust —en, to indulge in voluptuousn[illegible] wir pflogen abgerissenes Gespräch, we exchanged a few sentences now and then (*poet.*); Umgang mit einem —en, to have intercourse *or* be on terms of intimacy with s.o.; to associate with s.o.; gepflogene Unterhandlungen, negotiations conducted. II. *n.* (pflegte, gepflegt) to be accustomed to *or* in the habit of, to be given to, to be wont; to indulge in; er —te zu sagen, he used to say, he would say; er —t weite Spaziergänge zu machen, he is in the habit of taking long walks, he usually goes for long walks; er pflegte der Erste zu sein, he usually was *or* used to be the first; (*rarely irreg.*) sein Auge glomm heute grauser noch als sonst es pflag, to-day his eyes glowed even more terribly than was their wont (*poet.*). (*In careless speaking and writing* —en *is frequently accompanied by such* (*pleonastic*) *adverbs as* oft, häufig, gewöhnlich); er —te gewöhnlich zu sagen, he would usually say; so —t es häufig zu gehen, such is generally the case, that's the way of the world. —er, *m.* (—ers, *pl.* —er), —erin, *f.* fosterer; nurse; benefactor; guardian. —ling, *m.* (—lings, *pl.* —linge) *see* —e=kind. *Comp.* —e=amt, *n.* guardianship; office of a district-inspector. —e=bedürftig, *adj.* needing care. —e=befohlen, *adj.* committed to the care of; der, die —ebefohlene, charge, ward. —e=bruder, *m.* foster-brother. —e=eltern, *pl.* foster-parents. —e=haus, *n.* hospital. —e=kind, *n.* foster-child. —e=los, *adj.* neglected. —e=mutter, *f.* foster-mother; nurse. —e=schwester, *f.* foster-sister. —e=vater, *m.* foster-father.

Pflicht, *f.* (*pl.* —en) duty; allegiance; obligation; tax; oath of fealty; pledged word, promise; in — stehen, to be bound by oath, to be subject to; es für seine — halten, to think it one's duty (*to*); einem etwas zur — machen, to enjoin s.th. upon a p.; einen zu seiner — anhalten, to compel a p. to do his duty; in eines Herrn — stehen, to be the servant of a lord; seine — und Schuldigkeit, his bounden duty. *Comp.* —anker, *m.* sheet *or* main anchor. —brüchig, *adj.* perjured; disloyal; undutiful. —en=lehre, *f.* ethics, doctrine of morals. —en=streit, *m.* conflict of duties. —frei, *adj.* free from obligation. —gefühl, *n.* sense of duty. —gemäß, *adj. & adv.* conformable to duty, due; loyal, conscientious; as in duty bound. —gesetz, *n.* moral law. —leistung, *f.* performance of duty; oath of allegiance. —mäßig, *see* —gemäß. —schuldig, *adj.* bound in duty. —teil, *m.* legitimate *or* entailed portion. —treu, *adj.* true to duty. —treue, *f.* fealty; faithfulness to duty. —vergessen, *adj.* disloyal, undutiful, unfaithful, false; perjured. —vergessenheit, *f.* dereliction of duty; disloyalty, falsity. —verletzung, *f.* violation of duty. —widrig, *adj.* contrary to duty; undutiful, disloyal; —widrig handeln, to act counter to one's duty.

Pflock, *m.* (—es, *pl.* Pflö'cke) tent-peg; wooden pin, peg, nail; plug. *Comp.* —schießen, *n.* blasting of a rock.

Pflö'cken, *v.a.* to fasten with pegs; to peg.

Pflog; Pflö'ge, *1 & 3 pers. sing. imperf. ind.; 1 & 3 pers. imperf. subj. of* pflegen.

Pflü'cken, *v.a.* to pluck, gather, cull; to pluck (*fowls, etc.*); ich habe ein Sträußchen (Hühnchen) mit ihm zu —, I have a crow to pluck with him (*coll.*).

Pflug, *m.* (—es, *pl.* Pflü'ge) plough; drag (*for dredging*); Land unter dem —e, arable land. *Comp.* —baum, —balken, *m.* plough-beam. —dienst, *m.* socage. —eisen, *n.* coulter. —haupt, *n.* axle-tree of a plough. —kehre, *f.* turn of the plough. —land, *n.* arable land. —reitel, *m.*, —reute, *f.*, —rödel, *n.* plough-staff. —schar, *f.* ploughshare. —sterze, *f.* plough-staff, plough-handle. —stränge, *pl.* plough-traces. —treiber, *m.* plough-boy.

Pflüg'bar, *adj.* arable, ploughable.

Pflü'g—en, *v.a. & n.* (*aux.* h.) to plough; to till; to groove; to drag (*an anchor*); mit fremdem Kalbe —en, to plough with another man's heifer; den Sand —en, to plough the sands, to beat the air; halb —en, to half-plough, to rafter; zum erstenmal —en, to break up; zum zweitenmal —en, to plough a second time. —er, *m.* (—ers, *pl.* —er) ploughman.

Pfört'—chen, *n.* (—chens, *pl.* —chen) little door; wicket-gate. —ner, *m.* (—ners, *pl.* —ner) porter, door-keeper; turnkey; pylorus (*Anat.*). —nerin, *f.* female door-keeper.

Pfor't—e, *f.* (*pl.* —en) gate, door; port-hole, die Hohe *or* Ottomanische —e, the Sublime Porte. *Comp.* —angeln, *pl.* gate-hinges. —en=ring, *m.* knocker, port-ring. —segel, *n.* tarpaulin; port-sail.

Pfos'te, *f.* (*pl.* —n), —n, *m.* (—ns, *pl.* —n) post; jamb, pier (*of doors*); main-piece (*of rudders*).

Pfo'te, *f.* (*pl.* —n; *dim.* Pföt'chen) paw; scrawling handwriting; gieb Pfötchen! give your paw!

Pfriem, *m.* (—s, *pl.* —e), —e, *f.* (*pl.* —en), —en, *m.* (—ens, *pl.* —en) puncheon, punch; awl; bodkin; gun-piercer; broom (*Bot.*). —en, *v.a.* to punch, to bore. *Comp.* —en=förmig, *adj.* awl-shaped. —en=gras, *n.* feather-grass. —geld, *n.* primage (*C. L.*).

Pfropf, *m.* (—es, *pl.* —e, Pfröp'fe), —en, *m.* (—ens, *pl.* —en) stopper, cork; bung, plug; wad, wadding; tampion (*Artil.*); graft, scion.

—en, *v.a.* to cram, to stuff *or* thrust into; to cork; to plug; to graft. *Comp.* **—en=geld**, *n.* corkage. **—messer**, *n.* grafting-knife. **—reis**, *n.* graft, scion, shoot, slip. **—säge**, *f.* grafting-saw. **—spalt**, *m.* graft-slit. **—(en)=voll**, *adj.* full to overflowing (*coll.*). **—(en)=zieher**, *m.* corkscrew; wadhook.

Pfröpf'ling, *m.* (**—s**, *pl.* **—e**) recently grafted tree; shoot for grafting.

Pfrün'd—e, *f.* (*pl.* **—en**) benefice, living; prebend; place (*in a hospital, etc.*). **—ner**, *m.* (**—ners**, *pl.* **—ner**) beneficiary; prebendary; incumbent, beneficed clergyman. *Comp.* **—en=besetzungs=recht**, *n.* advowson. **—en=buch**, *n.* register of livings. **—en=ertrag**, *m.* income of a living. **—en=genuß**, *m.* impropriation (*of laymen*). **—en=handel**, *m.* simony. **—gut**, *n.* glebe lands. **—haus**, *n.* parsonage, rectory; hospital, institution.

Pfuhl, *m.* (**—s**, *pl.* **—e**) pool; puddle; **Sünden—**, sink of corruption; **Höllen—**, bottomless pit; **der feurige —**, hell (*B.*). **—icht** (*obs.*), **—ig** (*rare*), *adj.* full of pools, marshy, swampy.

Pfühl, *m.* (*& n.*) (**—s**, *pl.* **—e**) bolster; pillow; couch; torus, column-moulding. **—en**, *v.a.*; **weich gepfühlt**, softly-bedded.

Pfui! *int.* fie! shame! **— schäme dich!** fie upon you! **— über ihn!** out upon him! **—en**, *v.a.* to cry shame on.

Pfund, *n.* (**—es**, *pl.* **—e**) pound (*weight*); pound (*sterling*); talent (*B.*); **drei — Fleisch**, three pounds of meat; **sein — vergraben**, to hide one's talent. **—ig**, *see* **Pfündig**. *Comp.* **—birne**, *f.* large pear. **—böller**, *m.* pound-mortar. **—geld**, *n.* poundage. **—sohle**, *f.* stout sole. **—weise**, *adv.* by the pound.

Pfün'd—er, *m.* (**—s**, *pl.* **—**) weigher (*at the custom-house*); (*in comp.* =) pounder; **Sechs—er**, six-pounder (*Artil.*). **—ig**, *adj.* of one pound; (*in comp.* =) weighing (*so many*) pounds; -pounder; **ein sechs—iges Geschütz**, a six-pounder.

Pfu'sch—en, *v.* I. *a. & n.* (*aux.* **h.**) to carry on a trade without a license; to do badly, bungle, botch; to cheat (*at cards*); **in etwas** (*acc.*) **—en**, to meddle with, dabble in; **dem Gärtner ins Handwerk —en**, to dabble in gardening. II. *n.* (*aux.* **h.**) to hiss, whizz, flash (*of powder*). **—er**, *m.* (**—ers**, *pl.* **—er**) bungler, dabbler; cobbler; inferior tradesman; artisan working for himself; blunder; hissing, flashing (*of powder*). **—erei'**, *f.* bungling work; blunder; daub. **—er=haft**, *adj.* clumsy, bungling, unworkmanlike. *Comp.* **—arbeit**, *see* **—erei**. **—makler**, *m.* unlicensed broker.

Pfüt'z—e, *f.* (*pl.* **—en**) puddle, slough, pool; pool of water (*in a pit*). **—en**, *v.a.* to pump out water (*Min.*). **—ig**, *adj.* muddy, miry, full of puddles. *Comp.* **—en=wasser**, *n.* stagnant water, puddle water.

Phänome'n, *n.* (**—s**, *pl.* **—e**) phenomenon.

Phant—asie', *f.* (*pl.* **—asieen**) imagination, fancy; fantasia; chimera, whim; reverie. **—asie'ren**, *v.a. & n.* (*aux.* **h.**) to indulge in reveries *or* fancies; to rave; to improvise (*Mus.*). **—ast**, *m.* (**—as'ten**, *pl.* **—as'ten**) visionary; oddity. **—asterei'**, *f.* fancy, whim. **—as'tisch**, *adj.* fanciful; fantastic. *Comp.* **—asie=anzug**, *m.* fancy dress. **—asie=bild**, *n.* fanciful picture, picture of one's imagination, day-dream. **—asie=reich**, *adj.* imaginative, endowed with a strong imagination. **—asie=spiel**, *n.* play of fancy. **—asie=voll**, *adj.* imaginative. **—asmago'risch**, *adj.* phantasmagorial.

Phanto'm, *n.* (**—s**, *pl.* **—e**) phantom, chimera; manikin (*med.*).

Pharisä'—er, *m.* (**—s**, *pl.* **—**) Pharisee. **—isch**, *adj.* Pharisaical.

Pha'rospiel, *n.* faro.

Pharma—kopö'e, *f.* pharmacopœia. **—zeu't**, *m.* (**—zeuten**, *pl.* **—zeuten**) apothecary, druggist; student of pharmacy. **—zeu'tisch**, *adj.* pharmaceutical.

Philanthro'p, *m.* (**—en**, *pl.* **—en**) philanthropist. **—isch**, *adj.* philanthropic.

Philis't—er, *m.* (**—s**, *pl.* **—**) Philistine; vulgarian; townsman; landlord (*of the house in which a student lives*); any non-student (*Univ. sl.*); member of the town police (*obs.*); pedant; **—er und Studenten**, town and gown. **—erei'**, *f.* Philistinism; narrow-mindedness, pedantry. **—erhaft**, **—rö's**, *adj.* philistine, pedantic, narrow-minded. **—ertum**, *n.* (**—ertums**), **—e'rium**, *n.* (**—eriums**) (*sl.*) philistine life, ordinary citizen's life, humdrum existence, every-day routine; tradesmen; town.

Philolo'g, *m.* (**—en**, *pl.* **—en**) philologist, linguist; **alter —**, **klassischer —**, classical scholar, student of classics; **neuerer —**, modern language student, student of modern languages. **—ie'**, *f.* philology; **alte —ie**, classics; **neuere —ie**, modern languages; **Goethe —ie**, critical study of Goethe's life and writings. **—isch**, *adj.* philological; **—isch=historische Disciplinen**, linguistic and historical subjects, arts, humanities, humaniora.

Philoso'ph, *m.* (**—en**, *pl.* **—en**) philosopher; **— von Sanssouci**, King Frederick II. (the Great) of Prussia. **—e'm**, *n.* (**—ems**, *pl.* **—eme**) theorem, philosophical problem. **—ie'**, *f.* philosophy; **Doktor der —ie**, doctor of philosophy (**Dr. phil.** = Ph.D.). **—ie'ren**, *v.n.* (*aux.* **h.**) to philosophize. **—isch**, *adj.* philosophical.

Phio'le, *f.* (*pl.* **—n**) phial.

Phleg'ma, *n.* (**—s**) phlegm; apathy, dulness.

Phlegma'ti—ker, *m.* (**—kers**, *pl.* **—ker**) phlegmatic person. **—sch**, *adj.* phlegmatic.

Phon—e'tik, *f.* phonetics. **—e'tiker**, *m.* (**—etikers**, *pl.* **—etiker**) phonetician, student *or* teacher of phonetics. **—e'tisch**, *adj.* phonetic; **—etisches Laut(wert)zeichen**, phonetic symbol *or* character; **—etische Umschrift**, phonetic transcription, phonetic script; **—etische Schulung**, phonetic drill. **—ik** (*pron.* **Pho'nik**), *f.* acoustics, phonics.

Phosge'n, *n.* (**—s**) phosgene gas.

Phospha't, *n.* (**—s**) phosphate.

Phos'phor, *m.* (**—s**) (*abbr.* **P.**) phosphorus; **der — leuchtet im Dunkeln**, phosphorus is luminous in the dark. *Comp.* **—blei**, *n.* phosphuretted lead. **—blei=erz**, *n.*, **—blei=spat**, *m.* phosphate of lead. **—gehalt**, *m.* amount of phosphorus contained in (a mineral, *etc.*). **—pasta**, *f.* phosphorus paste. **—sauer**, *adj.* phosphoric; **—saurer Kalk**, phosphate of lime. **—wasserstoff**, *m.* phosphuretted hydrogen.

Photogra'ph, *m.* (**—en**, *pl.* **—en**) photographer. **—ie'**, *f.* (*pl.* **—ieen**) photograph; photography; **eine —ie hervorrufen**, to develop a photograph. **—ie'ren**, *v.a.* to photograph. **—isch**, I. *adj.* photographic. II. *adv.* by photography.

Phra'se, *f.* (*pl.* **—n**) phrase; **leere —n**, empty talk, clap-trap. **—n=drescher**, *m.* phrasemonger, empty talker. **—n=machen**, *n.* empty talk.

Phrenolo'g, *m.* (**—en**, *pl.* **—en**) phrenologist. **—isch**, *adj.* phrenological.

Phta'lsäure, *f.* phtalic acid.

Phys—i'k, *f.* *see* **Physik**. **—iogno'm**, **—iolo'g**, **&c.** *see* **Physiognom**, **Physiolog**, **&c.** **—isch**, (*pron.* **phy'sisch**) *adj.* physical.

Physi'k, *f.* physics; natural philosophy. **—a'lisch**, *adj. & adv.* physical. **—a't**, *n.* (**—ates**, *pl.* **—ate**) office of the chief physician of a town *or* district.

Phy'si—ker, *m.* (**—kers**, *pl.* **—ker**) physicist, student *or* teacher of physics. **—kum**, *n.* the first medical examination in Germany (*coll.*).

—kus, *m.* (—kus, *pl.* —ci) chief (*official*) physician of a town *or* district.

Physiogno'm, *m.* (—en, *pl.* —en) physiognomist. —ie', *f.* physiognomy. —isch, *adj.* physiognomic.

Physiolo'g, *m.* (—en, *pl.* —en) physiologist. —ie', *f.* physiology. —isch, *adj.* physiological. —us, *m.* bestiary.

Pian—i'no, *n.* (—inos, *pl.* —inos) cottage piano, upright piano, cabinet piano. —i'st, *m.* (—is'ten, *pl.* —is'ten), —is'tin, *f.* pianist. —o (*pron.* pia'no), I. *adv.* piano, gently. II. *n.*, (—o=for'te,) pianoforte; —os und —inos, pianofortes grand and upright; tafelförmiges —o, square *or* horizontal piano(forte). *Comp.* —o=sessel, *m.* piano-stool, music-stool.

Pi'ch—el, *m.* (—s, *pl.* —) slobbering-bib, feeder. —elei', *f.* tippling. —eln, *v.a.* & *n.* (*aux.* h.) to tipple, tope, bib; to drink eagerly, to quaff (*sl.*). —en, *v.a.* to pitch, smear with pitch. —ler, *m.* (—lers, *pl.* —ler) toper, tippler.

Pick, *m.* (—es, *pl.* —e) pick; pricking; puncture; stab; tick (*of a watch*). —e, *f.* (*pl.* —en) pickaxe, pick. —el, *m.* (—els, *pl.* —el) *see* —e & Pickel. —en, *v.a.* & *n.* (*aux.* h.) to peck, to pick; to tick. *Comp.* —hacke, *f.* pickaxe. —hammer, *m.* pickaxe, poll-hammer. —(e)nick, *n.* picnic.

Pi'ckel, *m.* (—s, *pl.* —) pimple; pickaxe, ice-axe. —ig, *adj.* pimply, pimpled, blotched.

Pi'ckelflöte, *f.* (*pl.* —n) piccolo, octave-flute.

Pi'ckelhaube, *f.* (*pl.* —n) spiked helmet; skull-cap.

Pi'ckelhering, *m.* (—s, *pl.* —e) bloater; Jack Pudding, merry Andrew, clown, buffoon.

Piedesta'l, *n.* (—s, *pl.* —e, —s) pedestal, base.

Piek, *f.* run (*Naut.*); topping-lift, peak (*Naut.*).

Piep! *int.* chirp! tweet! peep! nicht — sagen, not to utter a word, to be mum (*coll.*). —e, *adj.* das ist mir ganz —e, that 's all the same to me, I do not care (*sl.*). —(s)en, *v.n.* (*aux.* h.) to peep, chirp, cheep; to whine. —ig, —isch, *adj.* crying, piping; weakly, ailing, poorly (*coll.*). *Comp.* —gans, *f.*, —gössel, *n.* (*dial.*) gosling; cry-baby. —matz, *m.* (dickie-)bird (*coll.*).

Pie'sacken, *v.a.* to vex, worry, torment a p. (*sl.*).

Piet—ä't, *f.* piety, reverence. —i'st, *m.* (—is'ten, *pl.* —is'ten) pietist. —is'tisch, *adj.* & *adv.* sanctimonious. *Comp.* —ät'=voll, *adj.* reverent. —ät'=los, *adj.* irreverent.

Pik, *m.* (—es, *pl.* —e) peak; rancour, grudge. das —, spade (*at cards*). —a'nt, *adj.* piquant, biting, poignant; racy (*coll.*); highly seasoned, highly flavoured, hot, spicy; das —ante, piquancy, pungency. —e, *f.* rancour, grudge, pique; pike; auf einen einen — (*or* eine —e) haben, to have a spite against s.o., to bear s.o. a grudge (*coll.*) —enie'r, *m.* (—eniers, *pl.* —eniere) pikeman. —e't(t), *n.* (—et(t)s, —et(t)es, *pl.* —et(t)s, —et(t)e) picket (*Mil.*); piquet (*cards*). —ie'ren, *v.* I. *a.* to pique, nettle, annoy. II. *r.* to pique oneself (auf eine S., upon a th.); to make it a point (of honour) to do a th., to set one's mind on doing a th. *Comp.* —aß, *n.* ace of spades. —fein, *adj.* extremely elegant, tiptop (*coll.*).

Pi'k—e, *f.* pike; von der —e auf dienen, to rise from the ranks. —en, —sen, *v.a.* to prick (*coll.*). *Comp.* —eisen, *n.* iron point of a pike. —en=träger, *m.* pikeman. —schaft, *m.* pike-staff.

Pikrin'säure, *f.* picric acid.

Pil'ger, *m.* (—s, *pl.* —), —in, *f.* pilgrim. —n, *v.n.* (*aux.* h. & s.) to go on *or* make a pilgrimage; to wander; —schaft, *f.* pilgrimage. *Comp.* —fahrt, *f.* pilgrimage. —flasche, *f.* gourd bottle. —schar, *f.* troop of pilgrims. —tasche, *f.* pilgrims' scrip.

Pil'grim, *see* Pilger.

Pil'le, *f.* (*pl.* —n) pill; eine — vergolden, to sugar a pill. *Comp.* —n=dreher, *m.* apothecary *coll.*).

Pilo't, *m.* (—en, *pl.* —en) pilot; pilot-fish

Pilz, *m.* (—es, *pl.* —e) mushroom, fungus; upstart; in die —e gehen, to go mushroom-gathering; to run away, to disappear (*coll.*). —haft, —ig, *adj.* fungous, mushroom-like. *Comp.* —artig, *see* —ig. —säure, *f.* fungic acid.

Pime'nt, *n.* (—es, *pl.* —e) allspice, Jamaica pepper.

Pimpelei', *f.* complaining; effeminacy.

Pim'pel—ig, *adj.* effeminate; sickly; complaining. —n, *v.n.* (*aux.* h.) to whine, complain (*of every slight change of the weather*); to be sickly. *Comp.* —fritz, *m.*, —liese, *f.*, delicate, sickly person.

Pinakothe'k, *f.* (*pl.* —en) pinacotheca, picture gallery (*especially the one at Munich*).

Pinas'se, *f.* (*pl.* —n) pinnace.

Pin'guin, *m.* (—s, *pl.* —e) penguin (Fettgans).

Pi'nie, *f.* (*pl.* —n) pine-kernel (—n=kern); stone-pine (—n=kiefer).

Pin'ke, *f.* (*pl.* —n) vessel with high stern, pinky.

Pin'keln, *v.n.* to make water (*coll.*).

Pin'ken, *v.n.* (*aux.* h.) to hammer on an anvil.

Pin'kepank! *int.* cling! cling!

Pin'ne, *f.* (*pl.* —n) pinion-feather, quill; point; spindle (*of the capstan*); peg, tack; pivot; thin end of a hammer; tiller; centre-pin (*compass*).

Pin'scher, *m.* (—s, *pl.* —) fox-terrier, English terrier.

Pin'sel, *m.* (—s, *pl.* —) paint-brush; hair-pencil; style (*in art*); junger —, young simpleton, duffer, dunce. —ei', *f.* daubing; stupid trick; stupidity. —er, *m.* (—ers, *pl.* —er), Pins'ler, *m.* dauber. —haft, —ig, *adj.* silly, stupid. —n, *v.a.* & *n.* (*aux.* h.) to handle the brush; to touch (*with a brush*); to paint; to daub; to play the fool (*coll.*). *Comp.* —führung, *f.* method of handling the brush *or* pencil, touch. —stiel, *m.* paint-brush handle, hair-pencil holder. —strich, *m.* stroke of the brush, touch *or* dash of the pencil.

Pionie'r, *m.* (—s, *pl.* —e) pioneer (*Mil.*); die —e, the sappers and miners (*Mil.*).

Pi'pe, *f.* (*pl.* —n) pipe, butt, large vat; pipe (*dial.*); das ist mir (ganz) —, that is all the same to me, I do not care a rap about it (*sl.*).

Pips, *m.* (—(s)es) pip (*in fowls*).

Piqué', Pike', *m.* quilting; cotton fabric, piqué.

Pira't, *m.* (—en, *pl.* —en) pirate. —entum, *n.* piracy.

Pi'rol, *m.* (*also* Piro'l) (—s, *pl.*—e); Vogel—, golden oriole, thrush (*Orn.*).

Pirouet'te, *f.*; eine — schlagen, to pirouette.

Pirsch, *see* Birsch.

Pi'sang, *m.* (—s, *pl.* —e) banana, plantain (*tree*).

Pis'pern, *v.n.* (*aux.* h.) to whisper (*Poet.*).

Pis'se, *f.* urine. —n, *v.n.* (*aux.* h.) to urinate.

Pista'zie, *f.* (*pl.* —n) pistachio-nut: pistachio-tree.

Pisti'll, *n.* (—s, *pl.* —e) pistil (*Bot.*); pestle.

Pisto'l, *n.* (—s, *pl.*—e), —e, *f.* (*pl.* —en) pistol; wie aus der —e geschossen, all of a sudden, abruptly; eine Doppel —e, a double-barrelled pistol. *Comp.* —en=duell, *n.* duel with pistols. —en=griff, *m.* handle, butt-end of a pistol. —en=kappe, *f.* holster-cap. (in) —en=schuß=weite, *f.* (within) pistol-shot. —en=schütze, *m.* pistol-shot.

Pisto'n, *n.* (—s, *pl.* —s) piston; cornet-à-piston. *Comp.* —bläser, *m.* player on the cornet-à-piston.

Pit'sch(e)naß, *adj.* wet through, wet to the skin (*coll.*).

Pittore'sk, *adj.* picturesque.

Plack, *m.* (—es, *pl.* —e), —en, *m.* (—ens, *pl.*

—en) patch, piece; blot, stain; freshly ploughed land; plane surface, plaque. —a't, see Plakat. —en, v.a. to patch; to stick, post up; to placard; to flatten by beating, stamping; to line the walls with earth (*Fort.*).

Pla'ck—en, see Plagen. —er, m. (—ers, pl. —er) vexer; oppressor. —erei', f. vexation; toil drudgery; extortion, oppression.

Plad'dern, v.n. to pour down, rain heavily (*dial.*).

Pla'g—e, f. (pl. —en) plague, torment; vexation; misery; trouble; calamity; nuisance, annoyance; plague (*Med.*); jeder Tag hat seine —e, sufficient for the day is the evil thereof (*prov.*). —en, v.a. to plague, torment; to vex, annoy; to scourge; to worry, harass; sich —en, to toil and moil, to be troubled; sich —en mit, to take trouble about; to be afflicted with (*a disease*); durch —en bewegen zu, to worry into (*doing, etc.*); durch —en bringen um, to worry s.o. out of (*a thing*); geplagt werden von, to be afflicted with (*a disease*). —er, m. (—ers, pl. —er) vexer, tormentor. *Comp.* —e=geist, m. evil *or* mischievous spirit; tormentor; fury. —e=los, adj. untroubled.

Plag'ge, f. (pl. —n) sod. —n, v.a. to sod; to cut sods.

Plagia'—r, m. (—rs, pl. —re) plagiarist. —t, n. (—tes, pl. —te) plagiarism. —tor, m. (—tors, pl. —to'ren) plagiarist.

Plaid, n. (—s, pl. —s) rug. —halter, m., —hülle, —rolle, f. hold-all. —nadel, f. safety-pin.

Plaidie'ren, v.n. (*aux.* h.) to plead.

Plaka't, n. (—es, pl. —e) bill, placard; poster; hier dürfen keine —e angeklebt werden, stick no bills. *Comp.* —ankleber, m. bill-sticker, bill-poster. —anzeiger, m. handbill. —farbe, f. ink for placards.

Plan, I. adj. & adv. plane; plain; simple, clear. II. m. (—s, pl. —e, Plä'ne) plane; plain; arena; battle-field; clearing (*in a wood*); pleasure-ground, lawn; ground (*Paint.*); ground-plan (*Arch.*); (pl. Plä'ne) plan, design, project; ein tief durchdachter —, a carefully thought-out scheme, gedruckter —, prospectus; Pläne schmieden, to make plans; der grüne —, the green plain *or* field, meadow; auf dem —, on the (battle)field. *Comp.* —gemäß, adj. & adv. according to a fixed plan. —hammer, m. planishing hammer. —konvex, adj. plano-convex. —los, adj. & adv. without a regular plan, planless, purposeless. —losigkeit, f. want of design *or* purpose. —macher, Plä'ne=schmied, m. projector, planner, schemer. —mäßig, —voll, adj. planned, systematic, concerted, arranged. —zeichnen, n. plan-drawing.

Pla'n—e, f. awning, tilt (*of a cart*). *Comp.* —wagen, m. tilt-cart.

Pla'nen, v.a. & n. (*aux.* h.) to plane; to hover in the air; to plan, project.

Plane't, m. (—en, pl. —en) planet. —a'risch, adj. planetary. *Comp.* —en=aspekt, m. planetary aspect. —en=bahn, f. orbit of a planet. —en=jahr, n. planetary year. —en=stand, m. aspect (*Astrol.*). —en=system, n. planetary system.

Planie'r—en, v.a. to level, to plane; to size (*paper*). —ung, f. grading (*Railw.*). *Comp.* amboß, m. planishing anvil. —hammer, m planishing hammer. —maschine, f. road-roller. —presse, f. size-press. —wasser, n. size; glue-water.

Plan'k—e, f. (pl. —en) plank, board. —en, v.a. to plank. *Comp.* —eisen, n. caulking iron. —en=werk, n. planking; plank-fence; wainscotting.

Plänkelei', f. (pl. —en) skirmishing.

Plän'k—eln, v.n. (*aux.* h.) to skirmish. —ler, m. (—lers, pl. —ler) skirmisher, sharpshooter.

Plan'sche, Plant'sche, f. (pl. —n) ingot. *Comp.* —n=einguß, m. ingot mould.

Plan'schen, v.a. & n. (*aux.* h.) to splash (*coll.*).

Plapper—ei', f. (pl. —eien) babbling, babble. —er, m. (—ers, pl. —er) blab; gossip. —haft, adj. talkative, babbling. —haftigkeit, f. garrulity. —n, v.a. & n. (*aux.* h.) to babble. *Comp.* —liese, —lotte, f., —maul, n., —tasche, f. babbler, chatterbox, gossip.

Plär'ren, v.n. (*aux.* h.) to bleat, to low; to whimper, blubber; to bawl; to sing badly.

Plas't—ik, f. plastic art. —iker, m. sculptor. —isch, adj. plastic, formative.

Plata'ne, f. (pl. —n) plane-tree.

Plati'n, n. (—s), —a (*usually pron.* Pla'tina), f. platinum, platina. —ie'ren, v.a. to cover, combine *or* coat with platina. *Comp.* —chlo=ri'd, n. platinic chloride. —draht, m. platinum wire. —haltig, adj. platiniferous. —verbindung, f. platinous compound.

Plat'menage, f. cruet-stand, (set of) casters.

Plato'n—iker, m. (—ikers, pl. —iker) Platonist. —isch, adj. Platonic.

Platsch! int. splash! —en, v.n. (*aux.* h.) to splash; (*aux.* s.) to fall plump. *Comp.* —fuß, m. flat foot. —(e)naß, adj. dripping wet, drenched.

Plät'schern, v.n. (*aux.* h.) to splash, dabble; to ripple, murmur, plash.

Platt, I. adj. & adv. flat, plain, level; flat, dull; low, vulgar; plain, downright; low (*of a dialect*); astonished, amazed (*sl.*); —es Land, flat *or* open country; —es Gesicht, flat face; —e Scherze, low *or* vulgar jokes; —e Aussprache, broad pronunciation; —es Benehmen, boorish manners; —er Widerspruch, downright *or* flat contradiction; —e Wahrheit, plain, naked truth; ein —es Gespräch, a dull discourse; — abschlagen, to give a flat refusal; — auf der Erde liegen, to lie flat on the ground; das —e Gegenteil, quite the contrary; ich sagte es ihm — heraus, I told it him straight out; — schlagen, to flatten; ich war ganz —, I was quite taken aback (*sl.*); Segeln nach der —en Karte, plane sailing; —es Deutsch *or* —deutsch, low German, North German dialect(s). —e, f. (pl. —en) plate; dish; tray; salver; bald head; tonsure; clearing in a wood; plate, sheet (*of metal*); plinth (*Arch.*); smoothing-iron; stereotype plate; flaw (*in cloth*); flat top (*of a hat, nail, etc.*); small plateau; smooth slope of rock; sand-bank, leaf (*of a table*); in —en brechen, to flake off. —heit, f. flatness; levelness; flatness, insipidity; trite expression; (pl.) platitudes. —ie'ren, v.a. to plate; to cover (*hats*); mit Silber —iert, silver-plated. —ie'rer, m. (—ierers, pl. —ierer) plater. *Comp.* —bogig, adj. elliptical. —boot, n. flat-bottomed boat, barge. —deutsch, adj. & n. Low-German, the North German dialects. —en=abdruck, m. stereotyped proof. —en=druck, m. stereotyping, stereotypography. —en=förmig, adj. plate-shaped; lamelliform. —en=hammer, m. blacksmith's hammer. —en=kupfer, n. sheet-copper. —en=rüstung, f. plate-armour. —en=schläger, m. plate-maker. —en=schrift, f.; mit —enschrift drucken, to stereotype. —en=schwingung, f. vibration of plates (*Acoust.*). —er=dings, adv absolutely, positively, by all means; straight out; —erdings nicht, not by any means, in no case. —fisch, m. flatfish, plaice, flounder. —form, f. platform. —fuß, m. sole of the foot; flat foot. —füßig, adj. flat-footed. —garn, n. embroidery cotton. —gedrückt, adj. flattened. —ier'=kunst, f. art of plating. —kopf, m. flat head; shallow pate. —lot, n. apron (*Artil.*); cap of a gun. —schiff, n. barge, lighter. —schienen, pl. plate rails (*Railw.*). —stich, m. satin-stitch

—stickerei, *f.* satin-stitch embroidery. —strecken, *n.* stretching, pressing, dressing of felt. —ware, *f.* plates, *etc.* —we'g, *see* —zu. —zange, *f.* pliers. —ziegel, *m.* flat tile. —zu', *adv.* flatly, roundly, peremptorily.

Plätt'—bar, *adj.* laminable. —chen, *n.* (—chens, *pl.* —chen) small plate; lamella (*Bot.*); fillet (*Arch.*); membrane (*Med.*). —e, *f.* (*pl.* —en) ironing; flat-iron. —en, *v.a.* to iron (*linen, etc.*); *see* Platten. —er, *m.* (—ers, *pl.* —er), —erin, *f.* ironer. *Comp.* (*also* Platt—) —bolzen, —stahl, *m.* heater for a smoothing-iron. —brett, *n.* ironing board; a lean, flat-chested woman, a regular straight Jane (*coll.*). —eisen, *n.* smoothing-iron. —glocke, *f.* box-iron. —kissen, *n.* covered ironing-board. —ofen, *m.* stove for heating smoothing-irons. —zeug, *n.* linen (to be) ironed, fine linen.

Platt'eis, *m.*, **Platt'eise**, *f.* plaice, flat-fish.

Plat'ten, *v.a.* to flatten; to level; to plate, laminate (*wire*); to lay (*beams*) flat one on the other.

¹**Platz**, *m.* (—es, *pl.* Plät'ze) place, spot; room, space, place, stand; stand (*for carriages*); situation, appointment, place, post; ein fester —, a fortress; freier —, open space, esplanade, area; viereckiger, mit Häusern umgebener —, a square (*in a town*); hier ist kein — mehr, there is no more room here; — da! make way there! — nehmen, to sit down; — genommen! be seated! take a seat! wieder an seinen — thun, to put back, replace; jemandes Bitte — finden lassen, to grant a p.'s request; — machen, to make way, clear the way (*for*), to fall back; nicht am —e, irrelevant, out of place; 500 blieben auf dem —e, five hundred were slain; immer auf dem —e sein, to be always on the alert; to be ready for anything; auf dem —e! on the spot! at once! — greifen, to take root, to take effect. *Comp.* —adjutant, *m.* town adjutant. —bedarf, *m.* local wants. —geschäft, *n.* local business. —karte, *f.* seat-ticket. —kommandant, —major, *m.* commandant, major of a fortress. —meister, *m.* doorkeeper at theatres. —verkauf, *m.* sale on the spot. —verlust, *m.* loss on the spot. —wechsel, *m.* change of place; local bill.

²**Platz**, *m.* (—es, *pl.* Plät'ze) bun, yeast cake.

³**Platz**, I. *int.* smash, crack. II. *m.* (—es, *pl.* —e, Plät'ze) smash, crack, slap, clap, crash; explosion. *Comp.* —kugel, *f.* shell, bursting ball. —patrone, *f.*; mit —patronen schießen, to shoot with blank cartridge. —pulver, *n.* fulminating powder. —regen, *m.* sudden downpour of rain, pelting rain, heavy shower.

Plätz'—chen, *n.* (—chens, *pl.* —chen) little place; pastille, drop, lozenge. —en, *v.a.* & *n.* (*aux.* h.) to pop; to slap, smack; to blaze (*trees*).

Plat'zen, *v.n.* (*aux.* h.) to fall with a crash; to crack; crackle; (*aux.* s.) to burst, explode; einem ins Zimmer —, to burst into a p.'s room; (mit etwas) heraus —, to burst out with s. th., to blurt out s. th.

Plät'zewechseln, *n.* general post (*game*).

Plauder—ei', *f.* chattering; tittle-tattle, gossip. —er, *m.* (—ers, *pl.* —er) chatterer; chatterbox; gossip. —haft, *adj.* tattling, talkative, gossiping. —haftigkeit, *f.* loquacity. —n, *v.n.* (*aux.* h.) to babble, chatter, prate; to gossip. *Comp.* —hans, *m.*, —liese, *f.*, —maul, *n.*, —tasche, *f.* chatterbox; tattler. —stündchen, *n.* a cozy chat, an hour's chat.

Plau'schen, *v.n.* to chat (*dial.*).

Plausi'b—el, *adj.* plausible. —ilitä't, *f.* plausibility.

Plauz! *interj.* bounce, bang, smash! —en, *v.n.* to fall down with a bang (*coll.*).

Pleb—e'jer, *m.* (—ejers, *pl.* —ejer), —e'jerin, *f.* plebeian. —e'jertum, *n.* plebeians; plebeianism. —e'jisch, *adj.* plebeian. —iszi't, *n.* (—iszits, *pl.* —iszite) plebiscite, plebiscitum.

Plebs, *f.* plebs; common people, populace, mob.

Plei'te, *f.* bankruptcy (*sl.*). *adj.* bankrupt; — gehen, to go smash, fail (*in business*) (*sl.*); to get lost (*of things*); — gehen, — machen, to become bankrupt (*coll.*); so —, so —, in for a penny, in for a pound (*coll.*).

Pleja'den, *pl.* Pleiades.

Plem'pe, *f.* (*pl.* —n) short sword, spit (*mil. sl.*); bad beer *or* coffee (*vulg.*). —rn, *v.a.* to splash (*prov.*); to tope.

Ple'n—um, *n.* (—ums) full assembly. *Comp.* —ar'sitzung, *f.* full sitting (*of a court*); general meeting (*of shareholders, etc.*).

Pleonas'mus, *m.* (*pl.* —en) pleonasm.

Pleue'lstange, *f.* connecting-rod (*Mach.*).

Pli, *m.* (—s) easy deportment.

Plin'ke—(l)n, —rn, *v.n.* to blink, make signs with the eyes, to blink, wink (*coll.*).

Plin'se, **Plin'ze**, *f.* (*pl.* —n) thin fritter, pancake, fritter, omelette.

Plioce'n, *adj.* pliocene (*Geol.*).

Plom'b—e, *f.* (*pl.* —en) lead; filling (*for a tooth*). —ie'ren, *v.a.* to lead (*goods*), to affix leads to; to plug, to stop (*a tooth*).

Plöt'ze, *f.* (*pl.* —n) roach, bleak.

Plötz'lich, I. *adj.* sudden, abrupt. II. *adv.* all at once; etwas —, very quickly, without more ado (*sl.*). —keit, *f.* suddenness, abruptness.

Plu'derhosen, *pl.* wide trousers.

Plump, I. *adj.* coarse, heavy, clumsy; rude, blunt, illbred; —e Schmeichelei, gross flattery; ein —es Wesen haben, to have blunt manners. II. *m.* (—es, *pl.* —e) plump, heavy fall. —heit, *f.* coarseness, clumsiness; bluntness. *Comp.* —sack, *m.* game of the knotted handkerchief (*handkerchief twisted into a knot with which blows are dealt in a romping game*), the knot; clumsy person, lout; dreh' dich nicht um, der —sack geht 'rum, don't turn about, the knot is going round!

Plum'p—en, *v.n.* (*aux.* s.) to fall plump; to blurt out; to bounce (*into*). —sen, *v.n.* (*aux.* h. & s.) *see* —en.

Plun'der, *m.* (—s) lumber, trash, rubbish. *Comp.* —kammer, *f.* lumber-room. —kram, *m.* litter, lumber. —mann, *m.* rag-man. —markt, *m.* rag-fair. —wagen, *m.* baggage-waggon. —weisheit, *f.* useless knowledge.

Plün'derer, *m.* (—s, *pl.* —) plunderer.

Plün'der—n, *v.a.* to plunder, pillage, sack; to rob. —ung, *f.* plundering, sack, sacking; der —ung preisgeben, to give up to pillage, to allow to be sacked.

Pluralitä't, *f.* plurality.

Plus, *adv.* plus. *Comp.* —macher, *m.* financial schemer. —quamperfektum, *n.* pluperfect. —vorgaben, *pl.* received odds (*Tennis*). —zeichen, *n.* plus-sign (+).

Plüsch (*long* ü), *m.* (—es, *pl.* —e) plush; shag. —en, *adj.* plush.

Plutonis'mus, *m.* Plutonic theory.

Pneuma't—ik, *f.* pneumatics. —isch, *adj.* pneumatic; —ische Bremsen, pneumatic brakes.

Pö'bel, *m.* (—s, *pl.* —) mob, populace, rabble. —ei', *f.* vulgarity; low conduct *or* expression. —haft, *adj.* vulgar, low, plebeian; —haftes Benehmen, low conduct, coarseness of manner. —haftigkeit, *f.* lowness, vulgarity; coarseness. *Comp.* —ausdruck, *m.* vulgarism. —haufe, *m.* rabble. —herrschaft, *f.* mob-rule. —justiz, *f.* lynch-law. —sprache, *f.* vulgar language. —wort, *n.* low word, vulgarism.

Po'ch—en, *v.* I. *a.* to break, crush, pound. II. *a.* & *n.* (*aux.* h.) to knock; to stamp; to beat, throb; man —t, there is a knock at the door; mir —t das Herz, my heart beats *or* throbs; auf eine S. —en, to brag of, to boast, to presume upon a th. —er, *m.* (—ers, *pl.* —er) knocker; stamper; boaster, braggart. *Comp.* —brett, *n.* poke-board (*game*). —erz, *n.* ore rough from the mine. —herd, *m.* buddle. —kasten, *m.* pounding *or* stamping trough. —mehl, *n.* pulverized ore. —schlägel, *m.* ore-hammer. —spiel, *n.* poker (*game at cards*). —stempel, *m.* stamp (*Min.*). —werk, *n.* pounding machine, stamping-mill.

Po'ck—e, *f.* (*pl.* —en) pock; pock-mark; die —en, small-pox. —icht, (*obs.*) —ig, *adj.* pock-marked; variolous. *Comp.* —en=gift, *n.* small-pox virus. —en=grube, —en=narbe, *f.* pock-mark. —en=grübig, *adj.* pock-pitted. —en=impfung, *f.* vaccination. —en=krank, *adj.* ill with *or* suffering from the small-pox. —en=lymphe, *f.* variolo-vaccine.

Po'dagra, *n.* (—s) gout, podagra.

Poesie', *f.* (*pl.* —en) poetry; piece of poetry, poem. *Comp.* —los, *adj.* without poetry, unpoetical, prosaic, dull, commonplace.

Poe't, *m.* (—en, *pl.* —en) poet. —ik, *f.* theory of poetry, poetics. —isch, *adj.* poetic. —isie'ren, *v.n.* (*aux.* h.) to poetize, to write poetry.

Pog'ge, *f.* (*pl.* —n) (*dial.*) frog.

Pointie'ren, *v.* I. *a.* to point (*a gun, a telescope*); einen Gedanken —, to express an idea pointedly *or* to the point. II. *n.* (*aux.* h.) to punt (*at hazard, etc.*).

Poka'l, *m.* (—s, *pl.* —e) goblet, drinking-cup.

Pokulie'ren, *v.n.* (*aux.* h.) to drink, carouse.

Pö'kel, *m.* (—s) brine, pickle. —n, *v.a.* to salt, corn, pickle. *Comp.* —fleisch, *n.* salt meat, corned beef. —hering, *m.* pickled herring.

Pol, *m.* (—s, *pl.* —e) pole. —a'r, *adj.* polar. —arisie'ren, *v.a.* to polarize. —aritä't, *f.* polarity. *Comp.* —(ar)=bär, *m.* polar bear. —arisations=ebene, *f.* plane of polarization. —arisations=ströme, *pl.* currents of polarization (*Elect.*). —ar=länder, *adj.* arctic regions. —(ar)=kreis, *m.* polar circle. —ar=meer, *n.* Arctic ocean; südliches —armeer, Antarctic ocean. —(ar)=stern, *m.* polar star, lodestar (*poet.*). —ar=völker, *pl.* inhabitants of the polar regions. —ar=zone, *f.* frigid zone. —höhe, *f.* elevation of the pole; latitude; —höhe seiner Beliebtheit, zenith of his popularity. —stein, *m.* loadstone, lodestone. —stein=kraft, *f.* magnetic power.

Pol'der, *m.* (—s, *pl.* —) marshy ground reclaimed from fen-land *or* sea by canalization and protected by dikes.

Pole'm—ik, *f* polemics, controversy. —iker, *m.* (—ikers, *pl.* —iker) controversialist. —isch, *adj.* polemic. —isie'ren, *v.n.* to carry on a controversy; (gegen eine S.) to controvert (s.th.).

Polie'r—bar, *adj.* polishable. —en, *v.a.* to polish, brighten, burnish; to furbish; to French-polish. —er, *m.* (—ers, *pl.* —er) polisher; French-polisher; foreman-mason. *Comp.* —eisen, *n.*, —stahl, *m.* burnisher. —stock, *m.* polishing-stick; brazier's polishing anvil.

Politi'k, *f.* politics; policy.

Poli't—iker, *m.* (—ikers, *pl.* —iker) politician. —ikus, *m.* politician, diplomat, sly old fox. —isch, *adj.* & *adv.* political; politic.

Politu'r, *f.* (*pl.* —en) polish; varnish; er hat viel —, he is a man of the world, a very polished man.

Polizei', *f.* (*pl.* —en) police; police-station. —lich, *adj.* & *adv.* police; —lich verboten, contrary to police regulations; unter —licher Aufsicht stehen, to be under police supervision. *Comp.* —amt, —bureau, *n.* police-station. —beamte(r), *m.* police-officer. —behörde, *f.* police (authorities). —diener, *m.* policeman. —gericht, *n.* police-court. —leutnant, *m.* lieutenant of the police-force, inspector of police. —macht, *f.* constabulary force. —ordnung, *f.* police regulation. —reiter, *m.* mounted policeman. —richter, *m.* police magistrate. —spitzel, *m.* police spy. —staat, *m.* state ruled by the police. —stunde, *f.* closing hour for public-houses. —truppe, *f.* constabulary, police. —wache, *f.* police station. —wachtmeister, *m.* police sergeant. —wesen, *n.* police department. —widrig, *adj.* contrary to police regulations; —widrige Nase, enormous nose (*coll.*).

Polizi'st, *m.* (—en, *pl.* —en) policeman, constable; bobby (*sl.*).

Pol'ka, I. *adj.* (*obs.*) elegant, fashionable. II. *f.* (*pl.* —s) polka; — tanzen, to polk, to dance the polka.

Pol'ster, *n.* (—s, *pl.* —) cushion; bolster; hassock; stuffing; pad, padding. —n, *v.a.* to stuff, pad. *Comp.* —bank, *f.* cushioned bench. —bett, *n.* divan, ottoman. —förmig, *adj.* pulvinate (*Arch., Bot.*). —reifen, *m.* cushion tire. —stuhl, *m.* easy chair.

Pol'ter—er, *m.* (—ers, *pl.* —er) blustering person, bully, hector; roisterer, noisy person. —n, *v.n.* (*aux.* h. & s.) to make a noise by knocking *or* tumbling things about; to knock, rattle; to bluster, scold. *Comp.* —abend, *m.* nuptial eve (*celebrated by gay and noisy rites at the bride's home*). —geist, *m.* hobgoblin; noisy fellow. —kammer, *f.* lumber-room.

Poltro'n, *m.* (—s, *pl.* —) poltroon.

Poly—an'drisch, *adj.* polyandrous (*Bot.*). —ga'misch, *adj.* polygamous. —glot'te, *f.* polyglot. —gona'l, *adj.* polygonal, multangular. —gy'nisch, *adj.* polygynian (*Bot.*). —p (*pron.* Poly'p), *m.* (—pen, *pl.* —pen) polyp(e) (*Zoöph.*); polypus. —pho'nisch, *adj.* polyphonic. —tech'nik, *f.* polytechnics. —tech'niker, *m.* student at a polytechnic academy. —tech'nikum, *n.* polytechnic institute. —tech'nisch, *adj.* polytechnic. —thei'smus, *m.* polytheism.

Poma'd—e, *f.* (*pl.* —en) pomade; pomatum; coolness, ease (*sl.*); das ist mir —e, that is nothing to me; in der —e bleiben, to keep one's hair on (*sl.*). —ig, *adj.* phlegmatic, indifferent; easy-going; pomaded. *Comp.* —en=büchse, *f.* pomatum-pot. —en=hengst, *m.* dandy; fop. —isie'ren, *v.a.* to grease *or* scent with pomatum.

Pomeran'ze, *f.* (*pl.* —n) orange. *Comp.* —n=farben, —n=farbig, *adj.* orange-coloured. —n=schale, *f.* orange-peel; eingemachte —n=schale, candied orange-peel.

Pomp, *m.* (—s, *pl.* —e) pomp. —haft, *adj.* pompous, stately. —haftigkeit, *f.* pomp; pomposity. —ö's, *adj.* splendid, magnificent.

Ponie'ren, *v.a.*; drei Flaschen Wein —, to stand three bottles of wine (*sl.*).

Pontifika't, *n.* (—s, *pl.* —e) pontificate.

Ponto'n, *m.* (—s, *pl.* —s) pontoon. *Comp.* —brücke, *f.* pontoon bridge. —thor, *n.* floating gate of a dock.

Po'panz, *m.* (—es, *pl.* —e) bugbear, scarecrow.

Popul—ä'r, *adj.* & *adv.* popular; sich —är machen, to make o.s. a general favourite, to ingratiate o.s. with everyone; —är=wissenschaftliche Vorlesung, scientific lecture for the general public. —arisie'ren, *v.a.* to popularize. —aritä't, *f.* popularity.

Por—ö's, *adj.* porous. —ositä't, *f.* porosity.

Por'phyr, *m.* (—s, *pl.* —e) porphyry.

Port—ie'r, *m.* (—iers, *pl.* —iers) porter, door-keeper; stiller —ier, tablet hung up in the entrance hall of a house with the names, *etc.*, of the occupants. —o, *see* Porto. *Comp.* —e=chaise, *f.* sedan chair. —e=feuille, *f.* portfolio. —(e)=epée, *n.* sword-knot. —(e)=epée=fähnrich, *m.* ensign. —e=monnaie, *n.* purse.

Portio'n, *f.* (*pl.* —en) portion; plate (*of meat*); ration; eine — Thee und zwei Tassen, a pot of tea and two cups; **zwei —en Kaffee**, coffee for two. *Comp.* **—en=weise**, *adv.* in rations; by the plateful.

Por'to, *n.* (—s) postage; carriage. *Comp.* —**frei**, *adj.* free of postage; prepaid, post-free. —**freiheit**, *f.* exemption from postage. —**pflichtig**, *adj.* subject to postage. —**satz**, *m.* rate of postage. —**vergütung**, *f.* refunding of postage; **unter —vergütung**, repaying postage. —**zuschlag**, *m.* additional postage, extra stamp.

Porträ't, *n.* (—s, *pl.* —s) portrait, likeness. —**ie'ren**, *v.a.* to portray, take the likeness of, to paint a portrait of. *Comp.* —**maler**, *m.* portrait-painter. —**malerei**, *f.* portrait-painting.

Por'tugalle, *f.* (*pl.* —n) kind of Southern fruit.

Por'tulak, *m*, (—s) purslane (*Bot.*).

Porzella'n, *n.* (—s, *pl.* —e) (real) china, porcelain; **unechtes** —, earthenware; **Delfter** —, delft; **sächsisches** (*or* **Meißner**) —, Dresden china; **gemaltes** —, Japan china. —**en**, *adj.* porcelain, china. *Comp.* —**aufsatz**, *m.* china service. —**blau**, *adj.* china-blue. —**brennerei**, *f.* porcelain manufactory. —**gefäß**, *n.* china vase. —**glasur**, —**glätte**, *f.* enamel on china. —**handlung**, *f.* china shop. —**malerei**, *f.* painting on china.

Posame'nt, *n.* (—(e)s, *pl.* —e) gold *or* silver lace; gimp; galloon. —**ie'r**, *m.* (—iers, *pl.* —iere), —**ie'rer**, *m.* (—ierers, *pl.* —ierer) maker of gold lace, *etc.* *Comp.* —**ier'=arbeit**, *f.* lace-work, gimp *or* fringe-work.

Posau'n—e, *f.* (*pl.* —en) trombone; (large) trumpet; **die letzte —e**, the last trump(et), the trump of doom. *Comp.* —**en=bläser**, *m.* trombone-player. —**en=engel**, *m.* angel with puffed-out cheeks, chub-cheeked baby (*coll.*).

Posau'n—en, *v.a.* & *n.* (*aux.* **h.**) to play the trombone; to sound, proclaim aloud; **er —t seinen eigenen Ruhm aus**, he blows his own trumpet (*coll.*).

Po'se, *f.* (*pl.* —n) quill; pose; feather (*coll.*); **'raus aus den —n!** get out of (your) bed! get up! (*coll.*).

Positi'v, I. *adj.* positive; —**e Größe**, positive *or* affirmative quantity; —**es Recht**, statute law. II. *m.* (—s, *pl.* —e) positive (*degree*). III. *n.* (—s, *pl.* —e) portable organ, chamber-organ.

Positu'r, *f.* (*pl.* —en) posture; **sich in — setzen** *or* **stellen**, to put o.s. on one's guard; to square up.

Pos's—e, *f.* (*pl.* —en) drollery, buffoonery; jest; piece of fun; farce; —**en reißen**, to play the buffoon; —**en treiben mit**, to play tricks on; **einem etwas zum —en thun**, to do a thing to vex some one; —**en!** pshaw! nonsense! —**en=haft**, *adj.* droll, comic, farcical. —**ier'lich**, *adj.* odd; droll, comic, funny, waggish. —**ier'=lichkeit**, *f.* comicalness. *Comp.* —**en=macher**, —**en=reißer**, *m.* buffoon, jester. —**en=spiel**, —**en=stück**, *n.* farce (*Theat.*); stuff, nonsense.

Post, *f.* (*pl.* —en) post-office; post, mail; mail-coach; stage, relay; news, intelligence; **Reichs** —, Imperial (German) Post; **Haupt** —, General Post-Office; — **nehmen**, to post (*by horse*); **wie auf der — gehen**, to go post-haste; **mit der — fahren**, to travel by post; **mit der heutigen** —, by to-day's post; **mit umgehender** *or* **wendender** —, by return of post; **Hiobs**—, bad news; **Welt**—, universal postal union; **auf die — geben** *or* **tragen**, to (take *or* send to the) post. —**en**, *m.* (—ens, *pl.* —en) post, station, place; sentry, sentinel; picket; post, situation; entry, article, item; lot, parcel; (**Reh—en**) buck-shot, deer-shot; **ein kleiner** —, a small item (*C.L.*); **ein starker** —, a strong picket (*Mil.*); —**en zu Pferde**, vedette; (**auf**) —**en stehen**, to be on guard, to stand sentinel; **auf seinem —en sein**, to be at one's post; **nicht auf dem —en sein**, to feel out of sorts, seedy (*coll.*). —**ame'nt**, *n.* (—aments, *pl.* —amen'te) pedestal, base. —**ie'ren**, *v.a.* to post, place. —**illio'n**, *m.* (—illions, *pl.* —illione) postillion. —**o**, *m.* post, stand; —**o fassen**, to take one's stand. *Comp.* —**adreß=buch**, *n.* post-office directory. —**amt**, *n.* post-office; situation in the post-office; **fahrendes —amt**, travelling post-office. —**annahme=stempel**, *m.* date stamp, dated stamp. —**anschluß**, *m.* postal connection *or* communication. —**anstalt**, *f.* post-office. —**anwärter**, *m.* candidate. —**anweisung**, *f.* money order. —**auftrag**, *m.* order for collection of money. *See* —**nachnahme**. —**ausgabe=stempel**, *m.* stamp of delivery office. —**aushülfs=stelle**, *f.* sub-post-office (*often in a shop*). —**beamte(r)**, *m.* employee of the post-office. —**beförderung**, *f.* postal service; **der Zug hat —beförderung**, the train carries mails, is a mail train; —**beförderung auf Landwegen**, conveyance of mails by road. —**beförderungs=dienst**, *m.* mail service, conveyance of the mails. —**begleit=dienst**, *m.* travelling mail service. —**bericht**, *m.* post-office notice. —**bezirk**, *m.* postal district. —**bon**, *m.* postal order. —**bote**, *m.* postman, letter-carrier. —**dampfschiff**, *n.* mail packet. —**diebstahl**, *m.* mail robbery. —**dienst**, *m.* postal service, mail service, post-office duty. —**dienst=stunden**, *pl.* hours of attendance at a post-office. —**direktion**, *f.* general post-office. —**direktor**, *see* —**meister**. —**eile**, *f.* post-haste. —**einzahlung**, *f.* *see* —**anweisung**. —**eleve**, *m.* learner (at a post-office). —**en=kette**, *f.* chain of military posts. —**expedition**, *f.* post-office. —**felleisen**, *n.* pouch. —**frei**, *adj.* post-paid; post-free. —**gebühr**, *f.* postal charge. —**gebühren**, —**gefälle**, *pl.* revenues of the post-office. —**geld**, *n.* postage; fare. —**fuhrwesen**, *n.* horse post service (*not in Engl.*). —**gut**, *n.* goods conveyed by post. —**halter**, *m.* keeper of post-horses; mail contractor. —**halterei'**, *f.* posting establishment. —**haltestelle**, *f.* stage. —**handbuch**, *n.* post-office guide, book giving postal information. —**horn**, *n.* post horn, postillion's horn. —**hülfs=stelle**, *f.* sub-post-office. —**jacht**, *f.* advice-boat. —**karte**, *f.* post-card; **Ansichts —karte**, pictorial post-card. —**kasse**, *f.* chief postal cash office. —**kasten**, *m.* letter box. —**knecht**, *m.* postboy. —**kontravention**, *f.* infringement of the postal laws. —**kutsche**, *f.* mail-coach; post-chaise. —**lagernd**, *adv.* to be left (*at the P. O.*) till called for; poste-restante; —**lagernde Sendung**, to be kept till called for, poste-restante article. —**landkarte**, *f.* map of mail routes. —**lauf**, *m.* course *or* line of a post. —**leitheft**, *n.* schedule of departures and arrivals of mails. —**mandat**, *n.* *see* —**auftrag**. —**marke**, *f.* adhesive postage stamp. —**meister**, *m.* postmaster. —**nachnahme**, *f.*; **gegen —nachnahme**, (money) to be collected by the postal authorities *or* on delivery (*not done in England*). —**numerando**, *n.*; —**numerando bezahlen**, to pay after receipt. —**ordnung**, *f.* post-office regulation(s). —**ort**, *m.* post-town; stage. —**paket**, *n.* parcel sent by post. —**papier**, *n.* note-paper. —**quittung**, *f.* certificate of posting (*parcels*). —**regal**, *n.* post-office royalty, postal privilege. —**reise**, *f.* journey by mail-coach. —**reisende(r)**, *m.* passenger by the mail-coach. —**reiter**, *m.* courier. —**säule**, *f.* mile-stone. —**schaffner**, *m.* mail guard; —**schaffner im Bahndienst**, railway mail guard. —**schalter**, *m.* post-office counter *or* window. —**schein**, *m.* post-office receipt; certificate of posting (*in the case of parcels*); ticket for a mail coach. —**schiff**, *n.* advice-boat; packet-boat, mail packet. **—schiffahrts=linie,** *f.* packet-line, line of mail packets. **—schluß,** *m.;* **vor —schluß,** within post hours, before the mail goes out. **—schreiber,** *m.* post-office clerk. **—schwede,** *n.* post-office clerk *or* postman (*coll.*). **—sekretär,** *m.* post-office clerk; **Ober—sekretär,** chief clerk. **—sendung,** *f.* mail matter, postal article. **—sparkasse,** *f.* post-office savings-bank. **—station,** *f.* stage. **—stempel,** *m.* office stamp; *see* **—zeichen.** **—straße,** *f.* high road. **—stube,** *f.* waiting-room, travellers' room. **—stunden,** *pl.* hours of business at a post-office. **—tag,** *m.* mail day. **—tasche,** *f.* private bag. **—transport,** *m.* conveyance of mails. **—verbindung,** *f.* postal communication. **—verein,** *m.* postal union. **—verkehr,** *m.* postal traffic. **—verwalter,** *m.* chief clerk; deputy postmaster (*not in Engl.*). **—vorschuß,** *m. see* **—nachnahme.** **—wagen,** *m.* mail-coach, stage coach; mail car (*Engl.*), postal car (*Am.*); diligence. **—wechsel,** *m.* change of horses. **—wendend,** *adv.* by return of post. **—wertzeichen,** *m.* postage stamp; **gummiertes —wertzeichen,** adhesive postage stamp. **—wesen,** *n.* postal affairs *or* system; postal service. **—zeichen,** *n.* post-mark. **—zug,** *m.* mail-train; team of post-horses. **—zwang,** *m.* postal privilege.

Post—il'le, *f.* (*pl.* **—illen**) postil, book of family sermons. **—skrip'tum,** *n.* postscript (P.S.).

Postul—a't, *n.* (**—ats,** *pl.* **—ate**) postulate. **—ie'ren,** *v.a.* to postulate.

Po'tentat, *m.* (**—en,** *pl.* **—en**) potentate, monarch.

Pote'nz, *f.* (*pl.* **—en**) power; **zweite —,** square; **dritte —,** cube. **—ie'ren,** *v.a.* to raise to a higher power (*Math.*). **—ie'rung,** *f.* involution.

Pott, *m.* (**—es,** *pl.* **Pöt'te**) pot (*sl. & dial.*).

Pott— (*in comp.*) **—asche,** *f.* potash. **—erde,** *f.* potter's clay. **—lot,** *n.* black lead.

Potz— (*for* **Gott(e)s**) (*in comp.*) **—bli'tz! —tau'send! —wet'ter!** *int.* my goodness! good gracious! the deuce! I say!

Pou'le, *f.* pool (*game*).

Poussie'ren, *v.a.* to promote, patronize, push; **sich —,** to push one's way in the world; **ein Mädchen —,** to make love to, to flirt with a girl (*sl.*).

Prä, *n.* preference; **das — haben,** to come *or* rank first.

Präben'de, *see* **Pfründe.**

Prä—cede'nz, *f.* precedence. **—cedenz'fall,** *m.,* (**—cede'ns,** *n.,*) precedent. **—cipitatio'n,** *n.* precipitation. **—cipitie'ren,** *v.a.* to hasten, precipitate. **—ci's,** *adj.* precise; punctual. **—cisio'n,** *f.* precision; punctuality. **—desti=nie'ren,** *v.a.* to predestinate. **—dika'bel,** *adj.* predicable. **—dika'nt,** *m.* (**—dikan'ten,** *pl.* **—dikan'ten**) preacher. **—dika't,** *n.* (**—dikats,** *pl.* **—dikate**) predicate; title; (good *or* bad) note, report, marks. **—fe'kt,** *m.* (**—fek'ten,** *pl.* **—fek'ten**) prefect. **—fi'x,** *n.* (**—fixes,** *pl.* **—fixe**) prefix. **—judi'z,** *n.* (**—judizes,** *pl.* **—judize**) prejudice; **ohne —judiz,** without prejudice (*to the established custom*), reserving (*our*) rights. **—klusio'n,** *f.* foreclosure (*Law*). **—la't,** *m.* (**—laten,** *pl.* **—laten**) prelate. **—latu'r,** *f.* prelacy. **—limina'r,** *adj.* preliminary. **—limina'rien,** *pl.* preliminaries. **—ludie'ren,** *v.a. & n.* to prelude. **—lu'dium,** *n.* (**—ludiums,** *pl.* **—ludien**) prelude. **—mie,** *f.* (*pl.* **—mien**) premium, prize; premium *or* rate (*of insurance, etc.*); bonus; lottery-prize. **—mien=geschäfte,** *pl.* time-bargains, negotiations for time. **—mien=lotterie,** *f.* lottery with prizes. **—mien=schein,** *m.* premium-bond. **—mien=schießen,** *n.* shooting for prizes. **—mi'se,** *f.* (*pl.* **—missen**) premise. **—monstracen'ser,** *m.* (**—monstracensers,** *pl.* **—monstracenser**) Premonstrant (monk), white canon. **—numeran'do,** *adv.* in advance, beforehand. **—numera'nt,** *m.* (**—numeran'ten,** *pl.* **—numeran'ten**) subscriber. **—numeratio'n,** *f.* subscription. **—nume=rie'ren,** *v.a.* to subscribe. **—numerations'=liste,** *f.* subscription list. **—para'nd,** *m.* (**—paran'den,** *pl.* **—paran'den**) one being trained as a pupil in a training college for elementary teachers. **—para't,** *n.* (**—parates,** *pl.* **—parate**) preparation. **—positio'n,** *f.* preposition. **—rogati'v,** *n.* (**—rogativs,** *pl.* **—rogative**), **—rogati've,** *f.* (*pl.* **—rogativen**) prerogative. **—sens,** *n.* (*pl.* **—sen'tia**) present tense. **—se'nt,** *n.* (**—sen'tes,** *pl.* **—sen'te**) present, gift. **—senta'nt,** *m.* (**—sentan'ten,** *pl.* **—sentan'ten**) presenter, holder (*of a bill*); presenter (*to an office*). **—sentie'ren,** *v.a.* to present. **—sen=tier'teller,** *m.* tray, salver. **—se'nz,** *f.* presence. **—senz'liste,** *f.* list of members attending a meeting *or* congress; muster-roll (*Mil.*). **—senz'stärke,** *f.* effective (*peace*) force (*Mil.*). **—ses,** *m.* (**—ses,** *pl.* **—ses, —sides**), **—si=de'nt,** *m.* (**—siden'ten,** *pl.* **—siden'ten**) president; chairman; speaker (*Brit. Parl.*); moderator. **—siden'ten=stelle,** *f.* presidency. **—siden'ten=wahl,** *f.* election of a president. **—sidie'ren,** *v.n.* (*aux.* **h.**) to preside. **—si'=dium,** *n.* (**—sidiums,** *pl.* **—sidien**) presidency; chair. **—tende'nt,** *m.* (**—tenden'ten,** *pl.* **—tenden'ten**) claimant, pretender. **—te'ritum,** *n.* (**—teritums,** *pl.* **—terita**) preterite, past tense. **—toria'ner,** *pl.* prætorian guards. **—tu'r,** *f.* prætorship.

Pracht, *f.* pomp, state; splendour, magnificence; luxury; **das ist eine —!** that 's splendid! **das ist eine — von einem Becher,** that is a magnificent goblet. *Comp.* **—aufzug,** *m.* pageant. **—ausgabe,** (*abbr.* **Pr. A.**) *f.* édition de luxe. **—bau,** *m.,* **—gebäude,** *n.* splendid building. **—bett,** *n.* state-bed. **—einband,** *m.* sumptuous, choice binding. **—exemplar,** *n.* fine specimen, splendid copy (*of a book*). **—gesetze,** *pl.* sumptuary laws. **—grabmal,** *n.* mausoleum. **—himmel,** *m.* canopy. **—kerl,** *m.* splendid fellow, brick (*coll.*). **—liebe,** *f.* love of splendour. **—liebend,** *adj.* fond of show, ostentatious. **—los,** *adj.* unostentatious. **—stück,** *n.* choice piece, fine specimen, beauty (*coll.*). **—voll,** *adj.* gorgeous, magnificent. **—wagen,** *m.* state coach. **—werk,** *n.* splendid work, choice edition. **—zimmer,** *n.* stateroom.

Präch'tig, *adj. & adv.* magnificent, splendid; gorgeous; brilliant, superb, glorious; excellent, capital. **—keit,** *f.* magnificence; splendour.

Prä'g—en, *v.a.* to coin; to stamp; to impress. **—er,** *m.* (**—ers,** *pl.* **—er**) coiner, stamper. **—ung,** *f.* stamping, coining; coinage. *Comp.* **—(e)=recht,** *n.* right of coinage.

Pragma'tisch, *adj.* pragmatic; **—e Sanktion,** Pragmatic Sanction (1724).

Prägna'n—t, *adj.* pregnant (*with meaning*); significant, pithy, terse; precise, exact. **—z,** *f.* signification, terseness.

Prah'l—en, *v.n.* (*aux.* **h.**) to boast, brag, swagger; to shine, glitter with splendour; **mit einer S. —en,** to make a parade of, boast of, value o.s. upon a th. **—er,** *m.* (**—ers,** *pl.* **—er**) boaster, braggart, swaggerer. **—erei',** *f.* brag, boasting; ostentation. **—erisch,** *adj.* boastful, bragging; ostentatious; swaggering. *Comp.* **—hans,** *m.* swaggerer, boaster. **—sucht,** *f.* love of boasting, ostentation.

Prahm, *m.* (**—(e)s,** *pl.* **—e**) flat-bottomed, square-ended boat, punt. *Comp.* **—geld,** *n.* lighterage. **—spritze,** *f.* floating fire-engine.

Prak't—ik, *f.* (*pl.* **—iken**) practice; (*pl.*) machinations, mean tricks. **—ika'nt,** *m.* (**—ikan'ten,** *pl.* **—ikan'ten**) (medical) practitioner; assistant, supernumerary. **—iker,** *m.* practitioner;

practical man; expert. **—isch,** *adj. & adv.* practical. **—izie'ren,** *v.a. & n.* (*aux.* **h.**) to practise, exercise (*a profession, etc.*); **einem etwas aus der Tasche —izieren,** to extract s.th. from a p.'s pocket.

Prall, I. *adj.* tight, stretched; stuffed out; chubby; elastic, springy. II. *m.* (—**s**, *pl.* —**e**) bounce, rebound, recoil. **—heit,** *f.* elasticity; tightness, tension. *Comp.* **—kraft,** *f.* elasticity. **—schlag,** *m.* rebound; cushion-stroke (*Bill.*). **—schuß,** *m.* ricochet. **—stein,** *m.* curbstone. **—stoß,** *m.* rebound. **—triller,** *m.* mordent (*Mus.*). **—winkel,** *m.* angle of reflection.

Pral'len, *v.n.* (*aux.* **h.** & **s.**) to rebound, recoil; to be reflected; to ricochet (*Art.*).

Pran'gen, *v.n.* (*aux.* **h.**) to make a show; to sparkle, shine; to vaunt; to crowd on sail; **die Bäume — in vollem Blätterschmucke,** the trees are decked in rich foliage.

Pran'ger, *m.* (—**s**, *pl.* —) pillory, whipping-post; **an den — stellen,** to (put in the) pillory, to expose *or* disgrace publicly.

Pran'ke, *f.* (*pl.* —**n**) clutch; paw.

Pras'seln, *v.n.* (*aux.* **h.** & **s.**) to crack, crackle; to rustle; to rattle down.

Pras's—en, *v.n.* (*aux.* **h.**) to feast; to live in debauchery; to riot, carouse. **—er,** *m.* (—**ers**, *pl.* —**er**) reveller, spendthrift, rake. **—erei',** *f.* debauchery, dissipated life.

Pra'xis, *f.* practice; exercise (*of an art, etc.*).

Pre'dig—en, *v.a. & n.* (*aux.* **h.**) to preach; **Gelehrten ist gut —en,** a word to the wise (is enough) (*prov.*). **—er,** *m.* (—**ers**, *pl.* —**er**) preacher, clergyman, minister; **—er Salomo,** Ecclesiastes *or* the Preacher; **die Stimme des —ers in der Wüste,** the voice of one crying in the wilderness (*B.*). **—erin,** (**—er(s)=frau,**) *f.* pastor's wife. **—t,** *f.* (*pl.* —**ten**) sermon; lecture; **in die —t gehen, —t hören,** to go to church; **eine —t halten,** to preach a sermon; **einem eine tüchtige (Moral) —t halten,** to give a p. a good lecture. *Comp.* **—er=amt,** *n.*, **—er=stelle,** *f.* office of preacher, ministry. **—er=orden,** *m.* Dominican order. **—er=schule,** *f.* theological college. **—er=seminar,** *n.* theological seminary, training college for (*graduate*) students of divinity. **—er=witwe,** *f.* clergyman's widow. **—t=amt,** *n.* holy orders. **—t=buch,** *n.* collection of sermons. **—t=stuhl,** *m.* pulpit.

Prei'en, *v.a.* to hail (*a ship*).

[1]**Preis,** I. *m.* (—(**s**)**es**, *pl.* —(**s**)**e**) price, cost, charge; fee, fare; reward, prize; praise, glory; glory, jewel; booty, plaything (*in phrases only*); **der Skalden —,** praised by the poets, the object of the bards' praises; **sie aller Harfen —,** the best of all harps; **— und Ehre sei Gott!** praise and glory be to God! **um diesen —,** at this price *or* rate; **um jeden —,** at any price *or* sacrifice, at all costs; **um keinen —,** not for all the world; **feste —(s)e,** fixed prices; **civile —e,** fair, reasonable prices, moderate charges; **der geringste, äußerste —,** the lowest price; **unter dem —(s)e,** below cost (price) *or* the value; **zu jedem —(s)e losschlagen,** to sell at any price. II. *used as adv.*; **— geben,** to deliver up, expose, abandon; **eine Stadt — geben,** to give up a town to pillage; **einen der Schande — geben,** to expose a p. to shame; **alles — geben,** to let everything go to rack and ruin; **sich — geben,** to deliver o.s. up, to prostitute o.s.; **(dem) Wind und (den) Wellen — gegeben,** at the mercy of wind and waves. **—(s)en,** *ir.* (*& obs. reg.*) *v.a.* to praise, extol, laud; to glorify, praise (*God*); **Gott sei gepriesen!** glory be to God! **sie — (s)eten den Herrn,** they praised the Lord (*obs.*); **einen glücklich —(s)en,** to call s.o. happy. **—(s)er,** *m.* (—(**s**)**ers**, *pl.* —(**s**)**er**) praiser, extoller. **—lich,** *adj.* praiseworthy. *Comp.* **—angabe,** *f.*, **—ansatz,** *m.* quotation of prices; **ohne —angabe,** not priced, not marked. **—aufgabe,** *f.* (subject for a) prize essay. **—ausschreiben,** *n.* prize competition. **—ausstellung,** *f.* prize exhibition; prize competition; offering of prizes. **—austeilung,** *f.* distribution of prizes. **—bewerber,** *m.* competitor. **—courant,** *see* **—liste.** **—ermäßigung,** *f.* reduction of price; reduced price. **—fechter,** *m.* prize-fighter, champion. **—frage,** *f.* subject *or* question for a prize competition; matter of price. **—gebung,** *f.* surrender, abandonment; prostitution. **—gericht,** *n.* prize court, tribunal. **—gesang,** *m.* song of praise. **—lied,** *n.* song that competes for *or* wins the prize. **—liste,** *f.* price-current; priced catalogue; list of prices. **—richter,** *m.* judge, arbiter, umpire. **—satz,** *m.* valuation, estimate. **—schießen,** *n.* rifle-shooting (*for prizes*). **—schrift,** *f.* prize essay. **—spiel,** *n.* event (*Tennis*). **—wert, —würdig,** *adj.* praiseworthy; worth the money, good value, cheap (*at the price or for what it is*); marketable. **—verzeichnis,** *n. see* **—liste.**

[2]**Preis,** *m.* (—(**s**)**es**, *pl.* —(**s**)**e**), **—chen,** *n.* (—**chens**, *pl.* —**chen**), **Preise,** *f.* (*pl.* —**n**) staylace; stripe; wristband; **— am Hufe,** coronet.

Prei'ßelbeere, *f.* (*pl.* —**n**) cranberry.

Prel'le, *f.* (*pl.* —**n**) tossing in a blanket; blanket for tossing.

Prel'l—en, *v.* I. *a.* to make rebound; to toss (in a blanket); to humbug; to cheat, swindle. II. *n.* (*aux.* **h.** & **s.**) *see* **Prallen.** **—er,** *m.* (—**ers**, *pl.* —**er**) one who tosses; cheat, swindler; backstroke, rebound; slap, smack. **—erei',** *f.* cheating, taking-in, cheat, fraud; blanket-tossing. *Comp.* **—garn,** *n.* net for catching foxes. **—hammer,** *m.* sledge-hammer. **—klotz,** *m.* anvil. **—stein,** *m.* curb-stone, guard-stone.

Premier'leutnant, *m.*, (*now* **O'berleutnant,**) first lieutenant.

Presbyteria'nisch, *adj.* Presbyterian.

Presbyte'ri—um, *n.* (—**ums**, *pl.* —**en**) presbytery.

Pre'schen, *v.n.* to hurry, scurry (*sl.*).

Preß, *adj. & adv.* tight, close-fitting. **—bar,** *adj.* compressible. **—(ss)e, 2c.,** *see under* **Press—.** *Comp.* **—baum,** *m.* lever (*of a press*). **—brett,** *n.* pressing-board. **—frechheit,** *f.* insolence of journalists (*hum.*). **—freiheit,** *f.* liberty of the press. **—gesetzgebung,** *f.* press-laws. **—glanz,** *m.* gloss given by pressing. **—knebelungsgesetz,** *n.* law by which the press is muzzled. **—kohle,** *f.* briquette. **—prozeß,** *m.* action against a printer *or* editor of a newspaper. **—verein,** *m.* association for safeguarding and promoting the interests of the press. **—vergehen,** *n.* offence against the press laws. **—wand,** *f.* cheek of a press. **—zwang,** *m.* restriction *or* suppression of the freedom of the press.

Pres's—e, *f.* (*pl.* —**en**) press; pressure; stop, stay (*of windmills*); difficulty, dilemma; gloss, lustre; the press; place for cramming young men for examinations, cramming establishment, coaching-college; **in, unter der —e,** in the press, being printed; **die —e knebeln,** to restrict (*or* do away with) the liberty of the press, to muzzle the newspapers.

Pres's—en, *v.a.* to press, squeeze, strain; to press (*paper, etc.*); to stamp; to compress; to gloss; to urge, dun; to oppress; to cram; **durch ein Tuch —en,** to strain; **das preßt ihm Thränen aus den Augen,** that draws tears from him; **Matrosen —en,** to (im)press sailors; **gepreßt voll,** overcrowded, crammed full; **mit gepreßter Stimme,** in a choked voice. **—er,** *m.* (—**ers**, *pl.* —**er**), presser; crammer; dresser, finisher; one of the press-gang. **—ie'ren,** *v.a. & n.* (*aux.* **h.**) to hasten; to be urgent; to dun;

es —iert sehr, it is most urgent, there's no time to be lost. —ung, f. pressure, pressing; impressing; squeeze. *Comp.* —kolben, m. press-ram.

Pria'mel, f. special kind of short gnomic poem (*in which a number of parallel premises are summed up in one general epitome*) (*Poetry*).

Pri'ck—e, f. (*pl.* —en) prick, prickle; eel-spear. —el, m. (—els, *pl.* —el) prickle; prickling. —elig, *adj.* prickly. —eln, *v.a. & n.* (*aux.* h.) to prick; to itch; to sting; to goad, tease. —elnd, *p. & adj.* prickling; sharp, pungent; piquant.

Prie'che, f. (*pl.* —n) gallery (*in a church*).

Priem'chen, n. (—s, *pl.* —) quid, chew (*of tobacco*).

Pries, Prie'sest; Prie'se, *1 (& 3) & 2 pers. sing. imperf. ind.; 1 (& 3) pers. sing. imperf. subj. of* preisen.

Prie'ster, m. (—s, *pl.* —) priest. —in, f. priestess. —lich, *adj.* sacerdotal, priestly. —schaft, f. clergy; priesthood. —tum, n. priesthood. *Comp.* —amt, n. priesthood, priest's office. —bäffchen, n. clergyman's bands. —binde, f. fillet. —gewand, n. vestment. —hemd, n. alb, surplice. —herrschaft, f. hierarchy. —rock, m. priest's robe, cassock. —stand, m. priesthood. —weihe, f. ordination, consecration of a priest.

Pri'm—a, f. the first *or* highest class of a first grade secondary school for boys (= *VI. form in English schools*); first of exchange (*C. L.*). —a'ner, m. (—aners, *pl.* —aner) sixth-form boy. —ä'r, *adj.* primary. —as, m. (—as, *pl.* —a'ten) primate. —a't, n. (—ats, *pl.* —ate) primacy. —e, f. prime (*Eccl.*, *Typ.*, *Fenc.*); prima (*Mus.*). —el, f. (*pl.* —eln) primrose. —iti'v, *adj.* primitive, original; simple, poor. *Comp.* —a=sorte, f. first *or* prime quality. —a=vista, *adv.* at sight (*Mus.*). —a=wechsel, m. first (*bill*) of exchange. —är'=schule, f. primary *or* elementary school; board school. —geld, n. primage. —us, m. head (boy) *or* top (boy) *or* captain of the form; —us omnium, captain of the school. —zahl, f. prime number.

Prie'stern, *v.n.* to twitter (of sparrows).

Prinz, m. (—en, *pl.* —en) prince; — von Preußen, William I. (*before he became regent*); der rote —, Prince Frederick Charles of Prussia (*in his red hussar's uniform*). —es'sin, f. princess. —i'p, *see* Prinzip. —lich, *adj. & adv.* princely. *Comp.* —en=erzieher, —en=hofmeister, m. tutor to a prince. —essin=steuer, f. tax levied to raise a princess's dowry. —gemahl, m. Prince Consort. —metall, n. Prince Rupert's metal. —regent, m. Prince Regent.

Prinzi'p, n. (—s, *pl.* —e, —ien) principle; —ien, rudiments (*of a science*); im —, in principle, essentially. —a'l, m. (—als, *pl.* —ale) principal, chief; employer, head (*of a firm*), manager (*of a theatre*). *Comp.* —ien=frage, f. question of principle. —ien=reiter, m. stickler for his principles, dogmatist, pedant (*coll.*). —ien=reiterei', f. dogmatism, pedantry.

Pri'or, m. (—s, *pl.* —en) prior. —a't, n. (—ats, *pl.* —ate) priorate; *see* —ei. —ei', f. priory. —in, f. prioress. —itä't, f. priority. *Comp.* —itäts'=aktie, f. preference- *or* primacy-share. —itäts'=anleihe, f. loan on a mortgage.

Pri'se, f. (*pl.* —n) prize; pinch (*of snuff*). *Comp.* —n=gericht, n. prize court. —n=recht, n. law concerning prizes.

Pris'ma, n. (—s, *pl.* Prismen) prism; doppelt brechendes —, double-refracting prism.

Prisma'tisch, *adj.* prismatic.

Pritsch! *int.* away! gone! — sein, to be lost.

Prit'sch—e, f. (*pl.* —en) harlequin's wooden sword; ferule; bat, racket, battledore; back-seat (*of a sledge*); bench; parapet; guard-bed (*Mil.*). *Comp.* —meister, m. marker (*at rifle-shooting*); harlequin (*who drubs the people*).

Prit'schen, *v.a. & n.* (*aux.* h.) to slap, beat.

Priv—a't, *adj. & adv.* private. —a'tim, *adv.* privately; separately; private and confidential (*on letters*); ein Kolleg —atim lesen, to deliver a course of University lectures for which a fee is charged. —atisie'ren, *v.n.* (*aux.* h.) to live on one's own property, as a private gentleman. —atis'simum, n. (—atissimums, *pl.* —atissima) University lecture *or* class (*usually held free of charge*, gratis) to which students are admitted only with the lecturer's sanction; private instruction (*with* or *without fees*) at the professor's private residence (*Univ.*). —é', n. (—es, *pl.* —es) water-closet, privy. —ile'=gien, *rc.*, *see under* Privileg. *Comp.* —at'=abkommen, n., —at'=abmachung, f. private deed. —at'=dozent, m. teacher recognized by the University (*who must have graduated as a doctor in his faculty and must, in addition to his dissertation, produce a* Habilitationsschrift *and give a trial lecture* (Probevorlesung)). —at'=gelehrte(r), m. private scholar, literary man who does not hold an official appointment. —at'=kasse, f. privy purse. —at'=kolleg, n. a course of University lectures which must be paid for (*opposed to the* öffentliche Vorlesung, *which is free to all members of the university*). —at'=mann, m. private person. —at'=meinung, f. individual opinion. —at'=recht, n. civil law.

Privilegie'ren, *v.a.* to privilege.

Privile'gi—um, n. (—ums, *pl.* —en) privilege.

Proba't, *adj.* proved, tried; good, excellent.

Pro'b—e, f. (*pl.* —en), trial, experiment; probation, proof, test; exhibition; ordeal; assay; pattern, sample; rehearsal; mark, stamp; (die) —e halten *or* bestehen, to stand the test, to keep its colour; zur —e, by way of trial, on approbation, on approval; auf die —e stellen, to (put to the) test; auf (die) —, on trial; die —e machen auf eine S. *or* die Richtigkeit einer S., to prove a th. (*Arith.*); es gilt die —e! let us try it! *Comp.* —e=abdruck, m. proof-impression. —e=abzug, m. proof. —e=blatt, n. proof-sheet; pattern-sheet; specimen number. —e=bogen, m. proof-sheet. —e=druck, m. essay (*postage stamps*). —e=exemplar, n. specimen copy. —e=fest, —e=haltig, *adj.* proof. —e=gold, n. standard gold. —e=jahr, n. year of probation. —e=kandidat, m. probationer (*before being appointed* ordentlicher Lehrer). —e=ladung, f. proof-charge. —e=lehrling, m. probationer; apprentice on trial. —e=lektion, f. trial lesson, criticism, lesson. —e=maß, n. standard measure. —e=nummer, f. specimen number. —e=predigt, f. trial-sermon. —e=rolle, f. beginner's part, début (*Theat.*). —e=schießen, n. trial-shooting. —e=schrift, f. specimen of writing; draught. —e=stein, m. touch-stone. —e=stück, n. sample, pattern; specimen. —e=wage, f. assay-balance. —e=zeit, f. novitiate; time of probation.

Pro'b—en, *v.a.* to mark; *see* —ie'ren. —er, m. (—ers, *pl.* —er) assayer; gauge. —ier'=bar, *adj.* testable. —ie'ren, *v.a.* to try, test, prove, put to the proof; to taste; to try (*a piece of music, etc.*); to assay; Rollen —ieren, to rehearse; —ieren geht über Studieren, practice is better than theory (*prov.*). —ie'rer, m. (—ierers, *pl.* —ierer) assayer. *Comp.* —ier'=hahn, m. gauge-tap. —ier'=nadel, f. touch-needle. —ier'=ofen, m. assaying furnace. —ier'=röhre, f. test-tube. —ier'=stein, m. touch-stone. —ier'=tiegel, m. crucible.

Problema'tisch, *adj.* problematic.

Produ'kt, n. (—(e)s, *pl.* —e) produce; product.

—i'v, *adj.* productive. **—ivitä't**, *f.* productiveness. *Comp.* **—en=handel**, *m.* trade in home produce. **—en=karte**, *f.* map showing the products of different districts *or* countries. **—iv'=genossenschaft**, *f.* cooperative society.

Produz—e'nt, *m.* (**—en'ten**, *pl.* **—en'ten**) producer, grower; producer. **—ie'ren**, *v.a.* to produce, bring forward; to furnish proofs (*Law*); to grow; to yield; (*refl.*) **sich —ieren**, to perform, to appear in public.

Profa'n, *adj.* profane, secular. **—ie'ren**, *v.a.* to profane. **—ie'rung**, *f.* profanation. *Comp.* **—bau**, *m.* secular building.

Profe'ß, *m.* (**—(ss)es**, *pl.* **—(ss)e**) profession, vow (*Rel.*); **— thun**, to take vows, take the veil. *Comp.* **—haus**, *n.* religious house, nunnery.

Profess—io'n, *f.* (*pl.* **—ionen**) trade; profession; **ein Spieler von —ion**, a professional gambler. **—ioni'st**, *m.* (**—is'ten**, *pl.* **—is'ten**) tradesman, artisan.

Profes's—or, *m.* (**—ors**, *pl.* **—o'ren**) professor at a university (**Universitäts —or**); senior assistant master at first grade secondary schools (**Gymnasial—or**); **ordentlicher —or**, ordinary professor; **außerordentlicher —or**, professor, university lecturer. **—ora't**, *n.* (**—orats**, *pl.* **—orate**), **—u'r**, *f.* professorship, (professorial) chair; **deutsche —ur**, chair of German. **—orin**, *f.* (**Frau —**) wife of a professor.

Profi'l, *n.* (**—s**, *pl.* **—e**) profile. **—ie'ren**, *v.a.* to (sketch in) profile.

Profi't, *m.* (**—s**, *pl.* **—e**) profit, turn-out; net proceeds, clearance.

Profi't—chen, *n.* (**—s**) small profit; save-all (*for candles*). **—ie'ren**, *v.a. & n.* (*aux.* **h.**) to profit, gain. **—lich**, *adj.* profitable, advantageous.

Profo'ß, **Profo's**, *m.* (**—(s)es** *or* **—(s)sen**, *pl.* **—(s)se** *or* **—(s)sen**) provost; bailiff; **General —**, provost-marshal.

Progno's—e, *f.* (*pl.* **—en**) prognosis (*Med.*). **—tikon**, *n.* (**—tikons**, *pl.* **—tika**) prognostic. **—tizie'ren**, *v.a. & n.* (*aux.* **h.**) to prognosticate, predict, foretell.

Progra'mm, *n.* (**—s**, *pl.* **—e**) programme; annual report (in German schools) published at Easter, usually containing some scientific essay by one of the teachers. *Comp.* **—mäßig**, *adj. & adv.* according to programme. **—musik**, *f.* illustrative *or* descriptive music.

Pro'gymnasi—um, *n.* (**—ums**, *pl.* **—en**) lower and middle part of a classical school.

Prohibit—o'rium, *n.* (**—oriums**, *pl.* **—orien**) writ of prohibition. *Comp.* **—iv'=zoll**, *m.* prohibition duty.

Proje'kt, *n.* (**—(e)s**, *pl.* **—e**) project. **—ie'ren**, *v.a.* to project, plan. **—i'l**, *n.* (**—ils**, *pl.* **—ile**) projectile. **—io'n**, *f.* projection; **Mittelpunkts —ion**, gnomonic projection. *Comp.* **—e(n)=macher**, *m.* projector, schemer.

Projizie'ren, *v.a.* to project, raise a projection.

Proklamie'ren, *v.a.* to proclaim.

Proku'r—a, *f.* (*pl.* **—as**) procuration, proxy. **—a'tor**, *m.* (**—ators**, *pl.* **—ato'ren**) proctor; procurator. **—i'st**, *m.* (**—is'ten**, *pl.* **—is'ten**) agent empowered to sign in the principal's name *or* for the firm; confidential clerk.

Proletari—a't, *n.* (**—ats**) proletariat, proletarians collectively; the lower classes; rabble.

Proleta'rier, *m.* (**—s**, *pl.* **—**) proletarian.

Prolo'g, *m.* (**—s**, *pl.* **—e**) prologue.

Prolong—ie'ren, *v.a.* to prolong; to renew (*a bill*). *Comp.* **—ations'=gebühr**, *f.* continuation (*C.L.*).

Promemo'ria, *n.* (**—s**, *pl.* **—s**) memorandum; memorial; round robin. *Comp.* **—schreiber**, *m.* memorialist.

Promena'de, *f.* promenade, walk, stroll (*coll.*). *Comp.* **—n=anzug**, *m.* elegant walking dress; walking suit. **—n=konzert**, *n.* promenade concert.

Promo—tio'n, *f.* (*pl.* **—tionen**) promotion; graduation; proceeding to *or* taking of the doctor's degree (*Univ.*). **—vie'ren**, *v.* I. *a.* to promote; to confer a doctor's degree on. II. *n.* (*aux.* **h.**) to graduate; to take the doctor's degree. *Comp.* **—tions'=schrift**, *f.* dissertation (*for the doctor's degree*).

Prompt, *adj. & adv.* prompt, ready, quick; **— bezahlen**, to pay promptly, pay ready money; **Zucker ist — abzusetzen**, sugar commands a ready sale. **—heit**, *f.* promptitude.

Prono'm—en, *n.* (**—ens**, *pl.* **—ina**) pronoun.

Proph—e't, *m.* (**—eten**, *pl.* **—eten**) prophet; foreteller; **Moses und die —eten**, ready cash (*vulg.*); **die kleinen —eten**, the lesser prophets; **ein —et gilt nirgend weniger denn in seinem Vaterlande**, a prophet is not without honour save in his own country (*B.*). **—e'tin**, *f.* prophetess. **—e'tisch**, *adj.* prophetic. **—ezei'en**, *v.a.* to prophesy. **—ezei'ung**, *f.* prophecy.

Propon—e'nt, *m.* (**—en'ten**, *pl.* **—en'ten**) proposer, mover. **—ie'ren**, *v.a.* to propose, move.

Proportion—a'le, *f.* (*pl.* **—alen**); **mittlere —ale**, mean proportional. **—ie'ren**, *v.a.* to proportion. *Comp.* **—al'=größen**, *pl.* proportionals.

Propst, *m.* (**—es**, *pl.* **Pröp'ste**) provost; prior; clerical overseer; prefect. **—ei'**, *f.* jurisdiction and dwelling of a provost. *Comp.* **—gericht**, *n.* provostship.

Prorekto'r, *m.* (**—s**, *pl.* **—en**) vice-chancellor (*Univ.*).

Prorogie'ren, *v.a.* to prorogue.

Pro'sa, *f.* prose.

Prosa'—iker, *m.* (**—ikers**, *pl.* **—iker**), **—i'st**, *m.* (**—is'ten**, *pl.* **—is'ten**) prose-writer. **—isch**, *adj.* prosaic.

Prosce'niums=loge, *f.* stage-box, corner-box.

Proselh't, *m.* (**—en**, *pl.* **—en**) proselyte. **—is'=mus**, *m.*, (**—en=macherei**, *f.*) proselytism.

Pro'sit! Prost! *int.* bless you! much good may it do you! your health; **— (die) Mahlzeit**, (*lit.* **Prosit Mahlzeit**, may your meal be blessed!) bless you! you may whistle for it, you won't get it! (*coll.*); **— Jahrmarkt!** a pleasant fair to you! (*said by children on days of a fair to their parents and friends in asking for a fairing or for money to go to the fair*); **— Neujahr!** a Happy New Year to you! **ja, —!** don't you wish you may get it! (*coll.*).

Prosodie', *f.* prosody.

Proso'dik, *f.* science of prosody.

Prospe'kt, *m.* (**—es**, *pl.* **—e**) prospect; prospectus, syllabus; elevation, design. **—us**, *m.* prospectus.

Prostituie'ren, *v.r.* to offer o.s. to anybody; to make a fool of o.s. (*obs.*). **—ier'te**, *f.* prostitute.

Prote'st, *m.* (**—es**, *pl.* **—e**) protest; **mit — zurückkommen**, to be returned dishonoured (*C.L.*); **— einlegen**, to enter a protest (against); **— wegen Mangel an Annahme**, protest for non-acceptance. **—a'nt**, *m.* (**—an'ten**, *pl.* **—an'ten**), **—an'tin**, *f.* Protestant. **—an'tisch**, *adj.* Protestant; **—antische Union**, (*in the 19th century*) league of Lutherans and Calvinists. **—antis'mus**, *m.* Protestantism. **—ie'ren**, *v.* I. *n.* (*aux.* **h.**) (**gegen etwas**) to protest (*against*); to protest, declare. II. *a.* to protest (*a bill, etc.*); **einen Wechsel —ieren lassen**, to have a bill protested. *Comp.* **—an'ten=verein**, *m.* Protestant union of clergymen and laymen to resist the fanaticism of straight-laced (*Lutheran*) churchmen (*since 1863*). **—erhebung**, *f.* entering of a protest. **—kosten**, **—spesen**, *pl.* protest-charges.

Protoko'll, *n.* (**—s**, *pl.* **—e**) record, protocol.

minutes; im —, upon record; in das — eintragen, *see* —ieren; (das) — führen, to make a draft of the proceedings, take down the minutes, keep the register; zu — geben, to depose, to state in evidence, to register; zu — nehmen, to draw up an official report of, to take down (*a deposition, etc.*). —a'nt, *m.* (—an'ten, *pl.* —an'ten) actuary, recorder, clerk. —ie'ren, *v.a.* to register, record. *Comp.* —aufnahme, *f.*; eine —aufnahme fand statt, a report was drawn up. —buch, *n.* minute-book. —eintragung, *f.* minute. —führer, *see* —ant.

Protz, *m.* (—en, *pl.*—en) (rich) snob. —entum, *n.* snobbism, snobbishness, purse-pride. —en, *v.n.* to crack; to be a snob; to be purse-proud. —ig, *adj.* snobbish, insolent; purse-proud.

Prot'z—e, *f.* (*pl.* —en) limber (*Artil.*). —en, *v.a. see* Abprotzen, Aufprotzen. *Comp.* —gestell, *n.* limber-body. —kasten, *m.* ammunition-chest, caisson; auf dem —kasten fahren, to ride upon the caissons. —kette, *f.* gun-carriage chain. —wagen, *m.* limber, gun-carriage.

Provia'nt, *m.* (—s) provisions, victuals, provender; mit — versehen, —ie'ren, *v.a.* to provision, victual. *Comp.* —amt, *n.* store-office, commissariat. —haus, *n.* magazine, storehouse. —kammer, *f.* store-room. —meister, *m.* commissary (*Mil.*); caterer, steward; purser. —sack, *m.* haversack. —schiff, *n.* victualling ship. —wagen, *m.* provision waggon. —wesen, *n.* commissariat.

Provi'nz, *f.* (*pl.* —en) province; in der — sein, to be in the country. —ia'l, I. *adj.* provincial. II. *m.* provincial, superior of a religious order. —ialis'mus, *m.* (*pl.* —ialismen) provincialism, dialect word. —ie'll, *adj.* provincial, dialectal. *Comp.* —ia'l=landtag, *m.* provincial diet. —ia'l=rat, *m.* provincial counsellor, member of the provincial board of inspectors. —ial=schul'kollegium, *n.* provincial board of inspectors (*of schools*), (*Royal*) Provincial School Council, provincial board of inspection. —ial=schul'rat, *m.* member of the provincial board of instruction (*which supervises the schools of the district on behalf of the government*). —ia'l=stadt, *f.* provincial town.

Provis—io'n, *f.* (*pl.* —ionen) provision; commission, percentage. —or (*pron.* Provi'sor), *m.* (—ors, *pl.* —o'ren) provisor; dispenser; apothecary's assistant. —o'risch, *adj.* provisional. —o'rium, *n.* (—oriums, *pl.* —orien) provisional *or* temporary arrangement. *Comp.* —ions'=reisende(r), *m.* travelling agent, commercial traveller.

Provozie'ren, *v.a.* to provoke; to challenge.

Prozedu'r, *f.* procedure; proceeding (*at law*).

Proze'nt, *n.* (—s, *pl.* —e) per cent, percentage; zu sechs —, at six per cent; wie viel —? what percentage? zu hohen —en, at a high rate of interest. —ig, *adj.* of *or* yielding a certain percentage; drei —ige Rente, three per cent stock. *Comp.* —einnahme, *f.* percentage. —satz, *m.* percentage, rate of interest.

Proze'ß, *m.* (—(ss)es, *pl.* —(ss)e) process, operation; procedure; proceedings; action, process, law-suit; einen — anfangen mit, einem einen — anhängen, einen — gegen einen anhängig machen, to institute (legal) proceedings against a p.; im — liegen, to be at law; einem den — machen wegen, to put a p. on his trial for; einen — führen, to conduct a case; kurzen — mit einem machen, to make short work with s.o.; der — schwebt noch, the case is still pending *or* sub judice. —(ss)ie'ren, *v.n.* (*aux.* h.) to carry on a lawsuit. *Comp.* —akten, *pl.* minutes (*of a case, Law*). —fähig, *adj.* actionable. —führer, *m.* plaintiff; plaintiff's counsel. —krämer, *m.* litigious person. —ordnung, *f.* rolls of court. —sachen, *pl.* clauses, law business. —süchtig, *adj.* litigious. —wesen, *n.* system of legal proceedings.

Pru'del, *m.* (—s) steam; bubbling. —n, *v.n.* (*aux.* h.) to bungle; to sew (embroider, *etc.*) carelessly and badly (*coll.*); to steam; to bubble up.

Prü'f—en, *v.a.* to try, examine, test, prove; geprüft, (examined and) approved, passed (*in an examination*), certificated; tried, tested; geprüfte Lehrerin, certificated teacher; —et alles und das Beste behaltet, prove all things, hold fast that which is good; Herz und Nieren —en, to try the reins and the heart (*B.*). —er, *m.* (—ers, *pl.* —er) examiner, prover, tester. —erei', *f.* hyper-criticism. —ling, *m.* (—lings, *pl.* —linge) examinee, candidate. —ung, *f.* examination; proof; trial, test; temptation. *Comp.* —eisen, *n.* probe. —stein, *m.* touchstone, test, ordeal. —ungs=ausschuß, *m.*, —ungs=behörde, *f.* board of examiners. —ungs=beaufsichtigung, *f.* invigilation. —ungs=eid, *m.* test-oath. —ungs=hetzerei, *f.* hurry and worry of examinations. —ungs=kommission, *f.* board of examinations; board of examiners; Mitglied der wissenschaftlichen —ungskommission der Universität London, examiner to the University of London; Vorsitzender der —ungskommission, chairman of examiners. —ungs=stunde, *f.* hour of examination *or* trial. —ungs=vorschrift, *f.* regulation for an examination. —ungs=zeit, *f.* period of suffering; time of trial. —ungs=zeugnis, *n.* certificate, diploma.

Prü'gel, *m.* (—s, *pl.* —) cudgel, stick; drubbing; thrashing; eine Tracht —, a sound thrashing; mit einem — drein schlagen, to resort to violent measures. —ei', *f.* beating; fight, row. —n, *v.a.* to cudgel, cane, thrash; sich —n, to fight (*of boys*); der Teufel —t seine Großmutter, it is raining while the sun shines (*coll.*). *Comp.* —junge, —knabe, *m.* scapegoat. —strafe, *f.* corporal punishment; whipping, caning; birching. —suppe, *f.* a sound thrashing (*coll.*).

Prunk, *m.* (—es) pomp, splendour; ostentation; parade. —haft, *adj.* ostentatious, showy. *Comp.* —bett, *n.* bed of state. —gewand, *n.* gorgeous dress. —liebe, *f.* love of display. —los, *adj.* unostentatious, unpretentious. —saal, *m.* stately hall. —zimmer, *n.* state room.

Prun'k—en, *v.n.* (*aux.* h.); —en mit einer S., to make a show of a th., parade a th. —er, *m.* (—ers, *pl.* —er) showy person.

Pru'sten (*long* u), *v.n.* (*aux.* h.) to snort; to purr; to sneeze violently; to burst out laughing.

Psal—m, *m.* (—m(e)s, *pl.* —men) psalm. —ter, *m.* (—ters, *pl.* —ter) psalter; psaltery; third stomach of ruminants (*Zoöl.*). *Comp.* —m=singen, *n.* psalmody. —ter=spiel, *n.* playing on the psaltery.

Pseudony'm, I. *n.* false *or* feigned, fictitious, assumed name. II. *adj.* pseudonymous.

Psy'ch—isch, *adj.* psychical. —olo'g, *m.* (—ologen, *pl.* —ologen) psychologist. —olo'gisch, *adj.* psychological.

Pst! *int.* hush! stop! here! (*calling waiters in restaurants*).

Pubertä't, *f.* puberty.

Publi'k, *adj.* public.

Pub'likum, *n.* (—s, *pl.* —s) the public; audience; (*pl. also* Publica) open lecture; das große —, the general public.

Publiz—ie'ren, *v.a.* to publish; to make public, to promulgate; to prove (*a will*). —i'st, *m.* (—i'sten, *pl.* —i'sten) political writer, newspaper writer, journalist.

Pu'ckern, *v.n.* (*aux.* h.) to throb (*prov.*).

Pud, *n.* (—s, *pl.* —) pood (*Russian weight*).

Pud'del—n, I. *v.a.* to puddle (*metal*). II. *subst.n.*

puddling. *Comp.* —**eisen**, *n.* puddled iron. —**maschine**, *f.* puddler. —**walzwerk**, *n.* puddling rolls.

Pu'del, *m.* (—s, *pl.* —) poodle; shaggy-haired person; menial drudge; slattern; scapegoat; miss (*at nine-pins*); blunder, bungle; university beadle, bull-dog (*sl.*). —**n**, *v.n.* (*aux.* **h.**) to miss; to blunder. *Comp.* —**kopf**, *m.* shaggy, curly head of hair, mop (*coll.*). —**mütze**, *f.* fur cap. —**närrisch**, *adj.* playful; droll, funny. —**naß**, *adj.* drenched, wet through, sopping wet.

Pu'der, *m.* (—s, *pl.* —) powder (*for the face*). —**ig**, *adj.* powdered. —**n**, *v.a.* to powder. *Comp.* —**mantel**, *m.* peignoir. —**zucker**, *m.* powdered sugar.

Puff, I. *int.* puff! bang! II. *m.* (—es, *pl.* —e, **Püf'fe**) bump; cuff, thump, blow; nudge; puff; hoax; backgammon; mishap; **auf — nehmen**, to take on credit; **er kann einen (guten) — vertragen**, he can stand a good deal, he is thick-skinned. *Comp.* —**ärmel**, *m.* puffed sleeve. —**brett**, *n.* backgammon-board. —**spiel**, *n.* backgammon.

Puf'fe—n, *v.a.* & *n.* (*aux.* **h.**) to pop; to thump, whack, cuff; to puff; to play backgammon; **daß es pufft**, with a vengeance. —**r**, *m.* (—rs, *pl.* —r) pocket-pistol; buffeter. *Comp.* —**r=staat**, *m.* buffer-state.

Pul'le, *f.* (*pl.* —**n**) bottle (*dial.* & *vulg.*).

Puls, *m.* (—(s)es, *pl.* —(s)e) pulse; peal (*of bells*); **ein erhobener** —, a high pulse; **einem** (**an** *or* **auf** *or simply*) **den — fühlen**, to feel a person's pulse. —(**s**)**ie'ren**, *v.n.* (*aux.* **h.**) to pulsate. *Comp.* —**ader**, *f.* artery; **die große —ader**, aorta. —**schlag**, *m.* pulsation. —**stillstand**, *m.*, —**stockung**, *f.* stoppage of the pulse. —**wärmer**, *m.* mitten.

Pult, *n.* (—es, *pl.* —e) desk; master's desk; **Chor**—, lectern, reading desk, choir desk.

Pul'ver, *n.* (—s, *pl.* —) powder; gunpowder; **rauchloses**—, smokeless powder; **zu — und Blei verurteilt**, condemned to be shot; **er hat das — nicht erfunden**, he will never set the Thames on fire; **ein Schuß** —, a charge of powder; **keinen Schuß — auf einen geben**, to think little of a p.; **er ist keinen Schuß — wert**, he is not worth powder and shot, he is a worthless fellow; **er hat — gerochen**, he has seen service. —**icht**, (*obs.*) —**ig**, *adj.* powdery, powder-like. —**isier'bar**, *adj.* pulverizable. —**isie'ren**, *v.a.* to pulverize. —**n**, I. *v.a.* to pulverize, reduce to powder. II. *subst.n.* pulverization. *Comp.* —**ar=tig**, *adj. see* —**ig**. —**dampf**, *m.* powder-smoke. —**faß**, *n.* powder-barrel. —**horn**, *n.* powder-flask. —**kammer**, *f.* powder magazine; chamber. —**karren**, *m.* caisson. —**müller**, *m.* gunpowder-maker. —**sack**, *m.* chamber (*of a gun*). —**schaufel**, *f.* charger (*Artil.*); powder-shovel. —**scheu**, *adj.* timorous. —**schwamm**, *m.* powder-tinder. —**verschwörung**, *f.* Gunpowder Plot (*Nov. 5, 1605, in London, by Guy Fawkes*). —**wagen**, *m.* powder-cart.

Pum'mel, *m.* plump little person (*coll.*). —**ig**, *adj.* round, pretty, pleasant (*coll.*).

Pump, I. *int.* bump! bounce! II. *m.* (—es, *pl.* **Püm'pe**) hollow sound; thump; credit, trust, tick (*sl.*); **etwas von einem auf — nehmen**, to borrow s.th. from a p. (*sl.*). —**e**, *f.* (*pl.* —**en**) pump; **die —e schlägt**, the pump sucks *or* is dry; **die —e anheben, ansaugen lassen**, to fetch the pump; **Saug= und Druck—e**, suction and forcing pump. —**en**, *v.a.* & *n.* (*aux.* **h.**) to give *or* take on credit (*sl.*); to pump. —**er**, *m.* (—ers, *pl.* —er) pumper, lender, borrower. *Comp.* —**brunnen**, *m.* well with a pump. —**er=nickel**, *m.* (very dark) Westphalian rye-bread. —**hosen**, *pl.* wide, baggy breeches. —**ma=schine**, *f.* pumping engine. —**werk**, *n.* pump.

Pum'pen— (*in comp.*) —**ärmel**, *m.* hose. —**deckel**, *m.* valve. —**geck**, *n.*, —(**geck=**)**stock**, *m.* pump-handle. —**hub**, *m.* stroke. —**kasten**, *n.* pump-cistern (*Min.*). —**kleid**, *n.* pump-case. —**kolben**, *m.* piston. —**leder**, *n.* sucker of a pump. —**schlag**, *m.* stroke of a pump-handle. —**sonde**, *f.* pump-gauge. —**so(o)d**, *m.* pump-well. —**schwengel**, *m.* pump-handle. —**stange**, *f.* piston. —**stiefel**, *m.* barrel, chamber of a pump. —**wärter**, *m.* waterman, pitman. —**werk**, *n.* pump work.

Punkt, *m.* (—es, *pl.* —e) point; dot; period; full stop; article, head, topic; respect; — **für — durchgehen**, to examine point by point, to scan closely; **auf den** —, exactly; — **zehn**, on the stroke of ten; **das trifft auf den — zu**, that is right to a T, that hits the nail on the head; **ich war** (*or* **stand**) **auf dem —e aufzustehen**, I was just going to get up; **auf dem —e, wo die Sachen stehen**, as matters stand; **bis zu einem gewissen —e**, to a certain point *or* extent; **zarter** —, delicate, nice point; **hier macht man einen** —, here you put a full stop; **der wunde** —, the weak *or* sore point. —**atio'n**, *f.* heads, notes of a discourse, *etc.;* contract. —**ie'ren**, *v.a.* to point, dot; to punctuate; to tap (*Med.*); to stipple; **den Frieden —ieren**, to stipulate the conditions *or* draw up preliminaries of peace; —**ierte Noten**, dotted notes (*Mus.*). —**ie'rung**, *f.* punctuation; tapping (*Med.*). —**um**, *n.* full stop; end, ending; **und damit —um!** enough! let us have no more of it! and there's an end of it! —**u'r**, *f.* puncture; (*pl.*) points (*Typ.*). *Comp.* —**ier'=figur**, *f.* geomantic figure. —**ier'kunst**, *f.* geomancy; stippling. —**ier'=nadel**, *f.* stipple. —**ier'=rad**, *n.* dotting wheel. —**linie**, *f.* dotted line. —**reihe**, *f.* range of points (*Math.*). —**strich**, (**Strich**—,) *m.* semicolon. —**weise**, *adv.* point by point.

Pünkt'—chen, *n.* (—chens, *pl.* —chen) little point, dot. —**lich**, *adj.* punctual, precise, accurate; —**licher Gehorsam**, strict obedience. —**lichkeit**, *f.* punctuality.

Punsch, *m.* (—es, *pl.* —e) punch. *Comp.* —**essenz**, *m.* essence of punch (*made with rum, tea, sugar, lemon and water*). —**löffel**, *m.* punch-ladle. —**napf**, *m.*, *f.* punch-bowl.

Pun'z—e, *f.* (*pl.* —en), —**en**, *m.* (—ens, *pl.* —en) punch. —**en**, *v.a.* to punch (*leather*); to (en)chase, chisel, stamp, emboss.

Pupilla'risch, *adj.* pupillary.

Pupil'le, *f.* (*pl.* —**n**) ward; pupil (*of the eye*). —**n=erweiterung**, *f.* enlargement of the pupil. —**n=gelder**, *pl.* property of a ward *or* of a minor. —**n=gericht**, *n.* court of chancery.

Pup'p—e, *f.* (*pl.* —en) puppet; doll; lay figure; child; chessman; chrysalis; nice little creature; darling; float (*Angl.*); **über die** *or* **bis in die —en**, beyond all bounds, continually, without stopping (*sl.*). *Comp.* —**en=gesicht**, *n.*, —**en=larve**, *f.* doll's face. —**en=hülle**, *f.* cocoon. —**en=spiel**, *n.* puppet-show; puppet-play. —**en=zustand**, *m.* chrysalis condition.

Pup'pen, *v.* I. *a.* to wrap up. II. *n.* (*aux.* **h.**) to play with dolls; to change into a chrysalis.

Pup'pern, *v.n.* (*aux.* **h.**) (*dial.*) to throb; to tremble.

Pur, *adj.* pure, genuine; sheer (*curiosity, etc.*).

Purg—a'nz, *f.* (*pl.* —**an'zen**) purgative. —**ie'ren**, *v.a.* & *n.* (*aux.* **h.**) to purge. *Comp.* —**ier'=mittel**, *n.* purgative. —**ier'=moos**, *n.* Iceland moss. —**ier'=pille**, *f.* aperient pill.

Purita'n—er, *m.* (—ers, *pl.* —er), —**erin**, *f.* Puritan. —**isch**, *adj.* puritanical.

Pur'pern, *v.a. see* **Purpurn**; **sich** —, to turn purple (*rare*).

Pur'pur, *m.* (—s) purple; crimson, deep red· purple robe *or* mantle. —**isch** (*pron.* **pur-pu'risch**), (*obs.*) *adj.* purplish. —**n**, I. *adj.* purple, crimson, scarlet, deep red. II. *v.a.* to dye purple. *Comp.* —**braun**, puce. —**farben**,

—farbig, *adj.* purple, crimson. —glut, *f.* purple glow. —hut, *m.* cardinal's hat. —rot, *adj.* purple, crimson, deep red, scarlet.

Pur'ren, *v.* I. *n.* (*aux.* h.) to purr; to grumble. II. *a.* to call the watch (*Naut.*); to stir (*fire*).

Pur'zeln, *see* Burzeln.

Pu'schel, *see* Büschel.

Pus'seln, *v.n.* to potter about (*coll.*).

Pussie'ren, *v.a. see* Poussieren.

Pu'st—e, *f.* breath (*coll.*); er hat keine —e mehr, die —e geht ihm aus, he is out of breath (*coll.*). —en, *v.a. & n.* (*aux.* h.) to puff, blow, snort. *Comp.* —rohr, *n.* blow-pipe.

Pus'tel, *f.* (*pl.* —n) pustule.

Put! (Putt!) *int.* chuck! chuck! —chen, *n.* (—chens, *pl.* —chen) little turkey; duck, darling. —hahn, *m.*, —huhn, *n.* children's names for 'cock' and 'hen.'

Pu'te, *f.* (*pl.* —n) turkey-hen. —r, *m.* (—rs, *pl.* —r) turkey-cock. —rhaft, *adj.* strutting. *Comp.* —r=braten, *m.* roast turkey. —(r=) hahn, *m.* turkey-cock. —r=rot, *adj.* red as a turkey-cock.

Putsch, *m.* (—es, *pl.* —e) riot; unsuccessful insurrection *or* rising. —en, *v.n.* (*aux.* h.) to riot, to create a disturbance.

Put'ting, *f.* (*pl.* —en) link of the dead-eye chains. *Comp.* —eisen, *n.* chain-plate.

Putz, *m.* (—es) dressing, toilet; attire, dress; ornaments; finery; trimming; jewelry; plastering, rough-casting; im —, in full dress; dem — ergeben, fond of dress, dressy.

Put'ze, *f.* (*pl.* —n) snuffers.

Put'z—en, *v.a.* to clean; to brush, wipe; to polish, brighten, burnish; to dress, trim, adorn; to rebuke; to clear by eating up (*vulg.*); to snuff (*a candle*); to groom (*a horse*); to prune, lop; to plaster (*a wall*); to trim (*a lamp*); to pluck (*fowls*); die Sterne —en sich, the stars are shooting; Diamanten —en sehr, diamonds are very ornamental; sich (*dat.*) die Nase —en, to blow *or* wipe one's nose. —er, *m.* (—ers, *pl.* —er) scourer, cleaner; polisher; rebuke. —ig, *adj.* funny, queer, quaint, curious (*coll.*). *Comp.* —händlerin, *f.* milliner. —kästchen, *n.* dressing-case. —kram, *m.* millinery, finery; toilet wares. —macherei', *f.* millinery trade. —macherin, *f.* milliner. —maschine, *f.* scutching machine. —maurer, *m.* plasterer. —schachtel, *f.* bandbox. —schere, *f.* snuffers. —schuhe, *pl.* dress-shoes. —stock, *m.* cleaning-rod (*of a gun*). —sucht, *f.* love of dress *or* finery. —süchtig, *adj.* very fond of dress. —tisch, *m.* dressing-table. —waren, *pl.* millinery. —zeug, *n.* cleaning utensils *or* articles. —zimmer, *n.* dressing-room; state-room.

Pygmä'—e, *f.* (*pl.* —en) pigmy. —isch, *adj.* pigmy.

Pyramida'l, *adj.* enormous (*sl.*).

Pyrami'de, *f.* (*pl.* —n) pyramid; die Gewehre in —n (zusammen) setzen, to pile arms (*Mil.*).

Pyri't, *m.* (—es, *pl.* —e) pyrites.

Pyro—holz'säure, *f.* pyroligneous acid. —metrie', *f.* pyrometry. —phos'phorsäure, *f.* pyro-phosphoric acid. —tech'niker, *m.* pyrotechnist. —tech'nisch, *adj.* pyrotechnical.

Pythagor—ä'isch, —isch, (*pron.* Pythago'risch) *adj.* Pythagorean; —äischer Lehrsatz, Pythagorean theorem (*47th proposition of the first book of Euclid*).

Q

Q, q, *n.* Q, q; (*for abbreviations see the Index of abbreviations at the end of the German-English part*).

Quab'be, *see* Quappe.

Quab'b—el, *m.* (—els, *pl.* —el) flabby, trembling mass; fat lump of flesh; marshy, boggy land. —(e)licht, (*obs.*) —(l)ig, *adj.* flabby; unsavoury; mir ist —elig, I feel sick (*coll.*). —eln, *v.n.* (*aux.* h.) to be flabby; to wobble; to shake (*like jelly*); to move (*as boggy land*).

Quack—elei', *f.* (*pl.* —eleien) quacking (*of ducks, etc*); silly talk; irresolution; trifling, nonsense.

Qua'ck—eln, *v.n.* (*aux.* h.) to quack; to chatter, babble; to be irresolute, shilly-shally; to waver. *Comp.* —el=fritz, *m.*, —el=lotte, *f.* irresolute and fussy person (*coll.*). —salber, *m.* (—salbers, *pl.* —salber) quack. —salberei', *f.* quackery. —salbern, *v.n.* (*aux.* h.) to practise quackery; mit einer S. —salbern, to tamper with *or* to dabble in a th.; an einem herum —salbern, to doctor a p. with quack medicines.

Quad'del, *f.* (*pl.* —n) swelling of the skin left by the bite of an insect *or* the sting of a nettle.

Qua'd—er, *m.* (—ers, *pl.* —er) & *f.* (*pl.* —ern) hewn stone, squared stone; freestone. —ra't, I. *n.* (—rates, *pl.* —rate) square; natural (*Mus.*); quadrat (*Typ.*); block (*of houses*); zum *or* auf das —rat erheben, to square (*a number*). II. *adj. see* —ratisch. —rät'chen, *n.* M-quadrat (*Typ.*); halbes —rätchen, N-quadrat. —ra'tisch, *adj.* square, quadratic; —ratische Gleichungen, quadratic equations. —ratu'r, *f.* quadrature, squaring (*of the circle*). —rie'ren, *v.* I. *a.* to square (*Math.*). II. *n.* (*aux.* h.) to suit. —ril'le, *f.* (*pl.* —rillen) quadrille. —rillie'ren, *v.a.* to weave in checks. —rillio'n, *f.* (*pl.* —rillionen) the number expressed by a unit preceding 24 ciphers. —ru'pel, *adj.* quadruple. *Comp.* —er=maurer, *m.* (cut-) stone-mason. —er=stein, *see* —er. —er=stein=bruch, *m.* quarry. —er=werk, *n.* bound masonry. —rat'=förmig, *adj.* square. —rat'=meile, *f.* square mile. —rat'=meter, *n.* square metre. —rat'=rute, *f.* square perch (*14.21 square metres*). —rat'=schädel, *m.* blockhead (*coll.*). —rat'=schein, *m.* quartile (*Astr.*). —rat'=verhältnis, *n.* duplicate ratio. —rat'=wurzel, *f.* square root; die —ratwurzel ausziehen, to extract the square root. —rat'=zoll, *m.* square inch.

Quai, Kai, *m.* (—s, *pl.* —s) quay.

Quak, *m.* croak; quack. —en, *v.n.* (*aux.* h.) to croak; to quack; to groan.

Quä'k—en, *see* Quaken. —er, *m.* (—ers, *pl.* —er) Quaker; Friend. —erei', —ertum, *n.* Quakerism, Quakerdom. —erin, *f.* Quakeress. *Comp.* —er=bund, *m.* Society of Friends.

Qual, *f.* (*pl.* —en) torment, torture, pain; pang; great affliction. *Comp.* —voll, *adj.* very painful, excruciating, full of anguish, distressing.

Quä'l—en, *v.a.* to torture, afflict, distress; to harass, worry; molest; bore; zu Tode —en, to kill by (slow) torture, to worry the life out of a p.; sich zu Tode —en, to worry oneself to death; to toil and moil; die Farben —en, to deaden the colours. —er, *m.* (—ers, *pl.* —er) tormentor, torturer, afflicter, bore. —erei', *f.* tormenting; torments; vexation; persecution. *Comp.* —geist, *m.* tormentor, bore. —süchtig, *adj.* fond of tormenting.

Qualifizie'ren, *v.a.* to qualify, fit; to modify; sich — für eine *or* zu einer S., to be fit *or* suitable for a th.

Qualit—ä't, *f.* (*pl.* —äten) quality; von jeder —ät, of every description. —ati'v, *adj.* qualitative.

Qual'le, *f.* (*pl.* —n) jelly-fish, sea-jelly *or* blubber.

Qualm, *m.* (—s) thick smoke; smother; mist, vapour; exhalation. —en, *v.* I. *n.* (*aux.* h.) to steam; to smoke. II. *a.* to puff out smoke. —icht, (*obs.*) —ig, *adj.* vaporous; steaming; smoky. *Comp.* —bad, *n.* vapour-bath. —feuer, *n.* smouldering fire.

Quan'del, *m.* chimney (*in a kiln*).

Quän'geln, *see* Quengeln.
Quant—itä't, *f.* (*pl.* —itäten) quantity. **—i=tie'ren,** *v.n.* to measure the syllables, marking them as either long *or* short. **—um** (*pron.* Quan'tum), *n.* (—ums, *pl.* —a) quantity; share, portion.
Quants'weise, *adv.* for form's sake; as it were (*dial.*).
Quap'pe, *f.* (*pl.* —n) eel-pout; tadpole.
Quarantä'ne, *f.* quarantine; — **halten,** to undergo quarantine; **Schiffe aus G. werden — halten müssen,** ships arriving from G. will be subject to quarantine; **die — auferlegen,** to place in quarantine. *Comp.* **—maßregeln,** *pl.* measures prescribed during quarantine.
Quark, *m.* (—es) curd, curds; dirt; excrement; worthless thing, trifle; trash, rubbish; **den alten — aufrühren,** to rake up some old tale. **—ig,** *adj.* containing curds; dirty. *Comp.* **—brot,** *n.*, **—schnitte,** *f.* piece of bread spread with curd *or* soft cheese. **—käse,** *m.* whey-cheese.
Quarré', *n.* (—s) square (*Mil.*); set (*Danc.*); **offenes —,** hollow square.
Quar'r—e, *f.* (*pl.* —en) squalling *or* whining child; **erst die Pfarre, dann die —e,** have the means to keep a wife before marrying (*prov.*). **—en,** *v.n.* (*aux.* **h.**) to whine *or* squall; to grumble. **—ig,** *adj.* squalling; whining.
Quart, I. *n.* (—s, *pl.* —e, *dim.* Quärt'chen) quart (*measure containing* 1⅙ *litre*); quarto (*Typ.*). II. *f.* (*pl.* —en) *see* **—e.** **—a,** *f.* the highest form of the junior department (*in a secondary boys' school, corresponding to the English III.*). **—a'l,** *n.* (—als, *pl.* —ale) quarter (*of a year*); quarter-day; quarterly payment; quarterly meeting (*of mechanics, etc.*); **ein —al Hausmiete,** a quarter's rent. **—a'liter,** *adv.* quarterly, by the quarter, in quarterly instalments. **—a'ner,** *m.* (—aners, *pl.* —aner) third-form boy. **—a'nt,** *m.* (—an'ten, *pl.* —an'ten) *see* **band.** **—e,** *f.* (*pl.* —en) fourth, quarter; series of four; carte, quart (*Cards, Fenc.*); fourth (*Mus.*). **—e'tt,** *n.* (—et'tes, *pl.* —et'te) quartette. **—ier,** *see* Quartier. *Comp.* **—al'=geld,** *n.* quarterly allowance. **—al'=gericht,** *n.* quarter-sessions. **—al'=weise,** *adj.* & *adv.* quarterly. **—band,** *m.* (*volume in*) quarto. **—bogen,** *m.* sheet divided into four parts. **—ett'=abend,** *m.* evening on which string-quartettes are performed. **—ett'=musik,** *f.* music in four parts *or* for four (string) instruments. **—format,** *n.* quarto. **—stoß,** *m.* thrust in carte (*Fenc.*).
Quartie'r, *n.* (—s, *pl.* —e) quarters, lodging; quart; quarter; fourth part; quarter, district, ward; watch (*Naut.*); **in — liegen bei . . .,** to to be quartered upon . . .; **alle Stadt—e,** all quarters of the town; **um — bitten,** to call for quarter (*obs.*); **Sie sind im —,** your ball is in balk (*Bill.*). **—en,** *v.a.* to quarter, billet. **—ung,** *f.* quartering; quartation (*of gold*). *Comp.* **—meister,** *m.* quartermaster; alderman of a ward. **—träger,** *m.* one who has soldiers quartered upon him. **—zettel,** *m.* billet.
Quarz, *m.* (—es, *pl.* —e) quartz. **—ig,** *adj.* quartzy, of quartz. *Comp.* **—drüse,** *f.* crystallized quartz. **—fluß,** *m.* coloured, transparent quartz. **—haltig,** *adj.* quartziferous. **—schiefer,** *m.* gneiss.
Qua'si, *adv.* as it were, so to speak, in a way. *Comp.* **—gelehrte(r),** *m.* would-be scholar. **—modogeniti,** *m.* Quasimodo, Low Sunday.
Quas'sel—n, *v.a.* & *n.* (*aux.* **h.**) to prattle, chatter, talk foolishly (*sl.*). *Comp.* **—fritz,** *m.* foolish prattler.
Quast, *m.* (—es, *pl.* —e), **—e,** *f.* (*pl.* —en) hanging knot, tuft; tassel; mop; fellow, clown. **—ig,** *adj.* tasselled.
Quä'st—or, *m.* (—ors, *pl.* —o'ren) questor, university registrar(y). **—u'r,** *f.* (*pl.* —uren) questorship; questor's *or* university registrar(y)'s office.
Quat—em'ber, *m.* (—embers, *pl.* —ember) quarter-day; ember-days; (*in comp.* =) quarterly.
Quater'ne, *f.* quaternity; quire of 4 sheets.
Quatsch, I. *int.* squash! II. *m.* (—es, *pl.* —e) slap; squash; twaddle. III. *adj.* silly, stupid. **—en,** *v.* I. *n.* (*aux.* **h.** & **s.**) to splash, flop; (*aux.* **h.**) to talk trash, bosh. II. *a.* to crush, squash. *Comp.* **—kopf,** *m.* twaddler.
Que'cke, *f.* (*pl.* —n) couchgrass.
Queck'silber, *n.* (—s) quicksilver, mercury. **—n,** *adj.* mercurial, of quicksilver. *Comp.* **—auflösung,** *f.* solution of mercury. **—kapsel,** *f.* bulb (*of a thermometer*). **—oxyd,** *n.* mercuric oxide. **—oxydul,** *n.* mercurous oxide. **—salbe,** *f.* mercurial ointment. **—salpeter,** *n.* nitrate of mercury. **—säule,** *f.* column of mercury, mercurial column (*in a thermometer*). **—sublimat,** *n.* corrosive sublimate. **—wanne,** *f.* mercury trough.
Queh'le, *f.* (*pl.* —n) towel (*dial.*).
Quell, *m.* (—(e)s, *pl.* —e) (*Poet.*) *see* **—e.** **—e,** *f.* (*pl.* —en) spring; source, fountain, fountain-head; source; authority; **aus guter —e haben, wissen,** to have on *or* upon good authority.
Quel'l—en, I. *ir.v.n.* (*aux.* **s.** & **h.**) to spring, gush, well up; to issue, flow; to swell; to arise from. II. *reg.* & *ir.v.a.* to cause to swell; to soak; **gequollene Erbsen,** soaked peas. *Comp.* **—bottich,** *m.* steeping-vat. **—brunnen,** *m.* fountain, well, spring. **—en=forscher,** *m.* investigator of the sources. **—en=forschung,** *f.* study of the authorities, original research. **—en=mäßig,** *adj.* on good authority, according to the best sources, authentic. **—grund,** *m.* ground full of springs; quagmire. **—reich,** *adj.* abounding in springs. **—sand,** *m.* quicksand. **—wasser,** *n.* spring water.
Quen'del, *m.* (—s) wild thyme.
Quengelei', *f.* wrangling; plaint.
Quen'gel—haft, —ig, *adj.* grumbling, wrangling. **—n,** *v.n.* (*aux.* **h.**) to wrangle; to worry about trifles; to grumble, nag; to whine, lament.
Quent, *n.* (—es, *pl.* —e), **—chen,** *n.* (—chens, *pl.* —chen) drachm, dram.
Quer, I. *adj.* transverse, oblique, diagonal. II. *adv.* athwart, across; cross-wise; perversely; **—durch,** across; **—über,** over against; **—über einander legen,** to cross; **— gegenüber,** over against, (right) across, nearly opposite; **— über den Weg gehen,** to cross the road; **kreuz und —,** in all directions; **etwas — nehmen,** to take a th. amiss; **die Sachen gehen —,** matters are going wrong; **die Sache kommt mir —,** I am put out, annoyed by this, this matter crosses my plans, thwarts me. **—e,** *f.* diagonal; oblique direction, bias; **die —e, in die —e, der —e nach,** athwart, across, crossways, bias; **die Länge und die —e,** the length and breadth; **einem in die —e kommen,** to cross a p.'s path, to thwart s. o.'s designs. *Comp.* **—achse,** *f.* transverse axis. **—axt,** *f.* twibill. **—balken,** *m.* crossbeam, sleeper, transom; (**der große**) architrave. **—band,** *n.* transverse ligament (*Anat.*); rail (*of bridges*); traverse (*Her.*). **—baum,** *m.* crossbar. **—binde,** *f.* traverse. **—blick,** *m.* side-glance. **—bolzen,** *pl.* cross-bolts (*Artil.*). **—durchschnitt,** *m.* transverse section *or* diameter (*of a conic section*). **—faser,** *f.* transverse fibre. **—feldei'n,** *adv.* across the field. **—flöte,** *f.* German flute. **—flügel,** *m.* transept. **—frage,** *f.* cross-question; **—fragen thun,** to cross-examine. **—gang,** *m.* traverse, cross-way. **—gasse,** *f.* cross-street. **—gestein,** *n.* stones crossing a stratum. **—holz,** *n.* crossbar, transom. **—kopf,** *m.* oddity, odd fellow.

—köpfig, *adj.* odd, cross-grained. **—linie,** *f.* diagonal. **—naht,** *f.* cross-seam; transverse suture. **—pfeife,** *f.* fife. **—profil,** *n.* transverse section (*Survey.*). **—sack,** *m.* wallet. **—säge,** *f.* cross-cut saw. **—sattel,** *m.* side-saddle. **—saum,** *m.* cross-hem. **—schwelle,** *f.* cross-sleeper; traverse-beam, transom. **—schiff,** *n.* transept. **—schnitt,** *m.* cross-section. **—schwingung,** *f.* transverse vibration. **—sinnig,** *adj.* cross-grained. **—strich,** *m.* dash; break (*Typ.*); hyphen; cross-line (*dividing the different parts of a fraction*); ledger-line; bar; disappointment; **einen —strich durch eine S. machen,** to spoil a thing, thwart a design. **—wall,** *m.* traverse (*Fort.*). **—wand,** *f.* partition wall.

Querl, *m.* (**—es,** *pl.***—e**) a wooden kitchen utensil used in the same way as the English whisk, twirling stick; whorl (*Bot.*); one year's growth of firs; restless person. **—en,** *v.* I. *n.* (*aux.* **h.** & **s.**) to whirl about. II. *a.* to whisk (*eggs*).

Querulie'ren, *v.n.* (*aux.* **h.**) to be querulous, contentious *or* complaining.

Que'se, *f.* (*pl.* **—n**) blister from pressure *or* hard work (*e. g., from rowing*) (*dial.*); **ungewohnte Arbeit macht —n,** soft hand, heavy land (*prov.*).

Quet'sch—e, *f.* tool for crushing *or* squeezing; state of being pinched, crush; dilemma; **in der —e,** in a fix.

Quet'sch—en, *v.a.* to crush, bruise, squeeze; to pinch; to flatten by pressing; **einen Ball an die Bande —en,** to strike a ball against the cushion (*Bill.*). **—ung,** *f.* crushing; bruise; contusion. *Comp.* **—eisen,** *n.* curling-iron. **—falten,** *f.* ruche. **—hahn,** *m.* nipper-tap. **—hut,** *m.* opera hat. **—kartoffeln,** *pl.* mashed potatoes. **—laut,** *m.* combination of a dental with a hissing sound, *e.g.*, ch in church, g in gem, j in jam (*Phonet.*). **—maschine, —walze,** *f.* crushing machine. **—werk,** *n.* ore to be crushed; crushing mill. **—wunde,** *f.* wound caused by a contusion, by pinching; bruise.

Queu'e, *n.* (**—s,** *pl.* **—s**), *f.* (*pl.* **—s**) cue (*Bill.*); rearguard (*of an army*).

Quick, I. *adj.* & *adv.* lively, brisk. II. *m.* & *n.* (**—es**) quicksilver. *Comp.* **—born,** *m.* living spring, fountain of rejuvenescence; title of a famous collection of modern Low German poems (*by Klaus Groth*). **—brei,** *m.* amalgam. **—erz,** *n.* quicksilver ore. **—faß,** *n.*; **das rotierende —faß,** revolving amalgamation-cask. **—metall,** *n.* metal mixed with silver. **—mühle,** *f.* mill for amalgamating ore. **—wasser,** *n.* mercurial solution.

Qui'dam, *m.* (**—s,** *pl.* **—s**) a certain person, somebody, so and so.

Quiek, *int.* & *m.* (**—es,** *pl.* **—e**) squeak. **—en, —sen** (*coll.*), *v.n.* (*aux.* **h.**) to squeak.

Quiet'schen, *v.n.* to scream out (*coll.*); to creak (*coll.*); **die Thür quietscht,** the door creaks, makes a grating noise (*if not properly oiled*).

Quill; Quillst, Quillt, *imperat. sing.*; *2 & 3 pers. sing. pres. indic. of* **quellen.**

Quinkaillerie', *f.* hardware, ironmongery; fancy wares.

Quin't—a, *f.* fifth form in a German secondary school (*corresponding to the English II.*). **—a'ner,** *m.* (**—aners,** *pl.* **—aner**) scholar of the fifth class. **—e,** *f.* (*pl.* **—en**) fifth (*Mus.*); first string, E string (*of violins*); quinte (*Fenc.*); quint (*Cardp.*); trick, whim; **reine —e,** perfect fifth; **verminderte —e,** imperfect fifth. **—e'tt,** *n.* (**—etts,** *pl.* **—et'te**) quintette (*Mus.*). **—us,** *m.* fifth boy in a form; form master of the **Quinta,** master of a very low form (*obs.*). *Comp.* **—absatz,** *m.* pause on the fifth (*Mus.*). **—en=fortschreitung,** *f.* succession of fifths. **—en=sänger, —en=macher,** *m.* intriguer, tricky fellow. **—essenz,** *f.* quintessence, pith.

Quirl, —en, *see* **Querl, Querlen.**

Quitt, *adj.* (*only used as predicate with gen.*) quits, even; rid, free. **—ie'ren,** *v.a.* to receipt (*an account*); to quit, abandon. **—ung,** *f.* receipt.

Quit'te, *f.* (*pl.* **—n**) quince. *Comp.* **—n=brei,** *m.* stewed quinces. **—gelée,** *n.* quince marmalade *or* jam.

Quoll, Quoll'est; Quöl'le, *1 (& 3) & 2 pers. sing. imperf. ind.*; *1 (& 3) pers. sing. imperf. subj. of* **quellen.**

Quo't—e, *f.* (*pl.* **—en**) quota, share; contingent. **—ie'nt,** *m.* (**—ien'ten,** *pl.* **—ien'ten**) quotient. **—ie'ren,** *v.a.* to quote (*prices*).

R

R, r, *n.* R, r; *for abbreviations see the Index of abbreviations at the end of the German-English part;* **Zungen r,** lingual r; **Zäpfchen r (gutturales r),** uvular r (guttural r); **ein kräftiges r sprechen,** to trill *or* roll the r; **das — guttural sprechen,** to burr the r.

'Rab (*coll.*) *for* **Herab (Hinab).**

Rabas'teln, *v.* to move about noisily (*coll.*).

Raba'tt, *m.* (**—(e)s**) discount, deduction; reduction; **davon geht noch — ab,** discount to be deducted. **—e,** *f.* facing (*of a coat*); cuff; border, bed (*Hort.*). **—ie'ren,** *v.a.* to abate, deduct, allow for discount. *Comp.* **—berechnung,** *f.* (*calculation of the*) discount.

Rab'bi, *m.* (**—s,** *pl.* **—s**), **—ner** (*pron.* **Rabbi'ner**), *m.* (**—s,** *pl.* **—**) rabbi. **—na't,** *n.* office of rabbi. **—nisch** (*pron.* **rabbi'nisch**), *adj.* rabbinical.

Ra'be, *m.* (**—n,** *pl.* **—n**) raven; corvus (*Astr.*), **der — krächzt,** the raven croaks; **ein weißer —,** a rare bird, rara avis; **alt wie ein —,** as old as the hills; **er stiehlt wie ein —,** he steals like a magpie. *Comp.* **—n=aas,** *n.* carrion. **—n=eltern,** *pl.* unnatural parents. **—n=haar,** *n.* raven-black hair. **—n=krähe,** *f.* carrion crow. **—en=schlacht,** *f.* battle of Ravenna (*A.D. 476; famous in mediæval German romance*). **—n=schwarz,** *adj.* raven-black, jet-black, coal-black; **—nschwarze Locken,** raven locks; **—nschwarze Nacht,** pitch dark night. **—n=stein,** *m.* place of execution; belemnite (*Geol.*). **—n=vater,** *m.* unnatural father. **—n=volk,** *n.* thieves.

Rabuli'st, *m.* (**—en,** *pl.* **—en**) pettifogger, hedge-lawyer, brawling advocate. **—erei',** *f.* pettifogging.

Ra'ce, *see* **Rasse.**

Ra'ch—e, *f*, vengeance, revenge; **—e an einem nehmen,** to revenge oneself on a person. *Comp.* **—begier, —begierde,** *f.*, **—durst,** *m.*, **—lust, —sucht,** *f.* revengefulness; vindictiveness; thirst for revenge. **—e=akt,** *m.* revengeful act. **—e=engel,** *m.* avenging angel. **—e=geist,** *m.* spirit of revenge. **—e=göttin,** *f.* Fury. **—gierig,** *adj.* vindictive; resentful.

Ra'chen, *m.* (**—s,** *pl.* **—**) jaws (*of beasts*); throat; yawning abyss. *Comp.* **—bein,** *n.* jawbone. **—förmig,** *adj.* labiate (*Bot.*) **—höhle,** *f.* pharynx, pharyngeal cavity. **—muskel,** *m.* muscle of the throat. **—putzer,** *m.* bad wine (*coll.*); gum tickler (*brandy; coll.*). **—wand,** *f.* the side of the throat.

Rä'ch—en, (*rarely ir.*) *v.a.* to avenge, revenge; **sich wegen einer S. an einem —en,** to take revenge on a p. for something; **es wird sich an ihm —en,** it will come home to him. **—er,** *m.* (**—ers,** *pl.* **—er**) avenger. **—erisch,** *adj.* revengeful.

Ra'cker, *m.* (**—s,** *pl.* **—**) rogue, rascal, sly dog, pickle, young monkey (*said good-naturedly*). *Comp.* **—zeug,** *n.* rogues, rascals (*used good-naturedly*).

Ra'ckern, *v.n.* & *r.* to drudge, toil, fag (*coll.*).

Racke'tt, *see* Rakett.

Rad, *n.* (—s, *pl.* Rä'der) wheel; **gezahntes —**, cog(ged) wheel; lock (*of an arquebuse*); bicycle, cycle, machine; **das — an der Welle**, wheel and axle; **ein — schlagen**, to spread the tail (*of peacocks*); to turn a somersault; **das ist zum — schlagen**, that is enough to drive one silly; that is screamingly funny (*coll.*); **zum —e verdammen**, to condemn to be broken on the wheel; **aufs — flechten**, to bind on the whee ; **das — laufen lassen**, to coast (*cycl.*); **ein — aus dem Eingriff bringen**, to throw a wheel out of gear, to ungear; **das fünfte — am Wagen sein**, to be the fifth wheel to the cart, to be of no use whatever. *Comp.* **—achse**, *f.* axle-tree. **—arm**, *m.* spoke of a wheel. **—bewegung**, *f.* rotatory motion. **—bohrer**, *m.* wheel-auger. **—brunnen**, *m.* well worked by a wheel. **—dampfer**, *m.* paddle-steamer. **—(e)=brechen**, *v.a.* (*insep.*) to break on the wheel; **eine Sprache —(e)brechen**, to speak a language badly, to mangle *or* torture a language; **er —brechte Englisch**, he murdered the King's English. **—(e)=haspel**, *f.* windlass. **—(e)=haue**, *f.* hoe. **—(e)=macher**, *m.* wheelwright. **—fahren**, *v.a.* to cycle; to ride a bicycle *or* tricycle; to wheel, bike (*sl.*); **in rasender Eile —fahren**, to scorch (*coll.*); **bergab — fahren mit vorn aufgestemmten Füßen**, to coast. **—fahrer(in**, *f.*), *m.* cyclist, bicyclist, tricyclist, wheelman (*coll.*), wheelwoman (*coll.*), lady cyclist. **—fahr=beinkleider**, *pl.* (**für Damen**) bloomers. **—fahrer=anzug**, *m.* cycling suit *or* costume. **—fahrer=bahn**, *f.* bicycling ground, cycling path, cinder path. **—fahrer=verein**, *m.* cyclists' club *or* association. **—fahr=gamasche**, *f.* cycling gaiter. **—fahr=kniehose**, *f.* cycling knickerbockers. **—fahr=pelerine**, *f.* cycling cape. **—fahr=mütze**, *f.* cycling cap. **—fahr=sport**, *m.* cycling. **—felge**, *f.* felly. **—förmig**, *adj.* rotate (*Bot.*); wheel-shaped. **—gehäuse**, *n.* paddle-box. **—kranz**, *m.* shrouding; rim of a wheel. **—lauf**, *m.* rotation. **—linie**, *f.* cycloid (*Geom.*). **—reif**, *m.* tire. **—schaufel**, *f.* sweep (*of a water-mill*); paddle-float; (**bewegliche**) feathering paddle. **—scheibe**, *f.* ram's block, roll in a block *or* pulley. **—schiene**, *f.* iron clout; wheel-tire. **—schuh**, *m.* brake. **—speiche**, *f.* spoke. **—spur**, *f.* wheel-rut. **—stern**, *m.* star of spokes, centre of wheels. **—stuhl**, *m.* wheel frame. **—welle**, *f.* axle-tree. **—zahn**, *m.* cog.

Radau', *m.* (—s) noise, row. **—leben**, *n.* noisy life (*sl.*). **—machen**, *v.n.* to be very noisy; to kick up a row (*sl.*).

Räd—chen, *n.* (—chens, *pl.* —chen) small wheel; caster. **—eln**, *v.a.* to riddle; to wind (*silk*). **—ern**, *v.a.* to provide with wheels (*rare*); to break on the wheel; **wie gerädert sein**, to be worn out, to be quite knocked up. *Comp.* **—els=führer**, *m.* ringleader. **—er=fuhrwerk**, *n.* wheel-carriage. **—er=gehäuse**, *n.* paddle-box; watch- *or* clock-frame. **—er=tierchen**, *pl.* wheel-animalcules, rotatoria. **—er=übersetzung**, *f.* gearing, gear. **—er=werk**, *n.* wheelwork; clockwork-movement.

Ra'de, *f.* (*pl.* —n) corn-cockle.

Ra'd—eln, **—fahren**, *v.a.* to cycle, bicycle, to ride a bicycle *or* tricycle; to bike (*coll.*); **wollen Sie mit mir —eln?** will you come for a bicycle ride with me? **—ler**, *m.*, **—lerin**, *f.* cyclist. **—ler=anzug**, *m.*, **—ler=kostüm**, *n.* cycling dress *or* costume *or* suit. **—ler=verein**, *m.* cycling club; cyclist's touring club (*C. T. C.*).

Rä'delsführer, *m.* ringleader.

Rad—ie's, *n.* (—ieses, *pl.* —iese), **—ies'chen**, *n.* (—ieschens, *pl.* —ieschen) radish. **—ika'l**, *adj. & adv.* radical; **der —ikale**, radical. **—ie'ren**, *v.a.* to rub out, erase, to etch (*Engr.*). **—ius** (*pron.* **Ra'dius**) *m.* (—ius, *pl.* —ien) radius (*Math.*, *Anat.*). **—izie'ren**, *v.a.* to extract the square root of; to trace to the root. *Comp.* **—ien=winkel**, *m.* angle formed by two radii at the centre of a circle. **—ier'=eisen**, *n.* scalping-iron (*Surg.*). **—ier'=gummi**, *m.* india-rubber. **—ier'=kunst**, *f.* art of etching. **—ier'=messer**, *n.* scraping-knife. **—ier'=nadel**, *f.* etching needle. **—ier'=wasser**, *n.* tempered aqua fortis.

Raf'fel, *f.* (*pl.* —n) raffle-net (*for turbot*); rattle; iron-rake; flax-comb.

Raf'f—en, *v.* I. *a.* to sweep, snatch away, gather up; to collect hastily; **sich zusammen —en**, to collect o.s.; **das Kleid —en**, to gather up the dress. II. *n.* (*aux.* **h.**) **—en nach**, to snatch at. *Comp.* **—gier**, *f.* rapacity. **—gut**, *n.* stolen goods. **—holz**, *n.* windfallen wood.

Raffin—a'de, *f.* refined sugar. **—ie'ren**, *v.a.* (*aux.* **h.**) to refine. **—ier't**, *adj.* refined; artful, designing, cunning; **—ierte Grausamkeit**, refined *or* exquisite cruelty; **—ierte Bosheit**, studied malice. *Comp.* **—ier'=feuer**, *n.*, **—ier'=herd**, *m.* refinery furnace.

Ra'gen, (*poet.*) *see* **Hervorragen**, **Emporragen**.

Ragou't, *n.* (—s, *pl.* —s) stew, hotch-potch.

Ra'he, (**Raa**,) *f.* (*pl.* —n) yard; **große —**, main yard; **mit bloßen —n**, under bare poles, without sails. *Comp.* **—banden**, *pl.* robbins, rope-bands. **—haken**, *pl.* grappling irons. **—holz**, *n.*, **—leiste**, *f.* waist-rail. **—segel**, *n.* square sail; any sail rigged on a yard. **—tau**, *n* head-line.

[1]**Rahm**, *m.* (—s) cream; **— ansetzen**, to form cream; **— abnehmen**, to skim the cream. **—en**, *v.* I. *a. & n.* (*aux.* **h.**) to (yield *or* form) cream. II. *a.* to skim. *Comp.* **—farben**, *adj.* cream-coloured. **—käse**, *f.* cream cheese. **—kelle**, *f.* skimmer.

[2]**Rahm**, *m.* (—s) soot, dirt; **— fangen** *or* **— empfangen**, to get dirty *or* sooty.

Rah'men, I. *m.* (—s, *pl.* —) (*picture-*, *window-*, *embroidery-*, *etc.*) frame; casement (*of windows*); chase; rim, edge, border; tenter; welt (*Shoem.*). II. *v.a.* to frame. *Comp.* **—einfassung**, *f.* framing. **—erzählung**, *f.* number of stories forming one artistic unit and joined together by a common framework (*e.g.*, *Chaucer's 'Canterbury Tales' or Keller's 'Sinngedicht'*). **—haken**, *m.* tenter-hook. **—rohr**, *n.*; **oberes —rohr**, top tube (*cycl.*). **—rollen**, *pl.* sash-pulleys. **—spiegel**, *m.* framed mirror. **—stickerei**, *f.* frame-embroidery. **—tasche**, *f.* cyclist's bag.

Rain, *m.* (—s, *pl.* —e) balk, ridge (*between two fields*); limit, border (*poet.*). *Comp.* **—stein**, *m.* boundary stone. **—weide**, *f.* privet.

Raisonnie'ren, *v.n.* (*aux.* **h.**) to argue.

Rajo'len, *see* **Rigolen**.

Rä'keln, *see* **Rekeln**.

Rake'te, *f.* (*pl.* —n) rocket. *Comp.* **—n=batterie**, *f.* rocket- *or* ricochet-battery. **—n=feuer**, *n.* rocket-practice. **—n=hülse**, *f.* rocket paper.

Rake'tt, *n.* (—s, *pl.* —s) racket; battledore.

Ram'm—e, *f.* pile-driver; rammer, beetle. **—eln**, *v.* I. *a.* to ram in. II. *n.* (*aux.* **h.**) to buck, rut, be in heat; to roll about (*coll.*); to romp (*coll.*); to shake (*coll.*); to racket; **sich hin und her —eln**, to move about, be restless; **die Gänge —eln sich**, the lodes join. **—en**, *v.a.* to drive, ram in; to beat hard, stamp down (*the soil*). **—er**, *m.* (—ers, *pl.* —er) rammer, pile-driver. **—ler**, *m.* (—lers, *pl.* —ler) buck; ram; tomcat. *Comp.* **—arbeit**, *f.* pile-driving. **—bär**, *m.* ram-block, rammer. **—block**, *m.* pile-driver. **—bock**, *m.* ram.

Ram'pe, *f.* perron, ascent, broad sloping approach to the entrance of a palace or a railway station; foot-lights. *Comp.* **—n=lichter**, *pl.* foot-lights (*Theat.*).

Ramponie'ren, *v.a.* to spoil, injure (*coll.*).
Ramsch, *m.* (—**es**) odds and ends; job goods; **im —,** in the lump, in lots. *Comp.* **—bazar,** *m.*, **—verkauf,** *m.* jumble sale. **—geschäft,** *n.* junk-shop.
'Ran, *coll. for* **Heran**; **immer —,** come along, don't hesitate! (*coll.*). *Comp.* **—lootsen,** *v.a.* to induce a person to come up, to bring up (*sl.*). **—schlängeln,** *v.r.* to creep *or* slink up (*sl.*).
Rand, *m.* (—**es**, *pl.* **Rän'der**) edge, brink; brim, rim; crust; margin (*of a book, etc.*); ledge; border; lip (*of a wound*); **am —e des Verderbens,** on the verge of ruin; **am —e des Todes,** at death's door; **aus** (*or* **außer**) **— und Band sein,** to be out of all bounds, out of hand, to be unmanageable; **bis zum —e voll,** full to the brim, brimful; **das versteht sich am —e,** that's a matter of course (*sl.*); **zu —e kommen mit,** to accomplish a thing; **den — halten,** to hold one's tongue, to shut up (*sl.*). **—en,** *see* **Rändeln.** **—ig,** *adj.* margined. *Comp.* **—anmerkung, —bemerkung,** *f.* marginal note, gloss. **—lichter,** *pl.* footlights (*Theat.*). **—schrift,** *f.* edge-legend (*on coins*). **—schweifig,** *adj.* wavy-margined. **—ständig,** *adj.* marginal. **—stoß,** *m.* stroke from the cushion (*Bill.*). **—stück,** *n.* crust, outside piece. **—verzierung,** *f.* marginal embellishment; cartouche (*Arch.*). **—weisung,** *f.* marginal reference. **—zacken,** *m.* edging. **—zeichnung,** *f.* marginal illustration.
Randa'l, *m.* (—**s**, *pl.* —**e**) row, brawl (*sl.*); **— schlagen, —ie'ren,** *v.n.* to kick up a row (*sl.*).
Rän'd—eln, —en, —ern, *v.a.* to put a border, edge *or* brim to. **—erung,** *f.* engrailment.
Ranft, *m.* (—**es**, *pl.* **Ränf'te**) crust (*of bread*); edge, border (*poet.*).
Rang, Ran'gest; Rän'ge; *1* (*& 3*) *and 2 pers. sing. imperf. ind.*; *1* (*& 3*) *pers. sing. imperf. subj. of* **ringen.**
Rang, *m.* (—**es**, *pl.* **Rän'ge**) row, tier; degree, grade; rank; order, class; quality; precedence; **einem den — ablaufen,** to get ahead of a p., to outrun, outstrip, *or* outdo a p.; **ersten —es, vom ersten —e,** first-class, first-rate; **Loge im ersten —e,** box in the dress-circle (*Theat.*). *Comp.* **—klasse,** *f.* class. **—liste,** *f.* army-list. **—los,** *adj.* without rank. **—mäßig,** *adj. & adv.* according to rank. **—ordnung,** *f.* order of precedence; regulations regarding rank. **—stolz,** I. *adj.* proud of rank. II. *m.* pride of rank. **—streit,** *m.* dispute for precedence. **—stufe,** *f.* order, grade. **—sucht,** *f.* love of rank, ambition.
Ran'ge, I. *m.* (—**n**, *pl.* —**n**) young scapegrace; tall ungainly lad; **ungezogene —n,** naughty children, young scamps. II. *f.* (*pl.* —**n**) tomboy, romp.
Rangie'r—en, *v.* I. *a.* to arrange; to rank; to shunt (*trains*); **nach der Größe —t sein,** to be placed according to size. II. *n.* (*aux.* **h.**) to (have a certain) rank; **—en mit,** to be classed *or* to take rank with *or* among. *Comp.* **—bahnhof,** *m.* shunting station *or* yard (*Railw.*). **—geleise, —gleis,** *n.* siding (*Railw.*). **—maschine,** *f.* shunting engine (*Railw.*).
Rank, I. *adj.* winding; creeping; slender. II. *m.* (—**es**, *us. in the pl.* **Rän'ke**) crookedness, winding course; intrigue, trick, wile, artifice; **Ränke schmieden** *or* **spinnen,** to hatch plots, to intrigue. **—e,** *f.* (*pl.* —**en**) tendril, runner, shoot. **—en,** *v.r. & n.* (*aux.* **h.** & **s.**) to creep, to climb; to shoot forth tendrils. **—en,** *m.* hunch; **ein —en Schwarzbrot,** a chunk, hunch, of brown bread (*coll.*). **—ig,** *adj.* having tendrils. *Comp.* **—en=gewächs,** *n.* creeper, climber.
Rän'ke, *pl. see* **Rank** II. *Comp.* **—schmied,** *m.* intriguer, plotter. **—sucht,** *f.* spirit of intrigue. **—voll,** *adj.* intriguing.

Rann, Ran'nest; Rän'ne, *1* (*& 3*) *and 2 pers. sing. imperf. ind.*; *1* (*& 3*) *pers. sing. imperf. subj. of* **rinnen.**
Rann'te, Rann'test, *1* (*& 3*) *and 2 pers. sing. imperf. ind. of* **rennen.**
Ranun'kel, *f.* (*pl.* —**n**) ranunculus, buttercup, crowfoot.
Ran'zen, *m.* (—**s**, *pl.* —), **Rän'zel,** *or* **Ränz'=lein,** *n.* (—**s**, *pl.* —) knapsack, wallet; satchel (*of school children*); belly, paunch; **sein —el schnüren,** to pack and be off.
Ran'zig, *adj.* rancid, spoilt. **—keit,** *f.* rancidity.
Ranzio'n, *f.* (*pl.* —**en**) ransom. **—ie'ren,** *v.a.* to redeem, ransom; to demand a ransom.
Rapiditä't, *f.* rapidity.
Rapie'r, *n.* (—**s**, *pl.* —**e**) rapier, foil; **er führte ein gutes —,** he fenced well.
Rapie'ren, *v.a.* to grate, rasp; to scrape.
Rap'pe, *m.* (—**n**, *pl.* —**n**) black horse; **auf Schusters —n reiten,** to go on shank's mare; to trudge on foot (*coll.*).
Rap'pel, *m.* (—**s**) fit of madness; **er hat einen —,** he is cracked (*coll.*). **—ig,** *adj.* crazy. **—n,** *v.n.* (*aux.* **h.**) to rattle, make a noise; **es —t bei ihm im Oberstübchen,** he is out of his mind, cracked (*coll.*). *Comp.* **—kopf,** *m.* crazy person. **—köpfig,** *adj.* crack-brained.
Rap'peln, *v.r.* to make haste, bestir oneself, to stir; **sich zusammen —,** to pull oneself together (*coll.*); **er rührt und rappelt sich nicht,** he does not stir at all.
Rap'pen, *m.* (—**s**, *pl.* —) centime (old Swiss coin).
Rap(p)s, *m.* (—(**s**)**es**, *pl.* —(**s**)**e**) rape-seed.
Rapp'schnabel, *m.* pert young person, young jackanapes.
Rappu'se, *f.* scramble; **in die — geben,** to throw down to be scrambled for, to regard as lost.
Rap'tus, *see* **Rappel.**
Rapüns'chen, *n.* (—**s**, *pl.* —), **Rapun'zel,** *f.* lamb's lettuce; name of various plants used for salad.
Rapüsch'chen, *n.* little scramble game (*dial.*); *see* **Rappuse.**
Rar, *adj.* rare, scarce; **Sie machen sich sehr —,** you make quite a stranger of yourself, you never come to see us. **—itä't,** *f.* rarity; curiosity.
Rasau'nen, *v.n.* to run along noisily (*sl.*).
[1]**Rasch,** *m.* (—**es**, *pl.* —**e**) ras; serge.
[2]**Rasch,** *adj.* quick, swift; impetuous, hasty; lively; rash (*rare, poet.*). **—heit,** *f.* quickness, liveliness; rashness.
Ra'scheln, *v.n.* (*aux.* **h.**) to rustle.
[1]**Ra's—en,** *v.* I. *n.* (*aux.* **h.**) to bluster; to make a great noise; to rave, rage; to be mad; **Paule, du —est,** Paul, thou art beside thyself (*B.*); **er hatte auf dem Balle gerast,** he had danced like a madman at the ball; **er —t auf seinem Rade die Straße entlang,** he scorches along the road on his cycle. II. *a.* to do *or* say in passion *or* fury. **—end,** *adj. & adv.* raving; furious; mad, frantic; **—end hungrig,** furiously hungry; **einen —end machen,** to enrage a p.; **man möchte darüber —end werden, es ist um —end zu werden,** it is enough to drive one mad; **der, die —ende,** mad person. **—erei',** *f.* rage, frenzy; madness; mad act.
[2]**Ra's—en,** *m.* (—**ens**, *pl.* —**en**) turf, sward; sod; lawn, grass(plot); **auf dem —en,** on the lawn. **—ig,** *adj.* grassy, covered with turf. *Comp.* **—en=bank,** *f.* grassy seat. **—en=bekleidung,** *f.* turf-lining, sod-work (*Fort.*). **—en=hacke,** *f.* sod-cutter. **—en=platz,** *m.* lawn, grass-plot. **—en=stechen,** *n.* turf-cutting. **—en=walze,** *f.* roller.
Rasie'r—en, *v.a.* to shave; to raze (*Mil.*); **sich —en lassen,** to get shaved. *Comp.* **—becken,**

n. shaving basin. —messer, n. razor; —messer geschliffen und abgezogen, razors ground and set. —zeug, n. shaving things.

Ras'pel, (Ras'pe,) f. (pl. —n) rasp; instrument for stripping the grapes off a bunch. —n, v.a. to rasp; Süßholz —n, to say soft things, to flirt, spoon (coll.). Comp. —haus, n. house of correction. —späne, pl. filings.

Ras'se, f. (pl. —n) race, breed; von reiner —, thoroughbred; von gekreuzter (or Misch=) —, cross-bred. Comp. —n=kampf, m. racial struggle, conflict of races.

Ras'sel, f. (pl. —n) rattle. —n, v.n. (aux. h. & f.) to rattle, clatter; to clank; to rustle, to be ploughed (sl.); er ist in der Prüfung gerasselt, he has been ploughed in the examination (sl.).

Rast, f. (pl. —en) rest, repose; resting place; stage; foot-rest (Cycl.); rest (of a gun-lock); boshes (of a blast-furnace); halt; ohne — und Ruh, restlessly, never at rest. —en, v.a. & n. (aux. h.) to rest; wer —et rostet, if you rest you rust (prov.). Comp. —los, adj. restless. —losigkeit, f. restlessness. —ort, m. resting place, halting place. —tag, m. day of rest.

Rastra'l, n., (—s, pl. —e) pen for ruling music.

Rat, m. (—es) (pl. Rat'schläge; Berat'schlagungen) counsel, advice; deliberation, consultation; economy, prudence; help, provision, remedy (obs.); means, expedient; will, resolution; mind; (pl. Rats'versammlungen) senate, assembly, board, council; (pl. Rä'te) councillor, counsellor; (pl. Rats'herrn, rarely Rä'te) alderman, senator; etwas zu —e halten, to be economical of a th.; to be sparing of, to husband a th.; — schaffen, to help, to devise means; dazu kann — werden (des mag — werden (obs.)), that may be remedied, that can be helped; da ist guter — teuer, that is a very difficult case, it is a critical situation; lustiger —, jester (at a court), fool, merry Andrew; auf jemandes —, by s.o.'s advice; mit einem zu — gehen, to consult with a person; sich (dat.) —s erholen bei, to consult (a person); folg' meinem —e, be advised by me; da wußt' ich keinen — mehr, then I was at my wits' end; da ward er zu —, wieder umzuwenden, then he purposed to return (B.); guter — kommt über Nacht, good counsel comes overnight (prov.).

Rät, 3 pers. sing. pres. ind. of raten.

Ra't—a, f. rate, proportional share. —e, f. (pl. —en) rate; in —en, by instalments. Comp. —en=zahlung, f. payment by instalments.

Ra't—en, ir.v.a. & n. (aux. h.) to counsel, advise, exhort; to guess, conjecture; to solve; to help (obs.); einem etwas or zu einer Sache —en, to advise s.o. as to a th.; damit ist mir nicht geraten, that does not help me much; laß dir —en, be advised; er läßt sich von niemand —en, he will take no advice from any one; geschehenen Dingen ist nicht zu —en, what 's done can't be undone; ich wußte mir nicht zu —en, I did not know what to do; einem etwas zu —en geben, to give a p. something to think about or guess, to give a p. a nut to crack; geraten, advisable, advantageous; da wäre mir hinlänglich geraten, that would answer all my wants; wem nicht zu —en ist, dem ist auch nicht zu helfen, a wilful man must have his way, he that will not be counselled cannot be helped (prov.); geraten! you have guessed it, right! —er, m. (—ers, pl. —er) guesser. —s, see Rats in comp. —sam, adj. & adv. useful; advisable, expedient; prudent. —samkeit, f. advisableness, expediency; thriftiness. Comp. —geber, m. adviser, counsellor; counsel (Law). —haus, n. town-hall, guildhall. —los, adj. unadvised; perplexed, helpless; at sea. —schlag, m. advice, council; —schläge erteilen, to give advice, to advise. —schlagen, v.n. (aux. h.) (insep.) to deliberate; sie —schlagten, they consulted, they took counsel. —schluß, m. resolution, decision; decree; die —schlüsse der Vorsehung, the decrees of Providence; die —schlüsse Gottes sind unerforschlich, the ways of the Lord are inscrutable.

Ratifizie'ren, v.a. to ratify.

Rät—in, f. the counsellor's or senator's wife. —lich, see Ratsam. —sel, n. (—sels, pl. —sel) riddle; enigma; conundrum; puzzle; das ist mir ein —sel, that puzzles me, that beats me. —selhaft, adj. & adv. enigmatical; problematic; unintelligible; mysterious. Comp. —sel=deuter, m. guesser of riddles. —sel=dichter, m. riddle-maker. —sel=frage, f. puzzling or enigmatical question. —sel=spruch, m., —sel=wort, n. enigma, enigmatical or puzzling saying. —sel=voll, adj. enigmatical.

Ratio'n, f. (pl. —en) ration, portion.

Rationa'l, (Ratione'll,) adj. rational; —e Ackerwirtschaft, systematic agriculture. —is'mus, m. rationalism. —is'tisch, adj. rationalistic.

Rats— (in comp.) —befehl, m. order of the (town) council. —erlaß, m. decree of the council. —fähig, adj. eligible for election to a council. —herr, m. senator; alderman, town councillor. —kammer, f. council room or chamber. —keller, m. town-hall cellar. —kollegium, n. senate; board; council. —schreiber, m. recorder, clerk to the council, town clerk. —schreiberei, f. clerkship of a council; town clerk's office; the rolls. —sitzung, f. meeting of a council. —stube, f. council chamber. —tisch, m. council-board. —versammlung, f. meeting of council.

Rätst, 2 pers. sing. pres. ind. of raten.

Rat'te, Rat'z(e), f. (pl. —n) rat; er schläft wie eine —, he sleeps like a top. Comp. —en=fänger, m. rat-catcher; —enfänger von Hameln, the pied piper of Hamelin. —n=gift, —n=pulver, n. poison for rats. —n=kahl, (Ratze=kahl,) adj. bald as a rat, egg-bald, quite bare. —en=könig, m. several rats grown together by the tails; (fig.) ein wahrer —enkönig, a perfect maze. —en=schwanz, m. rat's tail (also Vet.); rat-tail file; anything like a rat's tail.

Ratz, m. (—es, pl. —e) marmot; dormouse; polecat; schlafen wie ein —, to sleep like a top.

Raub, m. (—es) robbery; plundering; rapine; prey, spoil, loot, booty; auf — ausgehen, to go out to plunder or prey; Jungfern—, rape; Kinder—, kidnapping; — zur See, piracy; gewaltsamer —, theft with violence; zu — gehen, to become a prey, get lost (rare); zum —e geben, to hand over to be plundered; einem zum —e werden, to fall a prey to a p., to become a p.'s victim. —en, v. I. a. to rob, steal, plunder, pillage; to ravish; to take away, deprive of. II. n. (aux. h.) to rob; to pillage; die —ende Rotte, a band or gang of robbers. Comp. —anfall, m. armed attack (of brigands, etc.). —bau, m. mine worked carelessly or without permission. —begierde, f. rapacity. —begierig, adj. rapacious. —fisch, m. fish of prey. —geflügel, n. birds of prey. —geschwader, n. pirate fleet. —gesindel, n. gang of robbers. —gier, f. rapacity. —gut, n. booty. —höhle, f. den of robbers. —krieg, m. predatory war. —mord, m. robbery with murder. —nest, n. see —höhle, castle of a robber-knight. —ritter, m. robber-knight. —schiff, n. pirate-ship, corsair. —schloß, n. castle of robbers or of a robber-knight. —staat, m. piratical state; die kleinen deutschen staaten, the smallest states of the German empire (hum.). —schütz, m. poacher. —stück, n. spoil. —sucht, f. rapacity. —süchtig, adj. rapacious. —tier, n. beast of prey. —vogel, *m.* bird of prey. **—wild,** *n.* beasts of prey. **—wut,** *f.* rapacious fury. **—zeug,** *n.* vermin (*Hunt.*). **—zug,** *m.* predatory incursion, marauding expedition, raid.

Räu'ber, *m.* (**—s,** *pl.* **—**) robber; thief; pirate; brigand; sucker (*Hort.*); candle-waster. **—ei',** *f.* robbery; depredation; brigandage. **—haft, —isch,** *adj. & adv.* robber-like; thievish; rapacious. *Comp.* **—bande,** *f.* gang of robbers. **—haupt'mann,** *m.* captain of brigands, robber chief. **—höhle,** *f.* den of robbers *or* thieves. **—pack,** *n.* gang of robbers.

[1]**Rauch,** *adj.* (*obs.; in compds.* =) hairy, shaggy; furred. *Comp.* **—färber,** *m.* fur-dyer. **—füßig,** *adj.* rough-footed; plumiped (*Orn.*). **—gar,** *adj.* dressed with the hair on. **—händler,** *m.* furrier. **—waren,** *pl.*, **—werk,** *n.* furs.

[2]**Rauch,** *m.* (**—es**) smoke; fume; soot; steam; fireside; **nach — schmecken,** to have a smoky taste; **in den — hängen,** to smoke-dry; **in — aufgehen,** to be burnt (up); to end in smoke, to come to nothing (*fig.*).

Rauch'bar, *adj.* smokable, good for smoking.

Rau'ch—en, I. *v.n.* (*aux.* **h.**) to smoke; **gern —en,** to be fond of smoking; **es —t,** there is a smoke (rising); **lernen, daß einem der Kopf —t,** to kill oneself with study (*coll.*). II. *v.a.* to smoke. III. *subst.n.;* **das —en ist hier verboten,** no smoking allowed here. **—er,** *m.* (**—ers,** *pl.* **—er**) smoker. **—ig,** *adj.* smoky. *Comp.* **—abteil,** *m.* smoking compartment. **—altar,** *m.* altar of incense. **—artig,** *adj.* smoky. **—bad,** *n.* fumigation; vapour-bath. **—coupé,** *n. see* **—abteil. —dicht,** *adj.*, smoke-proof. **—fang,** *m.* chimney, flue. **—fang=kehrer,** *m.* chimney-sweep. **—farben, —grau,** *adj.* smoke-coloured, dark gray. **—faß,** *n.* censer. **—fleisch,** *n.* smoked meat, hung beef. **—gar,** *adj.* thoroughly smoked. **—glas,** *n.* smoked glass. **—helm,** *m.* smoke(proof) helmet (*of firemen*). **—kammer,** *f.* smoking room; combustion chamber; smoke box (*in engines*). **—kanal,** *m.* smoke-flue, funnel. **—kohle,** *f.* live coal; half burnt charcoal. **—loch,** *n.* vent-hole for smoke. **—lokal,** *n.* smoking-room; tap-room. **—los,** *adj.* smokeless. **—massen,** *pl.* volumes of smoke. **—opfer,** *n.* incense offering. **—pfanne,** *f.* censer. **—pulver,** *n.* fumigating powder. **—rohr,** *n.*, **—röhre,** *f.* flue. **—säule,** *f.* pillar of smoke. **—schieber,** *m.* damper, register. **—schwarz,** *adj.* sooty-black. **—stube,** *f.* smoking-room. **—taback,** *m.* tobacco (for smoking). **—topas,** *m.* smoky topaz *or* quartz, cairngorm. **—topf,** *m.* censer. **—verbrennung,** *f.* consumption of smoke. **—verzehrend,** *adj.* smoke-consuming, fumivorous. **—werk,** *n.* incense (*for* **Räucherwerk**). **—wirbel,** *pl.* plumes of smoke. **—wolke,** *f.* cloud of smoke. **—zimmer,** *n.* smoking-room. **—zug,** *m.* flue.

Räu'cher—er, *m.* (**—ers,** *pl.* **—er**) fumigator; perfumer; smoker (*of meat*); censer-swinger. **—ig,** *adj.*, smoky; tasting of smoke; reeky.

Räu'cher—n, I. *v.a.* to fumigate; to smoke; to smoke-dry, cure; to perfume; **geräucherte Heringe,** smoked herrings, bloaters. II. *v.n.* (*aux.* **h.**) to burn incense *or* perfume. **—ung,** *f.* fumigation; smoking. III. *subst. n.* smoking, smoke-drying; curing; burning of incense, adulation. *Comp.* **—apparat,** *m.* fumigator. **—büchse,** *f,* incense- *or* perfume-box. **—essig,** *m.* aromatic vinegar. **—faß,** *n.* censer. **—kammer,** *f.* smoking-chamber (*for meat*). **—kerze,** *f.*, **—kerzchen,** *n.* fumigating candle, pastil. **—pfanne,** *f.* pastil burner. **—pulver,** *n.* fumigating powder. **—werk,** *n.* perfumes, scents, perfumery; frankincense.

Rau'de, *f.* (*pl.* **—n**) scab, scurf, scald.

Räu'd—e, *f.* scab (*of horses*), mange (*of dogs*), rubbers (*of sheep*). **—ig,** *adj.* scabby; mangy; **—ige Schafe,** black sheep (*of the family*) (*fig.*); **ein —iges Schaf verdirbt die ganze Herde,** one scabbed sheep will mar the flock (*prov.*).

'Rauf, *coll. for* **Herauf (Hinauf).** *Often in cpds. e.g.* **—kraxeln,** *v.a.* to climb *or* scramble up.

Rau'fe, *f.* (*pl.* **—n**) stable-rack; rack (*for guns, etc.*); flax-comb.

Rau'f—en, *v.a.* to pluck, pull, tear out; **einen —en,** to drag a p. about by the hair; **sich —en,** to fight, scuffle. **—er,** *m.* (**—ers,** *pl.* **—er**) brawler. **—erei',** *f.* scuffle, fight, fray. *Comp.* **—bold,** *m.* bully, brawler, inveterate duellist, swash-buckler, rowdy. **—degen,** *m.* rapier, long sword. **—handel,** *m.* brawl. **—sucht,** *f.* pugnacity.

Rauh, *adj. & adv.* rough; rugged, rude; inclement, raw; coarse; hoarse; harsh; inclement, cold; desert; **aus dem —en arbeiten,** to rough-hew; **das —e Haus,** house of correction (*at Hamburg*); **—er Stein,** rough stone; **—er Pfad,** rugged path *or* track; **—es Klima,** raw *or* inclement climate; **—e Nacht,** bleak night; **—er Wind,** rough, biting wind; **—e Stimme,** harsh voice; **—e Gegenden,** wild, mountainous *or* sterile countries; **—e Behandlung,** harsh treatment; **—e Sitten,** coarse manners; **—es Benehmen,** unceremonious ways; **—e Tugend,** austere virtue. **—e,** *f.* moulting time; *see* **—heit. —(h)eit,** *f.* roughness; rudeness, coarseness; harshness, hoarseness; inclemency; ruggedness; acerbity. **—en,** *v.* I. *a.* to roughen; to card, tease, nap, dress. II. *n.* (*aux.* **h.**) *& r.* to moult. **—igkeit,** *see* **—(h)eit.** *Comp.* **—bein,** *n.* churl, blackguard, blackleg (*vulg.*). **—futter,** *n.* hay, straw, *etc.*, as provender. **—gemäuer,** *n.* rough masonry. **—reif,** *m.* rime. **—stein,** *m.*, **—wacke,** *f.* compact carbonate of lime, red-land limestone (*Geol.*).

Raum, *m.* (**—s,** *pl.* **Räu'me**) room, space; place; chamber, room; space (*Mus., Typ.*); area; capacity; hold (*of a ship*); occasion, opportunity; **luftleerer —,** vacuum; **— zwischen den Verdecken,** the between-decks; **— geben,** to give way (*to*), to grant, yield, make room *or* way; **seinen Neigungen — geben,** to follow one's bent *or* one's inclinations. *Comp.* **—anker,** *m.* sheet-anchor. **—größe,** *f.* geometrical quantity. **—inhalt,** *m.* volume, cubature. **—maß,** *n.* measure of capacity. **—nadel,** *f.* priming-wire; gun-pick; borer.

Räu'm—en, *v.* I. *a.* to clear away, remove; to clear (*a place, etc.*); to quit, leave, evacuate; **aus dem Wege —en,** to remove (*obstacles*), to make away with (a p.); **bei Seite —en,** to put aside; **das Lager —en,** to decamp (*Mil.*); to clear *or* sell off; **das Feld —en,** to retreat; **einem sein Zimmer —en,** to give up one's room to a p. II. *n.* (*aux.* **h.**) to veer aft (*of the wind*). **—er,** *m.* (**—ers,** *pl.* **—er**) cleaner, scavenger; arranger; cleaning-rod. **—ig,** *adj.* spacious, roomy; capacious. **—lich,** *adj. & adv.* occupying *or* filling a certain space; relating to space, in space. **—lichkeit,** *f.* extent, space; spaciousness; locality. **—te,** *f.* offing; **die —te suchen,** to stand out to sea. **—ung,** *f.* removing, clearing, removal; evacuation. *Comp.* **—nadel,** *f.* needle, nail (*Min.*). **—ungs=ausverkauf,** *m.* clearance sale (at reduced prices).

Rau'nen, *v.a. & n.* (*aux.* **h.**) to whisper; **einem etwas ins Ohr —** *or* **zu —,** to whisper s.th. in a p.'s ear; **man raunt sich** (*dat.*) **ins Ohr,** it is whispered, there is a rumour.

Rau'p—e, *f.* (*pl.* **—en**) caterpillar; worm; grub; pad on the Bavarian military helmet, crest. *pl.* thick fringes on the epaulettes (*to distinguish higher officers*); whims, fancies, maggots. **—en,** *v.a.* to clear of caterpillars. *Comp.* **—en=fliege,** *f.* larva-fly. **—en=fraß,** *m.* blight (*of caterpillars*), damage done by caterpillars. **—en=helm,** *m.* Bavarian military helmet.

'Raus, *coll. for* **Heraus** (**Hinaus**).

Rausch, *m.* (**—es,** *pl.* **Räu'sche**) carouse; intoxication; delirium, transport; **einen — haben,** to be drunk; **im —e,** in one's cups; **sich** (*dat.*) **einen — trinken,** to get tipsy.

Rau'sch—en, *v.* I. *n.* (*aux.* **h.**) to rush; to rustle, sough, ripple; to roar; (*aux.* **s.**) to rush, [pass quickly. II. *a.*; **der Wald hat mir die alte Zeit wach gerauscht,** the rustling of the trees has brought back old times to me. **—end,** *p. & adj.* rustling; murmuring; noisy. *Comp.* **—beere,** *f.* cranberry. **—e=bart,** *m.* Rush-Beard (*nickname given to Count Eberhard of Wirtemberg* ('*der Greiner*') †*1392*). **—gold,** *n.* tinsel. **—mittel,** *n.* narcotic. **—pfeife,** *f.*, **—werk,** *n.* loud alto (*in organs*). **—silber,** *n.* silver tinsel.

Räu'spern, *v.r.* & (*rarely*) *n.* (*aux.* **h.**) to clear the *or* one's throat.

[1]**Rau'te,** *f.* rue (*Bot.*).

[2]**Rau't—e,** *f.* lozenge(-shaped figure); diamond; rhomb(oid); facet. **—en,** *v.a.* to cut into facets. **—ig,** *adj.* in squares, diamonds *or* facets. *Comp.* **—en=feld,** *n.* lozenge (*Her.*). **—en=fläche,** *f.* rhomb; facet. **—en=förmig,** *adj.* rhomboidal; quadrangular, lozenge-shaped; **—enförmig schneiden,** to cut in facets. **—en=glas,** *n.* glass cut in facets; square, pane. **—en=stein,** *m.* jewel with facets.

Rayo'n, *m.* (**—s,** *pl.* **—s**) ray; radius (*Fort.*).

Re, *adj.* (*dial.*) ready (to turn); **ein Schiff — machen,** to alter the course of a ship.

Rea'g—ens, *n.* (*pl.* **—en'tien**) reagent, test. **—ie'ren,** *v.a.* to react; to counteract. *Comp.* **—ens=papier,** *n.* test-paper. **—ier'=cylinder,** *m.* test-tube.

Reaktionä'r, *adj. & m.* (**—s,** *pl.* **—e**) reactionary.

[1]**Rea'l,** I. *adj.* real, substantial; material; **das —e,** reality, something real. II. *n.* (**—s,** *pl.* **—e**) reality. **—abiturient,** *m.* boy leaving a (‚**Realanstalt**' *or*) modern school. **—ien,** *pl.* realities; exact sciences; technical acquirements; facts *or* studies bearing on the institutions, life and customs of a nation. **—isie'ren,** *v.a.* to realize; to execute; **einen Verkauf —isieren,** to effect a sale. **—is'mus,** *m.* realism. **—is'tisch,** *adj.* realistic. **—itä't,** *f.* (*pl.* **—itäten**) reality; (*pl.*) real property. *Comp.* **—anstalt,** *f.* modern school. **—encyklopädie,** *f.* encyclopædia. **—gymnasium,** *n.* semi-classical secondary school (*9 years' course; teaching Latin but not Greek, corresponding to some extent to the modern sides of English first grade schools*). **—injurie,** *f.* outrage, assault and battery. **—katalog,** *m.* subject catalogue, catalogue in which the books are classified according to subjects. **—kenntnisse,** *pl.* knowledge of the exact and historical sciences. **—kredit,** *m.* loan, credit upon landed property. **—lexikon,** *n.* encyclopædia. **—progymnasium,** *n.* lower and middle part of a semi-classical secondary school (*6 years' course*). **—schule,** *f.* non-classical secondary school (*6 years' course*). **—wert,** *m.* actual value. **—wörterbuch,** *see* **—lexikon.**

[2]**Rea'l,** *m.* (**—s, —en,** *pl.* **—en**) real (*Spanish coin*).

[3]**Rea'l,** *n.* (**—s,** *pl.* **—e**) *see* **Regal.**

Re'b—e, *f.* (*pl.* **—en**) branch *or* tendril (*of the hop, vine, etc.*); vine. *Comp.* **—en=auge,** *n.* vine-bud. **—en=bedeckt,** *adj.* vine-clad. **—en=berg,** *m.* vineyard. **—en=geländer,** *n.* vine-trellis. **—en=gestade,** *n.* banks of a river rich in vines. **—en=gott,** *m.* Bacchus. **—en=hain, —(en)hügel,** *m.* hill covered with vines, vineyard. **—en=messer,** *n.* pruning-knife. **—en=reich,** *adj.* rich in vines. **—en=saft,** *m.* grape-juice; wine (*poet.*). **—en=stab,** *m.* thyrsus. **—en=stock,** *m.* vine. **—gewächse,** *pl.* vineworts, vitaceæ. **—gewinde,** *n.* festoon of vine-branches. **—holz,** *n.* (**das abgeschnittene**) cuttings of vines. **—huhn,** *n.* partridge. **—hühner=hund,** *m.* pointer. **—laus,** *f.* Phylloxera vastatrix. **—recht,** *adj.* unadulterated (*of wine*).

Rebe'll, *m.* (**—en,** *pl.* **—en**) rebel; mutineer. **—io'n,** *f.* rebellion. **—ie'ren,** *v.n.* (*aux.* **h.**) to revolt. **—isch,** *adj.* rebellious.

Re'chen, I. *m.* (**—s,** *pl.* **—**) rake; rack, row of pins; grate (*in a fishpond*); detent-wheel, ratch. II. *v.a.* to rake.

Re'chen—schaft, *f.* reckoning, account; **einem —schaft schuldig sein,** to be accountable to a p.; **einen zur —schaft ziehen, fordern,** to call a p. to account; **—schaft ablegen, geben,** to answer for, give an account of. *Comp.* **—aufgabe,** *f.* problem in arithmetic. **—brett,** *n.* blackboard; tally; abacus. **—buch,** *n.* primer of arithmetic, arithmetic book. **—fehler,** *m.* miscalculation. **—heft,** *n.* sum book, exercise book for arithmetical problems. **—kammer,** *f.* audit-office. **—knecht,** *m.* ready reckoner. **—kunst,** *f.* arithmetic. **—künstler,** *m.* arithmetician, person good at mental arithmetic. **—lehrer,** *m.* teacher of arithmetic. **—maschine,** *f.* calculating machine. **—meister,** *m.* arithmetician; accountant. **—pfennig,** *m.* counter (*at cards*). **—schafts=bericht,** *m.* statement of accounts. **—schafts=pflichtig,** *adj.* responsible; accountable. **—stunde,** *f.* arithmetic lesson. **—tafel,** *f.* slate; blackboard; abacus; multiplication-table. **—tisch,** *m.* counter (*in a shop*).

Rech'n—en, *v.a. & n.* (*aux.* **h.**) to count, calculate, reckon; to esteem, deem; to rank, class; (**auf eine S.** *or* **einen**) **—en,** to count, rely upon; to depend upon; **falsch —en,** to miscalculate; **an einer Aufgabe —en,** to work at a problem; **—en lernen,** to learn arithmetic; **Eins ins Andere gerechnet,** taking one with the other; **mit dazu gerechnet,** including, inclusive of; **Eins zum Andern —en,** to add to; **Alles in Allem gerechnet,** taking all in all, on the whole; **gegen einander —en,** to balance, to compare; **es sind hoch gerechnet 2 Meilen,** it is at the most 2 miles; **ich —e ihn als verloren,** I look upon him as lost. **—er,** *m.* (**—ers,** *pl.* **—er**) reckoner, arithmetician, calculator. **—ung,** *see* **Rechnung.**

Rech'nung, *f.* calculation, computation; arithmetic; account; bill, reckoning; calculus; opinion; **laufende —,** current account; **auf neue — stellen,** to place to a new account; **halbe —,** joint account, half share; **— ablegen,** to render an account; **eine — führen,** to keep an account; **auf jemandes — schreiben, stellen, in — bringen** *or* **stellen,** to place to a p.'s account; **soweit man seine — dabei findet,** as far as one's own interest is served; **er fand dabei nicht seine —,** the transaction did not pay him; **seine — bei einer S. finden,** to profit *or* benefit by a th., to reap advantage from a th.; **für — und Gefahr,** for account and risk; **in — stehen mit,** to have a running *or* ledger account with; **laut —,** as per account; **laut eingesandter —,** to account rendered; **eine — ausgleichen, aufgehen lassen,** to strike a balance; **die — ohne den Wirt machen,** to reckon without one's host; **sich auf etwas** (*acc.*) **— machen,** to count, rely upon; **er macht sich — befördert zu werden,** he counts on promotion; **eine — saldieren,** to settle an account; **einem einen Strich durch die — machen,** to frustrate a p.'s plans; **einer Sache** *or* **den Umständen — tragen,** to make allowance for *or* accommodate o.s. to a th. *or* to circumstances. *Comp.* **—s=abhörung, —s=abnahme,** *f.* audit(ing of accounts). **—s=ablage,** *f.* rendering of accounts. **—s=abschluß,** *m.* close *or* closing of accounts. **—s=art,** *f.*

method of calculation; **die vier —sarten**, the four species. **—s=artikel**, *m.* item. **—s=aufgabe**, *f.* arithmetical problem. **—s=aufseher**, *m.* auditor. **—s=auszug**, *m.* abstract *or* extract *or* statement of accounts. **—s=beamte(r)**, *m.* clerk in an audit-office. **—s=beleg**, *m.* voucher. **—s=betrag**, *m.* sum total of an account. **—s=buch**, *n.* account-book. **—s=fehler**, *m.* miscalculation. **—s=führer**, *m.* accountant, bookkeeper. **—s=jahr**, *n.* financial year. **—s=kammer**, *f.* chamber of accounts, audit office. **—s=liste**, *f.* statement of accounts. **—s=münze**, *f.*, **—s=pfennig**, *m.* fictitious coin, counter (*at cards*). **—s=pflichtig**, *adj.* responsible. **—s=prüfer**, *m.* auditor, comptroller. **—s=rat**, *m.* member of a council of finance; superior official in an audit-office. **—s=rest**, *m.* balance, remainder of an account. **—s=revisor**, *m.* auditor. **—s=tafel**, *f.* calculating table. **—s=wesen**, *n.* accounts; bookkeeping; audit-system. **—s=wissenschaft**, *f.* arithmetic.

Recht, I. *adj. & adv.* right; straight; proper, fitting, suitable; true, real, accurate, correct; genuine; pure; just, equitable, reasonable; lawful, legitimate; agreeable; right (*not left*); *only as adv.* in right condition; well; greatly, remarkably, very; actually; quite; downright; **mein —er Bruder**, my own brother (*opp. to half-brother*); **—e Ehefrau**, lawful wife; **wenn es Ihnen — ist**, if it is agreeable to you; **die —e Seite**, the right side, the off side; **zu —er Zeit**, in time, punctually; **Sie sind der —e**, you are the very man; **du bist mir auch der —e!** you're a fine fellow, indeed! (*iron.*); **Wittwen, welche —e Wittwen sind**, widows that are widows indeed; **ein —er Winkel**, a right angle; **—es Gold**, pure gold; **das geht nicht mit —en Dingen zu**, there's something not quite right there; **nicht halb —**, not half fair; **— und billig**, just and reasonable, fair; **nicht mehr als — und billig**, only fair; **mir ist alles —**, I am content with anything, I agree to everything; **mir ist nicht —**, I am not at ease, I am not well, I am not satisfied (*that*); **wenn, wo mir — ist**, if I mistake not; **wenn ich es — bedenke**, when I come to think about it, to consider it properly; **was dem einen — ist, ist dem andern billig**, sauce for the goose is sauce for the gander, what is fair for one is fair for all (*prov.*); **ich weiß nicht — wie . . .**, I don't quite know how . . .; **diese Stelle wäre mir —**, that place would just suit me; **es einem — machen**, to please *or* satisfy one; **ist es so —?** will that do? **da kommst du mir —!** that won't suit me at all! just what I expected! (*coll.*); **an den —en kommen**, to light on the right man; to meet with one's match; **komme ich hier — zu . . .? gehe ich hier — nach . . .?** is this right for . . .? does this lead to . . .? **sich zu — finden**, to find one's way; **er dünkt sich etwas —es**, he thinks himself somebody; **das ist auch 'was —(e)s!** that's something wonderful, I'm sure! **das half ihm auch 'was —es!** that helped him mightily, I'm sure! **— so! so —! ganz —!** quite right! true! hear, hear! **— gern**, very willingly; **es thut mir — leid**, I am truly sorry; **(so) — als ob**, just as if; **O bitte — sehr!** pray don't mention it! excuse me! **jetzt erst —**, now all the more, now more than ever; **jetzt erfahren Sie es erst — nicht**, now, less than ever, would I tell you. II. *n.* (**—es**, *pl.* **—e**) right; claim, title; law; justice; privilege; system of law; administration of justice; taxes, duties; **ausgehende —e**, export duties; **bürgerliches —**, civil code; **das gemeine —**, common law; **das geschriebene —**, statute law; **das peinliche —** penal code; **das Natur —** law of nature; **Student der —e**, law-student; **dem —e gemäß, nach dem —e**, according to law; **— über Leben und Tod**, power over life and death; **mit —**, justly; **er wurde böse und mit —**, he grew angry, as well he might; **mit noch größerem —e**, with still greater reason; **— behalten**, to be right in the end, to carry one's point; **zu — bestehen**, to be *or* continue valid; **einem — geben**, to acknowledge the justice *or* truth of a p.'s views, to decide in a p.'s favour, to admit that a p. is right; **ihm ist — geschehen**, he has got his due, justice has been done him; **— haben**, to be right; **sich** (*dat.*) **selbst — verschaffen**, to take the law into one's own hands; **einem — widerfahren lassen**, to do a p. justice; **dein — muß dir werden**, your claim must be admitted, justice must be done you; **von —swegen**, by right, in justice; **thue — und scheue niemand**, be just and fear not; do your duty, come what may (*prov.*). **—e**, *f.* the right hand; right side; the Conservatives, the Tories; **mit erhobener —en**, with the right hand uplifted; **zur —en**, on *or* to the right. **—en**, *v.n.* (*aux.* **h.**) to plead; to go to law; to contest, dispute; to remonstrate. **—ens**, (*obs.*) *gen. of* **das Rechte**; **ein Schein —ens**, a semblance of justice; **das ist bei uns —ens**, such is the law with us, that is the law of the land; **im Wege —ens**, by legal proceedings, by law; **den Weg —ens beschreiten**, to take legal proceedings. **—lich**, *adj. & adv.* just; honest, upright; lawful, judicial; legitimate; proper; **—licher Beistand**, counsel; **ein —liches Mädchen**, a respectable girl. **—lichkeit**, *f.* legality; integrity, honesty; fair play. **—s**, I. *adv.* on the right hand; to the right; **—s halten!** keep to the right! **gleich —s um die Ecke**, (take) the first turning to the right; **—s her**, from the right side; **—s hin**, towards *or* on the right; **—s um (kehrt)!** right (about) turn! II. *see* **Rechts** *in comp. Comp.* **—eckig**, *adj.* rectangular. **—fertig**, *adj.* just, righteous (*obs.*). **—fertigen**, *v.a.* (*insep.*) to justify, vindicate, exculpate. **—fertigung**, *f.* justification, vindication. **—gläubig**, *adj.* orthodox. **—gläubigkeit**, *f.* orthodoxy. **—haber**, *m.* dogmatic person; disputer. **—haberei'**, *f.* positiveness; disputatiousness. **—haberisch**, *adj.* positive, dogmatic. **—linig**, *adj.* rectilinear. **—los**, *adj.* unjust, illegal; outside the pale of the law, outlawed; illegitimate. **—losigkeit**, *f.* illegality; outlawry. **—mäßig**, *adj.* legal, legitimate; just. **—mäßigkeit**, *f.* legality; legitimacy. **—schaffen**, I. *adj.* righteous, upright, honest; solid, thorough. II. *adv.* righteously; very; vigorously; **— schaffen an einem handeln**, to deal honestly by s.o.; **bei diesem Buche habe ich mich — schaffen geplagt**, I have taken no end of trouble over *or* with this book. **—schaffenheit**, *f.* integrity, honesty, uprightness; thoroughness. **—schreibung**, *f.* orthography, (right) spelling; **Besserung der —schreibung**, spelling reform; **lautgetreue —schreibung**, phonetic script. **—sprechung**, *f.* administration of justice. **—sucher**, *m.* plaintiff. **—winkelig**, *adj.* rectangular. **—zeitig**, *adj. & adv.* opportune, seasonable; punctual; in time.

Rechts— (*in comp.*) **—altertümer**, *pl.* legal antiquities. **—amt**, *n.* court of justice. **—anhängig**, *adj.* pending judicial decision. **—anwalt**, *m.* counsel, solicitor; **vor Gericht plädierender —anwalt**, barrister-at-law (*in England*). **—ausschließung**, *f.* outlawry. **—beflissene(r)**, *m.* law-student. **—befugnis**, *f.* competency of a court. **—behörde**, *f.* law-court, legal authorities. **—beistand**, *m.* legal assistant, counsel. **—beständig**, *adj.* valid, legal. **—bewegung**, *f.* movement to the right (*Mil.*). **—beweis**, *m.* deduction. **—boden**, *m.* legal basis. **—buch**, *n.* law-book. **—eingriff**, *m.* encroachment upon a p.'s rights. **—einwand,** *m.* demurrer, traverse, plea. **—erfahren,** *adj.* versed in the law *or* in jurisprudence. **—fähig,** *adj.* competent; personal. **—fähigkeit,** *f.* competence, legal ability *or* rights. **—fall,** *m.* suit, case. **—form,** *f.*; **die strengste —form,** the strictest legal procedure. **—frage,** *f.* legal question, issue, point of law. **—gang,** *m.* legal procedure; proceedings. **—gelehrsamkeit,** *f.* jurisprudence. **—gelehrt,** *adj.* learned in the law, versed in jurisprudence. **—gelehrte(r),** *m.* lawyer, jurist. **—gemäß,** *adv.* according to law. **—gleichheit,** *f.* equality in the eyes of the law. **—grund,** *m.* legal argument. **—gültig,** *adj.* legal, valid, good in law. **—handel,** *m.* action, law-suit. **—hülfe,** *f.* legal aid *or* relief. **—kniff,** *m.* quibble, lawyer's dodge. **—konsulent,** *m.* legal adviser. **—kosten,** *pl.* costs (*of a suit*). **—kraft,** *f.* force of law; **—kraft erteilen,** to confirm, validate. **—kräftig,** *adj.* valid. **—mittel,** *n.* legal measure *or* remedy. **—pflege,** *f.* administration of justice. **—satz,** *m.* legal maxim. **—schluß,** *m.* judgment, decree. **—schule,** *f.* school of law; **—schulen** (*in London*), Inns of Court. **—schutz-verein,** *m.* society for the legal protection of its members. **—sinn,** *m.* love of justice, equity. **—sprache,** *f.* law terms, legal terminology. **—spruch,** *m.* sentence; judgment; verdict. **—staat,** *m.* constitutional state. **—stand,** *m.*, **—statt,** *f.* jurisdiction. **—streit,** *m.* action, lawsuit. **—tag,** *m.* court-day. **—titel,** *m.* legal title. **—urkunde,** *f.* legal document; patent. **—verdreher,** *m.* pettifogging lawyer, caviller. **—verdreherei,** *f.* pettifogging. **—verfahren,** *n.* legal proceedings; **peinliches —verfahren,** criminal prosecution. **—verfassung,** *f.* judicial system, code of laws, judicature. **—verständige(r),** *see* **—gelehrte(r).** **—verwalter,** *m.* administrator of justice. **—weg,** *m.* course of law; **den —weg beschreiten,** to go to law, to take legal steps. **—widrig,** *adj.* illegal. **—wissenschaft,** *f.* jurisprudence. **—wohlthat,** *f.* benefit of the law. **—wort,** *n.* legal term. **—zwang,** *m.* legal compulsion.

Reck, *n.* (—(e)s, *pl.* —e) horizontal bar (*Gymn.*). *Comp.* **—übung,** *f.* exercise on the horizontal bar.

Re'ck—en, *v.a.* to stretch, extend; to rack; **sich —en, die Glieder —en,** to stretch one's limbs, oneself; **den Kopf in die Höhe —en,** to toss one's head, to hold up one's head. *Comp.* **—bank,** *f.* rack. **—holz,** *n.* stretcher; (*pl.*) boot-trees. **—schmied,** *m.* smith working with a tilt-hammer.

Re'cke, *m.* (—n, *pl.* —n) renowned warrior, valiant hero, skilled swordsman; trusty vassal, thane, hero. **—nhaft, —nmäßig,** *adj.*, like one of the heroes of old, valiant, heroic, brave.

Redakt—eu'r, *m.* (—eurs, *pl.* —eure, —eurs) editor (*of a journal*). **—io'n,** *f.* (*pl.* —ionen) editorship; editor's office; editorial staff; drawing up (*of deeds, etc.*); **Auskunft erteilt die —ion dieser Blätter,** enquiries to be made *or* will be answered at the office of this paper.

Re'de, *f.* (*pl.* —n) speech; language, words; discourse, conversation; harangue, speech, oration; report, rumour; explanation, satisfaction; **eine undeutliche — haben,** to speak indistinctly; **an der — erkennen,** to recognize by the voice; **gebundene —,** verse, poetry; **ungebundene —,** prose; **gehobene —,** lofty language; elevated style; poetic style; **einem in die — fallen,** to interrupt a p.; **die — fiel auf diesen Gegenstand,** the conversation turned upon this subject; **der in — stehende Gegenstand,** the subject under discussion; **du mußt mir — stehen,** you must give me an account of it; **davon ist keine —,** that is out of the question; that goes without saying; **davon ist die — nicht,** that is not the question; **nicht der — wert,** not worth mentioning *or* talking about; **wovon ist die —?** what are you talking about? what is the matter? **einen zur — kommen lassen,** to let a p. speak; **nach seinen —n,** according to what he says; **um wieder auf unsere — zu kommen,** to return to what we were speaking of; **vergiß deine — nicht,** don't forget what you were going to say; **die — geht,** people say, it is said; **— und Antwort geben über** (*acc.*), to render an account of, to answer questions about; **einen über eine S. zur — setzen** *or* **stellen,** to call a p. to account with regard to something; to take some one to task; **— stehen,** to answer, account for; **eine — halten,** to deliver a discourse, make a speech.

Re'd—en, I. *v.a. & n.* (*aux.* **h.**) to speak; to talk; converse; to discourse; **ins Gelag** *or* **in den Tag hinein —en,** to talk at random; **er —et wie gedruckt,** he speaks like a book; **einem ins Gewissen —en,** to admonish a p. seriously, appeal to a p.'s conscience; **sich** (*dat.*) **einen Prozeß an den Hals —en,** to bring a lawsuit upon oneself by babbling; **Sie haben gut —en,** it is all very well for you to talk; **sich um den Hals —en,** to talk away one's life; **klug —en,** to play the wiseacre; **ein Langes und Breites über eine S. —en,** to discuss s.th. at great length; **mit sich —en lassen,** to listen to reason; **einem nach dem Munde —en,** to echo a p.'s opinion; **einem zu Munde —en,** to flatter s.o.; **über Politik —en,** to talk politics; **aus ihm —et die Verzweiflung,** this is the language of despair; **das Wort —en (einer Person oder Sache),** to put in a good word for, to defend, recommend; **—en Sie nur weiter,** go on; **wir wollen von etwas anderem —en,** let us change the subject. II. *subst.n.* talking, speaking; speech; **viel —ens von etwas machen,** to make a great talk *or* fuss about a th.; **all' Ihr —en ist umsonst,** you are wasting your words; **das —en wird ihm schwer,** he speaks with difficulty; **—en ist Silber, Schweigen ist Gold,** speech is silver, silence is golden (*prov.*). **—end,** *p. & adj.* speaking; expressive; **die —ende Person,** the interlocutor, speaker; **—ende Künste,** poetry and music; **—endes Wappen,** coat of arms with the name of the person bearing it. **—erei',** *f. see* **Gerede.** **—lich,** *adj. & adv.* honest; upright, honourable; straightforward, candid; just, fair. **—lichkeit,** *f.* honesty, probity, integrity, straightforwardness, candour. **—ner,** *see* **Redner.** **—selig,** *adj.* chatty; talkative, loquacious. **—seligkeit,** *f.* loquacity. *Comp.* **—e-accent,** *m.* rhetorical accent. **—e-begabt,** *adj.* eloquent. **—e-bild,** *n.* trope, figure of speech. **—e-fertig,** *adj.* of ready speech, of glib tongue. **—e-fertigkeit,** *f.* readiness of speech, gift of the gab (*coll.*). **—e-floskel,** *f.* figure of speech, metaphorical expression. **—e-fluß,** *m.* fluency of speech, volubility. **—e-form,** *f.* form of expression; mood (*Gram.*). **—e-fügung,** *f.* syntax. **—e-gabe,** *f.* faculty of speech, gift of the gab (*coll.*). **—e-gesang,** *m.* recitative. **—e-kunst,** *f.* rhetoric. **—e-künstler,** *m.* rhetorician, orator. **—e-lustig,** *adj.* talkative. **—ens-art,** *f.* expression, phrase; idiom; **nur so eine —ensart,** merely a figure of speech; **bloße —ensarten,** empty phrases. **—e-prunk,** *m.* oratorical pomp. **—e-satz,** *m.* period, sentence. **—e-scheu,** *adj.* shy of speaking, reticent, taciturn. **—e-schmuck,** *m.* rhetorical embellishment. **—e-schwulst,** *m.* bombast. **—e-schwung,** *m.* rhetorical flight. **—e-teil,** *m.* part of speech (*Gram.*). **—e-teilchen,** *n.* particle. **—e-ton,** *m.* rhetorical accent. **—e-übung,** *f.* exercise in speaking, declamation. **—e-verbindung,** *f.* context. **—e-verein,** *m.* debating society. **—e=weise,** *f.* manner of speech, mode of expression. **—e=zeichen,** *n.* stop.

Redigie'ren, *v.a.* to edit (*a journal, etc.*).

Red'ner, *m.* (—s, *pl.* —) orator; speaker. **—isch,** *adj.* oratorical, elocutionary. *Comp.* **—blumen,** *pl.* flowers of oratory. **—bühne,** *f.* pulpit; tribune; platform. **—kunst,** *f.* rhetoric. **—stuhl,** *m.* speaker's chair; pulpit. **—talent,** *n.*, **—gabe,** *f.* gift of eloquence, faculty of speech; gift of the gab (*hum.*).

Redou'te, *f.* (*pl.* —n) redoubt (*Fort.*); masquerade.

Reduktio'n, *f.* (*pl.* —en) reduction.

Reduzie'r—bar, *adj.* reducible. **—en,** *v.a.* to reduce (**auf** (*acc.*) to); **sich —en,** to be(come) reduced; **er sieht sehr —t aus,** he looks very shabby.

Ree'd—e, *f.* (*pl.* **—en**) road, roadstead; **auf der —e liegen,** to ride at anchor (*in the roads*).

Ree'd—en, *v.a.* to fit out ships. **—er,** *m.* (**—ers,** *pl.* **—er**) freighter, shipper; owner (*of a ship*). **—erei',** *f.* fitting out of a merchantman; shipping interest *or* trade; shipping; ship-owners; **—erei betreiben,** to be in the shipping trade.

Ree'll, *adj.* real, essential; safe, solid, respectable; honourable, just; **—e Behandlung,** fair dealing; **ein —es Geschäft,** a respectable *or* fair dealing firm; **—e Ware,** good article. **—itä't,** *f.* solidity (*C. L.*); honourableness.

Reep, *n.* (—s, *pl.* —e) rope.

Refekto'ri—um, *n.* (—ums, *pl.* —en) refectory.

Refer—a't, *n.* (—at(e)s, *pl.* —ate) report; review (*of a book*). **—enda'r,** *m.* (—endars, *pl.* —endare) (more formal is:) **—enda'rius,** *m.* (*pl.* —endarien) referendary; young barrister who, after having passed his first state examination in law, practises at a court without emolument, thus qualifying for his second professional examination for the post of 'Assessor.' **—e'nt,** *m.* (—en'ten, *pl.* —en'ten) reporter reviewer, writer, **—ent einer Deputation,** chairman. **—e'nz,** *f.* (*pl.* —en'zen) reference; information. **—ie'ren,** *v.a. & n.* (*aux.* **h.**) to report; to relate; to sum up.

Reff, *n.* (—s, *pl.* —e) basket for the back; dosser. *Comp.* **—träger,** *m.* pedlar.

[2]Reff, Reef, *n.* (—s, *pl.* —e) reef (*of a sail*).

Reflekt—ie'ren, *v.* I. *a.* to reflect. II. *n.* (*aux.* **h.**); **auf (eine S.) —ieren,** to think of, have in view; **über (eine S.) —ieren,** to reflect upon a thing; **hierauf —ierende mögen sich bei dem Herrn N. melden,** for further particulars apply to Mr. N.

Refle'x, *m.* (—es, *pl.* —e) reflex, reflection. **—io'n,** *f.* *see* **Reflex**; reflection, contemplation. **—i'v,** *adj.* reflective (*Gram.*). *Comp.* **—galvanometer,** *m.* reflecting galvanometer. **—ions'=strahl,** *m.* reflected ray. **—ions'=winkel,** *m.* angle of reflection.

Refo'rm, *f.* (*pl.* —en) reform. *Comp.* **—hose,** *f.* bloomers (= **Beinkleid für Damen**). **—kleid,** *n.*, **—rock,** *m.* divided skirt. **—kleidung,** *f.* (**für Damen**) rational dress.

Reform—atio'n, *f.* (*pl.* —ationen) reformation. **—a'tor,** *m.* (—ators, *pl.* —ato'ren) reformer. **—ato'risch,** *adj.* reformatory; **—atorische Bestrebungen,** reformatory efforts. **—ie'ren,** *v.a.* to reform. **—ier'te(r),** *m.* adherent of the Swiss reformers Zwingli and Calvin, Calvinist, member of the Reformed Church.

Refrai'n, *m.* (—s, *pl.* —s) burden (*of a song*); refrain; chorus (*fam.*).

Refrakt—io'n, *f.* refraction. **—or** (*pron.* **Refrak'tor**), *m.* (—ors, *pl.* —o'ren) refracting telescope.

[1]Reg—a'l, *n.* (—ales, *pl.* —ale, —alien) royal prerogative. **—alie'ren,** *v.a.* to regale (**mit,** with); to treat (**mit,** to). **—e'nt,** *see* **Regent.** *Comp.* **—al'=folio,** *n.* royal folio.

[2]Rega'l, *n.* (—s, *pl.* —e) book-case, book-rack, what-not; regal organ; organ-register; stand (*Typ.*).

Re'ge, *adj.* astir, in motion, lively; zealous; animated, brisk, active; industrious; **—machen,** to set in motion, stir up, excite; **wieder —machen,** to revive; **— sein,** to be up and doing; **der Wunsch wurde in ihm —,** he was seized with a desire to.

Re'gel, *f.* (*pl.* —n) rule; precept, principle, law; order, discipline; menses (*Med.*); **— de tri,** rule of three (*Arith.*); **in der —,** as a rule. **—n,** *v.a.* to regulate; **sich —n nach,** to be ruled by. *Comp.* **—los,** *adj.* without rule; **—n des Fußballspiels,** laws of football; irregular. **—losigkeit,** *f.* irregularity. **—mäßig,** *adj.* regular. **—mäßigkeit,** *f.* regularity. **—recht,** *adj.* regular, according to rule; normal; orderly; correct. **—widrig,** *adj.* contrary to rule, irregular.

Re'geling, *f.* (*pl.* —e) rail (*of a ship*).

Re'g—en, *v.* I. *a.* to move, stir; to animate; to touch on, mention. II. *r.* to stir, move, be in motion; to make itself felt; **er darf sich nicht —en,** he may not stir; **es —t sich kein Lüftchen,** not a breath of air is stirring. **—sam,** *adj. & adv.* active, nimble, agile, bustling, brisk. **—samkeit,** *f.* agility, activity. **—ung,** *f.* motion, movement; emotion, impulse, agitation. *Comp.* **—ungs=los,** *adj.* motionless; dead.

Re'gen, *m.* (—s) rain; shower; downpour; **feiner —,** drizzling rain; **kurzer —,** shower; **starker —,** heavy shower, pelting rain; **aus dem — in die Traufe,** out of the frying-pan into the fire; **wir werden — bekommen,** we shall have rain, it looks like rain. *Comp.* **—bad,** *n.* shower-bath. **—bö,** *f.* white squall (*Naut.*). **—bogen,** *m.* rainbow. **—bogen=farben,** *pl.* prismatic colours; **in —bogenfarben,** iridescent. **—bogen=haut,** *f.* iris (*Anat.*). **—dicht,** *adj.* waterproof. **—fang,** *m.* cistern. **—faß,** *n.* water-butt. **—guß,** *m.* violent shower of rain, downpour of rain. **—leder,** *n.* carriage-hood; carriage-apron. **—mantel,** *m.* water-proof (cloak), mackintosh. **—maß,** *n.*, **—messer,** *m.* rain-gauge. **—monat,** *m.* rainy month. **—pfeifer,** *m.* dotterel. **—rock,** *m.* mackintosh. **—schauer,** *n.* shower. **—schirm,** *m.* umbrella. **—schirm=förmig,** *adj.* umbelliferous. **—schirm=gestell,** *n.* skeleton, frame (*of an umbrella*). **—schirm=ständer,** *m.* umbrella stand. **—schnecke,** *f.* slug. **—strom,** *m.* torrent of rain. **—tag,** *m.* rainy day. **—vogel,** *m.* plover. **—wasser,** *n.* rain-water. **—wetter,** *n.* rainy weather; **anhaltendes —wetter,** spell of rain, succession of rainy days. **—wind,** *m.* rainy wind. **—wurm,** *m.* earth-worm, lob-worm. **—zeit,** *f.* rainy season.

Rege'nt, *m.* (—en, *pl.* —en) regent; administrator; reigning prince. **—in,** *f.* (female) regent. **—schaft,** *f.* regency, regentship.

Reg—ie', *f.* (*pl.* —ieen) public management, administration (*of dues, etc.*); stage management; **unter —ieverschluß,** in bond. **—ieren, &c.** *see under* **Regieren.** **—ime'nt,** *see* **Regiment.** **—isseu'r,** *m.* (—isseurs, *pl.* —isseure) stage-manager.

Regier'bar, *adj.* governable, manageable.

Regie'r—en, *v.* I. *a.* to manage, guide (*horses, etc.*); to steer (*ships*); to govern, rule, sway (*peoples*); to govern (*Gram.*). II. *n.* (*aux.* **h.**) to reign; to rule; **—ende Königin,** reigning queen, queen regent; **—ender Bürgermeister,** burgomaster in office; **—tes Wort,** regimen. **—er,** *m.* (—ers, *pl.* —er) ruler, governor; sovereign; **—er und Regierte,** sovereign and subjects. **—ung,** *f.* reigning; government, reign, sway; regency; power, authority; administration, executive power; management. *Comp.* **—ungs=advokat,** *m.* counsel for the crown. **—ungs=antritt,** *m.* accession (to the throne).

—ungs=bezirk, *m.* administrative district *or* area (*part of a Prussian province*). —ungs=blatt, *n.* official journal, organ of the government. —ungs=form, *f.* form of government. —ungs=gegner, *m.* member of the opposition. —ungs=los, *adj.* anarchical. —ungs=partei, *f.* ministerialists. —ungs=paß, *m.* Foreign-Office passport; government passport. —ungs=präsident, *m.* president of a government-board. —ungs=rat, *m.* member of a government board. —ungs=sache, *f.* state-affair. —ungs=sitz, *m.* seat of government. —ungs=verweser, *m.* regent. —ungs=wechsel, *m.* change of government.

Regime'nt, I. *n.* (—s, *pl.* —e) power, government; Pantoffel—, petticoat government; das — haben *or* führen, am — sein, to rule. II. *n.* (—s, *pl.* —er) regiment (*of soldiers*). *Comp.* —er=weise, *adv.* in regiments. —s=arzt, —s=chirurg, —s=feldscherer, *m.* army surgeon. —s=bureau, *n.* orderly room. —s=inhaber, —s=kommandeur, *m.* colonel of a regiment. —s=kapelle, —s=musik, *f.* band of a regiment, regimental band. —s=quartier=meister, *m.* regimental quartermaster. —s=stab, *m.* staff of a regiment. —s=tisch, *m.* officer's mess. —s=tambour, *m.* drum-major. —s=unkosten, *pl.* regimental expenses; auf —sunkosten leben, to live at the other people's expense (*coll.*).

Regis't—er, *n.* (—ers, *pl.* —er) register, record; table of contents, index; list, catalogue; register (*in organs; of chimneys, etc.; Typ.*); damper; stop (*organ*); alle —er ziehen, (*organ-playing*) to pull out all the stops; alle —er der Kunst sind hier gezogen, all that art can do is displayed here; ins alte —er gehören, to be obsolete, old fashioned *or* out of date; ich stehe bei ihr im schwarzen —er, I am in her black *or* bad books. —ran'de, *f.* (*pl.* —randen) register; order-book. —ra'tor, *m.* (—rators, *pl.* —rato'ren) registrar, recorder. —ratu'r, *f.* registry; record-office. —rie'ren, *v.a.* to register, record. *Comp.* —er=papier, *n.* large-sized, stout writing paper. —er=stimme, *f.*, —er=zug, *m.* register (*in organs*).

Reglementiererei', *f.* red-tapeism, craze for uniformity.

Reg'ler, *m.* (—s, *pl.* —) regulator (*of electric current*).

Reg'n—en, *v.a. & n.* (*aux.* h.) & *imp.* to rain; fein —en, to drizzle; es —et Prügel, blows are falling fast. —erisch, —icht (*obs.*), *adj.* rainy.

Regre'—ß, *m.* (—s'ses, *pl.* —s'se) recourse, remedy; —ß nehmen, to go back (to the drawer) (*C. L.*). —ssi'v, *adj.* regressive; analytic (*Log.*).

Regul—ä'r, *adj.* regular. —ati'v, *n.* (—ativs, *pl.* —ative) regulation, rule. —a'tor, *m.* (—ators, *pl.* —ato'ren) governor; regulator. —ie'ren, *v.a.* to regulate; to adjust. *Comp.* —ator=hebel, *m.* standard lever. —ier'=füll=ofen, *m.* moderator-stove, regulative stove. —ier'=hahn, *m.* regulating cock. —ier'=stange, *f.* regulator (*Mech.*). —ier'=ventil, *n.* regulator valve.

[1]**Reh**, *n.* (—s, *pl.* —e) roe; weibliches Reh, doe; ein Rudel —e, a herd of deer. *Comp.* —bock, *m.* roebuck; der —bock bellt, the roebuck bellows. —braten, *m.* roast venison. —fahl, —farben, —farbig, *adj.* fawn-coloured. —fell, *n.*, —haut, *f.* doe-skin. —fleisch, *n.* venison. —kalb, *n.*, —kitze, *f.* fawn. —keule, *f.*, —schlägel, *m.* haunch of venison. —leder, *n.* buck-skin. —posten, *pl.* buck-shot. —spießer, *m.* roebuck six months old. —wild, *n.* deer. —ziege, *f.* doe. —ziemer, *m.* loin of venison.

[2]**Reh**, —e, *adj.* foundered in the feet (*Vet.*).

Rei'be, *f.* (*pl.* —en) grater; rasp; tap.

Rei'b—en, *ir.v.a.* to rub, to grate; to grind (*colours*); to pulverize, triturate; to scour, clean by rubbing; to gall, fret; sich (*dat.*) die Hände wund —en, to rub the skin off one's hands; sich an einem —en, to tease, provoke a p.; einem etwas unter die Nase —en, to tell s.o. a thing plainly *or* to his face, to bring a th. home to him. —er, *m.* (—ers, *pl.* —er) rubber; grinder; brayer. —erei', *f.* provocation; bantering. —ung, *f.* rubbing; friction; abrasion; trituration; clash, collision. *Comp.* —(e)=eisen, *n.* grater. —(e)=fläche, *f.*; die —efläche auf der Schachtel, the rubber on the box. —(e)=kartoffeln, *pl.* mashed potatoes. —(e)=keule, *f.* pestle. —e=lappen, *m.* rubbing cloth. —e=laut, *m.* continuant *or* fricative (consonant), spirant; der tonlose labiale —elaut, the voiceless labial spirant (f). —(e)=stein, *m.* grinding-stone; ink-block (*Typ.*). —(e)=zeug, *n.* rubber. —(e)=zündhölzer, *pl.* lucifer-matches. —maschine, *f.* grating machine. —ungs=elektrizität, *f.* electricity by friction, frictional electricity. —ungs=kissen, *n.* rubber (*Elect.*). —ungs=maschine, *f.* common *or* friction electrical machine. —ungs=rad, *n.* friction-wheel. —ungs=widerstände, *pl.* resistance to friction.

Reich, I. *adj. & adv.* rich, wealthy; abundant; copious; opulent, ample, exuberant, plentiful, fertile, abounding in; powerful, mighty (*obs. poet.*); — an (*dat.*) rich in; — an Erfahrung, rich in experience; eine —e Anzahl, a large number; — und Arm, rich and poor; ein —er, a rich man; die —en, the well-to-do people, the wealthy. II. *n.* (—es, *pl.* —e) empire, kingdom, realm; reign; kingdom; Tier—, animal kingdom; Pflanzen —, vegetable kingdom; das heilige, römische — (deutscher Nation), the Holy Roman Empire (of the German Nation); das — der Mitte, the Celestial Empire, China. —lich, *adj. & adv.* ample, copious, plentiful; sein —liches Auskommen haben, to be well off. —lichkeit, *f.* plentifulness, abundance. —tum, *m.* (—tums, *pl.* —tümer) riches, wealth; opulence, abundance; affluence; richness, fulness, copiousness.

Rei'ch—en, *v.* I. *a.* to reach; (einem etwas) —en, to give, present, pass; das Abendmahl —en, to administer the sacrament; Almosen —en, to bestow alms; er —t ihm das Wasser nicht, he is not fit to hold a candle to him, he is no match for him; hier wird nichts gereicht, no alms given here. II. *n.* (*aux.* h.) to reach, extend to; to suffice, to last, hold out; —en nach, to stretch out one's hand for *or* towards; das —t, that will do; Fritz —t mit einen Glase, one glass is sufficient for Fred; —t das nicht? is that not enough? wer —t an ihn? who comes up to him? —ung, *f.* reaching; administering; offering.

Reichs— (*in comp.*) —acht, *f.* ban of the empire; in die —acht thun, to outlaw. —adel, *m.* peerage; nobility of the empire. —adler, *m.* imperial eagle. —amt, *n.*; —amt des Innern, Home Office; Minister im —amt des Innern, Home Secretary; Minister of the Interior; —amt des Äußern, Foreign Office. —angelegenheiten, *f.pl.* imperial affairs. —anzeiger, *m.* imperial *or* official gazette. —apfel, *m.* imperial globe *or* orb (*as emblem*). —archivar, *m.* master of the rolls. —bank, *f.* imperial bank (*at Berlin*). —behörden, *f.pl.* imperial authorities. —bote, *m. see* —tagsbote. —dampfer=linie, *f.* line of steamers subsidized by the Empire. —eisen=bahn=amt, *n.* imperial board of direction of railways. —erz=amt, *n.* high office of the empire (*obs.*). —fahne, *f.* national standard; flag of the empire. —fiskal, *m.* attorney-general (*for the empire*). —folge, *f.* imperial succession. —frei, *adj.* subject only to the emperor. —freiherr, —fürst, *m.* baron, prince of the Holy Roman Empire. —gericht, *n.* Imperial High Court of Justice, Supreme Court of the Empire (*at Leipzig*). —gesetzwidrig, *adj.* & *adv.* contrary to the laws of the empire. —heer, *n.* imperial army. —hülfe, *f.* subsidies granted by the imperial government. —kam'=mergericht, *n.* imperial chamber, supreme court (*obs.; formerly at Wetzlar*). —kanzlei, *f.* imperial chancery. —kanzler, *m.* chancellor of the empire. —kleinodien, *pl.* insignia of the empire, crown-jewels. —kreis, *m.* district of the (*old*) German empire (*obs.*). —krüppel, *m.* invalid (*wounded in the Franco-German war*) (*sl.*). —kursbuch, *n.* imperial railway guide. —land, *n.* territory of the German Empire; die —lande, the Imperial provinces (*Alsace & Lorraine*). —lehen, *n.* fief of the empire. —münze, *f.* coin of the empire *or* realm. —oberhaupt, *n.* head of the empire, emperor. —panier, *n.* imperial standard. —partei, *f.* Imperial party, Imperialists. —pfennig, *m.* (*German*) pfennig. —post, *f.* Imperial post. —post=dampfer, *m.* Imperial mail-packet. —post=meister, *m.* Postmaster General of the Empire. —rat, *m.* senate, council of the empire; senator. —ritter, *m.* knight of the empire. —schluß, *m.* decree of the Imperial Diet. —schreibung, *f.* Imperial (*German*) spelling (*introduced in 1902*). —stadt, *f.* imperial city; freie —stadt, free town of the Empire (*now only Hamburg, Bremen, Lübeck*). —stand=schaft, *f.* privileges of a state of the empire. —tag, *m.* Imperial Diet; (*now*) German Parliament, Reichstag. —tags=abschied, *m.* recess of an imperial diet. —tags=gesandte(r), —tags=bote, *m.* deputy to the Diet, member of (*the German*) Parliament, M.P. —truppen, *pl.* imperial troops; (*usually*) troops sent into the field by the various states forming the Holy Roman Empire in the XVI–XVIII centuries. —unfallversicherungs=gesetz, *n.* (*German*) accident insurance act; employers' liability act. —universität, *f.* University of Strasburg. —unmittelbar, *adj.* immediate (*subject only to the imperial government*); —unmittelbare Fürsten, princes subject directly to the Empire. —verfassung, *f.* constitution of the empire. —versammlung, *f.* assembly of the Imperial states. —ver=waltung, *f.* regency, administration. —ver=weser, *m.* regent, administrator of the empire. —währung, *f.* standard currency of the Empire. —wappen, *n.* imperial arms.

Rei'e, *m.* (—n, *pl.* —n) a lively country dance; den —n springen, to dance merrily.

¹**Reif**, *adj.* ripe, mature; — werden, to ripen, become ripe, to mature; to season, to mellow; ein Mann von —e(re)n Jahren, a middle-aged man. —e, *f.* maturity; ripeness; zur —e bringen, *see* —en I. —en, *v.* I. *a.* to ripen. II. *n.* (*aux.* s.) to mature, ripen, mellow; der Jüngling —t zum Manne, the youth ripens into manhood. —lich, *adj.* ripe, mature; nach —licher Überlegung, after careful *or* full consideration. —e=prüfung, *f.* leaving examination at the first grade secondary boys' schools (*entitling the successful candidate to matriculate without any further test at any German University*), examination for leaving certificates. —e=zeugnis, *n.* leaving certificate.

²**Reif**, *m.* (—es, *pl.* —e) hoarfrost; bloom (*on fruit*). —en, *v.n.* (*aux.* h.) & *imp.*; es hat stark gereift, there has been a sharp white frost.

³**Reif**, *m.* (—es, *pl.* —e) ring, circle, hoop; tire; fillet (*Arch.*); hoop (*Coop.*); zone; —e legen um, to hoop (*a cask, etc.*); den — schlagen, treiben, to trundle, drive a hoop. —eln, *see under* Reifel. —en, I. *subst. n.* (—ens, *pl.* —en) *see* Reif. II. *v.a.* to hoop; to put a rim on. *Comp.* —en=bahre, *f.* cage, cradle for a broken limb. —en=spiel, *n.* Les Graces (*game*); trundling the hoop. —en=springen, *n.* skipping. —rock, *m.* hoop(ed) petticoat.

Rei'gen, *m.* (—s, *pl.* —) round dance; row of dancers *or* singers; roundelay, song; dance and song; den — eröffnen, to lead the dance, to open the ball; den — führen, to take the lead (*fig.*).

¹**Rei'h—e**, *f.* (*pl.* —en) row, rank, line, file; tier; range; suite; series, succession; train (*of thought, etc.*); string; order; turn; innings (*Cricket*); in einer —e, in a row *or* line; nach der —e, in file, in rows, in *or* by turns; —' und Glied, rank and file; in —' und Glied stellen, to draw up (*in battle array*); die —e ist an mir, ich bin an der —e, it is my turn; Sie werden auch an die —e kommen, your turn will come too; bunte — machen, to pair off, to sit alternately (*ladies and gentlemen*).

²**Rei'he** (= Reihen = Reigen), *m.* (—n, *pl.* —n) round dance, linked dance; (*fig.*) circle, community, company; der nächtliche —, the nocturnal dance.

Rei'h—en, I. *subst. m.* (—ens, *pl.* —en) *see* Reigen. II. *v.n.* (*aux.* h.) to couple, pair. III. *v.a.* to put in a row; to string (*pearls, etc.*); to connect; to range, rank; to arrange, classify; to baste. *Comp.* —en=folge, *f.* succession; sequence, proper order; series; procession. —en=marsch, *m.* file-marching, marching in files (*Mil.*). —en=tanz, *m.* round dance. —en=weise, *adv.* in rows; by turns.

Rei'her, *m.* (—s, *pl.* —) heron. *Comp.* —beize, *f.* heron hawking. —busch, —stutz, *m.* tuft of heron's feathers. —falk(e), *m.* Falco peregrinus. —gras, *n.* feather-grass. —stand, *m.* heronry.

Reim, *m.* (—s, *pl.* —e) rhyme, rime.

Rei'm—en, *v.a.r.* & *n.* (*aux.* h.) to rhyme, rime to agree, tally; zusammen —en, to make out, piece together; rührender —, rhyme of words with the same spelling but different meaning (*lit.* rhyme striking the same chord again). —er, *m.* (—ers, *pl.* —er) rhymer, versifier. —erei', *f.* love of rhyming; bad verses. *Comp.* —art, *f.* kind of rhyme *or* verse. —chronik, *f.* chronicle in verse. —fall, *m.* cadence. —frei, —los, *adj.* blank, unrhymed. —gedicht, *n.* poem in rhyme. —kunst, *f.* art of rhyming. —rätsel, *n.* charade *or* enigma in verse. —schmied, *m.* rhymester. —silbe, *f.* rhyming syllable. —spruch, *m.* rhymed maxim *or* proverb. —weise, *adv.* in rhymes; in couplets. —wort, *n.* word which rhymes; word used in rhymes.

Rein, I. *adj.* clean, pure, clear; innocent; sound, whole, intact; net (*C.L.*); fair (*writing, etc.*); genuine; downright; —e Aussprache, correct pronunciation, good accent; —e Bahn machen, to clear the way, to clear away impediments, to make a clean sweep; —e Bilanz, clear balance; ein —er Bogen Papier, a blank sheet of paper; —e Gesichtsfarbe, clear complexion; —er Gewinn, real *or* net profit; eine —e Lüge, a downright lie; —en Mund halten, to hold one's tongue, keep a secret; einem —en Wein einschenken, to tell someone the plain truth; einen — sprechen, to absolve, pronounce a p. innocent; der, die —e, pure, guiltless person; dem —en ist alles —, to the pure all things are pure; mit sich selbst über eine S. ins —e kommen, to make up one's mind about a th.; etwas ins —e bringen, aufs —e kommen, to clear off embarrassments, to clear up, to settle; to fair-copy; mit einem ins —e kommen, to come to an understanding with s.o.; etwas ins —e schreiben, to make a fair copy of a th.; ich bin mit mir im —en, I have made up my mind. II. *adv.* quite, entirely; — heraus, plainly; es ist — aus mit uns, it is all over with us; —(e)weg, completely, altogether (*coll.*); das ist ja —eweg! but that is too much! (*sl.*) — unmöglich, quite impossible; — nichts, nothing whatever. —heit, *f.* purity; pureness, clearness. —igen, *see under* Reinig—. —lich, *adj.* clean, cleanly; neat. —lichkeit, *f.* neatness, *etc.* *Comp.* —druck, *m.* fair impression, clean proof. —ertrag, *m.* net profit. —geist, *m.* alcohol. —gewicht, *n.* net weight (*C. L.*). —gewinn, *m.* net profit. —kultur, *f.* bacilliculture. —schrift, *f.* fair copy.

'Rein, *coll. for* Herein (Hinein). *Often in cpds. e. g.* —fall, *m.* disappointment, failure (*sl.*). —fallen, *v.n.* to be disappointed, unsuccessful.

Rei'nig—en, *v.a.* to clean, cleanse; to purify; to purge; to refine; to clarify. —er, *m.* (—ers, *pl.* —er) cleanser; refiner; (*gas*) purifier; purist. —keit, *f.* purity, cleanness; chastity. —ung, *f.* purification; cleaning, cleansing; purging; refinement; disinfection; Mariä —ung, Purification (*of the Virgin*) (*R. C.*); monatliche —ung, menses. *Comp.* —ungs=eid, *m.* oath of purgation. —ungs=mittel, *n.* purgative. —ungs=opfer, *n.* lustration.

¹Reis, *n.* (—(s)es, *pl.* —(s)er) twig, sprig; shoot, scion, sucker. —(s)ig, *n.* (—(s)igs) twigs; brushwood; copse. —lein, *n.* little sprig. *Comp.* —besen, *m.*, —bürste, *f.* birch-broom. —bund, —bündel, —büschel, *n.* faggot. —holz, *n.* brushwood, copse.

²Reis, *m.* (—(s)es) rice. *Comp.* —bau, *m.* cultivation of rice. —branntwein, *m.* arrack. —brei, *m.* rice boiled in milk. —mehl, *n.* rice-flour, ground rice.

³Reis, *f. see* Reise. *Comp.* —laufen, *n.* enlistment in a foreign army (*dial.*). —läufer, *m.* (Swiss) mercenary.

Rei's—e, *f.* (*pl.* —en) journey; tour; trip; voyage (*on the sea*); passage (*across the sea*); (warlike) expedition (*obs.*); sich auf die —e begeben *or* machen, to set out; wo geht die —e hin? where are you going to *or* bound for? die Hin—e, the out journey; die Rück—e, the return journey; die doppelte —e, the journey there and back; glückliche —e! a pleasant journey to you! Vergnügungs—e, pleasure trip;—e ins Ausland, journey abroad.

Rei's—en, *v.n.* (*aux.* h. & s.) to travel, journey; to go to; to set out for; to go on travels; wir —ten über, we went by *or* via; wir —en morgen, we (shall) start to-morrow; aufs Land —en, to go into *or* to leave for the country; wir —ten neun Stunden nach Paris, we were nine hours going to Paris; auf eine Kunst —en, to make a professional tour, to travel for professional employment; mit der Eisenbahn —en, to go by rail; zur See —en, to go by sea. —end, *p. & adj.* travelling, itinerant; der, die —ende, traveller; ein —ender, a commercial traveller; unser —ender, our traveller, agent, representative; zwei —ende, two travellers. —ig, (*obs. & poet.*) *adj.* (*lit.*) ready for an expedition, mounted; —iges Pferd, trooper's horse; —iges Kriegesgeschwader, a troop of horse; der —ige, horseman, (mounted) trooper. *Comp.* —e=anzug, *m.* travelling costume. —e=apotheke, *f.* portable medicine-chest. —e=bedarf, *m.* travelling necessaries. —e=beschreiber, *m.* writer of travels. —e=beschreibung, *f.* book of travels. —e=bett, *n.* camp-bed. —e=buch, *n.* guide-book. —e=bündel, *n.* knapsack. —e=bureau, *n.* tourist agency office. —e=fertig, *adj.* ready to start. —e=fieber, *n.* mania for travelling; restlessness through fear of being late. —e=flasche, *f.* travelling-flask. —e=freund, *m.* tourist. —e=gefährte(r), *m.* fellow-traveller. —e=gefolge, *n.* suite. —e=geld, *n.* money for travelling. —e=gepäck, *n.* luggage. —e=gesellschaft, *f.* travelling party; travelling companions. —e=handbuch, *n.* travellers' guide. —e=karte, *f.* traveller's map. —e=koffer, *m.* travelling box *or* trunk; kleiner —ekoffer, portmanteau, travelling bag. —e=kosten, *pl.* travelling expenses. —e=küche, *f.* portable kitchen. —e=lust, *f.* love of travelling. —e=marschall, *m.* (royal) courier. —e=müde, *adj.* tired of travelling; tired out by travelling. —e=mütze, *f.* travelling cap. —e=onkel, *m.* commercial traveller (*hum.*); er ist ein alter —eonkel, he is an experienced traveller (*coll.*). —e=paß, *m.* passport. —e=pfennig, *m.* viaticum; charity to a traveller. —e=prediger, *m.* itinerant preacher. —e=sack, *m.* portmanteau. —e=segen, *m.* benediction on a parting traveller (*in old German poetry*). —e=spesen, *pl.* travelling expenses. —e=spiegel, *m.* pocket mirror. —e=stipendium, *n.* travelling scholarship *or* studentship. —e=tasche, *f.* satchel, wallet; travelling bag. —e=wetter, *n.* weather for travelling. —e=ziel, *n.* destination. —e=zug, *m.* caravan.

Rei'ß—en, I. *ir.v.a.* to tear, rend, slit; to pull, drag; to split up; to draw, eviscerate; to sketch, draw, delineate, design; to reprimand; to snap asunder; den Acker —en, to break ground; Koulissen —en, to rant (*Theat.*); Witze —en, to crack jokes; Zoten —en, to talk obscenely; an sich (*acc.*) —en, to drag towards one, to seize upon, usurp; sich an einer Nadel —en, to scratch oneself on a pin; aus der Gefahr —en, to rescue from danger; einen aus einem Irrtum —en, to disabuse a p.'s mind of an error; einen dahin —en, to hurry a p. on *or* along; es —t mich im Leibe, I have the colic; mit sich *or* fort —en, to carry off *or* along with one; sich —en um, to struggle, contend for; alles —t sich um sie, there is a general scramble for her; einen zu Boden —en, to pull *or* knock a p. down; sein Tod —t eine große Lücke, his death makes a great blank; sich (*dat.*) ein Loch —en, to tear one's (*coat, etc.*). II. *ir. v.n.* (*aux.* s.) to burst, split, crack, chap, snap, tear; to break loose; to move swiftly, sweep, rush along, tear along; (*aux.* h.) to pull, tear; wenn alle Stricke —en, if all means fail, if the worst come to the worst; mir —t's in allen Gliedern, I have pains in all my limbs; da riß mir die Geduld, at this I lost patience; das —t (sehr) ins Geld, that runs away with a lot of money (*coll.*). III. *subst.n.* bursting, rending; rupture; (in Gliedern) tearing, acute pains; (im Leibe) colic. —end, *p., adj. & adv.* rapid; impetuous; ravening; smarting, acute; —ende Gicht, flying gout; seine Kräfte nehmen —end ab, his strength is rapidly declining; —end abgehen, to have a rapid sale. —er, *m.* (—ers, *pl.* —er) grasper; phrase that tickles the ear of the public, that brings the house down (*Theat.*). *Comp.* —aus, *n.* running away, flight; —aus nehmen, to decamp. —blei, *n.* black-lead; drawing pencil. —bohrer, *m.* small auger. —brett, *n.* drawing-board. —feder, *f.* drawing-pen. —kasten, *m.* box of compasses. —kohle, *f.* charcoal crayon. —nagel, *m.* drawing-pin. —schiene, *f.* T square, drawing-rule. —stift, *m.* tracing-pencil. —zahn, *m.* laniary tooth. —zeug, *n.* (case of) mathematical instruments. —zirkel, *m.* drawing compasses.

Reit'bar, *adj.* fit for riding; —er Weg, good road, bridle-path.

Rei't—en, *ir.v.* I. *n.* (*aux.* h. & s.) to ride, go on horseback; —en durch *or* über, to pass on horseback; ſpazieren —en, to take a ride; geritten kommen, to come on horseback; auf einem herum —en, to abuse a p.'s good nature, to plague s.o.; auf einer S. herum —en, to be always harping on a subject; auf dem Apoſtelpferde —en, to go on shank's mare; Galopp, Schritt, Trab —en, to gallop, pace *or* amble, trot. II. *a.* to ride; to break in; to pirate; einen zu Boden —en *or* über den Haufen—en, to ride a p. down, ride over a p.; ein Pferd zu Schanden —en, to over-ride, to founder a horse; ſich (*acc.*) wund, ſich (*dat.*) einen Wolf —en, to gall oneself in riding; einen in die Tinte —en, to drive a p. into a corner; ein Prinzip —en, to have a fad; Wechſel —en, to keep oneself afloat by accommodation bills. III. *subst. n.* riding, equitation. —end, *p. & adj.* riding; mounted; —ende Artillerie, horse-artillery. —er, *m.* (—ers, *pl.* —er) rider, horseman; trooper; cross-beam; cavalier (*Fort.*); ſpaniſche —er, chevaux de frise (*Mil.*); ein Regiment —er, a regiment of cavalry, a cavalry regiment; leichte —er, light horse (*Mil.*). —erei', *f.* cavalry; cavalcade; riding; mode of riding. —erin, *f.* horsewoman. —erſchaft, *f.* horsemanship; riders; cavalry. —lings, *adv.* astride. *Comp.* —anzug, *m.* riding-habit *or* dress. —bahn, *f.* riding-school, manège; circus. —decke, *f.* saddle-cloth, housing. —er=aufzug, *m.* cavalcade. —er=degen, *m.* cavalry sword. —er=fahne, *f.* standard. —er=fähnlein, *n.* squadron (*of horse*) (*obs.*). —er=fähnrich, *m.* cornet. —er=gefecht, *n.* cavalry engagement. —er=haufen, *m.* troop of horse. —er=jacke, *f.*, —er=koller, *m.* doublet, jerkin. —er=künſte, *pl.* equestrian feats. —er=pferd, *n.* trooper's horse. —er=piſtole, *f.* horse-pistol. —er=regiment, *n.* cavalry regiment. —er=ſäbel, *m.* trooper's sabre. —er=ſchar, *f.* troop of horse, cavalcade. —ers=mann, *m.* horseman. —er=ſtandbild, *n.*, —er=ſtatue, *f.* equestrian statue. —(er=)ſtiefel, *pl.* jack-boots. —er=ſtückchen, *n.* daring feat of a horseman (*in war*), trooper's adventure. —er=wache, *f.* vedette. —gerte, *f.* riding-whip. —gurt, *m.* riding-belt; saddle-girth. —handſchuh, *m.* riding-glove. —hoſen, *pl.* riding-breeches, leather breeches. —inſtitut, *n.* riding-school. —kiſſen, *n.* pillion. —kleid, *n.* riding-habit (*for ladies*). —knecht, *m.* groom. —kunſt, *f.* horsemanship. —peitſche, *see* —gerte; einem die —peitſche geben, to horse-whip a p. —pferd, *n.* saddle-horse. —poſt, *f.* courier; mail sent by courier. —ſattel, *m.* riding-saddle. —ſchule, *f.* riding school, equitation institute; military riding academy. —ſchüler, *m.* riding pupil; soldier at a military riding academy. —ſtall, *m.* stable for saddle-horses. —ſtock, *m.* puppet. —ſtunden, *pl.* riding lessons. —wechſel, *m.* accommodation bill. —weg, *m.* bridle-path. —zeug, *n.* riding equipment.

[1]Rei'ter, *m. see* Reiten.

[2]Rei'ter, *f.* (*pl.* —n), *m.* (—s, *pl.* —) riddle, coarse sieve; durch die —(n) fallen, to be disappointed; to remain an old maid (*coll.*).

Reiz, *m.* (—es, *pl.* —e) charm, attraction, fascination, grace; attractiveness, allurement, enticement; incentive; irritation, provocation. —bar, *adj.* sensitive, susceptible; irritable; inflammable (*Med.*). —barkeit, *f.* susceptibility; irritability.

Rei'z—en, *v.a.* to excite; to provoke, irritate; to charm, attract; to entice, allure; —e ſie nicht zur Wut, do not exasperate them. —end, *p. & adj.* charming, delightful, delicious, bewitching; tempting; inflammatory; irritant, stimulant. —ung, *f.* irritation; provocation; enticement; inducement; charm, attraction. *Comp.* —fähigkeit, *f.* susceptibility; irritability (*Phys.*). —los, *adj.* unattractive. —loſigkeit, *f.* unattractiveness. —mittel, *n.* stimulant; stimulus. —voll, *adj.* charming, attractive.

Re'keln, Rä'keln, *v.r.* to stretch one's limbs in an unmannerly way, to loll about (*coll.*).

Rekla'm—e, *f.* (*pl.* —en) puff; (puffing) advertisement. —ie'ren, *v.a.* to claim.

Rekognoszie'r—en, *v.a.* to reconnoitre (*Mil.*); to recognize, acknowledge; to identify (*a corpse*). —ung, *f.* reconnoitring, reconnaissance, scouting.

Rekommandie'ren, *v.a.* to recommend; to register (*a letter, etc.*).

Rekredeti'v, *n.* (—s, *pl.* —e) letter of recall.

Rekru't, *m.* (—en, *pl.* —en) recruit; conscript. —ie'ren, *v.a. & n.* (*aux.* h.) to recruit. —ie'rung, *f.* recruiting; recruitment. *Comp.* —ierungs=weſen, *n.* recruiting service.

Rektio'n, *f.* (*pl.* —en) government (*Gram.*).

Rek't—or, *m.* (—ors, *pl.* —o'ren) rector (*of a university*); chancellor, vice-chancellor; headmaster (*of some public schools*). —ora't, *n.* office of (vice-)chancellor; headship (*obs.*). —orats'=rede, *f.* rectorial address, chancellor's address, vice-chancellor's speech.

Reku'rs, *m. see* Regreß; appeal.

Relati'v, I. *adj. & adv.* relative, respective. II. *n.* (—s, *pl.* —e), —um, *n.* (—ums, *pl.* —a) relative (*Gram.*).

Relegie'ren, *v.a.* to expel, to send down, rusticate (*a student*).

Relie'f, *n.* (—s, *pl.* —s) relief, relievo; foil, set off; Bas—, bas-relief.

Relig—io'n, *f.* (*pl.* —ionen) religion. —iö's, *adj.* religious. —ioſitä't, *f.* religiosity.

Religio'ns— (*in comp.*) —duldung, *f.* religious toleration. —eid, *m.* religious test; religious oath, oath of religion. —freiheit, *f.* religious liberty. —gebräuche, *pl.* rites. —geſellſchaft, *f.* religious society. —lehre, *f.* doctrine. —lehrer, *m.* teacher of religion; divine. —meinung, *f.* religious opinion. —ſatz, *m.* dogma. —ſchwärmer, *m.* fanatic. —ſpötter, *m.* scoffer at religion. —ſtreit, *m.* religious controversy. —trennung, *f.* schism. —unterricht, *m.* religious instruction. —verfolgung, *f.* religious persecution. —wiſſenſchaft, *f.* theology, divinity; vergleichende —wiſſenſchaft, science of comparative religion. —zwang, *m.* religious compulsion, religious intolerance.

Reli'quie, *f.* (*pl.* —n) relic. *Comp.* —n=dienſt, *m.* worship of relics. —n=käſtchen, *n.* reliquary. —n=ſtück, *n.* relic.

Remeſ'ſe, *f.* (*pl.* —n) remittance; — *or* Remiſſe per Saldo, remittance in balance.

Reminiſce'nz, *f.* (*pl.* —en) reminiscence.

Remi's, *adj.*; das Spiel iſt —, the game is drawn, it's a draw (*coll.*).

Remi'ſe, *f.* (*pl.* —n) coach-house; cover (*for game*). *Comp.* —wagen, *m.* job-carriage.

Remi'ß, *m.* (—(ſſ)es, *pl.* —(ſſ)e) prolongation, postponement of payment; discount.

Remitt—en'den, *pl.* remainders, surplus *or* return copies. —e'nt, *m.* (—en'ten, *pl.* —en'ten) remitter. —ie'ren, *v.a.* to return; to remit.

Remon't—e, *f.* supply of horses for cavalry; eine —e zureiten, to break in (*or* train) cavalry-horses. —ie'ren, *v.a.* to remount (*cavalry*). *Comp.* —e=pferd, *n.* remount.

Rem'peln, *v.a.* to knock against on purpose, jostle (*sl.*).

Rem'(p)ter, *m.* (—s, *pl.* —) refectory (*in castles, monasteries, etc.*).

Renaiſſan'ce, *f.* Renaissance, Renascence, (period of) revival.

Renda'nt, *m.* (—en, *pl.* —en) treasurer, paymaster, cashier.

Renega't, *m.* (—en, *pl.* —en) renegade

Ren'ken, *v.a.* to turn, twist, wrench.
Renn, —e, *see* Rinne (*dial.*).
Ren'n—en, I. *ir.v.n.* (*aux.* h. & s.) to run; to race; to course; **—en an** (*acc.*) *or* **wider,** to dash against; **mit dem Kopfe wider eine S. —en,** to run one's head against a th.; **mit einem um die Wette —en,** to run with s.o. for a wager. II. *v.a.* & *v.r.*; **sich außer Atem —en,** to run o.s. out of breath; **einen zu Boden —en,** to run s.o. over, knock a p. down by running, overturn a p.; **einem den Degen durch den Leib —en,** to run one's sword through a person's body. III. *v.a.* to make run, to smelt. IV. *subst. n.* running; race; race-course; **Kirchturm —en** *or* **—en mit Hindernissen,** steeple-chase; **—en ohne Hindernisse,** flat race; **ein totes —en,** a dead heat. **—er,** *m.* (**—ers,** *pl.* **—er**) runner; race-horse. *Comp.* **—anzug,** *m.* costume for the race-course. **—arbeit,** *f.* extraction of malleable iron by the direct process. **—bahn,** *f.* race-course; arena; career. **—boot,** *n.* racing boat, yacht, cutter. **—feuer,** *n.* smelting furnace. **—herd,** *m.* bloomery hearth. **—jagd,** *f.*, **—jagen,** *n.* hunt. **—lanze,** *f.* tilting-lance. **—maschine,** *f.* path racing safety (*Cycl.*). **—schiff,** *n.* yacht; cutter. **—schlitten,** *m.* sleigh. **—spiel,** *n.* running-match; tournament; merry-go-round. **—sport,** *m.* racing, the turf. **—sport=kämpfe,** *pl.* races. **—stein,** *m.* gutter; sink. **—tier,** *see* Rentier. **—wagen,** *m.* chariot for racing. **—ziel,** *n.* winning post.
Renn'tier, *n.* reindeer. *Comp.* **—flechte,** *f.* reindeer-moss. **—zeit,** *f.* reindeer-period (*Geol.*).
Renomm—ie'ren, *v.n.* (*aux.* h.) to boast, brag; to bully, hector. **—ie'rt,** *p.p.* & *adj.* renowned, well-known, of good repute. **—i'st,** *m.* (**—is'ten,** *pl.* **—is'ten**) bragger; braggadocio; bully. *Comp.* **—ier'=stock,** *m.* gorgeous walking-stick (*of a swaggering student*).
Renon'ce, *f.* (*pl.* **—n**) revoking (*a suit*) (*cards*).
Renovie'ren, *v.a.* to renew; to do up (*a house*).
Rent—a'bel, *adj.* profitable, lucrative. **—abilitä't,** *f.* profitableness.
Rent'bar, *adj.* yielding rent *or* revenue.
Ren't—e, *f.* (*pl.* **—en**) rent; income; revenue; interest; pension; (*pl.*) stocks; **er lebt von seinen —en,** he has a private income, lives on his means; **jährliche —e,** annuity; **auf —en legen,** to invest, put out at interest. **—ei',** *f. see* **—amt. —en, —ie'ren,** *v.n.* (*aux.* h.) to yield a rent *or* revenue; to pay; **das —iert sich nicht,** that does not pay. **—ie'r,** *m.*, **—ie're,** *f.* gentleman *or* lady of private means. **—ner,** *m.* (**—ners,** *pl.* **—ner**), **—nerin,** *f.* gentleman *or* lady of private means; capitalist. *Comp.* **—amt,** *n.* board of revenue; revenue-office; exchequer. **—en=ablösung,** *f.* liquidation of a rent, annuity *or* pension. **—en=anstalt,** *f.* office for securing life-annuities. **—en=haber,** *m.* annuitant. **—kammer,** *f.* board of revenue; exchequer. **—meister,** *m.* treasurer; steward. **—meisterei,** *f.* exchequer, treasurer's office. **—schreiber,** *m.* clerk in a revenue-office. **—verwalter,** *m.* trustee; guardian; steward.
Repar—ie'ren, *v.a.* to mend, repair. **—atu'r,** *f.* repair.
Repet—e'nt, *m.* (**—en'ten,** *pl.* **—en'ten**) lecturer at some South German colleges; private tutor, coach (*Univ.*). **—ie'ren,** *v.a.* & *n.* (*aux.* h.) to repeat. **—iteu'r,** *m.* (**—iteurs,** *pl.* **—iteurs**) repeater (*Naut.*). *Comp.* **—en'ten=stelle,** *f.* tutorship. **—ier'=uhr,** *f.* repeater. **—ier'=werk,** *n.* repeating works (*in a watch*).
Repli'k, *f.* (*pl.* **—en**) counter-plea.
Reponie'ren, *v.a.* to replace; to set (*a limb*); to reduce (*Surg.*).
Reposito'ri—um, *n.* (**—ums,** *pl.* **—en**) (set of) book-shelves; music-stand, canterbury.
Repräsent—a'nt, *m.* (**—an'ten,** *pl.* **—an'ten**) representative. **—ie'ren,** *v.a.* to represent. *Comp.* **—anten=verfassung,** *f.* representative *or* constitutional government.
Repressa'lien, *pl.* reprisals; **— ergreifen gegen,** to make reprisals on. *Comp.* **—briefe,** *pl.* letters of marque.
[1]**Reps,** *m.* (**—(s)es,** *pl.* **—(s)e**), (**—kohl,** *m.*) rape.
[2]**Reps,** *m.* (**—(s)es,** *pl.* **—(s)e**) rep.
Repti'l, *n.* (**—s,** *pl.* **—e** *or* **—ien**) reptile. *Comp.* **—ien=fonds,** *m.* secret-service fund. **—ien=presse,** *f.* press servile to the government (*coll.*).
Republi'k, *f.* (*pl.* **—en**) republic. **—a'ner,** *m.* (**—aners,** *pl.* **—aner**) republican. **—a'nisch,** *adj.* republican.
Reputier'lich, *adj.* & *adv.* reputable, respectable.
Requi—rie'ren, *v.a.* to demand, require; to requisition. **—si't,** *n.* (**—sites,** *pl.* **—siten**) requisite; (*pl.*) properties (*Theat.*).
Rese'da, Rese'de, *f.* (*pl.* **Rese'das, Rese'den**) mignonette.
Reserv—a'gen, *pl.* resists, reserves (*Calico-printing*). **—a't,** *n.* (**—ats,** *pl.* **—ate**) reservation. **—e** (*pron.* Reser've), *f.* (*pl.* **—en**) reserve. **—ie'ren,** *v.a.* to reserve. **—i'st,** *m.* (**—is'ten,** *pl.* **—is'ten**) reservist. **—oi'r,** *n.* (**—oirs,** *pl.* **—oire** *and* **—oirs**) reservoir, cistern, tank. *Comp.* **—age=druck,** *m.* reserve-style. **—e=bett,** *n.* spare-bed. **—e=fonds,** *m.* reserve-fund. **—e=gut,** *n.* spare sails and stores. **—e=leutnant,** *m.*, **—e=offizier,** *m.* lieutenant, officer in the reserve. **—e=mannschaft,** *f.* the reserve (*Mil.*); **die —emänner einberufen,** to call in the reserves. **—e=stücke, —e=teile,** *pl.* reserve *or* spare pieces.
Resid—e'nt, *m.* (**—en'ten,** *pl.* **—en'ten**) resident; resident ambassador *or* minister. **—e'nz,** *f.* (*pl.* **—en'zen**) residence; seat of the court, capital. **—enz'=stadt,** *f.* capital town, capital. **—ie'ren,** *v.n.* (*aux.* h.) to reside.
Resi'du—um, *n.* (**—ums,** *pl.* **—en**) residue.
Resinö's, *adj.* resinous.
Resona'nz, *f.* resonance. *Comp.* **—boden,** *m.*, **—decke,** *f.* sounding-board. **—kasten,** *m.* sounding-box. **—loch,** *n.* sound-hole.
Respe'kt, *m.* (**—s**) respect; **mit — zu melden,** *or* **zu sagen,** with all due respect, if I may be allowed to say so. **—a'bel, —ier'lich,** *adj.* respectable. **—ie'ren,** *v.a.* to respect, to honour (*bills*). **—i'v,** *adj.* respective. **—i've,** *adv.* respectively. *Comp.* **—tage,** *pl.* days of grace (*C.L.*). **—widrig,** *adj.* disrespectful.
Respi'ro, *n.* respite (*C.L.*).
Responso'rium, *n.* response; antiphon.
Resso'rt, *n.* department, administrative province *or* sphere; **das — eines Ministers,** the department of a minister.
Rest, *m.* (**—es,** *pl.* **—e**) rest, residue, remainder; remainder (*Arith.*); remnant; remains; balance; arrears, debt; **den — zur Hälfte tragen,** to split the difference; **das wird ihm den — geben,** that will do for him, settle him, finish him off. **—a'nt,** *m.* (**—an'ten,** *pl.* **—an'ten**) defaulter; (*pl.*) arrears. **—ie'ren,** *v.n.* (*aux.* h.) to remain, be left; to be in arrears; to owe. *Comp.* **—bestand,** *m.* remainder, remains, remnant. **—los,** *adj.* without a rest.
Restaurat—eu'r, *m.* (**—eurs,** *pl.* **—eure**) keeper of a restaurant. **—io'n,** *f.* (*pl.* **—ionen**) restoration; restaurant, dining-rooms.
Result—an'te, *f.* resultant. **—a't,** *n.* (**—ats,** *pl.* **—ate**) result, inference, outcome.
Retardie'r—en, *v.* I. *a.* to check, impede; **—endes Element, —endes Moment,** incident *or* character causing delay in the development of the plot, obstruction in the progress of the (dramatic) action. II. *n.* (*aux.* h.) to slacken one's pace; to go slow (*of watches, etc.*). *Comp.* **—werk,** *n.* stop, check.
Retentions'recht, *n.* lien (*Law*).

Retir—a'de, *f.* (*pl.* **—aden**) retreat; *see* **Abtritt.** **—ie'ren**, *v.n.* (*aux.* **h.**) to retreat, retire.
Retor'te, *f.* (*pl.* **—n**) retort (*Chem.*).
Retou'r, *adv.* back. **—en**, *pl.* empties; return cargoes. *Comp.* **—billet**, *n.* return-ticket. **—fracht**, *f.* return-freight. **—kutsche**, *f.* return-carriage; tu quoque! repartee merely repeating a previous remark; **—kutschen gelten nicht**, no silly repartees allowed. **—waren**, *pl.* returns. **—wechsel**, *m.* re-draft.
Retrai'te, *f.* retreat; tattoo; **die — blasen**, to sound the tattoo; to sound a retreat. *Comp.* **—schuß**, *m.* evening-gun; cannon-shot giving the signal for retreat.
Retrat'te, *f.* (*pl.* **—n**) re-draft (*C.L.*).
Rett'bar, *adj.* saveable, rescuable.
Ret't—en, *v.a.* to save, rescue, deliver; to preserve; **sich —en**, to escape, save oneself; **seine Ehre —en**, to vindicate one's honour. **—er**, *m.* (**—ers**, *pl.* **—er**) saver, deliverer; saviour. **—ung**, *f.* saving; deliverance, rescue; recovery; escape; **ohne —ung**, past help. *Comp.* **—ungs=anstalt**, *f.* house of refuge; Humane Society. **—ungs=apparat**, *m.* life-saving apparatus. **—ungs=boje**, *f.* life-buoy. **—ungs=boot**, *n.* life-boat. **—ungs=gürtel**, *m.* life-belt. **—ungs=los**, *adj. & adv.* irremediable, irretrievable, past help. **—ungs=medaille**, *f.* medal (awarded) for saving life. **—ungs=mittel**, *n.* remedy, expedient. **—ungs=versuch**, *m.* attempt at rescue.
Ret'tig, *m.* (**—s**, *pl.* **—e**) radish.
Reu'—e, *f.* repentance; regret; remorse. **—en**, *v.a. & n.* (*aux.* **h.**) *& imp.* to regret; to repent; **es —(e)t mich**, I am sorry for it; **es hat ihn gereut**, he has been sorry for it, he has repented it; **diese That —et mich**, [**es —t mich dieser That** (*obs.*)], I repent having done this deed! **—ig**, *adj. & adv.* penitent, contrite. *Comp.* **—e=thränen**, *pl.* tears of repentance. **—geld**, *n.*, **—kauf**, *m.* forfeit, penalty (*for non-performance*). **—los**, *adj.* impenitent. **—mütig**, *adj. see* **—ig.** **—mütigkeit**, *f.* disposition to repent.
Reu'se, *f.* (*pl.* **—n**) weir-basket, oyster-basket.
Reut'e, *f.* rooting out, clearing; hoe, mattock.
Reu't—en, *v.a.* to root out; to plough *or* turn up. *Comp.* **—feld**, *n.* newly reclaimed land; virgin soil. **—hacke**, **—haue**, *f.* hoe, mattock. **—spaten**, *m.* spud.
Reu'ter, *m.* (**—s**, *pl.* **—**) marauding trooper, mounted soldier (*obs.*).
Revan'ch—e, *f.* revenge; satisfaction; indemnification; **einem —e geben**, to give a p. his revenge. **—ie'ren**, *v.r.* to have one's revenge, be revenged.
Reverberie'r—en, *v.a. & n.* (*aux.* **h.**) to reverberate. *Comp.* **—lampe**, *f.* lamp with reflector.
Reverenz, *f.* (*pl.* **—en**) reverence; obeisance, bow; courtesy, curtsy.
Reve'rs, *m.* (**—(s)es**, *pl.* **—(s)e**) reverse (side); facing; counter-deed; reciprocal bond; declaration (*Law*); **einen — ausstellen**, to give a written undertaking.
Revidie'r—en, *v.a.* to revise. *Comp.* **—bogen**, *m.* proof-sheet for revision, revised proof.
Revie'r, *n.* (**—s**, *pl.* **—e**) quarter, district, region, ward; preserve, shooting *or* hunting ground; manor; **— bekommen**, to be put on the sick list (*Mil.*); **das waldige —**, the woodlands. *Comp.* **—förster**, *m.* district-ranger. **—kranke(r)**, *m.* soldier confined to his quarters on account of sickness.
Revis—io'n, *f.* (*pl.* **—ionen**) revision, review; revisal. **—or** (*pron.* **Revi'sor**), *m.* (**—ors**, *pl.* **—o'ren**) reviser; examiner, auditor (*of accounts*). *Comp.* **—ions'=befehl**, *m.* (**wegen Formfehler**) writ of error. **—ions'=bogen**, *m.* revise, fresh proof (sheet). **—ions'=hof**, *m.* revising barrister's court. **—or=amt**, *n.* auditorship.
Revol't—e, *f.* (*pl.* **—en**) revolt, insurrection. **—ie'ren**, *v.n.* (*aux.* **h.**) to revolt.
Revolutio'n, *f.* (*pl.* **—en**) revolution. **—ä'r**, *adj. & m.* (**—ärs**, *pl.* **—äre**) revolutionary.
Revozie'ren, *v.a.* to revoke, recall.
Revue', *f.* (*pl.* **—en**) review; muster; **— passieren**, to pass muster; **— passieren lassen**, to pass in review, to review.
Rezens—e'nt, *m.* (**—en'ten**, *pl.* **—en'ten**) critic, reviewer. **—io'n**, *f.* (*pl.* **—ionen**) critique, review; revisal (*of a text*). **—ie'ren**, *v.a.* to criticize, review.
Rezep—is'se, *n.* (**—isses**, **—**, *pl.* **—isses**) receipt, acquittance. **—t** (*pron.* **Reze'pt**), *n.* (**—ts**, *pl.* **—te**) receipt; recipe; prescription. **—tivitä't**, *f.* receptivity. **—tor** (*pron.* **Rezep'tor**), *m.* (**—tors**, *pl.* **—to'ren**) receiver, collector. **—tu'r**, *f.* receivership. *Comp.* **—tier'=kunst**, *f.* art of dispensing.
Reze'ß, *m.* (**—(ss)es**, *pl.* **—(ss)e**) recess; compact, treaty.
Re'zip—e, *n.* (**—es**, *pl.* **—es**) recipe. **—ie'ren**, *v.a.* to receive, admit. **—ro'k**, *adj. & adv.* reciprocal.
Rezit—ati'v, *n.* (**—ativs**, *pl.* **—ative**) recitative. **—ie'ren**, *v.a.* to recite.
Rhabar'ber, *f. & m.* (**—s**, *pl.* **—**) rhubarb.
Rhapso'd—e, *m.* (**—en**, *pl.* **—en**) rhapsodist. **—ie'**, *f.* rhapsody. **—isch**, *adj.* rhapsodical.
Rhede, *see* **Reede.**
Rheto'r—ik, *f.* rhetoric. **—iker**, *m.* (**—ikers**, *pl.* **—iker**) rhetorician. **—isch**, *adj.* rhetorical.
Rheuma't—isch, *adj.* rheumatic. **—is'mus**, *m.* (*pl.* **—ismen**) rheumatism.
Rhino'ceros, *n.* (**—**, *pl.* **—(s)se**) rhinoceros; blockhead, duffer (*coll.*).
Rhom'b—isch, *adj.* rhombic. **—us**, *m.* (**—us**, *pl.* **—en**) rhomb, rhombus.
Rhyth'm—isch, *adj.* rhythmical. **—us**, *m.* (*pl.* **—en**) rhythm; **aufsteigender —us**, rising, iambic rhythm; **absteigender —us**, falling, trochaic rhythm; **aufgleitender —us**, anapæstic rhythm; **abgleitender —us**, dactylic rhythm; **gemischter —us**, mixed rhythm, mixture of iambic and anapæstic feet; **versetzter** *or* **umgelegter —us**, reversed rhythm ('xx' *instead of* x'x', *very frequent in the classical German blank verse*).
Rich'te, *f.* direction; straight *or* direct line; shortest distance; normal *or* proper position; row; **wieder in die — bringen**, to adjust, to make straight again; **in die — gehen**, to take a short cut, go as the crow flies.
Rich't—en, *v.* I. *a.* to set right, adjust, arrange, put in order; to dress (*Cook.*, *Tan.*, *Mil.*, *etc.*); to regulate, set (*a watch*, *etc.*); to direct, turn; to address, to aim at, point, direct; to adjust, settle (*a dispute*, *etc.*); to straighten, flatten (*metals*, *etc.*); to trim (*sails*); to judge, try; to execute (*criminals*); **eine Frage —en**, to put a question, to ask; **ein Geschütz —en**, to point a gun; **—et den Weg des Herrn**, make straight the way of the Lord (*B.*); **das war auf mich gerichtet**, that was aimed at me; **den Blick gen Himmel —en**, to turn one's eyes towards Heaven; **in die Höhe —en**, to raise, erect; **ins Werk —en**, to accomplish, effect; **nach der Setzwage —en**, to level, plomb; **die Segel nach dem Winde —en**, to set the sails to the wind (*Naut.*), to trim (*Pol.*); **seinen Weg nach der Stadt —en**, to direct one's steps towards the town; **zu Grunde —en**, to ruin, destroy; **sich —en**, to rise, stand erect, to dress in line (*Mil.*); **—(e)t euch**! dress (*your ranks*)! **Augen rechts (links), —(e)t euch**! dress, right (left)! (*Mil.*); **sich auf eine S. —en**, to prepare for; **sich nach einer S. —en**, to conform to, follow,

go by; der Preis —et sich nach der Güte der Waren, the price is determined by the quality of the goods; das Eigenschaftswort —et sich nach dem Hauptworte, the adjective agrees with its noun; sich nach den Umständen —en, to be guided by circumstances. II. *a. & n.* (*aux.* h.) to judge; to criticize; to pass sentence on, condemn; —et nicht, auf daß ihr nicht gerichtet werdet, judge not, that ye be not judged (*B.*). —er, *m.* (—ers, *pl.* —er) judge; magistrate; umpire; one who directs, *etc.*; pointer (*of a gun, Artil.*); das Buch der —er, the Book of Judges (*B.*); sich zum —er aufwerfen, to constitute o.s. judge. —erisch, *adj. & adv.* as a judge, magisterial, censorious. —erlich, I. *adj.* judicial; judiciary. II. *adv.* as a judge, judicially. —ig, *see* Richtig. —ung, *f.* direction; directing; aim; course; tendency; bent, turn, drift, inclination; neuere —ung, modern methods, reform movement (*e.g. in lang. teaching*); in jeder —ung, in all directions; in gerader —ung, in a straight line, straight on; gerade —ung, alignment (*Mil.*); Zug in der —ung nach London, up train; Zug in der —ung von London, down train, London train. *Comp.* —balken, *m.* traversing beam (*of a flying-bridge*). —bank, *f.* dresser. —baum, *m.* pulley-beam. —beil, *n.* executioner's axe. —blei, *n.* plummet. —block, *n.* executioner's block. —bühne, *f.* scaffold. —eisen, *n.* straightening rod. —er=amt, *n.* judgeship. —er=kollegium, *n.* assembly, council of judges. —er=schwert, *n.* sword of justice. —er=spruch, *m.* judgment, sentence. —er=stand, *m.* body of judges *or* magistrates, the bench; position of a judge. —er=stuhl, *m.* tribunal; das gehört nicht vor seinen —erstuhl, that is not within his jurisdiction. —er=wage, *f.* scales of justice. —essen, —fest, *n.* feast given to the workmen when the framework of a house is completed. —e=weg, *see* —weg. —haus, *n.* court. —holz, *n.* ruler; straightening board. —kegel, *m.* frontlet (*Artil.*). —keil, *m.* quoin *or* wedge for pointing guns. —lot, *n.* plumb-line. —marsch, *m.* flank march (*Mil.*). —maß, *n.* standard; gauge. —pfennig, *m.* assay weight (*Mint.*). —platz, *m.* place of execution. —saal, *m.* judgment-hall; court (*of justice*). —schacht, *m.* perpendicular shaft. —scheffel, *m.* standard bushel. —scheit, *n.* ruler; level; batten; justifier (*Typ.*). —schnur, *f.* level; plumb-line, chalk-line; rule of conduct, standard, model, pattern; laß dir dies zur —schnur dienen, be guided by this. —schraube, *f.* adjusting screw. —statt, —stätte, *see* —platz. —ungs=flügelmann, *m.* marker (*Mil.*). —ungs=klappe, *f.* regulating valve. —ungs=linie, *f.* line of direction; alignment (*Mil.*). —ungs=rotte, *f.* leading file. —ungs=unteroffizier, *m.* soldier posted so as to show the direction. —ungs=winkel, *m.* angle of elevation. —wage, *f.* level. —weg, *m.* short cut; way to the place of execution.

Rich'tig, I. *adj. & adv.* righteous, right (*B.*); right, accurate, correct; true, just; straight; in order; settled; in tune; — rechnen, to calculate correctly; einen — nehmen, to treat a p. in the right way; geht Ihre Uhr —? is your watch right? ein —es Scepter, a sceptre of righteousness (*B.*); — machen, to put to rights, arrange, adjust; to pay up; es ist alles —, all is well; —er Londoner, regular cockney; (mit einem) — werden, to agree *or* come to an understanding (with a p.); Wilhelm und Maria sind mit einander —, William and Mary have come to an understanding, are engaged; es ist nicht — zu sagen, daß, it is wrong *or* not correct to say that; es ist nicht —, there is something wrong; es ist hier nicht —, this place is not safe, is haunted; das geht nicht — (mit —en Dingen) zu, there is something wrong, that is not quite as it should be; es ist nicht ganz — mit ihm, he is not quite right in the head; das —e, what is right, proper; das ist — und zweifelsohne, that is perfectly certain. II. *int. & part.* truly; right; certainly, *etc.*; —! ganz —! quite right! quite correct *or* true! er hat es — vergessen, of course he has forgotten it; ich sagte, „er kommt bald" und —! da trat er in die Thür, I said he would soon come, and, sure enough, the words were scarcely out of my mouth when he entered. —keit, *f.* correctness; accuracy; justness, justice; regularity; propriety (*of an expression*); in —keit bringen, to adjust, settle, to pay; es ist alles in —keit, everything is settled *or* arranged; die Sache hat ihre —keit, es hat damit seine —keit, it is quite true, it's a fact. *Comp.* —befinden, *n.*; nach —befinden, if found correct. —machung, *f.* arrangement, putting in order.

Ri'cinusöl, *n.* castor-oil.

Rick'e, *f.* (*pl.* —n) doe.

Rieb, Rie'best; Rie'be; *1* (*& 3*) *and* 2 *pers. sing. imperf. indic.*; *1* (*& 3*) *pers. sing. imperf. subj. of* reiben.

Riech'bar, *adj.* that may be smelt, perceptible.

Rie'ch—en, *ir. v.a. & n.* (*aux.* h.) to smell; to foresee, perceive, find out; nach einer S. —en, to smell of; an einer S. —en, to smell a thing; er —t aus dem Munde, his breath is unpleasant *or* offensive; es —t angebrannt, it smells burnt; ich kann es nicht —en, I cannot bear (the smell of) it; Lunte —en, den Braten —en, to smell a rat; er kann kein Pulver —en, he is a coward, he cannot bear the smell of powder; das kann man nicht —en, you can't know that; daran kannst du —en! put that in your pipe and smoke it! —end, *p. & adj.* redolent; touched, too high (*of meat*); fusty. —er, *m.* (—ers, *pl.* —er) one who smells *or* finds out things; nose (*coll.*); er hat einen guten —er, he has a good nose (*coll.*). *Comp.* —fläschchen, *n.* smelling-bottle. —nerv, *m.* olfactory nerve. —salz, *n.* smelling salt(s). —werkzeuge, *pl.* olfactory organs.

Ried, *n.* (—(e)s, *pl.* —e) boggy country; reed. *Comp.* —gras, *n.* sedge.

Rief, Rie'fest; Rie'fe; *1* (*& 3*) *and* 2 *pers. sing. imperf. ind.*; *1* (*& 3*) *pers. sing. imperf. subj. of* rufen.

Rie'fe, *f.* (*pl.* —n) groove; chamfer, channel; flute. —ln, —n, *v.a.* to chamfer, channel, flute; to groove; to rifle (*a gun*).

Rie'ge, *f.* section, division, set (*in gymnastics*). —l, *m.* (—ls, *pl.* —l) bolt, rail, bar; cross-bar bolt; cross-beam; transom (*Artil.*); loop; button-hole; ein —l Seife, a bar of soap; einem einen —l vorschieben, to check a p., put an obstacle in his way. —ln, *v.a.* to bar, bolt. *Comp.* —l=feder, *f.* bolt-spring. —l=fest, *adj.* (securely) bolted, barred. —l=holz, *n.* cross-bar. —l=nagel, *m.* bolt. —l=wand, *f.* wooden partition. —l=werk, *n.* framework.

[1]**Rie'men, Riem** (*obs.*), *m.* (—s, *pl.* —) strap, thong; belt; brace; string; shoe-string; reglet (*Arch.*); mit — peitschen, to lash; die — ziehen müssen, to have to loose one's purse-strings, to have to pay; aus anderer Leute Haut ist gut — schneiden, it is easy to pay at other people's expense. *Comp.* —betrieb, *m.* transmission, belt-gearing, belting. —bügel, *m.* swivel of a gun. —handpferd, *n.* off-leader. —kalk, *m.* cyanite. —loch, *n.* hole in a strap *or* stirrup-leather. —schuh, *m.* sandal. —werk, —zeug, *n.* straps, harness.

[2]**Rie'men**, *m.* (—s, *pl.* —) oar; die — klar machen, to ship the oars. *Comp.* —klampen,

pl. rowlocks. —**schlag**, *m.* stroke with the oar.

¹Rie′mer, *m.* (—s, *pl.* —) saddler, leather-cutter, belt- *or* harness-maker. —**ei′**, *f.* harness making, saddlery. *Comp.* —**handwerk**, *n.* trade of a saddler *or* harness-maker.

²Rie′mer, (—s, *pl.* —) (*in compds.*); **Acht**—, eight-oared boat, (an) eight (*race-boat; Univ. sl.*).

Ries, *n.* (—(s)es, *pl.* —(s)e) ream (*of paper*). —**weise**, *adv.* by reams.

Rie′s—e, *m.* (—en, *pl.* —en) giant, ogre; **Adam** —, see Index of Names. —**in**, *f.* giantess. —**enhaft**, —**ig**, *adj.* & *adv.* gigantic; immense; immensely; awfully (*coll.*); **ich habe mich —ig gefreut**, I was awfully pleased (*coll.*). —**enhaftigkeit**, —**igkeit**, *f.* gigantic proportions. *Comp.* —**en=ameise**, *f.* great black ant. —**en=arbeit**, *f.* immense piece of work. —**en=artig**, *adj.* enormous, gigantic, colossal. —**en=ball**, *m.* gigantic coil (of a dragon). —**en=bau**, *m.* gigantic structure, noble pile. —**en=bild**, *n.* colossal figure. —**en=damm**, *m.* Giant's Causeway. —**en=faultier**, *n.* megatherium. —**en=geschlecht**, *n.* race of giants. —**en=gestalt**, *f.* colossus. —**en=groß**, —**en=mäßig**, *adj.* colossal. —**en=karte**, *f.* gigantic (*pictorial*) post card. —**en=maß**, *n.* gigantic proportions. —**en=schlange**, *f.* boa-constrictor; python. —**en=schritt**, *m.* giant-stride; **mit —enschritten**, (*to go, etc.*) at a rapid pace. —**en=welle**, *f.* giant wave, huge breaker; gigantic swing (*at the horizontal bar*).

Rie′sel, *m.* (—s, *pl.* —) rippling, purling; drizzling. —**n**, *v.n.* (*aux.* **h.** & **s.**) to purl, ripple; to trickle; **es —t**, it drizzles; **ein Schauer —t mir durch's Gebein**, I am shuddering *or* shivering. *Comp.* —**feld**, *n.* irrigated field *or* meadow.

Ries′ling, *m.* (—s, *pl.* —e) a kind of Rhenish vine and the wine made from it.

Rie′ster, *m.* (—s, *pl.* —) wrist; instep; stilt of a plough; patch (*on a shoe, etc.*).

Riet, **Rie′test**; **Rie′te**; *1* (*& 3*) *and 2 pers. sing. imperf. indic.; 1* (*& 3*) *pers. sing. imperf. subj. of* **raten**.

Riff, *n.* (—es, *pl.* —e) reef, ridge; sand-bank. *Comp.* —**kette**, *f.* (rocky) ledge.

Rif′fel, *f.* (*pl.* —n) flax-comb, ripple; polisher. —**n**, *v.a.* to ripple (*flax*); to file, polish; to scold (*see* **Rüffeln**). *Comp.* —**baum**, *m.* flax-comb. —**blech**, *n.* channelled plate. —**holz**, *n.* polisher, burnisher. —**maschine**, *f.* fluting machine. —**walze**, *f.* fluted roller.

Rigo′le, *f.* (*pl.* —n) deep furrow; culvert. —**n**, *v.a.* to trench-plough.

Rigor—is′tisch, —**ö′s**, *adj.* & *adv.* rigorous, rigid, severe. —**o′sum**, *n.* (rigorous) examination for the doctor's degree (*Univ. sl.*).

Rikoschettie′ren, *v.n.* (*aux.* **h.**) to ricochet

Rikosche′ttfeuer, *n.* ricochet-fire (*Mil.*).

Ril′le, *f.* (*pl.* —n) rill; drill (*Agr.*); small groove.

Rimes′se, *f.* (*pl.* —n) remittance; — **per Saldo**, remittance in balance (*of accounts*). *Comp.* —**n=buch**, *n.* book of remittances.

Rind, *n.* (—es, *pl.* —er) bullock, neat, ox; cow; (*pl.*) (horned) cattle, head of cattle; bovine race; **das — brüllt**, the ox lows. *Comp.* —**er=braten**, *m.* roast beef. —**er=bremse**, *f.* gad-fly. —**er=herde**, *f.* herd *or* drove of cattle. —**er=hirt**, *m.* neat-herd; cow-keeper; cow-boy (*Amer.*). —**er=pest**, *f.* murrain, cattle-plague; rinderpest. —**er=pökelfleisch**, *n.* corned beef. —**er=talg**, *m.* beef-suet *or* tallow. —**fleisch**, *n.* beef. —**fleisch=brühe**, *f.* beef-tea. —**s=braten**, *m.* roast beef. —**s=zunge**, *f.* ox-tongue. —**vieh**, *n.* horned cattle; duffer (*vulg.*). —**vieh=zucht**, *f.* cattle-breeding.

Rind′—chen, *n.* (—chens, *pl.* —chen) little crust. —**e**, *f.* (*pl.* —en) rind; bark; crust. —**ig**, *adj.* covered with bark; crusty. *Comp.* —**en=artig**, *adj.* cortical. —**en=kahn**, *m.* bark-canoe. —**en=tiere**, *pl.* crustaceans. —**fällig**, —**schälig**, *adj.* shedding the bark.

Rin′dern, *v.n.* to desire the bull.

Ring, *m.* (—es, *pl.* —e) ring; link; circle, halo (*of the moon*); iris (*of the eye*); arena; market place (*prov.*); astragal (*Arch.*); coil (*of wire, etc.*); bundle, skein; ruff (*in pigeons*); clique; handle, ear; swivel; ferule, principal street (*boulevards*) of Vienna. —**el**, *m.* (—els, *pl.* —el) ring, circle; small ring; ringlet, curl; collar; stitch. —**elchen**, *n.* (—elchens, —elchen), —(e)lein, *n.* (—(e)leins, *pl.* —(e)lein) annulet, little ring. —**elicht**, (*obs.*) —**elig**, *adj.* annular. —**s**, *adv.* around, in a circle; —**s um**, —**s herum**, —**s umher**, round about, all round. *Comp.* —**bahn**, *f.* circular railway *or* tramway. —**band**, *n.* annular ligament. —**el=haar**, *n.* curled hair. —**el=locke**, *f.* ringlet. —**el=natter**, *f.* ringed snake. —**el=reihen**, *m.* round-dance, circular dance. —**el=reim**, *m.* refrain, chorus. —**el=rennen**, *n.* *see* —**rennen**. —**el=tanz**, *m.* ring-dance, round dance. —**el=taube**, *f.* ring-dove. —**feder**, *f.* bolt-spring (*on a gun*). —**förmig**, *adj.* annular. —**kämpfer**, *m.* pugilist. —**knorpel**, *m.* annular *or* cricoid cartilage. —**kragen**, *m.* gorget. —**mauer**, *f.* circular wall. —**ofen**, *m* annular kiln. —**rennen**, *n.* tilting at the ring. —**schießen**, *n.* target-shooting.

Rin′geln, *v.a.* to curl; to provide with a ring *or* rings; to encircle; to blaze (*trees*); **sich** —, to curl.

Rin′g—en, *ir.v.* I. *n.* (*aux.* **h.**) to struggle; to wrestle, grapple (**mit**, with); (**mit einem**) **um eine S.** —**en**, to contend for; —**en nach einer S.**, to strive after, to contend for a th. II. *a.* to wring (*one's hands, clothes, etc.*); **einem etwas aus der Hand —en**, to wrest s.th. out of a p.'s hand; **einen zu Boden —en**, to throw a p. (in wrestling); **mit dem Tode —en**, to be in the grip *or* throes of death, to be in one's last agony; **sich in die Höhe —en**, to struggle to one's feet. —**er**, *m.* (—ers, *pl.* —er) wrestler. *Comp.* —**kampf**, *m.* wrestling contest *or* match. —**platz**, *m.* wrestling-ground. —**schule**, *f.* (**der Alten**), palæstra.

Rin′n—e, *f.* (*pl.* —en) gutter, sewer; drain, trench; groove; channel. —**ig**, *adj.* grooved; running, bleared (*of eyes*). —**sal**, *n.* (—sals, *pl.* —sale) channel, bed of a river. *Comp.* —**äugig**, *adj.* blear-eyed. —**en=förmig**, *adj.* fluted. —**stein**, *m.* gutter; sink; sewer. —**stein=kehrer**, *m.* sewer-man.

Rin′nen, *ir.v.n.* (*aux.* **s.**) to run, flow; to trickle; to gush; to curdle; (*aux.* **h.** & **s.**) to leak, drop; to gutter (*of candles*).

Ripp′—chen, *n.* (—chens, *pl.* —chen) small rib; chop; cutlet. —**e**, *f.* (*pl.* —en) rib; **unter den —en befindlich**, sub-costal. —**ig**, *adj.* ribbed. —**s**, **Rips**, *m.* rep. *Comp.* —**en=braten**, *m.* roast-rib *or* fore-quarter. —**en=bruch**, *m.* fracture of a rib. —**en=fell**, *n.*, —**en=haut**, *f.* pleura (*Anat.*). —**enfell=entzündung**, *f.* pleurisy. —**en=knorpel**, *m.* costal cartilage. —**e(n)=speer**, *m.* roast ribs of pork. —**en=stoß**, *m.* nudge, poke in the ribs. —**en=stück**, *n.* rib of meat. —**en=weh**, *n.* pain in the side.

Rip′pen, *v.a.* to furnish with ribs; rib; to plait (*a frill, etc.*); **geripptes Papier**, ribbed paper.

Ri′s—iko, *n.* (—ikos, *pl.* —ikos) risk (*C. L.*). —(**s**)**kie′ren**, *v.a.* to risk.

Ris′pe, *f.* (*pl.* —n) panicle (*Bot.*); slanting beam (*Arch.*).

¹Riß, **Ris′sest**; **Ris′se**; *1* (*& 3*) *and 2 pers. sing. imperf. ind.; 1* (*& 3*) *pers. sing. imperf. subj. of* **reißen**.

Riß, *m.* (—(ss)es, *pl.* —(ss)e) tearing, laceration; lash, stroke, tear, rent, cleft, chink, gap; fracture, flaw; plan, elevation; design, drawing; draught, outline; schism, breach; **sich vor den — stellen**, *or* **vor den — treten**, to step *or* throw o.s. into the breach; **sein Tod hat einen großen — gemacht**, his death has made a sad blank. **—(ss)ig**, *adj.* torn, rent; cracked; —(ss)**ig werden**, to spring (*of wood*).

Rist, *m.* (—es, *pl.* —e) wrist; instep; withers.

Ritrat'te, *f.* (*pl.* —n) re-exchange, re-draft.

Ritsch, *int.*; — **ratsch**! slish, slash!

[1]**Ritt, Rit'test; Rit'te**; *1 (& 3) and 2 pers. sing. imperf. ind.; 1 (& 3) pers. sing. imperf. subj. of* **reiten.**

[2]**Ritt**, *m.* (—es, *pl.* —e) ride; **einen — machen**, to take a ride; **in einem —e**, at one time, at one pull, without a break. **—lings**, *adv.* astride; **—lings im Sattel**, astride (in) the saddle; **—lings auf einer S. sitzen**, to sit astride s.th. *Comp.* **—meister**, *m.* cavalry captain, captain of horse (*Mil.*); **—meister werden**, to get one's troop.

Rit'ter, *m.* (—s, *pl.* —) knight; cavalier; champion; **der letzte —**, the German Emperor Maximilian I. (†*1519*); **irrender, fahrender —**, knight errant; **deutsche —**, Teutonic Knight; **Tempel —**, (Knight) Templar; **Johanniter —**, Knight of St. John, Knight Hospitaller; — **des Malteserordens**, Knight of Malta; **der — ohne Furcht und Tadel**, the knight without fear and without reproach, Bayard; — **der traurigen Gestalt**, knight of the woeful countenance (*Don Quixote*); **einen zum — schlagen**, to create *or* dub a p. a knight; **arme —**, Devonshire toast, fritters; **arme — backen**, to live in poverty; **an einem zum — werden**, to gain one's spurs by overcoming an opponent; **an einem zum — werden wollen**, to try to provoke a person in order to show one's superiority. **—lich**, *adj. & adv.* knightly, chivalrous; valiant, equestrian, belonging to a knightly order; — **liche Gesellschaft des Mittelalters**, chivalry of the Middle Ages. **—lichkeit**, *f.* gallantry, chivalry. **—schaft**, *f.* knighthood; body of knights, chivalry. **—schaftlich**, *adj.* belonging to knighthood. **—tum**, *n.* chivalry. *Comp.* **—akademie**, *f.* (*military*) academy for young noblemen. **—alter**, *n.* age of chivalry. — **buch**, *n.* book *or* romance of chivalry. — **burg**, *f.* knight's castle. **—bürtig**, *adj.* of knightly descent. **—dienst**, *m.* knight-service, feudal-service; **einer Dame —dienste erweisen**, to do knightly service to a lady. — **gebrauch**, *m.* custom of chivalry. **—gedicht**, *n.* poem composed by a knight *or* of knightly adventure, poem of chivalry. **—geist**, *m.* spirit of chivalry. **—gut**, *n.* estate, manor. **—hof**, *m.* manor-house. **—kampf**, *m.* tournament. — **lehen**, *n.* fief held by knightly service, knight's fee. **—mäßig**, *adj. & adv.* like a knight, chivalrous. **—orden**, *m.* knightly order; **deutscher —orden**, Teutonic order; **geistlicher —orden**, religious order of knighthood (**Johanniter, Templer, Deutschherrn**). **—roman**, *m.* romance of chivalry. **—saal**, *m.* hall of knights. **—schlag**, *m.* dubbing, knighting. **—sitte**, *f.* courteous, knightly custom. **—sitz**, *see* **—hof**. **—spiel**, *n.* tournament. **—sporn**, *m.* larkspur (*Bot.*). **—stand**, *m.* knighthood; equestrian order (*in Rome*). **—that**, *f.* chivalrous deed of arms. **—treue**, *f.* knightly allegiance. — **wesen**, *n.* chivalry. **—wort**, *n.* word of a knight *or* gentleman. **—würde**, *f.* dignity of a knight; knightly rank. **—zeit**, *f.* age of chivalry, chivalric times. **—zug**, *m.* knightly expedition.

Ritual—is'mus, *m.* ritualism. **—i'st**, *m.* (—**is'ten**, *pl.* —**is'ten**) ritualist.

Ri'tus, *m.* (*pl.* **Riten**) rite.

Ritz, *m.* (—es, *pl.* —e), **—e**, *f.* (*pl.* —en) cleft, fissure, crack, crevice; chap; scratch; flaw. **—ig**, *adj.* cracked; crannied; scratched.

Rit'z—en, *v.a.* to scratch, graze; to tear; to notch; to split, crack. **—ung**, *f.* scratching; scratch.

Rival—isie'ren, *v.n.* (*aux.* **h.**) to rival. **—itä't**, *f.* rivalry.

Rob'be, *f.* (*pl.* —n) sea-calf, seal. *Comp.* **—n-fang**, *m.* seal-hunting. **—n-fell**, *n.* seal-skin.

Rob'ber, *m.* (—s, *pl.* —, —s) rubber (*of whist*).

Roch, Ro'chest; Rö'che; *1 (& 3) and 2 pers. sing. imperf. ind.; 1 (& 2) pers. sing. imperf. subj. of* **riechen.**

[1]**Ro'che**, *m.* (—n, *pl.* —n), **—n**, *m.* (—ns, *pl.* —n) ray, thorn-back; **der stachlichte —**, the prickly ray.

[2]**Ro'ch—e**, *m.* (—en, *pl.* —en) castle, rook (*at chess*). **—en, —ie'ren**, *v.n.* (*aux.* **h.**) to castle.

Rö'cheln, I. *v.n.* (*aux.* **h.**) to rattle, have a rattling in the throat. II. *subst. n.* death-rattle.

Rock, *m.* (—es, *pl.* **Rö'cke**) coat; dress, gown; robe; petticoat; skirt; **geteilter —**, divided skirt (*of ladies*); **des Königs —**, the uniform; **der bunte —**, the soldier's uniform; **den bunten — anziehen**, to don the King's uniform, to take the King's shilling, to enlist, to become a soldier; **im bunten —e stecken**, to be a soldier, to serve one's time. *Comp.* **—hose**, *f.* divided skirt which can be worn in the shape of knickerbockers. **—knopf**, *m.* coat-button. **—schoner, —schützer**, *m.* dress guard (*Cycl.*). **—schoß**, *m.* coat-tail. **—tasche**, *f.* coat-pocket.

Röck'chen, *n.* (—s, *pl.* —) infant's robe; little coat *or* dress.

[1]**Ro'cken**, *dial. for* **Roggen.**

[2]**Ro'cken**, *m.* (—s, *pl.* —) rock, distaff. *Comp.* **—band**, *n.* ribbon wrapped round the distaff. **—politik**, *f.* feminine politics. **—stube**, *f.* spinning-room. **—weisheit**, *f.* old wives' wisdom. **—zunft**, *f.* set of spinsters.

Ro'del—n, *v.a.* to toboggan. *Comp.* **—schlitten**, *m.* toboggan.

Rö'del— (*in comp'ds*) **—balken**, *m.* racking-balk. **—holz**, *n.* rack-stick. **—n**, *v.a.* to rack (down).

Ro'de—n, *v.a. & n.* (*aux.* **h.**) to root out, grub up, to make arable. *Comp.* **—land**, *n.* woodland turned into arable land.

Ro'gen, *m.* (—s) (hard) roe, spawn. **—er**, *see* **—fisch.** *Comp.* **—fisch**, *m.* female fish. — **stein**, *m.* oolite.

Rog'gen, *m.* (—s) rye. *Comp.* **—brot**, *n.* rye bread. **—wurm**, *m.* rye-weevil.

Roh, *adj. & adv.* raw; crude; rough; rude; coarse, gross; barbarous, brutal; vulgar; unbound (*of books*); unbleached, brown (*of linen*); —(er) **Betrag**, gross amount; **—er Schwefel**, native sulphur; **—e Pferde**, untrained horses; **—es Leder**, untanned leather; **einen behandeln wie ein —es Ei**, to treat a p. with the greatest delicacy and consideration. **—heit**, *f.* rawness; roughness; crudity; rudeness, brutality; (*pl.*) coarse, vulgar *or* brutal actions. *Comp.* **—arbeit**, *f.* raw-melting (*Found.*). — **bau**, *m.* ashlar; rubble-work; **—bau in Ziegeln**, brick-work. **—eisen**, *n.* pig-iron. — **einnahme**, *f.*, **—ertrag**, *m.* gross receipts, proceeds. **—erzeugnisse**, *pl.* raw products. **—material**, *n.* raw material. **—metall**, *n.* crude metal. **—ofen**, *m.* furnace for common ore. **—stoffe**, *see* **—erzeugnisse.** **—schwefel**, *m.* native sulphur. **—zucker**, *m.* raw sugar.

Rohr, *n.* (—s, *pl.* —e) reed, cane; tube, pipe; nose (*of bellows*); flue (*of chimneys*); reed (*Mus.*); barrel (*of guns*); **spanisches —**, Arundo donax; **indisches —**, bamboo; **gezogenes —**, rifle-barrel; **geschweißtes —**, welded tube; **ein schwankes —** a reed shaken with the wind

(*B.*); **sich auf ein schwaches — stützen,** to trust to a broken reed; **wer im — sitzt, hat gut Pfeifen schneiden,** he that sits among reeds cuts pipes when he pleases (*prov.*). **—en,** I. *adj.* of reed *or* cane. II. *v.a.* to cut the reeds of, clear of reeds (*a pond*). **—ig,** *adj.* reedy. *Comp.* **—besen,** *m.* flag-broom. **—bündel,** *n.* bundle of reeds. **—dach,** *n.* reed thatch. **—decke,** *f.* rush mat. **—dommel,** *f.* bittern; **die —dommel ruft, schreit,** the bittern booms, bellows, cries. **—drossel,** *f.* great reed-sparrow. **—flechte,** *f.*, **—geflecht,** *n.* reed-work. **—flöte,** *f.* reed-pipe. **—förmig,** *adj.* tubular. **—huhn,** *n.* moor-hen, coot. **—kolben,** *m.* reed-mace (*Bot.*). **—nagel,** *m.* tack. **—netz,** *n.* pipes, conduit. **—post,** *f.* pneumatic post. **—post=brief,** *m.* letter sent by the pneumatic post, tubular letter. **—sänger,** *m.* sedge-warbler. **—schleifer,** *m.* gun-barrel grinder. **—schmied,** *m.* gun-barrel-maker. **—spatz, —sperling,** *m.* tree-sparrow; reed-warbler; **wie ein —spatz schimpfen,** to abuse like a fishwife. **—stock,** *m.* cane; bamboo; **einen Schüler mit dem —stock prügeln,** to cane a boy, to give a boy a caning. **—stößer,** *m.*, **—stoße,** *f.* reed-cutting machine. **—stuhl,** *m.* cane-bottomed chair. **—weite,** *f.* bore. **—werk,** *n.* reed-work; reed-stop (*in organs*). **—zirkel,** *m.* gunsmith's compasses. **—zucker,** *m.* cane-sugar.

Röh'r—e, *f.* (*pl.* **—en**) pipe, tube; spout; siphon, nozzle; funnel; shaft; socket; canal, duct; flue; cylinder. **—icht** (*obs.*), **—ig,** I. *adj.* reed-like. II. **—icht,** *n.* (**—icht(e)s,** *pl.* **—ichte**) reed-bank. **—ig,** *adj.* tubular; containing pipes; fistular. *Comp.* **—bein,** *n.*, **—knochen,** *m.* tibia. **—brunnen,** *m.* fountain, jet. **—en=gang,** *m.* conduit, set of water-pipes. **—en=förmig,** *adj.* tubular. **—en=kraut,** *n.* dandelion. **—en=meister,** *m.* turn-cock; inspector of water-works. **—geschwür,** *n.* fistula. **—holz,** *n.* wood for pipes. **—wasser,** *n.* pipe-water.

Röh'ren, *v.n.* (*aux.* **h.**) to bellow, roar; to rut.

Ro'koko, *a.* & *n.* (**—s**) rococo. *Comp.* **—mäßig,** *adj.* in rococo style.

Roll'—bar, *adj.* that may be rolled; voluble. **—e,** *f.* (*pl.* **—en**) roll; cylinder; roller; pulley; mangle; calender; roll, twist, bundle, coil; list, register; scroll; roller, pulley (*of blinds*); caster (*on chairs, etc.*); frisette; rôle, part (*Theat.*); **auf —en laufend,** moving on rollers *or* casters; **aus der —e fallen,** to act out of character, betray o.s.; **eine —e spielen,** to act a part, to cut a (fine) figure; **er spielt eine traurige —e,** he cuts a poor figure; **treu seiner —e,** in character. *Comp.* **—baum,** *m.* windlass. **—bombe,** *f.* ditch- *or* wall-grenade. **—brett,** *n.* mangling-board. **—draht,** *m.* wire in hoops. **—eisen,** *n.* rolled iron. **—en=band,** *n.* roll of tape *or* ribbon. **—en=besetzung,** *f.* cast (*Theat.*). **—en=blei,** *n.* rolled lead; sheet-lead. **—en=förmig,** *adj.* trochlear. **—en=kette,** *f.* roller chain (*Cycl.*). **—en=macher,** *m.* pulley-maker. **—en=presse,** *f.* rolling-press. **—en=taback,** *m.* tobacco in rolls. **—en=welle,** *f.* roller. **—en=zug,** *m.* triangle with pulleys. **—fleisch,** *n.* rolled meat. **—fuhrmann,** *m.* drayman, carter. **—fuhrwerk,** *n.* truck; cart. **—geld,** *n.* cost of cartage; cost of calendering *or* mangling. **—holz,** *n.* rolling-pin. **—kloben,** *m.* pulley. **—maschine,** *f.* beetling-machine. **—material,** *n.* rolling stock (*Railw.*). **—messing,** *n.* sheet-brass. **—mops,** *m.* rolled-up herring (*in vinegar*), collared herring. **—muskel,** *m.* rotatory muscle. **—schlittschuh,** *m.* roller-skate. **—schlittschuh=bahn,** *f.* skating-rink **—stein,** *m.* garden-roller; (*pl.*) boulders. **—stuhl,** *m.* chair on casters, wheel-chair; **im —stuhl umhergefahren werden,** to be wheeled about in a bath-chair. **—thür,** *f.* sash-door. **—vorhang,** *m.* roller-blind. **—wagen,** *m.* truck; go-cart. **—wäsche,** *f.* clothes for mangling. **—werk,** *n.* machinery moved on rollers; cylinder mill: scroll-work (*Arch.*).

Rol'le—n, *v.a.* & *n.* (*aux.* **h.** & **s.**) to roll; to revolve; to trundle; to mangle *or* calender; **sich —n,** to roll up, to curl; **gerolltes r,** trilled r. **—r,** *m.* (**—rs,** *pl.* **—r**) roller, mangler; canary bird (*cock*); trochleary muscle (*Anat.*).

Roma'n, *m.* (**—s,** *pl.* **—e**) novel (*of considerable length*), work of fiction; **Ritter —,** romance; **kurzer —,** tale, novelette; **— aus dem Leben,** romance from real life; **ein spannender —,** an exciting novel; **der Ich=Roman,** novel written in the first person ('*Werther*,' '*David Copperfield*'). **—en=tum,** *n.* (**—en=tums**) Romanic institutions, nationality, the Neo-Latin peoples. **—haft,** *adj.* romantic. **—isch,** *adj.* Romanic; Romance; Romanesque; **—ische Philologie,** Romance philology; **—ische Nationen,** Romance nations. **—is'mus,** *m.* Romanism. **—i'st,** *m.* student *or* teacher of Romance philology *or* of Roman law. **—is'tik,** *f.* domain *or* study of Romance philology. **—tik,** *f.* romantic poetry. **—tiker,** *m.* (**—tikers,** *pl.* **—tiker**) romantic author *or* poet, romanticist; **der —tiker auf dem Throne Preußens,** King Frederick William IV. (†*1861*). **—tisch,** *adj.* romantic; romanesque. **—ze,** *f.* (*pl.* **—zen**) epic-lyric poem, romance; ballad. *Comp.* **—artig,** *adj.* like a novel, novelistic. **—dichter(in,** *f.*), **—schreiber(in,** *f.*), *m.* romance writer, novelist. **—dichtung,** *f.* novel writing. **—held,** *m.*, **—heldin,** *f.* hero, heroine of romance. **—lesen,** *n.* novel-reading. **—zeitung,** *f.* journal for tales of fiction.

Rö'mer, *m.* (**—s,** *pl.* **—**) Roman; drinking glass (*obs.*). *See the Index of Names.*

Ron'd—e, Run'd—e, *f.* (*pl.* **—en**) round, patrol. **—e'l,** *n.* (**—els.** *pl.* **—ele**) target; (*also* **Runde'l(l), —e'll,**) apse (*Arch.*); round tower; bastion.

Ro's—a, *adj.* rose-coloured. **—e,** *f.* (*pl.* **—en**; *dim.* **Rös'chen**) rose; rosette; rose (*Arch.*); start; burr (*on a stag's antlers*); erysipelas (*Med.*); starfish (*Icht.*); **die Zeit bringt —en,** all things come to them that wait; **keine —e ohne Dorn(en),** no rose without a thorn (*prov.*). **—et'te,** *f.* (*pl.* **—etten**) rosette; centre-piece (*of a ceiling*); rose-diamond. **—ig,** *adj.* rosy, roseate; **in der —igsten Laune,** in the happiest mood, in the best of tempers; **die Dinge im —igsten Lichte sehen,** to look at the brightest side of things, to be an optimist. *Comp.* **—en=artig,** *adj.* rosaceous; erysipelatous. **—en=blühend,** *adj.* blooming like a rose. **—en=brand,** *m.* rose-blight. **—en=busch,** *m.* rose-bush, rose-tree. **—en=dorn,** *m.* sweet-briar, dog-rose. **—en=duft,** *m.* scent *or* fragrance of roses. **—en=essenz,** *f.* attar of roses. **—en=farbig,** *adj.* rose-coloured. **—en=holder,** *m.* guelder-rose. **—en=holz,** *n.* rosewood. **—en=knospe,** *f.* rosebud. **—en=kranz,** *m.* garland of roses; rosary; **seinen —enkranz beten,** to tell one's beads. **—en=kreuzer,** *m.* Rosicrucian (*XVII. cent. mystics*). **—en=krieg,** *m.* War(s) of the Roses (*Engl. Hist.*). **—en=lippen,** *pl.* rosy lips. **—en=öl,** *n.* attar of roses. **—en=rot,** *adj.* rose-red, rosy. **—en=stein,** *m.* rose-diamond. **—en=stock,** *m.* rose-tree, standard rose; part of (*a stag's*) head on which the horns grow; **wilder —enstock,** eglantine. **—en=strauch,** *m.* rose-bush. **—en=strauß,** *m.* bunch of roses. **—en=wange,** *f.* rosy cheek. **—en=zeit,** *f.* time of roses; youth. **—en=zucht,** *f.* cultivation of roses. **—etten=fenster,** *n.* rose *or* wheel window.

Rosie'ren, *v.a.* to dye pink, to rose.

Rosi'ne, *f.* (*pl.* **—n**) raisin; **große —n,** plums; **kleine —n,** currants; **kleine kernlose —n,**

sultanas; **große —n im Kopfe** *or* **Sack haben**, to think a great deal of o.s.; to purpose great things; **setz dir man recht viel—n in'n Kopf!** wait and see what will become of all your fine schemes (*coll.*).

Rosmari'n, *m.* (—**s**) rosemary. *Comp.* —**öl**, *n.* oil of rosemary.

Rös'selsprung, *m.* knight's move (*Chess*).

[1]**Rost**, *m.* (—**es**, *pl.* —**e**) grate, fire-grate; gridiron; roaster, despatch; pile-work; roasting, grilling; **auf dem —e braten**, to broil, grill. *Comp.* —**braten**, *m.* broil, grill; roast-beef. —**förmig**, *adj.* gridiron-like. —**fläche**, *f.* cooking surface (*of a grate*). —**pendel**, *n.* gridiron pendulum (*Phys.*). —**rippchen**, *n.* grilled cutlet. —**schnitte**, *f.* fritter. —**träger**, *m.* the fire-bar bearer. —**werk**, *n.* pile-work (*Arch.*).

[2]**Rost**, *m.* (—**es**) rust; blight, mildew. —**ig**, *adj.* rusty, rusted. *Comp.* —**farbe**, *f.* rust-colour. —**fleck(en)**, *m.* iron-mould. —**fleckig**, *adj.* iron-moulded. —**papier**, *n.* polishing paper; sand *or* emery paper.

Röst'—e, *f.* roasting; steeping (*of flax*); flax-hole; *see* —**stätte**; dish of roasted potatoes. *Comp.* —**arbeit**, *f.* smelting process (*by affinity*). —**eisen**, *n.* toasting-rack. —**erz=werk**, *n.* grating. —**gabel**, *f.* toasting-fork. —**haus**, *n.*, —**hütte**, *f.*, —**ofen**, *m.* roasting-furnace. —**pfanne**, *f.* frying-pan. —**stätte**, *f.* place where ore is burnt; flax-hole.

Ros'ten, *v.n.* (*aux.* **h.** & **s.**) to rust, to get *or* become rusty.

Rös't—en, *v.a.* to roast; to broil; to toast; to smelt (*ore*); to steep (*flax*). —**er**, *m.* (—**ers**, *pl.* —**er**) roaster, torrefactor. —**ung**, *f.* roasting; frying; smelting, *etc.*

Rostra'l, (**Rastra'l**,) *n.* (—**s**, *pl.* —**e**) music pen.

Roß, *n.* (—**(ſ'ſ)es**, *pl.* —**(ſ'ſ)e**) steed, charger, horse. —**(ſ'ſ)e**, (*in comp.*) *see* **Roß** *in comp.* *Comp.* —**arzenei**, *f.* horse-physic. —**arzt**, *m.* veterinary surgeon. —**bändiger**, *m.* horse-breaker. —**bremse**, *f.* gad-fly, horse-fly. —**haar**, *n.* horse-hair. —**händler**, *m.* horse-dealer. —**kamm**, *m.* curry-comb; horse-dealer. —**lenker**, *m.* charioteer; driver, cabman, cabby (*coll., hum.*). —**markt**, *m.* horse-fair. —**schweif**, *m.* horse's tail; horse-tail standard. —**täuscher**, *m.* horse-dealer, horse-coper. —**trappe**, *f.* imprint *or* mark of a horse's hoof.

Roß'kastanie, *f.* horse-chestnut (*not connected with* **Roß**).

Rot, I. (**röter, rötest**) *adj.* red; ruddy, rubicund; — **machen**, to make red, to redden; to cause to blush, to put to the blush; — **werden**, to get red, to blush, to colour up; **heute —, morgen tot**, here to-day, gone to-morrow; —**e Dame**, queen of hearts *or* diamonds; **die —e Erde**, Westphalia; **die —e Internationale**, the International League of Anarchists; **Schwestern vom —en Kreuz**, field-hospital nurses; **der —e Prinz**, Prince Frederick Charles of Prussia (in the uniform of the hussars); —**e Ruhr**, dysentery; **er hat keinen —en Heller**, he has n't a brass farthing; **das —e**, red (*colour*). II. *n.* (—**(e)s**) red; redness; rouge; paint; hearts, diamonds (*Cards*). *Comp.* —**auge**, *n.* roach (*Icht.*). —**äugig**, *adj.* red-eyed. —**bäckig**, *adj.* ruddy. —**bart**, *m.* red-beard; **Kaiser —bart**, Frederick Barbarossa (†*1190*). —**blond**, *adj.* light-reddish, auburn. —**braun**, *adj.* red-brown, russet, bay (*horse*). —**brüchig**, *adj.* red-short. —**buche**, *f.* common beech. —**eisenocher**, *m.* red ochre. —**fahl**, *adj.* tawny, pale red. —**farbig**, *adj.* red; gules (*Her.*). —**fichte**, —**föhre**, *f.* spruce-fir. —**fink**, *m.* chaffinch; bullfinch. —**forelle**, *f.* species of salmon-trout. —**fuchs**, *m.* fox; bay horse. —**gar**, *adj.* tanned. —**gelb**, *adj.* orange. —**gießer**, *m.* brazier. —**glühend**, *adj.* red-hot. —**guß**, *m.* red-brass, bronze, copper goods. —**haarig**, *adj.* red-haired, sandy-haired, rufous. —**hals**, *m.* red-headed duck. —**haut**, *f.* red-skin, red Indian. —**holz**, *n.* Brazil wood; red-wood; camwood. —**hosen**, *pl.* the French soldiers. —**hut**, *m.* cardinal. —**käppchen**, *n.* little Red-Riding-Hood. —**kehlchen**, *n.* robin red-breast. —**kohl**, *m.*, —**kraut**, *n.* red cabbage. —**kopf**, *m.* red-haired person. —**köpfig**, *adj.* red-haired, sandy. —**lauf**, *m.* erysipelas; red murrain (*of pigs*). —**laufgürtel**, *m.* shingles. —**liegende(s)**, *n.* lower new red sandstone. —**nasig**, *adj.* red-nosed. —**röcke**, *pl.* red-coats, British soldiers. —**röckig**, *adj.* red-coated. —**rüster**, *f.* red elm (*of North America*). —**schimmel**, *m.* roan-horse. —**spohn**, *m.* claret (*sl.*). —**stein**, *m.* ruddle; red brick *or* tile. —**stift**, *m.* red crayon. —**strumpf**, *m.* cardinal. —**sucht**, *f.* nettle-rash. —**tanne**, *f.* spruce-fir, common spruce, picea excelsa. —**wälsch**, —**welsch**, *n.* slang, gibberish, thieves' language, gipsy language. —**wangig**, *adj.* rosy-cheeked. —**wild**, *n.* red deer, venison. —**wurst**, *f.* red sausage.

Rot—atio'n, *f.* rotation; (*in comp.* =) rotatory —**ie'ren**, *v.n.* (*aux.* **h.**) to rotate. *Comp* —**ations'=bewegung**, *f.* rotatory motion. —**ations'=dampfmaschine**, *f.* rotary steam-engine. —**ations'=pumpe**, *f.* rotary pump.

Röt—e, *f.* redness, red; flush; madder; **die —e steigt ihm ins Gesicht**, the colour rushes to his face, he colours up. —**el**, *m.* (—**els**) red chalk, red pencil. —**eln**, *pl.* German measles. —**lich**, *adj.* reddish. —**lich=blau**, *adj.* lilac. —**lich=gelb**, *adj.* buff. *Comp.* —**el=farbe**, *f.* ruddle. —**el=stift**, *m.* red chalk pencil.

Rö'ten, *v.* I. *a.* to make *or* colour red, to redden. II. *r.* to get red, to flush.

[1]**Rot'(t)e**, *f.* (*pl.* —**n**) mediæval musical instrument similar to a fiddle.

[2]**Rot't—e**, *f.* (*pl.* —**en**) troop, band, company; horde; pack, gang; rabble; party, faction; sect; company (*Mil. obs.*); division of an army in the battle-field, section, detachment, platoon, squad, line, file (*Mil.*); **in —en links!** left, file! *Comp.* —**en=aufmarsch**, *m.* deployment in line. —**en=feuer**, *n.* dropping fire, volley firing. —**en=führer**, *m.* front-rank man; file leader; corporal. —**en=geist**, *m.* factious spirit. —**en=macher**, *m.* mutineer, caballer. —**en=meister**, *m.* corporal. —**en=weise**, *adv* by gangs *or* squads; in files. —**meister**, *m.* overseer of a gang of workmen.

Rot'ten, *v.a.* & *r.* to troop, assemble together; to collect in a mob; to plot.

Rotz, *m.* (—**es**) mucus from the noes; glanders. —**ig**, *adj.* snivelly, snotty; glandered. *Comp.* —**behaftet**, *adj.* glandered. —**löffel**, *m.*, —**maul**, *n.* impudent young brat; dirty nose (*vulg.*). —**näschen**, *n.* baby (*hum.*).

Routinie'rt, *p.p.* & *adj.* experienced, versed, practised.

Royali'st, *m.* (—**en**, *pl.* —**en**) royalist. —**isch**, *adj.* loyal to the sovereign; royalist.

Rü'b—e, *f.* (*pl.* —**en**) rape; (**weiße**) turnip; **gelbe —e**, carrot; **rote —e**, beet-root; **durch einander wie Kraut und —en**, higgledy-piggledy. *Comp.* —**en=feld**, *n.* field of turnips. —**en=förmig**, *adj.* turnip-shaped. —**(en)=samen**, (**Rüb'sen**,) *m.* rape-seed. —**en=zucker**, *m.* beet-root sugar. —**öl**, *n.* rape-seed oil, colza oil.

Rubi'n, *m.* (—**s**, *pl.* —**e**) ruby.

Rub—ri'k, *f.* (*pl.* —**riken**) rubric, heading. —**rizie'ren**, *v.a.* to mark with red (*obs.*); to mark, endorse; to head a column, chapter *or* division.

Ruch'bar, (**Rucht'bar**, *obs.*,) *adj.* notorious; known, public; — **werden**, to get about, transpire, become known; — **machen**, to spread about. —**keit**, *f.* notoriety. *Comp.* —**machen**, *n.* noising abroad.

Ruch'los, *adj.* impious, wicked; infamous, profligate. —(**s**)**igkeit**, *f.* wickedness, profligacy, infamy; wicked act.

Ruck, *m.* (—**es**, *pl.* —**e**) jolt, jerk, shock, sudden movement; **einen** — **thun**, to jerk *or* pull; **mit einem** —, **auf einen** —, all at once, suddenly. *Comp.* —**weise**, *adv.* by fits and starts

Rück, *adv.* back. —**lings**, *adv.* from behind; backwards; —**lings gehen**, to go backwards; —**lings liegend**, lying on one's back. *Comp.* —**anspruch**, *m.* counter-claim. —**antwort**, *f.* reply. —**berufungs=schreiben**, *n.* letters of recall. —**bettung**, *f.* gun-platform. —**bewegung**, *f.* retrograde movement. —**bildung**, *f.* retrogressive movement; **zentrifugale —bildung**, retrogressive movement in favour of separatism. —**bleibsel**, *n.* residue, remainder. —**blick**, *m.* backward glance, retrospect; **einen —blick werfen auf eine S.**, to pass s.th. in review. —**blickend**, *adj.* retrospective. —**bürge**, —**bürgschaft**, *f.* collateral bail *or* security. —**denken**, *ir.v.n.* (*aux.* **h.**) to reflect. —**en=naht**, *f.* dorsal suture. —**erinnerung**, *f.* reminiscence. —**erstattung**, *f.* restitution. —**fahrt**, *f.* return-journey. —**fall**, *m.* reversion; relapse. —**fällig**, *adj.* revertible; relapsing; **ein —fälliger**, a backslider. —**fluß**, *m.* reflux. —**forderung**, *f.* reclamation. —**fracht**, *f.* return-freight. —**frage**, *f.* return-question; further enquiry. —**fuhre**, *f.* return-conveyance. —**gabe**, *f.* return, restitution. —**gang**, *m.* return, going back, retreat; backsliding; relapse; retrograde motion, retrogression. —**gängig**, *adj.* retrograde, retrogressive: —**gängig machen**, to break off, put an end to; —**gängig werden**, not to take place, to retrograde; **die Verlobung ist —gängig geworden**, the match has been broken off; **er hat die Verabredung —gängig gemacht**, he has cancelled the appointment. —**gängigkeit**, *f.* retrograde movement; miscarriage, failure; rupture. —**gehen**, *ir.v.n.* (*aux.* **s.**) to return; —**gehende Gelder**, returns (*C.L.*). —**halt**, *m.* restraint, reserve; prop, stay, support; reservation. —**halten**, *v.n.* to keep back, reserve; —**haltend(es) Weigern**, reserved *or* cold refusal. —**haltslos**, *adj.* unreserved, frank. —**kauf**, *m.* repurchase; redemption. —**käuflich**, *adj.* redeemable. —**kehr**, —**kunft**, *f.* return; **bei meiner —kehr nach Hause fand ich**, on returning home I found. —**kehrend**, *adj.* returning; homeward bound (*ship*). —**klang**, *m.* reverberation, echo. —**ladung**, *f.* return-cargo. —**lage**, *f.* reserve. —**lauf**, *m.* recurrence: recoil (*of guns, etc.*). —**läufig**, *adj.* retrograde; recurrent. —**lehne**, *f.* back (*of a chair, etc.*). —**marsch**, *m.* march(ing) back *or* home. countermarch. —**prall**, *m.* repercussion; recoil; reaction. —**prämie**, *f.* return of premium. —**reise**, *f.* return journey. —**ruf**, *m.* recall. —**schein**, *m.* (reciprocal) bond; reflection of light. —**schlag**, *m.* backstroke; recoil, rebound; retrogression, return to the original, reaction; **der —schlag kam**, the reaction set in. —**schluß**, *m.* conclusion a posteriori. —**schreiben**, *n.* rescript; answer. —**schritt**, *m.* retrogression; backstep (*Mil.*); relapse. —**schritts=partei**, *f.* retrograde party (*Pol.*). —**seil**, *n.* gun-tackle (*Naut.*). —**seite**, *f.* back; reverse. —**seitig**, *adj.* & *adv.* on the other side *or* page. —**sendung**, *f.* return (*of goods, etc.*). —**sicht**, *f.* respect, regard, consideration; notice; discretion; **aus —sicht gegen (für)**, in deference to, in consideration of; **mit —sicht auf** (*acc.*) with regard to; **ohne —sicht auf**, irrespective of; —**sicht nehmen auf** (*acc.*) to take into consideration, to regard. —**sichtlich**, *adv.* & *prep.* (*with gen. or* **auf**); with regard to, considering. —**sicht=nahme**, *f.* respect, consideration. —**sichts**, *adv.* & *prep.* (*with gen.*) with regard to. —**sichts=los**, *adj.* regardless, inconsiderate. —**sichts=losigkeit**, *f.* want of consideration. —**sichts=voll**, *adj.* considerate, thoughtful. —**sitz**, *m.* back-seat, seat with one's back to the horses *or* to the engine. —**sprache**, *f.* conference; —**sprache nehmen mit einem**, to discuss a matter with a p. —**sprung**, *m.* rebound, resilience; **einen —sprung thun**, to recant, withdraw, to backslide, to flinch (*from*). —**stand**, *m.* arrears; residue, remainder; **im —stand bleiben**, to be in arrears with s.th.; **im —stand sein**, to be behindhand, backward, *or* in arrears with s.th. —**ständig**, *adj.* in arrears. —**ständler**, *m.* defaulter. —**stands=rechnung**, *f.* balance-account. —**stoß**, *m.* recoil; repulsion. —**strich**, *m.* return of birds of passage. —**sturz**, *m.* fall backwards, overthrow. —**tritt**, *m.* retreat; return to (*something*); resignation (*of a post*). —**übersetzung**, *f.* retranslation, retroversion. —**umlaut**, *m.* absence of mutation (*in the imperf. of certain weak verbs, e.g.* **nannte** *as compared with* **nennen**). —**vergütung**, *f.* re-payment; (**des Import=Zollbetrages**) cocket. —**versicherung**, *f.* re-insurance, guarantee. —**wälzung**, *f.* rolling back. —**wand**, *f.* back. —**wärts**, *adv.* backward(s), back. —**wärts=lage**, *f.* reclining posture. —**wärts=liegen**, *n.* lying on the back. —**wärts=wirkend**, *adj.* retrospective; reciprocal. —**wechsel**, *m.* return-bill. —**weg**, *m.* return, way back. —**weichung**, *f.* recess. —**wirken**, *v.n.* (*aux.* **h.**) (*insep.*) to react; to have a retrospective force. —**wirkend**, *p.* & *adj.* reactive; retrospective. —**wirkung**, *f.* reaction; **eine —wirkung äußerte sich bald**, a reaction soon took place *or* set in. —**zahlung**, *f.* repayment. —**zoll**, *m.* drawback (*C.L.*). —**zöllig**, *adj.* entitled to drawback. —**zoll=güter**, *pl.* debenture goods. —**zoll=schein**, *m.* debenture. —**zug**, *m.* return; return *or* up-train; retreat (*Mil.*).

Rück'bar, *adj.* movable.

Ru'ckeln, *v.n.* to jerk, bump (*dial.*).

[1]**Rü'cken**, *m.* (—**s**, *pl.* —) back; ridge; bridge (*of the nose*); chine (*of beef*); rear (*Mil.*); reverse (*Fort.*); estrados (*Arch.*); — **an** —, addorsed (*Her.*); **mit dem — gegen einander gekehrt**, back to back; **einem den —en decken**, to cover, protect a p.'s rear; **sich** (*dat.*) **den —en frei halten**, to cover one's retreat; not to commit o.s. absolutely; **einem den — halten**, to back, encourage s.o.; **einen krummen — machen**, to cringe; **auf dem — schwimmen**, to swim *or* float (on one's back); **das Schiff sticht einen —**, the ship becomes cambered; **einem immer auf den — sitzen**, to be always boring *or* worrying a person; **etwas mit dem — ansehen müssen**, to have to give up a thing; **die Thür mit dem — ansehen müssen**, to be turned out of a room *or* a house. *Comp.* —**batterie**, *f.* battery for reverse fire. —**blatt**, *n.* back of an altar-piece *or* of a fireplace, reredos. —**darre**, *f.* spinal disease in which the marrow dries up. —**flosse**, *f.* dorsal fin. —**halter**, *m.* support for the back. —**lehne**, *f.* back of a chair. —**mark**, *m.* spinal marrow. —**marks=kranke(r)**, *m.* spinal patient, patient suffering from a spinal disease. —**ständig**, *adj.* dorsal. —**titel**, *m.* (**eines Buches**) lettering (on the back of a book). —**wind**, *m.* stern wind. —**wirbel**, *m.*, —**wirbel=bein**, *n.* dorsal vertebra.

[2]**Rü'ck—en**, *v.* I. *a.* & *n.* to jerk, pull; to move, stir, push along; to change the place of; to set *or* regulate (*a watch*). II. *n.* (*aux.* **h.** & **s.**) to move, go along; to proceed. march; to

rock, wriggle; **die Arbeit —t,** the work progresses; **näher —en,** to approach; **höher —en,** to rise (*in rank, etc.*); **voran —en,** to advance, go on; **ins Feld —en,** to take the field; **in ein Land —en,** to invade a country. **—er,** *m.* (**—ers,** *pl.* **—er**) advancer; regulating-plate.

Rück'grat, *n.* (*& m.*) backbone, spine, vertebral column. *Comp.* **—s=krümmung,** *f.* spinal curvature, curvature of the spine. **—(s)=los,** *adj.* without a backbone, devoid of character, weak (*fig.*). **—s=schmerz,** *m.* pain in the spine. **—s=tiere,** *pl.* vertebrates, vertebrate animals. **—s=wirbel,** *m.* spinal vertebra.

Ruck'sack, *m.* (**—s,** *pl.* **Rucksäcke**) loose knapsack, wallet (*slung over the shoulder*) (*dial.*).

Ruck'sen, *v.n.* (*aux.* **h.**) to coo (*said of pigeons*).

[1]**Rü'de,** *m.* (**—n,** *pl.* **—n**) large hound; the male of dogs, foxes, wolves.

[2]**Rü'de,** *adj.* rude, coarse; low; brutal.

Ru'del, *n.* (**—s,** *pl.* **—**) flock, herd, troop (*of horses and wild beasts*); egg-whisk; **ein — Rehe,** a herd of deer; **in —n gehen,** to be gregarious. **—n,** *v.r.* to assemble in herds.

Ru'der, *n.* (**—s,** *pl.* **—**) oar; rudder, helm; **am — sein,** to steer, to rule; to be at the helm *or* at the head of affairs; **ans — kommen,** to come into office *or* power. **—er,** *m.* (**—ers,** *pl.* **—er**) rower, sculler. **—ig,** *adj.* (*in comp.* =) -oared. *Comp.* **—bank,** *f.* thwart, sliding seat. **—federn,** *pl.* wing *or* tail feathers. **—fuß,** *m.* webbed foot. **—gat,** *n.* rowlock. **—griff,** *m.* oar-handle. **—knecht,** *m.* rower. **—pinne,** *f.* tiller. **—platte,** *f.* blade of an oar. **—rad=dampfschiff,** *n.* paddle-steamer. **—rad=gehäuse,** *n.* paddle-box. **—schiff,** *n.* galley. **—schlag,** *m.* stroke of the oar. **—schwanz,** *m.* caudal fin. **—sklave,** *m.* galley-slave. **—stange,** *f.* rowing pole. **—stuhl,** *m.* bridge.

Ru'dern, I. *v.a. & n.* (*aux.* **h.** & **s.**) to row; to swim; to use the arms in swimming; **auf Englisch —,** to feather; **lang —,** to pull a long stroke; **rückwärts —,** to back water; **mit den Armen —,** to wave the arms in walking. II. *subst.n.* rowing.

Ruf, *m.* (**—es,** *pl.* **—e**) call; cry; summons; exclamation; fame; vocation, calling; rumour; repute, reputation, character; vogue; **dem —e nach,** by reputation; **von —, im —e,** renowned; reputable; **in — kommen,** to come into fashion, *or* notice; **ein Gelehrter von Welt—,** a scholar of world-wide fame *or* reputation; **er steht in dem —e eines reichen Mannes,** he has the reputation of being a rich man; **der Professor hat einen — nach Berlin erhalten,** the professor has been offered a professorship at Berlin; **einen in den — bringen geizig zu sein** *or* **daß** (*or* **als ob**) **er geizig sei,** to give a p. the reputation of being avaricious; to give a p. a character for avarice; **in — bringen,** to bring into fashion *or* make renowned; **in übeln — bringen,** to defame; **dem guten —e nachteilig,** disreputable. *Comp.* **—glocke,** *f.* (electric) call-bell. **—pfeife,** *f.* bird-call. **—station,** *f.* call-station. **—taste,** *f.* bell-button, call-button. **—weite,** *f.*; **in —weite,** within call *or* earshot.

Ru'f—en, *ir.* (*and obs. and poet. reg.*) *v.a. & n.* (*aux.* **h.**) to call; **er rief mich,** he called me; **wer ruft mir,** who is calling for me? (*poet.*); (*with dat. Swiss dial.*) to call for; to bring about; **einen zu sich —en,** to summon a p.; **ins Gewehr —en,** to call to arms; **einem —en,** to call to a p. (*as warning, etc.*); **der Antrag rief einen längeren Erörterung,** the motion brought about a prolonged discussion (*dial.*); **etwas ins Leben —en,** to start a th.; **einen wieder ins Leben —en,** to recall s.o. to life; **einen —en lassen,** to send for a. p.; **wie gerufen kommen,** to come in the nick of time; **einem etwas ins Gedächtnis —en,** to recall a thing to a p.; **nach der Mutter —en,** to call for one's mother; **um Hülfe —en,** to cry for help. **—er,** *m.* (**—ers,** *pl.* **—er**) crier; caller; speaking-trumpet.

Rüf'fel, *m.* (**—s,** *pl.* **—**) reprimand (*coll.*). **—n,** *v.a.* to reprimand sharply, to blow a p. up (*coll.*).

Rüg'—bar, *adj.*, blamable; punishable; actionable. **—barkeit,** *f.* blamableness. **—e,** *f.* (*pl.* **—en**) censure; reprimand; denunciation; fine, punishment; offence, crime. *Comp.* **—en=amt, —en=gericht,** *n.* (inferior) court of justice, police court. **—en=sache,** *f.* offence to be brought before a **Rügengericht;** misdemeanour.

Rü'gen, *v.a.* to denounce; to reprove; to censure, blame; to punish, fine.

Ru'h—e, *f.* rest, repose; peace, quiet, calm; stillness; sleep; resting-place; fulcrum; rest (*of a gun*); **das Gewehr steht in —e,** the gun is at half-cock; **zur —e bringen,** to hush, calm; **sich zur —e begeben,** to go to rest; **zur —e eingehen,** to go to one's long home; **—e!** silence! **—e, —e!** order, order! **—e seiner Asche!** peace be with him! may he rest in peace! **ohne Rast und —,** restless, restlessly; **weder — noch Rast,** neither peace nor quiet; **sich zur —e setzen,** to retire (*from business, etc.*); **zur —e gesetzt,** retired, pensioned off; **laß mich in —e!** let me alone! **laß mich damit in —e!** don't bother me about that! **—e ist die erste Bürgerpflicht,** to keep the peace is the first duty of a citizen; **keine —e haben vor einem,** to have no peace with a p.; **er hat auf keinem Flecke —e,** he never can stay anywhere. **Sie werden uns doch die —e nicht mitnehmen,** I trust you will rest a little before you go; **einem eine angenehme —e wünschen,** to wish s.o. a good night; **er ist nicht aus seiner —e zu bringen,** nothing disturbs his equanimity.

Ru'h—en, *v.n.* (*aux.* **h.**) to rest, repose, sleep; to rest, pause; to be still; to lie fallow; **hier —t,** here lies; **sanft —e seine Asche!** may he rest in peace! **ich werde nicht eher —en als,** I shall not rest until; **ich wünsche Ihnen wohl zu —en,** I wish you a good night; **ich wünsche Ihnen wohl geruht zu haben,** good day, I hope you have slept well! **lasset die Toten —en!** let the dead be! **wir wollen die Sache jetzt —en lassen,** we will now leave the matter, let the matter drop for the present; **auf einer S. —en,** to be based on a th.; **nach der Arbeit ist gut —en,** rest is pleasant after work (*prov.*). **—end,** *p. & adj.* resting; quiescent; **—endes Kapital,** unused, uninvested capital. **—ig,** *adj. & adv.* quiet, tranquil, still; serene, peaceful; composed; **seien Sie (deshalb) —ig,** do not trouble about that; **bei —igem Blute, —iger Überlegung,** on reflection; **immer —ig Blut,** keep cool! steady! **—ig, Kinder!** silence! hush! *Comp.* **—e=bank,** *f.* couch, resting-place. **—e=bett,** *n.* sofa, couch. **—e=feld,** *n.* fallow field. **—e=geber,** *m.* consoler. **—e=gehalt,** *n.* retiring allowance, pension. **—e=kammer,** *f.* sleeping-room; the grave. **—e=kissen,** *n.* pillow. **—e=los,** *adj.* restless; changeable. **—e=losigkeit,** *f.* restlessness. **—e=ort, —e=platz,** *m.*, **—e=statt, —e=stätte,** *f.* resting-place. **—e=punkt,** *m.* centre of gravity; rest, pause (*Mus.*); cæsura; fulcrum; resting-place. **—e=sessel,** *m.* easy-chair. **—e=sitz,** *m.* bench (*in a garden, etc.*); retreat, retirement. **—e=stand,** *m.* state of rest; retired list; **in den —estand versetzen,** to superannuate; **in den —estand treten,** to retire (*from business or an office*), to resign (*a post*); **in den —estand versetzt werden,** to be retired (*compulsorily*). **—e=störung,** *f.* breach of the peace, disturbance, riot. —e=strom, *m.* continuous current. —e=stunde, *f.* hour of rest, leisure hour. —e=tag, *m.* day of rest; sabbath; holiday. —e=voll, *adj.* tranquil, peaceful. —e=zeichen, *n.* pause, rest (*Mus.*). —e=zeit, *f.* rest, leisure time.

Ruhm, *m.* (—es) glory; honour; fame; renown; reputation (*obs.*); sein — ist nicht fein, his reputation is not too good; den — muß man ihm lassen, daß . . ., it must be said in his favour, to his credit, that . . .; einem zum —e gereichen, to redound to a p.'s honour; es sich (*dat.*) zum —e machen, to take pride in, make it one's boast; wir sind euer —, gleichwie auch ihr unser — seid, we are your rejoicing, even as ye also are ours (*B.*). *Comp.* —be=deckt, *adj.* covered with glory. —(be)gier(de), *f.* desire of glory, ambition. —(be)gierig, *adj.* desirous of glory, ambitious. —es=halle, *f.*, —es=tempel, *m.* temple of fame, pantheon. —es=titel, *m.* claim to glory. —los, *adj.* inglorious, without fame. —redig, *adj.* vainglorious, boastful. —reich, *adj.* glorious. —sucht, *f.* passion for glory *or* fame. —voll, *adj.* famous, glorious. —würdig, *adj.* praiseworthy, glorious.

Rühm—en, I. *v.a.* to praise, extol, celebrate, glorify; to mention with praise; man —t ihn als tapfer, he is said to be brave; sich —en, to boast, blow one's own trumpet; sich einer Sache, sich mit *or* wegen etwas —en, to glory in, boast of, plume o.s. on a th.; ohne mich zu —en, without boasting; ich —e mich, sein Freund zu sein, I am proud to call myself his friend. II. *v.n.* to exult, shout with joy (*B.*). III. *subst.n.*; viel —ens (von einer S.) machen, to speak in very high terms (of a th.). —er, *m.* (—ers, *pl.* —er) praiser; boaster. —lich, *adj.* & *adv.* laudable, praiseworthy, glorious; honourable. —lichkeit, *f.* glory, gloriousness.

Ruhr, *f.* diarrhœa; dysentery; last ploughing *or* dressing (*of land*); weiße —, diarrhœa; rote —, dysentery. —en, *v.a.* to give the last dressing (*to land*). *Comp.* —anfall, *m.* attack of dysentery. —artig, *adj.* diarrhœtic. —krank, *adj.* suffering from dysentery.

Rührbar, *adj.* movable; impressible, sensitive; emotional. —keit, *f.* susceptibility.

Rüh'r—en, I. *v.n.*; —en an (*acc.*), to touch; —en in (*acc.*), to stir in *or* up; davon —t der Gebrauch her, hence the custom. II. *v.a.* to stir, move; to touch, to strike; to set in motion; to beat (*a drum*); to move (*the feelings*), affect; to beat *or* stir up; to turn up (*the ground*); to rake (*hay, etc.*); to temper, mix (*mortar*); kein Glied —en können, not to be able to move; vom Schlage gerührt, seized with apoplexy, seized with an apoplectic fit; vom Donner gerührt, thunderstruck; Sahne —en, to whip cream. III. *v.r.* to stir, move; to bestir oneself, be active, be up and doing; es —t sich sein Gewissen, his conscience pricks him; —t euch! bestir yourselves; be quick! stand at ease (*Mil.*); das —t mich nicht, that makes no impression on me. IV. *subst.n.* = —ung, *f.* affection; ein menschliches —en, human affection *or* feeling. —end, *p.* & *adj.* stirring, *etc.*; moving, touching, affecting, pathetic. —ig, *adj.* & *adv.* stirring; active; nimble, agile. —igkeit, *f.* activity; agility; stirring disposition. —ung, *f.* moving, stirring; feeling, emotion; sympathy; unter —ung der Trommeln, with drums beating. *Comp.* —ei, *n.* beaten-up egg; (*pl.*) scrambled eggs, buttered eggs. —faß, *n.* churn. —haken, *m.* stirring-pole. —kartoffeln, *pl.* mashed potatoes. —kelle, *f.* stirring-ladle; pot-ladle. —krücke, *f.* plumber's rake; mash-rake (*Brew.*). —kübel, *m.* mason's trough. —löffel, *m.* see —kelle. —mich=nicht=an, *n.* noli me tangere (*Bot.*); touchy person. —milch, *f.* buttermilk. —stange, *f.* paddle, rake (*Metal.*). —stück, *n.* pathetic, sensational piece; melodrama.

Rui'n, *m.* (—s) ruin, downfall, decay. —e, *f.* (*pl.* —en) ruins, a ruin. —en=haft, *adj.* tumble-down, in ruins, dilapidated. —ie'ren, *v.a.* to ruin, destroy.

Rülps, *m.* (—(s)es, *pl.* —(s)e) eructation, belch; lout. —(s)en, *v.n.* (*aux.* h.) to belch.

'Rum, *coll. for* Herum (Umher). *Often in compds.*: seht euch nicht um, der Plumpsack geht —, don't look round, the knot is passing round! (*a game*).

[1]**Rum'mel**, *m.* (—s) uproar, hubbub, row; noise, din, rumble; old lumber; der ganze —, the whole lot (*coll.*); im — kaufen, to buy in the lump, in the gross; er versteht den —, he knows what's what, he is pretty sharp (*coll.*). —ei', *f.* rumbling noise, old (*piece of*) lumber.

[2]**Rum'mel**, *m.* (—s, *pl.* —) point (*at piquet*).

Rum'meln, *v.n.* (*aux.* h.) to make a rumbling noise; (*aux.* s.) to rumble.

Rumo'r, *m.* (—s, *pl.* —e) rumour; noise, uproar. —en, *v.n.* (*aux.* h.) to make a noise *or* row.

Rumpelei', *f.* see Gerumpel.

Rum'p(e)lig, *adj.* see Holperig.

Rum'pel—n, *v.* I. *n.* (*aux.* h. & s.) to rumble, to jolt. II. *a.*; Alles durcheinander —n, to turn everything topsy-turvy. *Comp.* —kammer, *f.* lumber-room; carriage without springs *or* with bad springs; ästhetische —kammer, lumber-room of antiquated art theories. —kasten, *m.* lumber-chest; rumbling old coach; tumble-down (*of houses*); worn-out piano.

Rumpf, *m.* (—es, *pl.* Rüm'pfe) trunk (*of a tree, etc.*); body (*of a man, etc.*; *of a machine*; *of a shirt*); carcass (*of a fowl*); torso; hull (*of a vessel*); — des Hochofens, blast-furnace; mit — und Stumpf, root and branch, altogether, completely. *Comp.* —beuge, *f.* bending the body. —beugen=und=strecken, *n.* gymnastics for exercising the trunk of the body. —parlament, *n.* Rump Parliament (*1648 in London*; *1849 in Stuttgart*).

Rümp'fen, *v.a.* to wrinkle, pucker, curl; die Nase —, to sneer, to turn up one's nose.

Rund, I. *adj.* & *adv.* round; rotund, circular, spherical; smooth, flowing; bold, decisive; frank; puzzling; —es Geld, specie; eine —e Summe, a round sum; gib mir auf meine —e Frage eine —e Antwort, give me a plain answer to a plain question; —es Kleid, a round skirt (without a train); —e Zahl, round number; eine —e volle Stunde, a good hour; etwas — machen, to terminate a matter satisfactorily, bring s.th. about; das ist mir zu —, that is beyond me, too deep for me; — heraus, in plain terms; straight out; — und nett, plainly and bluntly; — abschlagen, to refuse flatly; — heraus gesagt, to speak plainly; zehn Meilen — umher, ten miles round. II. *n.* (—es, *pl.* —e) round object; globe, orb, sphere, circle; Erden —, face of the earth, terrestrial globe. —a, *n.* (*pl.* —as) burden of a folksong *or* students' song; song sung in chorus; short folksong (*dial.*). —e, *f.* round, circle; circular motion, rotation; circular dance; patrol, beat, rounds; die —e gehen, to go the rounds (*Mil.*); zehn Meilen in die —e, ten miles round; das Glas die —e machen (*or* in der [die] —e gehen) lassen, to pass round the glass; in der —e, around, round about. —heit, —igkeit, *f.* see Ründe. —lich, *adj.* roundish; plump; arched. —lichkeit, *f.* rotundity. *Comp.* —bäckig, *adj.* round-cheeked. —bau, *m.* circular building. —bogen, *m.* round arch, semicircular arch. —erhaben, *adj.*

convex. —fahrt, f.; eine —fahrt machen, to drive or sail round, to make a circular tour. —falte, f. puff. —gang, m. round (Mil., etc.); rotation, revolution. —gebäude, n. rotunda. —gedicht, n. roundelay. —gemälde, n. panorama. —gesang, m. round, roundelay, glee; catch. —hohl, adj. concave. —höhlung, f. concavity. —lauf, m. circular motion; orbit (of planets); circulation (of the blood, etc.); tour. —reim, m. refrain, burden (of a song). —reise, f. circular tour; circuit. —reise-billet, n., —reise-karte, f. circular (tour) ticket. —säge, f. circular saw. —säule, f. column; cylinder. —schau, m. panorama; review; politische —schau, political review or chronicle; litterarische —schau, literary review or magazine. —schreiben, n. circular; round robin. —stück, n. circular space or lawn; round cake, bun. —tanz, m. round dance. —um, adv. round about. —wacht, f. patrol. —weg, I. m. covered way (Fort.). II. adv. flatly, plainly. —werk, n. sculpture; roundel (Fort.). —zirkel, m. callipers.

Rün'd—e, f. roundness; rotundity; sphericity; curve (of an arch); finish. —en, see Runden. —ung, f. see Rundung.

Run'd—en, v.a. to make round, to round off; to finish; die Lippen —en, to round or protrude the lips (as in pronouncing Engl. oo, Germ. u), to labialize (Phonet.). —ung, f. rounding, curve; labialization, protruding (of lips); roundness; round thing; round; circular path; arch.

Ru'n—e, f. (pl. —en) rune, runic letter. —isch, adj. runic. Comp. —en-schrift, f. runic writing or characters; runic inscription. —en-stab, m. small piece of (beech) wood on which runic letters were scratched. —en-stein, m. runic stone, stone covered with runic writing.

Run'ge, f. rung (of a ladder); bolt, pin; brake.

Run'kel, Run'kelrübe, f. beet(-root).

'Run'ter, coll. for Herunter (Hinunter); often in comp'ds. —langen, v.a.; einem eine —langen, to give a p. a box on the ear (sl.).

Run'zel, f. (pl. —n) wrinkle, pucker, fold; —n um die Augen, crows' feet. —ig, adj. wrinkled; shrivelled. Comp. —häutig, adj. wrinkled.

Run'zeln, v.a. & n. (aux. h.) to wrinkle; to shrivel; die Stirn —, to knit the brows, to frown.

Rü'pel, m. (—s, pl. —) swarthy person; lout; der Junge ist ein rechter —, he is a regular boor, hobbledehoy, he is a most unmannerly boy. —ei', f. grossness; rudeness. —ig, —haft, adj. boorish, unmannerly.

Rup'f—en, v.a. to pluck, pull, pick; einen —en, to fleece a p.; sein Hühnchen —en, to feather one's nest; ein Hühnchen mit einem zu —en haben, to have a bone to pick with a p. (coll.). —er, m. (—ers, pl. —er) plucker (of fowls); (pl.) preliminary labour(-pains) (Med.). Comp. —wolle, f. wool in flocks.

Rupie', f. (pl. —n) rupee.

Rup'p—ig, adj. ragged, shabby; mean, niggardly. Comp. —sack, m. ragamuffin, mean fellow.

Rusch, m. (—es, pl. —e, Rü'sche) rush, reed; — und Busch, briars and brushwood.

Rü'sche (long ü), f. (pl. —n) ruche, ruching.

Ru'schel, m. (—s, pl. —) heedless person. —ig, adj. fidgety; hasty. Comp. —kopf, m. harum-scarum (coll.).

Ru'scheln, Ru'schen, Rü'schen, v.n. (aux. h.) to rush; to rustle, to be fidgety; to do hastily or carelessly.

Ruß, m. (—es, pl. —e) soot, smoke-black; thick foggy air (fig.). —ig, adj. sooty; —iges Silbererz, black silver ore. Comp. —braun, n., —farbe, f. bistre. —farbe, f. soot-colour, lamp-black. —kreide, f. black chalk. —schwarz, n. lamp-black.

Ru'ßen, v.a. to soot, smut, blacken.

Rüs'sel, m. (—s, pl. —) snout; trunk, proboscis. —icht (obs.), —ig, adj. proboscis-like; snouted. Comp. —tiere, pl. proboscidians.

Rüs'te, see Ruhe; zu or zur — gehen, to sink, to set (of the sun); to expire.

Rüs't—en, v. I. a. to prepare; to prepare for war; to fit out, equip, array, arm; sich —en zu, to prepare for; sich zum Kriege —en, to arm. II. n. (aux. h.) to make preparations, get ready (auf or zu, for); to put up a scaffolding; die Franzosen —en, the French are arming; zum Essen —en, to lay the cloth, to set the table. —er, m. (—ers, pl. —er) armer, equipper. —ig, adj. & adv. strong, vigorous, robust, active. —igkeit, f. vigour, activity. —ung, f. preparations (for war, a feast, etc.); arming, equipment; armour, armament; implements, apparatus; fowler's tackle; scaffolding; cross-bow; armature (of a magnet); in voller —ung, fully armed; vollständige —ung, suit of armour; complete armament. Comp. —haus, n. arsenal. —holz, n. prop, shore (Min.). —kammer, f. armoury; arsenal. —meister, m. overseer of an arsenal. —nägel, pl. scaffolding nails. —saal, m. armoury. —tag, m. day of preparation. —wagen, m. munition or baggage-waggon. —woche, f. Holy Week. —zeug, n. armour; tools, implements; crane; arms; auserwähltes —zeug, chosen vessel (of the Lord) (B.).

Rü'ster, f. (pl. —n) elm; maple (dial.). —n, adj. of elm.

Ru'te, f. (pl. —n) rod; switch; chastisement; pole, rod (as measure); brush (of foxes); penis (Anat.); er hat sich eine — auf den Rücken gebunden, he has made a rod for his own back; einem Kinde die — geben, to whip a child. Comp. —n-bündel, n. fasces, bundle of rods. —n-fischer, m. angler. —n-förmig, adj. virgate. —n-lang, adj. of the length of a rod. —n-schlag, —n-streich, m. stripe, stroke with a rod. —n-schwinger, m. wielder of the cane, schoolmaster (hum.).

Rutsch, m. (—es, pl. —e) push, shove; fall, slide, landslip; im —(e), in a trice. —e, f. sliding roller, slide. —en, I. v.n. (aux. h. & s.) to slide, glide, slip; zur Seite —en, to skid (cycl.). II. subst. glissade (mount.). —er, m. (—ers, pl. —er) slider; gallop (Danc.); aufs Land —en, to make an excursion into the country (coll.); die Sache —t, the affair is progressing. —er, m. (—ers, pl. —er) slider; gallop (Danc.). Comp. —bahn, f. slide. —partie, f.; eine —partie machen, to make a short strip.

Rüt't—eln, v.a. & n. (aux. h.) to shake; to jog, jolt; to winnow (corn); to press the seams (of gloves); gerüttelt voll, heaped; ein gerüttelt und geschüttelt Maß, a full or good measure. Comp. —stroh, n. loose straw, litter.

S

S, s, n. S, s; as abbr. S. = 1. Seite, page, folio; 2. (or St.) Sankt, saint; s. = siehe, see; s. = sive, or; 's = 1. das, as, ins Haus gehen, to go into the house; 2. es, as, geht's nicht? won't it do?

Sa, int. ho! hullo! courage! cheer up!

Saal, m. (—(e)s, pl. Säle, dimin. Säl'chen) hall, room, saloon; drawing-room; Tanz—, ball-room; Empfangs—, reception room; Vorlesungs—, lecture room; Speise—, dining-room. Comp. —einrichtung, f. furniture and decoration of a room. —theater, *n.* private theatre.

Saat, *f.* (*pl.* —en) sowing; seed; standing corn; green crops; die — steht schön, the crops look well; in — schießen, to run to seed; in — geschossen, run *or* gone to seed. *Comp.* —bestellung, *f.* sowing. —egge, *f.* seed-harrow. —feld, *n.* field sown with corn; corn-field. —gurke, *f.* cucumber. —hanf, *m.* seed hemp. —huhn, *n.* golden plover. —jahr, *see* Sabbat(h)=jahr. —kartoffel, *f.* seed-potato. —korn, *n.* seed(-*corn*), corn for sowing. —krähe, *f.* rook. —krähen=geniste, *n.* rookery. —lerche, *f.* skylark. —reihe, *f.* drill (*for seed*). —schote, *f.* seed-pod. —zeit, *f.* seed-time, sowing time.

Sab'bat(h), *m.* (—(e)s, *pl.* —e) sabbath; Sunday; den — heiligen, to keep the Sabbath; den — entheiligen, to break the Sabbath. —a'rier, *m.* (—ariers, *pl.* —arier) sabbatarian. —lich, I. *adj.* sabbatical. II. *adv.* every sabbath. *Comp.* —jahr, *n.* sabbatical year (among the Jews). —ruhe, *f.* Sabbath rest *or* quiet, Sunday rest. —schänder, *m.* sabbath-breaker. —tag, *m.* Sabbath, Sunday.

Sä'bar, *adj.* sowable.

Sab'b—eln, —en, —ern, *v.n.* (*aux.* h.) to slaver, drivel. —erei', *f.* slavering. —eler, —erer, *m.* (—erers, *pl.* —erer) slaverer; babbler. *Comp.* —el=fritz, *m.*, —el=liſe, *f.*, —el=matz, *m.* babbler. —el=pichel, *m.*, —el=tuch, *n.* (slobbering-)bib.

Sä'bel, *m.* (—s, *pl.* —) sabre, broadsword; kurzer —, cutlass; krummer —, scimitar. —n, *v.a.* to sabre; to cut *or* carve awkwardly; to carve too big slices. *Comp.* —bajonett, *n.* sword-bayonet. —bein, *n.* bow-leg. —beinig, *adj.* bandy-legged, bow-legged. —duell, *n.*, —mensur, *f.* duel with broadswords. —fisch, *m.* swordfish. —gefäß, *n.* sword-hilt. —gehenk, *n.* sword-belt. —hieb, *m.* sword-cut. —klinge, *f.* sabre-blade; scimitar-blade. —koppel, *f.* sword-belt. —korb, *m.* basket-hilt. —scheide, *f.* sabre-sheath, scabbard. —tasche, *f.* sabretache. —troddel, *f.* sword-knot.

Sa'bul, *m.* *hum. for* Säbel.

Sa'ch—e, *f.* (*pl.* —en) thing; cause; action, case; matter, affair, business, concern; event; fact; circumstance; (*pl.*) goods, furniture, luggage, clothes, *etc.*; (*pl.*) goings-on; was ist an der —e? is there anything in it? how much truth is there in it? das ist seine —e, that is his affair, that is his look-out (*coll.*); meine sieben —en, my belongings, bag and baggage, my goods and chattels; seine sieben —en packen, to pack up; to decamp; eine —e führen, to plead a cause; in —en des M. N., in the case of M. N. (*Law*); zur —e! to the point! to the business! Question (*Parl.*)! zur —e kommen, to come to the point; stets bei der —e bleiben, to stick to the point; seiner —e gewiß sein, to know what one is about; die —e ist, the fact is; gemeinschaftliche —e, common cause; die —e verhält sich so, the matter stands thus; so steht die —e, that 's how the matter stands; ich muß wissen, was an der —e ist, I must know how the matter stands, what is the truth of the matter; mit ganzer Seele bei der —e sein, to be heart and soul in a thing; nicht bei der —e sein, to be absent-minded; die —en gehen lassen, die —e laufen lassen wie sie läuft, to let things slide; nichts zur —e thun, to have nothing to do with the subject, to be irrelevant, beside the mark, to make no difference; unverrichteter —e zurückkommen, to return without having accomplished anything; die vorliegende —e, the subject in question; allerhand —en, all kinds of things; es ist nicht deine —e, an so etwas zu denken, you have no business to think of such things; kümmere dich um deine —en, mind your own business; lügen ist seine —e nicht, he is not given to lying, he hates lying; es ist nicht meine —e, mich in die —en anderer zu mischen, I am not fond of meddling with other people's affairs; jede — hat zwei Seiten, there are two sides to every question *or* to everything; seine —e auf nichts gestellt haben, to let things take their chance. —lich, *adj. & adv.* real, essential; pertinent; to the point; positive; objective. —lichkeit, *f.* reality, essentiality, objectivity. *Comp.* —bemerkung, *f.* remark to the point, pertinent remark. —beweis, *m.* objective proof. —dienlich, *adj.* relevant, pertinent, apt. —erfahren, *adj.* expert, versed in; professional. —erklärung, *f.* explanation of the thing; real definition. —fällig, *adj.* unsuccessful (*in a lawsuit*). —führer, *m.* agent; authorized representative; *see* —walter. —gedächtnis, *n.* memory for facts. —kenner, *m.* expert, connoisseur. —kenntnis, *f.* special knowledge (*of a subject*), knowledge of an expert. —klage, *f.* real action. —kundig, *adj.* *see* —erfahren. —lage, *f.* state of affairs. —register, *n.* table of contents, index. —reich, *adj.* copious, full of facts, circumstantial. —verhältnis, *n.*, —verhalt, *m.* circumstances, state of the case. —verständig, *adj.* versed, expert; ein —verständiger, a competent judge, an expert. —vorlage, *f.* statement. —walter, *m.* counsel, legal adviser, solicitor, attorney. —waltung, *f.* management. —wert, *m.* real value. —wort, *n.* substantive, noun. —wörterbuch, *n.* dictionary of general information, encyclopædia.

Sä'ch—elchen, *n.* (—elchens, *pl.* —elchen) little thing; (*pl.*) pretty little things. —lich, *adj.* neuter (*Gram.*).

Sach't(e), I. *adj. & adv.* soft, gentle, light; slow. II. *adv.* by degrees; cautiously; gently.

Sack, *m.* (—es, *pl.* —, Säcke) sack, bag; sac; purse; pocket; pucker (*in a dress, etc.*); pack (*of wool*); budget (*of news*); blind alley; sackcloth (*B.*); loose garment; zwanzig — Korn, twenty sacks of corn; zwanzig leere Säcke, twenty empty sacks; mit — und Pack, with bag and baggage, in heavy marching order; in — und Asche trauern, to mourn in sackcloth and ashes; einem den — geben, to send a p. away; einen in den — thun, to get the better of a p.; einen in den — stecken, to get s. o. into one's power; to do better than a p.; voll wie ein —, dead drunk; eine Katze im —e kaufen, to buy a pig in a poke; sie hat ihn zweimal im —e, she is worth two of him; einen im — haben, to have a p. in one's clutches; eine Faust im —e machen, to bear a secret grudge against s. o.; Lachen und Weinen in einem —e haben, to laugh and cry in one breath; den — schlagen und den Esel meinen, to strike one person through the other; viele Säcke sind des Esels Tod, too many sacks are the death of the ass; it 's the last straw that breaks the camel's back (*prov.*). —en, *v.* I. *a.* to sack, bag, pocket; to seize greedily upon; to stuff (*one's mouth, etc.*) with. II. *r.* to form a sac; to pucker, bag. *Comp.* —band, *n.* sack-string; purse-string. —drillich, *m.* drilling. —frucht, *f* sporangium. —garn, *n.* bag-net; *see* —zwirn. —gasse, *f.* blind-alley. —geige, *f.* pocket-fiddle. —geschwulst, *f.* encysted tumour. —grob, *adj.* exceedingly rude, like a bear. —hüpfen, *n.* sack-race, racing in sacks. —leinwand, *f.* sack-cloth, sacking. —nadel, *f.* packing needle. —netz, *n.* bag-net. —pfeife, *f.* bagpipe; auf der —pfeife gespielte Melodie pibroch. —pistole, *f.*, —puffer, *m.* pocket-pistol. —tuch, *n.* sacking; pocket-handkerchief. —tüchlein, *n.* pocket-handkerchief. —träger, *m.*; ein Esel schilt den andern —träger, the pot calls the kettle black. —weise, *adv.* by bagfuls. —zwillich, *m.* drilling. —zwirn, *m.* pack-thread.

Säck'—chen, *n.* (—chens, *pl.* —chen) little bag. —el, *see* Seckel. —en, *v.a.* to put in a bag; to drown in a sack.

¹**Sa'cken,** *v.a.* to put into sacks, to bag.

²**Sa'ck—en,** *v.r.* & *n.* (*aux.* h.) to sink, give way; sich —en, to settle (down); to get baggy. —ung, *f.* settlement (*of embankments, etc.*).

Sackerlo't! Sackerme'nt! *int.* the deuce! bother(ation)!

Sä'—en, *v.a.* & *n.* (*aux.* h.) to sow; mit der Hand —en, to sow broadcast. —er, *m.* (—ers, *pl.* —er) sower. *Comp.* —mann, *m.* sower. —maschine, *f.* sowing-machine, drill-plough. —tuch, *n.* seed-bag *or* cloth. —wetter, *n.* (gutes) (good) sowing weather. —zeit, *f.* seed-time.

Saf'fian, *m.* (—s, *pl.* —e) morocco leather.

Saf'(f)lor, *m.* (—s, *pl.* —e) safflower, bastard saffron. *Comp.* —rot, *adj.* safflower extract, carthamine.

Saf'ran, (—s, *pl.* —e) saffron. *Comp.* —farben, —farbig, *adj.* saffron-coloured, saffrony.

Saft, *m.* (—es, *pl.* Säf'te) juice; sap; syrup; liquor, moisture; humour (*Med.*); voll —, succulent; im — stehen, to be in sap; weder — noch Kraft haben, to be without strength *or* savour, to have no energy *or* backbone, stale, insipid; — der Beeren = Wein. —ig, *adj.* juicy, luscious, succulent; obscene (*vulg.*); thorough, goodly (*coll.*); eine —ige Ohrfeige, a good box on the ear; eine —ige Anekdote, a spicy anecdote. —igkeit, *f.* juiciness, succulence. *Comp.* —behälter, *m.* nectary (*Bot.*). —gang, *m.*, —gefäß, *n.* sap-duct; lacteal vessel. —grün, *n.* sap-green. —los, *adj.* sapless, juiceless; insipid. —pflanze, *f.* succulent plant. —reich, *adj.* juicy, succulent. —ring, *m.* sap-ring, annual circle. —röhre, *f.* sap-tube. —voll, *adj.* juicy, succulent. —zeit, *f.* spring-time.

Sag'bar, *adj.* utterable, expressable; es ist nicht —, wie . . ., I cannot tell you how . . .

Sa'ge, *f.* (*pl.* —n) saying; report, rumour; tale; fable, saga, legend; tradition; es geht die —, the story goes, it is rumoured.

Sä'ge, *f.* (*pl.* —n) saw. *Comp.* —blatt, *n.* blade of a saw. —block, *m.* log. —bock, *m.* sawing-trestle. —fisch, *m.* saw-fish. —förmig, *adj.* serrated. —gestell, *n.* saw-frame. —grube, *f.* saw-pit. —maschine, *f.* mechanical saw, sawing machine. —mehl, *n.* sawdust. —müller, *m.* owner *or* manager of a saw-mill. —schmied, *m.* maker of saws. —schnitt, *m.* kerf. —späne, *pl.* sawdust. —werk, *n.* saw-mill; serrated line; redan (*Fort.*). —zähnig, *adj.* serrate; —zähniger Rand, serrated edge.

Sa'g—en, I. *v.a.* to say, tell; to speak; to pronounce, declare, propose; to offer; to command; to mean; ich kann wohl —en, I may (well) say; einem —en lassen, to send a p. word; ich ließ mir das nicht zweimal —en, I jumped at it, I did not wait to be told twice; nun, das muß ich —en, well, I declare; indeed; wie man so zu —en pflegt, as the saying is; ich habe mir —en lassen, I am *or* have been told; was ich —en wollte, what I was going to say; er ist reich, wohlhabend, wollte ich —en, he is rich, I mean comfortably off; was Sie nicht —en! you don't say so! was —t man Neues? what is the news? das will ich nicht gesagt haben, I did not mean that, I don't wish it to be thought that I said that; ich will nichts gesagt haben, don't take what I have said into account; das —t man nicht, that is not to be said, that should not be said, that is not proper to say! man —t ihn tot, they say he is dead; gut —en für, to be responsible for; Dank —en, to thank; es hat nichts zu —en, it does not signify, it is not dangerous; das will nichts —en, that 's nothing; that 's of no consequence; das ist viel gesagt, that is saying a great deal; wenn ich etwas zu —en hätte, if I had any influence, anything to say in the matter; er kann von Glück —en, he may count himself lucky; das —en Sie, you are pleased to say so; das —en Sie nur so! you don't mean it! lassen Sie sich etwas —en, believe me; laß dir das gesagt sein, let it be a warning to you; es läßt sich nicht —en, there is no saying; er läßt sich (*dat.*) nichts —en, he will listen to no advice *or* to no one; Sie haben mir nichts zu —en, you have no right to give me orders; auf eine Bitte Nein —en, to refuse (*to comply with*) a request; auf alles etwas zu —en wissen, to be quick at repartee, to have an answer to everything, to be ready with an answer; wenn es nur eine Stunde vorher gesagt wird, at an hour's notice; gesagt, gethan, no sooner said than done; unter uns gesagt, between you and me, in confidence; beiläufig gesagt, by the way; richtiger gesagt, properly speaking, to speak more correctly; wie gesagt, as I said; er ist, offen (*or* gerade heraus) gesagt, ein Spitzbube, he is, to put it plainly, a thorough scoundrel; das Gesagte bleibt unter uns, you will not let things go any further, what I have said remains between ourselves. II. *subst.n.* saying, *etc.*; seinem —en nach, according to him. —enhaft, *adj.* legendary, mythical; traditional; ein —enhafter Held, a hero of romance. *Comp.* —en=buch, *n.* collection of popular legends *or* sagas. —en=dichtung, *f.* legendary poetry, poetry based on heroic legends. —en=forscher, *m.* student of popular legends. —en=forschung, *f.* study of legendary lore, folk-lore, investigation of popular legends. —en=geschichte, *f.* legendary history, folk-lore. —en=kreis, *m.* legendary cycle, great epic cycle (*of the Middle Ages*). —en=kunde, *f.* legendary lore; folk-lore. —en=kundige(r), *m.* one versed in legendary lore, student of popular traditions; folk-lorist. —en=reich, *adj.* rich in (popular) legends and traditions. —en=schatz, *m.* legends; folk-lore. —en=zeit, *f.* legendary, heroic age; fabulous age; mythical period.

Sä'g—en, *v.a.* & *n.* (*aux.* h.) to saw. —er, *m.* (—ers, *pl.* —er) sawyer, sawer.

Sa'go, *m.* (—s) sago, tapioca. *Comp.* —grütze, *f.*, —mehl, *n.* sago-flour.

Sah, Sä'he, *1 pers. imperf. indic.* & *subj. of* sehen.

Sa(h)l— (*in comp.*) —band, *n.* selvage; border; fag-end. —weide, *f.* Salix caprea (*Bot.*).

Sah'n—e, *f.* cream. —en, *v.* I. *a.* to skim the cream off; to fill with cream. II. *r.* to form a cream. —ig, *adj.* creamy. *Comp.* —en=kuchen, *m.* cream tart. —en=käse, *m.* cream cheese. —en=reich, *adj.* creamy.

Sai'gern, *see* Seigern.

Sai't—e, *f.* (*pl.* —en) string, chord (*of a violin, etc.*); besponnene —en, silver strings; die —en ändern, to change one's tone; strenge —en aufziehen, to assume a tone of severity, to become strict *or* severe; die —en zu hoch spannen, to take too high a tone, assume too much; gelindere —en aufziehen, to lower one's tone, to become more lenient, to come down a peg; in die —en fallen, to touch the chords; die —en schlagen *or* rühren, to touch the chords, to strike the chords. —ig, *adj.* stringed. *Comp.* —en=bezug, *m.* set of strings. —en=brett, *n.* sounding-board; *see*

—enhalter. —en=draht, m. piano-wire. —en=halter, —en=fessel, m. tail-piece (*of a violin, etc.*); the part of an instrument to which the strings are fastened. —en=instrument, n. string instrument, stringed instrument. —en=klang, m. music of strings, harp. —en=spiel, n. lyre; string music. —en=spieler, m. player on a string instrument, lute-player.

Sakrame'nt, n. (—(e)s, *pl.* —e) sacrament; consecrated host. —lich, *adj. & adv.* sacramental. *Comp.* —s=häuschen, n. tabernacle.

Sakrist—a'n, m. (—ans, *pl.* —ane) sacristan, sexton. —ei', *f.* vestry.

Säkula'r, *adj.* secular. —isie'ren, *v.a.* to secularize. *Comp.* —feier, *f.* centenary.

Salaman'der, m. salamander; einen — reiben (auf einen), to drink a p.'s health with due ceremony (*stud. sl.*); Feuer—, salamander.

Sal—ä'r, n. (—ärs, *pl.* —äre) salary. —arie'=ren, *v.a.* (einen) to pay a salary to a person.

Sala't, m. (—(e)s, *pl.* —e) salad; lettuce; den — anmachen, to dress the salad; da haben wir den —, we are in a nice mess! a pretty kettle of fish! (*coll.*). *Comp.* —beet, n. bed of lettuce. —blatt, n. leaf of lettuce. —bohne, *f.* French bean. —kopf, m. head of lettuce. —schüssel, *f.* salad bowl.

Sal'bader, m. (—s, *pl.* —) tedious proser, prater, bore; quack. —ei', *f.* interminable talking; twaddle. —n, *v.n.* (*aux.* h.) to prate, talk foolishly and tediously, drivel.

Sal'b—e, *f.* (*pl.* —en) ointment, salve, embrocation; scented oil, pomade; coating for a ship's bottom. *Comp.* —öl, n. anointing oil.

Sal'b—en, *v.a.* to anoint; to rub with ointment; to embalm; einem die Hände —en, to bribe a p. (*fig.*). —ung, *f.* anointing; unction. *Comp.* —en=büchse, *f.* ointment-box. —ungs=reich, —ungs=voll, *adj.* unctuous.

Sal'bei, m. (—s, *pl.* —e), *f.* (*pl.* —en) sage (*Bot.*). *Comp.* —strauch, m. sage-plant.

Sälb'ling, Säl'm'ling, m. (—s, *pl.* —e) salmon-trout.

Sald—ie'ren, *v.a.* to pay, balance, settle; to strike a balance; durch Gegenrechnung —iert, counterbalanced by. —ie'rung, *f.* balancing, settlement. —o (*pron.* Sal'do), n. (—os, *pl.* —os) balance of an account; —o vorgetragen, balance carried forward; —o zu unseren Gunsten, balance in our favour; per —o trassieren, to draw per appoint; per —o quittieren, to receipt in full. *Comp.* —ier'=buch, n. balance-book. —o=betrag, m. amount of balance. —o=guthaben, n. balance (in favour). —o=übertrag, m. balance from former account, amount carried forward. —o=vortrag, n. transfer of balance to new account. —o=wechsel, m. balance-draft, draft for the balance. —o=zahlung, *f.* payment per appoint, payment to square.

Salicylie'ren, *v.a.* to impregnate with salicylic acid.

Salicyl'säure, *f.* salicylic acid.

Sali'n—e, *f.* (*pl.* —en) salt works, salt pit. —isch, *adj.* saline.

Sa'lisch, *adj.* Salic.

[1]**Salm**, m. (—s, *pl.* —e) salmon.

[2]**Salm**, m. (—s) (*prov.*) see Psalm; langer —, rigmarole; einen langen — machen, to deliver a sermon *or* an oration, to spin a long yarn; mache keinen —! no sermon, please! no preachifying! come to the point! (*coll.*).

Salmia'k, m. (—s) sal-ammoniac. *Comp.* —geist, m. spirits of sal-ammoniac. —salz, n. sal volatile.

Salo'n, m. (—s, *pl.* —s) drawing-room; saloon (*in ships*). *Comp.* —fähig, *adj.* fit for (good) society. —löwe, m. carpet knight. —wagen, m. saloon carriage, Pullman car. —tiroler, m. carpet Tyrolese, sham Tyrolese.

Salpe'ter, m. (—s, *pl.* —) nitre, saltpetre. —haft, **Salpe'trig**, *adj.* nitrous, containing saltpetre. *Comp.* —artig, *adj.* nitrous. —bildung, *f.* nitrification; nitrous exhalation (*on walls, etc.*). —dampf, m. nitric vapour. —druse, *f.* crystallized saltpetre. —erde, *f.* nitrous earth. —fraß, m. injury done by saltpetre (*to walls, etc.*). —gas, n. nitrous gas, laughing gas. —geist, m. spirit of nitric ether, nitric acid, aqua fortis. —haltig, *adj.* nitrous, nitric. —hütte, *f.* saltpetre works. —sauer, *adj.* nitric; —saures Salz, nitrate; salpetrigsaures Kalium, potassium nitrite. —säure, *f.* nitric acid. —salzsäure, *f.* nitro-muriatic acid, aqua regia. —siederei', *f.* saltpetre manufactory.

Sal—utie'ren, *v.a. & n.* (*aux.* h.) to salute. —ve, (*pron.* Sal've), I. *int.* hail! II. *f.* (*pl.* —ven) salute, discharge of guns in a p.'s honour; volley; round (*of applause*); eine —ve geben, to fire a salute; to fire a volley. —ven=feuer, n. volley-firing.

Salz, n. (—es, *pl.* —e) salt; wit; flüchtige —e, volatile salts; das englische —, Epsom salts; basisches —, subsalt; ohne — und Schmalz, without seasoning, tasteless, insipid; — sieden, to prepare salt; einen ins — hauen, to slander, backbite s.o.; er hat einen Schinken bei mir im —e, I have a rod in pickle for him; im —e liegen, to be in a sad plight. —ig, *adj.* salty, salt; saline. *Comp.* —amt, n. salt-office. —abgabe, *f.* salt-tax. —artig, *adj.* saline. —äther, m. muriatic ether. —bäder, *pl.* salt *or* sea-water baths. —bildend, *adj.* salt-forming, halogenous. —bildung, *f.* salification. —blumen, *pl.* efflorescence of salt. —brühe, *f.* brine, pickle. —brunnen, m. saline spring. —bündnis, n. imperishable covenant (*B.*). —butter, *f.* salt butter. —erde, *f.* earth containing salt. —faß, n. salt-cellar; salt-box; barrel of salt. —fleisch, n. salt meat. —gehalt, m. saline matter. —geist, m. see —säure. —graf, —richter, m. overseer of salt-works. —grube, *f.* salt-mine. —gurke, *f.* pickled cucumber. —haltig, *adj.* saliferous. —handel, m. salt-trade. —hä=ring, m. salt herring. —korn, n. grain of salt. —kuchen, m. coarse wheaten *or* rye-cake. —lake, *f.* brine. —lecke, *f.* salt lick (*for cattle*). —lösung, *f.* salt solution. —messer, m. salimometer. —niederschlag, m. saline deposit. —sauer, *adj.* hydrochloric. —säule, *f.* pillar of salt. —säure, *f.* hydric chloride, hydrochloric acid, muriatic acid. —schreiber, m. clerk at salt-works. —siederei, *f.* salt-works. —sole, *f.* salt spring; brine, salt water. —spat, m. rock salt in bars. —steuer, *f.* salt-tax; salt-freight duty. —teich, m. pond of brackish water. —wage, *f.* salimeter, brine-gauge. —wasser, n. salt water; brine; —wasser kosten, to become a sailor. —werk, n. salt-works; salt-mine.

Sal'z—en, *irreg. & reg. v.a.* to salt; to pickle; to season (*with wit, etc.*); zu stark —en, to oversalt, to salt too much; gesalzen, piquant, spicy, strong; gesalzener Häring, salt herring.

Sa'm—e, m. (—en, *pl.* —en) [—en, m. (—ens, *pl.* —en)] seed; sperm; fry, spawn; posterity, children, descendants (*obs.* —ig, *adj.* containing seed *or* seeds. *Comp.* —en=ader, *f.* spermatic vein. —en=baum, m. tree kept for seed (*Hort.*). —en=behälter, m. seminal vessel; pericarp. —en=bruch, m. spermatocele. —en=drüse, *f.* prostate gland (*Anat.*). —en=ergießung, *f.* spermatism; discharge of semen. —en=fische, *pl.* young fry. —en=fluß, m. seminal fluid; gonorrhœa (*Med.*). —en=gärtner, m. nursery-man. —en=gefäß, n. spermatic vessel. —en=gehäuse, n. pericarp, core. —en=gewächs, n. seedling. —en=händler,

m. seedsman. —en=hülse, *f.* husk, shell, pod. —en=kapsel, *f.*, —en=knopf, *m.* capsule. —en=kern, *m.* sperm-nucleus. —en=knospe, *f.* ovule. —en=korn, *n.* grain of seed; sowing corn. —en=kuchen, *m.* placenta. —en=lehre, *f.* spermatology. —en=öl, *n.* rape-seed oil. —en=pflanze, *f.* seedling. —en=schnur, *f.*, —en=strang, *m.* spermatic cord. —en=schote, *f.* pod, shell, husk, seed-vessel. —en=schule, *f.* seed-plot. —en=staub, *m.* pollen. —en=stengel, *m.* seed-stalk. —en=stiel, *m.* funicle. —en=strang, *m.* seed-stalk; spermatic cord. —en=tierchen, *pl.* spermatic animalculæ, spermatozoa. —en=tragend, *adj.* seed-bearing, spermatophorous. —en=umgebung, *f.* perisperm. —en=zwiebel, *f.* seed-bulb.

Säm—erei', *f.* (*pl.* —ereien) seeds. —ling, *m.* (—lings, *pl.* —linge) seedling. *Comp.* —erei=händler, *m.* seedsman.

Sä'misch, *adj.* soft; chamois-dressed, shammy; —es Leder, wash-leather. *Comp.* —gerber, *m.* chamois-dresser. —leder, *n.* chamois leather.

Sam'm—eln, *v.* I. *a.* to gather, collect, amass, accumulate; to assemble; to concentrate; to treasure up; für die Armen —eln, to make a collection for the poor; Kräuter —eln, to gather herbs, botanize; aus fremden Büchern —eln, to compile; zerstreute Truppen —eln, to rally scattered troops; zum —eln blasen, das Ganze —eln, to sound the recall (*Mil.*). II. *r.* to collect, assemble, flock together; to increase; to converge; to collect one's thoughts, to regain one's self-possession *or* composure, come to o.s. —ler, *m.* (—lers, *pl.* —ler) collector. —lung, *f.* collection; collecting; compilation; set; miscellany; reunion; accumulation; composure, collectedness; —lung ausgewählter Stücke, collection of extracts *or* specimens; Muster—lung von Gedichten, anthology of poems; —lung um die Fahne, rallying round the colours. *Comp.* —el=bahnhof, *m.* junction, terminus. —el=band, *m.* volume containing a variety of essays. —el=becken, *n.* artificial pond *or* lake. —el=buch, *n.* commonplace book, scrap-book. —el=büchse, *f.* collecting-box. —el=cylinder, *m.* accumulator (*hydraulic lifting-machine*). —el=fleiß, (—ler=fleiß), *m.* industry in collecting (*materials*). —el=fracht, *f.*; in —elfracht, as by car-load. —el=gut, *n.* goods collected (by cart). —el=kasten, *m.* cistern; reservoir. —el=ladung, *f.* full (car-)load. —el=linse, *f.* convex lens (*Opt.*). —el=name, *m.* collective name. —el=platz, *m.* rendezvous. —el=punkt, *m.* rallying-point. —el=röhre, *f.* collecting pipe. —el=spiegel, *m.* concave mirror. —el=su'rium, *n.* *n.* medley, jumble, omnium-gatherum; stuff (*coll.*). —el=zahl, *f.* collective number.

Sam'met, Samt, *m.* (—es, *pl.* —e) velvet; gerissener —, cut velvet. —en, *adj.* velvety. *Comp.* —artig, *adj.* velvet-like. —band, *n.* velvet ribbon, ribbon velvet. —blümchen, *n.* pansy. —blume, *f.* velvet flower. —bürste, *f.* brush for velvet. —hühnchen, *n.* rallus aquaticus. —kette, *f.* nap *or* pile of velvet. —kleid, *n.* velvet dress. —manchester, *m.* cotton velvet, velveteen. —pelz(rock), *m.* fur-lined velvet cloak. —pfötchen, *pl.*; —pfötchen machen, to draw in the claws (*of the cat*); to be all smiles and bows; to play the hypocrite. —tapete, *f.* velvet hangings. —teppich, *m.*; (Brüsseler) ausgezogener —teppich, Brussels carpet. —weber, *m.* manufacturer of velvet. —weich, *adj.* velvety.

Sams'tag, *m.* (—s, *pl.* —e) Saturday.

Samt (*also* Sammt), I. *adv.*; — und sonders, alle —, collectively and individually, one and all, all to a man, all without exception. II. *prep.* (*with dat.*) with, together with, along with; mit —, together with.

Sämt'lich, (*also* Sämmt'lich,) I. *adj.* all, all together; complete, entire; collective. II. *adv.* collectively, in a body, as a whole, jointly.

Sa'mum, *m.* (—s, *pl.* —s, —e) simoom, simoon.

Sand, *m.* (—es) sand; grober —, gravel; auf dem —e sitzend, stranded; left in the lurch; einem — in die Augen streuen, to throw dust in a p.'s eyes, to deceive a p.; etwas in den — schreiben, to dismiss a thing from one's mind; etwas im —e verlaufen lassen, to let a thing slide; es verlief im —e, it came to nothing. —ig, *adj.* sandy, gravelly. *Comp.* —allee, *f.* gravel walk. —bad, *n.* sand-bath (*also Chem.*). —bank, *f.* sand-bank; sandy bar; layer, bed of sand, sandy deposit. —berg, *m.* sand-hill. —boden, *m.* sandy soil. —dünen, *pl.* sand hills, downs. —ebene, —fläche, *f.* sands; sandy plain. —flötz, *n.*, —fluhe, *f.* layer of sand. —gegend, *f.* sandy district. —glimmer, *m.* mica. —gries, *m.* fine gravel. —guß, *m.* casting in sand. —gut, *n.* scrubs (*C. L.*). —hase, *m.* white hare; dweller in a sandy country (*colloq.*); miss (*at nine-pins*). —huhn, *n.* sand-grouse. —kloß, *m.* round mass of sand; swollen testicle (*Med.*). —korn, *n.* grain of sand. —kraut, *n.* sand-wort. —krebs, *m.* craw-fish. —kresse, *f.* common cress. —kuchen, *m.* sponge-cake. —mann, *m.* sand-hawker; der —mann kommt ihm in die Augen, he is getting sleepy; —männchen kommt geschlichen, *or* stellt sich ein, the dustman is coming, Willie Winkie is coming on, it is time to go to the Land of Nod. —meer, *n.* sandy desert. —sack, *m.* sand-bag; engraver's cushion. —schimmel, *m.* roan horse. —schuß, *m.* sand-flood. —stein, *m.* sandstone. —strecke, *f.* stretch of sandy land. —sturm, *m.* sand-storm, sand-drift. —torte, *f.* madeira cake. —ufer, *n.* sandy beach. —uhr, *f.* hour-glass. —wahrsagerei, *f.* geomancy. —welle, *f.* small sand-bank. —wüste, *f.* sandy desert. —zucker, *m.* raw sugar.

Sanda'le, *f.* (*pl.* —n) sandal.

San'del, *m.* (—s, *pl.* —), (—holz, *n.*) sandal wood.

Sand'te, *1 & 3 pers. sing. imperf. of* senden.

Sanft, *adj. & adv.* soft; gentle, bland, mild; easy, smooth; placid; tender; ein —er Abhang, a gentle slope. —heit, *f.* softness; mildness, gentleness. *Comp.* —herzig, —mütig, *adj.* tender-hearted; gentle, mild, meek; selig sind die —mütigen, blessed are the meek (*B.*). —mut, *f.* good cheerful temper.

Sänf't—e, *f.* (*pl.* —en) gentleness, mildness (*obs.*); sedan-chair. —igen, *v.a.* to soften, mitigate, appease, assuage. *Comp.* —en=träger, *m.* sedan-chair man.

¹Sang, *m.* (—es, *pl.* Sän'ge) song, strain; singing; mit — und Klang, with singing and bands playing, with joyous music; ohne — und Klang, without a sound, very quietly, softly and silently (*coll.*); ohne — und Klang abziehen, to sneak off. —bar, *adj.* adapted for singing. *Comp.* —weise, *f.* melody.

²Sang, Sän'ge, *1 & 3 pers. sing. imperf. ind. & subj. of* singen.

Sän'ger, *m.* (—s, *pl.*—) singer: chanter, chorister; minstrel, bard, poet; warbler (*Orn.*). —ei', *f.* singing; bawling, bad singing. —haft, *adj.* as a singer. —in, *f.* songstress, singer; opera-singer, minstrel girl. —krieg, *m.* bards' contest, strife of the minnesingers (*on the Wartburg, 13th century*). —schaft, *f.* singers (*coll.*); singers' ways. *Comp.* —bund, *m.* choral society. —fest, *n.* festival of song, choral festival. —tum, *n.* minstrelsy.

Sanqui'n—iker, *m.* (—ikers, *pl.* —iker) person

of a sanguine temperament. —**isch**, *adj.* sanguine.
Sanitä't, *f.* health, sanitation, hygiene. —**lich**, *adj.* relating to health. *Comp.* —**s=beamte(r)**, *m.* officer of (public) health, medical *or* health officer. —**s=behörde**, *f.*, —**s=kollegium**, *n.* board of health. —**s=bericht**, *m.* medical report. —**kolonne**, *f.* ambulance corps. —**polizei**, *f.* sanitary police. —**s=rat**, *m.* member of the board of health; honorary title conferred by the Crown on German physicians. —**s=verein**, *m.* society for succouring the sick and wounded. —**s=wache**, *f.* guard for protecting the sick and wounded; infirmary; ambulance station. —**s=wagen**, *m.* ambulance(-cart). —**s=wesen**, *n.* hygienic *or* sanitary matters.
Sank, Sän'ke, *1 & 3 pers. sing. imperf. ind. & subj. of* **sinken**.
Sankt, *indec. adj.* (*abbr.* S., St.,) saint; — **Johannes**, St. John. —**ifizie'ren**, *v.a.* to sanctify. —**io'n**, *f.* (*pl.* —**ionen**) sanction. —**ionie'ren**, *v.n.* to sanction. —**ua'rium**, *n.* (—**uariums**, *pl.* —**uarien**) sanctuary.
Sann, Sän'ne (**Sön'ne**), *1 & 3 pers. sing. imperf. ind. & subj. of* **sinnen**.
Sans'krit, *f.* Sanscrit. —**isch** (*pron.* **sans=kri'tisch**), *adj.* Sanscrit(ic). *Comp.* —**forscher**, *m.* Sanscritist.
Sa'phir (*sometimes pron.* **Saphi'r**), *m.* (—**s**, *pl.* **Saphi're**) sapphire. —**en**, *adj.* sapphire; sapphire-blue.
Sap'p—e, *f.* (*pl.* —**en**) sap (*in sieges*). —**en**, *v.a.* to sap, undermine. —**eu'r**, *m.* (—**eurs**, *pl.* —**eure**, —**eurs**) sapper.
Sapper—lo't, —me'nt, *int.* Zounds! the deuce!
Sard—el'le, *f.* (*pl.* —**ellen**) anchovy. —**ellen=brötchen**, *n.* anchovy sandwich. —**ellen=brühe**, *f.* anchovy sauce. —**i'ne**, *f.* sardine; —**inen in Öl**, tinned sardines.
Sardo'nisch, *adj.* sardonic.
Sarg, *m.* (—**es**, *pl.* **Sär'ge**) coffin; shell. *Comp.* —**beschlag**, *m.* coffin-mounting. —**deckel**, *m.* coffin-lid. —**tuch**, *n.* pall.
Sark—as'mus, *m.* (—**asmus**, *pl.* —**asmen**) sarcasm. —**as'tisch**, *adj.* sarcastic.
Sarkopha'g, *m.* (—**s**, *pl.* —**e**) sarcophagus.
Sar'ras, Sar'raß, *m.* (—(**ss**)**es**, *pl.* —(**ss**)**e**) sabre, broadsword.
Sar'sche, *f.* (*pl.* —**n**) serge.
Sarsenet'band, *m.* sars(e)net (binding).
[1]**Saß** (*short* **a**), *m.* (—(**ss**)**en**, *pl.* —(**ss**)**en**), **Saſ'ſe**, *m.* (—**n**, *pl.* —**n**), **Saſ'ſin**, *f.* settler; inhabitant, freeholder (*obs. dial.*).
[2]**Saß** (*long* **a**), **Sä'ße**, *1 & 3 pers. sing. imperf. ind. & subj. of* **sitzen**.
Sa'tan, *m.* (—**s**, *pl.* —**e**), —**as**, *m.* (—**as**) Satan.
Sata'nisch, *adj.* Satanic.
Satelli't, *m.* (—**en**, *pl.* —**en**) satellite.
Sati'r—e, *f.* (*pl.* —**en**) satire. —**iker**, *m.* (—**ikers**, *pl.* —**iker**) satirist. —**isch**, *adj.* satirical. *Comp.* —**en=dichter**, *m.* satirical poet, satirist.
Satisfaktio'n, *f.*; — **geben**, to give satisfaction (*by accepting a challenge for a duel*), to accept a challenge, be willing to fight a duel. —**s=fähig**, *adj.* capable of giving satisfaction, of a rank *or* station to be challenged to a duel.
Satt, *adj. & adv.* satisfied with food *or* drink; filled to satiety, satiated; saturated; dark; **ich bin** —, I have had enough; **es** — **haben**, to have had enough of it; **sich** — **lachen**, to laugh one's fill *or* to one's heart's content; **ich kann mich daran nicht** — **sehen**, I cannot take my eyes off it; **eine Sache** — **bekommen**, **einer Sache** — **werden**, to weary, get weary, sick of a thing. —**heit**, *f.* satiety. —**sam**, *adj. & adv.* sufficing; sufficiently. *Comp.* —**blau**, —**grün**, *n.* dark blue, dark green.
Sat'te, *f.* (*pl.* —**n**) milk-pan *or* bowl.
Sat't—el, *see* **Sattel**. —**ler**, *m.* (—**lers**, *pl.* —**ler**) saddler; harness-maker. —**lerei'**, *f.* saddlery. *Comp.* —**ler=ahle**, *f.* stitching awl. —**ler=ware**, *f.* saddlery.
Sat'tel, *m.* (—**s**, *pl.* **Sättel**) saddle; limber-bolster (*Artil.*); ridge (*of a hill*); pass (*Mount.*); bridge (*of a violin, etc.*); zest (*in a walnut*); gallows (*Typ.*); bed (*Typ.*); transom (*Arch.*); **aus dem** — **heben**, to unhorse, throw, to dismount, to supplant, to supersede; **fest im** — **sitzen**, to have a firm seat; to know one's ground, be master of the situation *or* of one's subject; **in allen Sätteln gerecht sein**, to be fit and ready for anything, to be able to turn one's hand to anything. *Comp.* —**baum**, —**bogen**, *m.* saddle-bow. —**blech**, *n.* wither-band; ridge-plate (*Arch.*); bolster-plate of limber (*Artil.*). —**dach**, *n.* span-roof. —**decke**, *f.* saddle-cloth; caparison. —**federn**, *pl.* springs (*cycl.*). —**fertig**, *adj.* ready to mount. —**fest**, *adj.* firm in the saddle. —**gurt**, *m.* girth, belly-band. —**kammer**, *f.* harness-room. —**kissen**, *n.* saddle-pad; pillion. —**knecht**, *m.* groom. —**knopf**, *m.* pommel. —**pferd**, *n.* near horse, near-sider, saddle-horse, thill-horse. —**pisto=len**, *pl.* horse-pistols. —**polster**, *n.* pillion; saddle-holster. —**protze**, *f.* battering-train *or* heavy gun limber. —**ranzen**, *pl.* saddle-bags. —**riemen**, *m.* girth-leather. —**seite**, *f.* near side (*of a horse*). —**steg**, *m.* bridge of a saddle. —**stück**, *n.* saddle (*of mutton, etc.*). —**stütze**, *f.* seat-pillar (*cycl.*). —**tasche**, *f.* saddle-bag. —**tief**, *adj.* hollow-backed. —**wagen**, *m.* platform-carriage (*Artil.*). —**zeug**, *n.* saddle and harness, saddlery.
Sat'teln, I. *v.a.* to saddle, to put the saddle on. II. *subst. n.* saddling; **zum** — **blasen**, to sound the boot-and-saddle.
Sät'tigen, *v.a.* to satisfy, satiate; to saturate, impregnate; **sich** —, to satisfy one's hunger; **einen** —, to appease a p.'s hunger.
Saturna'lien, *pl.* saturnalia.
Sa'tyr, *m.* (—**s**, *pl.* —**s**, —**e**(**n**)) Satyr; Pithecus satyrus (*Zool.*). *Comp.* —**artig**, *adj.* satyric(al). —**drama**, *n.*, —**spiel**, *n.* satyric drama.
Satz, *m.* (—**es**, *pl.* **Sät'ze**) setting, putting, laying; leap, bound, start; vault; stake; pile (*of wood; galvanic pile*); set; nest (*of boxes, etc.*); report (*of a law case*); litter, fry; heap, pile; dregs; grounds, sediment; deposit; treat, entertainment; sentence, passage, period; proposition; tenet; phrase (*Mus.*); movement (*Mus.*); composition (*Typ., Mus.*); allowance, rate; theme, thesis; mixture, composition; fixed price; theorem, proposition (*Arith.*); draught; statement (*of an arithmetical or algebraic question*); **einen** — **machen** *or* **thun**, to jump, take a leap; **einen** — **geben**, to stand a treat, give an entertainment (*coll.*); **seinen** — **behaupten**, to maintain one's point; **kurzer, kernhafter** —, aphorism. —**ung**, *f.* statute; institution; maxim, precept, dogma; —**ungen eines Vereins**, articles of an association, rules of a club *or* society. *Comp.* —**accent**, *m.* sentence accent, sandhi. —**artig**, *adj.* sedimentary. —**bildung**, *f.* structure *or* formation of sentences. —**bord**, *m.* wash-board (*Naut.*). —**bohrer**, *m.* set of augers. —**fehler**, *m.* error in composition (*Typ.*). —**fisch**, *m.* spawn. —**fügungs=lehre**, *f.* syntax. —**hase**, *m.* doe-hare. —**lehre**, *f.* syntax. —**löffel**, *m.* iron spoon. —**mehl**, *n.* fecula, lees (*Chem.*); starch. —**stück**, *n.* part, article. —**teich**, *m.* breeding-pond (*for fishes*). —**teil**, *m.* part of a sentence. —**ungs=lehre**, *f.* dogmatics. —**ungs=recht**, *n.* statute law. —**weise**, *adv.* sentence by sentence; by sets; by fits and starts; in heaps; by periods. —**zeit**, *f.* breeding-time. —**zwiebel**, *f.* bulb for transplanting.

Sau, *f.* (*pl.* —**en**, **Säu'e**) sow, hog; wild sow, wild boar; filthy creature; blot (*of ink*); blunder, howler (*sl.*); pig (*of metal*); **er züchtet Säue und jagt —en**, he breeds sows and hunts wild boars; — **haben**, to be lucky (*sl.*). *Comp.* (*as the first part of compounds often* = very, highly (*dial.*)) —**apfel**, *m.* crab-apple. —**arbeit**, *f.* dirty work; disgusting work *or* business. —**beller**, *m.* boar-hound. —**bohne**, *f.* broad bean. —**borste**, *f.* hog's bristle. —**essen**, *n.*, —**fraß**, *m.* hog's wash, bad food. —**fleisch**, *n.* boar's flesh. —**glocke**, *f.*; **die —glocken läuten**, to talk obscenely. —**grob**, *adj.* very rude (*dial.*). —**hatz**, —**hetze**, *f.* boar-hunting. —**hirt**, *m.* swine-herd. —**hund**, *m.* boar-hound; swineherd's dog. —**kerl**, *m.* dirty fellow (*vulg.*); pig. —**jagd**, *f.* boar-hunting. —**koben**, *m.* pig-sty. —**lache**, *f.* pool for swine (to wallow in). —**leben**, *n.* hoggish, beastly life. —**mensch**, *n.* bad wench. —**mutter**, *f.* farrow-sow. —**park**, *m.* mountainous enclosure where wild boars are kept. —**rüde**, *m.* boar-hound. —**rudel**, *n.* herd of wild boars. —**rüssel**, *m.* swine's snout. —**rüssel=fisch**, *m.* porpoise. —**spieß**, *m.* boar-spear. —**stall**, *m.* pig-sty. —**trog**, *m.* pig's trough. —**wetter**, *n.* horrible *or* beastly weather (*coll.*). —**wirtschaft**, *f.* dirty place, filthy hole, piggery; bad, filthy management.

Sau'ber, *adj.* clean; neat, tidy; pretty; fine, nice *or* rare (*in irony*); —**e Dinge**, fine doings, nice goings-on; **ein —er Gast**, a queer guest! **eine —e Bescherung**, a fine mess, a pretty kettle of fish! **eine —e Abschrift**, a fair copy. —**keit**, *f.* cleanness, cleanliness, neatness.

Säu'ber—lich, *adj. & adv.* clean; soft, gentle; **fein —lich**, very neat and proper. —**n**, *v.a.* to clean, cleanse; to purge (*a cannon*). —**ung**, *f.* cleansing.

Sau'c—e, *f.* (*pl.* —**en**) sauce; gravy. —**ie're**, *f.* sauce-boat, butter-boat.

Saucis'chen, *n.* (—**s**, *pl.* —) (little) sausage.

Sau'en, *v.* I. *n.* (*aux.* **h.**) to be filthy; to talk obscenely. II. *a.* to dirty, soil.

Sau'er, I. *adj. & adv.* (**sau'rer, sau'erst**) (*when inflected gen'lly* **saur**) sour, acid; acetous; cross, morose, peevish, crabbed; hard, bitter, troublesome, painful; —**e Arbeit**, hard work, grind; —**e Probe**, hard, difficult task, trial; —**er Boden**, marshy land; —**er Schweiß**, sweat of the brow; —**e Gurken**, pickled cucumbers; **ich lasse es mir — werden**, I take great pains, I work very hard; **es sich** (*dat.*) **— werden lassen**, to toil and moil; **einem das Leben — machen**, to embitter a p.'s life; **das Arbeiten in gebückter Haltung wird ihm —**, he finds working in a stooping posture very trying; **in den —n Apfel beißen**, to swallow the bitter pill; **das viele Sprechen wird mir —**, talking much fatigues me greatly; **es kommt ihn — an**, he thinks it very hard, he finds it difficult; — **dazu sehen**, to frown at a th. II. *n. see* **Säure**; goose-giblets prepared with vinegar (*Cook.*); work paid beforehand (*Typ.*). *Comp.* —**ampfer**, *m.* sorrel. —**braten**, *m.* beef kept in vinegar for three or four days and then cooked in a stewpan. —**brunnen**, *m.* chalybeate spring. —**dattel**, *f.* tamarind. —**e=gurken=zeit**, *f.* dead *or* dull *or* silly season (*for business, newspapers*). —**honig**, *m.* oxymel. —**kirsche**, *f.* morella cherry. —**klee**, *m.* wood-sorrel. —**kraut**, *n.* pickled cabbage. —**ling**, *m.* acidulous substance. —**milch**, *f.* curdled milk. —**stoff**, *m.* oxygen. —**stoff=verbindungen**, *pl.* oxygen compounds. —**süß**, *adj.* bitter-sweet, sour, tartish. —**teig**, *m.* leaven. —**topf**, *m.* morose, grumpy fellow. —**töpfisch**, *adj.* peevish, crabbed, cross, sullen. —**wein**, *m.* verjuice.

Säu'er—bar, —**lich**, *adj.* sourish, acidulous, tart; acetous. —**lichkeit**, *f.* acidity. —**ling**, *m.* sour wine. —**n**, *v.a.* to acidulate; to leaven. —**ung**, *f.* acidification; leavening.

Sau'ern, *v.r. & n.* (*aux.* **h.** & **s.**) to turn sour, to curdle.

Sau'f—en, I. *ir.v.a. & n.* (*aux.* **h.**) to drink (*of beasts*); to drink to excess, swill; to tipple. II. *subst. n.*; **sich** (*dat.*) **das —en angewöhnt haben**, to be addicted to hard drinking. —**erei'**, *f.* drunkenness; *see* —**gelag**. *Comp.* —**aus**, *m.*, —**bold**, *m. see* **Säufer**. —**bruder**, *m.* boon-companion; toper. —**gelag**, *n.* drinking-bout, orgy. —**lied**, *n.* bacchanalian song. —**schwester**, *f.* female drunkard.

Säu'fer, *m.* (—**s**, *pl.* —) drunkard, toper. —**ei'**, *f.* drunkenness; hard drinking, orgy, carouse. *Comp.* —**nase**, *f.* tippler's nose (*coll.*). —**wahnsinn**, *m.* delirium tremens.

Säu'g—eln, *v.a.* to engraft (*Hort.*). —**en**, *v.a.* to suckle, nurse. —**er**, *m.* (—**ers**, *pl.*—**er**) sucking animal; mammal; (*pl. also* —**ers**) hanks (*Naut.*). —**erin**, *f.* wet-nurse. —**ling**, *m.* (—**lings**, *pl.* —**linge**) infant, suckling; graft. *Comp.* —**amme**, *f.* wet-nurse. —**e=tier**, *n.* mammal. —**e=zahn**, *m.* milk-tooth.

Sau'g—en, *ir.v.a. & n.* (*aux.* **h.**) to suck; to absorb, imbibe; **an sich —en**, to suck up, exhaust; **sich** (*dat.*) **etwas aus den Fingern —en**, to invent, make up a th.; **an den Klauen —en**, to be in great misery, starving; **in sich —en**, to absorb, imbibe. —**er**, *m.* (—**ers**, *pl.* —**er**) sucker; sucking animal; tube and nipple (*of a feeding bottle*); sucker (*of a pump, etc.*). *Comp.* —**ader**, *f.* absorbent vessel. —**ader=drüse**, *f.* lymphatic gland. —(**e**)=**ferkel**, *n.* sucking pig. —(**e**)=**flasche**, *f.*, —(**e**)=**glas**, *n.* baby's feeding-bottle. —**hahn**, *m.* suction-cock. —**heber**, *m.* siphon. —(**e**)=**leder**, *n.* sucker. —(**e**)=**mündung**, *f.* lower opening of a suction-pipe. —(**e**)=**pumpe**, *f.* suction-pump; — **und Druck=Pumpe**, suction and delivery pipe. —**rohr**, *n.*, —(**e**)=**röhre**, *f.* suction-tube *or* pipe, sucker. —(**e**)=**rüssel**, *m.* proboscis of insects. —(**e**)=**sand**, *m.* quicksand. —(**e**)=**schwamm**, *m.* sponge. —(**e**)=**werk**, *n.* organs of suction; suction-pump. —(**e**)=**warze**, *f.* nipple.

Säu'isch, *adj.* swinish, filthy; obscene.

Säul'—chen, *n.* (—**chens**, *pl.* —**chen**) little column *or* pillar. —**e**, *f.* (*pl.* —**en**) column; pillar; post, jamb, upright; prop, support; *see* **Bildsäule**; **galvanische** *or* **voltaische —e**, voltaic pile. —**ig**, *adj.* columnar; column-shaped; furnished with columns; **achtsäulig**, with eight columns in front. *Comp.* —**en=anlauf**, *m.* apophyge (*Arch.*). —**en=förmig**, *adj.* columnar. —**en=fuß**, *m.* base, pedestal of a column. —**en=gang**, *m.* colonnade, arcade, cloister. —**en=gesims**, *n.* cornice. —**en=halle**, *f.* portico; piazza; pillared hall. —**en=heilige(r)**, *m.* Stylites (St. Simon); stylite, pillarist, pillar-saint. —**en=knauf**, —**en=kopf**, *m.* capital of a column. —**en=kreis**, *m.* peristyle. —**en=laube**, *f.* portico, piazza. —**en=ordnung**, *f.* order (*of architecture*). —**en=platte**, *f.* abacus, plinth (*Arch.*). —**en=reihe**, *f.* row of columns; **ein Gebäude mit fünf —enreihen umgeben**, pentastyle. —**en=schaft**, *m.* shaft of a column. —**en=ständer**, *m.* pedestal. —**en=stuhl**, *m.* pedestal. —**en=weite**, *f.* intercolumniation. —**en=werk**, *n.* colonnade. —**en=würfel**, *m.* plinth.

[1]**Saum**, *m.* (—**s**, *pl.* **Säu'me**) hem, seam; border, edge; selvage; fillet (*Arch.*); brink; doubling (*of a sail*). *Comp.* —**baum**, *m.* tree on the borders of a wood. —**naht**, *f.* hem. —**stich**, *m.* hem-stitch.

[2]**Saum**, *m.* (—**s**, *pl.* **Säu'me**) burden; liquid measure (*gen'lly = 150 litres*). *Comp.* —**esel**, *m.* ass for carrying burdens. —**maultier**, *n.*

sumpter-mule. —pfad, *see* —weg. —pferd, *n.* pack-horse. —sattel, *m.* pack-saddle. —tier, *n.* sumpter-mule, beast of burden. —weg, *m.* mule-track *or* path; bridle-path.

¹Säu'm—en, *v.a.* to border; to hem. —er, *m.* (—ers, *pl.* —er) hemmer (*Sew.-mach.*). —erin, *f.* hemmer. —erei', *f.* hemming. —ung, *f.* hemming.

²Säu'm—en, *v.a.* to convey *or* transport by beasts of burden; to load with a pack-saddle. —er, *m.* (—ers, *pl.* —er) keeper of pack-horses, *etc.*; leader, driver of a pack-horse; beast of burden.

³Säu'm—en, *v.n.* (*aux.* h.) to delay, linger, tarry; to defer; to hesitate; wie lange willst du —en, how long are you going to delay? mein Heil —et sich nicht, my salvation shall not tarry (*B.*). —ig, *adj. & adv.* tardy, dilatory, slow; negligent. —igkeit, *f.* slowness; negligence. —nis, *f.* (*pl.* —nisse) & *n.* (—nisses, *pl.* —nisse) slowness; negligence; delay; obstacle. —ung, *f.* delaying, tarrying.

Saum'—sal, *f. & n.* dilatoriness, slowness, tardiness; negligence. —sälig, —selig, *adj.* dilatory, slow, slack, negligent, careless, indolent. —seligkeit, *f. see* Säumigkeit.

Säu're, *f.* (*pl.* —n) sourness, acidity, tartness; acid; — im Magen hervorrufen, to cause heartburn(ing). *Comp.* —erzeugend, *adj.* producing acidity *or* an acid. —haltig, *adj.* acetous, acidiferous. —messer, *m.* acetimeter.

Sau'rier, *pl.* saurians; zu den —n gehörig, saurian.

Saus, *m.* (—(s)es) rush, storm, bluster, rushing noise; riotous life; in — und Schmaus (*or* Braus) leben, to revel, live riotously.

Sau'se—n, *v.n.* (*aux.* h. & s.) to whistle, bluster, to howl, sough (*as wind*); to whistle, whiz (*as arrows*); to hum; to rush; mir —n die Ohren, I have a ringing in my ears; laß ihn —n, let him go! (*coll.*). *Comp.* —laut, *m.* sibilant. —wind, *m.* blustering wind; impetuous *or* blustering person, flighty young person.

Säu'seln, *v.a. & n.* (*aux.* h.) to rustle, murmur, whisper, sigh; to hum; to whiz, hiss; einen in Schlummer —, to lull a p. to sleep by song *or* murmur.

Savan'ne, *f.* (*pl.* —n) savanna(h). *Comp.* —nfieber, *n.* prairie-fever.

Savo'yerkohl, *m.* savoys (*cabbage*).

Scat, *m. see* Skat.

Sce'n—e, *f.* (*pl.* —en) scene; die —en, scenery (*Theat.*); in —e setzen, to enact; to mount (*a piece*). —erie', *f.* scenery. —isch, *adj.* scenic. *Comp.* —en=führung, *f.* scenic arrangement. —en=wechsel, *m.* shifting of scenes.

Scep'ter, *n.* (& *m.*) (—s, *pl.* —) sceptre; mace; das — tragen *or* führen, to bear *or* wield the sceptre. *Comp.* —träger, *m.* sceptred monarch, sovereign; mace-bearer.

Schaa, *see* Scha.

Schab'bes, *m.* (—) Sabbath (*Hebr.*) (*coll.*).

Scha'b—e, *f.* (*pl.* —en) scraper; cockroach; moth. —en, *v.a.* to scrape, grate, scratch, rasp; to etch; to scrub, rub; to pare; —en und kratzen, to act stingily, scrape and hoard; einem Rüben *or* Rübchen —en, to jeer at, make game of a p. —er, *m.* (—ers, *pl.* —er) stingy, mean person, skin-flint; scraper; parer, rasp, rake. —sel, *n.* (—sels, *pl.* —sel) shavings, scrapings, parings. *Comp.* —ab, *n.* scrapings, refuse; du bist —ab, you are refused, I refuse your love (*obs.*). —e=baum, —e=b(l)ock, *m.*, —e=brett, *n.* tanner's block *or* horse. —(e)=eisen, *n.* scraper. —e=fleisch, *n.* scraped meat; scrapings. —(e)=manier, *f.* mezzotinto. —(e)=messer, *n.* scraping-knife. —en=geist, *m.*, —en=gift, *n.* insect-destroyer. —er=nack, *m.* (—er=nacks) rough winter-hat; trick, hoax, practical joke, mischievous prank; practical joker, imp (*fig.*); er hat es mir zum —ernack gethan, he did it to annoy me, he played a practical joke on me. —er=nackisch, *adj.* fond of playing tricks. —e=wolle, *f.* glover's wool. —zieger, *m.* green cheese.

Schä'big, *adj.* scabby; mangy; shabby; mean, stingy; wretched. —keit, *f.* shabbiness; scabbiness; sordidness; wretchedness.

Schablo'n—e, *f.* (*pl.* —en) model, mould, form; pattern, copy; stencil; calibre; nach der —e arbeiten, to work mechanically *or* like a machine. —ie'ren, *v.a.* to copy, model from; to stencil. *Comp.* —en=mäßig, *adj. & adv.* mechanical, routine; as if made in a mould. —en=wesen, *n.* routine. —en=zeichnung, *f.* stencil drawing, copy.

Schabra'cke, *f.* (*pl.* —n) caparison, trappings; saddle-cloth, housings; bards (*obs.*).

Schach, I. *m.* (—s, *pl.* —s) shah. II. *n.* (—es, —s) chess; check; square; dem Könige — bieten, to give check to the king; — dem König! check! — (und) matt! checkmate! — der Königin! check to the queen! in — halten, to keep in check. *Comp.* —aufgabe, *f.* chess-problem. —brett, *n.* chess-board. —brett=förmig, *adj.* chequered; tesselated. —feld, *n.* square of a chessboard. —figur, *f.* chessman, piece. —förmig, *adj.* chequered, checked. —klub, *m.* chess-club. —matt, *adj.* checkmate; played out, knocked up, worn-out. —spiel, *n.* game of chess; chessboard and men. —spieler(in, *f.*), *m.* chess-player. —stein, *m. see* —figur. —zug, *m.* move at chess.

Scha'cher, *m.* (—s), —ei', *f.* chaffering, higgling; low trade; usury. —er, *m.* (—ers, *pl.* —er) chafferer, petty dealer. —n, *v.n.* (*aux.* h.) to chaffer, higgle; to carry on a low trade. *Comp.* —jude, *m.* petty Jew dealer; cheat.

Schä'cher, *m.* (—s, *pl.* —) robber; thief; scapegrace; armer —, poor devil, poor wretch (*obs.*); der gute —, the penitent thief (*obs.*). *Comp.* —kreuz, *n.* cross in the form of a Y.

Schacht, *m.* (—es, *pl.* Schäch'te) an opening (*into something*); shaft, pit (*Min.*); gorge; ditch; hollow; — eines Hochofens, fire-room. *Comp.* —bühne, *f.* landing-stage in a shaft. —erz, *n.* ore detached from the parent mass. —gestänge, *n.* water-engine rods. —haspel, *m.* windlass of a shaft. —holz, *n.* timber-work of a mine. —maß, *n.* measure of slightly over six cubic metres. —mütze, *f.* miner's cap. —meister, *m.* pit-overseer; foreman of navvies (*on a railway*). —ofen, *m.* cupola; blast-furnace. —werk, *n.* pit-work; a measure; *see* —maß. —zimmerung, *f.* shaft-timbering.

Schach'tel, *f.* (*pl.* —n) box, bandbox, case; alte —, old maid; ein junger Pinsel und eine alte —, a young fool and an old hag. *Comp.* —halm, *m.* shave-grass. —holz, *n.* wood for bandboxes. —krämer, *m.* dealer in bandboxes *or* toys. —männchen, *n.* Jack in the box.

Schach'teln, *v.a.* to pack (*coll.*).

Schäch'te—n, *v.a.* to slaughter (*cattle, among the Jews*); to cheat. —r, *m.* (—rs, *pl.* —r) Jewish butcher.

Scha'd—e, *m.* (—en, *pl.* —en), —en, *m.* (—ens, *pl.* Schäden) damage, loss; injury, harm, wrong, mischief; prejudice, detriment, disadvantage, hurt, sore, wound; es soll dein —e nicht sein, you shall not regret (*or* lose anything by) it; —en thun, bringen, to prejudice, damage; sich (*dat.*) —en thun, to hurt oneself; zu —en kommen, to be hurt, sustain losses, to come to grief, to miscarry; haben Sie —en dabei? are you a loser by it? mit —en verkaufen, to sell below cost price; wer den —en hat, darf für den Spott nicht sorgen, losers are always in the wrong, the laugh is always against the loser (*prov.*); sich seines —ens erholen, to recover from a loss; durch —en klug werden, to learn wisdom by experience; durch —en wird man klug, a burnt child dreads the fire (*prov.*); fort mit —en! 't is a good riddance! nach —en trachten, to devise mischief (*B.*); was hülfe es dem Menschen, so er die ganze Welt gewönne und nähme doch —en an seiner Seele, for what is a man profited if he shall gain the whole world and lose his own soul (*B.*); innerer —en, internal disease; offener —en, open sore; —e, (*used as int.*) a pity! es ist ewig —e! it is a thousand pities! —e, daß, ꝛc.! what a pity that, *etc.!* —e um die verlorene Zeit, it is a pity that so much time has been lost; es ist —e um ihn, it is a pity for him, I am very sorry for him. —haft, *adj.* damaged, injured; spoilt; decayed; ruinous; vicious, faulty; —hafte Kleider, tattered clothes; —haft werden, to get damaged, spoil, decay. —haftigkeit, *f.* damaged condition, unsoundness. *Comp.* —e=kauf, *m.* a losing bargain. —en=bringend, *adj.* hurtful. —en=ersatz, *m.* reparation, compensation, indemnification; als —enersatz, to make amends, as damages; einen auf —enersatz verklagen, to sue a p. for damages. —en=ersatz=klage, *f.* action for damages. —en=freude, *f.* malicious joy (*at another's misfortune*), gratification of pent-up envy, joy over the misfortune of those one has formerly cringed to and envied, malignity. —en=froh, *adj.* mischief-loving, malicious; ein —enfroher Mensch, a mischief-maker. —en=lust, *f.* = —enfreude. —en=preis, *m.* amount for damages. —en=rechnung, —en=schätzung, *f.* statement *or* estimate of damages. —los, *adj.* harmless; indemnified; —los halten, to indemnify. —los=bürgschaft, *f.* bond of indemnity. —los=haltung, *f.* indemnification; indemnity.

Schä'del, *m.* (—s, *pl.* —) skull, cranium, brain-pan; pate. *Comp.* —bohren, *n.* trepanning. —bohrer, *m.* trepan. —haut, *f.* pericranium. —höhle, *f.* skull, brain cavity. —lehre, *f.* phrenology. —naht, *f.* coronal suture. —stätte, *f.* Golgotha, place of a skull.

Scha'd—en, *v.n.* (*aux.* h., *dat.*) to harm, hurt, injure; to prejudice, damage; einem bei einem andern —en, to prejudice a person against another; das —et nichts, no matter, never mind; was —et es, wenn . . . ? what does it matter, if . . . ? what harm can it do? das —et dir nichts, warum bist du nicht vorsichtiger? that serves you right for being so thoughtless.

Schä'd—igen, *v.a. see* Beschädigen; to wrong. —igung, *f.* wrong; hurt; ohne —igung seiner Interessen, without prejudice to his interests. —lich, *adj.* prejudicial, disadvantageous, pernicious, destructive; dangerous; der Gesundheit —lich, injurious to health; unhealthy, unwholesome. —lichkeit, *f.* harmfulness, destructiveness, perniciousness, noxiousness; hurtful thing.

Schäd'ling, *m.* (—s, *pl.* —e) noxious person *or* animal.

Schaf, *n.* (—es, *pl.* —e) sheep; goose; stupid, silly fool; das — blökt (sagt Bä), the sheep bleats (says baa); Mutter —, ewe; ein gutes —, a stupid dolt. *Comp.* —artig, *adj.* sheep-like; sheepish. —blattern, *pl.* chickenpox. —bock, *m.* ram. —bremse, *f.* sheep-bot, gadfly. —fäule, *f.* rot. —fell, *n.* sheepskin. —fleisch, *n.* mutton. —garbe, *f.* yarrow (*Bot.*). —herde, *f.* flock of sheep. —hirt, *m.* shepherd. —hürde, *f.* sheep pen *or* fold. —husten, *m.* dry, hard cough. —kame(e)l, *n.* llama. —lamm, *n.* ewe-lamb. —laus, *f.* tick. —leber, *f.* sheep's liver. —lecke, *f.* salt lick (*for sheep*). —leder, *n.* sheepskin; (saffianähnliches) roan. —milch, *f.* ewe's milk. —mutter, *f.* ewe. —pelz, *m.* fleece; sheepskin; der Wolf im —pelze, the wolf in sheep's clothing. —pergament, *n.* parchment (*of sheepskin*). —räude, *f.* scab. —schenkel, *m.* leg of mutton; sprit-sail (*Naut.*). —schere, *f.* sheep-shears. —schur, *f.* sheep-shearing. —schwemmen, *n.* sheep-washing. —seuche, *f.* sheep-rot. —s=geschlinge, *n.* sheep's pluck. —s=gesicht, *n.* stupid-looking person, dolt. —s=kleid, *n.*, —s=kleidung, *f.* sheep's clothing. —s=kopf, *m.* sheep's head; blockhead; a game at cards. —s=köpfig, *adj.* sheepish, silly, stupid. —s=mäßig, *adj.* sheepish, stupid. —stall, *m.* sheep-fold. —stand, *m.* stock of sheep. —trift, —weide, *f.* sheep-walk, sheep-run. —wolle, *f.* sheep's wool. —zucht, *f.* sheep-breeding.

Schäf'—chen, *n.* (—chens, *pl.* —chen), —lein, *n.* (—leins, *pl.* —lein) little sheep; lambkin, lamb; fleecy clouds, cirri; white horses, crests of foam (*on waves*); es sind —chen am Himmel, the sky is dappled; sein —chen scheren *or* ins Trockene bringen, to feather one's nest. —er, *m.* (—ers, *pl.* —er) shepherd; swain, lover; verliebter —er, pastoral lover; amorous swain (*hum.*). —erei', *f.* sheep-fold; sheep-farm; sheep-walk *or* run; shepherd's cot; flock; pastoral poetry *or* poem; the world of shepherds. —erin, *f.* shepherdess. —ertum, *n.* shepherd's life. *Comp.* —er=gedicht, *n.* idyl, eclogue, pastoral. —er=hund, *m.* shepherd's dog. —er=hütte, *f.*, —er=karren, *m.* shepherd's hut. —er=lied, *n.* pastoral song. —er=mädchen, *n.* young shepherdess. —er=pfeife, *f.* pastoral pipe. —er=spiel, *n.* pastoral play. —er=stab, *m.* shepherd's crook. —er=stunde, *f.* happy hour of lovers, lovers' hour. —er=stückchen, *n.* pastoral air (*Mus.*). —er=tasche, *f.* shepherd's scrip. —er=welt, *f.* Arcadian age, golden age, Arcadia.

Schaf'f—en, I. *ir.v.a. & n.* (*aux.* h.) to create; to produce; für etwas geschaffen sein, to be made, destined for something; er ist für diesen Posten wie geschaffen, he is the very man for this post, he is cut out for this post. II. *reg.v.a.* to do, make, work; to procure, provide, furnish with; to let have; to bring, convey, transport; to order, command (*prov.*); was —st du? what are you doing! ich habe heute nicht viel ge—t, I have not done much to-day, I have not got through much work to-day; ich habe nichts damit zu —en, that is no concern of mine, I wash my hands of it; er macht mir viel zu —en, he gives me a great deal of trouble, he causes me much anxiety; meine Migräne macht mir viel zu —en, my headache troubles me greatly; sein liebes Bild machte ihr viel zu —en, his dear image was always in her thoughts; —, daß du bald fertig bist, mind that you are ready soon; etwas fertig —en, to finish a thing; den Brief zur Post —en, to take *or* send the letter to the post; nach Hause —en, to take *or* convey home; Linderung —en, to soothe; aus dem Wege —en, to remove, get rid of; bei (*or* auf die) Seite —en, to put aside; to get done; to finish off; einen über Seite —en, to get rid of a p.; nichts —en, to effect nothing; da werde ich Rat —en, I shall see to that, find a way, er weiß immer Rat zu —en, he is never at a loss; sich (*dat.*) einen vom Halse —en, to shake s. o. off, get rid of a p. III. *reg.v.n.* (*aux.* h.) to work, be busy; einem zu —en geben *or* machen, to give a p. occupation, give s. o. trouble, plenty to do; sich (*dat.*) mit etwas zu —en machen, to occupy o.s. with, to be busy about a th.; das —t! that will do! that will help! that is some good! IV. *subst.n.* creating, creation. **—end,** *p. & adj.* creative. **—ner,** *m.* (**—ners,** *pl.* **—ner**) keeper of the house, agent, manager; steward, administrator; purveyor; waiter; conductor; guard (*Railw.*). **—nerei',** *f.* stewardship; office *or* house of a 'Schaffner.' **—nerin,** *f.* keeper of the house, housekeeper, female manager. *Comp.* **—ens=drang,** *m.* creative impulse, desire to create. **—ens=kraft,** *f.* creative power, genius.

Schafo'tt, *n.* (**—s,** *pl.* **—e**) scaffold.

[1]**Schaft,** *m.* (**—es,** *pl.* **Schäf'te**) shaft (*of a lance, of a column, etc.*); stock (*of a gun*); handle; shank; leg (*of a boot*); trunk (*of a tree*); flower-stalk; cutwater (*of a ship*). *Comp.* **—anlauf,** *m.* apophyge (*Arch.*). **—förmig,** *adj.* scapiform. **—halm, —leisten,** *m.* boot-tree, ast. **—nadel,** *f.* stocking-weaver's turning-needle. **—rinne,** *f.* fluting of a column. **—schneider,** *m.* pin-cutter.

[2]**Schaft,** *suffix in comp.* = ship.

Schäf'ten, *v.a.* to furnish with a stock, a handle, *etc.*; to stock, mount (*guns*); to splice (*a rope*); to put new legs to boots.

Schah, *m.* (**—s**) shah.

Scha'kal, *m.* (**—s,** *pl.* **—e**) jackal.

Scha'ke, *f.* (*pl.* **—n**) link of wire in the form of an S; link of a chain; mesh of a net.

Schä'ker, *m.* (**—s,** *pl.* **—**) jester, wag; joke. **—ei',** *f.* badinage; joke, jest. **—haft,** *adj.* playful, waggish.

Schä'kern, *v.n.* (*aux.* **h.**) to jest, joke, play tricks; **mit einem Mädchen —,** to flirt *or* dally with a girl.

Schal, *adj.* stale, flat, dull; insipid, spiritless, commonplace; trite, hackneyed. **—heit,** *f.* (**—sein,** *n.*) insipidity; vapidity.

Schäl'bar, *adj.* that may be peeled.

Schäl'chen, *n.* (**—s,** *pl.* **—**) small dish; cup; saucer.

Schä'l—en, *v.* I. *a.* to pare, peel; to shell; to blanch (*almonds*); to peel off sods; to bark (*trees*); **sie (er) ist wie aus dem Ei geschält,** she is as fresh as a daisy; he looks as if he had just come out of a bandbox, he looks spick and span; **geschält,** shelled, peeled. II. *r.* to peel *or* scale off; to cast the shell; to exfoliate; to blister. **—ung,** *f.* peeling; skinning; blistering, *etc.* *Comp.* **—maschine,** *f.* peeling machine. **—pflug,** *m.* plough for paring turf, breast-plough. **—seife,** *f.* kitchen soap. **—zahn,** *m.* decaying tooth.

Scha'l—e, *f.* (*pl.* **—en**) shell; skin; peel, rind; pod, husk; shell (*of crustacea*); capsule; bark; outside; cup (*of acorns*); bowl; cone-shaped vessel, vase; cup *or* saucer; scale (*of a balance*); slice; clasp-knife handle; cover (*of a book*); superficies; cloven hoof; toe (*of ungulated animals*); (*pl.*) fishes *or* cheeks (*Naut.*). **—ig,** *adj.* scaly, with a shell, *etc.*; crustaceous. *Comp.* **—brett,** *n.*, **—diele,** *f.* outside plank of a tree. **—en=förmig,** *adj.* cup-shaped. **—en=frucht,** *f.* shell-fruit. **—en=gehäuse,** *n.* shell (*of snails*). **—en=guß,** *m.* case-hardening, chill casting. **—en=kalk,** *m.* peastone. **—en=kreuz,** *n.* (**Robinsons**) Robinson's anemometer. **—en=mehl,** *n.* unbolted flour. **—holz,** *n.* barked timber, planks. **—latte,** *f.* bolster-prop (*Arch.*). **—tier,** *n.* crustacean, testacean, crustaceous animal, shell-fish; *pl.* conchylia. **—tier=kunde,** *f.* conchology. **—wage,** *f.* scales. **—wand,** *f.* board partition; wainscotted wall. **—werk,** *n.* planking, lining with wood.

Scha'len, *v.a.* to put a handle to; to board, wainscot.

Schalk, *m.* (**—(e)s,** *pl.* **—e;** *dial.* **Schäl'ke**) wag; rogue, knave; sly fellow; servant (*obs.*); *see* **—haftigkeit; er (sie) hat den — im Nacken,** he (she) is a sly-boots (sly fox *or* puss); **der — sieht ihm aus den Augen,** he looks a rogue, you can see the rogue in his eyes, he has a roguish twinkle in his eye. **—erei',** *see* **—haftigkeit. —haft,** *adj.* roguish, sly; waggish; crafty, wily. **—haftigkeit, —heit,** *f.* roguishness, slyness; roguery; guile, subtlety (*B.*); wile, wily trick. *Comp.* **—s=auge,** *n.* roguish eye. **—s=freund,** *m.* false friend. **—s=knecht,** *m.* unfaithful servant, unfaithful steward (*B.*). **—s=narr,** *m.* buffoon. **—s=ohr,** *n.* artful listener, one who pretends to be deaf. **—s=rat,** *m.* deceitful counsel. **—s=sinn,** *m.* roguish disposition, roguishness. **—s=streich,** *m.* wily trick.

Schall, *m.* (**—es**) sound; ring; peal; noise. *Comp.* **—becken,** *n.* cymbal. **—boden,** *m.* sounding-board. **—brechung,** *f.* refraction of sound. **—brechungs=lehre,** *f.* diacoustics. **—brett,** *n.* wind-chest (*of an organ*). **—dämpfer,** *m.* sourdine. **—empfindung,** *f.* acoustic sensation. **—erreger,** *m.* sound-producer. **—erregung,** *f.* radiophony (*Teleph.*). **—fülle,** *f.* sonority. **—glas,** *n.* musical glass. **—horn,** *n.* trumpet; trombone; *see* **Schalmei. —lehre,** *f.* acoustics. **—loch,** *n.* sound-hole (*in violins, etc.*); louvre window (*in a belfry*). **—messer,** *m.* phonometer. **—nachahmend,** *adj.* onomatopoetic. **—nachahmung,** *f.* onomatopœia, echoism. **—öffnung,** *f.*, **—rohr,** *n.* speaking trumpet; wind-instrument. **—schwingung,** *f.* acoustic vibration. **—stück,** *n.*, **—trichter,** *m.* bell mouth (*of a trumpet*). **—welle,** *f.* wave of sound, acoustic vibration.

Schal'l—en, *reg. & ir. v.n.* (*aux.* **h. & s.**) to sound, resound, ring; **es —t sehr in diesem Saale,** there is a strong echo in this room; **ein —endes Gelächter,** a loud peal of laughter, a roar; **in (ein) —endes Gelächter ausbrechen,** to burst into a fit of laughter.

Schalmei', *f.* (*pl.* **—en**) shalm, shawm (*Mus.*).

Schalot'te, *f.* (*pl.* **—n**) shallot.

Schalt, Schal'test, *1 & 3, and 2 pers. sing. imperf. ind. of* **schelten.**

Schal't—en, *v.n.* (*aux.* **h.**) to direct, govern, rule; to deal with; to put in the circuit; **mit** *or* **über etwas —en (und walten),** to dispose of, do as one likes with a th.; **einen —en und walten lassen,** to let a p. do as he likes; **wenn ich frei —en könnte,** if I were my own master, if I could do as I liked. **—er,** *m.* (*f.n.*) (**—ers,** *pl.* **—er**) ruler, disposer, master; sliding shutter; wall letter-box; (**zur Lösung von Fahrkarten**) booking-office. **—ung,** *f.* disposal (*of*); putting in the circuit. *Comp.* **—brett,** *n.* commutator, electrical switch, switch-board. **—er=beamte(r),** *m.* clerk at the counter; ticket-clerk. **—er=brief,** *m.* letter posted in a letter-box *or* at the counter; letter delivered at the window. **—er=dienst,** *m.* window-delivery. **—er=öffnung,** *f.* ticket-window; opening of the ticket-window. **—jahr,** *n.* leap-year. **—klinke,** *f.* click. **—tag,** *m.* intercalary day. **—vorrichtung,** *f.*, **—werk,** *n.*, feeding-device; switch. **—wort,** *n.* interpolated word. **—zeug,** *n.* feeding device (*Mach.*).

Schalup'pe, *f.* (*pl.* **—n**) sloop; shallop; long boat.

Scham, *f.* shame; bashfulness, modesty; disgrace, ignominy; nakedness (*B.*); genitals, privy parts, pudenda; **vor — erröten,** to blush with shame; **vor — vergehen,** to die with shame; **aller — den Kopf abgebissen haben, aller — bar sein,** to be dead to all sense of shame, to be past shame. **—haft,** *adj.* modest; bashful; chaste. **—haftigkeit,** *f.* modesty; chastity; bashfulness. *Comp.* **—bändchen,** *n.* ligament of the vulva. **—bein,** *n.* os pubis. **—bug,** *m.*, **—leiste,** *f.* groin. **—erröten,** *n.* blush of shame. **—gang,** *m.* vagina. **—gefühl,** *n.* sense of shame. **—gegend,** *f.* regio pubis. **—glied,** *n.* penis. **—hügel,** *m.* mons

Veneris. —lefze, —lippe, *f.* wings *or* lips of the vulva, labia pudendi. —los, *adj.* devoid of shame, shameless, impudent, brazen. —losig=keit, *f.* shamelessness; impudence. —nerv, *m.* pudic nerve. —pflanze, *f.* sensitive plant. —ritze, *f.* vagina. —rot, *adj.* blushing with shame; —rot machen, to put to the blush; —rot werden, to blush, to colour up. —röte, *f.* blush. —teile, *pl.* genitals, privates, pudenda. —züngelchen, *n.* clitoris.

Schama'de, *f.* parley (*Mil.*); —schlagen, to sound a parley; to give in (*fig.*).

Schä'men, *v.r.* to be ashamed (über eine S., wegen einer S., *also with gen.*) schäme dich! for shame! you ought to be ashamed of yourself! are n't you ashamed of yourself? ich brauche mich deshalb nicht zu —, I have no reason to be ashamed of that; ich schäme mich deiner, I am ashamed of you; er schämte sich über seine voreilige Bemerkung, he felt ashamed of *or* on account of his rash remark; du brauchst dich wegen deiner Liebe nicht zu —, you need not be ashamed of your love; sich vor einem —, to feel ashamed in a person's presence; sich zu Tode —, to die of *or* with shame.

Schä'mig, *adj.*, bashful, coy; shamefaced.

Schamot'te, *f.* fire-proof clay, chamotte.

Schamvie'len, *v.a.* to damage by friction; sich —, to chafe (*of ropes*).

Schand'—bar, *adj.* shameful, disgraceful; abominable (*coll.*). —barkeit, *f.* infamy. —e, *f.* (*pl.* —en) shame, disgrace; infamy; affront, ignominy, outrage; detriment; sich zu —en arbeiten, to wear oneself out by work; to kill oneself with work, to work the skin off one's fingers; zu —en machen, to spoil, confound, foil, overthrow, defeat, ruin, destroy; eine Hoffnung zu—en machen, to frustrate *or* baffle a hope; zu—en reiten, to override, founder (*a horse*); zu —en gehen, to go to ruin, perish; in —e bringen, to disgrace, to dishonour, debauch; einem —e bringen, to disgrace a p.; zu —en prügeln, to beat black and blue; to maim, cripple; —en halber, for honour's sake; zu—en werden, to come to nought; to be confounded; zu —en werden lassen, to cause *or* allow to be lost; Armut ist keine —, poverty is no sin (*prov.*). *Comp.* —bube, *m.* scoundrel. —buch, *n.* obscene book. —bühne, *f.* pillory. —deck, *n.* gunwale (*Naut.*). —fleck, *m.* stain, stigma. —geld, *n.* scandalous price. —gemälde, *n.* obscene picture. —geschichte, *f.* scandalous story. —glocke, *f.* bell which is tolled at the execution of a criminal. —kauf, *m.* disgraceful purchase; um einen —kauf, dirt-cheap. —leben, *n.* life of infamy. —lied, *n.* obscene song. —mal, *n.* brand of infamy. —maul, *n.* scandalous tongue; slanderer. —name, *m.* term of opprobrium. —pfahl, *m.*, —säule, *f.* pillory. —schrift, *f.* lampoon, libel; infamous writing. —that, *f.* infamous action; zu jeder —that aufgelegt, ready to do anything (*hum.*).

Schän'd—en, *v.a.* to disfigure, spoil, damage; to dishonour, bring infamy upon, disgrace; to desecrate, prostitute (*an art, etc.*); to violate, profane; to revile, defame; to rape, ravish. —er, *m.* (—ers, *pl.* —er) ravisher, despoiler; slanderer, traducer; blasphemer; der —er meiner Ehre, the defiler of my honour. —lich, *adj. & adv.* shameful, infamous, dishonourable, scandalous; despicable, vile, base; disfigured, frightful, ugly; das ärgert mich —lich, that annoys me extremely (*coll.*); es ist —lich kalt, it is most awfully cold; es ist —lich teuer, it is dreadfully expensive. —lichkeit, *f.* infamy, ignominy, disgrace, baseness, disgraceful conduct; merry trick (*hum.*). —ung, *f.* disfiguring, spoiling; profanation; violation; rape; prostitution (*of talents, etc.*); desecration, sacrilege (*of a temple*).

Schank, *m.* (—es) license for selling wine, beer, *etc.*; retail trade; public house. *Comp.* —bier, *n.* draught beer. —gerechtigkeit, *f. see under* Schenk. —lokal, *n.* public house, tap-house. —mamsell, *f.*, —mädchen, *n.* bar-maid.

Schan'ker, *m.* (—s, *pl.* —) chancre (*Med.*).

[1]**Schan'z—e,** *f.* (*pl.* —en) bulwark, intrenchment; quarter-deck; geschlossene —e, redoubt, fort. —en, *v.* I. *n.* (*aux.* h.) to work in the trenches, at a fortification; to drudge, work hard, toil (*coll.*). II. *a.* to throw up as an intrenchment. *Comp.* —arbeit, *f.* work at a fortification; intrenchment. —gräber, *m.* sapper, pioneer. —gerät, *see* —zeug. —kleid, *n.* waist-cloth (*Naut.*). —korb, *m.* gabion (*Fort.*). —kunst, *f.* art of fortification *or* intrenchment. —pfahl, *m.* palisade. —sack, *m.* earth *or* sand-bag. —verkleidung, *f.* barricade (*Naut.*). —wehr, *f.* barrier. —werk, *n.* intrenchment, redoubt. —zeug, *n.* pioneering *or* intrenching implements.

[2]**Schan'ze,** *f.* (*pl.* —n) chance; hazard; in die — schlagen, to stake, risk, hazard; sein Leben in die — schlagen, to risk one's life; seine — warten, to bide one's time (*obs.*).

Schap'pel, *n.* chaplet, wreath for the head (*obs.*).

Schar, *f.* (*pl.* —en) (*plough-*)share; troop, band; herd, flock; host, multitude, crowd. —en, *v.* I. *a.* to collect. II. *r.* to assemble, to flock together, to form into bands; to congregate. *Comp.* —en=führer, *m.* leader, captain of a band. —en=weise, *adv.* in bands *or* troops. —kramme, *f.* cramp of the ploughshare. —riegel, *m.* ploughshare pin. —schmied, *m.* ploughshare maker; hatchet-cutter. —wache, *f.* patrol; watch. —wächter, *m.* soldier on patrol; watchman.

Schar'be, *f.* (*pl.* —n) cormorant, sea-raven.

Schar'b—en, (**Schär'ben,**) *v.a.* to chop, mince, cut small (*Cook.*). *Comp.* —e=brett, *n.* chopping-board. —e=messer, *n.* chopping knife.

Schar'bock, *m.* scurvy; mit — behaftet, scurvy-stricken. *See* Skorbut.

Schä'ren, *pl.* cliffs on the coasts of Sweden and Finland. *See* Schere.

Scharf, *adj. & adv.* (schär'fer, schärfst) sharp; biting; stinging; pungent; shrill; acrid; acute; pointed; keen; severe, rigorous, austere; strict, exact; quick; penetrating; —er Accent, acute accent; ein —es Ohr, a quick ear; —e Gesichtszüge, sharply cut features; —e Patrone, ball-cartridge; —e Kälte, biting cold; —e Untersuchung, searching examination; —e Luft, keen *or* strong air; —es Gift, strong poison; —e Frage, examination under torture; —gebautes Schiff, sharp-floored ship; —er Winkel, acute angle; —e Flüssigkeit, corrosive liquid; —e Zunge, sharp tongue; —e Antwort, cutting reply; —er Verweis, severe rebuke; ein —es Gesicht haben, —sehen, to be keen-sighted; to have judgment, see clearly; einen — ansehen, to look at a p. hard *or* closely; einem — zu Leibe gehen, to press a p. hard; — laden, to charge with ball; — beschlagen, to rough-shoe (*a horse*); — betonen, to accentuate strongly; hinter dem Gelde — her sein, to have an eye to the main chance, be good at making money; einen — anlassen, to snap a p. up; allzu — macht schartig, a bow long bent at last grows weak. *Comp.* —blätterig, *adj.* scabrous-leafed. —blick, *m.* piercing look; sharp-sightedness; acuteness, penetration. —eckig, *adj.* sharp-cornered; acute-angled. —eisen, *n.* calking-iron. —kantig, *adj.* sharp-edged; acute-angled. —macher, *m.* (mill-stone) dresser; firebrand, extremist (*fig.*). —rennen, *n.* tournament with sharp weapons. **—richter,** *m.* executioner. **—schmeckend,** *adj.* pungent. **—schuß,** *m.* shot with ball. **—schütze,** *m.* sharp-shooter, rifleman. **—sichtig,** *adj.* sharp-sighted; clear-sighted; penetrating; subtle. **—sichtigkeit,** *f* keenness of vision; perspicacity, penetration. **—sinn,** *m.* sagacity, acuteness, penetration; ingenuity. **—sinnig,** *adj.* clear-sighted, sagacious; ingenious. **—sinnigkeit,** *f.* sagacity; penetration; ingeniousness.

Schär'f—e, *f.* (*pl.* **—en**) edge; sharpness, keenness, fineness; acuteness, keenness; causticity; acidity; severity, rigour; exactness; point (*of epigrams, etc.*); acuteness (*of a vowel*).

Schär'f—en, *v.a.* to whet, sharpen; to heighten, aggravate; to mend (*a pen*), point (*a pencil*); to rough-shoe (*a horse*); to graze (*the skin*); to hoe; to pare; to dress, cut, edge; **einem das Gewissen —en,** to rouse a p.'s conscience; **einen Vokal —en,** to give the short, sharp sound to a vowel; **das Gedächtnis —en,** to strengthen the memory; **den Blick —en,** to strain one's eyes. **—ung,** *f.* sharpening, augmenting, strengthening. *Comp.* **—(e)=messer,** *n.* bookbinder's paring-knife.

Schar'lach, *m.* (**—s**) scarlet. **—en,** *adj.* scarlet. *Comp.* **—baum,** *m.* kermes-oak. **—blume,** *f.* scarlet lychnis. **—bohne,** *f.* scarlet runner. **—farben, —farbig,** *adj.* scarlet, vermilion. **—fieber,** *n.* scarlet fever; scarlatina.

Scharmüt'z—el, *n.* (**—els,** *pl.* **—el**) skirmish. **—eln, —ie'ren,** *v.n.* (*aux.* **h.**) to skirmish, to have a brush with the enemy. **—ler,** *m.* (**—lers,** *pl.* **—ler**) skirmisher.

Scharnie'r, *n.* (**—s,** *pl.* **—e**) hinge, joint. *Comp.* **—band,** *n.* joint-frame. **—stift,** *m.* joint-pin. **—zirkel,** *m.* joint *or* hinge compasses.

Schär'pe, *f.* (*pl.* **—n**) scarf, sash; sling.

Scharpie', Charpie', *f.* (**—,** *pl.* **—(e)n**), lint.

Schar're, *f.* (*pl.* **—n**) raking, scraping; rake; scraper; place raked *or* scraped; scrapings.

Schar'r—en, *v.a. & n.* (*aux.* **h.**) to scrape, scratch; to paw (*of horses*); to rake; to hoe; **etwas in die Erde —en,** to bury something in the ground; **in die** (*or* **der**) **Erde —en,** to paw the ground (*as horses*), to shuffle with the feet; **in der Vorlesung —en,** to make a noise with the feet at a lecture (*either as a mark of disapproval*, or *as greeting*, or *to intimate that the lecturer has not been understood*). **—er,** *m.* (**—ers,** *pl.* **—er**) scraper; skinflint; (*pl.*) gallinaceous birds. *Comp.* **—eisen,** *n.* scraper, scuffling-hoe. **—fuß,** *m.* claw of gallinaceous birds; awkward bow, scrape. **—vogel,** *m.* scratcher.

Schar't—e, *f.* (*pl.* **—en**) notch; fissure; chink; gap; ward (*of a key*); crack; **eine —e auswetzen,** to grind out a notch, to make amends, repair a damage; to square accounts, take one's revenge for; **Schieß—e,** loop-hole. **—ig,** *adj.* jagged, full of notches; battlemented. *Comp.* **—en=blende,** *f.* embrasure-shutter. **—en=zeile,** *f.* merlon (*Fort.*).

Scharte'ke, *f.* (*pl.* **—n**) wretched, musty old book; trashy publication; trumpery, trash, old stuff *or* thing.

Schar'te=partie, *f.* charter-party (*Naut.*).

Schar'werk, *n.* (**—s**) statute labour. **—en,** *v.a.* to do statute labour (*for the lord of the manor*), to fag, toil.

Schat't—en, *m.* (**—ens,** *pl.* **—en**) shadow, shade; shade, spirit; shelter; shade (*Paint.*); **in den —en stellen,** to place in the shade, to throw into the shade; **Fürst der —en,** Prince of Shades, Death; **das Reich der —en,** kingdom of Shades, of Death, Hades; (*Schiller: realm of forms, the ideal, art*); **er macht mir —en,** he stands in my light. **—en=haft,** *adj.* shadowy. **—ig,** *adj.* shady, shadowy. **—ie'ren,** *v.a. & n.* (*aux.* **h.**) to shade (*of colours, etc.*). **—ie'rung,** *f.* gradation of colour, shading; imperceptible transition; shade, tint. *Comp.* **—en=bild,** *n.* silhouette, outline; phantom; *pl.* fictions, poetic fancies (*poet.*). **—en=erz,** *n.* lead-ore. **—en=farbe,** *f.* umber. **—en=fernrohr,** *n.* sciatheric telescope. **—en=gang,** *m.* shady walk. **—en=gebend,** *adj.* shady. **—en=gebung,** *f.* shading of a picture. **—en=gestalt,** *f.* phantom. **—en=größe,** *f.* imaginary greatness. **—en=land,** *n.* = **—en=reich,** *n.* abode of the Shades *or* departed souls, Hades. **—en=leuchte,** *f.* magic lantern. **—en=licht,** *n.* chiaroscuro. **—en=linie,** *f.* outline. **—en=los,** *adj.* shadowless; shadeless. **—en=reich,** I. *adj.* umbrageous, shady. II. *n.* Hades. **—en=riß,** *m.* silhouette; outline. **—en=seite,** *f.* shady side (*of a street*); dark side; drawback; **—enseite an einer Sache,** drawback to a thing; **er sieht an allem nur die —enseite,** he always looks on the dark side of things. **—en=spiel,** *n.* phantasmagoria; magic lantern; (**chinesisches**) ombres chinoises. **—en=stufe,** *f.* shading, gradation of shade. **—en=uhr,** *f.* sun-dial. **—en=wesen,** *n.* phantom. **—en=zeiger,** *m.* gnomon (*of a dial, etc.*).

Schatul'l—e, *f.* (*pl.* **—en**) casket, strong box; (**—en=gelder, —gelder,** *pl.*) privy purse (*of a prince*). *Comp.* **—en=brief,** *m.* casket letter. **(en=)gut,** *n.* private estate of a prince.

Schatz, *m.* (**—es,** *pl.* **Schät'ze**) treasure; store; sweetheart, love, darling. **—bar,** *adj.* ratable, assessable; tributary. *Comp.* **—amt,** *n.* treasury, exchequer. **—anweisung,** *f.* treasury-bond, exchequer-bill. **—einnehmer,** *m.* treasurer. **—geld,** *n.* spare-money; rare coin; tax. **—gräber,** *m.* treasure-digger. **—kammer,** *f.* treasury; exchequer; jewel-room. **—kammer=schein,** *m.* bill of exchequer. **—kanzler,** *m.* chancellor of the exchequer. **—kasten,** *m.* casket; strong box, safe; royal coffers. **—kästchen, —kästlein,** *n.* collection of gems; cameos (*fig.*). **—meister, —verwalter, —verweser,** *m.* treasurer; chancellor of the exchequer. **—pflichtig,** *adj.* taxable, ratable. **—rat,** *m.* (member of a) revenue-board. **—schreiber,** *m.* clerk of the treasury. **—tafel,** *f.* tariff.

Schätz'bar, *adj.* valuable; estimable. **—keit,** *f.* worth, merit, preciousness.

Schätz'chen, *n.* (**—s,** *pl.* **—**) sweetheart, darling.

Schat'z—en, *v.a.* to tax, assess; *see* **Brandschatzen.** **—ung,** *f.* tax, assessment, taxation.

Schät'z—en, *v.a.* to value, appraise, estimate; to esteem, prize; to consider; **ich —e,** I am of opinion, I think, hold; **ich — nein,** I don't think so (*dial.*); **gering —en,** to think little of, despise; **es für eine Ehre** *or* **es sich** (*dat.*) **zur Ehre —en,** to esteem it an honour; **sich glücklich —en,** to think oneself fortunate; **wie alt —en Sie ihn?** how old do you suppose he is? **geschätzt,** esteemed, *etc.*, in request; **das geschätzte Ihrige** *or* **Ihr Geschätztes vom . . .,** your esteemed favour of (*such and such a date*). **—er,** *m.* (**—ers,** *pl.* **—er**) appraiser, valuer, rater. **—ung,** *f.* estimation, valuing, appraisement; tax; estimate; **Gering—ung,** disdain, disregard, contempt. *Comp.* **—ens=wert, —ens=würdig,** *adj.* estimable, precious. **—ungs=anschlag,** *m.* estimate, assessment. **—ungs=preis,** *m.* fixed price; valuer's fee. **—ungs=protokoll,** *n.* draft of estimate.

Schau, *f.* (*pl.* **—en**) show, sight, view; inspection, parade, review; exhibition; **nur zur —,** only for show; **zur — tragen,** to display, to make a boast *or* display of.

Schau'—en, *v.* I. *a.* to look at, gaze upon, behold, see; to examine, inspect. II. *n.* (*aux.* **h.**) to look, gaze, see; **auf etwas** (*acc.*) **—en,** to have regard to, take care of, to take as model; **in die Zukunft —en**, to look into *or* scan the future; **da — mal einer!** look here, now really, I say! (*coll.*). **—er**, *m.* (**—ers**, *pl.* **—er**) spectator, beholder; inspector; expert. *Comp.* **—amt**, *n.* office of inspection. **—begierig**, *adj.* eager to see. **—brot**, *n.* shew-bread. **—bühne**, *f.* stage. **—ende**, *n.* pattern, show-end (*of cloth*). **—fenster**, *n.* shop window, show-window. **—gebühr**, *f.* entrance-money; gate-money. **—gepränge**, *n.* pageantry, pomp. **—gericht**, *n.* show-dish, dish put on the table for show only; table-ornament. **—gerüst**, *n.* scaffold, stage; catafalque; gallery, stand. **—glas**, *n.* opera-glass; spy-glass. **—herr**, *m.* inspector (*of mines*). **—ins=land**, *m.* name given to certain mountains and watch-towers. **—kästchen**, *n.* showcase. **—lustig**, *adj.* curious (*to see*). **—münze**, *f.* medal. **—platz**, *m.* theatre, scene; **Kriegs—platz**, seat of war; **vom —platz abtreten**, to retire into private life, to die. **—spiel**, *n. see* **Schauspiel**. **—stellen**, *v.a.* to exhibit, to display. **—steller**, *m.* exhibitor. **—stellung**, *f.* exhibition. **—stufe**, *f.* fine specimen of ore. **—tag**, *m.* day of inspection. **—tisch**, *m.* table of the shew-bread (*B.*). **—turm**, *m.* belvedere; watch-tower. **—turnen**, *n.* gymnastic display. **—werk**, *n.* specimen, sample, show-goods.

Schaub, *m.* (**—(e)s**, *pl.* **—e**, **Schäu'be**) bundle of straw (*dial.*).

Schau'be, *f.* (*pl.* **—n**) mantle; cassock; petticoat.

Schau'der, *m.* (**—s**, *pl.* **—**) shuddering; shudder, horror. **—haft**, *adj.* horrible, terrible, frightful, atrocious; **—hafte Ausgabe**, frightful expense (*coll.*). **—haftigkeit**, *f.* horribleness, horror. **—ös**, *adj.* frightful (*sl.*).

Schau'der—n, *v.* I. *n.* (*aux.* **h.** & **s.**) & *imp.* to shudder, shiver; to feel dread of *or* awed; **mir —t bei dem Gedanken**, I shudder at the thought; **vor Kälte —n**, to shiver with cold. II. *a.* & *imp.* to cause to shudder, shiver *or* feel awe; **mich —t's vor**, I dread. *Comp.* **—gefühl**, *n.* feeling of dread. **—geschichte**, *f.* awful tale. **—scenen**, *pl.* ghastly scenes, scenes of horror.

1**Schau'er**, *m.* (**—s**, *pl.* **—**) shower (*of rain, etc.*); squall, storm; chill; thrill; attack, fit, paroxysm; shuddering, awe, terror; *see* **Schauder**; **heiliger —**, sacred awe. **—lich**, **—ig**, *adj. see* **Schauderhaft**, shivering, shuddering, chilly. **—lichkeit**, *f. see* **Schauderhaftigkeit**. **—n**, *v.n.* (*aux.* **h.**) to shudder, shiver; **es —t**, it is pouring, raining (*rare*). *Comp.* **—bad**, *n.* shower-bath. **—gefühl**, *n.* feeling of horror. **—kerl**, *m.* horrible fellow (*sl.*). **—roman**, *m.* penny dreadful, horrible story of knights and robbers. **—that**, *f.* atrocity. **—voll**, *adj.* dreadful, most awful.

2**Schau'er**, (*m.* &) *n.* (**—s**, *pl.* **—**) shed, shelter, pent-house (*dial.*).

Schau'erleute, *pl.* quay-porters, wharfingers, lightermen.

Schau'fel, *f.* (*pl.* **—n**) shovel; scoop, ladle; paddle; float-board; blade (*of an oar*); palm, fluke (*of an anchor*); *see* **—zahn**; palm-antlers. *Comp.* **—band**, *n.* dovetail-hinge. **—blatt**, *n.* pan of a shovel. **—förmig**, *adj.* shovel-shaped. **—gehörn**, **—geweih**, *n.* palmed antlers. **—hirsch**, *m.* fallow deer over two years. **—kasten**, *m.* paddle-box. **—kunst**, *f.* chain-pump. **—pflug**, *m.* moulding-plough. **—rad**, *n.* float-wheel; paddle-wheel. **—stück**, *n.* shoulder of venison. **—weise**, *adv.* by shovelfuls. **—zahn**, *m.* incisor.

Schau'feln, *v.a.* to dig, to shovel, to rake.

Schauf'ler, *m.* one who shovels *or* digs; grave-digger; fallow deer; incisor.

Schau'k—el, *f.* (*pl.* **—eln**) see-saw; swing. **—eln**, *v.* I. *n.* (*aux.* **h.**) to balance; to see-saw; to rock; to pitch (*of ships*). II. *a.* to swing; to rock; to dandle (*a child, etc.*); **sich auf einem Stuhle —eln**, to rock backwards and forwards, to balance oneself on a chair. *Comp.* **—el=brett**, *n.* see-saw. **—el=pferd**, *n.* rocking-horse, rocker. **—el=reck**, *n.* trapeze. **—el=stuhl**, *m.* rocking-chair.

Schaum, *m.* (**—(e)s**, *pl.* **Schäu'me**) foam, froth; scum; spume; lather; bubble, idle *or* deceitful vision; **Bier auf — schenken**, to pour out beer so that it froths; **zu — schlagen**, to beat up (*the white of an egg*); **Träume sind Schäume**, dreams are mere shadows (*prov.*). *Comp.* **—artig**, *adj.* & *adv.* frothy, foamy. **—bedeckt**, *adj.* covered with foam. **—blase**, *f.* bubble; delusion. **—geboren**, *adj.* sprung from the sea-foam (*of Venus*). **—gold**, *see* **Flittergold**. **—kelle**, *f.*, **—löffel**, *m.* skimming ladle. **—kette**, *f.* slavering *or* water-chain. **—los**, *adj.* without foam *or* froth; without a head, flat (*of beer*). **—tierchen**, *n.* frog-hopper. **—wein**, *m.* sparkling wine, sparkling hock.

Schäu'men, *v.* I. *n.* (*aux.* **h.**) to foam, froth; to spume; to produce a lather; to sparkle. II. *a.* to skim.

Schau'spiel, *n.* (**—s**, *pl.* **—e**) spectacle, sight, play, drama; **ins — gehen**, to go to the theatre. **—er**, *m.* (**—ers**, *pl.* **—er**) player, actor; **herumziehender —er**, strolling actor. **—erin**, *f.* actress. **—e(r)n**, *v.n.* (*aux.* **h.**) to act, play the actor; to go in for theatricals (*coll.*). *Comp.* **—artig**, *adj.* dramatic, theatrical. **—dichter**, *m.* playwright, dramatist, dramatic poet. **—dichtung**, *f.* dramatic poetry. **—haus**, *n.* theatre. **—kunst**, *f.* dramatic art. **—schreiber**, *m.* playwright.

Schau'te, *m.* (**—n**, *pl.* **—n**) fool (*sl.*).

Schebe'cke, *f* xebec (*Mediterranean three-master*).

Schech, *m. see* **Scheich**.

1**Scheck**, *m.* (**—en**, *pl.* **—en**), **—e**, *f.* (*pl.* **—en**) piebald horse (*or* other animal). **—ig**, *adj.* pied, piebald; dappled; spotted; **sich —ig lachen**, to split one's sides with laughing (*coll.*).

2**Scheck**, *m.* (**—s**, *pl.* **—s**) cheque.

Scheel, *adj.* oblique; askance, awry; squint-eyed; **— zu etwas sehen, etwas mit —en Augen ansehen**, to regard a th. with jealousy. *Comp.* **—auge**, *n.* squinting eye, evil eye. **—äugig**, *adj.* squinting; jealous. **—sucht**, *f.* envy. **—süchtig**, *adj.* envious, jealous.

Schef'fel, *m.* (**—s**, *pl.* **—**) bushel. **—n**, *v.n.* (*aux.* **h.**) to yield bushels *or* in abundance. *Comp.* **—macher**, *m.* cooper, bushel-maker. **—sack**, *m.* sack holding a bushel. **—steuer**, *f.* tax on every bushel of corn. **—weise**, *adv.* by the bushel.

Schegg, *m.* (**—es**, *pl.* **—e**) foremost part of the cutwater (*Naut.*); **— des Steuers**, after-piece of a rudder.

Scheib'—chen, *n.* (**—chens**, *pl.* **—chen**) little disk; little slice. **—e**, *f.* (*pl.* **—en**) disk; orb; slice (*of bread, etc.*); wafer; (*honey-*)comb; target; dial-plate; face (*of a clock, etc.*); quoit; wheel; sheave (*of a block*); pulley; coil (*of rope*); pane (*of glass*); **—e des Kompasses**, compass-card; **ja —e!** no, thank you! I should not think of such a thing! (*coll.*). **—ig**, *adj.* orbicular, round; **zwei—iger Block**, two-wheeled pulley. *Comp.* **—en=ähnlich**, **—en=artig**, *adj.* disk-shaped. **—en=bank**, *f.* drawing-plate. **—en=binde**, *f.* rhomb-shaped bandage. **—en=blei**, *n.* glazier's lead. **—en=blume**, *f.* discoid flower. **—en=bohrer**, *m.* cooper's turrel. **—en=büchse**, *f.* rifle, kind of arquebuse. **—en=drehbank**, *f.* surfacing lathe. **—en=honig**, *m.* honey in the comb. **—en=instrument**, *n.* astrolabe. **—en=könig**, *m.* best shot at a shooting-match; chief of a rifle-club. **—en=kunst**, *f.* chain-pump. —

en=maschine, *f.* plate-machine (*Elect.*). —**en=nagel,** *m.* nail in a target. —**en=pulver,** *n.* fine gunpowder. —**en=rohr,** *n.* rifle, gun. —**en=schießen,** *n.* target-shooting; rifle-match; ball-practice, target-practice (*Mil.*). —**en=schleier,** —**en=stand,** *m.* butt. —**en=umschalter,** *m.* plate-commutator. —**en=weise,** *adv.* in slices. —**en=werfen,** *n.* quoit-throwing. —**en=werk,** *n.* sheaves, pulleys.

Scheich, *m.* (—**s**, *pl.* —**s**) sheikh.

Scheid'—bar, *adj.* separable; divisible; that can be analyzed (*Chem.*). —**e,** *f.* (*pl.* —**en**) place *or* point of separation; boundary, limit; case, sheath; scabbard; vagina. *Comp.* —**e=los,** *adj.* sheathless. —**en=artig,** *adj.* sheath-like; vaginal. —**en=entzündung,** *f.* vaginitis. —**en=klappe,** *f.* hymen. —**en=mündung,** *f.* orifice of the vagina. —**en=schnitt,** *m.* vaginotomy.

Schei'd—en, I. *ir.v.r. & n.* (*aux.* **f.**) to separate; to depart; **das —ende Jahr,** the closing year. II. *ir.v.a.* to separate, divide, part; to analyze, refine; to decompose; to divorce; **so schieden wir,** thus we parted; **hier schieden sie von einander,** here they took leave of one another; **sich —en lassen,** to sue for a divorce, to obtain a judicial separation, to get divorced; **wir sind geschiedene Leute,** we have nothing more to do with one another; **aus diesem Leben —en,** to depart this life; **die Milch —et sich,** the milk turns, grows sour; **hier —en sich die Wege,** here the roads part, branch off; **der (die) Geschiedene,** divorced person. III. *subst.n.* parting, separation; **vor seinem —en,** before leaving; previous to his death; **—en (und Meiden) thut weh,** partings are sad things, parting is painful. —**er,** *m.* (—**ers**, *pl.* —**er**) separater; metal-refiner. —**ung,** *f. see* —**en** III.; divorce; clarifying; decomposition, chemical analysis; —**ung von Gold und Silber,** parting, refining of gold and silver. *Comp.* —**e=bank,** *f.* bench *or* table on which the ore is culled. —**e=brief,** *m.* farewell letter; bill of divorce. —**e=erz,** *n.* picked, culled ore. —**e=feuer,** *n.* refining furnace. —**e=gerüst,** —**e=gestell,** *n.* insulator (*Phys.*). —**e=glas,** *n.* separatory (*Chem.*). —**e=gruß,** *m.* farewell (*greeting*). —**e=herr,** *m.* arbitrator. —**e=kolben,** *m.* alembic. —**e=kunst,** *f.* analytical chemistry. —**e=künstler,** *m.* analyst. —**e=kuß,** *m.* parting kiss. —**e=linie,** *f.* line of demarcation; boundary. —**e=mauer,** *f.* partition wall. —**e=messer,** *n.* separatory (*Surg.*). —**e=münze,** *f.* small coin, copper coin, (small) change. —**e=punkt,** *m.* point of separation *or* divergence; boundary; diæresis. —**e=stunde,** *f.* hour of parting *or* death. —**e=wand,** *f.* partition-wall; barrier; septum (*of the heart, brain, etc.*). —**e=wasser,** *n.* aqua fortis. —**e=weg,** *m.* boundary; cross-road, place where roads meet; **am —ewege stehen,** to stand at the parting of the ways, to have to choose between two courses; to be undecided; **Herkules am —ewege,** the choice of Hercules. —**e=zeichen,** *n.* signal for parting; dying knell; diæresis (*Gram.*). —**ungs=erkenntnis,** *n.* decree nisi. —**ungs=kraft,** *f.* force of induction.

Schein, *m.* (—**s**, *pl.* —**e**) shine; light (*of the lamp, sun, moon, etc.*); splendour, lustre; aspect; appearance; show, outside; pretence, semblance; illusion; receipt, bond, bill, quittance; I.O.U.; certificate; glory, halo; blaze, glare; gleam, glimpse; **zum —e, des —es wegen,** for form's sake; **sie thun das nur zum —,** they only do it for show; it is all pretence; **den bösen — meiden, den — retten,** to save appearances; **unter dem —e der Freundschaft, (Rechtens),** under the pretence *or* cloak of friendship (*of justice*); **kein — von Hoffnung,** no glimmer of hope; **es hat den —, als ob . . .,** it looks as if . . .; **dem —e nach,** apparently; **sich** (*dat.*) **den — geben,** to pretend; **das ist alles nur —,** that is all pretence; **der — trügt,** appearances are deceitful, appearances often deceive (*prov.*). —**bar,** *adj.* apparent, seeming; ostensible, plausible; evident; showy, good-looking; **der —bare Horizont,** the sensible horizon. —**barkeit,** *f.* seemingness, likelihood, plausibility. *Comp.* (*gen'lly* = pretended, sham, pseudo; illusory; apparent.) —**angriff,** *m.* feigned attack, demonstration. —**behelf,** *m.* shift, evasion, specious excuse. —**bild,** *n.* illusion; phantom. —**buße,** *f.* feigned penitence. —**christ,** *m.* pretended *or* lip Christian. —**ding,** *n.* phantom, chimera. —**ehe,** *f.* pretended marriage, mock marriage. —**farben,** *pl.* accidental colours (*Phys.*). —**friede,** *m.* hollow peace. —**fromm,** *adj.* hypocritical. —**furcht,** *f.* pretended fear. —**gefecht,** *n.* sham-fight. —**gelehrt,** *adj.* would-be learned. —**gelehrsamkeit,** *f.* would-be learning, pretended erudition. —**gericht,** *n.* mock trial. —**glück,** *n.* seeming happiness. —**grund,** *m.* apparent reason; pretence; sophism. —**heilig,** *adj.* sanctimonious. —**heilige(r),** *m.* hypocrite. —**hoffnung,** *f.* delusive hope. —**klage,** *f.* mock action. —**krankheit,** *f.* feigned illness. —**leben,** *n.* semblance of life; empty life. —**mittel,** *n.* palliative (*remedy*). —**s=halber,** *adv.* to save appearances. —**spröde,** *adj.* apparently coy. —**tod,** *m.* apparent death, trance. —**tot,** *adj.* in a trance, asphyxiated. —**übel,** *n.* imaginary evil. —**verkauf,** *m.* pro forma sale, fictitious sale. —**wechsel,** *m.* accommodation-bill. —**werfer,** *m.* reflector; **elektrischer —werfer,** (*electric*) search light. —**wesen,** *n.* imaginary being, phantom.

Schei'n—en, *ir.v.n.* (*aux.* **h.**) to shine; to seem, appear, look; to suit, please; **die Sonne —t warm,** the sun is hot; **sie —en reich zu sein, es —t, als ob sie reich sind,** they seem to be rich; **wenn es Ihnen gut —t,** if it seems good *or* advisable to you, if you like; **ein Anderes ist —en, ein Anderes ist sein,** things are not always what they seem; **mir will es nicht recht —en,** it does not please me altogether; I cannot credit that; **wie —t dir die Geschichte?** what do you think of the story, do you think there is anything in it?

Schei'ß—en, *ir.v.a. & n.* (*aux.* **h.**) to go to stool, to void, excrete (*vulg.*). —**erei',** *f.* excrement; voiding (*of excrement*).

Scheit, *n.* (—(e)**s**, *pl.* —**e**, —**er**) log, billet; packer's stick; little board; **zu —ern gehen,** to go to ruin, to be wrecked. —**ern,** *v. n.* (*aux.* **h.** & **f.**) to run aground, become a wreck; to be frustrated, miscarry; **daran —ert meine (ganze) Kunst,** that is beyond me, beats me; **das Schiff ist gescheitert,** the ship was wrecked. *Comp.* —**er=haufen,** *m.* funeral pile, pyre; **einen zum —erhaufen verurteilen,** to condemn a p. to be burnt alive, to send a p. to the stake. —**flöße,** *f.* canal on which wood is floated. —**hauer,** *m.* woodcutter. —**holz,** *n.* log(s). —**maß,** *n.* log wood measure. —**meiler,** *m.* charcoal-burner's furnace for logs. —**recht,** *n.* straight (*Arch.*).

Schei'tel, *m.* (—**s**, *pl.* —) top, vertex, summit; crown of the head; parting (*of the hair*); origin of coördinates (*Math.*); **vom — bis zur Sohle,** from top to bottom, from head to heel; from top to toe, from head to foot, from the crown of one's head to the sole of one's foot; **zum — gehörig,** vertical. —**n,** *v.a.* to part the hair; **sich —n,** to part (*of the hair*); **die Gescheitelten und die Geschorenen,** the parsons and the priests, Protestant and Roman Catholic clergy. *Comp.* —**bein,** *n.* parietal bone. —**ecke,** *f.*

vertical angle, angle at the apex. **—fläche,** *f.* vertical plane. **—g(e)rade,** *see* **—recht.** **—käppchen,** *n.* skull-cap. **—kreis,** *m.* vertical circle, azimuth. **—linie,** *f.* vertical line. **—punkt,** *m.* vertex; zenith. **—recht,** *adj. & adv.* vertical; perpendicular. **—winkel,** *m.* vertical angle; azimuth; (*pl.*) vertical *or* opposite angles.

Schelch, *m.* (—(e)s, *pl.*—e) barge, lighter (*dial.*).

Schel'fe, Schil'fe, *f.* (*pl.* —n) husk, shell (of fruits); valve. **—n, —rn,** *v.n.* to peel off, to shell (off). **—r,** *f.* dandruff. **—rig,** *adj.* peeling off.

Schel'le, *f.* (*pl.* —n) little bell; bell; box on the ear (*rare*); manacle; diamonds (*at cards*); **wie eine klingende —,** as a tinkling cymbal (*B.*). *Comp.* **—n=bube,** *m.* knave of diamonds. **—n=geläut,** *n.* tinkling of bells; sleigh-bells; bell-harness. **—n=kappe,** *f.* fool's cap and bells, coxcomb. **—n=schlitten,** *m.* sledge with bells. **—n=trommel,** *f.* tambourine; timbrel. **—n=zug,** *m.* bell-pull.

Schel'len, *v.a. & n.* (*aux.* **h.**) to ring, ring the bell; to tinkle; **einem —,** to ring for s. o.; **— Sie!** ring the bell! **es hat geschellt,** there was the bell; **ich habe geschellt,** I have rung the bell.

Schell'fisch, *m.* haddock.

Schell'hammer, *m.* large hammer; oress-punch.

Schell'hengst, *m.* stallion.

Schell'lack, *m.* shellac. *Comp.* **—politur,** *f.* French polish.

Schelm, *m.* (—**es,** —**en,** *pl.* —**e,** —**en**) rogue, rascal, knave, swindler; **armer —,** poor wretch *or* fellow; **an einem zum — werden,** to betray a p.; **ein —, der mehr thut als er kann,** you must not expect impossibilities (*prov.*); **ein — giebt mehr als er hat,** you cannot give more than you have (*prov.*); **auf einen — gehören anderthalb,** set a thief to catch a thief; pay rogues in their own coin (*prov.*); **je ärger —, je besser Glück,** the greater the rogue, the greater his luck (*prov.*); **ein — der Schlechtes dabei denkt,** honi soit qui mal y pense; **den — im Nacken** *or* **hinter den Ohren haben,** to be a sly dog; **ihm sitzt der — im Nacken,** he is full of fun. **—erei',** *f.* roguery; villainy. **—in,** *f.* female rogue, roguish girl *or* woman; cunning woman, vixen. **—isch,** *adj.* roguish; knavish. *Comp.* **—(en)=gesicht,** *n.* knavish *or* roguish countenance; roguish-looking person. **—(en)=sprache,** *f.* thieves' slang. **—(en)=streich,** *m.*, **—(en)=stück,** *n.* knavish trick, piece of roguery, prank.

Schelt'—bar, *adj.* blamable. **—e,** *f.* (*pl.* —**en**) rebuke, reprimand; **—e bekommen,** to be scolded.

Schel't—en, *ir.v.a. & n.* (*aux.* **h.**) to blame; to reproach; to scold, chide, reprimand; to call, to nickname; **auf einen —en,** to scold a p., to inveigh against a p.; **einen einen Dummkopf —en,** to call a p. a blockhead *or* stupid. **—er,** *m.* (—**ers,** *pl.* —**er**) scolder, reviler. *Comp.* **—brief,** *m.* scolding letter. **—name,** *m.* opprobrious name; nickname. **—wort,** *n.* abusive word, insulting word, invective.

Sche'ma, *n.* (—**s,** *pl.* **Schemata**) scheme; model, pattern. **—tisch,** *adj.* (*pron.* **schema'tisch**) schematic, in accordance with a certain plan *or* pattern. **—tisie'ren,** *v.a.* to schematise.

Sche'mel, *m.* (—**s,** *pl.* —) footstool; treadle (*Weav.*); bolster (*Artil.*); banquette (*Fort.*).

Sche'men, *m.* (—**s,** *pl.* —) phantom, shadow.

Schenk, *m.* (—**en,** *pl.* —**en**) cup-bearer; lord butler; retailer of wines and spirits. **—bar,** *adj.* fit to be made a present of; fit to be retailed. **—e,** *f.* (*pl.* —**en**) inn, tavern, public-house. **—in,** *f.* female pouring out liquors, barmaid, waitress at an inn; innkeeper's wife. *Comp.* **—en=amt,** *n.* cup-bearer's office.

Schen'kel, *m.* (—**s,** *pl.* —) leg; thigh; shank; haunch; side (*of angles*); leg (*of a compass*); jamb. **—ig,** *adj.* having thighs, *etc.*, shanked; **gleich—ig,** isosceles. *Comp.* **—bein,** *n.* thigh-bone. **—blutader,** *f.* crural vein. **—bruch,** *m.* fracture of the thigh-bone; femoral hernia. **—hülfen,** *pl.* action of the legs (in riding). **—recht,** *adj.*; **—recht sein,** to be tractable, to obey the action of the rider's legs. **—zirkel,** *m.* pair of compasses.

Schen'k—en, *v.a.* to pour out, fill; to retail liquor; to give, present, bestow; to grant, accord; to impart; to remit (*a debt, a punishment, etc.*); to forgive; **etwas zu Weihnachten geschenkt bekommen,** to get s. th. as a Christmas-present; **wenn Gott mir das Leben —t,** if God grants me life; **es soll dir geschenkt sein,** I pardon you, I 'll let you off this time; **es soll dir nicht geschenkt sein,** you shall not escape with impunity; **den Rest der Geschichte (das Übrige) —e ich dir,** I will spare you the rest of the story; **ihm wurde nichts geschenkt,** he received his due, he was paid in full. **—er,** *m.* (—**ers,** *pl.* —**er**) donor, giver. **—ung,** *f.* donation; gift. *Comp.* **—bier,** *n.* beer sold on draught. **—gerechtigkeit,** *f.* public-house license. **—kanne,** *f.* pot, pint. **—mädchen,** *n.*, **—mamsell,** *f.* barmaid. **—stube,** *f.* taproom; coffee-room. **—tisch,** *n.* sideboard; bar. **—ungs=brief,** *m.*, **—ungs=urkunde,** *f.* deed of gift. **—wirt,** *m.* publican, landlord. **—wirtin,** *f.* landlady, innkeeper's wife.

Scher—bar, *adj.* shavable. **—e,** *f.* (*pl.* —**en**) scissors; shears; clippers; shafts, thill; claws (*of crabs, etc.*); tenaille (*Fort.*); (*pl.*) reef, rock, cliff (*especially on the Baltic*). **—en=boot,** *n.* small Swedish boat. **—en=flotte,** *f.* coasting flotilla. **—en=schleifer,** *m.* knife *or* scissors grinder. **—en=werk,** *n.* tenaille (*Fort.*). **—en,** I. *ir.v.a.* to shear, clip, cut, poll, lop, mow; to shave; to warp; to fleece, cheat; to plague, tease, vex; **geschorener Sammt,** cut *or* stamped velvet; **einem den Bart —en, einen —en,** to shave a p.; **laß mich ungeschoren!** let me alone! **was —t mich das?** what 's that to me? **was schert mich Weib, was schert mich Kind?** what care I for wife? what care I for children? **sie sind alle über einen Kamm geschoren,** they are all of the same stamp; **sich —en,** to go away, clear off (*vulg.*); **sich um (einen** *or* **eine Sache) —en,** to trouble oneself about, be concerned for, care about (*generally used negatively*); —(**e**) (*or* **schier**) **dich weg!** be off with you! you get away! **er mag sich zum Teufel —en,** he can go to Jericho! II. *subst.n.*; **das —en der Schafe,** sheep-shearing. **—er,** *m.* (—**ers,** *pl.* —**er**) shearer; barber; warper. **—erei',** *f.* trouble, vexation, annoyance; **einem —ereien machen,** to bother a person. *Comp.* **—becken,** *n.* shaving-basin. **—baum,** *m.* weavers' hind-beam. **—block,** *m.* warping-block (*Naut.*). **—flocken,** *pl.* flock. **—garn,** *n.* thread for the warp. **—maschine,** *f.* shearing-machine (*for cloth*). **—messer,** *n.* razor. **—rahmen,** *m.* great warp-reel. **—wolle,** *f.* shearings, fleece. **—zeit,** *f.* shearing-time. **—zeug,** *n.* shearing implements; shaving things.

Scher'be, *f.* (*pl.* —**n**), **—l, —n,** *m.* (—**ns,** *pl.* —**n**) fragment (*of glass, earthenware, etc.*); potsherd; débris; earthenware vessel; flower-pot; scarf (*of timber*); monocle, eye-glass (*sl.*). *Comp.* **—n=futter,** *n.* mould for tests (*Chem.*). **—n=gericht,** *n.* ostracism. **—n=gewächs,** *n.* pot-plant. **—n=haufe,** *m.* heap of fragments. **—n=kobalt,** *m.* native arsenic.

Scherf, *m.* (—(e)**s,** *pl.* —**e**), **—lein,** *n.* (—**leins,** *pl.* —**lein**) mite.

Scher'ge, *m.* (—**n,** *pl.* —**n**) beadle; constable, policeman; myrmidon; des Gesetzes —n, myrmidons of the law. *Comp.* —n=amt, *n.* office of a beadle. —n=volk, *n.* myrmidons.

Scherwen'zel, *m.* (—s, *pl.* —) awkward bow *or* scrape; jack-of-all-trades; toady; factotum; Scherwenzel (*game at cards*); knave (*in this game*). —n, *v.n.* (*aux.* h.) to be officious *or* obsequious; to fawn; to dance attendance on.

Scherz, *m.* (—es, *pl.* —e) jest, joke; pleasantry; raillery, chaff, fun; aus —, for fun; im —(e), jestingly, for fun; — bei Seite, joking apart; — verstehen, to understand *or* see a joke; er versteht keinen —, he has no sense of humour; einen — mit einem treiben, to make game of a p., turn a p. into ridicule. —haft, *adj.* jesting, joking, facetious; droll; sportive; jocose, jocular. —haftigkeit, *f.* jocularity, facetiousness; sportiveness. *Comp.* —gedicht, *n.* comic poem. —laune, *f.* sportiveness. —liebend, *adj.* waggish, fond of a joke. —macher, *m.* wag, wit. —name, *m.* nickname. —weise, *adv.* for fun, in jest. —wort, *n.* word spoken in jest, facetious word; joke; witticism.

Scher'zen, *v.n.* (*aux.* h.) to jest, joke, make fun; to banter; Sie — *or* Sie belieben zu —, you are joking, you don't mean it; er läßt nicht mit sich —, he cannot stand *or* does not see a joke, he is not to be trifled with; es ist nicht zum —, it is no joking *or* jesting matter.

Schet'ter, *m.* (—s, *pl.* —) buckram.

Scheu, I. *adj.* shy, timid, bashful, coy; skittish, shying; — machen, to startle, to frighten; — werden, to shy, to take fright (*at*), to run away (*of horses*). II. *f.* shyness; timidity; awe; aversion; eine heilige — tragen vor, to have a wholesome dread of.

Scheu'che, *f.* (*pl.* —n) scarecrow; bugbear. —n, *v.a.* to scare, frighten away.

Scheu'—en, *v.* I. *a.* to fear; to shun; to shrink from; sich —en vor, to be afraid of; to hesitate at, to have an aversion to; das Pferd —te sich vor einem Steine, the horse shied at a stone; thue Recht und —e niemand, do right and fear no one. II. *n.* (*aux.* h.) to be frightened; to shy. —heit, *f.* shyness. —sal, *n.* (—sals, *pl.* —sale) object of horror, monster, fright. —sälig, —selig, *adj. see* Scheußlich. *Comp.* —klappe, *f.*, —leder, *n.* blinker, winker.

Scheu'er, *f.* (*pl.* —n) barn, granary, shed.

Scheu'er—n, *v.a.* to scour, scrub; to wash; to chafe; to polish; das Hemd —t mir den Rücken, the shirt rubs the skin off my back. —er, Scheurer, *m.* (—ers, *pl.* —er), —erin, Scheurerin, *f.* scourer. *Comp.* —bürste, *f.* scrubbing-brush. —faß, *n.* washing-up tub. —frau, *f.* charwoman. —lappen, *m.* dishcloth; scouring cloth; mop, swab. —leiste, *f.* washboard. —magd, *f.* scullery maid. —papier, *n.* emery *or* sand paper. —sand, *m.* scouring-sand. —stein, *m.* holystone (*Naut.*). —tag, *m.* scouring day.

Scheu'ne, *f.* (*pl.* —n) barn, granary, shed. *Comp.* —n=tenne, *f.* threshing-floor.

Scheuß'lich, *adj.* horrible, frightful, abominable, hideous. —keit, *f.* hideousness; atrocity; horror; horribleness.

Schib'boleth, *n.* (—s, *pl.* —s) shibboleth.

Schicht, *f.* (*pl.* —en), —e, *f.* (*pl.* —en) layer, bed, stratum; class, rank (*in society, etc.*); pile; task, day's work; pause, rest; — machen, to leave off working; mit etwas — machen, to put an end to a thing; in einer —, uninterruptedly. —ig (*only in compounds, e. g.* viel—ig, with many layers; weit—ig, with layers wide apart; vast, extensive). *Comp.* —arbeit, *f.* job-work. —arbeiter, *m.* day-labourer. —en=ordnung, *f.* stratification. —fuge, *f.* grain (*in coal, etc.*). —gesteine, *pl.* stratified rocks. —holz, *n.* wood in piles. —meister, *m.* overseer of miners; assayer. —schreiber, *m.* clerk of the mines. —(en)=weise, *adv.* in layers, stratified, in rows *or* piles. —zahn, *m.* milk-tooth.

Schich't—en, *v.* I. *a.* to put into layers, strata *or* rows; to pile up; to divide, distribute; to classify. II. *n.* (*aux.* h.) to shed one's milk teeth. —ung, *f.* stratification; separation; arrangement; second dentition.

Schick, *m.* (—es) fitness; due order; tact; skill; a good bargain; advantage, profit; wieder in — bringen, to readjust, put in order again; er hat seinen rechten — nicht, he is not quite himself (*coll.*); er ist nicht auf dem —, he is out of sorts, he is seedy (*coll.*).

Schi'ck—en, *v.* I. *a.* to send, despatch; to send, ordain, direct; to send for (nach einem); ins Parlament —en, to return to parliament; der Zufall —te es, it so happened, it chanced; ein Buch in die Welt —en, to publish a book; denn das Volk hatte sein Herz noch nicht geschickt zu dem Gott ihrer Väter, for as yet the people had not prepared their hearts unto the God of their fathers (*B.*). II. *r.* to come to pass, to happen; to prepare (*for*); to suit, be fit (zu, for); to suit, become; to agree (*with*); to match, suit, blend; es —t sich nicht für ihn, it does not become him, it is not proper for him; it is not the proper thing for him to do; sich zusammen —en, to agree; sich in eine S. —en, to become reconciled to a th., to resign o.s. to a th.; sich in etwas (*acc.*) nicht —en können, not to get accustomed to a th., not to be able to understand a th.; sich in einen —en, to humour a p., accommodate o.s. to him; einen in den April —en, to make an April fool of s.o.; er versteht sich in die Leute zu —en, he knows how to get on with people; sie konnte sich nicht darein —en, she could not reconcile herself to it; sich in die Zeit —en, to go with the times; sich zu etwas —en, to be fit for a thing; nachdem es sich —t, according to circumstances; es wird sich schon —en, it will all come right some day; wie sich einer —', also hat er Glück, as you make your bed, so must you lie. —lich, *adj. & adv.* proper; becoming; appropriate; decent; nice, well-bred. —lichkeit, *f.* propriety; fitness; decorum; good breeding. —sal, *n.* (—sals, *pl.* —sale) destiny, fate; fortune, lot; wechselnde —sale, vicissitudes of life; Leben mit wechselndem —sal, chequered life *or* career. —ung, *f.* Providential arrangement, Providence, fate; *see* —sal; Gottes —ung, divine ordinance, the finger of God; ordinance, decree. *Comp.* —lichkeits=gefühl, *n.* tact; sense of propriety. —sal=reich, *adj.* chequered. —sals=gang, *m.* march of destiny. —sals=gefährte, —sals=genosse, *m.* companion in misfortune, fellow-sufferer; wir sind —sals=gefährten, we are in the same boat (*coll.*). —sals=glaube, *m.* fatalism. —sals=göttinnen, *pl.* the Fates, Destinies, the Parcæ. —sals=linie, *f.* line of fate (*in the palm*). —sals=prüfung, *f.* sore trial, ordeal, visitation. —sals=schlag, *m.* heavy blow, fatal blow; *pl.* buffets of fate, reverses. —sals=schwanger, *adj.* big with destiny, portentous. —sals=schwestern, *pl.* fatal *or* weird sisters. —sals=tag, *m.* day on which one's fate is decided. —sals=tragödie, *f.* tragedy of destiny. —sals=tücke, *f.* malice *or* treachery of fate, malignant fate, tricks of fortune. —sals=wechsel, *m.* change of fortune, vicissitude(s). —sals=wort, *n.* word *or* decree of fate *or* Providence; oracle.

Schick'sel, *n.* a Jewish girl, young Jewess (*coll.*).

Schie'be, *f.* (*pl.* —n) shovel; spud.

Schie'b—en, *ir. v.* I. *a. & n.* (*aux.* h. & s.) to shove, push; to slide; to move; Kegel —en, to play at nine-pins *or* skittles; das Brot in den Ofen —en, to put bread into the oven; bei Seite —en, to put aside; einen Stein im Dambrett —en, to make a move (*at draughts*); einem etwas in die Schuhe —en, to put s.th. to a person's account, make him appear responsible for it; die Schuld auf einen —en, to lay the blame on s. o.; einem etwas ins Gewissen —en, to appeal to a p.'s conscience; etwas in die Tasche (in den Sack) —en, to slip s.th. into one's pocket; einen über die Grenze —en, to send a p. out of the country; von einem Tage zum andern —en, to put off from day to day. II. *r.* to move off; to move, shift; to slide; sich weiter *or* fort —en, to shuffle along. **—er,** *m.* (—ers, *pl.* —er) pusher; shover; bowler; slide; lid; shove; oven-peel; bar, bolt; running-loop; movable slider (*on the Mauser-rifle*); slide-valve; slide-index; sash-bolt; slide (*on a necklace, of an umbrella, etc.*); leaf (*of a table*). **—ung,** *f.* push, pushing, shoving; slide; shuffle, shifting; bowling; —ungen machen, to shuffle; das ist alles nur —ung, this is mere shuffling, this is mere beating about the bush (*coll.*). *Comp.* **—brücke,** *f.* rolling bridge. **—deckel,** *m.* sliding lid. **—e=blinde,** *f.* spritsail-topsail. **—e=bühne,** *f.* traverser, sliding platform (*Railw.*). **—e=fenster,** *n.* sliding window; sash-window. **—(e)=karren,** *m.* (wheel-)barrow, hand-barrow. **—(e)=lampe,** *f.* slide lamp. **—e=lineal,** *n.* sliding rule. **—e=rad,** *n.* curb-wheel. **—e=rahmen,** *m.* sash frame, English casement. **—e=ring,** *m.* sliding ring. **—er=feder,** *f.* rifle-trapspring. **—er=nut,** *f.* sash-groove. **—er=stange,** *f.* valve-rod. **—er=ventil,** *n.* sliding-valve. **—er=weg,** *m.* stroke of the slide, slide-valve travel. **—e=schloß,** *n.* snap-lock. **—e=stange,** *f.* sliding *or* valve-rod. **—e=vorrichtung,** *f.* slide, shifter. **—e=wand,** *f.* side scene, movable partition (*Theat.*). **—lade,** *f.* drawer. **—stange,** *f.* pole; organ-stop; slider, see-saw. **—thür,** *f.* sliding-door. **—werk,** *n.* cog-wheeled machine. **—zeug,** *n.* cog-work (*of saw-mills*).

Schied, Schie'de, *1 & 3 pers. sing. imperf. ind. & subj. of* scheiden.

Schieds— (*in comp.*) **—gericht,** *n.* court of arbitration, of equity. **—gerichtlich,** *see* —richterlich. **—mann, —richter,** *m.* arbitrator, umpire. **—richterlich,** *adj. & adv.* by arbitration. **—spruch,** *m.*, **—urteil,** *n.* award, (arbitrator's) decision.

Schief, I. *adj. & adv.* crooked; oblique; sloping; bias; wry, distorted; wrong; jutting out (*Arch.*); —e Ebene *or* Fläche, inclined plane; —e Fahrt, oblique sailing; — gewickelt sein, to be all wrong, to be much mistaken (*coll.*); in einer —en Lage sein, to be in a false position; ein —es Maul ziehen, to make a wry face. II. *adv.* awry; across, crosswise; ill; etwas — anfangen, to set the wrong way to work; — gehen, to go all wrong, to turn out badly; — stehen, to be wrong; es steht — darum, there is something wrong about it; wenn etwas — gehen sollte, if anything should go wrong, *or* amiss; nur Mut, die Sache wird schon — gehn, don't be afraid, it is sure to turn out all right (*hum.*); — nehmen, to take amiss (*coll.*); seine Stiefel — laufen, to tread one's boots down at the heels; — segeln, to tack. **—e, —heit, —igkeit,** *f.* obliquity, obliqueness, crookedness; slope; wrongness, perversity. *Comp.* **—blatt,** *n.* begonia. **—geladen,** *adj.* tipsy (*coll.*). **—halsig,** *adj.* wry-necked. **—maß,** *n.* parallel ruler. **—rund,** *adj.* oval. **—segeln,** *n.* tacking. **—winkelig,** *adj.* oblique-angled.

Schie'fer, *m.* (—s, *pl.* —) slate, schist; splinter; flake, lamina. **—ig, Schiefrig,** *adj.* slate-like; slaty, schistous; splintery, scaly. *Comp.* **—artig,** *adj.* slaty, schistous. **—bedachung,** *f.* slating, slate-roof. **—blau,** *adj.* slate-coloured. **—bruch,** *m.* slate-quarry. **—dach,** *n.* slated roof. **—decker,** *m.* slater. **—platte,** *f.* slab, tablet of slate. **—stein,** *m.* slate. **—stift,** *m.* slate-pencil. **—tafel,** *f.* slate. **—thon,** *m.* slate-clay, shale. **—zahn,** *m.* scaly tooth.

Schie'fer—n, *v.r.* to peel off, scale. **—ung,** *f.* stratification, exfoliation.

Schie'l—en, *v.n.* (*aux.* h.) to squint; —en nach (*dat.*), auf (*acc.*), to leer at, cast furtive glances at; to have an eye to, to hanker after a th. **—end,** *p. & adj.* squint-eyed; ambiguous; leering; —ende Seide, shot silk; ein —endes Verfahren, one-sided proceedings; ein —ender Vergleich, an inappropriate comparison. **—er,** *m.* (—ers, *pl.* —er), **—erin,** *f.* squinting person. *Comp.* **—äugig,** *adj.* squint-eyed. **—brillen,** *pl.* goggles. **—haken,** *m.* instrument for operating on strabismus.

Schie'mann, *m.* (—s, *pl.* Schiemänner) quartermaster; boatswain's mate. *Comp.* **—s=garn,** *n.* spun yarn. **—s=maat,** *m.* quartermaster's mate.

Schien, Schie'ne, *1 & 3 pers. sing. imperf. ind. & subj. of* scheinen.

Schie'n—e, *f.* (*pl.* —en) splint; iron band; rail; tire; clout; greave; rib (*of umbrellas*); shin; breitbasige —e, flat-footed rail; —en legen to lay down rails; aus den —en kommen, to run off the rails, to leave the metals. *Comp* **—bein,** *n.* shin-bone, tibia. **—en=bahn,** *f.* railroad, railway. **—en=leger,** *n.* plate-layer (*Railw.*). **—en=nagel,** *m.* tire-clout nail. **—en=räumer,** *m.* safeguard, cow-catcher (*on engines*). **—en=reibung,** *f.* rolling-friction. **—en=strang,** *m.* track, railway line, metals. **—en=weg,** *m.* railway line, permanent way.

Schie'nen, *v.a.* to put in splints; to shoe, tire (*wheels*).

[1]**Schier,** *obs. imperat. sing. of* scheren.

[2]**Schier,** I. *adj. & adv.* clean, clear; smooth, plain; sheer, downright, pure; —es Fleisch, meat without fat *or* bones; —e Unmöglichkeit, sheer impossibility. II. *m.* Russian sheeting.

[3]**Schier,** *adv.* almost, nearly, in a high degree, all but; quite, totally.

Schier'ling, *m.* (—s, *pl.* —e) hemlock. *Comp.* **—s=becher,** *m.* cup of hemlock. **—s=tanne,** *f.* hemlock spruce-fir.

Schierst, Schiert, *2 and 3 pers. sing. pres. ind. of* scheren.

Schieß'bar, *adj.* within shot, within range.

Schie'ß—en, *ir.v.* I. *n.* (*aux.* s.) to shoot (*as stars*); to dart, rush rapidly; to spring; to burst forth, gush; auf etwas (*acc.*) herab —en, to dart down upon, rush at a th.; ein Habicht schoß auf eine Lerche, a hawk swooped down upon a lark; das Blut schoß ihm ins Gesicht, the blood rushed to his face; in die Höhe —en, to spring up; in Samen —en, to run to seed; —en lassen, to let go, let fly, let loose, pay out (*rope*); to give (a thing) up (*sl.*) seinen Begierden den Zügel —en lassen, to give the rein to one's desires; das schoß mir durch den Kopf, that suddenly occurred to me, struck me, crossed my mind. II. *a. & n.* (*aux.* h.) to shoot, to discharge (*a gun, an arrow, etc.*); to burst, blast; blind —en, to shoot with blank cartridge; to fire blank cartridges; scharf —en, to shoot with powder and ball; to fire ball cartridges; sich (*dat.*) eine Kugel durch den Kopf —en, to blow one's brains out; gut —en, to be a good shot; unfehlbar sicher —en, to be a dead shot; fehl, vorbei —en, to miss one's aim; fehl geschossen! wrong! weit —en, to carry far. III. *a.* to pilfer (*sl.*); den Ballast ins

Schiff —en lassen, to ballast a ship; die Sonne —en, to take the sun's altitude (*obs.*); Wolle —en, to pick wool; einen Vogel im Fluge —en, to shoot a bird on the wing; einen (groben) Bock —en, to make a (bad) mistake; einen Purzelbaum —en, to turn a somersault; Blicke —en, to dart glances; in Grund und Boden —en, to batter down; in Kolumnen —en, to remove the columns from the galley to the composing-stick; sich mit einem —en, to fight a pistol duel with a p. —er, *m.* (—ers, *pl.* —er) shooter; ovener; oven-peel. —erei', *f.* bad, aimless firing. *Comp.* —baum=wolle, *f.* gun-cotton. —bedarf, *m.* ammunition. —gatten, *pl.* loop-holes (*Naut.*). —gerechtigkeit, *f.* right *or* privilege of shooting over a preserve, shooting license. —gewehr, *n.* fire-arm; spiele nicht mit —gewehr, those who play with edged tools must expect to cut themselves (*prov.*). —hagel, *m.* shot. —hund, *m.* pointer, sporting-dog; aufpassen wie ein —hund, to follow with the closest attention, to watch like a lynx (*coll.*). —hütte, *f.* shooting-box. —instruktion, *f.* (*manual of*) musketry instruction. —kommando, *n.* shooting-detachment. —kugel, *f.* ball, bullet. —loch, *n.* loop-hole; port-hole; space between the platoons; blasting-hole. —mal, *n.* mark, butt, bull's eye. —mauer, *f.* mound, *etc.*, behind the target. —nadel, *f.* blasting needle. —patrone, *f.* cartridge, charge. —pferd, *n.* horse trained to stand firing. —platz, *m.* rifle-range, shooting-place; practice-ground. —pulver, *n.* gunpowder. —prügel, *m.* fire-arm, brown Bess. —scharte, *f.* loop-hole, embrasure. —scheibe, *f.* target. —schule, *f.* school of musketry *or* gunnery. —stand, *m.* place, stand for shooting. —tabelle, *f.* practice table (*Artil.*). —übungen, *pl.* rifle-practice; artillery-practice. —zeit, *f.* shooting season.

Schiff, *n.* (—(e)s, *pl.* —e) ship, vessel; scapha (*Anat.*); carina (*Bot.*); paint-pot; saucer; vessel for hot water in a stove; nave (*of a church*); shuttle (*Weav.*); car (*of a balloon*); galley (*Typ.*); zu —(e) gehen, to go on board (ship), to embark; zu —(e) versenden, to send by water; zu — gebracht, ship-borne (goods); ein nach Hause bestimmtes —, a home-bound vessel; ein nach auswärts bestimmtes —, an outward-bound ship; es ist ein gutes Segel—, she is a good sailing-boat; kleine —e, small craft; jagdmachendes —, chaser; gejagtes —, chase; — der Königlichen Marine, His (Her) Majesty's Ship (*H. M. S.*); schnell segelndes —, fast sailer; gepanzertes —, iron-plated ship, ironclad; — auf der Reede, roadster; — in Not, ship in distress. —bar, *adj.* navigable. —barkeit, *f.* navigableness. —chen, *n.* (—chens, *pl.* —chen) little vessel, skiff; carina (*Bot.*); shuttle. —lein, *see* —chen. —s, *see* Schiffs *in comp. Comp.* (*also often* Schiffs—) —bau, *m.* ship-building. —bauer, *m.* ship-builder. —bau=hof, *m.* shipbuilding-yard, dockyard, dry-dock, stocks. —bau=kunst, *f.* naval architecture. —bau=meister, *m.* master shipwright; naval architect. —beschlag, *m.* sheathing. —bruch, *m.* shipwreck. —brüchig, *adj.* shipwrecked. —brücke, *f.* bridge of boats, pontoon bridge, floating bridge. —er=ausdruck, *m.* nautical term. —er=knoten, *m.* sailor's knot. —er=lohn, *m.* passage-money. —er=sprache, *f.* nautical language. —er=stechen, *n.* naumachy; regatta. —fahrer, *m.* navigator. —fahrt, *f.* navigation; voyage; zur —fahrt gehörig, nautical, maritime; —fahrt treibend, seafaring. —fahrts=akte, *f.* Navigation-Act. —fahrts=kunst, *f.* art of navigation. —fahrts=sperre, *f.* embargo. —fracht, *f.* freight. —fracht=brief, *m.* bill of lading. —(s)=gerät=händler, *m.* ship's chandler. —gerippe, *n.* ribs of a ship, hulk. —(s)=grund, *m.* hold (*of a ship*). —leine, *f.* tow-rope. —männisch, *adj.* sailor-like. —mühle, *f.* ship mill, floating mill. —pferd, *n.* towing-horse. —rose, *f.* mariner's compass. —sand, *m.* sand serving as ballast. —seil, *n.* cable.

Schif'f—en, *v.* I. *a.* to ship (*goods, etc.*). II. *a.* & *n.* (*aux.* s.) to navigate, sail (*on*), go by water; to make water (*vulg.*). —er, *m.* (—ers, *pl.* —er) seaman, sailor; navigator; skipper; sailing-master (*Nav.*).

Schiffs— (*in comp.*) *see also* Schiff. —bedürfnisse, *pl.* naval stores. —befrachter, *m.* fitter-out, equipper of vessels; freighter, charterer. —befrachtung, *f.* freightage, chartering. —bekleidung, *f.* planking. —besen, *m.* swab, mop. —beute, *f.* prize. —bodenbrief, *m.* bottomry-bond. —breite, *f.* breadth of beam. —eigentümer, —eigner, *m.* ship-owner. —flagge, *f.* flag. —frachtbrief, *m.* bill of lading. —freund, *m.* part-owner of a ship. —geleite, *n.* convoy. —gerät, *n.* ship's rigging. —geschütz, *n.* ship's guns. —haken, *m.* grappling-iron, boat-hook. —hinterteil, *n.* poop, stern. —junge, *m.* cabin-boy. —kammer, *f.* cabin. —kapitän, *m.* captain; —kapitän eines kleinen —, skipper. —kiel, *m.* keel, bottom. —korb, *m.* crow's nest. —krahn, *m.* crane on a wharf. —küche, *f.* cook-room; galley. —kunst, *f.* navigation, piloting. —ladung, *f.* cargo. —lafette, *f.* naval gun-carriage. —last, *f.* tonnage; last (= *2 tons*). —laterne, *f.* poop-lantern. —leute, *pl.* crew, sailors. —luken, *pl.* hatches. —macht, *f.* naval force. —makler, *m.* ship-broker. —mannschaft, *f.* crew. —miete, *f.* freight. —mühle, *f.* mill built on a boat, floating mill. —partner, *see* —freund. —paß, *m.* passport; permit; certificate of health. —patron, *m.* ship-master. —pfandbrief, *m.* bottomry-bond. —prediger, *m.* naval chaplain. —rat, *m.* naval council. —raum, *m.* hold. —reeder, (—rheder,) *m.* ship-owner. —register, *n.* naval *or* ship's register. —rose, *f.* mariner's compass. —rüstung, *f.* naval equipment. —schnabel, *m.* cut-water; rostrum. —schraube, *f.* screw (*of a steamer*), screw propeller. —schreiber, *m.* naval *or* captain's clerk. —soldat, *m.* marine. —spiegel, *m.* stern. —spur, *f.* wake of a ship. —tagebuch, *n.* ship's journal, log-book. —tau, *m.* hawser; rope, cable. —tauwerk, *n.* rope-work, cordage. —treppe, *f.* ship's ladder; companion ladder (*to the cabins*). —vermietung, *f.* chartering, freighting. —verzollung, *f.* clearing out. —visitator, *m.* custom-house officer. —volk, *n.* crew. —vorderteil, *n.* prow, forecastle, bows. —vorräte, *pl.* stores of a ship. —wache, *f.* look-out; watch. —wanten, *pl.* shrouds. —werft, *f.* dockyard; dry-dock. —wesen, *n.* shipping concerns. —winde, *f.* capstan; windlass. —zeughaus, *n.* naval arsenal. —ziehen, *n.* towing; tracking. —zimmermann, *m.* ship's carpenter. —zoll, *m.* tonnage(-duty), freightage —zwieback, *m.* ship *or* sea-biscuit, hard tack.

Schika'n—e, *f.* (*pl.* —en) chicanery, trickery, subterfuge, underhand dealings. —ie'ren, *v.* I. *a.* to vex, *or* annoy by frivolous objections *or* subterfuges, to play tricks upon. II. *n.* to deal in an underhand way; über eine S. —ieren, to chicane about *or* cavil at a thing.

Schil'der, Schil'fer, see Schelfe.

Schild, I. *m.* (—es, *pl.* —e) shield, buckler; (e)scutcheon, coat of arms; shield, scutum (*Zoöl.*); den —ergreifen, to seize one's buckler; einen Eber im —e führen, to bear the wild boar in one's coat-of-arms; etwas im —e führen, to have a secret design (*fig.*): zum —e geboren sein, to be born to be a knight, to be of noble birth. II. *n.* (—es, *pl.* —er) signboard, (painted) board, (brass) plate; door-plate; breast-plate; name-plate (*on street corners*); badge, ticket (*of porters*); scutcheon (*Arch.*); etiquette (*on wine-bottles*); peak (*of a cap*); screen (*to protect sappers*); shell (*of tortoises*); das — aushängen (einziehen), to open (shut up) business *or* a shop. —erer, *m.* (—erers, *pl.* —erer) painter, delineator; calico-printer. *Comp.* —abteilung, *f.* quarter; quartering. —bogen, *m.* longitudinal arch. —bürtig, *adj.* of gentle birth. —dach, *n.* testudo (*Hist.*). —decke, *f.* mantle of the shield (*Her.*). —drüse, *f.* thyroid gland. —er=blau, *n.* pencil blue. —er=haus, *n.* sentry-box. —erhebung, *f.* armed rising. —es=amt, *n.* knighthood; office of a knight. —förmig, *adj.* shield-shaped, scutiform. —fuß, *m.* bottom, plain (*Her.*). —halter, *m.* shield-bearer, esquire; supporter (*Her.*). —haupt, *n.* chief (*Her.*). —jungfrau, *f.* battle maiden, Valkyria. —knappe, —knecht, *m.* shield-bearer, squire. —knorpel, *m.* thyroid cartilage, shield cartilage, Adam's apple. —kröte, *f.* tortoise, turtle. —kröten=schale, *f.* tortoise-shell. —kröten=suppe, *f.* turtle soup. —lehen, *n.* knight's fief. —patt, *n.* tortoise-shell. —rand, *m.* rim of a shield; bordure (*Her.*). —teilung, *f.* quartering (*Her.*). —träger, *m.* squire, shield-bearer. —wache, *f.* sentinel, sentry; —wache zu Pferde, vedette; —wache stehen, to stand as sentry; verlorene —wache, forlorn hope. —zapfen, *m.* trunnion (*Artil.*).

Schil'der—n, *v.* I. *a.* to paint; to colour; to depict, portray, describe. II. *n.* (*aux.* h.) to stand sentry, to walk up and down before a place. —ung, *f.* picture, painting; portrayal; description, representation. —ei', *f.* painting (*obs.*). —er, *m.* portrayer, describer.

Schilf, *n.* (—(e)s, *pl.* —e) reed; rush; bulrush; sedge. —ig, *adj.* reedy, sedgy. *Comp.* —artig, *adj.* arundinaceous, reedy. —dach, *n.* reed-thatch. —decke, *f.* rush-mat. —gras, *n.* reed-grass. —meer, *n.* reedy sea; Red Sea (*B.*). —rohr, *n.* reed; reeds. —schlag=röhre, *f.* reed-tube (*Artil.*).

Schil'ler, *m.* (—s, *pl.* —) play of colours; lustre, glistening splendour. —ig, *adj.* iridescent, changing. —n, *v.n.* (*aux.* h.) to change in colour, to play from one colour into another. —nd, *adj.* iridescent. *Comp.* —farbe, *f.* changing hue. —seide, *f.* shot silk. —taffet, *m.* shot taffeta.

Schil'ling, *m.* (—s, *pl.* —e) shilling.

Schilt, Schilt(e)st, *imperat. & 3 pers. sing. pres. ind.; 2 pers. sing. pres. ind. of* schelten.

Schim'mel, *m.* (—s, *pl.* —) mould, mildew; white film on liquids; white horse. —ig, *adj.* mouldy, musty. —n, *v.n.* (*aux.* h. & s.) to grow mouldy, to contract mould.

Schim'mer, *m.* (—s, *pl.* —) shimmer; glimmer, gleam; glitter; lustre; splendour; idea (*coll.*); coruscation; ich habe keinen — (davon), I have not the faintest notion (*coll.*). —n, *v.n.* (*aux.* h.) to twinkle, glimmer; to sparkle; to glitter. —nd, *p. & adj.* glistening; lustrous; tinsel. *Comp.* —licht, *n.* glimmer(ing light). —los, *adj. & adv.* lustreless; quiet.

Schimpan'se, *m.* (—n, *pl.* —n) chimpanzee.

Schimpf, *m.* (—(e)s, *pl.* —e) affront; insult, outrage; disgrace; abuse; joke, jest, fun (*obs.*); einem einen — anthun, to insult s. o.; einem — und Schande nachsagen, to say everything that is bad of a p.; einen — auf sich (*dat.*) sitzen lassen, to swallow an insult; —e, scolding (*vulg.*); — und Ernst, grave and gay (*title of a collection of XVI. cent. anecdotes*); — und Schande, opprobrium, disgrace. —lich, *adj.* insulting; outrageous; disgraceful, infamous. —lichkeit, *f.* disgracefulness, *etc.* *Comp.* —gedicht, —lied, *n.* lampoon. —name, *m.* opprobrious name *or* epithet; nickname. —rede, *f. see* —erei. —wort, *n.* abusive *or* insulting word, insult; invective.

Schim'pfe—n, *v.a. & n.* (*aux.* h.) to affront, insult; to abuse; to dishonour, disgrace; einen einen Schurken —n, to call a p. a rascal; —n auf (*acc.*) *or* über (*acc.*), to inveigh against. —r, *m.* (—rs, *pl.* —r) reviler. —rei', *f.* abusive language.

Schin'del, *f.* (*pl.* —n) shingle, splint; billet (*Her.*). —n, *v.a.* to cover *or* roof with shingles. *Comp.* —dach, *n.* shingle-roof. —sparren, *m.* rafter.

Schin'd—en, *ir.v.a. & n.* (*aux.* h.) to skin, flay; to scalp; to bark (*a tree*); to oppress; to harass, vex, worry; to fleece; to scrape, pinch, be miserly; to enjoy *or* use without paying (*sl.*); sich —en, to toil and moil, to slave, to wear the flesh off one's bones; Kolleg —en, to attend a University lecture without paying the fee (*sl.*); Lokal —en, to sit in a restaurant without ordering anything (*sl.*). —er, *m.* (—ers, *pl.* —er) flayer, knacker; hangman (*in curses, etc.*) —erei', *f.* knacker's yard; flaying; extortion. *Comp.* —aas, *n.* carrion. —anger, *m.*, —grube, *f.* flaying-place, carrion-pit. —er=karren, *m.* knacker's cart. —er=mäßig, *adj.* cruel, harsh, oppressive. —luder, *n.* carrion. —mähre, *f.* sorry jade.

Schin'ken, *m.* (—s, *pl.* —) ham; westfälischer —, smoked Westphalian ham; er hat einen — bei mir im Salze, I have a rod in pickle for him. *Comp.* —bein, *n.* ham-bone. —brötchen, —butterbrod, *n.* ham-sandwich. —schnitte, *f.* slice of ham.

Schin'nen, *pl.* scurf; pellicles.

Schip'pe, *f.* (*pl.* —n) shovel; (Schüp'pe) spade (*cards*).

Schir'bel, *m.* (—s, *pl.* —) bloom (*Metal.*).

Schirm, *m.* (—es, *pl.* —e) screen; umbrella; shelter, protection; protector (*fig.*), shade; Sonnen—, sunshade, parasol; Schutz und —, protection, protector, safeguard; unter seinem Schutz und —, under his patronage *or* protection. *Comp.* —brief, *m.* safe-conduct. —dach, *n.* pent-house; awning; shed. —förmig, *adj.* umbelliform (*Bot.*); umbrella-shaped. —futter, *n.* umbrella-case. —gestell, *n.* umbrella-frame. —herr, *m.* protector, patron. —herrschaft, *f.* protectorate. —leder, *n.* apron (*of a carriage*); top (*of a carriage*). —los, *adj.* defenceless. —macher, *m.* umbrella-maker. —meister, *m.* fencing-master. —palme, *f.* Corypha; Palmyra palm. —ständer, *m.* umbrella stand. —stock, *m.* umbrella stick. —wand, *f.* screen(ing wall). —werk, *n.* defences (*Fort.*). —zwinge, *f.* umbrella tip.

Schir'me—n, *v.a.* to screen, protect, defend to stand on guard, to fence (*obs.*). —r, *m.* (—rs, *pl.* —r) protector.

Schirr—en, *v.a.* to harness. *Comp.* —holz, *n.* carriage timber. —kammer, *f.* tool-house; harness-room. —kette, *f.* pole-chain. —macher, *m.* cartwright. —meister, *m.* head ostler (*in posting establishments*).

Schir'ting, *m.* (—s) shirting.

Schis'ma, *n.* (—s, *pl.* —s, —ta) schism

Schisma'tiker, *m.* (—s, *pl.* —) schismatic.

Schiß, *m.* (—(ſſ)es, *pl.* —(ſſ)e) voiding of excrement; excrement.

Schlab'be, *f.* (*pl.* —n) chops; blubber-lip. —rn, *v.n.* (*aux.* h.) to slobber, slaver; to babble, prate.

Schlacht, *f.* (*pl.* —en) battle, engagement, fight; regelmäßige —, pitched battle; — liefern, to engage, to give battle; — bei, battle of. —bar, *adj.* fit for killing. *Comp.* —berühmt, *adj.* famed in fight. —en=bummler, *m.* camp-follower; looker-on at manœuvres. —en=denker, m. strategist; der große —endenker, the great strategist (*Count Moltke*). —en=gott, m. God of battles. —en=maler, m. painter of battle-scenes. —feld, n. field of battle. —fertig, adj. ready for battle. —flotte, f. fleet of war-ships. —gesang, m. battle-song. —geschrei, n. war-cry. —geschwader, n. squadron. —getöse, —getümmel, —gewühl, n. mêlée. —haufen, m. battalion, body of fighting troops. —laterne, f. fighting-lantern (*Naut.*). —lied, n. battle-song. —linie, f. line of battle. —ordnung, f. order of battle, battle-array. —pferd, n. charger. —plan, m. plan of battle. —reihe, f. battle-array. —ruf, m. war-cry; signal. —schwert, n. broad-sword. —stück, n. battle-piece. —tag, m. day of battle. —verband, m. cock-pit (*Naut.*).

[1]Schlach't—en, v. I. a. to slaughter; to immolate (*a sacrifice*); to slay. II. n. (*aux.* h.). —er, m. (—ers, pl. —er) butcher. *Comp.* —bank, f. shambles; zur *or* auf die —bank führen, to have slain, to sacrifice. —e=fest, n. feast on killing a pig. —haus, n. slaughter-house. —und Mahl=steuer, f. town duties, octroi. —messer, n. butcher's knife. —opfer, n. victim, sacrifice. —tag, m. slaughtering day; day of battle. —vieh, n. cattle for the shambles. —zeug, n. butcher's tools. —zwang, m. obligation to kill the cattle at the slaughter-house.

[2]Schlach't—en, v.n. to take (nach, after) (*dial.*); er —et nach seinem Vater, he is a chip of the old block (*dial., coll.*).

Schläch'ter, m. (—s, pl. —) butcher. —ei', f. butcher's trade *or* shop; butchery; carnage.

Schla'ck—e, f. scoria, dross of metals; sediment, filth. —icht, (*obs.*) —ig, adj. sloppy, wet; full of dross. *Comp.* —en=bad, n. chalybeate bath. —en=blau, n. shining blue. —en=erz, n. vitreous matrix of silver, metal containing much dross. —en=förmig, adj., scoriform. —en=frei, adj. free from dross. —en=führer, —en=läufer, m. barrow-man who wheels away the slag. —en=kasten, m. cinder-box. —en=stein, m. slag-stone. —en=zange, f. cupel-tongs.

Schla'cke—n, v.n. (*aux.* h.) to give off scoria, dross (*in melting*); es —t, it is wet, sloppy weather. —rn, v.n. (*aux.* h.) to move loosely; es —rt, it rains continually. —rig, adj. sloppy. *Comp.* —r=wetter, n. sloppy weather.

Schlaf, I. m. (—es) sleep; slumber; fester —, sound sleep; er hat einen leichten —, he is a light sleeper; magnetischer —, hypnotism; ein kleines Kind in — wiegen (singen), to rock (lull) a baby to sleep; die ganze Nacht ist kein — in meine Augen gekommen, I have not slept a wink all night; (den) — befördern=des Mittel, soporific; das wäre mir nicht im —e eingefallen, I should never have dreamt of such a thing; sie hat einen bleiernen —, she sleeps like a top. II. m. (—es, pl. Schlä'fe) see Schläfe.

Schläf'—chen, n. (—chens, pl. —chen) doze, nap; ein —chen machen, to take a nap. —er, m. (—ers, pl. —er), —erin, f. sleeper. —(e)rig, adj. sleepy; stupid; indolent, sluggish; soporific. —ern, v. imp.; es —ert mich, I am sleepy. —rigkeit, f. drowsiness, etc.

Schlä'fe, f. (pl. —n) temple. *Comp.* —n=ader, f. temporal vein. —n=bein, n. temporal bone.

Schla'f—en, ir.v.n. (*aux.* h.) to sleep; to be asleep; to rest, repose; to be benumbed, dormant; to make careless blunders; gehen Sie —en? are you going to bed? —en Sie wohl! good night! sleep well! auswärts —en, to sleep out; ich will mich —en legen, I will go to bed; eine Sache —en lassen, to let a matter drop. —end, p. & adj. sleeping, dormant; —ende Kniee, lodging-knees (*Naut.*). *Comp.* —abteil, m. sleeping-compartment. —anzug, m. (für Herrn) pyjamas. —arznei, f. narcotic. —bringend, adj. soporific. —bursche, m. night-lodger, young workman (*who is out during the day and only sleeps at his lodgings*). —decke, f. blanket. —ens=zeit, f. bed-time. —fieber, n. lethargy. —gänger, m. somnambulist. —gast, m. traveller who stops the night only at an inn. —geld, n. price of a night's lodging. —gemach, n., —stube, f. bedroom. —genoß, —gesell, m. bedfellow. —gewand, n. night-dress, night-gown. —haube, f. night-cap. —kamerad, m. bedfellow. —kammer, f. (*small*) bedroom. —krankheit, f. somnolency. —lied, n. lullaby. —los, adj. sleepless, restless. —lust, f. drowsiness. —mädchen, n. working girl as a lodger (*who only sleeps in the house*), female night-lodger. —mittel, n. opiate. —mütze, f. night-cap; dull *or* lazy fellow. —mützig, adj. sleepy, slow. —ratte, —ratze, f., —ratz, m. sound sleeper, dormouse. —redner, m. somniloquist. —rock, m. dressing-gown. —saal, m. dormitory; Abteilungen im —saal, cubicles. —sessel, m. easy-chair. —sopha, n. bed sofa, box sofa, box couch. —stätte, —stelle, f. sleeping-place. —sucht, f. somnolence, stupor, lethargy. —süchtig, adj. somnolent. —trunk, m. sleeping-draught. —trunken, adj. overcome with sleep, very drowsy. —wachen, n. clairvoyance. —wagen, m. sleeping-car (*Railw.*). —wandeln, n. somnambulism. —wandelnd, adj. somnambulant. —wandler, m. sleep-walker, somnambulist. —zeit, f. bed-time. —zeug, n. night-things. —zimmer, n. bedroom; —zimmer mit zwei Betten, double bedroom.

Schlaff, adj. slack, loose, lax; flabby, flaccid; soft; remiss; feeble, weak, relaxed; limp; indolent; negligent; —e Grundsätze, lax principles; —es Seil, slack rope. —heit, f. slackness, laxness, flaccidity, *etc.*; atony (*Med.*).

Schläfst, Schläft, *2 and 3 pers. sing. pres. ind. of* schlafen.

Schlafitt'chen, n. collar (*coll.*); einen beim — erwischen, to (seize by the) collar, to catch a p. by the coat-tail; to call a p. to account.

Schlag, m. (—es, pl. Schlä'ge) blow; stroke; rap; (mit der flachen Hand) slap; beat, oscillation, pulsation, *etc.*; ticking (*of a watch, etc.*); kick (*of horses*); shock; clash, din; report, clap; stroke (*of pistons; of clocks, etc.*); song (*of birds*); rhythm; beat, measure (*Mus.*); grace-note (*Mus.*); coinage, stamping; stamp, race, kind, sort; stroke, fit of apoplexy; dove-cot; poultry-run; carriage door, coach door; wood-cutting; forest clearing; parcel (*of land*), strip, break; field; offered sum; turn, coil (*of a rope*); tack (*Naut.*); lathe, drawbridge (*rare*); lay (*Weav.*); beat-up (*Weav.*); sliding-door, shutter; chamber (*of a rocket, Pyr.*); return (*of a trench, Fort.*); horizontal works of a mine; erster —, toss, throw (*for first move, etc.*); mit dem —e *or* auf den — zehn, — zehn Uhr, upon the stroke of ten; ein — ins Wasser, a vain attempt, a wild-goose chase; ein kühner —, a bold stroke; ein kalter —, flash of lightning that strikes without setting on fire; Schläge bekommen, to get a (*good*) beating; ein unerwarteter —, an unexpected blow *or* misfortune; mit einem —e, at one blow, all at once; — auf —, blow upon blow, in rapid succession; auf den —, punctually; ohne einen — zu thun, without striking a blow; zum —e geneigt, apoplectic; von gleichem —e, of the same stamp *or* character; **von gutem —e,** of the right sort; **der gewöhnliche —,** the common run (*of men, etc.*); **er ist von einem anderen —e,** he is cast in a different mould; **sie sind zwei Herzen und ein —,** they are hand and glove; **ersten —es,** (diamond) of the first water; **schöner —Pferde,** fine breed of horses; **Einteilung in Schläge,** parcelling *or* distribution of crops; **— der Nachtigall,** warbling of the nightingale. **—bar,** *adj.* fit for felling.

Schla'g—en, I. *ir.v.a.* to beat, strike; to dash; to hit; to fell; to drive into; to wrap (**um sich,** around one); to toll; to pitch (*a camp*); to coin, stamp; to rout (*an enemy*); to take (*at draughts, etc.*); to touch (*a chord, etc.*), play; to clap, give a report; to hit in a certain direction; **eine Ader —en,** to open a vein; **Alarm —en,** to sound the alarm; **—en an** (*acc.*) to fasten to, nail on; **die Arme (Hände) in einander —en,** to cross one's arms (clasp one's hands); **die Augen zu Boden** *or* **nieder —en,** to cast down one's eyes, to look down; **die Augen in die Höhe —en,** to look up; **mit Blindheit —en,** to smite with blindness; **die Kugel war durch die rechte Brust ge—en,** the ball had passed through the right breast; **den Ball —en,** to strike the ball; **einen Purzelbaum —en,** to turn a somersault; **Eier zu Schaum —en,** to whisk the white of eggs; **Eier in die Suppe —en,** to stir eggs into the soup; **Falten —en,** to wrinkle, pleat; **in Falten —en,** to fold; **in Fesseln —en,** to put in irons; **er weiß, was die Glocke geschlagen hat,** he is a knowing fellow; **die Haare nach hinten —en,** to push, smooth back the hair; **einem etwas aus der Hand —en,** to knock s.th. out of a p.'s hand; **(etwas) von der Hand —en,** to refuse; **in die Höhe —en,** to knock up; **klein —en,** to cleave *or* break into small pieces; **Öl —en,** to press oil; **die Orgel —en,** to play the organ; **in Papier —en,** to wrap up in paper; **Schaum —en,** to beat *or* whisk the white of an egg to froth; **eine Schlacht —en,** to give battle; **durch ein Sieb —en,** to pass through a sieve; **wir müssen uns das aus dem Sinn —en,** we must not think any more about that; we must put that out of our minds; **diese Uhr schlägt die Stunden,** this clock strikes the hours; **ich ließe mich darauf tot —en,** I am as certain of it as that I am alive; **seine Unkosten auf die Ware —en,** to add one's expenses to the price of a thing; **sich** (*dat.*) **die Welt um die Ohren —en,** to go out into the wide world; **in den Wind —en,** to cast to the four winds, to disregard; **Wurzel —en,** to take root; **auf die Zeit —en,** to postpone, leave to time; **die Zinsen zum Kapital —en,** to add the interest to the capital; **ein geschlagener Mann,** a ruined man. II. *ir.v.r.* to fight; to turn; to pass; **sich** (*dat.*) **etwas aus den Gedanken —en,** to dismiss something from one's thoughts *or* mind; **sich ins Mittel —en,** to interpose; **sich auf die Seite der Verschworenen —en,** to take the part of, join the conspirators; **sich zu (einem) —en,** to side with, to go over to, to join; **sich links —en,** to turn to the left; **sich in die Büsche —,** to go into the brushwood. III. *ir.v.n.* (*aux.* **h.**) to strike, beat; to rap; to throb; to sing; to strike (*of clocks*); to clap, give a report; to kick; to belong to; to incline to; to beat, strike; (*aux.* **s.**) to fall; to turn out; **das Herz schlägt mir,** my heart is throbbing; **das Gewissen schlägt ihm,** his conscience pricks him; **die Uhr schlägt keinem Glücklichen,** time passes unobserved by the happy; **seine Stunde hat geschlagen,** his hour has come; **der Wagen schlägt,** the carriage jolts; **der Regen schlägt an** *or* **gegen die Fenster,** the rain beats against the windows; **liebliche Töne schlugen an mein Ohr,** sweet sounds fell upon my ear; **der Dampf schlägt mir auf die Brust,** the damp affects my chest; **aus der Art —en,** *see* **Art**; **die Tinte schlägt durchs Papier,** the ink runs through the paper; **in die Höhe —en,** to rise (*in price*); **die Flammen —en gen Himmel,** the flames shoot up towards the sky; **in die Art der Mutter —en,** to take after the mother; **der Blitz hat in die Eiche geschlagen,** the lightning has struck the oak; **das schlägt nicht in mein Fach,** that is not in my line; **der kalte Brand ist dazu geschlagen,** mortification has set in; **zur Fahne —en,** to beat to arms; **—ende Wetter,** fire-damps; **den ganzen geschlagenen Tag,** the livelong day. IV. *subst.n.* striking, beating; pulsation; song (*of birds*); kicking (*of horses*); fighting; construction (*of a bridge*); felling (*of timber*). **—er,** *m.* song *or* piece that takes well, favourite song, (theatrical) success, draw (*coll.*). *Comp.* **—ader,** *f.* artery. **—anfall,** *m.* apoplectic attack. **—artig,** *adj.* apoplectic. **—balken,** *m.* swipe (*of a drawbridge*); a kind of portcullis (*Fort.*). **—ball,** *m.* tennis ball; tennis; cricket ball. **—baum,** *m.* turnpike. **—brücke,** *f.* drawbridge. **—degen,** *m.* rapier. **—eisen,** *n.* fox-trap; stone-cutter's broad chisel. **—e=tot,** *m.* great swinging fellow, longshanks; bully, hector, brawler. **—falle,** *f.* pitfall. **—faß,** *n.* large cask. **—feder,** *f.* striking spring (*in clocks*); main spring (*in a gun*); beam-feather. **—fertig,** *adj.* ready (*to fight*); ready-tongued, sharp, quick-witted; quick at repartee. **—fertigkeit,** *f.* readiness for battle; ready wit; sharpness, acuteness, quickness of repartee. **—fittig,** *m.* wing; crab's tail. **—fluß,** *m.* apoplexy. **—gatter,** *n.* sliding gate, barrier. **—gewicht,** *n.* striking-weight. **—holz,** *n.* bat; copse; wood for felling. **—instrumente,** *pl.* percussion instruments. **—lawine,** *f.* heavy *or* overwhelming avalanche; avalanche (*consisting of the heavy frozen snow mixed with blocks of ice which melts in the spring and rolls down old beaten tracks, and strikes with terrible noise in the valleys*). **—licht,** *n.* strong *or* glaring light (*Paint.*). **—maschine,** *f.* batting machine. **—netz,** *n.* racket; clap net; seine. **—note,** *f.* semibreve. **—pulver,** *n.* fulminating powder. **—pumpe,** *f.* bilge-pump. **—regen,** *m.* pelting rain. **—reim,** *m.* tailed rhyme. **—riemen,** *m.* stroke-oar; check-string. **—ring,** *m.* plectrum, quill; knocker. **—röhre,** *f.* fuse. **—sahne,** *f.* whipped cream. **—schatten,** *m.* deep shadow, cast shadow (*Paint.*). **—schatz,** *m.* seigniorage; mintage. **—scheibe,** *f.* pallet of scapement (*Horol.*); tompion (*Artil.*). **—seite,** *f.* flat side (*of a hammer*); skin (*of a drum*); lapside (*Naut.*). **—sperre,** *f.* mute, damper (*Horol.*). **—spindel,** *f.* mandrel (*Mech.*). **—thür,** *f.* sluice-gate; trap-door. **—uhr,** *f.* repeater; striking-clock. **—wasser,** *n.* bilge water. **—weite,** *f.* striking distance. **—welle,** *f.* billow. **—werk,** *n.* clock-work; **das elektrische —werk,** the electric alarm. **—wort,** *n.* favourite expression, commonplace high-sounding phrase; **landläufige —wörter,** ordinary commonplaces. **—wunde,** *f.* wound caused by a blow.

Schlä'gel, *m.* *see* **Schlegel.**

Schlä'ge—r, *m.* (**—rs,** *pl.* **—r**) beater, *etc.*; batter; fighter, bully; kicker (*said of horses*); broadsword, rapier; racket (*tennis*); singing-bird, warbler. **—rei',** *f.* fighting; fray, brawl. *Comp.* **—faul,** *adj.* inured to blows, hardened; indolent. **—r=duell,** *n.*, **—r=mensur,** *f.* students' duel with rapiers.

Schlägst, Schlägt, *2 and 3 pers. sing. pres. ind. of* **schlagen.**

Schlamm, *m.* (—es) mud, slime, mire. —**en**, *v.n.* (*aux.* **h.**) to deposit mud. —**icht**, (*obs.*) —**ig**, *adj.* muddy, slimy, miry, oozy. *Comp.* —**bad**, *n.* mud-bath. —**boden**, *m.* slimy, muddy soil. —**grube**, *f.* slough. —**herd**, *m.* buddle (*Min.*). —**krücke**, *f.* mud-scraper. —**mühle**, *f.* dredging machine. —**pfütze**, *f.* bog, slough. —**werk**, *n.* ore-washing.

Schlämm'bar, *adj.* that can be cleansed.

Schläm'm—en, *v.a.* to cleanse from mud; to wash (*ore*); to whitewash. *Comp.* —**apparat**, *m.* cleansing apparatus. —**kreide**, *f.* whitening. —**stein**, *m.* washed tin-stone.

Schlampam'pen, *v.n.* (*aux.* **h.**) to gorge o. s. with food, to feast, to lead a jolly life.

Schlam'p—e, *f.* (*pl.* —en) slut, slattern; slovenly woman; (**Schlämpe**, *f.*) sloppy food for cattle. —**ig**, *adj.* sloppy; slovenly; dirty.

Schlam'p—en, (—**sen**,) *v.n.* (*aux.* **s.**) to be slovenly *or* dirty; (*aux.* **h.**) to dangle, hang loose. —**er**, *m.* (—ers, *pl.* —er) sloven.

Schlang, Schläng'ge, *1 & 3 pers. sing. imperf. ind. & subj. of* **schlingen.**

Schlan'ge, *f.* (*pl.* —n) snake, serpent; culverin (*usually* **Feldschlange**) (*Artil.*); hose (*of fire-engines*); worm (*of a still*); **die — zischt**, the snake hisses. *Comp.* —**n=adler**, *m.* snake-buzzard. —**n=anbetung**, *f.* worship of serpents. —**n=artig**, —**n=ähnlich**, *adj.* serpentine, snaky. —**n=balg**, *m.* serpent's skin. —**n=beschwörer**, *m.* snake charmer. —**n=brut**, *f.* brood of snakes; generation of vipers. —**n=geschlecht**, *n.* Ophidians. —**n=gezücht**, *see* —**n=brut.** —**n=gift**, *n.* serpent's venom. —**n=haar**, *n.* serpent locks (*of Medusa*). —**n=haut**, *f.* snake skin. —**n=klugheit**, *f.* wisdom of the serpent. —**n=linie**, *f.* serpentine *or* wavy line; spiral curve. —**n=pfad**, *m.* winding path. —**n=röhre**, *f.*, —**n=rohr**, *n.* worm (*of a still*). —**n=stab**, *m.* the caduceus (*of Mercury*). —**n=stein**, *m.* ophite. —**n=stich**, *m.* serpent's bite *or* sting. —**n=träger**, *m.* Ophiucus (*Astr.*). —**n=wandelnd**, *adj.* serpentine, winding, meandering (*poet.*). —**n=weg**, *m. see* —**n=pfad.** —**n=wurzel**, *f.* snake-root; snake-weed.

Schläng'gelicht, *adj.* serpentine, spiral (*obs.*).

Schläng'gel—n, *v.* I. *a.* to twist, wind; **geschlängelter Weg**, winding road, *etc.* II. *n.* (*aux.* **h.**) *& r.* to twist; **sich um etwas —n**, to twist, wind, coil round a th. —**nd**, *p. & adj.* meandering, winding, sinuous.

Schlank, *adj.* slim, slender; tall, lank, thin. —**heit**, *f.* slenderness. *Comp.* —**weg** (*us. pron.* **schlankwe'g**), *adv.* roundly, flatly; easily, without obstacles.

Schlapp, I. *adj.* (*coll.*) *see* **Schlaff.** II. *int.*; **schlipp — ist seine Suppe hin**, there, the soup is all gone. —**e**, *f.* (*pl.* —en) slap; blow, rebuff, check, reverse, defeat; loss; **in —en gehen**, to go slipshod; **eine —e erhalten, erleiden**, to be defeated *or* worsted, to sustain a reverse. *Comp.* —**hut**, *m.* soft *or* slouched hat. —**ohr**, *n.* flap ear. —**schwanz**, *m.* weakling, person without backbone (*vulg.*). —**seil**, *n.* slack rope.

Schlapp—s, *m.* slovenly person. —**sig**, *adj.* long and weakly; slovenly.

Schlaraf'fe, *m.*, (**Schlauraffe**, *obs.*,) (—n, *pl.* —n) sluggard, lazy lubber. *Comp.* —**n=land**, *n.* Lubberland, Land of Cocaigne, land of the idle. —**n=leben**, *n.* lazy, purposeless life.

Schlar'fen, Schlar'ren, *v.n.* (*aux.* **h.**) to shuffle, walk slipshod.

Schlau, *adj.* sly, cunning, crafty; subtle. —**heit**, —**igkeit**, *f.* slyness, cunning, subtlety. *Comp.* —**berger**, —**meier**, *m.* (sly) old fox, old dodger. —**kopf**, *m.* sly, knowing fellow.

Schlau'be, *f.* (*pl.* —n) husk (*dial.*).

Schlauch, *m.* (—es, *pl.* **Schläu'che**) leathern bottle *or* skin; leather tube; hose (*of fire-engines*); pipe, tube; funnel; ampulla, utricle (*Bot.*); corpulent person. —**en**, *v.a.* to fill (*barrels, etc.*) by a (leather) pipe.

Schlau'dern, *v.n.* (*aux.* **h.**) to move idly about, dangle; to bungle; to be unsteady; to have too much play (*of machinery*); to sell under price; *see* **Schleudern.**

Schlecht, I. *adj. & adv.* straight, plain (*obs. now replaced by* **schlicht**); bad, wicked, base; poor, sorry; wretched; —**e Papiere**, worthless papers *or* bills; —**e Zeiten**, hard times; —**er Trost**, sorry *or* poor comfort; **einen — machen**, to run a p. down, to speak evil of a p.; —**er Absatz**, heavy sale; **einem —en Dank wissen**, to give a p. no thanks for; — **und recht**, upright, honest, genuine; simply; clearly; **es steht — mit ihm**, he is in a bad way; he is badly off; **sich — behelfen**, to make shift to live; — **entzückt von etwas**, not delighted with a th.; **nicht —**, not bad, rather well, considerable; **der, die —e**, the wicked *or* naughty person; **das —e**, the bad, evil; **das —e an einer Sache**, the bad side, the worst of a matter; **von einem alles mögliche —e reden**, to say everything bad of a p. II. *adv.* ill; poorly; **mir ist —**, I feel ill. —**heit**, —**igkeit**, *f.* badness; baseness; wickedness; base *or* vile action. *Comp.* —**beschaffen**, *adj.* ill-conditioned. —**denkend**, *adj.* ill-disposed. —**er=dings** (*pron.* **schlechterdi'ngs**), *adv.* utterly; positively, by all means, absolutely; —**erdings unmöglich**, utterly impossible; —**erdings nicht**, not by any means, by no means. —**gelaunt**, *adj. & adv.* in a bad temper. —**hin**, *adv.* simply, plainly. —**we'g**, *adv.* plainly, without ceremony; briefly; absolutely.

Schle'cker, *m.* (—s, *pl.* —) dainty person. —**n**, *v.n. see* **Leckern.**

Schle'g—el, *m.* (—els, *pl.* —el) mallet, beater, sledge-hammer; beetle; drumstick (*Mus.*); racket, battledore, *etc.*; place where the miner works; egg-whisk; leg (*of veal, etc.*); sluice. —**eln**, *v.* I. *n.* (*aux.* **h.**) to limp, hobble; to blunder. II. *a.* to strike with a mallet *or* sledge-hammer. —**ler**, *m.pl.*; **die —ler**, League of South German nobles (in the 14th century). *Comp.* —**el=lahm**, *adj.*; **einen Hirsch —ellahm schießen**, to wound a stag in the leg.

Schleh—e, *f.* (*pl.* —en) sloe, wild plum. *Comp.* —**dorn**, —**en=baum**, *m.* sloe-tree, blackthorn. —**en=blüte**, *f.* sloe blossom. —**weiß**, *adj.* white as a sloe-blossom.

Schlei'che, *f.* (*pl.* —n) *see* **Blindschleiche**; (*pl.*) anguids.

Schlei'ch—en, *ir.v.* I. *r. & n.* (*aux.* **s.**) to slink; to crawl, creep; to move gently, glide, steal, slide, flow; **im Finstern —en**, to prowl, steal about in the dark; **sich davon —en**, to steal away, to slink off; **die Pestilenz, die im Finstern —t**, the pestilence that walketh in darkness (*B.*). II. *a.* to smuggle; to slip into. —**end**, *p. & adj.* sneaking; furtive; lingering, slow; creeping; —**endes Gift**, slow *or* lingering poison; —**endes Fieber**, slow *or* low fever. —**er**, *m.* (—ers, *pl.* —er) person who walks stealthily; sneak; creeper (*Bot.*). —**erei'**, *f.* sneaking; underhand dealing. *Comp.* —**handel**, *m.* smuggling trade. —**händler**, *m.* smuggler. —**patrouille**, *f.* secret patrol, reconnoitring detachment. —**ware**, *f.* contraband goods. —**weg**, *m.* secret path, hidden path, by-way; indirect means.

Schlei(e), *f.* (*pl.* —n) tench.

Schlei'er, *m.* (—s, *pl.* —) veil; pretence, cloak; **den — nehmen**, to take the veil, to become a nun; **den — über eine Sache ziehen**, to draw a veil over s.th., to hush s.th. up. —**haft**, *adj.* veil-like; veiled; mysterious, inexplicable.

—n, *v.a.* to veil. *Comp.* —eule, *f.* barn-owl. —flor, *m.* crape; veiling. —haube, —kappe, *f.* crape cap. —lawine, *f.* powdery avalanche. —lehen, *n.* petticoat hold. —leinwand, *f.* cobweb lawn. —los, *adj.* unveiled. —tanz, *m.* skirt-dance *or* dancing. —tänzerin, *f.* skirt-dancer. —taube, *f.* nun *or* helmet-pigeon. —tuch, *n.* *see* —flor; estamine. —umhüllt, *adj.* veiled; wrapped in mystery.

Schlei'fe, *f.* (*pl.* —n) slide; sliding-place; sledge; dray; slip-knot; bow, loop; favour; snare, noose; loop, mesh; trail, track; train (*of a dress*); handle (*of a wooden can*).

1**Schlei'f—en**, *v.* I. *n.* (*aux.* h. & s.) to slide; to glide, slip along. II. *a.* to drag, trail, draw, pull along; to convey on a sledge; to slur (*Mus.*); to bind (*Mus.*); to slide (*a step in dancing*); to raze, demolish (*a fortress*); to knot, tie in a bow; to put on a bow; to drawl (*words*); **Buchstaben —en**, to soften, to voice letters; to palatalise (*an l*); **die Festungswerke sollen geschleift werden**, the fortifications are to be razed, the fortress is to be dismantled. —er, *m.* slow waltz, shuffle (*Danc.*); coloratura, slurred note. —ung, *f.* razing, demolition; slurring (*Mus.*). *Comp.* —bahn, *f.* slide. —knoten, *m.* running knot (*Naut.*). —lade, *f.* sounding board (*of organs*). —lafette, *f.* sledge-carriage. —note, *f.* slurred note (*Mus.*). —schritt, *m.* sliding-step, glissade. —ungszeichen, *n.* slur (*Mus.*).

2**Schlei'f—en**, *ir.v.a.* to grind, polish, smooth; to whet, sharpen (*knives, etc.*); to polish, rub up; to cut (*gems, etc.*); **aus dem Groben —en**, to rough-hew; **dieser junge Mann muß erst noch geschliffen werden**, this young man wants polish. —er, *m.* (—ers, *pl.* —er) grinder, polisher; cutter. —ung, *f.* grinding. *Comp.* —bank, *f.* grinding-lathe. —baum, *m.* spar; trailing-beam (*Artil.*). —mühle, *f.* grinding-mill. —nadel, *f.* hair-pin. —rad, *n.* grinding-wheel. —stein, *m.* whet-stone, grinder. —zeug, *n.* grinding, polishing tool.

Schlei'he, *see* Schlei(e).

Schleim, *m.* (—s, *pl.* —e) slime; phlegm, mucus; mucilage (*Bot.*); **einen — auf einen haben**, to be angry with a p. (*dial.*); **Gersten—**, barley-gruel. —ig, *adj.* slimy, mucous, mucilaginous. *Comp.* —absonderung, *f.* mucous secretion. —auswurf, *m.* expectoration (*of mucus*). —blutig, *adj.* phlegmatic. —fieber, *n.* mucous fever. —fluß, *m.* blennorrhœa. —harz, *n.* gum-resin. —haut, *f.* mucous membrane. —husten, *m.* cough with expectoration of phlegm. —krankheit, *f.* catarrhal affection. —pfropf, *m.* polypus (*in the nose, etc.*). —sack, *m.* mucus-bag. —sauer, *adj.* mucous. —tiere, *pl.* mollusca.

Schlei'men, *v.* I. *n.* (*aux.* h.) to produce mucus; to become slimy (*in boiling, etc.*). II. *a.* to cleanse; to skim.

Schlei'ße, *f.* (*pl.* —n) splinter, splint; long strip of wood used as torch; quill of a feather; lint.

Schlei'ßen, *ir.v.* I. *a.* to split; to slit; **Federn —**, to strip quills. II. *n.* (*aux.* s.) to wear out.

Schlem'me—n, *v.* I. *n.* (*aux.* h.) to carouse; to gormandize. II. *a.* *see* Schlämmen. —r, *m.* (—rs, *pl.* —r) glutton, free liver. —rei', *f.* gluttony.

Schlen'd—er, *m.* (—ers) lounging gait; lounge; train of a dress; old way. —erer, *m.* (—erers, *pl.* —erer) lounger. —ern, *v.n.* (*aux.* h. & s.) to dawdle, lounge, saunter, stroll about. —rian, *m.* (—rians, *pl.* —riane) slow old humdrum way; lounger, loiterer; stick-in-the-mud, person of routine; **der alte —rian**, the old humdrum *or* sleepy ways; **am alten —rian festhalten**, to tread the beaten path; **zum alten —rian zurückgekehrt sein**, to have fallen back to one's old ways. *Comp.* —er=gang, *see* —er. —er=jan, *see* Schlendrian.

Schlen'kern, *v.* I. *n.* (*aux.* h.) to dangle; to shamble (*in walking*); to roll (*of ships*); to change about; **mit den Armen —**, to swing one's arms. II. *a.* to shake off, jerk, toss.

Schlep'pe, *f.* (*pl.* —n) train (*of a dress*); trail; truck; sledge.

Schlep'p—en, *v.* I. *a.* to drag, trail; to tug (*vessels*); to wear out (*a dress, etc.*); to drawl (*one's words*); to drag (*the anchor*). II. *r.* to move slowly; to be troubled *or* burdened with; to be prolix (*of style*). III. *n.* (*aux.* h.) to drag, trail. —end, *p.* & *adj.* spun out, tedious; drawling. —er, *m.* (—ers, *pl.* —er) one who drags, dragger, hauler, tracker; tow-rope; tout, decoy (duck). —erei', *f.* dragging, *etc.*; drudgery. *Comp.* —boot, *n.* tug, tow-boat. —dampfboot, *n.*, —dampfer, *m.* steam-tug. —en=träger, *n.* train-bearer; toady. —haken, *m.* towing-hook. —kleid, *n.* dress with a train. —netz, *n.* drag-net. —schiff, *n.* tow-boat. —seil, *n.* drag; *see* —netz; drag-rope (*Artil.*). —tau, *n.* hawser; **ins —tau nehmen**, to take in tow.

Schleu'der, *f.* (*pl.* —n) sling; thong (*of a scythe*); elater (*Bot.*). —er, *m.* (—ers, *pl.* —er) slinger; underseller.

Schleu'der—n, *v.* I. *a.* to sling; to throw, hurt; to dart, project, send, shoot. II. *n.* (*aux.* h.) to shake; to do hurriedly; to sell under price. *Comp.* —arbeit, *f.* bungling work. —buchhändler, *m.* bookseller who undersells other booksellers. —honig, *m.* strained honey. —konkurrenz, *f.* unfair competition. —mühle, *f.* centrifugal machine; (Carrs) Carr's disintegrating flour-mill. —preis, *m.* too low a price; **zu —preisen**, dirt cheap.

Schleu'nig, *adj.* & *adv.* quick, speedy, prompt, swift; immediate; hasty; **aufs —ste**, in all haste, as soon as possible, without delay. —keit, *f.* speed, haste.

Schleu'se, *f.* (*pl.* —n) sluice, lock; sewer. *Comp.* —n=bett, *n.*, —n=boden, *m.* bottom of a sluice. —n=flügel, *m.* leaf of a floodgate. —n=geld, *n.* lock-charges. —n=gerinne, *n.* channel of a sluice. —n=kammer, *f.* lock-chamber. —n=meister, *m.* sluice-keeper. —n=thür, *f.*, —n=thor, *n.* flood-gate, lock-gate. —n=zoll, *m.* *see* —ngeld.

1**Schlich**, *m.* (—(e)s, *pl.* —e) secret way; stealthy step; (*pl.*) tricks, artifices; **alle —e kennen**, to be an artful dodger, to know what 's what; **alle —e (in einem Hause) kennen**, to know every turn (*in a house*); **seine —e kennen**, to be up to a p.'s tricks; **hinter jemandes —e kommen**, to find somebody out, to discover a p.'s dodges.

2**Schlich**, *m.* (—es) grinder's dust *or* earth; slime, mud.

3**Schlich, Schli'che**, *1 & 3 pers. sing. imperf. ind. & subj. of* schleichen.

Schlicht, *adj.* & *adv.* plain, homely, simple; sleek, smooth; plain; straightforward, simple; **der —e Menschenverstand**, common sense; **—er Abschied**, unceremonious dismissal (*Mil.*); **—e Erzählung**, plain unvarnished tale; **ein —er Mann**, a plain, straightforward man; **—es Haar**, smooth hair. —bar, *adj.* that can be arranged. —e, *f.* *see* —heit; weaver's glue, dressing; cinder-paste.

Schlich't—en, *v.a.* to make straight *or* plain; to arrange; to plane, level, smooth; to dress (*Weav.*); to adjust, settle, make up (*quarrels, etc.*). —er, *m.* (—ers, *pl.* —er) planisher; dresser; mediator; arbiter. —heit, *f.* plainness, smoothness; simplicity. —ig, *adj.* sleek; even. —ung, *f.* settlement, amicable arrangement. *Comp.* —haarig, *adj.* with smooth hair. —hammer, *m.* planishing hammer. —**hobel**, *m.* long plane. —**maschine**, *f.* dressing *or* sizing machine. —**mond**, *m.* tanner's paring knife *or* hone. —**pinsel**, *m.* softening brush. —**rahmen**, *m.* tanner's stretching-frame. —**stahl**, *m.* broad chisel. —**zange**, *f.* tanner's stretching-pincers.

Schlick, *m.* (—**es**, *pl.* —**e**) slime, mud; clay. —**erig**, *adj.* muddy, slimy. *Comp.* —**grund**, *m.* fat and muddy soil, oozy bottom. —**watt**, *n.* stretch of muddy land left by the ebbing tide.

[1]**Schlief, Schlie'fe**, *1 & 3 pers. sing. imperf. ind. & subj. of* **schlafen.**

[2]**Schlief**, *m.* (—**s**, *pl.* —**e**) unbaked piece (*in bread, etc.*). —**en**, *ir.v.n.* (*aux.* **s.**) to slip, creep into (*obs. & dial.*). —**ig**, *adj.* soft, doughy.

Schließ'—bar, *adj.* that may be closed *or* locked; deducible, inferable; —**barer Kasten**, box with lock and key. —**e**, *f.* (*pl.* —**en**) bolt, peg, fastening; catch, staple (*of a lock*); shutter (*of a sluice, etc.*); book-clasp.

Schlie'ß—en, *ir.v.* I. *a.* to shut, close; to lock; to join; to stop (*rifle cocks*); to fold, clasp (*one's hands*); to press (*to one's heart*); to form (*a circle*); to close (*the ranks, Mil.*); to lock up (*a form, Typ.*); to enclose, close in (*a country*); to conclude (*an arrangement*); to contract (*a marriage, etc.*); to close (*a discussion, a paragraph, etc.*); to finish, end; to balance (*an account*); **er —t jetzt die dritte Ehe**, he is just about to marry for the third time; **hieran —en wir die Bemerkung**, to this we add the remark; **in die Arme —en**, to embrace; **daraus —e ich**, thence I conclude; **von sich selbst auf andere —en**, to judge others by oneself; **einen Winkel —en**, to subtend an angle; **einen Gefangenen —en**, to put a prisoner in chains; **einen krumm —en**, to bind a p. hand and foot; **die voltaische Säule —en**, to unite the two poles of electricity; **die Reihen —en**, to close the ranks, take close order; **geschlossene Reihen**, serried ranks; **eine geschlossene Jagd**, a hunt where the game is enclosed with nets, preserve; **geschlossene Gesellschaft**, private party, club; **geschlossenes Quarre**, solid square; **geschlossene Zeit**, close time (*Sport*); time of fasting (*R. C.*); **geschlossenes Ganze**, complete *or* absolute whole. II. *r.* to close, shut; to lock; to close (*as wounds*); to collapse; to end; **in sich —en**, to include, imply, comprehend, involve; **sich an einander —en**, to press close to one another, to crowd, to close the ranks (*Mil.*), to become intimate; **rechts —t euch!** close to the right! III. *n.* (*aux.* **h.**) to shut, close; to end, conclude; to fit well *or* close; to join well; **da** *or* **hiermit —t die Geschichte**, here the story ends; **die Schule schloß gestern**, yesterday the school broke up; **der Aktienverkauf begann mit 94 und schloß mit 94·85**, stocks opened at 94 and closed at 94.85; **der Schlüssel —t nicht**, the key does not fit the lock, does not work; **der Reiter —t, reitet geschlossen**, the horseman has a firm seat; **das Kleid —t**, the dress fits well. —**end**, *adj.* closing, concluding, final. —**er**, *m.* (—**ers**, *pl.* —**er**) doorkeeper; turnkey; storekeeper. —**lich**, I. *adj.* final, definitive. II. *adv.* finally, in conclusion. —**ung**, *f.* closing, close, conclusion; closure, cloture. *Comp.* —**balken**, *m.* iron bar (*for gates, Fort.*). —**baum**, *m.* bar; boom (*of a harbour*). —**blech**, *n.* rundle; hasp. —**bolzen**, *m.* joint-bolt. —**er=amt**, *n.* office of turnkey *or* porter. —**feder**, *f.* locking-spring, spring-catch; spring-bolt. —**hahn**, *m.* stop-cock. —**haken**, *m.* catch. —**kappe**, *f.* staple (*of a lock*). —**keil**, *m.* wedge. —**kette**, *f.* fastening chain. —**korb**, *m.* basket that can be locked. —**muskel**, *m.* sphincter muscle, contractor. —**nagel**, *m.* bolt-nail; bar (*Typ.*). —**quadrätchen**, *n.* M-quadrat (*Typ.*). —**riegel**, *m.* dead-bolt.

[1]**Schliff**, *m.* grinding; polishing; polish; edge; cutler's dust; **ein Mensch ohne —**, a man without manners, a boorish person.

[2]**Schliff, Schlif'fe**, *1 & 3 pers. sing. imperf. ind. & subj. of* **schleifen.**

Schlimm, *adj. & adv.* bad, ill; evil; sad, sorry; sore; unwell; **immer —er**, worse and worse; **um so —er**, all *or* so much the worse; —**stenfalls** *or* **im —sten Falle**, at the worst, if the worst comes to the worst; **der Kranke ist heute sehr —**, the patient is very low *or* ill to-day; **mir ist —**, I feel sick *or* unwell; —**e Augen**, sore eyes; —**er Geselle**, nasty fellow; **es geht ihm —**, he is in a bad way; **auf das —ste gefaßt sein**, to be prepared for the worst; **— nach etwas** *or* **hinter etwas her sein**, to be much set, bent upon something. *Comp.* —**bessern**, to correct for the worse, to make an unhappy alteration. —**besserung**, *f.* correction for the worse, unfortunate alteration, spoiling of a text.

Schlin'ge, *f.* (*pl.* —**n**) (*running*) knot; noose, loop; mesh; springe, gin, snare; tendril; sling (*Surg.*); **in die — gehen**, to fall into the snare; —**n legen**, to set snares; **sich aus der — ziehen**, to effect one's escape, get out of a scrape. —**l**, *m.* (—**ls**, *pl.* —**l**) clown; sluggard; rascal. —**lei'**, *f.* rascality. —**lhaft**, *adj.* rascally.

Schlin'g—en, I. *ir.v.a.* to wind, weave, twist; to entwine, intertwine; to sling; to swallow, devour, to engulf; **sich —en**, to coil, wind, twine, turn; **die Arme in einander —en**, to cross one's arms; **ein Band in eine Schleife —en**, to make a bow *or* knot of ribbon. II. *ir.v.n.* (*aux.* **s.**) to glide; to creep. III. *subst. n.* deglutition; gluttony; winding, entwining, *etc.* —**ern**, *v.n.* (*aux.* **h.**) to roll (*of ships*); *see* **Schlenkern**. *Comp.* —**faden**, *m.* tendril, clasper (*Bot.*). —**gewächs**, —**kraut**, *n.*, —**pflanze**, *f.* creeper, climber (*Bot.*).

Schlip'pe, *f.* space between houses, lane (*dial.*).

Schlippermilch, *f.* curdled milk (*dial.*).

Schlips, *m.* (—**(s)es**, *pl.* —**(s)e**) bow; cravat.

Schliß, Schlis'se, *1 & 3 pers. sing. imperf. ind. & subj. of* **schleißen.**

Schlit(t)a'ge, *f.* wear and tear (*of sails, ropes*).

Schlit'te—n, *m.* (—**ns**, *pl.* —**n**) sledge, sleigh; toboggan; cradle (*Naut.*); slide (*Mach.*); saw-mill-sledge; **unter den —n kommen**, to get into a scrape, to come off badly (*coll.*). —**rer**, *m.* (—**rers**, *pl.* —**rer**), —**rin**, *f.* slider. —**rn**, I. *v.n.* (*aux.* **h.** & **s.**) to slide. II. *subst. n.* slide. *Comp.* —**n=bahn**, *f.* sledging-way; sledging; **es wird bald —nbahn geben**, we shall soon have sledging. —**n=baum**, *m.* sledge-pole. —**n=fahrt**, *f.* sledge-drive. —**n=geläute**, *n.* sleigh-bells. —**n=partie**, *f.* sledging-party, tobogganing-party; sledge-excursion. —**r=bahn**, *f.* slide.

Schlitt'schuh, *m.* skate; **— laufen**, to skate. *Comp.* —**bahn**, *f.* skating ground. —**laufen**, *n.* skating. —**läufer**, *m.*, —**läuferin**, *f.* skater.

Schlitz, *m.* (—**es**, *pl.* —**e**) slit, slash; rift, cleft; glyph (*Arch.*); scar, seam; vulva. —**ig**, *adj.* slashed, having slits; **vier—ig**, with four slits. *Comp.* —**auge**, *n.* slit eye, Mongolian eye. *n.* **bruch**, *m.* longitudinal fracture. —**fenster**, — lancet window. —**mantel**, *m.* lady's cloak with armholes. —**messer**, *n.* lancet.

Schlit'zen, *v.a.* to slit, slash, cleave, rip, open.

Schloff, Schlöf'fe, *1 & 3 pers. sing. imperf. ind. & subj. of* **schliefen** (*obs.*).

Schloh'weiß, *adj.* snow-white (*for* **schloßweiß**, white as a hailstone).

[1]**Schloß**, *n.* (—**(ss)es**, *pl.* **Schlö(ss)er**) castle;

manor, seat; lock (*of firearms, doors, etc.*); clasp, snap (*of bracelets, etc.*); hinge (*of shells*); **unter — und Riegel,** under lock and key. **—(ss)er,** *see* **Schlosser.** *Comp.* **—aufseher,** *m.* castellan. **—bein,** *n.* hip-bone (*Anat.*). **—blech,** *n.* scutcheon (*of a lock*). **—feder,** *f.* spring of a lock. **—gefängnis,** *n.* dungeon. **—gesessene(r),** *m.* one enfeoffed with a castle. **—gewirr,** *n.* wards of a lock. **—graben,** *m.* castle-moat. **—hauptmann,** *m.* castellan; governor of a palace. **—hof,** *m.* castle-yard; court-circle. **—platz,** *m.* palace-yard. **—prediger,** *m.* court-chaplain. **—riegel,** *m.* bolt of a lock. **—stein,** *m.* key-stone. **—verwalter, —vogt,** *m.* castellan. **—wache,** *f.* guard of the palace *or* castle; castle-guard-house. **—zirkel,** *m.* reduction-compasses.

[2]**Schloß, Schlös'se,** *1 & 3 pers. sing. imperf. ind. & subj. of* **schließen.**

Schlöß'chen, *n.* (—s, *pl.* —) small castle; small lock; locket.

Schlo'ß—e, *f.* (*pl.* —en) hailstone; (*pl.*) hail. **—en,** *v.n.* (*aux.* **h.**) to hail. *Comp.* **—enkorn,** *n.*, **—en-stein,** *m.* hailstone. **—enwetter,** *n.* hailstorm. **—weiß,** *adj.* (*obs.*) *see* **Schlohweiß.**

Schlos'ser, *m.* (—s, *pl.* —) locksmith. **—ei',** *f.* locksmith's trade; locksmith's workshop. *Comp.* **—gesell,** *m.* journeyman-locksmith.

Schlot, *m.* (—(e)s, *pl.* —e, **Schlö'te**) chimney, flue; smoke-pipe. *Comp.* **—feger, —kehrer,** *m.* chimney-sweep. **—schwalbe,** *f.* house-swallow.

Schlot'terig, *adj. & adv.* loose, shaking; flabby; wobbly; slovenly; negligent; **— gehen,** to stagger, totter.

Schlot'ter—n, *v.n.* (*aux.* **h.**) to hang *or* fit loose; to shake, tremble, dangle; to slouch; to totter; to clash, knock together; **—nde Kniee,** shaking, trembling knees. *Comp.* **—füßig,** *adj.* unsteady in the legs, shambling. **—gang,** *m.* shuffling, unsteady gait.

Schlucht, *f.* (*pl.* —en) ravine, defile, glen, gorge.

Schluch'zen, I. *v.n.* (*aux.* **h.**) to sob. II. *subst.n.* sobbing.

Schluck, *m.* (—es, *pl.* —e, **Schlü'cke,** *as measure* —; *dimin.* **Schlück'chen,** *n.*) sip, gulp, mouthful, draught; **einen — über den Durst trinken,** to take a drop too much.

Schlu'ck—en, *v.* I. *a.* to swallow, gulp, drink down; **in sich —en,** to absorb, drink in, to pocket (*an insult, etc.*); **er wird nicht viel dabei —en,** he will gain but little by it. II. *n.* (*aux.* **h.**) to hiccough. **—er,** *m.* (—ers, *pl.* —er) swallower; hungry wretch; sponge; wretch; **armer —er,** poor starveling, poor devil. *Comp.* **—apparat,** *m.* organs of deglutition. **—auf,** *m.* hiccough. **—weise,** *adv.* by mouthfuls *or* draughts.

Schluft, *f.* (*pl.* —e, —en) *dial. for* **Schlucht.**

Schlug, Schlü'ge, *1 & 3 pers. sing. imperf. ind. & subj. of* **schlagen.**

Schlum'mer, *m.* (—s, *pl.* —) slumber; torpor; drowsiness. **—er,** *m.* (—ers, *pl.* —er) slumberer; *see* **—kopf.**

Schlum'mer—n *v.n.* (*aux.* **h.**) to slumber, doze, nap; to lie dormant. **—nd,** *p. & adj.* slumbering; dormant. *Comp.* **—betäubt,** *adj.* stupid with sleepiness. **—fieber,** *n.* lethargic fever. **—gott,** *m.* Morpheus. **—kissen,** *n.* (soft) pillow. **—kopf,** *m.* sleepy-head. **—köpfig,** *adj.* drowsy. **—körner,** *pl.* poppy seeds. **—lied,** *n.* lullaby. **—punsch,** *m.* night-cap (*coll.*) **—rolle,** *f.* round pillow, small bolster-shaped pillow.

Schlump, I. *m.* (—es, *pl.* —e) haste; hazard, chance. **—s,** *adv.* thoughtlessly, rashly. II. *f.*, **—e,** *f.* (*pl.* —en) slut, slattern, sloven. **—ig, —sig,** *adj.* slovenly.

Schlum'pe—n, *v.* I. *n.* (*aux.* **h.** & **s.**) to trail; to draggle, to dangle. II. *imp.* to succeed by chance; **es hat ihm geschlumpt,** he succeeded in it. **—r,** *m.* slovenly person. **—rn,** *v.n.* (*aux.* **h.** & **s.**) to dangle, trail.

Schlund, *m.* (—es, *pl.* **Schlün'de**) throat, œsophagus, gullet; gorge; abyss; mouth of a cannon; crater. *Comp.* **—bräune,** *f.* sore throat; pharyngitis. **—kopf,** *m.* pharynx. **—muskel,** *m.* muscle of the œsophagus. **—öffnung,** *f.* pharyngotomy. **—röhre,** *f.* œsophagus.

Schlup(e), *f.* (*pl.* —(e)n) sloop.

Schlupf, *m.* (—es, *pl.* **Schlüp'fe**) slipping; narrow place, place to creep into; refuge; running knot. *Comp.* **—gang,** *m.* haunt. **—hafen,** *m.* creek. **—käfer,** *m.* death-watch (*Ent.*). **—loch,** *n.* loophole (*for escape*); hiding-place. **—pforte,** *f.*, **—thor,** *n.* side-gate, postern. **—wespe,** *f.* ichneumon-fly. **—winkel,** *m.* secret recess; hiding place.

Schlüp'f—en, *v.n.* (*aux.* **s.**) to slip, slide, glide. **—(e)rig,** *adj.* slippery; delicate; dangerous; equivocal; changeable, unreliable; piquant racy; indecent, obscene. **—(e)rigkeit,** *f.* slipperiness, lubricity, ticklishness; indelicacy, obscenity, coarseness, lasciviousness.

Schlur'fen (*dial.*) *see* **Schlürfen,** II.

Schlür'fen, *v.* I. *a.* to sip, lap, quaff; to relish. II. *n.* (*aux.* **h.** & **s.**) to shuffle in walking, to go slipshod.

Schluß, *m.* (—(ss)es, *pl.* **Schlüs'se**) shutting, closing; end, conclusion; breaking-up (*of schools, etc.*); keystone (*of a vault*); hinge (*of a bivalve*); fit (*of doors, etc.*); end, conclusion; close; peroration; cadence, close (*of a period*); resolution; consequence; inference; syllogism (*Log.*); **Thür und Fenster haben keinen rechten —,** neither door nor window shuts tight, closes properly; **einen guten — haben,** to have a good *or* firm seat (*on horseback*); **eine Sache zum — bringen,** to terminate, settle a matter; **logischer —,** syllogism; **zum —,** finally, in conclusion. *Comp.* **—art,** *f.* method of reasoning. **—balken,** *m.* top-girder of a roof. **—bein,** *n.* hip-bone. **—bemerkung,** *f.* final observation; epilogue. **—bilanz,** *f.* annual balance. **—brett,** *n.* floodgate. **—ergebnis,** *n.* (final) result. **—fall,** *m.* cadence. **—fassung,** *f.* resolution, conclusion. **—folge,** *f.* chain of reasoning; conclusion; result. **—form,** *f.* form of a syllogism. **—gerecht,** *adj.* logical. **—kette,** *f.* chain of reasoning. **—kunst,** *f.* logic. **—(kurs)notie'rung,** *f.* closing quotation (*C.L.*). **—nagel,** *m.* pole-pin; perch-bolt (*Artil.*). **—prüfung,** *f.* final examination. **—punkt,** *m.* full stop, period; last point *or* head. **—rechnung,** *f.* final account, *see* **—bilanz**; proportion (*Arith.*). **—recht, —richtig,** *adj.* conclusive; logically correct. **—rede,** *f.* concluding speech; epilogue; syllogism. **—reif,** I. *m.* chime-hoop. II. *adj.* ready for judgment (*Law*). **—satz,** *m.* final proposition, conclusion; consequent (*of a syllogism*); finale (*Mus.*). **—stein,** *m.* keystone; (**des Gebäudes**) coping stone. **—widrig,** *adj.* inconclusive; illogical. **—zeichen,** *n.* sign of conclusion; double-bar, Fine (*Mus.*); full stop. **—zettel,** *m.* broker's memorandum *or* contract. **—zierat,** *m.* tail-piece (*Typ.*); crowning ornament.

Schlüs'sel, *m.* (—s, *pl.* —) key; **falscher —,** false key, skeleton key, picklock; **das Amt der —,** the power of the keys (*Eccl.*). *Comp.* **—ader,** *f.* sub-clavian vein. **—bart,** *m.* key-bit. **—bein,** *n.* collar-bone. **—blume,** *f.* cowslip, primula veris; **gelbe —blume,** primrose, primula vulgaris. **—bund,** *n.* bunch of keys. **—loch,** *n.* keyhole; bore of a key. **—rohr,** *n.* pipe of a key. **—schild,** *m.* key-plate, scutcheon. **—soldaten,** *pl.* papal soldiers.

Schlüs'ſ—ig, *adj.* resolved, determined; **—ig werden,** to make up one's mind.
Schmach (*long* **a**), *f.* insult, outrage, offence; disgrace. *Comp.* **—bedeckt, —beladen,** *adj.* covered with shame *or* ignominy. **—voll,** *adj.* disgraceful.
Schmach't—en, *v.n.* (*aux.* **h.**) to languish, pine (**vor,** with); **—en nach,** to long for, yearn after. *Comp.* **—blick,** *m.* languishing glance. **—hans, —lappen,** *m.* starved wretch; love-sick swain; **er ist ein —lappen,** he is love-sick, he is a sentimental fellow (*coll.*). **—locke,** *f.* love-lock. **—riemen,** *m.* belt for decreasing the size of the stomach.
Schmäch'tig, *adj.* slender, slim; lank; wasted, hectic. **—keit,** *f.* slenderness, slimness.
[1]**Schmack,** *m.* (—es) (*obs. & dial.*) *see* **Geschmack.** **—haft,** *adj.* tasty; savoury; relishable. **—haftigkeit,** *f.* savouriness; savour, taste.
[2]**Schmack(e),** *f.* (*pl.* **—en**) smack (*Naut.*)
Schmad'dern, *v.a.* to daub; to scrawl (*coll.*).
Schmä'h—en, *v.a. & n.* (*aux.* **h.**) to revile, abuse; to calumniate; **einen —en** *or* **auf, gegen** *or* **über einen —en,** to rail at, inveigh against, slander *or* insult s.o. **—er,** *m.* (—ers, *pl.* —er) reviler, slanderer. **—lich,** *adj.* ignominious, disgraceful; abusive; insulting; **es ist —lich heiß,** it is frightfully hot (*coll.*); **er hat sich —lich geärgert,** he was horribly vexed (*coll.*). **—ung,** *f.* (*pl.* **—ungen,** *used as pl. of* **Schmach**) abuse, invective, aspersion; **Klage wegen —ung,** action for libel. *Comp.* **—brief,** *m.* insulting letter. **—rede,** *f.* objurgation, diatribe. **—schrift,** *f.* libel; lampoon; abusive writings. **—sucht,** *f.* slanderous disposition. **—süchtig,** *adj.* slanderous. **—wort,** *n.* invective.
Schmal, *adj.* (—er, —st; *older and less common* **schmäler, schmälst**) small; poor, scanty; narrow; slender; **auf die —e Seite legen,** to lay edgewise; **—e Bissen haben,** to fare badly, to be on short commons; **bei ihnen geht es — her,** they are badly off, they have to pinch themselves very much. **—heit,** *f.* narrowness; scantiness, poverty. *Comp.* **—bäckig,** *adj.* lantern-jawed; narrow-faced. **—beet,** *n.* flower-border. **—bier,** *n.* small beer. **—brüstig,** *adj.* narrow-chested. **—hans,** *m.* lanky fellow; niggard; **heute ist —hans bei uns Küchenmeister,** we are on short commons to-day. **—leder,** *n.* (*tanned calf-skin used for*) upper leather. **—leibig,** *adj.* slender (-bodied), lank, slim. **—spur,** *f.* narrow gauge. **—spurig,** *adj.* narrow gauged; **—spurige Bahn,** narrow-gauge railway. **—tier,** *n.* hind in its second year. **—vieh,** *n.* small cattle (*sheep, goats, etc.*).
Schmä'len, *v.a. & n.* (*aux.* **h.**) to scold; **auf einen —,** to chide, scold, declaim against a p.
Schmä'ler—n, *v.a.* to lessen, diminish; to curtail; to intrench upon; to detract from; to narrow; straighten. **—ung,** *f.* lessening; narrowing; diminution; retrenchment; detraction.
Schmal't—e, *f.*, (**—blau,** *n.*) small-blue, azure.
Schmalz, *n.* (—es) melted fat *or* grease; dripping; (**Schweine—**) lard; **in — backen,** to fry in lard. **—ig,** *adj.* greasy. *Comp.* **—birn(e),** *f.* butter-pear. **—blume,** *see* **Butter-blume.** **—brot,** *n.* slice of bread and dripping. **—gebackene(s),** *n.* dripping *or* short cake, fry. **—grube,** *f.* rich land (*coll.*). **—kuchen,** *m. see* **—gebackenes.** **—pfanne,** *f.* frying pan.
Schmal'zen, Schmäl'zen, *v.a.* (*p.p. often* **geschmalzen**) to grease, to put dripping *or* lard (*into*).
Schmant, *m.* (—es, *pl.* —e) cream; cream-like substance (*dial.*).
Schmarot'z—en, *v.n.* (*aux.* **h.**) to sponge (**bei,** upon); to play the toady. **—er,** *m.* (—ers, *pl.* **—er**) parasite; sponge; toady; tuft-hunter. **—erei',** *f.* sponging; parasitism; toadyism; tuft-hunting. **—erhaft, —erisch,** *adj.* sponging. *Comp.* **—er-krebs,** *m.* hermit-crab. **—er-pflanze,** *f.* parasitic plant, parasite.
Schmar'r—e, *f.* (*pl.* **—en**) slash, scar. **—ig,** *adj.* scarred.
Schmar'ren, *m.* crust made of crumbs; kind of cake made of white bread, eggs, milk, etc. (*dial.*).
Schmatz, *m.* (—es, *pl.* —e) (*dim.* **Schmätz'chen**) smack, hearty kiss.
Schmat'zen, *v.a. & n.* (*aux.* **h.**) to smack (*the lips, etc.*); to kiss heartily, smack.
Schmauch, *m.* (—es, *pl.* —e) thick *or* dense smoke. **—en,** *v.a. & n.* (*aux.* **h.**) to smoke (violently), to blow a cloud (*coll.*).
Schmaus, *m.* (—(s)es, *pl.* **Schmäu'se**) feast, banquet; **Ohren—,** musical treat; **einem einen — geben,** to feast *or* treat a p., to give a dinner in a p.'s honour. **—(s)en,** *v.a. & n.* (*aux.* **h.**) to feast, banquet. **—(s)er,** *m.* (—(s)ers, *pl.* —(s)er) feaster; lover of good living. **—(s)erei',** *f.* feasting; banquet. **—(s)erisch,** *adj.* festive; extravagant.
Schmeck'bar, *adj.* appreciable by the taste.
Schme'ck—en, *v.* I. *a.* to taste; to try by tasting; to relish, enjoy. II. *n.* (*aux.* **h.**) to taste (*bitter, sweet*); to taste good, be pleasant to the taste; to smell (*dial.*); **fein —en,** to have a fine palate; to taste nice; **—en nach,** to savour, smack of; **dieser Wein —t mir,** I like this wine; **ihm will nichts —en,** he has no appetite, nothing is to his taste; **er läßt es sich —en,** he enjoys it *or* his meal; **es hat mir vortrefflich geschmeckt,** I have thoroughly enjoyed it; **ein Schluck Wein darauf wird —en,** a glass of wine would make a good finish; **das —t nach mehr,** it is so good that I should like some more of it; **Zimmt —t vor,** the predominating flavour is cinnamon; **diese Nachricht —te ihm gar nicht,** he did not relish *or* enjoy that piece of news at all; **wenn es am besten —t, soll man aufhören,** one should leave off with an appetite; when the jest is at its best, 't will be well to let it rest. **—er,** *m.* (—ers, *pl.* —er) taster; gourmand; man of taste.
Schmeer, *see* **Schmer.**
Schmeich—elei', *f.* flattery; adulation; coaxing, cajolery. **—elhaft,** *adj.* flattering; complimentary; coaxing. **—lerisch,** *adj.* flattering, adulatory, fawning.
Schmei'ch—eln, *v.* I. *n.* (*aux.* **h.**, *dat.*) to flatter; to cajole, caress, wheedle; to fawn upon; **einem Hunde —eln,** to pat, caress a dog. II. *a.*; **sich in eiteln Hoffnungen —eln,** to flatter oneself with foolish hopes. **—ler,** *m.* (—lers, *pl.* —ler), **—lerin,** *f.* flatterer; coaxer; sycophant. *Comp.* **—el-blick,** *m.* flattering, coaxing look. **—el-katze,** *f.* flatterer, wheedler. **—el-name,** *m.* pet-name. **—el-rede,** *f.*, **—el-wort,** *n.* flattering word *or* speech.
Schmeiß, *m.* (—es) dirt, excrement.
Schmei'ß—en, *ir.v.a.* to fling, cast, throw (*vulg.*); to deposit eggs; to stand (a bottle of wine) (*coll.*); **geschmissenes Fleisch,** fly-blown meat. *Comp.* **—fliege,** *f.* blow-fly, blue-bottle.
Schmelz, *m.* (—es) enamel; glass bead *or* bugle; **melodischer — einer Stimme,** melting sweetness of a voice. **—bar,** *adj.* fusible. **—barkeit,** *f.* fusibility. **—e,** *f.* melting; smelting; fusion; mass, charge (*of metal*); composition (*of glass*), foundry.
Schmel'z—en, I. *ir.v.n.* (*aux.* **s.**) to melt, dissolve, fuse; to diminish, melt away; **in Thränen —en,** to dissolve into tears; **das Regiment war auf 150 Mann (zusammen) geschmolzen,** the regiment was reduced to 150 men. II. *reg.*

& ir.v.a. to melt, dissolve, liquefy; to smelt; to blend. **—end**, *p. & adj.* melting, liquefying; touching; languishing; melodious, melting; **—ende Schönheit**, refining (*power of*) beauty, beauty in its moving influence. **—er**, *m.* (—ers, *pl.* —er) smelter. **—erei'**, *f. see* **—arbeit**, **—hütte**. **—ung**, *f.* melting, fusion; liquefaction. *Comp.* **—arbeit**, *f.* smelting; enamelling; enamel. **—blau**, *see* **Schmaltblau**. **—butter**, *f.* melted butter. **—eisen**, *n.* cast iron. **—farbe**, *f.* vitrifiable pigment, enamel-colour; **mit —farben malen**, to enamel. **—feuer**, *n.* smelting fire. **—form**, *f.* mould. **—gemälde**, *n.* enamel painting. **—glas**, *n.* enamel. **—grad**, *m.*, **—hitze**, *f. see* **—punkt**. **—hütte**, *f.* smelting-house, foundry. **—küche**, *f.* laboratory. **—kunst**, *f.* art of smelting; art of enamelling. **—laut**, *m.* liquid (*Gram.*). **—löffel**, *m.* ladle. **—maler**, *m.* enameller; painter in enamel. **—ofen**, *m.* furnace; forge. **—punkt**, *m.* melting point. **—röhrchen**, *n.* blow-pipe. **—silber**, *n.* silver for plating. **—tiegel**, *m.* crucible. **—topf**, *m.* melting-pot. **—wärme**, *f.* heat of fusion. **—wasser**, *n.* melting *or* melted snow. **—werk**, *n.* enamel-work; smelting-house.

Schmer, *n.* (—(e)s) fat, grease, suet. *Comp.* **—bauch**, *m.* (*person with a*) fat paunch. **—büchse**, *f.* greasebox (*for oiling the wheels*).

Schmer'gel, *m. See* **Schmirgel**.

Schmerl, *m.* (—es, *pl.* —e) merlin (*Orn.*). **—e**, *f.* (*pl.* —en) merlin; loach (*Icht.*).

Schmerz, *m.* (—es, (—ens) (*acc. also* —en) *pl.* —en) pain, ache, smart; woe, grief, affliction; **geteilter — ist halber —**, grief is half removed when it is shared; shared pain is half the pain (*prov.*).

Schmer'z—en, *v.* I. *a.* to pain; to afflict, grieve; **es —t mich, das zu sagen**, it pains me to say so. II. *n.* (*aux.* **h.**) to be painful, smart, ache; **mir (mich) —t der Kopf**, my head aches. **—haft**, **—lich**, *adj. & adv.* painful; grievous; **—lich weh thun**, to pain deeply, give great pain to. *Comp.* **—beladen**, **—belastet**, *adj.* deeply afflicted. **—ens=geld**, *n.* smart-money, compensation. **—ens=kind**, *n.* child of sorrow. **—ens=lager**, *n.* bed of suffering. **—ens=reich**, *adj.* deeply afflicted. **—lindernd**, *adj.* soothing; anodyne. **—los**, *adj.* painless; sluggish (*Med.*). **—stillend**, *see* **—lindernd**. **—voll**, *adj.* painful.

Schmet'terling, *m.* (—s, *pl.* —e) butterfly. *Comp.* **—blumen**, *pl.* papilionaceous flowers. **—fang**, *m.* butterfly-catching. **—käscher**, **—kescher**, *m.*, **—s=netz**, *n.* butterfly-net. **—sammlung**, *f.* butterfly-collection.

Schmet'tern, *v.* I. *n.* (*aux.* **h.** & **f.**) to crash, fall with a crash; to peal, bray, resound (*as a trumpet*); blare (*as a trumpet*) (*poet.*); to warble (*as birds*). II. *a.* to dash, crash, smash, throw down violently.

Schmied, *m.* (—s, *pl.* —e) smith; forger; author, architect; clickbeetle, Elater (*Ent.*); **jeder ist seines Glückes —**, every man is the architect of his own fortune (*prov.*). **—bar**, *adj.* malleable. **—barkeit**, *f.* malleability. **—e**, *f.* (*pl.* —en) smithy, forge; **vor die unrechte —e gehen**, to knock at the wrong door, to get into the wrong box.

Schmie'd—en, *v.a.* to forge, hammer; to fabricate; **in Eisen —en**, to fetter, put in irons; **zwei Nägel in einer Hitze —en**, to kill two birds with one stone; **sein eigenes Unglück —en**, to be the author of one's own misfortune. *Comp.* **—e=amboß**, *m.* anvil. **—e=arbeit**, *f.* smith's work. **—e=(blas)=balg**, *m.* forge-bellows. **—e=eisen**, *n.* wrought iron. **—e=eisern**, *adj.* made of wrought iron. **—e=esse**, *f.* forge. **—e=hammer**, *m.* sledge-hammer. **—e=knecht**, *m.* journeyman-smith. **—e=kohle**, *f.* small coal, forge coal. **—e=stock**, *m.* block of the anvil. **—e=ware**, *f.* hardware. **—e=werkstätte**, *f.* forge, smithy. **—e=zange**, *f.* blacksmith's tongs.

Schmie'ge, *f.* (*pl.* —n) bent, inclination; bevel; angle; slope.

Schmie'g—en, *v.a.* to bend, incline; to bevel; **sich —en**, to bend; **sich —en an** (*acc.*), to press close, cling to; **sich —en um**, to twine round; **sich —en vor**, to crouch before, to submit to, to cringe; **sich —en und biegen**, to give in on every point. **—sam**, *adj.* pliant, flexible, lithe, supple. **—samkeit**, *f.* pliancy, flexibility.

Schmie're, *f.* grease, wheel-grease; ointment; a thrashing; pack, set, troop; greasy dirt; bribery; strolling company, provincial show, third-rate theatre; **was kostet die ganze —?** what does the whole concern cost? (*vulg.*); **— stehen**, to keep watch (*sl.*).

Schmie'r—en, *v.a.* to smear, grease, oil; to anoint; to butter; to tar; to daub; to adulterate (*wine*); to scribble, scrawl; to tip heavily, to bribe; to thrash; **wer gut —t, der gut fährt**, money makes the mare go; grease well and speed well; **einem das Maul mit Honig —en**, to delude a p. with false hopes. **—er**, *m.* (—ers, *pl.* —er) greaser; dauber; scribbler. **—erei'**, *f.* greasy work; daubing; scribbling; scrawl, daub; **mit den Öllampen ist das eine ewige —erei**, you cannot help getting greasy if you have oil-lamps. **—ig**, *adj.* greasy, dirty; dauby; unctuous; viscous. *Comp.* **—apparat**, *m.* lubricator, oil-feeder. **—buch**, *n.* waste-book. **—büchse**, *f.* grease-box; oil-can, oil-feeder. **—bürste**, *f.* oil-brush. **—fett**, *n.* grease (*for lubricating*). **—fink**, *m.* dirty fellow (*fam.*). **—käse**, *f.* soft cheese. **—leder**, *n.* leather greased with train-oil. **—mittel**, *n.* unguent; liniment. **—öl**, *n.* lubricating oil. **—seife**, *f.* soft soap. **—stiefel**, *pl.* boots greased with train-oil. **—tasche**, *f.* flatterer. **—vorrichtung**, *f.* lubricator, oil-feeder. **—wolle**, *f.* dirty, greasy wool.

Schmilz, *imperat. sing.*; **Schmilzt**, *3 pers. sing. pres. indic. of* **schmelzen** (*intrans.*).

Schmin'ke, *f.* paint, rouge; cosmetic; make-up (*theat.*).

Schmin'k—en, *v.a.* to paint; to colour, gloss over; **sich —en**, to rouge, paint. *Comp.* **—arznei**, *f.* cosmetic. **—bällchen**, *n.* pad, ball of rouge. **—büchse**, **—dose**, *f.* rouge-pot. **—fleckchen**, **—läppchen**, *n.* rag for dabbing on colour. **—mittel**, *n.* cosmetic. **—pflästerchen**, *n.* beauty-patch. **—wasser**, *n.* cosmetic, wash. **—weiß**, *n.* pearl-white.

Schmirgel, *m.* (—s) emery. **—n**, *v.a.* to rub, polish, grind with emery.

[1]**Schmiß**, *m.* (—(ss)es, *pl.* —(ss)e) blow; cut, lash; wound from a lash.

[2]**Schmiß**, **Schmis'se**, *1 & 3 pers. sing. imperf. ind. & subj. of* **schmeißen**.

Schmitz, *m.* (—es, *pl.* —e) blow, cut; spot, blot. **—e**, *f.* whip-lash.

Schmit'zen, *v.* I. *a.* (*aux.* **h.**) to lash, whip; to blacken. II. *a. & n.* (*aux.* **h.**) to soil, stain; to blur (*Typ.*).

Schmö'ker, *m.* (—s, *pl.* —) old, well-worn book; story of knights and robbers. **—n**, *v.n.* (*aux.* **h.**) to read old books; **herum —n**, to ferret about.

Schmol'l—en, *v.n.* (*aux.* **h.**) to pout, be sulky; to smile complacently (*dial.*). *Comp.* **—lippe**, *f.* pouting lip. **—winkel**, *m.* sulking corner, retired spot; boudoir.

Schmol'lis, *n.*; **mit einem — trinken**, (**mit einem schmollie'ren**), to fraternize with a p. over a glass of beer *or* wine, to hob-nob with a p.; **ein — den Sängern!** to the very good health of the singers! (*stud. sl.*).

Schmolz, Schmöl'ze, *1 & 3 pers. imperf. ind. & subj. of* **schmelzen** (*intrans.*).

Schmo'r—en, *v.* I. *n.* (*aux.* **h.**) to roast, cook slowly; to be suffocated *or* parched with heat. II. *a.* to stew; to bake (*meat*). *Comp.* **—braten,** *m.* stewed meat; beef à la mode. **—pfanne,** *f.*, **—tiegel, —topf,** *m.* stew-pan; sauce-pan.

Schmu, Schmuh, *m.* unfair *or* illicit profit (*coll.*); **einen — machen,** to overcharge a person; to pocket marketings (*coll.*).

Schmuck, I. *m.* (—(e)s) ornament; decoration; jewels, ornaments; set of ornaments; finery; dress, attire; embellishment. II. *adj.* spruce, neat, smart, pretty, nice. **—heit,** *f.* smartness, elegance. *Comp.* **—arbeit,** *f.* ornamental work; jewelry. **—gerät,** *n.* ornaments. **—händler,** *m.* jeweller. **—kästchen,** *n.* jewel-box; **Ihr Haus ist ein wahres —kästchen,** you have got a jewel *or* a love of a house. **—laden,** *m.* jeweller's shop. **—los,** *adj.* simple, unadorned. **—losigkeit,** *f.* plainness, simplicity. **—nadel,** *f.* shirt pin; breast-pin, brooch. **—sachen,** *pl.* jewels, ornaments. **—voll,** *adj.* highly adorned. **—ware,** *f.* finery; trinkets. **—waren=händler,** *m.* jeweller.

¹Schmü'ck—en, *v.a.* to attire, dress; to decorate; to trim; to set off; to gloss over; to embellish, adorn; **die Tugend —t die Seele,** virtue adorns the mind; **sich —en,** to deck o. s. out. **—ung,** *f.* adorning, decoration, embellishment.

²Schmü'cken, *v.r.* to bend, to crouch (*obs.*).

Schmuddelei', *f.* uncleanliness (*coll.*).

Schmud'delig, *adj.* dirty, unclean (*coll.*).

Schmug'g—el, *m.* (—els, *pl.* —el), **—elei',** *f.* smuggling. **—eln,** *v.a. & n.* (*aux.* **h.**) to smuggle. **—ler,** *m.* (—lers, *pl.* —ler) smuggler.

Schmun'zeln, *v.n.* (*aux.* **h.**) to smirk; to look pleased.

¹Schmu'sen, *v.n.* (*aux.* **h.**) to talk *or* bargain with a p. (*coll.*).

²Schmu's—en, Schmu'ster—n, *v.n.* to gossip, chatter; to talk nonsense; **im Dustern ist gut —n,** the twilight hour is the best time for a chat (*prov.*). **—er,** *m.* talkative fellow, chatterbox.

Schmutz, *m.* (—es) filthiness; dirt, filth, smut, mud. **—en,** *v.n.* (*aux.* **h.**) to soil, get dirty (*easily*). **—erei',** *f.* dirty actions; low way of living; filthiness; obscenity. **—ig,** *adj.* dirty; muddy; soiled; base, sordid; obscene; niggardly; **—iger Abdruck,** smudged, uneven proof (*Typ.*); **—iger Eigennutz,** sordid *or* gross selfishness; **—ige Geschichte,** obscene story; **—iger Wucher,** filthy lucre; **—ige Wäsche,** soiled linen. **—igkeit,** *f.* filthiness, dirtiness, *etc.*; fouling (*of firearms*). *Comp.* **—ärmel,** *pl.* protecting sleeve (*to be worn over a coat during work*). **—blech,** *n.* mud-guard (*Cycl.*). **—bogen,** *m.* slur, waste sheet (*Typ.*). **—bürste,** *f.* scrubbing-brush. **—farbe,** *f.* mud colour; dark colour. **—fink(e),** *m.* dirty fellow (*vulg.*). **—fleck,** *m.* dirty spot, stain. **—kittel,** *m.* blouse *or* apron to protect from dirt. **—lappen,** *m.* clout; *see* **—fink(e).** **—loch,** *n.* mud-hole, man-hole; filthy hole. **—papier,** *n.* waste paper. **—titel,** *m.* paper cover title, outer title-page.

Schna'bel, *m.* (—s, *pl.* **Schnäbel**) bill, beak; nib; mouth (*vulg.*); snout (*Ent.*); nozzle; rostrum; (gas-)burner; cutwater (*of a ship*); socket (*of a lamp*); mouth-piece (*Mus.*); **das ist nichts für seinen —,** that is not to his taste, that is nothing for him, meat for his master; **seinen — an allem wetzen,** to poke one's nose into everything; **er spricht wie ihm der — gewachsen ist,** he speaks plainly, naturally, according to his lights. **—ie'ren,** (*also* **Schnabulie'ren,**) *see* **Schmausen.** *Comp.* **—eisen,** *n.* curling-tongs. **—förmig,** *adj.* beak-shaped; rostrate. **—schiff,** *n.* ship with beak-like prow. **—schuhe,** *pl.* pointed shoes. **—tier,** *n.* duck-bill. **—weide,** *f.* tit-bit, dainty, delicacy.

Schnäb—elei', *f.* billing and cooing **—eln,** *v.n.* (*aux.* **h.**) & *r.* to bill and coo; to caress. **—ler,** *m.* (—lers, *pl.* —ler) billed bird; **Dick—ler,** broad-billed bird.

Schnabulie'ren, *v.n.* to eat comfortably (*coll.*).

Schnack, *m.* (—es), chat (*coll. & dial.*); **ach —!** stuff and nonsense! fiddlesticks! **das ist ein ganz anderer —,** that is quite another thing. **—en,** *v.a. & n.* (*aux.* **h.**) (*dial. & coll.*) to chat; to chatter, gossip. **—ig,** *adj.* funny.

Schna'd—a=hüpfl, —er=hüpfel, —er=hüpferl, *n.* merry extempore popular ditty (*usually alternate*) of four short lines, the 2d and 4th lines rhyming, sung in the Bavarian and Austrian mountain-districts; challenge song *or* ditty.

Schnak, *m.* (—en, *pl.* —en), **—e,** *f.* (*pl.* —en) jest, merry tale, joke, piece of nonsense, fun **—isch,** *adj.* funny, amusing, comical.

Schna'ke, *f.* (*pl.* —n) gnat, midge; crane-fly.

Schnal'le, *f.* (*pl.* —n) buckle; latch, catch (*of a door*); fillip; hoax.

Schnal'len, *v.a.* to buckle; to strap; to fillip; **die Bügel länger —,** to lengthen the stirrup-leathers. *Comp.* **—dorn,** *m.* tongue, teeth of a buckle. **—schuh,** *m.* shoe with buckles.

Schnal'zen, *v.n.* (*aux.* **h.**) to crack, click, smack (*with the tongue*); to snap (*with the fingers*).

Schnapp, I. *int.* crack! snap! before you can say 'Jack Robinson'! II. *m.* (—s, *pl.* —e) snap; fillip; mouthful.

Schnap'p—en, *v.n.* (*aux.* **h.** & **s.**) to snap; to close with a snap; to snatch; to catch; to spring *or* fly up; **nach einer S. —en,** to snatch at, to seek eagerly, hanker after; **nach Luft —en,** to gasp for breath; **jetzt hat's aber geschnappt,** but now there is an end of it, I will not stand it any longer (*coll.*). **—s,** *see* **Schnaps.** *Comp.* **—feder,** *f.* catch-spring. **—hahn,** *m.* (mounted) highwayman. **—karren,** *m.* tumbrel. **—messer,** *n.* clasp-knife. **—sack,** *m.* knapsack. **—schloß,** *n.* snap; spring-lock. **—schuß,** *m.* snap-shot.

Schnäp'per, *m.* (—s, *pl.* —) snap, catch; trigger; cross-bow; cupping instrument; fly-catcher (*Orn.*).

Schnaps, *m.* (—(s)es, *pl.* **Schnäp'se**) dram; brandy, gin. *Comp.* **—bruder,** *m.* toper. **—bude,** *f.* gin-shop, public house. **—glas,** *n.* glass of brandy, dram-glass. **—kneipe,** *f.* gin-shop, tippling-house. **—nase,** *f.* (*person with a*) copper nose. **—säufer, —trinker,** *m.* dram-drinker, tippler, drunkard.

Schnap'sen, *v.n.* to take a drop, to tipple.

Schnar'ch—en, *v.n.* (*aux.* **h.**) to snore. **—er,** *m.* (—ers, *pl.* —er) snorer. *Comp.* **—ratze,** *f.* snorer. **—ventil,** *n.* snifting valve, throttle-valve.

Schnar're, *f.* (*pl.* —n) rattle; *see* **Wachtelkönig.**

Schnar'r—en, *v.n.* (*aux.* **h.**) to rattle, to spring a rattle; to (*speak with a*) burr; to whirr, hum; to utter a harsh, jarring sound; to growl, grumble; to scold; **‚Herr!' —te der Leutnant,** 'Sir!' the lieutenant said with a strong twang; **das —en des r,** the burr of the r. *Comp.* **—baß,** *m.* drone (*of the hurdy-gurdy, organs, etc.*). **—drossel,** *f.* missel-thrush. **—laut, —ton,** *m.* rattling *or* jarring sound. **—pfeife,** *f.* drone-pipe; reed-stop (*in organs*). **—ventil,** *see* **Schnarchventil.** **—werk,** *n.* reed-stops (*of an organ*).

Schnatterei', *f.* gabbling.

Schnat'ter—er, *m.* (—ers, *pl.* —er) chatterer, babbler. **—haft,** *adj.* babbling, chattering.

Schnat'tern, *v.n.* (*aux.* **h.**) to chatter, gabble; to quack; to cackle (*of geese*). *Comp.* **—maul,** *n.*, **—tasche,** *f.* chatterbox.

Schnau'ben, *reg. & ir.v.a. & n.* (*aux.* **h.** & **s.**)

to pant, puff, blow; to breathe heavily; to snort; **vor Zorn —**, to pant with rage; **nach Rache —**, to pant for revenge; **er schnaubte Rache**, he was breathing vengeance; **er schnaubte sich**, he blew his nose; **die Rosse schnoben**, the steeds snorted; **Roß und Reiter schnoben**, horse and rider were gasping for breath; **der Föhn schnob**, the south wind was blowing a gale.

Schnau'fen, *a little stronger than* **schnauben**; to breathe (*dial.*).

Schnau'z—e, *f.* (*pl.* **—en**) snout, muzzle; mouth; spout, lip; nozzle; gargoyle; **die —e halten**, to hold one's tongue (*vulg.*). **—en**, *v.n.* (*aux.* **h.**) to snap (*up*), to speak brusquely *or* rudely. *Comp.* **—bart**, *m.* moustache. **—bärtig**, *adj.* moustached; rude; coarse; **—bärtiges Wesen**, rude *or* gruff behaviour. **—kanne**, *f.*, **—krug**, *m.* can, pitcher with a spout.

Schnäuz'chen, *n.* (**—s**, *pl.* **—**) *dim. of* **Schnauze**.

Schnäu'zen, Schneuzen, *v.* I. *a.* to blow (*the nose*); to snuff (*a candle*). II. *r.* to blow one's nose; **da schnäuzt sich ein Stern**, there is a shooting star (*vulg.*).

Schne'cke, *f.* (*pl.* **—n**) snail, slug; cochlea (*of the ear*); volute (*Arch.*); fusee (*Horol.*); winding staircase; Archimedes' screw; worm of an endless screw. **—n=haft**, *adj.* snail-like; as slow as a snail; spiral. *Comp.* **—n=achse**, *f.* axis of a volute. **—n=auge**, *n.* centre of a volute (*Arch.*); centre of a helix (*Geom.*). **—n=bohrer**, *m.* screw-auger. **—n=feder**, *f.* main-spring (*of a watch*); spiral spring. **—n=fraß**, *m.* damage done by slugs. **—n=gang**, *m.* snail's pace; winding alley. **—n=garten**, *m.* snail-park, snailery. **—n=getriebe**, *n.* worm and wheel, screw and wheel. **—n=gewinde**, *n.* whorl. **—n=haus**, *n.* snail-shell. **—n=horn**, *n.* feeler, horn (*of a snail*). **—n=lehre**, *f.* conchology. **—n=linie**, *f.* spiral line. **—n=muschel**, *f.* conch-shell. **—n=post**, *f.* snail's pace, slow coach. **—n=rad**, *n.* balance-wheel (*Horol.*); tympanum, turbine-wheel. **—n=treppe**, *f.* spiral staircase, winding *or* cork-screw staircase. **—n=werk**, *n.* shell-work. **—n=zug**, *m.* slow procession; spiral line (*Arch.*); scroll (*of mouldings, etc.*).

Schnee, *m.* (**—s**) snow. **—ig**, *adj.* snowy; snow-covered. *Comp.* **—bahn**, *see* **Schlittenbahn**. **—ball**, *m.* snow-ball; guelder-rose. **—ballen**, *v.a. & r.* (*aux.* **h.**) (*insep.*) to snow-ball. **—bedeckt**, *adj.* covered with snow; snow-capped (*of mountains*). **—berg**, *m.* mountain of snow; snow-capped mountain. **—blume**, *f.* snowdrop. **—eule**, *f.* large white owl. **—flocke**, *f.* snowflake; snow-drop. **—gans**, *f.* Anas hyperborea; little goose (*fam.*). **—gestöber**, *n.* snow-storm. **—glöckchen**, *n.* snowdrop. **—grenze**, *f.* snow-line. **—hase**, *f.* Alpine hare. **—huhn**, *n.* white grouse. **—könig**, *m.* snow-man; **sich freuen wie ein —könig**, to be as merry as a cricket. **—koppe, —kuppe**, *f.* snowy mountain-summit. **—lawine**, *f.* avalanche. **—luft**, *f.* snowy air. **—menge**, *f.* snow-fall. **—milch**, *f.* whipped cream. **—pflug**, *m.* snow-plough (*also on locomotives*). **—regen**, *m.* sleet. **—schuh**, *m.* snow-shoe; **—schuh laufen**, to run on snow-shoes, to go ski-ing. **—treiben**, *n.* heavy snow-fall, blizzard. **—trift**, *f.* snow-drift. **—wehe**, *f.* snow-drift. **—wetter**, *n.* snowy weather; snow-storm. **—zeit**, *f.* snowy season.

Schnei'd—e, *f.* (*pl.* **—n**) edge (*of a knife, etc.*); cut; energy, dash. **—ig**, *adj. & adv.* cutting; energetic, spirited. **—igkeit**, *f.* energy, smartness, spirit; **—iger Offizier**, dashing officer.

Schnei'd—en, *ir.v.a. & n.* (*aux.* **h.**) to cut; to carve; to engrave; to intersect; **eine Feder —en**, to make a pen; **Fleisch —en**, to carve meat; **ins lebendige Fleisch —en**, to cut to the quick; **in Holz —en**, to cut, carve wood; **einem den Stein —en**, to perform an operation for stone (*Surg.*); **sich** (*dat.*) **die Nägel —en**, to cut one's nails; **sich** (*dat.*) **Pfeifen —en**, to feather one's nest; **Geld bei etwas —en**, to make money by a transaction; **das —et mir ins** (**durchs**) **Herz**, that cuts me to the heart; **es —et mir im Leibe**, I have the colic, the gripes (*coll.*); **mit der Dame —en**, to finesse the queen (*Whist*); **ein Gesicht —en**, to make a (wry) face; **Fratzen** *or* **Gesichter —en**, to make faces; **Kapriolen —en**, to cut capers; **einem Mädchen die Cour —en**, to pay court to a girl; **einer Dame Komplimente —en**, to pay compliments to a lady. II. *a.* to cut up, to chop; to castrate; **sich —en**, to blunder, to make a mistake, to be mistaken, to be disappointed; **der Krämer hat Sie geschnitten**, the shopkeeper has overcharged you (*coll.*); **ich fürchte Sie werden sich —en**, I fear you will be disappointed (*coll.*); **Brot in die Suppe —en**, to cut up bread into soup; **sich in den Finger —en**, to cut one's finger; **griechisch geschnittene Nase**, Greek profile; **er ist ihm wie aus den Augen geschnitten**, he is his very image. **—end**, *p. & adj.* cutting, sharp; piercing; penetrating; inharmonious; striking; violent; bitter, sarcastic; glaring, gaudy; keen, forcible; transversal; **—ende Gewaltthätigkeiten**, outrages. **—er**, *m.* (**—ers**, *pl.* **—er**) tailor; cutter; poltroon; Phalangium (*Ent.*); **—er, der ein Lager von Kleiderstoffen hält**, merchant tailor; **aus dem —er heraus sein**, to gain more than half the points (*Bill.*, *Cards*); **sie ist aus dem —er**, she is over thirty years old (*coll.*); **aus dem höheren —er sein**, to be considerably over thirty, to be no chicken (*coll.*); **wir froren wie die —er**, we were awfully cold (*coll.*). **—erei'**, *f.* tailoring; **wir haben heute —erei**, we have a dressmaker (*tailor*) in the house to-day. **—erin**, *f.* dressmaker, female tailor; tailor's wife. **—ern**, *v.n.* (*aux.* **h.**) to do *or* practise tailoring *or* dressmaking. *Comp.* **—e=bank**, *f.* cooper's (*chopping*) bench. **—e=bock**, *m.* chopping-block. **—e=bohnen**, *pl.* French beans. **—e=brett**, *n.* cutting-board. **—e=eisen**, *n.* chopping-knife, edge-tool; slit-iron. **—e=klotz**, *m.* plank, rafter. **—e=leder**, *n.* sole-leather. **—e=maschine**, *f.* cutting-machine; flax-breaking machine. **—e=mühle**, *f.* saw-mill. **—er=beine**, *pl.* crooked legs, bow-legs. **—er=meister**, *m.* master-tailor. **—er=muskel**, *m.* tailor's muscle. **—er=rechnung**, *f.* tailor's bill. **—er=ring**, *m.* tailor's thimble. **—er=seele**, *f.* cowardly soul. **—e=tisch**, *m.* chopping-board. **—e=walzen**, *pl.* cylindrical slitting-machine. **—e=zahn**, *m.* incisor. **—e=zeug**, *n.* cutting engine; cutting-edge-tools. **—werk**, *n.* slitting-mill.

Schnei'en, *v.n.* (*aux.* **h.** & **s.**) to snow; **es hat viel geschneit**, we have had much snow; **es hat ihm in die Hütte geschneit**, he has had a stroke of bad luck; **er ist uns ins Haus geschneit**, he dropped upon us as if from the clouds, he came to us quite unexpectedly.

Schnei'se, Schnei'ße, *f.* (*pl.* **—n**) glade (*in a forest*).

Schnei'teln, *v.a.* to lop, prune, trim.

Schnell, *adj. & adv.* rapid; swift, quick; prompt; sudden; hasty; brisk; presto (*Mus.*); **—!** be quick! **nicht so —!** gently! easy! **—er Umsatz**, quick returns; **—er Strom**, rapid stream.

Schnel'l—en, *v.* I. *n.* (*aux.* **s.**) to spring, snap, fly back with a jerk; **in die Höhe —en**, to tip up. II. *a.* to give a sudden impulse to; to let fly; to toss, jerk, dart; to snap one's fingers; to bamboozle, cheat; **das hat mich**

geschnellt, that has vexed me (*dial., coll.*). — **er,** *m.* (—**ers**, *pl.* —**er**) one who throws, darts, *etc.*; spring; hair-trigger; marble, taw; elater (*Bot., Ent.*); jerk, fillip; *see* —**galgen**; driver (*Weav.*). —**igkeit,** —**heit,** *f.* velocity; swiftness, speed; despatch; rapidity; quickness (*of a pulse*). *Comp.* —**balken,** *m.* chain and lever; swipe, plyer (*of a drawbridge*). — **bank,** *f.* catapult. —**bleiche,** *f.* chemical bleaching. —**brett,** *n.* spring-board. —**dampfer,** *m.* fast steamer. —**feder,** *f.* spring. —**feuer,** *n.* rapid fire, running *or* dropping fire, independent firing. —**feuer=kanone,** *f.*, —**feurer,** *m.* quick-firing gun, machine gun. —**feuer=zeug,** *n.* lucifer matches. —**füßig,** *adj.* nimble, agile. —**galgen,** *m.* T-shaped gibbet. —**ig=keit,** *f.* velocity, rapidity. —**käulchen,** — **kügelchen,** *n.* marble, taw. —**kraft,** *f.* elasticity, spring. —**kräftig,** *adj.* elastic. —**lader,** *m.* quick-loading gun *or* cannon. —**lauf,** *m.* (*foot*) race; gallop; **im —lauf,** at the double (quick) (*Mil.*). —**läufer,** *m.* racer. —**post,** *f.* mail(*-coach*); express. —**photographie,** *f.* instantaneous photography; instantaneous photograph, snap shot. —**post,** *f.* quick mail, express. —**presse,** *f.* fly-press; steam-press; mechanical press; rapid printing. —**schreibe=kunst,** *f.* art of rapid writing, shorthand, stenography. —**schreibe=maschine,** *f.* type-writing machine, type-writer. —**schreiber,** *m.* shorthand writer. —**schrift,** *f.* short-hand writing; stenography; tachygraphy. —**schritt,** *m.* quick march (*Mil.*). —**segler,** *m.* fast sailer *or* goer. —**sein,** *n.* promptitude. — **wage,** *f.* steel-yard. —**zug,** *m.* forced march; fast train, express. —**zünder,** *m.* quick-match (*Artil.*). —**züngig,** *adj.* voluble, fluent.

Schnep'fe, *f.* (*pl.* —**n**) snipe; woodcock; simpleton; disreputable woman, prostitute. *Comp.* —**n=dreck,** *m.* snipe-excrements; roast giblets (of a snipe *or* woodcock). —**n=fang,** *m.*, —**n=jagd,** *f.* snipe-shooting. —**n=strich,** **n=zug,** *m.* flock of snipes.

Schnep'pe, *f.* (*pl.* —**n**) nozzle, spout, lip; top, peak (*of a cap*); clasp (*of a girdle*).

Schneu'se, *see* **Schneise.**

Schneu'zen, *see* **Schnäuzen.**

Schnick'schnack, *m.* (—**es**) verbiage, stuff, fiddle-faddle.

Schnie'geln, *v.r.* to dress up, deck oneself out.

Schnie'pel, *m.* (—**s**, *pl.* —) dress-coat (*coll.*).

Schnipp, *int.* snap! —**chen,** *n.* (—**chens**, *pl.* —**chen**) snap (*with the fingers*); **einem ein —chen schlagen,** to snap one's fingers at a person, to make fun of a p. —**el,** *m.* (—**els**, *pl.* —**el**), —**sel,** *m.* (—**sels**, *pl.* —**sel**) snip, shred, morsel. —**eln,** —**seln,** *v.a.* to cut, chop up. —**en,** *v.* I. *a.* & *n.* (*aux.* **h.**) to snap; to move suddenly, jerk. II. *a.* to snip, cut up. —**isch,** *adj.* snappish, short, pert.

[1]**Schnitt,** *m.* (—**es**, *pl.* —**e**) cut; cutting, incision; operation; cut, form; reaping; section; slice (*of bread, meat, etc.*); pattern, model; edge (*of a book*); cut, engraving; half a measure, a half-glass; a small glass (*of beer*); small profit, perquisite; **seinen — bei etwas machen,** to make a profit out of a th. —**chen,** *n.* (—**chens**, *pl.* —**chen**) small slice; fritter; small profit. —**e,** *f.* (*pl.* —**en**) cut, slice (*of bread, etc.*); chop, steak. —**er,** *m.* (—**ers**, *pl.* —**er**) reaper, mower. —**ling,** *m.* (—**lings**, *pl.* —**linge**) cutting (*Bot.*); *see* **Schnitzel.** *Comp.* —**blumen,** *pl.* cut flowers. —**bohne,** *f.* French bean, Dutch kidney-bean. —**farbe,** *f.* colour for book edges. —**handel,** *m.* drapery-trade. —**lauch,** *m.* chive (*Bot.*). —**linie,** *f.* secant; intersecting line. —**messer,** *n.* pruning-knife; bistoury (*Surg.*). —**muster,** *n.* pattern (*to cut from*). —**ware,** *f.* drapery, dry goods. —**weise,** *adv.* by slices, by cuts. —**wunde,** *f.* cut (*wound*).

[2]**Schnitt, Schnit'te,** *1 & 3 pers. sing. imperf. ind. & subj. of* **schneiden.**

Schnitz, *m.* (—**es**, *pl.* —**e**) slice, cut; snip; chippings; chop, steak. —**el,** *n.* (—**els**, *pl.* —**el**) chip, shred, paring; collop, cutlet; (*pl.*) parings, shavings. —**elei',** *f.* cutting, *etc.*; carving. —**eln,** *v.a.* & *n.* (*aux.* **h.**) to carve, whittle, chip, cut finely. —**en,** *v.a.* & *n.* (*aux.* **h.**) to carve, cut. —**er,** *m.* (—**ers**, *pl.* —**er**) carver, cutter; carving-knife; graver, point; blunder, mistake. —**erei',** *f.* wood-carving; piece of carved wood. —**ern,** *v.n.* (*aux.* **h.**) to blunder. *Comp.* —**arbeit,** *f.* wood-carving; carved work. —**el=jagd,** *f.* paper-chase. — **kunst,** *f.* wood-carving. —**werk,** *n.* wood-carving, carved work.

Schnob, Schnö'be, *1 & 3 pers. sing. imperf. ind. & subj. of* **schnauben** (*obs.* **schnieben**).

Schno'b(b)ern, Schno'p(p)ern, *v.n.* (*aux.* **h.**) to snuff, sniff about.

Schnod'derig, *adj.* pert, insolent (*coll.*). —**keit,** *f.* pertness, insolence.

Schnö'd—e, *adj.* base, mean; vile, worthless; despicable; iniquitous; insolent, disdainful; —**er Gewinn,** vile profit; —**er Undank,** base ingratitude. —**igkeit,** *f.* baseness, vileness; worthlessness; disdain, insolence.

Schnör'kel, *m.* (—**s**, *pl.* —) spiral *or* twisted ornament; flourish (*in writing*); scroll, volute (*Arch.*). —**ei',** *f.* flourishes, superfluous ornaments. —**n,** *v.n.* (*aux.* **h.**) to flourish, make flourishes; to adorn with spiral ornaments, scrolls, *etc.*

Schnor're—n, *v.n.* (*aux.* **h.**) to beg (*vulg.*). —**r,** *m.* beggar, tramp (*coll.*).

Schnö'sel, *m.* (—**s**, *pl.* —) stuck-up prig (*sl.*).

Schnu'ck—e, *f.* (*pl.* —**en**) kind of small sheep. —**elchen,** —**chen,** *n.* darling, pet (*coll.*).

Schnüf'f—eln, Schnuf'f—eln, *v.n.* (*aux.* **h.**) to snuff, smell, sniff; to snuff about; to speak through the nose; to act the spy. —**ler,** *m.* (—**lers**, *pl.* —**ler**) snuffer; person speaking through his nose; inquisitive person; spy.

Schnup'f—en, I. *m.* (—**ens**, *pl.* —**en**) cold in the head; catarrh; **den —en bekommen, sich** (*dat.*) **einen —en holen,** to catch cold (*coll.*). II. *v.a.* & *n.* (*aux.* **h.**) to snuff, take snuff. III. *subst. n.*; **sich** (*dat.*) **das —en angewöhnen,** to get into the habit of taking snuff. —**er,** *m.* (—**ers**, *pl.* —**er**) snuff-taker. —**ig,** *adj.* having a cold; catarrhal. *Comp.* —**en=fieber,** *n.* feverish cold; influenza. —**tabak,** *m.* snuff. —**tabaksdose,** *f.* snuff-box. —**tuch,** *n.* pocket-handkerchief.

Schnup'pe, I. *f.* (*pl.* —**n**) snuff (*of a candle*); **Stern—,** shooting-star. II. *adj.*; **das ist mir (ganz) —!** that 's all the same to me, much I care! (*coll.*). —**rn,** *v.n.* (*aux.* **h.**) to snuff about; to sniff. *See* **Schnobern.**

[1]**Schnur,** *f.* (*pl.* **Schnü're,** *more recent and less good* —**en**) string, cord; lace; line; string (*of beads, etc.*); **nach der —,** by the line, straight as a line, regular; **nach der — leben,** to be strictly methodical; **mit Schnüren besetzen,** to lace, braid, trim; **am Schnürchen haben,** to have at one's fingers' ends; **einen am Schnürchen haben,** to have a p. under one's thumb; **wie am Schnürchen gehen,** to go like clock-work; **über die — hauen,** to overstep the line, to kick over the traces, run into excesses; **von der — leben,** to live on one's income *or* savings; **die Schnüre tragen,** to wear the cord-trimming on the epaulettes, to be a volunteer (**Einjährig Freiwilliger**) in the German army. *Comp.* —**annäher,** *m.* guide for sewing braid on dresses (*on sewing-machines*). —**besatz,** *m.* braid-trimming. —**feuer,** *n.* running fire (*Pyr.*). —**g(e)rade**

—gerecht, *adj. & adv.* straight as a line. —maschine, *f.* braiding machine. —stracks, *adv.* directly; at once; —stracks zuwider, diametrically opposed.

[2]Schnur, *f.* (*pl., rare,* Schnü're) daughter-in-law (*obs. & poet.*).

Schnü'r—en, *v.a.* to lace; to cord, strap (*a box, etc.*); to tie; to string; to tie up, to tie with a string; das —t mir das Herz zusammen, that wrings my heart; sein Bündel —en, to pack up; sich —en, to wear stays. —chen, *n.* (—chens, *pl.* —chen) *see* Schnur. *Comp.* —band, *n.* stay-lace; lace; string with a tag. —boden, *m.* rigging loft of a stage for scenical machinery. —brust, *f.* laced-bodice; stays. —haken, *m.* hook. —holz, *n.* bobbin. —kasten, *m.* clasp. —latz, *m.* stomacher. —leibchen, *n.* laced-bodice. —leib=macher, *m.* corset-maker. —loch, *n.* eyelet-hole. —nadel, *f.* bodkin; tag. —riemen, *m.* lace; strap. —rock, *m.* jerkin. —senkel, *m.* boot-lace. —stiefel, *m.* laced-boot. —stift, *m.* tag. —stock, *m.* upper roller (*Weav.*).

Schnurr'diburr, *adv.interj.* fluently, glibly.

Schnur'r—e, I. *f.* (*pl.* —en) anything humming; rattle; humming-top; policeman's *or* watchman's rattle (*obs.*); spinning wheel; joke, quip; piece of nonsense; funny tale; old hag; old lumber; snout. II. *m.* (—en, *pl.* —en) watchman; policeman (*obs.*). —a'nt, *m.* street musician. —en, *v.n.* (*aux.* h. & s.) to hum, buzz; to whirr; to purr; to go about begging; to shrivel; Katzen —en, cats purr. —er, *m.* tramp. —ig, *adj.* droll, funny, facetious; queer, odd. *Comp.* —bart, *m.* moustache. —bärtig, *adj.* moustached, wearing a moustache. —katze, *f.* humming cat (*a children's toy*). —pfeifer, *m.* travelling rag-man; wag. —pfeiferei', *f.* knick-knack, trifle, trash; twaddle, nonsense, fun.

Schnut—e, *f.* mouth (*dial. coll.*). —chen, *n.* little girl (*coll.*).

Schob, Schö'be, *1 & 3 pers. sing. imperf. ind. & subj. of* schieben.

Scho'ber, *m.* (—s, *pl.* —) stack, rick; cock; pile (*of books or of wood*); measure = 60 bundles *or* bottles (*of straw, etc.*). —n, *v.a.* to stack (*hay*). *Comp.* —hof, *m.* stack-yard.

Schock, *n.* (—es, *pl.* —e, —) heap, shock; threescore; a (*large*) quantity; zwei —, six score. *Comp.* —anschlag, *m.* valuation, assessment. —holz, *n.* faggot-wood, brushwood in bundles. —schwerenot, *int.* confound it! hang it (all)! —weise, *adv.* by three-scores; in bundles.

Scho'cken, *v.* I. *a.* to count by sixties; to place in heaps of sixties. II. *n.* (*aux.* h.) to yield in abundance.

Scho'fel (*vulg.*), I. *m. & n.* (—s, *pl.* —) trash, refuse, rubbish. II. —ig, *adj.* paltry, worthless, mean; shabby.

Schöf'fe, *m.* (—n, *pl.* —n) alderman, a kind of magistrate *or* juror who assists the judge; juryman (*of the 'Vehmgericht'*). *Comp.* —n=amt, *n.* juryman's office. —n=gericht, *n.* sheriff's court, court of jurors, judge and jury; local tribunal consisting of a petty judge and two jurymen (*for cases of slight misdemeanour*). —n=stuhl, *m. See* —n=gericht.

Schol—a'r, *m.* (*pl.* —aren) scholar, disciple, pupil. —a'rch, *m.* (—ar'chen, *pl.* —ar'chen) school-inspector; headmaster of a school. —a'st, *m.* (—as'ten, *pl.* —as'ten) scholar, student (*obs.*). —as'tik, *f.* scholastic divinity (*of the Middle Ages*). —as'tiker, *m.* school-divine, scholastic. —as'tisch, *adj.* scholastic. —ia'st, scholiast, annotator.

Scho'li—e, *f.* (*pl.* Scho'lien), —on, *n.* (—ons, *pl.* Scho'lia), scholium (*pl.* scholia), comment, annotation.

Schol'ken, *v.n.* (*aux.* h.) to splash, run high (*of waves*).

Scholl, Schöl'le, *imperf. sing. ind. & subj. of* schallen.

[1]Schol'l—e, *f.* (*pl.* —en) clod; sod; flake, lump (*of ice*). —ern, *v.n.* (*aux.* h. & s.) to roll *or* fall with a thud (*e.g.* earth on a coffin). —ig, *adj.* cloddy.

[2]Schol'le, *f.* (*pl.* —n) sole; plaice.

Schöl'te, *1 & 3 pers. sing. imperf. subj. of* schelten.

Schon, *adv. & part.* already, yet; besides; only, alone; certainly, indeed, no doubt; after all; wenn —, ob —, though, although; wenn —, denn —, as well done as ill done, what is worth doing at all is worth doing well; sind Sie — in London gewesen? have you been in London yet? have you ever been in London? — lange, long ago; ist es — Zeit zum Aufbruch? is it already time to start? es gibt des Elendes so — genug, there is enough misery in the world as it is; — den folgenden Morgen, the very next morning; was ist es — wieder? what is it again? wenn er doch nur — käme! if he would only come! er wird — kommen, he will be sure to come! es wird — gehen, no doubt it will turn out all right; — der Gedanke, the very thought; er wird — wissen, no doubt he will know; — gut! all right! very well; das ist — wahr, aber, that is quite true, but; that is all very well, only; er wird sein Unrecht — einsehen, he will surely see his error; Sie werden mich — verstehen, I am sure you know what I mean; ich will es — machen, never fear, I will manage it; er mußte — bekennen, he could not help confessing; ich helfe mir — selbst, I trust I shall be able to help myself; wenn *or* ob es — wahr ist, although it be true; muß ich es — thun, though I must do it; wollte ich — nachgeben, so kann ich es doch nicht, even if I wished to give in, yet I cannot do it; das wäre ihm — recht, aber, no doubt that would just suit him, but; — wegen, — weil, just because.

Schön, *adj. & adv.* beautiful, handsome; fine, fair, lovely (*of weather*); lofty, noble; pretty, fine (*ironically*); —e Seele, fair *or* beautiful soul; danke —! —en Dank! many thanks, best thanks; das ist — von Ihnen, that is very kind of you *or* you have done well; die —e Welt, the fashionable world; die —en Künste, the fine arts; die —en Wissenschaften, belles lettres; halte dich — warm, keep yourself nice and warm; grüßen Sie ihn —stens von mir, give him my kindest regards; das —e Geschlecht, the fair sex; — machen, to make fine, to clean up, to embellish; — thun, to mince, to be prim, affect great nicety; mit einem Mädchen — thun, to caress, cajole, to play the lover to a girl; das ist was —es! that's a pretty business! Sie werden was —es von mir denken! you will have a nice opinion of me! das wäre — gewesen! now, that would have been nice! a pretty thing indeed! da haben Sie etwas —es angerichtet, you have made a fine hash of it! das sind (mir) —e Sachen! pretty doings indeed! da sind wir — daran! well, we are in a nice fix! das klingt —, that sounds very nice; das werde ich — bleiben lassen, I shall take good care not to do that; Sie haben — lachen, it's all very well for you to laugh, (*but*); thun Sie das. —, do that. Yes, sir, certainly; er wird sich — erschrecken, he will get a nice fright; das wäre ja noch —er! that's getting better and better! certainly not! manch —es Mal, many a time. —e, I. *n.* the beautiful; das —e an diesem Stücke, what is beautiful in *or* the beauty of this piece. II. *f.* (*pl.* —en) beauty, splendour (*obs. poet.*)

beautiful woman, beauty. —**heit**, *f.* beauty, beautifulness; beauty, belle; (*pl.*) compliments. *Comp.* —**bartspiel**, *see* **Schönbartspiel**. —**busig**, *adj.*; —**busiges Weib**, fair-bosomed woman. —**dank**, *int.* many thanks! much obliged! —**druck**, *m.* prime (*Typ.*). —**fahrt=segel**, *n.* mainsail. —**färber**, *m.* dyer in fine colours; (*fig.*) one inclined to colouring; one given to embellishment. —**färberei'**, *f.* dyeing in fine colours; colouring, embellishment. —**fleckchen**, *n.* beauty-spot. —**geist**, *m.* wit, bel-esprit, polite scholar. —**geisterei**, *f.* wit; pretension to wit *or* culture. —**geistig**, *adj.* pretending to wit, affecting literary ways; æsthetic. —**heits=gefühl**, *n.* feeling for beauty, taste. —**heits=lehre**, *f.* theory of the beautiful, æsthetics. —**heits=linie**, *f.* line of beauty. —**heits=mittel**, *n.* cosmetic. —**heits=sinn**, *m.* sense of beauty, feeling for the beautiful, artistic feeling, taste. —**heits=wasser**, *n.* wash, cosmetic. —**pflästerchen**, *n.* beauty-patch. —**redend**, *adj.* fine-spoken. —**redner**, *m.* fine talker; rhetorician. —**schreibe=kunst**, *f.*, —**schreiben**, *n.* calligraphy. —**schreiber**, *m.* calligraphist. —**seligkeit**, *f.* exaggerated worship of the beautiful, exaggerated attention to the form, æstheticism. —**sicht**, *f.* (*as name*) Bellevue. —**thuend**, *adj.* affected; coquettish; flirting. —**thuerei'**, *f.* coquettish ways, flirtation; affectation. —**wissenschaftlich**, *adj.* literary.

Schön'bartspiel, *n.* masquerade, masked ball.

Scho'n—en, *v.* I. *a. seldom n.* (*aux.* **h.** *gen.*); to treat with consideration *or* indulgence; to be sparing of; to save, spare, preserve, husband, economize; to take good care of; to manage, regulate the management of (*woods*); **sich —en**, to take care of o.s., of one's health; **etwas nicht —en**, to be prodigal of, not to spare. II. *n.* (*aux.* **h.**, *gen.*) to have a slight limp *or* halt (*of horses*). —**er**, *m.* (—**ers**, *pl.* —**er**) preserver, sparer; antimacassar. —**ung**, *f.* management, care; sparing; consideration, regard, indulgence, forbearance; young plantation. *Comp.* —**ungs=brille**, *f.* sight-preservers. —**ungs=los**, *adj.* unsparing, pitiless. —**ungs=voll**, *adj.* sparing; indulgent, full of consideration. —**zeit**, *f.* close time (*Sport.*).

Schö'nen, *v.a.* to refine, to clarify.

Schoo'ner, Scho'ner, Schu'ner, *m.* (—**s**, *pl.* —) schooner.

Schooß, Schoo'te, *see* **Schoß, Schote**.

Schopf, *m.* (—**es**, *pl.* **Schöp'fe**) top of the head; tuft (*of hair on the top of the head*): tuft, crest, topknot (*of birds*); forelock (*of horses*); top, crest (*of trees, of mountains*); coma (*Bot.*); **beim —e halten**, to hold by the hair; **die Gelegenheit beim —e fassen**, to seize an opportunity, to take time by the forelock (*coll.*); **einen beim — nehmen**, to seize s. o. by the hair; to arrest a p.

Schöp'f—en, I. *v.a.* to draw (*water, etc.*); to ladle, scoop out; to leak, admit water; to draw (*breath*), to respire, inhale; to conceive, entertain (*suspicions*); to derive, obtain, draw (*information, etc.*); to take (*courage*); **Geduld —en**, to exercise patience, grow patient; **ein Faß leer —en**, to empty a cask; **Mut —en**, to take courage. II. *subst. n. see* —**ung**; drawing; dipping (*Pap.*). —**er**, *m.* (—**ers**, *pl.* —**er**) drawer (*of water*); dipper, vat-man (*Pap.*); creator. —**erisch**, *adj.* creative; generative; productive. —**ung**, *f.* creation; the universe, created things. *Comp.* —**brett**, *n.* ladle-board, float (*of a mill-wheel*). —**brunnen**, *m.* draw-well. —**bütte**, *f.* pulp-vat (*Pap.*). —**eimer**, *m.* bucket. —**er=geist**, —**er=sinn**, *m.* creative genius. —**er=kraft**, *f.* creative power *or* energy. —**gefäß**, *n.*, —**gelte**, *f.* scoop, ladle. —**kelle**, *f.*, —**löffel**, *m.* scoop; drainer; basting ladle. —**maschine**, *f.* chain-pump; chain of buckets for raising water. —**rad**, *n.* well-wheel; (**persisches**) Persian wheel; ratchet-wheel. —**ungs=geschichte**, *f.* history of (the) creation, genesis. —**ungs=tag**, *m.* day of creation. —**werk**, *n.* hydraulic machine, water-engine.

Schöpp'chen, *n.* small glass (*of beer, etc.*); **ein — Wein**, a small glass of wine.

Schöp'pe, **2c.**, *see* **Schöffe, 2c.**

[1]**Schop'pen**, *m. see* **Schuppen**.

[2]**Schop'pen**, *m.* (—**s**, *pl.* —) liquid measure, (*about a*) pint; **ein — Bier**, a glass, a pint of beer.

Schöps, *m.* (—(**s**)**es**, *pl.* —(**s**)**e**) wether; booby, simpleton. *Comp.* (*with a weak genit. not otherwise occurring*) —(**s**)**en=braten**, *m.* roast-mutton. —(**s**)**en=fleisch**, *n.* mutton. —(**s**)**en=keule**, *f.*, —(**s**)**en=schlägel**, *m.* leg of mutton.

Schor, Schö're, *1 & 3 pers. sing. imperf. ind. & subj. of* **scheren**.

Scho're, *f.* (*pl.* —**n**) prop, shore.

Schorf, *m.* (—(**e**)**s**) scurf, scab; **Kopf—**, dandruff. —**ig**, *adj.* scurfy, scabby.

Schörl, *m.* (—**es**, *pl.* —**e**) schorl, black tourmaline.

Schorn'stein, *m.* (—**s**, *pl.* —**e**) (*older* **Schor'=stein**) chimney; flue; **eine Schuld in den — schreiben**, to give up as a bad debt; to drop a claim. *Comp.* —**brand**, *m.* chimney on fire. —**feger**, *m.* chimney-sweep. —**haube**, *f.* chimney-cowl. —**kappe**, *f.* chimney-pot. —**kasten**, *m.* chimney-stack. —**mündung**, *f.* vent of a chimney. —**rohr**, *n.*, —**röhre**, *f.* chimney-flue.

[1]**Schoß** (*short* **o**), **Schös'se**, *1 & 3 pers. sing. imperf. ind. & subj. of* **schießen**.

[2]**Schoß** (*short* **o**), *m.* (—(**ss**)**es**, *pl.* —(**ss**)**e** *and* **Schös'se**) sprig, shoot, sprout; story (*Arch.*); tax, impost (*obs.*). —**bar**, *adj.* liable to taxation. *Comp.* —**frei**, *adj.* scot free; free from taxation. —**gesetz**, *n.* taxation law. —**kiel**, *m.* young blade (*of corn*). —**rebe**, *f.* vine-shoot. —**register**, *n.* register of assessments. —**reis**, *n. see* **Schößling**.

[3]**Schoß** (*long* **o**), *m.* (—**es**, *pl.* **Schö'ße**) lap; womb; bosom; flap, skirt (*of a coat*); **es ist ihm in den — gefallen**, it has come to him over night; **die Hände in den — legen**, to fold one's arms, to be idle; **im —e seiner Familie**, in the bosom of his family; **im —e der Kirche**, within the pale of the Church; **in den — der Kirche zurückkehren**, to return to the bosom of the Church; **das ruht im —e der Götter**, that lies on the knees of the gods. *Comp.* —**hund**, *m.* lap-dog, pet dog. —**jünger**, *m.* favourite disciple. —**kind**, *n.* pet (child), darling child. —**tasche**, *f.* skirt-pocket; coat-tail pocket.

Schöß'ling (*short* **ö**), *m.* (—**s**, *pl.* —**e**) shoot, sprig, sucker; stripling.

[1]**Scho'te**, *f.* (*pl.* —**n**, *dim.* **Schöt'chen**) pod, husk, shell, cod; (*pl.*) green peas. *Comp.* —**n=dorn**, *m.* acacia. —**n=erbse**, *f.* pea. —**n=förmig**, *adj.* pod-shaped. —**n=frucht**, *f.* legume, pod. —**n=früchtig**, *adj.* poddy, leguminous. —**n=gewächse**, *pl.* leguminous plants. —**n=klee**, *m.* bird's-foot trefoil. —**n=tragend**, *adj.* pod-bearing.

[2]**Scho'te**, *f.* (*pl.* —**n**) sheet, clew-line (*Naut.*). *Comp.* —**n=gat(t)**, **Schot'gat**, *n.* sheet-hole (*through which the mainsail is reefed*).

Schott, *n.* (—**es**, *pl.* —**e**) partition-wall; breast-work, bulkheads (*Naut.*); shutter (*in a stove, etc.*); flood-gate; knot in wood.

Schot'ter, *m.* (—**s**, *pl.* —) boulder; rubble-stone.

Schraffie'r—en, *v.a. & n.* (*aux.* **h.**) to hatch; **ins Kreuz —en**, to cross-hatch. —**ung**, *f.* hatching (*in drawing, etc.*).

Schräg, *adj.* oblique; slanting, sloping; bias; diagonal; awry; bevelled; **der —e Durchschnitt eines Kegels,** the oblique conic section. **—e,** *f.* (*pl.* **—en**) obliquity; slope, slant; bevel. **—heit,** *f. see* **—e.** *Comp.* **—balken,** *m.* bar, bend (*Her.*). **—fenster,** *n.* sky-light. **—feuer,** *n.* oblique firing (*Mil.*). **—fläche,** *f.* slope; bevel. **—kante,** *f.* chamfer. **—kreuz,** *n.* saltire (*Her.*). **—linie,** *f.* diagonal. **—maß,** *n.* bevel. **—schnitt,** *m.* diagonal cut; ellipse (*Geom.*).

Schrä'g—en, *v.a.* to slant, slope, bevel. **—ung,** *f.* sloping, slanting, bevelling, bevel.

Schra'gen, *m.* (**—s,** *pl.* **—**) trestle, frame, jack; couch; stall; stack (*of wood*).

Schram'm—e, *f.* (*pl.* **—en**) scratch; slash; scar. **—en,** *v.a.* to scratch; to graze (*the skin*); to scar. **—ig,** *adj.* scarred; scratched.

Schrank, *m.* (**—es,** *pl.* **Schrän'ke**) cupboard; press; wardrobe; cross-trace of deer; **Bücher —,** bookcase; **Kleider—,** wardrobe; **Porzellan —,** china-cabinet. **—e,** *f.* (*pl.* **—en**) barrier; rail, fence; bar (*Law*); starting-place; limit, bound; arena; place railed off, enclosure; (*pl.*) lists; **die —en überschreiten,** to go beyond (all) bounds; **die —en einhalten, in den —en bleiben,** to keep within bounds; **innerhalb der gesetzlichen —en,** within the pale of the law; **einer Sache —en setzen,** to set bounds to a th.; **in die —en treten,** to enter the lists; **in die —en fordern,** to defy, provoke, challenge; **vor den —en,** at the bar, before a jury; **—en ziehen,** to draw a line, to limit. *Comp.* **—en=effekten,** *pl.* bills, stocks, *etc.*, admitted to the list (*on the stock exchange*). **—en=los,** *adj.* boundless; unbridled, unrestrained; unlicensed. **—en=losigkeit,** *f.* boundlessness; license. **—en=wächter,** *m.* gate-keeper. **—en=werk,** *n.* barrier, railing, fence-work. **—piano,** *n.* cabinet piano.

Schrän'ken, *v.* I. *a.* to put crosswise, to cross; to fold one's arms; to fence in; to weave (*baskets*); to set (*a saw*); **geschränkte Zähne,** cross-cut teeth (*of a saw*). II. *n.* (*aux.* **h.**) to walk straddling.

Schran'ne, *f.* (*pl.* **—n**) stall; shambles; corn-exchange.

Schran'z(e), *m.* (*pl.* **—n**) parasite, sponger; sycophant, servile courtier; flunkey.

Schra'pe, *f.* (*pl.* **—n**) scraper. **—n,** *v.a.* to scrape.

Schrapne'll, *m.* (*& n.*) case-shot, shrapnel (*shell*). *Comp.* **—schuß,** *m.* round of case-shot.

Schrat, *m.* (**—s,** *dim.* **Schrät'lein, Schrä'tel**) hobgoblin, imp, incubus; **Wald—,** wood sprite.

Schrau'be, *f.* (*pl.* **—n**) screw (*also Naut.*); queer fish; **alte —,** old woman (*coll.*); **Archimedische —,** screw-propeller; **Doppel—,** double-threaded screw; **linksgängige —,** left-handed screw; **auf —n stehen,** to have an uncertain position, to be doubtful; **seine Worte auf —n stellen,** to speak *or* write in an affected way; to speak *or* write ambiguously; **in seinem Kopfe ist eine — los,** he has a screw loose.

Schrau'b—en, *reg. & ir.v.a.* to screw; to quiz, joke, mock, make game of; **einen —en,** to tease a p.; **einen um sein Geld —en,** to cheat a p. out of his money; **die Lampe herunter —en,** to lower the lamp; **seine Hoffnungen niedriger —en,** to lower one's expectations, to come down a peg; **seinen Stil —en,** to affect a high-flown style; **seine Worte —en,** to write *or* speak in a stilted way; **den Preis zu furchtbarer Höhe hinauf —en,** to run up, raise the price enormously; **geschraubt,** screwed, *etc.*; forced, unnatural. **—erei',** *f.* banter, quizzing. *Comp.* **—en=achse,** *see* **—enwelle.** **—en=blech,** *n.* screw-plate. **—en=bohrer,** *m.* screw-auger, screw-tap. **—en=boot,** *n.* propeller. **—en=dampfer,** *m.* screw-steamer. **—en=dreher,** *m.* turn-screw; winch. **—en=flügel,** *m.* blade of a screw. **—en=förmig,** *adj.* screw-formed. **—en=gang,** *m.*, **—en=gewinde,** *n.* thread, worm of a screw. **—en=hülse,** *f.* nut. **—en=kloben,** *m.* hand-vice. **—en=linie,** *f.* screw-line; spiral line. **—en=mutter,** *f.* female screw. **—en=nagel,** *m.* screw-nail, screw. **—en=presse,** *f.* screw-press. **—en=rahmen,** *m.* screw-chase (*Typ.*). **—en=rollen,** *pl.* screw-casters. **—en=schloß,** *n.* screw *or* jack-lock. **—en=schlüssel,** *m.* screw-key; key with a screw; (**englischer**) universal screw-wrench. **—en=schnecke,** *f.* helix (*Conch.*); Terebra (*Ent.*). **—en=schneidbank,** *f.* screw-cutting lathe. **—en=versenkbohrer,** *m.* counter-sink. **—en=welle,** *f.* propeller shaft. **—en=winde,** *f.* screw-jack. **—en=zange,** *f.* hand-vice. **—en=zeug,** *n.* tools for making screws. **—en=zieher,** *m.* screw-driver, turn-screw. **—en=zug,** *m.* set of pulleys. **—en=zwinge,** *f.* screw-clamp, holdfast. **—knecht,** *m.*, **zwinge,** *f.* holdfast. **—stiefel=stock,** *m.* boot-tree. **—stock,** *m.* vice.

Schreck, *m.* (**—(e)s**) *see* **—en** III. **—bar,** *adj.* fearful, easily frightened, timid. **—haft,** *adj.* fearsome, fearful, timid; terrible (*rare*). **—lich,** *adj. & adv.* frightful, terrible; dreadful, horrible; hideous; tremendous, excessive. **—lichkeit,** *f.* terribleness, frightfulness; horrible thing.

Schre'ck—en, I. *v.a.* to affright, frighten, alarm, terrify; to frighten away; to take the chill off (water, *etc.*); to pour water on something hot; to put something hot into cold water, *etc.* II. *ir.v.n.* (*aux.* **f.**) to experience a sudden change of temperature; to crack; to become frightened. III. *m.* (**—s**) terror, fright; fear, horror, dread; **einem —en einflößen, einjagen,** to strike terror into a p.; **in —en setzen,** to terrify, dismay. IV. *n.* (**—s**) object of awe, terrible thing *or* creature. **—nis,** *f.* (*pl.* **—nisse**) *& n.* (**—nisses,** *pl.* **—nisse**) horror; *see* **—en** III. *Comp.* **—bild,** *n.*, **—gestalt,** *f.*, **—gespenst,** *n.* frightful image *or* vision; terrible phantom, bugbear, fright. **—ens=bote,** *m.* bearer of evil tidings. **—ens=botschaft,** *f.* terrible news. **—ens=herrschaft,** *f.* reign of terror. **—ens=jahr,** *n.* terrible year. **—ens=mann,** *m.* terrorist. **—gespenst,** *n. see* **—bild.** **—mittel,** *n.* scarecrow, scare. **—schanze,** *f.* redoubt. **—schuß,** *m.* shot fired in the air to intimidate; false alarm. **—stein,** *m.* malachite; stone to protect corners from carriage-wheels. **—tuch,** *n.* rags used for a scarecrow.

Schrei, *m.* (**—(e)s,** *pl.* **—e**) cry, scream, shriek; **einen — thun** *or* **ausstoßen,** to utter a cry.

Schrei'b—en, I. *ir.v.a. & n.* (*aux.* **h.**) to write; to write down; to spell; **einem, an einen —en,** to write to s.o.; **ins Konzept, ins Unreine, in die Kladde —en,** to jot down, make a rough draft *or* copy of; **ins Reine —en,** to make a fair copy, to write out, to faircopy; **Diktat —en,** to write from dictation; **mit der Schreibmaschine —en,** to typewrite; **Noten —en,** to copy music; **die Zeitung —t,** the newspaper says; according to the newspaper; **den wievielten —en wir heute?** what day of the month is it? **das Wort sollte mit einem k geschrieben werden,** the word ought to be spelt with a k; **—en Sie sich das hinter die Ohren,** note that; **sich —en, seinen Namen —en,** to spell one's name; **seinen Namen darunter —en,** to subscribe *or* put one's name to a th.; **wie —en Sie sich?** how do you spell your name? what is your name? **es —t sich von meiner Mutter her,** I inherit it from my mother; **woher —en Sie sich?** where do you hail from? **wo schreibt er sich her?** what countryman is he? **wo —t sich dies her?** on what authority is this based? where does this come from? **können Sie**

Geschriebenes lesen? can you read writing? II. *subst. n.* writing; letter; diplomatisches —en, note; Ihr (geehrtes) —en, your favour (*C. L.*); das —en wird mir sauer, I write with difficulty. —er, *m.* (—ers, *pl.* —er) writer; penman, scribe; secretary; clerk; copyist; author. —erei', *f.* writing; scribbling; business of clerk *or* copyist. —ung, *f.* writing; orthography; phonetische —ung, phonetic script *or* transcription. *Comp.* —apparat, *m.* indicator (*Elect.*). —ärmel, *m.* sleeve to draw on when writing. —art, *f.* manner of writing, style; handwriting. —bedarf, *m.* writing materials. —(e)=brief, *m.* epistle. —(e)=buch, *n.* copy-book; exercise-book; scribbling-book; note-book. —er=amt, *n.*, —er=stelle, *f.* clerkship, writership. —faul, *adj.* disinclined for writing *or* corresponding; —faul sein, to be a bad correspondent. —feder, *f.* pen, quill. —fehler, *m.* mistake in spelling *or* writing, slip of the pen. —fertig, *adj.* ready to write; —fertig sein, to be a skilful penman, to have a ready pen. —fertigkeit, *f.* penmanship. —gebrauch, *m.* customary orthography, usual spelling. —gebühr, *f.*, —geld, *n.* copying *or* writing fees. —gerät, *n. see* —bedarf. —griffel, *m.* slate-pencil; style; calamus. —heft, *n.* scribbling-book, exercise-book. —kalender, *m.* diary, memorandum book. —kästchen, *n.* writing-case; pen-case. —kohle, *f.* plumbago. —krampf, *m.* writer's cramp. —(e)=kunst, *f.* calligraphy. —lehrer, *m.* writing-master. —lese=methode, *f.*, —lesen, *n.* system of teaching reading and writing simultaneously. —lustig, *adj.* fond of writing. —mappe, *f.* blotter; portfolio. —maschine, *f.* type-writer. —materialien, *pl. see* —bedarf; stationery. —materialien=händler, *m.* stationer. —papier, *n.* writing *or* note-paper; (gelblich weißes) cream note-paper. —pergament, *n.* vellum. —(e)=pult, *n.* writing desk, escritoire. —schrift, *f.* script; italics (*Typ.*). —schule, *f.* writing-school. —sekretär, *m.* bureau. —selig, *adj.* fond of writing. —stift, *m.* lead-pencil in holder; slate-pencil; style. —stube, *f.* office; counting-house. —stunde, *f.* writing lesson. —sucht, *f.* mania for writing. —tafel, *f.* slate; blackboard; pocket-book. —tisch, *m.* writing-table; study-table. —übung, *f.* practice in writing. —unterlage, *f.* blotter, blotting pad, desk pad. —verständige(r), *m.* expert (*in writing or deciphering writing*). —vorlage, —vorschrift, *f.* copy, head-lines. —zeug, *n.* writing apparatus; inkstand.

Schrei'—en, *ir.v.a. & n.* (*aux.* h.) to cry, shriek, scream; to bray (*as a donkey*); to caw; to hoot, screech (*as an owl*), to crow; to creak; aus vollem Halse —en, to shriek, bawl with all one's might; Ach und Weh —en, to utter loud cries, cry out; gen *or* zum Himmel —en, to cry aloud to heaven, to call heaven to witness; —en nach *or* um, to cry for; —en über (*acc.*), to cry out against; das ist zum —en, that 's enough to make you shriek with laughter (*fig.*). —end, *p. & adj.* crying, *etc.*; clamorous; glaring, flagrant; loud. —er, *m.* (—ers, *pl.* —er) crier; bawler; ranter. —erei', *f.* bawling; cries; clamour. *Comp.* —hals, *see* —er. —puppe, *f.* doll that can cry. —vögel, *pl.* Clamatores.

Schrein, *m.* (—s, *pl.* —e) cupboard; chest, coffer; shrine (*poet. & dial.*). —er, *m.* (—ers, *pl.* —er), joiner; Kunst—er, cabinet-maker. —er=geselle, *m.* journeyman joiner.

Schrei'ten, *ir.v.n.* (*aux.* s.) to stride, step, stalk; to proceed, advance, come *or* pass on (*to*); to have recourse (*to*); zur Abstimmung —, to proceed to a division, take the votes; zur Ehe —, to marry, to get married.

Schrie, Schrie'e, *1 & 3 pers. sing. imperf. ind. & subj. of* schreien.

Schrieb, Schrie'be, *1 & 3 pers. sing. imperf. ind. & subj. of* schreiben.

Schrift, *f.* (*pl.* —en) writing, hand; letters; script; type, letterpress; text; font (*Typ.*); writing, work, book, publication; paper, review, periodical; pamphlet; composition; inscription; legend; (*pl.*) writings; in lateinischer —, in Roman characters; phonetische —, phonetic script; die heilige —, the Holy Scriptures; eine monatliche —, a monthly publication; Lessings nachgelassene —en, the posthumous works of Lessing; vermischte —en, miscellaneous writings; Vierteljahrs —, quarterly; Kopf oder —? heads *or* tails? die — ablegen, to distribute the type; Abdruck vor der —, proof before the letter, proof-impression (*Engr.*). —lich, *adj. & adv.* written, in writing, in black and white; —licher (Gerichts) Befehl, writ; —lich abfassen, to put in writing, write down; laß mich deine Meinung —lich wissen, let me have your opinion in writing, write me what you think; ich gebe es Ihnen —lich, I 'll be bound for it, I warrant you; ich möchte lieber, daß Sie mir es —lich geben, I should prefer your giving it me in black and white. —tum, *n.* literature. *Comp.* —absatz, *m.* paragraph. —anzeige, *f.* bookseller's advertisement. —ausleger, *m.* expounder of the Holy Scriptures. —auslegung, *f.* exposition *or* interpretation of the Scriptures; exegesis. —band, *n.* label, scroll. —behältnis, *n.* set of pigeon-holes, *etc.*, for papers. —beweis, *m.* Scriptural proof (*adduced in support of doctrine*); Scripture evidence; written evidence. —bild, *n.* face (*of a letter*). —deutsch, *n.* literary German. —führer, *m.* secretary. —gelehrte(r), *m.* scribe (*B.*). —gießer, *m.* type-founder. —gießer=erz, —gießer=metall, *n.* type-metal. —gläubige(r), *m.* believer in Scripture. —guß, *m.* font of type. —kasten, *m.* letter-case (*Typ.*). —kegel, *m.* body *or* depth of a letter (*Typ.*). —kunde, *f.* Biblical knowledge; knowledge of Biblical criticism. —kürzung, *f.* abbreviation. —leiter, *m.* editor. —leitung, *f.* editorship; the editor(s). —mäßig, *adj.* scriptural, according to the Scriptures, biblical. —mäßigkeit, *f.* conformity to Scripture. —mutter, *f.* matrix (*Typ.*). —probe, *f.* specimen of writing *or* of type. —satz, *m.* composition. —setzer, *m.* compositor. —seite, *f.* page; reverse (*of a coin*). —sprache, *f.* written *or* literary language; Scriptural language. —sprachlich, *adj.* in accordance with the literary language. —steller, *m.* author; writer; elender —steller, wretched scribbler, literary hack; fruchtbarer —steller, prolific *or* voluminous author *or* writer. —stellerin, *f.* authoress, literary woman. —stellerei', *f.* authorship; literary profession. —stellerisch, *adj.* literary. —steller=verband, *m.* society of authors. —stempel, *m.* punch (*Typ.*). —stück, *n.* (literary) document; writing; packet (*Typ.*). —verdreher, *m.* distorter of the Scriptures. —verfälschung, *f.* interpolation; forgery. —wart, *m.* secretary (*to a society*). —wechsel, *m.* exchange of letters, correspondence. —widrig, *adj.* unscriptural. —zeichen, *n.* mark in writing; letter, character. —zeichen=setzung, *f.* punctuation. —zeug, *n.* type-metal. —zug, *m.* dash, stroke, flourish; character; deutsche —züge, German script *or* characters; geheimer —zug, cipher.

Schrill, *adj.* shrill. —en, *v.n.* (*aux.* h.) to utter a shrill cry; to chirp.

Schrin'den, *ir.v.n.* to chap, to get chappy; to split, crack.

Schrin'nen, *ir.v.n.* (*aux.* h. & s.) to smart, itch.

Schrip'pe, *f.* (*pl.* **—n**) a kind of French roll (*flat with pointed ends*); crease, crumple.

[1]**Schritt,** *m.* (**—es,** *pl.* **—e**) step; stride; pace; gait; **im —e gehen,** to walk, to pace (*of horses*); **— für** (*or* **vor**) **—,** step by step; **gleichen — mit einem halten,** to keep pace with a p.; **— halten,** to keep in step; **einen entscheidenden — thun,** to take a decisive step, to cross the Rubicon; **den ersten — thun,** to take the first step, to make the first move; to take the initiative; **zwei —e von,** within a stone's throw of; **aus dem —e kommen,** to get out of step; **es ist nur um den ersten — zu thun, der erste — ist immer der schwerste,** the difficulty is at the beginning; **die ersten —e zu ...,** the preliminary steps to ... **—lings,** *adv.* pacing; step by step; stridingly, straddlingly; astride; **—lings im Sattel sitzen,** to sit astride the saddle. *Comp.* **—gänger,** *m.* pacing horse. **—länge,** *f.* length of the pace. **—macher,** *m.* pace-maker. **—messer,** *m.* pedometer. **—schuh,** *m.* skate. **—stein,** *m.* stepping-stone. **—wechsel,** *m.* change of step (*Mil.*). **—weise,** *adv.* step by step.

[2]**Schritt, Schrit'te,** *1 & 3 pers. sing. imperf. ind. & subj. of* **schreiten.**

Schrob, Schrö'be, *1 & 3 pers. sing. imperf. ind. & subj. of* **schrauben.**

Schro'bel, *n.* (**—s,** *pl.* **—**) fine carding-comb. **—n,** *v.a.* to card (*wool*).

Schroff, *adj. & adv.* rough, rugged; steep, precipitous; uncouth; gruff, blunt, abrupt, harsh. **—heit,** *f.* ruggedness; roughness, rudeness.

Schröp'fe, *f.* (*pl.* **—n**) cropping (*of young corn, etc.*); cropped tops (*of corn*).

Schröp'f—en, *v.a.* to cup; to tap (*a tree*); to crop (*the young wheat, etc.*); to fleece, bleed, overcharge. **—er,** *m.* (**—ers,** *pl.* **—er**) cupper. **—ung,** *f.* cupping; cropping (*of corn, etc.*); fleecing. *Comp.* **—eisen,** *n.*, **—schnäpper,** *m.* cupping instrument, scarifier. **—glas,** *n.*, **—kopf,** *m.* cupping glass; **(einem) —köpfe setzen,** to cup a person.

Schrot, *m. & n.* (**—s,** *pl.* **—e**) piece cut off; small-shot, hail-shot; slugs, langrel, langrage (*Naut.*); log, block; cut, make, build; timber-work; lining (*of a shaft*); chips, clippings; groats; bruised grain; size *or* weight of coin; **von echtem** *or* **gutem (altem) — und Korn,** of standard weight and alloy, of the old stamp, of sterling worth; **von gleichem** *or* **vom selben —,** a chip of the old block. **—en,** *ir.v.a.* to cut, saw in pieces; to rough-hew; to rough-grind (*corn*); to bruise (*malt*); to gnaw (*as mice*); to shoot, lower, roll down (*casks, etc.*); to clip; to chip; **die Münzstücke —en,** to pare the edges of the coins. *Comp.* **—axt,** *f.* wood-cutter's axe. **—beutel,** *m.* shot-pouch (*Mil.*). **—büchse,** *f.* shot-case; fowling-piece, rifle. **—eisen,** *n.* chisel; cutting-knife (*Shoem.*). **—flinte,** *f.* fowling-piece. **—gießerei',** *f.* shot-manufactory. **—hobel,** *m.* jack-plane. **—holz,** *n.* skid. **—kasten,** *m.* bran-chest. **—kleie,** *f.* coarse bran. **—köcher, —koker,** *m.* canister for case-shot. **—korn,** *n.* groats; grain of shot. **—maß,** *n.* charge of shot. **—mehl,** *n.* groats, coarse meal. **—meißel,** *m.* turner's gouge; chisel. **—mühle,** *f.* bruising-mill. **—säge,** *f.* great-saw, pit saw; combmaker's cutter. **—schere,** *f.* shears; plate-shears. **—sieb,** *n.* sieve used in making shot. **—silber,** *n.* grains of silver. **—speck,** *m.* streaky bacon. **—stück,** *n.* shred, cutting; planchet (*Mint.*); heavy gun (*Artil.*). **—zeug,** *n.* paring tools.

Schröt—er, *m.* (**—ers,** *pl.* **—er**) gnawing-insect, beetle; canker worm; cutter; chisel (*for cutting metal*); gouge; drayman. **—ling,** *m.* (**—lings,** *pl.* **—linge**) piece cut off; planchet (*Mt.*).

Schrub'beln, *v.a.* to card (*wool*).

Schrub'be—(r)n, *v.a.* to scrub; to rough-plane. **—r,** *m.* (**—rs,** *pl.* **—r**) scrubber; swab; scrubbing-brush.

Schrul'le, *f.* whim, crotchet; **er hat seine —n,** he is whimsical; he is in one of his moods. **—nhaft,** *adj.* whimsical.

Schrumm, *int.* done, finished, stop! (*coll.*).

Schrum'p—el, *f.* (*pl.* **—eln**) (*coll.*) fold, wrinkle; **alte —el,** withered old woman. **—eln,** *v.n.* (*aux.* **s.**) *see* **Einschrumpfen.** **—fen,** *v.n.* (*aux.* **s.**) to shrivel, shrink; to crumple. **—fig, —f(e)lig,** *adj.* wrinkled, shrivelled.

[1]**Schrund,** *m.* (**—es,** *pl.* **Schrün'de**), **—e,** *f.* (*pl.* **—en**) cleft, crack, crevice, crevasse. **—ig,** *adj.* cracked, chapped; **—ig machen,** to split, crack; to chap.

[2]**Schrund, Schrün'de,** *1 & 3 pers. sing. imperf. ind. & subj. of* **schrinden.**

Schub, *m.* (**—es,** *pl.* **Schü'be**) shove, push, thrust; throw (*at throwing games*); batch (*of bread*); set (*of skittles*); compulsory conveyance (*of vagrants, etc.*) by the police; **einem einen — geben,** to push, shove a p.; **die Thür wurde um elf Uhr geöffnet und ich kam mit dem ersten — hinein,** the door was opened at eleven and I entered with the first batch (*of people*); **auf den — bringen,** to pass (*paupers, etc.*) to their parish. *Comp.* **—fach,** *n.* drawer. **—fenster,** *n.* sash-window. **—karren,** *m.* wheelbarrow. **—kasten,** *m.* set of drawers. **—lade,** *f.* drawer; set of drawers. **—laden-roman,** *m.* number of stories forming one artistic unit and joined together by a common framework. **—laden-stück,** *n.* comedy of episodes. **—paß,** *m.* order for the transport of paupers. **—riegel,** *m.* (sliding-)bolt. **—sack,** *m.* pocket. **—ventil,** *n.* sliding valve. **—weise,** *adv.* by shoves; gradually; in batches.

Schub'b(e)jack, *m.* (**—s,** *pl.* **—s**) ragamuffin, scamp, dirty wretch.

Schub'sen, Schup'sen, *v.a.* to push (*coll.*).

Schüch'tern, *adj.* shy, timid, bashful, coy. **—heit,** *f.* shyness, bashfulness, timidity.

Schuf, Schü'fe, *1 & 3 pers. sing. imperf. ind. & subj. of* **schaffen.**

Schuft, *m.* (**—es**) scamp, rascal; scrub; **ein —, wer Böses dabei denkt,** honi soit qui mal y pense. **—en,** *v.i.* to work hard, to slave (*vulg.*). **—ig,** *adj.* shabby; rascally; blackguard. **—igkeit,** *f.* shabbiness, baseness, mean trick.

Schuh, *m.* (**—es,** *pl.* **—e,** *as measure* **—**) shoe; foot (*of a boot; of a measure*); shoeing, ferrule, tip; socket (*of a pike*); **einem etwas in die —e schieben, gießen, schütten,** to lay (*a fault*) at a p.'s door; **einem die —e austreten,** to supplant a p.; **das habe ich (mir) längst an den —en abgelaufen,** I knew that long ago; **umgekehrt wird ein — daraus,** you are beginning at the wrong end; if you do just the opposite, you may succeed; **Sie wissen nicht, wo der — mich drückt,** you do not know where the shoe pinches me. *Comp.* **—absatz,** *m.* heel of a shoe or boot. **—ahle,** *f.* shoemaker's awl. **—anzieher,** *m.* shoeing-horn. **—band,** *n.* boot lace. **—blatt,** *n.* vamp. **—dehner,** *m.* shoe-stretcher. **—draht,** *m.* waxed end. **—eisen,** *n.* shoe-scraper. **—flicker,** *m.* cobbler. **—knöpfer,** *m.* button-hook. **—kratzer,** *m.* (door-)scraper. **—laden,** *m.* boot-shop. **—leisten,** *m.* last. **—macher,** *m.* shoemaker, bootmaker. **—pflock,** *m.* peg. **—putzer,** *m.* shoe-black. **—riemen,** *m.* shoe-lace; shoe-latchet (*B.*). **—schnalle,** *f.* shoe-buckle. **—schwärze,** *f.* (shoe-)blacking. **—wachs,** *n.* cobbler's wax. **—werk,** *n.* boots and shoes. **—wichse,** *f.* boot-polish, blacking. **—wichser,** *m.* shoeblack, boots. **—zwecke,** *f.* shoe-tack.

Schu'hu, *m.* (**—s,** *pl.* **—s**) owl.

Schuld, *f.* (*pl.* **—en**) debt; obligation; fault;

blame; offence; sin; crime; guilt; **die Sühnung der tragischen — in einem Stücke,** the Nemesis of a play; **tragische —,** the action of a hero of tragedy by which his ruin is brought about; **— und Gegen—,** debts active and passive; **sich in —en stürzen, —en machen,** to contract debts; **eine — abtragen,** to pay off a debt; **ich stehe in Ihrer —,** I am in your debt, under obligation to you; **einem die — beimessen, — geben,** to lay the blame on s.o., to ascribe the fault to a p.; **er hat — daran, es ist seine —, die — liegt an ihm,** it is his fault; **sich** (*dat.*) **etwas zu —en kommen lassen,** to incur blame, to become guilty of; commit (*a fault*); **— tragen an einer Sache,** to be guilty of a thing; **er hat sich Vieles dabei zu —en kommen lassen,** he has been very much to blame in the matter; **die schlechten Zeiten sind — daran,** the bad times are to blame for it; **vergib uns unsere —(en),** forgive us our debts (*B.*), forgive us our trespasses (*Prayer Book*). **—ig,** *adj.* due, owing, indebted; guilty, culpable, in fault; obliged; bound; **—ige Strafe,** just punishment; **—ig sein,** to owe, to be indebted *or* obliged; **einem die Antwort —ig bleiben,** not to answer a p.; **wie ich es —ig bin,** as I ought, as is fitting *or* due; **das ist man ihm —ig,** that is due to him; **das sind wir ihm schuldig,** that we owe to him; for that we have to thank him; **eines Fehlers —ig,** guilty of a fault; **sich —ig bekennen,** to acknowledge one's guilt, plead guilty (to); **er bleibt einem nichts —ig,** he gives as good as he gets, he gives tit for tat; Jack is as good as his master; **sie blieben einander nichts —ig,** they gave each other tit for tat. **—iger,** *m.* (**—igers,** *pl.* **—igere**) culprit; debtor; **wie wir vergeben unsern —igern,** as we forgive our debtors (*B.*), as we forgive them that trespass against us (*Prayer Book*). **—igkeit,** *f.* duty, obligation; due; **er hat nur seine —igkeit gethan,** he has only done his duty; **ich fragte den Wirt nach der —igkeit,** I asked the host how much I owed him. **—igst,** *adv.* most duly, as is most due, as is due and proper. **—ner,** *m.* (**—ners,** *pl.* **—ner**) debtor. *Comp.* **—abzahlung,** *f.* liquidation of debts. **—befleckt,** *adj.* stained with guilt. **—beladen, —belastet,** *adj.* laden with crime. **—beweis,** *m.* proof of guilt. **—bewußt,** *adj.* conscious of guilt. **—brief,** *m.* bond, promissory note. **—buch,** *n.* journal, ledger, account-book; memorandum-book; **unser —buch sei vernichtet!** let all old scores be wiped out! **—en=belastet,** *adj.* crippled with debts, deep in debt. **—en=frei,** *adj.* free from debt, unencumbered. **—en=last,** *f.* burden of debt. **—en=macher,** *m.* contracter of debts. **—en=masse,** *f.* aggregate amount of debt. **—en=tilgung,** *f.* liquidation of debt; sinking of the (national) debt. **—en=tilgungs=kasse,** *f.* sinking-fund. **—entum,** *n.* contracting of debts. **—en=wesen,** *n.* debtor's concerns, liabilities. **—erlaß,** *m.*, **—erlassung,** *f.* remission of a debt; forgiveness (*of sin, etc.*). **—forderer,** *m.* creditor. **—forderung,** *f.* claim, demand of payment; active debt. **—forderungs=sache,** *f.* action for debt. **—gefangene(r),** *m.* prisoner for debt. **—gefängnis,** *n.* debtor's prison. **—haft,** *f.* imprisonment for debt. **—ig=erklärung,** *f.* verdict of guilty. **—leute,** *pl.* creditors. **—los,** *adj.* guiltless, innocent. **—opfer** *n.* expiatory sacrifice. **—posten,** *f.* sum, item (*of a bill*). **—sache,** *f.* action for debt. **—schein,** *m.* debenture; promissory note, I O U. **—turm,** *m.* debtor's prison. **—überweisung,** *f.* delegation. **—verschreibung,** *f.* bond, I O U. **—voll,** *adj.* guilty.

Schul'den, *v.a.* to owe; to be guilty of.

Schu'l—e, *f.* (*pl.* **—en**) school; college; academy; **Fach —e,** professional school; **Fortbildungs —e,** continuation school; **Handels —e,** commercial school; **Handwerker —e,** mechanics' institute; **höhere —e,** secondary *or* intermediate school; **höhere Töchter —e,** high school for girls; **hohe —e, Hoch—e,** University; **technische Hoch—e,** Polytechnic Academy; **Internats —e,** boarding school; **Kleinkinder —e,** infant school; **lateinische —e, gelehrte —,** grammar school (*in England, not America*); **Privat—e,** private school; **städtische —e,** municipal school; **Vor—e,** preparatory school, preparatory department; **Stiftungs —e,** endowed school; **Volks —e, Elementar—e,** primary *or* elementary school; **hinter** *or* **neben die —e gehen, laufen, die —e schwänzen,** to play truant; **die —e fängt Freitag wieder an,** school re-opens on Friday; **man soll nicht aus der —e schwatzen,** tell no tales out of school; **heute ist keine —e,** there is no school to-day; **in die —e thun,** to put to school; **ein Pferd die —en machen lassen,** to put a horse through his paces; **die neue Lehrmeinung macht —e,** the new doctrine has found many adherents. **—en,** *v.a.* to school, teach; to train (*horses*). *Comp.* **—agent,** *m.* scholastic agent. **—agentur,** *f.* scholastic agency. **—aktus,** *m.* speech day. **—amt,** *n.* office of schoolmaster. **—amts=kandidat,** *m.* candidate for a mastership. **—anstalt,** *f.* school. **—arbeit,** *f.* lesson, task, home-work. **—aufseher,** *m.* inspector of schools. **—aufsicht,** *f.* inspection of schools. **—aufsichts=behörde,** *f.* School Board, Board of Education, Board of (school-)inspectors. **—ausdruck,** *m.* school-term. **—ausgabe,** *f.* school edition; **—ausgaben,** *pl.* school fees, expenses at a school. **—bank,** *f.* form, school bench. **—bekannte(r),** *m.* school-friend. **—besuch,** *m.* attendance at school. **—bibel,** *f.* school Bible, Bible for use in schools. **—bube,** *m.* pupil, schoolboy. **—buch,** *n.* school book, class book. **—bücher=verlag,** *m.* firm of educational publishers. **—deputation,** *f.* school committee. **—diener,** *m.* school porter. **—direktor,** *m.* headmaster, principal; **Stellung eines —direktors,** headmastership. **—ent=lassungs=zeugnis,** *n.* leaving certificate. **—ferien,** *pl.* (school-)holidays; **die —ferien beginnen,** the school is breaking up. **—fest,** *n.* school-treat. **—frage,** *f.* education question. **—frei,** *adj.*; **—freier Tag,** holiday; **—freier Nachmittag,** half-holiday. **—freund,** *m.* patron of schools; school-fellow, chum. **—fuchs,** *m.* assistant master, usher; pedant. **—fuchserei',** *f.* pedantry. **—fuchsig,** *adj.* pedantic. **—gebäude,** *n.* school-house. **—gebrauch,** *m.*; **für den —gebrauch,** for use in schools, for class-use. **—gehülfe,** *m.* usher, assistant-master. **—geld,** *n.* school-fees, schooling, terms. **—gelehrsamkeit,** *f.* book learning; erudition. **—gemäß, —gerecht,** *adj.* according to rule; well trained (*of horses*). **—gesetz,** *n.* school-regulation. **—haus,** *n.* school, college, school-premises. **—hof,** *m.* playground of a school. **—jahr,** *n.* scholastic year; (*pl.*) years spent at school *or* college. **—jugend,** *f.* school-children. **—kamerad,** *m.* school-fellow, chum (*fam.*). **—kenntnisse,** *pl.* knowledge acquired at school. **—klasse,** *f.* form. **—knabe,** *m.* schoolboy. **—kollegium,** *n.* staff (*of teachers*). **—konferenz,** *f.* meeting of teachers of the school. **—krank,** *adj.* shamming. **—krankheit,** *f.* sham illness. **—lehrer,** *m.* schoolmaster, assistant master. **—lehrer=anstalt,** *f.*, **—lehrer=seminar,** *n.* training college (*usually for elementary teachers*). **—lehrerin,** *f.* schoolmistress, assistant mistress.

—**lehrerstelle**, *f.* (*assistant*) mastership. —**lokal**, *n.* school; schoolroom. —**mann**, *m.* (*pl.* —**männer**) teacher, educationalist. —**mappe**, *f.* satchel, school-bag. —**mäßig**, *adj.* scholastic; *see* —**gerecht**. —**meister**, *m.* schoolmaster. —**meisterin**, *f.* schoolmistress. —**meisterisch**, *adj.* pedantic. —**meistern**, *v.a.* & *n.* (*aux.* **h.**) to be a schoolmaster; to keep a school; to play the schoolmaster, to be very censorious, to dogmatize, to play the pedant. —**ordnung**, *f.* school-regulations; school-discipline. —**pferd**, *n.* trained horse; riding-school horse. —**pflicht**, *f.* *see* —**zwang**. —**pflichtig**, *adj.* bound to attend school, of school-age. —**programm**, *m.* annual report of a (German) school, usually containing an essay by one of the masters. —**prüfung**, *f.* school-examination. —**ranzen**, *m.* school-bag, satchel. —**rat**, *m.* school-committee; School Board; H. M. Inspector of Schools. —**recht**, *adj.* *see* —**gerecht**. —**reise**, *f.* trip taken by a school *or* forms of a school. —**sache**, *f.* scholastic concern. —**sattel**, *m.* manège-saddle. —**schiff**, *n.* training-ship. —**schrift**, *f.* treatise on schools; school-book. —**schritt**, *m.* short pace (*of a horse*). —**schwänzer**, *m.* truant. —**sprache**, *f.* school-slang; language of schoolmen (*Philos.*). —**system**, *n.* scholastic system. —**stelle**, *f.* post in a school; mastership. —**stube**, *f.* school-room. —**stunde**, *f.* school-hour, period, lesson. —**tafel**, *f.* blackboard. —**tasche**, *f.* satchel. —**theologie**, *f.* scholastic divinity. —**ton**, *m.* dogmatic tone. —**übung**, *f.* school-exercise; task. —**unterricht**, *m.* school-teaching, instruction; **höherer** —**unterricht**, secondary *or* intermediate education. —**versäumnis**, *f.* non-attendance (*at school*). —**vogt**, *m.* school porter. —**vorstand**, *m.* school-committee; governing body of a school; School Board. —**vorsteher**, *m.* headmaster, principal of a school. —**weisheit**, *f.* philosophy of the Schools. —**wesen**, *n.* public instruction; school affairs. —**wissenschaften**, *pl.* humanities, polite literature. —**witz**, *m.* learned wit. —**zeit**, *f.* school-hours; school-days. —**zeugnis**, *n.* report on a boy's progress (at the close of each term), certificate. —**zimmer**, *n.* class-room (*in a school*); school-room (*in a private house*). —**zucht**, *f.* school-discipline. —**zwang**, *m.* compulsory attendance at school.

Schü'ler, *m.* (—**s**, *pl.* —), —**in**, *f.* school-boy, school-girl, pupil; scholar; student (*obs.*); disciple, follower; tyro; **ein früherer — der Anstalt**, an old boy; **in dieser Klasse sind zwanzig —innen**, there are twenty girls in this form; **er ist ein alter — von mir**, he is an old *or* a former pupil of mine; **er ist ein — der Prima**, he is a sixth-form boy; **ein — Christi**, a disciple of Christ; **ein fahrender —**, an itinerant scholar (*obs.*). —**haft**, *adj.* schoolboy-like. —**haftigkeit**, *f.* lack of experience, immaturity, boyishness; mediocrity, blundering ways. —**schaft**, *f.* discipleship; all the pupils *or* disciples. *Comp.* —**arbeit**, *f.* pupil's task; tyro's work. —**scene**, *f.* student scene, Mephistopheles and the freshman (*in 'Faust'*). —**spiele**, *pl.* boys' games; boys' sports.

Schul'ter, *f.* (*pl.* —**n**) shoulder; humerus (*Anat.*); **die — zucken, auf beiden —n tragen, ꝛc.**, *see* **Achsel**; **den Mantel auf beiden —n tragen**, to blow hot and cold; **einen über die —ansehn**, to look down upon a p. —**ig**, *adj.* (*in comp.* =) shouldered. *Comp.* —**band**, *n.* humeral ligament. —**blatt**, *n.* scapula, shoulder-blade. —**blech**, *n.* shoulder-piece (*of armour*). —**breite**, *f.* breadth of shoulders; shoulder-piece (*of shirts, etc.*). —**brett**, *n.* backboard. —**gehänge**, —**gehenk**, *n.* cross-belt (*Mil.*). —**gelenk**, *n.* shoulder-joint. —**höhe**, *f.* height of the shoulders; acromion (*Anat.*); **bis zur —höhe**, up to the shoulder. —**naht**, *f.* shoulder-seam; shoulder-piece. —**riemen**, *m.* shoulder-belt; cross-belt, shoulder-belt *or* strap (*Mil.*). —**tuch**, *n.* scapulary (*of monks*). —**wehr**, *f.* epaulement (*Fort.*).

Schul'tern, *v.a.* to shoulder (*arms, Mil.*); **mit geschultertem Gewehr**, with arms shouldered.

Schult'heiß, *m.* (—**en**, *pl.* —**en**), **Schul'ze**, *m.* (—**n**, *pl.* —**n**) village-mayor; chief magistrate of a village. *Comp.* —**n=gericht**, *n.* a farm with which the office of village-mayor was united, village-mayoralty.

Schum'meln, *v.a.* to cheat (*coll.*).

Schummerig, *adj.* dusky, dim (*coll.*).

[1]**Schund**, *m.* (—**es**) excrement; offal, refuse; trash; bad merchandise. *Comp.* —**feger**, —**könig**, *m.* night-man, scavenger. —**grube**, *f.* cess-pool.

[2]**Schund, Schün'de**, *imperf. ind. & subj. of* **schinden** (*rare*).

Schun'keln, *v.n.* to seesaw (*coll.*).

Schupp, (**Schupf**,) *m.* (—**es**, *pl.* —**e**) push, shove.

Schup'p—e, *f.* (*pl.* —**en**) scale; scurf; **die —en sind ihm von den Augen gefallen**, the scales have fallen from his eyes; **die —en fielen mir von den Augen**, my eyes were opened, I was undeceived. —**en**, *v.* I. *a.* to push, shove; to scale, strip of scales. II. *r.* to rub, scratch oneself (*prov.*); to slough, scale off. —**icht**, (*obs.*) *adj.* scaly. —**ig**, *adj.* scaly, scaled; squamous; scurfy; **blau—ig**, with blue scales. —**s, Schups**, *m.* (—(**s**)**es**, *pl.* —(**s**)**e**) push, shove (*coll.*). —(**s**)**en, Schupfen**, *v.a.* to push, shove (*coll.*). *Comp.* —**en=aussatz**, *m.* leprosy. —**en=eidechse**, *f.* scaly lizard. —**en=förmig**, *adj.* in the form of scales, scaly. —**en=grind**, *m.* scaly eruption. —**en=kette**, *f.* chin-strap of helmets. —**en=naht**, *f.* scaly suture, seam of the skull. —**en=panzer**, *m.* scale-armour, (scaly) coat of mail. —**en=pelz**, *m.* raccoon fur-coat. —**en=schlange**, *f.* scaly serpent. —**en=schnitt**, *m.* engrailing (*Her.*). —**en=tanne**, *f.* monkey-puzzle (*Araucaria imbricata*) (*Bot.*). —**en=tier**, *n.* scaly ant-eater, pangolin. —**en=weise**, *adv.* in scales, by flakes.

Schüp'pe, *f.* shovel; scoop; (*pl.*) spades (*Cards*); **die — bekommen**, to get shoved out, to be ousted.

Schup'pen, *m.* (—**s**, *pl.* —) shed; coach-house.

[1]**Schur**, *f.* shearing; sheep-shearing; fleece; clippings (*of hedges*); what is mown *or* shorn.

[2]**Schur**, *n.* shower, fit of anger, vexation (*dial.*); **einem etwas zum — thun**, to do s.th. to annoy a p.

Schü'r—en, *v.a.* to stir, poke, rake (*the fire*); to stir up; to trim (*a lamp*). —**er**, *m.* (—**ers**, *pl.* —**er**) poker; stoker; stirrer-up; poker (*for a furnace*). *Comp.* —**eisen**, *n.* poker. —**haken**, *m.* oven-rake; stithy-crook; poker. —**herd**, *m.* hearth of a kiln. —**holz**, *n.* wood for fuel (*Glassm.*). —**loch**, *n.* stoke-hole. —**schaufel**, *f.* fire-shovel. —**werkzeug**, *n.* fire-irons. —**zange**, *f.* tongs.

Schurf, *m.* (—**es**, *pl.* **Schür'fe**) cut, gash; scab; opening, hole (*in the ground*); passage (*to a mine*). *Comp.* —**arbeit**, *f.* burrowing *or* searching work, prospecting. —**eisen**, *n.* hoe, rake. —**schein**, —**zettel**, *m.* permit to make a passage (*Min.*).

Schür'f—en, *v.a.* to scratch, scrape; to rake; to burrow, uncover (*a mine*); to prospect (a district) for minerals, to costean; **tief —en**, to dig deep. —**er**, *m.* (—**ers**, *pl.* —**er**) miner who works at burrowing, prospector.

Schu'rigeln, *v.a.* to worry, harass, molest.

Schur'k—e, *m.* (—**en**, *pl.* —**en**) scoundrel, rogue; villain. —**erei'**, *f.* rascally trick; scoundrelism. —**isch**, *adj.* villainous, rascally.

Schur'ren, *v.n.* (*aux.* s. & h.) to glide along with a low sound, to slide.
Schurz, *m.* (—es, *pl.* Schür'ze) apron; mantel-piece. *Comp.* **—fell,** *n.* leathern apron.
Schür'ze, *f.* (*pl.* —n) apron; pinafore; woman (*coll.*); **hinter jeder — herlaufen,** to run after every petticoat. *Comp.* **—n=amt,** *n.* place obtained by petticoat influence. **—n=band,** *n.* apron-string; **ans —nband gebunden sein,** to be kept in leading strings (by a wife *or* mother). **—en=regiment,** *n.* petticoat-government. — **en=stipendium,** *n.* pecuniary assistance due to female influence.
Schür'zen, *v.a.* to tie (*a knot, etc.*); to complicate (*matters*); to tuck, pin up, shorten; **sich —,** to tuck up one's dress; **sich zu etwas —,** to gird up one's loins, to make ready for s. th.
Schuß, *m.* (—(ss)es, *pl.* Schüs'se, *as measure* —) rapid movement; rush (*of water, etc.*); precipitate career (*of horses, etc.*); élan, rapid flight, swoop; shoot, sprout; shooting up, rapid growth; shot; report (*of a gun*); charge; range; gun-shot wound; batch (*of bread*); throw, cast (*of money*); **scharfer —,** shot with ball; **in — kommen,** to get into working order, to move more and more rapidly; to get into the spirit of; **einem in den — laufen** *or* **kommen,** to come within shot (*of game*); to come across a p. *or* in a p.'s way; **einen — thun,** to fire a shot; **es fiel ein —,** a shot was fired; **der — geht los,** the gun goes off, is fired; — **der nicht losgeht,** hang-fire shot; — **aufs Geratewohl,** wild shot; — **ins Centrum,** (*shot into the*) bull's eye; — **ins Blaue,** random shot; — **aus dem Hinterhalt,** pot-shot; sniping-shot (*Mil.*); **der — sitzt** *or* **hat getroffen,** the shot has taken effect; **der — hat gefehlt,** the shot has missed its mark; **nicht alle Schüsse treffen,** not every shot tells; **sich zum — fertig machen,** to make ready to fire; **im —(ss)e sein,** to be in full swing, to be going on well, to be well started; **weit vom —,** wide of the mark; **weit davon ist gut vorm —,** always keep on the safe side; **ich möchte nicht zwei — Pulver daran wenden,** I would n't give two pins for it; **einen — haben,** to be a little cracked, to be hard hit (*in love*). *Comp.* **—bartel,** *m.* hot-headed person (*coll.*). **—fertig,** *adj.* ready to fire; cocked. **—fest,** *adj.* bullet- *or* shot-proof; invulnerable; **er ist —fest,** he bears a charmed life. **—frei,** *adj.* covered, protected; out of range. **—gatter,** *n.* flood-gate. — **gerecht,** *adj.* trained to stand fire (*of horses*); true (*of guns*); within range. **—geschwindigkeit,** *f.* rapidity of firing. **—leistung,** *f.* shooting powers, efficiency. **—licht,** *n.* light sufficient for shooting. **—linie,** *f.* line of fire, firing line, fire zone (*Artil.*). **—loch,** *n.* shot-hole; port-hole. **—mäßig, —recht,** *adj.* within range. **—scharte, —spalte,** *f.* loop-hole, embrasure. **—weise,** *adv.* by jerks; by fits and starts. **—weite,** *f.* range; **in —weite sein,** to be within range. **—wunde,** *f.* gun-shot wound.
Schus'sel, *m.* (—s) careless, slovenly person (*coll.*).
Schüs'sel, *f.* (*pl.* —n) dish, charger; dish (*of meat, etc.*); bowl; tureen. *Comp.* **—brett,** *n.* kitchen-dresser; plate-drainer *or* rack. — **förmig,** *adj.* dish-shaped. **—glocke, —stürze,** *f.* dish-cover. **—knecht,** *m.* dumb-waiter. — **korb,** *m.* plate-bucket. **—muschel, —schnecke,** *f.* limpet. **—ring,** *m.* dish-stand. **—rund,** *adj.* orbicular. **—schrank,** *m.* side-board. **—trage,** *f.* tray. **—wärmer,** *m.* plate-warmer. **—wasser,** *n.* dish-water.
Schus'ser, *m.* (—s, *pl.* —) marble, taw.
Schu'ster, *m.* (—s, *pl.* —) shoemaker; cobbler; — **bleib' bei deinem Leisten,** cobbler, stick to your last! (*prov.*); **auf —s Rappen reiten,** to go on Shanks' pony, to ride Shanks' mare. — **ei',** *f.* shoemaking-trade. *Comp.* **—draht,** *m.* waxed end. **—junge,** *m.* shoemaker's apprentice. **—kneif,** *m.* paring-knife. **—pech,** *n.* cobbler's wax. **—pfriem,** *m.* punch.
Schu'stern, *v.n.* (*aux.* h.) to be a shoemaker; to cobble; **sich** (*dat.*) **etwas zurecht —,** to put a th. together, to repair a th.
Schu'te, *f.* (*pl.* —n) barge (*Naut.*); large sun-bonnet.
Schutt, *m.* (—es) rubbish (*of buildings*); ruins; rubble; batch (*of malt*); bank of earth (*B.*); heap of corn (*as thresher's wages*); — **abladen,** to deposit rubbish. *Comp.* **—abladeplatz,** *m.* public dust-heap. **—ablagerung,** *f.* geological stratum formed from deposit. **—haufen,** *m.* heap of rubbish; **in einen —haufen verwandeln,** to lay in ruins. **—karren,** *m.* dust-cart. **—kärrner,** *m.* dustman, scavenger. — **kiste,** *f.* dust-bin.
Schüt'te, *f.* (*pl.* —n) heap, pile; truss (*of straw*); granary.
Schüt'tel—n, *v.a.* to shake; to make vibrate; to jolt; to jog; to wag; to shake off; **aus dem Ärmel —n,** to improvise, do on the spur of the moment; **einem die Hand —n,** to shake hands with a p.; **es —t mich,** it makes me tremble. **—ung,** *f.* shaking; jerk. *Comp.* **—frost,** *m.* feverish ague, shivering, rigor; **Anfall von —frost,** shivering fit, rigor. **—kopf,** *m.* head-shaker. **—rost,** *m.* grating with movable bars (*in steam-engines*). **—werk,** *n.* shaking-machine, fan.
Schüt't—en, *v.* I. *a.* to spill; to pour out; to throw (*water*); to shoot (*corn*); to drop (*lambs, etc.*); to pound (*cattle*); to raise, throw up (*a dam, etc.*); **leer (voll) —en,** to empty (fill); **Pulver auf die Pfanne —en,** to prime a gun. II. *n.* (*aux.* h.) to yield, produce; to litter, whelp. **—ung,** *f.* pouring out; dam, dyke. *Comp.* **—boden,** *m.* granary, corn-loft. — **gabel,** *f.* pitchfork. **—geld,** *n.* ransom for pounded cattle. **—ofen,** *m.* self-feeding stove. **—stroh,** *n.* litter. **—wasser,** *n.* back-water, dammed-up water.
Schüt'tern, *v.* I. *n.* (*aux.* h.) to vibrate, tremble, rock. II. *a.* to shake.
Schutz, *m.* (—es) defence, shelter, refuge, protection; care, keeping; safeguard; patronage; protection (*C. L.*); (*pl.* Schüt'ze) dam, sluice; — **und Schirm,** protection; **unter dem —e der Kanonen,** under cover of the guns; **sich in jemandes — begeben,** to seek shelter *or* take refuge with s. o.; **zu — und Trutz,** offensive(ly) and defensive(ly); — **suchen unter einem Baume,** to take shelter under a tree; **unter seinem —e einführen,** to patronize, introduce a p. *Comp.* **—amt,** *n.* protectorship, guardianship. **—ärmel,** *pl.* saving sleeves. **—baum,** *m.* protecting beam, supporting-joist. **—befohlene(r,** *m.,*) *f.* protégé(e); ward; client (*Rom. Hist.*). **—begleitung,** *f.* convoy. — **blattern,** *pl.* cow-pox, abortive small-pox. **—blech,** *n.* mud-guard (*Cycl.*). **—brett,** *n.* sluice, flood-gate, mill-dam. **—brief,** *m.* safe-conduct; protection (*in bankruptcy*). **—brille,** *f.* eye-preservers. **—bündnis,** *n.* defensive alliance. **—dach,** *n.* shed. **—damm,** *m.* inner dike, levee; dam. **—deck,** *n.* hurricane *or* bridge-deck. **—deckel,** *m.* cardboard box (*for the protection of books*). **—engel,** *m.* guardian angel. **—flügel,** *m.* jetty, breakwater. — **gatter,** *n.* portcullis; grate, barrier; flood-gate. **—gebiet,** *n.* protectorate; possession **—gehänge,** *n.* amulet. **—geist,** *m.* guardian spirit, tutelary genius. **—geländer,** *n.* railing, balustrade, breast-work. **—geld,** *n.* tax paid by protected *or* alien subjects. **—geleit,** *n.* safe conduct, escort, convoy. **—gerechtigkeit,** *f.* right of protection; protectorate. **—gitter,**

n. fire-guard. —**gott**, *m.* tutelary god. —**griff**, *m.* guard (*of a sword*). —**hafen**, *m.* harbour of refuge. —**heilige(r**, *m.*), *f.* patron-saint. —**heiligtum**, *n.* palladium. —**herr**, *m.* patron, protector. —**herrschaft**, *f.* protectorate. —**hütte**, *f.* shelter hut, refuge (*in the Alps*). —**jude**, *m.* nationalized *or* protected Jew (*obs.*). —**kind**, *n.* charge; ward. —**leistung**, *f.* protection. —**linie**, *f.* line of defence. —**los**, *adj.* defenceless, unprotected; shelterless, without protection; out in the cold (*coll.*). —**mann**, *m.* policeman; **berittene —leute**, mounted police(men). —**mannschaft**, *f.* police force, the constabulary. —**marke**, *f.* trade-mark; factory-mark. —**maßregel**, *f.* protective *or* precautionary measure, preventative. —**mauer**, *f.* rampart, bulwark. —**mittel**, *n.* preservative (*against*). —**ort**, *m.* asylum. —**patron(in**, *f.*), *m.* patron-saint. —**platte**, *f.* guard-plate. —**pocken**, *pl.* cow-pox. —(**pocken)gift**, *n.* vaccine lymph. —**rede**, *f.* apology, speech in defence. —**redner**, *m.* apologist. —**schachtel**, *f.* cardboard case (*for the protection of books*). —**truppe**, *f.* colonial force. —**=und=Trutz=bündnis**, *n.* alliance offensive and defensive. —**verwandte(r**, *m.*), *f.* stranger enjoying citizen's rights. —**wache**, *f.* escort; safeguard. —**waffen**, *pl.* defensive arms; means of defence. —**wand**, *f.* screen, shelter; snow-clearer (*Railw.*). —**wehr**, *f.* fence; bulwark, rampart, mantlet (*Fort.*); weir. —**zoll**, *m.* protective duty. —**zöllner**, *m.* protectionist. —**zoll=system**, *n.* protectionism.

Schütz, —**e**, *m.* (—**en**, *pl.* —**en**), —**in**, *f.* marksman, markswoman, shot; rifleman; member of rifle-club; shuttle; archer; guard, watchman (*of fields, woods*); **ein nie fehlender —e**, a dead shot. —**enschaft**, *f.* marksmanship; marksmen, riflemen; rifle-brigade *or* -club. *Comp.* —**en=aufzug**, *m.* parade of a rifle-corps. —**en=bataillon**, *n.* light-infantry battalion. —**en=brigade**, *f.* rifle-brigade. —**en=bruder**, *m.* fellow-marksman. —**en=fest**, *n.* festival of riflemen, riflemen's sports. —**en=gilde**, *f.* rifle-corps. —**en=graben**, *m.* rifle-pit. —**en=haus**, *n.* shooting gallery; club-house of a rifle-corps. —**en=kette**, *f.* skirmishing order, extended order, line of skirmishers; **die Kompanien gehen in —enketten vor**, the companies advance in skirmishing order. —**en=könig**, *m.* champion shot, winner of the first prize at a rifle-match. —**en=platz**, *m.* rifle-range; shooting-ground. —**en=übung**, *f.* rifle-practice. —**en=verein**, *m.* rifle-club.

Schüt'ze, *f.* sluice-board, lock-hatch, flood-gate.

Schüt'z—en, *v.a.* to protect, guard, defend; to shelter, to dam up; to shut off (*a mill-dam*); **Gott —e dich!** God protect you! **in dem Besitze —en**, to maintain in possession of. —**er**, *m.* (—**ers**, *pl.* —**er**) protector. —**ling**, *m.* (—**lings**, *pl.* —**linge**) protégé(e).

Schwa'bacher, (—**schrift**,) *f.* German italics.

Schwabbelei', *f.* babble; garrulity.

Schwab'bel—ig, *adj.* soft and quaking, wobbly, flabby. —**n**, *v.n.* (*aux.* **h.**) to babble, prate, gossip.

Schwab'ber, *m.* (—**s**, *pl.* —) swab (*Naut.*).

Schwa'be, *f.* (*pl.* —**n**) cockroach.

Schwä'beln, *v.n.* to speak in the Swabian dialect, to talk with a Swabian accent. *See* Schwabe *in the Index of Names.*

Schwach, *adj. & adv.* (**schwä'cher, schwächst**) weak, feeble; infirm; delicate; faint, dim, dull (*of sound, light*); **ein —es Zeitwort**, a weak verb; —**e Seite**, weak side; —**es Bier**, small beer; —**es Gedächtnis**, bad memory; **die Musik war —**, the music was poor; **er war so — zu . . .**, he had the weakness to . . .; **es wurde ihr —**, she became faint, fainted. —**heit**, *f.* weakness; weak fondness; frailty; debility; faint; debilitated condition; **sich** (*dat.*) —**heiten einbilden**, to get silly notions into one's head, to indulge in false hopes; **bilden Sie sich keine —heiten ein**, don't deceive yourself, don't cherish any delusions! *Comp.* —**äugig**, *adj.* weak-eyed. —**gläubig**, *adj.* weak in faith. —**heits=fehler**, *m.* fault from weakness of character. —**heits=sünde**, *f.* sin from natural frailty. —**herzig**, *adj.* faint-hearted. —**köpfig**, *adj.* weak-headed, silly. —**ma'tikus**, *m.* weakling; ignoramus (*in a branch of knowledge*). —**sinn**, *m.* feeble-mindedness; imbecility.

Schwä'che, *f.* (*pl.* —**n**) weakness; fragility; debility; frailty, infirmity; foible, weak side; (**männliche**) —, impotence.

Schwä'ch—en, *v.a.* to weaken, enfeeble, debilitate, enervate; to slow, slacken; to invalidate (*a witness*); to diminish the tone and slacken the time (*Mus.*); to seduce, ravish. —**er**, *m.* (—**ers**, *pl.* —**er**) weakener; seducer, ravisher. —**lich**, *adj. & adv.* feeble, weakly; sickly. —**lichkeit**, *f.* infirmity; delicacy. —**ling**, *m.* (—**lings**, *pl.* —**linge**) feeble person. —**ung**, *f.* weakening, debilitation; diminution; seduction, defloration, rape. *Comp.* —**e=zustand**, *m.* period debility, weakness, loss of vital power.

Schwad, *m.* (*& n.*), *see* [1]**Schwaden**.

[1]**Schwa'den**, *m.* (—**s**, *pl.* —) swath, row of mown corn *or* grass.

[2]**Schwa'den**, *m.* (—**s**, *pl.* —) vapour, exhalation; **feuriger —**, fire-damp, mine-gas. *Comp.* —**fang**, *m.* ventilating pipe, damp-shaft.

Schwadro'n, *f.* (*pl.* —**en**) squadron. —**en=weise**, *adv.* in *or* by squadrons. —**eu'r**, *m.* (—**eurs**, *pl.* —**eure**) braggart, swaggerer, blusterer, gascon. —**ie'ren**, *v.n.* (*aux.* **h.**) to talk big, brag, boast, swagger, draw the long bow; to hector.

Schwa'fel—n, *v.n.* to talk nonsense, to talk without thinking, without coming to the point; **was —t er da?** what nonsense is he talking?

Schwa'ger, *m.* (—**s**, *pl.* **Schwäger**) brother-in-law; good friend; postillion, coachman (*obs.*).

Schwä'ger—in, *f.* sister-in-law. —**schaft**, *f.* affinity by marriage; brothers- and sisters-in-law, relations by marriage.

Schwä'her, *m.* (—**s**, *pl.* —) father-in-law (*obs. & poet.*); brother-in-law (*rare, obs.*); **wir sind —**, our children are husband and wife, are united in marriage. —**in**, *f.* mother-in-law (*rare*).

Schwai'en, *v.* I. *n.* to swing round, to tend (*Naut.*). II. *a.* to swing (*the ship*) round.

Schwai'ge, *f.* dairy-farm (*dial.*).

Schwal'be, *f.* (*pl.* —**n**) swallow, martin(et); swift; box on the ear (*coll.*); **die — zwitschert**, the swallow twitters. *Comp.* —**n=flug**, *m.* flight of swallows. —**n=nest**, *n.* swallow's nest; —**n=nester der Spielleute**, bandsmen's shoulder-straps. —**n=schwanz**, *f.* swallow's tail; swallowtail coat; dovetailing; swallowtail work (*Fort.*); kite; swallowtail(ed butterfly).

Schwalch, *m.* (—(**e)s**, *pl.* —**e**) opening in a furnace through which the flame reaches the metal.

Schwä'len, *see* **Schwelen**.

Schwall, *m.* (—**es**) swell, undulation, surging; throng; confused mass; deluge, flood; sheet (*of flame*); — **von Worten**, torrent of words.

Schwamm, *m.* (—**es**, *pl.* **Schwäm'me**) sponge; fungus; mushroom; excrescence, growth, proud flesh; German tinder; spavin; dry-rot; — **drüber!** wipe it out, no more of it, let us forget it! (*sl.*); **der ganze —**, the whole concern (*sl.*). —**icht**, (*obs.*) —**ig**, *adj.* spongy, fungous. —**igkeit**, *f.* sponginess. *Comp.* —**artig**, *see* —**ig**. —**büchse**, *f.* tinderbox. —**gewächs**, *n.* fungous growth (*Surg.*); fungus (*Bot.*). —**halter**, *m.* sponge-holder. —**stein**, *m.* fossil sponge, fungite.

Schwan, *m.* (—(e)s) (*obs.* —en), *pl.* **Schwä'ne** (*obs.* **Schwa'nen**); *fem. sometimes* **Schwä'nin**; *dimin.* **Schwän'chen**) swan. *Comp.* **—en=bett,** *n.* swansdown bed *or* coverlet. **—en=brust,** *f.* **—en=busen,** *m.* swan-white bosom (*poet.*). **—en=daunen,** *pl.* swansdown. **—en=feder,** *f.* swan's quill *or* feather. **—en=gesang,** *m.*, **—en=lied,** *n.* swan's song; death-song. **—en=hals,** *m.* swan's neck; swan-bill (*Surg.*); tiller (*Naut.*); pivot (*of a swivel-gun*); fox-trap. **—en=jungfrau,** *f.* swan-maiden. **—en=ritter,** *m.* Knight of the Swan (*Lohengrin*). **—en=teich,** *m.* swannery. **—en=weiß,** *adj.* (as) white as a swan. **—en=züchter,** *m.* swan-keeper. **—s=feder,** *f.* swan's quill *or* feather; **—sfedern bekommen,** to get an inkling of a th.; to smell a rat (*dial.*); **mir wachsen —s=federn,** I have a presentiment (*dial.*).

Schwa'n—en, *v.n.* (*aux.* **h.**) *impers.*; **mir —t etwas,** I have a foreboding of something; **das hat mir von Anfang an geschwant,** I have had a presentiment of this from the beginning. **—ung,** *f.* presentiment.

Schwang, *m.* (—es) swing, swinging; **im —e, in —,** in motion, in full swing, in vogue, common, current; **in — kommen,** to become the fashion; **eine Glocke in — bringen,** to set a bell (a)ringing.

Schwan'ger, *adj.* pregnant, with child; **sie ist —,** she is in the family way; **(mit) Unheil —,** big with disaster; **hoch —,** far advanced in pregnancy; **mit etwas — gehen,** to brood over, to hatch, to teem with a th.; **mit großen Plänen — gehen,** to labour with grand projects. **—schaft,** *f.* pregnancy, being with child.

Schwän'ger—er, *m.* (—ers, *pl.* —er) one who impregnates, begetter, father. **—n,** *v.a.* to get with child, to get in(to) the family way; to impregnate; to fecundate; to saturate (*Chem.*). **—ung,** *f.* impregnation, fecundation.

Schwank, I. *adj.* pliable, flexible, supple; wavering, unsteady; slender; loose; vague; **ein —es Rohr im Winde,** a reed shaken by the wind (*B.*), a feeble vessel (*fig.*); **—es Seil,** slack rope. II. *m.* (—es, *pl.* **Schwän'ke**) prank, hoax; funny tale; farce; joke, jest; farcical comedy; **er steckt voller Schwänke,** he is full of fun; he knows a lot of funny stories. *Comp.* **—buch,** *n.* jest-book. **—macher,** *m.* jester. **—weise,** *adv.* in the form of a jest, as a joke.

Schwan'k—en, I. *v.n.* (*aux.* **h.**) to move to and fro, rock, shake; to roll, toss (*as a ship*); to toddle; to totter, to tremble; to oscillate; to wave, undulate; to be irresolute, vacillate, hesitate; to falter; to fluctuate; **die Preise —en,** the market fluctuates. II. *subst. n.* rocking; staggering; pitching, undulation; fluctuation; oscillation; nutation (*Astr.*); vacillation; perturbation; inconstancy. **—end,** *p. & adj.* tottering; unsteady; fluctuating (*of prices*); uncertain; unprincipled; precarious; vague; doubtful (*of quantity, Pros.*). **—ung,** *f.* variation (*of the barometer*); *see* **—en** II.

Schwanz, *m.* (—es, *pl.* **Schwän'ze**) tail; end; train, trail; retinue; tail (*of comets; of notes*); shank (*of screws*); penis (*sl.*); **— der Blocklafette,** block-trail; **den — eines Pferdes stutzen,** to dock a horse; **den — zwischen die Beine nehmen,** to take to one's heels; to sneak away; **einem den — streichen,** to flatter a p.; **Geld auf den — klopfen,** to cheat. *Comp.* **—blech,** *n.* trail-plate (*Artil.*). **—feder,** *f.* tail-feather. **—flosse,** *f.* caudal fin. **—meise,** *f.* long-tailed titmouse. **—riegel,** *m.* trail-transom (*Artil.*). **—riegel=blech,** *n.* transom-plate, trail-plate (*Artil.*). **—riemen,** *m.* crupper. **—schraube,** *f.* breech-pin (*of a gun*). **—spitze,** *f.* tip of the tail. **—stück,** *n.* tail-piece (*of a fish*); rump (*of beef*); trail (*Artil.*); breech (*of an air-gun*).

Schwän'z—chen, *n.* (—chens, *pl.* —chen) *dim. of* **Schwanz.** **—eln,** *v.n.* (*aux.* **h.**) to wag the tail, fawn on; to wheedle, flatter; to strut; to wriggle in walking, waddle. *Comp.* **—el=pfennig,** *m.*; **—elpfennige machen,** to pocket a part when marketing for one's master, to make a market-penny (*coll.*).

Schwän'zen, *v.* I. *a.* to provide with a tail; **die Schule —,** to play the truant; **die Kirche (eine Stunde) —,** to shirk church (a lesson); **eine Vorlesung —,** to cut a lecture; **geschwänzt,** with a tail, tailed. II. *n.* (*aux.* **h.**) to idle about.

Schwapp! Schwapps! *int.* slap! smack! dash! whack!

Schwap'pen, *v.n.* (*aux.* **h.**) (*colloq.*) to spill, spirt out; to burst (out); **—d voll,** full to overflowing.

Schwär, *m.* (—es, *pl.* —e), **—e,** *f.* (*pl.* —en) abscess, ulcer; **einem den — aufstechen,** to tell s. o. an unpleasant truth, to touch a sore point (*coll.*).

Schwä'r—en, I. *ir.v.n.* (*aux.* **h.** & **s.**) to suppurate, fester. II. *subst. n.* ulceration, formation of an abscess. **—ig,** *adj.* covered with sores *or* ulcers.

[1]**Schwarm,** *m.* (—es, *pl.* **Schwär'me**) swarm; troop, herd; flight, flock; host, crowd. *Comp.* **—hüter,** *m.* hiver of bees. **—weise,** *adv.* in swarms.

[2]**Schwarm,** *m.* (—es) object of enthusiasm *or* adoration, idol, hero, pet (*coll.*).

Schwär'm—en, *v.n.* (*aux.* **h.** & **s.**) to swarm; to fly about; to ramble, rove, wander; to riot, revel, carouse; to catch the wrong scent; to sprawl, skirmish (*Mil.*); to dream, muse; to rave, be enthusiastic (**für,** about); **es —t von Menschen auf der Straße,** the streets are thronged with people; **alles —t für sie,** everybody is mad about her, in raptures about her; **ich —e nicht sehr für ihn,** I do not admire him much, I do not much care for him. II. *subst. n.* swarming; roving; rioting; state of exaltation, enthusiasm. **—er,** *m.* (—ers, *pl.* —er), **—erin,** *f.* enthusiast, dreamer, visionary, fanatic; flirt; noisy reveller; rake; hound liable to lose the scent; sphinx (*Ent.*); cracker, serpent, squib (*Firew.*). **—erei',** *f.* roving about; enthusiasm; fanaticism; ecstasy; reverie, wild imaginings; wild devotion to; riotous living. **—erisch,** *adj. & a v.* enthusiastic; fanciful, visionary, wild; fanatical. *Comp.* **—attacke,** *f.* sprawling charge (*Mil.*). **—er=eifer,** *m.* fanaticism. **—er=kasten,** *m.* squib-case. **—er=rakete,** *f.* rocket discharging serpents. **—geist,** *m.* fanatical turn of mind; roving spirit; rake; fanatic. **—punkt,** *m.* object of enthusiasm, idol, hero, pet (*coll.*). **—zeit,** *f.* swarming time of bees.

Schwar't—e, *f.* (*pl.* —en) thick, hard skin; rind, skin, bark, slab, outside plank; sward; clay in sheets (*Pottery*); crust (*on earthenware*); **eine alte —e,** an old book bound in pigskin; an old daub; **daß die —e knackt,** vigorously (*coll.*). **—ig,** *adj.* thick-skinned. *Comp.* **—en=hals,** *m.* tramp, beggar (*obs.*). **—en=magen,** *m.* collared pork (head), sowmaw hamkin.

Schwarz, I. *adj. & adv.* (**schwär'zer, schwär'zest**) black; dark; gloomy; tanned; **—e Blattern,** malignant smallpox; **der —e Tod,** Black Death, the Plague; **das —e Gerüst,** scaffold; **—e Wäsche,** dirty linen; **—er Sonntag,** Judica; **—es Brett,** blackboard; **—es Brot,** brown *or* black bread; **—es Register,** police register; **die Kirche war — behängt,** the church was hung with black; **— machen,** to blacken; **bei einem — angeschrieben sein,** to be in a p.'s bad books. II. *n. indec.* black, black colour, blackness; **etwas — auf weiß haben,** to have a thing in black and white; **in —,** in black, in mourning. **—e,** I. *m.* (—en, *pl.* —en) negro;

the devil; **die —en**, the Ultramontane Roman Catholic clergy; fanatical bigots; **eine kleine —e**, a small cup of black coffee. II. *n.* black mark *or* spot; pupil (*of the eye*); bull's eye (*of a target*). *Comp.* **—amsel**, *f.* blackbird. **—bäcker**, *m.* baker of brown *or* black bread. **—blau**, *adj.* very dark blue; livid. **—blech**, *n.* sheet-iron. **—blei**, *n.* black-lead. **—blütig**, *adj.* melancholic. **—brot**, *n.* brown bread. **—druck**, *m.* impression in black (*Eng.*). **—elf**, *n.* malignant hobgoblin. **—färber**, *m.* dyer in black. **—fuchs**, *m.* dark bay horse with black points. **—gallig**, *adj.* melancholic, bilious. **—gar**, *adj.* tanned. **—gelb**, *adj.* dark, tawny yellow, black and yellow (*colours of the Austrian Empire*). **—holz**, *n.* pines. **—kunst**, *f.* black art, necromancy; mezzotinto (*Eng.*). **—künstler**, *m.* necromancer, magician. **—rock**, *m.* black-coat; parson, priest. **—rot**, *adj.* reddish-black, dark-red. **—rot=gold(en)**, *adj.* black, red and gold (*German colours before 1866, notably in 1848*). **—schimmel**, *m.* iron-gray horse. **—seher**, *m.* one who looks at the dark side of everything, pessimist. **—seherei'**, *f.* pessimism. **—stift**, *m.* black crayon. **—tanne**, *f.* Scotch fir. **—wald**, *m.* pine-wood; Black Forest. **—weiß**, *adj.* black and white, pepper and salt. **—weiß=rot**, *adj.* black, white and red (*the colours of the German Empire since 1871*). **—wild**, *n.* black game, wild boars.

Schwär'ze, *f.* (*pl.* —n) blackness; black stain; swarthiness; blacking; black; printer's ink; disease of the hop; Indian ink; atrocity, heinousness.

Schwär'z—en, *v.* I. *a.* to blacken, make black; to blacklead; to ink; to sully, defame; to darken; to smuggle. II. *r.* & *n.* (*aux.* **h.**) to grow black; to lower. **—er**, *m.* (—ers, *pl.* —er) smuggler; blackener. **—lich**, *adj.* blackish, darkish; tawny; **ins —liche spielen** *or* **fallen**, to incline to black, to be very dark.

Schwat'z—en, *v.a.* & *n.* (*aux.* **h.**) to chatter, babble, prate; to tattle; **ins Blaue hinein —en**, to talk at random, foolishly. **—haft**, *see* **Plauderhaft**. *Comp.* **—maul**, *n.* chatterbox; gossip. **—sucht**, *f.* love of gossip (*coll.*).

Schwät'ze—n, *see* **Schwatzen**. **—r**, *m.* (—rs, *pl.* —er), **—rin**, *f.* babbler, thoughtless talker; gossip.

Schwe'be, *f.*; **in der —sein**, to hang suspended, to be in suspense *or* undecided, in abeyance.

Schwe'b—en, *v.n.* (*aux.* **h.**) to soar; to hover, float in the air; to be poised *or* suspended, hang, swing; to be suspended (*Chem.*); to be pending; to be in suspense; **in Gefahr —en**, to be in danger; **auf der Zunge —en**, to be on the tip of one's tongue; **sein Bild —t mir immer vor Augen**, his image is always before my eyes, always before me; **zwischen Leben und Tod —en**, to hover between life and death; **das Luftschiff schwebte über der Stadt**, the balloon was hovering above the town; **das Mädchen —t über den Rasen**, the girl glides across the sward; **der Geist Gottes —te über dem Wasser**, the spirit of God moved upon the face of the waters (*B.*); **—ende Betonung**, hovering stress, level stress (*Prosod.*); **—ende Brücke**, suspension bridge; **—ende Frage**, pending question; **—ende Gärten**, hanging gardens; **—ende Pein**, agony of suspense (*poet.*); **—ende Schuld**, floating debt; **—ende Unterhandlungen**, pending negotiations; **—ender Schritt**, light, elastic step. **—ung**, *f.* tremor, tremolo-stop (*Org.*); **um eine —ung hinaufgehen**, to rise one fraction, point, a very little. *Comp.* **—e=bahn**, *f.* (electric) suspension railway. **—e=baum**, *m.* horizontal bar. **—e=künstler**, *m.* equilibrist. **—e=schritt**, *m.* balance-step (*Mil.*); balance, setting to one's partner (*Danc.*). **—e=stange**, *f.* rope-dancer's pole.

Schwe'fel, *m.* (—s) sulphur, brimstone; **plastischer —**, amorphous sulphur. **—bar**, *adj.* sulphurable. **—icht**, (**Schwef'licht**,) (*obs.*) **—ig**, (**Schwef'lig**,) *adj.* sulphurous; **schwefliges Salz**, sulphite. *Comp.* **—abdruck**, *m.* impression in sulphur. **—äther**, *m.* sulphuric ether. **—bad**, *n.* sulphur-bath; sulphurous springs. **—bande**, *f.* band of incendiaries; rascals (*coll.*). **—blei**, *n.* sulphuret of lead; lead sulphide. **—blumen**, *pl.* flowers of sulphur. **—faden**, *m.* thread dipped in sulphur, sulphurated match. **—farbe**, *f.* brimstone colour. **—gang**, *m.* vein, lode of sulphur. **—holz**, **—hölzchen**, *n.* lucifer match. **—kies**, *m.* pyrites. **—kohlenstoff**, *m.* carbon disulphide. **—leber**, *f.* sulphuret of potash. **—sauer**, *adj.*; **—saures Salz**, sulphate. **—säure**, *f.* sulphuric acid. **—sauer=kalk**, *m.* calcium sulphate. **—wasserstoff**, *m.* sulphide of hydrogen. **—zinn**, *n.* protosulphide of tin. **—zink**, *n.* zinc-sulphide.

Schwe'fel—n, *v.a.* to impregnate with sulphur, sulphurate; to smoke with sulphur; to bleach with sulphur; **den Kautschuk —n**, to vulcanize india-rubber; **geschwefelt**, sulphuretted. **—ung**, *f.* sulphuration.

Schweif, *m.* (—es, *pl.* —e) tail; train (*of dresses*); trail. *Comp.* **—haare**, *pl.* tail-hairs. **—huhn**, *n.* lyre-bird. **—riemen**, *m.* crupper. **—säge**, *f.* fret saw, compass saw. **—stern**, *m.* comet. **—träger**, *m.* train-bearer. **—wedeln**, I. *v.a.* to wag the tail; to fawn. II. *subst. n.* fawning.

Schwei'f—en, *v.* I. *n.* (*aux.* **h.** & **s.**) to roam about, rove, ramble, stray; **abwärts —en**, to stray away, wander (*of thoughts*) (*poet.*). II. *a.* to provide with a tail; to curve, cut into an arch; to chamfer; to fan, winnow; to warp; **schön geschweift**, with a handsome tail. **—ung**, *f.* curve, rounding; slant; bow; swell.

Schwei'g—en, I. *ir.v.n.* (*aux.* **h.**) to be silent, keep silence; to be quiet; to pause, to cease (*to speak*); **er mußte dazu —en**, he had to let it pass without saying a word, he could make no reply to it; **die Musik schwieg**, the music ceased; **—e!** hush! be quiet! silence! **auf eine Frage —en**, not to answer a question; **um zu —en von . . .**, not to speak of . . .; **—en Sie mir davon**, don't speak to me about it; **—end zuhören**, to listen in silence; **—en heißen**, to bid (a p.) be silent. II. *subst.n.* silence; **zum —en bringen**, to silence, to reduce to silence; **—en gebieten**, to order *or* impose silence. **—er**, *m.* (—ers, *pl.* —er) taciturn person; **der große —er**, *i.e.*, Count Helmuth v. Moltke (*coll.*). **—sam**, *adj.* taciturn; secretive; reserved; **Wilhelm der —same**, William the Silent. **—samkeit**, *f.* taciturnity. *Comp.* **—e=geld**, *n.* hush-money.

Schwein, *n.* (—s, *pl.* —e) hog, pig; blot; good luck (*sl.*); (*pl.*) swine; **das — grunzt**, the pig grunts; **enormes —**, **kolossales —**, ripping good luck (*sl.*); **— haben**, to be a lucky person, to fall on one's feet, to strike oil (*fam.*); **wildes —**, wild boar. **—chen**, *n.* (—chens, *pl.* —chen) little pig; **das —chen quiekt**, the little pig squeaks. **—erei'**, *f.* filthiness, piggishness; obscenity. **—isch**, *adj.* swinish. *Comp.* **—e=beschauer**, *m.* pig-sticker, butcher. **—e=braten**, *m.* roast pork. **—e=fett**, *n.* hog's lard; pork fat. **—e=fleisch**, *n.* pork. **—e=hirt**, *m.* swineherd. **—e=hund**, *m.* swineherd's dog; filthy fellow (*vulg.*). **—e=mast**, *f.* mast for swine. **—e=pökelfleisch**, *n.* salt pork. **—e=schmer**, *n.* hog's lard. **—e=stall**, *m.* pig-sty. **—e=treiber**, *m.* swineherd. **—e=trüffel**, *f.* hart's truffle. **—e=zucht**, *f.* pig-breeding; **es ist eine wahre —ezucht**, it is a regular scandal (*vulg.*). **—e=**

zungen=beschauer, *m.* examiner of pigs' tongues (*for signs of disease*). —hirt, *m.* swineherd. —hund, *m. see* —e=hund. —igel, *m.* hedgehog; dirty wretch; obscene talker. —igelei', *f.* beastliness, filthiness. —igeln, *v.n.* (*aux.* h.) to behave in a beastly way; to make smutty jokes. —s=borste, *f.* hog's bristle. —s=feder, *f.* boar-spear; spear (*Fort.*); (*pl.*) iron spikes (*on walls, etc.*). —s=hatz, —s=jagd, *f.* wild boar hunt. —s=keule, *f.* leg of pork. —s=kopf, *m.* hog's (*or* boar's) head. —s=rippchen, *pl.* pork-chops; spare-ribs. —s=rippe, *f.* spare-rib. —s=rüssel, *m.* pig's snout. —s=wurst, *f.* pork-sausage.

Schweiß, *m.* (—es, *pl.* —e) sweat, perspiration; moisture; exudation; blood (*Sport.*); ohn' — kein Preis, no gains without pains, no rose without a thorn (*prov.*); englischer —, sweating sickness; in — kommen, to get into a perspiration; das ist mein saurer —, that is the fruit of my hard toil. —bar, *adj.* that may be welded. —ig, *adj.* perspiring, moist; bloody (*Sport.*). *Comp.* —arbeit, *f.* welding. —ausbruch, *m.* bursting out of perspiration. —bad, *n.* vapour *or* Turkish bath. —blätter, *pl.* dress-preservers *or* shields. —drüse, *f.* perspiration gland. —fieber, *n.* sweating-fever. —fuchs, *m.* light-bay horse. —grube, *f.* pore (*of the skin*). —hitze, *f.* smelting heat. —hund, *m.* blood-hound. —loch, *n.* pore. —naht, *f.* seam where two iron bars are welded together. —pulver, *n.* flux. —treibend, *adj.* sudorific, diaphoretic. —tropfen, *m.* bead of perspiration. —tuch, *n.* handkerchief; sweating-cloth; winding-sheet; das —tuch Christi, the holy handkerchief, veronica, sudary. —tüchlein, *n.* handkerchief; napkin (*B.*).

Schwei'ß—en, *v.* I. *n.* (*aux.* h. & s.) to bleed (*Sport.*); to sweat; to begin to melt (*of iron, etc.*). II. *a.* to weld. —er, *m.* (—ers, *pl.* —er) welder. —ung, *f.* welding.

Schwei'zer, *m.* (—s, *pl.* —) doorkeeper, porter; Switzer; *see Index of Names.* —ei', *f.* Swiss dairy. *Comp.* —flöte, *f.* Swiss pipe *or* flute; flageolet-stop (*Org.*). —häuschen, *n.* Swiss cottage, châlet. —käse, *m.* Gruyère cheese. —krankheit, *f.* homesickness.

Schwe'l—en, *v.* I. *n.* (*aux.* h.) to smoulder, to burn without flame. II. *a.* to burn slowly; Teer —en, to extract *or* distil tar. *Comp.* —holz, *n.* resinous wood.

Schwel'g—en, *v.n.* (*aux.* h.) to feast, carouse, riot, revel; to gormandize; to run riot; in einer S. —en, to be intoxicated with, to revel in, delight in a th.; im Überfluß —en, to live on the fat of the land (*coll.*). —er, *m.* (—ers, *pl.* —er) person leading a life of luxury and enjoyment, reveller; glutton. —erei', *f.* life of pleasure and luxury, feasting; revelry; debauchery. —erisch, *adj. & adv.* voluptuous; gluttonous.

Schwel'le, *f.* (*pl.* —n) threshold; sill; sleeper (*Railw.*); architrave; ground-joist.

[1]**Schwel'l—en**, *ir.v.n.* (*aux.* s.) to swell, rise; to heave; to swell (*Mus.*), to increase. —ung, *f.* swelling, increase; tumefaction. *Comp.* —farbe, *f.* tanner's ooze. —holz, *n.* sill. —ton, *m.* crescendo.

[2]**Schwel'len**, *v.a.* to swell; to distend, to bloat.

Schwem'me, *f.* (*pl.* —en) horse-pond; watering-place (*cattle*); ein Pferd in die — reiten, to ride a horse to water; Vieh in die — treiben, to water cattle.

Schwem'm—en, *v.a.* to float (*wood, etc.*); to set afloat; to wash up, down *or* away, deposit; to water (*cattle, etc.*). *Comp.* —gebilde, *n.* alluvium. —klöße, *pl.* light dumplings. —land, *n.* alluvial land. —system, *n.* flushing-system. —teich, *m.* horsepond. —wiese, *f.* irrigation-meadow.

Schwen'gel, *m.* (—s, *pl* —) clapper (*of a bell*); handle (*of a pump*); swingle (*of a flail*); pendulum (*of a clock*); swingle-tree, swing-bar (*of a waggon*); plier (*of a drawbridge*); crank (*of a wheel*); bar, lever (*of a press, etc.*). *Comp.* —brücke, *f.* drawbridge with draw-beams, swing-bridge. —brunnen, *m.* well with a bucket-swipe. —kunst, *f.*, —werk, *n.* pump-work.

Schwen'k—en, *v.* I. *a.* to swing, shake about, wave to and fro; to flourish, brandish; to wave (*one's hat, etc.*); to toss, shake (*Cook.*); (klar) —en, to rinse (*a glass, etc.*). II. *r. & n.* (*aux.* h.) to turn, wheel about; to wheel (*Mil.*); to change one's mind. —ung, *f.* swinging, whirling; waving, brandishing; rinsing; change of front, turning about; change of mind; evolution; eine —ung machen, to wheel (to the right *or* left); to change one's mind. *Comp.* —becken, *n.* washing-up basin. —ungs=punkt, *m.* pivot.

Schwer, *adj. & adv.* heavy, weighty; ponderous; stout, strong; difficult, hard; grievous, serious; severe; oppressive; grave (*of crimes, etc.*); heavy, dull; strong (*of cigars*); —es Geschütz, heavy guns, siege-artillery; —er Wein, strong, full-bodied wine; —e Speisen, heavy food; —e Angst, great anxiety; confound it (you, *etc.*)! (*as curse*); —e Arbeit, difficult (piece of) work; —e Artillerie, heavy ordnance; —er Atem, shortness of breath; —es Geld, specie; —es Geld kosten, to cost much money; er hat ein —es Gehör, he is hard of hearing; —e That, heavy deed, evil deed, crime (*Poet.*); es wird — halten, daß ich komme, it will be difficult for me to come; er ist — verwundet, he is severely wounded; er ist — beschädigt, he is severely hurt; he is tipsy (*sl.*); sie hat eine —e Zunge, she has an impediment in her speech; —en Herzens, low-spirited, with a heavy heart; —e See, heavy *or* rough sea; — büßen, to pay dearly for; —e Not, epilepsy; hang it! botheration! (*sl.*); das wird ihm — eingehen, he will scarcely be able to understand that, he will not easily be reconciled to that; zu — gehen, to work hard, have too little play; — darnieder liegen, to be dangerously ill; es liegt mir — in den Gliedern, my limbs feel heavy, benumbed, stiff; es fällt mir —, I find it very hard; es kommt ihn — an, he finds it hard; zwei Pfund —, weighing 2 pounds *or* 2 pounds weight. —e, *f.* (*pl.* —en) burdensomeness, weight; gravity (*Phys.*); difficulty; heaviness; body (*of wine*); weight, full meaning (*of a word*). —lich, *adv.* hardly, scarcely. *Comp.* —atmig, *adj.* asthmatic. —blütig, *adj.* melancholic. —e=messer, *m.* hydrometer; aerometer, barometer. —e=mittelpunkt, *m.* centre of gravity. —e=nöter, *m.* rogue, young scamp; liebenswürdiger —enöter, ladies' man. —erde, *f.* baryta. —erworben, *adj.* hard-earned. —fällig, *adj.* heavy, ponderous; slow, sluggish; clumsy, awkward; unwieldy; dull. —fälligkeit, *f.* heaviness, clumsiness, *etc.* —flüssig, *adj.* difficult to fuse, refractory; reserved (*fig.*). —gläubig, *adj.* incredulous. —herzig, *adj.* depressed. —hörig, *adj.* hard of hearing, a little deaf. —kraft, *f.* gravitation, (force of) gravity. —leibig, *adj.* corpulent. —mut, *f.* melancholy, sadness, depression. —mütig, *adj.* dejected, sad. —punkt, *m.* centre of gravity. —spat, *m.* sulphate of baryta, heavy spar. —verdaulich, *adj.* indigestible. —verdientes Geld, *n.* hard-earned money. —verständlich, *adj.* difficult to understand; abstruse.

Schwert, *n.* (—es, *pl.* —er) sword; feuriges —, flaming sword; zum —e greifen, to draw one's sword; zum —e verurteilen, to condemn to be beheaded. —el, *m.* (—els, *pl.* —el) sword lily, gladiolus (*Bot.*). *Comp.* —bohne, *f.* French bean. —bruder, *m.* Knight of the Order of the Sword. —el=gras, *n.* sword-grass. —er=tanz, *m.* sword-dance. —feger, *m.* (sword-furbisher, *hence:*) sword-cutler, blade-smith. —feger=arbeit, *f.* sword-cutlery. —fisch, *m.* swordfish, grampus. —förmig, *adj.* sword-shaped. —hieb, *m.* sword-cut. —lehen, *n.* fief passing on the spear-side. —lilie, *f.* iris. —magen, *pl.* agnati. —schlag, —streich, *m.* stroke with the sword; ohne —streich, without striking a blow.

Schwes'ter, *f.* (*pl.* —n) sister; sister (*of charity, etc.*); trained nurse; leibliche —, full sister; barmherzige —, sister of mercy, hospital nurse; Kloster—, nun. —chen, *n.* (—chens, *pl.* —chen) (dear) little sister. —lich, *adj. & adv.* sisterly; sororal; meine —liche Liebe, my loving *or* dear sister (*hum.*). —lichkeit, *f.* sisterly conduct, feeling, *etc.* —schaft, *f.* sisterhood; female friendship. *Comp.* —kind, *n.* sister's child, nephew *or* niece. —liebe, *f.* sisterly love. —mann, *m.* brother-in-law. —(n)=paar, *n.* two sisters. —sohn, *m.* nephew. —sprache, *f.* sister language. —tochter, *f.* niece. —(n)=zunft, *f.* band of sisters; sisterhood; the Muses.

Schwib'bogen, *m.* arch(way); pier-arch.

Schwich'ten, *v.a.* to snake, wind one rope round another (*Naut.*).

Schwieg, Schwie'ge, *1 & 3 pers. sing. imperf. ind. & subj. of* schweigen.

Schwie'ger, *f.* (*pl.* —n) mother-in-law (*obs. & poet.*). —in, *f.* (*obs.*) *see* Schwägerin; *see* —mutter, —tochter. *Comp.* —eltern, *pl.* parents-in-law. —kind, *n.* son- *or* daughter-in-law. —mutter, *f.* mother-in-law. —sohn, *m.* son-in-law. —tochter, *f.* daughter-in-law. —vater, *m.* father-in-law.

Schwie'l—e, *f.* (*pl.* —en) callosity; weal, mark, stripe. —ig, *adj.* callous; marked with weals.

Schwie'm—el, *m.* (—els) giddiness; *see* —eler. —eler, —ler, *m.* (—(e)lers, *pl.* —(e)ler) rake, tippler, disorderly fellow. —elig, —lig, *adj.* dissolute. —eln, *v.n.* (*aux.* h. & s.) to reel; to lead a disorderly life.

Schwie'rig, *adj. & adv.* ulcerous (*obs.*); in fermentation, rebellious; discontented, refractory (*obs. & poet.*); fastidious, nice, tough (*fam.*); hard, difficult; eine —e Frage, a knotty question; —e Verhältnisse, trying circumstances; das —ste haben wir hinter uns, the worst is over; der Adel zeigte sich —, the nobles were refractory (*obs.*). —keit, *f.* difficulty; das macht gar keine —keit, there is no difficulty about that; —keiten machen, suchen, to raise difficulties, start objections.

Schwiert, *3 pers. sing. pres. ind. of* schwären (*obs.*).

Schwill; Schwillst, Schwillt, *imperat. sing.; 2 & 3 pers. sing. pres. ind. of* schwellen.

Schwimm'bar, *adj.* navigable for rafts, *etc.*

Schwim'm—en, *ir.v.n.* (*aux.* h. & s.) to swin; to float (*of wood, dead bodies, etc.*); to float (*about*); davon —en, to swim away, escape by swimming; das Brett ist ans Ufer geschwommen, the plank has drifted ashore; im Blute (in Thränen) —en, to be bathed in blood (in tears) mit dem Strom —en, to go *or* swim with the current; —ende Batterie, floating battery; —endes Gut, flotsam; —ende Häuser, ships; —ende Tische, floating tables (*in certain baths*). —er, *m.* (—ers, *pl.* —er) swimmer; float (*Mach.*). *Comp.* —anstalt, *f.* swimming-school. —bad, *n.* swimming bath; swim. —blase, *f.* air-bladder, swimming-bladder. —fähig, *adj.* able to swim, made for swimming. —feder, —flosse, *f.* fin. —fuß, *m.* webbed *or* palmated foot. —gürtel, *m.* life-belt, swimming-belt. —haut, *f.* web. —häutler, *pl.* web-footed animals, palmipeds. —hosen, *pl.* bathing-drawers. —jacke, *f.* swimming *or* cork jacket. —kleid, *n.* bathing costume. —kraft, *f.* buoyancy. —kunst, *f.* art of swimming. —lehrer, *m.* swimming master. —niveau, *n.* float. —platz, *m.* place for swimming, bathing sheds. —stoß, *m.* stroke. —stunde, *f.* swimming lesson. —vögel, *pl.* web-footed birds, palmipeds.

Schwin'de, *f.* (*pl.* —n) tetter; nettle-rash.

Schwin'd—el, *m.* (—els, *pl.* —el) giddiness, vertigo; extravagant project; charlatanism; swindling; fraud, cheat, humbug; den —el kenn' ich, I know that trick, I am up to that (*coll.*); der ganze —el, the whole lot *or* concern (*vulg.*); den —el bekommen, to turn giddy. —elei', *f.* extravagant, foolish project, swindling; cheat. —elhaft, —elicht (*obs.*), —(e)lig, *adj.* dizzy; causing giddiness; wild, extravagant; fraudulent, cheating.

Schwin'd—eln, *v.n.* (*aux.* h. *dat.*) & *imp.* to be giddy; to swindle, cheat; (ich —le), mir —elt, my head swims, my brain is reeling, I am giddy; er ist so mit Geschäften überhäuft, daß ihm davon —elt, he has so much to do that his head is almost turned; —elnde Höhe, dizzy height. —ler, *m.* (—lers, *pl.* —ler) swindler, extravagant projector; charlatan. —lerhaft, —lerisch, *adj.* fraudulent, cheating. *Comp.* —el=bank, *f.* swindling bank. —el=erregend, *adj.* dizzy, causing giddiness. —el=fieber, *n.* fever with vertigo. —el=firma, *f.* long firm (*Comm.*). —el=kopf, *m.* hare-brained *or* giddy-minded person. —el=köpfig, *adj.* hare-brained; humbugging. —el=sucht, *f.* vertigo; folly. —ler=bande, *f.* gang of swindlers.

Schwin'd—en, I. *ir.v.n.* (*aux.* s.) to become less, shrink, dwindle; to waste away; to vanish, disappear; to die away, decay; —en lassen, to abandon, give up, renounce; die Geschwulst —et, the swelling is going down; sein Mut —et mehr und mehr, his courage is dwindling away. II. *subst. n.* shrinkage (*of metals*); drying up. *Comp.* —grube, *f.* sink, drain. —sucht, *f.* consumption, phthisis. —süchtig, *adj.* consumptive. —suchts=kandidat, *m.* person with a tendency to consumption, consumptive person.

Schwin'ge, *f.* (*pl.* —n) swing; wing, pinion (*Poet.*); swingle (*for flax*); winnow, fan. —l, *m.* (—ls, *pl.* —l) swing (*Gymn.*); fescue-grass (*Bot.*).

Schwin'g—en, *ir.v.* I. *a.* to swing, whirl round; to brandish, wield, wave; to shake; to swing; to swingle, beat, break; to winnow, screen; to scutch; das Tanzbein —en, to dance, to go to a ball (*coll.*). II. *r.* to swing o.s., to spring, bound, vault, leap; to soar, rise; to ascend; sich hinten auf —en, to leap up behind; sich in den Sattel —en, to vault *or* jump into the saddle; sich auf den Thron —en, to raise oneself to the throne. III. *n.* (*aux.* h.) to swing; to oscillate, vibrate. —ung, *f.* swinging; oscillation; vibration; die Längsschwingung (Querschwingung) longitudinal (*transverse*) vibration. *Comp.* (*see also* Schwung—) —brett, *n.* swingle-board (*for flax*). —hang, *m.* suspension (*Gymn.*). —kolben, *m.* balancer, poiser (*Ent.*). —kraft, *f.* oscillating force. —seil, *n.* slack-rope, swing. —stock, *m.* flail, swingle. —ungs=bogen, *m.* arc of oscillation. —ungs=dauer, —ungs=zeit, *f.* time of oscillation. —ungs=fähig, *adj.* capable of vibrating *or* oscillating. —ungs=linie, *f.*, —ungs=raum, *m.* swing. —wanne, *f.* winnowing fan. —zeug, *n.* trapeze, swing (*Gymn.*).

Schwipp, I. *int.*; —, schwapp! flip, flop! II. *adj.* nimble, agile; pliant, flexible. —e, *f.* (*pl.* —en) lash (*of a whip*); switch; whipcord. —s, I. *int.* smack! slap! II. *m.* (—(s)es, *pl.* —(s)e) cut with a whip, lash; einen —s haben, to be half seas over (*coll.*).

Schwip'pen, *v.* I. *a.* to jerk, throw II. *n.*

(*aux.* h. & s.) to swing; to overflow, spill over; to jerk *or* jump about.

Schwir'ren, *v.n.* (*aux.* h. & s.) & *imp.* to whiz, whir; to whistle; to clang, grate, jar; to chirp; to buzz, hum; **herum —**, to flit about, fly hither and thither; **es schwirrt mir um die Ohren** (**vor den Augen**), I have a buzzing in my ears (a mist before my eyes); **das — der Kugeln**, the whizzing of the bullets.

Schwit'ze, *f.* sweating; **in die — bringen**, to pile up (*skins*, *Tann.*).

Schwit'zen, *v.* I. *n.* (*aux.* h.) to sweat, perspire; to toil; (*aux.* s.) to exude. II. *a.* to (*cause to*) sweat; **die Häute —**, to sweat the hides.

Schwö'de—n, *v.a.* to dress (*skins*) with lime-water. *Comp.* **—faß**, *n.*, **—grube**, *f.* lime-pit.

Schwoll, Schwöl'le, *1 & 3 pers. sing. imperf. ind. & subj. of* **schwellen.**

[1]**Schwor, Schwö're**, *1 & 3 pers. sing. imperf. ind. & subj. of* **schwären.**

[2]**Schwor, Schwö're**, *1 & 3 pers. sing. imperf. ind. & subj. of* **schwören.**

Schwö'r—en, *ir.v.a. & n.* (*aux.* h.) to swear; to take an oath; **vor Gericht —en**, to take the oath; **einen —en lassen**, to administer an oath to s.o.; **zur Fahne —en**, to take the military oath; **einem Rache —en**, to vow vengeance against a p.; **Huld und Treue —en**, to take the oath of allegiance; **ich könnte fast darauf —en**, I could almost swear to it; **zum Katholizismus —en**, to embrace Catholicism.

Schwül, *adj.* sultry, close; *see* **Schwul**; **mir wird — zu Mute, — ums Herz**, I feel very uneasy. **—e**, *f.* sultriness, closeness; oppression.

Schwul, *adj.* fearful, anxious (*coll.*). **—ibus**, *pl.*; **in —ibus**, in a scrape (*sl.*). **—itä't**, *f.* trouble, anxiety (*sl.*).

Schwulst, I. *f.* (*pl.* **Schwül'ste**) swelling; tumour (*obs.*). II. *m.* (**—es**) pompousness; **— im Stil**, high-flown style, bombast.

Schwül'stig, *adj.* swollen; bombastic, high-flown; **das —e**, bathos. **—keit**, *f.* bombastic style, pomposity.

Schwund, *m.* (**—es**) dying, withering away; disappearance, falling off (*of hair*); dropping (*of a vowel, etc.*); atrophy (*Med.*).

Schwung, *m.* (**—es**, *pl.* **Schwün'ge**) swing; oscillation, bound, spring, vault; play (*of imagination, etc.*); flight (*of fancy*); buoyancy (*of mind*); energy, impetus; emphasis; elevation; animation, warmth, ardour; counter-jumper (*coll.*); **in — bringen**, to cause to swing *or* vibrate, to set going; **er giebt den Dingen einen gewissen —**, he gives a certain turn to things; **diese Verse haben hohen** *or* **edeln —**, there is a lofty *or* noble strain in these verses; **im —e sein**, to be swinging, to be in vogue, be in train *or* flourishing. **—haft**, *adj.* swinging; full of movement; spirited, emphatic; lofty, soaring; flourishing (*business*), brisk (*trade*); fashionable. *Comp.* **—bewegung**, *f.* vibrating motion. **—brett**, *n.* spring-board. **—feder**, *f.* pinion. **—gewicht**, *n.* pendulum. **—kraft**, *f.* buoyancy; centrifugal power. **—los**, *adj.* dull, commonplace. **—maschine**, *f.* whirling apparatus. **—rad**, *n.* fly-wheel; balance-wheel (*Horol.*). **—riemen**, *pl.* main-braces, check-traces (*of a carriage*). **—seil**, *n.* slack-rope. **—voll**, *adj.* lofty, sublime; stirring, full of fire, spirited, emphatic.

Schwün'ge, *obs. 1 & 3 pers. sing. imperf. subj. of* **schwingen.**

Schwupp, —dich, —s, *int. see* **Schwipps** I.

[1]**Schwur**, *m.* (**—s**, *pl.* **Schwü're**) swearing; oath; vow; curse; **einen feierlichen — leisten**, to take a solemn oath. *Comp.* **—brüchig, —vergessen**, *adj.* perjured. **—finger**, *pl.* the fingers raised in swearing. **—gericht**, *n.* jury; court of assizes. **—zeuge**, *m.* sworn witness.

[2]**Schwur** (*also* **Schwor**), **Schwü're**, *1 & 3 pers. sing. imperf. ind. & subj. of* **schwören.**

Scl, Sco, *see* **Sk.**

Sech, *n.* (**—s**, *pl.* **—e**) ploughshare, coulter.

Sechs, I. *num. adj.* six; **mit —(s)en fahren**, to drive a coach and six, to drive six in hand; **— und neunzig**, ninety-six; **halb —**, half past five; **drei viertel —**, a quarter to six. II. *f.* (*pl.* **—(s)en**), **—(s)e**, *f.* (*pl.* **—(s)en**) the number six; card, *etc.*, bearing six. **—(s)er**, *m.* (**—(s)ers**, *pl.* **—(s)er**) number six; coin of six pfennig (*half a groschen, obs. equiv. to a half-penny*); soldier of the 6th regiment. **—t**, *num. adj.* (**der, die, das —te**) the sixth; **der —te, am —ten**, on the 6th; **zum —ten**, sixthly. **—tel**, *n.* (**—tels**, *pl.* **—tel**) sixth part, sixth. **—tens**, *adv.* sixthly, in the sixth place. *Comp.* **—achtel-takt**, *m.* six-eight time (*Mus.*). **—blätterig**, *adj.* hexaphyllous; hexapetalous. **—eck**, *n.* hexagon. **—(s)erlei**, *indec. adj. & adv.* of six kinds; six-fold. **—fach, —fältig**, *adj.* six-fold. **—flach**, *n.*, **—flächner**, *m.* hexahedron. **—füßig**, *adj.* with six feet; **—füßiger daktylischer Vers**, hexameter. **—hebig**, *adj.* containing six accented syllables (*a verse*). **—jährig**, *adj.* six years old, of six years. **—lötig**, *adj.* three-ounce. **—malig**, *adj.* six times repeated. **—monatig**, *adj.* lasting six months. **—monatlich**, *adj.* of six months, semi-annual, half-yearly. **—pfünder**, *m.* six-pounder (*Artil.*). **—saitig**, *adj.* six-stringed. **—säulig**, *adj.* hexastyle. **—schaufler**, *m.* three-year-old sheep. **—seitig**, *adj.* six-sided, hexagonal. **—silbig**, *adj.* of six syllables. **—spännig**, *adj.* with six horses. **—stimmig**, *adj.* for six voices (*Mus.*). **—stündig**, *adj.* of six hours, lasting six hours. **—stündlich**, *adj.* every sixth hour. **—tägig**, *adj.* lasting six days. **—te-halb**, *indec. adj.* five and a half. **—tel-kreis**, *m.* sextant. **—viertel-takt**, *m.* six-four time (*Mus.*). **—wink(e)lig**, *adj.* six-angled. **—wöchnerin**, *f.* woman lying-in. **—zeilig**, *adj.* six-lined; **—zeiliges Gedicht**, sextain.

Sech'zehn, I. *num. adj.* sixteen. II. *f.* the number sixteen. **—er**, *m.* (**—ers**, *pl.* **—er**) one of sixteen, soldier of the sixteenth regiment. **—t**, (**der, die, das —te**) *num. adj.* sixteenth; **der —te März**, the sixteenth of March. **—tel**, *n.* **—tels**, *pl.* **—tel**) sixteenth ($\frac{1}{16}$); semi-quaver (*Mus.*). **—tens**, *adv.* (**zum —ten**) in the sixteenth place. *Comp.* **—fach, —falt, —fältig**, *adj.* sixteen times as much. **—jährig**, *adj.* sixteen years old. **—lötig**, *adj.* weighing eight ounces; pure, genuine (*fig.*). **—te-halb**, *indec. adj.* fifteen and a half. **—tel-format**, *n. see* **Sedez**. **—tel-pause**, *f.* semi-quaver rest (*Mus.*).

Sech'zig, I. *num. adj.* sixty. II. *f.* (*pl.* **—e**) the number sixty; **er ist hoch in den —en** (*or* **er ist ein vorgerückter —er**), he is well advanced in the sixties. **—er**, I. *m.* (**—ers**, *pl.* **—er**), **—erin**, *f.* sexagenarian; pique (*Cards*). II. *indec. adj.* sixty; **die —er Jahre**, the sixties. **—st**, (**der, die, das —ste**) *num. adj.* sixtieth; **über das —ste Jahr hinaus sein**, to be on the wrong side of sixty. **—stel**, *n.* (**—stels**, *pl.* **—stel**) sixtieth part. **—stens**, *adv.* in the sixtieth place.

[1]**Se'ckel**, *m.* (**—s**, *pl.* **—**) purse, pouch; pocket; treasury. *Comp.* **—amt**, *n.* exchequer. **—meister, —wart**, *m.* treasurer. **—schneider**, *m.* cut-purse.

[2]**Se'ckel**, *m.* (**—s**, *pl.* **—**) shekel.

Sede'z(—format), *n.* sixteens, 16mo (*Typ.*).

Sedime'nt, *n.* (**—s**, *pl.* **—e**) sediment, deposit, settlings. **—ä'r**, *adj.* sedimentary, result of deposit. *Comp.* **—gebirge**, *pl.* sedimentary rocks (*Geol.*).

See, I. *m.* (—**s**, *pl.* —(**e**)**n**) lake. II. *f.* (*pl.* —(**e**)**n**) sea; **größere —**, ocean; **an der —**, by the sea(-side); **an die — gehen**, to go to the sea-side; **zur —**, by sea; **zur — gehen**, to go to sea, to become a sailor; **zur — gehörig**, marine; **in — gehen** *or* **stechen**, to put to sea; **auf hoher —**, on the high seas; **Kapitän zur —**, captain in the navy; **die — ging hoch**, the sea ran high. *Comp.* —**assekuranz**, *f.* marine insurance. —**ausdruck**, *m.* nautical term. —**bad**, *n.* sea-bath. —**bär**, *m.* ursine seal; **alter —bär**, old sea dog, old tar. —**bataillon**, *n.* battalion of marines. —**behörde**, *f.*; **oberste —behörde**, the (Board of) Admiralty. —**beine**, *pl.* sea-legs; **ihm wachsen die —beine**, he has found his sea-legs (*coll.*). —**beschädigt**, *adj.* damaged by the sea. —**beschreibung**, *f.* hydrography. —**beute**, *f.* prize (*Naut.*). —**brassen**, *m.* sea bream. —**brief**, *m.* sailing orders; (*pl.*) ship's papers. —**buch**, *n.* log-book; register of outward and home-bound ships. —**dienst**, *m.* service in the navy *or* at sea. —**distel**, *f.* sea-holly. —**ente**, *f.* puffin. —**fahrend**, *adj.* navigating, seafaring. —**fahrer**, *m.* sailor; seafarer; navigator; **Heinrich der —fahrer**, Henry the Navigator. —**fahrer=kunst**, *f.* navigation. —**fahrt**, *f.* navigation; voyage. —**fahrzeug**, *n.* ship. —**fest**, *adj.* seaworthy; not subject to sea-sickness. —**fischerei**, *f.* maritime fishing. —**frachtbrief**, *m.* bill of lading. —**frachtwesen**, *n.* carrying-trade by sea. —**freibeuter**, *m.* pirate. —**gang**, *m.* (motion of the) sea; **es ist schwerer —gang**, there is a heavy sea running; **der —gang nimmt zu**, the sea is getting up. —**gefahr**, *f.* risk at sea. —**gefecht**, *n.* naval engagement, naval action *or* combat. —**gegend**, *f.* maritime country. —**gemälde**, *n.* sea-piece. —**gericht**, *n.* maritime *or* naval court of law; Court of Admiralty. —**gerichtsbarkeit**, *f.* naval jurisdiction. —**geschäfte**, *pl.* shipping business. —**gesetz**, *n.* maritime law. —**gesetzbuch**, *n.* naval code. —**gras**, *n.* sea-weed. —**hafen**, *m.* sea-port. —**handel**, *m.* maritime commerce; shipping trade. —**heer**, *n.* naval force. —**herrschaft**, *f.* naval supremacy. —**hund**, *m.* seal (*Icht.*); sea-dog. —**hunds=fang**, *m.* seal-hunting *or* -fishing; **Schiff für den —hundsfang**, sealing vessel. —**hunds=fell**, *n.* seal-skin. —**igel**, *m.* sea-urchin. —**journal**, *n.* log-book. —**jungfer**, *f.* mermaid; siren. —**kabel**, *n.* submarine cable. —**kadett**, *m.* midshipman, middy (*coll.*). —**kadetten=schule**, *f.* naval school *or* college. —**kalb**, *n.* sea-calf, seal. —**karte**, *f.* (marine) chart. —**karten=zeichner**, *m.* hydrographer. —**kennung**, *f.* sea-marks; intelligence of the soundings. —**klippe**, *f.* shoal, reef. —**kohl**, *m.* sea-kale. —**krank**, *adj.* sea-sick; **ich werde nicht leicht —krank**, I am a good sailor. —**krankheit**, *f.* sea-sickness, nausea; **leiden Sie an —krankheit?** are you a good sailor? are you subject to sea-sickness? —**krebs**, *m.* lobster; craw-fish. —**krieg**, *m.* naval war. —**kriegskunst**, *f.* naval tactics. —**kuh**, *f.* sea-cow, walrus. —**kunde**, *f.* nautical science. —**kunst**, *f.* navigation. —**küste**, *f.* sea-shore. —**lage**, *f.*; **glückliche —lage**, favourable position as regards the sea. —**leuchte**, *f.* ship's lantern. —**leuchten**, *n.* phosphorescence of the sea. —**leute**, *pl.* sailors, seamen, mariners. —**liste**, *f.* marine list; shipping list (*Comm.*). —**macht**, *f.* naval forces; naval power. —**mächtig**, *adj.* powerful at sea. —**magazin**, *n.* naval store *or* arsenal. —**mann**, *m.* seaman, mariner, sailor. —**männisch**, *adj.* sailor-like; seafaring, navigating. —**mannschaft**, *f.* ship's crew. —**manns=heim**, *n.* sailors' home. —**manns=kunst**, *f.* seamanship, navigation. —**manns=stil**, *m.* sailor's fashion *or* custom; **nach —mannsstil**, ship-shape. —**marke**, *f.* sea-mark, buoy. —**meile**, *f.* nautical mile (*1855 metres*). —**minister**, *m.* minister of naval affairs; First Lord of the Admiralty. —**möve**, *f.* seagull. —**nebel**, *m.* fog at sea. —**not**, *f.* distress at sea. —**offizier**, *m.* naval officer. —**pferd**, *n.* sea-horse; *see* **Flußpferd** *and* **Walroß**. —**pflanze**, *f.* marine plant. —**polyp**, *m.* octopus. —**postdienst**, *m.* mail-service. —**rabe**, *m.* cormorant. —**rat**, *m.* *see* —**gericht**. —**ratte**, —**ratze**, *f.* old salt, ancient mariner. —**räuber**, *m.* pirate. —**räuberei'**, *f.*, —**raub**, *m.* piracy. —**recht**, *n.* maritime law; rules of the sea *or* navigation. —**reise**, *f.* (sea) voyage. —**richter**, *m.* judge in a maritime court, Admiralty judge. —**rose**, *f.* white water-lily. —**rüstung**, *f.* naval armament. —**sache**, *f.* naval affair. —**schaden**, *m.* loss suffered at sea, average. —**schadenberechnung**, *f.* adjustment of averages. —**schiff**, *n.* sea-going vessel. —**schlacht**, *f.* naval engagement *or* battle. —**schlange**, *f.* sea-serpent; fictitious story (*fig.*). —**schule**, *f.* naval school; **englische —schule**, Lake School (*of poetry*). —**soldat**, *m.* marine. —**sprache**, *f.* nautical language. —**stadt**, *f.* sea-side town. —**station**, *f.* naval station. —**stern**, *m.* star-fish. —**strand**, *m.* strand, beach. —**strich**, *m.* track of the sea. —**stück**, *n.* sea-piece, marine picture (*Paint.*). —**tang**, *m.* sea-weed. —**tonne**, *f.* buoy. —**torf**, *m.* marine turf. —**treffen**, *n.* *see* —**schlacht**. —**trift**, *f.* flotsam and jetsam. —**truppen**, *pl.* marines. —**tüchtig**, *adj.* seaworthy; suited for seafaring. —**ungetüm**, *n.* sea-monster. —**verkehr**, *m.* ocean traffic. —**volk**, *n.* maritime people; crew. —**wärts**, *adv.* out to sea, seawards. —**wasser**, *n.* salt-water; brine (*poet.*). —**weg**, *m.* sea route; **auf dem —wege**, by sea; —**weg nach Ostindien**, passage by sea to India. —**wehr**, *f.* marines, naval reserve. —**wesen**, *n.* naval *or* maritime affairs. —**wind**, *m.* sea-breeze. —**wissenschaft**, *f.* nautical science. —**wurf**, *m.* jetsam. —**zeughaus**, *n.* naval arsenal. —**zunge**, *f.* sole (*Icht.*).

See'l—e, *f.* (*pl.* —**en**) soul; mind; heart; human being; pith (*of a quill*); bore (*of a gun*); sounding post (*of a violin*); chamber (*of a shuttle*); bladder (*of a herring*); shaft, fire-room (*of a blast-furnace*); **das geht mir durch die —e, das thut mir in der —e weh**, that cuts me to the quick; **das ist mir in tiefster —e zuwider**, I detest that from the bottom of my heart; **von ganzer —e**, with all one's *or* my heart; **es war keine (menschliche) —e da**, there was not a (*living*) soul there; **sie ist eine —e von einem Mädchen**, she is a love of a girl; **es ist eine —e von Kind**, it is a darling child; **sie ist ihm an die —e gewachsen**, she has become very dear to him; **einem etwas auf die —e binden**, to enjoin s.th. upon s.o. very earnestly; **das liegt mir auf der —e**, that weighs heavily upon me; **Sie sprechen mir aus der —e**, you have guessed my (inmost) thoughts; **ein Herz und eine —e sein**, to be of one heart and mind; **schöne —en finden sich**, kindred spirits meet (*prov.*). —**en=haft**, *adj.* *see* —**envoll**. —**isch**, *adj.* psychical. *Comp.* —**en=achse**, *f.* axis of the bore. —**en=adel**, *m.* nobility of soul. —(**en**)=**amt**, *n.* office for the dead. —**en=angst**, *f.* anguish of soul, mental agony. —**en=braut**, *f.* mystical bride of Christ, the church. —**en=bräutigam**, *m.* Christ (as bridegroom of the human soul). —**en=drama**, *n.* drama of the soul. —**en=durchmesser**, *m.* calibre (*Artil.*). —**en=forscher**, *m.* psychologist. —**en=forschung**, *f.* psychology. —**en=freund**, *m.* bosom friend. —**en=froh**, *adj.* enraptured; heartily glad. —**en=größe**, *f.* greatness of soul, magnanimity.

—en(s)-gut, *adj.* thoroughly good; **ein —enguter Mensch,** a dear good soul, a kind-hearted person. **—en-heil,** *n.* salvation (*of a p.'s soul*), spiritual welfare. **—en-heilkunde,** *f.* medical treatment of mental disease. **—en-hirt,** *m.* spiritual shepherd, pastor. **—en-leiden,** *n.* suffering of the soul, mental disease. **—en-los,** *adj.* soulless; spiritless. **—en-messe,** *f.* mass for the dead. **—en-mut,** *m.* moral courage. **—en-not,** *f.* distress of mind. **—en-ruhe,** *f.* peace of mind. **—en-schwung,** *m.* mental flight. **—en-stärke,** *f.* strength of mind; energy. **—en-tag,** *m.*; **aller —entag,** All Souls' Day. **—entzückend,** *adj.* soul-entrancing. **—en-verkäufer,** *m.* (*coll.*) kidnapper; recruiting-sergeant; tipply boat, cockle-shell. **—en-vertraut,** *adj.* very intimate. **—en-verwandt,** *adj.* congenial (*in mind*), sympathetic. **—en-verwandte,** *pl.* kindred souls. **—en-verwandtschaft,** *f.* congeniality (*of souls*). **—en-wanderung,** *f.* transmigration of souls, metempsychosis. **—en-wärmer,** *m.* knitted shawl, woollen comforter. **—en-zahl,** *f.* number of souls, inhabitants, the population. **—en-zustand,** *m.* spiritual condition, state of the soul. **—erfreuend,** *adj.* soul-rejoicing. **—sorge,** *f.* care *or* cure of souls; ministerial *or* pastoral office. **—sorger,** *m.* spiritual adviser, clergyman, minister. **—sorgerisch,** *adj.* pastoral; spiritual.

Se'gel, *n.* (—s, *pl.* —) sail; ala (*Bot.*); **lose —,** spare sails; **alle — ausspannen, beisetzen,** to crowd all sail; **die — einziehen, streichen,** to reef the sails, to shorten sail, to strike sail; to give in; **unter — gehen,** to set sail. *Comp.* **—balken,** *m.* midship-beam. **—baum,** *m.* mast; boom. **—dampfschiff,** *n.* steaming and sailing ship. **—fertig,** *adj.* ready for sea. **—kahn,** *m.* sailing-boat. **—klar,** *see* **—fertig.** **—macher,** *m.* sailmaker. **—schiff,** *n.* sailing ship. **—spiel,** *n.* set of sails. **—spur,** *f.* wake (*of a ship*). **—stange,** *f.* (sail-)yard. **—tuch,** *n.* sail-cloth. **—werk,** *n.* sails. **—wind,** *m.* favourable wind.

Se'gel—n, *v.a. & n.* (*aux.* **h.** & **s.**) to sail; **längs einer Küste —n,** to coast along; **ein Schiff in den Grund —n,** to run down a ship; **mit halbem Winde —n,** to sail on a tack; **um ein Vorgebirge —n,** to double a cape; **vor dem Wind —n,** to run before the wind. **—er,** *see* **Segler.**

Se'gen, *m.* (—s, *pl.* —) blessing; benediction; grace (*before or after meals*); sign of the cross; spell, charm; **den — geben, erteilen, &c.,** to pronounce the benediction; **den — sprechen,** to say grace; **Gott gebe seinen — dazu!** God's blessing on it! **der apostolische —,** the Apostolic benediction; **das wird Ihnen keinen — bringen,** that will bring you no good luck; **an Gottes — ist alles gelegen,** God's blessing gained, all is obtained. *Comp.* **—los,** *adj.* unblessed, not prosperous; unfruitful. **—s-—formel,** *f.* formula of benediction; **heidnische —sformel,** charm. **—spendend,** *adj.* beneficial, blessing. **—sprechen,** *n.* benediction. **—(s)reich,** *adj.* prosperous, blessed. **—s-spruch,** *m.*, **—s-wunsch,** *m.* benediction.

Seg'ge, *f.* (*pl.* —n) sedge, rush.

Seg'ler, *m.* (—s, *pl.* —) sailor; swift (*Orn.*); sailer, ship; **Wolken! — der Lüfte,** ye (winged) clouds, aerial travellers.

Seg'n—en, *v.a.* to bless; to cross, make the sign of the cross on; to consecrate; to charm, enchant; **sich —en,** to cross o.s.; **einem das Bad —en,** (*iron.*) to put a p. into a great predicament, to make it hot for a p., to give a p. a good scolding; **das Zeitliche —en,** to depart this life, to die; **gesegneten Andenkens,** of blessed memory; **gesegnete Mahlzeit,** *see* **Mahlzeit; gesegneten Leibes, in gesegneten Umständen,** in the family way, pregnant. **—er,** *m.* (—ers, *pl.* —er) pronouncer of the benediction; blesser; charmer. **—ung,** *f.* blessing; exorcism.

Seh'bar, *adj.* visible, in sight. **—keit,** *f.* visibility.

Se'h—en, *ir.v.* I. *n.* (*aux.* **h.**) to see; to perceive; to look; to appear; **ich kann nicht mehr —en,** I can see no longer; **gut —en,** to have good eyes; **ich —e schlecht,** my (eye)sight is bad; **—en Sie mal!** look here! **ei, sieh' doch, Sie sind es!** what, it is you! **siehe oben, unten** (*abbr.* **s. o., s. u.**), see above, below; **auf eine S. —en,** to look at, to set one's eyes upon, to look at a th., attend to a th.; to be particular about; **—en Sie darauf!** look to it! **auf den Preis —e ich nicht,** I don't mind the price, I am not particular as to the price, the price is no consideration; **ihm sieht der Schelm aus den Augen,** he looks a rogue; **daraus ist zu —en,** hence it appears; **—en durch,** to look through; **einem ins Gesicht —en,** to look s. o. in the face; **in die Zukunft —en,** to dive into the future; **einem ins Spiel, in die Karten —en,** to discover a p.'s hidden motives; **durch die Finger —en,** to connive; **nach einer S. —en,** to look for a th.; to look after a th.; **nach dem** (*or* **zum**) **Rechten —en,** to see that everything is in order *or* is done properly; **und hast du nicht ge—en!** helter-skelter, in a twinkle (*fam.*); **haste nicht ge—en, fort war er,** he was gone before you could say Jack Robinson (*fam.*); **das Zimmer sieht nach der Straße,** the room faces the street; **zu etwas —en,** to see to, look after a th.; **einem ähnlich —en,** to resemble s. o.; **das sieht ihm ähnlich!** that is just like him! II. *a.;* **Gesellschaft bei sich —en,** to receive company; **man will ihn nirgend —en,** no one will receive him, all doors are closed against him; **gern (bei einem) gesehen sein,** to be a welcome guest; **ich —e ihn kommen,** I see him coming; **auf Gehalt wird nicht ge—en,** salary is no object; **auf gute Behandlung wird vor allem ge—en,** kind treatment is the first consideration; **—en lassen,** to let be seen, to show, to display; **sich —en lassen,** to appear, to make a show, to show oneself, to be visible; **sich mit etwas —en lassen können,** to have no need to be ashamed of a thing; **sollte jemand kommen, so lasse ich mich nicht —en,** if anyone calls, I am not at home; **es ist so schlecht, es läßt sich nicht —en,** it is too bad to be shown; **seine Freude** *or* **Lust an einer S. —en,** to look at a th. with pleasure; **ich will —en, ob ich es möglich machen kann,** I will try to do it, will see if I can bring it about; **du wirst ja —en, wie du es fertig bringst,** I dare say you will be able to manage it; **sich satt —en,** to feast one's eyes on, look as long as one likes (*at*); **es ist für Geld zu —en,** it can be seen by paying, it is exhibited for money. **—er,** *m.* (—ers, *pl.* —er) one who sees; seer, prophet; astronomer; *see* **Hellseher;** eye (*Sport.*). **—erin,** *f.* prophetess. *Comp.* **—achse,** *f.* axis of vision. **—ens-wert, —ens-würdig,** *adj.* worth seeing. **—ens-würdigkeit,** *f.* object of interest. **—er-blick,** *m.* prophetic eye *or* glance. **—er-gabe,** *f.* second sight. **—feld,** *n.* field of vision. **—kraft,** *f.* eye-sight; strength of vision. **—kunst, —lehre,** *f.* optics. **—linie,** *f.* line of collimation (*Ast.*); principal visual ray (*Persp.*). **—nerv,** *m.* optic nerve. **—organ,** *n.* organ of sight. **—punkt,** *m.* point of sight (*Persp.*); point of view. **—rohr,** *n.* telescope. **—strahl,** *m.* visual ray. **—weite,** *f.* field of vision, reach of sight. **—werkzeug,** *n.* organ of sight. **—winkel,** *m.* visual angle.

Se'hn—e, *f.* (*pl.* —en) sinew, tendon; nerve; string (*of a bow*); chord (*of an arc*). —icht (*obs.*), —ig, *adj.* sinewy, nervous, stringy. *Comp.* —en=band, *n.* ligament, tendon. —en=kunde, —en=lehre, *f.* tenology.

Se'hn—en, *v.r.* to long, yearn (*for*), desire passionately; sich nach Hause —en, to long for home, be homesick; ich sehne mich nach meiner Frau, I am longing for my wife; ich —e mich danach ihn zu sehen, I long to see him. —lich, *adj. & adv.* ardent, passionate, longing. *Comp.* —sucht, *f.* longing, ardent desire; hankering, yearning, pining. —süchtig, *adj.* longing, yearning; fond; passionate. —sucht=laut, *m.* expression of yearning.

Sehr, *adv.* very, much, greatly; recht —, greatly; wie — auch . . ., however much . . .; wenn er auch noch so — es verlangen sollte, however much he may wish for it; bitte —! oh! don't mention it!

Sei, *imperat. sing. of* sein.

[1]Sei'che, *f.* urine, water (*of horses, cows*) (*vulg.*).

[2]Sei'che, *f.* running water, stream.

Seicht, *adj.* shallow; low, flat; superficial; insipid; stupid; eine —e Stelle, a shoal. —e Redensarten, platitudes. —heit, —igkeit, *f.* shallowness.

Seid, *2 pers. pl. pres. ind. & imperat. of* sein.

Sei'de, *f.* silk; rohe, ungekochte *or* ungeschälte —, raw silk; dabei wird er keine — spinnen, he will not make much by that. —n, *adj.* silken; silky. *Comp.* —n=arbeiter, *m.* silk-weaver. —n=artig, *adj.* silky. —n=bau, *m.* rearing of silkworms. —n=ernte, *f.* gathering of the silkworm-cocoons. —n=fabrik, *f.* silk-factory. —n=faden, *m.* silk thread. —n=falter, *m.* see Seidenspinner. —n=garn, *n.* spun silk. —n=gehäuse, *n.* cocoon of the silkworm. —n=glanz, *m.* silky lustre. —n=händler, *m.* silk-merchant. —n=hase, *m.* Angora rabbit. —n=haspel, *m.* silk-reel. —n=papier, *n.* tissue paper. —n=raupe, *f.* silkworm. —n=rolle, *f.* silk-bobbin. —n=spinner, *m.* silk-moth (*Ent.*); silk-spinner *or* throw(st)er. —n=spitzen, *pl.* silk lace, blonde lace. —n=stickerei, *f.* embroidery in silk. —n=tüll, *m.* silk-net. —n=weich, *adj.* (as) soft as silk, silky. —n=winde, *f.* silk-winder. —n=wurm, *m.* silkworm. —n=zeug, *n.* silks. —n=züchter, *m.* rearer of silkworms, silk-grower. —n=zwirnen, *n.* silk-throwing.

Sei'del, *n.* (*sometimes m.*) (—s, *pl.* —) liquid measure (*gen'lly a little more than a pint*); beer-tankard; ein — Bier, a glass of beer.

Sei'et, *2 pers. pl. pres. subj. of* sein.

[1]Sei'f—e, *f.* soap; —e sieden, to boil *or* make soap; schwarze, weiche —e, soft soap; wohlriechende —e, scented soap; spanische —e, Castile soap; ein Stück —e, a cake of soap. —en, *v.a.* to soap. —icht (*obs.*), —ig, *adj.* soapy. *Comp.* —en=bildung, saponification. —en=blase, *f.* soap-bubble. —en=erde, *f.* saponaceous clay, fuller's earth. —en=haltig, *adj.* soapy, rich in soap. —(en)=lappen, *m.* washing-glove. —en=lauge, *f. see* —ensieder=lauge; soap-suds. —en=napf, *m.*, —n=tellerchen, *n.* soap-dish. —en=sieder, *m.* soap-boiler. —en=siederei, *f.* soap works. —en=sieder=lauge, *f.* caustic lye. —en=spiritus, *m.* spirit of soap. —en=stoff, *m.* saponine (*Chem.*).

[2]Sei'fe, *f.* diluvial ore; stream-works. —n, *v.n.* (*aux.* h.) to wash ore, to stream, buddle.

Sei'ge, *see* Seihe. —n, *see* Seihen & Mücke.

Sei'ger, I. *m.* (—s, *pl.* —) perpendicular; clock; hour-glass. II. *adj. & adv.* perpendicular. —n, *v.* I. *a. see* Seihen; to sink a shaft; to make perpendicular; to refine (*metals*). II. *n.* (*aux.* f.) *see* Sickern. *Comp.* —arbeiter, —abtreiber, *m.* refiner of metals. —blech, *n.* cheek (*Metal.*). —blei, *n.* lead added to the copper from which the silver is to be separated. —darr=ofen, *m.* roasting-furnace. —gang, *m.* clock-movement. —gekrätz, *n.* waste in metal refining. —gerade, *adj.* perpendicular. —glätte, *f.* litharge. —hütte, *f.* refining-house.

Sei'h—e, *f.* filtration; colander; strainer; filter; dregs. —en, *v.a.* to strain, to filter. *Comp.* —brühe, *f.* strained liquid (*as soup, jelly, gravy, etc.*). —kasten, *m.* paper-maker's size-filter. —sack, *m.* straining-bag; jelly-bag. —stein, *m.* filtering-stone. —trichter, *m.* strainer; funnel with a rose. —tuch, *n.* straining cloth.

Seil, *n.* (—s, *pl.* —e) rope, cord, line; cable; pulley; (*pl.*) traces (*of harness*); — und Treil, rigging; sich am (Narren=)—e führen lassen, to let oneself be led by the nose; an einem —e ziehen, to row in the same boat. *Comp.* —bahn, (Drahtseil=bahn,) *f.* (wire-)rope railway, funicular railway. —brücke, *f.* suspension-bridge made of ropes. —draht, *m.* wire-rope. —er=bahn, *f.* rope-walk. —er=kamm, *m.* rope-maker's hatchet. —er=rad, *n.* spinning-wheel. —er=schlitten, *m.* rope-sledge. —er=spule, *f.* spindle. —er=waren, *pl.* cordage. —fähre, *f.* ferry-boat. —kreuz, *n.* cabled cross (*Her.*). —ring, *m.* ring-bolt. —tanz, *m.* rope-dancing. —tanzen, I. *v.n.* (*aux.* h.) (*sep.*) to dance on the (tight *or* slack) rope. II. *subst. n. see* —tanz. —tänzer(in, *f.*), *m.* rope-dancer. —tänzerisch, *adj.* like a rope-dancer, funambulatory, break-neck, neck-breaking. —tänzer=stange, *f.* rope-dancer's (balancing-)pole. —werk, *n.* rope-work; rigging. —ziehen, *n.* rope-pulling, tug of war (*coll.*).

Sei'le—n, *v.a.* to warp the yarns; to rig; to fasten with rope. —r, *m.* (—rs, *pl.* —r) rope-maker; —rs Tochter, hangman's rope (*vulg.*). —rei', *f.* rope-making.

Seim, *m.* (—s, *pl.* —e) honey; viscous fluid; mucilage; cream, jelly (*Cook.*). —icht, (*obs.*) —ig, *adj.* mucilaginous.

Sei'men, *v.* I. *a.* to strain (*honey*); to boil down into a semi-liquid state. II. *n.* (*aux.* h.) to yield (*honey, cream, slime, etc.*).

[1]Sein, I. (—e, —) *poss. adj.* his, its, her; one's, your (*obs. to inferiors, see* Er); — Lehrer, his teacher; der Vogel und — Nest, the bird and its nest; das Schiff und — Kapitän, the ship and her captain; einer —er Freunde, one of his friends, a friend of his; mein und — Freund, my friend and his; Deutschland und —e Kolonien, Germany and her colonies; London und —e Umgebungen, London and its environs; —e Kleider anziehen, to put on one's clothes; —er Zeit (*adv. gen.*) in his *or* its time; in due time, in its proper time, duly; alles zu —er Zeit, all in good time, all in due course. II. *poss. pron.* (*for* —es, das —e), his; dies alles ist —, all this is his own, belongs to him; dieses Haus ist —, his house is his. III. — (*obs. & poet.*), —er, *gen. sing. of* er & es, of him, of it, of one; —er nicht mehr mächtig sein, to lose *or* have lost control of o.s.; ich erinnere mich —(er), I remember him. —e, (der, die, das —e), —er, —e, —es, —ige, (der, die, das —ige) *poss. pron.* his; das —ige, his property, his part *or* duty; jedem das —e, to every one his due; die —igen, his own family *or* people. *Comp.* —er=lei, *indec. adj.* of his kind. —er=seits, *adv.* on his side; for his part. —es=gleichen, *indec., adj. & pron.* of his kind, such as he; einen wie —es=gleichen behandeln, to treat a p. as an equal. (um) —et=halben, —et=wegen, —et=willen, *adv.* on his account, for his sake, as far as he is concerned; for aught he cares.

[2]Sein, I. *ir.v.n.* (*aux.* f.) to be; to exist; (*as aux.* =) to be, to have; was du bist, sei ganz, be either one thing or another; sind Sie es? is it you? es sind viele Leute angekommen, many people have come; er ist nicht zu sprechen, no one can see him; es ist ein Jahr, daß er abgereist ist, he set off a year ago; hier ist teuer leben or —, living is dear here; es sei! es mag —! be it so! granted! sei es drum! so be it! granted! es sei denn daß, es wäre denn daß, unless; dem sei, wie ihm wolle, be that as it may; ei, das wäre (noch schöner)! gracious! you don't say so! well! sei es . . ., whether; es sei denn, daß es sich so verhalte, unless it be thus; wäre er nicht gewesen, so würde ich hier gewesen —, but for him I should have been here; was soll das —? what does that mean? thust du es, so bist du des Todes, if you do it, you are a dead man; es sind unser drei, there are three of us; es ist mir um ihn, I am concerned for him; es ist mir als ob, I feel as if, I fancy, it seems to me that; mir ist warm, I feel warm; einem gut —, to like s. o., feel friendly towards a p.; jetzt weiß ich endlich, woran ich bin, now I know at last how I stand; wie ist Ihnen? how do you feel? mir ist schlecht, I feel unwell; was ist Ihnen? what is the matter with you? what ails you? der Ansicht —, to be of opinion. II. *subst.n.* being; existence; essence.

Seit, I. *prep.* (*with dat.*) since; for; — einiger Zeit, for some time past; — kurzem, of late, lately; — undenklicher Zeit, time out of mind; — Menschen(ge)denken, within the memory of man; — wann ist er fort? how long ago did he leave? when did he go? how long has he been away? II. *conj.* since. *Comp.* —dem, I. *adv.* since, since that time, ever since. II. *conj.* since. —her, *adv.* since then, from that time; hitherto. —herig, *adj.*; das —herige Wetter, the weather up to this time *or* until now.

Sei't—e, *f.* (*pl.* —en) side; page; flank; party, side; member (*of an equation*); verkehrte —e, reverse (*of coins*); eine —e Speck, a flitch of bacon; auf die —e bringen *or* schaffen, to put aside, to put out of the way; to finish off, to get done; to make away with; (einen) auf seine —e bringen, to bring over to one's party; sich auf die faule —e legen, to turn lazy; gelindere (*or* andere) —en aufziehen, to alter one's tone, to come down a peg; ich habe es von anderer —e her, I have it from another quarter; sich auf die —e machen, to get out of the way; einen auf die —e nehmen, to take a p. aside; bei —e, aside; ein Bei—e, an aside; bei —e legen, to put aside; einen bei seiner schwachen —e nehmen, to appeal to a p.'s weakness; Scherz bei —e, joking apart; die Hände in die —e stemmen, to set one's arms akimbo; in die —e fallen, von der angreifen, to attack (*an enemy*) in the flank; nach welcher —e hin Sie diese Sache auch betrachten mögen, from whatever side you look at this matter; nach dieser —e hin, on this side, in this direction; etwas von allen —en betrachten, to look at a th. from all sides; einen über (die) —e schaffen, to rid oneself of, to make away with a p.; von —en des Königs, on the part of the king; von —en seiner Mutter, on his mother's side; gute Atteste stehen ihm zur —e, he has good testimonials. —ens, *prep.* (*with gen.*) on *or* from the side (*of*); on the part of. —ig, *suffix* (*in comp.* =) -sided; viel—ig, many sided, of many parts; multifarious; zwölf—ig, twelve-sided. —lich, *adj.* lateral. —s, *suffix* (*in comp.*); mütterlicher—s, on the mother's side. *Comp.* —a'b, *adv.* aside, apart. —en=abriß, *m.* profile. —en=achse, *f.* diagonal. —en=angriff, *m.* flank attack. —en=ansicht, *f.* side-view; profile. —en=baum, *m.* cheek (*of the gun-carriage*). —en=blick, *m.* side-glance; scornful glance; sneer. —en=brustwehr, *f.* orillon. —en=chor, *n.* lateral choir (*Arch.*). —en=deckung, *f.* flank guard. —en=druck, *m.* lateral pressure. —en=erbe, *m.* collateral heir. —en=fleck, *m.* patch (*on a shoe*). —en=flügel, *m.* side-aisle; —en=flügel (*pl.*) einer Kreuzkirche, transepts. —en=gang, *m.* side-path *or* alley; slip (*Theat.*). —en=gebäude, *n.* wing (*of a building*). —en=gespräch, *n.* aside. —en=gewehr, *n.* side-arms; sword; das —engewehr aufpflanzen, to fix swords, to fix bayonets. —en=gleis, *n.* siding (*Railw.*). —en=hieb, *m.* side-cut; sly hit, taunt, innuendo. —en=hüter, *m.* catch word (*Typ.*). —en=joche, *f.* spur (*of a mountain*). —en=lehne, *f.* side rail; arm (*of a chair, etc.*); guard-iron (*Artil.*). —en=linie, *f.* collateral line; side (*Geom.*); second line of rail. —en=patrouille, *f.* flanking scouts. —en=schmerz, *m.* pain in the side. —en=sprung, *m.* side leap; double. —en=stechen, *n.* stitch in the side. —en=stoß, *m.* thrust in the side; flanconade (*Fenc.*). —en=stück, *n.* side-piece; counterpart, pendant; cheek (*of a gun-carriage*). —en=trieb, *m.* side growth. —en=verwandtschaft, *f.* collateral relationship. —en=wand, *f.* side-wall; cheek (*of a press; of a gun-carriage*); (*pl.*) side-scenes (*Theat.*). —en=wehr, *f.* epaulement (*Fort.*). —en=werk, *n.* outwork (*Fort.*); flank. —en=wind, *m.* side-wind, tack-wind. —en=zahl, *f.* number of a page; number of pages; Vieleck von ungerader —enzahl, unequal-sided polygon. —en=zimmer, *n.* side-room; adjoining room. —wärts, *adv.* aside; sideways; laterally; on one side.

Sekan'te, (—n=linie,) *f.* (*pl.* —n) secant.

Sekon'deleutnant, *m.* (—s, *pl.* —s) (second) lieutenant.

Sekre't, *n.* (—es, *pl.* —e) (*pl.*) secretions (*Physiol.*).

Sekret—ä'r, *m.* (—ärs, *pl.* —äre) secretary, clerk; bureau. —aria't, *n.* (—ariats, *pl.* —ariate) secretaryship; secretary's office.

Sekt, *m.* (—es) sack; dry wine; champagne (*coll.*). *Comp.* —propfen, *m.* cork of a champagne-bottle.

Sek't—e, *f.* (*pl.* —en) sect. —io'n, *f.* (*pl.* —ionen) section; dissection. —ie'rer, *m.* (—ierers, *pl.* —ierer) sectarian. —or, *m.* (—ors, *pl.* —o'ren) sector; eccentric catch (*Mach.*). *Comp.* —ions=aufriß, *m.* sectional elevation. —ions=feuer, *n.* sectional firing.

Sekun'd—a, *f.* (*pl.* —s, —en) second class from the top, second highest form (*of a German grammar school*), fifth form. —a'ner, *m.* (—aners, *pl.* —aner) second form boy (*in Germany*); fifth form boy. —a'nt, *m.* (—an'ten, *pl.* —an'ten) second (*in duels*). —ä'r, *adj.* secondary. —e, *f.* (*pl.* —en) second (*Mus., Fenc., Chron., Typ.*). —ie'ren, *v.* I. *a.* to second; to accompany. II. *n.* (*aux.* h.) to be a second (*Mus.*). —us, *m.* second boy (*in a class or set*). *Comp.* —a=wechsel, *m.* second (bill) of exchange (*C. L.*). —är=bahn, *f.* branch line. —är=schule, *f.* secondary school, intermediate school. —en=uhr, *f.* watch with a seconds-hand. —en=zeiger, *m.* seconds-hand (*of a watch*). —o=genitur, *f.* right of the younger son (*opp. to primogeniture*).

Sel., *abbrev. for* selig.

Se'la! *int.* selah! abgemacht, —! all right! done! settled! agreed!

Selb, *adj.*; zur —en Stunde, at that very hour. —e, —ige (der, die, das —e, —ige), —iger, —ige, —iges, *adj. & pron.* the same, the selfsame; zur —igen Stunde, at the same hour. —er, *indeclin. see* —st, I.; ich —er, I myself; die Mutter —er, the mother herself; die Kinder —er, the children themselves; even the children, the very children. —st, *see* Selbst.

Comp. —**an'der,** *pronominal adj.;* I and another, we two. —**dritt,** *pronominal adj.* myself with two others. —**sechst,** *pronominal adj.* I and five others; **wir gingen —sechst,** we went, six of us counting myself; I went with five others. —**ständig,** *adj.* self-supporting; independent; separate; —**ständige Forschung,** original research. —**ständigkeit,** *f.* independence.

Selbst, I. *indec. adj. or pron.* (*gen'lly used in apposition to a preceding noun or pron.*) self; myself, himself, yourself, *etc.;* **ich —,** I myself; **die Sache an und für sich —,** the thing in itself, abstractly considered; **— gethan ist wohl gethan,** what one does oneself is well done; **sie ist die Güte —,** she is kindness itself; **von —, aus sich —,** of oneself, alone, of one's own accord, voluntarily; **es bewegt sich von —,** it moves of itself; **er brachte den Ring von — zurück,** he brought back the ring of his own accord; **— gebackenes Brot,** home-made bread; **mit sich — reden,** to talk to o.s.; **es ist wohl von — gekommen!** it was the cat did it, of course; **das versteht sich von —,** that goes without saying; **— ist der Mann,** if you want a thing done, do it yourself; self do, self have (*prov.*); **er ist es —,** it is he himself. II. *n.* (*indec.*); **sein —,** his individuality, his own self; **sein ganzes —,** his whole being. III. *adv.* even; very; **— seine Freunde** *or* **seine Freunde —,** even his friends, his very friends; **bis zum Knochen —,** to the very bone; **— in der Luft, die man atmet,** in the very air we breathe. —**heit,** *f.* self, personality, ego, individuality; egoism; selfishness. —**isch,** *adj.* selfish; egotistic. —**ling,** *m.* (—**lings,** *pl.* —**linge**) egotist. *Comp.*—**achtung,** *f.* self-esteem. —**anklage,** *f.* self-accusation. —**aufopferung,** *f.* self-sacrifice. —**befruchtung,** *f.* spontaneous generation. —**beherrschung,** *f.* self-possession, self-restraint, —**bekenntnis,** *n.* voluntary confession; avowal of one's own guilt. —**beköstigung,** *f.* boarding oneself *or* at one's own expense. —**beobachtung,** *f.* introspection (*Philos.*). —**bestimmung,** *f.* determination of one's own destiny, disposal of o.s. —**bestimmungsrecht,** *n.* right of disposing of o.s.; self-government. —**bewegend,** *adj.* automatic. —**bewußt,** *adj.* self-conscious; conceited. —**bewußtsein,** *n.* self-consciousness, self-assurance; self-conceit. —**biographie,** *f.* autobiography. —**eigen,** *adj.* one's very own. —**einschätzung,** *f.* self-assessment, statement of income. —**entleibung,** *f.* suicide. —**entmannung,** *f.* voluntary emasculation. —**entsagung,** *f.* voluntary renunciation; self-denial. —**erhaltung,** *f.* self-preservation. —**fahrer,** *m.* motor-car, automobile. —**fahrer=wesen,** *m.* automobilism. —**gefällig,** *adj.* self-satisfied, self-complacent. —**gefälligkeit,** *f.* self-complacency. —**gefühl,** *n.* self-respect; self-reliance; self-consciousness. —**genügsam,** *adj.* self-sufficient; self-sufficing, self-contained. —**genügsamkeit,** *f.* contentment with oneself; self-sufficiency. —**gespräch,** *n.* monologue. —**geständnis,** *see* —**bekenntnis.** —**herrlich,** *adj.* autocratic. —**herrschaft,** *f.* self-command; autocracy. —**herrscher,** *m.* autocrat. —**herrscherisch,** *adj.* autocratic. —**hilfe,** —**hülfe,** *f.* self-help, self-defence; **zur —hülfe schreiten,** to take the law into one's own hands. —**käufer,** *m.* direct purchaser. —**klug,** *adj.* presumptuous; self-conceited. —**kocher,** *m.* self-acting boiler. —**kostenpreis,** *m.* net cost (*C.L.*). —**lader,** *m.* self-loader. —**laut(er),** *m.* vowel. —**liebe,** *f.* self-love. —**mord,** *m.* suicide; **—mord begehen,** to commit suicide. —**mörder(in,** *f.*), *m.* suicide; felo-de-se (*Law*). —**mörderisch,** *adj.* suicidal. —**öler,** *m.* self-acting lubricator. —**prüfung,** *f.* self-examination; trial of one's own powers. —**quäler,** *m.* self-tormentor. —**rache,** *f.* private revenge. —**redend,** *adj.* self-evident, (*as a matter*) of course, obvious. —**regulierend,** *adj.* self-acting, self-adjusting. —**schöpferisch,** *adj.* original. —**schuldner,** *m.* debtor in one's own name, on one's own account. —**schuß,** *m.* spring-gun. —**spanner,** *m.* self-cocking gun *or* action. —**spinnend,** *adj.* self-acting (*of a spinning machine*). —**ständig,** *see* **Selbständig.** —**sucht,** *f.* egotism; selfishness. —**süchtig,** *adj.* egotistic; selfish. —**thätig,** *adj.* self-acting; spontaneous. —**thätigkeit,** *f.* self-activity; spontaneity. —**trieb,** *m.* spontaneity. —**überhebung,** —**überschätzung,** *f.* overweening opinion of oneself; presumption. —**überwindung,** *f.* self-conquest, self-control. —**unterbrecher,** *m.* automatic circuit-breaker. —**unterricht,** *m.* self-instruction. —**verbrennung,** *f.* spontaneous combustion. —**vergessen,** *adj.* forgetful of o.s., self-forgetting, unselfish. —**vergötterung,** *f.* self-adulation. —**verlag,** *m.;* **im —verlage,** published by the author. —**verleger,** *m.* author and publisher. —**verleugnung,** *f.* self-abnegation. —**verschluß,** *m.;* **mit —verschluß,** self-closing. —**verschuldet,** *adj.* brought about by one's own guilt *or* fault. —**verständlich,** *adj. & adv.;* **das ist —verständlich,** that is a matter of course; —**verständlich!** of course! —**verstümmelung,** *f.* voluntary mutilation. —**vertrauen,** *n.* self-confidence. —**verwaltung,** *f.* self-government, autonomy. —**wille,** *m.* one's own will; self-will. —**zucht,** *f.* self-discipline. —**zufrieden,** *adj.* self-satisfied. —**zufriedenheit,** *f.* self-content, self-complacency. —**zündend,** *adj.* self-igniting, pyrophorous. —**zünder,** *m.* pyrophorus (*Chem.*). —**zweck,** *m.* end in itself, forming its own object.

Selek't—a, *f.* name of the highest form in some high schools for boys and girls, special class (*for senior pupils*). —**a'ner,** *m.* (—**aners,** *pl.* —**aner**) pupil of the highest form *or* of a special and advanced class. *Comp.* —**ions'=theorie,** *f.* (*Darwin's*) theory of natural selection.

Sele'n, *n.* (—**s**) selenium (*Chem.*). —**ogra'ph,** *m.* selenographer. *Comp.* (*in compds.* = selenic *or* selenide of). —**metalle,** *pl.* selenides. —**säure,** *f.* selenic acid.

[1]**Se'lig,** *adj. & adv.* blessed, happy, blissful; saved, in Heaven; deceased, late; tipsy; **einen — preisen,** to call a p. blessed; **Gott habe ihn —!** God rest his soul! **eines —en Todes sterben,** to die the death of a pious man *or* of a Christian; **— sprechen,** to pronounce blessed, beatify; **meine —e Mutter,** my deceased *or* late mother; **mein Vater —,** my deceased father; **ihr —er,** her late husband (*coll.*); **der —e König,** the late king; **—en Andenkens,** of blessed memory; **— werden,** to be saved (*in heaven*), to attain salvation; **dreimal —,** thrice blessed; **—e Tage,** blissful days; **in dem —en Bewußtsein, daß,** in the happy consciousness, that; **die Inseln der —en,** the happy islands; **die Gefilde der —en,** Elysium. —**keit,** *f.* happiness, bliss; **die ewige —keit,** everlasting bliss, salvation; **die ewige —keit erlangen,** to obtain salvation, to come to bliss. *Comp.* —**gesprochene(r),** *m.* beatified person, canonized saint. —**machend,** *adj.* beatific, (soul-)saving. —**macher,** *m.* Saviour. —**machung,** *f.* salvation; sanctification. —**preisung,** *f.;* **die —preisungen,** the Beatitudes. —**sprechung,** *f.* beatification.

[2]**Selig,** *as the second part of various compds. for* **=sälig,** *from* **=sal,** *e.g.:* **mühselig** *fr.* **Mühsal, trübselig** *fr.* **Trübsal,** *etc.*

Sel'lerie, *m.* (**—s**) *& f.* celery.

Sel'tēn, I. *adj.* rare, unusual; scarce; **das ist nichts —enes**, that is nothing extraordinary. II. *adv.* seldom; **nicht eben —en**, not very rarely, pretty frequently, now and again. —**enheit**, *f.* rarity, scarcity; unusualness; curiosity. —**sam**, *adj. & adv.* strange, unusual; odd, curious. —**samkeit**, *f.* strangeness; oddness.

Seman'tik, *f.* semantics, science of meaning (*of words*). —**er**, *m.* (—**ers**, *pl.* —**er**) student of semantics.

Semapho'r, *n.* (—**s**, *pl.* —**e**) semaphore (*Railw.*).

Semes'ter, *n.* (—**s**, *pl.* —) (term of) six months, half year; University term, half (year), session, semester; **Sommer —**, summer session; **Winter —**, winter session, winter half. *Comp.* —**schluß**, *m.* end of term *or* session.

Semina'r, *n.* (—**s**, *pl.* —**e** *and* —**ien**) training college, seminary (*for training priests*); training college (*for teachers; usually elementary teachers*); advanced class (*formed for specialised study, debate and independent investigation, under the guidance of a professor at a German university*); special class *or* classes added to a high school for girls (*with a view of training women teachers*); **das — arbeitet mit dem Professor von vier bis sechs**, the advanced class works with the professor from four to six; **er besucht ein — für Lehrer**, he goes to a training-college, he is a student at a training-college; **sie kommt ins —**, she is going to be trained, she will become a member of the training college for women teachers. —**i'st**, *m.* (—**is'ten**, *pl.* —**is'ten**) pupil of a training college (*for teachers or theologians*); member of an advanced class at a German university, advanced student. —**is'tin**, *f.* student at a training college for women teachers. —**is'tisch**, *adj.* concerning *or* obtained at a training college; —**istisch gebildet**, educated at a training college; —**istisch gebildet sein**, to have passed through a training college; —**istische Bildung**, education obtained at a training college. *Comp.* —**bibliothek**, *f.* reference library for the exclusive use of members of an advanced class at a German university; training college library. —**direktor**, *m.* headmaster of a training college. —**jahr**, *n.* year of professional training (*theory and practice of education, etc.*) for the teaching profession, following immediately after the University course and preceding the year of probation (**Probejahr**). —**kursus**, *m.* course of training at a (training) college. —**schüler**, *m.* student at a training college. —**übungen**, *pl.* exercises with a (limited) class of advanced students.

Sem'mel, *f.* (*pl.* —**n**) roll (*of wheaten flour*); **abgehen wie warme —n**, to be in great demand. *Comp.* —**blond**, *adj.* flaxen-haired. —**kloß**, *m.* yeast- *or* bread-dumpling. —**mehl**, *n.* wheaten-flour.

Sem'perfrei, *adj.* free-born, entitled to act as assessor of a synod.

Sena'r(ius), *m.* iambic verse of six feet.

Sena't, *m.* (—**s**, *pl.* —**e**) senate. —**or**, *m.* (—**ors**, *pl.* —**o'ren**) senator. —**o'risch**, *adj.* senatorial. *Comp.* —**s=ausschuß**, *m.* senatorial committee. —**s=würde**, *f.* senatorship.

Sen'd—en, *reg. & (usually) ir.v.a.* to send, despatch; to hurl; **nach einem —en**, to send for s. o. —**ling**, *m.* (—**lings**, *pl.* —**linge**) emissary; messenger. —**ung**, *f.* sending; mission; expedition; consignment; **eine —ung Weizen**, a consignment (*cargo*) of wheat. *Comp.* —**bote**, *m.* messenger; envoy; apostle. —**brief**, *m.*, —**schreiben**, *n.* despatch; circular; (open) letter.

Se'nes— (*in comp.*) —**baum**, *m.* senna-tree. —**blatt**, *n.* senna-leaf.

Se'neschall, *m.* (—**s**, *pl.* —**e**) seneschal, high-steward.

Senf, *m.* (—(**e**)**s**) mustard; **einen langen — machen über eine S.**, to descant at length upon a th., to twaddle; **seinen — dazu geben**, to put in one's word. *Comp.* —**büchse**, *f.* mustard-pot. —**brühe**, *f.* mustard-sauce. —**korn**, *n.* grain of mustard-seed. —**mehl**, *n.* ground mustard. —**pflaster**, *n.*, —**umschlag**, *m.* mustard-poultice *or* plaster. —**säure**, *f.* sinapic acid.

Sen'g—en, *v.* I. *a.* to singe, scorch; to burn; to bream (*Naut.*); —**en und brennen**, to burn and ravage (*a country*), to lay waste. II. *n.* (*aux.* **h.**) to burn, be singed. —(**e**)**rig**, *adj.* (*smelling or tasting*) burnt; fishy, dangerous (*fig.*).

Seniora't, *n.* (—**s**) seniority.

Senio'ren=konvent, *m.* (*abbrev. S.C.*) assembly of senior members *or* of chairmen; standing committee (*for the regulation of parliamentary business*).

Sen'ke, *f.* layering of vines; low ground; counter-sink; probe (*Surg.*). —**l**, *m.* (—**ls**, *pl.* —**l**) lace, string with a tag; clasp; plumb-line. —**ln**, *v.a.* to lace.

Sen'k—en, *v.* I. *a.* to cause to sink; to sink (*a shaft, etc.*); to let down, lower; to plunge; to lay (*vines*). II. *r.* to settle; to sink. —**er**, *m.* (—**ers**, *pl.* —**er**) countersink; layer (*Hort.*); sinker (*of a shaft, etc.*). —**ig**, *adj.* low (*of ground*). —**ung**, *f.* sinking; lowering, depression; dip; sunken place, hollow; declivity; thesis (*metre*). *Comp.* —**blei**, *n.* plummet, sounding lead. —**el=nadel**, *f.* tag. —**fäustel**, *n.* great beetle, sledge-hammer. —**garn**, *n.* trawl-net. —**grube**, *f.* sink, drain. —**kasten**, *m.* caisson (*Hydr.*). —**kolben**, *m.* countersink; bradawl; drill. —**leine**, —**linie**, *f.* fathom-line. —**loch**, *n. see* —**grube**; hole for planting vine-layers in. —**nadel**, *f.* probe (*Surg.*). —**pfahl**, *m.* prop (for a young vine). —**rebe**, *f.* layer of vine. —**recht**, *adj.* perpendicular, vertical; **eine —rechte Linie ziehen (fällen)**, to raise, draw, let fall a perpendicular; **nicht —recht stehen**, to be out of the perpendicular. —**schnur**, *f.* plumb-line. —**wage**, *f.* aerometer, hydrometer; levelling plummet. —**werk**, *n.* (sunken) hurdles for damming water. —**zeit**, *f.* season for taking layers.

Sen'n—e, *m.* (—**en**, *pl.* —**en**), —**er**, *m.* (—**ers**, *pl.* —**er**) Swiss *or* Bavarian cowherd; cheese-maker. —**e**, *f.* herd of cattle (*in Switzerland*); pasture-land; cowherd's cottage. —**en**, *v.n.* (*aux.* **h.**) to be a (Swiss) cowherd; to be a cheesemaker, to keep a dairy (*in the Alps*). —**erei'**, *f.* Alpine dairy; rearing of cattle. —(**er**)**in**, *f.* dairy-keeper, dairy-maid. *Comp.* —**hütte**, *f.* cow-keeper's hut, Alpine dairy.

Sen'nes, *see* **Senes**.

Sensa'l, *m.* (—**s**, —**en**, *pl.* —**e**, —**en**) licensed broker. *Comp.* —**gebühr**, *f.* brokerage.

Sensatio'n, *f.* (*pl.* —**en**) sensation; **— machen**, to create a sensation. *Comp.* —**s=bedürfnis**, *n.* desire for sensational news. —**s=nachricht**, *f.* sensational news. —**s=prozeß**, *m.* sensational case *or* law-suit. —**s=roman**, *m.* sensational novel; **billige —sromane**, shilling shockers, penny dreadfuls (*fam.*).

Sen'se, *f.* (*pl.* —**n**) scythe; **eine — dengeln**, to sharpen a scythe. *Comp.* —**n=eisen**, *n.* blade of a scythe. —**n=gerüst**, *n.* scythe-cradle. —**n=mann**, *m.* mower, reaper; man armed with a scythe; Polish soldier; Death. —**n=stein**, *m.* hone, whetstone. —**n=wagen**, *m.* scythed war chariot (*of the ancients*).

[1]**Sen'te**, *f.* (*pl.* —**n**) ribbon-line (*Naut.*).

[2]**Sen'te**, *f.* (*pl.* —**n**) herd of Alpine cows.

Sente'nz, *f.* (*pl.* —**en**) sentence; maxim; **in —en sprechen**, to be sententious. —**en=haft**, —**iö's**, *adj.* sententious.

Sentimenta'l, *adj.* sentimental; namby-pamby, milk-and-watery. **—isch,** *adv.* influenced by the writer's feeling, subjective; **—ische Dichtung,** subjective poetry. **—alitä't,** *f.* sentimentalism.

Separ—a't, *adj.* separate, special. **—ati'st,** *m.* (**—ati'sten,** *pl.* **—ati'sten**) sectary; seceder. **—ie'ren,** *v.a. & r.* to separate. **—ier'te(r,** *m.*), *f.* divorced person. *Comp.* **—at'=abdruck, —at'=abzug,** *m.* special print, off-print. **—at'=eingang,** *m.* private entrance. **—at'=konto,** *n.* special account.

Se'pia, *f.* cuttle-fish; sepia. *Comp.* **—zeichnung,** *f.* sepia-drawing.

Sept—em'ber, *m.* (**—embers,** *pl.* **—ember**) September. **—ima'ner,** *m.* (**—imaners,** *pl.* **—imaner**) pupil of the seventh class from the top, boy in the preparatory department.

Sep'time, *f.* (*pl.* **—n**) seventh, leading note (*Mus.*).

Seque'nz, *f.* (*pl.* **—en**) sequence.

Seques't—er, I. *n.* (**—ers,** *pl.* **—er**) sequestration. II. *m.* (**—ers,** *pl.* **—er**) sequestrator. **—rier'bar,** *adj.* subject to sequestration. **—rie'ren,** *v.a.* to sequestrate.

Serai'(l), (*m. &*) *n.* (**—s,** *pl.* **—s**) seraglio.

Sera'phisch, Seraphi'nisch, *adj.* seraphic.

Sergea'nt, *m.* sergeant (*Mil.*).

Se'rie, *f.* (*pl.* **—n**) series; **nach —n geordnet,** serial. *Comp.* **—n=system,** Gouin method (*of teaching languages*).

Sermo'n, *m.* (**—s,** *pl.* **—e**) sermon; tedious lecture *or* discourse (*usually iron.*).

Sero'ne, Suro'ne, *f.* (*pl.* **—n**) seroon (*bale covered with hide*).

Serö's, *adj.* serous.

Serpenti'n, *m.* (**—s,** *pl.* **—e**) serpentine(-stone), ophite (*Min.*).

Serpenti'n—e, *f.* (*pl.* **—en**) winding road, meandering walk. *Comp.* **—en=weg,** *m.* winding path *or* road. **—tanz,** *m.* skirt-dance. **—tänzerin,** *f.* skirt-dancer.

Serv—i'ce, *n.* service (*of plate*); service; *see* **—is. —iet'te,** *f.* (*pl.* **—ietten**) table-napkin. **—i'l,** *adj.* servile. **—ilis'mus,** *m.*, **—ilitä't,** *f.* servility. **—ie'ren,** *v.a. & n.* (*aux.* **h.**) to serve, wait (*at table*); to lay the cloth; to serve (*one's time*); **es ist —iert,** dinner is on the table. **—i's,** *n.* quartering-allowance (*Mil.*). **—itu't,** *f.* (*pl.* **—ituten**) compulsory service; obligation; charge upon an estate.

Se'sam, *m.* sesame; **—, —, thu dich auf!** open, sesame!

Ses'sel, *m.* (**—s,** *pl.* **—**) seat; arm-chair, easy-chair; **niedriger —,** low stool. *Comp.* **—macher,** *m.* manufacturer of arm-chairs, upholsterer. **—recht,** *n.* right of the tabouret, right of sitting in the presence of the sovereign.

Seß'haft, *adj.* settled; stationary; resident.

Ses'ter, *n.* (**—s,** *pl.* **—**) measure of about 12 bushels *or* 16 quarts, sester, sexter.

Sesti'ne, *f.* (*pl.* **—n**) sestine, sextain.

Set'z—en, I. *v.a.* to place, set, put, fix; plant; to erect; to arrange, settle; to lay down, prescribe (*obs.*); to wager, stake; to compose (*Mus.*, *Typ.*); to assume, suppose; to bring forth young, breed, spawn; **ein gesetzter junger Mann,** a steady young man; **—en an,** to put on, in, to *or* near, to apply, to expose to; **ans Land —en,** to put ashore; **einen Stuhl an den andern —en,** to draw two chairs together *or* near one another; **alles daran —en,** to stake one's all, to do one's utmost; **—en auf** (*acc.*), to put, place, set on; **sich aufs hohe Pferd —en,** to mount upon the high horse (*fig.*); **auf die Straße —en, an die Luft —en,** to turn out of doors; **auf die Probe —en** (*now usually* **stellen**), to put to the proof; **seinen Kopf auf eine S. —en,** to be bent on doing s. th.; **sich auf die Hinterbeine —en,** to resist, to defend o. s.; to be obstinate (*fam.*); **den Preis auf eine Mark —en,** to fix the price at a mark; **aus den Augen —en,** to neglect, disregard; **aus einander —en,** to explain, make clear; **sich mit seinen Gläubigern auseinander —en,** to compound with one's creditors; **sich mit seinen Kritikern auseinander —en,** to discuss the points raised by one's critics; **außer Kraft —en,** to invalidate; to repeal; **außer Stand —en,** to disable; **—en in** (*acc.*), to put, set in *or* into, to set at (*liberty, etc.*), to put to (*expense, etc.*), to put into (*a passion, etc.*), to carry into (*effect, etc.*); **einen in Angst —en,** to terrify a p.; **in Bewegung —en,** to move, set in motion; **Himmel und Hölle in Bewegung —en,** to move heaven and earth, to leave no stone unturned; **eine Truppe in Marsch —en,** to give orders to march; **einen in Bekanntschaft mit (einem** *or* **einer S.) —en,** to make s.o. acquainted with; **in Flammen —en,** to set on fire, to set fire to; **in Gang —en,** to set a-going; **sein Pferd** *or* **sich in Galopp —en,** to put one's horse to a gallop; **in Klafter —en,** to cord; **ein Stück in Scene —en,** to mount a play; **ein Stück neu in Scene —en,** to remount a piece (*Theat.*); **sich** (*dat.*) **etwas in den Kopf —en,** to take s.th. into one's head; **Mißtrauen in einen —en,** to mistrust a p.; **sich in Besitz —en,** to put oneself in possession of; **seinen Stolz darein —en,** to take a pride in it; **Kinder in die Welt —en,** to beget *or* bear children; **—en über** (*acc.*), to put, place over *or* above; to row, ferry over; to set over; to prefer to; **einen Punkt über das „i" —en,** to dot one's i's; **er wird uns übers Wasser —en,** he will take *or* put us across; **einen Schüler über die andern —en,** to place a boy above the others; **sich um das Feuer —en,** to sit round the fire; **einen unter die Heiligen —en,** to rank s.o. amongst the saints; **unter Wasser —en,** to submerge; **einen vor die Thür —en, einem den Stuhl vor die Thür —en,** to turn a p. out; **zur Rede —en,** to call to account; **zum Pfande —en,** to give as a pledge, to pawn; **zurecht —en,** to set right *or* to rights; **zum Richter —en,** to appoint, constitute judge; **den Bock zum Gärtner —en,** to set the fox to keep the geese (*prov.*); **sich zu Pferde —en,** to mount; **sich zu Tische —en,** to seat oneself at the table, to sit down to a meal; **sich zur Wehr —en,** to defend oneself, to show fight; **sich zu einem —en,** to sit down by s.o.; **sich zwischen zwei Stühle —en,** to fall between two stools; **seinen Wünschen Grenzen —en,** to limit one's desires; **wieviel —en Sie?** what will you wager? **man —t die Einer hin,** you put down the units (*Arith.*); **Interpunktion —en,** to punctuate; **fest —en,** to fix, appoint, determine; **einen fest —en,** to put a p. in prison; **den Fall —en,** to put the case, to suppose: **gesetzten Falls,** in the given case, suppose; **setzen wir also, daß,** let us therefore assume that; **gesetzt, es wäre so,** supposing it were so, granted that it is so; put the case (*assuming*) it be so. II. *v.r.* to seat oneself, take a seat; to perch; to sink (*of soil, etc.*); to settle, deposit dregs; to subside; to take up a position; to settle, establish oneself; to come to an arrangement (*for examples with prep.'s see above*). III. *v.n.* (*aux.* **h.** & **s.**) to run, spring, leap; to pass (*over*); to attack; **an den Feind —en,** to fall upon the enemy; **über einen Zaun —en,** to take a fence (*in riding*); **über einen Graben —en,** to jump (across) a ditch; **über einen Fluß —en,** to cross a river; **der Gang —t in (durch) das Gebirge,** the lode strikes into the rock. IV. *v.imp.*; **es wird Schläge —en,** there will be blows, it will come to blows; es —t schon Tropfen, it begins to rain; was hat es gesetzt? what has occurred? na, heute wird es etwas —en, well, to-day you will catch it hot (*coll.*). V. *subst.n.* setting (*at liberty, etc.*); settlement (*of buildings, etc.*); placing; composition (*Mus., Typ.*). —er, *m.* (—ers, *pl.* —er) staker; compositor (*Typ.*); composer (*Mus.*); ramrod. —erei', *f.* composing-room, compositor's room. —ling, *m.* (—lings, *pl.* —linge) cutting, slip, layer; plant, young tree; fry, spawn. *Comp.* —bord, *m.* wash-board (*Naut.*). —brett, *n.* letter-board, compositor's board (*Typ.*); riser (*of a stair*). —eier, *pl.* fried eggs; poached eggs (verlorene Eier). —eisen, *n.* blacksmith's cutter. —erde, *f.* sods. —(er)=fehler, *m.* typographical error. —er=maschine, *f.* composing machine. —haken, *m.* large drawing-hook (*Metall.*); crowbar; composing-stick (*Typ.*). —hase, *m.* doe-hare. —holz, *n.* dibble (*Hort.*). —karpfen, *m.* carp-fry. —kasten, *m.* letter-case (*Typ.*). —kolben, *m.* rammer (*Artil.*). —kunst, *f.* composition (*Mus.*); type-setting. —linie, *f.* reglet, composing *or* spacing rule (*Typ.*). —maschine, *f.* composing machine (*Typ.*); (—sieb, *n.*) machine-jigger (*Metall.*); —= und Ablegemaschine, machine for composing and distributing type. —rebe, *f.* vine-layer. —schiff, *n.* galley (*Typ.*). —teich, *m.* fish-(*breeding-*)pond. —wage, *f.* level. —zeit, *f.* breeding-time.

Seu'che, *f.* (*pl.* —n) contagious disease, epidemic; pestilence; protracted illness, lingering disease. *Comp.* —n=artig, *adj.* epidemic; contagious. —n=fest, —n=frei, *adj.* immune. —n=herd, *m.* centre of contagion. —n=stoff, *m.* contagious matter, virus.

Seuf'ze—n, I. *v.n.* (*aux.* h.) to sigh; to groan. II. *subst. n.* sighing, groaning. —r, *m.* (—rs, *pl.* —r) sigh, groan. *Comp.* —r=brücke, *f.* Bridge of Sighs.

Sex't—a, *f.* (*pl.* —en, —s) lowest form of any higher secondary Germ. school (*age of pupils between 9 and 10*), corresponds to the Engl. first form. —a'ner, *m.* (—aners, *pl.* —aner) sixth form boy (in Germany), first form boy (in England). —e, *f.* (*pl.* —en) sixth (*Mus.*); sequence of six (*Cards*); die kleine (große) —e, minor (major) sixth. —o'le, *f.* (*pl.* —olen) sextole, sextuplet (*Mus.*).

Seyn, *obs. spelling for* 2 Sein.

Sezessio'n, *f.* (*pl.* —en) secession.

Sezie'r—en, *v.a.* to dissect, to cut up (*fam.*). *Comp.* —besteck, *n.* case of dissecting instruments. —messer, *n.* scalpel.

Sgraffi'to, *n.* sgrafitto, scratch work.

Shawl, *m.* (—s, *pl.* —s) shawl; comforter.

She'rif, *m.* (—s, *pl.* —s) sheriff.

Sich, (*3 sing. or pl. dat. & acc. m. f. & n. of*) *refl. pron.* himself, herself, itself, themselves; yourself, yourselves (*where the 3 pers. is used in addressing*); one another; sie lieben —, they love themselves *or* each other; an —, in the abstract, of itself; der Magnet zieht das Eisen an —, the magnet attracts iron; Geld bei — haben, to have money about one; niemand bei — sehen, to see no company; — etwas zum Muster nehmen, to take s. th. for a model; das schickt — nicht, that is not proper *or* becoming, not nice; was hat das auf —? what does that matter? es hat wenig auf —, it is of little importance. *Comp.* (*infin. used as nouns, e.g.*) —gehenlassen, *n.* freedom from restraint. —selbst=überlassensein, *n.* isolation. —überheben, *n.* pride.

Si'chel, *f.* (*pl.* —n) sickle; sickle-shaped thing; crescent; falx (*Anat.*). —n, *v.a.* to cut with a sickle, reap; gesichelt, armed with a sickle, sickle-shaped. *Comp.* —artig, *adj.* sickle-shaped. —beinig, *adj.* bow-legged. —fest, *n.* harvest (*dial.*). —frohne, *f.* statute-reaping. —wagen, *m.* chariot armed with scythes.

Si'cher, *adj. & adv.* secure, safe; sure, certain; assured, without fear; trusty, trustworthy, true; — machen, to make (*a place*) secure, to make (*s.o.*) feel secure; — wissen, to know for certain, to be positive; um — zu gehen, in order to make quite sure, so as not to make any mistake, for sake of security; — vor, safe from *or* against; vor mir bist du —, you have nothing to fear from me; —es Geleit, safe-conduct; das Geld steht —, the money is safe; von —er Hand haben, to have on good authority; seiner Sache — sein, to know what one is about; to be certain of a thing; to be a proficient in a thing; — ist sie keine Schottin, one thing is certain: she is not a Scotchwoman; — auf einen rechnen, to count confidently upon a p.; er sitzt auf Numero —, he is safely locked up, he is in prison (*coll.*). —heit, *f.* certainty; trustworthiness; guarantee; security, safety; safeguard; etwas mit —heit behaupten, to affirm; —heit im Auftreten, self-possession, assurance. —lich, *adv.* surely, certainly, undoubtedly. —n, *v.* I. *a.* to ensure, make sure, guarantee; to indemnify. II. *n.* (*aux.* h.) to test the security of a place (*Sport*). —ung, *f.* securing, ensuring; guarantee; assurance. *Comp.* —heits=anstalt, *f.* institution for public security; insurance-company. —heits=arrest, *m.* precautionary arrest. —heits=ausschuß, *m.* committee of public safety. —heits=behörde, *f.* police. —heits=geleit, *n.* safe-conduct. —heits=lampe, *f.* (Davysche, Sir H. Davy's) safety-lamp. —heits=maßregeln, *pl.* precautionary measures. —heits=nadel, *f.* safety-pin. —heits=pfand, *n.* counter-pledge. —heits=schalter, *m.* safety-switch (*electr.*). —heits=ventil, *n.* safety-valve. —heits=zündhölzchen, *pl.* safety-matches. —stellig, *adj.* with sure aim; putting everything in its proper place (*rare, poet.*).

Sicht, *f.* sight; auf —, at sight; sieben Tage nach —, seven days after sight. —bar, *adj. & adv.* visible; —bar werden, to appear, to become visible, manifest *or* evident. —barkeit, *f.* visibleness. —barlich, *adv.* visibly. —lich, *adj. & adv.* visible, apparent; obvious. *Comp.* —bar=werden, *n.* appearance (*of a comet, etc.*). —korn, *n.* sight (*of a gun*). —note, *f.*, —wechsel, *m.* bill payable at sight. —tage, *pl.* days of grace.

Sich'te—n, *v.a.* to sift, winnow; to bolt (*flour*). —r, *m.* (—rs, *pl.* —r) sifter.

Si'cker—n, *v.n.* (*aux.* h. & s.) to trickle, drop, ooze; das Faß —t, the cask leaks. —ungen, (—schlitzen,) *pl.* spade-drams.

Side'risch, *adj.* sidereal.

Sie, I. *pers. pron.* **1.** (*3 sing. f. nom. & acc.*) she, her, (it); you (*used to women in an inferior position instead of* du). **2.** (*3 pl. m. f. & n. nom. & acc.*) they; them; (Sie) you (*in addressing*): — und ich werden zusammen abreisen, you and I will start together; — da, Mann! you there, fellow! I say! II. *f.* she, female (*usually of birds*); dieser Vogel ist eine —, it is a hen bird.

Sieb, *n.* (—es, *pl.* —e) sieve. *Comp.* —artig, *adj.* cribrose. —bein, *n.* ethmoid bone (*Anat.*). —kasten, *m.* box-riddle; cinder-sifter. — —läufer, *m.* rim of a sieve. —mehl, *n.* sifted flour, pollard. —staub, *m.* siftings. —tuch, *n.* straining-cloth.

[1]**Sie'ben,** *v.a.* to sift, bolt, riddle.

[2]**Sie'ben,** I. *num. adj.* seven; halb —, half-past six; meine — Sachen, my belongings, my goods and chattels; ein Buch mit — Siegeln, a book sealed with seven seals, a mysterious *or*

obscure book, a complete secret. II. *f.* number seven; card of seven; böse —, vixen, shrew. —er (—ers, *pl.* —er), Sieb'ner, *m.* soldier of the seventh regiment; the figure 7; one of seven; wine of 1807. —t, *num. adj.* (der, die, das —te) seventh; der —te (7) Februar, the 7th of February. —tel, *n.* (—tels, *pl.* —tel); ein —tel, a seventh (⅐). —tens, *adv.*, (zum —ten,) seventhly. —zig, *see* Siebzig. *Comp.* —eck, *n.* heptagon. —eckig, *adj.* heptagonal. —er=lei, Siebner=lei, *indec. adj. & adv.* of seven different kinds. —fach, —fältig, *adj.* seven-fold. —gestirn, *n.* Pleiades. —herrschaft, *f.* heptarchy. —hügel=stadt, *f.* city of the Seven Hills (*Rome*). —jährig, *adj.* seven years old; lasting seven years; der —jährige Krieg, the Seven Years' War (1756-63). —jährlich, *adj.* septennial, occurring every seven years. —mal, *adv.* seven times. —malig, *adj.* seven times repeated. —meilen=stiefel, *pl.* seven-league boots. —meilen=schritte, *pl.* giant's strides. —schläfer, *m.* one of the Seven Sleepers; great sleeper; sluggard, lie-a-bed, lazy-bones; dormouse. —stimmig, *adj.* for seven voices *or* parts. —stündig, *adj.* of *or* for seven hours. —tägig, *adj.* seven days old. —te=halb, *n.* six and a half. —thorig, *adj.* having seven gates. —zehn, *see* Siebzehn.

Sieb'zehn, *num. adj.* seventeen. —er, *m.* (—ers, *pl.* —er) the figure seventeen. —t, *num. adj.* (der, die, das —te) seventeenth. —tens, *adv.* seventeenthly. —tel, *n.* (—tels, *pl.* —tel) a seventeenth part ($\frac{1}{17}$).

Sieb'zig, *num. adj.* seventy. —er, *m.* (—ers, *pl.* —er), —erin, *f.* septuagenarian; ein vorgerückter —er, a man well advanced in the seventies; die —er Jahre, the years between 1870 and 1879, the seventies. —st, (der, die, das —ste) *num. adj.* seventieth. —stel, *n.* (—stels, *pl.* —stel) a seventieth part ($\frac{1}{70}$). *Comp.* —er=lei, *indec. adj. & adv.* of seventy kinds. —jährig, *adj.* of seventy years, septuagenarian.

Siech, *adj. & adv.* sickly; languishing with disease; pining away; infirm; ein —er, valetudinarian. —heit, *f.*, —tum, *n.* (—tums) sickliness, chronic ill health, (*permanent*) infirmity, valetudinarianism. *Comp.* —bett, *n.* sick-bed. —haus, —en=haus, *n.* infirmary; hospital for incurables. —korb, *m.* stretcher.

Sie'chen, *v.n.* to be a confirmed invalid; to languish away, to pine away.

Sie'de, *f.* boiling, seething, ebullition; in der — sein, to be boiling (hot).

Sie'deln, *see* ansiedeln.

Sie'de—n, *reg. & ir. v.* I. *n.* (*aux.* h.) to boil; mein Blut —te, my blood was boiling; —nd heiß, boiling hot. II. *a.* to boil, seethe; to stew; to blanch (*silver*); to refine (*sugar*); to make (*soap*); die Köchin sott das Huhn, the cook boiled the chicken; weich gesottene Eier, soft-boiled eggs. —r, *m.* (—rs, *pl.* —r) boiler, seether; refiner. —rei', *f.* boiling; boiling-place. *Comp.* —bottich, *m.* scalding-tub. —grad, *m.* boiling-point. —haus, *n.* salt-house; boiling-house. —hitze, *f.* boiling-heat. —kessel, *m.* boiler. —ofen, *m.* blanching furnace. —pfanne, *f.* boiling-pan; salt-pan; soap-pan. —punkt, *m.* boiling-point. —r=kessel, *m.*, —schale, *f.* boiler.

Sieg, *m.* (—es, *pl.* —e) victory; triumph; laurels, trophies; den — davon tragen, to carry the day; den — behalten, to be victorious. —haft, *see* —reich. *Comp.* —es=aufzug, *m.* triumphal procession, triumph. —es=bahn, *f.* career of victory. —es=bogen, *m.* triumphal arch. —es=dankfest, *n.* thanksgiving-festival, Te-Deum. —es=denkmal, *n.* monument in commemoration of a victory. —es=gewiß, *adj.* sure *or* confident of victory. —es=gepränge, *n.* triumphal pomp. —es=göttin, *f.* Victory. —es=lauf, *m.* course of victory, triumphal progress; —eslauf des Heeres, victorious advance of the army. —es=lied, *n.* song of triumph. —es=opfer, *n.* victim to a victory; sacrifice for a victory. —es=trunken, *adj.* flushed *or* elated with victory. —es=wagen, *m.* triumphal car. —es=zeichen, *n.* sign of victory; trophy. —es=zug, *m.* triumph, triumphal progress. —gewohnt, *adj.* accustomed to conquer. —reich, *adj.* victorious; triumphant.

Sie'gel, *n.* (—s, *pl.* —) seal; das geheime (Staats)—, privy seal; unter — legen, to seal; Brief und — über eine S. haben, to have under sign (*or* hand) and seal; das — lösen, to solve the mystery; unter dem — der Verschwiegenheit, under the seal of secrecy, in strict confidence; das ist für mich ein Buch mit sieben —n, that is a sealed book to me, that's all Greek to me. *Comp.* —bewahrer, *m.* keeper of the seal; (geheimer) Lord Privy Seal. —brief, *m.* letters patent. —erde, *f.* sealed *or* Lemnian earth. —gebühr, *n.* fees paid for affixing a seal. —lack, —wachs, *n.* sealing-wax. —lack=stange, *f.* stick of sealing-wax. —ring, *m.* signet-ring. —stecher, *m.* seal-engraver.

Sie'gel—n, *v.a.* to seal; to affix a seal. —ung, *f.* sealing.

Sie'ge—n, *v.n.* (*aux.* h.) to be victorious, triumph, gain the victory; —end, victorious, triumphant. —r, *m.* (—rs, *pl.* —r) conqueror, victor. *Comp.* —r=kranz, *m.* conqueror's (laurel) wreath, conqueror's crown.

Sie(h)l, *m.* (*& n.*) (—s, *pl.* —e) sluice in a dike; drain, sewer; creek, small inlet (*dial.*).

Sie'le, *f.* (*pl.* —n) horse-collar, breast piece of harness; belt *or* braces of a barrow-man; immer in den —n gehen, to be always in harness, to be continually slaving; wieder in die — gehen, to set to work again.

Sie'zen, *v.a.* to address a p. formally with Sie (*and not with* du).

Si'gle, *f.* (*pl.* —n) grammalogue; distinctive mark or notation.

Signa'l, *n.* (—s, *pl.* —e) signal. —isie'ren, *v.a.* to signal; to signalize. *Comp.* —apparat, *m.* signalling apparatus. —buch, *n.* code of signals. —feuer, *n.* signal fire; false signal. —flagge, *f.* Blue Peter. —geber, *m.* signaller. —glocke, *f.* warning *or* response bell (*at telegraph-stations*). —horn, *n.* signal-horn, bugle-(horn). —laternen, *pl.* signal-lights. —leine, *f.* bell-cord. —pfeife, *f.* signal-whistle; steam-whistle. —ruf, *m.* signal, call; bugle-call. —schuß, *m.* signal-gun; —schüsse thun, to fire signals. —stange, —station, *f.* semaphore (*Railw.*). —wärter, *m.* signal-man.

Signaleme'nt, *n.* (—s, *pl.* —s) personal description of a p. wanted by the police.

Signatu'r, *f.* (*pl.* —aturen) signature (*also Typ.*); sign; mark; stamp; label (*on a medicine-bottle, etc.*).

Signie'ren, *v.a.* to sign; to witness.

Si'grist, *m.* (—en, *pl.* —en) sacristan, sexton (*dial.*).

Sil'be, *f.* (*pl.* —n) syllable; vorletzte —, penult; drittletzte —, antepenult; —n stechen, to be precise about words, quibble; aus —n bestehend, syllabic; aus drei —n bestehend, trisyllabic. *Comp.* —n=abteilung, *f.* division into syllables. —n=fall, —n=tritt, *m.* rhythm. —n=klauber, *m.*, *see* —n=stecher. —n=maß, *n.*, n=rechnung, *f.* metre; quantity. —n=messung, *f.* prosody. —n=rätsel, *n.* charade. —n=stecher, *m.* verbal critic, petty critic. —n=stecherei, *f.* hypercriticism; hair-splitting; quibbling. —n=weise, *adv.* by syllables.

Sil'ber, *n.* (—**s**) silver; plate; **mit — belegt**, silver-plated, plated with silver; — **in Barren**, silver in ingots, bar- *or* rod-silver, bullion. —**ling**, *m.* (—**lings**, *pl.* —**linge**) piece of silver; shekel. —**n**, *adj.* (of) silver; —**ne Hochzeit**, silver wedding (*25th anniversary*); —**nes Zeitalter**, age of silver. *Comp.* —**ader**, *f.* vein of silver (*Min.*). —**arbeiter**, *m.* silversmith. —**artig**, *adj.* silvery, argentine. —**barre(n**, *m.*), *f.* bar, ingot of silver. —**beschlag**, *m.* silver fittings *or* mounting. —**blei**, *n.* argentiferous lead. —**blende**, *f.* galena of silver, mock silver ore. —**blick**, *m.* gleam of silver; silvery light (*poet.*). —**braut**, *f.*, —**bräutigam**, *m.* wife *or* husband celebrating the 25th aniversary of their wedding. —**brenner**, *m.* silver-refiner. —**buche**, *f.* white *or* American beech. —**diener**, *m.* servant *or* official in charge of the plate. —**drahtzieher**, *m.* silver-wire drawer. —**erz**, *n.* silver-ore. —**farben**, —**farbig**, *adj.* silvery (in colour). —**fasan**, *m.* silver pheasant. —**forelle**, *f.* salmon trout. —**gehalt**, *m.* proportion of silver in an amalgam; standard (*of coin*). —**geld**, *n.* silver money; **kleines —geld**, (small) change. —**gerät**, —**geschirr**, *n.* plate. —**glanz**, *m.* silvery lustre; silver-glance (*Min.*). —**gold**, *n.* electrum. —**grau**, *adj.* silvery gray. —**groschen**, *m.* silver piece ($\frac{1}{30}$ *of a thaler*) worth about one penny (*obs.*) —**hell**, *adj.* (as) bright as silver; —**helle Stimme**, silvery voice. —**kammer**, *f.* plate-room. —**kämmerer**, *see* —**diener**. —**klang**, *m.* clear, silvery sound. —**korn**, *n.* grain of silver; button (*Chem.*). —**krone**, *f.* crown-piece. —**laden**, *m.* silversmith's shop. —**licht**, *n.* silvery light (*of the moon*). —**locke**, *f.* silvery lock *or* curl. —**münze**, *f.* silver coin. —**oxyd**, *n.* oxide of silver. —**papier**, *n.* silver-paper. —**pappel**, *f.* white poplar, abele. —**plattierung**, *f.* silver-plating. —**salpeter**, *m.* nitrate of silver. —**schaum**, *m.* foliated silver. —**scheibe**, *f.* silvery disc (*of the moon*). —**scheider**, *m.* silver-refiner. —**schein**, *m.* silvery lustre. —**schiff**, *n.* (*Spanish*) galleon. —**schimmel**, *m.* silver-gray horse. —**schmied**, *m.* silversmith. —**schrank**, *m.* plate-chest. —**service**, *n.* service of plate. —**stickerei**, *f.* embroidery in silver. —**stoff**, *m.* silver brocade; silver cloth *or* tissue. —**tanne**, *f.* silver fir, abies pectinata. —**ton**, *m.* silvery sound. —**tresse**, *f.* silver lace. —**verbindungen**, *pl.f.* argentiferous compounds. —**waren**, *pl.* silver goods; plate. —**währung**, *f.* silver-standard; silver currency; **Anhänger der —währung**, bimetallist, silverite (*Amer.*). —**wäscher**, *m.* plate-cleaner. —**weide**, *f.* common white willow. —**weiß**, I. *adj.* silvery. II. *n.* shell-silver (*Paint.*). —**zahn** *m.* sprig of silver. —**zeug**, *n.* plate, household silver.

Sil'ge, *f.* milk-parsley.

Silhouettie'ren, *v.a.* to take silhouettes.

Sillabie'ren, *v.a.* to spell; to syllable.

Silla'bisch, *adj. & adv.* syllabic.

Silu'risch, *adj.* silurian.

Sim'pel, I. *adj.* simple; plain. II. *m.* (—**s**, *pl.* —) simpleton, blockhead, duffer (*coll.*).

Sims, *m.* (*& n.*) (—(**s**)**es**, *pl.* —(**s**)**e**) cornice, moulding; shelf. *Comp.* —**hobel**, *m.* moulding-plane. —**werk**, *n.* mouldings.

Simula'nt, *m.* (—**en**, *pl.* —**en**), —**in**, *f.* one who feigns illness in order to shirk duty or labour, sham-patient, malingerer (*milit.*).

Simulie'ren, *v.a. & n.* (*aux.* **h.**) to feign, simulate, sham; **er simuliert nur**, he is only shamming *or* pretending; **simulierte Rechnung**, pro-forma account; **auf eine S. —**, to brood over something, to plot something.

Simultan'=schule, *f.* school attended by children belonging to different religious communities, *e.g.* by Protestants and Catholics; **undenominational** school.

Sind, *1 & 3 pers. pl. pres. ind. of* **sein**.

Sinekü'r(e), *f.* (*pl.* —(**e**)**n**) sinecure.

Sing'bar, *adj.* singable; vocal.

Sin'g—en, I. *ir.v.a. & n.* (*aux.* **h.**) to sing; to ring, tingle; to chant (*the litany in church*) · to warble, carol (*of birds*); **in den Schlaf —en**, to sing, lull to sleep; **falsch —en**, to sing out of tune; **Sopran —en**, to have a soprano voice; to take the soprano part; **mehrstimmig —en**, to sing part songs, to sing in parts; **sein eignes Lob —en**, to chant one's own praises, to blow one's own trumpet (*coll.*); **dem Herrn —en**, to sing unto the Lord; **immer dasselbe Lied —en**, to be always harping on the same string; **dieser Sänger kann das hohe C —en**, this singer can take the high C; **seine Stimme —en**, to take a *or* one's part; **ein Tonstück mit Benennung der Noten —en**, to (sing) sol-fa; **vom Blatte weg en**, to sing at sight; **nach Noten —en**, to sing from music; **das ist gesungen wie gepfiffen**, that all comes to the same thing (*prov.*); **das ward mir an meiner Wiege nicht gesungen**, people little thought that I should ever come to this (*coll.*); **ich kann ein Liedchen davon singen**, I know by experience; **wie die Alten sungen, so zwitschern nun die Jungen**, as the old cock crows, the young one learns; as the old birds sing, the young ones twitter. II. *refl. & impers.*; **das Lied —t sich leicht**, this song is easy to sing; **es —t sich schön im Walde**, it is pleasant to sing in the woods; **es —t mir in den Ohren**, my ears are tingling. —**erei'**, *f.* perpetual singing. *Comp.* —**akademie**, —**anstalt**, *f.* singing-school. —(**e**)=**chor**, I. *m.* choir (*of singers*). II. *n.* choir (*Arch.*). —**drossel**, *f.* song-thrush. —**fertigkeit**, *f.* aptitude for singing; **große —fertigkeit haben**, to be a great singer. —**gedicht**, *n.* poetry *or* words for music, cantata. —**lehrer**, *m.* singing-master. —**meister**, *m.* teacher of singing; celebrated singer. —**oper**, *f.* grand opera. —(**e**)=**note**, *f.* musical note; *pl.* vocal music. —**saite**, *f.* treble string (*Violin*). —**sang**, *m.* sing-song. —**schlüssel**, *m.* clef (*Mus.*). —**schwan**, *m.* whistling swan, Cygnus musicus. —**spiel**, *n.* operetta; lyrical drama; musical comedy, vaudeville. —**spielhalle**, *f.* music-hall. —**stimme**, *f.* good voice for singing; vocal part (*Mus.*); **Lied für eine —stimme**, song for a single voice, solo song. —**stück**, *n.* song, ballad, air, cantata. —**verein**, *m.* choral society. —**vogel**, *m.* singing-bird, songster (*poet.*), warbler (*poet.*). —**weise**, *f.* style of singing; melody, tune, air.

Sin'grün, *n.* (—**s**) periwinkle (*Bot.*).

Sin'gular, *m.* singular (*number*) (*Gram.*).

Singulä'r, *adj.* strange, peculiar, odd.

Sin'ken, *ir.v.* I. *a.* to sink (*a shaft*). II. *n.* (*aux.* **s.**) to sink, give way, descend; to fall down, sink; to abate, diminish, decline; **in Ohnmacht —**, to faint away; **die Stimme — lassen**, to lower the voice; **bis in die —de Nacht**, till nightfall; **die Flügel nicht — lassen**, not to lose heart *or* courage; **der Mut sank ihm**, his heart failed him.

Sinn, *m.* (—**es**, *pl.* —**e**; *obs. & poet.* —**en**) sense, organ of perception; intellect, mind, intelligence; apprehension; memory; opinion; taste; disposition; tendency; wish; character; temper; import, meaning, signification; **hoher —**, highmindedness, magnanimity; — **für (etwas) haben**, to have a taste for, be susceptible to, take an interest in; — **für Litteratur**, interest in literature, literary taste; — **für Kunst**, taste for art; — **für Humor**, sense of humour; — **für Natur**, love of nature; **demütigen —es**, humble-minded; **in die —e fallen**, to appeal to the senses; **in die —e fallend**, perceptible, striking; **weder — noch Verstand**, neither rhyme nor reason; **seine fünf —e beisammen haben**, to have one's wits about one; **das sagen mir meine fünf —e**, my common sense tells me that; **nimm deine fünf — zusammen**, pull your wits together; **moralischer —**, moral sense; **fleischlicher —**, sensuality; **bildlicher —**, figurative sense; **im bildlichen —e**, figuratively; **im übertragenen —e**, metaphorically; **im eigentlichen —e**, literally, verbally; **in gewissem —e**, in a sense *or* way; **ihr vergingen die —e**, she lost consciousness; **sein — steht nach Höherem**, he has more ambitious views; **mit einem eines —es sein**, to be of one mind with, agree with a p.; **andern —es sein**, not to agree (*with a p.*); to differ (*from a p.*); **andern —es werden**, to change one's mind; **ich war meines —es voll es zu thun**, I was minded, felt inclined, had made up my mind to do it; **auf seinem — beharren**, to persist in one's intention *or* opinion; **ich kann es mir nicht aus dem —e schlagen, es will mir nicht aus dem —**, I can't get it out of my mind, can't forget it; **bei (von) —en sein**, to be in (out of) one's senses; **er ist kaum bei —en**, he is half-cracked; **durch den — fahren**, to strike, occur to s.o.; **es liegt mir im —e**, I have it in my mind, I can't get it out of my mind; **im —e behalten**, to carry (*Arith.*), to bear in mind; **(etwas) im —e haben**, to intend, meditate; **es will mir nicht in den —**, I can't conceive; **es kam mir in den —, daß**, it occurred to me that; **sich** (*dat.*) **in den — kommen lassen**, to take into one's head; **sich** (*dat.*) **aus dem —e schlagen**, to put out of one's mind; **in jemandes —e handeln**, to enter into another's ideas *or* plans; **er muß es nach seinem —e haben**, he must have it all his own way; **bist du von —en?** are you out of your senses? are you mad? **viel Köpfe, viel —e**, many men have many minds. **—ig**, *adj. & adv.* sensible, judicious; thoughtful, reflective; deliberate; ingenious; (*in comp.* =) -minded; **ein —iges Mädchen**, a thoughtful girl; **ein —iges Geschenk**, a well-devised gift. **—igkeit**, *f.* judgment, sense; thoughtfulness; ingenuity. **—lich**, *adj.* affecting the senses; material, physical, sensuous; perceptible; sensual, voluptuous; sentient (*Philos.*); **—liche Liebe**, sensual love; **—licher Mensch**, sensualist. **—lichkeit**, *f.* perceptive faculty; material nature; sensuality; **die —lichkeit reizen**, to appeal to the senses. *Comp.* **—bild**, *n.* symbol, type; allegory. **—bildlich**, *adj.* symbolic, emblematic; **—bildlich andeuten**, to be symbolical of. **—en=genuß**, *m.* sensual enjoyment. **—en=lust**, *f.* voluptuousness. **—en=rausch**, *m.* intoxication of the senses. **—en=welt**, *f.* material world. **—erklärung**, *f.* explanation of the sense *or* meaning. **—es=änderung**, *f.* change of mind; repentance, conversion. **—es=art**, *f.* character, disposition. **—es=kraft**, *f.* power of the senses; thinking faculty. **—es=organ**, *n.* organ of sense. **—es=täuschung**, *f.* illusion; hallucination. **—es=werkzeug**, *n.* organ of sense. **—gedicht**, *n.* epigram. **—gedicht=verfasser**, *m.* epigrammatist. **—leer**, *adj.* unmeaning, meaningless, devoid of meaning. **—los**, *adj.* deprived of the use of one's senses; thoughtless; mad; foolish, unmeaning. **—losigkeit**, *f.* want of perception; senselessness; absurdity; want of good sense. **—pflanze**, *f.* sensitive plant. **—reich**, *adj.* sensible; clever, witty; ingenious, talented; intellectual. **—rückhalt**, *m.* mental reservation. **—spruch**, *m.* witty *or* smart saying; maxim; motto. **—verwandt**, *adj.* synonymous; **—verwandtes Wort**, synonym. **—widrig**, *adj.* contrary to sense, nonsensical.

Sin'nen, I. *ir.v.n.* (*aux.* **h.** & **s.**) to think, meditate, reflect; to speculate (**über** (*acc.*), upon); **— auf** (*acc.*), to study, to scheme, contrive, devise, plot; **was sinnt ihr?** what are you thinking of? **gesonnen sein**, to be inclined, to intend, purpose; **gesinnt**, minded, inclined; **Gustav Adolf war protestantisch gesinnt und daher gesonnen, den deutschen Protestanten zu helfen**, G. A. was a Protestant and therefore intended to help the German Protestants. **—d**, *pres.p.* musing, pensive, thoughtful, contemplative, reflective; **—d aussehen**, to look thoughtful, absorbed in thought. II. *ir.v.a.* to cogitate, think out; to plot; to invent; **(auf) Rache —**, to meditate revenge. III. *subst.n.* thinking, planning; thoughts, aspirations.

Sinn'grün, *n. see* **Singrün**.

Sintema'l(en), *conj.* since, whereas (*obs.*).

Sin'ter, *m.* (**—s**) anvil-flakes (*of iron*); dross of iron; sinter, stalactite. **—n**, *v.n.* (*aux.* **s.**) to trickle, drop, ooze; to form stalactite deposits, to petrify; to coagulate.

Sint'flut, *f. obs. for* **Sündflut**.

Si'nus, *m.* sine (*Math.*); **— versus eines Bogens**, versed sine. *Comp.* **—bussole**, *f.* sine-compass. **—quadrant**, *m.* sinical quadrant.

Sip'p—e, *f.* (*pl.* **—en**) consanguinity, kin, kindred, relations; genus, tribe (*Zool.*); **die ganze —e**, all the kinsmen, the whole clan; **mit der ganzen —e**, with kith and kin. **—schaft**, *f.* consanguinity, kindred; set, lot, clique (*cont.*); **die ganze —schaft**, the whole lot *or* crew.

Sire'ne, *f.* (*pl.* **—n**) siren (*Myth.; Acoust.*).

Si'rup, *m.* (**—s**, *pl.* **—e**) syrup; treacle, molasses. *Comp.* **—artig**, *adj.* syrupy. **—s=prinz**, *m.* small retail shopkeeper (*contempt.*).

Sistie'r—en, *v.a.* to stop, inhibit. **—ung**, *f.* inhibition; summons (*Law*).

Sit't—e, *f.* (*pl.* **—en**) custom; habit; usage; practice; propriety, etiquette; (*pl.*) manners; (*pl.*) morals; **das ist so seine —e**, that is his way; **das ist bei uns nicht —e**, that is not our custom, we don't do that here; **feine —e**, good breeding. **—ig**, *adj. & adv.* modest, chaste; moral; polite; well-bred. **—lich**, *adj. & adv.* relating to *or* in accordance with manners *or* morals; customary; moral, ethical. **—lichkeit**, *f.* morality; **Verbrechen gegen die —lichkeit**, indecency, indecent assault. **—sam**, *adj.* modest; virtuous, chaste; well-behaved, proper. **—samkeit**, *f.* modesty, decency, coyness, bashfulness; **übertriebene —samkeit**, prudery. *Comp.* **—en=anmut**, *f.* charm of manner. **—en=buch**, *n.* book on morals; book on the manners and rules of good society, book on etiquette. **—en=gesetz**, *n.* moral code; moral law. **—en=lehre**, *f.* moral philosophy, ethics. **—en=lehrer**, *m.* moral philosopher, moralist. **—en=los**, *adj.* immoral, profligate, wicked; insulting, acting without consideration *or* restraint (*rare, poet.*). **—en=losigkeit**, *f.* immorality. **—en=polizei**, *f.* control of prostitutes, police surveillance. **—en=prediger**, *m.* moralizer. **—en=predigt**, *f.* moralizing sermon; **einem eine —enpredigt halten**, to read a p. a lecture. **—en=regel**, *f.* rule of conduct; moral precept. **—en=rein**, *adj.* pure (*morally*), chaste. **—en=reinheit**, *f.* purity of morals, chastity. **—en=richter**, *m.* censor, moralizer. **—en=richterlich**, *adj.* censorious. **—en=spruch**, *m.* moral maxim. **—en=strenge**, *f.* austerity (*of morals or manners*); **übertriebene —enstrenge**, rigorism. **—en=verderbend**, *adj.* demoralizing. **—en=verfall**, *m.* decay of manners *or* morals; depravity. **—en=verfeinerung**, *f.* (higher) culture, refinement of manners. **—en=zeugnis,** *n.* testimonial of good conduct *or* character. **—en=zwang,** *m.* etiquette, conventionalism. **—lich=keits=gefühl,** *n.* moral sense.

Sit'tich, *m.* (**—es,** *pl.* **—e**) (*small green*) parrot, popinjay.

Sit'tigen, *v.a.* to make well-behaved, to moralize; to civilize.

Situatio'n, *f.* (*pl.* **—en**) situation; **wir sind in derselben —,** we are in the same position; we are in the same boat (*coll.*); **auf der Höhe der — stehen,** to be equal to the occasion; **eine — ausnutzen,** to make the most of an opportunity. *Comp.* **—s=plan,** *m.* plot of situation, ground-plan; plan of site; topographical sketch. **—s=stück,** *n.* light comedy (*the interest in which lies in funny situations*). **—s=zeichnen,** *n.* topographical drawing.

Sitz, *m.* (**—es,** *pl.* **—e**) sitting; seat (*in all its senses*); residence; (*academic*) chair; (*episcopal*) see; form, lodge (*Sport.*); perch; box, dickey; **— und Stimme im Rate haben,** to have a seat and vote in the council; **seinen — an einem Orte aufschlagen,** to establish s. o. *or* to take up one's residence in a place.

Sitz—en, *ir.v.n.* (*aux.* **h.** & (*prov.*) **f.**) to sit; to stay, be situated, remain; to live; to be (*imprisoned, etc.*); to fit, suit; **der Hieb —t,** that 's a home thrust! (*Fenc.*); **gut zu Pferde —en,** to have a good seat (*in riding*); **der Nagel —t fest,** the nail is firmly in; **im Rate** (**Parlament**) **—en,** to be a member of council (parliament); (**einem Maler**) **—en,** to sit for a portrait, to give a sitting; **mir —t viel Schleim auf der Brust,** my chest is oppressed with phlegm; **das Schiff —t fest** (**auf dem Grunde**), the ship is aground; **zu Gericht —en,** to hold a council; **warm —en,** to be well off (*coll.*); **einem auf dem Nacken —en,** to be troublesome to a p., to pester *or* bore a p.; **ihm —t der Schelm im Nacken,** he is fond of a joke, he is full of fun *or* mischief; **—en bleiben,** to remain seated, to be deposited (*as sediment, etc.*); to be left without partners (*at a dance*); to be unsought in marriage; to lag behind, not to get on, to be neglected; not to get one's remove (*to a higher form in school*); **—en lassen,** to make (*a p.*) sit down; to keep on (*one's hat*); to abandon, to give the slip to, to disappoint; **sie ist beim Tanze —en geblieben,** she was a wall-flower (*coll.*); **der Mensch hat sie —en lassen,** the fellow has jilted her; **er hat mich —en lassen,** he has left me in the lurch; **er —t,** he is in prison; **der Mensch hat wiederholt gesessen,** that fellow has been repeatedly in jail; **lasset uns hierher —en,** let us sit down here (*dial.*); **einen Schimpf auf sich** (*dat.*) **—en lassen,** to pocket an affront; **da —t der Knoten!** there's the rub! **einen zum —en nötigen,** to ask a p. to sit down; **er kommt den ganzen Tag nicht zum —en,** he does not get a chance of sitting down all day. **—end,** *p. & adj.* seated; sedentary; sessile (*Bot.*); **—ende Lebensart,** sedentary (*mode of*) life. **—er,** *m.* (**—ers,** *pl.* **—er**) sitter; futtock. **—lings,** *adv.* sitting. **—ung,** *f.* sitting, session, meeting; seat; perch; **eine lange —ung bei Tische halten,** to sit a long time over one's dinner (*coll.*). *Comp.* **—anker,** *m.* buoy anchor. **—arbeit,** *f.* sedentary work. **—bad,** *n.* hip-bath. **—bein,** *n.* ischium. **—fleisch,** *n.* assiduity, steadiness in working; **er hat —fleisch,** he is very persevering, he sticks to his work; **er hat kein —fleisch,** he can't sit still, he does not persevere *or* stick to his work. **—fuß,** *m.* insessorial foot (*Orn.*). **—füßler,** *pl.* perchers, insessores (*Orn.*). **—geld,** *n.* prison fees. **—kasten,** *m.* box *or* boot (*of a coach*). **—klappe,** *f.* seat-cloth (*of a carriage*). **—redakteur,** *m.* dummy *or* pretended editor. **—ungs=berichte,** *pl.* (*reports of the*) proceedings (*of an academy or learned society*). **—ungs=dauer,** *f.* session. **—ungs=tag,** *m.* day of sitting (*of an assize, etc.*). **—ungs=zeit,** *f.* session, term. **—ungs=zimmer,** *n.* council-room, committee-room.

Six, *int.*; **meiner —,** upon my soul! upon my word! by Jove! (*coll.*). **—chen,** *see* **—.**

Ska'la, *f.* (*pl.* **Skalen**) gamut; scale; graduation.

Skal'de, *m.* (**—n,** *pl.* **—n**) scald, ancient Scandinavian poet *or* singer. **—n=tum,** *n.* profession of a scald; scalds (collectively). *Comp.* **—n=gesang,** *m.* scaldic poem. **—n=metrik,** *f.* metre of old Norse poetry, metrical rules observed by the old Norse poets.

Skalpe'll, *n.* (**—s,** *pl.* **—e**) scalpel (*Surg.*).

Skalpie'ren, *v.a.* to scalp.

Skanda'l, *m.* (**—s,** *pl.* **—e**) scandal; row, uproar; rag (*coll.*). *Comp.* **—geschichte,** *f.* (*piece of*) scandal. **—ie'ren,** *v.n.*; **auf einen —ieren,** to abuse a p. **—isie'ren,** *v.r. see* **—ieren; sich über eine S. —isieren,** to take offence at, to be shocked by a th. **—ö's,** *adj.* scandalous.

Skandie'r—en, I. *v.a.* to scan (*verses*). II. *subst. n.*, **—ung, Skansio'n,** *f.* scansion, scanning.

Skapulie'r, *n.* (**—s,** *pl.* **—e**) scapulary (*Eccl., Surg.*).

Skat, *m.* (**—s,** *pl.* **—e**) skat (*a German game at cards*).

[1]**Ska'ten,** *v.a.* to play 'skat' (*coll.*).

[2]**Ska'te—n,** *v.n.* (*aux.* **h.**) to rink, to skate on roller-skates (*rare*). **—r,** *m.* (**—rs,** *pl.* **—r**) rinker, rink-skater.

Skele'tt, *n.* (**—(e)s,** *pl.* **—e**) skeleton. **—artig,** *adj.* skeleton-like; reduced to a skeleton, all skin and bones.

Skep'—sis, *f.* doubt. **—tik,** *f.* doubt, scepticism. **—tiker,** *m.* (**—tikers,** *pl.* **—tiker**) sceptic. **—tisch,** *adj. & adv.* sceptical. **—tizis'mus,** *m.* scepticism.

Ski'laufen, *n.* ski-ing.

Skiz'z—e, *f.* (*pl.* **—en**) sketch. **—en=haft,** *adj.* sketchy. **—ie'ren,** *v.a.* to sketch; to make a rough draught of. *Comp.* **—en=buch,** *n.* sketch-book.

Skla'v—e, *m.* (**—en,** *pl.* **—en**), **—in,** *f.* slave. **—en=schaft,** *f.*, **—en=tum,** *n.*, **—erei',** *f.* slavery, servitude, bondage, thraldom; captivity. **—isch,** *adj.* enslaved, slavish, servile. *Comp.* **—en=arbeit,** *f.* slave-work; drudgery (*fig.*). **—en=aufseher,** *m.* overseer of slaves, slave-driver. **—en=aufstand,** *m.* revolt of slaves; Servile Insurrection (*Rom. Hist.*). **—en=dienst,** *m.* slavery; drudgery. **—en=furcht,** *f.* slavish fear. **—en=halter,** *m.* slave-owner. **—en=handel,** *m.* slave-trade. **—en=händler,** *m.* slave-dealer. **—en=krieg,** *m.* Servile War (*Rom. Hist.*). **—en=markt,** *m.* slave-mar(ke)t; slave-bazaar (*in Turkey*). **—en=schiff,** *n.* slave-ship, slaver. **—en=seele,** *f.* servile disposition, slavish mind. **—en=staaten,** *pl.* Slave States (*of America*). **—en=stand,** *m.* (state of) slavery.

Skont—ie'ren, *v.n.* to compensate, square, balance by comparing accounts. **—o,** *n. see* **Diskonto.**

Skon'tro, *n.* (**—s**) account-current book.

Skorbu't, *m.* (**—es**) scurvy. **—isch,** *adj.* scorbutic.

Skorpio'n, *m.* (**—s,** *pl.* **—e**) scorpion. *Comp.* **—stich,** *m.* sting of a scorpion.

Skrib—e'nt, *m.* (**—en'ten,** *pl.* **—en'ten**) writer, author; penman, scribbler, literary hack.

Skriptu'ren, *pl.* writings, papers.

Skro'f—eln, (**Skro'ph—eln,**) *pl.* scrofula. **—ulö's,** *adj.* scrofulous, strumous. *Comp.* **—el=kranke(r),** *m.* scrofulous person.

Skru'p—el, *m.* (**—els,** *pl.* **—el**) scruple (*also weight*); **sich** (*dat.*) **—el machen über eine S.,**

to have one's scruples about a th. —**ulö's**, *adj.* scrupulous.

Skurri'l, *adj.* scurrilous.

Smara'gd, *m.* (—(e)s, *pl.* —e) emerald. —**en**, *adj.* emerald.

Smir'gel (*usually* **Schmir'gel**), *m.* emery

Smo'king, *m.* (—s, *pl.* —s) dinner-jacket.

So, I. *adv.* so, thus, in this *or* in such a manner *or* degree; as; so (*poetical use*); **O Milon mein Gemahl — süß**, O Milo, husband mine, so dear; **ihr Harfenspiel, ihr Lied — süß**, her sweet harping and song; **ein Schloß — hoch und hehr**, a very high and noble castle; — **ein**, such a; — **einer, wie er**, such a one as he; — **etwas**, such a thing, that sort of thing; — **recht!** that will do! quite right! just so! **dem ist nicht** —, that is not so, not true; —? indeed? really? **es ist mir —, als wäre ich nicht müde**, I don't seem to feel tired; — **geht es, wenn man**, that's the way when one, that's what it is to; — **bin ich nun einmal**, that's my nature *or* way; — **ist das Leben**, such is life; — **sind die Menschen**, such are men; **wenn dem — ist**, if (*that be*) so; **er sprach** —, he spoke thus; **sein Betragen war —, daß**, his conduct was such as (to); **er spricht bald —, bald —**, he says now this, now that; **ich habe — großen Hunger!** I am so hungry; **ich habe — eine Ahnung, daß**, I have a kind of presentiment that; **er ist — eben gekommen**, he has just come; **das reicht nur — eben**, that is barely sufficient, just enough and no more; — **ziemlich**, pretty well; **Sie sagen das nur —**, those are but words, of course, you do not mean it; **er hat nicht — ganz Unrecht**, he is not so far wrong; **machen Sie es — wie ich**, do as I do; — **wie** —, anyhow, in any case, at any rate, already; **er ist — wie — böse auf mich**, he is angry enough with me as it is; — **oder —**, one way or another; **wer wird denn — sein?** who would behave in such a way? — . . . **wie** *or* **als**, as . . . as; — **sehr**, so much, in such a manner, to such a degree; — **sehr auch**, as much as; however much; — **viel**, so *or* as much, so *or* as many; **es waren nicht — viele**, there were not so many of them; — **viel ich weiß**, as far as I know, for aught I know; — **viel** *or* — **wie ich höre**, according to what I hear; — **lange (als)**, as long as, while; — **oft (als)**, as often as; **um — besser**, so much the better; **um — viel mehr**, so much the more; **noch einmal — viel**, as much again, twice as much; — **krank Sie auch sind**, ill as you are, however ill you may be; — **sehr sie auch Weib ist**, woman though she is; — **groß er war**, great as he was; — **groß er auch sein mag**, however great he may be; — **Geduld als Zeit**, patience as well as time: — **wahr ich lebe!** as (*sure as*) I live! — **lasset uns gehen**, let us go then; — **sehr ihr ihn liebt, — sehr haßt er euch**, just in proportion as you love him does he hate you. II. *adv. & conj.*; **Ihr Freund war nicht zu Hause, — war mein Gang vergebens**, your friend was not at home, so I had my walk for nothing; — **wollen Sie nicht?** you won't then? **er ist krank, — daß er nicht kommen kann**, he is too ill to come. III. *part.*; — **hören Sie doch!** do listen! do but hear! **ich ging im Walde — für mich hin**, I went in the wood just by myself; **wenn du Zeit hast, — schreibe mir**, when you have time, write to me; **da du Abhaltung hast, — werde ich selbst hingehen**, since you cannot come, I will go myself; **kaum warst du fort, — kam er zurück**, you were scarcely gone, when he returned; **er ist — schon böse auf mich**, he is angry enough already with me; **wir haben so der guten Freunde wenig**, we have too few friends already. IV. *int.* indeed! well, well! really! V. *obs. for rel. pron.* who, that, which; **diejenigen, — mich lieben**, those who love me; **der Sohn, — ihm der Herr gegeben**, the son whom the Lord had given him. VI. *conj.* if, in case; — **Gott will**, if it please God. *Comp.* (— *is usually not accented*) —**ba'ld**, I. *adv.* so soon; **du wirst es nicht —bald bekommen**, you will not get it in a hurry. II. *conj.* as soon as; —**bald es Ihnen bequem ist**, at your earliest convenience. —**da'nn**, *adv. & conj.* then, in that case. —**da'ß**, *conj.* so that. —**e'ben**, *adv.* just, but just. —**fe'rn**, I. *adv.* so far. II. *conj.* as far as; if; **in —fern**, inasmuch as. —**fo'rt**, *adv.* immediately, forthwith, at once. —**for'tig**, *adj.* prompt, instantaneous. —**ga'r**, *adv. or part.* even; **alle, —gar mein Bruder**, all, even my brother; **ja —gar**, yes, and what is more. —**genannt**, *adj.* so-called; pretended, would-be. —**glei'ch**, *see* —**fort**; coming! (*in reply to a call*). —**hi'n**, —**mi't**, —**na'ch**, *adv.* consequently, accordingly, then. —**so'**, *adv.* tolerably well, middling. —**than**, *adj.* such, this (*obs.*); **unter —thanen Umständen**, in the present circumstances, this being the case, as matters stand. —**viel**, *adv.* so *or* as much. —**weit**, *see* —**fern**. —**wie'**, *conj.* so as, according as, as also, as well as. —**wo'hl**, *adv.* so much; as well; **sie ist nicht —wohl schön als liebenswürdig**, she is charming rather than beautiful; (*with* **als**, *forming a conj.* = and); —**wohl er als sie**, he as well as she.

Soci—, *see* **Sozi—**.

So'cke, *f.* (*pl.* —n) sock (*opp. to* cothurnus); sock; short stocking; **sich auf die —n machen**, to go (*coll.*); to take to one's heels (*coll.*). —**l**, *m.* (—ls, *pl.* —l) socle, plinth; pedestal, base.

Sod, *m.* (—es, *pl.* —e, *rarely* **Sö'der**) boil, boiling; brew; heart-burn; spring, well (*dial.*); *see* **Brennen**. *Comp.* —**brennen**, *n.* heart-burn.

So'da, *f.* (carbonate of) soda (*Chem.*); **gereinigte** —, refined sofa *or* alkali. —**lis'ke**, *f.* barmaid in a soda-water stall (*sl.*). *Comp.* —**haltig**, *adj.* sodaic, containing soda. —**fabrikant**, *m.* alkali-maker. —**salz**, *n.* soda-ash. —**wasser=bude**, *f.* stall where soda-water is sold.

So'fa, *n.* (*& m.*) sofa, ottoman, divan; couch; **kleines** —, settee. *Comp.* —**bett**, *n.* sofa-bed. —**ecke**, *f.* corner of a sofa. —**lehne**, *f.* back of a sofa. —**schoner**, *m.* antimacassar.

[1]**Soff, Suff**, *m.* (—es) drunkenness; good draught, drink; inferior beverage, stuff.

[2]**Soff, Söf'fe**, *1 & 3 pers. sing. imperf. sing. ind. & subj. of* **saufen**.

Soffi't(t)e, *f.* soffit (*theat.*); —**n**, soffits, flies, borders, heavens (*coll.*).

Sog, Sö'ge, *1 & 3 pers. sing. imperf. sing. ind. & subj. of* **saugen**.

Sog'gen, *v.* I. *n. & r.* to crystallize (during evaporation) and sink to the bottom. II. *a.* to precipitate in crystals, to rake out the precipitated crystals; to salt down.

Soh'le, *f.* (*pl.* —n) sole (*of a foot, of a slipper, etc.*); sole, face (*of a plane*); foot (*of a plough*); splint, cradle (*Surg.*); bottom (*of a mine*); sill, plate; **auf leisen —n**, (treading) softly, gently; **mir brennen die —n**, the floor burns under my feet; **mach' dich auf die —n**, set off, go forth; **sich an eines Menschen —n** (*or* **einem an die —n**) **heften**, to follow close at a p.'s heels, to dog a p.; **sich** (*dat.*) **etwas an den —n abgelaufen haben**, to have known s.th. long ago. *Comp.* —**n=gänger**, *m.* sole-walker, plantigrade (*Zoöl.*). —**n=linie**, *f.* horizontal line. —**n=macher**, *m.* slipper-maker; sole-maker.

Soh'lig, Söh'lig, *adj.* level, horizontal (*Min.*).

Sohn, *m.* (—es, *pl.* **Söh'ne**, *dim.* **Söh'nchen**) son; **Schmidt** —, Schmidt junior; **Ihr Herr**

—, your son; — der Sünde, child of sin; des Menschen —, the Son of Man (*B.*); der verlorene —, the prodigal son (*B.*). —schaft, *f.* sonship; filiation (*Law*). *Comp.* —es=frau, *f.* daughter-in-law. —es=liebe, *f.* filial affection.

Söh'nerin, *f.* (*dial.*) daughter-in-law.

Soiree', *f.* (*pl.* —n) soirée, evening *or* dinner party.

Solar'=öl, *n.* inferior quality of petroleum.

So'la=wechsel, *m.* sole bill (*of exchange*).

Solch, I. *adj. & dem. pron.* (—er, —e, —es) such; ein —er Mensch, — ein Mensch, a man like him, such a man; ich habe —e, I have some of them. II. *adv.* ein —, *or* — ein häßliches Kind, such an ugly child, so plain a child. *Comp.* —en=falls, *adv.* in this case, in such a case. —er=gestalt, *adv.* in such a way, so, to such a degree; thus. —erlei, *indec. adj.* of such kind, such; such like.

Sold, *m.* (—es) pay; salary, wages; halber —, half-pay; der Minne —, reward *or* guerdon of love; der Tod ist der Sünde —, the wages of sin is death (*B.*); um — dienend, mercenary. *Comp.* —knechte, *pl.* hirelings. —truppen, *pl.* hired soldiers, mercenary troops, mercenaries. —zulage, *f.* supplement.

Solda't, *m.* (—en, *pl.* —en) soldier; military man; gemeiner —, private; gemeine —en, rank and file; — werden, to enlist, to enter the army; — zweiter Klasse, degraded private; — zu Fuß, foot-soldier; — zu Pferde, horseman, trooper; abgedankter —, discharged soldier; alter erfahrener —, veteran; ausgedienter —, time-expired man; freiwilliger —, volunteer. —enhaft, —isch, *adj.* soldierlike, soldierly; martial. —es'ka, *f.* the soldiery, soldiers (*coll.*). *Comp.* (*usually* = military) —en=arrest, *m.* military arrest. —en=art, *f.* ways of soldiers, military ways; nach —enart, as soldiers do. —en=aushebung, *f.* conscription, levy; recruiting. —en=bett, *n.* camp-bed. —en=dienst, *m.* military service. —en=eid, *m.* military oath. —en=geist, *m.* military *or* martial spirit. —en=geld, *n.* pay; tax for the maintenance of soldiers. —en=geschichte, *f.* story about soldiers *or* military life. —en=gesindel, *n.* military rabble, soldiery. —en=handwerk, *n.* profession of arms, military profession. —en=kost, *f.* soldiers' fare. —en=lied, *n.* soldier's song, martial air *or* tune. —en=pferd, *n.* trooper's horse. —en=pflicht, *f.* duty of a soldier, military duty. —en=rock, *m.* uniform; military cloak *or* overcoat. —en=schenke, *f.* canteen. —en=sprache, *f.* military language; soldiers' slang. —en=volk, *n.* military nation; soldiers; soldiery. —en=wesen, *n.* military affairs; army organization; manners of soldiers. —en=wirt, *m.* sutler. —en=zucht, *f.* military discipline.

Söld'—ling, *m.* (—lings, *pl.* —linge) hireling. —ner, *m.* (—ners, *pl.* —ner) hired soldier; mercenary. *Comp.* —ner=heer, *n.* army of mercenaries.

So'l—e, *f.* mother-water (*Chem.*). *Comp.* —bad, *n.* sea-water bath; sea-side place. —ei, *n.* egg cooked in salt-water. —salz, *n.* pit-salt. —spindel, *f.* brine-gauge.

Sole'nn, *adj.* solemn. —itä't, *f.* (*pl.* —itäten) solemnity.

Solfeggie'ren, *v.n.* (*aux.* h.) to sing sol-fa.

Soli'd, Soli'd—e, *adj.* solid, sterling; good, solvent (*of a firm*); settled, respectable, steady. —a'risch, *adj. & adv.* conjointly responsible; for one and all; —arische Verbindlichkeit, unlimited *or* joint liability; —arisch trockner Wechsel, promissory note. —aritä't, *f.* joint liability. —itä't, *f.* solidity; soundness; prudence, respectability.

Solitä'r, I. *adj.* solitary. II. *m.* (—s, *pl.* —s, —e) brilliant, solitaire, recluse.

Soll, *n.* positive order, command; debit; debtor's side (*of the ledger*); ins — eintragen, to debit (a p.'s account); (das) — und Haben, debit and credit. *Comp.* —bestand, *m.* presumed stock. —einnahme, *f.* supposed receipts, gross receipts. —posten, *m.* debtor's account.

Sol'l—en, *ir.v.* I. *a.* to owe. II. *n.* (*aux.* h.) to be obliged *or* bound in duty; to be *or* have to; to be in debt; to mean; to be of use for, be intended for; to be allowed, to be granted; to be said; to be believed, to pass for; (*as aux.* =) shall, should, owe, ought, must; du —st nicht töten, thou shalt not kill; Ihr Kinder —t etwas warten, you children are to wait a little; du —st deinen Vater und deine Mutter ehren, honour thy father and thy mother; wir thun nicht immer was wir —en, we do not always do what we ought; sagen Sie ihm, daß er kommen —, tell him to come, that he must come; ich hätt' es nicht thun —en, I ought not to have done it; man — nicht einmal mehr reden, one must not even speak now; was — ich? what am I to do? was — ich sagen? what shall I say? was —en diese Thorheiten? what is the meaning of these tomfooleries? wenn es regnen —te, if it should rain; —te er vielleicht krank sein? can he be ill, do you think he is ill? —te ich selbst zu Grunde gehen, though I myself perish; —te es die Katze gewesen sein? could it have been the cat? ich —te meinen Freund verraten! I betray my friend! nun, er — Recht haben, well, let him be right! Truppen —ten über den Fluß setzen, troops were to cross the river; er —te König werden, he was (*destined*) to be king; ich weiß nicht, was ich thun —, I don't know what to do; ich weiß nicht, was es bedeuten —, I do not know what it signifies; was —te ich dagegen machen? how could I help it? man —te meinen, one would think; es —te ein Witz sein, it was meant for a joke; was — das? what is the meaning of this? wem — das? for whom is that meant? was — mir das alles? what is all that to me? was — mir das (nützen)? what good does it do me? what is that to me? wozu — dieses? what is this for? er — die Wahrheit gesagt haben, he is supposed to have told the truth; er — gelehrt sein, he is said to be a scholar; nun — mich einer noch anklagen, daß . . ., now is some one's chance to accuse me of . . .; wie — man da nicht lachen? how could one help laughing? es hat nicht —en sein, it was not to be; man — nicht sagen können, daß ich . . ., no one shall say that I . . .; so einer — erst geboren werden, such a man is still to be born.

Söl'ler, *m.* (—s, *pl.* —) balcony; loft; top room; landing of top floor.

Solmisie'ren, *v.n.* (*aux.* h.) to sing sol-fa.

So'lo, I. *adv.* alone. II. *n.* (—s, *pl.* —s, Soli) solo. *Comp.* —geiger, *m.* solo violinist. —geigen=stück, *n.* violin-solo. —gesang, *m.* solo (*singing*). —partie, *f.* solo part. —sänger, *m.* solo singer, soloist. —stimme, *f.* solo part. —tanz, *m.* pas seul. —tänzer, *m.*, —tänzerin, *f.* first opera *or* ballet dancer.

Solözi'sm—us, *m.* (—us, *pl.* —en) solecism.

Som'mer, *m.* (—s, *pl.* —) summer; fliegender —, *see* —fäden. —haft, —lich, *adj.* summer-like; (*of*) summer; sich —lich kleiden, to put on summer clothes. —n, *v.* I. *n.* (*aux.* h.) & *imp.*; es —t, summer is drawing on; der Baum —t, the tree is sprouting. II. *a. also* Sömmern, to expose to the sun; to keep (*plants*) through the summer; to turn out (*cattle*) to graze; to lop, prune (*trees*); to sow (*a field*) for early crop. III. *r.*; die Hühner —n sich, the hens bask in the sun. *Comp.* —fäden, *pl.*

gossamer, spider's web. —**fahrplan**, *m.* summer time-table (*Railw.*). —**feld**, *n.* field of spring wheat. —**fleck**, *m.* freckle. —**frische**, *f.* summer holiday-resort. —**frischeln**, *v.n.* to take a summer-holiday. —**frischler**, *m.* visitor at a summer resort, holiday-maker. —**frist**, *f.* = —frische (*dial.*). —**gerste**, *f.* spring barley. —**getreide**, *n.* spring wheat. —**laden**, *m.* (Venetian) blind. —**mal**, *n.* freckle. —**nachts=traum**, *m.* Midsummer Night's Dream. —**obst**, *n.* early fruit. —**punkt**, *m.*, —**sonnenwende**, *f.* summer solstice. —**saat**, *f.* spring corn. —**seite**, *f.* south side. —**semester**, *n.* summer term, summer session. —**sprosse**, *f.* freckle. —**theater**, *n.* open-air theatre. —**vogel**, *m.* bird of summer; butterfly (*dial.*). —**zeug**, *n.* light stuff for summer dresses, material for summer wear.

Sona'te, *f.* (*pl.* —n) sonata.

Son'd—e, *f.* (*pl.* —en) probe; plummet (*Naut.*). —**ie'ren**, *v.a.* to probe; to sound, fathom. —**ie'rungen**, *pl.* soundings.

Son'der, I. *adj.* separate, special, peculiar. II. *prep.* (*with acc.*) without; — **Zweifel**, without doubt, no doubt, undoubtedly; — **Zahl**, countless. —**bar**, *adj.* & *adv.* singular, peculiar; strange, odd; droll; **etwas —bares**, something odd, peculiar; —**bar!** how strange! —**barkeit**, *f.* peculiarity, oddity, strangeness. —**heit**, *f.* peculiarity; speciality; **in —heit**, in particular. —**lich**, *adj.* & *adv.* special, peculiar, particular, remarkable; distinct, separate; **es ist nichts —liches daran**, there is nothing remarkable in that; **kein —licher Gelehrter**, no great scholar; **nicht —lich**, not specially, not much. —**ling**, *m.* (—lings, *pl.* —linge) odd person, original **den —ling spielen**, to affect eccentricity. —**n**, *conj.* but; **nicht nur gedacht, —n auch gesagt**, not only thought but said; **ich werde nicht sterben, —n genesen**, I shall not die, but recover. —**s**, *adv.* separately (*obs.*); **sammt und —s**, one and all, all together. *Comp.* —**abdruck**, —**abzug**, *m.*, separate impression; off-print; (special) pull. —**artig**, *adj.* odd, strange, singular. —**ausgabe**, *f.* special edition. —**bestrebung**, *f.* separatism, particularism. —**bund**, *m.* separate league; the Sonderbund; League of the Roman Catholic cantons of Switzerland (*1846*). —**bündler**, *m.* separatist. —**gesetzgebung**, *f.* special legislation. —**gelüste**, *pl.* particular desires. —**gericht**, *n.* special court. —**glei'chen**, *adj.* unequalled, unparalleled, matchless. —**gut**, *n.* separate property; the wife's fortune. —**interesse**, *n.* separate *or* exclusive interest; special *or* private interest. —**stellung**, *f.* exceptional *or* unique position. —**zug**, *m.* special train.

Son'der—n, *v.a.* to separate, sunder, part, sever; to sift; to sort; to distinguish; **sich —n**, to separate. —**ung**, *f.* separation, division; discrimination; **völlige —ung**, isolation. *Comp.*—**ungs=partikel**, *f.* disjunctive particle.

Sone'tt, *n.* (—(e)s, *pl.* —e) sonnet. —**i'st**, *m.* (—is'ten, *pl.* —is'ten) sonnet-writer, sonneteer, *Comp.* —**en=dichter**, *m.* see —ist.

Son'n—e, *f.* (*pl.* —en; *old gen. sing.* —en) sun, sunshine; **die —e schießen**, to take the sun's altitude; **die —e gleich austeilen**, to arrange combatants in tournaments so that neither shall face the sun (*obs.*); **'s ist nichts so fein gesponnen, es kommt ans Licht der —en**, everything comes to light in the end (*prov.*); **die —e sticht**, the sun is burning; **von der —e beschienen**, sunlit, sunny. —**enhaft**, *adj.* radiant; sun-like. —**ig**, *adj.* sunny, bright, radiant. *Comp.* (*often* = solar *or* helio). —**abend**, *m.* Saturday. —**abends**, *adv.* on Saturdays; on a Saturday. —**en=aufgang**, *m.* sunrise; the east. —**en=auge**, *n.* the sun; brilliant eye; opal; Heliopsis (*Bot.*). —**en=bahn**, *f.* ecliptic; brilliant career. —**en=ball**, *m.* orb of the sun. —**en=beglänzt**, —**en=beschienen**, *adj.* sunlit, sunny. —**en=beschreibung**, *f.* heliography. —**en=bild**, *n.* solar spectrum. —**en=blick**, *m.* glimpse of sun; sunny glance. —**en=blume**, *f.* sunflower. —**en=brand**, *m.* sun-burning. —**en=bruder**, *m.* homeless tramp (*sl.*). —**en=dach**, *n.* awning; sun-blind (*before a shop-window, etc.*). —**en=deck(e**, *f.*) *n.* awning (*Naut.*). —**en=dienst**, *m.* sun worship. —**en=durchmesser**, *m.* diameter of the sun. —**en=ferne**, *f.* distance from the sun; aphelion; very great distance (*fig.*). —**en=fernrohr**, *n.* solar telescope. —**en=fleck**, *m.* solar spot. —**en=finsternis**, *f.* solar eclipse. —**en=gebiet**, *n.* solar system. —**en=geflecht**, *n.* solar plexus (*Anat.*). —**en=glut**, *f.* blaze of the sun. —**en=gott**, *m.* sun-god, Helios, Phœbus, Sol. —**en=hell**, *adj.* bright like the sun; sunny; clear, evident. —**en=hof**, *m.* halo round the sun. —**en=höhe**, *f.* sun's altitude. —**en=höhen=messer**, *m.* back-staff (*used before the quadrant, Naut.*). —**en=jahr**, *n.* astronomical year. —**en=käfer**, *m.* lady-bird. —**en=klar**, *adj.* clear, evident; bright; **es ist —enklar**, it is as clear as daylight. —**en=kreis**, *m.* zodiac. —**en=licht=telegraph**, *m.* heliograph. —**en=los**, *adj.* sunless. —**en=messer**, *m.* heliometer. —**en=mythus**, *m.* solar myth. —**en=nähe**, *f.* proximity of the sun; perihelion. —**en=niedergang**, *m.* sunset. —**en=pfad**, *m.* orbit of the sun. —**en=reich**, *adj.* sunny. —**en=roß**, *n.* steed of the sun-god. —**en=scheu**, *adj.* shunning the light of the sun; heliophobic (*Bot.*). —**en=schirm**, *m.* sunshade, parasol. —**en=schuß**, *m.* sunstroke; staggers (*Vet.*). —**en=seite**, *f.* sunny side. —**en=stand**, *m.* solstitial point. —**en=stäubchen**, *n.* mote in a sun-beam; atom. —**en=stern**, *m.* fixed star. —**en=stich**, *m.* sun-stroke. —**en=stillstand**, *m.* solstice. —**en=system**, *n.* solar system. —**en=tierchen**, *n.* sun-animalcule (*Actinophrys*). —**en=uhr**, *f.* sun-dial. —**en=uhrkunst**, *f.* gnomonics. —**en=(uhr)zeiger**, *m.* gnomon (of a dial). —**en=untergang**, *m.* sunset. —**en=verbrannt**, *adj.* sun-burnt, tanned by the sun. —**en=wagen**, *m.* Phœbus' car. —**en=warte**, *f.* solar observatory. —**en=wende**, *f.* solstice; heliotrope. —**en=wendepunkt**, *m.* solstitial point. —**en=wirt**, *m.* landlord of the 'Sun' inn. —**en=zeiger**, *m.* dial plate. —**en=zeit**, *f.* solar time. —**en=zirkel**, *m.* ecliptic; cycle of the sun. —**tag**, *see* Sonntag. —**tägig**, *adj.* Sunday, taking place on a Sunday. —**täglich**, *adj.* happening every Sunday; **sich — täglich anziehen**, to put on one's Sunday dress.

Sön'ne, (Sän'ne,) *1 & 3 pres. sing. imperf. subj. of* **sinnen**.

Son'n—en, *v.* I. *a.* & *r.* to expose to the sun's rays, to sun, air; to warm, revive. II. *n.* (*aux.* **h.**); **es —t rings um dich**, the sun is shining brightly round you; **sich —en**, to bask in the sun; to take delight (in a th. *fig.*).

Sonn'tag, *m.* (—s, *pl.* —e) Sunday; **auf (den) —**, on Sunday; —**s**, on Sundays *or* a Sunday; **unser Dienstmädchen hat heute seinen —**, this is our maid's Sunday-out (*coll.*); **es ist nicht alle Tage —**, Sunday does not come every day. *Comp.* —**s=beilage**, *f.* Sunday supplement (*of a newspaper*). —**s=besuch**, *m.* Sunday visit *or* visitor(s). —**s=entheiliger**, *m.* Sabbath-breaker. —**s=kind**, *n.* Sunday child; child gifted with second sight; lucky *or* gifted person; **er ist ein —s=kind**, he was born with a silver spoon in his mouth. —**s=**

reiter, *m.* unskilful rider. **—s=ruhe,** *f.* Sabbath-rest, observance of the Sabbath. **—s=schule,** *f.* Sunday-school. **—s=staat,** *m.* Sunday finery. **—s=zeug,** *n.* Sunday clothes.

Sono'r, *adj.* sonorous. *Comp.* **—laut,** *m.* sonant.

Sonst, (**—en,** *obs.*) I. *adv.* else, otherwise; besides; in other respects; independently of that; moreover; formerly, of yore; **— niemand,** no one else; **— nichts,** nothing more *or* else; **wenn es — nichts ist,** if that is all; **— etwas,** something besides; **— war es anders hier, das war doch — nicht so,** things were different here in former times; **befehlen Sie — noch etwas?** can I get you anything else? what else can I do for you? **giebt es — etwas?** is there anything else? **—wo,** elsewhere, somewhere (*else*); **— sind wir gesund,** otherwise we are all well; **— woher,** from some other place; **wenn —,** if on the other hand, provided; **wie —,** as usual; **sie kommen nicht mehr so häufig wie —,** they come no longer so frequently as they used to; **es findet sich ja wohl — einmal eine Gelegenheit,** no doubt there will be an opportunity some time; **— habe ich noch zu berichten,** in addition I have to report. II. *n.* **das — und das Jetzt,** the past and present. **—ig,** *adj.* other, existing besides; former.

Soo'le, *f* see **Sole.**

Sophist—erei', *f.* sophistry. **—isie'ren,** *v.n.* (*aux.* **h.**) to be sophistical, talk sophistically.

Sopra— (*in comp.* =) super, extra, over.

Sopra'n, *m.* (**—s,** *pl.* **—e**) treble, soprano.

Sor'g—e, *f.* (*pl.* **—en**) care; uneasiness, anxiety, trouble, concern; sorrow (*prov.*); **—e für eine S. tragen,** to take care of, attend to, bestow care upon, to see to a thing; **man wird alle mögliche —e dafür tragen,** all possible care shall be taken (of it); **sich** (*dat.*) **—en machen, in —en sein um,** to trouble oneself about; **das ist meine geringste —e,** that gives me the least *or* but little concern; **außer —en,** reassured, unconcerned; **das lassen Sie meine —e sein,** I shall attend to that, leave that to me. **—lich,** *adj. & adv.* careful, anxious; sad; perilous. **—los,** *adj.* thoughtless, reckless, indifferent, negligent, careless. **—sam,** *adj.* careful, anxious; provident; cautious. **—samkeit,** *f.* carefulness. *Comp.* **—en=brecher,** *m.* care-drowner, banisher of care, wine, cup. **—en=frei,** *adj.* free from care, careless; sans-souci. **—en=schwer,** *adj.* overwhelmed with care. **—en=stuhl,** *m.* easy-chair. **—en=voll,** *adj.* full of cares *or* troubles, anxious. **—falt,** *f.* carefulness, heedfulness; care attention; neatness, scrupulosity; conscientiousness. **—fältig,** *adj.* anxious; careful, attentive; exact; scrupulous. **—fältigkeit,** *see* **—falt.**

Sor'ge—n, I. *v.n.* (*aux.* **h.**) to fear, be afraid; to be anxious, solicitous, troubled; to attend to, look after; to care for; to provide for; **für sich —n,** to take care of oneself; **man würde für dich —n,** you would be provided for; **dafür laß mich —n,** leave that to me! **lassen Sie mich nur dafür —n,** trust to me to see to it; **dafür hat er zu —n,** that is his look-out; **—en Sie nicht dafür,** don't trouble yourself about that; **— nicht, daß du zu spät kommst,** don't be afraid of coming too late; **—n Sie nicht, es wird alles gut gehen,** don't be afraid, all will go well. II. *v.r.* **sich um eine S. —en,** to trouble oneself about a th. III. *subst. n. see* **—.** **—r,** *m.* (**—rs,** *pl.* **—r**) one who cares for *or* is anxious about.

Sor'r—en, *v.a.* to lash, seize moor (*Naut.*).

Sor't—e, *f.* (*pl.* **—en**) kind, sort, species. **—ime'nt,** *n.* (**—iments,** *pl.* **—imen'te**) assortment; miscellaneous stock. **—imen'ter,** *m.* (**—imenters,** *pl.* **—imenter**) (retail) bookseller. **—ier'bar,** *adj.* sortable. **—ie'ren,** *v.a.* to assort; to put in order; to pick; to sift. **—ie'rer,** *m.* sorter. *Comp.* **—ier'=kasten,** *m.* sorting-chest (*Pap.*). **—iments'=buchhandel,** *m.* trade in books published by others, retail book-trade. **—iments'=buchhändler,** *see* **—imenter.** **—iments'=lager,** *n.* bookseller's stock in hand.

So'ße, *f.* (*pl.* **—n**) sauce; gravy. *See* **Sauce.**

Sott, Söt'te, *1 & 3 pers. sing. imperf. ind. & subj. of* **sieden.**

Souffl—eu'r, *m.* (**—eurs,** *pl.* **—eure**) prompter. **—eu'se,** *f.* female prompter. **—ie'ren,** *v.a.* to prompt. *Comp.* **—eur'=kasten,** *m.* prompter's box.

Soutachie'ren, *v.a.* to braid.

Souterrai'n, *n.* (**—s,** *pl.* **—s**) basement, cellar.

Souverä'n, I. *m.* (**—s,** *pl.* **—s, —e**) sovereign. II. *adj.* sovereign. **—itä't,** *f.* sovereignty. *Comp.* **—itäts=schwindel,** *m.* ridiculous pretensions to sovereignty.

Sozia'l, *adj.* social; **christlich —e Partei,** Christian Socialists. **—is'mus,** *m.* Socialism; **Katheder—ismus,** theoretic Socialism. **—is'tisch,** *adj.* socialist(ic). *Comp.* **—demokrat,** *m.* Socialist, Social-Democrat. **—demokratie,** *f.* Social Democracy, (*the growth of*) Democratic Socialism. **—demokratisch,** *adj.* socialist(ic); **—demokratischer Wahlverein,** Society for the promotion of Social-Democratic elections. **—is'ten=gesetz,** *n.* law against Socialists. **—wissenschaft,** *f.* sociology. **—wissenschaftlich,** *adj.* sociological.

Soz—ietä't, *f.* society; partnership. **—ius,** (*pron.* **So'zius**) *m.* (**—ius,** *pl.* **—ii**) partner; comrade; **stiller —ius,** sleeping partner. *Comp.* **—ietäts=handel,** *m.* trade carried on by a company. **—ietäts=kontrakt, —ietäts=vertrag,** *m.* deed of partnership.

Spaga't, *m.* (**—s,** *pl.* **—e**) string (*dial.*).

Spä'he—n, I. (*aux.* **h.**) to observe attentively; to peer, to pry into, lie in wait, watch. II. *v.a.* to search, explore; to spy out. **—r,** *m.* (**—rs,** *pl.* **—r**) spy; scout; prying person; speculator; explorer. *Comp.* **—r=blick,** *m.* searching glance.

Spa'hi, *m.* (**—s,** *pl.* **—s**) spahi, French African soldier.

Spalie'r, *n.* (**—s,** *pl.* **—e**) espalier, trellis; lane formed by people; **ein — machen,** to line each side of the way. **—en,** *v.a.* to furnish with an espalier; to train against a wall. *Comp.* **—obst,** *n.* espalier *or* wall-fruit. **—stange,** *f.* pole, prop for espaliers. **—werk,** *n.* trellis-work.

Spalt, *m.* (**—(e)s,** *pl.* **—e**) cleft, chink, slit, crack, fissure, crevice, crevasse. **—bar,** *adj.* that may be cleft. **—barkeit,** *f.* cleavage. **—e,** *f.* (*pl.* **—en**) *see* **Spalt;** column (*Typ.*); (*pl.*) boards (*Bookb.*). *Comp.* **—ader,** *f.* grain in wood. **—axt,** *f.* cleaver. **—bruch,** *m.* longitudinal fracture. **—en=reich,** *adj.* fissured. **—en=weise,** *adv.* in columns. **—en=zeile,** *f.* line of the column. **—fuß,** *m.* cloven-foot. **—füßig,** *adj.* cloven-footed. **—holz,** *n.* split wood, firewood. **—messer,** *n.* grafting-knife; cleaver. **—pfropfung,** *f.* stock-grafting. **—säge,** *f* long-saw, pit-saw. **—stück,** *n.* splinter. **—werk,** *n.* slitting-mill.

Spal't—en (*p.p.* **gespalten** *and* **gespaltet**). I. *v.a.* to split; cleave; to slit; to cut open; to crack; to decompose (*a ray of light*); to compose in columns (*Typ.*); to burst. II. *v.r. & n.* (*aux.* **s.**) to split; to gape, open; to divide; to branch off. III. *subst. n.* wood-cleaving, splitting; cleavage; decomposition (*of rays*). **—er,** *m.* (**—ers,** *pl.* **—er**) cleaver. **—ig,** I. *adj.* split, fissured; full of cracks; divided; (*also* **Spältig**) easily split *or* cracked. II. *suffix* (*in comp.* =) -cleft; having so many columns (*to a page, etc.*); **drei—ig,** three-columned. **—ung,** *f.* *see* **—en**

III.; fissure, split, crack; division, dissension, disunion, rupture; quarrel; schism (*eccles.*).

Span, *m.* (—s, *pl.* **Spä'ne**) chips; thin board; chip, shaving; splinter; reglet (*Typ.*); wedge (*Carp.*); split, division, disagreement (*prov.*); **Gedankenspäne**, detached thoughts, aphorisms; **aus einem —**, of one piece; **einen — auf einen** *or* **mit einem haben**, to squabble with a p., to have a spar with a p. (*coll.*); **wo man Holz haut, fallen Späne**, from chipping come chips (*prov.*); **machen Sie mir keine Späne**, don't make a fuss (*coll.*). *Comp.* —**holz**, *n.* chips. —**hut**, *m.* chip hat *or* bonnet.

Spä'neln, *v.a.* to whittle, to pare with a knife.

Spä'nen, *v.a.* to wean (*animals*).

Span'ferkel, *n.* sucking pig.

Span'ge, *f.* (*pl.* —**n**); **Arm—**, bracelet, clasp, buckle.

[1]**Spann**, I. *m.* (—(e)s, *pl.* —e) instep. II. *n. see* **Gespann**. —**bar**, *adj.* that can be stretched, extensible. —**e**, *f.* (*pl.* —**en**) span; short space of time; **nicht eine —e Boden**, not an inch of ground. *Comp.* —**dienst**, *m.* statute labour with teams. —**hoch**, *adj.* a span high *or* long.

[2]**Spann**, *1 & 3 pers. sing. imperf. ind. of* **spinnen**.

Span'n—en, *v.* I. *a.* to span; to strain, stretch, brace; to put into a vice; to tighten, make tense; to brace (*the nerves, etc.*); to put *or* keep on the stretch (*one's attention, etc.*); to work up, excite, intensify (*hopes, fears, interest*); to bend (*a bow*); to cock (*a gun*); to prick up (*the ears*); to harness, put to (*horses*); to fetter (*grazing cattle*); to screw up, tighten (*strings*); **die Oktave —en können**, to be able to stretch an octave; **etwas weit (eng) —en**, to stretch out (to compress, confine, contract); **Wasser —en**, to dam up water; **den Dampf —en**, to increase by heat the expansive power of steam; **die Pferde vor den Wagen —en**, to put the horses to the carriage; **die Pferde hinter den Wagen —en**, to put the cart before the horse (*prov.*); **auf die Folter —en**, to put to the rack; **die Saiten zu hoch —en, seine Forderungen zu hoch —en**, to demand too much, take too high a tone, make ridiculous pretensions; **er steht mit ihm auf gespanntem Fuße**, the relations between them are strained, there is a coolness between them; **ich bin sehr gespannt, davon zu hören**, I am very anxious to hear about it. II. *n.* (*aux.* **h.**) to be exciting *or* interesting; **dieser Roman —t sehr**, this novel is most exciting. —**er**, (**Spän'n—er**,) *m.* (—**ers**, *pl.* —**er**) bender, *etc.*; tensor (*muscle*); tenter (*for cloth*); packer; trigger; gaffle (*of a cross-bow*); span, chord (*of an arch*); Geometra (*Ent.*); **Einspänner**, one-horse vehicle. —**ung**, *f.* stretching, *etc.*; tension; stress, strain; arching; tone (*Med.*); suspense; close attention; discord; —**ung eines Gewölbebogens**, span of an arch; **die —ung zwischen den Familien**, the coolness *or* strained relations between the families. *Comp.* —**ader**, *f.* sinew; nerve. —**balken**, *m.* tie-beam. —**feder**, *f.* spring. —**haken**, *m.* tenter-hook. —**kraft**, *f.* elasticity; spring; expanding force, elasticity, tension (*Phys.*); tonic power, tone. —**muskel**, *m.* extensor. —**nagel**, *m.* pole-bolt; brace-pin, peg. —**rahmen**, *m.* tenter-frame; frame in water-mills. —**reif**, *m.* hoop. —**riemen**, *m.* shoemaker's knee-straps; tether. —**rolle**, *f.* tension-roller. —**seil**, *n.* fetter; iron cable, chain (*of a suspension-bridge*). —**stock**, *m.* templet (*Weav.*); dressing-stake. —**tau**, *n.* cable-painter (*of a boat*). —**ungs=apparat**, *m.* tension-regulator (*on sewing-machines*). —**ungs=kolben**, *m.* expansive piston (*Locom.*). —**weite**, *f.* span.

Spant, *n.* (—s, *pl.* —**en**) ship's frame.

Spa'r—en, I. *v.a.* to spare, save, economize, lay by; to spare; to put off. II. *v.n.* (*aux.* **h.**) to be thrifty, economical *or* penurious. III. *subst. n.*; —**en bringt Haben**, a penny saved is a penny gained. —**er**, *m.* (—**ers**, *pl.* —**er**) economical person, saver; **dem —er gehört ein Zehrer**, a miserly father begets a spendthrift son. —**sam**, *adj.* economical, saving; thrifty; frugal; *see* **Spärlich**; —**sam im Lobe sein**, to be chary of praise; —**sam mit etwas umgehen**, to use a th. sparingly, to economize *or* husband a th., to take good care of a th. —**samkeit**, *f.* economy; parsimony. *Comp.* —**büchse**, *f.* money box, savings box. —**einlage**, *f.* deposit in a savings-bank. —**endchen**, *n.* candle-end; save-all. —**geld**, —**gut**, *n.* savings. —**herd**, *m.* economical stove, kitchener. —**kalk**, *m.* plaster of Paris. —**kasse**, *f.* savings-bank. —**lampe**, *f.* economical lamp. —**pfennig**, *m.* (small) savings; money laid by for a rainy day. —**schatz**, *m.* savings. —**seide**, *f.* a kind of fine glossy thread used for silk. —**sucht**, *f.* parsimony. —**süchtig**, *adj.* parsimonious; close-fisted. —**verein**, *m.* savings club, savings-bank.

Spar'gel, *m.* (—s) asparagus. *Comp.* —**beet**, *n.* asparagus bed. —**messer**, *n.*, —**stecher**, *m.* asparagus-knife. —**zeit**, *f.* asparagus season.

Spär'lich, *adj.* scanty; bare, meagre, frugal; little; moderate; scarce; beggarly. —**keit**, *f.* scantiness, scarcity, rareness, rarity.

Spar'ren, *m.* (—s, *pl.* —) spar, rafter; chevron (*Her.*); **einen — zu viel haben**, to be not quite right in the upper story, to have a tile loose (*coll.*). *Comp.* —**feld**, *n.* square. —**holz**, *n.* rafter-wood. —**kopf**, *m.* modillion, mutule (*Arch.*); rafter-end. —**werk**, *n.* rafters.

Spaß (*long* **a**), *m.* (—**es**, *pl.* **Spä'ße**) jest; joke; fun, sport, amusement; **das ist ein — für ihn**, that is a trifle to him; **zum —**, for fun; **das war nur ein —**, it was only a joke; **es wäre ein —, wenn**, it would be a good joke if; — **beiseite!** joking apart! *see* **Scherz**.

Spa'ß—en, *v.n.* (*aux.* **h.**) to joke, jest, make fun; **Sie —en wohl**, you are joking, I suppose; **damit ist nicht zu —en**, that is no joking matter; **mit ihm ist nicht zu —en**, he is not to be trifled with; **Sie belieben zu —en**, you are pleased to be facetious. —**er**, *m.* (—**ers**, *pl.* —**er**) wag, joker. —**erei'**, *f.* jesting, jokes. —**haft**, **ꝛc.**, *see* **Scherzhaft**. —**ig**, *adj.* droll, funny, merry, jocose. *Comp.* —**angeber**, *m.* the life and soul of a party. —**liebend**, *adj.* fond of a joke *or* jokes. —**macher**, *m.* wag, joker; merry companion. —**vogel**, *m.* wag; buffoon. —**weise**, *adv.* in joke, jestingly.

Spät, (*obs. adv.* **Spat**,) *adj. & adv.* late; backward, behindhand, slow; **wie — ist es?** what o'clock is it? **bei —er Nacht**, late at night; **von früh bis —**, from morning till night; **wollen Sie mir, bitte, sagen, wie — es ist?** will you tell me the time, please? **der Zug kam zehn Minuten zu —**, the train was ten minutes late. —**e**, *f.* advanced hour; lateness. —**er**, *comp. of* **spät**; subsequent, after, later; —**ere Jahreszeit**, end of the season, latter part of the year; **in —eren Jahren**, in after years, in later life; **in —eren Zeiten**, at a later period; in the future. —**estens**, (**aufs —este**) *adv.* at the latest, at the farthest. —**ling**, *m.* (—**lings**, *pl.* —**linge**) animal born late in the year, late fruit; late, tardy production. *Comp.* —**gothik**, *f.* late Gothic style; perpendicular style (*Engl.*). —**herbst**, *m.* latter part of autumn. —**jahr**, *n.* end of the season, latter part of the year. —**reif**, *adj.* backward; late. —**sommer**, *m.* latter part of summer.

[1]**Spat** (*short* **a**), *m.* (—(e)s) spavin (*Vet.*). —**ig**, (—**lahm**,) *adj.* spavined.

[2]**Spat** (*long* **a**), *m.* (—(e)s, *pl.* —e) spar. —**ig**, *adj.* sparry. *Comp.* —**eisenstein**, *m.* sparry iron ore. —**fluß**, *m.* fluor spar. —**säure**, *f.* fluoric acid.

Spa'tel, *f.* (*pl.* —n) spatula, spattle, slice; scoop (*Med.*). *Comp.* —förmig, *adj.* spatulate.

Spa'ten, *m.* (—s, *pl.* —) spade; spades (*Cards*). *Comp.* —stich, *m.* spadeful; den ersten —stich thun, to turn the first sod.

Spa'tium, *n.* (—s, *pl.* Spatien) space; die Spatien einsetzen, to space (*Typ.*).

Spatz, *m.* (—es, —en, *pl.* —en) sparrow (*coll.*); das pfeifen die —en auf den Dächern, that is notorious; mit Kanonen auf —en schießen, to break butterflies on the wheel. —en=haft, *adj.* sparrow-like, insolent, libidinous. *Comp.* —en=kopf, *m.* empty, stupid fellow.

Spätz'le, *f.* favourite Swabian dish, brown roux.

Spazie'r—en, *v.n.* (*aux.* s.); —en *or* —en gehen (laufen), to take a walk, to go for a walk; —en fahren, to drive out, to take a drive; to go (out) in a boat; —en reiten, to go for a ride, to ride out; er geht gerade —en, he is just taking his walk. *Comp.* —fahrt, *f.* drive; sail, row, water-excursion. —gang, *m.* promenade; walk; einen —gang machen, to take a walk. —gänger(in, *f.*), *m.* walker. —platz, *m.* promenade, parade. —ritt, *m.* ride (on horseback). —stock, *m.* walking stick.

Specht, *m.* (—(e)s, *pl.* —e) woodpecker; der — pickt, the woodpecker pecks *or* taps.

Speck, *m.* (—(e)s) bacon; fat, lard; blubber; thrum (*Naut.*); paying work; mit — umwickeln, to wrap up in bacon; — auf den Rippen haben, to be well off; im — sitzen, to live in clover. —icht, (*obs.*) —ig, *adj.* bacon-like; fat. *Comp.* —artig, *adj.* lardy, bacon-like. —geschwulst, *f.* steatoma. —griebe, *f.* greaves, sediment of melted fat, tallow. —hals, *m.* fat neck. —händler, *m.* pork-butcher. —haut, *f. see* —schwarte; buff (*Med.*). —kuchen, *m.* cake made with lard. —messer, *n.* bacon-knife; larding knife. —schneider, *m.* blubber-cutter. —schnitte, *f.* slice of bacon. —schwarte, *f.* rind, skin of bacon. —schwein, *n.* fat pig. —seite, *f.* flitch of bacon; die (*or* mit der) Wurst nach der —seite werfen, to throw a sprat to catch a herring. —stein, *m.* steatite, soapstone.

Sped—ie'ren, *v.a.* to forward; to despatch, send on. —iteu'r, *m.* (—iteurs, *pl.* —iteure) forwarding agent, shipping agent, carrier. —itio'n, *f.* despatch, sending, forwarding (*of goods*). *Comp.* —itions=bureau, *n.* forwarding office, receiving office. —itions=gebühren, *pl.* carrier's charges. —itions=geschäft, *n.* carrier's trade *or* business, forwarding agency *or* business, transit trade. —itions=handel, *m.* carrying trade; —itionshandel und Verladungsgeschäft, forwarding agency and warehousing business.

Speer, *m.* (—(e)s, *pl.* —e) lance, spear; kurzer Wurf —, javelin; seinen — gegen einen schleudern, to hurl one's spear at a p. *Comp.* —förmig, *adj.* spear-shaped; lanceolate (*Bot.*). —gerassel, *n.* rattling of spears. —stich, *m.* stab with a spear. —träger, *m.* spearman. —wurf, *m.* throw of the spear, spear-thrust.

Spei'che, *f.* (*pl.* —n) spoke (*of a wheel*); radius (*Anat.*). —n, *v.a.* to spoke (*a wheel*). *Comp.* —n=blatt, *n.* blade, nave-end of a spoke. —n=hammer, *m.* hammer for fixing the spokes. —n=nerv, *m.* radial nerve. —n=ring, *m.* ferrule of the nave. —n=zapfen, *m.* sharp end of a spoke.

Spei'chel, *m.* (—s, *pl.* —) spittle, saliva. —n, *v.n.* (*aux.* h.) to spit, secrete *or* eject saliva; to dribble. *Comp.* —absondernd, *adj.* secreting saliva. —drüse, *f.* salivary gland. —fluß, *m.* flow of saliva. —gang, *m.* salivary duct. —kur, *f.* salivation (*Med.*). —latz, *m.* bib. —lecker, *m.* toady, sycophant; lickspittle (*obs.*). —leckerisch, *adj.* toadying, fawning. —stoff, *m.* ptyaline (*Chem.*).

Spei'cher, *m.* (—s, *pl.* —) granary; warehouse. —n, *v.a.* to store, lay up in a granary; to hoard, treasure up.

Spei'—en, *ir.v.a. & n.* (*aux.* h.) to spit; to spew out; to vomit (*vulg.*). —er, *m.* spitter. *Comp.* —becken, *n.*, —napf, —kasten, *m.* spittoon. —röhre, *f.* gutter-spout, gargoyle. —wurz, *f.* ipecacuanha.

Spei'ler, *m.* (—s, *pl.* —) skewer. —n, *v.a.* to skewer.

Spei'se, *f.* (*pl.* —n) food, nourishment; diet, fare; meal; dish; (*bell-*)metal; mortar; speiss; solder; (*dyers'*) lime-water; — zu sich nehmen, to take food; die —n abtragen, to clear the table; — der Augen, delight of the eyes.

Spei's—en, *v.* I. *a.* to give to eat, feed; to board; to entertain; einen mit leeren Hoffnungen —en, to feed a p. with vain hopes; einen —en, to give a p. food. II. *n.* (*aux.* h.) to eat, take food; to board; zu Abend —en, to sup; in welchem Gasthofe —en Sie? in what hotel do you take your meals? man —t gut in diesem Gasthof, you are well fed *or* the food is good at this hotel; (ich wünsche Ihnen) wohl zu —en! good appetite! (ich) wünsche wohl gespeist zu haben, I hope you enjoyed your dinner. —ung, *f.* eating; meal; feeding; boarding; food; —ung der 5000; feeding of the 5000. *Comp.* —e=amt, *n.* steward's office. —e=anstalt, *f.* eating-house, restaurant; städtische —eanstalt, public eating-house, people's kitchen. —e=bier, *n.* table-beer. —e=brei, *m.* chyme. —e=brett, *n.* tray. —e=eis, *n.* ice (-cream), ices. —e=fisch, *m.* edible fish; small fish for feeding other fish. —e=gang, *m.* alimentary canal. —e=graben, *m.* feeder (*of a canal*). —e=haus, *n.* restaurant, dining rooms. —e=kammer, *f.* larder; pantry. —e=karte, *f.* bill of fare, menu. —e=keller, *m.* underground restaurant. —e=kellner, *m.* dining-room waiter. —e=korb, *m.* provision basket, luncheon basket (*Railw.*); hamper. —e=kübel, *m.* hod (*Mas.*). —e=kunst, *f.* gastronomy. —e=maschine, *f.* tender (*of a locomotive*). —e=meister, *m.* steward, master-cook, chef. —en=folge, *f.* succession of the courses, menu, bill of fare. —e=opfer, *n.* oblation (*of first-fruits, etc.*) —e=ordnung, *f.* menu, order of meals. —e=pumpe, *f.* feeding pump. —e=rohr, *n.* feed-pipe. —e=röhre, *f.* feed-pipe, gullet; œsophagus. —e=röhren=schnitt, *m.* œsophagotomy. —e=saal, *m.* dining-room, dining-hall; refectory (*in monasteries*); mess-room (*for officers*); dining-saloon (*on steamers*). —e=saft, *m.* chyle. —e=schrank, *m.* cupboard; meat-safe. —e=tisch, *m.* dining-table. —e=vorrichtung, *f.* feeding-apparatus (*of steam-engines*). —e=wagen, *m.* dining-car (*Railw.*). —e=wärmer, *m.* apparatus for heating up food, meat-warmer. —e=wein, *m.* (*common*) dinner wine, table wine; sacramental *or* communion wine. —e=wirt, *m.* keeper of a restaurant. —e=wirtschaft, *f.* restaurant. —e=zettel, *m.* see —ekarte. —e=zucker, *m.* moist sugar.

Spek—ta'kel, I. *n.* (—takels, *pl.* —takel) show; play (*obs.*). II. *m.* noise, uproar, row (*coll.*). —ta'keln, *v.n.* (*aux.* h.) to make a row. —tra'l, *adj.* spectral. —trum, *n.* (—trums, *pl.* —tra) spectrum. —ula'nt, *m.* (—ulan'ten, *pl.* —ulan'ten) speculator. —ulatio'n, *f.* abstract *or* mental speculation (*Philos.*); commercial speculation, enterprise, venture. —ulati'v, *adj.* speculative. —ulie'ren, *v.n.* (*aux.* h.) to speculate (*Phil. & C. L.*); auf das Fallen (Steigen) der Kurse —ulie'ren, to speculate on a fall (*rise*) in stocks (*C.L.*). *Comp.* —takel=macher, *m.* rowdy. —takel=stück, *n.* grand spectacular piece (*Theat.*). —tral=analyse, *f.* spectrum analysis.

Spelz, (Spelt,) *m.* (—es) spelt. **—e,** *f.* glume. **—ig,** *adj.* chaffy; glumaceous; **drei—ig,** with three glumes (*Bot.*). **—en=artig,** *adj.* glumaceous.

Spen'de, *f.* (*pl.* **—n**) distribution; alms, charity; gift; bounty.

Spen'd—en, *v.a.* to dispense, deal out; to bestow; *see* **—ie'ren.** **—er,** *m.* (**—ers,** *pl.* **—er**) distributor, dispenser; benefactor. **—ie'ren,** *v.a.* (*coll.*) to give, make a gift of; to spend lavishly; **sich** (*dat.*) **etwas —ieren,** to treat o.s. to a th.; **einem etwas —ieren,** to stand a p. s.th., to treat a p. to s. th. **—ung,** *f. see* **—e;** administration (*of the Sacrament*).

Sper'ber, *m.* (**—s,** *pl.* **—**) sparrow-hawk. *Comp.* **—baum,** *m.* service-tree. **—beere,** *f.* service-berry. **—binde,** *f.* four-headed bandage (*Surg.*).

Speren'zien, *pl.* resistance, opposition (*coll.*); **machen Sie keine —!** don't make a fuss! no ceremony, please!

Sper'ling, *m.* (**—s,** *pl.* **—e**) sparrow; **der — zwitschert, zirpt,** the sparrow twitters, chirps. *Comp.* **—s=artig,** *adj.*; **—sartige Vögel,** passer(in)es. **—s=eule,** *f.* pygmy-owl, gnome-owl (*Amer.*). **—s=kraut,** *n.* red pimpernel. **—s=männchen,** *n.* cock-sparrow. **—s=schrot,** *n.* small shot. **—s=taube,** *f.* ground-pigeon. **—s=vogel,** *m.* passerine (bird); (*pl.*) passeres. **—s=weibchen,** *n.* hen-sparrow.

Sper're, *f.* (*pl.* **—n**) shutting, closing; block (*in streets, etc.*); blockade; obstruction; prohibition, embargo; bar; stop; impediment; catch, stop (*Horol.*); drag, shoe (*of a wheel*); **— des Verkehrs,** stoppage of the traffic; **Straßen—,** barricade; **Napoleons Kontinental —,** Napoleon's Continental System.

Sper'r—en, *v.* I. *a.* to spread open, stretch out *or* asunder; to sprawl, straddle; to (inter-)space (*a word, Typ.*); to shut, close; to bar, barricade, obstruct; to blockade; to lock, trig (*wheels*); **ins Gefängnis —en,** to put in prison; **einen aus dem Hause—en,** to shut the door in a p.'s face, to lock a p. out; **den Seehandel—en,** to blockade ports, lay an embargo on commerce; **einen Pfarrer—en,** to suspend a clergyman; **gesperrte Schrift,** spaced words *or* lines. II. *r.* to resist, oppose, struggle (*against,* **wider**); to bridle up. **—ig,** *adj.* stretched out, spread; wide open; unwieldy, cumbrous. **—ung,** *f.* spreading out, distension; interspacing; block, barricade; stoppage, prohibition; *see* **—.** *Comp.* **—angel=weit,** *adj.* gaping. **—baum,** *m.* bar (*of a gate*); turnpike. **—beinig,** *adj.* straddling. **—feder,** *f.* trigger-spring. **—fort,** *n.* outer fort. **—geld,** *n.* toll; entrance-money. **—gesetz,** *n.* prohibitive law; law suppressing ecclesiastical benefices. **—glocke,** *f.* curfew bell announcing the closing of the gates. **—hahn,** *m.* stop-cock. **—haken,** *m.* catch (*of a cog-wheel*); drag-hook; picklock; any hook that keeps itself *or* something open *or* shut. **—holz,** *n.* gag. **—kegel,** *m.* catch; stay; pin to stop motion. **—kette,** *f.* barring *or* door-chain; drag-chain. **—klappe,** *f.* organ-valve. **—rad,** *n.* cog-wheel; ratchet-wheel. **—riegel,** *m.* bolt. **—ring,** *m.* ferrule. **—sitz,** *m.* stall, reserved seat; **—sitz im Parquet,** orchestra-stall. **—weit,** *adj.* wide open. **—zeit,** *f.* closing-time.

Spe'sen, *pl.* charges, expenses, costs; **unter Zurechnung Ihrer —,** plus your expenses. *Comp.* **—frei,** *adj.* all expenses paid. **—nachnahme,** *f.* reimbursement for charges, charges following the goods, charges collected on delivery. **—vergütung,** *f.* reimbursement of expenses.

Spezerei', *f.* (*usually in the pl.* **—en**) aromatics, spices. *Comp.* **—gewölbe,** *n.,* **—handlung,** *f.* grocer's shop. **—händler,** *m.* grocer. **—lade,** *f.* spice-box. **—waren,** *pl.* grocer's wares, groceries.

Spezi—a'l, I. *adj.* special. II. *m.* (**—als,** *pl.* **—ale**) bosom friend (*dial.*). **—a'lien,** *pl.* details. **—alisie'ren,** *v.a.* to specialize, specify. **—ialitä't,** *f.* speciality. **—e'll,** *see* **—al** I.; **—ell angeben,** to specify; **—eller Freund,** particular friend. **—fisch,** *adj.* specific. *Comp.* **—al=arzt,** *m.* specialist. **—al=bericht,** *m.* particulars.

Spe'—zies, *f.* (*pl.* **—zies**) species; specie; **die 4 —zies,** the four first rules of arithmetic; **—zies facti,** the fact (*Law.*). **—zi'fisch,** *adj.* specific. **—zimen,** *n.* (**—zimens,** *pl.* **—zi'mina**) specimen. **—zies=dukaten,** *pl.* gold ducats. **—zies=geld,** *n.* specie.

Sphä'r—e, *f.* (*pl.* **—en**) sphere; globe. **—isch,** *adj.* spherical. *Comp.* **—en=harmonie,** *f.* music of the spheres.

Spi'ck—en, *v.a.* to lard; **den Beutel —en,** to fill one's purse; **einen —en,** to bribe a p.; **seine Rede —en,** to interlard one's discourse. *Comp.* **—aal,** *m.* smoked eel. **—gans,** *f.* smoked goose(-breast). **—nadel,** *m.* larding-pin. **—pfähle,** *pl.* small pickets (*Milit.*).

Spie, Spie'e, *imperf. ind. & subj. of* **speien.**

Spie'gel, *m.* (**—s,** *pl.* **—**) looking-glass, mirror; smooth surface; speculum (*Surg.*); tompion, wooden-shoe (*Artil.*); ring round the centre of a target; dapple (*on horses*); eye (*on feathers*); oval ornament (*Arch.*); panel (*of a door*); stern (*Naut.*); **das wird er nicht hinter den — stecken,** he will not boast of that, he will keep that secret; **das Bild ist wie aus dem — gestohlen,** it is a wonderful likeness. **—icht,** (*obs.*) **—ig,** *adj.* specular; smooth, bright; with large square meshes (*of nets*). *Comp.* **—becken,** *n.* barber's basin (*hung as sign*). **—belag,** *m.* tin foiling of a mirror. **—bild,** *n.* reflected image; mirage. **—braun,** *adj.* dappled-bay. **—decke,** *f.* mirrored ceiling. **—ei,** *n.* poached egg. **—eisen,** *n.* specular iron. **—erz,** *n.* specular iron-ore. **—fabrik,** *f.* looking-glass factory. **—fechter,** *m.* dissembler; juggler. **—fechterei',** *f.* sham-fight; pretence, humbug; feint; jugglery. **—feder,** *f.* peacock's feather. **—feld,** *n.* panel for a mirror. **—fenster,** *n.* plate-glass window; window with a movable mirror. **—fernrohr,** *n.* reflecting telescope. **—fläche,** *f.* smooth, glassy surface. **—folie,** *f.* tin-foil. **—gießerei,** *f.* plate-glass factory. **—glas,** *n.* plate-glass. **—glatt,** *adj.* as smooth as a mirror; glassy, unrippled. **—glätte,** *f.* perfect smoothness. **—granate,** *f.* (hand-)grenade. **—handel,** *m.* looking-glass trade. **—hell,** *adj.* as bright *or* clear as a mirror. **—hütte,** *f.* glass-works. **—karpfen,** *m.* dappled carp, king of the carps (*Icht.*). **—kasten,** *m.* dressing-table; box with a mirror; catoptric box (*Phys.*). **—klar,** *adj.* as clear as a mirror, glassy. **—lampe,** *f.* lamp with (a mirror for) a reflector. **—lehre,** *f.* catoptrics. **—leiste,** *f.* rim, border of a mirror. **—metall,** *n.* specular metal. **—netz,** *n.* net with large square meshes. **—pfeiler,** *m.* pier (*Arch.*). **—quadrant,** *m.* Hadley's (*reflecting*) quadrant. **—rappe,** *m.* black-dappled horse. **—rein,** *adj.* very pure. **—roche,** *m.* star-ray (*Icht.*). **—saal,** *m.* room hung with mirrors. **—scheibe,** *f.* mirror *or* plate-glass; (window) pane of plate-glass. **—schiefer,** *m.* porcelain-clay, specular schist. **—schiff,** *n.* square-sterned vessel. **—schirm,** *m.* reflector. **—schleifer,** *m.* mirror-polisher. **—sextant, —sextel=kreis,** *m.* reflecting sextant. **—stein,** *m.* mica. **—tafel,** *f.* sheet of plate-glass. **—taffet,** *m.* flowered taffeta. **—tischchen,** *n.* dressing-table; console-table. **—thür,** *f.* plate-glass door. **—wage,** *f.* reflecting level. **—wand,** *f.* mirrored wall; wall with a looking-glass. **—zeug,** *see* **—netz.**

Spie'gel—n, *v.* I. *n.* (*aux.* **h.**) to be bright, polished, shining; to sparkle. II. *a.* to reflect; to look at in a glass; to glaze (*a cake, etc.*). III. *r.* to be reflected; to look at oneself in a glass; **sich an einem —n**, to imitate, take example by a p.; **sich an einer S. —n**, to take warning from *or* by; **ein gespiegeltes Pferd**, a dappled horse. **—ung**, *f.* reflection; mirage.

Spie'k—anard, *m.* (**—anardes**, *pl.* **—anarde**) *see* **indische —e.** **—e**, *f.* (*pl.* **—en**) broad-leaved lavender; **indische —e**, spikenard, Valeriana spica. **—er**, *m.* (**—ers**, *pl.* **—er**) large nail. **—ern**, *v.a.* to nail, spike (*Naut.*).

Spiel, *n.* (**—s**, *pl.* **—e**) play, game, sport; playing, acting, performance; play, gambling; game; set; pack (*of cards, etc.*); playing (*of musical instruments, etc.*); manner of playing; touch (*Mus.*); drum; military music; play, motion, working; stroke (*of a piston, etc.*); plaything; affair; matter; **sein — mit einem treiben**, to play with a p., to make game of a p.; **einem gewonnen(es) — geben**, to throw up the game, to acknowledge oneself beaten by a p.; **gewonnen — haben**, to be sure of the game, to be out of danger, to have gained the day; **das — verloren geben**, to look on the game as lost, to throw up one's cards; **er hat gewiß die Hand im —e**, he is sure to have a finger in the pie; **leichtes — haben**, to have no difficulty (*in doing a th.*); **— zu vieren**, four-handed game (*Tennis*); **ich bin am —**, it is my turn to play; **aus dem — bleiben**, to take no part in an affair; not to be counted *or* mentioned; **aus dem —e lassen**, to leave out of the question, let alone; **sich ins — mischen**, to interfere; **in das — ziehen**, to compromise, entangle s.o.; **im —e sein**, to be implicated in the game, to meddle; **eine Dame ist mit** *or* **dabei im —e**, there is a lady in the case *or* involved in the matter; **laß mich aus dem —e**, do not drag me into that affair; **es war Eifersucht dabei im —e**, jealousy was at the bottom of it, it was a matter of jealousy; **aufs — setzen**, to stake; **das — hat sich gewandt**, the tables are turned; **ein gewagtes — spielen**, to play a bold *or* high game; **einem freies — lassen**, to leave the field clear for a p., give scope to s.o.; **das — rühren**, to beat the drum; **mit klingendem —e ausziehen**, to march out with the band playing, with drums beating and trumpets sounding; **dem —e ergeben**, addicted to gaming; **volles —**, full organ; **Glocken—**, carillon; **das — des Lebens**, the game of life; **das ist das — des Lebens**, such is life; **ein — der Wellen sein**, to be at the mercy of the waves; **— der Muskeln**, action of the muscles; **gute Miene zum bösen — machen**, to put a good face on the matter. **—bar**, *adj.* fit for representation. **—chen**, *n.* (**—chens**, *pl.* **—chen**); **ein —chen machen**, to have a quiet little game (*of whist, etc.*).

Spie'l—en, *v.a.* & *n.* (*aux.* **h.**) to play, sport, trifle; to play, gamble; to play, act, perform (*Theat.*); to play (*Mus.*); to glitter, sparkle (*as gems*); **vom Blatte —en**, to play music by sight; **—en lassen**, to spring (*a mine*), to fire off (*guns*), to display (*a flag*), to set a-going (*water-works, musical boxes, etc.*), to show off, exhibit (*one's talents, etc.*); **er läßt nicht mit sich —en**, he is not to be trifled with, he does not understand a joke; **die Augen über eine S. —en lassen**, to run the eyes over, glance at; **mit Worten —en**, to pun, play upon words, to equivocate; **einem etwas in die Hand —en**, to slip s. th. into a p.'s hand, to help a p. to a thing; **einem etwas aus den Händen —en**, to juggle something out of someone's hand; **den Krieg in ein Land —en**, to carry war into a country; **die Sache ins Weite —en**, to spin out a matter; **ins Rote —en**, to incline to red; **einander in die Hände —en**, to have a secret understanding, to play into one another's hands; **um Geld —en**, to play for money; **ich habe in der Lotterie gespielt**, I have tried my chance in the lottery; **es wird heute nicht gespielt**, the theatre is closed to-day, there will be no performance to-day; **das Stück spielt in . . .**, the scene is laid in . . .; **im Winde —en**, to flutter in the wind; **ins Loch —en**, to pocket a ball (*Bill.*); **vor Anker —en**, to ride at anchor. **—end**, I. *p.* & *adj.* playing; opalescent. II. *adv.* easily; **er thut es —end**, that is but play to him. **—er**, *m.* (**—ers**, *pl.* **—er**) player; actor; performer; gambler. **—erei'**, *f.* play, sport; jesting, dalliance; play-work, trifle; silly *or* childish tricks; toys. **—erig**, *adj.* playful; fond of playing. **—erin**, *f.* actress; player; performer. *Comp.* **—art**, *f.* manner of playing, play; style, touch (*Mus.*); variety (*Nat. Hist.*). **—ball**, *m.* ball, playing-ball; sport, plaything; **ein —ball der Winde und Wellen sein**, to be at the mercy of the winds and waves. **—bank**, *f.* gaming-table, casino. **—brett**, *n.* (*chess, draught, etc.*) board. **—bruder**, *m.* inveterate gambler; playfellow. **—bude**, *f.* gambling-booth; lottery-booth. **—dose**, *f.* musical box. **—feld**, *n.* court (*Tennis*). **—gefährte**, *m.* playfellow, playmate. **—gehülfe**, *m.* croupier. **—geld**, *n.* stake(s), pool; card-money. **—genosse**, *m.*, **—genossin**, *f.* playmate. **—gesellschaft**, *f.* card-party. **—gewinst**, *m.* winnings (*at play*). **—glück**, *n.* luck in play. **—haus**, *n.* gaming-house. **—hölle**, *f.* gambling-hell; silver-hell; pony-trap (*sl.*). **—karte**, *f.* playing card. **—kätzchen**, *n.* playful creature; frolicsome child; kitten. **—kränzchen**, *n.* small card-party; card-club, whist-club. **—leute**, *pl.* musicians; drums and fifes, band. **—mann**, *m.* musician; fiddler; (**mittelalterlicher**) **—mann**, (mediæval) minstrel, gleeman; **ein fahrender —mann**, a wandering gleeman. **—mannsdichtung**, *f.* minstrel poesy, poetry of the gleemen. **—marke**, *f.* counter, marker. **—oper**, *f.* grand opera. **—papier**, *n.* gambling-share, lottery-ticket. **—pfennig**, *m.* *see* **—marke.** **—plan**, *m.* programme; **—plan der Bühne**, repertory, répertoire. **—platz**, *m.* playground. **—ratte**, *f.* gambler (*coll.*). **—raum**, *m.* room for action *or* motion; (free) play, scope; elbow-room; windage (*Artil.*); *see* **—platz.** **—regeln**, *pl.* laws (*or* rules) of a game. **—rolle**, *f.* list. **—sache**, *f.* plaything, toy. **—sachen-händler**, *m.* toyman, owner of a toyshop. **—schuld**, *f.* gambling debt, debt of honour. **—schule**, *f.* infant school, kindergarten. **—stunde**, *f.* play-hour. **—sucht**, *f.* passion for playing *or* gambling. **—tag**, *m.* holiday. **—teller**, *m.* plate for the stakes, pool. **—teufel**, *m.* demon of play, passion for gambling. **—tisch**, *m.* gambing-table; card-table. **—trieb**, *m.* æsthetic pleasure, æsthetic contemplation, instinct of play (Schiller). **—uhr**, *f.* musical box. **—verderber**, *m.* spoil-sport, kill-joy, wet blanket. **—waren**, *pl.* toys. **—werk**, *n.* toy; child's play; peal (*of bells*). **—zeug**, *n.* plaything, toy; bauble. **—zeughandlung**, *f.* toy-shop. **—zimmer**, *n.* play-room; (day-)nursery; card-room, gambling-room.

Spiel'hahn, (*better:* **Spill'hahn**,) *m.* heath-cock, black-cock. *Comp.* **—feder**, *f.* heath-cock's plume.

Spier, I. *n.* (**—s**, *pl.* **—e**) thin stalk, blade of grass. II. *m.* (**—s**, *pl.* **—e**) Spiræa (*Bot.*). **—chen**, *n.*; **kein —chen**, not a bit, not in the very least (*coll.*). **—e**, *f.* (*pl.* **—en**) spar, boom (*Naut.*); Spiræa. **—(l)ing** *m.* (**—(l)ings**, *pl.* **—(l)inge**) *see* **Eberesche.**

Spieß, *m.* (—es, *pl.* —e) spit; pike; spear; lance; javelin; harpoon; peg, pick (*Typ.*); first year's antlers; **an den — stecken**, to spit; **den — umkehren**, to turn the tables. —**ig**, *adj.* pointed. *Comp.* —**braten**, *m.* meat roasted on a spit. —**bürger**, *m.* pikeman; narrow-minded townsman, commonplace fellow, philistine. —**bürgerlich**, *adj.* vulgar, commonplace, humdrum; —**bürgerliche Ansichten haben**, to be somewhat humdrum in one's ideas. —**bürgertum**, *n.* narrow-mindedness, bourgeois way of thinking, philistinism. —**dreher**, *m.* turn-spit. —**förmig**, *adj.* spear-shaped. —**gerte**, *f.* switch. —**gesell**, *m.* comrade, (*usually*) accomplice. —**glanz**, *m.* antimony. —**glanz=asche**, *f.* oxide of antimony. —**glanz=blei**, *n.* (schwarzes) antimonial sulphuretted lead-ore. —**glanz=erz**, *n.* sulphuret of antimony; bournonite. —**glanz=haltig**, *adj.* antimonial. —**glas**, *n.* *see* —**glanz**. —**hirsch**, *m.* young stag. —**rute**, *f.* rod, switch; (**durch die**) —**ruten laufen**, to run the gauntlet; **einen —ruten jagen**, to make a p. run the gauntlet. —**träger**, *m.* spearman, pikeman, halberdier.

Spie'ße—n, *v.a.* to spear; to spit; to empale. —**r**, *m.* (—rs, *pl.* —r) pikeman; *see* —**bürger**; young stag with first year's antlers.

Spill, *n.* (—es, *pl.* —e) capstan. —**e**, *f.* (*pl.* —en) pin (*of a windlass*); *see* **Spill** *and* **Spindel**. *Comp.* —**baum**, *m.* capstan-bar. —**gaten**, *pl.* bar-holes of a capstan.

Spill—e, *f.* (*dial.*) *for* **Spindel**, spindle; distaff. *Comp.* —**mag(e)**, *m.* relative on the female (*or* distaff) side (*obs.*). —**seite**, *f.* female (spindle *or* distaff) side, female line of descent (*obs.*).

Spil'ling, *m.* (—s, *pl.* —e) small yellow plum.

Spina't, *m.* (—(e)s, *pl.* —e) spinach.

Spind, (*m. &*) *n.* (—es, *pl.* —e), —**e**, *n.* (*pl.* —en) wardrobe, press.

Spin'del, *f.* (*pl.* —n) spindle; distaff; shaft; shank; mandrel; axis, axle-tree; pin; pivot, nut (*of a press*); worm (*of a screw*); radius (*Anat.*); newel (*Arch.*). *Comp. see* **Kunkel**. —**bank**, *f.* bobbin and fly frame. —**baum**, *m.* spindle-tree (*Bot.*); beam of a spindle. —**beine**, *pl.* spindle-shanks. —**dünn**, *adj.* very thin. —**dürr**, *adj.* dry as a bone, dried-up. —**förmig**, *adj.* fusiform, spindle-shaped. —**muskel**, *m.* radial muscle. —**presse**, *f.* screw-press. —**säule**, *f.* spindle-shaped column. —**treppe**, *f.* spiral stair-case. —**welle**, *f.* bobbin. —**zapfen**, *m.* pivot, axis, spindle. —**zug**, *m.* parabolic spindle.

Spine'tt, *n.* (—(e)s, *pl.* —e) spinet (*Mus.*).

Spinn'—bar, *adj.* textile. —**e**, *f.* (*pl.* —en) spider; **ich hasse ihn wie eine —e**, I hate him like poison; **pfui —e!** disgusting! shocking! (*coll.*); —**en sehen**, to have black spots floating before one's eyes.

Spin'n—en, *ir.v.a. & n.* (*aux.* **h.**) to spin; to spin *or* whirl round, to twist; to purr (*as a cat*); to (respond to a challenge to) drink (*stud. sl.*); **Verrat —en**, to plot treason; **der Kreisel —t**, the top spins round *or* sleeps; **er hat keine Seide dabei gesponnen**, he has not made much by it; **'s ist nichts so fein gesponnen, es kommt ans Licht der Sonnen**, everything is found out at last, murder will out (*prov.*). —**er**, *m.* (—ers, *pl.* —er) spinner; silkworm. —**erei'**, *f.* spinning; spinning-mill. —**erin**, *f.* spinner, spinster. *Comp.* —**e=feind**, *adj.* bitterly hostile, savage (*coll.*); **einem —efeind sein**, to hate a p. like poison, to be at daggers drawn with a p. —**en=artig**, *adj.* spider-like. —(**en**)=**gewebe**, *n.* cobweb; arachnoid membrane (*Anat.*). —**en=netz**, —**en=nest**, *n.*, —**e(n)=webe**, *f.* cobweb. —**er=lohn**, *m.* spinner's wages. —**e=web**, *n.*, —**e=webe**, *f.* cobweb; very thin gauze. —**flachs**, *m.* flax dressed for spinning. —**gesellschaft**, *f.* spinning party. —**haus**, *n.* spinning room; house of correction. —**hütte**, *f.* hut for silkworms. —**maschine**, *f.* spinning-jenny. —**meister**, *m.* foreman of a spinning-mill. —**rad**, *n.* spinning-wheel. —**rocken**, *m.* distaff. —**stube**, *f.* spinning-room; spinning party. —**stuben=erzählungen**, *pl.* stories told in the spinning-room; popular legends, old wives' tales. —**stuben=lieder**, *pl.* popular songs. —**warze**, *f.* spinning-pap (*of spiders*). —**wirbel**, *m.* whirl.

Spinö's, *adj.* spinous, spiny.

Spintisie'ren, *v.n.* (*aux.* **h.**) to ruminate; to subtilize.

Spio'n, *m.* (—s, *pl.* —e) spy; spy-glass; looking-glass outside a window. —**a'ge**, *f.*, —**en=tum**, *n.* (—en=tums) spying. —**ie'ren**, *v.n.* (*aux.* **h.**) to play the spy. —**iererei'**, *see* —**age**.

Spira'l, *adj.* spiral. —**e**, *f.* (*pl.* —en) spiral (*Math.*); coil; (—**feder**, *f.*) mainspring (*of a watch*). *Comp.* —**förmig**, *adj.* spiral; convolute (*Bot.*). —**gefäß**, *n.* spiral duct (*Bot.*). —**pumpe**, *f.* spiral pump. —**ständig**, *adj.* arranged in a spiral.

Spiritu—alis'mus, *m.* spiritualism. —**alitä't**, *f.* spirituality. —**e'll**, *adj.* spiritual. —**o'sen**, *pl.* spirituous liquors. —**s** (*pron.* **Spi'ritus**), *m.* spirit, alcohol; mettle; —**s asper**, rough breathing, voiceless glottal continuant *or* fricative; —**s lenis**, soft breathing. *Comp.* —**s=brennerei**, *f.* distillery. —**s=hospital**, *n.* hospital of the Holy Spirit. —**s=lampe**, *f.* spirit-lamp. —**s=wage**, *f.* alcohol-metre; spirit-level.

Spita'l, *n.* (—es, *pl.* **Spitäler**), **Spit'tel**, *m. & n.* (—s, *pl.* —) hospital. *Comp.* —**schiff**, *n.* hospital-ship. —**zug**, *m.* ambulance-train.

Spitz, I. *adj. & adv.* pointed; peaked; tapering; delicate; acute; sharp; —**er Winkel**, acute angle; — **auslaufen**, to terminate in a point; **ich kann es nicht — kriegen**, I can't make it out (*coll.*). II. *m.* (—es, *pl.* —e) Pomeranian dog; **einen (kleinen) — haben**, to be (somewhat) tipsy (*coll.*). —**chen**, *n.* (—chens, *pl.* —chen) little point; lace. —**e**, *f.* (*pl.* —en) point (*of a needle, knife, sword, thorn, etc.*); extremity; top, summit, peak; tip; nib (*of a pen*); vertex, apex (*Geom., Bot.*); peak (*of sails*); point (*of an epigram*); spire; head; (*pl.*) lace; —**en klöppeln**, to make (pillow-)lace; **erzgebirgische** *or* **sächsische —en**, Dresden lace; **Brüsseler —en**, Brussels lace; **geklöppelte —e**, bone- *or* pillow-lace; **die —en der Behörden**, the heads of the administration, the authorities; **an der —e stehen**, to be at the head (*of affairs*); **einem die —e bieten**, to oppose a p.; **auf die —e treiben**, to drive to extremities. —**el**, *m.* (**Polizei—el**, **Lock—el**) secret police agent, detective. *Comp.* —**ahorn**, *m.* Norway maple. —**amboß**, *m.* bickern. —**axt**, *f.* pickaxe. —**bart**, *m.* pointed beard. —**berg**, *m.* peak. —**blatter**, *f.* pointed pustule; (*pl.*) chicken-pox. —**bogen**, *m.* pointed arch; (*in comp.* =) pointed. —**bohrer**, *m.* gimlet, centre-bit; draw-point. —**bub(e)**, *m.* rascal; swindler; thief; rogue. —**buben=gesicht**, *n.* rascally countenance. —**buben=sprache**, *f.* cant of thieves. —**buben=streich**, *m.* piece of rascality, knavish trick. —**büberei**, *f.* rascality. —**bübisch**, *adj.* rascally. —**en=applikation**, *f.* application of lace. —**en=arbeit**, *f.* lace-work. —**en=bändchen**, *n.* lace-edging. —**endig**, *adj.* apiculate. —**en=einsatz**, *m.* insertion. —**en=kleid**, *n.* dress trimmed with *or* made of lace. —**en=klöpplerin**, *f.* lace-maker. —**en=stich**, *m.* lace stitch. —**en=werk**, *n.* laces; lace-work. —**en=zacken**, *m.* Van Dyke edging. —**findig**, *adj.* sharp; crafty, shrewd, ingenious; subtle; keen; cavilling, hypercritical, sophistical. —**findigkeit**. *f.* subtlety; keenness, sharpness; craftiness, captiousness; sophistry. —**flöte**, *f.* fusiform pipe (*Org.*). —**glas**, *n.* pointed wine-glass. —**hacke**, *f.* pickaxe. —**hammer**, *m.* pick. —**kopf**, *m.* long head. —**köpfig**, *adj.* long-headed; cute. —**kugel**, *f.* cone-shaped ball (*Artil.*). —**maul**, *n.* pointed mouth; Muræna myrus (*Icht.*). —**maus**, *f.* shrew-mouse. —**meißel**, *m.* triangular punch. —**name**, *m.* nickname. —**nasig**, *adj.* sharp-nosed. —**pfahl**, *m.* foundation-pile. —**rad**, *n.* wheel for pointing needles. —**säule**, *f.* obelisk. —**steine**, *pl.* gems cut in facets. —**winkelig**, *adj.* acute-angled. —**zahn**, *m.* dog-tooth.

Spit'z—en, *v.a.* to point; to tip; to whet; to sharpen; **eine Feder —en**, to make a pen; **einen Bleistift—en**, to sharpen a pencil; **seine Antwort —en**, to say something stinging in reply, to give a sharp answer; **das ist auf mich gespitzt**, that is aimed at me; **den Mund —en**, to purse up one's lips; **die Ohren —en**, to prick up one's ears; **sich auf eine S. —en**, to reckon upon a th., to look forward to s.th.; to set one's heart upon a th. —**ig**, *adj.* pointed; sharp; acute; delicate; sarcastic; *see* **Spitz** I. —**igkeit**, *f.* sharpness, pointedness; piquancy; sarcasm.

Splei'ß—e, *f.* (*pl.* —**en**) splinter; scale (*of iron*). —**ig**, *adj.* easily split.

Splei'ßen, *ir.v.a. & n.* (*aux.* **s.**) to split, splinter; to cleave; to crack; to refine (*copper*).

Splendi'd, *adj. & adv.* splendid, magnificent; liberal; wide, far apart (*Typ.*).

Splint, *m.* (—**es**, *pl.* —**e**) sap(wood), alburnum (*Bot.*); linch-pin.

[1]**Spliß**, *m.* (—(**ss**)**es**, *pl.* —(**ss**)**e**) cleft. —(**ss**)**en**, *v.a.* to splice. —(**ss**)**ig**, *adj.* having clefts *or* fissures. *Comp.* —**hammer**, *m.* splicing-hammer.

[2]**Spliß, Splis'se**, *1 & 3 pers. sing. imperf. ind. & subj. of* **spleißen**.

Split'ter, *m.* (—**s**, *pl.* —) splinter, chip, shiver; scale (*of metal, etc.*); mote (*B.*); **wir sehen den — in des Nächsten Auge und sehen nicht den Balken in unserm eigenen**, we see the mote in another's eye, but don't see the beam in our own. —**ig**, *adj.* splintery; shivered. *Comp.* —**holz**, *n.* chips of wood. —(**faden**)=**nackt**, *adj.* stark naked. —**kohle**, *f.* slaty coal. —**richten**, *v.a.* to criticize minutely; to carp, cavil at things. —**richter**, *m.* straw-splitter, carper. —**toll**, *adj.* stark mad.

Split'tern, *v.* I. *a.* to shatter, shiver. II. *n.* (*aux.* **s.**) to splinter, shiver, split.

Spond—a'ikus, *m.* (*pl.* —**aici**) spondaic verse. —**ä'isch**, *adj.* spondaic. —**ä'us**, *m.* (*pl.* —**äen**) spondee.

Spön'ne, *1 & 3 pers. sing. imperf. subj. of* **spinnen**.

Sponſ—a'lien, *pl.* espousals (*Law*). —**ie'ren**, to court, woo. —**ie'rer**, *m.* wooer, lover, amorous swain, ladies' man.

Sponta'n, *adj. & adv.* spontaneous.

Sponto'n, *m.* (—**s**, *pl.* —**s**) spontoon (*Mil.*).

Spora'disch, *adj.* sporadic.

Spo're, *f.* (*pl.* —**en**) sporule, spore. *Comp.* —**n=bildend**, *adj.* sporiferous, sporuliferous. —**n=bildung**, *f.* formation of spores, sporulation. —**n=kapsel**, *f.* spore-capsule.

[1]**Spo'ren**, *v.n.* (*aux.* **h.**) to dry up; to become mouldy; to rot.

[2]**Spo're—n**, *pl. of* **Sporn** *q. v.* —**r**, *m.* (—**rs**, *pl.* —**r**) spur-maker. *Comp.* —**n=stich**, *m.* spur, dig of a spur.

Sporn, *m.* (—(**e**)**s**, *pl.* **Spo'ren**) spur; ram; stimulus, incentive; **dem Pferde die Sporen geben**, to set spurs to one's horse; **sich** (*dat.*) **die Sporen verdienen**, to win one's spurs. *Comp.* —**blume**, *f.* larkspur; Centranthus. —**füße**, *pl.* spurred feet. —**halter**, *m.* heel-plate. —**leder**, *n.* spur-strap. —**rädchen**, *n.* rowel; spur-gear *or* -wheel; mullet (*Her.*). —**riemen**, *m. see* —**leder**. —**stätisch**, *adj.* restive. —**streichs**, *adv.* at full gallop *or* speed; post-haste, as fast as possible; at once; immediately.

Spor'nen, *v.a.* to spur, goad; to set spurs to.

Sport, *m.* (—**s**) sport. —**treibend**, *adj.* sporting. *Comp.* —**angelegenheiten**, *pl.* sporting matters. —**anzug**, *m.* sporting costume, flannels. —**ausdruck**, *m.* sporting term. —**liebhaber**, *m.* sporting man, sportsman. —**mäßig**, *adj.* sportsmanlike. —**neuigkeiten**, *pl.*, —**zeitung**, *f.* sporting news. —**welt**, *f.* sporting world.

Spor't—el, *f.* (*pl.* —**eln**) fee, perquisite. —**ulie'ren**, *v.n.* (*aux.* **h.**) to collect *or* levy fees. *Comp.* —**el=kasse**, *f.* fund of court-fees, fines, *etc.* —**el=taxe**, *f.* fixed scale *or* rate of fees.

Spott, *m.* (—**es**) mockery, ridicule; scorn; banter; (**Zielscheibe für den** —), butt, laughing-stock; **beißender** —, biting sarcasm; **witziger** —, satire; **seinen — mit etwas treiben**, to make fun (game *or* sport) of a th., to turn a th. into ridicule, to mock *or* scoff at a th.; **Schande und** —, shame and disgrace; **zum — werden**, to become the laughing-stock; **wer den Schaden hat, darf für den — nicht sorgen**, the laugh is always against the loser (*prov.*). *Comp.* —**benennung**, *f.* nickname. —**bild**, *n.* caricature. —**billig**, *adj.* ridiculously cheap. —**dichter**, *m.* satirical poet. —**drossel**, *f.* mocking-bird. —**gebot**, *n.* preposterous offer. —**geburt**, *f.* monstrosity, monster, abortion. —**gedicht**, *n.* squib; satirical poem. —**geist**, *m.* scoffing disposition; scoffer. —**gelächter**, *n.* scornful, derisive laughter. —**geld**, *n.* ridiculously low price; **um ein —geld**, for a trifling sum, for a song. —**laune**, *f.* ironical humour. —**lied**, *n.* satirical song; **ein —lied auf einen**, a song in ridicule of a p. —**lob**, *n.* ironical praise. —**name**, *m.* nickname. —**preis**, *m. see* —**geld**. —**schlecht**, *adj.* execrable. —**schrift**, *f.* satire, lampoon. —**schriftsteller**, *m.* satirical writer, satirist. —**süchtig**, *adj.* fond of mocking, quizzing; satirical. —**vogel**, *m.* mocking-bird; mocker; quiz. —**weise**, *adv.* mockingly, derisively, ironically. —**wohlfeil**, *adj.* dirt-cheap, ridiculously cheap.

Spött—elei', *f.* jeering; mockery, derision; raillery. —**eln**, *v.n.* (*aux.* **h.**) (**über eine S.**) to laugh, jeer, sneer at. —**er**, *m.* (—**ers**, *pl.* —**er**) mocker, scoffer; quiz. —**erei'**, *f.* raillery; jeering, derision; chaff; sarcasm; blasphemy. —**isch**, I. *adj.* mocking, scoffing, jeering; scornful; ironical, sarcastic; smart; caustic, stinging; disdainful. II. *adv.* in mockery, in scorn. —**lich**, *adj. see* —**isch**; shameful.

Spot't—en, *v.n.* (*aux.* **h.** *gen. or* **über** *with acc.*) to mock, jeer at, deride, ridicule; to trifle with; **er —et meiner** *or* **über mich**, he mocks me; **in einem Grade, der jeder Beschreibung —et**, to a degree that defies all description; (*also v.a.*); **Gott läßt seiner nicht —en**, God is not mocked (*B.*). —**ender=weise**, *adv.* tauntingly.

Sprach (*long* **a**), **Sprä'che**, *1 & 3 pers. sing. imperf. ind. & subj. of* **sprechen**.

Spra'ch—e, *f.* (*pl.* —**en**) speech, power of utterance; language, tongue; idiom; dialect; voice; accent; diction; style; **alte —en**, classical languages; **neuere —en**, modern languages *or* tongues; —**e der Bibel**, language of the Bible; —**e der Dichter**, poetical language; —**e der Diebe**, cant of thieves; —**e der Studenten**, students' slang; **mundartliche —e**, dialectic speech, provincial language; **vertrauliche —e**, familiar language; **Umgangs —e**, colloquial language; **gehobene —e**, elevated style *or* diction; **blumenreiche —e**, flowery style; —**e eines besonderen Gewerbes, einer besonderen Klasse**, technical language, slang; **der**

—e beraubt sein, to be bereft of speech; to be speechless; die —e wiedergewinnen, to recover one's speech; heraus mit der —e! say it out! out with it! speak out! mit der —e nicht recht heraus wollen, to be unwilling to explain oneself *or* to speak out; frei mit der —e herausgehen, to speak (*out*) freely; einem die —e benehmen, to deprive a p. of utterance, to strike s.o. dumb; zur —e bringen, to introduce, broach (*a subject*); die —e in seiner Gewalt haben, to be a good *or* voluble speaker, to have a great command of language; ich erkenne ihn an der —e, I know him by his voice *or* by his accent. —lich, *adj.* linguistic; grammatical; —liche Schönheit, beauty of diction *or* style. *Comp.* (*in cpds. often* = of language, linguistic) —ähnlichkeit, *f.* analogy (*of language*(*s*)). —armut, *f.* poverty of expression; poverty of a language. —art, *f.* idiom, dialect. —atlas, *m.* atlas of languages, linguistic maps. —bau, *m.* structure, character of a language. —beherrschung, *f.* command of a language. —bewußtsein, *n. see* —gefühl. —centrum, *n.* centre of speech. —denkmal, *n.* literary document, text; alte —denkmäler, literary remains, old texts, literary monuments. —eigenheit, —eigentümlichkeit, *f.* idiomatic peculiarity, idiom, idiotism; deutsche (englische, amerikanische, französische, lateinische) —eigentümlichkeit, Germanism (Anglicism, Americanism, Gallicism, Latinism). —en=gewirr, *n.* confusion of tongues. —en=verordnung, *f.* ordinance regulating the official use of languages. —fähig, *adj.* capable of speaking. —fehler, *m.* error in speech, grammatical mistake *or* blunder; defect of speech (*lisp*); impediment of speech (*stutter*). —fertig, *adj.* fluent, voluble. —fertigkeit, *f.* facility in speaking, fluency of speech; gift of tongues, proficiency in (*foreign*) languages. —forscher, *n.* student of the science of language, (*comparative*) philologist. —forschung, *f.* philology, linguistics; vergleichende —forschung, comparative study of languages, comparative philology. —führer, *m.* colloquial guide (*to a language*), phrase-book. —gebiet, *n.* country *or* district where a language is spoken; das gesamte deutsche —gebiet, all German-speaking countries. —gebrauch, *m.* colloquial usage; der heutige —gebrauch, the language of the present day, modern German (*English, etc.*). —gebräuchlich, *adj.* idiomatic. —gefüge, *n.* connected speech. —gefühl, *n.* linguistic feeling (*viz., an intuitive sense of what is correct and idiomatic in a language; hence*) intuitive sense of the language, instinct *or* natural feeling for a language. —gelehrte(r), —kundige(r), *m.* linguist; philologist. —genie, *n.* one who has a genius for learning languages. —gesellschaft, *f.* linguistic society; society for promoting purity and elegance of diction. —gewaltig, *adj.* endowed with a ready command of language. —insel, *f.* district where the language spoken is different from that of the surrounding country. —kenner, *m.* one who knows the language thoroughly; linguist; grammarian. —laut, *m.* speech-sound. —lehre, *f.* grammar. —lehrer, *m.* teacher of languages; grammarian. —los, *adj.* speechless; mute; —los vor Schrecken, speechless with fright. —mengerei, *f.* practice of introducing foreign words in speaking. —neuerer, *m.* neologist. —probe, *f.* specimen of language, selected piece, selected passage; altdeutsche —proben, specimens of Old German; Old German Reader. —regel, *f.* grammatical rule. —reinheit, *f.* purity of speech; purity of a language. —reiniger, *m.* purist. —reinigung, *f.* purification of a language. —richtig, *adj.* correct, grammatical. —richtigkeit, *f.* grammatical correctness. —rohr, *n.* speaking trumpet *or* tube; die —rohre der öffentlichen Meinung, the organs of public opinion; sich zum —rohr der öffentlichen Meinung machen, to make oneself the mouthpiece of public opinion. —schatz, *m.* vocabulary of a language. —schnitzer, *see* —fehler. —störung, *f.* impediment of speech. —stunde, *f.* lesson in a (*foreign*) language; deutsche —stunden, German lessons. —sünde, *f.* gross violation of grammar. —übung, *f.* exercise in speaking *or* in elocution. —unterricht, *m.* instruction in a language; deutschen —unterricht erteilen, to give lessons in German (conversation). —verbesserung, *f.* linguistic reform. —verein, *m.* linguistic society; philological society. —vergleichung, *f.* comparative philology. —vermögen, *n.* faculty of speech; linguistic capacity. —(en)=verwirrung, *f. see* —engewirr. —werkzeug, *n.* vocal organ, organ of speech. —widrig, *adj.* incorrect, ungrammatical. —wissenschaft, *f.* science of language, (comparative) philology.

Sprang, Spräng'ge, *1 & 3 pers. sing. imperf. ind. & subj. of* springen.

Spre'ch—en, *ir.v.* I. *a. & n.* (*aux.* h.) to speak, say; to talk; to converse; (*only v.a.*) to declare, pronounce (*judgment*); frei —en, to acquit, pronounce not guilty, absolve; aus dem Kopfe, frei —en, to speak extempore, without notes, on the spur of the moment; von etwas anderem —en, to change the subject; man spricht stark davon, it is much talked of; einen zu —en wünschen, to wish to see a p.; ist Herr N. zu —en? can I see Mr. N.? er läßt nicht mit sich —en, he wont listen to reason, it is no use reasoning with him; er ist nicht gut zu —en, he is anything but affable; er ist auf ihn nicht gut zu —en, he has not much good to say of him, he is very angry with him; ich bin heute für niemand zu —en, I am not at home to any one to-day; vor Gericht —en, to plead a cause; heilig —en, to canonize; den Segen über einen —en, to pronounce benediction upon a p., to bless a p.; wir werden uns darüber noch —en, we'll see about that. —end, *p. & adj.* speaking; —end ähnliches Bild, speaking likeness. —er, *m.* (—ers, *pl.* —er) speaker; spokesman; orator. *Comp.* —apparat, *m.* telegraph-receiver. —art, *f.* manner of speaking, diction, style; dialect. —gesang, *m.* recitative. —maschine, *f.* talking machine, phonograph. —oper, *f.* opera partly sung; comic opera; operetta. —strom, *m.* working current (*Tele.*). —stunde, *f.* reception hour; business hour; consultation hour; office hour; täglich im eigenen Hause von 2-4 —stunde haben, to be at home every day from 2 to 4. —süchtig, *adj.* talkative. —übung, *f.* exercise in speaking *or* conversing. —weise, *f. see* —art. —zimmer, *n.* parlour, consulting-room (*of medical men*).

Spreiß— (*in comp.*) —feder, *f.* pendulum-spring. —haken, *m.* charcoal-burner's raker.

Sprei'ten, *v.a.* to spread out, extend.

Sprei'ze, *f.* (*pl.* —n) stay, prop; stretcher; wedge.

Sprei'zen, *v.* I. *a.* to spread, stretch out; to straddle, spread wide (*the legs*); to prop, support; to skewer. II. *r.* to straddle, stretch oneself, sprawl; to swagger, strut; sich gegen etwas —, to resist, strive against a th.; sich mit etwas —, to boast of, plume o.s. on a th.

Spreng'bar, *adj.* capable of being blasted *or* blown up.

Spren'gel, *m.* (—s, *pl.* —) sprinkling brush (*for holy-water*); diocese; parish; district; jurisdiction.

Spren'g—en, *v.* I. *a.* to cause to spring, to make

jump; to sprinkle, strew, scatter; to water; to spring, burst, blow up, blast; to burst open; to disperse (*a mob, etc.*); to break (*a gaming bank, etc.*); to rupture (*a blood-vessel*); to throw down from the table (*a ball, Bill.*); to start (*game*); to marble (*the edges of books*); **den Garten —en,** to water the garden, to syringe the garden (*with a hose*); **sein Pferd über einen Graben —en,** to make one's horse take a ditch; **einen nach einem Orte hin —en,** to send s.o. running to a place. II. *n.* (*aux.* **s.**) to gallop, ride at full speed, dash, bound; **auf den Feind los —en,** to charge the enemy at full speed. III. *n.* (*aux.* **h.**) *& imp.*; **es hat nur gesprengt,** there were only a few drops, it only drizzled. **—er,** *m.* (**—ers,** *pl.* **—er**) sprinkler; blaster; started game; **einen —er machen,** to send a ball over the table (*Bill.*). **—ung,** *f.* springing, blasting, *etc.*; dispersion, scattering (*of a crowd*); headlong course; sprinkling. *Comp.* **—arbeit,** *f.* blasting. **—büchse,** *f.* petard (*Artil.*). **—eisen,** *n.* cracking-ring. **—gefäß,** *n.*, **—kanne,** *f.* watering-pot. **—geschoß,** *n.* explosive projectile, (bomb-) shell. **—graben,** *m.* mine. **—gräber,** *m.* sapper, miner. **—kessel,** *m.* holy-water vessel. **—kolben,** *m.* rose of a watering-pot. **—kugel,** *f.* bomb, shell. **—ladung,** *f.* explosive charge, charge of bursting-powder. **—maschine,** *f.* infernal machine. **—öl,** *n.* blasting oil, nitro-glycerine. **—patrone,** *f.* blasting cartridge. **—pinsel,** *m.* mason's sprinkling brush; marbling-brush (*Bookb.*). **—pulver,** *n.* blasting powder; percussion powder (*Artil.*). **—regen,** *m.* fine rain. **—schuß,** *m.* blasting shot. **—schutt,** *m.* débris of an explosion. **—stück,** *n.* splinter (*of a shell*). **—tonne,** *f.* powder-barrel. **—trichter,** *m.* rose of a watering-pot. **—wage,** *f.* splinter-bar (*of a carriage*). **—wedel,** *m.* sprinkling brush, holy-water sprinkler. **—werk,** *n.* ornamented lattice-work; strut-frame; explosives. **—wisch,** *m.* brush. **—zünder,** *m.* blasting fuse.

Spren'kel, *m.* (**—s,** *pl.* **—**) gin, snare; speckle, spot; freckle. **—icht,** (*obs.*) **—ig,** *adj.* speckled, spotted. **—n,** *v.a.* to speckle, spot; to dapple; to sprinkle (*Brew.*); to marble (*Bookb.*).

Spreu, *f.* chaff; husks; **wie — vor dem Winde,** as chaff before the wind. *Comp.* **—artig,** *adj.* chaffy; paleaceous (*Bot.*). **—blättchen,** *n.* palea (*Bot.*). **—regen,** *m.* drizzling rain

Sprich, *imperat. sing. of* **sprechen.**

Sprich— (*in comp.*) **—wort,** *n.* saying; proverb; maxim, adage; phrase, mocking phrase (*obs.*); **es ist sein —wort,** it is a saying of his; **zum —wort werden,** to become a byword, to become a proverb; **—wörter spielen,** to act proverbs. **—wörter=lexikon,** *n.* dictionary of proverbs. **—wörtlich,** *adj.* proverbial.

Sprichst, Spricht, *2 & 3 pers. sing. pres. ind. of* **sprechen.**

Sprie'gel, *m.* (**—s,** *pl.* **—**) thin piece of wood; hoop; head, top (*of cradles*); support of a tilt *or* awning; tilt; reed-work, cradling (*of walls, etc.*).

Sprie'ßen, *ir.v.n.* (*aux.* **s.**) to sprout.

Spriet, *n.* (**—es,** *pl.* **—e**) *see* **Gabelstange;** sprit, spar.

Spring, *m.* (**—(e)s,** *pl.* **—e**) spring, source; sheer (*of a deck*); **— auf dem Ankertau,** spring on the cable. **—el,** *m.* (**—els,** *pl.* **—el**) (wooden) vaulting-horse (*gymn.*).

Sprin'g—en, *ir.v.* I. *n.* (*aux.* **h.** & **s.**) to leap, spring, jump; to run, hasten (*dial.*); to spring, gush, spout; to crack, snap, burst, break; to burst, fall in pieces; to advance rapidly over open ground with occasional short halts (*Mil.*); to copulate, cover (the mare); **über einen Graben —en,** to leap a ditch; **zu einem hin—en,** to run up to a p.; **auf die Seite —en,** to leap aside; **die Thür sprang auf,** the door flew open; **das Schloß sprang auf,** the lock burst open; **eine Saite ist gesprungen,** a string has snapped; **mir ist, als sollte mein Kopf —en,** I have a splitting headache; **das —t in die Augen,** that is evident *or* obvious; **er muß —en,** he is turned off, dismissed; **die Wasserkünste —en lassen,** to make the fountains play; **über die Klinge —en lassen,** to put to the sword; **über die Zunge —en lassen,** to slander, calumniate; **Geld —en lassen,** to spend money freely; **eine Mine —en lassen,** to spring a mine; **sein Haus wird —en müssen,** he will have to sell his house; **zurück—en,** to rebound; **gesprungen kommen,** to come running. II. *r.* **sich müde —en,** to run till one is tired. **—er,** *m.* (**—ers,** *pl.* **—er**) jumper, leaper, vaulter; knight (*Chess*). **—erei',** *f.* repeated leaping, continual jumping. *Comp.* **—anker,** *m.* kedge anchor. **—ball,** *m.* india-rubber ball, elastic ball. **—bock,** *m.* springbok, Cape antelope. **—brett,** *n.* spring-board. **—brunnen,** *m.* fountain. **—faden,** *m.* brittle glass-thread; elater (*Bot.*). **—feder,** *f.* elastic spring. **—feder=matratze,** *f.* spring-mattress. **—fisch,** *m.* flying fish. **—flut,** *f.* spring-tide. **—frosch,** *m.* leap-frog (*a game*). **—glas,** *n.* anaclastic glass. **—hahn,** *m.* cock. **—hase,** *m.* jumping hare; jerboa. **—hengst,** *m.* stallion. **—ins=feld,** *m.* romp, mad-cap; hoyden (*of a girl*); whipper-snapper (*of a boy*). **—käfer,** *m.* click- *or* spring-beetle. **—kasten,** *m.* a kind of padded box used for jumping (*Milit.*). **—kraft,** *f.* elasticity. **—kräftig,** *adj.* elastic, springy. **—kunst,** *f.* art of vaulting *or* leaping. **—lade,** *f.* wind-chest (*Org.*). **—ladung,** *f.* explosive charge. **—maus,** *f.* jerboa. **—ochs,** *m.* bull kept for breeding purposes. **—pferd,** *n.* leaping horse, jumper. **—prozession,** *f.* dancing procession. **—quell(e,** *f.*,) *m.* spring. **—rohr,** *n.* jet-pipe (*of fountains*). **—schloß,** *n.* spring-lock. **—seil,** *n.* skipping-rope. **—spiel,** *n.* leaping, vaulting, tumbling; dancing on the tight rope. **—stange,** *f.*, **—stock,** *m.* balancing pole; leaping *or* jumping pole. **—stunde,** *f.* an hour's interval between two lessons. **—tau,** *n.* skipping rope. **—übung,** *f.* exercise in leaping *or* vaulting. **—wand,** *f.* spring-screen for catching birds. **—welle,** *f.* bore, large tidal wave. **—wurzel,** *f.* open sesame. **—zeit,** *f.* season of the highest spring-tides; coupling-time.

Sprit, *m.* (**—s,** *pl.* **—e**) spirit, alcohol.

Sprit'ze, *f.* (*pl.* **—n**) syringe, irrigator; squirt; watering engine; fire-engine; splash; Nautilus siphunculus (*Zool.*); trip (*coll.*); **bei der — sein,** to be at one's post; **erster Mann bei der — sein,** to be cock of the walk (*coll.*).

Sprit'z—en, *v.* I. *n.* (*aux.* **h.** & **s.**) to gush forth, spurt up; to play (*as fire-engines, etc.*); to splutter (*as a pen*). II. *a.* to squirt, spurt, syringe; to inject; to splash; to play (*the engines*); to make an excursion, trip (*coll.*). **—er,** *m.* (**—ers,** *pl.* **—er**) squirter, splasher; syringer; splash. *Comp.* **—arbeit,** *f.* work at the fire-engine; spatterwork (*Paint.*); marbled work (*Bookb.*). **—bad,** *n.* shower bath, douche. **—bewurf,** *m.* rough-cast, plastering. **—brett,** *n.* dash-board, splash-board. **—büchse,** *f.* squirt. **—en=haus,** *n.* engine-house, fire-engine station. **—en=leute,** *pl.* fire-men. **—en=macher,** *m.* fire-engine maker. **—en=meister,** *m.* head fireman; inspector of fire-engines. **—en=röhre,** *f.*, **—en=schlauch,** *m.* hose of a fire-engine. **—en=stock,** *m.* piston of a syringe. **—fahrt,** *f.* flying visit, pleasure excursion, trip (*coll.*). **—fisch,** *m.* beaked bandoleer-fish; dolphin; sperm whale. —**flasche**, *f.* wash-bottle. —**fleck**, *m.* splash. —**gebackene(s)**, *n.*, *see* —**kuchen**. —**hahn**, *m.* cock (*of a barrel*). —**kanne**, *f.* watering-pot. —**kuchen**, *m.* kind of fritter. —**leder**, *n.* splash-leather (*on carriages*). —**löcher**, *pl.* spout-holes. —**malerei**, *f.* spatterwork. —**mittel**, *n.* injection (*Med.*). —**nudeln**, *pl.* vermicelli. —**regen**, *m.* drizzle. —**röhre**, *f.* syringe; spout-hole; clyster-pipe. —**tour**, *f.* trip (*coll.*). —**wasser**, *n.* spray.

Sprö'd—e, I. *adj. & adv.* brittle; hard, inflexible, stubborn; dry; chapped (*of the skin*); coy; shy, demure; cold, disdainful; —**e sein**, to be reserved; **seien Sie nicht so —e!** do not be so shy *or* coy! —**e thun**, to affect shyness, to play the prude; —**e Tugend**, severe *or* prim virtue; —**e Dame**, prim lady. II. *f.* (*pl.* —**en**) prude. —**heit**, —**igkeit**, *f.* brittleness; hardness; dryness; demureness, coyness; prudery; reserve, coldness. *Comp.* —**glas=erz**, *n.* brittle, sulphureous silver-ore. —**hufig**, *adj.* brittle-hoofed (*of horses*). —(**e**)=**thun**, *n.* affected shyness, prudery.

¹**Sproß** (*short* **o**), *m.* (—(**ss**)**es**, *pl.* (—(**ss**)**en**) shoot, sprout(ing bud), sprig; descendant, offspring, scion; **sein erster —**, his first-born (child). *Comp.* —**vokal**, *m.* parasitic vowel.

³**Sproß** (*short* **o**), **Sprös'se**, *1 & 3 pers. sing. imperf. ind. & subj. of* **sprießen**.

¹**Spros's—e**, *f.* (*pl.* —**en**) *see* ¹**Sproß**; **Brüsseler —en**, Brussels sprouts; point, prong, start, branch (*hunt.*); **erste —e**, brow-antler, broach. *Comp.* —**en=bier**, *n.* (Danzig) spruce-beer. —**en=bildung**, *f.* prolification. —**en=extrakt**, *m.* extract of spruce-fir. —**en=fichte**, *f.* spruce-fir. —**en=kohl**, *m.* broccoli; **Brüsseler —en=kohl**, Brussels sprouts. —**en=tanne**, *f.* hemlock-spruce. —**en=tau**, *n.* knotted climbing rope (*gymn.*). —**en=tragend**, —**en=treibend**, *adj.* proliferous, prolific.

²**Spros'se**, *f.* (*pl.* —**n**) rung, round, rundle, step, stave; star, bar; peg; cross-bar (*of a window-frame*).

Spros'sen, *v.n.* (*aux.* **h.** & **s.**) to sprout, germinate, bud; to come from, to descend from. —**d**, *pres. p. & adj.* prolific.

Spros'ser, *m.* (—**s**, *pl.* —) thrush- *or* bastard-nightingale (*Luscinia major*).

Sprößling, *m.* (—**s**, *pl.* —**e**) sprout, shoot; scion, descendant.

Sprot'te, *f.* (*pl.* —**n**) sprat; **Kieler —n**, smoked sprats (from **Kiel**).

Spruch, *m.* (—(**e**)**s**, *pl.* **Sprü'che**) sentence, decree, judgment; verdict; saying; dictum; axiom; maxim, motto; aphorism, epigram; short gnomic poem; passage, text; **Sprüche Salomonis**, Proverbs of Solomon; **einen — thun**, to pass sentence, make an award. —**haft**, *adj.* sententious. *Comp.* —**artig**, *adj.* aphoristic. —**buch**, *n.* book of texts; book of aphorisms. —**dichter**, *m.* aphoristic poet; gnomic *or* sententious poet. —**dichtung**, *f.* epigrammatic *or* gnomic poetry. —**fähig**, *adj.* competent. —**fertig**, *adj.* sufficiently investigated (*Law*). —**gedicht**, *n.* rhymed maxim *or* proverb, gnomic poem, epigram. —**register**, *n.* concordance (to the Bible). —**reich**, *adj.* aphoristic, sententious. —**reif**, *adj.* ready for trial *or* judgment; **die Sache ist noch nicht —reif**, the matter has not yet been fully investigated. —**weise**, *adv.* in sentences; sententiously. —**weiser**, *m.* concordance (to the Bible).

Sprüch'wort, *see* **Sprichwort**.

Spru'del, *m.* (—**s**, *pl.* —) bubbling source, spring, well; hot spring.

Spru'del—n, *v.* I. *n.* (*aux.* **s.**) to bubble, effervesce; (*aux.* **h.**) to bubble *or* boil up; to sparkle (*as wine*); to gush; to flash, gleam, to be full of (*ardour, etc.*); to fume; to boil with (*anger, etc.*); to sputter (*in talking*); **der Witz —t von seinen Lippen**, he is bubbling over with wit. II. *a.* to spurt forth. —(**er**), **Sprud'l—er**, *m.* (—**ers**, *pl.* —**er**) sputterer. *Comp.* —**kopf**, *m.* hot-headed person. —**wasser**, *n.* bubbling water.

Sprü'h—en, *v.* I. *a.* to send forth in drops *or* sparks; to sprinkle; to scatter; to emit (*sparks, etc.*). II. *n.* (*aux.* **h.**) to fly out in sparks *or* drops; to sparkle, scintillate; to drizzle; to flash (*with anger, etc.*). *Comp.* —**auge**, *n.* flashing eye. —**feuer**, *n.* sparkling *or* (*rarely*) coruscating fire. —**funke(n)**, *m.* flying-spark. —**regen**, *m.* drizzling rain, drizzle. —**welle**, *f.* white-crested wave.

Sprung, *m.* (—**es**, *pl.* **Sprün'ge**) crack, fissure, split, chink; spring, leap, jump, bound; rebound; ricochet; skip; sudden transition; coition (*of animals*); (*pl.*) tricks, gambols, pranks; **in vollem —e**, at full speed; **mit einem —e**, at a bound; **— mit Anlauf**, running jump; **Sprünge machen**, to frisk, gambol; **es ist nur ein — bis dahin**, it is within a stone's throw, quite near; **einen — nach Hause machen**, to run home; **— ins Ungewisse**, leap in the dark; **er wird keine großen Sprünge machen (können)**, he won't be able to go far, *or* do much, he will have to keep within bounds; **einem auf die Sprünge helfen**, to set a p. right; **einem auf die** (*or* **hinter jemands**) **Sprünge kommen**, to find a p. out, to find out a p.'s tricks *or* secrets; **wieder auf seine alten Sprünge kommen**, to fall into one's old ways; **auf dem —e stehen**, to be on the point of. *Comp.* —**bein**, *n.* astragal, ankle-bone. —**brett**, *n.* spring-board, jumping board. —**fischerei**, *f.* trout-fishing. —**gelenk**, *n.* hock (*of horses*). —**kasten**, *m.* padded box used for jumping (*Mil.*). —**lauf**, *m.* gallop. —**riemen**, *m.* martingale. —**schlag**, *m.* half-volley (*Tennis*). —**weise**, *adv.* by bounds *or* leaps. —**weite**, *f.* leaping range.

Spu'ck—e, *f.* spittle, saliva. —**en**, *v.a. & n.* (*aux.* **h.**) to spit. *Comp.* —**kasten**, —**napf**, *m.* spittoon.

Spuk, *m.* (—(**e**)**s**, *pl.* —**e**) ghost, apparition, spectre, phantom, spook (*coll.*); hobgoblin; witchcraft; confusion, noise, uproar; a sad piece of business, a scandal; **es ist — dabei**, there is something not quite right, something uncanny in that. —**haft**, *adj.* ghostlike, ghostly. *Comp.* —**geist**, *m.* imp, hobgoblin. —**geschichte**, *f.* ghost-story. —**haus**, *n.* haunted house. —**stunde**, *f.* witching hour.

Spu'k—en, *v.n.* (*aux.* **h.**) & *imp.* to appear, walk (*as a ghost*), haunt (*a place*); to make a row; to make a noise; **es —t in diesem Hause**, this house is haunted; **der Wein —t in seinem Kopfe**, the wine has gone to his head; **es —t in seinem Kopfe**, he is not quite right in his head *or* his upper story. —**erei'**, *f.* apparitions; ghost-walking; disturbance.

Spu'l—e, *f.* (*pl.* —**en**) spool, bobbin; quill; coil (*electr.*). *Comp.* —**baum**, *m.* spindle-tree. —**draht**, *m.* spool-wire. —**eisen**, *n.* bobbin-iron. —**holz**, *n.* puppet (*Weav.*). —**kasten**, *m.* bobbin-chest. —**maschine**, *f.* jack-frame. —**rad**, *n.* spooling-wheel. —**röhrchen**, *n.* small bobbin for silk. —**wurm**, *m.* belly-worm; large round-worm.

Spu'l—en, *v.a.* to wind upon a reel *or* bobbin; to spin. —**er**, *m.* (—**ers**, *pl.* —**er**) winder; creel; reel-holder (*on sewing-machines*).

Spü'l—en, *v.* I. *a.* to wash, clean, scour; to rinse; **die Wogen —en das Ufer hohl**, the waves are undermining the shore. II. *n.* (*aux.* **h.**) to wash against, lap. —**icht**, (—**ig**,) *n.*

(—ichts, pl. —ichte), dish-water, slops; pig-wash, swill. Comp. —bank, f. sink, slop-stone; washing-place (on rivers). —faß, n. wash-tub. —frau, f. scullery-maid. —kammer, f., —küche, f. scullery. —napf, m. slop-basin; rinsing-basin. —wasser, n. water for washing up; sloppy water, slops, dish-water.

Spund, m. (& n.) (—es, pl. Spün'de) bung, plug; stopple; tompion (Artil.); bunghole; aperture (of an air-shaft); feather, tongue (Carp.); shutter (Hydr.); channel, groove. —en, v.a. see Spünden. Comp. —band, n. bung-hoop. —brett, n. thick board or plank. —geld, n. tax on liquors. —hefe, f. barm, yeast worked out at the bung-hole. —hobel, m. grooving-plane. —loch, n. bung-hole. —messer, n. cooper's hatchet. —nägel, pl. floor-nails. —tiefe, f. centre measurement (of a cask). —wand, f. sheet-piling (Hydr.). —zapfen, m. bung. —zieher, m. bung-pick.

Spün'd—en, v.a. to bung; to put into casks; to groove, fit (planks, etc.) into one another; to inlay. —er, m. (—ers, pl. —er) beer- or wine-porter. —ung, f. bunging; rabbet, rabbeting.

Spur, f. (pl. —en) trace, track; footstep; mark, sign, vestige, clue; remains; rut (of a wheel); wake (of a ship); trail, scent; track (Railw.); furrow, channel; point of intersection; aus der — bringen, to mislead; von der — abbringen, to throw off the scent; auf die — bringen, to put on the right scent or track; die — verschlagen, to double back; keine — von, not the least sign or trace of, not a bit of, not the faintest notion of, no . . . whatever. Comp. —breite, f. (width of) gauge (Railw.). —eisen, n. furrow-cutter. —herd, m. hearth of a forge. —kranz, m. flange, tire (of a wheel). —lehre, f. gauge (Railw.). —los, adj. trackless; —los verschwinden, to disappear without leaving a trace, to disappear completely, to vanish into space, to be hopelessly lost. —punkt, m. trace (Math.). —ritt, m. following the game on horseback. —stein, m. concentrated metal. —weite, f. width of the track (railway-)gauge.

Spu'ren, v.n. (aux. h.) to keep the track.

Spür'—en, v. I. a. & n. (aux. h.) to trace, track, follow the track of, scent out. II. a. to perceive; to discover; to feel, experience; to have an inkling of. —er, m. (—ers, pl. —er) see —hund. —erei', f. espionage. Comp. —gang, m. quest of game; tour of inspection. —hund, m. dog that hunts by scent, tracker, track-hound; spy. —kraft, f. keen scent; sagacity, penetration. —nase, f. tracking nose; prying or inquisitive person; eine gute —nase haben, to have a keen scent. —ohr, n. sharp ear. —schnee, m. newly fallen snow.

Spur're, f. Spanish plaintain.

Spüt'zen, v.a. to spit (obs.; B.).

Spu'ten, v.r. to make haste, hurry (up).

Ss, int. (onomat.) swish!

St, int. hush! sh! silence! be quiet!

Staat, m. (—s, pl. —en) state, parade, pomp; finery, dress; train equipage; state, country; government, body politic; condition; die Niederländischen —en, the Low Countries; die —en (= Stände), the (e)states; (= die General—en), the States-General; die Balkan—en, the Balkan States, Balkans; die Vereinigten —en (von Nordamerika), the United States, abbr. U. S. (A.); in vollem —e, in full dress; zum —e, for show; einen großen — machen, to live in great style; — machen mit, to make a parade of, boast of. —lich, adj. & adv. pertaining to or proceeding from the state, political; public; —liche Unterstützung, state help, subvention from public funds; —liche Einrichtungen, public institutions. Comp. —en=beschreibung, f. political geography. —en=bund, m. confederation. —en=geschichte, f. political history. —en=kunde, f. political science, politics. —en=recht, n. law of nations. —en=system, n. political system. —licher=seits, adv. on the part of the state. —s=abgaben, pl. (government-)taxes. —s=akten, pl. state papers; state records. —s=aktien, pl. government bonds or securities. —s=amt, n. government appointment, office under the crown; public office; civil service. —s=angehörige(r), m. subject of a state; ein deutscher —sangehöriger, a German subject; er ist kein deutscher (englischer, etc.) —sangehöriger, he is an alien, he is not a German (English) subject. —s=angehörigkeit, f. citizenship, nationality; die —sangehörigkeit erwerben, to become naturalized; die —sangehörigkeit verlieren or aufgeben, to become denaturalized. —s=anleihe, f. government loan. —s=anwalt, m. Attorney-General; public prosecutor. —s=anweisung, f. bond, exchequer-bill. —s=anzeiger, m. official advertiser or gazette; deutscher Reichs und —s=anzeiger, German Imperial and State Gazette. —s=archiv, n. public-record office. —s=archivar, m. keeper of the rolls; erster —sarchivar, master of the rolls. —s=ausgaben, pl. public expenditure. —s=bank, f. national bank. —s=beamte(r), —s=diener, m. civil servant, government official. —s=behörde, f. government authorities. —s=bürgerrecht, n. (rights of) citizenship; Verleihung des —sbürgerrechts, naturalization. —s=degen, m. sword of state. —s=dienst, m. see —samt. —s=einkommensteuer, f. income-tax. —s=einkünfte, pl. public revenues. —s=fach, n. politics. —s=gebäude, n. public building; the constitution; magnificent building. —s=gefährlich, adj. dangerous to the state. —s=gefängnis, n. state-prison. —s=gerichtshof, m. Supreme Court of Judicature. —s=geschäft, n. State affair. —s=gesetz, n. law of the land, constitutional law; statute law. —s=gewalt, f. supreme or executive power. —s=gläubige(r), m. public creditor; fundholder. —s=grundgesetz, n. fundamental law of a state; constitution. —s=grundsatz, m. political maxim. —s=gut, n. public property. —s=handel, m. political or public affair. —s=haushalt, m. finances, administration of revenue, ways and means. —s=haushalts=etat, m. budget. —s=kalender, m. official almanac, state-directory; (in England) Red Book. —s=kanzler, m. chancellor of a state; (in England) Lord Chancellor. —s=kasse, f. public exchequer, treasury. —s=kirche, f. national church, Established Church; Englische —skirche, Church of England, Anglican Church. —s=kleid, n. gala dress. —s=klug, adj. versed in state affairs, politic; diplomatic. —s=klugheit, f. political shrewdness; policy. —s=körper, m. body-politic. —s=kosten, pl. public expense; auf —skosten, at the public expense. —s=kredit=zettel, m. treasury-bill. —s=kunde, —s=kunst, f. political science, politics; statesmanship. —s=kutsche, f. state-coach. —s=lehre, f. political science. —s=mann, m. (pl. —s=männer) statesman, politician. —s=minister, m. (state-)minister (in England), secretary of state. —s=ökonomie, f. political economy; administration of the public revenue. —s=pächter, m. farmer of a branch of the public revenue. —s=papiere, pl. state-papers; government securities, public securities, funds, stocks, consols. —s=papier=handel, m. stock-jobbing. —s=prozeß, m. state trial. —s=prüfung, f. government examination; civil service examination. —s=rot, m. council of state; councillor of state;

geheimer —srat, Privy Council; Privy Councillor, member of the Privy Council. **—s=rätin,** *f.* wife of a councillor of state. **—s=recht,** *n.* right of a state; civic rights; public, constitutional *or* political law. **—s=rechts=wissenschaft,** *f.* political science. **—s=rechts=lehrer,** *m.* professor of public law. **—s=säckel,** *m.* public purse. **—s=schatz,** *m.* exchequer, public treasury. **—s=schuld,** *f.* national debt; **fundierte —sschuld,** consols, consolidated funds. **—s=schuldenverwaltung,** *f.* administration of the national debt. **—s=schuld=schein,** *m.* government bond. **—s=sekretär,** *m.* secretary of state. **—s=siegel,** *n.* official seal; **großes —ssiegel,** Great Seal. **—s=sozialismus,** *m.* state socialism. **—s=steuer,** *f.* government tax; inland revenue. **—s=streich,** *m.* coup d'état. **—s=umwälzung,** *f.* (political) revolution. **—s=unterhändler,** *m.* diplomatist. **—s=verbesserung,** *f.* political reform. **—s=verfassung,** *f.* political constitution. **—s=verwaltung,** *f.* administration of a state; government. **—s=wirtschaft,** *f.* political economy; administration of public money. **—s=wissenschaft,** *f.* political science; state-craft. **—s=zimmer,** *n.* state-room.

Stab, *m.* (—s, *pl.* Stä'be, *as measure* —) staff; stick; wand (*of a conjuror, of office, etc.*); mace, rod; bar (*of a grate, etc.; of metal*); perch (*for a bird*); crosier; (*marshal's*) baton; ell; metre; measure (*of length*); rib (*of an umbrella*); moulding, fillet (*Arch.*); astragal; torus; prop; support; the staff (*Mil.*); jurisdiction; (*pl.*) stumps, wicket (*Cricket*); **am —e gehen,** to walk with the help of a stick; **seinen — weiter setzen,** to continue one's journey; **den — über einen brechen,** to condemn a p. (to death); **ich stehe nicht unter Ihrem —e,** I am not under your authority; **geflügelter —,** caduceus (*Myth.*). *Comp.* **—einguß,** *m.* ingot-mould. **—eisen,** *n.* bar-iron, wrought iron. **—gereimt,** *adj.* alliterative. **—gold,** *n.* bar-gold. **—halter,** *m.* mace-bearer; beadle; president (*of a court of justice*); sergeant-at-arms; staff-holder (*Survey.*). **—hammer,** *m.* flattening hammer; slitting mill. **—holz,** *n.* stave. **—lehen,** *n.* episcopal fief. **—reim,** *m.* alliteration; **Gedicht in —reimen,** alliterative poem; **—reimend,** alliterative; **—reimender Vers,** alliterative line. **—s=arzt,** *m.* (surgeon-) major; staff-surgeon (*Naut.*); **General —s=arzt,** general in the medical department, (surgeon-)general. **—s=hoboist,** *m.* band-master. **—s=offizier,** *m.* staff-officer; flag-officer (*Naut.*); field-officer, regimental field-officer. **—s=quartier,** *n.* headquarters. **—s=quartiermeister,** *m.* quartermaster-general. **—s=trompeter,** *m.* trumpet-major. **—s=wache,** *f.* soldiers permanently attached to the mobile staffs of the German army. **—tierchen,** *n.* bacillus. **—träger,** *see* **—halter.**

Stäb'—chen, *n.* (—chens, *pl.* —chen) little wand; treble, long stitch. **—eln,** *v.a.* to stake (*peas*). *Comp.* **—el=erbsen,** *pl.* staked peas.

Stabi'l, *adj.* stable, steady. **—ität',** *f.* stability.

Stach (*long* a), **Stä'che,** *imperf. ind. & subj. of* **stechen.**

Sta'chel, *m.* (—s, *pl.* —n) prickle, prick; thorn; sting; spine; quill (*of porcupines*); point, prong (*of spurs*); beard (*of barley*); tongue (*of a buckle*); goad; **ein — im Auge,** a thorn in the flesh; **wider den — lecken** (*or* **löcken**), to kick against the pricks (*B.*). **—icht,** (**stach=licht**) (*obs.*), **—ig,** (**stachlig,**) *adj.* prickly, thorny; spinous; bristly; stinging, poignant. *Comp.* **—ähre,** *f.* French grass, esparcet. **—beere,** *f.* gooseberry. **—biene,** *f.* working-bee. **—draht,** *m.* barbed wire. **—draht=zaun,** *m.* barbed wire fence. **—fisch,** *m.* stickle-back; sea-urchin; globe- *or* porcupine-fish. **—flosse,** *f.* fin-spine. **—flosser,** *pl.* acanthopterygians (*Icht.*). **—förmig,** *adj.* thorn-like. **—frucht,** *f.* prickly fruit. **—halsband,** *n.* spiked dog-collar. **—los,** *adj.* without prickles; stingless. **—muskel,** *m.* spinous muscle. **—raupe,** *f.* prickly caterpillar, caterpillar of the swallow-tail butterfly. **—rede,** *f.* satirical, stinging speech. **—roche,** *m.* thorn-back. **—schnecke,** *f.* Venus' shell (*Mollusc.*). **—schwein,** *n.* porcupine. **—zaundraht,** *m.* barbed wire (*for fencing*).

Sta'chel—n, *v.a.* to arm *or* set round with points, thorns, stings, *etc.*; to prick, sting; to goad; to spur on; **ihn —t Ehrbegier,** the love of fame spurs him on.

Sta'del, *m.* (—s, *pl.* —) stall, shed (*dial.*).

Sta'den, *m.* (—s, *pl.* —) river bank, quay (*dial.*).

Sta'dium, *n.* (—s, *pl.* **Stadien**) stadium; stage (*of affairs, trade, a disease, etc.*).

Stadt, *f.* (*pl.* **Städ'te**) town; city; **die ewige —,** the Eternal City (*Rome*); **die heilige —,** the Holy City (*Jerusalem*); **in der — aufgewachsen,** town-bred; **das weiß die ganze —,** that is all over the town; **er ist mit mir aus einer —,** he is a fellow-townsman of mine. *Comp.* **—abgeordnete(r),** *m.* town-councillor; member for a borough. **—adel,** *m.* resident nobility; patricians. **—amt,** *n.* municipal office; mayoralty (*in Germany*). **—amtmann,** *m.* mayor (*in Frankfort a. M.*). **—bahn,** *f.* city-railway; **Londoner —bahn,** metropolitan (railway). **—bann,** *m.* district *or* jurisdiction of a town. **—baumeister,** *m.* municipal architect. **—beamte(r),** *m.* municipal officer. **—behörde,** *f.* municipal authorities. **—bekannt,** *adj.* generally known; **die Geschichte ist —bekannt,** the story is the talk of the town. **—bewohner,** *m.* townsman, dweller in a town. **—bezirk,** *m.* ward. **—brief,** *m.* letter sent by town-post. **—buch,** *n.* municipal register. **—bürger,** *m.* citizen. **—bürger=recht,** *n.* freedom of the city, civic rights. **—festung,** *f.* citadel. **—gebiet,** *n.* township. **—gefängnis,** *n.* city-jail. **—gegend,** *f.* quarter of a town. **—gemeinde,** *f.* city corporation, municipality. **—gericht,** *n.* magistrate's court. **—gerichts=barkeit,** *f.* municipal jurisdiction. **—gespräch,** *n.* town-talk. **—graben,** *m.* town-moat. **—gut,** *n.* municipal property. **—hauptmann,** *m.* captain of the civic guard *or* town militia. **—haus,** *n.* townhall, guildhall; town-house. **—kämmerer,** *m.* city-receiver. **—kind,** *n.* townsman, native of a town. **—klatsch,** *m.* talk of the town. **—klatsche,** *f.* town-gossip. **—kommandant,** *m.* governor of a (*fortified*) city. **—kreis,** *m.* district formed by a town. **—kundig,** *adj.* well acquainted with the town; well-known in town. **—leute,** *pl.* townspeople, townsfolk. **—miliz,** *f.* civic guard; town militia. **—neuigkeit,** *f.* local news. **—physikus,** *m.* medical officer of a town. **—post,** *f.* town-post, local post, local delivery. **—rat,** *m.* town-council; town-councillor, alderman. **—recht,** *n.* municipal law(s). **—richter,** *m.* judge in a magistrate's court, city-magistrate. **—säckel,** *m.* city treasury. **—schreiber,** *m.* town-clerk. **—schreiberei,** *f.* office of the town-clerk. **—schule,** *f.* municipal school, board school; town-school. **—schul=kommission,** *f.* local school-board. **—schul=rat,** *m.* member of school-board; inspector of (*board*) schools. **—soldat,** *m.* city-militiaman. **—steuer,** *f.* municipal rate. **—teil,** *m.* quarter, ward. **—verordnete(r),** *m.* town-councillor. **—verordneten=versammlung,** *f.* town-council. **—verordneten=vorsteher,** *m.* chairman of the town-council. **—verwaltung,** *f.* local administration. **—viertel,** *n.* ward. **—vogt,** *m.* high-bailiff, provost. **—vogtei',** *f.* city-jail.

—wache, *f.* municipal guard. —wage, *f.* public scales. —weide, *f.* town-common. —wesen, *n.* municipal concerns. —wohnung, *f.* town-residence.

Städt'—chen, *n.* (—chens, *pl.* —chen) small town. —er, *m.* (—ers, *pl.* —er) inhabitant of a town; townsman (townswoman); *pl.* townspeople; —er und Studenten, town and gown. —isch, *adj.* of a town *or* city; municipal; town-like. *Comp.* —e=bezwinger, *m.* conqueror of cities. —e=bund, *m.* league of cities. —e=ordnung, *f.* municipal statutes. —e=tag, *m.* meeting of the delegates of several towns. —e=wesen, *n.* civic *or* municipal concerns; das deutsche —ewesen, the German towns.

Stafet'te, *f.* (*pl.* —n) courier, express.

Staff—a'ge, *f.* figures (*persons, animals, etc.*) in a landscape (*Paint.*); decoration. —ie'ren, *v.a.* to garnish, dress, trim; to finish; to decorate; to enliven (*a picture*) with figures. —ie'rer, *m.* (—ierers, *pl.* —ierer) trimmer, dresser; decorator, *see* —ier=maler. —ie'rung, *f.* garnishing; decorating; trimming, *see* —age. *Comp.* —ier'=maler, *m.* decorator; painter of figures, groups, *etc.*, in landscape. —ier'=malerei, *f.* decorative painting. —ier'=naht, *f.* garnish-seam.

Staf'fel, *f.* (& *m. dial.*) (*pl.* —n) step, round (*of a ladder*); degree; echelon (*Mil.*). —ei', *f.* easel (*Paint.*). *Comp.* —aufstellung, *f.* echelon (*Mil.*). —bewegung, *f.* movement in echelon form. —förmig, *adj.* in steps; in echelon. —tarif, *m.* adjustable tariff.

Stag, *n.* (—(e)s, *pl.* —e) stay (*Naut.*); loses —, preventer stay. *Comp.* —fock, *f.* fore-stay sail.

Stagnie'ren, *v.n.* (*aux.* h.) to stagnate.

[1]**Stahl**, *m.* (—s, *pl.* —e *and* Stäh'le) steel; sword, dagger; any steel instrument; chisel; stamp; heater (*of an iron*). *Comp.* —artig, *adj.* steel(y); chalybeate. —bad, *n.* chalybeate bath. —blech, *n.* (thin) steel plate, sheet-steel. —brennen, *n.* conversion of iron into steel. —brunnen, *m.* chalybeate spring. —erz, *n.* sparry iron-ore. —fabrik, *f.* steel manufactory. —feder, *f.* steel-pen; steel-spring. —feder=halter, *m.* penholder. —feder=matratze, *f.* spring-mattress. —frischen, *n.* steel-fining (process). —geschoß, *n.* steel projectile. —geschütz, *n.* steel gun *or* cannon. —gewand, *n.* coat of mail, armour (*poet.*). —gewinnung, *f.* production of steel. —granate, *f.* steel shell; panzerbrechende —granaten, armour-piercing steel shells. —guß, *m.* toughened cast-iron. —haltig, *adj.* containing steel, chalybeate. —hammer, *m.* steel-hammer; steel forge. —hart, *adj.* hard as steel. —härtung, *f.* tempering of steel. —hütte, *f. see* —fabrik. —kammer, *f.* strong-room (*in large banking establishments*). —kopfschiene, *f.* steel-headed rail (*Railw.*). —pille, *f.* iron-pill. —pulver, *n.* steel filings; iron powder. —quelle, *f.* chalybeate spring. —roß, *n.*; das —roß tummeln, to ride a bicycle, to bike (*hum.*). —schuh, *m.* iron shoe, solleret. —stecher, *m.* steel engraver. —stecher=kunst, *f.* art of steel engraving. —stich, *m.* steel engraving, print. —tropfen, *pl.* iron-drops; —tropfen einnehmen, to take iron. —wasser, *n.* chalybeate water.

[2]**Stahl, Stäh'le** (**Stöh'le**), *1 & 3 pers. sing. imperf. ind. & subj. of* stehlen.

Stäh'l—en, *v.a.* to convert into steel; to harden; to temper; to impregnate (*fluids*) with steel; to steel (*the courage, one's heart*). —ern, *adj.* steel, steely. —ung, *f.* steeling; tempering.

Stak, *imperf. of* stecken (*if used intrans. obs.*).

Sta'ke, *f.* (*pl.* —n) stake; boat-hook, gaff. —n, I. *m.* (—ns, *pl.* —n) *see* Stake. II. *v.n.* (*aux.* h.) to hook (*with a boat-hook*).

Stake't(t), *n.* (—s, *pl.* —e) palisade; fence, railing; stockade.

Stal'hof, (**Stahl'hof**,) *m.* (—s) Steelyard (*old settlement of Hanseatic merchants in London*).

Stall, *m.* (—es, *pl.* Stäl'le) shed; stall; stable; sty; kennel; outhouse. *Comp.* —anzug, *m.* stable-dress. —bediente(r), *m.* stableman. —dienst, *m.* stable-work; stable-duty. —fütterung, *f.* stall-feeding. —gabel, *f.* dung-fork. —geld, *n.* stallage; stabling-money. —hengst, *m.* stallion. —junge, *m.* stable-boy. —knecht, *m.* hostler, groom. —meister, *m.* equerry, master of the horse; riding-master. —miete, *f. see* —geld.

Stal'l—en, *v.* I. *a.* to stall, stable. II. *n.* (*aux.* h.) to be in a stall *or* stable; to run well in harness together; to urinate (*of animals*). —ung, *f.* stabling; stables, sheds; preserve, enclosure.

Stami'n, *m.* (—s, *pl.* —s) estamine (*cloth*).

Stamm, *m.* (—es, *pl.* Stäm'me) stem, trunk; stalk; family; tribe; race, stock, breed; trunk; stem (*of words*); stock (*Agr.*); nucleus, officers; stake (*Cards*); card(s) left after dealing; capital; Holz auf dem —e kaufen, to buy standing trees; to buy timber at the stub; einen — Kegel schieben, to play a game of skittles; der — Juda, the tribe of Judah; die zwölf Stämme, the twelve tribes; die Stämme der Germanen, the Germanic tribes; von königlichem —e, of royal blood; die Stämme in Schottland, the Highland clans; der Apfel fällt nicht weit vom —, like father, like son (*prov.*). —en, *v.n.* (*aux.* s.) to be descended, sprung (*from*); to be derived (*from*). —haft, *adj. see* Stämmig. *Comp.* —aktie, *f.* original share. —bahn, *f.* trunk line, main line (*Railway*). —baum, *m.* genealogical tree. —bildung, *f.* formation of primary words. —buch, *n.* genealogical register; album; sich in ein —buch einschreiben, to write one's name (*a few lines or a poem*) in an album. —buch=blatt, *n.* leaf from an album. —buchstabe, *m.* radical letter. —buch=vers, *m.* verse(s) suitable for *or* written in an album. —burg, *f.* ancestral castle. —eltern, *pl.* progenitors; first parents. —ende, *n.* stump (*of a tree*). —erbe, *m.* heir-at-law; lineal representative. —folge, *f.* line of descent. —form, *f.* primitive form (*of a word*). —gast, *m.* habitué, constant visitor (*at an inn, etc.*). —geld, *n.* capital; stake. —genosse, *m.* member of the same race, tribe, clan. —halter, *m.* representative (*of a race*); eldest son of the family, heir. —haus, *n.* ancestral home. —holz, *n.* timber, trunk-wood. —kapital, *n.* capital, stock-fund. —kneipe, *f.* tavern *or* restaurant which a p. frequents regularly. —land, *n.* mother-country. —lehen, *n.* family-fief, fee-simple. —linie, *f.* chief branch; line, lineage. —liste, *f.* muster-roll. —los, *adj.* trunkless, stemless. —mutter, *f.* ancestress. —ochse, *m.* stock bull. —prioritätsaktie, *f.* preference share. —register, *n. see* —baum. —reihe, *f.* line of descendants. —reis, *n.* sucker. —rolle, *f.* register. —sage, *f.* tribal tradition. —schloß, *n.* ancestral castle. —seidel, *n.* beer mug reserved at a restaurant for a regular guest. —silbe, *f.* radical-syllable; *in some cases* = root-syllable. —sitz, *m.* ancestral seat; mother-country. —sprache, *f.* primitive language. —tafel, *f.* genealogical table. —tisch, *m.* table reserved for regular guests (*of an inn*). —vater, *m.* founder of a race, (*tribal*) ancestor. —verbindung, *f.* clanship. —vermächtnis, *n.* entail. —vermögen, *n.* capital. —verwandt, *adj.* akin, cognate, of kindred race. —verwandtschaft, *f.* community of race, kinship; affinity. —

volk, *n.* aborigines, primitive people *or* race. —**wappen**, *pl.* family arms. —**wort**, *n.* primitive word, stem, theme. —**zeit**, *f.* primitive tense.

Stam'm—eln, *v.a.* & *n.* (*aux.* **h.**) to stammer, stutter; to falter. —**ler**, *m.* (—**lers**, *pl.* —**ler**) stammerer.

Stäm'm—en, *see* **Stemmen**. —**ig**, *adj.* & *adv.* with a stem; full-grown; strong, sturdy; massive; vigorous. —**igkeit**, *f.* strength, sturdiness.

Stam'pfe, *f.* (*pl.* —**n**) stamping; crushing, pounding; stamp; pestle, beetle; beater, rammer; short and thick-stemmed wineglass.

Stam'pf—en, *v.* I. *a.* & *n.* (*aux.* **h.**) to stamp; to paw the earth, (*aux.* **s.**) to pitch (*of ships*); to march, stamp. II. *a.* to pound, crush, stamp, beat; to mash (*potatoes*); to bruise (*corn*); to express (*oil*). —**er**, *m.* (—**ers**, *pl.* —**er**) stamper, pounder; rammer; pestle; pawing, stamping horse; ship that pitches. *Comp.* —**bau**, *m.* pisé-building. —**büchse**, *f.* wooden mortar. —**eisen**, *n.* iron pestle. —**erde**, *f.* stamped clay *or* mud. —**gang**, *m.* crushing-mill. —**hammer**, *m.* stamp-hammer. —**kartoffeln**, *f. pl.* mashed potatoes. —**klotz**, *m.* pile-driver, rammer. —**mühle**, *f.* crushing-mill. —**reiten**, *v.n.* (*aux.* **h.**) to pitch at anchor (*Naut.*). —**see**, *f.* heavy sea over the bow. —**werk**, *n.* crushing-mill, stamping-mill. —**zucker**, *m.* crushed sugar.

[1]**Stand**, *m.* (—**es**, *pl.* **Stän'de**) act of standing; position; standing-place; post; state; station; profession; condition (*of things*); class, rank; stand, stall; pew, seat (*in church*); stall, crib; state, rate (*of exchange, etc.*); (*pl.*) estates of the realm; **seinen — einnehmen**, to take up one's stand; **— halten**, to withstand, resist, to hold one's own, stand firm; **ich habe hier keinen guten —**, I am not well placed here; —**in gutem —e**, in good condition; **außer —e zu**, not in a condition to, not able to; **zu —e kommen**, to take place, come to pass, come off; **etwas zu —e bringen, mit etwas zu —e kommen**, to bring about, accomplish something; **in (außer) — setzen**, to enable (disable, put out of one's power); **sich in — setzen**, to prepare oneself for; **in den vorigen — setzen**, to restore to a former condition; **von niederm —e**, of low degree; **Mann von —e**, man of position; **Leute von —e**, men of rank (*or* quality); **mit einem einen harten — haben**, to have a great deal of trouble with a p.; **er ist seines —es Advokat**, he is a lawyer by profession; **ein bedeutender Fasanen—**, good pheasant-shooting; **ehelicher —**, married state; **geistlicher —**, clergy. —**haft(ig)**, *adj.* steady, constant, steadfast, unflinching; resolute, firm; persevering; stoical. —**haftigkeit**, *f.* constancy; resoluteness; stoicism. *Comp.* —**barometer**, (*m.* &) *n.* stationary barometer. —**baum**, *m.* stall-bar. —**bild**, *n.* statue. —**es=adel**, *m.* old nobility. —**es=amt**, *n.* registrar's office. —**es=amtlich**, *adj.*; —**esamtliche Trauung**, marriage before a registrar *or* at a registrar's office. —**es=amts=buch**, *n.* register of births, marriages and deaths kept by the registrar. —**es=ausweis**, *m.* statement of a p.'s trade *or* profession. —**es=beamte(r)**, *m.* registrar of births, marriages and deaths. —**es=ehe**, *f.* marriage for position *or* rank. —**es=erhöhung**, *f.* raising in rank, ennobling. —**es=ehre**, *f.* professional honour. —**es=gebühr**, *f.* honour due to rank; **nach —esgebühr**, with all honour, according to one's rank. —**es=gemäß**, —**es=mäßig**, *adj.* in accordance with one's rank. —**es=genosse**, *m.* equal in station, compeer; **meine —es=genossen**, people of my own class. —**es=gleichheit**, *f.* equality of rank. —**es=herr**, *m.* peer; gentleman; mediatized prince. —**es=herrlich**, *adj.* lordly, baronial. —**es=person**, *f.* person of distinction. —**es=register**, *n.* book of the peerage. —**es=vorurteil**, *n.* caste-prejudice. —**geld**, *n.* stall-rent. —**krämer**, *m.* stall-keeper. —**lager**, *n.* settled quarters, cantonment. —**lehre**, *f.* statics (*Math.*). —**linie**, *f.* base-line, base. —**ort**, —**platz**, *m.* stand, station. —**pferd**, *n.* relay-horse. —**punkt**, *m.* position; station; point of view, standpoint; **überwundener —punkt**, out-of-date view, antiquated conception. —**quartier**, *n.* fixed quarters. —**recht**, *n.* lynch law; martial law. —**rede**, *f.* harangue, speech. —**riß**, *m.* elevation (*Art*). —**rohr**, *n.* heavy rifle; pipe *or* hose of a fire-engine. —**scheibe**, *f.* fixed target. —**uhr**, *f.* time-piece, pendulum-clock. —**wild**, *n.* game frequenting the same spot. —**wind**, *m.* steady wind.

[2]**Stand, Stän'de**, *1 & 3 pers. sing. imperf. ind.* & *subj. of* **stehen**.

Standar'te, *f.* (*pl.* —**n**) standard, ensign; brush (*of a fox, etc.*). *Comp.* —**n=stange**, *f.* flag-staff. —**n=junker**, —**n=träger**, *m.* ensign, cornet, standard-bearer.

Ständ'—chen, *n.* (—**chens**, *pl.* —**chen**) serenade. —**er**, *m.* (—**ers**, *pl.* —**er**) desk for standing at; pillar; post, pole; pedestal; upright (*of a mill*); water-tub. —**ig**, *adj.* fixed; permanent, settled; constant; stated, established; —**ige Anstellung**, permanent appointment, appointment for life; —**iger Begleiter**, constant companion; —**iges Einkommes**, fixed income; —**ige Wohnung**, permanent residence; —**iges Mitglied einer Bühne**, one of the stock company (*Theat.*). —**isch**, *adj.* belonging to the estates (*of a realm*). —**e=saal**, *m.* chamber of the diet, house of assembly. —**e=tag**, *m.* day of the meeting of the diet.

Stan'ge, *f.* (*pl.* —**n**) pole, perch; bar, rod (*of iron, etc.*); beam, rafter; stick, stake; handle, shaft; ingot; bar (*of a curb-bit*); shank (*of scissors*); sear (*of a gunlock*); stick (*of sealing-wax, licorice*); perch, roost; **gezahnte —**, rack; **bei der — bleiben**, to persevere, to stick to the point, maintain one's ground; **nicht bei der — bleiben**, to waver, wander from the point, digress; **einem die — halten**, to take a p.'s part. *Comp.* —**n=besen**, *m.* long-handled broom. —**n=bier**, *n.* beer in tall glasses. —**n=bohne**, *f.* kidney bean. —**n=blei**, *n.* lead in bars. —**n=bürste**, *f.* long-handled brush. —**n=eisen**, *n.* bar-iron; nail (*Min.*); split-rod; trap (*for foxes, etc.*). —**n=erbsen**, *pl.* climbing peas. —**n=gebiß**, *n.* cannon-bit. —**n=gitter**, *n.* bars. —**n=gold**, *n.* bar gold. —**n=holz**, *n.* paling; young copse-wood; twigs, sprays. —**n=kunst**, *f.* hydraulic engine with sweeps. —**n=lack**, *m.* sealing-wax in sticks. —**n=leiter**, *f.* pole-ladder. —**n=pferd**, *n.* wheeler; pole-horse. —**n=presse**, *f.* (lithographic) lever-press. —**n=quadrant**, *m.* gunner's quadrant. —**n=reiter**, *m.* wheel-horse rider; wheel-driver; driver of an ammunition-waggon (*Artil.*). —**n=schraube**, *f.* sear-screw. —**n=schwefel**, *m.* roll-sulphur, cane-brimstone. —**n=seife**, *f.* bar-soap. —**n=spargel**, *m.* asparagus served whole. —**n=stahl**, *m.* bar-steel. —**n=wage**, *f.* swing splinter-bar. —**n=werk**, *n.* rods. —**n=zaun**, *m.* pole-fence. —**n=zirkel**, *m.* beam-compasses.

[1]**Stank**, *m.* (—**es**) stench, stink. *Comp.* —**kugel**, *f.* suffocating ball.

[2]**Stank, Stän'ke**, *1 & 3 pers. sing. imperf. ind.* & *subj. of* **stinken**.

[1]**Stän'ker**, *m.* (—**s**, *pl.* —) stinker; stinking person *or* thing; skunk. —**ig, Stän'krig**, *adj.* stinking. —**n**, *v.n.* (*aux.* **h.**) to smell, stink.

[2]**Stän'ker**, *m.* (—**s**, *pl.* —) quarrelsome person; pryer, ferreter. —**ei'**, *f.* quarrel; wrangling. —**n**, *v.n.* (*aux.* **h.**) to pry about, ferret into; to wrangle, quarrel, be quarrelsome.

Stan(n)io'l, *m.* (—s) tinfoil. **—belegung,** *f.* coat of tinfoil.

Stan'z—e, *f.* (*pl.* **—en**) stanza; stanza (*of eight lines, ottave rime*); mould (*of metal*); metal stamp, die. **—en,** *v.a.* to stamp, to punch. *Comp.* **—en=ſtempel,** *m.* stamp for embossed work.

Sta'pel, *m.* (—s, *pl.* —) stake, staple, beam; pile; scaffolding; stocks (*for a ship*); emporium, mart; store-house; **vom — (laufen) laſſen,** to launch; to bring out, to publish. **—bar,** *adj.* subject to staple-laws; that may be piled up. **—n,** *v.* I. *a.* to pile up. II. *n.* (*aux.* **ſ.**) to stride, stalk. *Comp.* **—gerecht(ig)=keit,** *f.* staple-law *or* right. **—gut,** *n.* staple commodity. **—holz,** *n.* piled wood; stocks (*for a ship*). **—lauf,** *m.* launching, launch. **—ort, —platz,** *m.* staple market, emporium. **—ſtadt,** *f.* emporium.

Stap'fe, *f.* (*pl.* **—n**) footstep. **—n,** *v.n.* (*aux.* **h.** *&* **ſ.**) to walk with a heavy tread, to stamp.

[1]**Star,** *m.* (—(e)s *&* —(e)n, *pl.* —e *&* —en) starling. *Comp.* **—matz,** *m.* starling.

[2]**Star,** *m.* (—(e)s, *pl.* —e); **(grauer —)** cataract; **grüner —,** glaucoma; **ſchwarzer —,** amaurosis; **weißer —,** leucoma; **einem den — ſtechen,** to operate for cataract, to couch a cataract; to open s. o.'s eyes, to tell a p. the plain truth. *Comp.* **—artig,** *adj.* cataractous. **—blind,** *adj.* blind from a cataract. **—brille,** *f.* spectacles for couched eyes (*with convex glasses*). **—fell,** *n.* film of a cataract. **—nadel,** *f.* couching-needle. **—operation,** *f.*, **—ſtechen,** *n.* operation for cataract.

Stär, *m.* (—s, *pl.* —e) ram.

Starb, *1 & 3 pers. sing. imperf. ind. of* **ſterben.**

Stark, *adj. & adv.* (**ſtär'ker, ſtärkſt**) strong; robust; stout; vigorous; numerous, strong; thick; skilful, clever at, well versed in, violent, severe, heavy; hearty (*as an appetite, etc.*); long (*as a mile, etc.*); forte (*Mus.*); **—e Erkältung,** bad cold; **—er Eſſer,** hearty eater; **—es Fieber,** high fever; **—er Froſt,** hard frost; **—es Gedächtnis,** good memory; **das —e Geſchlecht,** the stronger sex; **—er Geiſt,** powerful mind; **der —e Gott,** the mighty God; **—er Regen,** heavy rain; **eine —e Meile,** rather more than a mile; **—er Hirſch,** warrantable stag; **—e Kälte,** severe *or* intense cold; **ein —es Stück,** a bold deed, a daring enterprise; **das iſt —er Tabak,** that's rather strong (*coll.*); **ein —er Schach=ſpieler,** a good chess-player; **wie — iſt Ihre Familie?** how large is your family? **man ſpricht — davon,** it is much talked of; **der Stärkſte hat Recht,** might is *or* goes before right; **das iſt etwas —!** that is rather strong, rather too much! **das iſt zu —!** that is too bad! **in —en Tagemärſchen,** by forced marches; **darin iſt er —,** he is great at that; **— an Reiterei,** strong in cavalry; **Einigkeit macht —,** union is strength. *Comp.* **—beleibt, —leibig,** *adj.* corpulent, stout. **—beſetzt,** *adj.* well-attended, crowded; full (*of an orchestra, etc.*). **—gläubig,** *adj.* staunch in faith. **—gliederig,** *adj.* strong-limbed. **—knochig,** *adj.* strong-boned; big-boned. **—ſtrom,** *m.* powerful (electric) current.

[1]**Stär'ke,** *f.* (*pl.* **—n**) heifer.

[2]**Stär'k—e,** *f.* strength, force, vigour, sturdiness; intensity, violence; stress, energy; stoutness, corpulence; magnitude, greatness; strong side; starch. *Comp.* **—e=artig,** *adj.* amylaceous. **—e=blau,** *n.* blue starch. **—e=fabrik,** *f.* starch-factory. **—e=fabrikant,** *m.* starch-maker. **—e=haltig,** *adj.* containing starch. **—e=kleiſter,** *m.* starch-paste. **—(e)=mehl,** *n.* starch-flour. **—(e)=mehl=artig,** *adj.* starchy, amylaceous. **—e=wäſche,** *f.* linen (*to be*) starched. **—e=zucker,** *m.* starch-sugar.

Stär'k—en, *v.a.* to strengthen, fortify; to cheer, comfort, console; to brace, invigorate; to corroborate, confirm; to starch. **—erin,** *f.* starcher, laundress, laundry-maid. **—ung,** *f.* strengthening, fortifying; bracing, invigorating; comfort; tonic; support, corroboration; starching. *Comp.* **—ungs=mittel,** *n.* restorative, tonic.

Staro'ſt, *m.* (**—en,** *pl.* **—en**) Polish governor of a district. **—ei',** *f.* starosty.

Starr, *adj.* stiff, motionless; fixed, staring; rigid, benumbed; inflexible, obstinate; **— von Erſtaunen,** transfixed with amazement; **— anſehen,** to look at fixedly, stare at.

Star'r—en, *v.n.* (*aux.* **h.**) *see* **— anſehen;** to stiffen, be benumbed *or* rigid; to run cold, curdle; to stand out, project; to bristle, stand on end; to bristle, abound, overflow with; to stare; **die Finger —en mir vor Kälte,** my fingers are benumbed *or* stiff with cold; **von Gold —en,** to be covered *or* to bristle with gold; **von Bajonetten —en,** to bristle with bayonets; **ſeine Hände —en von Schmutz,** his hands are filthy. **—heit,** *f.* stiffness, rigidity; numbness; inflexibility; obstinacy. *Comp.* **—äugig,** *adj. & adv.* staring, with fixed eyes. **—kopf,** *m.* stubborn person. **—köpfig,** *adj.* headstrong, stubborn, obstinate, mulish, pig-headed. **—köpfigkeit,** *f.* obstinacy, stubbornness, pig-headedness. **—krampf,** *m.* tetanus, cataleptic trance. **—ſinn,** *m.* obstinacy. **—ſucht,** *f.* catalepsy.

Stät, *adj.* fixed, stable; steady; constant. **—ig,** *adj.* constant, continual, perpetual; steady. **—igkeit,** *f.* steadiness; constancy; continuity; restiveness. **—iſch,** *adj.* restive (*of horses*); refractory. **—s,** *adv. see* **ſtets.**

Stat—a'riſch, *adj.* standing, progressing slowly; exegetical (*of lectures*), **—ariſche Lektüre eines Schulſchriftſtellers,** careful and slow reading of a school classic. **—ik** (*pron.* **Sta'tik**), *f.* statics. **—io'n,** *f.* (*pl.* **—ionen**) station; stage; station (*R. C.*); **freie —ion haben,** to have board and lodging free *or* found. **—ionä'r,** *adj.* stationary. **—iſch** (*pron.* **ſta'tiſch**), *adj.* statical. **—i'ſt,** *m.* (**—i'ſten,** *pl.* **—i'ſten**) mute (*person in a play*), supernumerary, walking gentleman (*Theat.*). **—i'ſtik,** *f.* statistics. **—i'ſtiker,** *m.* (**—iſtikers,** *pl.* **—iſtiker**) statistician. **—i'ſtiſch,** *adj.* statistical; **—iſtiſche Angaben,** statistics. **—i'v,** *adj.* tripod, stand, foot (*of a machine or instrument*). *Comp.* **—ions=gebäude,** *n.* railway-station. **—ions=ſchiff,** *n.* guard-ship. **—ions=vorſteher,** *m.* station master.

Statt, I. *f.* place, stead, lieu; **bleibende —,** fixed abode; **an Vaters —,** in the place of a father; **an Kindes — annehmen,** to adopt; **an Eides —,** in lieu of oath; **da hat das Schweigen beſſere —,** then, in such a case, it is better to be silent; **eine Bitte — finden laſſen,** to grant a request; **gebt nie dem tollen Wahn des Pöbels —,** never give way to the madness of the crowd; **— finden, — haben,** to take place, to come off, happen, to be permitted. II. *prep.* (*with gen.*) instead (of), in lieu (of), in the place (of); **an meiner —, — meiner,** instead of me, in my place; **— deſſen,** in place of that; (*gov'ng a clause*): **— daß er arbeiten ſollte,** instead of working; **— daß, (an — daß,)** while (*rare*). **—en,** *dat. pl. of* **Statt; von —en gehen,** to proceed, prosper, to go *or* come off, succeed; **zu —en kommen,** to stand in good stead, to be of use *or* advantage, to help. **—haft,** *adj.* admissible, allowable; valid, legal, legitimate. **—haftigkeit,** *f.* admissibility; validity. **—lich,** *adj. & adv.* stately, majestic; magnificent, grand; solemn; important, distinguished; portly. **—lichkeit,** *f.* elegance; magnificence; stateliness; portliness. *Comp.* **—finden, —halten,** *ir.v.n.* (*aux.* **h.**) (*sep.*) *see under* **Statt.** **—halter,** *m.* vicar, representative; viceroy; governor; Stadtholder (*in Holland*). **—halterei',** *f.* governorship, lieutenancy; district governed by a 'statthalter'; stadtholdership.— **halterin,** *f.* viceroy's *or* governor's wife. **—halterschaft,** *f.* lieutenancy; *see* **—halterei.**

Stät'te, *f.* (*pl.* **—n**) place, stead; abode; room.

Sta'tue, *f.* (*pl.* **—n**) statue; *pl.* statuary (*collect.*).

Stat—uie'ren, *v.a.* to maintain, affirm; to lay down, ordain, enact; to permit, tolerate; **an einem ein Exempel —uieren,** to make an example of a p. **—u'r,** *f.* (*pl.* **—uren**) height, figure, stature, size. **—us** (*pron.* **Sta'tus**), *m.* state; return; statement (*C. L.*); **die Dinge im —us quo belassen,** to leave things as they are *or* in statu quo. **—u't,** *n.* (*pl.* **—uten**) institution, regulation; statute, law. **—uta'risch,** *adj.* statutory, legal, according to statute. *Comp.* **—uten=buch,** *n.* statute-book. **—uten=mäßig,** *see* **—utarisch.** **—uten=recht,** *n.* statute-law.

Stau, *m.*; **das Wasser ist im —,** it is the turn of the tide; **das Wasser im — halten,** to dam up the water.

Staub, *m.* (**—es**) dust; powder; pollen; **zu — machen,** to reduce to powder *or* dust; **sich aus dem —e machen,** to abscond; **in den — ziehen (treten),** to drag through the mire; **den — niederschlagen,** to lay the dust.

Stäub'chen, *n.* (**—s,** *pl.* **—**) particle of dust; atom.

Stau'b—en, *v.n.* (*aux.* **h.**) to fly off *or* about like dust; to fall in spray; (*as v. imp.*) to be dusty. **—ig,** *adj.* dusty; powdery. **—igkeit,** *f.* dustiness. *Comp.* **—ähnlich, —artig,** *adj.* dust-like, powdery. **—bach,** *m.* waterfall in the mountains which is dispersed in spray before it reaches the ground; Staubbach (*in Switzerland*). **—behälter,** *m.* anther. **—besen,** *m.* dust-broom. **—beutel,** *m.* anther (*Bot.*). **—beutel=tragend,** *adj.* antheriferous. **—blüte,** *f.* male flower. **—boden,** *m.* place in a mill for receiving the finest part of flour. **—brand,** *m.* mildew, smut. **—brille,** *f.* travelling *or* dust-spectacles; wire-gauze spectacles, goggles (*coll.*). **—bürste,** *f.* clothes-brush; dust-brush. **—deckel,** *m.* false *or* inner case of a watch. **—erde,** *f.* dry mould. **—faden,** *m.* filament, stamen (*Bot.*). **—faden=los,** *adj.* sessile (*Bot.*). **—feder,** *f.* down. **—fege,** *f.* winnowing machine. **—flechte,** *f.* powdery lichen. **—flügel,** *m.* downy wing (*of a butterfly, etc.*). **—flügler,** *pl.* lepidoptera. **—geboren,** *adj.* earth-born. **—gefäß,** *n.* stamen. **—haar,** *n.* downy hair, down. **—hemd,** *n.* blouse, smock-frock. **—hülle,** *f.* the human body (*poet.*). **—kalk,** *m.* dry slaked lime. **—kamm,** *m.* small-tooth comb. **—kittel,** *m.* blouse. **—kohlen,** *pl.* small coal, slack. **—lappen,** *m.* duster. **—lawine,** *f.* avalanche of dry snow. **—mantel,** *m.* dust-cloak. **—mehl,** *n.* flour-dust. **—perle,** *f.* seed-pearl. **—regen,** *m.* fine rain, spray. **—säckchen,** *n.* pounce-bag. **—same,** *m.* pollen. **—sand,** *m.* very fine sand. **—schwamm,** *m.* puff-ball. **—sieb,** *n.* dust-sieve (*for wheat*). **—thee,** *m.* tea-dust. **—tuch,** *n.* duster. **—wedel,** *m.* dusting *or* feather-whisk. **—weg,** *m.* pistil. **—wirbel,** *m.* drift, whirlwind of dust. **—wolke,** *f.* cloud of dust, dust cloud.

Stäu'b—en, *v.* I. *n.* *see* **Stauben.** II. *a.* to powder; to strew, sprinkle with dust; to dust; to pounce (*Engr.*); to winnow (*corn*); **die Feinde auseinander —en,** to disperse the enemy; **die Brücke, welche —et,** the bridge which scatters spray, the bridge that hangs in showers of spray. **—er,** *m.* (**—ers,** *pl.* **—er**) duster; one who dusts; beagle, harrier. **—ern,** *v.* I. *a.* to dust; to start, dislodge, to disperse. II. *n.* (*aux.* **h.**) to rummage; **es —ert,** it drizzles, it is snowing hard (*prov.*). **—ling,** *m.* (*pl.* **—linge**) mortal (*rare*).

Stau'che, *f.* (*pl.* **—n**) bundle, little heap.

Stau'ch—en, *v.a.* to stem, dam up (*water*); to put in shocks, to stook (*corn, etc.*); to knock, shove, nudge; to strain, sprain; to jolt; to pack in, stow down; to shorten by forging. *Comp.* **—sieb,** *n.* brake-sieve (*Metall.*).

Stau'd—e, *f.* (*pl.* **—en**; *dim.* **Stäud'chen, Stäud'lein,** *n.*) shrub; bush; head (*of lettuce, etc.*). **—en,** *v.r.* & *n.* (*aux.* **h.** & **s.**) to grow like a shrub; to head (*as lettuce*). **—ig,** *adj.* shrub-like. *Comp.* **—en=artig,** *see* **—ig.** **—en=gebüsch,** *n.* copse. **—en=gewächs,** *n.* shrub. **—en=hopfen,** *m.* wild hop.

Stau'—en, *v.* I. *a.* to stow away (*goods*); to trim (*a ship*); to dam, stem (*water*); **schlecht gestaut,** out of trim. II. *r.* & *n.*; **das Wasser —t (sich),** the water is rising. **—er,** *m.* (**—ers,** *pl.* **—er**) stower (*Naut.*). *Comp.* **—er=lohn,** *m.* (*cost of*) stowage. **—wasser,** *n.* back-water.

Stau'nen, I. *v.n.* (*aux.* **h.**) to be astonished, amazed (at a th., **über eine S.**). II. *subst.n.* astonishment. *Comp.* **—s=wert, —s=würdig,** *adj.* astonishing, wonderful, amazing.

[1]**Stau'p—e,** *f.* (*pl.* **—en**) flogging; (**—besen,** *m.*) rod, scourge; **den —besen bekommen,** to be flogged.

[2]**Stau'pe,** *f.* (*pl.* **—n**) epilepsy; contagious disease; distemper.

Stäu'pe, *see* [1]**Staupe** **—n,** *v.a.* to flog, scourge.

Steari'n, *n.* (**—s**) stearine. *Comp.* **—licht,** *n.* stearine candle. **—säure,** *f.* stearic acid.

Ste'ch—en, I. *ir.v.a.* & *n.* (*aux.* **h.**) to prick; to pierce; to sting; to stab; to puncture; to bite (*as fleas*); to tilt; to stick, kill (*pigs, etc.*); tc lance; to couch; to burn, scorch (*as the sun*); to stitch; to quilt; to cut (*turf, grass, etc.*); to tap, draw off (*wine*); to engrave, cut; **um eine S. —en,** to cast lots for a th.; **mit einander —en,** to throw for conqueror; **nach dem Ringe —en,** to tilt; **eine Karte —en,** to trump *or* take a card; **—en müssen,** to be forced (*Cards*); **das sticht mir in die Augen,** that strikes my eye; **dieses Haus sticht ihm in die Augen,** he covets this house greatly; **mich sticht die Milz,** I am troubled with spleen; **es sticht mir in die Seite,** I have a stitch *or* shooting pain in my side; **der Hafer sticht ihn,** prosperity has spoiled him, success is making him reckless; **Silben —en,** to be punctilious about, pick one's words; **den Schneller —en,** to cock (*a gun*); **ins Rote —en,** to incline to red; **Tau —en,** to pay out cable; **Löcher in (eine S.) —en,** to pierce holes in; **durch und durch —en,** tc run *or* pierce through, to perforate; (*aux.* **s.**) **in See —en,** to put to sea. II. *subst.n.* (**das Lanzenstechen**) jousting, tourney. **—er,** *m.* (**—ers,** *pl.* **—er**) pricker, *etc.*; tilter; engraver; scoop, proof-stick; hair-trigger (*of a gun*). *Comp.* **—apfel,** *m.* thorn apple. **—bahn,** *f.* tilting-place; arcade (*Arch.*). **—baum,** *m.* holly. **—becken,** *n.* bed-pan. **—beitel, —beutel,** *m.* ripping chisel. **—bolzen,** *pl.* reef-earings (*Naut.*). **—eiche,** *f.* holm; ilex. **—eisen,** *n.* piercer. **—fliege,** *f.* biting *or* stinging fly; stable fly. **—gabel,** *f.* fish-spear; hay-fork. **—ginster,** *m.* thorny German broom; furze, gorse. **—heber,** *m.* plunging-siphon. **—karte,** *f.* winning card, trump(-card). **—kissen,** *n.* engraver's cushion; cushion *or* pillow on which German babies are carried. **—mücke,** *f.* gnat. **—nelke,** *f.* rose-campion. **—palme,** *f.* holly. **—ring,** *m.* tilting-ring. **—sattel,** *m.* jousting-saddle. **—scheibe,** *f.* target. **—schloß,** *n.* hair-trigger lock. **—seide,** *f.* embroidery-silk. **—stahl,** *m.* turner's chisel. **—torf,** *m.*

cut peat. **—vieh,** *n.* cattle for slaughter. **—zeug,** *n.* punching tools.

Ste'ck—en, I. *reg. & (sometimes) ir.v.a.* to stick; to put, place; to set, plant; to stick fast, fix; **in Brand —en,** to set on fire; **den Degen in die Scheide —en,** to sheathe one's sword; **mit Nadeln —en,** to pin; **los —en,** to unpin; **eine Haube —en,** to make a cap; **Geld in ein Geschäft —en,** to invest money in a business; **Grenzen —en,** to set bounds (to); **einem ein Ziel —en,** to set a p. a task; to set limits to one; **ins Loch —en,** to put in prison; **sich in Schulden —en,** to run into debt; **einen in den Sack —en,** to outdo a p.; to get the better of a p.; **einen unter die Soldaten —en,** to make s.o. a soldier; **zu sich —en,** to put in one's pocket; **einem etwas —en,** to confide a th. to a p., to inform s.o. secretly of; **sich hinter eine S. —en,** to get behind a th., to work a th. secretly; to hide behind a th.; **sich hinter einen —en,** to make a tool of s.o. II. *reg. & ir.v.n.* (*aux.* **h.**) to stick fast, be fixed; to be involved in; to hide, lie hidden; **in Elend —en,** to be in great want *or* misery; **in Schulden —en,** to be in debt; **im Gefängnisse —en,** to be in prison; **—en bleiben,** to stick fast, come to a dead stop; to break down (*in a speech*); **—en lassen,** to leave (*a p.*) in the lurch; **den Schlüssel —en lassen,** to leave the key in the door; **in dem Kerl —t etwas,** there's something in that fellow (*coll.*); **eine Frau —t dahinter,** there is a woman at the bottom of it; **es —t etwas dahinter,** there is more in it than meets the eye; **es —t ein Betrug dahinter,** there's some trickery about that; **wir wissen nicht, was ihm im Kopfe —t,** we don't know what he has got in his head; **es —t mir im Halse,** it sticks in my throat, I can't swallow it; there is something wrong with my throat; **wo —en Sie denn?** where are you? **voll —en (von),** to be full (of); **da —t's!** there's the rub! **ich möchte nicht** *or* **um keinen Preis in seiner Haut —en,** I would not be in his skin for a good deal; **er schreit, als ob er am Spieße stäke,** he screams as if he were being spitted; **mit einem unter einer Decke —en,** to have a secret understanding with a p. III. *subst.n.* setting, putting, *etc.* IV. *m.* (**—s,** *pl.* **—**) stick, staff, rod; pole (*dial.*). **—ling,** *m.* (**—lings,** *pl.* **—linge**) slip; cutting, layer, shoot. *Comp.* **—amboß,** *m.* stake. **—brief,** *m.* warrant of apprehension *or* arrest; **er wird —brieflich verfolgt,** warrants are out against him. **—en=bleiben,** *n.* stoppage; sticking fast; stand-still; break-down (*in a speech*). **—en=bündel,** *n.* bundle of sticks. **—en=pferd,** *n.* hobby-horse; hobby; fad, whim, crotchet, mania. **—en=zaun,** *m.* palisade, stick-fence. **—garn,** *n.* fowling-net. **—leuchter,** *m.* spiked candlestick. **—nadel,** *f.* pin. **—nadel=kissen,** *n.* pin-cushion. **—nagel,** *m.* jig-pin. **—reis,** *m. see* **—ling. —rübe,** *f.* turnip; Swedish turnip. **—zirkel,** *m.* draughting compasses (*with shifting points*). **—zwiebel,** *f.* bulb for planting.

Steg, *m.* (**—es,** *pl.* **—e**) foot-path, narrow path; small wooden bridge, plank; gangway; bridge, fret (*Mus.*); thwart; traverse; strap; furniture, reglet, *etc.* (*Typ.*); fillet, middle leg of a triglyph (*Arch.*); **Wege und —e,** roads and paths, ways and by-paths; ins and outs (*fig.*). *Comp.* **—fach,** *n.*, **—kasten,** *m.* furniture-case (*Typ.*). **—kreuz,** *n.* turnstile. **—lehne,** *f.* hand-rail *or* railing of a foot-bridge. **—reif,** *m.* stirrup; **aus dem —reife,** extempore, offhand, on the spur of the moment, without preparation; **aus dem —reif(e) reden,** to speak extempore *or* without notes, to improvise a speech; **Rede aus dem —reif,** extempore speech, impromptu speech. **—reif=dichter,** *m.* improvisator(e), extempore poet. **—reif=dichterin,** *f.* improvisatrice. **—reif=musiker,** *m.* improvisator(e) of music.

Ste'h—en, I. *ir.v.n.* (*aux.* **h.** *&* **s.**) to stand; to be situated; to remain; to be; to stand still, stop; to be pending; to point (*as dogs*); **einem —en,** to become, suit a p.; to hold one's ground against a person; to sit (*to a painter, etc.*); **wie ich gehe und —e,** just as I am; **es kam ihm teuer zu —en,** he had to pay dearly for it; **wie —t's?** how are you? how are matters getting on? how about (mit)? **wie —t's zu Hause,** how are all at home? **es —t schlimm mit seiner Gesundheit,** he is in poor health; **das —t Ihnen frei,** you are at liberty to do that; **das Geld —t sicher,** the money is safe, securely invested; **—en lassen,** to leave standing, to leave, to give (*one*) the slip; **einem Maler (als) Modell —en,** to serve as model to a painter; **der Artikel —t,** the article is retained, is used; **der Ort, wo er gestanden,** the place where he was employed, exercised his profession, *etc.*; **als Bürge —en,** to go security; **das Kleid —t ihr gut,** the dress suits her; **es —t geschrieben,** it is written; **dann —t das Blut augenblicklich,** then the blood is staunched *or* the bleeding stops at once; **—en auf,** to be upon; **es —t der Kopf darauf,** it is a capital crime; **die Aktien stehen auf 200%,** the shares, stocks are at 200 per cent; **der Dativ —t auf die Frage „wem",** the dative is used in answer to the question "to whom;" **auf eignen Füßen —en,** to be independent, self-supporting; **auf seinem eignen Kopfe —en,** to be wilful, obstinate; **es —t ein Preis auf seinem Kopfe,** a price is set upon his head; **da —en die Ochsen am Berge,** there we are brought to a standstill, here is a puzzle; **das Barometer —t auf Regen,** the barometer is low, points to rain; **auf die Füße zu —en kommen,** to fall on one's feet; **bei einem —en,** to stand by, help a p.; **bei einem in Arbeit —en,** to be in s. o.'s employment; **es —t bei Ihnen,** it rests with you; **gut bei einem —en,** to stand well, be on good terms with a p.; **er steht bei den Uhlanen,** he serves in the Lancers; **das Regiment steht in Hannover,** the regiment is garrisoned in Hanover; **dabei —en,** to be present; **bei seiner Meinung —en,** to adhere to one's opinion; **dahin —t mein Sinn nicht,** I have no inclination for that *or* that way; **(gut) —en für,** to stand, answer, vouch for; **sie —en für einen Mann,** they are conjointly responsible; **ich mußte selbst für alles —en,** I had to look after everything, I was responsible for everything; **auf dem Spiele —en,** to be at stake; **—en in,** to stand in, to be in (*garrison; a newspaper; one's power; doubt, etc.*); **in einem Amte —en,** to be in, to fill an office; **im fünften Jahre —en,** to be in one's fifth year; **im Verdachte —en,** to be suspected; **ich —e nicht allein mit meiner Meinung,** I am not alone in thinking so; **wie —t's mit seinem Prozesse?** how is his lawsuit getting on? **ich —e gut mit ihm,** I am on good terms with him; **es —t schlecht mit ihm,** he is in a bad way; **ich weiß nicht, wo mir der Kopf —t,** I do not know which way to turn; I am quite distracted; **—en nach,** to aspire to, seek after; **einem nach dem Leben —en,** to wish to kill a p., to attempt a p.'s life; **—en über,** to be above; **er —t über mir,** he is my superior; **—en unter,** to stand, be under; **es —t zu hoffen,** it is to be hoped; **es stand zu fürchten,** it was to be feared; **es —t nicht zu ändern,** it cannot be changed; **ich —e im Augenblicke zu Ihren Diensten,** I shall be at your service in a moment; **einem zur Seite**

—en, to help a p. II. *v.a.* seinen Mann —en, to hold one's own against, be a match for another; Rede und Antwort —en, to answer questions, to give an account (of oneself); Geld bei einem —en haben, to have placed money with s. o.; wie —en Sie sich mit einander? how do you get on with one another? on what terms are you with one another? er —t sich auf 3000 Mark, he has £150 a year. III. *subst. n.* standing, *etc.*; das —en fällt ihm schwer, he cannot stand long; —en unter dem Gewehre, to be under arms; zum —en bringen, to stop, stay, arrest; das Blut zum —en bringen, to staunch the blood. —end, *p. & adj.* standing; stationary; upright; vertical; continual; lasting; permanent; regular; —enden Fußes, at once, on the spot; —endes Wasser, stagnant water; —ende Redensarten, hackneyed *or* stock phrases; —ender Wind, settled wind; mit —enden Lettern gedruckt, stereotyped; —ende Schuld, consolidated debt. *Comp.* —auf, *m.*, —aufchen, —männchen, *n.* cork-tumbler. —bier=halle, *f.* bar. —bolzen, *pl.* stays (*of a boiler*). —kragen, *m.* stand-up-collar. —leiter, *f.* pair of steps. —platz, *m.* standing-place. —plätze, *pl.* standing room. —pult, *n.* standing-desk, high desk. —rahmen, *m.* print-holder —seidel, *n.* glass of beer drunk standing.

Stehl'bar, *adj.* stealable.

Steh'le—n, *ir.v.a. & n.* (*aux.* h.) to steal; to rob; to pilfer; dem lieben Gott die Zeit —n, to idle away one's time; sich davon —n, to steal away; das kann mir gestohlen werden, I don't care two straws for it (*coll.*); er kann mir mit seiner Musik gestohlen werden, he may go to Bath with his music (*coll.*). —r, *m.* (—rs, *pl.* —r) thief.

Steif, *adj. & adv.* stiff; wooden, ungraceful; rigid; benumbed; formal, pedantic, unbending; starched; straight-laced; thick; strong; firm, inflexible; obstinate; einen —en Daumen haben, to be avaricious; —e Kühlte, strong gale; —er Grog, strong grog; halten Sie die Ohren —! don't give in, keep up your courage! — und fest behaupten, to maintain obstinately. —e, *f.* stiffness; *see* —heit; stiffening, starch, size; starching; prop, buttress, support. —heit, *f.* stiffness; rigidity; awkwardness; formality. *Comp.* —hals, *m.* person with a stiff neck. —halsig, *adj.* stiff-necked. —leinen, *adj.*; ein —leinener Gesell, a strait-laced and pedantic fellow. —leinwand, *f.* buckram. —ofen, *m.* hat-dressing stove. —rock, *m.* stiff petticoat, crinoline. —stiefel, *m.* strong boot; jack boot. —werden, *n.* stiffening; erection (*Physiol.*).

Stei'f—en, *v.a.* to stiffen; to starch; to line with buckram, *etc.*; to prop, shore up, stay; sich auf eine S. —en, to take one's stand upon, to rely on, to insist upon a th.; sich —en gegen, to resist. —er, *m.* (—ers, *pl.* —er) stiffener. —ung, *f.* stiffening; starching; support.

Steig, *m.* (—es, *pl.* —e) path; footpath; steep *or* narrow way. —e, *f.* (*pl.* —en) steep stairs; ladder; foot-way, stile; steep path *or* ascent; palisade; hen-roost; coop; score, twenty.

Stei'g—en, I. *ir.v.n.* (*aux.* h. & s.) to mount, ascend: to climb, scale; to descend; to rise; to rear, prance; to soar; to mount up; to advance in price; auf einen Baum —en, to climb a tree; einem aufs Dach (*or* zu Dach) —en, to fly at, attack a p.; (vom) zu Pferde —en, to (dismount) mount; ans Land —en, to go on shore; aus dem (durch das) Fenster —en, to go out at (enter by) the window; aus dem (ins) Bett —en, to get out of (into) bed; über den Zaun —en, to climb, step, get over the fence; Baumwolle —t von Tag zu Tage, cotton is rising daily; —en lassen, to let off, to fly (*as a kite*); ein Lied —en lassen, to sing a song (*coll.*); es —t der Cantus, we now sing the song (*stud. sl.*); in den Kopf —en, to go to one's head; die Haare —en ihm zu Berge, his hair stands on end; wo —en Sie hin? where are you going? (*coll.*); mit —endem Alter, as one grows older; with increasing years; im Verhältnis —end, progressing; —ender Löwe, lion rampant. II. *subst. n.* rising; rise; advance; increase; im —en sein, to be rising, to be on the increase; das —en und Fallen, fluctuation (*of prices*). —er, *m.* (—ers, *pl.* —er) mounter; descender; master-miner; mine-inspector; fireman; rocket. —erer, *m.* (—erers, *pl.* —erer) auctioneer (*at auctions*). —ern, *v.a.* to raise, enhance, increase, heighten; to raise, advance; to strengthen; to screw up; to intensify; to run up; to work up (*passions*); to outbid; to buy at an auction; to compare, form the degrees of comparison (*Gram.*); den Mieter —ern, einen mit der *or* in seiner Miete —ern, to raise a tenant's rent. —erung, *f.* raising, enhancing; intensifying; gradation, climax (*Rhet.*); comparison (*Gram.*); auction. —ung, *see* —en II.; ascent; rising, height; incline; pitch; gradient (*Railw.*). *Comp.* —bügel, *m.* stirrup. —(bügel)riemen, *m.* stirrup-leather. —eisen, *n.* spurs; climbing-irons, crampons. —erungs=gegenstände, *pl.* articles sold at an auction. —erungs=grad, *m.*, —erungs=stufe, *f.* degree of comparison. —leiter, *f.* (*library*) steps. —rad, *n.* balance-wheel (*Horol.*). —rohr, *n.* ascension pipe. —röhre, *f.* upper tube (*of a pump*); suction-pump.

Steil, *adj.* steep; bluff, bold. —e, *f.* (*pl.* —en) steepness (*obs.*); steep place, acclivity (*obs.*). —heit, *f.* steepness. —schrift, *f.* vertical writing.

Stein, *m.* (—s, *pl.* —e) stone; rock; gem; block (*Typ., etc.*); man, piece (*Draughts, etc.*); kernel, stone; weight (*about 22 lbs.*); calculus (*Med.*); geschnittener —, intaglio (*when the design is cut out*); cameo (*when the design is raised*); geschnittene —e, gems; zu — machen, to petrify; es fällt mir ein — vom Herzen, a weight has been lifted off my mind; über Stock und — laufen, to run away over hedge and ditch, over bush and brake; einen — ansetzen, to play a domino; — der Weisen, philosopher's stone; bei einem einen — im Brett haben, to be in favour with some one; ein — des Anstoßes, a stumbling block; a rock of offence; — und Bein schwören, to swear by all that is holy, to swear most solemnly (*or* positively). —chen, *n.* (—chens, *pl.* —chen) little stone; kernel. —e(r)n, *adj.* stone; stony; der —erne Gast, the marble statue. —icht, *adj.* stonelike, stony. —ig, *adj.* abounding in stones, stony; gravelly; rocky; *see* —icht. —igen, *v.a.* to stone. —igung, *f.* stoning. *Comp.* —abdruck, *m.* lithograph(ic) print. —acker, *m.* stony field. —adler, *m.* golden eagle; imperial eagle. —alt, *adj.* very old, as old as the hills. —amsel, *f.* rock-thrush. —art, *f.* species of stone, mineral. —artig, *adj.* stonelike, stony. —bach, *m.* rocky stream. —bank, *f.* horizontal stone-bed (*Geol.*); stone-bench. —bau, *m.* stone building. —beschreibung, *f.* lithology. —beschwerde, *f.* calculous disease, the stone. —bild, *n.* statue. —bildung, *f.* lithiasis (*Med.*). —bock, *m.* bouquetin (*Capra Ibex*); capricorn (*Astr.*). —boden, *m.* stony soil; stone floor. —bohrer, *m.* stone-bore; stone-borer (*Mollusc.*) —brech, *m.* saxifrage. —brecher, *m.* quarryman. —bruch, *m* quarry. **—brücke,** *f.* stone-bridge. **—buche,** *f.* hornbeam. **—butt,** *m.*, **—butte,** *f.* turbot. **—damm,** *m.* stone pier *or* mole; paved road. **—druck,** *m.* lithography; lithograph(ic) print; **in —druck,** lithographed. **—drucker,** *m.* lithographic printer. **—druckerei,** *f.* lithographic printing-office. **—eiche,** *f.* evergreen oak; common oak. **—eppich,** *m.* stone-parsley. **—erbarmen,** *n.*; **das ist zum —erbarmen,** it is enough to melt a heart of stone. **—erzeugung,** *f.* lithiasis (*Med.*). **—esche,** *f.* ash-tree. **—flechte,** *f.* rock-lichen. **—forelle,** *f.* common trout. **—förmig,** *adj.* stone-shaped. **—frucht,** *f.* stone-fruit; fossil fruit. **—galle,** *f.* wind-gall (*Vet.*); stone-gall (*Min.*). **—geier,** *m.* stone-hawk. **—gerinne,** *n. see* **—rinne.** **—geschirr, —gefäß,** *n.* stone-vessel. **—gries,** *m.* gravel. **—grund,** *m.* stony ground; stony bottom. **—gut,** *n.* earthenware; **feines —gut,** half-china ware, faience; **gelbes —gut,** yellow ware. **—gut=fabrik,** *f.* pottery. **—händler,** *m.* lapidary, jeweller. **—hänfling,** *m.* linnet. **—haue,** *f.* stone-pick. **—hauer,** *see* **—metz.** **—haufe(n),** *m.* heap of stones. **—horst,** *m.* wood in a stony country. **—kenner,** *m.* lapidary, mineralogist. **—kern,** *m.* stone in burnt lime. **—kies,** *m.* sulphurous pyrites. **—kluft,** *f.* cleft in a rock. **—kohle,** *f.* coal, pit-coal; **entschwefelte —kohle,** coke. **—kohlen=bergwerk,** *n.* colliery. **—kohlen=gas,** *n.* coal-gas. **—kohlen=gebirge,** *n.* carboniferous group. **—kohlen=gräber,** *m.* collier. **—kohlen=schacht,** *m.* shaft of a coal-pit. **—kohlen=teer,** *m.* coal-tar, gas-tar. **—kolik,** *f.* gall-stone colic. **—krank,** *adj.* suffering from stone. **—krebs,** *m.* crawfish. **—kreide,** *f.* hard chalk. **—kresse,** *f.* wild cress. **—krug,** *m.* stone jar *or* bottle. **—kügelchen,** *n.* taw, marble. **—kümmel,** *m.* hartwort (*Bot.*). **—kunde,** *f.* lithology. **—lage,** *f.* layer of stones. **—löffel,** *m.* scoop (*Surg.*). **—malerei,** *f.* painting on stone; mosaic-work. **—marder,** *m.* stone-marten (*Zool.*). **—mark,** *n.* lithomarge, stone-marrow. **—meißel,** *m.* stone-cutter's chisel. **—mergel,** *m.* stone-marl. **—messer,** *n.* gorget (*Surg.*); stone knife. **—metz,** *m* stone-cutter, stone-mason. **—moos,** *n.* rock-lichen. **—mörtel,** *m.* cement, concrete. **—öl,** *n.* petroleum, rock-oil. **—operation,** *f.* lithotomy (*Surg.*). **—packung,** *f.* pitching (*with dry stone*). **—pappe,** *f.* fire-proof pasteboard; statuary pasteboard. **—pech,** *n.* fossil tar. **—pflanze,** *f.* lithophyte. **—pflaster,** *n.* stone pavement. **—pilz,** *m.* yellow (*eatable*) boletus. **—platte,** *f.* stone slab; flag. **—presse,** *f.* bench-press. **—pulver,** *n.* pulverized stone; powder for the stone. **—ramme,** *f.* rammer, paving-beetle. **—reich,** I. *n.* mineral kingdom. II. *adj.* stony, full of stones; enormously rich. **—rinde,** *f.* stone crust, crust of freestone. **—ring,** *m.* iron hoop. **—rinne,** *f.* stone drain. **—rose,** *f.* rock-rose. **—ruß,** *m.* dark slate-colour. **—säge,** *f.* saw for stone. **—salz,** *n.* rock-salt. **—salz=grube,** *f.* salt-mine. **—sand,** *m.* gravel. **—sarg,** *m.* sarcophagus. **—säure,** *f.* lithic acid. **—schalig,** *adj.* covered with a stony shell. **—schicht,** *f.* layer of stones; a course (*Arch.*). **—schlag,** *m.* broken stones. **—schleifer,** *m.* lapidary, stone-polisher. **—schleuder,** *m.* sling for throwing stones; mortar (*Artil.*). **—schloß,** *n.* flint-lock. **—schmerzen,** *pl.* suffering caused by the stone. **—schnecke,** *f.* triton (*Mollusc.*). **—schneiden,** *n.* stone-cutting; engraving on stone; lithotomy (*Surg.*). **—schneider,** *m.* engraver; lapidary. **—schnitt,** *m.* stone-cutting; lithotomy (*Surg.*). **—schrift,** *f.* inscription on stone; lapidary's style; uncial letters. **—schrot,** *m.* stone-chips, quarryings. **—schwalbe,** *f.* swift (*Orn.*). **—setzer,** *m.* stone-layer, paver. **—sinter,** *m.* stalactite. **—stoßen,** *n.* putting the stone (*Gym.*). **—ware,** *f.* stone-ware. **—waffen,** *pl.* stone-weapons. **—wahrsagerei',** *f.* divination by stones. **—wall,** *m.* stone rampart. **—wand,** *f.* rock; stone, *or* brick, wall. **—weg,** *m.* paved way, causeway. **—werk,** *n.* masonry, stone-work; grotto-work, rock-work. **—zange,** *f.* mason's iron tongue; grapnel. **—zeichnung,** *f.* lithograph. **—zeiger,** *m.* statuary's graver. **—zeit,** *f.* stone-age; **—zeitliche Keramik,** pottery of the stone-age. **—zeug,** *n.* stone-ware.

Steiß, *m.* (—es, *pl.* —e) rump, buttocks. *Comp.* **—bein,** *n.* coccyx (*Anat.*). **—flosse,** *f.* anal fin. **—fuß,** *m.* foot inserted near the anus; grebe (*Orn.*).

Stell—a'ge, *f.* (*pl.* **—agen**) stand. **—bar,** *adj.* movable. **—e,** *f.* (*pl.* **—en**) place; stand. position; room; situation, post, office, place; department; authority (*prov.*); passage (*in a book, etc.*); **eine harte —e,** a hard place *or* spot; **auf der —e,** on the spot, immediately; **an — dessen,** instead of that; **an meiner —e,** in my place; **wenn ich an Ihrer —e wäre,** if I were you, if I were in your place; **an Ort und —e sein,** to be on the spot; to be delivered (*of goods*); **jemandes —e vertreten,** to take the place of a p., to represent another; **nicht von der —e!** don't stir! **zur —e,** here.

Stel'l—en, *v.* I. *a.* to put, place, set, lay, arrange; to put right, set in order, regulate; to post, station; to stop (*wheels, etc.*); to spoil (*the appetite*); to trim (*sails*); to regulate (*a watch*); to put (*a question*); to point (*guns*); to set (*chairs; snares; a watch. etc.*); to furnish (*troops*); to produce (*witnesses*); to charge, fix (*a price*); **einen Antrag —en,** to move (*Parl.*), to bring an action, to petition (*Law*); **er —t sich dumm,** he pretends to know nothing about it; **eine Frage —en,** to ask a question; **ein Ziel —en,** to set an aim (before a p.); **den Champagner kalt —en,** to ice the champagne; **das Essen warm —en,** to keep the food hot; **ich —e es dir frei,** I leave it to your option *or* choice; **er ist schlecht gestellt,** he is not in a good (*lucrative*) situation; **dahin gestellt sein lassen,** to leave undecided; **einen Stellvertreter —en,** to find a substitute; **einem die Nativität —en,** to cast a p.'s nativity; **an einander —en,** to join; **ans Licht —en,** to set forth; **auf die Probe —en,** to put to the proof; **er ist ganz auf sich** (*acc.*) **selbst gestellt,** he is entirely dependent upon himself; **auf Krieg ist jedes Herz gestellt,** every one is bent on war; **ich habe meine Sache auf nichts gestellt,** I leave all to chance, I don't trouble myself about anything; **eine Uhr —en,** to regulate a clock; **eine Uhr richtig —en,** to set a watch right; **eine Behauptung richtig —en,** to correct a statement; **etwas in jemandes Belieben** *or* **Ermessen —en,** to leave s.th. to a p.'s pleasure *or* discretion; **ins Werk —en,** to execute; **welche wir Ihnen in Rechnung gestellt haben,** which we have charged to you; **einem nach dem Leben —en,** to wish to kill a p., to attempt a person's life; **zur Rede —en,** to call to account; **zur Verfügung—en,** to place at a p.'s disposal. II. *r.* to place *or* post o.s. take one's stand; to range o.s.; to appear, present o.s.; to turn out (*Mil.*), to feign, pretend, affect; **sich einem gleich —en wollen,** to wish to put o.s. on an equality with a p.; **die Sache —t sich günstiger als ich gedacht,** the matter is really not so bad as I thought; **es —t sich anders als ich gedacht,** it is different from what I thought; **ich kann mich mit ihm nicht —en,** I cannot get on with him; **der Hirsch —te sich gegen die Hunde,** the stag stood at bay; **sich**

-vor Gericht —en, to appear in court, to surrender to the court; vor ein Kriegsgericht gestellt werden, to be tried by court-martial; sich zu seinem Regimente —en, to join one's regiment; er —t sich nur so, he is only shamming; sich krank —en, to feign illness; sich ungeberdig —en, to behave unseemly (*B.*), to show anger, der Preis —t sich auf 8 Mark, the price is 8 marks; er —t sich gut dazu, he has a good way of doing it; he takes up a favourable attitude. —er, *m.* (—ers, *pl.* —er) one that sets, places, *etc.*; regulator (*Horol.*). —ung, *f.* putting, placing; arrangement, regulation; disposition; posture, attitude; guard (*Fenc.*); producing (*of witnesses, etc.*); furnishing (*of troops*); formation (*Mil.*); pointing (*of a gun*); position; station, constellation; situation, post; rank; —ung! attention; on your guard! —ung zur Disposition, placing at a p.'s disposal. *Comp.* —bottich, *m.* brewer's fermenting vat; dyer's settling vat. —dichein, *n.* meeting, rendezvous, tryst; einem ein —dichein geben, to appoint a meeting with a p. —en=jäger, *m.* place-hunter. —en=register, *n.* list of passages *or* quotations from books. —en=sammlung, *f.* collection of quotations; selections, anthology. —garn, *n.* stalker, net across a river. —hefe, *f.* dregs, lees; yeast. —holz, *n.* treadle, bridge-tree; rack. —hölzchen, *n.* bird-trap. —jagd, *f.*, —jagen, *n.* hunting with nets. —keil, *m.* coin (*Artil.*). —klappe, *f.* regulating valve. —macher, *m.* wheelwright. —pfahl, *m.* propping-hole. —rad, *n.* regulator (*Horol.*). —riegel, *m.* levelling-bolt (*Artil.*). —schraube, *f.* regulating-screw; lock screw (*Cycl.*). —ungs=nahme, *f.* the taking of an attitude, siding with. —ungs=befehl, *m.* order to present o.s. (*at a depot*). —ungs=kunst, *f.* tactics (*Mil.*). —ungs=pflichtig, *adj.* liable to military service. —ung=vermittlungsbureau, *n.* registry-office (for servants), appointments agency. —vertretend, *adj.* vicarious, representative; —vertretendes Leiden, vicarious suffering. —vertreter, *m.* deputy, representative; proxy; vicar; substitute; —vertreter Christi, the Vicar of Christ. —vertretung, *f.* representation; substitution, deputyship; mit der Wahrnehmung der Geschäfte in —vertretung beauftragt, charged with the conduct of affairs in place of *or* in the absence of . . . —wagen, *m.* stage-coach; omnibus; railway-carriage. —zeiger, *m.* pointer of the regulating plate (*Horol.*). —zirkel, *m.* compasses.

Stel'z—e, *f.* (*pl.* —en) stilt; short prop, shore (*Min.*); auf —en gehen, to walk on stilts; to be bombastic *or* stilted (*fig.*). *Comp.* —bein, *n.* spindle-leg; wooden leg. —en=gang, *m.* walk on stilts; stilted walk. —en=läufer, *m.* long-legged plover; long-legged person. —en=schritt, *m.* giant stride. —fuß, *m.* wooden leg. —vögel, *pl.* stilt-walkers, grallatores.

Stem'm—en, *v.a.* to cut away (*branches*); to fell; to stand firm against; to stem (*water, etc.*); to prop, support, lean firmly against; to work with the axe *or* chisel; die Arme in die Seite —en, to put one's hands on one's hips *or* (*coll.*) to set one's arms akimbo; die Füße gegen die Wand —en, to plant one's feet against the wall; sich —en, to oppose, resist. *Comp.* —axt, *f.* woodman's axe. —beitel, *m.*, —eisen, *n.* two-bevelled chisel; dreieckiges —eisen, burr. —leder, *n.* welt (*of a boot*), toe-piece. —maschine, *f.* mortise-machine. —meißel, *m.* double-bevelled chisel. —nadel, *f.* flat needle, awl. —ring, *m.* shoemaker's thimble. —thor, *n.* sluice-gate.

Stem'pel, *m.* (—s, *pl* —) stamp; die; marker; mark, stamp; trade-mark, brand; post-mark; impress; prop, shore; stemple (*Min.*); pestle, pounder; puncheon; piston (*Mach.*); pistil (*Bot.*); bookbinder's stamp. *Comp.* —abgabe, *f.* stamp-duty. —amt, *n.* stamp-office. —bogen, *m.* stamped sheet of paper. —eisen, *n.* stamp; punch. —farbe, *f.* ink for stamping. —förmig, *adj.* pistil-like (*Bot.*). —gebühr, *f.*, —geld, *n.* stamp-duty, stamping fee. —halter, *m.* letter-stamp. —hammer, *m.* stamping-hammer. —los, *adj.* without pistils, male (*Bot.*). —marke, *f.* duty-stamp; bill-stamp. —papier, *n.* stamped paper. —pochwerk, *n.* stamping-machine. —schneidekunst, *f.* art of stamp-cutting, *or* of die-sinking. —schneider, *m.* stamp-cutter, die-sinker. —zeichen, *n.* stamp, mark.

Stem'pel—n, I. *v.a.* to stamp; to mark; to seal; to set one's seal *or* mark to; to drive out (*a bolt*); to prop; einen —n, to instruct beforehand, prime. II. *subst. n.*, —ung, *f.* stamping; coining.

Stem'pler, *m.* (—s, *pl.* —) stamper.

Sten'del— (*in comp.*) —gewächse, *pl.* orchids.

Sten'ge, *f.* (*pl.* —n) topmast; die große —, main top-mast; Kreuz—, mizzen top-mast. —l, *m.* (—ls, *pl.* —l) stalk, stem; pedicel; stick; pole (*for hops, etc.*). —lig, *adj.* stalked. —ln, *v.* I. *a.* to stake (*peas, etc.*). II. *n.* (*aux.* h.) to run to stalk; to shoot up into stalk. *Comp.* —l=abschnitt, *m.* section of a branch. —l=artig, —l=förmig, *adj.* stem-formed, cauliform. —l=bohne, *f.* climbing-bean. —l=glas, *n.* wine glass (*with stem*). —l=los, *adj.* stemless.

Stenogra'—mm, *n.* (—mms, *pl.* —m'me) shorthand note, shorthand report. —ph, *m.* (—phen, *pl.* —phen) stenographer, shorthand writer. —phie', *f.* stenography, shorthand. —phie'ren, *v.a.* to write shorthand. —phisch, *adj.* stenographic(al), in shorthand.

Sten'torstimme, *f.* (stento'rische Stimme) stentorian voice, very loud voice.

Step'pe, *f.* (*pl.* —n) steppe. *Comp.* —n=bewohner, *m.* dweller in the steppes. —n=fuchs, *m.* (*Canis*) corsac; (*Canis*) caragan (*Zool.*). —n=wolf, *m.* prairie wolf.

Step'p—en, *v.a.* to quilt; to stitch with a machine. —er, *m.* (—ers, *pl.* —er) quilter. —erei', *f.* quilting. *Comp.* —bett, *n.* mattress. —decke, *f.* quilt, quilted cover, coverlet. —draht, *m.* shoemaker's *or* saddler's thread. —nadel, *f.* quilting needle. —naht, *f.* raised seam; stitched seam. —rock, *m.* quilted petticoat. —stich, *m.* stitch. —zwirn, *m.* quilting thread, flat thread.

Ster'b—en, I. *ir.v.n.* (*aux.* s.) to die; to die away; to perish; to become extinct; eines natürlichen Todes —en, to die a natural death; Hungers —en, to die of hunger; to be starving, to die of starvation; an der Pest —en, to die of the plague; sie starb an *or* bei ihrem ersten Kinde, she died in her first childbed; darauf will ich leben und —en! I will live and die in this faith! aus Gram —en, to die of grief; durch ihn ist sie gestorben, he was the cause of her death; über seinen Plänen —en, to die whilst maturing one's plans, *or* before one's plans are carried out; vor Langerweile —en, to be bored to death, to die of ennui. II. *subst. n.* dying; death; im —en liegen, to be dying, *or* on the point of death; auf Leben und —en, come life, come death. —lich, *adj. & adv.* mortal; —lich verliebt, desperately in love over head and ears in love. —lichkeit, *f.* mortality; Gott hat ihn aus dieser —lichkeit abgefordert, God has called him away from this earthly life. —ling. *m.* (—lings, *pl.*

—linge) frail mortal, one destined to early death (*rare*); sheep that dies of disease. *Comp.* **—e=bett,** *n.* death-bed. **—e=buch,** *n.* register of deaths. **—e=fall,** *m.* death; casualty. **—e=gebet,** *n.* prayer of *or* for a dying person. **—e=geld,** *n.* money paid in case of death; funeral expenses. **—e=gesang,** *m.* funeral dirge *or* hymn. **—e=gewand,** *n.* winding sheet, shroud. *pl.* grave-clothes. **—e=glocke,** *f.* funeral bell, passing bell. **—e=haus,** *n.* house in which a p. has died; house of mourning. **—e=hemd,** *n.* shirt in which a p. dies. **—e=jahr,** *n.* year of a person's death. **—e=kasse,** *f.* burial-club *or* fund. **—e=kleid,** *n.* shroud. **—e=lied,** *n.* *see* **—egesang.** **—e=liste,** *f. see* **—ebuch**; bill of mortality. **—ens=angst,** *f.* mortal anguish. **—ens=bange,** *adj.* in mortal terror. **—ens=krank,** *adj.* dangerously ill; sick unto death (*B.*). **—ens=langweilig,** *adj.* terribly dull. **—ens=seele,** *f.*; **keine —ensseele,** not a living soul. **—ens=wort,** *n.*; **kein —enswort,** not a single word. **—e=sakramente,** *pl.* last sacraments (*received before death*). **—e=stunde,** *f.* hour of a p.'s death, dying hour. **—e=zimmer,** *n.* room in which a p. dies, death-chamber.

Stereo—metrie', *f.* solid geometry, stereometry. **—me'trisch,** *adj.* relating to solids *or* solid geometry, stereometrical. **—sko'p,** *n.* (**—skops,** *pl.* **—skope**) stereoscope. **—sko'pisch,** *adj.* stereoscopic. **—ty'p,** *adj.* stereotyped; **—type Redensart,** stereotyped *or* stock phrase. **—typ'=ausgabe,** *f.* stereotype edition. **—typie',** *f.* stereotype printing. **—typie'ren,** *v.a.* to stereotype. **—ty'pik,** *f.* stereotypography.

Steri'l, *adj.* barren, unfruitful. **—isie'ren,** *v.a.* to sterilize. **—isie'rung,** *f.* sterilization. **—itä't,** *f.* sterility, barrenness.

Ster'ke, *f.* (*pl.* **—n**) heifer.

Ster'let, *m.* (**—s,** *pl.* **—e**) sterlet, small sturgeon.

Stern, *m.* (**—es,** *pl.* **—e**) star; white spot; **er hat weder Glück noch —,** he has no luck, the fates are against him; **der Hoffnung letzte —e,** the last rays of hope; **ein — erster Größe,** a star of the first magnitude. **—chen,** *n.* (**—chens,** *pl.* **—chen**) little star; asterisk. *Comp.* **—achat,** *m.* starred agate. **—ader,** *f.* caudal vein (of horses). **—anbetung,** *f.* star-worship. **—artig,** *adj.* star-like. **—beschreiber,** *m.* astrographer. **—bild,** *n.* constellation. **—blume,** *f.* star-shaped *or* stellate flower, China aster. *pl.* Asteraceæ. **—deuterei, —deuterkunst,** *f.* astrology. **—dienst,** *m.* worship of stars. **—en=banner,** *n.* star-spangled banner, stars and stripes. **—en=bühne,** *f.* starry vault of heaven. **—en=förmig,** *adj.* stellar. **—en=gucker,** *m.* star-gazer, astronomer (*hum.*). **—en=heer,** *n.* starry host. **—(en)=stunde,** *f.* sidereal hour; propitious hour. **—en=welt,** *f.* celestial sphere. **—gürtel,** *m.* Milky Way. **—hagelvoll,** *adj.* dead drunk (*vulg.*). **—haufe(n),** *m.* cluster of stars, constellation. **—hell,** *adj.* starry, star-bright. **—helle,** *f.* starriness. **—himmel,** *m.* starry sky *or* firmament. **—jahr,** *n.* sidereal year. **—kammer,** *f.* Star-chamber. **—karte,** *f.* celestial *or* astronomical chart. **—kegel,** *m.* astroscope. **—kenner,** *m.* astronomer. **—klar,** *adj.* starry, star-bright; **es ist —klar,** the stars are out *or* shining. **—klarheit,** *f.* starriness. **—kunde, —lehre,** *f.* astronomy. **—nudeln,** *pl.* star-macaroni. **—pflanze,** *f.* starwort. **—schanze,** *f.* star-fort *or* redoubt (*Fort.*). **—schnuppe,** *f.*, **—schuß,** *m.* shooting star. **—schnuppen=fall,** *m.* shower of meteors. **—seher,** *m.* observer of the stars, astronomer. **—stein,** *m.* asterite, star-shaped fossil. **—sucher,** *m.* astronomical telescope. **—tafel,** *f.* astronomical table. **—uhr,** *f.* sidereal dial. **—wahrsagerei',** *f.* astrology. **—warte,** *f.* observatory. **—wissenschaft,** *f.* astronomical science, astronomy. **—zeichen,** *n.* asterisk. **—zeit,** *f.* sidereal time.

Sterz, *m.* (**—es,** *pl.* **—e**) tail; rump; plough-handle *or* tail; windmill-handle; *see* **Steiß.**

Stet, *see* **Stät.** **—s,** *adv.* steadily, constantly continually; always; **—s Ihr, H. J.,** ever yours, H. J.

[1]**Steu'er,** *n.* (**—s,** *pl.* **—**) rudder, helm; **das — führen,** to be at the helm; **das — an Backbord!** port the helm!

[2]**Steu'er,** *f.* (*pl.* **—n**) tax; rate; duty; impost, assessment; aid (*obs.*); **Grund—,** land-tax ground-rent; **staatliche direkte —,** (income) tax; **die indirekten —n,** duties; **städtische —n,** local rates; **die gesamten —n,** rates and taxes **zur — der Wahrheit,** for the sake of truth. **—bar,** *adj.* assessable, liable to duty, liable to income tax *or* taxation, ratable; tributary. **—barkeit,** *f.* liability to be taxed. **—n,** *v.a.* & *n.* (*aux.* **h.**) to pay taxes; to contribute to. *Comp.* **—amt,** *n.* customs-office; inland-revenue office; board of inland revenue. **—anlage, —auflage,** *f.* imposition of a tax. **—anschlag,** *m.* assessment. **—beamte(r),** *m.* revenue-officer; tax-collector. **—bediente(r),** *m.* exciseman. **—befehl,** *m.* edict relating to a tax; money-bill (*Parl.*). **—befreiung,** *f* exemption from taxes. **—behörde,** *f.* board of assessment, inland revenue. **—bewilligung,** *f.* grant of supplies (*Parl.*). **—bezirk,** *m.* tax-collector's district. **—buch,** *n.* rate-book. **—einnehmer,** *m.* tax-collector. **—einschätzung,** *f.* assessment. **—erhebung,** *f.* collecting *or* levying of taxes. **—ermäßigung,** *f.* abatement of income tax. **—frei,** *adj.* exempt from taxation; free of duty. **—geld,** *n.* yield of an impost. **—kasse,** *f.* tax-collector's office. **—klasse,** *f.* class of tax-payers. **—kollegium,** *n.* board of revenue. **—kraft,** *f.* capacity for paying taxes. **—modus,** *m.* mode of taxation. **—pflichtig,** *see* **—bar**; liable to duty, subject to taxation; **der —pflichtige,** the rate-payer. **—satz,** *m.* rate. **—schein,** *m* tax-collector's receipt. **—verwaltung,** *f.* administration of the revenue. **—wesen,** *n.* taxation, taxes. **—zahler,** *m.* tax *or* rate-payer. **—zettel,** *m.* bill of taxes; *see* **—schein.** **—zuschlag,** *m.* increase of taxation; addition to a rate *or* tax.

Steu'er—n, *v.* I. *a.* to steer; to pilot, navigate. II. *n.* (*aux.* **h.** & **s.**) to steer; to stand for (*Naut.*); **einer Sache** (*dat.*) **—n,** to put restraint upon, to put a stop to, to check *or* stop s.th.; to help, aid something; **hart —n,** not to answer the helm readily; **nach London —n,** to direct a ship's course to London. **—ung,** *f.* steering; checking; regulating; distributing-regulator (*Mach.*); valve-gear; starting-gear; (*Stephenson's*) link-motion. *Comp.* **—bord,** *n.* starboard (*Naut.*). **—brücke,** *f.* helmsman's post *or* seat. **—ende,** *n.* stern, poop. **—mann,** *m.* helmsman; pilot. **—manns=maat,** *m.* second mate (*Naut.*). **—nagel,** *m.* linch-pin. **—rad,** *n.* (*steering*-)wheel. **—reep,** *n.* tiller-rope. **—rohr,** *n.* steering tube (*cycl.*). **—ruder,** *n.* rudder. **—ungs=hebel,** *m.* starting *or* distributing-lever (*Mach.*).

Ste'ven, *m.* (**—s,** *pl.* **—**); **Vor—,** stem (*Naut.*).

Stibit'zen, *v.ir.* to pilfer, to purloin (*coll.*).

[1]**Stich,** *m.* (**—es,** *pl.* **—e,** *as measure,* **—**) pricking; prick, puncture; sting; bite (*of an insect*); stab; thrust; sharp pain; stitch; engraving, print; trick (*at cards*); slight intoxication; barter; cut, taunt; knot (*Naut.*); **das ist mir ein — durch die Seele,** that cuts me to the heart; **— halten,** to hold firm, stand the test, to hold good (*as arguments*); **das hält nicht —,** that does not hold good; that won't hold water; **im —e lassen,** to leave in the lurch;

einen — haben, to have a screw loose; (*of beer*) to be turning sour; auf den — handeln, to barter; ein — Erde, a spadeful of earth; einen — ins Blaue, a tinge of blue; Doppel-Stepp-—, lock-stitch; Hinter—, back-stitch, stitching stitch; Kreuz—, cross-stitch, herring-bone-stitch; Vorder—, running-stitch; soll ich die Kappnaht mit Hinter—en nähen oder säumen? shall I back-stitch or fell the seam? —el, *m.* (—els, *pl.* —el) style; graving-tool (*Engr.*); burin; stamp (*Horol., etc.*); spade. —elei', *f.* sewing (*coll. and contemp.*); sarcasm, taunt, gibe; sarcastic language. —eln, *v.a. & n.* (*aux.* h.) to stitch, sew; to prick; to taunt, jeer, jibe, be sarcastic towards; auf einen — eln, to taunt, jeer at a p. —ler, *m.* (—lers, *pl.* —ler) giber, taunter. *Comp.* —blatt, *n.* guard (*of a sword*), hilt; protection; butt, laughing-stock; winning card, trump. —bohrer, *m.* wimble. —brett, *n.* tie-beam. —eisen, *n.* stoker's rod. —el=naht, *f.* stitched seam; run and back-stitch. —el=name, *m.* nickname. —el=rede, *f.* bitter speech, sarcasm, jibe. —entscheid, *m.* casting vote. —flamme, *f.* darting flame. —hahn, *m.* spigot. —haltig, *adj.* that will stand the test, sound; —haltige Gründe, sound arguments, solid reasons. —loch, *n.* needle-hole (*Sew.-mach.*), tapping-hole (*Metall.*). —ofen, *m.* blast-furnace. —platte, *f.* needle-plate (*Sew.-mach.*). —probe, *f.*; —proben machen, to try *or* test at random. —säge, *f.* key-hole saw, fret saw. —steller, *m.* stitch regulator (*Sew.-mach.*). —tag, *m.* day of grace. —waffe, *f.* pointed weapon, foil. —wahl, *f.* second *or* final ballot. —weise, *adv.* by stitches; in twinges. —wort, *n.* catch-word, key-word; cue (*Theat.*); party-cry. —wunde, *f.* stab, thrust, punctured wound.

[2]**Stich**, *imperat. sing.*; Stichst, Sticht, *2 & 3 pers. sing. pres. ind. of* stechen.

Stich'ling, *m.* (—s, *pl.* —e) stickleback (*Icht.*).

Sti'ck—en, *v.* I. *a. & n.* (*aux.* s.) to suffocate, choke. II. *a.* to embroider. —er, *m.*, —erin, *f.* embroiderer. —erei', *f.* embroidery. —ig, *adj.* stifling. *Comp.* —arbeit, *see* —erei. —fluß, *m.* choking catarrh. —garn, *n.* embroidery cotton. —gaze, *f.* canvas (*for rug-work*). —häkchen, *n.* crochet needle. —husten, *m.* hooping cough. —luft, *f.* close *or* stuffy air. —nadel, *f.* embroidery, rug-, *or* crewel-needle. —oxyd=gas, *n.* nitric oxide. —oxydul=gas, *n.* nitrous oxide, laughing-gas. —rahmen, *m.* embroidery-frame. —seide, *f.* embroidery-silk, crewel-silk. —silber, *n.* silver thread. —stoff, *n.* nitrogen. —stoff=haltig, *adj.* nitrogenous, azotized. —zeug, *n.* embroidery materials.

Stickst, Stickt, *2 & 3 pers. sing. pres. ind. of* sticken, *and of* stecken (*intrans. obs.*).

Stie'ben, *ir.v.* I. *a.* to start, set suddenly in motion; auseinander —, to disperse. II. *n.* (*aux.* h. & s.) to rise *or* fly about like dust; to rise up, disperse; es stiebt, it is dusty, it drizzles; Funken stoben, sparks flew about.

Stief, *prefix* (*in comp. gen'lly* =) step-. —bruder, *m.* step-brother. —geschwister, *pl.* step-brothers and sisters. —gesinnt, *adj.* malevolent, unkind (*poet.*). —kind, *n.* step-child. —mutter, *f.* step-mother. —mütterchen, *n.* pansy. —mütterlich, *adj. & adv.* like a step-mother; partially, unkindly —schwester, *f.* half-sister, step-sister. —sohn, *m.* step-son. —tochter, *f.* step-daughter.

Stie'fel, *m.* (—s, *pl.* —) boot; tube, shank (*of a pipe*); barrel (*of a pump*); manner, way; in —n und Sporen, booted and spurred; seinen guten — arbeiten, trinken, to work away, to drink hard (*sl.*); seinen guten — gehen, to step out at a fine rate (*coll.*); hoher —, Wellington boot. —chen, *n.* (—chens, *pl.* —chen) lady's boot; small boot. —et'te, *f.* (*pl.* —etten) gaiter; laced boot *Comp.* —absatz, *m.* boot-heel. —anzieher, *m.* boot-hook; shoe-horn. —appell, *m.* boot-inspection (*Mil.*). —band, *n.* boot-lace; boot-strap. —brett, —holz, *n.* boot-tree. —bürste, *f.* blacking-brush. —fabrikant, *m.* shoemaker. —fuchs, *m.* boots (*at an inn*); gyp (*Cambridge*), scout (*Oxford*). —geschäft, *n.* shoe-maker's business; boot-shop. —knecht, *m.* boot-jack —kolben, *m.* lower pump-box. —leisten, *m.* boot-last. —mündung, *f.* bore of the working-barrel (*Hydr.*). —putzer, *m.* boots (*at hotels*); shoeblack (*in the streets*). —quaste, *f.* tassel of a Hessian boot. —schaft, *m.* leg of a boot. —strippe, *f.* boot-strap. —stulpe, *f.* boot-top. —wichse, *f.* blacking.

Stie'feln, *v.* I. *a.* to provide with boots; gestiefelt, booted; gestiefelt und gespornt, road-ready; der gestiefelte Kater, Puss in boots. II. *n.* (*aux.* s.) to walk with great strides, to stalk along; wo — Sie hin? where are you going to? (*coll.*).

[1]**Stieg**, *m.* (—es, *pl.* —e) steep path *or* road; ascent, mounting, climb.

[2]**Stieg, Stie'ge**, *1 & 3 pers. sing. imperf. ind. & subj. of* steigen.

[1]**Stie'ge**, *f.* (*pl.* —n) staircase, (flight of) stairs.

[2]**Stie'ge**, *f.* (*pl.* —n) score (*of eggs*).

Stieg'litz, *m.* (—es, *pl.* —e) goldfinch, thistle finch.

Stiehl, *imperat. sing.*; **Stiehlst, Stiehlt**, *2 & 3 pers. sing. pres. ind. of* stehlen.

Stiel, *m.* (—s, *pl.* —e) haft, handle; stick (*of a broom*); peduncle, stalk, petiole; shank (*of a nail*); upright (*Carp.*); mit Stumpf und — ausrotten, to root out, extirpate, to destroy root and branch, to utterly exterminate. —en, *v.a.* to furnish with a handle. —ig, *suff.* (*in comp.* =) -stalked, -handled, -pedunculate. *Comp.* —äugig, *adj.* having peduncular eyes (*as the lobster*). —blatt, *n.* petiolate leaf. —durchschlag, *m.* punch *or* stamp with a handle. —loch, *n.* eye (*of a hatchet, etc.*). —los, *adj.* without a handle; sessile, stalkless. —rippe, *f.* main rib (*of a leaf*). —rund, *adj.* cylindrical, terete. —ständig, *adj.* growing on the stem, pedunculate.

Stie'per, *m.* (—s, *pl.* —) short prop; stanchion.

[1]**Stier**, *adj.* fixed, staring; —er Blick, vacant look. —en, *v.n.* (*aux.* h.) to stare, to look with a fixed *or* vacant gaze.

[2]**Stier**, *m.* (—s, *pl.* —e) bull, steer; Taurus (*Astr.*); verschnittener —, bullock; der — brüllt, the bull bellows; den — bei den Hörnern packen, to take the bull by the horns; der — von Uri, the bugler of Uri. *Comp.* —äugig, *adj.* bull-eyed. —fechter, *m.* bull-fighter; (berittener) toreador. —gefecht, *n.* bull-fight. —gespann, *n.* team, span of oxen. —hetze, *f.* bull-baiting. —hirsch, *m.* bubalus gnu. —haut, *f.* bull's hide; *pl.* —häute, bulls. —jagd, *f.* bull-hunt. —töter, *m.* matador (*at bull-fights*).

Stieß, Stie'ße, *1 & 3 pers. sing. imperf. ind. & subj. of* stoßen.

[1]**Stift**, *m.* (—es, *pl.* —e) brad, pin, peg, rivet, stub-nail; pivot; tack; stump (*of a tooth*); tooth (*of a comb*); crayon; little man; apprentice; bunte —, chalks; kleiner —, little chap (*coll.*). *Comp.* —farbe, *f.* pastel. —gemälde, *n.* crayon drawing. —halter, *m.* crayon-holder, pencil-holder. —kreide, *f.* white chalk. —macher, *m.* maker of tags, brads, pegs, *etc.*; pencil manufacturer. —uhr, *f.* watch with hook-escapement. —zahn, *m.* crown (*of a tooth*).

[2]**Stift**, *n.* (—es, *pl.* —e *and* —er) foundation; religious establishment, convent, monastery; chapter(-house); bishopric; seminary, train-

ing college (*for clergymen*); **Tübinger —,** theological seminary of Tübingen.

Stif't—en, *v.a.* to found, establish, institute; to originate, be the author of; to cause, make, excite; **eine Ehe —en,** to make a match; **Freundschaft zwischen zwei Personen —en,** to make two people friends; **Gutes —en,** to do good; **da haben Sie etwas Schönes angestiftet!** that 's a fine piece of work you have done! you have put your foot into it there! (*coll.*). **—er,** *m.* (**—ers,** *pl.* **—er**), **—erin,** *f.* founder; author, originator. **—isch,** *adj.* of *or* belonging to a foundation *or* chapter. **—ler,** *m.* member of a theological seminary. **—ung,** *f.* founding; establishment; foundation, institution; pious bequest; originating, causing, making; **fromme —ung,** religious foundation *or* establishment; **milde —ung,** charitable institution. *Comp.* **—s=amt,** *n.* chapter-court; canonicate. **—s=amtmann,** *m.* vidame. **—s=bauer,** *m.* tenant of a chapter. **—s=brief,** *m.* deed of foundation. **—s=dame, —s=frau,** *f.*, **—s=fräulein,** *n.* canoness. **—s=gebäude,** *n.* chapter-house. **—s=gemeinde,** *f.* congregation of a cathedral. **—s=gut,** *n.* chapter-property; ecclesiastical endowment. **—s=hauptmann,** *m.* vidame. **—s=haus,** *n.* chapter-house; institution. **—s=herr,** *m.* canon, prebendary. **—s=herrnstelle,** *f.* canonicate. **—s=hütte,** *f.* (Jewish) tabernacle. **—s=kanzler,** *m.* chancellor of a chapter. **—s=kirche,** *f.* collegiate church; cathedral. **—s=küster,** *m.* verger. **—s=mäßig,** *adj.* qualified for a canonship. **—s=mitglied,** *n.* member of a chapter *or* of a foundation. **—s=pfarre,** *f.* living, *etc.*, in gift of a chapter. **—s=pfründe,** *f.* prebend. **—s=propst,** *m.* provost of a collegiate church. **—s=schule,** *f.* foundation school; cathedral school. **—s=tag,** *m.* day of a chapter-meeting. **—s=versammlung,** *f.* meeting of a chapter. **—ungs=feier,** *f.*, **—ungs=fest,** *n.* foundation-festival, commemoration (day *or* festival). **—ungs=tag,** *m.* founder's day.

Stigmatisie'ren, *v.a.* to stigmatize.

Stil, *m.* (**—s,** *pl.* **—e**) style (*also Chron.*); **nach dem eingeführten —,** according to the established usage, customary. **—isie'ren,** *v.a.* to write; to look at, correct in the matter of style; **er —isiert gut,** he writes well. **—i'st,** (**—is'ten,** *pl.* **—is'ten**) writer; **ein guter —ist,** writer of a good style. **—is'tik,** *f.* art of composition. **—is'tisch,** *adj.*; **in —istischer Hinsicht,** in the matter of style.

Stile'tt, *n.* (**—(e)s,** *pl.* **—e**) stiletto.

Still, —e, *adj.* & *adv.* still, silent; quiet; hushed; calm; peaceable; secret; motionless; inanimate; stagnant; dead, dull (*C.L.*); **der —e Freitag,** Good Friday; **die —e Woche,** Passion week; **—es Gebet,** silent prayer; **—es Meer,** calm sea; Pacific (Ocean); **—er Associe, —er Teilhaber,** sleeping partner; **—e Hochzeit,** quiet *or* private wedding; **—e Liebe,** unavowed love; **bei —er Nacht,** at dead of night; **—e Mieter,** quiet lodgers; **—e Messe,** low mass; **—er Vorbehalt,** mental reservation; **—er Mensch,** quiet, inoffensive, silent *or* staid man; **—es Beileid,** unspoken sympathy; **wir bitten um —es Beileid,** no visits of condolence (desired) (*in announcement of a death*); **ein —es Glas leeren,** to drink in silence to the memory of one dead (*or* absent); **dem —en Trunk ergeben,** addicted to secret drinking; **—e Wasser sind tief,** still waters run deep (*prov.*); **—e Wohnung,** quiet lodgings, retired dwelling; **—! seid —!** hush! be quiet! (*to dogs*) lie down! **— davon!** no more of that! don't mention it! **—'mal!** be quiet, will you! **— gestanden!** (stand at) attention! (*Mil.*); **einen — bekommen,** to succeed in silencing a p.; **einen — machen,** to kill a p.; **— bleiben,** to be still *or* silent; **— halten (mit dem Wagen),** to draw up; **er kann den Mund nicht — halten,** he can't hold his tongue; **einem — halten,** to let s. o. do as he likes; **— liegen,** to lie quiet; to lie down; to lie to (*as a ship*); to stop; **die Geschäfte liegen** *or* **stehen —,** trade is dull, business is at a stand-still; **— stehen,** to stop, to be at a stand-still; **da steht mir der Verstand —,** that is beyond me; **zu etwas — schweigen,** to say nothing about, to take no notice of a th.; **sich — verhalten,** not to move, to keep quiet; **das —e,** quiet; **im —en,** quietly, in silence, secretly; **die —en im Lande,** the pious of the land. **—e,** *f.* calm, stillness, silence; tranquillity, repose; peace; pause; **in der —e, in aller —e,** *see* **im —en; in der —e abziehen,** to steal away; **tiefe —e,** profound silence; **in der —e leben,** to lead a retired life. *Comp.* **—beglückt,** *adj.* secretly happy. **—flöte,** *f.* soft flute-stop (*Org.*). **—halten,** *n.* stop, pause, halt. **—leben,** *n.* quiet life; still life (*Paint.*). **—schweigen,** *n.* silence. **—schweigend,** *adj.* & *adv.* silent; tacit, implied. **—stand,** *m.* stand-still, stop; cessation; stagnation (*of trade, etc.*); inactivity; station (*Astr.*); **—stand ist Rückgang,** he who does not advance goes backwards; **einen —stand machen,** to stop, to stand still; **Waffen —stand,** armistice. **—stehen,** *n.* stop. **—stehend,** *adj.* stationary; motionless, inactive; stagnant.

Stil'l—en, *v.a.* to quiet, appease, hush; to soothe, allay (*pain, etc.*); to stay, quench (*thirst, etc.*); to nurse, suckle; to silence; to staunch (*blood*); to gratify (*desires*). **—end,** *p.* & *adj.* soothing, sedative, lenitive. **—er,** *m.* (**—ers,** *pl.* **—er**) calmer, soother. **—ung,** *f.* stilling; appeasing; staunching; nursing. *Comp.* **—amme,** *f.* wetnurse.

Stimm'bar, *adj.* tunable, that may be tuned.

Stim'm—e, *f.* (*pl.* **—en**) voice; vote, voice, suffrage; stop (*of an organ*); opinion; part (*Mus.*); sound-post (*of a violin*); **nicht bei —e sein,** not to be in voice; **erste —e,** soprano; **zweite —e,** alto; **die —en austeilen,** to distribute the parts (*Mus.*); **entscheidende —e,** casting vote; **Sitz und —e haben,** to have a seat and vote; **seine —e abgeben,** to give one's vote *or* opinion, to vote; **einem seine —e geben,** to give one's vote to *or* in favour of a person; **ich will jetzt die —en sammeln,** I will now put the matter to the vote; **in dieser Sache habe ich keine —e,** I have no say *or* nothing to say in this matter; **mit einer —e,** with common consent, unanimously; **ohne eine —e dagegen,** without a dissentient voice, carried unanimously *or* nem. con. *Comp.* **—abgabe,** *f.* voting, vote. **—apparat,** *m.* vocal organ(s). **—band,** *n.* vocal cord, vocal ligament, ligament of the glottis (**falsches,** upper; **wahres,** inferior). **—berechtigt,** *adj.* entitled to a vote, enfranchised. **—berechtigung,** *f.* right of voting, franchise. **—bildung,** *f.* formation of the voice. **—en=einheit, —en=einhelligkeit,** *f.* unanimity; **mit —eneinheit,** unanimously, with no dissentient vote, nem. con. **—en=gleichheit,** *f.* equality of votes (for and against); **bei —engleichheit den Ausschlag geben,** to give the casting vote. **—en=mehrheit,** *f.* majority. **—en=minderheit,** *f.* minority. **—en=prüfung,** *f.* scrutiny, recounting of votes. **—en=sammler,** *m.* scrutineer, counter of votes. **—en=teilung,** *f.* splitting of votes; division. **—en=werber,** *m.* canvasser, solicitor of votes. **—en=werbung,** *f.* canvassing. **—en=zähler,** *m.* teller (*Parl.*). **—en=zählung,** *f.* counting of votes, scrutiny of the ballot-box. **—fähig,** *adj.* having a vote. **—führer,** *m.* leader (*of a choir*); spokesman;

leader. —gabel, *f.* tuning-fork. —geber, *m.* elector, voter. —haft, *adj.* voiced, sonant (*Phon.*). —hammer, *m.* tuning-hammer *or* -key. —holz, —hölzchen, *n.* sound-post (*of a violin*). —lage, *f.* regimen (*Mus.*). —los, *adj.* voiceless, surd (*Phon.*). —nerv, *m.* vocal nerve. —organ, *n.* vocal organ. —pfeife, *f.* tuning-pipe, pitch-pipe. —recht, *n.* right of voting, franchise; allgemeines — recht, universal suffrage. —ritze, *f.* glottis. —ritzen=deckel, *m.* epiglottis. —ritzen=verschlußlaut, *m.* glottal stop, glottal catch. —schlüssel, *m.* tuning-key. —wechsel, *m.* breaking of the voice (*in boys*).

Stim'm—en, *v.* I. *a.* to tune; to dispose, incline; to determine, induce; einen fröhlich —en, to put s. o. in good *or* in a gay humour; die Nachricht hat mich traurig gestimmt, the news has made me (feel) sad; —en gegen, to prejudice against; günstig für einen —en, to prejudice in favour of; seine Forderungen hoch —en, to make great demands; er ist heute schlecht gestimmt, he is in bad spirits *or* in a bad mood to-day. II. *n.* (*aux.* h.) to agree; to accord, agree in pitch and tone; to be in keeping with, to harmonize; to vote; der —ende, the voter; zu etwas —en, to accord with; (das) —t, (that is) all right. —er, *m.* (—ers, *pl.* —er) tuner. —ung, *f.* tuning; tune, pitch; —ung des Gemüts, mood, humour, state *or* frame of mind, temper; bei —ung, in tune; in good humour, in good spirits. *Comp.* —ungs=bild, *n.* landscape intended to produce a certain state of mind in the spectator. —ungs=voll, *adj.* & *adv.* in high spirits, buoyant(ly), elated, full of genuine feeling.

Stimulie'ren, *v.a.* to stimulate.

Stin'k—en, *ir.v.n.* (*aux.* h.) to stink, exhale a disagreeable odour; Eigenlob —t, self-praise is no recommendation; der Junge —t vor Faulheit, that boy is frightfully lazy. —end, *p.* & *adj.*, —ig, *adj.* stinking; fetid, rancid; —ende Lüge, odious lie. *Comp.* —loch, *n.* stinking hole. —ratz, *m.* pole-cat. —tier, *n.* skunk. —topf, *m.* stink-pot (*Artil.*, *Naut.*).

Stint, *m.* (—es, *pl.* —e) smelt (*Icht.*).

Stipendi—a't, *m.* (—aten, *pl.* —aten) exhibitioner, foundationer, (*Queen's*, *etc.*) scholar; ein —at werden von . . ., to be put on the foundation of . . ., to be made (*or* elected) a scholar (exhibitioner) of . . ., to be elected to a scholarship at . . ., to be awarded a scholarship at . . . —um, *n.* (—ums, *pl.* —en) scholarship, exhibition, allowance.

Stip'p—en, *v.a.* & *n.* (*aux.* h.) to steep, dip (*dial.*); to dot. *Comp.* —milch, *f.* sweet curdled milk (*dial.*). —visite, *f.* flying visit, short call (*dial.*).

Stipulie'ren, *v.a.* to stipulate.

Stirb, *imperat. sing.*; **Stirbst**, **Stirbt**, *2 & 3 pers. sing. pres. ind. of* sterben.

Stirn, —e, *f.* (*pl.* —en) forehead; brow; countenance, face; impudence, face; brow (*of a mountain*); crown, vertex (*of an arch*); tail (*of a counterfort*); eine eiserne —, an iron countenance; die — hoch tragen, to carry a high head; die — bieten, to show a bold front; dem Feinde die — bieten, to face, resist the enemy; das geht ihm wider die —, that goes against his grain. *Comp.* —arterie, *f.* frontal artery. —band, *n.* fillet, frontlet, bandeau. —blatt, *n.* frontal, plate of metal worn on the forehead. —bogen, *m.* frontal arch. —fläche, *f.* (*front-*)face of an arch. —haar, *n.* front hair *or* locks. —krankheit, *f.* mad staggers (*Vet.*). —löckchen, *pl.* front curls. —locke, *f.* forelock, curl on the forehead. —los, *adj.* barefaced, shameless. —rad, *n.* spur wheel, straight wheel. —riegel, *m.* breast-transom (*Artil.*). —riemen, *m.* forehead-band, head-piece (*of a bridle*). —runzeln, *n.* frown. —runzler, *m.* corrugator(*-muscle*); frowning person. —seite, *f.* façade, front (*Arch.*). —stück, *n.* frontlet; principal side (*Arch.*). —tuch, *n.* chaperon (*on horses*). —wand, *f.* principal wall, façade.

Sto'a, *f.* (*pl.* Stoen) stoa, porch; Zenos —, the Porch. *See* Stoiker.

Stob, **Stö'be**, *1 & 3 pers. sing. imperf. ind. & subj. of* stieben.

Sto'ben, **Sto'f[illegible]**, **Sto'ven**, *v.a.* to stew.

Stö'ber, *see* St[illegible]uber. —n, *v.n.* (*aux.* h.) to hunt, to search everywhere, rummage; es —t, a fine snow (*or* rain) is falling, there is sleet falling, it drizzles. *Comp.* —hund, *m.* beagle, sporting-dog. —wetter, *n.* sleety, rainy *or* snowy weather.

Sto'cher, *m.* (—s, *pl.* —) picker; toothpick; poker; Zahn—, toothpick.

Sto'chern, *v.a.* & *n.* (*aux.* h.) to pick (*one's teeth*); to poke, rake, *or* stir (*the fire*); to rummage.

Stöchiometrie', *f.* stochiometry, stoicheiometry.

[1]**Stock**, I. *m.* (—es, *pl.* Stö'cke) stick; cane; walking-stick; surveyor's pole *or* staff; stem (*of a plant*); stump, body (*of a tooth*); trunk, stem; stalk; stum[illegible] *of a tree*); staff; rod; cue (*Bill.*); stock, body (*of an anvil, etc.*); foot, pedestal (*of a column*); stocks (*for culprits*); plant, (*vine-*)stock; capital; stocks, funds; stock (*of cattle, etc.*); hat-maker's block; hollow chest *or* box; (*bee-*)hive; mountain-mass, mass (*of rock, etc.*); vignette (*Typ.*); (*pl.* Stöcker) block, stupid lout; in den — legen, to put in the stocks; einen Hut über den — schlagen, to put a hat on the block; über — und Stein, up hill and down hill *or* dale. II. *m.* (*pl.* —) floor, storey (*of a house*); wie viel — hat es? how many stories are in it? im ersten —(e), on the first storey *or* floor. *Comp.* (*before names denoting nationality — often = true, typical, to the core*) —adler, *m.* goshawk. —amboß, *m.* round anvil. —amerikaner, *m.* thorough American; true *or* regular Yankee (*coll.*). —blind, *adj.* stone-blind. —britte, *m.* typical *or* true-born Briton. —degen, *m.* sword-cane. —deutsche(r), *m.* true German, German to the backbone *or* to the core. —dumm, *adj.* utterly stupid. —dunkel, *adj.* pitch dark. —dürr, *adj.* dry as a bone. —erbse, *f.* field-pea. —erz, *n.* ore in masses. —fackel, *m.* pine-torch. —fäule, *f.* rotting of the grape on the vines. —fechter, *m.* single-stick fencer. —finster, *see* —dunkel. —fisch, *m.* stockfish; dried cod; blockhead. —fisch=fang, *m.* cod-fishing; ling-, hake-fishing. —fleck, *m.* damp-stain. —fleckig, *adj.* stained by damp, mouldy; foxy (*of paper*). —flinte, *f.* cane-gun. —fremd, *adj.* entirely strange. —geige, *f.* kit. —gelehrt, *adj.* pedantic. —glaube, *m.* blind faith, implicit belief. —halter, *m.* stand for sticks. —hamen, *m.* landing net (*with a handle*). —händler, *m.* dealer in sticks. —haus, *n.* jail. —holz, *n.* firewood (*of stumps, etc.*). —jude, *m.* regular *or* typical Jew. —kampf, *m.* cudgel-play, fighting with sticks. —kohle, *f.* small coal. —laterne, *f.* cresset (*Railw.*); Chinese-lantern on a stick. —leiter, *f.* beam-ladder. —leuchter, *m.* lamp mounted on a pole. —macher, *m.* cane-maker. —meister, *m.* jailer. —messer, *n.* pruning-knife. —narr, *m.* arrant fool. —pfeife, *f.* beaked flute. —pflug, *m.* wheel-plough. —presse, *f.* bookbinder's large press. —prügel, *pl.* drubbing, sound thrashing; caning, flogging. —reis, *n.* sprig, sprout. —rose, *f.* hollyhock. —scheit, *n.* log from a

trunk. —**schere**, *f.* shears fixed in a block, bench-shears. —**schirm**, *m.* umbrella used as a walking-stick. —**schläge**, *see* —**prügel**. —**schnupfen**, *m.* stoppage in the head from cold, obstinate cold (in the head). —**schraube**, *f.* screw of a vice. —**still**, *adj.* stock-still. —**taub**, *adj.* stone-deaf. —**viole**, *f.* stock-gilliflower; wallflower. —**wache**, *f.* guard of prisoners. —**werk**, *n.* storey, floor. —**werk-batterien**, *pl.* guns in tiers. —**werke**, *pl.* interlaced masses *or* veins (*Min.*). —**winde**, *f.* windlass. —**zwinge**, *f.* ferrule (*on a stick*).

[2]**Stock**, *m.* (—s, *no pl.*) mould.

Stöck'—chen, *n.* (—chens, *pl.* —chen) cane. —**erig**, *adj.* dry and thin as a rake. —**ig**, *suffix* (*in comp.* =) -storied; **zwei—iges Haus**, two-storied house. —**isch**, *adj.* obstinate, stiff.

Stock'—en, I. *v.a.* to prop, stake (*peas, etc.*); to stock (*an anchor*); to roll (*cloth*); to pile up (*wood*). II. *v.n.* (*aux.* h. & s.) to stop; to run slowly; to cease to run *or* circulate; to be dull, to stagnate; to thicken, coagulate; to set (*as jelly*); to turn mouldy *or* fusty; **das Blut —t in den Adern**, the blood does not circulate; **der Handel —t**, trade is dull; **die Sache —t, es —t mit der Sache**, the affair is at a stand-still; **im Reden —en**, to break down in a speech, to stammer, to falter, hesitate. III. *subst. n.* stopping, cessation; stagnation; interruption; **ins —en geraten**, to come to a stand-still. —**ig**, *adj.* mildewed, fusty; rotten; damp; obstinate; stiff. —**ung**, *f.* stopping; stoppage; cessation; stagnation; stand-still; congestion.

Stock—s, *pl.* stocks, funds. *Comp.* —**besitzer**, *m.* stockholder, shareholder. —**börse**, *f.* stock-exchange. —**mäkler**, *m.* stock-broker. —**s-reiterei'**, *f.* stock-jobbing.

Stoff, *m.* (—(e)s, *pl.* —e) matter; substance; subject, theme; material, stuff; beer (*stud.sl.*); **einfacher —**, elementary body, element; — **zum Lachen geben**, to furnish matter for laughter; **Körper ist die Menge von — in einer körperlichen Substanz enthalten**, body is the mass *or* quantity of matter contained in any material substance. —**lich**, *adj.* material. *Comp.* —**auswahl**, *f.* choice of subjects. —**bildend**, *adj.* plastic, forming tissue. —**gebiet**, *n.* range of subjects. —**halter**, *m.* cloth-presser (*on sewing-machines*). —**haltig**, *adj.* material, substantial. —**lehre**, *f.* chemistry; materialism. —**los**, *adj.* immaterial; flimsy; worthless. —**name**, *m.* concrete noun. —**reich**, *adj.* substantial; rich in matter. —**rüsche**, *f.* silk frilling. —**teilchen**, *n.* material particle; **kleinstes —teilchen**, molecule. —**trieb**, *m.* sensuous impulsion, natural impulse (*issuing from the physical existence of man*). —**vergeudung**, *f.* spilling of good stuff *or* beer (*sl.*). —**wahl**, *f.* selection of subject(-matter) for an essay, a speech *or* a poem. —**wechsel**, *m.* change *or* circulation of matter, assimilation (*of food*) by digestion.

Stöh'le, (**Stäh'le**,) *1 & 3 pers. sing. imperf. subj. of* **stehlen**.

Stöh'nen, *v.n.* (*aux.* h.) to groan (**über eine S.**, over, at a thing).

Sto'—iker, *m.* (—ikers, *pl.* —iker) Stoic. —**isch**, *adj.* Stoic. —**izis'mus**, *m.* stoicism. *See* **Stoa**.

Sto'l—a, *f.* (*pl.* —en) stola (*of the Romans*); stole, surplice (*R.C.*). *Comp.* —**gebühren**, *pl.* surplice fees.

Stol'le, *f. see* **Stulle**.

[1]**Stol'len**, *m.* (—s, *pl.* —) foot (*of a bedstead, etc.*); prop, post; baluster; caulk, sponge of a horse-shoe; cake *or* bun; level, stulm, gallery (*of a mine*); first half of an **Aufgesang** *i.e.* first half of the opening portion of a (*mediæval*) tripartite stanza. *Comp.* —**arbeit**, *f.* work at a stulm (*Min.*). —**firste**, *f.* top of a stulm (*Min.*). —**gerechtigkeit**, *f.* right of having adits *or* drains to a mine. —**hauer**, —**häuer**, *m.* miner working a gallery. —**schacht**, *m.* shaft of a pit. —**wagen**, *m.* truck. —**weise**, *adv.* in galleries; by the gangways (*Min.*).

[2]**Stol'len**, *v.a.* to furnish with props *or* posts; to stretch, soften (*skins*); to rough-shoe (*a horse*).

Stöll'ner, *m.* (—s, *pl.* —) stulm-maker, drift maker; proprietor of a mine.

Stol'per, *m.* (—s, *pl.* —), —**ei'**, *f.* stumbling, stumble; blunder. —**er**, *m.* (—ers, *pl.* —er) stumbler, blunderer. —**ig**, —**icht** (*obs.*), *adj.* stumbling; uneven, rough (*as a road*).

Stol'pern, I. *v.n.* (*aux.* h. & s.) to stumble; to trip; to blunder. II. *subst. n.* stumble, blunder.

Stolz, I. *adj. & adv.* proud; haughty; arrogant; presumptuous; splendid, superb; stately; **auf (eine S.) — sein**, to be proud of, take a pride in. II. *m.* (—es) pride; haughtiness; arrogance; boast; **seinen — in eine S. setzen**, to take a pride in a th., make it one's boast. —**ie'ren**, *v.n.* (*aux.* h.) to be proud; to flaunt, strut.

Stop'fe, *f.* (*pl.* —n) place filled up; darn(ed place).

Stop'f—en, *v.* I. *a.* to stuff (*chairs, etc.; fowls*); to fill (*a pipe; sausage-skins, etc.*); to cram; to darn; to plug, close, stop up, cork; to caulk (*a ship*); to stem; to check, stop, obstruct; to constipate; to stop firing; **diese Speise —t**, this dish *or* food is constipative; **gestopft voll**, filled to suffocation, crammed full. II. *r.* to stuff oneself, gorge; to be jammed by crowding; **einem den Mund** (*or* **das Maul**) —**en**, to put a p. to silence, to stop a p.'s mouth. —**er**, *m.* (—ers, *pl.* —er) stuffer, filler, stopper; cork, bung, plug; rammer; boxer (*of railway-sleepers*); anything that checks *or* stops; patcher, darner. *Comp.* —**arz(e)nei**, *f.* astringent medicine. —**büchse**, *f.* stuffing-box; rod-collar; piston-rod (*Mach.*). —**farbe**, *f.* colour for repairing a picture. —**fleck**, *m.* patch(ed place), darn. —**garn**, *n.* darning cotton. —**holz**, *n.* plug, pin. —**lappen**, *m.* rag to stop a hole with. —**nadel**, *f.* darning-needle. —**naht**, *f.* darn. —**nudel**, *f.* force-meat ball. —**stich**, *m.* darning-stitch. —**stück**, *n.* plug. —**töne**, *pl.* damped tones. —**wachs**, *n.* propolis. —**werk**, *n.* darning, darn.

Stop'p—el, *f.* (*pl.* —eln) stubble; (*pl.*) pin-feathers, young feathers. —**el-haft**, —**elig**, *adj.* stubbly, like stubble; —**eliges Haar**, scrubby hair. —**eln**, *v.a.* to glean, to compile. —**ler**, *m.* (—lers, *pl.* —ler), —**lerin**, *f.* gleaner; compiler. *Comp.* —**el-bart**, *m.* bristly *or* scrubby beard. —**el-butter**, *f.* autumn-butter. —**el-dach**, *n.* thatch. —**el-feder**, *f.* young feather on the skin of a plucked bird. —**el-feld**, *n.* stubble-field. —**el-gans**, *f.* goose fed in a stubble-field. —**el-gedicht**, *n.* patchwork poem; cento. —**el-gras**, *n.* after-grass. —**el-korn**, *n.* autumn-sown corn. —**el-mast**, *f.* stubble-grazing. —**el-rübe**, *f.* late turnip. —**el-sense**, *f.* stubble-scythe. —**el-vers**, *m.* cento. —**el-vogt**, *m.* overseer of reapers. —**el-weide**, *f.* pasturage after harvest. —**el-werk**, *n.* literary patch-work, compilation. —**el-zeit**, *f.* gleaning season, autumn.

Stop'p—en, *v.a.* to stop; to stopper; to stem. —**er**, *m.* (—ers, *pl.* —er) stopper. —**i'ne**, *f.* quick-match (*Artil.*).

Stöp'sel, *m.* (—s, *pl.* —) stopper, cork; plug; stumpy person. —**n**, *v.a.* to cork, stopper.

Stör, *m.* (—s, *pl.* —e) sturgeon. *Comp.* —**ei**, *n.*, —**rogen**, *m.* sturgeon's spawn, caviare.

Storch, *m.* (—es, *pl.* Stör'che) stork; **ägyptischer —**, ibis; **der — klappert**, the stork chatters; **da brat' mir einer einen —**, that beats everything! well, I never! (*coll.*). *Comp.* **—bein**, *n.* stork's leg; spindle-leg. **—beinig**, *adj.* spindle-legged. **—nest**, *n.* stork's nest. **—schnabel**, *m.* stork's bill; geranium; crane's bill (*Surg.*); pantograph (*Draw.*). **—weibchen**, *n.* female stork.

Stor'cher, *see* Storger.

Stör'ch—in, *f.* female stork. **—ling**, *m.* (—lings, *pl.* —linge) young stork.

Stö'r—en, *v.* I. *a.* to disturb; to interrupt; to trouble, annoy; to disorder, derange; **sich —en lassen**, to inconvenience oneself; **laß dich** *or* **lassen Sie sich doch nicht —en**, don't trouble (*yourself*), don't let me disturb you; **gestörte Ruhe**, broken sleep. II. *n.* (*aux.* **h.**) to stir, poke (**im Feuer**, the fire); to rummage; to pick (*one's teeth*). **—er**, *m.* (—ers, *pl.* —er) disturber; troublesome person, meddler; intruder; kill-joy; **—er des Friedens**, peace-breaker. **—erei'**, *f.* constant disturbance. **—ung**, *f.* disturbance; trouble; interruption; inconvenience, annoyance; disorder; derangement; putting out of order; disturbing, (*pl.*) perturbations (*of the needle*). *Comp.* **—eisen**, *n.* poker. **—en=fried**, *m.* peace-breaker, mischief-maker. **—stange**, *f.* boat-hook. **—stock**, *m.* poker; stirring stick; pot-stick.

Stö'rer, *m.* (—s, *pl.* —) travelling quack (*dial.*).

Stor'ger, *m.* (—s, *pl.*—) quack, mountebank, vagabond (*dial.*, *obs.*).

Storr, *adj.* stiff, unbending (*dial.*).

Stör'r—ig, **—isch**, *adj.* stubborn, headstrong; cross, peevish. **—igkeit**, *f.* stubbornness.

Stoß (*long* o), *m.* (—es, *pl.* Stö'ße) push, shove, thrust; knock, blow, hit; jog, nudge; jolt; jerk; collision; shock; kick; impact, stroke (*Bill.*); thrust, pass (*Fenc.*); blast, flourish (*of a trumpet*); swoop; onset; heap, bundle, file; pile, heap (*of wood*); breech (*of a gun*); bolt-pin; side of a shaft (*Min.*); end (*of a mine-gallery*); joining, seam; joint (*Railw.*); joint, seam (*Carp.*); facing (*of a petticoat*); skirt-braid; piece added *or* inserted, impetus, impulse; recoil; **— durch Übereinandergreifen**, lap-joint (*Mach.*); **stumpfer —**, butt-joint; **auf den — fechten**, to fence with foils; **der letzte —**, the finishing stroke; **das hat mir einen — gegeben**, that has given me a shock; **das hat seiner Ehre einen empfindlichen — gegeben**, it has seriously affected his honour.

Sto'ß—en, I. *ir.v.a.* to push, shove, thrust; to jostle; to jog, nudge; to strike, knock, hit; to butt; to kick; to stab; to pound, bruise, bray; to ram (*pavement, etc.*); to drive (*piles, etc.*); **Sie dürfen sich nicht daran —en**, you need not take offence at that; **Noten —en**, to sing, perform staccato; **sich** (*dat.*) **den Fuß lahm —en**, to lame oneself by a knock; **Geld zusammen —en**, to collect money; **einen Ball ins Loch —en**, to send a ball into a pocket; **wer stößt?** who plays? (*Bill.*); **Zähne —en**, to teeth; **an einander —en**, to push together; to join; **Gläser an einander —en**, to touch glasses; **an die Wand —en**, to knock against the wall; **es stößt sich an nichts weiter als**, the only difficulty is; **auf die Straße —en**, to turn into the street; **einen mit der Nase auf eine S. —en**, to place a thing under a person's very nose; **aus dem Hause —en**, to turn out; **ins Gefängnis —en**, to thrust into prison; **über den Haufen —en**, to overthrow; **er stieß ihm den Dolch ins Herz**, he thrust the dagger into his heart; **einen vor den Kopf —en**, to offend a p.; **vom Lande —en**, to push off, launch; **von sich —en**, to push away, turn off, reject, discard; **sein Weib von sich —en**, to repudiate, divorce one's wife. II. *ir.v.r.* to hit, strike (**an**, against); to hurt oneself by striking; to take offence (**an eine** *or* **einer S.** at a th.); to hesitate (*about*); **er stößt sich an der** *or* **die Rede**, he is offended at the speech; **— dich nicht daran!** don't take it amiss! don't take offence at that! **daran stößt es sich**, that's the difficulty, that's what makes him hesitate. III. *ir.v.n.* (*aux.* **h.** & **f.**) to thrust, push, knock, strike (**an, auf, gegen**, against); to jolt; to recoil; to swarm (*of bees*); to blow (**in ein Horn**, a horn); **mit dem Fuße an eine S. —en**, to stumble against s. th.; **wir stießen bei X. auf den Feind**, we encountered the enemy near X.; **das Regiment wird zu Ihrem Corps —en**, the regiment will join your corps; **ans Land —en**, to run ashore, to land; **an einander —en**, to strike against one another; **—en an**, to join, to touch, to border upon; **diese Zimmer —en an einander**, these rooms are adjoining; **auf eine S. —en**, to meet with unexpectedly, light upon; **der Wind stößt**, the wind comes in puffs; **die Flinte stößt**, the gun kicks. IV. *subst. n.* pushing, thrusting; trituration; jolting; recoil (*of a gun*); fermenting (*of beer*). *Comp.* **—apparat**, *m.* buffing-apparatus (*Locom.*). **—band**, *n.* facing braid. **—bewegung**, *f.* projectile, forward motion. **—bock**, *m.* battering-ram. **—bolzen**, *m.* breeching-bolt (*Artil.*). **—degen**, *m.* rapier; foil. **—erde**, *f.* stiff clay for pisé building. **—falk(e)**, *m.* hobby (*Orn.*). **—fechten**, *n.* fencing with foils. **—feld**, *n.* first reinforce (*of a cannon*). **—fuge**, *f.* upright joint. **—garn**, *n.* oakum. **—gebet**, *n.* ejaculatory prayer, short and fervent prayer. **—heber**, *m.* hydraulic lever. **Hieb= und —=waffen**, *pl.* cut- and thrust-weapons. **—hobel**, *m.* cooper's jointer. **—holz**, *n.* wooden pestle; wood in heaps. **—kante**, *f.* hem, edge, lining; gunwale (*Naut.*). **—keil**, *m.* launching-wedge (*Naut.*). **—klinge**, *f.* small-sword blade. **—kolben**, *m.* mace (*Bill.*). **—kraft**, *f.* impetus, impulsive force. **—maschine**, *f.* percussion-machine; slotting-machine. **—netz**, *n.* net for catching birds of prey. **—platte**, *f.* rail-ground-plate (*Railw.*); butt-plate (*covering a butt-joint*). **—polster**, *pl.* buffers (*Railw.*). **—rapier**, *n.* thrusting-sword. **—riegel**, *m.* breech transom-bolt (*Artil.*). **—riemen**, *m.* cheek-brace (*of a coach*). **—ring**, *m.* ferrule. **—säge**, *f.* hand-saw. **—seufzer**, *m.* pious ejaculation. **—ventil**, *n.* valve to control the wind in an organ, slider. **—vogel**, *m.* bird of prey. **—waffe**, *f.* thrust(ing)-weapon. **—weise**, *adv.* by starts *or* jerks; by fits and starts; joltingly. **—werk**, *n.* coining-press; escapement (*of a watch*). **—wind**, *m.* gust of wind, squall. **—winkel**, *m.* angle of incidence. **—zähne**, *pl.* tusks.

Stö'ß—el, *m.* (—els, *pl.* —el) pestle; rammer, beetle. **—er**, *m.* (—ers, *pl.* —er) knocker, kicker, *etc.*; pounder, compounder; bird of prey; *see* **—el**. **—ig**, *adj.* fond of butting, given to goring; vicious.

Stotterei', *f.* stammering.

Stot'ter—er, *m.* (—ers, *pl.* —er) stutterer, stammerer. **—ig**, *adj.* stuttering. **—n**, *v.n.* (*aux.* **h.**) to stammer, stutter.

Sto'ven, *v.a.* to steam, stew.

Strack, I. *adj.* straight; sleek; quick; direct; downright; resolute. II. *adv.* immediately; strictly. **—s**, *adv.* straightway; directly; outright.

Straf'bar, *adj.* punishable; culpable; criminal. **—keit**, *f.* punishableness; culpability.

Stra'fe, *f.* (*pl.* —n) punishment; penalty; fine; judgment; **bei — des Todes**, on pain of death; **bei hoher Geld— verboten**, forbidden under penalty of a heavy fine; **einen in — nehmen,** to punish *or* fine a p.; **ihm zur —,** to punish him; **seine — absitzen,** to expiate one's crime in prison; **Vorladung bei —,** subpœna.

Stra'f—en, *v.a.* to punish; to chastise, correct; to blame, reprove, rebuke (*obs.*); **einen an der Ehre —en,** to inflict a degrading punishment on a p.; **einen um Geld —en,** to fine a p.; **einen am Leben —en,** to punish a p. with death; **am Leibe —en,** to inflict corporal punishment; **er hat sich erkühnt mich Lügen zu —en,** he had the impudence to give me the lie; **solche Fehler —en sich selbst,** such faults bring their own punishment, meet with their due reward. **—end,** *p. & adj.* punishing, punitive; revengeful; threatening. **—er,** *m.* (**—ers,** *pl.* **—er**) punisher, chastiser. *Comp.* **—änderung,** *f.* commutation of sentence. **—androhung,** *f.* threat of punishment; commination (*Eccles.*). **—anstalt,** *f.* house of correction, convict-prison. **—antrag,** *m.* sentence proposed *or* demanded by the public prosecutor. **—appell,** *m.* punishment roll-call. **—arbeit, —aufgabe,** *f.* imposition (*at school*), lines. **—arrest,** *m.* detention (*in schools*); cell (*Mil.*). **—aufschub,** *m.* postponement of the execution of a sentence. **—bedingung,** *f.* penal clause. **—befehl,** *m.* order to inflict a punishment *or* a fine. **—befreiung,** *f.* amnesty. **—befugnis,** *f.* authority to punish, penal power. **—beispiel,** *n.* public example. **—bestimmung,** *f.* paragraph in the penal code. **—buch,** *n.* fine-book; black book (*Mil.*). **—büchse,** *f.* fine-box. **—engel,** *m.* avenging angel. **—erkenntnis,** *n.* sentence passed in a criminal case, judgment against a p. **—erlaß,** *m.* remission of punishment; (**allgemeiner**) **—erlaß,** amnesty. **—erleichterung,** *f.* mitigation of punishment. **—exerzieren,** *n.* punishment-drill. **—fall,** *m.* penal case; **schwerer —fall,** criminal case. **—fällig,** *adj.* punishable; **—fälliges Vergehen,** punishable offence. **—freiheit,** *f.* exemption from punishment. **—gebot,** *n.* order accompanied by threat of punishment. **—gefangene(r),** *m.* person detained in prison, convict. **—geld,** *n.* fine, money-penalty. **—genosse,** *m.* fellow-culprit. **—gerechtigkeit,** *f.* penal jurisdiction. **—gericht,** *n.* criminal court; judgment; **ihn traf des Himmels —gericht,** the judgment of God overtook him. **—gerichtsbarkeit,** *f.* criminal justice. **—gerichts=ordnung,** *f.* criminal code. **—gesetz,** *n.* penal law. **—gesetzbuch,** *n.* penal code. **—gesetz=gebung,** *f.* penal legislation. **—kasse,** *f.* exchequer into which *or* office where fines are paid. **—klage,** *f.* criminal proceedings. **—kläger,** *m.* crown prosecutor. **—klausel,** *f.* penal clause. **—kodex,** *m.* penal code. **—kolonie,** *f.* penal settlement. **—kompanie,** *f.* company of refractory soldiers. **—krieg,** *m.* punitive war. **—los,** *adj. & adv.* unpunished; exempt from punishment, guiltless. **—losigkeit,** *f.* impunity. **—maß,** *n.* punitive measure, amount of punishment; **höchstes —maß,** maximum penalty. **—milderung,** *f.* mitigation of a penalty, commutation of a sentence. **—mittel,** *n.* means of punishment. **—porto,** *n.* more to pay, additional postage. **—prediger,** *m.* censorious preacher, severe moralist. **—predigt,** *f.* severe sermon *or* lecture; **einem eine — predigt halten,** to give a p. a severe lecture, to blow a p. up (*sl.*). **—prozeß,** *m.* criminal procedure. **—recht,** *n.* *see* **—befugnis;** criminal jurisdiction; penal law. **—rechtlich,** *adj.* penal, criminal. **—rechts=kundige(r),** *m.* one versed in criminal law, criminalist. **—rechts=lehrer,** *m.* professor *or* teacher of criminal law. **—rede,** *f.* reprimand. **—richter,** *m.* judge in a criminal court. **—rute,** *f.* scourge. **—satz,** *m.* forfeit (*at games*); amount of punishment. **—urteil,** *n.* penal sentence; **—urteil über einen verhängen,** to pass judgment upon a p. **—verfahren,** *n.* criminal procedure. **—versetzung,** *f.* transfer for disciplinary reasons. **—vollziehung, —vollstreckung,** *f.*, **—vollzug,** *m.* infliction of punishment. **—würdig,** *adj.* deserving punishment; punishable, penal. **—zumessung,** *f.* award of punishment.

Straff, *adj. & adv.* stretched, tense, tight, dense, stiff; erect; close; austere, rigid; **—er Beutel,** well-filled purse; **— anliegen,** to fit tightly; **—e Haltung,** straight military bearing; **sich — halten,** to stand bolt upright; **—e Zucht,** strict discipline. **—en,** *v.a. & r.* to tighten; to stretch; to tauten (*Naut.*). **—heit,** *f.* tightness, tension. *Comp.* **—haarig,** *adj.* with bristly hair. **—seil,** *n.* tight rope. **—ziehen,** *n.* tension.

Sträf'—lich, I. *adj. & adv. see* **Strafbar;** severe. II. *adv.* severely, enormously; **das thut —lich weh,** that is terribly painful; **er ist —lich faul,** he is awfully lazy (*coll.*). **—ling,** *m.* culprit; convict.

Strahl, *m.* (**—s,** *pl.* **—en**) ray, beam; jet (*of water, etc.*); flash; radius; straight line; spoke (*of a wheel*); frog (*Vet.*); bolt; **Flüssigkeits—,** fluid vein (*Phys.*); **Wärme—,** ray of heat; **leuchtende —en,** luminous rays; **Röntgen —en,** X rays; **der Papst schleuderte seinen Bann—,** the Pope fulminated *or* thundered out an excommunication.

Strah'l—en, *v.* I. *n.* (*aux.* **h.**) to beam, radiate, emit rays of light; to shine, beam (*as the face*). II. *a.* to beam, shed forth. **—end,** *p. & adj.* radiant; beaming. **—icht** (*obs.*), **—ig,** *adj.* radiant. **—ung,** *f.* radiance; radiation. *Comp.* **—ader,** *f.* vein of the frog (*in a horse's foot*). **—douche,** *f.* shower-bath from a single jet of water. **—en=auge,** *n.* beaming eye. **—en=blume,** *f.* radiate flower. **—en=brechend,** *adj.* refractive (*Opt.*). **—en=brechung,** *f.* refraction. **—en=brechungs=lehre,** *f.* dioptrics. **—en=büschel,** *m.* (*& n.*), **—en=kegel,** *m.* pencil *or* cone of rays. **—en=förmig,** *adj.* radiate. **—en=glanz,** *m.* irradiance, irradiation, lustre. **—en=krone,** *f.* radiant crown; halo, glory, nimbus. **—en=los,** *adj.* rayless. **—en=spalter,** *m.* prism. **—en=werfen,** *n.* (ir)radiation. **—pumpe,** *f.* jet-pump. **—tierchen,** *n.* radiolarian, acantharian.

Strähn, *m.* (**—s,** *pl.* **—e**), (*usually*) **—e,** *f.* (*pl.* **—en**) lock of hair, plait; skein, hank; strand. **—ig,** *suffix* (*in comp.* =) of so many skeins *or* strands; **drei—ig,** three-skeined; of three strands.

Strami'n, *m.* (**—s**) fine canvas for tapestry work.

Stramm, *see* **Straff;** **—er Bursche,** vigorous, robust youth; **—es Mädel,** buxom lass; **—er Soldat,** smart soldier; **—e Zucht,** strict discipline; **— arbeiten,** to work hard; **einem Jungen die Hosen — ziehen,** to give a boy a flogging; **— stehen,** to stand at attention. **—heit,** *f.* *see* **Straffheit;** fine deportment (*coll.*); **preußische —heit,** Prussian rigour.

Stram'peln, *v.* I. *n.* (*aux.* **h.**) to fling, toss about; to kick. II. *r.*; **sich bloß —,** to kick the clothes off (*as children asleep*).

Strand, *m.* (**—es,** *pl.* **—e**) strand, beach, sea-coast; **auf den — laufen,** to run ashore.

Stran'd—en, *v.n.* (*aux.* **h.** *&* **s.**) to be stranded; to run ashore; to make shipwreck (*of one's life, etc.*). **—ung,** *f.* stranding. *Comp.* **—batterie,** *f.* coast-battery. **—bauer, —bewohner,** *m.* person dwelling on the sea-coast. **—dieb,** *m.* wrecker. **—fischerei,** *f.* fishing on the beach. **—gerechtigkeit,** *f.* jurisdiction over stranded goods. **—gut,** *n.* flotsam; stranded goods. **—hafer,** *n.* sand oats. **—herr,** *m.* proprietor of a shore, one who has the right to stranded goods. **—jäger,** *m.* arctic gull; wrecker; sea-shore sportsman. **—korb,** *m.* roofed wicker-chair for use on the beach. **—läufer,** *m.* sandpiper, dunlin (*Orn.*). **—pfeifer,** *m.* ringed plover, sandpiper. **—räuber,** *m.* wrecker. **—recht,** *n. see* **—gerechtigkeit.** **—reiter,** *m.* mounted coastguardsman; long-legged plover. **—ſtein,** *m.* shingle. **—vogt,** *m.* inspector of the sea-shore of coast-dikes. **—wache,** *f.*, **—wächter,** *m.* coast-guard.

Strang, *m.* (**—es,** *pl.* **Strän'ge**) rope, cord, line; halter; skein; trace (*of harness*); railroad; **alle Stränge anziehen,** to do one's utmost; **an einem —e ziehen,** to pull together, act in concert, **wenn alle Stränge reißen,** if the worst comes to the worst; **über die Stränge ſchlagen,** to kick over the traces; **er verdient den —,** he deserves hanging. **—ulie'ren,** *v.a.* to strangle. *Comp.* **—haken,** *m.* trace-hook. **—leder,** *n.* trace-leather.

Strapa'z—e, *f.* (*pl.* **—en**) fatigue; toil, hardship; **an —en gewöhnt,** inured to toil *or* hardship. **—ie'ren,** *v.a.* to tire; to harass; to knock *or* do up. **—iö's,** *adj.* tiring, fatiguing.

Strapezie'ren, *see* **Strapazieren.**

Stra'ße, *f.* (*pl.* **—n**) street; road, way; thoroughfare; highway; straits; firth; route; cut (*Min.*); **Heer—, Poſt—, Land—,** highroad; **— von Gibraltar,** Strait(s) of Gibraltar; **—e von Meſſina,** Strait of Messina; **die —e von Calais,** the (British) Channel; **geh' deine —!** go your ways! begone! **auf die — ſetzen,** to turn out of doors; **die breitgetretene — des Herkommens,** the beaten path *or* track of custom. *Comp.* **—n=anlage,** *f.* laying out of a street *or* road. **—n=arbeiter,** *m.* road-man. **—n=aufſeher,** *m.* road-surveyor. **—n=bahn,** *f.* tramway. **—n=bau,** *m.* road-making. **—n=beleuchtung,** *f.* lighting of the streets. **—n=damm,** *m.* causeway. **—n=dieb,** *m.* highwayman; pickpocket. **—n=eiſenbahn,** *f.* tramway. **—n=feger,** *m.* scavenger; crossing-sweeper. **—n=junge,** *m.* street-arab. **—n=kleid,** *n.* walking dress. **—n=kot,** *m.* mud. **—n=laterne,** *f.* street-lamp. **—n=lokomotive,** *f.* steam-roller; road-engine. **—n=räuber,** *see* **—n=dieb.** **—n=recht,** *n.* right to protection on the high-road. **—n=renner,** *m.* road-racer (*cycl.*). **—n=ſäule,** *f.* mile-stone; finger-post. **—n=ſperrung,** *f.* barricade; closing of a thoroughfare. **—n=thür,** *f.* street-door. **—n=weſen,** *n.* the streets, streets and highways. **—n=zoll,** *m.* toll.

Strate'g—e, *m.* (**—en,** *pl.* **—en**) strategist. **—ie',** *f.* strategy. **—iſch,** *adj.* strategic.

Sträu'b—en, *v.* I. *a.* to ruffle up; **der Anblick —te ihm das Haar,** the sight made his hair stand on end. II. *r.* to stand, bristle up; to struggle (*against*), resist, oppose; **die Feder —t ſich zu ſchildern . . .,** the pen refuses to describe . . . **—ig,** *adj.* bristling, stiff (*poet.*); contradictory, obstinate (*rare*).

Strau'b—ig, *see* **Sträubig.** *Comp.* **—fuß,** *m.* malanders (*Vet.*). **—rad,** *n.* undershot wheel, ladle wheel.

Strauch, *m.* (**—es,** *pl.* **Sträu'che, Sträu'cher**) shrub, bush. **—ig,** *adj.* bushy; covered with shrubs. *Comp.* **—artig,** *adj.* shrub-like. **—dieb,** *m.* ruffian, prowling thief, highwayman. **—läufer,** *m.* bushranger. **—werk,** *n.* shrubbery, shrubs; brushwood, underwood.

Strau'ch—eln, *v.n.* (*aux.* **h.** *&* **ſ.**) to stumble; to make a false step. **—ler,** *m.* (**—lers,** *pl.* **—ler**) stumbler; blunderer.

[1]**Strauß,** I. *m.* (**—es,** *pl.* **Sträu'ße**) crest, tuft, top-knot; bunch; nosegay, bouquet; thyrsus (*Bot.*). II. *m.* (**—es,** *pl.* **—e**) strife, struggle, combat. *Comp.* **—binderin,** *f.* flower-girl. **—blume,** *f.* umbelliferous flower. **—ſperling,** *m.* crested sparrow.

[2]**Strauß,** *m.* (**—es,** *pl.* **—e**) ostrich. *Comp.* **—(en)ei,** *n.* ostrich egg. **—feder,** *f.* ostrich feather. **—vogel,** *m.* ostrich.

Sträuß'chen, *n.* (**—s,** *pl.* **—**) nosegay, bouquet.

Straz'ze, *f.* (*pl.* **—n**) waste-book, daybook.

Stre'be, *f.* (*pl.* **—n**) strut, prop, stay; buttress; opposition.

Stre'b—en, I. *v. n.* (*aux.* **h.**) to strive, struggle, strain (**nach,** after); to aspire (*to*), aim (*at*); to strive, struggle; to tend (*towards*); to gravitate; **wider, gegen einen —en,** to struggle against, resist a p.; **nach etwas hin (von etwas weg) —en,** to have a tendency to approach (fly from); **nach dem (von dem) Mittelpunkte —ende Kraft,** centripetal (centrifugal) force. II. *subst.n.* striving, endeavour; aspiration; tendency; aim, effort. **—er,** *m.* (**—ers,** *pl.* **—er**) pushing fellow; place-hunter. **—ertum,** *n.* (**—s**) place-hunting. **—ſam,** *adj.* assiduous; aspiring; pushing. **—ſamkeit,** *f.* assiduity, perseverance. *Comp.* **—e=balken,** *m.* prop, shore; buttress, brace. **—e=band,** *n.* brace. **—e=bau,** *m.* long-wall method (*Min.*). **—e=bogen,** *m.* flying buttress. **—e=holz,** *n. see* **—ebalken, —eband.** **—e=mauer,** *f.* counterfort (*Fort.*). **—e=pfahl,** *m.* prop. **—e=pfeiler,** *m.* buttress, stay, pier. **—e=ſtange,** *f.* prop, stay, pier. **—e=ſtütze,** *f.* prop.

Streck'—bar, *adj.* that may be stretched; extensible; ductile; malleable. **—barkeit,** *f.* extensibility; ductility. **—e,** *f.* (*pl.* **—en**) tract, extent, stretch, way; distance; line of rail; extension; stretcher; (*pl.*) horizontal water-conduits; (*pl.*) galleries, passages (*Min.*); **in einer —e,** at a stretch; **eine gute —e Weges,** a good piece of the way; **zur —e bringen,** to shoot down, kill, (bring to) bag (*Hunt.*).

Streck'—en, *v.* I. *a.* to stretch, extend, spread; to draw, roll *or* beat out; to elongate; **zu Boden —en,** to fell to the ground; **die Hände gen Himmel —en,** to raise one's hands towards heaven; **das Gewehr, die Waffen —en,** to lay down one's arms, to surrender; **in geſtrecktem Galopp,** at full speed; **geſtreckter Winkel,** rectilinear angle. II. *r.* to stretch oneself; **ſich nach der Decke —en,** to cut one's coat according to one's cloth; **ſich zur Ruhe (nieder *or* hin=) —en,** to lie down to rest. **—er,** *m.* (**—ers,** *pl.* **—er**) stretcher; extensor(*-muscle*). **—ung,** *f.* stretching; extension; deployment. *Comp.* **—balken,** *m.* strut; stretcher; cross-beam (*of bridges*). **—bank,** *f.* bench for stretching. **—bett,** *n.* stretching *or* orthopœdic bed (*Surg.*). **—eiſen,** *n.* stretcher (*for hides, etc.*). **—en=förderung,** *f.* transport (*Min.*). **—en=geſchwindigkeit,** *f.* speed (*of a train*). **—en=verkehr,** *m.* local traffic (*Railw.*). **—en=wärter,** *m.* line-keeper; signalman. **—en=weiſe,** *adv.* here and there. **—en=zimmerung,** *f.* timbering of mines. **—hammer,** *m.* flattening hammer. **—maſchine,** *f.* drawing-frame (*Spin.*). **—muskel,** *m.* extensor muscle. **—rahmen,** *m.* stretching-frame. **—vers,** *m.* long line. **—walze,** *f.* laminating roller (*in mints*); drawing roller; steel roller. **—werk,** *n.* rolling- *or* stretching-machine.

Streich, *m.* (**—(e)s,** *pl.* **—e**) stroke; blow (*also fig.*); lash, stripe; trick, prank, joke; **von einem —e fällt keine Eiche,** a single stroke won't fell an oak; Rome was not built in a day; **auf einen —,** at one blow; **einem einen — beibringen,** to give a p. a blow; **einem einen —**

spielen, to play a p. a (nasty) trick; **ich könnte —e erzählen,** I could tell some fine stories; **das ist einer seiner dummen —e,** that is one of his foolish pranks *or* of his stupid tricks. —**eln,** *v.a.* to stroke; to caress; to flatter, coax. —**en,** I. *ir.v.n.* (*aux.* **h.** *&* **s.**) to stretch, extend (*towards, etc.*); to move, rush quickly past; to run, fly, sweep over; to wander, stroll, ramble; to migrate (*as birds*); to graze, touch in passing; to spawn; to rut; —**en lassen,** *see* **Fahren lassen; das Gebirge —t von Mittag nach Abend,** the mountain chain runs *or* stretches from south to west; **der Gang —t,** the load runs out; **auf dem Boden —en,** to trail on the ground (*of dresses*); **mit der Hand über das Gesicht —en,** to pass the hand over one's face; **das Schiff —t durch die Wellen,** the ship cuts through the waves. II. *ir.v.a.* to touch; to spread; to scrape, smooth; to whet (*a knife*), strop (*a razor*); to strike; to strike (*a match*); to rub; to stroke; to whip; to erase, expunge, cancel; to flatter, cajole; to strike, lower (*sails; a flag, etc.*); **glatt —en,** to smooth, polish; **Ziegel —en,** to make *or* mould tiles; **Lerchen —en,** to snare larks; **eine gestrichene Note,** note above (below) the line; **die Geige —en,** to play the violin; **Brot mit Butter (ein Butterbrot) —en,** to spread butter on the bread; **Gold auf dem Probirsteine —en,** to try gold on a touch-stone; **sich** (*dat.*) **die Haare aus dem Gesichte —en,** to push one's hair out of one's eyes *or* one's face; **den Schweiß von der Stirne —en,** to wipe the perspiration from one's forehead; **den Bogen —en,** to resin the bow; **mit Ruten —en,** to flog; **Wolle —en,** to card wool; **Eisen mit dem Magnete —en,** to magnetize iron; **Geld in die Tasche —en,** to pocket money; **heraus —en,** to extol; — **überall!** back water all! back astern! **die Riemen** *or* **Ruder —en,** to back water, hold water (*Naut.*); **die Segel —en,** to furl *or* lower the sails; to give in (*fig.*); **gestrichen voll,** full to the brim. III. *subst. n.* passing, *etc.;* bearing, direction (*Min.*); pass (*of a mesmerist*). —**er,** *m.* (—**ers,** *pl.* —**er**) rover, rambler; woolcomber; mould (*for bricks*); whet-stone; **Land—er,** tramp. *Comp.* —**bank,** *f.* carding-bench. —**baum,** *m.* stretching-tree, horse; work-roller (*Weav.*). —**brett,** *n.* smoothing-board; brickmaker's strike; mould-board. —**bürste,** *f.* whisk; colour-brush; size- *or* paste-brush. —**eisen,** *n.* sleeking-iron; heart-tool (*Bookb.*); rubber, straightening-plate (*for needles*); trowel for filling up crevices, *etc.;* paring-knife (*Tan.*). —**feuer,** *n.* flank fire (*Artil.*). —**fisch,** *m.* spawning fish. —**garn,** *n.* drag-net; tunnel net; carded yarn. —**holz,** *n. see* —**hölzchen**; strike, strickle; polisher (*Hatm.*); hone. —**hölzchen,** *pl.* (lucifer-) matches. —**hölzchen=kasten,** *m.* (*or* —**schachtel,** *f.*) match-box. —**instrumente,** *pl.* string instruments. —**kalk,** *m.* quick-lime. —**kamm,** *m.* carding-comb. —**leder,** *n.* strop. —**linie,** *f.* line of defence, flank (*Fort.*). —**maß,** *n.* mortise-gauge; close measure. —**meißel,** *m.* foundry-rake. —**messer,** *n.* spatula; pallet-slice; paring-knife. —**musik,** *f.* string-music. —**netz,** *n. see* —**garn.** —**platz,** *m.* second line of defence (*Fort.*). —**quartett,** *n.* string quartette. —**richtung,** *f.* horizontal direction. —**riemen,** *m.* razor-strop. —**schwamm,** *m.* phosphuretted tinder. —**spatel,** *m. see* —**messer.** —**stange,** *f.* putlog (*Arch.*); sleeper (*of coaches*). —**stein,** *m.* touchstone; hone, whetstone. —**vogel,** *m.* bird of passage. —**wehr(e),** *f.* flank, bulwark. —**werk,** *n.* flanking bastion. —**winkel,** *m.* flanking angle. —**wolle,** *f.* carded wool. —**zeit,** *f.* season for the migration of birds; spawning time (*of fishes*). —**zither,** *f.* zither played with a bow.

Streif, *m.* (—**es,** *pl.* —**e**) *see* —**en.** —**chen,** *n.* (—**chens,** *pl.* —**chen**) strip; fillet, bandelet (*Arch.*). —**e,** *f. see* —**zug.** —**en,** *m.* (—**ens,** *pl.* —**en**) stripe, streak; mark; rib (*in cloth*); fillet, band (*Arch.*); plate, sheet (*of metal*); vein (*in marble*); belt (*Astr.*); slip, scrap (*of paper*); slip-proof (*Typ.*); piping, edging, band, braid (*Tail.*); train (*of gunpowder*).

Strei'f—en, I. *v.a.* to streak, stripe; to variegate; to channel, flute; to rib; to touch slightly, graze, brush; to strip off; to take off; to flay; **die Ärmel in die Höhe —en,** to turn up one's sleeves; **den Ring vom Finger —en,** to take one's ring off. II. *v.n.* (*aux.* **h.** *&* **s.**) to ramble, rove, roam; to range, scour; to make raids; to graze, brush against; —**en an,** to border, trench upon; **auf Kundschaft —en,** to reconnoitre, to scout. —**er,** *m.* (—**ers,** *pl.* —**er**) ranger, scourer; scout; rambler. —**erei',** *f.* roaming, ramble, excursion; tour, trip; incursion (*Mil.*); expedition (*Mil.*). —**ig,** *adj.* striped. *Comp.* —**band,** *n.* postal wrapper, paper cover. —**blick,** *m.* glance. —**esel,** *m.* zebra. —**hieb,** *m.* grazing cut *or* blow, light blow. —**jagen,** *n.* hunting with hounds, coursing. —**kolonne,** *f.* flying column. —**korps,** *n.* flying column, scouting party. —**licht,** *n.* accidental light (*Paint.*). —**partie,** *f.* ramble; *see* —**korps.** —**reiter,** *m.* mounted scout, roving horseman. —**schuß,** *m.* shot that grazes; **er hat einen —schuß bekommen,** a bullet just grazed him. —**wache,** *f.* patrol. —**wunde,** *f.* scratch, slight wound. —**zug,** *m.* (roving) expedition; incursion, raid.

Streik, (—(e)s, *pl.* —**e** *and* —**s**), **Stri'ke,** *m.* (—**s,** *pl.* —**s**) strike, suspension of work. —**en,** *v.n.* to strike (*work*), to go out on strike. *Comp.* —**brecher,** *m.* blackleg, scab (*coll.*). —**kasse,** *f.* strike-fund.

Streit, *m.* (—**es,** *pl.* —**e** (*obs.*), —**igkeiten**) dispute, quarrel, strife, contention; lawsuit; combat, struggle; conflict (*of interest, etc.*); **Wort—,** controversy; **außer allem —e,** beyond all dispute; **im —e liegen,** to be at variance. —**bar,** *adj.* fit for fighting, effective; fighting; warlike; valiant; virile, manly. —**barkeit,** *f.* warlike spirit *or* character.

Strei't—en, *ir.v.* I. *n.* (*aux.* **h.**) to fight; to quarrel, to dispute, to wrangle; to disagree; to struggle, contend (*for*); to go to law (*about*); **darüber läßt sich —en,** that is a debatable point; **das —et gegen die gesunde Vernunft,** that is repugnant to common sense; **dieser Umstand —et für uns,** this circumstance tells in our favour. II. *a.;* **mit einem —en,** to fight a p.; **darüber ist nicht zu —en,** that is indisputable; **dagegen will ich nicht —en,** I will not dispute that; **sich —en,** to dispute, quarrel; **sich um des Kaisers Bart —en,** to quarrel over trifles; **die —ende Kirche,** the Church Militant; **die —enden Mächte,** the belligerent powers; **die —enden Parteien,** the opposing parties. —**er,** *m.* (—**ers,** *pl.* —**er**) combatant; fighter; disputant; champion. —**ig,** *adj.* contending, disputing; in dispute, debatable, questionable; contentious, quarrelsome; **die —ige Sache,** the matter in dispute; **einem etwas —ig machen,** to contend with s.o. for, dispute about a th.; **die Sache ist noch vor Gericht —ig,** the suit is still pending. —**igkeit,** *f.* dispute, controversy; quarrel; lawsuit; disputable character of a matter. *Comp.* —**axt,** *f.* battle-axe; war-hatchet; tomahawk, axe. —**begierde,** *f.* combativeness. —**fertig,** *adj.* ready to fight, prepared for battle. —**frage,** *f.* point of controversy, matter of dispute, vexed question, moot point. —**gegenstand,** *m.* matter in dispute; bone of contention (*fig.*). —**hammel,** *m.* quarrelsome fellow (*vulg.*).

—hammer, *m.* mallet, mace, pole-axe. **—handel,** *m.* lawsuit. **—handſchuh,** *m.* boxing-glove. **—hengſt,** *m.* war-horse, charger, steed. **—kolben,** *m.* club, mace. **—kräfte,** *pl.* fighting *or* military forces. **—kunſt,** *f.* art of fighting; art of debating. **—lehre,** *f.* controversial doctrine, polemics. **—luſt,** *f.* love of disputing; quarrelsomeness. **—luſtig,** *adj.* quarrelsome; litigious; desirous of fighting, pugnacious, disputatious, polemical. **—predigt,** *f.* controversial sermon. **—punkt,** *m.* point in dispute, controverted point. **—rede,** *f.* dispute. **—roß,** *n.* war-horse, charger. **—ſache,** *f.* matter in dispute; lawsuit. **—ſatz,** *m.* thesis, article of a dispute. **—ſchlichter,** *m.* peacemaker; arbitrator. **—ſchrift,** *f.* polemic treatise. **—ſchriften,** *pl.* controversial writings. **—ſucht,** *f.* love of dispute; quarrelsomeness, contentious disposition. **—theologie,** *f.* polemical theology. **—übung,** *f.* debate, practice of debating. **—wagen,** *m.* war-chariot.

Streng, —e, *adj. & adv.* severe, stern, austere; strict; harsh, rough, severe; hard; brittle; astringent; tart; sharp; acrid; **mit einem —e verfahren,** to be severe towards a p.; **im —ſten Winter,** in the depth of winter; **—er Arreſt,** close arrest (*Mil.*); **—e Haft,** close confinement; **—e Prüfung,** severe *or* stiff examination; **—e Maßregeln,** rigorous measures; **—e Regeln,** stringent rules; **— nach der Vorſchrift handeln,** to act in strict accordance with instructions; **im —ſten Sinne** (*or* **Verſtande) des Wortes,** in the very strictest acceptation of the word; **—ſtens verboten,** strictly prohibited; **aufs —ſte unterſagen,** to forbid most positively. **—e,** *f.* (*pl.* **—en**) sternness, austerity; severity; strictness; bitterness; **—e des Klimas,** rigour of climate; **—e des Geſchmacks,** sharpness of taste; **—e des Charakters,** austerity (*of character*); **Harn —e,** dysuria (*Med.*). *Comp.* **—flüſſig,** *adj.* difficult of fusion. **—fromm,** *adj.* strictly religious. **—gläubig,** *adj.* strictly *or* very orthodox. **—gläubigkeit,** *f.* orthodoxy.

Streu, *f.* (*pl.* **—en**) litter; bed (*of straw*). **—bar,** *adj.* that may be scattered *or* spread.

Streu'—en, *v.a.* to strew, scatter, sprinkle; to dredge; to disseminate; to yield straw; **dem Vieh —en,** to litter cattle; **die Flinte —t,** the gun spreads the shot; **ſie —ten ihr Blumen,** they strewed flowers in her path. **—ung,** *f.* strewing, scattering; littering. *Comp.* **—büchſe,** *f.* dredging box; pepper-(sugar-)caster. **—gabel,** *f.* dung *or* stable-fork. **—kügelchen,** *n.* (homœopathic) globule. **—mehl,** *n.* dredging-flour. **—pulver,** *n.* powder for (strewing on) wounds; violet *or* face powder. **—rechen,** *m.* hay-rake. **—ſand,** *m.* pounce. **—ſtroh,** *n.* litter-straw. **—zucker,** *m.* powdered sugar, caster-sugar. **—ungskegel,** *m.*, **—ungskreis,** *m.* cone of dispersion, cone of spread (*of projectiles*) (*Mil.*).

[1]**Strich,** *m.* (**—es,** *pl.* **—e**) stroke, line, dash; course, way, direction; touch; bar (*Mus.*); comma; hyphen; notch, score; streak, stripe; point of the compass; rhomb; course, way, direction; ship's course; track, rut; wake (*of a ship*); migration, flight (*of birds*); grain (*of wood, etc.*); boundary, limit; extent (*of country*); region, tract, district, county; space; latitude; climate, zone; flock, flight (*of birds*); fry (*of fish*); spawning time; touch (*Magnet.*); train (*of gunpowder*); flaw (*in glass*); measure (= *less than half an inch*); batch (*of bricks*); **Bogen—,** stroke with the fiddle-bow, bowing; **in einem —e,** all at once, at one stroke, continuously; **einen — unter eine S. machen,** to underline something; to put an end to something; **das macht uns einen — durch die Rechnung,** that upsets our calculations; **er hat ihm einen — durch die Rechnung gemacht,** he has balked, thwarted him; **wider den —,** against the grain; **es iſt ein guter — bis dahin,** it is a good way off; **auf den — gehen,** to go out to snare woodcock; to run after women (*sl.*); **einen — haben,** to be a fool; to be tipsy; **einen auf dem — haben,** to bear s.o. a grudge, to have a spite against s.o.; **das Schiff hält einen guten —,** the ship is a good sailer; **— von Eitelkeit,** touch of vanity; **kühner Pinſel—,** bold touch (*Paint.*); **— mit der Bürſte,** a brush; **guter Bogen—,** fine bowing (*Mus.*). **—eln,** *v.a.* to streak, mark with little lines. *Comp.* **—punkt,** *m.* semicolon. **—regen,** *m.* local rain, rain confined to a limited area. **—vogel,** *m.* bird of passage. **—weiſe,** *adv.* by lines *or* strokes; by dashes; in certain places, by zones; partially; in flocks *or* flights. **—zaun,** *m.* hurdled fence. **—zeit,** *f.* time of migration (*of birds*).

[2]**Strich, Stri'che,** *1 & 3 pers. sing. imperf. ind. & subj. of* **ſtreichen.**

Strick, *m.* (**—es,** *pl.* **—e**) cord, rope; line, string; leash; snare; halter, gallows; scapegrace; good-for-nothing, young rogue. **—bar,** *adj.* that can be knitted. *Comp.* **—leiter,** *f.* rope-ladder. **—ſchaukel,** *f.* rope-swing.

Strick'—en, *v.a.* to knit; to net; to ensnare; captivate, entwine; **Geſtrickte(s),** knitting, knitted work. **—er,** *m.* (**—ers,** *pl.* **—ers**), **—erin,** *f.* knitter. **—erei',** *f.* knitting. *Comp.* **—beutel,** *m.* knitting-bag. **—erlohn,** *m.* payment for knitting; cost of knitting. **—garn,** *n.* knitting yarn. **—haken,** *m.* hook for holding the thread when knitting. **—linie,** *f.* catenarian curve (*Math.*). **—maſche,** *f.* mesh. **—maſchine,** *f.* knitting-machine. **—muſter,** *n.* pattern for knitting. **—nadel,** *f.* knitting-needle. **—naht,** *f.* knitted seam; back-seam (*of stockings*). **—perle,** *f.* bead (for knitting). **—ſchule,** *f.* knitting-school. **—ſtrumpf,** stocking while it is being knitted. **—ſtuhl,** *m.* stocking(-maker's) loom. **—werk,** *n.* knitting; cordage, tackling, ropes. **—zeug,** *n.* necessaries *or* things for knitting; knitting.

Strie'gel, *m.* (**—s,** *pl.* **—**) curry-comb; flesh-brush. **—n,** *v.a.* to curry, comb, dress; to smooth, polish, clean; to cudgel; to ill-use, criticize, cut up.

Strie'm—e, *f.* (*pl.* **—en**) & *m.*, **—en,** *m.* (**—ens,** *pl.* **—en**) stripe; streak; mark *or* weal left by a whip *or* rod. **—ig,** *adj.* striped, streaked; covered with weals.

Strie'zen, *v.a.* to pilfer (*coll.*).

Striktu'r, *f.* (*pl.* **—en**) stricture (*Med.*).

Strip'pe, *f.* (*pl.* **—n**) (*dial.*) piece of string; string; strap, band.

Stritt, Strit'te, *1 & 3 pers. sing. imperf. ind. & subj. of* **ſtreiten.**

Stroh, *n.* (**—s**) straw; thatch; (**leeres**) **— dreſchen,** to waste one's words *or* labour; to flog a dead horse (*coll.*). **—e(r)n,** *adj.* of straw; empty, insipid, dull. **—ig,** *adj.* strawy. *Comp.* **—arbeit,** *f.* straw-work. **—band,** *n.* twist of straw. **—bett,** *n.* paillasse; straw-bed. **—blume,** *f.* artificial flower of straw; immortelle (*Bot.*). **—boden,** *m.* straw-loft. **—breche,** *f.* machine for breaking straw. **—bund,** *n.* truss of straw. **—butter,** *f.* winter butter. **—dach,** *n.* thatched roof; thatch. **—decke,** *f.* cover, layer of straw; straw-mat. **—decker,** *m* thatcher. **—fackel,** *f.* wisp of lighted straw **—farben, —farbig,** *adj.* straw-coloured. **—feilen,** *pl.* straw-packed files, German files. **—feuer,** *n.* fire of straw; fit of passion, transient ardour; **—feuer der Liebe,** short-lived love. **—flaſche,** *f.* flask *or* bottle in straw-case. **—flechter,** *m.* straw-plaiter. **—futter,** *n.* straw-fodder; straw-lining. **—gelb,** *see* **—farben.** **—halm,** *m.* blade of straw;

—hälmchen ziehen, to draw (straws as) lots; nach jedem —halme greifen, to catch at every straw. —hut, *m.* straw hat *or* bonnet. —hütte, *f.* thatched cottage. —junker, *m.* country squire. —kopf, *m.* simpleton, blockhead. —lade, *f.* splint cased in straw. —lager, *n.* straw bed. —latte, *f.* lath for a thatch. —leckwerk, *n.* graduation-house made of straw. —lehm, *m.* loam mixed with straw. —mann, *m.* man of straw; scarecrow; dummy (*at whist*); lay-figure. —pfeife, *f.* reed. —sack, *m.* paillasse; ach du gerechter —sack! good gracious! dear me! (*coll.*). —seil, *n.* straw-rope; matting (*Fort.*). —sitz, *m.* straw-bottom. —teller, *m.* table-mat; wicker plate-holder. —wein, *m.* sweet wine from grapes dried on straw, vin de paille. —wisch, *m.* whisk; wisp of straw (*put up as a warning*). —wittwe(r, *m.*) *f.* grasswidow(er); ich bin —wittwer, my wife is (away) from home.

Strolch, *m.* (—es, *pl.* —e(r)) idler, lounger; tramp, vagabond. —en, *v.n.* (*aux.* h. & s.) to stroll about (esp'lly in the comp'd. umher—en).

Strom, *m.* (—s, *pl.* Strö'me) large river; current, stream; flow, gush, flood; crowd; Berg —, torrent; Menschen —, throng of people; Ströme Blutes, streams of blood; Ströme von Thränen, flood of tears; elektrischer Strom, electric current; mit dem —e, with the stream; — von Worten, flow *or* volume of words; wider *or* gegen den — schwimmen, to swim against the stream. —er, *m.* (—ers, *pl.* —er) travelling craftsman *or* journeyman; tramp; farmer's apprentice *or* learner. *Comp.* —a'b, —ab'wärts, *adv.* down stream; with the tide *or* current, down the river. —anker, *m.* kedge-anchor. —anwohner, *m.* dweller near a river. —au'f, —auf'wärts, *adv.* up the river, against the stream. —aufseher, *m.* inspector of rivers. —bahn, *f.* deepest part, channel of a stream; line followed by the waters of a valley. —bau, *m.* anything built in a river. —enge, *f.* narrows of a river, gorge. —fall, *m.* descent of a river; cataract. —gang, *m.* current; sea-stream. —gebiet, *n.* bed of a river. —(geschwindigkeits)messer, *m.* galvanometer (*hydraulic gauge*). —karte, *f.* river-chart. —korb, *m.* weir. —kreis, *m.* circuit (*Electr.*). —regler, *m.* controller (in electric cars). —schiffer, *m.* waterman, boatman, ferryman. —schließer, *m.* circuit-closer (*Electr.*). —schnelle, *f.* rapidity of a current, rapid; (*pl.*) rapids. —stärke, *f.* intensity *or* force of a current (*Electr.*). —strecke, *f.* reach. —strich, *m.* axis of a stream; current of a stream. —sturz, *m.* cataract. —unterbrecher, *m.* circuit-breaker (*Electr.*). —weise, *adv.* in torrents. —wender, *m.* current-reverser, commutator (*Electr.*). —zeit, —tid (*dial.*), *f.* time of apprenticeship on a farm.

Strö'm—en, *v.n.* (*aux.* h. & s.) to stream, flow; to gush, run (*as blood*); to flock, crowd, rush; to pour; herab—en, to pour down; das Blut —te ihm nach dem Kopfe, the blood rushed to his head. —ling, *m.* small herring (*in the Baltic*). —ung, *f.* streaming; current; flood; revolutionäre —ung, revolutionary spirit *or* tendency.

Strontia'n, *m.* (—s) strontian; kohlensaurer —, strontianite; schwefelsaurer —, celestite.

Stron'tium, *n.* (—s) strontium (*Chem.*).

Stro'ph—e, *f.* (*pl.* —en) strophe; stanza, verse; —e und Gegen —e, strophe and antistrophe; sechszeilige —e, stanza consisting of six lines, sixain. —ig, *adj.*; ein drei —iges Gedicht, a poem consisting of three stanzas; ein gleich—iges Gedicht, a poem of similar stanzas. —isch, *adj.* strophic; consisting of stanzas; —ische und frei gebaute Gedichte, poems in stanzas and poems in irregular rhythms.

Stropp, *m.* (*pl.* —es, *pl.* —e) strop (*Naut.*).

Stros'se, *f.* (*pl.* —n) step, slope, gradation (*Min.*). *Comp.* —n=bau, *m.* working in reverse steps.

Strot'zen, *v.n.* (*aux.* h.) to be puffed up; to be swelled; to superabound; to abound in, swarm with, teem; to strut; to boast of, make a parade of; von Hochmut —, to be puffed up with pride. —d, *p.* & *adj.* swollen, distended; turgid; puffed up; exuberant; —de Segel, swelling sails; —d voll, crammed full, full to overflowing.

Stru'del, *m.* (—s, *pl.* —) eddy, whirlpool; vortex; rapids; gulf; abyss; pancake; — der Vergnügungen, whirl of amusements, round of pleasure.

Stru'del—n, *v.n.* (*aux.* h.) to boil, bubble; to whirl, eddy; to spout, gush; to bluster, fume; to proceed rashly, to muddle, blunder. *Comp.* —kopf, *m.* hot-headed person; hot-spur; muddler. —köpfig, *adj.* hot-headed; muddling.

Struktu'r, *f.* structure; texture (*of metals*). *Comp.* —formel, *f.* structural formula.

Strumpf, *m.* (—es, *pl.* Strüm'pfe) stocking; mantle (*incandescent gas*); sich auf die Strümpfe machen, to slip away, to make off; (*coll.*); Rot —, cardinal. *Comp.* —band, *n.* garter. —brett, *n.*, —form, *f.* stocking-stretcher. —fabrikant, *m.* stocking-maker. —flicker(in, *f.*), *m.* stocking-mender. —garn, *n.* yarn for knitting stockings. —handel, *m.* hosiery, stocking-trade. —händler, *m.* hosier. —handlung, *f.* hosiery shop. —hose, *f.* trousers and stockings combined, hose. —waren, *pl.* hosiery. —weber, —wirker, *m.* stocking-weaver. —wirkerei', *f.* hosiery. —(wirker)stuhl, *m.* stocking-loom.

Strunk, *m.* stalk (*of cabbage, etc.*); trunk; stump.

Struppie'rt, *adj.* disabled, lame, crippled.

Strup'p—ig, *adj.* rough, bristly; scrubby; shaggy, rugged. *Comp.* —bart, *m.* bristly, scrubby beard.

Struw'wel— (*in comp.*) —kopf, *m.* (*person with*) unkempt hair. —peter, *m.* shock-headed Peter.

Strychni'n, *n.* (—s) strychnine.

Stub'be, *f.* (*pl.* —n) stump of a tree; quart.

Stüb'chen, *n.* (—s, *pl.* —) little chamber; liquid measure. *Comp.* —vermieten, *n.* puss-in-the corner (*children's game*).

Stu'be, *f.* (*pl.* —n) room, chamber; sitting-room; that on which a building raised over a river rests; such a building itself; — und Kammer in eins, bed-sittingroom; die gute —, best room *or* parlour; the room to look at. *Comp.* —n=älteste(r), —n=aufseher, *m.* senior of the room (*Mil.*). —n=arbeit, *f.* work done in the house. —n=arrest, *m.* confinement to one's room; —n=arrest haben, to be confined to one's room. —n=bursche, *m.* room-mate, chum. —n=fliege, *f.* common fly. —n=gelehrsamkeit, *f.* book- *or* closet-learning. —n=gelehrte(r), *m.* book-worm. —n=genosse, *m.* fellow-lodger. —n=heizer, *m.* person who attends to the fires. —n=hocker, *m.* stay-at-home, stick-indoors. —n=leben, *n.* sedentary life, confined life. —n=luft, *f.* close *or* stuffy air. —n=mädchen, *n.* housemaid. —n=maler, *m.* house-decorator. —n=ofen, *m.* stove. —n=orgel, *f.* chamber-organ. —n=poesie, *f.* closet *or* artificial poetry. —n=rein, *adj.* of clean habits, clean (*of dogs*). —n=schlüssel, *m.* key of a room. —n=sitzer, *see* —n=hocker. —n=uhr, *f.* time-piece; clock.

Stü'ber, *m.* (—s, *pl.* —) stiver (*old coin*); filip.

Stuck, *m.* (—s) stucco.

Stück, *n.* (—es, *pl.* —e, *as measure* —) piece (*in*

all English senses); bit; fragment; action; trait, characteristic action; trick; item; narrative; point; circumstance; piece of business, affair; head (*of cattle*); number (*of a magazine*); article (*in a journal, etc.*); passage; plot, patch, butt (*of wine*); pat (*of butter*); (*piece of*) work; picture; salamander (*Metall.*); (*pl.*) title deeds; **aus einem —e bestehen,** to be all of one piece; **— für —,** piece by piece; **Zwei-Mark —,** two-mark piece; **ein gut(es) — Arbeit,** a good piece of work; **ein Musik —,** a piece of music; **sechs — Gläser,** 6 glasses; **wieviel Fische? acht —,** how many fishes? 8; **zwanzig — Vieh,** twenty head of cattle; (**wie viele Leute waren da?**) **ein —er sechzig,** (how many people were there?) about sixty (*vulg.*) [*lit.* **ein Stücker sechzig** *is short for* **ein Stück oder sechzig,** between one and sixty, right up to sixty, nearly sixty]; **ein —er tausend Dukaten,** some 1000 ducats (*vulg.*); **ein — von einem Gelehrten,** a bit of a scholar; **in vielen —en,** in many ways *or* points; **in diesem —e,** in this respect; **in einem —e (fort),** continuously, uninterruptedly, on the whole (*night, day, etc.*) through; **einem ein —(chen) spielen,** to play a p. a trick; **sich** (*dat.*) **große —e einbilden,** to think highly of o.s., to be conceited; **man hält große —e von ihm** *or* **auf ihn,** people have a high opinion of him; **du bildest dir zu große —e ein,** you are too conceited; **das ist kein hübsches — von ihm,** that is not nice of him; **Freundschafts—,** piece *or* act of friendship; **ein hübsches — Geld,** a nice little sum; **aus freien —en,** of one's own free will, voluntarily, spontaneously. **—chen,** *n.* (—**chens,** *pl.* —**chen**) little piece; scrap; pat (*of butter*); snatch; air (*Mus.*); trick; anecdote, characteristic story. **—ig,** *adj.* in pieces; **groß —ig,** in large pieces. *Comp.* **—arbeit,** *f.* work paid by the piece *or* job. **—bett,** *n.* **—bettung,** *f.* platform; battery (*Fort.*). **—bohrerei,** *f.* cannon-boring. **—(en)=butter,** *f.* butter in rolls *or* ½-pound pieces. **—faß,** *n.* butt, large cask (*of about 8 hogsheads*). **—fracht,** *f.* luggage, goods in packets *or* bales. **—gießerei,** *f.* cannon-foundry. **—gut,** *n. see* **—fracht**; gun-metal. **—hof,** *m.* park of artillery. **—hufe,** *f.* thirty acres of land. **—kappe,** *f.* apron (*Artil.*). **—keller,** *m.* casemate (*Fort.*); wine-cellar for barrels. **—kohle,** *f.* round coal. **—kugel,** *f.* cannon-ball. **—ladung,** *f.* gun-charge (*Artil.*). **—laffet(t)e,** *f.* gun-carriage. **—meister,** *m.* inspector of ordnance; gunner; master-workman. **—messing,** *n.* block-brass. **—metall,** *n.* gun-metal. **—patrone(n=hülse),** *f.* cartridge. **—pferd,** *n.* artillery horse. **—pforte,** *f.* port-hole. **—probe,** *f.* proving of a gun. **—richter,** *m.* cannon-pointer *or* lever. **—seil,** *n.* breeching-tackle (*Artil.*). **—verkauf,** *m.* retail selling *or* sale. **—verzeichnis,** *n.* inventory, schedule (*of artillery*). **—wagen,** *m.* tumbrel. **—wall,** *m.* battery. **—wärter,** *m.* storekeeper. **—weise,** *adv.* by the piece; piecemeal; retail. **—werk,** *n.* piece-work; imperfect work; **unser Wissen ist (nur) —werk,** our knowledge is very incomplete *or* but fragmentary. **—winkelmaß,** *n.* compass (*Artil.*). **—wischer,** *m.* sponge (*Artil.*). **—(en)=zucker,** *m.* lump sugar.

Stück'eln, *v.a.* to cut into small pieces.

Stü'cken, *v.a.* to cut in pieces, cut up; to piece, patch (*clothes*).

Stu'ckern, *v.n.* (*aux.* **h.**) to jolt.

Studen't, *m.* (—**en,** *pl.* —**en**) student, collegian; undergraduate; **— der Theologie,** student of divinity; **— der Rechte,** student of law; **— der Mathematik,** mathematical student; **— der alten Sprachen,** student of classics, classical student; **— der neueren Sprachen** *or* **Philologie,** student of modern languages, modern language student; **— der Naturwissenschaften,** science student; **eifriger —,** hard-working student, reading man. **—enhaft, —'isch,** *adj. & adv.* student-like. **—enschaft,** *f.* students (*coll.*); *see* **—entum. —entum,** *n.* (—**s**) student-life *or* habits. **—in,** *f.* (woman) student; **—en und —innen,** men and women students; **jede —in bezahlt,** each female student pays. *Comp.* **—en=futter,** *n.* almonds and raisins. **—en=kragen,** *m.* student's short cloak (*obs.*). **—en=jahre,** *pl.* years spent at college, undergraduate years, college days. **—en=mütze,** *f.* student's cap (*showing his club*); **—en=mütze und =mantel,** cap and gown. **—en=sprache,** *f.* students' slang. **—en=streich,** *m.* student's prank. **—en=tracht,** *f.* academicals; cap and gown (*esp. at Cambridge and Oxford*). **—en=verbindung,** *f.* students' club *or* association. **—en=zeit,** *f.* college time *or* days, undergraduate days.

Stu'd—ie, *f.* (*pl.* —**ien**) study (*of a painter*) (*pl.*) studies; pursuits. **—ie'ren,** I. *v.a. & n.* (*aux.* **h.**) to study; to be at college; **Medizin —ieren,** to study medicine; **er —iert die alten Sprachen,** he is reading classics; **wir —ierten zusammen,** we were at college together; **er —iert in Cambridge,** he is studying at Cambridge, he is a student at Cambridge; **auf eine S. —ieren,** to meditate (upon) s.th. (*obs.*); **er —iert unter Scherer,** he is attending Scherer's lectures. II. *subst.n.* studying. **—ie'rende(r),** *m.* student. **—ie'rt,** *p.p. & adj.* studied; premeditated, contrived; affected; **ein —ierter,** a man of education, a university man. **—io,** *m.* (—**ios,** *pl.* —**ios**), **—io'sus,** *m.* (—**iosus,** *pl.* —**iosen**) student; **Bruder —io,** student (*coll.*). **—ium,** *n.* (—**iums,** *pl.* —**ien,** —**ia**) (*obs.*) study, reading, literary pursuit; **eifriges —ium,** hard reading. *Comp.* **—ien=aufseher,** *m.* usher; superintendent of studies. **—ien=direktor,** *m.* director of studies; tutor, coach. **—ien=gang,** *m.* course of studies. **—ien=genosse,** *m.* fellow student. **—ien=jahre,** *pl.* years of study, college days. **—ien=kopf,** *m.* head for a study (*Paint.*). **—ien=rat,** *m.* educational council; member of an educational council. **—ien=reise,** *f.* artist's excursion *or* journey for the purpose of studying nature *or* works of art. **—ien=zeichnung,** *f.* study (*Draw., etc.*). **—ien=zeit,** *f.* time spent at college, undergraduate days; hours of reading, time allotted to study; term. **—ier'=lampe,** *f.* reading-lamp. **—ier'=stube,** *f.*, **—ier'=zimmer,** *n.* study; student's den (*coll.*). **—ier'=trieb,** *m.* love of study.

Stu'fe, *f.* (*pl.* —**n**) step, stair; degree; rank; grade; stage; shade, tint; notch, step (*cut in rock*); specimen (*of ore*); tuck; **eine hohe —,** a high degree; **—n der Komparation,** degrees of comparison; **—n der Töne,** musical intervals; **die höchste — des Glücks,** the height of happiness *or* good fortune; **erste — der Handlung,** first stage of the action (*dram.*). *Comp.* **—n=bahn,** *f.*, **—n=breite,** *f.* breadth of stairs. **—n=erz,** *n.* pure ore. **—n=folge,** *f.* gradation; flight of steps; scale; sequence. **—n=förmig,** *adj.* in the form of steps. **—n=jahr,** *n.* climacteric year. **—n=land,** *n.* land which rises terraces. **—n=leiter,** *f.* step-ladder; steps; scale. **—n=weise,** *adv.* by steps; by degrees, gradually.

Stuhl, *m.* (—**es,** *pl.* **Stüh'le**) seat; chair; stool; seat (*in a church*); close-stool; throne (*of the pope*); flag-staff, staff of a vane; truck (*Naut.*); evacuation of the bowels; **Dach—,** ridge-lead; **Glocken—,** belfry; **Kirchen—,** pew, seat; **Lehn —,** easy chair; **Lehr—,** chair, professorship.

Web—, loom; päpstlicher —, Holy See; Meister vom —e, master of the Lodge; einem den — vor die Thür setzen, to turn a p. out of doors, to break off abruptly all connection with a p.; nicht zu —e kommen können, to be unable to do *or* say what one wants (*sl.*). *Comp.* —bein, *n.* leg of a chair. —bezug, *m.* chair-covering. —drang, *m.* urgency to relieve the bowels. —entleerung, *f.* evacuation of the bowels. —feier, *f.*, —fest, *n.* festival of St. Peter. —flechter, *m.* cane-plaiter of chair-bottoms. —flecht=arbeit, *f.* caning of chairs. —gang, *m.* stool, excrement; action of the bowels. —geld, *n.* pew-rent. —gericht, *n.* secret tribunal. —herr, *m.* justiciary. —lehne, *f.* back of a chair. —macher, *m.* chair-maker. —meister, *m.* master of a lodge. —richter, *m.* presiding judge. —rolle, *f.* chair-caster. —schlitten, *m.* hand-sledge. —sitz, *m.* bottom of a chair. —trittleiter, *f.* library chair. —verhaltung, *f.* constipation. —vermieter(in, *f.*), *m.* person who lets out chairs. —wagen, *m.* basket-carriage; invalid chair. —zwang, *m.* obstruction in the bowels, tenesmus (*Med.*).

Stul'le, *f.* (*pl.* —n) slice of bread and butter; belegte (Butter) —, sandwich.

Stülp, (Stulp,) *m.* (—es, *pl.* —e) something turned up; brim (*of a hat*). —e, (Stulpe,) *f.* (*pl.* —en) *see* Stülp; boot-top; pot-lid; cuff. *Comp.* —handschuh, *m.* long glove *or* gauntlet; fencing-glove. —hut, *m.* hat with turned-up brim; cocked-hat. —nase, *f.* turned-up nose. —(en)=stiefel, *pl.* top-boots, boots with flexible tops.

Stül'p—en, *v.a.* to turn upside down *or* inside out; to turn up; to tilt (*a cart*); to put the lid on; den Hut auf den Kopf —en, to put one's hat carelessly on (one side of) the head.

Stumm, *adj.* dumb, mute; silent; ein —er, a mute; —es Spiel, by-play, dumb show; —es Klavier, dumb piano; —es h, silent h; diese Buchstaben sind —, these letters are not sounded *or* pronounced. —heit, *f.* dumbness.

Stum'mel, *m.* (—s, *pl.* —) stump; (fag-)end (*of a candle, etc.*); (—pfeife, *f.*) cutty pipe.

Stüm'per, *m.* (—s, *pl.* —) bungler, blunderer, dabbler. —ei', *f.* bungling, bad work. —haft, (—mäßig,) *adj.* unskilful, clumsy, bungling.

Stüm'pern, *v.a. & n.* (*aux.* h.) to bungle, botch; to strum.

Stumpf, I. *adj. & adv.* lopped, docked; stumpy; worn-out (*as a broom*); blunt, dull; obtuse; flat, flattened; insensible, apathetic; —er Reim, masculine rhyme; —er Versausgang, masculine ending of a line; —er Winkel, obtuse angle; für eine S. ganz — sein, to be quite indifferent to; die Zähne — machen, to set the teeth on edge; —er Kegel, truncated cone; —es Schwert, blunt sword; —e Stoß=rapiere, buttoned foils; — gerittenes Pferd, worn-out, used-up horse. II. *m.* (—es, *pl.* Stümp'fe) stump; short-end; — und Stiel, root and branch; mit — und Stiel ausrotten, to root out *or* destroy completely. —heit, *f.* bluntness, dulness; flatness; being on edge; stupidity. *Comp.* —eckig, *adj.* obtuse-angled. —ende, *n.* blunt end. —fuß, *m.* club-foot. —gasse, *f.* blind alley. —kegel, *m.* truncated cone. —näschen, *n.* little turn-up nose. —schwanz, *m.* docked tail. —sinn, *m.* stupidity. —sinnig, *adj.* dull, stupid. —werden, *n.* state of becoming blunt *or* dull; wearing off; loss of intellectual power and of interest in life. —winkelig, *adj.* obtuse-angled. —zahn, *m.* stump of a tooth.

Stund, Stün'de, *1 & 3 pers. sing. imperf. ind. & subj. of* stehen (*obs. & poet.*).

Stun'de, *f.* (*pl.* —n) hour; time, period; lesson; distance walked in an hour, about 2½ miles; in der elften —, at eleven; at the eleventh hour; von Stund' an, from that very hour, ever since then; zur Stund(e), now, at once; zu einer glücklichen —, in a happy hour; zur rechten —, at the right moment; —n geben, to give lessons, teach; — halten, to take, have a class; —n der Andacht, Pious Meditations (*title of a book*); die — hat geschlagen, the hour has struck; the day has come. *Comp.* —n=gebete, *pl.* the hours (*R. C.*). —n=geld, *n.* fee for instruction. —n=glas, *n.* hour-glass. —n=glocke, *f.* bell that rings out the hours. —n=kreis, *m.* horary circle (*Astr.*). —n=lang, *adj.* lasting one *or* several hours; for hours together. —n=lauf, *m.* course of time. —n=linie, *f.* meridian. —n=lohn, *m.* money paid for work by the hour. —n=plan, *m.* arrangement of one's time, (*school*) time-table. —n=rad, *n.* hour- *or* plate-wheel. —n=säule, *f.* cylindrical dial; mile-stone. —n=schlag, *m.* striking of the hour. —n=tafel, *f.* gnomonic table. —n=uhr, *f.* clock that marks the hours only. —n=weise, *adv.* by the hour; by lessons. —n=weiser, —n=zeiger, *m.* hour-hand; horoscope; dial. —n=winkel, *m.* horary angle (*Astr.*).

Stun'd—en, *v.a.* to time; einem eine Summe —en, to grant a p. delay in payment. —ung, *f.* respite, delay in paying. —ungs=frist, *f.* delay granted in the matter of payment. —ungs=gesuch, *n.* petition for respite of payment.

Stün'd—ig, *adj.* of an hour; vier —ig, lasting four hours. —lein, *n.* (—leins, *pl.* —lein) *dim. of* Stunde; Gott gebe ihm ein seliges —lein, God grant him an easy death. —lich, I. *adj.* hourly; vier—lich, every fourth hour. II. *adv.* from hour to hour.

Stür'be, *1 & 3 pers. sing. imperf. subj. of* sterben.

Sturm, *m.* (—es, *pl.* Stür'me) storm; tumult; rage, fury; rush, onset; assault (*Mil.*); —blasen, to sound the alarm; —läuten, to ring the alarm-bell; im —e sein, einen — haben, to be tipsy, to be beside oneself (*coll.*); — und Drang, irresistible ardour, impetuosity; Storm and Stress (*Lit.*); — laufen, to make an assault, to storm; eine Festung mit — nehmen, to take a fortress by storm; sie kamen — gelaufen, they advanced at the charge. *Comp.* —anlauf, *m.* charge, assault. —balken, —block, *m.* herisson (*Fort.*). —band, *n.* strap *or* string fastened to a cap *or* hat to keep it on. —block, —bock, *m.* battering-ram. —brett, *n.* storming-board, spring board (*Gymn.*). —brücke, *f.* bridge by which an attack is made. —dach, *n.* testudo (*Artil.*). —und=Drangperiode, *f.* revolutionary period in German literature (*from about 1770-1784*), period of Storm and Stress. —deich, *m.* breakwater. —fahne, *f.* banner *or* battle standard. —faß, *n.* fire-barrel (*used to defend a breach*). —fest, *adj.* tempest-proof. —flut, *f.* high tide raised by a storm. —frei, *adj.* sheltered from assault; ein —freies Fort, an unassailable fort. —glocke, *f.* tocsin, signal-bell. —haube, *f.* head-piece, morion (*Mil.*). —hut, *m. see* —haube; southwester; aconite (*Bot.*). —igel, *m.* spiked beam, herisson (*Fort.*). —klüver, *m.* storm-jib (*Naut.*). —kolonne, *f.* scaling-party. —laterne, *f.* wind-lantern. —laufen, *n.* assault; leaping from the storming-board (*gymn.*). —läufer, *m.* stormer; die —läufer, the assailers, storming-party. —leiter, *f.* scaling-ladder; quarter-ladder (*Naut.*). —lücke, *f.* breach in a wall. —marsch, *m.* march in double quick time, charge. —möwe, *f.* common gull. —pfahl, *m.* palisade. —pferd,

ten, *pl.* dead lights (*Naut.*). **—riemen,** *m.* chin-strap; *see* **—band.** **—schritt,** *m.* double quick step *or* march. **—schwalbe,** *f.*, **—vogel,** *m.* petrel, storm-bird; *pl.* procellarians. **—segel,** *n.* lug-sail. **—streichhölzer,** *pl.* wind-lucifers. **—voll,** *adj.* stormy, tempestuous. **—warnung,** *f.* storm-signal, storm-warning. **—wetter,** *n.* stormy weather; storm. **—wind,** *m.* storm, tempest, heavy gale.

Stür'm—en, *v.* I. *a.* to storm; to take by storm; to force; to pull down and destroy; to break (*images*). II. *n.* (*aux.* **h.**) to storm, be violent; to storm, advance to the attack; (*aux.* **s.**) to dash at, fall on; to storm about, rage; **in einen mit Bitten —en,** to besiege a p. with requests; **auf seine Gesundheit los —en,** to injure one's health, abuse one's constitution. **—end,** *p. & adj.* attacking; impetuous; violent; **die —enden,** the attacking party; **mit —ender Hand erobern,** to take by assault. **—er,** *m.* (**—ers,** *pl.* **—er**) assailant; violent *or* impetuous person; blusterer; bully; **—er und Dränger,** poets of the German Storm and Stress period (1770-1784). **—isch,** *adj. & adv.* stormy; impetuous.

Sturz, *m.* (**—es,** *pl.* **Stür'ze**) sudden fall, crash; somersault; waterfall, cataract; downfall, ruin; overthrow; disgrace (*of a minister, etc.*); lintel (*of doors, windows, etc.*); mantelpiece; stump (*of a tree, etc.*); broken shaft (*of a column*); impetuosity; **ein Glas auf einen — austrinken,** to empty a glass at one draught. *Comp.* **—acker,** *m.* land ploughed for the first time. **—bach,** *m.* torrent, rapid stream. **—bad,** *n.* shower-bath. **—furche,** *f.* first ploughing. **—güter,** *pl.* goods laden in bulk (*Naut.*). **—karren,** *m.* tumbrel. **—see,** *f.* heavy sea breaking over the deck. **—weg,** *m.* very steep path. **—wellen,** *pl.* breakers.

Stür'ze, *f.* (*pl.* **—e**) cover; lid; bell (*of a horn*); damper, extinguisher.

Stür'z—en, *v.a.* I. to hurl, throw, plunge, precipitate; to overturn; to overthrow; to pour, empty out; to tilt (*a cart*); to shoot (*rubbish*); to examine, count over (*cash*); to plough up (*land*); to put on (*a lid, etc.*); to toss off (*a glass*); to undo, ruin; **sie —te sich von einem Felsen herab,** she threw herself from a rock; **einen Minister, das Ministerium —en,** to overthrow a minister, the government; **ins Elend —en,** to ruin, to plunge into misery. II. *v.r. & n.* (*aux.* **s.**) to sink, be precipitous; to rush; to plunge; to fall upon; to gush; **sich in Schulden —en,** to plunge into debt; **Varus —te sich in sein Schwert,** Varus fell upon his sword; **sich in jemandes Arme (einem zu Füßen) —en,** to throw oneself into a person's arms (*at a p.'s feet*). III. *v.n.* (*aux.* **s.**) to fall (*suddenly and violently*); to tumble; to come down. IV. *subst. n.* violent fall; overthrow; breaking up (*of ground*).

Stu'te, *f.* (*pl.* **—n**) mare. **—rei',** *f.* (breeding-) stud. *Comp.* **—n=fohlen, —n=füllen,** *n.* foal, filly. **—n=knecht,** *m.* stud-groom.

Stutz, *m.* (**—es,** *pl.* **—e**) *see* **Stoß; auf den —,** all of a sudden, suddenly.

Stütz, *m.* (**—es,** *pl.* **—e**) turner's hand-rest. **—e,** *f.* (*pl.* **—en**) prop, stay, support; shore (*Naut.*); joist; sustainer, pillar, prop; **—(der Hausfrau),** lady's help. **—en,** *v.a.* to prop, stay, shore up; to sustain, support; to lean (*one's arm, etc.*); **sich auf eine S. —en,** to lean, depend, rest on, to rely on; **gestützt auf sein Recht,** strong in *or* relying on the justice of his cause. *Comp.* **—balken,** *m.* joist; wooden stay *or* support. **—brett,** *n.* supporting plank. **—gabel,** *f.* stay. **—holz,** *n.* prop, stay. **—mauer,** *f.* buttress; retaining-wall. **—pfeiler,** *m.* pillar, column; support. **—punkt,** *m.* fulcrum.

Stut'z—en, I. *v.n.* (*aux.* **h.**) to stop short; to hesitate; to be startled *or* taken aback; to prick up the ears (*as horses*); **bei, über etwas —en,** to stop short, be struck motionless with astonishment. II. *v.a.* to cut short; to lop (*trees, etc.*), crop (*dog's ears*); to cock (*a hat*); to put in order; to trim; to dress. III. *subst. n.* cropping, *etc.*; hesitation, stopping short. IV. *m.* (**—ens,** *pl.* **—en**) short rifle, carbine. **—er,** *m.* (**—ers,** *pl.* **—er**) fop, dandy; masher. **—erhaft,** *adj.* foppish. **—ern,** *v.n.* (*aux.* **h.**) to play the dandy. **—ertum,** *n.* habits of young men of fashion, dandyism. **—ig,** *adj.* startled; surprised, taken aback; **—ig machen,** to disconcert; **—ig werden,** to stop short, to prick up the ears. **—igkeit,** *f.* surprise; hesitation. *Comp.* **—ärmel,** *m.* short sleeve. **—bart,** *m.* turned up moustache. **—büchse,** *f.* short rifle, carbine; blunderbuss. **—degen,** *m.* hanger, short sword. **—flügel,** *m.* semi-grand piano-forte. **—glas,** *n.* low tumbler. **—handschuh,** *m.* mitten. **—kopf,** *m.* head with hair cut short; regulation-cut hair, short crop (*coll.*). **—lauf,** *m.* short rifled barrel (*of a gun*). **—nase,** *f.* snub nose. **—ohr,** *n.* cropped ear; animal with cropped ears. **—ohrig,** *adj.* crop-eared. **—perrücke,** *f.* bob-tail wig. **—rohr,** *n. see* **—büchse.** **—säbel,** *m.* cutlass. **—schere,** *f.* hedging-bill, garden shears. **—uhr,** *f.* mantel-piece clock, time-piece.

Styl, *see* **Stil.**

Sua'd—a, —e, *f.* (*pl.* **—en**), power of persuasion; gift of the gab; blarney.

Subalte'rn, *adj.* subaltern. **—e(r),** *m.* subaltern. *Comp.* **—offizier,** *m.* subaltern (*Mil.*).

Subhastatio'n, *f.* (*pl.* **—en**) sheriff's sale.

Subje'kt, *n.* (**—s,** *pl.* **—e**) subject (*Gram., Log.*); fellow; creature; **schlechtes —,** villain, blackguard. **—i'v,** *adj.* (*also* **sub'jektiv**) subjective; **—ives Verbum,** neuter verb. **—ivitä't,** *f.* subjectivity. *Comp.* **—s=kasus,** *m.* nominative case; case of the subject.

Subkutan'spritze, *f.* subcutaneous syringe.

Subli'm, *adj.* sublime. **—a't,** *n.* (**—ats,** *pl.* **—ate**) sublimate, mercuric chloride. **—ie'ren,** *v.a.* to sublimate (*Chem.*). *Comp.* **—ier'=ofen,** *m.* subliming furnace.

Submi'ß, *adj.* submissive. **—(ss)io'n,** *f.* submission; tender (*for a contract*). *Comp.* **—(ss)ions'=bedingungen,** *pl.* conditions attaching to a tender. **—(ss)ions'=offerte,** *f.* tender. **—(ss)ions'=strich,** *m.* line drawn lengthwise from the foot of a petition down to the signature(s). **—(ss)ions'=weg,** *m.*; **im —(ss)ions=wege vergeben,** to offer a contract by tender, to entrust the execution of some work to one who tenders for it, who submits the most satisfactory estimate.

Sub'rektor, *m.* sub-rector, vice-principal, senior assistant master at a grammar school (*obs.*).

Subsel'li—um, *n.* (**—ums,** *pl.* **—a** *or* **—en**) form, school bench, desk (*in schools*).

Subsi'dien, *pl.* subsidies. *Comp.* **—vertrag,** *m.* contract for, treaty with regard to subsidizing.

Subskrib—e'nt, *m.* (**—en'ten,** *pl.* **—en'ten**) subscriber (**auf eine S.,** to a th.). **—ie'ren,** *v.a.* (**auf eine S.**) to subscribe to a thing.

Subskriptio'n, *f.* (*pl.* **—en**) subscription. *Comp.* **—s=anzeige,** *f.* prospectus. **—s=schein,** *m.* receipt for subscription.

Substantie'll, *adj.* substantial.

Substa'nz, *f.* (*pl.* **—en**) substance, matter, stuff.

Sub'stantiv, *n.* (**—s,** *pl.* **—e**), **—um,** *n.* (**—ums,** *pl.* **—a**) substantive. **—isch,** *adj.* substantive.

Substituie'ren, *v.a.* (**einen einem**) to substitute (*one person for another*).

Subti'l, *adj. & adv.* subtile; subtle, cunning; delicate; **eine —e Behandlung,** a minute and careful treatment; **mit einem sehr — umge-**

hen müssen, to be obliged to treat a p. with great circumspection, to manage, humour s.o. **—itä't,** *f.* subtlety.

Subtra—hie'ren, *v.a.* to subtract. **—ktio'n,** *f.* subtraction.

Subven—ie'ren, *v.a.* to stay, help, assist, support. **—tionie'ren,** *v.a.* to subsidize.

Success—i'v, *adj.* successive. *Comp.* **—ions'=akte,** *f.* act of settlement (*Pol.*). **—ions'=berechtigt, —ions'=fähig,** *adj.* capable of inheriting *or* succeeding. **—ions'=krieg,** *m.* war of succession; **spanischer —ionskrieg,** war of the Spanish succession.

Succu'rs, *m.* (—(s)es) succour, help, reinforcements (*Mil.*).

Su'che, *f.* (*pl.* **—n**) search, quest; scent (*of dogs*); **auf die — gehen,** to go in search of.

Su'ch—en, *v.a.* & *n.* (*aux.* **h.**) to seek, search (*for*), go in quest (*of*); **ich habe, was Sie —en,** I have got what you want; **jemandes Verderben —en,** to plot a p.'s ruin; **was hast du hier zu —en?** what do you want here, what business have you here? **ich habe dabei nichts zu —en,** I have nothing to do with that; **das Weite —en,** to run away; **—! —!** at him! catch him! seek it out! **Händel mit einem —en,** to pick a quarrel with a p.; **das hätte ich nicht hinter** *or* **in ihm gesucht,** I did not think he could have done that; **(s)eine Ehre in einer S. —en,** to take a pride, glory in a th.; **er —t etwas darin, mich zu beleidigen,** he takes a pleasure in insulting me; **ich habe unter allen Menschen nach ihm gesucht,** I looked for him among all the people; **was —t er darunter?** what does he mean by that? **eine Stelle (ein Schreiber) wird gesucht,** Wanted, a situation (a clerk); **eine gesuchte Schreibart,** an elaborate *or* affected style; **das ist doch sehr ge—t,** that is surely very far-fetched; **gesuchte Waren,** fashionable goods; **das Gesuchte finden,** to find what one was looking for; **—et, so werdet Ihr finden,** seek and ye shall find (*B.*). **—er,** *m.* (**—ers,** *pl.* **—er**) seeker; probe; finder (*Opt.*). *Comp.* **—eisen,** *n.* probe. **—hund,** *m.* hound hunting by scent. **—ort,** *m.* passage dug between one shaft and another (*Min.*).

Sucht, *f.* (*pl. rarely* **Süch'te**) sickness, disease; passion, mania, rage; **fallende —,** falling sickness, epilepsy.

Süch'tig, *adj.* sickly, infirm, diseased; affected with a disease; malignant (*of ulcers*); having a mania for; **gelb—,** jaundiced; **eifer—,** jealous.

Su'ckeln, *v.a.* to go on sucking (*dial.*).

Sud, *m.* (**—es,** *pl.* **—e**) boiling; brewing; decoction. **—el,** *m.* (**—els,** *pl.* **—el**) puddle, pool; dirt, filth. **—elei',** *f.* dirty work; patching; patchwork; daubing; scribbling; filth. **—elhaft, —elig,** *adj.* dirty, filthy; slovenly. **—(e)ler,** *m.* (**—(e)lers,** *pl.* **—(e)ler**), **—lerin,** *f.* sloven, slut; dauber; bungler; scribbler; bad, sluttish cook.

Süd, *m.* (**—es**) (*poet. & in compds.*). **—en,** *m.* (**—ens,** *abbr.* **S.**) south; (*in comp.* =) south; southern; **— zum Osten,** south by east. **—lich,** *adj. & adv.* south, southern, meridional; **—liche Lage,** southern aspect; **—liche Richtung,** southerly direction; **—lichst,** southernmost; **—lich von Berlin,** (to the) south of B. *Comp.* **—bahn,** *f.* Southern railway. **—breite,** *f.* south latitude (*Geog.*). **—früchte,** *pl.* fruit from the South, tropical fruit. **—früchte=handlung,** *f.* Italian warehouse. **—grenze,** *f.* south(ern) frontier. **—kante,** *f.* southern bank *or* shore (*Naut.*). **—kreuz,** *n.* the Southern Cross. **—länder(in,** *f.*), *m.* inhabitant of a southern *or* tropical country. **—licht,** *n.* aurora australis. **—pol,** *m.* Antarctic pole. **—pol=expedition,** *f.* Antarctic expedition. **—polar'=länder,** *pl.* south polar regions. **—see,** *f.* Pacific (ocean); South Sea (*obs.*). **—see=länder,** *pl.* Australasia. **—sonne,** *f.* noon (*Naut.*). **—staaten,** *pl.* Southern States; **Krieg gegen die abgefallenen —staaten der Union,** War of Secession, American civil war (1861-1865). **—wärts,** *adv.* southward, to the south. **—wes'ter,** *m.* south-wester. **—west'lich,** *adj.* south-west(ern). **—wind,** *m.* south wind, southerly breeze.

Su'del—n, *v.a. & n.* (*aux.* **h.**) to do in a dirty *or* slovenly way; to daub; to scribble; to soil; to slur (*Typ.*). *Comp.* **—arbeit,** *f. see* **—elei.** **—koch,** *m.*, **—köchin,** *f.* sluttish cook. **—köcherei,** *f.* foul mess (*poet.*). **—wäsche,** *f.* linen got up dirtily.

Sud'=hütte, *f.* salt-works.

Suff, *m.* boozing, tippling (*sl.*); **an den — kommen,** to take to (*quiet*) boozing (*sl.*).

Süf'fig, *adj.* tasty, good (of wine *or* beer).

Suffi'x, *n.* (**—es,** *pl.* **—e**) suffix.

Suggerie'ren, *v.a.* to suggest; to influence a p.'s mind by suggestion.

Suggestiv'frage, *f.* leading question.

Suh'l—e, *f.* dirty puddle, wallow, slough. **—en, Süh'len,** *v.n. & r.* to roll o.s. *or* wallow in the mire; to befoul o.s.

Sühn'—bar, *adj.* expiable. **—barkeit,** *f.* possibility of being expiated. **—e,** *f.* atonement, expiation; reconciliation. **—en,** *v.a.* to conciliate; to expiate, atone for. **—er,** *m.* (**—ers,** *pl.* **—er**) atoner; expiater. **—ung,** *f.* reconciliation; propitiation, atonement. *Comp.* **—altar,** *m.* altar of expiation. **—bock,** *m.* scape-goat. **—e=versuch,** *m.* attempt at reconciliation. **—geld,** *n.* blood-money, money paid to atone for a murder. **—opfer,** *n.* expiatory sacrifice, atonement.

Sui'te, *f.* (*pl.* **—n**) suite; prank, lark, trick; **—n reißen,** to play tricks.

Sülf'meister, *see* **Sülzmeister.**

Sulph—(Sulf—)a't, *n.* (**—at(e)s,** *pl.* **—ate**) sulphate; salt-cake (*Chem.*). **—i'd,** *n.* (**—id(e)s,** *pl.* **—ide**) sulphide. **—ü'r,** *n.* (**—ürs,** *pl.* **—üre**) protosulphide (*of mercury*); protosulphuret (*of iron*). **—urö's,** *adj.* sulphurous.

Sul'tans— (*in comp.*) **—blume,** *f.* sultan-flower. **—laune,** *f.* a despot's whim. **—rosinen,** *pl.* sultanas.

Sul'z—e, Sül'z—e, *f.* salt liquor, pickle, brine; meat, *etc.*, pickled *or* salted; jelly; meat covered with a jelly; pickled pork; brawn; deer-lick; salt-works (*rare*). **—en,** *v.a.* to salt, pickle, corn; to preserve in jelly. *Comp.* **—er,** *m.* workman employed in salt-works. **—meister,** *m.* superintendent of salt-works.

Summ, Summ, *interj.* (*onomatopoetic*) buzz, buzz (*imitating the noise of insects*). *Comp.* **—mücke,** *f.* buzzing gnat *or* fly. **—vogel,** *m.* humming bird.

Sum'm—a, *f.* sum; **in —a,** in short, to sum up; **—a —arum,** sum total, grand total. **—a'nd,** *m.* (**—an'den,** *pl.* **—an'den**) term of a sum (*Alg.*). **—a'risch,** *adj.* summary; succinct; **—arisches Verfahren,** summary proceedings, short work. **—e,** *f.* (*pl.* **—en**) sum; amount; **eine fehlende —e ergänzen,** to make good a deficit; **die höchste —e,** maximum; **—e der Bewegung,** momentum. **—en, —ie'ren,** *v.a.* to sum up. *Comp.* **—episkopat,** *n.* (& *m.*) position as supreme head of the Protestant Church.

Sum'men, Sum'sen, *v.* I. *a. & n.* (*aux.* **h.**) to hum; **ein Liedchen —,** to hum an air. II. *n.* (*aux.* **h.**) to buzz; to ring; to tinkle.

Sumpf, *m.* (**—es,** *pl.* **Süm'pfe**) swamp, bog, marsh, fen, quagmire; sump (*Min.*); **— der Schändlichkeit,** sink *or* den of infamy; **eine Grube zu —e gehen lassen,** to flood a mine; **in den — geraten,** to get into bad ways (*fig.*); **im —e stecken,** to stick in the mud; **einen — austrocknen,** to drain a marsh **—ig,** *adj* marshy. *Comp.* **—bewohner**, *m.* dweller in a boggy *or* fen country. **—boden**, *m.* marshy ground. **—distel**, *f.* species of thistle (*Carduus palustris*). **—fieber**, *n.* malaria, marsh fever. **—gegend**, *f.* marshy country. **—huhn**, *n.* moor-hen; disorderly fellow, boozer (*sl.*). — **—lache**, *f.*, **—loch**, *n.* pool, quagmire. — **pflanze**, *f.* plant thriving on marshy ground. **—schild=kröte**, *f.* marsh turtle. **—schnepfe**, *f.* snipe. **—vogel**, *m.* wading bird, wader. — **wasser**, *n.* boggy water. **—wiese**, *f.* swampy meadow.

Süm'pfer, *m.* moulder (*in brick-making*).

Sums, *m.* (— (s)es) buzzing noise; empty talk, twaddle (*coll.*).

Sund, *m.* (—es, *pl.* —e) sound, strait; south (*dial.*).

Sün'd—e, *f.* (*pl.* —en) sin; offence. **—er**, *m.* (—ers, *pl.* —er) sinner; culprit; delinquent; **armer —er**, condemned criminal awaiting execution; **der Tod ist der —e Sold**, the wages of sin is death (*B.*); **es ist eine —e und eine Schande**, it is a wicked shame; **Gott verzeih mir die —e!** Heaven forgive me! **ich hasse ihn wie die —e**, I hate him like poison. **—haft**, **—ig**, *adj.* sinful, culpable; inclined to sin; **das —hafte**, iniquity. **—haftigkeit**, *f.* culpability, sinfulness. **—igen**, *v.a.* & *n.* (*aux.* h.) to (*commit a*) sin, to trespass; **was habe ich gesündigt?** what (wrong) have I done? **—iger**, *see* —er. **—igkeit**, *f.* sinfulness. **—lich**, *adj.* sinful; criminal; wrong; unlawful, impious. **—lichkeit**, *f.* iniquity, sinfulness. *Comp.* **—en=bahn**, *f.* way of sin, road to perdition. **—en=bock**, *m.* scape-goat. — **en=erlaß**, *m.* remission of sins, absolution. **—en=fall**, *m.* fall (*of man*). **—en=frei**, *adj.* free from sin. **—en=geld**, *n.* ill-gotten gain; very large sum of money (*coll.*). **—en=höhle**, *f.* the body (*obs.*). **—en=knecht**, *m.* slave of sin, hardened sinner. **—en=last**, *f.* burthen of sin. **—en=leben**, *n.* sinful *or* wicked life. **—en=lohn**, *m.* wages of sin. **—en=losigkeit**, *f.* innocence, sinlessness. **—en=lust**, *f.* love of sin *or* vice; sinful pleasure. **—en=maß**, *n.*; **sein —enmaß war voll**, the measure of his iniquities was full. **—en=register**, *n.* list of sins committed. **—en=schuld**, *f.* (sum of) trespasses. **—en=tilger**, *m.* Redeemer, Saviour. **—en=tilgung**, **—en=vergebung**, *f.* forgiveness of sins; absolution. **—en=voll**, *adj.* full of iniquity, sinful. **—er=glöcklein**, *n.* passing bell for a person to be executed. **—er=hemd**, *n.* hair shirt. **—flut**, *f.* the Flood; deluge; **vor der —flut**, **vor—flutlich**, antediluvian. **—opfer**, *n.* sin-offering. **—wasser**, *n.* water of purification.

Su'per—fein, *adj.* superfine. **—iorität**, *f.* superiority. **—intende'nt**, *m.* (*in Protestant churches*) superintendent (*a higher grade than the ordinary* '*Pastor*'). **—intendentu'r**, *f.* office of superintendent (*in Protestant churches*). **—kargo**, *n.* supercargo. **—klug**, *adj.* overwise; too shrewd; pert. **—lativ**, *m.* superlative. **—revision**, *f.* final revision; final proof (*Typ.*).

Supi'num. *n.* (—s, *pl.* —na) supine.

Sup'pe, *f.* (*pl.* —n) soup, broth; repast; **die rote —**, blood (*vulg.*); **die — ausessen müssen**, to have to abide by the consequences; **einem die — versalzen**, to spoil a p.'s pleasure, disappoint a p.; **einem eine — einbrocken**, to serve someone an ill turn; **einen Löffel — mit einem essen**, to take pot-luck with a p., to dine with a p. in a quiet way. *Comp.* **—n=anstalt**, *f.* soup-kitchen, people's kitchen. **—n=fleisch**, *n.* gravy-beef; meat from which soup is *or* has been made; boiled beef. **—n=koch**, *m.* maker of soups. **—n=kräuter**, *pl.* pot-herbs. **—n=löffel**, *m.* soup-ladle; table-spoon. **—n=marke**, *f.* ticket for a soup-kitchen (*for the poor*). **—n=napf**, *m.* soup-basin; soup-tureen. **—n=schüssel**, *f.* soup-basin. **—n=terrine**, *f.* soup-tureen. **—n=topf**, *m.* stock-pot; digester; pot for making soup; pot of soup.

Sup'pig, *adj.* souplike; soppy.

Supp—lik', *f.* petition. **—leme'nt=winkel**, *m.* supplementary angle. **—lizie'ren**, *v.a.* to supplicate, sue. **—onie'ren**, *v.a.* to think, presume, suppose.

Suprema't, *m.* & *n.* (—es), **—ie'**, *f.* supremacy.

Sur'de, *f.* (*pl.* —n) surd (*Math.*).

Suro'ne, **Sero'ne**, *f.* (*pl.* —n) seroon (*a kind of pannier or hamper of certain kinds of goods*).

Sur'ren, *v.n.* (*aux.* h.) to hum, buzz.

Surroga't, *n.* (—s, *pl.* —e) substitute; makeshift.

Surtou't, *m.* (—s, *pl.* —s) overcoat (*obs.*).

Suspen—die'ren, I. *v.a.* to suspend. II. *subst. n.* **—die'rung**, **—sio'n**, *f.* suspension. **—so'rium**, *n.* (—soriums, *pl.* —sorien) suspender; suspensory (*Surg.*).

Süß, *adj.* & *adv.* sweet; sweetened; **mein —es Lieb**, my darling love; **mein —es Herzblatt**, my own dear, my darling; **dein Leutnant ist —**, your lieutenant is a dear (*girls' sl.*); **—es Wasser**, fresh water; **—e Butter**, fresh butter; **—es Brot**, unleavened bread; **—e Speise**, sweets; pudding; **ein —es Herrchen**, a mealy-mouthed youth; a young fop, a namby-pamby fellow (*coll.*); **einem —e Worte geben**, to use sugared words; to speak s. o. fair; **—e Worte**, wheedling *or* winning words; **—e Thränen**, tears of joy. **—chen**, *n.* (—chens, *pl.* —chen) sweetmeat; sweetheart, darling. **—e**, *f.* sweetness. **—eln**, *v.n.* (*aux.* h.) to be nauseously sweet; to be fulsomely polite; to be insipid *or* prudish. **—en**, *v.a.* to sweeten. **—igkeit**, *f.* (*pl.* —igkeiten) sweetness; suavity; sweet thing. **—lich**, *adj.* sweetish; mawkish; fulsome. **—lichkeit**, *f.* sweetishness, lusciousness; sickening sweetness. **—ling**, *m.* (—lings, *pl.* —linge) flatterer, sweet-talking person; fop. *Comp.* **—apfel**, *m.* sweet apple. **—brot**, *n.* unleavened bread. **—flöte**, *f.* soft flute (*in organs*). **—holz**, *n.* licorice; **—holz raspeln**, to pay compliments, say soft things, to flirt. **—holz=raspler**, *m.* spoon(ey); (male) flirt. **—holz=wurzel**, *f.* licorice-root. **—liebchen**, *n.* darling. **—mandel=öl**, *n.* oil of sweet almonds. **—maul**, *n.* sweet-tooth. — **milch=käse**, *m.* cheese made from sweet milk. **—sauer**, *adj.* bittersweet, sour-sweet. **—teig**, *m.* unleavened dough. **—wasser**, *n.* fresh water.

Sykomo're, *f.* (*pl.* —n) Egyptian sycamore.

Sykopha'nt, *m.* (—en, *pl.* —en) sycophant. — **ie'**, *f.* sycophancy.

Syl'be, *see* Silbe.

Syllog—is'mus, *m.* (—, *pl.* —ismen) syllogism. **—is'tisch**, *adj.* syllogistic.

Syl'ph—e, **—i'de**, *f.* (*pl.* —en, —iden) sylph.

Sylves'ter=abend, *m.* New Year's Eve (*Pope Sylvester I. died Dec. 31, 335*). **—nacht**, *f.* New Year's Night.

Symbo'l—ik, *f.* symbolism. **—isch**, *adj.* symbolical. **—isie'ren**, *v.a.* to symbolize

Symmet—rie', *f.* symmetry. **—risch** (*pron.* symme'trisch), *adj.* symmetrical.

Sympath—e'tisch, *adj.* & *adv.* sympathetic; mysterious, miraculous. **—ie'**, *f.* sympathy. **—isch** (*pron.* sympa'thisch), *adj.* sympathetic, congenial, kindred-souled.

Symptoma'tisch, *adj.* symptomatic.

Synago'ge, *f.* (*pl.* —n) synagogue.

Synchron—is'mus, *m.* synchronism. **—is'tisch**, *adj.* synchronous.

Syndika't, *n.* (—s, *pl.* —e) syndicate.

Syn'dikus. (—, *pl.* —(ss)e), *m.* syndic.

Syn'kop—e, *f.* (*pl.* **—en**) syncope. **—ie'ren**, *v.a.* to syncopate (*Mus. etc.*).
Syno'd, *m.* (**—(e)s**, *pl.* **—e**) ecclesiastical council (*in Russia*). **—e**, *f.* (*pl.* **—en**) synod. **—isch**, *adj.* synodical (*Ast.*). *Comp.* **—al'=beschluß**, *m.* decision of a synod.
Synony'm—ik, *f.* synonymy, synonymics, study of synonyms. **—(isch)**, *adj.* synonymous, synonymic; **—isches Wörterbuch**, dictionary of synonyms.
Synop'tisch, *adj.* synoptic(al); **die —en Evangelien**, the synoptic gospels, the synoptics.
Syntak'tisch, *adj.* syntactical.
Synthe'—se, *f.* synthesis. **—tisch**, *adj.* synthetic.
Syste'm, *n.* (**—s**, *pl.* **—e**) system; jurisdiction (*Free-m.*). **—a'tiker**, *m.* (**—atikers**, *pl.* **—atikere**) systematic person. **—a'tisch**, *adj. & adv.* systematic. **—atisie'ren**, *v.a. & n.* (*aux.* **h.**) to systematize. *Comp.* **—los**, *adj.* unsystematic, unmethodical.
Sze'ne, *see* **Scene**.

T

For words not found under **T** *look under* **D**. *Many words formerly spelt with initial* **Th** *are now given* (*according to the new spelling*) *under simple* **T**. *See also the Preface.*

T, t, *n.* T, t; *for abbr. see the Index of abbreviations at the end of the German-English part. Comp.* **T=Binde**, T-bandage; **T=Schiene**, T-rail; **T=Schwelle**, T-sill; **T=Winkel**, T-square.
Tabagie', *f.* (*pl.* **—en**) smoking-room (in a public house), smoking-den (*obs.*).
Ta'bak, (**Taba'ck**, *obs.*,) *m.* (**—s**, *pl.* **—e**) tobacco; **Schnupf—**, snuff; **lang=geschnittener (kurz=geschnittener) —**, shag (cut tobacco); **von Anno —** (*or* **To'ba(c)k**) **her**, since the year 1; **das ist starker —**, that is hard to swallow *or* believe, that is rather too strong, that 's too much for me. *Comp.* **—(s)=bau**, *m.* cultivation of tobacco. **—(s)=beize**, *f.* tobacco-juice. **—(s)=beutel**, *m.* tobacco-pouch. **—(s)=bruder**, *m.* confirmed smoker. **—(s)=dose**, *f.* tobacco-box; snuff-box. **—(s)=gesellschaft**, *f.* smoking-party. **—(s)=händler**, *m.* tobacco-merchant; tobacconist. **—(s)=kollegium**, *n.* smokers' club; Tobacco Parliament of King Frederick William I. of Prussia. **—(s)=laden**, *m.* tobacconist's shop. **—monopol**, *n.* tobacco-monopoly. **—(s)=pfeife**, *f.* pipe. **—(s)=qualm**, *m.* tobacco-smoke. **—(s)=regie**, *f.* administration of the tobacco monopoly, levying tobacco-duties. **—spinner**, *m.* tobacco-dresser *or* twister. **—(s)=stube**, *f.* smoking-room.
Tabell—a'risch, *adj.* tabular, in form of tables; **—arische Übersicht**, tabulated view *or* statement.
Tabel'le, *f.* (*pl.* **—n**) table, index, synopsis; **in —n bringen**, to tabulate, make an index of.
Ta'bernakel, *n.* (**—s**, *pl.* **—**) tabernacle.
Tabul—a't, *n.* (**—ats**, *pl.* **—ate**) wooden floor; wainscotting. **—atu'r**, *f.* tablature (*Mus.*). **—e'tt**, *n.* (**—et'tes**, *pl.* **—et'te**) pedlar's box. *Comp.* **—ett'=kram**, *m.* pedlar's ware. **—ett'=krämer**, *m.* pedlar.
Tabure'tt, *n.* (**—(e)s**, *pl.* **—e**) foot-stool
Tachygraphie', *f.* tachygraphy, shorthand.
Ta'del, *m.* (**—s**) blame, censure, reproof, rebuke, reproach · reprimand, censure; fault; bad mark (*in schools*); **— finden an** (*dat.*) to find fault with; **Ritter ohne Furcht und —**, knight without fear or reproach (Bayard); **ohne —**, blameless, faultless. **—bar, —haft**, *adj.* blamable; faulty; reprehensible. **—ei'**, *f.* constant fault-finding; nagging. **—haftigkeit**, *f.* blamableness. *Comp.* **—frei, —los**, *adj.* irreproachable; excellent, splendid, perfect; **—lose Exemplare**, perfect specimens, perfect copies. **—losigkeit**, *f.* blamelessness. **—lust, —sucht**, *f.* love of fault-finding, censorious spirit. **—rede**, *f.*, **—wort**, *n.* reproof. **—s=votum**, *n.* vote of censure. **—süchtig**, *adj.* censorious; nagging.
Ta'deln, I. *v.a.* to blame, find fault with, censure; **einen wegen einer S. —**, to rebuke s. o. for something; **an allem etwas zu — finden**, to find fault with everything; **— ist leichter als Bessermachen**, it is easier to find fault than to do better. II. *subst.n.* blame, censure. *Comp.* **—s=wert, —s=würdig**, *adj.* blameworthy.
Tad'ler, *m.* (**—s**, *pl.* **—**), **—in**, *f.* fault-finder, critic.
Ta'fel, *f.* (*pl.* **—n**) table; tablet; slab; plate, sheet; roll; index, register; cake (*of chocolate*); plinth; flag-stone; panel; board; dinner-table, table; **Wand—**, blackboard; **große — bei Hofe**, court dinner-party; **bei —**, at table, at dinner; **freie — haben bei . . .**, to board free with . . .; **die — decken**, to lay the cloth *or* the table. *Comp.* **—arbeit**, *f.* panelling. **—artig**, *adj.* tabular. **—aufsatz**, *m.* centre-piece. **—besteck**, *n.* (*case containing*) knife, fork and spoon. **—blei**, *n.* sheet-lead. **—brot**, *n.* bread for the table, rolls. **—butter**, *f.* best butter (*for the table*). **—decker**, *m.* officer in a prince's household who has charge of the table linen and lays the table. **—diener**, *m.* waiter; (*at table*); footman. **—förmig**, *adj.* tabular; **—förmiges Klavier**, square piano. **—freuden**, *pl.* pleasures of the table. **—freund**, *m.* epicure, lover of good living. **—gedeck**, *n.* (*set of*) table linen. **—gelder**, *pl.* allowance for board, table money. **—geschirr**, *n.* dinner service, plate. **—glas**, *n.* plate-glass. **—klavier**, *n.* square piano. **—knecht**, *m.* dumb-waiter. **—land**, *n.* plateau, table-land. **—musik**, *f.* music played during a repast. **—obst**, *n.* dessert (*fruit*). **—runde**, *f.* Round Table; **unsere gewöhnliche gemütliche —runde**, our usual party. **—scheibe**, *f.* sheet *or* pane of glass. **—schiefer**, *m.* slate in slabs. **—service**, *f.* table-service, service of plate. **—stein**, *m.* table-cut precious stone. **—stift**, *m.* slate pencil. **—tuch**, *n.* table-cloth. **—weise**, *adv.* in tables. **—werk**, *n.* wainscotting. **—zeug**, *n.* table-linen; plate.
Tä'fel—chen, *n.* (**—chens**, *pl.* **—chen**) *dim. of* **Tafel**, *q.v.*; lozenge. **—n**, *v.a.* to floor, inlay a floor; to wainscot. **—ung**, *f.* inlaying (*of floors*); panelling; wainscotting. *Comp.* **—holz**, *n.* wainscotting; panelling. **—werk**, *n.* *see* **—ung**.
Ta'feln, *v.* I. *a.* to put on the table. II. *n.* (*aux.* **h.**) to dine, sup, banquet; **gern —**, to be fond of the pleasures of the table.
Taf'fet, Taft, *m.* (**—es**, *pl.* **—e**) taffeta. **—en**, *adj.* of taffeta. *Comp.* **—band**, *n.* sarsnet ribbon. **—weber**, *m.* manufacturer of taffeta.
Tag, *m.* (**—es**, *pl.* **—e**) day; daylight; open air; **es ist (heller) —**, it is broad day(light); **der jüngste —**, the Last Day, Doomsday; **der — des Herrn**, the Lord's day; **heutigen (heutiges) —(e)s**, at the present time; to-day; **einen — um den andern**, every other day; **eines —es**, once, one day; **eines schönen —es**, one fine morning; **den ganzen — über**, the whole day long; **— für —, einen — nach dem andern**, day after day, daily; **am hellen, lichten —e**, in broad daylight; **am —e liegen**, to be manifest, clear; **an den — bringen, legen**, to bring to light, disclose, make manifest; **an den — kommen**, to come to light; **zu —e streichen**, to crop out (*Min.*); **zu —e fördern**, to unearth, extract; to bring to light; **zweimal des —es**, twice a day; **es wird —**,

day is breaking; es ist noch früh am —e, it is still early; —s darauf, folgender —, morgiger —, the next day, the day after; den ganzen geschlagenen —, the livelong day; heute über acht —e, this day week; sich (dat.) einen guten — machen, to enjoy o.s., to take it easy; to take a holiday; er hat gute —e, he has a pleasant life, a fine time of it; er hat heute seinen guten —, he is in a good mood to-day; dieser —e, in diesen —en, one of these days; nächster —e, shortly, one of these days; in meinen —en, in my time; in den — hinein, at random, recklessly, from day to day; Jahr und —, a year and a day, a long time; vor Jahr und —, a long time ago; man soll den — nicht vor dem Abend loben, don't halloo till you are out of the wood (prov.). —es, see Tages (in comp.). Comp. (the forms with e are as a rule North German, those without e South German). —(e)=arbeit, f. day-labour; work by the day; daily task. —(e)=arbeiter, m. day-labourer. —(e)=arbeiterin, f. charwoman. —e=bau, m. open working (Min.). —(e)=blatt, n. daily paper; pl. dailies. —blind, adj. seeing only or best at night. —(e)=buch, n. day-book, journal; diary. —(e)=dieb, m. idler, sluggard. —ei'n, —au's, adv. every day of the week, daily. —(e)=falter, pl. butterflies. —(e)=futter, n. ration. —(e)=gelder, pl. daily allowance. —hell, adj. clear as day. —hemd, n. day-shirt (for men), chemise (for women). —(e)=lang, adj. for days (together). —e=lied, n., —e=weise, f. morning-song, alba (of the Minnesinger). —(e)=lohn, m. day's wages. —(e)=löhner, m. workman, labourer working by the day. —(e)=löhnerin, f. charwoman. —(e)=löhnern, v.n. (aux. h.) to work by the day. —(e)=marsch, m. day's march. —und=Nachtgleiche, f. equinox. —(e)=reise, f. day's journey; journey by day. —satzung, f. (Swiss) Diet. —(e)=schicht, f. day-shift (Min.). —täg'lich, adj. usual, daily, day in, day out. —täg'lichkeit, f. every-day occurrence. —(e)=wache, f. guard for the day; morning-watch (Naut.); die —ewache schlagen, to beat the reveille (Mil.). —s=über, adv. during the day. —weise, adv. by the day. —(e)=werk, n. day's work; daily task; measure of land.

Ta'ges— (in comp.) —an'bruch, m. break of day, daybreak. —angabe, f. date. —arbeit, f. day's work. —befehl, m. order of the day, general order. —bericht, m. daily report; news of the day. —billet, n. ticket (available) for the day. —büreau, n. box-office (Theat.). —fragen, pl. questions of the day. —grauen, n. dawn. —helle, f. light of day. —kasse, f. see —bureau; day's receipts. —kurs, m. rate of exchange on a day. —licht, n. daylight; ans —licht kommen, to appear, become known. —litteratur, f. current literature. —neuigkeiten, pl. news of the day. —ordnung, f. order of the day, agenda. —post, f. daily post. —zeit, f. time of day; zu jeder —zeit, at any hour; bei guter —zeit ankommen, to arrive early or at an early hour; einem die —zeit bieten, to say 'good morning' (afternoon, evening) to a person.

Tä'g—ig, suff. (in comp.); drei—ig, lasting three days; vierzehn —iges Kind, child fourteen days old, child of fourteen days. —lich, adj. & adv. daily; every day, per diem; quotidian; ordinary, every-day; vierzehn —liche Lieferung, fortnightly delivery or part.

Taifu'n, Teifu'n, m. (—s, pl. —e) typhoon.

Tail'l—e, f. (pl. —en) waist; bodice, body (of a dress); ein Mädchen um die —e fassen, to put one's arm round a girl's waist. —ie'ren, v.a. to cut (cards).

Ta'kel, n. (—s, pl. —) tackle (Naut.). —a'ge, f. see —werk. Comp. —garn, n. tarred twine. —haken, m. tackle-hook. —meister, m. rigger; boatswain. —werk, n. rigging, tackle. —zeug, n. riff-raff (coll.).

Takt, m. (—es, pl. —e) time, measure (Mus.); see —strich; tact; — halten, to keep time; nach dem —e tanzen, to keep good time in dancing; aus dem —e bringen, to put out of time; to disconcert; im —e marschieren, to march in time, keep in step; den — angeben or schlagen, to beat the time; ¾ —, three-four time. —ie'ren, v.a. & n. to beat time. Comp. —art, f. measure; time. —bezeichnung, f. time-signature, indication of the time. —einteilung, f. assigning the proper time-value to notes (Mus.). —fest, adj. steady in keeping time; firm of purpose, consistent. —festigkeit, f. steadiness with regard to time. —führer, m. conductor (Mus.). —gefühl, n. tactfulness, delicacy of feeling. —los, adj. tactless, without tact, indiscreet, injudicious, ill-advised, in bad taste. —losigkeit, f. want of tact, bad taste; indiscretion; eine — losigkeit begehen, to commit an indiscretion; to act in bad form (coll.). —mäßig, adj. in good time, well-timed; rhythmical (Mus., Danc.); regular. —messer, m. metronome. —note, f. semibreve (Mus.). —pause, f. bar-rest. —schlagen, n. beating time. —schritt, m. measured (or dance-)step. —stock, m. conductor's baton. —strich, m. bar. —voll, adj. tactful, discreet, judicious, of delicate feeling.

Tak'tik, f. tactics. —er, m. (—ers, pl. —er) tactician.

Tak'tisch, adj. tactical.

Tala'r, m. (—s, pl. —e) robe (of a lawyer); clergyman's gown.

Tale'nt, n. (—es, pl. —e) talent (money); talent (B.); talent, natural gift, aptitude, capacity; erworbenes —, acquirement, accomplishment; attainment; er hat kein — zu . . ., he has no talent or gift for . . . Comp. —los, adj. without talent or ability, not gifted. —voll, adj. talented, gifted, of great parts.

Talg, m. (—(e)s) tallow; grease; fat. —en, v. I. n. (aux. h.) to yield tallow; to form cakes of fat. II. a. to grease with tallow. —icht (obs.), —ig, adj. tallowy; covered with tallow or grease. Comp. —artig, adj. tallowy. —drüsen, pl. sebaceous glands. —fett, n. stearin(e). —grieben, pl. tallow-greaves. —händler, m. tallow-chandler. —licht, n. tallow candle. —säure, f. stearic or sebacic acid. —stoff, m. stearin(e).

Tal'je, f. (pl. —n) tackle; große —, main tackle. Comp. —reep, n. lanyard (Naut.).

Talk, m. (—(e)s, pl. —e) talc, talcum. Comp. —artig, adj. talcky, talcous, talcose, of the nature of talc. —erde, f. magnesia. —gebirge, —gestein, n. talc rocks. —glimmer, m. laminar talc. —schiefer, m. talc slate. —spat, m. magnesite. —stein, m. soapstone. —thon, m. talcous clay.

Tal'mi— (in comp.) —gold, n. Talmi-gold, Abyssinian gold; sham. —graf, m. sham-count, bogus-count, would-be aristocrat.

Tal'mud, m. (—s) Talmud.

Talmu'disch, adj. Talmudic(al).

Tamarin'de, f. (pl. —n) tamarind.

Tamaris'ke, f. (pl. —n) tamarisk.

Tam'bour, m. (—s, pl. —e) drummer; drum; tambour (Arch., Fort.). —i'n, n. (—ins, pl. —ine) tambourine (Mus.); small drum; tambour-frame. —ie'ren, v.a. to tambour. Comp. —in'=schläger, m. player on the tambourine. —ier'=nadel, f. tambour-needle, embroidery-needle. —major, m. drum-major.

Tand, m. (—es) toy; trifle, bauble; prattle, idle talk; nonsense; vanity.

Tändel—ei', *f.* dallying, trifling, toying; dawdling; flirtation, spooning. **—er, Tänd'l—er,** *m.* (**—ers**, *pl.* **—er**) trifler; dawdler. **—haft, —ig,** *adj.* trifling, dallying, playful; frivolous. **—n,** *v.n.* (*aux.* **h.**) to dally, to trifle; to flirt; to lounge, idle about; to dawdle; to flirt. *Comp.* **—markt,** *m.* rag-fair; jumble-sale. **—schürze,** *f.* fancy-apron. **—wochen,** *pl.* honey-moon.

Tang, *m.* (**—es**, *pl.* **—e**) sea-weed, fucus.

Tang—e'nt, *m.* (**—en'ten**, *pl.* **—en'ten**) jack (*of a harpsichord*). **—en'te,** *f.* (*pl.* **—enten**) tangent (*Math.*). **—ie'ren,** *v.a.* to touch; to touch upon. *Comp.* **—en'ten=bussole,** *f.* tangent-compass. **—en'ten=viereck,** *n.* quadrilateral (*or* four-sided figure) formed by the tangents of a circle.

Tann, *m.* (**—(e)s**, *pl.* **—e**) forest (*obs. & poet.*). **—e,** *f.* (*pl.* **—en**) (silver) fir, abies; **gemeine —e,** silver fir. **—en,** *adj.* fir. **—icht,** *n.* (**—ichts**, *pl.* **—ichte**) fir-plantation. **—ig,** *adj.* planted with firs; fir. **—i'n,** *n.* (**—ins**) tannin, tannic acid. *Comp.* **—en=baum,** *m.* fir-tree, abies alba. **—en=brett,** *n.* deal board. **—en=gehölz,** *n.* fir-grove. **—en=harz,** *n.* resin from fir-trees. **—en=holz,** *n.* fir-wood, deal. **—en=nadeln,** *pl.* needles of the fir. **—en=wald,** *m.* fir-wood. **—(en)=zapfen,** *m.* fir-cone.

Tan'tal, *n.* (**—s**) tantalum. *Comp.* **—säure,** *f.* tantalic acid.

Tan'te, *f.* (*pl.* **—n**, *dim.* **Tant'chen,** *n.*) aunt; **— Voß,** the Vossische Zeitung (*popular Berlin newspaper*) (*coll.*); **— Anstand,** Mrs. Grundy.

Tantieme, *f.* (*pl.* **—n**) share, portion; author's rights (*in a play*), royalty (*in a book*).

Tanz, *m.* (**—es**, *pl.* **Tän'ze**) dance; ball; brawl, fray; war, fight (*poet.*); row; **einen — mit einem wagen,** to engage in a contest with a p.; **da ging der — los,** then the row began (*coll.*); **der blutige —,** war; **zum —e auffordern,** to ask to dance; **— im Zimmer,** carpet dance. **—bar,** *adj.* danceable.

Tänz'—chen, *n.* (**—chens**, *pl.* **—chen**) little *or* quiet dance, hop. **—eln,** *v.n.* (*aux.* **h.**) to trip, skip, hop, caper; to amble (*of horses*). **—er,** *m.* (**—ers**, *pl.* **—er**), **—erin,** *f.* (dancing) partner; dancer. **—erei',** *f.* wild dancing. **—erlich,** *adj.*; **es war mir gar nicht —erlich (zu Mute),** I was not at all in a dancing mood. **—erschaft,** *f.* dancer's calling; dancers (*coll.*); corps de ballet.

Tan'z—en, *v.a. & n.* (*aux.* **h.** & **s.**) to dance; **nach der Geige —en,** to dance to the fiddle; **einen zu Boden —en,** to knock a p. down in dancing; **sich müde —en,** to tire oneself with dancing; **—en wollen, wenn die Musik aufhört,** to come a day after the fair (*prov.*). **—erei',** *f.* continual dancing. *Comp.* **—bär,** *m.* dancing bear. **—bein,** *n.*; **das —bein schwingen,** to dance, hop, to foot it (*coll.*). **—belustigung,** *f.* merry dance; (public) ball. **—boden,** *m.* dancing-room; public ball-room (*generally for artisans, peasants, etc.*). **—fest,** *n.* ball. **—gefährte,** *m.*, **—gefährtin,** *f.* partner (*at a dance*). **—gesellschaft,** *f.* dancing-party, dance. **—karte,** *f.* programme. **—klapper,** *f.* castanet. **—kneipe,** *f.* public-house where dancing is allowed. **—kränzchen,** *n.* dancing club. **—kunst,** *f.* art of dancing. **—lehrer,** *m.* dancing master. **—lied,** *n.* dancing-song. **—lokal,** *n. see* **—boden.** **—lust,** *f.* love of dancing. **—musik,** *f.* dance music. **—platz,** *m.* open space for dancing. **—schritt,** *m.* dance-step. **—schuh,** *m.* dancing shoe; pump. **—tour,** *f.* figure. **—unterricht,** *m.* dancing lessons. **—vergnügen,** *n.* ball (of the lower classes *or* of a very simple character); carpet dance. **—wut,** *f.* dancing mania.

Ta'perig, *adj.* awkward, clumsy (*coll.*).

Tape't, *n.* (**—s**) carpet; **aufs — bringen,** to broach *or* introduce a subject, to bring s.th. upon the tapis; **aufs — kommen,** to come under discussion. **—e,** *f.* (*pl.* **—en**) tapestry; paper-hangings, wall-paper, paper. *Comp.* **—en=bahn,** *f.* single breadth of wall-paper. **—en=behang,** *m.* tapestry; hangings, wall-paper. **—en=borte, —en=kante,** *f.* border of a wall-paper. **—en=fabrik,** *f.* manufactory of wall-paper. **—en=händler,** *m.* dealer in wall-paper; decorator. **—en=leiste,** *f.* paper-border. **—en=nagel,** *m.* tack; brass-headed nail. **—en=papier,** *n.* wall-paper. **—en=rahmen,** *m.* tapestry-frame. **—en=thür,** *f.* hidden door, door covered with paper. **—en=weber, —en=wirker,** *m.* tapestry-maker.

Tapezie'r, *m.* (**—s**, *pl.* **—e**), **—er,** *m.* (**—ers**, *pl.* **—er**) upholsterer; paperhanger. **—en,** *v.a.* to hang *or* fit with tapestry; to (hang with) paper; **neu —en,** to repaper. **—ung,** *f.* papering (*of walls, rooms*). *Comp.* **—arbeit,** *f.* upholstery; paper-hanging.

Tap'fer, *adj. & adv.* brave, valiant; bold, courageous; *see* **Tüchtig; — arbeiten,** to work with zeal, work hard; **einen — abprügeln,** to thrash a p. soundly; **halte dich —!** steady! don't flinch! **sich — wehren gegen,** to make a gallant stand against. **—keit,** *f.* bravery, valour.

Tapio'ka, *f.* (*pl.* **—s**) tapioca.

Ta'pir, *m.* (**—s**, *pl.* **—e**) tapir.

Tapisserie', *f.* (*pl.* **—en**) tapestry-work.

Tapp, I. *int.* tap! II. *m.* (**—es**, *pl.* **—e**) slap, blow; kick; foot-print; awkward fellow, clumsy lout. **—e,** *f.* (*pl.* **—en**) claw; paw; foot-step. **—eln,** *v.n.* to trip (*coll.*). **—en,** *v.n.* (*aux.* **h.** & **s.**) to poke about, to grope one's way; **im Dunkeln —en,** to grope in the dark; **im Dunkeln —end,** benighted. **—s, (Taps,)** *m.* (**—(s)es**, *pl.* **—(s)e**) *see* **Tapp.** **—sen (Tapsen),** *see* **—en.** **—sig,** *adj.* awkward.

Täp'pisch, *adj.* awkward, clumsy, heavy.

Ta'r—a, *f.* tare (*C.L.*). **—ie'ren,** *v.a.* to tare, ascertain *or* deduct the tare. *Comp.* **—a=rechnung,** *f.* tare-account. **—a=vergütung,** *f.* allowance for tare.

Taran'tel, *f.* (*pl.* **—n**) tarantula (*Ent.*); **wie von der — gestochen,** as if stung by an adder, like mad.

Tari'f, *m.* (**—s**, *pl.* **—e**) tariff. **—ie'ren,** *v.a.* to fix a tariff, levy duty on. *Comp.* **—ermäßigung,** *f.* reduction of the tariff. **—mäßig,** *adj.* according to the tariff.

Tarn— (*in comp.*) **—haut, —kappe,** *f.* cloak of invisibility.

Taro'ck, (Ta'rok,) *n.* (**—s**) taroc, tarot, a game at cards. **—ie'rt,** *adj.* chequered (*of cards*).

Tart'sche, *f.* (*pl.* **—n**) (*small*) round shield; target (*obs. poet.*).

Täsch'—chen, *n.* (**—chens**, *pl.* **—chen**) little pocket. **—ner,** *m.* (**—ners**, *pl.* **—ner**) purse-maker; trunk-maker.

Ta'sche, *f.* (*pl.* **—n**) pocket; purse; pouch; satchel, wallet; **etwas in die — stecken,** to pocket s.th.; **einen in die — stecken,** to be more than a match for *or* far superior to a p.; **aus jemandes — leben,** to live at another's expense. *Comp.* **—n=ausgabe,** *f.* pocket edition. **—n=buch,** *n.* pocket *or* memorandum book; small book. **—n=dieb,** *m.* pickpocket; **vor —ndieben wird gewarnt,** beware of pickpockets. **—n=diebstahl,** *m.* picking pockets, pocket-picking. **—n=feuerzeug,** *n.* pocket match-box. **—n=format,** *n.* pocket-size. **—n=geld,** *n.* pocket-money, (weekly *or* monthly) allowance. **—n=gesteck,** *n.* pocket-case. **—n=krebs,** *m.* crab-fish (*Cancer pagurus*). **—n=messer,** *n.* pocket-knife; clasp-knife; **zusammenklappen wie ein —nmesser,** to collapse (*coll.*) **—n=puffer,** *m.* pocket-pistol (*coll.*).

—n=spiegel, *m.* pocket-mirror, pocket-glass. **—n=spiel**, *n.* jugglery, sleight of hand. **—n=spieler**, *m.* juggler, conjurer. **—n=spielerei'**, *f.* legerdemain; jugglery. **—n=spieler=künste**, *pl.* juggler's *or* conjurer's tricks. **—n=tuch**, *n.* pocket-handkerchief. **—n=uhr**, *f.* watch. **—n=wörterbuch**, *n.* pocket-dictionary.

Tas'se, *f.* (*pl.* **—n**, *dim.* **Täß'chen**, *n.*) cup; (**Ober— und Unter—**) cup and saucer. *Comp.* **—n=kopf**, *m.* cup. **—n=schälchen**, *n.*, **—n=untersatz**, *m.* saucer (*dial.*).

Tast—atu'r, *f.* (*pl.* **—aturen**) keys, key-board (*of a piano, etc.*). **—bar**, *adj.* palpable; tangible. **—e**, *f.* (*pl.* **—en**) key (*of a piano, etc.*); **eine falsche —e anschlagen**, to strike a wrong note.

Tas't—en, I. *v.a. & n.* (*aux.* **h.**) to touch, feel; to grope, fumble; **nach einer S. —en**, to stretch out the hand for a th.; **—end gehen**, to grope one's way; **ein Blinder kann es —en**, a blind man can recognize it by the touch. II. *subst. n.* feeling, touching, touch; groping. **—er**, *m.* (**—ers**, *pl.* **—er**) feeler, antenna; one who feels *or* gropes; key, communicator (*Tele.*); **Gegensprech—er**, duplex-key (*Tele.*). *Comp.* **—empfindung**, *f.* sensibility of touch; **einzelne —empfindung**, sensation of touch. **—en=brett**, *n.* key-board. **—en=hebel**, *m.* key-lever. **—en=instrumente**, *pl.* keyed instruments. **—en=lager**, *n.* key-board. **—en=leiter**, *m.* (hand-)guide. **—en=werk**, *n.* key-action. **—er=förmig**, *adj.* feeler-like. **—er=zirkel**, *m.* calliper compasses. **—haken**, *m.* cant-hook. **—organ**, *n.* organ of touch. **—sinn**, *m.* (*sense of*) touch. **—spitzen**, *pl.* antennæ. **—wissenschaft**, **—lehre**, *f.* science of touch, haptics.

Tät'scheln, (**Tä'scheln**,) *v.a.* to pet.

Tat'terich, *m.* trembling (*of the hands*) (*sl.*).

Tät(t)owie'ren, *v.a.* to tattoo.

Tat'ze, *f.* (*pl.* **—n**) paw; claw. *Comp.* **—n=förmig**, *adj.* claw-like. **—n=hieb**, *m.* blow with a paw.

[1]**Tau**, *n.* (**—(e)s**, *pl.* **—e**) rope, cable; **die —e**, tackling, rigging; **dem Anker mehr — ausstechen**, to pay out more cable; **ein — schlagen**, to twist a rope. **—en**, *v.a.* to tow (*a ship, etc.*); to tow (*skins*). **—er**, *m.* (**—ers**, *pl.* **—er**) tower; dresser (*of skins*). **—erei'**, *f.* towing. *Comp.* **—anker**, *m.* sea-anchor, tow-anchor; **den —anker lichten**, to unmoor a ship. **—brücke**, *f.* rope-bridge. **—block**, *m.* pulley. **—länge**, *f.* cable's length. **—werk**, *n.* cordage; rigging; (**laufendes**) running gear; (**stehendes**) standing rigging.

[2]**Tau**, *m.* (**—(e)s**) dew; **gefrorener —**, hoar frost; **es fällt—**, the dew is falling. **—en**, *v.n.* (*aux.* **h.** *&* **f.**) *& imp.* to thaw; (*aux.* **h.**) to be covered with dew; **es —t**, the dew is falling it is dewy; **der Schnee ist von den Dächern getaut**, the snow has melted off (*or* fallen from) the roofs. **—icht** (*obs.*), **—ig**, *adj.* dewy. *Comp.* **—benetzt**, **—feucht**, *adj.* moist with dew, bedewed, dew-besprinkled. **—erde**, *f.* top soil. **—luft**, *f.* soft air, mild atmosphere. **—messer**, *m.* drosometer. **—perle**, *f.* dewy pearl. **—regen**, *m.* mild rain. **—schlag**, *m.* fallen dew. **—wetter**, *n.* thaw. **—wind**, *m.* warm wind, mild breeze.

Taub, *adj.* deaf; dead; unfeeling; torpid; numb; empty; sterile, barren; **— machen**, to deafen; **— auf einem Ohre**, deaf of one ear; **— sein bei (für, gegen, zu) jemandes Bitten**, to be deaf to a person's entreaties; **—en Ohren predigen**, to talk to the winds; **mit —en Ohren anhören**, to turn a deaf ear to; **—er Gang**, exhausted lode; **—es Gestein**, deads, dead heaps; **—es Gras**, weeds; **—e Nüsse**, empty (*blind*) nuts; **—es Ei**, addled egg. **—heit**, *f.* deafness; numbness; sterility. *Comp.* **—feld**, *n.* soil producing little ore. **—geboren**, *adj.* born deaf. **—hafer**, *m.* wild oats. **—kohle**, *f.* blind coal. **—nessel**, *f.* dead nettle. **—stumm**, *adj.* deaf and dumb. **—stummen=anstalt**, *f.* asylum for the deaf and dumb. **—stummheit**, *f.* deaf-and-dumbness.

Täub'—chen, *n.* (**—chens**, *pl.* **—chen**) little dove *or* pigeon; **mein —chen!** my darling, my love! **—er**, (**—erich**,) *m.* (**—ers**, *pl.* **—er**) *see* **Tauber**. **—in**, *f.* hen-pigeon.

Tau'be, *f.* (*pl.* **—n**) pigeon; dove (*certain kinds, high style, poet.*); **ein Flug —n**, a flight *or* flock of pigeons; **verirrte —**, stray pigeon; **Brief—**, carrier-pigeon; **Noahs —**, Noah's dove; **sanft wie eine —**, (as) gentle as a dove; **die — girrt**, the pigeon coos; **wo —n sind, fliegen —n hin**, to him that hath shall be given; **das Land der gebratenen —n**, a fool's paradise; Utopia; Land of Cocayne; **ihm fliegen die gebratenen —n in den Mund**, he gets all he wants without trouble, the larks fall to him ready roasted. **—n=haft**, *adj.* pigeon-like, dove-like, columbine. **—r**, *m.* (**—rs**, *pl.* **—r**) cock, cock-pigeon. *Comp.* **—n=einfalt**, *f.* dove-like simplicity. **—n=falk(e)**, *m.* goshawk. **—n=farben**, *adj.* dove-coloured. **—n=flug**, *m.* flight of a pigeon; flock, flight of pigeons. **—n=geier**, **—n=habicht**, *m.* goshawk. **—n=haus**, *n.* dove-cot. **—n=kropf**, *m.* pigeon's crop; fumitory (*Bot.*). **—n=liebhaber**, *m.* pigeon-fancier. **—n=loch**, *n.* pigeon-hole. **—n=paar**, *n.* a pair of pigeons *or* doves. **—n=pastete**, *f.* pigeon-pie. **—n=post**, *f.* conveyance of letters by (carrier-)pigeons. **—n=schlag**, *m.* dove-cot; house where people are continually coming and going *or* where the servants are frequently changed (*coll.*) **—n=stößer**, *m.* goshawk. **—n=zucht**, *f.* pigeon-breeding. **—n=züchter**, *m.* pigeon-breeder *or* fancier.

Tau'ch—en, *v.* I. *r. & n.* (*aux.* **h.** *&* **f.**) to dip *or* plunge (*into water*), dive; to disappear; **mit der Hand in die Schüssel —en**, to dip one's hand into the dish; **die Sonne —t (sich) ins Meer**, the sun sinks into the sea; **auf—en**, to emerge. II. *a.* to dip, slip; to duck, plunge; **Eisen —en**, to temper iron. **—er**, *m.* (**—ers**, *pl.* **—er**) diver; diving-bird, diver. *Comp.* **—batterie**, *f.* immersion battery (*Phys.*). **—ente**, *f.* mergus (*Orn.*). **—er=anzug**, *m.* diver's dress *or* outfit. **—er=glocke**, *f.* diving-bell. **—er=kolben**, *m.* plunger. **—er=schiff**, *n.* diving-ship. **—er=vögel**, *pl.* divers (*Orn.*).

Tau'fe, *f.* (*pl.* **—n**) baptism; christening; christening-feast; **ein Kind aus der — heben**, to stand sponsor to a child; **ein Kind über die — halten**, to present a child at the font *or* for baptism; **die — vornehmen** *or* **vollziehen**, to baptize; **die heilige —**, the holy baptism.

Tau'f—en, *v.a.* to baptize, christen; to dub, call; **Wein —en**, to water, adulterate wine; **er läßt alle Jahre —en**, he has a new baby every year. *Comp.* **—akt**, *m.* act *or* ceremony of baptism. **—amt**, *n.* ministry of baptism. **—becken**, *n.* (christening) font. **—buch**, *n.* baptismal register. **—bund**, *m.* baptismal covenant. **—formel**, *f.* form of baptism. **—gebühr**, *f.* christening-fee. **—gelübde**, *n.* baptismal vow. **—geschenk**, *n.* christening present. **—gesinnte(r)**, *m.* (ana)baptist. **—handlung**, *f. see* **—akt**. **—kapelle**, *f.* baptistery. **—name**, *m.* Christian name. **—patchen**, *n.* godchild. **—pate**, *m.* godfather; godchild. **—patin**, **—pate**, *f.* godmother; god-daughter. **—register**, *see* **—buch**. **—schein**, *m.* certificate of baptism. **—schmaus**, *m.* christening feast. **—stein**, *m.* (baptismal) font. **—wasser**, *n.* baptismal water. **—zeuge**, *m.* sponsor.

Täu'f—er, *m.* (—**ers**, *pl.* —**er**) baptizer; *see* **Wieder—er**; **Johannes der —er**, John the Baptist. —**ling**, *m.* (—**lings**, *pl.* —**linge**) infant (*or person*) receiving baptism; neophyte (*of grown-up persons*).

Tau'g—en, *v.n.* (*aux.* **h.**) to be of use; to answer, to do, to serve, to be good *or* fit for; **es —t (zu) nichts**, it is worthless; **er —t nichts**, he is a good-for-nothing fellow; **das —t nicht zur Sache**, that is no good *or* no us ; **wozu soll das —en**? of what use is that? —**lich**, *adj.* good, able, qualified, fit, useful; available. *Comp.* —**e=nichts**, *m.* a good-for-nothing, ne'er-do-weel; **ein ganzer —enichts**, an utter scamp.

Tau'mel, *m.* (—**s**) reeling, staggering; giddiness; intoxication; the staggers (*Vet.*); ecstasy; transport; frenzy; whirl. —**ig**, **Taum'lig**, *adj.* reeling; giddy.

Tau'mel—n, *v.n.* (*aux.* **h.** & **s.**) to reel, stagger; to be giddy; **er ist in das Zimmer getaumelt**, he staggered into the room; **er —t von diesem unverhofften Glücke**, this unexpected good fortune has turned his head. *Comp.* —**becher**, *m.* intoxicating cup. —**geist**, *m.* one who forms wild projects; revolutionary spirit *or* disposition. —**taube**, *f.* tumbler pigeon.

Tausch, *m.* (—**es**, *pl.* —**e**) exchange (*of goods*), barter; **im — gegen**, in exchange for; **einen — machen**, to effect an exchange. —**bar**, *adj.* exchangeable.

Tau'sch—en, *v.a.* & *n.* (*aux.* **h.**) to exchange; to barter; **ich möchte nicht mit Ihnen —en**, I would not change places with you, I should not like to be in your place. —**er**, *m.* (—**ers**, *pl.* —**er**) barterer. —**erei'**, *f.* exchange. *Comp.* —**handel**, *m.* barter; exchange trade. —**weise**, *adv.* by *or* in exchange.

Täu'sch—en, *v.a.* to deceive, delude; to cheat; to impose upon; to disappoint; **sich durch etwas —en lassen**, to let oneself be deceived by something; **einen um etwas —en**, to cheat a p. out of a thing; **in der Liebe getäuscht werden**, to be disappointed in love. —**end**, *p.* & *adj.* deceitful, illusory; —**ende Ähnlichkeit**, striking resemblance; **das ist —end nachgeahmt**, that is copied to the life. —**er**, *m.* (—**ers**, *pl.* —**er**) deceiver, cheat; (*horse-*)dealer. —**ung**, *f.* deception, fraud; illusion; disappointment; **man gebe sich darüber keiner —ung hin**, let no one deceive himself on that score.

Tauschie'ren, *v.a.* to inlay.

Tau'send, I. *num. adj.* thousand; **— und aber —**, thousands and thousands; thousands upon thousands; **nicht einer unter —**, not one in a thousand; **vor vielen — Jahren**, many thousand years ago; **— Mann**, a thousand men; **— und eine Nacht**, the Arabian Nights' (Entertainments). II. *n.* (—**s**, *pl.* —**e**) thousand; **bei, zu —en**, by thousands. III. *int.* **(ei,) der —! Potz —!** the deuce! dear me! good gracious! —**er**, *m.* (—**ers**, *pl.* —**er**) thousand; figure marking the thousands. —**st**, *num. adj.* thousandth; **das weiß der —ste nicht**, not one in a thousand knows that. —**stel**, *n.* (—**stels**, *pl.* —**stel**) thousandth part. —**stens**, *adv.* in the thousandth place. *Comp.* —**armig**, *adj.* thousand-armed. —**blatt**, *n.* milfoil. —**blätterig**, *adj.* thousand-leaved. —**eck**, *n.* polygon of a thousand sides, chiliagon. —**erlei'**, *indec. adj.* & *adv.* of a thousand kinds; —**erlei Dinge**, thousands of things; ever so many things. —**fach**, —**fältig**, I. *adj.* a thousand times, thousand-fold. II. *adv.* in a thousand ways. —**fuß**, *m.* milliped. —**güldenkraut**, *n.* centaury. —**jährig**, *adj.* of a thousand years, a thousand years old; millennial; **das —jährige Reich Christi**, the millennium. —**künstler**, *m.* conjurer, Jack of all trades. —**mal**, *adv.* a thousand times. —**sakrament**, *int.* the deuce (take it all), hang it. —**sappermenter**, *m.* devil of a fellow. —**schön(chen)**, *n.* daisy. —**sasa**, *m.*; **er ist ein —sasa**, he is a devil of a fellow, a marvellous person. —**weise**, *adv.* by thousands.

Tautolog—ie', *f.* tautology. —**isch**, *adj.* (*pron.* **tautolo'gisch**) tautological.

Tax—ame'ter=droschke, *f.* taxameter cab. —**a'tor**, *m.* (—**ators**, *pl.* —**ato'ren**) taxer, appraiser, valuer; **vereidigter —ator**, sworn appraiser *or* valuer. —**e**, *f.* (*pl.* —**en**) authorized charge *or* price; estimate, value; tax, rate, duty. —**ie'ren**, *v.a.* to appraise, value, estimate; to rate, tax; to put a fixed price on; **zu niedrig —iert**, rated *or* priced too low. —**ie'rung**, *f.* taxation, valuation. *Comp.* —**belegung**, *f.* levying of a tax. —**en=ermäßigung**, *f.* abatement of taxes, decrease in the tariff. —**gebühren**, *pl.* dues, fixed charges. —**ordnung**, *f.* tariff; regulation of assize; scale of fees *or* taxed costs (*in law-courts, etc.*). —**wert**, *m.* appraised value.

Ta'xus, *m.* (—, *pl.* —) yew. *Comp.* —**hecke**, *f.* yew hedge.

Tech'n—ik, *f.* science of technical terms; technics; technical art; execution. —**iker**, *m.* (—**ikers**, *pl.* —**iker**) technologist; one skilled in an art; engineer. —**isch**, *adj.* & *adv.* technical; —**ische Ausdrücke**, technical terms; technicalities; —**ische Hochschule**, Polytechnic (Academy); —**ische Mittelschule**, technical school *or* institute.

Tech'telmechtel, *n.* (—**s**, *pl.* —) love affair, entanglement, secret flirtation with a girl (*coll.*).

Teck'el, *m.* (—**s**, *pl.* —) dachs(hund), crook-legged German terrier.

Teer, *m.* (& *n.*) (—**s**) (**Steinkohlen=**) (coal-) tar; **mit — anstreichen**, to tar. —**en**, *v.a.* to tar. —**icht**, *adj.* tarry. —**ig**, *adj.* tarry; tarred. *Comp.* —**aufguß**, *m.* infusion of tar. —**baum**, *m.* Scotch fir. —**brenner**, *m.* tar-maker. —**büchse**, *f.* tar- *or* grease-box. —**farben**, *pl.* coal-tar *or* aniline colours. —**farbig**, *adj.* tar-coloured. —**faß**, *n.* tar-barrel. —**hütte**, *f.* tar-factory. —**jacke**, *f.* tarred vest; Jack Tar. —**pappe**, *f.* tarred pasteboard. —**pech**, *n.* artificial asphalt. —**pinsel**, *m.* tar-brush. —**quelle**, *f.* spring of mineral tar. —**schwelerei**, *f.* manufactory of tar. —**tonne**, *f.* tar-barrel. —**tuch**, *n.* tarpaulin. —**werg**, *n.* tarred tow *or* oakum.

Te'gel, *m.* (—**s**) species of bluish-green marl forming part of the tertiary strata (*Geol.*).

Tei'anker, *m.* small bower(-anchor).

Teich, *m.* (—**es**, *pl.* —**e**) pond, pool. *Comp.* —**binse**, *f.* bulrush. —**fenchel**, *m* water-milfoil. —**gitter**, *n.* sluice-grating. —**lilie**, *f.* water-lily. —**pflanzen**, *pl.* pond-plants. —**rohr**, *n.* reed. —**schilf**, *n.* reeds. —**zapfen**, *m.* lock (*of a sluice*).

Teifu'n, *see* **Taifun**.

Teig, I. *m.* (—(**e**)**s**, *pl.* —**e**) dough, paste. II. *adj.* mellow; overripe. —**ig**, *adj.* doughy; mellow; over-ripe. *Comp.* —**decke**, *f.* covering of paste *or* crust. —**holz**, *n.*, —**klöpfel**, *m.* rolling-pin. —**kratze(r**, *m.*), *f.*, —**scharre**, *f.* baker's scraper. —**messer**, *n.* dough-knife. —**mulde**, *f.* baker's trough. —**rädchen**, *n.* jagging iron. —**schüssel**, *f.* bake-board.

Teil, *m.* & *n.* (—**s**, *pl.* —**e**) part, share; part, division; party (*Law*); **der größte — der Menschen**, most people; **er hat sein — bekommen**, he has got his due; **wenn er nicht spricht, so denkt er sein —**, though he says nothing, he thinks the more; **ein gut — von etwas**, a good bit, a fair share; **sieben —e von**, seven parts of, 7/8 of; **drei —e von etwas**, three-fourths of s.th.; **zwei —e**, two-thirds; **großen —s**, in a great measure. to a large extent;

größten —s, for the most part; **zum —(e),** partly, in part; **einem zu — werden,** to fall to a p.'s lot *or* share; **einem etwas zu — werden lassen,** to admit s.o. to a share of a th.; to grant a p. s.th.; **— an einer S. — haben** *or* **nehmen,** to take part in a th., to interest oneself in a th.; to contribute to a th.; to join in a th.; **einen an einer S. — nehmen lassen,** to give a p. a share in a th.; to allow a p. to join in a th.; **beide —e,** both parties; **ich meines —s, für meinen —, an meinem —e,** I for my part, as for me; **ich halte es mit keinem —e,** I side with neither party; **andern —s,** on the other hand. **—chen,** *n.* (**—chens,** *pl.* **—chen**) particle. **—haft(ig),** *adj.* (*with gen.*) partaking of, sharing in; **sich (einer Sache) —haftig machen,** to participate in; (**einer Sache**) **—haftig werden,** to partake of, share. **—s,** *adv.* partly, in part; **—s in barem Gelde, —s in Wechseln,** partly in money (*coin*), partly in bills of exchange; **—s durch Gewalt, —s durch Politik . . .,** what with force, what with policy . . . *Comp.* **—begriff,** *m.* partial notion. **—besitzer,** *m.* part-owner. **—bruch,** *m.* partial fraction. **—habend,** *adj.* participating in. **—haber,** *m.* sharer, participator; joint-owner; partner; **—haber gesucht,** a partner wanted (*in newspapers*); **stiller —haber,** sleeping partner. **—kreis,** *m.* primitive *or* pitch-circle (*Mach.*). **—nahme,** *f.* participation, share; sympathy; interest; complicity; co-operation; **—nahme an einer Person (für eine P.),** interest in a person. **—nahmlos,** *adj.* unfeeling, indifferent. **—nahmlosigkeit,** *f.* indifference, want of sympathy. **—nehmend,** *adj.* sharing; sympathetic; tender; interested (*in*). **—nehmer,** *m.* participator; part-owner; sympathizer; accomplice. **—nehmung,** *f. obs. for* **—nahme.** **—quantum,** *n.* quota, split. **—scheibe,** *f.* divider (*Mach.*); graduator. **—strecke,** *f.* section of a railway *or* tramway. **—weise,** *adj. & adv.* partial; in part; in parts *or* numbers; **—weise Zahlung,** part-payment. **—zahl,** *f.*, **—zähler,** *m.* quotient (*Arith.*). **—zahlung,** *f.* part-payment, payment by instalments; **monatliche —zahlungen,** payment by monthly instalments. **—zirkel,** *m.* dividing compasses.

Teil'bar, *adj.* divisible, separable. **—keit,** *f.* divisibility.

Tei'l—en, *v.a.* to divide; to share; to separate; to participate, share in; **den Unterschied —en,** to split the difference; **hier —en sich die Wege,** here the roads divide; **jemandes Leiden —en,** to sympathize with a p., to share s.o.'s suffering *or* sorrow. **—er,** *m.* (**—ers,** *pl.* **—er**) divider; sharer; divisor (*Arith.*). **—erfremd,** *adj.* indivisible; **—erfremde Zahl,** prime number. **—ung,** *f.* division, separation; quartering (*Her.*); sharing; dismemberment (*of an empire*); parcelling out (*of lands*). **—ungs=artikel,** *m.* partitive article. **—ungs=ebene,** *f.* bisecting plane. **—ungs=glied,** *n.* divisional member. **—ungs=hahn,** *m.* branch-spout (*Hydr.*). **—ungs=linie,** *f.* dividing-line. **—ungs=punkt,** *m.* point of division; (*pl.*) diæresis. **—ungs=recht,** *n.* right of partition. **—ungs=verfahren,** *n.* mode of division *or* partition. **—ungs=vertrag,** *m.* treaty of partition. **—ungs=zahl,** *f.* dividend (*Arith.*). **—ungs=zeichen,** *n.* hyphen; mark of division. **—ungs=zirkel,** *m.* dividing-compasses.

Teint, *m.* (**—s,** *pl.* **—s**) complexion.

Tele—gra'mm, *n.* (**—gramms,** *pl.* **—gram'me**) telegram, telegraphic message, wire; **Kabel —gramm,** cablegram, cable. **—gra'ph,** *m.* (**—graphen,** *pl.* **—graphen**), telegraph; **optischer —graph,** optical telegraph, semaphore; **unterseeischer —graph,** submarine cable; **durch den —graphen,** by telegraph *or* wire. **—graphen=beamte(r),** *m. see* **—graphist.** **—graphen=bote,** *m.* telegraph-boy. **—graphen=draht,** *m.* telegraph-wire. **—graphen=kabel,** *n.* telegraph-cable. **—graphen=leitung, —graphen=linie,** *f.* telegraph-line. **—graphen=stange,** *f.* telegraph-pole. **—graphie',** *f.* telegraphy; **drahtlose —graphie,** wireless telegraphy; **Sonnen—graphie,** heliography. **—graphie'ren,** *v.a. & n.* (*aux.* **h.**) to telegraph, wire; to cable. **—gra'phisch,** *adj.* telegraphic. **—graphis't(in,** *f.*), *m.* telegraph clerk, telegraphist. **—ologie',** *f.* teleology. **—olo'gisch,** *adj.* teleological. **—pho'n,** (*also* **Te'lephon,**) *n.* (**—phons,** *pl.* **—phons**) telephone. **—phonie'ren,** *v.a. & n.* (*aux.* **h.**) to telephone. **—pho'nisch,** *adj.* telephonic; **—phonisch anfragen,** to ask by telephone. **—phon=leitung,** *f.* telephonic circuit. **—phoni'st(in)** *m.* (*f.*) man (woman) at the telephone. **—sko'p,** *n.* (**—skops,** *pl.* **—skope**) telescope.

Tel'ler, *m.* (**—s,** *pl.* **—**) plate; tray; salver; crown, disc (*Bot.*); plate, table (*of an air-pump*); palm of the hand (*rare*). **—chen,** *n.* (**—chens,** *pl.* **—chen**) little plate. *Comp.* **—artig,** *adj.* plate-shaped. **—bord, —brett,** *n.* plate-drainer; plate-rack. **—drehen,** *n.* twirling the trencher, My Lady's Toilet. **—förmig,** *adj.* plate-shaped. **—huf,** *m.* flat hoof. **—knecht,** *m.* dumb waiter. **—korb,** *m.* plate-basket. **—lecker,** *m.* lick-dish, lick-plate, toady. **—leckerei',** *f.* toadyism. **—schrank,** *m.* cupboard, sideboard. **—tuch,** *n.* (dinner-)napkin; dish-cloth. **—wärmer,** *m.* plate-warmer.

Tellu'r, *n.* (**—s**) tellurium; tellurion (*Ast.*). **—ig,** *adj.* tellurous. **—isch,** *adj.* telluric; terrestrial.

Tem'pel, *m.* (**—s,** *pl.* **—**) temple, place of worship; sanctuary; synagogue; game of chance (*Cards*); **einen zum — hinauswerfen,** to turn a p. out (*coll.*). **—n,** *v.n.* (*aux.* **h.**) to play at **Tempel**; to gamble. *Comp.* **—diener,** *m.* officer of the temple, priest. **—herr,** (**Templer,**) *m.* (Knight-)Templar. **—herrisch, —herrlich,** *adj.* belonging to *or* in the manner of the Templars. **—hof,** *m.* court of a temple; residence of the Knights-Templars, Temple, preceptory. **—hüter,** *m.* temple-ward. **—orden,** *m.* order of the Templars. **—raub,** *m.* sacrilege. **—räuberisch,** *adj.* sacrilegious. **—ritter,** *see* **—herr.** **—schänder,** *m.* desecrator of a temple. **—weihe,** *f.*; **Fest der —weihe,** (Jewish) Feast of Dedication.

Tem'pera, *f.* distemper, tempera.

Temper—ame'nt, *n.* (**—(e)s,** *pl.* **—e**) temperament; temper; **hitziges —ament,** hot temper. **—atu'r,** *f.* temperature; temperament (*Mus.*). **—ie'ren,** *v.a.* to temper, moderate, soften; to anneal; **—ierte Stimmung,** temperament (*Mus.*); **—iertes Wasser,** lukewarm water. *Comp.* **—aments'=fehler,** *m.* defect of temper; constitutional defect. **—atur'=erhöhung,** *f.* rise in temperature. **—atur'=grad,** *m.* degree of temperature. **—ir=messer,** *n.* palette-knife. **—ir'=wasser,** *n.* tempering-water.

Tem'pern, *v.a.* to temper, anneal, cool down.

Tem'p—o, *n.* (**—s,** *pl.* **—s, Tem'pi**) time, measure, pace, rate. **—ora'lien,** *pl.* temporalities, secular possessions; (clerical) living. **—orä'r,** *adj.* temporary. **—orisie'ren,** *v.n.* (*aux.* **h.**) to temporize; to delay. **—us,** *n.* (**—us,** *pl.* **—ora**) tense (*Gram.*).

Tena'kel, *n.* (**—s,** *pl.* **—**) leaf-holder (*Typ.*); tenaculum (*Surg.*).

Tend—e'nz, *f.* tendency. **—enziö's,** *adj.* having a marked tendency, uttered *or* written with a view to effect; biassed, prejudiced. *Comp.* **—enz=roman,** *m.* (**—enz'=stück,** *n.*) novel (drama) written with a purpose.

Ten'der, *m.* (**—s,** *pl.* **—**) advice boat; tender

(*of a railway-engine*). *Comp.* **—maschine,** *f.* tank-engine.

Ten'ne, *f.* (*pl.* **—n**) threshing-floor. *Comp.* **—n=patsche,** *f.*, **—n=schlägel,** *m.* beetle for making threshing-floors.

Ten'nis, *n.* lawn-tennis. *Comp.* **—schläger,** *m.* tennis racket. **—spiel=feld,** *n.* tennis-court. **—spiel=regeln,** *pl.* rules of lawn-tennis.

Teno'r, *m.* (**—s,** *pl.* **—e**) tenor. **—i'st,** *m.* (**—is'ten,** *pl.* **—is'ten**) tenor-singer. *Comp.* **—geige,** *f.* viola. **—partie,** *f.* tenor-part. **—stimme,** *f.* tenor-voice, tenor-part.

Tenta'men, *n.* (**—s,** *pl.* **Tentamina**) preliminary examination (*e.g.* **— physicum,** preliminary medical examination).

Te'nuis, *f.* (*pl.* **Tenues**) voiceless stopped consonant, voiceless stop; t, p, k; **schwache —,** weakly-articulated almost voiced stops.

Tenzo'ne, *f.* (*pl.* **—n**) trobador's tenzon, tenson.

Tep'pich, *m.* (**—es,** *pl.* **—e**) carpet; **Wand—,** tapestry; **Tisch—,** table-cover; **Brüsseler —,** Brussels carpet; **mit einem auf den breiten — treten,** to be joined in marriage to a person; **mit —en überziehen, belegen,** to carpet; **der grüne — der Wiesen,** the green (carpet of the) meadows, the green sward. *Comp.* **—arbeit,** *f.* tapestry. **—band,** *n.* carpet-binding. **—beet,** *n.* carpet-pattern, flower-bed. **—nagel,** *m.* tack. **—pflanzen,** *pl.* small plants suited for carpet-gardening. **—sticker(in,** *f.*) *m.* tapestry-worker. **—weber, —wirker,** *m.* carpet-manufacturer. **—zeug,** *n.* carpeting, carpet in the piece.

Termi'n, *m.* (**—s,** *pl.* **—e**) time, term; fixed day; term (*Law*); court-day; summons to appear on a fixed day; day of appearance; **ich habe morgen —,** I am (summoned) to appear (in court) to-morrow; **in vier —en zahlbar,** payable in four instalments; **die —e sollen richtig abgetragen werden,** the payments are to be made regularly; **seine Miete noch zwei —e schuldig sein,** to be two quarters in arrears with one's rent. **—a'lien,** *pl.* Roman festival in honour of the god Terminus. **—ie'ren,** *v.a.* to beg alms (*as the mendicant friars*). **—ologie',** *f.* terminology, technical language, nomenclature; notation. **—us,** *m.* the god Terminus; term; **—i technici,** technical terms. *Comp.* **—kalender,** *m.* almanac showing the terms, quarter-days, *etc.* **—weise,** *adv.* by instalments; by the term. **—(al')=zahlung,** *f.* payment by instalments *or* at fixed terms.

Termi'te, *f.* (*pl.* **—n**) white ant.

Terpenti'n, *m.* (**—s,** *pl.* **—e**) turpentine. *Comp.* **—geist,** *m.* (**—öl,** *n.*) spirits (oil) of turpentine.

Terr—ai'n, *n.* (**—ains,** *pl.* **—ains**) ground; country (*Mil. etc.*). **—as'se,** *f.* (*pl.* **—assen**) terrace; flat roof; foreground (*Paint.*). **—assie'ren,** *v.a.* to terrace; to step (*Railw.*). **—es'trisch,** *adj.* terrestrial. **—i'ne,** *f.* (*pl.* **—inen**) tureen. **—ie'ren,** *n.* claying (*of sugar*). *Comp.* **—assen=land,** *n.* country sloping in terraces.

Ter'rier, *m.* (**—s,** *pl.* **—**) terrier.

Terror—isie'ren, *v.a.* to terrorise, browbeat. **—is'mus,** *m.* terrorism. **—i'st,** *m.* (**—is'ten,** *pl.* **—is'ten**) terrorist.

Ter't—ia, *f.* (**—ia,** *pl.* **—ien**) third form (from the top) in a German higher secondary school, fourth form in an English grammar school; great primer (*Typ.*); tenth, great tierce (*Org.*); *see* **—iawechsel. —ia'l,** *n.* (**—ials,** *pl.* **—iale**), (University) term. **—ia'ner,** *m.* (**—ianers,** *pl.* **—**) third-form boy. **—iä'r,** *adj.* tertiary. **—ie,** *f.* third (*Mus.*); tierce. **—ius,** *m.* boy third in his form *or* set; third-form master (*obs.*). *Comp.* **—ian'=fieber,** *n.* tertian ague. **—ia=schrift,** *f.* great primer (*Typ.*). **—ia=wechsel,** *m.* third of exchange.

Terz, *f.* (*pl.* **—en**) third (*Mus.*); tierce (*Fenc.*); **kleine —,** minor third; **große —,** major third. **—ero'ne,** *m.* (**—eronen,** *pl.* **—eronen**) offspring of a white and a mulatto *or* mestizo. **—ero'l,** *n.* (**—erols,** *pl.* **—erole**) pocket-pistol. **—e'tt,** *n.* (**—etts,** *pl.* **—et'te**) trio, terzetto, three-part song. **—i'ne,** *f.* (*pl.* **—inen**) terzarima (*Poet.*). *Comp.* **—(en)=folge,** *f.* succession of thirds (*Mus.*). **—(en)=lauf,** *m.* run in thirds. **—hieb,** *m.* thrust in tierce.

Te'sching, *n.* & *m.* (**—s,** *pl.* **—e**) small rifle.

Test, *m.* (**—es,** *pl.* **—e**) test; cupel.

Testame'nt, *n.* (**—(e)s,** *pl.* **—e**) testament, will; **Altes (Neues) —,** Old (New) Testament; **ohne — sterben,** to die intestate *or* without leaving a will; **ein Anhang zu einem —,** a codicil to a will; **ein — umstoßen,** to cancel, set aside a will. **—lich, —a'risch,** *adj.* testamentary, by will. *Comp.* **—s=zusatz,** *m.* codicil. **—s=verfügung,** *f.* testamentary disposition. **—s=vollstrecker,** *m.* executor.

Testa't, *n.* (**—(e)s,** *pl.* **—e**) certificate (*of regular attendance, Univ.*).

Testie'r—en, *v.a.* & *n.* (*aux.* **h.**) to make a will; to bequeath; to testify; **über eine S. —ieren,** to bequeath s.th.; to testify s.th. **—er,** *m.* (**—ers,** *pl.* **—er**), **—erin,** *f.* testator, testatrix; one who certifies to attendance. *Comp.* **—bogen,** *m.* certificate of attendance (at lectures).

Testimo'ni—um, *n.* (**—ums,** *pl.* **—a**) certificate; testimonial; testimony.

Te'traeder, *n.* (**—s,** *pl.* **—**) tetrahedron.

Teu'er, *adj.* & *adv.* dear, costly; dear, beloved; precious; **wie — ist es?** how much is it? what does it cost? what price is it? **ich habe es — bezahlt,** I paid dearly for it; **in Hannover ist es nicht — zu leben,** living in Hanover is not expensive; **hier ist guter Rat —,** it is difficult to give good advice in this case, this is a very perplexing case; **das soll ihm — zu stehen kommen,** that will cost him dear, he shall smart for that; **hoch und — schwören,** to swear solemnly, to take a solemn oath; **es war im Lande —e Zeit,** there was a famine in the land. **—ung, Teu'rung,** *f.* dearth, famine; dearness.

Teu'fe, *f.* (*pl.* **—n**) depth (*Min.*). **—n,** *v.a.* to deepen shafts (*Min.*).

Teu'fel, *m.* (**—s,** *pl.* **—**) devil; demon; **eingefleischter —,** devil incarnate; **armer —,** poor devil, luckless beggar; **der hinkende —,** the devil on two sticks; **sie ist ein kleiner —,** she is a little fiend; **was zum —!** what the deuce! **was — giebt es?** what the deuce is wrong? **er fragt den — darnach,** he does n't care a straw about it; **Pfui —! — noch mal!** the deuce! **der — mag wissen warum,** the devil knows why; **er weiß den — davon,** he knows nothing whatever about it; **der — ist los!** here 's the devil to pay! **reitet euch der —? bist du des —s!** are you possessed (mad)? **man darf den — nicht an die Wand malen,** don't talk of the devil if you don't wish him to appear; **wenn man den — an die Wand malt, dann kommt er,** talk of the devil and he 'll appear; **es ist um des —s zu werden,** it is enough to drive one mad; **das heißt beim — zur Beichte gehen,** that is Satan reproving sin; **bei ihm geht alles zum —,** everything is going to rack and ruin with him. **—chen,** *n.* (**—chens,** *pl.* **—chen**) imp, little devil; **kartesianisches —chen,** cartesian devil. **—ei',** *f.* sorcery; devilry, devilment; devilish tricks *or* conduct; troublesome business. **—isch,** *see* **Teuflisch.** *Comp.* **—mäßig,** *adj. see* **Teuflisch. —s=arbeit,** *f.* devilish *or* tremendously hard work. **—s=bann,** *m.*, **—s=beschwörung,** *f.* exorcism. **—s=braten,** *m.* villain, rake, thorough scamp. **—s=braut,** *f.* witch. **—s=brut,** *f.* generation of vipers; bad lot. **—s=dreck,** *m.* as(s)afœtida. **—s=gestank,** *m.* infernal stench. **—s=inseln,** *pl.* the Bermudas. **—s=junge,** *m.*

devil of a boy, young imp *or* scamp; brick of a boy. **—s=kegel, —s=finger,** *m.* belemnite. **—s=kerl,** *m.* devil of a fellow. **—s=kind,** *n.* hardened sinner; scamp. **—s=kirsche,** *f.* berry of the belladonna. **—s=kunst,** *f.* sorcery, magic. **—s=lärm,** *m.* infernal noise. **—s=list,** *f.* diabolical cunning. **—s=streich,** *m.* diabolical trick. **—s=weib,** *n.* she-devil; witch. **—s=werk,** *n.* piece of devilment. **—s=zeug,** *n.* devilish tricks; damned nonsense.

Teuf'lisch, *adj.* devilish, diabolical, fiendish; infernal; **seine —e Herrlichkeit,** his Satanic Majesty.

Teutsch, *obs. for* **Deutsch.**

Te'xel, *m.* (—s, *pl.* —) adze.

Text, *m.* (—es, *pl.* —e) text; letterpress; words (*Mus.*); libretto; double pica (*Typ.*); **weiter im —e!** go on! (*coll.*); **einem den — lesen,** to lecture a p., to give s.o. a blowing up (*coll.*); **aus dem —e kommen,** to lose the thread of one's discourse, to be disconcerted, to get confused, to break down (*in a speech*). *Comp.* **—abbildung,** *f.* illustration of the letterpress. **—ausgabe,** *f.* edition containing the text only, edition without notes. **—berichtigung,** *f.* emendation *or* correction of the text. **—buch,** *n.* text-book; book of the words, libretto. **—gemäß, —mäßig,** *adj.* in conformity with the text. **—worte,** *pl.* words of the original.

Texti'l, *adj.* textile.

Textu'r, *f.* (*pl.* —en) texture.

Th . . .; *words not found under* **Th—** *should be looked for under* **T—**. *See also the Preface.*

Thal, Tal, *n.* (—s, *pl.* **Tä'ler** (*obs.:* **Ta'le**); *dim.* **Täl'chen**) valley, vale, dale; glen; **zu — fahren,** to descend a river; **zu —,** downwards. *Comp.* **—ab'wärts,** *adv.* downstream; downhill; valleywards. **—au's,** *adv.* out of a valley. **—bahn,** *f.* railway in a valley. **—buche,** *f.* red beech. **—ei'n,** *adv.* entering a valley. **—enge,** *f.* narrow pass entering a valley. **—fahrt,** *f.* descent. **—sohle,** *f.* bottom of a valley. **—sperre,** *f.* dam across a valley which bars *or* regulates a river; **dieses Fort bildet die —sperre,** this fort defends *or* closes the valley. **—weg,** *m.* road through a valley; channel of a river.

Tha'ler, *m.* (—s, *pl.* —) German coin (*no longer coined*) = 3 marks; **das ist ein schöner —,** that is a nice sum. *Comp.* **—fuß,** *m.*; **nach dem —fuße,** reckoning in thalers.

Than, *m.* (—s, *pl.* —e, —s) thane (*obs. poet.*).

¹**That, Tat,** *f.* (*pl.* —en) deed, act, action; fact; **eine große —,** a great achievement, a feat. **auf frischer —,** in the (very) act; **in der —,** in reality, indeed, in point of fact; **zur — schreiten,** to proceed to action; **ein Mann der —,** a man of action; **einem mit Rat und — beistehen,** to help a p. in every way, efficaciously; **die — leugnen,** to deny the charge; **er führt den Namen mit der —,** he lives up to his name, he is rightly so called; **Drohungen zur — machen,** to put threats into execution. *Comp.* **—bestand,** *m.* facts of a case; **einem den —bestand darlegen,** to lay the facts before a p.; **es auf die Frage über den —bestand ankommen lassen,** to join issue with regard to the facts of the case. **—beweis,** *m.* practical proof, proof by the fact. **—en=drang, —en=durst,** *m.* desire of achieving great things, restless activity, impulsiveness. **—(en)=los,** *adj.* idle, inactive. **—en=reich,** *adj.* active, having achieved much. **—fertig,** *adj.* ready to act. **—frage,** *f.* question of fact. **—handlung,** *f.* fact, deed of violence. **—kraft,** *f.* energy. **—kräftig,** *adj.* energetic. **—kundig,** *adj.* notorious. **—sache,** *f.* fact; (*pl.*) data. **—sächlich,** *adj.* & *adv.* real, positive, actual; founded on fact; matter-of-fact.

²**That; Tha'test,** *1 & 3; 2 pers. sing. imperf. indic. of* **thun; that** = *1 & 3 pers. sing. imperf. subj.* (*dial.*); **ich — ihr gleich nehmen** (= **ich thäte sie gleich nehmen**), I should take her at once.

Thä'te, *1 & 3 pers. sing. imperf. indic.* (*obsol. & poet.*) *& subj. of* **thun; da —n sie sich trennen,** then they separated; **ich — es gern,** I should like to do it.

Thä't—er, *m.* (—ers, *pl.* —er), **—erin,** *f.* doer, culprit; author, active agent; perpetrator. **—er=schaft,** *f.* guilt; **er kann die —erschaft nicht leugnen,** he cannot deny having done it. **—ig,** *adj.* active, energetic; efficacious; effective; active (*Gram.*); **immer — ig sein,** to be always busy; **nur immer —ig,** go on, exert yourself (*coll.*). **—igkeit,** *f.* activity; actuality; efficacy; **in —igkeit setzen,** to set going, to put in action; **außer —igkeit setzen,** to set aside, to pension off, to suspend. **—lich,** *adj.* & *adv.* founded upon fact; actual; violent; **einen —lich mißhandeln,** to offer violence to s.o.; **—lich werden,** to come to blows. **—lichkeit,** *f.* (*pl.* **—lichkeiten**) (*act of*) violence. *Comp.* **—igkeits=centrum,** *n.* centre of activity. **—igkeits=kreis,** *m.* sphere of activity. **—igkeits=wort,** *n.* transitive verb.

Thau, *see* **Tau.**

The . . .; *words not found under* **The** *should be looked for under* **Te.**

Thea't—er, *n.* (—ers, *pl.* —er) theatre; stage; **aufs —er gehen,** to go on the stage, to become an actor *or* actress; **ins —er gehen,** to go to the theatre. **—ra'lisch,** *adj.* theatrical, scenic, dramatic. *Comp.* **—er=bericht,** *m.* theatrical news, stage report. **—er=besuch,** *m.* going to the theatre. **—er=billet,** *n.* ticket for the theatre. **—er=dichter,** *m.* writer for the stage; dramatist, dramatic writer; playwright. **—er=effekt,** *m.* stage-effect. **—er=held,** *m.* stage-hero. **—er=inspizient,** *m.* superintendent in a theatre; stage-manager. **—er=kapelle,** *f.* orchestra (*of a theatre*). **—er=kasse,** *f.* theatrical funds; box-office; ticket-office. **—er=leben,** *n.* theatrical life *or* profession. **—er=loge,** *f.* box. **—er=maler,** *m.* scene-painter. **—er=manuscript,** *n.* acting copy. **—er=meister,** *m.* property-man. **—er=schwank,** *m.* farce. **—er=stück,** *n.* play (*for the stage*), drama. **—er=vorstellung,** *f.* theatrical performance. **—er=wesen,** *n.* theatrical concerns, the stage. **—er=zeitung,** *f.* theatrical journal. **—er=zensur,** *f.* censorship of plays. **—er=zettel,** *m.* play-bill.

Thee, Tee, *m.* (—s, *pl.* —e, *and* (C.L.) —s) tea; infusion; **der — muß noch ziehen,** the tea has not stood long enough; **wollen Sie bei uns — trinken?** will you take *or* have tea with us? *Comp.* **—artig,** *adj.* tea-like. **—bau,** *m.* tea-growing. **—brett,** *n.* tea-tray. **—brötchen,** *n.* muffin; thin slice of bread and butter. **—büchse,** *f.* tea-caddy. **—gesellschaft,** *f.* tea-party. **—händler,** *m.* tea-merchant. **—kanne,** *f.* tea-pot. **—kästchen,** *n.* tea-caddy. **—kessel,** *m.* tea-kettle; blockhead (*coll.*). **—kind,** *n.* pet, favourite (*coll.*). **—kiste,** *f.* tea-chest. **—klatsch,** *m.* (ladies') tea-party. **—kräuter,** *pl.* herbs used for tea. **—kuchen,** *m.* tea-cake. **—löffel,** *m.* tea-spoon. **—maschine,** *f.* tea-urn. **—mütze,** *f.* tea-cosy. **—rose,** *f.* tea-rose. **—service,** *n.* tea set *or* service. **—sieb,** *n.* tea-strainer. **—sorten,** *pl.* teas, kinds of tea. **—steuer,** *f.* duty on tea. **—stoff,** *m.* theine. **—strauch,** *m.* tea-plant. **—topf,** *m.* tea-pot. **—wasser,** *n.* hot water for tea. **—zeug,** *n.* tea-things.

Theer, *see* **Teer.**

Theil, *see* **Teil.**

Thei'n (*pron.* **The=i'n**), *n.* (—s) theine (*Chem.*).

Theis'—mus, *m.* theism. **—(ſ)t,** *m.* (**—ſ'ten,** *pl.* **—ſ'ten**) theist.

The'm—a, *n.* (**—as,** *pl.* **—as, —a'ta, —en**) theme, subject (*of a discourse, of music, etc.*); school composition.

Thema'tiſch, *adj.* thematic; **—es Verzeichnis,** list of music with a few bars printed from each composition.

Theodoli't, *m.* (**—en,** *pl.* **—en**) theodolite.

Theo—kratie', *f.* theocracy. **—lo'g,** *m.* (**—logen,** *pl.* **—logen**) theologian; **er iſt —log,** he is a student *or* professor of divinity; he is a clergyman. **—logie',** *f.* theology, divinity; **Profeſſor der —logie,** professor of divinity. **—lo'giſch,** *adj.* theological. **—ſo'ph,** *m.* (**—ſophen,** *pl.* **—ſophen**) theosophist.

Theor—e'm, *n.* (**—ems,** *pl.* **—eme**) theorem. **—e'tiker,** *m.* (**—etikers,** *pl.* **—etiker**) theorist. **—e'tiſch,** *adj. & adv.* theoretic(al). **—ie',** *f.* (*pl.* **—ieen**) theory; **eine —ie aufſtellen,** to start *or* put forward a theory; **die —ie iſt aufgegeben,** the theory is exploded.

Therapie', *f.* (*pl.* **—en**) therapeutics.

The'riak, *m.* (**—s**) theriaca (*Med.*); treacle.

Ther'm—en, (**—al'=quellen,**) *pl.* hot-springs. *Comp.* **—o=me'ter,** *n.* (*& m.*) thermometer; **das —ometer ſteht 3 Grad unter Null,** the thermometer stands three degrees below zero. **—o=meter=kugel,** *f.* bulb of the thermometer.

The'ſ—e, *f.* (*pl.* **—en**), **—is,** *f.* (*pl.* **—en**) thesis.

Theuer, *see* **Teuer.**

Thi . . .; *words not given under* **Thi . . .** *should be looked for under* **Ti . . .**

Thier, *see* **Tier.**

Thon, *m.* (**—s,** *pl.* **—e**) clay; **feuerfeſter —,** fire-clay; **— brennen,** to bake tiles. **—icht** (*obs.*), **—ig,** *adj.* clayey, argillaceous. *Comp.* **—ar=beiter,** *m.* worker in clay. **—artig,** *see* **—ig.** **—boden,** *m.* clayey soil. **—erde,** *f.* argillaceous earth; alumina. **—erde=metall,** *n.* aluminium. **—figur,** *f.* clay-figure. **—gefäß,** *n.* earthen vessel. **—geſtein,** *n.* argillaceous rock. **—grube,** *f.* clay-pit. **—haltig,** *adj.* argillaceous. **—kugel,** *f.* clay-pellet. **—lager,** *n.* clay-stratum. **—pfeife,** *f.* clay pipe. **—röhre,** *f.* tile pipe *or* conduit. **—ſauer,** *adj.*; **—ſaures Salz,** aluminate. **—ſchiefer,** *m.* red tile, clay-slate. **—ſchneide,** *f.* potter's knife. **—ſchneide=maſchine,** *f.* pugging-machine (*Pott.*). **—ſeiſe,** *f.* soap-earth. **—ware,** *f.* (piece of) pottery. **—ziegel,** *m.* clay-tile, roofing tile.

Thö'nern, *adj.* (of) clay, earthen; **—e Füße,** feet of clay; **—es Gefäß,** earthenware vessel.

[1]**Thor, Tor,** *n.* (**—s,** *pl.* **—e**) gate; gateway; **zum —e hinein gehen,** to enter at the gate; **zum —e hinauslaufen,** to run out of the gate *or* away; **vor das — gehen,** to take a walk outside the town. *Comp.* **—angel,** *m. & f.* hinge of a gate. **—flügel,** *m.* wing of a gate. **—geld,** *n.*, **—groſchen,** *m.* gate-money. **—glocke,** *f.* bell sounded at the closing of the gates. **—hüter,** *m.* gate-keeper, porter. **—kammer,** *f.* gate-chamber (*of a lock*). **—klappe,** *f.* small door in a gate. **—pfoſten,** *pl.* door-posts. **—ſchluß,** *m.* shutting of the gates; time of closing the gates; **vor —ſchluß** *or* **—es=ſchluß,** at the eleventh hour. **—ſchreiber,** *m.* receiver of town-dues *or* tolls; soldier in charge of the gate, sentry (*in a fortress*). **—ſperre,** *f.* *see* **—ſchluß.** **—ſtube,** *f.* porter's lodge. **—wächter, —wärter,** *m.* porter, gate-keeper. **—weg,** *m.* gateway. **—weit,** *adj.* very wide. **—zettel,** *m.* ticket, pass (*of admission or exit*).

Thor, *m.* (**—en,** *pl.* **—en**) fool. **—heit,** *f.* (*piece of*) folly; **Alter ſchützt vor —heit nicht,** age is not proof against folly (*prov.*).

Thö'r—icht, *adj. & adv.* foolish, silly, absurd. **—in,** *f.* foolish woman.

Thran, *m.* (**—s**) train-oil, blubber; **im — ſein,** to be in a state of apathy; to be drunk (*sl.*). **—icht, —ig,** *adj.* smelling *or* tasting of train-oil; containing train-oil. *Comp.* **—brennerei,** *f.* place where blubber *or* train-oil is boiled. **—ſeife,** *f.* soft soap. **—ſpeck,** *m.* blubber.

Thrä'ne, *f.* (*pl.* **—n**) tear; **in —n ſchwimmen,** to be bathed in tears. *Comp.* **—n=auge,** *n.* weeping eye; epiphora (*Med.*). **—n=bach,** *m.* torrent of tears. **—n=bein,** *n.* lachrymal bone. **—n=benetzt,** *adj.* bedewed with tears. **—n=drüſe,** *f.* lachrymal gland. **—n=feucht,** *adj.* wet with tears. **—n=feuchtigkeit,** *f.* lachrymal fluid. **—n=fluß,** *m.* flood, flow of tears; epiphora. **—n=gang,** *m.* lachrymal duct. **—n=geſchwür,** *n.* ægilops (*Med.*). **—n=grube,** *f.* lachrymal pit. **—n=krug,** *m.* lachrymatory. **—n=krüglein,** *n.* pitcher filled to overflowing with tears; person given to weeping (*hum.*). **—n=los,** *adj.* tearless, dry-eyed. **—n=quelle,** *f.* source of tears. **—n=ſack,** *m.* lachrymatory bag. **—n=thal,** *n.* vale of tears. **—n=voll,** *adj.* tearful. **—n=weide,** *f.* weeping willow. **—n=welt,** *f.* world of tears, miserable world. **—n=wert,** *adj.* deplorable.

Thrä'nen, *v.n.* (*aux.* **h.**) to be filled with tears; **die Augen — ihm,** tears are in his eyes; **mit — den Augen,** with tears in his (her) eyes.

Thron, *m.* (**—s,** *pl.* **—e**) throne; **den — beſteigen,** to ascend the throne; **vom —e ſtoßen,** to dethrone, depose; **auf den — erheben,** to raise to the throne; **ſeinen — aufſchlagen,** to establish one's authority *or* dominion. *Comp.* **—beſteigung,** *f.* accession to the crown. **—be=werber,** *m.* aspirant to the throne; competitor for the throne; pretender to a crown. **—erbe,** *m.* heir to the throne, heir apparent. **—erbin,** *f.* heiress apparent, female successor to the crown. **—erledigung,** *f.* demise. **—folge,** *f.* succession to the throne. **—folge=akte,** *f.* Act of Settlement (*in England*). **—himmel,** *m.* canopy. **—kandidatur,** *f.* candidature for a throne. **—räuber,** *m.* usurper. **—rede,** *f.* speech from the throne. **—ſaal,** *m.* throne-room; presence-chamber.

Thro'nen, *v.n.* (*aux.* **h.**) to be enthroned, to reign.

Thu—lich, *see* **Thunlich.** **—n,** *see* **Thun.** *Comp.* **—nichtgut,** *m.* ne'er-do-weel.

Thun, Tun, I. *ir.v.a.* to do, perform, make; to put; **das können Sie — und auch laſſen,** you can do that or not, as you please; **wie iſt's um dich gethan?** how fares it with thee? (*poet. obs.*); **das Seinige —,** to do one's part *or* duty; **des Guten zu viel —,** to go too far; **es iſt mir um mein Geld zu —,** I am anxious about my money; **öffentlich Abbitte —,** to make a public apology; **eine Bitte —,** to make a request; **Buße —,** to do penance; **einen Blick —,** to cast a glance (*at*); **einem einen Dienſt —,** to do s. o. a service; **Einſprache —,** to protest; **einen Eid —,** to take an oath; **eine Frage —,** to ask a question; **einen Fall —,** to have a fall, to fall; **einen Gang —,** to take a walk; **ein Gebet —,** to make *or* offer up a prayer; **Genüge —,** to satisfy; **alle Hände voll zu — haben,** to have one's hands full, to be very busy; **einem etwas zu Leide** (*or poet.* **ein Leides**) **—,** to injure a p.; **einen Schluck —,** to take a drink, a mouthful; **in die Schule —,** to put *or* send to school; **einen Schritt —,** to take a step; **einen Spruch —,** to pronounce sentence; **ich will den Teufel —!** devil take me if I do! (*vulg.*); **ein Übriges —,** to do more than is necessary; **einem Unrecht —,** to wrong a p.; to do a p. wrong; **er thut nichts,** he does nothing, he is idle; **das thut nichts,** that does not matter *or* signify, never mind; **was thut's?** what does it matter? **das thut's,** that will do, that is sufficient; **Waſſer thut es nicht,** water won't do, water is not sufficient;

er thut nichts als schimpfen, he does nothing but scold; etwas in den Sack —, to put s.th. into the bag; thu' es dort hin, put it down there; bei Seite —, to put aside; es thut not, there is need; das thut nichts zur Sache, that is nothing to the purpose, that does not alter things; etwas dazu *or* zur Sache —, to help, contribute to; was läßt sich dabei —? what can be done in the matter? II. *ir.v.n.* (*aux.* h.) to act, do; to pretend, to affect; to behave; Sie haben recht gethan, daß Sie, ꝛc., you did well to, *etc.* (in *etc.*); einem wohl —, to show a p. kindness; er thut (so), als ob er uns nicht sieht, he pretends not to see us; — Sie als ob Sie zu Hause wären, make yourself at home; er that so betrübt, he assumed such an air of sadness, he seemed so sad; böse —, to pretend to be angry; vertraut —, to affect intimacy; groß —, to affect superiority, give oneself airs; spröde —, to play the prude; man so —, to pretend (*coll.*); — Sie doch nicht so! don't make such a fuss! don't pretend! don't be so stuck-up; (mit einer Dame) schön —, to flirt (with a lady); zu wissen —, kund —, to give notice, to inform; sich (*dat.*) zu — machen mit, to occupy oneself with, to interfere, meddle with; es thäte gut wenn, it would be well if; jetzt haben wir beide mit einander zu —, now it rests with you and me, now you and I alone must settle this; es ist damit nicht gethan, the matter is not ended by that, that is not enough; es ist mir sehr darum zu —, it is of great importance to me; es thut mir leid, I am sorry, regret; es ist zu — um, it concerns; es ist mir um eine Woche zu —, I am anxious to gain a week; Sie thäten besser zu gehen, you had better go; (*used as an auxiliary* = do) loben thue ich ohne Bedenken, tadle ich aber . . ., where it is a matter of praising, I can do it readily, but when it comes to blaming . . .; loben that sie nicht viel, she did not praise much; *in the form* thät, thäten, *used* (*now only in poetry*) *to paraphrase the imperfect*; die Augen thäten ihm sinken, his eyes fell; (*used pleonastically*) ich thät das Reisen wählen, I chose to travel. III. *ir.v.r.*; sich — lassen, to be practicable, feasible; das läßt sich —, that can be done. IV. *subst. n.* doing; doings, conduct, action; sein — und Lassen, his actions, conduct; Sagen und — ist zweierlei, promising and performing are two different things. —lich, *adj.* feasible, practicable; expedient. —lichst, *adv.* as far as possible *or* practicable. —lichkeit, *f.* feasibleness; um die —lichkeit zu beweisen, to show that the thing can be done.

Thunfisch, *m.* (—es, *pl.* —e) tunny.

Thür, Tür, *f.* (*pl.* —en), —e, *f.* (*pl.* —en) door; zwei —en vor hier, the next door but one; mit der — ins Haus fallen, to let *or* blurt out, to say abruptly, to come out with a th. abruptly; sich nach der — umsehen, to seek to escape; einem die — weisen, to show a p. the door; einem die — vor der Nase zumachen, to slam the door in a p.'s face; vor der —, outside the door, at hand; zwischen — und Angel stecken, to be in a dilemma; hinter der —e Abschied nehmen, to take French leave; Politik der offnen —, policy of the open door; offne —n einrennen, to carry coals to Newcastle (*prov.*). —chen, *n.* (—chens, *pl.* —chen) little door; wicket; valve. *Comp.* —angel, *f.* hinge of a door. —beschlag, *m.* metal-work of a door, door-plate. —feld, *n.* door-panel. —flucht, *f.* space for the door to move in. —flügel, *m.* wing of a folding door. —gerüst, *n.* frame for a door; gallery-frame (*Min.*). —gewicht, *n.* weight causing a door to close of itself. —giebel, *m.* pediment (*of a door*). —griff, *m.* door-handle. —hüter(in, *f.*), *m.* door-keeper, porter. —klinke, *f.* latch. —klopfer, *m.* knocker. —kratzer, *m.* door-scraper. —pfoste(n, *m.*) *f.* door-post; (*pl.*) jambs. —platte, *f.* door-plate. —riegel, *m.* (door-)bolt. —schloß, *n.* lock of a door. —schwelle, *f.* door-sill, threshold. —spalte, *f.* chink of a door. —steher, *see* —hüter; usher (*Law*). —stein, *m.* corner-stone. —verkleidung, *f.* door-case. —vertiefung, *f.* embrasure of a door. —vorhang, *m.* door-curtain.

Thurm, Thurn, (*obs.*) *see* Turm.

1Tick, I. *int.* chuck, chuck! (*to fowls*). II. *m.* (—es, *pl.* —e) tap; home (*in a catching game*); flaw. —en, *v.* I. *a.* to tap. II. *n.* (*aux.* h.) to tick (*as a clock*). *Comp.* —tack, *adv.* tick-tack; pit-a-pat.

2Tick, *m.* (—s, *pl.* —s) whim, fancy, caprice; fad (*coll.*); einen — haben, to be whimsical; to be conceited; einen — auf einen haben, to have a grudge against a person.

Tief, *adj. & adv.* deep; innermost; profound; low; far; high; —er Teller, hollow plate *or* dish; — in Schulden, deep in debt; — atmen, to breathe heavily; — in der Nacht, far on in the night; im —sten Winter, in the depth of winter; —es Elend, extreme misery; in —en Gedanken, deep in thought; das —e Herz, the innermost heart; der —e Himmel, the dark blue sky; im —sten Norden, in the extreme north; —es Rot, dark red; die Augen liegen ihm — im Kopfe, his eyes are sunken; seinen Hut — in die Augen drücken, to pull one's hat over one's eyes; das Schiff geht sehr —, the ship draws much water; die Straße —er legen, to lower the street; ein Instrument —er stimmen, to lower the pitch of an instrument; aus des Herzens —em Grunde, from the bottom of the heart; das läßt — blicken, that gives (one) food for reflection. —e, *f.* (*pl.* —en) depth; profundity; lowness; deep place, abyss; gorge; depth (*of a battalion, etc.*); (*pl.*) soundings; —e des Zwischendecks, height between decks; —e des Herzens, depth of the heart, innermost heart; auf die —e fahren, to go out to sea. *Comp.* —aufschlag, *m.* underhand service (*Tennis*); —aufschlag *or* —anschlag mit Drehball, underhand twist service (*Tennis*). —äugig, *adj.* hollow-eyed. —bahn, *f.* underground railway. —bau, *m.* building underground. —bewandert, *adj.* profoundly versed. —bewegt, *adj.* deeply agitated *or* moved. —blau, *adj.* dark blue. —blick, *m.* penetrating glance penetration. —bohrer, *m.* squarer; auger. —ebene, *f.* (low) plain, lowland(s). —eindringend, *adj.* penetrating. —en-linie, *f.* current of a river. —en-messung, *f.* measuring of depths. —er-legung, *f.* lowering (*of level*). —ernst, *adj.* very grave, solemn. —gang, *m.* draught (*of vessels*); ein Schiff von 8 Zoll —gang, a ship drawing 8 inches of water. —gehend, *adj.* going deeply into; profound; thoroughgoing; deep-drawing (*Naut.*). —hammer, *m.* hollowing hammer. —land, *n.* low-lying country. —liegend, *adj.* deep-seated; sunken. —lot, *n.* deep-sea lead. —quart, *f.* low quarte (*fenc.*); lower fourth (*Mus.*). —ründe, *f.* concavity. —schäftig, *adj.* of the low-warp (*Weav.*). —see-lotung, *f.* deep-sea soundings, bathymetry. —see-schlamm, *m.* deep-sea slime, bathybius. —sein, *n.* depth. —sinn, *m.*, —sinnigkeit, *f.* profoundness; thoughtfulness; reverie; melancholy. —sinnig, *adj.* thoughtful; pensive; serious; profound. —stimmig, *adj.* deep-voiced, deep-mouthed. —ton, *m.* secondary accent (*opp. to* Hochton, *Pros.*). —tönend, *adj.* deep-sounding. —un-

terst, *adj.* the very deepest, bottom-most, nethermost. **—wurzelnd,** *adj.* deep-rooted.

Tie'fen, *v.a.* to deepen; to take soundings.

Tie'gel, *m.* (—s, *pl.* —) stew-pan; sauce-pan; crucible; smelting-pot; platen (*Typ.*). **—guß,** *m.* melting in crucibles. **—zange,** *f.* crucible tongs.

Tie'ne, *f.* (*pl.* —n) little tub.

Tier, *n.* (—s, *pl.* —e) animal; living creature; beast; brute; doe, hind; **er ist ein großes —,** he is a person of consequence, he is a big gun (*coll.*). **—chen,** *n.* (—chens, *pl.* —chen) little beast; little creature; animalcule; **jedes —chen hat sein Pläsirchen,** little things please little minds; every one has his own hobby; every man to his taste. **—heit,** *f.* animal nature; brutishness. **—isch,** *adj.* animal; bestial, brutish, beastly; **—ische Geister,** animal spirits; **—ischer Leim,** gluten. *Comp.* (*often* = zoo . . .) **—anbetung,** *f.* worship of animals; zoolatry. **—art,** *f.* species of animals. **—arznei=kunde,** *f.* veterinary science. **—arznei=schule,** *f.* veterinary college *or* school. **—arzt,** *m.* veterinary surgeon. **—ärztlich,** *adj.* veterinary. **—ausstopfer,** *m.* taxidermist. **—beschreibung,** *f.* zoography. **—buch,** *n.* book about animals. **—bude,** *f.* menagerie. **—chemie,** *f.* animal chemistry. **—epos,** *n.* animal epic, beast epic (*esp'lly of Reynard the fox*). **—garten,** *m.* preserve, park (for game); zoological gardens. **—geschichte,** *f.* natural history of animals. **—haus,** *n.* menagerie. **—heilkunde,** *f.* veterinary science. **—hetze,** *f.* chase. **—kalb,** *n.* young doe. **—kenner, —kundige(r),** *m.* zoologist. **—kohle,** *f.* animal charcoal. **—kreis,** *m.* zodiac (*Astr.*). **—kunde, —lehre,** *f.* zoology. **—leben,** *n.* animal life. **—maler,** *m.* animal-painter. **—pflanze,** *f.* zoophyte. **—quälerei,** *f.* cruelty to animals; **Verein gegen —quälerei,** society for the prevention of cruelty to animals. **—reich,** *n.* animal kingdom; animals (*coll.*). **—sage,** *f.* beast-legend cycle, beast epic. **—schau,** *f.* cattle-show. **—schutz,** *m.* protection of animals. **—schutz=verein,** *m.* society for the prevention of cruelty to animals. **—stück,** *n.* painting representing animals. **—versteinerung,** *f.* zoolite. **—wärter,** *m.* keeper (*of animals*). **—welt,** *f.* animals (*coll.*); animal kingdom. **—wesen,** *n.* animal; animality, brute nature.

Ti'ger, *m.* (—s, *pl.* —) tiger. **—in,** *f.* tigress. **—n,** *v.a.* to spot, to speckle; **getigert,** speckled; brindled; tabbied (*of cats*). *Comp.* **—decke, —haut,** *f.*, **—fell,** *n.* tiger-skin(-*rug*). **—farbig, —fleckig,** *adj.* spotted, striped like a tiger. **—hund,** *m.* striped dog. **—katze,** *f.* tiger-cat; tiger; panther; tortoiseshell cat. **—pferd,** *n.* zebra; spotted horse. **—tier,** *n.* tiger. **—weibchen,** *n.* tigress. **—wolf,** *m.* spotted hyena; wolf with tiger-like ferocity, ferocious wolf (*poet.*).

Tilg'—bar, *adj.* extinguishable, effaceable; redeemable. **—keit,** *f.* annullability; redeemableness.

Til'g—en, *v.a.* to extinguish; to efface, erase, blot out; to eradicate, destroy; to abolish; to cancel, annul; **eine Schuld —en,** to cancel a debt, to pay a debt. **—er,** *m.* (—ers, *pl.* —er) destroyer, exterminator; annuller; **—er der Sünde,** Redeemer. **—ung,** *f.* extermination; blotting out; cancelling; liquidation, payment (*of debts*); redemption (*of annuities*). *Comp.* **—ungs=fonds,** *m.*, **—ungs=kasse,** *f.* sinking fund. **—ungs=schein,** *m.* certificate of redemption, bill of amortization. **—ungs=zeichen,** *n.* dele (*Typ.*).

Tin'geltangel, *m.* low music-hall, café chantant (*coll.*).

Tingie'ren, *v.a.* to colour, tinge, dye; to extract (*essence, etc.*).

Tinktu'r, *f.* (*pl.* —en) tincture, infusion; dye.

Tin't—e, *f.* (*pl.* —en) ink; tint (*Paint.*); scrape; **halbe —e,** mezzotinto; **in der —e sitzen,** to be in a pretty mess; **in die —e kommen** *or* **geraten,** to get into a scrape; **er muß —e gesoffen haben,** he must be cracked (*sl.*). **—ig,** *adj.* inky; stained with ink; ink-like. *Comp.* **—en=beutel,** *m.* ink-bag of the cuttle-fish. **—en=faß,** *n.* inkstand. **—en=faß=feder,** *f.* self-feeding *or* fountain pen. **—en=fisch,** *m.* cuttle-fish. **—en=fisch=schwarz,** *n.* sepia. **—en=flasche,** *f.* ink-bottle. **—en=fleck,** *m.* blot, ink-stain. **—en=klecks,** *m.* ink-stain *or* blot. **—en=kleckser,** *m.* scribbler; dauber. **—en=sack,** *m.* *see* **—enbeutel.** **—en=stecher,** *m.* inkhorn (*obs.*). **—en=stift,** *m.* ink (lead) pencil; stylograph. **—en=strich,** *m.* line drawn with ink; stroke of the pen. **—en=wein, Tinto,** *m.* Tent-wine (*a Spanish port*). **—en=wischer,** *m.* penwiper.

Tip'p—el, *n.* & *m.* (—els, *pl.* —el) tittle, dot (*coll.*); **bis aufs —elchen wissen,** to know to the smallest detail. **—eln,** *v.* I. *a.* to dot; to stipple. II. *n.* (*aux.* s.) to tip-toe. **—en,** *v.a.* to touch gently, tap.

Tiraillie'ren, *v.n.* (*aux.* h.) to skirmish (*Mil.*)

Tisch, *m.* (—es, *pl.* —e) table; dinner- *or* supper-table; board, food; **— des Herrn,** communion table; **Scheidung von — und Bett,** judicial separation; **am —e, bei —e,** at table; during meal-time; **nach (vor) —e,** after (before) dinner *or* supper; **über** *or* **bei —(e),** during dinner *or* supper; **eine Dame zu —(e) führen,** to take a lady in (to dinner); **zu —(e) gehen,** to sit down to a meal, dinner, supper, *etc.*; **zu —e laden,** to ask to dine *or* to dinner; **ich blieb zu —,** I stayed for dinner; **den — decken,** to lay the cloth; **den — abdecken,** to clear the table; **den — bei einem haben,** to board with a p.; **einen guten — führen,** to keep a good table; **reinen — machen,** to make a clean sweep; **am grünen —e,** at the council-board; **Verordnungen vom grünen —e,** red tape ordinances. **—chen, —lein,** *n.* (—leins, *pl.* —lein) small table, stand; **—lein deck dich,** table spread, magic table. **—en,** *v.a.* & *n.* (*aux.* h.) to lay the cloth, prepare the table; to sit at table; to feast; **es ist nicht für mich getischt,** there is no cover laid for me. *Comp.* **—aufsatz,** *m.* service of glass, plate, *etc.*; cruet; centre-piece; dumb-waiter. **—besteck,** *n.* cover, knife and fork. **—blatt,** *n.* table-top; leaf of a table. **—bursch,** *m.* boarder. **—dame,** *f.* lady taken in to dinner. **—gänger,** *m.* boarder; regular diner at a restaurant. **—gast,** *m.* guest (*at dinner*). **—gebet,** *n.* grace; **das —gebet beten,** to say grace, return thanks. **—gedeck,** *n.* table-linen; dinner service. **—geld,** *n.* board-wages (*of servants*). **—genoß,** *m.* fellow boarder; messmate. **—gerät, —geschirr,** *n.* plate, glass for the table. **—gespräch,** *n.* table-talk. **—gestell,** *n.* trestle; frame of a table. **—glocke,** *f.* dinner-bell; gong. **—herr,** *m.* gentleman taking a lady in to dinner. **—karte,** *f.* name-card. **—kasten,** *m.* table-drawer. **—klopfen,** *n.* table-rapping, table-turning. **—korb,** *m.* plate-basket. **—läufer,** *m.* table-centre. **—platte,** *f.* table-top. **—reden,** *pl.* table-talk; speeches, toasts. **—rücken,** *n.* table-turning; house-warming (*dial.*). **—segen,** *see* **—gebet.** **—teppich,** *m.* table-cover. **—tuch,** *n.* table-cloth. **—wein,** *m.* ordinary table-wine. **—zeit,** *f.* meal-time. **—zeug,** *n.* table-linen. **—zucht,** *f.* rules to be observed during meal-time; **altdeutsche —zuchten,** old German books of courtesy.

Tisch'ler, *m.* (—s, *pl.* —) joiner, carpenter; cabinet-maker. **—ei',** *f.* carpentry; cabinet-making. **—n,** *v.a.* & *n.* (*aux.* h.) to do carpentry. *Comp.* —arbeit, *f.*, —handwerk, *n.* *see* —ei. —bank, *f.* joiner's bench. —gesell, *m.* journeyman joiner. —meister, *m.* master-joiner. —werkzeug, *n.* joiner's tools.

Tita'n, I., —e, *m.* (—en, *pl.* —en) Titan. II. *n.* (—s) titanium. —enhaft, —isch, *adj.* Titanic. *Comp.* —eisen, *n.* titanic iron, sandy, magnetic iron ore. —sauer, *adj.;* —saures Salz, titanate.

Ti'tel, *m.* (—s, *pl.* —) title; claim; bloßer —, mere *or* empty title; Sie werden es unter dem und dem — finden, you will find it under such and such a head(ing); Buch mit aufgedrucktem —, lettered book; den — Graf *or* eines Grafen führen, to have the title of count. *Comp.* —auflage, —ausgabe, *f.* edition with merely a new title-page. —bild, *n.* frontispiece. —bildchen, *n.* vignette. —blatt, *n.* title-page; title. —bogen, *m.* title-sheet (*Typ.*). —kopf, *m.* heading (*of an article*). —könig, *m.* titular king. —kupfer, *n.* frontispiece. —los, *adj.* without a title. —narr, *m.* person with a mania for titles. —sucht, *f.* fondness for titles, tuft-hunting. —vignette, *f.* head-piece. —wesen, *n.* (everything relating to) titles; (system of bestowing) titles. —wort, *n.* head-word. —zahl, *f.* number of titles; head number, number at the head of a chapter.

Titrie'r—en, *v.a.* to titrate. *Comp.* —apparate, *pl.* volumetric apparatus. —methode, *f.* titration.

Titul—a'r, *adj.* titulary; nominal, honorary; brevet (*Mil.*). —atu'r, *f.* styling; title(s). —ie'ren, *v.a.* to style; einen Herzog —ieren, to give a p. the title of duke.

Ti'voli(spiel), *n.* German billiards.

Toast, *m.* (—es, *pl.* —e) toast, health; toasted bread; einen — ausbringen, *see* —en; auf einen — antworten, to respond to a toast. —en, *v.a. & n.* (*aux.* h.) to propose a toast, to toast.

To'bak, (**Toba'ck**,) *m.* (—s, *pl.* —e) tobacco (*obs. see* Tabak); ein beizender —, stinging tobacco; seit anno —, from times immemorial (*sl.*).

To'bel, *m.* gorge, gully (*dial.*).

To'b—en, *v.n.* (*aux.* h.) to fume, storm, rage, bluster, rave; das —en, raving madness. *Comp.* —sucht, *f.* frenzy, delirium.

Toch'ter, *f.* (*pl.* Töchter) daughter; höhere —, high-school girl (*coll.*); — der Lust, prostitute; — Zion, daughter of Zion. *Comp.* —anstalt, *f.* branch-establishment. —herz, *n.* filial *or* daughter's heart; dear daughter. —kapelle, *f.* chapel of ease. —kind, *n.* daughter's child, grandchild. —kirche, *f.* chapel of ease. —land, *n.* colony. —liebe, *f.* filial *or* daughter's love. —loge, *f.* branch lodge, offshoot (*Freem.*). —mann, *m.* son-in-law. —sprache, *f.* derivative *or* daughter language. —staat, *m.* colony. —stadt, *f.* colonial town.

Töch'ter—chen, *n.* (—chens, *pl.* —chen) little daughter. —lich, *adj.* daughterly, filial. *Comp.* —anstalt, —schule, *f.* girls' school; höhere —schule, high school for girls, girls' college. —institut, *n.*, —pension, *f.* boarding-school for girls.

Tockie'ren, *v.a. & n.* (*aux.* h.) to paint in a bold style.

Tod, *m.* (—es, *pl.* —e, *often* To'desfälle) death; decease; auf den — gefangen sitzen, to be imprisoned for a capital offence; auf den — verwundet, mortally wounded; er ist mir (bis) in den — verhaßt, I hate him with a deadly hatred *or* like poison; bis in den — zuwider, utterly detestable; mit (dem) —e abgehen, to die; nach dem —e, after death, posthumous; der — läuft mir über das Grab, I shudder (*coll.*); sich zu —e ärgern, to be terribly vexed, to fret oneself to death; sich zu —e lachen, to die with laughing *or* laughter; einen zu —e quälen, to worry a p. to death; zum —e betrübt, grieved to death, mortally grieved; Geld oder — ! your money or your life! eines schönen —es sterben, to die nobly *or* well; du bist ein Kind des —es, wenn . . ., you are a dead man if . . .; ich will des —es sein, wenn . . ., may I die if . . .; ich will den — an dem Bissen essen, wenn . . ., may this be my last bite if . . .; umsonst ist (nur) der —, everything has its price *or* costs money; für den — kein Kraut gewachsen ist, there is no remedy against death (*prov.*); des einen — des andern Brot, one man's meat is another man's poison (*prov.*); nach unserm —e mag kommen, was da will! after us the deluge! — und Teufel! Zounds! *Comp.* —ähnlich, *adj.* death-like. —bange, *adj.* mortally terrified, frightened to death. —bringend, *adj.* inflicting death, deadly; fatal; mortal. —es=ahnung, *f.* foreboding of death. —es=angst, *f.* death-agony; mortal terror. —es=anzeige, *f.* announcement of a death, obituary notice; notification *or* notice of death. —es=art, *f.* manner of death. —es=becher, *m.* fatal cup. —es=block, *m.* fatal block (*of a scaffold*). —es=ende, *n.;* an —esenden sein, to be at death's door (*coll.*). —es=fackel, *f.* funeral torch. —es=fall, *m.* death; decease; casualty (*in war*); (*pl.*) deaths (*used as a pl. of* Tod). —es=feier, *f.* funeral solemnity; commemoration of a death. —es=gefahr, *f.* deadly peril, peril of one's life; in —esgefahr schweben, to be in imminent danger; einen aus —esgefahr retten, to save a p.'s life. —es=kampf, *m.* death-struggle, throes of death, last agony; mortal combat. —es=kandidat, *m.* one who has not long to live, dying man. —es=keim, *m.* germ *or* seeds of death. —es=not, *f.* peril of death; in —esnöten, struggling with death. —es=pein, *f.* pangs of death. —es=pfeil, *m.* fatal arrow. —es=pforte, *f.* death's door. —es=ritt, *m.* death-ride, last charge. —es=röcheln, *n.* death-rattle. —es=schlaf, *m.* sleep of the dead; deathlike *or* profound sleep. —es=schrecken, *m.* fear of death; deadly fright. —es=stoß, *m.* death-blow, finishing stroke. —es=strafe, *f.* capital punishment; bei —esstrafe, on pain of death; die —esstrafe erleiden, to suffer the death-penalty, to be executed. —es=stunde, *f.* hour of death; fatal *or* supreme hour. —es=tag, *m.* day of death; anniversary of a p.'s death. —es=urteil, *n.* sentence of death; ein —esurteil vollstrecken, to carry out a sentence of death. —es=verachtung, *f.* contempt *or* defiance of death. —es=verbrechen, *n.* capital crime. —es=wunde, *f.* mortal wound. —es=würdig, *adj.* deserving death. —feind, *m.* deadly enemy. —feindschaft, *f.* deadly enmity. —krank, *adj.* hopelessly ill; sick unto death (*B.*). —matt, —müde, *adj.* dead tired, completely worn out. —sünde, *f.* deadly sin.

Todt, *see* Tot.

Toilet'te, *f.* (*pl.* —n) toilet; dress; toilet-table; — machen, to dress, to make one's toilet.

Toler—a'nt, *adj.* tolerant (gegen, of). —a'nz, *f.* toleration. —ie'ren, *v.a.* to tolerate.

Toll, *adj. & adv.* mad; frantic; furious; nonsensical; absurd; erratic, extravagant, wild; intoxicating, stupefying; —er Hund, mad dog; —er Einfall, mad freak; es ist zum — werden, man möchte — werden, it is enough to drive one mad; einen — machen, to drive a p. mad; — und voll, dead drunk; — auf . . ., mad after . . .; er macht *or* treibt es zu —, he goes too far; das ist zu —, that's too bad; bist du —, are you out of your senses? ist das nicht —, is n't it absurd? das —ste dabei, the funniest part of it; je —er je besser, the madder the merrier; **das wird noch —er kommen,** the worst is yet to come. **—en,** *v.n.* (*aux.* **h.** & **s.**) to be boisterous *or* rollicking, to romp (*about*); to fool about, to make a row (*coll.*). **—heit,** *f.* madness, frenzy; rage, fury; mad trick *or* action, piece of folly; eccentricity. *Comp.* **—beere,** *f.* belladonna. **—haus,** *n.* lunatic asylum. **—häusler,** *m.* madman, maniac. **—kerbel,** *m.* wild chervil; hemlock. **—kirsche,** *f.* deadly nightshade, belladonna. **—kopf,** *m.* madcap; hot-headed person. **—köpfig,** *adj.* mad, harebrained, cracked; hot-headed. **—korn,** *n.* cockleweed, darnel. **—körner,** *pl.* seeds of the thorn-apple. **—kraut,** *n.* belladonna; Datura. **—kühn,** *adj.* foolhardy, rash. **—kühnheit,** *f.* foolhardiness, rashness. **—sucht,** *f.* madness. **—wut,** *f.* raving (*madness*); frenzy; hydrophobia (*of dogs*).

Tol′l—e, *f.* (*pl.* **—en**) tuft, crest; fringe (*of hair*); frill. **—en,** *v.a.* to crimp (*frills, etc.*); to frizzle (*the hair*). *Comp.* **—eisen,** *n.* crimping-iron, goffering-tongs. **—falte,** *f.* goffer. **—kragen,** *m.* goffered collar.

Töl′p—el, *m.* (**—els,** *pl.* **—el**), **Tol′patsch,** *m.* (**—es,** *pl.* **—e**) blockhead; booby; lout; gannet (*Orn.*); dodo (*Orn.*). **—elei′,** *f.* awkwardness, loutishness; boorish manners. **—elhaft, —isch,** *adj.* clumsy; doltish, stupid; loutish. **—elhaftigkeit,** *see* **—elei.** **—eln,** *v.n.* (*aux.* **h.**) to be awkward *or* clumsy in one's manners.

Toma′te, *f.* (*pl.* **—n**) tomato.

Tom′bak, *m.* (& *n.*) (**—s**) tombac, pinchbeck (*alloy of zinc and copper*).

Ton, *m.* (**—s,** *pl.* **Tö′ne**) sound; note (*Mus.*); (**—art**) key (*Mus.*); timbre (*Mus.*); tone (*Mus., Paint., Med., etc.*); strain; fashion, tone; stress, accent; air; tinge; **einen andern — anschlagen,** to change one's tone; **ein ernster —,** a serious word (*coll.*); **den — halten,** to keep in tune; **einen — von sich geben,** to utter a sound; **in spöttischem —e,** jeeringly; **es ist jetzt feiner — zu . . .,** it is now the fashion to, a mark of good-breeding to . . .; **das ist kein guter —,** that is not good form, that is not etiquette; **den — angeben,** to set the fashion; **in einem hohen —e,** in a high key, loftily; **Mann von gutem —e,** well-bred man; **eine Dame von gutem —,** a thorough gentlewoman. **—ika,** *f.* key-note, tonic (*Mus.*). **—isch,** *adj.* tonic (*Med.*). *Comp.* **—abstand,** *m.* interval (*Mus.*). **—abweichung, —ausweichung,** *f.* modulation (*Mus.*). **—angebend,** *adj.*; **—angebende Kreise,** leading *or* fashionable circles. **—angeber,** *m.* leader of fashion. **—art,** *f.* key, mode; tone. **—bad,** *n.* toning bath (*Photo.*). **—bild,** *n.* musical tableau; representation of something by music; symphony; phonetic figuration of a sound. **—bühne,** *f.* orchestra. **—dichter,** *m.* (*musical*) composer. **—dichtung,** *f.* musical composition. **—empfindung,** *f.* tone-sensation. **—fall,** *m.* cadence. **—farbe,** *f.* timbre. **—folge,** *f.* scale, succession of tones; melody. **—führung,** *f.* modulation. **—fülle,** *f.* volume of sound; melodiousness. **—gemälde,** *n. see* **—bild.** **—halle,** *f.* concert-hall. **—höhe,** *f.* musical pitch, pitch of a note. **—kunst,** *f.* music, musical art. **—künstler(in,** *f.*,) *m.* professional musician, virtuoso. **—lehre,** *f.* acoustics. **—leiter, —reihe,** *f.* gamut, scale. **—los,** *adj.* soundless; voiceless, surd; unaccented. **—losigkeit,** *f.* absence of sound; absence of stress. **—malerei,** *f.* imitative music. **—maß,** *n.* measure, metre; quantity (*Pros.*). **—messer,** *m.* tonometer. **—messung,** *f.* tonometry, prosody. **—satz,** *m.* phrase (*Mus.*). **—schluß,** *m.* cadence. **—schlüssel,** *m.* key, clef. **—schöpfung,** *f.* musical creation. **—schrift,** *f.* musical notation *or* notes. **—setzer,** *m.* (musical) composer. **—setzkunst,** *f.* art of composition. **—silbe,** *f.* accented syllable, stressed syllable. **—stäbe,** *pl.* abstracts (*Org.*). **—stärke,** *f.* force *or* stress of sound *or* tone. **—stück,** *n.* piece of music, composition. **—stufe,** *f.* pitch (*Mus.*); degree (*of a scale*). **—übergang,** *m.* change of key; modulation. **—umfang,** *m.* compass, range (*of a voice, etc.*). **—veränderung,** *f.* change of tone *or* accent; modulation. **—verhältnis,** *n.* inter-relation of sounds; rhythm. **—verschiebung,** *f.* shifting of accent. **—wahrnehmung,** *f.* tone-perception. **—welle,** *f.* sound-wave. **zeichen,** *n.* accent; note (*Mus.*).

Tö′nen, *v.* I. *n.* (*aux.* **h.**) to sound, resound; to ring. II. *a.* to time; to give voice to; to express by sound; to sing; **töne ins Horn,** sound the bugle (*poet.*).

Ton′ne, *f.* (*pl.* **—n,** *dim.* **Tönn′chen**) tun, butt; cask, barrel; ton (*weight of 1,000 kilograms, or about 2,205 pounds Avd.*); **eine — Häringe,** a cask of herrings. *Comp.* **—n-butter,** *f.* cask *or* barrelled butter. **—n-förmig,** *adj.* barrel-shaped; tubby. **—n-fracht,** *f.* freight per ton. **—n-gehalt,** *m.* ship's tonnage, burden. **—n-geld,** *n.* tonnage. **—n-gewölbe,** *n.* tunnel-vault. **—n-last,** *f.* ton (*weight*), tonnage. **—n-maß,** *n.* tonnage. **—n-reif,** *m.* cask-hoop.

Tonsu′r, *f.* (*pl.* **—en**) tonsure.

Topa′s, *m.* (**—(s)es,** *pl.* **—(s)e**) topaz. *Comp.* **—fels,** *m.* topaz-rock. **—fluß,** *m.* false topaz.

Topf, *m.* (**—es,** *pl.* **Töp′fe**) pot; (**Nacht**) **—,** chamber; **papinianischer —,** Papin's digester; (**Pflanzen**) **in den — einsetzen,** to pot (*plants*); **Alles in einen — werfen,** to treat all alike, to make no distinctions. *Comp.* **—binder,** *m.* mender of broken pots. **—blume,** *f.*, **—gewächs,** *n.* plant growing in a pot, potted plant. **—brett,** *n.* dresser; rack for pots and pans; flower-stand. **—deckel,** *m.* pot-lid. **—fabrik,** *f.* pottery. **—form,** *f.* mould. **—glasur,** *f.* potter's glaze. **—gucker,** *m.* a p. fond of poking about the kitchen, prying p. **—haken,** *m.* pot-hook. **—kuchen,** *m.* cake baked in an earthenware pan, sort of dough-cake. **—lappen,** *m.* kettle-holder; oven-cloth. **—lecker,** *m.* glutton, greedy person. **—macher,** *m.* potter. **—markt,** *m.* crockery fair. **—scherbe,** *f.* potsherd. **—schlagen,** *n.* an out-of-doors game (in which a blindfolded person is to strike a flower-pot). **—ständer,** *m.* flower-stand. **—stein,** *m.* pot-stone, soapstone. **—stürze,** *f.* pot-lid.

Töpf′—chen, *n.* (**—chens,** *pl.* **—chen**) small pot *or* jar; (**Nacht**)**—chen,** small chamber. **—er,** *m.* (**—ers,** *pl.* **—er**) potter. **—erei′,** *f.* pottery; ceramic art; pottery-trade. **—ern,** *v.a.* & *n.* (*aux.* **h.**) to make pottery. *Comp.* **—erarbeit,** *f.* potter's work. **—er-erde,** *f.* potter's clay. **—er-geschirr, —er-gut,** *n.* earthenware, pottery, crockery. **—er-gesell,** *m.* journeyman potter. **—er-scheibe,** *f.* potter's lathe. **—er-thon,** *m.* plastic earth, potter's clay. **—er-ware,** *f. see* **—ergut.**

To′p—ik, *f.* the art of finding arguments. **—isch,** *adj.* topical. **—ogra′ph,** *m.* topographer. **—ographie′,** *f.* topography. **—ogra′phisch,** *adj.* topographical.

¹**Topp,** *int.* done! agreed; all right! so be it!

²**Topp,** *m.* (**—es,** *pl.* **—e**) top, head; **vor — und Takel treiben,** to sail under bare poles. **—ena′nt,** *f.* (*topping*) lift (*Naut.*). *Comp.* **—auflanger,** *pl.* top-timbers. **—segel,** *n.* top-sail.

Tor, *n.* (**—s,** *pl.* **—e**) goal. **—wächter,** *m.* (**—s,** *pl.* **—**) goalkeeper.

Torf, *m.* (**—(e)s,** *pl.* **—e, Tör′fe**) peat; turf (*rare*); **— graben** *or* **stechen,** to cut peat. *Comp.* **—artig,** *adj.* peaty. **—asche,** *f.* peat-ashes. **—boden,** *m.* turfy ground, peat-bog; turf-shed *or* loft. **—bruch,** *m.* peat-bog *or* moss; turf-moss. **—erde,** *f.* peaty earth *or* mould. **—gräber,** *m.* peat-cutter. **—grube,** *f.* peat-pit. **—lager,** *n.* peat-bog. **—land,** *n.* moor.

—masse, *f.* peat. **—moor**, *n.* peat-moor. — **moos**, *n.* gray sphagnum, bog-moss (*Bot.*). — **presse**, *f.* peat-compressing machine. **—soden, —sohlen**, *pl.* sods of peat. **—staub**, *see* — **erde**. **—stechen**, *n.* peat-cutting *or* digging. **—stich**, *m.* peat-cutting.

Tor'fen, *v.a.* to manure with turfy mould.

Tor'kel, *m.* (—s) good luck (*sl.*). **—n**, *v.n.* (*aux.* **s.**) to reel, stagger (*coll.*).

Tornis'ter, *m.* (—s, *pl.* —) haversack; pouch; knapsack; satchel.

Torpe'd—er, *m.* (—ers, *pl.* —er) torpedo-worker, submarine-miner (*Naut.*). *Comp.* **—o=boot**, *n.* torpedo-boat; **unterseeisches —o=boot**, submarine torpedo-boat. **—o=(boots=) jäger**, *m.* torpedo-catcher. **—o=(boots=) zerstörer**, torpedo-destroyer.

Tort, *m.* (—s) wrong, injury; **einem zum —**, to spite a person.

Tor'te, *f.* (*pl.* —n, *dim.* **Tört'chen**) fancy-cake tart; (*dim.*) tartlet. *Comp.* **—n=bäcker**, *m.* pastry-cook. **—n=pfanne**, *f.* patty-pan. **—n=teig**, *m.* batter; paste for a tart *or* cake.

Tortu'r, *f.* (*pl.* —en) torture; **einen auf die — spannen**, to torture a person.

To'sen, *v.n.* (*aux.* **h.** & **s.**) to rage, storm, roar.

Tot, *adj.* dead; lifeless; stagnant, dull; uninvested, idle; **—e Zeit**, dull, dead season; **—e Hand**, mortmain; **an die —e Hand verkaufen**, to amortize; **—es Kapital**, unemployed capital; **—es Gebirge**, exhausted mines; **—es Wasser**, neap-tide; **—es Fleisch**, proud flesh; **sein Geld, (die Zeit) — schlagen**, to waste one's money (time); **ein —es Rennen**, a dead heat; **—es Wissen**, useless *or* unprofitable knowledge; **—e Befriedigung**, paling, railed fence; **der Wind ist — geregnet**, the rain has lulled the wind; **eine Sache — machen**, to hush up a matter; **das macht einen auch nicht —**, that is not a killing matter; **sich — arbeiten**, to kill o. s. by working *or* with work; **sich — lachen**, to split one's sides with laughter; **sie wollten sich — lachen**, they nearly died with laughter; **sich — schießen**, to blow out one's brains; **etwas — schweigen**, to hush up a matter. **—e(r)**, *m.*, **—e**, *f.* dead person; **die —en**, the dead; *see* **Toten** (*in* (*comp.*). — **enhaft**, *adj.* deathlike; cadaverous. *Comp.* — **geboren**, *adj.* still-born. **—lachen**, *n.;* **es ist zum —lachen**, it is enough to make one die with laughing, it is too funny for anything; **Geschichte zum —lachen**, screaming tale *or* story. **—liegende(s)**, *n.;* **das rote —liegende**, new red conglomerate. **—schießen**, *n.;* **es ist zum —schießen**, it is enough to make one blow one's brains out; it is too funny for anything, a capital joke *or* story (*coll.*). **—schlag**, *m.* homicide, manslaughter. **—schläger**, *m.* a p. guilty of manslaughter; loaded cane, life-preserver. **—schweigen**, *n.* hushing up (*of a matter*).

Tota'l, *adj.* & *adv.* total, whole. **—itä't**, *f.* totality. *Comp.* **—ansicht**, *f.* entire view. **—betrag**, *m.* sum total, whole amount. — **bilanz**, *f.* final balance (*C. L.*). **—summe**, *f.* sum total.

To'ten— (*in comp.*) **—acker**, *m.* burying-ground. **—amt**, *n.* burial-service; mass for the dead, requiem. **—bahre**, *f.* bier. **—begängnis**, *n.* obsequies, funeral. **—beschwörer**, *m.* necromancer. **—bett**, *n.* death-bed. **—blaß**, *adj.* pale as death. **—bläſſe**, *f.* deadly pallor. — **buch**, *n.* register of deaths. **—eule**, *f.* screech-owl. **—farbig**, *adj.* corpse-like, cadaverous (*complexion*). **—feier**, *f.* funeral rites; solemnity in honour of the dead. **—fest**, *n.* commemoration. **—flagge**, *f.* flag hoisted half-mast high. **—fleck**, *m.* livid spot (*on a corpse*). — **gebeine**, *pl.* bones of the dead. **—geläut(e)**, *n.* knell; passing-bell. **—geleit**, *n.* funeral train; **einem das —geleit geben**, to attend a person's funeral. **—gerippe**, *n.* skeleton. — **geruch**, *m.* cadaverous smell. **—gerüst**, *n.* catafalque. **—gesang**, *m.* funeral chant *or* dirge; funeral hymn. **—gespräch**, *n.* dialogue of the dead. **—gewand**, *n.* shroud. **—glocke**, *f.* funeral bell; knell. **—gräber**, *m.* grave-digger; necrophorus (*Ent.*). **—gruft**, *f.* vault. **—haus**, *n.* dead-house, mortuary. — **hemd**, *n.* shroud. **—hügel**, *m.* barrow, mound over the dead. **—käfer**, *m.* rare cellar-beetle. **—klage**, *f.* lamentation for the dead. **—kopf**, *m.* death's head; skull; caput mortuum (*Chem.*). **—krampf**, *m.* tetanus. — **kranz**, *m.*, **—krone**, *f.* funeral wreath. **—lied**, *n.* funeral chant, dirge. **—liste**, *f.* obituary, list of the dead; list of casualties. **—mahl**, *n.* funeral feast; wake. **—marsch**, *m.* funeral-march. **—maske**, *f.* death-mask. **—messe**, *f.* mass for the dead. **—opfer**, *n.* sacrifice to *or* for the dead. **—register**, *n.* see **—buch**. **—reich**, *n.* realm of the dead, Hades. — **schau**, *f.* coroner's inquest; post-mortem examination. **—schauer**, *m.* doctor who furnishes certificate of death; coroner. **—schein**, *m.* certificate of death. **—schild**, *n.* hatchment. **—schlaf, —schlummer**, *m.* deathlike sleep, trance; sleep of death, last sleep. **—stadt**, *f.* necropolis. **—starre**, *f.* rigidity of death. **—still**, *adj.* as still as death; **—still lag die See**, the sea was a dead calm. **—stille**, *f.* dead silence *or* calm. **—tabellen**, *pl.* bills of mortality. **—tanz**, *m.* dance of death, dance Macaber. **—träger**, *m.* corpse-bearer. — **uhr**, *f.* death-watch (*Ent.*). **—urne**, *f.* sepulchral urn. **—verbrennung**, *f.* cremation. **—vogel**, *m.* bird of death; white owl; flax-finch; wall-creeper. **—wache**, *f.* wake; death watch, watch by a dead body. **—wurm**, *m.* death-watch beetle; **der —wurm pickt**, the death-watch ticks.

Tö't—en, I. *v.a.* to kill; to destroy; to mortify (*the body*); to annul (*a contract*); to consume (*drink*); to extinguish (*fire*); to fix (*mercury*); **sich —en**, to commit suicide. II. *subst. n.* killing; fixing (*of quicksilver*); mortification (*of the flesh*). **—er**, *m.* (—ers, *pl.* —er) murderer; killer. **—lich**, *adj.* fatal; deadly; mortal; murderous; **—lich hassen**, to hate with a deadly hatred, to hate like poison. **—lichkeit**, *f.* deadliness, fatal nature. **—ung**, *f.* see **—en** II.; **fahrlässige —ung**, manslaughter.

Touchie'ren, *v.a.* to touch; to affect, to offend.

Tour, *f.* (*pl.* —en) tour; trip, excursion; round; turn (*Danc.*); turn in the conversation; coiffure; **zwei —en im Stricken**, two rounds in knitting; **einen Wagen auf die — nehmen**, to take a cab by distance; **außer der —**, out of one's turn, not according to seniority (*Mil.*); **in einer —**, at a stretch, continuously (*coll.*). **—i'st**, *m.* tourist. **—nü're**, *f.* see **Gewandtheit**; dress-improver. *Comp.* **—billet**, *n.* single ticket. **—en=rad**, *n.* roadster; **leichte —en=räder**, light roadsters. **—isten=(fahr)karte**, *n.* excursion-ticket.

Trab, *m.* (—es) trot; **im — gehen**, to trot; **in — setzen**, to put into a trot; **einen auf den — bringen**, to urge a p. on; **warte, ich werde dich auf den — bringen!** just wait a moment, I'll soon make you find your legs! **—a'nt**, *m.* (—an'ten, *pl.* —an'ten) gentleman-at-arms, satellite, myrmidon. *Comp.* **—gänger**, *m.* trotter. **—reiten**, *n.* trot. **—rennen**, *n.* trotting race.

Tra'ben, *v.n.* (*aux.* **h.** & **s.**) to trot; to jog; **hoch —**, to strut, carry a high head (*of persons*), to be a high stepper (*of horses*).

Trä'ber, *see* **Treber**.

Tracht, *f.* (*pl.* —en) dress, costume; load; yoke (*for pails*); course (*of dishes, etc.*); litter (*of* *puppies, etc.*); prop, support (*Arch.*); span (*of a beam*); yield, crop; **eine — Prügel**, a sound thrashing; **eine — Wasser**, a load of water, what can be carried at one time; **National—**, national dress *or* costume.

Trach'ten, I. *v.n.* (*aux.* **h.**); **nach einer S. —**, to strive, endeavour after, aspire to a th.; **einem nach dem Leben —**, to seek a p.'s life. II. *subst. n.* endeavour, aim, aspiration.

Träch'tig, *adj.* great with young, pregnant; having the due cargo (*Naut.*). **—keit**, *f.* pregnancy, gestation.

Tracie'ren, *v.a.* to trace, mark out (*Fort.*, *Arch.*); to map out (*a railway, etc.*).

Traf, Trä'fe, *1 & 3 pers. sing. imperf. indic. & subj. of* **treffen.**

Trag'—bar, *adj.* portable, easy to carry; wearable, fit to wear; bearable, supportable; fruitful, productive; **in der Tasche —bar**, that can be carried in the pocket; **ein noch —bares Kleid**, a decent wearing-dress. **—barkeit**, *f.* condition of being portable *or* wearable; burden, tonnage (*of a ship*). **—e**, *f.* (hand-)barrow; litter; yoke.

Trä'g—e, *adj.* slow; lazy, indolent, inactive; sluggish, dull; languid; inert. **—heit**, *f.* laziness, indolence; slowness; inactivity; inertia; **natürliche —heit**, phlegm. *Comp.* **—heits=gesetz**, *n.* law of inertia. **—heits=kraft**, *f.* vis inertiæ. **—heits=moment**, *n.* momentum of inertia.

Tra'g—en, I. *ir.v.a.* to bear, carry; to bear, support, sustain; to transport, take; to endure, suffer; to yield, produce, bear; to return, bring in (*a profit*), to bear, entertain (*a grudge, etc.*); to bear, have (*a name, etc.*); to wear (*clothes, etc.*); to carry, be with (*young*); to carry (*a sword, etc.*); to hold (*an office*); **Bedenken —en**, to scruple, hesitate; **seine Haut (ohne Bedenken) zu Markte —en**, to expose oneself (rashly) to danger; **einen Brief auf die Post —en**, to take a letter to the post-office; **Ekel vor einer S. —en**, to have an aversion to a th.; **einen auf den Händen —en**, to bear a p. up on one's hands, to treat s.o. with (*angelic*) kindness and the utmost care; **die Kosten —en**, to bear the expense, to pay the costs; **wer trägt die Schuld ?** who is to blame? **Sehnsucht nach . . . —en**, to yearn for . . .; **Sorge —en um**, to be anxious about; **die Stimme —en**, to slur one's notes; **die Verantwortung —en**, to be responsible for; **Verlust —en**, to bear the loss; **bei sich —en**, to have about one; **den Sieg davon —en**, to carry off the victory; **in ein Buch —en**, to enter in a book; **zur Schau —en**, to expose to view, to show (off), to exhibit publicly; **Zinsen —en**, to bring in *or* yield interest; **das Kapital trägt fünf vom Hundert**, the capital brings in five per cent; **getragene Töne**, slurred notes; **in einer getragenen Stimmung**, in an exalted *or* solemn frame of mind. II. *ir.v.r.*; **sich nach Hause —en**, to return home (*obs.*); **sich mit etwas herum —en**, to have one's mind occupied with, be always thinking of, brood over a th.; **man trägt sich mit dem Gerücht**, it is rumoured, the rumour goes; **sich gut —en**, to carry oneself well; **sich sauber —en**, to be always nicely dressed; **das Zeug trägt sich gut**, that is a good wearing material; **das trägt sich leicht fadenscheinig**, that soon grows threadbare; **es trägt sich unbequem**, it is difficult, inconvenient to carry. III. *ir.v.n.* (*aux.* **h.**) to carry; **so weit das Auge trägt**, as far as the eye can reach; **das Geschütz trägt . . .**, the gun has a range of . . . IV. *subst. n.* bearing; carriage; conveyance; wearing, wear; compass (*of voice*); range (*of guns*). *Comp.* **—altar**, *m.* portable altar. **—bahre**, *f.* stretcher, litter. **—(e)=balken**, *m.* beam, transom. **—band**, *n.* strap; brace; suspenders; sling (*Surg.*); truss; bracket; jamb. **—baum**, *m.* carrying-pole (*of a litter*); shaft; bearing-bar; tree (*Pap.*). **—bett(e)**, *n.* portable bed; stretcher. **—beutel**, *m.* suspensory (*Surg.*). **—binde**, *f.* sling. **—bock**, *m.* prop, trestle. **—butte**, *f.* mason's hod; dosser. **—fähig**, *adj.* capable of bearing. **—fähigkeit**, *f.* tonnage (*of a ship*); capacity of holding; productiveness. **—hebel**, *m.* portable lever. **—himmel**, *m.* canopy. **—holz**, *n.* yoke; bearing-wood. **—kapsel**, *f.* sling (*Surg.*). **—kiepe**, *f.* dosser, pannier. **—kleidchen**, *n.* long clothes (*pl.*) (*of a baby*). **—knospe**, *f.* gem; fruit-bud. **—korb**, *m.* hamper, basket, dosser. **—kraft**, *see* **—fähigkeit. —kranz**, *m.* pad for a weight carried on the head. **—lohn**, *m.* cost of transport. **—orgel**, *f.* portable organ. **—pfeiler**, *m.* pillar. **—pfosten** *m.* supporting beam. **—räder**, *pl.* trailing wheels. **—(e)=reff**, *n.* porter's knot. **—riemen**, *m.* strap; back-band (*of harness*); sling (*Mil.*); (*pl.*) main-braces (*of a coach*). **—sattel**, *m.* packsaddle. **—seil**, *n.* iron-wire rope (*of suspension-bridges*). **—sessel**, *m.* sedan-chair. **—stein**, *m.* keystone; springer (*Arch.*). **—stuhl**, *m.* sedan-chair. **—vermögen**, *n.* strength (*of a bridge, etc.*). **—weite**, *f.* range, reach; bearing, import(ance) (*fig.*). **—zeit**, *f.* time of gestation (*of animals*).

Trä'ger, *m.* (—**s**, *pl.* —) carrier, porter; bearer; stretcher-bearer; supporter; girder (*Carp.*); beam; post, pillar; holder (*of a bill of exchange*); stamen (*Bot.*); trestle; atlas (*Anat.*); **— der Litteratur**, the representative authors of a literary period. *Comp.* **—lohn**, *m.* porterage, carriage. **—muskel**, *m.* alloid muscle.

Tra'g—iker, *m.* (—**ikers**, *pl.* —**iker**) tragic poet. **—isch**, *adj. & adv.* tragic(al); **—ische Schuld**, guilt of the hero of a tragedy causing the catastrophe; **—ische Muse**, tragic muse, muse of tragedy. **—ö'de**, *m.* (—**öden**, *pl.* —**öden**), **—ö'din**, *f.* tragic actor (*or* actress), tragedian. **—ö'die**, *f.* tragedy. *Comp.* **—i=komisch**, *adj.* tragi-comic. **—ö'dien=dichter**, *m.* writer of tragedies, tragic poet.

Trail'le, *f.* (*pl.* —**n**) bar of trellis-work; banister.

Train, *m.* (—**s**, *pl.* —**s**) train; *see* **—jagd. —ie'ren**, I. *v.a.* to train. II. *subst.* training. *Comp.* **—inspektor**, *m.* inspector of the military train. **—kolonne**, *f.* column of artillery-drivers. **—soldat**, *m.* waggoner, soldier forming part of a convoy. **—wagen**, *m.* baggage-waggon, waggon belonging to a train of artillery (*Mil.*). **—wesen**, *n.* convoy, personnel and material of a train of artillery.

Trakt—ame'nt, *n.* (—**amen't(e)s**, *pl.* —**amen'te**) treatment; entertainment; (*military*) pay (*obs.*). **—a't**, *m.* (—**ats**, *pl.* —**ate**) treatise, essay, treaty; (*pl.*) negotiations. **—ät'chen**, *n.* (—**ätchens**, *pl.* —**ätchen**) tract; short treatise. **—ie'ren**, *v.a. & n.* (*aux.* **h.**) to treat; to entertain, give a treat to.

Tral(l)a' ! *int.* trolly ! derry-down (*as a refrain*).

Tra'lala ! *int.* trá-la-la ! tol-de-rol !

Träl'lern, *v.n.* (*aux.* **h.**) to hum, trill (*a tune*).

Tram— (*in comp.*) **—bahn**, *f.* tram-way, tram-road, tram-line. **—wagen**, *m.* tram-car.

Tram'pel, *m.* (—**s**, *pl.* —), *f.* clumsy person. **—n**, (**Tramp'sen**,) *v.n.* (*aux.* **h.**) to walk heavily; to trample; to stamp. *Comp.* **—tier**, *n.* dromedary; Bactrian (two-humped) camel.

Trampoli'n, *m. & n.* (—**s**, *pl.* —**e**) spring-board. **—sprung**, *m.* leap from a spring-board.

Tranch—ee', *f.* (*pl.* —**een**) trench (*Fort.*). **—ie'ren**, *v.a. & n.* (*aux.* **h.**) to carve, cut up. *Comp.* **—ee=arbeiter**, *m.* trencher. **—ier'=messer**, *n.* carving-knife.

[1]**Trank**, *m.* (—es, *pl.* Trän'ke) drink, beverage; potion; draught; decoction; Speise und —, meat and drink. *Comp.* —opfer, *n.* drink-offering, libation.

[2]**Trank, Trän'ke**, *1 & 3 pers. sing. imperf. indic. & subj. of* trinken.

Trän'k—e, *f.* (*pl.* —en) watering-place; horse-pond; swill; zur —e führen, to water (*cattle*).

Trän'k—en, *v.a.* to give to drink; to water (*cattle, the ground*); to suckle (*a child*); to saturate. *Comp.* —eimer, *m.*, —faß, *n.* drinking-tub for cattle; pig's trough. —signal, *n.* call to water. —trog, *m.* watering trough.

Transch, *m.* (—es, *pl.* —e) reproof, reproach, scolding (*coll.*); einem einen — machen, to give s.o. a thorough blowing-up (*coll.*).

Tran's—(s)itiv, *adj.* transitive. —(s)it=handel, *m.* transit *or* carrying-trade. —(s)it=lager, *n.* store-house for transit-goods, bonded warehouse. —(s)ito'risch, *adj.* transitory. —(s)it=portosatz, m. parcels' postage. —missions'=apparat, *m.* transmitter (*Tele.*). —pare'nt, *n.* (—paren'tes, *pl.* —paren'te) a transparency. —(s)piratio'n, *f.* perspiration. —(s)pirie'ren, *v.n.* (*aux.* h.) to perspire; to transpire; stark —spirieren, to perspire freely. —ponie'ren, *v.a.* to transpose. —po'rt, *m.* (—ports, *pl.* —por'te) transport, carriage; brought-over (*C. L.*); —port in Karren, wheeling in barrows. —port'=bureau, *n.* forwarding office. —port'=geschäft, *n.* carrying trade. —porteu'r, *m.* (—porteurs, *pl.* —porteure) carrier, shipper; protractor (*Geom.*). —portie'ren, *v.a.* to transport, carry; to transfer.

Trape'z, *n.* (—es, *pl.* —e) trapezoid (*Math.*); trapeze (*Gymn.*). —oe'der, *n.* trapezohedron. *Comp.* —förmig, *adj.* trapeziform, trapezoid. —künstler, *m.* trapezist.

Trapp, *m.* (—es, *pl.* —e) loud, heavy step; trap (*Min.*). —e, *f.* (*pl.* —en) footstep; trap; (*also m.*) bustard. —eln, *v.n.* (*aux.* h.) to tramp; to patter. —en, *v.n.* (*aux.* h. & s.) to walk heavily, tramp. —er, *m.* (—ers, *pl.* —er) trapper. —i'st, *m.* (—is'ten, *pl.* —is'ten) trappist; trapper. —sen, *v.n.* to walk heavily, to stamp. *Comp.* —gang, *m.* trap-vein (*Min.*) —is'ten=orden, *m.* order of La Trappe. —porphyr, *m.* trachyte, trachytic porphyry. —sand, *m.* coarse gravel.

Trass—a'nt, *m.* (—an'ten, *pl.* —an'ten) drawer (*of a bill*) (*C. L.*). —a't, *m.* (—aten, *pl.* —aten) drawee (*C. L.*). —ie'ren, *v.a. & n.* (*aux.* h.) to draw (*a bill*); —ierter Wechsel, *see* Tratte.

Trat, Trä'te, *1 & 3 pers. sing. imperf. indic. & subj. of* treten.

Tratsch, *m.* (—es) silly *or* empty talk. —en, **Trät'schen**, *v.a. & n.* (*aux* h.) to chatter, to talk nonsense.

Trat'te, *f.* (*pl.* —n) draft, bill of exchange.

Trau'b—e, *f.* (*pl.* —en) bunch of grapes; cluster. —ig, *adj.* clustered; grape-like. *Comp.* —en=abfell, *m.* husks of grapes. —en=artig, *adj.* grape-like, in clusters. —en=blut, *n.* juice of the grape, wine. —en=geländer, *n.* vine-trellis. —en=kamm, *m.* grape-stalk. —en=kirsche, *f.* cherry growing in a cluster; bird-cherry (tree). —en=krankheit, *f.* vine-disease. —en=lese, *f.* vintage. —en=nachlesen, *n.* gleaning in a vineyard. —en=papier, *n.* (großes) Royal, (kleines) small Royal. —en=reich, *adj.* abounding in grapes. —en=rosinen, *pl.* raisins in bunches. —en=saft, *m.* juice of the grape; wine. —en=säure, *f.* racemic acid. —en=schimmel, *m.* grape-mould, botrytis. —en=sieb, *n.* grape-funnel. —en=stock, *m.* vine. —en=tragend, *adj.* grape-bearing. —en=treter, *m.* treader of the wine-press. —en=zeit, *f.* time when the grapes are ripe, time of vintage. —en=zucker, *m.* grape-sugar, dextrose, (dextro-) glucose.

Trau'—en, *v.* I. *n.* (*aux.* h.); einem —en, to trust, have confidence in, rely on a p.; einer Sache nicht —en, not to trust to, not to believe in a thing; auf eine S. —en, to rely on, put one's trust in a thing; sich —en, to venture, to be so bold as; dem Frieden —e ich nicht, I have no confidence in the present state of things, this state of things cannot last; dem Glück ist nicht zu —en, fortune is fickle; —, schau, wem, take care in whom you trust; look before you leap, better known than trusted (*prov.*). II. *a.* to unite in marriage; einem Manne ein Weib —en, to marry a woman to a man (*obs., poet.*); sich —en lassen, to get married (*in church*). —lich, *adj.* familiar, intimate, cordial; homely; snug, cosy. —lichkeit, *f.* familiarity, intimacy, cordiality; cosiness, comfort. —ung, *f.* marriage-ceremony *or* -service, wedding. *Comp.* —altar, *m.* marriage-altar. —formel, *f.*, —formular, *n.* marriage-certificate. —gebühr, *f.*, —geld, *n.* marriage-fee. —handlung, *f.* marriage-ceremony, wedding. —rede, *f.* clergyman's address to the bride and bridegroom. —register, *n.* register of marriages. —ring, *m.* wedding-ring. —schein, *m.* certificate of marriage; marriage-license. —zeuge, *m.* marriage-witness (*especially, in England, he who gives the bride away and the bridegroom's best man*), who signs his name in the marriage-register.

Trau'er, *f.* grief, affliction; mourning; — anlegen um, to go into mourning for. *Comp.* (*often* = mournful, funeral *or* mourning-, death-) —anzeige, *f.* announcement of a death. —anzug, *m.* suit of mourning. —binde, *f.* crape (*for the hat, arm*). —birke, *f.* weeping birch. —botschaft, *f.* sad news, mournful tidings; news of a death. —brief, *m.* letter announcing sad news *or* a death. —decke, *f.* mourning-housings (*on horses*). —fahne, *f.* black flag. —fall, *m.* sad event; death. —farbe, *f.* black; mourning-colour. —flor, *m.* mourning-crape. —gedicht, *n.* elegy. —gefolge, —geleit, *n.* funeral procession. —geläut(e), *n.* tolling of the bells at a funeral; funeral knell, passing-bell. —gepränge, *n.* funeral pomp. —gesang, *m.* funeral hymn; dirge. —geschichte, *f.* sad tale. —geschrei, *n.* lamentations. —gestalt, *f.* doleful figure; knight of the rueful countenance. —gottesdienst, *m.* funeral service. —haube, *f.* widow's cap. —haus, *n.* house of mourning *or* of death. —hut, *m.* mourning-hat. —jahr, *n.* sad year, year of mourning. —kapelle, *f.* mortuary chamber *or* chapel. —kleid, *n.*, —kleidung, *f.* mourning dress; weeds. —kloß, *m.* dull *or* silly fellow, duffer (*coll.*). —kutsche, *f.* mourning coach. —leute, *pl.* mourners. —mahl, *n.* funeral repast. —mantel, *m.* mourning cloak; Camberwell beauty (*butterfly*). —marsch, *m.* funeral march. —musik, *f.* funeral music. —nachricht, *f.* mournful news *or* tidings. —nadel, *f.* mourning-pin. —papier, *n.* black-edged (note-)paper. —post, *f.* sad news. —prinz, *m.* dull fellow (*coll.*). —rede, *f.* funeral oration. —schläge, *pl.* knell of a funeral bell. —spiel, *n.* tragedy. —spiel=artig, *adj.* tragic. —stück, *n.* mournful drama; bad, wretched drama. —tuch, *n.* black cloth. —voll, *adj.* sad, mournful. —wagen, *m.* funeral car; mourning carriage. —weide, *f.* weeping willow. —zeit, *f.* time of mourning. —zug, *m.* funeral procession.

Trau'ern, *v.n.* (*aux.* h.) to mourn, lament, grieve; um einen —, to mourn for s.o., to wear mourning for a person.

Trau'f—e, *f.* (*pl.* —en) drip; gutter; eaves; aus dem Regen in die —e, out of the frying-pan into the fire. *Comp.* —**bad**, *n.* shower-bath. —**faß**, *n.* rain-water tub. —**gang**, *m.* passage between two buildings for the rain to run down. —**rinne**, *f.* gutter. —**röhre**, *f.* gutter-pipe, spouting. —**stein**, *m.* gutter-stone; stalactite. —**wasser**, *n.* rain-water.

Träu'f—eln, *v.* I. *n.* (*aux.* **h.** & **s.**) to trickle; to fall in drops, to drip; to gutter; to weep. II. *a.* to drop. —**en**, *v.* I. *a.* to let fall in drops; to shower down. II. *n.* (*aux.* **h.** & **s.**) to drop, drip, trickle.

Traum, *m.* (—**s**, *pl.* **Träu'me**) dream; vision, fancy; **quälender —**, nightmare; **— eines Wachenden**, day-dream; **er spricht im —e!** he is dreaming! **ich habe auch im —e nicht daran gedacht, das ist mir nicht im —e eingefallen**, I never dreamt of such a thing, it never entered my head; **einem aus dem —e helfen**, to undeceive a p., disabuse s.o.'s mind; **Träume sind Schäume**, dreams are empty; dreams are froth; **Träume treffen selten ein**, dreams seldom come true. —**haft**, *adj.* dreamlike. —**selig**, *adj.* somnambulistic. *Comp.* —**ausleger**, *m.* interpreter of dreams. —**bild**, *n.* vision; phantom; illusion. —**buch**, *n.* dream-book, fortune-book. —**deuter(in**, *f.*), *m.* fortune-teller, dream-interpreter. —**deuterei'**, —**deutung**, *f.* interpretation of dreams. —**gesicht**, *n.*, —**gestalt**, *f.* vision. —**gott**, *m.* god of dreams, Morpheus. —**leben**, *n.*; **er führt nur ein —leben**, he lives in a dream *or* in a cloud. —**spiel**, *n.* phantasmagoria. —**welt**, *f.* realm of dreams, world of fancy, dreamland.

Träu'm—en, *v.a.* & *n.* (*aux.* **h.**) & *imp.* to dream; **ich —te** *or* **es —te mir, mir —te**, I dreamt; **wachend —en**, to go about in a dream, to be given to day-dreaming; **das hätte ich mir nie —en lassen**, I should never have dreamt of such a thing. —**er**, *m.* (—**ers**, *pl.* —**er**) dreamer; visionary. —**erei'**, *f.* dreaming; fancy; daydream, reverie. —**erisch**, *adj.* dreaming; thoughtful; chimerical; —**erischer Mensch**, visionary.

Traun! *int.* (*for* **in Treuen**) indeed! faith! upon my word! forsooth!

Trau'rig, *adj.* sad, melancholy, sorrowful; dismal; wretched; **eine —e Belohnung**, a poor reward; —**er Ausruf**, doleful cry *or* exclamation. —**keit**, *f.* sadness; melancholy; grief.

Traut, *adj.* dear, beloved; cosy; intimate; —**es Mädchen**, —**chen**, —**el**, beloved, darling; sweetheart; —**es Plätzchen**, cosy *or* snug corner.

Travestie', *f.* (*pl.* —**en**) travesty. —**ren**, *v.a.* to travesty, burlesque.

Tre'ber, *pl.* husks (*of grapes*); draff, brewer's grains. *Comp.* —**wein**, *m.* after-wine.

Tre'ck—en, *v.a.* to drag; to pull; to tow (*a ship*). *Comp.* —**schute**, *f.* canal boat. —**seil**, *n.* towing-rope. —**weg**, *m.* towing-path.

Treff, *m.* (—(**e**)**s**, *pl.* —**e**) smart blow; shrewd *or* cutting remark; club (*at cards*).

Tref'f—en, I. *ir.v.a.* & *n.* (*aux.* **h.**) to hit, strike; to reach; to affect, touch, concern; to befall; to fall upon s.o., come to a p.'s turn; to find, light upon; to guess, hit upon, divine; to seize (*the sense of an author; a likeness, etc.*); to conclude (*a treaty, etc.*); to take (*measures*); to make (*a choice; arrangements; preparations, etc.*); to catch, take; to fall in with (*the enemy, etc.*); to encounter (*difficulties*); to strike (*the right note*); to burst upon (*the ear*); **das Ziel nicht —en**, to miss one's aim, fall short of the mark; **vom Blitze getroffen**, struck by lightning, thunderstruck; **jeder Schuß (Ausdruck) trifft**, every shot (word) tells; **gut —en**, to hit home; **es gut —en**, to be successful; **Sie haben es gut getroffen, daß Sie heute kommen**, it is lucky that you came to-day; **er trifft gut**, he is a good shot; **dies traf**, that went home; **sich getroffen fühlen**, to apply a p.'s remark to oneself, to feel hurt; **wen trifft die Schuld?** who is to blame? **wer sich getroffen fühlt, nehme sich bei der Nase**, let him whom the cap fits wear it; **das Los traf ihn**, the lot fell on him; **den Nagel auf den Kopf —en**, to hit the nail on the head; **die Reihe trifft dich**, it is your turn; **bin ich getroffen?** is it a good likeness? **der Maler hat Sie gut getroffen**, the painter has hit you off well; **Sie haben es getroffen!** you have hit it! **getroffen!** right, that 's just it, exactly so; **das Unglück traf mich**, I had the misfortune; **er traf es bei ihr**, he pleased her; **da trifft er ja Bekannte**, he is among friends there, of course; **wie sich das trifft!** how well that suits! how exactly that falls in with our plans! what a strange coincidence! **das trifft sich gut**, that 's lucky, that 's the very thing we want; **Vorsichtsmaßregeln —en**, to take precautions; **eine Wahl —en**, to make a choice; **auf einen —en**, to meet with, encounter a p.; **es traf sich, daß**, it so happened that. II. *subst. n.* encounter; battle; striking; meeting, finding; line of battle (*Mil., Naut.*); **ein —en liefern**, to offer battle; **es kam zum —en**, an engagement ensued *or* came about; **Mittel —en**, centre of an order of battle; **als es zum —en kam**, when it came to the scratch; —**en bei**, engagement, encounter at. —**end**, *p.* & *adj.* striking; pertinent; suitable; **das —ende Wort**, the right word; **seine Bemerkungen waren —end**, his remarks were to the point. —**er**, *m.* (—**ers**, *pl.* —**er**) homethrust, shot that hits the mark, good shot; hit, lucky chance; winning ticket; painter that catches a likeness; **viele —er haben**, to be lucky; —**er und Nieten**, prizes and blanks. —**lich**, *adj.* & *adv.* excellent, choice; first-rate; admirable. —**lichkeit**, *f.* excellence, perfection; excellent thing. *Comp.* —**aß**, *n.* ace of clubs. —**könig**, *m.* king of clubs. —**schuß**, *m.* shot that hits the mark, hit, bull's eye. —**sicherheit**, *f.* absolute certainty (*in shooting*), unerring aim.

Trei'b—en, I. *ir.v.a.* to drive, push; to put in motion, drive, propel; to spin, whip (*tops*); to carry on, exercise, do; to force (*Hort.*); to refine (*metals*); to emboss, chase; to extract (*ore*); to produce, cause; to put forth (*leaves, branches, etc.*); to run to (*leaves, etc.*); to occupy oneself with; to breed (*cattle*); to roll out (*paste*); **Kühe auf die Weide —en**, to drive cattle to pasture; **das Wild —en**, to beat game; **einen —en**, to drive, urge a p. on; **aufs Äußerste —en**, to push to extremes; **einen aus dem Besitze einer Sache —en**, to dispossess a p.; **in die Enge —en**, to press a p. hard; **ins Exil —en**, to exile; **in die Flucht —en**, to put to flight; **in die Hitze —en**, to put in a passion; **die Preise in die Höhe —en**, to raise the prices; **über das Ziel —en**, to carry, push too far; **von einander —en**, to separate violently; **vom Amte —en**, to make (a p.) lose, force out of an office; **einem das Haar zu Berge —en**, to make s.o.'s hair stand on end; **zur Verzweiflung —en**, to drive to despair; **so weit möchte ich es doch nicht —en**, I should not wish to go so far as that *or* to push matters to that extreme; **vorwärts —en**, to hasten (on); **es —t mich fort**, I feel compelled to go away; **das Pulver —t die Kugel**, the powder discharges the ball; **der Fluß —t Eis**, the river is blocked with floating ice; —**ende Kraft**, motive power; **der Wein —t sehr**, wine is in a high degree diuretic; **diese Arznei, —t den Schweiß**, this medicine promotes perspiration; **was —st du da?** what are you doing there? **was —t er jetzt?** what is he doing now? **was —t er für ein Handwerk?** what is his trade? **Musik —en,** to devote oneself to music; **deutsch —en,** to go in for German, to study German; **Kurzweil —en,** to amuse oneself; **ich lasse keinen Unsinn mit mir —en,** I will stand no nonsense; **er —t es zu arg,** he goes too far; **wie man's —t, so geht's,** as you make your bed so you must lie; do well and have well; as you sow, you shall reap (*prov.*); **Strecken —en,** to open galleries (*in a mine*); **den Teig —en,** to roll out the dough; **Häute —en,** to soak hides; **getriebene Arbeit,** embossed, raised work. II. *ir.v.n.* (*aux.* h. & s.) to drive, drift, float; to sprout; **ein Schiff trieb auf uns,** a ship ran foul of us; **es —t,** it is urgent; **das Bier —t aus dem Faß,** the beer overflows the cask; **der Saft —t im Holze,** the sap rises in the wood. III. *subst. n.* driving, *etc.*; germination; impulse; doings; life; activity; stir; movement; study; **das —en der Parteien,** the doings of (political) parties. **—er,** *m.* (—ers, *pl.* —er) driver; drover; beater (*Sport.*); spring, instigator; hastener, driver on; puffer (*at auctions*); driving-wheel, driver, propeller. **—erei',** *f.* driving; urging; forcing; forcing beds *or* houses. *Comp.* —**anker,** *m.* driving-anchor. **—asche,** *f.* cupel-ashes. **—baum,** *m.* driving-axle. **—(e)=beet,** *n.* hot-bed. **—bogen,** *m.* bow-drill. **—eis,** *n.* drift ice. **—hammer,** *m.* chasing-hammer; mallet. **—haus,** *n.* hothouse, greenhouse. —**haus=frucht,** *f.* hothouse fruit. **—herd,** *n.* cupelling-furnace, refining hearth. **—holz,** *n.* drift-wood; rolling-pin (*Cook.*); planer, shooting-stick (*Typ.*). **—kasten,** *m.* forcing-frame. **—keil,** *m.* wedge; planer (*Typ.*). **—kolben,** *m.* moving, driving piston. **—kraft,** *f.* motive power. **—ofen,** *m. see* **—herd. —rad,** *n.* driving-wheel. **—reis,** *n.* sprout. **—riemen,** *m.* driving-belt (*of machines*). **—sand,** *m.* drift-sand; quicksand. **—stangen,** *pl.* connecting-rods. **—stock,** *m.* rung, stave of a trundle (*Mach.*). **—welle,** *f.* main shaft (*of a machine*). **—werk,** *n.* engine, machine. —**wirt,** *m.* contractor undertaking the working of an engine.

Trei'del, *m.* (—s, *pl.* —) tow-line, towing-rope. **—n,** *v.a.* to tow.

Tre'ma, *n.* (—s, *pl.* —s & —ta) diæresis.

Tre'molo, *n.* (—s, *pl.* —s) shaking, tremolo.

Trem'se, *f.* (*pl.* —n) corn-flower (*dial.*).

Tremul—a'nt, *m.* (—an'ten, *pl.* —an'ten) trill, shake; tremolo-stop (*Org.*). **—ie'ren,** *v.n.* (*aux.* h.) to shake (*Mus.*), to sing with a tremolo.

Trenn'bar, *adj.* separable, divisible. **—keit,** *f.* separableness, divisibility.

Tren'n—en, *v.* I. *a.* to separate, divide, part; to sever, sunder, divorce; to detach; to break (*the ranks, Mil.*); to break up; to dissolve (*partnership; a marriage*); to pick out, rip up (*a seam*). II. *r.* to separate; to be divorced; to branch off (*as roads*). **—ung,** *f.* separation; dissolution, divorce. *Comp.* —**messer,** *n.* ripping-knife. **—punkt,** *m.* point of separation, diæresis. **—säge,** *f.* cutting-out saw. **—stift,** *m.* quadrat (*Typ.*). **—ungs=flächen,** *pl.* natural joints (*in crystals*). —**ungs=partikel,** *f.* disjunctive particle. —**ungs=schmerz,** *m.* pain of separation. —**ungs=zeichen,** *n.* diæresis; hyphen.

Tren'se, *f.* (*pl.* —n) snaffle, bridoon. **—n,** *v.a.* to worm (*a rope*) (*Naut.*).

Trepa'n, *m.* (—s, *pl.* —e) trepan. **—ie'ren,** *v.a.* to trepan (*Surg.*).

Trep'p—e, *f.* (*pl.* —en) staircase, (*flight of*) stairs; **—auf, —ab,** upstairs and downstairs; **die —e hinauf,** upstairs; **Schiffs —,** ladder; (**steinerne**) **—e vor dem Hause,** (*stone*) steps; **man hat ihn die —e hinunter geworfen,** they threw him down-stairs; **zwei —en hoch wohnen,** to live in the second story, on the second floor; **—en schneiden,** to cut (*the hair*) in steps, to chop a p.'s hair; **von der —en fallen,** to have one's hair cut (*coll.*). *Comp.* **—a'b,** *adv.* coming downstairs. **—au'f,** *adv.* going upstairs; **—auf, —ab,** upstairs and downstairs. **—en=absatz,** *m.* landing (*of a staircase*). **—en=bau,** *m.* construction of a staircase. **—en=baum,** *m.* spindle (*of a winding staircase*). **—en=förmig,** *adj.* in the form of stairs, rising like steps; in echelons (*Mil.*). **—en=geländer,** *n.* railing, balustrade, banisters. **—en=läufer,** *m.* stair-carpet. **—en=luke,** *f.* hatchway (*Naut.*). **—en=schacht,** *m.* shaft with steps cut in the rock (*Min.*). **—en=stufe,** *f.* step of a staircase. **—en=turm,** *m.* staircase turret, tower with winding staircase.

Treso'r, *m.* (—s, *pl.* —e) treasury; money-safe. *Comp.* **—schein,** *m.* treasury-note.

Tres'p—e, *f.* (*pl.* —en) brome-grass. **—ig,** *adj.* abounding in brome-grass.

Tres's—e, *f.* (*pl.* —en) lace, galloon; plait, braid (*of hair*). **—ie'ren,** *v.a.* to plait, braid (*hair*). *Comp.* **—en=hut,** *m.* laced hat. —**ier'=bank,** *f.*, **—ier'=stock,** *m.* wig-block.

Tres'ter, *pl.* residue (*of fruit*); grape-skins. *Comp.* **—wein,** *m.* wine made of the pressed skins of grapes, poor wine.

Tre't—en, *ir.v.* I. *n.* (*aux.* h. & s.) to tread, walk (*softly, etc.*); to step, walk; to take a step; to walk, go, pass over to; **—en an,** to step, to advance towards; **die Endung tritt an den Stamm,** the ending is joined to the stem; **an die Spitze —en,** to assume the leadership, to (take the) lead; **an jemandes Stelle —en,** to take a p.'s place, to replace a p.; **ans Licht —en,** to come to light, to appear, become known; **—en auf** (*acc.*) to mount, get upon, to walk on; **auf die Seite, bei Seite —en,** to step aside; **auf jemandes Seite —en,** to take a p.'s part; **auf der Stelle —en,** to mark time; **—en aus,** to step, go out, to stand out of (*the way, etc.*); **aus dem Dienste —en,** to retire from (*active*) service; **die Sonne tritt in den Löwen,** the sun enters Leo; **ins Haus —en,** to enter the house; **ins** *or* **unters Gewehr —en,** to take up arms; **in Kriegsdienste —en,** to enter the army; **in einen Orden —en,** to become a member of an order; **in den Ehestand —en,** to marry; **sie ist in ihr zehntes Jahr getreten,** she has entered her tenth year; **in Unterhandlung(en) —en,** to enter into negotiations; **in Wirksamkeit —en,** to take effect; **ins Mittel —en,** to interpose, mediate; **in Geschäftsverbindung —en,** to enter into a business connection; **in die Bresche, in** *or* **vor den Riß —en,** to throw oneself into the breach, to bear the brunt; **einem in den Weg —en,** to oppose a person, to stand in a p.'s way; **es traten ihm Thränen in die Augen,** the tears came into his eyes; **der Saft ist in die Bäume getreten,** the sap has risen in the trees; **das Podagra ist ihm in den Magen getreten,** the gout has gone to his stomach; **über die Schnur —en,** to go too far; **über die Ufer —en,** to overflow its banks; **tritt mir nie wieder unter die Augen!** never let me see your face again! **vor den Richterstuhl Gottes —en,** to appear before the judgment-seat of God; **ein Wölkchen trat vor den Mond,** a little cloud passed over the moon; **kalter Schweiß trat ihm auf die Stirn,** cold perspiration stood upon his brow; **zu einem —en,** to go up to a p.; to take a person's side; **zu Tage —en,** to appear, to become evident; **dazwischen —en,** to interpose, come between, to intercede; **daneben** *or* **fehl —en,** to make a false step; **leise —en,** to go softly, to be artful; **—en Sie hier herein,** step in here; **—en Sie näher, meine Herrn!** walk in, gentleman! step this way, gentlemen! **einer Frage näher —en,** to look more closely into a question; **einem zu nahe —en,** to wrong *or* malign a person, to injure a p.'s reputation; **ohne der Wahrheit zu nahe zu —en,** without any violation of truth; **ohne ihrer Bescheidenheit zu nahe zu —en,** without offence to her modesty. II. *a.* to tread, walk upon, trample; to tread (*grapes, etc.*); to knead; to temper (*clay*); to blow (*organ-bellows*); to mark (*time*); to tread cover (*of birds*); to trample under foot, treat with contempt; to dun (*sl.*); to kick; **entzwei —en,** to break by treading on; **sein Glück mit Füßen —en,** to act against one's own interests, to spurn one's good fortune; **mit Füßen —en,** to trample under foot; **einen —en,** to dun, to press a p. for payment (*vulg.*); **das Pflaster —en,** to lounge about the streets; **sich** (*dat.*) **einen Dorn in den Fuß —en,** to run a thorn into one's foot; **seine Schuhe schief —en,** to wear one's shoes crooked; **einen Wurm tot —en,** to tread *or* crush a worm to death; **einen Weg —en,** to follow a path (*poet.*). **—er,** *m.* (**—ers,** *pl.* **—er**) treader; kneader; bellows-blower (*Org.*); fuller (*of cloth*). *Comp.* **—brief,** *m.* dunning letter, letter calling in a debt (*vulg.*). **—butte, —kufe,** *f.* tub, vat in which the grapes are trodden. **—haspel,** *f.* wheel-capstan. **—mühle,** *f.* tread-mill; **die alte —mühle treten,** to work at the old tread-mill; **die alte —mühle des Berufs,** the humdrum round of duty *or* of one's profession. **—rad,** *n.* tread-wheel. **—schemel,** *m.* treadle of a loom (*Weav.*).

Treu, I. *adj. & adv.* faithful; true; sincere; loyal; conscientious; upright; retentive, good; **seinem Charakter — bleiben,** to be true to one's character; **ein —es Gedächtnis,** a good memory; **sein —es Schwert,** his trusty sword; **Du —er Gott,** Lord God of truth (*B.*); **es — mit einem meinen,** to mean well by a p.; **seinem Vorsatz — bleiben,** to adhere (*faithfully*) to one's purpose. II. *f. see* **—e**; **— und Glauben halten,** to keep one's word; **auf — und Glauben,** in good faith; **üb' immer — und Redlichkeit,** be always faithful and upright; **bei meiner —!** upon my honour! **—e,** *f.* fidelity, faithfulness; sincerity; honesty; loyalty; **—e brechen,** to break faith; **den Eid der —e ablegen,** to take the oath of allegiance. **—lich,** I. *adj. & adv. see* **Treu.** II. *adv.* truly, faithfully; conscientiously. *Comp.* **—bruch,** *m.* breach of faith; perfidy; disloyalty. **—brüchig,** *adj.* faithless, perfidious; disloyal. **—bündler,** *m.* enthusiastic loyalist, ultra conservative. **—ergeben, —gehorsam,** *adj.* truly devoted. **—gesinnt,** *adj.* loyal. **—herzig,** *adj.* sincere, true, loyal; candid; simple, naif. **—liebchen,** *n.* true-love. **—los,** *adj.* faithless, perfidious; disloyal; treacherous, traitorous. **—losigkeit,** *f.* faithlessness, perfidy; treachery.

Tri—agona'l, *adj.* triangular. **—angel** (*pron.* **Tri'angel**), *m.* (**—angels,** *pl.* **—angel**) triangle (*Mus., Math.*); fishing rod with three hooks (*dial.*). **—angulä'r,** *adj.* triangular, three-cornered. **—angulie'ren,** *v.a.* to draw plans, triangulate, survey ground by trigonometry. **—a'rier,** *m.* (**—ariers,** *pl.* **—arier**) triarian, veteran soldier (*Rom. Hist.*). **—as** (*pron.* **Tri'as**), *f.* triad; trias (*Geol.*). **—e're,** *f.* (*pl.* **—eren**) *see* **Dreiruderer.** **—gonometrie', —nitä't, —umvira't, —vium,** *see* **Trigonometrie, Trinität, Triumvirat, Trivium.** **—logie',** *f.* trilogy. **—me'ster,** *n.* (**—mesters,** *pl.* **—mester**) term of three months, quarter (*Univ.*). **—no'm,** *n.* (**—noms,** *pl.* **—nome**), **—no'mium,** *n.* (**—nomiums**) trinomial. **—no'misch,** *adj.* trinomial. **—o** (*pron.* **Tri'o**), *n.* (**—os,** *pl.* **—os**) trio. **—o'le,** *f.* triplet (*Mus.*). **—pel** (*pron.* **Tri'pel**), *m.* (**—pels,** *pl.* **—pel**) triple. **—pel=allianz,** *f.* triple alliance. **—pel=takt,** *m.* triple-time. **—pli'k,** *f.* (*pl.* **—pliken**) surrejoinder (*Law*). **—plie'ren,** *v.a.* to treble; to make the ball strike the cushion twice (*Bill.*). **—po'de,** *m.* (**—poden,** *pl.* **—poden**) tripod.

Tribulie'ren, *v.a.* to vex, harass.

Tribu'n, *m.* (**—s, —en,** *pl.* **—en**) tribune. **—a'l,** *n.* (**—als,** *pl.* **—ale**) tribunal, high court of justice. **—a't,** *n.* (**—ats,** *pl.* **—ate**) tribuneship, post *or* office of a tribune.

Tribü'ne, *f.* (*pl.* **—n**) platform, tribune; rostrum, gallery; stand (*for spectators*). *Comp.* **—n=billet,** *n.* balcony-ticket; ticket for a stand. **—n=platz,** *m.* seat in the balcony *or* on a stand.

Tribu't, *m.* (**—s,** *pl.* **—e**) tribute. **—ä'r,** (**—pflichtig,**) *adj.* tributary.

Trichi'ne, *f.* (*pl.* **—n**) trichina spiralis (*Zoöl.*).

Trich'ter, *m.* (**—s,** *pl.* **—**) funnel; opening into a mine; crater; species of limpet. **—n,** *v.a.* to pour by a funnel. *Comp.* **—förmig,** *adj.* funnel-shaped. **—öffnung,** *f.*, **—schlund,** *m.* crater. **—röhrchen,** *n.* ramrod-holder.

Trick'track(spiel), *n.* backgammon.

Trico't, (**Triko't,**) *n.* stockinet, (*pl.*) tights, fleshings (*of circus riders*). *Comp.* **—bluse,** *f.* jersey blouse. **—stoffe,** *pl.* hosiery. **—taille,** *f.* jersey (bodice). **—unterbeinkleid,** *n.* stockinet pants *or* drawers.

[1]**Trieb,** *m.* (**—s,** *pl.* **—e**) germinating power; sprout, young shoot; movement; moving force; host (*dial.*); flock(s) (*dial.*); impetus; instinct, impulse; inclination; liking; *see* **Trift; aus eignem —e,** instinctively, of one's own accord; **— zum Vaterlande,** love of one's country; **— zum Studieren,** love of study; **sinnliche —e,** sensual desires; **der Fluß hat einen starken —,** the river has a rapid current; **die Kanonenkugeln verlieren einen Teil ihres —es,** cannon-balls lose part of their momentum. **—el,** *m.* (**—els,** *pl.* **—el**) driver, mallet; winch (*on wheels*). *Comp.* **—artig,** *adj.* instinctive. **—feder,** *f.* spring; mainspring, motive; **die —feder von einer S. sein,** to be at the bottom of a th. **—feile,** *f.* pinion-file. **—kraft,** *f.* impetus, motive power; mechanical power; germinating power. **—maß,** *n.* pinion-gauge. **—rad,** *n.* driving-wheel; gear-wheel; cog-wheel; pinion (*Horol.*). **—sand,** *m.* quick-sand. **—stahl,** *m.* pinion-wire. **—stock,** *see* **Treibstock. —welle,** *f.* driving-shaft (*Locom.*). **—werk,** *n.* machinery, mechanism; springs, works (*of a machine*).

[2]**Trieb, Trie'be,** *1 & 3 pers. sing. imperf. indic. & subj. of* **treiben.**

Trie'f—en, *ir.v.n.* (*aux.* **h.** *&* **s.**) to drop, drip, trickle; to secrete a fluid (*Med.*); **die Augen —en ihm,** he has a running at the eyes, he is blear-eyed. **—end,** *p. & adj.*, **—ig,** *adj.* dropping, dripping. *Comp.* **—äugig,** *adj.* blear-eyed. **—naß,** *adj.* sopping *or* dripping wet.

Triegen, *obs. for* **Trügen.**

Trie'zen, *v.a.* to vex, worry, bother (*coll.*).

Triff; Triffst, Trifft, *imperat.; 2 & 3 pers. pres. indic. of* **treffen.**

Trift, *f.* (*pl.* **—en**) right of pasturage, pasture, common; passage, run (*for cattle*); drove, flock; floating (*of wood*); (*also m.* **—es,** *pl.* **—e**) drift (*Geol.*); (*also n.* **—es,** *pl.* **—e**) wreck, flotsam. **—ig,** *adj.* drifting, adrift; strong in growth (*of plants*); cogent, forcible, strong, conclusive, convincing; plausible; sound, valid; active; zealous; **—ig sein,** to drive (*of ships, etc.*). **—igkeit,** *f.* cogency (*of arguments*), validity, strength, soundness. *Comp.* **—gerechtigkeit,** *f.* right of pasture. **—strömung,** *f.* glacial current.

Trigonometrie', *f.* (*pl.* **—en**) trigonometry.

Trigonome'trisch, *adj.* trigonometrical.

[1]**Tril'ler**, *m.* (—s, *pl.* —) trill, shake (*Mus.*); **einen — schlagen**, to shake, trill. **—n**, *v.* I. *a.* to vary, ornament with trills. II. *a.* & *n.* (*aux.* **h.**) to shake, trill; to warble (*as birds*); to hum (*a song*).

[2]**Tril'ler**, *m.* (—s, *pl.* —) turnpike, toll-bar; turnstile; turning pillory (*obs. dial.*).

Trinit—a'rier, *m.* (—ariers, *pl.* —arier) Trinitarian. **—ä't**, *f.* Trinity. *Comp.* **—äts'=fest**, *n.*, (**Sonntag—a'tis**, *m.*) Trinity Sunday.

Trink'bar, *adj.* drinkable; ready for drinking; **nicht —**, undrinkable.

Trin'k—en, I. *ir.v.a.* & *n.* (*aux.* **h.**) to drink; to imbibe, absorb; to tipple, drink; **sich** (*dat.*) **einen Rausch, einen Haarbeutel, einen Zopf —en**, to get drunk; **der Wein läßt sich gut —en**, the wine is pleasant to drink; **ein Glas leer —en**, to empty a glass; **gern eins —en**, to be fond of one's glass; **einem Bescheid —en**, to pledge a person. II. *subst. n.* drink; drinking; drunkenness; **ein Trunkenbold läßt das —en nicht**, a thorough drunkard never gives up drinking. **—er**, *m.* (—ers, *pl.* —er) drinker; drunkard. *Comp.* **—becher**, *m.* goblet. **—gelag(e)**, *n.* drinking bout, carousal. **—geld**, *n.* gratuity (*to servants, coachmen, etc.*); tip (*coll.*); **einem ein —geld geben**, to tip a p. (*coll.*). **—geschirr**, *n.* drinking-vessel. **—gesellschaft**, *f.* wine-party; company of drinkers. **—glas**, *n.* wine-glass, beer-glass; tumbler. **—halle**, *f.* pump room (*at a watering place*). **—horn**, *n.* drinking-horn. **—lied**, *n.* drinking song. **—napf**, *m.* fountain (*in a bird-cage*). **—scene**, *f.* picture representing a drinking bout; orgy. **—schale**, *f.* goblet. **—spruch**, *m.* toast. **—stube**, *f.* tap-room, bar; refreshment-room. **—wasser**, *n.* drinking water.

Tri'pel, *m.* (—s, *pl.* —), (**—erde**, *f.*) rottenstone.

Trip'pel—n, *v.n.* (*aux.* **h.**) to trip; to mince one's steps; to trot (*with short, light steps*); **sie kam heran getrippelt**, she came tripping along. *Comp.* **—tritt**, *m.* patter, light, quick step.

Trip'per, *m.* (—s, *pl.* —) gonorrhœa (*Med.*).

Tripp'(sammet), *m.* mock-velvet.

[1]**Tritt**, *m.* (—es, *pl.* —e) step; pace; tread; trace, footprint; kick; tread; treadle; footboard; carriage-step; step (*of an altar, etc.*); pair of steps; estrade; flowerstand; footstool; **einem auf Schritt und — folgen**, to follow in a person's footsteps; **— vor —**, step by step; **gleichen Schritt und — halten**, to keep pace with; **ohne —**, at ease! **im —e!** (keep) time! **— wechseln**, change step! **— halten**, to keep step. *Comp.* **—brett**, *n.* treadle (*of a loom*); pedal (*of an organ*). **—harfe**, *f.* harp with pedals. **—leiter**, *f.* (pair of) steps. **—wechsel**, *m.* change of step.

[2]**Tritt; Trittst**, *imperat. & 3 pers. sing.*; *2 pers. sing. pres. indic. of* **treten**.

Triu'mph, *m.* (—s, *pl.* —e) triumph. **—ie'ren**, *v.n.* (*aux.* **h.**) to triumph (**über**, over); **die —ierende Kirche**, the Church triumphant. *Comp.* **—bogen**, *m.* triumphal arch. **—marsch**, *m.* triumphal march. **—wagen**, *m.* triumphal car. **—zug**, *m.* triumphal procession.

Triumvira't, *n.* (—s, *pl.* —e) triumvirate.

Trivialitä't, *f.* (*pl.* —en) triviality.

Trochä'—isch, *adj.* trochaic. **—us**, *m.* (—us, *pl.* —en) trochee.

Tro'ck—en, *adj.* & *adv.* dry; arid; barren; dull, uninteresting; chilly; blunt; **—enes Couvert**, dinner without wine; **—ener Empfang**, cool reception; **—ene Messe**, mass without the sacrament; **—ene Wahrheit**, plain truth; **einen mit —enem Munde (einen —en) sitzen lassen**, to offer a guest no refreshment; **—ener Wechsel**, bill drawn on oneself; **das —ene**, *see* **—ne; im —enen sitzen**, to be under cover, to be safe, to be well off; **auf dem —nen sitzen**, to be stranded, to be without money *or* resources; **—enen Fußes**, dryshod; **—en legen**, to drain; **—en pressen**, to dry by pressure. **—enheit**, *f.* dryness; aridity; barrenness; frigidity; dulness. **—ne**, *f.* dryness; dry land. **—nen**, *v.* I. *n.* (*aux.* **s.**) to dry, become dry. II. *v.a.* to dry; to air; to dry up, desiccate; to drain; **getrocknete Feigen**, dried figs. III. *subst.n.*, **—nung**, *f.* drying; desiccation; **zum —nen aufhängen**, to hang up to dry. *Comp.* **—en=apparat**, *m.* drying-apparatus, desiccator. **—en=boden**, *m.* drying-loft. **—en=brett**, *n.* clothes-horse; drying-stand. **—en=dock**, *n.* graving-dock, dry-dock (*Naut.*). **—en=fäule**, *f.* dry-rot. **—en=früchte**, *pl.* dried fruits. **—en=fütterung**, *f.* dry-feeding *or* fodder. **—en=gerüst**, **—en=gestell**, *n.* drying-stand; contrivance for drying. **—en=gewicht**, *n.* net weight. **—en=herd**, *m.* drying-ground. **—en=kammer**, *f.* drying-room. **—en=legung**, *f.* draining; drainage. **—en=legungs=maschine**, *f.* draining-machine. **—en=leine**, *f.* clothes-line. **—en=malerei**, *f.* crayon drawing. **—en=mittel**, *n.* siccative. **—en=ofen**, *m.* drying-stove *or* kiln. **—en=platz**, *m.* drying-ground. **—en=presse**, *f.* drying cylinders. **—en=rahmen**, *m.* tenter. **—en=stange**, *f.* drying-pole. **—en=stube**, *f.* drying-room *or* stove. **—en=verfahren**, *n.* drying-process. **—en=wohner(in**, *f.*), *m.* first tenant (*of a newly built house*) (*hum.*).

Trod'del, *f.* (*pl.* —n) tassel, bob. *Comp.* **—mütze**, *f.* nightcap, cap with a tassel.

Trö'd—el, *m.* (—els, *pl.* —el) old clothes; rubbish; lumber; second-hand goods; bric-à-brac; spree, lark (*coll.*); piece of fun; bustle, confusion. **—elei'**, *f.* frippery, old clothes; dawdling. **—eln**, *v.n.* (*aux.* **h.**) to deal in second-hand goods; to dawdle, loiter, waste one's time, to be slow; to have a spree. **—ler**, *m.* (—lers, *pl.* —ler), **—lerin**, *f.* dealer in old clothes *or* second-hand goods *or* bric-à-brac; dawdler. *Comp.* **—el=bude**, *f.* old-clothes-shop *or* -stall. **—el=frau**, *see* **—lerin**. **—el=hexe**, *f.* rag- and bone-hag (*poet.*). **—el=kram**, *m.* lumber; old clothes. **—el=leute**, *pl.* brokers, dealers in second-hand goods. **—el=markt**, *m.* place where second-hand goods are bought and sold; rag-fair. **—el=ware**, *f.* old clothes *or* furniture.

Troff, Tröf'fe, *1 & 3 pers. sing. imperf. indic. & subj. of* **triefen**.

Trof'fen, I. *obsol. past part. of* **treffen**. II. *1 & 3 plur. imperf. indic. of* **triefen**.

[1]**Trog**, *m.* (—es, *pl.* **Trö'ge**) trough; mason's hod; **schwingender —**, cradle (*for washing ore*). *Comp.* **—apparat**, *m.* galvanic trough.

[2]**Trog, Trö'ge**, *1 & 3 pers. sing. imperf. indic. & subj. of* **trügen** (*obs.* **triegen**).

Trol'le—n, *v.* I. *n.* (*aux.* **s.**) to toddle along, trudge. II. *r.* to go away, to march off; **—e dich**! be off! get away! away with you!

Trom'mel, *f.* (*pl.* —n) drum; tympanum (*Anat.*, *Mach.*); cylinder; sieve; barrel (*Horol.*); coffee-roaster; outwork (*Fort.*); tin-canister; barrel (*of a roasting-jack, etc.*); tambour; **die — rollt, wirbelt**, the drum rolls, beats. **—ei'**, *f.* continuous drumming; din. **—n**, *v.a.* & *n.* (*aux.* **h.**) to drum, to beat the drum; **es —t**, the drum is beating; **einen Marsch —n**, to beat a march on the drum. *Comp.* **—blech**, *n.* brass for drums. **—fell**, *n.* drum-skin, drum-head; drum of the ear, membrane of the tympanum (*Anat.*). **—fell=erschütternd**, *adj.* deafening, ear-splitting. **—gehäuse**, *n.*, **—kasten**, *m.* barrel of a drum. **—klöppel, —schlägel**, *m.* drumstick. **—rad**, *n.* tympan (*Mach.*). **—schlag**, *m.* beat of the drum; unter —schlag, with drums beating; bei gedämpftem —schlag, with muffled drums. —schlägel, —stock, m. drumstick. —schläger, m. drummer. —signal, n. drum-call. —sucht, f. tympanitis. —wirbel, m. roll of the drum.

Tromm'ler, m. (—s, pl. —) drummer.

Trommе'te, Drommete, f. trumpet (*both poetic*). —n, v.n. to sound the trumpet (*poet.*).

Trompe'te, f. (*pl.* —n) trumpet; die — *or* auf der — blasen, in die — stoßen, to blow *or* sound the trumpet; die — schmettert, bläst, the trumpet is sounded, the trumpet blares (*poet.*); eustachische —, eustachian tube. —n, v. I. *a.* to blow (*on the trumpet*), trumpet forth; einen aus dem Schlafe —n, to wake a p. by blowing a trumpet. II. *n.* (*aux.* h.); es hat —t, the trumpet has sounded. —r, m. (—rs, *pl.* —r) trumpeter. *Comp.* —n=bläser, m. trumpeter. —n=register, n. *see* —nzug. —n=schall, m. sound of the trumpet; unter —nschall bekannt machen, to publish by sound of trumpet *or* with trumpets sounding. —n=signal, n. trumpet-signal *or* call; —nsignal zum Satteln und Fertigmachen für das Aufsitzen, boot-and-saddle. —n=stoß, m. flourish of the trumpet. —n=tusch, m. flourish of trumpets. —n=zug, m. trumpet stop of an organ. —r=corps, n. brass band. —r=tisch, m. side-table.

Tro'p—e, f. (*pl.* —en) trope (*Rhet.*); (*pl.*) the tropics. —ikus, m. tropic, *see* Wendekreis. —isch, *adj.* tropical; metaphorical, figurative. *Comp.* —en=gegend, f. tropical country. —en=koller, m. frenzy produced by the heat of the tropics. —en=krankheiten, *pl.* endemic diseases of tropical climates. —en=lehre, f. tropology. —en=welt, f. tropical world; in der —enwelt, in the tropics.

Tropf, m. (—es, *pl.* Tröp'fe) ninny, booby, simpleton; armer —, armes Tröpfchen! poor wretch! —bar, *adj.* liquid, that can be dropped. —barkeit, f. liquidity. —en, I. *m.* (—ens, *pl.* —en) drop; tear; (*pl.*) drops (*Med.*). II. *v.a.* & *n.* *see* Tröpfeln; stetes —en höhlt den Stein, constant dropping wears the stone (*prov.*); es —t, a few drops are falling. *Comp.* —bad, n. shower-bath. —bern=stein, m. liquid amber. —brett, n. (plate-) drainer. —en=fall, m. drip, gutter, eaves. —en=weise, *adv.* by drops, drop by drop. —feuer, n. shower of drops (*Firew.*). —naß, *adj.* dripping wet. —öler, m. dropping oil-feeder. —pfanne, f. dripping-pan. —rinne, f. gutter. —stein, m. stalactite.

Tröpf'—chen, n. (—chens, *pl.* —chen) little drop. —eln, v. I. *n.* (*aux.* h. & f.) to drop, drip, trickle, fall in drops. II. *a.* to drop.

Trophä'e, f. (*pl.* —n) trophy.

Troß (*short* o), I. *m.* (—(ſ'ſ)es, *pl.* —(ſ'ſ)e) baggage (*Mil.*); baggage train; train of artillery; cavalcade; crowd; followers; gang, crew. II. *n.* (—(ſ'ſ)es, *pl.* —(ſ'ſ)e) & *f.* hawser (*Naut.*). *Comp.* —bube, —junge, —knecht, m. soldier in charge of baggage; camp-follower. —pferd, n. baggage-horse. —wagen, m. baggage-waggon.

Trost (*long* o), m. (—es) comfort, consolation, solace; einem — zusprechen, to comfort, console a p.; es gereicht mir zum —e, daß . . ., it is a comfort to me to think that . . .; bist du nicht bei —e? are you mad? du bist wohl nicht (recht) bei —e! you are mad, I think. *Comp.* —bedürftig, *adj.* needing consolation. —brief, m. letter of condolence. —bringend, *adj.* comforting, consolatory. —bringer, —geber, m. comforter. —fahren, n. consolation race (*cycl.*). —los, *adj.* comfortless; inconsolable, desperate; disconsolate. —rede, f. consolatory discourse, words of consolation. —reich, *adj.* consoling, comforting. —wort, n. word of comfort.

Tröst'bar, *adj.* consolable.

Trö'st—en, v.a. to comfort, console, solace; einen über eine S., wegen einer S. —en, to console a p. for something; sich mit . . . —en, to take comfort in . . ., to console oneself with; sich einer Sache (*gen.*) —en, to acquiesce in, be satisfied with a thing; Gott —e ihn! God rest his soul! —er, m. (—ers, *pl.* —er) comforter, consoler; the Comforter (*B.*); old book (*coll.*). —lich, *adj.* consoling, comforting; pleasant. —ung, f. consolation, comfort.

Trott, m. (—(e)s, *pl.* —e) trot; der gemeine, gewöhnliche —, the old jog-trot. —oi'r, n. (—oirs, *pl.* —oirs) pavement.

Trot'tel, m. (—s, *pl.* —) cretin (*dial.*); dunce, fool (*dial.*). —krankheit, f. cretinism.

Trotz, I. *m.* (—es) boldness, intrepidity; independence (*of spirit*); obstinacy; refractoriness; insolence; disdain; defiance; strength, (*cause of*) confidence (*B.*); — bieten, to set at defiance, defy; einem etwas zum —e thun, to do something in spite of a person; to do something to spite a person. II. *prep.* (*with dat. or gen.*) in spite of; despite; notwithstanding; — des schlechten Wetters, in spite of the bad weather; — dem, in spite of it, nevertheless; although, albeit, notwithstanding; — alledem, in spite of *or* for all that; — alledem und alledem, in spite of all that, whatever may be said, for all you may say; — einem, as well, as quick, as much as s. o.; er spricht — einem Gelehrten, he speaks as well as a scholar, he vies with any scholar in conversation.

Trot'z—en, v.n. (*aux.* h.) to bid defiance to, to defy; to brave; auf eine S. —en, to trust in, presume upon, be proud of, boast of a th.; mit einem —en, to be angry *or* sulky with a p. —er, m. (—ers, *pl.* —er) defiant, haughty *or* insolent person. —ig, *adj.* & *adv.* haughty, proud, overbearing; insolent; defiant; obstinate; refractory; sulky; (einen) —ig ansehen, to look at disdainfully, defiantly, haughtily. —iglich, *adj.* & *adv.* boldly. *Comp.* —kopf, m. stubborn *or* pig-headed person. —köpfchen, n. obstinate, perverse little thing. —köpfig, *adj.* obstinate; pig-headed; defiant. —wort, n. defiant word, disdainful expression.

Trou'badour, m. (—s, *pl.* —s) troubadour.

Trüb, (**Trü'b—e**,) I. *adj.* & *adv.* troubled, muddy, turbid, thick; opaque; dull, gloomy; dark; overcast; dull, dim; clouded (*of gems, etc.*); sad, gloomy, melancholy; die Lampe brennt —, the lamp burns dimly; im —en ist gut fischen, it is good fishing in troubled water (*prov.*); im —en fischen, to fish in troubled waters. II. *f.* (*pl.* —en) muddy, turbid state; dimness; opaqueness; gloom. —en, *v.a.* to trouble, make thick *or* muddy; to darken, dim; to cloud; to tarnish; to disturb, trouble; to sadden, cast a gloom over; der Himmel —t sich, the sky becomes overcast. —heit, *see* —e II. —sal, f. (*pl.* —sale) ((& *n.* —sals, *pl.* —sale)) affliction; trouble; distress; —sal blasen, to be in trouble, to be in the dumps (*coll.*). —selig, *adj.* troubled, afflicted; sad; miserable; —selige Stimmung, despondency, gloom; er ist in —seliger Stimmung, he is in the dumps (*coll.*). —seligkeit, f. sadness; affliction. —ung, f. darkening (*of vowels produced by*) rounding (*of the lips*). *Comp.* —sinn, m melancholy, dejection; pensiveness; gloom. —sinnig, *adj.* low-spirited; sad; sombre.

Tru'bel, m. (—s) trouble; upset, confusion.

Truch'seß (*long* u), m. (—(ſſ)en, *pl.* —(ſſ)en) Lord High Steward (*of a royal household*).

Truck'system, n. truck system, system of paying workmen in kind, in goods.

Tru'del. I. *m.* (—s, *pl.* —) loose *or* fast girl.

II. *f.* (*pl.* —n) dumpy girl, stumpy little woman. **—n**, *v.a.* & *n.* (*aux.* s.) to trundle.

Trüf'fel, *f.* (*pl.* —n) truffle. **—n**, *v.a.* to garnish *or* flavour with truffles. *Comp.* **—brut**, *f.* young truffles. **—hund**, *m.* dog that hunts for truffles. **—jagd**, *f.* truffle-hunting. **—leberpastete**, *f.* Périgord pie, Strasburg pie. **—zucht**, *f.* cultivation of truffles.

¹**Trug, Trü'ge**, *1 & 3 pers. sing. imperf. indic. & subj. of* **tragen**.

²**Trug**, *m.* (—es) deceit; imposture, deception, fraud; illusion; **ohne —**, fairly; **ein Mann ohne —**, a straightforward *or* upright man. *Comp.* **—bild**, *n.* phantom; dream; illusion. **—erfüllt**, *adj.* full of deceit. **—gebilde**, *n.*, **—gestalt**, *f.* phantom. **—gewebe**, *n.* tissue of lies. **—grund**, *m.* specious argument, sophism. **—los**, *adj.* artless, guileless. **—schluß**, *m.* false conclusion, fallacy; paralogism; delayed *or* interrupted cadence (*Mus.*). **—voll**, *adj.* deceptive; delusive **—werk**, *n.* deception, fraud, illusion.

Trü'g—en, *ir.v.a.* & *n.* (*aux.* h.) to deceive; **der Schein —t**, appearances are deceitful; **Gottes Wort kann nicht —en**, the word of God cannot fail; **der Schein —t**, appearances are deceptive; **das Lügen und —en**, lying and deceiving, falsehood and fraud. **—erisch, —lich**, *adj.* deceptive, deceitful; delusive; insidious; sophistical; unsafe (*as ice*). **—lichkeit**, *f.* deceitfulness; fallaciousness.

Tru'he, *f.* (*pl.* —n) trunk, chest; (clothes) press.

Trul'le, *f.* (*pl.* —n) plump, fat female.

Trumeau', *m.* (& *n.*) (—s, *pl.* —s) pier-glass.

Trumm, *m.* & *n.* (—(e)s, *pl.* **Trüm'mer**) end, stump (*of a candle, etc.*); end (of weaver's threads), thrum; fragment, piece; needleful (*of thread*).

Trüm'mer, *pl.* (*of* **Trumm**) fragments; wreckage, ruins; broken pieces; **zu —n** *or* **in —er gehen**, to go to rack and ruin; **zu —n schlagen**, to batter to pieces, to wreck. **—haft**, *adj.* ruinous, decayed. *Comp.* **—artig**, *adj.* like a heap of ruins, ruinous. **—besäet**, *adj.* strewn with débris. **—feld**, *n.* field covered with débris *or* ruins. **—gebäude**, *n.* building falling to ruins. **—gestein**, *n.* breccia, conglomerate. **—haufe(n)**, *m.* heap of ruins.

Trumpf, *m.* (—es, *pl.* **Trüm'pfe**) trump (*Cards*); **was ist —?** what are trumps? **Herz ist —**, hearts are trumps; **der letzte —**, the last resource; **einen — darauf setzen**, to play one's trump card, answer smartly; **seine Trümpfe ausspielen**, to beat *or* cap s. th.; **die Gesinnung ist —**, principle is everything; **einem zeigen, was — ist**, to show a p. what is what. **—en**, *v.a.* & *n.* (*aux.* h.) to trump; **einen —en (abtrumpfen)**, to snub a p. *Comp.* **—bube**, *m.* knave of trumps. **—farbe**, *f.* trump(-suit). **—karte**, *f.* trump-card.

Trunk, *m.* (—es, *pl.* **Trün'ke**) drinking; drink, liquor; draught; drinking-bout; drunkenness; **dem — ergeben**, addicted to drinking; **an den — kommen**, to take to drinking; **auf einen —**, at one gulp *or* draught. **—en**, *adj.* drunk, intoxicated; **sie waren —en vor Freude**, they were wild with joy; **sieges —en**, elated with victory. **—en=heit**, *f.* drunkenness. *Comp.* **—en=bold**, *m.* drunkard. **—sucht**, *f.* drunkenness, dipsomania. **—süchtig**, *adj.* given to drink(ing), dipsomaniac.

Trupp, *m.* (—(e)s, *pl.* —s) troop; band, gang; flock, herd. **—e**, *f.* (*pl.* —en) troop *or* body (*of soldiers*); troupe *or* company (*of actors*); **die —en**, the troops, (*military*) forces, soldiers, men. *Comp.* **—en=aushebung**, *f.* raising of troops. **—en=bewegungen**, *pl.* military movements *or* manœuvres. **—en=einschiffung**, *f.* embarkation of troops; entraining of soldiers **—en=gattung**, *f.* arm of the service. **—en=körper**, *m.*, **—en=korps**, *n.* body of troops. **—en=küche**, *f.* military kitchen. **—en=nachschub**, *m.* reinforcements. **—en=schau**, *f.* military review, parade. **—en=teil**, *m.* body of troops; arm of the service. **—en=übung**, *f.* manœuvre. **—weise**, *adv.* in troops; in bands.

Tru'sche, Trü'sche, *f.* lote, burbot (*Icht.*).

Tru't— (*in comp.*) **—hahn**, *m.* turkey(-cock); **der —hahn kollert**, the turkey gobbles. **—henne**, *f.*, **—huhn**, *n.* turkey(-hen). **—hühner**, *pl.* turkey-fowls.

Trut'schel, *f.* (*pl.* —n) plump girl; fat woman.

Trutz, *m.* (—es) *see* **Trotz**; **zu Schutz und —**, offensively and defensively. **—en, —ig**, *see* **Trotzen, Trotzig**. *Comp.* **—bündnis**, *n.* offensive alliance; **Schutz- und —bündnis**, offensive and defensive alliance. **—lied**, *n.* defiant song. **—waffen**, *pl.* weapons for attack

Tschahi', Tschaho'! *int.* fol-de-rol!

Tscha'ko, *m.* (—s, *pl.* —s) shako.

Tschi'buk, *m.* (—s, *pl.* —s) chibouque, chibouk, Turkish tobacco-pipe.

Tu'b—a, *f.* (*pl.* —en) a brass musical instrument; tuba. **—us**, *m.* (—us, *pl.* —usse, —en) tube; telescope.

Tuber'—kel, *f.* (*pl.* —keln) tubercle. **—kulö's**, *adj.* tubercular. **—kulo'se**, *f.* (*pl.* —kulosen) tuberculosis, tubercular disease; **—kulose der Lungen**, phthisis. *Comp.* **—kel=bildung**, *f.* tubercul(iz)ation.

Tuch (*long* u), *n.* (—es, *pl.* **Tü'cher**, *after numerals* —) cloth; piece of cloth; web; fabric; stuff; kerchief, shawl; (**Schnupf—**) pocket-handkerchief; sail; (**Hals—**) neck-tie; (**Hand—**) towel; rag, duster; (*pl.*) hunter's toils. (*pl.* —e) sort of cloth, woollen fabric. (*pl.* —e, *obs.*; **Tü'cher**) piece of cloth about 52 ells long; **zweierlei —, was in zweierlei — geht**, soldiers, the military. **—en**, *adj.* cloth. *Comp.* **—artig**, *adj.* cloth-like. **—bereiter**, *m.* cloth-dresser. **—fabrikant**, *m.* cloth-manufacturer. **—geschäft**, *n.* cloth-trade; woollen-draper's shop. **—halle**, *f.* drapers' hall. **—händler**, *m.* cloth-merchant, (woollen-)draper. **—handlung**, *f.* cloth-trade; *see* **—laden**. **—laden**, *m.* clothier's *or* woollen-draper's shop. **—lager**, *n.* cloth-warehouse. **—macher**, *m.* cloth-maker, cloth-worker. **—macher=innung**, *f.* cloth-workers' company. **—nadel**, *f.* shawl-pin; breast-pin. **—rahmen**, *m.* cloth-frame, tenter. **—rasch**, *m.* cloth-serge. **-rauher(in**, *f.*), *m.* carder. **—reisende(r)**, *m.* traveller for a cloth-factory *or* -warehouse; billiard-ball (*hum.*). **—rest**, *n.* remnant of cloth. **—sarsche**, *f. see* **—rasch**. **—scher=maschine**, *f.* cloth-shearing machine; carding *or* friezing-machine. **—schrot**, *n.* list (*of cloth*). **—stopfer**, *m.* fine-drawer (*of cloth*). **—walke**, *f.* fulling of cloth. **—walker**, *m.* fuller. **—waren**, *pl.* cloth goods. **—weberei**, *f.* cloth-manufacture; cloth-factory.

Tü'chelchen (*long* ü), *n.* (—s, *pl.* —) little piece of cloth; small neckerchief.

Tüch'tig, *adj.* & *adv.* fit, able, qualified; sound, hearty, good; thorough; clever; excellent; efficient; **— sein in einer S.**, to know a th. thoroughly, to be good at a th., **— zu nichts**, fit for nothing; **er wurde — durchgeprügelt**, he got a sound thrashing; **er hat etwas —es in der Schule gelernt**, he has had an excellent education at school; **er ist — in den neueren Sprachen**, he is good at modern languages; **er ist ein —er Übersetzer**, he is a skilful translator. **—keit** *f.* ability, fitness; solidity, soundness; excellence; proficiency.

Tück, (Tuck,) *m.* (—es, *pl.* **Tü'cke**), **—e**, *f.* (*pl.* —en) prank, trick; malice, malignity, spite;

knavery; **eine —e auf einen haben,** to have a spite against a p. **—(i)sch,** *adj.* malicious, spiteful; artful, insidious; **auf einen —isch sein,** to have a spite against a p. *Comp.* **—e=bold,** *m.* treacherous *or* spiteful person; mischievous imp (*hum.*).

Tuck, I. *int.* chuck! chuck! II. *m. see* **Tück.** **—en,** *v.n.* (*aux.* **h.**) to cluck (*of hens*).

Tuff, *m.* (—(e)s, *pl.* —e) tufa, tuff. *Comp.* —**kalk, —stein,** *m.* tufaceous limestone.

Tüftelei', (**Düftelei',**) *f.* hairsplitting, very punctilious way of doing things, subtleties. **—n,** *v.n.* to draw over-nice distinctions; to go in for subtleties.

Tu'gend, *f.* (*pl.* —en) virtue; chastity; excellence, good quality (*obs.*); **Jugend hat keine —,** youth has little grace, boys will be boys. **—haft, —sam,** (*obs.*) *adj.* virtuous. —**haftigkeit,** *f.* virtue. *Comp.* **—arm,** *adj.* possessing few virtues. **—bild,** *n.*, **—spiegel,** *m.* model of virtue. **—bold,** *m.* paragon of virtue (*iron.*). **—bund,** *m.* League of Virtue (*secret society of German students 1808—1816*). **—bündler,** *m.* member of the L. of V. *or* person in sympathy with it. **—held,** *m.* rigid moralist. **—lehre,** *f.* moral philosophy, morals, ethics. **—lehrer,** *m.* moralist. **—reich,** *adj.* very virtuous. **—weg,** *m.* path of virtue.

Tüll, *m.* (—(e)s, *pl.* —e) tulle; net. *Comp.* —**gardine,** *f.* net *or* lace-curtain. **—stuhl,** *m.* net-loom.

Tül'le, *f.* (*pl.* —n) spout, nozzle; socket.

Tul'pe, *f.* (*pl.* —n) tulip; tulip-shaped glass (*holding a pint* (Schnitt) *of beer*); name of several molluscs. *Comp.* **—n=baum,** *m.* tulip-tree. **—n=flor,** *m.* tulips in full bloom; profusion of tulips. **—n=glas,** *n.* tulip-shaped pint-glass. **—n=zucht,** *f.* tulip growing. **—n=zwiebel,** *f.* tulip-bulb.

Tum'mel, *m.* (—s) (*dial.*) giddiness; tumult; *see* **Rausch.**

Tum'm—eln, *v.* I. *a.* to turn round, to stir about; to give exercise to, to keep (a p.) moving; to wheel (*a horse*) round; **der Soldat muß erst recht getummelt werden,** the soldier must first be well drilled *or* exercised. II. *r.* to move, bustle about; to bestir oneself; to shake oneself; to hurry; **sich mit einem —eln,** to wrestle, scuffle with s.o. **—ler,** *m.* (—lers, *pl.* —ler) horse-breaker, trainer; tumbler, dancer; (*also* **Tümmler**) tumbler-pigeon; dolphin, porpoise. *Comp.* **—el=platz,** *m.* exercise-ground; riding-school; wrestling-ground; scene of action; place of combat, arena.

Tüm'pel, *m.* (—s, *pl.* —) pool; deep part of a lake.

Tumult—ua'nt, *m.* (—uan'ten, *pl.* —uan'ten) rioter. **—ua'risch,** (**—voll,**) *adj. & adv.* riotous, rioting. **—uie'ren,** *v.n.* (*aux.* **h.**) to riot.

Tün'ch—e, *f.* limewash, whitewash; plastering; plaster; varnish (*fig.*). **—en,** *v.a.* to whitewash; to plaster; to roughcast. **—er,** *m.* (—ers, *pl.* —er) whitewasher; plasterer. —**erei',** *f. see* **—e;** daubing. *Comp.* **—farbe,** *f.* (**weiße**) whitewash. **—pinsel,** *m.* whitewasher's brush. **—scheibe,** *f.* whitewasher's palette. **—werk,** *n.* whitewashing.

Tu'nik—a, *f.* (*pl.* —as, —en) tunic.

Tun'k—e, *f.* (*pl.* —en) sauce; soaking, sopping. **—en,** *v.a.* to dip; to steep; to sop (*bread, etc.*) in a fluid and eat it; **ein Schälchen Kaffee —en,** to take a cup of coffee by sopping bread *or* biscuits in it (*coll., dial.*). *Comp.* **—näpfchen,** *n.*, **—schale,** *f.* sauce-boat.

Tun'nel, *m.* (—s, *pl.* —s) tunnel; underground passage, subway; **einen — bohren,** to drive (*or* to cut) a tunnel (through). **—ie'ren, —isie'ren,** *v.a. & n.* (*aux.* **h.**) to tunnel. *Comp.* **—axe,** *f.* axis of a tunnel. **—bau,** *m.* tunnelling.

Tup'f—en, *v.a.* to touch lightly (*with something pointed*); to dot; to dab; **einen Stein —en,** to rough-hew a stone. *Comp.* **—bällchen,** *n.*, **—ballen,** *m.* printer's ball.

Tüp'fe—l, *m.* (—ls, *pl.* —l) dot; spot; iota. **—lig,** *adj.* dotted. **—ln,** *v.a.* to dot; to spot; to stipple, engrave *or* shade in dots; to punctuate. **—n,** *see* **Tupfen.**

Turbi'ne, *f.* (*pl.* —n) turbine, horizontal wheel. *Comp.* **—n=anlage,** *f.* turbine-plant. **—n=betrieb,** *m.* hydraulic power. **—n=rad,** *m.* horizontal water-wheel.

Türki'—s, *m.* (—ses, *pl.* —se) turquoise.

Turm, *m.* (—es, *pl.* **Tür'me**) tower; steeple (*of a church*); belfry (*of a castle*); dungeon; prison; rook, castle (*Chess*); **der babylonische —,** the tower of Babel. *Comp.* **—bau,** *m.* building of a tower. **—fahne,** *f.* vane. —**falk(e),** *m.* kestrel. **—hoch,** *adj.* towering, very high. **—höhe,** *f.* height of a tower. —**hüter,** *m.* warder of a tower; jailer. —**kanone,** *f.* turret-gun (*in a ship*). **—knopf,** *m.* knob on the top of a steeple. **—schiff,** *n.* turret-ship, monitor. **—schwalbe,** *f.* swift (*Orn.*). **—spitze,** *f.* top of a tower; spire. —**uhr,** *f.* tower-clock, church-clock. **—verließ,** *n.* dungeon, keep. **—wächter,** *see* **Türmer.** **—zinne,** *f.* battlement(s) of a tower.

Turmali'n, *m.* (—s, *pl.* —e) tourmaline (*Min.*).

Türm'chen, *n.* (—s, *pl.* —) little tower, turret.

Tür'men, *v.* I. *a.* to pile up. II. *r. & n.* (*aux.* **h.**) to tower up, rise high; **die —de Stadt,** the city towering aloft (*poet.*).

Tür'mer, *m.* (—s, *pl.* —) watchman on a tower; warder of a tower.

Turn, Thurn, *obs. for* **Turm.** **—er,** *obs. for* **Türmer.**

Tur'n—en, I. *v.n.* (*aux.* **h.**) to do *or* practise gymnastics. II. *subst.n.* gymnastics, gymnastic exercise(s); **—en für Mädchen,** cal(l)isthenics; **Schau—en,** gymnastic display. **—er,** *m.* (—ers, *pl.* —er) gymnast. **—erei',** *f.* gymnastic exercises. **—erisch,** *adj.* gymnastic. **—erschaft,** *f.* body of gymnasts. **—ie'r,** *n.* (—iers, *pl.* —iere), (*obs., poet.:* **—ei',** *n.*) tournament, jousting. **—ie'ren,** *v.n.* (*aux.* **h.**) to hold a tournament; to tilt, joust, contend in a tournament. **—us,** *m.* (—us, *pl.* —usse) turn; rotation. *Comp.* **—anstalt,** *f.* gymnasium. **—fahrt,** *f.* pedestrian tour of gymnasts. **—fest,** *n.* athletic sports. **—gerät,** *n.* gymnastic apparatus. **—halle,** *f.* gymnasium. —**kunst,** *f.* gymnastics. **—lehrer,** *m.* teacher of gymnastics. **—lehrerin,** *f.* teacher of cal(l)isthenics. **—platz,** *m.* athletic grounds. **—ier'=bahn,** *f.* the lists. **—ier'=dank,** *m.* prize of the tournament. **—ier'=fähig,** *adj.* qualified to tilt. **—ier'=mäßig,** *adj.* according to the rules of tilting. **—ier'=platz,** *m.* the lists. —**ier'=rennen,** *n.* passage of arms, tilting. —**ier'=richter,** *m.* umpire, marshal of the lists. **—ier'=sattel,** *m.* saddle used in tilting. —**ier'=schranken,** *pl.* barrier; the lists. **—ier'=spiel,** *n.* tournament. **—ier'=waffen,** *pl.* tilting weapons. **—saal,** *m.* gymnasium. **—spiel,** *n.*, **—spiele,** *pl.* athletics, athletic sports. **—vater,** *m.* father of gymnastics; **der deutsche —vater,** F. Ludwig Jahn (1778-1852). **—verein,** *m.* gymnastic *or* athletic club. **—wart,** *m.* leading gymnast, superintendent of gymnastic exercises. **—wesen,** *n.* gymnastics. **—zeug,** *n.* gymnastic apparatus.

Tur'nip, *m.* (—s, *pl.* —s) turnip.

Tur'teltaube, *f.* (*pl.* —n) turtle-dove.

[1]**Tusch,** *m.* (—(e)s, *pl.* —e) flourish of trumpets; **— blasen,** to sound a flourish (*of trumpets*).

[2]**Tusch,** *m.* (—(e)s, *pl.* —e) (slight) affront provoking a duel. **—e,** *f.* (*pl.* —en) Indian ink, China ink. **—en,** *v.a.* to draw in Indian ink *or* in water-colours; to paint with a child's paint-box. **—ie'ren,** *v.a.* to touch; to insult. *Comp.*

—**farbe,** *f.* water-colour. —**kasten,** *m.* paint- *or* colour-box. —**manier,** *f.* aquatint. —**napf,** *m.* saucer (for painting). —**pinsel,** *m.* brush for washing in Indian ink *or* water-colours. —**wort,** *n.* word provocative of a duel (*e.g.* **dummer Junge, komisch**).

Tusch, *m. int* hush! —**eln,** to whisper. —**en, Tü'schen,** *v.* I. *a.* to quell (*disturbance*). II. *a. & n.* (*aux.* **h.**) to silence, to hush.

Tüt'chen, *n.* small paper bag. *Comp.* —**dreher,** *m.* small shopkeeper *or* his apprentice (*coll.*).

Tu'te, Tü'te, *f.* (*pl.* —**n**) paper-bag; screw.

Tute'l, *f.* (*pl.* —**en**) guardianship.

Tu'ten, *v.a.* to blow (a horn), to toot (*coll.*).

Tüt'tel, *m.* (—**s,** *pl.* —) dot. —**chen,** *n.* (—**chens,** *pl.* —**chen**) tittle, jot.

Twie'te, *f.* narrow side lane, alley (*dial.*).

Twing, *m.,* = **Zwing,** *n.* citadel, stronghold.

Ty'p, *m.* (—(**e**)**s,** *pl.* —**e**(**n**)), —**us,** *m.* (—**us,** *pl.* —**en**) type. *Comp.* —**en=haft,** —**isch,** *adj.* typical.

Ty'p—e, *f.* (*pl.* —**en**) type, character. —**en,** *v.a.* to print (*rare*). *Comp.* —**en=drucktelegraph,** *m.* type-setting telegraph. —**en=ehrlich,** *adj.* careful in returning borrowed photographs (*sl.*). —**en=hebel,** *m.,* —**en=metall,** *n.* type-metal. —**ogra'ph,** *m.* (—**ographen,** *pl.* —**ographen**) typographer. —**ogra'phisch,** *adj.* typographic.

Typh—ö's, *adj.* typhous, typhoid. —**us,** *m.* (—**us**) typhus, camp-fever; typhoid fever. *Comp.* —**us=kranke(r),** *m.* one ill with typhoid fever.

Tyra'nn, *m.* (—**en,** *pl.* —**en**) tyrant, king; tyrant, despot(ic ruler). —**ei',** *f.* tyranny; despotism. —**isch,** *adj.* tyrannical; despotic. —**isie'ren,** *v.* I. *a.* to tyrannize over. II. *n.* to act the tyrant. *Comp.* —**en=herrschaft,** —**en=macht,** *f.* tyranny. —**en=joch,** *n.* yoke of despotism. —**en=laune,** *f.* caprice of a tyrant. —**en=mord,** *m.* murder of a tyrant, tyrannicide.

U

U, u, *n.* U, u; **einem ein X für ein U machen,** to deceive, humbug, cheat a person; *for abbr. see the Index of abbreviations.*

Ü'bel, I. *adj. & adv.* (**üb'ler, üb'le, üb'les;** *comp.* **übler**) evil, ill, bad; wrong; sick; ill; **nicht** —, not bad, rather nice; pretty well; **üble Aussprache,** faulty pronunciation; **kein übler Bissen,** a dainty morsel; **einem einen übeln Dienst erweisen,** to do s.o. an ill turn; **ich habe nicht — Lust dazu,** I am rather inclined for it *or* to do it; **einen in üble Nachrede bringen,** to slander a p., to give a p. a bad name; **einem Übles gönnen,** to wish s.o. ill; — **angebracht,** misplaced; **eine Sache — (auf)nehmen,** to take a th. amiss *or* in bad part; — **auslegen,** to misconstrue; **nehmen Sie es mir nicht —!** pardon me, no offence, I hope! **nehmen Sie es mir nicht —, daß ich,** don't be offended with me for (*or* if I); — **ankommen,** to catch a Tartar; **es wird ihm — bekommen,** he will have to suffer for that; **mir bekam es —,** I came off badly; — **deuten,** to misinterpret, put a wrong construction on; **es wird ihm — ergehen,** he will fare badly; he will not prosper; **einem — mitspielen,** to treat a p. badly; — **riechen,** to have a bad smell; — **schmecken,** to have a disagreeable taste; **mir ist** *or* **wird —, ich bin —,** I feel sick, queer, squeamish, I do not feel well (at all); **er befindet sich —,** he feels *or* is ill; **mir ist — zu Mute,** I feel not well; I feel uncomfortable; **dabei kann einem — werden,** it is enough to make one sick, it is sickening; — **daran sein,** to be in a bad way, to be badly off, to be in a fix *or* in difficulty; **das klingt nicht —,** that sounds rather nice; **es steht — mit ihm,** his affairs are *or* he is in a bad way, **nicht — Lust zu einer S. haben,** to have a good mind *or* a great wish to do a th.; **das wäre nicht —,** that would not be a bad thing *or* a bad plan, that would not be amiss, I should rather like that; **auf einen — zu sprechen sein,** to be ill disposed towards one, not to have a good word to say of a p.; **wohl oder —,** willy-nilly, willing or unwilling, whether one likes it or not. II. *n.* (—**s,** *pl.* —) evil; mischief; misfortune; sore; wound; malady; **was darüber ist, das ist vom —,** whatsoever is more cometh of evil. —**keit,** *f.* sickness, nausea; disgust (*fig.*); —**keit verursachen,** to bring about nausea, to turn the stomach; —**keit verursachend,** nauseous; —**keit verursachendes Mittel,** nauseant, emetic (*Med.*). *Comp.* —**befinden,** *n.* indisposition. —**berüchtigt,** *adj.* of ill fame. —**gelaunt,** *adj.* ill-humoured, out of humour, cross. —**klang,** *m* dissonance; cacophony. —**klingend,** —**lautend,** *adj.* dissonant. —**nehm(er)isch,** *adj.* easily offended, touchy. —**sein,** *n.* indisposition; nausea. —**stand,** *m.* disadvantage, inconvenience, drawback. —**that,** *f.* misdeed, bad action. —**thäter(in,** *f.*,) *m.* evildoer. —**thätig,** *adj.* mischievous, doing evil. —**thun,** *n.* wrong-doing. —**wollen,** *n.* ill-will, malevolence, enmity. —**wollend,** *adj.* malevolent, ill-disposed, spiteful.

Ü'b—en, *v.a.* to exercise, practise; to use, exert; to drill, train (*Mil.*); to show, exercise; to do, execute; **geübt,** disciplined, skilled, skilful, practised, well versed; **Barmherzigkeit an einem —en,** to show a p. mercy; **Betrug —en,** to practise deceit; **Geduld —en,** to have patience, be patient (*with*); **Gewalt —en,** to use violence; **ein Handwerk —en,** to pursue, carry on a trade; **eine im Schreiben wohl geübte Hand haben,** to be skilled in writing, to be a ready writer; **Rache an einem —en,** to take vengeance on a p.; **die Rechtspflege —en,** to administer justice. —**lich,** *adj.* usual, customary, in use; **das Wort ist nicht mehr —lich,** the word is obsolete, has gone out of use. —**lichkeit,** *f.* usage; customariness. —**ung,** *f.* exercise, practice; exercising; use; exercise, study (*Mus.*); dexterity; drilling, discipline (*Mil*); training, military manœuvres; —**ung macht den Meister,** practice makes perfect (*prov.*); **aus der —ung,** out of practice; **sich in der — ung erhalten,** to keep in training, to keep one's hand in; **er hat keine —ung mehr im Deutschsprechen,** his German has become rusty, he has had no practice in speaking German; **diese Sitte ist schon lange außer —ung,** this custom has long fallen into disuse. *Comp* —**ungs=aufgabe,** *f.* exercise. —**ungs=fähigkeit,** *f.* capacity for exercise. —**ungs=geschwader,** *n.* manœuvring squadron. —**ungs=haus,** *n.* drill-hall, fencing-school. —**ungs=lager,** *n.* training camp for soldiers. —**ungs=marsch,** *m.* practice in marching, test march. —**ungs=platz,** *m.* drill ground. —**ungs=spiel,** *n.* gymnastic exercise. —**ungs=stück,** *n.* exercise. —**ungs=zeit,** *f.* time for practising; drill time.

Ü'ber, I. *prep.* (*with acc. & dat.*) *with* **dat.** *when implying rest or a limited or circular motion,* over, above, higher than, superior to; in the process of, during, while; on account of, by reason of; (*Austrian dial.* = **gemäß**) in accordance with; — **Beschluß,** in accordance with the resolution; — **einem stehen,** to be above a p.; — **der Stadt schweben,** to be hovering over the town (*of a balloon*); — **der Arbeit sein,** to be at work; — **den Büchen sitzen,** to sit over one's books; **er war — dem Lesen eingeschlafen,** he had fallen asleep while reading;

— dem Essen, at meal times, during dinner, *etc.;* — einem Glase Wein, over, whilst drinking, a glass of wine; — dem Lärm etwas überhören, not to hear something on account of the noise; ein Schwert schwebt — seinem Kopfe, a sword hangs over his head; er wohnt — dem Meere, he lives on the other side of the ocean; man vergaß den Dichter — dem Menschen, one forgot the poet in the man; er vergißt — dem Spiele seine Geschäfte, he becomes so absorbed in playing that he forgets his business; — dem Zanken, whilst disputing. *with* **acc.** *when signifying transfer or motion to, over or past* (*often in answer to* **wohin?** whither?), across, from one side to another; beyond, on the further side of; after; by way of, viâ; *or, when used without any reference to motion, signifying* with regard to, as for, concerning, about; along, over; Thränen flossen ihr — die Wangen, tears trickled down her cheeks; — die Stadt fliegen, to fly *or* pass over the town (*of a balloon*); — ein Volk herrschen, to rule over a people; — einen Gewalt haben, to have power over a person; sie kann (vermag) viel — ihn, she has great influence over him; es — sich gewinnen, — sein Herz bringen, zu . . ., to bring oneself to, to find it in one's heart to . . .; — eine Brücke gehen, to cross a bridge; der Übergang — die Donau, the crossing of the Danube; — Paris nach Wien, to Vienna by (way of) *or* via Paris; — die Straße gehen, to cross the street; — das Knie herab reichen, to reach below the knee; eine Reise — See, a trip across the sea; — die Vierzig(e) hinaus sein, to have passed *or* be over forty; das geht — das Maß des Erlaubten, that goes beyond what is permissible, that goes too far; das geht — alles, that beats everything; es geht nichts — ein Glas Rheinwein, there's nothing like a glass of hock; das geht mir — alles andere, I prefer that to everything else; — die Kräfte gehen, to go beyond one's strength; Nichts geht — den Mut, there is nothing better than courage; Zufriedenheit geht — (den) Reichtum, contentment is better than riches; — Hals und Kopf, head over heels; — alles Erwarten glücklich, happy beyond all expectation; die Wahrheit — alles lieben, to love truth more than anything; — alle Maßen schön, incomparably beautiful; sich — eine S. freuen, to rejoice at *or* over s.th.; — Ungerechtigkeit klagen, to complain of injustice; er schreibt — Kunst, he writes on *or* about art; sich (*dat.*) — eine S. graue Haare wachsen lassen, to grow gray with worry over *or* about a th.; sich — einen lustig machen, to make fun of a p.; ich bin — die Neugierde weg, I am past *or* above curiosity; — Sprachvergleichung, essay on comparative philology (as title of a treatise); — die freien Künste, the Fine Arts (*as title of a book*); — Nacht, during the night; — kurz oder lang, sooner or later; Briefe — Briefe, letter after letter; einmal — das andere, again and again. *used elliptically as int.;* — den Narren! oh! what a fool! Fluch — dich! a curse upon you! O. — die Jugend! oh, youth! youth! *used before a numeral adverbially either govern'g the acc. or not affecting the case* = over, above, more than; heute — acht Tage, this day week; heute —s Jahr, in a year from to-day; zehn Minuten — zwölf, 10 minutes past 12; es ist noch — ein Meter davon da, there is still more than a metre left; — hundert Studenten, more than a hundred students. *with acc. or gen. of a subst. of time which it follows;* tag —, tags —, all day long, during the day. II. *adv. & sep. or* (*mostly*) *insep. pref.* over, above, too much in excess; — und —, over and over, through and through, out and out, completely; einem in etwas — sein, to surpass, excel s.o. in a thing; darin ist er mir —, in this he beats me (*coll.*); die Sache ist mir —, I am tired of it (*coll.*); das Fieber ist —, the fever is past (*coll.*); die Stadt ist —, the town has surrendered; *see* Vorüber, Gegenüber. [*Neuter verbs compounded with* **über** *are gen'lly insep.; most transitive verbs can be used as sep. & insep., when sep.* **über** *has the accent. Note the glottal stop in compounds the second part of which begins with a vowel, e.g.* **überall, überein.**]

überа'ckern, *v.a.* (*insep.*) to plough a field over again, to plough lightly.

überа'll, I. *adv.* everywhere; all over, throughout; at all times; positively; upon the whole, at all (*dial., rare*); —! all hands on deck! — her, from all quarters; — hin, everywhere, in every direction; — nicht, by no means, certainly not; — wo, wherever. II. *m.* Hans —, — und Nirgends, Paul Pry, busybody,

überanstreng—en, *v.a. & r.* (*gen'lly insep.*)(*p.p.* überangestrengt) to overwork. **—ung,** *f.* over-exertion, overstrain.

überant'worten, *v.a.* (*insep.*) to deliver up, give over, surrender.

überarbeit—en, *v.a.* (*sep.*) to work in excess; heute wird übergearbeitet, to-day we shall work overtime; (*insep.*) to do over again, to retouch, revise, to give the finishing touch; dies Wörterbuch ist von meinem Freunde überarbeitet, this dictionary has been revised by my friend; sich —en (*insep.*), to overwork, to overexert o.s., to work too hard. **—ung,** *f.* finishing off of a work; retouch(ing), touching up (*of a painting*); later modified text, transcript with alterations and additions.

Ü'berärmel, *m.* over-sleeve; false sleeve.

überau's, *adv.* exceedingly, excessively.

Ü'berbau, *m.* (—es, *pl.* —e, —ten) building built over another; superstructure; projection.

überbau—en, *v.* I. *a.* (*insep.*) to build over, raise above (*something*); sich —en, to ruin o.s. with building. II. *a. & n.* (*aux.* h.) (*sep.*) to build a projection (*over another building*); to build above; to build higher. **—ung,** *f.* superstructure; die —ung wurde beschlossen, it was agreed to build another story *or* to build higher.

ü'berbehalten, *ir.v.a.* (*sep.*) to keep on (*one's cloak, etc.*); to keep *or* have over.

Ü'berbein, *n.* (—s, *pl.* —e) exostosis (*Surg.*); ganglion (*in the sinews*); bone-spavin (*Vet.*).

Ü'berbett, *n.* (—es, *pl.* —en) (feather) coverlet.

ü'ber—beugen, —biegen, *ir.v.a.* (*sep.*) to bend above; to bend too much; sich —, to bend over.

überbieten, *ir.v.a. & n.* (*aux.* h.) (*sep.*) to offer in addition, more; er bot noch drei Mark über, he offered 3 marks more. II. *a.* (*insep.*) to outbid; to outdo, excel, surpass; to ask too much, overcharge; sie — sich in Höflichkeiten, they vie with each other in civilities.

überbil'd—en, *v.a.* (*insep.*) to over-educate, over-refine. **—et,** too highly educated, too refined *or* bookish (*for one's station in life*). **—ung,** *f.* over-refinement.

Überbinde (*pron.* Ü'berbinde), *f.* (*pl.* —n) upper (*or* outer) bandage (*Surg.*). **—n,** *ir.v.a.* (*sep.*) to bind over; (*insep.*) to dress (*a wound*), to tie *or* wrap up.

überblättern, *v.a.* (*insep.*) to cover with leaves; to overlook, miss (*in looking over a book, etc.*); (*sep. & insep.*) ein Buch —, to turn over the pages of a book.

überbleib—en, *ir.v.n.* (*aux.* f.) (*sep.*) to remain (over); (*insep.*) *gen'lly only in p.p.* überblieben, surviving. **—sel** (*pron.* Ü'berbleibsel), *n.* (—sels, *pl.* —sel) remainder, residue; vestige, remains; relic; wreck.

ü'berblick, *m.* survey, view; prospect; quickness of perception, width of view; sketch, review; synopsis, summary. **—en**, *v.a.* (*insep.*) to glance at, survey.

überblü'hen, *v.a.* (*insep.*) to cover *or* fill with flowers; to raise its blossoms above (*something*); **sich —**, to have too many blossoms; to fade, to outlive one's beauty.

überbreiten, *v.a.* (*sep. & insep.*) to spread, cover over; **sich —**, to spread everywhere.

ü'berbrettl, *n.* chanson, air sung *or* acted at a music hall, song performed at a 'varieties' theatre; kind of 'varieties' theatre.

überbrin'g—en, *ir.v.a.* (*insep.*) to bring to *or* over, to deliver. **—er**, *m.* (**—ers**, *pl.* **—er**) bearer, deliverer.

überbrü'cken, *v.a.* (*insep.*) to throw a bridge over.

ü'berbunt, *adj.* too gay *or* motley.

überbür'd—en, *v.a.* (*insep.*) to overload, to overburden. **—ung**, *f.* overburdening, overtasking, excessive amount of work *or* labour. **—ungs=frage**, *f.* question of lightening the school curriculum, question of overstrain; question of over-taxation.

überchlor'sauer, *adj.*; **—es Salz**, perchlorate.

ü'berdach, *n.* shed, penthouse, shelter. **—en**, (*pron.* **überda'chen**) *v.a.* (*insep.*) to cover with a roof, to shelter.

überdau'ern, *v.a.* (*insep.*) to outlast; to outlive, survive; *see* **überstehen** I.

ü'berdeck—e, *f.* upper cover, coverlet. **—en**, *v.a.* (*sep.*) to stretch over, spread out on; (*insep.*) to cover with; to make a ceiling over, to vault. **—ung**, *f.* spreading over, covering, cover.

überden'ken, *ir.v.a.* (*insep.*) to think s.th. over, to reflect, meditate, ponder on a th.; **wohl überdacht**, well considered, well balanced.

überdie's, *adv.* in addition to this, besides, moreover.

ü'berdruck, *m.* overprint, supernumerary sheets (*Typ.*); transfer (*of written matter to stone, etc.*); surcharge (*postage stamps*). **—en**, *v.a.* (*insep.*) to transfer.

ü'ber—druß, *m.* (**—drusses**) weariness, ennui; satiety; disgust. **—drüssig**, *adj. & adv.* (*with gen.*) weary, tired; satiated; disgusted; bored; **einer Person —drüssig werden**, to grow tired of a p., to feel bored by a person.

überdün'gen, *v.a.* (*insep.*) to manure; to manure too much.

ü'bereck(s), *adv.* across, diagonally; (**etwas**) **— bringen**, to put out of the way; **— gehen**, to go on in a disorderly fashion, to be topsy-turvy.

ü'bereil—e, *f.* precipitation. **—en**, (*insep. pron.* **überei'len**) *v.* I. *a.* to overtake; to hasten too much, to press; **—en Sie nichts**, don't hurry; **—en Sie die Sache nicht**, don't precipitate matters; **die Nacht —te uns**, night overtook us. II. *r.* to hurry too much; to act precipitately; **—en Sie sich nicht**, don't be in (too great) a hurry! **er hat sich —t**, an imprudent word escaped him; he has acted rashly *or* inconsiderately. **—t**, *p.p. & adj.* precipitate, rash, headlong; unguarded, thoughtless. **—ung**, *f.* precipitation; rashness; overhaste, heedlessness.

überei'n, *adv. & sep. pref.* in accordance; conformably, alike, agreeably (*to*); **das ist ganz —**, that is exactly the same thing. *Comp.* **—kommen**, I. *ir.v.n.* (*aux.* **s.**) to be conformable (*to*), agree (*with*), answer; to come to terms with; to stipulate; **über eine S. —kommen**, to agree on *or* about a th. II. *subst. n.*, **—kunft**, *f.* agreement; arrangement; contract; **ein —kommen treffen**, to make an agreement; **laut —kunft mit**, by agreement with; **gegenseitige —kunft**, mutual consent. **—stimmen**. *v.n.* (*aux.* **h.**) to agree (*in pitch and tone*); to accord; to agree, coincide, suit, sympathize with; to correspond (**mit**, to); **ich stimme damit —**, I agree to that; **das Adjektiv muß mit seinem Substantive im Geschlechte und in der Zahl —stimmen**, the adjective must agree with its substantive in gender and number. **—stimmig**, *adj.* agreed; agreeing; harmonious; conformable. **—stimmung**, *f.* accord; agreement; correspondence; concord, unison; conformity; **die Einnahme mit der Ausgabe in —stimmung bringen**, to make the receipts balance the expenses, to make both ends meet (*coll.*). **—treffen**, *ir.v.n.* (*aux.* **s.**) (**mit etwas**) to agree with; to correspond *or* answer to a thing.

übereinan'der, *adv.* one upon another; **— legen**, to lay one upon another, to pile up; **die Beine — schlagen**, to cross one's legs; **— schlagen, — stehen, — treffen**, to overlap. *Comp.* **—greifen**, *n.* overlapping. **—setzung**, *f.* superposition.

[1]**überei's—en**, *v.a.* (*insep.*) to cover with ice *or* hoar-frost; **—t**, covered with ice, frozen over; ice-clad (*poet.*); ice-glazed, frosted (*of cakes*).

[2]**ü'bereisen**, *n.* beak, crow's bill (*on the shoe of a lame horse*).

überessen, *ir.v.* I. *r.* (*insep.*); **er hat sich über(g)essen**, he has overeaten. II. *a.* (*sep.*) **sich** (*dat.*) **eine Speise —**, to take a loathing to s.th. by eating too much of it.

überfahr—en, *ir.v.* I. *n.* (*aux.* **s.**) (*sep.*) to pass (*drive, sail, etc.*) over. II. *a.* (*insep.*) to traverse, cross (*a stream, etc.*); to pass lightly, wash over; to pass (*a certain point*); to overdrive (*horses*); **es überfuhr kalt seinen Rücken**, a cold shiver ran down his back; (*sep.*) to transport over; (*sep. & insep.*) to drive over, crush by driving. **—t**, (*pron.* **Ü'berfahrt**) *f.* passage, crossing; place of passing over; ferry(-boat); **die —t nach Irland**, the crossing to Ireland; **wir hatten eine gute (abscheuliche) —t**, we had a smooth (dreadful) passage *or* crossing. *Comp.* **—ts=boot**, *n.* ferry-boat; railway-ferry.

überfall, *m.* (*pron.* **Ü'berfall**) unexpected attack, surprise; inroad, invasion; raid; overfall, weir. **—en**, *ir.v.* I. *a.* (*insep.*) to fall upon suddenly, surprise; to invade; to overtake (*as nightfall, illness, etc.*); **die Nacht überfiel uns**, night overtook us, we were benighted; **der Regen überfiel sie**, they were caught in the rain; **der Schlaf überfiel mich**, sleep stole upon me; **Schrecken überfiel uns**, we were seized with terror. II. *n.* (*aux.* **s.**) (*sep.*) to fall over. III. *imp. fig.* to have suddenly the feeling that . . ., to imagine; **plötzlich überfiel es ihn**, suddenly he fancied.

überfeilen, *v.a.* (*sep. & insep.*) to file over again; to retouch.

ü'berfein, *adj.* over-refined; superfine.

überflechten, *ir.v.a.* (*insep.*) to enclose in straw *or* wickerwork; (*sep.*) **Stroh über eine Flasche —**, to plait straw round a bottle.

überfliegen, *ir.v.* I. *n.* (*aux.* **s.**) (*sep.*) to fly over. II. *a.* (*insep.*) to cross flying, to pass swiftly across; to run *or* glance quickly over, to peruse (*a letter*); to outfly, soar beyond; to surpass, overstep (*fig.*); to cover, mantle; **ihr Antlitz überflog ein roter Schein**, the colour mounted to her face.

überfließen, *ir.v.* I. *n.* (*aux.* **s.**) (*sep.*) to flow over, overflow; to be overflowing with (joy, *etc.*, **vor Freude ꝛc.**). II. *a.* (*insep.*) to overspread, flow over.

überflü'gel—n, *v.a.* (*insep.*) to outflank (*Mil.*); to surpass, outstrip. **—ung**, *f.* outflanking.

ü'ber—fluß, *m.* (**—flusses**) overflow; superabundance; plenty, abundance; exuberance;

opulence, luxury; **—fluß haben an einer S.**, to abound in a th., to have plenty of a th.; **zum —**, superabundantly, over and above; **—fluß an Worten**, redundancy of expression; **—fluß bringt Überdruß**, abundance begets indifference (*prov.*). **—flüssig**, *adj. & adv.* abundant, profuse; superfluous; **ein volles, gedrücktes, gerütteltes und —flüssiges Maß**, good measure, pressed down and shaken together and running over (*B.*); **—flüssig machen**, to render unnecessary *or* superfluous, to supersede.

überfluten, *v.* I. *n.* (*aux.* **h.** & **s.**) (*sep.*) to overflow. II. *a.* (*insep.*) to inundate.

überfor'der—n, *v.a.* & *n.* (*aux.* **h.**) (*insep.*) to demand too much. **—ung**, *f.* exorbitant demand.

ü'berfracht, *f.* overfreight, overload; (charge for) excess luggage. **—en** (*pron.* **überfrach'ten**), *v.a.* (*insep.*) to overfreight.

überfres'sen, *v.r.* (*of animals*) *see* **überessen.**

überfrieren, *ir.v.n.* (*aux.* **s.**) (*sep.* & *insep.*) to freeze over.

überführ—en, I. *ir.v.a.* (*sep.*) to conduct across; to convey over; to bring over (*to an opinion*); (*insep.*) to convince, to convict (*of a crime, etc.*); to glut (*a market*). **—t**, *adj.* overstocked (*C.L.*). II. *subst. n.*, **—ung**, *f.* conviction; transportation; crossing; viaduct.

ü'berfüll—e, *f.* superabundance; exuberance (*of spirits, etc.*). **—en**, *v.a.* (*sep.*) to fill into another vessel, to decant; to transfuse; (*insep.*) to overfill; to surfeit; to overstock, to crowd to excess. **—ung**, *f.* overfilling; surfeiting; repletion.

überfüt'ter—n, *v.a.* (*insep.*) to overfeed. **—t**, *p.p.* & *adj.* gorged.

ü'bergabe, *f.* delivery; conveyance; surrender; transfer; **eine Stadt zur — auffordern**, to summon a town to surrender.

ü'bergang, *m.* passage, crossing; passage, ford; transition; desertion, going over (*to the enemy*); sudden shower; (*pl.*) nuances (*Paint.*, *Mus.*); **Niveau—**, level crossing (*Railw.*); **hier ist kein —!** No thoroughfare! *Comp.* **—s=bestimmungen**, *pl.* provisional, temporary arrangements. **—s=brücke**, *f.* foot-bridge; viaduct. **—s=gebirge**, *n.* transition *or* secondary rocks (*Geol.*). **—s=punkt**, *m.* crossing, passage. **—s=recht**, *n.* right of way. **—s=zeit**, *f.* transition-period. **—s=zustand**, *m.* state of transition, temporary arrangement.

ü'bergar, *adv.* overdone, too much cooked.

übergeben, I. *ir.v.a.* (*sep.*) (**einem etwas**) to put over (*a p.* e. g. *a shawl, cloak*); (*insep.*) to deliver over to; to give up to, remit; to give in charge; to leave *or* commit to; to surrender; **eigenhändig —**, to deliver personally. **—**, *p.p.* & *adj.* reckless, bad (*obs.*). II. *ir.v.r.* (*insep.*) to vomit; to surrender (*Mil.*).

ü'bergebühr, *f.* supererogation; extra charge. **—lich**, *adj.* supererogatory.

übergeh—en, I. *ir.v.n.* (*aux.* **s.**) (*sep.*) to flow, run over, overflow; to cross, pass over; to change sides; to desert; to turn, change (*to*); to run into; to surpass (*coll.*); to be transient; **die Augen gingen ihm über**, his eyes welled over, his eyes grew moist; **in Fäulnis —en**, to rot; **in eine schnellere Bewegung —en**, to quicken the time (*Mus.*); **eine Farbe geht in eine andere über**, the colours run into one another; **die Festung ist über(gegangen)**, the fortress has surrendered; **der Druckfehler ist in alle folgenden Ausgaben übergegangen**, the misprint has been retained in all subsequent editions; **das Regenschauer geht bald über**, the shower will soon pass over; **wes das Herz voll ist, des geht der Mund über**, out of the fulness of the heart the mouth speaketh (*B.*); **zu etwas —en**, to proceed to, to set about; **zu einer andern Religion —en**, to change one's religion. II. *ir.v.a.* (*insep.*) to skip, to pass over; to pass by; to violate, transgress; to glance at, run one's eye over; to run, go over; to revise; to omit; to overlook, not see; **sich —en**, to overtire oneself with walking. III. *subst.n.*, **—ung**, *f.* omission, neglect; passing over (*in silence*); passing over *or* by (*in advancing a soldier*); visiting (*of a field*).

ü'bergenug, *adv.* more than enough, ample; **— haben**, to have enough and to spare.

ü'bergewicht, *n.* overweight, excess of weight; preponderance, ascendancy; superiority; **das — bekommen**, to gain *or* get the ascendancy over; **das — behaupten**, to maintain one's superiority; **das — haben**, to predominate; **diese Meinung gewann das —**, this view prevailed.

übergießen, *ir.v.a.* (*sep.*) to pour over; to spill; to sprinkle; to pour (*from one vessel into another*); (*insep.*) to pour on; to sprinkle; to cover with; to suffuse; **mit Zucker —**, to candy, to ice with sugar, glaze; **es übergoß ihn purpurrot**, he grew crimson.

übergipsen, *v.a.* (*sep.* & *insep.*) to plaster over, to parget.

übergit'tern, *v.a.* (*insep.*) to cover with a trellis; to crosshatch, to divide into squares.

überglän'zen, *v.a.* (*insep.*) to throw a brilliant light on; to outshine, eclipse.

übergla'sen, *v.a.* (*insep.*) to glaze over.

übergletʼscher—n, *v.a.* (*insep.*) to cover with glaciers. **—ung**, *f.* formation of a layer of ice.

ü'berglücklich, *adj.* extremely happy; too happy.

übergol'den, *v.a.* (*imp.*) to gild (*all over*).

ü'ber—greifen, *ir.v.n.* (*aux.* **h.**) (*sep.*) to overlap; to shift, glide (*on a violin, etc.*); to encroach; **in jemandes Rechte —greifen**, to encroach on another's rights. **—griff**, *m.* (**—(e)s**, *pl.* **—e**) encroachment.

ü'bergroß, *adj.* too large; enormous; colossal.

ü'ber—guß, *m.* (**—gusses**, *pl.* **—güsse**) pouring over; crust.

ü'bergut, *adj.* exceedingly good; above the standard.

ü'berhaben, *ir.v.a.* (*sep.*) to have on (*over other things*); to have remaining, to have left; **eine S. —**, to be weary *or* sick of a th. (*coll.*).

ü'berhand, *adv.*; **— nehmen**, to gain ground, get the upper hand, prevail, spread, grow large, increase; **das Übel nimmt —**, the evil goes on increasing; **das Wasser nimmt —**, the water is rising very high; **die Krankheit nimmt —**, the disease is spreading. *Comp.* **—nehmen**, *n.* increase; prevalence.

ü'berhang, *m.* projection (*Arch.*); canopy, cover; cornice (*of snow*); overhanging rock, crag; something hanging over; great *or* excessive inclination (*fig.*, *rare*). **—en**, *ir.v.n.* (*aux.* **h.**) (*sep.*) to hang over; to overhang; to project over; to lean to one side.

ü'berhängen, (*sep.*) *v.* I. *a.* to hang, cover over; to put on; to sling over one's shoulder (*a gun, etc.*). II. *n.* (*aux.* **h.**) *see* **überhängen.**

ü'berharken, *v.a.* (*sep.*) to rake (lightly) over.

überhäu'fen, *v.a.* (*insep.*) to load, overwhelm (*with*); to overload; to oppress, weigh down; to glut (*the market, etc.*).

überhau'pt, *adv.* in general, generally; upon the whole; at all; especially, in particular (*dial.*); **du hättest es — nicht thun sollen, und besonders nicht jetzt**, you should not have done it at all, and especially not now.

überheb—en, I. *ir.v.a.* (*sep.*) to lift over; (*insep.*) **einen einer Sache** (*gen.*) **—en**, to exempt, excuse from; **einen einer Mühe —en**, to spare s.o. trouble; sich —en, to overstrain oneself (*by lifting*); sich wegen einer Sache —en, to be proud of, to boast of a thing. II. *subst.n.*, —ung, *f.* exemption; vanity, pride; presumption.

ü'berhemdchen, *n*, shirt-front; chemisette.

überhe'r, (*obs.*) *adv.* over; over and above; moreover.

überhi'n, *adv.* over; slightly, superficially; past (*obs.*); moreover (*dial.*); ein Buch nur — lesen, to skim a book.

überhobeln, *v.a.* (*sep. & insep.*) to plane over, rough-plane.

ü'berhoch, *adj.* too high; exceedingly high.

überhö'h—en, *v.a.*, to command; to surmount. —ung, *f.* command (*Fort.*); die —ung der äußern Schiene, the super-elevation of the outer rail (*Railw.*).

überholen, *v.a.* (*sep.*) to overhaul; to shift (*sails*); to take over; (*insep.*) to overtake; (*fig.*) to outstrip, surpass.

überhö'ren, *v.a.* (*insep.*) not to hear (*through inattention, etc.*); ich habe seine Bemerkung überhört, I have missed *or* I did not catch his remark; einen —, einem seine Aufgabe —, to hear a p. say *or* repeat a lesson, to hear a *p.*'s lesson.

ü'berhosen, *pl.* overalls (*trousers*).

überhüpfen, *v.* I. *n.* (*aux.* s.) (*sep.*) to hop over *or* across. II. *a.* (*insep.*) to skip, omit, pass over; to hop *or* leap over.

ü'berirdisch, *adj.* above the earth; supermundane; spiritual; celestial; supernatural; unearthly; divine.

überja'g—dbar, *adj.* too old, great (*of a deer*). —en, *v.* I. *a.* (*insep.*) to over-ride, overdrive; to outrun; to overtake; to chase across. II. *a. & n.* (*aux.* s.) (*sep.*) to hurry over *or* across.

ü'berjährig, *adj.* more than a year old; too old, superannuated.

überkalken, *v.a.* (*sep. & insep.*) to cover with lime.

überkau'fen, *v.r.* (*insep.*) to buy too dear; to ruin oneself in buying.

ü'berkippen, *v.* I. *n.* (*aux.* s.) (*sep.*) to tip over, tilt over, topple over. II. *v.a.* to overturn, upset.

überkleben, *v.a.* (*sep. & insep.*) to paste over.

ü'berkleid, *n.* upper garment; upper covering. —en, *v.a.* (*insep.*) to cover over, *see* Bekleiden.

ü'berklug, *adj.* overwise; too clever; self-sufficient; conceited; —er Mensch, wiseacre. —heit, *f.* too great sharpness *or* cleverness.

überknor'peln, *v.r. & n.* (*aux.* s.) (*insep.*) to get *or* become covered with cartilage.

ü'berkochen, *v.n.* (*aux.* s.) (*sep.*) to boil over; to boil (*with rage, etc.*).

überkoh'lensauer, *adj.* bicarbonate.

überkom'men, (*insep.*) *ir.v.* I. *a.* to get, receive; to take possession of, attack, seize; to be passed on *or* transmitted; eine plötzliche Angst überkam sie, they were seized with a sudden fear. II. *n.* (*aux.* s.); was ist dir —? what has come *or* been sent to you? III. *adj.* that which has been handed down, traditional; ein —es Verhältnis, traditional relations.

ü'berkraft, *f.* superior power, exuberant strength.

überkreu'z, *adv.* across, crossways, crosswise.

ü'berkultur, *f.* over-culture, over-civilization.

überkün'steln, *v.a.* (*insep.*) to employ too much art in doing, to overdo.

überladen, *ir.v.a.* (*sep.*) to remove, trans-ship, *etc.*; (*insep.*) to overload.

überla'nds— (*in comp.*) —eisenbahn, *f.* transcontinental railway; Pacific Railway (*Amer.*). —post, *f.* overland-mail. —reise, *f.* overland route.

ü'berlang, *adj.* too long. —e, *adv.* too *or* ever so long; —e ausbleiben, to be too slow in coming, to stay beyond one's time.

ü'berlangen, *v.a.* (*sep.*) to reach *or* hand over.

ü'berlaß, *m. see* Überbleibsel.

überlass—en, *ir.v.* I. *a.* (*sep.*) to let pass; to leave (*remaining*); (*insep.*) to leave (*to some one else*); to give up, relinquish; to cede, make over; zur Miete —en, to let; —en Sie das mir, leave that to me; das muß man der Beurteilung des Lesers —en, this must be left to the reader's discretion *or* judgment; es ist ihm —en, was er thun will, he is at liberty to do as he pleases; sich einer Sache (*dat.*) —en, to give oneself up *or* give way to a th. —er, *m.* (—ers, *pl.* —er) ceder, relinquisher. —ung, *f.* leaving; yielding up, cession.

ü'berlast, *f.* overweight, surcharge, overcharge; trouble, nuisance, vexation; sich selbst zur — sein, to be a burden to o. s. —en, *v.a.* (*insep.*) to overload.

ü'berlästig, *adj.* burdensome; troublesome, tiresome, importunate; —er Mensch, a bore.

überlaufen, *ir.v.* I. *a.* (*sep.*) to run over *or* down; (*insep.*) to spread over, overrun; to overflow, inundate; to run over, glance at; to pester, annoy, bore, importune (*with frequent visits, etc.*); to outstrip, outrun; einen mit dem Degen —, to run at a p. with drawn sword; es überläuft mich, I shudder; my blood runs cold; es überlief ihn ein kalter Schauer, a cold shudder seized him. II. *n.* (*aux.* s.) (*sep.*) to run over, overflow; to boil over; die Augen laufen ihm über, his eyes overflow with tears; zum Feinde —, to go over to the enemy, to desert.

ü'berläufer, *m.* (—s, *pl.* —) deserter (*Mil.*); apostate (*Rel.*); turncoat (*Pol.*).

ü'berlaut, *adj.* too loud; (too) noisy; clamorous; —es Lachen, horse-laugh.

überle'b—en, *v.a.* (*insep.*) to outlive, survive; to get out of fashion; —t sein, to be spent, to die; das —e ich nicht, that would (will) be my death-blow; seinen Ruhm —en, to outlive one's fame; das hat sich überlebt, that has had its day, that has gone out of fashion; der Tag ist —t, the day is done.

1**überle'gen**, *adj.* superior; er ist ihm —, he excels him, he is more than a match for him. —heit, *f.* superiority; ascendancy, preponderance.

2**überleg—en**, *v.a.* (*sep.*) to lay over *or* upon; to lean, bend over; Geld —en, to lay by money; das Ruder —en, to shift the helm; ein Kind —en, to whip a child (*coll.*); (*insep.*) to cover all over; to overburden; to reflect on, ponder over, weigh; bei sich —en, to consider; mit einem etwas —en, to consult with s. o. about a th.; ich werde es mir —en, I shall think the matter over, I shall think about it; alles wohl —t, taking everything into account, upon the whole. —end, *p. & adj.* deliberative. —sam, *adj. & adv.* deliberate, prudent; meditative. —t, *p.p. & adj.* well weighed, deliberate. —ung, *f.* reflection, deliberation; nach reiflicher —ung, upon mature consideration; nach besserer —ung, on reflection, on second thoughts; mit —ung verübtes Verbrechen, premeditated crime; ohne —ung, inconsiderate. *Comp.* —ungs=kraft, *f.* power of reflection, judgment.

ü'berleiten, *v.a.* (*sep.*) to lead over *or* across: to form a transition, lead (*from one argument to another*); to transfuse (*blood*), —des Zeitwort, transitive verb (*rare*).

überlernen, *v.a.* (*sep. & insep.*) to con; to go over (one's lesson) again.

überlesen, *ir.v.a.* (*sep. & insep.*) to read, run over; to overlook in reading; einem zu(m) — geben, to give to s. o. to read over; sich —, (*insep.*) to injure one's health by reading too much.

überlie'fer—n, *v.a.* (*insep.*) to deliver, hand over, give; to surrender; **der Nachwelt —n**, to hand down to posterity. **—ung**, *f.* delivering; delivery; surrender; tradition.

überlis'ten, *v.a.* (*insep.*) to overreach, outwit.

übermach—en, *v.a.* (*insep.*) (**einem etwas**) to make *or* hand over; to transmit; to consign; **Geld (durch Wechsel) —en**, to remit money (by cheque); **—te Summe**, the remittance; (*sep.*) to put over *or* upon. **—ung**, *f.* consignment, remittance, transmission, sending.

ü'bermacht, *f.* superior force; preponderance, supremacy, ascendancy; too great power.

ü'bermächtig, *adj.* superior, overwhelming, paramount; too powerful.

übermalen, *v.a.* (*sep.*) to paint over; (*insep.*) to paint out; to paint a new picture over another; to paint over, paint (*a room*); to touch up (a picture).

übermangan'sauer, *adj.* permanganic; **—es Salz**, permanganate.

überman'nen, *v.a.* (*insep.*) to overcome, master.

ü'ber—maß, *n.* (**—es**) excess; abundance; superfluity; **—maß im Essen**, gluttony. **—mäßig**, *adj.* & *adv.* extravagant; excessive; exorbitant; extreme, immoderate; **—mäßig arbeiten**, to work excessively *or* too hard; **—mäßig groß**, huge, enormous. **—mäßigkeit**, *f.* excess; exorbitancy.

überman'ern, *v.a.* (*insep.*) to cover with masonry, to wall up.

übermei'stern, *v.a.* (*insep.*) to master, subdue.

ü'bermensch, *m.* superhuman being, demigod. **—lich**, *adj.* superhuman, more than human; godlike, heroic; excessive, enormous (*coll.*); **sich —lich anstrengen**, to make superhuman efforts.

übermessen, *ir.v.a.* (*sep.*) to give over-measure of; to measure, pour out, *etc.*; (*insep.*) to measure *or* survey by the eye; to estimate in measuring.

übermit'tel—n, *v.a.* (*insep.*) to convey; to hand over, transmit. **—ung**, *f.* conveyance; delivery, transmission.

übermö'gen, *v.a.* (*insep.*) to overcome (*obs.*); to force, influence, decide a p. (*obs.*).

ü'bermorgen, *adv.* & *n.* the day after to-morrow; **ja, —!** you may wait a long time for it! (*coll.*). **—d**, *adj.* happening, *etc.*, the day after to-morrow; **der —de Tag = Übermorgen.**

übermü'd—en, *v.a.* (*insep.*) to overtire; to fag out; **übermüdet**, knocked up (*coll.*); **sich —en**, to overexert o. s., to become exhausted. **—ung**, *f.* overfatigue, exhaustion.

ü'ber—mut, *m.* wild spirits; wantonness, excessive joy *or* merriment; arrogance, insolence, haughtiness; presumption; bravado; **—mut thut selten gut**, pride goes before a fall (*prov.*). **—mütig**, *adj.* in high spirits; playful, wanton; haughty, supercilious; insolent; presumptuous.

ü'bernächst, *adj.* after the next, the next but one; **—e Woche**, the week after next, the next week but one; **am —en Tage**, the day after to-morrow.

überna'cht, *adv.* during the night.

übernach'ten, (*insep.*) *v.* I. *n.* (*aux.* **h.**) to pass the night. II. *a.* to lodge a p., to take a person in for the night.

ü'bernächtig, *adj.* kept for a night; lasting but one night; fleeting, transient; having stayed up all night, *or* having had too little sleep during the night, tired out, fatigued, worn, haggard; **—e Augen**, eyes weary with watching. **—keit**, *f.* fatigue from want of sleep; pale, weary look.

übernähen, *v.a.* (*sep.*) to sew over; (*insep.*) to cover with stitches; to overcast; to whip together.

ü'bernahm—e, *f.* the taking possession of; taking charge of; taking upon oneself; assumption; **bei der —e habe ich**, in taking possession of *or* in accepting s.th. I have; **—e eines Amtes**, entering upon an office; **—e einer Arbeit**, undertaking a work; **—e einer Erbschaft**, acceptance of a legacy, entering upon an inheritance. *Comp.* **—e=bedingungen**, *pl.* conditions of acceptance. **—e=liste**, *f.* inventory. **—s=schein**, *m.* certificate of shipment; bill of lading.

ü'bernaht, *f.* overseam; overcasting.

ü'bername, *m.* surname, nickname (*dial.*).

ü'bernatürlich, *adj.* supernatural, miraculous; **—es Ereignis**, miracle. **—keit**, *f.* supernaturalism, miraculousness.

übernehm—en, *ir.v.* I. *a.* (*sep.*) to take over *or* across; to cover oneself over with; to overtrump; to ship (*a sea*); (*insep.*) to take possession of; to receive; to undertake; to accept, assume (*responsibility, etc.*); to seize; to overcharge, exact too much; to oppress; **sich vom Zorne —en lassen**, to (allow o.s. to) be overcome with rage. II. *r.* (*insep.*) to undertake too much; to overexert o.s.; **sich im Essen und Trinken —en**, to overeat, to drink too much; **übernommene Gefahr**, risk subscribed (*C.L.*). **—er**, *m.* (**—ers**, *pl.* **—er**) receiver; transferee; undertaker. **—ung**, *see* **Übernahme.**

ü'berordnen, *v.a.* (*sep.*) to place above, to set over.

ü'beroxyd, *n.* (su)peroxide. **—ie'ren**, *v.a.* to peroxidize.

überpi'chen, *v.a.* (*insep.*) to pitch, cover with pitch.

überpinseln, *v.a.* (*sep.* & *insep.*) to paint *or* daub over.

ü'berproduktion, *f.* over-production, surplus production; overtrading.

überque'r, *adv.* across, crossways, crosswise, diagonally. **—en**, *v.a.* to cross, to traverse.

überra'gen, *v.a.* (*insep.*) to overtop, rise *or* tower above; to extend beyond; to overlook; to command (*a town*, *etc.*, *Fort.*); to hang over; to crown; to surpass, to excel.

überran'ken, *v.a.* (*insep.*) to cover with (its) tendrils.

überra'sch—en, *v.a.* (*insep.*) to surprise; to take unawares; to startle. **—ung**, *f.* surprise.

überrechn—en, *v.a.* (*insep.*) to calculate, reckon up; to compute; (*sep.*) to run through (*an account*); to examine (*an account*). **—ung**, *f.* calculation.

überre'd—en, *v.a.* (*insep.*); **einen —en, etwas zu thun, einen zu einer S. —en**, to persuade s.o. to do a th.; **sich durch Gründe —en lassen**, to allow o.s. to be persuaded, *or* convinced. **—end**, *p.* & *adj.* persuasive. **—ung**, *f.* persuasion. *Comp.* **—ungs=kraft**, *f.* power of persuasion. **—ungs=kunst**, *f.* art of persuading, gift of persuasion.

ü'berreich, *adj.* too rich; extremely rich; **— (an)**, abounding (in), teeming (with). **—lich**, *adj.* superabundant. *adv.* in profusion.

überreich—en, *v.* I. *n.* (*aux.* **h.**) (*sep.*) to extend over *or* beyond. II. *a.* (*sep.*) to stretch over *or* above; (*insep.*) to hand, reach over; to present, give in, deliver. **—ung**, *f.* handing over; presentation.

ü'berreif, *adj.* overripe. **—e**, *f.* over-ripeness.

[1]**überrei'fen**, *v.a.* (*insep.*) to ripen too much. to grow too ripe.

[2]**überrei'fen**, *v.a.* (*insep.*) to hoop (*a cask*).

[3]**überrei'f—en**, *v.a.* (*insep.*) to cover with hoar-frost: **—t**, hoary, pruinous.

überreiten, *ir. v.* I. *a.* (*insep.*) to overtake in riding; to override, ride too hard; to pass in riding; (*sep.*) to ride over (*a child, etc.*); to ride over (*a field, etc.*). II. *n.* (*aux.* ſ.) (*sep.*) to ride across *or* over.

ü'berreiz, *m.* excess of irritation. **—en,** *v.a.* (*insep.*) to over-excite; to irritate too much; **—te Nerven,** overstrained *or* unstrung nerves; **—tes Gehirn,** overtasked brain. **—theit, —ung,** *f.* over-excitement, excess of irritation.

überrennen, *ir.v.a.* (*sep. & insep.*) to run over; (*insep.*) to over-run; to outrun; to run upon; to run down; to pester, importune.

ü'berreſt, *m.* rest, remains, remnant; residue, remainder, balance; (*pl.*) fragments, scraps, shreds, waste; **getrümmerte —e,** detritus; **irdiſche —e,** mortal remains; ashes (*poet.*).

überrin'den, *v.a.* (*insep.*) to cover with bark, to crust.

ü'berrock, *m.* frock-coat (*of men*); skirt (*of women*); overcoat, greatcoat (*of men*); **langer —,** ulster; **waſſerdichter —,** waterproof, mackintosh; **im —(e),** in morning dress.

überrum'pel—n, *v.a.* (*insep.*) to surprise, take unawares. **—ung,** *f.* surprise; sudden attack, surprisal.

überſalzen, *v.a.* (*sep.*) to sprinkle lightly with salt; (*insep.*) to salt too much.

ü'ber—ſatt, *adj.* surfeited, cloyed; **—ſatt einer S.,** sick and tired of a th. **—ſät'tigen,** *v.a.* (*insep.*) to surfeit, pamper, fill to loathing; to oversaturate (*Chem.*).

ü'berſatz, *m.* leap over; attic story.

überſäu'ern, *v.a.* (*insep.*) to make too acid; to overoxidate (*Chem.*); **den Magen —,** to produce heartburn *or* acidity of the stomach.

überſchät'z—en, *v.a.* (*insep.*) to think too highly of, overrate, overestimate; to assess too heavily (*a house*); to overtax. **—ung,** *f.*; **—ung ſeiner ſelbſt,** overweening estimation of oneself; vanity, conceit.

ü'berſchau, *f.* see **Überſicht, Überblick.** **—en,** (*insep.*) see **Überblicken; dieſer Hügel —t das ganze Thal,** this hill commands a view of the entire valley.

überſchäumen, *v.n.* (*sep.*) to froth over; **—de Luſt,** exuberant mirth; (*insep.*) to cover with foam *or* spray.

ü'berſchicht, *f.* extra shift; over-stratum. **—en,** *v.a.* (*sep.*) to pile up, to stratify, to dispose into layers.

überſchi'cken, *v.a.* (*insep.*) to transmit, to send; to remit (*money*).

überſchießen, *ir.v.* I. *a.* (*insep.*) to shoot over (*a country*); to overshoot, shoot too high; to overshoot (*the mark*); to skip, pass over (*through haste*); to superadd, count (*in addition*); to count out *or* over (*money*). II. *n.* (*aux.* ſ.) (*sep.*) to shoot *or* fall over; to overbalance; to overflow; to exceed. III. *a. & n.* (*aux.* h.) (*sep.*) to shoot too high, shoot past; (*insep.*) **ſich —,** to turn head over heels.

überſchiffen, *v.* I. *a.* (*sep.*) to ship, send across; (*insep.*) to traverse, cross (*a sea, etc.*). II. *n.* (*aux.* ſ.) (*sep.*) to sail across; **nach England —,** to cross over to England.

überſchla'fen, *ir.v.a.* (*insep.*) to sleep on, advise with one's pillow about; to sleep longer than; **eine Zeit —,** to sleep past a time; **ſich —,** to oversleep oneself.

ü'berſchlag, *m.* tumbling over; turn (*of the scale*); bias, inclination; turned-down collar; band; facing (*on dresses*); cuff; band, border (*Arch.*); flap; cataplasm; rough calculation, estimate. **—en,** *ir.v.* I. *a.* (*sep.*) to throw over; to apply (*a poultice*); to fold over (*in p.p. sometimes insep.*) to cross (*one's legs*); (*insep.*) to beat too much; to turn over (*a leaf, etc.*); to overlook; to skip, miss; to calculate (*roughly*); to consider, think over; **einen Hund —en,** to make a dog timid by too much beating; **einen Poſttag —en,** to miss a post, not to write; **ſich —en,** to go head over heels, to turn a somersault. II. *n.* (*aux.* ſ.) (*sep.*) to turn over; to tumble over, fall down; to fall backwards; to incline; to descend (*as a scale*); to go over into; to fall, descend to; to dart up, shoot forth; **die elektriſchen Funken ſchlagen über,** the electric sparks flash out; (*insep.*) to grow mouldy; to become lukewarm; **—en laſſen,** to take the chill off. *Comp.* **—s=kragen,** *m.* turn-over collar. **—s=rechnung,** *f.* rough calculation, estimate.

überſchlei'chen, *ir.v.a.* (*insep.*) to steal upon.

überſchlei'ern, *v.a.* (*insep.*) to veil; to throw a veil over, wrap up, conceal, hide, mask.

überſchlucken, *v.r.* (*sep.*) to swallow down, gulp down; (*insep.*) to swallow too fast, to choke.

überſchmie'den, *v.a.* (*insep.*) to forge over again.

überſchnappen, *v.n.* (*aux.* h. & ſ.) (*sep. & insep.*) to snap, slip *or* jerk over; to snap to; to become crazy; to lose one's head; **mit der Stimme —,** to sing falsetto; **er iſt übergeſchnappt,** he is cracked, he is gone mad.

überſchnü'ren, *v.a.* (*insep.*) to string, to furnish with strings; to strap up.

überſchreib—en, *ir.v.a.* (*sep.*) to write (*something left out*) above *or* over the line; to transcribe; to carry over *or* forward (*C. L.*); (*insep.*) to superscribe, inscribe; to direct, address; to dedicate; to docket (*papers*); to label; **etwas —en,** to write the title on; **einen Brief —en,** to address a letter; **ſich —en,** to write too much, write oneself out (*as an author*). **—ung,** *f.* superscribing, superscription; transcribing, transcription; sum carried over, transfer.

überſchrei'en, *ir.v.a.* (*insep.*) to cry louder than, cry down; to fill with one's cries; **ſich —,** to overstrain one's voice.

überſchreiten, *ir.v.* I. *a.* (*insep.*) to step *or* stride over; to pass over, go across; to overstep; to exceed; to transgress; **das überſchreitet alles Maß,** that exceeds all bounds, goes too far; **ein Geſetz —,** to infringe a law; **ſein Guthaben —,** to overdraw one's balance. II. *n.* (*aux.* ſ.) (*sep.*) to step over.

ü'berſchrift, *f.* superscription, heading, title.

ü'berſchuh, *m.* galosh; clog (*over a hoof*).

überſchul'det, *p.p. & adj.* involved in debt.

ü'ber—ſchuß, *m.* surplus; residue; balance, premium, bonus (*C.L.*); excess (*Typ.*). **—ſchüſſig,** *adj.* projecting; surplus, remaining.

überſchütten, *v.a.* (*sep.*) to pour over; to spill in pouring; (*insep.*) to pour over, cover (*with*); to load, overwhelm.

ü'berſchwanken, *v.n.* (*aux.* h.) (*sep.*) to tilt, tumble over; to run over.

ü'berſchwappen, *v.n.* (*aux.* ſ.) (*sep.*) to spill, spirt out (*of water in a bucket, etc.*).

überſchwem'm—en, *v.a.* (*insep.*) to overflow, inundate; to submerge. **—te(r),** *m.* one suffering from a flood. **—ung,** *f.* inundation, flood.

überſchweng'lich, *adj.* superabundant, boundless, excessive; transcendental, rapturous, extravagant. **—keit,** *f.* excess, exuberance; transcendency, extravagance.

ü'berſchwer, *adj.* too heavy; extremely difficult.

ü'berſeeiſch, *adj.* transmarine; oversea.

überſegeln, *v.* I. *a.* (*insep.*) to sail faster than, outstrip in sailing; to run foul of, run down (*a ship*). II. *a. & n.* (*aux.* ſ.) (*sep.*) to sail over (*to*).

überſe'hbar, *adj.* visible at a glance; observable; in full view; that may be overlooked.

überſehen, *ir.v.* I. *a.* (*insep.*) to take in at a glance; to perceive; to overlook, survey; to run the eye over; to overlook, not see; to take no notice of; to overlook, to shut one's eyes to, to connive at (*a fault*); to make allowances for; to run, read over; **einen —**, to be superior to s.o. (**in einer S.**, in a th.); **Kindern zu viel —**, to over-indulge children; **solche Kleinigkeiten werden oft —**, such trifles often escape notice. II. *n.* (*aux.* **h.**) (*sep.*) to look over; **sich** (*dat.*) **etwas —**, to get tired of seeing *or* looking at a thing; **ich habe mir das übergesehen**, I have seen too much of it, I have seen it too often.

ü'bersein, *ir.v.n.* (*sep.*) to remain over; to be past; **die Festung ist über**, the fortress has surrendered; **das ist mir über**, I am weary of it, I am sick and tired of it; **er ist dir über**, he is superior to you, he beats you.

ü'berselig, *adj.* most happy, over-joyful.

übersend—en, *ir.v.a.* (*sep.*) to send over *or* across; (*insep.*) to send, transmit. **—er**, (*pron.* **Übersen'der**) *m.* (**—ers**, *pl.* **—er**) one who transmits *or* remits, sender, transmitter, remitter; forwarding agent. **—ung** (*pron.* **Übersen'dung**), *f.* transmission.

übersetz'—bar, *adj.* translatable. **—en**, *v.* I. *n.* (*aux.* **s.**) (*sep.*) to leap, bound over; to cross, pass over (*in a boat, etc.*). II. *a.* (*insep.*) to translate; to interpret; to transpose (*Mus.*); to crowd, overstock; to overload; to overcharge; **wörtlich** *or* **wortgetreu —en**, to translate literally; **frei —en**, to give a free rendering; **falsch —en**, to misinterpret, to mistranslate; **ins Deutsche —en**, to turn into German. **—er** (*pron.* **Übersetz'zer**), *m.* (**—ers**, *pl.* **—er**), **—erin**, *f.* translator. **—ung**, *f.* translation; gear (*cycl.*); **—ung in die Muttersprache**, translation; **—ung aus der Muttersprache**, composition; **—ung ins Lateinische**, Latin composition; **—ung aus dem Lateinischen**, Latin translation. *Comp.* **—ungs=aufgabe**, *f.* exercise, translation; **unvorbereitete —ungsaufgabe**, unseen (translation). **—ungs=fehler**, *m.* misrendering. **—ungs=kunst**, *f.* art of translating. **—ungs=recht**, *n.* right of translation *or* translating.

ü'bersicht, *f.* view, sight, prospect, survey; perspective; review; abstract; summary; abridgment; **zusammenstellende —**, synopsis. **—igkeit**, *f.* long-sightedness. **—lich**, *adj.* clear, distinct; affording a general view of the whole; synoptical. **—lichkeit**, *f.* clearness (*of arrangement*), lucidity (*of style*); perspicuity. *Comp.* **—s=karte**, *f.* general map, outline-map. **—s=plan**, *m.* general plan. **—s=tafel**, *f.* synoptical table.

ü'bersiedel—n, (*sep.* & *insep.*) *v.* I. *n.* (*aux.* **s.**) to emigrate (**nach**, to); to remove, move (*to new quarters*). II. (*insep.*) *a.* to transplant, take to another country. **—ung**, *f.* emigration; removal.

übersil'bern, *v.a.* (*insep.*) to silver over, plate.

übersin'gen, *v.* I. *a.* (*insep.*) to sing better *or* louder than someone else. II. *r.* to spoil one's voice by singing too much.

ü'bersinnlich, *adj.* supersensual; supernatural; abstract; metaphysical; transcendental; **—er Freier**, supersensual lover. **—keit**, *f.* immateriality; transcendentalism; abstractness.

übersom'mern, **übersöm'mern**, (*insep.*) *v.* I. *a.* to keep through the summer. II. *n.* (*aux.* **s.**) to pass the summer (*in a place*).

überspann—en, *v.a.* (*sep.*) to stretch over; (*insep.*) to spread over, cover; to overstrain, overexert; to stretch too far; to span (*with the hand*); to exaggerate; to overexcite (*the mind*), heat (*the imagination*). **—t** (*pron.* **überspa'nnt**), *p.p.* & *adj.* overstrained; extravagant, exaggerated; high flown, wild, eccentric. **—theit**, *f.* exaltation of mind, excitement, enthusiasm; extravagance, exaggeration. **—ung**, *f.* over-tension; over-excitement; exaggeration.

überspin'nen, *ir.v.a.* (*insep.*) to spin over, cover; **übersponnene Saiten**, spun music-strings, covered strings.

überspringen, *ir.v.* I. *a.* (*insep.*) to leap (*a ditch, etc.*); to pass over, omit; to pass over (*one's body*); to leap better, outleap; **das Fieber überspringt einen Tag**, the fever intermits, discontinues for a day; **sich —**, to hurt o.s. in leaping. II. *n.* (*aux.* **s.**) (*sep.*) to leap over; to pass over (*to*); to flit from one (*subject*) to another; to intermit; to become displaced, to start (*of a sinew*); **das —**, displacement, starting (*of a nerve, etc.*)

ü'bersprudeln, *v.n.* (*aux.* **h.** & **s.**) (*sep.*) to bubble over; **—der Witz**, sparkling wit; **—de Freude**, exuberant mirth.

ü'berständig, *adj.* that has stood too long, stale, flat, vapid; **—e Frucht**, overripe fruit.

ü'berstark, *adj.* exceedingly strong *or* powerful.

überstechen, *ir.v.a.* & *n.* (*aux.* **h.**) (*sep.* & *insep.*) to play a higher card, to beat, to (over)trump.

überstehen, *ir.v.* I. *a.* (*insep.*) to endure, overcome, support, surmount, stand; **eine Krankheit —**, to get over an illness. II. *n.* (*aux.* **h.**) (*sep.*) to stand out, project, hang over; to overlap (*as tiles*); to stand *or* remain too long; to stand, lie over.

übersteig'bar, *adj.* surmountable.

übersteig—en, *ir.v.* I. *a.* (*insep.*) to step, get over; to pass, cross (*a mountain*); to scale; to surmount, overcome; to exceed, surpass; **es —t seinen Verstand, alle Begriffe**, it passes his understanding, all belief; **sich —en**, to mount too high, to miss one's way in climbing; to overtire o.s. *or* knock o.s. up by climbing. II. *n.* (*aux.* **s.**) (*sep.*) to step over *or* across; to overflow. **—ern**, *v.a.* (*insep.*) to force up (*prices*); to outbid; **einen —ern**, to outbid s. p. **—lich**, *adj. see* **—bar**.

ü'berstich, *m.* residue, extra work (*Typ.*); higher trump (*Cards*).

übersti'cken, *v.a.* (*insep.*) to embroider over, cover with embroidery; to re-embroider.

überstim'men, *v.a.* (*insep.*) to tune too high, above concert-pitch (*Mus.*); to outvote, overrule.

überstop'fen, *v.a.* (*insep.*) to overfill, cram; (*also sep.*) to darn, mend (*thin places*).

überstrah'len, *v.a.* (*insep.*) to shine upon; to outshine, eclipse.

überstreichen, *ir.v.a.* (*sep.*) to spread *or* rub over; (*insep.*) to paint, wash, *etc.* over; **mit Firniß —**, to varnish; **mit Schwarz —**, to blacken.

überstreifen, *v.a.* (*sep.*) to put on, draw over (*sleeves, etc.*); (*insep.*) to streak.

überstreuen, *v.a.* (*sep.*) to strew, sprinkle over; (*insep.*) to cover all over.

überström—en, *v.* I. *a.* (*insep.*) to overflow, inundate, deluge. II. *n.* (*aux.* **s.**) (*sep.*) to stream, flow, run over; to overflow, abound; **sein Mund strömte über von ihrem Lobe**, he was loud in praise of her. **—ung** (*pron.* **Ü'berströmung**), *f.* overflowing. *Comp.* **—ungs=röhre**, *f.* waste-pipe, overflow-pipe.

ü'berstrumpf, *m.* gaiter; outer stocking.

überstudie'ren, *v.r.* (*insep.*) to study too hard to overtax one's brain.

ü'berstülpen, *v.a.* (*sep.*) to tilt *or* cover over.

ü'berstunde, *f.* extra hour *or* lesson; overtime.

überstürz—en, *v.* I. *a.* (*sep.*) to put on; (*insep.*) to overturn, upset; to cover (*with*); to tumble over; to precipitate; to do rashly, carry (*something*) out hastily. II. *n.* (*aux.* **s.**) (*sep.*) to capsize, upset, tumble over *or* backwards; to dash across *or* over. **—ung**, *f.* precipitation; **nur keine —ung!** don't act rashly! don't (be in a) hurry! take it easy!

ü'bersüß, *adj.* luscious, too sweet, oversweet.

übertä'feln, *v.a.* (*insep.*) to board, to wainscot.

übertäu'ben, *v.a.* (*insep.*) to drown (*one sound by another*); to stun, to deafen; to stifle.

ü'berteuer, *adj. & adv.* too dear, exorbitant.

überteu'ern, *v.a.* (*insep.*) to overcharge; to charge too high for.

überteu'feln, *v.a.* (*insep.*) to out-devil; **den Teufel —,** to be blacker than the devil himself.

überti'schen, *v.a.* (*insep.*) to put too many dishes on a table; **übertischtes Mahl,** a feast over-supplied with dishes, too ample a meal.

übertöl'peln, *v.a.* (*insep.*) to deceive, cheat.

übertö'nen, *v.a.* (*insep.*) to drown (*a sound*); **den Lärm —,** to rise above the noise; **den Schmerz —,** to be louder than the voice of grief.

ü'ber—trag, *m.* (**—trags,** *pl.* **—träge**) carrying over; sum carried over. **—trag'bar,** *adj.* transferable; infectious, contagious (*of an illness*); negotiable; translatable. **—trag'barkeit,** *f.* transmissibility, transferability; infectiousness (*Med.*); **leichte —tragbarkeit,** ease with which a thing can be transferred.

übertrag—en, *ir.v.a.* (*sep.*) to wear (*a dress, etc.*) over (*other dresses, etc.*); to carry over, bring forward (*C.L.*); to carry over, transport; (*insep.*) to transfer, transmit, convey; to assign; **einem die Besorgung von etwas —en,** to charge, commission s.o. with the care of a th.; to entrust a th. to a p.; **etwas auf einen —en,** to leave to s.o. to do, consign, entrust to a p.; **in ein anderes Buch —en,** to transcribe, enter in another book; **einen Artikel in das Hauptbuch —en,** to post, enter an item in the ledger; (**aus einer Sprache in die andere**) **—en,** to translate; **sein Eigentum —en,** to cede, make over one's property; **—ene Bedeutung,** figurative sense, metaphorical meaning; **sich —en,** to weary, injure oneself by carrying too much, to bear too much (*fruit*); **die Krankheit überträgt sich auf Menschen,** the disease communicates itself to men, is infectious. **—er,** *m.* (**—ers,** *pl.* **—er**) translator; transferrer. **—ung,** *f.* transfer, transference; transfer (*of book-debts, C. L.*); conveyance, transmission; endorsement (*of a bill of exchange*); cession; assignment; conferring (*of an office*); translating; translation; **—ung der Bewegung,** transmission of motion, gear (*Cycl.*). *Comp.* **—ungs=apparat,** *m.* transmitter, translator (*Tele.*). **—ungs=brief,** *m.*, **—ungs=urkunde,** *f.* deed of conveyance. **—ungs=papier,** *n.* transfer paper.

ü'berträger, *m.* (**—s,** *pl.* **—**) reporter; endorser (*of a bill*); conveyance, means of transmission.

übertreff'—bar, *adj.* surpassable. **—en,** *ir.v.a.* (*insep.*) to surpass, excel, outdo.

übertreib—en, *ir.v.* I. *a.* (*sep.*) to drive over; to force over; (*insep.*) to overdrive; to overwork, overexert; to carry too far; to exaggerate; to overact, overdo (*a part*); **aus übertriebenem Eifer,** through excessive zeal. II. *n.* (*aux.* **f.**) (*sep.*) to flow over. **—ung,** *f.* overdriving, *etc.*; exaggeration; overacting; excess; extravagance.

übertret—en, *ir.v.* I. *a.* (*sep.*) to tread down at heel, wear crooked (*shoes, etc.*); (*insep.*) to overstep; to transgress, violate, infringe upon; **sich** (*dat.*) **den Fuß —en, sich** (*acc.*) **—en,** to sprain one's ankle, to tread on one side. II. *n.* (*aux.* **f.**) (*sep.*) to step, pass over; to run over, overflow (*of rivers*); to go over, join (*a party, etc.*); to go too fast; **zur christlichen Kirche —en,** to become a Christian; **er ist zum Katholizismus übergetreten,** he has turned (*Roman*) Catholic. **—er,** *m.* (**—ers,** *pl.* **—er**) trespasser, transgressor; one who goes over to another party. **—ung,** *f.* transgression, trespass; violation (*of a law*); **sich einer —ung schuldig machen,** to act contrary to, to violate a law, to trespass, offend. *Comp.* **—ungs=fall,** *m.*; **im —ungsfalle,** in case of transgression.

ü'bertrift, *f.* right of way (*for cattle*); cattle run.

ü'bertritt, *m.* (**—es,** *pl.* **—e**) going over to, joining (*a party*); change (*of religion*), conversion.

übertrüm'mern, *v.a.* (*insep.*) to bridge over with fragments, to strew with ruins.

übertrumpfen, *v.a.* (*sep. & insep.*) to trump higher; to surpass, to outdo.

übertün'chen, *v.a.* (*insep.*) to whitewash; to plaster; to patch up; to gloss over; **die Wahrheit —,** to veil the truth; **Europens übertünchte Höflichkeit,** the surface civility *or* sham-politeness of the Old World.

ü'berverdienst, *m.* extra profit *or* gain.

übervöl'ker—n, *v.a.* (*insep.*) to over-populate. **—ung,** *f.* excess *or* surplus of population.

ü'bervoll, *adj.* too full, brim-full; overcrowded.

übervor'teilen, *v.a.* (*insep.*) to overreach; to make profit by; to impose on, cheat, defraud.

überwa'chen, *v.a.* (*insep.*) to watch over, superintend; **sich —,** to exhaust oneself by vigils.

überwachsen, *ir.v.*I. *a.* (*insep.*) to outgrow; **sich —,** to grow too fast, to outgrow one's strength (*of children*). II. *n.* (*aux.* **f.**) (*sep.*) to grow over.

überwallen, *v.n.* (*aux.* **f.**) (*sep. & insep.*) to boil over; to gush over; to overflow.

überwäl'tig—en, *v.a.* (*insep.*) to overcome, subdue, vanquish; to overpower; to overwhelm. **—er,** *m.* (**—ers,** *pl.* **—er**) conqueror, vanquisher, victor.

überwei'f—en, *ir.v.a.* (*insep.*) to convince; to convict; to assign, make over; to endorse (*a bill*); **einen eines Irrtums —en,** to convince a p. of his error. **—end,** *p. & adj.* convincing. **—ung,** *f.* attainting; conviction; assignment, cession. *Comp.* **—ungs=grund,** *m.* convincing proof *or* argument. **—ungs=urteil,** *n.* bill of attainder.

ü'berwendlich, *adj. & adv.* whipped, overcast; **— nähen,** to oversew.

überwerfen, *ir.v.a.* (*sep.*) to throw over; to cover over; **einen Mantel —,** to (*quickly*) put on a cloak; (*insep.*) *see* **Bewerfen; sich mit einem —,** to quarrel *or* fall out with s.o.; **einen —,** to surpass a p. in throwing.

ü'berwichtig, *adj.* too heavy; most important; **— sein,** to be overweight.

ü'berwickeln, *v.a.* (*sep.*) to wrap up, to tie up.

überwie'gen, *ir.v.a.* (*insep.*) to outweigh, weigh down; to preponderate; to surpass, excel. **—d,** *adj.* predominant, paramount; **—de Mehrzahl,** vast *or* overwhelming majority.

ü'berwind, *m.* sheltered place, lee; **— haben,** to be sheltered from the wind.

überwind'bar, *adj.* conquerable; (*fig.*) surmountable.

überwind—en, *ir.v.a.* (*sep.*) to wind over; to wind round; (*insep.*) to overcome, prevail over, conquer, subdue; to surmount (*obstacles*); to wrap up, lap; **ich kann mich nicht —en,** I cannot prevail on myself *or* bring myself to. **—er,** *m.* (**—ers,** *pl.* **—er**) conqueror. **—lich,** *adj. see* **—bar. —ung,** *f.* overcoming; victory; **Selbst—ung,** self-restraint; **es gehört viel —ung dazu,** it requires great self-control; **das hat mir —ung gekostet,** it cost me an effort, I did it with great reluctance.

überwin'tern, *v.* (*insep.*) I. *a.* to keep through the winter. II. *n.* (*aux.* **h.**) to winter, pass the winter.

überwölben, *v.* I. *a.* (*insep.*) to arch over. II. *a. & n.* (*aux.* **f.**) (*sep.*) to overhang, hang over.

überwöl'ken, *v.r.* (*insep.*) to cloud over, grow cloudy; **überwölkt,** overcast, cloudy.

überwu'chern, *v.a.* (*insep.*) to overgrow, overrun. II. *n.* (*aux.* **f.**) (*sep. & insep.*) to grow too luxuriantly.

ü'berwurf, *m.* shawl, wrap, wrapper; overall (*for children*).

ü'berzahl, *f.* surplus; superior numbers *or* forces (*Mil.*); numerical superiority, odds; **große** *or* **starke —**, heavy odds.

überzähl—en, *v.a.* (*usually insep.*); **ich habe das Geld zweimal —t** *or* **übergezählt**, I have counted the money twice over; **sich —en**, to make a mistake in counting.

ü'berzählig, *adj.* surplus; supernumerary; **etwas —es Geld**, some money left over. **—keit**, *f.* the state of being (a) supernumerary.

ü'berzahn, *m.* projecting tooth.

überzeu'g—en, *v.a.* (*insep.*) to convince; **sich mit eignen Augen von etwas —en**, to see with one's own eyes; **man —e sich selbst!** go and see for yourself! **—end**, *p. & adj.* convincing, conclusive. **—ung**, *f.* persuasion; conviction; **er ist der festen —ung**, he is thoroughly convinced. *Comp.* **—ungs=gabe**, *f.* persuasive eloquence. **—ungs=kraft**, *f.* power of convincing. **—ungs=treue**, *f.* fidelity to one's convictions, moral earnestness.

überzieh—en, I. *ir.v.a.* (*sep.*) to put *or* draw over; to put on; to cover; to tease, chaff (*dial. obs.*); **einem eins** *or* **einen (Hieb) —en**, to give s.o. a blow with a whip *or* a cane; (*insep.*) to cover over with; to overlay; to spread over; to overrun; to suffuse (*with blushes, etc.*); to line; **mit Zucker —en**, to sugar, candy, ice; **mit Gips —en**, to plaster; **einen Stuhl —en**, to cover a chair; **ein Land mit Krieg —en**, to invade *or* to wage war against a country; **der Himmel —t sich mit Wolken**, the sky becomes overcast; **ein frisch überzogenes Bett**, a bed with clean linen on it. II. *ir.v.n.* (*aux.* **f.**) (*sep.*) to pass over; to remove (*into a new house, etc.*); **nach Wien —en**, to remove to Vienna (*rare*). III. *subst. n.* removing, removal; covering; plating; overlaying; putting *or* drawing over. **—er**, *m.* (**—ers**, *pl.* **—er**) overcoat, greatcoat; cut right across the face (*Fenc.*); **langer —er**, ulster; **wasserdichter —er**, mackintosh, waterproof; **Sommer—er**, light overcoat, dust-coat. *Comp.* **—ärmel**, *m.* sleeve to draw on. **—jacke**, *f.* outside jacket; sweater.

überzin'ken, *v.a.* (*insep.*) to cover *or* line with zinc.

überzin'nen, *v.a.* (*insep.*) to cover *or* line with tin.

überzu'ckern, *v.a.* (*insep.*) to (cover with) sugar; to ice; to candy; **eine Pille —**, to gild a pill.

ü'berzug, *m.* passing over; removal; hostile invasion; cover; coverlet; case (*of a pillow*); coat, coating; lining; tick (*of a bed*); crust (*Min.*); — (**der Zunge**), fur, coating (*Med.*).

überzwe'rch, I. *adj.* slanting; diagonal (*C.L.*). II. *adv.* awry; athwart, across, aslant, crosswise, diagonally.

üb'lich, **—keit**, *see under* **Üb.**

ü'brig, *adj. & adv.* left over, remaining; superfluous, unnecessary; — **haben**, to have over, to have more than enough; **für diesen Menschen habe ich nichts —**, I do not care for *or* do not think much of this fellow (*coll.*); **keine Zeit — haben**, to have no time to spare; **ein —es thun**, to do more than is necessary; to go out of one's way to show a special kindness; **mein —es Geld**, the rest of my money; **die —en Tage meines Lebens**, the rest of my life; — **lassen**, to leave a remainder (*Arith.*), to leave (*over*); **es läßt nichts zu wünschen —**, it leaves nothing to be desired; **er ist nicht — gewissenhaft**, he is not over scrupulous (*coll.*); **die —en**, the others, the rest; **im —en.** *see* **—ens.** **—ens**, *adv.* as for the rest, moreover; besides; in other respects, however.

U'fer, *n.* (**—s**, *pl.* **—**) sea-coast, beach; shore (*of a lake*); edge, brink, bank (*of a river, etc.*). *Comp.* **—bahn**, *f.* railway along a river's banks *or* the seashore. **—bau=kunst**, *f.* art of building embankments. **—bewohner**, *m.* dweller by a river *or* the sea. **—bezirk**, *m.* sea-coast. **—damm**, *m.* quay. **—läufer**, *m.* sandpiper (Actitis). **—los**, *adj.* shoreless; boundless; too far-reaching, extravagant (*fig.*). **—pflanzen**, *pl.* plants growing on a river's banks *or* the seashore. **—schwalbe**, *f.* sand-martin (*Orn.*). **—schutz=bauten**, *pl.* embankment, dikes, seawalls. **—seite**, *f.* bank, riverside

Uhla'n, *m. see* **Ulan.**

Uh'le, *f.* (*pl.* **—n**) hair-broom (*dial.*).

Uhr, *f.* (*pl.* **—en**) clock; timepiece; (**Taschen —**) watch; time of the day, hour; **trockene (nasse) Gas—**, dry (wet) gas-meter; **wie viel — ist's?** what o'clock is it? **können Sie mir sagen, wie viel — es ist?** can you tell me the time? **es ist halb drei —**, it is half past two; **nach (an) meiner — ist's vier**, by my watch it is four o'clock; **die — ist abgelaufen**, the clock has run down; **seine — ist abgelaufen**, his time has come, his sands have run (*fig.*); **eine — stellen (nach)**, to set a watch, to regulate a timepiece (by); **wie nach der Uhr**, like clock-work; **Mann nach der —**, punctual man; **um wieviel —?** at what o'clock? *Comp.* **—band**, *n.* watch-cord. **—deckel**, *m.* outer case of a watch. **—en=fabrik**, *f.* watch-manufactory. **—en=fabrikation**, *f.* watch- and clock-making industry. **—en=handel**, *m.* trade in clocks, *etc.* **—en=steller**, *m.* clock-setter *or* regulator. **—feder**, *f.* watch-spring. **—futteral**, *n.* watch-case. **—gehänge**, *n.* trinkets on a watch-chain. **—gehäuse**, *n.* clock-case. **—getriebe**, *n.* pinion of a watch. **—glas**, *n.* clock *or* watch-glass; glass shade for a clock. **—glocke**, *f.* glass shade (over a clock); bell of a clock *or* repeater. **—haken**, *m* watch-hook; (*carbine-*) swivel. **—halter**, *m.* watch-stand, watch-holder. **—kette**, *f.* watch-chain *or* guard. **—macher**, *m.* watch- *or* clock-maker. **—platte**, *f.* dial-plate. **—schlüssel**, *m.* watch- *or* clock-key. **—schrank**, *m.* clock-case. **—schwengel**, *m.* pendulum. **—tasche**, *f.* watch-pocket. **—werk**, *n.* clock-work; works of a watch, *etc.* **—zeiger**, *m.* hand of a watch *or* clock.

U'hu, *m.* (**—s**, *pl.* **—s**) great horned owl; **der — schreit, uhut**, the owl hoots.

Uis'titi, *m.* (**—s**, *pl.* **—s**) ouistiti (*monkey*).

U'kas (*better:* **Uka's**), *m.* (**—(s)es**, *pl.* **—(s)e**) ukase.

Ukelei', **Ük(e)lei'**, *m.* (**—s**, *pl.* **—s**) alburn, bleak.

Ula'n, *m.* (**—en**, *pl.* **—en**) uhlan, lancer. **—ka**, *f.* (*pl.* **—kas**) lancer's uniform *or* tunic. *Comp.* **—en=attacke**, *f.* charge made by a body of lancers. **—en=tschapka**, *f.* lancer's cap.

Ulk, *m.* (**—es**, *pl.* **—e**) polecat; fun, trick, frolic, spree (*sl.*); row (*sl.*). **—en**, *v.n.* (*aux.* **h.**) to lark, to make fun (*sl.*). **—ig**, *adj.* frolicsome; **das war —ig**, that was great fun (*coll.*).

Ul'me, *f.* (*pl.* **—n**) elm. **—n**, *adj.* elm.

Ul'timo, I. *m.* last day, end of the month; — **August**, at the end of August. II. *adv.* ultimo. *Comp.* **—abschluß**, *m.* monthly settlement. **—geld**, *n.* money due end of this month. **—geschäft**, *n.* business (done) for the (monthly) settlement. **—liquidation**, **—regulierung**, *f.* settling at the end *or* on the last day of the month, monthly settlement.

Ul'tra, *m.* extremist, ultra. *Comp.* **—klein**, *f.* extreme left. **—mari'n**, *n.* ultramarine, lazulite blue. **—monta'n**, *adj.* ultramontane; **—montaner**, ultramontanist; **—montane Partei**, (extreme) Roman Catholic party (which accepts the authority of the Pope as supreme).

Um, I. *prep.* (*with acc.*) about; **— . . . herum,** about, round, around; round about; about, near, towards; about, with regard to, concerning; for, because of; for (to buy *or* sell a th.); for, in exchange for; by (*signifying the amount of difference*); at; alternately with, after; **— die Stadt (herum),** round about the town; **er ist immer — sie,** he is always hanging about her; **Sie wissen nicht, wie mir —s Herz ist,** you have no idea how (*sad*, *anxious*, *etc.*) I feel; **— eine Sache wissen,** to be privy to *or* informed of a matter; **— die sechste Stunde,** towards, about the 6th hour; **— sechs Uhr,** at 6 o'clock; **er ist der Angelpunkt — den sich alles dreht,** everything turns upon *or* depends on him; **sich — einen ängstigen,** to be anxious about s.o.; **— eine S. anhalten, bitten,** to sue, beg for something; **einen — seine Sanftmut lieben,** to love s.o. for his gentleness; **einen — sein Geld beneiden,** to envy a p. his money; **es ist Schade — den Verlust!** it 's a pity to have lost . . .! **wie steht's — euch?** how are you getting on? how are you? **wie steht es — die Sache?** how are things going on? how about . . .? **es ist eine ernste Sache — das Sterben,** it is a serious thing to die; **es ist eine schöne Sache — die Tugend,** virtue is a fine thing; **es ist doch ein wundersam Ding — die Liebe,** love is indeed a strange thing; **— Lohn arbeiten,** to work for money; **— bares Geld kaufen,** to buy for ready money *or* for cash; **Aug' — Auge,** an eye for an eye; **— alles in der Welt nicht,** not for all the world; **— zwei Jahre älter,** two years older; **— einen Kopf größer,** a head taller; **— die Hälfte mehr,** half as much again; **sich — zehn Mark verrechnen,** to miscalculate by ten marks, to be ten marks wrong in one's reckoning; **— so besser!** so much the better! **— so mehr,** so much the more; **— so viel mehr ist er zu beklagen,** all the more is he to be pitied; **— so weniger müssen Sie hingehen,** so much less reason is there for your going; **einen — hundert Mark strafen,** to fine a p. 100 marks (£5); **— etwas kommen,** to lose a thing; **einen — da(s) Leben bringen,** to cause a p.'s death, to kill a p.; **sich — das Leben reden,** to talk one's life away, pay for one's words with one's life; **es ist — ihn geschehen,** he is done for; **ausgesendet wird Bot' — Bote,** messenger after messenger is despatched; **einen Tag — den andern,** every other day; day by day, every day; **einen Tag — den andern regnet es,** day after day it rains; one day is fine, the next wet; **einer — den andern,** one after another, every other; alternately, by turns; (*with gen. and* **willen,** for the sake of) **— Gotteswillen!** for God's sake! for Heaven's sake! **was thut man nicht — des lieben Friedens willen?** what will one not do for the sake of peace? II. *conj.* **— zu,** (*with infin.*) so as, in order to; to; **er ist zu klug — seinen Ärger zu zeigen,** he is too prudent to show his anger; **— Ihnen zu beweisen,** in order to prove to you. III. *adv. & sep. prefix* (*or insep. indicating complete surrounding*) about; past, out, ended, over; over, upset; around, enclosing, surrounding; round about *or* over; (*in comp. with verbs, substantives & adverbs* **um** *signifies change, alteration, doing over again, turning, bringing to an end, completion, etc.*) **— und —,** all round about, from *or* on all sides; **wenn es — und — kommt,** when all comes to all; **— mit diesem Baume!** down with this tree! **rechts —!** right turn! (*Mil.*); **es ist wenigstens eine Meile —,** it is a round of at least a mile; **über Berlin zu reisen ist —,** it is out of the way to go by Berlin; **dieser Weg ist —,** this is a roundabout way, this is not the direct way; **— sein,** to have completed a revolution, to have expired; to have come to a close; **das Jahr ist —,** the year is gone; **seine Zeit ist —,** his time is over; **seine Dienstzeit ist —,** he has served his time. (*Verbs compounded with* **um** *when sep. have the principal accent on* **um,** *when insep. on the root of the verb. Note the glottal stop in compounds, the second part of which begins with a vowel, e.g.* **um'arbeiten**).

Um'ackern, I. *v.a.* (*sep.*) to plough up; to plough down (*a shrub*, *etc.*). II. *subst.n.* ploughing, tillage.

Um'ändern, *v.a.* (*sep.*) to change, transform.

Um'arbeiten, *v.a.* (*sep.*) to do over again; to remodel, recast; to revise; to plough *or* dig up; to alter.

Umar'm—en, *v.a.* (*insep.*) to embrace; to fold a p. in one's arms, to press a p. to one's breast; **einen fest und lange —en,** to hug a p.; **sie —ten einander** *or* **sich,** they embraced. **—ung,** *f.* embracing; embrace, clasp, hug.

Um'bau, *m.* rebuilding, reconstruction; alterations made in a house; new building, altered premises. **—en,** *v.a.* (*insep.*) to surround with buildings; (*sep.*) to build anew, to rebuild, reconstruct; to make alterations in.

Um'behalten, *ir.v.a.* (*sep.*) to keep on.

[1]**Um'ber,** *m.* (—s), (**—erde,** *f.*) umber.

[2]**Um'ber,** *m.* (—s), (**—fisch,** *m.*) umber.

Um'betten, *v.a.* (*sep.*) to put into another bed.

Um'biegen, *ir.v.a.* (*sep.*) to bend, turn back, round *or* down.

Um'bild—en, *v.a.* (*sep.*) to remould; to remodel; to transform; to reform. **—ung,** *f.* remodelling; transformation; reformation.

Umbinden, *ir.v.a.* (*sep.*) to tie, bind round; to tie over again; to re-bind (*books*); **ein Tuch —,** to knot a shawl round one's neck; **sich** (*dat.*) **eine Schürze —,** to put on an apron; (*insep.*) to bind round, tie up.

Um'blasen, *ir.v.a.* (*sep.*) to overturn by blowing, blow down; (*insep.*) **von den Winden — werden,** to be exposed to every wind that blows.

Umblättern, *v.a. & n.* (*aux.* **h.**) (*sep.*) to turn over leaves; *see* **Durchblättern.**

Um'blick, *m.* panorama; survey; glance back; retrospect. **—en,** *v.r. & n.* (*aux.* **h.**) (*sep.*) to look round; **sich nach einem** *or* **einer S. —en,** to look back to see, look round for *or* after a p. *or* a th.

Um'bra, *see* [1]**Umber.**

Um'brassen, *v.a.* (*sep.*) to brace at the other side.

Umbrechen, *ir.v.* I. *a.* (*sep.*) to break down; to break up (*a field*); (*insep.*) to make up into pages (*Typ.*); to over-run (*the page*). II. *n.* (*aux.* **s.**) (*sep.*) to break down (*under a weight*).

Um'bringen, *ir.v.a.* (*sep.*) to make away with, slay, kill, murder, destroy; to ruin; **sich —,** to kill oneself, to commit suicide.

Um'bruch, *m.* newly cleared *or* turned-up land; side-adit (*in a mine*).

Umdämmen, *v.a.* (*sep.*) to repave (*a street*); (*insep.*) to embank, to surround with a dike.

Umdecken, *v.a.* (*sep.*) to put a covering round; to re-cover, re-tile (*a roof*); to lay (*a table-cloth*) over again; (*insep.*) to cover all round.

Um'deuten, *v.a.* (*sep.*) to give a new interpretation *or* a new meaning to.

Um'deutschen, *v.a.* (*sep.*) to put into German.

Um'dichten, *v.a.* (*sep.*) to re-model, re-cast (*a poem*).

Umdrän'gen, *v.a.* (*insep.*) to press, crowd round.

Um'dreh—en, *v.a.* (*sep.*) to turn, twist round; to turn (*on a pivot*, *etc.*); to roll; **einem den Hals —en,** to wring a p.'s neck; **wie man die Hand —t,** in the turn of a hand, in a moment; **den Spieß —en,** to strike a p. with his own weapons, to turn the tables upon a p.; **das Blatt dreht sich um,** the tables are turned; **sich —en,** to turn round, to rotate, revolve; **alles dreht sich um,** everything goes (whirls) round. **—er,** *m.* (**—ers,** *pl.* **—er**) one who turns; rotator (*Anat.*). **—ung,** *f.* turning round; rotation; revolution. *Comp.* **—ungs=achse,** *f.* axis of rotation. **—ungs=bewegung,** *f.* rotatory motion. **—ungs=ellipsoid,** *n.* elliptic conoid; (**verlängertes**) oblong ellipsoid. **—ungs=punkt,** *m.* centre of rotation. **—ungs=zeit,** *f.* period of revolution.

Um'druck, *m.* reprint, transfer(-printing). **—en,** *v.a.* (*sep.*) to reprint, transfer.

Umdun'keln, Umdü'stern, *v.a.* (*insep.*) to darken, to cloud, to overshadow.

Um'expedieren, *v.a.* (*sep.*) to send (*by rail* or *ship*) to another place, to forward.

Umfa'hen, (*obs. & poet.*) see **Umfangen.**

Umfahr—en, *ir.v.* I. *a.* (*sep.*) to run down, drive over; (*insep.*) to drive, go round; to (sail) round, double; to evade (*a toll, etc.*) by driving round. II. *n.* (*aux.* **h.** & **s.**) to drive a roundabout way; to drive about. **—t,** *f.* round, circuitous way; circuit, tour; **eine —t halten,** to go upon circuit (*said of judges*); to make the round (*of a parish, etc.*). **—ung** (*pron.* **Umfah'rung**), *f.* circumnavigation.

Um'fall, *m.* fall; tumble; cattle-disease. **—en,** *ir.v.n.* (*aux.* **s.**) (*sep.*) to fall down, tumble; to overturn; to die (*of beasts*).

Um'falzen, *v.a.* (*sep.*) to fold over again (*Bookb.*).

Um'fang, *m.* circumference, circuit; precincts; girth; bulk, range, extent, compass; perimeter, circumference (*Geom.*); sphere, latitude; volume (*of sound*); compass (*of instruments*); extent (*of a business*); **— des Körpers,** width round the chest. **—en** (*pron.* **umfan'gen**), *ir.v.a.* (*insep.*) to surround, encircle, encompass; to embrace, to clasp. *Comp.* **—reich,** *adj.* wide, broad, extensive; voluminous; spacious. **—s=linie,** *f.* periphery. **—s=winkel,** *m.* (**des Kreises**) angle of the circumference.

Um'fänglich, *adj.* see **Umfangreich.**

Um'färben, *v.a.* (*sep.*) to re-dye.

Umfass—en, I. *v.a.* (*sep.*) to re-set (*jewels*); (*insep.*) to clasp round, enclose; to span; to embrace; to comprehend, include, comprise. II. *subst.n.*; **—en seiner Kniee,** clasping (embracing) his knees. **—end,** *p. & adj.* far-reaching; extensive; comprehensive. **—ung,** *f.* resetting; embrace; enclosure; enceinte (*Fort.*). *Comp.* **—ungs=mauer,** *f.* outer-wall, enclosure-wall.

Umflat'tern, *v.a.* (*insep.*) to float round (*one*); to flow loosely round; to flutter; to flutter about (*one*).

Umflechten, *ir.v.a.* (*sep.*) to twist, plait round; to plait anew; (*insep.*) to plait round, cover with wickerwork.

Umfliegen, *ir.v.a.* (*sep.*) to upset by flying against; (*insep.*) to fly round, about; to fly round.

Umflie'ßen, *ir.v.a.* (*insep.*) to flow (a)round, encircle; **von Licht umflossen,** in a blaze of light; **meerumflossen,** washed by the sea.

Umflo'ren, *v.a.* (*insep.*) to cover with crape; to veil; **umflorte Augen,** eyes dim with tears.

Umflü'geln, (*insep.*) to flap the wings round; to hover round; **der Morgenwind umflügelt die Bucht,** the early morning breeze plays round the bay.

Umflu'ten, *v.a.* (*insep.*) to flow round *or* about, to encompass with waves.

Um'formen, see **Umbilden.**

Um'frage, *f.* (*pl.* **—n**) general inquiry, inquiry all round; **— halten,** to inquire in every quarter, to inquire all round; **etwas in — bringen, zur — schreiten,** to take the general opinion upon, put to the vote. **—n,** *v.n.* (*aux.* **h.**) (*sep.*) to enquire all round.

Umfrie'd(ig)—en, *v.a.* (*insep.*) to enclose, fence in. **—ung,** *f.* enclosure, fence.

Um'führen, *v.a.* (*sep.*) to lead, conduct round about; to lead a circuitous way.

Um'füllen, *v.a.* (*sep.*) to pour out of one vessel into another; to transfuse

Um'gang, *m* going round *or* about; round, circuit; circuitous way; procession; passage, gallery (*Arch.*); rotation, revolution; intercourse, familiar acquaintance; connection; (*business or other*) relations · society, acquaintances; **mit einem — haben,** to be on visiting terms with a p., to see a great deal of a p., to associate with a p.; **durch vielen —,** by mixing much with people, by going much into society; **wir haben hier wenig —,** we have few friends here, we do not see many people here; **einen — halten,** to go in a procession; **von einer S. — nehmen,** to avoid, to forbear doing a th.; **ich konnte keinen — nehmen, ich mußte es ihm sagen,** I could not help it, I had to tell him; **fleischlicher, geschlechtlicher —,** sexual intercourse; **guten (schlechten) — haben** *or* **pflegen,** to keep good (bad) company; **eine Sprache aus dem —e lernen,** to acquire a language colloquially *or* by mixing with people who speak it. *Comp.* **—s=formen,** *pl.* forms of social intercourse, (*good*) manners, deportment. **—s=sprache,** *f.* familiar *or* colloquial language; **die deutsche —s=sprache,** conversational, colloquial *or* spoken German. **—s=weise,** *adv.* in *or* by intercourse. **—s=welt,** *f.* society, one's acquaintances, associates *or* friends.

Um'gänglich, *adj.* sociable; affable. **—keit,** *f.* sociability, pleasant ways; affability.

Umgar'nen, *v.a.* (*insep.*) to surround with nets; to ensnare, to enmesh, to trap.

Umgau'keln, *v.a.* (*insep.*) to hover, flit, flutter, dance, sport, play around.

Umgeb—en, *ir.v.a.* (*sep.*) **einem den Mantel —en,** to help s.o. on with his cloak; (*insep.*) to enclose, encompass, encircle, surround.

Umge'bung, *f.* surroundings, environs, neighbourhood; environment; sphere of life, circle of acquaintances; **er hat schlechte —ung,** he has evil surroundings, he keeps bad company.

Um'gegend, *f.* environs, neighbourhood.

Umgeh—en, *ir.v.n.* (*aux.* **s.**) (*sep.*) to go round; to revolve; to circulate; to make a circuit, go round; to change, shift (*of wind*); to go a roundabout way; to make a detour in going; to miss the direct *or* the nearest way; to go, walk, lounge about; to associate, have intercourse with; to haunt; to walk in one's sleep; **der Reihe nach —en,** to take it in turns; **sie lassen es unter sich —en,** they take it by turns; **einen Brief —en lassen,** to let a letter circulate; **in diesem Schlosse geht es um,** his castle is haunted; **wir sind eine Meile umgegangen,** we have gone a mile round *or* a mile out of our way; **gern mit einem —en,** to like a person's company; **er weiß mit Menschen umzugehen,** he knows how to get on with people *or* how to deal with people, he knows the (ways of the) world, is a man of the world; **mit etwas —en,** to be occupied with; **mit etwas umzugehen wissen,** to know how to manage a thing; **du gehst nicht recht damit um,** you go the wrong way to work; **mit einem Gedanken —en,** to turn over an idea in one's mind; **mit einem Plane —en,** to cherish a project; **mit Mord —en** to meditate murder; **mit Verrat —en,** to contemplate treachery; **damit umgehen, sich zu verheiraten,** to think of marrying; **sage mir, mit wem du —st, und ich will dir sagen,**

wer du bist, a man is known by the company he keeps, birds of a feather flock together (*prov.*); **mit einem hart —en,** to treat a p. harshly; **mit Betrug —en,** to practise deceit; **er geht mit seinem Sohne zu nachsichtig um,** he is too indulgent towards his son. II. *a.* (*insep.*) to walk round; to perambulate; to elude, evade, pass over, avoid; to turn (*the enemy's flank; Mil.*). **—end,** *p. & adj.* going about; alternate; prevalent; **—end,** *or* **mit —ender Post antworten,** to reply by return of post; **—ende Antwort dringend erbeten,** an answer by return is urgently requested. **—ung** (*pron.* **Umge'hung**), *f.* going round; evasion; omission.

Um'gestalten, *v.a.* (*sep.*) to transform, metamorphose; to reorganize.

Um'gießen, *ir.v.a.* (*sep.*) to pour from one vessel into another; to recast; to kill *or* beat down (*young plants*) by too heavy watering.

Umgit'tern, *v a.* (*insep.*) to surround with a grating *or* lattice-work.

Umglän'zen, *v.a.* (*insep.*) to irradiate, surround with splendour *or* lustre.

Umgraben, *ir.v.a.* (*sep.*) to dig, break up (*soil*); to dig over again; to dig up, cause to fall by digging round (*as trees*); (*insep.*) to dig round about; to surround with a ditch.

Umgrei'fen, *ir.v.a.* (*insep.*) to span, to grasp.

Umgren'z—en, *v.a.* (*insep.*) to encircle, enclose, bound; to circumscribe. **—ung,** *f.* boundary; enclosure; limitation, restriction.

Um'gucken, *v.r.* to look round; to be astonished, to be disappointed (*coll.*).

Umgür'ten, *v.a.* (*sep.*) to gird round *or* on; to gird anew; (*insep.*) **seine Lenden —,** to gird up one's loins.

Um'guß, *m.* transfusion; recasting; recast.

Um'haben, *ir.v.a.* (*sep.*) to have round (*one*), have (a cloak, *etc.*) on.

Um'hacken, *v.a.* (*sep.*) to hoe, dig up; to hew down.

Umhal'sen, *v.a.* (*insep.*) to embrace, hug.

Um'hang, *m.* (—**s**, *pl.* **Umhänge**) curtain; loose wrap; shawl; opera-cloak; mantle; cape.

Umhängen, *v.a.* (*sep.*) to throw on (*a shawl, etc.*); to hang anew; (*insep.*) to hang round (**mit,** with).

Umhauen, *ir.v.a.* (*sep.*) to hew *or* cut down; (*insep.*) to cut, notch all round.

Umhe'r, *adv. & sep. prefix,* about, up and down; all round; this way and that way; here and there; **wir gingen erst um den Dom herum und dann in ihm —,** we first walked round the cathedral and then walked about inside it; **sein Gerücht erscholl —,** his fame spread abroad; **— liegen lassen,** to leave littered *or* lying about. *Comp.* **—fahren,** *ir.v.* I. *n.* (*aux.* **s.**) to drive about; to go one's rounds (*of a doctor*); **mit der Hand —fahren,** to gesticulate. II. *a.* to send *or* drive from one place to another. **—fechten,** *ir.v.n.* (*aux.* **h.**) to fence; to gesticulate; to beg from door to door (*of journeymen-tradesmen*). **—führen,** I. *v.a.* to lead about. II. *subst. n.*; **beim —führen der Fremden in den Galerien,** in (when) conducting strangers through the galleries. **—gehen,** *ir.v.n.* (*aux.* **s.**) to go, walk, stroll about; to loaf about. **—schlendern,** *v.n.* (*aux.* **s.**) to lounge about (*coll.*). **—sitzen,** *ir.v.n.* (*aux.* **h.**, to sit about; to be settled in a neighbourhood. **—ziehend,** *p. & adj.* itinerant, strolling; **—ziehende Spielleute,** wandering minstrels *or* gleemen.

Umhi'n, *adv.*; **ich kann nicht —, zu,** I cannot help, I cannot but, I cannot refrain from.

Umhüll—en, *v.a.*; (*sep.*) **sich** (*dat.*) **ein Tuch —en,** to wrap oneself up in a shawl; (*insep.*) to envelop, cover, wrap up; to veil; to clothe. **—ung,** *f.* envelopment; cover, envelop. *Comp.* **—ungs=kurve,** *f.* envelope (*Math.*).

Um'kehr, *f.* turning back, return; conversion; (beginning of) peripetia (*Dram.*). **—bar,** *adj.* that can be turned round; convertible (*Log.*). **—en,** (*sep.*) *v.* I. *n.* (*aux.* **s.**) to turn back; to turn round; to return; to reform; **auf demselben Wege —en,** to retrace one's steps. II. *a.* to turn (*round or about, inside out, etc.*); to turn over *or* up; to turn upside down, overturn; to subvert; to invert (*Mus., Math., etc.*); to convert; to change; to throw into disorder; **den Braten —en,** to turn the spit (*the roast*); **wie man die Hand —t,** in a twinkling; **mit umgekehrter Hand,** with the back of the hand; **mir kehrt sich das Herz im Leibe um,** my heart is bleeding *or* breaking; **Shakespeare hat die Bühne umgekehrt,** Shakespeare revolutionized the stage; **um und um kehren,** to turn topsy-turvy; to overturn everything; **die Reihenfolge der Wörter —en,** to invert the order of the words; **einen Satz —en,** to convert a proposition; **einen Bruch —en,** to invert a fraction; **umgekehrte Seite (einer Münze),** reverse (of a coin); **in umgekehrter Ordnung,** in reverse order, inverted; **umgekehrt!** on the contrary! just the opposite! **in umgekehrtem Verhältnisse stehen,** to be in the inverse ratio; **die Zeiträume sind umgekehrt wie die Geschwindigkeiten,** the time is in inverse ratio to the velocity; **er ist ganz umgekehrt,** he is quite different, entirely changed; **das Umgekehrte,** the contrary, the reverse. **—ung,** *f. see* **Umkehr**; overturning; inversion; subversion; revolution; conversion.

Um'kippen, *v.a. & n.* (*aux.* **s.**) (*sep.*) to tip over, upset, overturn.

Umklaf'tern, *v.a.* (*insep.*) to encompass with extended arms.

Umklam'mern, *v.a.* (*insep.*) to clasp, embrace.

Um'kleiden, *v.a.* (*sep.*) to change the dress of; **sich —,** to change (one's dress); (*insep.*) to clothe; to decorate; to invest; **das —de,** drapery, hangings.

Um'knicken, *v.n.* (*aux.* **s.**) (*sep.*) to snap off, to break down; **der Fuß ist mir umgeknickt,** I have sprained my foot.

Um'kommen, *ir.v.n.* (*aux.* **s.**) (*sep.*) to perish, die; to fall (*in battle*); to spoil; to be lost; **vor Hunger —,** to die of hunger; **ich käme um, wenn ich noch länger dies Leben führen sollte,** this life would kill me if it were to continue.

Um'krämpe(l)n, Um'krempeln, *v.n.* (*aux.* **s.**) (*sep.*) to turn up *or* upside down, to disturb (*coll.*); **das ist zum —,** that 's enough to make you die with laughter (*coll.*); that is enough to drive a p. mad (*coll.*).

Umkrän'zen, *v.a.* (*insep.*) to wreathe, adorn with garlands.

Um'kreis, *m.* circle; circuit; circumference; extent; **im —(s)e von 5 Meilen,** for 5 (*German*) miles round. **—(s)en,** *v.a.* (*insep.*) to turn, revolve round; to enclose, encompass.

Um'lad—en, *ir.v.a.* (*sep.*) to load anew, to reload, to load on another carriage *or* ship; to tran(s)ship; to shift (*from one waggon to another*). **—ung,** *f.* loading anew; tran(s)shipment.

Um'lage, *f.* (*pl.* **—n**) assessment (*of taxes*); **städtische —n,** local rates.

Umlager—n, *v.a.* (*insep.*) to enclose, surround closely; to besiege; **einen —n, —t halten,** to assail, beset one; (*sep.*) to remove (*troops*) to another camp; **sich —n,** to change one's couch.

Um'lauf, *m.* turn, revolution; circulation; period (*of a planet*); **in — bringen** *or* **setzen,** to put into circulation, issue, circulate; to spread (*a rumour*); **im — sein,** to circulate; **das im**

— **befindliche Geld**, currency. —**en**, (*sep.*) *ir.v.* I. *a.* to run over, knock down in running. II. *n.* (*aux.* **s.**) to revolve; to circulate (*as blood, reports, money, etc.*); to pass (*of time*); to shift, change (*of wind*); **wir sind eine Meile umgelaufen**, we have gone a (*German*) mile out of our way. *Comp.* —**bewegung**, *f.* rotatory movement. —(**s**)=**kapital**, *n.* floating capital. —(**s**)=**mittel**, *n.* circulating medium, currency. —(**s**)=**schreiben**, *n.* circular letter. —(**s**)=**zeit**, *f.* period of revolution *or* rotation.

Um'laut, *m.* modification of a vowel (*as* **a**, **o**, **u**, *to* **ä** *or* **e**, **ö**, **ü**). —**en**, (*sep.*) *v.* I. *a.* to modify (*the radical vowel*); **ein ursprüngliches i der Endsilbe lautete ein wurzelhaftes a zu e um**, an original i of a final syllable modified a radical a to e. II. *n.* (*aux.* **s.**); **die Plurale auf „er" lauten gewöhnlich um**, plurals formed by the termination „**er**" usually modify the radical vowel; **der Diphthong lautet um**, the diphthong is modified.

Um'legekragen, *m.* turn-down collar.

Umlegen, *v.a.* (*insep.*) to surround (*with*); to garnish; (*sep.*) to lay *or* put round; to lay down; to put on (*a cloak, etc.*); to change the position of; to remove to other quarters (*Mil.*); to careen (*a ship*); to turn down (*an edge*); to bend; to re-lay (*a floor*); to repair (*a pavement*); **die Segel** —, to shift the sails; **sich im Bette** —, to turn in bed; **der Ostwind legte sich um**, the wind shifted *or* changed round to the west; **die Kosten (auf die einzelnen Teilnehmer)** —, to divide, apportion the expenses.

Um'leiten, *v.a.* (*sep.*) to lead another way, turn aside; to lead a roundabout way.

Um'lenken, *v.a. & n.* (*aux.* **h.** & **s.**) (*sep.*) to turn round; to change (*one's opinions*).

Um'lernen, *v.a. & n.* (*aux.* **h.**) (*sep.*) to change the method of study; to learn anew *or* differently.

Umleuchten, *v.* I. *a.* (*insep.*) to surround with light. II. *n.* (*aux.* **h.**) (*sep.*) to throw, shed light all round.

Um'liegen, *ir.v.n.* (*aux.* **s.**) (*sep.*) to lie around; to lie on the ground, lie about; —**d**, neighbouring; circumjacent; —**de Gegend**, country around, surrounding country.

Ummau'ern, *v.a.* (*insep.*) to wall in *or* round.

Um'messen, *ir.v.a.* (*sep.*) to measure over again.

Um'modeln, *v.a.* (*sep.*) to remodel, alter.

Um'münzen, *v.a.* (*sep.*) to recoin, new-mint.

Umnach'ten, *v.a.* (*insep.*) to shroud in darkness.

Umnähen, *v.a.* (*insep.*) to sew all round; to hem; (*sep.*) to sew otherwise *or* over again.

Umne'beln, *v.a.* (*insep.*) to wrap in fog; to cloud.

Um'nehmen, *ir.v.a.* (*sep.*) to take round one, put on.

Um'packen, *v.a.* (*sep.*) to repack, pack over again.

Umpan'zern, *v.a.* (*insep.*) to cover with mail; to cover with blinds (*Fort.*); **umpanzert**, steel-clad.

Umpfäh'len, *v.a.* (*insep.*) to surround with paling, palisade.

Umpflanzen, *v.a.* (*sep.*) to transplant, replant; (*insep.*) to plant all round (*with trees, etc.*).

Umpflastern, *v.a.* (*sep.*) to repave; (*insep.*) to pave round.

Um'pflügen, *v.a.* (*sep.*) to plough up.

Um'prägen, *v.a.* (*sep.*) to recoin *or* new-coin (money).

Um'quartieren, *v.a.* (*sep.*) to dislodge, to remove to fresh quarters.

Umrah'men, *v.a.* (*insep.*) to frame.

Umran'ken, *v.a.* (*insep.*) to enclose, surround with (*its*) tendrils; to clasp (round) (*fig.*); **epheuumrankt**, ivy-clad; **rebumrankt**, vine-clad.

Um'räumen, *v.a.* (*sep.*) to displace, remove.

Umrau'schen, *v.a.* (*insep.*) to rustle *or* roar round; **wellenumrauscht**, encircled by roaring waves.

Um'reise, *f.* (*pl.* —**n**) tour, circuit. —**n**, *v.* I. *a.* (*insep.*) to travel round, make the tour of. II. *n.* (*aux.* **s.**) (*sep.*) to turn aside in travelling; to travel a circuitous route.

Um'reißen, *ir.v.a.* (*sep.*) to pull down, to tear up, blow down (*trees, etc.*); to demolish; to pull about; to turn upside down; (*insep.*) to outline, sketch.

Umreiten, *ir.v.* I. *a.* (*insep.*) to ride round; to make a circuit riding; (*sep.*) to overturn, ride over. II. *n.* (*aux.* **s.**) (*sep.*) to make a detour in riding.

Um'rennen, (*sep.*) *ir.v.* I. *a. see* **Umlaufen** I. II. *n.* (*aux.* **s.**) to run round, make a detour.

Umrin'geln, *v.a.* (*insep.*) to entwine, twist round.

Umrin'gen, *ir.v.a.* (*insep.*) to close in, beset; to encircle; to encompass, surround.

Um'riß, *m.* (—(ss)es, *pl.* —(ss)e) outline, contour; sketch; ground-plan; **in kräftigen —(ss)en schildern**, to paint, sketch in bold outlines; **fließende, leicht hingeworfene —(ss)e**, rough sketch; —(**ss**)**e des Gesichts**, outline of the face.

Um'ritt, *m.* round (*on horseback*); cavalcade.

Um'rühren, *v.a.* (*sep.*) to stir up, stir round.

Um'rütteln, *v.a.* (*sep.*) to shake up.

Ums' = **um das** *and also* **um des**; —**Himmels willen**, for Heaven's sake.

Um'sacken, *v.a.* (*sep.*) to put into another sack.

Um'sägen, *v.a.* (*sep.*) to saw down.

Um'salzen, *v.a.* (*sep.*) to salt afresh *or* again.

Um'satteln, (*sep.*) *v.a.* to resaddle (*a horse*). II. *n.* (*aux.* **h.**) to leap into another saddle; to change one's way of life *or* opinions; to change one's ideas *or* opinion, to change sides; to change one's studies *or* profession.

Um'satz, *m.* (—**es**) sale; exchange; transaction business; **rascher** —, quick returns (*C.L.*).

Umsau'sen, *v.a.* (*insep.*) to roar, howl around.

Um'schaff—en, *ir.v.a.* (*sep.*) to transform; to remodel; **sich —en**, to reform. —**ung**, *f.* transformation, regeneration.

Um'schalt—en, *v.a.* (*sep.*) to switch, to reverse the current. —**er**, *m.* switch, commutator. —**ung**, *f.* commutation. *Comp.* —**ungs=schlüssel**, *m.* reversing-key.

Umschan'z—en, *v.a.* (*insep.*) to intrench, to circumvallate. —**ung**, *f.* intrenching; intrenchment, circumvallation. *Comp.* —**ungs=linie**, *f.* line of circumvallation.

Um'scharren, *v.a.* (*sep.*) to scratch up; (*insep.*) to scratch about.

Umschat'ten, *v.a.* (*insep.*) to shade, overshadow.

Um'schau, *f.* looking round; — **halten**, to look out *or* round (**nach einer S.**, for a th.).

Um'schauen, *v.r. & n.* (*aux.* **h.**) (*sep.*) to look about, around; **sich** —, to look round.

Um'schaufeln, *v.a.* (*sep.*) to turn up with a shovel; to trench (*potatoes, etc.*); to shovel, stir up (*corn*).

Umschei'nen, *ir.v.a.* (*insep.*) to shine from all sides *or* around; to bathe in a flood of light.

Um'schichtig, *adv.* in layers; alternately; in turns.

Umschießen, *ir.v.* I. *a.* (*insep.*) to fire at . . . from all sides; (*sep.*) to shoot down. II. *n.* (*aux.* **s.**) (*sep.*) to shift, change suddenly; to fall down suddenly (*coll.*); to chop about (*of wind*).

Umschiff'—bar, *adj.* circumnavigable. —**en**, *v.* I. *a.* (*insep.*) to sail round, circumnavigate; to round, double (*a cape*); (*sep.*) to tran(s)ship. II. *n.* (*aux.* **s.**) (*sep.*) to make a detour in sailing. —**ung**, *f.*; —**ung der Erde**, circumnavigation of the globe.

Um'schlag, *m.* (—**s**, *pl.* **Umschläge**) turning up or over; revulsion; sudden change (*of the weather, opinions*); turn; alteration; turning, getting sour; cover; wrapper; envelope; band, facing, hem (*on dresses*); cuff, collar; flap, turned-up brim; rim; turn-up card; poultice; **einen — machen um (einen Arm)**, to poultice (an arm). **—en**, (*sep.*) I. *ir.v.a.* to knock down *or* over; to turn over (*a page, etc.*); turn up (*a hem, cuff*), to turn down, over (*a collar*); to tuck, roll up (*sleeves*); to apply (*a poultice*); to turn up (*a card*); to wrap round, wrap up; **ein Tuch —en**, to put on a shawl, to wrap (*oneself*) up in a shawl; **Papier um ein Packet —en**, to tie *or* do up a parcel. II. *ir.v.n.* (*aux.* **s.**) to turn over, capsize, upset; to turn, change suddenly; to degenerate, grow worse; to shift, veer, change; to turn, grow sour; to spoil; to break (*of the voice*); **die Krankheit schlägt um**, the malady assumes a new aspect, has changed (for the worse); **in entscheidender Weise zum Guten —en**, to take a favourable turn; **das Boot war umgeschlagen**, the boat had been upset; **der Kranke ist wieder umgeschlagen**, the patient has had a relapse; **in etwas** (*acc.*) **—en**, to change into something else; **das Wetter schlug um**, the weather changed; **der Wind schlug um**, the wind shifted *or* veered round; **die Sache ist umgeschlagen**, the matter has assumed a different aspect. III. *subst. n.* sudden overthrow; overturning; change, crisis, turn; wrapping up; turning up; application (*of a poultice, etc.*); **—en des Glückes**, change of fortune. *Comp.* **—bogen**, *m.* sheet of packing paper; casing. **—bohrer**, *m.* wimble, centre-bit. **—deckel**, *m.* cover. **—(e)=kragen**, *m.* turn-down collar. **—e=papier**, *n.* wrapping *or* packing paper. **—(e)=tuch**, *n.* shawl.

Umschleichen, *ir.v.* I. *a.* (*insep.*) to sneak round about. II. *n.* (*aux.* **s.**) (*sep.*) to sneak about.

Umschlei'ern, *v.a.* (*insep.*) to veil, cover with a veil.

Umschließ—en, *ir.v.* I. *n.* (*aux.* **h.**) (*sep.*) to turn the key in the lock. II. *a.* (*insep.*) to inclose, surround; to invest, besiege; **mit seinen Armen —en**, to clasp in one's arms, embrace. **—ung**, *f.* embracing; embrace; inclosure; blockade (*Mil.*). *Comp.* **—ungs=linien**, *pl.* lines round a fortress.

Umschlingen, *ir.v.a.* (*sep.*) to twist, wind round; (*insep.*) to embrace, clasp round; to cling to.

Um'schmeißen, *ir.v.a. & n.* (*aux.* **s.**) (*sep.*) (*vulg.*) *see* **Umwerfen.**

Um'schmelzen, I. *ir.v.a.* (*sep.*) to melt again, recast, refound. II. *subst. n.* recasting; conversion of bullion *or* old coin into current coin.

Umschmieden, *v.a.* (*sep.*) to forge over again *or* afresh; (*insep.*) to forge, weld round.

Umschnallen, *v.a.* (*sep.*) to buckle on (*a sword*); to buckle differently; (*insep.*) to fasten all round.

Umschnüren, *v.a.* (*sep.*) to lace, strap round; to lace again *or* differently; (*insep.*) to cord, tie up.

Umschrän'ken, *v.a.* (*insep.*) to surround with a barrier; to confine, limit.

Umschreib—en, *ir.v.a.* (*sep.*) to re-write; to write all round; to transfer; **einen Wechsel —en**, to reindorse a bill; **ein Recht auf einen —en**, to transfer, make over a right to a p.; (*insep.*) to write an inscription on; to describe round, circumscribe with (*Math.*); to paraphrase; to write periphrastically, use circumlocution; **ein Dreieck mit einem Kreise —en**, to describe a circle round a triangle. **—ung**, *f.* transcription, transliteration; transfer; circumlocution, paraphrase. *Comp.* **—e=buch**, *n.* transfer-book.

Um'schrift, *f.* (*pl.* **—en**) (circular) inscription, legend (*on a coin*), device, motto; transcription, transcript; something re-written.

Um'schüren, *v.a.* (*sep.*) to stir, rake up.

Um'schütteln, *v.a.* (*sep.*) to shake up *or* about.

Umschütten, *v.a.* (*sep.*) to upset; to spill in pouring; to pour into another vessel; (*insep.*) to heap up *or* throw all round; **mit Erde —**, to earth up, cover round with earth.

Umschwär'men, *v.a.* (*insep.*) to swarm, buzz round; to harass (*Mil.*).

Umschwe'ben, *v.a.* (*insep.*) to hover (a)round *or* over, to float *or* flutter round.

Um'schweif, *m.* (**—s**, *pl.* **—e**) roundabout way, circumlocution; digression; verbosity; **ohne —e**, bluntly, point blank; **—e machen**, to digress, to beat about the bush.

Umschwei'fen, *v.a.* to wander round, to hover round.

Um'schwenken, *v.a. & n.* (*aux.* **h.**) (*sep.*) to turn round, wheel about.

Umschwir'ren, *v.a.* (*insep.*) to buzz round.

Um'schwung, *m.* (**—s**) rotation; revolution; wheeling; sudden change, turn; revulsion (*of feeling, etc.*); (*pl.*) vicissitudes (*of fortune*). *Comp.* **—s=punkt**, *m.* centre of rotation.

Umsegeln, *v.a.* (*sep.*) to run foul of, run down, to fall down (*coll.*); (*insep.*) to sail round, circumnavigate, to double (*a cape*).

Um'sehen, *ir.v.r.* (*sep.*) to look back, look round; to look about one; **hier kann man sich recht —** there is a wide prospect from this (*point, etc.*) **eh' man sich umsieht** *or* **im —**, in a twinkling **sich in der Stadt —**, to go about and see the town; **er hat sich viel in der Welt umgesehen**, he has seen a great deal of the world; **sich nach einem —**, to look about for a p., to look out for s.o.; **da kann er sich lange —**, he will have to wait a good while (*for that*).

Um'sein, *ir.v.n.* (*sep.*) to expire (*of a term*); to be over, to have come to an end; to be circuitous.

Um'seitig, *adj.* on the other page, overleaf.

Um'setz—bar, *adj.* convertible; marketable; exchangeable; negotiable; **in bares Geld —bar**, that can be realized. **—barkeit**, *f.* convertibility. **—en**, I. *v.a.* (*sep.*) to set *or* put round; to place otherwise; to transpose; to transplant; to exchange; to sell, convert into cash; to compose (*Mus.*); to re-compose (*Typ.*); to permute (*Math.*); **ein Musikstück in eine andere Tonart —en**, to transpose a piece of music (*into another key*); **sich —en**, to change. II. *subst. n.*, **—ung**, *f.* placing differently; change of place; transposition: transplantation; permutation (*Math.*); *see* **Umsatz.**

Um'=sich=greifen, *n.* progress; spreading, spread.

Um'sicht, *f.* looking about; panorama, prospect round about; circumspection: prudence; tact. **—ig**, *adj.* circumspect; prudent; cautious. **—ige(r)**, *m.* prudent, far-seeing person. **—ig=keit**, *f.* circumspection, prudence, deliberation.

Um'sinken, *ir.v.n.* (*aux.* **s.**) (*sep.*) to sink down.

Umso'nst, *adv.* for nothing, without pay, gratuitously, gratis; aimlessly; to no purpose, in vain; **er giebt nichts —**, he gives nothing for nothing; **er sagte das nicht —**, he had some design in saying that; **sich — bemühen**, to lose one's labour; **— ist der Tod**, nothing for nothing; no pay, no work (*prov.*); **das soll er nicht — gethan haben**, he shall pay for that; he shall not have done that in vain.

Umspannen, *v.a.* (*sep.*) to stretch round; to change (*horses*); to re-string; (*insep.*) to surround, encompass.

Umspin'nen, *ir.v.a.* (*insep.*) to wrap round in a web, spin all round.

Umspringen, *ir.v.* I. *a.* (*sep.*) to overturn by leaping against; (*insep.*) to jump about, round (*one*). II. *n.* (*aux.* **s.**) (*sep.*) to jump about; to change, veer, chop about, shift; **mit einem (einer S.) umzuspringen wissen**, to know how to manage a person (thing); **damit werde ich bald —**, I shall soon settle that.

Umspü'len, *v.a.* (*insep.*) to lave, wash, beat against.

Um'stand, *m.* (**—s**, *pl.* **Umstände**) circumstance; consideration; condition, situation; (*pl.*) particulars, details, circumstances; (*pl.*) formalities, ceremonies; **die näheren Umstände**, further particulars; **sich in einzelne Umstände einlassen**, to enter into particulars; **die kleinsten Umstände**, minutiæ; **in andern (gesegneten) Umständen sein**, to be with child, to be in an interesting condition; **(viele) Umstände machen**, to be formal, ceremonious; **sie werden nicht lange Umstände mit ihm machen**, they will make short work of him; **machen Sie keine Umstände**, don't put yourself about; **unter allen Umständen**, in any case, at all events; **unter keinen Umständen**, on no account; **ohne Umstände**, without ceremony, do not stand on ceremonies; **ohne viele Umstände**, without much ado; **das kommt auf die Umstände an**, that depends on circumstances; **aus dem —, daß . . .**, from the circumstance of (*or* that) . . .; **in guten Umständen**, well to do, well off; **Kaffee mit Umständen**, coffee with cake, *etc.* *Comp.* **—s=brötchen**, *n.* sandwich (*dial.*). **—s=kasten**, **—s=kommissarius**, **—s=krämer**, *m.* fussy *or* pedantic person. **—s=korsett**, *n.* stays for a woman who is with child. **—s=satz**, *m.* subordinate sentence of condition. **—s=wort**, *n.* adverb.

Um'ständlich, *adj.* & *adv.* circumstantial; minute, detailed; ceremonious; **—er Bericht**, detailed account; **— erzählen**, to detail, particularize, give the details of; **das ist mir viel zu —**, that is far too much trouble for me. **—keit**, *f.* circumstantiality; ceremoniousness; (*pl.*) formalities.

Um'stauen, *v.a.* (*sep.*) to stow differently, to rummage the hold.

Um'stechen, *ir.v.a.* (*sep.*) to stir, turn up with a fork; to cut, engrave again.

Umstecken, *v.a.* (*sep.*) to put on and fasten with a pin; to pin *or* fasten differently; (*insep.*) to plant around; **mit Näglein umsteckt**, with pinks fastened all around.

Umstehen, *ir.v.* I. *a.* (*insep.*) to stand round *or* about, surround. II. *n.* (*aux.* **h.**) (*sep.*) to stand about; to turn sour, to spoil. **—d**, *p. adj.* & *adv.*; **—de Seite**, the next page; **—d**, on the following *or* opposite page; **die —den**, the bystanders; **wie —d**, as stated overleaf.

Um'steig—en, *ir.v.n.* (*aux.* **f.**) to change carriages *or* horses; **nach Hannover—en!** change for Hanover! (*Rail.*). *Comp.* **—billet**, *n.*, **—karte**, *f.* through ticket.

Umstell—en, *v.a.* (*sep.*) to place differently; to transpose; to invert, reverse (*Arith.*); **sich —en**, to change places; (*insep.*) to surround, encompass. **—ung**, *f.* change of position; permutation.

Um'stempeln, *v.a.* (*sep.*) to re-stamp, to stamp again *or* afresh; to change a p.'s views.

Umsteuern, *v.a.* (*insep.*) to steer round; to avoid; (*sep.*) to reverse (*an electric current*).

Um'stimm—en, *v.a.* (*sep.*) to re-tune, tune to another pitch (*Mus.*); **einen —en**, to make a p. change his opinion *or* mind, to bring a p. round. **—ung**, *f.*; **ihre —ung war leicht gemacht**, it was easy to convert them.

Um'stoßen, *ir.v.a.* (*sep.*) to overturn, overthrow, knock down; to subvert, overturn; to abolish (*laws*); to revoke, annul; to invalidate (*an agreement*); **ein Erkenntnis —**, to quash a judgment.

Um'stößlich, *adj.* that may be overthrown; reversible; annullable.

Umstrah'len, *v.a.* (*insep.*) to surround *or* enwrap with rays, to shine round.

Umstricken, *v.a.* (*insep.*) to knit round; to ensnare, entangle; (*sep.*) to knit differently *or* afresh.

Umströ'men, *v.a.* (*insep.*) to flow, stream round.

Um'stülpen, *v.a.* (*sep.*) to turn upside down, to tilt over.

Um'sturz, *m.* falling down, fall; downfall, overthrow; revolution; subversion; ruin. *Comp.* **—bestrebungen**, **—ideen**, *pl.* subversive, revolutionary, anarchical ideas. **—partei**, *f.* anarchists; revolutionary party (*Pol.*). **—vorlage**, *f.* bill against the spreading of anarchism, social order preservation bill.

Um'stürz—en, (*sep.*) *v.* I. *a.* to turn over; to overthrow, upset, overturn; to subvert; to demolish, destroy. II. *n.* (*aux.* **f.**) to fall down, tumble. **—ler**, *m.* revolutionary, anarchist. **—lerisch**, *adj.*; **—lerische Bestrebungen**, revolutionary tendencies.

Um'taufen, *v.a.* (*sep.*) to re-baptize; **einen (etwas) —**, to give a p. (a thing) a new name.

Um'tausch, *m.* exchange. **—en**, *v.a.* (*sep.*) to exchange; **sich —en**, to change (*one's nature*).

Um'thun, *ir.v.a.* (*sep.*) to put on; **sich nach einer S. —**, to put oneself about for a th., to look about for a th.; **sich bei Leuten —**, to make inquiries; **habt ihr euch sonst schon umgethan?** have you yet made any inquiry elsewhere?

Umto'ben, *v.a.* (*insep.*) to rage *or* storm round.

Umtö'nen, *v.a.* (*insep.*) to sound *or* echo round.

Um'treiben, *ir.v.a.* (*sep.*) to drive round; to propel.

Um'treten, (*sep.*) *ir.v.* I. *a.* to tread down, tread under foot. II. *n.* (*aux.* **h.**) to change one's step.

Um'trieb, *m.* constant movement; activity; circulation; thorough, systematic cultivation of a wood; (*pl.*) intrigues, plots, agitation, machinations.

Um'trunk, *m.* drinking in turn, all round; **— halten**, to pass the goblet all round.

Umwach'sen, *ir.v.a.* (*insep.*) to grow round, surround; **epheuumwachsen**, ivy-clad.

Umwal'l—en, *v.a.* (*insep.*) to surround with ramparts; to float around. **—ung**, *f.* circumvallation.

Um'wälzen, *v.a.* (*sep.*) to roll, whirl round; to overturn; to revolutionize.

Umwandel—n, *v.* I. *a.* (*sep.*) to change, turn, metamorphose; *sometimes* = **nachtwandeln**, to walk about in a dream; **sich —n**, to become assimilated (*Physiol.*). II. *n.* (*insep.*) to walk slowly round. **—ung**, **Um'wandlung**, *f.* change, transformation. *Comp.* **—ungs=prozeß**, *m.* metamorphosis.

Umweben, *ir.v.a.* (*insep.*) to surround with a web, weave a web round; (*sep.*) to weave over again; to weave round.

Um'wechseln, (*sep.*) *v.* I. *a.* to change, exchange (*money; one's clothes; books*). II. *n.* (*aux.* **h.**) to change places, alternate, take in turn.

Um'weg, *m.* roundabout way, detour; by-way, by-path; **auf —en**, indirectly; in a roundabout way; **—e machen**, to take a circuitous route, to shuffle, employ evasions; **ohne —e**, straight to the point.

Umwehen, *v.a.* (*sep.*) to blow down; (*insep.*) to blow around, to fan (*with breezes*).

Um'wendbar, *adj.* reversible.

Um'wenden, (*sep.*) I. *reg.* & *ir.v.a.* to turn, to turn round *or* about; to reverse; to invert; to turn over; to turn up; **wie man eine Hand umwendet**, in a twinkling; **einen —**, to make a p. change his views; **es wendet mir das Herz um**, it wrings my heart; **mit umgewandter Hand**, with the back of the hand **das Blatt wendet sich um**, the tables are turned; die umgewandte Seite, the wrong side (*of cloth, etc.*), the other side *or* page (*of a leaf*); bitte umzuwenden! please turn over (*abbr.:* P. T. O.)! II. *ir.v.n.* (*aux.* h. & s.) *see* Umkehren; es sind schon etliche umgewandt, some are already turned aside after Satan (*B.*).

Umwer'ben, *ir.v.a.* (*insep.*) to court, woo; sie ist viel umworben, she has many admirers *or* suitors.

Um'werfen, (*sep.*) *ir.v.* I. *a.* to overturn, upset; to throw round, throw, put on; to overthrow, subvert; to turn, break up (*a field*); to reverse (*a judgment*). II. *n.* (*aux.* h. & s.) to overturn, upset; to break down; to fail; to change (*of the weather*).

Um'wert—en, *v.a.* (*sep.*) to ascribe a different value to things, to alter one's own *or* other people's appreciation of things. **—ung,** *f.*; **—ung alter Werte,** change of attitude towards old-established conceptions (*Philos.*).

Umwickeln, *v.a.* (*sep.*) to wrap round; to wrap over again *or* differently; (*insep.*) mit etwas —, to wrap up in.

Umwinden, *ir.v.a.* (*insep.*) to twine around, to encircle; (*sep.*) to twist around; to wind otherwise; to turn, twist.

Umwir'beln, *v.a.* (*insep.*) to envelop (*in a whirl, cloud, etc.*).

Umwit'tern, *v.n.* to hover round, to envelop; to encompass (*in the form of an atmospheric influence*); von meinem Hauch umwittert, surrounded by the atmosphere of my breath.

Umwo'gen, *v.a.* (*insep.*) *see* Umströmen; (*sep.*) to overturn by its waves.

Umwoh'n—en, *v.a.* (*insep.*) to live, dwell around; die —enden (*pron.* Um'wohnenden), *see* —er. **—er** (*pron.* Um'wohner), *pl.* the neighbours, persons living in the neighbourhood.

Umwöl'ken, *v.a.* & *r.* (*insep.*) to cloud, darken.

Umwühlen, *v.a.* (*sep.*) to grub up (*as swine the earth*); to root up, to turn over, rake up; to rummage; to overturn (*in rummaging*); ein Bett —, to tumble a bed; (*insep.*) to rummage round, grub about.

Um'zählen, *v.a.* (*sep.*) to count over again; to count round.

Um'zapfen, *v.a.* (*sep.*) to tap, draw off (*beer*).

Umzäu'n—en, I. *v.a.* (*insep.*) to enclose, hedge round, fence in. II. *subst.n.*, **—ung,** *f.* enclosing; enclosure, hedge, fence.

Umzeichnen, *v.a.* (*sep.*) to draw over again; to mark (*goods*) differently; (*insep.*) to surround with designs.

Umziehen, *ir.v.* I. *a.* (*sep.*) to pull down; to put on; ein Kind —, to change a child's clothes, linen, *etc.*; sich (*dat.*) die Schuhe —, to change one's shoes; die Kleider —, sich —, to change (one's clothes); (*insep.*) to move, walk, travel about; to go round (*a mountain, etc.*); to surround; to draw the outlines of; to cover, hang with; to envelop; der Himmel hat sich umzogen, the sky has become overcast. II. *n.* (*aux.* s.) (*sep.*) to remove, change one's dwelling; to change one's situation; to go round about; dreimal umgezogen ist einmal abgebrannt, three removals are as bad as a fire (*prov.*).

Umzin'geln, *v.a.* (*insep.*) to surround, encircle.

Umzir'ken, Umzir'keln, *v.a.* to encircle.

Um'zug, *m.* wandering about; change of dwelling, removal; change of place *or* service; procession; cover, case (*of a pillow, etc.*). *Comp.* **—s=kosten,** *pl.* cost of removal.

Un, *negative particle used as prefix* (*in comp. with subst.'s, adj.'s, adv.'s and past participles* =) un-, in-, im-, dis-, ir-, not, non-. *The principal meanings of* un= *are:* (1) *absolute negation; e.g.* Unglück, unwahr; (2) *a bad sort of; e.g.* Unmensch, Untier; (3) *excessive amount: e.g.* Unmenge, Unsumme. *Only the most important of the numberless comp'ds with* un= *can be given here. The meaning of others will be obvious when* un-, in-, *or* not *are prefixed to the equivalent of the second part of the compound. If the second word is a participle, see the verb to which it belongs. In case it is a derivative in* =bar, =lich *or* =sam *look out the verb from which it is derived. The accentuation of the comp'ds with* un= *is in some cases doubtful; the usual one has been indicated. As a rule it may be noted that in the case of comp'ds with nouns* (Un'sinn) *and adjectives* (un'treu) *the principal accent is on the prefix* un=, *especially if the word without* un= *is of frequent occurrence. In other cases it is possible to place the accent so as to emphasize either the negation or the second part of the compound. Note the* (*slight*) *glottal stop in those compounds in which the second part begins with a vowel; e.g.,* unabsichtlich.

Unabän'derlich, *adj.* invariable; unalterable; immutable, unchangeable; irrevocable. **—keit,** *f.* unchangeableness.

Unabbüß'lich, *adj.* inexpiable.

Unab'gelöscht, *adj.* unquenched; quick (*of lime*).

Unab'gemacht, *adj.* unsettled, unpaid; unfinished; not agreed upon, not arranged.

Unab'gerechnet, *adv.* without taking into account.

Un'abhängig, *adj.* & *adv.* independent; absolute (*Gram.*). **—keit,** *f.* independence. *Comp.* **—keits=erklärung,** *f.* Declaration of Independence.

Un'abkömmlich, *adj.* indispensable; not disposable (*Mil.*). **—keit,** *f.* indispensableness.

Unabläs'sig, Unabläß'lich, *adj.* & *adv.* incessant.

Unablös'lich, *adj.* undetachable; irredeemable (*mortgage*), perpetual (*loan*); —e Anleihe, consolidated fund.

Unabseh'bar, (Unabseh'lich,) *adj.* beyond the reach of the eye; immeasurable; interminable; incalculable. **—keit,** *f.* immensity, immeasurableness.

Unabsetz'bar, *adj.* irremovable.

Un'absichtlich, *adj.* unpremeditated; chance.

Unab'stellbar, *adj.* unchangeable, irremediable; that cannot be turned off *or* stopped, ever flowing, ever burning.

Unab'tretbar, *adj.* untransferable.

Unabweis'bar, Unabweis'lich, *adj.* not to be refused; pressing; urgent; peremptory, imperative.

Unabwend'bar, *adj.* inevitable; appointed by fate.

Un'achtsam, *adj.* inattentive, careless, negligent; thoughtless, heedless. **—keit,** *f.* carelessness; heedlessness; aus —keit, through inattention.

Un'ähnlich, *adj.* unlike, dissimilar. **—keit,** *f.* unlikeness, dissimilarity.

Unanfecht'bar, *adj.* incontestable.

Unan'gebaut, *adj.* uncultivated.

Unan'gefochten, *adj.* & *adv.* undisputed; unmolested; laß mich —! let me alone! let me be!

Un'angemessen, *adj.* unsuitable; improper; incongruous; incompatible. **—heit,** *f.* unsuitableness, impropriety.

Un'angenehm, *adj.* unpleasant, disagreeable; er hat etwas —es an sich, there is something disagreeable about him.

Unan'gerührt, *adj.* intact; untouched.

Un'angesehen, I. *adj.* not looked at; undistinguished; disregarded. II. *prep.* (*with gen.*) regardless of.

Unangreif'bar, *adj.* unassailable; unimpeachable.

Unannehm'bar, *adj.* unacceptable.

Un'annehmlichkeit, *f.* disagreeableness, unpleasantness; inconvenience; (*pl.*) annoyances.

Un'ansässig, *adj.* non-resident; without domicile, without a settled home.

Un'ansehnlich, *adj.* mean-looking, poor-looking, plain; inconsiderable, insignificant. **—keit**, *f.* plainness, smallness; insignificance.

Un'anständig, *adj.* improper; indecent; unmannerly, unbecoming, unseemly; shocking; **es ist dem König —**, it is not suitable for the king (*obs.*). **—keit**, *f.* impropriety; indecency, unmannerliness.

Un'anstellig, *adj.* awkward, clumsy, maladroit.

Un'anstößig, *adj.* inoffensive, giving no offence.

Unantast'bar, *adj.* that may not be touched; inviolable; unimpeachable.

Unanwend'bar, *adj.* inapplicable; inopportune. **—keit**, *f.* inapplicability.

Un'appetitlich, *adj.* not appetizing; disgusting.

Un'art, I. *f.* bad conduct; ill breeding, bad manners; rudeness; incivility; bad habit; naughtiness (*of children*); peculiarity, vagary, trick. II. *m.* (**—s**, *pl.* **—e**) naughty child; rude person. **—ig**, *adj.* ill-behaved; naughty; ill-bred; rude; disobliging; improper; vicious (*of horses*). **—igkeit**, *f. see* **Unart** I.

Un'artikuliert, *adj.* inarticulate.

Un'ästhetisch, *adj.* not æsthetic; vulgar.

Unauffind'bar, *adj.* that cannot be found.

Un'aufgefordert, *adj.* unprovoked; uncalled for; unasked, of one's own accord.

Un'aufgeklärt, *adj.* unsolved, unexplained, mysterious; unenlightened.

Un'aufgelöst, *adj.* undissolved; unexplained.

Un'aufgeräumt, *adj.* disorderly, untidy; in low spirits; sulky.

Un'aufgeschnitten, *adj.* (*with*) uncut (*edges*).

Unaufhalt'—bar, —sam, *adj.* not to be stopped *or* checked; irresistible; impetuous; incessant.

Unaufheb'bar, *adj.* not to be abrogated.

Un'aufhörlich, Unaufhör'lich, *adj.* incessant, uninterrupted, perpetual; endless.

Unauflös'—bar, —lich, *adj.* not dissolvable; indissoluble; inexplicable.

Un'aufmerksam, *adj.*, inattentive; absent-minded. **—keit**, *f.* inattention.

Un'aufrichtig, *adj.* insincere, deceitful.

Unaufschieb'—bar, —lich, *adj.* pressing, urgent.

Un'ausbleiblich, Unausbleib'lich, *adj.* unfailing; certain; inevitable.

Unausbeut'bar, *adj.* that cannot be worked *or* exploited; that cannot be used.

Unausdehn'bar, *adj.* not extensible; non-ductile.

Unausführ'bar, *adj.* impracticable, impossible.

Unaus'gebildet, *adj.* uncultivated, unpolished; undeveloped, rudimentary.

Unaus'gefertigt, *adj.* not made out *or* drawn up.

Unaus'geführt, *adj.* unfinished; not carried out.

Unaus'gefüllt, *adj.* not filled up; blank.

Unaus'gemacht, *adj.* undecided; uncertain; not settled, questionable.

Un'ausgesetzt, *adj.* uninterrupted, constant.

Unaus'gesprochen, *adj.* not *or* never uttered; unutterable, ineffable.

Unausgleich'bar, *adj.* that cannot be compensated *or* atoned for.

Unausklag'bar, *adj.* irrecoverable (*of debts*).

Unauslösch'—bar, —lich, *adj.* & *adv.* inextinguishable; indelible; unquenchable; **—liche Dankbarkeit**, lasting gratitude; **—liche Schrift**, indelible characters; **—liche Tinte**, permanent ink; **—liche Erinnerung**, permanent memory.

Unaussprech'—bar, *adj.* unpronounceable, that cannot be articulated. **—lich**, *adj.* inexpressible; unutterable; ineffable; **die —lichen**, inexpressibles, trousers (*coll.*).

Unaussteh'lich, *adj.* & *adv.* insupportable, intolerable; odious.

Unaustilg'bar, *adj.* ineradicable; ineffaceable.

Unausweich'—bar, —lich, *adj.* inevitable.

Un'band, *m.* (**—es**, *pl.* **Unbände**) unruly child, unmanageable person, *see* **Unart** II.

Un'bändig, *adj.* unruly, intractable; excessive (*coll.*); furious (*coll.*); **er hat sich — gefreut**, he was frightfully *or* awfully pleased (*coll.*).

Un'barmherzig, *adj.* & *adv.* unmerciful, pitiless; hard; cruel. **—keit**, *f.* harshness, cruelty.

Un'bärtig, *adj.* beardless. **—keit**, *f.* beardlessness.

Un'beabsichtigt, *adj.* unintentional, undesigned.

Un'beachtet, *adj.* unnoticed; disregarded.

Unbeans'standet, *adj.* not objected to, unopposed; unimpeached; uncontested (*at elections*).

Unbeant'wortet, *adj.* unanswered.

Unbear'beitet, *adj.* unwrought, undressed rough, raw; that has not been treated (*of a subject*).

Unbebau'—bar, *adj.* not to be cultivated, that cannot be cultivated. **—t**, *adj.* uncultivated; **—ter Platz**, ground not built on, vacant plot.

Un'bedacht, —sam, (Unbedächtig,) *adj.* inconsiderate; thoughtless; indiscreet; rash; **—erweise**, inconsiderately, thoughtlessly, foolishly.

Un'bedeckt, *adj.* uncovered; **mit —em Haupte**, bareheaded.

Un'bedenklich, *adj.* unobjectionable; harmless; *adv.* without hesitation.

Un'bedeutend, *adj.* insignificant; unimportant; trifling; trivial. **—heit, Unbedeutenheit**, *f.* insignificance.

Un'bedingt, *adj.* unconditional, unqualified, absolute; **—er Gehorsam**, implicit obedience

Un'beeidigt, *adj.* without having taken an oath

Un'beeinflußt, *adj* not influenced; unbiassed, unprejudiced.

Unbeein'trächtigt, *adj.* unimpaired.

Un'beendigt, *adj.* unfinished, incomplete.

Un'beerbt, *adj.* without heirs, without issue.

Un'befähigt, *adj.* incompetent, unqualified.

Unbefahr'—bar, *adj.* impracticable. **—en**, *adj.* untraversed, trackless; **—enes Volk**, inexperienced sailors, green hands.

Un'befangen, *adj.* & *adv.* unprejudiced; impartial; disinterested; unembarrassed, unconstrained; calm, dispassionate; artless; unaffected; ingenuous. **—heit**, *f.* impartiality; freedom from bias; ease, unrestrainedness; unaffectedness; simplicity, naïveté; candour.

Un'befestigt, *adj.* unfortified, open.

Un'befiedert, *adj.* without feathers, unfledged; **—er Pfeil**, unfeathered arrow.

Unbefleck'—bar, *adj.* that cannot be sullied. **—t**, *adj.* unsullied, unspotted; pure, virgin; immaculate; **—te Empfängnis**, immaculate conception. **—theit**, *f.* purity, spotlessness.

Un'befördert, *adj.* undespatched, not forwarded; not promoted.

Un'befrachtet, *adj.* unfreighted, empty.

Un'befriedig—end, *adj.* unsatisfying, unsatisfactory; insufficient. **—t**, *adj.* unsatisfied; dissatisfied; disappointed; unappeased. **—theit**, *f.* dissatisfaction.

Un'befugt, *adj.* unauthorized; incompetent; **—erweise**, without authority.

Un'begangen, *adj.* unfrequented; untrodden.

Un'begeben, *adj.* unsold; uninvested; undisposed of; unmarried.

Unbegreif'lich, *adj.* inconceivable, incomprehensible; inexplicable. **—keit**, *f.* incomprehensibility; incomprehensible thing; mystery.

Unbegrenz'—bar, *adj.* illimitable. **—t**, *adj.* boundless. **—theit**, *f.* boundlessness.

Un'begriffen, *adj.* not comprehended *or* understood.

Un'begründet, *adj.* unfounded. **—heit**, *f.* groundlessness; **er behauptet die völlige —heit unserer Ansprüche**, he maintains that our claims are absolutely without foundation.

Un'begütert, *adj.* without landed property; not rich; not well off.

Un'behaart, *adj.* without hair; hairless; bald; smooth; smooth-leaved (*Bot.*); glabrous.
Un'behag—en, *n.* (**—ens**) discomfort, uneasiness; displeasure. **—lich,** *adj. & adv.* unpleasant; uncomfortable, uneasy. **—lichkeit,** *f.* uneasiness, uncomfortableness; constraint.
Un'behelligt, *adj.* unmolested, undisturbed.
Un'behende, *adj.* heavy, clumsy, awkward.
Un'behindert, *adj.* unrestrained, unhindered.
Un'beholfen, *adj.* clumsy, awkward; heavy, ungainly; embarrassed. **—heit,** *f.* awkwardness; heaviness; unwieldiness.
Un'behülflich, (**Un'behilflich,**) *adj.* helpless; unwieldy; not helpful; *see* **Unbeholfen. —keit,** *see* **Unbeholfenheit.**
Un'beirrt, *adv.* without being disconcerted, calmly.
Un'bekannt, *adj.* unknown; ignorant (**mit,** of), unacquainted (*with*), a stranger (*to*); obscure; **er ist mir —,** I do not know him; **es wird dir nicht — sein . . .,** you know, of course . . .; **ich bin hier —,** I am a stranger here. **—schaft,** *f.* unfamiliarity; ignorance.
Unbekehr'bar, *adj.* that cannot be converted.
Un'bekümmert, *adj.* untroubled, unconcerned, careless.
Un'beladen, *adj.* unladen, without cargo.
Un'belaubt, *adj.* leafless, without foliage.
Un'belebt, *adj.* lifeless, inanimate; apathetic, dull. **—heit,** *f.* lifelessness; dulness; apathy.
Un'beleckt, *adj.*; **von der Kultur —,** without any trace of culture, uncivilised.
Un'belesen, *adj.* unread, unlettered, illiterate.
Un'beliebt, *adj.* disliked; **beim Volke —,** unpopular. **—heit,** *f.* unpopularity.
Un'bemannt, *adj.* unmanned (*Naut.*).
Unbemerk'—bar, *adj.* imperceptible. **—t,** *adj. & adv.* unperceived, unnoticed.
Un'bemittelt, *adj.* not rich; without fortune; poor.
Un'benamt, *adj.* nameless; anonymous.
Un'benannt, *adj.* nameless; anonymous; unknown (*Math.*); **—e Zahl,** abstract number.
Un'benommen, *adj.* permitted; rough (*Mint.*); **es ist (bleibt) Ihnen — zu . . .,** you are (still) quite at liberty to . . .
Un'benutzt, *adj.* unused, unemployed; profitless; idle (*of money*); **das wird er nicht — lassen,** he will not fail to profit by it, to make (good) use of it.
Un'bequem, *adj.* inconvenient; inopportune; uncomfortable; embarrassing. **—lichkeit,** *f.* inconvenience, *etc.*
Un'beraten, *adj.* ill-advised; bewildered, puzzled; in a bad condition *or* state.
Unbere'chenbar, *adj.* incalculable; **er ist ganz —,** there is no telling what he will do.
Un'berechnet, *adj.* free of charge.
Un'berechtigt, *adj.* unauthorized, without authority; not entitled (*to*); unqualified.
Un'berichtigt, *adj.* uncorrected; unsettled, unpaid.
Un'beritten, *adj.* not broken in (*of horses*); unmounted (*of cavalry*); **einen — machen,** to dismount s.o., take a p.'s horse away.
Un'berücksichtigt, *adj.* not taken into account.
Un'berufen, *adj.* unbidden, uncalled for; officious; intrusive; without the inward call *or* natural vocation; **— !** (*lit. without invoking ill-luck*); **— und unbeschrieen !** Heaven preserve it (*or* us) from harm! may no evil ensue! absit omen! (*a superstitious exclamation to ward off evil after speaking favourably of something*).
Un'berühmt, *adj.* not celebrated, obscure. **—heit,** *f.* want of fame, obscurity.
Un'berührt, *adj.* untouched; intact; virgin (*forest, soil*); unnoticed; passed over in silence.
Un'beschadet, *prep.* (*with gen.*) not detrimental to, without detriment to, without prejudice to.
Un'beschädigt, *adj.* uninjured; safe and sound; in good condition (*C. L.*).
Un'bescheiden, *adj.* wanting in modesty; immodest; arrogant, insolent; bold; exaggerated, unreasonable.
Un'bescheinigt, *adj.* uncertified, unreceipted.
Un'beschlagen, *adj.* unshod (*of horses*); without mountings, not mounted; unskilled, not versed in (*a science, etc.*).
Un'beschnitten, *adj.* uncircumcised; unshorn; unclipped (*of coin*); uncut (*of books, etc.*).
Un'bescholten, *adj.* irreproachable, blameless; of good reputation. **—heit,** *f.* blamelessness.
Unbeschränk'—bar, *adj.* not to be limited, illimitable. **—t,** *adj.* boundless, unlimited; absolute; uncontrolled; discretionary. **—theit,** *f.* limitlessness; absoluteness.
Unbeschreib'lich, I. *adj. & adv.* indescribable; beyond all description. II. *adv.* inexpressibly
Un'beschrieben, *adj.* blank; unwritten, undescribed.
Un'beschrieen, *adj.* not disparaged; uncharmed; *see* **Unberufen.**
Un'beschuht, *adj.* unshod, without shoes.
Un'beschwert, *adj.* unburdened, easy, light (*conscience*).
Un'beseelt, *adj.* soulless; lifeless, inanimate.
Un'besehen, *adj. & adv.*, **—s,** *adv.* without looking at it; unseen; just as it is; **etwas — kaufen,** to buy a pig in a poke.
Un'besetzt, *adj.* unoccupied; free; vacant; untrimmed; **die Droschke ist —,** the cab is disengaged; **der Stuhl ist —,** the chair is not taken. **—heit,** *f.*, (**—sein,** *n.*) vacancy.
Unbesieg'—bar, —lich, *adj.* invincible; insuperable. **—t,** *adj.* unconquered.
Un'besoldet, *adj.* unsalaried, unpaid, honorary
Un'besonnen, *adj.* thoughtless, inconsiderate; heedless, giddy; rash; indiscreet. **—heit,** *f.* imprudence, thoughtlessness, rashness, (*fam.*) giddiness.
Un'besorgt, *adj.* easy, unconcerned; not executed, unfulfilled; **seien Sie (deswegen) — !** don't trouble yourself, make your mind easy (about that)!
Unbesprech'bar, *adj.* unfit for discussion.
Un'bestand, *m.* instability, changeableness; inconstancy.
Un'beständig, *adj.* inconstant; unstable, unsteady; variable; fickle; versatile; unequal. **—keit,** *f.* inconstancy; versatility.
Unbestech'—bar, —lich, *adj.* incorruptible. **—barkeit,** *f.* incorruptibleness, integrity.
Unbesteig'bar, *adj.* that cannot be climbed. **—keit,** *f.* inaccessibility (*of a mountain-peak*).
Unbestell'—bar, *adj.* returned through the dead letter office, 'addressee unknown,' dead (*letter*); that cannot be tilled (*of fields*). **—t,** *adj.* not ordered *or* bespoken; undelivered (*of letters*); untilled (*of fields*).
Unbestimm'—bar, *adj.* indeterminable; vague. **—t,** *adj.* indeterminate, undefined; indefinite; undecided; doubtful; indistinct; vague; confused, uncertain; **—es Geschlechtswort,** indefinite article; **—tes Zahlwort,** indefinite numeral (*as* **viel, einige, ꝛc.**); **—te Aufgabe,** unlimited problem. **—theit,** *f.* infiniteness; indecision; vagueness; uncertainty.
Un'bestochen, *adj.* unbribed, incorrupted; unbiassed; upright, honest.
Unbestreit'bar, *adj.* incontestable, indisputable.
Un'bestritten, *adj.* undisputed, unquestionable.
Un'besucht, *adj.* unfrequented, unvisited, lonely.
Un'beteiligt, *adj.*; **bei etwas —,** not interested *or* concerned in, having no share in a thing.
Un'betont, *adj.* unaccented, without (an) accent.
Un'beträchtlich, *adj.* inconsiderable, of little importance.
Un'betreten, *adj.* untrodden (*path*), unbeaten (*track*); unembarrassed, easy.

Un'beugsam, *adj.* inflexible; obstinate, firm. **—keit**, *f.* inflexibility.
Un'bewacht, *adj.* unwatched, unguarded; **—er Augenblick**, unguarded moment.
Un'bewaffnet, *adj.* unarmed; unaided; thornless (*Bot.*); **mit —em Auge**, with the naked eye.
Un'bewährt, *adj.* not proved *or* confirmed; untried.
Un'bewandert, *adj.* inexperienced; unskilled.
Unbeweg'—lich, *adj.* immovable; fixed; motionless; real (*property*); apathetic; inflexible; **—liche Schrift**, stereotype. **—lichkeit**, *f.* immovableness; inflexibility. **—t**, *adj.* unmoved; motionless.
Un'bewehrt, *adj.* unarmed, defenceless. **—heit**, *f.* defencelessness.
Un'beweibt, *adj.* unmarried, single. **—heit**, *f.* wifeless condition; bachelorhood.
Un'beweint, *adj.* unwept (*for*), unlamented.
Unbeweis'—bar, **—lich**, *adj.* not provable.
Un'bewiesen, *adj.* not proved; not proven (*Scotch Law*).
Unbewohn'—bar, *adj.* uninhabitable. **—t**, *adj.* uninhabited; vacant; desert. **—theit**, *f.*; **er zeigte die —heit dieses Planeten**, he showed that this planet must be uninhabited.
Un'bewußt, *adj.* unknown; unconscious; involuntary; instinctive; **es wird Ihnen nicht — sein**, you know, of course; **sich** (*dat.*) **einer Sache — sein**, not to be conscious *or* aware of a thing; **es ist mir nichts weniger als —**, I know it very well; **Philosophie des —en**, Philosophy of the Unconscious.
Unbezahl'—bar, *adj.* beyond price, that cannot be paid *or* requited. **—t**, *adj.* unpaid.
Unbezähm'bar, *adj.* untamable, indomitable.
Un'bezeugt, *adj.* unattested; **und zwar hat er sich selbst nicht — gelassen**, nevertheless he left not himself without witness (*B.*).
Un'bezogen, *adj.* uninhabited; unhung, uncurtained; unstringed, without strings (*Mus.*); **—es Kopfkissen**, uncased pillow.
Un'bezweifelt, *adj.* undoubted, unquestioned.
Unbezwing'—bar, **—lich**, *adj.* invincible, indomitable; insuperable; impregnable; irresistible.
Un'biblisch, *adj.* not biblical, unscriptural.
Un'biegsam, *adj.* inflexible, unbending, stiff; stubborn.
Un'bilde, *f.* (*pl.* **—n**) injury, hardship; wrong, injustice; **—n der Witterung**, inclemency of the weather; **—n des Winters**, rigour *or* severity of winter; *see* **Unbill**.
Un'bild—sam, *adj.* not plastic; inflexible; not pliant. **—ung**, *f.* want of cultivation.
Un'bill, *f.* (**—s**) iniquity; wrong, injustice; insult. **—ig**, *adj.* unfair, unjust; unreasonable; iniquitous; **—iges erträgt kein edles Herz**, a noble mind will not suffer injustice. **—igkeit**, *f.* iniquity; injustice; unjust act.
Un'blutig, *adj.* not bloody, bloodless, without shedding blood, not stained with blood.
Un'botmäßig, *adj.* insubordinate. **—keit**, *f.* (*no pl.*) insubordination.
Un'brauchbar, *adj.* inapplicable; useless; good for nothing, bad. **—keit**, *f.* uselessness; incompetence. *Comp.* **—machung**, *f.* spoiling, rendering unserviceable; dismounting (*cannon*).
Un'bürgerlich, *adj.* uncitizen-like.
Un'bußfertig, *adj.* impenitent; obdurate.
Un'christ, *m.* not a Christian; unbeliever, infidel; heathen. **—lich**, *adj.* unchristian.
Und, *conj.* and; *in old popular songs it often appears almost redundant; it used to give to demonstrative pronouns a relative sense:* **ich ritt — da mein Feinslieb saß**, I rode to where my love sat; **an dem — dem Platze, da — da**, at such and such a place; **kein Brot — kein Geld haben**, to have neither bread nor money; **— ?** and then? and afterwards? well? **er — Furcht haben!** he afraid! **— wenn**, even if; **— ich auch nicht**, nor I either; **fort — fort**, on and on; **für — für**, continually, incessantly.
Un'damm, *m.*; **auf dem — sein**, to feel shaky, not to feel well, to be seedy (*coll.*).
Un'dank, *m.* ingratitude; **— ist der Welt Lohn**, the world pays with ingratitude (*prov.*); **— macht Wohltaten krank**, ingratitude turns away benevolence. **—bar**, *adj.* ungrateful. **—barkeit**, *f.* ingratitude.
Un'datiert, *adj.* undated.
Undefinier'bar, *adj.* indefinable.
Undehn'bar, *adj.* inductile; inextensible; inelastic.
Undeklinier'bar, *adj.* indeclinable.
Undenk'—bar, *adj.* inconceivable, unimaginable. **—lich**, *adj.*; **seit —licher Zeit**, from time immemorial.
Un'deutlich, *adj.* & *adv.* indistinct; obscure, vague; confused; undecided; unintelligible; difficult to read. **—keit**, *f.* indistinctness; obscurity, *etc.*
Un'dicht, *adj.* not water-tight, leaky.
Un'dienlich, *adj.* unserviceable; unsuitable; inopportune.
Un'ding, *n.* (**—es**, *pl.* **—e**) chimera; something non-existent; absurdity; **es ist ein — davon zu reden**, it is absurd to talk of it.
Un'diszipliniert, *adj.* undisciplined.
Un'duldsam, *adj.* intolerant. **—keit**, *f.* intolerance.
Undulie'ren, *v.n.* (*aux.* **h.**) to undulate.
Undurchdring'lich, *adj.* impenetrable; water-tight, waterproof. **—keit**, *f.* impenetrability.
Un'durchforscht, *adj.* unexplored, not investigated.
Un'durchsichtig, *adj.* not transparent, opaque.
Un'eben, *adj.* uneven, rough, rugged; unsuitable, unseemly; **nicht —**, not amiss, not bad, rather good, acceptable. **—heit**, *f.* unevenness; inequality; ruggedness. *Comp.* **—bürtig**, *adj.* inferior rank, not equal in birth.
Un'echt, *adj.* not genuine; false, spurious; imitation; artificial; not fast (*of colours*); improper (*Arith.*); illegitimate. **—heit**, *f.* artificiality; spuriousness.
Un'edel, *adj.* common, vulgar; ignoble; base.
Un'ehelich, *adj.* illegitimate, natural (*child*).
Un'ehr—bar, *adj.* dishonourable; dishonest; disgraceful; immodest, improper. **—barkeit**, *f.* dishonesty; immodesty. **—e**, *f.* dishonour, disgrace. **—lich**, *adj.* dishonest; dishonourable; disgraceful, ignominious; disloyal. **—lichkeit**, *f.* dishonesty; infamy; bad faith. *Comp.* **—erbietig**, *adj.* disrespectful.
Un'eigennützig, *adj.* disinterested, unselfish.
Un'eigentlich, *adj.* & *adv.* not literal, figurative; improper (*of fractions, etc.*).
Un'eingebunden, *adj.* unbound; in sheets.
Un'eingedenk, *adj.* (*with gen.*) forgetful *or* unmindful of; regardless of.
Un'eingenommen, *adj.* unprejudiced; not prepossessed, unbiassed; untaken, unconquered.
Un'eingeschränkt, *adj.* unlimited, unrestrained.
Un'eingeweiht, *adj.* uninitiated; **der —e**, outsider, one who is not in the secret.
Un'einig, *adj.* disunited; at variance; **— sein**, to disagree, to be at variance with a p.; **— werden**, to quarrel, disagree; **ich bin mit mir selber noch —**, I have not quite made up my mind yet. **—keit**, *f.* disunion; dissension; discord.
Uneinnehm'bar, *adj.* impregnable.
Un'einträglich, *adj.* unprofitable, not lucrative.
Uneintreib'bar, *adj.* irrecoverable (*of debts*).
Un'empfänglich, *adj.* not susceptible (**für**, to), unimpressionable.
Un'empfindlich, *adj.* insensible; cold; unfeel-

ing; apathetic; hardhearted; stoical; **für Liebe —sein**, to be insensible to love. **—keit**, *f.* coldness; insensibility, unfeelingness.
Unend'lich, *adj.* & *adv.* endless; infinite; immense; **— klein**, infinitesimal; **eine — kleine Größe**, an infinitesimal quantity. **—e(s)**, *n.* that which is infinite; **ins —e**, ad infinitum; **das geht ins —e**, there is no end to it; **die Teilbarkeit der Materie ins —e**, the infinitesimal divisibility of matter. **—keit**, *f.* infinity; endlessness.
Unentbehr'lich, *adj.* indispensable, absolutely necessary.
Unentgelt'lich, *adj.* & *adv.* free (of charge), gratis, gratuitous.
Un'enthaltsam, *adj.* incontinent, intemperate. **—keit**, *f.* incontinence, intemperance.
Unentleer'bar, *adj.* that cannot be emptied.
Unentrinn'bar, *adj.* inevitable.
Un'entschieden, *adj.* undecided; doubtful; pending; **—e Schlacht**, (**—es Spiel**) drawn battle (game); **—e Frage**, open question. **—heit**, *f.* indecision.
Un'entschlossen, *adj.* undecided; irresolute.
Unentschuld'bar, *adj.* inexcusable.
Unentweg'—bar, —t, *adj.* firm; **seinem Ziele —t zustreben**, to be firmly resolved on attaining one's object.
Un'entwickelt, *adj.* undeveloped, in embryo.
Unentwirr'bar, *adj.* inextricable.
Unentziff'erbar, *adj.* undecipherable.
Unentzünd'bar, *adj.* not inflammable.
Un'erachtet, *see* **Ungeachtet** II.
Un'erbaulich, *adj.* unedifying; low, vulgar.
Unerbitt'lich, *adj.* inexorable, pitiless.
Un'erbrochen, *adj.* intact, unentered; unbroken (*of the seal of a letter*).
Un'erfahren, *adj.* inexperienced; unskilled; raw.
Un'erfindlich, *adj.* undiscoverable, mysterious; **es ist mir —**, I cannot make it out.
Unerforsch'—bar, *adj.* that cannot be explored. **—lich**, *adj.* impenetrable, inscrutable.
Un'erfreulich, *adj.* unpleasant, unsatisfactory; joyless; disagreeable; afflicting; vexatious.
Unerfüll'—bar, *adj.* unrealizable, chimerical. **—t**, *adj.* unfulfilled; not executed *or* accomplished.
Un'ergiebig, *adj.* unproductive, sterile, barren.
Un'ergründ—et, *adj.* unfathomed; unfathomable. **—lich**, *adj.* unfathomable, bottomless; impenetrable, profound.
Un'erheblich, *adj.* insignificant, trifling; light; slight, small; indifferent.
Unerhö'rt, *adj.* unheard, not granted; unheard of; fabulous; exorbitant.
Un'erinnerlich, *adj.* that one cannot recall; **es ist mir —**, it has escaped my memory.
Un'erkannt, *adj.* unrecognized.
Unerkenn'—bar, *adj.* not recognizable. **—tlich**, *adj.* ungrateful. **—tlichkeit**, *f.* ingratitude.
Unerklär'—bar, —lich, *adj.* inexplicable; unaccountable.
Un'erkünstelt, *adj.* unaffected, natural; sincere; true.
Un'erläßlich, *adj.* indispensable; essential.
Un'erlaubt, *adj.* unlawful, illicit; forbidden. **—heit**, *f.* unlawfulness; illegality.
Unermeß'lich, *adj.* immense; infinite; immeasurable.
Un'ermüd—et, *adj.* unwearied, active, stirring. **—lich**, *adj.* indefatigable. **—lichkeit**, *f.* indefatigableness.
Un'erörtert, *adj.* undebated, undiscussed.
Un'erquicklich, *adj.* unpleasant; disagreeable.
Unerreich'—bar, *adj.* unattainable; inaccessible. **—t**, *adj.* unattained, unrivalled.
Unersätt'lich, *adj.* insatiable; devouring.
Unerschöpf'lich, *adj.* inexhaustible.
Un'erschrocken, *adj.* intrepid; undaunted. **—heit**, *f.* intrepidity.
Unerschüt'ter—lich, *adj.* immovable; imperturbable; unflinching, firm, steady. **—t**, *adj.* unshaken, steadfast.
Unerschwing'lich, *adj.* unattainable; exorbitant; **das ist mir —**, I cannot afford it, it is too dear for me.
Unersetz'—bar, —lich, *adj.* irreparable, irretrievable, irrecoverable.
Un'ersichtlich, *adj.* not apparent, not clear, mysterious.
Un'ersprießlich, *adj.* unprofitable, useless.
Un'ersteiglich, *adj.* inaccessible; unscalable.
Unerträg'lich, *adj.* intolerable, insufferable.
Un'erwachsen, *adj.* immature, young.
Un'erwartet, *adj.* unexpected; sudden.
Unerweich'—bar, —lich, *adj.* not to be softened; inflexible.
Unerweis'lich, *adj.* that cannot be demonstrated *or* proved.
Un'erwidert, *adj.* unanswered (*letter*); unreturned, unrequited (*love*).
Un'erwiesen, *adj.* unproved; not proven (*Scotch Law*).
Un'erwünscht, *adj.* unwished for; unwelcome.
Un'erzeugt, *adj.* unbegotten.
Un'erzogen, *adj.* uneducated; unmannerly, ill-bred.
Unexplodier'bar, *adj.* non-explosive, inexplosive.
Un'fähig, *adj.* incapable (*of*), unfit (*for*); incompetent; **— zu zahlen**, insolvent.
Un'fall, *m.* accident; misfortune, disaster. *Comp.* **—versicherung**, *f.* insurance against accidents. **—versicherungs=gesetz**, *n.* act dealing with accident insurance, Workmen's Compensation Act.
Un'farbig, *adj.* colourless; uncoloured, undyed.
Unfaß'—bar, —lich, *adj.* unseizable, difficult to grasp, unintelligible; incomprehensible.
Unfehl'bar, *adj.* & *adv.* unfailing; infallible; certain, sure. **—keits=dogma**, *n.* dogma of infallibility.
Un'fein, *adj.* coarse; indelicate; boorish, unmannerly, rude.
Un'fern, I. *adj.* & *adv.* near. II. *prep.* (*with gen., dat. or* **von**) near, not far from.
Un'fertig, *adj.* unfinished; unprepared.
Un'flat, *m.* (**—es**) filth, dirt; dirty person.
Un'flät—er, *m.* (**—ers**, *pl.* **—er**) dirty, beastly person. **—erei'**, *f.* filthiness; nastiness; lewdness. **—ig**, *adj.* filthy; nasty; lewd. **—igkeit**, *see* **—erei**.
Un'fleiß, *m.* want of application; indolence. **—ig**, *adj.* indolent; not industrious.
Un'folgsam, *adj.* disobedient, wilful, wayward (*of children*).
Un'form, *f.* deformity; deformed person; monster.
Un'förm—ig, —lich, *adj.* misshapen; shapeless; irregular; unwieldy. **—lichkeit**, *f.* deformity; (*pl.*) monstrosities.
Un'freigebig, *adj.* illiberal, parsimonious.
Un'freisinnig, *adj.* illiberal, narrow-minded.
Un'freiwillig, *adj.* involuntary, compulsory.
Un'freund—lich, *adj.* unfriendly; unkind; disobliging; ungracious; cold; unpleasant. **—lichkeit**, *f.* unfriendliness; disobligingness; unkindness; repulsiveness; inclemency (*of the weather*). **—schaftlich**, *adj.* unfriendly.
Un'fried—e, *m.* (**—ens**, [*less good:* **—en**, *m.* (**—ens**)] discord, disunion, want of harmony. **—lich**, *adj.* discordant; quarrelsome.
Un'fruchtbar, *adj.* unfruitful, unproductive; barren; **auf —en Boden fallen**, to fall upon stony ground, to produce no effect *or* impression upon a person.
Un'fug, *m.* (**—s**) wrong; mischief, disorder, disturbance; misconduct; nuisance; **grober**

—, gross misconduct, disorderly conduct. *Comp.* —**paragraph**, *m.* Riot Act.

Un'fügsam, *adj.* unyielding, unaccommodating; intractable.

Unfühl'bar, *adj.* impalpable, intangible.

Un'fürstlich, *adj.* unprincely.

Un'galant, *adj.* ungallant, discourteous; ungentlemanly.

Ungang'bar, *adj.* impassable, impracticable; unfrequented; unusual, obsolete; not current (*of coins*); unsaleable.

Un'gar, *adj. & adv.* underdone, insufficiently done *or* cooked; raw.

Un'gastlich, *adj.* inhospitable. —**keit**, *f.* inhospitality.

Un'geachtet, I. *adj.* disregarded, not esteemed. II. *prep.* (*with preceding or following gen. or dat.*) notwithstanding, in spite of; **dessen** — in spite of, for all that. III. *conj.* though, although.

Un'geahndet, *adj.* unpunished, unrevenged.

Un'geahnt, *adj.* unthought of, unsuspected; unexpected.

Un'gebahnt, *adj.* unbeaten; untrodden.

Un'gebändigt, *adj.* untamed, unbroken; unsubdued.

Un'gebärd—e, *f.* (*pl.* —**en**) unruliness, turbulence. —**ig**, *adj.* unruly.

Un'gebaut, *adj.* unbuilt; untilled, uncultivated.

Un'gebeten, *adj.* uninvited; unasked; of one's own accord; —**er Gast**, intruder, sponger.

Un'gebeugt, *adj.* unbent, uncurbed. —**heit**, *f.* indomitable spirit, courage, fortitude.

Un'gebildet, *adj.* unformed; uncultivated, rude; unmannerly; uneducated, unlettered.

Un'gebleicht, *adj.* unbleached.

Un'geblümt, *adj.* without a pattern, plain.

Un'gebräuchlich, *adj.* unusual; unused.

Un'gebraucht, *adj.* unused, quite new.

Un'gebühr, *f.* injustice; abuse; indecency, impropriety; excess; **zur** —, unduly, to excess. —**end**, —**lich**, *adj.* undue, excessive; unsuitable; improper; indecent; unwarrantable. —**lichkeit**, *f.* impropriety, unsuitableness.

Un'gebunden, *adj.* unbound, in sheets (*often abbr.* **ungeb.**); free, unrestrained; loose, unbridled; licentious; —**e Rede**, unrestrained speech; prose. —**heit**, *f.* freedom, unrestraint, free and easy way(s); liberty; dissoluteness, looseness, licentiousness.

Un'gedeckt, *adj.* uncovered; unprotected; **der Tisch ist noch** —, the table is not yet laid.

Un'gedeihlich, *adj.* unprofitable; thriftless; not nourishing, unwholesome.

Un'geduld, *f.* impatience; impatient person. —**ig**, *adj.* impatient.

Un'geeignet, *adj.* unsuitable, unfit; inopportune. —**heit**, *f.* unsuitableness, unfitness, inappropriateness.

Un'gefähr, I. *adj. & adv.* casual, accidental; probable; approximate; **ein** —**er Stoß**, a chance blow. II. *adv.* casually, by chance; about, near, almost; **vor** — **einem Monate**, about a month ago; **das war es** —, **was er mir sagte**, that was pretty much what he said to me. III. *n.* (—**s**) chance; **es auf das** — **ankommen lassen**, to leave to, to let things take their chance; **von** —, by chance, by accident; **er fragte von** —, he chanced to ask.

Un'gefährdet, *adj.* safe, not endangered.

Un'gefährlich, *adj.* not dangerous, safe.

Un'gefällig, *adj.* discourteous, unaccommodating; disobliging; disagreeable.

Un'gefärbt, *adj.* undyed; colourless; unpainted; unvarnished, true, sincere; —**e Seide**, raw silk, Tussah silk.

Un'geflügelt, *adj.* wingless, apterous.

Ungefrier'bar, *adj.* uncongealable.

Un'gefüg—e, —**ig**, *adj.* unpliant, unyielding; disobliging; ill-shaped, clumsy, huge.

Un'gegliedert, *adj.* without joints *or* limbs; unorganized; inarticulate.

Un'gegohren, *adj.* unfermented.

Un'gegründet, *adj.* unfounded; false; imaginary.

Un'gehalten, *adj.* unkept, unfulfilled; not sustained; displeased; angry; indignant; **über eine S., auf einen — sein**, to be angry at something, with some one; — **werden**, to become angry, to fly into a passion.

Un'geheißen, I. *adj.* unbidden, not ordered. II. *adv.* voluntarily, of one's own accord.

Un'geheuchelt, *adj.* unfeigned, sincere.

Un'geheuer, I. *adj.* monstrous; huge, colossal; enormous; atrocious; frightful; **das** —**e dieses Krieges**, the atrocity of this war. II. *n.* (—**s**, *pl.* —) monster. —**lich**, *adj.* monstrous. —**lichkeit**, *f.* monstrous character, atrocity; enormity.

Un'gehobelt, *adj.* not planed *or* polished; rude, rough, uncouth, boorish.

Un'gehofft, *adj.* unhoped for, undreamt of.

Un'gehörig, *adj.* undue; unseemly, improper; impertinent. —**keit**, *f.* impropriety; irregularity.

Un'gehorsam, I. *adj.* disobedient, intractable; insubordinate; **wegen** —**en Ausbleibens vor Gericht verurteilt werden**, to suffer judgment to go by default. II. *m.* (—**s**) disobedience; insubordination.

Un'gehudelt, *adj.* undisturbed, in peace.

Un'geistlich, *adj.* unspiritual; worldly; lay; unclerical, secular.

Un'gekränkt, *adj.* unvexed; in peace; unhurt; **der Vorwurf läßt mich** —, that reproach does not mortify *or* disturb me.

Un'gekünstelt, *adj.* unaffected, simple, natural, frank. —**heit**, *f.* artlessness, unaffectedness.

Un'geladen, *adj.* not loaded, empty; uninvited, unbidden.

Un'geläutert, *adj.* unclarified, unpurified, unrefined.

Un'geleckt, *adj.* unlicked, unpolished; shapeless, rough; —**er Bär**, unlicked cub, regular bear. —**heit**, *f.* boorishness.

Un'geleg—en, *adj.* inconvenient; inopportune; unsuitable. —**enheit**, *f.* inconvenience; trouble; unseasonableness; **einem** —**enheiten machen**, to inconvenience a p., to give a p. trouble. —**t**, *adj.* unlaid; —**te Eier**, unhatched projects.

Un'gelehr—ig, *adj.* indocile; not quick in learning; unintelligent. —**t**, *adj.* unlearned, illiterate. —**theit**, *f.* want of learning, ignorance.

Un'geleimt, *adj.* unsized; unglued.

Un'geleitet, *adj.* not guided; unaccompanied, by oneself.

Un'gelenk, *adj.* inflexible, not supple; stiff; awkward, clumsy. —**heit**, *f.* stiffness; awkwardness.

Un'gelöscht, *adj.* unquenched; —**er Kalk**, unslaked lime, quick-lime.

Un'gemach, *n.* (—(e)**s**) privation, hardship; trouble; toil; evil; calamity; — **der Witterung**, inclemency of the weather.

Un'gemächlich, *adj.* toilsome; uncomfortable, troublesome. —**keit**, *f.* inconvenience, discomfort.

Un'gemein, *adj.* extraordinary; uncommon; — **bewegt**, deeply affected, strangely moved; — **erfreut**, exceedingly pleased *or* glad.

Un'gemessen, *adj.* unmeasured; boundless; immense; immoderate. —**heit**, *f.* (*pl.* —**heiten**) excess; boundlessness.

Un'gemünzt, *adj.* uncoined; —**es Gold (Silber)**, bullion.

Un'genannt, *adj.* anonymous; nameless.

Un'geneigt, *adj.* disinclined; unfriendly. —**heit**, *f.* disinclination; illwill.

Ungenie'rt, *adj.* unembarrassed, free and easy;

unceremonious. —**heit**, *f.* unconstraint, free and easy way(s); unceremoniousness.
Un'genießbar, *adj.* unenjoyable; unpalatable; uneatable; insipid; dull, tedious; unbearable; — **sein**, to be in a bad humour; to be no good (*coll.*).
Un'genossen, *adj.* untasted.
Un'genüg—end, *adj.* insufficient. —**sam**, *adj.* exacting; insatiable. —**samkeit**, *f.* exactingness, unreasonableness; insatiability.
Un'genützt, *adj.* unprofited by; unused.
Un'geordnet, *adj.* disorganized; unarranged; —**er Lebenswandel**, dissolute life.
Un'geprüft, *adj.* unexamined; untried, untested; unaudited; —**er Lehrer**, uncertificated teacher.
Un'geputzt, *adj.* uncleaned; untrimmed (*of lamps*); unadorned, simple.
Un'gerächt, *adj.* unrevenged; unavenged, unpunished.
Un'g(e)rad—e, *adj.* not straight; uneven; odd; —**er Takt**, triple time. *Comp.* —**zählig**, *adj.* uneven.
[1]**Un'geraten**, *adj.* abortive, checked in growth; stunted; that has failed, unsuccessful; spoiled; depraved; —**er Sohn**, undutiful *or* unnatural son; —**e Kinder**, spoiled undutiful children.
[2]**Un'geraten**, *adj.* not guessed, unsolved.
Un'gerecht, *adj.* unjust, unrighteous. —**igkeit**, *f.* injustice.
Un'gerechtfertigt, *adj.* unjustified, unwarranted.
Un'gereimt, *adj.* unrhymed; absurd; unreasonable; preposterous.
Un'geritten, *adj.*; —**es Pferd**, horse that has never been ridden.
Un'gern, *adv.* (*comp. sometimes* —**er**) unwillingly; regretfully; **ich sehe** —, I am sorry to see; **gern oder** —, willy-nilly, whether you like it or not.
Un'gerochen, *adj. see* **Ungerächt**.
Un'gerügt, *adj.* unblamed, uncensured; **ich kann nicht** — **lassen** . . ., I cannot help censuring . . .
Un'gerupft, *adj.* unplucked; — **davon kommen**, to get off without loss *or* with a whole skin, to get off unfleeced.
Un'gesagt, *adj.* unsaid; **das will ich** — (**sein**) **lassen**, I don't wish to speak of that.
Un'gesäuert, *adj.* unleavened, azymous.
[1]**Un'gesäumt**, *adj.* seamless.
[2]**Un'gesäumt**, I. *adj.* prompt, immediate. II. *adv.* without delay, at once, immediately.
Un'geschehen, *adj.* undone; **man kann das nicht** — **machen**, it cannot be undone.
Un'gescheut, *adj.* fearless; intrepid; bold, audacious.
Un'geschichtlich, *adj.* unhistorical, not historical; fictitious.
Un'geschick, I. *n.* (—(e)s) adverse fate (*rare*); awkwardness. II. *m.* (—es) awkward person (*rare*). —**lichkeit**, *f.* awkwardness; gaucherie; ineptitude, incapacity.
Un'geschickt, *adj.* awkward; gauche; stupid, inept; clumsy; — **läßt grüßen**! how awkward you are! what a clever thing to do (*iron.*).
Un'geschlacht, *adj.* uncouth; clumsy; boorish, rude; uncivilized; coarse.
Un'geschliffen, *adj.* unpolished; blunt; rough; rude; coarse. —**heit**, *f.* impoliteness, roughness.
Un'geschmack, *m.* tastelessness; bad taste.
Un'geschmälert, *adj.* undiminished; whole; intact.
Un'geschmeidig, *adj.* not malleable; inductile; not supple; unpliant; inflexible, intractable.
Un'geschminkt, *adj.* unpainted; unvarnished, plain; undisguised, true, sincere.
Un'geschoren, *adj.* unshorn; uncut (*of velvet*); unmolested; **lassen Sie mich** —! let me alone! leave me in peace!
Un'geschwächt, *adj.* unweakened; unimpaired; **mit** —**en Mitteln**, with undiminished means; **mit** —**en Kräften**, vigorously, energetically.
Un'geschworen, *adj.* & *adv.* unsworn; **ich glaube es Ihnen** —, I take your word for it.
Un'gesell—ig, *adj.* unsociable, unsocial; shy; misanthropic. —**schaftlich**, *adj.* anti-social.
Un'gesetz—lich, *adj.* illegal. —**lichkeit**, *f.* illegality. *Comp.* —**mäßig**, *adj.* illegitimate, illegal.
Un'gesittet, *adj.* unmannerly; illbred; rude. —**heit**, *f.* rudeness, unmannerliness.
Un'gesprächig, *adj.* taciturn, silent.
Un'gestalt, I. *adj.* shapeless; misshapen. II. *f.* deformity. —**et**, *see* **Ungestalt** I. —**heit**, *f.* deformity; monstrosity.
Un'gestempelt, *adj.* unstamped; undefaced (*stamps*).
Un'gestielt, *adj.* without a handle; stalkless, sessile (*Bot.*).
Un'gestillt, *adj.* unappeased; unstanched (*bleeding*); unsatisfied (*wish*); unquenched (*thirst*).
Un'gestört, *adj.* & *adv.* untroubled; uninterrupted; peaceful. —**heit**, *f.* tranquillity.
Un'gestraft, *adj.* not punished. *adv.* with impunity. —**heit**, *f.* impunity.
Un'gestüm, I. *adj.* stormy; blustering; raging; violent; impetuous; **durch das** —**e Wetter**, by stress of weather. II. *n.* impetuosity, violence.
Un'gesucht, *adj.* unsought; natural, artless. —**heit**, *f.* absence of affectation, artlessness, naturalness.
Un'gesund, *adj.* unhealthy; sickly; unwholesome.
Un'geteilt, *adj.* undivided; one, entire; general.
Un'getrübt, *adj.* untroubled; serene, unclouded; clear.
Un'getüm, *n.* (—s, *pl.* —e) monster.
Un'gewandt, *adj.* wanting in agility, awkward, slow.
Un'gewaschen, *adj.* unwashed; dirty; absurd; —**es Zeug**! stuff and nonsense! —**es Maul**, insolent *or* pert tongue; slanderous tongue.
Un'gewiß, *adj.* uncertain, doubtful; tottering; precarious; irresolute; problematic; depending on circumstances; **aufs** —(**ss**)**e**, at random —(**ss**)**enhaft**, *adj.* unconscientious. —**heit**, *f.* doubt, uncertainty; **einen in** —**heit halten**, to keep a p. in suspense.
Un'gewitter, *n.* (—s, *pl.* —) violent storm.
Un'gewitzigt, *adj.* silly, inexperienced.
Un'gewogen, *adj.* unweighed; unfavourable; **einem** — **sein**, not to care for s.o., to dislike a p. —**heit**, *f.* dislike, ill-will.
Un'gewohn—heit, *f.* unwontedness, desuetude. —**t**, *adj.* unaccustomed; unusual. —**theit**, *see* —**heit**.
Un'gewöhnlich, *adj.* unusual, exceptional; extraordinary; rare; strange.
Un'gezählt, *adj.* unnumbered, uncounted, untold; in the lump.
Un'gezähmt, *adj.* untamed; unbridled (*passions*).
Un'gezähnt, *adj.* imperforate (*of postage stamps*)
Un'gezäumt, *adj.* unbridled, unrestrained.
Un'geziefer, *n.* (—s, *pl.* —) vermin; noxious insects.
Un'geziemend, *adj.* unseemly; improper.
Un'gezogen, *adj.* badly brought up; ill-bred; rude, uncivil; insolent; indecorous! —**es Kind**, naughty, disobedient child. —**heit**, *f.* naughtiness; rudeness.
Un'gezügelt, *adj.* unbridled, unrestrained.
Un'gezwirnt, *adj.* untwisted.
Un'gezwungen, *adj.* & *adv.* unconstrained, free; natural, unaffected; easy; **etwas** — **thun**, to do s.th. naturally *or* spontaneously, of one's own accord.
Un'glaub—e, *m.* (—**ens**) incredulity; unbelief. —**lich** (*us. pron.* **unglaub'lich**), *adj.* incredible. —**lichkeit**, *f.* incredibility. *Comp.* —**würdig**, *adj.* unworthy of belief, incredible, unlikely, unauthenticated.

Un'gläubig, *adj.* incredulous, sceptical; unbelieving, irreligious; infidel. **—e(r),** *m.* unbeliever; sceptic; incredulous person.

Un'gleich, I. *adj.* unequal; unlike, dissimilar; uneven, odd; disproportionate; variable, changeable; incompatible; **ein —er Handschuh,** an odd glove. II. *adv.* incomparably, much; **— besser,** far better; **— schöner,** much more beautiful. **—heit,** *f.* inequality; dissimilarity; difference; disproportion; (*pl.*) uneven places; (*pl.*) variations. *Comp.* **—artig,** *adj.* of a different kind; heterogeneous; uncongenial. **—artigkeit,** *f.* dissimilarity of nature; heterogeneousness. **—blätterig,** *adj.* heterophyllous. **—förmig,** *adj.* not uniform; dissimilar; irregular; unsymmetrical; uneven (*as timber*). **—mäßig,** *adj.* disproportionate; unequal. **—namig,** *adj.* having different names. **—seitig,** *adj.* with unequal sides, inequilateral; scalene (*of triangles*).

Un'glimpf, *m.* (—(e)s) rigour, harshness; injustice; disrespect; insult, outrage. **—lich,** *adj.* ungentle; harsh; insulting; **einen —lich behandeln,** to deal harshly with a person.

Un'glück, *n.* (—(e)s, *no pl.; replaced by* **Unglücksfälle**) mishap; misfortune; ill-luck; piece of ill-luck; adversity; calamity; disaster; distress; misery; **zum —(e),** unfortunately; **kein — so groß, es hat ein Glück im Schoß,** it is an ill wind blows no one any good (*prov.*); **das — davon ist,** the worst of it is; **ein — kommt selten allein,** misfortunes seldom come singly; one misfortune brings on another; it never rains but it pours. **—lich,** *adj. & adv.* unhappy; unlucky; unsucessful; disastrous; sad; fatal; **—lich ablaufen,** to turn out badly, to miscarry, to end disastrously; **—licherweise,** unluckily; **—lich spielen,** to have a run of ill-luck, to be unlucky (*at play*); **das Erste, was —lich ging,** the first thing that went wrong. **—selig,** *adj.* unhappy; unfortunate; disastrous. **—seligkeit,** *f.* misery; calamitousness. *Comp.* **—s=bote,** *m.* bringer of bad tidings; bird of ill omen. **—s=brief,** *m.* letter containing ill news. **—s=fall,** *m.* misfortune; casualty, (fatal) accident. **—s=fälle,** *pl. often used as pl. of* **Unglück** *q.v.* **—s=genoß, —s=gefährte,** *m.* companion in misfortune. **—s=kind,** *n.* child of woe; unlucky wight. **—s=prophet,** *m.* prophet of evil; croaker. **—s=rabe,** *m.* bird of ill omen, croaker. **—s=schwanger,** *adj.* big with misfortune. **—s=schwer,** *adj.* calamitous. **—s=stifter(in,** *f.*) *m.* mischief-maker. **—s=stunde,** *m.* unlucky hour. **—s=vogel,** *m.* bird of ill omen. **—s=wurm,** *m.* wretched, miserable creature (*coll.*).

Un'gnade, *f.* displeasure; dislike; **in —,** in disgrace, out of favour; **sich** (*dat.*) **jemandes — zuziehen,** to incur a p.'s displeasure, to get into his bad books.

Un'gnädig, *adj. & adv.* ungracious; unfavourable; harsh; unkind; cross; angry; **— aufnehmen,** to take amiss.

Un'göttlich, *adj.* ungodly; unworthy of God *or* of a god.

Un'grammatisch, *adj.* ungrammatical, contrary to the rules of grammar.

Un'grund, *m.* groundlessness, baselessness.

Un'gründlich, *adj.* superficial, shallow. **—keit,** *f.* superficiality, shallowness.

Un'gültig, *adj.* not current; invalid; worthless; inadmissible; not available (*as a ticket*); **für — erklären, — machen,** to annul. **—keit,** *f.* invalidity, nullity; uselessness. *Comp.* **—machung,** *f.* invalidation.

Un'gunst, *f.* disfavour; unkindness; **— der Verhältnisse,** unpropitiousness of circumstances; **— des Wetters,** inclemency of the weather; **zu seinen —en,** against him.

Un'günstig, *adj.* unfavourable; disadvantageous; **einem — sein,** to be ill-disposed towards s.o.; **—er Bericht,** unfavourable report.

Un'gut, *adj.;* **für — nehmen,** to take amiss; **nehmen Sie es nicht für —, wenn ich Ihnen sage,** don't think it unkind of me to tell you; **nichts für —!** no offence! no harm meant!

Un'gütig, *adj. & adv.* unfriendly, unkind; **— aufnehmen,** to take amiss.

Unhalt'bar, *adj.* not durable; untenable, indefensible (*of a position*); that cannot be kept (*of promises*). **—keit,** *f.* want of durability; untenableness.

Un'heil, *n.* (—s) harm, hurt; disaster; evil; **— stiften, anrichten,** to cause mischief. *Comp.* **—bringend,** *adj.* hurtful, mischievous; sad; unlucky; fatal. **—schwanger,** *adj.* fraught with misfortune. **—stifter,** *m.* mischief-maker. **—voll,** *adj.* harmful; pernicious; calamitous.

Unheil'bar, *adj.* incurable; irreparable.

Un'heilig, *adj.* unholy; profane; worldly.

Unheil'sam, *adj.* unsalutary; insalubrious.

Un'heim—isch, *adj.* strange, foreign, exotic. **—lich,** *adj.* uncomfortable, uneasy; gloomy; sinister; very (*coll.*); **es ward ihm dabei —lich zu Mute,** he grew uneasy at this; **ein —lich gelehrtes Haus,** an awfully learned chap (*coll.*); **—lich viel Geld,** lots of money (*coll.*).

Unheiz'bar, *adj.;* **ein —es Zimmer,** a room without a stove *or* fireplace, a room that cannot be heated.

Un'höflich, *adj.* impolite, uncivil.

Un'hold, (**Un'holdig** (*rare*),) I. *adj.* ungracious; unfriendly; unkind; ill-disposed, hostile. II. *m.* (—s, *pl.* —e) repulsively ugly person; monster; malicious foe; evil spirit; demon; sorcerer. **—in,** *f.* fiend; witch; vixen.

Unhör'bar, *adj.* inaudible, imperceptible.

Unie'r—en, *v.a.* to unite; **—te,** members of the union; members of the United Protestant Church (*in Prussia: Lutherans and Calvinists*).

Uni—fo'rm, *adj. & f.* (*pl.* **—formen**) uniform; **in großer —form,** in full uniform, in full-dress regimentals, in full war-paint (*coll.*); **kleine —,** undress uniform; **nicht in —,** in plain clothes. *Comp.* **—formie'ren,** *v.a.* to dress in uniform; to render uniform. **—formie'=rung,** *f.* giving of uniforms; making uniform. **—formitä't,** *f.* uniformity. **—ge'nitus,** *adj* only-begotten. **—kum** (*pron.* **U'nikum**), *n.* (**—kums,** *pl.* **—ka**) unique instance; unique example *or* copy. **—o'n,** *f.* (*pl.* **—onen**) union. **—oni'st,** *m.* (**—onis'ten, —onis'ten**) unionist; (*pl.*) federals. **—so'n,** *adj.* monotone, monotonous. **—so'no,** I. *n.* unison. II. *adv.* in unison. **—ta'rier,** *m.* (**—tariers,** *pl.* **—tarier**) Unitarian. **—ta'risch,** *adj.* Unitarian. **—versa'l, —verse'll,** *adj.* universal. **—versitä't,** *see* **Universität.** **—versal'=erbe,** *m.* sole heir; residuary legatee. **—versal'=genie,** *n.* universal genius, all round man; jack of all trades (*iron.*). **—versal'=mittel,** *n.* panacea, specific. **—ver'sum,** *n.* (**—versums**) universe.

Un'intereff—ant, *adj.* uninteresting. **—ie'rt,** *adj.* uninterested, not interested. **—iert'heit,** *f.* want of interest.

Universitä't, *f.* (*pl.* **—en**) university; **die — Cambridge beziehen,** to go to the University of Cambridge; **die — verlassen,** to leave the university, to go down; **zur — kommen,** to come up. *Comp.* **—s=druckerei,** *f.* University Press. **—s=ferien,** *pl.* vacation; **die großen —sferien,** the long vacation. **—s=freund,** *m.* college friend; fellow-student. **—s=gebühren,** *pl.* university fees *or* dues. **—s=jahr,** *n.* academical year. **—s=kasse,** *f.* university chest. **—s=leben,** *n.* life at the university; college life; college days. **—s=lehrer, —s=**

professor, *m.* professor, reader, lecturer at a university; **außerordentlicher —sprofessor (der deutschen Sprache und Litteratur)** university lecturer (in German). **—s=pedell**, *m.* proctor's man, vice-chancellor's man, beadle, bull-dog (*sl.*). **—s=rektor**, *m.* chancellor of the university; vice-chancellor of the university. **—s=richter**, *m.* member of the university court of discipline; proctor. **—s=unterricht**, *m.* university instruction *or* teaching. **—s=vorlesung**, *f.* university lecture. **—s=wesen**, *n.* university affairs, university management. **—s=zeit**, *f.* time spent at the university, college years.

Un'ke, *f.* (*pl.* **—n**) orange-speckled toad; croaker, grumbler, prophet of evil (*coll.*). *Comp.* **—n=gesang**, *m.* croaking of toads. **—n=ruf**, *m.* ominous croaking, ominous cry.

Un'kennt—lich, (**Un'kennbar**,) *adj.* that cannot be recognized; **—lich machen**, to disguise. **—lichkeit**, *f.* irrecognizable condition. **—nis**, *f.* ignorance; **einen in —nis über eine S. (er)halten**, to keep a p. in the dark about a th.

Un'keusch, *adj.* unchaste, lascivious, impure, lewd. **—heit**, *f.* unchastity, lewdness.

Un'kindlich, *adj.* unchildlike, precocious; disingenuous; unfilial, undutiful.

Un'kirchlich, *adj.* secular, worldly; not attached to the church; anticlerical. **—keit**, *f.* worldliness.

Un'klagbar, *adj.* not indictable, not actionable; that cannot be recovered by law.

Un'klar, *adj.* not clear; muddy, thick; foul; misty; foggy; unintelligible; obscure; uncertain. **—heit**, *f.* want of clearness, obscurity.

Un'klug, *adj.* imprudent; impolitic; thoughtless, silly.

Un'königlich, *adj.* unkingly; disloyal to the king.

Un'körperlich, *adj.* incorporeal; immaterial; spiritual. **—keit**, *f.* immateriality; incorporeity.

Un'kosten, *pl.* expense(s); costs; **nach Abzug aller —**, all charges (expenses) being deducted *or* paid; **auf meine —**, at my expense; **einen in — stürzen**, to put a p. to expense, to plunge a person into expense.

Un'kräftig, *adj.* weak, feeble; inefficacious; invalid; low, sloppy (*of diet*).

Un'kraut, *n.* weed, weeds; **— vergeht nicht**, ill weeds grow apace (*prov.*).

Un'kriegerisch, *adj.* not martial; peaceful.

Un'kultur, *f.* want of culture *or* civilization.

Unkünd'bar, *adj.* not redeemable, consolidated; **—e Papiere**, consolidated stocks, consols. **—barkeit**, *f.* irredeemableness.

Un'kund—e, *f.* want of knowledge *or* acquaintance with, ignorance. **—ig**, *adj.* (*with gen.*) ignorant of, unacquainted with; **des Griechischen —ig**, knowing no Greek.

Unland'bar, *adj.* inaccessible by sea.

Un'längst, *adv.* of late; recently, the other day.

Un'lauter, *adj.* impure; ignoble; self-interested.

Unleid'lich, *adj.* intolerable, unbearable.

Unlenk'—bar, **—sam**, *adj.* unmanageable; intractable. **—samkeit**, *f.* unruliness.

Unle'serlich, (**Unles'bar**,) *adj.* illegible; unreadable; **— schreiben**, to scrawl. **—keit**, *f.* illegibility.

Unleug'bar, *adj.* undeniable, incontestable; evident. **—keit**, *f.* undeniableness.

Un'lieb, *adj.* vexatious, unpleasant; not dear; **das ist mir —**, I am sorry for it; **es ist mir nicht — zu hören**, I am glad to hear that; **deshalb ist es mir nicht —er**, I don't like it the worse for that. **—sam**, *adj.* disagreeable.

Un'löblich, *adj.* not praiseworthy; blameworthy.

Un'logisch, *adj.* illogical.

Unlös'bar, **Unlös'lich**, *adj.* insoluble; indissoluble; inextricable. **—keit**, *f.* insolubility.

Unlöt'bar, *adj.* that cannot be soldered.

Un'lust, *f.* dislike, disinclination; ennui; discomfort; repugnance; aversion; disgust. **—ig**, *adj.* & *adv.* sad; dull; morose; disinclined, averse; disagreeable.

Un'manier, *f.* see **Unart** I. **—lich**, *adj.* & *adv.* unmannerly, boorish; awkward; **sich —lich aufführen**, to behave in an ill-bred *or* ungentlemanly way. **—lichkeit**, *f.* unmannerliness; awkwardness.

Unmann'bar, *adj.* not come to puberty; unmarriageable (*of girls*). **—keit**, *f.* impuberty.

Un'männlich, *adj.* unmanly; effeminate; cowardly. **—keit**, *f.* unmanliness; weakness; effeminacy.

Un'masse, *f.* enormous quantity *or* number.

Un'maßgeblich, *adj.* not authoritative *or* dictatorial; **nach meiner —en Meinung**, speaking under correction, in my humble opinion.

Un'mäßig, *adj.* immoderate; intemperate; excessive, enormous; dissolute. **—keit**, *f.* excess; intemperance, *etc.*

Un'menge, *see* **Unmasse**.

Un'mensch, *m.* inhuman person; monster; **was für ein —**, what a feelingless brute! **ich bin kein —**, I will let myself be moved, I will do it, I will fall in with it (*hum.*). **—lich**, *adj.* inhuman; barbarous; (*pron.* **unmensch'lich**) superhuman; vast, prodigious; exorbitant, tremendous (*coll.*); **—liche Kraft**, superhuman strength. **—lichkeit**, *f.* inhumanity, cruelty, barbarousness, ferocity.

Unmerk'—lich, *adj.* imperceptible; insensible; latent. **—lichkeit**, **—barkeit**, *f.* imperceptibleness.

Unmeß'bar, *adj.* immeasurable.

Unmit'teil—bar, *adj.* incommunicable. **—barkeit**, *f.* incommunicableness. **—sam**, *adj.* uncommunicative, reserved, taciturn. **—samkeit**, *f.* reserve.

Un'mittelbar, *adj.* immediate, direct; proximate; **—er Sinn**, literal sense (*of a passage*); **sich — an einen wenden**, to apply directly to a person; **—e Reichsstände**, immediate states of the empire. **—keit**, *f.* directness.

Un'modern, **Un'modisch**, *adj.* old-fashioned, unfashionable, out of fashion, antiquated.

Unmög'lich, *adj.* & *adv.* impossible; **ich kann es — thun**, it would be impossible for me to do that; **Schiff — vor Montag**, no vessel till Monday (*C. L.*); **—es kann man von niemand verlangen**, one must not expect impossibilities. **—keit**, *f.* impossibility.

Un'monarchisch, *adj.* contrary to monarchical principles, not monarchical.

Un'moralisch, *adj.* immoral.

Un'motiviert, *adj.* devoid of a motive *or* reason, uncalled for; not sufficiently motived.

Un'mündig, *adj.* minor, not of age; **—es Kind**, young infant. **—keit**, *f.* minority.

Un'musikalisch, *adj.* unmusical, not musical.

Un'mut, *m.* ill-humour; depression, displeasure. **—ig**, *adj.* angry, displeased, annoyed, put out. *Comp.* **—s=voll**, *adj.* gloomy, dejected.

Unnachahm'—bar, *adj.* not to be imitated. **—lich**, *adj.* inimitable.

Un'nachgiebig, *adj.* inflexible, hard; stubborn.

Unnachläß'lich, *adj.* not to be remitted; irremissible; unpardonable.

Un'nachsichtig, *adj.* unrelenting, strict, severe.

Unnah'bar, *adj.* inaccessible, unapproachable. **—keit**, *f.* inaccessibility.

Un'natur, *f.* unnaturalness; monstrosity.

Un'natürlich, *adj.* unnatural; monstrous; affected, forced. **—keit**, *f.* unnaturalness; anomaly; constraint; affectation.

Unnenn'bar, *adj.* unutterable; inexpressible.

Un'nötig, *adj.* unnecessary, superfluous; useless.

Un'nütz, *adj.* & *adv.* useless, unprofitable, vain; superfluous; good-for-nothing; **—es Geschwätz**, idle talk; **—es Zeug**, trash, nonsense; **den Namen Gottes — im Munde führen**, to take the name of God in vain; **sich — machen**, to make o.s. obnoxious, to be forward. **—lich**, *adj.* useless; idle. **—lichkeit**, *f.* uselessness, fruitlessness.

Un'ord—entlich, *adj. & adv.* disorderly; confused; untidy. **—nung**, *f.* disorder; confusion; **in —nung bringen**, to put out of order, to throw into confusion, to disorder, confuse, disorganize.

Un'organisch, *adj.* inorganic.

Un'—ort, *m.* unsuitable place (*poet.*). **—ört=lich**, *adv.* in the wrong place (*rare*).

Un'orthographisch, *adj.* wrongly spelt, misspelt.

Un'paar, *adj.* uneven; (*also* **—ig**) not paired; odd, without a fellow. **—igkeit**, *f.* inequality, imparity.

Un'partei—isch, —lich, *adj.* impartial, disinterested. **—ische(r)**, *m.* umpire. **—lichkeit**, *f.* impartiality.

Un'passend, *adj.* unsuitable; improper; indiscreet; misplaced, inopportune.

Unpassier'bar, *adj.* impracticable, impassable; unfordable (*of rivers*). **—keit**, *f.* impracticability.

Un'paß, *adv. & adj. used predicatively, see* **Unpäßlich**; **die Königin ist —**, the queen is indisposed *or* ailing.

Un'päßlich. *adj.* unwell, ailing. **—keit**, *f.* indisposition.

Un'paßlichkeit, *f.* unfitness; impropriety.

Un'persönlich, *adj.* impersonal; transferable (*ticket*).

Un'politisch, *adj.* non-political; impolitic.

Un'praktisch, *adj.* unpractical; impracticable.

Unpreß'bar, *adj.* incompressible.

Un'proportioniert, *adj.* not well proportioned, out of proportion; disproportionate.

Un'pünktlich, *adj.* unpunctual, irregular, inexact.

Un'qualifizierbar, *adj.* unqualifiable.

Un'rat, *m.* trash, rubbish, refuse; ordure; excrement; garbage; trouble; **— merken** *or* **wittern**, to scent mischief, to have a suspicion, to smell a rat. **—sam**, *see* **Unrätlich**. *Comp.* **—s=haufen**, *m.* rubbish heap. **—s=kanal**, *m.* sewer. **—s=kasten**, *m.* dust-bin. **—s=kehrer**, *m.* scavenger.

Un'rationell, *adj.* irrational.

Un'rätlich, *adj.* unadvisable, inexpedient; unsuitable; profuse, wasteful.

Un'recht, I. *adj. & adv.* wrong; incorrect; unsuitable; undue, improper; unjust; **komme ich jetzt —?** have I come inopportunely *or* at the wrong time? **—e Seite**, wrong side (*of stuff*); **an den —en kommen**, to catch a tartar; **seine Bemerkungen waren ganz am —ten Orte**, his remarks were quite out of place; **— ankommen**, to get into the wrong box; **es ist in —e Hände gekommen**, it has not been delivered to the person for whom it was intended; **das ist der —e**, that is not the man (*I am looking for*); **es ist mir etwas in die —e Kehle gekommen**, I have swallowed something the wrong way; **das ist hier am —en Orte angebracht**, that is misplaced, it does not apply here; **—er Gesichtspunkt**, wrong point of view; **das geht mit —en Dingen zu**, there is s.th. uncanny *or* queer about it; **— Gut gedeiht nicht**, ill gotten gain never thrives (*prov.*). II. *n.* (**—es**) wrong; injustice; error; **einem — thun**, to wrong a p.; **— haben, im — sein**, to be wrong, mistaken; **sie hatten nicht sehr —**, they were not very far wrong *or* out (*coll.*); **mit —**, unjustly; **einem — geben**, to decide against a p.; **bei dir bekommt er nie —**, in your opinion he is never wrong. **—lich**, *adj.* unjust, wrongful; illegal; dishonest; unrighteous. **—lichkeit**, *f.* injustice, dishonesty; illegality. *Comp.* **—mäßig**, *adj.* illegal; usurpatory; unrighteous. **—mäßigkeit**, *f.* illegality.

Un'redlich, *adj.* dishonest. **—keit**, *f.* dishonesty.

Un'regelmäßig, *adj.* irregular; anomalous; abnormal; informal; erratic. **—keit**, *f.* irregularity; anomaly.

Un'reif, *adj.* unripe; immature; crude. **—e, —heit**, *f.* unripeness; immaturity; crudity.

Un'rein, *adj.* unclean, dirty, impure; foul; obscene; false; **ich habe es erst im —en (ins —e) geschrieben**, I have only jotted it down roughly, made a rough copy; **—e Luft**, impure *or* vitiated air; **—e Küste**, foul coast; **—er Stil**, bad style; **—er Ton**, false note. **—heit**, *f.* uncleanness; impurity. **—igkeit**, *f. see* **—heit**; (*pl.*) ordure. **—lich**, *adj.* unclean; dirty. **—lichkeit**, *f.* dirtiness, impurity.

Unrett'bar, *adj.* irredeemable, past recovery; **— verloren**, irretrievably lost.

Un'richtig, *adj.* unjust; false; incorrect; irregular; **diese Uhr geht —**, this watch does not go right. **—keit**, *f.* injustice; incorrectness; falsity; inexactitude.

Un'ritterlich, *adj.* unknightly, unchivalrous. **—keit**, *f.* unchivalrous conduct *or* action.

Un'ruh—e, *f.* (*pl.* **—en**) unrest, disquietude, uneasiness; anxiety; agitation; trouble; embarrassment; alarm; bustling, restless person; pendulum (*of a clock*); (*pl.*) disturbances; (*pl.*) riots. **—ig**, *adj.* unquiet, restless; agitated; turbulent; **—iger Mensch**, restless, fidgety person. *Comp.* **—scheibe**, *f.* balance-ring (*Horol.*). **—stifter**, *m.* mischief-maker; disturber of the public peace; seditious person. **—uhr**, *f.* balance-watch. **—voll**, *adj.* restless, uneasy, unsettled; troubled.

Un'rühmlich, *adj.* inglorious. **—keit**, *f.* ingloriousness.

Uns, *pers. pron.* (*acc. & dat. of* **wir**) us; to us; ourselves; to ourselves; **wir werden — wiedersehen**, we shall meet again; **ein Freund von —**, a friend of ours, one of our friends; **er gehört zu —**, he is one of us (*of our party*); **unter — gesagt**, between ourselves; **grüßen Sie ihn von — allen**, remember us all to him; **mit herzlichsten Grüßen von — beiden**, with kindest regards from both of us.

Un'saftig, *adj.* wanting in sap, not juicy.

Unsäg'lich, Unsag'bar, *adj. & adv.* unspeakable, unutterable.

Un'sanft, *adj.* ungentle, harsh, rough.

Un'sauber, *adj.* unclean; impure; untidy.

Un'säuberlich, *adj.* dirty; **— behandeln**, to treat harshly.

Unschad'haft, *adj.* undamaged, sound, intact.

Un'schädlich, *adj.* innocuous; harmless. **—keit**, *f.* harmlessness. *Comp.* **—machung**, *f.* (**eines Giftes**) neutralization (*of a poison*).

Unschätz'bar, *adj.* inestimable. **—keit**, *f.* pricelessness.

Unschein'bar, *adj.* not bright; plain-looking; insignificant-looking; simple; homely, unpretentious; dull, dark; **— werden**, to tarnish, to lose brightness. **—keit**, *f.* dimness; humbleness, insignificance.

Un'schicklich, *adj.* unbecoming, unseemly; improper; indecent. **—keit**, *f.* impropriety; unsuitableness.

Un'schiffbar, *adj.* not navigable.

Un'schlitt, *n.* (—(e)s) grease, suet, tallow.

Un'schlüssig, *adj.* wavering; irresolute; perplexed. **—keit**, *f.* indecision; irresolution; perplexity.

Un'schmackhaft, *adj.* tasteless, insipid. **—igkeit**, *f.* insipidity.

Un'schön, *adj.* unlovely; ungracious; ugly.

Un'schuld, *f.* innocence; purity, chastity; harmlessness; **der Angeklagte beteuerte seine —**, the defendant protested his innocence, pleaded "not guilty"; **ich wasche meine Hände in —**, I wash my hands of it; **der Mensch im Stande der —**, man before the fall, man in the state of primitive innocence; **in aller —**, quite innocently, no harm being meant, without any evil design. **—ig**, *adj.* innocent, guiltless; guileless; pure; harmless; ingenuous. *Comp.* **—s=miene**, *f.* air of innocence. **—s=probe**, *f.* ordeal. **—s=voll**, *adj.* innocent.

Un'schwer, *adj.* easy; not difficult; **ich errate es —**, I have no difficulty in guessing it.

Un'segen, *m.* adversity, ill success; curse.

Un'selig, *adj.* unhappy; unlucky; fatal; wretched.

Unser, I. *pers. pron.* (*gen. of* **wir**) of us; **— eins, — einer**, one of us, such as we, such as I, men like me, people like us; **wir** (*or* **es**) **waren — vier**, there were four of us; **Vater —, der Du bist im Himmel**, Our Father which art in Heaven (*B.*); **Herr erbarme dich —!** Lord, have mercy upon us! II. *poss. adj.* (**unser, uns(e)re, unser**) our; **die Schriftsteller —er Zeit**, the writers of our time. III. — *or* **Uns(e)rer, Uns(e)re, Uns(e)res, (der, die, das —e** *or* **—ige)**, *poss. pron.* ours; our property; our duty; **die —igen** *or* **Unsrigen**, our family, our party, our men, our soldiers. *Comp.* **—t=halben —t=wegen, (um) —t=willen**, *adv.* for our sake, on account of us.

Un'sicher, *adj.* uncertain; insecure; not to be depended on, doubtful, precarious; unsteady; unsafe; **—es Gedächtnis**, bad, treacherous memory. **—heit**, *f.* insecurity; precariousness; uncertainty.

Un'sichtbar, *adj.* invisible, imperceptible, lost to view. **—keit**, *f.* invisibility.

Un'sinn, *m.* nonsense, stuff; folly; madness; **barer** *or* **blühender —**, downright nonsense; **— angeben**, to play the fool, to fool about; **zum — lieben**, to be madly in love with, to love to distraction. **—ig**, *adj.* nonsensical, absurd, irrational, foolish; mad. **—igkeit**, *f.* absurdity; extravagance, folly; madness.

Un'sinnlich, *adj.* spiritual, supersensual; not sensual; **—e Liebe**, Platonic love.

Un'sitt—e, *f.* bad habit *or* custom. **—lich**, *adj.* immoral; immodest; indecent. **—lichkeit**, *f.* immorality; indecency; immoral act.

Un'soldatisch, *adj.* unsoldierlike, unmilitary.

Un'sre, (Un'srige,) *see* **Unser**. *Comp.* **—r=seits**, *adv.* as for us, for *or* on our part.

Un'stät, Un'stet, *adj.* inconstant; unsteady; variable; restless; wandering; not fixed. **—ig**, *see* **Unstät**; **—ige Größe**, variable quantity. **—igkeit**, *f.* inconstancy; changeableness; unsettled condition.

Un'statthaft, *adj.* inadmissible; forbidden; illegal; insufficient; invalid; unsuitable.

Unsterb'lich, *adj.* immortal; **sich — machen**, to immortalize oneself. **—keit**, *f.* immortality.

Un'stern, *m.* unlucky star; misfortune, disaster.

Un'stet, Un'stetig, *see* **Unstät**.

Unstill'bar, *adj.* unappeasable; insatiable; unquenchable.

Unstör'bar, *adj.* imperturbable; impassive; **— im Besitze**, in incommutable possession.

Unstraf'bar, Unsträf'lich, *adj.* unpunishable; irreproachable, blameless.

Un'streitig, *adj.* incontestable, unquestionable. *adv.* no doubt, doubtless.

Unsühn'bar, *adj.* inexpiable; irreconcilable.

Un'summe, *f.* enormous *or* immense sum.

Un'sünd—ig, *adj.* innocent; sinless. **—igkeit**, *f.* sinlessness. **—lich**, *adj.* not sinful; *see* **—ig**.

Un'symmetr—ie, *f.* want of symmetry.

Unsymme'trisch, *adj.* unsymmetrical.

Unta'del—haft, —ig, *adj.* irreproachable, blameless, free from blame.

Untast'bar, *adj.* impalpable, intangible.

Un'tauglich, *adj.* unfit; unsuitable; unserviceable; useless; bad. **—keit**, *f.* uselessness.

Unteil'bar, *adj.* indivisible. **—keit**, *f.* indivisibility.

Un'teilhaft(ig), *adj.* (*with gen.*) having no part *or* share in, not partaking of.

Un'teilnehmend, *adj.* unsympathetic; indifferent.

Un'ten, *adv.* below, beneath, underneath, at the end, bottom *or* foot; downstairs; **— a'n**, at the foot *or* bottom, at the end; **— a'n gehen**, to go last; **— am Berge**, at the foot of the hill; **— auf der Erde**, here below, down on the ground; **— auf dem Boden des Wassers**, at the bottom of the water; **— durch**, down through, through underneath, under there; **nach —**, downwards; **— im Fasse**, at the bottom of the cask; **— im Lande**, in the valley, in the plain; **von oben bis —**, from top to bottom; **von — an** *or* **auf**, right up from below; **er hat von — auf gedient**, he has risen from the ranks; **weiter —**, further down; **siehe —**, (*abbr.* **s.u.**), see below; **ich habe — drei Zimmer**, I have three rooms on the ground-floor. *Comp.* **—an**, *adv. see* **Unten**. **—benannt**, *adj.* hereafter mentioned, mentioned further down, named at foot. **—hi'n**, *adv.* downwards, near the bottom. **—liegend**, *adj.* lying below, inferior; underlying. **—stehend**, *adj.* undermentioned, mentioned below.

Un'ter, I. *prep.* (*with acc. or dat.*) **1.** *with* **dat.** *implying rest or being in a place, or in answer to* **wo?** *where?* under, below, beneath, underneath, among, amongst, during; by; under, on; in the room below; **— vier Augen**, tête-à-tête; **was verstehst du — diesem Ausdrucke?** what do you understand by this expression? **— dieser Bedingung**, on this condition; **— jeder Bedingung**, (up)on any terms; **— dem dreißigsten Breitengrade**, in 30° (N.)L.; **sie zogen ihn — dem Bette hervor**, they dragged him out from under the bed; **— vier Dukaten waren drei zu leicht**, of four ducats three were too light; **— heutigem Dato**, under date of to-day; **— einem sein**, to be inferior *or* to be subject to a p.; **er wohnt — mir**, he lives in the room below mine; **— dem Gebete**, during prayer(s); — **— dem Gesetze stehen**, to be subject to the law; **— Glockengeläute**, amidst a peal of bells, with bells ringing; **— andern Gründen**, amongst other arguments; **— der Hand**, secretly; **etwas — den Händen haben**, to have something in hand; **— freiem Himmel**, in the open air, under the blue sky; **— den Kanonen sein**, to be under cover of the guns; **das ist — aller Kanone**, that is beneath contempt (*sl.*); **— dem Donner der Kanonen**, amidst the roar of artillery; **— Kaution**, under bond; **— der Kirche**, during church time, while the service is going on; **das ist — aller Kritik**, that is beneath criticism; **ich kann es Ihnen nicht — 50 Mark geben**, I cannot give it to you for less than 50 marks; **— dem Mittagessen**, during dinner; **— drei Monaten**, in less than 3 months; **— dem Namen S. bekannt sein**, to be known by the name of S.; **— seinen Papieren**, amongst his papers; **— Pari**, below par; **ein Buch — der Presse**, a book in the press; **— der Regierung von**, in *or* during the reign of; **— dem Schutze der Batterien**, under cover of the batteries; **— seinem Stande heiraten**, to marry beneath one's social position; **— Thränen**, with tears in his eyes, weeping; **— zwei Übeln das kleinste wählen**, of two evils to choose the least; **— solchen** (*or* **so bewandten**) **Umständen**, under these circumstances, this being the case, in this case; **— uns**, among ourselves, between ourselves; **— uns gesagt**, between ourselves, it must go no further; —

uns kommt es nicht darauf an, it is of no consequence to either you or me; **der Größte — uns,** the tallest of us; **keiner — uns,** not one of us; **— dem Wasser schwimmen,** to swim beneath the *or* under water; **— der Zeit,** meanwhile. **2.** *with acc. signifying motion towards or in answer to* **wohin?** *whither?* under; beneath; underneath; among; **einen einem — Augen stellen,** to confront one person with another; **— die Erde bringen,** to bury, to be the death of (*s.o.*); **viele Köpfe — einen Hut bringen wollen,** to try to bring many people to the same way of thinking; **wenn's — die Leute kommt,** if it gets abroad; **— die Räuber geraten,** to fall among thieves; **— Schloß und Riegel bringen,** to put under lock and key; **— die Soldaten gehen,** to enlist; **— den Tisch fallen,** to fall under the table; to be neglected, forgotten; **— das Wasser tauchen,** to dive; **— Wasser setzen,** to inundate. II. *adj.* (*sup.* **—st**) under; underneath; lower; low; **—st,** the lowest, the last; **zu —st,** in the lowest part, at the bottom; **der —ste in der Klasse,** the lowest boy in his form *or* set; **das —ste zu Oberst kehren,** to turn everything topsy-turvy *or* upside down. III. *m.* (**—s, —n,** *pl.* **—n**) knave (*Cards*). IV. *adv.* (*gone*) below, under. V. *sep. & insep. pref.* below, beneath, under; among; amid (*verbs in comp. with* **unter** *when sep. have the principal accent on* **unter,** *when insep. on the root of the verb. Note the glottal stop in cpds. the second part of which begins with a vowel, e.g.* **Unter'arm**). *Comp.* **—abart,** *f.* sub-variety. **—abteilung,** *f.* subdivision. **—admiral,** *m.* vice-admiral. **—arm,** *m.* fore-arm. **—ärmel,** *m.* undersleeve; lower part of the sleeve. **—art,** *f.* sub-species. **—arzt,** *m.* doctor's assistant; junior surgeon. **—aufseher,** *m.* sub-inspector; under-manager. **—balken,** *m.* lower beam; crosspiece, winter (*Typ.*); architrave. **—band,** *n.* under-bandage (*Surg.*). **—bau,** *m.* substructure; subway; foundation; earthworks; **gemeinsamer —bau,** common basis. **—bauch,** *m.* hypogastrium, abdomen. **—bauen,** *v.a.* (*sep.*) to build beneath; (*insep.*) to undermine; to furnish with a new substructure; to underpin. **—baum,** *m.* under-beam; shaft, side-piece (*of vehicles*). **—beamte(r),** *m.* subordinate official *or* civil officer. **—befehlshaber,** *m.* second in command, subordinate officer. **—behörde,** *f.* inferior court. **—beinkleid,** *n.* drawers (*of women*), pants (*of men*); **ein —beinkleid,** a pair of drawers. **—bilanz,** *f.* deficit. **—binden,** I. *ir.v.a.* (*sep.*) to tie underneath; (*insep.*) to bind up tightly (*so that the blood, etc., cannot circulate, Surg.*); to tie *or* take up (*a vein*), to apply a ligature to (*a vein*); **einem die Lebensader —binden,** to undo a p., to make it impossible for a p. to live. II. *subst.n.*, **—bindung,** *f.* ligature. **—bischof,** *m.* suffragan. **—blatt,** *n.* lower leaf; foil (*Jew.*); lower blade (*of shears*). **—bleiben,** I. *ir.v.a.* (*insep.*) not to take place, to be left undone; not to be repeated; to discontinue; **ich hoffe, das wird in Zukunft —bleiben,** I trust this will not occur again. II. *ir.v.n.* (*aux.* **s.**) (*sep.*) to remain below. III. *subst.n.* cessation, discontinuance. **—boden,** *m.* under floor; lower plate (*of a watch*); base, mould (*of buttons*). **—bogen,** *m.* subarch, archvault (*Arch.*). **—brechen,** I. *ir.v.a.* (*insep.*) to interrupt; to discontinue, stop; to intercept. II. *subst.n.*, **—brechung,** *f.* interruption; cessation, stop. **—brecher,** *m.* interrupter. **—breiten,** *v.a.* (*sep.*) to spread under; (*insep.*) to present, lay before, submit to (*for examination, judgment*). **—bringen,** *ir.v.a.* (*sep.*) to shelter, house, bring under shelter; to lodge; to provide (*a place*) for; to dispose of (*in marriage*); to invest; to negotiate (*bills*); to sell, dispose of; **Pferde —bringen,** to stable horses; **einen —bringen,** to get a p. a situation; to lodge a person; **ein Kätzchen —bringen,** to find a home for a kitten. **—chlorsäure,** *f.* hypochloric acid. **—dampf,** *m.* steam acting from below. **—deck,** *n.* lower deck. **—decke,** *f.* undercoverlet, blanket. **—de's, —des'sen,** *adv. & conj.* meanwhile, in the meantime. **—drücken,** *v.a.* (*sep.*) to push under; (*insep.*) to repress, restrain; to suppress; to stifle; to crush, quell. **—drü'cker,** *m.* oppressor, tyrant. **—drü'ckung,** *f.* oppression; suppression; compression. **—ducken,** *v.a.* (*sep.*) to duck, dive under. **—einander,** *adv.* (*pron.* **untereinan'der**) mutually, reciprocally; pell-mell, confusedly; one with another, together; **alles —einander werfen,** to throw everything topsy-turvy; (*pron.* **un'tereinander**) one under another. **—erdgeschoß,** *n.* underground story. **—fahren,** *ir.v.* I. *a. & n.* (*aux.* **s.**) (*sep.*) to drive under cover. II. *a.* (*insep.*) to pass (*one's hand*) under s.th.; to cut a p. short (*rare*). **—faktor,** *m.* printer's sub-foreman, second overseer. **—fangen,** I. *ir.v.r.* (*insep.*) (*gen.*) to attempt, venture on, (*dare to*) undertake. II. *subst.n.* bold enterprise; pluck, boldness. **—fassen,** *v.a.* (*sep.*) to put one's hand under, hold up; **einen —fassen,** to take a p.'s arm. **—feldherr,** *m.* general who is second in command. **—flechten,** *ir.v.a.* (*sep.*) to entwine; to interweave; (*insep.*) to interlace; to mix, mingle. **—fuß,** *m.* lower part of the foot, sole. **—futter,** *n.* lining. **—futtern,** *v.a.* (*sep. & insep.*) to line; **einen tüchtig —futtern,** to rule over a p., to keep a p. down (*coll.*). **—gährung,** *f.* fermentation from below, sedimentary fermentation. **—gang,** *m.* goingdown; setting, sinking; the west; fall; ruin; destruction; decay; **—gang eines Schiffes,** shipwreck; **—gang eines Reiches,** downfall of an empire. **—gattung,** *f.* sub-species. **—geben,** *ir.v.a.* (*sep.*) to give something that may be placed under; to put out, provide for; (*insep.*) to commit, intrust to; to subordinate, subject; **einem —geben sein,** to be under a p.'s care or control. **—gebene(r),** *m.* subaltern; subordinate. **—gebenheit,** *f.* subordination, subjection; inferiority (*in office*). **—gehen,** *ir.v.n.* (*aux.* **s.**) (*sep.*) to sink, be submerged; to be swallowed up; to sink, be wrecked; to go to ruin; to perish; to set (*of the sun*); to be lost *or* annihilated; to go under; **der Heuwagen ging nicht —,** the waggon of hay would not go under (*a shed*); **—gegange Tiere,** extinct animals. **—gehölz,** *n.* underwood, copse. **—gehülfe,** *m.* under-assistant. **—geordnet,** *p.p. & adj.* subordinate, auxiliary. **—geordnete(r),** *m.* subordinate; inferior. **—gericht,** *n.* inferior court. **—gerichtsbarkeit,** *f.* jurisdiction of an inferior court. **—geschoben,** *adj.* counterfeit, spurious; interpolated; **—geschobenes Kind,** substituted child. **—geschoß,** *n.* groundfloor. **—gestell,** *n.* underpart of a trestle *or* stand; underpart of the frame of a carriage. **—gewand,** *n.* under-garment. **—gewehr,** *n.* sword, side arm. **—gewicht,** *n.* light weight. **—glied,** *n.* lower limb; minor proposition (*Log.*). **—graben,** *ir.v.a.* (*sep.*) to dig in (*as manure*); (*insep.*) to undermine, sap; to destroy; to corrupt, eat away; **—grabene Gesundheit,** shattered health. **—grund,** *m.* subsoil; lower stratum; underground. **—grund=bahn,** *f.* underground railway; **die —grundbahn benutzen,** to go by the underground. **—grund=pflug,** *m.* sub-soil plough. **—haben,** *ir.v.a.* (*sep.*) to have (*on*) underneath; to have in one's hands, have the management of; to have conquered; to be superior to; to tease, make sport of a p. —**haken**, *v.a.;* **einen —haken**, to take a p.'s arm (*coll.*). —**halb**, *prep.* (*with gen.*) below; at the lower end of; under. —**halt**, *m.* maintenance, support, livelihood; **seinen —halt verdienen**, to earn one's living *or* livelihood. —**halten**, I. *ir.v.a.* (*sep.*) to hold under; (*insep.*) to support, stay up; to maintain, sustain; to keep up (*a correspondence*); to entertain, amuse; to cultivate (*an acquaintance*); **sich —halten mit (über eine S.)**, to converse with (upon a th.); **ein Mädchen** *or* **Frauenzimmer —halten**, to keep a mistress. II. *subst. n.*, —**haltung**, *f.* keeping up, maintenance; conversation; **leichte —haltung**, small talk, society talk. —**haltungs=blatt**, *n.* comic paper, family magazine; literary supplement to a newspaper. —**haltungs=gabe**, *f.* conversational gift. —**haltungs=kosten**, *pl.* expenses of entertainment. —**haltungs=lektüre**, *f.* light reading, novels. —**haltungs=weise**, *adv.* by way of conversation. —**handeln**, *v.a. & n.* (*aux.* **h.**) (*insep.*) to negotiate (*a peace, etc.*); to parley; **mit einem wegen einer Sache** *or* **über eine S. —handeln**, to confer with s. o. about s.th. —**händler**, *m.* negotiator; mediator; broker, agent; bearer of a flag of truce (*Mil.*). —**handlung**, *f.* negotiation, transaction; mediation; (*with accent on* **unter**) joint-stock sale; **sich in —handlungen einlassen, in —handlung treten**, to enter into negotiations, to treat with, to parley. —**handlungs=kunst**, *f.* diplomacy. —**hauen**, *ir.v.a.* (*sep.*) to hew underneath *or* below; (*insep.*) to hollow out from below, to excavate (*Min.*). —**haus**, *n.* lower part of a house; Lower Chamber; Lower House, House of Commons. —**hefe**, *f.* yeast deposited at the bottom of a cask. —**hemd**, *n.* under-vest *or* -shirt. —**hof**, *m.* back yard; lower part of a yard; inferior court. —**höhlen**, *v.a.* (*insep.*) to undermine; to wear away. —**holz**, *n. see* —**gehölz**; wood serving as base *or* foundation. —**hosen**, *pl.* drawers (*of women*), pants (*of men*). —**irdisch**, *adj.* underground, subterraneous, subterranean; infernal; —**irdische Begräbnisstelle**, catacomb; —**irdischer Gang**, subway; cellar way, tunnel; —**irdische Kirche**, crypt; —**irdische Leitung**, underground transmission (*Telegr.*). —**jacke**, *f.* undervest. —**jochen**, *v.a.* (*insep.*) to subjugate, subdue; to enslave. —**kammerherr**, *m.* vice-chamberlain. —**kellner**, *m.* underwaiter. —**kiefer**, *m.* lower jaw. —**kinn**, *n.* double chin. —**klasse**, *f.* lower class; —**klassen**, lower forms of German secondary schools (*Sexta, Quinta, Quarta; age of boys 9–13 years*). —**kommen**, I. *ir.v.n.* (*aux.* **f.**) (*sep.*) to find shelter, *or* accommodation; to find employment, to be taken in. II. *subst.n. see* —**kunft**. —**könig**, *m.* viceroy. —**körper**, *m.* lower part of the body. —**kötig**, *adj.* festering underneath; —**kötige Geschichte**, a bad business. —**kriechen**, *ir.v.n.* (*aux.* **f.**) (*sep.*) to crawl under; **er sucht ein Plätzchen, wo er —kriechen kann**, he seeks a corner to crawl into. —**kriegen**, *v.a.* (*sep.*) to conquer; **laß dich nicht —kriegen von . . .**, do not allow yourself to be beaten by . . ., do not give in to . . . (*coll.*). —**kunft**, *f.* shelter; lodging; situation. —**kunfts=hütte**, *f.* shelter-hut for travellers (*in the Alps, etc.*). —**kunfts=lose(r)**, *m.* homeless *or* houseless person. —**lage**, *f.* anything laid underneath to support some other thing; prop, stay, support; wedge, bracket; trestle; base, foundation; substratum; subsoil; foil (*Jewelry*); base (*Chem.*); stand (*under casks*); foot *or* base of a column; lining; under-blanket; railway-sleeper; bearer (*Typ.*); —**lage eines Hebels**, fulcrum. —**land**, *n.* lowland(s), low country. —**ländisch**, *adj.* lowland. —**laß**, *m.;* **ohne —laß**, without intermission, unceasingly, continually. —**lassen**, *ir.v.a.* (*insep.*) to leave off, discontinue; to fail, omit to do; to forbear; to abstain (*from doing*); **ich werde nicht —lassen Ihnen das Ergebnis mitzuteilen**, I shall not fail to let you know the result; (*sep.*) to let (*go or come*) under, below. —**lassung**, *f.* omission, cessation. —**lassungs=fall**, *m.* case of omission *or* neglect. —**lassungs=sünde**, *f.* sin of omission. —**last**, *f.* ballast. —**lastig**, *adj.* insufficiently laden, with too little ballast. —**lauf**, *m.* lower course (*of a river*). —**laufen**, *ir.v.* I. *n.* (*aux.* **f.**) (*sep.*) to run under (*for shelter, etc.*); to run in among, mix with; (*insep.*) to run, be suffused underneath the surface (*of the skin, etc.*); **mit Blut —laufen sein**, to be blood-shot, suffused under the skin; —**laufenes Blut**, extravasated blood; **ein mit Blut —laufenes Mal**, a livid, bruised spot. II. *a.* (*insep.*) to run between s.o's legs; to trip a p. up. —**läufer**, *m.* smuggler; interloper; assistant salt-maker. —**leder**, *n.* sole-leather; underleather. —**lege=decke**, *f.* cover between the saddle and the horse, saddle-cloth. —**lege=keil**, *m.* wedge to stop the motions of wheels, scotch. —**legen**, I. *v.a.* (*sep., rarely insep.*) to lay, put under *or* to; to attribute (*to a person*) motives *or* words, to credit (*a p.*) with s. th.; **einem Huhne Eier zum Brüten —legen**, to put eggs under a hen; **einem Kinde frische Windeln —legen**, to change a baby's linen; **einer Melodie einen Text, Worte —legen**, to put (*new*) words to a tune; **einem Worte einen anderen Sinn —legen**, to put a new construction upon, give another meaning to a word; **Pferde —legen**, to have relays of horses on a journey; (*insep.*) to trim, put under. II. *p.p. see* —**liegen**. —**lehen**, *n.* mesne fief. —**lehrer**, *m.* junior (assistant) master; master in charge of the more elementary subjects, master taking a form in the junior *or* preliminary department; usher (*obs., contempt.*). —**leib**, *m.* abdomen; bowels; belly. —**leibs=krankheit**, *f.*, —**leibs=leiden**, *n.* abdominal complaint, enteric disease. —**leibs=schmerzen**, *pl.* pain in the abdominal region. —**leibs=typhus**, *m.* enteric (fever). —**leutnant**, *m.* sub-lieutenant, second lieutenant. —**liegen**, *ir.v.n.* (*aux.* **f.**) (*insep.*) to succumb; to be overcome, defeated; **das —liegt keinem Zweifel**, there is not the slightest doubt about that; (*aux.* **h.**) (*sep.*) to be at the bottom of, serve as a basis for. —**lieutenant**, *m. see* —**leutnant**. —**lippe**, *f.* under-lip. —**luft**, *f.* lower stratum of air. —**m**, *abbr. for* —**dem**. —**magd**, *f.* under-servant; second housemaid; nursery maid, undernurse; kitchen *or* scullery-maid. —**malen**, *v.a.* (*sep.*) to paint (*one's name, etc.*) under; (*insep.*) to prepare the canvas; to lay the first *or* ground colour on; to sketch roughly. —**ma'lung**, *f.* preparation of the canvas; laying on of the ground-colours; rough sketch. —**mann**, *m.* left-hand man. —**maß**, *n.* insufficient measure; —**haben**, to be . . . short. —**mäßig**, *adj.;* —**mäßig sein**, to be below a certain standard. —**mauern**, *v.a.* (*sep.*) to underpin; (*insep.*) to build a foundation to. —**mengen**, *v.a.* (*sep.*) to mix into *or* among; (*insep.*) to intermix. —**minieren**, *v.a.* (*insep.*) to undermine. —**n**, *abbr. for* —**den**. —**nehmen**, *ir.v.a.* (*insep.*) to undertake; to attempt. —**nehmend**, *p. & adj.* enterprising, bold. —**nehmer**, *m.* person engaged in an enterprise; contractor. —**nehmung**, *f.* enterprise. —**nehmungs=geist**, *m.* enterprising spirit. —**offizier**, *m.* non-commissioned officer, corporal, sergeant. —offiziers=dienst=thuer, *m.* private doing duty as a corporal. —ordnen, *v.a.* (*sep.*) to subordinate. —pacht, *f.* sublease; subtenancy. —pächter, *m.* subtenant. —pfand, *n.* pledge; security; mortgage; gerichtliches —pfand, judicial mortgage; ein Gut zum —pfand inne haben, to have the right of foreclosure over an estate. —pfändlich, *adj.* as security, as a mortgage. —pfarre, *f.* vicarage. —pfarrer, *m.* vicar; curate. —pflasterbahn, *f.* underground railway. —phosphorig, *adj.* hypophosphoric. —prima, *f.* lower-sixth form. —primaner, *m.* lower-sixth form boy. —reden, *v.r.* (*insep.*) to converse, confer (with, mit). —redung, *f.* conversation; conference; parley (*Mil.*). —richt, *m.* (—(e)s) instruction, lessons; er giebt guten —richt, he teaches well. —richten, *v.a.* (*insep.*) to teach, instruct; to inform of, acquaint with, apprise of; to warn; sich von einer S. *or* über eine S. —richten, to obtain information about s.th. —richter, *m.* instructor; (*pron* un'terrichter) inferior, puisne judge. —richtlich, *adj.* referring to education, educational. —richts=anstalt, *f.* educational establishment; school, college, academy. —richts=briefe, *pl.* correspondence lessons; englische —richtsbriefe, correspondence lessons in English. —richts=erlaubnis=schein, *m.* teacher's diploma, certificate of efficiency. —richts=fach, *n.* special subject, special branch of instruction. —richts=fähig, *adj.* capable of teaching; teachable. —richts=lokal, *n.* class-room; school. —richts=minister, *m.* minister of education; President of the Board of Education (*England*). —richts=methode, *f.* educational method, method of instruction *or* teaching. —richts=ministerium, *n.* department of public instruction; Board of Education (*England*). —richts=wesen, *n.* public instruction. —rock, *m.* petticoat; alle —röcke, womenfolk, womankind, the female world (*hum.*). —roßarzt, *m.* assistant veterinary surgeon. —s, *abbr. for* —das. —sagen, *v.a.* (*insep.*) to forbid, prohibit. —salpetersauer, *adj.* hyponitrite. —saß, *m.* (—(ss)en, *pl.* —(ss)en) vassal; subject; copyholder. —satz, *m.* support; stand; trestle; socle (*Arch.*); flower-pot saucer; tray; dumb-waiter; minor proposition (*Log.*). —schale, *f.*, —schälchen, *n.* saucer. —schätzen, *v.a.* (*insep.*) to undervalue, underrate, depreciate. —schätzung, *f.* underestimate, undervaluation. —scheidbar, *adj.* distinguishable. —scheiden, *ir.v.a.* (*insep.*) to distinguish; to discern; to discriminate; to separate; to differentiate. —scheidend, *p.* & *adj.* distinctive; characteristic; diagnostic. —scheidung, *f.* distinction; discrimination. —scheidungs=begriff, *m.* difference (*Log.*). —scheidungs=gabe, —scheidungs=kraft, *f.*, —scheidungs=vermögen, *n.* power of discrimination, discernment. —scheidungs=lehre, *f.* diagnosis. —scheidungs=zeichen, *n.* distinctive mark, characteristic; point, stop; criterion. —scheidungs=zug, *m.* distinguishing trait, characteristic. —schenkel, *m.* (lower segment of the) leg. —schicht, *f.* lower stratum. —schieben, *ir.v.a.* (*sep.*) to push under; (*sep.* & *insep.*) to substitute; to interpolate; to forge; to foist upon; den Worten einen falschen Sinn —schieben, to put a wrong construction on words. —schiebung, *f.* substitution (*of one child for another, etc.*); interpolation; forging. —schied, *m.* (—s, *pl.* —e) separation; distinction, difference; dissimilarity; zum —schiede von, in contradistinction to, unlike; in opposition to; ohne —schied, without distinction, indiscriminately. —schieden, *p.p.* & *adj.* different; distinct; diverse; auf —schiedene Art, in a different manner. —schiedlich, *adj.* different; divers, several; —schiedliches, many a thing, various things. —schlächtig, *adj.* undershot (*of a mill-wheel*). —schlagen, *ir.v.a.* (*sep.*) to cross (*the arms, etc.*); einem ein Bein —schlagen, to trip s.o. up; (*insep.*) to line (*with silk, etc.*); to steal, embezzle; to intercept (*a letter, etc.*); to suppress (*a will, etc.*). —schleif, *m.* embezzlement; fraud; smuggling; —schleif treiben, to embezzle (*money*), to smuggle. —schreiben, *ir.v.a.* (*sep.*) to write under; (*insep.*) to sign; to subscribe, put one's name to. —schreiber, *m.* underclerk; signer (*of a cheque, etc.*); subscriber. —schrift, *f.* signature; paraph; inscription (*under a picture, etc.*); eigenhändige —schrift, sign manual; falsche —schrift, forged signature. —schule, *f.* primary school. —schwefelsäure, *f.* dithionic acid. —schweflig, *adj.*; —schweflige Säure, thio-sulphuric acid. —schwelle, *f.* (ground-) sill; sleeper (*Railw.*). —see=boot, *n.* submarine boat. —seeisch, *adj.* submarine. —see=mine, *f.* submarine mine. —segel, *n.* lower sail; *pl.* courses. —segel=gehen, *n.* setting sail. —sein, *ir.v.n.* (*sep.*); die Sonne ist —, the sun has set. —sekunda, *f.* lower fifth (form) (*in a grammar-school*). —setzen, *v.a.* (*sep.*) to put under; to put (*one's name*) to; (*insep.*) to prop, underprop; to line, strengthen (*a seam, etc.*). —setzt, *p.p.* & *adj.* square-built, thick-set, short and thick. —setztheit, *f.* squareness of build; see Gedrungenheit. —siegeln, *v.a.* (*insep.*) to affix one's seal to; to seal. —speisemeister, *m.* under-steward *or* -caterer. —spülen, *v.a.* (*insep.*) to wash away underneath. —staatssekretär, *m.* under-secretary of state. —stadt, *f.* lower town. —ständig, *adj.* inferior (*Bot.*). —statthalter, *m.* deputy governor (*of a province*). —stecken, *v.a.* (*sep.*) to put *or* stick under; to put in among; to join to; to incorporate (*soldiers with another regiment, etc.*); (*insep.*) to trim with (*something laid under*). —stehen, *ir.v.* I. *n.* (*aux.* s.) (*sep.*) to be, stand under; to shelter under. II. *r.* (*insep.*) to dare, presume, to be so bold as to; —steh dich nicht, das zu thun, do not dare *or* attempt to do that! —steiger, *m.* second master-miner. —stelle, *f.* inferior situation. —stellen, *v.a.* (*sep.*) to put, place under; to put under cover *or* shelter; einen Wagen —stellen, to put up a carriage (*in a coach-house*); sich —stellen, to take shelter; (*sep.* & *insep.*) to suppose, to impute (*prov.*); das lasse ich mir nicht —stellen, I will not have that imputed to me; einem —stellt sein, to be under s.o., to be a p.'s subordinate. —stellung, *f.* supposition. —stempel, *m.* under-die (*Mint.*). —steuermann, *m.* second mate. —stock, *m.* groundfloor; under-back (*Brew.*). —streichen, *ir.v.a.* (*insep.*) to underline. —strömung, *f.* under-current. —stützen, *v.a.* (*sep.*) to underprop, shore up; (*insep.*) to support; to prop; to sustain, strengthen; to aid; to protect, patronize; to favour; ein Theater mit einer Geldhülfe —stützen, to grant a subvention to a theatre; mit Rat und That —stützen, to assist (a p.) by word and deed. —stützer, *m.* support, stay, patron. —stützung, *f.* propping, under-propping; support; assistance; stay. —stützungs=anstalt, *f.* charitable institution. —stützungs=bedürftig, *adj.* in need of support. —stützungs=gesuch, *n.* application for relief. —stützungs=kasse, *f.* benevolent fund; endowment; friendly society. —stützungs=mauer, *f.* bearing-wall. —stützungs=punkt, *m.* fulcrum. —stützungs=trupp, *m.* reinforcements. —stützungs=verein, *m.* friendly society. —suchen, *v.a.* (*insep.*) to inquire, search into; to examine; to sound; to probe; to explore; to verify; to prove;

to review, inspect. —**sucher**, *m.* examiner; investigator explorer. —**suchung**, *f.* examination; inquiry; investigation; research; inspection; sounding, probing; **gerichtliche —suchung**, judicial inquiry, inquest; **chemische —suchung**, chemical analysis; **philosophische —suchungen**, philosophical researches. —**suchungs=akten**, *pl.* (minutes of) proceedings at an inquest. —**suchungs=anstalt**, *f.* public analyst's office, testing station. —**suchungs=ausschuß**, *m.* commission of inquiry; visiting committee. —**suchungs=bescheid**, *m.* award of a court of inquiry (*Law*). —**suchungs=gefangene(r)**, *m.* prisoner upon trial. —**suchungs=kammer**, *f.* court of inquiry. —**suchungs=richter**, *m.* examining magistrate. —**taille**, *f.* petticoat bodice. —**tasse**, *f.* saucer. —**tauchen**, (*sep.*) *v.* I. *n.* (*aux.* **h.** & **s.**) to plunge, dip, duck, dive. II. *a.* to plunge, immerse, dip. —**tertia**, *f.* lower third (form) (*in a grammar school*). —**tertia'ner**, *m.* lower-third form boy. —**than**, I. *p.p.* & *adj.* subject (*to*); dependent; **seid einander —than in der Furcht Gottes**, submit yourselves one to another in the fear of God (*B.*); **sich** (*dat.*) **—than machen**, to subdue. II. *m.* (—**thans**, —**thanen**, *pl.* —**thanen**) subject. —**thanen=pflicht**, *f.* allegiance. —**thanen=treue**, *f.* loyalty. —**thanen=verhältnis**, *n.* relationship of a subject *or* vassal to a lord *or* sovereign. —**thanen=verstand**, *m.*; **beschränkter —thanenverstand**, the short-sighted views of the multitude. —**thänig**, *adj.* submissive; subject; dutiful; **—thänigster Diener**, (your) most humble servant; **ich bitte —thänigst**, I most respectfully beg. —**thänigkeit**, *f.* submission; submissiveness; humility. —**teil**, *m.* (& *n.*) lower part; base; underpart. —**thor**, *n.* gate of the lower town. —**thun**, *ir.v.a.* (*sep.*) to put under. —**treten**, *ir. v.* I. *a.* (*sep.*) to tread down; (*insep.*) to trample on; to oppress. II. *n.* (*aux.* **s.**) (*sep.*) to step under; to shelter under. —**verband**, *m.* (**der Vorschußvereine**) branch (of a loan-fund). —**verdeck**, *n.* orlop-deck. —**vormund**, *m.* deputy-guardian; person appointed to be a check upon a guardian. —**vorsteher**, *m.* sub-rector (*of a college*). —**wachsen**, *adj.* with an undergrowth; streaky (*of bacon, etc.*); interlarded; **eine mit wildem Fleische —wachsene Wunde**, a wound with proud flesh in it; **mit Unkraut —wachsenes Getreide**, weedy corn. —**wagen**, *m.* truck (*Railw.*). —**wald**, *m.* brushwood, copse. —**wall**, *m.* lower part of ramparts, false trench. —**wärts**, I. *adv.* downwards, underneath. II. *prep.* (*with gen.*) on the lower side of. —**waschen**, *ir.v.a.* (*sep.*) to lay bare (*the foundations*) by washing against. —**wasser**, *n.* back-water. —**we'g(e)s**, *adv.* on the way; **—wegs lassen**, to leave undone, to abandon; **—wegs bleiben**, to be passed over; not to take place. —**weisen**, *ir.v.a.* (*insep.*) to instruct, teach. —**weiser**, *m.* instructor. —**weisung**, *f.* instruction; **—weisung abwarten**, await instructions. —**welt**, *f.* the nether world, lower regions; Hades. —**werfen**, *ir.v.a.* (*sep.*) to throw under; (*insep.*) to subjugate, bring into subjection; to submit to one's judgment, refer to; **sich —werfen**, to submit, yield, resign oneself to; **einer Sache —worfen sein**, to be subject *or* exposed to something. —**werfung**, *f.* subjecting; subjection; submission; acquiescence (*in*). —**werk**, *n.* lower work (*Fort.*). —**wertig**, *adj.* below value; **—wertige Qualität**, inferior quality. —**wind**, *m.* undercurrent of air; under-grate blast. —**winden**, *see* —**fangen**. —**wölben**, *v.a.* (*insep.*) to arch under. —**wuchs**, *m.* brushwood. —**wühlen**, *v.a.* (*sep.*) to bury by burrowing and throwing up earth; (*insep.*) to hollow under, excavate; to undermine. —**würfig**, *adj.* subject; submissive; obsequious, subservient; **sich** (*dat.*) **einen —würfig machen**, to bring a person into subjection. —**würfigkeit**, *f.* subjection; submissiveness; servility. —**zahn**, *m.* bottom tooth. —**zeichnen**, *v.a.* (*sep.*) to draw underneath; (*insep.*) to sign; to ratify; **ich —zeichnete(r)**, I, the undersigned —**zeichne(te)r**, *m.* signer; subscriber. —**zeichnung**, *f.* signing; signature; ratification. —**zeug**, *n.* underclothing. —**ziehen**, *ir.v.a.* (*sep.*) to draw, put under; to shelter; to put in *or* under (*a beam*); to put on underneath (*as a petticoat*); **Leinwand —ziehen**, mount on canvas; **die Schildkröte ziehet Kopf und Füße —**, the tortoise draws in its head and feet; (*insep.*) to furnish with something underneath; **sich einer Sache** (*dat.*) **—ziehen**, to take a th. upon o.s., to undertake; to undergo, to submit to (*an operation, etc.*). —**zug**, *m.* horizontal beam; summer; stay, prop.

Un'that, *f.* monstrous crime, outrage, atrocity.

Un'thätig, *adj.* inactive; idle; unoccupied; indolent. —**keit**, *f.* inactivity; inaction; slothfulness.

Un'thunlich, *adj.* impracticable, impossible. —**keit**, *f.* impossibility.

Un'tief, *adj.* shallow; of little depth. —**e**, *f.* (*pl.* —**en**) shallowness; shallow place; shoal, sandbank; bottomless abyss.

Un'tier, *n.* monster; brute.

Untilg'bar, *adj.* inextinguishable; indelible; indestructible; not payable, irredeemable.

Untrag'bar, *adj.* unwearable (*too shabby, etc.*).

Untrenn'bar, *adj.* & *adv.* inseparable. —**keit**, *f.* inseparableness.

Un'treu, *adj.* unfaithful, faithless; **einen seiner Pflicht — machen**, to turn a p. from the path of duty; **seinen Schwüren — werden**, to break one's oath. —**e**, *f.* faithlessness, inconstancy; **—e schlägt ihren eignen Herrn**, treachery will come home to the traitor (*prov.*).

Untröst'—bar, **—lich**, *adj.* inconsolable; not consoling. —**lichkeit**, *f.* disconsolateness.

Un'trüglich, *adj.* certain; infallible; indubitable. —**keit**, *f.* infallibility; certainty.

Un'tüchtig, *adj.* incapable; incompetent, inefficient; impotent; good for nothing. —**keit**, *f.* incapacity, incompetence; impotence.

Un'tugend, *f.* defect; vice; bad habit.

Un'überdacht, **Un'überlegt**, *adj.* rash, thoughtless, inconsiderate.

Unüberschreit'bar, *adj.* insurmountable, impassable; insuperable.

Unüberseh'—bar, *adj.* immense, vast; incalculable. —**barkeit**, **—lichkeit**, *f.* immensity, vastness.

Unübersetz'—bar, **—lich**, *adj.* untranslatable. —**barkeit**, *f.* untranslatability. —**t**, *adj.* untranslated.

Unübersteig'—bar, **—lich**, *adj.* insurmountable.

Unübertrag'bar, *adj.* inalienable; intransmissible (*of diseases*); untransferable; not transferable (*on tickets*); unassignable (*Law*); untranslatable.

Unübertreff'—bar, **—lich**, *adj.* unsurpassable; unrivalled, incomparable.

Un'übertroffen, *adj.* unsurpassed, unexcelled.

Un'überwindlich, *adj.* unconquerable, invincible; impregnable; insurmountable.

Un'überwunden, *adj.* unvanquished, untamed.

Un'üblich, *adj.* unusual, not customary.

Unumgäng'lich, *adj.* unsociable; indispensable; inevitable; **—e Notwendigkeit**, absolute necessity. —**keit**, *f.* unsociableness; inevitableness.

Un'umschränkt, *adj.* unlimited; absolute, sovereign. —**heit**, *f.* unboundedness; absoluteness; despotic authority.

Unumstöß'lich, *adj.* irrefragable, incontestable; irrefutable; decisive; irrevocable. **—keit**, *f.* immutability; irrefragability; incontestableness; irrevocableness.

Un'umwunden, *adj.* candid, frank, plain. **—heit**, *f.* candour, frankness.

Un'unterbrochen, *adj. & adv.* uninterrupted; continuous; incessant.

Ununterscheid'bar, *adj.* undistinguishable.

Un'unterschrieben, *adj.* unsigned, not signed.

Un'untersucht, *adj.* unexamined, not examined; not investigated; not gone into; **ich werde es — lassen, ob . . .**, I shall not inquire if . . .

Un'väterlich, *adj.* unfatherly, unnatural; **— handeln**, not to act like a father.

Unverän'der—lich, *adj.* unchangeable; invariable; incorruptible. **—lichkeit**, *f.* immutability, *etc.* **—t**, *adj.* unchanged; **—t lassen**, to leave as it was.

Unverant'wortlich, *adj.* irresponsible; unjustifiable, inexcusable. **—keit**, *f.* irresponsibility; inexcusableness.

Un'verarbeitet, *adj.* not worked up, unmanufactured, raw; not worked *or* thought out.

Unveräu'ßerlich, *adj.* inalienable. **—keit**, *f.* inalienableness.

Unverbes'serlich, *adj.* incorrigible; irreclaimable; that cannot be mended; perfect. **—keit**, *f.* incorrigibility; perfection.

Un'verbindlich, *adj.* not binding *or* obligatory; disobliging; impolite, uncivil.

Un'verblümt, *adj.* not figurative, without ornament; plain; direct. *adv.* unequivocally, openly, bluntly; **er sagte es ihm —**, he told him plainly.

Un'verboten, *adj.* not forbidden, allowable.

Unverbrenn'—bar, —lich, *adj.* non-combustible. **—barkeit**, *f.* incombustibility, incombustibleness.

Un'verbrüchlich, *adj.* not to be broken, inviolable; firm, steadfast, lasting; **—es Schweigen**, absolute secrecy.

Un'verbunden, *adj.* disjoined; unconnected; not dressed (*of wounds*).

Un'verbürgt, *adj.* unwarranted, not authenticated; **die Nachricht ist noch —**, the news has not yet been confirmed.

Un'verdächtig, *adj.* unsuspected; trustworthy. **—keit**, *f.* trustworthiness.

Un'verdammlich, *adj.* not condemnable.

Un'verdau—lich, *adj.* indigestible. **—lichkeit**, *f.* indigestibleness; crudity; indigestion. **—t**, *adj.* not digested; crude.

Un'verderblich, *adj.* incorruptible; unspoilable. **—keit**, *f.* incorruptibility.

Un'verdient, *adj.* unmerited; undeserved; unjust; **Sie klagen uns —erweise an**, you accuse us undeservedly *or* unjustly.

Un'verdorben, *adj.* unspoiled, uncorrupted; undamaged; untainted, sound; pure, blameless, upright, honest. **—heit**, *f.* unspoiled condition, uprightness, honesty; soundness.

Un'verdrossen, *adj.* indefatigable, unwearied; assiduous; patient; cheerful. **—heit**, *f.* assiduity, indefatigableness; cheerfulness.

Un'verehelicht, *adj.* unmarried; **M. Smith, —**, M. Smith, spinster; **die —e M.**, Miss M., M. spinster (*Law*).

Un'vereidet, Un'vereidigt, *adj.* unsworn.

Un'vereinbar, *adj.* incompatible; repugnant (*to*); incongruous (*with*). **—keit**, *f.* incompatibility.

Un'verfälscht, *adj.* unadulterated; real, genuine; candid, true. **—heit**, *f.* genuineness.

Un'verfänglich, *adj.* not captious; natural, simple; artless. **—keit**, *f.* simplicity of nature.

Un'verfroren, *adj.* unfrozen; unabashed, imperturbable, bold; pert, daring, audacious. **—heit**, *f.* imperturbability; boldness, impudence.

Unverfüg'bar, *adj.* that cannot be disposed of or bequeathed.

Un'vergänglich, *adj.* imperishable; immortal. **—keit**, *f.* imperishableness; immortality.

Un'vergessen, *adj.* unforgotten; unforgetting.

Unvergeß'lich, *adj.* not to be forgotten; ineffaceable: **das wird mir —(ß)lich bleiben**, I shall never forget that; **mein —(ß)licher Lehrer**, my teacher whose memory will ever live in my heart. **—(ß)lichkeit**, *f.* memorableness.

Unvergleich'—bar, —lich, *adj.* matchless, incomparable; unique. **—lichkeit**, *f.* incomparableness.

Un'vergolten, *adj.* unrewarded, unrecompensed.

Un'verhältnismäßig, *adj.* disproportionate, inadequate, excessive. **—keit**, *f.* disproportion.

Un'verheiratet, *see* **Unverehelicht**.

Un'verhofft, *adj.* unhoped (*for*); unexpected; **— kommt oft**, it is always the unforeseen that occurs (*prov.*).

Un'verhohlen, *adj.* unconcealed, open, frank, candid; without reserve, unreserved(ly).

Unverjähr'—bar, *adj.* imprescribable. **—t**, *adj.* not lost by prescription, still in force.

Un'verkäuflich, *adj.* unsaleable; unmarketable; not negotiable; a drug in the market; not up for sale, not in the market.

Un'verkauft, *adj.* unsold, remaining on hand.

Unverkenn'bar, *adj.* unmistakable; obvious, evident; **es ist —**, there is no mistaking it.

Un'verkürzt, *adj.* uncurtailed; unabridged; intact.

Unverletz'—bar, —lich, *adj.* invulnerable; inviolable. **—barkeit, —lichkeit**, *f.* invulnerability; inviolability. **—t**, *adj.* unhurt, uninjured, safe; inviolate; intact.

Unverlier'bar, *adj.* that cannot be lost, safe.

Un'verloren, *adj.* not lost; in safety, safe.

Unvermeid'—bar, —lich, *adj.* inevitable; unavoidable. **—lichkeit**, *f.* inevitableness, absolute necessity.

Un'vermerkt, *adj.* unperceived; imperceptible.

Un'vermietet, *adj.* not let, unlet, untenanted.

Un'vermindert, *adj.* undiminished, unabated; entire.

Unvermisch'—bar, *adj.* that cannot be mixed. **—t**, *adj.* unmixed; pure.

Un'vermögen, *n.* powerlessness, incapacity; impotence; **— zu bezahlen**, insolvency. **—d**, *adj.* incapable, incompetent; feeble, powerless; impotent; poor; impecunious; **—d etwas zu thun**, incapable of doing something. *Comp.* **—s=fall**, *m.*; **im—sfalle**, in case of insolvency.

Un'vermutet, *adj.* unthought of, unexpected.

Unvernehm'—bar, —lich, *adj.* indistinct; inaudible, unintelligible. **—barkeit, —lichkeit**, *f.* inaudibleness, indistinctness.

Un'vernunft, *f.* unreasonableness, absurdity; **das ist die höhere —!** that is the height of absurdity!

Un'vernünftig, *adj.* irrational; void of reason; unreasonable, absurd; **—e Tiere**, (dumb) brutes.

Un'verpackt, *adj.* unpacked.

Un'verrichtet, *adj.* unperformed, unexecuted; **—er Dinge, —er Sache**, without having effected one's object.

Un'verrückt, *adj.* unmoved, in its place; steady, fixed. *adv.* fixedly, uninterruptedly.

Unversäum'bar, *adj.* not to be neglected; peremptory.

Un'verschämt, *adj.* shameless, impudent; brazen; saucy, pert; cheeky (*coll.*); **Sie sind ein —er! — läßt grüßen!** impudent fellow! well, you are brazen-faced! **—e Lüge**, barefaced lie. **—heit**, *f.* impudence; effrontery; cheek (*coll.*); **sich mit —heit durchhelfen**, to get off by audacity, to brazen it out (*coll.*).

Un'verſchieblich, *adj.* not to be put off, not to be postponed, urgent.
Unverſchließ'bar, *adj.* that cannot be locked.
Un'verſchnitten, *adj.* uncut; undressed (*Hort.*); entire (*of horses*).
Un'verſchuldet, *adj.* unmerited; not in debt, unencumbered; **—erweiſe,** undeservedly.
Un'verſchwiegen, *adj.* indiscreet, outspoken, that cannot keep a secret. **—heit,** *f.* indiscretion.
Unverſe'hen, *adj.* unexpected, unforeseen; surprising; unprovided (*with*); unintentional. **—s,** *adv.* unexpectedly, unawares, all of a sudden; unintentionally.
Unverſehr'—bar, *adj.* inviolable; that cannot be injured. **—t,** *adj.* uninjured; intact, entire. **—theit,** *f.* entirety.
Unverſieg'bar, *adj.* inexhaustible, that never dries up; ever flowing.
Un'verſiegelt, *adj.* not sealed up, without a seal, open.
Un'verſöhn—lich, *adj.* irreconcilable; implacable. **—lichkeit,** *f.* irreconcilableness; implacability. **—t,** *adj.* unreconciled.
Un'verſorgt, *adj.* unprovided for; without means.
Un'verſtand, *m.* want of understanding *or* judgment; imprudence; inconsiderateness; folly; foolish action *or* thing. **—en,** *adj.* not understood; misunderstood.
Un'verſtänd—ig, *adj.* imprudent; unwise; silly, stupid, absurd. **—lich,** *adj.* unintelligible; obscure, enigmatic; indistinct. **—lichkeit,** *f.* unintelligibility, incomprehensibility.
Un'verſteuerbar, *adj.* not liable to duty.
Un'verſteuert, *adj.* not taxed; not paying taxes.
Un'verſucht, *adj.* inexperienced; untried, unattempted; **ich habe nichts — gelaſſen,** I have left no stone unturned.
Un'verteidigt, *adj.* undefended; abandoned.
Un'verteilt, *adj.* undivided, undistributed.
Unvertilg'bar, *adj.* indelible; ineradicable; indestructible. **—keit,** *f.* indelibility.
Un'verträglich, *adj.* irreconcilable; unsociable; incompatible; intolerant. **—keit,** *f.* unsociableness, quarrelsomeness; incompatibility.
Un'verwahrt, *adj.* unguarded.
Un'verwandt, *adj.* unmoved; immovable, fixed; unrelated (**mit,** with); heterogeneous; **ſeine Blicke — auf eine S. richten,** to look steadfastly at *or* to fix one's eyes on a th.
Un'verwehrt, *adj.* unforbidden, permitted; **es iſt Ihnen — zu . . .,** you are at liberty to . . .
Unverwei'gerlich, *adj.* not to be refused *or* denied.
Un'verweilt, *adv.* without delay, promptly, immediately, at once, forthwith.
Unverwelk'lich, *adj.* unfading; always young; immortal. **—keit,** *f.* unfadingness; immortality. **—t,** *adj.* unfaded, blooming.
Un'verwelſcht, *adj.* unfrenchified, thoroughly German.
Unverwerf'lich, *adj.* unexceptionable; irrefragable. **—keit,** *f.* unexceptionableness; irrefragability.
Unverwes'lich, *adj.* incorruptible. **—keit,** *f.* incorruptibility.
Unverwiſch'bar, *adj.* ineffaceable, indelible.
Un'verworren, *adj.* unembroiled, not entangled, not confused.
Unverwund'bar, *adj.* invulnerable. **—keit,** *f.* invulnerableness.
Unverwüſt'lich, *adj.* indestructible; imperturbable. **—keit,** *f.* indestructibleness; imperturbability.
Un'verzagt, *adj.* undaunted, undismayed; intrepid; bold; without fear. **—heit,** *f.* intrepidity; boldness, courage.
Unverzeih'lich, *adj.* unpardonable. **—keit,** *f.* unpardonableness.

Unverzins'—bar, —lich, *adj.* paying no interest; **—bares Darlehen,** free loan.
Un'verzollt, *adj.* without paying duty; duty unpaid *or* off, unentered; in bond.
Unverzüg'lich, I. *adj.* immediate, instant. II. *adv.* without delay, forthwith.
Un'vollbracht, Un'vollendet, *adj.* unaccomplished, unachieved; unfinished.
Un'vollkommen, *adj.* imperfect, defective. **—heit,** *f.* imperfection; defect.
Un'vollſtändig, *adj.* incomplete; defective; imperfect. **—keit,** *f.* incompleteness; defectiveness.
Un'vollſtreckt, *adj.* not executed, unperformed.
Un'vollzählig, *adj.* incomplete. **—keit,** *f.* incompleteness.
Unvollzieh'bar, *adj.* that cannot be accomplished, not to be carried out.
Unvorausſehbar, *adj.* not to be foreseen.
Unvor'bereitet, *adj.* & *adv.* unprepared; not ready; extemporaneous, extempore; **—e Überſetzung,** unseen (translation); **auf den Krieg —,** unprepared for war.
Un'vordenklich, *adj.* immemorial; **ſeit —er Zeit,** time out of mind, from time immemorial.
Un'vorgreiflich, *adj.* without prejudice to; impartial; *see* **Unmaßgeblich.**
Unvorher'geſehen, *adj.* unforeseen, unexpected; **—er Schickſalsſchlag,** bolt from the blue.
Un'vorſätzlich, *adj.* unpremeditated, unintentional; involuntary.
Un'vorſichtig, *adj.* improvident; inconsiderate; unwise; incautious. **—keit,** *f.* want of foresight, improvidence; imprudence; thoughtlessness; **aus —keit,** from carelessness, from lack of caution, inadvertently.
Unvor'teilhaft, *adj.* disadvantageous, unprofitable; **einen —en Handel ſchließen,** to make a bad bargain, to buy *or* sell at a loss.
Un'wachſam, *adj.* unwary, unwatchful, wanting in vigilance. **—keit,** *f.* want of vigilance.
Unwäg'bar, *adj.* imponderable. **—keit,** *f.* imponderability.
Unwähl'bar, *adj.* ineligible. **—keit,** *f.* ineligibility.
Un'wahr, *adj.* false, untrue; lying; fictitious; hypocritical. **—haft,** *adj.* untrue, false; untruthful; not reliable. **—haftigkeit,** *f.* want of truth; inaccuracy; falseness. **—heit,** *f.* falsehood; inaccuracy; lie, false assertion; fiction.
Un'wahrnehmbar, *adj.* imperceptible.
Un'wahrſcheinlich, *adj.* improbable. **—keit,** *f.* unlikeliness, improbability.
Unwan'delbar, *adj.* immutable, unchangeable; constant, eternal; indeclinable (*Gram.*). **—keit,** *f.* immutability, unchangeableness; constancy.
Un'wegſam, *adj.* impracticable; pathless, untrodden. **—keit,** *f.* impracticable condition (*of roads*).
Un'wehrhaft, *adj.* defenceless.
Un'weib, *n.* hag, fury; virago, dragon, termagant. **—lich,** *adj.* unwomanly. **—lichkeit,** *f.* unwomanliness, unwomanly behaviour.
Unwei'gerlich, *adj.* unresisting, unhesitating; unrefusable, undeniable. **—er Gehorſam,** unquestioning *or* implicit obedience.
Un'weiſe, *adj.*, (**Un'weislich,** *adv.*,) unwise, foolish.
Un'weit, *adv.* & *prep.* (*with gen.*) not far off *or* from, near, close by; **— von hier,** not far from here, in the neighbourhood of this place, close by.
Un'wert, I. *adj.* unworthy; worthless; not esteemed, not valued. II. *m.* worthlessness; futility.
Un'weſen, *n.* disorder; abuse; row; disgrace-

ful state of things; excess; scandalous conduct; monster.

Un'wesenhaft, *adj.* immaterial, unreal, unsubstantial.

Un'wesentlich, *adj.* unessential, immaterial; accidental, accessory; **—e Dinge**, non-essentials. **—keit**, *f.* non-essentiality; unimportance.

Un'wetter, *n.* bad weather, stormy weather; storm.

Un'wichtig, *adj.* unimportant, insignificant, trifling. **—keit**, *f.* insignificance; **eine —keit**, a trifle.

Unwiderleg'—bar, **—lich**, *adj.* unanswerable, irrefutable. **—barkeit**, **—lichkeit**, *f.* unanswerableness, irrefutability.

Unwiderruf'lich, *adj.* irrevocable; irremovable; **die Sache ist —**, the affair is past recall; **— letzte Aufführung**, positively the last performance (*Theat.*).

Unwidersprech'lich, *adj.* incontestable, undeniable. **—keit**, *f.* incontestability.

Unwidersteh'lich, *adj. & adv.* irresistible; **—er Wunsch**, overpowering desire; **sich — zu einem hingezogen fühlen**, to feel o.s. irresistibly attracted by *or* drawn towards a p. **—keit**, *f.* irresistible force, impetuosity.

Unwiederbring'lich, *adj. & adv.* irreparable, irretrievable; **— dahin** *or* **verloren**, irretrievably lost, gone for ever. **—keit**, *f.* irretrievableness, irreparableness.

Un'will—e(n), *m.* indignation; displeasure, anger; annoyance, vexation; reluctance. **—ig**, *adj.* indignant; reluctant, unwilling; **—ig über (eine S.)**, indignant at, angry at (a th.). *Comp.* **—fährig**, *adj.* disobliging *or* uncomplying. **—fährigkeit**, *f.* want of compliance. **—kommen**, *adj.* unwelcome; disagreeable; troublesome. **—kürlich**, *adj.* involuntary. **—kürlichkeit**, *f.* involuntariness.

Un'wirk—lich, *adj.* not real *or* existing. **—sam**, *adj.* ineffectual; inefficacious; inoperative; null, void. **—samkeit**, *f.* inefficacy; inefficiency.

Un'wirsch, *adj.* cross; morose; brusque. **—heit**, *f.* bad temper; brusqueness.

Un'wirt—bar, **—lich**, **—sam**, *adj.* inhospitable; waste, barren; dreary. **—schaftlich**, *adj.* unthrifty, extravagant. **—schaftlichkeit**, *f.* wastefulness, extravagance, thriftlessness.

Un'wissen—d, *adj.* ignorant; not cognizant of; **mir —d**, unknown to me; **ein —der Mensch**, an ignoramus. **—heit**, *f.* ignorance. **—schaftlich**, *adj.* unscientific. **—schaftlichkeit**, *f.* want of scientific method, unscientific ways of studying. **—tlich**, *adj.* not cognizant of, unconscious of. *Comp.* **—heits=fehler**, *m.* mistake due to ignorance.

Un'wohl, *adj.* unwell, indisposed; out of sorts, seedy (*coll.*); **mir ist —, ich bin —, ich fühle mich —**, I don't feel well; I feel unwell *or* poorly, I feel queer *or* out of sorts (*coll.*). *Comp.* **—sein**, *n.* indisposition; menses.

Un'wohn—bar, **—lich**, *adj.* uninhabitable.

Un'wort, *n.* ghost word.

Un'würdig, *adj.* unworthy; **er wird nichts thun, was seiner — wäre**, he will do nothing unworthy of his character *or* position; **Lobes —**, undeserving of praise. **—keit**, *f.* unworthiness.

Un'zahl, *f.* excessively large number; **eine —**, an endless number, an infinity, a legion.

Unzahl'bar, *adj.* not payable; not due.

Unzähl'—bar, **—ig**, *adj.* innumerable, numberless; **—ige Male**, times without number. **—barkeit**, *f.* numberlessness.

Unzähm'bar, *adj.* untamable, indomitable. **—keit**, *f.* ferocity.

Un'zart, *adj.* not tender; indelicate, rough, rude; devoid of tact. **—heit**, *f.* rudeness; want of delicacy *or* tenderness.

[1]**Un'ze**, *f.* (—n) ounce; **— Gold**, ounce of gold; **eine halbe —**, half an ounce.

[2]**Un'ze**, *f.* (—n) ounce, Felis onca (*Zool.*).

Un'zeit, *f.* wrong time; **zur —**, inopportunely. **—ig**, *adj.* untimely, unseasonable; ill-timed; immature, unripe; premature; **—ige Geburt**, abortion, child, *etc.*, prematurely born. **—igkeit**, *f.* unseasonableness. *Comp.* **—gemäß**, (*pron.* **unzeit'gemäß**) *adj.* old-fashioned, unfashionable; behind the times; not time-serving, independent; inopportune.

Unzerbrech'lich, *adj.* unbreakable; infrangible.

Unzerleg'bar, *adj.* undecomposable; **—er Körper**, element, simple substance.

Unzerreiß'—bar, **—lich**, *adj.* untearable, solid.

Unzersetz'bar, *see* **Unzerlegbar**.

Unzerstör'—bar, **—lich**, *adj.* indestructible; imperishable. **—barkeit**, *f.* indestructibleness.

Unzerteil'—bar, *adj.* indivisible. **—barkeit**, *f.* indivisibility. **—t**, I. *adj.* undivided. II. *adv.* jointly.

Unzertrenn'—bar, **—lich**, *adj.* inseparable; **—liche Eigenschaften**, inherent qualities. **—lichkeit**, *f.* inseparableness, indissolubleness.

Unzial'buchstabe, *m.* uncial letter.

Un'ziem—end, **—lich**, *adj.* unbecoming, unseemly; indecent. **—lichkeit**, *f.* indecorum, unseemliness.

Un'zier, **—de**, *f.* blemish, stain; disfigurement. **—lich**, *adj.* inelegant, ungraceful. **—lichkeit**, *f.* inelegance.

Un'zinsbar, *adj.* not tributary.

Un'zivilisiert, *adj.* uncivilized, barbarous.

Un'zucht, *f.* unchastity; prostitution, lewdness.

Un'züchtig, *adj.* unchaste; lewd; obscene; lascivious. **—keit**, *f.* immodesty; dissoluteness.

Un'zufrieden, *adj.* dissatisfied, discontented; **der —e hat nie genug**, a discontented mind is never satisfied. **—heit**, *f.* discontent; dissatisfaction.

Un'zugänglich, *adj.* inaccessible; not affable; intractable. **—keit**, *f.* inaccessibility.

Un'zulänglich, *adj.* insufficient, inadequate. **—keit**, *f.* insufficiency.

Un'zulässig, *adj.* inadmissible. **—keit**, *f.* inadmissibility.

Un'zünftig, *adj.* not belonging to a guild, outsider.

Un'zurechnungsfähig, *adj.* irresponsible; weak-minded, imbecile; **die Leidenschaft macht ihn —**, passion has blinded his judgment. **—keit**, *f.* want of judgment; imbecility; irresponsibility.

Un'zureichend, *adj.* insufficient.

Un'zusammenhängend, *adj.* unconnected, disconnected, disjointed; incoherent; inconsecutive.

Un'zuständig, *adj.* incompetent (*Law*).

Un'zuträglich, *adj.* disadvantageous, unprofitable; prejudicial; unhealthy.

Un'zuverlässig, *adj.* unreliable, untrustworthy; shuffling; uncertain; inaccurate. **—keit**, *f.* untrustworthiness, unreliability; precariousness.

Un'zweckmäßig, *adj.* unsuitable, not to the purpose; irrelevant; injudicious; improper. **—keit**, *f.* unsuitableness, inadequacy. *Comp.* **—keits=lehre**, *f.* dysteleology.

Un'zweideutig, *adj.* unequivocal, unambiguous. **—keit**, *f.* unequivocalness, unambiguity.

Unzwei'felhaft, *adj.* undoubted, indubitable; **—e Thatsache**, established fact; **es ist — wahr**, it is beyond question, there can be no doubt about it.

Üp'pig, *adj.* luxuriant, rank; exuberant; rude; sensual; voluptuous; lascivious; sumptuous; (= **übermütig**) overbearing; in high spirits (*coll.*); **ihr —er Wuchs**, her full *or* fully developed figure *or* bust; **—er Haarwuchs**, exuberant growth of hair; **—es Mahl**, sumptuous repast; **—es Unkraut**, rank weeds.

—keit, *f.* luxuriant growth, exuberance; richness; luxury; sensuality; sensual pleasures; voluptuousness; lasciviousness.

[1]Ur, *m.* (—(e)s, *pl.* —e) species of wild ox, ureox; *see* Auer. *Comp.* —ochs, *m.* aurochs.

[2]Ur (*always long* u *except in:* Urteil), *prefix of nouns & adj.'s originally denoting 'out of' and now gen'lly implying* primitiveness, origin *or* extreme antiquity; *sometimes it merely adds an intensive force; it is equivalent to the prefix* „er," *which was originally the same word, and occurred in unaccented syllables while* ur *occurred in words in which the prefix was accented* (*see* Urteil *and* erteilen, Urlaub *and* erlauben).

Ur'ahn, *m.* (—en, *pl.* —en), —e, *f.* (*pl.* —en), (—herr, *m.*, —frau, *f.*) great-grandfather, great-grandmother; ancestor, ancestress.

Ur'alt, *adj.* extremely old; very ancient, primeval, as old as the hills.

Ura'n, *n.* (—s), (—erz, *n.*) uranium.

Ur'an—fang, *m.* the very beginning. —fänglich, *adj* original, primeval.

Ur'anlage, *f.* original disposition.

Urä'usschlange, *f.* uræus, serpent used as royal symbol in Egypt.

Urba'n, *adj.* urbane, polite. —itä't, *f.* urbanity.

Ur'bar, I. *adj.* arable, capable of cultivation; cultivated. II. *n.* revenue; copyhold, estate, land. *Comp.* —machen, *n.*, —machung, *f.* clearing, bringing into cultivation. —macher, *m.* breaker(-up of the ground).

Ur'bedeutung, *f.* original meaning.

Ur'beginn, *m.* (—es) *see* Uranfang.

Ur'begriff, *m.* primitive notion; —e einer Wissenschaft, rudiments of a science.

Ur'bestandteil, *m.* primitive element.

Ur'bewohner, *m.* original inhabitant; (*pl.*) aborigines.

Ur'bild, *n.* original; archetype, prototype; ideal. —lich, *adj.* original; ideal.

Ur'christ, *m.* primitive Christian. —entum, *n.* primitive Christianity, the early Church; the early Christians.

Ur'deutsch, *adj.* ancient *or* thorough(ly) German, German to the core.

Ur'eigen, *adj.* original; very exacting (*colloq.*). —heit, *f.*, —tümlichkeit, *f.* originality.

Ur'eltern, *pl.* ancestors; first parents.

Ur'enkel, *m.*, —in, *f.* great-grandchild.

Ur'evangelium, *n.* original gospel.

Ur'fehde, (*obs. spelling:* Ur'phede,) *f.* oath to keep the peace, oath of truce.

Ur'fels, *m.* primitive rock.

Ur'form, *f.* original form, prototype, archetype.

Ur'gebirge, *f.* primitive mountains *or* rocks.

Ur'geist, *m.* original spirit; uncreated being; the Eternal, the Deity.

Urgie'ren, *v.a.* to urge, insist upon.

Ur'groß— (*in comp.*) —eltern, *pl.* great-grandparents. —mutter, *f.* great-grandmother. —vater, *m.* great-grandfather.

Ur'grund, *m.* first cause, original cause.

Ur'heber, *m.*, —in, *f.* author, originator. —schaft, *f.* authorship, parentage. *Comp.* —recht, *n.* copyright (an Werken der Litteratur, of literary productions).

Uri'n, *m.* (—s) urine. —ie'ren, *v.n.* (*aux.* h.) to urinate, to make water.

Ur'kanton, *m.* original (*Swiss*) Forest Canton.

Ur'keim, *m.* first germ.

Ur'kirche, *f.* primitive church.

Ur'komisch, *adj.* excessively comic, extremely funny.

Ur'—kraft, *f.* original force. —kräftig, *adj.* very *or* most powerful; of original force.

Ur'kund—e, *f.* (*pl.* —en) deed, document; charter; voucher; record; attestation; diploma; zu —e dessen, in witness whereof. —lich, I. *adj.* documental, documentary; authentic; —lich dessen habe ich Obiges geschrieben, in proof of which I have written the above. *Comp.* —en=bewahrer, *m.* keeper of the records; registrar; master of the rolls. —en=beweis, *m.* documentary proof. —en=buch, *n.* record, register. —en=fälschung, *f.* forgery *or* falsification of documents. —en=forscher, *m. see* —enkenner. —en=gewölbe, —en=haus, *n.* record-office, archives. —en=kenner, *m.* one skilled in diplomatics, palæographer. —en=kenntnis, *f.* knowledge of ancient documents; diplomatics. —en=lehre, *f.* diplomatics; palæography. —en=sammlung, *f.* archives, collection of documents. —en=werk, *n.* register *or* collection of documents, *etc.*

Ur'laub, *m.* (—s) leave of absence, furlough; auf —, on furlough; — nehmen, to take leave (of absence). —er, *m.* (—ers, *pl.* —er) soldier on furlough, ticket of leave man.

Ur'laut, *m.* primitive sound.

Ur'mensch, *m.* the first man; original (person).

Ur'mutter, *f.* first mother, mother of mankind.

Ur'ne, *f.* (*pl.* —n) urn· water-bottle; spore-case of mosses.

Ur'ning, *m.* pederast.

Ur'phede, *see* Urfehde.

Ur'plötzlich, I. *adj.* sudden. II. *adv.* all at once.

Ur'quell, *m.* (—s, *pl.* —e), —e, *f.* (*pl.* —en) fountain-head; primary source, origin.

Ur'sach—e, *f.* (first) cause, (original) motive, ground, occasion; aus welcher —e? aus was für einer —e? for what reason? why? keine —e, don't mention it, no need (*for thanks*), pray don't apologize; man hat —e zu glauben, there is reason to believe; kleine —en, große Wirkungen, great events often come from little causes (*prov.*).

Ur'sächlich, *adj.* causal; causative. —keit, *f.* causality.

Ur'sage, *f.* ancient tradition, original legend.

Ur'satz, *m.* axiom.

Ur'schicht, *f.* primitive stratum.

Ur'schrift, *f.* original text; original; first sketch, notes (*of an article*); autograph. —lich, *adj.* autographic.

Ur'sitz, *m.* family seat; ancestral home.

Ur'sprache, *f.* primitive language; original speech.

Ur'sprung, *m.* (first) source; origin; beginning; principle, element; seinen — haben *or* nehmen von, to take its rise from, to descend from; deutschen —s, native of Germany; made in Germany. *Comp.* —s=depesche, *f.* forwarded telegram. —s=land, *n.* country of origin; producing country. —s=nachweis, *m.*, —s=schein, *m.*, —s=zeugnis, *n.* certificate of origin.

Ur'sprünglich, *adj.* primitive; first; primary; original; — aus Deutschland herstammen, to be a native of Germany, of German origin; to be made in *or* to come from Germany. —keit, *f.* primitiveness.

Ur'stamm, *m.* original stock; primitive race.

Ur'stand, (*poet.*) *see* Urzustand.

Ur'stende, Ur'ständ(e), *f.* resurrection (*obs.*).

Ur'stoff, *m.* primary *or* original matter; principle, element. *Comp.* —lehre, *f.* atomic theory. —teilchen, *n.* atom.

Ur'teil (*short* u), *n.* (—s, *pl.* —e) judgment, decision; judicial sentence; opinion; ein — über eine S. fällen, to pass sentence upon, to give an opinion upon a th.; meinem —(e) nach, in my opinion; sich dem —(e) unterwerfen, to submit to a judicial decision; einem das — sprechen, to pass judgment on a p.; nach dem —(e) von Sachverständigen, in the opinion of experts. *Comp.* —s=eröffnung, *f.* publication of a judgment *or* sentence. —s=fähig, *adj.* competent to form an opinion *or* to pass judgment. —s=kraft, *f.* (power of) judgment, discernment; Kants Kritik der —skraft, Kant's critique of the æsthetic faculties. —s=spruch, m. judgment, sentence, decree. —s=vermögen, n. see —skraft. —s=vollstreckung, f. carrying out of a sentence.

Ur'teilen, v.n. (aux. h.) to judge; nach seinen Reden or seiner Sprache nach zu —, according to him; darüber kann er nicht —, he is no judge of such matters.

Ur'tel, (dial. & poet. for) Urteil.

Ur'text, m. original text.

Ur'tier, n. primitive or antediluvian animal. —e, —chen, pl. protozoa.

Ur'=ur— (in comp.) —ahn, m. progenitor, great-great-grandfather. —eltern, pl. forefathers, first parents, early ancestors. —enkel(in, f.), m. great-great-grandchild.

Ur'vater, m. first parent, forefather.

Ur'väter—lich, adj. primitive; ancestral. Comp. —hausrat, m. ancestral furniture; ancestral lumber. —zeit, f. olden times, days of yore.

Ur'vernunft, f. fount of reason, divine reason.

Ur'verwandt, adj. cognate (of words). —schaft, f. primitive affinity, cognation.

Ur'volk, n. primitive or prehistoric people; aborigines.

Ur'vorfahr, m. (first) ancestor, forefather.

Ur'wahl, f. preliminary election (of electors).

Ur'wähler, m. primary elector. Comp. —versammlung, f. assembly of primary electors, primary (assembly).

Ur'wald, m. primeval or virgin forest; westliche Urwälder Amerikas, backwoods.

Ur'weib, n. first or primitive woman; type of a woman, ideal woman.

Ur'welt, f. primeval world. —lich, adj. primitive; antediluvian.

Ur'wesen, n. first or primordial being; first principle.

Ur'wort, n. primitive (word).

Ur'wüchsig, adj. original, native; natural, racy.

Ur'zeit, f. primitive times, primeval age.

Ur'zeugung, f. equivocal or spontaneous generation.

Ur'zustand, m. primitive state, original condition.

Ur'zweck, m. original aim, first purpose.

Us—an'ce, Üsan'ce, f. usage, custom; nach —ance or Üsance, see —ancenmäßig. —o, m. (—o, pl. —i) usance (C.L.); auf zwei —o, at double usance. —ukapie'ren, v.a. to acquire by prescription. —us, see Gebrauch. Comp. —ancen=mäßig, üsancen=mäßig, adv. as is customary. —o=wechsel, m. bill at usance (C.L.).

Usurp—a'tor, m. (—ators, pl. —ato'ren) usurper. —ato'risch, adj. usurping. —ie'ren, v.a. to usurp.

U'tang, see Orangutang.

Utilita'r—ier, m. (—iers, pl. —ier), —isch, adj. utilitarian.

Utilitä't, utility. Comp. —s=prinzip, n. utilitarian principle. —s=rücksichten, pl. considerations of utility.

Utopie', f. Utopianism, Utopian scheme or notion.

Uto'pisch, Utopis'tisch, adj. Utopian.

Utraquis't, m. (—en, pl. —en) Bohemian Protestant (17th century).

Ut'zen, U'zen, (long u) v.a. to mock, tease (coll.).

V

V, v, V, v; *for abbreviations see the Index at the end of the German-English part.*

Vaccinie'ren, v.a. to vaccinate.

Vademe'cum, n. vademecum, guide-book.

Vag, adj. & adv. vague, loose. —abun'd, m. (—abun'den, pl. —abun'den), —abun'din, f. vagabond, vagrant, tramp. —abun'denhaft, adj. vagabond. —abun'dentum, n. (—abundentums) vagabondage, vagrancy; tramps, vagabonds (coll.). —abundie'ren, v.n. (aux. h. & s.) to lead a vagabond or vagrant life. —a'nt, m. mediæval wandering scholar. —an'ten=poesie, f. Latin poetry (mostly rhymed songs in popular style) composed by the wandering scholars.

Vaka'n—t, adj. vacant, void. —z, f. (pl. —zen) vacancy; vacation, holidays (dial.); recess (Law, etc.).

Va'k—at, adj. blank; wanting (in lists); vacant (of offices). —uum, n. (—uums, pl. —ua) vacuum (Phys.). Comp. —uum=pumpe, f. air-pump.

Vale't, n. (—s, pl. —s) farewell, adieu, valediction; — geben, to dismiss; — sagen, to bid farewell or adieu, to take leave. Comp. —sagen, n. leave-taking, adieux. —schmaus m. farewell banquet.

Val—idie'ren, v. I. a. to make valid (C.L.); to effect (an insurance, etc.). II. n. to be valid; eine Summe —idieren lassen gegen, to place a sum against, set off one sum against (another); die Assekuranz —idiert auf . . ., the insurance is effected on . . . —idie'rung, f. a rendering valid. —u'ta, f. value; currency; beständige —uta, standard (C.L.). —utie'ren, —vie'ren, v.a. to value, valuate. —vatio'n, f. valuation. Comp. —vatio'ns=tabelle, f. table of values.

Vam'pir, (Vam'pyr,) m. (—s, pl. —e) vampire.

Vanadi'n, n. (—s) vanadium (Chem.).

Vanil'le, f. vanilla. Comp. —n=schokolade, f. vanilla chocolate. —n=sahne, f. vanilla cream.

Va'rek, m. (—s, pl. —s) kelp, sea-wrack (Bot.).

Va'ri—a, pl. sundries, different or miscellaneous things. —an'te, f. variant reading, varia lectio (in books or MSS). —anten=apparat, m. synopsis of all the various readings. —atio'n, f. variation. —etä't, f. variety. —ie'ren, v.a. & n. (aux. h.) to vary; ein Thema —ie'ren, to compose or play variations on an air. Comp. —ations'=fähig, adj. variable. —ations'=rechnung, f. calculus of variations.

Vasa'll, m. (—en, pl. —en), —in, f. vassal, liege(man), man, retainer. —enschaft, f., —entum, n. vassalage; vassals (coll.). Comp. —en=dienst, m. feudal service; homage. —en=eid, m. oath of vassalage, vassal's oath of allegiance. —en=staat, m. tributary (state)

Va'se, f. (pl. —n) vase. Comp. —n=förmig, adj. like a vase, vascular (Bot.).

Va'ter, m. (—s, pl. Väter) father; (male) parent; sire (Poet. & Zööl.); governor (sl.); papa; dad(die) (childr. lang.); unsre Väter, our forefathers, ancestors; die Väter der Stadt, the mayor and aldermen, the town councillors; ehrwürdiger —, Most Reverend Father (in God), Reverend Sir. —schaft, f. paternity, fatherhood; Nachforschung über die —schaft, affiliation case (Law). Comp. —bruder, m. paternal uncle. —freuden, pl. paternal joys. —haus, n. the paternal roof, home of one's childhood. —land, n. native country, fatherland; engeres —land, fatherland in a more limited sense, native province or district; fürs —land sterben, to die for one's country. —ländisch, adj. relating to one's country; national, vernacular. —lands=freund, m. patriot. —lands=liebe, f. patriotism. —lands=los, adj. without a fatherland; unpatriotic. —lands=verteidiger, m. soldier (often hum.). —los, adj. fatherless. —mord, m. parricide. —mörder, m. parricide; (old-fashioned) stand-up collar (coll.). —(s)=name, m. father's name; patronymic; maiden name. —schafts=klage, f. affiliation case. —s=

schwester, *f.* father's sister, paternal aunt. **—s=schwester=sohn,** *m.*, **—s=schwester=tochter,** *f.* first cousin (*on the father's side*). **—stadt,** *f.* native town. **—teil,** *n.* patrimony. **—= und mutterlos,** *adj.* orphan. **—un'ser,** *n.* the Lord's Prayer, Pater-noster (*R. C.*); **ein —unser beten,** to say a paternoster (*R. C.*); **ein —unser lang,** while one could repeat a paternoster, for a minute.

Vä'ter—chen, *n.* (**—chens,** *pl.* **—chen**) (*dear*) papa *or* father; daddie dear (*children's lang.*). **—lich,** *adj.* paternal. *Comp.* **—gruft,** *f.* ancestral vault. **—saal,** *m.* ancestral hall. **—sitte,** *f.* manners of our fathers *or* forefathers.

Vatika'n, *m.* (**—s**) Vatican, the see of Rome. **—isch,** *adj.* Vatican (*as, Vatican Council, etc.*).

Ve'da, *see* **Weda.**

Veget—abi'lien, *pl.* vegetables. **—abi'lisch,** *adj.* vegetable. **—a'rier,** (*less good:* **—aria'=ner,**) *m.* (**—ariers,** *pl.* **—arier**) vegetarian. **—a'risch,** (*less good:* **—aria'nisch,**) *adj.* vegetarian. **—ari(ani)s'mus,** *m.* vegetarianism. **—ie'ren,** *v.n.* (*aux.* **h.**) to vegetate.

Veheme'nz, *f.* vehemence, impetuosity.

Vehi'kel, *n.* (**—s,** *pl.* **—**) vehicle; medium, vehicle (*Med.*).

Vehm, *ꝛc.*, *see* **Fehm, ꝛc.**

Veil'chen, *n.* (**—s,** *pl.* **—**) violet (*Bot.*). *Comp.* **—blau,** *adj.* & *n.* violet. **—farbig,** *adj.* violet-coloured. **—fresser,** *m.* ladies' man; fop. **—moos,** *n.* red byssus (*Bot.*). **—stein,** *m.* iolite (*Min.*). **—wurz,** *m.*, **—wurzel,** *f.* orris-root, root of Florentine iris (*Pharm.*).

Veli'n, *n.* (**—s**), **—papier,** *n.* vellum.

Velleitä't, *f.* (*pl.* **—en**) faint desire, penchant, vacillation, velleity.

Ve'lo, *n.* (*short for* **—ciped**) (**—s,** *pl.* **—s**) cycle. *Comp.* **—sport,** *m.* cycling.

Velo—cipe'd, *n.* (**—cipeds,** *pl.* **—cipede**) velocipede (*obs.*); (bi)cycle; machine. **—cipe'disch,** *adj.* cycling. **—cipedi'st,** *m.* (**—cipedis'ten,** *pl.* **—cipedis'ten**), **—cipedis'tin,** *f.* cyclist, woman cyclist. **—dro'm,** *m.* track for cyclists, cycling school.

Ve'n—e, *f.* (*pl.* **—en**) vein (*Anat.*). **—ö's,** *adj.* venous. *Comp.* **—en=blut,** *n.* venous blood.

Venera'bile, *n.* the consecrated wafer, the Host.

Vene'risch, *adj.* venereal.

Venti'l, *n.* (**—s,** *pl.* **—e**) valve; **Klappen—,** clack-valve; **Kegel—,** conical valve; **Kolben —,** piston-valve; **Kugel—,** ball-clack. **—a=tio'n,** *f.* ventilation; discussion (*of a question*). **—a'tor,** *m.* (**—ators,** *pl.* **—ato'ren**) ventilator; fan. **—ie'ren,** *v.a.* to ventilate; to discuss (*a question*). *Comp.* **—bewegung,** *f.*, **—gehäuse,** *n.* valve-casing. **—getriebe,** *n.* valve-gearing. **—deckel,** *m.* lid of a valve. **—horn,** *n.* key-bugle. **—klappe,** *f.* clack, flap-valve. **—kolben,** *m.* valve-piston. **—trom=pete,** *f.* key-bugle. **—steuerung,** *f.* valve-motion.

Ve'nus, *f.* (*pl. coll.* **Venusse**) Venus. **—haft,** *adj.* like (a) Venus. *Comp.* **—berg,** *m.* mons Veneris (*Anat.*); Venusberg, Hörselberg near Eisenach (*German Legends*). **—durchgang,** *m.* transit of (the planet) Venus. **—feste,** *pl.* aphrodisia. **—flie'genfalle,** *f.* Venus' fly-trap (*Bot.*). **—gürtel,** *m.* girdle of Venus; Venus's basin (*Bot.*). **—haar,** *n.* maidenhair (*Bot.*). **—stern,** *m.* (*the planet*) Venus.

Ver—, *insep. prefix added to verbs and to the nouns and adjectives derived from them, with the idea of* removal, loss, untoward action, using up, change, reversal, *etc. Its general force will be gathered from the following examples;* **das Mehl ver=backen,** to use up all the flour for baking bread; **die Karten ver=geben,** to make a misdeal (*Cards*) (*idea of doing something wrong*); **ver=brausen,** to cease to roar *or* to ferment (*idea of cessation*): **ver=hängen (einen Spiegel),** to cover up (a looking-glass); **ver=achten,** to despise (*idea of opposite of that which is denoted by the simple verb*); **ver=plaudern,** to chat *or* talk away the time, to pass (the time) in chatting (*idea of loss of time*); **ver=dursten,** to perish with thirst (*idea of loss of life*). *But frequently it is used to form verbs from nouns, adjectives and other verbs, sometimes to denote change and sometimes without modifying the meaning, e.g.* **ver=ursachen,** to cause; **ver=edeln,** to ennoble; **ver=größern,** to enlarge.

Verab'folg—en, *v.a.* to deliver, send, remit; to give up, surrender; **nicht —en (lassen),** to retain, keep back. **—ung,** *f.* delivery; remitting

Verab'reden, *v.a.* to concert, agree upon; **sich —,** to come to an understanding; to make an appointment (**mit** with); **verabredetermaßen,** according to agreement, as agreed upon.

Verab'reichen, *v.a.* (**einem etwas**) to give; to hand over; to furnish; to administer (*chastisement*); **einem eins —,** to let a p. have s.th.; to strike at someone; **einem eine Ohrfeige —,** to give a p. a box on the ear.

Verab'säumen, *v.a.* to neglect, omit, forget; **eine Gelegenheit —,** to let an opportunity slip.

Verab'scheu—en, I. *v.a.* to abhor, abominate, detest. II. *subst. n.*, **—ung,** *f.* detestation. *Comp.* **—ungs=wert, —ungs=würdig,** *adj.* abominable, detestable, execrable.

Verab'schied—en, *v.a.* to dismiss, discharge, send away; to disband, discharge (*soldiers*); to decide, decree; **sich von** (*or* **bei**) **einem —en,** to take leave of a p., to bid goodbye to a person. **—ung,** *f.* dismissal; decreeing.

Veracci'sen, *v.a.* to pay excise duty on.

Verach't—en, *v.a.* to despise, scorn, disdain, slight. **—ung,** *f.* disdain, contempt. *Comp.* **—ungs=wert,** *adj.* contemptible, mean.

Veracht'fachen, *v.a.* to increase eight-fold.

Veräch't'lich, *adj.* contemptuous, disdainful; contemptible, abject. **—keit,** *f.* contemptuousness, disdainfulness; abjectness; despicableness.

Veräch'zen, *v.a.* to pass (*one's time, life, etc.*) away in groaning.

Verakkordie'ren, *v.a.* to contract for.

Verallgemei'ner—n, *v.a.* to generalize. **—ung,** *f.* generalization.

Veral't—en, *v.n.* (*aux.* **s.**) to grow old; to become obsolete. **—et,** *p.p.* & *adj.* old, antiquated; superannuated; obsolete.

Veran'da, *f.* (*pl.* **—s, Veran'den**) veranda.

Verän'der—lich, *adj.* changeable, mutable, liable to change; unsteady, unstable, fickle; fluctuating; change (*on barometers*); variable (*Gram., Math., etc.*). **—lichkeit,** *f.* variability, changeableness; instability, inconstancy, fickleness. **—n,** *v.* I. *a.* to change, alter; to vary; to modify; **seine Wohnung —n,** to remove; **die Religion —n,** to apostatize, change one's religion; **auf nachteilige Art —n,** to change for the worse. II. *r.* to change; to vary, to leave a service and take another place (*of servants*); to get married (*coll.*); **die Witterung hat sich —t,** the weather has changed. **—ung,** *f.* changing; change; alteration; variation; modification; breaking (*of the voice*). *Comp.* **—ungs=halber,** *adv.* for a change; on account of a change.

Veran'kern, *v.a.* to fasten with grappling irons.

Veran'lagen, *v.a.* to arrange; **die Steuern —,** to assess taxes; **gut veranlagter Mann,** a man of many parts, a highly gifted man.

Veran'lass—en, *v.a.* to cause, occasion, bring about, entail, effect, call forth; **einen zu einer S. —en,** to induce, *or* cause a p. to do something; **das veranlaßte ihn zu denken,** that made him think; **das hat mich zu dem Glauben veranlaßt,** that has led me to believe. **—er,** *m.* (—ers, *pl.* —er), **—erin,** *f.* author, cause. **—ung,** *f.* cause, occasion; motive, inducement; **—ung geben,** to cause, give rise *or* occasion to; **auf —ung von . . .,** at the instance, instigation of . . .

Veran′schaulich—en, *v.a.* to render clear *or* conspicuous, to illustrate, be illustrative of. **—ung,** *f.* demonstration. *Comp.* **—ungs=apparat,** *m.* apparatus to illustrate s.th.

Veran′schlag—en, *v.a.* to value, rate; to estimate, to make an estimate (of). **—ung,** *f.* valuation, estimate; rate.

Veran′stalt—en, *v.a.* to prepare; to contrive, arrange, bring about; to manage. **—er,** *m.* (—ers, *pl.* —er) arranger, organizer, disposer. **—ung,** *f.* preparation; arrangement; management; **—ungen treffen,** to arrange, prepare, make arrangements (*for*).

Verant′wort—en, *v.a.* to answer for, account for; to defend, vindicate; **das will ich schon —en,** I will be answerable for that, leave that to me; **er hat viel zu —en,** he has much to answer for; **sich (wegen einer S.) bei einem —en,** to justify one's conduct, vindicate oneself to a person. **—lich,** *adj.* responsible for, accountable; justifiable; **gegenseitig —lich,** mutually, jointly responsible; **ich bin nur meinem Gewissen und meinem Gott —lich,** I am accountable to none but my conscience and my God. **—lichkeit,** *f.* responsibility; **—lichkeit für eine Schuld,** accountability for a debt; **gegenseitige —lichkeit,** solidarity. **—ung,** *f.* responsibility; justification, vindication, excuse; **thun Sie es auf meine —ung,** do it and let me be answerable for it, do it and I will be responsible *or* take the responsibility; **die —ung auf sich laden,** to incur the responsibility; **auf seine —ung,** at his (own) peril, on his own responsibility; **einen zur —ung ziehen,** to call a p. to account. *Comp.* **—ungs=los,** *adj.* irresponsible. **—ungs=rede,** *f.* (speech made in) defence, apology. **—ungs=schrift,** *f.* apology; defence (*Law*). **—ungs=voll,** *adj.* involving great responsibility, responsible.

Verar′beit—en, *v.a.* to work, to manufacture; to use, work up; to use, employ; to work off; to ponder over, assimilate, to inwardly digest; to spend in working; **einen —en,** to pitch into a p., to pull s.o. to pieces (*coll.*). **seine Sorgen —en,** to work off one's troubles; **—etes Silber,** wrought silver. **—ung,** *f.* manufacturing; working up; digestion; elaboration, working out.

Verar′gen, *v.a.* to take amiss, misconstrue; **einem etwas —,** to blame a p. for a thing; **ich verarge es Ihnen gar nicht,** I don't blame you for it at all; **das kann mir niemand —,** no one can find fault with me *or* think the worse of me for that.

Verar′m—en, *v.n.* (*aux.* **s.**) to become poor, to be reduced to poverty. **—ung,** *f.* impoverishment, pauperization.

Veräs′t—e(l)n, *v.* I. *a.* to ramify. II. *r.* & *n.* (*aux.* **s.**) to branch out; to grow together (*Anat.*). **—elung,** *f.* ramification.

Veratri′n, *n.* (—s) veratrine (*Chem.*).

Verauktionie′ren, *v.a.* to put up for auction; to sell by auction; **verauktioniert werden,** to be put to the hammer, to be sold by auction.

Veraus′gab—en, *v.a.* to spend, pay out. **—ung,** *f.* paying away; **—ung falschen Geldes,** passing counterfeit money.

Veräu′ßer—lich, *adj.* alienable; saleable. **—n,** *v.a.* to alienate, to sell; **Kirchengüter können nicht —t werden,** church lands cannot be alienated. **—ung,** *f.* alienation: sale.

Verb, *n.* (—s, *pl.* —en), **—um,** *n.* (—ums, *pl.* —en *or* —a) verb. **—a′l,** *adj.* verbal. *Comp.* **—al′=injurie,** *f.* insult, invective, libel.

Verba′cken, *reg.* & *ir.v.* I. *a.* to consume in baking; to make bread of, bake into. II. *a.* & *n.* (*aux.* **s.**) to spoil in baking; **das Brot ist —,** the bread is spoilt, badly baked.

Verbal′lasten, *v.a.* to (provide with) ballast.

Verball′horn—en, —isie′ren, *v.a.* to make worse by attempting to correct, to correct badly; to Bowdlerize.

Verba′nd, *m.* (—es, *pl.* **Verbän′de**) a binding, joining; a fastening together; that by which anything is bound *or* joined; bond; joint; ligature; bandage, dressing; union, alliance; club; **— der Arbeiter,** workmen's union; **— der Gewerbetreibenden,** trade-union, **gesellschaftlicher —,** social tie, society; club. *Comp.* **—anlegen,** *n.* dressing, bandaging (*of a wound*). **—apparat,** *m.* appliances for bandaging *or* dressing (*a wound*). **—holz,** *n.* framing timber. **—kasten,** *m.* surgeon's dressing case. **—läppchen,** *n.* compress, bandage. **—platz,** *m.* field-hospital, dressing-station (*Mil.*). **—s=kasse,** *f.* funds of a society. **—s=mitglied,** *n.* member of a society *or* an association. **—stoffe,** *pl.*, **—zeug,** *n.* articles used in dressing wounds, bandages.

Verban′n—en, *v.a.* to banish, exile; to banish, dispel. **—te(r),** *m.* exile. **—ung,** *f.* banishment, exile; **freiwillig in die —ung gehen,** to expatriate o.s. *Comp.* **—ungs=ort,** *m.* place of exile.

Verbarrikadie′ren, *v.a.* to barricade; to block (*up*); **sich —,** to intrench oneself.

Verbau′—en, *v.a.* to shut out, obstruct, build up; to use up in building; to spend in building; to build badly; **einen Durchgang —en,** to close, build up a thoroughfare; **einem Hause die Aussicht —en,** to spoil the view from a house; **sich —en,** to ruin oneself by building; to make a mistake in building; **die Zeche —t sich,** the mine pays (*its expenses*). **—ung,** *f.* obstruction; building up.

Verbau′ern, *v.n.* (*aux.* **s.**) to adopt rustic *or* boorish manners, to become like a peasant, to become countrified *or* boorish.

Verbei′ßen, *ir.v.* I. *a.* to close one's teeth so as to repress s.th.; to swallow, stifle, suppress; **sich** (*dat.*) **das Lachen —,** to stifle (*one's*) laughter; **seinen Ärger —,** to conceal one's annoyance, to put a brave face on matters; **mit schlecht verbissenem Grimm,** with ill-concealed warth; **eine Beleidigung —,** to swallow an insult; **sich** (*dat.*) **die Zähne —,** to spoil one's teeth by biting. II. *r.* to lock the teeth in biting; **sich in eine S. —, sich auf eine S. —,** to stick obstinately to a th., to be set on *or* be mad after a th. (*coll.*).

Verbe′ne, *f.* (*pl.* —n) verbena (*Bot.*).

Verber′g—en, *ir.v.* I. *a.* to hide, conceal; **etwas** (*accus.*) **einem** (*or* **vor einem**) **—en,** to hide a thing from a person. II. *r.* to hide; to abscond; **sich vor einem —en,** to hide from a person. **—ung,** *f.* concealment; absconding; covert, shelter (*B.*).

Verbes′ser—er, *m.* (—ers, *pl.* —er), **—in,** *f.* improver, corrector; reformer. **—lich,** *adj.* improvable; reparable. **—n,** *v.a.* to improve, amend; to correct; to rectify; to redress; to repair; to reform; **der Kranke —t sich,** the patient is improving, mending, getting better; **seine Umstände haben sich —t,** his circumstances have improved; **ein zu —nder Fehler,** an error (which ought) to be corrected. **—ung,** *f.* improvement; amendment; correction; emendation (*of a corrupted passage*); reform, reformation; amelioration. *Comp.* **—ungs=antrag,** *m.* amendment. **—ungs=blatt,** *n.*

proof-sheet; sheet of errata. **—ungs=fähig,** *adj.* capable of improvement.

Verbeu'g—en, *v.r.* to bow. **—ung,** *f.* reverence, obeisance, bow.

Verbie'gen, *ir.v.a.* to bend; to twist; to spoil by bending; **sich —,** to warp.

Verbie'ten, *ir.v.a.* to forbid, prohibit; **die Herausgabe einer Schrift —,** to suppress a pamphlet, a journal; **einem bei Todesstrafe etwas —,** to forbid a p. something on pain of death.

Verbil'd—en, *v.a.* to form wrongly; to spoil; to train *or* educate badly; to pervert. **—lichen,** *v.a.* to represent under an image, to symbolize, personify. **—ung,** *f.* malformation; perversion; wrong direction; improper education; **eine —ung seines Charakters war die Frucht dieser Erziehung,** his character was quite perverted by this kind of education.

Verbil'ligen, *v.a.* to make cheaper, to reduce in price, to cheapen.

Verbin'd—en, *ir.v.a.* to bind; to unite, join; to connect; to combine (*Chem.*); to unite (*Mus.*); to dress (*wounds*); to tie, bind up; to piece, to join end to end; to league, ally; to pledge, engage; to bind wrongly; to transpose the sheets in binding; to use up in binding *or* tying; **einen zu etwas —en,** to bind a p. to s.th.; **einen Begriff mit einer S. —en,** to attach an idea to a th.; **meine Interessen sind mit den deinen eng verbunden,** my interests are closely bound up with yours; **sich geschäftlich mit einem —en,** to associate (in business) with a p., to go *or* enter into partnership with a p.; **sich chemisch —en,** to combine (chemically); **mit dieser Stelle sind folgende Vorteile verbunden,** this post has these (the following) advantages; **mit verbundenen Augen,** blindfolded; **sich ehelich —en (mit einem Mädchen),** to marry (a girl); **durch Heirat verbunden,** connected by marriage; **sich zu großen Unternehmungen —en,** to combine in (*or* make common cause for undertaking) great enterprises; **ich bin Ihnen sehr verbunden,** I am greatly obliged to you; **meine Schuldigkeit verband mich dazu,** I was bound in duty to do it; **dem Ochsen das Maul —en,** to muzzle the ox (*B.*). **—lich,** *adj.* binding, obligatory; compulsory; bound, obliged; obliging, courteous; **sich —lich machen zu . . .,** to bind oneself, engage to . . .; **sich gerichtlich —lich machen,** to enter into recognizances; **das ist für mich nicht — lich,** that does not bind me; **einem etwas —liches sagen,** to pay a p. a compliment; **danke —lichst,** many thanks, much obliged! **—lichkeit,** *f.* binding force *or* power; the state *or* quality of being obligatory; obligation; liability; obligingness; favour, kindness; pleasant manner; **ohne —lichkeit,** without liability *or* responsibility; **mündliche —lichkeit,** verbal promise; **mit gegenseitiger —lichkeit,** mutually binding; **seinen —lichkeiten nachkommen,** to meet *or* fulfil one's engagements; to pay one's way; **einem eine —lichkeit schuldig sein, gegen einen eine —lichkeit haben,** to be under an obligation to a p.; **die —lichkeit, womit er es mir sagte,** the polite way in which he said it to me. **—ung,** *f.* binding, joining, connecting; misplacing leaves in binding; union; (*students'*) club *or* association; league, alliance; connection; marriage; relation; combination (*of letters, etc.; of chemicals, etc.*); conjunction; engagement; binding up, bandaging, dressing (*Surg.*); inosculation (*Anat.*); joint (*Tele.*); junction; communication; **chemische —ungen,** chemical compounds; **eine gesättigte —ung,** a saturated compound; **religiöse —ung,** religious community, brotherhood; **studentische —ungen,** students' clubs *or* associations; **schlagende —ung,** students' club in which duels are fought (with rapiers); **in —ung stehend,** communicating, connected; **in —ung stehen,** to be connected with, to communicate with, to correspond with; **in —ung treten,** to enter into connection *or* correspondence with; **in eine —ung einspringen,** to join a students' association, to become a member of a students' club; **die —ung zu Wasser ist unterbrochen,** the communication by water is interrupted; **nach mehreren Orten die —ung vermitteln,** to connect several different places; **es ist keine —ung zwischen diesen Begriffen,** there is no connection between these ideas. *Comp.* **—ungs=bahn,** *f.* branch- *or* junction-line. **—ungs=damm,** *m.* connecting dam. **—ungs=gang,** *m.* connecting passage *or* duct. **—ungs=geleise,** *n.* junction-rails. **—ungs=gewicht,** *n.* combining weight. **—ungs=glied,** *n.* connecting link. **—ungs=hund,** *m.* large dog, mastiff belonging to a students' club. **—ungs=linie,** *f.*, **—ungs=weg,** *m.* line of communication. **—ungs=mittel,** *n.* means of communication; binding substance used in cooking (*as eggs, etc.*). **—ungs=mütze,** *f.* distinctive cap of a students' club. **—ungs=punkt,** *m.* juncture. **—ungs=rohr,** *n.*, **—ungs=röhre,** *f.* connecting tube *or* pipe. **—ungs=stelle,** *f.* joining; juncture; joint. **—ungs=stange,** *f.* connecting rod. **—ungs=strich,** *m.* hyphen. **—ungs=stück,** *n.* tie, coupling (*Arch.*). **—ungs=thür,** *f.* door of communication. **—ungs=verhältnis,** *n.* combining proportion (*Chem.*). **—ungs=wort,** *n.* copula; conjunction; conjunctive particle.

Verbis'sen, *p.p. & adj.* suppressed; morose, sullen, crabbed. **—heit,** *f.* sullenness, sourness of temper.

Verbit'ten, *ir.v.a.; sich (dat.) etwas von einem —,* to beg to decline, to beg a p. not to do a th.; **ich verbitte mir die Ehre,** I beg to decline the honour; **solche Bemerkungen verbitte ich mir,** I don't permit such remarks to be made to me; **sich** (*dat.*) **einen Besuch —,** to decline a visit; **das verbitte ich mir (für die** *or* **in Zukunft)!** don't do that again! that must not occur again; **Beileid verbeten,** no cards and no flowers by request, no visitors will be received.

Verbit'tern, *v.* I. *a.* to embitter; **einem das Leben —,** to embitter a person's life. II. *r.* & *n.* (*aux.* **s.**) to grow bitter, become soured.

Verbla'sen, I. *ir.v.a.* to blow away; to use up in blowing (*glass*); to blow badly; to spoil in blowing; to refine (*metals*); **die Farben —,** to dilute the colours in painting, to blend, shade off the colours. II. *subst.n.; durch — des Nebels,* by scattering, dispelling the fog.

Verblas'sen, *v.n.* (*aux.* **s.**) to grow, turn pale; to lose colour, fade.

Verblät'tern, *v.a.; eine Stelle im Buche —,* to lose one's place in turning over the leaves of a book.

Verblei'b, *m.* (—**s**) place where a thing is kept or left; **ich weiß nichts über den — dieser Papiere,** I don't know where those papers are *or* have gone to.

Verblei'ben, I. *ir.v.n.* (*aux.* **s.**) to remain in a certain condition; to remain; **bei seiner Meinung —,** to persist, persevere in one's opinion; **lassen wir es dabei —,** let the matter rest there, let us go no further; **ich verbleibe hochachtungsvoll, &c.,** I (have the honour to) remain most respectfully, *etc.*; **es verblieb mir noch eine ziemliche Summe,** I had still a considerable sum left. II. *subst.n.* *see* **Verbleib; es hat dabei sein —,** there the matter rests.

Verblei'chen, *ir.v.n.* (*aux.* **s.**) to grow (deadly) pale; to fade; to wash out; **des Todes —,** to die (*poet.*); **der, die Verblichene,** the deceased-

Verblei'en, *v.a.* to lead; to seal with lead; to alloy with lead.

Verblen'd—en, *v.a.* to blind, dazzle; to delude, beguile; to face (*a wall*); to plaster, roughcast; to mask (*live lodes in a mine*); to cover over, screen; **die Fachwand —en**, to face the bay *or* framework with bricks; **einen über eine S. —en**, to delude a p. with regard to a thing; **durch sein Glück —et**, dazzled by his good fortune. **—er**, (**—klinker**,) *m.* (**—ers**, *pl.* **—er**) brick *or* tile for facing (*a wall, etc.*). **—ung**, *f.* blinding, dazzling; facing (*Mas.*); delusion, infatuation, fascination.

Verblüf'f—en, *v.a.* to disconcert, nonplus, dumfound, confuse. **—end**, *adj.* startling; stupendous. **—t**, abashed, puzzled, dumfounded; **—t dastehen**, to be dumfounded; **er machte eine sehr —te Miene**, he looked quite taken aback. **—theit**, *f.* stupefaction.

Verblü'hen, I. *v.n.* (*aux.* **h.** & **s.**) to cease blossoming; to fade, to wither; to decay; **die Rosen sind verblüht**, the roses are over; **eine verblühte Schönheit**, a faded beauty. II. *subst. n.;* **im — sein**, to begin to fade, to be fading away.

Verblü'm—en, *v.a.* to cover with flowers; to cover, disguise; **etwas —en**, to speak in figurative language, to speak darkly, to hint. **—t**, *p.p., adj. & adv.* figurative, allegorical; covert; indirectly, in covert words; **etwas —t zu verstehen geben**, to hint at a th.

Verblu't—en, *v.* I. *a.;* **sein Blut für einen —en**, to shed one's blood for a person. II. *r. & n.* (*aux.* **s.**) to bleed profusely; to bleed to death; **die Sache hat sich —et**, the matter is no longer spoken of, has died a natural death; **—en lassen**, to bleed (*to death*). **—ung**, *f.* loss of blood; hemorrhage; bleeding to death.

Verboh'len, *v.a.* to plank, to board (*up*).

Verboh'r—en, *v.a.* to join, fasten with pins *or* wooden nails, to pin (*Carp.*); to bore; to bore badly. **—t**, *p.p. & adj.* badly bored; crazy, cracked, foolish, senseless.

Verboll'werken, *v.a.* to barricade, block up, close, defend by bulwarks or bastions.

[1]**Verbor'gen**, *v.a.* to lend out, to give on credit.

[2]**Verbor'gen**, *p.p. & adj.* hidden, secret; clandestine; obscure; (**—wirkend**) latent (*Phys.*); occult; **er lauert im —**, he lieth in wait secretly (*B.*). **—heit**, *f.* concealment; privacy, retirement; secrecy; obscurity; **in der —heit leben**, to live in retirement *or* obscurity; **die —heit suchen**, to retire from society. *Comp.* **—er=weise**, *adv.* secretly, by stealth.

Verbö'sern, *v.a.* to make worse; **sich —**, to get worse, to deteriorate.

Verbo't, *n.* (**—es**, *pl.* **—e**) prohibition; inhibition (*Law*); suppression (*of a book, etc.*); veto. **—en**, *p.p. & adj.* forbidden; illicit; **—ene Waren**, contraband goods.

Verbra'cht, *p.p.;* **Verbrach'te**, *imperf. of* **verbringen**.

Verbrä'm—en, *v.a.* to garnish, border, edge, trim; to embellish; **mit Spitzen —t**, laced (*coat, etc.*). **—ung**, *f.* border, trimming.

Verbra'nd, *m.* (**—es**) fuel, firewood.

Verbra'ten, *ir.v.* I. *a.* to use in roasting. II. *a. & n.* (*aux.* **s.**) to spoil in roasting.

Verbrau'ch, *m.* (**—s**) consuming; consumption; **übermäßiger —**, waste. *Comp.* **—s=steuer**, *f.* tax, duty upon articles of consumption; excise.

Verbrau'ch—en, *v.a.* to use, consume; to spend; to exhaust; to use up; **—t**, worn out, hackneyed, trite.

Verbrau—en, *v.a.* to use in brewing; **alles Malz ist —t**, all the malt has been used for the beer.

Verbrau'sen, *v.n.* (*aux.* **h.** & **s.**) to cease fermenting; to cease roaring; to subside, to calm down.

Verbre'ch—en, I. *ir.v.a.* to commit a crime *or* an offence, to do something wrong; to break off, to shorten by breaking off; to break; **das Leben —en**, to forfeit one's life (*through misdeeds*); **was habe ich verbrochen?** what have I done wrong? **verbrochener Schacht** *or* **Stollen**, choked gallery (*Min.*). II. *subst. n.* crime; misdeed; violation of an oath; **leichtes —en**, venial offence. **—er**, *m.* (**—ers**, *pl.* **—er**) criminal; delinquent; **jugendlicher —er**, youthful offender; **schwerer —er**, desperate criminal. **—erisch**, *adj.* criminal; sinful. *Comp.* **—er=kolonie**, *f.* penal settlement, convict colony. **—er=laufbahn**, *f.* career of a criminal. **—er=leben**, *n.* criminal life. **—er=physiognomie**, *f.* guilty countenance, hangdog look. **—er=wahnsinn**, *m.* moral insanity.

Verbrei't—en, *v.a.* to spread; to shed; to disseminate; to circulate, spread abroad (*a report, etc.*); to propagate (*opinions*); **weit —ete Ansichten**, widely spread, very common views; **—eter Gebrauch**, common usage, general custom; **sich über eine S. —en**, to enlarge upon a matter. **—er**, *m.* (**—ers**, *pl.* **—er**) publisher; propagator. **—ung**, *f.* propagation; dissemination; circulating.

Verbrenn'—bar, **—lich**, *adj.* combustible. **—barkeit**, **—lichkeit**, *f.* combustibility.

Verbren'n—en, *ir.v.* I. *a.* to burn, consume by fire; to roast; to scorch; to cremate (*the dead*); to scald; to blast (*corn*); **zu Asche —en**, to reduce to ashes; **sich** (*dat.*) **die Finger —en**, to burn one's fingers; **sich** (*dat.*) **die Hände an den Nesseln —en**, to sting one's hands with nettles; **von der Sonne verbrannt**, sunburnt. II. *r. & n.* (*aux.* **s.**) to burn, to burn away, be burnt up. **—ung**, *f.* burning; combustion; cremation (*of the dead*). *Comp.* **—ungs=apparat**, *m.* crematory furnace, crematorium (*for dead bodies*). **—ungs=ofen**, *m.* furnace for cremating bodies. **—ungs=prozeß**, **—ungs=vorgang**, *m.* (*process of*) combustion.

Verbrie'f—en, *v.a.* to furnish with documents; to confirm *or* recognize by a document; to mortgage *or* pledge by writing; to make known in writing; to charter; **versiegelt und —t**, quite certain; **sich —en**, to bind oneself by a deed; **sich für einen —en**, to stand security, give a written guarantee for a p. **—t**, *p.p. & adj.* chartered, documented; **—te Rechte**, vested rights; **—te Schulden**, obligations. **—ung**, *f.* written pledge, bond, confirmation by charter.

Verbrin'g—en, I. *ir.v.a.* to spend, pass (*time*); to squander, waste. II. *subst. n.*, **—ung**, *f.* spending; consumption, waste.

Verbrö'ckeln, *v.a.r. & n.* (*aux.* **s.**) to crumble away.

Verbrü'der—n, *v.a.* to unite closely; **sich mit einem —n**, to fraternize with a person. **—ung**, *f.* fraternization.

Verbrüh'—en, *v.a.* to scald; **—te Stelle**, scald.

Verbuh'l—en, *v.a.* to squander in debauchery. **—t**, *p.p. & adj.* amorous; lascivious; debauched. **—theit**, *f.* debauchery, wantonness.

Ver'bum, *n.* (**—s**, *pl.* **Verba**) verb; **— finitum**, finite verb.

Verbum'meln, *v.* I. *a.* to spend, waste (*money*); to idle away (*time*); to forget (*sl.*). II. *n.* (*aux.* **s.**) to be ruined by idleness; **ein verbummeltes Genie**, a man of talent without any (*moral*) backbone, an artist *or* student who has come down in the world.

Verbu'nd, *m.* (**—s**, *pl.* **Verbün'de**) compound (*Techn.*). *Comp.* **—(dampf=)maschine**, *f.* compound steam-engine.

Verbun'den, *p.p. & adj. see* **Verbinden**; **—es Mauerwerk**, bound masonry.

Verbün'd—en, *v.a.* to unite in a league, ally; **sich —en**, to make *or* form an alliance, to enter into a confederacy; **die —eten**, the allies, the confederates, the allied forces, the allied powers. —ung, *f.* alliance, confederation.

Verbür'g—en, *v.a. & r.* to guarantee; sich für . . . —en, to answer for, guarantee, to give security for . . . —t, *p.p. & adj.* authentic(ated), well-warranted, well-founded.

Verbü'ß—en, *v.a.* to atone for, pay the penalty of; seine Strafzeit —en, to undergo one's term of imprisonment *or* confinement. —ung, *f.;* die —ung seiner Strafe wurde zwei Monate hinausgeschoben, his term of imprisonment was postponed until two months later.

Verda'cht, *m.* (—es) suspicion; einen in — bringen, to cause s.o. to be suspected; einen wegen einer Sache in — haben, to suspect s.o. of something; in — kommen, to incur suspicion; im —e stehen, to be suspected; — schöpfen, to become suspicious. *Comp.* —s=grund, *m.* reason for suspecting.

Verdäch'tig, *adj.* suspected, suspicious, questionable; equivocal; not to be trusted; einen — machen, *see* —en. —en, *v.a.* to cause a p. to be suspected; sich selbst —en, to inculpate oneself. —keit, *f.* suspiciousness. —ung, *f.* rendering suspected; inculpation, accusation.

Verdam'm—en, *v.a.* to condemn; to anathematize; to damn; zum Tode —en, to condemn to death; —t, condemned, reprobate; ewig —t, damned; —t! damn it! damnation! er ist —t pfiffig, he is devilish sly (*coll.*); das ist seine —te Schuldigkeit, that is his bounden duty (*coll.*). —lich, *see* —enswert. —nis, *f.* (*pl.* —nisse) damnation; perdition. —ung, *f.* condemnation; damnation; ewige —ung, eternal damnation. *Comp.* —enswert, —ens=würdig, *adj.* blamable; damnable; criminal. —ungs=urteil, *n.* sentence of condemnation. —ungs=würdig, *see* ens=würdig.

Verdam'pf—en, *v.* I. *a.* to cause to evaporate; *see* Abkühlen; viel Taback —en, to smoke a great deal of tobacco. II. *n.* (*aux.* s.) to evaporate. —ung, *f.* evaporation.

Verdan'ken, *v.a.* (einem etwas) to owe (s.th. to a p.), to be obliged (to a p. for a th.); to thank a p. (*dial.*); seinem Rate ist es zu — daß . . ., it is owing to his advice that . .

Verda'rb, *1 & 3 p. sing. imperf. indic. of* verderben.

Verdau'—en, *v.a.* to digest; diese Speisen —en sich leicht, these dishes are easily digested *or* very digestible. —lich, *adj.* digestible; schwer —lich, indigestible, rich (*food*). —lich=keit, *f.* digestibleness. —ung, *f.* digestion; die —ung befördernd, digestive, promoting digestion. *Comp.* —ungs=beschwerden, *pl.* indigestion; pains *or* inconvenience arising from indigestion. —ungs=besuch, *m.* visit paid to the hostess within a week after a dinner party (*coll.*). —ungs=drüse, *f.* organ of digestion. —ungs=ferment, *n.* pepsin. —ungs=gang, *m.* walk for the sake of promoting digestion, constitutional. —ungs=kanal, *m.* alimentary canal. —ungs=los, *adj.* dyspeptic. —ungs=mittel, *n.* stomachic, digestive. —ungs=saft, *m.* gastric juice. —ungs=schwäche, *f.* weak digestion, dyspepsia. —ungs=schwierigkeiten, *pl.* difficulties in digesting. —ungs=stoff, *m.* pepsin. —ungs=störung, *f.* indigestion; bilious attack.

Verde'ck, *n.* (—s, *pl.* —e) covering; awning; hood (*of a carriage*); deck (*Naut.*); — der Offiziere, quarter-deck. *Comp.* —leder, *n.* leather hood of a carriage. —planken, *pl.* deck-planks. —sitz, *m.* seat on the outside of an omnibus; deck-chair. —zelt, *n.* awning. —zeug, *n.* waggon *or* rig cloth.

Verde'ck—en, *v.a.* to cover; to hide, conceal, mask, veil; to dissemble; to palliate. —t, *p.p. & adj.* covered; covert; masked (*battery*); —te Kanone, hidden *or* masked gun; —ter Weg, covert way; —te Schüssel, cover-dish. —ung, *f.* covering; concealing; occultation.

Verden'ken, *v.a.* to blame, take amiss, find fault.

Verde'rb, *m.* (—es) ruin; destruction; decay.

Verder'b—en, I. *reg. & ir.v.a.* to spoil; to deteriorate; to corrupt; to destroy, to undo, ruin; einem die Freude —en, to spoil a p.'s pleasure; sich (*dat.*) den Magen —en, to disorder one's stomach; er hat sich (*dat.*) den Magen verdorben, he suffers from indigestion; sich (*dat.*) die Augen —en, to spoil *or* ruin one's eyes; die Preise —en, to bring down prices; böse Beispiele —en gute Sitten, evil communications corrupt good manners; er will es mit keinem —en, he tries to please everybody; es mit einem —en, to fall out *or* quarrel with one, to incur s.o.'s displeasure; an ihm ist ein Schauspieler verdorben, a good actor is lost in him, he was cut out for an actor; er ist zum Schauspieler verdorben, he will *or* would never make a good actor, he has not the making of an actor. II. *ir.v.n.* (*aux.* s.) to spoil; to perish; to go to ruin; to fail; to be damaged (*at sea*). III. *subst.n.* spoiling, corruption; ruin; der Weg des —ens, the road to ruin; sich ins —en stürzen, to rush into destruction; einen ins —en stürzen, to ruin a p.; einem zum —en gereichen, to prove a p.'s ruin. —er, *m.* (—ers, *pl.* —er) destroyer, corrupter. —lich, *adj.* corruptible; easily spoiled, perishable; pernicious; ruinous; unfortunate, fatal. —lichkeit, *f.* corruptibility; perniciousness, destructiveness, ruinousness. —nis, *f.* (*pl.* —nisse) & *n.* (—nisses, *pl.* —nisse) corruption, taint, spoiled condition; depravity, perversion. —t, *p.p. & adj.* perverse, corrupt(ed), depraved, vicious. —theit, *f.* spoiled condition; corruptness; perverseness, depravity, vice. *Comp.* —en=bringend, *adj.* fatal, ruinous, destructive. —en=schwanger, —en=trächtig, *adj.* big with ruin, portentous. —en=stifter, *m.* author of evil, destroyer.

Verdeut'lichen, *v.a.* to elucidate, render clear.

Verdeut'sch—en, *v.a.* to translate into German, to explain (*fig.*). —ung, *f.* translation into German; German version.

Verdicht'—barkeit, *f.* condensability. —en, *v.a.* to thicken, condense, compress; to fix (*a gas*). —er, *m.* (—ers, *pl.* —er), (—ungs=apparat, *m.*) condenser. —ung, *f.* condensation (*Phys.*); solidification.

Verdi'ck—en, *v.a.* to thicken; to inspissate (*Chem., etc.*); to solidify, condense; —te Fleischbrühe, broth turned into jelly (*Cook.*). —ung, *f.* thickening. *Comp.* —s=mittel, *n.* thickening ingredient.

Verdie'len, *v.a.* to board, plank.

Verdie'n—en, *v.a.* to earn; to gain; to get, win; to merit; man —t dabei nicht das Salz zur Suppe, that brings in next to nothing; Geld muß wieder Geld —en, money ought to make money; das habe ich um Sie nicht —t, I have not deserved that from you; ein —ter Mann, a deserving man; mehr Glück —en als haben, to be more deserving than lucky; er hat sich um das Vaterland —t gemacht, he has deserved well of his country. —st, *m. & n.* (—stes, *pl.* —ste) (*gen'lly m.*) gain, profit; (*gen'lly n.*) merit; deserts; das ist mein ganzer —st dabei, that is all I get *or* make by it; das —st des Generals besteht in . . ., the merit of the general consists in . . .; die —ste dieses Mannes um die Stadt, the service which this man has rendered to the town; darin liegt kein —st, there is no merit in that; es ist vorzüglich sein —st, daß . . ., to him the credit is principally due that . . .; wie das —st, so der Ruhm, honour (*is given*) to whom honour is due; **das —ſt wird ſelten belohnt,** desert seldom meets with its reward; **man wird ihn nach —ſt behandeln,** he will be treated according to his deserts; **ſich** (*dat.*) **etwas zum —ſte anrechnen,** to make a merit of s.th. **—ſtlich,** *adj. & adv.* profitable; meritorious, deserving. **—ſtlichkeit,** *f.* meritoriousness. *Comp.* **—ſt=kreuz,** *n.*, **—ſt=medaille,** *f.* cross, medal for distinguished service. **—ſt=los,** *adj.* undeserving; unprofitable. **—ſt=orden,** *m.* distinguished service order, badge of honour. **—ſt=voll,** *adj.* meritorious.

Verdi'kt, *n.* (**—es,** *pl.* **—e**) verdict.

Verdi'ng, *n.* (**—es,** *pl.* **—e**) act of letting out on hire *or* hiring out; the contracting for work; agreement, contract; **auf — übernehmen,** to contract for.

Verdin'g—en, *reg. & ir.v.a.* to hire out; to contract for; to bind (*as apprentice*); to put out (*to board*); **ſeinen Sohn als Diener bei einem —en,** to put one's son to service with a p.; **ſich als Diener —en,** to take a situation; **Arbeiten —en,** to let out work by contract; **den Bau eines Hauſes —en,** to contract for the building of a house. **—ung,** *f.* hiring, agreement, contract.

Verdir'b, *imperat.;* **Verdir'bſt,** *2 p. sing. pres. ind.;* **Verdir'bt,** *3 p. sing. pres. ind. of* **verderben.**

Verdol'metſch—en, *v.a.* to interpret

Verdon'ner—n, *v.a.* to condemn (*coll.*); **er wurde —t,** judgment was pronounced against him (*coll.*). **—t,** *p.p. & adj.* thunderstruck; confounded. *adv.* enormously.

Verdop'pel—n, *v.a.* to double; **den Eifer —n,** to double one's zeal; **ſeine Schritte —n,** to quicken one's pace. **—ung,** *f.* doubling; duplication.

Verdor'ben, *p.p. & adj., see* **Verderben;** tainted, unsound; spoilt, rotten; **dazu iſt er —,** he is spoiled for that. **—heit,** *f.* spoiled *or* ruined condition; rottenness; depravity.

Verdor'ren, *v.n.* (*aux.* **ſ.**) to dry up.

Verdrän'gen, *reg. & ir.v.a.* to crowd out; to displace; to supplant; to suppress.

Verdrän'gung, *f.* displacement (*of a ship*).

Verdre'h—en, *v.a.* to twist, wrench; to sprain; to force; to distort; to put a false construction on; to warp, pervert; **ſich** (*dat.*) **den Arm —en,** to sprain one's arm; **die Augen —en,** to roll one's eyes; **das Geſicht —en,** to make a grimace; **einem den Kopf —en,** to turn a person's head; **das Recht —en,** to pervert justice. **—t,** *p.p. & adj.* twisted, distorted; forced; odd, queer, cracked, crazy. **—theit,** *f.* distortedness; craziness. **—ung,** *f.* twisting, distortion; sprain; contortion; forced construction, misrepresentation; perversion.

Verdrei'fachen, *v.a.* to treble.

Verdrie'ß—en, *ir.v.a.* to grieve, vex, annoy, trouble; **es —t mich,** it annoys me, vexes me; **ich bin darüber verdroſſen,** I am vexed at it; **geſtern verdroſſeſt du mich,** yesterday you made me angry; **ſich etwas —en laſſen,** to be vexed *or* hurt at something; **er läßt ſich nichts —en,** he lets nothing daunt him, nothing discourages him; **er ließ ſich keine Mühe —en,** he spared no pains; **ſich keine Mühe und Koſten —en laſſen,** to grudge neither pains nor expense. **—lich,** *adj.* vexed, annoyed; peevish, cross; out of humour; vexatious; annoying, irksome, disagreeable. **—lichkeit,** *f.* bad temper; peevishness, crossness; disagreeableness; irksomeness; vexatious matter, annoyance; **mit einem in —lichkeiten geraten,** to quarrel with a p.

Verdro'ß, *1 & 3 p. sing. imperf. ind.;* **Verdröſ'ſe,** *1 & 3 p. sing. imperf. subj. of* **verdrießen.**

Verdroſ'ſen, *p.p. &* I. *adj., see* **Verdrießen;** cross, peevish; vexed, annoyed; out of temper; loath, disinclined; indolent; listless. II. *adv.* unwillingly. **—heit,** *see* **Verdrießlichkeit;** unwillingness, reluctance, indolence.

Verdru'cken, *v.a.* to print badly, misprint; to transpose (*words, etc.*) in printing; to use (*paper, etc.*) in printing.

Verdrü'cken, *dial. for* **Zerdrücken.**

Verdru'ß, *m.* (—(ſſ)es) ill humour; displeasure; chagrin, vexation; discontent; disgust; annoyance; quarrel; **einem etwas zum — thun,** to do a thing in order to spite *or* vex a p.; **allen Menſchen zum —,** in spite of everybody, to every one's annoyance; **einem — machen,** to vex, annoy, irritate s.o.; **ich thue dies mit —,** I do this reluctantly; **zu meinem — finde ich,** I am annoyed to find; **es wird (einen) — geben,** it will cause trouble; **einen — haben,** to be deformed, crook-backed (*coll.*).

Verduf'ten, *v.r. & n.* (*aux.* **ſ.**) to exhale, evaporate; to disappear, vanish, to slip away (*coll.*).

Verdum'm—en, *v.* I. *a.* to make stupid, besot, brutalize. II. *n.* (*aux.* **h.**) to become stupid *or* brutalized. **—ung,** *f.* sinking into a state of ignorance; stupefying; brutalization. *Comp.* **—ungs=ſyſtem,** *n.* stupefying, brutalizing system, anti-educational system.

Verdum'pfen, *v.n.* (*aux.* **ſ.**) to grow damp *or* musty; to grow dull; to rumble, mutter (*as thunder*); to grow dull *or* callous.

Verdun'kel—n, *v.a.* to darken; to obscure, cloud; to eclipse, throw into the shade; **der Himmel —t ſich,** the sky becomes clouded *or* overcast; **er ſoll deinen Ruhm —n,** your glory shall pale beside his; **der Kommentar —t den Text,** the commentary obscures the sense of the text. **—ung,** *f.* darkening; obscuring; eclipse; **—ung des Geſichts,** the growing dim of the eye-sight.

Verdünn'—bar, *adj.* that may be thinned *or* diluted; dilutable; rarefiable. **—barkeit,** *f.* dilutableness (*of liquids*), rarefiableness (*of air*). **—en,** *v.a.* to thin; to attenuate; to rarefy; to dilute; to temper (*colours*); **eine —te Säule,** a diminished column. **—ung,** *f.* thinning, attenuation; dilution; rarefaction.

Verdunſt'bar, *adj.* that can be evaporated.

Verdun'ſt—en, *v.* I. *n.* (*aux.* **ſ.**) to evaporate. II. *a.*, (**Verdün'ſten,**) to cause to evaporate. **—ung,** *f.* evaporation; volatilization; exhalation. *Comp.* **—ungs=apparat,** *m.* evaporating apparatus. **—ungs=kälte,** *f.* cold due to evaporation.

Verdür'be, *1 & 3 p. sing. imperf. subj. of* **verderben.**

Verdur'ſten, *v.n.* (*aux.* **ſ.**) to die of *or* with thirst.

Verdü'ſter—n, *v.* I. *a.* to darken; to deepen; to wrap in gloom. II. *r. & n.* (*aux.* **ſ.**) to grow dark *or* gloomy. **—ung,** *f.* darkening, gloom.

Verdut'z—en, *see* **Verblüffen;** **—t machen,** to disconcert, abash, nonplus, confound; **—t ſein,** to be taken aback; **—t ausſehen,** to look sheepish. **—theit,** *see* **Verblüfftheit.**

Vere'd—eln, *v.a.* to bring to greater perfection, to improve (*trees, horses*); to refine; to ennoble; to cultivate; to raise, dignify, exalt. **—elung, —lung,** *f.* perfecting; ennobling; improvement; refinement, cultivation.

Vere'helich—en, *v.a. & r.* to marry; **eine Tochter —en,** to give one's daughter in marriage; **Marie N., —te W.,** Mary N. (by marriage *or* now) Mrs. W. **—ung,** *f.* marriage.

Vereh'r—en, *v.a.* to venerate, respect, reverence; to adore; to honour; **einem etwas —en,** to make a p. a present of a thing. **—er,** *m.* (**—ers,** *pl.* **—er**) reverer, votary, worshipper; devoted admirer, lover; partisan; **die Goethe—er,** the Goethe worshippers; **er iſt ein großer —er Schillers,** he admires Schiller very much. **—lich,** *adj.* honourable, venerable:

Ihr—liches Schreiben, your esteemed *or* kind letter; in Beantwortung Ihres —lichen Schreibens, in reply to your favour. —ung, *f.* respect, veneration, reverence; adoration; honour; honorarium, compliment, present (*obs.*). *Comp.* —ungs=wert, —ungs=würdig, *adj.* respectable, venerable, honourable; —ungswürdiger Mann, (*obs.*) honoured Sir.

Verei'd(ig)en, *v.a.*; einen —, to put a p. to *or* on his oath, to administer an oath to a p., to swear a p. in.

Verei'n, *m.* (—s, *pl.* —e) union, coalition; confederation; association, society; club; partnership, company; im — mit meinen Freunden, together with my friends. —bar, *adj.* combinable; that can be united; compatible, consistent. —baren, *v.a.* to unite, join, connect; to reconcile; sich über eine S. —baren, to agree, come to an understanding with regard to a matter; zu —bartem Lohn, in return for pay previously agreed upon. —barkeit, *f.* compatibility. —barung, *f.* agreement, arrangement; —barungen mit einem treffen, to make an agreement *or* to arrange with a person. —en, *see* —igen. —igen, *v.a.* to unite, join; to connect; to combine; to embody; to concentrate, centre; to ally; to associate; to reconcile; to assort; zwei Ämter in sich —igen, to unite two offices in one's own person; ich kann es mit seinem Charakter nicht —igen, I cannot reconcile it with his character; mit —ten Kräften, with (*our, their, etc.*) united strength; at (*our, etc.*) joint expense; sich —igen, to unite, join, to combine, to agree, accord, to assemble, to form a coalition, coalesce; sich über eine S. —igen, *see under* —baren; sich —igen lassen mit..., to be compatible *or* consistent with...; —igte Staaten, United States. —igung, *see* Vereinigung. *Comp.* —s=gebiet, *n. see* —s=länder. —s=gesetz, *n.* law concerning societies *or* (trade) unions. —s=haus, *n.* club(-house). —s=länder, *pl.* states, territories belonging to the 'Zollverein' *or* German Customs Union. —s=kasse, *f.* funds of a society. —s=leitung, *f.* management of a society, association *or* club, executive committee of an association. —s=und=Versammlungs=recht, *see* —igungsrecht. —s=vermögen, *n.* funds of a club, capital of a co-operative society. —s=wesen, *n.* co-operative system *or* movement; trade-unionism (of workingmen) —s=zimmer, *n.* club room.

Verein'fach—en, *v.a.* to simplify. —ung, *f.* simplification.

Verei'nigung, *f.* (*pl.* —en) union; meeting; junction; combination; alliance; association; confederation; incorporation; concentration; reconciliation; agreement. *Comp.* —s=akte, *f.* Act of Union (by which the crowns of Scotland and England were united). —s=fähig, *adj.* capable of being united; capable of concentration. —s=haut, *f.* conjunctiva (*Anat.*). —s=ort, *m.* place of assembly *or* meeting. —s=punkt, *m.* point of union; focus (*Phys.*); rallying-point; rendezvous. —s=recht, *n.* right of forming unions *or* companies; right of assembly. —s=ruf, *m.* rallying-word (*Mil.*); (*bugle-, etc.*) call (*Mil.*). —s=zeichen, *n.* signal for assembling.

Verein'nahmen, *v.a.* to take, receive (*money*).

Verein'sam—en, *v.* I. *a.* to isolate. II. *n.* to become isolated. —t, *p.p. & adj.* solitary, lonely. —ung, *f.* isolation.

Verein'zel—n, *v.a.* to isolate; to insulate; to separate, detach; to dismember; to dispose of singly *or* piece by piece; to take separately; Zusammengehöriges —n, to separate *or* spoil a pair *or* set; —t auftretend, sporadic (*Med.*). —ung, *f.* isolation; detachment, separation; dismemberment. *Comp.* —ungs=zeichen, *n.* diæresis.

Verei'f—en, *v.* I. *n.* (*aux.* h.) to be converted into ice, to glaciate, freeze. II. *a.* to convert into ice, to congeal. —t, glaciated. —ung, *f.* freezing, congelation, glaciation.

Verei'tel—n, *v.a.* to make vain *or* fruitless; to frustrate, baffle, balk, disappoint; to defeat; jemands Hoffnungen —n, to disappoint a p.'s hopes; die Nützlichkeit —n, to mar the usefulness; das Unternehmen ist —t, the undertaking has miscarried. —ung, *f.* disappointment; discomfiture; frustration.

Verei'tern, *v.r. & n.* (*aux.* s.) to fester, suppurate.

Vere'keln, *v.a.*; einem etwas —, to render a th. loathsome to a p., to disgust a p. with a thing (*coll.*).

Veren'den, *v.n.* (*aux.* h. & s.) to die (*of game*).

Veren'ge(r)n, *v.a.* to narrow, contract; wo das Land sich verengt, where the land narrows.

Vereng'lischen, *v.a.* to translate *or* put into English; to anglicize.

Verer'b—en, *v.* I. *a.* (einem etwas *or* etwas auf einen) to leave, bequeath; to transmit (*diseases, etc.*). II. *r. & n.* (*aux.* s.) to devolve (on, auf); to be hereditary. —lich, *adj.* inheritable; transmissible, hereditary. —t, *p.p. & adj.* hereditary. —ung, *f.* bequeathing (to); devolving (on); hereditary transmission. *Comp.* —pachten, —rechten, *v.a.* to grant a long lease of s.th. —ungs=fähigkeit, *f.* right to bequeath inheritance. —ungs=gesetz, *n.* law of succession; law of heredity (*Physiol.*). —ungs=theorie, *f.* (theory of) heredity (*Physiol.*).

Verer'den, *v.* I. *a.* to convert into earth; to oxidize. II. *n.* (*aux.* s.) to turn to earth; to become oxidized.

Verer'z—en, *v.* I. *a.* to mineralize. II. *n.* to change into ore. —ung, *f.* mineralization.

Vere'wig—en, *v.* I. *a.* to perpetuate; to immortalize. II. *r.* to inscribe one's name (*on benches, stones, etc.*) (*coll.*). —t, *p.p. & adj.* deceased, late; immortalized. —ung, *f.* immortalization; perpetuation.

Verfah'r—en, I. *ir.v.n.* (*aux.* h. & s.) to act, behave, proceed; mit einem —en, to treat, use a p.; redlich —en, to deal honestly; mit Nachsicht —en, to act with leniency, be indulgent; gerichtlich gegen einen —en, to take legal proceedings against a p.; womit Sie nach Bericht zu —en belieben, of which you will dispose according to advices *or* orders (*C. L.*). II. *ir.v.a.* to spend on driving *or* carriages *or* transport; to convey, transport; to export, to elude (*by driving about*): den Zoll —en, to defraud the customs; die Chausseehäuser —en, to avoid paying toll by driving round *or* another way; den Weg —en, to miss the road; to cut up the road by driving; einen Gang —en, to work a mine; seine Schicht —en, to finish one's task (*Min.*); eine Sache —en, to muddle, jumble, embroil s.th., to render a matter intricate. III. *ir.v.r.* to lose one's way; to get entangled *or* locked. IV. *subst.n.* proceeding; procedure, behaviour, conduct; treatment; management; gerichtliches —en, legal proceedings. —ung, *f.* transport, conveyance; exportation. *Comp.* —ungs=art, —ungs=weise, *f.* manner of proceeding. —ungs=lehre, *f.* treatise on (science of) method.

Verfa'll, *m.* (—s) decay, dilapidation; decline; break-up; downfall, ruin; deterioration; decadence, degeneracy; corruption; in — geraten kommen, to go to ruin, to decay, to decline, to deteriorate; to become dilapidated; in — bringen, to ruin; — der Kräfte, decline of physical strength; — der Sitten, corruption of morals, moral decay, depravity; — des Reiches, decline of the empire; der — eines Wechsels, maturity of a bill; **bei** —, when due; **bis** —, till maturity, till due; — **einer Klage**, nonsuit; — **eines Rechtes**, forfeiture, loss of a right. *Comp.* —**buch**, *n.* bill book. —**erklärung**, *f.* confiscation. —**frist**, *f.*, —**tag**, —**termin**, *m.*, —**zeit**, *f.* day on which a bill becomes due, day of payment; **zur —zeit**, when due; **bis zur —zeit**, until maturity, till due; **vor der —zeit**, before due. —(**s**)=**recht**, *n.* right of confiscation. — **zeit**, *f. see* —**frist**, **rc.**; period of decay.

Verfal'len, I. *ir.v.n.* (*aux.* **s.**) *see* **in Verfall geraten**, to fall, sink (*into folly, vice*); to expire, elapse; to fall due; to lapse, be forfeited; **auf eine S.** —, to fall upon, hit upon, conceive, chance to think of a th.; **auf den wäre ich nicht** —, I should never have thought of him; **einem** —, to fall to a p.'s lot *or* share, to devolve on s.o.; **ein Pfand für — erklären**, to foreclose a mortgage; **das Pfand ist** —, the pledge is forfeited, has lapsed; —**e Güter**, confiscated property; —**es Vermächtnis**, lapsed legacy; **in (eine S.)** —, to fall, run into; **in Nachdenken** —, to grow pensive; **in eine Krankheit** —, to fall ill; **in eine Geldstrafe** —, to incur a penalty, to be fined; **die Klage ist** —, the plaintiff has been non-suited; —**e Gesichtszüge**, worn features. II. *subst. n. see* **Verfall**; — **eines Pfandes**, foreclosure.

Verfäl'sch—en, *v.a.* to falsify; to adulterate; to forge; to interpolate; to debase (*coin*). —**er**, *m.* (—**ers**, *pl.* —**er**) forger; adulterater; interpolater. —**ung**, *f.* falsification; forging; adulteration; —**ung des Textes**, interpolation *or* corruption of the text.

Verfan'gen, *ir.v.* I. *r.* to be caught; to become entangled; to commit oneself; to suffer oneself to be caught, to get *or* be caught; to get foundered (*of horses*); — **sein**, to be forfeited; **der Wind hat sich im Schornstein** —, the wind has got down into the chimney; **sich im Reden** —, to contradict o.s., to get entangled *or* confused in speaking. II. *n.* (*aux.* **h.**) & *imp.* to operate, take effect; **bei ihm verfängt nichts**, nothing produces any effect upon him; **Gewalt würde hier nichts** —, force would avail nothing *or* be of no use here.

Verfäng'lich, *adj.* captious, fallacious, artful, deceitful; insidious, delusive, illusory. —**keit**, *f.* insidiousness; artifice.

Verfär'ben, *v.* I. *a.* to use in dyeing; to spoil in dyeing. II. *r.* & *n.* (*aux.* **h.**) to change colour; to grow pale.

Verfas's—en, *reg.* & *ir.v.a.* to compose; to write (*a book*); to draw up (*a document*); to set (*jewels*) badly. —**er**, *m.* (—**ers**, *pl.* —**er**), —**erin**, *f.* author. —**erschaft**, *f.* authorship. —**ung**, *f.* composing; composition; condition; situation, state; frame of mind; system of government; constitution; organization. *Comp.* —**ungs=bruch**, *m.* violation of the constitution. —**ungs=freund**, *m.* constitutionalist. — **ungs=gebend**, *adj.* constituent. —**ungs=los**, *adj.* without a constitution, unchartered. — **ungs=mäßig**, *adj.* constitutional. —**ungs=partei**, *f.* constitutional party. —**ungs=staat**, *m.* constitutional state. —**ungs=urkunde**, *f.* charter of the constitution. —**ungs=widrig**, *adj.* unconstitutional.

Verfaul'—bar, *adj.* putrescible. —**en**, *v.n.* (*aux.* **s.**) to rot. —**enzen**, *v.a.* to idle away.

Verfech't—en, *ir.v.a.* to fight for, stand up for; to defend; **wer verficht's**, who will stand up for it? **was verficht's**, what does it matter? (*obs.*). —**er**, *m.* (—**ers**, *pl.* —**er**) defender, champion. —**ung**, *f.* defending, defence.

Verfeh'len, *v.a.* to fail; to miss; to mistake (*one's way, etc.*); **kein Wort (von ihm) verfehlt den Eindruck**, every word (of his) tells; **diese Nachricht wird nicht —, Aufsehen zu machen**, this news will not fail to make a sensation; **ich werde nicht — Sie zu besuchen**, I shall be sure to call on you; **ihre Stellung war verfehlt**, she was in a false position; **er hat seinen Beruf (Zug) verfehlt**, he has missed his vocation (train); **es war eine verfehlte Geschichte**, it was a failure.

Verfeh'men, *v.a.* to proscribe, outlaw.

Verfein'de—n, *v.a.* to make an enemy of, **mit einem —t sein**, to be at daggers drawn with a p.; **sie sind mit einander —t**, there is no love lost between them; **sich mit einem —n**, to quarrel *or* fall out with a person.

Verfei'ner—n, *v.a.* to refine; to polish; to purify; to improve; **sich —n**, to grow (more) refined, to become (more) polished, to improve. —**ung**, *f.* refinement; improvement; polish.

Verfer'tig—en, *v.a.* to make, fabricate; to manufacture; to prepare (*medicines*); to construct. —**er**, *m.* (—**ers**, *pl.* —**er**) fabricator; manufacturer; maker; compiler. —**ung**, *f.* making; fabrication, manufacture.

Verfeu'ern, *v.a.* to burn; to use up (*powder or ammunition*); to burn out (*game*).

Verfil'zen, *v.a.* to felt, make felt of; **die Haare** —, to mat the hair.

Verfin'ster—er, *m.* (—**ers**, *pl.* —**er**) obscurer; obscurant. —**n**, *v.a.* to darken, obscure; to eclipse. —**ung**, *f.* darkening; eclipse (*of the sun, moon*); darkness.

Verfir'sten, *v.a.*; **ein Dach** —, to ridge a roof.

Verfla'chen, *v.* I. *a.* to flatten, to level. II. *r.* & *n.* (*aux.* **s.**) to become flat; to become shallow; to slope down.

Verfla'ckern, *v.n.* (*aux.* **s.**) to flicker away, flare out.

Verflech't—en, *ir.v.a.* to entwine, interlace, plait in; to involve, implicate; to entangle in; to use up in plaiting; to plait, twist badly. — **ung**, *f.* interlacing, interweaving; complicity; —**ung von Umständen**, combination of circumstances.

Verfle'cken, *v.a.* to heel (shoes).

Verflei'schen, *v.a.* to change into flesh; **sich** —, to become flesh, to carnify.

Verfli'cken, *v.a.* to use up in patching.

Verflie'gen, *ir.v.n.* (*aux.* **s.**) to fly away; to escape; to exhale, evaporate; to pass rapidly away; **sich** —, to lose oneself, fly too far; **verflogene Tauben, Bienen**, stray pigeons, bees.

Verflie'ßen, *ir.v.n.* (*aux.* **s.**) to flow away; to subside; to flow on, elapse; to expire (*of a term*); **verflossen sein**, to be over; **das verflossene Jahr**, the past year; **die Farben — in einander**, the colours run into one another, blend.

Verfli'xt, *adj.* (= **verflucht**) confounded (*fam.*); blessed (*iron.*); **eine —e Geschichte**, a damned business; a nice mess, a pretty kettle of fish; —**er Kerl**, a devil of a fellow.

Verflö'ßen, *v.a.* to cause to float.

Verflu'ch—en, *v.a.* to curse; to anathematize; to execrate; **er sei —t!** let him be accursed! —**t**, *p.p.*, *adj.* & *adv.* accursed; execrable; devilish (*coll.*); —**t!** confound it! damnation! —**t witzig**, devilish(ly) witty; **sein —te Schuldigkeit**, no more than his duty, his bounden duty; —**ter Bengel**, devil of a fellow, sly dog (*sl.*). —**ung**, *f.* malediction; anathema; anathematization. *Comp.* —**ens=würdig**, *adj.* execrable.

Verflüch'tig—en, *v.a.* to volatilize, cause to evaporate; to dissipate, dissolve; **sich —en**, to pass off in vapour, evaporate; to vanish. —**ung**, *f.* volatilization; evaporation.

Verflüs'sig—en, *v.a.* to liquefy, turn to a fluid; to fuse (*by heat*). —**ung**, *f.* liquefaction.

Verfo'lg, *m.* (—**es**) course, progress; sequel; **im —e Befehls**, in pursuance of orders. —**bar**, *adj.* that may be pursued; actionable, suable.

Verfol'g—en, *v.a.* to pursue; to follow; to persecute; to prosecute; to continue, carry on; **einen Gegenstand —en,** to pursue, follow up a subject; **sein Vorhaben bis ans Ende —en,** to carry out a project to the (*bitter*) end. **—er,** *m.* (**—ers,** *pl.* **—er**) pursuer; persecutor. **—ung,** *f.* pursuit; chase; persecution; pursuance, continuation; result, sequel. *Comp.* **—ungs=geist,** *m.* spirit of persecution. **—ungs=linie,** *f.* curve *or* line of pursuit. **—ungs=süchtig,** *adj.* bent on persecution. **—ungs=wahnsinn,** *m.* persecutional mania.

Verfrach't—en, *v.a.* to pay the carriage of; to send *or* carry goods; to hire out, to charter (*a vessel*), let it to freight. **—er,** *m.* (**—ers,** *pl.* **—er**) charterer, owner (*of a ship*). **—ung,** *f.* hiring out, letting; freighting; sending (*by carriage*).

Verfres'sen, *ir.v.a.;* **sein Vermögen —,** to squander one's fortune (*vulg.*); **sich —,** to eat too much (*vulg.*).

Verfrie'ren, *ir.v.n.* (*aux.* **s.**) to perish with cold.

Verfrü'h—en, *v.a.* to do before the time, to precipitate, hasten; to anticipate. **—t,** *p.p.* & *adj.* premature.

Verfüg'bar, *adj.* at one's disposal, available.

Verfü'g—en, *v.* I. *a.* to dispose, order, arrange; to ordain, decree; to provide; to enact; **durch ein Testament —en,** to dispose of by will. II. *r.;* **sich (nach einem Orte** *or* **zu einem Menschen) —en,** to betake oneself to a p. *or* a place; **sich nach Hause —en,** to go home. III. *n.* (*aux.* **h.**) **über (eine S.) —en,** to dispose of; **—en Sie über mich,** I am at your disposal, command me. **—er,** *m.* (**—ers,** *pl.* **—er**) disposer, arranger. **—lich,** *see* **—bar. —ung,** *f.* disposal, disposition; arrangement; order; decree; statute; enactment; **—ungen über (eine S.) treffen,** to take steps, give orders with regard to; **zu meiner —ung,** subject to my order; at my disposal; **weitere —ungen abwarten,** to await further orders *or* instructions; **zur —ung stellen,** to place at (*s.o.'s*) disposal; **ich stehe Ihnen ganz zur —ung,** I am quite at your disposal.

Verfüh'rbar, *adj.* transportable, conveyable; that may be seduced, seducible, corruptible.

Verfüh'r—en, *v.a.* to transport, convey; to lead astray, mislead; to seduce; to corrupt; to suborn (*witnesses*); to induce, gain over; **einen fürchterlichen Lärm —en,** to make a dreadful noise, kick up a terrible row (*coll.*); **ein —tes Mädchen,** a girl who has been seduced, who has lost her honour. **—er,** *m.* (**—ers,** *pl.* **—er**) tempter, seducer, gay Lothario, Don Juan. **—erisch,** *adj.* seducing; seductive; tempting; **—erisches Weib,** siren, Circe. **—ung,** *f.* transportation, conveyance, carriage, exportation; enticing away (*from duty, etc.*); corruption; seduction; subornation. *Comp.* **—ungs=kunst,** *f.* art of seduction; wile, artifice. **—ungs=mittel,** *n.* means of seduction.

Verfül'len, *v.a.* to pour from one vessel into another; to pour into the wrong vessel; to fill by mistake; to spoil in filling, by overfilling

Verfünf'fachen, *v.a.* to increase fivefold.

Verfut'tern, Verfüt'tern, *v.a.* to use up as fodder *or* provender; to overfeed (*cattle, etc.*).

Vergaf'fen, *v.r.;* **sich in einen —,** to fall in love with, to be smitten with a person.

Vergäh'nen, *v.a.;* **(die Zeit) —,** to yawn away.

Vergäh'ren, *ir.v.n.* (*aux.* **h.**) to cease fermenting; to ferment thoroughly; to ferment too much.

Vergäl'len, *v.a.* to break the gall bladder (*of a fowl, etc.*); to embitter; **sich** (*dat.*) **das Leben —,** to spoil one's own life, become embittered; **die ganze Welt ist mir vergällt,** I have lost all pleasure in life.

Vergalop(p)ie'ren, *v.r.* to go too fast, to blunder by overhaste; to overshoot the mark; to make a rash statement, to allow one's tongue to run away with one.

Vergan'gen, *p.p.* & *adj. see* **Vergehen;** past, gone; recent; last; **—e Dinge aufrühren,** to rake up bye-gones; **—e Woche,** last week. **—heit,** *f.* the past; preterite, past tense.

Vergäng'lich, *adj.* fleeting, passing, transitory; perishable, frail. **—keit,** *f.* perishableness, frailty; instability; transitoriness.

Vergan'ten, *v.a.* to sell by public auction (*prov.*); **einen —,** to declare s.o. a bankrupt.

Verga'—sen, *v.a.* to convert into gas. **—sbar,** *adj.* capable of being converted into gas. **—sung,** *f.* gasification.

Vergaf'ten, *v.n.;* **die Zeit** (*or* **Gezeit**) **vergaftet,** it is low water, the tide is turning *or* slacking.

Verga'ß, Vergä'ße (*long* **a, ä**), *1 & 3 sing. imperf. ind. & subj. of* **vergessen.**

Vergat'ter—n, *v.a.* to inclose with trellis-work *or* with a grating; **Soldaten —n,** to assemble soldiers by beat of drum. **—ung,** *n.* lattice-work, trellis; grating; assembly (*of soldiers*); **die** (*or* **zur**) **—ung schlagen,** to call together by beat of drum; **—!** sound the assembly! (*Mil.*).

Vergau'keln, *v.a.;* **die Zeit —,** to trifle away one's time.

Verge'b—en, *ir.v.a.* to give away, dispose of, confer, bestow; to cede, yield up, resign; to forgive, pardon; to compromise, to do despite to; to misdeal (*Cards*); **ein Amt an einen —en,** to appoint a p. to an office, to bestow an office on a p.; **ein Amt zu —en haben,** to have an office *or* charge in one's gift; **die Stelle ist noch nicht —en,** the place is still vacant; **die Pfarre wird vom Bischof —en,** the living is in the gift of the bishop; **die Hand seiner Tochter —en, seine Tochter —en,** to give one's daughter in marriage; **ihre Hand ist schon —en,** she is engaged to be married; **sich** (*dat.*) **nichts —en,** not to compromise one's dignity; **sich** (*dat.*) **etwas —en,** to forget oneself, not to maintain one's dignity; **vergieb dir nur, dem Ort vergiebst du nichts,** you may well compromise yourself, you cannot compromise this place; **sich** (*dat.*) **von seiner Würde etwas —en,** to compromise one's dignity; **sich** (*dat.*) **von seinem Rechte etwas —en,** to allow one's rights to be infringed; **sein Recht —en,** to cede one's rights; **er hat seiner Würde etwas —en,** he has compromised his dignity; **seiner Ehre** *or* **sich** (*dat.*) **nichts —en,** to be jealous of one's honour, to allow of no disrespect towards o.s.; **einem eine Sünde —en,** to forgive a p. a sin; **einen** *or* **einem —en,** to give poison to a p. (*obs.*); **sich —en,** to ruin oneself by over-generosity; to make a mistake in giving s.th.; **es ist —en,** it is a misdeal (*Cards*); **—ener Wunsch,** vain, useless desire. **—ens,** *adv.* in vain, to no purpose, fruitless; without reward, gratis (*obs.*). **—er,** *m.* (**—ers,** *pl.* **—er**) donor; collator, patron. **—lich,** *adj.* & *adv.* vain, idle, fruitless, to no purpose; pardonable, venial; **sich** (*dat.*) **—liche Mühe machen,** to lose one's labour. **—lichkeit,** *f.* uselessness, fruitlessness (*of a step*). **—ung,** *f.* bestowal (*of an office, etc.*); collation (*to a benefice*); cession (*of a right*); forgiveness; misdeal; **um —ung!** excuse me! I beg your pardon! pardon me!

Vergegenwär'tig—en, *v.a.* to represent, bring home to a p.'s mind; to realize; **sich** (*dat.*) **etwas —en,** to picture s.th. to o.s., to realize. **—ung,** *f.* realization.

Verge'h—en, I. *ir.v.n.* (*aux.* **s.**) to pass, slip away; to elapse; to vanish, disappear; to be lost; to diminish, fail, waste away, wear out, fade; to pass away, perish; **vor etwas —en,** to die of; **vor Gram —en.** to pine away;

wehe mir, ich —e, woe is me, for I am undone (*B.*); der Himmel wird —en, aber Du bleibest, the heavens shall perish, but thou shalt endure (*B.*); meine Tage sind vergangen wie ein Rauch, my days are consumed like smoke (*B.*); es verging ihm Hören und Sehen, he lost sight and hearing, he was quite stunned; der Appetit ist mir vergangen, I have lost my appetite; die Lust dazu ist mir vergangen, I have lost all desire for it; mir —t das Gesicht, my eye-sight is failing; Butter —en lassen, to melt butter; sich (*dat.*) die (steifen) Beine —en, to stretch one's legs, to walk off the stiffness in one's legs, to take exercise. II. *ir.v.r.* to go astray, go wrong; to err, fail in one's duty, commit a fault; sich an einem, wider *or* gegen einen —en, to insult *or* injure s.o.; sich gegen das Gesetz —en, to transgress against *or* to infringe the law; sich thätlich an einem —en, to assault a person. III. *subst.n.* disappearance; flight, lapse (*of time*); offence, crime. —ung, *f.* fault, offence, transgression; misdemeanour; trespass; sin.

Vergei'stig—en, *v.a.* to spiritualize, etherealize; to extract a spirit from, alcoholize. —ung, *f.* spiritualization.

Vergelt'bar, *adj.* remunerable.

Vergel't—en, *v.a.* (einem etwas) to requite, repay; to reward, recompense; Gott —e es Ihnen! may God reward you for it! einen Dienst —en, to repay a service, a kindness; Gleiches mit Gleichem —en, to give tit for tat; Gutes mit Bösem —en, to return evil for good. —er, *m.* (—ers, *pl.* —er) recompenser; remunerator; revenger. —ung, *f.* requital, return; reward, recompense; retaliation; reprisal. *Comp.* —ungs=recht, *n.* right of reprisal *or* retaliation, lex talionis. —ungs=tag, *m.* day of retribution; day of judgment.

Vergesell'schaft—en, *v.a. & r.* to associate, unite with. —ung, *f.* association.

Vergeß'bar, *adj.* forgettable, easily forgotten.

Verges's—en, I. *ir.v.a.* to forget; to neglect; auf sein Versprechen hatte er —en, he had forgotten his promise (*dial.*); ja, daß ich nicht —e . . ., oh! lest I forget . . .; ich habe das Wort beim Schreiben —en, I left out that word in writing; er vergißt darüber Essen und Trinken, he is so absorbed that he forgets to eat or drink; etwas bei einem —en, to leave something behind at a person's house; du sollst deine Sorgen —en, you shall forget your cares; ich will meiner Plage —en, I will forget my complaint (*B.*); mein ist —en im Herzen wie eines Toten, I am forgotten as a dead man out of mind (*B.*); vergiß mich nicht, vergiß mein (*obs. poet.*) nicht, do not forget me! so etwas vergißt sich leicht, such things are easily forgotten. II. *subst. n.* forgetting, oblivion. —enheit, *f.* forgetfulness; oblivion; negligence, neglect; in —enheit geraten, to fall (*or* to sink) into oblivion. —lich, *adj.* forgetful; easily forgotten. —lichkeit, *f.* forgetfulness; negligence. *Comp.* —en=sein, *n.* oblivion.

Vergeu'd—en, *v.a.* to squander (*away*); to dissipate, waste. —er, *m.* (—ers, *pl.* —er) squanderer, spendthrift. —ung, *f.* a squandering; extravagance; (*pl.*) waste, dissipation.

Vergewal'tige—n, *v.a.* to use force with, offer violence to; to commit a rape (on a woman). —r, *m.* (—rs, *pl.* —r) oppressor, tyrant.

Vergewis'ser—n, *v.a.* to confirm; to make sure, assure; einen einer Sache (*gen.*) —n, einen über eine S. —n, to convince a p. of a th.; sich einer Sache —n, to assure o.s. *or* make sure of (*the truth of*) a th., to ascertain —ung, *f.* confirmation; assurance.

Vergie'ß—en, *ir.v.* I. *a.* to spill, shed, pour out; to spill, pour wrongly; to spoil by watering, to drown (*as flowers*); to cast wrong; to spoil in casting; to use up in casting; to fix with molten lead, to solder; to stop up by pouring (*wax, etc.*) into. II. *r.* to make a mistake in pouring out; to cast badly. —ung, *f.* effusion, shedding (*of blood, etc.*).

Vergif't—en, *v.a.* to poison; to envenom; to taint, infect. —er, *m.* (—ers, *pl.* —er), —erin, *f.* poisoner. —ung, *f.* poisoning.

Vergil'ben, *v.n.* to turn yellow.

Vergi'ß, *imper. sing.;* **Vergis'sest, Vergi'ßt,** *2 p. sing. pres. ind.;* **Vergi'ßt,** *3 p. sing. pres. ind. of* vergessen.

Vergiß'meinnicht, *n.* forget-me-not (*Bot.*).

Vergit'ter—n, *v.a.* to inclose with lattice-work *or* a trellis; to grate (up). —ung, *f.* lattice-work, trellis; grating.

Verglas'—bar, *adj.* capable of being made into glass, vitrifiable. —barkeit, *f.* vitrifiability. —(s)en, *v.* I. *a.* to vitrify; to glaze (*a window*); —t, glazed (*eyes*). II. *n.* (*aux.* h.) to turn into glass; to become glazed. —(s)ung, *f.* vitrification; glazing.

Verglei'ch, *m.* (—es, *pl.* —e) agreement; contract, covenant, stipulation; arrangement; composition with creditors; comparison; parallel; einen — schließen, to conclude an arrangement, to come to terms; ein gütlicher —, an amicable settlement; ein — auf Termine, an arrangement to pay by instalments; über allen —, beyond comparison, incomparably, without making any comparison; das ist nichts im — mit *or* zu, that is nothing to *or* compared with; einen — anstellen *or* machen, to institute *or* make a comparison; den — aushalten, to bear comparison. —bar, *adj.* comparable (mit, *to*). —barkeit, *f.* comparableness.

Verglei'ch—en, *ir.v.* I. *a.* to make equal *or* even; to smooth, level, straighten; to adjust; to settle (*disputes*); to reconcile (*contending parties, etc.*); to compensate; to compare; to draw a comparison (*between or with*); etwas Streitiges —en, to arrange, settle a quarrel; Niemand ist mit ihm zu —en, no one is comparable to him, can be compared to him; Handschriften mit einander —en, to collate manuscripts; einen Saldo —en, to ascertain a balance. II. *r.* to compound; to come to an arrangement; to become reconciled; sich mit einem über eine S. *or* wegen einer S. —en, to agree upon s. th. with a p.; sich mit einem —en, to compare oneself with a person; diese Dinge lassen sich nicht —en, these things are not comparable. —end, *p. & adj.* comparative; —ende Sprachwissenschaft, comparative philology. —ung, *f.* adjustment, equalization; smoothing; comparison, parallel; collation; in —ung mit, in comparison with. *Comp.* —s=mäßig, *adj.* according to agreement, stipulated. —s=punkte, *pl.* articles of an agreement. —s=termin, *m.* day of settlement; love-day. —s=weise, *adv.* comparatively, by way of comparison; by agreement. —ungs=gabe, *f.* bump of comparison (*Phren.*). —ungs=grad, *m.*, —ungs=stufe, *f.* degree of comparison; erster, zweiter, dritter —ungsgrad, positive, comparative, superlative degree. —ungs=punkt, *m.* point of comparison. —ungs=weise, *adv.* comparatively.

Verglet'scher—n, *v.a. & n.* (*aux.* s.) to turn into a glacier. —ung, *f.* formation of glaciers, glacierization.

Verglim'men, *ir.v.*(*r.*) *& n.* (*aux.* s.) to die out gradually, to become *or* be slowly extinguished; sich —, to burn out slowly.

Verglü'h—en, I. *v.n.* (*aux.* s.) to cease glowing; to cool down; to die out gradually; to be consumed by fire. II. *v.a.* to spoil by heat; das Porzellan —en, to fire porcelain. III. *subst.n.*

biscuit-baking (*of porcelain*). **—er,** *m.* (**—ers,** *pl.* **—er**) brick- *or* porcelain-burner. *Comp.* **—ofen,** *m.* biscuit-kiln.

Vergnü'g—en, I. *v.a.* indulge; to content, (*dial., poet.*) satisfy; to please, gratify; to divert, amuse; **sich an einer S. —en,** to find amusement, take pleasure in a th. II. *subst.n.* pleasure, delight, enjoyment; amusement; satisfaction, comfort; joy; **etwas zum —en thun,** to do a thing for pleasure; **ländliche —en,** rural sports; **—en an einer S. finden,** to find pleasure, take delight in something; **machen Sie mir das —en und besuchen Sie mich,** give me the pleasure of a visit (from you); **es macht mir viel —en,** it gives me much pleasure; **wenn es Ihnen —en macht,** if you like it. **—lich,** *adj. & adv.* contented, easily pleased; satisfactory; pleasant; amusing. **—lichkeit,** *f.* pleasingness, agreeableness; contentment, satisfaction. **—t,** *p.p. & adj.* pleased; joyous, glad; cheerful, contented, satisfied (*dial.*). **—ung,** *f.* pleasure; amusement; recreation; **—ungen im Freien,** field-sports, outdoor games. *Comp.* **—ungs=kommissär,** *m.* maître de plaisir, arranger of entertainments (*at a holiday resort*). **—ungs=lokal,** *n.* place of amusement. **—ungs=ort,** *m.* place of entertainment; holiday-resort. **—ungs=reise,** *f.* pleasure-trip. **—ungs=reisende(r),** *m.* tourist, holiday-maker, tripper (*coll.*). **—ungs=sucht,** *f.* (*inordinate*) love of amusement. **—ungs=zug,** *m.* excursion-train.

Vergol'd—en, *v.a.* to gild; to cover; **galvanisch —en,** to electro-plate with gold. **—er,** *m.* (**—ers,** *pl.* **—er**) gilder. **—ung,** *f.* gilding; plating with gold; **trockene —ung,** leaf-gilding; **—ung mit Blattgold,** burnished gilding; **galvanische —ung,** electro-gilding. *Comp.* **—e=brettchen,** *n.* pallet. **—e=firnis,** *m.* gold-lacquer. **—e(r)=kunst,** *f.* gilding. **—e=lappen,** *m.* bookbinder's gold-rag. **—e=messer,** *n.* gilder's knife. **—e=pinsel,** *m.* gilder's tip. **—e=stein,** *m.* agate-burnisher; blood-stone.

Vergön'nen, *v.a.* to grant, permit, allow.

Vergöt'ter—er, *m.* (**—ers,** *pl.* **—er**) idolizer, adorer. **—n,** *v.a.* to deify; to idolize, adore. **—ung,** *f.* deification; adoration, idolatry.

Vergra'ben, *ir.v.a.* to bury; to hide in the ground; to intrench, furnish with a trench; **sich —,** to burrow (*of animals*); **sich in (ein Kloster) —,** to shut o.s. up in (a convent).

Vergrä'me(l)n, *v.a.* to pass in grief and sorrow; to fret (*one's time*) away; **einen —,** to grieve a p., give trouble to a p.; **sich —,** to pine away; **vergrämt,** care-worn, woe-begone; soured (*with grief*).

Vergra'sen, *v.* I. *a.*; **das Getreide —,** to cut the blades of young corn. II. *n.* (*aux.* **s.**) to be overgrown *or* covered with grass.

Vergrei'f—en, *ir.v.* I. *a.* to seize *or* touch wrongly; **die Saite —en,** to touch the wrong string; **eine Ware —en,** to seize upon, buy up an article; **diese Ware war bald vergriffen,** this article was soon bought up, sold out; **die Auflage des Buches ist vergriffen,** the edition of the book is exhausted, sold out; **das Buch ist —,** the book is out of print; **sich** (*dat.*) **die Hand —en,** to hurt, sprain one's hand. II. *r.* to seize wrongly, mistake in seizing; **sich an einem —en,** to lay violent hands upon a p.; **sich mit Worten an einem —en,** to insult a p.; **sich an einer Sache —en,** to steal s.th.; **sich an den Gesetzen —en,** to violate *or* infringe the law; **sich an geheiligten Sachen —en,** to commit sacrilege, profane holy things; **er vergriff sich an dem Herrn, seinem Gott,** he transgressed against the Lord his God (*B.*); **sich an dem Namen Gottes —en,** to take the name of God in vain; **sich an der Majestät —en,** to be guilty of high treason; **sich auf dem Klavier —en,** to touch a wrong note on the piano. **—ung,** *f.* wronging; violation; profanation.

Vergrif'fen, *p.p. adj. see* **Vergreifen.**

Vergrö'bern, *v.a.* to make coarse(r); **sich —,** to become coarser *or* ruder.

Vergrö'ßer—n, *v.* I. *a.* to enlarge; to increase, augment; to extend; to magnify; to aggravate; to exaggerate; **in —tem Maßstabe darstellen,** to draw on a larger scale. II. *r.* to aggrandize oneself; to extend one's power; (*also n.*) to grow larger. **—ung,** *f.* enlargement; increase; aggrandizement; **zur —ung seines Unglücks,** in extension of his misfortunes. *Comp.* **—ungs=camera,** *f.* copying *or* enlarging camera. **—ungs=fähig,** *adj.* that may be increased, capable of extension. **—ungs=fähigkeit,** *f.* capacity for increasing. **—ungs=glas,** *n.* magnifying glass. **—ungs=kraft,** *f.* magnifying power. **—ungs=laterne,** *f.* magic lantern. **—ungs=linse,** *f.* magnifying lens. **—ungs=plan,** *m.* plan of aggrandizement. **—ungs=spiegel,** *m.* concave mirror. **—ungs=silbe,** *f.* augmentative syllable. **—ungs=verfahren,** *n.* enlarging process (*Phot.*). **—ungs=wort,** *n.* augmentative.

Vergrü'beln, *v.a.* to lose (*one's time*) in ruminating; to spoil by subtleties; **sich —,** to be lost in gloomy meditations.

Vergrü'nen, *v.n.* (*aux.* **s.**) to lose the green colour, to fade; to become green (*of petals*).

Vergu'cken, *v.r.* to make a mistake in looking; **sich in einen —,** to let o.s. be dazzled by a p., to fall in love with a p. *See* **Vergaffen.**

Vergül'den, *obs. for* **Vergolden.**

Vergu'nst, *f.* permission; **mit —,** with your kind permission, by your leave.

Vergün'stigung, *f.* (*pl.* **—en**) permission; privilege; rebate, favour.

Vergü't(ig)—en, *v.a.* to make amends, restore; to compensate; **einem etwas —en,** to indemnify, compensate a p. for a thing; **einem die Auslagen —en,** to reimburse a p. (for outlay); **es wird den Eigentümern —et,** the owners will receive compensation; **ich werde Ihnen Ihre Mühe —en,** I shall make it worth your while. **—ung,** *f.* compensation, amends; indemnification, indemnity; reimbursement.

Verha'ck, *m.* (**—(e)s,** *pl.* **—e**) abattis, barrier of trees cut down (*Fort.*).

Verha'cken, *v.a.* to chop, cut up, to mince; **das Lager —,** to fence round the camp with an abattis *or* breastwork of felled wood.

Verha'ft, *m.* (**—(e)s**) arrest; custody; imprisonment; pledge (*obs.*); **in —,** under arrest, in custody; **in — nehmen,** to seize, arrest; **— auf eine S. legen,** to lay an embargo on a th.

Verhaf't—en, *v.a.* to arrest, apprehend, take into custody; to imprison; to stake; to mortgage; **einem —et sein,** to be indebted to a person (*rare*); **ein unterpfändlich —etes Gut,** a mortgaged estate; **—en lassen,** to have a p. arrested, to give a p. in charge, to send a p. to prison. **—ung,** *f.* arrest; imprisonment. *Comp.* **—s=befehl, —s=brief,** *m.* warrant, writ of arrest; **einen —sbrief gegen einen erlassen,** to issue a warrant for the apprehension of a p.

Verha'geln, *v.n.* (*aux.* **s.**) to be spoilt by hail; destroyed, ruined, brought to naught (*fig.*); **ihm ist die Petersilie verhagelt,** he has had (a stroke of) bad luck; he is very downcast.

Verhä'keln, *v.a.* to join, fasten with little hooks; **viel Seide —,** to use up a great deal of silk in crocheting.

Verhal'len, *v.n.* (*aux.* **s.**) to die *or* fade away, be lost; **langsam —d,** lingering.

Verhal't—en, I. *ir.v.a.* to keep back; to stop (*one's mouth, etc.*); to hold in (*one's breath*); to retain (*urine*); to repress; to master, control; to hide, dissimulate; **das Blut —en,** to stanch blood; **das Lachen —en,** to restrain one's laughter. II. *ir.v.r. & n.* (*aux.* s.) to stop, remain. III. *ir.v.r.* to tarry, linger (*prov.*); to be in a certain condition, be circumstanced, situated, be; to be in proportion, have a certain relation to; to demean, conduct, comport oneself; **wissen Sie, wie sich die Sache** *or* **wie es sich damit verhält?** do you know how the matter stands? **wenn es sich so verhält,** if that be the case; **sich —en zu,** to be in proportion to; **die Höhe verhält sich zur Breite wie fünf zu zwei,** the height is to the breadth as 5 to 2; **es verhält sich mit mir wie mit Ihnen,** it is with me as with you; **wie verhält sich Blei im Feuer?** what change does lead undergo in fire? **sich ruhig —en,** to keep quiet, to keep the peace; **—en Sie sich passiv,** maintain a passive attitude; **ich weiß nicht, wie ich mich dabei —en soll,** I don't know how to act in this case; **—ene Dünste,** pent-up vapours; **—ene Winde,** flatulency; **—ene Erregung,** suppressed excitement. IV. *subst.n. see* **—ung**; conduct, behaviour; attitude (*towards one, etc.*); procedure; method of acting, tactics; relation(s); **das —en einer Säure gegen ...,** the reaction of an acid upon ... **—ung,** *f.* suppression; retention; concealment. *Comp.* **—ungs=art,** *f.* manner of behaving. **—ungs=befehl,** *m.* instructions; orders; **mit —ungs-befehlen versehen,** to instruct, give orders to. **—ungs=maßregeln,** *pl.* instructions.

Verhält'nis, *n.* (—(ss)es, *pl.* —(ss)e) relation, bearing; proportion, ratio; (*gen'lly pl.*) situation, condition, circumstances; love-affair; **— zu,** relation with; **in freundschaftlichem —(ss)e mit einem stehen,** to be on friendly terms with a p.; **das — des Sohnes zu seinem Vater war das denkbar Schönste,** the son's relations with his father were the best imaginable; **ein sträfliches — mit einem haben** *or* **unterhalten,** to have illicit intercourse with a p.; **im — zu,** in proportion to; **im** *or* **nach —,** accordingly, proportionately, relatively, comparatively; **und alles Übrige im —,** and all the rest, everything else accordingly, in keeping, in the same style, proportionately; **im — von zwei zu vier,** in the ratio of 2 to 4; **in umgekehrtem —,** in inverse ratio; **in — stehend mit,** proportioned to, proportional, in proportion to; **nach — der Bevölkerung,** in proportion to the population; **nach —, im —(ss)e zahlt er mehr, als wir,** he pays more in proportion than we do; **das richtige —,** the right *or* due proportion, symmetry; **er lebt in angenehmen —(ss)en,** he lives in easy circumstances; he is very pleasantly situated; **seine —(ss)e haben sich gebessert,** his circumstances have improved; **unter solchen —(ss)en,** such being the case, under these circumstances. *Comp.* **—anteil,** *m.* quota, share. **—anzeiger,** *m.* exponent (*Math.*). **—linie,** *f.* proportion- *or* setting-rule (*Typ.*). **—los,** *adj.* having no relation *or* proportion. **—mäßig,** I. *adj.* proportionate, proportional. II. *adv.* in proportion; comparatively (speaking). **—mäßigkeit,** *f.* proportion(ateness). **—regel,** *f.* rule of three *or* proportion (*Arith.*). **—widrig,** *adj.* disproportioned, disproportionate. **—wort,** *n.* preposition. **—zahl,** *f.* proportional number.

Verhan'd—eln, *v.* I. *a. & n.* (*aux.* h.) to treat; to discuss, debate, deliberate upon; to negotiate; (**über**) **den Frieden —eln,** to negotiate, a peace; **einen Wechselbrief —eln,** to negotiate a bill; **gerichtlich —eln,** to try (a case). II. *a.* to sell, dispose of, barter away; to lose in speculation; **er hat sein ganzes Vermögen —elt,** he has lost everything he had in trade; **er hat seine eigene Tochter an diesen Lüstling —elt,** he has sold his own daughter to this rake. **—lung,** *f.* discussion, deliberation; argument; parley, conference; negotiation; treaty, transaction; proceeding; pleading (*Law*); **—lungen der (philologischen) Gesellschaft,** proceedings of the (philological) society. *Comp.* **—lungs=bericht,** *m.*, **—lungs=buch, —lungs=heft,** *n.*, **—lungs=schrift,** *f.* minutes, minute-book. **—lungs=papiere,** *pl.* records, acts, minutes. **—lungs=saal,** *f.* court, session-hall.

Verhän'g—en, *v.a.* to cover with a curtain, to veil, conceal; to hang up in a wrong way *or* place; to decree, ordain; to send; to inflict (a punishment); **einem Pferde den Zügel —en,** to give a horse his head; **mit —tem Zügel,** at full gallop; **die Todesstrafe über einen —en,** to condemn a p. to death; **wie es Gott —t,** as God ordains. **—nis,** *n.* (—nisses, *pl.* —nisse) fate, destiny; the powers that be, Fate; **durch ein sonderbares —nis,** by a strange fatality. *Comp.* **—nis=glaube,** *m.* belief in fate, fatalism. **—nis=gläubige(r),** *m.* fatalist. **—nis=voll,** *adj.* fatal, unhappy; fateful, ominous, portentous.

Verhär'm—en, *v.a.* to spend in sorrow; **—tes Gesicht,** care-worn, woe-begone face.

Verhar'ren, *v.n.* (*aux.* h. & s.) to remain; to continue (*in the same state, way of thinking*), to remain unchanged, to hold out; to persevere, persist (*in*); **auf** *or* **bei seiner Ansicht —,** to maintain, persist in one's opinion.

Verhar'sch—en, *v.* I. *n.* (*aux.* s.) to form a crust; to close (*of wounds*). II. *a.* to skin *or* crust over. **—ung,** *f.* crusting, incrustation; closing.

Verhär't—en, *v.* I. *a.* to harden, make hard, indurate; **den Leib —en,** to constipate the bowels. II., (**Verhar'ten,**) *n.* (*aux.* s.) to harden, grow hard; to become obdurate. **—et,** *adj.* (*fig.*) obdurate, callous. **—ung,** *f.* hardening; induration; callosity; hardness, obduracy.

Verhar'zen (*long* **a**), *v.* I. *a.* to close up, smear over *or* join with resin. II. *r. & n.* (*aux.* s.) to become resinous, turn to resin.

Verhas'peln, *v.a.* to use up in winding; to entangle in winding; **sich beim Reden —,** to become confused, embarrassed in speaking.

Verha'ßt, *adj.* odious, detestable, hateful, obnoxious; hated.

Verhät'scheln, *v.a.* to over-indulge, spoil, pamper.

Verhau', *m. see* **Verhack.**

Verhau'en, *ir.v.a.* to cut, hew down; to cut off, mutilate; to lop; to prune; to cut up (*wood*); to hack, spoil by cutting; to use up in cutting; **einen —,** to thrash s.o. soundly (*vulg.*); **das Tuch —,** to crop, pare cloth; **den Weg —,** to barricade, bar the way with felled wood; **einem den Weg —,** to put obstacles in a p.'s way; **sich —,** to make a false cut (*in fencing*), to expose o.s.; **sich (im Reden) —,** to blunder (*coll.*).

Verhe'ben, *ir.v.a.* to lift in a wrong way; to cut wrong (*Cards*); **sich —,** to strain o.s. in lifting; **sich** (*dat.*) **den Arm —,** to sprain one's arm by lifting (*a burden*).

Verhed'dern, *v.r.* to get entangled (*coll. & dial.*).

Verhee'r—en, *v.a.* to ravage, devastate, lay waste. **—er,** *m.* (—ers, *pl.* —er) devastator, destroyer. **—ung,** *f.* devastation.

Verhef'ten, *v.a.* to sew up, draw together (*a wound, etc.*); to use up in sewing; to stitch wrong, transpose (*the leaves of a book*) in sewing.

Verheh'l—en, *v.a.* to hide, conceal, dissemble to receive (*stolen goods*). **—t, Verhoh'len,** *p.p. see* **Verhohlen.** **—ung,** *f.* concealing, hiding; concealment; dissimulation; receiving (*of stolen goods*).

Verheim'lich—en, *v.a.* to conceal, hide, keep secret; to disguise, dissemble; to receive (*stolen goods*); **einem etwas —en,** to conceal a thing from a person. **—ung,** *f.* concealment;

dissimulation; receiving (*stolen goods*); **—ung des einer Person bekannt gewordenen Hochverrats,** misprision of (high) treason.

Verhei'rat—en, *v.* I. *a.* to marry, give in marriage, to settle (*a daughter, etc.*); to perform the marriage ceremony. II. *r.* to marry; **sich mit einem —en,** to marry a person; **sich wieder —en,** to marry again *or* a second time; **sich glücklich —en,** to marry happily; **sich günstig —en,** to make a good match, to be comfortably settled; **sich unter einander —en,** to intermarry. **—ung,** *f.* marriage; settlement; **—ung unter verschiedenen Rassen,** intermarriage.

Verhei'ß—en, *ir.v.n.* to promise; **das —ene Land,** the Promised Land. **—ung,** *f.* promise.

Verhel'fen, *ir.v.n.* (*aux.* **h.**); **einem zu einer S. —,** to help s.o. to a th. *or* to get a th., to procure a th. for a p.

Verhen'kert, *adj.* devilish, confounded (*vulg.*).

Verherr'lich—en, *v.a.* to glorify, extol, exalt. **—er,** *m.* (**—ers,** *pl.* **—er**) glorifier (*rare*); (*fig.*) herald. **—ung,** *f.* glorification.

Verhet'z—en, *v.a.* to incite, instigate, stir up; to goad on, exasperate, irritate; to chase away; **einen gegen eine Person —en,** to set s.o. against a p., incite s.o. to attack a p.; **einen, ein Tier —en,** to hunt a p. *or* a beast to death. **—ung,** *f.* setting on; incitation, instigation.

Verhe'xen, *v.a.* to bewitch, enchant; to cast an evil eye on.

Verhim'mel—n, *v.* I. *a.* to deify. II. *n.* to be lost in ecstasy, admiration; **—t sein,** to be in raptures. **—ung,** *f.* rapture; ecstasy; puffing up; adulation.

Verhin'der—n, *v.a.* to hinder, prevent; to obstruct; **einen an einer S. —n,** to prevent a p. from doing something; **wie willst du (es) —n, daß er es erfährt?** how will you prevent his learning (*hearing*) it? **jemandes Fortschritte —n,** to impede s.o.'s progress; **den Umlauf des Blutes —n,** to stop the circulation (of the blood). **—ung,** *f.* hindering; prevention; obstacle, impediment.

Verhof'fen, I. (*obs.*) *v.n.* (*aux.* **h.**) *see* **Hoffen.** II. *subst.n.* hope; **wider alles —,** contrary to all expectation, contrary to all hopes.

Verhoh'len, *p.p. of* **verhehlen,** concealed (*obs.*). *adj.* secretive; underhand, clandestine.

Verhöh'n—en, *v.a.* to scoff, laugh at, deride; to jeer, mock, make game of, turn into ridicule; to snap one's fingers at; to hiss; **die Vernunft —en,** to insult reason. **—er,** *m.* (**—ers,** *pl.* **—er**) scorner, derider. **—ung,** *f.* derision, mockery; insult.

Verhö'r, *n.* (**—s,** *pl.* **—e**) judicial examination; trial; **ein — anstellen,** to institute an inquiry; **einen zum — ziehen,** to bring a p. up for examination; **ins — nehmen,** to interrogate, cross-examine; **ein — bestehen,** to stand one's trial. **—bar,** *adj.* that can be interrogated *or* examined.

Verhö'r—en, *v.a.* to hear, try, examine (*an accused person*); to hear say *or* repeat (*as pupils their lessons*); not to hear; **er —te kein Wörtchen,** he did not lose a syllable; **sich —en,** to hear wrong *or* misunderstand a p.'s words. *Comp.* **—gemach,** *n.* court; room where the trial is held. **—protokoll,** *n.* minutes of a trial. **—termin,** *m.* day of (the) trial.

Verhu'deln, *v.a.* to spoil by want of care, to bungle, daub, botch.

Verhüll—en, I. *v.a.* to cover, veil, wrap up; to muffle (*a knocker, a bell*); **in —enden Worten,** in veiled language, euphemistically; **er —te sich in seinen Mantel,** he wrapped himself closely in his cloak; **unser Schicksal ist in Dunkelheit —t,** our fate is wrapped in obscurity. II. *subst. n.*, **—ung,** *f.* covering, veiling, disguise.

Verhun'dert—fachen, —fältigen, *v.a.* to multiply by a hundred.

Verhun'gern, *v.n.* (*aux.* **s.**) to die of hunger; **ganz verhungert aussehen,** to look famished *or* half-starved; **— lassen,** starved.

Verhun'zen, *v.a.* to spoil (*by bad workmanship*); to bungle, daub, botch; to disfigure; **die englische Sprache —,** to murder the King's English.

Verhu'rt, *adj.* lewd, debauched.

Verhüt'bar, *adj.* preventable.

Verhü't—en, *v.a.* to avert, ward off; to prevent; **ein Unglück —en,** to avert a calamity; **das —e Gott!** God forbid! **was Gott —e!** which God forbid (*in the middle of a sentence*). **—ung,** *f.* prevention; **die —ung von Druckfehlern ist schwer,** it is difficult to avoid printer's errors. *Comp.* **—ungs=maßregel,** *f.* preventive measure. **—ungs=mittel,** *n.* preventive, preservative.

Verhütt—en, *v.a.* to work (off), smelt. **—ung,** *f.* smelting.

Verhut'zelt, *adj.* small, tiny, shrivelled up (*coll.*); spoilt, disfigured (*dial.*).

Verifizie'r—en, *v.a.* to verify. **—ung,** *f.* verification.

Verin'nerlich—en, *v.a.* to intensify, to render more sincere. **—ung,** *f.* deepening, intensification.

Verin'nigen, *v.a.* to increase the intensity of; to make more intimate, unite more closely; **sich —,** to become more intimate *or* cordial.

Verinteressie'ren, *v.a.* to pay interest on *or* for; **sich —,** to yield interest, to pay.

Verir'r—en, *v.r. & n.* (*aux.* **s.**) to err, go astray, lose one's way; to wander about; **—te Kugel,** stray bullet. **—ung,** *f.* going astray, losing one's way; aberration; wandering; error.

Verja'g—en, *v.a.* to drive away; to expel; to dispel (*fig.*); to dislodge, drive out, put to flight (*Mil.*). **—ung,** *f.* expulsion; dislodgment.

Verjähr'bar, *adj.* prescriptible (*Law*).

Verjäh'r—en, *v.n.* (*aux.* **s.**) to grow old, become superannuated, to go out of date *or* fashion; to become rooted *or* inveterate; (*also r.*) to fall under the statute of limitations; to become null and void through disuse. **—t,** *p.p. & adj.* time-honoured (*obs.*); inveterate, deep-rooted; prescriptive (*Law*); obsolete; **ein —tes Recht,** a prescriptive right; **eine —te Schuld,** a prescriptive debt. **—ung,** *f.* superannuation; inveterateness; prescription (*Law*). *Comp.* **—ungs=frist,** *f.* term of limitation *or* prescription. **—ungs=gesetz, —ungs=recht,** *n.* statute of limitations.

Verjam'mern, *v.a.* to pass in lamentation.

Verjau'chen, *v.n.* to become sanious.

Verjauch'zen, Verju'beln, *v.a.* to pass (*one's time, etc.*) in merriment *or* rejoicing; **sein Geld verjubeln,** to waste one's fortune in gaiety *or* dissipation, to make ducks and drakes of one's money.

Verju'den, *v.* I. *a.* to Judaize. II. *n.* (*aux.* **s.**) to turn Jew, to adopt Jewish habits.

Verjün'g—en, *v.* I. *a.* to rejuvenate; to make and keep young (*rare*); to reduce to a smaller scale; to lessen, diminish; **in —tem Maßstabe,** on a small *or* reduced scale, in miniature; **—te Probe,** small assay (*Smelt.*); **—te Sparren,** supporting rafters *or* joists. II. *r.* to grow young again; to diminish (*of columns*). **—ung,** *f.* rejuvenescence; reduction; diminution; small model. *Comp.* **—ungs=kunst,** *f.* art of rejuvenating. **—ungs=maßstab,** *m.* reduced scale. **—ungs=mittel,** *n.* means of restoring youth. **—ungs=prozeß,** *m.* process of restoring youth, rejuvenating process. **—ungs=quelle,** *f.* fountain of youth. **—ungs=vierecke,** *pl.* squares for reducing designs.

Verju'xen, (*coll.*) *see* **Verjubeln.**

Verkal'ben, *v.n.* (*aux.* **h.**) to calve before the time.

Verkalk'—bar, *adj.* calcinable. **—en,** *v.* I. *a.* to calcine. II. *r.* & *n.* (*aux.* **f.**) to turn to chalk, calcine. **—ung,** *f.* calcination.

Verkalkulie'ren, *v.r.* to miscalculate.

Verkap'p—en, *v.a.* to put a coping to, cope (*a wall*); to hoodwink (*a hawk*); to muffle up; to mask, disguise; **sich —en,** to disguise oneself. **—t,** *p.p.* & *adj.* disguised, secret; undeveloped (*illness*); **ein —ter Schriftsteller,** a writer under an assumed name; **—ter Freidenker,** a freethinker in disguise *or* at heart. **—ung,** *f.* masking, disguising; disguise.

Verkap'seln, *v.r.* to become encysted (*Med.*).

Verkar'sten, *v.n.* (*aux.* **f.**) to become desolate and barren.

Verkau'f, *m.* (—**s**, *pl.* **Verkäu'fe**) sale; **zum —e aussetzen, ausstellen,** to put up for sale; **es steht zum —e,** it is to be sold, it is for sale. **—bar,** *see* **Verkäuflich.** *Comp.* **—s=automat,** *m.*, **—s=maschine,** *f.* automaton, penny-in-the-slot machine. **—s=bedingungen,** *pl.* terms *or* conditions of sale. **—s=buch,** *n.* sales-book, day-book. **—s=bude,** *f.* stall, booth (*of a vendor*). **—s=lokal,** *n.* shop; sale-room. **—s=preis,** *m.* selling price. **—s=recht,** *n.* right to sell.

Verkau'f—en, *v.a.* to sell; **mit Gewinn —en,** to sell to advantage; **mit Schaden —en,** to sell at a loss; **nichts mehr zu —en haben,** to be at one's wits' end (*coll.*); **zu —en sein,** to be for sale. II. *r.* to sell; **es —t gut,** to sell well; **das —t sich schwer,** that is a drug in the market, difficult to dispose of; **an guter Ware —t man sich nie,** a good article is never dear.

Verkäu'f—er, *m.* (—**ers**, *pl.* —**er**), **—erin,** *f.* seller, vendor; **—er im Kleinen,** retail dealer; **—erin im Laden,** shopwoman, shopgirl, saleswoman. **—lich,** I. *adj.* for sale; saleable; venal, mercenary; negotiable (*of bills*); **schwer — liche Ware,** drug in the market. II. *adv.* by sale; **einem etwas —lich überlassen,** to sell a th. to a p. **—lichkeit,** *f.* saleableness; venality.

Verke'geln, *v.a.* to play at skittles for; to lose at skittles.

Verke'hr, *m.* (—**s**) traffic; intercourse; connection; commerce, trade; train- *or* coach-service between places, communication; **eine Bahn dem — übergeben,** to open a railway (line) to traffic; **geselliger —,** social intercourse; **anregender —,** interesting friends; **mit einem — haben, in — mit einem stehen,** to have intercourse *or* dealings with a p.; **freier —,** open communication, free trade; **wir stehen im Zeichen des —s,** the signature of our time is commerce; **Handel und —,** trade and commerce; **— mit dem Auslande,** foreign trade. *Comp.* **—s=ader,** *f.* thoroughfare, (chief) artery (of a town). **—s=einrichtungen,** *f.pl.* arrangements for traffic. **—s=erleichterungen,** *pl.* facilities for traffic *or* trade. **—s=freiheit,** *f.* free trade. **—s=gebiet,** *n.* area traversed by a railway. **—s=mittel,** *n.* currency; means of communication. **—s=ordnung,** *f.* traffic regulations. **—s=platz,** *m.* commercial centre; town of transit. **—s=störung,** *f.* interruption of communication *or* traffic, block, breakdown. **—s=straße,** *f.* high road of commerce, trade route; line of communication. **—s=truppen,** *pl.* military cyclists; aeronauts; military railway and telegraph departments. **—s=wesen,** *n.* traffic, train-service.

Verkeh'r—en, *v.* I. *a.* to turn the wrong way; to turn upside down; to turn topsy-turvy; to turn, change, convert into; to roll (*one's eyes*); to overturn, overthrow; to reverse; to pervert (*the law; people's minds, etc.*); **die Freude in Leid —en,** to change mirth into sadness; **jemandes Worte —en,** to put a wrong construction upon a p.'s words. II. *r.* to change (*into*). III. *n.* (*aux.* **h.**) to come and go, to frequent; to have intercourse (*with*): to trade, traffic; to carry on *or* do business; **regelmäßig (zwischen zwei Orten) —en,** to ply between (*of ships*); **Lokal, in dem viele Schiffer —en,** house frequented by boatmen, sailors; **mit einem —en,** to have intercourse with a p.; **viel mit einem —en,** to see much *or* a good deal of a p.; **bei einem —en,** to visit, *or* to be a frequent visitor at a p.'s house. **—t,** *p.p.* & *adj.* & *adv.* turned the wrong way; inside out; upside down; inverted; wrong; perverse; wrongheaded; absurd, preposterous; **—te Seite,** wrong side; **mit —tem Gewehr,** arms reversed (*Mil.*); **Schlag mit der —ten Hand,** backhanded blow; **—te Pumpe,** forcing-pump; **—te Welt,** world turned topsy-turvy, upside down; **—te Ordnung,** inverted order; **—t anfangen,** to go the wrong way to work, set about badly; to put the cart before the horse. **—theit,** *f.* perversity, absurdity, awkwardness; preposterousness. **—ung,** *f.* *f.* overturning; inversion (*of an order, etc.*); perversion; inverse proposition.

Verkei'len, *v.a.* to wedge tight, fasten with a wedge; to drive up the quoins (*Typ.*); **(einen) —,** to thrash (*sl.*); **(etwas) —,** to sell (*at any price*) (*sl.*).

Verkenn'bar, *adj.* easily mistaken *or* misunderstood.

Verken'n—en, *ir.v.a.* to mistake, take for another; to misunderstand, misjudge, have a false idea of, fail to appreciate; to fail to recognize; to cut (*an acquaintance*); **verkanntes Genie, verkannter Mensch,** unrecognized, misunderstood genius. **—ung,** *f.* mistaking; want of appreciation.

Verket't—eln, *v.a.* to attach by a little chain. **—en,** *v.a.* to chain; to link together, form a chain of; to connect. **—ung,** *f.* chaining; chain-work; concatenation, (connected) series.

Verket'zer—er, *m.* (—**ers**, *pl.* —**er**) one who accuses another of heresy; zealot. **—n,** *v.a.* to accuse of heresy; to decry as heretical; to calumniate. **—ung,** *f.* charge of heresy.

Verkirch'lichen, *v.a.* to put under clerical *or* ecclesiastical management, to subject to the authority of the church.

Verkit't—en, *v.a.* to cement, lute; to stop up with cement. **—ung,** *f.* cementation, puttying.

Verklag'bar, *adj.* actionable, suable, indictable.

Verkla'g—en, *v.a.* to accuse, impeach; to sue, bring an action against; to inform against; **einen wegen einer Schuld —en,** to sue a p. for debt; **einen des Hochverrats —en,** to accuse s.o. of high treason; **seine Tage, sein Geld —en,** to spend one's days in complaining, one's money in litigation. **—te(r),** *m.*, **—te,** *f.* accused, defendant; respondent. **—ung,** *f.* accusation; prosecution.

Verklä'ger, *m.* (—**s**, *pl.* —) accuser, plaintiff.

Verklam'mern, *v.a.* to clamp, fasten with cramp-irons.

Verklä'r—en, *v.a.* to make bright *or* luminous; to clarify; to transfigure; **—te Leiber,** glorified bodies; **—tes Antlitz,** countenance refulgent with celestial bliss; **—ter Blick,** serene *or* radiant look; **ein —tes Aussehen haben,** to look radiant. **—ung,** *f.* transfiguration.

Verklat'schen, *v.a.* to babble, gossip away (*time*); to waste in gossiping; to defame, slander, backbite (*a p.*).

Verklau'sel—n, Verklausulie'r—en, *v.a.* to guard *or* insure by clauses, to insert clauses in; to stipulate, make special provision about. **—t,** *p.p.* & *adj.* specially provided *or* stipulated. **—ung,** *f.* stipulation.

Verkle'b—en, *v.a.* to plaster up, cement; to close up (*a wound*) with plaster; to loam up; to glue, gum up. **—ung,** *f.* a sticking together; agglutination.

Verkleck'sen, *v.a.* to waste in daubing *or* scribbling; to ink, to spoil with ink-stains.

Verklei'd—en, *v.a.* to cover, to face *or* case (*with*); to line (*shafts*); to board, to wainscot; to disguise (*by a change of dress*); to veil (*an insult, etc.*); to plank a ship; **als Spanier —et,** disguised as a Spaniard. **—ung,** *f.* covering, facing, lining; wainscotting; panelling; window- *or* door-case; revetment (*Fort.*); disguising; disguise; **die obere —ung einer Thür,** lintel.

Verklei'nerer, *m.* (—s, *pl.* —) belittler, detractor.

Verklei'ner—n, *v.a.* to make smaller; to diminish, reduce; to disparage; to detract from; to slander, calumniate; **einen Bruch —n,** to reduce a fraction; **den Wert von etwas** *or* **einer S. —n,** to depreciate the value of a thing; **einen, jemandes Verdienst —n,** to disparage a person's merit *or* services. **—ung,** *f.* diminution; extenuation (*of a fault, etc.*); reduction; detraction; disparagement. *Comp.* **—ungs=endung,** *f.* diminutive ending. **—ungs=glas,** *n.* concave lens, diminishing glass. **—ungs=wort,** *n.* diminutive (*Gram.*).

Verklei'stern, *v.a. see* **Verkleben**; to patch up, cover over; **einem die Augen —,** to throw dust in a p.'s eyes (*fig., coll.*).

Verklin'gen, *ir.v.n.* (*aux.* **s.**) to be lost, die *or* fade away (*of sounds*); to be forgotten.

Verklop'pen, *v.a.* to sell, dispose of (*sl.*).

Verknack'sen, *v.r.*; **sich** (*dat.*) **den Fuß —,** to sprain one's foot.

Verknal'len, *v.* I. *n.* (*aux.* **s.**) to explode; to go off with a report. II. *a.* to fire off at a wrong time, wrongly.

Verknei'fen, *ir.v.* I. *a.* to pinch, hide by pinching; **sich** (*dat.*) **etwas —,** to deny o.s. s.th., to forego s.th. (*sl.*). II. *r.* to err, to be mistaken.

Verknei'pen, *v.a.*; **sein Geld —,** to waste one's money at the public house (*sl.*).

Verknis'tern, *v.n.* to decrepitate.

Verknit'tern, *v.a.* to rumple up, crumple.

Verknö'cher—n, *v.* I. *a.* to change into bone, to ossify; to dry up, make hard. II. *n.* (*aux.* **s.**) to ossify; to grow hard, narrow, selfish. **—ung,** *f.* ossification; formation of bone; hardening.

Verknor'peln, *v.r. & n.* (*aux.* **s.**) to turn into cartilage.

Verknüp'f—en, *v.a.* to knot, tie, bind; to knot up, to tie, get in(to) knots; to connect, combine, unite; to annex, attach to; **mit Übelständen —t sein,** to be attended with, accompanied by drawbacks; **logisch —te Ideen,** logically connected ideas; **mit wenig Kosten —t,** causing little expense; **—te Kinder,** scrofulous, rickety children. **—ung,** *f.* knotting; tying together; uniting; bond; combination; connection. *Comp.* **—ungs=wort,** *n.* connective; copula.

Verknur'ren, *v.a.* to condemn, fine (*stud. sl.*).

Verknu'sen, *v.n.* to stomach, put up with, stand (*sl.*); **ich kann ihn nicht —,** I hate the sight of him.

Verko'chen, *v.* I. *a.* to use in cooking; to cook too much. II. *n.* (*aux.* **s.**) to spoil in cooking; to cook to rags; to boil away; **sein Zorn verkochte bald,** his anger soon cooled down.

Verkoh'l—en, *v.a. & n.* (*aux.* **s.**) to char; to carbonize. **—ung,** *f.* carbonisation, charring.

Verko'k—en, *v.a.* to convert into coke. **—ung,** *f.* coke-burning. *Comp.* **—ungs=meiler,** *m.* coking mound.

Verkom'men, I. *ir.v.n.* (*aux.* **s.**) to decay; to go to ruin; to go down in the world; to become demoralized. II. *p.p. & adj.* decayed; degenerate, depraved. **—heit,** *f.* depravity, demoralization.

Verkop'peln, *v.a.* to couple, join together.

Verkor'ken, *v.a.* to cork (up).

Verkör'per—n, *v.a.* to embody; to clothe in flesh and blood, to materialize; to personify. **—ung,** *f.* embodiment, personification.

Verköf'tigen, *v.a.*; **einen —,** to board s.o.

Verkra'chen, *v.n.* to become bankrupt, to fail, to go to smash (*sl.*).

Verkra'men, *v.a.* to mislay, misplace a thing.

Verkrie'chen, *ir.v.r.* to crawl away (*and hide*); to sneak off; **sich in das Bett —,** to creep into one's bed; **sich in ein Loch —,** to creep into a hole, to burrow (*of animals*); **er verkriecht sich vor jedem,** he shuns everyone; **er muß sich vor ihm** *or* **gegen ihn —,** he is no match for him.

Verkrü'meln, *v.a. & n.* (*aux.* **s.**) to crumble away; to waste little by little, to dissipate; **sein Geld —,** to fritter away one's money; **sich —,** to be mislaid, to be lost (*coll.*).

Verkrüm'm—en, I. *v.a.* to curve, crook, bend; to spoil by bending; to deform; **sich —en,** to grow crooked. II. *subst.n.*, **—ung,** *f.* crookedness, bend; **—ung der Wirbelsäule,** curvature of the spine.

Verkrüp'peln, *v.* I. *a.* to cripple; to stunt; to mutilate. II. *n.* (*aux.* **s.**) to become deformed, crippled; to be stunted.

Verküh'len, *v.r.* to cool down.

Verküm'mer—n, *v.* I. *a.* to stunt; to spoil; to seize, sequester (*Law*); to stop (*a person's salary*); **jemandes Freude —n,** to embitter, spoil a p.'s pleasure; **jemands Rechte —n,** to encroach upon another's rights. II. *n.* (*aux.* **s.**) to become stunted; to pine *or* wear away; to languish; **in Traurigkeit —n,** to pine away with grief. **—ung,** *f.* deprivation, degeneration.

Verkün'd—en, —igen, *v.a.* to announce; to make known, publish, proclaim; to preach (*the gospel*); to pronounce (*a judgment*); **im voraus —(ig)en,** to foretell, forewarn, prophesy; **ein Brautpaar (von der Kanzel) —igen,** to publish the banns (*prov.*). **—(ig)er,** *m.* (**—(ig)ers,** *pl.* **—(ig)er**), **—(ig)erin,** *f.* announcer, harbinger, herald; prophet; proclaimer; messenger. **—igung,** *f.* announcement; proclamation; preaching (*of the gospel*); prophecy, prediction; pronouncing (*of a sentence*); **Mariä—igung,** the Annunciation, Lady-day.

Verkund'schaften, *v.a.* to reconnoitre (*obs.*).

Verkün'stel—n, *v.a.* to over-refine, spoil by too much art *or* care. **—t,** *p.p. & adj.* affected, artificial, stilted. **—ung,** *f. see* **Künstelei.**

Verkup'fern, *v.a.* to copper.

Verkup'peln, *v.a.* to couple, pair; to make a match; to pander, procure.

Verkür'z—en, *v.a.* to shorten; to abridge; to curtail; to lessen, diminish; to prejudice, do an injury to; **einen —en,** to do a person a wrong, to encroach upon a p.'s rights; **einem den Mundvorrat —en,** to cut a p. short in provisions; **sich —en,** to contract, shrink (*as a muscle*); **die Zeit —en,** to beguile *or* while away the time; **einem das Leben —en,** to shorten a p.'s life; **—t,** contracted, syncopated. **—ung,** *f.* shortening, abridgement; abbreviation; foreshortening (*Paint., etc.*); retrenchment; stinting; wrong, injury; contraction, syncope (*Gram.*).

Verla'chen, *v.a.* to laugh at (*a th. or p.*); to laugh away (*the time*).

Verla'd—en, *ir.v.a.* to load, lade, ship; to export; to despatch, forward (*goods by train, etc.*); to load (*a gun*) badly; to spoil in loading. **—er,** *m.* (**—ers,** *pl.* **—er**) shipping-agent; carrier; exporter. **—ung,** *f.* lading; shipping, shipment; carriage, forwarding (*of goods*). *Comp.* **—ungs=kosten,** *pl.* charges for loading; shipping-charges. **—ungs=platz,** *m.*, **—ungs=schein,** *m.* bill of lading.

Verla'g, *m.* (—s) funds, capital (*of a business undertaking*); publication (*of a book*); stock, publications; **im —e von Cassell und Co.,** published by Cassell & Co., **in — nehmen,** to undertake the publication of; **dies Buch kommt in**

Cassell und Co.'s — heraus, this book is published by Cassell & Co.; dieser Buchhändler hat nur einen juristischen —, only law books are published by this bookseller. *Comp.* —s=artikel, *m.* publication. —s=bücher, *pl.* publications, books published. —s=buchhandel, *m.* publishing business. —s=buchhändler, *m.* publisher. —s=(buch)handlung, *f.* publishing house. —s=katalog, *m.* publisher's catalogue. —s=kosten, *pl.* expenses of publication. —s=recht, *n.* copyright. —s=zeichen, *n.* publisher's mark *or* monogram.

Verlan'g—en, *v.* I. *a.* to demand, claim; to require; to desire; zur Ehe —en, to ask in marriage; Genugthuung —en, to demand satisfaction; der Magen —t Nahrung, the stomach requires food; was —en Sie von mir? what do you want of me? what do you wish me to do? man —t zu wissen, information is desired; das ist zu viel —t, that is asking too much; mehr kann man nicht —en! one cannot expect more *or* wish for more; (*used impers'lly*) mich —t zu wissen, I am anxious *or* I want to know; es soll mich —en, wie die Sache abgelaufen ist, I long to know how it has all ended. II. *n.* (*aux.* h.) to desire; wish, long for, crave; nach einem —en, to long for, ask for a p.; nach etwas —en, das man verloren hat, to regret the loss of a thing. *Comp.* —ens=wert, *adj.* desirable.

Verlän'ger—n, *v.a.* to lengthen, elongate; to protract; to prolong, extend; to delay, spin out; to defer (*Law*). —ung, *f.* lengthening, extension, elongation; prolongation; production (*Geom.*); something added to lengthen *or* eke out; process (*Anat.*). *Comp.* —ungs=fähig, *adj.* capable of extension, protractile. —ungs=punkt, *m.* dot (*Mus.*). —ungs=stück, *n.* lengthening piece. —ungs=zettel, *m.* rider (*to a bill of exchange*).

Verlang'samen, *v.a.* to slacken, to slow down, to retard, delay.

Verläp'pern, *v.a.* (*coll.*) to waste on trifles; to trifle away, to squander, fritter away.

Verlar'v—en, *v.a.* & *r.* to disguise, put on a mask. —ung, *f.* masking; masquerade.

Verla'sch—t, *p.p.* & *adj.*; —ter Stoß, fish-joint (*Railw.*). —ung, *f.* fishing (*Railw.*).

Verla'ß, *m.* (—(ss)es, *pl.* —(ss)e) reliance, trust, confidence; es ist kein — auf diesen Menschen, auf den ist kein —, there 's no relying on that man, that man cannot be trusted.

Verlas'sen, I. *ir.v.a.* to leave, quit; to leave behind; to relinquish; to forsake, abandon, desert; seine Kräfte — ihn, his strength fails him; sich auf einen —, to rely on, trust to, depend upon a p.; sich wegen einer S. auf einen —, to entrust s.th. to a p., confide it to his care, to look to s.o. for s.th.; darauf kannst du dich —! trust me for that! never fear! I will see to that. II. *p.p.* & *adj.* deserted, forsaken, abandoned; forlorn; helpless; desert; von aller Welt —, forsaken by every one. —heit, *f.* forlorn condition, abandonment; destitution. —schaft, *f.* bequest, legacy; property left at a person's death.

Verläs'tern, *v.a.* to calumniate, slander.

Verlau'b, *m.*; mit —, with your permission, by your leave; excuse me.

Verlau'f, *m.* (—s) lapse, expiration, course (*of time*); course, progress (*of a matter*); outcome; nach — einiger Tage, in the course of a few days, after some days; der — einer Krankheit, the progress of a disease; der ganze — der Sache, the whole history of the affair.

Verlau'f—en, *ir.v.* I. *a.* to pass, spend in running; to dispel by running *or* walking, walk, run off; den ersten Becher —en, to digest the morning draught (*at mineral springs*) by walking; einem den Weg —en, to obstruct a p.'s way, to stop a p.; sich (*dat.*) das Kopfweh —en, to walk off a headache. II. *r.* (*aux.* h.) & *n.* (*aux.* s.) to lose one's way, go astray; to scatter, be dispersed; to flow away; to subside; to pass (*of time*); to blend (*of colours*); to descend, sink, slope, incline; to take a certain turn *or* course; wir haben uns —en, we have lost our way; das Gewässer verlief sich von der Erde, the waters returned from off the earth (*B.*); die Menge verlief sich, the crowd dispersed; wie ist die Sache —en? how has the affair turned out? III. *r.* to pocket one's own ball, make a losing hazard (*at billiards played with pockets*); to lose oneself *or* send one's ball off the table without striking another (*at billiards without pockets*); to go astray, sin; wie haben Sie sich hierher —en? what made you come here? ich werde mich nicht weit —en, I shan't go far. IV. *n.* (*aux.* s.); die Zeit verläuft, time passes quickly, runs away; die Krankheit verläuft normal, the disease is taking its regular course; ein —ener Kerl, a vagrant, a vagabond; ein —enes Mädchen, an abandoned girl; ein —ener, a runaway, a refugee.

Verläu'fer, *m.* (—s, *pl.* —) one who goes astray; one who has lost his way; ball that is pocketed *or* lost, losing hazard.

Verläug'nen, *see* Verleugnen.

Verlaut'—baren, *v.* I. *a.* to divulge; to publish, notify. II. *n.* (*aux.* h. & s.) to transpire; to be divulged. —en, *v.n.* (*aux.* h. & s.) *see* —baren II.; —en lassen, to give to understand, to say, to hint; nichts von der Sache —en lassen, to let nothing of the matter leak out *or* be(come) known; sie ließen (sich) —en, they were heard to say; wie —et, according to report, as it is rumoured, as people say, as the story goes.

Verle'b—en, *v.a.* to pass (*time*); to waste, wear out (*one's constitution*); den Sommer auf dem Lande —en, to pass the summer in the country. —t, *p.p.* & *adj.* worn out, broken down; decrepit; dead.

Verle'ckern, *v.a.* to squander on dainties; to make (*children*) dainty, to pamper.

[1]**Verle'g—en,** I. *v.a.* to remove to another place; to misplace; to mislay; to arrange wrongly; to stop, hinder; to bar, cut off (*the way*); to put off, delay, postpone; to lay an embargo on; to furnish, supply (*with goods, money, etc.*); to publish; sein Geschäft nach London —en, to remove one's business to London; auf einen andern Tag —en, to postpone to another day; eine Feier auf eine spätere Zeit —en, to put off a celebration to a later date; die Sitzung auf einen spätern Tag —en, to adjourn the meeting; seinen Schwerpunkt nach . . . —en, to transfer the centre of gravity to . . .; einem den Weg —en, to bar the way, to throw obstacles in a person's way; sich auf eine S. —en, to apply oneself to something. II. *p.p. of* verliegen, *see below* Verlegen. —er, *m.* (—ers, *pl.* —er) publisher (*of a book*); retail dealer (*dial.*); one who finances a business. —ung, *f.* removal; transportation; mislaying (*of keys*); stopping; barricading; publication (*of a book*).

[2]**Verle'gen,** *p.p.* & *adj.* spoiled, damaged by lying; embarrassed, confused, perplexed; disconcerted; um eine S. — sein, to be at a loss for s.th.; um Geld sehr — sein, to be very short of cash; er ist nie —, he is never at a loss; sie ist nicht um einen Mann —, she is at no loss for a husband. —heit, *f.* embarrassment; difficulty, dilemma, straits; scrape; in —heit setzen, to embarrass, perplex; einem —heiten bereiten, to embarrass a p.; sich aus der —heit ziehen, to extricate oneself, get out of a scrape.

Verlei'de—n, *v.a.* to spoil; to disgust; einem etwas —n, to spoil s.o.'s pleasure in, disgust s.o. with, give a p. a distaste for a th.; das

Landleben war ihm —t, he had taken a dislike to life in the country, he had lost all pleasure in country-life; es ist mir alles —t, I am sick of everything.

Verleih'bar, *adj.* that can be lent *or* imparted.

Verlei'h—en, *ir.v.a.* to lend; to hire out; to invest with (*a fief, etc.*); to give, grant, bestow, confer; **Geld auf Zinsen —en,** to lend money at interest; **einem eine Pfründe —en,** to give a p. a living; **einem ein Amt —en,** to appoint a p. to an office; **einem Hülfe —en,** to render s.o. assistance; **wenn Gott mir Leben und Gesundheit —t,** if God grant me life and health; **Gott —e uns seinen Segen,** may God grant us his blessing! **—er,** *m.* (**—ers,** *pl.* **—er**), **—erin,** *f.* lender; hirer out; granter, patron, bestower; collator. **—ung,** *f.* lending; loan; hiring out; conferring, bestowing; grant; bestowal. *Comp.* **—institut,** *n.* lending library.

Verlei't—en, *v.a.* to lead astray, mislead; to seduce; to suborn; **einen Soldaten zur Desertion —en,** to induce a soldier to desert. **—ung,** *f.* misleading; temptation; seduction; subornation (*of witnesses*); **—ung zum Bösen,** incitement *or* instigation to wrong(doing); **—ung zur Fahnenflucht,** incitement to desertion (*Mil.*); **—ung zum Meineid,** inducement to perjury (*Law*).

Verler'nen, *v.a.* to unlearn, forget what one has learnt; to spend in learning *or* study.

Verles, *m.* (—(s)es, *pl.* —(s)e) roll-call (*dial.*).

Verle's—en, I. *ir.v.a.* to pass (*the day*) in reading; to read out; to read badly, misread, make a mistake in reading; to pick (*out*); to read (*a bill in Parliament*); **die Namen —en,** to call over the names, to call the roll; **sich —en,** to make a mistake in reading; to become absorbed in a book; to read too much. II. *subst.n.*; **das —en der Namen,** the roll-call. **—ung,** *f.* reading aloud.

Verletz'—bar, —lich, *adj.* vulnerable; damageable; susceptible, touchy; frail, brittle. **—barkeit, —lichkeit,** *f.* vulnerability; susceptibility.

Verlet'z—en, *v.a.* to wound; to damage, injure; to violate; to break, infringe (*laws*); **jemandes guten Namen —en,** to injure a p.'s reputation; **jemandes Ehre —en,** to wound a p.'s honour; **jemandes Interessen —en,** to wrong a p., injure a p.'s interests; **er fühlte sich —t,** he felt (himself) aggrieved; **leicht —t,** sensitive, easily offended. **—ung,** *f.* wounding; hurt, damage; violation, infraction; injury, damage; wrong; offence; insult.

Verleug'n—en, *v.a.* to deny; to disown, disavow; to belie (*one's profession, etc.*); not to follow suit, to revoke (*Cards*); to act contrary to, act against; **seine Unterschrift, einen Freund —en,** to disown one's signature, a friend; **seinen Glauben —en,** to renounce one's belief; **er —ete seinen Herrn,** he said his master was not at home; **sich —en lassen,** to have o.s. denied (to visitors); **sie ließ sich für ihre besten Freunde —en,** she was not "at home" to her best friends; **sich selbst —en,** to practise self-denial. **—er,** *m.* (**—ers,** *pl.* **—er**) disowner, denier. **—ung,** *f.* denial; disavowal; disclaimer; abnegation; revoking (*a suit, at cards*); **Selbst —ung,** self-denial, self-effacement; unselfishness.

Verleum'd—en, *v.a.* to calumniate, slander, traduce; to backbite. **—er,** *m.* (**—ers,** *pl.* **—er**), **—erin,** *f.* calumniator, slanderer; libeller; backbiter. **—erisch,** *adj.* slanderous, defamatory. **—ung,** *f.* calumny, slander, backbiting, defamation; **giftige** *or* **böswillige —ungen,** malicious aspersions. *Comp.* **—ungs=prozeß,** *m.* action for defamation of character, action for libel.

Verlie'b—en, *v.r.*; **sich in einen —en,** to fall in love with a person. **—t,** *p.p. & adj.* in love (*with*), enamoured (*of*); amorous; **närrisch, sterblich,** *or* **bis über die Ohren in einen —t sein,** to be madly *or* desperately in love with a p.; **—te Augen machen,** to cast amorous glances, to make sheep's eyes (*at*); **von —ter Natur,** of an amorous disposition; **ein —ter Auftritt,** a love-scene; **ein —ter Schäfer,** an amorous swain. **—theit,** *f.* amorousness (*of disposition*).

Verlie'derlichen, *v.* I. *a.* to squander in debauchery; to ruin by dissipation. II. *n.* (*aux.* **s.**) to become impoverished *or* ruined by dissipation; to go down in the world.

Verlie'gen, *ir.v.a.* to pass (*time*) lying; to neglect (*doing something*), to lose by lying too long; **den guten Wind —,** to miss a favourable wind. II. *n.* (*aux.* **s.**) to spoil through lying too long (*in a shop, etc.*); **sich —,** *see* **Verliegen—**; to lose all activity (*obs.*).

Verlier'bar, *adj.* that can be lost, easily lost.

Verlie'r—en, *ir.v.* I. *a.* to lose; **den Grund —en,** to get out of one's depth; **den Kopf —en,** to lose one's self-control, lose one's head; **da ist keine Zeit zu —en,** there is no time to be lost; **ich habe viel Geld an dieser Ware verloren,** I have lost a lot of money on *or* by this article; **Sie haben an ihm einen guten Freund verloren,** you have lost a good friend in him; **einen aus den Augen —en,** to lose sight of a p.; **alle Bitten waren bei ihm verloren,** all entreaties were lost on him; **etwas für verloren achten, etwas verloren geben,** to regard a th. as lost, give a th. up as lost; **ich gebe das Spiel verloren,** I throw the game up, I acknowledge myself beaten, I give in; **verloren gehen,** to be lost, to get lost, to go astray, miscarry (*of letters*), to founder, go down (*of ships*). II. *n.* to fall off (*in value*); **die Blume hat etwas an Duft verloren,** the flower has lost something of its sweetness. III. *r.* to lose oneself, lose one's way, go astray; to disperse; to disappear; to melt into; **sich in Gedanken —en,** to be lost in thought; **die Menge —t sich,** the crowd disperses; **die Töne —en sich,** the sounds die away; **die Schmerzen —en sich,** the pains are subsiding; **diese Farbe —t sich ins Grüne,** this colour melts into green; **sich an einen Ort (hin) —en,** to lose o.s. to a place; to find o.s. at a place (unexpectedly). **—er,** *m.* (**—ers,** *pl.* **—er**), **—erin,** *f.* loser.

Verlie'ß, *n.* (**—es,** *pl.* **—e**) underground prison, dungeon, keep.

Verlo'b—en, *v.a.* to engage, affiance, betroth; **sich —en,** to become engaged; **einem seine Tochter —en,** to betroth one's daughter to a man; **—t sein mit . . .,** to be engaged to . . .; **—ter Bräutigam (—te Braut), der (die) —te,** the betrothed; **das —te Paar, die —ten,** the engaged couple; **ihr —ter, seine —te,** her fiancé *or* intended (husband), his fiancée *or* intended (wife). **—ung,** *f.* betrothal; ceremony of betrothal; **eine —ung aufheben,** to break off an engagement. *Comp.* **—ungs=anzeige,** *f.* (public) announcement of an engagement. **—ungs=fest,** *n.* festivity in celebration of a betrothal. **—ungs=ring,** *m.* engagement-ring.

Verlo'ck—en, *v.a.* to entice away, allure, seduce. **—ung,** *f.* enticement, allurement; seduction.

Verlo'gen, *p.p. & adj. see* **Verlügen**; mendacious, untruthful. **—heit,** *f.* habit of lying, untruthfulness.

Verloh'nen, *v.a. imp.*; **es verlohnt die** (*or* **es verlohnt sich der**) **Mühe,** it is worth the trouble, it is worth while.

Verlo'r, *1 & 3 p. sing. imperf. ind.*, **Verlö're,** *1 & 3 p. sing. imperf. subj.*; **Verlo'ren,** *p.p of* **verlieren.**

Verlo'ren, *p.p. & adj. see* **Verlieren**; lost; **—er Kopf,** sink(ing)-head (*Smelt.*); **—e Arbeit,** labour lost; **der —e Sohn,** the prodigal son;

—e Eier, poached eggs; —e Schildwache, —er Posten, out-of-the-way post; —er Haufe, forlorn hope (*body of men who attack first and make a passage for the rest*) (*obs.*); —e Hoffnung, vain hope; mit —er Schnur vermessen, to take a rough measurement of; —er Schuß, random shot, stray bullet; mit —en Stichen anschlagen, to baste; — thun, to do roughly *or* superficially; des Menschen Sohn ist gekommen, selig zu machen, das — ist, the Son of Man is come to save that which was lost (*B.*); in Gedanken —, lost in thought; das —e Paradies, Paradise Lost; —er Zapfen, peg buried in the wood. —heit, *f.* lost condition. *Comp.* —gehen, *n.* loss, miscarriage (*of letters, etc.*). —gehen=lassen, *n.* loss through carelessness. —heften, *n.* basting, tacking.

Verlösch'bar, *adj.* extinguishable.

[1]**Verlö'sch—en**, *v.a.* to extinguish; to rub *or* blot out, obliterate, efface. —ung, *f.* extinction.

[2]**Verlö'schen**, I. *ir.v.n.* (*aux.* s.) to be extinguished, go out; to become extinct; to expire, die out; verloschene Kohlen, dead coals; verloschene Inschriften, effaced inscriptions. II. *subst.n.*; im —en sein, to be dying away; to be going out (*of a candle*).

Verlo's—en, *v.a.* to dispose of by lot; to raffle; to cast lots for; to apportion, share. —ung, *f.* drawing lots for; raffling, disposing of by lot; apportionment. *Comp.* —ungs=bazar, *m.* bazaar (*at which goods are raffled for*). —ungs=blatt, *n.* lottery-advertiser *or* -journal.

Verlö'ten, *v.a.* to solder (*up*).

Verlot'tern, Verlu'dern, *see* Verliederlichen.

Verlü'gen, *v.a.* to tell lies of, to slander (a p.).

Verlum'p—en, *v.* I. *a.* to wear to rags; to ruin by dissipation. II. *n.* (*aux.* s.) to go to rags; to go to ruin; —ter Mensch, ragged fellow, ragamuffin, tatterdemalion.

Verlu'st, *m.* (—es, *pl.* —e) loss; damage, injury; waste; prejudice, disadvantage; *pl.* casualties (*in war*); bei —, with loss of, with forfeiture of, under pain of. —ig, *adj.* (*used predic'ly with gen.*) deprived of, without; einer Sache —ig gehen, to lose a thing; einen einer Sache für —ig erklären, to declare a p. devoid of all claims to a th.; sich einer Sache —ig machen, to incur the loss of a th. *Comp.* —bringend, *adj.* prejudicial. —liste, *f.* list of casualties; casualty returns (*Mil.*). —tragende(r), *m.*, —tragende, *f.*, —träger(in, *f.*), *m.* loser. Gewinn=und=—konto, *n.* profit-and-loss account.

Verlustie'ren, *v.r.* to amuse o.s., have fun (*coll.*).

Verma'chen, *v.a.*; einem etwas —, to make over *or* bequeath a thing to a p.; der Gang ist bedeckt und mit Glas vermacht, the passage is roofed and covered in with glass.

Vermächt'nis, *n.* (—(ss)es, *pl.* —(ss)e) testament; legacy; ohne — sterben, to die intestate. *Comp.* —erbe, *m.*, —erbin, *f.*, —nehmer(in, *f.*), *m.* legatee. —nahme, *f.* acceptance of a legacy.

Vermah'len, *ir.v.a.* to grind (down); to grind badly, spoil in grinding.

Vermäh'l—en, *v.* I. *a.* to marry, give in marriage (*a princess, etc.*); to unite. II. *r.* to espouse, wed; sich mit einem Mädchen —en, to wed *or* marry a girl. —ung, *f.* nuptials, wedding. *Comp.* —ungs=feier, *f.*, —ungs=fest, *n. see* Hochzeit. —ungs=tag, *m.* wedding day.

Vermah'n—en, *v.a.* to admonish, exhort. —ung, *f.* admonition, exhortation.

Vermaledei'en, *v.a.* to curse, to execrate.

Verma'len, *v.a.* to use in painting; ein Bild —, to spoil a picture, to paint it badly.

Verman'nig—fachen, —fältigen, *v.a.* to diversify, vary, variegate; to multiply; to reproduce.

Vermar'ken, *v.a.*; die Grenzen eines Feldes —, to mark out the boundaries of, to enclose a field.

Vermau'ern, *v.a.* to employ in building; to surround with a wall; to wall up; to fill up with masonry; to immure.

Vermehr'bar, *adj.* augmentable; that can be augmented *or* increased. —keit, *f.* augmentability.

Vermeh'r—en, *v.a.* to increase, augment, to add to, extend, enlarge; to propagate; dies —t meinen Kummer, this adds to my grief; sich —en, to increase, multiply; eine —te Auflage, an enlarged edition. —ung, *f.* increase; multiplication; propagation. *Comp.* —ungs=fähigkeit, *f.* power of multiplying, augmentability. —ungs=organe, *pl.* organs of propagation. —ungs=trieb, *m.* procreative instinct. —ungs=zahl, *f.* multiplier, factcr (*Arith.*).

Vermeid—bar, *adj.* avoidable. —en, *ir.v.a.* to avoid, shun, evade, elude; to escape (*from*). —ung, *f.* avoidance; bei —ung unserer Ungnade, under pain of (incurring) our displeasure.

Vermei'n—en, *v.a.* to think, believe; to imagine; to presume; deem, consider. —tlich, *adj.* supposed, presumed, presumptive; would-be, pretended.

Vermel'den, I. *v.a.* (einem etwas) to announce, notify; to send (*a p.*) word *or* an account of; es ist ihnen vermeldet worden, they have been informed; — Sie ihm meinen Gruß, give my compliments (kind regards) to him; mit Respekt zu —, with all due deference to you, saving your presence. II. *subst. n.*; mit dem —, daß . . ., whilst adding that . . .

Vermen'g—en, *v.a.* to mingle, mix, blend; to mix up, confuse; sich mit etwas —en, to meddle with a matter; er ist mit darein —t, he is involved in *or* mixed up with that affair. —ung, *f.* mixture, medley; confusion.

Vermensch'lichen, *v.a.* to represent under a human form; to civilize, humanize; die Gottheit —, to clothe Divinity with a human form.

Verme'rk, *m.* (—(e)s, *pl.* —e) observation, note, remark. —en, *v.a.* to perceive, observe, remark; to note down; to take, receive, interpret; etwas übel —en, to take a th. amiss, take offence at a thing.

Vermeß'bar, *adj.* measurable.

Vermes's—en, I. *ir.v.a.* to measure, take the measurement of; to survey; to measure, deal out, distribute. II. *r.* to make a mistake in measuring; to presume, have the audacity (*to*); to boast; sich einer Sache (*gen.*) —en, sich —en etwas zu thun *or* daß man etwas thun will, to venture, dare to undertake a thing, to boast of doing *or* that one can do a thing; sich zu viel —en, to be too self-confident, to take too much upon oneself; er vermaß sich, es zu vollbringen, he boasted that he would accomplish it; er sagte aber zu etlichen, die sich selbst vermaßen, and he spake unto certain which trusted in themselves (*B.*); sich hoch und teuer —en, daß . . ., to promise, protest solemnly that . . . III. *p.p. & adj.* daring, presumptuous; bold, rash; arrogant. —enheit, *f.* boldness; self-confidence; arrogance, presumptuousness, audacity; insolence. —ung, *f.* measuring; measurement; survey; mistake in measuring. *Comp.* —ungs=arbeit, *f.* surveyor's work, measuring. —ungs=bureau, *n.* surveyor's office. —ungs=karte, *f.* ordnance-survey map. —ungs=kunst, *f.* art of surveying. —ungs=revisor, *m.* surveyor. —ungs=tabelle, *f.* tables of survey.

Vermiet'bar, *adj.* that can be let, rentable.

Vermie't—en, *v.a.* to let, to hire out; *see* Verfrachten; ein Haus zu —en, a house to (be) let; Pianos zu —en, pianos on hire; sich bei einem —en, to enter a person's service; solche Häuser —en sich bald. houses like these let readily. **—er,** *m.* (**—ers,** *pl.* **—er**), **—erin,** *f.* letter (*of a house*), hirer out, lessor, landlord; house-agent; hirer out (*of a ship*). **—ung,** *f.* letting, leasing; hiring (*out*); freighting (*a merchant-vessel*). *Comp.* —(**ungs**)**=bureau,** *n.* labour-office; registry-office (*for servants*); house-agent's office. —(**ung**)**s=zettel,** *m.* bill (*of advertisement of a house*).

Vermin'der—n, *v.a.* to lessen, diminish, decrease; to abate; to impair; **jemandes Einkommen —n,** to reduce a person's income; **an Zahl —n,** to reduce *or* decrease in number; **um die Hälfte —n,** to reduce by the half; **seine Kräfte —n,** to impair one's strength; **sich —n,** to grow less, decrease, abate; **sein Eifer —t sich,** his zeal is abating; **die —nde Zahl,** subtrahend. **—t,** *p.p. & adj.* lessened, reduced; **die —te Terz,** diminished third (*Mus.*). **—ung,** *f.* diminution, decrease; reduction; abatement; depreciation (*of value, etc.*); retrenchment. *Comp.* **—ungs=wort,** *n.* diminutive.

Vermisch'bar, *adj.* mixable.

Vermi'sch—en, *v.a.* to mix, to blend (*colours, teas, etc.*); to cross, interbreed (*races, etc.*); to alloy; **sich —en,** to mix, mingle, blend with; **Metalle mit einander —en,** to alloy metals; **sich gut —en lassen,** to blend well, to amalgamate easily, to go well together; **sich mit einem Weibe fleischlich —en,** to have carnal *or* sexual intercourse with a woman; to cohabit with a woman; **—te Nachrichten, —tes,** Miscellaneous News (*heading of items in newspapers, etc.*). **—ung,** *f.* mixture, intermixture; alloy (*of metals*); crossing *or* interbreeding (*of races*); medley; **fleischliche —ung,** sexual intercourse, cohabitation, coition.

Vermis'sen, I. *v.a.* to miss; to regret; **man vermißt ihn,** he is missing; he is missed, his absence is (*greatly*) felt. II. *subst.n.*; **schmerzliches —,** deep regret.

Vermit't—eln, *v.a.* to mediate; to adjust, arrange (*a difference, etc.*); to negotiate (*a peace; a loan, etc.*); **den Handel mit einem Volke —eln,** to obtain a commercial treaty; to carry on trade with a people; **widerstreitende Ideen —eln,** to reconcile conflicting ideas; **einen Widerspruch —eln,** to reconcile a (seeming) contradiction; **—elnd eintreten,** to interpose. **—els, —elst,** *prep.* (*with gen.*) by means of, with the help of, through. **—(e)lung,** *f.* mediation, interposition, intervention; adjustment (*of differences*); conveyance (*of sound*); **durch jemands —(e)lung,** by a p.'s good offices *or* instrumentality. **—ler,** *m.* (**—lers,** *pl.* **—ler**), **—lerin,** *f.* mediator, mediatrix; reconciler; agent, go-between. *Comp.* **—(e)lungs=geschäft, —(e)lungs=institut,** *n.* (commission-)agency. **—(e)lungs=stelle,** *f.* (telephone) exchange. **—(e)lungs=versuch,** *m.* attempt to effect a reconciliation. **—(e)lungs=vokal,** *m.* intermediate vowel. **—(e)lungs=vorschlag,** *m.* proposal for the adjustment of a dispute.

Vermö'beln, (*coll.*) *v.a.*; **etwas —,** to sell, turn s.th. into cash; to sell at any price; to waste; **einen —,** to give a p. a good thrashing (*sl.*); to cry s.o. down (*sl.*).

Vermo'dern, *v.n.* (*aux.* **f.**) to moulder, to (fall into) decay; to rot.

Vermö'ge, *prep.* (*with gen.*) in virtue of, in pursuance of, upon the strength of, in conformity with, according to; **— unserer Abrede,** in virtue of our agreement.

Vermö'g—en, I. *ir.v.a.* to be able, have the power *or* capacity to do; **wir —en nicht hinaufzuziehen,** we are not able to go up; **Gott vermag dem Abraham aus diesen Steinen Kinder zu erwecken,** God is able of these stones to raise up children unto Abraham (*B.*); **ich will thun, was ich kann und vermag,** I will do all that lies in my power; **viel bei einem —en,** to have great influence with a person; **viel über einen —en,** to have great influence over a person; **sie vermochte alles bei ihrem Vater,** she could do anything with her father; **wenn er es über sich vermag,** if he can bring himself to do it; **einen zu etwas —en,** to induce, prevail upon s.o. to do s.th. II. *subst.n.* ability; power; capacity, strength; means; fortune, wealth, riches, property; **das geht über mein —en,** that is beyond me *or* my power; **alles, was in meinem —en ist** *or* **steht,** all that lies in my power; **—en erwerben,** to make a fortune; **er hat zehntausend Pfund im —en,** his fortune amounts to £10000, he is worth £10000 (*coll.*). **—end,** *p. & adj.*, **—lich,** *adj.* capable of, able; rich; well off, well-to-do. *Comp.* **—ens=abschätzung, —ens=aufnahme,** *f.* valuation of property, assessment; census (*Rom. Hist.*). **—ens=absonderung,** *f.* division of wealth, separation of the estate. **—ens=bestand, —ens=betrag,** *m.* amount of property; assets. **—ens=bilanz,** *f.* balance. **—ens=los,** *adj.* without fortune, impecunious. **—ens=losigkeit,** *f.* want of fortune, indigence. **—ens=masse,** *f.* estate. **—ens=nachweis,** *m.* detailed information concerning a p.'s financial position. **—ens=rechtlich,** *adj. & adv.* in right of one's fortune *or* property; *adv.* in money matters; **—ensrechtliche Ansprüche,** action for recovery of one's property. **—ens=steuer,** *f.* property tax. **—ens=umstände, —ens=verhältnisse,** *pl.* financial position, means. **—ens=verwalter,** *m.* administrator of an estate, trustee.

Vermu'ckern, *v.n.* (*aux.* **f.**) to grow saintly *or* sanctimonious, to become goody-goody (*coll.*).

Vermum'm—en, —eln (*coll.*), *v.a.* to muffle up; to mask, disguise. **—ung,** *f.* masquerade, mummery.

Vermu't—en, I. *v.a.* to conjecture, presume, suppose, imagine; to expect; to suspect; to foresee; (**sich,** *dat.*) **nichts Arges —en,** to suspect no harm, nothing wrong. II. *subst.n.* supposing, expectation; **meinem —en nach,** I think; as I expected. **—lich,** *adj.* presumable, probable, likely. **—ung,** *f.* supposition, conjecture, presumption; suspicion; **gegen alle —ung,** contrary to all expectation; **aller —ung nach,** to all appearances; **die —ung ist stark gegen ihn,** appearances are strongly against him.

Vernach'lässig—en, *v.a.* to neglect; to slight; to take little care of. **—ung,** *f.* negligence; neglect (**einer S.** *or* **von einer S.,** of a th.).

Verna'geln, *v.a.* to nail, stud with nails; to peg, to nail (*up or down*); to nail badly; to injure (*a horse*) in shoeing; **eine Kanone —,** to spike a gun (*Mil.*); **vernagelt sein (im Kopfe),** to be wooden-headed, dense, stupid (*coll.*).

Vernä'hen, *v.a.* to use in sewing; to sew up; to spend in sewing.

Vernar'ben, *v.* I. *a.* to heal over, cicatrize. II. *r. & n.* (*aux.* **f.**) to heal up leaving a scar.

Vernar'r—en, *v.r.*; **sich (in einen** *or* **etwas) —en,** to become infatuated with, fall madly in love *or* to be smitten with; **sie ist in das Kind —t,** she dotes on the child. **—theit,** *f.* infatuation.

Verna'schen, *v.a.*; **sein Geld —,** to waste one's money on dainties.

Vernehm'bar, *adj.* audible, perceptible. **-keit,** *f.* audibility, sonority.

Verneh'm—en, I. *ir.v.a.* to hear; to perceive; to understand; to hear, learn; to examine, interrogate; **sie vernahmen aber nicht, daß er ihnen von dem Vater sagte,** they understood not that he spake to them of the Father (*B.*); **ich habe nichts davon vernommen,** I have heard nothing of it; **vernimm mein Ge-**

bet! hearken to my prayer! sich —en lassen, to express oneself, intimate, declare; der Vater hatte manchmal die Gefälligkeit uns eine Beschreibung des . . . —en zu lassen, our father often had the kindness to give us a description of . . .; in einem Singchore hören wir auch die schwächste Stimme, aber wir —en sie nicht (einzeln heraus), in a chorus we hear even the weakest voice, only we do not distinguish it; sich aus einer S. —en, to understand (*or* make sense of) a th.; ich kann mich nicht daraus —en, I can't make it out, can't understand it; sich mit einem —en, to come to an understanding with a p.; einen Gefangenen —en, to examine, question a prisoner. II. *subst.n.* hearing; perceiving; intelligence; examination (*Law*); understanding; terms; dem —en nach, according to report; gutem —en nach ist er schon fort, we have it on good authority that he is already gone; das gute —en, friendly terms, good understanding; in einem heimlichen —en stehen, to have a secret understanding. —lich, *adj.* audible; distinct, clear; intelligible. —lichkeit, *f.* audibility, sonority, clearness, intelligibility. —ung, *f.* hearing; examination, trial. —ungs=fähig, *adj.* able to undergo an examination *or* a trial.

Verneiʹg—en, *v.r.* to bow; to courtesy. —ung, *f.* bow, obeisance; courtesy.

Verneinʹbar, *adj.* deniable.

Verneiʹn—en, *v.a.* to deny; to answer in the negative; to disown, disavow; to contradict. —end, *p. & adj.* negative; privative; —ende Partikel, negative particle; eine —ende Antwort, an answer in the negative. —ung, *f.* denial, contradiction, negation. *Comp.* —ungs=fall, *m.*; im —ungsfalle, in case of an answer in the negative. —ungs=satz, *m.* negative clause. —ungs=wort, *n.* negative.

Vernichtʹbar, *adj.* that can be annihilated.

Vernichʹt—en, *v.a.* to annihilate; to annul, nullify, declare null and void; to revoke; to abolish, abrogate (*laws*); to destroy, demolish; to ruin, undo; to exterminate; to overthrow; to quash; to disappoint (*hopes*); durch Feuer —en, to burn down, destroy by fire. —end, *p. & adj.* destroying; exterminating; annulling; injurious. —er, *m.* (—ers, *pl.* —er) destroyer; annihilator; annuller. —ung, *f.* annihilation, destruction; annulling; abrogation; abolition. *Comp.* —ungs=kampf, —ungs=krieg, *m.* war of extermination.

Vernieʹt—en, I. *v.a.* to rivet, clinch. II. *subst.n.*, —ung, *f.* riveting; versenkte —ung, countersunk riveting. —er, *m.* (—ers, *pl.* —er) riveter.

Vernunʹft, *f.* reason; understanding; judgment; discernment, sense; intelligence; die gesunde —, common sense; bei guter — sein, to be in one's senses; wider die gesunde — handeln, to act in defiance of common sense; einen zur — bringen, to bring a p. to his senses, make s.o. listen to reason; die Jahre der — erreichen, to come to years of discretion; das geht über die —, that is beyond the reach of reason; ich habe vielleicht nicht so viel Verstand wie Sie, aber mehr gesunde —, I am, perhaps, not so clever as you, but I have more common sense. *Comp.* —begabt, *adj.* endowed with reason, reasonable, rational, sensible. —begriff, *m.* idea (*founded on reason*). —beweis, *m.* proof founded on reason. —ehe, *f.* prudential match. —gemäß, *adj. & adv.* conformable to reason, rational, logical. —gemäßheit, *f.* reasonableness. —glaube, *m.* rationalism. —gläubige(r), *m.* rationalist. —grund, *m.* argument founded on reason; aus —gründen, a priori (*Log.*). —heirat, *f.* marriage prompted by reason *or* prudence, prudential match. —lehre, *f.* logic, science of reason. —los, *adj.* (de)void of reason, unreasonable, senseless; irrational; unreasoning. —losigkeit, *f.* want of reason; irrationality. —recht, *n.* law of reason, natural right *or* law. —religion, *f.* rational religion. —satz, *m.* proposition demonstrable by reason. —schluß, *m.* reason(ing), ratiocination; (schulgerechter) syllogism. —wahrheit, *f.* truth founded on reason. —wesen, *n.* rational being. —widrig, *adj.* contrary to reason, unreasonable, irrational, illogical. —wissenschaft, *f.* logic, (mental) philosophy.

Vernünftelei', *f.* (*pl.* —en) sophistry; subtlety, over-refinement in reasoning.

Vernünfʹt—eln, *v.n.* (*aux.* h.) to reason too nicely; to subtilize. —ig, *adj.* reasonable, sensible, rational; wise, judicious; good (*of children*); logical; —ige Wesen, rational beings; ein —iger Mann, a man of sense; —ig handeln, to act reasonably, wisely. —igkeit, *f.* reasonableness, rationality; goodness; good sense. —ler, *m.* (—lers, *pl.* —ler) subtle reasoner; sophist.

Veröʹd—en, *v.* I. *a.* to lay waste, devastate; to depopulate. II. *n.* (*aux.* s.) to become waste, desolate *or* deserted. —ung, *f.* desolation; devastation; depopulation.

Veröfʹfentlich—en, *v.a.* to publish; to make public; ein Gesetz —en, to promulgate a law. —ung, *f.* publication, public announcement; promulgation.

Verordʹn—en, *v.a.* to order, prescribe; to decree, enact; to nominate, appoint; to institute; einem etwas —en, to order a p. something, prescribe something for s.o. (*Med.*); wo Obrigkeit ist, die ist von Gott —et, the powers that be are ordained of God. —er, *m.* (—ers, *pl.* —er), —erin, *f.* one who orders, ordains, prescribes. —ung, *f.* order; prescription (*Med.*); ordinance; precept, decree, mandate; ordination, nomination, appointment; institution. *Comp.* —ungs=blatt, *n.* official list, gazette. —ungs=gemäß, —ungs=mäßig, *adj.* according to order *or* appointment.

Verpachtʹ—bar, *adj.* that can be let *or* farmed. —en, *v.a.* to let on lease; to farm out. —er, Verpächter, *m.* (—s, *pl.* —) letter of a farm, lessor. —ung, *f.* farming out, letting on lease.

Verpaʹck—en, *v.a.* to pack up; to use in packing; to mislay in packing. —er, *m.* (—ers, *pl.* —er) packer. —ung, *f.* packing-up; packing (*cloth*); innere —ung, under wrapper. *Comp.* —ungs=art, *f.* manner of packing. —ungs=leinwand, *f.* bale-cloth, packing.

Verpanʹzern, *v.a.* to cover with a coat of mail; to sheet with iron, to casemate (*Mil.*).

Verpäpʹpeln, *v.a.* to pamper, spoil (*a child*).

Verpasʹsen, *v.a.* to pass waiting; to pass over through negligence, let slip, miss, lose; to wait till s.th. is over; to pass (*Cards, etc.*); die Flut —, to miss the tide; den günstigen Augenblick —, to miss one's chance; er hat seinen Zug verpaßt, he has missed *or* lost his train.

Verpesʹt—en, *v.a.* to infect, poison, taint. —ung, *f.* infection.

Verpfähʹl—en, *v.a.* to palisade, pale; to fence in with stakes; to throw up a stockade *or* palisade (*Fort.*). —ung, *f.* palisading; stockade (*Fort.*); paling.

Verpfänʹd—en, *v.a.* to pledge; to pawn; to mortgage. —ung, *f.* pledging; pledge.

Verpfefʹfern, *v.a.* to spoil with pepper; to spoil entirely (*fig. coll.*); einem sein Vergnügen —, to spoil a p.'s pleasure (*coll.*).

Verpflanzʹ—bar, *adj.* transplantable. —en, *v.a.* to transplant; to replant (*trees, etc.*). —er, *m.* (—ers, *pl.* —er) transplanter. —ung, *f.* transplanting.

Verpfleʹg—en, *v.a.* to take care of; to support, provide for; to foster; einen Kranken —en, to nurse an invalid. —ung, *f.* feeding, alimentation; maintenance, support; nursing;

diet (*Med.*); Natural—ung, payment in kind; Wohnung mit —ung, board and lodging. *Comp.* —ungs=amt, *n.* poor-law board, office of the guardians of the poor; commissariat-department (*Mil.*). —ungs=anstalt, *f.* charitable institution; hospital; infant home. — ungs=beamte(r), *m.* commissariat-officer. — ungs=entschädigung, *f.* allowance for board (and lodging); board-wages (*of servants*). — ungs=haus, *n. see* —anstalt. —ungs=kosten, *pl.* cost of maintenance, charge for board and lodging; sustenance; aliments. —ungs=mittel, *pl.* victuals, provisions. —ungs=vorschuß, *m.* advance-money (*Mil.*). —ungs=wesen, *n.* relief of the poor; commissariat. —ungs=zuschuß, *m.* extra allowance for board.

Verpflich'—en, *v.a.* to bind by obligation *or* duty; to oblige; einen eidlich —en, to bind a p. by an oath; zu Dank —en, to lay s.o. under an obligation; sich zu etwas —en, to bind oneself *or* to engage to do a th. —ung, *f.* obligation, duty; engagement; eine —ung, —ungen eingehen, to enter into an engagement; seinen —ungen nachkommen, to keep one's engagements, fulfil one's duties; —ung(en) haben gegen, to be under an obligation to.

Verpflö'cken, *v.a.* to peg; to peg *or* plug up.

Verpfu'schen, *v.a.* to bungle, botch, murder.

Verpi'chen, *v.a.* to pitch *or* tar, to stop with pitch.

Verpim'peln, *v.a.* to make soft (*coll.*).

Verplap'pern, Verplau'dern, *v.a.* to pass (*time, etc.*) in chattering *or* chatting; to neglect through talking *or* chatting; sich —, to blab out a secret, to betray (*oneself*); so verplaudert sich die Zeit, so the time runs away when one is chatting.

Verplem'pern, *v.a.* to splash, spill; to fritter away; to waste foolishly; sich —, to enter rashly into an engagement, to be caught (in a woman's toils), to get hooked (*coll.*).

Verpö'nen, *v.a.* to forbid (*under severe penalties*); to proscribe.

Verpras'sen, *v.a.;* sein Vermögen —, to waste one's property in dissipation.

Verproviantie'ren, *v.a.* to supply with provisions.

Verpu'deln, *v.a.* to spoil (*by awkwardness*) (*coll.*).

Verpuf'fen, *v.* I. *a.* to let off, explode; to lose by carelessness, to throw away, to waste. II. *r.* to use all one's powder; to spend all one's money. III. *n.* (*aux.* s.) to detonate, explode, to fulminate.

Verpul'vern, *v.a.* to pulverize; to squander, waste (*coll.*).

Verpum'pen, *v.a.* to lend, give on credit (*sl.*).

Verpup'p—en, *v.r. & n.* to change into a chrysalis, to withdraw, retire into one's shell (*coll.*). —ung, *f.* transformation into the chrysalis condition.

Verpu'sten, *v.r.* to draw breath (*sl.*).

Verpu'tz, *m.* (—es) coating, coat, plaster.

Verput'zen, *v.a.* to spend in finery; to bedizen; to eat, polish off (*coll.*); sein Geld —, to squander one's money.

Verqual'men, *v.* I. *a.* to cause to evaporate *or* go off in smoke; to spend in tobacco (*coll.*). II. *n.* (*aux.* s.) to pass off in vapour *or* smoke, evaporate.

Verquel'len, *v.n.* (*aux.* s.) to swell up; to warp, get warped (*by moisture*); to close by swelling; to well up, bubble forth; verquollenes Fenster, warped window.

Verqui'ck—en, *v.a.* to amalgamate (*with*). — ung, *f.* amalgamation.

Verram'm—e(l)n, *v.a.* to ram up, bar, barricade, to block up. —elung, *f.* barricade.

Verra'nnt, *p.p. see* Verrennen. *adj.* stubborn, obstinate, prejudiced. —heit, *f.* stubbornness, bigotry.

Verra't, *m.* (—s) treason; treachery; einen — an einem begehen, to betray a person.

Verra't—en, *ir.v.a.* to betray; to divulge, disclose, reveal; es verrät eine Meisterhand, it bespeaks, betrays the hand of a master; seine Bücher —en große Belesenheit, his books give evidence of wide reading; einen für Geld —en, to sell a person; ein Geheimnis —en, to divulge a secret; seinen Angriffsplan —en, to unmask one's batteries (*fig.*); sich —en, to betray *or* commit oneself.

Verrä'ter, *m.* (—s, *pl.* —), —in, *f.* traitor, traitress; betrayer, informer; er ist ein — an der Königin, he is a traitor to the queen. —ei', *f.* treason; treachery. —isch, *adj.* treacherous; traitorous; faithless, perfidious; treasonable. —ischerweise, *adv.* treacherously, traitorously.

Verrau'ch—en, *v.* I. *a.* to smoke; to smoke up; to spend in smoking; to pass, beguile (*the time*) in smoking; to burn; to cause to evaporate; to cool. II. *n.* (*aux.* s.) to exhale, evaporate; to pass off in smoke; to evaporate, lose its strength (*of wine*); die Suppe —en lassen, to let the soup grow cool; sein Zorn —te, his anger passed away; seinen Zorn —en lassen, to calm down. —t, *p.p. & adj.* smoky, smoke-dried, browned with smoke. —ung, *f.* evaporation.

Verräu'chern, *v.* I. *a.* to burn, consume in burning (*incense, etc.*); ein Zimmer —, to fumigate a room. II. *n.* (*aux.* s.) to become smoky.

Verrau'schen, *v.n.* (*aux.* s.) to cease roaring; to rush away, rush along; to roll on, pass away (*of time*); to die away, subside (*fig.*).

Verrech'n—en, *v.* I. *a.* to reckon, to charge, to place to account. II. *r.* to make a mistake in calculating; Sie werden sich sehr —en, you will be very much mistaken (in your calculations); you will be sadly disappointed; er hat sich um 20 Mark verrechnet, he was £1 out in his accounts. —ung, *f.* placing to account; reckoning up, calculation; error in calculation.

Verre'cken, *v.n.* (*aux.* s.) to die (*of cattle and, vulgarly, of people*).

Verre'd—en, *v.* I. *a.* to take a vow against, forswear, abjure. II. *r. & n.* (*aux.* h.) to make a mistake in speaking; to make a slip of the tongue; to betray oneself, let slip something indiscreetly. —ung, *f.* renunciation; slip of the tongue; mistake; indiscreet remark.

Verreg'nen, *v.a.* to spoil *or* mar by rain.

Verrei'ben, *ir.v.a.* to grind *or* rub well; to use up by rubbing; to rub away; to grind down.

Verrei'sen, *v.* I. *a.* to spend (*money or time*) in travelling. II. *n.* (*aux.* s.) to travel, go on a journey; to set out (nach, for); oft —, to travel about a great deal; wie lange ist er verreist? how long has he been travelling? how long has he been away from home?

Verrei'ten, *ir.v.a.* to spend (*time; money, etc.*) in riding; to ride out; to ride off (*anger, etc.*).

Verren'k—en, *v.a.* to dislocate, sprain, put out of joint. —ung, *f.* dislocation, sprain.

Verren'nen, *ir.v.a.* to spend in running; to hinder, embarrass; einem den Weg —, to bar, stop s.o.'s way, to stand in a p.'s way; sich —, to run too far, to run the wrong way, to get into a corner; sich in eine Streitfrage —, to get involved in a dispute.

Verrich't—en, *v.a.* to do, perform, execute, accomplish; to acquit oneself of; seine Dienste —en, to officiate, do duty (*of persons*), to work well, answer the purpose (*of things*); seine Andacht —en, to perform one's devotions, to say one's prayers; schwere oder langweilige Arbeit —en, to do drudgery, to slave; Geschäfte —en, to transact business; einen Auftrag —en, to execute a commission; seine Notdurft —en, to ease nature. —ung, *f.* doing, performance, execution; manner of doing, executing, *etc.*; accomplishment, achievement; discharge of (*business*); affair; office; action, function (*of the organs of the body, etc.*); **—ung mit der Hand**, manipulation; **ich wünsche Ihnen gute —ung**, I wish you much success; **ich bin mit seiner —ung zufrieden**, I am satisfied with what he has done *or* the way in which he has done it.

Verrie'chen, *ir.v.r. & n.* (*aux.* **s.**) to lose its odour; to become vapid *or* flat.

Verrie'geln, *v.a.* to bolt, bar up; **einen —**, to bolt a p. in.

Verrin'gern, *v.a.* to diminish, lessen, reduce; to extenuate; to depreciate; **die Münzen —**, to lower the value *or* standard of money; **sich —**, to diminish, grow less.

Verrin'nen, *ir.v.n.* (*aux.* **s.**) to run off, run out; to run away, elapse (*of time*).

Verrö'cheln, *v.a.* (*aux.* **h.**) to breathe one's last, to expire.

Verros't—en, *v.n.* (*aux.* **s.**) to rust; **—et**, rusty. **—ung**, *f.* rusting; rust.

Verrot'te—n, *v.n.* (*aux.* **s.**) to rot; **—te Ansichten**, exploded ideas; **—te Zustände**, rotten *or* antediluvian conditions.

Verru'cht, *adj.* infamous; atrocious; rascally; heinous; **—er Mensch**, abandoned wretch. **—heit**, *f.* infamy; atrocity; atrociousness, wickedness; wicked, infamous action.

Verrück'bar, *adj.* movable; loose.

Verrü'ck—en, *v.a.* to displace; to disarrange; to put back *or* on (*the hand of the clock*); to derange, disturb, unsettle; **jemandes Plan, einem den Plan —en**, to disturb, frustrate a p.'s plans; **einem den Kopf —en**, to turn a p.'s head; **den Witwenstuhl —en**, to marry again (*obs.*). **—t**, *p.p. & adj.* wrong, out of order (*of clocks, etc.*); mad, crazy; cracked; foolish; funny, droll (*coll.*); **ein —ter**, a lunatic, madman; **du bist wohl —t**, are you mad? you do not mean it (*coll.*). **—theit**, *f.* mental derangement; madness; frenzy; mad *or* foolish action. **—ung**, *f.* displacement; derangement.

Verru'f, *m.* (**—s**) obloquy; ill repute; **in — bringen**, to bring into discredit; **in — sein (kommen)**, to be in (fall into) disrepute; **einen in — erklären** *or* **thun**, to send a p. to Coventry, cut s.o., to (socially) boycott a person.

Verru'f—en, I. *ir.v.a.* to cry down, condemn; to give a bad name to; to decry, declare (*coins*) not current; withdraw (*coin*) from circulation; to discredit. II. *p.p. & adj.* notorious, infamous, in bad repute. **—ung**, *f.* decrial, defamation, depreciation.

Verrüh'ren, *v.a.* to whip, beat up (*eggs, etc.*).

Vers, *m.* (—(s)es, *pl.* —(s)e) verse; couplet; strophe, stanza; verse (*of the Bible*); **in —(s)e bringen**, to put into verse; **er kann sich** (*dat.*) **keinen — daraus machen**, he can't make it out, can't understand it; **ich kann mir keinen — daraus** (*or* **darauf**) **machen**, I can make neither head nor tail of it. *Comp.* **—abschnitt**, *m.* hemistich. **—accent**, *m.*, **—betonung**, *f.* metrical accent, rythmical stress. **—art**, *f.* kind of verse, metre. **—bau**, *m.*, **—bildung**, *f.* structure of the verses, versification. **—einschnitt**, *m.* cæsura. **—fuß**, *m.* (metrical) foot. **—kunst**, *f.* (art of) versification; poetic art. **—fürstler**, *m.* versifier; poetaster. **—lehre**, *f.* prosody. **—machen**, *n.* versification. **—macher**, *m.* verse-maker, rhyme(ste)r. **—maß**, *n.* metre, poetic measure; rhythm; **nach dem —maße lesen**, to scan. **—messung**, *f.* scanning, scansion. **—weise**, *adv.* in verses; verse by verse. **—wut**, *f.* mania for writing verse. **—zeichen**, *n.* verse-mark (*Typ.*). **—zeile**, *f.* metrical line, line of poetry, verse.

Versa'g—en, I. *v.a.* to deny, refuse; to promise, engage (*implying refusal to others*), **einem einen Dienst —en**, to refuse to do one a service; **die Beine —en mir den Dienst**, my legs fail me, refuse to carry me; **der wird mich Dir nicht —en**, he will not withhold me from thee (*B.*); **dieses Glück ist mir —t**, this happiness is denied me; **sich** (*dat.*) **etwas —en**, to deny oneself, deprive oneself of a thing; **ich bin schon (anderwärts) —t**, I am already engaged (*elsewhere*); **die Stelle war schon —t, als er sich meldete**, the appointment had been made when he applied for it; **diese Plätze sind —t**, these seats are taken, bespoken; **sie ist (bereits) —t**, she is (already) promised in marriage, she is engaged. II. *v.n.* (*aux.* **h.**) to fail (*of the voice, strength, etc.*); to miss fire, not to go off (*of a gun*). III. *subst.n.*, **—en, —ung**, *f.* refusal, denial; failure to act; miss-fire. **—er**, *m.* (**—ers**, *pl.* **—er**) denier; miss-fire.

Versal'buchstabe, *m.* (**—n**, *pl.* **—n**, **Versa'lien**) capital letter (*Typ.*).

Versal'zen, *v.a.* to spoil with salt; **einem ein Vergnügen —**, to spoil a p.'s pleasure *or* fun.

Versam'm—eln, *v.* I. *a.* to assemble, bring together, collect; to convoke, convene; **die zerstreuten Truppen —eln**, to rally the scattered troops; **zu seinen Vätern —elt werden**, to be gathered to one's fathers. II. *r.* to meet, assemble, collect; to muster (*Mil.*). **—lung**, *f.* assembling; convening; assembly; concourse, gathering, meeting; congregation; convention, convocation; company, party. *Comp.* **—lungs=haus**, *n.* house of assembly; meeting-house, club; casino. **—lungs=ort, —lungs=platz**, *m.* meeting-place; rendezvous. **—lungs=recht**, *n.* right of assembling *or* holding meetings. **—lungs=zimmer**, *n.* green-room (*Theat.*).

Versa'nd, *m.* (—(e)s) despatch, sending off; export(ation). *Comp.* **—artikel**, *m.* article for exportation; *pl.* exports. **—bier**, *n.* beer for exportation. **—buch**, *n.* shipping book. **—fertig**, *adj.* ready for exportation. **—geschäft**, *n.* export business. **—rechnung**, *f.* bill of shipping; forwarding-expenses. **—station**, *f.* despatch-station.

Versan'd—en, *v.* I. *a.* to cover *or* fill up with sand; to sand. II. *r. & n.* (*aux.* **s.**) to be covered *or* choked up with sand; to run on a sandbank. **—ung**, *f.* collection of sand; sand-bank.

Versati'l, *adj.* versatile. **—itä't**, *f.* versatility.

Versa'tz, *m.* (**—es**, *pl.* **Versätze**) pledging; pledge; alloy; deposit (*of milk*); filling up (*with rubbish, etc.*); rubbish, refuse; *see* **—mauer**; **in — geben**, to pledge, to pawn, to mortgage. *Comp.* **—amt**, *n.* pawn-shop, loan-bank. **—hölzer**, *pl.* slides (*in sluices*). **—mauer**, *f.* partition-wall, enbankment (*Min.*). **—stück**, *n.* movable scenery (*Theat.*).

Versau'er—n, I. *v.n.* (*aux.* **s.**) to turn sour; to get rusty *or* stale, to vegetate. II. *v.a.* (*better* **Versäuern**) to make too acid; to sour; to spoil, embitter. III. *subst.n.*, **—ung**, *f.* turning sour; **das —n ist sehr leicht**, it (*or* one) soon grows rusty.

Versau'fen, *ir.v.a.* (*vulg.*) to waste in drinking; **seinen Verstand —**, to muddle one's brains with drink, to fuddle o.s.; **versoffen**, drunken, given to hard drinking; **versoffner Kerl**, drunkard.

Versäu'm—en, *v.* I. *a.* to omit, miss, let slip (*an opportunity, etc.*); to neglect; to fail, be absent, to forget; to stop; **den Appell —en**, to miss the roll-call, be missing at the muster (*Mil.*); **ich habe keine einzige (Lehr)stunde —t**, I have not missed a single lesson; **den Zug —en**, to miss the train; **ich will dich nicht verlassen noch —en**, I will never leave thee nor forsake thee (*B.*). II. *r.* to neglect oneself. **—nis**, *f.* (*pl.* **—nisse**) & *n.* (**—nisses**, *pl.* **—nisse**) neglect, negligence; loss occasioned by neglect; loss of time. **—ung**, *f.* neglect, negligence; omission; absence (*at muster*). *Comp.* **—nis=kosten**, *pl.* costs occasioned by non-appearance. **—nis=liste**, *f.* list of the absent. **—nis=urteil**, *n.* judgment by default (*Law*).

Verscha'chern, *v.a.* to sell, chaffer away; to hawk.

Verschaf'f—en, I. *v.a.* (**einem etwas**) to procure, supply with, provide; **einem Recht —en**, to see that justice is done to a p.; **sich** (*dat.*) **selbst Recht —en**, to take the law into one's own hands; **dies wird Ihnen Linderung —en**, this will give you relief; **sich** (*dat.*) **—en**, to obtain, acquire. II. *subst.n.*, **—ung**, *f.* furnishing, providing; **die —ung von Geld ist mit Schwierigkeiten verbunden**, it is difficult to raise (*procure*) money.

Verschä'kern, *v.a.* to dally away; to spend in playing.

Verscha'l—en, *v.a.* to furnish with a shell *or* cover; to furnish (*knives*) with handles; to line with boards, board; **die Decke eines Zimmers —en**, to ceil a room. **—ung**, *f.* lining; **Bretter —ung**, lining of boards.

Verschal'len, *ir.v.n.* (*aux.* **f.**) to cease to sound, die away; to disappear; to disappear from men's minds, to sink into oblivion, to be forgotten; **verschollen**, lost sight of, forgotten, looked upon as dead; **er ist verschollen**, no one knows anything of him; he has passed out of ken, has disappeared *or* never been heard of again; **in verschollenen Jahrhunderten**, in ages long past; **selbst die Sage davon ist verschollen**, even the tradition of it is forgotten.

Verschä'mt, *adj.* ashamed; modest; abashed, confused; timid; **—e Arme**, deserving poor. **—heit**, *f.* confusion; timidity; bashfulness.

Verschan'z—en, *v.a.* to intrench, fortify; **sich —en**, to intrench o.s., to throw up intrenchments *or* earthworks; to take up a fixed position (*fig.*). **—ung**, *f.* intrenching; intrenchment, fortification; **den Feind aus seinen —ungen treiben**, to dislodge the enemy from his trenches *or* his intrenched position. *Comp.* **—ungs=arbeiten**, *pl.* trenches, earthworks. **—ungs=linie**, *f.* line of trenches.

Verschär'fen, *v.a.* to render more severe, heighten, aggravate; to heighten (*the colour, etc.*); to sharpen, render more acute.

Verschar'ren, *v.a.* to bury without ceremony, to cover with earth.

Verschat'ten, *v.a.* to overshadow; to shade (*Paint.*).

Verschäu'men, *v.* I. *a.* to bubble up. II. *n.* (*aux.* **f.**) to cease frothing; to froth, foam away, boil over; to vanish in spray.

Verschei'den, I. *ir.v.n.* (*aux.* **f.**) to depart (this life); to die, expire. II. *subst.n.* death; **im — liegen**, to breathe one's last, to be on the point of death.

Verschen'ken, *v.a.* to give away (as a present); **Getränke —en**, to retail drinks.

Verscher'z—en, I. *v.a.* to spend, pass (*time*) in joking; **etwas —en**, to lose s.th. through folly; **sein Glück —en**, to trifle away one's happiness *or* fortune. II. *subst.n.*, **—ung**, *f.* loss (*caused by folly or neglect*).

Verscheu'chen, *v.a.* to chase, scare away; to banish (*fig.*).

Verschie'b—en, I. *ir.v.a.* to move out of its place, remove, shift; to displace; to disarrange; to postpone; **verschobenes Viereck**, lozenge (*Math.*); **verschobene Menschen**, deformed people; **ihm ist der Kopf verschoben**, he is cracked. II. *subst.n.*, **—ung**, *f.* displacement, disarrangement; dislocation; delay; procrastination; prorogation (*of parliament*).

Verschie'den, I. *p.p. see* **Verscheiden**. II. *adj.* & *adv.* different; unlike; distinct; (*pl.*) several, sundry, various, divers; **himmelweit —**, as different as day from night; **vier —e Armeen**, four separate armies; **die Anlagen sind —**, dispositions differ; **da hört (sich denn) doch —es auf!** that is really too much, too bad! **—heit**, *f.* difference; diversity, variety; disparity, dissimilarity, discrepancy; **—heit der Ansichten**, diversity of views, difference of opinion. **—tlich**, I. *adj.* different. II. *adv.* differently; in different ways; at different times, more than once. *Comp.* **—artig**, *adj.* of a different kind, nature *or* species, heterogeneous, dissimilar. **—artigkeit**, *f.* heterogeneousness, difference of nature *or* kind. **—blätterig**, *adj.* heterophyllous. **—er=lei**, *indec. adj.* of different kinds, various, sundry. **—farbig**, *adj.* of different colours, variegated, parti-coloured. **—gestaltet**, *adj.* heteromorphous.

Verschie'ßen, *ir.v.* I. *a.* to shoot off *or* away; to shoot wrong; to shade off, to degrade; to transpose, impose wrongly (*Typ.*); **seine Munition, sein Pulver —, sich —**, to exhaust one's (stock of) ammunition, use up one's powder; to come to the end of one's tether, exhaust one's resources. II. *r.* to make a mistake, miss in shooting; **sich in einen —**, to fall madly in love with a person; *see under* I. III. *n.* (*aux.* **f.**) to flow rapidly down *or* away; to fade; to become discoloured; to run, come off, wash out (*of colours*).

Verschiff'—bar, *adj.* that can be shipped *or* sent by water. **—en**, *v.a.* to ship, to send *or* transport by water; to export; to lade; **—en von Truppen mit der Bahn**, to entrain. **—ung**, *f.* shipping; shipment, exportation; entraining (*of troops*).

Verschim'mel—n, *v.n.* (*aux.* **f.**) to grow mouldy, mould; **—t**, mouldy. **—ung**, *f.* mouldiness.

Verschim'pfen, *v.a.* to disfigure; to disgrace, insult; to spoil entirely.

Verschimpfie'ren, *v.a.* to spoil entirely (*coll.*).

Verschi'ß, *m.*; **einen in — erklären** *or* **thun**, to send a p. to Coventry (*stud. sl.*).

Verschla'cken, *v.r.* & *n.* (*aux.* **f.**) to turn into dross.

Verschla'fen, I. *ir.v.a.* to spend, pass in sleeping; to miss, lose by sleeping; to sleep off *or* away (*weariness, anger, etc.*); **sich** *or* **die Zeit —en**, to oversleep oneself. II. *p.p.* & *adj.* sleepy, drowsy. **—heit**, *f.* sleepiness, drowsiness.

Verschla'g, *m.* (**—s**, *pl.* **Verschlä'ge**) boarded partition; wooden screen; compartment; cubicle; alcove; wainscotting.

Verschla'gen, I. *ir.v.a.* to use up in hammering, carpentering, *etc.*; to spoil by hammering, *etc.*; to spoil by beating; to fasten with nails, nail up; to board up; to board off, partition off (*a room*); to strike, send too far *or* wrong; to blunt (*tools*); **viele Nägel —**, to use many nails (*in hammering s.th.*); **mit Nägeln —**, to stud with nails, to nail; **zum Blattgold werden meist Dukaten —**, ducats are mostly used in making gold leaf; **mit Brettern —**, to board (*up*); **ein Zimmer —**, to board *or* partition off a room; **den Ball —**, to lose a ball, strike it beyond bounds; **ein Schiff von der Fahrt —**, to drive a ship out of her course; **der Sturm verschlug uns nach Indien**, the storm drove us to the coast of India; **die Stelle in einem Buche —**, to lose one's place in a book; **sich** (*dat.*) **etwas —**, to lose *or* miss by carelessness *or* by one's own fault; **sich** (*dat.*) **die Kunden —**, to drive away one's customers; **sich** (*acc.*) **—**, to miss, to lose oneself. II. *ir.v.n.* (*aux.* **f.**) to become lukewarm; to be lukewarm (*of hot or cold drinks*); (*aux.* **h.**) (*used with neuter subject only in negative and interrogative sentences*) to avail, to be of use, to prove effective; to be of consequence, to matter; **kalte Getränke — lassen**, to take the chill off (of cold drinks); **er darf nur —es**

Wasser trinken, he is allowed only tepid water to drink; durch den Sturm verschlugen wir nach Norwegen, the storm drove us on the Norwegian coast; das verschlägt nichts, that does not matter; was verschlägt Ihnen das? what does that matter to you? nichts will bei ihm —, nothing does him any good, has any effect on him; es will nichts —, it will be of no use, it will not do. III. *p.p.* & *adj.* cunning, crafty, sly; cast-away, adrift. **—heit,** *f.* craft, subtlety, cunning.

Verschlam'men, *v.n.* (*aux.* f.) to get filled *or* choked up with mud.

Verschläm'men, *v.a.* to fill *or* cover with mud.

Verschlech'ter—n, *v.a.* to deteriorate, make worse; to spoil, to corrupt; sich —n, to become worse, deteriorate. **—ung,** *f.* deterioration, degradation, degeneration.

Verschlei'chen, *ir.v.r.* & *n.* (*aux.* f.) to slip away; to crawl along (*of time*).

Verschlei'er—n, *v.a.* to veil; to palliate, gloss over. **—ung,** *f.*; die —ung der Thatsachen hilft nichts, concealment of facts does no good.

Verschlei'f—en, I. *reg.* & *ir.v.a.* to spoil *or* wear out by dragging; to spoil in sharpening; to grind badly; to draw out, lengthen, drag; to slur (*notes*). II. *subst.n.*; durch —en der Töne, by slurring the notes (*Mus.*). **—ung,** *f.*; —ung der Silben, the running together of two syllables, synalœpha.

Verschlei'm—en, I. *v.a.* to fill with slime; to cover with phlegm *or* mucus; to fill with mucous matter; to coat, fur (*the tongue*); to thicken; to congest; ein Gewehr —en, to foul, choke up a gun with dirt. II. *v.r.* & *n.* (*aux.* f.) to be filled with slime, phlegm, *etc.*; to be stopped up, to be congested; to foul (*of guns*); —t sein, to have one's chest congested; —te Zunge, foul tongue. III. *subst.n.*, **—ung,** *f.* obstruction caused by phlegm *or* mucous matter; fouling (*Mil.*); coating (*of the tongue*).

Verschlei'ß, *m.* (—es, *pl.* —e) retail-trade.

[1]**Verschlei'ß—en,** *v.a.* to sell by retail. **—er,** *m.* (—ers, *pl.* —er) retailer, retail dealer.

[2]**Verschlei'ßen,** *ir.v.n.* & *r.* to get worn out *or* used up, to wear out; verschlissen, worn out, threadbare.

Verschlem'men, *v.a.* to spend, waste in carousing.

Verschlen'dern, *v.a.* to idle, lounge away (*time*).

Verschlep'p—en, I. *v.a.* to remove, move to another place; to misplace, mislay; to hide, conceal; to embezzle, purloin; to protract, draw out, delay; to wear out (*clothes*); sich —en, to drag oneself along; eine Krankheit irgendwohin —en, to carry (the seeds of) a contagious disease to some place. II. *subst.n.*, **—ung,** *f.* removing; misplacement; hiding, *etc.*; spread (*of disease*); delay; obstruction; durch das —en dieser Sache, by letting this slide, by the neglect of this matter. *Comp.* —ungs=politik, *f.* policy of obstruction (*Parl.*).

Verschleu'derer, *m.* (—s, *pl.* —) squanderer, lavish person, spendthrift.

Verschleu'der—n, *v.a.* to throw, hurl (*a stone, etc.*); to throw away; to squander, dissipate; to waste (*time*); Waren —n, to sell goods below cost. **—ung,** *f.* wasting, squandering, prodigality; selling under (cost-)price.

Verschließ'bar, *adj.* that can be closed *or* locked, provided with lock and key.

Verschlie'ß—en, *ir.v.a.* to close, shut; to lock up *or* away; to obstruct, blockade (*a port, etc.*); to hide (*feeling*); einem sein Herz —en, to hide one's feelings from a p.; to steel one's heart against a p.; sein Ohr der Verleumdung —en, to close one's ears to slanderous reports; sich —en, to lock o.s. up; sich in sich selbst —en, to turn in on o.s., to wrap oneself up in oneself; bei ihr ist alles verschlossen, everything is under lock and key at her house. **—ung,** *f.* locking; closing up; keeping under lock and key; bolt.

Verschlim'mern, *v.* I. *a.* to make worse; to do harm to; to deprave; to aggravate. II. *r.* & *n.* (*aux.* f.) to deteriorate, grow worse.

[1]**Verschlin'g—en,** *ir.v.a.* to swallow (down) eagerly, to gorge (down); to gulp down (*drinks*), to devour (*food*); das —t viel Geld, that swallows up *or* runs away with a lot of money; ich wollte, die Erde verschlänge ihn, I wish the earth would open and swallow him, I wish he was at Jericho; ein Buch begierig —en, to devour a book greedily; er sieht aus, als wollte er einen —en, he looks as if he would eat a person; einen mit den Augen —en, to stare at a p. open-mouthed. **—er,** *m.* (—ers, *pl.* —er) devourer. **—ung,** *f.* devouring, swallowing up.

[2]**Verschlin'g—en,** *ir.v.* I. *a.* to interlace, (inter-)twine, entwine, twist, coil. II. *r.* to become interlaced *or* entangled; to be welded together; to blend; verschlungene Pfade, winding paths; verschlungene Buchstaben, intertwined letters. **—ung,** *f.* entwining, interlacing; festoon; intricacy, maze.

Verschlos'sen, *p.p.* & *adj. see* Verschließen; very reserved, uncommunicative; taciturn; bei —en Thüren, with closed doors; —er Brief, closed *or* sealed letter; einen —en Leib haben, to be constipated; —er Mensch, taciturn, reserved person. **—heit,** *f.* great reserve, taciturnity.

Verschlu'ck—en, *v.a.* to swallow; to absorb (*Chem.*); to swallow, slur over (*one's words*); die Erde —t das Wasser, the earth sucks up, drinks in the water; sich —en, to swallow the wrong way; ich habe mich —t (*also* —ert), something has gone down the wrong way.

Verschlum'mern, *v.a.* to pass, spend in sleeping.

Verschlu'ß, *m.* (—(ss)es, *pl.* Verschlüs'se) closing; locking; closure; lock; bolt; clasp; seal; confinement, custody; closed place; den, cage; etwas unter — haben, to have under lock and key. *Comp.* —apparat, *m.*, —vorrichtung, *f.* locking apparatus. —kopf, *m.* movable top *or* head (*on firearms*). —laut, *m.* stop, explosive (*Phonet.*); stimmhafter —laut, voiced stop, sonant. —kapsel, *f.* closing-capsule. —schraube, *f.* end-screw. —stück, *n.* plug; breech-block. —ventil, *n.* waste-valve.

Verschmach't—en, *v.* I. *a.*; sein Leben —en, to drag on a lingering existence. II. *n.* (*aux.* f.) to languish; to pine away; to faint; vor Durst —en, to be parched with *or* dying of thirst; ich —e vor Hitze, I am suffocated with (the) heat; die Menschen werden —en vor Furcht, men's hearts will be failing them for fear (*B.*); einen —en lassen, to let a p. perish *or* starve (*to death*). **—ung,** *f.* languishing existence, slow death; languor.

Verschmä'h—en, *v.a.* to disdain, reject (*with scorn*); er —t die Arbeit, he scorns *or* refuses to work; —te Liebe, despised love. **—te,** *f.* forsaken *or* deserted girl, jilted sweetheart.

Verschmä'lern, Verschmä'lerung, (*obs.*) = schmälern, Schmälerung.

Verschmau'chen, *v.a.* to spend, consume in smoking.

Verschmau'sen, *v.a.* to spend, consume in feasting.

Verschmel'z—en, *reg.* & *ir.v.* I. *a.* to melt away, use up in melting; to blend; etwas mit *or* in etwas —en, to blend, run into one another; to melt down together; gut verschmolzene Farben, well-blended colours. II. *n.* (*aux.* f.) to melt, blend; to dissolve. **—ung,** *f.* melting, fusion; blending; melting away; die —ung der Farben, the gradation of colours.

Verschmer'z—en, *v.a.* to console oneself for, get

over; to put up with, make the best of; **den Verlust werde ich nicht so leicht —en,** I shall not get over that loss so easily.

Verschmie'den, *v.a.* to consume, use up in forging; to spoil in forging.

Verschmie'ren, *v.a.* to smear over, stop up (*with clay, plaster, etc.*); to use up in greasing, smearing *or* daubing; to daub; to glue up; **viel Geld —,** to spend large sums of money (*in bribery*); **die Mühlsteine — sich,** the millstones get clogged; **Papier —,** to waste paper in scribbling.

Verschmi'tzt, *adj.* wily, cunning, crafty, sly. **—heit,** *f.* craftiness, cunning, wiliness.

Verschmo'ren, *v.* I. *a.* to parch; to use up (*butter, etc.*) in cooking. II. *n.* (*aux.* **s.**) to be parched; to be smothered with heat; to be over-done, too much cooked.

Verschnap'pen, *v.r.* to say a word too many, to let the cat out of the bag.

Verschnar'chen, *v.a.* to snore, sleep away (*time*).

Verschnau'ben, Verschnau'fen, *v.r. & n.* (*aux.* **s.**) to draw breath, breathe, respire; **die Pferde — lassen,** to breathe the horses.

Verschnei'den, *ir.v.a.* to cut away; to cut off; to cut up, use up in cutting; to spoil in cutting; to prune, lop; to castrate, geld; **Wein —,** to adulterate wine; **einem die Flügel —,** to clip a person's wings; **sechs Meter Stoff zu einem Kleide —,** to use six metres of material for a dress; **der Verschnittene,** eunuch; **verschnittener Hahn,** capon; **verschnittener Stier,** bullock; **verschnittenes Tier,** gelding.

Verschnei'en, *v.a.* to cover with snow, snow up.

Verschnup'f—en, *v.a.* to use in snuffing; to spend on snuff; **der schnelle Temperaturwechsel —t leicht,** the sudden change in the temperature is likely to give one a cold; **ich bin —t,** I have a cold in my head; **das —t ihn,** that annoys, nettles him (*coll.*); **durch eine S. —t werden,** to be put out *or* nettled by a th. (*coll.*); **es hat mich gehörig —t,** I feel much vexed at it (*coll.*).

Verschnü'ren, *v.a.* to trim with cord *or* lace; to tie up; to spoil with (tight) lacing.

Verschol'len, *p.p. & adj. see* **Verschallen. —heit,** *f.* disappearance; prolonged absence. *Comp.* **—heits=erklärung,** *f.* declaration that a missing person is dead in the eyes of the law.

Verscho'n—en, *v.a.;* **einen** *or* **etwas** (*obs.* **eines** *or* **einer Sache**) **—en,** to spare a p. *or* a th.; **einen mit etwas —en,** to exempt, dispense, excuse a p. from s.th.; **—en Sie mich doch mit solchen Reden,** pray spare me such language; **ich bitte Sie, mich mit diesem Auftrage zu—en,** I beg you will excuse me from executing this commission. **—ung,** *f.* forbearance, exemption.

Verschö'n—en, *v.* I. *a.* to beautify, embellish, adorn. II. *r.* to grow beautiful. **—erer,** *m.* (**—erers,** *pl.* **—erer**) adorner, beautifier. **—ern,** *v.a.* to beautify, embellish, adorn. **—erung,** *f.* embellishment. **—erungs=verein,** *m.* society for the improvement of urban scenery, paths, *or* public parks.

[1]**Verschos'sen,** *v.n.* to stop budding *or* shooting.

[2]**Verschos'sen,** (*p.p. of* **verschießen,**) *adj.;* **er ist in sie —,** he has fallen madly in love with her, he is quite wrapped up in her (*coll.*).

Verschrän'ken, *v.a.* to cross, fold (*the arms*); to entwine, interlace.

Verschrau'b—en, *reg. & ir.v.a.* to screw up, close with a screw; to screw on *or* in; to twist, screw wrong. **—ung,** *f.* screwing.

Verschrei'b—en, *ir.v.* I. *a.* to consume, use (*ink*) in writing; to spend (*time*) in writing; to write wrong; to order, write for; to prescribe; **einem etwas —en,** to give a p. a written promise of a thing, to prescribe s.th. for a p.; **ein Wort —en,** to miswrite a word. II. *r.* to make a mistake in writing; to bind oneself, give one's bond; to make o.s. over to; **sich dem Teufel —en,** to sell o.s. to the devil; **ich habe mich verschrieben,** I have made a slip of the pen *or* in writing. **—ung,** *f.* consumption (*of ink*); error in writing; order; prescription; written promise *or* engagement.

Verschrei'en, *ir.v.a.* to decry, cry down; to give a bad name to; to cast an evil eye on, bewitch; **verschrieenes Geld,** base money.

Verschro'ben, *p.p. & adj. see* **Verschrauben;** twisted, distorted; perverse; intricate; confused; queer; preposterous; **ein —er Mensch,** an eccentric *or* crazy person, a wrong-headed, perverse person. **—heit,** *f.* perverseness; eccentricity; duplicity; confusion.

Verschro'ten, *v.a.* to grind up.

Verschrum'pfen, Verschrum'peln (*coll.*), *v.* I. *a. & n.* (*aux.* **s.**) to shrink, shrivel up; to wither. II. *n.* (*aux.* **s.**) to be blasted, blighted.

Verschüch'tern, *v.a.* to intimidate, to scare.

Verschul'd—en, I. *v.a.* to involve in debt, load, encumber with debts; to commit, be guilty of; to incur (*blame*), to merit; to be the cause of; to recompense, return (*prov.*); **einem —et sein,** to be under great obligation to a p.; **was habe ich —et?** what (*wrong*) have I done; **das haben wir an unserm Bruder —et,** we are guilty concerning our brother (*B.*); **das hat er an ihr —et,** that was the consequence of his treatment of her; **sich an einem** *or* **wider einen —en,** to act wrongly towards a p., to wrong a p. II. *subst.n.*, **—ung,** *f.* involving in debt; encumbering, mortgaging; wrong, fault, guilt; **ohne mein —en,** through no fault of mine.

Verschüt'ten, *v.a.* to spill; to fill *or* choke up with earth, *etc.*; to block up, obstruct (*with rubbish, etc.*); to bury, overwhelm; **er hat es bei ihm verschüttet,** he has got into his bad books, has incurred his displeasure; **sich** (*dat.*) **alles —,** to make a mess of it; **der Brei ist verschüttet,** the fat is in the fire; **das Kind mit dem Bade —,** to throw away the good with the bad (*prov.*).

Verschwä'ger—n, *v.a.* to ally by marriage; **—t,** related by marriage. **—ung,** *f.* relationship by marriage, alliance.

Verschwär'men, *v.* I. *a.* to pass (*the night, etc.*) in revelry *or* debauchery. II. *r.* to get scattered in swarming; to fly away (*of bees*); to weary o.s. with revelry. III. *n.* (*aux.* **h.**) to cease to swarm.

Verschwär'zen, *v.a.* to blacken; to dirty; to asperse; **Waren —,** to smuggle goods.

Verschwat'zen, Verschwät'zen, *v.* I. *a.* to pass in chatting *or* gossiping; to drive away, to forget (*sorrow, etc.*) in chatting; to blurt out, divulge; to calumniate, backbite. II. *r.* to blunder in speaking; to betray oneself, to let the cat out of the bag (*fig.*); to let the time slip in gossiping.

Verschwei'g—en, *ir.v.a.* to keep secret, conceal; to pass over in silence; to suppress; **einem etwas —en,** to hide a th. from a p. **—ung,** *f.* silence (*regarding something*); concealment; reticence.

Verschwem'men, *v.a.* to wash *or* sweep away; to flood, inundate; to blend colours (*Paint.*).

Verschwen'd—en, *v.a.* to waste, lavish, squander. **—er,** *m.* (**—ers,** *pl.* **—er**) spendthrift, extravagant person; prodigal. **—erisch,** *adj.* wasteful, prodigal; lavish; extravagant; sumptuous; **—erisch mit etwas umgehen,** to be lavish *or* prodigal of a th. **—ung,** *f.* prodigality.

Verschwie'gen, *p.p. & adj. see* **Verschweigen;** suppressed, kept secret; close; discreet; reserved; taciturn. **—heit,** *f.* silence; secrecy; reserve; **unter dem Siegel der —heit,** under the seal of secrecy.

Verschwie'len, *v.n.* (*aux.* **s.**) to grow callous, hard *or* horny.

Verschwie'mel—n, *v.a.* to waste (time *or* money) (*sl.*). **—t,** *adj.;* **—tes Gesicht,** seedy look (*sl.*).

Verschwim'men, *ir.v.n.* (*aux.* **s.**) to dissolve, fade away; to grow hazy; to merge *or* melt into one another; to mingle, blend (*as fluids*); **in einander —**, to blend.

Verschwin'd—en, *ir.v.n.* (*aux.* **s.**) to vanish, disappear; to be evanescent; to pass away; **das macht unsere Hoffnungen —en,** that puts our hopes to flight. **—ung,** *f.* disappearance; loss (*of strength*). *Comp.* **—e=punkt,** *m.* vanishing point. **—scheibe,** *f.* vanishing target.

Verschwis'ter—n, *v.a.* to make brothers and sisters, unite by the ties of fraternity; to unite intimately; **wir sind (alle) —t,** we are (all) brother(s) and sister(s), brothers *or* sisters; **sich mit . . . —n,** to enter into brotherly *or* sisterly relations with . . .; **—te Seelen,** sympathetic souls, kindred spirits. **—ung,** *f.* brotherly *or* sisterly union, close relationship.

Verschwit'zen, *v.* I. *a.* to exhale by perspiring; to get rid of by perspiring; to spoil by perspiring; to spend (*time*) perspiring; to forget, unlearn (*coll.*). II. *n.* (*aux.* **s.**) to pass off in perspiration.

Verschwom'men, *p.p. & adj. see* **Verschwimmen,** indistinct, hazy; indefinite, vague; dissolving; **—e Bilder,** dissolving views. **—heit,** *f.* vagueness, uncertainty; gradual disappearance.

Verschwö'r—en, *ir.v.* I. *a.* to curse; to forswear, abjure; **das Spiel —en,** to renounce gambling. II. *r.* to conspire, form a conspiracy; to swear, protest with oaths; to bind oneself by an oath; **sich zu etwas —en,** to plot s.th. **—er,** *m.* (—ers, *pl.* —er) conspirator. **—ung,** *f.* conspiracy, plot; solemn oath; curse, malediction; abjuration, renunciation.

Verschwo'rene(r), *m.* conspirator, plotter.

Versechs'fachen, *v.a.* to increase six-fold, to multiply by six; to sextuple.

Verse'hen, I. *ir.v.a.* to provide, furnish with, supply; to stock (*a farm, a pond, etc.*); to discharge *or* perform the duties of an office; to administer; to overlook, neglect, fail to do, omit, miss; to make a mistake, err; to do wrong; **einen mit Lebensmitteln —,** to supply a p. with victuals; **eine Stadt mit Lebensmitteln —,** to stock a place with provisions, to victual a place; **ein Rad mit Speichen —,** to spoke a wheel; **einen Mann mit Vollmacht —,** to invest a p. with full power(s); **ein Haus mit Hausgerät —,** to furnish a house; **wohl —es Lager,** well-assorted stock; **mit Mitteln reichlich — sein,** to have ample means, to have plenty of money; **mit Accept —,** accepted, honoured, to accept (*C. L.*); **den Wechsel mit dem Giro —,** to endorse a bill *or* a cheque; **ein Amt —,** to perform the duties of an office; **er versah dort das Amt des Lehrers,** he was a teacher there; **den Dienst eines andern —,** to take another's place, to discharge the duties of another man; **eine Pfarre für einen andern —,** to take charge of a parish; **einen Sterbenden —,** to administer the last sacrament to a p.; **Geschäfte —,** to transact business, to look after the business; **den Gottesdienst —** to hold divine service; **die Küche —,** to do the cooking; **Unteroffiziersdienste —,** to do the work of a sergeant; **die Wirtschaft —,** to keep house, do the housekeeping; **es —, etwas —,** to mistake a th., to err *or* blunder in a th.; **es bei einem —,** to incur a p.'s displeasure; **er hat es bei ihr —,** he is in her bad books; **ich habe es darin —, daß ich . . .,** I have made a mistake in . . . (-ing); **ich habe das —,** I have overlooked that (*rare*). II. *r.* to make a mistake, to blunder, to go wrong, to commit an error; **er hatte sich wohl —,** very likely he made a mistake; **— ist auch verspielt,** who makes a mistake loses, a miss is as good as a mile (*prov.*); **sich eines Dinges zu einem —,** to look (confidently) to a p. for a th., to expect s.th. of a p. (*obs.*); **ich versehe mich eines Bessern zu euch,** I expect better things of you; **wes** *or* **wessen soll man sich zu euch — ?** what is one to expect from you? **ich versehe mich zu dir alles Guten,** I look to you for all that is good, expect nothing but kindness from you (*obs.*); **ehe er sich dessen versah, ehe er sich's versah,** before he was aware of it, in the twinkling of an eye; **ehe man sich's versieht,** all of a sudden, before you realize what you are doing, before you can say Jack Robinson (*coll.*); **sich (an einer Sache) —,** to be frightened *or* nervously impressed (by s.th.), to take fright (at a th.), have a shock (from a th.). III. *subst.n.* oversight, omission; mistake, blunder, slip; **Sprech —,** slip of the tongue; **Schreib—,** slip of the pen; **— der Schwangern,** fright during pregnancy; **aus —,** through inadvertence, inadvertently, by mistake, erroneously.

Verseh'ren, *v.a.* to wound, injure, damage.

Versei'fen, *v.* I. *a.* to saponify, make into soap; to soap (*all over*). II. *n.* (*aux.* **s.**) to turn to soap.

Versend'bar, *adj.* transportable.

Versen'd—en, *ir.v.a.* to send, despatch, forward; **ins Ausland —en,** to export. **—er,** *m.* (—ers, *pl.* —er) shipper; carrier; exporter; consigner; forwarder. **—ung,** *f.* sending away *or* off; consignment; conveyance, transmission, transport; carriage. *Comp.* **—ungs=art,** *f.* mode of transmission. **—ungs=fähig,** *adj.* that can be sent, transportable, suitable for transport *or* exportation. **—ungs=güter,** *pl.* goods for transport *or* exportation.

Versen'gen, *v.a.* to singe, burn; to parch.

Versen'k—en, *v.a.* to (cause to) sink; to lower, let down; to submerge; to ruin, destroy; to overwhelm; **sich —en,** to plunge, dive into (*meditations, etc.*); **ein Schiff —en,** to sink *or* scuttle a ship; **in tiefe Gedanken —t,** absorbed in thought. **—ung,** *f.* sinking; submersion; lowering; hollow (*in ground*); trap-door (*Theat.*).

Verses'sen, *p.p. & adj.; see* **Versitzen; auf eine S. — sein,** to be mad after a th. (*coll.*).

Versetz'bar, *adj.* that may be removed; movable; transposable; transplantable; that can be given in pledge, that can be pawned.

Verset'z—en, *v.* I. *a.* to change the place of; to displace; to remove; to transplant; to misplace; to advance, promote (*an officer, etc.*); to transpose (*words, etc.*); to permute (*Math.*); to put (*into a certain condition*); to reduce; to throw; to deal (*a blow, etc.*); to obstruct, bar up, put an obstacle in the way of; to dam up; to pledge, pawn, mortgage; to mix up, temper, to alloy; **—te Betonung,** alteration of the accentuation; **er wurde von Woolwich nach Portsmouth —t,** he was transferred from Woolwich to Portsmouth; **die Schüler unter einander —en,** to rearrange the forms *or* sets in a school; **einen Schüler in eine höhere Klasse —en,** to promote a scholar to a higher form *or* class; **unter die Götter —en,** to raise to the rank of a god; **—en Sie sich in meine Lage,** put yourself in my place; **das —t mich in die Notwendigkeit,** that reduces me to the necessity (*of doing, etc.*); **einen in große Angst —en,** to alarm, terrify a p. greatly; **etwas —en,** to put a th. in pledge, to pawn a th.; **Wein mit Wasser —en,** to mix wine with water; **eine Krone mit Diamanten —en,** to set a crown with diamonds (*prov.*); **einem einen Schlag —en,** to give a p. a blow; **er hat ihm einen (*or* eins) —t,** he has dealt him a (sudden) blow; **das —t mir den Atem,** that takes my breath away; **der Glaube —t Berge,** faith removes mountains; **den Eingang mit Steinen —en,** to block up the entrance with stones; **eine Geldsorte gegen eine andere —en,** to exchange money. II. *r.* to change its place, to shift; to curdle; to earth (*of badgers, etc.*); **der Krankheitsstoff —t sich,**

the morbid matter changes its place; **der Strom —t sich**, the stream changes its bed *or* course. III. *a.* & *n.* (*aux.* **h.**) to answer, to (say in) reply. **—ung**, *f.* displacing, removal; putting, placing (*in a certain condition*); transposition; transplantation; promotion; change, inversion (*of words*); metathesis; permutation (*Math.*); metastasis (*Med.*); curdling (*of milk in the breast*); retention (*of urine*); flatulence; alloy; pledging; repartee; **—ung eines Bischofs**, translation of a bishop. *Comp.* **—amt**, *n.* pawn-shop. **—schienen**, *pl.* switches (*Rail.*). **—schwärmer**, *m.* squib. **—stücke**, *pl.* movable scenery, shifting *or* side scenes. **—ungs=befehl**, *m.* order of transfer (*Mil.*). **—ungs=examen**, *n.* examination for promotion (*to a higher form*). **—ungs=kapsel**, *f.* cylinder. **—ungs=regel**, *f.* rule of alligation. **—ungs=zeichen**, *n.* sign of transposition (*Mus.*).

Verseuf'zen, *v.a.* to pass in sighing.

Versich'er—bar, *adj.* that may be insured. **—er**, *m.* (**—ers**, *pl.* **—er**) insurer; underwriter.

Versi'cher—n, *v.* I. *a.* to insure, assure, protest; to aver, assert; to make sure, certify; to insure; to give security for; **einem etwas, einen einer Sache** (*gen.*) *or* (*rarely*) **von einer Sache —n**, to assure *or* convince s.o. of a thing; **ich —e dir** *or* (*less good*) **dich**, I assure you; **mir wird versichert**, I have been assured; **der König —te das Mädchen seiner Gnade**, the king assured the maiden of his favour; **er —te mir das Gegenteil** *or* **—te mich des Gegenteils**, he assured me of the contrary; **seien Sie —t, daß**, you may depend upon it that; **seien Sie meines Eifers —t**, be assured of my zeal; **an Eides Statt —n**, to affirm; **auf die Hin=und=Herreise —n**, to insure (the) out and home (journey). II. *r.* to assure oneself of, obtain certainty about; to ascertain; to insure one's life; **sich einer Person —n**, to make sure of a p.; to arrest a p. **—ung**, *f.* insurance (*against fire, hail*), assurance (*of life*); security; assurance, protestation; guarantee; **eine —ung abschließen**, to effect an insurance; **die —ung erlischt**, the policy expires; **—ung gegen Einbruch**, insurance against burglary. *Comp.* **—ungs=agent**, *m.* agent for an insurance company. **—ungs=betrag**, *m.* amount insured. **—ungs=gebühr**, *f.* insurance fee. **—ungs=gesellschaft**, *f.* insurance company. **—ungs=prämie**, *f.* premium of insurance. **—ungs=schein**, *m.* policy (of insurance). **—ungs=wesen**, *n.* insurance matters.

Versicht'baren, *v.a.* to show, render visible.

Versi'ckern, *v.n.* (*aux.* **s.**) to leak out, trickle away.

Versie'chen, *v.n.* (*aux.* **s.**) to languish, pine away in sickness.

Versie'den, *reg.* & *ir. v.* I. *a.* to boil away; to use in boiling; to spoil by boiling too much. II. *n.* (*aux.* **s.**) to boil away, evaporate; to cease boiling.

Versieg'—bar, *adj.* liable to run dry. **—en**, *v.n.* (*aux.* **s.**) to dry up; to be exhausted; to fail.

Versie'gel—n, *v.a.* to seal (*up*). **—ung**, *f.* sealing; setting a seal to.

Versifizie'r—en, *v.a.* to versify, make verses. **—ung**, *f.* versification.

Versil'ber—er, *m.* (**—ers**, *pl.* **—er**) one who plates *or* silvers; seller (*coll.*). **—n**, *v.a.* to plate, silver over; to realize, to turn to cash, make money of (*coll.*); to pawn (*coll.*). **—ung**, *f.* silvering, plating; selling (*coll.*); realization.

Versim'pel—n, *v.n.* (*aux.* **s.**) to become imbecile (*coll.*). **—t**, *p.p.* & *adj.* dull, stupid.

Versin'gen, *ir.v.* I. *a.* to pass (*time, etc.*) in singing. II. *r.* & *n.* (*aux.* **h.**) to sing false, out of tune, make a mistake in singing.

Versin'k—en, *ir.v.n.* (*aux.* **s.**) to sink, be swallowed up; to sink, founder, go down (*of ships*); **in Laster —en**, to plunge into vice; **ich hätte in die Erde —en mögen**, I could have sunk into the earth; **in einen Abgrund —en**, to become engulfed; **in Gedanken versunken sein**, to be lost *or* absorbed in thought. **—ung**, *f.* sinking into, immersion; submersion.

Versinn'bild(lich)en, *v.a.* to symbolize, allegorize.

Versinn'lichen, *v.* I. *a.* to render tangible *or* perceptible to the senses, to materialize; to convey a clear idea of, to illustrate; to sensualize. II. *n.* (*aux.* **s.**) to become sensual.

Versin'ter—n, *v.n.* to incrust. **—ung**, *f.* incrustation.

Versitt'lichen, *v.a.* to improve the morals of, to civilize.

Versit'zen, *ir.v.a.* to pass (*time, etc.*) sitting *or* seated; to neglect *or* miss by sitting too long *or* by sitting idle; to spoil by sitting on; **sich —**, to grow pale from leading a sedentary life.

Ver'so, I. *adv.* (*abbr.* V°) on the other side, next page. II. *n.*; **auf dem —**, see overleaf.

Versoh'len, *v.a.* to sole; **einem die Haut, einen —**, to flog *or* thrash a p. thoroughly (*vulg.*).

Versof'fen, *pp.* & *adj.* drunken (*vulg.*).

Versöh'n—en, *v.a.* to conciliate, reconcile; to propitiate; to appease (*anger*); to atone for, expiate (*one's sins*); **—end**, expiatory. **—er**, *m.* (**—ers**, *pl.* **—er**) reconciler, mediator. **—lich**, *adj.* inclined to reconciliation, one who can be propitiated, forgiving. **—lichkeit**, *f.* forgiving *or* conciliatory spirit. **—ung**, *f.* reconciliation; propitiation; expiation, atonement. *Comp.* **—ungs=bund**, *m.* covenant of grace. **—ungs=fest**, *n.*, **—ungs=tag**, *m.* day of reconciliation; day of atonement (*of the Jews*). **—ungs=lehre**, *f.* doctrine of atonement. **—ungs=opfer**, *n.* expiatory sacrifice; scapegoat; expiatory victim. **—ungs=tod**, *m.* expiatory death.

Verson'nen, *adj.* lost in thought *or* reverie (*eyes*).

Versor'g—en, *v.a.* to provide, supply, furnish; to provide for, maintain; to establish, settle (*in life*); **er ist lebenslänglich —t**, he is provided for for the rest of his life. **—er**, *m.* (**—ers**, *pl.* **—er**), **—erin**, *f.* maintainer, supporter; patron(ess); foster-parent. **—ung**, *f.* providing for; maintenance; provision; settlement; situation; furnishing, supplying with; provisioning; supply. *Comp.* **—ungs=anstalt**, *f.*, **—ungs=haus**, *n.* charitable institution, asylum. **—ungs=bureau**, *n.* registry-office; labour-bureau.

Verspa'ren, *v.a.* to save, spare; to postpone.

Verspä't—en, *v.* I. *a.* to make late; to retard, keep back, delay. II. *r.* to come too late; to tarry, loiter; **er hat sich um einen Tag —et**, he arrived a day too late; **—et**, late, behind time, belated. **—ung**, *f.* delay, stop, retardment; coming too late; **der Zug hat 20 Minuten —ung**, the train is 20 minutes late *or* overdue.

Verspei'sen, *v.a.* to eat up, consume; to polish off (*coll.*).

Verspekulie'ren, *v.r.* to make a bad speculation.

Versper'r—en, *v.a.* to bar, barricade, obstruct, block up; to shut, close up; **einem die Aussicht —en**, to obstruct a person's view. **—ung**, *f.* barring, barricading; barricade, obstruction; blockade (*of a port*); closing up; closing (*of the game at dominoes*).

Verspie'kern, *v.a.* to spike (*Naut.*).

Verspie'len, *v.a.* to pass (*an evening, etc.*) in playing; to lose, gamble away; to raffle; **ihr habt es verspielt**, you have lost the game; **er hat (es) bei ihr verspielt**, he has lost her favour; **Geld —**, to lose money at play.

Verspin'nen, *ir.v.a.* to use up (*flax*) in spinning; **sich —**, to become entangled, get into a difficulty.

Versplit'tern, *v.a.* to squander, trifle away.

Verſpot't—en, *v.a.* to scoff, deride, ridicule; to jeer at. **—er**, *m.* (—ers, *pl.* —er) jeerer, scoffer, mocker. **—ung**, *f.* scoffing; derision, ridicule.

Verſpre'ch—en, I. *ir.v.a.* to promise; to bind oneself, engage; to give promise of, bid fair; **einem etwas —en**, to promise a p. something; **ſich** (*dat.*) **etwas —en**, to anticipate, hope for a th.; **es war ein junger Menſch, der viel verſprach**, he was a very promising youth; **der Knabe verſpricht ein großer Maler zu werden**, the boy promises *or* bids fair to become a great painter; **ſie ſind verſprochen**, they are engaged; **ich —e mir nicht viel davon**, I don't expect much from it, I have no great hopes of it; **bei Treu und Glauben —en**, to pledge one's honour *or* word. II. *ir.v.r* to promise; to make a mistake in speaking, to let slip (*something*); to become engaged; to engage oneself; **verſpricht ſich doch der Prediger auf der Kanzel**, even Homer occasionally nods; **ich habe mich ſchon für den nächſten Tanz verſprochen**, I am engaged for the next dance; **das ſchöne Mädchen hat ſich ſchon verſprochen**, that beautiful girl is already engaged to be married. III. *subst. n.*, **—ung**, *f.* promise; engagement; **einem das —en abnehmen**, to exact a promise from a p.; **ein ſchriftliches —en**, a written promise, a promissory note; **einen ſeines —ens entbinden**, to release a p. from a promise.

Verſpren'gen, *v.a.* to scatter, disperse (*troops, etc.*); to blow up, blast; to strike a ball off the table (*Bill.*); **verſprengtes Korps**, commando cut off from the main body.

Verſprin'gen, *ir.v.* I. *a.* to caper away, spend (*time*) in jumping; **ſich** (*dat.*) **den Fuß —**, to sprain one's foot in jumping. II. *r.* to lose one's way, to get off the track.

Verſprit'zen, *v.* I. *a.* to squirt out; to spill, shed; **ſein Blut —**, to shed one's blood. II. *r.*; **ſich an den Felſen —**, to dash furiously against the rocks.

Verſpü'len, *v.a.* to wash away; to sweep past; to wash (*colours*).

Verſpun'den, Verſpün'den, *v.a.* to bung up (*a cask*); to fill up; to join by grooves.

Verſpü'ren, *v.a.* to feel, perceive, be aware of; to become aware of, to experience.

Verſtaat'lich—en, *v.a.* to acquire for the state, to make the property of the state. **—ung**, *f.* absorption *or* acquisition by the state.

Verſtäh'len, *v.a.* to steel; to tip with steel; to harden.

Verſtam'pfen, *v.a.* to crush, pound; to trample, tread down.

Verſta'nd, *m.* (—es) understanding, mind, intellect; intelligence; sense, discernment; judgment; sagacity; sense, signification, meaning; **der geſunde (Menſchen=)—**, (sound) common sense; **er iſt nicht (recht) bei —**, he is not in his right mind, he is a little crazy; **der Kranke blieb bei —e**, the patient retained his mental faculties; **zu —e kommen**, to arrive at years of discretion; **wieder zu —e kommen**, to recover one's senses, come to oneself again; **einen um den — bringen**, to drive a p. out of his senses; **ihm ſteht der — ſtille**, he is at his wits' end; **mir ſtand dabei der — ſtille**, it was beyond my comprehension; **das geht über meinen —**, that is beyond me **einen klaren — haben**, to have a good head, to be clear-headed; **— kommt nicht vor den Jahren**, reason comes with years (*prov.*); **— iſt beſſer als Reichtum**, wisdom is better than riches; **nach meinem geringen —**, in my humble opinion; **— eines Wortes**, acceptation of a term; **in jedem —e**, in every respect, in whatever way you take it (*obs.*). *Comp.* **—es=begriff**, *m.* (*abstract*) idea. **—(e)s=kaſten**, *m.* head, head-piece; very sensible *or* matter-of-fact person (*coll.*). **—es=kraft**, *f.* intellectual power. **—es=mäßig**, *adj.* reasonable; that appeals to the understanding. **—es=menſch**, *m.* matter-of-fact person. **—es=ſchärfe**, *f.* penetration, sagacity, judgment. **—es=ſchwäche**, *f.* imbecility; feebleness of intellect, weak-mindedness. **—es=ſtörung**, *f.* mental derangement. **—es=thätigkeit**, *f.* intellectual work. **—es=welt**, *f.* intellectual world. **—es=weſen**, *n.* intelligent being.

Verſtan'den, *p.p. of* **verſtehen**.

Verſtän'd—ig, *adj.* reasonable, rational, sensible; intelligent; clever; wise, prudent, judicious; **—iges Alter**, years of discretion; **—iger Einfall**, good *or* sensible idea. **—igen**, *v.a.* (**einen von etwas**) to give (a p.) notice of, to acquaint (s.o.) with, inform of; (**einen über eine S.**) to enlighten (a p. upon s.th.); to undeceive (a p.), disabuse a (p.'s) mind; **ſich mit einem —igen**, to come to an understanding with s.o.; **ſich mit einem über eine S. —igen**, to discuss, come to an arrangement with a p. about a th. **—igkeit**, *f.* wisdom, sensibleness, good sense. **—lich**, *adj.* intelligible, clear, comprehensible; distinct; **allgemein —lich**, popular, intelligible to every one; **ſich —lich ausdrücken**, to express o.s. clearly; **ſich —lich machen**, to make o.s. understood; **einem etwas —lich machen**, to make a p. comprehend a th.; **—licher Vortrag**, clear delivery; lucid exposition. **—lichkeit**, *f.* intelligibility, clearness, lucidity. **—nis**, *n.* (—niſſes, *pl.* —niſſe) comprehension; understanding, intelligence; agreement, understanding, concord; terms of intercourse; **ſceniſches —nis haben**, to have a feeling for scenic effect; **—nis für eine S. haben**, to appreciate s.th., to be capable of comprehending a th.; **einem das —nis einer Sache eröffnen**, to explain, render something intelligible to a person; **ein heimliches —nis**, a secret understanding; **in einem guten —nis mit einem leben**, to be on friendly terms with a p. *Comp.* **—nis=innig**, *adj.* with profound understanding; of deep meaning; significant, speaking volumes; **ein —nisinniger Blick**, a glance of mutual understanding, a knowing glance; **—nisinnige Worte**, appreciative words. **—nis=los**, *adj.* devoid of understanding, imbecile, unappreciative. **—nis=loſigkeit**, *f.* want of comprehension. **—nis=voll**, *adj.* intelligent; appreciative; knowing (*coll.*).

Verſtär'k—en, I. *v.a.* to strengthen, fortify; to augment; to reinforce; to aggravate; to corroborate; to swell (*a note*); to raise (*the voice*); to concentrate (*liquids*); **die Farben —en**, to give more depth *or* richness to the colours; **—end**, strengthening; intensi(ti)ve. II. *subst.n.* the toning (*of a photograph*). **—ung**, *f.* strengthening, *etc.*; increase; concentration; corroboration; aggravation; elevation (*of the voice*); reinforce (*of a gun*); (*pl.*) reinforcements, supplies (*Mil.*). *Comp.* **—ungs=flaſche**, *f.* Leyden jar. **—ungs=partikel**, *f.* augmentative *or* intensitive (*particle*). **—ungs=truppen**, *pl.* reinforcements (*Mil.*). **—ungs=wort**, *n.* augmentative *or* intensive word.

Verſtat'ten, *v.a.* to allow, permit, grant.

Verſtau'ben, *v.* I. *a. see* **Verſtäuben**. II. *r. & n.* (*aux.* ſ.) to be covered with dust; to fly off as *or* in dust.

Verſtäu'b—en, *v.a.* to cover with dust; to reduce to dust *or* powder. **—er**, *m.* (—ers, *pl.* —er), (**—ungs=apparat**, *m.*) spray-diffuser. **—ung**, *f.* reduction to powder, pulverization.

Verſtau'chen, *v.a.*; **ſich** (*dat.*) **die Hand —**, to sprain one's hand.

Verſtau'en, *v.a.* to stow away.

Verſte'chen, I. *ir.v.a.* to stitch together; to patch (*a hole, etc.*); to break (*a lance in tilting*); to adulterate (*wine*); **ſeine Trümpfe —**, to trump, to play out one's trumps.

Verste'ck, *n.* (& *m.*) (—s, *pl.* —e) hiding, concealing; hide-and-seek (*game*); hiding-place; ambush; ambuscade (*Mil.*).

Verste'ck—en, *v.a.* to hide, conceal; **sich —en,** to hide, to get out of the way; **sich vor einem —en müssen,** to be no match for a p. **—t,** *p.p.* & *adj.* hidden; indirect; deep; close, sly; **—te Anspielungen,** covert hints *or* references; **—ter Vorwurf,** covert reproach; **—ter Mensch,** close, secretive person; sly, cunning person. **—theit,** *f.* dissimulating spirit; closeness, secretiveness. *Comp.* **—ens=spielen, —spiel,** *n.* hide-and-seek.

Verste'hen, *ir.v.* I. *a.* to understand, comprehend; to mean; **Deutsch —,** to know German; **den Rummel —,** to have the knack of it, to know what's what (*sl.*); **einem etwas zu — geben,** to give a p. to understand, to intimate to a p.; **jeder macht's wie er's versteht,** every one acts according to his lights; **Sie — mich falsch,** you misunderstand me; **er verstand das Ding unrecht,** he took it ill, took it in bad part; **er versteht keinen Spaß,** he cannot take *or* does not see a joke; **will man dadurch zu — geben, daß ...,** if that is to say that ...; **etwas —,** to understand a thing, know (*all*) about it; **aus dem Grunde —,** to know thoroughly; **— Sie das?** do you understand? do you follow? **verstanden?** do you follow? did you understand *or* hear what I said? **das — Sie nicht,** you don't understand, what do you know about that? **was — Sie darunter?** what do you understand by that? **wohl verstanden,** let it be understood; **mit darunter verstanden,** included, comprehended. II. *r.* to understand o.s.; to understand one another; **sich mit einem —,** to come to an understanding *or* to agree with a p.; **das versteht sich von selbst** *or* (*sl.*) **am Rande,** that is understood, is a matter of course; **(das) versteht sich!** of course! **sich auf eine S. —,** to understand, know a thing well, to be an expert at s.th.; **sich auf seinen Vorteil —,** to know where one's own interest lies *or* which side one's bread is buttered; **sich zu einer S. —,** to consent, agree to, to lend oneself to, to condescend to do a thing; **der Wohnungspreis versteht sich auch für Morgenkaffee,** the rent of the lodgings includes coffee in the morning.

Verstei'g—en, I. *ir.v.r.* to climb too high (*so as not to be able to return*), to lose o.s. among precipitous mountain peaks; to fly high; to go too far; to attempt too much, to lose oneself; to get lost, absorbed in a th.; **so hoch habe ich mich nie verstiegen,** I have never ventured as high as that; **dieser Autor —t sich zu hoch,** this author soars too high; **sich im Reden —en,** to lose oneself, get out of one's depth in speaking; **er verstieg sich zur Behauptung ...,** he went so far as to maintain, he had the presumption to assert ... II. *subst.n.*; **die Gefahren des —ens,** the danger of flying *or* climbing too high.

Verstei'gerer, *m.* (—s, *pl.* —) auctioneer.

Verstei'ger—n, *v.a.* to (*sell by*) auction, to bring under the hammer. **—ung,** *f.* auction.

Verstei'ner—n, *v.a.*, *r.* & *n.* (*aux.* **f.**) to petrify. **—ung,** *f.* petrifaction; fossil. *Comp.* **—ungs=fähig,** *adj.* that can be petrified. **—ungs=kunde,** *f.* science of fossils, palæontology.

Verstell'bar, *adj.* movable, adjustable. **—keit,** *f.* movability, mobility, adjustableness.

Verstel'l—en, I. *v.a.* to put one thing in the place of another; to remove, change the place of; to misplace; to disarrange; to arrange badly; to bar, block up, obstruct (*a way*); to disfigure, deform; to disguise; to pretend, counterfeit; **man hat mir alle Bücher —t,** all my books have been disarranged; **die Handschrift —en,** to disguise one's handwriting, to write in a feigned hand. II. *v.r.* to disguise o.s.; to dissemble; to feign, pretend, sham; **sich gegen einen —en,** to use *or* practise dissimulation towards a p.; **sich zu —en wissen,** to know how to dissemble, to be a good dissembler; **sich gut —en,** to play one's part well; **—t,** pretended, disguised, insincere, sham, fictitious. III. *subst.n.*, **—ung,** *f.* change of place, removal; displacement; barrier, barricade; disarrangement; dissembling; dissimulation, pretence make-believe; disguise; make-up, fictitious tale; hypocrisy. *Comp.* **—ungs=kunst,** *f.* art of feigning *or* dissembling, dissimulation, hypocrisy.

Verster'ben, *ir.v.n.* (*aux.* **f.**) to die; to breathe one's last; to expire, be extinguished; **verstorben,** dead, deceased, late; **längst verstorben,** dead and gone; **meine verstorbene Mutter,** my mother, who is dead; **der (jüngst) Verstorbene,** the deceased; **die Verstorbenen,** the dead, the departed.

Versteu'ern, *v.a.* to pay duty on; to steer a wrong course; **auf eine S. versteuert** (*usually* **gesteuert**) **sein,** to have a yearning for a thing.

Verstie'ben, *ir.v.n.* (*aux.* **f.**) to be scattered as dust; to fly off as dust; to fly away; to disappear.

Verstie'gen, *p.p. of* **versteigen;** *adj.* high-flown, extravagant. **—heit,** *f.* extravagance, eccentric character.

Verstie'len, *v.a.* to furnish with a handle.

Verstim'm—en, *v.a.* to put out of tune; to put out of sorts, into a bad temper; **—tes Klavier,** piano out of tune; **—t sein,** to be out of humour, in a bad temper; **sich —en,** to get out of tune; to get out of temper, to be in low spirits. **—theit, —ung,** *f.* discord; being out of tune; ill humour; depression of spirits.

Versto'ck—en, *v.* I. *a.* to harden. II. *n.* (*aux.* **f.**) to grow musty, rot. III. *r.* & *n.* (*aux.* **f.**) to grow hard, obdurate, impenitent. **—theit, —ung,** *f.* obduracy, stubbornness, hardness of heart; callousness, insensibility.

Verstoh'len, *adj.* stealthy, furtive, secret, clandestine; surreptitious; thievish.

Verstol'len, *v.a.* to tunnel (*a hill*); **ein Bergwerk —,** to make galleries in a mine.

Verstop'f—en, *v.a.* to stop, plug up, close; to choke, obstruct; to fill up (*a canal, etc.*); to constipate (*Med.*); **die Ritzen einer Thür —en,** to fill up the chinks of a door; **sein Ohr vor ... —en,** to close one's ears to ... **—ung,** *f.* stopping, obstructing; filling up; stoppage, obstruction; constipation; **an —ung leiden,** to be constipated.

Verstö'r—en, *v.a.* to trouble, disturb, disquiet; to disperse, scatter, dissipate; to confuse, bring into disorder; **—t,** troubled, disconcerted, agitated; **mein Kopf war zu —t,** my head (*mind*) was too confused; **ein ganz —tes Gesicht haben, ganz —t aussehen,** to have a haggard, wild look, an air of consternation, to look troubled, agitated; **die Diebe —en,** to put the thieves to flight. **—theit,** *f.* haggard appearance; trouble, agitation, consternation.

Versto'ß, *m.* (—es, *pl.* **Verstö'ße**) offence; mistake; error, blunder, slip; **einen — gegen etwas machen,** to offend against a th., to violate a thing.

Versto'ß—en, *ir.v.* I. *n.* (*aux.* **h.**); **gegen eine S. —en,** to give offence to, to offend against, to transgress in the matter of, to wound; **wider einen —en,** to be wanting in respect to a p.; **das Bier verstößt,** the beer ceases to ferment. II. *a.* to push, turn away; to repel, repulse; to reject; to repudiate, divorce (*a wife*); to disown, cast off, disinherit (*a son, etc.*); to dispossess, turn out; **einen aus einer Gesellschaft —en,** to expel a p. from a company;

eine Ader —en, to start a vein; **der, die —ene,** the outcast. **—ung,** *f.* expulsion; rejection; banishment; repudiation; casting off, disinheriting; blunder (*obs.*); **grobe —ungen wider die historische Wahrheit,** serious breaches of historic truth, serious misrepresentations of historical facts; *see* **Verstoß.**

Verstrei'ch—en, *ir.v.* I. *a.* to spread, do over (*with some soft substance*); to use up in spreading; to close up; to joint, grout (*joints*); **eine Mauer mit Mörtel —en,** to rough-cast, plaster, parget a wall; **verstrichene Fugen,** joints filled up with mortar; **ein Faß mit Pech —en,** to pitch a cask. II. *n.* (*aux.* **s.**) to glide, slip away (*of time*); to expire, elapse; **der Termin ist verstrichen,** the term has expired. **—ung,** *f.* flight of time; expiration (*of a term*); pargeting *or* rough-casting (*of a wall*).

Verstrei'ten, *ir.v.a.* to spend (*time*) in quarrelling; to spend (*money*) in litigation.

Verstreu'—en, *v.a.* to scatter; to strew about; to spread abroad; to litter; to use for litter; **—te Felsblöcke,** erratic blocks (*Geol.*).

Verstri'cken, *v.a.* to use up in knitting; to spend (*time*) in knitting; to knit wrong; to ensnare, entangle; to bind with cords; to unite closely; **sich —,** to make a mistake in knitting; to be caught; **in einer S. verstrickt sein,** to be involved in an affair; **in eine S. verstrickt werden,** to get mixed up *or* entangled in a thing.

Verströ'men, *v.n.* (*aux.* **s.**) to flow off *or* away; to gush forth; to pass, roll on.

Verstudie'ren, *v.a.* to spend in studying; **seine Gesundheit —,** to injure one's health by overstudy.

Verstu'fen, *v.a.* to jag, notch, mark (*Min.*).

Verstüm'm—eln, *v.a.* to mutilate, maim, mangle; to curtail, garble; to cut down; **—elte Glieder,** maimed limbs; **—elter Bericht,** garbled account; **sich —eln,** to maim *or* mutilate oneself. **—elung,** *f.* mutilation. **—ler,** *m.* (**—lers,** *pl.* **—ler**), **—lerin,** *f.* mutilator.

Verstum'm—en, *v.n.* (*aux.* **s.**) to hold one's tongue, be silent; **vor Erstaunen —en,** to be struck dumb with astonishment. **—ung,** *f.* loss of speech.

Versu'ch, *m.* (—(e)s, *pl.* —e) attempt, trial, endeavour, essay; experiment; proof; effort; **—e anstellen,** to experiment, to try, attempt; **einen — mit einer S. machen,** to prove s.th., to give s.th. a trial, to experiment upon a thing; **ein — kann nicht schaden,** it can do no harm to try; **es kommt auf einen — an,** it depends upon how it turns out, how it stands the test; **erster —,** first attempt; début (*Theat.*); **erster — im Reden,** maiden speech. *Comp.* **—s=bataillon,** *n.* trial battalion (*for experiments with guns*). **—s=feld,** *n.* field for (*scientific*) experiments. **—s=kaninchen,** *n.* rabbit used for vivisectional experiments, experimentation rabbit *or* guinea-pig; object of (scientific) experiments (*coll.*); **ich will kein —skaninchen sein,** I refuse to be the object of an experiment (*coll.*). **—s=ladung,** *f.* proof charge (*Artil.*). **—s=objekt,** *n.* object of scientific experiment; *corpus vile;* butt, laughing-stock (*coll.*). **—s=schießen,** *n.* trial gun *or* artillery practice. **—s=station,** *f.* station for (scientific) experiments *or* for experimental farming. **—s=weise,** *adv.* by way of trial, as an experiment.

Versu'ch—en, *v.a.* to attempt; to try, put to the test, experiment on; to tempt, entice, allure; to seduce; **es mit etwas —en,** to give a thing a trial; **sein Äußerstes —en,** to do one's utmost; **sein Glück im Kriege —en,** to try the chances of war; **einen zu überreden —en,** to attempt to persuade a p.; **sein Heil, sein Glück —en,** to seek one's fortune; **er hat sich in der Welt —t,** he has seen life, has had great experience. **—er,** *m.* (**—ers,** *pl.* **—er**) tempter; seducer; the devil (*B.*). **—ung,** *f.* temptation; **in —ung führen,** to lead into temptation; **in —ung kommen,** to be tempted.

Versu'deln, *v.a.* to soil, besmear, bedaub.

Versum'pf—en, *v.n.* (*aux.* **s.**) to become marshy, boggy; to stagnate; to come down in the world (*sl.*); **die ganze Gegend ist —t,** the whole district is a swamp *or* bog.

Versün'dig—en, *v.r.* to sin; **sich an einem —en,** to sin against *or* offend a person. **—ung,** *f.* sin; **—ung an Gott,** sin against God.

Versun'ken, *p.p. & adj.; see* **Versinken. —heit,** *f.* stagnation, depression (*of trade, etc.*); degradation, demoralization; absorption (*in thought*), engrossment (*fig.*).

Versü'ßen, *v.a.* to sweeten; to edulcorate (*Chem.*); to make too sweet.

Verta'g—en, *v.a.* to adjourn, put off; to prorogue (*parliament*); **—ter Wechsel,** bill that has fallen due. **—ung,** *f.* adjournment; prorogation.

Vertän'deln, *v.a.* to trifle *or* fritter away (*time*); to fritter away (*money*).

Vertan'zen, *v.a.* to pass in dancing; to dance off *or* away (*sorrow, ill humour, etc.*).

Vertau'meln, *v.a.* to spend in a whirl of pleasure *or* gaiety.

Vertausch'bar, *adj.* exchangeable, permutable. **—keit,** *f.* exchangeability.

Vertau'sch—en, *v.a.* to exchange, barter; to interchange; to change (*places*); to confound, mistake; **etwas gegen, für, mit** *or* **um etwas —en,** to exchange one thing for another; **ein Wort mit dem andern —en,** to use *or* put one word for another; **Berlin mit Leipzig —en,** to leave Berlin for Leipsic. **—ung,** *f.* exchange; barter; permutation (*of livings*); substitution: confounding one thing with another.

Vertau'send—fachen, —fältigen, *v.a.* to increase a thousandfold; to multiply by a thousand.

Ve'rte, (*imper. of Latin*) turn over (*P. T. O.*).

Vertei'dig—en, *v.a.* to defend; to maintain, justify, vindicate; to stand up for, stand by; to advocate; to excuse; **einen Satz —en,** to maintain a proposition; **eine schlechte Sache —en,** to defend a weak *or* bad cause; **sich —en,** to stand up for one's rights, to defend, justify, vindicate oneself. **—er,** *m.* (**—ers,** *pl.* **—er**) defender; advocate; supporter (*of a proposition*); **Vaterlands —er,** soldier (*coll.*). **—ung,** *f.* defence; vindication, justification; advocacy; apology; maintenance, support; **zur —ung dienend,** justificatory, defensive; **zur —ung meiner Ehre,** in defence of my honour. *Comp.* **—ungs=anstalten,** *pl.* defensive measures, preparations for defence. **—ungs=bündnis,** *n.* defensive alliance. **—ungs=grund,** *m.* ground for defence, justificatory reason. **—ungs=los,** *adj.* defenceless. **—ungs=linie,** *f.* line of defence (*Fort.*). **—ungs=mittel,** *n.* means of defence; defence (*Law*). **—ungs=rede,** *f.* apology, speech (*in defence*). **—ungs=schrift,** *f.* apology, written defence. **—ungs=stand,** *m.; eine* **Festung in —ungsstand setzen,** to put a fortress in a state of defence, render it defensible. **—ungs=waffen,** *pl.* defensive weapons. **—ungs=weise,** I. *f.* method of defence. II. *adv.* by way of defence; on the defensive; **—ungsweise verfahren,** to act upon the defensive. **—ungs=werke,** *pl.* defensive works (*Fort.*). **—ungs=zustand,** *m.; see* **—ungsstand.**

Vertei'en, Verteu'en, *v.a.* to moor (*a boat*).

Verteil'bar, *adj.* distributable.

Vertei'l—en, I. *v.a.* to distribute, divide; to allot, apportion; to dispense; to assess (*the taxes*); to dispose, lay out, arrange; to distribute (*Paint.*); **milde Gaben unter die Armen —en,** to distribute money, to dispense charity among the poor; Steuern —en, to assess taxes; die Rollen —en, to assign *or* cast the parts (*Theat.*); ein Schauspiel mit —ten Rollen lesen, to read a play with the rôles assigned to different persons; die Geschwulst —t sich, the tumour dissolves *or* subsides. II. *subst.n.; see* —ung. —er, *m.* (—ers, *pl.* —er) divider, distributor. —ung, *f.* distribution; cast (*of the characters in a play*); apportionment; assessment (*of taxes*); revolution (*Med.*); division; —ung in die Quartiere, quartering (*of troops*).

Verteu'ern, *v.a.* to raise the price, make dearer.

Verteu'felt, *adj. see* Verflucht; devilish, deuced, infernal; confounded; enormous; marvellous; was für ein —es Geschäft! what a deuced business *or* confounded bother; ein —er Kerl, a devil of a fellow; einem — mitspielen, to play the devil with a person.

Vertbu'—er, *m.* (—ers, *pl.* —er) spendthrift, extravagant person. —erisch, —lich, *adj.* extravagant; prodigal. —n, *ir.v.* I. *a.* to spend foolishly, lavish, waste; to put away; to give away; to scatter. II. *n.* (*aux.* h.) to do one's duty.

Vertie'f—en, *v.* I. *a.* to deepen; to sink deeper; to sink; in Gedanken —t, lost *or* absorbed in thought; eine Schüssel —en, to hollow out a vessel. II. *r.* to become deeper; to deepen; sich in eine S. —en, to plunge into, give oneself up to a thing; sich in seine Gedanken —en, to bury oneself in one's own thoughts. —ung, *f.* deepening; depth; cavity, hollow.

Vertie'r—en, *v.* I. *n.* (*aux.* s.) to grow brutal. II. *a.* to brutalize; to animalize (*Physiol.*). —t, *adj.* brutish, bestial.

Vertika'l, *adj.* vertical.

Vertilg'bar, *adj.* exterminable, eradicable, destructible.

Vertil'g—en, *v.a.* to destroy; to extirpate; to exterminate; to efface, blot out; to finish off, polish off, consume (*sl.*). —er, *m.* (—ers, *pl.* —er), —erin, *f.* exterminator, destroyer. —ung, *f.* extermination, extirpation, destruction. *Comp.* —ungs=krieg, *m.* war of extermination, war to the knife.

Vertö'nen, *v.n.* (*aux.* s.) *see* Verklingen.

Vertra'ckt, *adj.* distorted, twisted, deformed; odd, strange; vexatious; cursed, confounded; —e Gebärden, odd movements, strange gestures.

Vertra'g, *m.* (—s, *pl.* Verträ'ge) accord, agreement; covenant, compact, stipulation, bargain; treaty, cartel; convention.

Vertra'g—en, *ir.v.* I. *a.* to carry away; to carry away and hide; to carry to a wrong place, misplace; to wear out; to digest; to bear, suffer, endure, tolerate, brook; to make peace between, reconcile; to settle (*disputes*); to conclude (*a treaty*); —et mich, daß ich auch rede, suffer me that I may speak (*B.*); —et einer den andern in der Liebe, forbearing one another in love (*B.*); diese Speise kann ich nicht —en, this food *or* dish does not agree with me; ich kann nicht viel Wein —en, I can't stand much wine; die Hitze —en, to bear the heat; er kann nicht viel —en, he can't stand much; he has little forbearance *or* endurance; das kann ich nicht —en, I can't stand that; this does not agree with me; mit dem Feinde —en, to treat with the enemy. II. *r.* to live, get on (*well or ill*) together; to agree; to be compatible *or* consistent; to suit; sich mit einem (wieder) —en, to come to an understanding with, to be reconciled to s.o.; sich mit einander —en, to agree, get on (*well*) with one another; sie —en sich wie Hund und Katze, they live a cat-and-dog life; Grün und Blau —en sich nicht, green and blue don't go well together; es verträgt sich mit meiner Pflicht nicht, it is incompatible with my duty. *Comp.* —s=artikel, *m.* article *or* term of agreement. —s=bruch, *m.* breach of a contract. —s=brüchig, *adj.* defaulting (in a contract). —schließend, *adj.*; —schließende Teile, contracting parties. —s=mäßig, *adj.* according to (an) agreement, (as) stipulated. —s=mäßigkeit, *f.* conformity with the agreement. —s=recht, *n.* right of concluding a treaty; right accorded by a treaty. —s=widrig, *adj.* contrary to the terms of an agreement *or* to the provisions of a treaty.

Verträg'lich, *adj.* conciliatory; friendly; peaceable; good-natured; tractable; accommodating; compatible, consistent. —keit, *f.* sociableness; easy temper; conciliatory spirit; tractableness; compatibility.

Verträl'lern, *v.a.* to hum away (*care, etc.*); to pass (*time, etc.*) in humming.

Vertrau'—en, I. *v.a.* to confide, entrust; einem etwas —en, to entrust, confide something to a p. *or* to a p.'s care; sich einem —en, to open one's heart *or* unbosom o.s. to a person. II. *v.n.* (*aux.* h.) (einem, auf einen *or* etwas) to trust *or* confide in, to rely upon; —e mir, trust me. III. *subst.n.* confidence, trust; reliance; —en auf einen *or* zu einem haben, to trust, rely on, have faith in a p.; sein —en auf einen setzen, einem sein —en schenken, to trust, to bestow one's confidence on a person; etwas im —en sagen, to say something in confidence; im —en gesagt, between ourselves; im —en auf deine Güte, relying on *or* trusting to your kindness. —lich, *adj. & adv. see* —ensvoll; familiar; intimate; confidential; mit einer Sache —lich werden, to familiarize o.s. with a th.; er thut sehr —lich, he is rather familiar, is very much at home; auf einem sehr —lichen Fuß mit einem leben, —lich mit einem umgehen, to be on very familiar terms *or* on terms of great intimacy with a p.; —licher Stil, familiar style; —liche Mitteilung, confidential communication; —lich! private and confidential (*on a letter*); —liche Sitzung, private meeting. —lichkeit, *f.* intimacy; familiarity; confidence; sich (*dat.*) gewisse —lichkeiten herausnehmen, to allow oneself certain liberties *or* familiarities. —t, *p.p. & adj.* intimate; familiar; *see* —ensvoll; mit einem —t sein, auf —tem Fuße mit einem stehen, to be very familiar, to be on terms of intimacy with a p.; mit einer S. wohl —t sein, to be well acquainted *or* fully conversant with a th., to be well versed in s.th.; sich mit etwas —t machen, to make oneself (thoroughly) familiar with a thing; —ter Freund, trusty friend, confidential, intimate friend, chum (*coll.*). —te(r), *m.* intimate friend; confidant. —theit, *f.* intimacy, familiarity; thorough knowledge of *or* acquaintance with. *Comp.* —ens=amt, *n.*, —ens=posten, *m.* confidential post, trust. —ens=bruch, *m.* breach of confidence; grober —ensbruch, gross breach of confidence. —ens=selig, —ens=voll, *adj.* full of confidence, confident. —ens=seligkeit, *f.* blind confidence. —ens=würdig, *adj.* worthy of confidence.

Vertrau'ern, *v.a.* to pass (*one's life, etc.*) in mourning; sich —, to pine away.

Verträu'men, *v.a.* to pass (*time*) in dreaming; to dream away; sein Glück —, to miss one's opportunity by dreaming; verträumte Augen, eyes lost in reverie, dreamy eyes.

Vertrei'b—en, *ir.v.a.* to drive away, expel; to disperse; to dislodge, turn out; to make pass; to soften, shade down; to kill, beguile (*time*); to retail; einen aus dem Lande —en, to banish, exile a p.; einen aus seinem Besitze —en, to dispossess s.o.; einen aus seiner Wohnung —en, to eject a p., turn a p. out of house and home: Gewalt mit Gewalt —en, to repel force by force; **der Wind —t die Wolken,** the wind disperses the clouds; **die Furcht hat ihn vertrieben,** fear has driven him away; **eine Krankheit —en,** to cure a disease; **sich** (*dat.*) **die Zeit —en,** to amuse, divert oneself, to beguile the time; **einem den Rausch —en,** to sober a p.; **einem den Kitzel —en,** to knock the nonsense out of a p.'s head; **die Farben —en,** to blend, sweeten, soften the colours; **die Umrisse —en,** to soften, round off the outlines; **Waren —en,** to sell, dispose of wares. **—ung,** *f.* expulsion; banishment; dispersion; dispossession; eviction; cure (*Med.*); selling, disposing of; softening (*Paint.*). *Comp.* — **bürste,** *f.* softening-brush. **—pinsel,** *m.* pencil *or* brush for blending the colours (*Paint.*).

Vertre't—en, *ir.v.a.* to injure by treading on, over *or* down; to tread out (*traces*); to bar, obstruct by stepping in the way; to stop; to supply the place of another, stand in his stead, to represent (*a person; a district, in parliament, etc.*); to appear for *or* plead for a person; **sich** (*dat.*) **den Fuß —en, sich** (*acc.*) **—en,** to sprain one's foot; **sich** (*dat.*) **die Beine —en,** to stretch one's legs (*by walking*); **einem den Weg —en,** to stand in a p.'s way, to stop s.o.; **einen —en, jemandes Stelle —en,** to supply a p.'s place, to act as a p.'s substitute; **auf dem Markte nicht —en sein,** to have no representative, not to be represented at the fair; **er vertritt den Staat nach außen,** he represents the state in foreign affairs, in its relations with foreign countries; **einen bei einem —en,** to intercede with s.o. for s.o., to defend a p.; **jemandes Sache vor dem Richter —en,** to plead a p.'s cause before a judge; **die Kinderschuhe —en haben,** to have left off childish ways; **jemandes Interesse —en,** to look after a person's interests. **—er,** *m.* (**—ers,** *pl.* **—er**) representative, substitute, proxy; deputy; intercessor; advocate; champion; agent. — **er=schaft,** *f.* representative body; advocacy, defence. **—ung,** *f.* treading down; representation, acting for; intercession; advocacy, defence; sprain; **die —ung des beurlaubten M. übernimmt Herr N.,** Mr. N. will undertake duty for *or* act as substitute for Mr. M. now on leave (*of absence*); **Schauspieler in —ung des Hauptdarstellers,** understudy; **in —ung des . . .,** representing . . . *Comp.* **—ungs=körper,** *m.* representative body. **—ungs=kosten,** *pl.* expenses of representation *or* of supplying the place of another. **—ungs=recht,** *n.* right of representation *or* of being represented.

Vertrie'b, *m.* (**—s**) sale, market; **der — dieser Ware ging stark,** this article had a brisk sale.

Vertrie'ben, *p.p. of* **vertreiben. —e(r),** *m.* one driven out, banished person, exile.

Vertrin'ken, *v.a.* to spend in drinking.

Vertrock'nen, *v.n.* (*aux.* **s.**) to dry up; to be parched; to wither.

Vertrö'deln, *v.a.* to idle away, waste (*one's time*); to hawk about; to sell to dealers.

Vertrö'st—en, *v.a.* to console, appease; to feed with hope, give fair words, put off; **einen auf eine S. —en,** to console a p. (*for present misfortune*) by holding out hopes for the future; **seine Gläubiger von einem Tage auf den andern —en,** to put off one's creditors from day to day. **—ung,** *f.* holding out hopes; vain promise.

Vertrum'pfen, *v.a.*; **alle seine Trümpfe —,** to play out all one's trumps.

[1]**Vertu'schen, Vertu'scheln,** *v.a.* to hide *or* conceal s.th., to keep s.th. secret *or* quiet; to hush s.th. up; to stifle *or* smother.

[2]**Vertu'schen,** *v.a.* to wash (a drawing) with Indian ink.

Verü'beln, *v.a.* to take amiss; **einem etwas —,** to blame s.o. for a thing.

Verü'b—en, *v.a.* to commit, perpetrate. **—er,** *m.* (**—ers,** *pl.* **—er**) perpetrator, author. — **ung,** *f.* perpetration; commission (*of a crime*).

Verun'ähnlichen, *v.a.* to make unlike.

Verun'edeln, *v.a.* to degrade, debase; **sich —,** to deteriorate; to become poor (*Min.*).

Verun'ehren, *v.a.* to dishonour, disgrace; to profane.

Verun'einigen, *v.a.* to disunite, set at variance; **sich —,** to fall out, to quarrel.

Verun'glimpf—en, *v.a.* to bring into discredit, defame, cast a blot upon; to disparage; to slander, blacken, calumniate, traduce, libel, revile. **—ung,** *f.* defamation, disparagement, calumny.

Verun'glück—en, *v.n.* (*aux.* **s.**) to meet with an accident *or* misfortune; to perish (*through an accident*); to suffer shipwreck; to fail, miscarry, come to grief; **er —te beim Radeln,** he was killed through a cycling accident; **das Schiff ist —t,** the vessel has been lost; **der Plan —te,** the scheme failed; **der —te,** the victim, unfortunate person; **die —ten,** the victims of the disaster, the killed and wounded. **—ung,** *f.* failure, miscarriage; non-success; casualty, (*fatal*) accident; loss through an accident.

Verun'reinigen, *v.a.* to dirty; to defile, pollute; to taint; to infect (*the air*); to profane (*a temple*); **dieser Ort darf nicht verunreinigt werden,** commit no nuisance.

Verun'stalt—en, *v.a.* to disfigure, deform; to make ugly; **—et,** misshapen, deformed, ugly. **—ung,** *f.* deformity; ugliness.

Verun'treu—en, *v.a.* to embezzle, to defraud; **Gelder —en,** to embezzle money, to defalcate. **—er,** *m.* (**—ers,** *pl.* **—er**) embezzler, fraudulent person; thief. **—ung,** *f.* breach of trust; embezzlement, fraud; **—ung öffentlicher Gelder,** defalcation *or* embezzlement of public money.

Verun'zieren, *v.a.* to disfigure, deface, spoil, mar.

Verur'sach—en, *v.a.* to cause, occasion, bring about, produce; to provoke; to give rise to. **—er,** *m.* (**—ers,** *pl.* **—er**) author. **—ung,** *f.* causing, causation; cause, occasion.

Verur'teil—en, *v.a.* to condemn, sentence; **gerichtlich —ter Mensch,** condemned person; **einen zum Tode —en,** to sentence a p. to death; **einen zu einer Geldstrafe von 20 Mark —en,** to fine a p. twenty shillings. — **te(r),** *m.* condemned person. **—ung,** *f.* condemnation, doom, sentence.

Verviel'—fachen, —fältigen, *v.a.* to multiply; to reproduce; to diversify. **—fältiger,** *m.* (**—fältigers,** *pl.* **—fältiger**) multiplier. **—fachung, —fältigung,** *f.* multiplication; reproduction.

Vervier'fachen, *v.a.* to quadruple; **sich —,** to increase *or* multiply fourfold.

Vervoll'komm=n—en, *v.a.* to perfect. **—er,** *m.* (**—ers,** *pl.* **—er**) perfecter. **—ung,** *f.* perfecting; perfection; completion. *Comp.* — **ungs=fähig,** *adj.* capable of being perfected; perfectible. **—ungs=patent,** *n.* patent for improvement.

Vervoll'ständigen, *v.a.* to complete; to make up the full number; **das Lager wieder —,** to replenish the stock.

Verwa'chen, *v.a.* to pass (*nights*) in watching.

Verwach's—en, *ir.v.* I. *a.* to outgrow, grow out of; to lose in growing; **er hat seine Narbe ganz —en,** his scar has quite disappeared; **sich —en,** to lose (*in symmetry, appearance, etc.*), to deteriorate in growing, to grow too fast. II. *n.* (*aux.* **s.**) to be overgrown, grown over (*with*); to close, heal up; to fill up, disappear (*as a scar*); to join in growing, grow together; to interlace, entwine; to grow crooked, deformed; to grow too fast; **die Wunde verwächst,** the wound is healing up. **—enheit,** *f.* (**—en=hei**

n.) adhesion, cohesion, growing together; deformity. —ung, *f.* cicatrization; interlacing; defective growth; deformity.

Verwä'gen, *v.* I. *a.* to weigh out. II. *r.* to make a mistake in weighing; **sich einer Sache —**, to dare, to have the effrontery to (*rare*); to give up (*obs.*).

Verwa'hr—en, *v.a.* to guard, secure; to keep, preserve; to put in a place of safety; **vor** *or* **gegen etwas —en**, to guard, preserve from, to secure against; **einem Geld zu —en geben**, to entrust money to a p.'s care; **gut —t**, well preserved, well kept, carefully packed; **sich gegen eine S. —en**, to take precautions against a th., to secure oneself against a th.; to protest (*against*); **sich gegen die rauhe Witterung** *or* **vor der Kälte —en**, to provide against the inclement weather, to protect oneself from the cold; **sich** *or* **sein Recht —en**, to reserve to o.s. one's rights, to protest; **den Tempel mit Schlössern und Riegeln —en**, to furnish the temple with locks and bolts. **—er**, *m.* (**—ers**, *pl.* **—er**) keeper; guardian, trustee; depositary. **—lich**, *adj.* that may be kept safe; **—lich niederlegen**, to deposit, lodge in trust (**bei einem**, with s.o.), commit to (*a p.'s*) care. **—ung**, *f.* guarding, keeping; guard, care, custody; preservation; protest (*Law*); reservation; depot; **einen in —ung nehmen**, to take a p. into custody, put s.o. in prison; **—ung gegen eine S. einlegen**, to protest, enter a protest against a th.; **einem etwas in —ung geben**, to give a th. into s.o.'s care, trust s.th. to a p.; **ein Mittel zur —ung gegen . . .**, a preservative against . . .; **in —ung liegen**, to be deposited. *Comp.* **—losen**, *v.a.* to neglect; to spoil by neglect. **—losung**, *f.* neglect, negligence; injury caused by neglect. **—ungs=gebäude**, *n.* repository, warehouse. **—(ungs)=geld**, *n.* deposit (*of money*); security for costs (*Law*). **—haft**, *f.* detention, custody (*dial.*). **—ungs=mittel**, *n.* preservative; protest (*Law*). **—ungs=ort**, *m.* place where things are kept, dépôt. **—ungs=kontrakt**, *m.* deposit-contract.

Verwai'f—en, *v.* I. *a.* to make an orphan; to orphan. II. *n.* (*aux.* **f.**) to become an orphan, to lose one's parent(s); to be deserted, abandoned. **—t**, *pp. & adj.* orphan(ed); fatherless, motherless, bereft of one's parents; deserted; destitute; **doppelt —t**, fatherless and motherless; **Das —te Dorf**, The Deserted Village. **—ung**, *f.* orphaned state.

Verwal't—en, *v.a.* to administer, manage, conduct, superintend; to govern, rule; to fill, hold, discharge the duties of (*an office*); **für einen —en**, to hold in trust for, to manage for; **übel —en**, to mismanage, misgovern; **die Regierung —en**, to hold the reins of government. **—er**, *m.* (**—ers**, *pl.* **—er**) administrator; manager, director, steward; superintendent; trustee; curator. **—erin**, *f.* administratrix, female manager, stewardess; steward's *or* manager's wife. **—ung**, *f.* administration; management; stewardship; government; exercise (*of an office*); trusteeship; **Treue in der —ung paarte sich mit Weisheit in der Verfassung**, faithfulness in the administration was joined with prudence in the government. *Comp.* (**—ungs=** *is often to be rendered by* '*administrative*'). **—ungs=abteilung**, *f.* administrative department. **—ungs=amt**, *n.* managership; post in the administrative department. **—ungs=ausschuß**, *m.* committee of management, executive committee. **—ungs=beamte(r)**, *m.* official employed in the administration; magistrate. **—ungs=behörde**, *f.* board of directors, board of management; government-board. **—ungs=bezirk**, *m.* administrative district, jurisdiction. **—ungs=dienst**, *m.* public service. **—ungs=fach**, *n.* department *or* branch of the administration. **—ungs=kosten**, *pl.* expenses of administration *or* management. **—ungs=maßregel**, *f.* administrative measure. **—ungs=rat**, *m.* board *or* committee of management, working *or* executive committee (*in joint-stock companies*); managing director, trustee. **—ungs=recht**, *n.* administrative law. **—ungs=weg**, *m.*; **auf dem —ungswege**, administratively, through the administration. **—ungs=wesen**, *n.* administration. **—ungs=zweig**, *m.* department *or* branch of the administration.

Verwan'delbar, *adj.* transmutable, convertible. **—keit**, *f.* transmutability; convertibility.

Verwan'd—eln, *v.a.* to change; to transform, transmute, transfigure, metamorphose; to commute (*penalties, etc.*); to reduce (*Arith.*); to transmute (*metals*); **in einen Aschenhaufen —eln**, to reduce to (a heap of) ashes; **in Geld —eln**, to turn into money, realize; **in den Leib und das Blut Christi —eln**, to change into the body and blood of Christ; **sich —eln**, to change, alter, turn, to be converted. **—lung**, *f.* act of changing; alteration, change; conversion; transformation; metamorphosis; transsubstantiation; commutation (*of a punishment*); changing one figure *or* quantity into another equal to it (*Math.*); **—lung auf dem Theater**, shifting of scenes.

Verwa'ndt, *adj.* related, kin; allied; congenial; kindred (*of languages, etc.*); cognate; analogous, like; sympathetic; **er ist mit mir —**, he is a relative of mine; **wir sind nahe —**, we are near relations; **wie sind Sie mit ihm — ?** on which side *or* in what way are you related to him? **Malerei und Dichtkunst sind miteinander —**, painting and poetry are kindred arts; **er ist mir mit 10 Mark —**, he owes me 10 marks (*coll.*); **mit —er Hand**, with the back of the hand. **—e(r)**, *m.*, **—e**, **—in**, *f.* (male, female) relative; **der nächste —e**, the next of kin. **—schaft**, *f.* relationship; consanguinity; sympathy, congeniality; connection; affinity; relations (*coll.*); **—schaft von väterlicher Seite**, relationship on the father's side; **—schaft der Stämme und Sprachen**, affinity of race and language; **chemische —schaft**, chemical affinity; **—schaft von Begriffen**, affinity of ideas. **—schaftlich**, *adj.* kindred, allied; kinsman-like, as a relation; congenial. *Comp.* **—en=besuch**, *m.* visit from relatives. **—schafts=beziehung**, *f.* points of relationship. **—schafts=grad**, *m.* degree of relationship. **—schafts=kraft**, *f.* force of affinity (*Chem.*). **—sein**, *n.* relationship; affinity; sympathy.

Verwar'n—en, *v.a.* to warn. **—ung**, *f.* warning, caution, notice.

Verwa'schen, I. *v.a.* to use up in washing; to wash away *or* wash out (*stains, etc.*); to wear out *or* spoil through washing; to wash (*Paint.*). II. *p.p. & adj.* washed-out, faded; spoiled in washing; undecided, characterless, wishy-washy (*coll.*); vague, pale. **—heit**, *f.* paleness, indecision (*of colour*).

Verwäs'sern, *v.* I. *a.* to water too much; to spoil by watering; to dilute; to make vapid, insipid, *or* watery; **verwässerte Schreibart**, milk-and-water style. II. *n.* (*aux.* **f.**) to soak too long; to become weak *or* insipid.

Verwe'ben, *reg. & ir.v.a.* to consume in weaving; to weave up; to weave into, interweave, complicate; to cover with cobwebs; **Wahrheit mit Dichtung —**, to interweave truth with fiction.

Verwech'selbar, *adj.* changeable, convertible, interchangeable.

Verwech'sel—n, I. *v.a.* to change, exchange; to mistake, change by mistake, take one for another; **er —t stets die Namen**, he is always making mistakes about names; **wir haben un-**

ſere Hüte —t, we have exchanged hats; die Soll=und=Haben=Seite beim Eintragen —n, to enter on the wrong side of the ledger; Begriffe —n, to confound, confuse ideas; Geld —n, to change money. II. *subst.n.*, —ung, *f.* confusion (*of names*); exchange; mistake; permutation; ſie ſehen einander zum —n ähnlich, they are so much alike as to be mistaken for one another.

Verwe'gen, *adj.* bold, daring; rash, foolhardy; determined; forward; presumptuous; insolent; saucy. —heit, *f.* temerity; audacity; boldness; bold action.

Verwe'h—en, *v.* I. *a.* to blow *or* drive away; to blow about; ein Schiff —en, to blow a ship out of her course; der Wind hat den Weg mit Schnee —t, the wind has covered the path with snow. II. *n.* (*aux.* ſ.) to blow over; to be scattered; ſeine Hoffnungen ſind —t, his hopes are dead, are blighted.

Verweh'ren, *v.a.* (einem etwas) to hinder, prevent, restrain (a p. from doing a th.), to forbid.

Verwei'ch—en, I. *v.a.* to render too soft, steep too much. II. *v.n.* (*aux.* ſ.) to soak too long, to become too soft. —lichen, *v.a.* to render weak *or* effeminate, to enervate. —lichung, *f.* weakening; effeminacy.

Verwei'ger—n, *v.a.* (einem etwas) to refuse, deny (a th. to a p.). —ung, *f.* denial, refusal. *Comp.* —ungs=fall, *m.* case of denial; im —ungsfalle, if refused.

Verwei'len, *v.* I. *a.* to stop, delay; to keep back, to cause to stay, to detain (*obs.*). II. *n.* (*aux.* h.) to stay, tarry, stop; to sojourn; bei einem Gegenſtande —, to dwell upon a subject.

Verwei'nen, *v.a.* to pass (*time*) in weeping; to shed (*tears*), to weep, cry (*one's grief, etc.*) away; ſeine Augen —, to injure one's eyes with weeping; verweinte Augen, eyes swollen with crying, red with tears; verweintes Geſicht, tear-stained countenance.

Verwei's, *m.* (—(ſ)es, *pl.* —(ſ)e) reprimand, rebuke, censure; lecture, rating; einem wegen etwas einen — geben, to reprove, censure a p. for a th.; einen derben — geben, to give a sharp rebuke *or* a severe reprimand.

[1]**Verweiſ—en,** *ir.v.a.* to reprove, to rebuke, reprimand a p. (for s.th.), to reproach *or* upbraid a p. (with s.th.); einem etwas —en, to reprimand *or* censure a p. for s.th. —ung, *f.* censure, reproach, rebuke.

[2]**Verwei'ſ—en,** *v.a.* to refer to; to send to; to banish to; einen an einen —en, to refer s.o. to a person; einen aus dem Lande (des Landes) —en, to banish a p.; er iſt verwieſen worden, he has been expelled (*from school*) *or* exiled (*from his native country*); (einen) auf eine Inſel —en, to relegate to an island. —ung, *f.* reference (auf, to); return; banishment, exile; proscription; relegation (auf, to); wechſelſeitige —ung, cross-reference.

Verwel'ken, *v.n.* (*aux.* ſ.) to fade, wither, droop.

Verwel'ſchen, *v.a.* to Frenchify; to Italianize.

Verwelt'lich—en, *v.* I. *a.* to make worldly *or* frivolous; to secularize. II. *n.* (*aux.* ſ.) to become worldly. —ung, *f.* secularization.

Verwend'bar, *adj.* available (*for*), applicable (*to*), suitable (*for*). —keit, *f.* applicability; suitability.

Verwen'd—en, *reg. & ir.v.* I. *a.* to turn away *or* aside; to turn; to turn, reduce *or* convert into; to metamorphose; to apply to; to bestow upon; to employ in *or* for; er verwandte kein Auge von ihr, he never lifted his eyes from her face, he kept his eyes steadfastly fixed on her; viel Sorgfalt auf eine S. —en, to bestow much care upon a th.; etwas zu einem beſonderen Gebrauch —en, to assign a th. to a particular use; ſeine Zeit zu . . . —en, to employ one's time in . . .; die nötige Zeit auf eine S. —en, to give the time necessary to a th.; (etwas) zu ſeinem Nutzen —en, to apply to one's own profit; mit der —eten *or* verwandten Hand, with the back of the hand. II. *r.* to use one's influence on behalf of; ſich für einen bei einem —en, to intercede with s.o. on behalf of a p. —ung, *f.* use, application, employment, expenditure; converting; appropriation; intercession.

Verwer'f—en, *ir.v.* I. *a.* to make a mistake in throwing; to throw into a wrong place; to throw, cast away; to disperse, scatter about; to cast away (*B.*); to reject; to disallow, disavow; to condemn; to repudiate; to spurn, als parteiiſch —en, to challenge (*juries, etc.*); eine Klage —en, to dismiss a summons *or* bill; die Anklage wurde verworfen, the indictment was quashed; eine Einwendung als ungültig —en, to overrule an objection. II. *r.* to throw badly, make a mistake in throwing; to miss (the mark); to throw out wrongly, discard (*Cards*); to bowl wide; to warp (*of wood*). —lich, *adj.* that may be rejected; worthy of being rejected, objectionable; blamable, reprehensible; bad. —lichkeit, *f.* objectionableness. —ung, *f.* throwing *or* turning away; rejection; refusal; reprobation; condemnation; exception (*Law*); casting (*of the young by beasts*); dislocation (*of an arm*); fault, shift (*Min.*).

Verwer't—en, *v.a.* to convert into money, realize; to turn to good account, to make use of. —ung, *f.* realization; making profit by; ich habe keine —ung dafür, I cannot make any use of it, I cannot do anything with it.

Verwe'ſ—en, *v.* I. *n.* (*aux.* ſ.) to cease to exist, to perish; to decay, moulder, rot. II. *a.* to act as substitute for another; to administer, manage, conduct. —er, *m.* (—ers, *pl.* —er) administrator; manager; substitute; vicar; vicegerent. —(s)lich, *see* Verweslich. —ung, *f.* decomposition; putrefaction. *Comp.* —ungs=prozeß, *m.* (*process of*) putrefaction.

Verwes'lich, *adj.* corruptible, liable to decay. —keit, *f.* corruptibility, perishableness.

Verwet'ten, *v.a.* to bet, stake; to lose by betting.

Verwet'ter—n, *v.a.*; *see* Verfluchen. —t, *p.p. & adj.* destroyed by the weather, weather-beaten, tanned; blasted; damned, confounded.

Verwi'chen, *p.p. of* (*obs.*) verweichen; *adj.* past, late; —e Zeiten, former times; —es Jahr, last year.

Verwich'ſen, *v.a.* to stop up with wax; to use in waxing *or* blacking; to thrash soundly (*sl.*).

Verwi'ckel—n, *v.a.* to entangle, implicate; to complicate; to involve; to embarrass, perplex; ſich in (einer S. *or*) eine S. —n, to get entangled in, to engage, embark in, to be concerned in; ſich in ſeinen eigenen Worten —n, to get involved in one's own words *or* utterances. —ung, *f.* entangling; entanglement; tangle; complication; intricacy; plot (*of a play*); embarrassment.

Verwie'ſen, *p.p. of* verweiſen. —e(r), *m.* exile; outlaw.

Verwil'der—n, *v.r. & n.* (*aux.* ſ.) to grow wild *or* savage *or* intractable; to become depraved *or* brutalized; to run wild; to fall out of cultivation (*fields*); —n laſſen, to let run to waste, to neglect the culture *or* education of. —t, *p.p. & adj.* wild; savage; unruly. —ung, *f.* return to a wild *or* savage state, want of culture; wildness; barbarism; brutalization; wilderness.

Verwil'ligen, *v.a.* to allow, grant.

Verwin'den, *ir.v.a.* to intertwine, interlace; to overcome, get the better of; to get over, recover from; er wird es nie —, he will never get over it.

Verwir'k—en, *v.a.* to forfeit, lose (*through wrong-doing*); to merit, incur (*a punishment*); to commit (*a crime*); to work, use up, consume; to knead up; ein Vasall —t sein Leben, a vassal forfeits his fief. —ung, *f.* loss, forfeiture.

Verwirk'lich—en, *v.* I. *a.* to realize. II. *r.* to be realized, to come true. —ung, *f.* realization.

Verwir'r—en, *ir.v.a.* to entangle (*thread, etc.*); to put into disorder; to complicate; to make intricate; involve; to embarrass, confuse, disconcert; to bewilder, perplex; to embroil; to trouble; einem die Frisur —en, to tumble, disarrange a p.'s hair; einen —t machen, to embarrass, bewilder a p., to put a p. out; einem den Kopf —en, to make one quite confused; durch den Versuch die Sachen zu ordnen, hat er sie nur noch mehr —t, in trying to arrange matters, he has only complicated them still more; —te Blicke, wild looks. —ung, *f.* entanglement; confusion, disorder; complication; perplexity; derangement, craziness; in —ung bringen (geraten), to throw (*get*) into disorder.

Verwirt'schaft—en, *v.a.* to waste *or* lose (*by bad management*), dissipate. —ung, *f.* dissipation (*of one's property*).

Verwisch'bar, *adj.* effaceable, easily wiped out.

Verwi'sch—en, *v.a.* to wipe away, efface, blot out, obliterate; to rumple, disarrange; to stump, soften (*a drawing*); sich —en, to become effaced, to be lost. —ung, *f.* effacement.

Verwit'ter—n, *v.* I. *n.* (*aux.* s.) to decompose, to become disintegrated; to become dilapidated; to be weatherbeaten; to effloresce (*Chem.*); —ter Kalk, air-slacked lime; im Wasser —t, water-worn. II. *a.* to decompose. —ung, *f.* decomposition, disintegration; efflorescence (*Chem.*); weathering (*Geol.*).

Verwitt'w—en, *v.* I. *a.* to widow. II. *n.* (*aux.* s.) to become a widow(er). —et, *p.p. & adj.* widowed; die —ete Königin, the queen-dowager, the widowed queen; die —ete Lady C., the dowager Lady C.; die —ete Frau Brown, the widow of the late Mr. Brown. —ung, *f.* loss of one's husband *or* wife, widowhood; seit ihrer —ung, since she became a widow.

Verwo'gen, I. *v.n.* (*aux.* s.) to cease to sound; to flow away. II. *p.p. & adj.* desperate; foolhardy.

Verwoh'nen, *v.a.* to spoil (*a room*) by living in it.

Verwöh'n—en, *v.a.* to spoil (*a child*); to pamper (*the appetite, etc.*); sich —en, to contract luxurious habits, over-indulge o.s., to get spoilt. —theit, *f.* bad habits, spoiled condition. —ung, *f. see* —theit; pampering, spoiling; die —ung der Kinder ist gefährlich, it is dangerous to indulge children; —ung im Essen, fastidiousness as to food.

Verwor'fen, *p.p. & adj. see* Verwerfen; depraved, vile, infamous; reprobate (*Theol.*). —heit, *f.* depravity, vileness; infamy; reprobation.

Verwor'ren, *p.p. & adj. see* Verwirren; confused; intricate; der —e Bericht eines verwirrten Menschen, the confused account of a bewildered person. —heit, *f.* entanglement, confusion, muddled state, disorder (*of ideas*).

Verwund'bar, *adj.* vulnerable; soft, delicate; —e Stelle, weak point, sore spot. —keit, *f.* vulnerability.

Verwun'd—en, *v.a.* to wound, to hurt; to cut; auf das Schmerzlichste —en, to wound to the quick. —et, *p.p.* wounded, hit; leicht, schwer, gefährlich —et, slightly, severely, dangerously wounded. —ung, *f.* wound; wounding; being wounded; tötliche —ung, mortal wound.

Verwun'der—lich, *adj.* astonishing, wonderful, strange.

Verwun'der—n, I. *v.a.* to surprise, astonish; sich —n, to be astonished, to wonder; er —te sich, mich dort zu sehen, he was surprised to see me there; es —t mich, I wonder; sich —t stellen, to feign *or* affect surprise. II. *subst. n.*, —ung, *f.* astonishment, surprise; das ist zum —n, that is remarkable; in die höchste —ung setzen, to throw into the greatest astonishment. *Comp.* —ungs-ausruf, *m.* exclamation of surprise. —ungs-brille, *f.*; die —ungsbrille aufsetzen, to affect astonishment (*coll.*). —ungs-stuhl, *m.* stool of repentance (*game*). —ungs-voll, *adj.* full of astonishment. —ungs-zeichen, *n.* note of admiration.

Verwün'sch—en, *v.a.* (*p.p. sometimes* verwunschen; der —ene Prinz, the enchanted prince) to wish ill to, to curse, execrate; to bewitch, enchant, cast a spell on. —t, *p.p. &* I. *adj.* cursed, confounded; damned; execrable; das —te Geld, that confounded money; —ter Spaß, abominable joke; —t gescheit, awfully clever. II. *int.* —t! confound it! —ung, *f.* enchantment; spell; curse, malediction; —ungen gegen einen ausstoßen, to curse a p., hurl imprecations at a person.

Verwür'zen, *v.a.* to season, spice too much; to make unsavoury *or* insipid; to spoil.

Verwü'st—en, *v.a. see* Verheeren. —er, *m.* (—ers, *pl.* —er) destroyer, devastator.

Verza'g—en, I. *v.n.* (*aux.* s.) to despond, despair (an einer S., of a th.); to lose courage; uns ist bange, aber wir —en nicht, we are perplexed but not in despair. II. *subst.n.* despair, despondency (*B.*). —t, *p.p. & adj.* discouraged, despondent, dejected; disheartened; fearful, hopeless; pusillanimous; —t machen, to dishearten, discourage; —t werden, to despond, to lose courage. —theit, *f.* despair, despondency; pusillanimity; fearfulness; cowardice.

Verzäh'l—en, *v.r.* to make a mistake in counting. —ung, *f.* error in counting.

Verzah'n—en, *v.a.* to tooth, cog (*a wheel, etc.*); to indent, notch, jag; sich in einander —en, to lock *or* work into each other, to dovetail; —te Balken, joggle pieces. —ung, *f.* indentation, notch, jag; joggling; dovetailing; toothwork.

Verzap'f—en, *v.a.* to sell (*beer, etc.*) on draught; to join by a mortise and tenon; to give out (*sl.*); es wird nichts (mehr) —t, no use, you will get nothing (*sl.*). —ung, *f.* retailing on draught; mortise and tenon joint *or* joining.

Verzap'peln, *v.r. & n.* (*aux.* s.) to struggle; to be exhausted with struggling; einen — lassen, to let s.o. perish *or* despair.

Verzär'tel—n, *v.a.* to spoil by over-tenderness; to coddle, pamper; —t, pampered, spoilt. —ung, *f.* over-indulgence; pampering; effeminacy.

Verzau'ber—n, *v.a.* to charm, bewitch, enchant; —ter Prinz, enchanted prince. —ung, *f.* enchantment.

Verzäu'nen, *v.a.* to surround with a fence *or* hedge, to fence in.

Verze'chen, *v.a.* to spend in drinking.

Verzehn'fachen, *v.a.* to increase ten-fold.

Verzeh'rbar, *adj.* eatable, edible; consumable.

Verzeh'r—en, *v.a.* to consume, eat up; to consume, absorb; to waste; to spend, expend (*money*); was habe ich —? what have I to pay, what does my bill come to? sich —en, to be consumed (vor, with), to fret, waste away; —end, consumptive. —er, *m.* (—ers, *pl.* —er) consumer. —ung, *f.* consumption (*also Med.*); absorption.

Verzeich'n—en, *v.a.* to draw wrong *or* badly; to sketch, trace out; to note down, record, register; to mark, specify; to take an inventory of; sich —en, to make a mistake in drawing; zu dem —eten Kurs, at the price quoted (*C. L.*). —is, *n.* (—isses, *pl.* —isse) list; statement; catalogue; specification; inventory; index, register; bill; invoice; price-list; —is von

Soldaten, muster-roll; **—is der Einkünfte**, rent-roll; **—is der Druckfehler**, list of errata *or* printer's errors; **—is des Inhalts**, table of contents; **—is der Anmerkungen**, index of notes; **—is der Verstorbenen**, obituary; **—is der vom Papst verbotenen Bücher**, (expurgatory) index. **—ung**, *f.* error in drawing; incorrect drawing; drawing, sketch; memorandum, note; specification; abstract.

Verzei'h—en, *ir.v.a.* (**einem etwas**) to forgive, pardon; to excuse; to remit (*sins*); to pass over (*a fault*); **—en Sie!** excuse me! pardon me! I beg your pardon! **es ist zu —en**, it is excusable; **es soll dir diesmal noch verziehen werden**, you shall be forgiven this time. **—lich**, *adj.* pardonable; excusable; venial. **—lichkeit**, *f.* pardonableness. excusableness; veniality. **—ung**, *f.* pardon, remission (*of sins*); **einen um —ung bitten**, to beg a p.'s pardon; **um —ung!** I beg your pardon! excuse me! please forgive me.

Verzer'r—en, *v.a.* to distort, twist, pull out of shape; to pull out, fray (*cloth*); **sich —en**, to make a grimace, roll one's eyes, distort the countenance; **den Mund —en**, to make a wry mouth. **—ung**, *f.* distortion, twisting; contortion, grimace; fraying out (*of cloth*).

Verzet'teln, *v.a.* to spill; to scatter, disperse; to crumble; to waste, squander; to mislay.

Verzi'cht, *m.* (—(e)s) renunciation, resignation, act of disclaiming; **auf eine S. — leisten** *or* **thun**, *see* **verzichten**. *Comp.* **—brief**, *m.* act *or* deed of renunciation. **—leistung**, *f.* renunciation.

Verzich'ten, *v.n.* (*aux.* **h.**) (**auf eine S.**) to renounce, resign, to give up all claim to, to desist from, to forego (a thing).

Verzie'h—en, *ir.v.* I. *a.* to draw wrong; to distort, twist (up); to warp; to train badly, spoil (*children*); to put off, delay; to prolong; **den Mund —en**, to make a wry mouth; **den Mund zum Lachen —en**, to force a smile *or* laugh; **er verzog keine Miene**, he did not move a muscle; **verzogener Name**, initials (*obs. for* **Namenszug**); **Gicht hat seine Glieder verzogen**, gout has twisted his limbs; **sich** (*dat.*) **eine Sehne —en**, to strain a sinew; **einen Stein** (*or* **sich**) **—en**, to move the wrong piece, make a false move (*in draughts, etc.*); **eine Grube —en**, to measure a mine. II. *r.* to draw away; to withdraw; to disperse, be dispersed; to pass away; to disappear; to subside, be lost gradually; to warp; to be twisted; to hang badly, to pucker, to drag (*of dresses, etc.*); to drag on, be protracted; **das Gewitter —t sich**, the storm is passing over. III. *r. & n.* (*aux.* **s.**) to move, remove; **in die Stadt —en**, to move into town; **Herr Herford ist von A. nach M. verzogen**, Mr. Herford has removed from A. to M. IV. *n.* (*aux.* **h.**) to delay, tarry (*obs.*). **—ung**, *f.* distortion, contortion; spoiling, bad bringing up (*of children*); change of residence; subsiding, scattering (*of a tumour*); delay.

Verzie'r—en, *v.a.* to adorn, ornament, decorate; to embellish; to trim; to over-charge with ornament; **ein Buch mit Kupfern —en**, to illustrate a book; **—ter Kontrapunkt**, figurate counterpoint. **—er**, *m.* (—ers, *pl.* —er) decorator; trimmer; adorner. **—ung**, *f.* decoration, ornamentation; ornament, embellishment; illustration; trimming; (*pl.*) decoration; **sämmtliche —ungen an einem Bauwerke**, decoration of a building; **musikalische —ungen**, flourishes, variations, grace-notes.

Verzim'mern, *v.a.* to fit up, furnish with timberwork; to line (*a mine*) with timberwork; to refit, repair (*a ship*).

Verzin'ken, *v.a.* to zinc.

Verzin'n—en, *v.a.* to tin; to blanch (*pins, etc.*); **—tes Eisenblech**, tin plate, tinned sheet-iron. **—er**, *m.* (—ers, *pl.* —er) tinker, tin-man. **—ung**, *f.* tinning. *Comp.* **—kolben**, *m.* soldering iron. **—stoff**, *m.* melted zinc.

Verzin's—en, *v.a.* to pay interest on *or* for s.th.; **eine Summe zu 3 % —en**, to pay (an interest of) 3 per cent. on a sum; **sich —en**, to yield interest; **es —t sich nicht**, it yields no interest, it does not pay; **das Kapital —t sich zu 3 %**, the capital yields *or* bears an interest of 3 per cent. **—(s)lich**, *adj.* bearing interest; **—(s)lich austhun** *or* **anlegen**, to put out at interest, to invest; **—sliches Darlehen**, loan on interest; **—slich vom ersten Oktober**, interest (to be) paid from October 1. **—ung**, *f.* (yielding) interest; payment of interest; **zur —ung ausleihen**, to put out at interest.

Verzö'ger—n, *v.* I. *a.* to delay, defer, retard; to procrastinate; to protract, lengthen, spin out. II. *r.* to delay, to be protracted. **—ung**, *f.* delay; adjournment; retardation.

Verzoll'bar, *adj.* liable to duty, excisable.

Verzol'l—en, *v.a.* to pay toll *or* duty on; **—t**, duty paid; **haben Sie etwas zu —en?** have you anything to declare? **Waren —en**, to clear goods at the custom-house. **—ung**, *f.* payment of duty *or* toll, clearance of goods.

Verzot'teln, *v.a.* to disarrange; to scatter.

Verzu'ck—en, *v.a.* to contract, draw, pull; to convulse. **—ung**, *f.* convulsion.

Verzü'ck—en, *v.a.* to fill with rapture *or* enthusiasm, to ravish. **—t**, *p.p. & adj.* enraptured, rapt, ravished, in raptures, in transports, in ecstasy. **—ung**, *f.* ecstasy, rapture; transport; trance.

Verzu'g, *m.* (—s, *pl.* **Verzü'ge**) delay; postponement; darling, spoilt child; **es ist Gefahr im —e**, there is danger in delay; **ohne —**, forthwith; **der Junge ist unser kleiner —**, the boy is our pet. *Comp.* **—s-zinsen**, *pl.* interest for delay, penal interest.

Verzup'fen, *v.a.* to pluck, ravel out (*for lint*).

Verzwei'f—eln, I. *v.n.* (*aux.* **h.** & **s.**) to despair (**an einer S.**, of a th.); to despair, despond; **eine —elte Geschichte**, a desperate story; a dreadful, hopeless story; a dreadful business (*coll.*). II. *subst.n.*, **—(e)-lung**, *f.* despair; **es ist zum —eln**, it is enough to drive one to despair; **einen in** *or* **zur —(e)lung bringen**, to reduce a p. to despair; **in —(e)lung geraten**, to (sink into) despair. *Comp.* **—lungs-wut**, *f.* desperation, rage of despair. **—lungs-voll**, *adj.* despairing; desperate.

Verzwei'g—en, *v.r.* to branch out. **—ung**, *f.* ramification; derivation (*Phys.*). **—ungs-punkt**, *m.* branch point.

Verzwer'gen, *v.n.* (*aux.* **s.**) to become dwarfed; to grow stunted; **verzwergt**, dwarfish; stunted.

Verzwi'ck—en, *v.a.* to pinch, nip off; to wrench; to entangle, confuse; to clench, rivet; to fill up with rubble, packing, *etc.* (*Mas.*); **den Weinstock —en**, to prune the vine. **—t**, *p.p. & adj.* nipped, clipped; queer, odd; whimsical; puzzling, confused; awkward; intricate, difficult. **—theit**, *f.* oddness; difficulty.

Ves'per, *f.* (*pl.* —n) evening; vespers; light afternoon meal, high tea; **zur —essen**, *see* **—n**; **sizilianische —**, Sicilian Vespers (*March 30, 1282*); **die — schlägt**, the evening bell sounds (*signal for leaving off work*). *Comp.* **—brot**, *n.* light afternoon meal. **—gesang**, *m.* even-song. **—glocke**, *f.*, **—läuten**, *n.* vesper-bell. **—predigt**, *f.* afternoon sermon. **—stunde**, **—zeit**, *f.* evening-time, afternoon; hour for vespers.

Ves'pern, *v.n.* (*aux.* **s.**) to have a light afternoon meal, to take afternoon-tea *or* high-tea.

Vest (*see* **Fest**); **die —e**, stronghold (*esp'lly of natural defences or a natural fortress*); castle; firmament (*B.*).

Vesta'lin, *f.* (*pl.* **—nen**) vestal (virgin).

Vetera'n, *m.* (**—en,** *pl.* **—en**) veteran (soldier). **—enschaft,** *f.* condition of a veteran; veterans (*coll.*).

Veterinä'r, I. *m.* (**—s,** *pl.* **—s, —e**) veterinary surgeon. II. *adj.* veterinary.

Ve'to, *n.* (**—s,** *pl.* **—s**) veto; **aufschiebendes —,** suspensive veto; **gegen eine S. sein — einlegen,** to veto a th., to protest against a th.; **gegen diese Beschlüsse wurde von einer starken Mehrheit ein — eingelegt,** these proposals were vetoed *or* negatived by a large majority.

Vet'tel, *f.* (*pl.* **—n**) slut, dirty creature; **alte —,** old hag; **liederliche —,** jade.

Vet'ter, *m.* (**—s,** *pl.* **—n**) male cousin. **—lich,** *adj.* cousinly, cousinlike. **—n,** *v.a.* to treat as a cousin; **sich —n, einander —n,** to call one another cousin. **—schaft,** *f.* cousinship; cousins (*coll.*). *Comp.* **—(n)=gunst,** *f.* nepotism, favour shown to relations.

Vexie'r, *n.* (**—s,** *pl.* **—e**) catch, surprise, puzzle. **—en,** *v.a.* to vex, tease; to quiz, banter; to puzzle, mystify; to catch, hoax, take in. **—erei',** *see* **Fopperei.** *Comp.* **—becher,** *m.* surprise-cup, puzzle-cup. **—ei,** *n.* mock-egg. **—glas,** *n.* anaclastic glass. **—ring,** *m.* puzzle-ring. **—schloß,** *n.* puzzle *or* permutation lock. **—spiegel,** *m.* deceptive mirror, conjuring mirror. **—stück,** *n.* surprise, puzzle. **—uhr,** *f.* clock-puzzle.

Vezie'r, *m.* (**—s,** *pl.* **—e**) vizier.

Viadu'kt, *m.* (**—s,** *pl.* **—e**) viaduct.

Via'tikum, *n.* (**—s,** *pl.* **Viatica**) viaticum; charity bestowed on poor journeymen *or* tramps; extreme unction (*Rel.*).

Vibrie'ren, *v.n.* (*aux.* **h.**) to vibrate.

Vi'ce— (*in comp.*) **—korporal,** *m.* lance corporal. **—graf,** *m.* viscount. **—gräfin,** *f.* viscountess. **—kanzler,** *m.* vice-chancellor. **—könig,** *m.* viceroy, lord lieutenant. **—königs=würde,** *f.* vice-royalty. **—präsident,** *m.* vice-president; deputy-chairman. **—statthalter,** *m.* deputy-governor. **—wirt,** *m.* landlord's agent; caretaker.

Vidimie'ren, *v.a.* to attest (*by signing one's name*) the correctness of (*a copy, etc.*); to authorize; to legalize, render valid; to confirm, corroborate.

Vieh, *n.* (**—(e)s**) cattle; beast, brute; live stock (*on farms*); **zwei Stück —,** two head of cattle; **eine Herde** *or* **Trift —,** a drove of cattle; **Menschen und —,** men and beasts; **zum — machen,** to brutalize. **—heit,** *f.* brutishness, bestiality. **—isch,** *adj.* brutal, bestial. *Comp.* **—arz(e)nei,** *f.* medicine for cattle. **—arzt,** *m.* veterinary surgeon. **—ausstellung,** *f.* cattle-show. **—besitzer,** *m.* cattle raiser, owner of cattle. **—bremse,** *f.* horse-fly, gad-fly. **—diebstahl,** *m.* cattle-stealing. **—dumm,** *adj.* brutishly stupid. **—futter,** *n.* food for cattle; forage, provender. **—handel,** *m.* trade in live stock, cattle trade. **—händler,** *m.* cattle-dealer, live-stock dealer. **—herde,** *f.* herd of cattle. **—hirt(in,** *f.*), *m.* cattle herd, herdsman, herdswoman, tender of cattle. **—hof,** *m.* yard for cattle; stock-farm, cattle-run, farm for raising stock. **—hürde,** *f.* cattle-pen. **—knecht,** *m.* man who tends the cattle, cattle-breeder's man; dairyman. **—magd,** *f.* maid for tending cattle; cowmaid; dairy-maid. **—markt,** *m.* cattle *or* stock market; cattle-fair. **—mäßig,** *adj. see* **—isch. —mast,** *f.* fattening of cattle; mast *or* food for cattle. **—mäster,** *m.* grazier; cattle-fattener. **—pacht,** *f.* lease of live stock. **—schaden,** *m.* loss of cattle; damage done by cattle. **—schwemme,** *f.* watering-place for cattle, horse-pond. **—seuche,** *f.* cattle disease, murrain, foot and mouth disease; cattle-plague, rinderpest. **—seuchen=gesetz,** *n.* Contagious Diseases (Animals) Act. **—sperre,** *f.* prohibition to import cattle. **—stall,** *m.* cow-house; stable. **—stamm,** *m.* breed *or* stock of cattle. **—stand,** *m.* (**auf einem Gute**) stock of cattle, live stock (*on a farm*). **—sterben,** *n. see* **Seuche. —steuer,** *f.* tax on live stock, cattle tax. **—tränke,** *f. see* **—schwemme. —trift,** *f.* cattle-run, right of way for cattle; pasturage. **—wagen,** *m.* cattle-truck; cattle-van; stock-car (*Amer.*). **—weide,** *f.* pasture ground, cattle-range; *pl.* pasturage. **—zoll,** *m.* duty on cattle. **—zucht,** *f.* stock farming, cattle breeding. **—züchter,** *m.* stock farmer, cattle-breeder.

Viel, (**mehr, meist,**) *adj. & adv.* much; (*pl.* **—e**) many; **—e sind berufen, aber wenige sind auserwählt,** many are called, but few are chosen (*B.*); **— Geld,** much money, a great deal of money; **das —e Geld,** all that money; **trotz seines —en Geldes,** in spite of all his riches; **seine —en Geschäfte,** his numerous affairs, the multiplicity of his affairs; **er hat — gelesen,** he has read a great deal; he is widely read; **es fehlt — (daran), daß . . .,** much is wanting (to) . . .; **es kamen ihrer —e,** many of them came; **die —en Menschen, welche . . .,** the great number of people who . . .; **das will — sagen,** that is saying a great deal; **wenn es (sehr) — ist,** at the most; **nicht —es, sondern —,** non multa, sed multum; **ohne ihn würde ich —es nicht wissen,** without him I should be ignorant of many things; **ein bischen —, etwas —, ein wenig —,** rather too much; **eben so —,** (*just*) as much; **gar —,** a great deal; **gar —e,** very many; **nicht —,** not much; **es hätte nicht — gefehlt, so hätte er . . .,** a little more and he would have . . .; **es ist nicht — los damit,** there is not much in it (*coll.*); there is not much to fear from it (*coll.*); **recht —, sehr —,** very much, a great deal; **sehr —e,** many people; **so —,** as much; **so und so —,** such and such a number; **so —e Male wie nötig,** as often as necessary; **so — ich gehört habe,** as far as I have heard; **so — ich weiß,** for aught I know; **nein, so — ich weiß,** not so far as I know; **der so und so —te Teil,** such and such a part; **wie —,** how much *or* many; **wie — er auch gelernt haben mag,** however great may be his learning; **wie — Kinder er auch haben mag,** however many children he may have; **ziemlich —,** a good deal; **das ist zu —,** that is too much, that is going too far! **des Guten zu — thun,** to go too far, overdo it, give (*a p.*) too much of a good thing; **—(e) hundert,** many hundreds; **ich weiß —!** much I know about it! what do I know about it? **ich frage — nach euerm Gelde!** what do I care about your money! **mit —em hält man Haus, mit Wenigem kommt man aus,** if one has much one uses it, if little, one makes it do. **—heit** *f.* plurality; multiplicity; multitude. *Comp.* (*in cpds.* **viel—** *often corresponds* to many-, multi-, poly-). **—arm,** *m.* polype (*Zool.*). **—armig,** *adj.* many-armed. **—artig,** *adj.* multifarious, varied, diverse. **—ästig,** *adj.* branched. **—bändig,** *adj.* voluminous, of many volumes. **—bedeutend,** *adj.* having many significations; very significant; influential. **—beinig,** *adj.* many-legged. **—beschäftigt,** *adj.* much occupied, very busy. **—betreten,** *adj.* much trodden; **—betretener Pfad,** well-beaten path. **—blätt(e)rig,** *adj.* many-leaved; polypetalous. **—blumig,** *adj.* many-flowered; **—blumige Aurikel,** polyanthus. **—blütig,** *adj.* multiflorous. **—brüderig,** *adj.* polyadelphous. **—deutig,** *adj.* having many significations; ambiguous. **—deutigkeit,** *f.* ambiguity. **—eck,** *n.* polygon; polyhedron. —**eckig**, *adj.* many-cornered, polygonal. —**ehig**, *adj.* polygamous. —**erlei**, *indec. adj.* many, divers, multifarious, of many sorts *or* kinds; **zu—erlei Geschäfte haben**, to have too many irons in the fire. —**essen**, *n.* —**esserei**, *f.* gluttony; voracity. —**fach**, I. *adj.* manifold, multifarious; various; multitudinous; reiterated. II. *adv.* often, frequently; in many ways. —**fächerig**, *adj.* many-celled (*Bot.*); having several compartments. —**fachheit**, —**fältigkeit**, *f.* diversity, multiplicity. —**fältig**, *adj. see* —**fach**; abundant. —**farbig**, *adj.* many-coloured, variegated. —**fingerig**, *adj.* polydactylous. —**flach**, *n.*, —**flächner**, *m.* polyhedron. —**flüg(e)lig**, *adj.* polypterous (*Ent.*). —**förmig**, *adj.* multiform, polymorphous, Protean. —**förmigkeit**, *f.* polymorphism. —**fraß**, *m.* glutton, voracious eater; glutton, wolverine, Gulo borealis (*Zool.*). —**frucht**, *f.* polychorion. —**früchtig**, *adj.* polycarpous. —**fuß**, *m.* animal with many feet; centiped, milleped (*Ent.*). —**geliebt**, *adj.* well-beloved. —**genannt**, *adj.* often-named; renowned. —**gereist**, *adj.* widely travelled. —**geschäftig**, *adj.* much-occupied; bustling; —**geschäftiger Mensch**, busybody; **sich —geschäftig anstellen**, to pretend to be extremely occupied. —**geschäftigkeit**, *f.* bustling ways; many-sided activity. —**gestaltig**, *see* —**förmig**. —**gliederig**, *adj.* with *or* composed of many members; polynomial (*Math.*). —**götterei**, *f.* polytheism. —**griff(e)lig**, *adj.* having many styles. —**herrschaft**, *f.* polycracy. —**hufer**, *m.* multungulate, animal with many hoofs. —**jährig**, *adj.* of many years, many years old; —**jähriger Freund**, friend of many years' standing. —**kantig**, *adj.* many-sided; polygonal. —**kapselig**, *adj.* multicapsular. —**kernig**, *adj.* having many pips *or* kernels. —**klappig**, *adj.* many-valved. —**köpfig**, *adj.* polycephalous. —**körnig**, *adj.* having many grains conglomerate (*Anat.*). —**lei'cht**, *adv.* perhaps, may be, perchance; **wenn er —leicht kommen sollte**, should he chance to come; **Sie haben —leicht Recht**, you may be right. —**lieb**, *adj.* very dear (*obs.*). —**lieb'chen**, *n.* darling, sweetheart, love; fillipeen (*corrupted fr. the Gm.*); **guten Morgen, —liebchen**, bon jour, Philippena; **ein —liebchen (mit einem Mädchen) essen**, to eat a fillipeen (*with a girl*). —**lippig**, *adj.* many-lipped. —**löcherig**, *adj.* riddled with holes. —**malig**, *adj.* often-repeated, reiterated; frequent. —**mal(s)**, *adv.* often, frequently, oftentimes; **ich danke Ihnen —mals**, I thank you very much, many thanks; **einen —mals grüßen lassen**, to send one's kind regards to a p. —**männerei'**, *f.* polyandry (*also Bot.*). —**me'hr**, I. *adv.* rather, much more. II. *conj.* rather; on the contrary. —**pfündig**, *adj.* of many pounds. —**räd(e)rig**, *adj.* many-wheeled. —**reder**, *see* —**sprecher**. —**reihig**, *adj.* multiserial. —**sagend**, *adj.* very expressive *or* significant, highly suggestive; meaning. —**saitig**, *adj.* many-stringed. —**samig**, *adj.* polyspermous. —**säulig**, *adj.*; **ein —säuliges Gebäude**, a polystyle. —**schreiber**, *m.* writer of many books, voluminous *or* prolific author; bookmaker; quill-driver, scribbler. —**schreiberei'**, *f.* mania for writing *or* for rushing into print; quill-driving, endless scribbling, voluminous writing. —**seitig**, *adj.* multilateral; polygonal; many-sided, of varied talents *or* acquirements; extensive; complex; —**seitiger Körper**, polyhedron. —**seitigkeit**, *f.* many-sidedness; versatility (of talent). —**silbig**, *adj.* polysyllabic; **silbiges Wort**, word of many syllables, polysyllable. —**spaltig**, *adj.* multifid. —**sprachig**, *adj.* of many tongues, in many languages, polyglot. —**sprecher**, *m.* great talker, person given to much talking. —**stimmig**, *adj.* for many voices; many voiced, polyphonic; —**stimmiger Satz** polyphony, counterpoint (*Mus.*). —**teilig**, *adj.* multipartite, composed of many parts; multinominal (*quantity*). —**thätigkeit**, *f.* many-sided activity. —**thuer**, *m.* bustling, fussy person, busybody. —**thuerei**, *f.* fussiness, officiousness. —**tönig**, *adj.* many-toned, composed of many sounds, multisonous. —**umfassend**, *adj.* vast, comprehensive. —**verheißend**, *adj.* promising much. —**vermögend**, *adj.* very influential, powerful. —**versprechend**, *adj.* very promising, of great promise. —**weiberei'**, *f.* polygamy; **einer, der in —weiberei lebt**, polygamist. —**weibig**, *adj.* polygynian (*Bot.*). —**wink(e)lig**, *adj.* with many angles. —**wissen**, *n.* varied knowledge *or* learning; great learning. —**wisser**, *m.* erudite man; smatterer, sciolist; walking encyclopædia, polyhistor. —**wisserei**, *f.* smattering of many things, sciolism. —**züngig**, *adj.* many-tongued; polyglot.

Vier, I. *num. adj.* (*nom. & acc. rarely* —**e**; *dat.* —**en** *when used substantively*) four; **unter — Augen**, tête-à-tête; confidentially, in strict confidence; **je — und —**, by fours; **zu je —en vorhanden**, quaternary (*Bot.*); **wir waren zu —en**, there were four of us; **mit — Pferden, mit —en fahren**, to drive four-in-hand; **auf allen —en gehen**, to go on all fours; **alle —e von sich strecken**, to stretch all fours (*of animals*); to stretch o.s. full length on the floor (*coll.*); **um halb —**, at half past three; — **und siebzig**, seventy-four; — **Wochen**, a month; **in seinen — Pfählen** *or* **Wänden**, at home. II. *f.* (*pl.* —**en**), —**e**, *f.* (*pl.* —**en**) the number four; the figure four; four (*at cards, etc.*). —**er**, *m.* (—**ers**, *pl.* —**er**) anything characterized by 4; one of (a council of) four; soldier of the 4th regiment; wine of the year (18)04. —**t**, I. *num.adj.* (**der, die, das** —**e**) fourth; —**tes Kapitel**, fourth chapter; **das —te Gebot**, the fifth commandment. II. *n.* quart (*measure*). —**tel**, *see* **Viertel**. —**tens**, *adv.* fourthly, in the fourth place. —**ung**, *f.* quadrature (*of the circle*); *see* **Gevierte** II.; intersection (*of the nave and transepts*). —**zig**, *see* **Vierzig**. *Comp.* —**armig**, *adj.* four-armed. —**beinig**, *adj.* four-legged. —**blatt**, *n.* quartette of friends, four comrades; a German game of cards in which 4 cards are dealt to each player (*Cards*); quatre-foil (*Arch.*); quadrifolium (*Bot.*). —**blätterig**, *adj.* four-leaved. —**bund**, *m.* quadruple alliance. —**draht**, *m.* stuff woven of four-threaded yarn; linsey-woolsey. —**eck**, *n.* square; quadrangle; quadrilateral figure; **geschobenes —eck**, rhomb, lozenge; **rechtwinkeliges —eck**, rectangle; **gleichläufiges, längliches —eck**, parallelogram; **Festungs—eck**, quadrilateral (*Fort.*). —**eckig**, *adj. & adv.* square, quadrangular, quadrate, four-cornered; —**eckig machen**, to square; —**eckig gewundene Schraube**, square-threaded screw. —**eck-schanze**, *f.* redoubt (*Fort.*). —**fach**, *adj.* quadruple; **um das —fache vermehren**, to quadruple. —**fächerig**, *adj.* four-celled. —**falt**, —**fältig**, *adj.* four-fold. —**felder-wirtschaft**, *f.* (—**feldrige Wirtschaft**) four-course system, rotation of crops. —**flächig**, *adj.* tetrahedral. —**fürst**, *m.* tetrarch. —**füßig**, *adj.* four-footed; —**füßiges Tier**, quadruped. —**füßler**, *m.* quadruped. —**gesang**, *m.* four-part song, quartette. —**gespann**, *n.* team of four (*horses, oxen, etc.*); four-in-hand; quadriga, four-horse chariot. —**gespann-fahrer**, *m.* four-in-hand driver. —**gestrichen**, *adj.* four-tailed (note); (note) in altissimo; **ein** —

gestrichenes F, F in altissimo, F of the sixth octave; **das Klavier geht bis ins —gestrichene F**, it is a six-octaved piano. **—gliederig**, *adj.* with four members *or* parts; quadrinomial (*Alg.*). **—händig**, *adj.* four-handed; **—händige Tiere**, quadrumana; **—händiges Tonstück**, piece arranged as a duet *or* for four hands; **—händig spielen**, to play duets *or* a duet on the piano. **—jährig**, *adj.* of four years; lasting four years; **—jähriges Kind**, child of four (years). **—jährlich**, *adj.* recurring every fourth year *or* once in every four years, quadrennial; **—jährliches Fest**, quadrennial celebration (*e.g. Olympic games*). **—klappig**, *adj.* quadrivalvular. **—mal**, *adv.* four times. **—malig**, *adj.* repeated four times. **—pfünder**, *m.* four-pounder. **—schrötig**, *adj.* square; square-built; thick-set. **—seitig**, *adj.* four-sided, quadrilateral. **—silbig**, *adj.* of four syllables, four-syllabled, tetrasyllabic; **—silbiges Wort**, word of four syllables, tetrasyllable. **—silbler**, *m.* tetrasyllable. **—sitzig**, *adj.* with four seats; holding four persons. **—spännig**, *adj.* drawn by four horses; **—spännig fahren**, to drive in a carriage and four; to drive four-in-hand. **—spiel**, *n.* quartette; quadrille (*Cards*). **—sprachig**, *adj.* in four languages, tetraglossic. **—stimmig**, *adj.* composed for four voices *or* parts; **—stimmiges Stück**, four-part song; quartette, quartet(to). **—stündig**, *adj.* lasting four hours; **—stündige Überfahrt**, crossing that takes four hours; **—stündiges Kolleg**, university lecture held four times a week. **—stündlich**, *adj.* once every four hours. **—stöckig**, *adj.* four-storied. **—tägig**, *adj.* of four days; lasting four days; **—tägiges Fieber**, quartan ague. **—täglich**, *adj.* recurring *or* happening every fourth day. **—te-halb**, *adj.* three and a half. **—teilen**, *v.a.* to divide into four parts; to quarter (*a criminal*). **—teilig**, *adj.* quadripartite; quadrinomial; quartered (*Her.*). **—undsechzigstel**, *n.* one sixty-fourth. **—undsechzigstel-note**, *f.* demisemiquaver. **—viertel-takt**, *m.* common time (*Mus.*). **—wink(e)lig**, *adj.* quadrangular. **—zahl**, *f.* quarternary number. **—zehig**, *adj.* four-toed. **—zehn**, *see* **Vierzehn**. **—zeilig**, *adj.* four-lined, of four lines; **—zeilige Strophe, —zeiliger Vers**, stanza of four lines; quatrain (if the rhymes are alternate).

Vier'tel, I. *n.* (—s, *pl.* —) fourth part; quarter; quarter, ward; district; **ein — (auf) vier**, a quarter past three; **drei — (auf) vier**, a quarter to four; **ein — Wein**, a quarter (of a litre), a glass of wine; **akademisches Viertel**, quarter of an hour after the full hour (*time when a German University lecture begins*). II. *adj.*; **eine — Elle**, a quarter of an ell. **—n**, *v.* I. *a.* to quarter (*also Her.*). II. *n.* (*aux.* **h.**) to strike, sound the quarters. *Comp.* **—bogen**, *m.* quarter of a sheet. **—elle**, *f.* quarter of an ell. **—faß**, *n.* quarter-barrel, quarter-cask; firkin (*for butter*). **—flut**, *f.* first-quarter tide. **—form, —größe**, *f.* quarto. **—hundert**, *n.* quarter of a hundred. **—jahr**, *n.* three months; quarter; **drei —jahre**, nine months. **—jährig**, *adj.* three months old, lasting three months. **—jährlich**, *adj.* every three months, once in three months, quarterly. **—jahrs-gehalt**, *n.* (**—jährliches Gehalt**) quarterly allowance, quarter's salary *or* stipend. **—jahrschrift**, *f.* quarterly (*journal, review*). **—meile**, *f.* quarter of a mile. **—note**, *f.* crotchet. **—pause**, *f.* crotchet-rest. **—pfund**, *n.* quarter of a pound. **—stunde**, *f.* quarter of an hour; distance *or* walk (*drive, etc.*) of a quarter of an hour. **—stündig**, *adj.* lasting a quarter of an hour. **—stündlich**, *adj.* happening every fifteen minutes. **—takt**, *m.* fourth of a bar. **—ton**, *m.* quarter of a tone, half a semitone, fourth; **durch —töne fortschreitend**, enharmonic. **—wendung**, *f.* quarter wheel (*Mil.*).

Vier'zehn, I. *num. adj.* fourteen; **— Tage, Zeit von — Tagen**, a fortnight; **heute über — Tage**, this day fortnight; **vor — Tagen**, a fortnight ago. II. *f.* the number fourteen. **—er**, *m.* (**—ers**, *pl.* **—er**) anything characterized by 14; soldier of the 14th regiment; wine of (18)14. **—t**, *adj.* (**der, die, das —e**) the fourteenth. **—tel**, *n.* (**—tels**, *pl.* **—tel**) fourteenth part. **—tens**, *adv.* in the fourteenth place. *Comp.* **—ender**, *m.* stag with fourteen tines. **—fach**, *adj.* fourteenfold; *adv.* fourteen times. **—lötig**, *adj.* of seven ounces. **—tägig**, *adj.* of *or* lasting fourteen days. **—täglich**, *adj.* (recurring) every fortnight, fortnightly.

Vier'zig, I. *num. adj.* forty; **Alter von — Jahren**, the age of forty, the forties; **er ist bald — Jahre alt**, he is getting on towards forty. II. *f.* the number forty. **—er**, *m.* (**—ers**, *pl.* **—er**) anything of which forty is the characteristic; wine of (18)40; soldier of the 40th regiment; (**—erin**, *f.*) person in the forties; **in den —ern, in den —er Jahren**, between 1840 and 1850, in the forties. **—st**, *num.adj.* (**der, die, das —ste**) fortieth. **—stel**, *n.* (**—stels**, *pl.* **—stel**) fortieth part. **—stens**, *adv.* in the 40th place. *Comp.* **—fach, —fältig**, *adj.* forty-fold. **—stündig**, *adj.* of *or* lasting forty hours. **—tägig**, *adj.* of *or* lasting forty days; **—tägige Fastenzeit vor Ostern**, Lent.

Vigil—a'nz, *f.* (*pl.* **—an'zen**) vigilance. **—ie**, (*pron.* **Vigi'lie**) *f.* vigil; eve (*of a feast*); one of the four (*Roman*) watches of the night. **—ie'ren**, *v.n.* (*aux.* **h.**); **auf einen —ieren**, to search *or* watch (for a p.), keep an eye (on a p.).

Vignet'te, *f.* (*pl.* **—n**) vignette (*Typ.*).

Vigog'ne, *f.* (*pl.* **—n**) vicu(g)na (*Zool.*). *Comp.* **—tuch**, *n.* vicu(g)na-cloth. **—wolle**, *f.* vicu(g)na-wool.

Vika'r, *m.* (**—s**, *pl.* **—e**) curate; vicegerent, substitute (*of a prelate*). **—ia't**, *n.* (**—iats**, *pl.* **—iate**) office of a curate, curacy; vicegerency; temporary office. **—ie'ren**, *v.n.* (*aux.* **h.**) to officiate as a p.'s substitute, to act as curate.

Vikto'ria, *f.* victory; **— rufen**, to shout victory. *Comp.* **—chaise**, *f.* victoria (*carriage*). **—schießen**, *n.* celebration of victory by firing of guns.

Viktorisie'ren, *v.n.* to be victorious (*obs. poet.*).

Viktua'lien, *pl.* victuals, provisions. *Comp.* **—händler**, *m.* provision-merchant, purveyor.

Vil'l—a, *f.* (*pl.* **—en, —as**) villa; country-house *or* residence; **kleine —a**, cottage. *Comp.* **—en-artig**, *adj.* like a villa. **—en-bewohner**, *pl.* inhabitants of villas. **—en-kolonie**, *f.*, **—en-viertel**, *n.* suburb of villas.

Villegiatu'r, *f.* stay in the country (during the summer holidays), villeggiatura.

Vindizie'ren, *v.a.* to claim, to lay claim to, to assert one's right to; to vindicate.

Vio'l—e, *f.* (*pl.* **—en**) *see* **Veilchen**; viol (*Mus.*). **—e'tt**, *adj.* & *n.* (**—etts**, *pl.* **—et'te**) violet; **dunkel —ett**, purple; **ins —ette spielen**, to shade into violet. **—i'ne**, *f.* (*pl.* **—inen**) violin; **die erste —ine spielen**, to be (*play*) the first violin, to lead; to take first fiddle (*fig.*). **—ini'st**, *m.* (**—inis'ten**, *pl.* **—inis'ten**), **—inis'tin**, violinist. **—once'll**, *n.* (**—oncells**, *pl.* **—oncells**) violoncello. *Comp.* **—ett-strumpf**, *m.* prelate, papal dignitary. **—in-bauch**, *m.* belly of a violin. **—in-bogen**, *m.* violin-bow. **—in-futteral**, *n.*, **—in-kasten**, *m.* violin-case. **—in-schlüssel**, *m.* treble-clef (*Mus.*). **—in-schule**, *f.* method of teaching the violin, violin-method; violin-exercises. —in=spieler, *m.* violinist. —in=steg, *m.* bridge of the violin. —in=stimme, *f.* violin-part. —in=virtuose, *m.*, —in=virtuosin, *f.* virtuoso, masterly performer on the violin.

Vi'per, *f.* (*pl.* —n) viper, adder. *Comp.* —(n)=artig, *adj.* like a viper; viperous, viperish (*fig.*). —(n)=biß, *m.* bite *or* sting of a viper.

Viril'stimme, *f.* man's voice; single vote.

Virtuo's, I. *adj.* masterly. II. *m.* (—(s)en, *pl.* —(s)en), —(s)in, *f.* virtuoso, masterly *or* professional performer. —(s)enhaft, *adj.* masterly, as a virtuoso. —(s)enschaft, *f.*, —(s)entum, *n.* (—s) professional skill, artistic perfection, masterly style; airs of a virtuoso; all virtuosi. —(s)ität, *f.* great perfection, mastery.

Vi's—a, *n.* (—as, *pl.* —as) visa, official endorsement (*of a passport*); signature. —a'ge, *f.* (—agen) face (*contempt.sl.*). —i(e)r, *see* Visi(e)r. —io'n, *f.* (*pl.* —ionen) vision. —ionä'r, *adj.* visionary. —itatio'n, —itie'=ren, *see under* Visit. —um, *n.* (—ums, *pl.* —a) *see* —a.

Visie'r, *n.* (—s, *pl.* —e) visor, beaver; sight (*of a gun*); sight-vane (*Opt.*); sight-hole; das — aufschlagen, to lift one's visor; mit offnem —, fearlessly, in the face of the world.

Visie'r—en, *v.* I. *a.* to visa, examine and endorse (*passports*); to adjust; to take the level of; to gauge. II. *n.* (*aux.* h.) nach einer S. —en, to take aim at a th. —bar, *adj.* capable of being gauged *or* sighted. —er, *m.* (—ers, *pl.* —er) gauger. —ung, *f.* visa; adjustment; gauging. *Comp.* —ebene, *f.* plane of direction (*Artil.*). —eisen, *n.* searcher (*Artil.*); probe (*at the custom-house*). —ge=bühr, *f.*, —geld, *n.* cost of gauging, gauger's fee. —instrument, *n.* diopter. —kappe, *f.* sight cover. —kette, *f.* measuring-chain. —korn, *n.* sight (*of a gun*). —lineal, *n.* dioptric rule. —linie, *f.* line of sight, aim (*Artil.*); line of sight *or* collimation (*Opt.*); bearing. —maß, *n.* gauge-measure, standard. —punkt, *m.* point of sight. —ring, *m.* gauge-ring. —scheibe, *f.* sliding vane (*Surv.*). —schraube, *f.* levelling screw. —schuß, *m.* point-blank shot (*Artil.*). —stab, —stock, *m.* gauging-rod; ranging pole (*Artil.*). —vorrichtung, *f.* sights.

Visit—atio'n, *f.* (*pl.* —ationen) visitation, visit of inspection; search, enquiry. —a'tor, *m.* (—ators, *pl.* —ato'ren) inspector; excise-officer. —e, *f.* (*pron.* Visi'te) (*pl.* —en) visit. —ie'ren, *v.a.* to visit; to inspect, search; eine Wunde —ie'ren, to probe a wound. —ie'rung, *see* —ation. *Comp.* —en=karte, *f.* visiting-card. —en=karten=täschchen, *n.* card-case. —en=tag, *m.* at-home day; visiting-day. —en=zimmer, *n.* drawing-room, reception-room. —ier=eisen, *n.* custom-house officer's probe. —ier=ronde, *f.* counter-round (*Mil.*).

Vis'ta, *f.* (*pl.* Vis'ten) view; vista; sight (*Mus.*); a —, at sight (*C.L.*).

Visü'r, *f.*; die Vor—, the fore-sight; die Rück—, the back-sight (*Surv.*).

Vitrio'l, *m.* & *n.* (—s, *pl.* —e) vitriol. *Comp.* —erz, *n.* vitriolic ore. —geist, *m.* diluted sulphuric acid. —hütte, *f.* vitriol-works. —machen, *n.* vitriolization. —öl, *n.*, —säure *f.* oil of vitriol, sulphuric acid; —sauer, *adj.* sulphuric; —saure Salze, sulphates. —wasser, *n.* vitriolic water.

Vi'vat, I. *n.* (—s, *pl.* —s) cheer, shout of acclamation; einem ein — bringen, to cheer a p. II. *int.* hurrah! — der König! long live the king!

Vivisektio'n, *f.* (*pl.* —en) vivisection.

Vlies, *n.* (—(s)es, *pl.* —(s)e), skin, hide; fleece.

Vo'cativus, *m. see* Vokativus.

Vo'gel, *m.* (—s, *pl.* Vögel) bird; fowl; falcon; any winged insect (*coll.*); fellow, chap, customer, dog (*coll.*); der — singt, zwitschert, the bird sings, twitters; — Bülow, yellow thrush; — Strauß, ostrich; ein loser —, a sly dog, a good-for-nothing scamp; arger, durchtriebener —, sly, cunning fellow; lustiger —, jolly dog; seltener —, rara avis; gerupfter —, one who has been fleeced (*at gaming*); Vögel von gleicher Feder fliegen zusammen, birds of a feather flock together; einen — haben, to be somewhat crazy, cracked; es ist ihm so wohl, wie dem — im Hanfsamen, he is in clover, he was born with a silver spoon in his mouth; Vögel, die zu früh singen holt am Abend die Katze, don't halloo till you are out of the wood (*prov.*); friß — oder stirb, root, hog, or die; kill or cure; you must sing or sink; es ist ein schlechter —, der sein eigen Nest beschmutzt, it is an ill bird that fouls its own nest; jeder — singt, wie ihm der Schnabel gewachsen ist, every bird sings as it is beaked *or* is known by its note; einem jeden — gefällt sein Nest am besten, there is nothing like your own home (*prov.*); wie der — so das Ei, a wild goose never laid a tame egg (*prov.*); nach und nach baut der — sein Nest, drop by drop fills the tub (*prov.*); den — abschießen, to carry off the prize. —er, **Vogler,** *m.* (—s, *pl.* —) fowler, bird-snarer. *Comp.* —abwerfen, *n.* game at knocking down a wooden bird with a stick. —art, *f.* species of bird. —artig, *adj.* birdlike, of the nature of a bird. —bauer, *n.* bird-cage; aviary. —beer=baum, *m.* mountain-ash. —beere, *f.* berry of the mountain-ash; mountain-ash. —beize, *f.* falconry. —deuter, *m.* augur. —deuterei, *f.* divination by the flight of birds. —dunst, *m.* small shot. —ei, *n.* bird's egg. —fang, *m.* fowling; bird-catching. —fänger, *see* —er. —flinte, *f.* fowling-piece. —flug, *m.* flight of birds; flock of birds. —frei, *adj.* outlawed; free as a bird; für —frei erklären, to outlaw. —fuß, *m.* bird's foot; Ornithopus (*Bot.*). —futter, *n.* food for birds. —garn, *n.* fowler's net. —(ge)sang, *m.* song, warbling of birds. —handel, *m.* bird-trade. —händler, *m.* bird-seller. —haus, *n.* aviary. —hecke, *f.* breeding-time (*of birds*); breeding-cage *or* place. —herd, *m.* fowling-floor. —kenner, *m.* ornithologist. —kirsche, *f.* bird-cherry; common wild cherry; black cherry. —kunde, *f.* ornithology; divination by the flight of birds. —kundig, *adj.* ornithological; able to augur from the flight of birds. —leicht, *adj.* light as a feather. —leim, *m.* bird-lime. —mist, *m.* bird-dung; guano. —napf, *m.* seed-box, drawer of a bird-cage. —netz, *see* —garn. —nest, *n.* bird's nest. —nester=ausnehmen, *n.* bird-nesting. —perspektive, *f.* bird's-eye view; aus der —perspektive entworfener Plan, bird's-eye sketch; Berlin aus der —perspektive, a bird's-eye view of Berlin. —pfeife, *f.* bird-call; flageolet. —schau, *f.* bird's-eye view; augury from the flight of birds. —schauer, *m.* augur. —scheuche, *f.* scarecrow. —schrot, *see* —dunst. —spieß, *m.* spit for roasting birds. —stange, *f.* perch (*in a bird-cage*); lime-twig; pole for a wooden bird. —stellen, I. *v.n.* (*aux.* h.) to catch, snare birds. II. *subst. n.* fowling, bird-catching. —steller, *m.* bird-catcher, fowler, decoy-man. —strich, *m.* flight (arrival *or* departure) of birds of passage. —wahrsager, *m.* augur. —wahrsagerei, *f.* ornithomancy. —wärter, *m.* bird-keeper. —weibchen, *n.* female bird, hen bird. —weid(e), *f.* bird-catching, falconry. —weide, *f.* place (*often* clearing in a wood) where birds are kept *or* caught (*obs.*); fowler's hut (in such a place). —wildpret, *n.* wild fowl. —zucht, *f.* breeding of birds; bird fancying. —züchter, *m.* bird-fancier, rearer of birds.

Vö'gelchen, Vög'lein, *n.* (—s, *pl.* —) little bird, birdie; **ich habe ein — singen hören,** a little bird told me.

Vogt, *m.* (—es, *pl.* Vög'te) overseer; bailiff; warden; prefect, governor; provost; steward; curator; policeman, constable; superior; principal; magistrate (Armen—) beadle; patron, guardian. **—ei',** *f.* (*pl.* **—eien**) office, duties, jurisdiction, residence *or* income of a vogt; prefecture, bailiwick; prison (*prov.*). **—ei'lich,** *adj.* belonging to a bailiwick; relating to the office *or* jurisdiction of a bailiff.

Voka'bel, *f.* (*pl.* **—n**) word, vocable. *Comp.* **—buch,** *n.* vocabulary. **—lernen,** *n.* learning words.

Vokabula'r(ium), *n.* (—s, *pl.* **Vokabula're**) vocabulary.

Voka'l, I. *m.* (—s, *pl.* —e) vowel; **reine —e,** pure vowels, oral vowels (without nasal resonance); **gutturale —e,** back *or* guttural vowels; **palatale —e,** front vowels; **gerundete Palatal—e,** front vowels with lip rounding (ü, ö). II. *adj.* vocal. **—isch,** *adj.* vocalic; **—ischer Laut,** vowel sound; **—ischer Auslaut,** vowel ending, word *or* syllable ending with a vowel. **—isie'ren,** *v.n.* (*aux.* **h.**) to vocalize; to sol-fa (*Mus.*). **—isie'rung,** *f.* (*pl.* **—isierungen**) vocalization; sol-fa-ing. **—is'mus,** *m.* vocalism; vowel-system. *Comp.* **—anlaut,** *m.* initial vowel. **—auslaut,** *m.* final vowel. **—inlaut,** *m.* intermediate vowel. **—merkmale,** *pl.* vowel points (*Stenog.*). **—musik,** *f.* vocal music, singing. **—partie,** *f.* vocal part. **—punkt,** *m.* vocal point (*Gram.*). **—resonanz,** *f.*; **die tiefste —resonanz,** the lowest pitch of all vowels. **—satz,** *m.* vocal composition, musical phrase for singing. **—steigerung,** *f.* gradation of vowels, guna. **—umlaut,** *m.* mutation.

Vokatio'n, *f.* (*pl.* **—en**) nomination to an office.

Vo'kativ, *m.* (—s, *pl.* —e) vocative (case).

Vo'kativus, *m.* wonderful person; sly dog (*coll.*).

Volk, *n.* (—s, *pl.* **Völ'ker**) people; nation; soldiery, troops; men, crew; race; troop, herd (*of beasts*); flock, covey; **das gemeine —,** the vulgar, the common people, the common herd, the lower classes; **viel —,** great multitude; — (*also* **Völker**), soldiery, soldiers, men (*poet.*); **ein — Wachteln,** a bevy of quails; **ein — Bienen,** a swarm of bees; **zwei —** *or* **Völker (Reb)hühner,** two coveys of partridges. **—s=tum,** *n.* (—s=tums, *pl.* —s=tümer) nationality; **sein —stum bewahren,** to preserve one's national characteristics. **—s=tümeln,** *v.a.* to court popularity. **—s=tümlich,** *adj.* popular; national; vulgar; **—stümliche Dichtung,** popular national poetry. **—s=tümlichkeit,** *f.* nationality; national trait *or* characteristic; popularity; (*pl.*) popular things. *Comp.* **—arm,** *adj.* thinly peopled. **—leer,** *adj.* desert. **—reich,** *adj.* populous, thickly populated. **—s=aberglaube,** *m.* popular superstition. **—s=abstimmung,** *f.* plebiscite, vote obtained by universal suffrage. **—s=anwalt,** *m.* people's advocate. **—s=aufruhr, —s=aufstand,** *m.* popular rising, riot; insurrection. **—s=aufwiegler,** *m.* agitator (of the people), demagogue. **—s=ausdrücke,** *pl.* common expressions, popular phrases and expressions. **—s=beliebt,** *adj.* popular. **—s=beschluß,** *m.* plebiscite, decree of the people. **—s=beschwerde,** *f.* national grievance. **—s=bewaffnung,** *f.* arming of the people. **—s=bewegung,** *f.* national movement. **—s=bildung,** *f.* popular education; national education. **—s=bildungsverein,** *m.* society for popular education *or* for the education of the masses, society for the extension *or* promotion of popular education. **—s=blatt,** *n.* popular paper. **—s=buch,** *n.* national book *or* work; book for the million; popular prose romance; chap book; **die deutschen —s=bücher,** the German popular prose romances. **—s=dichter,** *m.* popular poet; national poet. **—s=dichtung,** *f.* popular poetry; national poetry. **—s=epos,** *n.* national epic, primitive *or* naive epic. **—s=etymologie,** *f.* popular etymology. **—s=feind,** *m.* enemy of the people. **—s=feindlich,** *adj.* hostile to the people. **—s=fest,** *n.* national festival; people's fête, public holiday *or* merry-making. **—s=freund,** *m.* people's friend. **—s=freundlich,** *adj.* friendly to the people, popular. **—s=führer,** *m.* leader of the people; demagogue. **—s=gebrauch,** *m.* popular usage; national custom. **—s=gefühl,** *n.* national feeling. **—s=geist,** *m.* national spirit, public mind. **—s=genosse,** *m.* (fellow-)countryman. **—s=glaube,** *m.* popular belief. **—s=gunst,** *f.* popularity. **—s=halle,** *f.* free library. **—s=haufe,** *m.* the mob, populace; crowd of people. **—s=heer,** *n.* national army, army raised by universal conscription. **—s=herrschaft,** *f.* democracy. **—s=hochschule,** *f.* people's university; university extension. **—s=hymne,** *f.* national anthem. **—s=justiz,** *f.* mob-justice; lynch law. **—s=klasse,** *f.* class of people; **die höheren —sklassen,** the upper classes. **—s=krieg,** *m.* national war. **—s=küche,** *f.* public soup kitchen, people's kitchen. **—s=kunde,** *f.* folk-lore; **Verein für —skunde,** folk-lore society. **—s=lehrer,** *m.* teacher of the people; elementary *or* primary teacher. **—s=lied,** *n.* national song; popular song, ballad. **—s=mann,** *m.* popular man; democrat. **—s=märchen,** *n.* popular (fairy) tale, fairy tale. **—s=mäßig,** *adj.* popular; **—smäßig machen,** to popularize. **—s=meinung,** *f.* public opinion *or* feeling. **—s=melodie,** *f.* popular air. **—s=menge,** *f.* crowd throng; mob. **—s=name,** *m.* name of a people. **—s=poesie,** *see* **—sdichtung.** **—s=redner,** *m.* popular speaker; tub-orator. **—s=regierung,** *f.* popular government; democracy. **—s=sage,** *f.* national legend, popular tradition. **—s=schicht,** *f.* class of people, social stratum. **—s=schrift,** *f.* popular book *or* writing. **—s=schriftsteller(in,** *f.*), *m.* popular author(ess) *or* writer. **—s=schule,** *f.* elementary *or* primary school, board-school. **—s=schul=lehrer,** *m.* primary teacher, elementary *or* board-schoo lteacher. **—s=schul=lehrer=seminar,** *n.* training college for elementary teachers. **—s=schul=wesen,** *n.* system of primary education; system of national education. **—s=souveränetät,** *f.* sovereignty of the people. **—s=sprache,** *f.* language of a people, national speech *or* idiom; vernacular; vulgar tongue. **—s=stamm,** *m.* tribe, race. **—s=stimme,** *f.* public voice, voice of the people. **—s=stimmung,** *f.* public spirit; public feeling *or* opinion. **—s=stück,** *n.* popular play *or* drama; **—sstück mit Musik,** melodrama. **—s=tracht,** *f.* national costume *or* dress. **—s=tribun,** *m.* tribune of the people. **—s=überlieferung,** *f.* popular tradition *or* legend. **—s=unterricht,** *m.* national education; public instruction. **—s=verein,** *m.* people's club, working-men's club. **—s=versammlung,** *f.* national assembly (*of representatives*); assembly of the people, public meeting. **—s=vertreter,** *m.* deputy, representative of the nation *or* the people. **—s=vertretung,** *f.* representation of the people; representatives (*coll.*). **—s=wirt,** *m.* political economist. **—s=wirtschaft,** *f.* political economy. **—s=wirtschaftslehre,** *f.* system of political economy. **—s=wirtschaftlich,** *adj.* politico-economic. **—s=wohlstand,** *m.* wealth of the nation, national wealth. **—s=zähler,** *m.* census-taker. **—s=zählung,** *f.* census (of the people). **—s=zeitung,** *f.* people's paper; national gazette.

Völk'—chen, *n.* (—chens, *pl.* —chen) tribe; se

(*of people*); **mein —chen**, my little ones; **ein lustiges —chen**, a merry party. **—erschaft**, *f.* people; tribe; colony. *Comp.* **—er=beschreibung**, *f.* ethnography. **—er=hirt(e)**, *m.* sovereign (*poet.*). **—er=krieg**, *m.* international war. **—er=kunde, —er=lehre**, *f.* ethnology. **—er=name**, *m.* name of a people. **—er=recht**, *n.* international law. **—er=rechtlich**, *adj.* international; **—er=rechtlich vertreten**, to represent in international relations. **—er=schlacht**, *f.* the battle of Leipsic (Oct. 16–18, 1813). **—er=stamm**, *m.* race. **—er=wanderung**, *f.* migration of nations.

Voll, I. *adj.* (*usually followed by a gen. or* **von** *with dat.*) full; filled; complete, whole, entire; rounded; replete (*with*), fraught (*with*); drunk; **des Lobes —**, full of praise; **der Mond ist —**, the moon is full; **ein Glas — Wein**, a glass *or* a glassful of wine; **mit —em Rechte**, with perfect right; **er sagte mit —em Rechte**, he was quite right in saying; **in —er Arbeit**, in the midst of work; **—e Börse**, well-filled purse; **aus —er Brust**, heartily; **aus —em Herzen**, from the bottom of my (his, her, *etc.*) heart; **in —em Trabe**, at full trot; **der Wagen ist —!** all full (inside)! **die —e Summe**, the entire sum; **die —e ganze Wahrheit sagen**, to tell the whole truth; **im —en Sinne des Wortes**, in the fullest sense of the word; **für — annehmen**, to accept (coins) as current; **die Aktien sind — eingezahlt**, the shares are fully paid-up; **er ist —e vierzig Jahr(e alt)**, he is fully forty, quite forty years old; (*with verbs*) **sich** (*dat.*) **den Leib — ärgern**, to grow very angry (*coll.*); **— füllen, — gießen, — packen, — schenken**, to fill; **sich recht — gegessen haben**, to have eaten one's fill, to have been stuffing; **er gilt noch nicht für —**, he is not considered grown up yet; he is hardly to be taken seriously; **einen für — ansehen**, to treat a p. as a reasonable *or* responsible being; to take a p. seriously; **im —en leben**, to live in abundance; **— machen**, to fill, to complete; **das Maß — machen**, to make up the sum; **um das Unglück — zu machen**, to crown everything, as the last straw; **sich — machen**, to dirty o. s.; **für — nehmen, rechnen**, to take, count at its nominal value; **sich** (*dat.*) **den Kopf mit lateinischen und griechischen Brocken — pfropfen**, to stuff one's head with Latin and Greek; **einem den Buckel — schlagen**, to thrash a p. soundly; **einem den Hinteren — geben**, to whip a p.; **sich** (*dat.*) **den Leib — schlagen**, to eat as much as one can; **die Uhr hat — geschlagen**. the clock has struck the full hour; **einen Bogen — schmieren**, to scribble all over a sheet; **einem die Ohren — schreien**, to deafen a p. with shouting *or* crying; **sich — trinken**, to drink too much; **von** (einer S.) **— werden**, to be filled with; **aus dem —en wirtschaften**, not to be sparing; not to stint o.s.; **aus dem —en schöpfen**, to draw freely from one's store of information, ideas *or* wealth. II. *insep. prefix signifying completion, accomplishment, etc.; also* = full. *The inseparable verbs compounded with* **voll** *have the accent on the root of the verb.* **—ends**, *adv.* entirely, wholly, completely; altogether; finally; on the top of it, to crown everything; moreover; **das wird ihn —ends zu Grunde richten**, that will be the end of him, will complete his ruin. **—er**, I. *indec. adj.* (*stereotyped nom. sing. masc.*) *in the sense of* **voll von**, *see* **Voll**); **er (sie) ist —er List**, he (she) is full of cunning; **unsre Kinder sind —er Freude**, our children are full of joy *or* delighted; **—er Freundlichkeit und Komplimente**, all smiles and bows; **—er Sorge**, full of care. II. *Comparative of* **voll. —heit**, *f.* fulness, completeness. *Comp.* **—ährig**, *adj.* full-eared. **—aktie**, *f.* paid-up share. **—au'f**, *adv.* abundantly, plentifully; **—auf zu thun haben**, to have one's hands full *or* plenty to do; **er hat —auf**, he is in affluence, very well to do. **—bad**, *n.* complete bath, plunge-bath. **—bahn**, *f.* main line. **—bart**, *m.* (full) beard, beard and moustache. **—berechtigt**, *adj.* fully authorized *or* qualified. **—besitz**, *m.* full possession. **—blütig**, *adj.* full-blooded, plethoric; sanguine. **—blütigkeit**, *f.* redundancy of blood, plethora. **—blut=pferd**, *n.* thorough-bred horse. **—bringen, 2c.**, *see* **Vollbring—**. **—brüstig**, *adj.* full-breasted; with well-developed bust. **—bürger**, *m.* citizen possessing full civil and political rights. **—bürtig**, *adj.* of the same parents, whole-blood; **bürtige Geschwister**, full brothers and sisters. **—dampf**, *m.* full (-pressure) steam; **—dampf voraus!** full steam ahead! **—druck**, *m.*; **mit —druck**, at full pressure (*Loco.*). **—enden 2c.** *see under* **Vollend—**. **—führen**, *see* **Vollführen**. **—gefühl**, *n.* (full) consciousness. **—gehalt**, *m.* good alloy, full weight and value. **—gehaltig**, *adj.*, of good alloy, of full weight and value; of sterling value; **—gehaltige Münze**, standard coin. **—gemessen**, *adj.* justly measured, plenty. **—genuß**, *m.* full enjoyment. **—gepfropft, —gerammt**, (*vulg.*) **—gerüttelt**, *adj.* crammed fully, closely packed, crowded. **—gespritzt**, *adj.* splashed all over. **—gestopft**, *see* **—gepfropft**. **—gewalt**, *f.* full power; absolute power; power of attorney. **—gewicht**, *n.* full weight. **—gültig**, *adj.* of full value, sterling; valid, unexceptionable. **—haarig**, *adj.* hairy, shaggy. **—haltig**, *adj.* of full value, standard; rich (*of a language*). **—hufig**, *adj.* hoof-bound. **—inhaltlich**, *adj.* complete. *adv.* all round, in all points. **—jährig**, *adj.* of full age. **—jährigkeit**, *f.* majority, full age; **seine —jährigkeit erlangen**, to come of age, to attain one's majority. **—kantig**, *adj.* (fully-) squared. **—klang**, *m.* full chord; sonorous sound. **—kommen**, *see* **Vollkommen**. **—körnig**, *adj.* full-grained. **—kraft**, *f.* full strength *or* vigour, energy. **—kugel**, *f.* round shot. **—lautend**, *adj.* sonorous. **—leibig**, *adj.* corpulent, stout. **—leibigkeit**, *f.* stoutness, corpulence, obesity. **—macht**, *f.* full power *or* authority; fulness of power; power of attorney; warrant; proxy, procuration; **einem —macht geben**, to empower, authorize a p. **—macht=geber**, *m.* mandator, constituent. **—macht=haber**, *m.* mandatory; proxy, procurator. **—machts=brief**, *m.* procuration; permit. **—matrose**, *m.* able-bodied seaman. **—mond**, *m.* full moon; **wir haben —mond**, the moon is full. **—monds=gesicht**, *n.* full round face. **—pfropfen**, *v.r.* to stuff, to eat too much; **—gepfropft**, crammed full. **—reifen**, *m.* non-pneumatic tire. **—saftig**, *adj.* very juicy; full of sap; **—saftig (sein)**, replete (*with humours*), plethoric; full blooded. **—saftigkeit**, *f.* abundance of sap; abundance of humours (*Med.*), plethora. **—schiff**, *n.* full-rigged ship. **—ständig**, *adj.* complete, entire, total, whole, integral; perfect; unmixed; **—ständig besetzt sein**, to be full (*of omnibuses, etc.*); **das Unglück —ständig machen**, to crown everything. **—ständigkeit**, *f.* completeness; integrity; **die —ständigkeit des Werkes wird verbürgt**, the work is guaranteed complete; **mit —ständigkeit**, completely. **—stimmig**, *adj.* for full orchestra *or* chorus; **—stimmiges Tonstück**, symphony. **—strecken 2c.** *see under* **Vollstreck—**. **—tönend, —tönig**, *adj.* full-sounding, full-toned, sonorous, rich. **—wertig**, *adj.* of full value, sterling, precious; valid. **—wichtig**, *adj.* of full weight; weighty, forcible; important. **—wichtigkeit**, *f.* full weight. **—wüchsig**, *adj.*

full-grown. **—zählig,** *adj.* complete. **—zähligkeit,** *f.* completeness, fulness. **—ziehen** *rc.* *see under* Vollzieh—en. **—zug,** *m. see* **—ziehung.**

Vollbrin'g—en, *ir.v.a.* (*insep.*) to accomplish, achieve; to complete; to consummate; to execute, fulfil, perform fully; to carry out; to perpetrate. **—er,** *m.* (**—ers,** *pl.* **—er**) one who accomplishes *or* achieves; performer. **—ung,** *f.* accomplishment, achievement; execution; consummation; performance; perpetration.

Vollen'd—en, *v.* I. *a.* (*insep.*) (*aux.* **h.**) to bring to a complete close; to finish; to achieve; to complete; to consummate; to perfect. II. *r.* & *n.* (*aux.* **h.**) to die. **—er,** *m.* (**—ers,** *pl.* **—er**) achiever, finisher. **—et,** *p.p.* & *adj.* accomplished, achieved; consummate; perfect; **er hat —et,** he has passed away, his race is run, he is dead (*elev. style*); **die früh Vollendete,** the woman (girl) that died so young. **—ung,** *f.* completion, ending; consummation; perfection; **nach — ung dieses . . .,** at the end of this . . ., having done *or* achieved this.

Völ'ler, *m.* (**—s,** *pl.* **—**) glutton, drunkard. **—ei',** *f.* intemperance, gluttony.

Völ'lig, *adj.* & *adv.* full, entire, complete; thorough; sufficient; full, too wide; **—er Narr,** downright fool; **—er Ablaß,** plenary indulgence; **—e Unwahrheit,** downright untruth; **ich bin nicht — Ihrer Meinung,** I do not quite agree with you; (**einem etwas**) — **abschlagen,** to give a flat refusal (to a p.).

Voll'kommen, *adj.* perfect; full, complete, entire; finished; consummate; accomplished; perfect; too wide, rather large (*of clothes*); **—e Gewalt,** absolute power; **—e Zahl,** perfect number. **—heit,** *f.* perfection; completeness.

Vollstre'ckbar, *adj.* executable. **—keit,** *f.* possibility of carrying out a sentence. *Comp.* **—keits=erklärung,** *f.* declaration that a sentence can be carried out.

Vollstre'ck—en, *v.a.* (*insep.*) to execute, put into effect, carry out. **—er,** *m.* (**—ers,** *pl.* **—er**) executor. **—erin,** *f.* executrix. **—ung,** *f.* execution. *Comp.* **—ungs=befehl,** *m.* writ of execution (*of a mandate*), warrant.

Vollzie'h—en, *ir.v.a.* (*insep.*) *see* **Vollstrecken**; to accomplish, consummate; to ratify; **sich —en,** to be effected, to take place; **ein Urteil —en,** to execute a sentence; **—ende Gewalt,** executive (*power*); **ihre vollzogene eheliche Verbindung zeigen an . . .,** so and so announce their marriage; **eine Heirat —en,** to consummate a marriage. **—er,** *m.* (**—ers,** *pl.* **—er**) executer, accomplisher; executor. **—ung,** *f.* execution; accomplishment; fulfilment.

Volontä'r, *m.* (**—s,** *pl.* **—s, —e**) volunteer; *see* **Freiwilliger;** supernumerary, unsalaried clerk.

Volt, *n.* (**—s,** *pl.* **—**) volt, unit of electro-motive force. *Comp.* **—messer,** *m.* volt-meter.

Vol'taisch, *adj.*; **der —e Strom,** the voltaic current.

Vol'te, *f.* (*pl.* **—n**) volt (*Fenc.*, *Equest.*); sleight of hand; **die — schlagen,** to make the pass (*Cards*).

Voltigeu'r, *m.* (**—s,** *pl.* **—s**) vaulter, tumbler.

Voltigie'r—en, *v.n.* (*aux.* **h.**) to vault. *Comp.* **—kunst,** *f.* art of vaulting. **—meister,** *m.* master of a troop of equestrians. **—pferd,** *n.* (*wooden*) vaulting horse.

Volubilitä't, *f.* volubility.

Volu'm—en, *n.* (**—ens,** *pl.* **—ina**) volume; **die Abnahme (Zunahme) des —ens,** the diminution (increase) of volume. **—inö's,** *adj.* voluminous. *Comp.* **—gesetz,** *n.* the Gay-Lussac law of volumes (*Chem.*).

Vomi—e'ren, *v.n.* (*aux.* **h.**) to vomit. **—ti'v,** *n.* (**—tivs,** *pl.* **—tive**) emetic.

Von, *prep.* (*with dat.*) of; from; by; in; on, upon; concerning. *Before family names* **von** *is a sign of nobility, and may be left as* **von** *or translated by* de. I. **von** = of: **1.** *to denote possession or used for the genitive;* **Vater — dem (vom) Kinde,** the father of the child (*coll.*); **ein Freund — mir,** a friend of mine; **ein Kaufmann — London,** a merchant of London, a London merchant; **die Belagerung — Paris,** the siege of Paris; **die Lage — Paris,** the situation of Paris; **der Herr vom Hause,** the master of the house. **2.** *to express the partitive genitive;* **zwei — uns,** two of us; **— allen Wanderern aus dem deutschen Lande . . .,** of all German travellers . . .; **trinken Sie — diesem Weine,** drink some of this wine. **3.** *before numerals;* **eine Frau — vierzig Jahren,** a woman of forty. **4.** *to denote quality or material;* **ein Mann — edelm Sinne,** a man of noble mind; **ein Geschäft — Wichtigkeit,** an affair of importance; **Lehre — der Buße,** doctrine of repentance; **klein — Person,** small of stature; **ein Engel — einem Weibe,** an angel of a woman; **Schurke — einem Bedienten,** rascal of a servant; **— ehrlichen Leuten geboren,** born of honest parents; **— Holz,** of wood; **ein Monument — Marmor,** a monument of marble. **5.** *before a proper name which is part of a title;* **Königin — England,** Queen of England; **Herzog Johann — Schwaben,** Duke John of Suabia. **6.** *to denote the worth or price*; **— gutem Schrot und Korne,** of due weight and alloy, of sterling worth. **7.** *to denote the subject treated of;* **— wem sprechen Sie?** of whom are you speaking? *also to denote various other relations;* **es ist nicht recht — ihm,** it is not right of him; **— denen wir voraussetzen, daß sie Ihnen passen,** taking for granted that these will be convenient to you; **— selbst,** of one's own accord, spontaneously. II. = from; off: **1.** *when used with an adv. or prep. following, as* **an, auf, aus, her, herab,** *rc.*; **— außen,** from without; **— oben,** from above; **— oben herab,** from on high; **— hinnen,** hence; **— hinten,** from behind; **— hinten hervor,** out from behind; **— heute an,** from this day forward; **— der Kanzel herab,** from the pulpit; **— wo aus,** from whence; **— da an,** from thence forward; **— nun an,** henceforth. **2.** *to denote motion from;* **— Berlin kommen,** to come from Berlin. **3.** *with verbs signifying separation or privation;* **ich behalte 2 Mark — dieser Summe,** I am keeping 2 marks out of this sum; **etwas — jemandes Gehalte abziehen,** to take something off a p.'s salary; **nehmen Sie das vom Tische weg,** take that away (from the table); **— einem gehen,** to go away from, leave one; **— wem haben Sie das Geld geliehen?** from whom did you borrow the money? **gut — statten gehen,** to go well, prove a success; **etwas vom Original abschreiben,** to copy from the original; **— etwas trennen, unterscheiden,** to separate from, distinguish between; **— der Arbeit ruhen,** to rest from work; **leiden —,** to suffer from. III. **von** *is variously translated in other cases, as in the following idioms:* **— Gottes Gnaden,** by the grace of God; **— Seiten jemandes,** on the part of some one; **— Sinnen kommen,** to lose consciousness; to lose one's head, go crazy, **was wollen Sie — mir?** what do you want with *or* from me? **— allen geliebt,** beloved of *or* by all; **ein Spieler — Profession,** a gamester by profession; **Kinder — der zweiten Frau,** children of *or* by the second wife; **— dem verstorbenen Herrn N. gebaut,** built by the late Mr. N.; **gedruckt und im Verlage — Herrn C.,** printed and published by Mr. C.; **eine Schottin — Geburt,** by birth a Scotchwoman; **ein Deutscher — Geburt,** a native of Germany; **— seinem Handel leben,** to live by one's trade; **— seinen Einkünften leben.** to live on one's income; man kann nicht — der Luft leben, one cannot live on air; Zinsen — Zinsen, compound interest; — allen Seiten, on all sides, from every side; — Rechtswegen, by right; according to law; er kann — Glück sagen, he may consider himself lucky, thank his stars; — neuem, anew, afresh. *Comp.* —einander *see* Auseinander. —nöten, *adv.*; —nöten haben, to stand in need of; —nöten sein, to be needful, necessary; ich habe es —nöten, I need it. —wannen, *adv.* from whence. —wegen, *prep.* because, on account of, for the sake of (*obs. & coll.*).

Vor, I. *prep.* (*with dat. implying rest or in answer to the question* wo?; *with acc. implying motion or in answer to the question* wohin?) —'m = vor dem; —s = vor das; before (*in time or place*), in front of, antecedent to, ere; in presence of; for; on account of, through, because of, with; from, against (*with verbs of protecting, warning, etc.*); in preference to, more than, above; (*denoting time* =) since, ago; das Subjekt steht — dem (stellt man — das) Zeitwort, the subject precedes (is placed before) the verb; — einem da sein, to exist *or* be at a place before somebody else; der Tag — dem Feste, the day before the feast *or* festival; er steht — dem Bankerott, he is on the verge of bankruptcy; die See — sich (*dat.*) haben, to have the sea before one *or* opposite; einem eine Kugel — den Kopf schießen, to lodge a ball in a p.'s head; sich (*dat.*) eine Kugel — den Kopf schießen, to blow one's brains out; — das Thor gehen, to go out of the gate; — dem Thore wohnen, to live outside the gate; — der Thüre sein, to be at the door; to be at hand; einen — die Thüre werfen, to turn a p. out; einem die Thüre — der Nase zuschlagen, to shut the door in a p.'s face; — allen Augen verborgen, hidden from all eyes; — Augen haben, to have before one's eyes, in view, to intend, purpose; — jemands Augen, before a p.'s very eyes; — Gott, in the presence of God, in the eyes of God; — allen Dingen, above all; Gewalt geht — Recht, might is stronger than right; — uns, ahead of us; er erhielt es — jedem andern, he obtained it in preference to every one else; sich — einem auszeichnen, to distinguish o.s. above another; Achtung — dem Gesetz, respect for the law; Furcht, Scheu — etwas (*dat.*) haben, sich — einem, einer S. fürchten, to be afraid of, to fear s.th. *or* s.o.; ich habe keine Geheimnisse — Ihnen, I have no secrets from you; ich habe keine Ruhe — ihm, I never have a moment's peace with *or* owing to him; — einem warnen, to warn against a p.; — einer S. geschützt, sicher, in Sicherheit sein, to be safe, secure from s.th.; Schutz — dem Winde, shelter from the wind; sein Herz — einer S. verschließen, to close one's heart to *or* against s.th.; sich — einem verstecken, to hide from a p.; er sieht den Wald — lauter Bäumen nicht, he cannot see the wood for trees; he does not see what is obvious; — Angst, — Aufregung, — Kälte zittern, to tremble with fear, with excitement, with cold; ich sterbe — Kälte, I am perishing with cold; ich konnte — dem Lärm nicht schlafen, I could not sleep because of the noise; — Freude weinen, to weep with joy; — Alter, — Angst, — Hunger ꝛc. sterben, to die of old age, of anxiety, of starvation, *etc.*; Schritt — Schritt, step by step; sie hat — ihrer Schwester den Vorrang, she takes precedence of her sister; — alters, of yore; heute — acht Tagen, a week ago to-day; — Zeiten, formerly; — alten Zeiten, in old times; — der Zeit, prematurely, in advance (*as payment*). II. *n.*; das — und Nach, the Before and After. III. *adv. & sep. prefix;* before; formerly; nach wie —, now as before; Schützenketten —, skirmishers forward *or* advance! —ig, *adj.* former, last, preceding, previous; —iges Jahr, last year; Ihr wertes Schreiben vom 5ten —igen Mts, your (esteemed) favour of the 5th ult. *Comp.* —a'b, *adv.* above all, before all, especially; besides. —abend, *m.* eve; evening before. —ächzen, *v.a.* (einem etwas) to sigh *or* groan out (*one's*) complaints to *or* in the presence of a p. —adami(ti)sch, *adj.* preadamite. —ahnen, *v.a.* to have a presentiment *or* foreboding of. —ahnung, *f.* presentiment. —an, *see* Voran. —anschlag, *m.* computation, previous *or* rough calculation, estimate. —anstalt, *f.* preparatory arrangement *or* measure; preparatory institution. —anzeige, *f.* preliminary announcement. —arbeit, *f.* previous labour *or* work; (*pl.*) preliminary studies. —arbeiten, *v.a.& n.* (*aux.* h.) to work in preparation, prepare work; to show (einem, a p.) the way to work; to pave the way (einem andern, for s.o.); ich habe auf morgen —gearbeitet, I have done (part of) my work for to-morrow. —arm, *m.* fore-arm; foreleg (*of horses*). —ärmel, *m.* false sleeve *or* cuff (*to protect the dress-sleeve*). —auf, *see* —an. —aus, *see* Voraus. —bau, *m.* front building, (*shop-*)front, fore-part of a building; building in front of another; screen (*Arch.*). —bauen, *v.a.* to build before something; to build out; einer Sache (*dat.*) —bauen, to obviate, prevent, preclude (*the possibility of, etc.*), to take precautions against a thing. —bauung, *f.* the building out *or* before; precaution, prevention. —bedacht, *m.* forethought, premeditation; mit —bedacht, deliberately, on purpose. —bedächtig, I. *adj.* full of forethought; cautious; deliberate; prudent. II. *adv. see* mit —bedacht. —bedenken, *ir.v.a.* to premeditate. —bedeuten, *v.a.* to forebode, presage. —bedeutung, *f.* foreboding, omen, augury. —bedingen, *ir.v.a.* to stipulate beforehand. —bedingung, *f.* preliminary condition. —begriff, *m.* preliminary notion, preconception. —behalt, *m.* reservation, restriction, proviso; mit —behalt meiner Rechte, without prejudice to my rights; unter —behalt aller Rechte, all rights reserved; ohne —behalt, without reserve, unconditionally; der stille —behalt, mental reservation. —behalten, *ir. v.a.* to keep back, keep in reserve, withhold; to stipulate for; to lay up for; to keep on (*an apron*); sich (*dat.*) etwas —behalten, to reserve s.th. to o.s.; ich behalte mir diese Ehre bis nächsten Montag —, I reserve this honour for next Monday. —behaltlich, *prep.* (*with gen.*) reserving, with the reservation of, save. —behaltung, *f. see* —behalt. —bei, *see* Vorbei. —bekommen, *ir.v.a.*; sie bekam eine Schürze —, she had to put on a pinafore; ich habe 10 Points von ihm —bekommen, he has given me 10 points. —bemeldet, —benannt, *adj.* afore-mentioned, previously referred to. —bemerkung, *f.* prefatory notice, preamble. —bereiten, ꝛc., *see under* Vorbereit—. —berg, *m.* spur of a mountain. —bericht, *m.* introduction, preface, prefatory notice. —bescheid, *m.* preliminary decree, interlocutory judgment; summons, subpœna. —bestellen, *v.a.* to order (engage, book, bespeak) beforehand. —bestellung, *f.* ordering in advance, subscription. —bestraft, *adj.* previously convicted. —bestrafung, *f.* previous conviction. —beten, *v.a. & n.* (*aux.* h.) (einem ein Gebet) to repeat, recite a prayer before s.o.; to expound at length (*coll.*). —beter, *m.* he who recites the prayers before the congregation (*of the Jews.*

etc.). —**beugen**, *v.* I. *a.* to bend forward. II. *n.* (*aux.* **h.**) to hinder, prevent, obviate (**einem Übel** 2c., an evil, *etc.*). —**beugend**, *p.* & *adj.* preventive; prophylactic (*Med.*) —**beuger**, *m.* pronator (*muscle of the fore-arm*). —**beugung**, *f.* bending forward; preventing; prevention. —**beugungs=mittel**, *n.* preservative; prophylactic (*Med.*). —**bild**, *n.* model, pattern, standard; prototype; original; (*beau*) ideal, type; symbol, prefiguration. —**bilden**, *v.a.* to prepare, give a preparatory education to; to foreshadow, typify; to represent. —**bildlich**, *adj.* typical; prefigurative; representative (**für**, *of*); model, ideal. —**bildung**, *f.* preparation; preparatory instruction; training; **allgemeine —bildung**, general education. —**bildungs=anstalt** *or* =**schule**, *f.* preparatory school. —**binden**, *ir.v.a.* to tie before, put on; to show how to tie; to bind (*sheaves, etc.*) faster than another; **dem Buche das Inhaltsverzeichnis —binden**, to put the table of contents at the beginning of a book; **sich** (*dat.*) **etwas —binden**, to set about a thing in earnest (*coll.*). —**bitte**, *f.* prayer against (*something*); intercession (*for*). —**blasen**, *ir.v.a.* to blow, play (*the flute, etc.*) before *or* to (*one*). —**bleiben**, *ir.v.n.* (*aux.* **s.**) to remain before *or* in advance; **die Schürze bleibt —!** you are to keep on your apron! —**bohren**, *v.a.* to open with a gimlet *or* auger; to make borings before s.o. —**bohrer**, *m.* auger, gimlet. —**börse**, *f.* coulisse, unauthorized part of the exchange. —**bote**, *m.* precursor, forerunner, harbinger, herald; sign, indication, presage; symptom. —**bramrahe**, *f.* fore-topgallant yard. —**bramsegel**, *n.* fore-topgallant sail. —**bramstenge**, *f.* fore-topgallant mast. —**bramstengestag**, *n.* fore-topgallant stay. —**bramstengestagsegel**, *n.* flying jib. —**brennen**, *ir.v.n.* (*aux.* **h.**) to flash in the pan. —**bringen**, *ir.v.a.* see **Hervorbringen**; to bring forward, adduce, allege; to advance, put forward (*an opinion, etc.*); to state; to propose; **Beweise —bringen**, to produce proofs; **er konnte kein Wort —bringen**, he could n't utter *or* say a word; **er wußte nicht, was er zu seiner Entschuldigung —bringen sollte**, he did not know what excuse to offer; **eine Anklage —bringen**, (**gegen**) to prefer a charge (against). —**bruch**, *m.* a bursting forth; outbreak; eruption. —**buchstabie'ren**, *v.a.* (**einem etwas**) to spell out before *or* to. —**bühne**, *f.* proscenium (*Theat.*). —**christlich**, *adj.* pre-Christian, before the Christian era. —**dach**, *n.* projecting roof; eaves. —**datie'ren**, *v.a.* to antedate. —**deich**, *m.* outer dike. —**de'm**, *adv.* formerly, in former times, of old. —**demonstrie'ren**, *v.a.* to demonstrate. —**der**, 2c. *see* **Vorder** 2c. —**drängen**, *v.a.* & *r.* to press *or* push forward; **sich —dränge(l)n**, to thrust oneself forward. —**dringen**, *ir.v.n.* (*aux.* **s.**) to push on, advance, force one's way onward; to gain ground. —**dringlich**, *adj.* forward; importunate, intrusive; pert; inquisitive; penetrating. —**druck**, *m.* first pressure; wine of the first pressure; first *or* original impression (*Typ.*); printed form. —**drucken**, *v.a.* to prefix. —**drücken**, *v.a.* to press forward, force on. —**ebbe**, *f.* beginning of the ebb-tide. —**eid**, *m.* oath of probity (*Law*). —**eilen**, *v.n.* (*aux.* **s.**) to hasten on before; to outrun, outstrip; to precede. —**eilig**, *adj.* hasty, precipitate, rash; premature; precocious. —**eiligkeit**, *f.* precipitation, rashness, overhaste. —**eilungs=winkel**, *m.* angle of the lead (*Loco.*). —**eingenommen**, *adj.* prejudiced, biassed. —**eingenommenheit**, *f.* prejudice, (*previous*) bias. —**eltern**, *pl.* ancestors, forefathers. —**empfinden**, *ir.v.a.* to feel beforehand; to have a presentiment of; to anticipate, surmise. —**empfindung**, *f.* presentiment. —**enthalten**, *ir. v.a.* (**einem etwas**) to withhold, keep back (*from a p. what is his due*). —**enthaltung**, *f.* withholding, retention. —**erinnerung**, *f.* preliminary notice *or* admonition; preliminary discourse, preamble, preface. —**erklärung**, *f.* preliminary explanation. —**ernte**, *f.* first harvest. —**e'rst**, *adv.* first of all, before all; firstly. —**erwählen**, *v.a.* to choose beforehand; to elect, predestinate. —**erwähnt**, *adj.* before-mentioned, aforesaid. —**erzählen**, *v.a.* (**einem etwas**) to relate, recount to. —**essen**. I. *ir.v.a.* to eat beforehand; *see* —**gegessen**. II. *subst. n.* entrée; first course of meat. —**exilisch**, *adj.* before the exile (of Babylon). —**fabel**, *f.*; **die —fabel eines Dramas**, events bearing on *or* throwing light on the action of a drama which have happened before the opening of the play. —**fabeln**, *v.a.* (**einem etwas**) to tell fables *or* lies (to). —**fahr**, *m.* (—**s** and —**en**, *pl.* —**en**) ancestor progenitor; **mein —fahr**, (one of) my ancestor(s). —**fahren**, *ir.v.n.* (*aux.* **s.**); **bei einem —fahren**, to drive up to, stop at a p.'s door, to call (*when driving*) on a p.; **den Wagen —fahren lassen**, to have the carriage brought round; **einem —fahren**, to drive past s.o.; **der Wagen fuhr uns —**, the carriage stopped in front of us, blocked up our way. —**fall**, *m.* occurrence; event, incident; conjuncture; case; falling forward; prolapsus (*Med.*); detent (*of a clock*); —**fall der Krystalllinse**, exophthalmy; **seltsamer —fall**, strange occurrence; **ein an —fällen merkwürdig leeres Leben**, a life singularly destitute of incidents. —**fallen**, *ir.v.n.* (*aux.* **s.**) to fall (*down*) before; to fall forward; to become misplaced (*Med.*); to happen, occur, take place; **bei —fallender Gelegenheit**, at the first opportunity, as occasion offers; **thun Sie, als wenn nichts —gefallen wäre**, act as if nothing had occurred. —**fassen**, *v.a.* to preconceive; —**gefaßte Meinung**, preconceived idea *or* opinion, prejudice, bias. —**fasten**, *pl.* Shrove-tide. —**fechten**, *ir.v.n.* (**einem**) to show how to fence; to fight for *or* in defence of. —**fechter**, *m.* champion, advocate; fencing-master. —**fegefeuer**, *n.* foretaste of purgatory. —**feier**, *f.* preliminary celebration of a festival; eve of a festival. —**fenster**, *n.* front window; outside window. —**finden**, *ir.v.* I. *a.* to find (*present*); to light upon. II. *r.* to be in existence; to be forthcoming. —**fliegen**, *ir.v.n.* (*aux.* **s.**) to fly forth *or* before; to outstrip in flying. —**flöße**, *f.* right of first floatage. —**flunkern**, *v.a.* (**einem etwas**) to tell s.o. a lie *or* a fib (*coll.*). —**flut**, *f.* coming-in tide; young flood. —**fordern**, *v.a.* to summon to appear, cite. —**frage**, *f.* preliminary question; **die —frage stellen**, to move the previous question (*Parl.*). —**fragen**, *reg.* & *ir.v.a.*; **bei einem —fragen ob . . .**, to call (*at a p.'s house*) to inquire if . . . —**freude**, *f.* anticipated joy, pleasure enjoyed beforehand. —**frucht**, *f.* green crop (*preceding the main produce of a field*). —**frühling**, *m.* beginning of *or* early spring; premature spring. —**fühlen**, *v.a.* to feel beforehand; to anticipate; to have a foreboding of. —**führen**, *v.a.* to bring forward, carry, lead before, to produce; **dem Richter einen Verbrecher —führen**, to lead out a criminal before the judge. —**führung**, *f.* bringing forth *or* out; introduction; production. —**gabe**, *f.* points *or* odds given *or* allowed; start. —**gabe=rennen**, *n.* handicap (race). —**gang**, *m.* proceeding; occurrence, incident, event; transaction; precedence, priority; example; model; precedent; **einem den —gang lassen**, to yield the precedence to s.o.

—gänger, *m.* leader; forerunner; predecessor. —gängig, *adj.* preliminary, preparatory; previous. —garten, *m.* front garden. —gaukeln, *v.a.* (einem etwas) to deceive (a p.) by false promises *or* hopes. —gebäude, *n.* forepart of a building; porch, vestibule. —geben, *ir.v.a.* to give (*a farce, etc.*) before (*the principal piece*); to give an advantage, to give points (*at billiards, etc.*); to put on (*as a pinafore*); to assert, advance, allege; to pretend; to plead; wie viel geben Sie mir — ? how many points will you allow *or* give me? Sie geben dies nur —, um Ihre unbesonnene That zu bemänteln, you only pretend this in excuse of your thoughtless action. —gebirge, *n.* hills at the foot of a mountain-chain; cape, foreland; promontory; headland. —geblich, I. *adj.* pretended; ostensible; so-called, would-be. II. *adv.* according to him (*her, etc.*), ostensibly. —gedacht, *adj. see* —erwähnt. —gefaßt, *adj.* preconceived. —gefecht, *n.* preliminary skirmish. —gefühl, *n.* presentiment; anticipation. —gegessen, *p.p. of* —essen; eaten *or* enjoyed beforehand; —gegessenes Brot, bread already eaten, bread bought with borrowed money; das ist — gegessenes Brot, that is counting one's chickens before they are hatched. —gehen, *ir.v.n.* (*aux.* f.) to go too fast (*of watches, etc.*); to go before, precede; to go first, take the lead; to march (upon, auf); to proceed, take measures to; to jut out, stand out; to outstrip (einem, one); to take precedence of; to surpass, excel (einem, a p.); to serve as model (einem, for s.o.); to show the way, to happen, go on, take place; bei einem —gehen, to call on s.o. (*on business*); bitte, gehen Sie —, ich folge, pray, lead the way, I will follow; Geschäfte gehen —, dann erst das Vergnügen, business first, pleasure afterwards; Ihr Unterrock geht —, your petticoat shows; was geht hier — ? what is going on here? was ist —gegangen? what has happened? es geht mir —, it occurs to me, I feel as if; ich weiß nicht, was in mir —ging, I don't know what I felt, what went on in my mind. —geigen, *v.a.* (einem ein Stück) to play (s.o. a piece) on the violin; to lead. —geiger, *m.* leader (*of the orchestra*). —gelege, *n.* communicator, fireplace, chimney, *etc.* (*prov.*); inneres —gelege, wheelwork with internal pinion. —gemach, *n.* anteroom. —gemeldet, —genannt, *adj.* aforementioned, before-mentioned. —genuß, *m.* foretaste of pleasure, anticipated enjoyment. —gericht, *see* —essen II. —gesang, *m.* introductory song; anthem. —geschichte, *f.* prehistoric times; history of the times preceding any epoch; previous history; antecedents. —geschichtlich, *adj.* prehistoric. —geschmack, *m.* foretaste. —gesetzte(r), *m.* chief; superior; principal, employer, master. —gestern, *adv.* the day before yesterday. —gestrig, *adj.* of the day before yesterday. —gestülpt, *adj.* protruded. —gethan, *see* —thun. —giebel, *m.* front gable (*Arch.*). —glänzen, *v.n.* (*aux.* h.) to appear in splendour, shine forth; einem —glänzen, to be a brilliant example to a person. —graben, *m.* avant-fossé, outer ditch. —greifen, *ir.v.n.* (*aux.* h.) to stretch out in front; to grasp, seize in front *or* before; to anticipate, forestall; to encroach, intrench upon (einem, a person's rights); den Ereignissen — greifen, to ancipate the events; einer Frage — greifen, to prejudge a matter; jemandes Urteil (*dat.*) —greifen, to forestall a p.'s judgment. —greiflich, *adv.* in anticipation. —greifung, *f.* anticipation, forestalling; encroachment; preoccupation. —haben, I. *ir.v.a.* to have before one; to have on, wear; to have in view; to purpose, intend; to be engaged on, occupied with, to be about; to examine, try; to call to account; to rebuke, chide, reprimand; sie hatte eine blaue Schürze —, she wore a blue apron; ich habe ihn schon — gehabt, I have already questioned *or* reprimanded him; was hat er — ? what is he after? was habt ihr mit einander — ? what are you quarrelling about? sie wußten nicht, mit wem sie es — hatten, they did not know with whom they had to do; er hat etwas Böses —, he is plotting some mischief, he means some evil; haben Sie für morgen etwas — ? have you made any plans for to-morrow? ich hatte — einen Brief zu schreiben, I intended to write a letter; was hast du mit ihm — ? what do you intend to do with him? what is your intention with regard to him? ich habe es gut mit Ihnen —, I wish you well. II. *subst. n.* intention, design, project, purpose; des —habens sein, to intend; das dient nicht zu unserm —haben, that does not suit our purpose; Gott segne Ihr —haben! God bless your work! —hafen, *m.* outer port. —halle, *f.* porch, vestibule; entrance hall; — halle einer Wissenschaft, the rudiments of a science. —halt, *m.* reproach; remonstrance, representation; retardation (*Mus.*). —halten, *ir.v.* I. *a.* (einem etwas) to hold before; to hold up to; to represent; to charge, reproach with. II. *n.* (*aux.* h.) to hold out; to wear, endure, stand; so lange das Geld —hält, as long as the money lasts. —hand, *f. see* Vorderhand; right hand, precedence; lead (*Cards*); einem die —hand lassen *or* geben, to give a p. the lead; to give *or* allow a p. the refusal (of a th.); wer hat die —hand? who has the lead? —han'den, *adj. & adv.* at hand, ready, present; actual, existent, extant; that can be found; —handen sein, to be, exist, to be on hand; es ist nichts mehr davon —handen, there is no more of it. —handen=sein, *n.* existence, presence. —hang, *m.* curtain. —hänge=blatt, *n.*; *see* —legeblatt. —hänge=schloß, *n.* padlock. —hangen, *v.n.* (*obs. dial.*) *see* —hängen, I. — hängen, *v.* I. *n.* (*aux.* f.) to hang before; to project. II. *a.* to hang before. —hauen, *ir.v.a.* to rough-hew; to prepare by hewing *or* cutting; ein Loch —hauen, to drill, bore a hole. —haupt, *n. see* Vorderhaupt; forehead. — haus, *n.* vestibule. —haut, *f.* foreskin; prepuce. —heizer, *m.* apparatus for heating (*the feed*-)water. —hemdchen, *n.*, —hemd(e), *n.* (false shirt-)front, dickey (*coll.*); chemisette (*for women*). —hemd=knopf, *m.* stud. —her, *see* Vorher. —herbst, *m.* beginning of autumn; early autumn. —herrschen, *v.n.* (*aux.* h.) to prevail, predominate. —heucheln, *v.a.* (einem etwas) to pretend, feign, sham; einem Treue —heucheln, to pretend fidelity to a person. —heulen, *v.a.* to howl, whine (einem, to *or* before s.o.). —himmel, *m.* fore-court of heaven; foretaste of heaven. — hi'n, *adv.* before, heretofore; a short time ago; erst —hin, just now. —historisch, *see* —geschichtlich. —hof, *m.* outer court; vestibule porch (*of a church, etc.*); vestibule (*of the ear*) ventricle (*of the heart*). —hölle, *f.* entrance to hell; limbo. —homerisch, *adj.* pre-Homeric. —hören, *v.* I. *a.*; man hört ihre Stimme unter allen —, her voice is heard above all the others. II. *n.* (*aux.* h.) to go and ask *or* find out. —hut, *f.* right of first pasturage; advanced guard, vanguard (*Mil.*). — jagen, I. *v.a.* to drive forth; to drive before. II. *n.* (*aux.* f.) to run in front; einem —jagen, to run before a p., to outstrip a p. in hunting *or* driving. —jahr, *n.* preceding year. — jährig, *adj.* of last year. —jammern, *v.a.* (einem etwas) to complain to (s.o.), trouble (a p.) with lamentations. —kammer, *f.* anteroom; auricle (*of the heart*). —**kämpfen**, *v.n.* (*aux.* **h.**) to fight before (**einem**, a p.); to fight in the front rank, the van; to set an example to other combatants. —**kämpfer**, *m.* fighter in the front rank; champion, advocate. —**kauen**, *v.a.* to chew previously (**einem Kinde**, for a child); **man muß ihm alles —kauen**, everything must be repeated over and over again, be made very plain to him (*coll.*). —**kauf**, *m.* forestalling; preemption; **den —kauf haben**, to have the refusal of. —**kaufen**, *v.a.* to buy before others; to forestall. —**käufer**, *m.* first purchaser; forestaller. —**kaufs=preis**, *m.* preemption price. —**kaufs=recht**, *n.* right of preemption. —**kehr**, *f.* provision, precaution, preventive measure; **weise —kehr der Natur**, wise provision of nature; **—kehr treffen**, to make arrangements, to provide for. —**kehren**, *v.a.* to sweep forth; to turn out; to provide (*against* or *for*), to take preventive measures, use precaution; **das Nötige —kehren**, to take the necessary steps; **Notwendigkeit —kehren**, to plead necessity. —**kehrung**, *see* **—kehr**. —**kenntnis**, *f.* previous knowledge. —**kenntnisse**, *pl.* elementary knowledge; rudiments; **gute —kenntnisse von einer S. besitzen**, to be well grounded in a subject; **keine —kenntnisse im Deutschen haben**, to have no previous acquaintance with German. —**kette**, *f.* secondary *or* lower chain (*of mountains*). —**kirche**, *f.* porch *or* vestibule of a church. —**klassisch**, *adj.* previous to the classic period, pre-classic(al). —**kleben**, *v.a.* to paste *or* glue before *or* on. —**klimpern**, *v.a.* (**einem etwas**) to strum a piece (*on a piano, etc.*) to a p. —**klingen**, *ir.v.n.* (*aux.* **h.**) to sound louder than the rest; to sound in one's ears; to sound beforehand. —**klö(h)nen**, *v.a.* (**einem etwas**) to talk to (a p.) at great length about trifles (*coll.*). —**kommen**, I. *ir.v.n.* (*aux.* **s.**) to come forth, out, on; to come sooner than another, get the start of; to come forward, appear; to look in, to call; to surpass, outstrip; to be admitted; to outrun; to be tried *or* heard (*Law*); to be moved, proposed, brought forward for discussion; to happen, occur, take place; to seem; to offer, present itself, fall in a p.'s way; to prevent, obviate; to be presented (*of bills*); **bei einem (mit) —kommen**, to give a p. a call in passing, call on s.o.; **kommen Sie nächsten Sonntag bei mir —**, give me a call *or* look in on me next Sunday; **die Sache kam —**, the matter was touched on; **dergleichen kommt nicht alle Tage —**, such things don't occur every day; **so etwas ist mir noch nicht —gekommen**, I have never heard of (*or* met with) such a thing before; **es kam mir recht wunderlich —**, it seemed very strange to me; **er schlug, was ihm —kam**, he struck everyone that came in his way; **einem etwas —kommen**, to pledge a person, to drink a p.'s (*good*) health (*stud. sl.*); **sind Ihnen meine Bücher nicht —gekommen?** have n't you seen my books? **das kommt Ihnen wohl spanisch —**, that strikes you, no doubt, as very strange; **das ist dir gewiß im Traume —gekommen**, you must have dreamt that; **ich weiß nicht, wie du mir heute —kommst**, I don't know what to make of you, I cannot make you out to-day. II. *subst. n.* occurrence; presence. —**kommnis**, *n.* occurrence, event. —**konferenz**, *f.* preliminary meeting *or* conference. —**können**, *ir.v.n.* (*aux.* **h.**) to be able to advance; to be able to come forth. —**korrektur**, *f.* indoor *or* rough proof; reading of indoor proof. —**kost**, *f.* hors d'œuvre, entrée; provisions, victuals, pulse and flour. —**kost=händler**, *m.* provision-dealer *or* merchant. —**kost=handlung**, *f.* provision shop, pulse and flour shop. —**kratze**, *f.* breaking-card (*Spin.*). —**kriegen**, *v.a.* to take to task, examine; to blow (a p.) up. —**lade=gewehr**, *n. see* **Vorderlader**. —**laden**, I. *ir.v.a.* to load at the muzzle. II. *ir. & reg.v.a.* to summon, subpœna (*a witness*). —**lader**, *m.* summoner. —**ladung**, *f.* I. loading in front *or* at the muzzle; wadding, wad (*Artil.*). II. citation, summons. —**ladungs=befehl**, *m.*, —**ladungs=schreiben**, *n.* summons to appear, citatory letter. —**ladungs=zettel**, *m.* summons (to appear). —**lage**, *f.* something laid before something else (*to prevent its rolling, etc.*); subject *or* matter (*brought forward for discussion, etc.*); bill (*Parl.*); text, copy; receiver (*in distilleries*); hydraulic main (*gas-works*); recipient, receiving vessel (*Chem.*); *see* —**legeblatt**; **eine gemeinsame —lage**, a common source (*of texts, mss.*). —**lager**, *n.* front, head of a camp (*Mil.*). —**lagern**, *v.r.* to sit down, pitch one's tent before (*s.th.*); to extend before, stretch out in front of. —**lallen**, *v.a.* (**einem etwas**) to mumble (s.th. to a p.). —**land**, *n.* foreland, foreshore; mud-flat; **die österreichischen —lande**, the Swabian provinces of Austria (now belonging to Baden). —**längst**, *adv.* long ago, long since. —**laß**, *m.* admission, access; unpressed wine. —**lassen**, *ir.v.a.* to suffer to go *or* come forward; to allow a p. to get the start of one; to let out of; to admit; **ich wurde (— ihn) —gelassen**, I was admitted (to his presence), I received an audience (of him). —**lassung**, *f.* admission, admittance; precedence. —**lauf**, *m.* start (*in a race*); first runnings, unpressed wine; the strongest distilled spirits; **—lauf von Apfelmost**, strong cider. —**laufen**, *ir.v.n.* (*aux.* **s.**) to run forward; to run in front; **einem —laufen**, to run in front of a p., to outstrip, pass a p. in running, to surpass s.o. —**läufer**, *m.*, —**läuferin**, *f.* forerunner; messenger; harbinger; precursor, symptom (*Med.*). —**läufig**, I. *adj.* previous, preliminary, preparatory, introductory; provisional; **—läufige Angabe beim Zoll**, prime entry. II. *adv.* as a preliminary (*measure, etc.*); previously; first of all; for the present, provisionally; in the mean time. —**laut**, *adj.* giving tongue too soon (*Hunt.*); noisy, forward; saucy, pert; hasty; **—lautes Wesen**, pertness, forwardness; **—laut sein**, to babble (*of dogs*). —**leben**, I. *v.n.* (*aux.* **h.**) to live previous to; **einem —leben**, to set an example to s.o. II. *subst.n.* former life; previous career *or* history, early life, antecedents. —**legbar**, *adj.* presentable; that may be propounded. —**lege=blatt**, *n.* drawing-copy, study; writing-copy. —**lege=gabel**, *f.* large fork; carving-fork. —**lege=kelle**, *f.* ladle; fish-slice. —**lege=löffel**, *m.* gravy-spoon; soup-ladle. —**lege=messer**, *n.* carving-knife; bread-knife. —**legen**, *v.a.* to put *or* lay before *or* in front; to put on; to put to (*horses, etc.*); to display, exhibit; to produce; to propose, offer, submit; to serve with, help (o.s. *or* s.o.) to (*a dish*); **dem Vieh Heu —legen**, to give the cattle hay; **Waren zum Verkauf —legen**, to expose goods for sale; **etwas weiter —legen**, to push something forward; **er hat gut —gelegt**, he has eaten a lot (*fam.*). —**leger**, *m.* person who carves, carver. —**lege=schloß**, *n.* padlock. —**legung**, *f.* laying before; exhibition, production; carving; representation; proposition. —**leiern**, *v.a.* (**einem etwas**) to play to a p. in a monotonous way; to din something into a person's ears. —**lesbar**, *adj.* fit for reading aloud. —**lese**, *f.* beginning of the vintage; vintage gathered in before others; **einem die —lese lassen**, to give a p. the first choice. —**lesen**, *ir.v.a.* to read aloud, read to; to gather the first ripe grapes; to gather in before others; **er läßt sich den Faust —lesen**, he has Faust read aloud to him. —**leser**, *m.*, —**leserin**, *f.*

reader (*to others*). —**lesung**, *f.* reading aloud; lecture, University lecture; **Wiedereröffnung der —lesungen am . . .**, lectures will begin again on . . .; courses will be resumed on . . .; —**lesungen über** (*acc.*) **halten**, to lecture (*on*), to give *or* deliver a course of lectures (*on*); —**lesungen hören**, to attend lectures; —**lesungen belegen**, to enter one's name for a course of lectures, to join a class (*on*); —**lesungen nachschreiben**, to take lecture notes; —**lesungen schwänzen**, to cut lectures; —**lesungen ausarbeiten**, to write out one's notes taken at a lecture; **eine öffentliche —lesung**, an open lecture, a lecture open to all students without payment of a fee; **eine Privat —lesung**, professor's lecture for which a fee is charged but open to all students; **eine Privatissime —lesung**, a lecture (free *or* otherwise) which cannot be attended without permission from the professor. *Comp.* —**lesungs=gebühr**, *f.* lecture fee. —**lesungs=verzeichnis**, *n.* lecture list. —**lesungs=zimmer**, *n.* lecture room, lecture hall. —**letzt**, *adj.* last but one; penultimate. —**leuchten**, *v.n.* (*aux.* **h.**) (**einem**) to carry a light *or* a torch before a p., to light (*a p.*); to be a brilliant example, set an example to. —**leuchter**, *m.* one who lights (*another*); torch-bearer; example. —**lieb**, *see* **Fürlieb**. —**liebe**, *f.* predilection, preference, bias, partiality. —**liegen**, *ir.v.n.* (*aux.* **h.**) to lie before; to be; **das Haus liegt —**, the house is in front; **einem —liegen**, to be under a p.'s eye, to be submitted to s.o.; **es liegt heute nichts —**, there is nothing to be discussed *or* considered to-day; **es muß hier ein Irrtum —liegen**, there must be some mistake here. —**lügen**, *v.a.* (**einem etwas**) to tell a p. lies. —**machen**, *v.a.* to put, place before; **einem etwas —machen**, to do before, show a p. how to do s.th.; to impose on a p.; to take a p. in; **einem einen blauen Dunst —machen**, to humbug a p. —**macht**, *f.* leading power. —**macht=stellung**, *f.* position of *or* as a leading power. —**magen**, *m.* crop (*of birds*); omasum (*Zool.*). —**mähen**, *v.n.* (*aux.* **h.**) to mow first; to show how to mow. —**malen**, *v.a.* (**einem etwas**) to draw *or* paint before; to show s.o. how to paint; to paint for (a p.); to describe, paint (to s.o.). —**malig**, *adj.* former. —**mals**, *adv.* formerly; once upon a time. —**mann**, *m. see* **Vordermann**; first player; foreman; —**mann eines Indossanten**, preceding endorser. —**mars**, *m.* the foretop (*Naut.*). —**marsch**, *m.* advance, march forward. —**marschieren**, *v.n.* (*aux.* **s.**) to advance. —**märzlich**, *adv.* before (the revolution of) March, 1848 (*said of old-fashioned reactionary institutions and views*). —**mast**, *m.* foremast. —**mauer**, *f.* outer wall, avant-mure (*Fort.*); barricade, bulwark, bastion; rampart. —**mauern**, *v.a.* to build a wall in front of. —**merken**, *v.a.* to mark in front; to perceive beforehand; to note down, take a note of, bespeak; **vorgemerkte Theaterbillets**, seats booked beforehand. —**merkung**, *f.* note; booking beforehand; memorandum. —**messen**, *ir.v.a.* (**einem etwas**) to measure in presence of. —**mittag**, **2c.**, *see* **Vormittag**, **2c.** —**mitternacht**, *f.* the time before midnight. —**mund**, **2c.**, *see* **Vormund**, **2c.** —**müssen**, *ir.v.n.* (*aux.* **h.**) to be obliged to come forth, advance, go out *or* appear. —**nageln**, *v.a.* to nail before. —**nahme**, *f.* undertaking, proceeding; design. —**name**, *m.* first name; Christian name. —**nehm**, **2c.**, *see* **Vornehm**, **2c.** —**nehmen**, *v.a.* (**eine S.** *or* **einen**) to take up, to work at a th.; to take a p. to task, to give a p. a piece of one's mind; **sich** (*dat.*) —**nehmen**, to intend *or* propose to do. —**neigen**, *v.a.* to bend forwards, to incline; **sich —neigen**, to bend forward, bow. —**neigung**, *f.* inclination, bending forward; predilection. —**ofen**, *m.* mouth of the oven; front of (a) furnace. —**ort**, *m.* place chosen by a society *or* association for its next general meeting, central place for the executive of an association; directorial canton in Switzerland. —**parlament**, *n.* preliminary parliament (*which met at Frankfort on the Main after the revolution of 1848*). —**pfeifen**, *ir.v.a.* (**einem etwas**) to whistle (*an air, etc.*) to. —**plappern**, *see* —**plaudern**. —**platz**, *m.* place before something; front garden; esplanade; landing (*of a staircase*); hall, vestibule; porch. —**plaudern**, *v.a.* (**einem etwas**) to chat, prattle to; to tell, make (a p.) believe (a thing that is not true). —**posten**, *m.* outpost, advanced post (*Mil.*); outlying picket; **auf —posten**, on outpost duty; —**posten ausstellen**, to place outposts; to throw out pickets. —**posten=dienst**, *m.* outpost-duty. —**posten=gefecht**, *n.* skirmish of outposts; engagement of advanced guards. —**posten=kette**, *f.* chain of outposts. —**posten=linie**, *f.* line of outposts, picket-line. —**prahlen**, *v.a.* (**einem etwas** *or* **von einer Sache**) to boast of a th. to *or* before (one). —**predigen**, *v.a.* (**einem etwas**) to preach to (s.o. upon a th.); to sermonize. —**prüfen**, *v.a.* to examine previously. —**prüfung**, *f.* previous examination, preliminary examination; **Universitäts —prüfung**, matriculation examination. —**ragen**, *v.n.* (*aux.* **h.**) to be prominent, to project, to jut out; to overtop. —**ragend**, *adj.* prominent, salient. —**rang**, *m.* pre-eminence, superiority, precedence; **den —rang vor einem haben**, to have *or* take precedence of s.o. —**rat**, *see* **Vorrat**. —**rechnen**, *v.a.* to compute, calculate in presence of; to enumerate; **ich kann Ihnen leicht —rechnen, was ich dabei verdiene**, I can easily show you how much I make by it. —**recht**, *n.* privilege, prerogative. —**recken**, *v.a.* to stretch forward. —**rede**, *f.* preliminary observation, prefatory discourse; preface; —**rede spart Nachrede**, a word before is worth two after (*prov.*). —**reden**, *v.a.* (**einem etwas**) to tell (s.o. s.th.); to speak (a p.) fair; to talk into *or* over; **sich** (*dat.*) **etwas —reden lassen**, to let oneself be talked over, be humbugged. —**redner**, *m.* he who speaks before another; **mein (geehrter Herr) —redner**, the honourable gentleman who has just spoken *or* sat down (*parl.*). —**reiben**, *ir.v.a.* to rub, pound, grind previously; **einem etwas —reiben**, to cast something in a p.'s teeth. —**reif**, *adj.* premature, precocious. —**reigen**, —**reihen**, *m.* opening of a ball; first row of dancers; **den —reihen haben**, to lead off (*the dance*). —**reißen**, *ir.v.a.* to tear violently forth; to make a first sketch of; to trace, sketch; **einem Witze —reißen**, to retail bad jokes for a p.'s amusement. —**reißer**, *m.* tracer; gardener's dibble; *see* —**walze**. —**reiten**, *ir.v.* I. *a.*; **ein Pferd —reiten**, to put a horse through its paces; **einem etwas —reiten**, to make a parade *or* show of; to display a th. before a p.; **einen Ball —reiten**, to expose oneself, one's ball (*Bill.*). II. *n.* (*aux.* **s.**) (**einem**) to ride before; to ride forward; to outride; to show (a p.) how to ride; to expose one's ball (*Bill.*). —**reiter**, *m.* outrider, mounted courier; postillion. —**rennen**, *ir.v.n.* (*aux.* **s.**) to run on; to outrun (**einem**, one). —**richten**, *v.a.* to bring, push forward; to prepare, make ready; to fit up; to put on (*a watch, etc.*). —**richtung**, *f.* preparation, arrangement; contrivance; mechanism; (*pl.*) preparations. —**riß**, *m.* first sketch, rough draught. —**ritt**, *m.* riding out *or* forward; exposed ball. —**rücken**, *v.* I. *a.* to put, push forward (*a chair; a watch, etc.*); **einem etwas —rücken**, to reproach *or* charge a p. with a th. II. *n.* (*aux.* **s.**) to advance, to be promoted; to push on; **Truppen —rücken lassen**, to order troops to advance, to push the troops forward. **—rufen**, *ir.v.a.* to call forth; to call up. **—rüsten**, *v.a.* to prepare, equip (*beforehand*). **—saal**, *m.* entrance-hall; ante-chamber; waiting-room. **—sagen**, *v.a.* to say beforehand: **einem etwas —sagen**, to tell a p. a thing, to rehearse *or* recite something to s.o., to say something to deceive s.o., to prompt a p., to dictate to s.o.; **einem viel Schönes —sagen**, to make pretty speeches to a p.; **das kann ich kaum glauben, du sagst mir das wohl nur so —**, I can scarcely believe it, you are only saying so (*to see if I will believe it, etc.*). **—sager**, *m.* prompter. **—sänger(in**, *f.*), *m.* leader of a choir; precentor; officiating minister (*in a synagogue*). **—satz**, *m.* design, project, plan; resolution; **mit —satz**, on purpose, with premeditation; **mit —satz lügen**, to tell a deliberate lie. **—sätzlich**, *adj. & adv.* intentional, done designedly. **—schanze**, *f.* outwork, advanced redoubt. **—schein**, *m.*; **zum —schein kommen**, to appear; **wieder zum —schein kommen**, to turn up again; **zum —schein bringen**, to produce. **—schieben**, *ir.v.a.* to push *or* shove forward; to slip (*a bolt*); to hinder, prevent; to interpose; to cover (*by pushing something before*); to plead (*as excuse*); **—geschobene Forts**, advanced forts, outlying fortifications; **zu weit —geschoben**, too far advanced. **—schieber**, *m.* slide-bolt; sliding door; iron tie *or* clamp (*Arch.*). **—schiebung**, *f.* feed (*Sew-mach.*). **—schießen**, *ir.v.* I. *a.*; **einem eine Summe Geld —schießen**, to lend *or* advance a p. a sum of money; **einen Saum —schießen**, to put a hem on a dress. II. *n.* (*aux.* **h.**) to shoot in presence of (**einem**, a p.); to show (**einem**, a p.) how to shoot; to shoot before (**einem**, s.o.); (*aux.* **s.**) to dart, rush forth; to shoot up, to project; to surpass, excel. **—schlag, ꝛc.**, *see* **Vorschlag, ꝛc.** **—schläger**, *m.* bird that teaches others to sing; forge-man. **—schmack**, *m.* foretaste. **—schmecken**, *v.* I. *a.* to taste beforehand; to have a foretaste of. II. *n.* (*aux.* **h.**) to predominate (*of a flavour*). **—schmeicheln**, *v.a.* to flatter a person. **—schneide=brett**, *n.* trencher. **—schneide=messer**, *n.* carving-knife. **—schneiden**, *ir.v.a.* to carve, cut up (*fowls, etc.*); to cut in presence of; **einem Gesichter —schneiden**, to make faces at a p. **—schneider**, *n.* carver. **—schnell**, *see* **—eilig**. **—schrauben**, *v.a.* to screw forward *or* out. **—schreiben**, *ir. v.a.* to set (**einem**, s.o.) a copy; **etwas vor eine S. —schreiben**, to write s.th. before *or* in front of something else; (**einem etwas**) **—schreiben**, to dictate, prescribe, lay down (*as a rule*), to order, direct; **ich lasse mir nichts —schreiben**, I will not be dictated to (*by any one*); **Sie haben mir nichts —zuschreiben**, I am not under your orders, not bound to obey you. **—schreien**, *ir.v.a.* (**einem etwas**) to shout, cry, bawl in s.o.'s ears. **—schreiten**, *ir.v.n.* (*aux.* **s.**) to step forth; to advance, march on; **einem —schreiten**, to step before a p., to precede, to outstrip s.o. (*in walking*); **—geschrittenes Stadium**, advanced stage (*of an illness*). **—schrift**, *f.* writing-copy; recipe; prescription; direction, precept, rule; order, instructions; regulation; **nach —schrift**, as prescribed. **—schriften=buch**, *n.* copy-book; book of written instructions. **—schrifts=mäßig**, *adj.* according to instructions; as ordered; regulation (*Mil.*). **—schrifts=widrig**, *adj.* contrary to directions *or* to regulations *or* to orders. **—schritt**, *m.* step forward, advance. **—schub**, *m.* first throw *or* bowl (*at skittles*); the lead, first stroke (*Bill.*); help, assistance, aid, support; **einem —schub leisten**, to help *or* abet a p.; **einer Sache —schub leisten** *or* **thun**, to further a matter. **—schuh**, *m.* vamp, upper leather (*of a boot*). **—schuhen**, *v.a.* to put new feet (*to boots*); to put new vamps (*on boots*). **—schule**, *f.* preparatory school, junior department; introduction to (*a science, etc.*); elementary course. **—schul=klasse**, *f.* class *or* form in a preparatory school. **—schüler**, *m.* pupil in a preparatory school. **—schürze**, *f.* apron. **—schuß**, *see* **Vorschuß**. **—schütten**, *v.a.* to raise (*dikes*); to throw down, give (*provender*). **—schützen**, *v.a.* to throw up as a defence; to shelter behind; to pretend; to allege as excuse; **Unwissenheit —schützen**, to plead ignorance. **—schwarm**, *m.* first swarm (*of bees*). **—schwatzen**, *see* **—plaudern**. **—schweben**, *v.n.* (*aux.* **h.**, *& now obs.*, **s.**) to swim, hover before; **das schwebt mir dunkel —**, I have a confused notion *or* recollection of it. **—schwimmen**, *ir.v.n.* (*aux.* **s.**) to swim in front; to swim quicker than s.o. (**einem**); to show (**einem**, a p.) how to swim. **—schwindeln**, *v.a.* (**einem etwas**) to try to make (a p.) believe, to cheat a p. by telling fibs. **—segel**, *n.* foresail. **—segeln**, *v.n.* (*aux.* **s.**) to sail in front; to sail on; **einem Schiffe —segeln**, to outsail a vessel. **—sehen**, *ir.v.* I. *a.* to foresee; to consider; to provide for; **der Fall ist im Gesetze nicht —gesehen**, this case is not provided for by the law. II. *r.* to take care, be mindful of, be on one's guard; **seht euch —!** **—gesehen!** look out! take care! (*on packing-cases*) glass, with care! **sich auf eine S. —sehen**, to take precautions against a th.; **sich vor einem —sehen**, to be on one's guard against a p. **—sehung**, *f.* providence; **die göttliche —sehung**, (Divine) Providence. **—sein**, *ir.v.n.* to be in advance, on before; to have the first chance; to be discussed; to be tried; to stand out; **weit in Jahren —sein**, to be advanced in years; **was ist jetzt —?** what is on now? (*coll.*); what is now under consideration? **da sei Gott —!** God forbid! **—setz—, ꝛc.**, *see* **Vorsetz—, ꝛc.** **—sich=gehend**, *adj.* proceeding, progressing. **—sich=hin=lächeln**, *n.* smiling to o.s., silent smile. **—sich=hin=sprechen**, *n.* talking to o.s., monologue. **—sicht**, *f.* foresight; prudence, caution, circumspection; providence; **—sicht!** look out! have a care! with care! (*on boxes*); **mit vieler —sicht zu Werke gehen**, to act very cautiously; **—sichtig**, *adj.* cautious, prudent, wary, circumspect; discreet; wise; **—sichtig sein**, to be cautious, to take care. **—sichtigkeit**, *f.* caution, circumspection. **—sichts=maßregeln**, *pl.* precautionary measures, measures of prudence. **—silbe**, *f.* prefix. **—singen**, *ir.v.a.* to sing to *or* before (**einem**, a p.); to lead the singing. **—singer**, *see* **—sänger**. **—sitz**, *m.* presidency, the chair; **den —sitz haben, führen**, to preside, to be in the chair; **den —sitz (bei einer Versammlung) übernehmen**, to take the chair (at a meeting). **—sitzen**, *ir.v.n.* (*aux.* **h.**) to preside; **einem —sitzen**, to have precedence of s.o. **—sitzer, —sitzende(r)**, *m.* president, chairman; **—sitzer und Beisitzer**, chairman and committee, **—sitzender der Prüfungskommission**, chairman of the board of examiners; **mit Dr. Jackson als —sitzer** *or* **—sitzendem**, with Dr. Jackson in the chair. **—sommer**, *m.* early summer. **—sorge**, *f.* foresight, care; precaution; provision; providential care; **—sorge tragen** *or* **treffen, daß ...**, to take care that, to provide for; **—sorge verhütet Nachsorge**, prevention is better than cure (*prov.*). **—sorgen**, *v.n.* (*aux.* **h.**) to take (*the necessary*) precautions; to provide for, take care that; **—gesorgt ist halb gethan**, well begun is half done (*prov.*). **—sorglich**, *adj. & adv.* provident, careful; as a precaution. **—spann**, *m.* relay, fresh horses. **—spannen**, *v.a.* to stretch in front of; to put horses to *or* in a carriage. **—spann=pferd**, *n.* fresh horse;

additional horse. **—spiegeln,** *v.a.* (**einem etwas**) to dazzle s.o.'s eyes with, present in a dazzling light (to a p.); to deceive (s.o.) by false show. **—spiegelung,** *f.* illusion, sham, mockery, misrepresentation; promise founded on illusions. **—spiel,** *n.* prelude (*Mus.*); short piece before the principal one (*Theat.*); prologue. **—spielen,** *v.a.;* (**einem etwas**) to play before *or* to (a p.). **—spinnen, —gespinnst,** *n.* roving (*Spin.*). **—spinn=maschine,** *f.* frame used in spinning, roving-frame. **—sprechen,** *ir.v.* I. *a.* (**einem etwas**) to pronounce to *or* for (s.o.); to teach (a p.) how to pronounce. II. *n.* (*aux.* **h.** & **s.**); **bei einem —sprechen,** to call on s.o., to look in at a p. **—sprengen,** *v.n.* (*aux.* **h.**) to gallop forward. **—springen,** *ir.v.n.* (*aux.* **h.**) to leap before (a p., **einem**); (*aux.* **s.**) to leap forward; to leap further than (s.o., **einem**); to jut out, project. **—sprung,** *m.* projection, ledge; start, lead; advantage; **den —sprung gewinnen, einem den —sprung abgewinnen,** to get the start of a p., to have the advantage over a p. **—spuk,** *m.* omen, portent, ghostly warning. **—spuken,** *v.n.* (*aux.* **h.**) to appear as a portent, to forebode, to serve as an omen. **—stadt,** *f.* suburb. **—städter,** *m.* resident in a suburb. **—städtisch,** *adj.* suburban. **—stand,** *m.* board of directors, managing *or* executive committee; director. **—stand=schaft,** *f.* directorship, directorate. **—stands=dame,** *f.* lady member of the executive committee, (lady) patroness. **—stands=mitglied,** *n.* director, member of the managing *or* executive committee. **—stands=sitzung,** *f.* meeting of a board of directors; meeting of the executive *or* managing committee. **—stands=wahl,** *f.* election of the committee *or* directors. **—stechen,** *ir.v.* I. *a.* to prick *or* pierce before. II. *n.* (*aux.* **h.**) to stand out; to jut forth, be prominent; to outdo, outshine; **das Rot sticht —,** the red predominates. **—stecher,** *m.* punch, stamp; piercer. **—steck—, ꝛc.,** *see* **Vorsteck—, ꝛc. —steh—, ꝛc.,** *see under* **Vorsteh—, ꝛc. —stellbar, ꝛc.,** *see under* **Vorstell—. —stenge,** *m.f.* foretopmast. **—stopfen,** *v.a.* to put before (*a hole*) in order to stop it. **—stoß,** *m.* push forward; forward movement, advance (*Mil.*); eking-piece; projection; adapter (*Chem.*); beak (*of an alembic*); detent (*Horol.*); piping, raised seam (*Carp.*); braid; binding; bee-glue. **—stoßen,** *ir.v.* I. *a.* to push forward; **einen Saum —stoßen,** to welt, make a raised seam. II. *n.* (*aux.* **s.**) to push forward, march against; to rush out and fall upon; to project. **—strecken,** *v.a.* to stretch forward *or* out; to stretch in front of; to put forth, poke out; to extend; to advance, lend (*money*). **—streckung,** *f.* stretching forth; extension; advancement (*of money*). **—streichen,** *ir.v.a.* to rub, stroke forward. **—streuen,** *v.a.* to strew, scatter (*before*). **—strich,** *m.* front ward (*of a key*). **—stück,** *n.* piece in front; piece before another (*Theat.*); (*pl.*) bow-chaser. **—stufe,** *f.* first step; step in front; introduction (*to a science, etc.*). **—stülpen,** *v.a.* to protrude (*the lips*). **—stürzen,** *v.n.* (*aux.* **s.**) to rush forward. **—suche,** *f.* quest, search. **—suchen,** *v.a.* to search for; to bring forth by searching; to draw a cover (*Sport*). **—sündflutlich,** *adj.* antediluvian. **—tanzen,** *v.* I. *a.* to dance (*a waltz, etc.*) before one. II. *n.* (*aux.* **h.**) to lead off a dance. **—tänzer(in,** *f.*), *m.* leader of the dance; one that shows how to dance (*a certain step or figure*). **—teil,** *see* **Vorteil. —thun,** *ir.v.* I. *a.* to put before; to put on; to do beforehand; to do hastily, inconsiderately; to show how to do; **es einem —thun,** to surpass s.o. in doing; **die Pferde —thun,** to harness, put in the horses; **—gethan und nachgedacht hat manchem schon groß Leid gebracht,** it's no use to shut the stable door after the steed is stolen, look before you leap (*prov.*). II. *r. see* **Hervorthun. —thür(e),** *f.* outer door (*of a double door*). **—trab,** *m.* vanguard, advanced guard; skirmishers. **—traben,** *v.n.* (*aux.* **s.**) to trot on in front. **—trag, ꝛc.** *see* **Vortrag, ꝛc. —treff'lich,** *adj.* excellent, admirable, first-rate, splendid, capital. **—treff'lichkeit,** *f.* excellence. **—treiben,** *ir.v.a.* to drive before; to drive on *or* forth; **eine Galerie —treiben,** to push forward a trench *or* mine (*Mil.*). **—treppe,** *f.* first *or* short flight of stairs (*before another*); flight of steps outside a house. **—treten,** *ir. v.n.* (*aux.* **s.**) to step before; to step forward, come forth, advance; to project; to come out; to appear before (**einem**, one); **mit etwas nicht —treten wollen,** not to be willing to produce a th. **—trinken,** *ir.v.a. & n.* (*aux.* **h.**) to drink before (**einem**, a p.); to drink more quickly than (**einem**, s.o.); **einem —trinken,** to pledge a p. **—tritt,** *m.* first step; step forward; precedence; **den —tritt vor einem haben,** to take precedence of a p. **—trupp,** *m.* front rank *or* troop of the vanguard. **—truppen,** *pl.* advanced troops, troops of the advanced guard. **—tuch,** *n.* apron; bib; handkerchief worn in front. **—turnen,** *v.n.* (*aux.* **h.**) to lead *or* teach a squad of gymnasts. **—turner,** *m.* leader of a squad *or* section of gymnasts. **—über, ꝛc.** *see* **Vorüber, ꝛc. —untersuchung,** *f.* preliminary trial *or* inquiry *or* investigation. **—urteil, ꝛc.,** *see* **Vorurteil, ꝛc. —vater,** *m.* forefather, ancestor, progenitor. **—vergangenheit,** *f.* pluperfect (*Gram.*); antecedents, previous career. **—verhör,** *n.* preliminary examination. **—verkauf,** *m.* advance sale; booking in advance (*Theat.*); **im —verkauf,** if booked in advance. **—versammlung,** *f.* preliminary meeting. **—vordern,** *pl.* ancestors. **—vorgestern,** *adv.* three days ago. **—vorig,** *adj.* last but one. **—vorletzt,** *adj.* last but two; antepenultimate. **—wache,** *f.* advanced guard. **—wagen,** *v.r.* to venture forward. **—wahl,** *f.* preliminary election, nomination. **—wall,** *m.* outer rampart. **—walten,** *v.n.* (*aux.* **h.**) to predominate, prevail; to be, to (actually) exist. **—walze,** *f.* (**der Dubliermaschine**) licker-in, taker-in; (*pl.*) roughing-rolls. **—walzen,** *v.a.* to rough down. **—wand,** *m.* pretext, subterfuge, excuse; shelter; colour; **unter dem —wand,** on the plea. **—wärts, ꝛc.,** *see* **Vorwärts, ꝛc. —we'g,** *adv.* before; from before; from the beginning; beforehand; **—weg genießen,** to anticipate enjoyment; **—weg sein (mit der Zunge),** to be too free with one's tongue, to let one's tongue wag too freely (*coll.*). **—weg'=nahme,** *f.* anticipation; taking before another; previous deduction. **—weg'=nehmen,** *ir.v.a.* to deduct, take away beforehand; to anticipate (*a p. in*). **—wein,** *m.* unpressed wine. **—weinen,** *see* **—jammern. —weisen,** *ir.v.a.* to exhibit, show (forth), display, produce. **—welt,** *f.* former ages, antiquity; primitive world; our forefathers. **—weltlich,** *adj.* of former ages; of a primitive world. **—wenden,** *reg. & ir.v.a.* to allege, pretend, give out. **—werfen,** *ir.v.a.* to throw out; to cast before, throw to; **einem (etwas) —werfen,** to cast in a p.'s teeth, to reproach a p. with; **einem seine Faulheit —werfen,** to reproach a p. with laziness; **sie haben einander nichts —zuwerfen,** the one is as bad (*or* as good) as the other. **—werk,** *n.* farm (*adjacent to the manor*); outwork (*Fort.*); **—werke einer Festung,** advanced forts. **—wiegen,** *ir.v.* I. *a.* (**einem etwas**) to weigh in (s.o.'s) presence; to weigh out (to a p.). II. *n.* (*aux.* **h.**) to preponderate, prevail; to predominate. **—wimmern, —winseln,** *see* **—jammern.**

—**wind**, *m.* wind astern. —**winter**, *m.* beginning of winter; early winter. —**wissen**, *n.* foreknowledge; (*previous*) knowledge; **es geschah mit meinem —wissen**, it happened with my full knowledge and consent; **ohne mein —wissen**, without my knowing (it), unknown to me. —**witz**, *m.* curiosity, inquisitiveness; forwardness, impertinence; inquisitive person (*coll.*); **was deines Amtes nicht ist, da lasse deinen —witz**, don't meddle with what does n't concern you. —**witzig**, *adj.* inquisitive, prying; forward, pert, impertinent. —**wort**, *n.* preface; preamble. —**wurf**, *m.* reproach; blame; remonstrance; subject, theme (*of drama or painting*) (*obs.*); lure, bait. —**wurfs=frei**, —**wurfs=los**, *adj.* irreproachable, blameless. —**wurfs=voll**, *adj.* reproachful. —**zählen**, *v.a.* (**einem etwas**) to count out to, to count before; to enumerate. —**zahn**, *m.* projecting tooth. —**zeichen**, *n.* omen, prognostic; sign (*Math.*); signature (*Mus.*). —**zeichnen**, *v.a.* to draw *or* sketch before; to show how to draw (*something*); to point out; to mark, indicate; to trace out; to chalk out; to sketch; to put the sign of the clef, prefix sharps and flats (*Mus.*). —**zeichner**, *m.* sketcher, designer. —**zeichnung**, *f.* drawing before (*a p.*); drawing-copy, model, design; pattern; key-signature. —**zeigen**, *v.a.* to show, display; to produce. —**zeiger**, *m.*; —**zeiger dieses**, the bearer of this (*note, etc.*). —**zeigung**, *f.* production, exhibition. —**zeit**, *f.* antiquity, days of yore. —**zei'ten**, *adv.* formerly. —**zeitig**, *adj.* premature, before its proper time, all too soon, precocious; anticipated. —**ziehbar**, *adj.* preferable. —**ziehen**, *ir.v.* I. *a.* to draw forward *or* forth; to draw before; to prefer, give the preference to; **ich werde es dir bringen, wenn du nicht —ziehst, es zu holen**, I shall bring it to you, unless you would rather fetch it yourself. II. *n.* (*aux.* **s.**) to march before; to go on, advance; to remove to the front. —**zimmer**, *n.* anteroom, antechamber; lobby. —**zug**, *m.* preference; excellence; superiority; priority; prerogative; advantage; merit; privilege; train running in advance of the regular train, pilot train; **den —zug vor einem haben**, to be preferred to a p., to have the advantage over a p.; to surpass, excel a p. —**züglich**, *adj.* preferable; (*pron.* **vorzüg'lich**) superior; first-rate; excellent; remarkable; **der, die, das —züglichste**, the first, best, most excellent; **das —züglichste Stück**, the principal piece; —**züglicher als einer**, superior to a p. —**züg'lichkeit**, *f.* superiority, excellence, superior quality. —**zugs=aktien**, *pl.* preference shares. —**zugs=preis**, *m.* exceptional price, special price. —**zugs=recht**, *n.* privilege. —**zugs=tage**, *pl.* days of grace *or* respite. —**zugs=weise**, *adv.* preferably, by preference.

Vora'n, *adv. & sep. prefix*, before, on, onwards; at the head, in front, foremost, first; **nur —!** go on! pass on! go ahead! *Comp.* —**eilen**, *v.n.* (*aux.* **s.**), —**laufen**, *ir.v.n.* (*aux.* **s.**) to run, hasten on before. —**gehen**, *ir.v.n.* (*aux.* **s.**) to go before; to take the lead; **gehen Sie —!** go first! lead on, lead the way! **einem —gehen**, to precede a p.; **mit gutem Beispiel —gehen**, to set a good example. —**schicken**, *v.a.* to send on before; to put at the head of. —**schreitend**, *adj.* progressive.

Voran's, I. *adv. & sep. prefix*, in advance; in front, on ahead, before the rest; previously; in preference; **er ging —**, he went on in front; **ich habe mein Gepäck —geschickt**, I have sent my luggage in advance; **er ist vor seinem Alter —**, he is precocious; **etwas vor einem — haben**, to have an advantage over another; **im** *or* **zum —**, in advance, by anticipation; proleptically (*Gram.*). II. *n.* advantage greater *or* extra share. *Comp.* —**bedenken**, *ir.v.a.* to think of beforehand, to premeditate. —**bedingen**, *reg. & ir.v.a.* to stipulate beforehand; **sich** (*dat.*) **etwas —bedingen**, to reserve to oneself (*a right, etc.*). —**bestimmung**, *f.* predetermination (*of man's will*); predestination. —**bezahlen**, *v.a.* to pay in advance; to prepay. —**bezahlung**, *f.* payment in advance. —**beziehung**, *f.* drawing beforehand *or* in advance (*one's salary, etc.*). —**empfangen**, *ir. v.a.* to receive in advance. —**empfinden**, *ir.v.n.* (*aux.* **h.**) to feel beforehand, have a presentiment of. —**fahren**, *ir.v.* I. *a.* to drive before. II. *n.* (*aux.* **s.**) to precede. —**gehen**, *ir.v.n.* (*aux.* **s.**) to go before; **dem Regimente —gingen . . .**, the regiment was preceded by . . . —**laufen**, *ir.v.n.* (*aux.* **s.**) to run before. —**nahme**, *f.* anticipation, forestalling. —**nehmen**, *ir.v.a.* to take in advance; to anticipate, forestall. —**reisen**, *v.n.* (*aux.* **s.**) to travel on before *or* in advance. —**reiten**, *ir.v.n.* (*aux.* **s.**) to ride on ahead. —**sage**, *f.* prediction, prophecy; **die ärztliche —sage**, prognosis. —**sagen**, *v.a* to prophesy, predict. —**schicken**, *v.a.* to send on before; to say beforehand, to give notice, to premise; **dies —geschickt, gehen wir zur Sache über**, this being premised, let us pass on to the matter in hand. —**sehen**, *ir.v.a.* to foresee, forebode. —**setzen**, *v.a.* to suppose, presume. —**setzung**, *f.* supposition; hypothesis; **zur —setzung haben**, to presuppose; **zur —setzung machen**, to make the basis of, to take for granted. —**sicht**, *f.* foresight, prudence. —**sichtlich**, *adj.* probable, presumable, to be expected.

Vorbei', *adv. & sep. prefix*, along, by; past; passing before; past, over, done with; **an, neben, vor einer S. — gehen**, to pass something, to pass near, to pass in front of something; **es ist mit ihm —**, it is all over with him; **— ist —**, gone is gone, the past cannot be recalled; **drei Schüsse —!** missed three times (*to hit the target*)! *Comp.* —**eilen**, *v.n.* (*aux.* **s.**); **an einem —eilen**, to hasten past a p. —**fahren**, *ir.v.n.* (*aux.* **s.**) to drive past. —**fliegen**, *ir.v.n.* (*aux.* **s.**) to fly past. —**fließen**, *ir.v.n.* (*aux.* **s.**); **an der Mauer —fließen**, to flow at the foot of the wall, flow by the wall. —**gehen**, I. *ir.v.n.* (*aux.* **s.**), (**an einem**, *or* (*obs. poet.*) **einen**) *see under* **Vorbei**. II. *subst.n.* passing; **im —gehen**, in passing. —**gelingen**, *v.n.* (*sl.*) not to be successful; **es ist ihm —gelungen**, he has failed (*sl.*). —**kommen**, *ir.v.n.* (*aux.* **s.**) to pass before, pass by. —**können**, *ir.v.n.* (*aux.* **h.**) to be able to pass. —**lassen**, *ir.v.a.* to let pass, let go past. —**marsch**, *m.* defiling, march past; passage. —**marschie'ren**, *v.n.* (*aux.* **s.**) to march past. —**müssen**, *ir.v.n.* (*aux.* **h.**) to be obliged to pass. —**reisen**, *v.a.* (**an einem** *or* (*obs. poet.*) **einen**). —**reiten**, *ir.v.n.* (*aux.* **s.**) to ride past. —**schießen**, *ir.v.n.* (*aux.* **s.**) to shoot past; to dart quickly past; (*aux.* **h.**) to miss (*in shooting*). —**werfen**, *ir.v.n.* (*aux.* **h.**) to miss (*in throwing*). —**ziehen**, *ir.v.n.* (*aux.* **s.**) to pass; to march past.

Vor'bereit—en, *v.a.* to prepare, get ready beforehand; **einen für eine S. —en**, to prepare, fit, make a p. disposed for a thing; **auf eine S. —et sein**, to be prepared for a th.; **sich auf eine S.** *or* **zu einer S. —en**, to make preparations, get ready for a th.; **einem eine Überraschung —en**, to prepare a surprise for a p.; —**end**, preliminary, predisposing; **er hat sich auf die Prüfung sorgfältig —et**, he has prepared himself carefully *or* he has read hard for his examination. —**ung**, *f.* preparation.

training; (*pl.*) preparations, arrangements, preliminaries. *Comp.* **—ungs=klasse**, *f.* class for preparation; elementary class. **—ungs=schule**, *f.* preparatory school. **—ungs=zimmer**, *n.* dark room (*Photog.*); initiatory room (*Freem.*).

Vor'der, *adj.* fore, forward, anterior, front; foremost; **der —ste**, the furthest advanced, the first; **—e Seite**, front. *Comp.* **—ansicht**, *f.* front view. **—arm**, *m.* fore-arm. **—blatt**, *n.* fore-quarter (*of a beast*); shoulder (*of mutton*); fore-part (*of a stocking*); vamp (*of a shoe*). **—brust**, *f.* front part of the chest. **—bug**, *m.* shoulder (*of mutton, etc.*). **—chor**, *n.* front part of the choir (*Arch.*). **—deck**, *n.* fore-deck. **—eck**, *n.* first skittle. **—eisen**, *n.* front shoe of a horse; coulter (*of a plough*). **—fassade**, **—façade**, **—front**, *f.* front (*Arch.*). **—fläche**, *f.* anterior surface. **—flagge**, *f.* bowsprit-flag. **—fleck**, *m.* fore-end of the sole, half sole. **—fuß**, *m.* fore-foot; front part of the foot, metatarsus; **der linke —fuß eines Pferdes**, the near fore-foot of a horse. **—gang**, *m.* front corridor. **—gebäude**, *n.* front of a building, front building. **—geschirr**, *n.* breast-harness (*of four-in-hand harness*). **—gestell**, *n.* fore-carriage; front wheels and frame (*of a carriage*), gallows and wheels (*of a plough, etc.*). **—glied**, *n.* fore-limb; front rank; antecedent, first term (*Arith.*); major (*Log.*); antecedent (*Log.*). **—grund**, *m.* foreground, front; **in den —grund stellen**, to place in the front *or* foreground, to take first into consideration, to throw into relief. **—hand**, *f.* fore part of the hand; metacarpus; fore paw; lead (*at cards*). **—haupt**, *n.*, **—kopf**, *m.* fore part of the head, forehead; sinciput. **—lader**, *m.* muzzle-loader (*Gun.*). **—lauf**, *m.* fore-leg (*Hunt.*); fore-end (*of the barrel of a gun*). **—leib**, *m.* front of the body. **—leute**, *pl.* (*men in the*) front ranks; **ich habe noch zehn —leute**, there are still ten ahead of (*or* before) me. **—mann**, *m.* front-rank man; file-leader; preceding endorser; **—mann halten**, to keep in line *or* file. **—mast**, *m.* fore-mast. **—maschine**, *f.* receiver (*Mach.*). **—mauer**, *f.* front wall. **—perron**, *n.* front platform (*on tram cars*). **—pferd**, *n.* leader, leading horse. **—rad=gabel**, *f.* front fork (*Cycl.*). **—rad=schutzblech**, *n.* front mud guard (*Cycl.*). **—reihe**, *f.* front rank. **—satz**, *m.* protasis (*Gram.*); antecedent; (*pl.*) premises (*Log.*). **—seite**, *f.* front; frontispiece, façade (*Arch.*); obverse (*Typ.*); face (*of a coin*) recto (*in manuscripts*). **—sitz**, *m.* front seat. **—stelle**, *f.* front *or* first place. **—steven**, *m.* stem (*of a ship*); cut-water (*Naut.*). **—stich**, *m.* running stitch (*Sew.*). **—teil**, *n.* (*& m.*) front; prow (*of a ship*). **—thor**, *n.* flood-gate; front gate. **—thür**, *f.* house-door, front door. **—treffen**, *n.* first line (*of battle*). **—wagen**, *m.* fore-carriage (*Artil.*). **—wand**, *f.* front of a wall.

Vorhe'r, *adv. & sep. prefix*, beforehand, in advance; before, previously; on before, in front; **am Abend —**, (*on*) the previous evening; **kurz —**, a little while before. **—ig**, *adj.* previous, preceding, antecedent, former, last. *Comp.* **—bedenken**, *ir.v.a.* to think, consider beforehand; to premeditate. **—bestimmen**, *v.a.* to determine, settle beforehand; to preordain; to predestine. **—bestimmung**, *f.* pre-determination; predestination. **—bestimmungs=lehre**, *f.* doctrine of predestination. **—dasein**, *n.* pre-existence. **—empfinden**, *ir.v.a.* to have a presentiment (of). **—erkennen**, *ir.v.a.* to recognize beforehand. **—gehen**, *ir.v.n.* (*aux.* **s.**); **einer Sache —gehen**, to precede, happen before s.th.; **—gehend**, preceding, anterior, previous; **aus dem —gehenden folgt, daß . . .**, it follows from what has already been said that . . .; **die —gehenden Seiten**, the foregoing pages; **im —gehenden ist schon davon die Rede gewesen**, the matter has been already discussed, has been touched upon before; **die —gehenden Umstände erwägen**, to take the preceding circumstances into consideration; **ohne —gegangene Warnung**, without previous notice. **—geschehen**, *ir.v.n.* (*aux.* **s.**) to take place previously, to precede. **—merken**, *v.a.* to have a presentiment of. **—sagen**, *see* **Voraussagen**. **—sagung**, *f.* prediction, prophecy. **—sehen**, *ir.v.a.* to foresee. **—verkündigen**, *v.a.* to predict, foretell, announce beforehand. **—verkündigung**, *see* **—sagung**. **—wissen**, *ir.v.a* to foreknow, know beforehand.

Vor'mittag, *m.* (**—s**, *pl.* **—e**) morning, forenoon. *Comp.* **—s=prediger**, *m.* morning preacher. **—s=stunde**, *f.* morning hour; morning lesson. **—s=wache**, *f.* forenoon watch (*Naut.*). **—s=zeit**, *f.* forenoon-time.

Vor'mittäg—ig, *adj.* in the forenoon, before noon, antemeridian; **—iger Besuch**, morning call. **—lich**, *adj.* of every morning.

Vor'mund, *m.* (**—es**, *pl.* **Vor'münder**), **—münderin**, *f.* guardian; trustee. **—schaft**, *f.* guardianship; trusteeship; tutelage; **unter —schaft stehen (stellen)**, to be (place) under the care of a guardian. **—schaftlich**, *adj.* relating to a guardian's duty *or* affairs of guardianship. *Comp.* **—s=bestellung**, *f.* appointment of a guardian. **—schafts=amt**, *n. see* **—schaftsgericht**. **—schafts=gelder**, *pl.* trust-money, property of a ward. **—schafts=gericht**, *n.* court for the protection of wards, Court of Chancery (*in England*). **—schafts=ordnung**, *f.* order in Chancery; law regarding guardianship. **—schafts=rechnung**, *f.* account of guardianship, of a ward's estate *or* of trust-money. **—schafts=wesen**, *n.* (*everything relating to*) guardianship, trusteeship.

Vorn, (**—e**,) I. *adv.* in front; in the forepart, before; **ganz —**, right in front; **nach — heraus wohnen**, to live in the front (*part of the house* facing the street; **— an sitzen**, to sit in front; **— im Buche**, at the beginning of the book; **— und hinten**, before and behind, fore and aft; **— und hinten sein**, to be everywhere; **er ist überall hinten und —**, he is here, there and everywhere; **jetzt nennen sie sie „Fräulein" — und hinten**, everybody is Miss now-a-days; **Zimmer nach — hinaus**, front rooms, rooms facing the street; **von —**, opposite, facing; **ich sah sie von —**, I saw her face; **von — gesehen**, seen in front; **von — anfangen**, to begin at the beginning; **wieder von — anfangen**, to recommence, start afresh, begin all over again; **von — herein**, at first; to start with, at once, of itself, as a matter of course. II. *n.*; **das — und hinten**, the front and back.

Vor'nehm, *adj.* of superior rank, genteel, refined, distinguished; eminent; aristocratic, grand; principal; **die —en (Leute)**, people of rank, distinguished people; **die —sten in einer Stadt**, the leading *or* chief people in a town; **die —e Welt**, the world of fashion, (*good*) society; **—es Äußere**, distinguished appearance; **—es Wesen**, air of superiority; **—er Anstrich**, aristocratic air *or* bearing; **—es Haus**, aristocratic house, fine *or* grand house; **dies ist das —ste und größte Gebot**, this is the first and greatest commandment; **— thun**, to give oneself airs, affect superiority, live in great style. **—heit**, *f.* (*air of*) distinction; superiority; rank. **—lich**, *adv.* particularly, above all. *Comp.* **—thuerei**, *f.* airs and graces, giving o.s. airs, assuming haughty manners, affectation of superiority, superciliousness.

Vor'nehmen, I. *ir.v.a.* to take before; to put on *or* before o.s.; to take in hand, take up, undertake; **sich** (*dat.*) **etwas —**, to propose to o.s., to intend, design, purpose; **ich habe mir vor-**

genommen, I have made up my mind, I propose to; **wieder —,** to resume (*an interrupted work*); **einen —,** to call a p. to account, to upbraid, chide, reprimand a p. (*coll.*); **Ihre Sache wird heute vorgenommen,** your case comes on to-day (*Law*). II. *subst.n.* undertaking; project.

Vor'rat, *m.* (—s, *pl.* **Vor'räte**) store, provision, supply; assortment; stock; **im —,** in store, in reserve; **sich** (*dat.*) **einen — verschaffen,** to provide o.s. with, take in a supply, stock, store (*of*); **— nimmer schadt,** store is no sore (*prov.*). *Comp.* **—s=achse,** *f.* spare axle-tree (*Artil.*). **—s=haus,** *n.* store(-house), warehouse. **—s=kammer,** *f.* storeroom. **—s=schleuse,** *f.* lock on a canal. **—s=schrank,** *m.*, **—s=spind,** *n.* larder, pantry; side-board; meat-safe. **—s=verzeichnis,** *n.* inventory. **—s=wagen,** *m.* tender (*Rail.*).

Vor'rätig, *adj.* in store, in stock, on hand; in reserve; **— haben,** to stock (an article), to have *or* keep in stock; **nicht mehr — haben,** not to have in stock, to be out of; **— bei allen Buchhändlern,** to be had of all booksellers.

Vor'schlag, *m.* (—s, *pl.* **Vor'schläge**) proposition, proposal; motion; offer; price, demand; overcharge, amount put on to the price to be afterwards deducted (as discount); appoggiatura, grace-note (*Mus.*); initial weak element of a sound; anacrusis; something placed before another thing (*to protect or support it*); iron stays (*Min.*); first blow *or* stroke; wadding (*Artil.*); the blank space on the first page of a book (*Typ.*); templet (*Bookb.*); **Vorschläge machen** (*or* **thun**), to make proposals; **in — bringen,** to propose, to move; **auf einen — eingehen,** to agree to a proposal; **— zur Güte,** conciliatory proposal; good way out of the difficulty, excellent proposal (*coll. hum.*); **das englische j hat den Laut eines zh mit dem — eines d,** the English j sounds like zh with a d before it; **durch — eines e,** by sounding an e before it, prefixing an e. **—bar,** *adj.* proposable. *Comp.* **—s= und Geldbewilligungs=kommission,** *f.* finance committee. **—s=liste,** *f.* list of persons proposed for an appointment (*Mil.*). **—s=note,** *f.* appoggiatura (*Mus.*). **—s=recht,** *n.* right of nominating *or* presenting (to an office). **—zieher,** *m.* worm (*Artil.*).

Vor'schlagen, I. *ir.v.a.* to put forward, propose; to propound; to offer; to move; to overrate, overprize; to overcharge, ask too much; to strike, beat, thrust, throw forward; to strike, nail on; **einem etwas —,** to propose s.th. to a p.; **einen zu einem Amte —,** to propose a p. for *or* nominate s.o. to an office; **auf eine Ware 3 Mark —,** to ask 3 marks too much for s.th.; **einem den Takt —,** to beat time for a p. II. *ir.v.n.* (*aux.* **s.**) to fall, rush headlong forward; *see* **Vorwalten; die Zunge schlägt vor,** the tongue *or* needle inclines (*in weighing*); **eine Note schlägt vor,** a note is out of time, is struck before its time; **der —de,** the proposer, mover, presenter; **der Vorgeschlagene,** the nominee. III. *subst.n.*; **das — ist nicht meine Art,** I am not in the habit of overcharging, of asking more than I mean to take; **— zu einem Amte,** presentation, nomination (*to an office, etc.*).

Vor'schuß, *m.* (—(ss)es, *pl.* **Vorschüsse**) (*cash-*) advance; payment in advance; first shot; first stroke; **um 100 Mark im — sein,** to be 100 marks in advance, to be 100 marks to the good; **Vorschüsse machen** *or* **thun,** to advance money; **ein Buch auf — drucken,** to print a book by subscription; **Sie haben den —,** you have the lead. *Comp.* **—bewilligung,** *f.* grant of an advance. **—verein,** *m.* lending *or* loan society. **—weise,** *adv.* as an advance, by way of advance. **—zahlung,** *f.* payment in advance.

Vor'setz—en, *v.a.* to set before; to place in front, set over, place at the head of; to prefer; to prefix (to); **darf ich Ihnen etwas —en,** may I offer you anything (*to eat, etc.*) or any refreshments? **sich** (*dat.*) **einen Zweck —en,** to propose, to do, to aim at s.th., to intend, resolve to do a th., to determine upon s.th.; **einen einem Amte —en,** to appoint a p. to an office; **einer Note ein Kreuz** (**ein B**) **—en,** to mark a note with a sharp (a flat); **eine hohe Karte —en,** to cut a high card (*for trump*); **einen Stein —en,** to cover a man (*Chess*); **einem Worte eine Silbe —en,** to prefix a syllable to a word; **vorgesetzte Behörde** the proper authorities, those in authority **seine Vorgesetzten** *or* **seine vorgesetzte Behörde,** his superior officers, his superiors. **—er,** *m.* (—ers, *pl.* —er) something put before something else; movable cover (*Glassw.*); hurdle and basket (*Metall.*); outside window-blind; fire-screen, stove-screen. **—ung,** *f. see* **—ungszeichen; durch die —ung eines Kreuzes vor eine Note,** by prefixing a sharp to a note. *Comp.* **—blatt,** *n.* fly-leaf (*of a book*). **—blech,** *n.* iron plate placed before an opening; strainer *or* grating placed before the fire-hole of a furnace (*in foundries, etc.*). **—deckel,** *m.* lid. **—fenster,** *n.* outer (half of a double) window. **—gitter,** *n.*, **—laden,** *m.* shutter. **—partikel, —silbe,** *f.* prefix. **—ungs=zeichen,** *n.* signature (*Mus.*); sign (*Math.*). **—wort,** *n.* prefix (*of a compound word*). **—zeichen,** *n.* signature (*Mus.*); sharp (♯) *or* flat (♭).

Vor'steck—en, *reg. & ir.v.* I. *a.* to stick *or* put before; to fasten on before; to poke, stick out; to mark out beforehand; to appoint beforehand; to prefix, mark, appoint; **den Kopf —en,** to put, poke out one's head; **sich** (*dat.*) **ein Ziel —en,** to set s.th. before o.s., to aim at s.th.; **das vorgesteckte Ziel erreichen,** to attain one's object, to hit the mark. **—er,** *m.* (—ers, *pl.* —er) something stuck on *or* into s.th. else to fasten it; pin, peg; **—er eines Artilleriewagens,** transom-bolt; **—er vor einem Rade,** linch-pin, axle-pin. *Comp.* **—ärmel,** *m.* sleeve-protector. **—blume,** *f.* button-hole (*flower*). **—latz,** *m.* stomacher. **—lätzchen,** *n.* pinafore. **—lünse,** *f.* linch-pin. **—nadel,** *f.* breast-pin. **—nagel,** *m.* pin, peg, key of a round bolt; fore-lock. **—pflock,** *m.* stud (*Horol.*). **—schlips,** *m.* necktie, cravat.

Vor'steh—en, *ir.v.n.* (*aux.* **h.**) to stand before (*a thing*); to jut out, project, overhang; to precede; to superintend, oversee, preside over; to be at the head of, manage, direct, administer; to appear (*in a court of justice*); **der Hund steht vor,** the dog points, sets; **einem, einer Sache —en,** to look after a p., a th.; **dem Hause —en,** to manage the house, keep house; **einem Amte —en,** to hold *or* administer an office. **—er,** *m.* (—ers, *pl.* —er), **—erin,** *f.* chief, principal; administrator, director, manager; superintendent; inspector; head-master (*of a school*); superior (*of a convent*); warden, master (*of a college*); foreman; lady principal; mother superior; head-mistress; manageress. *Comp.* **—er=amt,** *n.* office of overseer, administrator, manager, superintendent. **—hund,** *m.* pointer, setter.

Vor'stellbar, *adj.* that may be represented; presentable; imaginable, conceivable.

Vor'stell—en, *v.a.* to place before; to put in front of; to put forward; to present, introduce; to represent, act; to personate; to put forward, plead; to demonstrate; to remonstrate, protest; **einen Schirm vors Licht —en,** to put a shade in front of the candle; **einem Verschiedenes zur Wahl —en,** to give a person the choice between several things; **darf ich Sie meiner Schwester —en?** may I introduce you to my sister? **eine Rolle —en,** to play a part, to act the character; etwas —en, was man nicht ist, to set up for what one is not (*coll.*); etwas Großes —en wollen, to wish to be thought somebody, give oneself airs; er stellt etwas vor, his appearance is striking; er stellt wenig vor, he is not much to look at; was stellt das vor, was soll das —en? what is (*the meaning of*) that? sich (*dat.*) etwas —en, to imagine s.th.; stellen Sie sich meine Freude vor, fancy my joy, imagine my delight. —ig, *adj.*; einem etwas —ig machen, to explain, demonstrate, make s.th. clear to a p., to remonstrate; (bei einer Behörde) —ig werden, to present a petition, to memorialize. —ung, *f.* presentation (*at court, etc.*); performance; representation; description; plea, remonstrance; expostulation; memorial; idea, notion, conception, image; —ung einer Truppe, review (*Mil.*); das geht über alle —ung, that passes the bounds of imagination; sich (*dat.*) eine —ung machen von . . ., to form an idea of . . .; keine —ung! the theatre is closed (*for to-day, etc.*). *Comp.* —ungs=fähigkeit, *f.* power of imagination. —ungs=vermögen, *n.* imaginative faculty, imagination. —ungs=weise, *f.* way of looking at things; way of putting things.

Vor'teil (*short* o), *m.* (—s, *pl.* —e) advantage, profit, benefit, interest; emolument; — des Windes, weather-gauge; einem den — abgewinnen, to get the better of a p.; einem zum — gereichen, zu jemandes — ausschlagen, to turn out to one's advantage; — ziehen, to derive advantage from, to turn to account; auf seinen — sehen, to have an eye to one's own interests; im — sein, to have the advantage; der — ist auf seiner Seite, the odds are on his side; jeder — gilt, all 's fair in love and war (*prov.*). —haft, *adj.* advantageous; profitable; lucrative; favourable; eine —hafte Gelegenheit, a favourable opportunity. *Comp.* —bringend, *see* —haft. —suchend, *adj.* self-seeking.

Vor'trag, *m.* (—s, *pl.* Vor'träge) diction, delivery, utterance, enunciation; elocution; execution (*Mus.*); lecture, discourse; recital; explanation, exposition; report; proposal; balance carried forward (*C.L.*); den — haben, to be the spokesman, to speak; — beim Könige haben, to present a report to the king, have an audience of the king; einen — halten über (*acc.*), to lecture *or* give a lecture on; in — bringen, to bring forward for discussion, to propose, to report on; der Redner hat einen deutlichen —, the speaker has a clear delivery. *Comp.* —s=art, —s=weise, *f.* manner of speaking; elocution, delivery. —s=kunst, *f.* art of delivery, declamation, elocution.

Vor'trag—en, I. *ir.v.a.* to carry *or* bring forward *or* before; to carry forward (*the balance*); to explain, expound; to lay before a p.; to propose; to speak (*of*), discourse *or* lecture (*on*); to report on; to deliver (*a speech, etc.*); to execute (*Mus.*); —ender Rat, councillor who makes reports; eine Arie —en, to sing a tune *or* air; den Saldo auf neue Rechnung —en, to carry forward the balance. II. *subst. n.*, —ung, *f.* carrying before; reporting; delivery; elocution; explanation, *etc.*; unter —ung des Kreuzes, the cross being carried in front.

Vorü'ber, *adv. & separable prefix*, before *or* in front; along by, past; gone by, over, finished, done with; den Kopf — beugen, to bend the head forward; der Regen ist —, the rain is over; sein Ruhm war schnell —, his fame soon passed away, was but transient. *Comp.* —fliegen, *ir.v.n.* (*aux.* s.) to fly past *or* across. —fliehen, *ir.v.n.* (*aux.* s.) to hurry past. —gehen, I. *ir.v.n.* (*aux.* s.); to pass; an einem (*poet.* einem *or* einen) —gehen, to go past a p., to pass by a p.; to pass over, neglect one. II. *subst.n.*; im — gehen, in passing; by the way. —gehend, *p. & adj.* passing; transitory; migratory; die —gehenden, the passers-by. —können, *ir.v.n.* (*aux.* h.) to be able to pass. —kutschie'ren, *v.n.* (*aux.* s.) to drive past. —ziehen, *ir.v.n.* (*aux.* s.) to pass (by).

Vor'urteil, *n.* (—s, *pl.* —e) prejudice, prepossession; von —en eingenommen, prejudiced; biassed; sich von seinen —en freimachen, to get the better of one's prejudices; einem —e einflößen, to prejudice a p. *Comp.* —s=frei, —s=los, *adj.* unprejudiced, unbiassed. —s=losigkeit, *f.* freedom from prejudice, open-mindedness, impartiality. —s=voll, *adj.* prejudiced, full of prejudice.

Vor'wärts, *adv. & sep. prefix*, forward, onward, on; in front; towards the front, forwards; in advance; —! forward! march! move on! go on! go ahead! right away! sich — bewegen, to move forward, advance; — gehen, to go on; es will nicht (mit ihm) — gehen, he does not get on; sich (*dat.*) — helfen, to make one's way in the world; — kommen, to advance, make one's way, make headway; to get on; langsam kommt man auch —, slow and sure wins the race, more haste less speed (*prov.*); Marschall —, Marshal "Vorwärts," Field Marshal Blücher. *Comp.* —beuge, *f.* bending forward (*Gymn.*). —kommen, —schreiten, *n.* progress, advance. —streben, *n.* progresssive tendency, push (*coll.*).

Vo't—a, *pl. see* Votum. —ie'ren, *v.n.* (*aux.* h.) to vote; die —ierenden, the voters. —um, *n.* (—ums, *pl.* Vota) vote; vow. *Comp.* —iv'=bild, —iv'=gemälde, *n.* votive offering, votive picture. —iv'=kirche, *f.* votive church. —iv'=tafel, *f.* votive tablet; *pl.* (*title of a series of philosophical poems in distichs by Schiller*).

Vulg—ä'r, *adj.* vulgar. —a'ta, *f.* Vulgate.

Vul'g—o, *adv.* commonly. —us, *m.* populace, mob.

Vulka'n—isch, *adj.* volcanic. —isie'ren, *v.a.* to vulcanize (*india-rubber*). —isie'rung, *f.* vulcanization. —is'mus, *m.* vulcanism (*Geol.*). —i'st, *m.* (—is'ten, *pl.* —is'ten) vulcanist.

W

W, w, *n.* W, w; *for abbreviations see the index of abbreviations at the end of the German-English part.*

Wa'be, *f.* (*pl.* —n), (*sometimes* —n, *m.* (—ns, *pl.* —n)) honey-comb. *Comp.* —n=honig, *m.* honey in the comb. —n=zelle, *f.* honey-cell.

Waber—n, *v.n.* to flicker, blaze. *Comp.* —lohe, *f.* flickering flame, magic fire.

Wach, *adj.* awake; on the alert; — werden, to awake. —sam, *adj.* vigilant, watchful; attentive; alert; ein —sames Auge auf eine S. haben, to keep a sharp eye on something; —sam auf (über) eine S. sein, to watch over a thing. —samkeit, *f.* vigilance.

Wa'ch—e, *f.* guard, watch; sentinel, sentry; the men on guard, the guard, watch; watch-house; sentry-box; station-house; watch (*of four hours on deck*); —e haben *or* thun, auf Wache sein, to be on guard; auf —e ziehen, die —e beziehen, to mount guard; —e stehen, to stand sentinel; von der —e abziehen, to come off duty, be relieved; —e 'raus! turn out, guard! —e halten, to keep guard, to be on the lookout, to watch; bei einem —e halten, *see* —en. *Comp.* —aufzug, *m.* mounting guard, parade (*of the soldiers on guard*). —bett, *n.* nurse's bed; camp-bed, stretcher. —frei, *adj.* exempt from mounting guard. —geld, *n.* salary for sitting up with a patient. —habend, *adj.* (being) on guard, on duty. —haus, *n.* watch-house; guard-house; binnacle (*Naut.*). —häuschen, *n.* sentry-box. —**loch**, *n.* guard-room; lock-up. —**sucht**, *f.* sleeplessness.

Wa'chen, *v.n.* (*aux.* **h.**) to watch, sit up; to be awake; to guard, watch; **bei einem** —, to sit up with a p., to nurse an invalid.

Wachol'der, *m.* (—**s**, *pl.* —) juniper; *see* —**branntwein**. —**n**, *adj.* (of) juniper. *Comp.* —**branntwein**, *m.* gin. —**geist**, *m.* juniper-spirit. —**harz**, *n.* gum-juniper.

Wachs, *n.* (—(s)es, *pl.* —(s)e) wax. *Comp.* —**abdruck**, *m.* impression in wax. —**artig**, *adj.* waxy, wax-like; waxen. —**bild**, *n.* wax figure *or* image. —**blume**, *f.* wax-flower; honey-wort (*Bot.*). —**decke**, *f.* oil-cloth. —**farbe**, *f.* wax-colour. —**figur**, *f.* wax figure. —**figuren=kabinett**, *n.* wax-works. —**firnis**, *m.* wax-varnish. —**form**, *f.* wax mould. —**händler**, *m.* dealer in wax. —**haut**, *f.* cere (*of a bird's bill*). —**kerze**, *f.* wax candle; taper. —**leinen**, *n.*, —**leinwand**, *f.* oil-cloth. —**licht**, *n.* wax candle. —**malerei**, *f.* wax-painting; **eingebrannte** —**malerei**, encaustic painting, cerography. —**perle**, *f.* wax bead; artificial pearl. —**pflaster**, *n.* cerate. —**röhrchen**, *n.* catheter (*Surg.*). —**salbe**, *f.* cerate. —**scheibe**, *f.* cake of wax. —**schmelze**, *f.* melting-house for wax. —**sonde**, *f.* bougie (*Surg.*). —**stock**, *m.* roll of wax tapers. —**stock=leuchter**, *m.* taper-stand, taper-holder. —**streichholz**, *n.* wax vesta. —**tafel**, *f.* cake of beeswax; wax tablet. —**taffet**, *m.* oil-skin. —**tuch**, *n.* oil-cloth. —**zieher**, *m.* wax-chandler. —**zündhölzchen**, *n.* wax vesta.

Wach'sen, I. *ir.v.n.* (*aux.* **s.**) to grow; to wax, increase; to grow up; to thrive; to come up (*of plants*); to advance; **sehr ins Kraut** —, to run to leaf; **in die Breite** —, to grow broad, to extend, stretch out; **in die Höhe** —, to grow tall, to shoot up; **schief** —, to grow crooked; **das Wasser wächst**, the water is rising; **der Mond wächst**, the moon is on the increase; **an Weisheit** —, to grow in wisdom; **Sie sind aber gewachsen!** how you have grown! **er ist ihm ans Herz gewachsen**, he is very dear to him; **er ist aus den Kleidern gewachsen**, he has outgrown his clothes; **einem über den Kopf** —, to get beyond a p.'s control; **ihm wächst der Kamm**, he is getting angry; he is getting overbearing; **einem gewachsen sein**, to be a match for s.o.; **einer Sache gewachsen sein**, to be equal to s.th., to be able to bear a thing; **bist du der Sache gewachsen?** are you equal to it, competent to undertake it? II. *subst.n.* growing; growth; increase, augmentation; rising (*of water*); development; **das** — **in den Beinen haben**, to have growing pains. —**d**, *p.* & *adj.* growing; crescendo (*Mus.*).

Wäch'se—n, *v.a.* to wax, to coat *or* treat with wax. —**rn**, *adj.* waxen; **einem eine** —**rne Nase drehen**, to lead a p. by the nose, to humbug a p.

Wächst, *2 & 3 p. sing. pres. ind. of* **wachsen**.

Wachs'tum, *n.* (—**s**) growth; vegetation; increase; **Wein, mein eignes** —, wine of my own growing; **übermäßiges** —, overgrowth.

Wacht, *f.* (*pl.* —**en**) watch (*Naut.*); guard (*Mil.*); watch-house, sentinel's post; **die** — **am Rhein**, the watch on the Rhine. *Comp.* (*see also* **Wach** *in comp.*) —**boot**, *n.* guard-boat. —**dienst**, *m.*; —**dienst haben**, to be on guard. —**feuer**, *n.* watch fire, bivouac fire. —**habend**, *adj.* on duty. —**kommandant**, *m.* commander of the guard; **die Funktion eines** —**kommandanten ausübender Korporal**, corporal of the guard. —**mannschaft**, *f.* men on guard, picket, (men on) watch. —**mantel**, *m.* sentinel's cape; watchman's cloak. —**meister**, *m.* sergeant-major (of cavalry). —**offizier**, *m.* officer of the guard. —**parade**, *f.* parade of the soldiers on mounting guard; **Potsdamer** —**parade**, Prussian soldiers (*iron.*, *obs.*). —**posten**, *m.* post, watch; sentinel. —**pritsche**, *f.* guard-bed. —**schiff**, *n.* guard-ship; revenue-cutter. —**stube**, *f.* guard-room. —**turm**, *m.* watch-tower.

Wach'tel, *f.* (*pl.* —**n**) quail; **die** — **schlägt** *or* **ruft**, the quail calls. *Comp.* —**falk(e)**, *m.* lanner(et). —**garn**, *n.* quail-net. —**hund**, *m.* spaniel. —**hündchen**, *n.* King Charles' spaniel. —**könig**, *m.* land-rail, corn-crake. —**pfeife**, *f.* bird-call. —**schlag**, *m.* call of the quail. —**streichen**, *n.*, —**strich**, *m.* quail-catching with nets; migration *or* passage of quails.

Wäch'ter, *m.* (—**s**, *pl.* —) watch, guard; care-taker; attendant; keeper; guardian; look-out man (*Naut.*). —**in**, *f.* sick-nurse; matron; keeper; care-taker. *Comp.* —**geld**, *n.* watchman's wages. —**häuschen**, *n.* watch-box; signalman's box. —**ruf**, *m.* watchman's call *or* cry. —**lied**, *n.* watchman's (morning-)song, aubade.

Wa'ck—e, *f.* (*pl.* —**en**) wacke, toadstone. —**ig**, *adj.* containing wacke.

Wa'ck—elig, *adj.* & *adv.* shaky, tottering; loose; rickety; rocking. —**eln**, I. *v.n.* (*aux.* **h.**) to shake; to wag, rock, reel, totter, waddle; to be loose; **mit dem Kopfe** —**eln**, to shake one's head; **es** —**elt mit seiner Gesundheit**, his health is rather shaky (*coll.*); (*aux.* **s.**) **er ist die Straße hinauf gewackelt**, he tottered *or* waddled up the street. II. *subst.n.* shakiness; looseness; vacillation. —**ler**, *m.* (—**lers**, *pl.* —**ler**), —**lerin**, *f.* waddler. *Comp.* —**el=kopf**, *m.* palsied head.

Wa'cker, I. *adj.* valiant, brave, gallant; good; honest. II. *adv.* bravely; well; thoroughly; zealously (*coll.*).

Wad, *n.* (—**s**) wad, manganese ore.

Wa'de, *f.* (*pl.* —**n**) calf (*of the leg*). *Comp.* —**n=bein**, *n.* fibula; shin. —**n=krampf**, *m.* cramp in the leg. —**n=nerv**, *m.* peroneal (*nerve*).

Waf'f—e, *f.* (*pl.* —**en**) (*obs.* —**en**, *n.* (—**ens**, *pl.* —**en**)) weapon, arm; tusk, fang, *etc.*; (*pl.*) arms; **das Volk in** —**en**, armed nation; **einem die** —**en abnehmen**, to disarm a p.; **unter den** —**en**, under arms; **zu den** —**en greifen**, to take up arms (*against*); **die** —**en strecken**, to lay down one's arms, surrender. —**nen**, *v.a.* to arm; **mit gewaffneter Hand**, by force of arms; **sich gegen einen** —**nen**, to arm o.s. *or* to take up arms against a p. *Comp.* —**en=arbeit**, *f.* war. —**en=bruder**, *m.* companion in arms. —**en=dienst**, *m.* military service. —**en=fabrik**, *f.* manufactory of arms. —**en=fähig**, *adj.* capable of bearing arms. —**en=gang**, *m.* passage of arms. —**en=gattung**, *f.* kind of arms; **bei welcher** —**engattung dient er?** to what arm of the service does he belong? —**en=gerüst**, —**en=gestell**, *n.* stand for arms. —**en=geschmeide**, *n.*, —**en=schmuck**, *m.* warlike accoutrements. —**en=gewalt**, *f.* force of arms, armed force. —**en=haus**, *n.* arsenal. —**en=herold**, *m.* herald, king-at-arms. —**en=könig**, *m.* warrior king; king-at-arms. —**en=kundig**, *adj.* experienced in arms; warlike. —**en=los**, *adj.* unarmed. —**en=rock**, *m.* tunic (*Mil.*); coat-of-arms (*obs.*). —**en=ruhe**, *f.* cessation *or* suspension of hostilities. —**en=ruhm**, *m.* military glory. —**en=rüstung**, *f.* armour. —**en=schmied**, *m.* armourer. —**en=schmiede**, *f.* armourer's workshop. —**en=schmuck**, *m.* warlike accoutrements; **in vollem** —**enschmuck**, in full armour. —**en=stillstand**, *m.* truce, armistice; *see* —**enruhe**. —**en=streckung**, *f.* laying down of arms, surrender. —**en=stück**, *n.* arm; feat of arms. —**en=tanz**, *m.* war-dance; war, battle; tournament, display. —**en=that**, *f.* feat of arms, military exploit. —**en=tragen**, *n.* carrying of arms; **das** —**entragen ist verboten**, it is forbidden to carry arms. —**en=träger**, *m.* armed man; armour-bearer, esquire. —**en=übung**, *f.* military exercise, drill. —**en=wache**, *f.* knight's watch by his armour.

Waf'fel, *f.* (*pl.* **—n**) waffle, wafer. *Comp.* **—eisen,** *n.* gauffering-iron; waffle-iron.

Wäg'bar, *adj.* ponderable, weighable. **—keit,** *f.* ponderability.

Wa'g—e, *f.* (*pl.* **—en**) balance, weighing machine; Libra (*Astr.*); areometer; level; pendulum; weigh-house; balance-wheel; horizontal position; equilibrium; splinter-bar, swingle-tree; **Brief—e,** letter-balance; **Brücken—e,** weigh-bridge; (**einem** *or* **einer Sache**) **die —e halten,** to counterbalance, balance, keep even with, play up to; **in der —e halten,** to hold in equilibrium; **eine feine —e giebt auf** $\frac{1}{115200}$ **der Belastung einen Ausschlag,** a fine balance turns with $\frac{1}{115200}$ of the load; **die —e gleich machen,** to adjust the balance; **auf die —e legen,** to weigh; **das Zünglein der —e,** the needle of the balance; **die Sonne tritt in die —e,** the sun enters Libra; **Vorteil und Nachteil halten einander die —,** the pros and cons counterbalance one another. *Comp.* **—(e)=amt,** *n.* public weighing-office. **—(e)=balken,** *m.* (*scale-*) beam. **—(e)=geld,** (**Wäge=geld,**) *n.* weighing-toll *or* fee. **—(e)=halter,** *m.* balance-stay. **—(e)=haus,** *n.* weigh-house. **—(e)=meister,** *m.* weigh-master, public weigher; inspector of weights and measures. **—(e)=recht,** *adj.* horizontal, level. **—(e)=schale,** *f.* balance-scale; (*pl.*) scales; **die —schale sinken machen,** to preponderate, outweigh; **seine Worte auf die —schale legen,** to weigh one's words. **—(e)=schwebe,** *f.* see-saw. **—(e)=zettel,** *m.* certificate of weight. **—(e)=zunge,** *f.*, **—(e)=zünglein,** *n.* index *or* needle of a balance.

Wa'ge, *f.* (*obs.*) *see* **Wag'nis.**

Wä'gelchen, *n.* (**—s,** *pl.* **—**) little carriage.

Wa'g—en, *v.a.* to venture, risk; to dare, attempt; **sich an eine S. —en,** to venture upon an undertaking *or* s.th.; **sich unter die Leute —en,** to venture into society; to show o.s.; **es mit einem —en,** to cross swords with, *or* measure one's strength with a p.; **wer nicht —t, der nicht gewinnt,** nothing venture, nothing have; **alles —en,** to risk everything; **frisch gewagt ist halb gewonnen,** well begun is half done; fortune favours the brave (*prov.*); **ich will es darauf —en,** I'll risk it; **es sei frisch gewagt!** let us take our chance! **gewagt,** risky, hazardous, dangerous, daring, bold. **—er,** *m.* (**—ers,** *pl.* **—er**) venturesome person, venturer, daring person. **—lich,** *adj.* that may be risked; hazardous. **—nis,** *n.* (**—nisses,** *pl.* **—nisse**) hazardous enterprise, risky undertaking; chance, risk. *Comp.* **—(e)=hals,** *m.* foolhardy *or* rash person. **—(e)=halsig,** *adj.* rash; bold; foolhardy. **—e=spiel,** *n.* game of chance. **—(e)=stück,** *n.* bold attempt, daring enterprise.

Wä'g—en, *ir.v.a.* to weigh; to poise, balance; **er wog das Schwert in der Hand,** he poised the sword in his hand; **du hast deine Worte wohl gewogen,** you have well weighed *or* considered your words; **erst —en, dann wagen,** *or* **erst wäg's, dann wag's,** look before you leap (*prov.*). **—er,** *m.* weigher. *Comp.* **—e=amt,** *n. see* **Wageamt.** **—e=kunst,** *f.* statics.

Wa'gen, *m.* (**—s,** *pl.* **—**) vehicle; (*also* **Waggon**) waggon, cart; carriage; coach; chariot; Charles' Wain (*Astr.*); **unter den — kommen,** to be worsted (*coll.*); **der Hintersitz eines —s,** dickey, rumble; **die Pferde hinter den — spannen,** to put the cart before the horse; **— erster Klasse,** first-class carriage; **Salon—,** saloon carriage; **Pullmann—,** Pullman-car; **Gepäck—,** luggage-van, baggage-car (*Amer.*); **offener (gedeckter) Güter—,** truck, lorry, goods van, freight car (*Amer.*); **der große (kleine) —,** the Great (Lesser) Bear (*Astr.*). **—er,** *see* **Wagner.** *Comp.* **—abteil,** *m.* compartment (of a railway carriage). **—achse,** *f.* axle-tree. **—bau,** *m.* coach-building. **—bauer,** *m.* cartwright; coach-builder. **—baum,** *m.* carriage-pole *or* perch. **—brücke,** *f.* floating-bridge. **—burg,** *f.* barricade of waggons, laager; (**Jerusalem**) **sie werden eine —burg um dich schlagen,** they will cast a trench around thee and encompass thee (*B.*). **—decke,** *f.* carriage-head; tilt for a cart; tarpaulin. **—deichsel,** *f.* carriage-pole; cart-shaft. **—fabrikant,** *m.* coach-maker *or* -builder. **—führer,** *m.* waggoner; coachman, driver; charioteer. **—gedränge,** *n.* block of carriages. **—geleise,** *n.* carriage-rut. **—gestell,** *n.* frame of a carriage. **—gestirn,** *n.* Ursa Major. **—kämpfer,** *m.* warrior fighting from a chariot. **—klasse,** *f.* class; **ein Billet erster —klasse,** a first-class (*railway-*)ticket. **—korb,** *m.* hamper. **—ladung,** *f.* carriage-load, cart-load. **—leiter,** *f.* cart-rails. **—lenker,** *m.* charioteer. **—macher,** *see* **—bauer.** **—meister,** *m.* owner *or* inspector of waggons; *see* **Schirrmeister.** **—remise,** *f.* coach-house. **—schlag,** *m.* coach-door. **—schmiere,** *f.* wheel-grease. **—schuppen,** *m.* coach-house; shed for carts. **—sport,** *m.* coach-driving. **—spur,** *f.* track of carriage-wheels. **—straße,** *f.* carriage-road. **—wechsel,** *m.* change of carriages. **—winde,** *f.* draw-beam, jack. **—zug,** *m.* train (*Railw.*).

Waggo'n, *m.* (**—s,** *pl.* **—s**) *see* **Wagen.**

Wag'ner, *m.* (**—s,** *pl.* **—**) cartwright.

[1]**Wahl,** *f.* (*pl.* **—en**) choice; selection; option; election (*of a member of parliament, etc.*); alternative; **direkte —en,** elections by direct suffrage; **— durch Kugeln oder geheime Stimmzettel,** ballot; **aus freier —,** of one's own (free) choice; **einem die — lassen,** to leave the option to a p.; **auf — begründet,** elective; **eine — treffen,** to make a choice; **auf der — stehen,** to be a candidate; **auf der engeren — stehen,** to be on the select list, to be one of the selected candidates; **jemands — billigen,** to approve of a person's choice. *Comp.* **—abstimmung,** *f.* polling, balloting for the election of officers *or* for the return of members of parliament. **—abt,** *m.* elective abbot. **—akt,** *m.* election. **—akten,** *pl.* election returns (*Parl.*). **—amt,** *n.* elective office. **—aufruf,** *m.* electoral manifesto, manifesto to the electors *or* constituents. **—ausschreiben,** *n.* writ(s) for an election. **—bedingung,** *f.* condition of election. **—befehl,** *m. see* **—ausschreiben.** **—berechtigt,** *adj.* entitled to vote. **—bericht,** *m.* return. **—bestechung,** *f.* electoral corruption. **—bewegung,** *f.* electioneering. **—bezirk,** *m.* ward. **—bude,** *f.* polling-booth. **—bühne,** *f.* hustings. **—fähig,** *adj.* eligible; *see* **—berechtigt.** **—fähigkeit,** *f.* eligibility; electoral qualification; franchise. **—frei,** *adj.* optional; **—freie Fächer,** optional subjects. **—fürst,** *m.* elective prince; princely elector. **—handlung,** *f.* election; the poll. **—herr,** *m.* elector. **—kaisertum,** *n.* elective empire. **—kapitulation,** *f.* terms upon which a German emperor was elected, imperial capitulation. **—kasten,** *m.* ballot-box. **—kind,** *n.* adopted child. **—kommissär,** *m.* returning officer. **—königtum,** *n.* elective kingship. **—körper,** *m.* electoral body, constituency. **—kreis,** *m.* ward. **—kugel,** *f.* voting-ball, ballot. **—liste,** *f.* register of (the) electors. **—lokal,** *n.* polling-booth *or* place. **—mann,** *m.* delegate; voter, elector. **—männer=wahl,** *f.* election of delegates. **—modus,** *m.* method of conducting an election. **—ort, —platz,** *m.* place of election, polling-place. **—protokoll,** *n.* polling register, election returns. **—prüfung,** *f.* verification of the poll, scrutiny. **—recht,** *n.* right to vote, electoral franchise; **allgemeines —recht,** universal suffrage; **Entziehung des —rechts,** disfranchisement. **—reich,** *n.* elective empire *or* kingdom. **—spruch**

m. device, motto. **—stimme,** *f.* vote. **—tag,** *m.* day of election. **—umtriebe,** *pl.* electioneering practices, canvassing. **—urne,** *f.* ballot-box. **—vater,** *m.* adoptive father. **—verein,** *m.* electoral association. **—versammlung,** *f.* electoral assembly; caucus (*Amer.*). **—verwandt,** *adj.* congenial; **—verwandte Seelen,** kindred spirits. **—verwandtschaft,** *f.* congeniality; elective affinity (*Chem.*). **—zettel,** *m.* voting-paper. **—zeuge,** *m.* teller, scrutineer (*at elections*). **—zimmer,** *n.* room in which an election is held. **—zimmer der Kardinäle,** conclave.

[2]**Wahl,** *n.* (*in cpds.*) see **Wal.**

Wähl'bar, *adj.* eligible; **nicht —,** ineligible. **—keit,** *f.* eligibility.

Wäh'l—en, *v.a.* to choose, make a choice; to elect; to pick out; **sie —ten ihn zu ihrem Führer,** they chose him for their leader; **einen bleibenden Wohnsitz —en,** to choose a place to settle in; **zum Präsidenten —en,** to choose for a president, to vote into the chair; **ins Parlament —en,** to return to parliament; **gewählte Gesellschaft,** select society; **gewählte Sprache,** choice or refined language, high style. **—er,** *m.* (**—ers,** *pl.* **—er**) chooser; elector. **—erei',** *f.* prolonged selection; electioneering; **was nützt die lange —erei?** what is the good of taking so long to choose? **—erisch,** *adj.* dainty. **—erschaft,** *f.* body of electors, constituency.

Wäh'lig, *adj.* comfortable, at ease.

Wahn, *m.* (**—s**) false, erroneous opinion; illusion; delusion; fancy; madness, folly; mirage; (unconfirmed) idea, notion, opinion (*obs.*). *Comp.* (*in many compounds there is confusion between* **Wahn** *and* (*the obsolete adjective*) **wan** (*Eng.* wan *in* wanhope).) **—bild,** *n.* chimera, vision, phantom. **—glaube,** *m.* superstition, false belief. **—hoffnung,** *f.* vain hope. **—holz,** *n.* back-sided timber. **—korn,** *n.* empty grain. **—sinn,** *m.* insanity, frenzy; madness; delirium; **stiller —sinn,** melancholia, melancholic madness; **es wäre —sinn, so zu handeln,** it would be madness to act so; **dichterischer —sinn,** poetic frenzy. **—sinnig,** *adj.* insane, crazy, mad; frantic; **es ist zum —sinnig werden,** it is enough to drive one mad. **—witz,** *m.* delirium; *see* **—sinn.** **—witzig,** *adj.* senseless, absurd, extravagant; *see* **—sinnig.**

Wäh'nen, I. *v.a.* & *n.* (*aux.* **h.**) to think, believe, fancy, suppose; to believe (*erroneously*), fondly imagine. II. *subst.n.* illusion, fancy, vain hope.

[1]**Wahr,** *adj.* & *adv.* true; real, genuine; correct; proper; **—er Freund,** true friend; **nicht —?** is it not so? **nicht —, Sie kommen?** you will come, will you not? **ich habe es gesagt, nicht —?** I said so, did I not? *or* don't you think so? **so — ich lebe!** as sure as I'm here, as I live! **so — Gott lebt!** as true as there is a God above! **so — mir Gott helfe!** so help me God! **es ist kein —es Wort darin,** there is not a word of truth in it; **etwas für — halten,** to believe a th. to be true, to believe in a th.; **das muß — sein!** upon my word! well, I never! **der —e Gesichtskreis,** the rational horizon; **das —e (an) der Sache ist,** the fact of the matter is; **eine —e Null,** a mere cipher; **— werden,** to be realized; **— machen,** to make true, realize, fulfil; **er hat das Sprichwort — gemacht,** he has proved the truth of the saying; **er will es nicht — haben,** he will not admit it. **—haft,** *adj.* true, genuine; real; veracious. **—haftig,** I. *adj.* see **—haft.** II. *adv.* (*usual pron.* **wahrhaf'tig**) truly; really, indeed; **—haftig!** upon my honour! you don't say so! truly! **—haftigkeit,** *f.* veracity. **—heit,** *f.* truth; truism, fact; **einem derb die —heit sagen,** to tell a p. the plain truth, speak plainly to s.o.; **im Wein ist —heit,** wine reveals the truth, has no secrets; **der —heit gemäß,** faithfully, in accordance with truth. **—lich,** *adv.* truly; **—lich!** well, really! indeed! upon my word! **—! —! ich sage euch,** verily, verily, I say unto you (*B.*). *Comp.* **—heits-eifer,** *m.* zeal for truth. **—heits-gemäß, —heits-getreu,** *adj.* faithful, in accordance with truth. **—heits-liebe,** *f.* love of truth. **—heits-liebend,** *adj.* truthful. **—machung,** *f.* verification. **—sagen,** *rc.*, *see under* **Wahrsag—.** **—scheinlich,** *rc.*, *see* **Wahrscheinlich,** *rc.* **—spruch,** *m.* verdict (*of a jury*).

[2]**Wahr,** *adj.* (*obs. surviving only in cpds.*). *Comp.* **—nehmbar,** *adj.* perceptible. **—nehmbarkeit,** *f.* perceptibility. **—nehmen,** *ir.v.* I. *a.* (*sep.*) to notice, observe, perceive; to look after, give attention to; to profit by, make use of, avail oneself of; **die Gelegenheit —nehmen,** to make use of an opportunity; **seinen Vorteil —nehmen,** to look after one's interests. **—nehmung,** *f.* perception; observation. **—nehmungs-vermögen,** *n.* perception; powers of observation. **—zeichen,** *n.* mark, token, sign; omen; signal; landmark.

Wah'ren, *v.a.* to notice, observe (*obs.* & *dial.*); to watch over, take care of, keep safe, preserve; **einen vor etwas —,** to preserve a p. from a th.

Wäh'r—en, *v.n.* (*aux.* **h.**) to last, continue, endure, hold out; **die Erinnerung an ihn wird ewig —en,** his memory will never die; **es kann noch lange —en, ehe ...,** it may be a (good) long time before ...; **es —te nicht lange, so brach der Krieg los,** it was not long before war broke out; **was lange —t, wird gut,** good work takes time (*prov.*). **—end,** I. *p.* & *adj.* lasting; **ewig —end,** everlasting; **—endes Krieges,** during the war (*obs.*); **(in) —ender Arbeit,** whilst working. II. *prep.* (*usually takes the gen. but the dative if the gen. has the same form as the nom. and acc. and also in uneducated and coll. speech*) during, in the course of, pending. III. *conj.* during the time that, whilst; **—end doch** *or* **hingegen,** whilst (*on the other hand*). **—ung,** *f.* duration; fixed value *or* standard, currency; importance, worth; **Doppel-—ung,** bimetallism.

Wahr'sag—en, *v.a.* & *n.* (*aux.* **h.**) (*insep.*) to prophesy, predict, foretell; to tell fortunes; to augur; **sich** (*dat.*) **etwas —en lassen,** to have one's fortune told. **—er,** *m.* (**—ers,** *pl.* **—er**) soothsayer, prophet; augur; fortune-teller. **—erei',** *f.* divination; fortune-telling. **—erin,** *f.* fortune-telling woman; prophetess. **—erisch,** *adj.* soothsaying; **—erische Künste,** fortune-telling tricks. *Comp.* **—e-geist,** *m.* spirit of divination; prophetic spirit. **—e-kunst,** *f.* (*art of*) divination.

Wahr'scheinlich (*also pron.* **wahrschein'lich**), *adj.* & *adv.* probable, likely; plausible. **—keit,** *f.* probability, likelihood; plausibility. *Comp.* **—keits-rechnung,** *f.* calculation *or* theory of probabilities.

Waid, *m.* (**—s**) dyer's woad, blue dye.

Wai'se, *f.* (*pl.* **—n**), *sometimes* (*in case of a boy*) *m.* (**—n,** *pl.* **—n**) orphan; **zum —n machen,** to orphan. *Comp.* **—n-gelder,** *pl.* money of orphans *or* wards. **—n-haus,** *n.* orphan-asylum, orphanage. **—n-knabe,** *m.* orphan-boy. **—n-mädchen,** *n.* orphan girl. **—n-mutter,** *f.* matron in an orphan asylum. **—n-rat,** *m.* council for taking charge of orphans; member of such council; Master in Chancery. **—n-stand,** *m.* orphaned condition, orphanhood. **—n-vater,** *m.* superintendent in an orphanage.

Wa'ke, *f.* (*pl.* **—n**) hole cut in the ice.

[1]**Wal,** *m.* (**—s,** *pl.* **—e**) whale (= **Walfisch**); (*pl.* **—e**) cetacea; balænidæ; (**—fisch,** *m.*) whale; (*pl.*) cetacea; balænidæ; **der —fisch sprudelt,** the whale blows. *Comp.* **—fisch-ähnlich, —fisch-artig,** *adj.* cetaceous. **—fisch-bein,** *n.*

whalebone. —fisch=boot, *n.* whaler. —fisch=fahrer, *m.* whale fisher; whaler. —fisch=fang, *m.* whale-fishing, whaling. —fisch=fett, *n.* blubber. —fisch=laich, *m.* spermaceti. —fisch=thran, *m.* train-oil. —rat, *m.* & *n.*, —rat=fett, *n.* spermaceti. —roß, *n.* walrus.

²Wal, *n.* (*now only in compounds, often spelt* Wahl—). —feld, *n.*, —platz, *m.*, —statt, *f.* battle-field. —hal'la, *f.* Valhalla; hall of immortality, memorial hall (*fig.*). —kü're, *f.* (—küren) Valkyria, swan-maiden, battle-maiden of Odin who conducted the warriors slain on the battle-field to Valhalla. *Comp.* —küren=ritt, *m.* ride of the Valkyries.

³Wal (*now only in cpds., sometimes spelt* Wall—). —nuß, *f.* (*large*) walnut.

Wald, *m.* (—es, *pl.* Wäl'der) wood, forest; woodland; (*pl.*) collected poems (*obs.*); in Wäldern lebend, sylvan; wie man in den — hinein ruft, so schallt's heraus, as the question, so the answer; er sieht den — vor lauter Bäumen nicht, he cannot see the wood for the trees. —ig, *adj.* wooded, woody; overgrown with shrubs and trees. —ung, *f.* wood; woodland, wooded country. *Comp.* —ameise, *f.* red ant. —amsel, *f.* ring-ousel. —bach, *m.* forest-brook. —bau, *m.* silviculture, tree-planting. —baum=schule, *f.* nursery of forest trees. —bau=schule, *f.* school of forestry. —bedeckt, *adj.* well-wooded, covered with forests. —bereiter, *m.* mounted ranger *or* forester. —biene, *f.* wild bee. —blume, *f.* flower of the woods, wild flower. —brand, *m.* forest-fire. —bruder, *m.* hermit living in a wood. —(es)=dunkel, *n.* forest-gloom. —ei'n, *adv.* into the forest. —einsamkeit, *f.* solitude of the woods. —erdbeere, *f.* wild strawberry. —esel, *m.* wild ass. —eule, *f.* long-eared owl. —frevel, *m.* mischief done in a forest; breach of forest-laws. —gebirge, *n.* range of wooded hills. —gegend, *f.* woodland, well-wooded country. —geist, *m.* spirit of the woods, wood goblin, sylvan spirit; faun, satyr. —geschrei, *n.* hunting cry. —glöckchen, —glöcklein, *n.* blue-bell. —gott, *m.* sylvan god; faun, satyr. —göttin, *f.* wood-nymph, dryad. —(es)=grün, *n.* verdure of the woods. —honig, *m.* wild honey. —horn, *n.* bugle(-horn); French horn. —hüter, *m.* forest-keeper, ranger. —kapelle, *f.* chapel in a forest. —kirsch(en)=baum, *m.* wild-cherry tree. —kultur, *f.* forestry, sylviculture. —landschaft, *f.* woodland scenery. —leute, *pl.* forest-folk; inhabitants of the Four (old Swiss Forest) Cantons. —mann, *m.* woodman, forester; dweller in a wood; satyr; sporting dog; dog's name. —männchen, *n.* forest-sprite, wood goblin. —maus, *f.* field mouse. —meister, *m.* forest-ranger; woodruff (*Asperula odorata*). —mensch, *m.* wild man (*of the woods*); satyr; orang-outang. —mühle, *f.* mill in a forest. —nymphe, *f.* nymph of the woods, dryad. —ordnung, *f.* forest laws. —rauch, *m.* peat smoke. —rebe, *f.* clematis. —recht, *n.* forest laws; rights of the owner of a forest. —reich, *adj.* rich in forests, well-wooded. —reiter, *m.* mounted wood ranger. —revier, *n.* preserve. —schaden, *m.* damage done in a forest. —schloß, *n.* castle in a forest. —schnepfe, *f.* wood-cock. —schrat, *m.* wood-goblin, forest sprite. —schütze, *m.* wood-ranger. —stadt, *f.* town surrounded by woods. —stätte, *pl.*; die vier —stätte, the Four (Swiss) Forest Cantons. —streu, *f.* litter collected from woods. —strom, *m.* torrent. —teufel, *m.* wood-demon; baboon, mandrill (*Zool.*). —wärts, *adv.* towards the wood. —weg, *m.* forest-road *or* path. —weib, *n.* woman of the woods. —weide, *f.* forest-pasture. —wiese, *f.* forest-glade. —wiesel, *n.* ferret. —winde, *f.* wood-bine. —wirtschaft, *f.* forestry. —wolle, *f.* pine-needle wool. —zeichen, *n.* mark on forest-trees, blaze.

Wäld'chen, *n.* (—s, *pl.* —) little wood, grove.

Wa'len, *v.n.* (*aux.* h.) to vacillate (*of the magnetic needle, etc.*); to have no steerage-way.

Wal'ke, *f.* (*pl.* —n) fulling; fulling-machine; pile (*of skins*); felting stick.

Wal'k—en, *v.a.* to full, mill (*cloth*); to felt (*hats*); to tread (*skins*); to thrash, cudgel. —er, *m.* (—ers, *pl.* —er) fuller. —erei', *f.* fulling; drubbing; fulling-mill. *Comp.* —(er)=erde, *f.* fuller's earth. —er=thon, *m.* fulling clay. —faß, *n.* fulling-trough. —haare, *pl.* waste hair in the fulling-trough. —hammer, *m.* fulling-hammer. —holz, *n.* felting-stick. —mühle, *f.* fulling-mill. —wolle, *f.* felted wool.

¹Wall, *m.* (—es, *pl.* Wäl'le) rampart; mound; bank; embankment, dam, dike; coast, shore; einen — aufwerfen, to throw up an embankment. *Comp.* —anker, *m.* shore-anchor. —arbeit, *f.* rampart-work. —auftritt, *m.* banquette (*Fort.*). —bruch, *m.* breach in a rampart. —büchse, *f.* rampart-gun. —gang, *m.* walk on the ramparts. —graben, *m.* rampart ditch, moat. —keller, *m.* casemate. —lafette, *f.* standing-bed *or* carriage (*of a rampart-gun*). —meister, *m.* inspector of ramparts. —schild, *n.* ravelin (*Fort.*).

²Wall, *m.* (—es, *pl.* —e) boiling; bubbling up; einen — thun lassen, to boil up.

³Wall, *see* Wallfaß.

Wal'lach, *m.* (—s, —en, *pl.* —e, —en) Wallachian horse, gelding. —en, *v.a.* to geld.

¹Wal'l—en, *v.n.* (*aux.* h.) to undulate; to move backwards and forwards, move like waves; to float; to heave; to bubble, boil up; to be agitated, to boil; ihm —t das Blut, his blood boils, his blood is up; es —et und siedet und brauset und zischt, it bubbles and seethes and hisses and roars; —ende Gewänder, flowing garments. —ung, *f.* ebullition; undulation; flow; undue excitement; agitation; sein Puls ist in —ung, his pulse is high; in —ung geraten, to become agitated, to fly into a passion.

²Wal'l—en, I. *v.n.* (*aux.* s.) to walk, wander about; to go on a pilgrimage. II. *subst.n.* pilgrimage. —er, *m.* (—ers, *pl.* —er) pilgrim. *Comp.* —bruder, —fahrer(in, *f.*), *m.* pilgrim. —fahrt, *f.* pilgrimage. —fahrten, *v.n.* (*aux.* s.) (*insep.*) to go on *or* make a pilgrimage. —fahrts=ort, *m.* place of pilgrimage.

Wäl'len, *v.a.* to (let) boil; to (let) simmer.

Wall'faß, *m.* barrel of fourscore herrings.

Wall'fisch, *see* ¹Wal.

Wall'nuß, *see* ³Wal.

Walm, *m.* (—es, *pl.* —e) slope, hip (*Arch.*). —en, *v.a.* to slope (*a roof*). *Comp.* —dach, *n.* hip-roof.

Wal'te—n, I. *v.n.* (*aux.* h.) to rule, govern, sway; hold the reins of government; schalten und —n, to govern absolutely, to rule, command; der Vater —t im Hause, the father rules the house; einen —n lassen, to let a p. do as he pleases; Gnade —n lassen, to show mercy; — deines Amtes! discharge the duties of your office! das (*or obs.* des) — Gott! (may) God grant it! amen, so let it be! II. *n.* rule, government; management.

Wal'ze, *f.* (*pl.* —n) cylinder; roller; barrel; auf der — sein = auf der Wanderschaft sein (*coll.*).

Wal'z—en, *v.* I. *a.* to roll; to roll out (*dough, etc.*); to form into a cylinder; to mill (*iron*). II. *r.* & *n.* (*aux.* h.) to waltz. —ende(r), *m.* waltzer. —er, *m.* (—ers, *pl.* —er) waltz. *Comp.* —blech, *n.* rolled plate. —blei, *n.* sheet-lead. —eisen, *n.* rolled iron. —en=apparat, *m.* rolling-frame. —en=brechmaschine, *f.* flax-dressing machine. —en=druck, *m.* cylinder-printing. —en=förmig, *adj.* cylindrical. —en=gerüst, *n.* housing frame of a roller (*Agr.*).

—en=kessel, *m.* cylindrical boiler. —en=presse, *f.* rolling-press. —en=stein, *m.* wheel-stone. —holz, *n.* roller (*Glassw.*). —hütte, *f.* rolling-mill. —rad, *n.* double wheel, caster. —stahl, *m.* rolled steel. —werk, *n.* rollers, rolling-mill. —zapfen, *m.* round spike. —zinn, *n.* laminated tin.

Wäl'z—en, I. *v.a.* to roll, trundle. II. *v.r.* to wallow; to welter; to revolve; seine Tonne —en, to go through the daily routine (*coll.*); von sich —en, to release, exonerate oneself from; die Schuld —en auf einen, to throw the blame upon a p.; er —t sich vor Lachen, he is splitting *or* convulsed with laughter. III. *subst. n.* rolling; das ist zum —en, it is enough to make a cat laugh (*coll.*). —er, *m.* (—ers, *pl.* —er) roller; heavy mass; ponderous book. *Comp.* —maschine, *f.* finishing engine (*for rounding*).

Wam'me, *f.* (*pl.* —n) paunch; belly (*in furs*); belly, entrails (*of beasts*); flank; dewlap; fat.

Wams, (*dim.* Wäms'chen, *n.*,) *n.* (& *m.*) (—(s)es, *pl.* Wäm'ser) doublet, jerkin; camisole; jersey. —(s)en, *v.a.* to provide with doublet *or* jersey; to thrash, drub.

[1]Wand, *1 & 3 p. sing. imperf. indic.*; Wän'de, *1 & 3 p. sing. imperf. subj. of* winden.

[2]Wand, *f.* (*pl.* Wän'de) wall; partition; side (*of a mountain*); back (*of a chimney*); side, inside, wall (*of a gun-barrel*); bed (*of a gun-carriage*); cheek (*of a press*); coat (*of the stomach*); wall side (*of rock, Min.*); quarter (*of a horse's hoof*); row of clap-nets; rib (*of venison*); shroud (*Naut.*); panel (*of a carriage*); die Wände haben Ohren, walls (*or* pitchers) have ears; man soll den Teufel nicht an die — malen, speak of the Devil and you see his hoofs (*prov.*); mit dem Kopfe durch die — rennen, to run one's head against a wall; es ist um an den Wänden *or* (die Wände) hinaufzulaufen, it is enough to drive one mad (*coll.*); etwas den Wänden vorerzählen, to talk to the winds; der Horcher an der — hört seine eigne Schand, listeners never hear good of themselves (*prov.*); spanische —, folding-screen, Japanese screen. —ung, *f.* wall, partition. *Comp.* —anstrich, *m.* painting. —bank, *f.* bench fastened to the wall. —bekleidung, *f.* wainscotting, (*paper*) hangings. —bewurf, *m.* plaster, parget. —fest, *adj.* fixed to the wall. —gemälde, *n.* fresco, mural painting. —gestell, *n.* bracket. —getäfel, *n.* wainscotting. —kalender, *m.* almanac to be hung up on the wall; sheet *or* block-almanac. —karte, *f.* wall-map. —laus, *see* Wanze. —leuchter, *m.* candlestick affixed to a wall; gas bracket. —malerei, *f. see* —gemälde. —nachbar, *m.* inhabitant of the neighbouring room. —pfeiler, *m.* pillar inserted in a wall, pilaster. —pianoforte, *n.* cottage *or* upright piano. —putz, *m.* parget, plaster. —säule, *f.* upright post (*in a screen, etc.*); wall-pillar. —schirm, *m.* folding screen. —schrank, *m.* cupboard. —spiegel, *m.* mirror fixed to a wall, pier-glass. —tafel, *f.* blackboard. —teller, *m.* decorative plate. —uhr, *f.* wall-clock; hall- *or* kitchen-clock.

Wan'del, *m.* (—s) walking, going; progress; walk; change, mutation; way of living, conduct, behaviour, walk; social intercourse; traffic; Handel und —, trade, commerce; einen tugendhaften — führen, to lead a virtuous life; ohne —, not subject to change, unchangeable; unblemished; irreproachable; wer ohne — einhergehet, he that walketh uprightly (*B.*); Gottes Wege sind ohne —, as for God, his way is perfect (*B.*). —bar, *adj. & adv.* changeable, variable, fickle; current; practicable, passable; fragile, perishable; ruinous, decayed. —barkeit, *f.* changeableness; vicissitude. —haft, *adj.* changeable; fragile; disordered, in disorder.

Wan'd—eln, I. *v.a. & r.* to change; (sich) —eln in, to turn into. II. *v.n.* (*aux.* h. & s.) to go, walk; to wander, travel; handeln und —eln, to trade, traffic; (*in scriptural lang.*) to live; unsträflich —eln, to lead an irreproachable life. III. *subst.n.* walking; walk; change; *see* —lung; im Handeln und —eln, in trade, commerce. —ler, *m.* (—lers, *pl.* —ler) wanderer; walker; pilgrim. —lung, *f.* change, alteration, transformation; transubstantiation. *Comp.* —el=bahn, *f.* covered walk, arcade. —el=bild, *n.* phantom; —elbilder, dissolving views. —el=dekoration, *f.* shifting scenery. —el=gang, *m.* gallery; promenade, corridor; die —elgänge der Kammer, the lobbies of the house (*Parl.*). —el=halle, *f.* corridor. —el=skala, *f.* sliding scale. —el=stern, *m.* planet. —el=wand, *f.* shifting scene.

Wan'der—er, *m.* (—ers, *pl.* —er), —in, *usually* Wan'drerin, *f.* wanderer, pedestrian, traveller (*on foot*); tourist; pilgrim.

Wan'der—n, *v.n.* (*aux.* s.) to travel (*on foot*), go, walk; to wander, ramble, roam; to travel; to migrate (*of birds*); to walk (*of ghosts*); to move, to be shifting (*of sand, etc.*); ins Gefängnis —n, to go to prison (*coll.*); seines Weges —n, to go one's way; seine Uhr ist aufs Leihhaus gewandert, his watch has gone to the pawnshop. —nd, *p. & adj.* itinerant; strolling; nomadic; migratory; circulating (*of a library*); erratic (*Geol.*); movable (*kidney*); shifting (*sand hills*). —schaft, *f.* travelling; travels, tour; auf die —schaft gehen, to go travelling; auf der —schaft sein, to be on one's travels (*of journeymen*). —ung, *f.* travelling; trip, tour; travels; migration; excursion; Fuß —ung, pedestrian tour. *Comp.* —blöcke, *pl.* erratic blocks (*Geol.*). —buch, *n.* travelling-journeyman's book. —bursch, —gesell, *m.* travelling journeyman. —falk(e), *m.* peregrine falcon. —heuschrecke, *f.* migratory locust. —jahre, *pl.* journeyman's years of travel (*following his* Lehrjahre); er hat seine —jahre vollendet, he has completed his travels. —lager, *n.* travelling vender's booth *or* shop. —leben, *n.* wandering, nomadic life. —lehrer, *m.* itinerant teacher; extension lecturer, touring lecturer. —lust, *f.* desire to travel *or* to see the world. —niere, *f.* movable kidney. —prediger, *m.* itinerant preacher. —ratte, *f.* brown *or* Norway rat. —raupe, *f.* palmer worm (Bombyx processionea). —redner, *m.* itinerant lecturer, extension lecturer. —s=mann, *m.* (*pl.* —s=leute) traveller. —stab, *m.* pilgrim's staff; den —stab ergreifen, zum —stabe greifen, to set out (*on one's travels*), to go abroad; den —stab weiter setzen, to go on, continue on one's way. —stamm, *m.* nomadic tribe. —taube, *f.* passenger pigeon. —vögel, *pl.* birds of passage. —zeit, *f. see* —jahre.

Wand'te, *1 & 3 p. sing. imp. ind. of* wenden.

Wan'g—e, *f.* (*pl.* —en) cheek; cheek, sidepiece; —en, notchboards (*of a staircase*); cheeks (*of a press*); vans, wings (*of an hydraulic engine*); —en des Mastes, fishes (*Naut.*). —ig, *suff.* (*in cpds.* =) -cheeked; rot—ig, rosy-cheeked. *Comp.* —en=bein, *n.* cheek-bone. —en=grübchen, *n.* dimple in the cheek. —en=rot, *adj.* rosy-cheeked. —en=scheibe, *f.* honeycomb from the sides of the hive.

Wan'kel (*obs.*), —haft, *adj.* unstable, fickle, inconstant. *Comp.* —mut, *m.* vacillation; fickleness, inconstancy. —mütig, *adj.* fickle, changeable. —rede, *f.* undecided, wavering speech.

Wan'ken, *v.n.* (*aux.* h. & s.) to stagger, reel, totter; to waver, vacillate; to flicker; to hesitate; to flinch; to tumble about; in der Treue —d machen, to shake (*a p.'s*) allegiance; weder weichen noch —, to stand firm, not to flinch.

Wann, I. *adv.* when; seit —? since when? how long? dann und —, now and then. II. *conj.* when; es sei — es wolle, whenever *or* whatever time it may be.

Wan'ne, *f.* (*pl.* —n) winnowing fan; tub; pail; bath. —n, *v.a.* to winnow. *Comp.* —n=bad, *n.* bath in a tub.

Wan'nen, *adv.*; von —, (from) whence.

Wanst, *m.* (—es, *pl.* Wän'ste) belly, paunch.

Want, *f.* (*pl.* —en) shroud (*Naut.*); die großen —en, the main shroud. *Comp.* —klampen, *pl.* shroud-cleats. —tau, *n.*, —troß, *f.* shroud.

Wan'z—e, *f.* (*pl.* —en) bug; (metal) clip. —ig, *adj.* buggy. *Comp.* —en=kraut, *n.* bug-wort.

Wap'pen, *n.* (—s, *pl.* —) (*coat of*) arms, escutcheon, armorial bearings; — ohne Beizeichen, plain coat of arms; — im Siegel, crest, signet; im — führen, to bear. *Comp.* —amt, *n.* herald's office. —ausleger, *m.* herald. —auslegung, *see* —erklärung. —balken, *m.* fesse (*Her.*). —berechtigt, *adj.* authorized to bear a coat of arms. —bild, *n.* figure in an escutcheon, heraldic figure. —buch, *n.* book of heraldry. —decke, *f.* pavilion. —erklärung, *f.* blazonry, heraldry. —farben, *pl.* armorial colours. —feld, *n.* field, quarter. —halter, *m.* supporter (*Her.*). —helm, *m.* helmet. —herold, —könig, *m.* herald, king-at-arms. —kunde, *f.* armoury, heraldry, heraldic science. —kundige(r), *m.* expert in heraldry. —kunst, *f.* heraldic art. —mantel, *m.* mantling (*Her.*). —schild, —schildchen, *n.* escutcheon. —spruch, *m.* heraldic motto, device. —zierde, *f.* accompaniment (*Her.*).

Wapp'nen, *v.a.* to arm (*obs. & poet.*); der Gewappnete, man-at-arms (*obs. & poet.*).

War, *1 & 3 p. sing. imperf. ind.*; **Wä're,** *1 & 3 p. sing. imperf. subj. of* sein.

Warb, *1 & 3 p. sing. imperf. ind. of* werben.

Ward, *1 & 3 p. sing. imperf. ind. of* werden.

Ward—ei'n, *m.* (—eins, *pl.* —eine) assayer, mint warden. —ie'ren, *v.a.* to assay coin.

Wardst, *2 p. sing. imperf. ind. of* werden.

Wa're, *f.* (*pl.* —n) ware, merchandise, article, commodity, goods; piece of goods (*fig.*); ordinäre —, rough, low class goods; grüne —, herbs, vegetables; irdene —, pottery; seidene, wollene, baumwollene —, silks, woollens, cottons; verbotene —, contraband goods; kurze —, small wares, hardware; —n ausführen, to export goods; —n beziehen, to import goods; das ist teure —, that's a luxury. *Comp.* —n=absender, *m.* sender of goods, consigner, forwarding agent, shipper, *etc.* —n=abschluß, *m.* contract in goods. —n=adreß=zettel, *m.* docket, label. —n=ausfuhr, *f.* exportation of merchandise. —n=bestand, *m.* stock (*C. L.*). —n=bestellungs=buch, *n.* order book. —n=bezieher, *m.* importer. —n=deklaration, *f.* declaration (*specification*) of merchandise at the custom-house. —n=einsender, *m.* consigner. —n=empfänger, *m.* consignee. —n=fälschung, *f.* adulteration of goods. —n=gattung, *f.* description *or* kind of goods. —n=gewölbe, —n=haus, *n.* shop; warehouse. —n=kenntnis, *f.* knowledge of goods; er besitzt große —n=kenntnis, he is well *or* intimately acquainted with the articles. —n=konto, *n.* current-account book. —n=kunde, *f.* knowledge of articles of commerce; Commercial Dictionary (*as title of a book*); knowledge of goods. —n=lager, *n.* stock in trade; store, warehouse. —n=lieferant, *m.* contractor, purveyor. —n=mäkler, *m.* broker, agent. —n=niederlage, *f.* magazine, warehouse. —n=preis, *m.* current price of goods; mark (*on goods*). —n=probe, *f.* sample; pattern; inspection of wares. —n=rechnung, *f.* invoice, bill. —n=stempel, *m.* trade-mark, manufacturer's mark. —n=steuer, *f.* duty. excise. —n=verkaufsbuch, *n.* sale-book. —n=verzeichnis, *n.* price-list; invoice; docket; bill of lading. —n=vorrat, *m.* stock (*C. L.*). —n=zoll, *m.* custom-house duty.

Warf, *1 & 3 p. sing. imperf. indic. of* werfen.

Warm, *adj. & adv.* (wär'mer, wärmst) warm; hot; mir ist —, I am warm; — auftragen, to serve up hot; — baden, to take warm baths; sich — halten, to keep o.s. warm, dress warmly; die Sonne scheint —, the sun is hot; — sitzen, to be in easy circumstances; man muß das Eisen schmieden, wenn es noch — ist, strike while the iron is hot; nicht — nicht kalt, neither one thing nor another; — stellen, to put on the fire; (sich, *dat.*) einen — halten, to cultivate a p.'s acquaintance, to do all one can to oblige a p.; einem — machen, to make it warm *or* unpleasant for a p.; es ging da — her, there was hot work there; einem den Kopf — machen, to excite a p., to provoke a p., stir a p. up; — werden, to warm up to, to get hot *or* excited over, to get into a passion (für, about). *Comp.* —bad, *n.* thermal springs. —blütig, *adj.* warm-blooded. —halter, *m.* plate-warmer; oven. —herzig, *adj.* warm-hearted. —luft=heizung, *f.* heating with hot air, hot-air pipes. —wasser=heizung, *f.* heating by hot-water pipes.

Wär'm—e, *f.* warmth; heat, ardour; —e wird gebunden, heat becomes latent; freie —e, sensible heat (*Phys.*); strahlende —e, radiant heat; zwölf Grad —e, 12 degrees of heat; —e durchlassen, to transmit heat. *Comp.* —apparat, *m.* plate-warmer; stove. —e=äquator, *m.* thermal equator. —e=äquivalent, *n.*; das mechanische —eäquivalent, the mechanical equivalent of heat. —e=einheit, *f.* thermal unit. —e=elektrizität, *f.* thermo-electricity. —e=erzeugend, *adj.* calorific. —e=grad, *m.* degree of heat; hoher (niederer) —egrad, high (low) temperature. —e=kapazität, *f.* calorific capacity. —e=kraftlehre, *f.* thermodynamics. —e=lehre, *f.* science of heat. —e=leitend, *adj.* heat-conducting. —e=leiter, *m.* conductor. —e=magnetismus, *m.* thermo-magnetism. —e=messer, *m.* thermometer. —e=stoff, *m.* caloric. —e=theorie, *f.* theory of heat. —e=tragend, *adj.* caloriferous. —e=zeiger, *m.* thermoscope. —flasche, *f.* hot-water bottle. —korb, *m.* basket with warming pan for underlinen. —kraft, *f.* heating power. —ofen, *m.* stove for keeping things hot. —pfanne, *f.* warming-pan; chafing-dish; copper; pan; heater. —stein, *m.* hot brick.

Wär'm—en, *v.a.* to warm, heat; to make warm *or* hot; sich —en, to warm oneself, to bask; sich (*dat.*) die Hände —en, to warm one's hands. —er, *m.* (—ers, *pl.* —er) warmer, stove; warming-pan. —ung, *f.* warming, heating; calefaction.

War'n—en, I. *v.a.* (einen vor einem) to warn *or* caution (a p. against s.o.); to advise, admonish; vorher gewarnt, vorher gewaffnet, forewarned is forearmed (*prov.*). II. *subst.n. see* —ung. —er, *m.* (—ers, *pl.* —er) admonisher; monitor. —ung, *f.* warning; caution, admonition; laßt euch das zur —ung dienen, let this be a warning to you; das soll mir eine —ung sein, it shall be a warning *or* a lesson to me. *Comp.* —ruf, *m.* warning cry. —ungs=anzeige, *f.* public warning. —ungs=tafel, *f.* notice-board, caution.

War'pen, *v.a.* to tow.

Wart, *m.* (—es, *pl.* —e) warder (*as the second pt. of compounds, see* Kassenwart, Schriftwart, Turnwart). —e, *f.* (*pl.* —en) look-out; watch-tower; observatory; belfry.

Wär'tel, *m.* warder of a watch tower (*obs.*).

War't—en, I. *v.n.* (*aux.* h.) to wait, stay; to abide; to await, be in expectancy *or* on the look-out; (gen'lly with **auf einen** or **eine S.**, rarely with gen.) to await, wait for; to wait on, attend, serve; **da können Sie lange —en,** you may wait till doomsday, you may whistle for it (coll.); **—'! wenn ich dich erwische!** just wait till I catch you! **—e nur!** you will catch it! (coll.); **er läßt immer auf sich —en,** he is never ready in time; **einen —en lassen,** to keep a p. waiting; **er kann —en,** let him wait; **mit dem Essen auf einen —en,** to keep dinner waiting for s.o.; **seines Amtes, seiner Arbeit —en,** to discharge one's duties, to attend to one's work. II. v.a. to attend to, tend, nurse. III. subst.n. waiting; tending; **ich bin des —ens müde,** I am tired of waiting. **—ung,** f. nursing, tending; attendance. Comp. **—e=frau,** see **Wärterin.** **—e=geld,** n. attendant's wages; compensation for loss of time; allowance (for waiting); half pay; **auf —egeld setzen,** to put on half-pay. **—(e)=saal,** m. waiting-room (Railw.). **—e=turm,** m. watch-tower. **—e=zeit,** f. demurrage, time of waiting (before lovers can marry or before a ship is allowed to unload). **—(e)=zimmer,** n. waiting-room (of a doctor, etc.); see **—esaal.**

Wär'ter, m. (—s, pl. —) keeper, attendant. **—in,** f. female attendant; sick-nurse; caretaker. Comp. **—haus, —häuschen,** n. signalman's box or hut.

Wärts, adv. towards; (in comp. =) -wards.

Waru'm, adv. & conj. wherefore, why, on what account, for what reason; **— nicht?** why not? **— nicht gar!** you don't say so! dear me! by no means! **— bin ich nicht gestern gekommen?** why did I not (or if I had only) come yesterday!

Wär'wolf, see **Werwolf.**

War'z—e, f. (pl. —en) wart; nipple; teat; tubercle (Bot.); knob; crank-pin. **—ig,** adj. warty. Comp. **—en=aloe,** f. warted aloe. **—en=artig,** adj. warty; papillary. **—en=förmig,** adj. papillary. **—en=fortsatz,** m. papillary tubercle; mastoid process. **—en=mittel,** n. remedy for warts. **—en=ring,** m. areola of the nipple.

Was, I. inter. pron. what; what a lot, how many (with the gen. obs.); why; whatever; **—?** what did you say? what? (vulg.); **—, schon wieder!** what, again! **— bekommen Sie?** how much is it? the bill, please; what is your fare? **— rennt das Volk?** why are the people running? **— dann, — weiter?** what then? is that all? **— Sie sagen!** you don't say so! really! **— für?** what? **— für ein?** what sort of? **das zeigt, — für ein Mensch er ist,** that shows what sort of a man he is; **— das für ein lästiger Mensch ist!** what a bore that man is! **— für ein Unglück!** what a misfortune! **— ist Ihnen denn?** what is wrong, what ails you? **— hilft's?** of what use is it? **— der Junge doch fährt!** how well the lad drives! (coll.); **— haben wir gelacht!** how we have laughed! did n't we laugh? **— da der edeln Garben auf allen Feldern lag,** how many noble sheaves lay on all the fields (obs. & poet.); **ach —!** bah! pshaw! II. rel. pron. what; that which; whatever; **er läuft — er (nur) kann,** he runs as hard as he can; **— mich betrifft,** as for me; **— Ihr auch immer thut,** whatever or no matter what you do; **— ich euch sage,** I assure you. III. coll. for **etwas; ich will dir mal — sagen,** I will tell you something; **das ist auch — Rechts!** I don't think much of that! **so — lebt nicht!** such a thing has never been heard of; well, I never! **ein unbekanntes —,** an undefined something. IV. coll. for **— (meinen Sie?); ein bischen kalt heute, —?** rather cold to-day, don't you think? Comp. **—maßen,** conj. seeing that, in as much as (obs.).

Wasch'bar, adj. washable, fast (of colours).

Wä'sch—e, f. washing; wash; linen, etc., for or from the wash; (under-)linen; place where ore is washed; **das Hemd ist in der —e,** the shirt is being washed, is in the wash; **morgen haben wir (große) —e,** to-morrow is washing-day; **—e zeichnen,** to mark linen; **die —e wechseln,** to change; **in die —e thun, schicken,** to send to the wash, to have washed; **schmutzige —e,** soiled linen. **—er,** m. (—ers, pl. —er) washer, washerman. **—erei',** f. washing; laundry. **—erin,** f. washerwoman, laundress. Comp. **—(e)=beutel,** m. soiled-clothes bag. **—(e)=fabrik,** f., **—geschäft,** n. linen-drapery, under-clothing business. **—kammer,** f. linen-cupboard. **—(e)=kiste,** f. linen-chest. **—korb,** m. (soiled) linen basket. **—(e)=mangel, —rolle,** f. mangle. **—er=lohn,** m. money paid for washing; laundry-maid's wages. **—(e)=rollen,** n. mangling. **—schrank,** m. linen-press. **—(e)=trockenständer,** m. clothes-horse. **—waren,** pl. under-clothing.

Wa'sch—en, I. ir.v.a. & n. (aux. **h.**) to wash; to chatter (coll. dial.); **eine Hand wäscht die andere,** one good turn deserves another (prov.); **wir —en heute,** this is washing-day; **sich —en lassen,** to bear washing, wash (well); **sich** (dat.) **das Gesicht, die Hände —en,** to wash one's face, hands, etc.; **ich —e meine Hände in Unschuld,** I wash my hands of it; **einen (einem den Kopf) —en,** to blow a p. up; **das hat sich gewaschen!** that is capital or A1! II. subst.n., **—ung,** f. washing. Comp. **—amber,** m. yellow amber. **—anstalt,** f. public laundry. **—apparat,** m. washing apparatus; washing machine; purifier (Chem.). **—arznei,** f. wash (Med.). **—bank,** f. washing stand or bench; laundry-boat. **—bär,** m. raccoon; person very fond of washing (coll.). **—becken,** n. washing or hand basin. **—blau,** n. washing-blue. **—bleuel,** m. washing-beetle. **—bock,** m. washing-stool, bidet. **—bütte,** f., **—faß,** n. washing-vat. **—echt,** adj. fast (in colour), genuine, true, thorough (fig.). **—fleck,** m. stain that shows after washing. **—frau,** f. washerwoman, laundress. **—geld,** n. money or charge for washing. **—gerät, —geschirr,** n. utensils used in washing; wash-stand set. **—gold,** n. river-gold; gold obtained by washing. **—handschuhe,** pl. gloves that bear washing. **—haus,** n. washing house, laundry. **—herd,** m. floor of the buddle, sump (Min.). **—kessel,** m. copper (for boiling linen). **—klammer,** f. clothes-peg. **—korb,** m. clothes-basket. **—küche,** f. see **—haus.** **—lappen,** m. dishcloth; weakling, milksop. **—lauge,** f. lye. **—leder,** n., **—ledern,** adj. wash-leather, shammy; **—lederne Handschuhe,** shammy gloves. **—leine,** f. clothes-line. **—maschine,** f. washing-machine, washer. **—maul,** n. gossip, babbler; scandal monger. **—mittel,** n. lotion. **—platz,** m. washing-place (of a village, etc.); lavatory. **—pritsche,** f. washing stand or boat (at the edge of a stream, etc.). **—schwamm,** m. sponge. **—seife,** f. common soap. **—tisch,** m., **—toilette,** f. washing-stand. **—topf,** m. basin for washing up in. **—trog,** m. washing-trough; cradle (Min.). **—wanne,** f. wash-tub; foot-pail. **—wasser,** n. water for washing; wash, cosmetic; lotion; dish-water. **—weib,** n. laundress; see **—maul.** **—zettel,** m. washing-bill; washing-list. **—zeug,** see **—gerät.** **—zimmer,** n. lavatory (at stations), dressing room. **—zuber,** m. see **—faß.**

Wä'schest, Wäschst, 2 p.; **Wäscht,** 3 p. sing. pres. ind. of **waschen.**

Wa'sen, m. (—s, pl. —) sod, turf, grass; lawn; bundle of brushwood (dial.); steam (dial.) see **Brasen.** Comp. **—stück,** n. grass-plot.

Was'ser, n. (—s, pl. —) water; piece of water; **destillie'rtes —,** distilled water; **gebranntes**

—, brandy, liqueur; **fließendes —,** running water; **stehendes —,** stagnant water; **Kölnisches —,** eau de Cologne; **Selters —,** seltzer water; **Meer—,** sea water; **Süß—,** fresh water; **weiches —,** soft water; **Trink—,** drinking-water; **verschlagenes (laues) —,** tepid water; **einem nicht das — reichen,** to be far inferior to, not to be compared to, unable to hold a candle to a p.; **— ins Meer** *or* **in den Rhein tragen,** to carry coals to Newcastle (*prov.*); **bei — und Brot sitzen,** to be fed on bread and water; **sich mit Not über dem — erhalten,** to have difficulty in keeping o.s. afloat *or* in making both ends meet; **— fahren,** to carry water; to take a trip on the water; **bis dahin wird noch viel — ins Meer fließen,** many things may happen before that; **der Hund geht ins —,** the dog takes to the water; **ein schönes — haben,** to be of a fine water (*of diamonds*), to be prettily watered (*of silks, etc.*); **sein — abschlagen,** to make water; **das — läuft ihm im Munde zusammen,** his mouth waters; **zu — werden, ins — fallen,** to melt away, come to naught, to fall to the ground; **alle seine schönen Pläne wurden zu —,** all his fine schemes ended in smoke; **zu — machen,** to bring to naught; **unter — setzen,** to inundate, submerge; **die Augen stehen voll —,** the eyes are suffused with tears; **das war — auf seine Mühle,** that was grist to his mill; **das — auf seine Mühle leiten,** to feather one's nest; **er spricht Deutsch wie —,** he speaks German fluently; **zu — und zu Lande,** by sea and land; **das — hat keine Balken,** the sea is treacherous, the sea is not planked over, beware of the water (*prov.*); **er sieht aus als könnte er kein Wässerchen trüben,** he looks as if butter would not melt in his mouth; **stille — sind tief,** still waters run deep (*prov.*). *Comp.* **—ablaß,** *m.* draining; drainage. **—ablauf-rinne,** *f.* gutter, spouting (*on a roof*). **—ableitung,** *f.* diversion of water *or* a water-supply. **—abschlag,** *m.* outlet for water. **—abzugsröhre,** *f.* drain. **—arm,** *adj.* not well supplied with water, arid. **—armut,** *f.* want *or* scarcity of water. **—arzt,** *m.* hydropathic doctor. **—auge,** *n.* dropsy of the eye. **—barometer,** *m.* & *n.* hydro-barometer. **—bau,** *m.* water-work; hydraulic structure. **—bau-direktor,** *m.* chief engineer *or* constructor of water-works. **—baukunst,** *f.* hydraulics, hydraulic architecture *or* works. **—baumeister, —techniker,** *m.* hydraulic engineer. **—becken,** *n.* reservoir, basin. **—behälter,** *m.* reservoir; cistern; boiler; well (*of a steam-engine*). **—beschreiber,** *m.* hydrographer. **—beschreibung,** *f.* hydrography. **—blase,** *f.* bubble. **—blattern,** *pl.* Varicella (*Med.*). **—blau,** *adj.* marine blue. **—blume,** *f.* aquatic flower. **—brei,** *m.* pap; paste. **—bruch,** *m.* hydrocele (*Med.*). **—damm,** *m.* dam, dike. **—dicht,** *adj.* water-tight; water-proof. **—doktor,** *m.* see **—arzt;** quack. **—eimer,** *m.* water-pail, bucket. **—faden,** *m.* stream of water; conferva (*Bot.*). **—(fahr)rad,** *n.* water-bicycle. **—fahrt,** *f.* boating, excursion by water. **—fall,** *m.* cascade, waterfall; (**großer —fall**) cataract. **—fang,** *m.* cistern, reservoir. **—farbe,** *f.* colour of water; water-colour, distemper. **—farben-malerei,** *f.* water-colour painting, painting in water colours. **—farbig,** *adj.* water-coloured. **—feuerwerk,** *n.* fireworks on the water, aquatic fireworks. **—fläche,** *f.* water-surface; sheet of water. **—flasche,** *f.* carafe, water-bottle. **—flut,** *f.* flood, deluge. **—fracht,** *f.* carriage by water, freight. **—frei,** *adj.* containing no water; anhydrous. **—freund(in,** *f.*), *m.* lover of water; lover of aquatic sports. **—gang,** *m.* aqueduct; canal; drain. **—gebläse,** *n.* hydrostatic blast. **—gefahr,** *f.* danger from water; danger of inundations. **—gefäß,** *n.* water-cask *or* tub; water-jar; lymphatic vessel (*Anat.*). **—geflügel,** *n.* water-fowl. **—geist,** *m.* water-sprite. **—gerechtigkeit,** *f.* laws *or* rules relating to water. **—gesetzgebung,** *f.* laws relating to rivers and canals. **—gewächs,** *n.* aquatic plant. **—glas,** *n.* tumbler, water-glass; soluble glass. **—gleich,** *adj.* aqueous; level, horizontal. **—gott,** *m.* Neptune. **—graben,** *m.* drain; moat. **—grube,** *f.* cistern. **—guß,** *m.* downpour (*of rain*); sink; gargoyle. **—haltig,** *adj.* containing water; hydrated (*Chem.*). **—hart,** *adj.* dried in the air, half dry (*of pottery*). **—hebemaschine,** *f.* engine for raising water, hydraulic engine, water-wheel. **—heilanstalt,** *f.* hydropathic establishment. **—heilkunde,** *f.* hydropathy. **—heizung,** *f.* heating by hot-water pipes. **—hose,** *f.* water-spout. **—huhn,** *n.* coot. **—jungfer,** *f.* dragon-fly; water-nymph; **—jungfern werfen,** to throw ducks and drakes. **—käfer,** *m.* aquatic beetle. **—kanne,** *f.* water-jug; ewer. **—karte,** *f.* hydrographic chart. **—kasten,** *m.* cistern. **—kessel,** *m.* caldron, copper; kettle. **—kitt,** *m.* hydraulic cement. **—klee,** *m.* marsh trefoil. **—kluft,** *f.* fissure filled with water. **—kopf,** *m.* hydrocephalus; person suffering from hydrocephalus. **—kothurn,** *m.* skate (*poet.*). **—kraft,** *f.* water *or* hydraulic power. **—kraft-maschine,** *f.* water-power engine. **—krafts-lehre,** *f.* hydrodynamics. **—kresse,** *f.* water-cress. **—krug,** *m.* water-pitcher. **—kuh,** *f.* sea-cow. **—kultur,** *f.* regulation of the water-supply of a country. **—kunst,** *f.* water-work; fountain; draining engine (*Min.*); hydraulic engine; hydraulics. **—kur,** *f.* water-cure, hydropathic treatment. **—lache,** *f.* pool. **—lauf,** *m.* water-course; drain. **—leer,** *adj.* dry, arid. **—leitung,** *f.* aqueduct, canal; water laid on (*in a house*); water-supply *or* service; **—leitung ins Haus bekommen,** to have the water laid on; **die —leitung abschneiden,** to cut off the water-supply. **—leitungs-hauptrohr,** *n.* (water-) main. **—leitungs-röhre,** *f.* water-pipe, conduit-pipe. **—lilie,** *f.* (white) water-lily. **—linie,** *f.* high-water mark; load-water line. **—linse,** *f.* duckweed. **—loch,** *n.* cesspool; hole with water; well. **—luftgebläse,** *n.* air and water blast. **—malerei,** *see* **—farbenmalerei.** **—mangel,** *m.* dearth of water. **—mann,** *m.* water-carrier, water-bearer; water-sprite; Aquarius (*Astr.*). **—marke,** *f.* water-mark, water-line; *see* **—zeichen.** **—maschine,** *f.* hydraulic engine. **—menge,** *f.* amount of water. **—messer,** *m.* hydrometer; water-metre. **—meßkunst,** *f.* hydrometry. **—molch,** *m.* (water-)newt. **—mühle,** *f.* water-mill. **—müller,** *m.* owner of a water-mill. **—nabelbruch,** *m.* hydromphalon (*Med.*). **—napf,** *m.* water-bowl. **—nymphe,** *f.* naiad. **—not,** *f.* dearth *or* scarcity of water, drought. **—orgel,** *f.* water-organ. **—partie,** *see* **—fahrt.** **—paß,** I. *adj.* level, horizontal. II. *m.* level of the water. **—perle,** *f.* imitation pearl. **—pest,** *f.* (**kanadische**) water weed, Elodea canadensis (*Bot.*). **—pfahl,** *m.* pile in the water. **—pferd,** *n.* hippopotamus. **—pflanze,** *f.* aquatic plant. **—pfuhl,** *m.*, **—pfütze,** *f.* pool. **—pocken,** *see* **—blattern.** **—pumpe,** *f.* water-pump. **—rabe,** *f.* cormorant. **—rad,** *n.* water-wheel; aquatic girandole (*Firew.*); **ober- (unter-) schlägiges —rad,** overshot- (*undershot-*) water-wheel. **—ratte,** *f.* water-rat; person very fond of the sea *or* of bathing (*coll.*); **alte —ratte,** old sea-dog. **—recht,** I. *adj. see* **paß.** II. *n.* legislation with regard to water. **—reich,** I. *adj.* abounding in rivers, lakes, *etc.* II. *n.* watery kingdom. **—reise,** *f.* aqueduct, pipes *or* gutters for the supply of drinking water from a distance; journey by water, sea voyage. —rinne, *f.* gutter. —riß, *m.* ravine. —rose, *f.* (white) water-lily. —rotte, *f.* steeping (*of flax*). —rübe, *f.* turnip. —sack, *m.* watery cyst; space between the float-boards; sump (*Min.*). —säugetier, *n.* aquatic mammal. —säulen=gebläse, *n.* hydrostatic blast. —säulen=maschine, *f.* water-pressure engine. —schacht, *m.* draining-shaft, water-shaft (*in a mine*). —schaden, *m.* injury done by floods *or* by water. —schaufel, *f.* baling-scoop; Dutch shovel; float (*on a water-wheel*). —scheide, *f.* water-shed. —scheu, I. *adj.* dreading water; affected with hydrophobia. II. *f.* dread of water; hydrophobia. —schiff, *n.* brewing-vat. —schlange, *f.* water-snake; ringed snake; Hydra (*Astr.*). —schlauch, *m.* water-hose; bladder-wort (*Bot.*). —schlund, *m.* gulf, whirlpool. —schnepfe, *f.* curlew; snipe. —schraube, *f.* hydraulic screw. —schutz, *m.* grating (*in a pond, etc.*); weir. —schwalbe, *f.* sand-martin. —schwärmer, *m.* water-serpent (*Firew.*). —schwere, *f.* specific gravity of water. —semmel, *f.* kind of roll. —s=not, *f.* distress *or* injury caused by flood, inundation. —spiegel, *m.* surface of the water; expanse of water. —sprudel, *m.* bubbling of water. —stand, *m.* state of the tide, high *or* low water; water-level. —stand=glas, *n.* glass-gauge, water-glass (*on locomotives*). —stand=zeiger, *m.* water-gauge. —stiefel, *m.* waterproof thigh boot, mud boot, fishing boot. —stoff, *m.* hydrogen. —stoff=haltig, *adj.* hydrogenated. —stoff=verbindung, *f.* compound of hydrogen. —strahl, *m.* jet of water; stream. —straße, *f.* channel (*of a river*); water-way. —strecke, *f.* water-course (*Min.*); expanse of water. —streif(en), *m.*, —strich, *m.*, —strieme, *f.* streak of water; watery streak (*in bread*). —strudel, *m.* whirlpool. —stube, *f.* water-chamber (*in waterworks*). —sturz, *m.* waterfall. —sucht, *f.* dropsy. —süchtig, *adj.* dropsical. —suppe, *f.* water-gruel; soup maigre. —teilchen, *n.* aqueous particle, molecule of water. —tiere, *pl.* aquatic animals. —turm, *m.* water-castle (*Hydr.*). —topf, *m.* water-pot, jug; water-receiver. —tracht, *f.* (*ship's*) draught of water. —träger, *m.* water-carrier. —trans=port, *m.* conveyance by water. —treibend, *adj.* diuretic. —trense, *f.* watering-bit; snaffle. —treten, *n.* treading the water. —trog, *m.* water-trough. —uhr, *f.* clepsydra. —umschlag, *m.* cold-water bandage. —(stoff)=verbindungen, *pl.* compounds of hydrogen. —versorgung, *f.* water-supply. —vögel, *pl.* water-fowl, aquatic birds. —wage, *f.* water-level (*Surv.*); hydrostatic balance (*Phys.*); gauge. —wägekunst, *f.* hydrostatics. —wägung, *f.* taking the level; hydrostatic operation. —weide, *f.* common osier; white willow. —welt, *f.* the watery world. —werk, *n.* water-work; hydraulic engine. —wirbel, *m.* eddy; water-spout. —wirtschaft, *see* —kultur. —woge, *f.* large wave, billow. —wüste, *f.* watery waste. —wut, *f.* mania for water. —zeichen, *n.* water-mark (*in paper*); mit —zeichen, watermarked.

Wäs'ser—chen, —lein, *n.* little water, rivulet, brook. —icht, (*obs.*) *adj.* aqueous, watery; serous (*Med.*). —ig, *adj.* watery; serous; insipid; diluted, weak; einem den Mund (nach etwas) —ig machen, to make a p.'s mouth water (for a th.). —igkeit, *f.* wateriness; liquidity; insipidity; washiness; serosity.

Wäs'ser—n, *v.* I. *a.* to water, irrigate; to mix with water; to soak, steep (*in water*); to water (*silk, etc.*); gewässert, watered; hydrated (*Chem.*). II. *n.* (*aux.* h.) to water; ihr —ten die Augen, tears came into her eyes; der Mund —t mir darnach, it makes my mouth water —ung, *f.* watering; irrigation.

Wat, *f.* garment, clothing, dress (*obs. & poet.*).

Wa'te, *f.* (*pl.* —n) scoop-net, seine.

Wa't—en, *v.n.* (*aux.* h. & s.) to wade. *Comp.* —vogel, *m.* wading bird.

Wat'schel—ig, *adj.* waddling. —n, *v.n.* (*aux.* h. & s.) to waddle.

Watt, *n.* (—(e)s, *pl.* —e), —e, *f.* (*pl.* —en) shallow place in sea only covered at high tide; (*pl.*) banks of sand *or* clay, flats, muddy shallows. *Comp.* —en=fahrer, *m.* barge, smack, coasting vessel. —en=fischerei, *f.* shoal-fishing. —en=meer, *n.* shallow sea, shoals, shallows.

Wat't—e, *f.* (*pl.* —en) wadding; fleece (*Spin.*). —ie'ren, *v.a.* to wad, line with wadding. *Comp.* —en=macher, *m.* manufacturer of wadding.

Wat't(i)sch, *adj.*; —es Parallelogramm, Watt's parallel motion (*Locom.*).

Wau, *m.* (—es) dyer's weld, yellow weed (*Bot.*).

Wauwau', I. *int.* bow-wow. II. *m.* dog (*children's lang.*); bugbear.

Web'—bar, *adj.* textile. —e, *f.* (*pl.* —en) web.

We'bel, *see* Weibel.

We'b—en, I. *reg. & ir.v.a.* to weave, fabricate; to weave, entwine; to hatch, plot; to cause, bring forth; to move, stir up; to wave (*B.*). II. *reg. v.n.* (*aux.* h.) to move; to wave, float; to blow (*B.*); in Ihm leben, —en und sind wir, in Him we live and move and have our being; alles lebt und —t, everything is full of activity; alles lebt und —t an ihr, she is full of life. —er, *m.* (—ers, *pl.* —er) spinner, weaver; Bombyx (*Ent.*). —erei', *f.* weaving; texture; tissue; fabric, web. *Comp.* —e=art, *f.* mode of weaving. —e=baum, *see* —erbaum. —e=faser, *f.* textile fibre. —e=garn, *n.* yarn, thread, cotton. —er=arbeit, *f.* weaving; web, tissue. —er=baum, *m.* weaver's beam, warp beam, yarn-roller. —er=einschlag, —er=eintrag, *m.* woof, weft. —er=gesell, *m.* journeyman weaver. —er=glas, *n.* magnifying *or* counting-glass (*used in examining the texture of fabrics*). —er=kamm, *m.* weaver's reed, comb. —er=karde, *f.* card, carding-machine. —er=kunst, *f.* art of weaving. —er=lade, *f.* batten, lathe of the loom. —er=schiffchen, *n.* shuttle. —er=schlichte, *f.* weaver's dressing *or* starch. —er=schule, *f.* school of weaving. —er=schütze, *f. see* —erschiffchen. —er=spule, *f.* spool, bobbin. —er=tritt, *m.* treadle. —er=zettel, *m.* warp. —e=stoff, *m.* textile fabric. —(e)=stuhl, *m.* weaver's loom. —e=waren, *pl.* textile fabrics.

Wech'sel, *m.* (—s, *pl.* —) vicissitude; change; rotation (*of crops, etc.*); variation; changing; turn; interchange; exchange (*also C. L.*); bill of exchange; student's allowance for a term, session *or* year; place where game pass, haunt of game; joint; der Hand—, promissory note; gezogener — (auf zwei Monate Ziel) bill (*drawn at two months*), draft; indossierter —, endorsed bill (of exchange); offener —, letter of credit, L/C; — auf Sicht, bill of exchange payable at sight; — auf den Aussteller selbst, eigener —, trockener —, note of hand, promissory note; einen — ausstellen auf, to draw a bill on; langer —, long-dated *or* sighted bill of exchange; kurzer —, bill at short date; Inhaber eines —s, holder of a bill; ich habe einen —, der auf Sie ausgestellt und an meine Ordre addressirt ist, I have a bill of exchange drawn upon you and endorsed to my order. —bar, *adj.* that may be changed; changeable. —ei', *f.* continual changing; exchange business. *Comp.* —accept, *n.* acceptance of a bill. —agent, *m.* bill broker. —agio, *n.* exchange. —bank, *f.* bank doing exchange business; discount-house. —begriff, *m.* reciprocal *or* equivalent idea. —bewegung, *f.* reciprocal movement. —beziehung, *f.*, —

bezug, *m.* correspondence, correlation. —**brief**, *m.* bill of exchange. —**bude**, *f.* exchange. —**bürge**, *m.* surety for the payment of a bill. —**cötus**, *m.* parallel division (*in schools*). —**fähig**, *adj.* entitled to draw bills of exchange. —**fall**, *m.* case of exchange; alternative; alternate fall. —**fälle**, *pl.* (*gen'lly used as pl. of* Wechsel *in the same sense*) vicissitudes, changes. —**fälschung**, *f.* forgery of bills. —**forderung**, *f.* claim founded on a bill *or* note of hand. —**frist**, *f.* usance (*C. L.*). —**geber**, *m.* drawer (*of a bill*). —**gebrauch**, *m.* usance. —**gebühr**, *f.* commission; discount. —**geld**, *n.* exchange, agio; bank-money. —**gericht**, *n.* court regulating exchange-matters. —**geschäft**, *n.* banking *or* brokerage transaction; banking business; exchange business. —**gläubiger**, *m.* creditor holding a bill of exchange. —**handel**, *m.* bill-oroking; banking. —**händler**, *m.* bill-broker; banker; discounter of bills. —**handlung**, *f. see* —geschäft. —**haus**, *n.* bank. —**inhaber**, *m.* holder of a bill of exchange. —**klage**, *f.* action arising out of a bill of exchange. —**recht**, *n.* right of exchange; laws regarding exchange. —**reiten**, *n.*, —**reiterei**, *f.* bill-jobbing; speculation in accommodation-bills, kite-flying. —**reiter**, *m.* speculator in bills, bill-jobber. —**schuld**, *f.* debt founded on a bill of exchange. —**seitig**, *adj.* reciprocal, mutual; alternate; interchangeable. —**sendung**, *f.* remittance. —**sensal**, *m.* bill-broker. —**stempel**, *m.* exchange-stamp. —**verjährung**, *f.* prescription of a bill of exchange. —**voll**, *adj.* subject to change. —(**s**)=**weise**, *adv.* reciprocally; alternately. —**winkel**, *pl.* alternate angles.

Wech'sel—n, *v.* I. *a.* & *n.* (*aux.* **h.** & **f.**) to change; to issue, draw bills, correspond, carry on banking business; (**sich**) —**n mit**, to alternate with, to replace, change places with; **die Kleider—n**, to change one's clothes; **die Zähne —n**, to get one's new teeth. II. *a.* to exchange; to interchange; **Worte mit einem—n**, to bandy words with a p.; **Briefe mit einem—n**, to correspond with a p.; —**n Sie mir diese Mark**, give me change for this mark. III. *n.* to frequent; to pass and repass; to pass down by (*of game*); to double, dodge (*Sport.*). *Comp.* —**armig**, *adj.* with alternating arms. —**balg**, *m.* changeling, elfish child; monster; imp. —**fieber**, *n.* intermittent fever. —**gesang**, *m.* alternate chant *or* song. —**gespräch**, *n.* dialogue. —**hang**, *m.* suspension by first one arm, then the other (*Gym.*). —**konto**, *n.* account of exchange, bill account. —**kurs**, *m.* course of exchange; **Verrechnung, Vergleichung verschiedener —kurse, —kursberechnung**, *f.* arbitration of exchange. —**makler**, *m.* bill-broker. —**marder**, *m.* fraudulent bill-broker (*coll.*). —**nehmer**, *m.* taker *or* buyer of a bill of exchange. —**noten**, *pl.* appoggiatura (*Mus.*). —**ordnung**, *f.* law regarding bills of exchange. —**platz**, *m.* place of exchange, exchange market. —**protest**, *m.* (*abbr. p.*) protest. —**provision**, *f.* change. —**rechnung**, *f.* banker's account; exchange-account. —**rede**, *f.* dialogue; reply. —**reime**, *pl* alternate rhymes. —**satz**, *m.* dilemma (*Log.*). —**schrift**, *f.* controversy; correspondence. —**ständig**, *adj.* alternating, alternate. —**station**, *f.* junction (-station). —**streit**, *m.* conflict, dispute; dispute regarding exchange-matters. —**strom**, *m.* alternating current (*of electricity*). —**tag**, *m.* day on which a change is made; critical day. —**verhältnis**, *n.* reciprocal relation. —**wirkung**, *f.* reciprocal action *or* effect; **in —wirkung mit einander stehen**, to act and react on one another. —**wirtschaft**, *f.* rotation-system in farming. —**zersetzung**, *f.* double decomposition. —**zustand**, *m.* reciprocity.

Wechs'ler, *m.* (—**s**, *pl.* —) money-changer; banker.

Weck, *m.* (—(**e**)**s**, *pl.* —**e**), —**e**, *f.* (*pl.* —**en**), —**en**, *m.* (—**ens**, *pl.* —**en**) roll of fine white bread.

We'ck—en, I. *v.a.* to awake, waken. II. *subst. n.* awaking, awakening. —**er**, *m.* (—**ers**, *pl.* —**er**) awakener, one who wakes (*others*); alarum-clock; alarm arrangement in a clock; warning-bell *or* whistle. *Comp.* —(**er**)=**uhr**, *f.* alarum-clock. —**er=vorrichtung**, *f.* alarum apparatus, works in an alarum clock. —**glocke**. *f.* alarm-bell.

We'd—a, (**Ved—a**,) *m.* (—**a**(**s**), *pl.* —**as** *and* **We'den**) Veda, scriptures of the ancient Hindus. —**isch**, *adj.* Vedic. *Comp.* —**en=forschung**, *f.* study of the Vedas.

We'del, *m.* (—**s**, *pl.* —) sprinkling-brush, sprinkle; fly-brush; duster; tail; brush (*of foxes, etc.*); frond (*Bot.*). *Comp.* —**förmig**, *adj.* fan-shaped.

We'del—n, *v.a.* & *n.* (*aux.* **h.**) to wag the tail; to fawn, crawl, cringe; to fan. *Comp.* —**affe**, *m.* species of green monkey (*Calithrix*). —**bürste**, *f.* sprinkling-brush, whisk, feather-brush.

We'der, *conj.* neither; than (*B.*); — **er noch ich**, neither he nor I; **Weisheit ist besser — Gold**, wisdom is better than gold (*obs. B.*); — . . . — . . ., neither . . . nor (*rare*).

Weg, I. (*long* e) *m.* (—**es**, *pl.* —**e**) way, road; course, route; passage; manner; means; distance; direction; errand, business; **bedeckter —**, covert-way (*Fort.*); — **unter der Straße**, subway; **Mitte des —es**, midway; **eine Meile —es**, a mile distant, distance of a mile; **am —e**, by the roadside; **auf dem —e**, on the way; approaching, at hand; in a fair way; **auf halbem —e stehen bleiben**, to stop half way; **einem etwas (mit) auf den — geben**, to give a p. s.th. for his journey; **auf dem —e der Güte**, by fair means, amicably; **auf dem ganzen —e**, all the way; **sich auf den — begeben**, to set off *or* out; **er machte sich auf den — nach der Stadt**, he set out for the town; **einem auf halbem —e entgegen kommen**, to meet a p. half way; **die Sache ist auf gutem —e**, the matter is making progress; **auf den rechten — bringen**, to put in the right way; **Glück auf den —!** good luck! good journey to you! **aus dem —e gehen**, to go *or* get out of the way, stand aside; **der durchlaufene —**, the space described; **der gerade — ist der beste**, honesty is the best policy (*prov.*); **das liegt aus (außer) meinem —e**, that is not in my way, I know nothing of that; **bei —e sein**, to be up, to be visible; **gut bei** (*or* **zu**) **—e sein**, to be well, in good health; — **und Steg** *or* —**e und Stege kennen**, to know one's way well, to know all the ins and outs; **im —e Rechtens**, by law; **einem in den — laufen** *or* **kommen**, to come in a p.'s way; to befall, to occur; to thwart, oppose; **er wird mir schon in den — kommen**, never fear, I shall come across him yet **sich** (*dat.*) **selbst im —e stehen**, to stand in one's own light; **einem etwas in den — legen**, to throw *or* put s.th. in a p.'s way, to embarrass s.o., to oppose a p.; **einem in den — treten, sich einem in den — stellen**, to thwart, oppose a p.; **ich traue ihm nicht über den —**, I trust him no further than I can see, I do not trust him out of sight; **von —en jemands**, on the part of some one; **zu —e bringen**, to bring about, accomplish; **mit etwas zu —e kommen**, to complete, finish s.th.; **hier geht kein —! verbotener —!** no thoroughfare! private! **einen falschen — betreten**, to mistake the way; **seinen ruhigen — fortgehen**, to go on in one's own way quietly; **er weiß Mittel und —e**, he has ways and means of accomplishing his ends; **das hat gute —e**, it is all right; **das hat** *or* **es hat damit gute —e!** there is no need to trouble about it (yet); that will not easily come off! **er sieht aus wie sieben Meilen schlechter —**, he has a very evil countenance; **desselben —es mit einem gehen**, to go the same way as another; **er steht mir im —e**, he is in my way; **geht Eures —es!** go your way! **geh deiner —e**, go about your business! **woher des —s?** whence do you come? **wohin des —es**, whither are you going? **lassen Sie ihn seiner —e gehen!** let him alone! **einem seine —e weisen**, to send a p. about his business; **viele —e führen nach Rom**, there are many roads to Rome, there are more ways than one of doing a thing (*prov.*); **wer am Wege baut, hat viele Meister**, he who builds by the roadside has many masters (*prov.*). II. (*short* e) *adv.*, *part. & sep. prefix*, away; gone; lost; off; — **ist er**, he is gone; **der Reiz ist —**, the charm has gone; **das Haus liegt weit — von der Straße**, the house stands far back from the street; **ganz — sein, rein — sein**, to be quite beside o.s. (**vor**, with) (*coll.*); **über eine S. — sein**, to be beyond, have passed s.th.; **darunter — sein**, to be a laughing-stock, an object of contempt (*coll.*); — **wie der Blitz**, off like a shot; **frisch —!** gaily! smartly! look alive! **dreist —, flott —**, boldly; **frei —!** forward, march! **schlecht —**, simply, plainly; **in einem —**, without stopping, continually; **fünf Jahre in einem —**, five consecutive years. III. *int.* (*pron. short* e) — **da!** be off there! look out! **Kopf —!** look out for your head! — **mit den Komplimenten!** a truce to compliments! **—sam** (*pron. long* e), *adj.* passable, practicable. *Comp.* **—arbeiten**, *v.a.* to work off *or* away. **—ätzen**, *v.a.* to remove by caustics, cauterize. **—begeben**, *ir.v.r.* to go away, set off. **—beißen**, *ir.v.a.* to eat away; to supplant (*a p.*) (*coll.*). **—beizen**, *see* **—ätzen**. **—bekommen**, *ir.v.a.* (*coll.*) to succeed in removing, get off; to bring about, accomplish; learn to do, see; **er kann es nicht —bekommen**, he can't manage (learn, *etc.*) it; **eins —bekommen**, to get a blow. **—beten**, *v.a.* to get rid of by prayer. **—blasen**, *ir.v.a.* to blow off *or* away. **—bleiben**, *ir.v.n.* (*aux.* **ſ.**) to remain *or* stay away; to be omitted, left out; **bleiben Sie davon —!** don't meddle with it! leave it alone! **—blicken**, *v.n.* (*aux.* **h.**) to look away. **—brechen**, *ir.v.a.* to break off *or* away; to pull down. **—brennen**, *ir.v.* I. *a.* to destroy by burning; to cauterize. II. *n.* (*aux.* **ſ.**) to be burnt down. **—bringen**, *ir.v.a.* to bring away, remove; **mit Citronensaft bringt man Tintenflecke —**, lemon-juice takes out ink-stains. **—denken**, *ir.v.a.* to transport in imagination; **sich —denken**, to imagine o.s. as being (far) away. **—dürfen**, *ir.v.n.* (*aux.* **h.**) to be allowed *or* to venture to go away. **—drängen**, *v.a.* to press *or* force away. **—e=amt**, *n.* surveyors' office, office of public ways. **—e=aufseher**, *m.* road-inspector, surveyor of the roads and highways. **—e=bau**, *m.* road-making. **—e=bau=meister**, *m.* civil engineer. **—e=geld**, *n.* turnpike-money, toll. **—eilen**, *v.n.* (*aux.* **ſ.**) to hasten away; to hurry (over, **über**); to touch (on, **über**). **—e=kehre**, *f.* serpentine. **—e=lag(e)rer**, *m.* waylayer, highwayman, brigand. **—e=lagerung**, *f.* highway robbery. **—(e)=los**, *adj.* pathless, impracticable. **—e=macher**, *m.* road-maker. **—e=messer**, *m.* odometer; log (*Naut.*). **—e=recht**, *n.* right of way *or* of passage; highway regulations. **—e=säule**, *f.* milestone; finger-post. **—e=scheid(e)**, *f.* cross way. **—essen**, *ir.v.a.* to eat away (greedily); **einen —essen**, to give a p. a farewell dinner (*coll.*). **—e=strecke**, *f.* length *or* piece of the way. **—e=stunde**, *f.* league. **—(e)=warte**, *f.* chicory. **—e=zehrung**, *f.* travelling expenses, viaticum. **—fahren**, *ir.v.* I. *a.* to carry away in a carriage. II. *n.* (*aux.* **ſ.**) to drive away, to sail away. **—fall**, *m.* suppression, omission; abolition; **in —fall bringen**, to abolish, suppress. **—fallen**, *ir.v.n.* (*aux.* **ſ.**) to fall away; to be omitted; to be suppressed; to come to nothing, not to take place. **—fischen**, *v.a.* to fish away; **einem etwas —fischen**, to snatch something away from under a person's nose. **—führen**, *v.a.* to lead away, carry off. **—führung**, *f.* carrying off; abduction. **—gabeln**, *v.a.* to snatch away. **—gang**, *m.* going away, departure; **beim —gang aus der Kirche**, on going out of church. **—geben**, *ir. v.a.* to give away; to let go; to send away (*to school, etc.*). **—gehen**, *ir.v.n.* (*aux.* **ſ.**) to go away; to leave; **einen —gehen heißen**, to bid a p. be gone; **über eine S. —gehen**, to pass over a thing. **—gewöhnen**, *v.a.*; **einen von einem Orte —gewöhnen**, to wean a p. from a place, to accustom a p. to stay away from a place. **—gießen**, *ir.v.a.* to pour *or* throw out. **—haben**, *ir.v.a.* to have received one's share; to have a hold of; to understand readily, comprehend; to guess; **Sie haben es —**, you have hit it; **er hat es gleich —**, he sees it at once; **jetzt habe ich ihn —**, now I know what to think of him; **es (einen Schaden) —haben**, to get the worst of it, to catch it; **ich habe den Tod —**, it will be my death. **—halten**, *ir.v.a.* to keep, hold off; to turn away. **—hängen**, *v.a.* to hang in another place. **—heben**, *ir.v.a.* to lift and carry away; **hebe dich —!** begone! (*obs.*). **—helfen (einem)**, *ir.v.n.* (*aux.* **h.**) to help (*a p.*) to get away. **—holen**, *v.a.* to fetch away. **—jagen**, *v.* I. *a.* to drive away; to expel. II. *n.* to gallop off. **—kapern**, *v.a.* to snatch away; to capture. **—kehren**, *v.a.* to brush away; to turn off *or* away. **—kommen**, *ir.v.n.* (*aux.* **ſ.**) to get away; to go out; to be lost *or* missing; **am schlimmsten —kommen**, to get the worst of it; **über eine S. —kommen**, to get over a trouble *or* a grief; **es sind mir verschiedene Sachen —gekommen**, several things of mine are missing, have been lost. **—können**, *ir.v.n.* (*aux.* **h.**) to be able to get away. **—kriegen**, *v.a. coll. for* **—bekommen**; to learn; to understand readily, make out; **er hat dabei einen Stoß —gekriegt**, he got a blow by it. **—lassen**, *ir.v.a.* to leave out, omit; to let go. **—legen**, *v.a.* to put aside, lay down; to lay past. **—leihen**, *ir.v.a.* to lend out. **—leugnen**, *v.a.* to deny, disavow. **—loben**, *v.a.* to get rid of an unpleasant colleague by recommending him for another office (*coll.*). **—locken**, *v.a.* to entice away. **—machen**, *v.a.* to take away, remove; to take out (*stains*); to obliterate; **sich —machen**, to get off (*coll.*). **—mögen**, *ir.v.n.* to wish *or* like to go away. **—müssen**, *ir.v.n.* (*aux.* **h.**) to be obliged to go away; **das muß —**, that must be removed; **ich muß —**, I must be off. **—nahme**, *f.* taking away; seizure; confiscation; capture. **—nehmen**, *ir.v.a.* to take away; to remove, carry off; to seize upon; to confiscate; to take out (*stains, etc.*); to take up, occupy (*room, space, etc.*). **—packen**, *v.a.* to pack *or* put away; **sich —packen**, to pack off (*vulg.*). **—putzen**, *v.a.* to brush away, remove by cleaning; to polish off, finish up (*vulg.*). **—radieren**, *v.a.* to erase, scratch out. **—raffen**, *v.a.* to carry off (*of disease*). **—räumen**, *v.a.* to clear away; to remove. **—reisen**, *v.n.* (*aux.* **ſ.**) to depart, set out. **—reißen**, *ir.v.a.* to tear snatch away; to demolish, pull down. **—rücken**, *v.* I. *a.* to move away, remove. II. *n.*

(*aux.* s.) to make way, move aside, go back. **—schaffen,** *v.a.* to clear away, carry off; to get rid of; to make away with; to turn off, dismiss; to sell; to eliminate (*Math.*). —**scheren,** *ir.v.a.* to cut off *or* away. **—scherzen,** *v.a.* to turn off with a joke, to drive away by joking. **—schießen,** *ir.v.a. & n.* (*aux.* s.) to shoot away. **—schlüpfen,** *v.n.* (*aux.* s.) to slip off; **—schlüpfen über,** to slip over, glide over. **—schnappen,** *v.t.* (**einem etwas**) to snatch away (s.th. from a p.), to carry off. —**schneiden,** *ir.v.a.* to cut away *or* off; to retrench; to amputate. **—schnellen,** *v.a.* to jerk *or* fling off. **—schwemmen,** *see* **Fortschwemmen. —sehen,** *ir.v.n.* (*aux.* h.) to look away; **über eine S. —sehen,** to shut one's eyes to a th. **—sehnen,** *v.r.* to long to depart. **—setzen,** *v.* I. *a.* to put away; **einen über eine S. —setzen,** to make a p. independent of, place s.o. above a thing; **sich über andere —setzen,** to think o.s. superior to other people; **sich über eine S. —setzen,** not to trouble about a th. II. *n.* (*aux.* s.) to jump (**über,** over). —**sollen,** *v.n.* to be obliged to leave *or* go away. **—stechen,** *ir.v.a.* to remove with a pointed instrument; to carry off (*the ring in tilting*). —**sterben,** *ir.v.n.* (*aux.* s.) to die *or* be carried off (*rapidly*). **—stoßen,** *ir.v.a.* to push away; to knock off; to repel. **—streichen,** *ir.v.* I. *a.* to smooth away *or* off; to erase; to strike out, take off (*a number, an item*). II. *n.* (*aux.* s.) to fly away, depart. **—thun,** *ir.v.a.* to put *or* take away; to set aside; to remove; to turn away, dismiss; to lay away; to sell; (**thut die Hände**) **—!** (take your) hands off! **—treiben,** *v.* I. *a.* to drive away. II. *n.* to drift away. **—treten,** *ir.v.* I. *a.* to wear away by treading on. II. *n.* (*aux.* s.) to step aside, retire; to break the ranks; **— getreten!** break the ranks! (*Mil.*)- **—überführung,** *f.* overbridge (*Railw.*). **—unterführung,** *f.* underbridge. **—weisen,** *ir.v.a.* to send away, turn off, dismiss; to refuse; to direct to another place. **—weiser,** *m.* guide; finger-post. —**wenden,** *ir.v.a.* to turn away, off *or* aside; **mit —gewandtem Gesichte,** with averted face. **—werfen,** *ir.v.a.* to throw away; to reject; to throw out (*cards*); to elide, cut off (*a letter*); **sich —werfen,** to throw o.s. away, degrade o.s. **—werfend,** *a. & adv.* disparaging, disdainful, supercilious, contemptuous; **sich —werfend über einen äußern,** to speak disparagingly of a p. **—wollen, —wünschen,** *see* **Fortwollen. —ziehen,** *ir.v.* I. *a.* to draw away *or* off; to draw aside. II. *n.* to move (from one place to another), to change one's home; **mein Lieb war —gezogen,** my love had left the town (*village, house*). **—zug,** *m.* drawing off; removal; migration; departure.

We'gen, *prep.* (*with preceding or following gen., sometimes dat.;* **von** — (*obs. for* —)) because of, on account of; for the sake of, for; on behalf of; with regard to; in consideration of; **der Kürze** —, for the sake of brevity, to be short; (**von**) **meinet** —, for my sake; **von Polizei** —, by order of the police; **von rechts** —, by right.

We'gerich, *m.* (—s, *pl.* —e) plantain (*Bot.*).

Weh, —e, I. *int.* alas! woe! **au —!** oh! oh! you have hurt me! **— mir!** woe to me! woe is me! **— ihm, wenn er . . .!** woe to him if he . . .! **ach und — schreien,** to utter loud lamentations. II. *adj. & adv.* painful, sore; aching; sad; **es ist mir — zu Mut, zu Sinn, ums Herz,** my heart aches; **mir thut der Kopf —,** my head is aching; **das thut mir im Innersten —,** that cuts, pains me to the heart; **einem — thun,** to hurt a p.; to offend *or* wrong a p.; **ich that mir damit an den Augen —,** I hurt my eyes with it; **ihm thut kein Zahn mehr —,** he is beyond the reach of pain; **es ist ihm — darnach,** he longs for it. III. *n.* (—(e)s) plaint, lamentation; misery; calamity, misfortune; woe; pain; **Zahn—,** toothache. **—e,** *f.* (*pl.* **—en**) labour-pains, travail. *Comp.* **—frau,** *f.* midwife. —**gefühl,** *n.* feeling of grief *or* pain. **—geheul,** *n.* howl, loud wailing. **—gesang,** *m.* song of lamentation. **—klage,** *f.* lamentation, wail. **—klagen,** *v.a. & n.* (*aux.* h.) (*insep.*) to lament, bewail. **—leidig,** *adj.* woebegone, sorry for oneself (*coll.*), querulous. **—mut,** *m.* pensive melancholy. **—mütig,** *adj.* sad, melancholy. —**mutter,** *f.* midwife. **—stand,** *m.* sad condition.

We'he, *f.* drift (*of snow*). **—n,** *v.* I. *a.* to blow along, drift. II. *n.* (*aux.* h.) to blow; to flutter, wave.

Wehl, *n.* (—s) hollow wrought by sea-water under a dike.

[1]**Wehr,** *f.* (*pl.* **—en**) defence, resistance; arm, weapon; protection; bulwark, fortification; corps, body (*of armed men*); **sich zur — setzen,** to resist, put o.s. in an attitude of defence; **mit — und Waffen,** fully armed *or* equipped. —**haft,** *adj.* capable of defending o.s. *or* of bearing arms; valiant; **—haft machen,** to arm. —**haftigkeit,** *f.* capability of defending o.s. *or* of bearing arms; valour. *Comp.* **—anstalten,** *pl.* preparations for defence. **—bezirk,** *m.* military district. **—fähig,** *adj. see* **—haft;** fit for military service. **—gehänge, —gehenk,** *n.* shoulder-belt; sword-belt. **—gesetz,** *n.* law regarding military service. **—gestell,** *n.* gun-rack, stand for arms. **—kraft,** *f.* defensive force, army and navy. **—los,** *adj.* unarmed; defenceless. **—los=machung,** *f.* disarming. **—mann,** *m.* warrior; soldier; militiaman. **—ordnung,** *f.* law regarding military organization. **—pflicht,** *f.* obligation to serve in the army; **allgemeine —pflicht,** universal compulsory military service, universal conscription. **—pflichtig,** *adj.* liable to military service. **—stand,** *m.* military profession, the army. **—verfassung,** *f.* military organization. **—zahn,** *m.* tusk.

[2]**Wehr,** *n.* (—(e)s, *pl.* —e) weir (*of a mill*), dam. *Comp.* **—bau,** *m.* dam, dike. **—baum,** *m.* barrier; weir-beam. **—damm,** *m.* mole. **—gatter,** *n.* grating, lattice-work of a weir.

Weh'ren, *v.* I. *a. & n.* (*aux.* h.) to arrest, prevent; to oppose; to suppress; to control, keep down, check. II. *a.* (**einem etwas**) to hinder, prevent (*a p. from*); to forbid (*s.o. to do a th.*); (**etwas von einem**) to protect, ward off; **wer will es —?** who is to prevent it? **sie wehret den Knaben,** she checks the boys. III. *r.* to defend o.s.; to resist; **sich mit Hand und Fuß —,** to make a fierce resistance; **sich seines Lebens, seiner Haut —,** to defend one's life, protect one's skin.

Wehrgeld, *see* **Wergeld.**

Weib, *n.* (—es, *pl.* —er) woman; wife; **zum —e nehmen,** to marry; **zum —e geben,** to give in marriage. **—chen,** *n.* (**—chens,** *pl.* **—chen**) little wife *or* woman; wifie, darling; hen bird, she (*of birds, etc*). **—erhaft,** *adj.* womanlike, feminine; effeminate. **—ig,** *suff.* (*in comp.* =) -pistiled; **drei—ig,** having three pistils. **—isch,** *adj.* womanish, effeminate. **—lich,** *adj.* womanly, feminine; female. **—lichkeit,** *f.* womanliness; feminine reserve *or* delicacy; feminine weakness. **—ling,** *m.* (—lings, *pl.* —linge) milksop, old woman. **—sen,** *n.* woman, female, wench (*vulg.*); (*pl.* **—sen**) women(folk) (*hum.*). *Comp.* (*see also the cpds. with* **Frauen—**) **—er=art,** *f.* women's way. **—er=feind,** *m.* misogynist. —**er=geklatsch, —er=gewäsch,** *n.* feminine gossip. **—er=gelüst,** *n.* feminine desire; (**krankhaftes**) longing incident to pregnancy. **—er=gunst,** *f.* favour *or* good graces of women; **—ergunst ist wie Aprilwetter,** women are as changeable as April weather (*prov.*). **—er=hand,** *f.* woman's hand; handwriting of a woman. **—er=hasser,**

m. misogynist. —er=haß, m. hatred of women or of the female sex, misogyny. —er=haus, n. harem; brothel. —er=held, m. lady-killer, ladies' man. —er=hemd, n. chemise. —er=herrschaft, f. female sway or influence, petticoat government. —er=kenntnis, f. knowledge of, acquaintance with women. —er=kleid, n. woman's dress. —er=knecht, m. ladies' man, man devoted to woman. —er=krankheit, f. disease of women. —er=lehen, n. petticoat hold. —er=narr, m. dangler after women, amorous fellow. —er=raub, m. abduction, rape. —er=regiment, —er=reich, n. see —erherrschaft. —er=rock, m. petticoat; woman's dress. —er=stamm, m. female line. —er=stimme, f. female voice; contralto or soprano. —er=toll, adj. mad after women. —er=volk, n. women(-folk). —er=zwinger, m. harem. —s=bild, n. hussy, wench; strumpet; hag. —s=leute, pl. women (coll.; also contempt.). —s=person, f., —s=stück, n. see —sbild. —s=volk, n. women(folk), women.

Wei'bel, m. (—s, pl. —) sergeant (obs.).

Weich, adj. & adv. soft; tender; smooth; delicate; soft, effeminate, weak; impressible, soft (-hearted); ductile; supple; melodious; minor; liquid (sound); — gesottene or gekochte Eier, soft-boiled eggs; Fleisch — kochen, to boil meat until tender; mir wird ganz — ums Herz, I feel deeply touched; —e Hirnhaut, pia mater (Anat.); —es Wetter, sloppy weather; —es Herz, gentle heart, faint heart (B.). —e, f. (pl. —en) softness (poet.); sweetness (poet.); delicacy (poet.); flank, side; weak side; steep, soak; (pl.) groin. —heit, f. softness; tenderness; sweetness; gentleness; flaccidity; sensibility. —lich, adj. & adv. somewhat soft, tender; feeble; insipid; effeminate, weak; delicate; nice; indolent, inactive; tame, spiritless. —lichkeit, f. softness, etc.; delicacy; effeminacy. —ling, m. (—lings, pl. —linge) effeminate man; voluptuary. Comp. —blei, n. refined lead. —en=band, n. Fallopian ligament. —en=gegend, f. inguinal region. —erz, n. silver-glance. —faß, n. steeping tub. —flosser, m. malacopterygian (Icht.). —geschaffen, adj. sensitive, sympathetic. —haarig, adj. soft-haired. —häutig, adj. soft-skinned. —herzig, adj. tender-hearted. —kübel, m. see —faß. —mäulig, adj. tender-mouthed. —pflaster, n. poultice, emollient plaster. —tiere, pl. mollusca. —wasser, n. steep, water for soaking.

Weich'bild, n. (jurisdiction of a) town, outskirts of a town; precincts, boundary, enclosure; enceinte (Fort.).

Wei'che, f. (pl. —n) siding, switch, shunt; die —n stellen, to shift the points. Comp. —n=bahn, f. siding, shunting line. —n=bock, m. switch-box (Railw.). —n=schiene, f. movable rail. —n=signal, n. switch signal changing the line. —n=stellung, f. shifting of the points. —n=steller, —n=wärter, m. pointsman. —n=wechsel, m. change of line.

[1]**Wei'chen**, I. v. a. to soften, steep, soak. II. v. n. (aux. h. & s.) to become soft, grow tender or mellow.

[2]**Wei'chen**, I. ir.v.n. (aux. s.) to yield, give way; to sink in; to flinch, waver; to yield; to decline, fall (of prices); nicht von der Stelle —, not to budge an inch; aus dem Wege —, to make room, give way; aus den Fugen —, to get out of joint; von einem —, to leave, abandon, desert a p. II. subst. n. zum — bringen, to push back, repel; die Kurse sind im —, the rate of exchange is falling.

Weich'sel— (in comp.) —kirsche, f. Cerasus vulgaris (Bot.). —rohr, n. stem of tobacco pipe made out of cherry wood.

Weich'selzopf, m. elflock; Plica polonica.

[1]**Weid**, m. see Waid.

[2]**Weid**, f. hunt, chase. —bar, adj. affording pasture. [1]—e, f. (pl. —en) pasture, grazing; food; pasture-land; auf die —e treiben, to turn out to grass, drive to pasture. —lich, I. adj. & adv. brave, stout, strong; vigorous; lively; valiant (B.). II. adv. very much, thoroughly; see Tüchtig. —ner, m. hunter (obs., poet.). Comp. —e=acker, m. pasture-ground. —e=berechtigt, adj. having the right of pasturage. —e=darm, m. rectum. —e=land, n. pasture land; good grazing country. —e=platz, m. grazing-place, pasturage. —gerecht, adj. skilled in hunting; broken-in, trained. —geschrei, n. tally-ho; hue and cry. —geselle, m. fellow-huntsman. —leute, pl. huntsmen. —mann, m. huntsman; —manns Heil! hunter's greeting. —männisch, adj. sportsmanlike. —manns=sprache, f. language of the chase, hunters' slang. —messer, n. hunting-knife. —ruf, m. tally-ho. —sack, m. game-bag. —sprosse, f. antler. —spruch, m. huntsmen's greeting; password among sporting men. —tasche, f. see —sack. —werk, n. chase, sport, hunt; huntsmanship; game; niederes —werk, small game; das edle —werk, the noble sport of hunting. —wund, adj. wounded or shot in the intestines.

[2]**Wei'de—e**, f. (pl. —en) willow, osier. —en, adj. willow. —erich, m. (—erichs, pl. —eriche) willow-herb. —icht, n. (—ichts, pl. —ichte) willow-plot. Comp. —en=asche, f. willow-ashes. —en=bach, m. brook bordered or fringed with willows. —en=band, n. band or rope of willow; osier-twig; withe. —en=baum, m. willow-tree. —en=bitter, n. salicine. —en=bohrer, m. willow-weevil. —en=gebüsch, —en=gehölz, n. willow-plantation. —en=geflecht, n. wicker-work. —en=gerte, f. osier-switch. —en=holz, n. willow(-wood). —en=kätzchen, n. willow-catkin. —en=korb, m. wicker-basket. —en=röschen, n. willow-herb. —en=rute, f. see —engerte; (pl.) wicker-work.

Wei'de—n, v. I. a. to graze; to lead to pasture; to tend, feed (a flock); to feast one's eyes on (a th.); sie —t sich an meinem Unglück, she gloats over my misfortune; sich in Hoffnungen —n, to live in hopes.

Wei'fe, f. (pl. —n) reel. —n, v.a. & n. (aux. h.) to wind, reel.

Wei'gand, m. (—s, pl. —e) warrior, hero (obs.).

Wei'ger—n, v. I. a. (einem etwas) to refuse, deny, object to. II. r. to refuse; ich —e mich dessen nicht, I do not refuse it, do not object to it; sich —n etwas zu thun, to refuse to do a thing. —ung, f. refusal. Comp. —ungs=fall, m.; im —ungsfalle, in case of refusal.

Weih, m. (—en, pl. —en), —e, m. (—en, pl. —en) & f. (pl. —en) kite, hen-harrier (Orn.).

Wei'he, f. consecration; ordination; inauguration; sacred fire, inspiration (of a preacher, etc.); initiation (Freem.); einem die —(n) erteilen, to ordain a p., to bestow holy orders on a p.

Wei'h—en, v.a. to consecrate; to dedicate; to ordain; to sanctify; to inspire; sich —en lassen, to take (holy) orders; geweiht, consecrated, sacred, votive. —ung, see —e. Comp. —altar, m. holy or consecrated altar. —becken, n. holy-water basin; font. —bild, n. sacred image; votive offering. —bischof, m. suffragan (bishop). —e=frühling, m. consecrated spring, ver sacrum. —e=stunden, pl. sacred or hallowed hours. —e=voll, adj. solemn, hallowed, holy; —evolle Stimmung, solemn mood. —gabe, f. see —geschenk. —gelübde, n. (ordination) vow; votive offering. —geschenk, n. oblation. —kelch, m. chalice. —kessel, m. see —becken. —messe, f. mass of consecration. —

nacht, *f.*, —nachten, *pl.* (*also sing.n.*) Christmas; *abbr.* Xmas. —nachts=abend, *m.* Christmas-eve. —nachts=baum, *m.* Christmas-tree. —nachts=feier, *f.* celebration of Christmas. —nachts=fest, *n.* festival of Christmas; Christmas feast. —nachts=geschenk, *n.* Christmas present *or* gift; Christmas box. —nachts=kind, *n.* the child Jesus. —nachts=lied, *n.* Christmas carol. —nachts=mann, *m.* father Christmas, Santa Claus. —nachts=messe, *f.* Christmas matins; Christmas-fair. —nachts=stollen, *m.* Christmas cake. —nachts=tag, *m.*; der zweite —nachtstag, Monday after Christmas, Boxing day. —rauch, *m.* incense; einem —rauch streuen, to laud *or* flatter a p. —räuchern, *v.n.* (*aux.* h.) (einem) to extol, flatter (a p.). —rauch=faß, *n.* censer. —wasser, *n.* holy water. —wedel, *m.* holy water sprinkle *or* sprinkler; sprinkling-brush; aspergill

Wei'her, *m.* (—s, *pl.* —) fish-pond.

Weil, *conj.* because, since; while, as long as (*obs.* & *poet.*); freut euch des Lebens — noch das Lämpchen glüht, enjoy life while it is still yours; schmiede das Eisen — es warm ist, wärme dich — das Feuer brennt, strike while the iron is hot, make hay while the sun shines (*prov.*). —and, (*obs.*) *adv.* formerly, of old, quondam; late, deceased. —chen, *n.* (—chens, *pl.* —chen) little while. —e, *f.* a while, a (*space of*) time; leisure; eile mit —e, more haste less speed; (*prov.*) lange —e, *see* Langweile; eine geraume —e, a long time; über eine kleine —e, a short time afterwards; damit hat es gute —e, there is no hurry, we 'll see; Zeit und —e mit etwas verlieren, to lose time over a thing; gut Ding will —e haben, nothing good is done in a hurry, more haste less speed (*prov.*); bei nächtlicher —e, during the night.

Wei'len, *v.n.* (*aux.* h.) to stay, stop; to tarry, to linger; to sojourn; wo mag sie jetzt —? I wonder where is she now?

Wei'ler, *m.* (—s, *pl.* —) hamlet.

Wein, *m.* (—es, *pl.* —e) wine; vine; — keltern, to press the grapes; den — lesen, to gather in the grapes; — bauen, to grow wine, cultivate the vine; Rot—, claret; Weiß—, hock; Schaum—, sparkling wine *or* hock; champagne; gebrannter —, brandy; wilder —, Virginia creeper; — auf Bier rat' ich dir, Bier auf — laß hübsch sein, wine upon beer is very good cheer; beer upon wine, you 'll repine (*prov.*); einem klaren — einschenken, to tell a p. the whole truth, to speak plainly. —es, (*in comp.*) *see* Wein (*in comp.*). —haft, —ig, *adj.* vinous. *Comp.* —arm, *adj.* producing little wine. —artig, *adj.* vinous. —bau, *m.* wine *or* vine-growing. —bauer, *m.* wine-grower. —becher, *m.* goblet, wine-cup. —beere, *f.* grape. —bekränzt, *adj.* vine-clad. —bereitung, *f.* wine-making. —berg, *m.* vineyard, vine-hill. —blatt, *n.* vine-leaf. —blume, *f.* bouquet (*of wine*). —butte, *f.* wine-coop, wine-tub. —ernte, *f.* vintage. —faß, *n.* wine-cask; wine-bibber, toper. —flasche, *f.* wine-bottle. —frohne, *f.* service due to the lord of the manor during the vintage. —gährung, *f.* fermentation of wine; vinous fermentation (*Chem.*). —garten, *m.* vineyard. —gärtner, *m.* vine-dresser. —gebirge, *n.* hills of vines, vineyards. —gegend, *f.* wine(-growing) district. —gehalt, *m.* vinosity. —geist, *m.* spirits of wine; alcohol. —gelag, *n.* wine-party. —geländer, *n.* trellis for vines. —geruch, *m.* flavour *or* bouquet of wine. —geschmack, *m.* winy taste *or* flavour. —gott, *m.* Bacchus. —grün, *adj.* vine-leaf green; seasoned (*of casks*). —gut, *n.* vineyard. —hacke, *f.* vineyard-hoe. —haltig, *adj.* vinous. —händler, *m.* wine-merchant. —handlung, *f.* wine-shop, wine-merchant's offices; bodega. —haus, *n.* wine-merchant's shop, warehouse *or* business; tavern. —heber, *m.* siphon. —hefe, *f.* dregs of wine. —jahr, *n.* (*good*) wine-year; year's wine-crop, vintage. —kalteschale, *f.* cold wine-soup; claret-cup. —karte, *f.* wine-list, price-list of wines. —kauf, *m.* purchase of wine; earnest-money (*given on the conclusion of a bargain*). —keller, *m.* wine-cellar; vaults. —kellner, *m.* cellarman. —kelter, *f.* winepress. —kenner, *m.* connoisseur of wine. —kirsche, *f.* vinous cherry, *see* Weichselkirsche. —krankheit, *f.* vine-disease; illness from wine. —krug, *m.* wine-flagon. —kufe, *f.* wine-tub. —küfer, —küper, *m.* cooper. —kühler, *m.* wine-cooler, refrigerator. —lager, *n.* stand for casks (*in cellars*); stock of wine; wine-store. —land, *n.* wine(-growing) country. —laub, *n.* vine-leaves, foliage. —laube, *f.* vine-arbour. —laune, *f.* merry mood caused by drinking wine; in —laune sein, to be in one's cups. —lese, *f.* vintage; —lese halten, to gather in the grapes. —leser(in, *f.*) *m.* vintager. —lied, *n.* drinking song. —meier, —meister, *m.* surveyor of vineyards; cellarer, butler; vine-dresser. —messer, I. *m.* wine-gauge. II. *n.* pruning-knife. —met, *m.* vinous mead. —monat, *m.* vintage month, October. —most, *m.* must. —palme, *f.* toddy palm. —pan(t)scher, *m.* adulterator of wine, one who doctors wine. —pfahl, *m.* vine-prop. —pflaume, *f.* vinous plum. —presse, *f.* wine-press. —ranke, *f.* vine-branch *or* tendril. —rebe, *f.* vine. —reich, *adj.* vinous; abounding in wine. —reis, *n.* vine-shoot. —reisende(r), *m.* traveller for a wine-business. —rose, *f.* eglantine, sweet briar. —rot, *adj.* ruby *or* claret-coloured. —sauer, *adj.* acid (*as wine*); —saures Salz, tartrate. —säure, *f.* acidity of wine; tartaric acid. —schank, *m.* retail of wine; wine-shop. —schenk, *m.* publican; vintner; butler. —schenke, *f.* wine tavern. —schenkin, *f.* girl serving at a wine-shop. —schlauch, *m.* wine-skin; wine-bibber. —schröter, *m.* wine-merchant's porter. —schuld, *f.* debt for wine. —schwefel=säure, *f.* sulphovinic acid; vinic acid. —selig, *adj.* elevated with wine; one who has had too much wine; in his cups. —= und Speisewirt, *m.* restaurant-keeper licensed to sell wine. —stein, *m.* tartar; tartar (*of the teeth*). —stein=artig, *adj.* tartaric. —stein=sauer, *adj.* tartaric; tartrate of. —stein=säure, *f.* tartaric acid. —stock, *m.* vine. —stube, *f.* wine-room (in a tavern); wine-shop. —tragend, *adj.* wine-bearing. —traube, *f.* bunch of grapes. —treber, —trester, *pl.* skins *or* husks of pressed grapes. —trunken, *adj.* intoxicated with wine, in his cups. —umrankt, *adj.* vine-clad. —verfälschung, *f.* adulteration *or* doctoring of wine. —vorrat, *m.* store of wine. —wachs, *m.* growth of wine; einen guten —wachs haben, to produce good *or* much wine. —wage, *f.* wine-gauge. —wetter, *n.* favourable weather for the vines. —wirt, *m.* landlord, tavern-keeper. —zeichen, *n.* tavern-sign. —zieher, *m. see* —bauer, siphon. —zoll, *m.* duty on wine. —zwang, *m.* obligation at some restaurants to take wine with one's meal.

Wei'n—en, I. *v.a.* & *n.* (*aux.* h.) to weep, to cry; um einen —en, to weep for (*the loss of*) s.o.; vor Freude —en, to weep for joy; sich (*dat.*) die Augen rot —en, to make one's eyes red with weeping; sich (*acc.*) blind —en, sich (*dat.*) die Augen aus dem Kopfe —en, to cry one's eyes out; heftig —en, to sob and cry. II. *subst.n.* weeping, tears; zum —en bringen, to make weep, to move to tears. —erei', *f.*

continual weeping. **—erlich,** *adj.* inclined to weep; whining, crying; tearful; **ihm ist —erlich zu Mute,** he is in a crying mood, he feels inclined to weep; **in —erlichem Tone,** in a whimpering tone; **—erliches Lustspiel,** pathetic comedy, comédie larmoyante. **—erlichkeit,** *f.* crying mood; tearful nature; whining tone. *Comp.* **—krampf,** *m.* crying fit, convulsive *or* hysterical sobbing.

Weis, *adj.;* **einem etwas — machen,** to tell a p. stories, to make a p. believe, hoax a p.; **das machen Sie andern — !** don't tell me that! tell that to the marines!

Wei'ſ—e, I. *adj.* wise; prudent; sagacious, discerning, judicious; **—e Frau,** midwife; wise woman, sorceress, enchantress; fortune-teller; **—e anordnen,** to manage wisely; **der —e,** the wise man, sage, philosopher; **Stein der —en,** philosopher's stone; **die sieben —en Griechenlands,** the seven wise men of Greece; **die —en aus dem Morgenlande,** the (three) wise men from the East, the Magi. II. **—e,** *f.* (*pl.* **—en**) manner, mode, way; method; style, rate; habit, custom; condition; mood (*Gram.*); melody, air; tune; motif (*Mus.*); **auf welche —e?** in what way? **auf keine —e, in keiner —e,** in no wise, by no means, not at all; **auf diese —e, in dieser —e,** in this way, like this; **auf jede (alle) —e,** in every way; in any case; **jeder nach seiner —e,** every one in his own way; **das ist so seine —e,** that is his way; **Wort und —e,** text and tune, words and melody; (*used with an adjective in the genitive forming an adverb*); **ausschließlicher —e,** exclusively; **irrtümlicher —e,** by mistake; **glücklicher —e,** happily, fortunately; **natürlicher —e,** naturally, of course; (*used as suff. of a noun, forming an adv.*) **haufen—e,** by heaps; **kreuz—e,** in the form of a cross, cross-wise; **massen —e,** in large numbers, plentifully. **—heit,** *f.* wisdom; knowledge, learning; science; philosophy; **—heit auf der Gasse,** wisdom in the street (*a designation of proverbs*); **er denkt, er habe die —heit mit Löffeln gegessen,** he imagines himself a great sage; **mit seiner —heit zu Ende sein,** to be at one's wits' end. **—lich,** *adv.* wisely, prudently. *Comp.* **—heits=dünkel,** *m.* intellectual conceit. **—heits=lehre,** *f.* philosophy. **—heits=voll,** *adj.* very wise. **—heits=zahn,** *m.* wisdom-tooth; **die —heitszähne bekommen,** to cut one's wisdom-teeth.

Wei'ſ—en, I. *ir.v.a.* to show; to direct; to point; to instruct; to reprove; to send (a p.) to *or* from (*a place*); **einen an einen *or* etwas —en,** to direct, refer s.o. to a person *or* thing; **aus dem Lande —en,** to banish from a country, to exile; **etwas von sich, von der Hand —en,** to refuse, reject a th.; **einem die Thür —en,** to show a p. the door; **einem die Wege —en,** to bid s.o. begone; **mit den Fingern —en auf,** to point out; **mit Fingern auf einen —en,** to point at a p. (*derisively*); **die Uhr —t auf zwölf,** the hand of the clock points to 12; **er will sich nicht —en lassen,** he will not listen to reason. II. *r.* **sich —en,** to become apparent, to show. **el,** *m.* (**—els,** *pl.* **—el**) queen-bee. **—er,** *m.* (**—ers,** *pl* **—er**) pointer; guide; teacher; queen-bee; hand (*of a clock, etc.*); *see* **Wegweiser.** **—ung,** *f.* direction; instruction, order; money-order; reprimand.

Weissag—en, *v.a. & n.* (*insep.*) to foretell, predict, prophesy; to forebode; **sie hat dem Matrosen geweissagt,** she has told the soldier his fortune. **—end,** *p. & adj.* prophetic. **—er(in,** *f.*), *m.* prophet(ess), fortune teller. **—ung,** *f.* prophecy, prediction.

Weis'tum, *n.* (**—s,** *pl.* **Weis'tümer**) legal sentence *or* document, precedent, record law (*obs.*).

[1]**Weiß,** *1 & 3 p.;* **Weißt,** *2 p. sing. pres. ind. of* **wissen.**

[2]**Weiß,** I. *adj.* white; clean; blank; hoary; argent (*Her.*); **— sieden,** to blanch; **— lassen,** to leave blank; **— machen,** to blanch, bleach; **sich — brennen,** to clear o.s., to assert one's innocence; **einen — waschen,** to prove a p.'s innocence; **— nähen,** to do plain sewing; **— kleiden,** to dress in white; **die —e Frau,** the Woman in White; **—e Wäsche,** clean linen; **—er Sonntag,** Sunday after Easter, Low Sunday; **—er Kupferrauch,** sulphate of zinc; **ein —er,** a white man; **eine —e,** a white woman; **eine (Berliner) —e,** a measure of sweet (Berlin) pale ale; **die —en,** the white races, Caucasians; **das —e,** the white (*of the eye, egg*). II. *n.* white; **— auflegen,** to paint, put on white. **—e,** I. *f.* whiteness; whitewash. II. *see under* **Weiß** I. **—en,** *v.a. & n.* (*aux.* **ſ.**) to whiten; to whitewash; to blanch; to refine (*cast-iron*). **—er,** *m.* I. (**—ers,** *pl* **—er**) bleacher, whitener; whitewasher. II. *see under* **Weiß** I. **—lich,** *adj.* whitish. **—ling,** *m.* (**—lings,** *pl.* **—linge**) whiting (*Icht.*); species of agaric (*Agaricus Georgii*). *Comp.* **—anstreichen,** *n.* painting white; whitewashing. **—armig,** *adj.* with *or* having white arms. **—backen,** *adj.;* **—backenes Brot,** fine, white bread. **—bäcker,** *m.* baker of wheaten bread, fancy baker. **—bier,** *n.* light and sweet pale ale. **—binder,** *m.* cooper making tubs; whitewasher, house-painter. **—blätterig,** *adj.* white-leaved. **—blau,** *adj.* pale blue. **—blech,** *n.* tin, white metal. **—blech=schmied,** *m.* whitesmith. **—blech=waren,** *pl.* tin-ware. **—bleiche,** *f.* bleaching of cotton. **—brennen,** *n.* blanching, bleaching; exculpation. **—brot,** *n.* white bread *or* loaf. **—buche,** *f.* hornbeam. **—busig,** *adj.* white-bosomed. **—dorn,** *m.* hawthorn, may. **—erde,** *f.* pipe-clay. **—fichte,** *f.* (variety of) spruce-fir. **—fleckig,** *adj.* white-spotted. **—fluß,** *m.* leucorrhœa (*Med.*). **—fuchs,** *m.* silver fox; light sorrel horse. **—füßig,** *adj.* white-footed. **—gallerte,** *f.* blancmange. **—gar,** *adj.* tawed. **—gelb,** *adj.* light yellow, flaxen. **—gerben,** *v. a.* to taw. **—gerber,** *m.* tawer. **—gerberei',** *f.* tawer's trade *or* workshop. **—gewaschen,** *adj.* clean-washed. **—glühend,** *adj.* at a white heat, welding hot, incandescent. **—glüh=hitze,** *f.* white heat, incandescence. **—gold,** *n.* platinum. **—grau,** *adj.* light gray. **—gülden=erz, —gültig=erz,** *n.* white silver-ore. **—haarig,** *adj.* white-haired. **—kirsche,** *f.* white-heart cherry. **—kohl,** *m.* white cabbage. **—kram,** *m.* linen-drapery. **—krämer,** *m.* linen-draper. **—= und Kuchen=bäckerei,** *f.* pastry-cook's shop. **—kupfer,** *n.* German silver, plated silver. **—mehl,** *n.* fine flour. **—nä(t)herei,** *f.* plain needle-work. **—nä(t)herin,** *f.* plain seamstress, needlewoman. **—ofen,** *m.* refining furnace. **—pinsel,** *m.* whitewash-brush. **—schnabel,** *m.* white-billed woodpecker; greenhorn. **—sieden,** *ir.v.a.* to blanch, to whiten. **—specht,** *m.* spotted woodpecker. **—spieß=glanz=erz,** *n.* white antimony. **—sticken,** *n.,* **—stickerei',** *f.* white embroidery, muslin embroidery. **—tanne,** *f.* silver fir. **—tüncher,** *m.* whitewasher. **—waren,** *pl.* linens, cottons, white goods. **—waren=engros=geschäft,** *n.* wholesale linen-draper's business. **—waren=handlung,** *f.* linen-draper's shop, linen-warehouse. **—wein,** *m.* white wine, hock. **—werden,** *n.* whitening, bleaching. **—zeug,** *n.* (household) linen. **—zeug=kammer,** *f.* linen-cupboard.

Weit, *adj. & adv.* wide; broad; large; extended, spacious, ample; long; (*only as adv.*) off; far; much, greatly; far off, distant, remote; far on, advanced; **in die —e Welt**

gehen, to go out into the world, to go abroad; **alle Herzen wurden —,** all hearts expanded; **ein drei Fuß —es Gefäß,** a vessel 3 feet wide; **eine Meile —,** a mile off; **von so — als ich ihn hören konnte,** (from) as far off as I could hear him; **— davon ist gut vorm Schuß,** prudence is the better part of valour (*prov.*); **mit der Zeit kommt man auch —,** many a little makes a mickle (*prov.*); **wie — sind Sie mit Ihrer Arbeit?** how far have you got with your work? **so — ist es noch nicht,** it has not come to (such a pass as) that yet; **— her,** from afar, far off; **— hin,** far off; to a great distance; **nicht — her sein,** to be of little value; **das ist nicht — her,** that is not (worth) much; **es ist nicht — her mit ihm,** he is of no importance, he does not count; **die Verzweiflung kann einen so — bringen, daß,** despair can bring one (even) to; **ist es so — gekommen?** has it come to this? **es zu — treiben,** to pass all bounds, go too far; **Geld reicht —,** money goes a long way; **mein Freund ist bisweilen sehr — weg,** my friend is at times very absent-minded (*coll.*); **ein — größerer Abstand,** a much *or* far greater distance; **— gefehlt!** far from it! not at all! **in so —,** in so far; **so — ist es mir gelungen,** I have so far succeeded, up to this point I have succeeded; **so — Sie es für gut finden,** in so far as you think well; **so — ich zurückdenken kann,** as far back as I can remember; **er hat so — recht, aber . . .,** there is some truth in what he says, still . . .; **vier Fuß — von der Wand,** four feet from the wall; **— und breit,** far and wide; **—e Reise,** long journey; **—er Umweg,** very circuitous route; **—es Gewissen,** elastic conscience; **— aus** (*or* **von**) **einander,** far apart, at long intervals; **— nach Hause haben,** to be a long way from home; **die Zeit ist nicht mehr —,** the time is drawing near; **die Sache liegt im —en,** the matter is uncertain; **bei —em nicht so schlecht als . . .,** not nearly so bad as . . .; **des —en und Breiten etwas erzählen,** to relate in detail, at length; **darüber belehrt uns die Geschichte des —ern,** history gives us further information on this point; **—er entfernt,** more distant; **am —esten zurück,** the furthest back, most backward; **—er lesen,** to go on reading, to continue reading; **—er! nur —er!** continue! go on! **immer —er,** on and on; **nicht —er!** stop! not any further, no more (of this)! **Ausflüchte werden nicht —er geduldet,** evasions will no longer be tolerated; **hören Sie —er!** hear what follows! **unsere Verwandten, und wer —er?** our relatives and who else? **—er niemand,** no one else; **und —er?** and then? **was —er?** and what after that? and what else? **und so —er (u. s. w.),** and so on (*etc.*); **—er habe ich nichts zu sagen,** I have nothing to add, nothing further to say; **—er hat es keinen Zweck,** it has no other aim, that is all that is desired; **das hat —er nichts zu sagen,** that does not signify *or* is of no consequence; **es wird mir nicht —er helfen,** it will be of no use to me; **das bringt mich nicht —er,** that does not help me much; **einen Schüler —er bringen,** to make a pupil get on; **—er geben,** to pass on (*to others*); **—er gehen,** to walk on, to continue walking; **er ging —er,** he continued his walk *or* went on; **sie sang —er,** she went on singing; **einem —er helfen,** to help a p. on; **—er kommen,** to get on, to advance; **nicht —er können,** to be obliged to stop (short); **der Zug konnte nicht —er,** the train came to a standstill *or* stopped short; **—er sagen,** to repeat; **—er schicken,** to send on; **ohne —eren Aufschub,** without further delay; **in —eren Kreisen,** widely; **ohne —ere Umstände,** without further *or* more ado, unceremoniously; **das —ere,** what follows, the remainder, further particulars; **das —ere morgen,** the rest to-morrow; **bis auf —eres,** for the present, until further notice; **ohne —eres,** without further ceremony. **—e,** I. *f.* (*pl.* **—en**) distance; width, breadth; size; capacity; extent; amplitude (*Astr.*); length; range (*of a shot*); bore (*of a gun*); **in die —e ziehen,** to go out into the world, to go abroad, travel; **in die —e spielen,** to protract. II. *n.* open space; **ins —e,** far away; *see* **Weit.** *Comp.* **—ästig,** *adj.* with spreading branches. **—au's,** *adv.* far off; by far, much. **—ausſehend,** *adj.* extensive, vast, far-reaching (*projects, etc.*). **—berühmt,** *adj.* illustrious, famous. **—beschreit,** far-famed (*obs.*). **—bewundert,** *adj.* much admired. **—blickend,** *adj.* far-seeing. **—erbeförderung,** *f.* sending on; transmission; despatch; **zur —erbeförderung an Herrn M.,** to be forwarded to Mr. M. **—erbildung,** *f.* (further) development; continuation of education, improvement; derivation (*Gram.*). **—erfracht,** *f.* forwarding carriage *or* freight. **—ermarsch,** *m.* continuation of the march. **—erreise,** *f.* continuation of the journey; **auf der —erreise,** in continuing the journey, further on. **—erschreiten,** *n.* advance. **—erumsichgreifen,** *n.* spreading (*of fire, etc.*). **—gehend,** *adj.* vast; *see* **—aussehend.** **—hi'n, —hinau's,** *adv.* far off. **—her'geholt,** *adj.* far-fetched. **—läuf(t)ig,** *adj.* & *adv.* distant; copious; vast; scattered; rambling, diffuse, prolix; long-winded, lengthy; detailed; **sie sind —läuf(t)ig verwandt,** they are distantly related; **die Sache ist sehr —läuf(t)ig,** the matter is very complicated. **—läuf(t)igkeit,** *f.* wideness; vast extent; diffuseness, prolixity; copiousness; (*pl.*) ceremonies, difficulties; **ohne —läuftigkeiten zu machen,** without making difficulties. **—maschig,** *adj.* with wide meshes. **—reichend,** *adj.* far-reaching. **—schichtig,** *adj.* far apart (*of layers*); large, vast. **—schichtigkeit,** *f.* vast extent. **—schweifig,** *adj.* wide, vast diffuse, verbose, prolix. **—schweifigkeit,** *f.* verbosity, prolixity. **—sichtig,** *adj.* long sighted; far-seeing, clear-sighted. **—sichtigkeit,** *f.* long-sightedness; perspicacity. **—spurig,** *adj.* wide-tracked. **—tragend,** *adj.* carrying to a great distance; of long range (*of fire-arms*). **—umfassend,** *adj.* comprehensive, extensive. **—verbreitet,** *adj.* widely spread, wide-spread, prevalent, general. **—verzweigt,** *adj.* widely ramified, extensive. **—vorstehend,** *adj.* jutting (far) out, prominent.

Wei't—en, *v.* I. *a.* to widen, expand, enlarge. **—ern,** *v.a.* to widen, enlarge; to dilate. **—erung,** *f.* extension; length; (*pl.*) difficulties, formalities. **—ung,** *f.* enlargement; distance; space; **—ung einer Treppe,** room under a staircase; **—ungen** (*pl.*) hollows, excavations (*Min.*).

Wei'zen, *m.* (**—s**) wheat; corn; **der türkische —,** maize; **mein — blüht,** I am in luck's way, fortune smiles on me. *Comp.* **—acker,** *m.* wheat-field. **—artig,** *adj.* frumentaceous. **—boden,** *m.* soil adapted for wheat-growing; granary. **—brand,** *m.* black rust. **—gries,** *m.* grits of wheat. **—mehl,** *n.* wheaten flour.

Welch, I. *inter. adj.* which; what; **—er Mann?** which man? **—e Frau?** which woman? **—es Ding gefällt dir?** which of the things pleases you? **—er** (*or* **—ein**) **Erfolg!** what (a) success! **— eine Tiefe der Weisheit Gottes!** what a depth of divine wisdom! II. (**—er, —e, —es**) *inter. pron.* which, what; **—e dieser** *or* **von diesen Damen?** which of these ladies? **wer hat es gethan? einer meiner Brüder; —er?**

who did it? one of my brothers; which one? —es sind ihre Kinder? which are her children? III. *rel. pron.* (*gen. sing. m. & n.* dessen; *f.* deren; *gen. pl.* deren) which, what, that, who; derjenige, —er, he who; die Bücherei, —e prächtig ist, the library, which is a splendid one; die Dame, —er wir geschrieben haben, the lady to whom we wrote; die Bücher, ohne —e ich meine Arbeit nicht vollenden kann, the books, without which I cannot finish my work; es ist keiner, —er nicht weiß, there is no one but knows; (*used indefinitely*); —er auch (immer), who(so)ever, whichever; —es auch immer Ihre Ansprüche sein mögen, whatever your claims may be, let your claims be what they may. IV. *rel. adj.* 100 Mark, —e Summe Sie einliegend finden, 100 marks, which (*sum*) I enclose; —e Tugenden er auch haben mag, whatever virtues he may possess; und —en Preis nun auch mein Werk erhält, euch dank' ich ihn, and whatever praise my work receives, it is to you I owe it; von —er Art auch, of whatever kind, whatsoever. V. *indef. pron.* some (*coll.*); haben Sie Zucker? ich habe —en, have you sugar? yes, I have some; wenn Sie Geld haben, so geben Sie mir —es, if you have money, give me some; eine Masse Menschen, —e zu Pferde und —e zu Fuß, a lot of people, some on horseback and some on foot. *Comp.* —er=gestalt, *adv.* in what form *or* manner; in consequence of which. —er=lei, *indec. adj. & adv.* of what kind *or* sort; —erlei Gründe er auch haben mag, —erlei Art seine Gründe auch sein mögen, what kind of reasons he may have, of what kind his reasons may be. —ermaßen, *adv.* in what form *or* manner.

Welf, *n.* (—(e)s, *pl.* —er), *also m.* (—(e)s, *pl.* —e) whelp, cub (*Hunt.*). II. *m.* (—en, *pl.* —en); Guelph (*see index of names*). —en, *v.n.* (*aux.* h.) to cub, have young (ones) (*Hunt.*).

Welk, *adj.* withered, faded; shrivelled; flabby, flaccid; insipid; languid; dried (*prov.*); —machend, withering. —en, *v.a. & n.* (*aux.* f.) to wither, fade (away), dry (up). —heit, *f.* fading condition, withered state; flabbiness, flaccidity.

Well—e, *f.* (*pl.* —en) wave; billow; swell; ripple; surge; breaker; wave, undulation (*of light, sound, etc.*); axle-tree, shaft; roller; cylinder; barrel (*Mach.*); faggot, bundle of brushwood; bottle (*of straw*); circling *or* revolution round the horizontal bar, grinder (*Gymn.*); liegende —e, horizontal shaft; gebrochene —e, crank-shaft; stehende (senkrechte) —e, vertical shaft, crab, capstan; —en schlagen, to rise in waves, to surge; die —en durchschneiden, to plough the waves; eine —e machen, to revolve round the bar (*Gymn.*); das Rad an der —e, wheel and axle. —ern, *v.a.* to build with mud; to build *or* plaster with loam and straw. —ig, *adj.* wavy, undulating. *Comp.* —bank, *f.* lathe-bench; pivot *or* axle-end of a water-wheel. —baum, *m.* shaft; axle-tree (*of a mill*); beam (*of a bell*); tumbler-axle (*Gun.*); arbor (*Horol.*). —blech, *n.* corrugated iron *or* plate. —daumen, *m.* cog of an axle-wheel. —en=artig, *adj.* wave-like, undulating, undulatory. —en=atmend, *adj.* breathing waves, *i.e.* breathing the coolness of the lake *or* breathing in the waves (*poet.*). —en=bad, *n.* sea-bath, plunge bath. —en=baum, *m.* arbor *or* shaft (*of a mill*); axle-tree. —en=bewegung, *f.* undulatory motion, undulation; —enbewegung der Erdoberfläche, earth pulsation. —en=binder, *m.* faggot-maker. —en=brecher, *m.* breakwater. —en=förmig, *see* —enartig. —en=gebirge, *n.* mountains formed of undulated strata. —en=gekräusel, *n.* rippling of the waves. —en=holz, *n.* brushwood, faggot-wood. —en=länge, *f.* length of an undulation, wave-length. —en=linie, *f.* wavy line. —en=schlag, *m.* beating of the waves against the shore, surging of the waves; succession of waves; prächtiger hoher —en=schlag, splendid dashing of the great waves. —en=schwingung, *f.* undulation. —en=theorie, *f.* wave-theory (*of light, etc.*). —rad, *n.* wheel and axle. —zapfen, *m.* pin, pivot.

Wels, *m.* (—(s)es, *pl.* —(s)e) shad (*Icht.*).

Welt, *f.* (*pl.* —en) world; society; humanity; die ganze —, the whole world, everybody; alle —, all the world, every one, everybody; die große —, society, the upper ten; die junge —, youth, young people; das Licht der — erblicken, auf die — kommen, to be born; zur — bringen, to give birth to, to bear, produce; so geht es in der —, das ist der — Lauf, that is the way of the world; (viel) — haben, to be well-bred; da ist die — mit Brettern vernagelt, that's beyond the wit of man (to find out); einen aus der — bringen, schaffen *or* räumen, to do away with a p., to put a p. to death, despatch s. o.; aber was in aller — dachten Sie? but what in all the world were you thinking of? wie in aller — geht das zu? but how in the name of wonder does that come about? das geht mich in aller — nichts an, I have no earthly concern in it; er muß sich durch die — schlagen, he must make his way in the world; das ist so der — Lauf, that's the way of the world; in aller — nicht, most certainly not; er thut auf Gottes — nichts, he does absolutely nothing. —lich, *adj.* of the world, mundane; worldly; secular; lay; profane; temporal; —liche Güter, temporal possessions, temporalities; am —lichen hängen, to be fond of the things of this world; —lich machen, to secularize. —lichkeit, *f.* secular state; civil power; worldliness, worldly-mindedness; (*pl.*) temporal rights *or* possessions. —ling, *m.* (—lings, *pl.* —linge) worldling. *Comp.* —abgeschieden, *adj.* separated from the world, lonely, secluded. —achse, *f.* earth's axis. —all, *n.* universe. —alter, *n.* age of the world; age. —anschauung, —ansicht (*obs.*), *f.* conception of the world, world-philosophy. —ausstellung, *f.* international exhibition, World's Fair (*Amer.*). —ball, *m.* the globe. —bau, *m.* structure of the world; cosmic system, the universe; the world. —begebenheit, *f.* great event in the history of the world. —bekannt, *adj.* generally known, notorious. —berühmt, *adj.* of world-wide fame. —beschreibung, *f.* cosmography. —bezwinger, *m.* conqueror of the world. —blatt, *n.* paper *or* magazine known throughout *or* read all over the world. —bummler, *m.* globe-trotter (*coll.*). —bürger(in, *f.*), *m.* citizen of the world, cosmopolitan; ein kleiner —bürger ist angekommen, an infant has been born. —bürgerlich, *adj.* cosmopolitan. —bürgersinn, *m.*, —bürgertum, *n.* cosmopolitanism. —chronik, *f.* chronicle-romance (*of the middle ages, usually pretending to give a history of the world down to the authors' own times*). —dame, *f.* woman of the world, fashionable woman, lady. —diener, *m.* worldling. —ehre, *f.* worldly honour. —en=bildung, *f.* cosmogony. —en=lehre, *f.* cosmology. —entstehung, *f.* formation of the universe; Lehre von der —entstehung, cosmogony. —ereignis, *n.* event of world-wide importance. —erfahren, *adj.* experienced in the (ways of the) world. —erfahrung, *f.* experience of the world. —erschütternd, *adj.* world-shaking. —**fern,** *adj.* at a great distance; retired from the world. —**fremd,** *adj.* solitary, out of the world; ignorant of the ways of the world. —**gebäude,** *n. see* —**bau.** —**gegend,** *f.* region, quarter, part of the world. —**geist,** *m.* spirit of the age; the spirit ruling the universe (*poet.*). —**geist=liche(r),** *m.* secular priest. —**geistlichkeit,** *f.* secular clergy. —**gericht,** *n.* last judgment; judgment of humanity. —**geschichte,** *f.* universal history; profane history. —**ge=wandt,** *adj.* knowing the (ways of the) world. —**handel,** *m.* international trade, world's commerce. —**händel,** *pl.* worldly affairs; political struggles. —**kabel,** *pl.* cables of the world. —**karte,** *f.* map of the world. —**kennt=nis,** *f.* knowledge of the world, savoir-vivre. —**kind,** *n.* worldling, child of this world. —**klug,** *adj.* worldly-wise, prudent, politic. —**klugheit,** *f.* worldly wisdom, policy, prudence, discretion. —**körper,** *m.* heavenly body, sphere. —**kreis,** *m.* world. —**kugel,** *f.* globe; world. —**kundig,** *adj. see* —**bekannt;** knowing the world. —**lage,** *f.* political situation, state *or* condition of public affairs. —**lauf,** *m.* course of the world. —**lich=machung,** *f.* secularization. —**licht,** *n.* light of the world, luminary, the sun. —**liebe,** *f.* love of the world; worldliness. —**litteratur,** *f.* universal literature. —**lust,** *f.* worldly *or* sensual pleasure. —**mann,** *m.* man of the world, man accustomed to society. —**männisch,** *adj.* well-bred, gentlemanly. —**markt,** *m.* international market. —**meer,** *n.* ocean. —**müde,** *adj.* weary of the world, tired of life. —**ordnung,** *f.* system of the universe; constitution of the world; natural laws; **die jetzige —ordnung,** the world as now constituted; **die sittliche — ordnung,** the moral order in the universe; ethical laws. —**politik,** *f.* world-policy, policy taking into consideration the political situation of the whole world. —**post,** *f.* international postal union. —**post=karte,** *f.* Postal Union post-card, foreign post-card. —**post=verein,** *m.* universal Postal Union. —**priester,** *m.* secular priest. —**raum,** *m.* space. —**ruf,** *m.* world-wide reputation. —**scheu,** *adj.* misanthropic; recluse. —**schmerz,** *m.* (*affected*) weariness of life, pessimism, pessimistic melancholy. —**schmerzeln,** *v.n.* (*aux.* **h.**) (*sep.*) to be inclined to pessimism; to profess pessimism. —**schmerzler(in,** *f.*), *m.* pessimist. —**schmerz=lich,** *adj.* pessimistic. —**schöpfer,** *m.* Creator. —**seele,** *f.* all-pervading spirit of the universe. —**sprache,** *f.* universal language. —**stadt,** *f.* great and important city. —**stellung,** *f.* great position in the world. —**strich,** *m.* region of the world, meridian, climate. —**teil,** *m.* continent, quarter, part of the world. — **umsegler,** —**umreiser,** *m.* circumnavigator of the globe. —**umseg(e)lung,** *f.* circumnavigation of the globe; journey *or* trip (*coll.*) round the world. —**untergang,** *m.* end *or* destruction of the world. —**verbesserer,** *m.* reformer of the world, social reformer. —**vergessen,** *adj.* forgetful of the world, forgetting the world, solitary. —**verkehr,** *m.* international commerce *or* intercourse, the world's traffic. —**verlassen,** *adj.* deserted by the world, solitary, lonely. —**weise(r),** *m.* philosopher. — **weisheit,** *f.* philosophy; worldly wisdom. —**wirtschaft,** *f.* international commerce. — —**wunder,** *m.* wonder of the world; prodigy.

Wem, *dat. of* **wer;** to whom? **von** —? from whom? *Comp.* —**fall,** *m.* dative case.

Wen, *acc. of* **wer;** whom; — **man auch wählen mag,** whoever may be chosen; **für** —? for whom? *Comp.* —**fall,** *m.* accusative case.

Wen'de, *f.* (*pl.* —**n**) turning; turn; turning-point; change; beginning of a new epoch, era, period; — **des Jahrhunderts,** beginning of a new century.

Wen'd—en, *reg. & ir.v.a. & n.* (*aux.* **h.**) to turn; to turn over (*hay*); to turn up earth; to plough (*a field*) for the second time; to change; to turn away; **jemands Sinn —en,** to change a p.'s opinion; **plötzlich —en,** to double (*Sport*); **sich —en,** to turn, to turn away *or* round, to veer; **sich an einen —en,** to turn, apply to, have recourse to a p.; **für nähere Auskunft —e man sich an,** for particulars apply to; **viel Geld an eine S. —en,** to spend much money on a th.; **seine Kräfte, seine Zeit auf eine S. —en,** to devote one's strength, one's time to s.th.; **etwas auf sich** (*acc.*) **—en,** to spend on o.s.; **die Augen auf eine S. —en,** to glance at a th.; **das Gespräch —ete sich auf den Gegen=stand,** the conversation turned upon the subject; **sich gegen einen —en,** to turn to *or* towards, to go in the direction of, to direct one's attacks against a p.; **die Sonne —ete sich gegen Abend,** the sun began to decline; **sich von etwas —en,** to turn away from a th.; **er wandte kein Auge von mir,** he kept his eye steadily on me; **er —e sich vom Bösen,** let him eschew evil (*B.*); **sich zum Guten —en,** to turn over a new leaf; **sich zur Rechten —en,** to turn to the right; **mit —ender Post,** by return (of post); **ein Schiff —en,** to put a ship about. —**er,** *m.* (—**ers,** *pl.* —**er**) clearer (*Spin.*). —**ung,** *f.* action of turning; turn; turning (*of a street, etc.*); winding (*of a river*); volt (*Fenc.*); turn, change; turn (*of expression, etc.*); wheeling (*Mil.*); tacking, going-about (*Naut.*); **entscheidende —ung,** crisis, catastrophe (*Dram.*); **einer Sache eine andere —ung geben,** to give a new turn to a matter **eine andere —ung nehmen,** to take a new turn, to change; **glückliche —ung,** favourable turn; **—ung zur Besserung,** change for the better; **—ung der Hand und des Degens,** guard (*in fencing*). *Comp.* —**e=hals,** —**e=hals=vogel,** *m.* wry-neck (*Orn.*). —**e=kreis,** *m.* tropic (**des Krebses,** of Cancer; **des Steinbocks,** of Capricorn); **zwischen den —ekreisen liegend,** intertropical. —**el=baum,** *m.* axle-tree, winch; newel (*of a winding staircase*). —**el=steig,** *m.* winding path. — **el=treppe,** *f.* winding stairs, spiral staircase; Scalaria pretiosa (*Mollusc.*). —**e=pflug,** *m.* double-swing plough. —**e=platz,** *m.* place (*for carriages*) to turn; turn-table (*for a steam-engine*). —**e=punkt,** *m.* critical moment, turning-point, crisis; solstitial point (*Astr.*). —**e=rohr,** *n.* movable tube (*of a fire-engine*). —**e=säule,** *f.* quoin (*of a lock*). —**e=stock,** *m.* glove-stretcher.

We'nig, *adj. & adv.* little, small; (*pl.*) few; **mein —es,** the little I have; **sein —es Geld,** the little money he has; **die —en Male, daß,** the few times that; **einige —e,** a few, some few, a small quantity; **meine —e Hoffnung ihn zu retten,** the small hope I have (*or* had) of saving him; **die —en,** the few (*persons, etc.*); **das —e, was ich habe,** the little I have; **ein — Wasser,** a little water; **ein — schneller,** a little quicker; **es fehlte —, so wäre ich getö=tet worden,** I was nearly killed; **eben so — als,** as little as; **in —en Worten,** in a few words; **in nicht —en andern Ländern,** in not a few *or* in many other countries; **so — auch,** however little; **ich war nicht — überrascht,** I was not a little surprised; **er ist so — arm, daß er vielmehr . . .,** so far from being poor he is rather . . .; —**er,** less; **das kostet nicht —er als . . .,** that costs no less than . . .; **sie ist nichts —er als schön,** she is anything but beautiful; **nichts desto —er,** nevertheless, notwithstanding; **desto** (*or* **um so**) **—er darf**

er verschwenden, he ought to be all the less extravagant; **sechs —er eins,** six minus one; **am —sten,** least of all; **zum —sten,** at least. **—keit,** *f.* the few; small quantity; the little; trifle; **meine (eigene) —keit,** my humble self, your humble servant. **—stens,** *adv.* at least, at all events.

Wenn, I. *conj.* when; if; in case, provided, whilst, whereas (*rare*); though, although; **— die Zeit da ist, müssen wir fort,** when the time comes we must be off; **— Fritz vor mir stirbt, so wird mir das Haus gehören,** if Fred should die before me, the house will be mine; **— ich es wüßte, würde ich es Ihnen sagen,** if I knew it, I should tell you; **— der Feind uns angriffe und besiegt würde,** if the enemy attacked us and were beaten; **— man ihn hört, sollte man glauben . . .,** to hear him, one would think . . .; **es ist nicht gut, — man zu viel schläft,** it is not good to sleep too much; **es soll mich freuen, — ich erfahre . . .,** I shall be delighted to learn . . .; **— ich Ihnen die Wahrheit sagen soll,** to tell you the truth; **allemal —,** whenever; **sie jammert als** (*or* **wie**) **— alles vorbei wäre,** she mourns as if all was over *or* lost; **nicht als — das nicht häufig vorkäme,** it is not as if it was a rare occurrence; **außer —,** unless; **— nur, — anders,** provided that; **(und) — auch, — gleich,** although, even if; nevertheless; what of that, what does it matter? **selbst —, und —,** even if, although, even if that be the case, what then; **— er auch König ist,** king though he be; **— es auch noch so wenig ist,** little though it be; **selbst — ich es könnte,** even if I could; **mir graut, — ich nur daran denke,** I shudder at the very thought of it; **Sie müssen das kaufen, und — es noch so teuer wäre,** were it twice as dear, you must buy it; **— man doch einmal sterben soll,** since one must die some time; **— nicht,** if not, unless, but that; **— man kein Narr ist,** unless one is a fool; **— nichts dazwischen kommt,** unless something unforeseen happens; **— nur im Geringsten,** if even in the least, however little; **— er schon nicht viel gelernt hat,** even if he has not learned much; **— schon, denn schon,** if it must be, let it be; **Ihr Anblick giebt den Engeln Stärke — keiner sie ergründen mag,** its aspect gives might to the angels though no one can fathom it (*i.e., the universe*); **des Mimen Kunst geht schnell und spurlos an dem Sinn vorüber, — das Gebild des Meißels, der Gesang des Dichters nach Jahrtausenden noch leben,** the actor's art passes by our minds quickly and without leaving a trace, whilst the creations of the chisel and the songs of the poet are still living after thousands of years. II. *n.*; **die —s,** the "ifs."

Wen'zel, *m.* (**—s**) knave (*Cards*); *see Index of names.*

[1]**Wer,** I. *inter. pron.* who; **— ist größer, er oder sein Bruder?** which is the taller, he or his brother? **— von euch?** which of you? **— da?** who goes there? **— bist du, der du . . .?** who are you that . . .? **— kommt denn alles?** who are all the people who are coming? (*coll.*). II. *rel. pron.* who; he who *or* that; **— auch,** who(so)ever; **— nur immer,** whoever; **— es auch sei,** whoever it may be. III. *indef. pron. used coll. for* **jemand; ist —, der's leugnen will,** if any one will deny it; **ich höre wen rufen,** I hear some one calling; **es ist — an der Thür,** there is somebody at the door. *Comp.* **—da,** I. *int.* who goes there? II. *n.* sentinel's call *or* challenge.

[2]**Wer—,** (*meaning* '*man,*' *only survives in cpds. It is often spelt* **Wär** *or* **Wehr**). *Comp.* **—geld,** *n.* bloodgelt, weregeld, mulct for homicide. **—wolf,** *m.* wer(e)wolf, wolf-man.

Wer'b—en, I. *ir.v.a. & n.* (*aux.* **h.**) (**um einen** *or* **etwas**) **—en,** to sue for, to solicit, to court; **um ein Mädchen —en,** to seek a girl in marriage, to woo, court, to propose to a girl; **für einen andern —en,** to ask a girl in marriage for somebody else; **nach einer Sache —en,** to aspire to, seek after a th. (*obs.*); **einen zu etwas —en,** to enlist a p.'s sympathies for a th., to win a p. over to a th., to engage a p. for s.th.; **zum Kriegsstand —en,** to recruit for the army; **Rekruten —en,** to raise, levy, enlist recruits; **mit Gewalt —en,** to press; **—endes Kapital,** capital bearing interest. II. *subst. n. see* **—ung. —er,** *m.* (**—ers,** *pl.* **—er**) recruiting officer; wooer; proselytizer. **—ung,** *f.* (*pl.* **—en**) wooing; solicitation; levying, recruiting. *Comp.* **—e=amt, —e=büreau,** *n.* recruiting office. **—e=geld,** *n.* earnest paid on enlistment, king's (*or* queen's) shilling. **—e=liste,** *f.* list of recruits. **—e=offizier,** *m.* recruiting officer. **—e=platz,** *m.* recruiting place. **—e=trommel,** *f.*; **die —etrommel rühren,** to beat up for recruits.

Wer'de, *n.*; **das —,** the word of creation, the Creator's fiat *or* word.

Wer'de—n, I. *ir.v.n.* (*the past part. is* **geworden;** *the older* **worden** *now only survives in the auxiliary and in obs. and poetical lang.*) (*aux.* **s.**) to become; to come to be, grow; to turn out, prove; to come into existence, to be; **und Gott sprach, es — Licht! und es ward Licht,** and God said, let there be light! and there was light; **alle Tage, die Gott —n läßt,** every day which God gives; **was soll aus ihm —n?** what will become of him, what is he going to be? **man weiß nicht, was noch —n mag,** there is no knowing what may yet happen; **was nicht ist, kann noch —n,** what is not may yet be; **der Kranke wird wieder,** the patient begins to mend (*coll.*); **die Sache wird —,** the matter is making headway, *or* is getting on; the affair will come off (*coll.*); **glaubst du, daß aus der Sache was wird?** do you think anything will come of it? (*coll.*); **es wird schon —n,** it will surely turn out all right; **nun, wird's (bald)?** well, will you soon have done? will it soon be ready? will you do it *or* come soon? **aus Kindern —n Leute,** children grow into men and women; **aus dir wird nichts,** nothing will ever be made of you; **aus ihm wird nichts —n,** he will come to no good; **daraus wird nichts,** it is out of the question; nothing will come of it; **aus dem Nebel ward Regen,** the fog turned (in)to rain; **was würde daraus —n?** what would be the consequence? **was wird mir dafür?** what shall I get by it? (*obs. & poet.*); **drei Fräulein fein, soll mir die ein' nicht —n, so gilt's das Leben mein,** fair damsels three, falls not the one to me for her I dead will be (*obs. & poet.*); **Recht soll euch —n,** justice shall be done you; **Ihr Wertes vom 8ten dieses Monats ist mir erst heute geworden,** your letter of the 8th only reached me to-day (*obs.*); **so gut ist es mir nie geworden,** I have never had such luck; **heute muß die Glocke —n,** to-day the bell must be made *or* cast (*poet.*); **einem zu Teil —n,** to fall to one's share *or* lot; **klug —n,** to grow wise; **Arzt —n,** to become a doctor; **er ist katholisch geworden,** he has turned Roman Catholic; **adelig —n,** to be ennobled; **ärger —n,** to grow worse; **bekannt —n,** to become notorious, get abroad; **mit einem bekannt —n,** to make a p.'s acquaintance; **böse —n,** to grow angry; **einig —n,** to agree, come to an understanding; **es wird noch alles gut —n,** it will all come right (*in the end*); **es wird hell,** day is breaking, it is growing light; er ist krank geworden, he has fallen ill; er ist König geworden, he has become king; wie wird die Ernte —n? how will the harvest turn out? man möchte des Teufels —n, it is enough to drive one mad; so kann es nicht bleiben, es muß anders —n, it cannot go on thus, it must change; es wird jetzt früh dunkel, the days are growing short; morgen wird es jährig, it will be a year tomorrow; es wird nötig, (Zeit,) daß wir aufbrechen, we must (it is high time for us to) set off; es wird mir, I feel; wie wird mir? what do I feel? what is it I feel? du kannst denken, wie mir zu Mute wurde, you can imagine what I felt; mir wurde bange; jetzt wird mir wieder wohl, I began to feel afraid, now I begin to feel happy again; etwas *or* zu etwas —n, to change, turn (in)to; zum Gelächter —n, to become a laughing stock; der Schnee wird zu Wasser, the snow is melting; das Holz wurde zu Stein, the wood turned to stone, was petrified; alle seine schlauen Pläne wurden zuschanden, all his cunning devices were foiled; meine Pläne sind zu Wasser geworden, my plans have fallen through. *As auxiliary:* **1.** (*forming the future and conditional tenses*) ich — es ihm gleich sagen, I shall tell him at once; er würde es mir gesagt haben, he would have told me; wo — ich nur den Schlüssel haben? where can I have put the key? es wird ihm doch nichts passiert sein? I trust no evil has befallen him. **2.** (*forming the passive voice, the p. part. being* worden) ich —e geliebt, I am loved; ich bin geliebt worden, I have been loved; das Haus wird eben gebaut, the house is just being built; die Glocke wurde geläutet, the bell was rung; diese Früchte —n im Winter gegessen, this fruit is for winter eating. III. *subst.n.* the state of growing *or* coming into existence; gradual development; evolution, formation; genesis, rise, growth, origin; noch im —n sein, to be in embryo; große Dinge sind im —n, great things are preparing. *Comp.* —gang, *m.* development, evolution. —lust, *f.* bliss of developing into a higher being, joy of entering upon a new existence. —prozeß, *m.* process of evolution, development. —zeit, *f.* period of growth *or* development.

Wer'der, *m.* (—s, *pl.* —) (*in cpd. names* — werder, —wert(h), —wört(h)) small river island, plot of land surrounded by water.

Wer'f—en, I. *ir.v.a. & n.* (*aux.* h.) to throw, cast, fling; Anker —en, to cast anchor; Falten —en, to pucker, wrinkle; den Feind —en, to beat back the enemy, to put the enemy to flight; ein Kalb —en, to calve; Junge —en, to bring forth young; einen Kaufmann —en, to ruin a merchant; das Los —en, to cast lots (über eine Sache, for a thing); einen Gegner im Turnier —en, to unhorse one's adversary in a tournament; Schatten —en, to cast a shadow, to give shade; Strahlen —en, to dart forth beams, to beam forth; einem Steine an den Kopf —en, to throw stones at a p.'s head; die Augen auf eine S. —en, to fix one's eyes on a th.; sich auf ein Studium —en, to give o.s. up *or* to apply o.s. to the study of a th., to take up a subject; einen Verdacht auf einen —en, to suspect a p.; to throw suspicion on s.o.; einen aus dem Hause —en, to turn a p. out of doors; etwas bei Seite —en, to throw a th. aside; durch einander —en, to jumble together, throw into confusion; einen die Treppe hinunter —en, to throw a p. downstairs; Besatzung in die Stadt —en, to throw a garrison into the town; sich in die Brust —en, to swagger, to strut; alles in einen Topf —en, to treat all things alike; die Flinte ins Korn —en, to throw up the sponge *or* the game, to lose heart; sich ins Zeug —en, to exert o.s.; über den Haufen —en, to upset, overthrow; unter einander —en, to jumble up, throw into disorder; mit Geld um sich —en, to scatter money about; mit französischen Brocken um sich —en, to spice one's discourse with French phrases; mit Beleidigungen um sich —en, to insult people all round; Sie —en zuerst, you have the first throw; sich —en, to warp (*of wood*). II. *subst.n.* distorting (*Found.*). [1]—t, *m. & n.* (—tes, *pl.* —te) woof, weft; (*also* —e, *f.*) winnowing machine.

[2]**Werft**, *m. & n.* (—es, *pl.* —e), *also f.* (*pl.* —en), —e, *f.* (*pl.* —en) wharf; dockyard; dock.

Werg, *n.* (—(e)s) tow; oakum.

Werk, *n.* (—(e)s, *pl.* —e) work, act, deed; performance; work, production, composition; business; undertaking; enterprise; mechanism, works; (*pl.*) fortifications; frit (*Glassw.*); *see* —blei; ans — gehen, sich ans — machen, to set to work; ins — setzen, to set going, to bring about, to put into practice, to effect, to accomplish; es ist etwas (Großes) im —e, something great is being prepared; es ist etwas im —e, there is something in the wind; zu —e gehen, to set about (a thing); das — lobt den Meister, the master is known by his work. —chen, —lein, *n.* little work; opusculum. *Comp.* —bank, *f.* work-bench. —blei, *n.* crude *or* workable lead; lead-plate. —brett, *n.* cutting-board. —el=tag, *m.* working-day, week-day. —führer, *m.* foreman. —heilige(r), *m.* sanctimonious person, one trusting to good works. —heiligkeit, *f.* sanctimoniousness, outward piety; hypocrisy. —hof, *m.* timber yard. —leute, *pl.* workpeople, workmen. —meister, *m.* overseer; foreman. —meisterin, *f.* forewoman. —ofen, *m.* glass-furnace; melting furnace. —schuh, *m.* foot (*as a measure*). —seide, *f.* floss silk. —silber, *n.* silver extracted from lead ore; silver for bullion. —statt, —stätte, —stelle, *f.* workshop; (artist's) studio. —stein, *m.* freestone. —stuhl, *m.* loom. —täglich, *adj. & adv.* work-a-day. —(el)=tagskleid, *n.* everyday dress. —thätig, *adj.* active; industrious; practical; efficacious; —thätige Liebe, charity. —thätigkeit, *f.* activity, industry; realization, accomplishment. —tisch, *m.* work-table. —zeug, *n.* tool, implement; organ. —zeug=maschinen, *pl.* machine tools. —zeug=tasche, *f.* tool-bag.

Wer'mut, *m.* (—s) wormwood; bitterness, gall. *Comp.* —artig, *adj.* absinthian. —becher, —kelch, *m.* cup of bitterness.

Wer'pen, *v.n.* (*aux.* h.) to tow (*Naut.*).

Wer're, *f.* (*pl.* —n) mole-cricket; eyesore (*prov.*).

Werst, *f.* (*pl.* —, —e *and* —) verst (*Russian measure = 1.0668 kilometres or about 1170 yards*); die nächste Stadt war zwanzig — entfernt, the nearest town was twenty versts off.

Wert, I. *adj.* dear; honoured, worthy; worth; deserving; er ist mir lieb und —, I love and esteem him, he is very dear to me; — halten, — schätzen, to honour, value, appreciate, hold dear, to make much of; wie ist Ihr —er Name? to whom have I the honour of speaking? may I ask your name? Ihr —es Schreiben, your esteemed favour (*C. L.*), your letter; Sie und Ihre —e Familie, you and your family; das ist nicht der Rede —, that is not worth speaking of; please do not mention it (*coll.*); achtens—, achtungs—, estimable; er ist es nicht —, daß man . . ., he does not deserve . . .; keinen Schuß Pulver —, not worth a straw; das ist viel Geld —, that is worth a lot of money; einer ist so viel — wie der andre, one is as good as the other; das ist viel —. that is a great thing, that is very valuable; er ist seine 100,000 Mark —, he is worth 100,000 marks (£5,000). II. *m.* (—es) worth, value; import; price, rate; estimation, appreciation; standard (*of coin*); großen — auf eine S. legen, to set great value on a th., to attach great importance to a th.; der — der unbekannten Größe, the value of the unknown quantity; von gleichem —e, equivalent (*to*); in gleichem —e, at par (*C. L.*); — erhalten, value received (*on bills of exchange*); der — in Faktura, value as per invoice; — bei Verfall, value when due; — in Waren, value received in goods. —en, *v. a.* to value, appraise; to appreciate. —ig, *suff. as in* gleichwertig, of equal value, equivalent; minderwertig, of inferior quality. —igkeit, *f.* atomicity (*Chem.*) —ung, *f.* valuing, appraising; valuation, estimation, appreciation. *Comp.* —angabe, *f.* declaration of value, declared value. —begriff, *m.* conception of value. —bestimmung, *f.* valuation, taxation. —betrag, *m.* amount of value (*of a letter, etc.*). —brief, *m.* letter containing money. —ersatz, *m.* equivalent. —geschätzt, *adj.* esteemed. —herabsetzung, *f.* depreciation. —los, *adj.* worthless; undeserving; futile. —losigkeit, *f.* worthlessness. —messer, *m.*; das ist der —messer für . . ., that gives the value of, is the standard for, of . . . —nehmer, *m.* giver of a bill. —papier, *n.* bill; note; cheque, money-order. —regulator, *m.* standard of value. —schätzung, *f.* esteem, regard, value. —sendung, *f.* consignment of valuables; remittance. —verhältnis, *n.* proportion of value, ratio. —verringerung, *f.* depreciation of value. —versicherung, *f.* premium of insurance. —voll, *adj.* valuable, precious. —zeichen, *n.* paper money; postage-stamp.

Wes (*older spelling:* Weß), *gen. sing. of* wer, was, (*now usually replaced by*) Wessen; —Brod ich ess', des Lied ich sing, whose bread I eat, his opinion I hold (*prov.*); — das Herz voll ist, des gehet der Mund über, out of the abundance of the heart the mouth speaketh (*B.*). *Comp.* —fall, *m.* genitive case. —halb, —wegen, *adv. & conj.* on account of which; wherefore, why; therefore, so; ich traf ihn nicht, —halb ich weiter reiste, I did not meet him, so I went on.

We'sen, *n.* (—s, *pl.* —) being, existence; reality; essence; being, creature, living thing; state, condition; nature, character, disposition; conduct; demeanour, bearing; manners; affairs, concerns (*coll.*); property, economy; organization; system, arrangement, concern; thing; affair, stirring affair, bustle, noise, row; das gehört zum — der Sache, that is an essential part, belongs to the nature of the thing; sein — mißfällt mir, his manners displease me; gesetztes —, quiet demeanour; gezwungenes —, affected air, affectation, constraint of manner; das gelehrte —, the world of letters, literature; sein — treiben, to go on in one's own way; to play one's pranks, to be at it again (*coll.*); das gemeine —, commonwealth; Finanz—, finance, the finances; das höchste —, the Supreme Being; ohne viel —s zu machen, without much ado *or* ceremony; nicht viel —s mit einem machen, to treat a p. unceremoniously; was ist das für ein — hier? what does all this row mean? (*coll.*). —haft, *adj.* real. —heit, *f.* being, essence; substance; reality, essentiality; being. —tlich, *adj.* essential; real; substantial; fundamental, intrinsic; principal; das —tliche, that which is essential, the vital point; —tlicher Inhalt eines Buches, the substance of a book. —tlichkeit, *f.* essentiality, reality, essential thing. *Comp.* —(s)=einheit, *f.* consubstantiality (*of the Father and the Son*). —(s)=gleich, *adj.* identical. —(s)=gleichheit, *f.* identity. —kette, *f.* scale of beings. —(s)=lehre, *f.* ontology. —los, *adj.* unreal, shadowy, idle, vain. —losigkeit, *f.* unreality. —reich, *n.* visible *or* living world.

Wes'pe, *f.* (*pl.* —n) wasp. *Comp.* —n=ähnlich, *adj.* wasplike. —n=nest, *n.* wasp's nest; in ein —nnest stechen, to put one's foot into it (*coll.*). —n=stich, *m.* wasp's sting.

Wes'sen, *gen. sing. of* wer *and of* was, whose; — Schwert hat ihn erschlagen? whose sword slew him? — klagt man dich an? what are you charged with? in — Hause wohnst du? in whose house do you live? — er mich anklagt, that of which he accuses me, what he accuses me of.

West, *m.* (—s, *pl.* (*rare & poet.*) —e) west; west wind. —en, *m.* (—ens *or* —en) the West; nach —en zu, gegen —en, westward, towards the west. —lich, *adj. & adv.* westerly; —lich von, to the west of. *Comp.* —grenze, *f.* western boundary *or* frontier. —punkt, *m.* west point. —römisch, *adj.*; —römisches Reich, Western *or* Occidental Empire. —seite, *f.* west(erly) side. —wärts, *adv.* westward. —wind, *m.* west(erly) wind; zephyr.

Wes'te, *f.* waistcoat; vest; feste auf die —! give it him! let him have it (*coll.*). *Comp.* —n=futter, *n.* waistcoat lining.

Wett, *adj. & adv.* equal, even; etwas — machen, to square *or* balance a th.; wie soll ich ihm das je — machen? how am I ever to make it up to him? nun sind wir —, now we are quits.

Wet'te, *f.* (*pl.* —en) bet, wager; eine — eingehen, to make a bet; gilt es eine —e? will you bet? was gilt die —? what do you bet? die — gilt! done! agreed! um die —, in emulation; sie boten mir um die — ihre Dienste an, they vied with one another in their offers of assistance; um die — laufen, to race for a wager, to race one another.

Wet't—en, *a. v. & n.* (*aux.* h.) to bet, wager, stake; es läßt sich Hundert gegen Eins —en, daß . . ., it is a hundred to one that . . .; ich —e so hoch Sie wollen, I'll bet you what you like; auf eine S. —en, to bet on s.th.; für einen —en, to back a p.; ich —e, daß Sie es nicht können, I bet you cannot do it, I defy you to do it; für und wider —en, to hedge; um einen ungleichen Satz —en mit . . ., to take odds with . . .; ich —e fünf Pfund gegen Sie, I hold (bet) you £5; so haben wir nicht gewettet, that is not what we agreed upon, that is not fair. —er(in, *f.*), *m.* better, wagerer. *Comp.* —bewerb, *m.* competition. —buch, *n.* betting book; book (*of horse-racers*). —eifer, *m.* emulation, rivalry; competition. —eiferer, *m.* rival; competitor. —eifern, *v.n.* (*aux.* h.) (*insep.*) to emulate; to contend (*with*); mit einem in Höflichkeitsbezeigungen —eifern, to try not to let o.s. be outdone by another in politeness. —fahren, I. *ir. v.n.* (*aux.* s.) (*insep.*) to race (*in driving, etc.*) II. *subst.n.* chariot-racing; (zu Wasser) boat-racing. —fahrt, *f.* driving *or* cycling race; boat-race; regatta. —gehen, I. *ir.v.n.* (*aux.* s.) to walk for a wager. II. *subst. n.* walking-match. —gesang, *m.* singing-match. —kampf, *m.* prize-fight; contest, match. —kämpfer, *m.* prize-fighter, champion, athlete. —lauf, *m.* (foot-)race, running-match. —laufen, *ir.v.n.* (*aux.* s.) (*insep.*) to race, run for a prize. —läufer, *m.* runner. —rennen, I. *ir.v.n.* (*aux.* s.) (*insep.*) to race, run. II. *subst.n.* racing (*of men, horses, etc.*); horse-racing; race. —rudern, I. *v.n.* (*aux.* s.) (*insep.*) to row in a race. II. *subst.n.* boat-racing; boatrace. —segeln, *n.* regatta. —spiel, *n.* match. —streit, *m.* contest, match, prize-fighting; sich mit einem in einen —streit einlassen, to enter the lists with a p., to enter into competition with a p.

Wet'ter, *n.* (—s, *pl.* —) weather; storm, tempest; lightning; air, atmosphere; **was ist heute für —?** what sort of day is it? **wir bekommen anderes —,** the weather is going to change, there will be a change (in the weather); **ein — zieht sich zusammen,** a storm is gathering; **es ist schönes —,** it is a fine day, is fine weather; **alle —! Donner und —! — noch einmal!** good gracious! confound it! — **auch!** damnation! **ihn soll doch das —!** deuce take him! **es ist bei mir nicht das — darnach,** I am in no mood for that; **böse —,** choke-damp; **die Grube hat böse —,** the mine is badly ventilated; **schlagende —,** fire-damp; **der Schacht, in welchen (aus welchem) die — einfallen (ausziehen),** downcast (upcast) shaft. *Comp.* —**beobachter,** *m.* meteorologist. —**beobachtung,** *f.* meteorological observation. —**bericht,** *m.* meteorological report; forecasts of the weather. —**bube,** *m.* young imp; splendid chap, devil of a boy. —**dach,** *n.* shed; eaves; shelter (*Build.*;) louvre-roof (*Arch.*). —**fahne,** *f.* vane, weather-cock. —**fest,** *adj.* weather-proof, accustomed to inclement weather. —**führung,** *f.* ventilation of mines. —**geläut,** *n.* ringing of bells during a storm. —**glas,** *n.* barometer. —**hahn,** *m.* weather-cock. —**karte,** *f.* meteorological chart. —**kenner,** *m.* meteorologist. —**kunde,** *f.* meteorology. —**kundig,** *adj.* versed in meteorology, weatherwise. —**launisch,** *adj.* fickle (*rare*). —**läuten,** *see* —**geläut.** —**leuchten,** I. *v.n.* (*aux.* **h.**) *imp.* (*insep.*); **es —leuchtet,** it lightens, there is summer lightning. II. *subst. n.* sheet-lightning. —**loch,** *n.* draughty place: quarter from which storms come. —**lotte,** *f.* air-escape. —**männchen,** *n.* figure which indicates the weather. —**maschine,** *f.* mine-ventilator. —**prognose,** *f.* weather forecast. —**prophet,** *m.* weather-prophet; barometer. —**schacht,** *m.* air-shaft (*Min.*). —**schaden,** *m.* damage done by a storm. —**scheide,** *f.* meteorological limit, line over which thunder-clouds separate. —**schirm,** *m.* screen, shelter against a storm; shed. —**segen,** *m.* prayer *or* charm against a storm. —**seite,** *f.* weather-side. —**stange,** *f.* lightning-conductor (*poet.*). —**stein,** *m.* belemnite (*Geol.*). —**strahl,** *m.* flash of lightning. —**sturm,** *m.* tempest. —**thür,** *f.* trap-door (*Min.*). —**wechsel,** *m.* change of weather; current of air (*in mines*). —**wendisch,** *adj.* fickle, capricious, (as) changeable as the weather. —**wolke,** *f.* storm-cloud, thunder-cloud. —**zeichen,** *n.* meteorological sign, sign of approaching bad weather.

Wet'tern, I. *v.n.* (*aux.* **h.** & **s.**) *& imp.* to thunder and lighten; to curse and swear; to storm, bluster; **es hat gewittert und gewettert,** there was storm, thunder and lightning. II. *subst.n.;* **es war ein fortwährendes —,** it never ceased thundering and lightening.

Wet'z—en, *v.* I. *a.* to whet, sharpen. II. *n.* (*aux.* **h.**) to brush (*against*). *Comp.* —**spule,** *f.* needlemaker's bobbin for sharpening needles. —**stahl,** *m.* steel for sharpening knives. —**stein,** *m.* whetstone, hone.

Wich, *1 & 3 p. sing. imperf. ind.;* **Wi'che,** *1 & 3 p.sing. imperf. subj. of* **weichen.**

Wichs, *m.* (—(s)es, *pl.* —(s)e) full dress; one's best; **sich in — werfen,** to deck oneself out; **in vollem (höchstem) —,** decked out, in full dress, in gala attire; (*fam.*) in full fig (*students' sl.*). —**(s)e,** *f.* (*pl.* —**(s)en**) blacking, polish (*for shoes*); wax-paste; drubbing, thrashing (*sl.*). —**(s)en,** *v.a.* to black, polish (*boots, etc.*); to wax (*thread, a floor, etc.*); to thrash (*sl.*); **gewichst,** decked out. —**(s)ie'r,** *m.* (—**(s)iers,** *pl.* —**(s)iers**) boot-black (*vulg.*). *Comp.* —**bürste,** *f.* blacking-brush. —**glanz,** *m.* boot-polish. —**lappen,** *m.* rubbing-cloth.

Wicht, *m.* (—**es,** *pl.* —**e**) wight, creature, being; ragamuffin; little child, chit; chap; girl (*dial.*); **armer —,** poor wretch. —**chen,** *n.* (—**chens,** *pl.* —**chen**) little ragamuffin; young urchin. *Comp.* —**el=männchen,** *n.* brownie.

Wich'tig, *adj.* weighty; important, momentous, serious; — **thun, sich —ig machen,** to assume an air of importance. —**keit,** *f.* weight, heaviness; importance, consequence; matter of importance. *Comp.* —**keits=krämer,** *m.* consequential fellow. —**thuerei,** *f.* consequential manner; pompousness.

Wi'cke, *f.* (*pl.* —**n**) vetch; tare; **wohlriechende —n,** sweet peas; **in die —n gehen,** to disappear, to run away; to come down in the world (*coll.*) *Comp.* —**n=brot,** *n.* vetch-bread. —**(n=)futter,** *n.* fodder mixed with vetches.

Wi'ckel, *m.* (—**s,** *pl.* —) roll; curl-paper; paper rolled round the end of a candle; distaff-full (*of flax*); winder (*for cotton, etc.*); hair; wig; (*also f. pl.* —**n**) *see* —**zeug; einen beim — kriegen,** to catch hold of, to collar a p. (*sl.*).

Wi'ck—eln, *v.a.* to roll, roll up, twist; to wind (*wool, etc.*); to put (*hair*) in papers; to swathe, swaddle (*a child*); to roll *or* make (*cigars*); **etwas in eine S. —eln,** to wrap up a th. in a th.; **zu einem** *or* **in ein Knäuel —eln,** to roll into a ball; **(Zusammengewickeltes) auseinander —eln,** to untwist, undo, disentangle; **sich aus dem Handel —eln,** to get out of the scrape; **schief gewickelt,** in error, much mistaken (*sl.*). —**ler,** *m.* (—**lers,** *pl.* —**ler**) roller, wrapper-up; winder; *see* —**elraupe.** *Comp.* —**el=band,** *n.* roller, swaddling band. —**el=blatt,** *n.* wrapper, outside leaf (*of cigars*). —**el=kind,** *n.* child in swaddling clothes, child in long clothes, baby. —**el=maschine,** *f.* winder (*for wool, etc.*); lap-machine (*Spin.*). —**el=puppe,** *f.* baby-doll. —**el=ranke,** *f.* tendril. —**el=raupe,** *f.* tortricid caterpillar. —**el=schwanz,** *m.* prehensile tail. —**el=tisch,** *m.* table on which a newborn babe is swathed. —**el=tuch,** *n.* wrapper; baby's roller. —**el=zeug,** *n.* baby-colthes, swaddling-clothes.

Wid'der, *m.* (—**s,** *pl.* —) ram; battering-ram, Aries; **hydraulischer —,** hydraulic ram. —**chen,** *n.* (—**chens,** *pl.* —**chen**) (—**schwärmer,** *m.*) Zygaena (*Ent.*). *Comp.* —**fell,** *n.* ram's skin; **das goldene —fell,** the golden fleece. —**punkt,** *m.* vernal point. —**schiff,** *n.* ram (*war-vessel*).

Wi'der, I. *prep.* (*with acc.*) against, contrary to, in opposition to; — **Willen,** against his will, unwillingly; **das Für und —,** the pros and cons. II. *adv. & insep. or* (*obs.*) *sep. pref.* against; in opposite direction; back again; (*gen'lly spelt* **Wieder**) again, anew, once more; in return; **hin und —,** there and back again, to and fro; now and then, at times. —**lich,** *adj. & adv.* offensive, repugnant, loathsome, disgusting; hostile, repulsive (*obs.*). —**lichkeit,** *f.* loathsomeness; repulsiveness. *Comp.* —**christ,** *m.* antichrist (*obs.*). —**christlich,** *adj.* antichristian (*obs.*). —**druck,** *m.* counterpressure, reaction (*Phys.*); counter-proof (*Engr.*); reprint (*Typ.*). —**fah'ren,** *ir.v.n.* (*aux.* **s.**) (*insep.*) to happen, fall to a p.; **mir ist viel Ehre —fahren,** great honour has been done me; **das kann Ihnen auch —fahren,** the same may happen to you; **jedem sein Recht — fahren lassen,** to give everyone his due. —**gabe,** *f.* rendering; **ihre —gabe der Beethovenschen Sonate,** her reading of Beethoven's sonata. —**haarig,** *adj.* perverse, refractory —**häkchen,** *n.,* —**haken,** *m.* barb, barbed hook. —**hakig,** *adj.* barbed. —**hall,** *m.* echo. —**hallen,** *v.n.* (*aux.* **h.**) (*sep. & insep.*) to resound, re-echo. —**halt,** *m.* support, prop; purchase. —**haltig,** *adj.* resisting. —**halt=kette,** *f.* pole-chain. —**kehren** (*gen'lly* **Wieder-**

kehren, *v.n.* (*aux.* s.) (*sep.*) to come back, return; to repeat itself. **—lager,** *n.* abutment; counterfort, buttress. **—leg'bar,** *adj.* refutable. **—le'gen,** *v.a.* (*insep.*) to refute, disprove, negative; **seine eignen Worte —legen,** to give the lie to one's own words; **durch das Leben —legen,** to live down. **—natürlich,** *adj.* unnatural; monstrous. **—part,** *m.* adversary, opponent; opposition; **einem —part halten,** to oppose a p. **—prall,** *m.* rebound; reflection. **—ra'ten,** *ir.v.a.* (*insep.*) (**einem etwas**) to dissuade from, advise against. **—rechtlich,** *adj. & adv.* unjust, unrighteous; illegal; iniquitous. **—rede,** *f.* contradiction; **ohne —rede,** without contradiction, opposition, *or* objection. **—reden,** *v.n.* (*sep. & insep.*) *see* **—sprechen.** **—rist,** *m. & n.* withers (*Vet.*). **—ruf,** *m.* recantation; disavowal; countermand. **—ruf'bar,** *adj.* revocable. **—ru'fen,** *ir.v.a.* (*insep.*) to revoke, recant, retract, withdraw; to contradict (*a report*); to disavow. **—ruf'lich,** *adj.* revocable; uncertain (*tenure of office, etc.*). **—sacher,** *m.* adversary, opponent. **—schein,** *m.* reflection. **—schlagen,** *ir.v.a.* (*sep.*) to strike back, return a blow. **—set'zen,** *v.r.* (*insep.*) (*dat.*) to oppose, to combat; to disobey (*the law*). **—setz'lich,** *adj.* refractory, insubordinate; disobedient. **—setz'lichkeit,** *f.* insubordination. **—sinn,** *m.* opposite sense; contradiction, paradox; nonsense; spirit of contradiction. **—sinnig,** *adj. & adv.* repugnant to common sense, absurd; abnormal; cross-grained; recalcitrant; **eine Rede —sinnig verstehen,** to misunderstand a speech. **—sinnigkeit,** *f.* contrary sense; absurdity. **—spenstig,** *adj.* refractory, unruly; obstinate, perverse. **—spenstigkeit,** *f.* refractoriness; disobedience. **—spiel,** *n.* reverse, contrary, opposition; **einem das —spiel halten,** to act in opposition to a p. **—spre'chen,** *ir.v.a. & n.* (*aux.* h. *dat.*) (*insep.*) to contradict; to be at variance with; to oppose; **diese Sätze —sprechen einander,** these propositions are contradictory. **—sprecher,** *m.* gainsayer, arguer. **—spruch,** *m.* contradiction; opposition; disagreement; **—spruch erheben gegen (wider eine S.),** to raise an objection to; **heftigen —spruch bei einem finden,** to provoke violent opposition on the part of s. o.; **einen —spruch reimen,** to reconcile a contradiction. **—spruchs=geist,** *m.* spirit of contradiction. **—spruchs=voll,** *adj.* full of contradiction, (self-) contradictory; inconsistent. **—stand,** *m.* opposition, resistance; **wesentlicher —stand (der Batterie),** battery-resistance (*Elect.*); **—stand leisten,** to resist, to offer resistance. **—stands=fähigkeit,** *f.* power of resistance *or* of holding out. **—stands=moment,** *n.* momentum of resistance. **—ste'hen,** *ir.v.n.* (*aux.* h.) (*dat.*) (*insep.*) to oppose, resist, withstand; to be repugnant to; **nicht —stehen,** to succumb to. **—stoß,** *m.* countershock. **—stoßen,** *ir.v.a.* (*sep.*) to return a knock *or* push. **—stre'ben,** I. *v.n.* (*aux.* h., *dat.*) (*insep.*) to resist, oppose; to be repugnant to (a p.). II. *subst.n.* opposition, resistance; repugnance; **mit —streben,** reluctantly, against one's will; **ohne —streben,** readily, with a good grace; **da hilft kein —streben,** all resistance is useless. **—streit,** *m.* opposition; conflict. **—strei'ten,** *ir.v.n.* (*aux.* h., *dat.*) (*insep.*) to conflict (*with*), to clash (*with*), to be contrary (*to*), militate (*against*). **—strom,** *m.* counter-current. **—wärtig,** *adj. & adv.* disagreeable; perverse, cross; offensive, disgusting; repugnant; contrary, adverse. **—wärtigkeit,** *f.* disagreeableness; offensiveness; perversity; untoward event, accident, calamity; reverse (*of fortune*). **—wille,** *m.* repugnance, antipathy; disgust; ill-will; hatred; **mit —willen,** reluctantly, with a bad grace. **—willig,** *adj. & adv.* reluctant. **—wind,** *m.* adverse wind.

Wi'der—n, *v.n.* (*aux.* h.); **es —t mir** (*now usually* **es —t mich an**), it is repugnant to me (*obs., poet.*); **es —t mir davor,** I loathe it.

Wid'm—en, *v.a.* to dedicate; to devote; to consecrate. **—er,** *m.* (**—ers,** *pl.* **—er**) dedicator. **—ung,** *f.* dedication; **die —ung seines Buches war mir sehr angenehm,** I was much gratified by his dedicating his book to me. *Comp.* **—ungs=schrift,** *f.* dedicatory epistle.

Wi'drig, *adj. & adv.* adverse, untoward; inimical; *see* **Widerlich, Widerwärtig; bundes—,** contrary to the treaty of alliance; **im —en Falle, —enfalls,** otherwise, in the contrary case, failing which. **—keit,** *f. see* **Widerlichkeit;** unpleasantness; untoward event; **allerlei —keiten,** all sorts of unpleasantnesses.

Wie, I. *adv.* how; in what way; in what degree; **— geht's?** how are you? how are things getting on? **— kommt es, daß . . .?** how is it that . . .? **— denn anders?** how else? how could it be otherwise? of course; **— macht der Hund? wau=wau,** what does the dog say? bow-wow; **und — sie alle heißen mögen,** whatever their names may be; **— stark war die Gesellschaft?** how many people were there? **— schwer es mir auch ankommt,** however much it may cost me; **— ? — beliebt? — sagten Sie?** I beg your pardon? what did you say? Sir? Madam? **— so denn?** why so? but why? how is it? **ein Mann — er,** such a man as he; **— wäre es, wenn er nun gar nicht käme?** what if he should not come at all? **— schlau sie auch waren,** crafty as they were, however cunning they were; **— leicht läßt man sich täuschen!** how easily one is deceived! **— häßlich ist (nicht) die Undankbarkeit!** how hateful is ingratitude! **—! hat sie es wirklich gesagt?** what! did she really say so? II. *conj.* how; as, like; as, for instance, as if, such as; as, when, when once; **so — ich bin,** such as I am; **— sich's gebührt** *or* **gehört,** as is proper; **schön — ein Engel,** beautiful as an angel; **ich weiß nicht, — ich handeln soll,** I don't know how to act; **— man mir gesagt hat,** as I have been told; **— die Sachen jetzt stehen,** as matters now stand; **— du mir, so ich dir,** as you treat me so I shall treat you, claw me and I'll claw thee, measure for measure, tit for tat; **das Geschick ist Ihnen günstig, — es mich verfolgt,** fate is as favourable to you as it is unfavourable to me; **schlau — er ist, wird er . . .,** cunning as he is *or* with all his cunning he will . . .; **— er's macht, treibt,** at the rate he is going, in the way he is going on; **— man's treibt, so geht's,** as you make your bed, so you must lie (*prov.*); **— er dies hörte, ging er weg,** on hearing this, he went away; **— gesagt so gethan,** no sooner said than done; **— auch, — nur, — immer,** however, howsoever; **— dem auch sei,** be that as it may; **— auch immer,** in whatever way; **er sagte uns, — sehr er bedaure, daß . . .,** he told us how much he regretted . . . III. *n.* (*gen. & plur.* —s); **das — und das Warum,** the why and the wherefore; **auf das — kommt es an,** it all depends on the way in which it is done *or* said. *Comp.* **—fern,** *adv.;* **in —fern?** in what respect? **—so',** *adv.;* **—so weißt du das?** how is it that you know that? **—viel,** *adv.* how much; how; **um —viel mehr wird er es jetzt thun!** how much rather will he do it now! **—viel unnütze Mühe geben Sie sich!** what needless trouble you give yourself! **das —viel,** the how-much; **der —vielte ist er in seiner Klasse?** what place has he in his class? **den —vielten haben wir heute?** what day of the month is it? der —vielte war diese Kandidat? what was the place of this candidate? —wo'hl, *conj.* although.

Wie'de, *f.* (*pl.* —n) withe, willow-twig.

Wie'dehopf, *m.* hoopoe (*Orn.*).

Wie'der, I. *adv.* again, anew; back again; in return; einem —etwas zu Gefallen thun, to return a p.'s favours; reden wir nicht — davon, don't let us talk any more about it, we won't mention the subject again; *see* Wider. II. *pref. mostly sep.* (*when insep. it will be stated; the accent in this case is on the root*) *gen'lly* = once more, again. *Comp.* —abdruck, *m.* reprint, reimpression. —abdrucken, *v.a.* to reprint. —abgeben, *ir.v.a.* to return. —abschreiben, *ir.v.a.* to copy out again, to recopy. —abteilen, *v.a.* to subdivide. —abtreten, *ir.v.* I. *a.* to cede again. II. *n.* to retire. —abtretung, *f.* retrocession. —anfang, *m.* recommencement; reopening (*of school, etc.*). —anfassen, *v.a.* to handle again. —angehen, *ir.v.n.* (*aux.* s.) to recommence; die Schule geht — an, school reopens. —anknüpfen, *v.a.* to renew. —anmachen, *v.a.* to tie, fasten again; to rekindle (*a fire, etc.*). —annehmen, *ir.v.a.* to reassume. —anschaffen, *v.a.* to procure anew. —anstellen, *v.a.* to reappoint, reinstate. —anziehung, *f.* reattraction (*Phys.*). —aufbau, *m.* reconstruction. —aufbringen, *ir.v.a.* to revive (*a fashion, etc.*). —auferwecken, *v.a.* (vom Tode) to resuscitate. —auffindung, *f.* recovery of something lost. —aufforstung, *f.* reforesting. —aufgehen, *ir. v.n.* (*aux.* s.) to reopen. —aufkommen, *ir.v.n.* (*aux.* s.) to recover (*from an illness, etc.*). —aufleben, I. *v.n.* (*aux.* s.) to revive, to show new signs of life. II. *n.* resurrection; revival (*of learning, etc.*). —auflegen, *v.a.* to reprint (*a book*). —aufmachen, *v.a.* to reopen. —aufnahme, *f.* resumption. —aufnehmen, *ir.v.a.* to resume. —aufstellen, *v.a.* to put back in its place. —aufthun, *ir.v.a.* to reopen. —auftreten, *ir.v.n.* (*aux.* s.) to reappear. —aufwärmen, *v.a.* to warm up again. —ausbruch, *m.* fresh outbreak; recommencement; renewal (*of hostilities*). —ausgrabung, *f.* disinterment. —aussöhnung, *f.* reconciliation. —bekommen, *ir.v.a.* to recover, get back. —beleben, *v.a.* to reanimate, call back to life, revive. —belebungs-versuch, *m.* attempt to restore to life. —besetzen, *v.a.* to reoccupy (*a country*); to repeople; to restock (*a pond*); to fill again (*a vacant professorial chair, etc.*). —besinnen, *ir.v.r.* to call to mind again; to recollect o.s.; to recover one's senses. —besitzergreifung, *f.* taking possession of again. —besohlen, *v.a.* to put a new sole on, resole. —betretungs-fall, *m.*; im —betretungsfalle, in case of a repetition (*of the offence*). —bringen, *ir.v.a.* to bring back; to restore, return to. —einführen, *v.a.* to bring in again, reintroduce. —eingehen, *v.n.* to come in again (*of money*). —einlenken, *v.a. see* Einrenken; to turn again (*into a track, etc.*); to amend; to resume (*a topic, etc.*). —einnehmen, *ir.v.a.* to retake, recapture. —einrichten, *v.a.* to rearrange, reorganize; to refurnish; to reset (*a limb*); to reduce (*a sprain, etc.*). —einschlafen, *ir.v.n.* (*aux.* s.) to fall asleep again; die Sache ist —eingeschlafen, the affair has again fallen into oblivion, has again been shelved. —einsetzen, *v.a.* to replace; to reinstate. —eintreten, *ir.v.n.* (*aux.* s.) to reenter; to rejoin (*the army, etc.*); to happen again, recur. —erkennen, *ir.v.a.* to recognize. —ersetzen, —erstatten, *v.a.* to return, restore; to refund. —erzeugen, *v.a.* to reproduce; to regenerate. —gabe, *f.* restitution, return; reproduction. —geben, *ir.v.a.* to give again; to give back, return, restore. —geburt, *f.* regeneration, new birth. —genesen, *ir.v.n.* (*aux.* s.) to recover. —grüßen, *v.a.* to return a bow. —gutmachen, *n.* reparation. —haben, *ir.v.a.* to become again possessed of. —hall, *see* Widerhall. —her'stellung, *f.* thorough repair, restoration; readjustment; revival (*of learning, etc.*); reinstatement; reduction (*Chem.*). —her'stellungs-zeichen, *n.* natural, quadrant, (♮ *Mus.*). —holen, I. *v.a.* (*sep.*) to bring, *or* carry back; (*insep.*) to repeat, reiterate, say again; to rehearse (*a lesson*); kurz —holen, to sum up, recapitulate; beständig —holen, to be constantly repeating *or* telling; sich —holen, to repeat o.s., to recur, occur again *or* frequently; das läßt sich nicht —holen, that won't bear repeating. II. *subst. n.*, —ho'lung, *f.* repetition; reiteration; recapitulation. —ho'lentlich, —holterma'ßen, *adv.* repeatedly, again and again. —ho'lungs-zeichen, *n.* sign of repetition; repeat (*Mus.*). —kauen, —käuen, *v.a. & n.* (*aux.* h.) (*sometimes insep.*) to ruminate; to repeat (*oneself*). —käuer, *m.* ruminant; one who always tells the same story. —kauf, *m.* repurchase; redemption (*of an estate*). —kehr, *f. see* Rückkehr; —kehr in gewissen Zeiträumen, periodic return; die 25-jährige —kehr des Tages von Sedan, the 25th anniversary of the battle of Sedan. —kehren, *see* Widerkehren. —kunft, *f.* return. —nahme, *f.* recapture. —sammeln, *v.a.* to reassemble; to rally (*troops*). —schaffen, I. *ir.v.a.* to recreate. II. *reg. v. a.* to get *or* find again. —schall, *see* Widerhall. —schein, *see* Widerschein. —scheinen, *ir.v.n.* (*aux.* h.) to be reflected. —schimpfen, *v.a.* to abuse in return. —schlagen, *see* Widerschlagen. —schlimmer-werden, *n.* relapse. —sehen, I. *ir.v.a.* to see again. II. *subst. n.*; auf —sehen! till we meet again! au revoir! —taufe, *f.* rebaptizing, second baptism. —täufer, *m.* anabaptist. —trauen, *v.a.* to remarry. —thun, *ir.v.a.* to do again, to repeat; daß du das nicht —thust! don't (let me see you) do that again! —um, I. *adv.* again, anew, afresh; on the other hand; on the contrary; in (his, her, their) turn. —um'kehren, *v.n.* (*aux.* s.) to turn back, retrace one's steps. —vereinigen, *v. a.* to reunite; to reconcile. —wahl, *f.* reëlection. —wählbar, *adj.* eligible for reëlection. —zahlen, *v.a.* to pay again; to repay. —zählen, *v.a.* to count again. —zulassung, *f.* readmission. —zustellen, *v.a.* to return.

Wie'ge, *f.* (*pl.* —n) cradle; *see* —messer. *Comp.* —n-angebinde, *n.* birthday-gift. —n-band, *n.* string by which a cradle is rocked; cradle-band (*to keep the coverlet, etc. on*). —n-druck, *m.* incunabulum (*Typ.*). —n-fest, *n.* birthday (-celebrations); sein —nfest begehen *or* feiern, to celebrate one's birthday (*high style*). —n-kind, *n.* young infant, infant in the cradle. —n-korb, *m.* bassinette. —n-lied, *n.* lullaby.

Wie'ge—n, I. *ir.v.a. & n.* (*aux.* h.) to weigh. II. *reg. v.a.* to rock; to rock a cradle; to move gently; to shake; to chop (*meat, etc.*); to scrape, roughen (*the plate, Engr.*); in (den) Schlaf —n, to rock to sleep; sich —n in (*dat.*), to lull *or* delude o.s. with (*vain hopes, etc.*); einen —nden Gang haben, to waddle; in einer Sache gewiegt, well versed in, skilled in. —r, *m.* (—rs, *pl.* —r) weighing-machine *or* apparatus. *Comp.* —brett, *n* chopping board. —maschine, *f.* mincing machine. —messer, *n.* chopping-knife. —stempel, *m.* stamp of the weight. —vorrichtung, *f.* arrangement (*at a railway station*) for weighing.

Wie'hern, I. *v.n.* (*aux.* h.) to neigh; to bawl, roar, shout noisily; —des Gelächter, horse laugh; roaring laughter. II. *subst. n.* neighing, neigh.

Wiek, *f.* (*pl.* —en) creek, bay (*dial.*).

Wie'ke, *f.* (*pl.* —n) piece of lint, tent.

Wie'men, *m.* (—s, *pl.* —) roost (*of hens*) (*dial.*).

Wienertränk'chen, *n.* infusion of senna.

Wies, *1 & 3 p. sing. imperf. ind.*; **Wie'se**, *1 & 3 p. sing. imperf. subj. of* weisen.

Wie's—e, *f.* (*pl.* —en) meadow; pasture-land, green field; mead (*poet.*). *Comp.* —en=bach, *m.* meadow-stream. —en=bau, *m.* cultivation of meadows. —en=egge, *f.* harrow for meadows. —en=feld, *n.* grass-land, meadow. —en=gras, *n.* meadow-grass. —en=grund, *m.* meadow-land; meadow at the bottom of a valley. —en=hopfen, *m.* wild hop. —en=kresse, *f.* meadow-cress. —en=kümmel, *m.* common caraway. —en=plan, *m.* meadow; prairie. —en=quelle, *f.* meadow-spring. —en=raute, *f.* meadow rue. —en=schaumkraut, *n.* meadow cress. —en=schilf, *n.* meadow reedgrass. —en=teppich, *m.* grassy carpet. —e=wachs, (Wieswachs,) *m.* herbage; grass-crop, hay-crop.

Wie'sel, *n.* (—s, *pl.* —) weasel. *Comp.* —artig, *adj.* weasel-like; musteline. —fell, *n.* weasel-skin.

Wi'king, *m.* (—s, *pl.* —er) viking. *Comp.* —er=balk, *m.* vikings' law. —er=schiff, *n.* viking ship.

Wild, I. *adj. & adv.* wild, savage; uncultivated; uncivilized; growing naturally; unruly, intractable; ferocious, fierce; rude; noisy, turbulent; unrestrained; angry; —e Bäder, mineral springs, baths; —er Boden, virgin soil; —e Ehe, unlawful marriage, concubinage; —es Fleisch, proud flesh; —e Flucht, headlong flight, rout; —e Gegend, rugged country; —es Geflügel, wild fowl; —es Gestein, dead rock; —es Haar, dishevelled *or* unkempt hair; —e Jagd, wild chase; troop *or* swarm of noisy persons; uproar; —er Jäger, wild huntsman; —es Leben, wild *or* disorderly life; —es Volk, savage people; —er Mann, wild man of the woods; protector of wild animals; — wachsend, growing naturally, not sown; —es Pferd, ungovernable horse; — machen, to enrage, exasperate; ein Tier — machen, to frighten an animal, make it shy; seid nicht so —! don't make so much noise! II. *n.* (—es) wild animals; game; a head of game; deer; Rot—, venison; Schwarz—, black game; hohes —, large game, deer, *etc.* —e, *f. obs. & poet. for* —heit, —nis; das —e in seinem Aussehen, the wildness of his appearance; eine —e, a savage woman. —e(r), *m.* savage; candidate for a school leaving certificate examination without having attended the school; student belonging to no club *or* college, non-collegiate student; deputy *or* parliamentary representative not belonging to any party. —erei', *f.* poaching. —erer, *m.* poacher. —ern, *v.n.* (*aux.* h.) to be in a wild *or* savage state; to run *or* become wild; to poach. —heit, *f.* wildness, savagery; rudeness; ferocity; anger, fury; rude action; barbarous act; sterility, deadness (*of rocks, etc.*). —ling, *m.* (—lings, *pl.* —linge) wild stock *or* tree; wild beast; untrained animal; savage; boor; Goth. —nis, *f.* wilderness; desert; jungle; savage state. *Comp.* —acker, *m.* preserve in a park. —bad, *n.* natural mineral bath *or* watering-place. —bahn, *f.* preserve, chase, hunting ground; road through a preserve. —bann, *m.* exclusive right of chase; preserve; game-regulations. —braten, *m.* roast venison *or* other game. —bret (*older spellings also* —brett, —brät, —pret(t)), *n.* game, venison. —bret=geschmack, *m.* taste of venison, gamy flavour. —bret=pastete, *f.* venison-pie. —dieb, *m.* poacher. —dieben, *v.n.* (*aux.* h.) (*insep.*) to poach. —dieberei', *f.* poaching. —fang, *m.* deer-stalking; snaring; tamed horse; romp, unruly child. —fleisch, *n.* venison. —fremd, *adj.* quite strange *or* unknown; ein —fremder, an utter stranger; unter —fremden Leuten, among perfect strangers. —garten, *m.*, —gehege, *n.* park; preserve, game-cover. —geruch, *m.* smell of venison. —geschmack, *m.* gamy taste. —graf, *m.* Wildgrave (*title of counts in the Rhine and Nahe districts*). —grube, *f.* snare, pitfall. —heuer, *m.* one who mows grass on mountain-ridges (*dial. & poet.*). —hüter, *m.* game-keeper. —kalb, *n.* fawn. —knecht, *m.* game-keeper's man. —leder, *n* deerskin, buckskin. —meister, *m.* head game-keeper, ranger. —park, *see* —garten. —pret, *see* —bret. —recht, *n.* quarry. —reich, *adj.* abounding in game. —ruf, *m.* call (*Sport.*). —schaden, *m.* injury done by game. —schur, *f.* fur-coat (*with the hair outside*). —schütz(e), *m.* poacher; sportsman, shot. —schwein, *n.* wild boar. —schweins=kopf, *m.* boar's head. —schweins=rüssel, *m.* snout of a wild boar. —wachsend, *adj.* growing wild, wild-growing. —wasser, *n.* torrent. —werk, *n.* game. —zaun, *m.* paling of a preserve *or* park.

Wilden'zen, *v.n.* to taste of *or* like venison; to smell *or* taste high *or* gamy.

Will, *1 & 3 p. sing.*; **Willst**, *2 p. sing. pres. ind. of* wollen.

Wil'l—e, *m.* (—ens, *pl.* —en) will; volition; design, purpose; pleasure; wish, inclination; mit —en, on purpose, designedly; nach —en, as one pleases; wider —en, unwillingly; aus freiem —en, mit gutem —en, voluntarily; ohne meinen —en, without my consent, against my will; mit dem guten —en vorlieb nehmen, to take the will for the deed; darin geschieht unser —e, such is our will and pleasure; es ging ihm nach —en, he had his wish; ich ließ ihm seinen —en, I let him have his own way; einem zu —en sein, jemandes —en thun, einem seinen —en thun, to do as s.o. wishes, to humour a p.; man muß ihm zu —en sein, his wish must be gratified; das Mädchen war ihm zu —en, the girl allowed him to do as he pleased; wenn es Ihr —e ist, if you wish it; es war ja dein eigener —e, but it was your own wish, you know; —ens sein, to be willing, disposed, have a mind, intend, wish; um Gottes (Himmels) —en, for God's (Heaven's) sake. —entlich, *adj.* intentional. —ig, *adj.* willing; voluntary; ready; docile; —ig thun, to do willingly, readily; sich zu einer S. —ig finden lassen, to show o.s. willing to do, to be disposed for s.th. —igen, *v.n.* (*aux.* h.); in eine S. —igen, to consent to, to acquiesce in a th. —igkeit, *f.* willingness, readiness; good-will. *Comp.* —en=los, *adj.* having no will of one's own; weak-minded, characterless; undecided, wavering, hesitating. —en=losigkeit, *f.* want of will-power, indecision. —ens=änderung, *f.* change of mind. —ens=bestimmung, *f.* testamentary disposition, will. —ens=erklärung, *f.* declaratory act. —ens=freiheit, *f.* free will, freedom of will. —ens=kraft, *f.*, —es=vermögen, *n.*, faculty of volition. —ens=meinung, *f.* will, pleasure. —ens=stärke, *see* —enskraft. —fahren, *v.n.* (*aux.* h.) (*dat.*) to accede to, to comply with, to grant; to humour; einem in einer S. —fahren, to concede, grant something to o.s.; ich —fahrte seinem Wunsche, I acceded to his wish, I complied with his demand. —fährig, *adj.* obliging, complaisant; compliant. —fährigkeit, *f.* obligingness; compliance; complaisance. —**komm**, *see* **Willkomm**, **2c.** —**kür**, *see* **Willkür**, **2c.**

Willko'mm, *m.* (—**s**, *pl.* —**en**) cup of welcome; *see* —**en** II. —**en**, I. *adj.* welcome; acceptable, gratifying; **seien Sie —en!** (be) welcome! **einen —en heißen**, to bid a person welcome, to welcome a p.; —**ene Kunde**, welcome news. II. *m.* (—**ens**, *pl.* —**en**) welcome, reception.

Will'kür, *f.* free will; option, choice; discretion; caprice; arbitrariness, despotism; **ich lasse das in Ihre — gestellt, handeln Sie nach Ihrer —**, I leave that to you, act according to your own discretion; **nach —**, at will, as one pleases; in an arbitrary manner. —**lich**, *adj.* arbitrary, despotic. —**lichkeit**, *f.* arbitrariness; arbitrary act. *Comp.* —**herrschaft**, *f.* despotism; tyranny. —**verfahren**, *n.* arbitrary proceeding.

Willt, **Wilt**, *obs. for* **Willst.**

Wim'meln, *v.n.* (*aux.* **h.** & **s.**) to swarm, to be crowded; to abound, teem (**von**, with), to be filled (**von**, with).

Wim'mer—n; *v.n.* (*aux.* **h.**) to whimper, whine, cry, lament (*over*). *Comp.* —**holz**, *n.* inferior violin (*with a screechy and twangy sound*) (*coll.*).

Wim'pel, *m.* (—**s**, *pl.* —) pennon *or* pennant, streamer. *Comp.* —**fall**, *m.* pendant halliards. —**stock**, *m.* staff for a pennant.

Wim'per, *f.* (*pl.* —**n**) eye-lash. —**ig**, *adj.* ciliate. —**n**, *v.n.* (*aux.* **h.**) to wink; **gewimpert**, fringed with eyelashes, ciliated. *Comp.* —**haar**, *n.* ciliary hair; eyelash. —**rand**, *m.* ciliary edge.

Wim'perg, *m.* (—**s**, *pl.* —**e**), —**e**, *f.* (—, *pl.* —**en**) gabled hood-moulding; gable-board.

[1]**Wind**, *m.* (—**es**, *pl.* —**e**) wind; hint; scent; emptiness, humbug; flatulence; **starker —**, high wind; **kühler —**, cool wind; breeze (*Mar.*); **beständiger**, **stehender —**, steady wind; **unbeständiger —**, choppy wind; **halber —**, side wind; **lauer**, **sanfter**, **lieblicher —**, gentle breeze; **es geht ein starker —**, there is a gale blowing; **bei — und Wetter**, in all weathers, in storm and rain; **der — kommt von Osten**, the wind is in the east; **woher weht der —?** in what quarter is the wind? **dicht beim —e segeln**, to sail close to the wind, to hug the wind; **gegen den — segeln**, to sail against the wind, to go right in the wind's eye; **guten — haben**, **den — im Rücken haben**, **vor dem —e segeln**, to run before the wind, have the wind astern; **in den — reden**, to talk to the wind; **in den — säen**, to build castles in the air; **in den — schlagen**, to disregard, set at nought, pay no heed to; **über den — kommen**, to gain the wind; **unter dem —e**, under the lee; **die Inseln unter dem —e** (**Antillen**), the Leeward Isles; **vom —e abkommen**, to fall to leeward; — **von etwas bekommen**, to get scent of s.th.; — **machen**, to boast, bluster, swagger; —! fudge! stuff, verbiage! **Passat—e**, trade winds; **den Mantel nach dem —e hängen**, to trim one's sails to the wind; to comply with the times; **es ist lauter —**, **was er spricht**, it is all smoke that he is talking, he is beating the air; **das ist ja alles —**, that is all humbug *or* moonshine; **ich habe — davon bekommen**, I have got scent of it. —**en**, *v.n.* (*aux.* **h.**) to catch the scent; **es —et**, it is stormy, there is a high wind (*rare*). —**ig**, *adj.* windy, breezy; exposed to the wind; airy; thoughtless, heedless; unreliable; visionary; vain; **es sieht —ig um ihn (mit ihm) aus**, he seems in a bad way; **damit sieht es —ig aus**, there is nothing in it. —**igkeit**, *f.* windiness, airiness, emptiness; blustering, boasting. *Comp.* —**ball**, *m.* small air-balloon. —**beschädigung**, *f.* damage done by a storm. —**beutel**, *m.* kind of puff; windbag; empty-headed fellow; boaster, braggart; one who promises much and does little. —**beutelei'**, *f.* idle boasting, braggadocio. —**beuteln**, *v.n.* (*aux.* **h.**) (*insep.*) to brag, boast, talk big. —**blattern**, *pl.* chicken-pox. —**blume**, *f.* anemone. —**bruch**, *m.* windfallen wood; pneumatocele (*Med.*). —**brüchig**, *adj.* wind-fallen. —**büchse**, *f.* air-gun. —**drehung**, *f.* change of wind. (**Doves**)—**drehungs=gesetz**, *n.* Dove's law of rotation of winds. —**dürr**, *adj.* air-dried; lean. —**ei**, *n.* addled *or* barren egg; soft-shelled egg. —**fackel**, *f.* torch that is not extinguished by the wind. —**fahne**, *f.* weathercock. —**fang**, *m.* air-hole; ventilator; porch; projection (*before a door*). —**frei**, *adj.* sheltered. —**geschwulst**, *f.* emphysema. —**hafer**, *m.* wild oats. —**harfe**, *f.* Æolian harp. —**hetze**, *f.*, —**hetzen**, *n.* coursing. —**hund**, *m.* greyhound; thoughtless *or* empty-headed lad; **wie ein —hund rennen**, to run like mad. —**kanal**, *m.* windpipe (*in organs*). —**karte**, *f.* pilot's chart. —**kessel**, *m.* air-vessel, air-regulator (*of a forcing-pump, etc.*). —**klappe**, *f.* valve (*of bellows*). —**kolik**, *f.* windy colic. —**lade**, *f.* wind-chest, sounding-board; ventilator. —**laden**, *m.* window-shutter. —**lawine**, *f.* wind avalanche, drift-snow avalanche. —**lehre**, *f.* anemology. —**licht**, *n.* candle protected from the wind by a globe. —**loch**, *n.* air-hole; draughty place. —**lotte**, *f.* air passage *or* pipe. —**macher**, *m.* fan, punkah; brag; humbug; charlatan. —**macherei'**, *f.* charlatanry; empty bluster. —**maschine**, *f.* ventilator; wind-engine. —**messer**, *m.* anemometer, manometer. —**mühle**, *f.* windmill. —**mühlen=flügel**, *m.* sail of a windmill. —**ofen**, *m.* wind-furnace, draught-furnace. —**orgel**, *f.* musical anemometer. —**pocken**, *see* —**blattern.** —**rad** *n.* ventilator-wheel. —**rose**, *f.* anemone; rhomb-card, compass card. —**s=braut**, *f.* raging (of) wind, strong gust of wind, hurricane, whirlwind, squall. —**schacht**, *m.* air-shaft. —**schief**, *adj.* warped, askew, awry; —**schief werden**, to warp; —**schief sitzen**, to be put awry; —**schiefe Ansichten**, warped views (*coll.*). —**schirm**, *m.* screen. —**schnell**, *adj.* quick as lightning. —**seite**, *f.* exposed side, weather-side. —**spiel**, *n.* greyhound. —**still**, *adj.* calm. —**stille**, *f.* calm. —**stock**, *m.* cover of organ-pipes. —**stoß**, *m.* blast of wind. —**strich**, *m.* current of air; rhomb. —**strom**, *m.*, —**strömung**, *f.* current of air. —**sturm**, *m.* heavy gale, squall. —**sucht**, *f.* tympanitis. —**thür**, *f.* ventilating door; wind-gate (*Mining*). —**wärts**, *adv.* windward. —**wehe**, *f.* snow-drift. —**wirbel**, *m.* whirlwind. —**zeiger**, *m.* anemoscope. —**zug**, *m.* draught, current of air; ventilator; Æolian attachment (*in a piano*).

[2]**Wind**, *adj.* writhing with pain (*obs.*) (*esp'lly in the phrase* — **und weh**, utterly miserable).

Win'de, *f.* (*pl.* —**n**) bindweed, wild convolvulus; reel; winder; windlass; winch; lift; worm (*of a screw*). —**l**, *f.* (*pl.* —**ln**) swaddling clothes; roller; napkin. —**ln**, *v.a.* to swaddle. *Comp.* —**l=band**, *n.* baby's roller, swaddling band. —**l=bohrer**, *m.* wimble, centre-bit; round punch. —**l=kind**, *n.* young infant. —**l=weich**, *adj.*; —**lweich schlagen**, to beat to a jelly. —**n=artig**, *adj.* of the convulvulus family (*Bot.*). —**n=schwärmer**, *m.* convolvulus hawk-moth (*Ent.*).

Win'd—en, *ir.v.* I. *a.* to wind; to reel, wind off; to twist, wring, wrench; to twine; **in die Höhe —en**, to hoist; **einem etwas aus den Händen —en**, to wrest s.th. out of a p.'s hands. II. *r.* to wind, twist, turn; to writhe; to wriggle; to meander (*of streams, rivers*); **sich vor Schmerz —en**, to writhe with pain.

—ig, —isch, *adj. & adv.* spiral (*rare*). —ung, *f.* winding, twisting; twist, turn; coil; sinuosity; meandering (*of a stream*); whorl (*of a shell*); worm (*of a screw*); die —ungen der Schneckenlinie am jonischen Kapitäl, the circumvolutions of the Ionic volute. *Comp.* —e=baum, *m.* beam (*of a windlass, etc.*). —e=eisen, *n.* joint-hook (*Tele.*). —e=seil, —e=tau, *n.* rope of a pulley *or* drawbeam.

Wink, *m.* (—(e)s, *pl.* —e) sign; wink; nod; beckoning (*with the hand*); hint; twinkling; einem einen — geben, to sign *or* beckon to a p.; to drop a p. a hint, to give some friendly advice (*fig.*); ein — mit dem Laternenpfahl *or* Zaunpfahl, a broad hint.

Win'kel, *m.* (—s, *pl.* —) angle; corner; nook; privacy (*fig.*), humble condition of life (*fig.*); *see* —haken, —maß; in den — bringen, to square; im —, in secret, privately, clandestinely; äußerer —, external angle; auswärtsgehender —, salient angle; spitzer (stumpfer) —, acute (obtuse) angle. —ig, wink'lig, *adj.* angular; full of angles *or* corners; bent, cornered; twisted; spitz—ig, acute-angled. *Comp.* —advokat, *m.* pettifogging lawyer, hedge-lawyer (*coll.*). —blatt, —blättchen, *n.* small local newspaper. —bogen, *m.* arc subtending an angle. —börse, *f.* unlicensed exchange, place where exchange-business is done outside the ordinary exchange. —börsen=spekulant, *m.* speculator outside the stock-exchange. —dach, *n.* square roof. —drucker, *m.* secret *or* unlicensed printer. —druckerei, *f.* secret press; clandestine printing. —ehe, *f.* clandestine marriage. —förmig, *adj.* angular, corner-shaped. —funktion, *f.* circulating function (*Math.*). —gasse, *f.* secluded lane; blind alley. —haken, *m.* instrument for measuring and adjusting angles; square; justifier (*Typ.*); composing-stick (*Typ.*). —kirche, *f.* conventicle. —klammer, *f.* bent-clamp. —konsulent, *m.* hedge-lawyer. —linie, *f.* diagonal. —makler, *m.* unlicensed broker. —maß, *n.* square (*Carp.*). —messer, *m.* instrument for measuring angles. —meßkunst, —messung, *f.* measurement of angles, goniometry. —münze, *f.* base, illegal coin; illegal mint. —münzer, *m.* coiner of base money. —naht, *f.* lambdoidal suture (*Anat.*). —presse, *see* —druckerei. —recht, I. *adj.* rectangular. II. *adv.* at right angles. —scheibe, *f.* astrolabe (*Astr.*). —schenke, *f.* unlicensed ale-house; low tavern. —schule, *f.* small private school, dame-school, hedge-school. —schul=lehrer, *m.* teacher not duly qualified; teacher at a —schule. —spiel, *n.* puss-in-the-corner. —ständig, *adj.* axillary. —treppe, *f.* private staircase. —züge, *pl.* subterfuges, shifts, pretexts, tricks; —züge machen, to use subterfuges *or* evasions, to prevaricate, shuffle.

Win'ken, I. *v.a. & n.* (*aux.* h.) to wink, to sign, beckon, nod; (einem) etwas —, to enjoin by a sign; einem mit den Augen —, to wink to a p.; einem mit dem Zaunpfahl *or* Scheunenthor —, to give a p. a broad hint; einem — heranzukommen, to beckon to a p. to approach; einem Stillschweigen —, to make signs to a p. to keep silent. II. *subst.n.* winking; sign, wink.

Win'sel—ei, *f.* continuous whining; lamentation. —er, *n.* (—ers, *pl.* —er) whiner, moaner. —ig, *adj.* whining, plaintive. —n, *v.n.* (*aux.* h.) to whine, whimper, moan; einem die Ohren voll —n, to deafen a p. with plaints. *Comp.* —affe, *m.* weeping ape, capuchin. —stimme, *f.* whining *or* moaning voice.

Win'ter, *m.* (—s, *pl.* —) winter; mitten im —, in the depth of winter; den — verbringen, to pass the winter; to hibernate (*of birds*). —haft, —lich, I. *adj.* winter, wintry. II. *adv.* as in winter. —n, *v.a. & n.* (*aux.* h.) to winter; es —t, it is winter; it grows wintry (*rare*). —ung, *f.* wintering; hot-house; winter-crop. *Comp.* —bestellung, *f.* winter-fallowing. —feldzug, *m.* winter-campaign. —fenster, *n.* outer window. —frucht, *f.* winter-crop. —gerste, *f.* autumn-sown barley. —getreide, *n.* *see* —frucht. —grün, *n.* periwinkle (*Bot.*); wintergreen. —hafen, *m.* winter-harbourage. —hart, *adj.*; —harte Pflanzen, hardy plants. —haus, *n.* winter-house; hothouse. —holz, *n.* fuel for winter. —könig, *see* Zaunkönig; king for one winter (*name given in mockery to Frederick V., Elector Palatine, King of Bohemia* (*1619–20*)). —korn, *n.* *see* —frucht. —mäßig, *see* —haft. —punkt, *m.* winter-solstice. —quartiere, *n.pl.* winter-quarters. —saat, *f.* sowing of winter-corn; winter-crop. —schein, *m.* new moon in November. —schlaf, *m.* hibernation. —schläfer, *m.* hibernating animal. —seite, *f.* northern side. —sonnenwende, *f.* *see* —punkt. —überzieher, *m.* winter-overcoat. —weizen, *m.* wheat sown in autumn. —wetter, *n.* wintry weather.

Win'zer, *m.* (—s, *pl.* —), —in, *f.* vintager; vine-dresser. *Comp.* —hacke, *f.* vineyard-hoe. —lied, *n.* vintager's song. —messer, *n.* vine-knife.

Win'zig, *adj.* tiny, diminutive; petty; scanty; contemptible. —keit, *f.* diminutiveness; pettiness.

Wip'fel, *m.* (—s, *pl.* —) (*tree-*)top; top, summit. —ig, *adj.* peaked, with a top. —n, *v.* I. *a.* to lop (*trees*). II. *r. & n.* (*aux.* h.) to rise aloft.

Wip'p—chen, *n.* (*coll.*) (—chens, *pl.* —chen) trick, shift, evasion; pretence; joke, fun; mache mir keine —chen vor, don't try to throw dust in my eyes, none of your tricks with me (*coll.*). —e, *f.* (*pl.* —en) brink (*of a fall, etc.*); critical point; see-saw; seat (*of a swing*); crane; swipe; strappado; tumbrel; gibbet; whip (*Naut., etc.*); windlass (*of a crossbow*); pliable pole (*Gymn.*); bow (*of a drill*); heading-machine (*for needles*); (*money-*)clipping; auf der —e stehen, to be ready to fall, to be on the point of falling.

Wip'p—eln, *v.a. & n.* (*aux.* h.) to rock; to move up and down. —en, *v.* I. *a.* to rock; to see-saw; to tip over, tilt up, overturn; to strappado (*criminals*); Münzen kippen und —en, to clip coin. II. *r. & n.* (*aux.* h.) *see* —eln. —er, *m.* (—ers, *pl.* —er) money-clipper. —erei', *f.* money-clipping. *Comp.* —galgen, *m.* gibbet, estrapade. —seil, *n.* rope for tying to the estrapade.

Wir, *pers. pron.* (*1st pers. pl.*) we; — sind es, it is we; —, Wilhelm, von Gottes Gnaden . . . , We, William, by the grace of God.

Wirb, *imperat. sing.*; Wirbst, Wirbt, *2 & 3 p. sing. pres. ind. of* werben.

Wir'bel, *m.* (—s, *pl.* —) rapid rotation, whirl; whirlpool, vortex, eddy; whirlwind; wreath (*of smoke*); giddiness; intoxication; whirl (*of passion; of business*); place where the hair parts, crown (*of the head*); vertebra; ball-and-socket joint; peg (*of violins, etc.*); spigot (*of a cock*); button, bolt (*of a window*); trill (*Mus.*); roll (*of a drum*); warbling (*of birds*); einen — schlagen, to beat *or* sound a roll; vom — bis zur Zehe, from top to toe. —haft, —icht, (*obs.*) —ig, *adj.* eddying, whirling; wild, impetuous, giddy. *Comp.* —bein, *n.* vertebra. —(blut)ader, *f.* vertebral artery. —brett, *n.* peg of a violin, *etc.* —förmig, *adj.* whirling; vertebra-like; vertebrate; spindle-shaped. —kasten, *m.* *see* —brett. —knochen, *m.* *see* —bein. —los, *adj.* invertebrate. —säule, *f.* spine, vertebral column. **—stock,** *m.* screw-plate of a piano. **—tiere,** *pl.* vertebrate animals.

Wir'bel—n, *v.a. & n.* (*aux.* **h.** *&* **s.**) to whirl, turn round; to warble; to trill; **auf der Trommel —n,** to beat the drum; **das Zeichen zum Rückzuge —n,** to beat the retreat *or* recall; **der Kopf —t mir,** my head is in a whirl; **gewirbelt,** vertebrate. *Comp.* **—atom,** *n.* whirling atom. **—sturm,** *m.* hurricane; tornado. **—wind,** *m.* whirlwind.

Wird, *3 p. sing. pres. ind. of* **werden.**

Wirf, *imperat. sing.;* **Wirfst; Wirft,** *2; 3 p. sing. pres. ind. of* **werfen.**

Wir'k—en, (*obs.* **Wür'ken,**) I. *v.a.* to effect; to work; to bring about, produce; to weave (*stockings, etc.*); to knead (*dough*); **Speise —en,** to labour for meat (*B.*); **eine Reue —en,** to work repentance (*B.*); **Salz —en,** to boil salt; **den Huf —en,** to pare the hoof (*of a horse*). II. *v.n.* (*aux.* **h.**) to work, operate (upon), act (upon); to affect; **jedes Wort —te,** every word told, produced an effect; **auf einen —en,** to work on, influence a p.; **an einer Schule (als Lehrer)—en,** to teach in a school; **nachteilig auf eine S. —en,** to have an injurious effect upon a th., to tell upon (a p.'s nerves, health); **auf die Sinne —en,** to affect the senses; **gut auf Schüler —en,** to influence pupils for good; **nachhaltig auf die Gemüter —en,** to produce a lasting impression on the minds; **gegen einander —en,** to counteract each other; to react. III. *subst.n.* acting, working; activity, effort, endeavour, acts, works; operation; weaving, *etc.; see* **—ung.** **—end,** *p. & adj.* operating; efficacious; efficient, effective (*cause*); active (*poison*); drastic. **—er,** *m.* (**—ers,** *pl.* **—er**) worker, agent, cause; weaver, embroiderer; kneader; (*salt-*)maker. **—erei',** *f.* weaving; embroidering; weaver's workroom. **—lich,** *adj. & adv.* actual, real; true; genuine; acting, in activity; effective; effectual; (*South Gm. dial.*) exactly, quite; already, as much as; now; **—lich vorhanden,** effective (*Mil.*); **—licher Bestand,** effective force; **—licher geheimer Rat,** acting privy-councillor; **—liche Schuld,** real debt; **—lich?** really? actually? do you mean it? **—lich machen,** to realize; **—lich werden,** to be *or* become realized. **—lichkeit,** *f.* reality, actuality; actual fact; **in —lichkeit,** in reality. **—sam,** *adj.* producing the (desired) effect, effective, efficacious, instrumental; working, operative, powerful (*Med.*); **gegen eine S. —sam,** good for a th. **—samkeit,** *f.* efficacy; virtue; effect; **in —samkeit sein,** to be in operation; to perform one's duties; to be in working order; **außer —samkeit setzen,** to suspend (*a law*). **—ung,** *f.* effect; operation, action; force; efficacy; result; impression produced; **auf einen eine —ung ausüben,** to produce an effect upon a p., to affect a p.; **ohne —ung bleiben,** to prove ineffectual, to produce no effect; **keine —ung ohne Ursache,** no effect without cause, no smoke without a fire (*prov.*). *Comp.* **—bank,** *f.*, **—brett,** *n.* board on which the dough is kneaded. **—eisen,** *n.* paring-knife (*for hoofs*). **—meister,** *m.* master-weaver; baker's foreman. **—stuhl,** *m.* loom. **—tafel,** *f.*, **—tisch,** *m.*, *see* **—brett.** **—ungs=art,** *f.* mode of acting *or* operation. **—ungs=grad,** *m.* efficiency (*of a machine*). **—ungs=kraft,** *f.* efficacy; virtue; force. **—ungs=kreis,** *m.* sphere of activity; province, domain; **dies schlägt nicht in unsern —ungskreis,** this is beyond our province *or* sphere, this is not in our line (*coll.*), we do not go in for this (*coll.*). **—ungs=los,** *adj.* ineffectual, futile; inefficient; inactive; without effect; **—los bleiben,** to produce no effect (upon), to be lost (**bei,** upon). **—ungs=losigkeit,** *f.* inefficacy. **—ungs=voll,** *adj.* efficacious, effective; telling.

Wirr, *adj.* confused; entangled; **—e Haare,** dishevelled hair, hair in disorder; **—es Durcheinander,** chaos, confusion. **—e,** *f.* (*pl.* **—en**) tangle; (*pl.*) disturbances; troubles, disorders, agitations; complications; **kirchliche —en,** agitations in the church. **—sal,** *n.* (**—sals,** *pl.* **—sale**) confusion; perplexity. *Comp.* **—garn,** *n.* tangled yarn. **—haar,** *n.* tangled hair. **—kopf,** *m.* ruffled *or* unkempt hair; confused thinker. **—seide,** *f.* silk-refuse; tangled silk. **—stroh,** *n.* short straw, litter. **—warr,** *m.* jumble, chaos, disorder, confusion, hubbub; **in —warr bringen,** to throw into confusion.

Wir'r—en, *v.a.* (*p.p. sometimes* **geworren**) to entangle, twist; to jumble, mix up; to confound; to perplex; **auseinander —en,** to disentangle. **—nis,** *f.* (*pl.* **—nisse**) *&* *n.* (**—nisses,** *pl.* **—nisse**) confusion, perplexity. **—ung,** *f.* entanglement, confusion; disturbance, trouble.

Wir'singkohl, *m.* crisped *or* curly cabbage, savoy.

Wirst, *2 p. sing. pres. ind. of* **werden.**

Wirt, *m.* (**—(e)s,** *pl.* **—e**) [**—in,** *f.*] head of a house *or* family; host, (hostess); husband, (wife) (*obs., poet.*); landlord, (landlady); tavern- *or* restaurant-keeper; lodging-house keeper; housekeeper; manager, economist; **den — machen,** to preside, do the honours; **die Rechnung ohne den — machen,** to reckon without one's host. **—bar,** *adj.* hospitable; habitable. **—lich,** *adj.* frugal; thrifty, economical; *see* **—bar; —liche Kenntnisse,** knowledge of housekeeping. **—lichkeit,** *f.* frugality; economy; housewifery; hospitality. **—schaft, 2c.,** *see* **Wirtschaft, 2c.** *Comp.* **—s=haus,** *n.* tavern, public-house. **—s=haus=leben,** *n.* life in restaurants and hotels. **—s=haus=tisch,** *m.* ordinary, table d'hôte. **—s=junge,** *m.* pot-boy. **—s=leute,** *pl.* innkeepers; lodging-house keepers; hosts. **—s=stube,** *f.* private parlour of a public-house, coffee room. **—s=tafel,** *f.*, **—tisch,** *m.* ordinary, table d'hôte.

Wir'tel, *m.* (**—s,** *pl.* **—**) whorl.

Wirt'schaft, *f.* domestic economy; management of affairs; administration; working; husbandry; innkeeping; public-house; household, establishment; doings, goings on; row, disturbance; mess (*coll.*); **— treiben,** to keep an inn; **die — gut verstehen,** to be a good manager *or* housekeeper; **polnische —,** topsyturvydom (*coll.*); **die ganze —,** the whole show (*coll.*); **was ist das für eine —?** what's going on here? **eine schreckliche** *or* **schauderhafte —,** a terrible mess *or* confusion (*coll.*). **—en,** *v.n.* (*aux.* **h.**) to keep house; to manage (*a house, farm, business*); to keep an inn *or* public-house; to administer (*property*); to make a noise; **(arg, übel)** to make sad havoc, ravage, destroy, plunder; to live wildly; **gut —en,** to manage well, husband (*one's income*), to economize. **—er,** *m.* (**—ers,** *pl.* **—er**) manager; housekeeper; steward; economist. **—erin,** *f. see* **—er;** manageress, steward's wife. **—lich,** *adj.* economical, thrifty; orderly, regular; economic, domestic; belonging to a household; agricultural. **—lichkeit,** *f.* economy, husbandry, good management. *Comp.* **—s=amt,** *n.* stewardship, management of a farm *or* an estate. **—s=aufseher,** *m.* manager; steward, bailiff. **—s=beamte(r),** *m.* steward, bailiff *or* agent of an estate. **—s=betrieb,** *m.* cultivation, agriculture, farming. **—s=buch,** *n.* housekeeper's book. **—s=gebäude,** *n.* farm-buildings, offices; steward's office. **—s=geld,** *n.* household money, housekeeping-money. **—s=gerät.** *n.* household utensils. —**s=inspektor,** *m.* steward; overseer of an estate. —**s=kunst,** *f.* husbandry; economy. —**s=lehre,** *f.* economics. —**s=politik,** *f.* political economy. —**s=rechnung,** *f.* household account. —**s=regel,** *f.* economic rule. —**s=verwalter,** *m.* steward, manager. —**s=wesen,** *n.* political economy.

Wisch, *m.* (—(e)s, *pl.* —e) rag, clout; wisp; scrap of paper, waste paper; trashy writing.

Wi'sch—en, I. *v.a.* to wipe; to rub; to stump (*drawings*). II. *v.n.* (*aux.* **s.**) to whisk, slip off; **vorbei —en,** to whisk past. III. *subst.n.*; **das —en der Augen ist schädlich,** rubbing the eyes is bad for them. **—er,** *m.* (—ers, *pl.* —er) wiper; cloth, clout; stump (*for drawing*); sponge (*Artil.*); sharp reprimand, rebuff, rebuke (*coll.*). *Comp.* **—gold,** *n.* gold-leaf. **—kolben,** *m.* sponging-rod (*Artil.*). **—lappen,** *m.* rag for wiping *or* cleaning; dish-cloth; duster. **—tuch,** *n.* duster; dish-cloth. **—wasch,** *m.*, **—iwaschi,** *n.* gabble, twaddle, stuff, nonsense.

Wis'mut, *m.* & *n.* (—s) bismuth. **—en,** *v.a.* to solder with bismuth. *Comp.* **—asche,** *f.* oxide of bismuth. **—blei=erz,** *n.* bismuthic silver-ore. **—butter,** *f.* chloride of bismuth. **—oxid,** *n.* oxide of bismuth.

Wis'pel, *m.* (—s, *pl.* —) measure of corn (*of about 1300 litres or 24 bushels*) (*obs.*).

Wis'pe—ln, —rn, *v.a.* & *n.* (*aux.* **h.**) to whisper.

Wiß'—bar, *adj.* knowable. *Comp.* **—bedürfnis,** *n.* desire of knowledge. **—begier(de),** *f.* craving *or* thirst for knowledge; curiosity. **—begierig,** *adj.* desirous of knowledge; inquisitive.

Wis'sen, I. *ir.v.a.* to know; to have knowledge of; to be aware *or* informed of; to understand, to know how to; **das weiß Gott! das mag Gott —!** God knows! **nicht —, wo aus noch ein,** not to know which way to turn *or* what to do; **aus Erfahrung —,** to know by experience; **so viel ich weiß,** so far as I know, for aught I know; **was ich nicht weiß, macht mich nicht heiß,** what the eye does not see the heart rues not (*prov.*); **nicht daß ich wüßte,** not that I am aware of; **einen etwas — lassen, einem etwas (kund und) zu — thun,** to let a p. know, send word, tell s.o.; **kund und zu — sei hiemit,** be it known by these presents; **etwas auf** *or* **gegen einen —,** to know s.th. against a p.; **einem Dank —,** to be grateful to a person; **sich** (*dat.*) **viel mit einer S. —en,** to pride o.s. on a thing; **er thut, als wäre er wer weiß was,** he behaves as if he were ever so grand a person; **ich will das beendet —,** I want to see that finished; **nichts mehr von sich selbst —,** to have lost consciousness; **sich** (*dat.*) **keinen Rat —,** not to know what to do; **— Sie es gewiß?** are you sure of it? **wenn Sie es doch — wollen,** if you insist upon knowing it; **von** *or* **um etwas —,** to be acquainted with a th.; **mit um eine S. —,** to be privy to a thing; **er weiß von keiner Sorge,** he knows no care; **ich weiß mir kein größeres Vergnügen,** I know of no greater pleasure; **ich will von ihm nichts —,** I don't wish to hear anything about him, I will have nothing to do with him; **davon will er nichts —,** he will not hear of it; **etwas gethan — wollen,** to wish that a thing be done; **er will ihn glücklich —,** he wishes him to be happy; **ich weiß mich zu verteidigen,** I can defend myself; **er weiß sich in alles zu finden,** he knows how to adapt himself to all circumstances; **er wußte davon zu kommen,** he contrived to escape; **weißt du** *or* **— Sie was?** do you know? I'll tell you what; **damit du es nur weißt,** remember, understand; **—d,** knowing, initiated. II. *subst.n.* knowledge, learning; **ohne mein —,** unknown to me; **mit — und Willen,** intentionally, on purpose; **meines —s ist er nicht angekommen,** he has not come, so far as I know; **er spricht wider besseres — (und Gewissen),** he says it, though he knows the contrary to be true; he speaks against his better judgment; **mit seinem — ist es nicht weit her,** his learning is not great. **—schaft,** *f.* science; learning; knowledge; **die schönen —schaften,** belles-lettres, polite literature; **exakte —schaften,** the exact sciences; **philologisch-historische —schaften,** arts, humanities; **ich habe keine —schaft davon,** I know nothing of it (*obs.*); **—schaft ist Macht,** knowledge is power (*prov.*); **Jünger der —schaft,** man of science. **—schaft(l)er,** *m.* (—schaft(l)ers, *pl.* —schaft(l)er) man of science, learned man, true scholar; **Natur-—schaftler,** scientist. **—schaftlich,** *adj.* scientific; scholarly; learned; **das —schaftliche Studium der neueren Sprachen,** the scientific study of modern languages; **—schaftliche Bildung haben,** to have received a scholarly training, to be a scholar; **—schaftlich gebildet,** learned, scholarly. **—schaftlichkeit,** *f.* scientific method, character *or* arrangement. **—tlich,** *adj.* knowing, conscious; wilful, deliberate. *Comp.* **—schafts=drang, —schafts=durst,** *m.* thirst *or* craving for knowledge. **—schafts=lehre,** *f.* theory of sciences, philosophy. **—s=drang, —s=durst,** *m.* desire for knowledge. **—s=wert, —s=würdig,** *adj.* worth knowing, interesting. **—s=würdigkeit,** *f.* value or interest of a science; interesting fact. **—s=zweig,** *m.* branch of knowledge *or* learning.

Wis'ser, *m.* (—s, *pl.* —) one who knows.

Wißmut, *see* **Wismut.**

Wit—frau, *f. see* **—we. —ib,** *f.* (*obs.*) *see* **—we. —mann,** *m.* (*rare*) *see* **—wer. —tum,** *n.* (—tums, *pl.* —tume *and* —tümer) widow's jointure, dowry, settlement. **—we,** *f.* (*pl.* —wen) widow; dowager; **zur —we gemacht** *or* **geworden,** widowed; **Kaiserin —we,** empress dowager. **—wen=schaft,** *f.*, **wen=tum,** *n.* widowhood. **—wer,** *m.* (—wers, *pl.* —wer) widower. *Comp.* **—wen=gehalt,** *n.* widow's jointure, allowance *or* pension. **—wen=jahr,** *n.* year of mourning; *see* **Gnadenjahr. —wen=kasse,** *f.* widows' fund. **—wen=kleid,** *n.* widow's weeds. **—wen=schatz,** *m.* dower. **—wen=sitz,** *m.* dowager's estate. **—wen=stand,** *m.* widowhood. **—wen=stuhl,** *m.*; **den —wen-stuhl verrücken,** to marry again (*said of a widow*) (*obs.*). **—wen=trauer,** *f.* widow's weeds. **—wen=verbrennung,** *f.* (**in Indien**), suttee. **—wer=leben,** *n.* life of a widower.

Wit'ter—n, *v.a.* & *n.* (*aux.* **h.**) to scent, smell, perceive; **nach einer S. —n,** to smell about for s.th.; **etwas —n,** to scent s.th. out; **er —t überall nur Sünde,** he is always suspecting evil, is on the lookout for iniquity; **ich —e Morgenluft,** I scent the morning air; **Unrat —n,** to smell a rat. **—ung,** *f.* weather, state of the atmosphere; temperature; scent; trail; **bei günstiger —ung,** (wind and) weather permitting; **von einer S. —ung bekommen,** to get scent of a th. *Comp.* **—ungs=anzeichen,** *n.* meteorological sign. **—ungs=bericht,** *m.* meteorological report. **—ungs=einwirkung,** *f.* influence of the weather. **—ungs=forscher, —ungs=kundiger,** *m.* meteorologist. **—ungs=kunde, —ungs=lehre,** *f.* meteorology. **—ungs=verhältnisse,** *pl.* atmospheric *or* meteorological conditions. **—ungs=wechsel,** *m* change of weather.

Witz, *m.* (—es, *pl.* —e) wit, wittiness, esprit; sense, understanding; witticism, joke, pun; witty sally, repartee; imagination, inventive faculty, literary faculty (*obs.*); drinking-bout (*sl.*); dance; affair; **schlagfertigen — haben,** to be good at repartee, have a ready wit; **faule**

—e machen, to make bad jokes; to play silly practical jokes; alter —, stale joke; guter —, capital joke; beißender —, caustic wit, sarcasm; einen — reißen *or* machen, to crack a joke; das ist ja eben der —, that 's the fun of it; das ist der ganze —, that 's all, that is the point of it (*coll.*). —elei', *f.* attempted wit; continual (*forced*) jesting; bad pun *or* joke. —eln, *v.n.* (*aux.* h.) to affect wit; to laugh at, turn into ridicule; to pun; über einen —eln, to be witty at another's expense. —ig, *adj.* witty; having esprit, bright, intelligent, clever; brilliant; piquant; —iger Einfall, witty idea; —ige Entgegnung, clever repartee; —iger Kopf, bel esprit, man of letters, wit, person interested in literature (*obs.*). —igen, *v.a.* to make wiser, teach a lesson. —igung, *f.* (*obs.* —ung) teaching (a p.) wit; warning; example, lesson. —ler, *m.* (—lers, *pl.* —ler), —ling, *m.* (—lings, *pl.* —linge) would-be wit. *Comp.* —blatt, *n.* comic journal *or* paper. —bold, *m.* witty fellow, wit, wag; punster. —(es)=funke(n), *m.* flash of wit. —los, *adj.* wanting in wit *or* intelligence; stupid, insipid, tame, dull. —reißer, *see* —bold. —wort, *n.* bon-mot, witty remark.

Wo, I. *inter. adv.* where; in what place; how (*sl.*); ich weiß, — er ist, I know where he is, I know his whereabouts; — sie auch sein mögen, wherever they may be; — werd' ich so dumm sein? do you think I'm a fool? (*sl.*); i —! what are you thinking of? I should never think of such a thing! (*sl.*). II. *rel. adv.* (= *a rel. pron. & prep.*) where; in, on, at which (*place, etc.*); at which (*time*), when, that; if, in which case; das Haus, — ich wohne, the house in which I live; er wandte sich nach England, (als) — die meiste Freiheit ist, he turned to England as the country enjoying the greatest liberty; zu einer Zeit, — Sie abwesend waren, at a time when you were absent; den Augenblick, — sie im Garten ist, ist er auch da, the moment she is in the garden, he is there too; — man singt, da laß dich ruhig nieder, in a place where people sing you may quietly settle. III. *ind. pronominal adv.;* ich habe es — gefunden, I found it somewhere (*coll.*). IV. *conj.;* — nicht, if not, unless; — ich nicht irre, if I am not mistaken; — du das thust! take care not to do it! (*coll.*). V. *n.* es kommt auf das — an, it depends on where it is. *Comp.* —bei', *inter. & rel. adv.* (= *inter. or rel. pron. with prep.*) whereby, whereat, near, at *or* in connection with which *or* what (= bei welchem, 2c.); es geschieht nichts, —bei nicht sein Name ins Spiel käme, nothing is done without his name appearing; —bei mir einfällt, and that brings to my mind; — bei es sein Bewenden hatte, and there the matter ended. —du'rch, *inter. & rel. adv.* (= *rel. pron. with prep.*) whereby, through *or* by means of which *or* what (= durch was, welches, 2c.). —fe'rn, *conj.* if, in case of, provided that, so far as. —fü'r, *inter. & rel. adv.* (= *inter. or rel. pron. with prep.*) wherefore; for which, for what; (= für was welches 2c.); —für ist das gut? what is that good for? —für halten Sie mich? what do you take me for? —für er auch gehalten wird, whatever one may think of him; er ist das nicht, —für er angesehen sein will, he is not what he wishes to pass for. —ge'gen, *inter. & rel. adv.* (= *inter. or rel. pron. with prep.*) against which, what; in return *or* exchange for which *or* what; (= gegen was, welches, welche(n)). —he'r, *inter. & rel. adv.* (= *inter. or rel. pron. with prep.*) whence, from whence, from which *or* what place; how; —her wissen Sie das? how do you know that? —her er auch kommen mag, wherever he may come from. —hi'n, *inter. & rel. adv.* (= *inter. or rel. pron. with prep.*) whither, what way, to *or* toward what place; —hin gehen Sie, *or* (*more usually*) wo gehen Sie hin? where are you going to? der Ort —hin ich gehe, the place I am going to; (*as n.*) diese Präposition regiert den Accusativ auf die Frage „—hin?" this preposition governs the accusative in answer to the question "whither?" —hina'b, *inter. & rel. adv.* (= *inter. or rel. pron. with prep.*) down which *or* what, at the foot of which *or* what. —hinau's, *inter. & rel. adv.* (= *inter. or rel. pron. with prep.*) to what place, which way; out at what place; —hinaus das führen soll, weiß ich nicht, I don't know where that will lead to *or* end. —hinge'gen, *conj.* whilst, whereas. —hin'ter, *inter. & rel. adv.* (= *inter. or rel. pron. with prep.*) behind *or* after what *or* which; (= hinter was, welchem, 2c.). —mi't, *inter. & rel. adv.* (= *inter. or rel. pron. with prep.*) wherewith, with *or* by which *or* what; (= mit welchem, 2c.); das ist's —mit ich nicht zufrieden bin, that is what I am not satisfied with. —na'ch, *inter. & rel. adv.* (= *inter. or rel. pron. with prep.*) whereafter, whereupon, after *or* towards *or* according to which *or* what (= nach welchem, 2c.); —nach fragt er? what is he asking for *or* about? —ra'n, —rau'f, —ri'n, *see* Wor—. —se'lbst, *adv.* where. —vo'n, *inter. & rel. adv.* (= *inter. or rel. pron. with prep.*) whereof, of *or* concerning which *or* what (= von welchem, 2c.). —vo'r, *inter. & rel. adv.* (= *inter. or rel. pron. with prep.*) of, from *or* before which *or* what (= vor welchem, 2c.); —vor fürchtest du dich? what are you afraid of? —zu', I. *inter. & rel. adv.* (= *inter. or rel. pron. with prep.*) whereto, to what purpose; why; to, for, at *or* in addition to what *or* which (= zu was, welchem, 2c.); —zu das? what is that for? why that? —zu man Lust hat, what one is inclined for. II. *ind. pron.* wir müssen uns —zu entschließen, we must decide on something (*coll.*).

Wob, *1 & 3 p. sing. imperf. ind.;* **Wö'be,** *1 & 3 p. sing. imperf. subj. of* weben.

Wo'che, *f.* (*pl.* —n) week; künftige —, next week; stille —, Passion week; ich habe die —, it is my week (*to serve, etc.*); in (den) —n sein, die —n halten, to be confined, lie in; in die —n kommen, to be brought to bed, to be confined; in die —n kommen mit einem Sohne, to be delivered of a son. *Comp.* —n=besuch, *m.* visit paid to a woman newly confined. —n=bett, *n.* childbed. —n=blatt, *n.* weekly paper; advertiser. —n=blättchen, *n.* local weekly newspaper. —n=einnahme, *f.* receipts during a week. —n=fieber, *n.* puerperal fever. —n=geld, *n.* weekly allowance *or* wages. —n=gesell, *m.* journeyman engaged by the week. —n=kind, *n.* newly-born child. —n=kleid, *n.* every-day dress. —n=lang, *adv.* for weeks (together). —n=lohn, *m.* weekly pay *or* wages. —n=prediger, *m.* week-day preacher. —n=predigt, *f.* week-day sermon. —n=rechnung, *f.* weekly bill. —n=schrift, *f.* weekly publication *or* magazine. —n=schüler, *m.* weekly boarder at a school. —n=stube, *f.* lying-in-room. —n=suppe, *f.* gruel, soup for a woman lying-in. —n=tag, *m.* week-day, day of the week.

Wöch—entlich, *adj. & adv.* weekly; every week; by the week; dreimal —entlich, three times a week; vier —entlich, recurring every 4 weeks, monthly; letzt—entlich, last week's. —ig, *adj.* (*only in cpds.*); vier—ig, lasting 4 weeks; 4 weeks old. —ner, *m.* (—ners, *pl.* —ner) person on (weekly) duty. —nerin, *f.* woman in child-bed; Hospital für —nerinnen, lying-in hospital.

Wo'cke(n), *m.* (—(e)s, *pl.* —(n)) distaff (*dial.*).

Wog, *1 & 3 p. sing. imperf. ind.;* **Wö'ge**, *1 & 3 p. sing. imperf. subj. of* wägen; wiegen.

Wo'g—e, *f.* (*pl.* —en) wave, billow. **—en**, *v.n.* (*aux.* h.) to surge; to heave; to fluctuate; to undulate. **—ig**, *adj.* wavy, billowy; surging. *Comp.* **—en=drang**, *m.* rushing of waves. **—en=getöse**, *n.* roars of waves. **—en=prall**, *m.* dashing of waves. **—en=schwall**, *m.* surging of waves. **—en=weise**, *adv.* in waves.

Wohl, (*sometimes spelt* Wol). I. (—er & besser, am —sten) *adv.* (*accented*) well; — bekomm's (Ihnen)! much good may it do you! leben Sie —! farewell! — berechnet, well calculated; ein Wirt hat sich — in Acht zu nehmen, a landlord has to be on his guard *or* very careful; wieder — werden, to recover from an illness; sich (*dat.*) 's — sein lassen, to enjoy o.s.; ich fühle mich am —sten, wenn ich allein bin, I am happiest when alone; — oder übel, Sie müssen mitkommen, whether or no, you must come with us; es thut mir —, wenn, it does me good when, I feel happy when; ich sehe —, I see clearly; ich wünsche Ihnen — zu schlafen, I wish you a good night; — ihm, daß er das nicht erlebt hat! well for him that he has not lived to see that; — dem, der . . ., happy he, who . . .; den Toten ist —, the dead are happy —; —! (*sailor's answer to a command of the boatswain*) aye, aye, sir! all right, sir! II. *part.* (*without any stress*) indeed; to be sure; forsooth; perhaps, probably; I wonder; I presume, I daresay; es sind — drei Jahre, daß . . ., it is about three years since . . .; es waren ihrer — zwanzig, there were probably twenty of them; du hättest — kommen können, you might very well have come; dies ist — Ihr Bruder? this is your brother, I presume? ich verstehe mich — selbst nicht, very likely I don't understand myself; er hat — Geld, aber . . ., it is true that he has money, but . . .; siehst du —, daß ich Recht hatte? do you see now that I was right? heute nicht, — aber morgen, not to-day, but perhaps to-morrow; das könnte — sein, es kann — sein, that may well be, that is very possible; ich möchte — wissen, I should like to know; er irrt sich —, he is probably wrong, I fear he is mistaken; ich habe es — gedacht, I thought as much; er wird es — nicht mit Fleiß gethan haben, he did not do it intentionally, I suppose; ob er mich — noch kennt! I wonder whether he still knows me! ob er — krank ist? I wonder if he is ill? ja —! surely, of course, yes, indeed. III. *n.* (—s) weal, welfare, well-being, advantage; prosperity; health; auf Ihr —! to your very good health! here 's to you! das gemeine —, the common weal, the good of the commonwealth; — und Wehe, weal and woe. **—ig**, *adj.* happy, cheerful, content; nice; pleasant, comfortable. *Comp.* **—achtbar**, *adj.* right honourable; worshipful. **—a'n**, I. *adv.* boldly. II. *int.* come on! well! now then; —an, es sei darum! done! all right! **—an=ständig**, *see* Anständig. **—anständigkeit**, *f.* decorum, propriety. **—au'f**, I. *adv.*; er ist —auf, he is well. II. *int.* cheer up! come on! well then! arouse ye! up! **—bedacht**, I. *adj.* well thought on *or* over, well considered, deliberate. II. *adv.* deliberately, on purpose, considerately. III. *n.*; mit —bedacht, after mature reflection. **—bedächtig**, *see* —bedacht I. **—befinden**, *n.* good health; well-being. **—befugt**, *adj.* well qualified, justly entitled. **—begabt**, *adj.* richly endowed, highly gifted. **—begütert**, *adj.* well off, rich. **—behagen**, *n.* feeling of comfort *or* ease. **—behalten**, *adj.* safe and sound; in good condition. **—belaubt**, *adj.* leafy. **—beleibt**, *adj.* corpulent, stout, fat. **—beschaffen**, *adj.* well-conditioned. **—bestallt**, *adj.* duly installed. **—edel(geboren)**, *adj.* honourable, high and noble. **—ehrwürden**, *f.*; Ew. (Euer) —ehrwürden, your Reverence. **—ehrwürdig**, *adj.* reverend. **—erfahren**, *adj.* (thoroughly) experienced. **—ergehen**, *n.* prosperity. **—fahrt**, *f.* welfare, weal; öffentliche —fahrt, general welfare, common weal. **—fahrts=ausschuß**, *m.* committee of public safety (*Hist.*). **—fahrts=einrichtungen**, *pl.* workingmen's benefit institutions. **—fahrts=polizei**, *f.* board of sanitary inspectors. **—feil**, *adj.* cheap; am —feilsten, at the lowest price; —feil ist nicht billig, bargains are costly (*prov.*); —feilen Kaufs davon kommen, to get off cheaply *or* easily. **—feilheit**, *f.* cheapness. **—geartet**, *adj.* well-disposed; well-bred. **—gebaut**, *adj.* well-made. **—gebildet**, *adj.* well-shaped. **—geboren**, *adj.*; —geborener Herr! sir! Sr. (Seiner) —geboren dem Herrn W. B., W. B., Esq. **—gefallen**, *n.* pleasure, satisfaction; sich in —gefallen auflösen, to finish to every-one's satisfaction; to come to nothing, to end in smoke (*coll.*). **—gefällig**, *adj.* agreeable; satisfactory; etwas —gefällig aufnehmen, to take a thing well, receive with pleasure; etwas Gott —gefälliges, a thing well pleasing to God. **—gefühl**, *n.* pleasant feeling. **—gemeint**, *adj.* well-intentioned; friendly. **—gemut**, I. *adj.* joyous, gay. II. *n.* common marjoram. **—geneigt**, *adj.* well-disposed, well-affected, favourable, kind. **—geruch**, *m.* pleasing odour, sweet scent, perfume. **—geschmack**, *m.* pleasant taste, flavour; —geschmack bringt Bettelsack, a lordly taste makes a beggar's purse (*prov.*). **—gesinnt**, *adj.* well disposed. **—gesittet**, *adj.* well-mannered, well brought up. **—gestalt**, *f.* fine shape *or* form. **—gestalt(et)**, *adj. see* —gebildet. **—getroffen**, *adj.* very successful; strikingly like, speaking (*of pictures*); well-met; well-hit. **—gewogen**, *see* —geneigt. **—gewogenheit**, *f.* kindness, affection. **—habend**, *adj.* wealthy, well-to-do, well-off. **—habenheit**, *f.* easy circumstances, affluence. **—häbig**, *adj.* wealthy. **—klang**, *m.* pleasing sound; euphony, harmony, melody. **—klingend**, *adj.* harmonious, musical; sonorous; euphonious. **—laut**, *see* —klang. **—lautend**, *adj.* euphonious. **—leben**, *n.* life of pleasure; luxury, good living. **—löblich**, *adj.* highly esteemed. **—meinend**, *adj.* well-meaning, friendly. **—redend**, *adj.* eloquent. **—redenheit**, *f.* facility in speaking; eloquence. **—riechend**, *adj.* sweet-scented, fragrant, perfumed; —riechende Wicken, sweet peas; —riechende Öle, perfumes. **—schmeckend**, *adj.* savoury, nice, delicate, tasty, palatable. **—sein**, *n.* good health. **—stand**, *m.* well-being; wealth, comfort. **—that**, *f.* benefit, kindness, favour; good deed; what does one good; bei solcher Hitze ist ein Bad eine wahre —that, a bath in such hot weather is a real blessing. **—thäter(in**, *f.*), *m.* benefactor (benefactress). **—thätig**, *adj.* beneficent; charitable; salutary. **—thätigkeit**, *f.* charity, beneficence. **—thätigkeits=anstalt**, *f.* charitable institution. **—thätigkeits=verein**, *m.* benevolent society, charity organization society. **—thuend**, *adj.* salutary, comforting. **—thun**, *ir.v.n.* (*aux.* h.) (*sep.*) to benefit; to do good; to be pleasing to; das thut einem —, that does one good, is pleasant; —thun trägt Zinsen, he who gives to the poor lends to the Lord (*prov.*). **—verdient**, *adj.* just, well-merited. **—verhalten**, *n.* good conduct. **—weise**, *adj.* most wise. **—weislich**, *adv.* prudently, prudentially. **—wollen**, I. *ir.v.n.* (*aux.*

h.) (*sep.*) (einem) to wish a p. well. II. *subst.n.* good-will, benevolence, kind feeling; —wollen hegen gegen . . ., to cherish kind feelings towards . . . —wollend, *adj.* kind, benevolent.

Wohn'bar, *adj.* habitable. —keit, *f.* habitable condition.

Woh'n—en, *v.* I. *n.* (*aux.* h.) to dwell, lodge, live, reside; to exist, to be (*obs.*); er —t bei meinem Bruder, he lives at my brother's, with my brother; vorigen Sommer —ten wir auf dem Lande, last summer we stayed in the country; Vögel —en auf Bäumen, birds lodge in trees; die Hoffnung —t in seinem Herzen, hope lives in his heart; so wahr ein Gott im Himmel —t, as true as there is a God in Heaven; es —et Lieb bei Liebe darzu groß Herzeleid, there is joy connected with love, but also great sorrow. II. *r.;* es —t sich dort sehr angenehm, living there is very pleasant. —bar, *adj.* habitable. —barkeit, *f.* habitable condition. —haft, *adj.* living, dwelling, resident; sich an einem Orte —haft niederlassen, to settle in a place; —haft sein, to be an inhabitant of, to dwell *or* reside in. —lich, *adj.* comfortable, commodious. —lichkeit, *f.* comfort, commodiousness (*of a house, etc.*). —ung, *f.* dwelling, residence, habitation; house, mansion; lodgings, rooms. *Comp.* —gebäude, —haus, *n.* dwelling-house; manor-house. —ort, *m.* place of residence, dwelling-place, home. —sitz, *m.* fixed dwelling, residence; seat. —stätte, *f. see* —ort. —stube, *f.*, —zimmer, *n.* sitting-room. —ungs=anzeiger, *m.* directory. —ungs=geber, *m.* lodging-house keeper. —ungs=geld=zuschuß, *m.* allowance for lodging *or* rent. —ungs=kosten, *pl.* rent of house *or* rooms. —ungs=los, *adj.* houseless, homeless. —ungs=nachweis, *m.* information as to lodgings. —ungs=vermieter, *see* —ungsgeber. —ungs=(ver)änderung, *f.* change of house *or* lodgings, removal, change of address. —zins, *m.* rent.

Woi'lach, *m.* (—s, *pl.* —e) horse rug, folded saddle-blanket, thick blanket (*Mil.*).

Woiwo'de, *m.* (—n, *pl.* —n), voivode, waywode.

Wol, 2c., *see* Wohl, 2c.

Wöl'b—en, *v.a.* to vault, arch; sich —en, to arch, vault, spring; einen Weg —en, to raise a road in the centre, to barre a road; gewölbt, arched, vaulted, convex; gewölbter Gang, arched passage; gewölbter Keller, vault. —ung, *f. see* Gewölbe; arch, bow, bend; convexity; —ung des Gaumens, roof of the mouth. *Comp.* —(e)=dach, *n.* vaulted roof. —fläche, *f.* (äußere) extrados; (innere) intrados. —höhe, *f.* curve, elevation of an arch. —stein, *m.* voussoir; keystone. —stütze, *f.* centring (*Arch.*).

Wolf, *m.* (—es, *pl.* Wöl'fe) wolf; abrasion (*of the skin*); whitlow; lump, pig (*of metal*); devil (*Metall.*); square hole (*Metall.*); surplus metal (*Metall.*); snuff (*of a candle*); rammer, pile-driver; ridge-beam (*of a roof*); lower counter (*of a ship*); willow, wool-cleaner; cotton-opener; der — heult, the wolf howls; reißende Wölfe, ravening wolves; Wolf im Schafspelz, wolf in sheep's clothing; wenn man den — nennt, so kommt er gerennt, *or* wenn man vom —e spricht, ist er nicht weit, speak of the devil and he appears (*prov.*); sich (*dat.*) einen — reiten, to chafe the skin by riding; Schaf und —, (game of) fox and geese; mit den Wölfen muß man heulen, to do at Rome as the Romans do (*prov.*); den — zum Hirten machen, to set the wolf to guard the sheep. —en, *v.a.* to clean (*cotton or wool*) with the willow, to willow. *Comp.* —s=angel, *f.* wolf-trap, caltrop (*Sport*). —s=art, *f.* wolfish nature; species of wolf. —s=balg, *m.* wolf's skin. —s=bohne, *f.* lupine. —s=brut, *f.* pack of young wolves. —s=eisen, *n.* wolf-trap; caltrop; spear; bloom-iron. —s=falle, *f.* wolf-trap. —s=gebiß, *n.* bit for hard-mouthed horses. —s=grube, *f.* pit for catching wolves; pitfall; covered pit (*Fort.*). —s=hetze, *f.* wolf baiting. —s=hund, *m.* wolf-dog. —s=hunger, *m.* canine appetite, ravenous hunger. —s=jäger, *m.* wolf-hunter, wolfer. —s=kirsche, *f.* deadly nightshade (*Bot.*). —s=lager, *n.* wolf's haunt *or* den. —s=magen, *m.* wolf's stomach; ravenous appetite (*fig.*). —s=milch, *f.* wolf's milk; spurge (*Bot.*). —s=pelz, *m.* wolf's fur. —s=rachen, *m.* malformation of the palate (*Med.*). —s=schlucht, *f.* wolves' glen. —s=sucht, *f.* lycanthropy.

Wöl'f—chen, *n.* (—chens, *pl.* —chen) little *or* young wolf, wolf's cub. —in, *f.* she-wolf. —isch, *adj.* wolfish. —lein, *n. see* —chen.

Wol'fram, *n.* (—s) wolfram, tungsten (*Chem.*). *Comp.* —sauer, *adj.* tungstic.

Wölk'—chen, *n.* (—chens, *pl.* —chen) little cloud; film, nebula; weiße —chen, fleecy clouds. —en, *v.a. & n.* (*aux.* h.) to cloud; sich —en, (*usually* sich be —en,) to become cloudy *or* overcast.

Wol'k—e, *f.* (*pl.* —en) cloud; cloud (*for wrapping the head, etc. in*); er war wie aus den —en gefallen, he was thunderstruck, utterly astonished, amazed; he was taken aback. —en=haft, —ig, *adj.* clouded, cloudy; cloudlike. *Comp.* —en=artig, *adj.* cloudlike. —en=bildung, *f.* cloud formation. —en=bruch, *m.* cloudburst, downpour of rain. —en=himmel, *m.* cloudy region, welkin skies; cloudy sky. —en=hoch, *adj.* (as) high as the clouds. —en=kratzer, *m.* sky-scraper, very high house (*coll.*). —en=kukuksheim, *n.* cloudland; Utopia; Nephelococcygia (*in the 'Clouds' of Aristophanes*). —en=leer, —en=los, *adj.* cloudless. —en=maschine, *f.* cloud-apparatus (*Theat.*). —en=säule, *f.* pillar of cloud (*B.*). —en=schieber, (*coll.*) *m.* scene-shifter (*Theat.*); three-cornered hat. —en=umgeben, *adj.* cloud-capped, surrounded by clouds. —en=verhangen, *adj.* covered with clouds. —en=zerstreuend, *adj.* cloud-dispelling. —en=zug, *m.* passage of the clouds.

Wol'l—e, *f.* (*pl.* —en *in comm. lang., usually* Wollarten) wool; down, hair (*of rabbits, hares, etc.*); down, cotton (*Bot.*); *see* Flaum' —e spinnen, to spin wool; to pick oakum (*of prisoners*); in der —e gefärbt, ingrained; true, staunch (*fig.*); —e aufwerfen, to throw up, show nap; in der —e sitzen, to be very well off, to live in clover; keine —e bei einer S. spinnen, to gain nothing by a th.; —e lassen müssen, to come off a loser, to be fleeced; viel Geschrei und wenig —e, great boast, small roast; much ado about nothing (*prov.*). —en, *adj.* woollen. —icht, *adj.* (*obs.*) woolly; fleecy; downy; curly. —ig, *adj. see* —icht; cotton-bearing. *Comp.* —arbeit, *f.* wool-work; woollen stuff. —arbeiter, *m.* worker in wool; wool-picker, wool-dresser. —baum, *m.* wool-bearing tree; silk-cotton tree (*Bombax*). —bereiter, *m.* wool-dresser. —blume, *f.* Anthyllis (*Bot.*). —en=atlas, *m.* satin-cloth. —en=band, *n.* worsted binding *or* braid. —en=fabrik, *f.* cloth-factory, manufactory for woollen goods. —en=tuch, *n.* tweed. —(en=)waren, *pl.* woollen goods. —en=zeug, *n.* woollen cloth. —färber, *m.* wool-dyer. —faser, *f.* downy fibre. —garn, *n.* woollen yarn, wool. —gras, *n.* cotton-grass. —haar, *n.* woolly hair; single hair of wool. —handel, *m.* wool-trade. —hase, *f.* viscacha (*Zool.*). —industrie, *f.* wool-industry. —kamm, *m.* carding-comb. —kämmer, *m.* wool-carder. —kämm=maschine, *f.* wool-combing machine.

—**krämpel=maschine,** *f.* carding-machine. —**kratze,** *f.* wool-card. —**markt,** *m.* wool-market. —**reich,** *adj.* woolly. —**reißer,** *m.* wool-carder. —**sack,** *m.* sack *or* bag of wool; woolsack (*H. of Parl.*). —**scheere,** —**schur,** *f.* sheep-shearing. —**spinner,** *m.* wool-spinner; Liparis (*Ent.*). —**spinnerei',** *f.* wool-spinning; wool-factory. —**stickerei',** *f.* tapestry; wool-work, crewel-work. —**tapete,** *f.* flock-paper.

Wol'l—en, I. *ir.v.a.* to wish; to will, be willing; to please, desire, like, choose; to want, desire; to will, ordain; to intend; to have a mind; to be about (*to*), on the point (*of*); to require; to maintain, assert, insist upon; **lieber —en,** to prefer; **ich will, daß dies geschehe,** I wish that may come to pass *or* may be done; **er will gethan wissen,** he wishes *or* orders to be done; **das will ich 'mal sehen,** I should like to see that; **was —en Sie von mir?** what do you want of me? **einem wohl —en,** to wish a p. well; **wo willst du hin,** where do you wish to go to, where are you going to? **er —te nach England,** he wished to go to England; **sie —te ihn nicht,** she would not have him (*coll.*); **zu wem —en Sie?** whom do you want to see? **ich will mich gern geirrt haben,** I should be glad to think I was mistaken, perhaps I was mistaken, I hope so; **—te Gott!** would to God! **Gott will es,** God wills it (*Crusaders' cry*); **das —e Gott nicht!** God forbid! **so Gott will,** please God; **weitere Auskunft —e man einholen bei . . .,** for (further) particulars apply to . . .; **das will ich meinen,** I should think so indeed; **ich will gern glauben, daß Sie nicht gelogen haben,** I am ready to believe you have not told a lie; **er mag —en oder nicht,** willy-nilly, whether he likes it or not; **ich —te gern zufrieden sein,** I should be quite willing to be content; **mir will scheinen,** it seems to me; **ich will nicht hoffen, daß er es thut,** I hope he will not do it; **ich will nur hoffen, daß er . . .,** I do hope that he . . .; **das will mir nicht in den Sinn,** I can't understand that; **es will mir nicht aus dem Sinn,** I can't forget it, I can't get it out of my mind; **die Sache will nicht recht vom Flecke, nicht vorwärts,** the affair does not progress; **der Deckel will nicht ab,** the lid won't come off; **ich will lieber, ich —te lieber,** I would rather, I should prefer; **ich —te lieber Steine klopfen als . . .,** I had rather break stones than . . .; **macht was Ihr —t,** do what you like, do your worst; **was willst du damit sagen?** what do you mean by that? **ohne es zu —en,** unintentionally; **er will sich schlagen,** he has a mind *or* intends to fight; **ich —te eben ausgehen, als . . .,** I was on the point of going out when . . .; **sie —te umsinken,** she was about to faint *or* on the point of fainting; **es will Nacht werden,** night is coming on; **dieser Baum will fetten Boden,** this tree requires a rich soil; **eine solche Arbeit will Zeit haben,** such work demands time; **Sie —en zu viel für diese Ware,** you want too much for this article; **er will es selbst gesehen haben,** he maintains (pretends) that he has seen it himself; **ich will es nicht gehört haben,** I shall pretend not to have heard it; **ich will nichts gesagt haben,** let it be as if I had not spoken, never mind what I have been saying; **wart'! dich will ich,** just wait! I'll soon give it you; **dem sei wie ihm —e,** be that as it may; **es sei, wo es —e,** wherever it may be; **es geschehe was da —e,** whatever may happen, happen what may; **wie gern ich auch —te,** however much I should like it; **einem in die Haare, (zu Leibe) —en,** to fall upon, attack a p.; **hoch hinaus —en,** to have grand projects; **das will etwas (nichts) sagen, heißen, &c.,** that is something, (nothing); **wir —en gehen,** let us go; *as aux.* (= **müssen,** *with negative* = **dürfen**); **diese Sache will mit Klugheit ausgeführt werden,** this affair must be carried out with prudence; **Eigensinn will früh ausgerodet werden,** obstinacy must be rooted out early; (= **werden,**) **was —en wir sagen, wenn er uns fragt,** what shall we say *or* what are we going to say if he asks us? (= **können**) **was will ich machen?** what can I do? **ich —te es schon malen,** I could paint it; **wie wollt' es euch zu Ohren kommen?** how could you (possibly) hear of it? II. *after an inf.* = *p.p.* **gewollt; ich habe nur scherzen —en,** I only intended to joke, I was only joking. III. *subst. n.* will, volition; inclination; **—en habe ich wohl, aber Vollbringen des Guten finde ich nicht,** to will is present with me, but how to perform that which is good I find not (*B.*).

Wol'l—ust, *f.* (*pl.* **—üste**) delight, bliss (*obs.*); sensual pleasure; voluptuousness; lasciviousness; lust, debauchery; **der —ust nachhängen,** to be given to sensuality *or* debauchery. —**üstig,** *adj.* voluptuous; lewd, lascivious, wanton. —**üstling,** *m.* (—**üstlings,** *pl.* —**üstlinge**) sensual person; sensualist, voluptuary; debauched person, libertine.

Won'ne, *f.* (*pl.* **—n**) joy; rapture, ecstasy; bliss; **in — schweben** *or* **schwimmen,** to be enraptured. —**sam, Wonnig, Wonniglich,** *adj.* delightful, delicious, blissful. *Comp.* —**bebend,** *adj.* trembling *or* quivering with delight. —**gefühl,** *n.* feeling of delight *or* bliss. —**graus,** *m.* shudder of delight, blissful tremor. —**kloß,** *m.* baby (*coll.*). —**leben,** *n.* blissful life. —**leer,** —**los,** *adj.* joyless. —**monat,** —**mond,** *m.* month of May (*orig.* month of pastures). —**rausch,** *m.* transport, delirium of bliss. —**schauer,** *m.* tremor of delight. —**taumel,** *m.* rapturous intoxication, ecstasy. —**thränen,** *pl.* tears of joy *or* delight. —**trunken,** *adj.* intoxicated *or* overbrimming with bliss, enraptured. —**voll,** *see* —**sam.**

Wor, *see* **Wo** (*used as* **wo** *and instead of it in cpds. with a prep. beginning with a vowel; in older German not unfrequently in cpds. with a prep. beginning with a cons., e.g.* **wormit** *for which see* **womit,** *etc.; such cpds. equalling a case of the inter. or rel. pron.* **wer, was, welcher, der,** *governed by the prep. with which it is compounded. As a rule the prep. bears an equal or stronger accent than* **wor,** *but* **wor** *takes the stress if the interrogative force is to be specially emphasized, e.g.* **woran denken Sie?** what are you thinking of? **wo'ran denken Sie?** what is it you are thinking of? —**an,** I. *inter. & rel. adv.* whereon, whereat, on, of, against *or* by which *or* what; **das Buch, —an ich arbeite,** the book which I am engaged in writing; **ich weiß nicht, —an ich mit ihm bin,** I don't know what to make of him; **—an bin ich?** where have I got to? where did I leave off? **der Kasten, —an er sich mit dem Kopfe gestoßen,** the chest against which he struck his head; **—an liegt es, daß . . .?** what is the cause that (*or* of) . . .? **—an hat er mich erkannt?** by what (*how*) did he recognize me? **—an hielt es?** what was it fastened to? II. *ind. pron.;* (*coll.*) **du mußt doch —an gedacht haben,** but you must have thought of something. —**auf,** *inter. & rel. adv.* whereupon, upon, to *or* at which *or* what; —**auf sinnst du?** what are you meditating on? **—auf alle fort gingen,** whereupon every one went away. —**aus,** *inter. & rel. adv.* by, out of *or* from which *or* what, whence. —**ein,** *inter. & rel. adv.* (*now rare and usually replaced by* **wohinein, in was, in den**) whereinto, into which *or* what; das ist etwas —ein ich mich nicht mische, that is a thing I don't meddle with; der Schrank —ein ich es verschlossen habe, the cupboard in which I have locked it up. —in, *inter. & rel. adv.* whereat, in which *or* what. —über, *inter. & rel. adv.* wherein, whereof, of, at, over *or* upon which *or* what; —über lachst du? what are you laughing at? das ist es, —über ich mich wundere, that is what astonishes me; —über ich sehr ärgerlich war, at which I was very angry. —um, *inter. & rel. adv.* for which; —um handelt es sich? what is it about? what is the matter? —unter, *inter. & rel. adv.* in, under, among *or* betwixt which *or* what; —unter hatte er sich versteckt? under what had he concealed himself? —unter soll ich Sie zählen? where (*in what row, rank, etc.*) shall I put you? die verbotenen Bücher, —unter auch dieses gehört, the prohibited books, of which this is one; die Papiere —unter, the papers among which.

Wor'den, *p. p. of* werden.

Wor'f—el, *f.* (*pl.* —eln) winnowing shovel. —e(l)n, *v.a.* to fan, winnow. —ler, *m.* (—lers, *pl.* —ler) winnower. *Comp.* —maschine, *f.* fan, winnowing-machine. —schaufel, *f.* winnowing-shovel. —tenne, *f.* winnowing-floor.

Wort, *n.* (—es, *pl. when signifying* single unconnected words *usually* Wörter; *in all other cases* Worte) word; term; expression; speech; saying; word of honour, promise, pledge; language; scripture; watchword (*Mil.*); Word (*B.*); ein — von etwas fallen lassen, to let fall a word, drop a hint of s. th.; das — führen, to be spokesman; das große — haben, to speak authoritatively, to lead the conversation; das große — führen, to swagger, boast, draw the long bow; nicht zu —e kommen, not to get an opportunity of speaking; einen nicht zu —e kommen lassen, not to allow a p. to put a word in; das — ergreifen, to begin to speak; ums — bitten, to beg permission to speak (*Parl. etc.*); das — erhalten, to be allowed to speak; to catch the Speaker's eye (*Parl. etc.*); das — haben, to be in possession *or* have the ear of the House (*Parl.*); einem das — entziehen, to refuse a p. the permission to continue; das — abtreten, to allow another person to speak; mit einem —e, in a word; mit wenigen —en, in a few words, briefly; man kann sein eigenes — nicht hören, one can't hear one's own voice; ein gutes — findet einen guten Ort, a good (kind) word is never lost (*prov.*); einem (einer Sache) das — reden, to speak for, in favour of, defend a p. (a th.); kein sterbendes — *or* Sterbens —, not a single word, not a sound, not a whisper; ein — gab das andere, one word produced another; einem das — im Munde verdrehen, to misinterpret what s.o. says; ein Edelmann im wahrsten Sinne des —es, a nobleman in the truest sense of the word; kein — über eine S. verlieren, to waste no words about a matter; ohne viele —e zu machen, to cut a long story short; er macht nicht viele —e, he is a man of few words; er läßt ein — mit sich reden, he listens to reason; das — an einen richten, to address a p.; er will es nicht — haben, he will not own it; ich will Ihnen besser — halten, als Sie es mir gehalten haben, I will keep my promise to you, better than you kept yours to me; nicht — halten, to break one's word; ein Mann, ein —! word of honour! honour bright! aufs —, on one's word, on trust, on parole; auf seine —e hin, according to him; auf jemandes — schwören, to pin one's faith to a p., to believe implicitly in the statements of a p.; aufs — gehorchen, to obey implicitly; ich komme nur auf ein paar —e, I only come to have a few words with you, may I have just a word with you? ich verlasse mich auf Ihr —, I rely on your word, I depend on your promise; er gab mir sein — darauf, daß er 2c., he gave me his word that he would, *etc.*; er nahm mich beim —e, he took me at my word; bei diesen —en, at these words; einem ins — fallen, to interrupt a p. in speaking; er brach in die —e aus, he cried, he burst out; mit ausdrücklichen —en, in express terms; mit dürren —en, dryly, clearly, explicitly; nach den —en, die unter uns gefallen sind, after the words that have passed between us; den —en nach verstehen, to take literally; er ist ein Mann von —, he is as good as his word; ein — zu seiner Zeit, a word spoken in season; seinen Gedanken —e leihen, to clothe one's thoughts in words; kein — mehr! not another word! dein — in Ehren, aber es ist schwer zu glauben, with due deference to you, I can scarcely believe it; das — des Rätsels, the solution of the enigma; geflügelte —e, household words, familiar quotations. *Comp.* —ableitung, *f.* derivation of words, etymology. —accent, *m.* accent of the word, natural accent (*as distinguished from* Versaccent, *metrical accent*). —ähnlichkeit, *f.* affinity of words, resemblance between words (of different languages). —arm, *adj.* poor *or* deficient in words. —armut, *f.* poverty of words. —art, *f.* part of speech (*Gram.*); kind of word. —bau, *m.* structure of words. —bedeutung, *f.* meaning *or* significance of words. —bedeutungs-lehre, *f.* science of the meaning and changes of meaning of words, semantics. —betrug, *m.* sophism. —biegung, *f.* accidence, inflection. —bildung, *f.* word-formation; etymology. —bruch, *m.* breach of one's word. —brüchig, *adj.* false to one's word; — brüchig werden, to break one's word. —brüchigkeit, *f.* faithlessness; breach of promise (*Law*). —erklärung, *f.* verbal explanation; definition. —fechterei', *f.* haggling about words. —folge, *f.* order *or* sequel of words. —forscher, *m.* philologist, etymologist. —forschung, *f.* study of words, etymology. —fügung, *f.* syntax, structure of phrases. —fügungslehre, *f.* syntax. —führer, *m* speaker; spokesman; foreman (*of a jury*). —fülle, *f.* verbosity; richness of vocabulary. —gefecht, *n.* dispute, debate. —geklingel, *n.* jingle of words. —gepränge, *n.* bombast. —geschichte, *f.* history of a word; etymology. —getreu, *adj.* word for word, literal. —gläubig, *adj.* having faith, trusting in what is written, said; orthodox, believing the scripture. —habend, *adj.* being the speaker; presiding. —halter, *m.* speaker, first representative of a town council. —kampf, *m. see* —gefecht. —karg, *adj.* laconic, taciturn. —kargheit, *f.* taciturnity. —klauber, *m.* hypercritic, pedant. —klauberei', *f.* dabbling in words. —kram, *m.* verbiage, windy, wordy talk; verbosity. —krämer, *m.* verbose person; windy talker. —künstelei', *f.* affectation of style *or* in language; subtlety, sophistry. —laut, *m.* the wording (*of a document, etc.*), text, terms; sound of a word. —macher, *m.* word-coiner; verbose speaker; idle talker. —macherei', *f.* verbiage, big talk. —mangel, *m. see* —armut. —rätsel, *n.* enigma. —register, *n.* vocabulary; index of words. —reich, *adj.* abundant in words; fluent; wordy, verbose. —schatz, *m.* vocabulary, words in use (*by a people, etc.*). —schwall, *m.* verbosity; balderdash, bombast, fustian. —schwulst, *m.* tall talk, bombast; balderdash. —sinn, *m.* literal sense. —spiel, *n.* play upon words, pun. —stellung, *f.* order of words. —streit, *m.* controversy; dispute about words. —tarif, *m.* tariff according to the number of words (*Tele.*) —verderber.

m. corrupter of language. —**verdreher,** m. distorter, perverter of words. —**verdrehung,** f. distortion of the meaning of a word or words. —**versetzung,** f. transposition of words, inversion. —**verstand,** m. literal sense. —**verwechselung,** f. mistaking one word for another, confusion of terms. —**verzeichnis,** n. see —**register.** —**vorrat,** m. see —**schatz.** —**wechsel,** m. exchange of words, discussion; altercation, dispute. —**witz,** m. see —**spiel.**

Wört'—chen, n. (—**chens,** pl. —**chen**) little word; **unabänderliches —chen,** particle. —**lich,** adj. literal, verbal, word for word; —**liche Beleidigung,** verbal insult. —**lichkeit,** f. literalness, literal character. *Comp.* —**er=buch,** n. dictionary; vocabulary; glossary; **deutsch=englisches —erbuch,** German-English dictionary; —**erbuch des allgemeinen Wissens,** enyclopædia (*of general information*). —**er=buch=schreiber,** m. lexicographer. —**er=verzeichnis,** n. list of words, vocabulary.

Wrack, I. adj. cast off, waste. II. n. (—(e)**s,** pl. —**e,** —**s**) wreck, wreckage of a stranded ship; **treibendes —,** derelict; (**Wrak, Wraking,** f.) drift, leeway. *Comp.* —**gut,** n. wrecked goods, jetsam. —**recht,** n. right of salvage. —**schiff,** n. wrecked vessel, stranded craft.

Wra'sen, m. steam (*of soup, punch*) (*dial.*).

Wri'cke—n, v.a. to scull (*a boat*), to paddle astern. —**r,** m. sculler (*from the stern*).

Wrin'g—en, v.a. to twist; to wring. *Comp.* —**maschine,** f. wringing-machine, wringer.

Wu'cher, m. (—**s,** pl. —) usury; interest; gain, profit; — **treiben,** to practise usury; **von — leben,** to live on usury; **mit — vergelten,** to repay *or* return with interest. —**ei',** f. usury, business of a usurer. —**er, Wuch'rer,** m. usurer; Jew. —**haft,** —**isch, Wuch'risch,** adj. usurious; —**isch aufkaufen,** to forestall. —**ung,** f. extuberance (*Med.*). *Comp.* —**frei,** adj. without interest *or* usury. —**geschäft,** n. usurious trade. —**gesetz,** n. law of usury. —**gierig,** adj. usurious, grasping. —**handel,** m. see —**geschäft.** —**zins,** m., —**zinsen,** pl. usurious interest.

Wucher—n, v. I. n. (*aux.* **h.**) to grow luxuriantly, to be rampant; to produce abundantly; to give a good return; to practise usury, to seek gain; to make the most of; **mit dem Gelde —n,** to lend money at usurious interest; to speculate in stocks. II. r.; **sich reich —n,** to enrich o.s. by usury. *Comp.* —**blume,** f. chrysanthemum. —**jude,** m. Jew money-lender. —**pflanze,** f. rank weed.

[1]**Wuchs** (*usually pron. with long* **u**), m. (—(s)**es,** pl. **Wüch'se**) growth; development; form, figure, shape; height; growth, shoot; **von schönem** —(s)**e,** well-grown, well-made, finely-shaped.

[2]**Wuchs,** *1 & 3 p. sing. imperf. ind.*; **Wüch'se,** *1 & 3 p. sing. imperf. subj. of* **wachsen.**

Wüch'sig, adj. that will grow well; growing, in its growth; **hoch—,** of high stature, tall.

Wucht, f. (pl. —**en**) weight, pressure, burden; bulk; fulcrum, (lever-)prop. —**en,** v. I. n. (*aux.* **h.**) to weigh heavy, lie *or* press heavily upon. II. a. to lift with difficulty, raise by lever (*rare*). —**ig,** adj. weighty, heavy.

Wüh'l—en, v.a. & n. (*aux.* **h.**) to root, grub up (*as swine the ground*); to burrow, turn up the ground; to hollow, to wash away; to rummage, to rake; to agitate, stir up; to rage; **sich in die Erde —en,** to scrape, burrow a hole for o.s. in the earth; **das Wasser hat hier gewühlt,** the water has excavated a hole here; **sich** (*dat.*) **in den Haaren —en,** to run one's hands through one's hair; **in einer Wunde —en,** to probe a wound; **der Schmerz —t mir in den Eingeweiden,** pain is gnawing at my vitals; **in seinen eigenen Eingeweiden —en,** to rage against o.s. —**er,** m. (—**ers,** pl. —**er**) one who roots up; stump orator, political agitator; revolutionary spirit, insurgent; (*pl.*) rooting animals. —**erei',** f. constant rooting *or* turning up; political agitation. —**erisch,** adj. inflammatory, seditious, mutinous.

Wu(h)'ne, f. (pl. —**n**) hole cut in the ice, ice-hole.

Wulst, m. (—**es,** pl. **Wül'ste**) & f. (pl. **Wül'ste**) swelling; pad; roll, ring (*for the head when carrying weights*); dress-improver, bustle; chignon, frisette (*for hair*); torus (*Arch.*); coussinet (*Arch.*); —**von zusammengeschlungenen Haaren im Genick,** coil of hair, chignon. —**en,** v. I. a. to form into a pad *or* roll; to puff, swell II. r. & n. (*aux.* **s.**) to puff, swell. —**ig,** adj. pad- *or* roll-shaped; stuffed, padded; puffed up, swelled. —**ige Lippen,** blubber-lips, thick lips. *Comp.* —**förmig,** adj. roll-shaped. —**haar,** n. hair rolled up in a coil.

Wund, adj. sore; galled, chafed; wounded; **sich** (*dat.*) **die Füße — gehen,** to make one's feet sore by walking; **einen — schlagen,** to beat a p. black and blue; **sich — liegen,** to get bed-sores; —**er Punkt,** sore point, weak point; —**e Stelle,** a sore spot. —**e,** f. (pl. —**en**) wound; sore; bruise, hurt; cut; **eine —e sondieren** *or* **untersuchen,** to probe a wound; **es wird seinem Kredit eine —e schlagen,** it will injure his credit. —**heit,** f. state of being wounded, sore *or* ulcerated state. *Comp.* —**arz(e)nei'=kunst,** f. surgery, surgical art. —**arz(e)nei'lich,** adj. surgical. —**arz(e)nei'=schule,** f. school of surgery. —**arzt,** m. surgeon; dresser (*in a hospital*). —**ärztlich,** adj. surgical. —**balsam,** m. vulnerary balsam. —**eisen,** n. probe. —**en=frei,** adj. unwounded, unhurt; unscathed (*poet.*). —**enmal,** n. mark of a wound, scar. —**fäden,** pl. lint. —**fieber,** n. wound-fever. —**gedrückt,** adj. galled. —**gehen,** v.r. to become footsore. —**gelaufen,** adj. foot-sore. —**mal,** see —**mal.** —**mittel,** n. surgical remedy *or* application. —**schere,** f. probe-scissors. —**schorf,** m. scab. —**sein,** n. soreness, excoriation. —**wasser,** n. lotion (*for wounds*). —**zettel,** m. surgeon's bulletin.

Wun'der, n. (—**s,** pl. —) wonder, surprise, astonishment; marvel; miracle; **es nimmt mich —, daß . . .,** I am surprised that . . .; **es sollte mich nicht — nehmen, wenn . . .,** I should not be at all surprised if . . . **es ist kein —, daß . . .,** it is no wonder that . . .; —**s halber,** for curiosity's sake; **er denkt — was er thut,** he thinks he is doing ever so much, is doing something wonderful; **ich dachte —, was es wäre,** I was all curiosity to see what it was, I expected to see wonders; **er bildet sich — 'was ein,** he thinks an extraordinary amount of himself, he considers himself a great swell; **er bildet sich —'was darauf ein,** he prides himself ever so much on it; **ich hielt sie für — wie klug,** I thought her wonderfully clever; **sein blaues — an einer S. sehen,** to marvel, be amazed at a th. —**bar,** (—**barlich,** *rare*,) adj. wonderful, amazing, surprising; marvellous; supernatural, miraculous; strange, odd; admirable. —**barkeit,** f. wonderfulness; wonder, strange thing. —**lich,** adj. strange, odd, singular, curious; whimsical, wayward; eccentric; —**licher Kauz,** odd fish, queer chap; **es ist ihm —lich ergangen,** he has met with a strange adventure; **mir wurde —lich zu Mute,** I felt very strange. —**lichkeit,** f. oddness, strangeness; whimsicality; eccentricity. —**n,** v.a. & n. (*aux.* **h.**) to wonder, marvel at; **sich über eine S. —n,** to be surprised at a th.; **ich —e mich zu hören,** I am surprised to hear; **das —t mich,** I am astonished at that, I wonder; **es soll mich doch —n, ob . . .,** I am curious to know if . . . ; **mich —t's, ob . . .**, I wonder whether . . . ; **sie —ten sich der Rede**, they were astonished at the words (*obs.*). **—sam**, *see* **—bar.** *Comp.* **—alt**, *adj.* exceedingly old. **—apfel**, *m.* balsam-apple. **—bau**, *m.* wonderful building, admirable structure. **—bild**, *n.* wonderful picture; wonderworking image. **—bilderbuch**, *n.* transformation toy-book. **—blume**, *f.* marvel of Peru (*Bot.*). **—ding**, *n.* marvel, prodigy; **—dinge von einem erzählen**, to tell wonderful things of a p. **—doktor**, *m.* quack-(doctor). **—erde**, *f.* stone-marrow, lithomarge. **—erklärung**, *f.* explanation of miracles. **—geschichte**, *f.* marvellous tale; history of miracles. **—geschöpf**, *n.* prodigy. **—glaube**, *m.* belief in miracles; miracle-working faith. **—gleich**, *adj.* miraculous; wonderfully like. **—groß**, *adj.* colossal. **—hold**, *adj.* very charming; most gracious; **das Blümchen —hold**, modesty. **—horn**, *n.* enchanted horn; **des Knaben —horn**, the Boys' Magic Horn (*collection of German popular poems, by Arnim and Brentano*). **—hübsch**, *adj.* lovely, exceedingly pretty. **—kind**, *n.* youthful prodigy. **—lampe**, *f.* magic lamp. **—lieblich**, *adj.* most lovable; most lovely. **—mann**, *m.* wonderful *or* strange man; miracle-worker. **—märe**, *f.* wonderful news, wondrous news. **—reich**, I. *adj.* wonderful, full of wonders; wonderfully rich. II. *n.* land of wonders. **—salz**, *n.* miraculous salt; Glauber's salts. **—schild**, *m.* miraculous shield. **—schön**, *adj.* wondrously beautiful, exquisite. **—selten**, *adj.* very rare (*poet.*). **—spiegel**, *m.* magic mirror. **—that**, *f.* miracle; wonderful exploit; doughty deed. **—thäter(in**, *f.*), *m.* miracle-worker; saint. **—thäterisch**, *adj.* thaumaturgical. **—thätig**, *adj.* miraculous, wonder-working. **—thätigkeit**, *f.* miraculous virtue; gift of working miracles. **—tier**, *n.* wonderful beast; monster; prodigy (*coll.*); **einen wie ein —tier anstaunen**, to look upon a p. as a prodigy. **—voll**, *adj.* wonderful; marvellous; wondrous (*poet.*). **—welt**, *f.* enchanted world; world of wonders. **—werk**, *n.* marvellous work, wonder; miracle; **ein —werk aus einer S. machen**, to make a wonder of a th. **—zeichen**, *n.* miraculous sign, portent, supernatural incident.

Wun'niglich, (*poet.*) see **Wonnig.**

Wunsch, *m.* (**—es**, *pl.* **Wün'sche**) wish, desire; thing wished for; **mir geht alles nach —**, everything is going on as well as I could wish; **einen — ausdrückend**, optative (*Gram.*); **dies Haus war schon lange mein —**, I have long wished for this house. *Comp.* **—erfüllung**, *f.* realization of one's desires. **—form**, *see* **—weise** II. **—mädchen**, *n.*, **—maid**, *f.* Valkyria. **—partikel**, *f.* optative particle. **—satz**, *m.* clause expressing a wish. **—weise**, *adv.* in the form of a wish. **—zettel**, *m.* list of what one would like for birthday *or* Christmas gifts.

Wünsch'bar, *adj.* desirable.

Wün'sch—en, *v.a.* to wish, to desire; to long for; to wish for, wish to possess; **ich —e nicht, daß er es erfährt**, I should not like him to know it; **ich —e es (Ihnen) von (ganzem) Herzen**, I wish it (for you) it with all my heart; **ich —e Ihnen einen guten Morgen**, I wish you good morning; **ich —e (Ihnen) wohl zu ruhen**, I wish you a good night's rest; **ich —e wohl geruht zu haben**, I hope you have slept well; **sich** (*dat.*) **etwas —en**, to wish for a thing; **ich —te mir einige tausend Mark mehr**, I wished I had a few thousand marks more; **einem zu etwas Glück —en**, to congratulate a p. on a thing; **sich wohin —en**, to wish to be somewhere. *Comp.* **—el=hut**, *m.*, **—el=hütlein**, *n.* wishing-cap. **—el=rute**, *f.* wishing wand, divining-rod. **—ens=wert**, **—ens=würdig**, *adj.* to be desired. desirable; **es wäre mir —enswert zu wissen**, I should much like to know.

Wupp(s), *int.* slap! bang!

Wür'be, *1 & 3 p. sing. imperf. subj. of* **werben.**

Wur'de, *1 & 3 p. sing. imperf. ind.*; **Wür'de**, *1 & 3 p. sing. imperf. subj. of* **werden.**

Wür'd—e, *f.* (*pl.* **—en**) dignity; majesty; propriety; post (of honour), office, honour, merit; **seiner —e etwas vergeben**, to compromise one's dignity *or* character; **zu den höchsten —en erhoben**, raised to the highest honours; **—en sind Bürden**, honour brings bother (*prov.*); **ich halte es unter meiner —e, ihm zu schmeicheln**, I consider it beneath me *or* my dignity to flatter him; **akademische —e**, academic honour *or* degree; **die Sache ist unter aller —e**, the matter is beneath contempt; **nach —en**, worthily; **in Amt und —en**, holding an office; in a good post, a comfortable position. **—ig**, *adv.* worthy; estimable; merited, deserving (of, *gen.*); **er ist dessen nicht —ig**, he does not deserve it. **—igkeit**, *f.* merit; dignity. **—iglich**, *adv. see* **—ig.** *Comp.* **—en=träger**, *m.* dignitary.

Wür'dig—en, *v.a.* (*acc. & gen.*) to deign, vouchsafe; to value, rate, estimate; **der du mir zu erscheinen —test**, thou who didst deign to appear to me (*obs.*); **er —te mich keiner Antwort**, he vouchsafed no answer; **er —te mich seiner Freundschaft**, he honoured me with his friendship; **nach seinem Werte —en**, to rate at one's *or* its true value; **zu —en wissen**, to know how to value, to appreciate fully. **—ung**, *f.* appreciation, estimation.

Wurf, *m.* (**—es**, *pl.* **Wür'fe**) throw, cast (*of balls, dice, a net*); line, direction, way; projection; dropping (*of young*); brood, litter; **einem in den — kommen, laufen, rennen**, to run in a p.'s way, come across s.o., fall into a p.'s hands; **einen — thun**, to throw; **Sie sind am —e**, it is your throw; **der — ist gethan, gefallen, geschehen**, the die is cast; **wem der große — gelungen, eines Freundes Freund zu sein**, whosoever has had the great fortune to be a friend unto a friend; **alles auf einen — setzen**, to stake all on one throw, to put all one's eggs in one basket; **aus einem schlimmen — den besten Vorteil ziehen**, to make the best of a bad bargain; **der — des Ungefährs**, the lottery of chance, the vicissitudes of life. *Comp.* **—angel**, *f.* fishing-line. **—anker**, *m.* kedge-anchor. **—bewegung**, *f.* projectile motion. **—blei**, *n.* sounding-lead. **—eisen**, *n.* harpoon. **—erde**, *f.* earth thrown up *or* out, rubbish, refuse. **—garn**, *n.* casting-net. **—geschoß**, *n.* projectile. **—geschütz**, *n.* mortar; catapult, ballista (*obs.*). **—haken**, *m.* grapnel. **—kraft**, *f.* projectile force. **—linie**, *f.* projectile curve, line of projection. **—maschine**, *f.* winnowing-machine; catapult. **—pfeil**, *m.* dart; javelin. **—riemen**, *m.* leash (*Falc.*). **—ring**, *m.*, **—scheibe**, *f.* quoit. **—schaufel**, *f.* round shovel, winnowing shovel *or* fan. **—scheibe**, *f.* quoit. **—speer**, **—spieß**, *m.* javelin, dart. **—stein**, *m.* stone for throwing; **flacher —stein**, quoit. **—waffe**, *m.* missile; arrow, spear, javelin. **—weise**, *adv.* in lots *or* heaps. **—weite**, *f.* stone's throw; range (*Artil.*).

Wür'fe, *1 & 3 p. sing. imperf. subj. of* **werfen.**

Wür'f—el, *m.* (**—els**, *pl.* **—el**) die; cube; hexahedron; **falsche —el**, cogged *or* loaded dice; **glückliche —el**, lucky dice, cogged dice; **—el spielen**, to play at dice; **die —el kneipen**, to cog the dice; **die —el sind gefallen**, the die is cast. **—icht**, *see* **—elförmig.** **—elig**, *adj.* cubical; checkered; crossbarred; tesselated. *Comp.* **—el=becher**, *m.* dice-box. **—el=brett**, *n.* draught-board, backgammon-board. **—el=bude**, *f.* booth in a fair where dice-playing is carried on. —el=fall, *m.* fall of the dice; number thrown. —el=form, *f.* cubic form. —el=förmig, *adj.* cubical, cube-shaped. —el=inhalt, *m.* cubic contents. —el=pasch, *m.* pair-royal. —el=spat, *m.* cubic spar, boracite. —el=spiel, *n.* game at dice; dice-playing. —el=stein, *m.* cubic stone; boracite. —el=thon, *m.* potter's clay. —el=wurzel, *f.* cube-root. —el=zahl, *f.* cube (*of a number*). —el=zoll, *m.* cubic inch.

Wür'f—eln, I. *v.n.* (*aux.* h.) to play at dice; um eine S. —eln, to throw for s.th. II. *v.a.* to cut into little squares *or* dice; to checker; gewürfelt, *see* —elig; gewürfelter Fußboden, tesselated floor *or* pavement. III. *subst.n.* dice-playing. —ler, *m.* (—lers, *pl.* —ler) dice-player.

Würg'bar, *adj.* that may be slaughtered *or* exterminated.

Wür'g—en, I. *v.n.* (*aux.* h.) & *r.* to choke; to gulp, struggle with s.th. in the throat; to retch; er —t (sich) an diesem Bissen, dieser Bissen —t ihn im Halse, this piece has stuck in his throat; an einer Arbeit —en, to work hard, laboriously at s.th. II. *v.a.* to choke; to take by the throat; to slaughter, massacre; to strangle, throttle, suffocate; etwas hinunter —en, to swallow, gulp something down. III. *subst.n.*, —ung, *f.* choking; strangling; killing; efforts made to swallow *or* to vomit; nausea; mit Hängen und —en (*coll.*), with no end of trouble, with unheard-of efforts. —er, *m.* (—ers, *pl.* —er) strangler, throttler; exterminator, destroyer; murderer. —erei', *f.* strangling, massacre. —erisch, *adj.* murderous, slaughtering. *Comp.* —birne, *f.* choking-pear. —engel, *m.* destroying angel; *see* —birne. —knebel, *m.* gag. —leine, —linie, —schnur, *f.* choking-line (*for fireworks*). —schwert, *n.*, —stahl, *m.* exterminating sword; murderous steel *or* weapon.

Wür'ken, (*obs.*) *see* Wirken.

Wurm, *m.* (—es, *pl.* Wür'mer; Wür'me (*obs.* & *poet.*)) worm; grub; vermin; serpent, snake, dragon (*obs.*, *poet.*); fancy, whim, crotchet; diseases formerly supposed to be due to a worm; whitlow; farcy; (*often n.*) helpless little child, little mite, poor little creature; auch ein — krümmt sich, even a worm will turn; einem die Würmer aus der Nase ziehen, to draw a p. out, pump a p. (*vulg.*); das war der Kopf des —es, that was where the danger lay, that was the critical point; du armes — (Würmchen)! poor little mite! den — haben, to be attacked by grubs (*Hort.*). —ig, *adj.* worm-eaten; wormy; worm-like; vexed (*obs.*); odd, eccentric. *Comp.* —abtreibend, *adj.* anthelmintic, good for acting against worms; —abtreibendes Pulver, worm-powder. —ähnlich, *adj.* worm-like. —artig, *adj.* of the nature of a worm. —arz(e)nei, *f.* vermifuge. —doktor, *m.* quack. —fieber, *n.* fever caused by worms. —förmig, *adj.* vermicular, worm-shaped. —fraß, *m.* damage done by worms; das Holz hat —fraß, the wood is worm-eaten. —fräßig, *adj.* worm-eaten. —geschwür, *n.* worm-ulcer (*in horses*). —krank, *adj.* suffering from worms. —kuchen, *m.* worm-biscuit, worm-tablet. —loch, *n.* worm-eaten hole. —mehl, *n.* worm-dust. —mittel, *n.* vermifuge, worm-medicine. —moos, *n.* anthelmintic moss. —nudeln, *pl.* vermicelli. —pille, *f.*, —plätzchen, —pulver, *n.* worm-pill, powder. —rinde, *f.* worm-bark. —samen, *m.* worm-seed, semen contra. —stich, *m.* worm-hole. —stichig, *adj.* worm-eaten, wormy. —tod, *m.* wormwood. —treibend, *see* —abtreibend.

Würm'—chen, *n.* (—chens, *pl.* —chen) little worm; poor little mite *or* chit. *Comp.* —erlehre, *f.* vermeology.

Wur'm—en, *v.a.* *usually imp.*; das *or* es —t mich, it vexes me, annoys me, I am vexed at it: das wurmt und frißt so weiter, that vexes me and goes on worrying me.

Wurst, *f.* (*pl.* Wür'ste) sausage; pudding; roll, pad; saucisson, saucisse (*Art.*, *Fort.*); fascine (*Hydr.*); dough for rolls; *see* —wagen: (*pl.* —en) piece of old cable, junk (*Naut.*); Blut—, black pudding; — machen, to make sausages; es ist mir völlig — *or* (Wurscht), it is all one to me (*sl.*); — wider —, tit for tat; brätst du mir die —, so lösch' ich dir den Durst, scratch me and I'll scratch you, one good turn deserves another; die — nach dem Manne braten, to cut one's coat according to one's cloth, to treat a p. according to his merit; mit der — nach der Speckseite werfen, to throw a sprat to catch a salmon. —eln, —en, *v.* I. *n.* (*aux.* h.) to make sausages. II. *a.* to shape like a sausage; es wird so weiter gewurstelt, we go on in the old jog-trot way (*coll.*). —erei', *f.* pork-butcher's shop (*dial.*). —ig, *adj.* *see* Wulstig, (*coll.*) indifferent, callous. —igkeit, *f.*; Zustand allgemeiner —igkeit, (*coll.*) state of complete indifference. *Comp.* —blech, *n.*, —bügel, *m.* filler for sausages. —darm, *m.* intestine, skin for sausages. —el=prater, *m.* part of Vienna Prater where popular amusements take place. —fabrikation, *f.* sausage manufacture. —fett, *n.* sausage-fat. —fleisch, *n.* sausage-meat. —händler, *m.* pork-butcher. —horn, *n.* sausage-filler. —kessel, *m.* sausage-pan, frying-pan; jetzt sitze ich im —kessel, now I am in a nice scrape (*coll.*). —kraut, *n.* seasoning-herb for sausages; marjoram. —laden, *m.* pork-butcher's shop. —lippig, *adj.* blubber-lipped. —macher, *m.* pork-butcher, sausage-maker. —maul, *n.* blubber-lipped mouth; person with thick lips. —stopf=maschine, *f.* filler for sausages. —wagen, *m.* long, narrow carriage; ammunition box of horse-artillery (*coll.*). —waren=handlung, *f.* *see* —laden.

Würst'chen, *n.* (—s, *pl.* —) small sausage; Wiener—, small Germans (*coll.*).

Wurz, *f.* (*pl.* Wür'ze), —el, *f.* (*pl.* —eln) root (*Bot.*, *Gram.*, *Math.*); foot (*of a mountain*); *see* Fuß—el, Hand—el; gelbe —eln, carrots; —el schlagen, treiben, fassen, to take *or* strike root; die —el ausziehen, to extract the root (*Math.*); mit der —el ausreißen, ausrotten, to uproot, pull up by the root(s); to eradicate. —elhaft, *adj.* radical. —(e)lig, *adj.* *see* —elartig; full of roots; rugged, uneven (*road*, *etc.*). —eln, I. *pl.* *see* Wurzel. II. *v.n.* (*aux.* h. & s.) to take *or* strike root; to send out roots; in einer S. . . . —eln, to have its root in a th. . . .; sich fest —eln, to take deep root (*in*). *Comp.* —el=artig, *adj.* of the nature of a root, rootlike. —el=ausschlag, *m.* suckers, shoots thrown out by a root. —el=ausziehen, *n.* extraction of a root. —el=auszieher, *m.* stump-forceps (*of a dentist*). —el=bildung, *f.* formation of roots. —el=blatt, *n.* radical leaf. —el=buchstabe, *m.* radical letter. —el=echt, *adj.* ungrafted. —el=exponent, *m.* exponent (*Math.*). —el=faser, *f.* rooty fibre, rootlet. —el=fest, *adj.* root-bound. —el=förmig, *adj.* root-shaped. —el=fressend, *adj.* living on roots. —el=gewächs, *n.* plant with edible roots; bulbous plants. —el=haft, *adj.* radical. —el=keim, *m.* radicle. —el=knollen, *m.* tuber, bulb. —el=knospe, *f.* turio (*Bot.*). —el=los, *adj.* without a root. —el=mehl, *n.* flour prepared from roots; cassava flour. —el=messer, *n.* root-cutter. —el=ranke, *f.* runner (*Bot.*). —el=rebe, *f.* layer from a vine. —el=reis, *n.* shoot, sucker, sprig. —el=schoß, —el=schößling, *m.* sucker, runner, layer. —el=silbe, *f.* root syllable (*Gram.*). —el=sprosse, *f.* sucker of a tree *or* shrub. —el=sprossend adj. putting forth suckers, soboliferous. —el=ständig, *adj.* radical; growing from the root. —el=stock, *m.* root-stock, rhizome. —el=stoff, *m.* radical principle *or* element, base. —el=werk, *n.* roots (*coll.*). —el=wort, *n.* radical word, root. —el=zahl, *f.* root (*of a number*). —el=zeichen, *n.* radical sign (√).

Wür'z—e, *f.* (*pl.* —en) spice; seasoning, (*brewer's*) flavouring, dressing; wort (*Brew.*); **Hunger ist die beste —e**, hunger is the best sauce (*prov.*); **Kürze ist des Lebens —e**, brevity is the soul of wit (*prov.*). **—elchen**, *n.* (—elchens, *pl.* —elchen) radicle. **—en**, *v.a.* to spice; to season; to give an aromatic odour to. **—haft**, **—ig**, *adj.* aromatic. *Comp.* **—brühe**, *f.* highly seasoned sauce. **—büchse**, *f.* spice-box. **—duft**, *m.* aroma. **—garten**, *m.* kitchen garden. **—geruch**, *m.* aromatic smell. **—kräuter**, *pl.* pot-herbs, aromatic *or* sweet herbs. **—los**, *adj.* flavourless; unspiced. **—mittel**, *n.* spice. **—stoff**, *m.* seasoning. **—weihe**, *f.* consecration of herbs (on Assumption Day). **—wein**, *m.* spiced *or* mulled wine; medicated wine.

Wusch (*usually with long* u), *1 & 3 p. sing. imperf. ind.;* **Wü'sche**, *1 & 3 p. sing. imperf. subj. of* **waschen**.

Wust (*usually with long* u), *m.* (—es) confused mass, chaos; rubbish; disgusting object; filth, dirt.

Wüst, *adj. & adv.* desert, waste, uncultivated; confused; wild, disorderly; dissolute; filthy (*prov.*); ugly (*prov.*); bad (*prov.*); **— liegen**, to lie waste; **die Erde war — und leer**, the earth was without form and void (*B.*); **der Kopf ist mir —(e) vom vielen Schreiben**, my head is quite confused with writing so much; **ein —es Leben führen**, to lead a dissolute life. **—e**, *f.* (*pl.* —en) desert, wilderness; **ein Prediger in der —e**, a voice crying in the wilderness. **—en**, *v.n.* (*aux.* h.) to live wildly (*rare*). **—enei'**, *f.* desert. **—heit**, *f.* wildness, deserted condition; wildness; dissoluteness; badness; brutality; dizziness (*of the head, etc.*). **—ling**, *m.* (—lings, *pl.* —linge) libertine, dissolute person. *Comp.* **—en=bewohner**, *m.* inhabitant of the desert. **—(en)=gerinne**, *n.* waste leat (*Hydr.*).

Wuß'te, *1 & 3 p. sing. imperf. ind.;* **Wüß'te**, *1 & 3 p. sing. imperf. subj. of* **wissen**.

Wut, *f.* rage, fury; madness; mania; **in — geraten**, to get into a rage, to fly into a passion; **in — setzen**, to enrage; **seine — an einem auslassen**, to vent one's fury on a person. *Comp.* **—anfall**, *m.* fit of rage. **—entbrannt**, *adj.* inflamed with rage, enraged. **—geschrei**, *n.* cry, howl *or* yell of rage. **—gift**, *n.* rabic poison. **—gier**, *f.* frenzy. **—krankheit**, *f.* rabies. **—schnaubend**, *adj.* breathing rage, infuriated, furious. **—voll**, *adj.* full of rage, furious.

Wü't—en, I. *v.n.* (*aux.* h.) to rage, be furious; to rage (*of disease, a storm, etc*). II. *subst. n.* raging, fury. **—end**, *p. & adj.* enraged, furious; mad, rabid; **einen —end machen**, to enrage a p. **—erich**, *m.* (—erichs, *pl.* —eriche) furious, frantic person; cruel, ruthless tyrant; butcher; barbarian. **—ig**, *adj.* furious, raging; mad, rabid.

X

X, x, *n.* X, x; unknown quantity, x (*Math.*); secret; **ein — für ein U machen**, to throw dust in a p.'s eyes, to humbug a p., (lit. to change a Five (V) into a Ten (X) by lengthening the two arms of a V below the line so as to make an X; the letter V in mediæval orthography often denotes a U); **man kann ihm kein — für ein U machen**, he is not easily taken in; **sich** (*dat.*) **ein — für ein U machen lassen**, to let o.s. be cheated; **ich lasse mir kein — für ein U machen**, I was not born yesterday; **ich habe es ihm —mal gesagt**, I have said it to him I don't know how many times, I have told him ever so often *or* for the hundredth time; **ich habe ihn —mal gewarnt**, I have warned him over and over again; *for other abbreviations see the index at the end of the German-English part.* **—t**, *adj.;* **die —te Potenz**, the xth power; **zum —ten Male**, for the hundredth time, ever so often. *Comp.* **—=Beine**, *pl.* turned-in legs. **—beinig**, *adj.* in-kneed, knock-kneed. **—beliebig**, *adj.* any, whoever, whatever; **eine —beliebige Linie**, any line you please. **—mal**, *adv.* at any moment (*coll.*); an unknown number of times. **—=Strahlen**, X rays, Röntgen rays.

Xe'ni—e, *f.* (—e, *pl.* —en), **—on**, *n.* (—ons, *pl.* —en) epigram (*after the model of Martial*); satirical epigram in the form of a distich by Schiller and Goethe on contemporary writers, first printed in their **Musenalmanach** (‚**Xenienalmanach**') for 1796. *Comp.* **—en=dichter**, *m.* writer of xenia, epigrammatist. **—en=jahr**, *n.* (*1796*), **—en=kampf**, *m.*, **—en=streit**, *m.* controversy raised by the xenia of Goethe and Schiller.

Xylogra'ph, *m.* (—en, *pl.* —en) wood-engraver. **—ie'**, *f.* wood-engraving. **—ie'ren**, *v.a.* to engrave on wood. **—isch**, *adj.* xylographic.

Y

Y, y, *n.* Y, y; ypsilon; Noctua gamma (*Ent.*); second unknown quantity (*Math.*).

Y'a(u)en, *v.n.* (*aux.* h.) to bray.

Y'sop, *m.* (—s, *pl.* —e *or* —s) hyssop.

Ya'tagan, *m.* (—s, *pl.* —s) *m.* yataghan.

Yt'ter=erde, *f.* yttria, oxide of yttrium.

Yucc'a, Yuk'ke, *f.* yucca (*Bot.*).

Z

Words not found under Z must be looked f under C.

Z, z, *n.* Z, z; third unknown quantity (*Math.*); **von A bis Z**, from beginning to end; *for abbreviations see the index at the end of the German-English part.*

Zacherli'n, *n.* (—s), zacherlin, insect powder.

Zäck'chen, *n.* (—s, *pl.* —) little point; scalloping, pinking (*on dresses, etc.*); burr (*on coins*); edging, purl (*of lace*). *Comp.* **—macherin**, *f.* lace-worker, maker of edging.

Za'ck—e, *f.* (*pl.* —en), **—en**, *m.* (—ens, *pl.* —en) scallop; scalloping (*on dresses, etc.*); point, peak, tongue (*of land*); prong (*of a fork*); tooth (*of a comb*); sharp point (*of crystals*); notch (*on coins*); crenel. **—ig**, *adj.* pointed; notched, indented, jagged; pronged; branched (*of a deer's head*); crenate (*Bot.*); **—ig ausschneiden**, to pink, to scallop. *Comp.* **—en=blatt**, *n.* indented leaf. **—en=fels**, *m.* jagged rock. **—en=garnitur**, *f.* edging; pinking, scalloping. **—en=haupt**, *n.* forked *or* jagged peak (*of a mountain*). **—en=krone**, *f.* indented crown. **—en=linie**, *f.* notched *or* serrated line; line of a redan. **—en=meißel**, *m.* sculptor's notched chisel. **—en=striche**, *pl.* indentations (*on wood, stone, etc.*). **—en=walze**, *f.* notched roller, clod-crusher. **—en=werk**, *n.* scalloping, pinking; redan (*Fort.*).

Za'cken, *v.a.* to furnish with points *or* teeth; to indent; to scallop, pink; to jag; **sich —**, to form in zig-zag, to be jagged.

Zackerie'ren, *v.n.* (*aux.* **h.**) to squabble, quarrel (*coll.*).

Zag, *see* **—haft.** **—en,** I. *v.n.* (*aux.* **h.**) to lack (*or* be lacking in) courage; to be faint-hearted, timorous; to fear; to hesitate. II. *subst.n.* fear, timidity; hesitation; **mit Zittern und —en,** with great trepidation, tremblingly, quaking in one's shoes (*coll.*). **—haft,** *adj.* faint-hearted; fearful, timorous, afraid; shy, timid; irresolute. **—haftigkeit,** *f.* timidity, fear; timorousness; irresolution.

Za'gel, *m.* (**—s,** *pl.* —) (*dial.*) tail; top (*of a tree*); penis.

Zäh, —e, *adj.* tough; tenacious; viscous, sticky; ductile; fine, refined (*of metal*); obstinate; **—er Wein,** ropy, oily wine; **—e Beharrlichkeit,** unwavering perseverance; **ein —es Leben haben,** to be tenacious of life, to have the nine lives of a cat. **—igkeit,** *f.* tenacity.

Zahl, *f.* (*pl.* **—en**) number; cipher, figure; **um die — voll zu machen,** to make up the number; **benannte —,** denominate quantity, concrete number; **unbenannte —,** abstract number; **ganze** *or* **natürliche —,** whole *or* integral number; **gebrochene —en,** fractional numbers; **gerade und ungerade Zahl,** even and odd number; **ungleiche —en,** odds (*pl.*); **Fünf eine g(e)rade — sein lassen,** not to be over-particular; **—en beweisen,** numbers are conclusive *or* convincing (*prov.*); **—en sprechen,** numbers are eloquent; **ohne —,** numberless; **an der —,** in number; **auf —en bezüglich,** numerical; **—, welche sich durch zehn vermittelst der Teilung aufheben läßt,** number divisible by 10 without remainder; **—, welche eine andere vielmal in sich enthält,** a multiple of a number; **einfache —,** singular number; **mehrfache —,** multiple; **vier stellige —,** number of four digits. **—bar,** *adj.* payable, due; **—bar werden,** to fall due; **—bar auf** *or* **bei Sicht, a Vista,** payable at sight. *Comp.* **—adverbium,** *n.* numeral adverb (*as* **sechsmal,** six times). **—bruch,** *m.* fraction of a number. **—buchstabe,** *m.* numeral letter, Roman numeral. **—en=arithmetik,** *f.* arithmetic. **—en=aussprechen,** *n.* numeration. **—en=folge,** *f.* numerical series. **—(en)=größe,** *f.* number, numerical quantity. **—en=kunst, —en=lehre,** *f.* arithmetic, theory of numbers. **—en=lotterie,** *f.* lottery with numbers. **—en=mensch,** *m.* matter-of-fact man. **—en=rechnung,** *f.* arithmetic, calculation of numbers. **—en=schreiben,** *n.* numeration. **—en=schloß,** *n.* letter lock, secret lock. **—en=sinn,** *m.* talent for calculation *or* figures; arithmetical faculty. **—en=system,** *n.* numerical *or* arithmetical system. **—en=verhältnis,** *n.* numerical proportion. **—en=wert,** *m.* numerical value. **—figur,** *f.* figure, cipher. **—los,** *adj.* numberless; innumerable. **—losigkeit,** *f.* numberlessness. **—reich,** *adj.* numerous. **—wort,** *n.* numeral (*adjective, etc.*). **—zeichen,** *n.* figure, cipher, numeral.

Zah'l—en, *v.a.* to count (out in payment); to pay; to pay for, atone for; **nicht(s) —en können,** to be insolvent; **Kinder —en die Hälfte,** children half price; **Kellner, —en!** waiter! the bill, please; **einen Wechsel (mit Protest) —en,** to meet (to protest) a bill. **—er,** *m.* (**—ers,** *pl.* **—er**) payer; **er ist ein säumiger —er,** he is slow in his payments; **schlechter —er,** one who pays badly; defaulter. **—ung,** *f.* payment; receipt; acquittance; **mangels —ung,** for want of payment; for non-payment; **—ung leisten,** to pay; **um —ung bitten,** to solicit payment, to solicit the favour of a cheque; **einen (zwangsweise) zur —ung anhalten,** to enforce payment on a p.; **die —ung einstellen,** to suspend payment; **Mangel an —ung,** non-payment; **eine —ung in Terminen leisten,** to pay by instalments; **Teil—ung,** part-payment, instalment; **—ung erhalten,** paid, settled (*at the foot of bills*); **er hat die —ung eingestellt,** he has stopped payment; **gegen bar(e) —ung,** for cash; **nur gegen bar(e) —ung,** on the cash *or* ready money system. *Comp.* **—amt,** *n.* treasury, pay-office. **—fähig,** *adj.* solvent. **—kammer, —kasse,** *f. see* **—amt.** **—kellner,** *m.* waiter who makes out the bills at cafés, cashier. **—meister,** *m.* treasurer; cashier; paymaster; purser, bursar. **—meister=amt,** *n.* treasurership; paymastership. **—muschel,** *f.* cowry. **—perlen,** *pl.* round beads used in counting. **—pfennig,** *m.* counter. **—pult,** *n.* pay-desk, counter. **—schein,** *m.* promissory note; cheque. **—stelle,** *f.* pay-office, cashier's office; pay-counter (*in banks, etc.*). **—tag,** *m.* pay-day, settling-day; account-day. **—tasche,** *f.* purse, money bag. **—ungs=anweisung,** *f.* order; draft, cheque, order; (pay) ticket (*Mil., Nav.*). **—ungs=aufschub,** *m.* delay of payment. **—ungs=bedingungen,** *pl.* terms (*of payment*). **—ungs=befehl,** *m.* ready-money order. **—ungs=einstellung,** *f.* suspension of payment. **—ungs=fähig,** *adj.* solvent. **—ungs=fähigkeit,** *f.* solvency. **—ungs=frist,** *f.* date *or* term of payment. **—ungs=mittel,** *n.* (**gesetzliches,** legal) tender. **—ungs=statt,** *f.*; **an —ungsstatt,** instead of payment, in lieu of cash. **—ungs=termin,** *m.* day, date of payment; instalment. **—ungs=unfähig,** *adj.* insolvent. **—ungs=unfähigkeit,** *f.* insolvency. **—ungs=verbindlichkeit,** *f.* liability for payment. **—ungs=vermögen,** *n. see* **—ungsfähigkeit.** **—woche,** *f.* week for payment, settling-week.

Zähl'bar, *adj.* computable, numerable.

Zäh'l—en, *v.a. & n.* (*aux.* **h.**) to number, count, reckon; **die Bevölkerung —en,** to take the census of the population; **die Stimmzettel —en,** to tell the votes, examine the ballot-box; **wenn ich mich zu Ihren Freunden —te,** were I a friend of yours; **auf einen —en,** to rely on a p.; **er sieht aus, als könnte er nicht drei —en,** he looks as if he could not say Bo to a goose; **ehe man drei —en konnte,** in a twinkling, before one could say Jack Robinson. **—er,** *m.* (**—ers,** *pl.* **—er**) counter, reckoner; teller; (*billiard-*)marker; numerator (*Arith.*); counter (*on the spinning-jenny, etc.*); person of importance; **die Fürsten waren die —er, das Volk die Nullen,** only the princes counted, the people were mere ciphers. **—ung,** *f.* counting; calculation; census. *Comp.* **—apparat,** *m.* counter (*on machines*). **—bezirk,** *m.* district in which an enumeration *or* census takes place. **—brett,** *n.* counter. **—kandidat,** *m.* minority candidate. **—karte,** *f.* census-paper; counting-card (*Cards*). **—maschine,** *f.* numbering machine. **—methode,** *f.* method of reckoning; system of numeration. **—stab,** *m.* fish (*cards*); arrow (*surveying*). **—tisch,** *m.* counter. **—ungs=kommission,** *f.* commission appointed to take a census. **—zettel,** *m.* census paper.

Zahm, *adj.* tame; domestic; arable (*of land*); tractable, docile; peaceable; **—e Fische,** fish kept in ponds; **—er Baum,** seedling, ungrafted (*fruit*) tree; **—e Erze,** not refractory metals, fusible, malleable metals; **— machen** to tame. **—heit,** *f.* tameness.

Zähm—bar, *adj.* tamable. **—barkeit,** *f.* tamableness. **—en,** I. *v.a.* to tame; to domesticate; to break in (*a horse*); to subdue, check, curb, master, restrain. II. *subst.n.*, **—ung,** *f.* taming; domestication. **—er,** *m.* (**—ers,** *pl.* **—er**) tamer; subduer.

Zahn, *m.* (—s, *pl.* **Zäh'ne**) tooth; fang; tusk; dentil (*Arch.*); tooth (*of a comb, saw, rake, etc.*); prong (*of a fork*); cog, tooth (*of wheels*); fly (*Horol.*); (*pl.*) teeth-range (*Horol.*); **die Zähne betreffend,** dental; **schlechter —,** bad *or* decayed tooth; **mit schwarzen Zähnen,** black toothed; **der Abstand der Zähne,** distance between the teeth (*Mech.*); **Zähne schneiden in eine S., etwas mit Zähnen versehen,** to notch, cog, cut teeth in a th.; **Zähne bekommen,** to cut one's teeth; **die Zähne stumpf machen,** to set one's teeth on edge; **die Zähne fletschen** (*obs.* **blecken**), to show one's teeth; **der — der Zeit,** the ravages of time; **einen — auf einen haben,** to owe a p. a grudge; **einem auf den — fühlen,** to sound a person; **(einem) die Zähne zeigen,** to show one's teeth; to show fight (*fig.*); **Haare auf den Zähnen haben,** to know what's what, to be wide-awake; **einem etwas aus den Zähnen reißen,** to snatch a th. out of a p.'s grip; **einem etwas in die Zähne rücken,** to cast a thing in a p.'s teeth. **—ig,** *adj.* toothed, indented; (*in comp.* =) with (*so many*) teeth. *Comp.* **—arm,** *adj.* having few teeth. **—arterie,** *f.* dental artery. **—artig,** *adj.* tooth-shaped, tooth-like. **—arz(e)nei,** *f. see* **—mittel. —arz(e)nei=kunde, —arz(e)nei=kunst,** *f.* dental surgery. **—arzt,** *m.* dentist, dental surgeon. **—ärztlich,** *adj.* concerning dental surgery; **—ärztliche Behandlung,** dentist's professional attendance. **—bildung,** *f.* formation *or* growth of teeth. **—brecher,** *m.* tooth-drawer. **—bürste,** *f.* tooth-brush. **—fäule,** *f.* caries of the teeth. **—feile,** *f.* dentist's file; watch-maker's file. **—fieber,** *n.* fever accompanying teething. **—fistel,** *f.* fistula in the gum. **—fleisch,** *n.* gum(s). **—förmig,** *adj.* tooth-shaped, dentiform; odontoid. **—füllung,** *f.* stopping. **—geschwür,** *n.* alveolar abscess, abscess on the tooth. **—heilkunde,** *f.* dentistry. **—hobel,** *m.* tooth-plane (*Carp.*). **—höhle,** *f.* socket of a tooth; cavity in a decayed tooth. **—kitt,** *m.* plastic filling for teeth. **—künstler,** *m.* maker of artificial teeth; dentist. **—laut,** *m.* dental (sound), dental (consonant). **—lehre,** *f.* dentology. **—= und Lippen=laut,** *m.* dentolabial, labiodental (sound). **—los,** *adj.* toothless; **—lose Tiere,** edentata. **—lücke,** *f.* space between two teeth, gap where teeth are wanting; metope, space between the dentils (*Arch.*). **—meißel,** *m.* dentist's scraper. **—mittel,** *n.* remedy for toothache; dentifrice. **—nerv,** *m.* nerve of a tooth. **—operation,** *f.* dental operation. **—plombe,** *f.* stopping, filling. **—pulver,** *n.* tooth-powder. **—rad,** *n.* cogged *or* toothed wheel; cog-wheel; **—rad mit innerer Verzahnung,** internally toothed wheel. **—rad=bahn,** *f.* cog-wheel railway, rack-railway. **—räder=werk,** *n.* tooth-gearing. **—reihe,** *f.* row *or* set of teeth, dental arch; denture (*of artificial teeth*); teeth-range; indent. **—reinigend,** *adj.* teeth-cleaning. **—salbe,** *f.* tooth-paste. **—schlüssel,** *m.* key-instrument of dentists. **—schmerz,** *m.* toothache. **—schnitt,** *m.* denticulation; row of dentils (*Arch.*). **—sichel,** *f.* toothed sickle. **—stange,** *f.* rack; **—stange und Getriebe,** rack and pinion. **—stift,** *m. see* **—stumpf;** peg *or* pin for fastening in artificial teeth. **—stocher,** *m.* tooth-pick. **—stumpf,** *m.* stump of a tooth. **—technik,** *f.* science of dentistry. **—wasser,** *n.* tooth-wash, mouth lotion. **—wechsel,** *m.* second dentition. **—weh,** *n. see* **—schmerz. —weinstein,** *m.* tartar. **—werk,** *n.* tooth-work (*Horol.*); rack-work (*of machines*); toothwork, jagging; teeth-range (*of wheels*). **—wurm,** *m.* caries of the teeth. **—zange,** *f.* dentist's forceps.

Zah'n—en, I. *v.a.* to indent, notch; **gezahnt,** toothed, notched, denticulate. II. *v.n.* (*aux.* **h.**) to teeth, to be teething, to cut one's teeth. III. *subst. n.* teething, dentition. **—ung,** *f.* toothing, cogs; number of cogs, teeth-range (*Horol.*).

Zäh'neklappern, *n.* chattering of teeth.

Zäh'nung, *f.* perforation (*of postage stamps*).

Zäh're, *f.* (*pl.* **—n**) tear (*obs. high style & poet.*).

Zain, *m.* (—s, *pl.* **—e**) ingot, wedge, bar; ribbon, fillet, slip (*Mint.*). **—en,** *v.a.* to make into bars *or* ingots. **—er,** *m.* (**—ers,** *pl.* **—er**) forger of bars, master-smith. *Comp.* **—eisen,** *n.* iron in bars; nail-rods. **—hammer,** *m.* forge, slitting-mill. **—silber,** *n.* silver in bars.

Zam'pel, *m.* (—s, *pl.* —) simple, loom on which figured stuffs are made (*Weav.*).

Zan'der, *m.* (—s, *pl.* —) giant pike-perch.

Zan'ge, *f.* (*pl.* **—n**) tongs; pincers; tweezers; pliers; forceps; vice; claw (*of a hammer*); palp (*Ent.*); (*pl.*) fore-teeth (*of horses*); tenail (*Fort.*). *Comp.* **—n=artig, —n=förmig,** *adj.* pincer-like. **—n=befestigung,** *f.* redan *or* tenail-system of fortification. **—n=linie,** *f.* tenail front *or* line. **—n=ring,** *m.* sliding ring, coupler. **—system,** *n.* redan-system. **—n=schanze,** *f.*, **—n=werk,** *n.* tongs-shaped trench, tenail. **—n=winkel,** *m.* flanking angle.

Zän'g—(el)chen, *n.* (**—(el)chens,** *pl.* **—(el)chen**) pincers; tweezers. **—en,** *v.a.* to shingle.

Zank, *m.* (**—es**) quarrel, wrangle, brawl; strife, contention, dispute; **mit einem — suchen,** to pick a quarrel with a p. **—haft,** *adj.* quarrelsome; irritable. *Comp.* **—apfel,** *m.* apple of discord, bone of contention. **—duett,** *n.* duet of abuse; mutual recrimination. **—geist,** *m.* quarrelsome spirit. **—lust,** *f.* quarrelsomeness. **—stifter,** *m.* mischief-maker, fire-brand. **—sucht,** *f.* mania for quarrelling, quarrelsomeness. **—süchtig,** *adj.* quarrelsome, contentious. **—teufel,** *m.* wrangler, termagant, shrew.

Zan'ken, *v.r. & n.* (*aux.* **h.**) to quarrel; **sie — über** (*acc.*) **Kleinigkeiten, um des Kaisers Bart,** they quarrel over trifles; **wo sich Zweie —, gewinnt der Dritte,** where two fall out the third wins (*prov.*).

Zän'k—er, *m.* (**—ers,** *pl.* **—er**), **—erin,** *f.* quarrelsome person, squabbler, bickerer, shrew. **—erei',** *f. see* **Gezänk(e). —isch,** *adj. see* **zankhaft**

Zäpf'chen, (Zäpf'lein,) *n.* (—s, *pl.* —) *dim. of* Zapfen, *q. v.;* uvula. *Comp.* **—entzündung,** *f.* inflammation of the uvula. **—=R,** *n.* uvular r (*Northumbrian burr*). **—schnitt,** *m.* staphylotomy, cutting of the uvula.

Zap'fen, *m.* (—s, *pl.* —) peg; plug; pin; tenon (*Carp.*); cock, tap; bung, spigot; sluice, lock; pivot; trunnion (*Artil.*); hook (*of a tile*); tear, drop (*Arch.*); cone; fruit of the hop; *see* **Zäpfchen; stehender —,** pivot; **— von Tropfstein,** stalactite; **Eis—,** icicle; **Tannen —,** cone; **der Cylinder hängt auf —,** the cylinder is suspended on trunnions (*Locom.*). *Comp.* **—artig, —ähnlich,** *adj.* plug-like, cone-shaped. **—bäume,** *pl.* conifers. **—bohrer,** *m.* tap-bore; pivot-drill. **—feile,** *f.* pivot file. **—feld,** *n.* trunnion-ring. **—frucht,** *f.* cone. **—geld,** *n.* ale-house impost (*obs.*). **—gelenk,** *n.* spigot-joint. **—lager,** *n.* rest, socket; bed (*Artil.*); pillow-block. **—loch,** *n.* bung-hole; faucet-hole; mortise. **—loch=maschine,** *f.* mortising machine. **—streich,** *m.* tattoo, retreat (*Mil.*); **großer —streich,** tattoo beaten by all the military bands of a garrison (*drums and whistles*); **den —streich schlagen,** to beat the tattoo, to beat to quarters. **—träger,** *pl.* conifers.

Zap'fe—n, *v.a.* to tap (*a cask; a dropsical pa-*

rient); to mortise. —r, m. (—rs, pl. —r) tapster, beer drawer.

Zap'pelig, *adj.* struggling, fidgety, restless.

Zap'pel—n, *v.n.* (*aux.* h.) to move convulsively; to kick, sprawl, flounder, writhe; to fidget (about); mit Händen und Füßen —n, to struggle with hands and feet, kick and strike about one; einen —n lassen, to keep s.o. in suspense, to tantalize a p. *Comp.* —fritze, *m.* fidgety boy, fidget (*coll.*). —mann, *m.* jumping Jack, tumbler (*a toy*).

Zar, *m.* (—en, *pl.* —en, *also* —e), czar, tsar. —ewitsch, *m.* czarevitch. —ewna, *f.* czarevna. —in, *f.* czarina, czariza.

Zar'ge, *f.* (*pl.* —n) border, edge, rim, brim; groove; hoop; frame, case; setting (*of a jewel*); sides of the violin, guitar, *etc.*; holdfast, cramp; chime (*Carp.*). *Comp.* —zieher, Zarg'zieher, *m.* cooper's turrel.

Zart, (—er, —est; (*obs.* also zär'ter, zär'test)) *adj.* tender; soft, delicate; fragile, frail; fine, nice; slender, slight; soft, delicate, subdued, pale (*of colours*); sensitive; loving, fond; —e Gesichtsfarbe, delicate complexion; —es Fleisch, tender meat; —er Wink, gentle hint. —heit, *f.* tenderness; delicacy; softness; weakness; morbidezza (*Paint.*). *Comp.* —fühlend, —fühlig, *adj.* sensitive; with fine feelings; full of tact *or* sympathy; delicate, considerate. —gefühl, *n.* delicacy of feeling. —glied(e)rig, *adj.* with slender limbs, delicate-limbed. —rosa, *adj.* pale pink. —sinnig, *see* —fühlend. —sinn(igkeit, *f.*), *m. see* —gefühl.

Zärtel—ei', *f.* affectation of sensitiveness. —n, *v.a.* to fondle, pet; to ponder.

Zärt'lich, *adj.* tender; soft; delicate; loving, fond; sensitive; weak; — thun, to affect tenderness, to play the lover. —keit, *f.* tenderness; delicacy (*obs.*); (*pl.*) loving speeches.

Zärt'ling, *m.* (—s, *pl.* —e) delicate person; weakling, effeminate fellow; milksop.

Za'ser, ꝛc., *see* Faser.

Zas'pel, *f.* (*pl.* —n) skein, hank; reel *or* bundle of 20 skeins.

Zau'ber, *m.* (—s, *pl.* —) spell; charm; magic, witchcraft; magic effect *or* power; enchantment, glamour, fascination; fauler —, humbug, bosh (*coll.*); der ganze —, the whole concern (*coll.*). —ei', *f.* magic, sorcery; spell, enchantment. —er, *m.* (—ers, *pl.* —er) magician, sorcerer; juggler. —erin, Zaubrerin, *f.* sorceress, witch. —haft, —isch, *adj.* magical, enchanted; illusive, fairy-tale, juggling; bewitching, enchanting; marvellous.

Zau'ber—n, *v.* I. *a.* to charm, to cast a spell on *or* over; einen jung —n, to make a p. young (again) by magic (art); das Geld aus dem Beutel des einen in den des andern —n, to charm money out of one person's purse into that of another; sich (*dat.*) etwas in den Är=mel —n, to charm s.th. down one's sleeve. II. *n.* (*aux.* h.) to conjure, to practice magic *or* witchcraft, to work charms; to do juggling tricks; —n können, to be able to conjure. *Comp.* —apparat, *m.* box of conjuring tricks, juggler's apparatus. —bild, *n.* magic image, talisman; enchanting image *or* creature. —blick, *m.* magic glance; fascinating look. —brunnen, *m.* enchanted fountain. —buch, *n.* book of charms; conjuring book. —dose, *f.* magic box. —flöte, *f.* magic flute. —formel, *f.* magic formula, incantation, charm, spell, conjuration. —garten, *m.* enchanted garden. —gehenk, *n.* amulet. —insel, *f.* enchanted isle. —kasten, *m.* box of conjuring tricks. —kraft, *f.* magic power. —kräftig, *adj.* magical. —kunst, *f.* magic art, witchcraft, sorcery. —künste, *pl.* conjuring tricks, jugglery. —land, *n.* enchanted country; fairyland. —laterne, *f.* magic lantern. —lehrling, *m.* apprentice *or* novice in the art of magic, magician's apprentice. —macht, *see* —kraft. —märchen, *n.* fairy tale. —märchenland, *n.* fairyland. —mittel, *n.* charm. —nacht, *f.* enchanted night. —pferd, *n.* magic steed. —posse, *f.* fairy play, pantomime. —reich, I. *n. see* —land. II. *adj.* full of enchantment. —ring, *m.* magic ring. —rute, *f.* magic wand. —segen, *m. see* —spruch. —spiegelung, *f.* mirage. —spruch, *m.* incantation, charm; exorcism. —stab, *m.* magic wand. —stück, *n. see* —posse; conjuring trick. —trank, *m.* magic potion, philtre. —wald, *f.* enchanted forest. —werk, *n. see* —ei. —wesen, *n.* magic, sorcery; fairy being; bewitching creature. —wort, *n.* magic word; sein Name war ein —wort, his (name) was a name to conjure with. —zeichen, *n.* magic sign.

Zau'der—er, Zaudrer, *m.* (—ers, *pl.* —er), —in, Zaudrerin, *f.* dilatory person; irresolute person; temporizer, procrastinator. —haft, *adj.* hesitating, irresolute, vacillating; slow, dilatory. —haftigkeit, *f.* hesitation; irresolution; dilatoriness. —n, I. *v.n.* (*aux.* h.) to hesitate; to delay, procrastinate, temporize; to waver, dally; mit etwas —n, to hesitate about a th. II. *subst. n.* procrastination; delay.

Zaum, *m.* (—s, *pl.* Zäu'me) bridle; rein; ligament; im —e halten, to keep a tight rein on, to keep in check, to curb, restrain. *Comp.* —geld, *n.* purchaser's tip to the ostler. —los, *adj.* unbridled. —recht, *adj.* accustomed to the bridle. —zeug, *n.* horse's head-gear.

Zäu'm—en, *v.a.* to bridle, to put the reins *or* bit on; to curb, bridle, keep in check. —ung, *f.* bridling.

Zaun, *m.* (—s, *pl.* Zäu'ne) hedge, fence; separation; toter —, fence; lebendiger —, quickset hedge; geflochtener —, plashed hedge; das ist nicht hinter jedem — zu finden, that is not to be met with every day; eine S. vom —e brechen, to seize the first opportunity *or* excuse to do a th.; die Gelegenheit zu einem Streite vom —e brechen, to pick a quarrel; hinterm —e sterben, to die in a ditch; durch den — stechen, not to play fair. *Comp.* —dürr, *adj.* as thin as a lath. —könig, *m.* wren. —pfahl, *m.* hedge-pole *or* stake, pale; einem mit dem —pfahl winken, to give s.o. a broad hint. —rebe, *f.* Virginia creeper; white bryony. —rübe, *f.* white bryony. —ruten, *pl.* twigs *or* boughs for hedges. —schlüpfer, *m.* wren; großer —schlüpfer, hedge-sparrow. —wicke, *f.* bush-vetch. —winde, *f.* bindweed.

Zäu'nen, *v. a.* to fence in, provide with a fence.

Zau'seler, *m.* (—s, *pl.* —) willow.

Zau'sen, *v.a.* to pull (about), to tug; to touse, tousle; sie haben einander gehörig gezaust, they have pulled each other about very thoroughly.

Ze'bra, *n.* (—s, *pl.* —s) zebra.

Ze'bu, *m.* (—(s), *pl.* —s) Indian bull, zebu.

Ze'ch—e, *f.* (*pl.* —en) rotation, order (*obs.*); turn; succession; (*obs.*) share; bill, reckoning (*in an inn*); club; repast, party where each person pays a share of the expenses (*obs.*); banquet; drinking-bout (*obs.*); guild, corporation; mine, mining company; die —e bezahlen, to pay the bill, to bear the expense; die —e machen, to make up the bill, to present the bill; die —e ohne den Wirt machen, to reckon without one's host; wer bezahlt die —e? who pays the piper? um die —e, nach der —e, in succession, in turns (*obs.*). —en, *v.a.* & *n.* (*aux.* h.) to drink freely, carouse; to banquet, feast; to run up a bill at an inn. —er, *m.* (—ers, *pl.* —er) one who drinks (hard), drinker; toper; carouser, reveller; der alte —er, that old reveller. —erei', *f.* carousing; drinking bout, drinking party. *Comp.* **—bruder,** *m.* boon companion, toper, tippler. **—en=haus,** *n.* miner's place of meeting. **—en=holz,** *n.* timber in a mine. **—frei,** *adj.* free of expense; **einen —frei halten,** to pay a p.'s score. **—gast,** *m.* drinking companion. **—gelag,** *n.* carouse. **—genoß,** *m.* boon companion. **—gesellschaft,** *f.* drinking-party. **—preller,** *m.* one who shirks paying his score. **—prellerei,** *f.* cheating an innkeeper of the amount due. **—schuld,** *f.* tavern score, debt for drink. **—schwester,** *f.* tippler, woman who drinks. **—stein,** *m.* zechstein (*Min.*).

Zechi'ne, *f.* (*pl.* **—n**) sequin.

Zeck, *n.* (**—s**), game of running and catching.

Ze'cke, *f.* (*pl.* **—n**) tick (*Ent.*).

Ze'drach, *m.* (**—s,** *pl.* **—e**) bead-tree, pride of India.

Zeh, *m.* (**—(e)s,** *pl.* **—en**), **—e,** *f.* (*pl.* **—en**) toe; root (*of ginger*); stick (*of celery*); **auf den —en gehen,** to walk on tiptoe, on one's toes. *Comp.* **—en=entzündung,** *f.* dactylitis. **—en=gang,** *m.* walking on the toes *or* on tiptoe. **—en=gänger,** *m.* digitigrade (*lion, cat, etc.*). **—en=spitze,** *f.* point of the toe, tiptoe. **—en=stand,** *m.* standing on tiptoe (*Gymn.*). **—en=strecker,** *m.* extensor of the toes.

Zeh'(e)nt, I. *num. adj. see* **Zehnt.** II. (**—en,** *pl.* **—en**) *m.* tithe; tenth; **mit —en belegen,** to tithe; **den —en entrichten,** to pay tithe (**von,** on). *n.* number of ten, decade. **—bar,** *adj.* subject to tithe. **—e,** *m.* (**—en,** *pl.* **—en**) *see* **Zeh(e)nt** II. **—en,** *v.a.* to tithe; to pay tithe. **—er,** *m.* (**—ers,** *pl.* **—er**) tithe-owner. *Comp.* **—acker,** *m.* field under tithe. **—einnehmer,** *m.* tithe-collector. **—frei,** *adj.* exempt from paying tithe. **—herr,** *see* **—er.** **—land,** *n.* tithable land. **—pflichtig,** *adj.* tithable, subject to pay tithe. **—rechnung,** *f.* decimal calculation *or* arithmetic. **—recht,** *n.* right to levy tithe.

Zehn, (**Zehen,** *obs. poet.*) I. *num. adj.* ten; **es ist dreiviertel —,** it is a quarter to ten; **es ist halb —,** it is half past nine; **ein Stücker —,** about ten, ten or so (*coll.*); **Anzahl von —,** decade; **Klasse der Pflanzen mit — Staubfäden,** decandrians. II. *f.* (*pl.* **—en**) the figure ten; the number ten. III. *n.* ten, decade. **—er,** *m.* (**—ers,** *pl.* **—er**) a ten, half a score; number ten; a ten-pfennig piece; member of a council *or* committee of ten; ten (*at cards*); wine of the year 1810; the figure ten; soldier of the tenth regiment; **in den —en stehen,** to be in one's teens. **—t,** I. *num. adj.* (**der, die, das —te**) tenth; **der —te August,** August the tenth (August 10th), the tenth of August; **—tes Kapitel,** chapter the tenth (chapter X.); **im —ten Kapitel,** in the tenth chapter; **morgen ist der —te,** to-morrow will be the tenth; **das kann der —te nicht vertragen,** not one in ten can stand it. II. *n.* space of ten years, decennium. **—tel,** *n.* (**—tels,** *pl.* **—tel**) a tenth ($\frac{1}{10}$). **—tens,** *adv.* tenthly, in the tenth place. *Comp.* **—eck,** *n.* decagon. **—eckig,** *adj.* having ten angles *or* corners. **—ender,** *m.* stag with ten antlers. **—er=lei,** *adv.* of ten kinds. **—er=reihe,** *f.* column of tens (*Arith.*). **—fach, —fältig,** *adj.* tenfold. **—füßig,** *adj.* ten-footed, decapod. **—herr,** *m.* member of the council of Ten (*at Venice*); (*Roman*) decemvir. **—herrschaft,** *f.* decemvirate. **—jährig,** *adj.* ten years old, of ten years. **—jährlich,** *adj.* decennial; happening every ten years. **—lötig,** *adj.* of five ounces. **—mal,** *adv.* ten times. **—männ(er)ig,** *adj.* decandrian. **—markstück,** *n.* ten-mark piece, half a sovereign. **—silbig,** *adj.* ten-syllabled, decasyllabic. **—silbler,** *m.* decasyllabic verse, line of ten syllables. **—stemp(e)lig,** *adj.* with ten pistils (*Bot.*). **—teilig,** *adj.* composed of ten parts. **—tel=meter,** *n.* (*& m.*) decimetre. **—weib(er)ig,** *adj.* decagynous.

Zeh'r—en, *v.* I. *n.* (*aux.* **h.**) to eat and drink; to live; to board; to waste, become less; to make thin; to waste, evaporate; to give an appetite; (*aux.* **h.** *&* **s.**) to grow thin; **bei einem Wirte —en,** to have one's meals at a hotel *or* restaurant; **auf die Kreide —en,** to live on credit; **von seinen Zinsen —en,** to live on one's income; **ich —e an dem Anblicke meines kleinen Gärtchens,** I feed *or* feast my eyes on my little bit of garden; **wir haben drei Wochen an diesem Schinken gezehrt,** we have been eating at this ham for three weeks; **der Wein, der Thee, das Wasser —t,** wine, tea, water gives no nourishment, makes thin; **die Seeluft —t,** the sea-air gives an appetite. II. *r.;* **der Kummer —te sich immer tiefer in ihr Herz,** grief continued to gnaw at her heart (*rare*). **—end,** *p. & adj.* eating and drinking; wasting, consumptive, hectic; **am Leben —end,** life-consuming. **—er,** *m.* (**—ers,** *pl.* **—er**) consumer, spender; wasteful person, spendthrift. **—ung,** *f.* living; expenses of living; bill (*at an inn*); score; waste, evaporation; grease (*for wheels*); *see* **Auszehrung; die letzte** *or* **heilige** (**Wege=**) **—ung,** viaticum, extreme unction. *Comp.* **—fieber,** *n.* hectic fever. **—frei,** *adj.* with free board; **einen —frei halten,** to give a p. free board (*obs.*). **—geld,** *n.*, **—pfennig,** *m.* money for provisions, board-expenses; travelling expenses *or* allowance. **—ungs=kosten,** *pl. see* **—geld.** **—ungs=steuer,** *f.* duty on articles of food.

Zei'chen, *n.* (**—s,** *pl.* **—**) mark, token, sign; indication; proof, testimony; signal; symptom (*Med.*); marker; brand, stamp; sign (*Alg.; Mus.; of inns*); beacon (*Naut.*); signature (*Typ.*); badge; profession; sign (*Astr.*); omen; **zum —, daß . . .,** as a proof that . . .; **ein — geben,** to give *or* make a sign, to sign to, signal; **unter einem glücklichen — geboren,** born under a lucky star; **welches —s sind Sie?** what is your trade?; **ich bin meines —s ein Tischler,** I am a joiner by trade. *Comp.* **—deuter,** *m.* interpreter of signs; astrologer; augur; prophet. **—deuterei, —deutung,** *f.* interpretation of signs; divination; astrology. **—erklärung,** *f.* key to the marks *or* signs (*on a map, etc.*). **—setzung,** *f.* punctuation. **—sprache,** *f.* language of signs, pantomime; cipher, (telegraphic) code. **—telegraph,** *m.* optical telegraph, semaphore.

Zeich'—nen, I. *v.a. & n.* (*aux.* **h.**) to mark, set a mark on; to brand; to sign; to subscribe; to draw, sketch; to delineate, represent; **von der Seite —nen,** to draw in profile; **nach dem Leben —nen,** to draw from (the) life; **der Hund —net die Fährte,** the dog draws on the scent; **eine Schrift —nen,** to sign a paper; **und —ne (mich) hochachtungsvoll ergebenst A. B.,** I have the honour to remain, Sir (*or* Madam), your obedient servant *or* yours faithfully, A. B.; **zu einem Denkmal hundert Mark —nen,** to subscribe 100 marks towards the erection of a monument. II. *subst. n.* drawing, *etc.;* **—nen aus freier Hand,** free-hand drawing. **—ner,** *m.* (**—ners,** *pl.* **—ner**), **—nerin,** *f.* drawer, designer, draughtsman; subscriber. **—nerisch,** *adj.* with regard to drawing; according to the rules of drawing; **—nerischer Trieb,** instinct for drawing. **—nerei',** *f.* poor, bad drawing. **—nung,** *f.* drawing; design, sketch; diagram; subscription. *Comp.* **—en=brett,** *n.* drawing-board. **—en=buch,** *n.* sketch-book. **—en=feder,** *f.* drawing-pen. **—en=garn,** *n.* marking-thread. **—en=hammer,** *m.* marking-hammer. **—en=kreide,** *f.*

chalk for drawing *or* marking; crayon. —**en=kunst**, *f.* art of drawing, designing. —**en=lehrer**, *m.* drawing-master. —**en=lineal**, *n.* flat ruler. —**en=papier**, *n.* drawing-paper. —**en=saal**, *m.* class-room for drawing. —**en=schule**, *f.* school of design. —**en=stift**, *m.* crayon. —**en=talent**, *n.* gift for drawing. —**en=unterricht**, *m.* drawing lessons. —**en=vorlage**, *f.* drawing copy.

Zei'del—er, Zeidl—er, *m.* (—**ers**, *pl.* —**er**) keeper of bees (*prov.*). —**n**, *v.a.* & *n.* (*aux.* **h.**) to cut the honeycombs (from the hives). *Comp.* —**bär**, *m.* common bear. —**baum**, *m.* tree in which wild bees make their hives. —**heide**, *f.* heath where bees feed. —**meister**, *m.* bee-master, keeper of bees. —**messer**, *n.* knife for cutting the hives.

Zei'gbar, *adj.* that may be shown, ostensible, presentable.

Zei'g—en, *v.* I. *a.* to show, point out; to exhibit, display; to discover (*Theat.*); to demonstrate; to prove; **das wird sich bald —en**, it will soon appear *or* be seen, we shall soon see; **es —t sich, daß . . .**, it appears that . . ., we see that . . .; **sich —en**, to make one's appearance, to emerge, come to light, to turn out; **er kann sich überall —en**, he may go wherever he likes, may appear in any society; **da hat er sich recht gezeigt**, there he has shown what he could do; **seine Unschuld wird sich zuletzt —en**, his innocence will become apparent at last; **darin —t er sich als der Mann, der er immer war**, in that he shows himself the man he always was; **das Thermometer —t 20 Grad**, the thermometer stands at 20°. II. *n.* (*aux.* **h.**); **auf eine S. —en**, to point at s.th.; **die Magnetnadel —t nach Norden**, the needle points to the north. —**er**, *m.* (—**ers**, *pl.* —**er**) one who shows; any instrument for showing *or* pointing; pointer (*on scales*); hand (*of clocks, watches*); gnomon (*of a dial*); needle (*of a compass*); indicator (*Artil.*); index (*Math.*); style, index, needle (*Tele.*); —**er dieses**, the bearer (of this note, paper) (*C. L.*); **der große —er**, the big hand (*of a clock*). *Comp.* —**e=finger**, *m.* forefinger, index. —**e=stock**, *m.* pointer. —**er=muskel**, *m.* extensor of the forefinger. —**er=rad**, *n.* dial-wheel. —**er=stange**, *f.* style, gnomon. —**er=telegraph**, *m.* dial-telegraph, needle-telegraph. —**er=werk**, *n.* works that move the hands of a clock, *etc.* —**er=uhr**, *f.* clock that does not strike. —**e=tisch**, *m.* show-table.

Zei'hen, *ir.v.a.* (**einen einer S.**) to accuse a p. of a thing (*obs. & high style*).

Zei'le, *f.* (*pl.* —**n**) line (*of letters; of buildings*); row; rank, file; **zwischen den —n lesen**, to read between the lines; **zwischen zwei —n geschrieben**, interlinear. —**n**, *v.a.* to arrange in rows; to sew together (*several skins*) in a row. *Comp.* —**n=schreiber**, *m.* penny-a-liner. —**n=weise**, *adv.* in lines, by rows.

Zei'sig, *m.* (—**s**, *pl.* —**e**) siskin (*Orn.*); scamp; **lockerer —**, fast fellow, loose fish. *Comp.* —**grün**, *adj.* canary-green.

Zeis'lein, *n.* (—**s**, *pl.* —) little siskin.

Zeit, *f.* (*pl.* —**en**) time (*also Mus.*); epoch; period, age; season; term; period (*Med.*); time of delivery; tense (*Gram.*); weather (*prov.*); tide (*Naut.*); **gegenwärtige, vergangene, zukünftige —**, present, past and future tense (*Gram.*); **vor langer —**, long ago, a long time ago; **lange — vorher**, long before this; **die — her**, ever since; **die ganze — her, durch** *or* **über**, all along, ever since; **eine — lang**, for some time; **das währt nur eine — lang**, that will only last for a time; — (**seines**) **Lebens**, during (his) lifetime, so long as he lives; **er war seiner — ein tüchtiger Schauspieler**, he was a good actor in his day; **ich werde dir das seiner — mitteilen**, I will tell you that in due time *or* at a suitable moment; **O du meine** *or* **liebe —!** good heavens! well, I never! **es ist — genug**, there is time enough *or* plenty of time; **es ist die höchste —**, it is high time; **das hat —, damit hat es gute —**, there is no hurry about that; **es hat — bis . . .**, it need not be done, is not wanted until . . .; **es hat —, bis er die Stelle bekommt**, it will be some time before he gets the place; **die — abpassen**, to bide one's time; **eine — festsetzen**, to appoint a date, fix a time *or* term; **man muß sich zu allem — lassen**, everything requires time; **mit der — fortschreiten**, to keep pace with the times; **mit der — geizen**, to economize time; **harte, schwere —**, hard times; **mir wird die — lang**, time hangs heavy on my hands; **andre —en, andre Sitten**, other times bring other manners (*prov.*); — **gewonnen, alles gewonnen**, time is everything (*prov.*); **wer nicht kommt zur rechten —, der muß essen was übrig bleibt**, last come, last served (*prov.*); **jedes Ding währt seine —**, there is an end to everything (*prov.*); **alles zu seiner —**, there is a time for everything (*prov.*); **gerade zur rechten —**, in the nick of time; **kommt —, kommt Rat**, time brings wisdom (*prov.*); **spare in der —, so hast du in der Not**, make hay while the sun shines (*prov.*); **es ist an der —**, it is time, the moment has come (*for*); **dies ist nicht mehr an der —**, that is out of season; the right time for that is past; **wie viel** *or* **wie hoch ist es an der —?** what o'clock is it? what is the time?; **es ist früh an der —**, it is early; **auf eine kurze — will ich es Ihnen leihen**, I will lend it to you for a short time; **auf ewige —en**, for ever and ever, in perpetuity; **bis auf diese —**, up to now, hitherto; **aus der — der Republik**, from *or* of the time of the Republic; **außer der —**, out of season; **bei —en**, in (good) time, early; **bei guter —**, early, at the right time, in good time; **bei diesen unseren —en**, nowadays; **für alle —en**, for all time, lasting; **in der —** *or* **in den —en der Völkerwanderung**, at the time of the migration of nations; **in kurzer —**, in a short time; **mit der —**, with time, in the end; **mit der — pflückt man Rosen**, all things come to him who waits (*prov.*); **nach einiger —**, some time afterwards; **seit längerer —**, for a long time; **es sind schon zwei Tage über die —**, it is now two days past the time; **um die — der Ernte**, about harvest time; **übers Jahr um dieselbe —**, about the same time next year; **von — zu —**, from time to time; **vor kurzer —**, a short time ago; **vor der gehörigen —**, before the (proper) time; **vor —en**, formerly, in olden times; **vor grauen —en**, in gray antiquity, in days of yore; **vor undenklichen —en**, time out of mind; **während der —, daß . . .**, whilst . . .; **zu allen —en, zu jeder —**, at any time, always; **zu —en Schillers, zu Schillers —en**, in the time of Schiller; **noch zu gehöriger —**, still in (good) time; **zu gleicher —**, at the same time; **zu ungelegener —**, unseasonably, at the wrong time; **zu —en**, now and then, at times; **zu meiner —**, in my time *or* day; (**grade**) **zu rechter —**, in the nick of time, à propos. —**ig**, *adj.* early; ripe, mature; coming at the right time, opportune, seasonable; for the time being, present, actual. —**igen**, *v.* I. *a.* to mature, ripen, bring to maturity; to bring to a head. II. *n.* (*aux.* **s.**) to mature, grow ripe. —**lich**, *adj.* & *adv.* temporal; secular; earthly; passing, transient; **das —liche segnen**, to depart this life (*high style*). —**lichkeit**, *f.* this life;

temporal power; (*pl.*) temporalities; **aus dieser (irdischen) —lichkeit abscheiden**, to pass from time to eternity, to depart this life. *Comp.* **—abschnitt**, *m.* period; epoch; moment, portion of time. **—alter**, *n.* age; generation, era; **in unserem —alter**, in our (own) days. **—angabe**, *f.*; **ohne —angabe**, without date, undated. **—anwendung**, *f.* employment of time. **—bedürfnis**, *n.* needs of the time. **—begebenheit**, *f.* event of the time; contemporary event. **—behelf**, *m.* temporary expedient. **—berechnung**, **—bestimmung**, *f.* chronology. **—beschreibung**, *f.* chronography, chronicle-writing. **—buch**, *n.* chronicle, annals. **—differenz**, *f.* difference in time; difference between the local times of two places. **—droschke**, *f.* cab hired by the hour. **—einheit**, *f.* unity of time. **—folge**, *f.* chronological order. **—(en)=folge**, *f.* concord of tense. **—form**, *f.* tense. **—forscher**, *m.* chronologist. **—forschung**, *f.* chronology. **—geist**, *m.* spirit of the age. **—gemäß**, *adj.* in keeping with the spirit of the age; seasonable; opportune. **—gemäßheit**, *f.* seasonableness; opportuneness. **—genoß**, **—genosse**, *m.*, **—genossin**, *f.* contemporary. **—geschäft**, *n.* time-purchase *or* bargain; option business; call (*of stocks*). **—geschichte**, *f.* contemporary history. **—geschmack**, *m.* prevailing taste, fashion. **—gewinn**, *m.* economy of time. **—grund**, *m.* background of time. **—hafen**, *m.* tidal harbour. **—kunde**, *f.* chronology. **—kundig**, *adj.* versed in chronology. **—kürzend**, *adj.* amusing, entertaining. **—lauf**, *m.* course of time, course of events; lapse of time, period. **—läuf(t)e**, *pl.* (occurrences of the) times, conjunctures, junctures. **—le'bens**, *adv.* during life; **Pension auf —lebens**, annuity, pension for life. **—lehen**, *n.* temporary fief. **—lose**, *f.* common meadow-saffron. **—maß**, *n.* measure of time; space of time; time (*Mus.*); measure, quantity (*Pros.*). **—messer**, *m.* chronometer; metronome (*Mus.*). **—meßkunst**, **—messung**, *f.* measurement of time. **—ordnung**, *f.* chronological order. **—pacht**, *f.* lease for a certain time. **—punkt**, *m.* moment. **—raubend**, *adj.* requiring *or* taking up much time; tedious, wearisome. **—raum**, *m.* period, time. **—rechner**, *m.* chronologist. **—rechnung**, *f.* chronology; style, reckoning; **christliche —rechnung**, Christian era. **—rechnungs=fehler**, *m.* chronological error. **—register**, *n.* chronological table. **—rente**, *f.* annuity. **—schrift**, *f.* periodical (publication), journal, magazine. **—tafel**, *f.* chronological table. **—umstände**, *pl.* circumstances (of the time); juncture(s), coincidences; **bei den augenblicklichen —umständen**, in the present state of affairs. **—verderb**, *m.* waste of time. **—verhältnisse**, *see* **—umstände**. **—verlauf**, *m.* course, lapse of time. **—verlust**, *m.* loss of time; **ohne —verlust**, without losing time, without delay. **—verschwendung**, *f.* waste of time. **—vertreib**, *m.* pastime, amusement; **zum —vertreib**, to pass the time, for (the sake of) amusement. **—vertreibend**, *adj.* entertaining. **—weilig**, *adj.* temporary; for the time being, actual. **—weise**, *adv.* at times, from time to time; for a time. **—widrig**, *adj.* unseasonable. **—wind**, *m.* periodical wind. **—wort**, *n.* verb. **—zünder**, *m.* time-fuse (*Artil.*).

Zei'tung, *f.* (*pl.* —en) newspaper, paper; gazette; news, intelligence (*obs.*); **sich** (*dat.*) **eine — halten**, to take in a newspaper; **in die — setzen**, to insert in a newspaper, advertise, to gazette; **eine angenehme — bekommen**, to get a pleasant piece of intelligence (*obs.*). *Comp.* **—s=amt**, *n.* office of a journal. **—s=anzeige**, *f.* advertisement. **—s=artikel**, *m.* article in a newspaper, newspaper article; press notice. **—s=ausschnitt**, *m.* newspaper cutting. **—s=blatt**, *n.* leaf of a journal; newspaper. **—s=beilage**, *f.* supplement of *or* to a newspaper. **—s=berichterstatter**, *m.* newspaper correspondent; reporter. **—s=ente**, *f.* canard, newspaper hoax. **—s=expedition**, *f. see* **—s=amt**. **—s=junge**, *m.* newspaper-boy. **—s=kiosk**, *m.* news-stall (*where newspapers are sold in Germany*). **—s=krieg**, *m.* newspaper war. **—s=lesehalle**, *f.* news-room; free library. **—s=notiz**, *f.* notice, item, paragraph in a newspaper. **—s=papier**, *n.* news (*Comm. Lang.*); old newspapers. **—s=redakteur**, *m.* editor of a (news)paper. **—s=reklame**, *f.* puff. **—s=rubrik**, *f.* newspaper column. **—s=schreiber**, *m.* journalist. **—s=stil**, *m.* newspaper language, journalese (*coll.*). **—s=umschlag**, *m.* newspaper wrapper. **—s=verkäufer**, *m.* newsvender. **—s=wesen**, *n.* journalism, the daily press.

Zel'l—e, *f.* (*pl.* —en) cell (*of a nunnery or prison; of bees; Anat., etc.*); alveolus (*Anat.*); vesicle (*in vegetable and animal bodies*); bucket (*of water-wheels*. **—ig**, *adj.* cellular; full of cells; **—ige Beschaffenheit**, cellularity. *Comp.* **—bruder**, *m.* hermit; monk. **—en=anhäufung**, *f.* mass of cells. **—en=faser**, *f.* cellular fibre. **—en=fäule**, *f.* potato-rot. **—en=förmig**, *adj.* cellular, alveolate. **—en=gang**, *m.* cellular duct (*Anat.*); corridor (*in prisons, etc.*). **—en=gefangene(r)**, *m.* prisoner condemned to solitary confinement. **—en=gefängnis**, *n.* cellular prison, prison on the solitary system. **—en=pflanzen**, *pl.* vascular plants. **—en=rad**, *n.* bucket-wheel. **—en=system**, *n.* system of solitary confinement (in cells), Pennsylvania system. **—gewebe**, *n.* cellular tissue. **—knoten**, *m.* cellular node. **—masse**, *f.* cellular substance. **—stoff**, *m.* cellulose, celluline, protoplasm(a).

Zelo't, *m.* (—en, *pl.* —en) zealot; fanatic. **—entum**, *n.* (—s) fanaticism. **—isch**, *adj.* fanatical; (*rarely*:) zealotical.

[1]**Zelt**, *n.* (—es, *pl.* —e) tent; pavilion; awning; tabernacle; vault of heaven; tentorium (*Anat.*); **sein — aufschlagen**, to pitch one's tent. *Comp.* **—baracken**, *pl.* tent-barracks. **—baum**, *m.* tent-pole. **—bett**, *n.* canopy-bed. **—bude**, *f.* tent-stall. **—dach**, *n.* roof of a tent, awning; tent-shaped roof. **—decke**, *f.* marquee. **—haus**, *n.* pavilion. **—knopf**, *m.* the hook at the top of a tent to support the cloth. **—lager**, *n.* camp (formed of tents). **—leinwand**, *f.* tent-cloth. **—pfahl**, *m.* tent-pole. **—pflock**, *m.* tent-peg. **—stuhl**, *m.* camp-stool. **—wagen**, *m.* baggage-waggon; waggon with an awning.

[2]**Zelt**, *m.* (—es) amble. **—en**, *v.n.* to amble, to pace. **—er**, *m.* (—ers, *pl.* —er) palfrey. *Comp.* **—gang**, *m.* amble, ambling pace.

[3]**Zelt**, *m.* (—es, *pl.* —e), **—chen**, *n.* (—chens, *pl.* —chen), **—el**, *n.* (—els, *pl.* —el) tablet, lozenge, drop.

Zeni'th, *m.* (*n.*) (—s) zenith, vertical point.

Zent'ner, *m.* (—s, *pl.* —) hundred-weight, fifty kilograms. *Comp.* **—gewicht**, *n.* hundred-weight. **—last**, *f.* burden weighing a hundred-weight; heavy burden (*fig.*). **—schwer**, *adj.* weighing a hundred-weight; very heavy.

Zer—, *prefix* (*before verbs*) *usually denotes* 'to pieces,' 'away,' 'asunder,' *etc., also* 'to spoil by.' *For verbs not given in the following lists see the simple verbs. Words beginning with a vowel after the prefix* **zer** *must be pronounced with the glottal stop.*

Zerar'beiten, *v.a.* to destroy by working; to crush; **sich —**, to work o.s. to death.

Zerbei'ßen, *ir.v.a.* to crunch; to crack; to break with the teeth *or* with the beak.

Zerber'sten, *ir.v.n.* (*aux.* **s.**) to burst, split asunder.

Zerbla'sen, *ir.v.a.* to destroy by blowing; to blow away.

Zerblät'tern, *v.a.* to strip, despoil of leaves; **sich** —, to lose *or* shed its leaves; to exfoliate.

Zerbleu'en, *v.a.* to beat *or* thrash soundly.

Zerbre'ch—bar, *see* **—lich**. **—en**, *ir.v.* I. *a.* & *n.* (*aux.* **s.**) to break in pieces, to shatter, to smash to pieces, to shiver (*to atoms*); to snap; **sich** (*dat.*) **den Kopf —en**, to rack one's brains; **sich** (*dat.*) **das Kreuz —en**, to break one's back. II. *a.* to put out of joint; to disjoint. **—lich**, *adj.* brittle, fragile; breakable; with care (*on boxes*). **—lichkeit**, *f.* fragility.

Zerbrö'ckel—n, *v.a.* & *n.* (*aux.* **s.**) to crumble away *or* to pieces, to moulder. **—ung**, *f.* crumbling to pieces, mouldering.

Zerdre'schen, *ir.v.a.* to thrash to pieces; to thrash soundly.

Zerdrü'cken, *v.a.* to crush; to crumple; to squash.

Zerfah'ren, *ir.v.* I. *a.* to crush, break *or* destroy by driving over; (**die Wege**) —, to spoil by heavy carting. II. *n.* (*aux.* **s.**) to burst, fly asunder; to dissolve; **das Ei ist** —, the yolk of the egg is mixed up with the white; — **sein**, to be careless, confused, distracted, heedless, absent-minded; **—er Mensch**, scatter-brain. **—heit**, *f.* desultoriness; carelessness; unsteadiness; looseness.

Zerfa'll, *m.* (**—s**) ruin, decay; decadence (*fig.*).

Zerfal'len, I. *ir.v.a.* to break *or* crush by a fall; **sich** (*dat.*) **den Kopf** —, to hurt one's head by a fall. II. *ir.v.n.* (*aux.* **s.**) to fall to pieces, fall to ruin; to decompose; to disintegrate; to come to grief; **in mehrere Teile** —, to fall under several heads, be divided into several branches; **in Stücke** —, to crumble away *or* to pieces; **mit einem** —, to quarrel with a p. III. *p.p.* & *adj.* in ruins, dilapidated; at variance, at war. IV. *subst.n.* ruin; decomposition, dilapidation.

Zerfäl'len, *v.a.* to split up, cleave (asunder).

Zerfa'ser—n, *v.a.* to reduce to fibres *or* threads, to unravel; to fray (out). **—ung**, *f.* unravelling; close analysis.

Zerfei'len, *v.a.* to file through; to spoil by filing; to file down, file to powder.

Zerfet'zen, *v.a.* to tear up, tear in pieces; to slash, hack in pieces; to mangle, mutilate; **einem das Gesicht** —, to give a p. a cut *or* cuts across the face.

Zerflat'tern, *v.n.* (*aux.* **s.**) to be scattered (*in fluttering*), to flutter away.

Zerflei'sch—en, *v.a.* to lacerate; to tear to pieces, to mangle. **—ung**, *f.* laceration.

Zerflie'gen, *ir.v.n.* (*aux.* **s.**) to fly asunder *or* to pieces; to disperse and fly away.

Zerflie'ß—bar, *adj.* deliquescent. **—en**, *ir.v.n.* (*aux.* **s.**) to melt, dissolve, liquefy, melt away; to disperse; to deliquesce; **in Thränen —en**, to melt into tears. **—ung**, *f.* melting away, liquefaction.

Zerfol'tern, *v.a.* to (put to the) rack, torture.

Zerfran'sen, *v.a.* to pick to pieces, fray (out).

Zerfres'sen, *ir.v.a.* to eat *or* gnaw away; to corrode; to cauterize; **—d**, corrosive; septic.

Zerfrie'ren, *ir.v.n.* (*aux.* **s.**) to be broken by the frost, to freeze to pieces, to crack.

Zerge'hen, *ir.v.n.* (*aux.* **s.**) to melt, dissolve, liquefy; **der Nebel zergeht**, the mist disperses; **in Nichts** —, to dwindle to nothing.

Zergei'ßeln, *v.a.* (& *r.*) to scourge (o.s.).

Zerglie'der—er, *m.* (**—ers**, *pl.* **—er**) anatomist, dissector; analyst. **—n**, *v.a.* to dissect; to dismember; to analyze; to cut up. **—ung**, *f.* dissection, anatomy; dismemberment; analysis; **—ung lebender Tiere**, vivisection. *Comp.* **—ungs-kunst**, *f.* anatomy. **—ungs-messer**, *n.* dissecting-knife. **—ungs-saal**, *m.* dissecting-room.

Zergrä'men, *v.r.* to be consumed with grief, to pine away.

Zerha'ck—en, *v.a.* to hack, mince, chop, cut in pieces; **—te Eisenstücke**, case-shot, canister-shot.

Zerhau'en, *ir.v.a.* to cut asunder; to cut in pieces; to hew, chop, cut up; **den (gordischen) Knoten** —, to cut the Gordian knot.

Zerkau'en, *v.a.* to masticate *or* chew well *or* thoroughly.

Zerklei'ne(r)n, *v.a.* to reduce to small pieces; to pulverize, triturate.

Zerklop'fen, *v.a.* to beat, to pound, to knock to pieces, to smash.

Zerklüft—et, *p.p.* & *adj.* cleft, rifted, riven, disrupted, fissured; rugged. **—ung**, *f.* cleft, disruption, fissure, crevice, crevasse.

Zerkna'cken, *v.a.* to crack, break with the teeth *or* with the beak.

Zerknaut'schen, *v.a.* to rumple, tumble, ruffle.

Zerkni'cken, *v.a.* to crack, crush, snap (off).

Zerknir'sch—en, *v.a.* to crush, crunch; to bruise, squash; to overwhelm with regret *or* sorrow; **—t**, deeply contrite. **—theit**, **—ung**, *f.* broken-heartedness, contrition.

Zerknit'tern, *v.a.* to crumple, rumple, wrinkle.

Zerko'chen, *v.a.* & *n.* (*aux.* **s.**) to boil to rags; to boil down.

Zerkra'chen, *v.n.* to burst with a noise.

Zerkrat'zen, *v.a.* to scratch, to spoil with scratches.

Zerkrü'meln, *v.a.* to crumble away; to pulverize.

Zerlas'sen, *ir.v.a.* to melt, dissolve; to liquefy.

Zerlau'fen, *ir.v.* I. *n.* (*aux.* **s.**) *see* **Zerfließen**; to disperse; **die Landschaft zerläuft in ein breites Grasmeer**, the landscape melts into a vast prairie. II. *a.*; **sich** (*dat.*) **die Stiefel** —, to wear out one's boots with walking.

Zerle'g—bar, *adj.* that can be decomposed; that can be taken to pieces. **—en**, *v.a.* to decompose; to reduce (*a polygon to triangles, etc.*); to dissect; to analyze; to cut up; to divide; to take to pieces; **in zwei Teile —en**, to divide in two. **—er**, *m.* (**—ers**, *pl.* **—er**) carver; dissector; one who takes to pieces. **—ung**, *f.* taking to pieces, *etc.*; dissection; decomposition; analysis; **—ung der Kräfte**, resolution of forces. *Comp.* **—ungs-vermögen**, *n.* dispersive power (*Phys.*).

Zerle'sen, *ir.v.a.* to destroy by *or* in reading; **ein —es Buch**, a well-thumbed book.

Zerlu'mpt, *adj.* in rags, ragged, tattered and torn; **—er Mensch**, ragamuffin. **—heit**, *f.* ragged state.

Zermah'len, *ir.v.a.* to grind to pieces *or* to powder.

Zermal'm—en, I. *v.a.* to bruise, crush, dash in pieces; to grind to powder, pulverize; to crunch. II. *subst.n.*, **—ung**, *f.* crushing, bruising; crashing; crunching; pulverization.

Zermar'tern, *v.a.* to torment, torture; to torture to death; **sich** (*dat.*) **das Gehirn** —, to rack one's brains.

Zermü'rbt, *adj.* broken down (*in body and spirit*).

Zerna'gen, *v.a.* to gnaw *or* eat away; to erode; to corrode.

Zerpflü'cken, *v.a.* to pluck to pieces; to spoil in plucking.

Zerplat'zen, *v.n.* to burst asunder *or* in pieces.

Zerpres'sen, *v.a.* to overpress, spoil by pressing.

Zerprü'geln, *v.a.* to thrash soundly.

Zerquet'schen, *v.a.* to crush, squash, jam.

Zerrau'fen, *v.a.* to tear *or* pull off; **sich** (*dat.*) **das Haar** —, to tear one's hair; **einem das Haar** —, to tear a person's hair out.

Zerreib'—bar, *adj.* friable, triturable. **—en**, *ir. v.a.* to rub away; to grind down; to pulverize, triturate, pound. **—ung**, *f.* grinding, trituration.

Zerrei'ß—bar, *adj.* that may be torn *or* lacerated. **—en,** *ir.v.* I. *a.* to rend; to tear up, tear in pieces; to break up; to dismember; to break; to split, snap; to lacerate, mutilate, mangle; to worry; to rend (*a country by factions*); to break (*a p.'s heart*); to wear out (*clothes*); to break (*an alliance*); to rupture (*Med.*); **sich —en,** to overwork o.s.; **seine Ketten —en,** to break one's chains; **ich würde mich für ihn —en lassen,** I would die for him; **er ließe sich lieber in Stücke —en,** he would rather be torn to pieces. II. *n.* (*aux.* **s.**) to break; to burst asunder; to wear out. **—ung,** *f.* rending, breaking, tearing; laceration; rupture.

Zer'r—en, *v.a.* to pull, tug, drag, haul about; to tease, worry; **etwas in den Kot —en,** to drag a th. through the mud; **einem die Kleider vom Leibe —en,** to tear the clothes off a p.; **sich mit andern (herum)—en,** to scuffle. *Comp.* **—bild,** *n.* caricature. **—gestalt,** *f.* grotesque figure, caricature.

Zerren'n—en, *ir.v.a.* to break by running against; to remelt, dissolve, refine. *Comp.* **—herd,** *m.* finery.

Zerrin'gen, *v.a.* to wring to pieces, to spoil *or* hurt by wringing; **sich** (*dat.*) **die Hände —,** to wring one's hands in utter despair.

Zerrin'nen, *ir.v.n.* (*aux.* **s.**) to melt; to melt away, disappear, come to nothing; **in ein Nichts —,** to vanish away; **wie gewonnen, so zerronnen,** soon got, soon gone (*prov.*).

Zerris'sen, *p.p. see* **Zerreißen;** *adj.* melancholy, pessimistic (*obs.*). **—heit,** *f.* torn *or* tattered condition; raggedness; dismemberment, want of union; pessimism (*obs.*).

Zerrup'fen, *see* **Zerpflücken.**

Zerrüt't—en, *v.a.* to disarrange, unsettle, disturb; to throw into confusion; to overturn; to ruin; to shatter (*the health, etc.*); to unhinge (*the mind*). **—et=heit, —ung,** *f.* disorder, confusion; trouble; ruin.

Zersä'gen, *v.a.* to saw up, saw in pieces.

Zerschel'len, *v.* I. *a.* to dash in pieces; to shatter, shiver. II. *n.* (*aux.* **s.**) to go to pieces, to be dashed to pieces, to be shattered.

Zerschie'ßen, *ir.v.* I. *a.* to shoot to pieces; to riddle with shot. II. *n.* (*aux.* **s.**) to burst (*rare*).

Zerschla'gen, I. *ir.v.a.* to beat, break, dash to pieces; to batter; to bruise; to beat unmercifully; to cut up, to destroy; to parcel out (*an estate*); **ich bin an allen Gliedern —, alle Glieder sind mir (wie) —,** I feel as if I had been beaten black and blue, I am quite done up. II. *ir.v.r.* to break off; to divide (*into smaller veins, Min.*); to be dispersed; to be broken off; to come to nothing; to be disappointed.

Zerschlei'ßen, *ir.v.n.* to wear off, grow tattered.

Zerschlit'zen, *v.a.* to slit, slash, rip up.

Zerschmei'ßen, *ir.v.a.* to dash in pieces, smash.

Zerschmel'zen, *reg. & ir.v.a. & n.* (*aux.* **s.**) to melt (away), to dissolve.

Zerschmet'tern, *v.* I. *a.* to shatter, smash, crash, crush; to overwhelm, confound. II. *n.* (*aux.* **s.**) to be shattered.

Zerschnei'den, *ir.v.a.* to cut in pieces, cut up; to cut out; to carve; to mince; to dissect; **einem das Herz —,** to break a p.'s heart; **eine von Straßen zerschnittene Gegend,** a country intersected by roads.

Zerschnipp'(s)eln, *v.a.* to cut into shreds, shred, chip.

Zerschro'ten, *v.a.* to cut asunder; to cut in pieces; to grind coarsely; to bruise.

Zerset'z—bar, *adj.* decomposable, soluble. **—en,** *v.a.* to decompose; to dissolve; to digest; to break up; to disintegrate. **—ung,** *f.* decomposition. *Comp.* **—ungs=fieber,** *n.* putrid fever. **—ungs=kunst,** *f.* analysis. **—ungs=prozeß, —ungs=vorgang,** *m.* process of decomposition.

Zersin'gen, *v.a.* to alter *or* spoil by frequent singing, to change the original character (of a song).

Zerspal'ten, I. *v.a. & n.* (*aux.* **s.**) to cleave, split up, slit. II. *ir.p.p. of* **zerspalten.**

Zerspel'len, *v.a.* (*poet.*) *see* **Zerspalten.**

Zersplit'ter—n, *v.* I. *a.* to break into splinters; to shiver to pieces; to scatter, disperse, dissipate; to waste, lose; **seine Truppen —n,** to divide, disperse one's troops; **seine Zeit —n,** to fritter away one's time; **sich** *or* **seine Kräfte —n,** to have too many irons in the fire. II. *n.* (*aux.* **s.**) to burst, fly into fragments; to scatter about. III. *subst.n.*, **—ung,** *f.* comminuted fracture (*Surg.*); violent rupture; division into fragments; waste.

Zerspren'gen, *v.a.* to burst, spring open, blow up, explode; **eine Menschenmenge —,** to disperse a crowd.

Zersprin'gen, *ir.v.n.* (*aux.* **s.**) to fly to pieces, break, burst; to slit, crack; to explode; **der Kopf will mir —,** my head is splitting.

Zerstamp'fen, *v.a.* to pound; to trample, tread down; **zu Pulver —,** to reduce to powder.

Zerstäu'b—en, *v.* I. *a.* to pulverize; to disperse. II. *n.* (*aux.* **s.**) to turn to dust. **—er,** *m.* (**—ers,** *pl.* **—er**) (**—ungs=apparat,** *m.*) pulverizer; pestle and mortar; spray-diffuser *or* apparatus.

Zerste'chen, *ir.v.a.* to cut; to perforate; to pierce, to prick, to sting all over.

Zerstie'ben, *ir.v.n.* (*aux.* **s.**) to turn to dust, moulder; to be scattered as dust; to disperse, scatter; to vanish away.

Zerstör'bar, *adj.* perishable, destructible. **—keit,** *f.* perishableness, destructibility.

Zerstö'r—en, *v.a.* to destroy; to overthrow, demolish; to ruin; to ravage; to disorganize; **—te Gesundheit,** broken *or* shattered health; **ein —ender Grundsatz,** a destructive principle; **—te Hoffnungen,** blighted hopes; **einander gegenseitig —end,** mutually destructive. **—er,** *m.* (**—ers,** *pl.* **—er**) destroyer, devastator. **—ung,** *f.* destruction; overthrow, ruin; disorganization. *Comp.* **—ungs=geist,** *m.* spirit of destruction, subversive spirit. **—ungs=werk,** *n.* work of destruction.

Zersto'ßen, *ir.v.a.* to knock *or* beat to pieces; to bruise, to break; to pound.

Zerstreu'—en, *v.* I. *a.* to disperse, dissipate, scatter, dispel; to distract; to amuse. II. *r.* to disperse, scatter; to break up; to amuse o.s. **—t,** *p.p. & adj.* dispersed, scattered; loose; detached; wandering; sporadic; **—t sein,** to be absent-minded; **sich —en lassen,** to allow one's attention to be distracted, to allow o.s. to be diverted. **—theit,** *f.* distraction; preoccupation (*of mind*). **—ung,** *f.* dispersion; divergence, dispersion (*Opt.*); dissemination; distraction; diversion; **sich** (*dat.*) **—ung machen,** to divert, amuse o.s. *Comp.* **—ungs=linse,** *f.* diverging *or* dispersing lens (*Opt.*). **—ungs=prisma,** *n.* dispersing prism. **—ungs=punkt,** *m.* point of dispersion, focus of divergence. **—ungs=spiegel,** *m.* convex mirror. **—ungs=sucht,** *f.* fondness for amusements, dissipation.

Zerstü'ck—(e)ln, *v.a.* to cut into little pieces; to mangle, dismember; to divide, cut up; to parcel out; **mein armer Sinn ist mir —t,** my poor mind is distracted *or* shattered.

Zertan'zen, *v.a.* to wear out in dancing.

Zer'te, *f.* (*pl.* **—n**) indented duplicate of a record, *etc.*; situation of a ship on the nautical chart; plan of a ship. **—r,** *m.* (**—rs,** *pl.* **—r**) *see* **Zerte.** *Comp.* **—partie,** *f.* charter-party (*Naut.*).

Zerteil'bar, *adj.* divisible. **—keit,** *f.* divisibility.

Zertei'l—en, *v.a.* to divide, separate, disjoin; to dissolve; to disperse; to distribute; to resolve; to cut up; **in Brüche —en,** to reduce to fractions. **—ung,** *f.* division; dismemberment; separation; decomposition; resolution (*Med.*); resolution (into factors).

Zertram'peln, Zertrap'pe(l)n, *v.a.* to trample under foot, to trample down.

Zertren'nen, *see* **Trennen** *and* **Zerteilen.**

Zertre'ten, *v.a.* to crush *or* trample down *or* under foot.

Zertrüm'mer—er, *m.* (—ers, *pl.* —er) destroyer. **—n,** I. *v.a.* to destroy, crush, shatter; to lay in ruins; to demolish, overthrow. II. *v.n.* (*aux.* **s.**) to shatter, be wrecked *or* ruined. III. *subst. n.*, **—ung,** *f.* ruin, destruction.

Zerwir'ken, *v.a.* to skin and cut up (*a deer*).

Zerwüh'len, *v.a.* to root up; to rummage *or* grub about (in); to dishevel (hair).

Zerwürf'nis, *n.* (—(ss)es, *pl.* —(ss)e) difference, quarrel; strife; **in — bringen,** to embroil.

Zerzau'sen, *v.a. see* **Zausen**; to tumble, crumple; to dishevel (hair); to pull to pieces; **einen tüchtig —,** to handle a p. roughly.

Zerzup'fen, *v.a.* to pull to pieces; to unravel, fuzz.

Ze'ter, I. *n.* (—s, *pl.* —) cry of distress *or* murder, cry for help, yell. II. *int.* murder! **— schreien,** to cry murder, cry for help; **— über einen schreien,** to raise a hue and cry after a p., to cry shame upon s.o. **—n,** *v.a. see* **—schreien.** *Comp.* **—geschrei,** *n.* shouts for help; cry of murder; loud outcry. **—mordio,** *n. see* **Zeter.**

[1]**Zet'tel,** *m.* (—s, *pl.* —) scrap of paper; paper; note; memorandum; ticket; bill; playbill; placard; label; docket; etiquette (*on bottles*); pattern. **—n,** *v.a.* to scatter, strew; to make plots, to intrigue; to label. **—ung,** *f.* machination, plot, intrigue. *Comp.* **—ankleber, —anschläger,** *m.* bill-sticker. **—anschlagen,** *n.* bill-sticking; **das —anschlagen ist verboten,** stick no bills! **—aussuchen,** *n.* sorting of papers *or* tickets. **—bank,** *f.* bank of issue. **—träger,** *m.* person who carries *or* distributes bills *or* tickets; sandwich-man.

[2]**Zet'tel,** *m.* (—s, *pl.* —) chain, warp (*Weav.*). *Comp.* **—baum,** *m.* beam for the warp (*Weav.*). **—ende,** *n.* fag-end.

Zeuch! *imper. sing;* **Zeuchst, Zeucht,** *2 & 3 pers. sing. pres. ind. of* **ziehen** (*obs. & poet.*).

Zeug, *n.* (*& dial. m.*) (—es, *pl.* —e) stuff, substance, matter; material; cloth, fabric, stuff; clothes; stuff (*Pap.*); implements, tools; apparatus; utensils; pots and pans, crockery; dough; baking powder; type-metal; fishing-tackle; cast metal; artillery, ordnance (*obs.*); accoutrements; equipage; harness, trappings; hunting-apparatus; nets, toils; rigging, tackle, *etc.* of a ship; stuff, bosh, nonsense; trash; refuse(*-type, etc.*); **Ganz—,** pulp (*Pap.*); *see* **Gezeug, Leinzeug, Weißzeug; das — haben zu,** to have the required ability for; **er hat das — dazu,** he is cut out for it, made for it; **er hat das — zu einem Künstler,** he has the stuff for an artist in him; **was das — hält** *or* **(nur) halten will,** as much as possible; **einem etwas am —e flicken,** to pick a hole in a p.'s coat, pull s.o. to pieces; **ins — gehen,** to set to work with a will; **allerhand —(s),** all sorts of things; **albernes** *or* **dummes —,** stuff and nonsense; **mach' kein dummes —,** don't play the fool! **das ist schönes —!** pretty stuff that! **—e,** *m.* (—en, *pl.* —en), **—in,** *f.* witness; **ich habe sie zu —en genommen** *or* **angerufen,** I have summoned them to appear as witnesses; **einen —en stellen,** to produce evidence. **—enschaft,** *f.* testimony, deposition, evidence; the witnesses. **—nis,** *n.* (—(ss)es, *pl.* —(ss)e) testimony, evidence; deposition; certificate, testimonial; character; discharge; authority; **—nis ablegen,** to bear testimony, vouch (*for*); **einem ein —nis ausstellen,** to write a p. a testimonial; **ein hinreichendes —nis von . . .,** a sufficient proof *or* test of . . .; **Du sollst kein falsch —nis reden wider Deinen Nächsten,** thou shalt not bear false witness against thy neighbour; **buchhändlerische —nisse sind nicht zulässig,** bookseller's certificates are not admissible; **Schul—nis,** school-report. *Comp.* **—amt,** *n.* board of ordnance. **—baum,** *m.* weaver's beam. **—bütte,** *f.* pulp-vat (*Pap.*). **—drucker,** *m.* printer on calico, linen, woollen stuffs, *etc.* **—druckerei,** *f.* print-works. **—en-aussage,** *f.* deposition, testimony. **—en-bestechung,** *f.* suborning of witnesses. **—en-beweis,** *m.* proof afforded by evidence. **—en-eid,** *m.* oath administered to witnesses. **—en-eidlich,** *adj.*; **—eneidliche Vernehmung,** taking of a deposition made on oath. **—en-verhör,** *n.*, **—en-vernehmung,** *f.* hearing of witnesses. **—fabrik,** *f.* manufactory of textile fabrics. **—hauptmann,** *m.* captain of the artillery dépôt. **—haus,** *n.* arsenal, armoury; hut for spare guns, ammunition (*Hunt.*). **—haus-verwalter,** *m.* arsenal superintendent. **—jagd,** *f.* chase, hunt with nets, *etc.* **—kammer,** *f.* tool-room, armoury. **—kasten,** *m.* linen-chest; stuff-chest, room *or* box in which the ground rags are kept (*Pap.*); case for rejected type. **—knecht,** *m.* man that has the care of the hunting-equipage, keeper. **—leutnant,** *m.* lieutenant of the artillery dépôt. **—meister,** *m.* inspector-general of ordnance; overseer of hunting requisites. **—nis-ablegung,** *f.* deposition. **—nis-brief,** *m.* testimonial, certificate. **—nis-zwang,** *m.* obligation to give evidence. **—offizier,** *m.* officer of the artillery dépôt. **—presse,** *f.* clothes-press, calender. **—pressen,** *n.* calendering. **—probe,** *f.* pattern of material. **—rolle,** *f.* calender; mangle. **—schmied,** *m.* edge-tool maker. **—schreiber,** *m.* arsenal-clerk. **—sergeant,** *m.* sergeant in the artillery-dépôt. **—stiefel,** *pl.* cloth boots. **—tapete,** *f.* tapestry. **—wagen,** *m.* cart for carrying the hunting-requisites. **—wärter,** *m.* inspector *or* guard of an arsenal *or* of artillery; keeper of hunting-requisites. **—weber, —wirker,** *m.* stuff-manufacturer.

[1]**Zeu'gen,** *v.n.* to bear witness *or* testimony, to testify, depose, give evidence (of).

[2]**Zeu'g—en,** *v.a.* to engender, beget, procreate; to give being to; to produce. **—er,** *m.* (—ers, *pl.* —er), (**—erin,** *f.*) procreator, generator, begetter, father, (mother). *Comp.* **—mutter,** *f.* alma mater, Nature. **—ung,** *f.* generation, begetting, procreation. **—ungs-apparat,** *m.* genital organs. **—ungs-fähig,** *adj.* capable of begetting, procreative. **—ungs-kraft,** *f.* generative faculty *or* power. **—ungs-organe,** *pl.* genital organs, privy parts. **—ungs-stoff,** *m.* matter of generation. **—ungs-trieb,** *m.* sexual instinct, procreative impulse. **—ungs-unfähig,** *adj.* impotent; sterile. **—ungs-unfähigkeit,** *f.* impotence; sterility.

Zib'be, *f.* (*pl.* —n) (*coll.*) ewe-lamb; little nanny goat; young doe-hare *or* doe-rabbit.

Zibe'be, *f.* (*pl.* —n) largest sort of raisin.

Zi'beth, *m.* (—(e)s, *pl.* —e) civet. *Comp.* **—katze,** *f.* civet cat. **—ratte,** *f.* musk-rat. **—tier,** *n.* musk-weasel.

Zi'ck—e, *f.* (*pl.* —en) (*prov.*) *see* **Ziege.** **—el** *n.* (—els, *pl.* —el), **—lein,** *n.* (—leins, *pl.* —lein) kid. **—eln,** *v.n.* (*aux.* **h.**) to kid.

Zick'zack, *m.* (—s, *pl.* —e) *& adv.* zigzag; **im — fahren,** to zigzag, flutter (*of lightnings*); **im — laufen,** to (run) zigzag, to crankle; to double (*of hares*); **im — segeln,** to tack about. **—ig,** *adj.* zigzag. *Comp.* **—förmig,** *adj.* (*going*) zigzag.

Zie'ge, *f.* (*pl.* —n) goat; she-goat; Cyprinu cultratus (*Icht.*); **die — meckert,** the goa bleats. *Comp.* **—n=artig,** *adj.* goat-like, goatish. **—n=auge,** *n.* goat's eye; ægilops (*Med.*). **—n=bart,** *m.* goat's beard. **—n=bock,** *m.* he-goat; snip (*nickname for a tailor*). **—n=fell,** *n.* goatskin; gegerbtes —nfell, kid (-leather). **—n=fleisch,** *n.* goat, goat's flesh. **—en=füßig,** *adj.* goat-footed; —enfüßiger Gott, satyr. **—n=hären,** *adj.* of goat's-hair. **—n=hirt,** *m.* goatherd. **—n=käse,** *m.* cheese made from goat's milk. **—n=lamm,** *n.* kid. **—n=leder,** *n.* kid(-leather). **—n=melker,** *m.* milker of goats; goatsucker (*Orn.*). **—n=peter,** *m.* mumps.

Zie'gel, *m.* (—s, *pl.* —) brick; tile; — brennen, to burn bricks; hohler —, pantile; mit —n decken, to tile. **—ei',** *f.* brick-works, brick-yard; tile-works, tilery. *Comp.* **—anstrich,** *m.* brickwork, inlaying *or* facing with bricks *or* tiles. **—arbeit,** *f.* brickwork; laying down of bricks. **—bau,** *m.* bricklaying; brick building. **—brenner,** *m.* brickmaker, tilemaker; owner of a brick-kiln. **—dach,** *n.* tiled roof. **—decker,** *m.* tiler. **—erde,** *f.* brick-clay *or* -earth, loam. **—erz,** *n.* tile-ore. **—farbe,** *f.* brick- *or* tile-colour. **—farbig,** *adj.* brick-coloured. **—händler,** *m.* brick and tile merchant. **—hütte,** *f.* brick-kiln, tile-kiln. **—mehl,** *n.* brick-dust. **—meister,** *see* **Ziegler.** **—ofen,** *m.* brick-kiln; tile-furnace. **—presse,** *f.* brick-press. **—rohbau,** *m.* (visible) brickwork. **—rot,** *adj.* brick-red. **—stein,** *m.* brick; tile. **—streichen,** *n.* moulding of tiles *or* bricks, brickmaking. **—streicher,** *m.* moulder of bricks *or* tiles. **—thon,** *m.* brick-clay, loam. **—werk,** *n.* brickwork, brick masonry.

Zie'ger, *m.* (—s, *pl.* —) whey; (—käse,) whey cheese.

Zieg'ler, *m.* (—s, *pl.* —) brickmaker.

Zieh, Zie'he, *1 & 3 pers. sing. imperf. ind. & subj. of* zeihen.

Zieh'bar, *adj.* ductile. **—keit,** *f.* ductility.

Zie'h—en, I. *ir.v.a.* to draw (*a carriage; a line; the sword; conclusions; water, etc.*); to pull, haul, tug; to pull, ring (*the bell*); to tow; to take off (*one's hat*); to move (*at draughts, etc.*); to attract (*iron, etc.*); to extract (*teeth*); to obtain, bring; to bring up, rear, nurture; to train; to erect; to describe (*a circle, etc.*); to rifle (*a gun*); to prepare by drawing (*as gold, wire, etc.*); to dip (*candles*); to drawl (*one's words*); to warp (*wood*); to prepare (*quills*); **die Achsel —en,** to shrug the shoulders; **die Bilanz —en,** to draw up, make out the balance-sheet (*C. L.*); **Blasen —en,** to raise blisters; **Flachs —en,** to pull flax, (**durch die Hechel —en**) to hackle flax; **Gesichter —en,** to make faces; **ein Gesicht —en,** to pull a (*long*) face; **einen Graben —en,** to dig a ditch, throw up trenches; **einem einen Hieb —en,** to give a p. a smart blow; **den Hut vor einem —en,** to raise one's hat to a p.; **den Kürzeren —en,** to come off a loser, get the worst of it; **das Los —en,** to draw lots; **eine Mauer —en,** to build a wall; **den Mund —en,** to twist the mouth, put on a wry face; **Narben —en,** to grain leather; **eine Niete —en,** to draw a blank; **Nutzen, Gewinn, Vorteil (von** *or* **aus einer S.) —en,** to derive profit, advantage (*from a th.*); **Pflanzen —en,** to cultivate plants; **eine Senkrechte —en,** to erect a perpendicular; **die Stirne —en, das Gesicht in Falten —en,** to frown; **Wirbel —en,** to eddy; **die Sonne —t Wasser,** the sun sucks up water, moisture; **das Schiff —t Wasser,** the vessel leaks; **einen Vergleich —en,** to draw *or* make a comparison; **einen am Arme —en,** to drag a p. by the arm; **einen an** (*or* **bei**) **den Haaren —en,** to drag a p. by the hair; **an sich** (*acc.*) **—en,** to attract, draw to o.s., to absorb, imbibe, to draw back, to withdraw, to draw together, collect, to engross, monopolize, absorb, to win over to one's side; **mit Gewalt an sich —en,** to seize upon; **ein Boot ans Land —en,** to haul a boat ashore; **etwas ans Licht —en,** to bring something to light, make a th. known; **einen am Ärmel —en,** to pluck a p. by the sleeve; **an demselben Seile —en,** to play the same game; **auf die Seite —en,** to draw aside; **auf seine Seite —en,** to win over to one's side; **Saiten auf eine Geige —en,** to string a violin; **Wein auf Flaschen —en,** to bottle wine; **einen Wechsel auf einen —en,** to draw a bill on s.o.; **alle** *or* **aller Augen auf sich —en,** to attract universal attention; **die Aufmerksamkeit auf eine S. —en,** to direct attention to something; **jemandes Ungnade auf sich —en,** to incur a p.'s displeasure; **den Kork aus der Flasche —en,** to take the cork out of the bottle; **den Kopf aus der Schlinge —en,** to slip the collar, to make one's escape, to extricate o.s.; **Nutzen aus etwas —en,** to derive profit from a th., turn a th. to one's own account; **Schlüsse aus etwas —en,** to conclude *or* draw conclusions from a th.; **aus der Verlegenheit —en,** to extricate from a difficulty; **wie aus dem Wasser gezogen,** drenched; **Pflanzen aus Stecklingen —en,** to raise plants from layers; **die Wurzel aus einer Zahl —en,** to extract the root of a number; **etwas aus einander —en,** to draw a th. out (*as elastic*), to pull asunder; **aus einem Geschäft viel Geld —en,** to make a great deal of money by a business, to draw large profits from a business; **ich bin bei den Haaren dazu gezogen worden,** I have been forced to do it; **durch den Schmutz —en,** to drag through the dirt; **in Beratung —en,** to take into consideration, deliberate on; **in die Enge —en,** to contract, narrow; **in die Höhe —en,** to draw *or* pull up, to raise; **ins Geheimnis —en,** to take *or* let into the secret; **einen in sein Interesse —en,** to attach a p. to one's interests; **er —t alles ins Lächerliche,** he turns everything into ridicule; **in die Länge —en,** to draw out lengthways, to spin out; **in sich —en,** to soak up, imbibe, absorb; **einen ins Unglück —en,** to involve a p. in misfortune; **in Verdacht —en,** to suspect; **ins Vertrauen —en,** to take into one's confidence; **in Zweifel —en,** to call in question, doubt; **mit hinein —en,** (**in eine S.**) to involve (in a th.); **nach sich —en,** to draw after one *or* along with one; to cause, bring about, to be attended with; **ernste Folgen nach sich —en,** to have serious consequences; **ein Kleid über das andere —en,** to put on one dress over another; **einem das Netz** (*or* **Garn**) **über den Kopf —en,** to ensnare a p.; **einem das Fell über die Ohren —en,** to fleece s. o.; **vor Gericht —en,** to summon before a court of law; **einem die Larve vom Gesicht —en,** to tear the mask from a p.'s face; (**einen**) **Gewinn** *or* **Vorteil von etwas —en,** to derive profit from a th.; **der Abzug der Baiern zog die Preußen vor Frankfurt,** the departure of the Bavarians caused the Prussians to march upon Frankfort; **einen zu sich —en,** to attract a p.; **einen zu Boden —en,** to throw a p. down; **ein Kind zum Guten —en,** to bring up a child in the right way; **einen zu Rate —en,** to consult (with) a p.; **zur Rechenschaft —en,** to call to account; **einen zur Tafel —en,** to invite, to summon someone to dinner, *etc.*; **sich** (*dat.*) **etwas zu Herzen, zu Gemüte —en,** to take a th. to heart; **einen zur Strafe —en,** to punish a p., inflict a penalty on a p. II. *ir.v.r.* to move, to draw (*towards*); to march (*towards*); to stretch, extend; to be elastic, stretch; to warp; to penetrate, soak in; **das Gebirge**

—t sich weit ins Meer, the mountains run far out into the sea; **der Wald —t sich längs den Bergen hin,** the wood extends along the mountains; **sich ins Enge —en,** (*fig.*) to limit one's expenses; **die Strümpfe —en sich nach dem Fuße,** the stockings give to the feet; **sich in die Länge —en,** to grow long; to last long, to be protracted; **der Handel zog sich sehr in die Länge,** the affair took a long time to settle; **der Krieg —t sich außerordentlich in die Länge,** the war drags on for a very long time; **sich ins Blaue —en,** to have a tinge of blue; **das Brett hat sich gezogen,** the board has warped; **die Sache wird sich zurecht —en,** the matter will be arranged. III. *ir.v.n.* **1.** (*aux.* **h.**) to prove attractive, to draw, to attract the public; to swallow, drink; **die Wage ist so empfindlich, daß selbst ein so kleines Gewicht —t,** the balance is so nicely adjusted that even so small a weight turns the scale; **der neue Professor —t,** the new professor draws large audiences, proves a success; **dieser Grund —t bei mir nicht,** this reason does not weigh with me; **mit dem König —en,** to move, play the king (*Chess*); **es —t hier,** there is a draught here; **es —t durch diese Thür,** a draught comes from that door; **es —t mich in der Schulter,** I have a twitching, a slight pain in my shoulder (*coll.*); **der Thee hat jetzt genug gezogen,** the tea has now drawn sufficiently *or* has stood long enough; **—en, wer Karten giebt,** to cut *or* draw for deal; **die Löcher —en,** the pockets attract (*the balls*); **der Ofen —t gut,** the stove draws well. **2.** (*aux.* **s.**) to advance slowly; to march, go; to migrate; to change one's residence; to remove; to change one's place (*as a servant*); **das Gewitter ist südwärts gezogen,** the storm has passed over to the south; **gezogen kommen,** to arrive; **die Kreuz und Quer —en,** to journey in a zig-zag line; **auf ein anderes Zimmer —en,** to change one's room; **die Wolken —en aus Süden,** the clouds come from the south; **der Rauch —t ins Zimmer,** the smoke is coming into the room; **durch die Stadt —en,** to pass through the town; **in einen Dienst —en,** to enter a p.'s service; **in die Fremde —en,** to go abroad *or* to a strange country; **in den Krieg —en,** to go to the war; **übers Meer —en,** to cross the sea; **laß mich —en,** let me go *or* depart; **in die Stadt —en,** to remove to the town; **aufs Land —en,** to go to live in the country; **in ein Haus —en,** to move into a house; **zu einem —en,** to go to live with a p.; **zu Felde, ins Feld —en,** to take the field; **gezogener Federkiel,** dressed quill; **gezogene Lichte,** dip candles; **gezogenes Rohr,** rifled barrel. IV. *subst.n.* drawing; pulling; cultivation; rearing; migration; draught; removal; attraction; rheumatic pain, twinges in the limbs; surveying (*for a mine*). **—er,** *m.* (**—ers,** *pl.* **—er**) drawer, tower; drawer (*of a bill*); any instrument used for drawing; siphon; trigger. **—ung,** *f.* drawing (*of lots, etc.*). *Comp.* **—band,** *n.* string by which anything is drawn; iron hoop *or* cramp for binding things together. **—bank,** *f.* wire-drawing frame; machine for rifling guns. **—bilderbuch,** *n.* movable toy-book. **—brunnen,** *m.* draw-well, bucket-well. **—deckel,** *m.* file for papers, manuscripts, *etc.* **—eisen,** *n.* draw-plate, wire-plate; screw (*of a cork-screw*). **—fenster,** *n.* sash-window. **—garn,** *n.* large net for catching birds. **—gewicht,** *n.* bumper. **—haken,** *m.* draught-hook; tire-dog. **—harmonika,** *f.* accordion. **—hund,** *m.* dog used for drawing. **—kind,** *n.* foster-child. **—klimmen,** *n.* rise and fall (*Gymn.*); climbing a ladder with the aid only of one's hands (*Gymn.*). **—klinge,** *f.* scraper; slice (*Typ.*). **—klinke,** *f.* draw-latch. **—kraft,** *f.* power of drawing; attraction. **—leine,** *f.* cord for drawing *or* pulling; tow-rope. **—maschine,** *f.* wire-drawing machine; stretching-machine. **—pferd,** *n.* draught-horse. **—pflaster,** *n.* blister. **—rad,** *n.* glazier's vice. **—schacht,** *m.* shaft by which the ore is taken out, working-shaft (*Min.*). **—seil,** *n.* towing-line; hauling-rope; trace used in drilling. **—stange,** *f.* pump-gear; beam of a plough. **—stengel,** *m.* cigar (*sl.*). **—tag,** *m.* (**—zeit,** *f.*) day (time) of removal. **—topf,** *m.* pot for boiling clothes in. **—ungs-liste,** *f.* list (*in newspapers*) of the prizes in a lottery. **—ungs-tag,** *m.* day appointed for the drawing of a lottery. **—wage,** *f.* steelyard. **—weg,** *m.* towing-path. **—werk,** *n.* machine for drawing *or* pulling. **—zange,** *f.* wire-pincers, pliers; forceps (*Med.*).

Ziel, *n.* (**—s,** *pl.* **—e**) limit, boundary, extremity; end; goal; destination; butt, target; winning-post; term; aim, scope, object; **seinem Ehrgeize ein — setzen,** to set limits to one's ambition; **Maß und — halten,** to keep within bounds; **das — überschreiten,** to overstep the limits; **am —e seines Lebens sein,** to be at the end of one's life, to have lived one's life; **auf drei Monate —,** having three months to run, at 3 months' credit; **— einer Reise,** goal of a journey; **ohne — umhergehen,** to wander aimlessly about; **am — seiner Wünsche angelangt sein,** to have attained one's desire *or* object; **auf diesem Weg sind wir noch weit vom —e,** by this road we are still far from our destination *or* our goal; **er ist weit vom —e,** he is quite beside the mark; **einem das — verrücken,** to frustrate a p.'s designs; **sich** (*dat.*) **ein hohes — stecken** *or* **setzen,** to aim at something great; **— des Schützen,** mark, butt, object aimed at; **das — treffen,** to hit the mark; **das — aufsitzen lassen,** to put the foresight below the object aimed at; **die Pferde kamen zu gleicher Zeit ans —,** the horses came in neck and neck. **—en,** *v.n.* (*aux* **h.**) to aim; **auf eine S. —en,** to aim at, to drive at, to tend to, to strive towards, to allude *or* refer to a th.; **nach einer S. —en,** to aim at a th. **—er,** *m.* (**—ers,** *pl.* **—er**) one who aims; person that marks the shots on the target; artilleryman that points the gun. *Comp.* **—bewußt,** *adj.* conscious of one's aim, systematic, methodical. **—leistung,** *f.* aim of instruction (*in schools*), knowledge *or* aptitude to be expected from pupils at the end of the instruction. **—los,** *adj.* aimless, purposeless. **—punkt,** *m.* goal; bull's eye, white spot (*in a target*). **—scheibe,** *f.* target, butt, aim; **—scheibe (für die Geschosse) des Witzes,** laughing-stock, butt. **—tafel,** *f.* slide (*Surv.*).

Zie'm—en, *v.r. & n.* (*aux.* **h.,** *dat.*) to beseem, become, to suit, be fitting for; **es —t sich nicht, das zu thun,** it is not the proper thing to do it; **es —t sich nicht, daß du . . .,** it is not becoming for you to . . . **—lich,** I. *adj.* fit, suitable, becoming; reasonable (*of price*); moderate, tolerable, pretty considerable *or* large; **eine —liche Strecke,** a considerable distance; **eine —liche Anzahl Leute,** a goodish *or* good number of people. II. *adv.* pretty, tolerably; **—lich gut,** pretty good, tolerably well; **—lich natürlich,** natural enough; **—lich spät,** rather late; **—lich weit,** a rather long way (off); **es waren —lich viel Fremde da,** there were a good many strangers there; **er ist so —lich von meinem Alter,** he is about the same age as I am, he is about my age.

Zie'mer, *m.* (**—s,** *pl.* **—**) buttock, hind-quarter (*of animals*); haunch (*of venison*); yard, pizzle.

Zie'pen, *v.a.;* **einen an den Haaren —**, to pull, drag a p. by the hair (*prov.*).

Zier, *f.* (*pl.* **—en**) *see* **—de. —at**, *m.* (**—ats**, *pl.* **—ate**) ornament, decoration, embellishment; flourish. **—de**, *f.* (*pl.* **—den**) ornament, decoration; ornament, honour (*to one's country, etc.*). *Comp.* **—aten=macher**, *m.* ornament-maker, decorator (*Arch.*). **—aten=maler**, *m.* decorator, decorative painter.

Zie'r—en, *v.* I. *a.* to ornament, adorn, be an ornament to; to decorate, embellish, deck, set off; to garnish. II. *r.* to be affected, behave affectedly; to mince (*one's words*); to be prim, prudish *or* coy; to pretend to refuse; to refuse from affectation, to make formalities; **geziertes Wesen**, affectation, prudishness; **—en Sie sich nicht so!** do not be so affected! do not give yourself airs! **nehmen Sie es nur und —en Sie sich nicht!** just take it and do not stand upon ceremony! **—erei'**, *f.* airs and graces, affectations. **—lich**, *adj.* decorative, ornamental, elegant; neat; fine, nice, pretty, dainty, delicate; polite. **—lichkeit**, *f.* grace; elegance; nicety; fineness; politeness; pretty thing. *Comp.* **—äffchen**, *n.*, **—affe**, *m.* fop, coxcomb; affected person; dressed-up fop *or* dolly of a girl. **—blume**, *f.* decorative ornamental plant. **—buchstabe**, *m.* ornamental letter. **—druck**, *m.* decorative printing. **—garten**, *m.* pleasure-grounds, flower-garden. **—gärtner**, *m.* ornamental *or* fancy gardener. **—kunst**, *f.* decorative art. **—leiste**, *f.* tringle; tail-piece (*Typ.*). **—pflanze**, *f.* decorative plant. **—puppe**, *f.* affected person. **—schriften**, *pl.* ornamental type.

Ziest, *m.* (**—es**, *pl.* **—e**) hedge-nettle (*Stachys*).

Zies'tig, *m.* (**—s**) Tuesday (*dial.*).

Zif'fer, *f.* (*pl.* **—n**) figure, numeral; cipher, secret character; **—n auf der Uhr**, figures marking the hours on the clock, *etc.;* **mit** *or* **in —n schreiben**, to write in cipher; **mit —n bezeichnen**, to figure. **—ig**, *adj.;* **eine vier —ige Zahl**, a number of four digits, running into four figures. **—n**, *v.a. & n.* (*aux.* **h.**) to cipher; to figure (*Mus.*). *Comp.* **—blatt**, *n.* face, dial-plate (*of a clock*). **—brief**, *m.* letter written in cipher. **—kunst**, *f.* art of writing in cipher. **—n=mäßig**, *adj.* numeral, absolutely exact; **etwas —nmäßig beweisen**, to prove s.th. by figures. **—rechnung**, *f.* arithmetic, numeral calculation. **—schlüssel**, *m.* key to cipher. **—schrift**, *f.* cipher code. **—system**, *n.* numerical notation. **—telegramm**, *n.* code telegram, cipher telegram.

Zigar're, *see* **Cigarre**.

Zigeu'ner, *m.* (**—s**, *pl.* **—**) gipsy; Romany. **—in**, *f.* female gipsy, gipsy woman *or* girl. **—haft, —isch**, *adj.* gipsylike, gipsy; Bohemian; vagrant. **—n**, *v.n.* (*aux.* **h.**) to lead a gipsy life; to rove, wander about; to lead a vagrant life. **—tum**, *n.* (**—s**) Bohemianism, gipsies' ways, gipsyism. *Comp.* **—bande**, *f.* band *or* gang of gipsies. **—bursche**, *m.* young gipsy. **—kunde**, *f.* gipsology. **—lager**, *n.* gipsy encampment. **—leben**, *n.* life of a gipsy, wandering *or* vagrant life. **—mädchen**, *n.* gipsy girl. **—sprache**, *f.* language of the gipsies, Romany. **—volk**, *n.* the gipsies; gipsydom. **—wagen**, *m.* gipsy van. **—wesen**, *n.* gipsyism, gipsy calling.

Zika'de, *f.* (*pl.* **—n**) grasshopper.

Zil'le, *f.* (*pl.* **—n**) little boat, skiff.

Zim'bel, *f.* (*pl.* **—n**) cymbal (*Mus.*).

Zim'mer, *n.* (**—s**, *pl.* **—**) room, chamber; timber; timbered building; woodwork of a mine; packet of forty skins (*Furr.*); **Arbeits—**, work-room, study; **Wohn—**, sitting room; **möblierte —**, furnished apartments; **unmöbliertes —**, unfurnished room; **Haus mit elf —n**, eleven-roomed house; **— mit zwei Betten**, double-bedded room; **— nach vorn hinaus**, front-room; **— nach hinten hinaus**, a back room; **— nach der Straße hinaus**, room looking into the street. **—chen**, *n.* (**—chens**, *pl.* **—chen**) little room, closet. *Comp.* **—bekleidung**, *f.* furniture of a room; wainscotting. **—decke**, *f.* ceiling. **—douche**, *f.* bath in one's room. **—jungfer**, *f.*, **—mädchen**, *n.* chambermaid, housemaid. **—kellner**, *m.* waiter who attends on visitors in their rooms. **—pflanzen**, *pl.* indoor plants. **—reich**, *adj.* roomy. **—reihe**, *f.* suite of rooms. **—spiel**, *n.* indoor game, parlour game. **—stück**, *n.* painting of, scene in an interior. **—vermieter(in**, *f.*), *m.* lodging-house keeper. **—verzierer**, *m.* decorator.

Zim'mer—n, *v.a. & n.* (*aux.* **h.**) to cut, frame and join timber; to frame, make, build; to carpenter; to fabricate. **—ung**, *f.* carpentering; timber-work. *Comp.* **—arbeit**, *f.* carpenter's work; timber-work. **—beil**, *n.* carpenter's axe, adze. **—bock**, *m.* carpenter's trestle. **—gerät**, *n.* carpenter's tools; furniture; upholstery. **—gesell**, *m.* journeyman-carpenter. **—handwerk**, *n.* carpentry; carpenter's trade. **—hof**, *m.* carpenter's yard, timber-yard. **—holz**, *n.* timber, wood for building. **—mann**, *m.* (*pl.* **—leute**) carpenter; **einem zeigen, wo der —mann das Loch gelassen** *or* **gemacht hat**, to show a p. the door (*coll.*). **—meister**, *m.* master-carpenter; master-builder. **—nagel**, *m.* carpenter's nail; peg, pin. **—polier, —polierer**, *m.* foreman, head journeyman-carpenter. **—späne**, *pl.* chips. **—werk**, *n. see* **—arbeit.**

Zim'met, Zimt, *m.* (**—s**) cinnamon. **—en**, *adj.* cinnamon. *Comp.* **—baum**, *m.* cinnamon-tree; (**weißer**) Canella alba. **—blüte**, *f.* cinnamon-flower. **—braun, —farben**, *adj.* cinnamon-brown. **—mandeln**, *pl.* almonds covered with candied cinnamon. **—nägelein**, *n.* clove of cinnamon. **—rinde**, *f.* bark of the cinnamon-tree. **—röhrchen**, *n.* cinnamon-stick. **—rose**, *f.* cinnamon-rose. **—säure**, *f.* cinnamic acid.

Zim'per—lich, *adj.* prim, prudish; affected; finicking. **—lichkeit**, *f.* affectation. **—n**, *see* **Zieren** II. *Comp.* **—liese**, *f.* prude, prudish girl, bread-and-butter miss.

Zin'del, *m.* (**—s**, *pl.* **—**) (**—taffet**, *m.*) light taffeta.

Zin'gulum, *n.* (**—s**) girdle (*of a R. C. priest*).

Zink, *m. & n.* (**—(e)s**) zinc; **— beschlägt an der Luft**, zinc tarnishes in the air. *Comp.* **—artig**, *adj.* of the nature of zinc. **—asche**, *f.* dross of zinc. **—ätzung**, *f.* zincography. **—blech**, *n.* sheet-zinc. **—blende**, *f.* zinc sulphide. **—blumen**, *pl.* oxide of zinc. **—butter**, *f.* chloride of zinc. **—dach**, *n.* roof covered with zinc. **—erz**, *n.* zinc-ore. **—gewinnung**, *f.* extraction of zinc. **—haltig**, *adj.* containing zinc. **—kalk**, *m. see* **—asche. —ographie'**, *f.* zincography. **—salbe**, *f.* zinc ointment. **—vitriol**, *m.* (*& n.*) sulphate of zinc. **—wasser**, *n.* zinc lotion.

Zin'k—e, *f.* (*pl.* **—en**), **—en**, *m.* (**—ens**, *pl.* **—en**) prong (*of a fork, etc.*); spike; tooth (*of a comb*); tenon, dove-tail (*Carp.*); cornet. **—enist'**, *m.* (**—enis'ten**, *pl.* **—enis'ten**) *see* **—enbläser. —ig**, *adj.* pronged, toothed. *Comp.* **—en=bläser**, *m.* player on the cornet *or* bugle. **—en=register**, *n.*, **—en=zug**, *m.* cornet-register (*Org.*).

Zin'ken, *v.a.* to play the cornet; to furnish with prongs; to join by means of mortise and tenon; **dreigezinkte Gabel**, three-pronged fork.

Zinn, *n.* (**—(e)s**) tin; pewter; tin-ware. **—e(r)n**, *adj.* tin, pewter. *Comp.* **—asche**, *f.* tin-ashes, (tin-) putty. **—bad**, *n.* melted tin. **—bergwerk**, *n.* tin-mine. **—block**, *m.* bar of tin. **—erz**, *n.* tin-ore. **—geschirr**, *m.* pewter *or* tin-vessel. **—folio**, *n.* tin-foil. **—geschrei**, *n.* creaking of tin. **—gießer**, *m.* tin-man. **—haltig**, *adj.* containing tin, stanniferous. **—inseln**, *pl.*

Cassiterides (*on the west coast of England*). —**kies**, *m.* tin-pyrites, stannine. —**oxyd**, *n.* stannic oxide. —**oxydul**, *n.* stannous oxide. —**salz**, *n.* stannic salt. —**sand**, *m.* grain-tin. —**säure**, *f.* stannic acid. —**seife**, *f.* stream-tin. —**ver=bindung**, *f.* compound of tin. —**waren**, *pl.* tin-ware(s), tins. —**werk**, *n.* tin-works, stannary.

Zin'ne, *f.* (*pl.* —**n**) pinnacle; spire; battlement; pointed rocky peak (*Mount.*); Heaven (*in old miracle plays*); **mit —n versehen**, crenel(l)-ated, embattled. *Comp.* —**n=förmig**, *adj.* crenel(l)ated. —**n=lücke**, *f.* notching, loophole, crenelle. —**n=werk**, *n.* embattled work.

Zin'nel—n, *v.a.* to embattle, crenel(l)ate. —**ung**, *f.* (em)battlement.

Zinno'ber, *m.* (—**s**) cinnabar. *Comp.* —**blume**, *f.* scarlet lychnis. —**rot**, *adj.* vermilion. —**spat**, *m.* crystallized cinnabar.

Zins, *m.* (—(s)es, *pl.* —(s)e) tribute; ground-rent; rent; (*pl.* —(s)en) interest; **Geld auf —(s)en geben** *or* **(aus)leihen**, to lend money on interest; **einem etwas mit —(s)en zurückge=ben**, to return a p. s.th. with usury; **die —(s)en laufen von**, the interest is payable from; **von seinen —(s)en leben**, to live on the interest of one's money; **—(s)en ausrechnen**, to cast the interest; **— vom —**, compound interest. —**bar**, *adj.* tributary; subject to rent. —**barkeit**, *f.* liability to rent *or* tribute, obligation to pay rent. *Comp.* —**abzug**, *m.* discount. —**acker**, *m.* land subject to field-rent. —**bauer**, *m.* peasant who pays certain duties to his lord; tenant; copyholder. —**brief**, *m.* copyhold lease. —**buch**, *n.* rent-roll. —**buße**, *f.* fine for non-payment of ground-rent. —**ei**, *n.* tributary egg, duty-egg. —(s)**en=ausgleich**, *m.* balance of interest. —(s)**es=zins**, *m.* compound interest. —**frau**, *f.* lady of the manor. —**frei**, *adj.* exempt from paying rent, rent-free; not tributary; freehold; **Kapital —frei leihen**, to lend money free of interest; **—freies Gut**, freehold. —**fuß**, *m.* rate of interest. —**garbe**, *f.* field-rent; tithe-sheaf. —**groschen**, *m.* tribute money (*B.*). —**gut**, *n.* copyhold, rented property. —**hafer**, *m.* avenage. —**hahn**, *m.* duty fowl; **rot wie ein —hahn**, as red as a turkey-cock. —**heber**, *m.* rent-collector; capitalist. —**henne**, *f.* hen given as rent, duty fowl. —**herabsetzung**, *f.* reduction of interest. —**herr**, *m.* lord of the manor. —**koupon**, *m.* coupon, dividend-warrant. —**lehen**, *n.* copyhold fief. —**mann**, *m.* (*pl.* —**leute**) copyholder; tenant; feudatory. —**pacht**, *f.* renting. —**pächter**, *m.* copyholder. —**pflicht**, *see* —**barkeit**. —**rechnung**, *f.* interest (*Arith.*). —**schein**, *m. see* —**koupon**. —**ta=belle**, *f.* table of interest. —**tag**, *m.* rent-day; quarter-day. —**weise**, *adv.* as rent; as interest.

Zin'sen, *v.* I. *a. & n.* (*aux.* **h.**) to pay rent *or* tribute. II. *n.* to yield rent *or* interest.

Zi'onswächter, *m.* watchman upon Mount Zion; fanatical divine, zealous minister, zealot (*iron.*).

Zip'fel, *m.* (—**s**, *pl.* —) tip, point, end; corner; (*of a kerchief, etc.*); lappet; **eine S. beim rechten — anfassen**, to set the right way to work; **etwas bei allen vier —n anfassen**, to go cautiously to work; **etwas bei allen vier —n haben**, to be sure of a thing. —**ig**, *adj.* pointed, having points *or* ends. *Comp.* —**mütze**, *f.* peaked nightcap. —**pelz**, *m.* skin-cloak, *etc.*, made of sheeps' tails. —**tuch**, *n.* fichu.

Zipol'le, *f.* (*pl.* —**n**) small onion, scallion.

Zipp— (*in comp.*) —**ammer**, *f.* foolish bunting. —**drossel**, *f.* song-thrush.

Zip'per—lein, *n.* (—**s**) gout (*coll.*). —**n**, *v.n.* (*aux.* **f.**) to trip, move with quick, tripping steps.

Zir'bel, *m.* (—**s**, *pl.* —) & *f.* (*pl.* —**n**) stone pine, pinus cembra. *Comp.* —**drüse**, *f.* pineal gland (*Anat.*). —**kiefer**, *f. see* **Zirbel**.

Zir'k—el, *see* **Zirkel**. —**umfle'x**, *m.* (—**umflexes**, *pl.* —**umflexe**) circumflex (*accent*). —**us**, *m.* (—**uses**, *pl.* —**usse**) circus. *Comp.* —**us=reiterin**, *f.* circus-girl.

Zir'kel, *m.* (—**s**, *pl.* —) circle (*Geom.*, *Log.*); circle, company, society; revolution, course (*of the seasons, etc.*); circuit; pair of compasses; **der goldne —**, the crown (*poet.*); **Lese—**, reading-society, book-club; **er hat sich in den besten —n bewegt**, he has moved in the best circles *or* society; **alles mit dem — abmessen**, to do everything by rule and compass; **es ist heute — bei Hofe**, there is a drawingroom (*or* levée) to-day. *Comp.* —**abschnitt**, *m.* segment. —**beweis**, *m. see* —**schluß**. —**bewe=gung**, *f.* circular motion. —**bogen**, *m.* arc. —**bogig**, *adj.* arched. —**kasten**, *m.* box of compasses, set of compasses. —**säge**, *f.* circular saw. —**spitze**, *f.* point of the compasses. —**schluß**, *m.* vicious circle (*Log.*). —**schnur**, *f.* carpenter's line. —**vierung**, *f.* quadrature of the circle. —**wurm**, *m.* worm under the tongue of dogs. —**zahl**, *f.* circular number. —**zug**, *m.* circular trace, line *or* mark drawn by compasses.

Zir'keln, *v.a.* to measure with compasses; to revolve around; to (move in a) circle; to do everything with the utmost exactness.

Zir'kon, *m.* (—**s**, *pl.* —**e**) zircon (*a precious stone*). *Comp.* —**erde**, *f.* zirconia.

Zir'pe, *f.* (*pl.* —**n**) cricket; grasshopper. —**n**, *v.n.* (*aux.* **h.**) to chirp (*as grasshoppers, crickets etc.*); to cheep (*as young birds*).

Zisch, *m.* (—**es**, *pl.* —**e**) hiss, whiz. —**elei'**, *f.* whispering. —**eln**, *v.a. & n.* (*aux.* **h.**) to speak in an undertone, to whisper. —**en**, I. *v.a. & n.* (*aux.* **h.** & **f.**) to hiss, whiz (*as arrows*); to sputter; **Schlangen —en**, serpents hiss; **Kugeln —en**, bullets whiz; **—end Stille gebieten**, to cry 'hush'; **—end sprechen**, to sibilate. II. *subst. n.* hiss(ing), whi(zzing), whir, ping; **—en (im Theater** *or* **bei einem Vortrage)**, hisses, hootings, groans. —**er**, *m.* (—**ers**, *pl.* —**er**) whisperer. *Comp.* —**laut**, *m.* hissing sound, sibilant; **labialisierter —laut (sch)**, hushing sound (sh); **mit —laut sprechen**, to sibilate. —**ton**, *m.* hissing sound.

Zis—, **Zit—**. *For words beginning thus and not given here look under* **C**.

Zi'ther, *f.* (*pl.* —**n**) zither, zithern; cithara (*of the ancients*). *Comp.* —**ring**, *m.* quill; plectrum. —**schlagen**, *n.* zither-playing. —**schläger**, *m.* zitherist, zither-player; citharist (*of the ancients*).

Zit'terer, *m.* (—**s**, *pl.* —) trembler, quaker, shaker.

Zit'ter—n, *v.n.* (*aux.* **h.**) to tremble, shake, shudder; to quiver, waver (*as light*); to vibrate; **mit —n und Zagen**, with great fear, shaking with fear; **vor Kälte —n**, to tremble with cold; **—n und beben**, to tremble and shake; **mir —n alle Glieder**, I am shaking in every limb; **er —t an allen Gliedern**, he is trembling *or* shaking all over; **es —t alles vor ihm**, all tremble before him. *Comp.* —**aal**, *m.* electric eel. —**esche**, —**espe**, *f.* aspen. —**fisch**, *m.* torpedo, electric ray. —**gold**, *see* **Flittergold**. —**gras**, *n.* quaking-grass. —**laute**, *pl.* tremulants, R-sounds. —**nadel**, *f.* ornamental pin that quivers, aigret(te). —**pappel**, *f.* aspen, trembling poplar. —**roche(n)**, *m.* torpedo, electric ray. —**spiel**, *n.* spillikins. —**stimme**, *f.* trembling voice. —**tierchen**, *n.* vibrio(n). —**welle**, —**woge**, *f.* vibrating wave. —**wels**, *m.* electric cat-fish.

Zit'wer, *m.* (—**s**) zedoary (*Bot.*).

Zitz, *m.* (—**es**, *pl.* —**e**) chintz, print, printed calico. —**en**, *adj.* (of) chintz.

Zit'ze, *f.* (*pl.* —**n**) nipple, teat, udder. *Comp.* —**n=förmig**, *adj.* nipple-shaped; mammiform.

—n=fortsatz, *m.* mastoid process. —n=los, *adj.* udderless. —n=tiere, *pl.* mammals mammalia.

Zivi'l, *see* Civil.

Zo'bel, *m.* (—s, *pl.* —) sable; sable-fur. *Comp.* —balg, *m.*, —fell, *n.* sable-skin. —fang, *m.* sable-hunting. —pelz, *m.* sable (*robe, mantle*). —schwänze, *pl.* sable tails *or* tips.

Zo'ber, *see* Zuber.

Zo'ckeln, *v.n.* (*aux.* s.) to toddle (along) (*dial.*).

Zodiaka'l, *adj.* zodiacal.

Zodi'akus, (—, *no pl.*) *m.* zodiac.

Zo'fe, *f.* (*pl.* —n; *dim.* Zöf'chen) lady's maid, waiting-woman. *Comp.* —n=haft, *adj.* like a lady's maid.

Zog, Zö'ge, *1 & 3 pers. sing. imperf. ind. and subj. of* ziehen.

Zö'g—erer, *m.* (—erers, *pl.* —erer) lingerer, dilatory person, procrastinator. —ern, *v.n.* (*aux.* h.) to linger, loiter, tarry; to defer, to hesitate; ich werde nicht —ern, Ihre Bitte zu erfüllen, I shall lose no time in complying with your request. —ernd, *p. & adj.* hesitating; dilatory; slow. —erung, *f.* delay; hesitation; ohne —erung, without delay, unhesitatingly.

Zög'ling, *m.* (—s, *pl.* —e) pupil.

¹Zoll, *m.* (—(e)s, *pl.* —, —e) inch; digit (*Astr.*); vier — breit, four inches broad *or* wide; in —e einteilen, to inch; auf — und Linie, exactly, in every respect; jeder — ein König, every inch a king; — für —, inch by inch. *Comp.* —breit, *adj.* inch-wide. —dick, *adj.* inch-thick. —maß, *n.* measure(ment) in inches, inch-measure. —stab, —stock, *m.* rule; yard-stick; (mit Auszug) sliding rule. —weise, *adv.* by inches, inch by inch.

²Zoll, *m.* (—es, *pl.* Zöl'le) toll, custom, duty; debt (*of nature, of gratitude, etc.*); custom-house; passage-money (*of travellers*); am — sitzen, to be sitting at the receipt of custom (*B.*), to collect duties; — geben von, to pay duty on; beim — angeben, to enter at the custom-house; hohe (Eingangs)zölle, high tariffs; Ausfuhr—, export duties. —bar, *adj.* liable to duty. —barkeit, *f.* liability to duty. *Comp.* —amt, *n.* custom-house; board of customs. —amtlich, *adj.*; —amtliche Behandlung von Warensendungen, inspection of goods. —angabe, *f.* entry, declaration at the custom-house; bill of entry. —anschluß, *m.* accession to a customs-union. —aufschlag, *m.* increase in duty, additional duty. —aufseher, *m.* customs-inspector. —beamte(r), *m.* customs *or* custom-house officer; revenue-officer. —direktor, *m.* director of customs. —einnehmer, *m.* collector, receiver of customs. —flagge, *f.* revenue-flag. —frei, *adj.* free of duty; Gedanken sind —frei, thought is free (*prov.*); —freier Verkehr, exemption from duty, free trade. —freiheit, *f.* exemption from duty; free trade. —freischein, *m.* pass, permit. —gebiet, *n.* customs-district. —gefälle, *n.* customs-revenue. —geleitschein, *m.* permit. —gesetz, *n.* law relating to duties. —haus, *n.* custom-house. —inspektor, *m.* customs-inspector, custom-house overseer. —linie, *f.* custom-house line. —niederlage, *f.* bonded *or* bonding warehouse, store; Waren in die —niederlage bringen, to bond goods, to have goods bonded. —passierzettel, *m.* export permit. —pflichtig, *adj.* liable to duty. —politik, *f.* customs-policy. —quittung, *f.* clearance. —rechnung, *f.* bill of customs. —revision, *f.* customs revision *or* examination. —schein, *m.* customs receipt, permit; certificate of clearance. —schiff, *n.* revenue-cutter. —schreiber, *m.* custom-house clerk. —sicherheit, *f.* custom-house sealing. —siegel, *n.* cocket. —speicher, *m.* bonded warehouse, customs-warehouse. —stätte, —stelle, *f.* custom-house. —straße, *f.* turnpike road. —system, *n.* custom-house system. —tafel, *f.*, —tarif, *m.* tariff, list of duties. —verband, —verein, *m.* customs union, commercial league, tariff union; Deutscher —verein, the Zollverein, the German Customs Union. —vereins=gewicht, *n.* standard weight of the Zollverein. —vergünstigungen, *pl.* facilities granted by the custom(-house); preferential tariff. —verschluß, *m.* customs seal, leads, bond; unter —verschluß lassen, to leave in bond. —wächter, *m.* tide-waiter, subordinate custom-house officer. —wesen, *n.* custom-house affairs; customs department.

Zol'len, *v.a.* to pay duty on; to render what is due; einem Achtung —, to show due respect to a p.; einem Thränen —, to shed tears for s.o., pay the tribute of tears to a p.'s memory; einem Dank —, to thank a person.

Zöl'lig, *adj.* of an inch; drei—, three-inch.

Zöll'ner, *m.* (—s, *pl.* —) *see* Zolleinnehmer; publican (*B.*).

Zo'ne, *f.* (*pl.* —n) zone; die heiße, kalte, gemäßigte —, the torrid, frigid, temperate zone. *Comp.* —n=einteilung, *f.* division into zones. —n=linsen, *pl.*; —nlinsen für Leuchttürme, echelon lenses for lighthouses. —n=tarif, *m.* zone-tariff.

Zoo—lo'g, *m.* (—logen, *pl.* —logen) zoologist. —lo'gisch, *adj.* zoological. —phy't, *n.* (& *m.*) (—phyten, *pl.* —phyten) zoophyte, animal plant.

Zopf, *m.* (—es, *pl.* Zöp'fe) (*long*) plait of hair, tress; pigtail; cue; tuft; tree-top; (symbol of) antiquated ways; foolish pedantry; sie trägt Zöpfe, she wears her hair plaited, plaits her hair; des Mädchens lange Zöpfe, the girl's long tresses; einem einen — anstecken, machen, drehen, to impose upon *or* humbug a p.; einem auf den — kommen, to treat a p. harshly, reprimand s.o. sharply. —ig, *adj.* like a pigtail; wearing a pigtail; antiquated, old-fashioned; pedantic. —tum, *n.* (—tums) antiquated, old-fashioned ways, stupid pedantry *or* conservatism. *Comp.* —band, *n.* ribbon for tying a pigtail, hair-ribbon. —ende, *f.* top (of a tree). —holz, *n.* top-branches. —lerche, *f.* crested lark. —mensch, *m.* pedant; red-tapist. —perücke, *f.* wig with a cue. —stil, *m.* antiquated *or* pedantic style; rococo style of architecture. —zeit, *f.* age of pig-tails; Georgian era.

Zöpf'—chen, *n.* (—chens, *pl.* —chen) little pigtail. —en, *v.a.* to plait in a pigtail, to dress (*the hair*) in a long plait; to top (*trees*). —ig, *adj. see* Zopfig.

Zorn, *m.* (—s) anger, wrath; choler; passion, rage; indignation; irritation; seinen — an einem auslassen, die Schale seines —s über einen ausgießen, to vent one's anger, to pour out the vials of one's wrath upon a p.; einen in —bringen, to enrage *or* exasperate a person. —ig, *adj.* angry; in a temper (*coll.*); passionate; hot, hasty (*words, etc.*); —ig werden, to get angry, to fly into a passion. *Comp.* (*often with* —es=) —anfall, —ausbruch, *m.* fit of anger, passion. —(es)=blick, *m.* angry look *or* glance. —entbrannt, —glühend, *adj.* furious; inflamed with anger. —entflammend, *adj.* inflammatory. —mütig, *adj.* irascible, choleric. —(es)=röte, *f.* flush of anger. —rute, *f.* rod, chastisement of God. —wütig, *adj.* raging, furious.

Zo't—e, *f.* (*pl.* —en) obscenity, indecent *or* filthy expression (word *or* joke). —enhaft, —ig, *adj. & adv.* obscene, foul, filthy, smutty, lewd. *Comp.* —en=lied, *n.* obscene *or* smutty song. —en=reißen, n. habit of talking indecently; obscenity, ribaldry. —en=reißer, —olo'g, m. (—ologen) (*sl.*) person who is fond of telling obscene stories *or* jokes.

Zo'ten, Zo'teln, *v.n.* to talk smut.

Zot't—e, *f.* (*pl.* —en) lock, tuft; matted tuft, tangle. —elig, *adj.* in tufts. —eln, *v.* I. *a.* *only used in p.p.*, gezottelt, *see* —elig. II. *n.* (*aux.* s.) to hang down in tufts, hang loosely; to shuffle *or* move in a heavy shuffling way. —ig, *adj. see* —elig; shaggy; downy, hairy (*Bot.*). *Comp.* —el=bär, *m.* shaggy bear. —el=bart, *m.* shaggy beard. —el=haar, *n.* shaggy hair (*or coat*). —el=kopf, *m.* person with matted *or* shaggy hair.

Zu, I. *prep.* (*with dat.*) to, unto; in addition to, along with; at; in; at the rate of; on; by; for, in order to; for; — Abend speisen, to dine *or* sup, to take dinner *or* supper; — Anfang, at the beginning; for a beginning; —m Beispiel (z. B.), for instance, *e. g.;* das dient —m Beispiel, that serves as an example; — Berg fahren, to go up hill *or* up the mountains; to go up stream *or* against the stream; —m Besten, for the best; es geriet nicht —m Besten, it did not succeed as well as was expected; es geschieht — deinem Besten, it is for your good; — Bett gehen, to go to bed; Gott schuf den Menschen ihm —m Bilde, God created man in his own image; — Boden fallen, to fall to the ground, fall down; er geht — seinem Bruder, he is going to his brother's; — Deutsch, in German; — Dritt, three of us, three of them; — ebener Erde wohnen, to live on the ground floor; einem —r Ehre gereichen, to redound to a p.'s honour; einen — etwas ermuntern, to exhort *or* encourage a p. to do a th.; Wasser — etwas gießen, to water, pour water on a th.; — Ende sein, to be at an end, to be over, to be exhausted; to have done *or* finished; —m ersten, in the first place; —m ersten! —m andern! —m dritten! going! going! gone! Lust — einer S. haben, to have a liking *or* inclination for a th.; — einer S. lachen, to laugh at a th.; — einer S. schweigen, to take no notice of, be silent respecting a th.; —r Fährte kommen, to get the scent; sich (*dat.*) einen —m Feinde machen, to make an enemy of a p.; — Felde ziehen, to take the field; Brot —m Fleisch essen, to eat bread with one's meat; einen —m Freunde haben, to have s.o. for a friend; er setzte sich — seinem Freunde, he came and sat down by his friend; —m Fenster hinaussehen, to look out of the window; einem — Füßen fallen, to throw o.s. at a p.'s feet; einen — Gaste bitten, to invite a p. (*to dinner, to stay, etc.*); die Hochschule — G, the university of G; mir — Gefallen, to please me, for my sake; einem etwas — Gemüte führen, to remind a p. of a th.; etwas —r Genüge haben, to have sufficient of a th.; — Gesicht bekommen, to catch a sight of; —m Glücke, fortunately, happily; — Grunde gehen, to be ruined, be lost; —r Hälfte, by half, half of it; ein Musikstück — vier Händen, a piece arranged for four hands, a pianoforte duet; —r Hand sein, to be at hand; zu seiner rechten Hand sitzen, to sit on *or* at a p.'s right hand; — Hause kommen, (*dial.*) to come home; — Hunderten, by hundreds; einen —m König machen, to make a p. king; — Kreuze kriechen, to humble o.s., to eat humble pie; er rüstet sich —m Kriege, he is preparing for war; einem — Leibe gehen, to attack a p.; mir ist nicht —m Lachen, I am in no laughing mood; — Lande, by land; on the land; — guter Letzt, as a last treat (*obs.*); finally, to finish up with; er hat es Ihnen — Liebe, aus Liebe — Ihnen gethan, he did it out of love to you; — London wohnen, to live in London; —m Lohne für, in return for, as a reward for; —m letzten Male, for the last time; — sechs Mark das Stück, at six marks each; — Mittag speisen, to dine, to lunch; sich (*dat.*) —m Muster nehmen, to take as pattern; ihm ist schlecht — Mute, he is in a bad mood; — Nacht, by night, in the night time, at night; —m Narren werden, to be made a fool of, grow foolish *or* crazy; —r Not, in case of necessity, if (absolutely) necessary, if need be; —r Ordnung rufen, to call to order; — Paaren, in couples; — Paaren treiben, to rout; —r Rechten, on the right hand (side); —r Rede setzen *or* stellen, to call to account; Tuch — einem Rocke, cloth for a coat; — Schaden kommen, to meet with an accident, to sustain an injury; mir zum Schaden, to my hurt; —r See, at sea; einem —r Seite sitzen, to sit at a p.'s side; —r Stadt kommen, to come to town; — stande bringen, to bring about, accomplish; es ist —m Sterben, it is enough to kill a p.; — Staub werden, to turn to dust; — Sumpfe treiben, to neglect the working of a mine; — Tage bringen, to bring to light, make known; — ganzen Tagen, for whole days; — Tage ausgehen, to crop up, lie on the surface (*of layers, etc.*); — Thal fahren, to go down the hills; to go downstream *or* with the stream; —m Teil, in part, partly; —m Thore hinaus gehen, to go out at the gate; — Tisch gehen (führen), to go (take in) to dinner, *etc.;* Wasser —m Trinken, drinking-water; einem —m Trotz, in spite (defiance) of a p.; better than a p.; er liest —r Unterhaltung der Gesellschaft ein Buch vor, he reads aloud for the entertainment of the company; —r Unzeit, at an unsuitable time, unseasonably, prematurely; — seiner Verteidigung, in his defence; im Verhältnis —, in proportion to; wie sechs — vier, as six to four; ich habe kein Geld —m Verspielen, I have no money to lose; — Wasser und — Lande, by sea and land; — Wasser werden, to turn to water; to come to nothing; er hat sie —m Weibe, she is his wife; —m wenigsten, at least; — Werke gehen, to set to work, to begin; —r Zeit, at the time, at present; in time; — rechter Zeit, in (due) time; — Zeiten, at times; — welchem Zwecke? for what purpose? — zweien, by twos; — zweit, two of us *or* them; sechs verhält sich — zwölf wie zwei — vier, 6 is to 12 as 2 to 4; (*used with verbs of naming, choosing, appointing, making and the like*) der König ernannte ihn —m General, the king raised him to the rank of *or* made him general; der Zwang der Zeiten machte mich — ihrem Gegner, the pressure of the times made me her adversary; (*as sign of the infinitive, forming a supine*) ich habe — arbeiten, I have to work; anstatt selbst hin — gehen, instead of going himself; ich erinnere mich, ihn gesehen — haben, I remember seeing him; — geschweigen, daß . . ., not to mention that . . .; es steht — hoffen, it is to be hoped; eine gute Ernte ist — hoffen, a good harvest may be hoped for; der Brief ist — schreiben, the letter is to be (*or* must be) written; es ist schwer — thun, it is hard to do; was ist — thun? what is to be done? um mich — täuschen, in order to deceive me; es ist — unterscheiden, a distinction must be made; das Haus ist — verkaufen, the house is to be sold; ohne — wissen, without knowing (*it*); (*with p. forming a kind of future passive participle or gerundive*) ein — verbessernder Fehler, an error requiring correction; ein —

verkaufendes Haus, a house to be sold; **eine nicht — ertragende Hitze,** an unendurable heat; **ein nach — ahmendes Beispiel,** an example worthy of imitation. II. *adv. & sep. prefix,* to; towards; together; closed; (*preceding an adj. or adv.*) too; overmuch; — **neugierig,** over-inquisitive; — **sehr,** too much; **gar —,** far too; **er ist ein gar — ehrgeiziger Mann,** he is much too ambitious; **ein — großes Glück ist selten dauerhaft,** too great happiness seldom lasts long; **auf eine S. — gehen,** to go towards a th.; **auf einen — laufen,** to run up to a p.; **die Thür ist nicht —, mach' sie —,** the door is not closed, shut it; **ab und —,** at times, now and then; **geh —! immer —!** go on! get on! on! **Glück —!** good luck! God speed you! **schreibe nur —!** go on writing! write away! **schieß —!** fire away! **schlag —,** strike!

Zu'ackern, *v.* I. *a.* to cover up by ploughing. II. *n.* (*aux.* **h.**) to plough on, to go on ploughing.

Zu'arbeiten, *v.* I. *n.* (*aux.* **h.**) to work on, labour on, to continue working; to make haste. II. *a.* to add, join on to.

Zua've, *m.* (**—n,** *pl.* **—n**) zouave.

Zu'bauen, *v.a.* to build up, close (up) by building; to add to by building, add to a building.

Zu'behalten, *ir.v.a.* to keep shut *or* closed.

Zu'behör, *n.* (*m.*) (**—s**) belongings; appurtenances; accessories; appendages; adjuncts; **Arbeit und —,** work and materials *or* stuff; **Wohnung von sechs Zimmern mit —,** six-roomed house with offices *or* all conveniences; **— zu den Speisen,** trimmings; dressing (*for salad*), seasoning, relish.

Zu'beißen, *ir.v.a. & n.* (*aux.* **h.**) to snap at, to (have *or* take a) bite at; **tüchtig —,** to eat away with a good appetite (*coll.*).

Zu'bekommen, *ir.v.a.* to get in addition; to succeed in closing (up) *or* fastening.

Zu'benam(s)en, *v.a.* to surname.

Zu'ber, *m.* (**—s,** *pl.* **—**) (two-handled) tub; firkin (*for butter*).

Zu'bereit—en, *v.a.* to prepare, dress, get ready; to season; to adjust; to fit; **—etes Pelzwerk,** dressed furs. **—er,** *m.* (**—ers,** *pl.* **—er**) preparer, dresser. **—ung,** *f.* preparation; dressing, cooking (*of food*).

Zu=bet'te=gehen, *n.* going to bed, turning in; **beim —,** on going to bed *or* retiring to rest.

Zu'billigen, *v.a.* (**einem etwas**) to grant, allow, concede, adjudge (s.th. to s.o.).

Zu'binden, *ir.v.a.* to bind *or* tie up; **einem die Augen —,** to bandage a p.'s eyes, to hoodwink a person.

Zu'biß, *m.*; **ein Glas Wein mit einem —,** a glass of wine with a morsel of something to eat.

Zu'blasen, *ir.v.* I. *n.* (*aux.* **h.**) to go on blowing. II. *a.* to close by blowing; to blow towards; to whisper, suggest, prompt.

Zu'bläser, *m.* (**—s,** *pl.* **—**), **—in,** *f.* prompter.

Zu'bleiben, *ir.v.n.* (*aux.* **s.**) to remain shut *or* closed.

Zu'blinken, *v.n.* (*aux.* **h.**) to wink at; **einem —,** to glitter before a p.'s eyes, to shine in s.o.'s eyes.

Zu'blinze(l)n, *v.n.* (*aux.* **h.**); **einem —,** to wink at a p., to make a sign to a p.

Zu'brennen, *ir.v.a.* to close by burning; to cauterize; to roast, refine (*metal*).

Zu'bringen, *ir.v.a.* to bring, carry, take to; to pass, spend; to succeed in closing; **einem eins** *or* **einen Trunk —,** to pledge a p.; **das Zugebrachte,** separate personal estate, dowry; **zugebrachte Kinder,** children by a previous marriage; **die Zeit mit Lesen —,** to spend one's time reading; **sie hat drei Jahre damit zugebracht,** she has spent three years at it, it has taken her three years to do it.

Zu'brocken, *v.a.* to contribute of one's own; *see* **Brocken** II; **etwas zu — haben,** to have s.th. to live upon, to have the wherewithal to live.

Zu'brüllen, *v.a.*; **einem —,** to shout to a person.

Zu'buß—e, *f.* (*pl.* **—en**) (additional) contribution, share; extraordinary call *or* payment, supplementary contribution. *Comp.* **—zettel.** *m.* list of expenses.

Zu'büßen, *v.a.* to contribute, pay (*one's share*); to spend, lose.

Zucht, *f.* (*pl.* **—en**; *for* **Züch'te** *see below*) breeding, rearing (*of cattle, etc.*); rearing (*of plants, etc.*); breed, race; brood, flock, young stock; education; discipline; chastisement, correction; propriety; modesty; chastity; good breeding *or* manners; **die —en dieses Jahres,** the breeds of this year; **in** *or* **mit Züchten,** courteously, modestly; **zur — halten,** to keep for breeding; **Mangel an —,** want of discipline *or* good breeding; **sich an — und Ordnung halten,** to discipline o.s., live an orderly, well-regulated life; **in — und Ordnung halten,** to discipline, to keep discipline; **er nimmt keine — an,** he is not amenable to discipline, he is utterly intractable; **unter jemandes — stehen,** to be under a p.'s care; **in — und Ehre(n),** with due propriety, in all modesty; **verwirf die — des Herrn nicht,** despise not the chastening of the Lord; **der — entwachsen sein,** to have outgrown the rod; **sich der — unterwerfen,** to yield to discipline; **in aller —,** in all modesty *or* propriety, in all honour; **das ist ja eine nette —!** a pretty way of going on, indeed! why, this is Bedlam let loose! **was ist das für eine —!** what sort of conduct is this! *Comp.* **—arbeit,** *f.* forced work, hard labour. **—biene,** *f.* queen-bee. **—eber,** *m.* stock boar. **—esel,** *m.* stallion (ass). **—fähig,** *adj.* capable of reproducing the race; disciplinable. **—füllen,** *n.* sucking foal. **—gesetz,** *n.* disciplinary law. **—gestüt,** *n.* stud. **—gewohnt,** *adj.* accustomed to discipline, well-trained *or* disciplined. **—haus,** *n.* house of correction, convict prison, bridewell; **er erhielt zehn Jahr —haus,** he got ten years' penal servitude; **im —hause sitzen,** to be imprisoned with hard labour, to undergo a sentence of penal servitude, to pick oakum (*coll.*). **—haus=arbeit,** *f.* prison work. **—haus=aufseher,** *m.* inspector, overseer of a house of correction. **—haus=gefangene(r), —häusler, —häusling,** *m.* convict. **—haus=strafe,** *f.* penal servitude. **—hengst,** *m.* stallion, entire, stud-horse. **—huhn,** *n.* brood-hen. **—hund,** *m.* stock-dog. **—kalb,** *n.* (**—kuh,** *f.*,) calf (cow) kept for breeding. **—los,** *adj.* insubordinate; undisciplined; intractable; dissolute, loose, licentious. **—losigkeit,** *f.* want of discipline; insubordination; disorderly ways. **—meister,** *m.* taskmaster; governor of a house of correction; jailer; severe master, disciplinarian. **—mittel,** *n.* mode of correction, corrective. **—pferd,** *n.* stud horse. **—polizei,** *f.* correctional police. **—polizei=gericht,** *n.* police court. **—polizeilich,** *adj.* correctional. **—rute,** *f.* rod of correction; ferule. **—schaf,** *n.* sheep kept for breeding, ewe. **—schäferei,** *f.* farm for raising sheep, sheep-run. **—schule,** *f.* seminary. **—schwein,** *n.* store-pig. **—stier,** *m.* bull kept for breeding. **—stute,** *f.* brood-mare. **—tiere,** *pl.*, **—vieh,** *n.* animals kept for breeding, breeding cattle, breeders. **—wahl,** *f.*; **natürliche —wahl,** natural selection.

Züch't—en, *v.a.* to breed, raise (**von,** from); to cultivate, to train, bring up, discipline. **—er,** *m.* (**—ers,** *pl.* **—er**) breeder, cultivator. **—ig,** *adj.* chaste, modest, coy; proper, discreet. **—igen,** *v.a.* to chastise, correct, discipline;

to whip, scourge; to punish; **mit Worten —igen**, to censure, reprove; **sein Fleisch —igen**, to mortify one's flesh. **—iger**, *m.* (**—igers**, *pl.* **—iger**) chastiser, chastener, corrector. **—igkeit**, *f.* chastity, modesty; propriety; bashfulness. **—iglich**, *adv. see* **—ig.** **—igung**, *f.* chastisement, correction. **—ling**, *m.* (**—lings**, *pl.* **—linge**) *see* **Zuchthäusler.** **—ung**, *f.* breeding; rearing; discipline, growing, cultivation.

Zuck, I. *m.* (**—(e)s**, *pl.* **—e**) short, quick movement; twitch; start; shrug; trice. II. *int.* bang! crack! **—eln**, *v.n.* (*aux.* **f.**) to jog, to trot (*coll.*, *hum.*).

Zu'ck—en, I. *v.n.* (*aux.* **h.**) to move with a short, quick motion, convulsively; to jerk, to start; to palpitate, quiver; to thrill; **der Blitz —te durch die Luft**, the lightning flashed through the air; **mit den Augen —en**, to blink, wink; **er —t mit den Augenlidern**, his eyelids quiver; **das —te ihm durch alle Glieder**, it sent a thrill all through him; **das Herz —t noch**, the heart still beats. II. *v.a. & n.* to move suddenly, quickly; to jerk; to tug; **die Achseln (mit den Achseln) —en**, to shrug one's shoulders. II. *subst. n. see* **—ung.** **—end**, *p. & adj.* jerky; convulsive, spasmodic; palpitating. **—ung**, *f.* jerk, convulsive movement; thrill; quiver; palpitation; **—ungen bekommen**, to be seized with convulsions.

Zü'cken, *v.a.* to draw quickly; **den Degen auf einen —**, to draw one's sword upon a person.

Zu'cker, *m.* (**—s**) sugar; **roher —**, raw sugar, moist sugar; **gestoßener —**, pound sugar; **— in Broten** *or* **Hüten**, loaf-sugar; **ein Stück —**, a lump of sugar; **in — verwandeln**, to convert into sugar, to saccharify; **in — einmachen**, to preserve, to candy. **—ig, Zuckrig**, *adj.* sugary, saccharine; sugar. **—n**, I. *v.a.* to sugar, sweeten. II. *adj.* of sugar. *Comp.* **—apfel**, *m.* a kind of sweet apple. **—artig**, *adj.* sugary, saccharine. **—bäcker(in**, *f.*), *m.* confectioner. **—bäckerei'**, *f.* confectionery; confectioner's shop. **—backwerk**, *n.* confectionery, sweetmeats; pastry. **—bau**, *m.* cultivation of the sugar-cane. **—bildung**, *f.* *f.* formation of sugar, saccharification. **—bonbon**, *n.* sweet. **—brot**, *n.* pastry, sweet biscuit, cake; *see* **—hut.** **—büchse, —dose**, *f.* sugar-basin. **—dicksaft**, *m.* molasses. **—erbsen**, *pl.* sweet peas (*Bot.*); comfits, sugar-plums. **—erde**, *f.* sugar-boiler's clay. **—fabrik**, *f.* sugar-refinery. **—fabrikant**, *m.* sugar-refiner. **—form**, *f.* sugar-mould. **—gährung**, *f.* saccharine fermentation. **—gast**, *m.* sugar-mite. **—gebackene(s)**, *n. see* **—backwerk.** **—gehalt**, *m.* proportion *or* percentage of pure sugar contained in s.th. **—geist**, *m.* sugar-spirit; rum. **—guß**, *m.* sugar-icing. **—haltig**, *adj.* containing sugar. **—hammer**, *m.* hammer for breaking sugar. **—handel**, *m.* sugar-trade. **—harnruhr**, *f. see* **—krankheit.** **—hefen**, *pl.* refuse of sugar. **—honig**, *m.* molasses, treacle. **—hut**, *m.* sugar-loaf, loaf *or* cone of sugar. **—kand**, *m.* sugar-candy; **brauner —kand**, (**der Karamel**) caramel. **—kind**, *n.* sweet child, darling, pet. **—kiste**, *f.* sugar-box; cask for sugar. **—kisten=holz**, *n.* Havana cedar. **—krank**, *adj.* diabetic, affected with diabetes. **—krankheit**, *f.* diabetes. **—kuchen**, *m.* sugared cake. **—kügelchen**, *n.* dragée, (sugar-) pill. **—küpe**, *f.* sugar-vat. **—mandeln**, *pl.* sugared almonds; burnt almonds. **—maul**, *n.* sweet-tooth. **—mehl**, *n.* powdered sugar. **—melone**, *f.* sweet melon. **—messung**, *f.* saccharometry. **—mund**, *m.* honied lips (*with reference to the sweet words which fall from them; coll.*). **—papier**, *n.* paper for covering sugar-loaves. **—pflanzung**, *f.* sugar-plantation. **—plätzchen**, *n.* (sugar-)drop, comfit; lozenge. **—püppchen**, *n.*, **—puppe**, *f.* sugar-doll; darling, pet (*coll.*). **—raffinerie**, *f.* sugar-refinery, sugar-works. **—rinde**, *f.* coat of sugar. **—rohr**, *n.* sugar-cane. **—rübe**, *f.* sweet turnip; beetroot. **—ruhr**, *f. see* **—krankheit.** **—sachen**, *pl. see* **—werk.** **—saft**, *m.* juice of the sugar-cane, cane-juice, syrup. **—satz**, *m.* molasses. **—sauer**, *adj.* saccharic; **—saures Salz**, saccharate. **—säure**, *f.* oxalic acid; saccharic acid. **—schale**, *f. see* **—büchse.** **—schoten**, *pl.* sweet peas. **—sieden**, *n.* sugar-refining. **—sieder**, *m.* sugar-refiner. **—siederei'**, *f. see* **—fabrik.** **—sirup**, *m.* molasses, treacle. **—steuer**, *f.* duty on sugar. **—stoff**, *m.* saccharine matter. **—stoff=haltig**, *adj.* saccharine. **—streu=büchse**, *f.* sugar caster. **—streuer**, *m.* sugar-sifter. **—süß**, *adj.* sweet as sugar; honied. **—tüte**, *f.* screw of sugar-plums. **—verbindungen**, *pl.* saccharates. **—waren**, *pl.* confectionery, sweetmeats, sweets. **—wasser**, *n.* water with sugar in it. **—werk**, *n.* confectionery. **—zange**, *f.* sugar-tongs.

Zu'dämmen, *v.a. see* **Zudeichen; ein Loch im Pflaster —**, to stop, join, close a hole *or* break in the pavement.

Zu'decken, *v.a.* to cover up; to cloak, conceal; to thrash (*sl.*); to drink (*a p.*) under the table (*coll.*).

Zu'deichen, *v.a.* to dam up; to enclose with a dike.

Zude'm, *adv.* besides, moreover, in addition.

Zu'denken, *ir.v.a.* to destine, intend for; to add to in thought; **dies hatte ich dir zum Geschenk zugedacht**, I had intended this as a present for you.

Zu'diktieren, *v.a.* to decree; **einem eine Strafe —**, to award s.o. a punishment, to sentence a person to something.

Zu'drang, *m.* a crowding *or* thronging to; crowd, throng pressing towards; rush (*on a bank, etc.*).

Zu'drängen, *v.r.* to throng *or* crowd to; to press forward; to thrust oneself into, to intrude.

Zu'drehen, *v.a.* to shut *or* fasten by turning; to turn; to turn off (*by a cock, etc.*); **einem den Rücken —**, to turn one's back on a person.

Zu'dringlich, *adj. & adv.* importunate, obtrusive; forward; officious, tiresome, impertinent. **—keit**, *f.* importunity, obtrusiveness.

Zu'drücken, *v.a.* to shut, close by pressure; to continue to press; **ein Auge bei einer S. —**, to connive, wink at, to overlook, excuse a th.

Zu'eign—en, *v.a.* (**einem etwas**) to adjudge; to attribute, ascribe; to dedicate (*a book*); **sich** (*dat.*) **etwas —en**, to appropriate (*to o.s.*), to claim; **sich** (*dat.*) **widerrechtlich —en**, to arrogate to o.s.; to usurp, assume. **—er**, *m.* (**—ers**, *pl.* **—er**) one who appropriates; dedicator. **—ung**, *f.* adjudication; dedication, dedicatory poem; appropriation. *Comp.* **—ungs=schrift**, *f.* dedicatory epistle.

Zu'eilen, *v.n.* (*aux.* **f.**, *dat. or* **auf** *& acc.*) to run towards *or* up to, hasten towards; **seinem Verderben —**, to hasten to one's ruin *or* destruction.

Zu'erkenn—en, *ir.v.a.* to adjudge, adjudicate, award; to decree; to acknowledge; **einem eine Ehre —en**, to confer an honour *or* dignity on s.o.; **einem einen Preis —en**, to award a p. a prize; **einem den Vorzug —en**, to give the preference to a p.; **mit gutem Gewissen kann ich Ihnen nicht das Recht es zu thun —en**, I cannot conscientiously admit your right to do it; **—end**, adjudicating. **—ung**, *f.* award, adjudication. *Comp* **—ungs=urteil**, *n.* adjudicative sentence.

Zue'rst, *adv.* firstly, in the first place, at first;

first of all; above all, especially; foremost; — **erholen Sie ſich,** before everything else, get well; **gleich** —, at the very beginning.

Zu'eſſen, *ir.v.a. & n.* (*aux.* **h.**) to continue eating; **iß zu!** eat away! go on eating!

Zu'fächeln, *v.a.* (**einem etwas**) to fan to *or* towards; **ſich** (*dat.*) **Luft** —, to fan oneself.

Zu'fahren, *ir.v.n.* (*aux.* **h.** & **ſ.**) to drive *or* sail on; to drive faster; to drive fast; to approach; to shut of itself(*of a door*); **fahr zu, Kutſcher!** drive on, coachman! **auf das Land** —, to sail straight for land, to run ashore; **dem Dorfe** —, to drive to *or* in the direction of the village; **auf einen** —, to fly, rush at, fall upon a p.; **gleich blind** —, **blind auf eine S.** —, to rush blindly, headlong at *or* upon a th.; **gut** —, to drive at a brisk pace; **die Thüre iſt zugefahren,** the door has slammed.

Zu'fall, *m.* (—**s**, *pl.* **Zu'fälle**) chance; fortune; contingency; casual event, incident, occurrence; accident, casualty; attack (*Med.*); **der — wollte daß . . .,** as good (*or* bad) luck would have it; **den Launen des —s unterworfen,** uncertain, subject to the caprice of fortune; **ein bloßer** —, a mere chance; **ein glücklicher** —, a lucky chance, a piece of good luck; **widriger** —, misfortune, piece of ill-luck.

Zu'fallen, I. *ir.v.n.* (*aux.* **ſ.**) to fall towards; to close, fall to; to rush upon; to fall to one's lot, devolve on; to join with, adhere to (**einem,** a p.); **die Augen fallen ihm zu,** his eyes are closing with sleep; **die Schuld fällt ihm zu,** the blame rests with him; **der Beweis hiervon fällt ihm zu,** the burden of proving this rests with him; **ihm iſt eine Erbſchaft zugefallen,** he has inherited some property. II. *subst. n.* **um das — der Thür zu verhüten,** to prevent the slamming of the door.

Zu'fällig, *adj. & adv.* accidental, fortuitous, casual, occasional, contingent, uncertain; non-essential; accidental (*Phil.*, *Mus.*); **—erweiſe,** by chance, by accident, casually, as chance would have it; **ein —er Kunde,** a chance customer; **wir waren — da,** we happened to be there; **ich traf ihn** —, I happened *or* chanced to meet him, I met him accidentally *or* by chance. **—keit,** *f.* fortuitousness, contingency; chance; unforeseen occurrence, accident, incident; *see* **Zufall.**

Zu'falten, *v.a.* to fold, to fold up (*a letter*, *etc.*).

Zu'fertigen, *v.a.* (**einem etwas**) to despatch, send (s.th. to a p.).

Zu'flattern, *v.n.* (*aux.* **ſ.**) to fly *or* flutter towards (**einem,** a p.).

Zu'flechten, *ir.v.a.* to close by wickerwork *or* hurdles; to weave, twist together.

Zu'flicken, *v.a.* to mend, patch, repair.

Zu'fliegen, *ir.v.n.* (*aux.* **ſ.**) to fly to *or* towards; to continue flying; **die Thür flog zu,** the door slammed, closed with a bang.

Zu'fliehen, *ir.v.n.* (*aux.* **ſ.**) to flee towards; to flee on; to hurry *or* fly towards (*obs.*).

Zu'fließen, *ir.v.n.* (*aux.* **ſ.**) to flow to *or* towards; to flow in, throng upon a p.; **einem etwas — laſſen,** to bestow s.th. upon a p., to grant s.th. to a p.; **die Worte fließen ihm** (**nur ſo**) **zu,** he has a great flow of language, is never at a loss for words; **ein Gewinn fließt ihm zu aus . . .,** he derives (a) profit from . . .

Zu'flucht, *f.* refuge, shelter; recourse; **zu** (**einem** *or* **einer S.**) **ſeine — nehmen,** to have recourse to, apply to, take refuge with (in); **ſeine — zu den Waffen nehmen,** to appeal (*as a last resource*) to arms; **einem eine — gewähren,** to afford a p. a refuge. *Comp.* **—s=haus,** *n.* house of refuge. **—s=ort,** *m.*, **—s=ſtätte,** *f.* place of refuge, retreat, asylum, sanctuary; retirade (*Fort.*).

Zu'fluß, *m.* (**Zu'fluſſes,** *pl.* **Zu'flüſſe**) flowing in, influx; concourse (*of people*); flow (*of ideas*); (*pl.*) resources, means of subsistence; **die Zuflüſſe des Rheins,** the tributaries of the Rhine; **Abfluß und — des Meeres,** ebb and flow of the tide; **— von Blut nach dem Kopfe,** flow of blood to the head; **— friſcher Luft,** supply of fresh air; **— von Fremden,** influx of foreigners. *Comp.* **—bach,** *m.* tributary brook. **—graben,** *m.* feeder (of a pond). **—röhre,** *f.* feeding-, service-, supply-pipe.

Zu'flüſter—n, *v.a.* (**einem etwas**) to whisper to; to inform of; to prompt; to insinuate. **—ung,** *f.* whispering; whisper; insinuation.

Zufol'ge, *prep.* (*with dat. when following, with gen. when preceding the case governed*) in consequence of; in pursuance of; in virtue of; according to; — **ſeines Verſprechens,** in virtue of his promise; **ſeinen Worten** —, according to his words.

Zufrie'den, *adj.* content, pleased, satisfied; happy; peaceable; **ſich — geben,** to calm o.s., grow calm, to acquiesce (**mit,** in), to bear with contentedly; **er wollte ſich nicht eher — geben, als bis . . .,** he would not rest satisfied until . . .; **einen — ſprechen,** to calm s.o., to satisfy a p.; **einen — ſtellen,** to content, satisfy a p.; **ich bin damit** —, I am satisfied with it, I agree to it; **ich bin es** (*old gen.*) —, all right, well and good; **Urſache haben, mit etwas — zu ſein,** to have cause to be satisfied (with a th.); **der —e hat immer genug,** contentment is better than riches. **—heit,** *f.* contentment, satisfaction.

Zu'frieren, *ir.v.n.* (*aux.* **ſ.**) to freeze up *or* over, be covered with ice; to congeal.

Zu'fügen, *v.a.* to add to; to do, cause; **einem** (**ein**) **Leid** —, to pain s.o., cause a p. sorrow; **einem Schaden** —, to do a p. an injury.

Zu'fuhr, *f.* (*pl.* **—en**) conveying; conveyance; importation; supply, stock, store; supplies, provisions; convoy (*Mil.*); **wir haben hier eine ſtarke — von Waren,** we have here a large supply of goods; **einer Feſtung die — abſchneiden,** to cut off the supplies of a fortress.

Zu'führ—en, *v.a.* to conduct, lead, bring to; to convey, transport; to import; to waft over (*sounds*, *etc.*); to send in, supply; to enlarge (*a gallery in a mine*, *etc.*); **einem eine Braut —en,** to procure a wife for a p.; **einem einen Freund —en,** to introduce a friend to a p.; **einen ſeinem Untergang —en,** to be the cause of a p.'s ruin; **einem Heere Lebensmittel —en,** to provision an army. **—end,** *p. & adj.* conducting; **—ende Gefäße,** deferents (*Anat.*), ducts (*Bot.*). **—er,** *m.* (**—ers,** *pl.* **—er**) one that brings *or* conveys; procurer; duct. **—ung,** *f.* conveyance, importation, supplying; **ich veranlaßte die —ung von . . .,** I made them supply *or* bring in . . .; **—ung von Lebensmitteln,** victualling, supplying with food; food-supply. *Comp.* **—ſchlauch,** *m.* supply-hose. **—tiſch,** *m.* feeder, travelling-table (*Mech.*). **—walzen,** *pl.* feeding rollers.

Zu'füllen, *v.a.* to fill up; to pour to.

Zug, *m.* (**—es,** *pl.* **Zü'ge**) drawing, pulling; pull, tug; march, marching; passage (*through a country*), progress; expedition; excursion; passage (*of birds*), flight, migration; herd, flock (*of birds*, *etc.*); shoal (*of herrings*); flight, course (*of clouds*); current (*of water*); channel, bed (*of a river*); draught, strong current (*of air*); blast (*at the mouth of a furnace*); train, retinue, procession; file (*Mil.*); cavalcade; range (*of mountains*); row (*of houses*); migration, removal; troop; platoon, squad, part of a company (*Mil.*); team, couple, span; string, train (*of artillery*, *etc.*); railway-train; band.

gang; flue; stroke, dash (*of a pen*); line; touch; feature, lineament; trait (*of character*); move (*at chess, etc.*); draught (*of fish*); bias; attraction, sympathy; bent, leaning; impulse; disposition; characteristic; the power of drawing; draught, pull (*in drinking*); whiff (*of smoke*); set (*of strings, chords, etc.*); a (*wire, string, etc.*) contrivance to open a street-door *or* gate from within; (*bell-*)pull; pulley; extension (*Mech.*); wire-drawing; implements for wire-drawing; stop, register (*in organs*); pedal (*of a piano*); slide (*of a flute, etc.*); drawer, joint (*of telescopes*); piston; drawing-string (*in dresses, etc.*); dress-pulleys (*by which a skirt can be lifted*); (*pl.*) grooves, rifling (*in gunbarrels, etc.*); (*pl.*) shelves (*in a stove*); (*pl.*) agonies of death; **ankommender (abgehender) —, der nach (von) der Hauptstation fahrende —**, up-train (down-train); **durchgehender —**, through train; **ein gepanzerter —**, an armoured train; **— mit dem Zügel**, jerk with the bridle; **— gegen die Sarazenen**, expedition against the Saracens, crusade; **seinen — nehmen durch**, to pass through; **auf dem —e sein**, to be on the march, to be on the way; **im vollen —e**, in full march, on the march; **im —e sein**, to be moving, passing, marching, to be under weigh, to be in the vein; **in — bringen**, to set a-going, to start, to give an impetus to; **ich bin mit der Arbeit im —e, die Arbeit ist im —e**, I have the work in hand; **im besten —e, so recht im —e sein**, to be quite in the vein, to be in full activity; **im —e stehen**, to stand in a draught; **der Ofen hat einen guten —**, the stove draws well; **die Cigarre hat keinen —**, the cigar does not draw; **feine Züge**, delicate features; **ein ehrlicher Zug im Gesicht**, an honest expression of countenance; **ein — seines Charakters**, a feature of his character, a characteristic of his; **volle, dicke Züge**, broad, thick strokes; **— einer Büchse**, rifle of a gun-barrel; **der — ist an mir**, it is my (*turn to*) move; **einen — thun**, to (*make a*) move; **wer ist am —e?** whose move is it? **das ist ein — der Zeit**, that is a characteristic of the times; **der — des Herzens ist des Schicksals Stimme**, the dictates of the heart are the voice of fate, one's character is one's fate; **dem —e des Herzens folgen**, to follow one's impulses *or* the promptings of one's heart; **es ist kein — im Geschäfte**, trade is very dull; **er thut alles ohne rechten —**, he does everything in a half-hearted way; **— um — handeln**, to trade for ready money; **— um —, — für —**, taking with one hand and giving with the other; **in** *or* **mit einem —e**, at one pull, at once, uninterruptedly; **kleine Züge thun**, to sip; **einen — aus dem Glase thun**, to take a drink out of the glass; **das Glas auf einen — austrinken**, to empty the glass at one draught; **in langen Zügen trinken**, to take deep draughts; **keinen — thun**, not to move; **in den letzten Zügen liegen**, to be at the last gasp, in the agonies of death, to be dying; **elastischer — am Stiefel**, side-elastic. **—ig**, *adj.* draughty. *Comp.* **—ameise**, *f.* migratory ant. **—angel**, *f.* night-line. **—anker**, *m.* iron brace *or* clamp (*Arch.*). **—artikel**, *m.* article to attract the public, very salable article, draw. **—band**, *n.* strap *or* ribbon for pulling by; boot-strap. **—blatt**, *n.* tail-piece (*of a violin*); breast-collar. **—breite**, *f.* front of a platoon (*Mil.*). **—brücke**, *f.* draw-bridge. **—brunnen**, *m.* draw-well. **—erz**, *n.* ore extracted by machinery. **—feder**, *f.* draw- *or* drag-spring (*in engines*). **—festigkeit**, *f.* tensile strength. **—fisch**, *m.* migratory fish. **—feuer**, *n.* platoon-firing. **—führer**, *m.* file-leader; officer commanding a platoon; (railway-)guard (*in charge of a train*). **—garn**, *n.* drag-net. **—geschirr**, *n.* harness. **—haspel**, *m.* (*f.*) windlass, pulley; crane. **—heuschrecke**, *f.* passage-locust. **—kette**, *f.* coupling-chain (*on trains*). **—klappe**, *f.* damper; leaf (*of a drawbridge*). **—kraft**, *f.* tractive power; force of attraction. **—kräftig**, *adj.* in vogue, attractive. **—leine**, *f.* towing-rope. **—linie**, *f.* line of march (*Mil.*); column (*Mil.*); catenarian curve, trajectory. **—loch**, *n.* vent-hole, ventilator; draught-hole. **—luft**, *f.* current of air, draught. **—maschine**, *f.* drawing-frame; (traction) engine, locomotive. **—material**, *n.* the part of railway-machinery employed in drawing. **—mittel**, *n.* attraction, method of attracting (*a crowd, etc.*); vesicatory (*Med.*). **—netz**, *n.* drag-net. **—ochs**, *m.* draught-ox. **—ofen**, *m.* air-furnace, blast-furnace. **—personal**, *n.* personnel (*driver, stoker, guard, etc.*) of a railway-train. **—pferd**, *n.* draught-horse. **—pflaster**, *n.* plaster; blister. **—ramme**, *f.* common pile-engine. **—riemen**, *m.* pulling strap; trace, tug-strap (*of horses*). **—rohr**, *n.*, **—röhre**, *f.* passage for air; air-pipe; vent-hole, ventilator. **—rolle**, *f.* pulley. **—schnur**, *f.* string (*of a purse, etc.*). **—seil**, *n.* drawing-rope; trace, towing-line. **—stange**, *f.* pole for drawing up; pole (*of a draw-well*); swipe (*of a pump*); drawing-rod, spreader (*of trains*). **—stiefel**, *m.* elastic boot, boot with elastic, congress boot (*Am.*). **—stück**, *n.* piece that draws full houses (*Theat.*). **—telegraph**, *m.* portable telegraph. **—tiere**, *pl.* draught-animals, beasts of burden. **—vogel**, *m.* bird of passage; vagrant. **—weise**, *adv.* in flocks *or* troops; in squads, in platoons. **—wind**, *m.* draught, current of air. **—winde**, *f.* pulley. **—winkel**, *m.* angel of traction.

Zu'gabe, *f.* (*pl.* —n) what is given in addition; extra; overweight; make-weight; adjunct; supplement; **als —**, into the bargain, to boot, extra; **als — geben**, to give *or* throw in.

Zu'gang, *m.* admittance, access; approach; entrance; avenue, way to.

Zu'gänglich, *adj.* accessible, approachable; affable; **— für eine S.**, susceptible to a th.; **— machen**, to render accessible, to throw open, open out; to popularize; **er ist vernünftigen Gründen stets —**, he is always open to conviction. **—keit**, *f.* accessibility; affability. *Comp.* **—machung**, *f.* rendering accessible, throwing open, opening up; popularization.

Zu'geben, *ir.v.a.* to add; to give into the bargain; to grant, concede, admit; to suffer, allow; to agree to; to own, confess; to follow suit (*Cards*); **klein —**, to humble o.s., eat humble pie (*coll.*); to follow suit with a low card; **zugegeben**, granted, admitting.

Zuge'gen, *indec. adv.* present; **— sein bei**, to be present at.

Zu'gehen, *ir.v.n.* (*aux.* **s.**) to close; to freeze over *or* up; to go up to; to move towards; to face, front, meet; to go on faster; to take place, happen; **gut —**, to go on well; **spitzig —**, to end in a point; **einem —**, to reach a p.; **einem etwas — lassen**, to forward s.th. to a p.; **der Brief ist mir eben zugegangen**, the letter has just reached me; **wie geht es zu, daß . . .?** how is it that . . .? how does it happen *or* come about that . . .? **es geht sonderbar zu in dieser Welt**, queer things go on in this world, this is a queer world; **in diesem Hause geht es bunt zu**, in this house things are all in confusion; **bei ihm geht alles ehrlich zu**, with him everything is done in an honest way; **dort geht es lustig zu**, there it goes merrily; they keep it up; **es müßte mit dem Teufel —, wenn . . .**, the devil must be in it if . . .; es müßte seltsam —, wenn ich es nicht erhielte, it will be a strange thing if I don't get it; im Kriege geht es nicht anders zu, such is war.

Zu'gehör, *n.* (*m.*) (—s) *see* Zubehör. —**ig**, *adj.* appertaining, belonging to; attached to; proper; nicht —ig, unattached, detached; —ige Briefumschläge, envelopes to match. —**igkeit**, *f. see* Zubehör; sphere of action, business.

Zu'gehören, *v.n.* (*aux.* h.) to belong, to appertain to.

Zü'gel, *m.* (—s, *pl.* —) rein, reins; bridle; check, curb; den *or* die — anziehen, to rein in (*a horse*); mit verhängtem — reiten, to ride full speed; dem Pferde die — schießen lassen, to give the horse his head; seinen Leidenschaften die — schießen lassen, to give full rein *or* free vent to one's passions; einem den — (schießen) lassen, to let a p. do as he likes; ein Pferd am — führen, to lead a horse by the bridle; einem den — kurz halten, to keep a tight hand over s.o.; die — der Regierung in den Händen haben, to hold the reins of government. —**n**, *v.a.* to put on a bridle; to bridle, curb, check. *Comp.* —**bar**, *adj.* restrainable. —**fabrikant**, *m.* saddler. —**hand**, *f.* bridle-hand, left hand. —**los**, *adj.* unbridled; unrestrained. —**losigkeit**, *f.* licentiousness; libertinism; licentious action; —losigkeit der Sitten, looseness of morals. —**ring**, *m.* bridle-ring. —**schieber**, *m.* bridle-slide.

Zu'gemüse, *n.* vegetables served with meat; garnish(ing), trimming.

Zu'genannt, *adj.* surnamed.

Zu'geordnet, *p.p.* & *adj. see* Zuordnen, Beiordnen.

Zu'gesellen, *v.a.* & *n.* to associate; er ist mir zugesellt worden, he has been associated with me; sich —, to join.

Zu'geständnis, *n.* (—(ss)es, *pl.* —(ss)e) concession, admission; gegenseitiges —, compromise.

Zu'gestehen, *ir.v.a. see* Gestehen I.; (einem) etwas —, to grant, concede, admit s.th.; zugestanden! granted! zugestandenermaßen, admittedly.

Zu'gethan, *p.p.* & *adj.* attached to; fond of; einem —, devoted to s.o., having a strong affection for a person.

Zu'gewandt, *p.p.* & *adj. see* Zuwenden; die Schweiz mit ihren —en Orten, Switzerland with its confederate districts *or* its dependencies (*dial.*).

Zu'gießen, *ir.v.* I. *a.* to pour to; to fill up (by pouring in). II. *n.* to keep on pouring; to continue to pour; gieß zu! pour on! pour away!

Zu'gittern, *v.a.* to close (in) with a grate *or* bars; to rail in *or* up.

Zuglei'ch, *adv.* at the same time, together, along (*with*), conjointly (*with*); die Briefe kamen — an, the letters arrived at the same time; sie standen alle — auf, they all rose in a body.

Zu'graben, *ir.v.a.* to cover with earth, dig in; to bury.

Zu'greifen, *ir.v.n.* (*aux.* h.) to lay hold of, lay hands on; to seize; to help oneself to, to fall to; to take up (*arms*); to bear a hand; (allzu) leicht —, to be light-fingered; der Anker greift zu, the anchor bites; er braucht nur zu —, he has only to stretch out his hand for it, it is within his grasp; lassen Sie sich nicht nötigen, greifen Sie zu, don't wait to be asked, help yourself, fall to!

Zugrun'de— (*in comp.*) —**gehen**, *n.* destruction, ruin, loss. —**legung**, *f.* the taking as a base (*or basis*); mit —legung von . . ., taking . . . as a base (*or basis*). —**richten**, *n.* destruction, demolition.

Zu'gucken, *v.n.* (*aux.* h.) (*coll.*) *see* Zusehen.

Zu'gürten, *v.a.* to gird up, enclose with a girdle.

Zu'guß, *m.* (—(ss)es, *pl.* Zu'güsse) pouring to; liquid added; infusion.

Zu=guter=let'zt, *adv.* finally, in the end, at last, in conclusion.

Zu=gu'te=thun, I. *ir.v.r. sep.* to indulge, pamper oneself; sich (*dat.*) auf eine S. etwas —, to be proud of s.th. II. *subst. n.* indulgence.

Zu'haben, *ir.v.a.* to keep *or* keep shut *or* locked up; den Rock —, to have one's coat buttoned up; er will (beim Tausch) noch Geld —, he insists on having money besides (in an exchange).

Zu'häkeln, **Zu'haken**, *v.a.* to hook, close by hooking; to clasp.

Zu'halte—n, I. *ir.v.a.* to keep shut; to close (*one's eyes or ears*); to clench (*one's fist*). II. *ir.v.n.* (*aux.* h.) to keep (*one's promise, prov.*); auf eine S. —n, to rush at, go straight for a th.; mit einem —n, to have an understanding with, have (*illicit*) relations with a p.; er hält sich die Taschen zu, he keeps his pockets tight. III. *ir.v.r.* to make haste, bestir o.s. IV. *subst. n.*; das —n der Thür ist nötig, the door must be kept shut.

Zu'hälter, *m.* (—s, *pl.* —) fancy-man, bully, pouncey. —**in**, *f.* kept mistress, concubine.

Zu'hämmern, *v.a.* to hammer down, to close by hammering.

Zuha'nd, *adv.* at once (*dial.*). —**en**, *adv.* close at hand, ready; in hand, to hand.

Zu'hängen, *v.a.* to cover with a curtain *or* drapery; to hang, to drape.

Zu'hauen, *ir.v.* I. *a.* to strike; to cut up (*a pig, etc.*); to rough-hew; to dress, trim; to cut in shape. II. *n.* (*aux.* h.) to continue to strike; auf einen —, to strike a p.; hau nur zu! hit away!

Zuhau'f, (*poet.*) *see* Zusammen.

Zu'hefteln, *see* Zuhäkeln.

Zu'heften, *v.a.* to stitch, sew up.

Zu'heilen, *v.n.* (*aux.* s.) to close, heal up.

Zu'herrschen, *v.a.*; einem etwas —, to speak imperiously to a p., to say s.th. to a p. in an imperious manner.

Zuhil'fenahme, *f.*; mit (*or* ohne) — von, by (*or* without) the aid of *or* having recourse to.

Zuhin'terst, *adv.* at the very end, last of all.

Zu'horchen, *v.n.* (*aux.* s.) to listen to (*attentively*); heimlich —, to eavesdrop.

Zu'höre—n, *v.n.* (*aux.* h., *dat.*) to listen (*to*); to attend (*to*); einer Erzählung —n, to listen to a tale. —**r**, *m.* (—rs, *pl.* —r) listener, auditor; hearer; *pl.* attendance, audience; der Professor hat viele —r, the professor's lectures are well attended; dieser Prediger hat viele —r, this preacher is greatly run after. —**rschaft**, *f.* audience. *Comp.* —**r=raum**, *m.* place for the audience, lecture-room, auditory.

Zuin'nerst, *adv.* innermost, in the very heart, quite in the interior.

Zu'jagen, *v.* I. *a.*; einem ein Wild —, to drive game towards a p. II. *n.* (*aux.* s.) to gallop towards *or* to; (*aux.* h.) jag' zu! gallop on! ride *or* drive at full speed!

Zu'jauchzen, **Zu'jubeln**, *v.a.* & *n.* (*aux.* h.) to hail, shout to; to salute with shouts of joy, cheer; einem Beifall —, to applaud a p. with loud acclamations.

Zu'kaufen, *v.a.* to buy in addition; to buy more.

Zu'kehren, *v.a.* to turn towards; to sweep towards; to stop (*a hole*) by sweeping (*sand, etc., into it*); einem das Gesicht —, to turn one's face towards a person.

Zu'keilen, *v.a.* to close with a wedge, to plug.

Zu'ketteln, *v.a.* to lock with a small chain, chain up.

Zu'kitten, *v.a.* to cement, putty up.
Zu'klappen, *v.* I. *a.* to close. II. *n.* (*aux.* s.) to bang, slam, close with a snap.
Zu'klatschen, *v.a. & n.* (*aux.* h.) (**einem —**) to clap one's hands to a p.; **einem Beifall —**, to clap *or* applaud a person.
Zu'kleben, Zu'kleistern, *v.a.* to paste *or* glue up.
Zu'klemmen, *v.a.* to close by pressing.
Zu'klinken, *v.a.* to latch, close by a latch.
Zu'knöpfen, I. *v.a.* to button up *or* to. **Zugeknöpft**, *adj.* buttoned up; reserved (*coll.*); **er ist etwas zugeknöpft**, he is somewhat reserved. II. *subst.n.*; **zum —**, to button, that buttons.
Zu'knüpfen, *v.a.* to tie up; **enger —**, to tie tighter.
Zu'kommen, *ir.v.n.* (*aux.* s.) to come to, approach, arrive; to come to hand, reach (**einem**, a p.); to belong to (**einem**, a p.); to become, behove, be suitable for; to fall to s. o.'s share *or* lot; to cover (*of horses*); **auf einen —**, to come to, approach a p.; **einem etwas — lassen**, to let a p. have s.th., to accommodate *or* furnish s.o. with, to pass, send *or* communicate s.th. to a p.; **es ist mir zugekommen**, it reached me, I received it; **es kommt dir nicht zu, so zu sprechen**, it is not for you *or* becoming in you to speak thus; **das kommt ihm nicht zu**, he has no right to that; **es kommt mir nicht zu**, it is not within my province; **jedem, was ihm zukommt**, to every one his due; **den Teig — lassen**, to let the dough ferment.
Zu'können, *ir.v.n.* (*aux.* h.); **zu etwas —**, to be able to get near *or* to a thing.
Zu'korken, *v.a.* to cork (*up*).
Zu'kost, *f.* something eaten with bread *or* meat, *as* vegetables, preserves; seasoning, condiment, spice (*fig.*).
Zu'kratzen, *v.a.* to fill *or* cover up by scratching.
Zu'kriegen, *v.a.* *see* (*coll.*) **Zubekommen**; to succeed in closing (*coll.*).
Zu'kunft, *f.* future, time to come; future tense; return (*obs.*); coming (*obs.*); (**— Christi**) Advent; **in —**, in future, for the future, henceforth, from this time; **Mann der —**, coming man, rising star; **ob dies ein geeigneter Schritt ist oder nicht, muß die — lehren**, whether this is a wise step or not remains to be seen. *Comp.* **—ahnend, —schauend**, *adj.* foreseeing, anticipating the future. **—s=musik**, *f.* the music of the future; Wagnerian music; dreams of the future, castles in the air (*fig.*). **—s=pläne**, *pl.* plans for the future.
Zu'künftig, I. *adj.* future, to come; **—e Zeit**, time to come; future tense; **meine —e**, my future wife, my wife that is to be, my intended. II. *adv.* in future, for the future.
Zu'lächeln, *v.a. & n.* (*aux.* h.); **einem —**, to smile at a p.; **einem Beifall —**, to smile approval, smile on a person.
Zu'lage, *f.* (*pl.* **—n**) addition, augmentation, increase of salary; extra pay; allowance; make-weight; timber-work (*for a house*); upper timber-work (*of bridges*); **einem eine — geben**, to raise a p.'s salary, make a p. an allowance.
Zu'langen, *v.* I. *a.*; **einem etwas —**, to reach, hand s.th. to a p. II. *n.* (*aux.* h.) to stretch out the hand for; to help o.s. to; to suffice, be sufficient *or* long enough; to reach.
Zu'länglich, *adj.* sufficient. **—keit**, *f.* sufficiency.
Zu'laß, *m.* (**—(ss)es**, *pl.* **Zu'lässe**) *see* **—(ss)en** II. **—(ss)en**, I. *ir.v.a.* to leave closed, not to open, to admit; to grant, concede, permit; to turn on (*steam*); to let cover (*of horses*); **jemandes Entschuldigung —(ss)en**, to accept a p.'s excuse; **einen zu einem Amte —(ss)en**, to admit s.o. to an office, to receive, pass a p.; **diese Erklärung läßt zwei Deutungen zu**, this explanation admits of two interpretations, may be taken in two ways. II. *subst.n.*, **—(ss)ung**, *f.* admission; permission, concession; **um —(ss)ung zum Examen anhalten**, to apply for admission to an examination. *Comp.* **—(ss)ungs=gesuch**, *n.* application for admission. **—(ss)ungs=schein**, *m.* ticket of admission, pass.
Zu'lässig, *adj.* admissible, permissible; granted; **nicht —**, inadmissible; objectionable. **—keit**, *f.* admissibility.
Zu'lauf, *m.* crowd, rush, influx, throng; concourse; **einen — von Kunden haben**, to have many customers, a large custom; **großen — haben**, to be much run *or* sought after, to be in vogue; to draw large audiences (*of professors*) *or* large congregations (*of preachers*).
Zu'laufen, I. *ir.v.n.* (*aux.* s.) to run quickly, run on; to run towards *or* up (**auf einen**, to a p.); to run out into (*a point, etc.*); to crowd, throng to (**einem**, a p.; **einer Sache**, a th.); **lauf zu!** be quick, run on! II. *subst.n.*; **das Ab= und —**, the going and coming, the running to and fro.
Zu'lege—n, *v.* I. *a.* to close (*a hole with boards, etc.; a knife, etc.*) to superadd, add to; to prepare (*the timberwork for a house, etc.*); **einen Brief —n**, to fold a letter; **einen Riß —n**, to prepare, sketch a design; **es wurden ihm 300 Mark zugelegt**, his salary was increased by 300 marks; **dafür kann ich es Ihnen nicht geben, Sie müssen noch etwas —n**, I cannot let you have it at that price, you must give a little more; **sich** (*dat.*) **—n**, to provide, procure for o.s., indulge o.s. with (*coll.*); **ich werde mir einen neuen Rock —n**, I shall get myself a new coat (*coll.*); **sich einen Wagen —n**, to set up a carriage (*coll.*). II. *n.* (*aux.* h.) to continue adding; to grow stouter, to put on flesh. *Comp.* **—messer**, *n.* claspknife.
Zu'leimen, *v.a.* to cement, glue up.
Zu'leit—en, *v.a.* to lead, conduct, direct towards *or* to. **—ung**, *f.* conducting (*water*). *Comp.* **—ungs=graben**, *m.* ditch for conveying sea-water to a salt-marsh. **—ungs=kanal**, *m.* lateral drain; canal for conducting water to a place.
Zu'lernen, *v.a.* to add to one's stock of knowledge, to go on learning, learn in addition.
Zulet'zt, *adv.* finally; (*for*) the last time; ultimately, eventually; after all; **— kommen**, to arrive last.
Zu'lispeln, *see* **Zuflüstern**.
Zu'löten, *v.a.* to solder up.
Zum, *short for* **zu dem**.
Zu'machen, *v.* I. *a.* to close, shut up; to put down (*an umbrella*); to button up (*a coat*); to stop up (*a hole*); to fasten (*a dress, etc.*); to fold up (*a letter*); to close *or* seal (*a letter*); to cork (*a bottle*); **eine Thür fest —**, to fasten a door, shut it tight; **in einem zugemachten Wagen fahren**, to ride in a close(d) carriage; **mach zu!** shut it! II. *n.* (*aux.* h.) to make haste; **mach zu!** be quick!
Zuma'l, *adv.* above all, particularly, especially; *see* **Zugleich**; **— da . . .**, especially as . . .
Zu'mauern, *v.a.* to close up *or* enclose with brickwork; to build *or* wall up.
Zumei'st, *adv.* mostly, for the most part.
Zu'messen, *ir.v.a.* to measure, mete out; to ascribe, impute to; to assign (*a task*) to; to apportion (*a share*) to; **eine sehr kurze Zeit ward uns zugemessen**, a very short time was allowed us *or* was allotted to us; **der zugemessene Teil**, the apportioned share *or* part.
Zu'mut—en, *v.a.* to demand, exact, require, expect (**einem etwas**, s.th. of a p.); to burden (*s.o.*) with; to require (*a p.*) to do; to ascribe, attribute to; **er mutet mir viel zu**, he demands

a great deal from me, he expects me to do a great deal; **das kann ich ihm nicht —en,** I cannot expect it of him; **einem zu viel —en,** to overburden, overtask a p.; **sich** (*dat.*) **zu viel —en,** to attempt too much, to make too great demands upon a p.('*s health, talents*). **—ung,** *f.* demand, expectation; imputation; presumption.

Zum=Vor'scheinkommen, *n.* coming to light, appearance on the scene.

Zunä'chst, I. *adv.* next; first of all, above all, chiefly; **er wohnt hier —,** he lives next door. II. *prep.* (*with dat. or gen.*) next to; **— des Eingangs** *or* **dem Eingange,** close to the entrance.

Zu'nageln, *v.a.* to nail up; to nail down.

Zu'nähen, *v.a.* to sew up *or* together, to sew to.

Zu'nahme, *f.* (*pl.* **—n**) increase, growth; augmentation; advancement, improvement; progress.

Zu'name, *m.* (**—ns,** *pl.* **—n**) family-name; surname.

Zünd'bar, *adj.* inflammable. **—keit,** *f.* inflammability.

Zün'd—en, *v.* I. *n.* (*aux.* **h.**) to take fire; to kindle, ignite. II. *a.* to set on fire, set fire to; to kindle; to inflame, stir up. **—end,** *adj.* inflammable, combustible; burning; inflammatory, stirring, rousing, electrifying; **—ende Ansprache,** stirring speech *or* address. **—er,** *m.* (**—ers,** *pl.* **—er**) lighter; match; spill; train of gunpowder, match; fusee (*of a bomb, etc.*). **—ung,** *f.* kindling; priming (*Firew.*). *Comp.* **—deckel,** *m.* cap over the touch-hole of a cannon. **—dose,** *f.* fuse-cartridge. **—er=höhle,** *f.* cap. **—er=klotz,** *m.* fuse-block *or* socket. **—feld,** *n.* vent-field. **—fertig,** *adj.* primed. **—holz, —hölzchen,** *n.* match; **schwedische —hölzchen,** safety matches. **—holz=büchse,** *f.* match-box. **—hütchen,** *n.* percussion-cap. **—kanal,** *m.* nipple-bore; priming. **—kegel,** *m.* nipple. **—korn,** *n. see* **—lochstollen.** **—kraut,** *n.* priming-powder; **—kraut aufschütten,** to prime. **—kugel,** *f.* fire-ball; bomb, grenade. **—licht,** *n.* linstock (*Artil.*). **—loch,** *n.* touch-hole; vent. **—loch=aufräumer, —loch=bohrer,** *m.* priming-iron (*for guns*). **—loch=stollen,** *m.* (*copper-*)bouche. **—maschine,** *f.* apparatus for lighting, inflaming machine. **—nadel,** *f.* needle (*of a needle-gun*). **—nadel=gewehr,** *n.* needle-gun. **—papier,** *n.* touch-paper; spill. **—pfanne,** *f.* touch-pan. **—pfannen=deckel,** *m.*, **—pille,** *f.* primer. **—pulver,** *n.* priming powder. **—röhre,** *f.* see **—kanal;** quick-match tube. **—rute,** *f.* linstock, match. **—satz,** *m.* priming-composition. **—schnur,** *f.* quick-match. **—schwamm,** *m.* tinder. **—spiegel,** *m.* fulminating priming. **—stift,** *m.* nipple; hammer. **—stoff,** *m.* igniting agent, primer; inflammable matter; seeds of discontent (*fig.*). **—strick,** *m.* quick-match, match-rope (*Artil.*). **—waren,** *pl.* inflammables, combustibles, explosives; matches. **—wurst,** *f.* saucisse, saucisson (*Artil.*); powder-hose (*Min.*).

Zun'der, *m.* (**—s,** *pl.* **—**) (*German*) tinder; touchwood; fuse; smouldering fire. *Comp.* **—büchse,** *f.* tinder-box. **—holz,** *n.* touchwood.

Zu'nehmen, I. *ir.v.a.* to take in addition, take more; to increase (*the number of stitches in knitting*). II. *ir.v.n.* (*aux.* **h.**) to increase, augment, grow larger; to rise, swell; to improve, thrive, prosper; to grow worse (*of an evil*); to get stouter; to get longer (*of the days*); to increase (*in knitting*); **an Kräften —,** to grow stronger; **an Jahren —,** to advance in years; **an Zahl —,** to increase in number; **in der Lehre —,** to increase in learning (*B.*); **in dem Werke des Herrn —,** to abound in the work of the Lord (*B.*); **nach und nach —d,** progressing, progressive; **—de Geschwindigkeit,** accelerated velocity, acceleration; **bei —den Jahren,** with advancing years, as one grows older; **der —de Mond,** the waxing *or* crescent moon. III. *subst.n. see* **Zunahme; der Mond ist im —,** the moon is waxing *or* increasing; **ein beständiges — der Geschwindigkeit,** a constant increase in velocity.

Zu'neig—en, *v.a. & n.* to lean, incline towards. **—ung,** *f.* affection, attachment; partiality (*to*); sympathy (*with*); **—ung zu einem fassen,** to take a liking to a person.

Zunft, *f.* (*pl.* **Zünf'te**) body, company, society; guild, corporation; craft, profession, fraternity; club; sect, clique; gang, band; tribe; **geschlossene Zünfte,** close craft-guilds; **die — der Gelehrten,** the learned fraternity, the scholastic world; **— der Handwerker,** trade-union; **in eine — aufnehmen,** to make a member of a corporation; **sämmtliche Zünfte Londons,** all the London guilds. *Comp.* **—brief,** *m.* charter of a guild *or* city company. **—geist,** *m.* esprit de corps. **—gelehrte(r),** *m.* member of a learned profession; pedant. **—gemäß,** *adj.* in conformity with, according to the statutes of a corporation. **—genosse,** *m.* member of a guild *or* corporation; one of the same craft *or* trade. **—haus,** *n.* hall *or* meeting-place of a guild. **—meister,** *m.* master of a guild, warden of a corporation. **—sprache,** *f.* professional *or* technical language, cant. **—wesen,** *n.* everything relating to guilds *or* corporations (*the rules and statutes, charter, the freemen and masters, etc.*); trade-unionism. **—zwang,** *m.* obligation imposed upon artisans to join a guild.

Zünf't—ig, *adj. see* **Zunftgemäß;** belonging to a corporation; incorporated; **—ig werden,** to receive the freedom of a company, be received into a corporation. **—igen,** *v.a.* to admit as member of a guild; to instruct in the usages, *etc.*, of a corporation. **—igkeit,** *f.* corporateness. **—ler,** *m.* (**—lers,** *pl.* **—ler**) *see* **Zunftgenosse;** partisan of (*the system of*) guilds.

Zun'g—e, *f.* (*pl.* **—en**) tongue; language; palate (*fig.*); anything tongue-shaped; languet (*Org.*); reed, mouth-piece (*of wind instruments*); tongue, catch (*of a buckle, etc.*); head of the galley (*Typ.*); sole (*Icht.*); **eine feine —e haben,** to have a delicate taste *or* palate; **eine schwere —e haben,** to have a hesitation *or* an impediment in one's speech, to speak thick; **einem das Wort von der —e nehmen,** to take the words out of a p.'s mouth; **es schwebte mir auf der —e,** I had it on the tip of my tongue; **die — klebt mir am Gaumen,** my tongue cleaves to the roof of my mouth; **sagen, was einem auf die —e kommt,** to say whatever comes uppermost; **der Tod sitzt ihm auf der —e,** he is at death's door; **einen über die —e springen lassen,** to backbite, pull a p. to pieces (*hum.*); **es geht ihr glatt von der —e, sie hat eine geläufige —e,** she has a glib tongue; **sie trägt das Herz auf der —e,** she wears her heart on her sleeve, she is unreserved, very outspoken; **die Gabe fremder —en,** the gift of tongues. **—ig,** *see* **Züngig.** *Comp.* **—en=ader,** *f.* lingual vein. **—en=band,** *n.* ligament of the tongue; (*pl.*) vocal chords. **—en=bein,** *n.* tongue-bone, hyoid bone (*Anat.*). **—en=blatt,** *n.* blade of the tongue (*the part of the surface which lies behind the point*); common adder's tongue (*Bot.*). **—en=blütig,** *adj.* ligulate(d) (*Bot.*). **—en=buchstabe,** *m.* lingual (*letter*). **—en=drescher,** *m.* babbler; caviller. **—en=drescherei,** *f.* babble, foolish talk, pettifogging. **—en=drüse,** *f.* lingual gland. **—en=**

entzündung, *f.* inflammation of the tongue. **—en=faul**, *adj.* tongue-tied. **—en=fehler**, *m.* defect in speaking; lapsus linguæ. **—en=fertig**, *adj.* voluble, flippant. **—en=fertigkeit**, *f.* volubility; **—enfertigkeit besitzen**, to have a ready tongue, to have the gift of the gab. **—en=förmig**, *adj.* tongue-shaped. **—en=frei**, *adj.*; **—enfreies Mundstück**, cannon-bit (*bit arched in the middle*). **—en=freiheit**, *f.* liberty of the tongue; arched space in a (*cannon-*)bit. **—en=häutchen**, *n.* epidermis of the tongue; ligament of the tongue. **—en=held**, *m.* babbler; braggadocio. **—en=hieb**, *m.* cut, bitter *or* harsh remark. **—en=krebs**, *m.* cancer of the tongue. **—en=laut**, *m.* lingual sound; *pl.* linguals. **—en=löser**, *m.* anchylotome (*for cutting the tongue-ligament*). **—en=pfeife**, *f.* reed-pipe (*Org.*). **—en=register**, *n.* flute-stop (*Org.*). **—en=schlag**, *m.*; **einen guten —enschlag haben**, to have the tongue well hung (*sl.*). **—en=spitze**, *f.* tip of the tongue; **—enspitzen=r**, lingual r, trilled r. **—en=vorfall**, *m.* glossocele (*Med.*). **—en=wurzel**, *f.* root *or* base of the tongue.

Zün'g—elchen, *n.* (**—elchens**, *pl.* **—elchen**) little tongue; tab; point (*Typ.*). **—eln**, *v.n.* (*aux.* **h.**) to play with the tongue; to flatter; to hiss (*of serpents*); to fork (*as flames*). **—elnd**, *adj.* lambent (*of flames*). **—ig**, *suff.* (*in comp.* =) -tongued. **—lein**, *n. see* **—el=chen**; **—lein der Wage**, tongue *or* index of the balance.

Zunich't(e), *adv.* ruined, destroyed, undone, wasted; **— machen**, to ruin, destroy utterly; **einen — schlagen**, to beat a p. to death *or* unmercifully.

Zu'nicken, *v.a. & n.* (*aux.* **h.**) (**einem**) to nod (*to a person*); to intimate by a nod.

Zuo'berst, *adv.* quite at the top, uppermost.

Zu'ordn—en, *v.a.* to adjoin, to associate with; **zugeordnet**, allied, confederate (*states*), co-ordinate (*Math.*). **—ung**, *f.* co-ordination.

Zu'peitschen, *v.n.* (*aux.* **h.**) to whip, lash on; **auf einen —**, to lash a p. furiously; **peitsch zu, Kutscher!** whip up the horses, coachman.

Zup'f—en, *v.a.* to pull, tug, pluck; to pick (*wool*); to ravel out; **Leinwand zu Charpie —en**, to prepare lint; **—en Sie sich doch an Ihrer eigenen Nase**, sweep before your own door, mind your own business. *Comp.* **—leinwand**, *f.* lint. **—seide**, *f.* ravelled-out silk, silk ravellings. **—wolle**, *f.* picked wool, wool-pickings.

Zu'pfeifen, *v.n.* (*aux.* **h.**) (**einem**) to whistle to a p., to signal to a p. by a whistle.

Zu'pflastern, *v.a.* to cover up by paving over; to plaster up *or* over.

Zu'pflöcken, *v.a.* to plug up.

Zu'pflügen, *see* **Zuackern**.

Zu'pfropfen, *v.a.* to cork *or* bung up.

Zu'pichen, *v.a.* to cover *or* fill up with pitch.

Zu'pressen, *v.a.* to press, close by pressing.

Zur, *short for* **zu der**.

Zu'raten, I. *ir.v.a. & n.* to advise, counsel; **einem zu einer S. —en**, to advise *or* persuade a p. to (do) a th.; **ich will dir weder zu noch abraten**, I don't wish to advise (persuade) you one way or the other. II. *subst.n.*; **auf sein —en**, by his advice, at his suggestion.

Zu=ra'te—haltung, *f.* economy. **—ziehung (einer P.)**, *f.* consultation (with a p.).

Zu'raunen, *see* **Zuflüstern**.

Zur=Disposition'stellung, *f.* putting (*an officer, etc.*) on half-pay; placing at a p.'s disposal.

Zu'rech=n—en, *v.a.* to add (*in an account*); to put to (*a person's account*); to ascribe, attribute to. **—ung**, *f.* imputation, ascription; **mit —ung aller Kosten**, including all charges. *Comp.* **—ungs=fähig**, *adj.* accountable, responsible (*for one's actions*), of sound mind. **—ungs=fähigkeit**, *f.* sound state of mind, sound judgment; accountability, responsibility.

Zure'cht, *adv. & sep. prefix*, in order, aright; to rights; in the right place; as it ought to be; **— bringen**, to put to rights, arrange, set right; **sich — finden**, to find one's way; **einem — helfen**, to come to a p.'s aid, to help s.o. out of a difficulty; **mit etwas — kommen**, to get on well with s.th., to succeed in doing s.th., to manage s.th.; **mit einer S. schlecht — kommen**, to make a mess of a th.; **ich kann mit ihm nicht — kommen**, I cannot get on with him; **wie kommt er — ?** how does he make shift, how is he getting on (*with things*)? **— legen**, to lay in order, to put out; to interpret (*fig.*); **sich** (*dat.*) **eine S. — legen**, to explain a th. to o.s., to account for a th. to o.s.; **— machen**, to get ready, prepare, arrange, adjust, to do up (*a garden, clothes, etc.*); to trim up, to fit up (*houses*); to dress (*food*); to trim (*a lamp*); **sich — machen**, to get (o.s.) ready; **den Salat — machen**, to dress the salad; **— rücken**, to put in order, put to rights; **einem den Kopf — rücken**, to bring s.o. to his senses; **— setzen, — stellen**, to put right, put in order, arrange; **einem den Kopf — setzen**, to bring a p. to reason *or* to his senses, to give a p. a good lecture; **den Tisch — setzen**, to lay the table; **einen — weisen**, to put a p. in the right way, to set s.o. right, to instruct; to reprimand, rebuke; to disabuse a p.'s mind of an error. *Comp.* **—hämmern**, *v.a.* to hammer into shape. **—legung**, *f.* arrangement. **—machen**, *n.* putting to rights, doing up; dressing, cooking. **—weisung**, *f.* setting right, guidance, instruction; reprimand, reproof.

Zu'rede, *f.* (*pl.* **—n**) *see* **—n** II.

Zu'reden, I. *v.n.* (*aux.* **h.**) (**einem**) to advise *or* urge a p. to do s.th.; to exhort; to try to console; **ich habe ihm nicht zu= und nicht abgeredet**, I have neither persuaded him nor dissuaded him; **er läßt sich** (*dat.*) **nicht —**, he is not to be persuaded, he does not listen to any one. II. *subst.n.* persuasion; encouragement, exhortation; entreaties; **auf vieles — seiner Freunde that er es**, he did it at the urgent request of his friends; **— hilft**, a little persuasion is often of use.

Zu'reichen, *v.* I. *n.* (*aux.* **h.**) to suffice; **es reicht nicht zu**, it won't do; **—d**, sufficient, (just) enough; **—der Grund**, sufficient *or* conclusive reason. II. *a.* (**einem etwas**) to reach, hand (s.th.) over to (a p.).

Zu'reisen, *v.a.* to travel to(wards) a place; **zugereist kommen**, to arrive; **Zugereiste**, new comers, new arrivals. **—de**, *pl.* people coming here, new arrivals.

Zu'reite—n, *ir.v.* I. *a.* to break in, train (*a horse*); **nicht zugeritten**, untrained, unbroken. II. *n.* (*aux.* **s.**) to gallop, ride quickly; **einem Orte (auf einen) —n**, to ride to a place (up to a p.); **tüchtig —n**, to gallop on, ride quickly on. **—r**, *m.* (**—rs**, *pl.* **—r**) rough-rider, trainer, horse-breaker.

Zu'rennen, *ir.v.n.* (*aux.* **s.**) to run to *or* towards.

Zu'richt—en, *v.a.* to turn towards; to prepare, make ready; to do up; to dress, cook; to square, cut (*timber, stone*); to dress (*leather, cloth, etc.*); to make (*the form*) ready (*Typ.*); to smooth (*needles, stones, wood, etc.*); **zugerichtet**, in good register (*Typ.*); **das Brot —en**, to leaven the dough; **einen übel —en**, to use a p. badly, maltreat s.o.; **seine Kleider übel —en**, to soil one's clothes; **die Küpe —en**, to prepare the vat (*Dye*); **die Ballen —en**, to knock up, make balls (*Typ.*); **wie hast du dich zugerichtet!** what have you done with yourself! you have made a pretty mess of yourself! **er ist übel zugerichtet**, he has been badly treated; he is in a sad plight; **im Register zugerichtet**, in good register. **—er**, *m.* (**—ers**, *pl.* **—er**) one who prepares *or* dresses s.th.; maker-ready, feeder (*Typ.*); (*leather-*) currier. **—ung**, *f.* preparation, dressing; finish (*of stuffs*); leaven (*Bak.*); making ready (*for press*, *Typ.*). *Comp.* **—(e)=bogen**, *m.* register-sheet (*Typ.*). **—(e)=hammer**, *m.* pavior's dressing-hammer. **—(e)=maschine**, *f.* dressing-machine; twisting-machine (*for silk*). **—(e)=zimmer**, *n.* finishing-room.

Zu'riegeln, *v.a.* to bolt (*up*).

Zür'nen, *v.n.* (*aux.* **h.**) **über** *or* **um eine S.**, **wegen einer Sache —**, to be irritated, angry at something; (**mit**) **einem**, **auf einen —**, to be angry with a p.; **er zürnte mit sich und mit der** (**ganzen**) **Welt**, he was angry with himself and with everybody else.

Zu'rollen, *v.* I. *a.* & *n.* (*aux.* **h.**) to roll towards. II. *a.* to roll up, to close by rolling up.

Zu'rosten, *v.n.* (*aux.* **s.**) to get stopped up, become covered with rust, to close with rust.

Zurschau'stellung, *f.* exhibition, display, parading.

Zurü'ck, **—e**, *adv.* & *sep. prefix*, back, backward(s), behindhand, in the rear, in arrears; **er ist noch nicht —**, he has not returned yet. *Comp.* **—arbeiten**, *v.n.* (*aux.* **h.**) to work the opposite way, be reversed (*of machinery*). **—beben**, *v.n.* (*aux.* **s.**) to start back; to recoil (**vor**, from). **—begeben**, *v.r.* to return (**an einen Ort**, to a place). **—begehren**, *v.* I. *a.* to demand back. II. *n.* (*aux.* **h.**) to desire to return. **—begleiten**, *v.a.* to conduct, escort back; to show out, see to the door. **—behalten**, *ir.v.a.* to keep back, detain; to reserve, retain. **—behaltung**, *f.* retaining; detention, keeping back. **—behaltungs=recht**, *n.* right of reservation *or* retaining. **—bekommen**, *ir.v.a.* to get back; to recover. **—berufen**, *ir.v.a.* to recall, call back. **—beugen**, *see* **—biegen**. **—beuger**, *m.* supinator (*Anat.*). **—bezahlen**, *v.a.* to pay back, repay. **—beziehen**, *ir.v.r.* to refer back; to be reflexive (*Gram.*). **—bezüglich**, *adj.* reflexive (*Gram.*). **—biegen**, *ir.v.a.* to bend, fold, curve back. **—bleiben**, *ir.v.n.* (*aux.* **s.**) to remain behind; to fall behind *or* back; to stay behind; to survive; to remain at home; to lose, go slow; to be late (*of fruit*); **hinter einer S. —bleiben**, to fall short of, not come up to s.th.; **auf der Rennbahn —bleiben**, to be out-distanced in the race; **meine Uhr bleibt —**, my watch is slow; **er mußte in der Schule —bleiben**, he was kept in. **—blicken**, *v.* I. *n.* (*aux.* **h.**) to look back. II. *a.* to recall, review (*the past*, *etc.*); **—blickend**, retrospective. **—bringen**, *ir.v.a.* to bring back *or* bring again; to reduce (*Arith.*); **einen von einem schlechten Leben —bringen**, to reclaim, reform a p.; **von Irrtümern —bringen**, to convince of error, undeceive; **zum Gehorsam —bringen**, to reduce to obedience; **einen ins Leben —bringen**, to bring a p. back to life; **diese Verluste haben ihn sehr —gebracht**, these losses have reduced him greatly, have brought him very low. **—bugsieren**, *v.a.* to tow back; to bring back. **—datie'ren**, I. *v.a.* to date back, antedate. II. *subst. n.*; **das —datieren des Konkurses**, antedating a bankruptcy. **—denken**, *ir.v.n.* (*aux.* **h.**) to reflect, think of the past; **an seine Jugend —denken**, to recall one's youth. **—diskontieren**, *v.a.* to discount again. **—drängen**, *v.a.* to dress, push, drive back; to repel; to restrain (*tears*, *etc.*), repress (*one's feelings*). **—drehen**, *v.a.* to turn back. **—dürfen**, *ir.v.n.* (*aux.* **h.**) to be allowed to return. **—eilen**, *v.n.* (*aux.* **s.**) to hurry *or* hasten back. **—erbitten**, *ir.v.a.* to ask, beg back; **darf ich den Einschluß —erbitten?** may I ask you to return the inclosure? **—erhalten**, *see* **—bekommen**. **—erinnern**, *v.a.*; **sich an eine S. —erinnern**, to remember, recollect a th.; **so weit ich mich —erinnern kann**, as far as I can remember, as far as my memory serves me. **—erinnerung**, *f.* recollection. **—erobern**, *v.a.* to reconquer. **—erstatten**, *v.a. see* **Wiedererstatten**. **—fahren**, I. *ir.v.n.* (*aux.* **s.**) to drive, sail, *etc.*, back; to return; to dart back; to recoil, fly back, rebound; (**erschreckt**) **—fahren über** (**vor**), to start at (from). II. *ir.v.a.* to drive, row, *etc.*, back; **—fahren über** (*acc.*), to recross (*a river*, *bridge*); to travel *or* go back by *or* via; **wir fuhren über die Schweiz —**, we came back by Switzerland. III. *subst.n.* return-drive, drive home; **das —fahren einer Kanone**, the recoil of a gun. **—fahrt**, *f.* return, return-journey. **—fallen**, I. *ir.v.n.* (*aux.* **s.**) to fall back; to be reflected; to relapse; **in denselben Fehler —fallen**, to fall back into the same error; **in eine Krankheit —fallen**, to suffer a relapse; **die Schande davon ist auf uns —gefallen**, the disgrace redounds upon us; **an einen —fallen**, to revert to s.o., fall to a p. by reversion. II. *subst.n.* relapse; reversion; falling back; reflection. **—finden**, *ir.v.r.* & *n.* (*aux.* **h.** & **s.**) to find the way back. **—fliegen**, *ir.v.n.* (*aux.* **s.**) to fly back. **—fliehen**, *ir.v.n.* (*aux.* **s.**) to flee back; to withdraw hastily. **—fließen**, I. *ir.v.n.* (*aux.* **s.**) to flow, run back; **auf welche die Wohlthat —floß**, who reaped the benefit of the kindness. II. *subst. n.* reflux. **—fordern**, *v.a.* to demand back, claim again; to reclaim. **—forderung**, *f.* reclamation. **—führbar**, *adj.* that can be brought back, reducible. **—führen**, *v.a.* to lead back, reconvey, reconduct; **auf eine S. —führen**, to bring *or* trace back to s.th.; **auf seinen wahren Wert —führen**, to reduce to its true value. **—führung**, *f.* leading back; reduction (*Arith.*); **—führung auf das Unmögliche**, reductio ad absurdum (*Log.*); **—führung des Heeres auf den Friedensstand**, reduction of the army to a peace-footing. **—gabe**, *f.* returning, giving back; restoration; surrender. **—geben**, *ir.v.a.* to return, restore, give back; to deliver up; to surrender; **einem eine Beleidigung —geben**, to retaliate on a p., retort, return an insult. **—gehen**, *ir.v.n.* (*aux.* **s.**) to return; to go back, retrograde; to fall; to go down; to double (*as a hare*); to be broken off, not to succeed *or* take place, to come to nothing; to trace back (*to its origin*); **Waren —gehen lassen**, to return goods; **auf die Quelle, den Ursprung —gehen**, to trace to its source; **es geht mit ihm —**, his affairs are in a bad way; **seine Geschäfte gehen —**, his business is going down; **die Verlobung ist —gegangen**, the match has been broken off; **der Handel geht —**, the bargain is off; trade is getting worse. **—geleiten**, *v.a.* to lead back. **—gezogen**, *adj.* & *adv.* retired, secluded; **—gezogen leben**, to lead a retired life. **—gezogenheit**, *f.* privacy, seclusion, retirement, solitude. **—greifen**, *ir.v.n.* (*aux.* **h.**) to snatch, grasp at s.th. behind; **weiter —greifen**, to begin farther back. **—haben**, *ir.v.a.* to have back; **er möchte sein Wort —haben**, he would like to recall his words. **—halten**, I. *ir.v.a.* to hold back, to detain, delay, stop; to curb, check, hold in; to keep (*a schoolboy*, *etc.*) in (*detention*); to hold (*one's breath*); to suppress (*cries*, *etc.*); to restrain (*tears*, *etc.*); to reserve, suspend (*one's opinion*, *etc.*); to conceal (*a design*, *etc.*); **einen —halten, etwas zu thun**, to (*try to*) keep a p. from doing s.th.; **seine Gefühl —halten**, to repress one's feelings; **sich —halten**, to restrain o.s., to refrain (*from*), to keep back, keep behind; **er konnte nicht kommen, Krankheit hielt ihn zurück**, illness prevented him from coming.

II. *ir.v.n.* (*aux.* h.); **mit einer S. —halten,** to keep back, to conceal, reserve; **die Käufer halten sehr —,** customers are holding back. III. *subst.n.* the holding back; repression; reserve. **—haltend,** *p. & adj.* reserved, cautious, discreet; shy; retentive. **—haltung,** *f. see* **—halten** III.; retention; detention; reserve; cautiousness; modesty, reserve; propriety, discretion; retention (*Med.*); retardation (*Mus.*). **—holen,** *v.a.* to fetch back. **—jagen,** *v.* I. *a.* to drive back. II. *n.* (*aux.* ſ.) to gallop furiously back. **—kämmen,** *v.a.* to comb back. **—kaufen,** *v.a.* to buy back. **—kehren,** *v.n.* (*aux.* ſ.) to return, go back; to come back; to recur (*to one's memory*); to return (*to one's duty*); **nach Hause —kehren,** to return home. **—kommen,** *ir.v.n.* (*aux.* ſ.) to return, come back; to go down in the world; **von etwas —kommen,** to return from (*a place*), to recover from (*alarm, surprise, etc.*), to retrieve (*past errors*), to abandon (*one's vices, failings; a project*); **von seiner Meinung —kommen,** to alter one's opinion, to change one's mind; **auf eine S. —kommen,** to return, revert to a th.; **ich komme nachher auf diesen Punkt wieder —,** I shall return to this subject later on; **ich komme immer wieder darauf —, es wäre besser gewesen, wenn . . .,** I repeat what I have always said: it would have been better if . . .; **er ist in seinen Vermögensverhältnissen sehr —gekommen,** he is very much reduced in circumstances. **—können,** *ir.v.n.* (*aux.* h.) to be able to return; to be able to withdraw (*from a position*); to be able to retract. **—kunft,** *f.* coming back *or* home, return. **—lassen,** *ir.v.a.* to leave behind; to allow to return. **—laufen,** *ir.v.n.* (*aux.* ſ.) to run back; to ebb, flow back; to recoil; to retrograde. **—legen,** *v.a.* to place behind; to lay *or* put back; to lay aside, reserve; to lay by (*money*); to shelve; to travel, go over; to live, pass; **einen Weg** *or* **eine Strecke —legen,** to pass over, walk, travel a certain distance; **eine gute Strecke Weges —legen,** to get over a good deal of ground; **nach —gelegtem achtzehnten Lebensjahre,** after having completed one's eighteenth year; **das dreißigste Jahr —gelegt haben,** to have attained the age of 30; **die Schulzeit —gelegt haben,** to have gone through a complete school course, to have done with school. **—leiten,** *v.a.* to lead back; **zu etwas —leiten,** to lead up to, reduce to a th. **—lenken,** *v.a.* to turn back. **—leuchten,** *v.n.* (*aux.* h.) to light (**einem,** a p.) back, to be reflected. **—liefern,** *v.a.* to send back; return. **—marschieren,** *v.n.* (*aux.* ſ.) to march back. **—melden,** *v.a.* to reply; **sich vom Urlaub —melden,** to report o.s. after a furlough. **—mögen,** *ir.v.n.* (*aux.* h.) to like *or* wish to return, to wish o.s. back. **—müssen,** *ir.v.n.* (*aux.* h.) to be obliged to return; **das Buch muß —,** the book must be returned; **der Tisch muß —,** the table must be moved back. **—nahme,** *f.* the taking back, resumption; withdrawal; recantation; recall; revocation (*of an edict, etc.*); **ich hoffe, daß Sie die —nahme nicht beanstanden,** I hope you will not refuse to take (*it*) back; **—nahme eines gegebenen Versprechens,** the retracting of a promise. **—nehmen,** *ir.v.a.* to take back; to recall, retract; to revoke; to cancel (*an order*); **einen Schüler aus der Schule —nehmen,** to take a pupil away from school; **er wird das, was er Ihnen gesagt hat, —nehmen,** he will withdraw what he has said to you; **sein Wort —nehmen,** to go back from one's word, to retract one's promise; **denselben Weg —nehmen,** to go back the same way as one came. **—nötigen,** *v.a.* to force to return. **—prallen,** *v.n.* (*aux.* ſ.) to rebound, recoil, fly back; to be reflected; to reverberate; to start back (**vor,** from). **—rechnen,** *v.a. & n.* (*aux.* ſ.) to reckon back, go over an account; **zur Deckung dieses Vorschusses bevollmächtigen wir Sie, die gleiche Summe auf unsere Expedition in B. — zu rechnen,** to cover this advance, we authorize you to draw upon our house in B. for a like amount (*C. L.*). **—reise,** *see* **Rückreise.** **—reisen,** *v.n.* (*aux.* ſ.) to journey back, return. **—reiten,** *ir.v.n.* (*aux.* ſ.) to ride back. **—rollen,** *v.a.* to roll back. **—rücken,** *v.a. & n.* (*aux.* ſ.) to move *or* push back. **—rudern,** *v.n.* (*aux.* ſ.) to row back; to back-water. **—rufen,** I. *ir.v.a.* to call back; to recall. II. *subst.n.*, **—rufung,** *f.* recall. **—sagen,** *v.a.* to say in return; to reply; to return (*an answer, a compliment, etc.*); **—sagen lassen,** to send back word. **—schaffen,** *v.a.* to convey back. **—schallen,** *v.n.* (*aux.* ſ.) to resound, reecho. **—schaudern, —schauern (vor einer Sache),** *v.n.* (*aux.* ſ.) to recoil, shrink back with horror (from a thing). **—schaunen,** *v.n.* (*aux.* h.) *see* **—sehen.** **—scheuchen,** *v.a.* to scare, frighten away. **—schicken,** *v.a.* to send back, to return (*by post, etc.*). **—schieben,** *ir.v.a.* to push back; to repulse; to reduce (*a dislocation*); to pass over (*in appointing to an office*); to return, retort; to defer, postpone, delay; to turn the tables (*upon an opponent*); to throw back (*a charge upon the accuser*). **—schiffen,** *v.* I. *n.* to return in a ship. II. *a.* to row back; to bring *or* send back in a boat. **—schlagen,** *ir.v.* I. *a.* to strike, drive back; to repel, repulse; **eine Decke —schlagen,** to turn down, throw off a coverlet; **die Haare —schlagen,** to smooth back the hair; **den Mantel —schlagen,** to throw open one's mantle; **—geschlagener Wagen,** open carriage; **einen Ball —schlagen,** to return a ball (*Tennis*). II. *n.* (*aux.* ſ.) to fall violently backward; to be suppressed, driven in (*of diseases, perspiration, etc.*); **die Preise sind —geschlagen,** prices have fallen (still lower); **auf die Lunge —schlagen,** to be driven in on the lungs. **—schleichen,** *ir. v.r. & n.* (*aux.* ſ.) to crawl, creep back. **—schleppen,** *v.a.* to drag back. **—schleudern,** *v.a.* to hurl back. **—schließen,** *ir.v.n.* (*aux.* h.) to reason a posteriori, use an a posteriori argument. **—schneiden,** *ir.v.a.* to cut back, lop, prune. **—schnellen,** *v.* I. *a.* to dart, cast back. II. *n.* (*aux.* ſ.) to rebound. **—schrecken,** *v.* I. *a.* to frighten back; to discourage; to deter from. II. *n.* (*aux.* ſ.); **von einer Sache —schrecken,** to shrink back from (*doing*) a thing. **—schreiben,** *ir.v.a.* to send a written reply, to write back; to put on the list of reserves (*Mil.*) **—schreiten,** *ir.v.n.* (*aux.* ſ.) to step *or* go back. **—schwimmen,** *ir.v.n.* (*aux.* ſ.) to swim back. **—sehen,** *ir.v.n.* (*aux.* h.) to look back, look behind one; to reflect on, review (*the past, etc.*). **—sehnen,** *v.r.;* **er sehnt sich —,** he wishes himself back, he longs to return; **er sehnt sich nach dem Lande, &c. —,** he sighs for, regrets the country (*which he has left, etc.*). **—sein,** *ir.v.n.* to be behind, to be back, to have come back *or* returned; to be too slow; to be behindhand; to be backward (*in knowledge, etc.*); to be in arrears; **man ist in dieser Provinz sehr —,** the people in this province are very much behind the times; **der Junge ist in der Schule sehr —,** the boy is very backward in school; **wir sind in unserm Fache an dieser Universität sehr —,** we are not at all up to date in our department in this university. **—setzen,** *v.* I. *a.* to set, place back *or* behind; to replace; to put in the background (*fig.*); to neglect, slight; to remove into a lower class, to degrade (*in office*); to reduce (*in circumstances*); to set aside (*something for a p.*); to throw aside (*as useless, unsaleable, etc.*); **das Datum eines Briefes —**

ſetzen, to antedate a letter; —geſetzte Waren, refuse articles; ſich —geſetzt fühlen, to feel o.s. slighted, not treated with proper respect. II. *n.* (*aux.* ſ.); über einen Graben —ſetzen, to spring, jump back over a ditch. —ſetzung, *f.* slight, disregard, neglect. —ſinken, *ir.v.n.* (*aux.* ſ.) to sink, fall back; in Laſter —ſinken, to fall back into vicious ways. —ſollen, *ir.v.n.* (*aux.* h.) to be obliged to come back, to be bound to return; to be obliged *or* ordered to retire; er ſollte —, he was to return. —ſpiegeln, *v.a.* to reflect. —ſpielen, *v.a.* to play, send back (*a ball*). —ſprengen, *v.n.* (*aux.* ſ.) to gallop back. —ſpringen, *ir.v.n.* (*aux.* ſ.) to leap, spring back; to jump back; to run back; to spring back, rebound; to start back, recoil; to be reflected; to stand back, stand out of the line; —ſpringend, springing back, rebounding; resilient. —ſtecken, *v.a.* to put *or* place behind, to put back. —ſtehen, *ir.v.n.* (*aux.* ſ.) to stand back *or* behind; to be inferior to; —ſtehen müſſen, to be obliged to stand behind, to have to wait. —ſtellen, *v.a.* to put back, replace; to return; to put aside; to put back (*a watch*); to replace; to adjourn; einen Militärpflichtigen —ſtellen, to send back a conscript for military service for a year *or* until fully qualified (*Mil.*). —ſtellung, *f.* replacement; —ſtellung wegen zeitlicher Untauglichkeit, temporary rejection (*Mil.*). —ſtoßen, *ir.v.a.* to thrust back; to repel, repulse; to retort. —ſtoßend, *p. & adj.* repulsive, repellent. —ſtoßung, *f.* pushing back, *etc.*; repulsion (*Phys., etc.*). —ſtoßungs-kraft, *f.* power of repulsion. —ſtrahlen, *v.* I. *n.* (*aux.* ſ.) to be reflected, shine back. II. *a.* to cause to reflect *or* reverberate. —ſtreichen, *ir.v.* I. *a.* to stroke back, smooth back; to strike up (*the nap of cloth*). II. *n.* (*aux.* ſ.) to fly back (*of migratory birds*). —ſtreifen, *v.a.* to turn up, put back (*the sleeves, etc.*). —ſtrömen, *v.n.* (*aux.* ſ.) to flow, come back. —ſtürzen, *v.n.* (*aux.* ſ.) to fall violently back; nach Hauſe —ſtürzen, to rush (*back*) home. —taumeln, *v.n.* (*aux.* ſ.) to reel back. —telegraphieren, *v.a.* to telegraph *or* wire back, reply by telegraph. —thun, *ir.v.a.* to put back, replace; einen Schritt —thun, to (take a) step back. —tragen, *ir.v.a.* to carry back; to carry away back with one. —traſſieren, *v.a.* to make a redraft, redraw (auf, upon). —treiben, *ir.v.a.* to drive back; to drive home; to drive in (*perspiration, etc.*). —treten, *ir.v.n.* (*aux.* ſ.) to step back; to return (*to*); to recede; to go back, return to its place; to subside, return to its channel (*of a river*); to retire; to subside, to be checked (*of a disease, etc.*); in den Heeresdienſt —treten, to re-enter military service; in das Privatleben —treten, to return to private life; von einer Bewerbung —treten, to withdraw from a candidature; von ſeinem Amte —treten, to resign *or* give up one's post; to resign one's office. —tretend, *p. & adj.* stepping back, *etc.*; reentrant (*of angles*). —überſetzen, *v.a.* to retranslate. —verlangen, *see* —fordern, —ſehnen. —verſetzen, *v.a.* to put back; to restore to a former state; to put into a lower class, put down; to degrade (*Mil.*); ſich in eine Zeit —verſetzen, to go back, be carried back in imagination to a former time. —verweiſen, *v.a.* to refer back. —wälzen, *v.a.* to roll, push back. —wandern, *v.n.* (*aux.* ſ.) to return. —weichen, I. *ir.v.n.* (*aux.* ſ.) to give way, fall back, recede, retreat; to recoil; to withdraw; to shade off (*Paint.*); mutig weicht — der Starke, the strong can yield without cowardice. II. *subst.n.* recoil (*of a gun*); retreat; ebb (*of the sea*). —weiſen, *ir.v.a.* to show (*the way*) back; to send (*a p.*) back, make signs (*to a p.*) to go away; to refuse; to repulse; to retort; to reject; den Leſer auf eine frühere Anmerkung —weiſen, to refer the reader to a preceding note. —wenden, *ir.v.a.* to turn back. —werfen, *ir.v.a.* to throw back; to cast aside; to throw, send back (*a ball*); to reflect (*rays of light*); to repulse (*an enemy*); den Kopf —werfen, to throw back one's head; in das Elend —werfen, to cast back into (*his, etc.*) misery. —wirken, *v.n.* (*aux.* h.); auf eine S. —wirken, to react upon something. —wirkung, *see* Rückwirkung. —wollen, *ir.v.n.* (*aux.* h.) to wish to return. —wünſchen, *v.a.* to wish for the return of; to wish in return; ſich —wünſchen, to desire to be back. —zählen, *v.a.* to count back *or* backwards; to deduct, take off. —ziehen, I. *ir.v.a.* to draw back; to withdraw; to retract, recant; to move back again (*at chess, etc.*); to redeem (*a pledge*); to take no more part in, to be no longer interested in; ſich —ziehen, to retire, withdraw; ſich auf (*or* in) ſich ſelbſt —ziehen, to retire into oneself, become self-absorbed; ſich auf . . . —ziehen, to fall back upon . . .; einen Poſten —ziehen, to withdraw (an outpost), to order a sentry to fall back. II. *ir.v.n.* (*aux.* ſ.) to return, retire to; to retreat; in ſeine alte Wohnung —ziehen, to move back again into one's old lodgings *or* house. III. *subst.n.*, —ziehung, *f.* retreat (*Mil.*); das —ziehen der Gelder, the withdrawal of the money; —ziehung eines Verſprechens, withdrawal, retracting of one's promise; das (Sich-)—ziehen, recession, retirement, retreat. —zieher, *m.* screw (*Bill.*).

Zu'ruf, *m.* (—(e)s, *pl.* —e) shout, call; acclamation, cheer. —en, *ir.v.a. & n.*; einem etwas —en, to call s.th. to a p.; einem Beifall —en, to cheer, applaud a person.

Zu'runden, *v.a.* to round off; to enlarge, increase.

Zu'rüſt—en, *v.a.* to fit out, equip; to prepare, make *or* get ready. —ung, *f.* fitting out, equipment; preparation; —ungen treffen, to make preparations.

Zu'ſäen, *v.a. & n.* (*aux.* h.) to sow on *or* more.

Zu'ſage, *f.* (*pl.* —n) promise, pledge; assent.

Zu'ſagen, *v.* I. *a.* (einem etwas) to promise; einem etwas auf den Kopf —, to tell a p. plainly, maintain it to s.o.'s face. II. *n.* (*aux.* h.) to meet, suit a p.'s wishes; to be to s.o.'s taste; to agree with a p. (*of food*); einem nicht —, not to be to a p.'s mind; dieſer Mann ſagt mir nicht zu, I do not like this man, this man does not suit me; das ſagt mir nicht zu, that is not my taste; ich habe zugeſagt, I have promised; I have accepted (*an invitation*).

Zuſam'men, *adv. & sep. prefix*, together, jointly, all in all, all together; alle —, all in a body, all together; das macht 100 Mark —, that makes a total of 100 marks. *Comp.* —arbeiten, *v.* I. *a.* to work together; to exercise (*a horse*) well. II. *n.* (*aux.* h.) to work together, in company, to co-operate. —ballen, *v.a & r.* to form into a ball; die Fäuſte —ballen, to clench the fists. —ballung, *f.* agglomeration; conglomerate. —bauen, *v.a.* to build together, unite, join by building. —begeben, *ir.v.r.* to assemble. —bekommen, *ir.v.a.* to (*manage to*) get *or* scrape together. —berufen, *ir.v.a.* to convoke, call together. —beſtehen, *ir.v.n.* (*aux.* h.) to be consistent, compatible (mit, with). —betteln, *v.a.* to get together *or* collect by begging. —binden, *ir.v.a.* to bind together; to tie up. —blaſen, *ir.v.a.* to summon by trumpet; to unite with the blow-pipe; to blow down. —borgen, *v.a.* to get together by borrowing. —brauen, *v.a.* to brew, mix; es braut ſich etwas —, something is brewing, is being concocted. —**brechen,** *ir. v.* I. *n.* (*aux.* **s.**) to break (*in pieces*); to break down; to smash; **seine Knie brechen unter ihm —,** his knees give way under him. II. *a.* to break in pieces; to fold (*up*) (*a letter, etc.*). —**bringen,** *ir.v.a.* to bring together, join, unite; to collect, gather together; to rally (*troops*); to bring together, introduce; **seine Gedanken —bringen,** to collect one's thoughts; —**gebrachtes Vermögen,** joint property; —**gebrachte Kinder,** half-brothers and sisters. —**drängen,** *v.a.* to press together; to put close together; to compress; to condense. —**drehen,** *v.a.* to twist, twine, weave. —**drückbar,** *adj.* compressible. — **drückbarkeit,** *f.* compressibility. —**drucken,** *v.a.* to print together; **in ein Werk —drucken,** to print as one work, in one volume. — **drücken,** *v.a.* to compress. —**fahren,** *ir.v.* I. *n.* (*aux.* **s.**) to drive, travel together; to come into collision, rush against one another; to curdle; to shrivel, shrink up; **vor Schreck —fahren,** to start back in alarm; —**fahrende Sonnenstrahlen,** converging rays of the sun. II. *a.* to collect in a conveyance. —**falten,** *v.a.* to fold (*up*); to furl (*sails*). —**fassen,** *v.a.* to grasp, seize; to embrace, include, comprise; to collect (**sich,** oneself, one's thoughts, *etc.*); **das Ganze noch einmal —fassen,** to recapitulate; —**fassen in . . .,** to compress (*into*), reduce (*to*), narrow (*a question, etc.*) to . . .; **kurz —fassen,** to sum up, to abridge, compress; **um es kurz — zu fassen,** to sum up, to be brief. —**finden,** *ir.v.* I. *a.* to find together, to find assembled. II. *r.* to meet (*together*). —**flechten,** *v.a.* to braid *or* twine together. —**flicken,** *v.a.* to patch together. —**fließen,** I. *i.v.n.* to flow together, to flow in *or* into the same channel; to fuse. II. *n.* —**fluß,** *m.* confluence, junction (*of two rivers*); fusion (*of colours*); re-union; —**fluß von Umständen,** juncture; —**fluß von Menschen,** concourse, crowd, assemblage of people; —**fluß von Verbrechen,** complication of crimes. — **frieren,** *ir.v.n.* (*aux.* **s.**) to freeze together, to congeal; to shrink with cold *or* in freezing. —**fügen,** *v.a.* to join together, unite; to fit into one another; to pair, match; to mortise; to clamp; to articulate (*Surg.*); to construe (*Gram.*); to sew together, join; **was Gott zusammengefügt hat, das soll der Mensch nicht scheiden,** what God hath joined together, let no man put asunder. —**geben,** *ir.v.a.* to join in wedlock, marry. —**gehen,** *ir. v.n.* (*aux.* **s.**) to go together, belong to one another, to suit one another, to match; to shrink, get smaller, diminish; to melt down; to coincide, concur; to shut close; to communicate (*of rooms*); to get lower (*of supplies*). — **gehören,** *v.n.* (*aux.* **h.**) to belong to one another; to match, be fellows, form a pair. — **gehörig,** *adj.* belonging to one another; homogeneous. —**geraten,** *ir.v.n.* (*aux.* **s.**) to encounter; to fall out, attack one another. — **gesetzt,** *p.p. & adj.* composed, compound, complex; composite (*Bot.*, *Arch.*); compound (*Mus.*, *Gram.*, *Arith.*); complex (*being; idea; term; fraction*). —**halt,** *m.* holding together; consistence; cohesion; union; agreement; concert; tie, bond. —**halten,** *ir.v.* I. *a.* to hold together, to place one thing by the side of the other; to compare; **wenn wir die beiden Berichte —halten,** in comparing the two accounts. II. *n.* (*aux.* **h.**) to hold together; to cohere. —**hang,** *m.* coherence, connection, association; cohesion (*Phys.*); continuity; context; **aus dem —hange kommen,** to lose the thread of the *or* one's discourse, to get confused; **aus dem —hange gerissene Wörter,** words separated from their context; —**hang der Begriffe,** association of ideas; **dieser Gedanke steht nicht im —hange mit den vorhergehenden,** this idea has no connection with the previous train of thought; **Mangel an —hang,** incoherence; **ohne —hang,** incoherent, disconnected, loose (*of style*); **er denkt nicht im —hange,** his thoughts are disconnected; **ich will Ihnen den ganzen —hang der Sache erzählen,** I will tell you the whole story *or* the ins and outs of the matter. —**hangen,** *ir.v.n.* (*aux.* **h.**) to hang together *or* side by side, to be connected; to cohere; to be continuous; **sagen Sie mir doch wie die Geschichte —hing,** please give me some particulars of the matter; **wie hängt das — ?** how is this to be explained? —**hängen,** *v.* I. *a.* to hang together; to connect. II. *n.* (*aux.* **h.**) *see* —**hangen.** —**hangslos,** *adj.* disconnected, incoherent, disjointed, inconsistent; rambling (*fig.*). —**hangslosigkeit,** *f.* incoherence, disconnectedness, inconsistency. —**hauen,** *ir.v.a.* to mince, chop up; to cut to pieces; to thrash. —**häufung,** *f.* heaping up, accumulation; aggregation; heap. —**heilen,** *v.* I. *n.* (*aux.* **s.**) to heal, close up; to consolidate. II. *a.* to join, close up (*a wound, etc.*). —**hetzen,** *v.a.* to set a p. against another, to set persons at variance. —**holen,** *v.a.* to bring together. — **kauern,** *v.r.* to cower, squat, roll o.s. up. — **kaufen,** *v.a.* to buy up; to forestall. —**ketten,** *v.a.* to chain together. —**kitten,** *v.a.* to cement. —**klammern,** *v.a.* to fasten together with cramp-irons. —**klang,** *m.* accord, consonance, harmony, concert. —**klappen,** *v.* I. *a.* to put together; to fold up; to close (*a knife, fan, etc.*). II. *n.* (*aux.* **h.**) to agree, fit; **seine Zähne klappten —,** his teeth chattered; **er ist recht —geklappt,** he has shrunk to a skeleton (*coll.*). —**klauben,** *v.a.* to scrape together; to compile. —**kommen,** *ir.v.n.* (*aux.* **h.**) to come together; to assemble; to meet; **scharf mit einem —kommen,** to have a sharp altercation with a p., to quarrel. —**können,** *v.n.* to be able to meet. —**koppeln,** *v.a.* to couple together. —**krachen,** *v.n.* to fall *or* break down with a crash. — **kriechen,** *ir.v.n.* (*aux.* **s.**) to creep together; to shrivel, creep up. —**kunft,** *f.* assembly, convention; meeting, reunion; interview; rendezvous; conference; conjunction (*Astr.*). —**läppern,** *v.r.* to mount up imperceptibly *or* by small sums (*coll.*). —**lassen,** *ir.v.a.* to allow to be together, to leave together; to let (come) together, to cause to be united. —**lauf,** *see* —**fluß.** — **laufen,** *ir.v.n.* (*aux.* **h.**) to run together; to crowd together in a mob; to congregate, collect, meet; to converge, tend to meet in a point; to blend, run into one another (*Paint.*); to shrink up; to curdle; **auf, in einen Punkt —laufen,** to meet in a point, converge; **mit den Köpfen —laufen,** to knock their heads together, run against one another. —**laut,** *m.* consonance, harmony. —**läuten,** *v.* I. *n.* (*aux.* **h.**); **alle Glocken —läuten lassen,** to have all the bells rung at the same time; to set all the bells ringing. II. *a.* to assemble by ringing the bells. —**leben,** I. *v.n.* to live together; to be fellow lodgers; to cohabit (*sexually*); **mit einem —leben,** to live with a p. II. *n.* living together; companionship; social life; cohabitation. —**legen,** *v.a.* to place, put together; to fold up; to close (*a penknife*); to club together, contribute (*money*). —**leihen,** *ir.v.a.*; **sich** (*dat.*) **eine Summe —leihen,** to collect a sum of money by borrowing. —**lesen,** *ir.v.* I. *a.* to gather *or* pick together; to collect by reading. II. *a. & n.* to read together. —**liegen,** *ir.v.n.* (*aux.* **h.**) to lie together; to be quartered in the same place (*Mil.*). — **löten,** *v.a.* to solder (up). —**machen,** *v.a.* to make in company with others; to put together; **8 und 4 machen — 12,** 8 and 4 makes 12. — **nähen,** *v.a.* to sew up *or* together. —**nehmen,** *ir.v.a.* to take together, take conjointly with; to gather, tuck up (*one's clothes, etc.*); to take collectively; to take up (*one's cards*); to hold up, gather (*a horse*); to husband (*one's strength, time, etc.*); **seine Gedanken, den Verstand —nehmen,** to collect one's thoughts, oneself; **alles —genommen,** taking one thing with another, all things considered, upon the whole; **alle Umstände —nehmen,** to take all the circumstances into consideration; **sich —nehmen,** to collect o.s., to make an effort, to summon up all one's strength, control one's feelings, pluck up courage, give heed, take great care; **nimm dich —!** be a man! pluck up courage! **nimm dich — oder . . .,** look out, be careful, take care or . . . **—ordnen,** *v.a.* to arrange together, classify. **—packen,** *v.a.* to pack up (*together*). **—passen,** *v.* I. *n.* (*aux.* **h.**) to suit together; to match, go well together; to agree; **sie passen gut —,** they are well matched, they are a good match; **sie passen schlecht —,** they are ill assorted. II. *a.* to adjust, match, assort. **—pfarren,** *v.a.* to unite, form into one parish. **—pferchen,** *v.a.* to fold, pen up together. **—pressen,** *v.a.* to press together. **—raffen,** *v.* I. *a.* to sweep, rake up together; to snatch up; to hurry together; to tuck up (*one's clothes*); **die Kräfte —raffen;** *see* **—raffen** II. II. *r.* to collect *or* rouse o.s., to make a desperate exertion. **—rechnen,** *v.a. & n.* (*aux.* **h.**) to reckon up; to compute; to do one's accounts together; **alles —gerechnet,** *see* **alles —genommen; mit einem —rechnen,** to settle accounts with, come to an understanding with a p. **—reimen,** *v.a. see* **Reimen; reimen Sie das —, wenn Sie können,** make that out, reconcile that if you can; **ich kann es mir nicht —reimen,** I cannot make head or tail of it, it beats me altogether, it is beyond me. **—reiten,** *v.a.;* **ein Pferd —reiten,** to override, knock up a horse. **—rennen,** *ir.v.n.* to run together; to run against one another; **mit einem —rennen,** to quarrel with a p. (*coll.*). **—rotten,** *v.a.* to gather in a mob *or* troop; **sich —rotten,** to collect together, band, conspire. **—rücken,** *v.a. & n.* (*aux.* **ſ.**) to approach, draw nearer to; to draw closer, to close; **nach rechts —rücken,** to move to the right (*Mil.*). **—rufen,** *ir.v.a.* to call together, convoke, summon. **—schau(d)ern,** *v.n.* (*aux.* **ſ.**) to shudder with horror. **—schaufeln,** *v.a.* to shovel (*up*) together. **—schichten,** *v.a.* to pile, heap up; to crowd, squeeze together; to pile up in layers. **—schießen,** *ir.v.* I. *a.* to shoot down; to batter down with a gun; **eine Summe —schießen,** to make up a sum by contributions; **—geschossen,** destroyed, battered down, ruined; crippled; made up by contributions. II. *n.* (*aux.* **ſ.**) to shoot at the same time; to dart together; to crystallize. **—schlagen,** *ir.v.* I. *n.* (*aux.* **ſ.**) to strike against one another; to fall down with a crash; to close with a bang *or* crash; **die Wellen schlugen über ihm —,** the waves closed over him. II. *a.* to strike together; to beat up; to clap (*one's hands*); to smash up (*a hostile force*); to beat down (*the earth*); to pound; to unite (*estates*); to fold up (*a letter, napkin*); to wrap (*one's mantle*) around one; to put up (*a bed*); to gather (*Typ.*); to baste up; **vor Verwunderung die Hände über dem Kopf —schlagen,** to throw up one's hands in astonishment; **die Kosten —schlagen,** to lump the expenses; **Geld aus etwas —schlagen,** to turn s.th. into money. **—schließen,** *ir.v.* I. *a.* to chain (*prisoners, etc.*) together; **die Reihen —schließen,** to close the ranks. II. *n.* (*aux.* **h.**) to unite, join. **—schmelzen,** *v.* I. *n.* (*aux.* **ſ.**) to melt; to melt away. II. *a.* to melt together, fuse. **—schmieden,** *v.a.* to weld together. **—schmieren,** *v.a.* to scribble off, to puddle together (*vulg.*). **—schnüren,** *v.a.* to lace, tie together; to brace; to pack up; to cord, tie up; to strangle; **das schnürt mir das Herz —,** that oppresses me, wrings my heart. **—schreiben,** *ir.v.a.* to compile; to write in one word; to gain by writing; **sich** (*dat.*) **ein Vermögen —schreiben,** to make a fortune by one's books *or* one's writings; **was der Mann alles —schreibt!** what a scribbler (bookmaker) he is! **—schrumpfen,** *v.n.* (*aux.* **ſ.**) to shrivel, shrink up; to curl up; to wrinkle. **—schustern,** (*coll.*) *see* **—flicken. —schütteln,** *v.a.* to shake up well. **—schütten,** *v.a.* to pour together, to mix up together. **—schweißen,** *v.a.* to weld (*together*). **—setzbar,** *adj.* that can be put together *or* composed, compoundable. **—setzen,** I. *v.a.* to put together; to compose; to compound; to combine; to construct; **eine Maschine —setzen,** to put up, put a machine together; **die Gewehre —setzen,** to pile arms; **sich —setzen,** to sit down together; to be composed of, to consist of; *see* **—gesetzt.** II. *subst. n.*, **—setzung,** *f.* composition; combination; construction, formation; union, joining; synthesis. **—setzer,** *m.* one who makes up, compounder; mounter (*of machinery*), fitter; tool used for putting together (*watches*), watch-holder. **—singen,** *ir.v.a. & n.* (*aux.* **h.**) to sing together; **sich** (*dat.*) **ein Vermögen —singen,** to make a fortune by singing. **—sinken,** *ir.v.n.* (*aux.* **ſ.**) to sink down, fall, collapse; to sink into ruin. **—sparen,** *v.a.* to save up, amass by economy. **—spiel,** *n.* playing together, acting in unison, collective acting, ensemble (*of instruments or actors*). **—sprechen,** *ir.v.a.;* (**ein Brautpaar**) **—sprechen,** to unite in marriage. **—stallen,** *v.a.* to put into the same stable. **—stecken,** *v.* I. *a.* to stick together, to fasten *or* pin together; **sie steckten die Köpfe —,** they put their heads together. II. *n.* (*aux.* **h.**); **immer —stecken,** to be always together. **—stehen,** *ir.v.n.* (*aux.* **h.**) to stand together, be together; to side with one another; to unite for a common cause. **—stellen,** *v.a.* to place together; to place beside one another, compare to group; to assort; to compile; **das Wahlergebnis —stellen,** to inspect the ballot-box. **—stimmen,** *v.n.* (*aux.* **h.**) to accord, to harmonize; to suit, be congruous; to vote together; **nicht —stimmen,** to disagree, not to harmonise. **—stopfen,** *v.a.* to cram together; to darn. **—stoppeln,** *v.a.* to glean; to compile badly. **—stoppelung,** *f.* hash-up, medley. **—stoß,** *m.* striking together; shock; collision (*on a railway*); hostile encounter, conflict, clash. **—stoßen,** *ir.v.* I. *a.* to push, knock against one another; to pound up together; to join (*by pushing or knocking*); to join (*the pieces of a coat*); to overturn, knock down; to break up; **die Gläser —stoßen,** to touch glasses. II. *n.* (*aux.* **h.** & **ſ.**) to dash against one another; to become locked (*in one another*); to meet, encounter; to collide, cause a collision (*Railw.*); to effect a junction (*Mil.*); **—stoßend,** contiguous, adjacent, abutting (*on*). **—streichen,** *ir.v.a.* to cut down (*e.g. a play*); **Geld —streichen,** to amass, rake money together. **—strömen,** *v.n.* (*aux.* **ſ.**) to join, flow together; to converge; to crowd together. **—tragen,** *ir.v.a.* to bring, carry together; to collect; to compile. **—treffen,** I. *ir.v.n.* (*aux.* **ſ.**) to meet, encounter; to coincide; **zu etwas —treffen,** to assist in, co-operate in, work together at; **mit etwas —treffen,** to agree, coincide with s.th.; **es trifft nicht mit unseren Erwartungen —,** it does not answer our expectations. II. *subst.n.* meeting, encounter; concurrence (*of circumstances*), coincidence; (*hostile*) encounter; inosculation (*of veins*); identity (*of thoughts*). **—treiben,** *ir.v.a.* to drive together; to beat up (*game*). **—treten,** *ir.v.* I. *a.* to tread down; to tread to pieces. II. *n.* (*aux.* **ſ.**)

to meet, join; to unite; to combine; to coalesce; to agree. **—tritt,** *m.* coalition; meeting (*of parliament; of creditors*). **—wachsend,** *adj.* coalescent. **—werfen,** *ir.v.a.* to throw together; to confound; to make into a heap; to mix *or* jumble up; to throw down, overthrow. **—wirken,** I. *v.n.* (*aux.* **h.**) to act, work together; to co-operate; **—wirkend,** co-operative. II. *subst.n.* combined efforts; co-operation. **—würfeln,** *v.a.* to throw together; **es war eine bunt —gewürfelte Gesellschaft,** it was a motley assembly. **—zählen,** *v.a.* to count *or* add up. **—ziehbar,** *adj.* contractible. **—ziehen,** *ir.v.* I. *a.* to draw together; to tighten; to contract, to abridge, epitomize; to gather, assemble; to contract (*the brows*); to purse up (*the lips*); to oppress (*the chest*); to draw (*the mouth*); **—gezogene (Wort)formen,** contracted forms, contractions. II. *r.* to collect; to draw to a head; to contract; to gather; **es zieht sich ein Gewitter —,** a storm is gathering; **—ziehende Mittel,** astringents. III. *n.* (*aux.* **s.**) to take lodgings together, to become fellow-lodgers; to share rooms; to go off together. **—ziehung,** *f.* contraction; mustering, concentration (*of troops, etc.*); contracted word. **—ziehungszeichen,** *n.* hyphen; sign of contraction. **—zwängen,** *v.a.* to force together.

Zu'satz, *m.* (**—es,** *pl.* **Zusätze**) addition; adjunct; appendix; postscript; supplement; codicil (*to a will*); alloy (*Chem.*); additional note; amplification; corollary (*Log.*). *Comp.* **—steuer,** *f.* additional tax.

Zu'schanzen, *v.a.* (**einem etwas**) to procure (something) secretly for (a person) (*coll.*).

Zu'schärf—en, *v.a.* to point, sharpen; to thin, feather off. **—ung,** *f.* pointing, sharpening; thinning off; basil (*of a crystal*).

Zu'scharren, *v.a.* to cover *or* fill up by scraping (*something*) over.

Zu'schaue—n, *v.n.* (*aux.* **h.**, *dat.*) to look on at; **einem —n,** to watch a p. (*working or playing*). **—r,** *m.* (**—rs,** *pl.* **—r**), **—rin,** *f.* spectator; witness. **—rschaft,** *f.* spectators; the public. *Comp.* **—r=plätze,** *pl.* places for the spectators. **—r=raum,** *m.* house (*opp. to stage*).

Zu'schaufeln, *v.a.* to shovel up; to cover by shovelling.

Zu'schicken, *v.a.* (**einem etwas**) to send to, transmit to; **Geld —,** to remit money; **Waren —,** to consign goods.

Zu'schieb—en, *ir.v.a.* to shove *or* push towards *or* to; to shut, close by pushing; to make over to (a p.), give to secretly; **einem etwas —en,** *see* **Zuschanzen**; to shuffle s.th. off on to another; to turn the tables upon a p.; **den Riegel —en,** to shoot the bolt, bolt (*the door, etc.*); **einem den Eid —en,** to tender the oath to a p., to put a p. upon oath. **—ung,** *f.* feeding apparatus (*Mach.*); **selbstthätige —ung,** self-acting feed.

Zu'schießen, *ir.v.* I. *n.* (*aux.* **h.**) to shoot (away), fire; (*aux.* **s.**) to come (*of milk*); **auf einen —,** to rush at a p. II. *a.* to supply, add, furnish with in addition; **einem einen Blick —,** to give a p. a rapid look, to dart a glance at s.o.

Zu'schlag, *m.* (**—s,** *pl.* **Zuschläge**) the knocking down to a bidder (*at auctions*); additional payment; extra charge; addition; increase; flux. *Comp.* **—s=fahrkarte,** *f.* additional ticket. **—s=gebühr,** *f.* extra charge, extra fare, additional fee *or* payment.

Zu'schlag—en, I. *ir.v.a.* to slam; to strike, drive towards; to nail up *or* down; to knock down to (*a bidder*); to close; to dispose of, sell (*to*); to strike a bargain; to add as a flux (*Found.*); *see* **Zuhauen**; **einem die Thür vor der Nase —en,** to bang the door in a p.'s face. II. *ir.v.n.* (*aux.* **h.**) to strike, hit hard; to strike away, lay on; to agree with; to suit, benefit; to turn out well; (*aux.* **s.**) to bang. III. *subst.* **—en,** *n.*, **—ung,** *f.* striking towards, *etc.*; blows; **das —en der Thüren ist unerträglich,** the slamming of doors is unbearable.

Zu'schläger, *m.* (**—s,** *pl.* **—**) beater, striker (*smith's assistant*).

Zu'schleifen, I. *ir.v.a.* to sharpen, whet; to point; to polish; (**einen Stein**) **vieleckig —,** to cut (a stone) into facets. II. *reg.v.a.* to tie, knot together, fasten with a knot.

Zu'schleppen, *v.a.* to drag, haul towards *or* to; to convey to, let have (*privately*).

Zu'schließen, *ir.v.a.* to lock up, shut up, close.

Zu'schmeißen, *ir.v.a.* to throw to; to slam, bang to.

Zu'schmelzen, *ir.v.a.* to close by melting; to seal hermetically.

Zu'schmieren, *v.a.* to smear on, over *or* up; to plaster up.

Zu'schnappen, *v.a.* (*aux.* **h.**) & *n.* (*aux.* **s.**) to close with a snap, snap to.

Zu'schneide—n, *ir.v.a.* to cut up; to cut out (*a dress, etc.*); **aus dem Gröbsten —n,** to rough-hew; **einem das Brot, die Bissen (kärglich) —n,** to keep a p. on short allowance. **—r,** *m.* (**—rs,** *pl.* **—r**), **—rin,** *f.* cutter-out. **—rei',** *f.* (*tailor's etc.*) cutting-out room; cutting-out; bad cut. *Comp.* **—brett,** *n.* cutting-out board (*of tailors, saddlers, etc.*). **—kunst,** *f.* art of cutting out. **—messer,** *n.* shoe-maker's knife for cutting out. **—tisch,** *m. see* **—brett.**

Zu'schneien, *v.a.* (*aux.* **h.**) to snow up, to close with snow. II. *n.* (*aux.* **s.**) to close with snow; **zugeschneit sein,** to be snowed up, to be covered *or* closed up with snow.

Zu'schnitt, *m.* (**—es,** *pl.* **—e**) cut (*of a dress, etc.*); style; arrangement; nature; ways; **dieser Mensch hat einen sonderbaren —,** this man has something very odd about him, is eccentric; **der häusliche — ist zu großartig,** the household arrangements are on too grand a scale; **es schon im — versehen,** to go wrong *or* make a mistake at the very outset.

Zu'schnüren, *v.a.* to lace together, lace up; **einem die Kehle —,** to strangle a p.; **mir war die Kehle wie zugeschnürt,** I felt choked, I could not utter a single word, I felt a lump in my throat (*coll.*); **in ihrem Betragen war etwas Zugeschnürtes,** there was an air of constraint in her manner.

Zu'schrauben, *reg.* & *ir.v.a.* to screw down, to fasten with a screw; to screw up.

Zu'schreibbar, *adj.* attributable, imputable.

Zu'schreiben, I. *ir.v.a.* to write to; to dedicate; to add in writing; to assign, attribute, put down to, impute to; to put to one's credit; to confer (*on a p.*) by a deed, charter, *etc.*; **das schreibe ich seiner Unwissenheit zu,** I attribute that to his ignorance. II. *subst. n.*; **durch vieles — hat er die Arbeit verdorben,** he has spoilt the work by adding so much to it.

Zu'schreien, *ir.v.a.* & *n.* (*aux.* **h.**) to cry out, scream *or* shout out; **einem etwas —,** to call out s.th. to a person.

Zu'schreiten, *ir.v.n.* (*aux.* **s.**); **auf einen —,** to stride, step towards *or* up to a p.; **tüchtig —,** to step out well, to walk on briskly.

Zu'schrift, *f.* (*pl.* **—en**) letter; address; dedication; **amtliche —,** official communication. **—lich,** *adv.* by letter.

Zu'schüren, *v.a.* to stir, poke (*the fire*).

Zu'schuß, *m.* (**—(ss)es,** *pl.* **Zu'schüsse**) contribution, additional supply; extra allowance. *Comp.* **—bogen,** *m.* extra sheet (*Typ.*). **—mahl,** *n.* picnic. **—papier,** *n.* waste (*Typ.*). **—steuer,** *f.* additional tax *or* duty. **—summe,** *f.* additional sum. **—tage,** *pl.* epacts.

Zu'schütten, *v.a.* to fill up with; to pour to; to heap on; **einen Brunnen —,** to fill up a well.

Zu'schwären, *v.n.* (*aux.* **s.**) to close through suppuration.
Zu'schwellen, *ir.v.n.* (*aux.* **s.**) to close by swelling.
Zu'schwören, *ir.v.a.* (**einem etwas**) to swear (to a person).
Zu'segeln, *v.a.* to sail to *or* towards, to make for; to go on sailing; **segle zu!** sail on!
Zu'sehen, I. *ir.v.n.* (*aux.* **h.**) to look on at, watch; to witness; to look after, look to, oversee; to wait, delay; to connive *or* wink at; to look to, take heed; **das — haben,** to be left without a share, to have no part in the game; **einem beim Spiele —,** to watch a p. playing; **einer Sache ruhig —,** to look on at a th. calmly *or* unmoved, to tolerate; **noch ein wenig —,** to be patient, wait a little longer; **sieh zu, daß du nicht fällst,** take care lest you fall; **da hat er zu —,** that is his look-out; **seht für euch selbst zu!** look to yourself! II. *subst. n.* view, looking on; part of spectator. **—d(s),** *adv.* visibly, evidently, noticeably, obviously.
Zu'sein, *ir.v.n.* (*aux.* **s.**) to be shut *or* closed.
Zu'senden, *ir.v.a. see* **Zuschicken.**
Zu'setzen, *v.* I. *a.* to add to; to put, set to; to put on, over (*the fire*); to put to, to affix; to contribute; to stake higher; to alloy with; to lose (*money*); to sacrifice (*one's health, etc.*); to close (*a stove, etc.*); to obstruct, block up, close; to close the game (*at dominoes*); **er hat sein ganzes Vermögen dabei zugesetzt,** he has lost all his money by it; **er hat dabei zugesetzt,** he has been a loser by it; **bei diesem Geschäfte muß man —,** it is a losing concern. II. *n.* (*aux.* **h.**); **einem hart —,** to press a p. hard, pursue s.o. closely, to attack a p. vigorously; **einem mit Bitten —,** to overwhelm s.o. with entreaties, importune a p.; **einem so —, daß er nicht mehr aus noch ein weiß,** to put a p. into a corner, to nonplus a person.
Zu'sicher—n, *v.a.* (**einem etwas**) to assure (*a p. of a th.*); to secure s.th. for (*s.o.*). **—ung,** *f.* assurance, promise.
Zu'siegeln, *v.a.* to seal up.
Zu'speise, *f. see* **Zukost.**
Zu'sperren, *v.a.* to close, bar up, shut up.
Zu'spielen, *v.a.* (**einem etwas**) to play (*the ball, etc., to a p.*); to serve (*at tennis*); to play to one's partner (*Cards*); to convey to (*secretly*).
Zu'spitz—en, *v.a.* to point, cut to a point; to give a conical form to; to taper; to close (*a stocking in knitting*); to point (*needles*); to point, make (*an arch*) more pointed; **sich —en,** to taper to a point; **epigrammatisch —en,** to give an epigrammatic turn to, to turn into an epigram. **—er,** *m.* (**—ers,** *pl.* **—er**) pointer (*of pins, needles, etc.*). **—ung,** *f.* pointing, sharpening; tapering off; point.
Zu'sprache, *f.* (*pl.* **—n**) *see* **Zuspruch.**
Zu'sprechen, *ir.v.* I. *a.* (**einem etwas**) to instil, impart by speaking; to award, adjudge; **einem Mut —,** to cheer s.o. up, encourage a p.; **einem Trost —,** to comfort a p. II. *n.* (*aux.* **h.**) (*dat.*) to address, accost; to exhort, encourage, comfort; to suit, agree with; to please; **der Flasche fleißig —,** to partake freely of the bottle, to drink copiously; **einem Gerichte wacker —,** to do ample justice to a dish, to eat heartily of a dish.
Zu'springen, *ir.v.n.* (*aux.* **s.**) to spring towards; to snap, spring to (*of locks*); **auf einen —,** to run up to *or* towards a p.; **einem —** (*usually* **einem beispringen**), to run to a p.'s aid.
Zu'spruch, *m.* (**—es,** *pl.* **Zusprüche**) words addressed (*to a p.*); exhortation; encouragement; consolation; call, short visit; **viel — haben,** to have plenty of customers, have a great run (*of custom*), to be much resorted to.
Zu'spunden, *v.a.* to bung, close up (*a barrel*).
Zu'stand, *m.* (**—es,** *pl.* **Zustände**) condition, state; situation; position; lot; **in segelfertigem —e,** in sailing trim *or* order; **in elendem —e,** in wretched condition *or* plight; **— des Gemüts,** frame of mind.
Zustan'de—, *in compds. see* **Stand. —bringen,** *n.* bringing about, accomplishment, realization, achievement; restoration (*dial.*); **das —bringen dieser Sache wird schwer halten,** there will be considerable difficulty in accomplishing this. **—kommen,** *n.* taking place; **das —kommen des Kongresses ist gesichert,** the meeting of the congress will take place, the congress is sure to meet, the congress will certainly come off (*coll.*).
Zu'ständ—ig, *adj.* belonging to, appertaining; duly qualified, competent (*of judges, tribunals, etc.*); **—ige Stelle** *or* **Behörde,** proper quarters *or* authorities; **nicht —ig,** incompetent, not duly qualified. **—igkeit,** *f.* competence; appurtenance. **—lich,** *adj.* neuter, not active.
Zu'stechen, *ir.v.n.* (*aux.* **h.**) *v.* I. *a.* to stitch up. II. *n.*; **auf einen —,** to make a thrust (*with a sword*) at a p.; **immer —,** to spur on, to stitch on, to go on stabbing *or* stitching.
Zu'stecken, *v.a.* to slip a th. into a p.'s hand *or* pocket, to give a p. a th. secretly; to pin up; **einer Dame das Kleid —,** to fasten a lady's dress by pins, to pin a lady's dress together.
Zu'stehen, *ir.v.n.* (*aux.* **h.**) (**einem**) to belong to; to be the duty of, be incumbent upon; to become, suit; **das steht dir nicht zu,** it is not for you, that is not your business, that is not within your province.
Zu'stellen, *v.a.* to close, block up by putting something before; (**einem etwas**) **—,** to hand to, deliver up to, to present.
[1]**Zu'steuern,** *v.a.* to contribute, help by contributions.
[2]**Zu'steuern,** *v.n.* (*aux.* **s.**); **auf eine S. . . . —** to steer *or* make for a th.; **der Küste —,** to steer for the coast; **immer —,** to steer straight ahead.
Zu'stimm—en, *v.n.* (*aux.* **h.**) to assent, consent *or* agree to, to concur with. **—ung,** *f.* assent, consent; **nach erfolgter —ung,** consent having been obtained; **unter —ung von,** with the consent of.
Zu'stopfen, *v.a.* to stop up, close, fill up; to stop (*the ears*); to mend, darn (*a hole*).
Zu'stöpseln, *v.a.* to cork up.
Zu'stoßen, *ir.v.* I. *a.* to push towards; to push to, close (*the door*). II. *n.* (*aux.* **h.**) to push, thrust on; to push away; (*aux.* **s.**) **einem —,** to befall a p., to happen to s.o.; **falls mir irgend etwas Unglückliches — sollte,** in case of any misfortune overtaking me *or* happening to me.
Zu'streben, *v.n.* (*aux.* **h.**); (**einem Ziele**) **—,** to strive for *or* after, to endeavour to reach *or* attain; **dies ist das Ziel, dem alle Ereignisse —,** this is the goal towards which all events are tending.
Zu'streichen, *ir.v.* I. *n.* (*aux.* **h.**); **auf ein Ziel —, dem Ziele —,** to aim at, tend towards a goal. II. *a.* to close up by spreading on, smearing over.
Zu'stricken, *v.a.* to close (*a stocking*).
Zu'strömen, I. *v.n.* (*aux.* **s.**) to pour, stream in *or* towards. II. *subst. n.* influx.
Zu'stülpen, *v.a.* to cover with a lid.
Zu'stürmen, *v.n.* (*aux.* **h.**); **auf einen —,** to rush at a p. impetuously.
Zu'stürzen, *v.n.* (*aux.* **s.**); **auf einen —,** to rush upon *or* towards a p.
Zu'stutzen, *v.a.* to fashion, polish, dress up; to instruct, train, drill, discipline; **einen Baum —,** to train a tree; **ein Stück für die Bühne —,** to adapt a piece for the stage *or* for acting; **einen Hut —,** to trim, brush up a hat; **einen Bedienten —,** to train a servant.

Zuta'gestreichen, *n.* cropping-out (*of strata*).
Zu'tappen, *v.n.* (*aux.* **h.**) to grope, go gropingly; to fumble, lay hold of awkwardly; to act rashly, blunder.
Zu'täppisch, *adj.* awkward, clumsy.
Zu'teilen, *v.a.* (**einem etwas**) to assign, allot; to distribute, give a share of, apportion; to adjudge; to grant; **die ihm zugeteilte Rolle**, the part allotted to him; **einem etwas in reichem Maße —**, to lavish s.th. on a person.
Zu'that, *f.* (*pl.* **—en**) trimmings (*of a dress, etc., as lining, silk, braid, etc.*); trimming, ornamentation; ingredient; raw material; garnishing; **—en einer Speise**, ingredients of a dish.
Zu'thulich, *adj.* obliging, assiduous; officious; complaisant; insinuating. **—keit**, *f.* complaisance; officiousness; insinuating manner.
Zu'thun, *ir.v.a.* to add to; to furnish material for; to close, shut; **ich habe die ganze Nacht kein Auge zugethan**, I have not slept a wink the whole night; **er hat die Augen zugethan**, he has closed his eyes on this world (*is dead*); **ein Auge bei einer S. —**, to wink at a th.; **sich —**, to close (*of itself*); **sich einem** *or* **bei einem —**, to insinuate o.s. into a p.'s good graces; *see* **Zugethan**. II. *subst. n.* assistance, cooperation; **es geschah ohne mein —**, I had nothing to do with it; it was not of my seeking; **es geschah durch sein —**, it was (by) his doing he had a finger in the pie (*coll.*).
Zu'thunlich, *see* **Zuthulich**.
Zu'traben, *v.n.* (*aux.* **h.**) to trot on; **auf . . . (*acc.*) —**, to trot towards *or* up to . . .; **trab zu!** trot on!
Zu'tragen, *ir.v.* I. *a.* to carry, bring to; to carry (*tales*) to, report (*news*), whisper. II. *r.* to happen, take place; **wenn es sich — sollte, daß wir gewönnen**, if we should happen to win. III. *n.* (*aux.* **s.**) to be productive (*of trees*).
Zu'träg—er, *m.* (**—ers**, *pl.* **—er**), **—erin**, *f.* reporter; informer; tell-tale; whisperer, scandalmonger, evil gossip. **—erei'**, *f.* talebearing; informing; tittle-tattle. **—lich**, *adj.* productive (*of*); beneficial, advantageous; useful; salutary, wholesome; advisable; **nicht —lich sein**, not to be advantageous for, to disagree with (*one*); **der Gesundheit —lich**, healthful, salubrious. **—lichkeit**, *f.* advantageousness; wholesomeness; salubrity.
Zu'trau—en, *v.a.*; **einem etwas —en**, to believe a p. capable of, give a p. credit for, expect from s.o.; **einem —en**, to trust, confide in, rely upon a p.; **ich traue ihm alles Böse zu**, I believe him capable of any wickedness; **ich traue ihm nicht viel zu**, I do not think much of him; **sich** (*dat.*) **nicht viel —en**, to have no high opinion of o.s., *or* of one's powers, to be diffident. **—lich**, *adj. & adv.* confiding; familiar; **sprechen Sie —lich mit ihm**, be frank with him, speak to him without reserve! **—lichkeit**, *f.* confidingness, trust, confidence. *Comp.* **—en=erweckend**, *adj.* inspiring confidence. **—ens=voll**, *adj.* full of confidence. **—ens=wert**, *adj.* trustworthy.
Zu'treffen, I. *ir.v.n.* (*aux.* **h.**) to fit, tally, agree with; to prove right; to be conclusive; (*aux.* **s.**) to happen, take place; **es traf alles zu**, it all turned out to be true; **dies trifft gerade auf seinen Charakter zu**, this is exactly in keeping with his character; **auf ein Haar —**, to be right to a hair; **—d**, to the point, apt, just, suitable, corresponding, pertinent, striking, decisive; **—de Bemerkung**, just observation. II. *subst.n.*; **das — der Beweise**, the conclusiveness of the evidence.
Zu'treiben, *ir.v.* I. *a.* to drive towards *or* to; to drive on; to drive into (*s.th.*); **einem Kunden —**, to send a p. customers; **sich** (*dat.*) **Kunden —**, to tout for customers; **die Pferde —**, to whip up the horses. II. *n.* (*aux.* **s.**) to be driven, to be floating, to drift on.
Zu'treten, *ir.v.* I. *a.* to trample over, close up (*a hole*) by treading. II. *n.* (*aux.* **s.**) to approach; to intervene, interpose; to supervene; to join.
Zu'trieb, *m.* (**—s**, *pl.* **—e**) overplus of silver gained in refining; arrival (*of cattle in the market*).
Zu'trinken, *ir.v.n.* (*aux.* **h.**) to drink to, pledge (**einem**, a p.).
Zu'tritt, *m.* (**—s**, *pl.* **—e**) access; admission; **— haben**, to be received, have access (*to a p.*); **bei einem (freien) — haben**, to be received, to be readily admitted, be permitted to visit at s.o.'s house; **einem freien — verschaffen**, to procure s.o. a ticket of admission, a free pass.
Zuun'terst, *adv.* quite at the bottom, below all the others.
Zu'verlässig, *adj.* reliable, trustworthy, dependable, to be relied on; certain, credible, positive; safe, solid; **er ist nicht —**, he is not to be trusted. **—keit**, *f.* reliability; trustworthiness; solidity; certainty, credibility.
Zu'versicht, *f.* confidence (**auf eine S.**, in a th.), reliance, dependence (*on*); certainty, complete conviction; **— zu Gott**, trust in God; **ich hege die —**, I trust; **er hegte die feste —**, he confidently expected. **—lich**, *adj.* confident, undoubting; unshaken, steady; *see* **Zuverlässig**. **—lichkeit**, *f.* trust, confidence; positiveness; assurance.
Zuvie'l, I. *adv.* = **zu viel**; **was — ist, ist —**, more than enough is too much (*prov.*). II. *n.* excess.
Zuvo'r, I. *adv.* before, previously; once; beforehand; formerly. II. *n.*; **das — und Hernach**, the before and after. *Comp.* **—bedenken**, *ir.v.n.* (*aux.* **h.**) to reflect (*on s.th.*) beforehand. **—einnehmen**, *ir.v.a.* to preoccupy. **—erwägen**, *ir.v.a.* to examine, consider previously. **—kommen**, *ir.v.n.* (*aux.* **s.**) to get in front of (*a p.*); to take the lead; **einem —kommen**, to anticipate s.o., get the start of, steal a march upon a p.; **einer Sache —kommen**, to prevent, obviate s.th. **—kommend**, *p. & adj.* anticipatory, anticipating; obliging; civil, courteous, kind. **—kommenheit**, *f.* complaisance, obligingness; civility; kindness. **—laufend**, *p. & adj.* outstripping. **—thun**, *ir.v.a.*; **es einem (in einer S.) —thun**, to surpass, outdo a p. (*in s.th.*); **es einem — zuthun suchen**, to endeavour to excel a p., to vie with a p.
Zuvor'derst, *adv.* in the front rank, foremost, before everybody *or* all others.
Zuvör'derst, *adv.* first of all, in the first place, before doing anything else; before everything else, first and foremost, to begin with.
Zu'wachs, *m.* (**—(s)es**) growth, increase by natural growth, accretion; produce; increase, accession, augmentation (**an Ruhm**, of glory); expansion; **einen Rock auf (den) — machen**, to make a coat so as to allow for growing; **auf — berechnet**, allowing for expansion.
Zu'wachsen, *ir.v.n.* (*aux.* **h.**) to heal up, grow together (*of wounds*); to grow for the use of; to accrue (**einem**, to s.o.); **dem Landmanne wachsen die Früchte zu**, the earth supplies the farmer with its fruits; **ihm ist dieses Jahr viel Vieh zugewachsen**, his livestock has greatly increased this year.
Zu'wage, *f.* (*pl.* **—n**) make-weight; what is thrown in.
Zu'wägen, *ir.v.a.* to add in weighing out; **einem etwas —**, to weigh out, to mete out s. th. to a p., to dispense s.th. to s.o.
Zu'wälzen, *v.a.* to roll towards *or* to; to throw, lay (*the blame, etc.*) upon; **den Eingang der Höhle mit einem Felsstücke —**, to close up the mouth of the cave by rolling a stone before it.

Zu'wandern, *v.n.* (*aux.* s.) to wander *or* migrate towards; **zugewandert kommen,** to immigrate; **ein Zugewanderter,** an immigrant.
Zu'wanken, *v.n.* (*aux.* s.) to reel, totter towards.
Zu'warten, *v.a.* (*aux.* h.) to wait; **die —de Politik,** the policy of laisser-faire; **sich —d verhalten,** to wait for things to develop, to play the waiting game.
Zuwe'ge, *adv.;* **— bringen,** to bring about, accomplish, effect; **gut — sein,** to be flourishing.
Zu'wehen, *v.n.* to blow towards *or* to; to fill up by blowing into; **einem Luft —,** to fan a p.; **der Wind hat die Wege mit Schnee zugeweht,** the wind has choked up the roads with snow.
Zuwei'len, *adv.;* sometimes, at times, now and then.
Zu'weisen, *ir.v.a.;* (**einem etwas**) to assign *or* allot (s.th. to s.o.); **einem Kunden —,** to send, recommend customers to a p.
Zu'wenden, *ir.v.a.* to turn towards; **einem etwas —,** to let a p. have s.th., procure s.th. for s.o., throw s.th. in a p.'s way; **einem das Gesicht —,** to turn one's face towards a p.; **einem seine Liebe —,** to give one's love to a p.; to love a p.; **seine Freundlichkeit wandte ihm alle Herzen zu,** his kindliness won him all hearts; **seine ganze Kraft einem Gegenstande —,** to expend all one's strength *or* one's whole force on an object.
Zu'werfen, *ir.v.a.* to throw to *or* towards; to close, fill up (*with earth*); to throw in a p.'s way; to throw down, play (*Cards*); **einem Blicke —,** to cast glances at s.o.; **die Thür —,** to slam the door.
Zuwi'der, *adv. & prep.* (*with dat.*) contrary to, against; repugnant, odious, offensive; **das Glück war uns —,** fortune was against us; **die ihrer Pflicht — waren,** which conflicted with her duty; **das ist mir —,** I loathe, hate that, I have a great dislike to that; **er ist mir in den Tod —,** I detest him mortally; I hate the very sight of him; **der gesunden Vernunft —,** opposed to reason; **— handeln,** to act in opposition to, to act against, to offend against, infringe, violate; **er suchte meinem Plane — zu handeln,** he tried to act in opposition to my plan; **— laufen,** to run counter *or* contrary to; **es wird Ihnen nicht — sein, wenn . . .,** you will have no objection if . . .
Zu'winken, *v.n.* (*aux.* h.); **einem —,** to make signs to a p., to nod, beckon to a person.
Zu'wölben, *v.a.* to arch over.
Zu'zahlen, *v.a.* to pay in addition, over and above.
Zu'zählen, *v.a.* to add (*to*); **einem etwas —,** to count s.th. out to a person.
Zu'zieh—en, I. *ir.v.a.* to close by drawing; to draw together, draw tight; to tie; to draw, drag towards *or* to, to admit, allow to share, to invite, call in; to cause; to incur; to rear, raise (*in addition*); **die Vorhänge —en,** to draw the curtains; **zur Beratung —en,** to consult; **einen zweiten Arzt —en,** to call in *or* consult a second doctor; **sich** (*dat.*) **Händel —en,** to involve o.s. in altercations; **sich** (*dat.*) **einen Tadel —en,** to incur blame; **sich** (*dat.*) **eine Krankheit —en,** to contract a disease, catch an illness; **sich** (*dat.*) **einen Verdacht —en,** to bring suspicion upon o.s., to lay o.s. open to suspicion; **er hat sich** (*dat.*) **die Äußerung zugezogen,** he has taken the remark as meant for *or* applicable to himself; **einem die Kehle —en,** to strangle, choke a p.; **die Schleife zieht sich zu,** the knot tightens. II. *ir.v.n.* (*aux.* s.) to move towards, to remove to; to march to (*the aid of*); to go to a new place (*of servants*); (*aux.* h.) to pull on; **kräftig —en,** to pull hard, to pull away. **—ung,** *f.* drawing together; tying; incurring; calling in, aid, assistance; **mit —ung einiger Nachbarn,** with the aid of one *or* two neighbours; **unter —ung Ihrer Spesen,** including your expenses; **mit** *or* **unter —ung eines Arztes,** with the advice of a doctor, a doctor having been consulted; **ohne jemandes —ung,** without help from any one.
Zu'zug, *m.* (—**s**) marching to s.o.'s aid; reinforcements, contingent.
Zu'zügler, *m.* (—**s**, *pl.* —) volunteer; newcomer, recent settler; (*pl.*) auxiliary forces, reinforcements.
Zu'zwängen, *v.a.* to close with an effort, force to (*a door*).
Zwa'ck—en, *v.a.* to pinch; to tease, worry, torment; to fleece. *Comp.* **—eisen,** *n.* pincers (*in glass-works*).
[1]**Zwang,** *m.* (—(e)s) coercion, compulsion, force; constraint; restraint; want of freedom *or* ease; control; constriction, tenesmus (*Med.*); yoke, servitude; jurisdiction; **ohne —,** unconstrained(-ly); **einem — anthun,** to use violence to, compel, constrain a p.; **sich** (*dat.*) *or* **seinen Gefühlen — anthun,** to do violence to one's feelings; **dem Gesetze — anthun,** to wrest, pervert the law; **dem —e weichen,** to yield to compulsion. *Comp.* **—(s)=anleihe,** *f.* forced loan. **—(s)=arbeit,** *f.* compulsory labour; **zu lebenslänglicher —(s)arbeit verurteilen,** to condemn a p. to penal servitude for life. **—(back)ofen,** *m.* common *or* parish oven (*obs.*). **—(s)=dienst,** *m.* compulsory service. **—(s)=enteignung,** *f.* forced expropriation. **—(s)=gerechtigkeit,** *f.* banality (*obs.*). **—(s)=gesetz,** *n.* coercive law, coercion law. **—(s)=gewalt,** *f.* compulsory power. **—(s)=jacke,** *f.* strait-jacket. **—(s)=kurs,** *m.* forced currency (*of paper-money*). **—lage,** *f.* condition of constraint. **—los,** *adj.* unconstrained, unrestricted, free; unconventional, easy, natural; **in —losen Heften,** appearing in occasional numbers. **—losigkeit,** *f.* freedom, unconstraint; ease; laisser-aller. **—(s)=maßregel,** *f.* coercive measure; **—(s)maßregeln anwenden,** to employ coercive measures, to use force. **—mittel,** *n.* violent means, means of coercion, force; **gerichtliches —mittel der Güterbeschlagnahme,** distress-warrant. **—(s)=paß,** *m.* compulsory passport describing the route to be followed. **—(s)=pflicht,** *f.* compulsory duty. **—(s)=recht,** *n.* right of coercion; banality (*obs.*). **—(s)=schiene,** *f.* check-rail. **—stellung,** *f.* constrained position. **—(s)=verfahren,** *n.* coercive proceeding *or* measures. **—versteigerung,** *f.* forced sale, bankrupt sale (*by auction*). **—(s)=vollstreckung,** *f.* distraint, execution. **—s=weise,** *adv.* compulsorily, forcibly, by (main) force.
[2]**Zwang, Zwän'ge,** *1 & 3 pers. sing. imperf. ind. & subj. of* **zwingen.**
Zwän'gen, *v.a.* to pinch, squeeze; to constrain; to bend with force; to force; **gezwängt bei Tische sitzen,** to be close-packed, crowded at table; **das Recht —,** to do violence to the law.
Zwan'zig, I. *num. adj.* twenty. II. *f.* (*pl.* —**en**) (*number*) twenty, a score; **zu —en,** by scores, in twenties, by groups of twenty; **in den —en sein,** to be in the twenties, between twenty and thirty (*years of age*); **sie ist über die — hinaus,** she is over *or* turned twenty. **—er,** *m.* (—**ers**, *pl.* —**er**) the figure 20; thing of 20 units; coin of 20 pfennigs *or* kreutzers; person 20 years old; wine of the year '20; soldier of the 20th regiment. **—st,** *num. adj.* (**der, die, das —ste**) twentieth; **den —sten März,** the 20th of March, March the twentieth, March 20th. **—stel,** *n.* (—**stels**, *pl.* —**stel**) twentieth part; **drei —stel,** three twentieths. **—stens,** *adv.* in the 20th place. *Comp.* **—eck.**

n. polygon having 20 sides. —erlei, *indec. adj. or adv.* of 20 different kinds; auf —erlei Art, in twenty (*different*) ways. —fach, —fältig, *adj.* twenty-fold. —flächig, *adj.* having 20 faces, icosahedral. —flächner, *m.* icosahedron (*Cryst.*). —mark=stück, *n.* 20-mark piece.

Zwar, *adv.* indeed, truly, certainly; of course, it is true, to be sure, I admit; er that es —, aber ungern, he did it, certainly, but unwillingly; er gestand —, doch erst als es zu spät war, he confessed, it is true, but only when it was too late; und —, and that, and so; er ist ein Bösewicht und — von der gefährlichsten Art, he is a villain and that of the most dangerous kind.

Zweck, *m.* (—es, *pl.* —e) peg; sprig, wooden nail; (centre peg in the) target, bull's eye, butt; aim, end, object, design, goal; mit dem —e, with a view to, with the object of; for this purpose, with this end in view; zu welchem —e? for what purpose? with what view? to what intent? zum —e einer Unterredung, for the purpose of holding a conversation *or* conference; seinen — in sich selbst habend, autotelic; der — heiligt die Mittel, the end justifies the means; sonst hat es keinen —, there is nothing else in it, and that is all (*coll.*); seinen — erreichen, zu seinem —e kommen, to attain one's ends, carry one's point. —e, *f.* (*pl.* —en) peg; hob-nail (*for shoes*); carpet-tack; sprig; mit —en beschlagen, pegged, hob-nailed. —en, *v.a.* to peg; to tack; to fasten with pegs *or* tacks. —s, *prep.* (*with gen.*); *see above* mit dem —e, zum —e. *Comp.* —dienlich, *adj.* to the purpose, suitable, useful; efficacious. —dienlichkeit, *f.* utility, suitableness, efficacy, efficiency, fitness. —entsprechend, *adj.* answering its purpose, proper to the end in view. —essen, *n.* public dinner given for some special reason, complimentary dinner, public banquet. —gemäß, *adj. see* —entsprechend, —mäßig. —los, I. *adj.* aimless, objectless; purposeless, useless. II. *adv.* to no purpose, at random. —losigkeit, *f.* aimlessness; uselessness. —mäßig, *adj.* answering the purpose, suitable for the object in view; practical; useful; fit. —mäßigkeit, *f.* suitableness of the means to the end; usefulness; appropriateness; fitness; opportuneness; finality (*Phil.*). —widrig, *adj.* inappropriate; injudicious; not suited to the end in view.

Zween, (*obs.*) *num. adj.* (*orig. only masc., the fem. being* zwo, *the neuter* zwei. *This latter has now replaced the old masc. and fem.*) two, twain; Niemand kann — Herren dienen, no man can serve two masters (*B.*).

Zweh'le, *f.* (*pl.* —n) towel (*dial.*).

Zwei, I. *num. adj.* (*gen.* —er, *when no subst. follows or before a subst. not preceded by an art. or adj. showing the case; dat.* —en, *when no subst. follows*) two; — und zwanzig, two and twenty, twenty-two; es ist halb —, it is half-past one; um drei Viertel auf —, at a quarter to two; aus —(en) bestehend, in — zerfallend, binary; zu —(en) stehend, double (*Bot.*); das Geschlecht steht auf — Augen, the race *or* family is represented by one man; in — Exemplaren ausgefertigte Verhandlung, deed of which there is a duplicate; — und —, zu —en, two and two, by twos; mit —en fahren, to drive a pair of horses; das Spiel läßt sich zu —en spielen, two can play at that game; ich habe es —en gesagt, I said it to two persons; Tagebuch —er Kinder, diary of two children; durch —er Zeugen Mund, by the mouth of two witnesses; die Aussage dieser — Zeugen, the evidence of these two witnesses. II. *f.* (*pl.* —en) two; deuce; *see* —heit. III. *n.* pair, couple. —er, *m.* (—ers, *pl.* —er) the figure two (2); any thing *or* person characterized by the number two, as a coin of two units, a soldier of the 2d regiment, etc. —heit, *f.* duality, dualism. —t, *see* Zweit. *Comp.* —achselig, *adj.* ambidextrous; two-faced, double-dealing. —armig, *adj.* with two arms *or* branches. —bahnig, *adj.* of two breadths (*of cloth, etc.*). —basisch, *adj.* having two bases (*Chem.*). —blätterig, *adj.* two-leaved, diphyllous; dipetalous. —blumig, —blütig, *adj.* biflorate. —brüderig, —bündelig, *adj.* diadelphian (*Bot.*). —bund, *m.* dual alliance *or* league. —decker, *m.* two-decker (*obs.*). —deutelei', *f.* ambiguity; (habit of) equivocating. —deuteln, *v.n.* (*aux.* h.) to be ambiguous; to equivocate. —deutig, *adj. & adv.* ambiguous, with a double meaning; double-dealing; doubtful, suspicious; untruthful; —deutig reden, to equivocate. —deutigkeit, *f.* ambiguity; duplicity of character. —doppelt, *adj.* double, two-fold (*coll.*); binate (*Bot.*). —drittel=majorität, *f.* majority of two-thirds. —drittel=takt, *m.* two-three time. —ehig, *adj.* bigamous (*Bot.*). —erlei, *indec. adj.* of two kinds; two-fold, different; das ist —erlei, those are two very different things; die Herren von —erlei Tuch, the military (*coll.*). —fach, *adj.* double, two-fold; binate; —fache Intervalle, *pl.* compound intervals (*Mus.*). —fächerig, *adj.* having two compartments; with two cells (*Bot.*). —falter, *m.* butterfly (*obs.*). —fältig, *adj.* twofold. —farbig, *adj.* of two colours; —farbiger Druck, bi-coloured impression (*stamps, etc.*). —felder=wirtschaft, *f.* farming with (a rotation of) two crops. —flügelig, *adj.* two-winged; dipterous; eine —flügelige Thür, a folding door. —flügler, *pl.* diptera, dipterans (*Ent.*). —fünftel=schein, *m.* biquintile aspect (*Astr.*). —füßig, *adj.* with two feet, biped. —füß(l)er, *m.* biped. —gesang, *m.* duet. —geschlechtig, *adj.* of double sex, hermaphrodite, bisexual, androgynous. —gespann, *n.* carriage with two horses; two-horsed team; ein —gespann führen, to drive a (*carriage and*) pair. —gestrichen, *adj.* twice marked *or* accented; —gestrichene Note, semiquaver. —geteilt, *adj.* bipartite. —gliederig, *adj.* having two members; binomial (*Alg.*); biarticulate (*Zoöl.*); in two ranks (*Mil.*). —händig, *adj.* bimanous; two-handed (*of a sword*); ambidextrous; —händiges Stück, piece for two hands. —henkelig, *adj.* with two handles. —herr, *m.* duumvir. —herrschaft, *f.* duumvirate. —höckerig, *adj.* two-humped; —höckeriges Kameel, dromedary. —hörnig, *adj.* two-horned. —hufer, *m.* cloven-footed animal. —hufig, *adj.* cloven-footed, bisulcate. —hundert, *num. adj.* two hundred. —hundert=jährig, *adj.* lasting two hundred years; —hundertjähriger Geburtstag, the bicentennial anniversary of the birth of. —jährig, *adj.* of two years, two years old; lasting two years. —jährlich, *adj.* occurring every two years, biennial. —kammer=system, *n.* system of two (*legislative*) chambers. —kampf, *m.* single combat; duel; einen zum —kampf herausfordern, to challenge a p. to a duel, to call a p. out. —kämpfer, *m.* duellist. —kapselig, *adj.* bicapsular. —klappig, *adj.* bivalve, bivalvular. —lappig, *adj.* two-lobed (*Bot.*). —lebig, *adj.* amphibious. —lötig, *adj.* of one ounce (*weight*). —mächtig, *adj.* didynamian (*Bot.*). —mal, *adv.* twice, double; (auf) —mal, at two times *or* twice; —mal im Jahre, twice a year, half-yearly; er wird sich das nicht —mal sagen lassen, he will need no second telling. —malig, *adj.* done *or* repeated twice. —männerig, *adj.* diandrian (*Bot.*). —master, *m.* two-masted vessel; brig. —monatig, *adj.* lasting two months; —monatiger Urlaub, two months' leave (*of absence*). —monatlich, *adj.* occurring every two months; —monatliche Lieferung, delivery every second month. —pasch, *m.* double-two; two at either end (*in dominoes*). —pfünder, *m.* two-pounder (*Artil.*). —polig, *adj.* bi-polar. —rad, *n.* bicycle, bike (*coll.*); —rad für Touren, roadster; —rad für Wettfahrten, racer. —räderig, *adj.* two-wheeled; —räderiger Wagen, two-wheeler, hansom, cart. —radfahrer, *m.* bicyclist, cyclist. —reihig, *adj.* having two rows; bifarious (*Bot.*); double-breasted, with two rows of buttons. —ruderig, *adj.* two-oared; having two tiers of rowers. —schalig, *adj.* bivalve, bivalvular. —schattig, *adj.* amphiscian; —schattige Völker, amphiscii. —schläf(e)rig, *adj.*; —schläf(e)riges Bett, double bed, bed for two persons. —schneidig, *adj.* two-edged; die Bemerkung ist —schneidig, that observation cuts both ways. —schuhig, *adj.* two feet long. —schürig, *adj.* that is shorn *or* cut twice a year; —schürige Wolle, wool of the second shearing. —seelen-theorie, *f.* theory of two souls in one body. —seitig, *adj.* bi-lateral. —silbig, *adj.* two-syllabled, dissyllabic; —silbiges Wort, dissyllable. —silbigkeit, *f.* dissyllabism. —sitzer, *m.* tandem (*bicycle*). —sitzig, *adj.* with two seats, double-seated. —spaltig, *adj.* doubly-cleft; bifid (*Bot.*); in double columns (*Typ.*). —spänner, *m.* see —gespann. —spitzig, *adj.* two-pointed. —sprachig, *adj.* in two languages, bilingual; —sprachiger Mann, bilinguist. —spurig, *adj.* double-tracked. —stimmig, *adj.* two-voiced; —stimmiger Gesang, song for two voices, duet. —stündig, *adj.* lasting two hours; two hours old. —stündlich, *adj.* every second hour. —teilig, *adj.* bipartite. —teilung, *f.* division into two parts; bifurcation; bipartition; bisection. —und-dreißigstel-format, *n.* 32mo. —und-dreißigstel-note, *f.* demisemiquaver. —und-dreißigstel-pause, *f.* demisemiquaver rest. —viertel-note, *f.* minim. —viertel-pause, *f.* minim rest. —viertel-takt, *m.* two-four time (*Mus.*). —weiberei, *f.* bigamy. —weibig, *adj.* having two pistils (*Bot.*). —wöchentlich, *adj.* occurring every two weeks, fortnightly. —wöchig, *adj.* two weeks old, lasting two weeks. —wüchsig, *adj.* rickety; not ripening at the same time. —zack, *m.* two-pronged instrument. —zackig, *adj.* two-pronged; bifurcated. —zahl, *f.* number two; dual (*number*). —zahn, *m.* Bidens (*Bot.*); sea-hedgehog. —zähnig, *adj.* having two teeth; bidentate (*Bot.*). —zeilig, *adj.* of two lines; two-lined; —zeilige Gerste, long-eared barley. —zeitig, *adj.* dichronous, having two periods; —zeitige Silbe, doubtful syllable. —züngig, *adj.* double-tongued; insincere. —zweitel-takt, *m.* time of two minims in a bar.

Zwei'en, *v.r.* to go together in pairs, to pair (off) (*obs.*). *See* sich entzweien.

Zwei'fel, *m.* (—s, *pl.* —) doubt; uncertainty, hesitation; in — (stellen) ziehen, to call in question, to doubt; ohne *or* sonder —, without doubt, doubtless, unquestionably; es ist kein —, daß . . ., there is no doubt but that . . .; über allen — erhaben, beyond all doubt; außer —, beyond (a) doubt. —haft, *adj.* undecided, irresolute; doubting; dubious, questionable; suspicious; darüber bin ich nicht —haft, I have no doubt about that; etwas —haft machen, to cast a doubt upon, throw suspicion on a thing. *Comp.* —fall, *m.* doubtful case. —(s)-frei, *adj.* free from doubt. —geist, *m.* spirit of doubt, scepticism. —(s)-grund, *m.* reason for doubt. —los, I. *adj.* indubitable, certain. II. *adv. see* —sohne. —mut, *m.* irresolution; uncertainty. —mütig, *adj.* irresolute, wavering. —s-ohne, I. *adv.* doubtless, without doubt. II. *adj. used predic'ly* (*prov.*) indubitable; richtig und —sohne, sure and certain. —sucht, *f.* scepticism. —süchtig, *adj.* sceptical.

Zwei'fel—n, *v.n.* (*aux.* h.) to doubt, to suspect; an einer S., an einem —n, to doubt, a th., a p.; ich zweifle nicht daran, I do not doubt it; er —te, was er thun sollte, he was in doubt as to what he should do; ich zweifle, ob es passend ist, I doubt whether it is proper; eine Zeit lang —te man an seinem Aufkommen, his life was despaired of for a time. —nd, *p. & adj.* doubting; sceptical.

Zweif'ler, *m.* (—s, *pl.* —) doubter, sceptic.

Zweig, *m.* (—(e)s, *pl.* —e) branch, bough; scion; department, section; line; spur (*of a mountain-chain*); sprig (*in embroidery*); kleiner —, twig, spray, sprig; er wird nie auf einen grünen — kommen, he will never get on in the world, he will never prosper. —lein, *n.* (—leins, *pl.* —lein) sprig, little twig. *Comp.* —abteilung, *f.* section. —anstalt, *f.* branch institution. —bahn, *f.* branch line (*Railw.*). —geschäft, *n.* branch business. —gesellschaft, *f.* joint-stock company. —leitung, *f.* service-pipe (*for gas*). —station, *f.* station on a branch line, local branch. —verein, *m.* affiliated society.

Zweit, *num. adj.* (der, die, das —e) second; next; der —e des Monats, the 2d (*of the month*); der —e Mai, May the 2d; den —en Tag darauf, the next day but one; mein —es Ich, my other self, my alter ego; ein —er Alexander, a second Alexander; wir waren zu —, there were two of us. —el, *n.* (—els, *pl.* —el) second part, half. —ens, (zum —en,) *adv.* secondly, in the second place. *Comp.* —älteste(r), *m.* second-eldest. —best, *adj.* second-best. —edelst, *adj.*; das —edelste Metall, the most precious metal after gold. —geboren, *adj.* second, younger. —höchst, *adj.* second in height, highest but one. —instanzlich, *adj.* in the court of appeal. —jüngste(r), *m.* youngest but one. —letzt, *adj.* last but one. —nächst, *adj.* next but one; der —nächste Tag, the next day but one.

Zwerch, *adj. & adv.* athwart, across. *Comp.* —fell, *n.* midriff, diaphragm; einem das —fell erschüttern, to make a p.'s sides split with laughing. —fell-erschütterung, *f.* fit *or* outburst of laughter (*fig.*).

Zwerg, *m.* (—(e)s, *pl.* —e), —in, *f.* dwarf, diminutive person, pygmy, little mite; manikin (only *m.*); brownie. —haft, —ig, *see* —artig. —haftigkeit, —heit, *f.* dwarfishness. *Comp.* —apfel, *m.* dwarf apple. —apfelsine, *f.* tangerine. —artig, *adj.* dwarfish, of diminutive size *or* stature, pygmy, pygmean. —bildung, *f.* dwarfishness. —bohne, *f.* dwarf kidney-bean. —fledermaus, *f.* pipistrel. —kiefer, *f.* dwarf-pine. —könig, *m.* dwarf king, king of dwarfs; petty king, kinglet. —maus, *f.* harvest-mouse. —mensch, *m.* pygmy. —palme, *f.* dwarf fan-palm. —trappe, *f.* lesser bustard. —völker, *pl.* dwarf tribes. —wuchs, *m.* stinted growth. —wüchsig, *adj.* dwarfish, very small, stinted in growth.

Zwet'sch(g)e, *f.* (*pl.* —n) (*egg-shaped small*) plum; gedörrte —, prune.

Zwick, *m.* (—es, *pl.* —e) *see* Zwecke; pinch, nip; tweak; twinge; whip-lash; cut with a whip. —e, *f.* (*pl.* —en) clip. —el, *m.* (—els, *pl.* —el) wedge (*for splitting wood, etc.*); clock (*of a stocking*); gusset, gore; gusset (*Mach.*); queer fish *or* fellow. —eln, *v.a.* to clock (*stockings*), to gore (*skirts*); **gezwickelt**, with clocks. **—en**, *v.a.* to pinch; to twitch, tweak; to gripe; to peg; to disturb, torment, worry; **—en und zwacken**, to worry, harass; **es —t mich im Leibe**, I have the colic; **den Bart —en**, to trim the beard. **—er**, *m.* (**—ers**, *pl.* **—er**) one that pinches, twitches, *etc.*; faucet; eye-glasses, pince-nez; *see* **—zange.** *Comp.* **—bohrer**, *m.* gimlet, wimble. **—el=bart**, *m.* imperial. **—el=strumpf**, *m.* stocking with clocks. **—mühle**, *f.* double mill (*in a game*); double resource, two strings to one's bow; **eine —mühle machen**, to see-saw, play for one's partner to trump (*at whist*). **—nagel**, *m.* tack, small nail. **—steine**, *pl.* stones for filling up the inside of a wall, rubble. **—zange**, *f.* pincers, tweezers.

Zwie'—bel, *see* **Zwiebel.** **—fe.**, *see* **Zwiesel.** *Comp.* **—back**, *m.* rusk; biscuit. **—brache**, *f.* double ploughing. **—brachen**, *v.a.* (*insep.*) to plough a second time, to twi-fallow (*a field*). **—fach**, *adj.* twofold, double. **—fältig**, *adj.* twofold, double. **—gespräch**, *n.* dialogue, colloquy, private talk, (confidential) chat. **—laut**, *m.* diphthong. **—licht**, *n.* twilight; **im —licht**, at twilight, in the dusk. **—spalt**, *m.* disunion, discord, dissension; schism. **—spaltig**, **—spältig**, *adj.* disunited, divided. **—tracht**, *f.* discord, dissension. **—trächtig**, *adj.* discordant, at variance. **—trachts=stifter**, *m.* originator of discord, maker of mischief.

Zwie'bel, *f.* (*pl.* **—n**) onion; bulb; turnip (*of a big watch*). **—n**, *v.n.* (*aux.* **h.**) to smell (*or* taste) of onions. II. *a.* to rub with onions; to season with onion; **einen —n**, to plague, torment a p., to treat a p. harshly; to try a p.'s patience. *Comp.* **—artig**, *adj.* bulbous; onion-like. **—beet**, *n.* bed of onions. **—brühe**, *f.* onion-sauce. **—brut**, *f.* young bulbs. **—fische**, *pl.* fish dressed with onions; pie (*Print.*) **—förmig**, *adj.* bulbous. **—geruch**, *m.* smell of onions. **—gewächs**, *n.* bulbous plant. **—gras**, *n.* bulbous meadow-grass. **—knollen**, *m.* bulb. **—lauch**, *m.* chives; onion. **—sauce**, *see* **—brühe.** **—suppe**, *f.* onion soup. **—tragend**, *adj.* bulbiferous. **—wurzel**, *f.* bulb.

Zwier, *num. adv.* twice (*obs., poet.*).

Zwie'sel, *f.* (*pl.* **—n**) birfurcation; having a forked branch; fork; fetlow (*of cattle*). **—ig**, *adj.* forked, bifurcate. **—n**, *v.n. & r.* to fork, bifurcate. *Comp.* **—bart**, *m.* forked beard.

Zwie'sel—n, *v.n.* to chirp, twitter (*dial.*). *Comp.* **—beere**, *f. see* **Vogelbeere.**

Zwil—lich, *m.* (**—lichs**, *pl.* **—liche**), **—ch**, *m.* (**—ches**, *pl.* **—che**) ticken, ticking, coutil. **—lichen**, **—lchen**, *adj.* of ticking *or* coutil. **—ling**, *see* **Zwilling.** *Comp.* **—lich=kittel**, **—lich=rock**, *m.* smock *or* cassock of coutil *or* coarse cotton stuff. **—lich=weber**, *m.* ticking-weaver.

Zwill'ing, *m.* (**—s**, *pl.* **—e**) (**—s=knabe**, *m.*, **—s=mädchen**, *n.*) twin (*boy or girl*). *Comp.* **—s=apfel**, *m.* twin-apple. **—s=artig**, *adj.* didymous. **—s=bildung**, *f.* congemination. **—s=bruder**, *m.* twin-brother. **—s=geburt**, *f.* birth of twins. **—s=geschwister**, *pl.* twins. **—s=gestirn**, *n.* Gemini, Castor and Pollux. **—s=kristall**, *m.* twin crystals. **—s=muskeln**, *pl.* gemini (*Anat.*).

Zwing, *m.* (**—s**) fort, castle, keep, donjon (*obs., poet. for* **Zwinger, Zwingburg**).

Zwin'ge, *f.* (*pl.* **—n**) vice; clamp, holdfast; coupling-plates (*Mach.*); ferrule (*on sticks, canes, etc.*); tip (*of an umbrella*); round ring.

Zwin'g—en, *ir.v.a.* to force, constrain, compel; to master, overcome, vanquish; **einen zu etwas —en**, to compel a p. to (*do, etc.*), to force s.o. into (*doing, etc.*); **einen in Fesseln —en**, to put a p. in irons by force; **mit Gewalt —en**, to do violence to, force; **in eine S. hinein —en**, to force, drive into a th.; **durch Hunger —en**, to reduce by starvation; **sich —en**, to constrain o.s., to do violence to *or* restrain one's feelings, to make a great effort; **man braucht ihn nicht dazu zu —en**, he will do it of himself; **das läßt sich nicht —en**, that is not accomplished by violence, force *or* effort is of no use there; **er läßt sich nicht —en**, he won't yield to force, he can't bear constraint; **sich zum Lachen —en**, to force o.s. to laugh; **ich muß mich —en, seine Briefe zu lesen**, I have to force myself (it costs me an effort) to read his letters; **sich zur Freundlichkeit —en**, to make an effort *or* force o.s. to appear pleasant; **gezwungen**, forced, not natural, hypocritical; **gezwungenerweise**, compulsorily, by compulsion; **gezwungenes Wesen**, stiff, constrained manner; **gezwungen lachen**, to force a laugh. **—end**, *p. & adj.* forcing; compulsory; constraining; cogent, conclusive. **—er**, *m.* (**—ers**, *pl.* **—er**) one who forces *or* constrains; narrow and confined space between the main wall of a mediæval castle or city and the encompassing moat and outer walls; cage, den (*for wild beasts*); kennel; bear-pit; arena; donjon, tower, fort; barbacan (*Mil.*). *Comp.* **—burg**, *f.* citadel, fortress (*erected for the subjugation of a people*). **—herr**, *m.* despot, tyrant. **—herrschaft**, *f.* despotism, tyranny. **—schraube**, *f.* ferrule-screw; (**—stange**, *f.*) veneering-stick. **—stock**, *see* **Schraubstock.** **—uri**, *n.* Fortress of Uri (*poet.*).

Zwin'ke(r)n, *v.n.* (*aux.* **h.**) to wink, to blink.

Zwir'beln, *v.a.* to twirl.

Zwirn, *m.* (**—s**, *pl.* **—e**) (*linen*) thread; twine; twisted yarn; ideas, fancies (*sl.*); **sie hat — im Kopfe**, she 's no fool; **Gott mag wissen, was der Kerl für — im Kopfe hat**, the Lord only knows what notions the fellow has got in his head (*coll.*). **—en**, I. *adj.* of thread. II. *v.n.* (*aux.* **h.**) to purr (*of cats*); **die Wolle —t**, the wool sticks together, grows stringy. III. *v.a.* to twist (*wool or cotton*); to twine; to throw (*silk*); **gezwirnt**, double-threaded; **gezwirnte Seide**, silk-twist; **doppelt gezwirnte Seide**, thrown silk. **—er**, *m.* (**—ers**, *pl.* **—er**) thrower (*of silk*); twister, twiner. *Comp.* **—band**, *n.* linen tape. **—brett**, *n.* twining-board. **—fabrikation**, *f.* thread-making. **—(s)=faden**, *m.* thread; very thin person (*fig.*). **—gardinen**, *pl.* thread curtains. **—gaze**, *f.* very fine lawn. **—handschuh**, *m.* thread glove. **—haspel**, *f. & m.* reel. **—litze**, *f.* thread-bobbin. **—maschine**, *f.* twisting frame. **—mühle**, *f.* twisting frame, doubler; spinning-mill. **—saal**, *m.* twisting-mill. **—seide**, *f.* twisted silk. **—spitze**, *f.* thread- *or* tape-lace. **—tasche**, *f.* thread-case, housewife. **—wickel**, *m.* thread-paper.

Zwi'schen, I. *prep.* (*with dat. in answer to* **wo?** where? *with acc. in answer to* **wohin?** whither, where to?) between, betwixt; among, amongst; **— Thür und Angel stecken**, to be in a dilemma *or* in a fix; **— Himmel und Erde**, between *or* 'twixt heaven and earth; **er saß — mir und ihm**, he sat between me and him; **er setzte sich — mich und ihn**, he seated himself between us (*him and me*); **— den Bäumen hervorblicken**, to peep out between the trees; **— die Menge hineintreten**, to step right into the midst of the crowd; **es ist kein Unterschied — ihm und seinem Bruder**, there is no difference between him and his brother; **wählen Sie — diesen Büchern**, choose amongst these books; **es ist Unkraut — dem Weizen**, there are tares amongst the wheat; **Unkraut — den Weizen säen**, to sow tares among the wheat; **— (mehreren) Völkern**, international; **— Meeren**, interoceanic; **— Kolonien**, intercolonial; **Wettrudern — Universitäten**, inter-university boat race. II. *adv. see* Dazwischen. *Comp.* —akt, *m.* interval between the acts. —akts=musik, *f.* music between the acts *or* during the interval. —akts=vorhang, *m.* drop-scene. —balken, *m.* mid-beam. —band, *n.* intervertebral ligament. —begebenheit, *f.* episode. —bemerkung, *f.* incidental remark, remark thrown in; digression, aside. —bescheid, *m.* provisional reply. —blatt, *n.* interleaf, blank. —deck, *n.* between-decks, steerage. —decks=passagier, *m.* steerage passenger. —ding, *n.* intermediate thing, cross; hybrid; cross-breed. —durch, *adv.* through, in the midst; at times; between whiles, at intervals. —essen, *see* —gericht. —fabel, *f.* episode (in a drama). —fall, *m.* incident, episode; plötzlicher —fall von entscheidender Wirkung, sudden blow, bolt from the blue; coup de théâtre. —farbe, *f.* half-tint. —gebäude, *n.* intermediate building, wing joining one building to another. —gericht, *n.* side-dish; entrée; extra dish. —gesang, *m.* incidental song. —geschäft, *n.* business done in the midst of one's ordinary business, incidental business. —geschoß, *n.* intermediate stor(e)y. —glied, *n.* intermediary *or* connecting link. —hafen, *m.* trading port. —hand, *f.* mediation; durch die hansische —hand, by Hanseatic middlemen. —handel, *m.* carrying trade; commission business; intermediate trade; *see* —fall. —händler, *m.* (commission) agent, intermediary, middleman. —handlung, *f.* episode, incident; intermediate action. —he'r, *adv.* in the interval, in the mean time, meanwhile. —hi'n, *adv.* right into the *or* their midst. —in'ne, *adv.* in the midst of, between the two. —kiefer(=knochen), *m.* intermaxillary bone. —klage, *f.* bill of interpleader. —knoten, *m.* internode. —königtum, *n.* interregnum. —kunft, *f.* intervention. —latte, *f.* lath for filling up. —liegend, *adj.* intermediate. —magazin, *n.* store; bonded warehouse. —mahl(zeit, *f.*), *n.* luncheon; afternoon tea; light repast. —maschine, *f.* communicator. —mauer, *f.* party-wall. —mischung, *f.* intermixture. —mittel, *n.* medium (*Phys.*). —musik, *f.* incidental music. —pause, *f.* interval. —person, *f.* agent, intermediary, middleman; go-between. —pfeiler, *m.* pillar placed between two others. —pfosten, *m.* middle post. —platz, *m.* intermediate place; staple-town. —raum, *m.* intermediate space; interstice; distance between; pore (*Phys.*); space (*Typ.*); interval; gauge (*Railw.*); in langen —räumen, at long intervals; in —räumen wiederkehrend, intermittent, periodical; Anordnung der —räume, spacing. —rede, *f.* interruption; digression. —redner, *m.* interlocutor. —regierung, *f.* interregnum. —reich, *n.* kingdom situated between two others; interregnum. —reihe, *f.* intermediate *or* middle row. —ruf, *m.* loud interruption, exclamation. —satz, *m.* insertion; parenthesis; incidental proposition. —speise, *f. see* —gericht. —spiel, *n.* intermezzo; interlude; by-play. —stab, *m.* fillet (*Arch.*). —stand, *m. see* —stellung. —ständer, *m.* middle post. —station, *f.* intermediate station, way-side station. —stellung, *f.* interposition, intervention; intermediate position. —stock(werk), *see* —geschoß. —streifen, *m.* insertion (*embroidery*). —stück, *n.* piece inserted; insertion; intermediate piece, interlude (*Theat.*). —stunde, *f.* interval; pause; recreation-time. —ton, *m.* intermediate tone. —träger(in, *f.*), *m.* go-between; meddler; tell-tale. —trägerei, *see* Zuträgerei. —umstand, *m.* incidental circumstance. —vorhang, *m.* curtain at the end *or* in the middle of a scene, drop-scene; drop-curtain. —wall, *m.* partition wall, curtain (*Fort.*). —wand, *f.* partition. —weite, *f.* distance between; space. —wort, *n.* interjection. —zaun, *m.* partition- *or* boundary-fence. —zeile, *f.* space between lines; words inserted; space-line (*Typ.*). —zeilig, *adj.*; —zeilige Übersetzung, interlinear translation. —zeit, *f.* intervening time, interval; in der —zeit, in the mean time, during the interval. —zustand, *m.* intermediate state.

Zwist, *m.* (—es, *pl.* —e) dissension, discord, disunion; quarrel; twist, double shoot (*Weav.*); sie gerieten darüber in —, they began to quarrel about it. —ig, *adj.* discordant, disagreeing; in dispute. —igkeit, *f.* dissension, quarrel.

Zwit'schern, *v.* I. *a. & n.* (*aux.* h.) to twitter, chirp, warble; ein Lied —, to warble a song; so wie die Alten sungen, so — auch die Jungen, as the old cock crows the young one learns, like father, like son (*prov.*).

Zwit'ter, *m.* (—s, *pl.* —) mongrel, hybrid; bastard, hybrid (*Bot.*); hermaphrodite; crystallized tin ore; black-lead ore. —haft, —ig, *adj.* hybrid; mongrel; hermaphrodite, androgynal. —haftigkeit, —schaft, *f.*, —tum, *n.* (—s) hybrid character, mongrelism. *Comp.* —art, *f.* hybrid species. —artig, *see* —haft. —bildung, *f.* hybridation, hermaphrodism. —blume, —blüte, *f.* hermaphrodite flower. —geschlecht, *n.* hybrid stock; mongrel *or* degenerate race. —geschöpf, *n.*, —gestalt, *f.* hermaphrodite; bastard; mongrel. —pflanze, *f.* bastard plant. —wesen, *n.* hybrid *or* hermaphrodite nature *or* condition; hybrid; hermaphrodite; mongrel. —wort, *n.* hybrid (word).

Zwo, (*obs. fem.*) *num. adj.* two; *see* Zween. —te, (*obs. for* Zweite, *e.g.* —te Auflage) second.

Zwölf, I. *num. adj.* (*nom. & acc.* —e, *obs. and poet. dat.* —en) twelve; a dozen; um — (mittags), at twelve o'clock, at noon; um — (nachts), at midnight; um ¾ auf —, at a quarter to twelve. II. *f.* the number twelve; a dozen. —er, *m.* (—ers, *pl.* —er) the figure twelve (12); member of a council of twelve; wine of the year '12; soldier of the twelfth regiment. —t, *num. adj.* (der, die, das —e) twelfth; Karl der —te, Charles the Twelfth; der —te des Monats, the 12th of the month; die —ten, the twelve days (*or nights*) between Christmas and Epiphany, Twelfthtide; zum —ten, *see* —tens. —tel, *n.* (—tels, *pl.* —tel) twelfth part; sieben —tel, seven twelfths. —tens, *adv.* in the 12th place. *Comp.* —achtel=takt, *m.* twelve-eight time. —eck, *n.* dodecagon. —eckig, *adj.* twelve-sided, dodecagonal. —er=ausschuß, *m.* committee of twelve. —erlei, *indec. adj. or adv.* of 12 different kinds, in 12 different ways. —fach, —fältig, *adj.* twelve-fold. —fin'ger=darm, *m.* duodenum (*Anat.*). —flach, *n.*, —flächner, *m.* dodecahedron. —griff(e)lig, *adj.* dodecagynian (*Bot.*). —jährig, *adj.* twelve years old; of *or* lasting twelve years. —jährlich, *adj.* recurring every twelve years. —lötig, *adj.* of six ounces. —malig, *adj.* repeated twelve times. —männ(er)ig, *adj.* dodecandrian. —pfünder, *m.* twelve-pounder (*Artil.*). —seitig, *adj.* having twelve sides *or* faces; dodecahedral. —spaltig, *adj.* in twelve columns; dodecapartite (*Bot.*). —stündig, *adj.* lasting twelve hours; of *or* in twelve lessons. —stündlich, *adj. & adv.* happening every twelve hours. —tel=format, *n.* duodecimo (size *or* book). —teilig, *adj.* consisting of twelve parts; dodecafid; duodecimal. —teiligkeit, *f.* duodecimal system. —weib(er)ig, *adj.* dodecagynian. —zahl, *f.* number twelve, duodecimal.

INDEX OF NAMES.

GEOGRAPHICAL AND PROPER NAMES.

In the subjoined list of Geographical and Proper Names the following classes of words have, as a rule, been *omitted*:—

1. Those in which the German and English forms correspond exactly: e.g. Alfred, Alfred; Richard, Richard; London, London; Hamburg, Hamburg, etc., etc.

2. Those names of countries in which the German terminations -ien, -ika, correspond to the English -ia, -ica: e.g. Asien, Asia; Indien, India; Skandinavien, Scandinavia, etc., etc.

It should also be noticed that where the difference between the English and German forms is very slight, the names usually occur in the English-German part only. Names of *rivers* which are the same in both languages appear in the English-German part, where the German gender is shown.

A

Aa'chen, *n.* Aix-la-Chapelle.

Aar'gau, *m.* Argau, Argovia. **—er**, *m.*, **—erin**, *f.* Argovian.

Abderi't, *m.*, **—in**, *f.* Abderite; Gothamite. **—en-streich**, *m.* act of folly.

A'bendland, *n.* West, Occident. **—ländisch**, *adj.* Western.

Abessi'n—ien, *n.* Abyssinia. **—ier**, *m.*, **—ierin**, *f.*, **—isch**, *adj.* Abyssinian.

A'braham, *m.* Abraham; in —s Schoß sitzen, to be in Abraham's bosom; (*fig.*) to enjoy ease and prosperity.

Abruz'zen, (die) *pl.* the Abruzzi Mts.

Ac'con, *n.* Acre.

Achä'—er, *m.*, **—erin**, *f.* Achæan, Greek. **—isch**, *adj.* Achæan.

Achi'll, *m.* Achilles.

A'dalbert, *m.* Albert, Bert(ie), Ethelbert.

A'dam, *m.* Adam. **—s-apfel**, **—s-biß**, *m.* Adam's apple, thyroid cartilage. **—s-feige**, *f.* sycamore.

A'debar, *m.* name of the stork, as bringer of children.

Adel—bert, *m. see* Adalbert. **—heid**, *f.* Adelaide.

Ade'le, *f.* Adela.

Admiralitäts'inseln, *pl.* the Admiralty Islands (*pl.*).

A'dolf, *m.* Adolphus.

A'dria, *f.*, **Adria'tisches Meer**, *n.* Adriatic (Sea).

Afrikan'd—er, *m.*, **—erin**, *f.* Africander.

Afrika'n—er, *m.*, **—erin**, *f.*, **—isch**, *adj.* African.

Agä'isches Meer, *n.* Ægean Sea, Archipelago.

Aga'the, *f.* Agatha.

Äga'tische Inseln, *pl.* the Ægades, Egates; Egadi Islands.

Ägi'dius, *m.* Giles.

Ägyp't—en, *n.* Egypt. **—er** (*obs.* —ier), *m.*, **—erin**, *f.* Egyptian; gipsy (*obs.*). **—isch**, *adj.* Egyptian; der —ische Geier, Pharaoh's chicken.

Ahasve'r, *m.* Ahasuerus.

Aka'dien, *n.* Acadia, Nova Scotia.

Ala'nus, *m.* Alan.

A'larich, *m.* Alaric.

Al'ba, Herzog von —, Duke of Alva.

Alba'ner, *m.* inhabitant of Alba Longa. **—gebirge**, *n.* the Alban Mount.

Alba'n—er, **—e'se**, *m.*, **—erin**, **—e'sin**, *f.* Albanian. **—isch**, Albanian.

Al'berich, *m.* Alberic, Aubrey.

Alberti'ne, *f.* Alberta.

Al'brecht, *m.* Albert, Bert(ie).

Aleman'n—e, *m.* Aleman. **—isch**, *adj.* Alemannic.

A'lex (*dim. for* Alexander), *m.* Alick, Sandy.

Alexandri'ner, *m.* Alexandrian; Alexandrine.

Ale'xie, *f.* Alice, Alison.

Al'fons, Alfon'so, *m.* Alphonso.

Al'gier, *n.* Algeria (*the country*); Algiers (*the town*). **—er**, *m.*, **—erin**, *f.* Algerian. **—isch** (*pron.* algie'risch), *adj.* Algerian, Algerine.

Al(l)'gäu, *n.* Algau, a district in S. W. Bavaria and the adjoining parts of Würtemberg and the Vorarlberg.

A'lois, *m.* Aloysius.

Al'pen, (die) *pl.* the Alps. **—rose**, *f.* rhododendron. **—sohn**, **Älpler**, *m.* Swiss.

Alpi'nisch, *adj.* Alpine.

Älp'ler, *m.*, **—in**, *f.* inhabitant of the Alps, mountaineer.

Al't—england, *n.* Old England. **—englisch**, *adj.* Old English, Anglo-Saxon. **—griechisch**, *adj.* Ancient Greek. **—hochdeutsch**, *adj.* Old High German. **—nordisch**, *adj.* Old Norse. **—russe**, *m.*, **—russisch**, *adj.* Muscovite. **—sächsisch**, *adj.* Old (Continental) Saxon.

Alwi'ne, *f.* Albina.

Ama'lie, *f.* Amelia, Amy.

Amazo'ne, *f.* Amazon. **—n-haft**, *adj.* Amazonian. **—n-strom**, *m.* Amazons River, the river Amazon.

Ambro'si—us, *m.* Ambrose. **—a'nisch**, *adj.* Ambrosian.

Ame'lie, *f. see* Amalie.

A'melung, *m.* descendant of the (*East Gothic*) King Amala; (*especially applied to*) Dietrich von Bern and his followers; noble Goth. **—en-lied**, *n.* cycle of epic songs on Dietrich von Bern and his Gothic thanes.

Amerika'n—er, *m.* inhabitant of the United States of America. **—isch**, *adj.* American (*usually restricted to the United States*). **—is'mus**, *m.* (*pl.* —is'men) Americanism (*in language*). **—ertum**, *n.* Americanism.

Am'rei, *f.* (*short for* Anna Marie) Mary Ann.

Am'sel (*dim. of* Agnes), *f.* Aggie, Aggy.

Anakreon't—iker, *m.* Anacreontic poet, writer of Anacreontic poetry. **—isch**, *adj.* Anacreontic.

Andalu'sisch, *adj.* Andalusian.

An'den, *pl.* Andes.

Andre'as, Andres, *m.* Andrew. **—kreuz**, *n.* St. A.'s cross, saltier cross, Scotch cross. **—nacht**, *f.* eve of St. Andrew's, St. Andrew's eve. **Andre(a)stag**, *m.* St. Andrew's day (Nov. 30).

Äne'—as, *m.* Æneas. die **—i'de**, *f.* the Æneid.

An'gel, *m.* Angle. **—n**, I. *pl.* the Angles. II. *n.* Anglia. **—sachse**, *m.*, **—sächsin**, *f.* Anglo-Saxon. **—sächsisch**, *adj.* Anglo-Saxon.

An'gers, *n.* Angiers.

An'glisch, *adj.* Anglian.

An'jou, *n.* Anjou; die **Einwohner von —**, the Angevins.

An'na, *f.* Anna, Anne, Ann.

Annami'tisch, *adj.* Annamese.

Änn'chen (*dim. of* Anna), *n.*, **Annet'te**, *f.* Annie, Nancy.

Ans'bach, *n.* Anspach.

Antili'banon, *m.* Anti-Lebanon.

Antil'len, *pl.* (Is.) Antilles; die kleinen —, the Leeward Isles. **—meer**, *n.* Caribbean Sea.
Antioche'nisch, *adj.* Antiochian.
Antio'chien, *n.* Antioch.
An'ton, **Anto'n(ius)**, *m.* Anthony, Antony, Tony. **Anto'niusfeuer**, *n.* St. Anthony's fire, erysipelas. **Anto'nie**, *f.* Antonia.
Ant'werpen, *n.* Antwerp.
Ä'ol—us, *m.* Æolus, the God of the Winds. **—s=harfe**, *f.* Æolian harp.
Apala'chen, *pl.* Ap(p)alachian Mts.
Apenni'nen, (die) *pl.* Apennines (*pl.*), Apennine Mts.
Ap'pische Straße, *f.* Appian Way (from Rome to Capua).
Apu'lisch, *adj.* Apulian.
Äqua'tor, *m.* (the) Equator.
Aquita'nien, *n.* Aquitaine.
A'raber, *m.*, **—erin**, *f.* Arab. **Ara'bisch**, *adj.* Arabian, Arab.
Arago'n—ien, *n.* Aragon. **—isch**, *adj.* Aragonese.
Archipe'l(agus), *m.* (the) Archipelago.
Arden'nerwald, *m.* Forest of Ardennes.
Arela'tisches Reich, *n.* Arelatum, old Burgundian kingdom.
Areopa'g, *m.* (the) Areopagus.
Argi'visch, *adj.* Argive, Greek.
Argon'nerwald, *m.* Forest of Argonne(s).
Aria'n—er, *m.*, **—isch**, *adj.* Arian.
A'ri—er, *m.*, **—sch**, *adj.* Aryan.
Ariovi'st, *m.* Ariovistus.
Aristo'tel—es, *m.* Aristotle. **Aristote'liker**, *m.* Aristotelian.
Är'melmeer, *n.* English Channel.
Arme'nisch, *adj.* Armenian.
Armo'risch, *adj.* Armorican.
Ar'tus (König), King Arthur. **—gedicht**, *n.* poem on the Arthurian legend. **—ritter**, *m.* Knight of the Round Table (die Tafelrunde). **—sage**, *f.* Arthurian legend.
Aschan'ti, *n.* Ashanti.
A'schen—brödel, **—puttel**, *n.* Cinderella.
Äscula'p, Æsculapius; physician (*coll.*).
Asia't—e, *m.*, **—isch**, *adj.* Asiatic. **Halb—e**, *m.* Eurasian.
A'sowsches Meer, *n.* Sea of Azov.
As'sam—er, *m.*, **—e'sisch**, *adj.* Assamese.
As'sur, *m.* Asshur.
Assy'r—ier, *m.*, **—isch**, *adj.* Assyrian.
Astar'te, *f.* As(h)taroth (Phœnician goddess).
Astu'rien, *n.* the Asturias.
Athe'n, *n.* Athens; *also* town of the muses, town of letters (*e.g.* **Spree —**). **—er** (*obs.* **—ien'ser**), *m.*, **—erin**, *f.*, **—isch**, *adj.* Athenian; Eulen nach —tragen, to carry coals to Newcastle.
Äthio'p—e, *m.* Ethiop(ian). **—ien**, *n.* Ethiopia.
Atlan'tisches Meer, the Atlantic (ocean).
At'lasgebirge, *n.* Atlas Mountains.
Ät'na, *m.* Mt. Etna.
Au'gias, *m.* Augeas; Stall des —, Augean stable.
Augs'burgische Konfession, *f.* the Augsburg Confession.
Au'gust, *m.* Augustus, Gus, Gussie (*the person*). **Augu'st**, *m.* August (*the month*). **Augus'te**, *f.* Augusta. **—e'isch**, *adj.* Augustan.
Au'gustin, *m.* Augustine, Austin. **Augusti'ner=mönch**, *m.*, **—nonne**, *f.* Austin friar, nun.
Austra'l—ier, *m.*, **—isch**, *adj.* Australian.
Ava'ren, (die) *pl.* (the) Avars.
Azo'ren, (die) *pl.* the Azores (*pl.*).
Azte'ke, *m.* Aztec.

B

Ba'den, *n.* Baden (*the Grand-Duchy*). **Baden=Ba'den**, *n.* Baden (*the town*). **—er**, (*less good*: **—ser**, *pron.* Baden'ser) *m.*, **—erin**, (**—serin**) *f.*, **—isch**, **—sisch** (*pron.* baden'sisch), *adj.* of Baden.
Bai'er, *m.*, **—in**, *f.*, *etc.*, *s.* Bayer.
Bajuva'r(e), *m.* Bavarian.
Bak'tr—er, *m.*, **—isch**, *adj.* Bactrian.
Bal'der, *m.* Baldur.
Bal'duin, *m.* Baldwin.
Balea'ren, (die) *pl.* the Balearic Isles.
Bal'kan—halbinsel, *f.* Balkan peninsula; die —länder, the Balkans. **—staaten**, *pl.* Balkan States, Balkans.
Bal'thasar, **Bal'zer**, *m.* Balthazar.
Bal'tische(s) Meer, *n.* (*poet.*) the Baltic. *See* Ostsee.
Barba'den, (die) *pl.* the Barbados (*pl.*).
Bar'bara, *f.* Barbara, Babbie, Babs.
Barbar—ei', (die) *f.* Barbary; —es'ken Staaten, the Barbary States.
Barbaros'sa, *m.* Barbarossa, Redbeard (*Emperor Frederic I. of Germany*).
Bar'b—e, *f.*, **—chen**, *n.*, **Bärbelchen**, *n.* (*dim. for* **Barbara**), Babbie, Babs.
Bar'füßer, *m.* Franciscan friar.
Bar'nabas, *m.* Barnaby.
Bar't(h)el, *m. see* Bartholomäus; er weiß, wo — den Most holt, he knows what 's what, he knows a thing or two (*prov.*).
Bartholomä'us, *m.* Bartholomew; —nacht, die St. Barthelemi, (*poet.*) (Massacre of) St. Bartholomew('s eve), Aug. 23–24, 1572.
Baschki're, *m.* Bashkir. **—n=land**, *n.* Bashkiria.
Ba'sel, *n.* Basle, Bâle.
Basi'lius, *m.* Basil.
Bas'k—e, *m.*, **—isch**, *adj.* Basque.
Bata'v(i)er, *m.* Batavian.
Bath'seba, *f.* Bathsheba.
Bay'—er, *m.*, **—erin**, *f.*, **—(e)risch**, *adj.* Bavarian. **—ern**, *n.* Bavaria.
Bea'trix, *f.* Beatrice.
Be'da, *m.* (the venerable) Bede.
Bedui'n—e, *m.*, **—isch**, *adj.* Bedouin.
Bel'g—ien, *n.* Belgium. **—(i)er**, *m.*, **—isch**, *adj.* Belgian.
Bel'grad, *n.* Belgrade.
Bel'isar, *m.* Belisarius.
Belle=Alliance; **Schlacht bei —**, Battle of Waterloo.
Belsa'zar, *m.* Belshazzar.
Belt, *m.* Baltic (Sea) (*poet.*); großer —, Great Belt; kleiner —, Little Belt.
Be'nedikt, *m.* Benedict, Benedick, Bennet. **—i'=ner**, *m.* Benedictine friar; Benedictine (liquor).
Benga'l—e, *m.* Bengali, Bengalese. **—en**, *n.* Bengal. **—isch**, *adj.* Bengal(ese), Bengali.
Berber—ei', *f. s.* Barbarei. **—roß** (*pron.* Ber'berroß), *n.* Barbary horse.
Berg'—partei, *f.* Mountain (in the first French Revolution). **—schotte**, *m.* (Scotch) Highlander. **—straße**, *f.* the mountainous district between Darmstadt and Heidelberg, the Odenwald.
Be'ringstraße, *f.* Bering Strait.
Berli'ner, *m.* inhabitant of Berlin, Berlinian; — Zimmer, room with but one window; dark, gloomy room. **—blau**, *n.* Berlin blue, Prussian blue. **—blau=säure**, *f.* Prussic acid.
Bern, *n.* Bern(e); Verona (*poet.*); Dietrich von —, Theodoric of Verona. **—er**, *m.*, **—erin**, *f.*, **—(er)isch**, *adj.* Bernese; —er Oberland, Bernese Alps, Highlands; —er Wäglein, waggonette.
Bern'hard, *m.* Bernard; der Große St. —, the Great St. Bernard. **—i'ner(hund)**, *m.* St. Bernard dog. **—i'nerm(önch)**, *m.* Bernardine (monk).
Ber'saba, *n.* Beersheba.
Ber'thel, *s.* Barthel; *s.* Bertha.
Betha'nia, *n.* Bethany.
Bet'ty, *f.* (*dim. of* **Elisabeth**) Betsy, Bess.
Bi'leam, *m.* Balaam.

Bin'nenafrika, *n.* Central Africa.
Bir'ma, *n.* Burmah. **Birma'n—e**, *m.*, **—in**, *f.*, **—isch**, *adj.* Burman, Burmese.
Biska'ya, *n.* Biscay; Meerbusen von —, Bay of Biscay.
Blan'ka, *f.* Blanche.
Bla'sius, *m.* Blaise.
Blind'heim, *n.* Blenheim.
Blocks'berg, *m.* the Brocken, the highest peak of the Harz Mountains, where, according to popular belief, witches and devils used to celebrate the Walpurgisnacht; einen auf den — wünschen, to wish s.o. at Jericho.
Bo'densee, *m.* Lake of Constance.
Bö'heim, *n.* (*poet. for* **Böh'men**, *n.*) Bohemia.
Bohe'mer, *m.* (*poet.*) Bohemian, gipsy.
Böhma'(c)ke, *m.* (*dial. for* **Böh'me**, *m.*) Bohemian; stubborn fellow (*coll.*).
Böh'm—en, *n.* Bohemia. **—er-brüder**, **—ische Brüder**, *pl.* Bohemian Brethren, Moravians. **—er-wald**, *m.* Bohemian Forest. **—er-weib**, *n.* gipsy-woman. **—isch**, *adj.* Bohemian; das sind ihm —ische Dörfer, that 's all Greek to him.
Bologne's—er, *m.*, **—isch**, *adj.* of Bologna, Bolognese. **—er Wurst**, *f.* Bologna sausage, polony.
Bonifa'z(ius), *m.* Boniface.
Bors'dorfer, *m.* a Borsdorf pippin; er hat Backen wie ein — Apfel, he has cheeks like an apple, he has rosy *or* ruddy cheeks.
Borus'se, *m.* Prussian (*archaic form*); member of the students' club 'Borussia.'
Bosn—ia'ke, **—ier**, *m.*, **—isch**, *adj.* Bosnian.
Bot't—en, *n.* Bothnia. **—nisch**, *adj.* Bothnian; —nischer Meerbusen, Gulf of Bothnia.
Brahm—a'ne, **—i'ne**, *m.*, **—a'nisch**, **—i'nisch**, *adj.* Brahmin. **—ais'mus** (*4 syllables*), *m.* Brahminism.
Brasi'l—ien, *n.* Brazil. **—ier** (*less good:* **—ia'ner**, *m.*), **—isch**, *adj.* (*less good:* **—ia'nisch**) Brazilian.
Braun, *m.* Bruin (the Bear, *in the Beast Epic*).
Braun'schweig, *n.* Brunswick.
Brei'te (*dial. for* **Brigit'te**), *f.* Bridget, Bride.
Bre'm—er (*less good:* **—en'ser**), *m.* of Bremen.
Bretag'ne, (**die**) *f.* Brittany; in der —, in Brittany.
Brigit'te, *f.* Bridget, Bride.
Britan'nien, *n.* Britain. **Brit'(t)e**, *m.*, **Brit(t)in**, *f.* Briton; Englishman, Englishwoman.
Brit—an'nisch, **—(t)isch**, *adj.* British; Britannic; English; Brythonic.
Bro'cken, *m.* Mt. Brocken (*highest peak of the Harz Mts.*), *see* Blocksberg. **—gespenst**, *n.* spectre of the Brocken.
Brüg'ge, *n.* Bruges.
Brüs'sel, *n.* Brussels. **—er Kohl**, *m.* Brussels sprouts. **—er Spitzen**, *pl.* Brussels lace.
Bu'charei, *f.* Bukhara; der Amir der —, the Ameer of Bukhara.
Bu'karest, *n.* Bucharest.
Bulga'r—e, *m.*, **—isch**, *adj.* Bulgarian.
Bün'd—en, **—ner**, *s.* Graubünden.
Bu'ren, *pl.* Boers. **—freund**, *m.*, **—freundlich**, *adj.* pro-Boer.
Burgon'den, *pl.* (*poetic and obs. for* **Burgunder**) Burgundians.
Burgu'nd, *n.* Burgundy. **—er**, *m.* Burgundian; Burgundian wine, Burgundy. **—isch**, *adj.* Burgundian.
Busch'männer, (**die**) *pl.* Bushmen.
Buxtehu'de, *n.* small North German town near Stade; (*fig.*) Gotham.
Byza'n—z, *n.* Byzantium, Constantinople. **—ti'ner**, *m.*, **—ti'nisch**, *adj.* Byzantine.

C

See also under K, Z.

Ca'dix, *n.* Cadiz.
Cäci'lie, *f.* Cecilia, Cecil(y), Cicely, Cis.
Calvi'n, *m.* Calvin. **—is'mus**, *m.* Calvinism. **—is'tisch**, *adj.* Calvinistic(al).
Ca'petinger, *pl.* Capetians.
Capulet'ti, *pl.* the Capulets.
Cä'sar, *m.* Cæsar. **Cäsa'risch**, *adj.* Cæsarean.
Cas'sel, *see* Kassel.
Catala'nisch, *adj.* Catalan.
Catalau'nisch, *adj.* Catalaunian; die —en Gefilde, the Catalaunian Fields (*battle 451* A. D.).
Caudi'nisch, *adj.*; die —en Pässe, the Caudine Forks.
Chaldä'—a, *n.* Chaldæa. **—er**, *m.*, **—isch**, *adj.* Chaldee, Chaldæan.
Champag'ne, (**die**) *f.* Champagne (*province*). **—r**, *m.* Champagne (*wine*).
Chauvin—is'mus, *m.* Chauvinism, Jingoism. **—i'st**, *m.* Chauvinist, Jingo.
Cherso'ne's, *m.* the Chersonese (peninsula).
Cherus'k—er, *m.* Cheruscan; *pl.* the Cherusci (*an old Germanic tribe*). **—isch**, *adj.* Cheruscan.
Ches'terkäse, *m.* Cheshire cheese.
Chile'n—e, *m.*, **—in**, *f.*, **—isch**, *adj.* Chilian.
Chi'n—a, *n.* China. **—e'se**, *m.* Chinaman, Chinese. **—e'sentum**, *n.* Chinese ways and customs. **—e'sisch**, *adj.* Chinese.
Chi'narinde, *f.* Peruvian bark.
Chlod'wig, **Chlo'dowech**, *m.* Clovis.
Christ, *m.*, **—in**, *f.* Christian; Christ (*obs.*). **—lich**, *adj.* Christian. **—us** (*gen.* —i, *dat.* —o, *acc.* —um, *or all cases in* —us), Christ; vor (nach) —i Geburt, before (after) Christ (B. C., A. D.); —i Himmelfahrt, the Ascension; Ascension Day. **—woche**, *f.* Christmas week.
Chris'tel, *f.* (*dim. of* **Christia'ne**) Chrissie, Christie.
Chris'toph, *m.* Christopher, Kit.
Cim'bern, (**die**) *pl.* the Cimbri.
Cirkas's—ier, *m.*, **—isch**, *adj.* Circassian.
Cis—alpi'nisch, *adj.* Cisalpine. **—leitha'nien**, *n.* that part of the Austro-Hungarian monarchy this side of the River Leitha. **—leitha'nisch**, *adj.* Cisleithan. **—pada'nisch**, *adj.* Cispadane (*this side of the River Po*).
Cistercien'ser(mönch), *m.* Cistercian, Benedictine friar.
Cle'mens, **Kle'mens**, *m.* Clement. **Klementi'ne**, *f.* Clementina.
Cluniacen'ser, *m.* Cluniac monk.
Cölesti'n, *m.* Celestine (*man's name*). **—a**, *f.* Celestine (*woman's name*). **—er(mönch)**, *m.* Celestine friar.
Cöln, *n. see* Köln.
Co'mersee, *m.* Lake Como.
Constan'tia, *f.* Constance.
Corn'wallis, *n.* Cornwall.
Cykla'd—en, (**die**) *pl.*, **—ische Inseln**, *pl.* the Cyclades (*pl.*).
Cy'per—n, *n.* Cyprus. **—wein**, *m.* Cyprus wine.
Cyprio't, *m.* Cypriot(e).
Cy'prisch, *adj.* Cyprian.
Cyril'l(us), *m.* Cyril.
Cze'ch—e, *m.* Czech. **—isch**, *adj.* Czech.

D

Daho'me, *n.*, Dahomey.
Dalai La'ma, *m.* the Dalay *or* Grand Lama.
Dalma'tisch, *adj.* Dalmatian.
Damasce'ner, *m.* Damascene, inhab. of Damascus. *adj.* Damascene, damask.
Da'naer, *pl.* Danaans, old Greeks. **—geschenk**, *n.* gift from the Greeks, treacherous gift.
Dä'n—e, *m.*, **—in**, *f.* Dane. **—e-mark**, *n.* Denmark. **—isch**, *adj.* Danish. **—en-steuer**, *f.* Danegeld.
Dan'zig, *n.* Dantzig, Dantzic; —er Lachs, a kind of brandy made at the Dantzic distillery called 'the Salmon.'
Dardanel'len(straße), *f.* (Straits of) the Dardanelles.
Däum'(er)ling, *m.*; der kleine —, Tom Thumb.
Dauphine', (**die**) *f.* Dauphiny.
Delf'ter Geschirr, *n.* Delft (Dutch) ware.

Del'phisch, *adj.*, Delphic; —e Weisheit, Delphic oracle; oracular wisdom.
Deoda't(us), *m.* Deodate.
Der'wisch, *m.* Dervish.
Des'sauer, der alte, *m.* Leopold I., Prince of Anhalt-Dessau (*1676–1747*).
Deutsch, *adj.* German; Teuton. **—e**, *m. & f.* German; —er Ritterorden, Order of Teutonic Knights; —er Volksstamm, Germanic race, old German tribe. **—heit**, *f.* German character, nationality. **—herren**, *pl.* knights of the Teutonic order. **—herrlich**, *adj.* belonging to the Teutonic order. **Hoch- und —meistertum**, *n.* Grand-Mastership of the Teutonic order. **—tum**, *n.* German nationality. **—tümelei'**, *f.* Teutomania, Germanomania, German chauvinism.
Die'trich, *m.* Theodoric, Derrick. — von Bern, Theodoric (the Great) of Verona (*hero of romance*).
Di'na, *f.* Dinah, Di.
Ding'—erich(s), **—s-da**, **—s-kirchen** (**Herr-**, **Frau-**) *m.*, *f.* (Mr., Mrs.) Thingamy, What-do-you-call-him? What 's-his-name?
Diony's(ius), *m.* Dionysius, Dennis.
Diosku'ren, (die) *pl.* the Dioscuri (*Castor and Pollux*).
Dnje'pr, (der) *m.* R. Dnieper.
Dnje'str, (der) *m.* R. Dniester.
Domi'nik—us, (der heilige) *m.* St. Dominic. **—a'ner**, *m.* Dominican, Black friar.
Don, (der) *m.* R. Don; die do'nischen Kosaken, the Cossacks of the Don.
Do'nau, (die) *f.* R. Danube. **—fürstentümer**, *pl.* Danubian principalities.
Dor'chen (*long* o), *n.*, **Doret'te**, **Do'ris** (*dim. of* Dorothea), *f.* Doris, Dora, Dolly, Dot.
Dorn'röschen, *n.* The Sleeping Beauty.
Dorothe'a, *f.*, **Dort'chen** (*long* o), *n.* **Dörte**, *f.* **Dürten**, Dorothea, Dorothy, Doll(y), Dot.
Drau, (die) *f.* R. Drave.
Dreikä'sehoch, *m.* Tom Thumb (*coll.*)
Drui'd—e, *m.*, **—in**, *f.* Druid. **—entum**, *n.* Druidism. **—isch**, *adj.*, Druidical.
Due'ro, (der) *m.* R. Douro.
Dum'merjan, **Dumm'rian**, *m.* Simple Simon, Tom Noddy.
Dü'na, (die) *f.* (Southern) River Dwina.
Dün'kirchen, *n.* Dunkirk.
Dür'ten, *n.* (*dim. of* Dorothea), Dolly, Dot.
Dwi'na, (die) *f.* (Northern) River Dwina.

E

E'berhard, *m.* Everard; — der Greiner, — der Rauschebart, Everard the Quarreller, Rushbeard (one of the Counts of Würtemberg, †1392); — im Bart (first Duke of Würtemberg, †1496).
Ebrä'er, *etc. see* Hebräer.
E'ckart, der getreue, *m.* a legendary hero, ally of Dietrich von Bern; also kind-hearted old mountain sprite warning mortals to get out of the way of the Wild Huntsman.
E'di, *n.* (*dim. of* Eduard), Ned.
E'du(ard), *m.* Edward, Ned, Neddy; — der Bekenner, Edward (the Confessor).
E'ger, *n.* Egra.
Ei'der, (die) *f.* Eider R.; — dänen, Danish politicians (*before 1864*) who wished Denmark to be extended to the river Eider (thus incorporating the Duchy of Schleswig with Denmark).
Eis'meer, *n.* Polar Sea; Nördliches —, Arctic Ocean; Südliches —, Antarctic Ocean.
Elb'florenz, *n.* (*students' slang for*) Dresden.
Eleono're, *f.* Eleanor.
Eleusi'nisch, *adj.* Eleusinian.
Eli'a(s), *m.* Elias, Elijah (*B.*).
Eli'sa, *m.* Elisha (*B.*).
Eli's—a, —e, *f.* (*dim. of* Elisabeth), Elsie, Eliza.
Eli'sabeth, *f.* Eliza(beth), Lizzie, Bess(ie), Betty, Betsy, Elsie.
El'sa, *f.* I. Elsa. II. *dim. of* Elisabeth.
El'saß, *n.* Alsace. **—-Lothringen**, *n.* Alsace and Lorraine.
El'säss—er, *m.*, **—erin**, *f.*, **—isch**, *adj.* Alsatian.
Els'beth, *f.*, **—chen**, *n.* (*dim. of* Elisabeth), Elsie.
El'se, *f.* I. Elsa, Alison, Alice. II. *dim. of* Elisabeth.
Elysä'isch, *adj.* Elysian.
Emma'nuel, *m.* Emmanuel.
E'mil, *m.* Emilius, Emile. **Emi'lie**, *f.* Emily.
Em'm—a, —i, *f.* (*dim.*), **—chen**, *n.* (*dim.*) Emma, Em(mie).
Em'merich, *m.* Emery, Merick.
E'nak, *m.* Anak. **—s-kind**, *n.*, **—s-sohn**, *m.*, **—s-tochter**, *f.* child of Anak, giant.
En'gelsburg, *f.* Castle of St. Angelo (*in Rome*).
Eng'länder, *m.* Englishman; horse with docked tail. **—in**, *f.* Englishwoman. **—ei'**, *f.* Anglomania. **—scheu**, *f.* Anglophobia.
Eng'lisch, *adj.* English; —e Krankheit, rickets; —es Pflaster, court-plaster; —es Salz, Epsom salts.
Epiku'r, *m.* Epicurus. **—ä'er**, *m.* Epicure(an). **—(ä)'isch**, *adj.* Epicurean.
E'rich, *m.* Eric.
Erl'könig, *m.* the Elf-king, fairy-king.
Er'melind, Vixen, wife of Reynard the Fox.
Ernst, Er'ni, *m.* Ernest, Ernie.
Erz'gebirge, *n.* Erzgebirge (*mountains in the kingdom of Saxony*).
Erz'jude, *m.* Hebrew Jew.
Esa'ias, *m.* Isaiah.
Escuria'l, *m.* the Escorial.
Es'ra, *m.* Ezra.
E'sther, *f.* Esther, Hester.
Esth'—land, *n.* Esthonia. **—nisch**, *adj.*, Esthonian.
Etrus'k—er, *m.*, **—isch**, *adj.* Etruscan.
Etsch, (die) *f.* River Adige.
Et'zel, *m. poet. for* Attila (*King of the Huns*).
Euge'n, *m.* Eugene. **—ie**, *f.* Eugenia.
Eukli'd(es), *m.* Euclid.
Eu'lenspiegel, Owlglass, Howleglass. **—ei'**, *f.* merry trick, practical joke.
Eu'phrat, (der) *m.* R. Euphrates.
Euro'p—a, *n.* Europe. **—ä'er**, *m.*, **—ä'isch**, *adj.* European. **—ä'isch-asia'tisch**, *adj.* Eurasian. **Halb—äer**, *m.* Eurasian.
Eusta'—chius, —sius, *m.* Eustace.
E'v—a, —e, *f.* Eve, Eva. **—askind**, *n.* human being, mortal.
Ev'chen, *n. dim. of* Eva, Eveline.
Eze'chiel, *m.* Ezekiel.

F

Fa'bier, *pl.* the Fabians.
Fan'chon, Fan'ny, *f.* Frances, Fanny.
Farö'er-Inseln, *pl.* Faroe Islands.
Faust, *m.* Faustus.
Fel'sengebirge, *n.* Rocky Mountains (*pl.*).
Fe'n—ier, *m.*, **—isch**, *adj.*, Fenian. **—iertum**, *n.* Fenian movement, Fenianism.
Fen'riswolf, *m.* wolf Fenris (*Mythol.*).
Fernambu'k(o), *n.* Pernambuco. **—holz**, *n.* Brazil-wood.
Feu'erl—and, *n.* Tierra del Fuego. **—änder**, *m.*, **—ändisch**, *adj.* Fuegian, Patagonian.
Fich'telgebirge, *n.* the Fir Mountains, Fichtelgebirge (*Middle Germany*).
Fid'schi, *n.* Fiji (Islands).
Fi(e)k'chen, *n.* (*dim. of* Sophie) Sophy.
Fin'n—e, —länder, *m.* Finn, Finlander. **—isch**, *adj.* Finnish; —ischer Busen, Gulf of Finland. **—land**, *n.* Finland.
Flam'—länder, *m.*, **—länderin**, *f.* Fleming, Flamand. **—isch**, *adj.* Flemish, boorish.
Flan'd—ern, *n.* Flanders. **—risch**, *adj.* Flemish, from Flanders.
Flie'gengott, *m.* Beelzebub.

Floren'tia, *f.* Florence, Flossie, Flo.
Florenti'n—er, *m.*, **—isch**, *adj.*, Florentine.
Flore'nz, *n.* Florence (*town*).
Fortuna't, *m.* Fortunatus; —s Wünschelhut, Fortunatus' wishing-cap; —s Glückssäckel, Fortunatus' purse.
Fran'k—e, *m.* Frank, Franconian; Salische —en, Salian Franks. **—en(land)**, *n.* Franconia. **—en=reich**, *n.* Francia, the Frankish Kingdom. **—reich**, *n.* France; wie der Hergott in —reich leben, to live like a fighting-cock (*coll.*).
Frank'furt, *n.* Frankfort; Frankfurt a/M *or* a/O, Frankfort on the Main *or* on the Oder. **—er Messe**, *f.* Frankfort fair.
Frän'kisch, *adj.* Frankish, Franconian; (*poet.*) French.
Franz, *m.* Francis, Frank; — von Assisi, St. Francis of Assisi. **—is'kus**, *see* Franz. **—is'ka**, *f.* Frances, Fanny. **—iska'ner**, *m.* Franciscan friar.
Fränz'chen, *n.* (*dim. for* **Franziska**) Fanny.
Franz'—mann, (*poet.*) **—o'se**, *m.* Frenchman. **—ö'sin**, *f.* Frenchwoman. **—ö'sisch**, *adj.* French. **—ösisch=deutsch**, *adj.* Franco-German. **—öse=lei'**, *f.* Gallomania. **—o'senhaß**, *m.* Gallophobia. **—wein**, *m.* French wine.
Freund'schafts=Inseln, *pl.* Friendly Islands.
Friau'l, *n.* Friuli.
Fri'da, *f.* (*dim. of* **Friederi'ke**) Freda, Freddie.
Fried'—chen, *n.*, **—el**, *m. dim. of* **Gottfried**.
Friedericia'nisch, *adj.* of Frederick the Great.
Friederi'ke, *f.* Frederica, Freda, Freddie.
Fried'land, *n.*; Herzog von —, der Friedländer, Wallenstein, Duke of Friedland.
Fried'rich, *m.* Frederic, Frederick, Fred(dy); — der Große, Frederick the Great.
Frie's—e, *m.* Frieslander, Frisian. **—isch**, *adj.* Frisian. **—(s)land**, *n.* Friesland, Frisia.
Fritz, *m.*, **—chen**, *n.* (*dim. of* **Friedrich**) Freddie, Fred; der alte —, Frederick the Great.

G

Gabrie'le, *f.* Gabrielle.
Ga'later, (die) *pl.* the Galatians.
Gä'l—e, *m.* Gael. **—isch**, *adj.* Gaelic.
Gale'n, *m.* Galen(us).
Galilä'—a, *n.* Galilee. **—er**, *m.*, **—isch**, *adj.* Galilean.
Gali'zien, *n.* Galicia.
Gal'len, St., *n.* St. Gall (*town*).
Gal'l—ien, *n.* Gaul, Gallia. **—ier**, *m.* Gaul. **—icis'mus**, *m.* gallicism. **—ikanisch**, **—isch**, *adj.* Gallic(an), Gaulish.
Gal'lus, der heilige, St. Gall (*saint*).
Gambri'nus, *m.* patron of (Bavarian) beer and conviviality.
Gascog'n—e, (die) *f.* Gascony. **—er**, *m.*, **—isch**, *adj.* Gascon.
Gel'd—ern, *n.* Geldern (*the town*), Gelderland (*the country*).
General'staaten, *pl.* States General of Holland.
Genf, *n.* Geneva. **—er**, *m.* Genevan. **—er See**, *m.* Lake of Geneva. **—erisch**, *adj.* Genevan.
Genove'va, *f.* Geneviève.
Gent, *n.* Ghent.
Ge'nu—a, *n.* Genoa. **—e'se(r)**, *m.*, **—e'sisch**, *adj.* Genoese.
Geo'rg, *m.* George, Georgie. **—isch**, *adj.* Georgian.
Georgi'ne, *f.* Georgina, Georgiana, Georgie.
Ger'hard, *m.* Gerard.
Germa'n—e, *m.* Teuton. **—isch**, *adj.* Germanic. Teutonic. **—i'st**, *m.* German scholar, student of Germanic philology; student of German law.
Ge'rold, *m.* Gerald.
Gertrau'de, *usually* **Ger'trud**, *f.* Gertrude, Gertie.
Gerva'sius, *m.* Gervase, Jarvis.
Ge'ten, (die) *pl.* the Getæ.
Geu'sen, *pl.* the Gueux, the Beggars (*nickname given to Dutch nobles of the 16th century*).
Gibral'tar, *n.*; Straße von —, Straits of Gibraltar.
Gie'remund, *f.* Erswyn, name of the she-wolf in the Beast Epic.
Glar'ner (*long* a), *pl.* inhabitants of the Swiss canton Glarus.
Glau'bersalz, *n.* Glauber's salts.
Goe'the, *m.*, **—forscher**, *m.* student of Goethe. **—forschung**, *f.* study of Goethe's life and writings. **—gesellschaft**, *f.* Goethe Society. **—jahrbuch**, *n.* yearly periodical devoted to the study of Goethe's life and works.
Göhr'de, *f.* large forest in the province of Hanover.
Gol'gatha, *n.* Golgotha, Mount Calvary (*B.*).
Go'liath, *m.* Goliath; langer—, longshanks (*coll.*).
Gor'disch, *adj.* Gordian.
Görg, *s.* Georg.
Go'sen, *n.*; das Land —, the land of Goshen (*B.*).
Go't—e, *m.* Goth. **—isch**, *adj.* Gothic. **—ische Schrift**, *f.* black letter type.
Gott'fried, Götz, *m.* Godfrey, Geoffrey.
Gott'hard, *m.* Goddard; St. —, St. Gothard.
Gott'—hold, —lieb, *m.* Theophilus.
Gottseibei'uns, *m.* the Evil one, the Devil.
Grac'chen, (die) *pl.* the Gracchi.
Gral, *m.* (the) Sangreal, Holy Grail. **—sage**, *f.* legend of the Holy Grail.
Graubün'd—en, *n.* the Grisons (*Swiss canton*). **—ner**, *m.*, **—nerisch**, *adj.* Grison.
Gra'velingen, *n.* Gravelines.
Gre'gor, Grego'rius, *m.* Gregory. **—ia'nisch**, *adj.* Gregorian.
Gre't—e, *f.*, **—el**, **—chen**, **—elchen**, *n.* (*dim. of* **Margarethe**) Madge, Margery, Meg, Peggy. **—chen=tasche**, *f.* chatelaine.
Grie'ch—e, *m.*, **—in**, *f.*, **—isch**, *adj.* Greek, Grecian, Hellenic. **—isch=katholisch**, *adj.* belonging to the Greek Church. **—en=land**, *n.* Greece; König von —enland, king of the Hellenes. **—en=tum**, *n.* Hellenism.
Gries'gram, *m.* Peter Grievous.
Grisel'dis, *f.* Griselda: patient Grizel.
Grön'land, *n.* Greenland. **—fahrer**, *m.* whaler.
Großbritan'nien, *n.* Great Britain.
Großer Ozean, *m.* Pacific (Ocean).
Grü'neberger, *m.* a poor wine (*from Grüneberg in Silesia*).
Grünes Vorgebirge, *n.* Cape Verde.
Grüt'li, *n. see* **Rütli**.
Gui'do, *m.* Guy.
Gün'ther, *m.* Gunther.
Gus'tav, *m.* Gustavus, Gustave. **Gusta've**, *f.*, **Gust'chen**, *n.* Gustava.

H

Haag, (der) *m.* the Hague; **er kam vom —**, he came from the Hague.
Ha'benichts, *m.*; Jungfer von —, Miss Penniless.
Ha'besch, *n.* (*for* **Abessinien**) Abyssinia.
Ha'bichtsinseln, *pl.* the Azores.
Habs'burg, *n.* Hapsburg. **—er**, *m.* a member of the Hapsburg family; die **—er**, the Hapsburg dynasty.
Hadria'n, *m.* Hadrian, Adrian.
Had'wig, *f. obs. form of* **Hedwig**.
Haff, *n.* haff, lagoon (along the Prussian shore of the Baltic and connected with the Baltic Sea).
Hain, *s.* **Hein**.
Hall—en'ser, *m.*, **—isch**, *adj.* of Halle. **—o're**, *m.* workmen at the saltworks of Halle.
Ha'meln, *n.* Hamelin; der Rattenfänger **von —**, the Pied Piper of Hamelin.
Häm'mer—lein, —ling, *m.* Puck; Meister —lein, Meister —ling, Jack Ketch; the Devil.

Hammo'nia, *poet. for* **Hamburg.**
Hann'—chen, *n.*, —e, *f.*, —ele, *n.* (*dim. of* **Johanne**) Hannah, Jane, Jenny.
Hanno'ver (*the usual pronunciation of the name of the town is* Hanno'fer), *n.* Hanover. **—a'ner**, *m.*, **Hanno'versch, Hannö'versch**, *adj.* Hanoverian.
Hans, *m.* (*pl.* Han'sen *or* Hänse) Jack. **1.** (*dim. for* **Johann**) Jack. **2.** fellow. **3.** nickname of Dutchman. **4.** Dobbin (*name for a cart-horse*). — in allen Gassen, Jack-of-all-trades, Paul Pry, busy-body; — Guck in die Luft, Johnnie Head-in-air; — hinter der Mauer, coward; — Hasenfuß, coward; — im Glück, John in luck; — oben im Dorfe, the great man, first fiddle; — Liederlich, libertine; — Narr, Tom-fool, dunce; — Ohnesorge, careless fellow; — und Grete, Jack and Jill; — und Kunz, so and so, Dick, Tom, and Harry; großer —, grand gentleman, tall fellow; die großen Hansen, (*pl.*) the big-wigs; — Dampf, blusterer, fussy coxcomb; — Sachte, slow-coach, idler; (Hans) Prahl —, John Boaster; Fasel —, driveller; Hätschel —, spoilt boy; darling boy; Schab —, curmudgeon; — bleibt —, Jack will never be a gentleman (*prov.*); was Hänschen nicht lernt' (*or* versäumt'), holt — nimmer ein, you can't teach an old dog new tricks (*prov.*); das Ding heißt —, it is all right, very well (*prov.*). **Häns'chen, Hän'sel** (*dim. of* **Hans**), *n.* Jack. **—mäßig**, *adj.* buffoon-like. **—wurst**, *m.* Jack Pudding, Merry Andrew, clown. **—wurstia'de**, *f.* buffoonery.
Han's—a, —e, *f.*, **—a=bund**, *m.* Hansa, Hanse, Hanseatic Union *or* League. **—e=stadt**, *f.* Hanse-town. **—ea't**, *m.* Hansard. **—isch** *or* **—ea'tisch**, *adj.* Hanseatic.
Han'sei, Han'sel, Hän'sel, *m.* (*n.*) (*dim. of* **Hans**) Jack, Johnnie.
Harz, *m.*, **—gebirge**, *n.* Harz Mts. **—er**, *m.* dweller in the Harz Mts.
Havan'na, *f.* Havana.
Ha'vel, (die) *f.* Havel. **—seen**, *pl.* Havel lakes.
Hebrä'—er, *m.*, **—isch**, *adj.* Hebrew.
Hebri'den, (die) *pl.* the Hebrides (*pl.*).
Hed'schra, *f.* Hegira.
Hed'wig, *f.* Hedwiga.
Hegelia'ner, *m.* Hegelian.
Heidu'ck, *m.* Heyduk, Hungarian foot-soldier.
Hein, *m.;* Freund —, Death (*coll.*).
Hein'—rich, *m.* (*dim.* —e, —i, —z) Henry, Harry, Hal. **—rich der Finkler**, Henry the Fowler. **—rich der Seefahrer**, Henry the Navigator.
He'len—a, Hele'n—e, *f.* Helen(a), Ellen, Nell(ie).
Hel'goland, *n.* Heligoland.
Hel'las, *n.* Hellas, Greece.
Helle'n—e, *m.* Hellene, Greek. **—en=volk**, *f.* Greek nation. **—isch**, *adj.* Hellenic.
Helo't(e), *m.* Helot.
Helsingö'r, *n.* Elsinore.
Helve't—ier, *m.* Helvetian, Swiss; (*pl.*) Helvetii. **—isch**, *adj.* Helvetian, Swiss.
Hen'negau, *m.* Hainault.
Hen'ning, *m.* Chanticleer (*the cock in the Beast Epic*).
He'noch, *m.* Enoch.
Henriet'te, *f.* Henrietta, Harriet, Hetty.
He'rakles, *m.* Hercules.
Herakli't, *m.* Heraclitus.
Hercy'nisch, *adj.* Hercynian, Thuringian.
Herku'lisch, *adj.* Herculean.
Her'man(n), *m.* Herman; Arminius; — der Cherusker, Arminius the Cheruscan. **—s=schlacht**, *f.* battle in the Forest of Teutoburg (*where A. defeated the Romans under Varus in the year 9 A. D.*). **—ia'de**, *f.* patriotic epic on Arminius.
Hero'des, *m.* Herod.
Herrnhu'ter, *m.*, **—isch**, *adj.* Moravian.
Hese'kiel (*4 syll.*) *m. see* **Ezechiel.**
Hes's—e, *m.* Hessian; blinder —e, person as blind as a bat; dense, stupid fellow. **—en**, *n.* Hessia, Hesse. **—en=Darmstadt**, *n.* Hesse-Darmstadt. **—en=fliege**, *f.* Hessian fly. **—isch**, *adj.* Hessian.
Heu'lemeier, *m.* Peter Grievous (*coll.*).
Heu'ne, *poet. for* **Hunne.**
Hiber'nien, *n.* Hibernia, (*poet. for*) Ireland.
Hiero'nymus, *m.* Hieronymus, Jerome.
Hie'sel, *m.* (*South Germ. dim. of* **Matthias**), Mat.
Hila'rius, *m.* Hilary.
Hil'de, —gard, *f.* Hilda.
Hin'du, *m.* Hindoo. **—stan**, *n.* Hindostan. **—isch, —a'nisch**, *adj. & n.* Hindostani.
Hin'ter—indien, *n.* Further India, Indo-China. **—pommern**, *n.* Further Pomerania. **—rhein**, *m.* the most southern of the three head streams of the Rhine.
Hinz, *m.* (*dim. of* **Heinrich**) Hal; — und Kunz, Dick, Tom, and Harry; Smith and Brown.
Hin'ze, *m.* Tom (*name of the tom-cat*).
Hi'ob, *m.* Job. **—s=bote**, *m.* bringer of bad news. **—s=post**, *f.* bad news.
Hiski'a, *m.* Hezekiah (*B.*).
Hispa'nien, *n. obs. & poet. for* **Spanien.**
Hoch'—alpen, *pl.* High Alps. **—deutsch**, *n.*, *adj.* High German. **—lande**, *pl.* (Scotch) Highlands.
Hoch'heimer, *m.* Hock (*a white Rhenish wine*).
Hohenstau'fen, *m.pl.;* Haus der —, House of Hohenstaufen, mediæval Swabian dynasty.
Hohenzol'ler—n, *n.* Hohenzollern (*country and castle*). **—n, (die)** *pl.* (*Prussian monarchs of the old Swabian*) House of (Hohen)zollern.
Hol'land, Holland; jetzt ist — in Not, now we (they) are in a nice mess, danger is impending (*prov.*).
Hol'länd—er, *m.*, **—erin**, *f.* Dutchman, Dutchwoman; der fliegende —er, the Flying Dutchman, the Phantom Ship; die —er, the Dutch. **—isch**, *adj.* Dutch. **—erei'**, *f.* Dutch farm, dairy farm. **—isches Dach**, *n.* Dutch (*hipped or Italian*) roof.
Hol'le (Frau), Lady Holle.
Hol'ste, *m.* (*obs. a high style for*) **Holsteiner.**
Hol'stein—er, *m.*, **—isch**, *adj.* of Holstein.
Home'r, *m.* Homer. **—i'de**, *m.* Homerid. **—isch**, *adj.* Homeric.
Hono'ria, Honoria, Honour.
Hora'—tier, —zier, *pl.* the Horatii.
Hora'—tius, —z, *m.* Horace. **—zisch**, Horatian.
Hose'as, *m.* Hosea (*B.*).
Hospita'liter, *m.* Knight of St. John, Hospitaller.
Hu'go, *m.* Hugo, Hugh.
Hul'de, (Hulda,) *f.* kindly spirit (*poet.*); witch, sorceress.
Hum'fried, *m.* Humphrey.
Hun'garn, *n. obs. for* **Ungarn.**
Hun'n—e, *m.* Hun. **—isch**, *adj.* Hunnish.
Huro'nensee, *m.* Lake Huron.
Hussi't, *m.* Hussite. **—en=krieg**, *m.* Hussite war.

I

Ibe'rier, *m.* Iberian; Spaniard, Portuguese.
Igna'tius, Igna'z, *m.* Ignatius.
Ilia'de, I'lias, *f.* the Iliad.
Illy'r—ier, *m.*, **—isch**, *adj.* Illyrian.
Il'se, *f.* (*dim. of* **Elisabeth**), Lizzie, Alice, Elsie, Prinzessin —, Lady *or* Princess Ilse (*personification of a stream in the Harz Mountains*).
Imma'nuel, *m. see* **Emanuel.**
In'd—er, *m.* (Asiatic) Indian, Hindoo. **—ia'ner**, *m.* (American) Red Indian. **—ien**, *n.* India; the Indies. **—ienfahrer**, *m.* East Indiaman (*ship*). **—ier**, *m.* Indian. **—(ia'n)isch**, *adj.* Indian; —ische Kompanie, East India Company.

Indo—europä'isch, —germa'nisch, *adj.* Indo-European, Indo-Germanic.
In'nocenz, *m.* Innocent.
Jo'nisch, *adj.* Ionian, Ionic; —es Meer, Ionian Sea.
I'r—e, —länder, *m.* Irishman. **—in,** *f.*, **—länderin,** *f.* Irishwoman. **—land,** *n.* Ireland. **—isch, —ländisch,** *adj.* Irish; Erse (*language*).
Iroke'se, *m.* Iroquois.
Ischa'rioth, *m.* Iscariot.
Isabel'la, *f.* Isabella, Isabel.
I'sebel, *f.* Jezebel.
I'segrim, *m.* Isengrim, Gaunt Grim (*the Wolf in the Beast Epic*); surly fellow, grumbler, bear (*fig.*).
Is'—land, *n.* Iceland. **—länder,** *m.* Icelander. **—ländisch,** *adj.* Icelandic.
Ismaeli't, *m.* Ishmaelite.
Israeli't, *m.*, **—isch,** *adj.* Israelite, Hebrew.
Ita'l—ien, *n.* Italy. **—ie'ner,** *m.*, **—ie'nerin,** *f.*, **—ie'nisch,** *adj.* Italian. **—isch,** *adj.* Italic.
It'zig, *m.* popular (contemptuous) name for a Jew.

J

Ja(h)n, *m.* **1.** *see* **Johann. 2.** fellow (*as second part of compds.*).
Ja'kob, *m.* Jacob, James, Jem(my), Jim(my); das ist der wahre —, that is the real Simon Pure (*coll.*)! **—i'ne,** *f.* Jaqueline, Jemina. **—i't,** *m.* Jacobite. **—(i't)isch,** *adj.* Jacobean, Jacobite.
Jaku'te, *m.* Yakut.
Ja'pan, Japa'n, *n.*, **—er, —e'se,** *m.* Japanese, Jap (*coll.*). **—(e's)isch,** *adj.* Japanese.
Jeanne d'Arc, *f.* Joan of Arc.
Je'men, *n.* Yemen.
Je'nisei, *m.* R. Yenisei.
Jeremi'as, *m.* Jeremiah, Jeremy, Jerry.
Jero'beam, *m.* Jeroboam.
Jesa'ia(s), *m.* Isaiah.
Je'sus, *m.* Jesus; im Namen Jesu, in Jesu's name; das Buch — Sirach, Ecclesiasticus.
Jett'—chen, *n.*, **—e,** *f.* (*dim. of* **Henriette**), Harriet, Hetty.
Jo'achim, Jo'chen, *m.* Joachim.
Jo(b)st, *m. for* **Jodo'kus.**
Jodo'k—a, *f.* Joyce. **—us,** *m.* Jocelyn, Joyce.
Joha'nn, *m.* John, Johnnie, Jack(ie), Jock.
Johan'n—a, —e, *f.* Johanna, Joan, Jane(t), Jenny, Jinny; die Päpstin —a, Pope Joan.
Johan'n—es, *m.* John; der heilige —es, St. John; —es der Täufer, John the Baptist. **—is=beere,** *f.* currant. **—is=fest,** *n.*, **—is=tag,** *m.* Midsummer Day. **—i'ter,** *m.* Knight of St. John, Hospitaller.
Jo'na(s), *m.* Jonah; das Buch —, the book of Jonah.
Jop'pe, *n.* Joppa, Jaffa.
Jörg, *m.* (*dim. of* **Georg**) Georgie.
Jörn, *m. see* **Jürgen.**
Jo'saphat, *m.* Jehoshaphat.
Jo's—ef, —eph, *m.* Joseph, Joe(y). **—e'pha, —efe, —ephi'ne,** *f.* Josephine.
Jo'sias, *m.* Josiah.
Jost (*long* o), *m.* Jocelyn.
Jo'sua, *m.* Josh(ua), Jos.
Ju'da, *m.* Judah. **—ismus,** *m.* Judaism.
Judä'a, *n.* Judæa.
Ju'das, *m.* Judas, Jude; einem den armen — singen, to scold a p. thoroughly for his faithlessness (*coll., obs.*). **—kuß,** *m.* traitor's kiss. **—schweiß,** *m.* extreme anguish *or* remorse.
Ju'd—e, *m.* Jew; der ewige —e, the Wandering Jew. **Jü'din,** *f.* Jewess. **Jü'disch,** *adj.* Jewish. **Erz—e,** *m.* Hebrew Jew. **—en=christ,** *m.* convert from Judaism. **—en=deutsch,** *n.* Jewish slang. **—en=genosse,** *m.* Jewish proselyte. **—en=gasse,** *f.*, **—en=viertel,** *n.* Jewry. **—en=schaft,** *f.* Jewish community, the Jews. **—en=staat,** *m.* state governed by Jews. **—entum,** *n.* Judaism, Jewishness.
Ju'l—e, *f.*, **—chen,** *n.*, **—ia'ne, —ie, —iet'te,** *f.* Julia, Juliet, Gilian, Gil(l), Jill, Juliana.
Ju'lische Alpen, *pl.* Julian Alps.
Ju'lius, *m.* Julius, Jule.
Juno'nisch, *adj.* Juno-like.
Jür'g—(en), Jörn, *m. see* **Georg.**
Jü't—e, *m.*, **—in,** *f.* **—länder,** *m.*, **—länderin,** *f.* Jute. **—land,** *n.* Jutland.
Jut't—a, —e, *f.* (*for* **Johanna**) Janet, Joan.

K

Kad'mos, *n.* Cadmus.
Kaf'f—er, *m.* Kaffir. **—ern=land,** *n.* Kaffraria. **—risch,** *adj.* Kaffrarian.
Ka'in, *m.* Cain. **—s=zeichen,** *n.* mark of Cain.
Kai'phas, *m.* Caiaphas.
Kalabre's—e, *m.*, **—isch,** *adj.* Calabrian, Calabrese. **—er,** *m.* (Calabrian) broad-brimmed hat, slouched hat.
Kala'brien, *n.* Calabria.
Kaledo'nisch, *adj.* Caledonian, Scottish.
Kali'f, *m.* Khalifa, Caliph. **—a't,** *n.* Caliphate.
Kalifor'n—ien, *n.*, California. **—ier,** *m.*, **—isch,** *adj.* Californian.
Kalmü'cken, (die) *pl.* Calmucks, Kalmucks.
Kalva'rienberg, *m.* Mt. Calvary.
Kameru'n, *n.* Kamerun, the Cameroons.
Kamtschada'l—e, *m.*, **—in,** *f.* Kamchatkan, inhab. of Kamchatka.
Ka'na, *n.*; Simon von —, Simon the Canaanite.
Ka'n—aan, *n.* Canaan. **—ani'ter,** *m.* Canaanite. **—anä'isch, —ani'tisch,** *adj.* Canaanitish.
Kana'd—ier, *m.*, **—isch,** *adj.* Canadian.
Kana'l, *m.* the (English) Channel.
Kana'r—ien=sekt, *m.* canary (wine). **—ien=vogel,** *m.* canary(-bird). **Die —ischen Inseln,** *pl.* the Canary Islands, the Canaries.
Kap—kolonie, *f.*, **—land,** *n.* Cape Colony. **—stadt,** *f.* Cape Town.
Kaper'naum (*4 syll.*); der Hauptmann von —, the centurion (at Capernaum).
Kapito'l(ium), *n.* the Capitol.
Karai'b—e (*4 syllables*), *m.* Carib(bee). **—isch,** *adj.* Caribbean.
Karl, *m.*, **—chen,** *n.*, Charles, (Charlie); — der Große, Charlemagne. **—i'st,** *m.*, **—i'stisch,** *adj.* Carlist. **—mann,** *m.* Carloman(n).
Karmeli'ter, *m.* Carmelite *or* White friar.
Kärn't—en, (*obs.* **Kärn'then,**) *n.* Carinthia. **—ner,** *m.*, **—nerisch,** *adj.* Carinthian.
Karoli'ne, *f.* Caroline, Carrie.
Ka'roling—er, *m.*, **—isch,** *adj.* Carolingian, Carlovingian.
Karpa'then, (die) *pl.* Carpathian Mts.
Kartha'g—o, *n.*, Carthage. **—er,** *m.*, **—isch,** *adj.* Carthaginian.
Kart(h)äu'ser(mönch), *m.* Carthusian friar.
Kasch'mir, *n.* Cashmere.
Kas'p—ar, *m.*, **—er,** *n.* Jasper, Gaspard. **—erle,** *dim.* Jack Pudding. **—erle=theater,** *n.* Punch and Judy show; —erle und Kätchen, Punch and Judy.
Kas'pische(s) Meer, *n.* Caspian Sea.
Kas'sel, *n.* Cassel; ab nach —, go to Jericho! (*coll.*) (*alluding to Napoleon the Third's imprisonment at Wilhelmshöhe near Kassel*).
Kasti'l—ien, *n.* Castile. **—i(a'n)er,** *m.*, **(—ia'n=)isch,** *adj.* Castilian.
Katalo'n—ier, *m.*, **—isch,** *adj.* Catalan.
Kät(h)'—chen, *n.*, **—e,** *f.* (*dim. of* **Katharina**), Kate, Kitty.
Kath—ari'na, —(a)ri'ne, *f.* Katherine, Catherine, Kate, Katie, Kit(ty), Kathleen.

Katilina'risch, *adj.* Catilinarian; die —e Verschwörung, the conspiracy of Catiline.
Kau'derwelsch, *adj.* argot, Romany; gibberish.
Kauka's—ier, *m.*, **—isch**, *adj.* Caucasian.
Kau'kasus, *m.* Caucasus Mts.
Kel't—e, Cel't—e, *m.* Kelt, Celt. **—isch**, *adj.* Keltic, Celtic.
Keltibe'r—ier, *m.*, **—isch**, *adj.* Celtiberian.
Kirgi's—e, *m.*, **—in**, *f.*, **—isch**, *adj.* Kirghiz.
Kla'ra, *f.*, *dim.* **Klär'chen**, *n.*, **Klä're**, *f.* Clara, Clar(ri)e.
Kla(u)s, *m.*, *see* Nikolas.
Klein—a'sien, *n.* Asia Minor. **—rußland**, *n.* Little Russia. **—städter**, *m.* inhab. of small provincial town, Gothamite.
Kle'mens, Cle'mens, *m.* Clement.
Kleo'patra, *f.* Cleopatra.
Kleve, *n.* Cleves.
Knut, *m.* Canute.
Ko'blenz, *n.* Coblence.
Köln, Cöln, *n.* Cologne. **—er**, *m.* inhab. of C. **—isches Wasser**, *n.*, **—er-wasser**, *n.* eau-de-Cologne.
Kolos'ser, *pl.* the Colossians.
Kolum'bien, *n.* Colombia.
Konfut'se, *m.* Confucius.
Königsgrä'tz, *n.* Sadowa; Schlacht bei —, battle of Sadowa.
Kon'rad, (*older* **Kun'rad**,) *m.* Conrad; der arme —, name of a (XVIth cent.) Peasants' League. **—in**, *m.* Conradine.
Konstan'tia, *f.* Constance, Connie.
Kon'stantin(—us), *m.* Constantine. **—o'pel**, *f.* Constantinople. **—opolita'ner**, *m.*, **—opolita'nisch**, *adj.* Constantinopolitan.
Kon'stanz, *n.* Constance (*town*).
Konstan'ze, *f.* Constance, Connie.
Kop't—e, *m.*, **—isch**, *adj.* Coptic.
Kordille'ren, (die) *pl.* the Cordilleras, *pl.*
Kor'd—ova, *n.* Cordova. **—ua'nisch**, *adj.* Cordovan. **—uan**, *m.*, **—uan-leder**, *n.* Spanish leather, cordwain.
Korin'th—er, *m.*, **—isch**, *adj.* Corinthian.
Korne'lie, *f.* Cornelia.
Kor's—e, *m.* Corsican; Napoleon I. **—ika**, *n.* Corsica. **—ika'ner**, *m. see* **—e**.
Kosa'k, *m.*, **—isch**, *adj.* Cossack.
Kost'nitz (*obs. for* **Konstanz**), *n.* Constance (*the town*); —er See, Lake of Constance.
Kräh'wink—el, *n.* name given to an imaginary provincial town, Gotham; (Muggleton-on-Swamp). **—ler**, *m.* Gothamite, Muggletonian. **—elei'**, *f.* foolish proceedings; vestry-politics; der —ler Landsturm, militia of Gotham, poor soldiery.
Kra'in (*2 syllables*), *n.* Carniola.
Kra'kau, *n.* Cracow. **—er**, *m.*, **—isch**, *adj.* Cracovian.
Krat'zefuß (Frau), *f.* Dame Partlet (*hen in the Beast Epic*).
Kreml, *m.* the Kremlin.
Kre't—a, *n.* Crete, Candia. **—er, —en'ser**, *m.* Cretan. **—isch**, *adj.* Cretan.
Kre'thi und Ple'thi, *pl.* the Cherethites and Pelethites (*David's body-guard*); rag-tag and bob-tail.
Krim, (die) *f.* Crimea; in der —, in the Crimea. **—krieg**, *m.* Crimean war. **—mer**, *m.* Crimean lambskin, astrakan.
Kroa't—e, Croa't, *m.*, **—ien**, *n.* Croatia. **—isch**, *adj.* Croatian.
Krö'sus, *m.* Crœsus.
Kunigun'de, *f.* Cunegund.
Kunz, Kuo'ni, *m.* (*dim. of* **Kunrad, Konrad**) Conrad.
Kur—bayern, *n.* Electorate of Bavaria. **—hessen**, *n.* Electorate of Hesse. **—land**, *n.* Courland. **—pfalz**, *f.* the Palatinate. **—sachsen**, *n.* Electorate of Saxony.
Kurt, *m.* (*dim. of* **Kunrad, Konrad**) Conrad.
Kyff'häuser, *m.* Kyffhauser (*hill between the Harz and Thuringian mountains*).

L

La'ban, *m.*; ein langer —, a tall fellow.
Lacedämo'n—ier, *m.*, **—isch**, *adj.* Lacedæmonian.
Lam'brecht, Lam'precht, *m.* Lambert.
Lam'pe, *m.* Puss (*the Hare in the Beast Epic*).
Lap'p—e, *m.*, **—isch**, *adj.* Lap(p); Lappish, Laplandish. **—land**, *n.* Lapland. **—ländisch**, *adj.* Lapp.
Latei'n(—isch), *adj.* Latin; —ische Buchstaben, Roman characters; —(ische) Schule, grammar school; —isches Segel, lateen sail; —ische Spracheigentümlichkeit, Latinism; —ische Volkssprache, Vulgar Latin, Low Latin. **—er**, *m.* inhab. of Latium, Latin; Latin scholar; Roman Catholic (*obs.*).
Lati'n—er, *m.* inhab. of Latium. **—i'st**, *m.* Latinist, Latin scholar.
Lauren'tius, *m.*; der heilige —, St. Lawrence.
Lau'sitz, (die) *f.* Lusatia. **—er**, *m.*, **—isch**, *adj.* Lusatian.
Lea, *f.* Leah.
Leipzig, *n.* Leipsic.
Len'chen (*long* e), *n.* (*dim. of* **Helene, Magdalene**) Nellie.
Leno're, Leono're, *f.* Leonora, Eleanor, Nora(h), Ellen, Nell(ie).
Leon'hard, *m.* Leonard, Len(nie).
Let't—e, *m.* Lett. **—isch**, *adj.* Lettic.
Levan't—e, (die) *f.* the Levant. **—isch**, *adj.* Levantine.
Levi't, *m.* Levite. **—isch**, *adj.* Levitical.
Li, *f.* (*dim. of* **Elisabeth**) Lizzie.
Li'banon, *m.* Mount Lebanon; Zedern des —, cedars of Lebanon.
Li'bysch, *adj.* Libyan.
Lies'—chen, *n.*, **—e, —el**, *f.* (*dim. of* **Elisabeth**) Lizzie.
Li'ga, *f.* the (Catholic) League (17th century).
Lil(l)i, *f.* (*for* **Elise, Liesbeth**) Lilian, Lilias, Lil(y), Lizzie.
Li'n—a, *f.*, **—chen**, *n.* (*dim. of* **Karoline**) Carrie.
Links'rheinisch, *adj.* on the left bank of the Rhine.
Lipa'rische Inseln, *pl.* Lipari Islands.
Lips, *m.* (*dim. of* **Philipp(us)**) Phil.
Li's—(a)beth, *f.*, **—chen**, *n.*, **—et'te**, *f.* (*dim. of* **Elisabeth**) Lizzie.
Lissabo'n, *n.* Lisbon.
Li'tau—en, (*obs.* **Lithauen**) *n.* Lithuania. **—er**, *m.*, **—isch**, *adj.* Lithuanian.
Liut'pold, *m.* Leo(pold).
Li'vius, *m.* Livy.
Liv'—land, *n.* Livonia. **—länder**, *m.* Livonian. **—ländisch**, *adj.* Livonian.
Livor'no, *n.* Leghorn.
Lofo'ten, *pl.* Lofoden Islands.
Lo'(lo), *f.* (*dim. of* **Lotte, Charlotte**) Lottie.
Lombar'd—e, *m.* Lombard. **—ei'**, (die) *f.* Lombardy. **—isch**, *adj.* Lombard.
Lon'doner, *adj.* of London; — Stadtkind, cockney; — Spracheigenheit, cockneyism; — Stadtbahn, metropolitan railway.
Longobar'd—e, *m.*, **—isch**, *adj.* Lombard, Langobard.
Lor'—chen (*long* o), *n.*, **—e**, *f.* (*dim. of* **Lenore**) Eleanor.
Lo'relei, *f.* Lorelei (*a siren who haunted a dangerous rock of the same name on the right bank of the Rhine, between Bingen and Koblenz*).
Lo'renz, Laurence. **—strom**, *m.* St. Lawrence River.
Lotha'r, *m.* Lothario, Lothair.
Loth'ring—en, *n.* Lorraine. **—er**, *m.*, **—isch**, *adj.* Lothringian.
Lott'—chen, *n.*, **—e**, *f.* (*dim. of* **Charlotte**) Lottie.

Lö'wen, *n.* Louvain.
Lö'wenherz, *m.* Richard the Lion-hearted, Cœur de Lion.
Lübisch, *adj.* of Lubeck.
Lu'cas, *m. see* Lukas.
Lu'dolf, *m.* Ludolphus.
Ludovi'ca, *f.* Louisa, Lou(ie), Lu.
Lud'wig, *m.* Lewis, Louis.
Luga'nersee, *m.* Lake Lugano.
Lui'se, *f.* Louisa.
Lu'kas, *m.* Lucas, Luke; der heilige —, St. Luke. **—evangelium**, *n.* Gospel according to St. Luke.
Lukre'tia, *f.* Lucrece, Lucretia.
Lukre'tius, *m.* Lucretius.
Lur'lei, *f. see* Lorelei.
Lusita'nien, *n.* Lusitania, Portugal.
Luthera'ner, *m.* Lutheran.
Luthe'risch, **Lu'ther(i)sch**, *adj.* Lutheran.
Lu'thertum, *n.* Lutheranism.
Lüt'tich, *n.* Liege.
Luze'rn, *n.* Lucerne.
Lu'zie, *f.* Lucy.
Lyo'n, *n.* Lyons. **—er, —e'se(r)**, *ri.* inhabitant of Lyons.

M

Mäan'der, *m.* R. Meander.
Maas, *f.* R. Meuse.
Macchiavelli'st, *m.*, **—isch**, *adj.* Machiavellian.
Macedo'n—ier, *m.*, **—isch**, *adj.* Macedonian.
Madegas'se, *m.* Malagasy, Madagascan.
Magdale'n—a, —e, *f.* Magdalen(e), Maudlin, Madeleine, Maud. **—en=stift**, *n.* Magdalen-asylum.
Ma'gier, *pl.* the Magi.
Magya'risch, *adj.* Magyar.
Mahl'strom, *m.* Maelstrom.
Ma'homed, *m. see* Mahomet, Mohammed.
Mahrat'te, *m.* Mahratta. **—n=staaten**, *pl.* Mahratta States.
Mäh'r—e, *m.* Moravian. **—en**, *n.* Moravia. **—isch**, *adj.* Moravian; das —ische Gesenke, the Moravian mountains.
Mai'land, *n.* Milan.
Mai'länd—er, *m.*, **—isch**, *adj.* Milanese.
Main, *m.* R. Main. **—linie**, *f.* the line of the Main roughly dividing Germany into a northern and a southern half; südlich der —linie, South German.
Mainz, *n.* Mayence.
Makkabä'er, (die) *pl.* the Maccabees.
Malai'—e, *m.*, **—isch**, *adj.* Malay, Malayan.
Mal'chen (*long* a), *f.* (*dim. of* **Amalie**), Amelia.
Malea'chi, Malachi (*B.*).
Maledi'ven, *pl.* Maldive Islands, the Maldives.
Mal't—a, *n.* Malta; von —a, Maltese. **—e'ser**, *m.*, **—esisch**, *adj.* Maltese.
Mamelu'ck, *m.* Mameluke.
Manches'ter—tum, *n.* Manchester school (*of free traders*). **—theorie**, *f.* theory of free trade.
Mandschur—ei', (die) *f.* Manchuria. **—isch** (*pron.* mandschu'risch), *adj.* Manchurian.
Manichä'er, *m.* Manichee.
Marg(a)re'te, *f.* Margaret, Margery, Marjory, Mag(gie), Meg, Madge, Peg(gy).
Mär'gen, Mer'gen, *n.* (*dial. for* **Marien**), Mary (*in* St. Märgen, *and other S. German names*).
Mari'a, *f. see* Marie; die blutige —, Bloody Mary; — There'sia, Maria Theresa.
Marian'ne, *f.* Marian, Mary Ann.
Marie', *f.*, **—chen**, *n.* Mary, May, Moll(y), Poll(y).
Mark, (die) *f.* the March; — Brandenburg, (march of) Brandenburg.
Mär'k—er, *m.* inhab. of the mark Brandenburg. **—isch**, *adj.* belonging to the electorate of Brandenburg; **die —ische Schweiz**, hills N.E. of Berlin.

Mar'kus, *m.* Mark. **—evangelium**, *n.* Gospel according to St. Mark.
Mar'marameer, *n.* Sea of Marmora.
Marokka'n—er, *m.* Moor (of Morocco). **—isch**, *adj.* Moorish.
Marok'ko, *n.* Morocco.
Marseil'le, *n.* Marseilles.
Märt'—chen, —el, *n.* (*dim. of* **Martha**), Matty, Patty.
Mär'ten, Mer'ten, *m. dial. for* **Martin**.
Mar'th—a, —e, *f.* Martha, Matty, Patty.
Mar'tins—fest, *n.* Martinmas. **—abend**, *m.* St. Martin's eve (*Nov. 10*). **—gans**, *f.* Martinmas goose. **—korn**, *n.* ergot. **—tag**, *m. or* **Marti'ni**, *m.* St. Martin's day (*Nov. 11*). **—vogel**, *m.* St. Martin's bird, goose.
Mas'tricht (*long* a), *n.* Maestricht.
Mathil'de, *f.* Matilda, Tilda.
Matth—ä'us, —i'as, *m.* Matthew, Mat.
Matz, *m.*, **Mätz'chen**, *n.* (*dim. of* **Matthäus, Matthias, Matthes**), Mat; Dicky (bird).
Mau'r—e, *m.*, **—isch**, *adj.* Moorish; —ische Sprache, Morisco.
Me'chel—n, *n.* Mechlin, Malines; —er Spitzen, (*pl.*) Mechlin lace.
Mecht'hild(e), *f.* (*obs.*) *for* **Mathilde**.
Me'd—er, *m.* Mede. **—isch**, *adj.* Median.
Medice'ische Venus, *f.* Venus of Medici.
Meer'busen, *m.* gulf; arabischer —, gulf of Arabia; der persische —, the Gulf of Persia; der — von Biscaya, the Bay of Biscay.
Mei'dinger (*writer of a French grammar full of anecdotes*), Joe Miller (*a hackneyed story*).
Mei'ninger, *pl.* actors of the Duke of Meiningen.
Mei'ßen, *n.* Meissen, Misnia. **—er, Meiß'ner**, *m.* Misnian; —er Deutsch, Misnian German; —er Porzellan, Dresden china. **—isch, Meiß'nisch**, *adj.* Misnian.
Merku'r, *m.* Mercury.
Mer'lin der Wilde, Merlin of the Wood.
Me'rowing—er, *m.*, **—isch**, *adj.* Merovingian; die —ischen Herrscher, the Merovingians.
Messi'as, *m.* Messiah.
Messi'na=Apfelsine, *f.* blood-orange.
Me'ta, *f.* (*dim. of* **Margareta**), Peggy.
Methu'salem, *m.* Methuselah; das ist so alt wie —, that is as old as Methuselah *or* the hills.
Met'ze, *f.* (*obs. dim. of* **Mathilde**), Mattie, Matty, Meg, Peg, Tilly.
Meyer, Müller, und Schulze, Brown, Jones, and Robinson.
Mi'cha, *m.* Micah (*B.*).
Mi'chael, Michel, *m.* Michael, Mick(y), Mike; der deutsche —, plain honest German; nickname for a typical German (*cp. John Bull*); grober —, rude fellow (*coll.*).
Mie'k—e, *f.*, **—chen**, *n.* (*dim. of* **Marie**), May, Polly, Poll, Molly, Moll.
Miez'(chen), *n.* Puss(y), name of cat.
Mie'ze, *f.* (*dim. of* **Marie**), *see* **Mieke**.
Mi'mi, *f.* (*dim. of* **Emilie**), Millie.
Mi'n—a, *f.*, **—chen**, *n.* (*dim. of* **Mina, Wilhelmine**), Minnie.
Mit'tel—asien, *n.* Central Asia. **—euro'pa**, *n.* Central Europe. **—europä'isch**, *adj.* Central European; —europäische Zeit, time of the Middle European zone. **—hochdeutsch**, *adj.* Middle High German. **—ländisches Meer**, *n.* Mediterranean (Sea).
Mo'ham(m)ed, *m.* Mahomet.
Mohika'ner, *m.* Mohican.
Mohr, *m.* Moor. **—in**, *f.* Moorish woman, negress. **—en=fürst**, *m.* Moorish prince. **—en=land**, *n.* Ethiopia.
Mok'ka, *n.* Mocha.
Mol'dau, (die) *f.* Moldavia. **—er**, *m.*, **—isch**, *adj.* Moldavian.
Moluk'ken, (die) *pl.* the Moluccas.
Mond'gebirge, *n.* Mountains of the Moon.

Mongol—ei', (die) *f.* Mongolia. **—isch** (*pron.* mongo'lisch), *adj.* Mongolian.
Mor'genland, *n.* East, Orient.
Mo'ritz, *m.* Maurice, Morris.
Mo'sel, *f.* Moselle. **—a'ner,** *m.* inhabitant of the banks of the Moselle.
Mo'ses, *m.* Moses; — und die Propheten haben, to be wealthy (*coll.*).
Mos'k—au, *n.* Moscow. **—owi't(er),** *m.*, **—owi'tisch,** *adj.* Muscovite.
Mos'lem, *m.* (*pl.* —in) Moslem, Mussulman.
Mö'sogot—e, *m.* Mœso-Goth, Mœsogoth.
Mu'hamed, *m.* Mahomet, Mohammed. **—a'ner,** *m.*, **—a'nisch,** *adj.* Mahometan, Mohammedan.
Mulat't—e, *m.* mulatto. **—in,** *f.* mulattress.
Mül'hausen, *n.* Mulhausen.
Mün'ch—en, *n.* Munich. **—ner,** *n.* inhabitant of Munich; (*short for*) Munich beer.
Mur'ner, *m.* Tom-cat.
Mu'selmann, *m.*, **Mu'selmännin,** *f.*, **Mu'selmännisch,** *adj.* Moslem, Mussulman.
Myke'nisch, *adj.* Mycenæan.

N

Nann—et'te, —i, *f.* (*dim. of* **Anna**), Nancy.
Na'seweis, *m.* Jack Sauce; Jungfer —, Miss Pert.
Nasirä'er, *m.* Nazarite.
Natha'nael, *m.* Nathaniel, Nat.
Nazar—ä'er, *m.*, **—e'nisch,** *adj.* Nazarene.
Na'zi, *m.* (*dim. of* **Ignatius**), Ignatius.
Nea'pel, *n.* Naples.
Nebukadne'zar, *m.* Nebuchadnezzar.
Ne'ger, *m.* negro. **—in,** *f.* negress.
Neme'isch, *adj.* Nemean.
Ne'pomuk, der heilige —, St. John of Nepomuk; **heiliger —!** good gracious!
Ner'vier, (die) *pl.* the Nervii.
Nett'chen, *n.* (*dim. of* **Annette**), Nancy.
Neu'enburg, *n.* Neuchatel.
Neu—fu'ndland, *n.* Newfoundland. **—hol'land,** *n.* Australia, New Holland (*obs.*). **—see'land,** *n.* New Zealand. **—schott'land,** *n.* Nova Scotia. **—südwa'les,** *n.* New South Wales.
Ni'belunge, *pl.* the Nibelungs. **—n-hort,** *m.* Nibelung treasure. **—en-lied,** *n.* Lay of the Nibelungs. **Der** (*gen. pl.*) **—e Not,** *f.* tragedy *or* tragical end of the Nibelungs; also an alternative name for Nibelungenlied.
Nic—ä'a, *n.* Nicea. **—ä'isches** *or* **—e'nisches Glaubensbekenntnis,** *n.* Nicene creed.
Nie'der—deutsch, *n.* Low German. **—deutschland,** *n.* Lower *or* North Germany. **—lande,** *pl.* Netherlands; Low Countries. **—länder,** *m.* Dutchman; Netherlander (*obs.*). **—rhein,** *m.* Lower Rhine. **—sachsen,** *n.* Lower Saxony. **—wald-Denkmal,** *n.* monument of Germania on the Niederwald near Rüdesheim.
Ni'kola(u)s, *m.* Nicholas, Nick; **der heilige —,** Santa Claus.
Nil, *m.* R. Nile. **—pferd,** *n.* hippopotamus.
Nim'wegen, *n.* Nimeguen.
Ni'nive, *n.* Nineveh.
Nir'gendheim, *n.* Nowhere, Utopia.
Niz'za, *n.* Nice.
Noachi'den, *pl.* descendants of Noah.
No'bel, *m.* Noble (*the Lion in the Beast Epic*).
Nord'deutscher Bund, *m.* North German Confederation (1866–1871).
Nord'häuser, *m.* German whiskey (*from* **Nordhausen**).
Nor'd—isch, *adj.* Norse, Northern. **—mann,** (*poet.*) *m.* Norseman.
Nord'kap, *n.* North Cape. **—see,** *f.* North Sea, German Ocean.
Normandie', (die) *f.* Normandy.
Norman'n—e, *m.*, **—isch,** *adj.* Norman; **die —ischen Inseln,** the Channel Islands.
Nor'weg—en, *n.* Norway. **—er,** *m.*, **—isch,** *adj.* Norwegian.
Nu'b—ier, *m.*, **—isch,** *adj.* Nubian.
Numi'dische Jungfrau, *f.* Numidian crane.
Nürn'berg, *n.* Nuremberg; **—er Spiel-sachen** (-waren), (*pl.*) German toys; **—er Trichter,** Nuremberg filter (for pouring in knowledge), (hence:) any method of instruction which does not presuppose any exertion on the part of the learner (*orig. title of book professing to teach the Art of Poetry in 6 hours*).

O

Oba'd—ias, —ja, *m.* Obadiah (*B.*).
O'ber—ägypten, *n.* Upper Egypt. **—bayern,** *n.* Upper Bavaria. **—deutschland,** *n.* Upper Germany (*mountainous part, south of the Main*). **—italien,** *n.* North Italy. **—österreich,** *n.* Upper Austria. **—sachsen,** *n.* Kingdom of Saxony, (Upper) Saxony.
O'derbruch, *m.* low fertile country along the western bank of the Oder from **Lebus** to **Schwedt.**
Odyssee', *f.* Odyssey.
O'fen, *n.* Buda; **Ofen-Pesth,** Buda-Pesth.
Öl'berg, *m.* Mount of Olives.
O'livier, *m.* Oliver, Noll.
Oly'mp, *m.* Mt. Olympus. **—ia'de,** *f.* space of 4 years, Olympiad.
Ora'nien, *m.* Orange.
Oran'je-Freistaat, *m.* Orange Free State, (*now*) Orange River Colony.
Ore'st, *m.* Orestes.
Ori'genes, *m.* Origen.
Ork—a'den, *pl.*, **—a'dische Inseln, Ork'ney-Inseln,** *pl.* Orkney Islands, Orcades (*obs.*).
Os'kar, *m.* Oscar; **frech wie —,** very insolent, most impudent (*sl.*); devil-may-care (*sl.*).
Osma'n—e, *m.*, **—isch,** *adj.* Ottoman; **—isches Reich,** Ottoman empire.
O'st-angeln, *n.* East Anglia.
Ost—a'sien, *n.* Eastern Asia, the Far East. **—asia'tisch,** *adj.* in *or* for the Far East. **—en'de,** *n.* Ostend. **—frie'se,** *m.*, **—friesin,** *f.*, **—friesisch,** *adj.* East Frisian. **—fries'land,** *n.* East Frisian. **—gote,** *m.* East Goth, Ostrogoth. **—in'dien,** *n.* the East Indies, *pl.* **—indischer Archipel,** *m.* the Malay Archipelago. **—indische Kompanie,** *f.* East India Company. **—see,** *f.* the Baltic (Sea). **—see-provinzen,** *pl.* Baltic provinces.
Ö'st(er)reich, *n.*, Austria. **—er,** *m.*, **—isch,** *adj.* Austrian. **—-Ungarn,** *n.* Austria-Hungary. **—isch-ungarisch,** Austro-Hungarian.
Otahai't—ier, *m.*, **—isch,** *adj.* Tahitian.
Otran'to, *n.*; **Straße von —,** Straits of Otranto.
Ottoma'n—e, *m.*, **—isch,** *adj.* Ottoman, Turk(ish).
O'zean, *m.*; **Großer** (*or* **Stiller**) **—,** Pacific (Ocean).
Ozea'nien, *n.* Oceania, Australasia.
Ozea'nier, *m.* South Sea Islander.

P

Palästi'n—a, *n.* Palestine. **—en'sisch,** *adj.* Palestinian.
Pa'li, *n.* Pehlevi (*ancient Persian dial.*).
Pari's, *n.* Paris (*city*). **Pa'ris,** *m.* Paris (*of Troy*). **—er,** *m.*, **—erin,** *f.*, **—isch,** *adj.* Parisian. **—er Bluthochzeit,** *f.* (*Massacre of*) St. Bartholomew's Eve, 1572; **klein —,** Leipzig (*poet.*).
Parna'ß, *m.* Parnassus.
Pa'r—os, *n.* (*island of*) Paros. **—isch,** *adj.* Parian (*marble*), of Paros.
Par'se, *m.* Parsee.
Par'th—er, *m.*, **—isch,** *adj.* Parthian.
Par'zen, (die) *pl.* the Parcæ, Fates.
Par'zival, *m.* Percival.
Pas'sah, *n.* Passover.
Passat'winde, *pl.* trade-winds.
Patago'n—e, —ier, *m.*, **—isch,** *adj.* Patagonian.
Patri'cius, *m.* Patrick, Pat, Paddy.

Pauli'ne, *f.* Paulina.
Pau'l(us), *m.* Paul. (die) **—i'nischen Briefe**, *pl.* Pauline epistles, Epistles of St. Paul.
Pelas'ger, *pl.* the Pelasgians.
Peloponne's, *m.* Peloponnese.
Pend'schab, *n.* Punjab.
Pe'pi, *m.* (*dim. of* **Joseph**) Joe.
Per's—er, *m.*, **—isch**, *adj.* Persian.
Pe'ter, *m.*, **—chen**, *n.* Peter, Pete, Peterkin, Perkin; dummer —, Peter Simple, Simple Simon; langweiliger —, a bore; schwarzer —, Black Peter *or* Old Maid (*card game*). **—s=kirche**, *f.* St. Peter's (*Rome*). **—s=pfennige**, *pl.* Peter's pence. **—s=vogel**, *m.* Mother Carey's chicken.
Petrar'ca, *m.* Petrarch.
Pe'trus, *m. see* Peter; house-key, latch-key (*sl.*).
Petz, *m.* (*dim. of* **Bernhard**), Bruin (*the Bear*).
Pfalz, (die) *f.* the Palatinate; Kurfürst von der —, Elector Palatine. **Pfäl'zer**, *m.* inhab. of the Palatinate. **Pfäl'zisch**, *adj.* of the Palatinate, Palatine. **—graf**, *m.* Count Palatine, Palsgrave.
Pfef'fer—küste, *f.* Grain Coast. **—land**, *n.* Jericho (*hum.*).
Pforte, (die Hohe —) *f.* the (Sublime) Porte.
Pha'rao, *m.* Pharaoh.
Phi'lipp, *m.* Philip, Phil. **—er** (Philip'per), Philippians. **—i'ne**, *f.* Philippa. **—ika** (*pron.* Philip'=pika), *f.* Philippic. **—o'pel**, *n.* Philippopolis.
Philis't—er, *m.* Philistine; philistine, townsman (*opp. to student*); uncultured person. **—erei'**, *f.* philistinism, narrow-mindedness. **—erhaft**, **—rö's**, *adj.* narrow-minded.
Philome'le, *f.* Philomela; nightingale.
Phö'be, *f.* Phœbe, the moon.
Phöni'z—ier, *m.*, **—isch**, *adj.* Phœnician.
Pi'emont, *n.* Piedmont. **—e'se**, *m.*, **—e'sisch**, *adj.* Piedmontese.
Pik'te, *m.* Pict. **—n=wall**, *m.* Picts' Wall.
Pila'tus, *m.* Pilate; Pilatus (*a Swiss mountain*).
Pipi'n, *m.* Pepin.
Plato'ni—ker, *m.* Platonist. **—sch**, *adj.* Platonic.
Platt'deutsch, *adj.* Low German.
Pli'nius, *m.* Pliny.
Po, *m.* the River Po.
Pola'ck—e, *m.*, *see* Pole; Polish horse. **—ei'**, *f.* (*obs. & hum.*) *see* Polen.
Polar'kreis, *m.*; nördlicher —, Arctic Circle; südlicher —, Antarctic Circle.
Po'l—e, *m.* Pole. **—en**, *n.* Poland. **—nisch** (*pron.* pol'nisch, *short* o), *adj.* Polish; der —nische Bock, the rack; ein —nischer Reichstag, eine —nische Wirtschaft, disorderly doings, riot and confusion, Donnybrook fair.
Polichine'll, *m.* Punchinello.
Pom'mer, *m.* Pom(m)eranian; Pomeranian dog; thick-set fellow; piece of good luck (*sl.*); der hat —, he is a lucky fellow (*sl.*). **—n**, *n.* Pomerania.
Pompe'j—us, *m.* Pompey. **—a'ner**, *m.*, **—a'nisch**, *adj.* Pompeian. **—i**, Pompeii.
Ponti'nisch, *adj.* Pontine.
Pon'tius; von — zu Pilatus laufen, to be sent from pillar to post.
Portugie's—e, *m.*, **—isch**, *adj.* Portuguese.
Prag, *n.* Prague. **—er**, *m.* inhab. of Prague; Bohemian musician (*obs.*).
Prämonstraten'ser, *m.* Premonstrant (monk).
Preu'ß—e, *m.* Prussian. **—en**, *n.* Prussia. **—entum**, *n.* Prussianism **—isch**, *adj.* Prussian.
Pri'amus, *m.* Priam.
Proko'p, *m.* Procopius.
Prote'isch, *adj.* Protean.
Provenza'l—e, *m.*, **—in**, *f.* Provençal. **—isch**, *adj.* Provençal.
Ptolomä'us, *m.* Ptolemy.
Py'thisch, *adj.* Pythian.
Pyrenä'—en, *pl.* Pyrenees, *pl.* **—isch**, *adj.*; —ische Halbinsel, Iberian peninsula.
Pyr'rhus=sieg, *m.* Pyrrhic victory.

Q

Quichot't—e, **Quijo't—e**, *m.* Quixote. **—isch**, *adj.* Quixotic.
Quinti'n, *n.* Quentin.

R

Ra'benschlacht, *f.* Battle of Ravenna (*poet.*).
Radschpu'te, *m.* Rajput.
Ra'hel, *f.* Rachel.
Rai'mund, *m.* Raymond.
Raub'staaten, *pl.* Barbary States (in North Africa).
Rau'schebart, *m. see* Eberhard.
Rebek'ka, *f.* Rebecca, Becky.
Re'gensburg, *n.* Ratisbon, Regensburg.
Reha'beam, *m.* Rehoboam.
Reichs'lande, *pl.* the Imperial Provinces of Alsace and Lorraine.
Rei'nald, *m. see* Reinhold.
Rei'n—eke, **—hard**, *m.* Re(y)nard (the Fox).
Rein'—hold, **—wald**, *m.* Reginald, Reggie.
Reuß—, *see* Ruß—. **—e**, *m. & adj.* Russian; Selbstherrscher aller —en, autocrat *or* Czar of all the Russias (*de toutes les Russies*).
Rhein, *m.* R. Rhine. **—bayern**, *n.* Rhenish Bavaria. **—bund**, *m.* Confederation of the Rhine (1806-1813). **—bundstaaten**, *pl.* (16) German States forming the Confederation of the Rhine (*under the protectorate of Napoleon I. 1806-1813*). **—dampfer**, *m.* steamer on the Rhine. **—fahrt**, *f.* trip up *or* down the Rhine. **—fall**, *m.* Falls of the Rhine (at Neuhausen near Schaffhausen). **—fränkisch**, *adj.* Rheno-Franconian. **—graf**, *m.* Rhinegrave. **—lande**, *pl.* Rhinelands. **—länder**, *m.* Rhinelander; a dance. **—pfalz**, *f.* Palatinate (of the Rhine). **—preußen**, *n.* Rhenish Prussia. **—provinz**, *f.* Rhine province (*of Prussia*). **—schiffahrt**, *f.* navigation of the Rhine; shipping trade on the Rhine. **—strom**, *m.* (the river) Rhine. **—wein**, *m.* Rhenish wine, hock.
Rho'd—ier, *m.* inhabitant of the island of Rhodes, Rhodian. **—iser=Ritter**, *m.* Knight of Rhodes. **—us**, *n.* Rhodes (*island*).
Ri'chard, *m.* Richard, Dick.
Ries, *n.* Ries (*a fertile south German lowland district in the southeastern portion of Würtemberg and the southwestern portion of Bavaria*).
Rie'se (*really* **Ryse**) was the author of a much used arithmetic published in 1559; nach Adam —, according to Cocker.
Ri(e)'k—e, *f.*, **—chen**, *n.* (*dim. for* **Friederike**), Freddie.
Riesen=damm, *m.* Giant's Causeway. **—gebirge**, *n.* Riesengebirge, Giants' Mountains (in Silesia and Bohemia).
Ri'gischer Busen, *m.* gulf of Riga.
Ripua'risch, *adj.*; —e Franken, Ripuarian Franks.
Ro'bert, *m.* Robert, Robin, Rob, Bob.
Ro'derich, *m.* Roderic, Rod(e)rigo, Rory.
Ro'land, *m.* Roland, Rowland; der — auf dem Marktplatze, (*of Bremen and other ancient German towns*) stone figure of an armed warrior (*symbol of jurisdiction*).
Rom, *n.* Rome.
Rö'm—er, *m.* (—ers, *pl.* —er) Roman; rummer (*glass*); the town-hall at Frankfort-on-the Main. **—isch**, *adj.* Roman; das heilige —ische Reich (deutscher Nation), the Holy Roman Empire. **—ling**, *m.* Papist, ultramontanist, Romanist. *Comp.* **—er=straße**, *f.* Roman road; very old road. **—er=zug**, *m.* procession *or* expedition to Rome of the mediæval German emperors. **—isch=katholisch**, *adj.* Roman Catholic.
Roma'n—en, *pl.* the Romance nations, the Neo-Latin peoples. **—e'sk**, *adj.* Romanesque. **—isch**, *adj.* Romance. **—i'st**, *m.* scholar of

Romance philology; student of Roman law; Catholic, adherent of the Pope (*obs.*).
Romau'nsch, *adj. & n.* Romans(c)h (*the Romance dialect spoken in part of the Grisons*).
Ro'sa, *f.*, **Rös'chen**, **Rö'sel**, *n.* Rosa, Ros(i)e.
Rosamun'de, *f.* Rosamond.
Ro'senkreuzer, *m.* Rosicrucian.
Rot'—bart, *m.* Barbarossa. **—häute**, *pl.* redskins. **—käppchen**, *n.* Little Red-Riding-Hood. **—kehlchen**, *n.* Robin Redbreast. **—es Meer**, *n.* Red Sea.
Ru'ben, *m.* Reuben.
Rü'bezahl, Rape-tail, Old Nip (*wrongly rendered by* '*Number Nip*,' *for* Zahl = Zagel '*tail*,' *not* Zahl '*number*;' nip *stands for* turnip) (*name of a waggish mountain sprite in the Riesengebirge*). **—s Reich = das Riesengebirge.**
Rü'diger, *m.* Roger.
Ru'dolf, *m.* Rudolph(us), Ralph.
Ru'klas, *m.* *compound of* (Knecht) Ruprecht *and* St. Niklas = Santa Claus.
Rumä'n—ien, *n.* Roumania. **—e**, *m.*, **—isch**, *adj.* Roumanian.
Rume'lien, *n.* Roumelia.
Ruo'di, *m.* (*dim. of* Rudolf (*dial.*)), Ralph.
Ru'precht, *m.* Rupert, Bob(bie); Knecht —, Santa Claus, St. Nicholas.
Rus's—e, *m.*, **—in**, *f.*, **—isch**, *adj.* Russian; —ische Schaukel, swing-boat. **—isizie'ren**, *v.a.* to Russianize. **—isch-französisch**, *adj.* Russo-French, Franco-Russian. **—land**, *n.* Russia.
Rüt'li (*long* ü), *n.* the meadow above the Lake of Lucerne where the three founders of the Swiss Confederation concluded their secret union.

S

Sa'ba, *n.* Sheba.
Sachar'ja, *m.* Zachariah (*B.*).
Sach's—e, *m.*, **Säch'sin**, *f.*, **säch'sisch**, *adj.* Saxon; Sächsische Kaiser, the House of Saxony (*Low German Emperors 919–1024* A. D.); Sächsische Könige, Saxon kings (*since 1806*); Sächsische Schweiz, Saxon Switzerland, mountainous district south of Dresden. **Säch'seln**, *v.n.* to speak in the Saxon dialect. **—en**, *n.* Saxony. **—en-gänger**, *m.* (Saxony-goer), itinerant labourer, migratory Polish labourer who works in Germany in the summer and autumn. **—en-spiegel**, *m.* code of Old Saxon (*Low German*) laws. **—en-Koburg-Go'tha**, *n.* Saxe-Coburg-Gotha. **—en-Mei'ningen**, *n.* Saxe-Meiningen. **—en-Wei'mar**, *n.* Saxe-Weimar.
Sagu'nt, *n.* Saguntum.
Salmanas'sar, *m.* Shalmaneser.
Sa'lomo, *m.* Solomon; das hohe Lied —nis, the Song of Solomon; Prediger (*m.*) —nis, Ecclesiastes; Sprüche (*pl.*) —nis, Proverbs (of Solomon).
Sa'miel, *m.* Zamiel.
Samoje'de, *m.* Samoyed(e).
San'herib, *m.* Sennacherib.
San'sibar, *n.* Zanzibar.
Sa'ra(h), *f.* Sarah; Sal(ly).
Saraze'n—e, *m.*, **—isch**, *adj.* Saracen.
Sardanapa'l, *m.* Sardanapalus.
Sar'd—e, **—i'nier**, *m.*, **—i'nisch**, *adj.* Sardinian.
Sau, **Sa've**, *f.* R. Save.
Sau'erland, *n.* South Westphalia.
Savoy', **—en**, *n.*, Savoy. **—ar'd(e)**, *m.*, **—isch**, *adj.* Savoyard, inhabitant of Savoy.
Schel'de, *f.* R. Scheldt.
Scherwen'zel, *m.* Jack-of-all-work; Jack (at cards); toady.
Schif'ferinseln, *pl.* Navigator Islands, Samoa.
Schil'd—a, *n.* Gotham. **—bürger**, *m.* Gothamite, Wise Man of Gotham.
Schlaraf'fenland (*older:* **Schlauraffenland**), *n.* Fool's Paradise, Lubberland, Land of Cocaygne.
Schle's—ien, *n.* Silesia. **—ier**, *m.*, **—isch**, *adj.* Silesian.
Schles'wig, *n.* Sleswick.
Schmalkal'd—en, *n.* Schmalkalden. **—ische(r) Bund**, *m.* League of Schmalkalden, Schmalkaldic League (1531).
Schmuhl, **Schmul**, *m.* (contemp.) name for a Jew.
Schneewitt'chen, *n.* Little Snow-white.
Scho'nen, *n.* Scania.
Schöp'penstädter, *m.* Gothamite.
Schot't—e, (**—länder**,) *m.* Scot, Scotchman; die —en, the Scotch; the Scots (*hist.*). **—in**, (**—länderin**,) *f.* Scotchwoman. **—isch**, *adj.* Scottish, Scotch; (der) —ische, Scotch dance; der —ische Dichter, the Scottish bard; das —ische Volk, the Scottish people; eine —ische Zeitung, a Scotch paper; der —ische Eilzug, the Scotch express, the flying Scotsman.
Schwa'bacher (**Schrift**), *f.* German italics.
Schwa'b—e, *m.*, **Schwä'bin**, *f.*, **Schwä'bisch**, *adj.* Swabian; Schwä'bisches Meer, Lake Constance (*obs.*). **—en**, *n.* Swabia. **Schwä'beln**, *v.n.* to talk in the Swabian dialect *or* with a strong Swabian accent. **—en-alter**, *n.* 40 years; the age of discretion. **—en-land**, *n.* Swabia, Würtemberg. **—en-spiegel**, *m.* ancient law code of Swabia. **—en-streich**, *m.* act of folly perpetrated by a grown-up person.
Schwar'z—es Meer, *n.* Black Sea, Euxine. **—füßler**, *m.* Blackfoot (Indian). **—wald**, *m.* Black Forest; **—wälder Uhr**, German clock, cuckoo clock.
Schwe'd—e, *m.*, **—in**, *f.* Swede; alter —e, old boy, old man, old chap (*fam.*). **—en**, *n.* Sweden. **—isch**, *adj.* Swedish; **hinter —ischen Gardinen**, behind iron bars, in prison. **—en-kopf**, *m.* a closely cropped head of hair; short, frizzled head of hair. **—en-trank**, *m.* drink of torture causing violent pains (*obs. XVIIth century*).
Schweiz, (**die**) *f.* Switzerland; in der —, in Switzerland. **—er**, *m.* Swiss; Switzer, member of the (French) bodyguard. **—erin**, *f.* Swiss woman. **—erisch**, *adj.* Swiss. **—er-bund**, *m.* Swiss Confederation.
Scy'th—e, *m.*, **Skyth—e**, **—isch**, *adj.* Scythian.
Sebad'ja, *m.* Zebadiah (*B.*).
See'land, *n.* Zealand.
Se'ladon, *m.* Celadon, amorous swain.
Seld'schucke, *m.* Seljuk (Turk).
Sem, *m.* Shem (*B.*).
Sepp, **Sep'perl**, **Sep'pi**, *m.* (*dial. dim. of* **Joseph**) Joe(y).
Ser'b—ien, *n.* Servia. **—e**, **—ier**, *m.* Serb, Servian. **—isch**, *adj.* Servian.
Seschel'len, (**die**) *pl.* the Seychelles.
Seven'nen, *pl.* the Cevennes.
Sevil'l—a, *n.* Seville. **—a'nisch**, *adj.* Sevillian.
Sibi'r—ien, *n.* Siberia. **—ier**, *m.*, **—isch**, *adj.* Siberian.
Sibyl'le, *f.* Sibyl(la).
Si'chem, *n.* Shechem.
Si'di, *f. dim. of* **Posidonia.**
Siebenbür'g—en, *n.* Transylvania. **—e**, *m.*, **—isch**, *adj.* Transylvanian.
Sie'bengebirge, *n.* the Seven Hills, Siebengebirge (*near Bonn*).
Sieg'mund, **Si'gismund**, *m.* Sigismond.
Si'mon, *m.* Simon, Sim(my), Simpkin; — **von** Kana, Simon the Canaanite.
Sim'son, *m.* Samson.
Singapu'r, *n.* Singapore.
Sipoy, *m.* sepoy.
Si'rach, *m.* (*see* Jesus —) Ecclesiasticus.
Si'si, *f. dim. of* **Posidonia.**
Sit'ten, *n.* Sion (*in the Rhone valley*).
Sixti'nisch, *adj.* Sistine.
Sizi'l—ien, *n.* Sicily. **—i(a'n)er**, *m.*, **—(ia'n)isch**, *adj.* Sicilian.
Skla'venküste, *f.* Slave Coast.

Sla'w—e, *m.*, **—in**, *f.* Slav, Slavonian. **—isch**, *adj.* Slav, Slavonic, Slavonian. **—isie'ren**, *v.a.* to Slavonize, to Russify. **—o'nien**, *n.* Slavonia. **—o'nier**, *m.*, **—isch**, **—o'nisch**, *adj.* Slav(onic). **—en=freund**, *m.* Slavophil. **—en=reich**, *n.* Slavonic empire; allgemeines —enreich, Pan-slavonic empire. **—en=tum**, *n.* Slavdom.

Slowa'k—e, *m.*, **—isch**, *adj.* Slovak, Slovac.

Slowe'n—e, *m.*, **—isch**, *adj.* Slovenian.

Sneewitt'chen, *n.* *see* Schneewittchen.

Sokra'tisch, *adj.* Socratic.

Sophie', *f.* Sophia.

Spaa, *n.* Spa (in Belgium).

Spa'n—ien, *n.* Spain. **—ier**, *m.*, **—ierin**, *f.* Spaniard. **—isch**, *adj.* Spanish; es kommt mir —isch vor, it appears odd *or* strange to me, it is all Greek to me; —ischer Erfolgekrieg, War of the Spanish Succession; —ische Fliege, Spanish fly, cantharis, *pl.* cantharides; blister; einem eine —ische Fliege setzen, to put a blister on a p.; einen in —ische Stiefel einschnüren, to lace a p. in Spanish boots, to torture a p.; —ischer Pfeffer, red pepper; —ische Reiter, chevaux-de-frise; —isches Rohr, Bengal cane; —ischer Stiefel, boot (*as torture*); —ische Wand, folding screen. **—io'l**, *m.* (**—iols**), Spanish snuff. **—io'le**, *m. hum. for* **—ier.**

Spart—a'ner, **—er**, (*poet.*), **—ia't**, *m.*, **—a'nisch**, *adj.* Spartan.

Spei'er, *n.* Spires, Speyer.

Spree'=Athen, *n.* (*students' slang for*) Berlin.

Stam'bul, *n.* Constantinople.

Stau'f—er, *m.* Stauffer, emperor of the (Hohen-) staufen line. **—isch**, *adj.* belonging to the Stauffers, of Hohenstaufen. *Comp.* **—er=zeit**, *f.* the Hohenstaufen period (*1138–1254*).

Stax, *m. dim. of* **Eustachius.**

Stef'fen, *m. see* Stephan.

Stei'er—mark, *f.* Styria. **—märker**, **Stei'rer**, *m.*, **—(märk)isch**, *adj.* Styrian.

Ste'phan, *m.* Stephen, Steve. **—s=bote**, *m.* German postman (*coll.*) called after the first postmaster-general of the German Empire, Dr. H. V. Stephan.

Still—er O'zean, **—es Meer**, Pacific (Ocean).

Stin'chen (*long* i), *n.* (*dim. of* **Christine** *or* **Augustina**), Chrissie, Chris.

Stof'fel, *m.* (*dim. of* **Christoph**), Kit.

Sto'i—ker, *m.* Stoic. **—sch**, *adj.* stoic(al).

Stre'l—itz, *n.* Strelitz. **—it'ze**, *m.* soldier of the old Muscovite militia.

Stru(w)'welpeter, *m.* Shock-headed Peter, Touseled Peter.

Stüf'fi, *m. dim. of* **Justus.**

Süd—A'frika, *m.* South Africa; —afrika'nische Republik, South African Republic, Transvaal.

Suda'n, *m.* Sudan. **—e'se**, **—e'sisch**, *adj.* Sudanese.

Sude'ten, (**die**) *pl.* the Sudetes; Sudetic Mts.

Sü'd—see, *f.* South Sea. **—wales**, *n.* South Wales.

Sue'ven, *pl.* (the) Suevi.

Sulei'ka, *f.* Zuleikah.

Sund, *m.* (the) Sound.

Su—san'ne, *f.*, **—schen**, *n.*, **—se**, *f.* Susan, Susie, Sue; —se, silly goose, stupid creature (*coll.*).

Syraku's, *n.* Syracuse.

Sy'r—(i)er, *m.* Syrian. **—isch**, *adj.* Syrian, Syriac. **—isch=phönizisch**, *adj.* Syro-Phœnician.

Syr'te, *f.* the Syrtis; Große —, Syrtis Major; Kleine —, Syrtis Minor.

T

Tabori't, *m.* Taborite.

Ta'fel—berg, *m.* Table Mt. **—runde**, *f.* the Round Table (of King Arthur).

Tahei'ti, *n.* Tahiti.

Ta'jo, *m.*P. Tagus.

Ta'merlan, *m.* Tamerlane, Tamburlaine.

Tamu'l—e, *m.*, **—in**, *f.*, **—isch**, *adj.* Tamil.

Tan'ger, *n.* Tangier.

Tare'nt, *n.* Tarentum, Taranto.

Tarpe'jisch, *adj.* Tarpeian.

Tar'ser, *m.* inhab. of Tarsus.

Tau'rische Halbinsel, *f.*, **Tau'ris** (*poet.*), **Tau'rien**, *n.* Tauric Chersonese.

Ta(r)ta'r, *m.* Tartar. **—ei'**, (**die**) *f.* Tartary.

Teer'jacke, *f.* Jack Tar.

Te'lemach, *m.* Telemachus.

Tem'pelritter, **Temp'ler**, *m.* (Knight-)Templar

Tere'nz, *m.* Terence.

Tessi'n, *m.* Ticino, Tessin.

Teuto'n—e, *m.*, **—in**, *f.* Teuton. **—isch**, *adj.* Teutonic.

Teutsch, *adj. obs. for* **Deutsch.**

Theb—ai'de, *f.* Thebaid (*poem*). **—a'is**, *n.* Thebaid (*district*). **—a'ner**, *m.*, **—a'nisch**, *adj.* Theban. **The'ben**, *n.* Thebes.

Them'se, *f.* R. Thames.

The'odor, *m.* Theodore, Theo.

Theo'dorich, **Theodorik**, *m.* Theodoric.

Theokri't, *m.* Theocritus.

There's—e, (**—ia**,) *f.* T(h)eresa; **Maria —ia**, Maria Theresa.

Thermopy'len, (**die**) *pl.* the pass of Thermopylæ.

Thessa'l—ien, *n.* Thessaly. **—ier**, *m.*, **—isch**, *adj.* Thessalian. **—o'nicher**, *m.* Thessalonian.

Tho'mas, *m.* Thomas, Tommy, Tom.

Thra'c—ien, *n.* Thrace. **—ier**, *m.*, **—isch**, *adj.* Thracian.

Thraso'nisch, *adj.* Thrasonic, swaggering.

Thur'gau, *m.* Thurgau, Thurgovia.

Thü'ring—en, *n.* Thuringia. **—er**, *m.*, **—isch**, *adj.* Thuringian. **—er=wa'ld**, *m.* Thuringian Mountains.

Tibu'll, *m.* Tibullus.

Til'de, *f.* (*dim. of* **Mathilde**), Tilly, Tilda.

Timo'theus (*4 syll.*), *m.* Timothy, Timmy, Tim.

Ti'mur, *m.* *see* **Tamerlan.**

Ti'nchen (*long* i), **Ti'ne** (*dim. of* **Christine**), *n.* Tina, Tinie.

Tiro'l (*long* o), *n.* the Tyrol; in —, in the Tyrol. **—er**, *m.*, **—isch**, *adj.* Tyrolese.

Ti'tan, *m.* Titan (sun-god). **Tita'ne**, *m.* Titan (*giant*). **—en=haft**, **—isch**, *adj.* Titanic. **—en=kampf**, *m.* battle of the Titans (*against the gods*), Titanomachy.

Ti'zian, *m.* Titian. **Tizia'nisch**, *adj.* of Titian.

Tobi'—as, **—es**, *m.* Tobiah, Tobias, Toby; das Buch Tobiä, Book of Tobit (*apocryphal*).

Töf'fel, *m.* (*dim. for* **Stöffel**, **Stoffel**, *for* **Christoph(el)**), Christopher; blockhead.

Tokai'er, *m.* Tokay wine.

To'ni, *m.f.* (*dim. of* **Anton**, **Antonia**), Tony.

Ton'kin, *n.* Tonquin.

Toska'n—a, *n.* Tuscany. **—er**, *m.*, **—isch**, *adj.* Tuscan.

Transatlan'tiker, *m.* American (*hum.*).

Transvaa'l, *m.* the Transvaal; **in —**, in the Transvaal.

Trapezu'nt, *n.* Trebizond.

Trau'gott, *m.* Trust in God.

Trau'wohl, *m.* Good Faith (*iron.*).

Tri(d)e'nt, *n.* Trent. **—i'ner Konzil**, *n.* Council of Trent. **—i'nisch**, *adj.* Tridentine.

Trier, *n.* Treves. **—isch**, *adj.* Treviran.

Trie'st (*2 syllables*), *n.* Trieste.

Tri'n—e, *f.*, **—chen**, *n.* (*dim. of* **Katharine**), Kitty; dumme —e, silly girl, silly goose; faule —e, slut, sloven.

Tri'polis, *n.* Tripoli.

Tris'tan, *m.* Tristram, Tristrem.

Tro'—as, *n.* the Troad. **—ja**, *n.* Troy. **—ja'ner**, *m.*, **—ja'nisch**, *adj.* Trojan.

Tru'd—e(l), *f.*, **—chen** (*long* u), *n.* (*dim. of* **Gertrud**), Gertie.

Tsche'ch—e, *m.* Czech. **—isch**, *adj.* Czech.
Tscherkes's—e, *m.*, **—in**, *f.*, **—isch**, *adj.* Circassian.
Tul'lius, *m.* Tully.
Tune'sisch, *adj.* Tunisian.
Tura'nisch, *adj.* Turanian.
Turi'n—er, *m.*, **—isch**, *adj.* of Turin, Turinese.
Tür'k—e, *m.* (*pl.* —en), **—in**, *f.* Turk, Turkish woman; Groß —e, the Grand Turk. **—ei'**, (**die**) *f.* Turkey; in der —ei, in Turkey. **—isch**, *adj.* Turkish; —ische Bohne, French bean; —ische Ente, Muscovy duck; —ischer Teppich, Turkey carpet; —ischer Weizen, Indian corn. **—entum**, *n.* Turkish manners; Mahommedanism; the Turks. **—en-bund**, *m.* turban; Turk's cap (*lily*), martagon (*lily*) (*Bot.*). **—en-gebet**, *n.* prayer against the Turks. **—en-glaube**, *m.* Mahommedanism. **—en-kopf**, *m.* Saracen's head. **—en-krieg**, *m.* war against the Turks. **—en-predigt**, *f.* sermon against the Turks. **—en-säbel**, *m.* scimitar. **—en-zug**, *m.* expedition against the Turks. **—isch-ägyptisch**, *adj.* Turco-Egyptian. **—isch-blau**, *n.* dark blue. **—isch-rot**, *n.* Turkey red.
Tur'ko—, *m.*, (*pl.* —s) Turco, Zouave. **—ma'ne**, *m.* Turcoman.
Tyrrhe'nisches Meer, *n.* Tyrrhenian Sea.
Ty'r—us, *n.* Tyre. **—(i)er**, *m.*, **—isch**, *adj.* Tyrian.

U

U'l—i, *m.* (*poet. dial.*), **—rich**, Ulric. **—ri'ke**, *f.* Ulrica.
Um'br—ier, *m.*, **—isch**, *adj.* Umbrian.
Unde'ne, Undi'ne, *f.* water-sprite, nymph.
Un'gar, *m.*, **—in**, *f.*, **—isch**, *adj.* Hungarian. **—n**, *n.* Hungary.
Un'g—er, *m. obs. for* **Ungar**. **—(e)risch**, *obs. for* **Ungarisch**. **—ern**, **—erland**, *obs. for* **Ungarn**.
Unter den Linden, *n.* avenue of lime-trees (*in Berlin*), principal street of Berlin.
Un'ter—franken, *n.* Lower Franconia. **—rhein**, *m.* Lower Rhine. **—wäldner**, *m.* inhab. of Unterwalden.
Ura'lgebirge, *n.* Ural Mountains.
Ura'nia, *f.* Urania. **—säule**, *f.* advertising-pillar with clock (*at Berlin*) erected by the Urania, a kind of Polytechnic.
Uri'a(s), *m.* Uriah. **—sbrief**, *m.* a treacherous letter.
U'rian, *m.*; Herr —, Mr. What 's-his-name; the Devil; Meister —, Old Harry, old Nick.
Ur'kantone, *pl.* cantons of Uri, Unterwalden, Schwyz.
Ur'sel, *f.* (*dim. of* **Ursula**) Ursula, Ursly.
Ursuli'nerin, *f.* Ursuline nun.
Utraqui'st, *m.* (—en, *pl.* —en) Bohemian Protestant (*XVI. cent.*).

V

Va'land, *m. see* **Voland**.
Va'lentin, *m.* Valentine.
Vanda'l—e, *m.* Vandal; barbarian. **—isch**, *adj.* Vandal-like. **—is'mus**, *m.* Vandalism.
Vandie'menslānder, *m.* Tasmanian.
Veit, *m.* Vitus, Guy; the devil; Bruder —, nickname given to a German Landsknecht (*XVI. cent.*). *Comp.* **—s-tanz**, *m.* St. Vitus's dance.
Vel'ten, *m.* Valentine; potz —, good gracious; the deuce!
Veltli'n, (das) *n.* Valtelline, Valtellina.
Vende'—er, *m.* **—isch**, *adj.* Vendean.
Vene'—dig, *n.* Venice; Republik —, Venetian Republic, Republic of Venice. **—disch**, **—tia'nisch**, *adj.*, **—tia'ner**, *m.* Venetian. **—tien**, **—zien**, *n.* Venetia.
Venezue'lisch (*less good:* **Venezola'nisch**), *adj.* Venezuelan.

Verei'nigte Staaten, *pl.* United States (of North America), U. S. A.
Vergi'l, *m.* Virgil.
Vesu'v, *m.* Mt. Vesuvius.
Vier'l—ande, (die) *pl.* a district (*of four parishes*) belonging to Hamburg. **—änderin**, *f.* peasant woman from the Vierlande selling fruit, etc., at Hamburg.
Vierwaldstättersee', *m.* Lake of the Four Cantons, Lake of Lucerne.
Vin'cenz, Vincen'tius, *m.* Vincent.
Vitru'v, *m.* Vitruvius.
Vlä'me, *m. see* **Flamländer**.
Vlis'singen, *n.* Flushing.
Voge'sen, *pl.* Vosges Mts.
Vo'land, *m.*; Junker —, the Devil, Satan.
Völ'kerschlacht, *f.* Battle of Leipzig, 1813.
Vor'alpen, *pl.* the lower Alps.
Vor'der—asien, *n.* Western Asia. **—indien**, *n.* India (*proper*), Hindustan. **—österreich**, *n.* (*obs.*) the Austrian Forelands. **—pommern**, *n.* Hither Pomerania.
Vor'wärts, *m.*; Marschall —, Field Marshal Blucher.
Vre'nel—e, —i, *n.* (*dim. of* **Veronica**), Veronica.

W

Waadt'—(land), *n.* (*Canton de*) Vaud. **—länder**, *m.*, **—isch**, *adj.* Vaudois.
Waal, *m.* R. Vaal.
Wagneria'ner, *m.* Wagnerite, enthusiastic admirer of Richard Wagner.
Waib'ling(er), *m.* Ghibelline, adherent of the Staufer (Hohenstaufen).
Walden'ser, *m.* Waldensian.
Wald'stätte, *pl.* Forest Cantons (Uri, Unterwalden, Schwyz, and Lucerne).
Walkü're, *f.* Valkyrie, Walkyrie, swan-maiden. **—n-ritt**, *m.* ride of the Valkyries.
Wal(l)—achei', (**die**) *f.* Wallachia. **—a'che**, *m.*, **—a'chisch**, *adj.* Wallachian.
Wal'li, Wäl'ti (*dim. of* **Walther**), Wat.
Wal'l—is, *n.* le Valais; (*sometimes*) Wales. **—i'sisch**, *adj.* Valaisan; Welsh, Cambrian. **—i'ser**, *m.* Valaisan; Welshman; —iser Eisenbahnen, Cambrian Railways.
Wallo'n—e, *m.*, **—isch**, *adj.* Walloon.
Walpur'gisnacht, *f.* eve of May-day (*when witches hold a meeting on the Brocken*).
Wälsch, *adj. see* **Welsch**.
Wal'ther, Wal'ter, *m.* Walter, Walt.
Wanda'le, *m.* Vandal; *see* **Vandale**.
War'schau, *n.* Warsaw.
Wart'burg, *f.* castle of landgraves of Thuringia near Eisenach, now belonging to the Grand Duke of Saxe-Weimar. **—krieg**, *m.* famous legendary musical contest held in the Wartburg (*XIII. cent.*).
Was'gau, *n.*, **Waskenwald, Wasgenwald**, *m.* (*obs. & poet.*) the Vosges.
Was'sergeusen, *pl.* Gueux of the Sea; *see* **Geusen**.
Was'serpolacke, *m.* Pole of Upper Silesia.
We'da, Ve'da, *m.* (*pl.* **We'den**), Veda.
Weich'sel, *f.* R. Vistula.
Welf, Wel'f—e, *m.* Guelph; **die —en**, the Guelph party, party in favour of reinstating the Guelph dynasty in Hanover (*after 1866*); Hie —, Hie Waibling! Here, Guelphs! There, Ghibellines! **—en-fonds**, *m.* confiscated property of the late (*Guelph*) King George V. of Hanover (*1866*). **—en-tum**, *n.* the Guelph spirit *or* party. **—isch**, *adj.* Guelph(ic).
Welsch, *adj.* Welsh, Italian, French; die —en, the French, (*rarely*) the Italians; —e Bohne, French bean; —er Hahn, capon; —e Nuß, walnut; —e Schweiz, French Switzerland. **—kohl**, *m.* Savoy cabbage. **—korn**, *n.* maize. **—land**, *n.* Italy. **—tiro'l**, *n.* Italian Tyrol. **—tum**, *n.* foreign (*esp. French*) manners and customs.

Wen'd—e, *m.*, **—isch**, *adj.* Wend.
Wen'dekreis, *m.* Tropic; — **des Kreb'ses**, Tropic of Cancer; — **des Stein'bocks**, Tropic of Capricorn.
Wen'zel, *m.* Wenceslas; knave (*at cards*).
West—fa'len, *n.* Westphalia. **—fa'le**, *m.*, **—fä'lin**, *f.*, **—fä'lisch**, *adj.* Westphalian. **—fries'land**, *n.*, **—frie'sische Inseln**, *pl.* West Frisian Islands. **—gote**, *m.* West Goth, Visigoth. **—in'dien**, *n.* the West Indies (*pl.*). **—indien=fahrer**, *m.* West-Indiaman. **—phalen**, *obs. for* **—falen**. **—rich**, *m.* western part of the Vosges district.
Wicliffi't, *m.* Wicliffite, follower of Wiclif.
Wie'land der Schmied, *m.* Wayland Smith.
Wien, *n.* Vienna. **—er**, *m.*, **—erisch**, *adj.* Viennese; **—er Kongreß**, Congress of Vienna; **—er Tränkchen**, **—er Wasser**, infusion of senna.
Wi'king, Wi'kinger, *m.* Viking.
Wil'fried, *m.* Wilfred.
Wil'helm, *m.* William; — **der Eroberer**, William the Conqueror; — **der Rote**, William Rufus; — **der Siegreiche**, William I. (*of Germany*). **—i'ne**, *f.* Wilhelmina. **—s=höhe**, *f.* castle near Kassel (*surrounded by beautiful woods, where Napoleon III. was imprisoned after the battle of Sedan*). **—straße**, *f.* (*at Berlin*) street in which the German Ministry of Foreign Affairs is situated, hence: the Ministry of Foreign Affairs. Cp. Downing Street.
Wil'li, *m.* (*dim. of* **Wilhelm**) Bill.
Winfre'da, *f.* Winifred, Winnie.
Win'golf, *m.* Vingolf (*probably 'wine hall;' usually taken to mean 'hall of friendship'*); a large association of German students. **—i't**, *m.* a member of the Vingolf club.
Wisch'nu, *m.* Vishnu.
Wi'sigote, *m.* Visigoth (visi *is etymologically* NOT *connected with* west).
Wla'dislaus, *m.* Ladislaus.
Wo'dan, *m.* Odin, Woden.
Wol'ga, *f.* R. Volga.
Wolkenku'kuksheim, *n.* Utopia; Fool's Paradise.
Wür'temberg, (*obs.* **Wir'temberg**,) *n.* Wurtemberg.

X

Xanthip'pe, *f.* Xantippe; shrew.
Xa'ver, *m.* (*also* **Xave'r**) Xavier.

Y

Yan'keeartig, *adj.* Yankeefied.
Y'pern, *n.* Ypres; **aussehn wie der Tod von —**, to look as pale as death.

Z

Za(a)r, *m.* Czar.
Za'bern, *n.* Saverne.
Zachari'as, *m.* Zachariah, Zachary.
Zachä'us, *m.* Zaccheus (*B.*).
Ze'baoth, *m.* Sabaoth (*B.*); **der Herr(e)—**, the Lord of Sabaoth, the Lord of Hosts.
Zebedä'us, *m.* Zebedee (*B.*).
Zend'—volk, *n.* the Zends, the ancient Persians. **—sprache**, *f.* Zend.
Zigeu'ner, *m.*, **—in**, *f.* Gipsy, Romany.
Zinn'inseln, *pl.* Cassiterides.
Zi'on, *n.* Zion; **Tochter —**, daughter of Zion. **—s=wächter**, *m.* guardian of Mt. Zion; zealous and fanatic divine (*fig.*).
Zol'ler, *m.*, **—n**, *m.* *see* **Hohenzoller(n)**.
Zui'dersee, *m.* Zuyder Sea.
Zürich, *n.* Zurich.

INDEX OF THE MOST COMMON GERMAN ABBREVIATIONS.

A., **acceptiert**, accepted (*on bills of exchange*).
a., aus, from, out of; an, am, an der, on, on the (*before names of rivers*).
a. a. O., am angeführten Orte, *loco citato*, in the before-mentioned place.
abgk., **abk.**, abgekürzt, abbreviated.
Abh., Abhandlung, treatise.
Abschn., Abschnitt, paragraph.
a. c., *anni currentis*, (of) this year.
a. Ch., *ante Christum*, Before Christ, B. C.
a. D., außer Dienst, retired, on half pay (*mil.*); **a. d.**, *anno domini*, in the year of the Lord, A. D.; **a. d.**, *a dato*, from (this) date.
A. G., Aktiengesellschaft, joint stock company.
A. H., alter Herr, former member of a (*students'*) club; *pl.* **AA. HH.**, alte Herren.
ahd., althochdeutsch, Old High German.
a. L., an der Lahn, on the Lahn; *e.g.* Marburg a/L.
allg., **allgm.**, allgemein, general.
a. M., am Main, on the Main; *e.g.* Frankfurt a/M.
Anm., Anmerkung, note.
Anz., Anzeigen *or* Anzeiger, advertisements *or* advertiser.
a. O., an der Oder, on the Oder; *e.g.* Frankfurt a/O.
a. Rh., am Rhein, on the Rhine; *e.g.* Köln a/Rh.
Art., Artikel, article.
a. S., an der Saale, on the Saale; *e.g.* Halle a/S.
a. St., alten Stils, old style (*in calendars*).
A. T., altes Testament, Old Testament.
Aufl., Auflage, edition.
ausgel., ausgelassen, omitted.
Ausspr., Aussprache, pronunciation.

B

B., Baß, bass; Briefe, bills, papers (*in opposition to* G(eld), *money*); Band, volume; Buch, book; Bericht, report; Beispiel, example, z. B. zum Beispiel, for instance.
b., bei, beim, bei dem, at, with, by, near; *e.g.* Gohlis b. Leipzig, Gohlis near Leipzig. **b.**, at the end of a word stands for: **1.** Bau, *e. g.* **Bergb.**, Bergbau, mining. **2.** ber, *e. g.* **Färb.**, Färber, dyer.
BA., Bankaktie, share.
Bair., Bay(e)r, Bayrisch, Bavarian.
BB., (*also* **Bde.**), Bände, volumes.
Bd., Band, volume; **Bde**, Bände, volumes; **Frzbd**, Franzband, binding in calf.
Bdtg., Bedeutung, meaning.
Bearb., Bearbeiter *or* Bearbeitung, editor *or* version.
bed., bedeutet, signifies; **Bed.**, Bedeutung, meaning.
Beibl., Beiblatt, supplement.
beif., **beiflgd.**, beifolgend, (*sent*) herewith.
beil., beiliegend, enclosed.
Ber., Bericht, report.
bes., besonders, especially.
best., bestimmt, destined.
betr., betreffend, betreffs, concerning.
bev., bevollmächtigt, authorized, plenipotentiary.
bez., bezüglich, with reference to.
bezw., **bzw.**, beziehungsweise, respectively, or.
B. G., Breitengrad, degree of latitude.
bibl., biblisch, biblical.
bildl., bildlich, figuratively, metaphorically.
bisch., bischöflich, episcopal.
bisw., bisweilen, sometimes.
Bl., Blatt, paper (**Bll.**, Blätter, papers); Ballen, bale.
Bmk., Bankomark, mark-banko.
Bmk., **Bmkg.**, Bemerkung, observation, note.
B. N., Banknote, banknote.
Bo., Bogen, sheet.
Br., breit, wide; broschiert, stitched; brutto, gross weight.
B. W., Buchhändler Währung, booksellers' currency.

C

C. *for* Carbon (*chem.*), Consul; Centrum, centre; Conto, account: Courant, current, currency.
Ca., Calcium (*chem.*).
C. A. (*also* **K. A.**), Cassenanweisung (Kassenanweisung), **1.** cash-note. **2.** bank-note.
ca., *circa*, about.
cart., cartonniert, boards (*binding*).
Chr., Chronik, chronicle(s).
crt., *currentis*, current.

D

d. *or* **dd.**, *dedit*, presented, paid.
das., daselbst, in the same place.
dass., dasselbe, the same.
dd., **ddo.**, *de dato*, dated, from the date.
d. G., durch Güte, by favour (*of Mr.*).
dgl., dergleichen, desgleichen, similarly; **u. dgl.**, und dergleichen, and so on, etc.
d. Gr., der Große, the Great.
d. h., das heißt, that is, viz.
d. i., das ist, that is.
d. J., dieses Jahres, (*of*) this year.
d. l. M., des laufenden Monats, of the current month.
d. M., dieses Monats, (*of*) this month; **de** 16te d. M., the 16th inst.
d. O., der Obige, the above.
Dr. Ing., Doktor Ingenieur, Doctor of Engineering.
D. R. P., Deutsche Reichspost, Imperial German Post; Deutsches Reichspatent, Imperial Patent.
Dr. phil., *Doctor philosophiae*, Ph. D.
Dr. u. j., *Doctor utriusque juris*, LL. D.
Dr. u. Vrl., Druck und Verlag, publisher, printed and published (*by*).
dtsch., deutsch, German.
Dtz., Dutzend, dozen.
Durchl., Durchlaucht, Serene Highness.
d. Vf., der Verfasser, the author.
D. W., **D. Wb.**, **D. W. B.**, Deutsches Wörterbuch, German Dictionary.
D.-Zug, Durchgangszug, through train; corridor train.

E

e., ein, einer, eins, one.
E. B., Eisenbahn, railway.
ebd., **ebds.**, ebenda, ebendaselbst, in the same place.
E. E. *or* **Ew. E.**, Euer Ehrwürden, Your Reverence; **von E. zu E.**, von Ewigkeit zu Ewigkeit. from everlasting to everlasting.
eig., **eig(en)tl.**, eigentlich, properly, really.
Eigenn., Eigenname, proper name.

Einl., **Einltg.**, Einleitung, introduction.
Einz., Einzahl, singular.
einz., einzeln, separate, single.
Em., Eminenz; **Ew. Em.**, Eure Eminenz, Your Eminence.
engl., englisch, English.
entspr., entsprechend, corresponding.
ep., episch, epic.
erg., ergänze, supply, add.
Erl., Erläuterung, explanation, (*explanatory*) note.
Et. Wb., Etymologisches Wörterbuch, etymological dictionary.
ev., eventuell, perhaps, possibly.
Ew., Euer, Eure, Eurer, your.
exkl., exklusive, except(ed), not included.

F

F., Fahrenheit.
f., für, for; **f. d. J.**, für dieses Jahr, for this year.
ff., folgende, the following; sehr fein, extra fine; *see also page 188*.
F. f., Fortsetzung folgt, to be continued.
fg., **flgd.**, folgend, following; **fgg.**, **flgde.**, folgende, the following.
Fl., (Florin), Gulden, florin.
Fl. Bl., Flugblatt, Fliegendes Blatt (*pl.* **Fll. Bll.**, Flugblätter), fly-sheet, broadsheet.
Flugschr., Flugschrift, pamphlet.
Fol., **fol.**, Folio, page.
Forts., Fortsetzung, continuation.
fr., franko, post free, paid.
Fr., Frau, Mrs.; **Fr. v.**, **Frau von**, Mrs., Madame de.
franz., französisch, French.
frdl., freundlich, kind.
Frl., Fräulein, Miss; **Frl. v.**, **Fräulein von**, Miss, Mademoiselle de.
Frzbd., Franzband, calf binding.
Fußn., Fußnote, footnote.

G

G., **Geld**, (*on bills of exchange*) bid, money wanted, inquired after; **Käufer**, buyers, takers.
g., Gramm, gramme.
g. D., gehorsam(st)er Diener, (most) obedient servant.
geb., geboren, born.
ged., gedichtet, written; **Ged.**, **Gedicht**, poem.
gef., gefälligst, if you please, kindly.
geh., geheftet, stitched.
Geh. R., Geheimrat, privy councillor.
geistl., geistlich, spiritual.
gek., gekürzt, abbreviated.
gen., genannt, mentioned; surnamed; geneigt, kind; **zur gen. Ans.**, zur geneigten Ansicht, for kind inspection, on approval.
Ges., Gesang, canto; Gesellschaft, society; club; company.
geschr., geschrieben, written.
gespr., gesprochen, spoken.
gest., gestorben, died, late.
gew., gewöhnlich, usually.
gez., gezeichnet, signed.
Gg., Goldgulden, florin (*gold*); **g. G.**, gut Geld, good money.
Ggew., **Ggw.**, **gGew.**, gut Gewicht, full (*correct*) weight.
G. J., Goethe Jahrbuch, Goethe Annual.
gleichbd., gleichbedeutend, synonymous.
gl. N., gleichen Namens, of the same name.
G. m. b. H., Gesellschaft mit beschränkter Haftung, limited (liability company).
gr., groß, great.
Gr., Grad, degree (*of longitude or latitude*).
Gr., Groschen, an old small silver piece (*value* 1*d.*).
Grdr., Grundriß, outline, sketch; compendium.

H

H., Haben, (Gut)haben, credit; Hoheit, Highness (*pl.* **H. H.**, Hoheiten); Hydrogen (*Chem.*); **HH.** (*pl. of* **Hr.**), Herren, Messrs.
h., **hl.**, **heil.**, heilig, holy, saint; **h.** *at the end of a compound word*, Hütte *or* Handwerk, *e.g.* **Eisenh.**, Eisenhütte, iron works; **Schmiedeh.**, Schmiedehandwerk, smith's handicraft.
Hapag, Hamburg=Amerika Paketfahrt Aktien=Gesellschaft.
hd., hochdeutsch, High German.
Hfrzbd., Halbfranzband, half calf binding.
holl., holländisch, Dutch.
Hptw., Hauptwort, noun, substantive.
Hr., Herr, Mr. (*pl.* **H. H.**, Herren, Messrs.).
hrsg. *or* **hsgb.**, herausgegeben, edited.
Hs., Handschrift, manuscript (*pl.* **Hss.**, **Handschriften**, MSS.).
Hsgbr., Herausgeber, editor.

I

J., Ihre, your, their; **J. M.**, Ihre Majestät, Her Majesty; **J. J. M. M.**, Ihre Majestäten, Their Majesties.
i., in, im, in, in the, into, into the; **ist**, is; **d. i.**, das ist, that is, viz.
J., Jahr, year; Jod (*Chem.*).
i. a., im allgemeinen, in general.
i. A., im Auftrage, by order.
i. b., im besondern, in particular.
i. d. J., in diesem Jahre, in this year.
i. J., im Jahre, in the year, anno.
J. K. H., Ihre Königliche Hoheit, Her Royal Highness; *see under* **J.**
inkl., inklusive, inclusively, included.
Inlt., Inlaut, medial sound; **inltd.**, **inlautend**, medially.
i. V., in Vertretung, on behalf of; by order; by proxy, as a substitute.

K

k., kaiserlich, Imperial; königlich, Royal; *at the end of a syll. for* —keit, —kunde, —kunst, *e.g.* **Ewigk.**, Ewigkeit, eternity; **Heilk.**, Heilkunde, medical science; **Bauk.**, Baukunde, Baukunst, architecture.
K., Kap, cape; **Kapitel**, chapter; **Kalium** (*Chem.*); Kirche, church; **König**, king.
kais., kaiserlich, Imperial.
Kap., Kapitel, chapter.
kgl., königlich, Royal.
kgswgs., keineswegs, in no way, by no means.
k. J., kommenden Jahres, of the following year, of next year.
k. k., **K. K.**, kaiserlich (und) königlich, Imperial and Royal.
Kl., Klasse, class; form.
kl., klein, small.
K. L., **Konv. Lex.**, **Konversationslexikon**, encyclopædia.
km., **kn.**, keinem, keinen, none.
km., Kilometer, kilometre.
k. M., künftigen Monats, (of) next month.
Kr., Kreuzer, Austrian copper coin (*value* $\frac{1}{5}$–$\frac{1}{4}$*d.*).

L

L., Lied, song; Länge, length; longitude (*Geog.*); Lot, $\frac{1}{12}$ ounce; **L. Zug**, see below.
l., lies, read; lieb (*in any case or number*), dear; —lich, like, -ly (*e.g.* **jährl.**, yearly, **frdl.**, freundlich, friendly) *or* —lung (*e.g.* **Handl.**, business, firm, shop).
l., Liter, litre.

l. a., *lege artis*, according to the rules of the art (*Pharm.*).
landschaftl., landschaftlich, provincial.
lauf. Mon., laufenden Monats, of this month.
L. Bl., Litteraturblatt, literary *or* critical magazine.
l. c., *loco citato*, in the place quoted, see above.
Ldr., Louis d'or; Leder, leather.
Ldrb., Lederband, calf binding.
Ldrr., Lederrücken, leather back, half calf.
L. F., Lieber Freund, Liebe Freunde, Dear . . .
Lfrg., Lieferung, delivery; instalment, part.
L. G., Längengrad, degree of longitude (*Geog.*).
Lic., Licentiat, Lizentiat, licentiate.
Lit., Literatur, literature.
l. J., laufenden Jahres, (of) this year.
l. M., laufenden Monats, (of) this month.
L. S., lange Sicht, long sight (*Comm.*).
L. S., *loco sigilli*, instead of a seal.
Lwd., Leinwand, canvas, calico, cloth.
Lwdb., Leinwandband, cloth(-binding).
L. Zug, Luxuszug, *train de luxe*, saloon-train.

M

M., Mark, mark (*about 1 shilling*); Meile, mile; Meter, metre; Mittelsorte, medium kind *or* quality; Modell, model; Monat, month.
m., merke, note; mit, with; männlich, masculine (*gender*); —m, (*final*), —macher, *e.g.* **Schuhm.**, Schuhmacher, boot-maker.
M. A., Miniatur Ausgabe, miniature edition.
Mag., Magazin, magazine.
m. B., **m. Bed.**, meines Bedünkens, in my opinion.
M.D.R., Mitglied des deutschen Reichstags, member of the Imperial diet (*cp.* M.P.).
m. E., meines Erachtens, in my opinion.
Mehrz., Mehrzahl, plural.
M. E. Z., Mitteleuropäische Zeit, time of the middle European zone (*1 hour in advance of English* (*Greenwich*) *time*).
mg., Milligramme, milligramme.
m. G., mit Goldschnitt, gilt edges.
mhd., mittelhochdeutsch, Middle High German.
m. l., mein lieber, meinem lieben, (to) my dear.
mm., Millimeter, millimetre.
mm. HH., meine Herrn, gentlemen.
m. s., man sehe, see, compare; **Ms.**, Manuskript, manuscript; **Mss.**, Manuskripte, manuscripts.
Mschr., Monatsschrift, monthly (*periodical*).
m. w., machen wir, it shall be done (*sl.*).
m. W., meines Wissens, as far as I know.
m. Z., mangels Zahlung, in default of payment (*Comm. Lang.*).

N

n., **nach**, after; **neu**, new.
N., Name, name; Nord(en), north; Nachmittag(s) *or* Nacht(s), afternoon *or* night, P. M. (*Railw.*); Nitrogen, nitrogen (*Chem.*).
N. A., neue Ausgabe *or* Auflage, new edition.
Nachm., nachmittags, in the afternoon, P. M.
Nachn., Nachnahme, reimbursement.
näml., nämlich, that is to say.
namtl., namentlich, especially.
N. B., nördliche Breite, northern latitude.
Nbf., Nebenform, byform.
n. Chr., nach Christo, nach Christi Geburt, After Christ, A. D.
N. F., neue Folge, new series.
nhd., neuhochdeutsch, New High German.
n. M., nächsten Monats, (of) next month.
N. N., *nescio nomen*, name unknown to me; Herr N. N., Mr. so and so.
no., **ntto.**, netto, net.
No., **Nro.**, numero, number; **Nros.**, numbers.
Nr., Numero, number.
N. S., Nachschrift, postscript, P. S.
N. S., **N. St.**, neuen Stils, New Style.
N. T., Neues Testament, New Testament.
num., numero, number.
Num., Numismatik, numismatics.

O

O., Order, order; **Ort**, place; **Osten**, east; **Oxygen**, oxygen.
o., oben, above; **vgl. o.**, vergleiche oben, see above.
ö. *or* **österr.**, österreichisch, Austrian.
Oct., **Okt.**, Oktav, octavo.
Oct., **Octbr.**, Oktober, October.
od., oder, or.
öff. Bll., öffentliche Blätter, public papers *or* press.
ö. L., östliche Länge, east longitude.
o. O. u. J., ohne Ort und Jahr, without date *or* place (*of publication*).
O. P. A., Oberpostamt, General Post Office (G. P. O.).
ord., ordinär, ordinary, common.
org., organisch, organic(ally).
o. U. d. B., ohne Unterschied der Bedeutung, without difference in meaning.
Oxh., Oxhoft, hogshead.

P

p., per, par, pro, by, for.
P., Phosphor, phosphorus.
p. A., **p. Adr.**, per Adresse, care of (*on letters*).
p. Ct., pro Cent, per cent.
Pf., Pfennig(e); **50 Pf.**, (*nearly*) 6d.
Pfd., Pfund, pound, pounds.
p.p., pianissimo; der p.p. Miller, the (afore)said Miller, Mr. Miller (*obs.*).
P. P., *praemissis praemittendis*, premising what is to be premised, omitting all titles, Sir, Madam, (*on business letters*).
Pr., Presse, press; preußisch, Prussian.
Pred., Prediger *or* Predigt, preacher *or* sermon.
Prgr., Programm, program.
Prof., Professor, professor; **Prof. Ord.**, Professor Ordinarius, (ordinary) professor.
p. t., *pro tempore*, for the time being.

Q

Q., Quadrat, square.
Q. F., Quadratfuß, square foot.
Qkm., Quadratkilometer, square kilometre; myriare.
Q. M., **Qm.**, Quadratmeile, square mile.
Qm., Quadratmeter, square metre.
Q. R., Quadratrute, square perch (*14.21 square metres*).

R

R., Reaumur, Réaumur; **Recht**, law; **Römisch**, Roman; Rute, pole, perch.
r., rund, round.
Rab., Rabatt, discount.
R. A. O., Roter-Adler-Orden, Order of the Red Eagle.
Rbl., Rubel, rouble.
Ref., Referent, referee.
Rel., Religion, religion.
Rep., Repertorium, handbook.
resp., respective, respectively.
rglm., regelmäßig, regular(ly).
Rh., Rhein, rheinisch, the Rhine, Rhenish.
Rhn., rheinisch, Rhenish.
Rim., Rimesse, remittance.
Rmk., Reichsmark, (*about*) one shilling.
Röm., Römisch, Roman.
Roman., **Romanisch**, Romance.

Rthlr., Reichsthaler, (*about*) 3 shillings.
Rttgt., Rittergut, manor.
Rum., Rumänisch, Roumanian.
R. W., Reichswährung, Imperial currency.

S

S., Seite, page; Sankt, Saint.
s., siehe, see; 's, es, it; of it.
s. a., siehe auch, see also.
Sächs., Sächsisch, Saxon.
Sarsb., Sarsenetband, bound in sarsenet.
sch., **schw.**, schwach, weak.
s. d., siehe dies, siehe dort, see above.
s. d. v(or), siehe das Vorige, see above.
Se., **Sr.**, Seine, Seiner, His.
sel., selig (*in all cases, genders and numbers*), late.
Ser., Serie, series.
sg., **sog.**, sogenannt, so called.
Skt., Sankt, Saint.
s. l., seinem lieben, to his dear (*in dedications*).
S. M., Seine Majestät, His Majesty.
S. M. S., Seiner Majestät Schiff, his Majesty's Ship, H. M. S.
s. o., siehe oben, see above.
spr., sprich, pronounce.
st., stark, strong.
St., Stück, piece; Stamm, stem; Sankt, Saint; Stil, style.
s. u., siehe unten, see below.
s. v. a., **s. v. w.**, **so viel als**, **so viel wie**, as much as.
s. Z., **seiner Zeit**, in due time; at the *or* that time.

T

T., Tonne, tun, cask; Tasche(n), pocket.
T. A., Taschenausgabe, pocket edition.
T. B., **Tb.**, Taschenbuch, pocket-book.
T. Bl., Tageblatt, daily (paper); **T. Bll.**, Tageblätter, dailies.
T. F., Taschenformat, pocket size.
teilw., teilweise, partly.
term. techn., *terminus technicus*, technical expression.
Th., Thema, subject.
Thlr., Thaler, dollar (*silver coin worth abt. 3 shillings*).
T. Wb., Taschenwörterbuch, pocket dictionary.

U

U., **u.**, **und**, and; **unter**, among, amongst; **U.**, Uhr, hour; o'clock.
u.a., unter anderm, amongst other things; **und** andere, and others.
u. a. a. O., und an andern Orten, and elsewhere, and in other passages.
u. Ä. (m.), und Ähnliches (mehr), and the like, and such like, and more of the kind.
u. a. m., **und andere mehr**, **und anderes mehr**, and others, and other things besides.
u. A. w. g., um Antwort wird gebeten, *or* **u. gefl. A. w. g.**, um gefällige Antwort wird gebeten, (the favour of) an answer is requested, an answer will oblige, R. S. V. P.
übhpt., überhaupt, in general, generally speaking.
übtrgn., übertragen, transcribed; translated; metaphorical.
u. drgl. m., **und dergleichen mehr**, and more of the (same) kind.
u. e. a., und einige andere, and some others.
ult., ultimo, letzten Monats, (of) last month; **am** Letzten des Monats, on the last day of the month.
unbest., unbestimmt, uncertain.
unfl., unflektiert, uninflected, undeclined.
unr., **unreg.**, unregelmäßig, irregular.
u. ö., **und öfter**, and oftener, and in other places.
urspr., ursprünglich, originally.
u. s. f., **u. s. w.**, **und so fort**, **und so weiter**, and so forth, and so on, etc.
u. v. a., und viele andere, and many others.
u. W., unseres Wissens, as far as we know.

V

V., Vers, line, verse; **vormittags**, before noon, A. M.
v., von, by, from, of.
Vbdg., Verbindung, conjunction.
verb., verbessert, improved, revised.
verd., verderbt, corrupt; verdoppelt, doubled.
vereinf., vereinfacht, simplified.
Verf., **Vf.**, Verfasser, author; **Verff.**, Verfasser, (*pl.*) authors.
verfl. J., verflossenen Jahres, (of) last year.
verk., verkürzt, abbreviated.
verl., verlängert, extended, lengthened.
Verl., Verleger, Verlag, publisher.
verm., vermehrt, enlarged, increased.
versch., verschieden, different.
verst., verstärkt, strengthened; **verstorben**, dead, late.
verw., verwandt, related.
vgl., vergleiche, compare, see; vergleichend, comparative.
v. H., vom Hundert, per cent.
viell., vielleicht, perhaps.
vielm., vielmehr, rather.
v. J., voriges Jahr, vorigen Jahres, (of) last year; von Jahre, of (this) year.
Vjs., Vierteljahrschrift, quarterly (magazine).
v. M., vorigen Monats, (of) last month, during the last month.
v. o., von oben, from the top.
Volksl., Volkslied, folksong.
vor., vorig, (of) last, late.
Vorm., Vormittag, vormittags, before noon, A. M.
v. R. w., **von Rechts wegen**, by right(s), according to the law, according to justice.
v. u., **von unten**, from the bottom.

W

W., Währung, standard; Westen, west; Wechsel, bill (*of exchange*); Werst, verst; Wolfram (*chem.*).
—w. (*final as the second part of a compound*), —weise, -ly, *e.g.* **teilw.**, teilweise, partly; *s.* bzw.
Wb., Wörterbuch, dictionary; **Wbb.**, Wörterbücher, dictionaries.
Wbl., Wochenblatt, weekly (paper).
w. o., wie oben, as above.
W. S. g. u., Wenden Sie gefälligst um, please turn over, P. T. O.
Würt., Würtemberg, Wurtemberg.
W. W., Wiener Währung, Viennese standard *or* currency.
Wwe., Witwe, widow.
W. W. W., die drei W's (= Wehs, woes), Würfel, Weib, Wein, cp. the 3 D's (dice, damsels, drink).
Wz., Wurzel, root.

X

Xber., **Dezember**, December.
Xr., **Kreuzer**, kreutzer.

Z

Z., Zeile, line; Zeit, time; **Zoll**, inch.
z., **zu**, (**zum**, **zur**,) to, (to the), by, per.
z. B., **zum Beispiel**, for instance, *e. g.*
Z. B., **Zur Beurkundung**, in witness (whereof)

z. D., zur Disposition, at (a p.'s) disposal; one half pay (*Mil.*).
z. d. St., zu der *or* dieser Stelle, (referring) to that place, about this passage.
z. E., zum Exempel, for instance, e. g.
Z. F., Zinsfuß, rate of interest.
Z. f. *or* **Zs. f.**, Zeitschrift für, periodical for . . ., journal of . . .
Zg., **Ztg.**, Zeitung, newspaper.
z. H., zu Handen, zu Händen, to be delivered to, care of, c/o.
Zs., **Ztschr.**, Zeitschrift, periodical; **Zss.**, Zeitschriften, periodicals.
zsgs., zusammengesetzt, compound.
zsgz., zusammengezogen, contracted.
z. s. Z., zu seiner Zeit, at its time; in due time.
z. T., zum Teil, partly.
Ztg., Zeitung, newspaper.
Ztr., Zentner, hundredweight, cwt.
Ztw., Zeitwort, verb.
zus., zusammen, together.
Zus., **Zszg.**, Zusammensetzung, compound.
zuw., zuweilen, sometimes.
zw., zwischen, between.
z. Z., zur Zeit, at the time, at present, now acting (e.g. secretary).

LIST OF GERMAN IRREGULAR VERBS

INCLUDING ALL VERBS OF THE STRONG AND ANOMALOUS CONJUGATION AS WELL AS THOSE OF THE WEAK WHICH ARE IN ANY WAY CONJUGATED IRREGULARLY.

The p.p. *of the auxiliary verbs of mood* (dürfen, müssen, wollen, mögen, ꝛc.) *is changed into the* Inf. *in the past compound tenses when it is immediately preceded by an infinitive; this is also the case with* lassen *used as an auxiliary as well as with the verbs,* heißen, helfen, sehen, hören, lehren, lernen.

† = to be avoided. * = obsolete or poetical. ‡ = colloquial or dialectic.	Forms not enclosed in parentheses are of fairly equal value. Forms enclosed in parentheses are less common or not so good.	For compounds with be=, er=, ge=, miß=, ver=, zer=, emp=, ent=, voll=, and other prefixes see the simple verbs where not otherwise given.

INFINITIVE.	PRESENT INDIC.	IMPERF. INDIC.	IMPERF. SUBJ.	IMPERATIVE.	PAST PART.
auslöschen (also trans. & weak)	(das Licht) } lischt (die Kerze) } aus	(das Licht) losch aus	(das Licht) lösche aus	S lisch aus P löscht aus	ausgeloschen
backen (also weak in the meaning 'to stick to,' 'to clot')	2 bäckst 3 bäckt	buk	büke	S backe P backt	gebacken
befehlen	2 befiehlst 3 befiehlt	befahl	beföhle (†befähle)	S befiehl P befehlt	befohlen
(sich) befleißen	2 befleißest or befleißt (dich) 3 befleißt (sich)	befliß (sich)	beflisse (sich)	S befleiß(e) (dich) P befleißt (euch)	beflissen
beginnen	2 beginnst 3 beginnt	begann (*begonnte)	begönne	S beginn(e) P beginnt	begonnen
beißen	2 beißest or beißt 3 beißt	biß	bisse	S beiß(e) P beißt	gebissen
bergen	2 birgst 3 birgt	barg	bärge (*bürge)	S birg P bergt	geborgen
bersten	2 birstest or birst 3 birst	barst (*borst) (†berstete)	bärste or börste	S berste or birst P berstet	geborsten
betrügen (*betriegen)	2 betrügst 3 betrügt	betrog	betröge	S betrüg(e) P betrügt	betrogen
bewegen (to induce any one to do anything) (in the meaning 'to move,' physically or when used metaphorically, the verb is weak)	2 bewegst 3 bewegt	bewog	bewöge	bewege	bewogen
biegen	2 biegst 3 biegt	bog	böge	bieg(e)	gebogen
bieten	2 biet(e)st (*beutst) 3 bietet (*beut)	bot	böte	biet(e) (*beut)	geboten
binden	2 bindest 3 bindet	band	bände	bind(e)	gebunden
bitten	2 bittest 3 bittet	bat	bäte	bitte	gebeten
blasen	2 bläst (*bläsest) 3 bläst (*bläset)	blies	bliese	blas(e)	geblasen
bleiben	2 bleibst 3 bleibt	blieb	bliebe	bleib(e)	geblieben
bleichen (to grow pale, to fade) (in the meaning 'to bleach' it is weak)	2 bleichst 3 bleicht	blich	bliche	bleich(e)	geblichen
braten	2 brätst 3 brät	briet	briete	brat(e)	gebraten
brechen	2 brichst 3 bricht	brach	bräche	S brich P brecht	gebrochen
brennen	2 brennst 3 brennt	brannte	brennte	brenne	gebrannt (‡gebrennt)
bringen	2 bringst 3 bringt	brachte	brächte	bring(e)	gebracht

Infinitive.	Present Indic.	Imperf. Indic.	Imperf. Subj.	Imperative.	Past Part.
denken	2 denkst 3 denkt	dachte	dächte	denk(e)	gedacht
dingen	2 dingst 3 dingt	dingte	dingte	ding(e)	gedingt or gedungen
dreschen	2 drischest (†dresch(e)st) 3 drischt (†drescht)	drasch or drosch	drösche	S drisch P drescht	gedroschen
dringen	2 dringst 3 dringt	drang	dränge	dring(e)	gedrungen
dünken (1 refl. to consider o.s.; 3 Impers.)	1 ich dünke mich 3 mich dünkt or es dünkt mich (mir) or 3 (†däucht, deucht)	däuchte (deuchte) (†dünkte)	däuchte (deuchte) (†dünkte)	dünke (dich)	gedäucht (gedeucht) (†gedünkt)
dürfen	1 & 3 darf 2 darfst 1 wir dürfen &c.	durfte	dürfte		gedurft
(empfehlen, see befehlen)					
erlöschen (to become extinguished)	2 erlisch(e)st 3 erlischt	erlosch	erlösche	S erlisch P erlöscht	erloschen
erschrecken (intrans.) (weak when trans. = to frighten)	2 erschrickst 3 erschrickt	erschrak	erschräke	S erschrick P erschreckt	erschrocken
erwägen	2 erwägst 3 erwägt	erwog	erwöge	erwäg(e)	erwogen
essen	2 ißt (*issest) 3 ißt (*isset)	aß	äße	S iß P eßt	gegessen (*gessen)
fahren	2 fährst 3 fährt	fuhr	führe	fahr(e)	gefahren
fallen	2 fällst 3 fällt	fiel	fiele	fall(e)	gefallen
fangen	2 fängst 3 fängt	fing (†fieng)	finge (†fienge)	fang(e)	gefangen
*fah(e)n (see fangen)					
fechten	2 fichtst 3 ficht	focht	föchte	S ficht P fechtet	gefochten
finden	2 findest 3 findet	fand	fände	find(e)	gefunden
flechten	2 flichtst 3 flicht	flocht	flöchte	S flicht P flechtet	geflochten
fliegen	2 fliegst (*fleugst) 3 fliegt (*fleugt)	flog	flöge	flieg (*fleug)	geflogen
fliehen	2 flieh(e)st (*fleuchst) 3 flieht (*fleucht)	floh	flöhe	flieh (*fleuch)	geflohen
fließen	2 fließest or fließt 3 fließt (*fleußt)	floß	flösse	fließ(e) (*fleuß)	geflossen
fragen	2 fragst (†frägst) 3 fragt (†frägt)	fragte (†frug)	fragte (†früge)	frag(e)	gefragt
fressen	2 frißt (*frissest) 3 frißt (*frisset)	fraß	fräße	S friß P freßt	gefressen
frieren	2 frierst 3 friert	fror	fröre	frier(e)	gefroren
gären (weak when used figuratively)	2 gärst or gierst 3 gärt or giert	gor or gärte	göre or gärte	gär(e)	gegoren or gegärt
gebären	2 gebierst (†gebärst) 3 gebiert (†gebärt)	gebar	gebäre	S gebier (†gebäre) P gebärt	geboren
geben	2 gibst 3 gibt	gab	gäbe	S gib P gebt	gegeben
gedeihen	2 gedeihst 3 gedeiht	gedieh	gediehe	gedeih(e)	gediehen
gehen	2 gehst 3 geht	ging (†gieng)	ginge (†gienge)	geh(e)	gegangen (‡gangen)
gelingen (Impers.)	3 (es) gelingt (mir)	gelang	gelänge	geling(e)	gelungen
gelten	2 giltst 3 gilt	galt	gälte or gölte	gilt	gegolten
genesen	2 genesest or genest 3 genest	genas	genäse	genese	genesen
genießen	2 genießest or genießt (*geneußt) 3 genießt (*geneußt)	genoß	genösse	genieß(e) (*geneuß)	genossen
geraten	2 gerätst 3 gerät	geriet	geriete	gerat(e)	geraten

INFINITIVE.	PRESENT INDIC.	IMPERF. INDIC.	IMPERF. SUBJ.	IMPERATIVE.	PAST PART.
geschehen (Impers.)	3 geschieht (*geschicht)	geschah	geschähe		geschehen
gewinnen	2 gewinnst 3 gewinnt	gewann	gewänne or gewönne	gewinn(e)	gewonnen
gießen	2 gießest or gießt (*geuß(es)t) 3 gießt (*geußt)	goß	gösse	gieß(e) (*geuß)	gegossen
gleichen (trans. is weak)	2 gleichst 3 gleicht	glich	gliche	gleich(e)	geglichen
gleißen	2 gleißest or gleißt 3 gleißt	gleißte (*gliß)	gleißte (*glisse)	gleiß(e)	gegleißt
gleiten	2 gleit(e)st 3 gleitet	glitt (†gleitete)	glitte	gleit(e)	geglitten (†gegleitet)
glimmen	2 glimmst 3 glimmt	glomm or glimmte	glömme or glimmte	glimm(e)	geglommen or geglimmt
graben	2 gräbst 3 gräbt	grub	grübe	grab(e)	gegraben
greifen	2 greifst 3 greift	griff	griffe	greif(e)	gegriffen
haben	1 habe 2 hast 3 hat	hatte (*hätte)	hätte	S hab(e) P habt	gehabt
halten	2 hältst 3 hält	hielt	hielte	halt(e)	gehalten
hängen (*hangen)	2 hängst or hang(e)st 3 hängt or hangt	hing (†hieng)	hinge (†hienge)	hang(e)	gehangen
hauen	2 hau(e)st 3 haut	hieb (†haute)	hiebe (†haute)	hau(e)	gehauen
heben	2 hebst 3 hebt	hob (*hub)	höbe (*hübe)	heb(e)	gehoben
heißen	2 heißest or heißt 3 heißt	hieß	hieße	heiß(e)	geheißen (†gehießen)
helfen	2 hilfst 3 hilft	half	hülfe (†hälfe)	S hilf P helf(e)t	geholfen
kennen	2 kennst 3 kennt	kannte	kenn(e)te	kenne	gekannt
kiesen	2 kiesest or kiest 3 kiest	kor (*kieste)	köre (*kieste)	kiese	(gekoren)
‡klieben	2 kliebst 3 kliebt	klob	klöbe	klieb(e)	gekloben
klimmen	2 klimmst 3 klimmt	klomm	klömm	klimm(e)	geklommen
klingen	2 klingst 3 klingt	klang	klänge	kling(e)	geklungen
kneifen	2 kneifst 3 kneift	kniff	kniffe	kneif(e)	gekniffen
kommen	2 kommst (†kömmst) 3 kommt (†kömmt)	kam	käme	komm(e)	gekommen
können	1 kann 2 kannst 3 kann 1 pl. können, &c.	konnte	könnte	könne	gekonnt
kriechen	2 kriechst (*kreuchst) 3 kriecht (*kreucht)	kroch	kröche	kriech(e) (*kreuch)	gekrochen
laden (= aufladen)	2 lädst 3 lädt	lud	lüde	lad(e)	geladen
laden (= einladen) (orig. only weak)	2 ladest or lädst 3 ladet or lädt	lud (*ladete)	lüde (*ladete)	lad(e)	geladen
lassen	2 läßt or lässest 3 läßt	ließ	ließe	laß	gelassen
laufen	2 läufst 3 läuft	lief	liefe	lauf(e)	gelaufen (*geloffen)
leiden	2 leid(e)st 3 leidet	litt	litte	leid(e)	gelitten
leihen	2 leihst 3 leiht	lieh	liehe	leih(e)	geliehen
lesen	2 liest (†liesest) 3 liest	las	läse	S lies P lest	gelesen
liegen	2 liegst 3 liegt	lag	läge	lieg(e)	gelegen
*löschen (*v.n.* to be extinguished)	2 lischst 3 lischt	losch	lösche	S lisch P löscht	geloschen
lügen	2 lügst (*leugst) 3 lügt (*leugt)	log	löge	lüg(e) (*leug)	gelogen
meiden	2 meidest 3 meidet	mied	miede	meid(e)	gemieden

Infinitive.	Present Indic.	Imperf. Indic.	Imperf. Subj.	Imperative.	Past Part.
melken	2 melkſt 3 melkt	melkte (*molk)	melkte (*mölke)	melk(e) (*milk)	gemelkt or ge molken (friſc gemolkene Milch)
meſſen	2 mißt (*miſſeſt) 3 mißt (*miſſet)	maß	mäße	S miß P meßt	gemeſſen
mögen	1 mag 2 magſt 3 mag 1 pl. mögen	mochte	möchte		gemocht
müſſen	1 muß 2 mußt 3 muß 1 pl. müſſen	mußte	müßte		gemußt
nehmen	2 nimmſt 3 nimmt	nahm	nähme	S nimm P nehmt	genommen
nennen	2 nennſt 3 nennt	nannte	nennte	nenn(e)	genannt
pfeifen	2 pfeifſt 3 pfeift	pfiff	pfiffe	pfeif(e)	gepfiffen
pflegen	2 pflegſt 3 pflegt	pflegte (*pflog or *pflag)	pflegte (*pflöge)	pfleg(e)	gepflegt (*gepflogen)
preiſen	2 preiſeſt or preiſt 3 preiſt	pries (*preiſte)	prieſe (*preiſte)	preiſ(e)	geprieſen (*gepreiſt)
quellen	2 quillſt 3 quillt	quoll	quölle	S quill P quellt	gequollen
raten	2 rätſt 3 rät	riet	riete	rat(e)	geraten
reiben	2 reibſt 3 reibt	rieb	riebe	reib(e)	gerieben
reißen	2 reißeſt or reißt 3 reißt	riß	riſſe	reiß(e)	geriſſen
reiten	2 reit(e)ſt 3 reitet	ritt	ritte	reit(e)	geritten
rennen	2 rennſt 3 rennt	rannte (*rennte)	renn(e)te	renn(e)	gerannt (*gerennet)
riechen	2 riechſt 3 riecht	roch	röche	riech(e)	gerochen
ringen	2 ringſt 3 ringt	rang	ränge	ring(e)	gerungen
rinnen	2 rinnſt 3 rinnt	rann	ränne	rinn(e)	geronnen
rufen	2 rufſt 3 ruft	rief (*rufte)	riefe	ruf(e)	gerufen
ſalzen	2 ſalzeſt 3 ſalzt	ſalzte	ſalz(e)te	ſalze	geſalzen or geſalzt
ſaufen	2 ſäufſt 3 ſäuft	ſoff	ſöffe	ſauf(e)	geſoffen
ſaugen	2 ſaugſt 3 ſaugt	ſog	ſöge	ſaug(e)	geſogen (†geſaugt)
ſchaffen (to create) (in the meaning 'to do, be busy,' the verb is weak)	2 ſchaffſt 3 ſchafft	ſchuf	ſchüfe	ſchaff(e)	geſchaffen
ſchallen	2 ſchallſt 3 ſchallt	ſcholl or ſchallte	ſchölle or ſchallte	ſchall(e)	geſchallt (*erſchollen)
ſcheiden	2 ſcheideſt 3 ſcheidet	ſchied	ſchiede	ſcheid(e)	geſchieden
ſcheinen	2 ſcheinſt 3 ſcheint	ſchien	ſchiene	ſchein(e)	geſchienen
ſcheißen	2 ſcheißeſt or ſcheißt 3 ſcheißt	ſchiß	ſchiſſe	ſcheiß(e)	geſchiſſen
ſchelten	2 ſchilt(e)ſt 3 ſchilt	ſchalt	ſchölte	S ſchilt P ſcheltet	geſcholten
ſcheren	2 ſcherſt (*ſchierſt) 3 ſchert (*ſchiert)	ſchor (†ſcherte)	ſchöre (†ſcherte)	ſchier or ſcher(e)	geſchoren
ſchieben	2 ſchiebſt 3 ſchiebt	ſchob	ſchöbe	ſchieb(e)	geſchoben
ſchießen	2 ſchießeſt or ſchießt 3 ſchießt	ſchoß	ſchöſſe	ſchieß(e)	geſchoſſen
ſchinden	2 ſchindeſt 3 ſchindet	ſchund or ſchin= dete	ſchünde or ſchindete	ſchind(e)	geſchunden
ſchlafen	2 ſchläfſt 3 ſchläft	ſchlief	ſchliefe	ſchlaf(e)	geſchlafen
ſchlagen	2 ſchlägſt 3 ſchlägt	ſchlug	ſchlüge	ſchlag(e)	geſchlagen
ſchleichen	2 ſchleich(e)ſt 3 ſchleicht	ſchlich	ſchliche	ſchleich(e)	geſchlichen

Infinitive.	Present Indic.	Imperf. Indic.	Imperf. Subj.	Imperative.	Past Part.
ſchleifen	2 ſchleifſt 3 ſchleift	ſchliff	ſchliffe	ſchleif(e)	geſchliffen
ſchleißen	2 ſchleißeſt or ſchleißt 3 ſchleißt	ſchliß	ſchliſſe	ſchleiß(e)	geſchliſſen
*ſchliefen	2 ſchliefſt 3 ſchlieft	ſchloff	ſchlöffe	ſchlief(e)	geſchloffen
ſchließen	2 ſchließeſt or ſchließt (*ſchleußeſt or ſchleußt) 3 ſchließt (*ſchleußt)	ſchloß	ſchlöſſe	ſchließ(e) (*ſchleuß)	geſchloſſen
ſchlingen	2 ſchlingſt 3 ſchlingt	ſchlang (*ſchlung)	ſchlänge	ſchling(e)	geſchlungen
ſchmeißen	2 ſchmeißeſt or ſchmeißt 3 ſchmeißt	ſchmiß	ſchmiſſe	ſchmeiß(e)	geſchmiſſen
ſchmelzen (v.n.)	2 ſchmilzeſt 3 ſchmilzt	ſchmolz	ſchmölze	S ſchmilz P ſchmelz(e)t	geſchmolzen
ſchnauben	2 ſchnaubſt 3 ſchnaubt	ſchnob or ſchnaubte	ſchnöbe or ſchnaubte	ſchnaub(e)	geſchnoben or geſchnaubt
ſchneiden	2 ſchneid(e)ſt 3 ſchneidet	ſchnitt	ſchnitte	ſchneid(e)	geſchnitten
ſchrauben	2 ſchraubſt 3 ſchraubt	ſchrob or ſchraubte	ſchröbe or ſchraubte	ſchraub(e)	geſchroben or geſchraubt
*ſchrecken (v.n.)	2 ſchrickſt 3 ſchrickt	ſchrak	ſchräke	S ſchrick P ſchreckt	geſchrocken
ſchreiben	2 ſchreibſt 3 ſchreibt	ſchrieb	ſchriebe	ſchreib(e)	geſchrieben
ſchreien	2 ſchreiſt 3 ſchreit	ſchrie	ſchriee	ſchrei(e)	geſchrieen
ſchreiten	2 ſchreit(e)ſt 3 ſchreitet	ſchritt	ſchritte	ſchreit(e)	geſchritten
*ſchrinden	2 ſchrind(e)ſt 3 ſchrindet	ſchrand	ſchründe	ſchrind(e)	geſchrunden
ſchwären (Impers.)	3 (es)ſchwärt (*ſchwiert)	ſchwor or ſchwärte	ſchwöre	S ſchwier or ſchwäre P ſchwär(e)t	geſchworen
ſchweigen (= 'to be silent' is intrans. & strong) (= 'to silence' is trans. & weak)	2 ſchweigſt 3 ſchweigt	ſchwieg	ſchwiege	ſchweig(e)	geſchwiegen
chwellen	2 ſchwillſt 3 ſchwillt	ſchwoll	ſchwölle	S ſchwill P ſchwellt	geſchwollen
chwimmen	2 ſchwimmſt 3 ſchwimmt	ſchwamm	ſchwömme or ſchwämme	ſchwimm(e)	geſchwommen
chwinden	2 ſchwindeſt 3 ſchwindet	ſchwand	ſchwände	ſchwind(e)	geſchwunden
chwingen	2 ſchwingſt 3 ſchwingt	ſchwang	ſchwänge	ſchwing(e)	geſchwungen
chwören	2 ſchwörſt 3 ſchwört	ſchwor or ſchwur	ſchwüre	ſchwör(e)	geſchworen
ehen	2 ſiehſt 3 ſieht (*ſicht)	ſah	ſähe	S ſieh(e) P ſeh(e)t	geſehen
ein	S 1 bin 2 biſt 3 iſt P 1 ſind 2 ſeid 3 ſind	war (*was)	wäre	S ſei P ſeid	geweſen
enden	2 ſendeſt 3 ſendet	ſandte or ſendete	ſendete	ſend(e)	geſandt or geſendet
eden	2 ſiedeſt 3 ſiedet	ſott or ſiedete	ſötte or ſiedete	ſied(e)	geſotten or geſiedet
ingen	2 ſingſt 3 ſingt	ſang	ſänge	ſing(e)	geſungen
nken	2 ſinkſt 3 ſinkt	ſank	ſänke	ſink(e)	geſunken
nnen	2 ſinnſt 3 ſinnt	ſann	ſänne or ſönne	ſinn(e)	geſonnen
tzen	2 ſitzeſt 3 ſitzt	ſaß	ſäße	ſitz(e)	geſeſſen
ollen	1 ſoll 2 ſollſt (*ſollt) 3 ſoll pl. 1 ſollen, &c.	ſollte	ſollte		geſollt
palten	2 ſpalt(e)ſt 3 ſpaltet	ſpaltete	ſpaltete	ſpalt(e)	geſpalten or geſpaltet
peien	2 ſpeiſt 3 ſpeit	ſpie	ſpiee	ſpei(e)	geſpieen (*geſpeit, cf. *beſpeit)

INFINITIVE.	PRESENT INDIC.	IMPERF. INDIC.	IMPERF. SUBJ.	IMPERATIVE.	PAST PART.
ſpinnen	2 ſpinn(e)ſt 3 ſpinnt	ſpann	ſpönne (†ſpänne)	ſpinn(e)	geſponnen
*ſpleißen	2 ſpleißeſt or ſpleißt 3 ſpleißt	ſpliß or ſpleißte	ſpliſſe or ſpleißte	ſpleiß(e)	geſpliſſen
ſprechen	2 ſprichſt 3 ſpricht	ſprach	ſpräche	S ſprich P ſprech(e)t	geſprochen
ſprießen	2 ſprießeſt or ſprießt 3 ſprießt	ſproß	ſpröſſe	ſprieß(e)	geſproſſen
ſpringen	2 ſpringſt 3 ſpringt	ſprang	ſpränge	ſpring(e)	geſprungen
ſtechen	2 ſtichſt 3 ſticht	ſtach	ſtäche	S ſtich P ſtecht	geſtochen
*ſtecken	2 ſtickſt 3 ſtickt	ſtak	ſtäke		
ſtehen	2 ſtehſt 3 ſteht	ſtand (*ſtund)	ſtände (*ſtünde)	ſteh(e)	geſtanden
ſtehlen	2 ſtiehlſt 3 ſtiehlt	ſtahl	ſtöhle (†ſtähle)	S ſtiehl P ſtehl(e)t	geſtohlen
ſteigen	2 ſteigſt 3 ſteigt	ſtieg	ſtiege	ſteig(e)	geſtiegen
ſterben	2 ſtirbſt 3 ſtirbt	ſtarb	ſtürbe	S ſtirb P ſterb(e)t	geſtorben
ſtieben	2 ſtiebſt 3 ſtiebt	ſtob (or ſtiebte)	ſtöbe	ſtieb(e)	geſtoben
ſtinken	2 ſtinkſt 3 ſtinkt	ſtank	ſtänke	ſtink(e)	geſtunken
ſtoßen	2 ſtößt 3 ſtößt	ſtieß	ſtieße	ſtoß(e)	geſtoßen
ſtreichen	2 ſtreichſt 3 ſtreicht	ſtrich	ſtriche	ſtreich(e)	geſtrichen
ſtreiten	2 ſtreiteſt 3 ſtreitet	ſtritt	ſtritte	ſtreit(e)	geſtritten
thun, *see* tun					
tragen	2 trägſt 3 trägt	trug	trüge	trag(e)	getragen
treffen	2 triffſt 3 trifft	traf	träfe	S triff P treff(e)t	getroffen
treiben	2 treibſt 3 treibt	trieb	triebe	treib(e)	getrieben
treten	2 trittſt 3 tritt	trat	träte	S tritt P tretet	getreten
triefen	2 triefſt (*treufſt) 3 trieft (*treuft)	troff	tröffe	trief(e) (*treuf)	getroffen
trinken	2 trinkſt 3 trinkt	trank	tränke	trink(e)	getrunken
trügen (*triegen)	2 trügſt 3 trügt	trog	tröge	trüg(e)	getrogen
tun (old spelling: thun)	S 1 tue 2 tuſt 3 tut P 1 & 3 tun 2 tut	tat (S 3 *tät) P 1 & 3 taten) (*täten)	täte	tu(e)	getan
verderben (v.n.)	2 verdirbſt 3 verdirbt	verdarb	verdürbe	S verdirb P verderb(e)t	verdorben
verdrießen	2 verdrießeſt or verdrießt 3 verdrießt	verdroß	verdröſſe	verdrieß(e)	verdroſſen
vergeſſen	2 vergißt (vergiſſeſt) 3 vergißt	vergaß	vergäße	S vergiß P vergeßt	vergeſſen
verhehlen	2 verhehlſt 3 verhehlt	verhehlte	verhehlte	verhehle	verhehlt or verhohlen
verlieren	2 verlierſt 3 verliert	verlor	verlöre	verlier(e)	verloren
verlöſchen (v.n.)	(das Feuer) verliſcht	verloſch	verlöſche	verliſch	verloſchen
verſchallen	2 verſchallſt 3 verſchallt	verſcholl	verſchölle	verſchalle	verſchollen
wachſen (meaning to grow)	2 wächſt 3 wächſt	wuchs	wüchſe	wachſ(e)	gewachſen
wägen	2 wägſt 3 wägt	wog or wägte	wöge or wägte	wäg(e)	gewogen or gewägt
waſchen	2 wäſch(e)ſt or wäſcht 3 wäſcht	wuſch	wüſche	waſch(e)	gewaſchen
weben	2 webſt 3 webt	webte or wob	webte or wöbe	web(e)	gewebt or gewoben
weichen	2 weichſt 3 weicht	wich	wiche	weich(e)	gewichen

Infinitive.	Present Indic.	Imperf. Indic.	Imperf. Subj.	Imperative.	Past Part.
weisen	2 weisest or weist 3 weist	wies	wiese	weis(e)	gewiesen
wenden	2 wendest 3 wendet	wandte or wen= dete	wendete	wend(e)	gewendet or gewandt
werben	2 wirbst 3 wirbt	warb	würbe	S wirb P werb(e)t	geworben
werden	2 wirst 3 wird	wurde (*ward)	würde	werde	geworden (*worden)
werfen	2 wirfst 3 wirft	warf	würfe	S wirf P werf(e)t	geworfen
wiegen (to weigh, v.n.) (wiegen, to rock, v.a. is weak)	2 wiegst 3 wiegt	wog	wöge	wieg(e)	gewogen
winden	2 windest 3 windet	wand	wände	wind(e)	gewunden
wissen	S 1 & 3 weiß 2 weißt P 1 wissen	wußte	wüßte	wisse	gewußt
wollen	S 1 & 3 will 2 willst (*willt) P 1 wollen	wollte	wollte	wolle	gewollt
zeihen	2 zeihst 3 zeiht	zieh	ziehe	zeih(e)	geziehen
ziehen	2 ziehst (*zeuchst) 3 zieht (*zeucht)	zog	zöge	zieh(e) (*zeuch)	gezogen
zwingen	2 zwingst 3 zwingt	zwang	zwänge	zwing(e)	gezwungen

TABLE OF GERMAN COINS, MEASURES AND WEIGHT REDUCED TO ENGLISH MONEY, MEASURES AN WEIGHTS.

Mk.	Pf.	s.	d.	Mk.	Pf.	s.	d.	Mk.	Pf.	s.	d.
0	4	0	½	5	0	5	0	13	0	13	0
0	8	0	1	6	0	6	0	14	0	14	0
0	25	0	3	7	0	7	0	15	0	15	0
0	50	0	6	8	0	8	0	16	0	16	0
1	0	1	0	9	0	9	0	17	0	17	0
2	0	2	0	10	0	10	0	18	0	18	0
3	0	3	0	11	0	11	0	19	0	19	0
4	0	4	0	12	0	12	0	20	0	20	0

ITINERARY MEASURE.

Meter (ten-millionth part of the arc of a meridian between the pole and the equator)	3·2808992	feet.
Decameter (10 meters) ..	32·808992	feet.
Kilometer (1,000 meters) ..	1093·633	yards.
Myriameter (10,000 meters)..	6·2138	miles.

LONG MEASURE.

Decimeter (10th of a meter) ..	3·937079	inches.
Centimeter (100th of a meter)..	0·393707	inch.
Millimeter (1000th of a meter)..	0·03937	inch.

SUPERFICIAL MEASURE.

Are (100 square meters)	0·098845 rood.
Hectare (10,000 square meters) ..	2·471143 acres.
Centiare (1 square meter) ..	1·196033 sq.yd.

MEASURE OF CAPACITY.

Liter (1 cubic decimeter)	1·760773 pint.
Decaliter (10 liters)	2·2009668 gallon
Hectoliter (100 liters)	22·009668 gallons 2·7512 bushels.
Kiloliter (1000 liters)	3·426 quarters.
Deciliter (10th of a liter)	0·1760773 pint.
Centiliter (100th of a liter)	0·01760773 pint.

WEIGHTS.

Gramme (weight of 1 cubic centimeter in its state of maximum density, or 39½° Fahr., or 4° C.)	15·4325 grai troy.
Decagramme (10 grammes)	6·43 dwt.
Hectogramme (100 grammes)	3·527 oz. avo or 4·183 oz. tro
Kilogramme (1000 grammes)	2·2055 lbs. avoir. or 2·6803lbs.tr
Centner (50 kilogrammes)	110 lbs. avo
Meter-centner (100 kilogrammes)	220 lbs. avo
Decigramme (10th of 1 gramme)	1·5432 grain
Centigramme (100th of 1 gramme)	0·15432 grai
Milligramme (1000th of 1 gramme)	0·015432 gra

THERMOMETER.

0°	Centigrade	Melting Ice	32°	Fahrenhe
100°	,,	Boiling Water	212°	,,
0°	Réaumur	Melting Ice	32°	,,
80°	,,	Boiling Water	212°	,,

TABLE OF ENGLISH COINS, MEASURES AND WEIGHT REDUCED TO GERMAN MONEY, MEASURES AN WEIGHTS.

Pound. Shil. Pence.	Mk.	Pf.	M.	Pf.	M.	Pf.	Feet.	Metres.	Inches. Centimeters.
1	20	0	1	0	0	08	1	0·30479449	2·539954
2	40	0	2	0	0	17	2	0·60953898	5·079908
3	60	0	3	0	0	25	3	0·91438348	7·619862
4	80	0	4	0	0	33	4	1·21917796	10·159816
5	100	0	5	0	0	42	5	1·52397245	12·699770
6	120	0	6	0	0	50	6	1·82876694	15·239724
7	140	0	7	0	0	58	7	2·13356143	17·779678
8	160	0	8	0	0	67	8	2·43835592	20·319632
9	180	0	9	0	0	75	9	2·74315041	22·859586
10	200	0	10	0	0	84	10	3·0479449	25·399540
11	220	0	11	0	0	92	11	3·3527394	27·939494
12	240	0	12	0	1	0	12	3·6575338	30·479448

TROY WEIGHT.

Grain	=	0·064798 grammes.
Pennyweight	=	1·55517 ,,
Ounce	=	31·1035 ,,
Pound	=	0·373242 kilogrammes.

LONG MEASURE.

3 Feet (1 Yard)	=	0·914383 meters.
Fathom (2 Yards)	=	1·828766 ,,
Pole, Rod (5½ Yards)	=	5·02911 ,,
Furlong (220 Yards)	=	201·16437 ,,
Mile (1,760 Yards)	=	1609·3149 ,,

AVOIRDUPOIS WEIGHT.

Dram	=	1·17718 grammes.
Ounce	=	28·3495 ,,
Pound	=	0·4535926 kilogramm
Quarter	=	12·6956 ,,
Hundredweight	=	50·802 ,,
Ton	=	1016·048 ,,

MEASURE OF CAPACITY.

Pint	=	0·5679 liters.
Quart	=	1·1359 ,,
Gallon	=	4·543458 ,,
Peck	=	9·086916 ,,
Bushel	=	36·34766 ,,
Sack	=	1·0904 hectoliters.
Quarter	=	2·90781 ,,
Chaldron	=	13·08516 ,,

A

GENERAL ENGLISH-GERMAN DICTIONARY.

A

A, a, *n.* A, a; A, la (*Mus.*). *For abbreviations see the Index at the end of the English-German part.*

A, (**An**, *before a vowel or silent h*), *ind. art.* ein, eine, ein; (*used distributively*) der, die, das; two minutes at — time, zwei Minuten hintereinander; many — man, mancher Mann; half — day, ein halber Tag; 2 shillings — pound, zwei Mark das Pfund; 3 shillings — day, täglich drei Mark; — hundred soldiers, hundert Soldaten; — few (some) einige; (not many) wenige; — great deal, sehr viel; — little, etwas; — while, eine zeitlang.

A, I. *prepositional prefix* (= on, in, at, etc.); —-bed, im Bette; —-foot, zu Fuße. II. *prep. in comp. with the so-called participial substantive or verbal noun in -ing;* to go —-begging, betteln gehen; the house is —-building, das Haus ist im Bau begriffen, wird gebaut; to fall —-weeping, zu weinen anfangen. III. *prefix* (= *Old English* ge-) aweary of the world, der Welt überdrüssig. IV. *For words formed with the English prefix* a (*as* awake, alight) *and the Latin prefix* a, ab (*as* avert, absolve) *see below.*

'A = he (*obs.*); I (*prov.*); have (*vulg.*); of (*obs.*).

Aback, *adv.* zurück, rückwärts, hinten; mastwärts (*Naut.*); taken —, überrascht, bestürzt, verblüfft, in Verlegenheit.

Abacus, *s.* das Rechenbrett; die Säulenplatte, Kapitäldeckplatte (*Arch.*).

Abaft, *adv.* hinterwärts, nach hinten, hinten.

Abandon, *v.a.* (give up) aufgeben; (forsake, leave forever) verlassen; (surrender, deliver up) preisgeben, überlassen; to — o.s. to . . ., sich einer S. . . . hingeben, überlassen; to — a p. to his fate, einen seinem Schicksale überlassen; to — all hope, alle Hoffnung aufgeben *or* fahren lassen. **—ed,** *p.p. & adj.* verlassen; aufgegeben; (profligate) lasterhaft, verworfen. **—ment,** *s.* das Verlassen; das Aufgeben, die Aufgabe; die Verlassenheit.

Abase, *v.a.* niederlassen (*obs.*); (humiliate) demütigen; (degrade) erniedrigen. **—ment,** *s.* das Niederlassen; die Demütigung, Erniedrigung (*fig.*); (dejection) die Niedergeschlagenheit.

Abash, *v.a.* beschämen, verlegen machen; to be —ed (at a th.), verlegen *or* betreten sein (über eine S.).

Abate, *v.* I. *a.* nachlassen, herabsetzen (*the price*); mildern (*pain, etc.*); (diminish) vermindern; to — a nuisance, etwas Ungebührliches, Schädliches abschaffen. II. *n.* nachlassen, an Stärke verlieren, abnehmen; the wind —s, der Wind legt sich. **—ment,** *s.* (diminution) die Verminderung, Abnahme; der Nachlaß, Abzug, die Herabsetzung (*in price, etc.*).

Abatis, (Abattis,) *s.* der Verhau (*Mil.*).

Abb—acy, *s.* die Würde und Rechte eines Abts. **—ess,** *s.* die Äbtissin. **—ey,** *s.* die Abtei. **—ot,** *s.* der Abt.

Abbreviat—e, *v.a.* abkürzen; reduzieren (*fractions, etc.*); auf den kleinsten Nenner bringen (*Math.*). **—ion,** *s.* die Abkürzung (*also Mus.*).

Abdicat—e, *v.a. & n.* niederlegen, aufgeben, entsagen; to —e the throne, dem Throne entsagen, abdanken. **—ion,** *s.* die Niederlegung, Abdankung; —ion of the throne, die Thronentsagung, Regierungsniederlegung.

Abdom—en, *s.* der Unterleib. **—inal,** *adj.* zum Unterleibe gehörig, Unterleibs=.

Abduct, *v.a.* abziehen; entführen. **—ion,** *s.* die Abziehung (*Anat.*); die Entführung (*Law*). **—or,** *s.* der Abziehmuskel (*Anat.*); der Entführer.

Abed, *adv.* zu Bett, im Bette.

Aberration, *s.* die Abweichung (*of light*); der Irrgang, Irrweg, falsche Weg (*fig.*); die Abirrung (*Astr.*); — of mind, die Geistesverwirrung; chromatic —, chromatische Abweichung.

Abet, *v.a.* (urge on) anhetzen, antreiben, aufmuntern; (aid) helfen, unterstützen. **—ment,** *s.* die Anhetzung, Anstiftung; der Beistand, die Unterstützung. **—tor,** *s.* der Anhetzer, Anstifter; der Unterstützer, Helfer; der Mitschuldige.

Abeyance, *s.* der ungewisse Aufschub; die Anwartschaft (auf eine S.); in —, noch nicht gerichtlich zugewiesen, herrenlos (*of lands*); unentschieden, anstehend, in der Schwebe (befindlich).

Abhor, *v.a.* verabscheuen. **—rence,** *s.* der Abscheu, die Verabscheuung; to hold in —rence, verabscheuen. **—rent,** *adj.* zuwider (to, *dat.*); unvereinbar (to, mit).

Abid—e, *ir.v.* I. *n.* (dwell) wohnen; (remain, stay) verweilen, bleiben; (last) fortdauern; —e by, verharren bei (*an opinion, etc.*); sich begnügen mit (*a decision, etc.*); halten (*a promise*); (insist on) bestehen auf; to —e by the consequences, die Folgen auf sich (*acc.*) nehmen. II. *a.* (endure) aushalten, leiden, ertragen; I cannot — him, ich kann ihn nicht ausstehen *or* leiden. **—ing,** *adj.* dauernd. *Comp.* **—ing-place,** *s.* der Wohnort; die Ruhestätte.

Abilit—y, *s.* das Vermögen, die Fähigkeit, die Geschicklichkeit; to the best of my —y, nach besten Kräften. **—ies,** *pl.* (Geistes=)Anlagen.

Abject, *adj.*, **—ly,** *adv.* (servile) kriechend, unterwürfig; (despicable) verächtlich, niedrig; (base, vile) niederträchtig; (worthless) verworfen; in — misery, im äußersten Elend. **—ness,** *s.* die Niedrigkeit; die Niederträchtigkeit.

Abjure, *v.a.* abschwören; (give up) entsagen (einer S.), verschwören (eine S.).

Ablative, *s.* der Ablativ; — absolute, der unabhängige Ablativ, Ablativus absolutus.

Able, *adj.*, **Ably,** *adv.* (capable) fähig; (clever) geschickt; (efficient) tüchtig; to be —, können, im stande sein; — to pay, zahlungsfähig; as one is —, nach seinen Mitteln. *Comp.* **—-bodied,** *adj.* stark, handfest; dienstfähig, tauglich; —-bodied seaman, der Vollmatrose.

Ablution, *s.* die Abwaschung, Abspülung; to perform one's —s, sich waschen.

Abnegat—e, *v.a.* ableugnen, verneinen. **—ion,** *s.* die Ableugnung, Verneinung; self —ion, die Selbstverleugnung.

Abnormal, *adj.* regelwidrig; ungewöhnlich, abnorm.

Aboard, *adv.* an Bord; — a ship, an Bord eines Schiffes; — a balloon, in der Gondel eines Luftschiffs; to go —, sich einschiffen.

[1]**Abode,** *s.* (dwelling) die Wohnung; (stay) der Aufenthalt; der Aufenthaltsort, Wohnsitz

[2]**Abode,** *imperf. of* Abide.

Aboli—sh, *v.a.* aufheben, abschaffen; (annul) vertilgen, vernichten; (abrogate) abschaffen; (suppress) unterdrücken. **—tion,** *s.* die Abschaffung, Aufhebung; die Vernichtung

tionist, *s.* Freund der Aufhebung der Sklaverei, Gegner der Sklaverei (*Amer.*).

Abomina—ble, *adj.*, **—bly**, *adv.* abscheulich, scheußlich; unrein (*B.*). **—te**, *v.a.* verabscheuen; I —te it, es ist mir ein Greuel. **—tion**, *s.* (horror) die Verabscheuung, der Abscheu; object of —tion, der Greuel.

Aborigin—al, *adj.* ursprünglich, ureingesessen, einheimisch. **—es**, *pl.* die Ureinwohner.

Aborti—on, *s.* das Mißgebären; (that which is produced) die Frühgeburt, Fehlgeburt; die Mißgeburt. **—ve(ly)**, *adj.* (*adv.*) unzeitig, zu früh geboren; verunglückt; to prove —ve, fehlschlagen, mißglücken. **—veness**, *s.* das Mißlingen (*fig.*).

Abound, *v.n.* (possess abundantly) Überfluß haben (an einer S.), übervoll sein *or* wimmeln von einer S.; (be abundant) im Überfluß *or* überreichlich vorhanden sein.

About, I. *prep.* (round) um, herum; (towards) gegen, um; (on account of) wegen, über, um; (concerning) über, in Beziehung auf, betreffend; the fields — the town, die Felder um die Stadt; he looked round — him, er sah um sich her; I care nothing — it, ich frage nichts danach; there is no mistake — it, so und nicht anders stehen die Sachen; he is — the house, er ist irgendwo im Hause; he went out — three o'clock, er ging etwa um drei Uhr aus; — the streets, in den Straßen umher; I have no money — me, ich habe kein Geld bei mir; my opinion — it, meine Meinung darüber; to talk —, reden über (*acc.*); the quarrel was — a trifle, der Streit war wegen einer (über eine) Kleinigkeit; to set — a thing, etwas anfangen; what are you —? was macht ihr? was habt ihr vor? mind what you 're —! nehmt euch in acht! (*coll.*); look — you! nehmen Sie sich in acht! to have one's wits — one, seine Gedanken beisammen haben; to send a p. — his business, einen fortschicken, einem (gehörig) heimleuchten; there is some mystery — it, da steckt etwas dahinter; don't bother me — it, bleiben Sie mir damit vom Leibe (*coll.*); he troubles his head — it, er macht sich Gedanken darüber; I feel uneasy — it, mir ist übel dabei zu Mute; shall I send him word — it? soll ich ihn davon benachrichtigen? there is something wrong — it, das geht nicht mit rechten Dingen zu; dabei ist etwas nicht in Ordnung; you make too much fuss — it, Sie machen zu viel Wesens davon; to beat — the bush, auf den Busch klopfen. II. *adv.* herum, umher, ringsherum; (round) in der Runde; (in circumference) im Umfange; (aside) abwegs; (nearly) ungefähr, etwa; (everywhere) überall; to be — to do a th.; im Begriffe sein etwas zu tun; he was — to write, er war im Begriffe *or* eben dabei zu schreiben; I must be — at cock-crow, ich muß beim ersten Hahnenschrei auf den Beinen sein; a long way —, ein großer Umweg; to be — as high, etwa, beinah, fast so hoch sein; to look —, sich umsehen; to put a ship —, ein Schiff wenden; to be lying —, hier und da zerstreut liegen, herumliegen; — a year later, etwa ein Jahr später; — 300 souls, an die dreihundert *or* gegen dreihundert Seelen; how came that —? wie ging das zu? to bring —, zustande bringen, fertig bringen; to come —, geschehen; right —, turn! rechts um, kehrt!

Above, I. *prep.* über; — all things, vor allen Dingen, vor allem; he has been waiting for me — twenty minutes, er hat über 20 Minuten auf mich gewartet; — praise, über alles Lob erhaben, höchst lobenswert; to be — a p. in a th., einem in einer S. überlegen sein, einen an einer S. übertreffen, höher als einer stehen; it is — me, das geht über meinen Verstand; he is — nothing, er hält nichts für unter seiner Würde; he is — it, er ist darüber erhaben, setzt sich über so etwas hinweg; he is — taking advice, er ist zu stolz, (um) Rat anzunehmen; they have privileges — other countries, sie haben Vorrechte vor andern Ländern; those — me, meine Oberen; — 300 mehr als 300. II. *adv.* oben; darüber; over and —, oben drein; the powers —, die himmlischen Mächte; — mentioned, oben erwähnt the —, der, die, das Obige; since writing the —, seitdem ich Obiges geschrieben habe. *Comp* **—-board**, *adv.* offen, ohne Arg, unversteckt.

Abrasion, *s.* das Abschaben, Abreiben; das Abgeriebene, Schabsel; die Hautabschürfung.

Abreast, I. *adv.* neben einander, Seite an Seite: they walked three —, sie gingen drei nebeneinander; the ship was — of the cape, das Schiff lag auf der Höhe des Kaps; formed —, in Schlachtlinie, Frontenlinie; to keep — of the progress of science, sich in der Wissenschaft auf der Höhe halten. II. *attrib.*; — line, die Schlachtlinie.

Abridg—e, *v.a.* abkürzen, verkürzen; zusammenziehen; einschränken, vermindern (*privileges, etc.*). **—ment**, *s.* die Abkürzung; der Abriß, Auszug (*of a book, etc.*).

Abroad, *adv.* draußen, außer dem Hause; im Freien; im Auslande; auswärts; weithin; at home and —, in und außer dem Hause; im eignen Lande und im Auslande; to go —, in die Fremde ziehen; ins Ausland reisen, außer Landes gehen; to live —, im Ausland leben; how did that matter get —? wie kam die Sache aus? the thing has got —, die Sache ist ruchbar geworden; there is a report —, es ist ein weit verbreitetes Gerücht, es geht die Rede.

Abrogat—e, *v.a.* aufheben, zurückrufen, abschaffen. **—ion**, *s.* die Aufhebung, Abschaffung

Abrupt, *adj.*, **—ly**, *adv.* abgerissen, abgebrochen; jäh; plötzlich; (curt) schroff, kurz; an — style, eine abgebrochene, kurze Schreibart; an — departure, eine plötzliche, unvermittelte Abreise. **—ness**, *s.* das Unzusammenhängende; die Abgebrochenheit (*of style*); die Jähe (*of a declivity*); das Ungeschliffene, die Rauhheit (*of a p.'s manner*); die Eile, Übereilung (*of s.o.'s departure*).

Abscess, *s.* die Eitergeschwulst, das Geschwür.

Abscond, *v.n.* sich verbergen; entweichen, sich heimlich davon machen. **—er**, *s.* der heimlich Entweichende, Flüchtling.

Absen—ce, *s.* die Abwesenheit; das Ausbleiben, Nichterscheinen (*Law*); (want) der Mangel; —ce of mind, die Zerstreutheit, Zerstreuung; leave of —ce, der Urlaub. **—t**, I. *adj.* abwesend; long —t, soon forgotten, aus den Augen, aus dem Sinn (*prov.*). II. *v.r.* (to —t oneself) sich entfernen; ausbleiben. **—tee**, *s.* Abwesende(r). **—teeism**, *s.* das Außerlandeswohnen. **—t-minded**, *adj.* zerstreut. **—t-mindedness**, *s.* die Geistesabwesenheit, Zierstreutheit.

Absinth(e), *s.* der Wermut; der Wermutgeist.

Absol—ute, *adj.* unumschränkt, unbeschränkt, eigenmächtig; (complete) vollkommen, vollständig; (unconditional) unbedingt; an —ute fool, ein völliger Narr; the case —ute, der unabhängige Kasus; —ute space, der unbeziehliche Raum. **—utely**, *adv.* unumschränkt; (actually) in der Tat, wirklich; (unconditionally) unbedingt; (positively) bestimmt; (indispensably) durchaus; (wholly) ganz, völlig; it is —utely necessary for him to . . ., er muß durchaus, es ist unbedingt notwendig *or* unumgänglich erforderlich, daß er . . .; he is —utely certain, er ist fest überzeugt. **—uteness**, *s.* die Unumschränktheit. **—ution**, *s.* die Absolution (*Theol.*); die Freisprechung. **—ve**, *v.a.* (acquit) lossprechen, freisprechen; entbinden (*from a promise, vow*); absolvieren (*Theol.*); to —ve a p. from a vow, einen eines Schwurs entbinden.

Absorb, *v.a.* verschlucken, einsaugen, in sich ziehen; (swallow up) verschlingen; gänzlich beschäftigen, in Anspruch nehmen (*the attention, etc.*); an sich ziehen (*the population, etc. of a place*); absorbieren (*Chem.*); —ed in thought, in Gedanken vertieft; the all —ing topic of conversation, der allbeherrschende Gesprächsgegenstand; to — s. o.'s whole interest, jemandes Interesse vollauf in Anspruch nehmen; —ing power, das Aufsaugevermögen. **—ent,** *adj.* einsaugend, absorbierend. **—ents,** *pl.* Lymphgefäße (*Anat.*); Absorptionsmittel (*Chem.*).

Absorption, *s.* das Einsaugen; die Aufsaugung; (disappearance) das Absterben, Verschwinden; die Absorption (*Chem.*); die Vertiefung (*in thought*), das in Gedanken Versunkensein.

Abstain, *v.n.* sich enthalten (from, von *or gen.*). **—er,** *s.* der sich Enthaltende, der Enthaltsame; total —er, der Mäßigkeit(s=verein)ler; einer, der keine geistigen Getränke trinkt.

Abstemious, *adj.*, **—ly,** *adv.* enthaltsam; (temperate) mäßig. **—ness,** *s.* die Enthaltsamkeit; die Mäßigkeit.

Abstention, *s.* die Enthaltung, Zurückhaltung (from, von); der Verzicht (from a th., auf eine S.); die Entbehrung, das Fasten.

Abstergent, I. *adj.* reinigend (*Bot.*); abführend (*Med.*). II. *s.* das Abführungsmittel.

Abstinen—ce, *s.* die Enthaltsamkeit; das Fasten; day of —ce, der Fasttag. **—t(ly),** *adj.* (*adv.*) enthaltsam; mäßig.

Abstract, I. *v.a.* (withdraw) abziehen; (separate) absondern; abstrahieren; abziehen, absondern (*Chem.*); (steal) (heimlich) entwenden; (epitomize) in einen Abriß bringen, sich (*dat.*) einen Auszug machen (aus einer S.). II. *adj.* abgezogen, abgesondert; (not concrete) abstrakt, rein begrifflich (*Log.*); (general) allgemein (*Log. etc.*); rein (*Math.*); (profound) tiefsinnig, schwer verständlich; an — idea, ein abstrakter *or* abgezogener Begriff; an — number, eine unbenannte Zahl; an — quantity, eine abgezogene Größe, eine Größe für sich allein betrachtet; the — sciences, die reinen *or* abstrakten Wissenschaften. III. *s.* der Abriß, Auszug (*from a book*); der Inbegriff, die kurze Übersicht, der Hauptinhalt (*of a speech, etc.*); die Liste (*obs.*); (— idea) der abgezogene Begriff; in the —, an sich betrachtet, rein begrifflich. **—ed,** *adj.* abgesondert, getrennt, abgezogen; (refined) verfeinert; (abstruse) schwer verständlich; (inattentive) geistesabwesend, unaufmerksam, zerstreut; abstrakt. **—edly,** *adv.* in der Zerstreuung. **—edness,** *s.* die Abgezogenheit; die Zerstreuung. **—er,** *s.* der Entwender, Dieb; der Zusammenfasser, Verfasser eines Abrisses. **—ion,** *s.* die Abziehung, Absonderung; das Abziehen; das Abgesondertsein; die Abstraktion; der abstrakte Begriff, etwas bloß Gedachtes; (faculty of —ion) das Absonderungsvermögen; der abstrakte Gegenstand; (—ion of mind) die Geistesabwesenheit, Zerstreuung. **—ly,** *adv.* abstrakt, an sich. **—ness,** *s.* die abstrakte Beschaffenheit, das Abstrakte. **—s,** *pl.* die Abstrakten (*Org.*).

bstruse, *adj.*, **—ly,** *adv.* dunkel, schwerverständlich; (profound) tief, tiefsinnig. **—ness,** *s.* die Dunkelheit, Unverständlichkeit.

bsurd, *adj.*, **—ly,** *adv.* (foolish) albern, töricht, abgeschmackt; (unreasonable) ungereimt, vernunftwidrig; (laughable) lächerlich. **—ity,** *s.* die Ungereimtheit, Albernheit, Abgeschmacktheit.

bund—ance, *s.* die Fülle; der Überfluß; in —ance (—antly), vollauf; —ance of friends, der Überfluß an Freunden, eine Menge Freunde; —ance of wit, viel Verstand; to live in —ance, im Überfluß leben. **—ant(ly),** *adj.* (*adv.*) reichlich, genugsam, übergenug; (overflowing) überflüssig; this will —antly suffice to show, dies wird völlig hinreichen zu zeigen *or* zur Genüge beweisen.

bus—e, I. *v.a.* (misapply) mißbrauchen; (scold) schimpfen; (speak ill of a p.) (einem) Böses nachsagen; (violate) schänden; (beat, etc.) mißhandeln; täuschen, betrügen (*a p.'s hopes, a p.'s confidence, etc.*); to —e s. o.'s kindness, die Güte jemandes mißbrauchen. II. *s.* der Mißbrauch; die Beschimpfung; falsche Anwendung (*of a word, term, etc.*); (public wrong) das Unrecht; the —e of justice, die Verletzung des Rechts. **—er,** *s.* der, welcher mißbraucht, der Mißbraucher; der Schimpfer; der Lästerer; der Verführer; der Betrüger. **—ive(ly),** *adj.* (*adv.*) schimpfend, schmähend; —ive language, Schimpfworte, gemeine Ausdrucksweise; he used —ive language, er schimpfte, bediente sich gemeiner Schimpfworte.

Abut, *v.n.* angrenzen, anstoßen (upon a th., an eine S.). **—ment,** *s.* die Angrenzung; der Strebepfeiler; das Widerlager (*of a bridge*). **—ting,** *p. & adj.* angrenzend; (salient) hervorragend, ausgehend.

Abyss, (*poet.* **Abysm,**) *s.* der Abgrund, Schlund.

Acacia, *s.* die Akazie, der Akazienbaum.

Academ—ic, —ical(ly), *adj.* (*adv.*) akademisch; zur Akademie gehörig; **—ic dress,** die offizielle Professorentracht *or* Studententracht an Hochschulen. **—ician,** *s.* der Akademiker; der Platoniker, der akademische Philosoph. **—y,** *s.* die Akademie; die Hochschule; der Künstlerverein, Gelehrtenverein; (school) die höhere Lehranstalt, Sekundärschule (*in Scotland*); member of the —y, der Mitglied der Akademie.

Acanth—aceous, *adj.* dornig, stachelig (*Bot.*). **—us,** *s.* die Bärenklau; der Akanthus; das (Säulen)laubwerk (*Arch.*).

Accede, *v.n.* (— to) bewilligen (*a request*); besteigen (*a throne*); to — to the proposed terms, den vorgeschlagenen Bedingungen beitreten, sie bewilligen *or* in dieselben einwilligen; to — to a treaty, an einem Vertrage teilnehmen.

Accelerat—e, *v.a.* beschleunigen. **—ion,** *s.* die Beschleunigung.

Accent, I. *v.a. see* —uate. II. *s.* der Ton, Wortton, die Betonung; der Akzent, das Tonzeichen (*Gram.*); (pronunciation) die Aussprache; acute —, gestoßener Akzent; a circumflex —, ein Dehnungszeichen; ein geschleifter Akzent; dynamic —, stress —, dynamischer Akzent, (Tonstärke); musical —, pitch —, musikalischer Akzent, (Tonhöhe); fluctuating, intermittent —, — points, zweigipfliger Akzent. **—uate,** *v.a.* betonen, akzentuieren. **—uation,** *s.* die Betonung, Akzentuation; die Tonbezeichnung.

Accept, *v.a.* annehmen; nehmen, akzeptieren (*C. L.*); (favour) begünstigen, vorziehen (*B.*), gnädiglich ansehen (*B.*); to — defeat, (eine) Niederlage hinnehmen; to — the terms, die Bedingungen annehmen, auf die Bedingungen eingehen; — £30, nehme £30 (*C. L.*); how is this phrase to be —ed? wie ist diese Redensart zu verstehen? (*obs.*). **—able,** *adj.*, **—ably,** *adv.* annehmbar, annehmlich; (agreeable) angenehm; (welcome) willkommen, erwünscht. **—ability, —ableness,** *s.* die Annehmlichkeit, Annehmbarkeit. **—ance,** *s.* die Annahme; die gute Aufnahme, die Annahme, das Akzept (*of a bill*); qualified —ance, bedingtes Akzept; —ance under protest, Interventionsakzept; to beg a p.'s —ance of a th., einen bitten, etwas anzunehmen; to find —ance, angenommen werden, Annahme *or* Geltung finden; my proposals did not meet with —ance from him, er ging nicht auf meine Vorschläge ein. **—ation,** *s.* die Annahme; die freundliche Aufnahme; *see* —ableness; die angenommene Bedeutung (*of a word, etc.*). **—ed,** *adj.* angenommen; (sanctioned, usual) üblich; —ed before God, Gott angenehm. **—er, —or,** *s.* der Annehmer, der, welcher etwas annimmt; der Akzeptant, Annehmer (*of a bill*); God is not an —er of persons, vor Gott gilt kein Ansehen der Person.

Access, *s.* der Zugang, Zutritt; die Audienz; (increase) der Zuwachs, die Zunahme, Vermehrung; der Anfall, Eintritt (*of fever, etc.*);

easy of —, zugänglich; be not denied —, laß dich nicht abweisen. —**ibility**, *s.* die Zugänglichkeit. —**ible**, *adj.* zugänglich; erreichbar, ersteigbar (*as a place*). —**ion**, *s.* der Zuwachs, die Vermehrung, das Hinzukommen (*of property, etc.*); der Beitritt (*to a treaty, etc.*); der Eintritt (*of fever, etc.*), die Annäherung; —ion to the crown, die Thronbesteigung. —**ory**, I. *adj.* (additional) hinzugefügt, hinzukommend, beiläufig, zusätzlich, akzessorisch; beitragend; nebensächlich, untergeordnet; (abetting) teilnehmend, mitschuldig; —ory parts, das Beiwerk; —ory phenomenon, die Begleiterscheinung; —ory nerves, die Beinerven, Hülfsnerven; —ory proof, der Nebenbeweis; to be —ory to, beitragen zu. II. *s.* der Teilnehmer, Mitschuldige; —ory after the fact, der Hehler; —ory before the fact, der Anstifter. —**ories**, *pl.* das Beiwerk (*Paint.*); (something added) das Zubehör, die Zugabe; die Begleiterscheinung(en).

Acciden—ce, *s.* die Wortbiegungslehre, Flexionslehre (*Gram.*). —**t**, *s.* (chance occurrence) der Zufall, das zufällige Ereignis; (mishap) der Unfall; der Unglücksfall; das Zufällige, die zufällige Eigenschaft, das Unwesentliche, die Akzidenz (*Log. etc.*); die Ableitung, Endung (*of a word*) (*obs.*); by —t, zufälligerweise, zufällig; he met with an —t, ihm stieß ein Unfall zu; it was by mere —t that I met him, es war der reine Zufall, daß ich ihm begegnete; ich traf ihn rein zufällig; the —t of his birth, der Zufall seiner Geburt; the —ts of life, die Zufälligkeiten des Lebens. —**tal**, I. *adj.* zufällig; (non-essential) unwesentlich; —tal sharp, zufälliges Kreuz, die neu hinzutretende Vorzeichnung (*Mus.*); —tal lights, Nebenlichter. II. *s.* das Zufällige; das Unwesentliche; das Versetzungszeichen (*Mus.*). —**tally**, *adv.* *see* by —t; durch Zufall.

Acclaim, I. *s. see* Acclamation. II. *v.* (einem) zurufen, Beifall rufen.

Acclamat—ion, *s.* der laute Beifall, Zuruf (*of approval*); das Freudengeschrei, Zujauchzen; elected by —ion, durch Zuruf gewählt. —**ory**, *adj.* zurufend, zujauchzend.

Acclimatiz—ation, *s.* die Akklimatisierung, Eingewöhnung (in ein fremdes Klima), Einbürgerung (in fremde Verhältnisse). —**e**, *v.a.* an ein Klima gewöhnen, eingewöhnen, einbürgern, heimisch machen; to become —ed, sich an ein fremdes Klima gewöhnen, sich in einem fremden Klima einbürgern, heimisch werden.

Acclivity, *s.* (hill) die (steile) Anhöhe, der Hügel; (ascent) die aufsteigende Höhe, Auffahrt (of a hill); (slope) die Böschung.

Accolade, *s.* die Umhalsung (beim Ritterschlag), der Ritterschlag; die Bindeklammer (*Typ. etc.*).

Accommodat—e, *v.a.* (adapt) passend machen, anbequemen, anpassen (to a th., einer S.); schlichten (*a quarrel*); (lodge) unterbringen, logieren, bewirten; to —e a p. with s.th., einen mit etwas versehen, versorgen; to —e o.s. to circumstances, sich in die Umstände fügen *or* schicken, sich den Verhältnissen anpassen; to —e s.o. with money, einem Geld leihen; to be well —ed, bequem wohnen, eine gute Wohnung haben. —**ing**, *adj.* gefällig, entgegenkommend. —**ion**, *s.* (adaptation) die Anpassung; die Beilegung, Ausgleichung der gütliche Vergleich (of a dispute); die Akkomodation (*Opt.*); (conveniences) die Bequemlichkeit; (help, etc.) die Aushülfe; (space, room) Räumlichkeit; (lodgings) Wohnung; to have good —ion, eine bequeme Wohnung haben, behaglich wohnen, bequem eingerichtet sein (*as a hotel*); —ion for cyclists, Unterkunft für Radfahrer; to find —ion in a place, an einem Orte unterkommen; I found —ion for the night, ich fand ein Unterkommen für die Nacht; —ion bill, der Gefälligkeitswechsel (*C. L.*).

Accompan—iment, *s.* die Begleitung. —**ist**, *s.* der Begleiter. —**y**, *v.* I. *a.* & *n.* begleiten (*Mus.*). II. *a.* (einen) begleiten, geleiten, (einem) Gesellschaft leisten.

Accomplice, *s.* der Mitschuldige, Teilhaber; they are —s, sie spielen *or* stecken unter einer Decke.

Accomplish, *v.a.* vollenden, ausführen, vollführen, zustande bringen (*a task*); erfüllen (*a promise, etc.*); vollenden (*a period*); erlangen, erreichen (*one's object, etc.*); (reach) erlangen. —**ed**, *adj.* ausgebildet; a highly —ed lady, eine Dame von feiner *or* hoher Bildung; an —ed violinist, ein vorzüglicher Geiger. —**ment**, *s.* die Ausführung (*of an object*); die Vollendung (*of a task, etc.*) die Erfüllung (*of a prophecy, of a duty, etc.*); (*pl.*) vielseitige Bildung, Talente; Fächer, welche nicht notwendige Bestandteile des Unterrichts ausmachen; she has many —ments, sie ist sehr fein gebildet, vielseitig gebildet *or* ausgebildet.

Accord, I. *s.* (agreement in opinion) die Übereinstimmung; (union) die Eintracht, Einigkeit; der Einklang, Accord (*Mus.*); with one —, einstimmig; of one's own —, aus eignem *or* freiem Antriebe, freiwillig; of its own —, von selbst. II. *v.a.* übereinstimmend machen; in Einklang bringen; vergleichen, vereinigen, versöhnen; bewilligen (*a request*); gewähren (*praise*). III. *v.n.*; — with, übereinstimmen mit. —**ance**, *s.* die Übereinstimmung; in —ance with your wishes, Ihren Wünschen gemäß. —**ant**, *adj.* im Einklang; gemäß, übereinstimmend. —**ing**, *adj.* (*rare*); —ing **as**, *conj.*, je nachdem, so wie. —ing **to**, *prep.*; gemäß, zufolge, nach; —ing to circumstances, nach der Beschaffenheit der Umstände; to cut one's coat —ing to one's cloth, sich nach der Decke strecken; —ing to custom, wie es der Gebrauch mit sich bringt; —ing to law, rechtgemäß, gesetzmäßig; —ing to reason, der Vernunft gemäß; —ing to report, wie das Gerücht geht wie es heißt; —ing to the latest intelligence, den letzten Nachrichten zufolge; —ing to your orders, Ihren Aufträgen zufolge *or* gemäß. —**ingly**, *adv.* danach, folglich, demnach, demgemäß, also.

Accost, *v.a.* sich annähern (einem); anreden, ansprechen. —**able**, *adj.* (*rare*) zugänglich, umgänglich; not —able, unnahbar.

Accoucheur, *s.* der Geburtshelfer.

Account, I. *s.* (calculation) die Rechnung; die Berechnung (*of expenses*); (bill) die Rechnung, Note; (number) die Zahl, Anzahl (*obs.*); (report) der Bericht; (narrative) die Erzählung; (list) die Liste, das Verzeichnis; die Rechenschaft (*of a p.'s doings, etc.*); (reason, cause) der Grund, die Ursache; (advantage) der Vorteil; (importance) die Wichtigkeit, der Wert, das Ansehen; das Konto, die Rechnung (*C. L.*); bank —, das Bankkonto, die Bankrechnung; cash —, die Kassenrechnung; profit and loss —, das Gewinn und Verlustkonto; — agreed upon, der Rechnungsabschluß; giving in —s, die Rechnungsablage, Rechnungsablegung; to balance an —, ein Konto saldieren; for — and risk, für Rechnung und Gefahr; to have an — with a p., mit einem in Rechnung stehen; — current, die laufende Rechnung, das Kontokorrent; joint —, gemeinschaftliche Rechnung; to s.o.'s —, auf jemandes Rechnung; on —, auf Rechnung, auf Abschlag; to keep an — of, Rechnung führen über (*acc.*), (auf)zählen; to keep —s, die Bücher führen, Buch halten; an open —, eine offene, unbezahlte Rechnung; to make out a p.'s —, jemandes Rechnung ausstellen; to place (s.th.) to a p.'s —, einem (etwas) in Rechnung bringen *or* stellen, einem (etwas) gutschreiben; to place to a new —, auf neue Rechnung bringen; payment on —, die Zahlung auf Abschlag, Abschlagszahlung, Anzahlung; to pay on —, abschläglich, auf Abschlag bezahlen; to settle —s, Rechnungen bezahlen; each on his own —, jeder für sich; on no —, auf keinen Fall; on — of, um . . . willen, wegen; on his —, um seinetwillen, seinetwegen; on that —, darum, deswegen; on another —, (besides) zudem; of no —, ohne Geltung, unbedeutend; to make no — of, nicht achten; to call to —, zur Rechenschaft ziehen; to be sent to one's —, vor Gottes Richterstuhl gestellt werden; to give an — (*of one's actions*), Rechenschaft ablegen (von einer S.); (*of o.s.*) Rechenschaft ablegen, sich rechtfertigen; (*of an occurrence*) erzählen, Bericht erstatten; to take into —, in Betracht ziehen, bedenken; by all —s, nach allen Nachrichten; according to Mr. N's —, nach der Aussage des Herrn N; from the latest —s, den spätesten Nachrichten zufolge; to turn to —, sich (*dat.*) zu Nutze machen; he gave a good — of himself in India, er benahm sich in Indien vorzüglich; he turned this to good —, er benutzte dies aufs beste. II. *v.n.*; to — for, (answer for) Rechenschaft von einer S. ablegen *or* geben, für eine S. stehen; (explain) den Grund davon angeben, erklären; I can't — for his conduct, ich kann mir sein Betragen nicht erklären; there is no accounting for taste, über den Geschmack läßt sich nicht streiten. III. *v.a.* to — it as, es betrachten als, es halten für. **—ability**, *s.* die Verantwortlichkeit. **—able**, *adj.* verantwortlich. **—ant**, *s.* der Rechnungsführer; der Buchhalter; der Bücherrevisor; chartered —ant, geprüfter Rechnungsrevisor. *Comp.* **—ant-general**, *s.* der Hauptrechnungsführer. **—-book**, *s.* das Rechnungsbuch, Kontobuch.

Accoutre, *v.a.* ausrüsten, ausstatten. **—ment**, *s.* (*gen'lly* **—ments**, *pl.*) der Anzug, Aufputz; die Ausrüstung, Bewaffnung (*Mil.*).

Accredit, *v.a.* beglaubigen, akkreditieren; (authorize) ermächtigen; (empower) bevollmächtigen.

Accr—etion, *s.* das Wachstum; der Zuwachs, Anwachs. **—ue**, *v.a.* anwachsen, zuwachsen; zufallen, erwachsen (*as property, etc.*); (arise) entstehen (aus); considerable advantage will thus —ue to science, bedeutende Vorteile werden der Wissenschaft auf diese Weise erwachsen.

Accumulat—e, *v.* I. *a.* (an)häufen, zusammenhäufen. II. *n.* sich anhäufen, sich ansammeln, zunehmen **—ing**, *p. & adj.* zunehmend, sich häufend. **—ion**, *s.* die Anhäufung, der Haufe; (the act of —ing) das Anhäufen. **—ive**, *adj.* anhäufend, sich häufend, zuwachsend. **—or**, *s.* der Sammler, Ansammler, Kraftsammler, Akkumulator (*Techn.*); der Anhäufer.

Accura—cy, *s.* die Genauigkeit; die Pünktlichkeit (*in time*); (correctness) die Richtigkeit. **—te(ly)**, *adj.* (*adv.*) genau, sorgfältig; pünktlich; getreu (*as a narrative*); fehlerfrei, richtig.

Accurs—ed, **—t**, *p.p. & adj.* verflucht, verwünscht; fluchwürdig; (abominable) verabscheuenswert.

Accus—able, *adj.* anklagbar (of, wegen). **—ation**, *s.* die Anklage, Beschuldigung; die Klage (*Law*). **—ative**, *s.* (—ative case) der Wenfall, der Akkusativ. **—atory**, *adj.* anklagend. **—e**, *v.a.* anklagen (of a th., einer *or* wegen einer Sache), beschuldigen; (einen einer S.) zeihen (*of sin, etc.*); (reproach) (einem eine S.) vorwerfen; to —e a p. of a crime, einen eines Verbrechens beschuldigen. **—ed**, *s.* der, die Beschuldigte, Angeklagte. **—er**, *s.* der Ankläger.

Accustom, *v.a.* gewöhnen; to — o.s. to a th., sich an eine S. gewöhnen; to — one's mind to s. th. (unpleasant), sich in eine S. finden. **—ed**, *p. p. & adj.* (in the habit) gewohnt; (trained) gewöhnt; (usual) gewöhnlich.

Ace, *s.* das As, die Eins; to be within an — of doing a thing, ganz nahe daran sein, etwas zu tun; within an —, um ein Haar, ums Haar; I was within an — of falling from the ladder, es fehlte nicht viel, so wäre ich von der Leiter gefallen.

Acephalous, *adj.* kopflos, ohne Kopf.

Acerbity, *s.* die Herbigkeit, der herbe Geschmack; die Härte, Strenge, Rauhheit (*of manner, etc.*).

Acet—ate, *s.* das Acetat, essigsaures Salz. **—ic**, *adj.* acetisch; —ic acid, die Essigsäure; —ic ether, der Essigäther. **—ify**, *v.a.* sauer machen, in Essig verwandeln. **—ous**, *adj.* essigsauer; säuerlich; —ous fermentation, die Essigsäuregährung. **—ylene**, *s.* das Acetylen, Äthin.

Ach—e, I. *s.* der Schmerz; head—, das Kopfweh, der Kopfschmerz. II. *v.n.* schmerzen, weh tun; my head —es, ich habe Kopfweh *or* Kopfschmerzen, mir tut der Kopf weh; my heart —ed for her, ihrethalben tat mir das Herz weh. **—ing**, I. *adj.* schmerzhaft. II. *s.* das Schmerzen.

Achieve, *v.a.* (accomplish) ausführen, zustande bringen, vollenden; (perform) verrichten; (gain) gewinnen, erlangen. **—ment**, *s.* die Ausführung; (work) das große Werk; das Wappenschild (*Her.*); great —ment, die bedeutende *or* hervorragende Leistung, Großtat; heroic —ment, die Heldentat.

Achromatic, *adj.* achromatisch, farblos.

Acicular, *adj.* nadelförmig.

Acid, I. *adj.* sauer. II. *s.* die Säure. **—ify**, *v.a.* ansäuern, in Säure verwandeln (*Chem.*). **—ity**, *s.* die Säure. **—ulate**, *v.a.* säuern, säuerlich machen. **—ulous**, *adj.* säuerlich; —ulous water, der Sauerbrunnen.

Acknowledg—e, *v.a.* (recognize) erkennen, anerkennen; (admit) zugeben; (confess) bekennen, gestehen; (notify) anzeigen; (be grateful for) mit Dankbarkeit erkennen, erkenntlich sein für; —e the truth of this, ich erkenne die Wahrheit hiervon an; to —e the receipt of a letter, den Empfang eines Briefes bestätigen *or* anzeigen; to —e the receipt of a remittance, den Empfang einer Rimesse bescheinigen *or* bestätigen. **—ment**, *s.* die Anerkennung; das Bekenntnis, Geständnis (*of a fault*); die Empfangsbescheinigung, Empfangsanzeige, Quittung, der Empfangsschein (*of payment, etc.*); —ments, der Dank, die Erkenntlichkeit.

Acme, *s.* der Gipfel, die Spitze.

Aconite, *s.* der Eisenhut (*Bot.*); das Akonit (*Pharm.*); tödliches Gift (*poet.*).

Acorn, *s.* die Eichel.

Acoustic, *adj.* akustisch, zur Schallehre gehörig, das Gehör betreffend; — effect, die Schallwirkung, Klangwirkung; — nerve, der Gehörnerv; — vibrations, Schallschwingungen. **—s**, *s.* die Lehre vom Schall, Akustik; das gehörstärkende Mittel (*obs.*) (*Med.*).

Acquaint, *v.a.* bekannt machen; (announce) berichten, melden, benachrichtigen; to be —ed with s.th., etwas kennen; to become —ed with a p., einen kennen lernen; to — o.s. with . . ., sich mit . . . bekannt machen. **—ance**, *s.* die Bekanntschaft (*with persons and things*); (knowledge) die Kenntnis; (person) der, die Bekannte; I know who the man is, but have no —ance with him, ich kenne den Mann, habe aber mit ihm keine nähere Bekanntschaft; an —ance of mine, eine(r) meiner Bekannten.

Acquiesce, *v.n.* einwilligen (in eine S.), sich (*dat.*) (etwas) gefallen lassen, sich (bei etwas) beruhigen, sich (in eine S.) fügen, schicken. **—nce**, *s.* (submission) die Ergebung; (consent) die Einwilligung (in), Zustimmung (zu), Genehmigung (zu). **—nt**, *adj.* ergeben, geduldig, nachgiebig.

Acquir—able, *adj.* erlangbar. **—e**, *v.a.* erlangen, erwerben; erlernen, lernen (*a language, etc.*); the body —es strength by exercise, der Körper gewinnt durch Übung Stärke; no honour is to be —ed by that, damit läßt sich keine Ehre einlegen. **—ement**, *s.* die Erwerbung, Erlangung; (object gained) das Erlangte, Erworbene; die erworbene Fertigkeit; —ements, Kenntnisse, erworbene Bildung. **—er**, *s.* der Erwerber.

Acquisit—ion, *s.* die Erwerbung; der Erwerb; die Erlernung (*of a language, etc.*); (gain) der Erwerb, das Erworbene, das erworbene Gut, die Eroberung. —**ive**, *adj.* habsüchtig, erwerbslustig. —**iveness**, *s.* der Erwerbstrieb.

Acquit, *v.a.* befreien, freisprechen, lossprechen (*a p. accused*); abtragen, quittieren (*a debt*); to — o.s. of a duty, etc., sich einer Pflicht, &c., entledigen, seine Pflicht, &c, tun; to — (of) an obligation, eine Verbindlichkeit erfüllen; to — a p. of evil intentions, einen von schlechten Absichten freisprechen; to — o.s. well, sich gut halten, sich tapfer benehmen. —**tal**, *s.* die Lossprechung, (discharge of duties) die Erledigung. —**tance**, *s.* die Freisprechung; die Empfangsbescheinigung, Quittung.

Acre, *s.* (measure) der Morgen Landes (= 4840 Quadrat-Yards *or* 0.404671021 Hektare); der Acker.

Acrid, *adj.* scharf, beißend.

Acrimon—ious(ly), *adj.* (*adv.*) scharf, beißend, bitter (*also fig.*). —**y**, *s.* die Bitterkeit.

Across, I. *adv.* kreuzweise, in die Quer(e). II. *prep.* quer durch, quer über; mitten durch; — Channel, über den Kanal hinüber; a short cut — the fields, ein Richtweg durch die Felder; I have come — him, ich bin ihm begegnet; it flashed — my mind, es fiel mir plötzlich ein.

Acrostic, *s.* das Akrostichon.

Act, I. *s.* (deed) die Handlung, Tat, das Werk; (action) das Handeln; der Aufzug, Akt (*of a play*); —s, Akten; — of parliament, die Parlamentsakte, das Gesetz, Statut; the —s (of the Apostles), die Apostelgeschichte; — of settlement, das Staatsgesetz von 1713 über die englische Thronfolge; in —, (about to) im Begriff, auf dem Punkt; to be taken in the (very) —, auf frischer Tat ertappt werden. II. *v.a.;* to — a part, eine Rolle spielen; sich verstellen; to — a piece, ein Stück aufführen; Mr. G. —ed the part of Hamlet, Herr G. spielte *or* machte *or* gab den Hamlet. III. *v.n.* wirken, tätig sein; (behave) sich betragen, handeln; spielen (*on the stage, etc.*); (operate) wirken; to — cautiously, vorsichtig zu Werke gehen; to — up to, (einer Sache) gemäß handeln; to — upon, wirken auf (*acc.*); to — upon a p.'s advice, nach jemandes Rat handeln. —**ing**, I. *s.* das Handeln; das Spiel; die Schauspielkunst. II. *adj.* handelnd, wirkend; (officiating) wirklich, fungierend; self —ing, selbstwirkend, selbsttätig, selbstbeweglich; —ing partner, der dirigierende Teilhaber (*C.L.*). —**ion**, *s.* die Wirkung, wirkende Kraft; die Handlung; der Gang (*of a horse, etc.*); die Handlung (*of a poem, etc.*); die Stellung, Haltung, Bewegung (*Paint.*); der Rechtshandel, Prozeß, die Klage; das Treffen, Gefecht, die Schlacht; das Geberdenspiel, die Geberdung (*of an orator*); double —ion, doppelte Wirkung; to bring an —ion against a p., einen gerichtlich verklagen; an —ion for debt, eine Schuldklage; to be in —ion, in Bewegung, tätig sein, wirken; ready for —ion, gerüstet, kampfbereit; klar zum Gefecht (*Naut.*); in full —ion, handgemein; to fight an —ion, eine Schlacht liefern. —**ionable**, *adj.* prozeßfähig, klagbar, strafbar. —**ionary**, *s.* der Aktieninhaber (*C.L.*). —**ive(ly)**, *adj.* (*adv.*) tätig; emsig, rührig, geschäftig; wirkend; (agile) behend, flink; (practical) praktisch, wirklich; aktiv, tätig (*Gram.*); —ive bonds, Prioritäts-Obligationen; —ive commerce, der Aktivhandel; —ive property, das Vermögen an barem Gelde *or* Waren, Aktivvermögen; —ive debts, die Außenstände; in —ive service, im (aktiven) Dienste stehend; an —ive life, ein tätiges Leben; an —ive partner, ein wirklicher Teilhaber; the market has been very —ive, der Markt war sehr lebhaft, der Umsatz war sehr stark. —**ivity**, *s.* die Tätigkeit; die Wirksamkeit (*also Phys.*); (nimbleness) die Behendigkeit; (industry) die Betriebsamkeit; in full —ivity, in vollem Gange *or* Betrieb; sphere of —ivity, der Wirkungskreis. —**or**, *s.* der Täter, Handelnde: der Schauspieler. —**ress**, *s.* die handelnde Person; die Schauspielerin. —**ual(ly)**, *adj.* (*adv.*) wirklich; (present) jetzig, gegenwärtig; —ual sin, die von der Person begangene Sünde; —ual state of matters, wirkliche Sachlage. —**uality**, *s.* die Wirklichkeit. —**uary**, *s.* der Aktuar, Gerichtsschreiber; Buchhalter, Rechnungsführer; Mathematiker bei Versicherungsgesellschaften. —**uate**, *v.a.* in Bewegung setzen; antreiben; —uated by the purest motives, von den reinsten Absichten beseelt.

Actin—ic, *adj.* den Aktinismus betreffend; —ic power of light, die Fähigkeit des Lichts, Stoffwechsel zu erzeugen. —**ism**, *s.* die chemische Wirkung der Sonnenstrahlen.

Acu—men, *s.* der Scharfsinn, die Scharfsinnigkeit. —**te(ly)**, *adj.* (*adv.*) spitzig; scharf, stechend (*of pain*); scharf, fein (*of the senses*); scharfsinnig, verschmitzt, schlau; —te accent, der scharfe Akzent, Akut; —te angle, spitzer Winkel; —te disease, heftige Krankheit. —**teness**, *s.* die Schärfe; der Scharfsinn, die Feinheit (*of the intellect*); die Feinheit (*of the hearing*); die Heftigkeit (*of a disease*).

Adage, *s.* das Sprichwort.

Adagio, I. *adv.* adagio, langsam (*Mus.*). II. *s.* das Adagio, der langsame Satz.

Adamant, *s.* sehr harter Stein; die Härte; der Diamant, Demant (*obs. poet.*); der Magnet (*obs.*). —**ine**, *adj.* hart wie ein Diamant; demanten.

Adapt, *v.a.* anpassen, anpassend machen, anbequemen. —**ability**, *s.* (applicability) die Anwendbarkeit; die Anpaßbarkeit, Anpassungsfähigkeit. —**able**, *adj.* anwendbar; paßlich. —**ation**, *s.* die Anwendung; die Anpassungsfähigkeit; die Herrichtung, Bearbeitung (*of a book, etc.*). —**ed**, *p.p. & adj.* angepaßt; (suitable) passend (für). —**er**, *s.* der Vorstoß (*Chem.*). —**ive**, *adj.* anpassungsfähig.

Add, *v.a.* hinzutun, hinzufügen, beifügen, beitragen; (increase) vermehren, erhöhen, steigern; zusammenzählen, addieren (*Arith.*); to — up, (alles) zusammenzählen; to — the interest to the capital, die Zinsen zum Kapital schlagen; to — fuel to the fire, Öl ins Feuer gießen. —**endum**, *s.* (*pl.* —enda) der Zusatz, Nachtrag. —**ition**, *s.* die Hinzutuung, Hinzusetzung, der Zusatz; die Vermehrung; die Zusammenzählung, Addition (*Arith.*); in —ition to this, noch dazu; an —ition to our happiness, eine Vergrößerung unseres Glückes. —**itional**, *adj.* hinzugesetzt, beigefügt, nachträglich; neu; an —itional pleasure, ein ferneres Vergnügen; —itional charges, Nebenkosten; —itional clause, die Zusatzklausel; —itional freight, die Frachtzulage; —itional subject, der Extragegenstand. —**itionally**, *adv.* als Zusatz, als Zugabe; mit dabei.

Adder, *s.* die Natter.

Addict, *v.a.;* to — o.s., sich ergeben; —**ed to . . .**, dem . . . ergeben.

Addle, *v.a.* unfruchtbar machen; verwirren (*the brains*); an —d egg, ein Windei. *Comp.* —**-brained**, —**-pated**, *adj.* dumm, leerköpfig.

Address, I. *s.* die Anrede; die Rede; die Ansprache; die Adresse, Aufschrift (*on a letter*); (dexterity) die Gewandheit, Geschicklichkeit; (manner) das Benehmen, die Manier, die Haltung; die Zuschrift, Dankschrift, Bittschrift; Vorstellung; to pay one's —es to a lady, einer Dame den Hof machen, sich um eine D. bewerben. II. *v.a.* anreden (einen, a p.); adressieren, überschreiben (*a letter*); richten (*a petition*); to — a meeting, an eine Versammlung eine Ansprache halten; to — a petition to the senate, eine Bittschrift an den Senat richten *or* beim Senate einreichen; to — o.s. to a p., sich an einen wenden; to — o.s. to (a journey, etc.), sich zu (einer Reise, &c.) anschicken *or* bereit machen.

Adduc—e, *v.a.* anführen, beibringen (*proofs, witnesses, etc.*). —**ible**, *adj.* anführbar, anziehbar. —**tor**, *s.* der Anziehmuskel.

Adept, I. *adj.* gelehrt, erfahren; geschickt. II. *s.* der Eingeweihte Adept; der Meister; der Goldmacher; an — in, geschickt in (einer S.).

Adequa—cy, *s.* die Gemäßheit, Hinlänglichkeit, Angemessenheit. **—te(ly)**, *adj.* (*adv.*) angemessen, entsprechend; hinreichend, zureichend; my means are not —te to my wants, meine Mittel sind meinen Wünschen nicht entsprechend *or* für meine Wünsche nicht ausreichend. **—teness,** *see* —cy.

Adhere, *v.n.* anhangen, ankleben; to — together, zusammen hangen; to — to an opinion, bei einer Meinung bleiben, an einer Ansicht festhalten; to — to a party, einer Partei angehören *or* zugetan sein; to — to orders, seine Vorschrift(en) genau befolgen; — to our directions, halten Sie sich an unsere Vorschriften. **—nce,** *s.* das Anhängen, Ankleben; (attachment) die Anhänglichkeit (an). **—nt,** I. *adj.*, **—ntly,** *adv.* anhängend; anhängig (*fig.*). II. **—r,** *s.* der Anhänger.

Adhesi—on, *s.* die Anhaftung, Adhäsion; das Anhangen; die Adhäsionskraft (*Phys.*); die Reibung; die Anhänglichkeit; der Anschluß, Beitritt; the —on to an opinion, das Festhalten an einer Meinung; to give in one's —on to . . ., sich für . . . erklären. **—ve(ly),** *adj.* (*adv.*) anklebend; —ve envelopes, gummierte Briefumschläge; —ve plaster, das Heftpflaster; —ve stamp, aufklebbare Brief- (oder Stempel-)marke; —ve postage stamp, gummiertes Postwertzeichen, die Freimarke. **—veness,** *s.* die Klebrigkeit; die Zähigkeit.

Adieu, I. *adv. & int.* lebe wohl! Gott befohlen; behüt' dich Gott! II. *s.* das Lebewohl, der Abschiedsgruß; to bid *or* say —, Abschied nehmen, Lebewohl sagen.

Adipose, *adj.* fett, feist (*Anat.*).

Adjacen—cy, *s.* die Angrenzung, das Naheliegen. **—t,** *adj.* anliegend, angrenzend, benachbart; —t angles, Nebenwinkel.

Adjectiv—al, *adj.* das Beiwort betreffend. **—e,** I. *s.* das Eigenschaftswort, Beiwort, Adjektiv. II. *adj.* beiwörtlich, adjektivisch. **—ely,** *adv.* als Beiwort.

Adjoin, *v.n.* anliegen, angrenzen, anstoßen; the —ing room, das Nebenzimmer; —ing gardens, anstoßende Gärten; hotel —ing the station, unmittelbar am Bahnhof *or* in unmittelbarer Nähe des Bahnhofs gelegenes Hotel.

Adjourn, *v.* I. *a.* auf einen andern Tag verschieben, vertagen; (delay) aufschieben, verschieben; to — a meeting, eine Versammlung vertagen. II. *n.*; sich vertagen, die Sitzung aufheben; parliament —ed at six o'clock, das Parlament vertagte sich um 6 Uhr. **—ment,** *s.* die Vertagung, Verschiebung, der Aufschub.

Adjud—ge, *v.a.* zuerkennen, zusprechen; verurteilen; dafür halten; the prize was —ged to the victor, der Preis wurde dem Sieger zuerkannt. **—icate,** *see* —ge. **—ication,** *s.* die Zuerkennung, Zusprechung; der Entscheid, das Urteil. **—icator,** *s.* der Schiedsrichter.

Adjunct, *s.* der Zusatz; die unwesentliche Eigenschaft, Zutat; das Adjunktum (*Gram.*); der Amtsgehülfe, Beigeordnete, Adjunkt.

Adjur—ation, *s.* die Vereidigung, Auferlegung des Eides; die Beschwörung, dringende Bitte; die Eidesformel. **—e,** *v.a.* (einem) den Eid auferlegen (einen) vereidigen; beschwören, auf das Dringendste bitten; I —e thee by the living God, ich beschwöre dich bei dem lebendigen Gott.

Adjust, *v.a.* zurecht machen, ordnen; anpassen, passend machen; berichtigen (*accounts*); abmachen, schlichten (*disputes*); adjustieren, einer Münze das richtige Gewicht geben; eichen (*a measure*); —ing scale, die Justier- *or* Münzwage; —ing screw, die Stellschraube. **—able,** *adj.* stellbar, verschiebbar, regulierbar. **—ment,** *s.* das Anordnen; die Einrichtung, Zurechtmachung, Anordnung; die Berichtigung, Ausgleichung; die Schlichtung, Beilegung (*of a quarrel*); das Fertigmachen, Justieren; das Eichen; —ment of the parts of a machine, die Einrichtung der Teile einer Maschine.

Adjutan—cy, *s.* das Amt eines Adjutanten. **—t,** *s.* der Adjutant (*Mil.*); der Amtsgehülfe.

Admeasurement, *s.* die Zumessung (*Law*); das Abmessen; das Maß, der Gehalt; bill of —, der Maßbrief.

Administ—er, *v.* I. *a.* (manage) verwalten; handhaben (*justice*); erteilen, geben (*relief, etc.*); ausspenden, erteilen (*the sacraments*); to —er an oath, (einem) einen Eid abnehmen; to —er the law, Recht sprechen. II. *n.* behülflich sein; als Testamentsvollzieher walten. **—ration,** *s.* die Verwaltung; die Regierung, das Ministerium; die Handhabung (*of justice*); die Ausspendung (*of the sacraments*); die Dauer der Verwaltungszeit; die Verwaltung der Güter eines Verstorbenen; —ration of the public revenue, Verwaltung der Staatsfinanzen. **—rative,** *adj.* verwaltend; behülflich; —rative difficulties, Verwaltungsschwierigkeiten, Schwierigkeiten in der Verwaltung. **—rator,** *s.* der Verwalter; der Testamentsvollstrecker, Testamentsvollzieher. **—ratorship,** *s.* Amt eines Verwalters. **—ratrix,** *s.* die Verwalterin; die Testamentsvollstreckerin.

Admir—able, *adj.*, **—ably,** *adv.* bewundernswert, bewunderungswürdig, herrlich, vortrefflich. **—ableness,** *s.* die Vortrefflichkeit. **—ation,** *s.* die Bewunderung. **—e,** *v.a.* bewundern. **—er,** *s.* der Bewunderer; der Anbeter, Verehrer (*of a lady*). **—ingly,** *adv.* bewundernd, mit *or* voll Bewunderung.

Admiral, *s.* der Admiral (*also Ent.*); vice-—, Vizeadmiral; rear-—, Konteradmiral; — of the Fleet, Flottenadmiral. **—ty,** *s.* die Admiralität; High Court of —ty, das Admiralitätsgericht; first Lord of the —ty, der (englische) Marineminister. *Comp.* **—-ship,** *s.* das Admiralsschiff, Flaggschiff.

Admissi—bility, *s.* die Zulässigkeit. **—ble,** *adj.* zulässig. **—on,** *s.* die Zulassung, Aufnahme; (concession) das Zugeständnis, die Einräumung.

Admit, *v.* I. *a.* einlassen, zulassen, den Zutritt gestatten; (receive) aufnehmen; gestehen, erkennen, zugeben, gestatten; I will — that, das lasse ich gelten; to — a thought, einem Gedanken Raum geben; this ticket —s two persons to the theatre, auf diese Karte können zwei Personen in das Theater gehen. II. *n.*; it —s of no excuse, es läßt sich nicht entschuldigen; that —s of no dispute, darüber ist nicht zu streiten; the words do not — of this construction, die Worte lassen diese Auslegung nicht zu. **—tance,** *s.* der Eintritt, Eingang; no —tance! verbotener Eingang! Eintritt verboten!

Admixture, *s.* die Hinzumischung, Beimischung; die Mischung, das Gemischte.

Admoni—sh, *v.a.* ermahnen; warnen. **—sher,** *s.* der Ermahner; der Warner. **—tion,** *s.* die Ermahnung; die Warnung; der Verweis. **—tory,** *adj.* ermahnend; verweisend.

Ado, *s.* das Tun, Aufsehen, der Lärm; die Mühe; much — about nothing, viel Lärm um nichts; to make much — about nothing, um des Kaisers Bart streiten; with no great —, ohne sonderliche Mühe; without more —, ohne Weiteres; without much —, ohne viel(e) Umstände.

Adolescen—ce, *s.* das Jünglingsalter. **—t,** *adj.* jugendlich, heranwachsend, groß werdend.

Adopt, *v.a.* an Kindesstatt annehmen, adoptieren; annehmen; —ed child, angenommenes Kind; —ed son, der angenommene Sohn, Adoptivsohn; his —ed country, sein neues Vaterland, seine neue Heimat. **—er,** der Adoptivvater. **—ion,** *s.* die Annahme (an Kindesstatt), Adoption; die Annahme (*of an opinion*); country of —, neue selbstgewählte Heimat, neues Vaterland. **—ive,** *adj.* angenommen; nicht eingeboren, fremd.

Ador—able, *adj.*, **—ably**, *adv.* anbetungswürdig. **—ation**, *s.* die Anbetung, Verehrung. **—e**, *v.a.* anbeten, verehren; (love) leidenschaftlich lieben. **—er**, *s.* der Anbeter, Verehrer.

Adorn, *v.a.* schmücken, zieren, putzen; (mit Worten) ausschmücken, verschönern. **—ing**, **—ment**, *s.* der Schmuck, Zierat; die Verzierung.

Adrift, *adv.* losgetrieben, treibend, dahin schwimmend, Wind und Wellen preisgegeben; to set —, (ein Fahrzeug) treiben lassen; I was turned —, ich wurde ins Weite gestoßen; he is all —, er weiß nicht, woran er ist; er hat allen Halt verloren.

Adroit, *adj.*, **—ly**, *adv.* geschickt, gewandt. **—ness**, *s.* die Gewandtheit.

Adulat—ion, *s.* die Schmeichelei. **—or**, *s.* der Schmeichler. **—ory**, *adj.* schmeichelhaft.

Adult, I. *adj.* erwachsen. II. *s.* der Erwachsene.

Adulter—ate, *v.a.* verfälschen; verderben (*fig.*). **—ation**, *s.* die Verfälschung; —ation of food, Verfälschung der Nahrungsmittel. **—er**, *s.* der Ehebrecher. **—ess**, *s.* die Ehebrecherin. **—ous**, *adj.* ehebrecherisch. **—y**, *s.* der Ehebruch.

Adumbrat—e, *v.a.* durch Schattenrisse darstellen; flüchtig entwerfen, skizzieren. **—ion**, *s.* die Abschattung, Darstellung durch Schattenrisse.

Advance, I. *v.n.* vorrücken, anrücken, sich nähern; Fortschritte machen; steigen (*in price, rank, etc.*); —d thinker, ein vorgeschrittener Denker; at an —d age, in vorgerücktem Alter. II. *v.a.* vorausbezahlen (*payment*); (lend) vorschießen; (elevate) erhöhen; (push forward) vorrücken; aufstellen, äußern (*an opinion*); to — a claim, Anspruch machen auf (eine S.); to — against, vorbringen gegen; to — a p.'s interests, jemands Interesse befördern *or* jemandes Interessen Vorschub leisten; to — a p. in office, einen befördern. III. *s.* das Anrücken; der Fortschritt; die Beförderung (*in office*); der Vorschuß (*of money*); general —, allgemeiner Vormarsch; to pay in —, im Voraus bezahlen; prices are on the —, die Preise steigen *or* sind im Steigen begriffen; to make —s to s.o., einem entgegen kommen, die ersten Schritte tun; to be in — of a p., einem voraus sein. IV. *adj.;* — guard, die Avantgarde, der Vortrab, die Vorhut. **—ment**, *s.* das Vorrücken; die Beförderung; der Fortschritt.

Advantage, *s.* der Vorteil; die Überlegenheit; to have the — of a p., einem überlegen sein, einem gegenüber im Vorteil sein; einen kennen, ohne von ihm erkannt zu sein; to take — of a th., etwas vorteilhaft benutzen, sich (*dat.*) etwas zu Nutze machen; it would be no — to me, ich würde nichts dabei gewinnen; with —, mit Nutzen; to the best —, auf das Vorteilhafteste; to turn to —, sich (*dat.*) zu Nutze machen; personal —, körperliche Vorzüge; — set, die Partie mit Spielvor (*Lawn Tennis*). **—ous(ly)**, *adj.* (*adv.*) vorteilhaft; Gewinn bringend; günstig.

Advent, *s.* der Advent (*Eccl.*); die Ankunft. **—itiously**, *adj.* (*adv.*) zufällig. **—ure**, I. *s.* das Abenteuer; (exploit) das gewagte Unternehmen, Wagestück; (unusual occurrence) das Ereignis; (venture) die Spekulation; at all —ures, auf jeden Fall. II. *v.a.* wagen. **—urer**, *s.* der Abenteurer, Glücksritter; der Spekulant. **—urous(ly)**, *adj.* (*adv.*) abenteuerlich; kühn; verwegen; waghalsig.

Adverb, *s.* das Umstandswort, Adverb(ium). **—ial(ly)**, *adj.* (*adv.*) adverbialisch.

Advers—ary, *s.* der Gegner, Feind, Widersacher; der Teufel (*B.*). **—ative**, *adj.* entgegensetzend, einen Gegensatz bezeichnend (*Gram.*). **—e(ly)**, *adj.* (*adv.*) zuwider, widerwärtig, widrig; feindlich; —e winds, widrige Winde; —e party, die Gegenpartei; —e fate, das Mißgeschick. **—eness**, *s.* die Widrigkeit. **—ity**, *s.* die Widerwärtigkeit, das Elend, die Not, Trübsal.

Advert, *v.n.;* — to, hinweisen auf, erwähnen, anspielen auf (*acc.*). **—ise**, *v.a.* öffentlich anzeigen; (inform) in Kenntnis setzen, benachrichtigen, warnen. **—isement**, *s.* die Anzeige, Ankündigung, das Inserat; die Benachrichtigung; office for —isements, die Anzeigenannahme; —isements cost per line, der Zeilenpreis für Inserate beträgt **—iser**, *s.* der Anzeiger; das Anzeigeblatt.

Advice, *s.* der Rat; der Bericht, Avis (*C. L.*); das Gutachten; die Meldung; to take *or* ask a p.'s —, sich (*dat.*) bei einem Rats erholen; to follow *or* take —, einem Rat folgen, einen Rat befolgen; to take — (upon a th.), einen Juristen, Arzt ꝛc. (über eine S.) konsultieren; take my —, lassen Sie sich von mir raten, folgen Sie meinem Rate; he will not take any —, er läßt sich nichts sagen *or* sich nicht raten; as per —, laut Bericht, laut Aufgabe; according to —s from Rome, nach Berichten aus Rom; for want of —, wegen Mangel an Bericht; letter of —, der Avisbrief. *Comp.* **—-boat**, *s.* das Avisboot *or* -schiff, der Aviso, das Depeschenschiff.

Advis—able, *adj.* ratsam. **—ableness**, *s.* die Ratsamkeit. **—e**, *v.* I. *a.* raten (eine S. *or* zu einer S.); beraten; benachrichtigen, melden; be —ed by me, laß dir von mir raten, folge meinem Rate; he —ed me, er riet mir, er beriet mich, gab mir seinen Rat; to —e s. o. to the contrary, einem (von etwas) abraten; as —ed, laut Aufgabe, laut Bericht. II. *n.* überlegen, bedenken; to —e with one's pillow, etwas beschlafen; to —e with o. s., mit sich zu Rate gehen. **—ed**, *adj.;* ill —ed, unbedachtsam, unklug, schlecht beraten; well —ed, wohlbedächtig. **—edly**, *adv.* mit Bedacht *or* Überlegung; absichtlich. **—er**, *s.* der Ratgeber, Berater.

Advoca—cy, *s.* die Verteidigung. **—te**, I. *s.* der Advokat; der Verteidiger; der Fürsprecher; I am a great —te of, ich halte große Stücke auf (*acc.*). II. *v.a.* verteidigen.

Advowson, *s.* das Pfründenbesetzungsrecht, das kirchliche Patronat.

Adze, I. *s.* die Krummaxt, das Breitbeil; (hollow —) der Deißel, Dechsel. II. *v.a.* deißeln, mit dem Breitbeil bearbeiten.

Ægis, *s.* die Ägis; (*fig.*) die Ägide, der Schutz.

Æolian harp, *s.* die Äolsharfe, Windharfe.

Aer—ated, *adj.* kohlensauer; —ated water, kohlensaures Wasser; —ated bread, mit Kohlensäure locker gemachtes Brot; —ated bread company (*abbr. A. B. C.*), Gesellschaft zur Herstellung lockeren kohlensauern Brotes, Verkaufsstelle von solchem Brot (zugleich von Tee, Kaffee u. a. leichten Erfrischungen). **—ial**, *adj.* luftig; ätherisch; in der Luft, hoch; —ial voyage, die Luftreise; —ial locomotion, die Luftschiffahrt. **—iform**, *adj.* gasartig; luftförmig. **—olite**, *etc.*, *see under* Aero—.

Aerie, *s.* der (Adler-)Horst, das Nest eines Raubvogels; erhöhter Standpunkt *or* Wohnort; junge Brut. *See also* Eyrie.

Aero—dynamics, *s.* die Aerodynamik. **—lite**, *s.* der Meteorstein, Aerolith. **—meter**, *s.* der Luftmesser. **—naut**, *s.* der Luftschiffer. **—nautics**, *pl.* die Luftschiffahrtskunde. **—static**, *adj.* aerostatisch. **—statics**, *pl.* die Aerostatik, Luftschwebekunst, Luftgleichgewichtslehre. **—station**, *s.* die Luftschiffahrtskunst.

Æsthet—e, *s.* der Ästhetiker; der ästhetisch gebildete Mensch; der gezierte, das Stilvolle übertreibende Mensch. **—ic**, *adj.* ästhetisch. **—ics**, *s.* die Schönheitslehre, Lehre vom Schönen, Ästhetik; der Kunstsinn.

Afar, *adv.* fern, von fern, weit entfernt; to come from —, weither *or* aus weiter Ferne kommen.

Affab—ility, *s.* die Leutseligkeit, Umgänglichkeit, Freundlichkeit, das liebreiche Wesen. **—le**, *adj.*, **—ly**, *adv.* leutselig, umgänglich, freundlich.

Affair, *s.* das Geschäft, die Angelegenheit; (matter) die Sache; (skirmish) das Treffen; love —, der Liebeshandel; — of honour, die Ehrensache, das Duell; family —s, Familienverhältnisse; their —s were in disorder, ihre Verhältnisse waren in Unordnung; —s of state, Staatsangelegenheiten; mercantile —s, kaufmännische Angelegenheiten; to take part in the management of —s, an den Geschäften tätigen Anteil nehmen; minister for foreign —s, Minister der auswärtigen Angelegenheiten *or* des Äußeren.

Affect, *v.a.* auf (eine S.) wirken, Eindruck machen; rühren, bewegen (*the passions, etc.*); angreifen (*the eyes, etc. injuriously*); (influence) Einfluß üben auf (einen *or* eine S.); lieb haben; begehren; (er)heucheln; (imitate) nachahmen; sitting up late will — your health, das (zu) späte Aufbleiben wird Ihre Gesundheit angreifen; your objection does not in the least — my assertion, Ihr Einwurf entkräftet meine Behauptung keineswegs; he —s good society, er liebt die vornehme Gesellschaft; to — modesty, Bescheidenheit heucheln. **—ation**, *s.* das gezwungene Wesen, die Ziererei, Affektation. **—ed**, *p.p. & adj.* (moved) gerührt; behaftet (*by a disease*); (injured) angegriffen; (full of affectation) geziert, gezwungen, affektiert; (pretended) erheuchelt; gesinnt, geneigt (towards a p., gegen einen); an —ed style (*in writing*), eine gezierte Schreibart; we were all more or less —ed by the failure, von der Zahlungseinstellung des Hauses wurden wir alle mehr oder minder betroffen. **—edly**, *adv.* gezwungen, geziert. **—ing**, *adj.* rührend. **—ion**, *s.* (emotion) die Gemütsbewegung, der Affekt; (love) die Zuneigung, Liebe; (inclination) die Neigung, der Hang; (disposition of mind) das Gefühl, der Gemütszustand; die Krankheit, der krankhafte Zustand; —ion for one's children, Liebe zu seinen Kindern; to set one's —ions upon a th., sein Herz an eine S. hängen. —**ionate(ly)**, *adj.* (*adv.*) ergeben, herzlich, zugetan, liebevoll; yours —ionately, herzlichst *or* in Liebe Ihr(e). **—ionateness**, *s.* das liebevolle Wesen; die Zärtlichkeit.

Affiance, I. *v.a.* verloben; —d bride, die Verlobte. II. *s.* das Verlöbnis; das Vertrauen.

Affidavit, *s.* die beschworene schriftliche Zeugenaussage; — of documents, die Reihe beschworener Dokumente; to make an —, durch schriftlichen Eid erhärten *or* bezeugen.

Affiliat—e, *v.a.* affiliieren; an Kindesstatt annehmen; (als Mitglied) aufnehmen; —ed institution, die (einer Universität) angegliederte Anstalt. **—ion**, *s.* die Angliederung, Affiliation; die Annahme an Kindes Statt; das Aufnehmen, die Aufnahme.

Affinity, *s.* die Verwandtschaft; die Verschwägerung; die Verwandtschaft, Affinität (*Chem.*), die Ähnlichkeit (*of languages, etc.*); elective —, Wahlverwandtschaft (*Chem.*).

Affirm, *v.* I. *a.* (confirm) bestätigen, bekräftigen; (assert) behaupten. II. *n.* feierlich erklären. **—ation**, *s.* die Bestätigung, Bekräftigung; die Erklärung (*by Quakers, etc.*); die Behauptung. **—ative**, I. *adj.* bejahend; positiv (*Math.*). II. *s.* to answer in the —ative, eine bejahende Antwort geben, bejahend antworten. **—atively**, *adv.* mit Ja, bejahend.

Affix, I. *v.a.* anheften, anschlagen; anhängen; to — one's seal, one's signature to a document, einer Urkunde sein Siegel beidrucken, eine Urkunde unterschreiben. II. *s.* das Affixum.

Afflatus, *s.* der Windhauch; die Eingebung; divine —, die göttliche Begeisterung, Inspiration.

Afflict, *v.a.* betrüben, niederschlagen; (torment) quälen, plagen, peinigen; he was —ed at the tidings, er war sehr betrübt bei der Nachricht; to — o.s., sich grämen, sich bekümmern (about a th., über eine S.); to be —ed with a disease, von einer Krankheit heimgesucht werden; the —ed, die Betrübten, Heimgesuchten; —ed with, krank an (einer S.). **—ing**, *p. & adj.* betrübend. **—ion**, *s.* die Betrübnis, Kümmernis, Trübsal; das Leiden, der Kummer.

Affluen—ce, *s.* der Überfluß; der Reichtum; der Zusammenfluß. **—t**, I. *adj.* zufließend; überflüssig, reich. II. *s.* der Nebenfluß.

Afflux, *s.* der Zufluß, Zulauf.

Afford, *v.a.* (yield) hervorbringen; (give) geben, gewähren; this consideration —s me great comfort, diese Betrachtung gewährt mir viel Trost; he can — it, er hat die Mittel dazu; I can't — it, ich kann es mir nicht leisten (*coll.*); he would n't do it, if he could n't — it, er würde es nicht tun, wenn seine Mittel es ihm nicht erlaubten; I can't — to waste my time thus, ich darf meine Zeit nicht so verschwenden.

Afforest, *v.a.* aufforsten. **—ation**, *s.* die Aufforstung; das aufgeforstete Land.

Affray, *s.* (fight) die Schlägerei, der Streit, das Handgemenge; (disturbance) der Auflauf.

Affricate, *s.* die Affrikata (*e. g. the German* z).

Affright, *v.a.* erschrecken; to be —ed at a th., erschrecken *or* sich entsetzen vor einer S.

Affront, I. *s.* die Beleidigung, der Schimpf; to pocket an —, eine Beleidigung einstecken *or* verschlucken; to take — at s.th., sich über eine S. beleidigt fühlen (*coll.*). II. *v.a.* beleidigen.

Affusion, *s.* das Begießen, Übergießen; das Besprengen (*at a baptism*).

Afield, *adv.* im Felde; ins Feld, in die Schlacht; von Hause fort, in die Weite, draußen; far —, weit und breit; further —, weiter hinaus; to go —, to look —, sich weiter umtun *or* umschauen.

Afloat, *adv.* schwimmend, flott; the rumour is —, das Gerücht verbreitet sich, es geht ein Gerücht; to set —, in Gang setzen *or* bringen.

Afoot, *adv.* zu Fuß; in Bewegung, im Gange.

Afore, *adv. & prep. see* Before. *Comp.* **—mentioned**, *adj.* vorher erwähnt. **—named**, *adj.* vorher genannt, obig. **—said**, *adj.* vorher erwähnt; obgemeldet (*Law*).

Afraid, *adj.* fürchtend, besorgt, bange; to be — of a thing, sich vor einer S. fürchten.

Afresh, *adv.* von neuem, von frischem, aufs neue, wieder, abermals.

Aft, *adv.* hinten am *or* im Schiffe; fore and —, vorn und hinten. **—er**, *see* After.

After, I. *prep.* nach (*of time*); (behind) nach, hinter; (according to) nach, zufolge, gemäß; (in imitation of) nach; — the storm a calm, auf Regen folgt Sonnenschein; — supper, nach dem Abendessen; the day — to-morrow, übermorgen; the week — next, die übernächste *or* zweitnächste Woche; one — another, einer nach dem andern; day — day, Tag für Tag; — that, nachdem; — all, am Ende, bei alledem, schließlich; what are you —? was habt ihr vor? (*coll.*); — having said so, he went away, nachdem er dies gesagt hatte, ging er fort; I'll go — him, ich will ihm nach (*coll.*). II. *adv.* hinterher; nachher, darauf; some time —, einige Zeit darauf; the day —, den Tag darauf; (*as adj.*) — ages, die Nachwelt, Zukunft; — life, der Rest des Lebens; das zukünftige Leben; — swarm, der Nachschwarm; — taste, der Nachgeschmack; in — years, in späteren Jahren. III. *conj.* nachdem; — I had done my business, I prepared to return, nachdem ich meine Geschäfte abgemacht hatte, machte ich mich zur Rückreise bereit; — having seen him, nachdem ich ihn gesehen hatte. **—wards**, *adv.* nachher, hernach, darauf, in der Folge. *Comp.* **—-birth**, *s.* die Nachgeburt. **—-dinner**, *s.* der Nachtisch (*obs.*). *adj.* an —-dinner nap, ein Nachmittagsschläfchen; an —-dinner conversation, ein Gespräch nach Tische; —-dinner speech, die Nachtischrede, Verdauungsrede (*coll.*); die politische Tischrede. **—-grass**, **—-math**, *s.* die Nachmahd; die Nachernte. **—-named**, *adj.* weiter unten genannt. **—noon**, *s.* der Nachmittag; good —noon, guten Tag, guten Abend. **—-pains**, *pl.* die Nachwehen. **—-piece**, *s.* das Nachstück (*Theat.*). **—thought**, *s.* der nachträgliche Einfall. **—time**, *s.* die Folgezeit, Zukunft; die Überstunden.

Again, *adv.* wieder, wiederum, nochmals, noch einmal; (back) zurück; (moreover) ferner, außerdem; (on the other hand) dagegen; — and —, wieder und wieder, immer wieder; as much —, noch einmal so viel; to come —, wiederkommen.

Against, *prep.* gegen; wider; (by) gegen, an, bis; (on, close to) an; to run — a pillar, gegen eine Säule laufen, stoßen; — the grain, gegen den Strich, wider Willen, ungern; a crime — the state, ein Verbrechen gegen den Staat; he that is not with me is — me, wer nicht für mich ist, ist wider mich (*B.*); it hangs — the wall, es hängt an der Wand; a lecture — pride, eine Vorlesung gegen den Stolz; he left a letter for me — my arrival, er ließ einen Brief für mich zurück, wenn ich ankäme; — death there is no remedy, für den Tod ist kein Kraut gewachsen; the laugh is always — the loser, wer den Schaden hat, braucht für den Spott nicht zu sorgen; — the end of the week, gegen Ende der Woche; over —, gegenüber; I am not — it, ich habe nichts dagegen.

[1]**Agape**, *adj. & adv.* gaffend, mit offnem Munde.

[2]**Agape**, *s.* das Liebesmahl (*of the early Christians*).

Agate, *s.* der Achat, Agat.

Age, *s.* das Alter; (period) das Zeitalter, die Zeit; (century) das Jahrhundert; (generation) das Geschlecht; old —, das hohe Alter, Greisenalter; to be of —, mündig sein; to come of —, mündig werden; under —, unmündig; at the — of 16 (years), im Alter von 16 Jahren; six years of —, sechs Jahre alt; he is my —, er ist so alt wie ich, er ist in meinem Alter; he does not look his —, man sieht ihm sein Alter nicht an; the — of Goethe, das Zeitalter Goethes. —**d**, *adj.* alt, bejahrt; middle-—d, von mittlerem Alter; —d forty, vierzig Jahre alt, vierzigjährig; the —d poor, die alten Armen. —**s**, *pl.;* the Middle —s, das Mittelalter; —s yet unborn, noch ungeborene Geschlechter; former —s, frühere Zeitalter *or* Zeiten; the —s of Shakespeare and of Schiller, die Zeiten Shakespeares und Schillers.

Agen—cy, *s.* (action) die Wirkung; (intervention) die Vermittelung; die Agentur, Agentenstelle; scholastic —cy, die Schulagentur; —cy business, das Kommissionsgeschäft. —**da**, *pl.* die Agende (*Eccl.*); das Denkbuch, der Schreibkalender; die Tagesordnung, die Verhandlungsgegenstände. —**t**, *s.* das Agens, die wirkende Kraft; der Agent; der Geschäftsträger, Vertreter; physical —ts, physikalische Kräfte.

Agglomerat—e, *v.* I. *a.* zusammenballen. II. *n.* sich zusammenballen, zusammenlaufen. —**ion**, *s.* das Zusammenballen; die Anhäufung.

Agglutina—nt, *adj.* anklebend, verbindend. —**te**, *v.* I. *a.* zusammenleimen, verbinden; agglutinieren (*Med. Gram.*). II. *n.* sich in Leim verwandeln. III. *adj.* zusammengeleimt, verbunden; agglutiniert, zusammengesetzt. —**tion**, *s.* das Zusammenkleben *or* =leimen; die Anheilung. —**tive**, *adj.* bindend; agglutinierend (*of languages*).

Aggrandize, *v.a.* vergrößern; erheben; he sought to — his family, er strebte darnach, seine Familie zu erhöhen. —**ment**, *s.* das Vergrößern; die Vergrößerung, Erhebung.

Aggravat—e, *v.a.* erschweren, ärger *or* schlimmer machen, verschlimmern; (provoke) ärgern, erzürnen; that only —es my woe, das vermehrt nur meinen Kummer; it is —ing, es ist ärgerlich, verdrießlich. —**ion**, *s.* die Erschwerung, Verschlimmerung; die Erzürnung, Aufreizung.

Aggregat—e, I. *v.a.* zusammenhäufen. II. *adj.* angehäuft; vereint; zusammengenommen; —e amount, der Gesamtbetrag. III. *s.* das Aggregat, der Haufe; in the —e, im ganzen, im allgemeinen, überhaupt. —**ion**, *s.* die Häufung, Anhäufung; *see* —e III.

Aggress—ion, *s.* der erste Angriff, Anfall. —**ive**, *adj.* den ersten Angriff machend, angreifend; zum Angriff geneigt; feindlich; —ive war, der Angriffskrieg. —**or**, *s.* der angreifende Teil.

Aggrieve, *v.a.* betrüben; —d, gekränkt; to feel —d, sich verletzt *or* gekränkt fühlen.

Aghast, *adj.* entsetzt, aufs höchste bestürzt.

Agil—e, *adj.* behend, flink, hurtig, gelenkig. —**ity**, *s.* die Behendigkeit, Hurtigkeit.

Agio, *s.* das Aufgeld, Agio; der Aufschlag.

Agitat—e, *v.a.* bewegen, in Bewegung bringen, schütteln, lebhaft hin und her bewegen; aufregen, beunruhigen (*the mind, etc.*); aufwiegeln; debattieren (*a question*). —**ion**, *s.* die Bewegung; Erschütterung; die Gemütsbewegung, Störung; die Unruhe; die Beratschlagung; der Aufruhr. —**or**, *s.* der Aufwiegler, Wühler, Aufruhrstifter.

Aglow, *adv.* glühend, gerötet (with, von, vor).

Agnate, *adj.* von männlicher *or* väterlicher Seite verwandt, agnatisch, vom gleichen Vorfahr abstammend. —**s**, *pl.* die Agnaten, Verwandten im Mannesstamme.

Agnostic, I. *adj.* agnostisch. II. *s.* der Agnostiker, agnostische Philosoph. —**ism**, *s.* die Anschauung und Lehre der Agnostiker.

Ago, I. *adj.* (*after a noun*) vergangen, vorüber, her, vor; a year —, vor einem Jahre; a fortnight —, vor vierzehn Tagen; a little while —, vor kurzem; many years —, vor vielen *or* langen Jahren; some time —, vor einiger Zeit. II. *adv.;* long —, lange her; vor langen Jahren; not long —, vor kurzem; how long — is that? wie lange ist das her? I saw him no longer — than yesterday, ich habe ihn erst gestern noch gesehen.

Agog, *adj. & adv.* (*coll.*); all —, ganz erpicht; to set a p.'s curiosity —, jemandes Neugierde erregen.

A-going, *adv.;* to set —, in Gang setzen *or* bringen; in Bewegung bringen.

Agon—ize, *v.* I. *a.* quälen, martern. II. *n.* qualvolle Schmerzen erdulden; mit dem Tode ringen. —**izing**, *adj.* höchst schmerzlich. —**y**, *s.* der Todeskampf; der größte Schmerz, die höchste Pein; die Seelenangst; —y of sorrow, unbeschreiblicher Schmerz; —y of tears, Strom von Tränen; —y column, (*coll.*) die zweite Spalte der (Londoner) Tagesblätter (Familiennachrichten, Liebesgrüße, Bitten, Mahnungen).

Agrarian, *adj.* agrarisch, die Äcker, Felder betreffend; — law, das Agrargesetz, Ackergesetz; — party, agrarische Partei, Bund der Landwirte; the —s, die Agrarier.

Agree, *v.n.* übereinstimmen; übereinkommen; (as to *or* on a th.) einig werden, sich einigen (über eine S.); gut zusammenstimmen, harmonieren (*Mus.*); gut bekommen (*of food*); (suit) stimmen, passen (zu); (— to a th.) annehmen (eine S.), eingehen (auf eine S.); (— on a th.) (etwas) gemeinsam beschließen, sich (über eine S.) verständigen; (— upon a th.) einwilligen (in eine S.), sich einigen (auf eine S.); to — for a th. at a certain price, zu einem bestimmten Preise handelseinig werden; I see we shall never — on this point, ich sehe, über diesen Punkt werden wir nie einig werden *or* übereinkommen; I have —d to act as you wished, ich habe mich bereit erklärt, so zu handeln, wie Sie es wünschten; it is difficult to — with him, es ist schwer mit ihm auszukommen; they — like cat and dog, sie vertragen sich wie Katze und Hund; at length he —d to this request, endlich willfahrte er dieser Bitte; they all —d that . . ., sie kamen alle überein, daß . . .; it was —d nem. con. that, es wurde der einmütige Beschluß gefaßt; this story does not — with what was reported yesterday, diese Geschichte paßt nicht zu dem gestrigen Gerücht; — with thine adversary quickly, sei willfährig deinem Widersacher bald (*B.*); wine does not — with me, Wein bekommt mir nicht; as —d upon, wie verabredet; —d! abgemacht! topp! es gilt! gut! —**able**, *adj.*, —**ably**, *adv.* übereinstimmend, gemäß, angemessen; angenehm, gefällig; —able, —ably to, zufolge, in Gemäßheit mit; I am —

able to it, ich bin es zufrieden. —**ableness,** —**ability,** *s.* die Annehmlichkeit, Anmut. —**ment,** *s.* die Übereinstimmung; der Einklang; die Ähnlichkeit; der Vertrag, Kontrakt, das Bündnis; die Zustimmung; to come to an —ment, (über eine S.) einig werden; articles of —ment, die Vergleichungspunkte; to make an —ment, eine Übereinkunft treffen.

Agricultur—al, *adj.* landwirtschaftlich, Ackerbau= ; the —al depression, das Darniederliegen der Landwirtschaft, die landwirtschaftliche Notlage ; an —al people, ein Ackerbau treibendes Volk; —al show, die landwirtschaftliche Ausstellung; —al society, der landwirtschaftliche Verein; —al wages, ländliche Arbeitslöhne ; —al labourer, der Landarbeiter. —**e,** *s.* der Feldbau, die Landwirtschaft; the Board of —e, der Landwirtschaftsrat. —**ist,** *s.* der Landwirt, Ackerbauer, Ökonom.

Aground, *adv.* auf dem Grunde, gestrandet ; to run (a ship) —, stranden, (ein Schiff auf den Strand setzen) ; British cruiser —, britischer Kreuzer festgefahren *or* gestrandet.

Agu—e, *s.* der Fieberfrost, Schüttelfrost ; —e fit, der Fieberfrost, Schauerfrost ; fever and —e, das Wechselfieber. —**ish,** *adj.* fieberhaft ; kalt, frostig.

Ah, *int.* ah ! ach ! —**a,** *int.* aha !

Ahead, *adv.* vorwärts, voraus, weiter vor ; straight —, gerade aus ; to go —, vorausgehen; sich rühren, vorwärts schreiten.

Aid, I. *s.* die Hülfe, der Beistand ; die Hülfssteuer ; to come to a p.'s —, einem zu Hülfe kommen. II. *v.a.* helfen, unterstützen, beistehen. —**er,** *s.* der Gehülfe, Helfer.

Aide-de-camp, *s.* der Adjutant (eines Generals).

Aigrette, *s.* der Strauß, Federbusch.

Ail, *v.* I. *n.* unpäßlich sein, Schmerzen haben. II. *imp.* weh tun, schmerzen; what —s him ? was fehlt ihm ? was sicht ihn an ? —**ing,** *adj.* unwohl, leidend, kränklich. —**ment,** *s.* das Leiden.

Aim, I. *s.* (direction) die Richtung ; das Ziel, die Zielscheibe ; der Zweck, die Absicht, das Vorhaben (*fig.*) ; to take — at a th., zielen auf eine S.; to miss one's —, das Ziel verfehlen, fehlschießen; seinen Zweck verfehlen, nicht erreichen; the end and —, der Zweck und das Ziel. II. *v.n.;* — at, zielen auf (*acc.*) *or* nach; seine Absicht auf eine S. richten; the end at which he —s, das Ziel seines Strebens ; that was —ed at me, das galt mir, war auf mich abgesehen ; he —s too high, er spannt die Saiten zu hoch, er steckt sich (*dat.*) ein zu hohes Ziel; he boldly —s at it, er geht kühn darauf los. III. *v.a. ;* to — a blow, einen Schlag richten, führen (at a p., auf *or* gegen einen). —**less(ly),** *adj.* (*adv.*) ohne Ziel, ziellos, zwecklos.

Air, I. *s.* die Luft ; die Arie, Melodie (*Mus.*) ; das Lied (*Mus.*); (breeze) das Lüftchen ; (appearance) das Aussehen, Ansehen, der Schein ; (manner) die Miene, das Ansehen ; der Duft, Dunst ; to take the —, frische Luft schöpfen ; to let a little — into the room, das Zimmer ein wenig auslüften ; to sleep in the open —, unter freiem Himmel schlafen ; without a breath of —, ohne ein Lüftchen, ohne daß sich ein Lüftchen regt ; an — of assurance, eine kecke, dreiste Miene ; there is an — of sadness about him, er hat ein trübes Aussehen ; to give o.s. —s, vornehm tun, sich aufs hohe Pferd setzen, sich zieren ; none of your —s ! komm mir nicht mit deiner Geziertheit ! change of —, die Luftveränderung ; castles in the —, Luftschlösser. II. *attrib.;* — bubble, die Luftblase; — cushion, das Luftkissen ; — lock, die pneumatische Schleuse; — passage, der Luftkanal. III. *v.a.* lüften, der Luft aussetzen ; auslüften (*a room, etc.*); trocknen, wärmen (*linen, etc.*). —**iness,** *s.* die Luftigkeit ; der Leichtsinn. die Leichtigkeit. —**ing,** *s.* das Lüften; der Spaziergang (*on foot*), Spazierritt (*on horseback*), die Spazierfahrt (*in a carriage*); to take an —ing, sich ins Freie begeben, an die Luft gehen, ausgehen, ausfahren. —**y,** *adj.* luftig ; hoch; aus Luft bestehend; (—**ily,** *adv.*) luftig, flüchtig, leicht ; windig ; leichtsinnig. *Comp.* —-**balloon,** *s.* der Luftballon. —-**bladder,** *s.* die Luftblase ; die Schwimmblase (*Icht.*). —-**engine,** *s.* der Kunstschacht; Ericsson's (hot-) —-engine, die Ericssonsche Heißluftmaschine. —-**gun,** *s.* die Windbüchse. —-**hole,** *s.* das Luftloch; die Zugröhre (*in a furnace*). —-**pipe,** *s.* die Luftröhre. —-**pump,** *s.* die Luftpumpe. —-**shaft,** *s.* der Wetterschacht (*Min.*). —-**tight,** *adj.* luftdicht. —-**tube,** *s.* der Luftschlauch (*Cycl.*). —-**vessel,** *s.* das Luftgefäß (*Bot.*); der Rezipient (*of a fire engine*).

Aisle, *s.* das Seitenschiff einer Kirche ; der Chorgang.

Aitch, *s.* der Buchstabe h ; to drop one's —es, das h (in Anlaut) nicht aussprechen.

Ajar, *adv.* halb offen, angelehnt ; (*fig.*) in Zwiespalt; to leave —, angelehnt *or* halb offen lassen; to set —, anlehnen.

Ajog, *adv.* im Paß, in langsamem Schaukeltrab.

Ajutage, *s.* die Ansatzröhre.

Akimbo, *adv.* ; in die Seite gestemmt; with arms —, die Arme in Seite gestemmt.

Akin, *adj.* verwandt ; — to, verwandt mit.

Alabaster, I. *s.* der Alabaster. II. *adj.* alabastern ; — glass, das Milchglas.

Alack, (— **a day,**) *int.* O weh ! Lieber Himmel !

Alacrity, *s.* die Munterkeit, die Frohsinn ; (readiness) die Bereitwilligkeit, Dienstfertigkeit.

Alarm, I. *s.* der Lärm, (call to arms) das Lärmgeschrei, der Waffenruf ; (fear) die Angst, Unruhe ; der Tumult, Aufruhr (*obs.*) ; der Wecker (*in a clock*) ; der Appell (*Fenc.*); to sound an —, Lärm blasen *or* schlagen ; to take — at, über eine S. in Angst geraten; the electric — *or* alarum, das elektrische Schlagwerk. II. *v.a.* Lärm blasen *or* schlagen; erschrecken, beunruhigen, in Furcht setzen. —**ing,** *adj.* beunruhigend. —**ist,** *s.* der Lärmbläser, der Bangemacher. *Comp.* —-**clock,** *s.* die Weckuhr, die Weckeruhr.

Alas, *int.* leider ! ach ! o weh ! — the day ! ach ! unglücklicher Tag !

Alb, *s.* die Albe, das Chorhemd. —**ino,** *s.* der Kakerlak, Albino. —**um,** *s.* das Stammbuch, Album. —**umen,** *s.* das Eiweiß ; vegetable —umen, Pflanzeneiweiß. —**uminate,** *s.* die Verbindung mit Eiweißstoff. —**uminous,** *adj.* eiweißartig. —**urnum,** *s.* das Alburnum.

Albatross, *s.* der Albatros.

Albeit, *conj.* (*also :* — that) obgleich, wiewohl.

Alchem—ical(ly), *adj.* (*adv.*) alchemistisch. —**ist,** *s.* der Goldmacher, Alchemist. —**y,** *s.* die Goldmacherkunst, Alchemie.

Alcohol, *s.* der rektifizierte Weingeist, Alkohol. —**ic,** *adj.* alkoholisch, spiritusartig. —**ization,** *s.* die Alkoholisierung. —**ism,** *s.* der Alkoholismus, die Alkoholkrankheit. —**ometer,** *s.* der Alkoholmesser; centesimal —ometer, das hundertteilige Alkoholometer.

Alcove, *s.* der Alkoven ; die Nische.

Alder, I. *s.* die Erle. II. *adj.* von Erlenholz, erlen; — tree, der Erlenbaum, die Erle.

Alderman, *s.* der Ratsherr, Stadtrat, Aldermann. —**ic,** *adj.* ratsherrlich ; würdevoll.

Ale, *s.* englisches Bier, Ale; ländliches Fest (*obs.*), pale —, helles englisches Bier; — brewer, der Bierbrauer; — pitcher, (großer) Bierkrug; — vat, der Braubottich. *Comp.* —-**bench,** *s.* die Bierbank. —-**house,** *s.* das Bierhaus, die Bierschenke *or* =kneipe; —-house politician, der Bierbank=Politiker, politischer Kannegießer; —-house keeper, der Schenkwirt.

Alee, *adv.* unter dem Winde, leewärts.

Alembic, *s.* der Brennkolben, Destillierkolben.

Alert, *adj.* wachsam ; (active) flink, behend ; on

the —, auf der Hut, wach. —**ness**, *s.* die Wachsamkeit; die Behendigkeit.
Alexandrine, *s.* der Alexandriner (*metre*).
Alexipharmic, Alexipharmac, I. *adj.* als Gegengift dienend. II. *s.* das Gegengift.
Algae, *pl.* die Algen.
Algaroth, *s.*; — powder, das Algarotpulver.
Algebra, *s.* die Algebra, Buchstabenrechnung. —**ic(al)**, *adj.*, —**ically**, *adv.* algebraisch. —**ism**, *s.* algebraischer Ausdruck; algebraisches Zeichen. —**ist**, *s.* der Algebraiker.
Alias, I. *adv.* sonst, anders; John Smith — Thomson, John Smith, genannt Thomson. II. *s.* angenommener Name; to go under an —, einen zweiten, falschen Namen führen.
Alibi, *s.* das Alibi, die Abwesenheit; to prove an —, sein Alibi nachweisen (*Law*).
Alien, I. *adj.* fremd, ausländisch; fremd, unangemessen (*to a purpose*); it is — to my purpose to dwell upon this, es entspricht nicht meiner Absicht, bei diesem hier zu verweilen. II. *s.* der Fremde, Ausländer. —**able**, *adj.* veräußerlich. —**ate**, *v.a.* veräußern (*property*); (estrange) entfremden. —**ation**, *s.* die Veräußerung; die Entfremdung (*of affection*); mental —ation, —ation of mind, die Geistesstörung.
[1]**Alight**, *v.n.* sich niederlassen (on, auf); absteigen, herabsteigen (*from a horse*); aussteigen (*from a carriage*); to — on, sich setzen auf (*acc.*).
[2]**A-light**, *adv.*; to be —, angezündet sein, brennen.
Alignment, *s.* die Abmessung nach der Schnur (*Carp.*); die Absteckline (*Mil.*); die Trace (*Surv.*).
Alike, I. *adj.* gleich, ähnlich; they are very much —, sie sind einander sehr ähnlich. II. *adv.* gleichmäßig, auf dieselbe Weise.
Alim—ent, *s.* die Nahrung, Speise. —**entary**, *adj.* zur Nahrung gehörig; nahrhaft; nährend; —entary canal, der Darmkanal; —entary duct, der Speisegang. —**entation**, *s.* die Ernährung(-sgelder); der Unterhalt. —**ony**, *s.* die Alimentation.
Aliqu—ant, *adj.* ungleich teilend (*Arith.*). —**ot**, *adj.* gleich teilend, ohne Rest aufgehend (*Arith.*).
Alive, *adj.* lebend, lebendig, am Leben; lebhaft, munter; — to, empfänglich für, aufmerksam auf (*acc.*); look —! munter! lebhaft! rege! nur lebendig! he is still —, er lebt noch; there 's not a man — who can . . ., kein Sterblicher kann . . .; he is the best man —, er ist der beste Mann der Welt, *or* der beste Mensch unter der Sonne; he was — to the danger, er war sich (*dat.*) der Gefahr bewußt; I am fully — to the necessity of, ich würdige vollständig die Notwendigkeit zu; he was — to the advantage, er nahm den Vorteil wahr; the shore was — with spectators, der Strand wimmelte von Zuschauern.
Alkali, *s.* das Alkali, Laugensalz; — maker, der Sodafabrikant. —**ne**, *adj.* laugensalzig; —ne salts, alkalische Salze.
All, I. *adj. & pronominal adj.* all; ganz; — men, alle Menschen; — good men, alle guten Menschen; — the good women of P., alle guten Weiber von P.; — the events of his stay, alle Erlebnisse seines Aufenthaltes; — the men who were saved, alle die Männer, welche gerettet wurden; — the officials, sämmtliche Beamten; — of us, wir alle; — and every one, one and —, alle mit einander, alle insgesammt; after —, am Ende, bei alle dem; above —, vor allen Dingen; it 's — one to me, es ist mir (ganz) einerlei, es ist mir alles gleich; once for —, ein für allemal; for good and —, gänzlich, für immer; for — that, dessen ungeachtet, trotzdem; — the world, die ganze Welt; — the world over, die ganze Welt hindurch; for — the world, durchaus, gerade; he looked for — the world as if, etc., er sah gerade so aus, als ob, 2c.; I would not for — the world, etc., um alles in der Welt möchte ich nicht, 2c.; by — means, gewiß, auf jeden Fall; to — intents and purposes, in jeder Hinsicht; that is —, das genügt; genug für heute; weiter nichts; they are only shouting for joy, that 's —, sie schreien nur vor Freude, weiter nichts; if that be —, wenn's weiter nichts ist; and — that (sort of thing), und dergleichen; he is — things to — men, er ist allen alles; with — speed, in aller Eile; — in vain, vergebens; — Europe, ganz Europa; — but, fast; "— but" saves many a man, „Beinahe" schützt so manchen (*prov.*). II. *adv.*, *or part. forming with another word an adverb*, all-, ganz, gar, gänzlich, völlig; an — absorbing occupation, eine alles in Anspruch nehmende Beschäftigung; — admiring, allbewundernd; — bounteous, — bountiful, allgütig; — destroying, alles zerstörend; — devouring, alles verschlingend; — efficient, allwirksam; — embracing, allumfassend; — just, allgerecht; — merciful, allbarmherzig; — sufficient, allgenugsam; — sustaining, alles unterhaltend; — along, die ganze Zeit über, die ganze Länge; — the better, um so besser, desto besser; — at once, auf einmal, plötzlich; — over, ganz über, ganz durch, ganz und gar; — over the town, durch die ganze Stadt verbreitet; to tremble — over, am ganzen Leibe zittern; at —, überhaupt, durchaus; if he does it at — he will do it well, wenn er es überhaupt tut, wird er es gut machen; not at —, keineswegs, ganz und gar nicht; nothing at —, gar nichts; nowhere at —, nirgends; — in a muddle, in völliger Unordnung *or* Verwirrung; — to pieces, in lauter Stücke; it 's — up with him, es ist aus mit ihm (*vulg.*); — too dear, viel zu teuer; — hail! heil dir! — right! richtig! recht! schön! sehr wohl! einverstanden! alles in Ordnung! he was — for himself, er dachte nur auf seinen eigenen Vorteil; to be — there, sehr gescheit sein (*coll.*). III. *n.* das Ganze; das All, Alles; my —, mein Alles; my — is at stake, alles steht bei mir auf dem Spiele; when — comes to —, wenn es um und um kommt; you are — in — to him, Sie gelten alles bei ihm; —'s well! Alles wohl! gute Wache! —'s well that ends well, Ende gut, alles gut (*prov.*). *Comp.* —**-fools'-day**, *s.* der Allernarrentag, erste April. —**-fours**, *s.*; to go on —-fours, auf allen Vieren kriechen. —**-hallow mass**, —**-hallow tide**, *s.* Zeit um Allerheiligen (1 November). —**-hallows eve**, *s.* der Allerheiligenabend. — **saints day**, *s.* der Allerheiligen(tag) (1 November). — **souls**, *s. pl.* (das Fest) Allerseelen (2 November). —**spice**, *s.* der Nelkenpfeffer.
Allay, *v.a.* lindern, dämpfen, mäßigen (*pain*); stillen (*thirst*); beruhigen (*fears*).
Alleg—ation, *s.* die Behauptung; die Anführung, Vorbringung; false —ation, falsche Angabe, fälschliche Beschuldigung. —**e**, *v.a.* (bring forward) anführen; (assert) behaupten.
Allegiance, *s.* die Pflicht *or* Treue der Untertanen; die Lehnspflicht; oath of —, der Huldigungseid; to do — to a prince, einem Fürsten huldigen *or* den Huldigungseid leisten.
Allegor—ical(ly), *adj.* (*adv.*) sinnbildlich, allegorisch. —**ize**, *v.* I. *a.* sinnbildlich darstellen; durch eine Allegorie ausdrücken. II. *n.* Allegorien brauchen. —**y**, *s.* (*pl.* —ies) die Allegorie, das Sinnbild.
Allegro, I. *s.* das Allegro. II. *adv.* allegro, munter.
Allelujah, Alleluia, *s.* das Hallelujah.
Allevia—te, *v.a.* erleichtern, lindern, mildern. —**tion**, *s.* die Erleichterung, Linderung.
Alley, *s.* die Allee, der Baumgang; das Seitengäßchen, Gäßchen; blind —, die Sackgasse.
Alli—ance, *s.* (treaty) das Bündnis, der Bund; die Verbindung (*of states*); die Verwandtschaf (by marriage, durch Heirat); an offensive and defensive —ance, ein Schutz-und-Trutz-Bündnis; to make an —ance, to enter into an —ance, sich verbinden; sich vermählen; matrimonial —ance, eheliche Verbindung. —**ed**, —**es**, *see* Ally.

Alligation, *s.* die Verbindung; die Mischung, Legierung; the rule of —, die Mischungsregel, Alligationsregel; — medial, die Durchschnittsrechnung.

Alligator, *s.* der Alligator, Kaiman; North American —, der hechtsköpfige Kaiman.

Alliterat—e, *v.a.* stabreimen, alliterieren. **—ion**, *s.* der Stabreim, die Alliteration. **—ive**, *adj.* stabreimend, alliterierend; —ive poetry, die Stabreimdichtung.

Allocat—e, *v.a.* stellen; jedem das Seinige zuerteilen. **—ion**, *s.* die Verteilung (*of shares*); (assignment) die Anweisung; die Zahlungsanweisung (*by the exchequer*).

Allodi—al, *adj.* allodial, erbeigen, zinsfrei; —al lands, Allodialgüter. **—um**, *s.* das Allodium, Allodialgut, freies Erbgut.

Allot, *v.a.* (assign) anweisen, zuteilen, bestimmen; (distribute) austeilen. **—ment**, I. *s.* (share) der Anteil, Teil; die Verteilung *or* Ausgabe (von Aktien); die Landparzelle; on —ment, bei Ausgabe, wenn die Verschreibungen zur Ausgabe gelangen; letter of —ment, der Interimsschein (*C. L.*). II. *attrib.*; —ment holder, der Tagelöhner mit einem Stück Feld.

Allow, *v.a.* (grant) zugeben, zuerkennen; (permit) erlauben, gestatten; (give) geben, bestimmen; (admit) gelten lassen, einräumen; his conduct —s of no excuse, sein Betragen läßt sich nicht entschuldigen; I — that you have done more than I, but you must — that I have effected more than you, ich gestehe, daß Ihr mehr getan habt als ich, Ihr müßt aber einräumen, daß ich mehr zustande gebracht habe, als Ihr; I — my cousin thirty pounds a year, ich lasse meinem Vetter jährlich 30 Pfund zukommen; he —ed three hours for the work, er bestimmte 3 Stunden für die Arbeit, er setzte 3 Stunden für die Arbeit an; — me one word, gestatten Sie mir ein Wort; they would not — that he had any talent, sie wollten nicht zugeben, daß er irgendwelches Talent habe, sie sprachen ihm alles Talent ab; she is generally —ed to be, etc., sie gilt im allgemeinen für, 2c.; to — for, Rücksicht auf (eine S.) nehmen; —ing for, wenn man abrechnet; —ing for his want of education, seinen Mangel an Erziehung abgerechnet. **—able**, *adj.* zulässig, zulaßbar; richtig, rechtmäßig; in a man of your age it is —able, ein Mann Ihres Alters darf es tun. **—ableness**, *s.* die Zulässigkeit; die Rechtmäßigkeit. **—ance**, I. *s.* die Einräumung, Zulassung; (approval) die Genehmigung, Gutheißung; die Erlaubnis; der bestimmte Teil, das Ausgesetzte; das Taschengeld; die Nachsicht, Schonung; der Abzug (*C.L.*); die Entschädigung (*C.L.*); yearly (monthly) —ance, das Jahrgeld (Monatsgeld); der Wechsel (*stud. lang.*); to put upon short —ance, auf knappe Rationen setzen, beschränken; to make —ance, Nachsicht üben; to make —ance for s.th., etwas in Anschlag bringen *or* in Betracht ziehen, auf eine S. Rücksicht nehmen; you must make some —ance for his years, Sie müssen ihm seine Jugend zu gute halten; to make s.o. an —ance, einem eine bestimmte Summe, ein Taschengeld (Jahrgeld, Monatsgeld), aussetzen *or* zukommen lassen. II. *v.a.* portionsweise austeilen.

Alloy, *s.* die Legierung, Vermischung; die Vermischung (*fig.*); — of gold, Goldlegierung; gold without —, echtes Gold; happiness without —, ungemischte Freude, vollkommenes Glück.

Allude, *v.n.* anspielen (to a thing, auf eine Sache); sich beziehen (auf); the person —d to, die Person, auf die man angespielt hat.

Allur—e, *v.a.* anlocken, anreizen; —ed by, bezaubert von, angezogen von; verführt von. **—ement**, *s.* die Lockung, Anreizung; der Reiz. **—er**, *s.* der Anlocker; der Verführer, die Verführerin. **—ing(ly)**, *adj.* (*adv.*) lockend, reizend; (seductive) verlockend, verführerisch.

Allusi—on, *s.* die Anspielung, Hindeutung (to a th., auf eine S.). **—ve**, *adj.* anspielend.

Alluvi—al, *adj.* angeschwemmt, angespült; —al detritus, die Geschiebbänke (*Geol.*). **—on**, **—um**, *s.* die Anspülung, Anschwemmung; das angeschwemmte Land, die Ablagerung.

Ally, I. *v.a.* verbinden, vereinigen (*by marriage, etc.*); allied to *or* with, verbunden, verwandt mit. II. *v.n.* eng verbunden sein, sich verbinden. III. *s.* der Verbündete, Bundesgenosse.

Almanac, *s.* der Almanach, Kalender.

Almight—iness, *s.* die Allmacht, Allmächtigkeit. **—y**, I. *adj.* allmächtig. II. *s.* der Allmächtige.

Almond, *s.* die Mandel (*also Anat.*); milk of —s, die Mandelmilch; —s of the throat, Halsmandeln. *Comp.* **—-tree**, *s.* der Mandelbaum.

Almoner, *s.* der Almosenpfleger, Almosenier.

Almost, *adv.* fast, beinahe.

Alms, *s.* (*often used as pl.*) das Almosen; die milde Gabe. *Comp.* **—-box**, *s.* der Almosenkasten, die Armenbüchse. **—-deed**, *s.* die Wohltat, das Almosen, die milde Gabe; das Liebeswerk. **—-giver**, *s.* der Almosenspender, der milde Geber. **—-giving**, *s.* das Almosenspenden, die Armenpflege. **—-house**, *s.* das Armenhaus. **—-people**, *pl.* von Almosen (oder im Armenhause) lebende Leute.

Aloe, *s.* die Aloe. *pl.* das Aloeholz (*B.*); der Aloesaft (*Pharm.*). **—tic**, *adj.* aloehaltig. *Comp.* **—s-wood**, *s.* das Aloeholz.

Aloft, *adv.* hoch oben, in der Höhe; empor; im Tauwerk, in der Takelung; himmelwärts; to mount —, in die Höhe steigen; he is —, er ist oben in dem Tauwerk (*Naut.*).

Alone, *adj. & adv.* allein; (solitary) einsam; (unique) einzig; to leave —, allein lassen, verlassen; to let a p. —, einen in Ruhe lassen, zufrieden lassen; to let a thing —, eine Sache unterlassen, eine Sache nicht anrühren; let that book —, laß das Buch liegen; let that —, laß das bleiben *or* sein; let —, geschweige (denn), abgesehen davon; let well —, was dich nicht brennt, das blase nicht (*prov.*); he is not — in it, er ist hierin nicht der Einzige; utterly —, mutterseelen allein; all —, ganz allein.

Along, I. *adv.* längs, der Länge nach; all —, der ganzen Länge nach, überall; die ganze Zeit hindurch; I knew all — that he was telling an untruth, ich wußte die ganze Zeit über, daß er die Unwahrheit sprach; — with, mit, in Gesellschaft mit, zugleich mit; come — with (me), komm mit (mir); go —! geh doch! let me go — with you, laßt mich mit euch gehen; as we go —, unterwegs; he drove —, er fuhr dahin; take that — with you, nehmt das mit; get — with you! packe dich! II. *prep.* längs, entlang; we walked — the river, wir gingen längs des Flusses, am Fluß entlang; — the road, die Straße entlang; — the forest, am Walde entlang *or* hin; to sail — the coast, die Küste entlang *or* an der Küste hin segeln. *Comp.* **—side**, *adv.* nebenan, auf der Seite; close —side, Bord an Bord; to lay —side of, anlegen bei.

Aloof, *adv.* fern, weitab; to keep — from, meiden, sich fern halten von; keep —, bleib mir vom Leibe! **—ness**, *s.* das Sichfernhalten.

Aloud, *adv.* laut, vernehmlich, mit lauter Stimme.

Alpaca, *s.* das Pako, Alpaka, die (peruanische) Kamelziege (*Zool.*); die Alpakawolle; der Alpakastoff.

Alphabet, *s.* das Alphabet; die Buchstabenfolge; (*fig.*) das A B C, die Anfangsgründe. **—ical**, *adj.* alphabetisch; —ical order, die Buchstabenfolge; in —ical order, nach der Buchstabenfolge **—ically**, *adv.* in alphabetischer Ordnung.

Alp—ine, I. *adj.* alpin(isch); die Alpen betreffend; auf den Alpen wachsend; sehr hoch; —ine boots, die Bergschuhe, Nagelschuhe; —ine club, der Alpenklub; —ine crow, die Alpenkrähe; —ine pole, der Alpenstock. II. *s.* der Älpler, Alpenbewohner;

die Alpenpflanze. —**ist**, *s.* der Alpenbesteiger, Alpendurchstreifer. —**s**, *pl.* die Alpen.
Already, *adv.* bereits, schon.
Also, *adv.* (likewise) auch, ebenfalls, gleichfalls; (moreover) ferner, noch außerdem.
Altar, *s.* der Altar. —**age**, *s.* das Altargeld, Opfergeld. *Comp.* —**-cloth**, *s.* das Altartuch, die Altardecke. —**-piece**, *s.* das Altarstück, Altargemälde. —**-screen**, *s.* der Altarschrein.
Alter, *v.* I. *a.* ändern, verändern. II. *n.* anders werden, sich (ver)ändern. —**able**, *adj.* veränderlich, abänderlich, wandelbar. —**ation**, *s.* die Änderung, Veränderung. —**ative**, I. *adj.* alterierend. II. *s.* das alterierende Mittel. —**cation**, *s.* der Wortwechsel, Zank. —**nate**, I. *v.a.* wechselweise verrichten *or* verändern, abwechseln lassen. II. *v.n.* abwechseln; abwechselnd folgen. III. *adj.* abwechselnd; wechselseitig; wechselweise gestellt (*Bot.*); on —nate days, einen Tag um den andern; —nate angles, Wechselwinkel. —**nately**, *adv.* wechselweise. —**nation**, *s.* die Abwechselung, wechselseitige Folge; das Versetzen, die Permutation der Zahlen (*Math.*); das Abwechseln (beim Chorgesang). —**native**, I. *s.* die Wahl (zwischen zwei Dingen), das Entweder-Oder, die Alternative. II. *adj.*, —**natively**, *adv.* abwechselnd; —native proposition, der Wechselsatz.
Although, *conj.* obgleich, obschon, wenngleich; — he is not clever, obgleich er nicht klug ist.
Alt—imetry, *s.* die Höhenmessung. —**itude**, *s.* die Höhe; meridian —itude, Mittagshöhe; to take the sun's —itude, die Sonne schießen, die Sonnenhöhe messen. —**o**, I. *s.* der Alt. II. *adj.;* —o key, der Altschlüssel; —o voice, die Altstimme. *Comp.* —**o-relievo**, *s.* das Hochrelief.
Altogether, *adv.* zusammen, allesammt; (wholly) gänzlich, ganz und gar, völlig, durchaus.
Altruis—m, *s.* die Nächstenliebe, Selbstlosigkeit, Uneigennützigkeit. —**t**, *s.* der selbstlose, uneigennützige Mensch. —**tic**, *adj.* auf das Wohl anderer bedacht, selbstlos, uneigennützig.
Alum, I. *s.* der Alaun; — earth, die Alaunerde. II. *v.a.* mit Alaun bearbeiten, alaunen; to — silks, Seidenzeuge beizen. —**inate**, *s.* das Aluminat. —**inium**, *s.* das Aluminium. —**inous**, *adj.* alaunartig; alaunhaltig.
Alveol—ar, *adj.* zu den Zahnzellen gehörig, alveolar (*Anat.*); —ar continuant, der Alveolarlaut, Alveolarkonsonant (*produced by pressing the tongue against the ridge above the upper teeth*). —**ate**, *adj.* mit kleinen Fächern versehen. —**i**, *pl.* Bienenzellen; Zahnzellen (*Anat.*).
Always, *adv.* immer, stets, beständig, allezeit.
Am, *first pers. pres. indic. of* to be, bin; werde; I — to go, — I not? ich soll gehen, nicht wahr? I — to see him to-morrow, ich soll ihn morgen sehen; I — told, man sagt mir, man berichtet mir, ich höre; you are old, so — I, Sie sind alt, ich auch.
Amain, *adj.* mit aller Kraft, heftig, frisch; (quickly) hurtig; let go —! laßt die Segel nieder, laßt laufen!
Amalgam, *s.* das Amalgam. —**ate**, *v.* I. *a.* amalgamieren. II. *n.* sich vereinigen; (*fig.*) sich verquicken, vermischen, verschmelzen. —**ation**, *s.* das Anquicken (*Metall.*); die Amalgamation, das Amalgamieren (*Chem.*); die Vermischung, innige Verbindung (*fig.*); der Zusammenschluß, die Verschmelzung (*fig.*).
Amanuensis, *s.* der Gehilfe, wissenschaftliche Hilfsarbeiter (eines Gelehrten).
Amaranth, *s.* der Amarant, das Tausendschönchen; (*fig.*) unverwelkliche Blume; die Amarantfarbe, das Purpurrot. —**ine**, *adj.* amaranten.
Amaryllis, *s.* die Amaryllis, Narzissenlilie.
Amass, *v.a.* (zusammen)häufen; aufhäufen; to — wealth, Reichtümer sammeln *or* aufhäufen.
Amat—eur, I. *s.* der Liebhaber (der Kunst), Kunstfreund; der Dilettant; der Stümper (*contempt.*). II. *adj.;* —eur concert, das Dilettantenkonzert; —eur theatricals, das Liebhabertheater, die Dilettantenaufführung. —**eurish**, *adj.* dilettantisch; stümperhaft. —**eurishness**, *s.* der Dilettantismus; die Stümperhaftigkeit. —**iveness**, *s.* der Hang zur Liebe, die Sinnlichkeit. —**ory**, I. *adj.* erotisch, die Liebe betreffend, verliebt; die Liebe erregend. II. *s.* der Liebestrank.
Amaurosis, *s.* der schwarze Star.
Amaz—e, I. *v.a.* erstaunen, in höchstes Staunen (ver)setzen; (astound) verdutzen, bestürzt machen; to be —ed at a th., er staunt sein *or* erstaunen über eine S. II. *s.;* in —e, bestürzt (*obs.*). —**ement**, *s.* das größte Erstaunen, die höchste Verwunderung. —**ing**, *adj.* höchst erstaunlich, erstaunenswert, wunderbar. —**ingly**, *adv.* erstaunlich, außerordentlich.
Amazon, *s.* die Amazone. —**ian**, *adj.* amazonenhaft; unweiblich, von männlichen Wesen.
Ambassad—or, *s.* der Botschafter, (*in very important capitals*) (*usually*) der Gesandte, (ein Gesandter). —**orial**, *adj.* gesandtschaftlich. —**ress**, *s.* die Botschafterin, die Gemahlin des Gesandten.
Amber, I. *s.* der Bernstein; — dropping, ambertränfend. II. *adj.* (aus) Bernstein, bernsteinen; — beads, Bernsteinkorallen. —**gris**, *s.* der graue Amber, die Ambra. *Comp.* —**-seed**, *s.* die Bisamkörner. —**-tree**, *s.* der Ambrabaum.
Ambidext—er, *s.* einer, der die linke Hand eben so gut wie die rechte gebrauchen kann; der Achselträger. —**rous**, *adj.* rechts und links (zugleich); achselträgerisch; falsch.
Ambi—ent, *adj.* umgebend, umfließend. —**guity**, *s.* die Zweideutigkeit; der Doppelsinn; die Ungewißheit, Dunkelheit; there should be no —guity about the words used, es sollten Wörter gebraucht werden, welche keines Doppelsinnes fähig sind. —**guous(ly)**, *adj.* (*adv.*) zweideutig, doppelsinnig; dunkel.
Ambitio—n, *s.* die Ehrsucht, Ehrbegier, der Ehrgeiz. —**us**, *adj.*, —**usly**, *adv.* ehrbegierig, ehrgeizig; hochstrebend, prunkend (*of style*); —us of glory, ruhmbegierig.
Ambl—e, I. *s.* der Paß, Paßgang. II. *v.n.* den Paß gehen. —**ing**, *adj.* den Paß gehend; —ing nag, der Paßgänger, Zelter; —ing pace, der Paßgang.
Ambrosia, *s.* die Götterspeise, Ambrosia; das Ambrosienkraut (*Bot.*). —**l**, *adj.* ambrosisch; (*fig.*) köstlich, erfrischend.
Ambula—nce, I. *s.* das Feldlazarett (*Mil.*). II. *attrib.;* —ance society, der Verein vom roten Kreuz. —**nt**, *adj.* umherwandernd, herumziehend. —**tory**, I. *adj. see* —nt; herumziehend, Wander-; die Kraft besitzend, sich fortzubewegen. II. *s.* der bedeckte Gang in einem Kloster.
Ambuscade, **Ambush**, I. *s.* der Hinterhalt, Versteck; to lay an ambush, einen Hinterhalt legen. II. *v.a.* aus dem Hinterhalt überfallen; our men were —ed, unsre Leute wurden aus einem ihnen gelegten Hinterhalt überfallen. III. *v.n.* im Hinterhalt liegen.
Ameer, **Amir**, *s.* der Amir (Titel des Herrschers von Afghanistan).
Ameliorat—e, *v.a.* verbessern. —**ion**, *s.* die Verbesserung; die Wendung zum Bessern, das Besserwerden.
Amen, I. *int.* Amen. II. *s.* das Amen; I say —, ich spreche Amen dazu, ich bin es zufrieden.
Amenable, *adj.* willfährig, biegsam, leitsam; — to reason, Vernunftgründen zugänglich, vernünftig; — to law, straffällig, verantwortlich.
Amend, *v.* I. *a.* bessern, verbessern; (correct) berichtigen; to — one's conduct, sein Betragen bessern. II. *n.* sich bessern, besser werden; genesen (*in health*). —**ment**, *s.* die Besserung, Verbesserung; der Verbesserungsantrag, das Amendement; to move an —ment, einen Verbesserungsantrag stellen *or* einbringen. —**s**, *s.* der Ersatz, die Vergütung, Genugtuung; to make

—s for a th., etwas ersetzen, vergüten, wieder gut machen, aufwiegen; to make a p. —s for a th., einem für eine S. Schadenersatz leisten, einen für eine S. entschädigen *or* schadlos halten, einem etwas vergüten.

Amenity, *s.* die Annehmlichkeit; die Anmut.

Amerc—e, *v.a.* eine Geldstrafe auflegen. **—iable**, *adj.* straffällig, strafbar. **—ement**, *s.* die Geldstrafe, Geldbuße.

Amethyst, I. *s.* der Amethyst; die Amethystfarbe, das Violett. II. *adj.* amethystfarben, violett.

Ami—able, *adj.*, **—ably**, *adv.* liebenswürdig; holdselig; to do the —able, (*coll.*) den Liebenswürdigen *or* liebenswürdigen Schwerenöter spielen. **—ableness**, **—ability**, *s.* die Liebenswürdigkeit. **—cable**, *adj.*, **—cably**, *adv.* freundschaftlich, friedlich; —cable settlement, gütlicher Vergleich. **—cableness**, *s.* die Freundlichkeit, Friedlichkeit. **—ty**, *s.* die Freundschaft, das gute Einvernehmen.

Amianthus, *s.* der Amiant, das Federweiß.

Amice, *s.* das Achseltuch des Meßpriesters.

Amid, **—st**, *prep.* mitten in, mitten unter (*dat.*), inmitten (*gen.*). *Comp.* **—ships**, *adv.* mittschiffs, in der Mitte des Schiffs.

Amiss, *adj. & adv.* verkehrt; übel, unrecht; to do —, unrecht handeln, Übles tun; to take —, übel nehmen; I should be sorry if I had done anything —, es sollte mir leid tun, wenn ich es in irgend etwas versehen hätte; if anything should happen —, wenn etwas schief gehen sollte (*coll.*); it would not be — for you to, etc., es könnte nicht schaden, wenn Sie, 2c.; not far —, gar nicht übel; nothing comes — to him, er nimmt mit allem fürlieb, er nimmt alles mit; the horse was —, das Pferd war in schlechtem Zustande.

Ammoni—a, *s.* das Ammoniak; liquor —a, der Salmiakgeist. **—ac**, *s.*; sal —ac, der Salmiak. **—acal**, *adj.*; —acal liquor, das Ammoniakwasser. **—ated**, *adj.* mit Ammoniak gemischt; —ated quinine, Chinin mit Ammoniak. **—um**, *s.* das Ammonium.

Ammunition, I. *s.* der Kriegsvorrat, der Schießbedarf, die Munition. II. *attrib.*; — bread, das Kommißbrot; — chest, der Munitionskasten; — waggon, der Munitionswagen.

Amnesty, I. *s.* (allgemeiner) Gnadenerlaß, die allgemeine Vergebung, Amnestie. II. *v.a.* begnadigen, Straflosigkeit versprechen (für politische Verbrechen, u. s. w.).

Amok, *see* Amuck.

Among, **—st**, *prep.* (mitten) unter, zwischen; from —, aus; aus . . . hervor, aus der Mitte heraus.

Amorous, *adj.*, **—ly**, *adv.* verliebt; zur Liebe geneigt; — airs, verliebte Liedchen, Liebeslieder; of an — nature, (von) verliebter Natur. **—ness**, *s.* die Verliebtheit.

Amorphous, *adj.* gestaltlos, amorphisch.

Amortis—able, *adj.* tilgungsfähig, abschreibbar. **—ation**, *s.* die Tilgung, Heimzahlung, Amortisation; bill of —ation, der Tilgungsschein. **—e**, *v.a.* tilgen, heimzahlen; abschreiben.

Amount, I. *s.* der Belauf, Betrag; die Summe; der Bestand; what is the —? wie viel macht *or* beträgt es? the — of these entries, das Fazit dieser Posten; to the — of, im Betrage von, betragend; the greatest — of nonsense, der größte Unsinn. II. *v.n.* sich belaufen (to, auf, acc.) betragen; auf eine S. hinauslaufen (*fig.*); the whole sum —s to . . ., die ganze Summe beträgt . . ., das Ganze beläuft sich auf (*acc.*) . . .

Amour, *s.* der Liebeshandel, die Liebschaft.

Amphi—bia, *pl.* Amphibien. **—bious**, *adj.* beidlebig; amphibisch; —bious animals, Amphibien, beidlebige Tiere. **—scians**, **—scii**, *pl.* die Zweischattigen, Bewohner der heißen Zone. **—theatre**, *s.* das Amphitheater.

Ampl—e, *adj.*, **—y**, *adv.* weit, breit; weitläufig; (specious) geräumig, umfänglich; (stout) groß, breit; (abundant) reichlich; the —e *or* —y-spread board, der reichlich versehene *or* gefüllte Tisch; —e means, reichliche Mittel; —e satisfaction, völlige Genugtuung; it's —e, es genügt vollständig. **—eness**, *s.* die Geräumigkeit; die Weite, Größe; (extent) die Ausdehnung; (abundance) die Fülle, Reichlichkeit. **—ification**, *s.* die Erweiterung, Vergrößerung; Ausdehnung; die ausführliche Schilderung; die weitere, umständlichere Ausführung. **—ify**, *v.a.* erweitern, ausdehnen; ausführlich darstellen. **—itude**, *s.* der Umfang; die Größe, Weite; eastern —itude, die Morgenweite; western —itude, die Abendweite; —itude of oscillation, die Schwingungsweite; —itude of the range, die Schußweite, Wurfweite.

Amputat—e, *v.a.* abschneiden, abnehmen, amputieren (*Med.*). **—ion**, *s.* die Abschneidung, Ablösung, Abnahme, Amputation (*Med.*).

Amuck, *adv.*; to run —, mit blinder Wut anfallen; einen Anfall von Mordraserei haben.

Amulet, *s.* das Amulett, Schutzmittel.

Amus—e, *v.a.* vergnügen, unterhalten, belustigen; (entertain) unterhalten, die Zeit vertreiben; to —e o.s. with, sich an einer S. ergötzen, sich mit einer S. unterhalten; to be —ed by, Spaß haben an (*dat.*), sich freuen über (*acc.*); it —es me, es macht mir Spaß. **—ement**, *s.* die Unterhaltung, der Zeitvertreib. **—ing(ly)**, *adj.* (*adv.*) unterhaltend; ergötzlich.

Amylaceous, *adj.* stärkehaltig, stärkemehlartig.

[1]**An**, *indef. art. used instead of* a (*q.v.*) *before a word commencing with a vowel or silent h.*

[2]**An, an'** (*for* and) *conj.* und (*dial.*); wenn (*obs.*).

Ana—baptist, *s.* der Wiedertäufer, Anabaptist; —baptist movement, wiedertäuferische Bewegung. **—chronism**, *s.* der Anachronismus. **—chronistic**, *adj.* anachronistisch. **—clastic**, *adj.*; —clastic glasses, Vexiergläser. **—glyph**, *s.* halberhabene Arbeit. **—gogical**, *adj.* geheimsinnig; geisterhebend; mystisch. **—gram**, *s.* die Buchstabenversetzung, das Buchstabenrätsel, Anagramm. **—grammatical(ly)**, *adj.* (*adv.*) anagrammatisch. **—lecta**, *pl.* die Analekten. **—logical(ly)**, *adj.* (*adv.*) analogisch. **—logous**, *adj.* ähnlich, analog(isch). **—logue**, *s.* etwas Entsprechendes, in mancher Beziehung Ähnliches. **—logy**, *s.* die Analogie, Ähnlichkeit. **—lyse**, *v.a.* analysieren, auflösen; zergliedern (*the plot of a play*). **—lyser**, *s.* der Analytiker; das Auflösungsmittel; der Analysator, das Zerstreuungsprisma (*Opt.*). **—lysis**, *s.* die Analyse, Auflösung, Zerlegung; die Zergliederung, die Darlegung des Hauptinhaltes (*of a book, etc.*); volumetric —lysis, Maßanalyse. **—lyst**, *s.* der Analytiker. **—lytic**, **—lytical(ly)**, *adj.* (*adv.*) analytisch; —lytical chemist, der Chemiker. **—lytics**, *s.* die Analytik. **—pæst**, *s.* der aufgleitende Versfuß, Anapäst. **—pæstic**, *adj.* aufgleitend, anapästisch. **—thema**, *s.* das Anathema; (excommunication) der Bannfluch. **—thematize**, *v.a.* den Bannfluch schleudern (gegen), verfluchen; mit dem Bannfluche belegen, in den Kirchenbann tun. **—thematizer**, *s.* der den Bannfluch Aussprechende *or* Schleudernde. **—tomical(ly)**, *adj.* (*adv.*) anatomisch. **—tomist**, *s.* der Anatom. **—tomize**, *v.a.* zergliedern, zerlegen. **—tomy**, *s.* die Anatomie, Zergliederungskunst.

Anæm—ia, *s.* der Blutmangel, die Blutarmut. **—ic**, *adj.* blutarm.

Anæsthe—sia, *s.* die gänzliche Unempfindlichkeit, Empfindungslosigkeit; Gefühllosigkeit, Anästhesie. **—tics**, *pl.* anästhetische Mittel, Gefühllosigkeit hervorrufende Mittel.

Ananas, *s.* die Ananas.

Anarch—ical, *adj.* umstürzlerisch, anarchisch. **—ist**, *s.* der Anarchist, Umstürzler, Umsturzmann. **—y**, *s.* die Anarchie, Gesetzlosigkeit, der Umsturz (der gesellschaftlichen Ordnung).

Ancest—or, *s.* der Vorfahr; der Ahn (*poet.*); (*pl.*) Voreltern, Ahnen. **—ral**, *adj.* angestammt, von den Ahnen her; altererbt; —ral castle, die Stammburg, das Ahnenschloß; —ral estate, das Erbgut; —ral right, das Erbrecht. **—ress**, *s.* die Stammmutter; die Ahne (*poet.*). **—ry**, *s.* die Ahnen, Voreltern, Vorfahren; (descent) die Abstammung; (race) der Stamm.

Anchor, I. der Anker; bow —, Buganker; kedge —, Katanker, Springanker; shore —, Wallanker; sheet —, Hauptanker (*also fig.*); to cast —, ankern, sich vor Anker legen, den Anker auswerfen, Anker werfen; the — bites, der Anker greift zu; the — has got a good hold, der Anker hält; the — is apeak, der Anker ist auf und nieder; to weigh —, den *or* die Anker lichten; the — drags, der Anker ist triftig; to lie *or* ride at —, vor Anker liegen. II. *v.n.* ankern, vor Anker liegen. **—age**, *s.* der Ankergrund; das Hafengeld, Ankergeld.

Anchoret, **Anchorite**, *s.* der Einsiedler, Klausner, Waldbruder, Anachoret.

Anchovy, I. *s.* die An(s)chovis; die Sardelle. II. *adj.;* — paste, die Sardellen-Paste; — toast, mit Sardellen-Paste bestrichenes Brötchen.

[1]**Ancient**, *adj.* alt; ehemalig, vormalig, von alten Zeiten herstammend; this — seat of learning, diese altehrwürdige Bildungsstätte; the —s, die alten Griechen und Römer, die alten Klassiker; that is — history, das ist eine altbekannte *or* längst abgetane Geschichte; — of Days, Gott der Vater (*B.*). **—ly**, *adv.* ehedem, vormals, vor Alters. **—ness**, *s.* das Alter.

[2]**Ancient**, *obs. for* Ensign.

Ancillary, *adj.* eine Dienstmagd betreffend; untergeordnet, ergänzend, Hülfs-.

And, *conj.* und; a coach — four, eine Kutsche mit vier Pferden; a little more — he would have been killed, es fehlte nicht viel, so wäre er getötet worden; how can you go out — not take him with you? wie können Sie ausgehen, ohne ihn mitzunehmen? worse — worse, later — later, immer schlimmer, immer später; both you — I, Sie sowohl wie ich; to walk two — two, paarweise gehen; go — see, sehen Sie nach; it is nice — warm here, es ist hübsch warm hier; will you come — take a walk? wollen Sie mit uns (mir) spazieren gehen?

Andante, I. *adv.* andante. II. *s.* das Andante.

Andiron, *s.* der (metallene) Feuerbock, Kaminbock.

Anecdot—al, *adj.* anekdotisch; anekdotenreich. **—e**, *s.* das Geschichtchen, die Anekdote, der Witz. **—ical**, *adj.* anekdotenartig, aus Anekdoten bestehend; gern Anekdoten erzählend, redselig. **—ist**, *s.* der Anekdotensammler.

Anele, (*obs.*) *v.a.* salben, die letzte Ölung geben.

Anemo—meter, *s.* das Anemometer, der Windmesser; Robinson's —meter, Robinsons Schalenkreuz. **—scope**, *s.* der Windzeiger. **—ne**, *s.* das Windröschen, die Anemone (*Bot.*).

Anent, *prep.* in gleicher Linie mit, neben (*obs.*); gegen, gegenüber (*obs. dial.*); in Betreff, betreffs, bezüglich (*dial.*).

Aneroid, *adj.;* — barometer, das Aneroïd-Barometer; pocket — barometer, das Taschenaneroïd.

Aneurism, *s.* die Pulsadergeschwulst.

Anew, *adv.* von neuem, aufs neue; wieder; to begin —, wieder *or* von frischem anfangen.

Angel, *s.* der Engel; (coin) der Engeltaler (*obs.*). **—ic(ally)**, *adj.* (*adv.*) engelgleich, wie ein Engel. **—us**, *s.* das Angelusläuten; die Angelusglocke; das Angelusgebet.

Ang—er, I. *s.* der Zorn, Unwille, Ärger, Verdruß. II. *v.a.* erzürnen, aufbringen; böse machen. **—ered**, *p.p. & adj.* erzürnt, aufgebracht. **—rily**, *adv.*, **—ry**, *adj.* zornig, böse, aufgebracht; entzündet (*of a wound*); to be —ry with a p., auf einen böse sein, einem gram sein; to be —ry at a th., böse über eine S. sein; to have an —ry look, böse aussehen; to make a p. —ry, einen ärgern, böse machen; the —ry flood, die stürmische Flut; an —ry frown, ein verdrießlicher Blick; an —ry word, ein ärgerliches *or* im Zorn ausgestoßenes Wort.

Ang—le, I. *s.* der Winkel; (fishing) die Angel; right, acute, obtuse —le, rechter, spitzer, stumpfer Winkel; —le of incidence, Einfallswinkel; —le of refraction, gebrochener Winkel; —le of reflection, Absprungswinkel; —le of elevation, Elevationswinkel; —le of sight, visual —le, Sehwinkel. II. *v.n.* angeln (for, nach). **—led**, *adj.* (*in comp.* =) -angled, wink(e)lig. **—ler**, *s.* der Angler; der Seeteufel (*Icht.*). **—ling**, *s.* das Angeln. **—ular(ly)**, *adj.* (*adv.*) winkelig, eckig, steif, ungelenk; **—ular** velocity, die Winkelgeschwindigkeit; an —ular person, ein eckiger, ungelenker Mensch. **—ularity**, *s.* das Winkelige; die Ungelenkheit, Steifheit (des Benehmens).

Anglic—an, *adj.* anglikanisch; hochkirchlich (gesinnt). **—e**, *adv.* auf Englisch, ins Englische übersetzt. **—ize**, *v.a.* anglisieren, englisch machen; to become —ized, englisch werden, zum Engländer werden. **—ism**, *s.* der Anglicismus.

Angor, *s.* heftiger Schmerz, die Herzbeklemmung, Angst (*Med.*).

Anguish, *s.* die Angst, Pein, Qual; — of mind, die Seelenpein, Herzensangst, Seelenqual.

Anhydr—ide, *s.* das Anhydrid (*Chem.*). **—ite**, *s.* der Anhydrit (*Min.*). **—ous**, *adj.* wasserfrei.

Anil—e, *adj.* altersschwach; altweibermäßig. **—ity**, *s.* das Altweiberhafte, Altweibermäßige.

Anim—adversion, *s.* die Anmerkung, Bemerkung; der Tadel, Verweis. **—advert**, *v.n.* den Geist auf eine S. richten, Betrachtungen machen (über eine S.); —advert upon a th., tadelnde Betrachtungen machen über eine S., etwas rügen, verweisen, tadeln. **—al**, I. *s.* das Tier. II. *adj.* animalisch, tierisch; —al chemistry, die Zoochemie; —al kingdom, das Tierreich; —al food, die Fleischnahrung; —al functions, tierische Verrichtungen; —al economy, das animalische System; —al spirits, Lebensgeister; full of —al spirits, voller Lebenskraft. **—alcule**, *s.* das Tierchen. **—alism**, *s.* die physische Tätigkeit; die grobe Sinnlichkeit, der tierische Trieb (des Menschen); der Animalismus; die Lehre, daß der Mensch nichts als ein Tier ist. **—ate**, I. *v.a.* beleben, beseelen; ermuntern, aufmuntern. II. *adj.* lebendig. **—ated**, *adj.* belebt, beseelt; lebhaft, munter; seelenvoll. **—ateness**, *s.* das Belebtsein, Leben. **—ation**, *s.* die Belebung, Beseelung; das Leben, die Belebtheit, Lebhaftigkeit; to bring some —ation into a company, Leben in eine Gesellschaft bringen; to give —ation to a th., einer Sache Leben, Lebhaftigkeit, Schwung verleihen, eine Sache beleben. **—osity**, *s.* der Unwille, die Abneigung; der Haß, die Feindseligkeit, Erbitterung. **—us**, *s.* (intention) die Absicht; (hostility) die Feindseligkeit. *Comp.* **—al-charcoal**, *s.* die Tierkohle.

Anight, *adv.* nachts, in der Nacht, zur Nachtzeit.

Aniline, *s.* das Anilin; — dyes, Anilinfarbstoffe.

Anis—e, *s.* der Anis. **—eed**, *s.* der Anissame. **—ette**, *s.* das Aniswasser, der Anislikör.

Ankle, I. *s.* der Fußknöchel, Enkel; he has sprained his —, er hat sich (*dat.*) den Fuß verstaucht. II. *adj.;* — bone, der Fußknöchel. **—t**, *s.* der Schmuck für den Knöchel. *Comp.* **—deep**, *adj.* knöcheltief, bis über die Knöchel.

Annal—ist, *s.* der Annalist, Annalenschreiber. **—s**, *pl.* die Annalen, Jahrbücher, die Chronik.

Anneal, *v.a.* ausglühen, brennen; anlassen (*metal*); kühlen (*glass*); —ing furnace (*for glass*), der Kühlofen; —ing colour, die Anlauffarbe; to — bricks, Ziegel brennen.

Annex, I. *v.a.* anhängen, beifügen, hinzufügen; at the —ed cash prices, zu beigefügten (beigesetzten) Barpreisen; he —ed a province, er annektierte eine Provinz; we — a report for your perusal, wir schließen Ihnen einen Bericht zur Durchsicht bei. II. *s.* das Beigefügte, der Anhang; das Nebengebäude, der Anbau. **—ation**, *s.* die Beifügung, Anhängung; die Vereinigung, Verbindung; die Annektierung, Einverleibung, Wegnahme.

Annihilat—e, *v.a.* vernichten, zerstören. **—ion**, *s.* die Vernichtung.

Anniversary, *s.* der Jahrestag, die Jahresfeier; to keep an —, ein Jahresfest feiern; 25th — of the battle of Sedan, 25jährige Wiederkehr des Jahrestages der Schlacht bei Sedan.

Annotat—e, *v.a.* mit Anmerkungen versehen, kommentieren; to —e a work, Anmerkungen zu einem Werke machen, —ed edition, kommentierte Ausgabe, Ausgabe mit Anmerkungen. **—ion**, *s.* das Versehen mit erläuternden Anmerkungen, das Kommentieren; die Anmerkung, Glosse, Note. **—or**, *s.* der Erklärer, Kommentator.

Announce, *v.a.* ankündigen, verkündigen, ansagen, melden; bekannt machen; to — an arrival, einen Besuch anmelden; to — o.s., sich anmelden; to have one's name —d, sich (an)melden lassen. **—ment**, *s.* die Anzeige, Ankündigung, Bekanntmachung; a newspaper —ment, eine Anzeige in den öffentlichen Blättern. **—r**, *s.* der Verkündiger.

Annoy, *v.a.* beunruhigen; (disturb) stören; (trouble) belästigen; (tease) quälen, plagen; (vex) Verdruß verursachen. **—ance**, *s.* der Verdruß; die Störung; die Plage, das Plagen.

Annu—al, I. *adj.* jährlich; jährlich wiederkehrend; einjährig; —al balance, die Schlußbilanz. II. *s.* die einjährige Pflanze (*Bot.*); die Jahresschrift, das Jahrbuch. **—ity**, *s.* die jährliche Leibrente. **—itant**, *s.* der Leibrentner.

Annul, *v.a.* (abrogate, abolish) ungültig machen, aufheben; (destroy) vernichten; (blot out) tilgen.

Annul—ar, *adj.* ringförmig; —ar kiln, der Ringofen. **—et**, *s.* der kleine Ring, das Ringlein, Ringelchen (*Her.*, *Arch.*).

Annunciation, *s.* die Verkündigung; — of the Virgin, Mariä Verkündigung.

Anodyne, I. *adj.* schmerzstillend. II. *s.* schmerzstillendes Mittel.

Anoint, *v.a.* salben; the Lord's —ed, der Gesalbte des Herrn (*B.*). **—ing**, *s.* die Salbung.

Anomal—ous, *adj.* unregelmäßig, von der Regel abweichend. **—y**, *s.* die Unregelmäßigkeit; —y in nature, die Naturwidrigkeit.

Anon, *adv.* gleich, sogleich; (soon) bald; (by and by) nachher; ever and —, immer wieder; immer fort; of this more —, hiervon bald mehr.

Anonym—ity, *s.* die Namenverschweigung, Anonymität. **—ous**, *adj.* ohne Namen, namenlos, ungenannt, anonym; —ous author, ungenannter Verfasser; —ous pamphlet, ohne Namen des Verfassers herausgegebene Flugschrift.

Another, *adj.* verschieden; noch ein(e); ein anderer, ꝛc., *see* Other; — time, ein anderes Mal; — way, anders; we have one form of government, France —, wir haben eine Regierungsform, Frankreich eine andere; I am of — way of thinking, ich denke anders; it is one thing to promise, — to perform, Versprechen und Halten sind zweierlei; take — cup, nehmen Sie noch eine Tasse; — attempt, ein zweiter Versuch; make — attempt, machen Sie noch einen Versuch, versuchen Sie es noch einmal; you ought to love one —, ihr solltet einander lieben; they injure one —, sie schaden einander; one with —, eins ins andere gerechnet, zusammen gerechnet; one after —, einer nach dem andern, nach einander; one from —, von einander; they are so much alike you can hardly distinguish them from one —, sie sehen einander so ähnlich, daß man sie kaum unterscheiden kann; we are often taken for one —, wir werden oft mit einander verwechselt; one upon —, eins aufs andere; yet —? noch einer? just such —, gerade so einer.

Anserine, *adj.* gänseartig, Gänse ; albern.

Answer, I. *s.* die Antwort; die Lösung, Auflösung (*Math.*); die Antwort, Replik (*Law*); der Gegengruß (*Naut.*); — in the affirmative (negative), eine bejahende (verneinende) Antwort; — to a question, Antwort auf eine Frage. II. *v.a.* beantworten; (suit) passen; (fulfil) erfüllen; entsprechen; (satisfy) genügen, befriedigen; (agree with) übereinstimmen (mit); lösen (*a riddle, etc.*); he —ed in the negative, er verneinte es; he —ed my question in the affirmative, er bejahte meine Frage; to — a question, eine Frage beantworten, auf eine Frage antworten; to — a p.'s expectations, jemandes Erwartungen entsprechen; to — the purpose, dem Zwecke entsprechen; it —s no purpose, es hilft zu nichts; to — a summons, einer Vorladung Folge leisten (*Law*); to — the bell, auf die Glocke hören; beim Ton der Klingel kommen; die Haustür aufmachen, *etc.;* the ship —s the helm readily, das Schiff lüstert gut aufs Ruder; to — back, erwidern. III. *v.n.* antworten; gelingen, von Erfolg sein, anschlagen; to — for, Rede stehen für, verantworten, Rechenschaft geben von, bürgen für; this plan will never —, dieser Plan wird sich nie ausführen lassen, ist unausführbar; the invention does n't —, die Erfindung entspricht dem Zwecke nicht; it does n't — (to) the description, es stimmt nicht mit der Beschreibung überein; these articles don't — in our market, diese Waren rentieren nicht auf unserm Markte; I'll — for it, dafür bürge ich *or* stehe ich (gut). **—able**, *adj.* beantwortbar (*of a question, etc.*); löslich (*of a problem, etc.*); (responsible) verantwortlich; to be —able for a p., für einen einstehen müssen *or* verantwortlich sein. **—ableness**, *s.* die Beantwortbarkeit.

Ant, *s.* die Ameise. *Comp.* **—-eater**, *s.* der Ameisenfresser. **—-hill**, *s.* der Ameisenhaufen. **—-lion**, *s.* der Ameisenlöwe (*Ent.*).

Antagonis—m, *s.* der Widerstand, das Widerstreben; die Feindschaft; der Antagonismus. **—t**, *s.* der Gegner. **—tic**, *adj.* widerstreitend, einander entgegengesetzt, gegnerisch.

Antarctic, *adj.* den Südpol betreffend, antarktisch; — circle, der südliche Polarkreis; — expedition, die Südpolexpedition.

Antarthritic, *adj.* gichtheilend.

Ante—cedence, *s.* das Vorhergehen, das frühere Vorhandensein; der Rücklauf, die scheinbare Bewegung eines Planeten gegen Westen. **—cedent**, I. *adj.* vorhergehend; früher, vorig; an event —cedent to his marriage, ein vor seiner Heirat geschehenes Ereignis. II. *s.* das Vorhergehende; der Vordersatz (*Log.*); das Vorderglied (*Math.*); das Antecedens (*Gram.*); his —cedents, sein früherer Lebenswandel *or* Lebenslauf, seine Antecedenzien. **—rior**, *see* Anterior. *Comp.* **—chamber**, *s.* das Vorzimmer, Vorgemach. **—chapel**, *s.* der nicht abgeschorene vordere Teil einer Kapelle, die Vorhalle einer Kapelle. **—date**, *v.a.* zurückdatieren, früher datieren; zum Voraus nehmen, vorgenießen. **—diluvian**, *adj.* vorsündflutlich, antediluvianisch. **—diluvians**, *pl.* vorsündflutliche Menschen. **—meridian**, *adj.* vormittägig. **—natal**, *adj.* vor der Geburt(geschehen(d) *or* liegend). **—nuptial**, *adj.* vorhochzeitlich, vor der Ehe. **—penult**, *s.* die drittletzte Silbe. **—room**, *s.* das Vorzimmer.

Antelope, *s.* die Hirschziege, Antilope.

Anterior, *adj.* vorhergehend, vorangehend, früher, älter; my claim is — to his, meine Forderung ist älter als die seinige.

Anthelion, *s.* die Nebensonne.

Anthem, *s.* der Wechselgesang (zwischen Priester und Gemeinde); die Hymne; national —, die Nationalhymne, Volkshymne.

Anther, *s.* der Staubbeutel. **—iferous**, *adj.* Staubbeutel tragend (*Bot.*).

Anthology, *s.* die Blumensammlung (*rare*); die Gedichtsammlung, Mustersammlung (*fig.*).

Anthracite, *s.* der Anthracit, die Glanzkohle.
Anthrax, *s.* der Karbunkel; der Milzbrand.
Anthropo—biology, *s.* die Entstehungsgeschichte des Menschen. **—logist**, *s.* der Anthropolog. **—logy**, *s.* die Anthropologie, Lehre vom Menschen, Menschenkunde. **—metrical**, *adj.* zur Menschenmessung dienend. **—metry**, *s.* die wissenschaftliche Messung des menschlichen Körpers. **—morphism**, *s.* der Anthropomorphismus; die Vermenschlichung. **—morphous**, *adj.* menschenähnlich, von menschenähnlicher Gestalt. **—phagi**, *pl.* die Menschenfresser, Kannibalen.
Anti—c, I. *adj. see* Antique; grotesk, possierlich. II. *s.* die Posse, Fratze; —cs, (*pl.*) Possen. **—quarian**, I. *adj.* antiquarisch, altertümlich; —quarian society, Verein der Altertumsfreunde *or* Altertumsforscher. II. *s.*, **—quary**, *s.* der Antiquar, der Altertumskenner, Altertumsforscher. **—quarianism**, *s.* die Altertümelei. **—quated**, *adj.* veraltet. **—que**, I. *adj.* alt, antik; altmodisch. II. *s.* die Antike, das Altertumsstück, die alte Kunstarbeit. **—quities**, *pl.* die Altertümer, Antiquitäten. **—quity**, *s.* die Vorzeit; das Altertum; die Antiquität; das Alter; (people of old) die Alten.
Anti—christ, *s.* der Antichrist. **—christian**, *adj.* widerchristlich. **—cipate**, *etc.; see under* Anticipate. **—climax**, *s.* die Gegensteigerung, Antiklimax. **—dote**, *s.* das Gegenmittel, Gegengift. **—-dyspeptic**, *adj.* gut gegen Unverdaulichkeit. **—febrile**, I. *adj.* fieberheilend. II. *s.* das Fiebermittel. **—-ministerialist**, *s.* der Gegner des Ministeriums. **—monarchical**, *adj.* antimonarchisch, der Monarchie feindlich (gesinnt). **—monial**, *adj.* spießglasig. **—mony**, *s.* das Antimon(ium), Spießglas, der Spießglanz. **—nephritic**, *adj.* antinephritisch. **—nomian**, *adj.* gesetzwidrig; zu der Sekte der Antinomisten gehörig. **—nomianism**, *s.* der Antinomismus. **—pathy**, *s.* die Antipathie, natürliche Abneigung, der Widerwille, Abscheu; die Unverträglichkeit (zweier Körper, *Phys.*). **—-pestiferous**, *adj.* pestbekämpfend. **—phon**, *s.* der kirchliche Wechselgesang. **—phonal**, *adj.* antiphonisch. **—phony**, *s.* der Gegengesang, Wechselchor. **—podal**, *adj.* gegenfüßlerisch, antipodisch. **—podes**, *pl.* die Gegenfüßler, Antipoden. **—pope**, *s.* der Gegenpapst. **—-Semitic**, *adj.* judenfeindlich. **—pyrin**, *s.* das Antipyrin. **—septic**, *adj.* Fäulnis verhindernd, antiseptisch. **—social**, *adj.* dem geselligen Zustande zuwiderlaufend. **—spasmodic**, *adj.* krampfstillend (*Med.*). **—splenetic**, *adj.* milzsuchtwidrig (*Med.*). **—strophe**, *s.* die Antistrophe, Gegenstrophe (*Poet.*); die Retorsion (*Rhet.*). **—thesis**, *s.* die Antithese (*Rhet.*); die Entgegensetzung, der Gegensatz (*Log.*). **—thetical**, *adj.* entgegengestellt. **—type**, *s.* das Gegenbild. **—-vibrator**, *s.* Erschütterungsverhüter (*Cycl.*).
Anticipat—e, *v.a.* vorausnehmen, vorwegnehmen, vorgreifen; (get beforehand) zuvorkommen; vor der Zeit tun; vorausgenießen; (forebode) ahnen, vorempfinden; (expect) erwarten; to —e payment, vor der Zeit Zahlung leisten; why should we —e (our) sorrows? warum sollen wir uns vor der Zeit Kummer machen? he always —es his salary, er verzehrt immer sein Gehalt, ehe es fällig ist; er nimmt von seinem Gehalt immer etwas im Voraus auf; she always —es my wishes, sie kommt meinen Wünschen immer zuvor; an —ed bill of exchange, ein vor der Verfallzeit eingelöster Wechsel. **—ion**, *s.* die Vorausnahme; das Zuvorkommen; das Vorgreifen; das Vorgefühl, der Vor(ge)schmack; die Vorempfindung; die Anticipation (*C. L., Mus.*); by —ion, vorweg, im voraus; payment by —ion, die Zahlung auf Abschlag, Abschlagszahlung. **—ory**, *adj.* vorgreifend, vorwegnehmend.

Antler, *s.* die Augensprosse am Geweih; (*pl.*) das (Hirsch-)Geweih. **—ed**, *adj.* gehörnt, geweihtragend, mit einem Geweih geschmückt.
Anus, *s.* der After, die Aftermündung.
Anvil, *s.* der Amboß; rising —, der zweispitzige Amboß, das Speerhorn; face of an —, die Amboßbahn; to be on the —, im Werke sein, sich auf dem Ambos befinden.
Anxi—ety, *s.* (fear) die Angst, Bangigkeit, Beängstigung, Furcht; (uneasiness) die Unruhe, Sorge, Besorgnis; die Beklemmung (*Med.*). **—ous(ly)**, *adj.* (*adv.*) ängstlich, bange, unruhig, besorgt (for, about, um, wegen); eifrig bemüht; I am —ous to see him, ich bin begierig, ihn zu sehen; I am —ous to find him at home, mir liegt daran ihn zu Hause zu finden; I am —ous to hear your opinion, ich möchte sehr gern Ihre Meinung erfahren; he was most —ous to make no mistake, er gab sich viele Mühe, keinen Fehler zu machen; I feel very —ous about the result, wegen des Ergebnisses bin ich sehr besorgt.
Any, I. *adj.* irgend ein, eine, ein; jeder, jede, jedes; irgend welch, welche, welches; ein wenig, etwas; ein nennenswerter, ein bemerkenswerter; one part only had — success, nur ein Teil hatte einen nennenswerten Erfolg; not —, keiner, keine, keins; are there — witnesses present? sind irgend welche Zeugen da? have you — wheat to sell? haben Sie Weizen zu verkaufen? is there — hope? ist noch Hoffnung vorhanden? I don't see — reason, why . . ., ich sehe nicht ein, warum . . .; take — you please, nehmen Sie, was Ihnen beliebt; — person that pleases, wer Lust hat. II. *adv.* irgend; — longer, (noch) länger; I will not tire you — longer, ich will Sie nicht länger ermüden; will you have — more? wollen Sie noch mehr, noch ein wenig haben? not — more, nichts mehr. *Comp.* **—body**, *s.* irgend einer; jeder(-mann); —body can do that, jedermann kann das tun. **—how**, *adv.* irgendwie, auf irgend eine Weise; es sei, wie es wolle; —how, I will try it, probieren will ich es auf jeden Fall; there 's no getting hold of him —how, man kann ihm durchaus nicht beikommen. **—one**, *see* —body; not —one, niemand, nicht einer. **—thing**, *s.* irgend etwas; alles; she is —thing but pretty, sie ist nichts weniger als hübsch; *see* — I.; have you —thing to say? haben Sie etwas zu sagen? for —thing I know, so viel ich weiß; not for —thing, um keinen Preis; —thing will do for him, er ist mit allem zufrieden. **—thingarians**, *pl.* die Indifferentisten (in der Religion). **—way**, *adv.* irgend wie; he would not —way consent, er wollte durchaus nicht einwilligen; —way, he would not consent, wie dem auch sei, wollte er nicht darauf eingehen. **—where**, *adv.* irgendwo. **—whither**, *adv.* irgendwohin. **—wise**, (in —wise) auf irgend eine Weise.
Aorta, *s.* die große Puls- *or* Schlag-ader.
Apace, *adv.* geschwind, schnell, eilig; ill weeds grow —, das Unkraut wuchert; night draws on —, die Nacht rückt eilig heran; our society is growing —, unser Verein wächst rasch *or* zusehends.
Apart, *adv.* beiseits, bei Seite, für sich; (separately) abgesondert, einzeln; — from, abgesehen von; I have set — this hour for study, ich habe diese Stunde zum Studieren bestimmt. **—ment**, *s.* das Zimmer; —ments, die Wohnung; furnished —ments, möblierte Zimmer, möblierte Wohnung; suite of —ments, eine Reihe Zimmer.
Apath—etic(ally), *adj.* (*adv.*) gefühllos, unempfindlich. **—y**, *s.* die Unempfindlichkeit (gegen), Gefühllosigkeit (für); (indifference) die Gleichgültigkeit (gegen).
Ap—e, I. *s.* der Affe. II. *v.a.* nachäffen; to —e a p., einem nachäffen. **—ish(ly)**, *adj.* (*adv.*) äffisch, affenmäßig; närrisch.
Apeak, *adv.* auf der Spitze; senkrecht (*Naut.*).

to set the yards —, die Raaen kaien; the anchor is —, der Anker ist auf und nieder.
Aper—ient, I. *adj.* öffnend, abführend. II. *s.* das Abführungsmittel. **—ture**, *s.* die Öffnung.
Apetalous, *adj.* blumenblattlos.
Apex, *s.* die Spitze, der Gipfel.
Aphelion, *s.* die Sonnenferne, das Aphelium.
Aphoris—m, *s.* der kurze Denkspruch, Gedankensplitter, Aphorismus. **—tic(ally)**, *adj.* (*adv.*) aphoristisch, abgerissen, kurz hingeworfen.
Apiar—ist, *s.* der Bienenzüchter. **—y**, *s.* der Bienenstand.
Apical, *adj.* gipfelständig, an der Spitze; apikal (*Phonet.*); — formation, durch den vorderen Zungensaum gebildete Enge (*Phonet.*).
Apices, (**Apexes**,) *pl. see* Apex.
Apiece, *adv.* für das Stück, jedes Stück; für jede Person, für jeden; here 's sixpence — for you, hier hat jeder von euch ein Fünfzigpfennigstück; they had to pay a shilling —, jeder mußte eine Mark zahlen.
Apo—calypse, *s.* die Offenbarung Johannis, die Apokalypse. **—cope**, *s.* die Endverkürzung (eines Wortes), Apokope. **—crypha**, *s.* die Apokryphen, die apokryphischen Bücher (der Bibel). **—cryphal**, *adj.* apokryphisch; ungewiß, verdächtig; zweifelhaft; falsch. **—dictic**, *adj.* apodiktisch. **—dosis**, *s.* die Apodosis, der Nachsatz (*Gram.*). **—gee**, *s.* das Apogäum, die größte Erdferne des Mondes. **—logetic(ally)**, *adj.* (*adv.*) entschuldigend, verteidigend, apologetisch **—logist**, *s.* der Schutzredner, Verteidiger. **—logize**, **—logise**, *v.n.* eine Entschuldigung vorbringen, (sich) entschuldigen; um Vergebung bitten (wegen, for; bei, to); you must —logize for your conduct, Sie müssen sich wegen Ihres Benehmens entschuldigen; he shall —logize for it, er soll dafür Abbitte tun *or* um Entschuldigung bitten. **—logue**, *s.* der Apolog, die Lehrfabel. **—logy**, *s.* die Entschuldigung, Abbitte; (defence) die Schutzrede, Verteidungsrede; die Ehrenerklärung; make no —logies, entschuldigen Sie sich nicht, es bedarf keiner Entschuldigungen; he wrote me an —logy, er leistete mir schriftlich Abbitte, bat mich brieflich um Entschuldigung. **—plectic**, *adj.* apoplektisch; an —plectic habit of body, eine zum Schlagfluß geneigte Körperbildung. **—plexy**, *s.* die Apoplexie, der Schlagfluß; to have a fit of —plexy, den Schlag bekommen, vom Schlage gerührt werden. **—stasy**, *s.* die Apostasie, der Abfall von einer Partei(ansicht), Glaubensabfall, die Abtrünnigkeit. **—state**, I. *s.* der Apostat, Abtrünnige. II. *adj.* abtrünnig; falsch. **—statize**, *v.n.* abtrünnig werden, von seinem Glauben abfallen. **—stle**, *etc.*, *see under* Apost—. **—strophe**, *s.* die Apostrophe, Anrede (*Rhet.*); der Apostroph, das Auslassungszeichen (*Gram.*). **—strophize**, **—strophise**, *v.a.* anreden, sich (an jemand) wenden. **—thecary**, *s.* der Apotheker; —thecary's shop, die Apotheke. **—thegm**, *s.* der Kernspruch. **—theosis**, *s.* die Vergötterung, Apotheose.
Apodal, *adj.* ohne Füße (*Zool.*); ohne Bauchflossen (*Icht.*).
Apost—le, *s.* der Apostel; —les' creed, das apostolische Glaubensbekenntnis. **—leship**, *s.* das Apostolat, apostolische Amt. **—olic(ally)**, *adj.* (*adv.*) apostolisch. *Comp.* **—le-spoon**, der Apostel-Löffel, Löffel mit kleiner Apostelfigur am Griff.
Appal, *v.a.* erschrecken, entmutigen; bleich machen. **—ling(ly)**, *adj.* (*adv.*) erschreckend, schrecklich.
Appanage, *s.* das Leibgedinge, Jahrgeld eines Fürsten, die Apanage; (dependency) das abhängige Gebiet.
Appar—atus, *s.* der Apparat, (utensils) die Vorrichtung; die Werkzeuge. **—el**, I. *s.* die Kleidung, der Anzug. II. *v.a.* kleiden, bekleiden, schmücken; ausrüsten (*Naut.*).

Appar—ent(ly), *adj.* (*adv.*) scheinbar, sichtbar; (evident) deutlich, augenscheinlich; (certain) unzweifelhaft; the heir —ent, der unbestreitbare Erbe, Erbprinz; —ently, wahrscheinlich; —ently healthy, anscheinend gesund. **—ition**, *s.* die Erscheinung; das Gespenst; die Lichtperiode (*Astr.*). **—itor**, *s.* der Gerichtsbote, Ratsdiener.
Appeal, I. *v.n.* appellieren; sich berufen (to a p., auf einen); sich (um Hülfe *or* Bekräftigung) wenden (to a p., an einen); to — to arms, zu den Waffen greifen; she cast an —ing glance at me, sie warf mir einen flehenden Blick zu; to — to the country, an das Volk appellieren (*Parl.*). II. *s.* die Appellation; die Berufung, Anrufung; action upon —, die Appellationsklage; to give notice of —, Appellation einlegen; the — was allowed, die Berufung wurde angenommen; a court from which there is no —, ein Gerichtshof, welcher in letzter Instanz entscheidet; the court of —, das Appellationsgericht; His Majesty's High Court of —, das Königliche Oberappellationsgericht; a fresh — is made to all students of Northern literature, wir wenden uns nochmals an alle Freunde der nordischen Litteratur (mit der ernsten Bitte). **—er**, *s.* der Appellant. **—ing(ly)**, *adj.* (*adv.*) flehend.
Appear, *v.n.* erscheinen, zum Vorschein kommen; auftreten; scheinen; den Anschein haben; it now —s that . . ., es stellt sich jetzt heraus, daß . . .; he —s quite satisfied, es hat den Anschein, als sei er ganz zufrieden; to — in print, im Druck erscheinen; to — against a p., wider einen (öffentlich) auftreten; to make —, beweisen, sichtbar machen; he —ed in the character of Othello, er trat als Othello auf. **—ance**, *s.* die Erscheinung; das Auftreten; der Anschein; der Schein; (air, outside) das Ansehen, Aussehen, Äußere, die Persönlichkeit; (likelihood) die Wahrscheinlichkeit; to make one's —ance, zum Vorschein kommen; (on the stage, auf der Bühne) auftreten; for the sake of —ances, um den Schein zu wahren; to keep up —ances, den Schein retten; to all —ance, allem Anscheine nach; to put in an —ance, sich zeigen, erscheinen, kommen; don't judge by —ances, urteilen Sie nicht nach dem äußern Scheine; —ances are deceitful, der Schein trügt (*prov.*); —ances are against you, der Schein ist gegen Sie; she thinks a great deal of her personal —ance, sie hat eine hohe Meinung von ihrer äußeren Erscheinung; with her —ance is everything, bei ihr gilt der äußere Schein alles.
Appeas—able, *adj.* versöhnlich, zu beruhigen. **—e**, *v.a.* beruhigen, besänftigen, stillen, befriedigen; löschen (*thirst*).
Appella—nt, I. *adj.*; party —nt, appellierende Partei. II. *s.* der Appellant (*Law*); der Ankläger; der Herausforderer. **—te**, I. *adj.*; party —te, die Partei, gegen welche appelliert wird; —te jurisdiction, die Appellationsgerichtsbarkeit. II. *s.* der Appellat. **—tion**, *s.* die Benennung, der Name. **—tive**, I. *adj.* appellativ(isch); noun —tive, das Gattungswort. II. *s.* der Gattungsname, das Gattungswort, Appellativ(um).
Append, *v.a.* anhängen, an (eine S.) hängen; beifügen (*a seal, etc.*). **—age**, *s.* der Anhang, das Anhängsel; das Zubehör; *see* Appurtenance. **—ant**, I. *adj.* anhängend, zugehörig, verbunden. II. *s.* der Anhang. **—icitis**, *s.* die Blinddarmentzündung. **—ix**, *s.* der Appendix, Anhang, Zusatz; der Fortsatz (*Med.*).
Appercepti—on, *s.* die bewußte Wahrnehmung, die Apperzeption. **—ive**, *adj.* mit Bewußtsein wahrnehmend.
Appertain, *v.n.* zugehören, zustehen; things —ing to this life, die zeitlichen Güter.
Appet—ence, **—ency**, *s.* die Begierde, das Gelüst; die fleischliche Lust; (instinct) der Naturtrieb. **—ite**, *s.* der Appetit, die Eßlust, der Hunger; die Begierde, das leidenschaftliche Ver-

langen; to raise, provoke, give an —ite, den Appetit reizen; to take away a p.'s —ite, einem den Appetit benehmen, einem die Eßlust verderben. —**izing**, —**ising**, *adj.* appetitlich, appetitreizend, lecker.

Applau—d, *v.a.; to* —d a p. *or* a th., einem *or* einer Sache Beifall geben *or* spenden, einen *or* etwas preisen, loben; (clap) einen *or* etwas beklatschen. —**se**, *s.* das Beifallklatschen, Händeklatschen; der Beifallsruf; der Beifall.

Apple, I. *s.* der Apfel; — of the eye, der Augapfel; bob — (*a game*), der Hasche-Apfel, das Apfeltründeln. II. *attrib.;* — core, der Gröbs *or* Griebs. *Comp.* —**-dumpling**, *s.* der Apfelkloß. —**-pie**, *s.* die Apfelpastete; in —-pie order, in der größten Ordnung (*coll.*). —**-sauce**, *s.* die Apfelsauce; der Apfelbrei, das Apfelmus. —**-tart**, *s.* die Apfeltorte. —**-woman**, *s.* die Apfelhändlerin, Apfelverkäuferin, Apfelfrau.

Appli—ance, *s.* die Anwendung; (thing applied) das Angewandte, (Hülfs-)Mittel, Gerät. —**capability**, *s.* die Anwendbarkeit. —**cable**, *adj.* anwendbar (to a th., auf eine S.); the argument is not —cable to this case, der Beweisgrund paßt nicht auf diesen Fall. —**cant**, *s.* der Bittsteller, Bewerber. —**cation**, *s.* die Auflegung, Anlegung (*of poultices, etc.*); (employment) die Anwendung, Nutzanwendung, der Gebrauch; das Gesuch, die Bewerbung (*for a place, etc.*); (industry) der Fleiß, die Emsigkeit, Geistesanstrengung; —cation to a case, die Anwendung auf einen Fall; upon the —cation of . . ., auf das Gesuch des . . .; close —cation is necessary, großer Fleiß ist erforderlich, man muß sich sehr anstrengen; lists will be sent on —ation, Verzeichnisse werden auf Ersuchen (*or* auf Wunsch) gesandt; to injure one's health by too close —cation to study, durch übertriebenen Lernfleiß der Gesundheit schaden; point of —cation, der Angriffspunkt (*Phys.*). —**ed**, *p.p. & adj.* angewandt; *see* Apply.

Apply, *v.* I. *a.* anlegen, auflegen; (employ) anwenden, gebrauchen, verwenden; to — colours, Farben auftragen; applied mathematics, angewandte Mathematik; to — to a p. (*for assistance, etc.*) sich an einen (um Hülfe, 2c.) wenden; do you — that to me? wenden Sie dies auf mich an? I intend to — this sum to the purchase of books, ich werde diese Summe zum Ankauf von Büchern verwenden; to — a th. to a certain use, eine Sache zu einem gewissen Zwecke anwenden; to — o.s. to, sich beschäftigen mit, sich auf (eine S.) legen; sich widmen (einer Sache), sich (einer S.) befleißigen; to — o.s. to the study of an art, sich dem Studium einer Kunst widmen; to — to a lawyer for advice, sich bei einem Rechtsgelehrten Rats erholen. II. *n.* passen, sich schicken, sich anwenden lassen; nachsuchen, sich bewerben (for, um); the remark did not in the least — to me, die Bemerkung hatte nicht den geringsten Bezug auf mich.

Appoint, *v.a.* bestimmen, festsetzen (*a day, a meeting, etc.*); ernennen; bestellen; verabreden; (equip) ausrüsten; I —ed to meet him to-day, ich habe mit ihm verabredet, ihn heute zu treffen; he was —ed to the vacant librarianship, ihm wurde die erledigte Stelle des Bibliothekars übertragen; he was —ed guardian, er wurde zum Vormund bestellt *or* ernannt; they will most likely — him professor, höchst wahrscheinlich werden sie ihn zum Professor ernennen; well —ed, gut, geschmackvoll eingerichtet; wohl gerüstet; well —ed carriages, bequeme Wagen. —**ment**, *s.* die Bestimmung, Festsetzung; das Rendezvous; die Stelle; —ments, die Einrichtung, das Mobiliar; to make an —ment, eine Stelle besetzen; to make an —ment with, sich verabreden mit; to keep an —ment, einer Verabredung pünktlich nachkommen; by —ment, der Verabredung gemäß, durch Bestellung; by special —ment to H. R. H. the Prince of Wales, Hoflieferant S. K. H. des Prinzen von Wales; the —ment is in the gift of . . ., die Ernennung zu der Stelle hängt ab von . . ., die Stelle wird vergeben von . . .; he held many important —ments, er hat viele wichtige Ämter bekleidet *or* Stellen innegehabt.

Apportion, *v.a.* in gerechte Teile teilen, verhältnismäßig verteilen, zuteilen; abmessen (*time*). —**ment**, *s.* die verhältnismäßige Verteilung.

Apposit—e, *adj.*, —**ely**, *adv.* passend, treffend, angemessen; the reply was —e, die Antwort war angemessen; paßte gut (auf die Bemerkung, 2c.). —**eness**, *s.* die Schicklichkeit, Angemessenheit. —**ion**, *s.* die Apposition (*Gram.*); der Zusatz; die Ansetzung.

Apprais—e, *v.a.* schätzen, abschätzen, den Wert bestimmen; anschlagen, taxieren. —**ement**, *s.* die Schätzung, Abschätzung, das Taxat. —**er**, *s.* der (angestellte) Taxator; der Schätzer.

Appreci—able, *adj.*, —**ably**, *adv.* schätzbar; (noticeable) merklich. —**ate**, *v.a.* (hoch *or* wert) schätzen, preisen, würdigen. —**ation**, *s.* die Würdigung, Schätzung, Wertschätzung.

Apprehen—d, *v.a.* anfassen; gefangen nehmen, verhaften (*a prisoner, etc.*); begreifen, einsehen (*an idea, etc.*); fürchten, befürchten. —**sible**, *adj.* faßlich, begreiflich. —**sion**, *s.* (seizure) das Ergreifen, Einfangen, die Gefangennehmung, Ergreifung; (power of —sion) die Fassungskraft; (faculty of —sion) die Auffassung, Wahrnehmung, der Begriff; (fear) die Besorgnis, Furcht; their action is regarded with —sion, ihr Vorgehen wird mit Besorgnis betrachtet; quick of —sion, schnell fassend *or* begreifend; dull of —sion, schwer von Begriffen, langsam auffassend; to be under —sion of, (etwas) befürchten. —**sive**, *adj.* besorgt, furchtsam; we were —sive of serious consequences, wir fürchteten ernste Folgen.

Apprentice, I. *s.* der Lehrling, Lehrbursche. II. *v.a.* in die Lehre geben *or* tun; he was —d to Mr. D., er war bei Herrn D. in der Lehre. —**ship**, *s.* die Lehrzeit, die Lehrjahre; die Lehre; to be out of one's —ship, aus der Lehre sein; to serve one's —ship, seine Lehrzeit durchmachen, in der Lehre sein.

Apprise, *v.a.* unterrichten, benachrichtigen, in Kenntnis setzen.

Approach, I. *v.n.* (heran)nahen, sich nähern; nahe kommen. II. *v.a.* nähern; Pope —es Virgil in the smoothness of his versification, in der Glätte seines Versbaus reicht Pope fast an Vergil; to — a subject, einen Gegenstand erwähnen, an einen Gegenstand herantreten; the colour —es green, die Farbe spielt ins Grüne; we —ed the castle, wir kamen dem Schlosse nahe; the minister was —ed, man wandte sich an den Minister. III. *s.* das Herannahen; die Annäherung; der Zutritt (*to kings, etc*); die Auffahrt, der Zugang (*Arch., etc.*); lines of —, —es, die Annäherungswerke, Laufgräben (*Mil.*); method of —es, die Approximation, Annäherungsmethode (*Math.*); to make the first —es, die ersten Schritte tun; grafting by —, die Ablaktation. —**able**, *adj.* erreichbar; zugänglich.

Approbation, *s.* die Billigung, der Beifall; it has my unqualified —, es hat meinen ungeteilten Beifall; on —, *see* Approval, on.

Appropriat—e, I. *v.a.* zueignen, widmen, bestimmen (*to a special use*); to —e s.th. (to o.s.), sich (*dat.*) etwas aneignen. II. *adj.* zweckmäßig, angemessen, passend. —**eness**, *s.* die Angemessenheit. —**ion**, *s.* die Aneignung; (dedication) die Zueignung; (application) die Anwendung, Verwendung. —**or**, *s. see* Impropriator; der Anwender; der, welcher zueignet.

Approv—able, *adj.* löblich. —**al**, *s.* die Billigung, der Beifall; on —al, auf Probe zur Ansicht, ohne Kaufzwang (*C.L.*). —**e**, *v.a.* &

n. billigen, genehmigen, gutheißen; (prove) beweisen; he did not —e of my conduct, er billigte mein Betragen nicht, er war mit meinem Verhalten unzufrieden; I —e of your quickness, ich lobe Ihre Geschwindigkeit. **—ed,** *p.p. & adj.* anerkannt, erprobt. **—er,** *s.* der Billiger; der geständige Verbrecher und Angeber seiner Mitschuldigen. **—ing(ly),** *adj.* (*adv.*) billigend, genehmigend, beistimmend.

Approximat—e, I. *adj.* annähernd; ungefähr; nahe, dicht (to, bei, an). II. *v.n.* sich nähern *or* nahen. **—ion,** *s.* die Näherung, Annäherung; die Approximation (*Math.*); by —ion, annähernd. **—ive,** *adj.* annähernd.

Appurtenan—ce, *s.* das Zugehör, Zubehör. **—ces,** *pl.* die Pertinenzstücke. **—t,** *adj.* zugehörig.

Apricot, *s.* die Aprikose.

April, *s.* der April. *Comp.* **—-fool,** *s.* der Aprilnarr; —-fool's day, der erste April; I made an —-fool of him, ich habe ihn in den April geschickt.

Apron, *s.* die Schürze; das Schurzfell (*of a smith*); die Bauchhaut (*of a goose, etc.*); das Schoßleder, Schutzleder (*on carts, etc.*); das Blattlot (*of a gun*); die Plankenbettung, der Schleusenboden (*of a dock*); die Binnenvorsteven (*Shipb.*). *Comp.* **—-string,** *s.* das Schürzenband; he is tied to her —-strings, sie hält ihn unter dem Pantoffel; he is tied to his mother's —-strings, er ist ein Muttersöhnchen.

Apropos, I. *adv.* gelegen, zu rechter Zeit; passend, schicklich. II. **— of,** *prep.;* — of that matter, betreffs jener Sache. III. *int.* ja so! dabei fällt mir ein! ehe ich es vergesse!

Aps—e, *s.* die Chornische, Apsis, halbkreisförmige Altarnische. **—is,** (*pl.* —ides) die Apside, der Wendepunkt in der Bahn der Planeten.

Apt, *adj.* (suitable) passend; (prone to) geneigt; (capable) geschickt, fähig; (accustomed) gewohnt; an — scholar, ein fähiger Schüler, ein Schüler, der leicht faßt; — to learn, gelehrig; — to teach, lehrhaft; it is — to disagree with one, es macht (einen) leicht krank; he is — to become excited, er wird leicht aufgeregt; we are — to like those who praise us, wir sind geneigt, diejenigen leiden zu mögen, welche uns loben; — to quarrel, streitsüchtig. **—itude,** *s.* die Geneigtheit, Neigung, der Hang; (talent for) die Fähigkeit, die Anlage(n); die Angemessenheit. **—ly,** *adv.* (justly) mit Recht; (suitably) passend angemessen, gemäß; (readily) schnell, fertig. **—ness,** *s.* die Paßlichkeit, Angemessenheit (*of an expression, etc.*); die Neigung, der Hang; die Tendenz; die Fertigkeit; —ness in learning, die Gelehrigkeit.

Apter—a, *pl.* flügellose Insekten. **—ous,** *adj.* flügellos.

Aqua—-fortis, *s.* das Scheidewasser. **—marine,** *s.* der Aquamarin; das Meergrün. **—-regia,** *s.* das Königswasser. **—rium,** *see* Aquarium. **—tic,** I. *adj.* im Wasser lebend; auf dem Wasser betrieben. II. *s.* die Wasserpflanze. **—tics,** *pl.* Wasservergnügungen, der Wassersport. **—tint,** *s.* die Aquatintamanier (*Engr.*).

Aquarell—e, *s.* das Aquarell, Gemälde in Wasserfarben; die Aquarell-Malerei. **—ist,** *s.* der (die) Aquarell-Maler(in).

Aquarium, *s.* das Aquarium; der Wassertierbehälter.

Aque—duct, *s.* die Wasserleitung. **—ous,** *adj.* wässerig; —ous humour of the eye, wässerige Feuchtigkeit des Auges; —ous vapour, der Wasserdampf.

Aquiline, *adj.* dem Adler gehörig, adlerartig; scharf gebogen; — nose, die Adlernase.

Arabesque, *s.* die Arabeske.

Arable, *adj.* pflügbar, anbaubar, urbar.

Arachnoid, *adj.* spinnwebartig; — tunic, die Spinnewebehaut, die Haut des Gehirns.

Arbit—er, *s.* der Schiedsrichter; der Gebieter, einer der entscheidet (*s.o.'s fate, etc.*). **—rament,** *s.* der freie Wille, die freie Wahl; die Entscheidung, der schiedsrichterliche Ausspruch. **—rarily,** *adv. see* —rary. **—rariness,** *s.* die despotische Gewalt, Unumschränktheit, Willkür. **—rary,** *adj.* willkürlich, despotisch; (capricious) launenhaft. **—rate,** *v.a. & n.* schiedsrichterlich entscheiden; einen Schiedsspruch tun; entscheiden, urteilen. **—ration,** I. *s.* der Schiedsspruch, die Entscheidung; court of —ration, das Oberschiedsgericht; to submit a disputed point to —ration, einen Streitpunkt einem schiedsrichterlichen Spruchunterwerfen; —ration of exchange, die Wechselarbitrage. II. *attrib.;* —ration bond, die Kompromißakte; —ration treaty, das Schiedsabkommen. **—rator,** *s.* der Schiedsrichter.

Arbor, *s.* der Baum; die Spindel, Welle, Achse, der Drehbaum (*Mech.*). **—escence,** *s.* die baumartige Krystallisation. **—escent,** *adj.* baumartig, baumähnlich. **—etum,** *s.* die Baumschule, Baumpflanzung. **—iculture,** *s.* die Baumzucht, Baumkultur. *Comp.* **—-vitae,** *s.* der Lebensbaum.

Arbour, Arbor, *s.* die Laube; der Laubengang, schattige Gang (*obs.*); der Baumgarten (*obs.*).

Arbutus, *s.* der Erdbeerbaum.

Arc, *s.* der Bogen, das Segment eines Kreises. **—ade,** *s.* der Bogengang, die Arkade. **—h,** *see* Arch. *Comp.* **—-boutant,** *s.* der Strebepfeiler. **—-lamp,** *s.* die Bogenlampe (*Electr.*).

Arcan—um, (*pl.* —a) *s.* das Geheimnis.

[1]**Arch,** I. *s.* der Bogen, Schwibbogen, das Gewölbe; fire —es, die Fritteöfen (*Glass*); triumphal —, Triumphbogen; Court of —es, das Oberkonsistorialgericht. II. *v.a.* wölben, überwölben, Bogen machen; —ed, gewölbt, geschweift; —ed roof, das Bogendach. III. *v.n.* sich wölben. **—er,** *s.* der Bogenschütze. **—ery,** *s.* das Bogenschießen; die Kunst des Bogenschießens. *Comp.* **—way,** *s.* der Bogengang.

[2]**Arch,** I. *adj.,* **—ly,** *adv.* schalkhaft, schelmisch. II. *adj. & pref.* oberst, vornehmst, erst; (*in comp. often* =) Erz-. **—aism, —æology, —etype, —i,** *etc., see* Archa—, Archæ—, Archetyp—, Archi—, etc. **—ness,** *s.* die Schelmerei, Schalkhaftigkeit. *Comp.* **—angel,** *s.* der Erzengel. **—bishop,** *s.* der Erzbischof. **—bishopric,** *s.* das Erzbistum. **—deacon,** *s.* der Archidiakonus. **—-druid,** *s.* (of Wales) der Erzdruide (von Wales). **—duke,** *s.* der Erzherzog. **—-enemy,** *s.* der Erzfeind. **—-fiend,** *s.* der alte böse Feind, der Teufel.

Archæolog—ical, *adj.* archäologisch, die Altertumsforschung betreffend. **—ist,** *s.* der Archäolog, Altertumsforscher. **—y,** *s.* die Altertumskunde, Altertumsforschung, Archäologie.

Archai—c, *adj.* altertümlich, veraltet. **—sm,** *s.* das veraltete Wort; der altertümliche *or* veraltete Ausdruck, der Archaismus.

Archetyp—al, *adj.* urbildlich. **—e,** *s.* das Urbild, der Urtypus.

Archi—diaconal, *adj.* zum Archidiakonat gehörig. **—episcopal,** *adj.* erzbischöflich. **—tect,** *s.* der Baumeister, Architekt; der Begründer, Stifter; he was the —tect of his own fortune, er war seines eignen Glückes Schmied. **—tectural,** *adj.* die Baukunst betreffend, architektonisch, baukünstlerisch. **—tecture,** *s.* die Baukunst; military —tecture, die Befestigungskunst; naval —tecture, der Schiffsbau, die Schiffsbaukunst. **—trave,** *s.* der Architrav, Unterbalken, Bindebalken. **—ves,** *see* Archives. **—volt,** *s.* der Unterbogen.

Archives, *pl.* das Archiv, die Urkundensammlung; die Urkunden; keeper of the —, der Urkundenbewahrer, Archivar.

Arctic, *adj.* am Nordpol gelegen, arktisch; — circle, nördlicher Polarkreis; — pole, der Nordpol; — expedition, die Nordpolexpedition, Nordpolfahrt; — fox, der Eisfuchs.

Ard—ency, *s.* die Hitze, Glut; die Innigkeit. **—ent(ly),** *adj.* (*adv.*) heiß, glühend, brennend, feurig, inbrünstig; —ent spirits, der Branntwein, Weingeist. —**our**, *s.* die Hitze, Heftigkeit; die Inbrunst, der (glühende) Eifer.

Arduous, *adj.*, —**ly**, *adv.* steil; schwierig, mühsam. —**ness**, *s.* die Schwierigkeit, Mühseligkeit.

Are, *1st, 2d, and 3d pl. pres. ind. of the verb* to be, wir sind, ihr seid, sie sind.

Are—a, *s.* die (Grund=)Fläche; der freie, offene Platz; der Flächeninhalt; der (kleine) Hof vor dem Hause, vertiefter Raum vor Häusern; das Feld (*Min.*); the —a of a building (of a circle), der innere Flächenraum eines Gebäudes (der Flächeninhalt eines Kreises); —a steps, die Treppe, welche vom Vorhof nach dem Kellergeschoß eines Wohnhauses führt, Kellertreppe.

Arena, *s.* die Arena, der Kampfplatz; der Harngries (*Med.*). —**ceous**, *adj.* sandig.

Areola, *s.* die Areole; der Hautring, Brustwarzenring.

Areometer, *s.* der Aräometer, die Senkwage.

Areopag—ite, *s.* der Areopagit. —**us**, *s.* der Areopag; (*fig.*) der Gerichtshof.

Argent, *adj.* silberfarbig, glänzend, silbern; silberweiß (*Her.*).

Argillaceous, *adj.* tonartig, tonig.

Argosy, *s.* das Handelsschiff, Kauffahrteischiff.

Argu—e, *v.* I. *a. & n.* erörtern; beweisen; disputieren; verraten; to —e sagacity, Scharfsinn verraten; so many laws —e so many sins, so viele Gesetze deuten auf so viele Sünden. II. *n.* Schlüsse machen, Gründe anführen; streiten, disputieren; you may —e with him a whole week without convincing him, man kann eine ganze Woche hindurch ihm seine Gründe auseinandersetzen und ihn doch nicht überzeugen; he —ed well against the proposition, er hat den Satz tüchtig bestritten; I won't be —ed out of that, das lasse ich mir nicht abstreiten. —**er**, *s.* der Wortkämpfer, Streiter, Disputant. —**ment**, *s.* der Beweis(=grund), die Beweisführung; der Streit, Wortstreit, das Disputieren; der Schluß (*Log.*); (subject of dispute) die Streitfrage, Sache; die gedrängte Inhaltsübersicht, Inhaltsangabe, der Hauptinhalt; das Argument, der Abstand (*Astr.*); to hold an —ment, disputieren; the drama holds the following —ment, der Inhalt des Dramas ist in Kürze der folgende. —**mentation**, *s.* das Beweisen; die Beweisführung. —**mentative(ly)**, *adj.* (*adv.*) disputierend; streitsüchtig. —**mentativeness**, *s.* die Streitsucht.

Arid, *adj.* dürr, trocken. —**ity**, *s.* die Dürre, Trockenheit.

Aries, *s.* der Widder; der Sturmbock, Mauerbrecher.

Aright, *adv.* recht, richtig; zurecht.

Arise, *v.n.* sich erheben, aufstehen (*from bed, etc.*); aufsteigen, aufgehen; aufstehen, sich erheben *or* empören (against, gegen); entstehen, entspringen (from, von); auferstehen (*from the dead*); aufgehen (*as the sun*); your misfortunes — from your idleness, euer Unglück entsteht aus eurer Trägheit; a dispute arose, ein Wortwechsel erhob sich *or* entstand; I will — and go to my father, ich will mich aufmachen und zu meinem Vater gehen (*B.*); whence —s this difference of opinion? woher kommt diese Meinungsverschiedenheit?

Aristocra—cy, *s.* der Adel, die Aristokratie; die Adelsherrschaft. —**t**, *s.* der Edelmann, Aristokrat. —**tic(ally)**, *adj.* (*adv.*) vornehm, edel, adlig, aristokratisch.

Arithmetic, *s.* die Rechenkunst, Arithmetik. —**al(ly)**, *adj.* (*adv.*) arithmetisch. —**ian**, *s.* der Rechenmeister, Rechner.

Ark, *s.* die Lade, der Kasten; Noah's —, die Arche Noahs; — of the covenant, die Bundeslade.

[1]**Arm**, *s.* der Arm; *see* [2]Arm; (power) die Macht; (branch) der (Baum=)Ast; — of the sea, der Meeresarm; the — of a glove, das Armstück an einem Handschuhe; to go — in —, Arm in Arm gehen; at —'s length, auf Armes Länge, in guter Entfernung; to keep a p. at —'s length, einen von sich abhalten, sich (*dat.*) einen vom Leibe halten; to hold at —'s length, vor sich ausgestreckt halten; within —'s reach, im Bereich der Arme, in unmittelbarer Nähe; the secular —, die weltliche Macht. —**let**, *s.* das Armband, die Armspange. *Comp.* —**-chair**, *s.* der Lehnsessel, Armstuhl. —**ful**, *s.* der Armvoll. —**hole**, *s.* das Armloch. —**pit**, *s.* die Achselgrube, Achselhöhle.

[2]**Arm**, I. *s.* die Waffe; die Truppengattung (*Mil.*). II. *v.a.* waffnen (*Mil.*); bewaffnen (*Mil.*, *Phys.*); (aus=)rüsten (*Mil.*, *Naut.*); armieren (*a magnet*). III. *v.n.* sich waffnen; they were —ed to the teeth, sie waren bis an die Zähne bewaffnet. —**ada**, *s.* die Kriegsflotte; die Armada. —**adillo**, *s.* das Armadill, Gürteltier. —**ament**, *s.* die Kriegsrüstung; (forces, *etc.*) die Kriegsmacht; die Bewaffnung, Schiffsrüstung; das schwere Geschütz (*of a ship*); naval —ament, die Kriegsflotte. —**ature**, *s.* die Rüstung; die Armatur (*of a magnet*). —**istice**, *s.* der Waffenstillstand. —**orial**, *adj.* zum Wappen gehörig; —orial bearings, das Wappen(=schild). —**our**, I. *s.* die Rüstung, der Harnisch. II. *v.* panzern; —oured, gepanzert; an —oured train, ein gepanzerter Zug, Panzerzug. —**ourer**, *s.* der Waffenschmied, Harnischmacher; der Waffenaufseher. —**oury**, *s.* die Rüstkammer, Gewehrkammer; (arsenal) das Zeughaus; die Waffen. —**s**, *pl.* die Waffen; der Krieg (*Poet.*); coat of —s, das Wappen; bred to —s, zum Waffenhandwerk herangezogen; fire-—s, Schießgewehre; —s of defence (offence), Schutzwaffen (Trutzwaffen); stand of —s, eine völlige Soldatenrüstung; to take up —s, die Waffen ergreifen; to take up —s in a p.'s defence, sich zum Verteidiger eines andern aufwerfen; to be under —s, unter den Waffen sein, stehen; the men stood to their —s, die Mannschaft trat unters Gewehr; companion in —s, der Waffenbruder; man-at-—s, der Soldat; serjeant-at-—s, der Stabträger (*Parl.*); the profession of —s, der Soldatenstand; to lay down one's —s, die Waffen strecken, sich ergeben; capable of bearing —s, waffenfähig; by force of —s, mit gewaffneter Hand; to —s! an die Gewehre! shoulder —s! Gewehr auf! slope —s! Gewehr über! stand to —s! an die Gewehre! ground *or* order —s! Gewehr ab! present —s! präsentiert das Gewehr! pile —s! setzt die Gewehre zusammen! with —s reversed, mit umgekehrtem *or* gesenktem Gewehr; all up in —s, (*fig.*) in hellem Zorn, in vollem Aufruhr. —**y**, *s.* das Heer, die Armee; an —y of women and children at his heels, eine Menge von Frauen und Kindern auf den Fersen; the vanguard, body and rear of an —y, der Vortrab, das Gros und der Nachtrab eines Heeres; an —y agent, ein Armeelieferant. *Comp.* —**our-bearer**, *s.* der Waffenträger, Schildknappe. —**our-plated**, *adj.* gepanzert; —our-plated ship, das Panzerschiff.

Armillary, *adj.* aus Ringen bestehend, ringförmig.

Aroint, (*obs.*) *int.* weg! fort! — thee! — ye! fort mit dir! packt euch!

Aroma, *s.* der würzige Duft, das Aroma; die Würze. —**tic**, *adj.* aromatisch, würzig.

Arose, *imperf. of* Arise.

Around, I. *adv.* rund herum, im Kreise, rings umher; they danced —, sie tanzten rundherum. II. *prep.* um . . . herum, (rings) um; they danced — the Maypole, sie tanzten um den Maibaum (herum).

Arouse, *v.a.* (auf)wecken; aufregen; aufrütteln; —d by, aufgeregt von, vorsichtig gemacht durch.

Arquebus—e, *s.* die Arkebuse, Hakenbüchse. —**ier**, *s.* der Arkebusier.

Arrack, *s.* der Arrak.

Arraign, *v.a.* anklagen, beschuldigen (*fig.*); vor Gericht führen; in Ordnung bringen (a writ, eine Klage). **—ment**, *s.* das Stellen, die Stellung vor Gericht; die Anklage, Beschuldigung; clerk of the —s *or* —ments, der Gerichtsaktuar, der die Klage fertigt.

Arrange, *v.a.* ordnen, in Ordnung bringen, einrichten; (order) anordnen; festsetzen (*a day*); arrangieren (*music*); he tried to — the quarrel, er bemühte sich, den Streit auszugleichen; the matter has been —d, die Sache ist abgemacht *or* beigelegt. **—ment**, *s.* die Anordnung, Einrichtung; (contrivance) die Einrichtung; das System, die Einteilung (*of plants, etc.*); die Stellung; (measure) die Vorkehrung; (settlement) der Vergleich, die Übereinkunft; die Abmachung (*of a plan*); das Arrangement (*of music*); a friendly —ment, ein gütlicher Vergleich; to come to an —ment, sich vergleichen, zu einem Vergleich gelangen; to make an —ment with, ein Übereinkommen treffen mit; to come to an —ment with one's creditors, (mit seinen Gläubigern) akkordieren; preliminary —ments, Vorbereitungen. **—r**, *s.* der Anordner; der Schlichter (*of a quarrel*).

Arrant, *adj.* arg, durchtrieben; Erz-; an — knave, ein Erzbösewicht.

Arras, *s.* gewirkte Tapete, der Tapetenbehang.

Array, I. *s.* kleiden, schmücken; herbeibringen (*testimony*); in Reih' und Glied ordnen, aufstellen; in Ordnung bringen; to — a panel, die Geschwornen aufrufen, ernennen (*Law*). II. *s.* die Ordnung (in Reih' und Glied); die Kleidung, der Anzug; die Musterung; die Ernennung und das Verzeichnis (der Geschwornen); die waffenfähige Mannschaft; (procession) der Zug; to set in — against, rüsten (*B.*); (einem) entgegenstellen; battle —, die Schlachtordnung; in rich —, festlich gekleidet, in prächtigen Gewändern.

Arrear, *s.* der Rückstand; —s, rückständige Summe, Rückstände; in —s, im Rückstande, rückständig (mit der Bezahlung); —s of rent, rückständige Miete.

Arrest, I. *s.* der Arrest, Verhaft, die Verhaftung; (stoppage) die Hemmung, Stockung; (check) der Einhalt, Aufhalt; die Beschlagnahme, der Beschlag (*of goods, etc.*); — of judgment, der Hemmungsspruch, die Aufschiebung des Urteils (*Law*); to move in — of judgment, als Aufschubsgrund vorbringen; to place under —, verhaften; close —, Stubenarrest (*Mil.*). II. *v.a.* verhaften, in Verhaft nehmen; aufhalten (*the current of a river, etc.*); hindern (*an inquiry, etc.*); zurückhalten (*the hand of death, etc.*); (stop) anhalten; hemmen (*Mach.*); to — s.o.'s attention, jemandes Aufmerksamkeit auf sich ziehen.

Arrière-ban, *s.* der Heerbann; der Landsturm.

Arriv—al, I. *s.* die Ankunft; die Anlandung; —als, die Zufuhren (*C.L.*), die ankommenden Personen oder Dinge; on —al, nach Ankunft, bei (meiner, *etc.*) Ankunft. II. *attrib.*; —al platform, der Ankunftsbahnsteig. **—e**, *v.n.* ankommen, anlangen; gelangen; (happen) geschehen; he —ed at this place, er kam an diesem Orte an; he has —ed at Berlin, er ist in Berlin angekommen; a despatch has just —ed, eine Depesche ist soeben eingelaufen; he has —ed at the highest perfection, er hat die höchste Vollkommenheit erreicht; to —e at a conclusion, zu einem Schlusse gelangen.

Arroga—nce, **—ncy**, *s.* die Anmaßung, Vermessenheit; der Übermut. **—nt(ly)**, *adj.* (*adv.*) anmaßend, vermessen; hochmütig. **—te**, *v.a.* sich (*dat.*) aneignen *or* anmaßen.

Arrow, *s.* der Pfeil; der Zählstab (*Surv.*); a shower of —s, ein Hagel von Pfeilen; straight as an —, pfeilgerade; swift as an —, pfeilgeschwind. **—y**, *adj.* aus Pfeilen bestehend; pfeilförmig; pfeilschnell. *Comp.* **—-head**, *s.* die Pfeilspitze; das Pfeilkraut (*Bot.*); —-headed characters, die Keilschrift. **—root**, *s.* die Pfeilwurz; das Pfeilwurzelmehl. **—-stone**, *s.* der Donnerkeil, Belemnit.

Arsenal, *s.* das Zeughaus; floating —, das Zeugschiff.

Arsen—ate, **—iate**, *s.* arsensaures Salz; —iate of lead, arsensaures Blei. **—ic**, *s.* der Arsenik; native —ic, gediegener Arsenik. **—ical**, *adj.* arsenisch, Arsenik enthaltend; —ical pyrites, der Arsenikkies. **—ite**, *s.* arseniksaures Salz.

Arsis, *s.* die Hebung, der Aufschlag im Takte (*Mus.*)

Arson, *s.* die Brandstiftung.

Art, I. *s.* die Kunst; (skill) die Kunst, Geschicklichkeit; (cunning) die Feinheit, List, Verschlagenheit, Kunst; the fine —s, die schönen Künste; the useful, the mechanical —s, die nützlichen, die handwerksmäßigen Künste, Handwerke; the liberal —s, die freien Künste; the black —, die schwarze Kunst; by —, durch Kunst, künstlich; master of —s (*abbr. M. A.*), Magister der freien Künste; bachelor of —s (*abbr. B. A.*), Baccalaureus der (freien) Künste; there is no — in that, das ist keine Kunst! an —s degree, ein Grad in der philosophisch-historischen Fakultät (B.A., M.A., Litt. D.); —s and sciences, Kunst und Wissenschaft; die philosophisch-historischen und die naturwissenschaftlich-mathematischen Fächer; a work of —, ein Kunstwerk. II. *attrib.*; — school, die Kunstschule. **—ful(ly)**, *adj.* (*adv.*) künstlich; listig, fein, schlau. **—fulness**, *s.* (skill) die Kunst; die List, Schlauheit. **—ifice**, *s.* der Kunstgriff; die List; by —ifice, durch List. **—ificer**, *s.* der Künstler; der Handwerker; der Stifter, Urheber. **—ificial(ly)**, *adj.* (*adv.*) künstlich; erkünstelt, nachgemacht, unecht; —ificial flowers, künstliche *or* nachgemachte Blumen; —ificial tears, erheuchelte Tränen; —ificial teeth, falsche Zähne. **—illery**, *s.* die Artillerie, das Geschütz. **—illerymen**, *pl.* die Artilleristen. **—isan**, *s.* der Handwerker. **—ist**, *s.* der (die) Künstler(in); —ist's proof, der Künstlerdruck, erste Abzug eines Kupferstichs (oft mit der eigenhändigen Unterschrift des Künstlers). **—istic(ally)**, *adj.* (*adv.*) künstlerisch. **—less(ly)**, *adj.* (*adv.*) kunstlos; natürlich, einfach, ungekünstelt; arglos. **—lessness**, *s.* die Kunstlosigkeit; die Einfachheit, Aufrichtigkeit; die Arglosigkeit. *Comp.* **—ist-like**, *adj.* künstlerisch. **—-union**, *s.* der Kunstverein.

Arter—ial, *adj.* die Pulsader betreffend, arteriell; —ial blood, das Pulsaderblut. **—iology**, *s.* die Lehre von den Arterien, die Arteriologie. **—iotomy**, *s.* die Arterienöffnung. **—y**, *s.* die Arterie, Pulsader, Schlagader.

Artesian, *adj.*; — well, artesischer Brunnen.

Arthritic, *adj.* gichtisch, arthritisch.

Artichoke, *s.* die Artischocke; Jerusalem —, die Erdartischocke, Erdbirne.

Artic—le, I. *s.* das Stück; (head) der Artikel, Punkt, Teil; die Klausel, Bedingung (*of an agreement*); der Absatz (*of a discourse, etc.*); der Aufsatz (*in a journal, etc.*); die Kritik; der Gegenstand, Artikel; (item) der Posten; das Gelenk, Glied (*Bot.*); der Artikel (*Gram.*); under —les, kontraktlich verpflichtet; —les of association, Statuten der Aktiengesellschaft; —le of commerce, der Warenartikel; —le of faith, der Glaubensartikel; a prime —le, eine extra gute Sache; —le of clothing, das Kleidungsstück; leading —le, Leitartikel. II. *v.a.* artikelweise abfassen; Punkt für Punkt darlegen; —le against, schriftlich anklagen; kontraktlich verbinden *or* übergeben; I have —led my son to an attorney, ich habe meinen Sohn (unter kontraktlichen Bedingungen) einem Advokaten in die Lehre gegeben; —led clerk, Kommis, der für seine Ausbildung Lehrgeld zahlt und sich auf eine Reihe von Jahren verpflichtet. III. *v.n.* Bedingungen machen. **—les** *pl.* die Gerätschaften; die Kontraktsbedingungen; —les of agreement, die Übereinkunftspunkte; —les of association, die Vereinsstatuten; to surrender upon —les, sich auf Bedingungen übergeben. **—ulate**, I. *v.a.* zusammenfügen (*bones*); deutlich aussprechen, artikulieren, sprechen, hervorbringen; —ulated animals, gegliederte Tiere, Gliedertiere. II. *adj.* deutlich, vernehmlich, klar (*of speech*); zusammengefügt. —**ulately**, *adv.* deutlich, vernehmbar. —**ulateness**, *s.* die Deutlichkeit, Vernehmbarkeit. —**ulation**, *s.* die deutliche Aussprache, die Artikulation; die Knochenfügung, Gelenkfügung (*Anat.*); das Gelenk; die Abgliederung, Abteilung in Glieder, der Knoten (*Bot.*); die Artikulation (*Paint.*).

As, I. *adv. & conj.* als wie; so, sowie, ebenso; sofern; da; indem; cold — ice, so kalt wie Eis; it's — broad — it is long, die Sache ist so lang, wie sie breit ist; — sound — a roach, so gesund wie ein Fisch; they are — like — two peas, sie sehen einander sehr ähnlich; she is — beautiful — a picture, sie ist zum Malen schön; — clear — day, so klar wie der Tag; twice — far, noch einmal so weit; — big again, noch einmal so dick *or* groß; — large — life, in Lebensgröße; — little — you please, so wenig Sie wollen; do — I do, machen Sie es so wie ich; — you like it, wie es euch gefällt; — a father, als Vater; — far — I know, so viel ich weiß; — far — I am concerned, was mich betrifft, meinetwegen; — for me, was mich betrifft; according —, je nachdem; — things fall out, je nachdem die Sachen ausfallen; do — I bid you, tun Sie, wie ich Ihnen sage; — far —, bis; — well —, so gut als, sowohl . . . als auch; — yet, bis jetzt; — though, als ob; — sure — I live! so wahr ich lebe! — I hope to be saved! so wahr ich selig zu werden hoffe! — you love me, be still! wenn du mich liebst, sei still; — you regard . . ., bei der Achtung vor . . .; — long — I live, so lange ich lebe; I did not so much — see him, ich sah ihn nicht einmal; I thought — much, das dachte ich mir; great men, — Cæsar, große Männer, wie *or* zum Beispiel Cäsar; — follows, wie folgt; — good luck would have it, glücklicherweise; — per bill of lading, laut Verladungsschein; — how? auf welche Weise? old — I am, so alt ich auch bin; — we went along, unterwegs; he trembled — she spoke, er zitterte, während sie sprach; — it were, so zu sagen, gewissermaßen, gleichsam; — 't were by accident, gleichsam als wäre es durch Zufall geschehen; — you will not come, we must go without you, da Sie nicht kommen wollen, müssen wir ohne Sie gehen; his conduct was such — to deserve punishment, sein Betragen war der Art, daß es Strafe verdiente. II. *used with* to *and* for *as prep.*; — to the day, I was mistaken, ich hatte mich in dem Tage geirrt; — for me, was mich betrifft; — for him, in Bezug auf ihn. III. *rel. pron.*; such — come shall be welcome, diejenigen, welche kommen, sollen willkommen sein; such — I like, die, welche mir gefallen.

Asafetida, *s.* der Stinkasand, stinkende Asant.

Asbestos, *s.* der Asbest.

Ascari—s, *s.* (*pl.* —des) der Eingeweidewurm.

Ascend, *v.* I. *n.* aufwärtssteigen, hinaufsteigen, aufsteigen, auffahren; zurückgehen; our inquiries — into the remotest antiquity, unsere Nachforschungen gehen bis in das graue Alter zurück. II. *a.* besteigen, ersteigen. —**ancy**, *see* —ency. —**ant**, I. *adj.* aufsteigend (*Astr.*); —ant over, überlegen. II. *s. see* —ency; der Aufgang eines Sternes; his star is in the —ant, sein Glück ist im Steigen. —**ency**, *s.* die Gewalt, Überlegenheit, der große Einfluß: to obtain an —ency over a p., große Gewalt über einen gewinnen.

Ascen—sion, *s.* das Aufsteigen (*also Astr.*); die Auffahrt; —sion of Christ, die Himmelfahrt Christi; —sion Day, der Himmelfahrtstag. —**t**, *s.* das Aufsteigen, Hinaufsteigen, der Aufstieg; die Anhöhe; die Steigung (*Surv.*); balloon —t, der Aufstieg des Luftschiffs *or* im Luftschiff.

Ascertain, *v.a.* ermitteln, in Erfahrung bringen, erfahren; sich erkundigen; sich (einer Sache) vergewissern; Gewißheit (über eine S.) erlangen; (inquire) festsetzen, bestimmen; to — the pric of an article, sich genau nach dem Preise eine Artikels erkundigen, den Preis in Erfahrun bringen; I could not — whether . . ., ich konnt nicht erfahren ob . . .; to — a balance, eine Saldo vergleichen; an —ed fact, eine sicher Tatsache. —**able**, *adj.* erforschbar, bestimmbar ermittelbar. —**ment**, *s.* die Vergewisserung Ermittelung.

Ascetic, I. *adj.*, —**ally**, *adv.* aszetisch, büßend enthaltsam. II. *s.* der Aszet, Büßer. —**ism** *s.* die Aszese, strenge Bußübung, enthaltsam Lebensweise; das Büßertum, der Aszetismus.

Ascrib—able, *adj.* zuschreibbar; it is —able, es ist . . . zuzuschreiben, es kommt von . . . —**e** *v.a.* zuschreiben; beilegen; it may be —ed t various causes, es läßt sich verschiedenen Ursache zuschreiben.

[1]**Ash**, I. *s.* die Esche; das Eschenholz; mountai —, die gemeine Eberesche, die Vogelbeere. II —, —**en**, *adj.* eschen, aus *or* von Eschenholz.

[2]**Ash**, I. *s.*, —**es**, *pl.* die Asche. II. *attrib.*; — colour das Aschgrau. —**en**, —**y**, *adj.* aschig; aschfarben aschgrau. *Comp.* —-**coloured**, *adj.* aschgrau aschfarbig. —-**pan**, *s.* das Aschenfaß; de Aschenkasten. —-**pit**, *s.* die Aschengrube. —-**tray**, *s.* der Aschenbecher. —-**Wednesday**, *s* der Aschermittwoch. —**y-pale**, *adj.* aschfahl (*fig.*) totenbleich.

Ashamed, *adj.* beschämt; to make —, beschämen to be *or* feel — of a th., sich einer Sache schämen I am — of you, ich schäme mich deiner; you ough to be — of yourself, du solltest dich schämen; ar you not — to look me in the face? schämen Si sich nicht, mir in die Augen zu sehen?

Ashlar, *s.* der Bruchstein. —**ing**, *s.* Stützen de Dachverschalung.

Ashore, *adv.* am Ufer, am Lande; ans Ufer ans Land; to bring —, ans Land bringen; t get —, landen, ans Land schaffen; to go — ans Land gehen; to run *or* to be driven —, stranden, auflaufen; the ship is —, das Schiff ist au den Strand aufgelaufen *or* gestrandet.

Aside, I. *adv.* seitwärts, auf der Seite; bei Seite (privately) für sich (*Theat.*); (in a different direction) abwärts; to put a th. —, etwas bei Sei setzen *or* legen; she has laid — her mourning sie hat die Trauer abgelegt; to lay — a project ein Vorhaben aufgeben; the court of appeal set this judgment —, das Appellationsgericht ho dies Urteil auf; he took him — and told hi . . ., er nahm ihn bei Seite und sagte ihm . . . to turn — from the path of virtue, vom Pfad der Tugend abweichen; he has put s.th. — for rainy day, er hat etwas für schlechte Zeiten zurückgelegt. II. *s.* das Beiseite, bei Seite Gesprochene.

Asinine, *adj.* eselhaft; zum Esel gehörig, Esels=

Ask, *v.* I. *a.* fragen (*a question*); verlangen; forder (*a price*); bitten; einladen; to be —ed in churc aufgeboten, von der Kanzel abgelesen werde (*coll.*); I should like to — you, ich möchte Si gern fragen; may he — you a question? darf e dich um etwas fragen? darf er eine Frage a dich richten? may I — you to pass me the bread darf ich Sie bitten, mir das Brot zu reichen darf ich Sie um das Brot bitten? to — permission, um Erlaubnis bitten; to — the way, na dem Wege fragen, sich nach dem Wege erkundigen — me and I will tell you all, frage mich und i will dir alles sagen; he —s more than we ca grant, er begehrt mehr *or* bittet um mehr als w gewähren können; he has —ed me to dinne next Tuesday, er hat mich auf nächsten Diensta zum Mittagessen gebeten *or* eingeladen; he —e us in, er nötigte uns herein; to — a p.'s advice einen um seinen Rat fragen. II. *n.*; — **about**, si erkundigen nach; — **after**, fragen nach; — afte a p.('s health), sich nach jemandes Befinden er kundigen; — **for**, bitten um; how much do yo

— for it, wieviel fordern Sie dafür? has anybody —ed for me? hat jemand nach mir gefragt? —**er**, *s.* der Bittende; der Fragende. —**ing**, *s. see* Ask; it can be had for the —ing, man kann es bekommen, wenn man nur darum bittet; second time of —ing, das zweite Aufgebot.

Ask—ance, —**ant**, *adv.* seitwärts; to look —ance at a p., einem einen Seitenblick zuwerfen, einen von der Seite ansehen, einen mißtrauisch betrachten; to eye —ance, scheel, schief ansehen. —**ew**, *adv.* schief.

Aslant, *adv.* schief, schräge, quer.

Asleep, *adv.* schlafend, im Schlafe; to be —, schlafen; to fall —, einschlafen; to put —, einschläfern; to be fast —, in tiefem Schlafe liegen, fest schlafen; my foot has fallen —, der Fuß ist mir eingeschlafen; half —, halb schlafend, halb im Schlaf.

Aslope, *adv.* (obliquely) schief; (aslant) abschüssig.

Asp, *s.* die Natter. —**ic**, *s. see* Asp; der Zwölfpfünder (*Artil.*); die Spieke (*Bot.*); die Gallertspeise, der Aspic (*Cook.*).

Asparagus, *s.* der Spargel.

Aspect, *s.* (sight) der Anblick; (appearance) das Ansehen, Aussehen; (situation, view) die Aussicht, Lage, Richtung; der Aspekt (*also Astr.*); das Licht; the house has a southern —, das Haus liegt nach Süden; the — of affairs has improved, die Aussichten sind besser geworden; to consider a question in its true —s, eine Frage vom richtigen Gesichtspunkt aus betrachten.

Aspen, I. *s.* die Espe, der Espenbaum, die Zitterpappel. II. *adj.* espen; to tremble like an — leaf, wie Espenlaub zittern.

Asperity, *s.* die Rauheit; die Härte, Strenge, Schroffheit; die Unfreundlichkeit, Widerwärtigkeit.

Aspers—e, *v.a.* (mit Weihwasser) besprengen (*obs.*); bespritzen; beschuldigen, verleumden, in übeln Ruf bringen. —**ion**, *s.* die Besprengung (*R.*), Bespritzung (*obs.*); die Verleumdung, Anschwärzung; he cast —ions upon his master's honour, er hat seines Herrn Ehre befleckt.

Asphalt, I. der Asphalt, das Erdpech, Erdharz. II. *adj.* asphaltisch, aus Erdpech.

Asphodel, *s.* der Affodill, Asphodill.

Asphyxia, *s.* der Scheintod, die Asphyxie.

Aspir—ant, *s.* der Bewerber, Kandidat; der Emporstrebende; einer, der nach etwas trachtet; —ant to an office, Bewerber (um ein Amt), Amtsbewerber. —**ate**, I. *v.a.* aspirieren. II. *adj.* aspiriert. III. *s.* die Aspirata, der Hauchlaut; der aspirierte Verschlußlaut (*e.g.* t^h, k^h, p^h). —**ation**, *s.* die Aspiration, Aussprache mit einem Hauchlaut; das Streben, Trachten, die Sehnsucht (after, nach). —**e**, *v.n.* verlangen, trachten, streben (after, to, nach); emporstreben; sich erheben; to —e to s.th., etwas heftig verlangen, nach einer S. streben. —**er**, *see* —ant. —**ing**, *adj.* hochstrebend.

Ass, *s.* der Esel; the — brays, der Esel iaht; she —, die Eselin; —'s milk, die Eselsmilch; —'s colt, das Eselsfüllen. —**like**, *see* Asinine.

Assail, *v.a.* angreifen, anfallen, bestürmen. —**able**, *adj.* angreifbar. —**ant**, *s.* der Angreifer.

Assassin, *s.* der Meuchelmörder; the would-be —, der Verüber des Mordversuchs. —**ate**, *v.a.* meuchelmörderisch umbringen, morden. —**ation**, *s.* der Meuchelmord, die Ermordung.

Assault, I. *v.a.* angreifen, anfallen; bestürmen. II. *s.* der Angriff, Anfall; die Bestürmung, der Sturm; der Versuch tätlicher Mißhandlung; die Drohung mit Tätlichkeiten (*Law*); — of (*or* at) arms, das Kontrafechten; die Fechtübung; Fechtvorstellung; indecent —, das Sittlichkeitsverbrechen. —**er**, *s.* der Angreifer.

Assay, I. *s.* der Versuch; die Probe, Prüfung; — of ores, die Erzprobe; mechanical —, mechanische Probe; — of weights and measures, Prüfung der Maße und Gewichte; to take the —, den Wert, die Reinheit der Metalle prüfen; — of alloys, die Probe, das Probieren der Legierungen; mark of —, das Probezeichen. II. *v.a.* versuchen; prüfen, probieren; wardieren (*Chem.*); to — by the cupel, abtreiben. —**er**, *s.* der Münzwardein; der Probierer. —**ing**, *s.* die Probierkunst. *Comp.*—-**balance**, *s.* die Probierwage. —-**master**, *s. see* —er. —-**test**, *s.* die Probierscherbe.

Assembl—age, *s.* die Versammlung, Sammlung; die Verbindung, Zusammenfügung (*Carp.*). —**e**, *v.* I. *a.* versammeln; zusammenberufen (*parliament, etc.*); zusammenziehen (*troops, etc.*). II. *n.* sich versammeln. —**y**, *s.* die Versammlung; die Gesellschaft; das (zweite) Zusammentrommeln; der Sammelruf (*Mil.*); to sound the —y, zum Sammeln blasen; house of —y, der Kongreß, die Repräsentantenkammer; General —y, (of the Scotch church) das höchste, geistliche Gericht in Schottland, der geistliche Konvent in Schottland. *Comp.* —**y-room**, *s.* das Versammlungslokal, der Saal.

Assent, I. *s.* die Zustimmung, Genehmigung; the bill has received the royal —, der Gesetzentwurf ist vom Könige genehmigt worden; without my knowledge and —, ohne mein Wissen und Willen; she nodded —, sie gab durch Kopfnicken ihre Einwilligung zu erkennen, sie nickte ein ‚ja'. II. *v.n.* beistimmen, beipflichten, zustimmen, genehmigen, billigen; I — to your proposals, ich billige Ihre Vorschläge, ich nehme sie an.

Assert, *v.a.* behaupten; verteidigen; geltend machen; to — o.s., sich geltend machen; human nature at last —ed its rights, die menschliche Natur machte endlich ihre Rechte geltend; to — one's rights, seine Rechte verteidigen; the witness —ed that he did not know, der Zeuge sagte aus, daß er es nicht wisse. —**ion**, *s.* die Behauptung, Versicherung; die Aussage; you cannot deny the truth of his —ion, die Wahrheit dessen, was er behauptet hat, können Sie nicht in Abrede stellen; —ion is no proof, Behaupten ist nicht Beweisen (*prov.*). —**ive**, *adj.* bestimmt, ausdrücklich, peremptorisch. —**ively**, *adv. see* —ive; bejahend. —**or**, *s.* der Behaupter; der Verteidiger, Verfechter.

Assess, *v.a.* einschätzen, abschätzen, schätzen; taxieren, besteuern; anschlagen; to — damages, die Entschädigungssumme bestimmen; I am —ed at twenty-five pounds, ich zahle an Steuer fünfhundert Mark. —**able**, *adj.* schätzbar, steuerbar; steuerpflichtig. —**ment**, *s.* die Einschätzung (für direkte Steuern); die Steuer, Abgabe; das Festsetzen (einer Entschädigung); die Schätzung. —**or**, *s.* der Assessor; der Beisitzer; der Steuerrat, Abschätzer, Einschätzer.

Assets, *pl.* der Nachlaß; die Aktiva, der Vermögensbestand eines Falliten; — and debts, — and liabilities, Aktiva und Passiva, das Aktiv- und Passiv-Vermögen; no —, kein Guthaben (*on cheques*).

Asseverat—e, *v.a.* beteuern, bestimmt behaupten. —**ion**, *s.* die Beteuerung.

Assidu—ity, *s.* die Emsigkeit, unverdrossene Tätigkeit; die Unverdrossenheit; die Beharrlichkeit, der ausdauernde Fleiß. —**ous**(**ly**), *adj.* (*adv.*) unablässig, emsig, fleißig; unverdrossen; —ous attentions, unablässige Aufmerksamkeiten.

Assign, I. *v.a.* anweisen, zuteilen (*a share, etc.*); (fix, point out) bestimmen; angeben (*a reason*); (sign over) übertragen, übermachen; (appoint) ernennen. II. *s. see* —ee. —**able**, *adj.* bestimmbar; anweisbar; übertragbar. —**ation**, *s.* die Bestellung an einen gewissen Ort, zu einer gewissen Zeit, das Stelldichein; die Übertragung, Abtretung. —**ee**, der, dem etwas übertragen wird; der Kurator (der Masse eines Falliten); der Bevollmächtigte, Zessionar. —**er**, *s.* der Bestimmende, Anweiser; der Abtreter, Übertragende. —**ment**, *s.* die Anweisung, Bestimmung; die Angabe (*of reasons, etc.*); die Übertragung; die Tratte (*C. L.*); deed of —ment, die Abtretungsurkunde.

Assimilat—e, *v.* I. *a.* ähnlich machen, verähnlichen; einverleiben, in Nahrungsstoff verwandeln, verdauen (*Med.*); sich aneignen, in sich aufnehmen. II. *n.* ähnlich werden. —**ion**, *s.* die Assimilation, Angleichung, Anpassung, Einverleibung, Umwandlung.

Assist, *v.a.* (succour) beistehen; (help) helfen; (contribute to) beitragen. —**ance**, *s.* der Beistand, die Hülfe; der Helfer. —**ant**, I. *s.* der Helfer, Gehülfe, Beistand, Hülfs=. II. *adj.;* —ant librarian, der Unterbibliothekar; —ant master, ordentlicher Lehrer an einer Schule; —ant secretary, der Hülfssekretär, der zweite Schriftführer; —ant surgeon, der Assistenzarzt, Unterarzt; —ant teacher, *see* —ant master.

Assize, *s.* das Assisen(=gericht); (*pl.* —s) das Geschworenengericht; der Gerichtstag; die öffentliche Gerichtssitzung; (*obs.*) die öffentliche Festsetzung von Maß und Preis, der festgesetzte Preis, die Taxe, Taxordung; das festgesetzte Gewicht und Maß; — of bread, die Brodtaxe; court of —(s), der Assisenhof; to hold the —s, die Assisen abhalten.

Associat—e, I. *v.a.* zugesellen, gesellen. II. *v.n.* sich gesellen zu, sich verbinden; (keep company) Umgang haben. III. *s.* der Gefährte, Kamerad, Genosse, Gesellschafter; das nicht vollberechtige Mitglied eines Vereins oder eines Standes; der Teilhaber (*C.L.*). —**ion**, *s.* die Verbindung; (society) der Verein; die Gesellschaft, Handelsverbindung; (union) die Genossenschaft, das Bündnis; articles of —ion, Satzungen des Vereins, Statuten der Aktiengesellschaft; —ion of ideas, die Ideenverbindung; I have many pleasant —ions connected with that place, es knüpfen sich für mich viele angenehme Erinnerungen an jenen Ort. *Comp.* —**ion-football**, *s.* eine Art Fußballspiel (in dem u. a. der Ball nur vom Hüter des Grenzmals mit den Händen berührt werden darf).

Assona—nce, *s.* der Anklang, der vokalische Gleichklang, die Assonanz. —**t**, *adj.* nur vokalisch gleichlautend, anklingend, assonierend.

Assort, *v.* I. *a.* (zusammen=)ordnen, sortieren. II. *n.* übereinstimmen, passen; an ill —ed couple, ein schlecht zu einander passendes Ehepaar; this does not — with my ideas, dies stimmt mit meinen Ideen nicht überein *or* verträgt sich nicht mit meinen Anschauungen. —**ment**, *s.* das Assortiment, Sortiment; das Zusammenordnen.

Assuage, *v.* I. *a.* mildern, lindern, besänftigen; mäßigen; to — angry passions, aufgebrachte Leidenschaften beruhigen; to — pain, Schmerzen lindern. II. *n.* nachlassen, abnehmen, sich verlaufen (*of water*); the waters —d, die Gewässer verliefen sich. —**ment**, *s.* die Linderung.

Assum—e, *v.* I. *a.* annehmen, sich (*dat.*) aneignen, übernehmen (*responsibility, etc.*); voraussetzen, annehmen (as true, etc., als wahr, ꝛc.); (usurp) sich (*dat.*) anmaßen, sich (*dat.*) herausnehmen; sich (*dat.*) beilegen (*a title, etc.*); to —e a haughty air, eine stolze, hochmütige Miene annehmen; to —e the reins of government, die Zügel der Regierung in die Hand nehmen. II. *n.;* to be —ing, anmaßend sein, groß tun. —**ption**, *s.* die Aneignung; (presumption) die Anmaßung; die Voraussetzung; die Übernahme (*of government, etc.*); das Postulat (*Log.*); der Untersatz (*Log.*); the —ption of the Blessed Virgin, Mariä Himmelfahrt.

Assur—ance, I. *s.* die Zusicherung, Versicherung; (confidence) die Zuversicht, das feste *or* sichere Vertrauen; (conviction) die feste Überzeugung; (steadfastness) die Festigkeit; (boldness) die Kühnheit; (self-confidence) das Selbstvertrauen; (arrogance) die Anmaßung, Unverschämtheit; (calmness) die Gemütsruhe; die Assekuranz (*C. L.*); —ance of manner, sicheres Benehmen; die Dreistigkeit; an air of —ance, eine dreiste Miene, in full —ance of faith, in völligem Glauben. II. *attrib.;* —ance society, die Versicherungsgesellschaft. —**e**, *v.a.* versichern; (guarantee) zusichern; (make sure) sichern, sicher machen; (encourage) aufmuntern; versichern (*one's life, etc.*); he —ed me that he was sincere, er versicherte mir (*or* mich), daß er aufrichtig sei; I have been —ed that it is so, man hat mir die Versicherung gegeben, daß es so sei; (you may) rest —ed of it, Sie können sich darauf verlassen; the king —ed the officer of his favour, der König versicherte den Offizier seiner Gnade. —**edly**, *adv.* sicherlich, gewiß, unzweifelhaft. —**edness**, *s.* die Gewißheit. —**er**, *s.* der Versicherer; der sich Versichernde.

Astatic, *adj.;* — needle, astatische Magnetnadel; — system, astatisches Nadelpaar (*Magnet.*).

Ast—er, *s.* die Aster (*Bot.*). —**erisk**, *s.* das Sternchen (*Typ.*). —**eroid**, *s.* der Asteroid (*Astr.*). —**ral**, *adj.* zu den Sternen gehörig; sternig; —ral lamp, die Astrallampe.

Astern, *adv.* hinten am Schiffe, am *or* im Hinterteile des Schiffes; (nach) achtern, achteraus (of, vom); hinter dem Schiffe; nach hinten, hinterwärts; rückwärts; to drop *or* fall —, zurückbleiben; the wind is —, der Wind ist von achtern; to be — of one's reckoning, mit dem Bestecke voraus sein.

Asthma, *s.* die Kurzatmigkeit, Engbrüstigkeit, das Asthma. —**tic**, *adj.* engbrüstig, kurzatmig, asthmatisch.

Astonish, *v.a.* in Erstaunen setzen, verwundern; to be —ed, erstaunen, sich verwundern, in Erstaunen geraten; I was —ed at his boldness, ich erstaunte über seine Kühnheit. —**ing**(**ly**), *adj.* (*adv.*) erstaunend, erstaunlich, zum Erstaunen; the —ing part of the matter is . . ., das Erstaunliche dabei *or* bei der Geschichte ist . . . —**ment**, *s.* das Erstaunen, die Verwunderung.

Astound, *v.a. see* Astonish; betäuben.

Astraddle, *adv.* rittlings, sperrbeinig; — of, rittlings auf, reitend auf.

Astragal, *s.* der Reif, Ring, Rundstab (*Arch.*); der Gurt, das Band (*on fire-arms*); der Astragal, das Sprungbein (*Anat.*).

Astray, *adv.* vom rechten Wege ab, irre; to lead —, verleiten, verführen, irre führen; to go —, sich verirren; vom Pfade der Tugend abweichen.

Astride, *adv.* mit gespreizten Beinen, rittlings, — of, rittlings auf (*dat.*).

Astringen—cy, *s.* die zusammenziehende Kraft. —**t**, I. *adj.* zusammenziehend, a(d)stringierend herb. II. *s.* das zusammenziehende Mittel.

Astro—labe, *s.* das Astrolabium. —**loger**, *s.* der Astrolog, Sterndeuter. —**logical**, *adj.* astrologisch. —**logy**, *s.* die Astrologie, Sterndeuterei. —**nomer**, *s.* der Astronom, der Sternkundige. —**nomical**, *adj.* astronomisch; —nomical tables, astronomische Tafeln. —**nomy**, *s.* die Astronomie, Sternkunde. —**scope**, *s.* das Astroskop, der Sternkegel.

Astute, *adj.*, —**ly**, *adv.* listig, schlau, verschlagen; scharfsinnig. —**ness**, *s.* der Scharfsinn; die Schlauheit, Verschlagenheit.

Asunder, *adv.* auseinander, voneinander; besonders; getrennt; (in two) entzwei.

Asylum, *s.* das Asyl, der Zufluchtsort; das Hospital; — for the insane, das Irrenhaus.

Asymptot—e, *s.* die Asymptote (*Math.*). —**ic**(**al**), *adj.* asymptotisch.

Asyndeton, *s.* das Asyndeton, die Auslassung des Bindeworts.

At, *prep.* an; auf; aus; bei; für; gegen; in; mit; nach; über, um; von; vor; zu; — court, am Hofe; there is a beggar — the door, es steht ein Bettler an der Tür; — the mouth of the river.

an der Mündung des Flusses; — the point of death, an Todesenden, im Sterben; — the beginning, am Anfang, zu Anfang, anfangs; — all events, auf jeden Fall, jedenfalls; — my expense, auf meine Kosten; — stake, auf dem Spiele; all — once, auf einmal; — the university, auf der Universität; — a ball, auf einem Balle; — his country-seat, auf seinem Landgute; — my suit, auf mein Gesuch; he ran — him, er stürzte auf ihn los; — this command, auf diesen Befehl; — sight, auf Sicht; — second hand, aus der zweiten Hand; — hand, bei der Hand; — the sight of her child, beim Anblick ihres Kindes; — daybreak, bei Tagesanbruch; — table, bei Tische; we have been — work the whole morning, wir sind den ganzen Morgen bei der Arbeit gewesen; to take a p. — his word, einen beim Wort nehmen; — half price, für den halben Preis; — a low price, für wenig Geld; — what time shall I see you? — about six in the evening, um welche Zeit werde ich Sie sehen? etwa gegen sechs Uhr abends; — large, im Freien; in Freiheit; frei, los; — school, in der Schule; when I was last — Paris, als ich zuletzt in Paris war; to be — a standstill, stocken, in Verlegenheit sein; — liberty, in Freiheit; — peace, im Frieden; — the very moment when . . ., gerade in dem Augenblicke, wo . . .; he was — fault, er befand sich im Irrtum; you can do this — your leisure, Sie können dies nach Muße tun; — my time of life, in meinem Lebensalter; — the age of sixteen, im Alter von sechzehn Jahren; — pleasure, nach Belieben; to throw —, werfen nach; he aims — perfection, er strebt nach Vollkommenheit; angry —, erzürnt über (*acc.*); to laugh —, lachen über (*acc.*); I was surprised — your refusal, ich wunderte mich über Ihre Weigerung; — five o'clock, um fünf Uhr; — how much the piece? um wieviel das Stück? — his hands, von ihm; I did not expect such treatment — your hands, solche Behandlung erwartete ich von Ihnen nicht; I live — . . ., ich wohne zu . . .; I am — home and — your service every evening, ich bin alle Abende zu Hause und stehe dann immer zu Ihren Diensten; to look in — the window, zum Fenster hereinsehen; — the right moment, im rechten Augenblick; — Michaelmas, zu Michaelis; — any minute, zu jeder Minute, jeden Augenblick; — reduced prices, zu herabgesetzten Preisen; (*the preposition suppressed or expressed in composition*) — night, des Nachts; — all, ganz und gar, durchaus, überhaupt; I think I shall not go — all, ich glaube nicht, daß ich überhaupt hingehe; I don't like him — all, ich kann ihn durchaus nicht leiden; not — all, durchaus nicht, keineswegs; nothing — all, (ganz und) gar nichts; my patience is now — an end, jetzt reißt mir die Geduld; — first, zuerst; — last, zuletzt; — length, endlich; — (great) length, weitläufig, ausführlich; — least, wenigstens; — the most, höchstens; — no time, niemals; — one, einer Meinung, einstimmig; to be always — a p., einen fortwährend bestürmen, dringend um eine S. bitten (*coll.*); are you — leisure for an hour? haben Sie eine Stunde frei? — times, zuweilen, bisweilen, manchmal; he is hard — work, er arbeitet tüchtig; he is good — telling a story, er erzählt gut; to be — law, prozessieren; to be laughed —, ausgelacht werden; to be — one's wits' end, sich (*dat.*) nicht mehr zu raten wissen, in der größten Verlegenheit sein; what are you — there? was macht Ihr dort? (*coll.*); I now saw what she was driving —, jetzt sah ich, worauf sie hinzielte, was sie haben wollte (*coll.*); I was — a loss what to say, ich wußte nicht, was ich sagen sollte; to be — the expense of . . ., die Kosten von . . . tragen; to be — great expense, viel ausgeben müssen; to play — whist, chess, *etc.*, Whist, Schach, u. s. w. spielen; you are — liberty to go, Sie dürfen gehen, können nach Belieben gehen; the house is close — hand, das Haus steht ganz nahe; — a distance, von ferne; weitab.

Ate, *imperf. of* Eat.

Atheis—m, *s.* die Gottesleugnung, der Atheismus. **—t**, *s.* der Gottesleugner. **—tic(al)**, *adj.*, **—tically**, *adv.* atheistisch.

Athenæum, *s.* das Athenäum; der Verein für Kunst und Wissenschaft.

Athirst, *adj.* (*poet.*) durstig; begierig (for, nach).

Athlet—e, *s.* der Wettkämpfer, Athlet; körperliche Übungen liebender Mensch; he is a great —e, er ist in allen körperlichen Übungen ausgezeichnet. **—ic(ally)**, *adj.* (*adv.*) athletisch; stark, kräftig, körperliche Übungen liebend; an —ic form, eine kräftige Gestalt; —ic sports, athletische Wettkämpfe *or* Wettspiele. **—icism**, *s.*, **—ism**, *s.* Pflege körperlicher Übungen, Vorliebe für körperliche Übungen und Wettkämpfe.

Athwart, I. *prep.* querüber, über; durch; dwars (*Naut.*); — hawse, quer vor dem Bug; to stand — the waves, dwars See liegen; — ships, querschiffs; to come —, in die Quere kommen. II. *adv.* schräg, schief; verkehrt, ungelegen.

Atilt, *adv.* mit gefällter Lanze, vorwärts gebeugt; kippend; to set a cask —, ein Faß kippen.

Atlas, *s.* der Atlas (*Myth.*); die Landkartensammlung, das Kartenwerk, der Atlas; der Atlas, Träger (*Anat.*); (*pl.* Atlantes) der Atlant, Träger (*Arch.*); das Atlasgebirge (*Geog.*); das Atlas-Format, Groß-Folio.

Atmospher—e, *s.* die Atmosphäre, der Dunstkreis, Luftkreis. **—ic(al)**, *adj.* atmosphärisch; —ic brake, die Luftbremse; —ic churn, das Luftbutterfaß; —ic pressure, der Luftdruck; —ic railway, die Luftdruckeisenbahn.

Atoll, *s.* das Atoll, die ringförmige Koralleninsel.

Atom, *s.* das Atom, das unteilbare kleinste Teilchen; das Ur(stoff)teilchen (*Phys.*); das Sonnenstäubchen; to break a thing into —s, eine Sache kurz und klein brechen. **—ic**, *adj.* atomi(sti)sch, von Atomen, aus Atomen; —ic theory, die Atomentheorie; —ic weight, das Atomgewicht. **—icity**, *s.* die Atomigkeit, Wertigkeit. **—ism**, *s.* die Atomenlehre. **—istic**, *adj.* aus Atomen *or* Urteilchen bestehend; die Atome betreffend.

Atone, *v.* I. *n.* Ersatz bieten, büßen (für); aufwiegen, genug tun. II. *a* (*obs.*) vereinigen, versöhnen, in Einklang bringen; to — for, abbüßen, ersetzen, vergüten; his kindness —s for his ugliness, seine Herzensgüte entschädigt für seine Häßlichkeit; he —d for his faults by his death, er büßte mit dem Tode für seine Fehler *or* büßte seine Fehler mit dem Tode. **—ment**, *s.* die Versöhnung (*B.*); die Buße, die Abbüßung; die Vergütung; (reconciliation) die Versöhnung, Sühne; to make —ment for, etwas versöhnen (*B.*); etwas abbüßen, sühnen.

Atony, *s.* die Erschlaffung, Laxität; die Kraftlosigkeit, Schwäche.

Atop, *adv.* oben (hin-)auf, oben.

Atrabilarian, Atrabiliar(y), Atrabilious, *adj.* schwarzgallig; schwermütig.

Atroci—ous(ly), *adj.* (*adv.*) gräßlich, schauderhaft, abscheulich. **—ty**, *s.* die Gräßlichkeit, Grausamkeit, Scheußlichkeit; das Scheusal.

Atrophy, *s.* die Abzehrung, Auszehrung, Atrophie.

Attach, *v.a.* anheften, anbinden (to, an); (fasten) befestigen; (subjoin) beifügen, verknüpfen; beilegen (*a condition, etc.*); an sich ziehen, fesseln; in Verhaft nehmen (*Law*); mit Beschlag belegen (*C. L.*); to — blame to a p., einem Schuld beimessen *or* zurechnen, einen tadeln (wegen einer S.); I — no value to his remarks, ich lege seinen Äußerungen keinen Wert bei *or* keinen Wert auf seine Äußerungen; he was —ed to the regiment, er wurde dem Regimente attachiert; to — o.s. to a p., (einem) anhängen; we have become —ed to these people, wir haben diese Menschen lieb gewonnen. **—able**, *adj.* verknüpfbar; was mit Beschlag belegt werden kann (*C. L.*). **—ment**, *s.* die Fesselung; die Anhänglichkeit, Neigung, Liebe; die Verhaftung, Inhaftnahme (*Law*); die Beschlagnahme; foreign —ment, Beschlag auf das Eigentum eines Ausländers.

Attack, I. *v.a.* angreifen, anfallen; we —ed the enemy vigorously, wir sind gehörig auf den Feind losgegangen, wir sind dem Feinde tüchtig auf den Leib gegangen (*coll.*). II. *s.* der Angriff (*of the enemy*), Anfall (*of influenza, etc.*); a false —, ein blinder, verstellter Angriff. **—able**, *adj.* angreifbar. **—er**, *s.* der Angreifer; der angreifende Teil.

Attain, *v.* I. *a.* erreichen, erlangen; to — one's end, seinen Zweck erreichen; zum Ziele gelangen. II. *n.* gelangen (zu), erreichen. **—able**, *adj.* erreichbar. **—der**, *s.* (taint) die Befleckung, der Makel, Schandfleck; die Verurteilung, Überführung (wegen Hochverrats *or* eines Kapitalverbrechens, welche die Einziehung des Eigentums und den Verlust der bürgerlichen Ehrenrechte zur Folge hat); bill of —der, Entwurf eines Gesetzes zur Bestrafung des Hochverrats. **—ment**, *s.* die Erlangung, Erreichung; —ments, die Kenntnisse und Fertigkeiten. **—t**, I. *v.a.* beflecken; eines Hauptverbrechens überführen, überweisen; für schuldig erkennen. II. *s.* der Makel; der Schlag, die Wunde am Pferdefuße; die Klage wegen falschen Spruchs der Geschwornen (*Law*).

Attar, *s.* die Blumenessenz; —of roses, das Rosenöl.

Attemper, *v.a.* mäßigen; gehörig mischen; anpassen; mäßigen, lindern.

Attempt, I. *v.a.* versuchen, unternehmen; don't — it! wagen Sie es nur nicht! to — a p.'s life, einem nach dem Leben stellen *or* trachten, einen Mordanfall auf einen verüben; Bismarck's life was several times —ed, es wurden mehrere Mordversuche *or* Attentate auf Bismarck gemacht. II. *s.* der Versuch, die Unternehmung; you have at least made the —, Sie haben wenigstens den Versuch gemacht; to make an — on a p.'s life, sich an jemandes Leben vergreifen, auf einen ein Attentat *or* einen Mordversuch machen.

Attend, *v.* I. *a.* begleiten, folgen; im Gefolge sein; aufwarten, bedienen; pflegen; ärztlich behandeln; (await) erwarten; (be present) beiwohnen, zugegen sein; great calamity —s war, der Krieg führt große Übel in seinem Gefolge; —ed with difficulties, mit Schwierigkeiten verknüpft; let me — you to your house, lassen Sie mich Sie nach Hause begleiten; this lady —ed me in my illness, diese Dame pflegte mich in meiner Krankheit; Doctor A. —s our family, Doktor A. behandelt unsere Familie, ist unser Hausarzt; to — school, die Schule besuchen; to — divine service, dem Gottesdienste beiwohnen; to — a lecture, eine Vorlesung besuchen *or* hören; to — the sessions, bei der Sitzung anwesend sein. II. *n.* merken, achten, hören (auf); folgen; to — on a p., einen warten, pflegen; (serve, wait) einen bedienen, einem aufwarten; to — to business, das Geschäft betreiben, besorgen; this would not have happened if you had —ed to what I said to you, dies wäre nicht geschehen wenn Sie auf das, was ich Ihnen sagte, Acht gegeben hätten; — to his words! merke auf seine Worte! — to the words of truth, hört mit Aufmerksamkeit auf die Worte der Wahrheit; to be well —ed to, gut gepflegt sein (*of gardens, etc.*); the theatre was but poorly —ed, das Theater war nur schlecht besetzt; the lecture was well —ed, die Vorlesung war stark *or* gut besucht; to — to one's devotions, seine Andacht verrichten; to — to the children, auf die Kinder achten, passen, nach den Kindern sehen; — to the children, sehen Sie nach den Kindern! to — (to) the door, die Haustür aufmachen, wenn geklopft oder geschellt wird; rely on me, I will — to it myself, verlassen Sie sich auf mich, ich will es selbst besorgen *or* mich selbst darum bekümmern. **—ance**, *s.* die Bedienung (*at a restaurant*); die Dienerschaft, das Gefolge; die Anwesenheit, der Besuch (*at lectures*); die Zuhörerschaft, das Auditorium (*at a lecture*); in —ance, diensttuend; to be in —ance, den Dienst haben; aufwarten; Doctor D. is in —ance, Doktor D. behandelt ihn; the doctor is in daily —ance, der Arzt besucht ihn täglich; doctor's professional —ance, die ärztliche Behandlung; —ance at church, der Kirchenbesuch; regular —ance at University lectures, regelmäßiger Besuch der Universitätsvorlesungen; to dance —ance on *or* upon a p., einem demütig aufwarten; to dance —ance on a lady, einer Dame den Hof machen; the —ance at the meeting was good, die Versammlung war zahlreich besucht; the —ance (at a restaurant, etc.) was bad, die Bedienung (in einer Restauration, ꝛc.) war schlecht; —ance list, namentliches Verzeichnis der bei einer Versammlung oder Prüfung anwesenden Personen. **—ant**, I. *adj.* begleitend; aufwartend. II. *s.* der Aufwartende; der Diener; der Begleiter; der Helfer; der Wärter (*in hospitals and asylums*); —ants, (*pl.*) die Dienerschaft, das Gefolge; shame is the —ant of vice, die Schande begleitet das Laster; his —ants never leave him, seine Begleitung läßt ihn nie allein.

Attenti—on, *s.* die Aufmerksamkeit; —on! stillgestanden! Achtung! to pay —on to a p., einem Höflichkeiten erweisen; he is paying Miss N. —ions, er macht Fräulein N. den Hof. **—ve(ly)**, *adj.* (*adv.*) aufmerksam (to a p., auf einen); an —ve ear, ein aufmerksames Ohr.

Attenuat—e, *v.a.* verdünnen, verringern, verkleinern; verjüngen, spitz auslaufen lassen. **—ed**, *p.p. & adj.* verdünnt; abgemagert; vermindert; spitzig zulaufend (*Bot.*). **—ion**, *s.* die Verdünnung; die Verminderung; die Abmagerung; die Verjüngung; die Verwitterung (des Gesteins); die Attenuation (*Brew.*).

Attest, *v.a.* bezeugen; bescheinigen; beweisen, dartun. **—ation**, *s.* das Zeugnis; die Bezeugung. **—or**, *s.* der Zeuge.

Attic, I. *adj.* attisch; — story, *see* —s; — base, der attische Säulenfuß; — order, die attische Säulenordnung (*obs.*). II. *s.* die Dachstube, das Mansardenzimmer; der Übersatz, das halbe Stockwerk (*Arch.*); —s, das Dachgeschoß. **—ism**, *s.* der Atticismus.

Attire, I. *s.* die Kleidung, der Anzug; der Putz; das Geweih (*of stags*). II. *v.a.* ankleiden, kleiden; schmücken.

Attitud—e, *s.* die Stellung, Haltung. **—inize**, *v.n.* sich in Positur setzen.

Attorney, *s.* der (nicht plaidierende) Anwalt; der Sachwalter; —general, der Ober-Staatsanwalt; — under power, bevollmächtigter Rechtsanwalt; power of —, die schriftliche Vollmacht. *Comp.* **—-general**, *s.* der Staatsanwalt; der Generalfiskal.

Attract, *v.a.* anziehen; an sich ziehen, auf sich (*acc.*) ziehen; the magnet —s iron, der Magnet zieht das Eisen an; to — attention, Aufmerksamkeit erregen. **—able**, *adj.* anziehbar. **—ile**, *adj.* anziehend. **—ion**, *s.* die Anziehung; das Reizende, Lockende; die Zauberkraft; power of —ion, die Anziehungskraft; to exert —ion, Anziehung ausüben; capillary —ion, die Kapillar-Attraktion; centre of —ion, der Anziehungsmittelpunkt; —ion of gravity, die Schwerkraft; the great —ion of the evening, das, was dem Abend seine Zugkraft verlieh, die Glanznummer des Abends. **—ive(ly)**, *adj.* (*adv.*) anziehend; she is very —ive, sie ist sehr reizend. **—iveness**, *s.* der Reiz, die Anziehung, das Anziehende, Reizende.

Attribut—able, *adj.* zuzuschreiben, beizulegen. **—e**, I. *v.a.* beilegen, zuschreiben, beimessen. II. *s.* (characteristic) das Attribut, die Eigenschaft;

(sign, symbol) das Zeichen, Kennzeichen; das Merkmal, Beizeichen (*Paint.*, *etc.*); das Ausgesagte, die Aussage, das Attribut (*Log.*) **—ion**, *s.* die Zuschreibung, Beimessung; die beigelegte Eigenschaft. **—ive**, I. *adj.* beilegend. II. *s.* das Attributiv, Beilegewort.

Attrition, *s.* das Abreiben, die Abnutzung; das Wundreiben der Haut; die unvollkommene Reue.

Attune, *v.a.* stimmen; harmonisch machen.

Auburn, *adj.* rotbraun, kastanienbraun, feuerblond.

Auction, *s.* die öffentliche Versteigerung, Auktion; to put up for — (to —, *v.a.*), in die Auktion geben, öffentlich versteigern, meistbietend verkaufen. **—eer**, *s.* der öffentliche Versteigerer, Auktionator.

Audaci—ous(ly), *adj.* (*adv.*) (daring) verwegen, keck, dreist, vermessen; (impudent) unverschämt, frech; (brave, bold) kühn. **—ty**, *s.* die Verwegenheit; die Frechheit, Unverschämtheit; die Kühnheit.

Audi—bility, *s.* die Hörbarkeit, Vernehmbarkeit. **—ble**, *adj.*, **—bly**, *adv.* hörbar, vernehmbar, laut. **—bleness**, *s.* die Hörbarkeit, Vernehmlichkeit. **—ence**, *s.* die Anhörung, Audienz, das Gehör; die Zuhörerschaft; he had an —ence of the Emperor, er hatte eine Audienz beim Kaiser; to grant *or* give an —ence to a p., einem eine Audienz erteilen *or* gewähren. **—t**, I. *s.* die Rechnungsuntersuchung. II. *v.a.* eine Rechnnug *or* Rechnungen untersuchen, prüfen. III. *attrib.*; —t ale, besonders starkes feines Bier; —t dinner, festliches Mahl am Tage der alljährlichen Rechnungsablage. **—tor**, *s.* der Zuhörer; der Rechnungsprüfer. **—torship**, *s.* das Amt eines Rechnungsrevisors. **—tory**, I. *adj.* das Gehör betreffend; —tory nerves, Gehörnerven. II. *s.* die Zuhörerschaft; (**—torium**,) der Hörsaal, das Auditorium. *Comp.* **—ence-chamber**, *s.* der Audienzsaal. **—ence-court**, *s.* Audienz-Gericht, geistliches Obergericht (des Erzbischop von Canterbury).

Auger, *s.* der große Bohrer, Schülpbohrer, Stangenbohrer; screw —, der Schneckenbohrer.

Aught, *s. pron.* etwas, irgend etwas; for — I care, meinetwegen; for — I know, for — that I can tell, so viel ich weiß; if — be wanting, wenn irgend etwas fehlen sollte.

Augment, I. *s.* das Augment (*Gram.*). II. *v.a.* vermehren; vergrößern. III. *v.n.* zunehmen. **—able**, *adj.* vermehrbar. **—ation**, *s.* die Vermehrung; (addition) der Zusatz; (growth) das Wachstum; (increase) die Zunahme; die Augmentation (*Mus.*); —ation of a p.'s salary, die Gehaltserhöhung. **—ative**, *adj.* vermehrend, vergrößernd. **—er**, *s.* der Vermehrer.

Augur, I. *s.* der Augur, Wahrsager. II. *v.a.* weissagen; deuten auf (*acc.*), bedeuten. III. *v.n.* weissagen; mutmaßen. **—ship**, *s.* das Augurenamt. **—y**, *s.* die Wahrsagung; das Anzeichen, die Vorbedeutung.

August, I. *adj.* erhaben, herrlich, hehr. II. *s.* der (Monat) August.

Auk, *s.* der Alk, Papageitaucher (*Orn.*).

Aulic, *adj.* zu einem Hofe gehörig; — council, ein aus Hofräten bestehendes Gericht.

Aunt, *s.* die Tante; great —, die Großtante; maiden —, unverheiratete Tante; — Mary, Tante Marie; — Sally, Wurfspiel mit Kokosnüssen. **—hood**, *s.* die Tantenschaft. **—y**, *s.* Tantchen.

Aur—ate, *s.* das Goldsalz. **—ic**, *adj.* das Gold betreffend, Gold-; —ic acid, die Goldsäure; —ic chloride, das Goldchlorid. **—iferous**, *adj.* goldhaltig. **—ous**, *adj.*; —ous chloride, das Goldchlorür.

Auri—cle, *s.* das äußere Ohr; —cle of the heart, das Herzohr. **—cula**, *s.* die Aurikel. **—cular**, *adj.* zu den Ohren gehörig, das Ohr betreffend Ohr-; (durch das Ohr) hörbar, Ohren-; heimlich; ohrförmig; —cular confession, die Ohrenbeichte. **—form**, *adj.* ohrförmig. **—scope**, *s.* der Ohrenspiegel. **—st**, *s.* der Ohrenarzt.

Aurochs, *s.* der Auerochs.

Auscultation, *s.* das (Zu-)Hören; die Auskultation, Behorchung (*Med.*).

Auspic—es, *pl.* die Auspizien, der Schutz, Beistand; die Vorbedeutung; das Wahrsagen aus dem Fluge und Geschrei der Vögel; under favourable —es, unter günstigen Vorbedeutungen; under the —es of Mrs. N., unter dem Schutze, Beistand, der Leitung der Frau N. **—ious(ly)**, *adj.* (*adv.*) günstig, glücklich.

Auster—e(ly), *adj.* (*adv.*) herb; streng, hart; an —e look, ein strenger Blick. **—ity**, *s.* die Strenge.

Austral, *adj.* südlich. **—ia**, *s. see the Index of Names.*

Auth—entic(ally), *adj.* (*adv.*) authentisch, glaubwürdig, zuverlässig; echt (*of documents, etc.*); rechtskräftig (*Law*); —entic melodies, richtige Melodien (*Mus.*). **—enticate**, *v.a.* als echt dartun, beglaubigen, bekräftigen, beurkunden. **—entication**, *s.* die Beglaubigung, der Beweis der Echtheit einer Sache. **—enticity**, *s.* die Authentizität, die Echtheit, die Glaubwürdigkeit. **—or**, **—ority**, *etc.*, *see* Author, etc.

Author, *s.* der Stifter, Urheber (*of mischief, etc.*); die Ursache; der Verfasser, Autor; der Schriftsteller; a great —, ein großer Schriftsteller; he is the — of, er ist der Verfasser von; she is the — of Romola, sie ist die Verfasserin von Romola; the — of my being, mein Schöpfer; —s' society, der Schriftstellerverband; his profession as an —, sein Schriftstellerberuf. **—ess**, *s.* die Verfasserin; die Schriftstellerin. **—ise**, **—isation**, *see* —ize, —ization. **—itative(ly)**, *adj.* (*adv.*) die nötige, gehörige Autorität *or* Gewalt habend; (authorized) bevollmächtigt; (commanding) gebieterisch; (peremptory) absprechend. **—itativeness**, *s.* das gebieterische Wesen, Wichtigtun. **—ity**, *s.* die Autorität, gesetzmäßige, rechtmäßige Macht und Gewalt; (influence) die moralische Gewalt, der Einfluß, das Gewicht; (prestige) das Ansehen; das Zeugnis (*drawn from documents, etc.*); (credibility) die Glaubwürdigkeit, Autorität; (sanction) die Genehmigung; (warrant) die Befugnis, Vollmacht; der Gewährsmann, die Quelle, der Beleg; the —ities, die Behörde, Obrigkeit; the police —ities, die Polizei(-Behörde); to be in —ity, die Gewalt in Händen haben; he is a great —ity on such matters, darin ist er ein großer Sachverständiger; he is a great —ity on bubonic plague, er ist ein bedeutender Spezialist über Beulenpest; he has no —ity over his pupils, er hat keine Macht über seine Schüler, er hat seine Schüler nicht in der Gewalt; and here he hath —ity from the chief priests to bind all that call on thy name, und er hat allhier Macht von den Hohenpriestern, zu binden alle, die Deinen Namen anrufen (*B.*); angels and —ities and powers, die Engel und die Gewaltigen und die Kräfte (*B.*); I have it on the best —ity, ich habe es aus der besten Quelle; I know it on good —ity, ich weiß es aus sicherer Hand; he had it on very good —ity, er erfuhr es aus vorzüglicher *or* durchaus zuverlässiger Quelle; on the —ity of, berechtigt durch, im Auftrage von; there is no —ity for such a proceeding, es giebt nichts, wodurch ein solches Verfahren gerechtfertigt werden kann; signed on —ity, amtlich bescheinigt; printed by —ity, mit obrigkeitlicher Erlaubnis gedruckt; published by —ity, amtlich bekannt gemacht *or* bekannt gegeben, offiziell. **—ization**, *s.* die Bevollmächtigung, Autorisation. **—ize**, *v.a.* bevollmächtigen, ermächtigen, berechtigen; billigen; gültig machen; für rechtmäßig erklären; durch Autorität einführen; —ized agent, der bevollmächtigte Unterhändler *or* Vertreter, der Bevollmächtigte; —ized capital, das Stammkapital; an —ized expression, ein durch den Gebrauch zulässig gewordener Ausdruck. —**ship**, *s.* die Autorschaft, Verfasserschaft; Schriftstellerei.

Auto—biographical, *adj.* autobiographisch. —**biography**, *s.* die selbstverfaßte Lebensbeschreibung, Selbstbiographie, Autobiographie. —**cracy**, *s.* die Selbstherrschaft, Autokratie; die Selbstbeherrschung (*Philos.*). —**crat**, *s.* der Selbstherrscher, unumschränkte Gebieter. —**cratic**, *adj.* allein herrschend, selbstherrlich. —**da-fé**, *s.* das Autodafe, Ketzergericht (der Inquisition). —**graph**, *s.* das Autograph, die eigene Handschrift, Selbstschrift, Urschrift; an —graph letter, ein mit eigener Hand *or* eigenhändig geschriebener *or* unterzeichneter Brief. —**graphic**, *adj.* eigenhändig geschrieben, autographisch. —**matic**, *adj.* automatisch, selbstbeweglich; maschinenmäßig. —**maton**, *s.* (*pl.* —mata) das Automat, die sich selbst bewegende Maschine. —**mobile**, *s.* das Auto, der Selbstfahrer, Triebwagen. —**mobilism**, *s.* der Selbstfahrersport. —**nomous**, *adj.* unabhängig, selbstherrschend. —**nomy**, *s.* die Selbstregierung, Selbstgesetzgebung; die Willensfreiheit der Menschen; die (vernünftige) Alleinherrschaft (*Philos.*). —**psy**, *s.* die Selbstschau, der Augenschein; die Leichenöffnung, Autopsie (*Med.*). —**telic**, *adj.* autotelisch, seinen Zweck in sich selbst habend. —**type**, I. *s.* der Faksimiledruck. II. *v.a.* mittelst Autotypie vervielfältigen.

Autumn, *s.* der Herbst. —**al**, *adj.* herbstlich.

Auxiliar—ies, *pl. see* —y forces. —**y**, I. *adj.* helfend, beistehend; —y verb, das Hilfszeitwort; —y forces *or* troops, die Hilfstruppen. II. *s.* der Hilfeleistende; das Hilfszeitwort.

Avail, I. *v.a.;* to — o.s. of a th., sich einer Sache bedienen, sich (*dat.*) eine Sache zu Nutze machen; I — myself of the opportunity, ich benutze die Gelegenheit. II. *v.n.* nützen, helfen; what —s it? was nützt es? it will — nothing, es wird nichts helfen *or* zu nichts nützen. III. *s.* der Nutzen; all was of no —, es half alles nichts. —**able**, *adj.*, —**ably**, *adv.* anwendbar (*obs.*); verfügbar; gültig; all —able troops, alle verfügbaren Truppen; return ticket —able for 3 days, Rückfahrkarte mit dreitägiger Gültigkeit; not —able to-day, heute nicht erhältlich (*C.L.*).

Avalanche, *s.* der Schneesturz, die Lawine.

Avant—-fosse, *s.* der Vorgraben einer Festung. —**-guard**, *s.* der Vortrab, die Vorhut.

Avaric—e, *s.* die Habsucht, der Geiz. —**ious**, (—**iously**,) *adj.* (*adv.*) habsüchtig, geizig.

Avast, *int.* genug! halt! (*Naut.*).

Avatar, *s.* die Menschwerdung eines Gottes (besonders des Wischnu); die Herabfahrt.

Avaunt, (*obs.*) *int.* fort! weg da! packe dich!

Ave, *s.* (— Maria,) das Ave Maria.

Avena, *s.* der Hafer (*Bot.*). —**ceous**, *adj.* haferartig.

Avenge, *v.a.* rächen; ahnden, strafen; to — o.s. on a p., sich rächen an einem; to — a murder, einen Mord rächen *or* (*poet.*) ahnden; für einen Mord Rache nehmen. —**r**, *s.* der Rächer.

Avenue, *s.* der Gang, die Allee; die (mit Bäumen besetzte) breite Straße; die Anfahrt.

Aver, *v.a.* (als wahr *or* mit Zuversicht) behaupten. —**red**, *imperf. & p.p. see* Aver.

Average, I. *adj.* durchschnittlich; — price, der Durchschnittspreis. II. *v.a.* den Durchschnitt finden; einen Durchschnittspreis machen; the fall of snow —d full 20 inches, der Schnee lag im Durchschnitt genommen volle 20 Zoll hoch; to — a loss, den Betrag eines Schadens in verhältnismäßige Teile teilen. III. *v.n.* durchschnittlich ausmachen; the price —s . . ., der Preis beträgt im Durchschnitt . . .; these spars — ten feet (in length), diese Spieren haben eine Durchschnittslänge von 10 Fuß. IV. *s.* der Seeschaden, die Havarie (*Naut.*); der Durchschnitt, das mittlere Verhältnis; der Durchschnittspreis; das Primgeld; petty —, die kleine, ordinä[re] Havarie; general *or* gross —, die große Havari[e]; simple *or* particular —, die einfache *or* besonde[re] Havarie; on an —, im Durchschnitt, durchschnit[t]lich, eins ins andre gerechnet; adjustment [of] —s, die Dispache.

Avers—e, *adj.* abgeneigt, abhold; ungünstig; am —e to it, es ist mir zuwider; my father wa[s] —e to my going, mein Vater war nicht geneig[t] mich gehen zu lassen. —**eness**, *s.* die Abg[e]neigtheit. —**ion**, *s.* die Abneigung, der Wide[r]wille, Abscheu; der Abscheu, Gegenstand d[es] Abscheus.

Avert, *v.a.* abwenden, ablenken, wegkehren; t[o] — a calamity, ein Unglück abwenden, verhüten with —ed gaze, mit abgewandten Blicken.

Aviary, *s.* das Vogelhaus.

Avidity, *s.* die Gier, Begierde (of, for, nach).

Avocation, *s.* das abhaltende Geschäft; Berufs[-]geschäft; die (einen in Anspruch nehmende) Be[-]schäftigung.

Avoid, *v.a.* (shun) meiden, vermeiden; (evade) ausweichen; (escape) entgehen; (leave) verlassen vereiteln, ungültig machen (*Law*); *see* Void; h[e] —s me, er meidet mich, geht mir aus dem Wege hält sich mir fern; these unpleasantnesse[s] would have been —ed if you had stayed away Sie würden diesen Unannehmlichkeiten entgange[n] sein, wenn Sie weggeblieben wären. —**able** *adj.* vermeidlich. —**ance**, *s.* das Meiden, Ver[-]meiden, die Vermeidung; *see* Voidance.

Avoirdupois, *s.* das schwere Handelsgewicht (1[6] Unzen auf das Pfund).

Avouch, *v.a.* behaupten, versichern, zu Gunste[n] einer Person anführen, anrufen.

Avow, *v.a.* offen bekennen; gestehen; anerkennen —**al**, *s.* das Bekenntnis, Geständnis. —**ed**, *p.p. & adj.* anerkannt; offen. —**edly**, *adv.* offen unverstellt, öffentlich; eingestandenermaßen seiner eignen Versicherung nach.

Await, *v.a.* abwarten; erwarten; entgegensehen what reward —s the good? welche Belohnun[g] erwartet die Guten? he is anxiously —ing you[r] answer, er sieht Ihrer Antwort gespannt ent[-]gegen; — instructions, Anweisung abwarten (*C. L.*).

Awake, I. *v.a.* wecken, erwecken, aufwecken. II *v.n.* erwachen, aufwachen. III. *adj.* wach, wachend; to be wide —, vollkommen wach sein; au[f] der Hut sein, schlau sein, sich vorsehen; to kee[p] —, wach bleiben; wach erhalten. —**n**, *v.a. & n see* Awake. —**ner**, *s.* der Wecker, Erwecker. —**ning**, I. *adj.* erwachend. II. *s.* das Erwachen das Erwecken; die religiöse Erweckung.

Award, I. *v.a.* zuerkennen, gerichtlich zusprechen II. *s.* das Urteil, der Ausspruch, Schiedsspruch die Zuerkennung, die Prämie; highest possi[-]ble —s, höchstmögliche Prämien; exhibits and —s Ausstellungsgegenstände und Prämien. —**er** *s.* der Schiedsrichter, der Preisrichter.

Aware, *adj.* gewahr; von etwas wissend; to b[e] —, wissen; to become — of a th., eine(r) S. ge[-]wahr werden; he is — of it, er weiß es, es ist ihm bekannt; I am quite — that she is your cousin ich weiß sehr wohl, daß sie eine Cousine vo[n] Ihnen ist; before I was —, ehe ich mich's versah.

Away, *adv.* weg, hinweg, fort; abwesend; t[o] send —, wegsenden, fortschicken; to go —, fort[-]gehen; to run —, weglaufen; to throw —, weg[-]werfen, vergeuden; to trifle —, vertändeln take the things —, nimm (die Sachen) weg decke ab; I was — at that time, damals wa[r] ich abwesend; — with him! fort *or* weg mi[t] ihm! whither — so fast? wohin so eilig? com[e] —! komm nur her! laugh —! lacht nur zu lacht nur tüchtig drauf los! (*coll.*); fire — schieß los! (*coll.*); eat —! eßt nur drauf los, nur zugegessen! to make — with o.s., sich (*dat.*) das Leben nehmen, sich ums Leben bringen; h[e] has made — with the money, er hat das Geld (über die Seite *or*) bei Seite gebracht; he has made — with all his fortune, er hat sein ganzes Vermögen verschwendet; to do — with a th., etwas abschaffen; to fall —, abfallen.

w—e, I. *s.* die Furcht, Scheu; die Ehrfurcht, heilige Scheu; to stand in —e of a p., sich vor einem scheuen; to command —e, Ehrfurcht gebieten; to inspire *or* strike a p. with —e (of a th.), einem Scheu einflößen (vor einer S.), einem Furcht einjagen. II. *v.a.* (heilige) Scheu einflößen; einschüchtern; einem Furcht einjagen; to —e s.o. into silence, einen durch Furcht zum Stillschweigen bringen. **—ful**, *adj.*, **—fully**, *adv.* ehrfurchterregend; furchtbar, furchterregend, feierlich, erhaben; sehr, höchst, schrecklich (*coll.*); an —fully cold day, ein schauderhaft *or* schrecklich kalter Tag. **—fulness**, *s.* (terribleness) die Furchtbarkeit; (venerableness) die Ehrwürdigkeit; (solemnity) die Feierlichkeit. *Comp.* **—e-inspiring**, *adj.* Ehrfurcht einflößend. **—e-struck**, *adj.* von Ehrfurcht ergriffen.

.weary, *adj.* müde, abgespannt.

.while, *adv.* eine Weile, auf kurze Zeit.

.wkward, *adj.*, **—ly**, *adv.* ungeschickt, linkisch, unbeholfen, tölpisch; (inconvenient) ungelegen; (annoying) widrig, verdrießlich; it makes me feel —, es geniert mich sehr; an — affair, eine dumme *or* fatale Geschichte. **—ness**, *s.* das tölpische, linkische, unbeholfene Wesen; die Ungeschicklichkeit, Ungeschlachtheit; the —ness of the situation suddenly struck him, das Heikle der Lage ging ihm plötzlich auf.

wl, *s.* die Ahle, der Pfriem (*Shoem. etc.*); der Spitzbohrer (*Carp.*); der Grünspecht. *Comp.* **—-shaped**, *adj.* pfriemenförmig.

.wn, I. *s.* die Granne, Achel. II. *v.a.* entgrannen.

.wning, *s.* das Schirmdach, Sonnenzelt; die ausgespannte Decke über Boote 2c., das Sonnendeck; die Marquise.

.woke, *imperf. of* Awake, *q. v.*

.wry, *adj.* schief; verkehrt (*fig.*).

.xe, *s.* die Art, das Beil; boarding —, Enterbeil; butcher's —, Fleischerbeil, der Schlägel. *Comp.* **—-head**, *s.* das Eisen der Axt. **—-helve**, *s.* das Axtstiel. **—-shaped**, *adj.* beilförmig. **—-stone**, *s.* der Beilstein.

xil, **—la**, *s.* die Achselgrube; der Blattwinkel (*Bot.*). **—lary**, *adj.* zur Achselgrube gehörig; achselständig (*Bot.*).

xiom, *s.* das Axiom, der allgemein anerkannte Grundsatz, Ursatz. **—atic**, *adj.*, **—atically**, *adv.* unumstößlich, durch sich selbst erwiesen, allgemein anerkannt, zweifellos, gewiß.

x—is, (*pl.* Axis *and* Axes) die Achse (*Geom. etc.*); der zweite Rückenwirbel (*Anat.*); die Achse (*Bot.*); der Wellbaum; principal —is, Hauptaxe; secondary —is, Nebenaxe; —is of the earth, Weltaxe. **—le**, *s.* (**—le-tree**, *s.*) die Achse; wheel and —le, das Rad an der Welle; —le-tree of a plough, das Pflughaupt. *Comp.* **—le-bed**, *s.* das Achsenfutter. **—le-pin**, *s.* der Achsennagel, die Lünse.

y, **—e**, *adv.* ja; the —es and the Noes, die Stimmen dafür und dawider; the —es have it, die Mehrheit ist für den Antrag, der Antrag ist angenommen; to —, (*Parl.*) mit ‚ja' stimmen.

yah, *s.* ostindisches Kindermädchen.

ye, *adv.* immer; for ever and —, auf immer.

zimuth, *s.* der Azimut.

zoic, *adj.* ohne Leben (*Geol.*).

zot—e, *s.* der Stickstoff. **—ed**, *adj.* mit Stickstoff verbunden. **—ic**, *adj.* Stickstoff enthaltend. **—ize**, *v.a.* mit Stickstoff schwängern.

zure, I. *adj.* himmelblau; azurn (*Poet.*). II. *s.* der Azur, die Smalte (*Min.*); das Himmelblau; das blaue Feld (*Her.*). *Comp.* **—-stone**, *s.* der Lasurstein. **—-tinted**, *adj.* himmelblau gefärbt.

zyma, *s.* das Fest der ungesäuerten Brote.

B

B, **b**, das B, b; h (*Mus.*); — flat, b (*Mus.*); — sharp, his, c (*Mus.*); *for abbreviations see the Index at the end of the English-German part;* he does n't know a — from a bull's foot, er ist so dumm, er kann keine fünf zählen (*coll.*).

Baa, I. *s.* das Blöcken. II. *v.n.* blöcken.

Babble, I. *v.n.* schwatzen, plaudern; murmeln, plätschern (*of brooks*); stammeln; undeutlich artikulieren; (vorlaut) anschlagen (*Sport.*). II. *v.a.* ausschwatzen. III. *s.* das Geschwätz; das Geplapper, Geplauder. **—r**, *s.* der Schwätzer.

Babe, *s.* kleines Kind (*B. & poet.*).

Baboon, *s.* der Pavian.

Baby, I. *s.* (*pl.* Babies) das kleine Kind, Kindlein, Kindchen; der Säugling. II. *attrib.;* — linen, — clothes, das Kinderzeug, die Kleinkinderwäsche. **—ish**, *adj.*, **—ishly**, *adv.* kindisch. **—hood**, *s.* die frühe Kindheit. *Comp.* **—-house**, *s.* das Puppenhaus.

Baccalaureate, *s.* das Baccalaureat.

Bacchanal, *s.* der Bachant; der Schwelger, Zechbruder; das Zechgelage, Bacchusfest. **—ia**, **—s**, *pl.* die Bacchusfeste, Bacchanalien. **—ian**, *adj.* bacchantisch, bacchanalisch; schwelgerisch; —ian song, das Bacchuslied, Trinklied.

Bacci—ferous, *adj.* beerentragend. **—vorous**, *adj.* beerenfressend.

Bachelor, *s.* der Junggesell; der Baccalaureus (*of arts, etc.*); — woman, weiblicher Hagestolz; old —, alter Hagestolz; —'s button, gemeine Lychnis (*Bot.*); der Wiesen-Hahnenfuß (*Bot.*). **—hood**, *s.* der Junggesellenstand; der Rang eines Baccalaureus.

Back, I. *s.* der Rücken; das Kreuz (*of a horse*); die Rückseite; die Kehrseite; — of the head, das Hinterteil des Kopfes; —s of the Colleges, the —s, Parkseite der (Cambridger) Colleges; — of a chair, die Lehne eines Stuhls; — of the chimney, die Kaminplatte; behind a p.'s —, hinter jemandes Rücken, heimlich; the — of a coach, die Rückseite einer Kutsche; — of the hand, Rückseite der Hand, die umgekehrte Hand; — of the neck, der Nacken; — of the rudder, die Fütterung *or* Verdoppelung des Steuerruders; — of a sword, der Rücken eines Schwertes; — to —, mit dem Rücken gegen einander gekehrt, Rücken gegen Rücken; a book with gilding on the —, ein auf dem Rücken vergoldetes Buch; to lay (a burden, etc.) upon s.o.'s —, einem (etwas) aufbürden; he has n't a shirt to his —, er hat kein Hemd auf dem Leibe; to turn one's —, sich abwenden; he had no sooner turned his —, than . . ., kaum war er fort, als . . .; to turn one's — upon a p., einem den Rücken kehren, ihn im Stiche lassen; he has completely turned his — upon them, er hat sie gänzlich aufgegeben, er will nichts mehr mit ihnen zu schaffen haben; his — is up, er ist sehr aufgebracht, er wird böse; the cat puts up her —, die Katze krümmt den Rücken. II. *adv.* zurück, hinterwärts; (— again), wieder, wiederum, wieder zurück; I shall be — again directly, ich werde gleich wieder da sein; he will be — to-morrow, morgen kommt er wieder; to come —, zurückkommen, wieder kommen; to go —, zurückgehen; to go — from one's engagements, seine Verbindlichkeiten nicht erfüllen; to keep —, zurückbehalten, nicht verabfolgen lassen; to look —, zurückblicken; in die Vergangenheit zurückblicken; a few years —, vor einigen Jahren. III. *v.a.;* to — a horse, ein Pferd besteigen (*Poet.*); zurücktreten lassen, zurückziehen; to — a (racing) horse, auf einen Renner wetten; to — (up), (support) a p., einen unterstützen, einem behülflich sein; he —ed me up manfully, er stand mir wacker bei; to — a letter, auf die Rückseite eines Briefes schreiben; to — a warrant, einen Verhaftsbefehl indossieren; to — the oars, die Rieme.

streichen, rückwärts rudern; to — the sails, die Segel backbrassen, backlegen; to — water, rückwärts rudern. IV. *v.n.* zurück treten, rückwärts gehen; to — out of an affair, sich aus einem Handel zurückziehen. V. *adj.;* — part, der hintere Teil; — parting, der Scheitel am Hinterkopf; — pedal, gegentreten (*Cycl.*); — pressure, der Gegendruck; the — numbers of a newspaper, die vorhergehenden Nummern eines Blattes; — room, die Hinterstube; — step, der Rücktritt; — stitch, hintersteppen, mit Hinterstichen nähen; — stroke, der Hub rückwärts (*Locom.*); — sweep, (— sweep of the waves) die Wiedersee; — tools, die Fileten (*Bookb.*); — yard, der Hinterhof. **—ed**, *adj.;* broad-—ed, breitrückig; broken-—ed, kreuzlahm. **—er**, *s.* der Unterstützer, einer der auf einen ꝛc. wettet; Cambridge —ers, Leute, die auf den Sieg von C. wetten. **—ward**, I. *adj.* spät (*in ripening*); träge; zurückgeblieben; schwerfällig; abgeneigt; this boy is —ward in learning, dieser Knabe lernt sehr schwer; he is rather —ward in school, er ist in der Schule ziemlich weit zurück; to be —ward in doing one's duty, seine Pflicht vernachlässigen; —ward children, Kinder, welche in ihrer Entwickelung zurückgeblieben sind; —ward course, der Rücklauf; —ward stroke, der Rückgang (*Mach.*). II. *adv.*, **—wards**, *adv.* rückwärts, zurück, nach dem Rücken zu; rückgängig; verkehrt; —wards and forwards, hin und her; to go —wards, rückwärts gehen. **—wardation**, *s.* der Deport (*C. L.*). **—wardness**, *s.* die Abgeneigtheit, der Widerwille; die Langsamkeit, Trägheit; langsame *or* späte Entwickelung, das Zurückbleiben. *Comp.* **—bite**, *v.a.* (die Abwesenden) verleumden, (ihnen) übel nachreden. **—biter**, *s.* der Verleumder. **—biting**, I. *adj.* verleumderisch. II. *s.* das Verleumden. **—board**, *s.* das Rückenbrett (for improving the carriage, um die Haltung junger Leute zu verbessern); die Rücksteife (*Bookb.*). **—bone**, *s.* der *or* das Rückgrat, der Rücken, die Charakterstärke, Festigkeit; he has no —bone, er hat keine Schneid *or* rechte Willenskraft; er ist ein Waschlappen (*contempt.*). **—door**, *s.* die Hintertür. **—gammon**, *s.* das Puffspiel. **—ground**, *s.* der Hintergrund; die Vertiefung (*Paint.*); to keep in the —ground, im Hintergrunde bleiben; to keep s.th. in the —ground, eine Sache wissentlich zurückhalten. **—-hand**, *s.* die Rückhand; (*in cpds.*) mit Rückhand gespielt (*L.T.*). **—-handed**, *adj.* mit umgewandter Hand; a —-handed blow, ein mit umgewandter Hand versetzter Schlag; schief, doppelsinnig; a —-handed compliment, ein spöttisches Kompliment. **—-settlements**, *pl.* die Binnenkolonien. **—side**, *s.* die Hinterseite (*of a house*); der Hintere (*vulg.*). **—sight**, *s.* das Visier, hintere Absehen (*on a gun*). **—slide**, *v.n.* zurückweichen, abfallen, abtrünnig werden. **—slider**, *s.* der Abtrünnige. **—sliding**, I. *p. see* —slide. II. *s.* das Abfallen, der Abfall, die Abtrünnigkeit. **—-staff**, *s.* der Sonnenhöhenmesser. **—stairs**, *pl.* die Hintertreppe, Geheimtreppe; —stairs influence, geheimer Einfluß. **—stay**, *s.* die Lünette (*Carp.*); (*pl.*) die Pardunen (*Naut.*). **—-stitch**, *s.* der Hinterstich, Steppstich. **—sword**, *s.* der Haudegen. **—water**, *s.* das Stauwasser. **—woods**, *pl.* die Wälder im Westen Nordamerikas. **—woodsman**, *s.* der weiße Bewohner solcher Wälder, Hinterwäldler.

Bacon, *s.* der Speck; flitch of —, die Speckseite; gammon of —, der Schinken; a slice of —, eine Speckschnitte; fried eggs and —, Spiegeleier und Speck; to save one's —, mit heiler Haut davon kommen (*vulg.*). *Comp.* **—-faced**, *adj.* mit rundem Vollmondsgesicht. **—-fed**, *adj.* fett, speckgenährt.

Bad, (Worse, Worst,) *adj.*, **—ly**, *adv.* schlecht; schlimm; böse; übel; schädlich; krank (*coll.*); sehr stark, bedeutend; a — cold, eine schlimme *or* starke Erkältung; a — heart, ein schlecht[es] Herz; a — finger, ein böser (schlimmer) Finge[r]; — blood (*fig.*), böses Blut; that 's — form, d[as] schickt sich nicht; he is in a — way, es steht schlim[m] mit ihm; er ist sehr krank; to be —ly in wa[nt] of food, an Nahrungsmitteln starken Mang[el] leiden; things are going —ly with me, es g[eht] mir schlecht *or* schlimm; — debts, schlechte, zwe[i]felhafte Schulden; — fortune, das Unglüc[k]; with a — grace, widerwillig, unfreundlich; a — job, ein schlimmer Handel; — courses, ways [of] life, der schlechte Lebenswandel; to mend one['s] — ways, sich bessern; — news, schlechte Na[ch]richt(en); — language, (oaths, *etc.*) Flüche, (o[b]scenities) Zoten; to use — language, sich g[e]meiner Redensarten bedienen, schimpfen, fluchen; this is a — match in colour for . . ., die Farbe paßt nicht gut zu . . .; reading in t[he] dark is very — for the eyes, das Lesen i[m] Dunkeln ist den Augen sehr schädlich; that [is] too —, das ist zu arg, zu stark; it was too — [of] you to go away, es war nicht schön von di[r] wegzugehen; matters went from — to wors[e], die Sache wurde schlimmer und schlimmer; [he i]s quite gone to the —, er ist völlig auf Abwe[ge] geraten, ist gänzlich verdorben (*coll.*). **—nes[s]**, *s.* die Schlechtigkeit; der schlechte Zustand; d[ie] Lasterhaftigkeit; die Bosheit.

Bade, *imperf. of* Bid.

Badge, *s.* das Kennzeichen, Abzeichen, Zeichen; d[as] Ordenszeichen; good conduct —, das Ehren[-] zeichen für gute Führung (*Mil.*).

Badger, I. *s.* der Dachs (*Zool.*); der privilegier[te] Kornhändler. II. *v.a.* hetzen, plagen. **—in[g]**, *s.* die Quälerei. *Comp.* **—-baiting**, *s.* d[ie] Dachshetze. **—-legged**, *adj.* dachsbeinig.

Badigeon, *s.* der Gipsmörtel, Steinkitt.

Badinage, *s.* das leichte, scherzhafte Gespräch; d[er] Scherz; die Neckerei.

Baffl—e, *v.a.* vereiteln; verwirren, in Verwi[r]rung bringen; täuschen; to —e pursuit, d[ie] Verfolgung (eines Feindes, ꝛc.) vereiteln; to — the designs of an enemy, die Pläne ein[es] Feindes vereiteln; he was —ed, er geriet [in] Verwirrung. **—ing**, *p. & adj.* vereitelnd, täu[]schend; —ing winds, unstäte, widrige Winde.

Bag, I. *s.* der Beutel, die Tasche; der Sack; d[er] Ballen; a — of wool, ein Ballen (240 Pf[d.]) Wolle; the gentlemen of those days wore — (*i.e.* bag-wigs), die Herren der damaligen Zeit trugen Haarbeutel; to make a good —, vi[el] Wild erlegen, viel Jagdglück haben (*Sport.*). [II.] *attrib.;* — frame, der metallene Bügel einer Reis[e]tasche. III. *v.a.* in einen Sack tun, einsacken; ei[n]stecken. IV. *v.n.* bauschen, aufschwellen. **—ful**, einen Sack voll; by —fuls, säckeweise, in (ganze[n]) Säcken. **—gy**, *adj.* sackartig, bauschig, falte[n]werfend. *Comp.* **—-clasp**, **—-fastener**, *s.* d[ie] Schließvorrichtung. **—-fox**, der zur Jagd ei[n]gefangene und dann aus dem Sack gelasse[ne] Fuchs. **—man**, *s.* der Handelsreisende (*vulg.*). **—pipe**, I. *s.* die Sackpfeife, der Dudelsack. I[I.] *v.a.;* to —pipe the mizzen, das Besansegel ba[ck] legen (*Naut.*). **—piper**, *s.* der Dudelsackpfeife[r].

Bagasse, *s.* das ausgepreßte Zuckerrohr.

Bagatelle, *s.* die Kleinigkeit; das Bagatellspiel.

Baggage, *s.* das Gepäck; das Heergerät; d[as] Mensch, Weibsbild; bag and —, Sack und Pa[ck].

Baggings, *s.* das Packleinen.

Bagnio, I. *s.* das Badehaus; das Bordell (*rare*); das Sklavenhaus (*in Turkey*). II. *attrib.;* — keeper, der Bademeister; der Bordellwirt.

Bail, I. *s.* der Bürge; die Bürgschaft; to go — stand — for a p., Bürgschaft für einen leiste[n], für einen bürgen; to give —, einen Bürg[en] stellen; excessive —, übertrieben hohe Bür[g]schafts-forderung (*or* -leistung); out upon — auf Bürgschaft aus dem Gefängnisse entlasse[n], losgebürgt; no — allowed, Bürgschaft abg[e]lehnt; — accepted, gegen Bürgschaft freigelasse[n].

II. *v.a.* Bürgschaft leisten für, Bürge werden für, gegen Bürgschaft frei geben. **—able,** *adj.* verbürgbar, was gegen Bürgschaft entlassen werden kann. **—ee,** *s.* der Depositar, Verwahrer. **—er, —or,** *s.* der Deponent (*Law*). **—iff,** *s.* der Amtmann, Landvogt; (special —iff) der Gerichtsdiener; der Verwalter, Renteneinnehmer (*on estates*). **—iwick,** *s.* der Amts- *or* Gerichtsbezirk eines Bailiff; die Vogtei, das Schulzengericht. *Comp.* **—bond,** *s.* der Bürgschaftsschein.

Bairn, *s.* das Kind (*Scotch*).

Bait, I. *s.* der Köder, die Lockspeise; die Mahlzeit *or* Erfrischung auf der Reise (*for horses, etc.*); die Lockung (*fig.*); live —, der Köderfisch; to take the —, sich ködern lassen; auf den Leim gehen; livery and — stables, Ställe, in denen fremde Pferde versorgt werden, Unterkunft für Pferde; at — with, eingestellt bei (*of horses*). II. *adj.;* — house, das Wirtshaus an der Landstraße (wo die Pferde gefüttert werden). III. *v.a.* ködern, ankörnen; (harass) quälen, plagen; auf der Reise füttern; to — one's hook with a th., etwas an die Angel stecken; to — a bull, einen Stier mit Hunden hetzen. IV. *v.n.* Erfrischung zu sich nehmen, füttern. **—ing,** I. *s.;* bull —ing, die Stierhetze. II. *attrib.;* —ing place, die Einkehr.

Baize, *s.* der Boi, roter *or* grüner Fries; Überzug, Vorhang; grüner Tisch, die Spielbank.

Bak—e, *v.* I. *a.* backen; härten; brennen; this bread is well —ed, dies Brod ist gut gebacken; the bricks are not well —ed, die Steine sind nicht gut gebrannt. II. *n.* backen. **—er,** *s.* der Bäcker; a —er's dozen, dreizehn; —er's shop, der Bäckerladen. **—ery,** *s.* die Bäckerei. **—ing,** I. *s.* das Backen; das Brennen; (batch) ein Ofen voll, das Gebäck; at one —ing, was auf einmal gebacken wird; bread of the first —ing, Brod vom ersten Gebäck. II. *attrib.;* —ing dish, die Backschüssel. *Comp.* **—ehouse,** *s.* das Backhaus. **—e-meat,** *s.* die Fleischpastete; das Backwerk.

Balance, I. *s.* die Wage; das Gleichgewicht (*also fig.*); der Saldo, die Bilanz (*C. L.*); (surplus) der Überschuß; Libra (*Astr.*); die Unruhe (*Horol.*); in the —, in der Schwebe (*fig.*); to strike a —, eine Rechnung ausgleichen, einen Saldo ziehen; — (in favour of a p.), das Saldo gut haben (einer P.); to have a — in one's favour, eine Summe gut haben; a trifle will turn the —, eine Kleinigkeit in der Wage wird den Ausschlag geben; his life hung in the —, er schwebte zwischen Tod und Leben; that threw his cool judgment off its —, das brachte sein (sonst so) kühles Urteil aus dem Gleichgewicht; — of accounts, der Rechnungsabschluß; — of torsion, die Torsionswage; — of trade, Handelsbilanz; — of power, das politische Gleichgewicht; the hydrostatic —, hydrostatische Wage; assay —, Probierwage; spring —, Federwage. II. *attrib.;* — account, das Bilanzkonto. III. *v.a.* wägen, abwägen; erwägen (*arguments, etc.*); im Gleichgewicht halten, aufwiegen, ausgleichen; bilanzieren, abschließen, saldieren (*C.L.*); the pleasure is more than —d by the danger, die Gefahr überwiegt bei weitem das Vergnügen; to — an account, eine Rechnung abschließen, saldieren; to — the amount of an invoice, den Betrag einer Faktura ausgleichen, saldieren; to — accounts with a p., mit einem Abrechnung halten; to — the ledger, das Hauptbuch schließen; the expenses — the receipts, die Ausgaben betragen eben so viel wie die Einnahmen; balancing thereby my account, womit Sie meine Rechnung ausgleichen *or* begleichen wollen; a rope-dancer, who does not — his body, ein Seiltänzer, der seinen Körper nicht im Gleichgewichte hält; balancing pole, die Balancierstange. **—ers,** *pl.* die Schwingkolben (*Ent.*). *Comp.* **—-sheet,** *s.* der Bilanzbogen. **—-wheel,** *s.* das Steigrad an der Unruhe.

Balcony, I. *s.* der Söller, Balkon, Austritt; die Hintergallerie (*Naut.*). II. *attrib.;* — stalls, numerierte Balkonplätze (*Theat.*).

Bald, *adj.,* **—ly,** *adv.* kahl; nackt; schmucklos, dürftig (*fig.*): a — translation, eine kahle, trockene Übersetzung; — buzzard, der Fischadler; — eagle, weißköpfiger Seeadler. **—ness,** *s.* die Kahlheit. *Comp.* **—-head,** *s.* der Kahlkopf. **—-headed,** *adj.* kahlköpfig. **—-pate,** *see* —-head.

Baldachin, *s.* der Baldachin, Thronhimmel.

Balderdash, *s.* der Mischmasch, das Gewäsch, das dumme Geschwätz, die Salbaderei.

Baldric, *s.* der Gürtel; das Wehr-, Degen-Gehenk.

[1]**Bale,** I. *s.* der Ballen; a — of cotton, ein Ballen Baumwolle; — goods, Güter in Ballen. II. *v.a.* in Ballen verpacken, emballieren.

[2]**Bale,** *v.a. & n.* Wasser mit Eimern ausschöpfen; to — (out) a boat, ein Boot ausschöpfen.

[3]**Bale,** *s.* das Elend, Unglück (*obs.*). **—ful,** *adj.,* **—fully,** *adv.* elend; unheilbringend.

[4]**Bale,** *s.* das Signalfeuer, Freudenfeuer (*rare*); der Scheiterhaufen (*obs. poet.*). *Comp.* **—-fire,** *s.* das Signalfeuer; der Scheiterhaufen.

Balister, *s.* die Armbrust; der Armbrustschütze.

Balk, I. *s.* der Furchenrain (Rain)-balken, Rain (*Agr.*); der Balken (*Arch.*); der Querstrich (*fig.*); (disappointment) die Täuschung; my ball is in —, mein Ball ist im Quartier, innerhalb des Striches (*Bill.*). II. *v.a.* aufhalten, hemmen; täuschen, vereiteln; (einem) Hindernisse in den Weg legen; übergehen, meiden; als einen Rain lassen. III. *v.n.* (*of horses*) scheuen (at a th., vor einer S.).

[1]**Ball,** *s.* der Ball; die Erdkugel; die Kugel (*Artil.*); der Ballen (*Typ. etc.*); a billiard —, eine Billardkugel; a cricket —, tennis —, ein Spielball; a — of yarn, ein Garnknäuel; — of the foot, der Ballen am Fuß; the — and socket joint, das Kugelscharnier; to take the — at the rebound (*fig.*), die Gelegenheit wahrnehmen; to keep the — rolling (*fig.*), das Gespräch im Gang erhalten, gegenseitig fortsetzen; to pocket a —, einen Ball machen, ins Loch spielen (*Bill.*); to hole one's own —, sich verlaufen (*Bill.*); to miss the —, einen Kicks machen (*Bill.*); to strike a — off the table, einen Ball versprengen; to leave a — against the cushion, einen Ball dicht an die Bande legen, spielen; to have a game at —, Ball spielen. **—oon, —ot,** *see* Balloon, Ballot. *Comp.* **—-cartridge,** *s.* die Kugelpatrone. **—-cock,** *s.* der Zulaß- und Absperrhahn. **—-valve,** *s.* das Kugelventil.

[2]**Ball,** *s.* der Ball, die Tanzgesellschaft; are you going to this —? werden Sie auf diesen Ball gehen?

Ballad, *s.* die Ballade; das Volkslied, Gassenlied. *Comp.* **—-monger,** *s.* der Balladenschmierer, Dichterling; der Balladenkrämer. **—-singer,** *s* der (die) Balladensänger(in), Bänkelsänger(in).

Ballast, I. *s.* der Ballast; in —, ohne Schiffsladung, nur mit Ballast versehen. II. *v.a.* ballasten, mit Ballast beladen; als Ballast dienen; im Gleichgewicht erhalten.

Ballet, *s.* das Ballet.

Ballist—a, *s.* die Ballista, Wurfmaschine. **—ic,** *adj.* ballistisch. **—ics,** *pl.* die Ballistik.

Balloon, I. *s.* der Ballon, Luftballon, das Luftschiff. II. *attrib.;* — ascent, der Aufstieg im Ballon.

Ballot, I. *s.* die Stimmkugel, Ballotierkugel; der Stimmzettel; die Kugelwahl, Kugelung; voting by —, das Ballotieren, die geheime Abstimmung durch Stimmzettel. II. *attrib.;* — ball, die Wahlkugel. III. *v.n.* durch Kugeln abstimmen, losen, wählen, ballotieren. *Comp.* **—-box,** *s.* die Wahlurne, das Stimmkästchen.

Balm. *s. see* Balsam; **wohlriechende Salbe;**

schmerzstillendes Mittel ; der Trost (*fig.*) ; — of Gilead, der Mekkabalsam. —**y**, *adj.* balsamisch; lindernd; —y breath, sanfter Hauch; —y slumbers, ruhiger Schlaf.

Balsam, *s.* der Balsam ; die Balsamine (*Bot.*) ; — of sulphur, der Schwefelbalsam. —**ic**, *adj.* würzig, erquickend, balsamisch. —**ine**, *s.* die Balsamine (*Bot.*). *Comp.* —-**apple**, *s.* der Balsamapfel; die Balsamgurke.

Balust—**er**, *s.* die Geländersäule. —**rade**, *s.* die Balustrade, Brustlehne ; das Geländer, Treppengeländer, Brückengeländer.

Bamboo, I. *s.* der Bambus. II. *attrib.;* — cane, das Bambusrohr (*Bot.*), der Bambusstock.

Bamboozle, *v.a.* betrügen, beschwindeln (*coll.*).

Ban, I. *s.* die öffentliche Bekanntmachung ; der Bann, die Acht ; der Fluch ; das feierliche Verbot ; —s, *see* —ns ; — of the empire, die Reichsacht ; he was placed under the — of the empire, er wurde in die Reichsacht erklärt ; the — of the church was pronounced against him, der Kirchenbann wurde über ihn ausgesprochen. II. *v.a.* in den Kirchenbann tun ; verfluchen ; verbieten. —**ns**, *pl.* das (kirchliche) Aufgebot (vor der Heirat) ; their —ns have already been published, sie sind schon aufgeboten worden; she forbade the —ns, sie tat gegen die Heirat Einspruch.

Banana, *s.* die Banane. *Comp.* —-**tree**, *s.* der Bananenbaum, Pisangbaum.

Band, I. *s.* das Band, die Binde ; (tie) die Schnur; die Plinte, Leiste, der Streif (*Arch.*) ; die Musik(-antentruppe), Musikkapelle, die Kapelle ; (bond) die Fessel, Bande ; (troop) die Bande, Rotte, Schar, Kompagnie ; —s, das Bäffchen ; der Priesterkragen ; — of robbers, Räuberbande ; military —, Militärmusik, Militärkapelle ; German —, umherziehende Musikanten; regimental —, die Regimentsmusik ; — of (*itinerary*) musicians, die Musikantentruppe. II. *v.n.;* to — together, sich vereinigen, sich zusammentun, sich zusammenrotten. —**age**, I. *s.* die Binde, der Verband. II. *v.a.* verbinden. —**it**, *s.* (*pl.* —its, —itti) der Bandit, der Straßenräuber. —**oleer**, *s.* das Bandelier; die Patrontasche. —**rol**, *s.* das Fähnchen. *Comp.* —**box**, *s.* die Hutschachtel, der Pappkasten; he looks as if he had come out of a —box, er sieht aus wie aus dem Ei geschält, er ist immer geschniegelt und gebügelt. —-**master**, *s.* der Kapellmeister, Musikdirektor (*Mil.*). —**sman**, *s.* der Militärmusiker.

Bandog, *s.* der Kettenhund, Bullenbeißer.

Bandy, I. *s.* ein gekrümmter Stock ; das Ballspiel (mit gekrümmten Stöcken). II. *v.a.;* to — words with s.o., Worte mit einem wechseln, hin und her streiten ; her name was freely bandied about, ihr Name war in aller Leute Munde. *Comp.* —-**legged**, *adj.* krummbeinig.

Bane, *s.* das Gift ; das Verderben (*fig.*) ; her brother has been the — of her existence, ihr Bruder hat ihr das Leben vergiftet *or* war der Fluch ihres Lebens. —**ful**, *adj.* verderblich, tödlich; giftig.

Bang, I. *s.* der heftige Schlag, Schmiß ; das Zuschmeißen; der Klapp, Knall ; — went the door, bums *or* klappsflog die Tür zu. II. *v.a.* schlagen ; zuwerfen (*a door, etc.*) ; to — a p. about, einen mißhandeln, puffen, knuffen.

Bangle, *s.* der Arm- *or* Fuß-ring, die Arm- *or* Fuß-spange.

Banian, *s.* der indische Kaufmann. *Comp.* —-**days**, *pl.* magere Tage (an welchen die Matrosen kein Fleisch bekommen), Fasttage (*coll.*).

Banish, *v.a.* verbannen, des Landes verweisen; to — sorrow, die Sorgen verscheuchen ; to — the thought of . . ., die Gedanken an . . . aus der Seele vertreiben *or* verbannen, sich (*dat.*) aus dem Sinne schlagen. —**ment**, *s.* die Verbannung.

Banister, *see* Baluster ; the —s, das Geländer.

Banjo, *s.* die Negerguitarre, der Banjo.

Bank, I. *s.* (mound of earth) die Erderhöhung, Anhöhe ; der Damm (*of a road*) ; das Ufer, Gestade (*of a river*) ; die Bank (*C. L.*) ; — of a river, das Ufer eines Flusses ; — of violets, ein Veilchenbeet ; — of oars, die Ruderbank ; sculptor's —, der Bossierstuhl ; — of England, die englische Bank, Bank von England ; — of issue, Zettelbank ; — of circulation, Girobank ; joint stock —, Aktienbank ; the sand —s, die Sandbänke ; the —s of London, die Banken Londons ; the —s of the Thames, die Ufer der Themse ; to keep the —, die Bank halten (*Gam.*) ; to break the —, die Bank sprengen ; to have an account in the —, Geld bei der Bank stehen haben. II. *v.a.* in die Bank einlegen ; dämmen. III. *v.n.* Bankgeschäfte machen. —**er**, *s.* der Bankier. —**ing**, I. *s.* das Bankgeschäft; the —ing (up) of the fire, die Dämpfung des Feuers (*Locom. etc.*). II. *attrib.;* —ing business, das Bankgeschäft, Wechselgeschäft; —ing house, das Bankhaus, Bankgeschäft, die Bank ; —ing transactions, Wechselgeschäfte. —**rupt**, I. *s.* der Bank(e)rottier(er), Zahlungsunfähige ; to become —rupt, Bankerott machen, seine Zahlungen einstellen ; to declare o.s. a —rupt, sich als zahlungsunfähig angeben ; mass of a —rupt's estate, die Konkursmasse. II. *adj.* bankerott, bankbrüchig, zahlungsunfähig, fallit ; —rupt in health, bankerott an Gesundheit ; poor —rupt heart, armes, gebrochenes Herz. —**ruptcy**, *s.* der Bank(e)rott, das Falli(sse)ment ; fraudulent —ruptcy, betrügerischer Bankerott ; court of —ruptcy, das Konkursgericht ; statute of —ruptcy, das Bankerottmandat ; he filed a petition in —ruptcy, er beantragte die Bankerotterklärung. *Comp.* —-**account**, *s.* das Bankkonto ; to open a —-account, sich (*dat.*) bei einer Bank ein regelmäßiges Konto einrichten, Geld bei einer Bank stehen lassen. —-**bill**, *s.* der Bankwechsel ; die Banknote (*Amer.*). —-**holiday**, *s.* der Bankfeiertag. —(**ing**)-**book**, *s.* das Bankbuch. —-**note**, *s.* die Banknote. —-**stock**, *s.* die Bankaktie(n).

Banlieu, *s.* die Bannmeile, das Weichbild.

Banner, I. *s.* das Banner, die Fahne ; das Fähnlein, Fähnchen (*on a lance; also Bot.*). II. *attrib.;* — screen, der Vorhang vor dem Kamin mit eingesticktem Wappen. —**et**, *s.* das Fähnchen ; der Bannerherr.

Bannock, *s.* ein schottischer Kuchen, Haferkuchen.

Banquet, I. der Schmaus, das Festmahl, Bankett ; (*also* —te) das Bankett (*Railw., etc.*) ; die Wallbank (*Fort.*). II. *v.n.* schmausen. —**er**, *s.* der Schmauser. —**ing**, I. *s.* das Schmausen. II. *attrib.;* —ing room, das Festzimmer. *Comp.* —**ing-house**, *s.* die Festhalle.

Banshee, *s.* weiblicher Geist, der nach irischem (und schottischem) Volksglauben durch klägliche Töne den Tod eines Familiengliedes vorhersagt.

Bantam, I. *s.* das Bantamhuhn, Zwerghuhn ; der Zwerg, Knirps. II. *adj.* winzig.

Banter, I. *s.* der Scherz, die Neckerei. II. *v.a.* necken, hänseln, aufziehen. —**er**, der Necker.

Bantling, *s.* das kleine Kind, der kleine Balg.

Banyan, *s.*, —-**tree**, *s.* der indische heilige Feigenbaum, der Banianbaum.

Bapti—**sm**, *s.* die Taufe. —**smal**, *adj.* zur Taufe gehörig ; —smal service, die Taufhandlung ; —smal font, der Taufstein ; —smal vow, der Taufbund. —**st**, *s.* der Täufer ; der Taufgesinnte ; John the —st, Johannes der Täufer. —**stery**, *s.* das Baptisterium, die Taufkapelle. —**ze**, —**se**, *v.a.* taufen. —**zer**, —**ser**, *s.* der Täufer.

Bar, I. *s.* die Stange (*of wood or metal*), Barre ; (bolt) der Riegel ; das Querholz (*of a cask, etc.*) ; (*of a watch*) Knebel ; die Zugwage (*of a carriage, etc.*) ; der Taktstrich (*Mus.*) ; das Hindernis, der Querstrich (*fig.*) ; (sand —) die Sandbank, -barre ; die Schranken eines Gerichtshofes ;

das Gericht; die Rechtsanwälte, welche vor Gericht plaidieren dürfen, die Sachwalter; der Advokatenstand; der Schenktisch, das Büffet; die Schenke, der Ausschank; der Schrägbalken (*Her.*); the bench and the —, Richter und Sachwalter; a — of gold, eine Goldbarre; the prisoner at the —, der Gefangene vor den Schranken; the — of God, das letzte Gericht; to bring before the — of public opinion, vor die Schranken der Öffentlichkeit bringen, dem Urteil der Welt unterwerfen; a — to further proceedings, ein Hemmschuh für weiteres Vorgehen; die peremptorische Einrede, welche die Aktion des Klägers völlig hemmt (*Law*); he was educated for the —, er hat Jura studiert; he is at the —, er ist Jurist; he was called to the —, er wurde in den Advokatenstand *or* unter die Advokaten aufgenommen; he was summoned before the — of the court, er wurde vor das Gericht gefordert; to cross the —, die vor der Einfahrt in den Hafen liegende Sandbank überschreiten, ins offne Meer hinauskommen; toll —, der Schlagbaum; harbour —, der Hafenbaum; window —s, Fensterstäbe; — of a grate, der Roststab; in cross —s, karriert. II. *v.a.* sperren, versperren; aufhalten, hemmen, hindern (*fig.*); riegeln, zuriegeln, verrammeln (*a door, etc.*); (forbid) verbieten; every doorway —red and loopholed, jeder Torweg verrammelt und mit Schießscharten versehen; —ring accidents, von unvorhergesehen Zufällen abgesehen; —ring mistakes, Irrtümer abgerechnet; to — out, aussperren. III. *prep.* außer, ausgenommen. **—red**, *adj.*; a 5- —red gate, ein Tor mit 5 Stangen. **—rel**, **—ricade**, **—rier**, **—rister**, *see* Barrel, Barricade, Barrier, Barrister. *Comp.* **—-iron**, *s.* das Stangeneisen, Stabeisen. **—-keeper**, *s.* der Schenkwirt, die Schenkwirtin. **—man**, *s.* der Kellner in einer Schenke. **—maid**, *s.* das Schenkmädchen, die Schenkmamsell. **—-parlour**, *s.* die Schenkstube. **—-sinister**, *s.* linker Schrägbalken.

[1]Barb, I. *s.* der Bart (*also Bot.*); der Widerhaken (an einem Pfeil, einer Angel). II. *v.a.* mit Widerhaken versehen; —ed, mit Widerhaken versehen; —ed wire, der Stachelzaundraht. **—ate**, *adj.* bärtig. **—el**, *s.* die Barbe (*Icht.*). **—er**, *s.* der Barbier; surgeon —er, Barbier und Chirurg.

[2]Barb, *s.* das Berberroß, Roß (*poet.*).

Barbacan, *see* Barbican.

Barbar—ian, I. *adj.* fremd; barbarisch; roh, ungesittet. II. *s.* der Ausländer; der Barbar, wilde Mensch; der rohe Mensch. **—ic**, *adj.* barbarisch; ausländisch, fremd. **—ism**, *s.* die Rohheit, Wildheit; der Barbarismus; die Sprachwidrigkeit. **—ity**, *s.* die Grausamkeit, Unmenschlichkeit; die Rohheit. **—ous**, *adj.*, **—ously**, *adv.* barbarisch; ungesittet, roh; grausam.

Barbecue, I. *s.* das Holzgerüst zum Braten oder Räuchern von Fleisch; großer Bratrost, auf dem ganze Tiere gebraten werden; ganzes gebratenes Tier (*e.g.* Spanferkel, Ochs); die Terrasse, auf der Kaffeebohnen geröstet werden (*Amer.*). II. *v.a.* räuchern, dörren; ein Tier ganz braten; Kaffeebohnen rösten (*Amer.*).

Barberry, *s.* die Berberitze; die Berberitzenbeere.

Barbican, *s.* der Wachtturm; das Außenwerk; die Schießscharte.

Bard, *s.* der Barde, keltischer Sänger; Sänger (*poet.*); Dichter (*poet.*).

[1]Bare, I. *adj.* nackt, bloß, entblößt; (wanting) bar, leer; (scanty) arm, dürftig; the — facts, die nackten Tatsachen; at the — mention of it, bei der bloßen Erwähnung davon; the plot was laid —, die Verschwörung wurde entdeckt; the ladies appeared with — necks, die Damen trugen ausgeschnittene Kleider; the — necessaries of life, die äußersten Bedürfnisse des Lebens; to scud under — poles, vor Tag und Takel treiben (*Naut.*). II. *v.a.* entblößen; when the prince passed, the people —d their heads, als der Fürst vorbeikam, nahmen die Leute die Hüte ab; he —d his breast, er entblößte seine Brust. **—ly**, *adv.* nackt; kaum; nichts als; —ly 3 feet, knapp 3 Fuß, kaum 3 Fuß. **—ness**, *s.* die Nacktheit, Blöße; die Armut, Dürftigkeit. *Comp.* **—bones**, *s.* der abgemagerte Mensch (*coll.*). **—-chested**, **—necked**, *adj.* mit bloßer Brust, mit bloßem Halse. **—faced**, *adj.*, **—facedly**, *adv.* frech, unverschämt; a —faced falsehood, eine schamlose Lüge. **—facedness**, *s.* die Dreistigkeit, Schamlosigkeit, Frechheit. **—footed**, *adj.* barfuß. **—headed**, *adj.* barhaupt, mit bloßen Kopfe, mit entblößtem Haupte. **—legged**, *adj.* barbeinig, mit bloßen Beinen.

[2]Bare, *obs. imperf. of* Bear.

Baret, *see* Barret.

Bargain, I. *s.* der Handel, Kauf; der Vertrag; der billige Einkauf; das Gekaufte; to get a thing a dead (*or* cheap) —, etwas spottwohlfeil kaufen; to make a good —, ein gutes Geschäft machen *or* abschließen; billig einkaufen; a bad (losing) —, ein böser (unvorteilhafter) Handel; the — was struck, der Handel wurde geschlossen; to make the best of a bad —, sich so gut wie möglich aus einem schlechten Handel ziehen; it's a (great) —, es ist spottbillig; a chance —, ein zufälliger, billiger Kauf; to drive a hard — with . . ., streng handeln mit . . .; a —'s a —, Kauf ist Kauf; 't is a —! topp! abgemacht! es bleibt dabei! into the —, in den Kauf, obendrein. II. *v.n.* handeln; (chaffer) feilschen; to — for, bedingen, um etwas handeln; this was more than I —ed for, dieses habe ich nicht erwartet; to — away, verhandeln; by —ing I got the book 3 marks cheaper, ich habe 3 Mark vom Preise des Buches abgehandelt; as —ed for, wie verabredet. **—er**, der Handelnde.

Barge, *s.* das große Boot, Flußschiff; langes, breites Lastschiff; das Prachtschiff; großer Vergnügungswagen, Kremser (*Amer.*); coal —, das Kohlenschiff. **—e**, *s.* der Bootsmann. *Comp.* **—master**, *s.* der Bootseigentümer.

Barilla, *s.* die Barilla, rohe Soda.

[1]Bark, I. *s.* die Borke, Rinde; Peruvian —, Chinarinde; tanner's —, die Lohe. II. *v.a.* abrinden, entrinden (*trees, etc.*); to — a p.'s shins, einem die Haut des Schienbeins abstoßen. *Comp.* **—ing-iron**, *s.* das Schäleisen.

[2]Bark, *see* Barque.

[3]Bark, I. *v.n.* bellen; to — at, anbellen; to — when one cannot bite, den Mond anbellen; great —ers are no biters, bellende Hunde beißen nicht. II. *s.* das Gebell; his — is worse than his bite, er ist nicht so böse wie er aussieht.

Barley, *s.* die Gerste; die Graupen; pearl —, Perlgraupen. *Comp.* **—-brake**, *s.* ein ländliches Spiel. **—-broth**, *s.* die Gerstensuppe; die Graupensuppe. **—-corn**, *s.* das Gerstenkorn; $\frac{1}{3}$ Zoll. **—-mow**, *s.* die Gerstenmahd. **—-sugar**, *s.* der Gerstenzucker. **—-water**, *s.* der Gerstenschleim.

Barm, *s.* die Hefe, Bärme. **—y**, *adj.* hefig.

Barn, I. *s.* die Scheune, Scheuer, der Kornboden. II. *attrib.*; — floor, die Dreschtenne, Tenne. *Comp.* **—-door**, I. *s.* das Scheunentor. II. *attrib.*; —(-door) fowls, Hühner. **—-owl**, *s.* die Schleiereule.

[1]Barnacle, *s.* die Entenmuschel; *see* Bernicle.

[2]Barnacle, *s.* die Bremse, der Nasenknebel (*for unruly horses*). **—s**, *pl.* die Brille, der Kneifer, Zwicker (*coll.*).

Baromet—er, *s.* das Barometer, Wetterglas. **—ric**, *adj.* barometrisch; —ric variations, Barometerschwankungen.

Baron, *s.* der Baron, Freiherr; —s of the exchequer, die vier Richter im Schatzkammergerichte; — of beef, die zwei ungeteilten Lendenstücke des Ochsen. **—age**, *s.* die Freiherrschaft; die Barone und Pairs (*coll.*). **—ess**, *s.* die Baronin, Freifrau, Freiin. **—et**, *s.* der Baronet.

—etage, *s.* die Baronetswürde; die Baronets (*coll.*); Verzeichnis der Baronets. **—etcy**, *s.* die Baronetswürde, Freiherrnwürde, der Freiherrnstand. **—ial**, *adj.* einem Baron gehörig, Barons . . ., freiherrlich. **—y**, *s.* die Besitzung *or* Würde eines Freiherrn.

Barouche, *s.* die Barutsche.

Barque, *s.* das Barkschiff, ein dreimastiges Fahrzeug.

Barrack, I. *s.* die Barracke. II. *attrib.;* — yard, — square, der Kasernenhof. **—s**, *pl.* die Kaserne. *Comp.* **—-master**, *s.* der Kaserneninspektor.

Barrage, *s.* der Damm, die Buhne.

Barrel, I. *s.* das Faß, die Tonne; der Lauf einer Flinte, der Gewehrlauf; die Trommel einer Uhr, der Cylinder; die Walze (*of an organ, etc.*); der Stiefel (*of a pump*); die Welle (*of the capstan*); — of the boiler, der zylindrische Rumpf des Kessels; fire —s, Feuerfässer; earth —, der Schanzkorb; thundering —s, Brandfässer auf Brandern; a double —led gun, eine zweiläufige Flinte; — of a pen, der Federkiel. II. *v.a.* in ein Faß tun, einpacken. *Comp.* **—-organ**, I. *s.* die Drehorgel. II. *attrib.;* —-organ grinder, der Orgeldreher.

Barren, *adj.* unfruchtbar; wüst, arm; eitel. **—ness**, *s.* die Unfruchtbarkeit; der Mangel (an einer S.); —ness of intellect, die Geistesleere.

Barret, (**Baret**,) *s.* das Birett (*R. C.*).

Barricade, I. *s.* die Verschanzung, Verrammelung, Barrikade; (— of trees), der Verhau. II. *v.a.* verrammeln, sperren, verschanzen.

Barrier, *s.* die Schranke; das Fallgatter; der Schlagbaum; die Verschanzung, Schutzwehr; die Grenzwehr; die Barriere (*Railw.*); (obstacle) das Hindernis, der Einhalt. **—s**, *pl.* die Schranken (*at a tournament*).

Barrister, **—-at-law**, *s.* der (vor Gericht plaidierende) Rechtsanwalt, Sachwalter, Advokat.

[1]**Barrow**, *s.* die Trage, Bahre. *Comp.* **—man**, *s.* der Schubkärrner.

[2]**Barrow**, *s.* der Grabhügel; das Hünengrab, der Tumulus.

[3]**Barrow**, **—-pig**, *s.* geschnittenes Schwein.

Barter, I. *s.* der Tausch, Tauschhandel. II. *v.a.* vertauschen; to — for, austauschen gegen. **—er**, *s.* der Tauschhändler.

Baryt—a, *s.* die Schwererde. **—es**, *pl.* der Baryt.

Barytone, (**Baritone**,) *s.* der Bariton.

Basalt, *s.* der Basalt. **—ic**, *adj.* basaltisch; basalt, Basalt-, aus *or* von Basalt.

Base, I. *adj.*, **—ly**, *adv.* niedrig; niederträchtig, gemein, verächtlich (*fig.*); gering, unedel (*of metals*); (illegitimate) unehelich; falsch; — treachery, schändlicher Verrat; — coin, falsches Geld, geringhaltige Münze. II. *s.* die Grundlage, Basis, der Grund; der Fuß, das Fußgestell (*Arch.*); die Grundfläche (*of a solid*); die Grundlinie (*of a triangle, etc.*); die Basis, Grundzahl (*Arith.*); die Basis (*Mil.*); die Base (*Chem.*); prisoner's —, das Barlaufspiel. III. *v.a.* gründen; to be —ed on, auf eine S. gegründet sein, auf eine S. sich gründen, auf einer S. basieren. **—less**, *adj.* grundlos. **—lessness**, *s.* die Grundlosigkeit. **—ment**, *s.* das Fundament; —ment story, das Kellergeschoß, vertieftes Erdgeschoß. **—ness**, *s.* die Niedrigkeit (des Standes); die Gemeinheit, Niederträchtigkeit; die Schändlichkeit; die Falschheit (*of coin*); the —ness of his birth, seine niedrige (*or* seine uneheliche) Geburt. *Comp.* **—-ball**, *s.* der Grundball (*L.T.*); der Baseball (*Amer.*). **—-born**, *adj.* niedrig von Geburt; unehelich. **—-burner**, *s.* der Füllofen. **—-line**, I. *s.* die Standlinie (*Surv.*); die Grundlinie (*L.T.*). II. *adj.;* —-line game, das Spiel an der Grundlinie (*L.T.*). **—-minded**, *adj.* niedrig gesinnt. **—-mindedly**, *adv.* niedrigen Sinnes. **—-souled**, *adj.* von gemeiner Seele.

Bashful, *adj.*, **—ly**, *adv.* schamhaft, verschämt; schüchtern, blöde, scheu; a — girl, ein schüchternes Mädchen. **—ness**, *s.* die Schamhaftigkeit; die Schüchternheit, Blödigkeit.

Basi—c, *adj.* die Base betreffend, basisch. **—s**, *s.* (*pl.* Bases), die Grundlage, Basis.

[1]**Basil**, I. *s.* die Schräge, die zugeschärfte Kante (*Carp.*). II. *v.a.* schräg zuschleifen.

[2]**Basil**, *s.* braunes Schafleder.

[3]**Basil**, *s.* das Basilienkraut (*Bot.*); field —, (— weed), die Wirbeldoste, Weichdoste; sweet —, die Basilienmünze. **—ica**, *s.* die Basilika (*Arch.*). **—isk**, *s.* der Basilisk (*Myth.*, *Artil.*); die Kron-Eidechse, der Basilisk (*Zool.*); transfixed by the eye of a —isk, vom Basiliskenblick getroffen.

Basin, *s.* das Becken (*also Geol. & Anat.*); die Schale; der Wasserbehälter; der Kessel (*Geog.*); das Flußgebiet (*of a river*); die Docke, das Becken, der kleine Hafen (*Naut.*); die Schleifschale (*Glassw.*); das Steiferblech (*for hats*); — of a dock, die Kumme bei einer Docke; — of a port, der Binnenhafen; washing —, das Waschbecken; rinsing —, die Spülschüssel, das Spülschälchen. *Comp.* **—-shaped**, *adj.* beckenförmig.

Bask, *v.n.* sich sonnen, sich wärmen. *Comp.* **—ing-shark**, *s.* der Riesenhai.

Basket, I. *s.* der Korb; der Steinkorb (*Artil.*); *see* Gabion; work —, Arbeitskorb. II. *attrib.;* — handle, der Korbhenkel. **—s**, *pl.* die Korbwaren (*C.L.*). **—ful**, *s.* der Korbvoll; by —fuls, korbweise, in Körben. *Comp.* **—-carriage**, *s.* die Korbchaise, der Korbwagen. **—-hilt**, *s.* der Säbelkorb. **—-hilted**, *adj.* mit überflochtenem Korbe versehen. **—-woman**, *s.* die Korbträgerin, Höferin. **—-work**, *s.* die durchbrochene Arbeit; das Flechtwerk (*Fort.*).

Bas-relief, *s.* das Basrelief, die flach *or* halberhabene Bildhauerarbeit (*Sculp.*).

[1]**Bass**, I. *s.* der Baß (*Mus.*). II. *adj.;* — clef, der F-Schlüssel, Baßschlüssel; — singer, der Bassist; — string, die Baßsaite; — voice, die Baßstimme. **—oon**, *s.* das Fagott, die Baßpfeife. **—oonist**, *s.* der Fagottist. *Comp.* **—et-horn**, *s.* das Bassethorn. **—-viol**, *s.* die Baßgeige.

[2]**Bass**, *s.* der (Linden-)Bast; die Bastmatte. *Comp.* **—-mat**, **—-matting**, *s.* die Bastmatte.

[3]**Bass**, *s.* der Barsch.

[4]**Bass**, *s.* der Kohlenschiefer.

Bast, *s.* der Bast; das Bastseil; *see* [2]Bass.

Bastard, I. *s.* der Bastard, Bankert; (mongrel) der Mischling. II. *adj.* unehelich; (false) unecht, falsch, verfälscht; von außerordentlich großem *or* kleinem Kaliber (*Artil.*); — file, die Bastardfeile, Vorfeile; — oats, der Wildhafer; — title, der Schmutztitel (*Typ.*). **—ize**, **—ise**, *v.a.* als Bastard erklären, der unehelichen Geburt überführen. **—y**, *s.* die uneheliche Geburt, Bastardschaft. *Comp.* **—-wing**, *s.* der Afterflügel.

[1]**Bast—e**, *v.a.* (einen Braten) mit Fett begießen, betröpfeln; (beat) durchprügeln (*coll.*); —ing ladle, der Begießlöffel. **—inade**, **—inado**, I. *s.* die Bastonnade, Prügelstrafe. II. *v.a.* die Bastonnade geben.

[2]**Bast—e**, *v.a.* mit weiten Stichen lose nähen, zusammenheften; —ing thread, der Anschlagefaden. **—ion**, *s.* die Bastei, das Bollwerk. **—ioned**, *adj.* bastioniert, mit Bastionen versehen.

[1]**Bat**, *s.* die Fledermaus (*Zool.*); as blind as a —, stockblind.

[2]**Bat**, I. *s.* der Knüttel; der Schlägel, das Schlagholz (*Crick.*); das Schlagholz (*of hatmakers*). II. *v.n.* schlagen, den Schlägel handhaben (*Crick.*). **—let**, *s.* der Waschbleuel. **—on**, *s.* der Dirigenstab, Taktstock. **—ten**, *see* Batten. **—ting**, *s.* das Schlagen. *Comp.* **—-fowling**, *s.* die (nächtliche) Vogeljagd; (mittels Netz und Licht) Fackeljagd; der Gimpelfang, die Schwindelei. **—ting-machine**, *s.* die Schlagmaschine. **—sman**, (**—ter**,) *s.* der Schläger; he is a good —sman *or* —ter, er schlägt vortrefflich.

Batch, *s.* das Gebäck, der Schub (*Bak.*); der Satz (*Pott.*); die Quantität auf einmal verfertigter

Dinge von derselben Art; the first —, die Vorschicht (*Found.*); the whole — of them, die ganze Sippschaft *or* Gesellschaft.

Bate, *see* Abate; with —d breath, mit verhaltenem Atem; he won't — an inch, er will nicht das Geringste nachlassen.

Bath, *s.* das Bad; Order of the —, der Bathorden; the —s, das Badehaus, die Badeanstalt. **—e**, *v.n. & a.* baden; to be—ed in tears, in Tränen schwimmen. **—er**, *s.* der Badende. **—ing**, I. *p.* badend. II. *s.* das Baden. III. *attrib.*; —ing accommodation, die Badegelegenheit; —ing place, der Badeplatz; der Badeort; —ing season, die Badezeit, Badesaison. *Comp.*—**ing-costume**,—**ing-dress**, *s.* das Badekostüm. **—ing-drawers**, *pl.* die Badehose. **—ing-gown**, *s.* der Bademantel. **—ing-machine**, *s.* der Badewagen, die Badekutsche. **—-room**, *s.* die Badestube, das Badezimmer. **—-tub**, *s.* die kleine tragbare Badewanne.

Bathos, *s.* das Schwülstige in der Schreib- und Sprechart, das Bathos; der Schwulst; das Niedrigkomische; die Herabwürdigung.

Batrachian, I. *adj.* Frosch-. II. *s.* das Froschtier.

Batta, *s.* die Soldzulage für ostindische Truppen im Kriegszustande.

Battalion, *s.* das Bataillon.

Battels, *s.* die Ausgabeberechnung eines Studenten zu Oxford für Verpflegung im College.

[1]**Batten**, I. *s.* die dünne, schmale Latte; die Lade (*Weav.*); —s of the hatches, die Lukenschalken (*Naut.*). II. *v.a.* mit Latten versehen, bekleiden (*a wall*); to — down, zunageln, verschalmen (*Naut.*); —ed door, (—-door,) die Leistentür. **—ing**, *s.* das Verlatten, die Verlattung.

[2]**Batten**, *v.* I. *n.* fett werden, gedeihen; — on, sich mästen (an *or* mit einer S.), schwelgen (in einer S.). II. *a.* mästen; düngen, fruchtbar machen (*land*).

Batter, I. *s. see under* Bat; der Schlagteig (*Cook.*); — pudding, ein Pudding von geschlagenen Eiern, Mehl und Milch. II. *v.a.* schlagen; zerschlagen; bestürmen (*Mil.*); abnutzen; to — down, niederschießen, zusammenschießen, niederschmettern; to — in, einschießen; an old —ed hat, ein alter, abgetragener Hut; a —ed shield, ein zerhackter Schild. **—er**, *s.* der Zertrümmerer, Schläger. **—y**, *s.* die Schlägerei; die tätliche Mißhandlung (*Law*); die Batterie (*Mil.*); die Batterie (*Phys.*); die Walkkammer (*of hatmakers*); action for assault and —y, Klage wegen Tätlichkeiten; Daniell's —y, die Daniellsche Säule; immersion —y, Tauchbatterie; magnetic —y, magnetisches Magazin; voltaic —y, die Voltaische Säule; to raise a —y, eine Batterie aufwerfen; to arm a —y, die Kanonen aufpflanzen; —y of field-artillery, bewegliche Batterie; —y of horse-artillery, reitende Batterie; floating —y, schwimmende Batterie. *Comp.* **—ing-ram**, *s.* der Sturmbock. **—ing-train**, *s.* der Stückzug, die Belagerungslaffette.

Battle, I. *s.* die Schlacht; small —, das Gefecht, Treffen; naval —, die Seeschlacht; the — of Waterloo, die Schlacht bei Waterloo; the — of the Pyramids, die Schlacht bei den Pyramiden; to join —, die Schlacht anfangen, den Feind angreifen; to offer —, eine Schlacht anbieten; to give —, die Schlacht liefern; angreifen; pitched —, eine regelmäßige Schlacht; to fight one's own —, sich ohne fremde Hülfe durchschlagen; — royal, die allgemeine Schlägerei; — of words, das Wortgefecht. II. *v.n.*; to — for, streiten um; to — it out, es auskämpfen (*coll.*). **—ment**, *s.* die Brustwehr mit Zinnen, Festungsmauer; —ments, die Zinnen. **—mented**, *adj.* mit Zinnen versehen, zinnengekrönt. **—-array**, *s.* die Schlachtordnung. **—-axe**, *s.* die Streitaxt, das Enterbeil. **—-cry**, *s.* der Schlachtruf, das Kriegsgeschrei. **—-field**, *s.* das Schlachtfeld. **—-piece**, *s.* das Schlachtgemälde.

Battledoor, Battledore, *s.* das Rakett, der Federballschlägel; — and shuttlecock, das Federball(spiel).

Battue, *s.* die Treibjagd; das Treibjagen.

Bauble, Bawble, *s.* das Spielzeug; die Nippsache, der Tand; die Spielerei, Kleinigkeit; die Narrenpritsche.

Baulk, *see* Balk.

Bawbee, *s.* der halbe Penny (*Scotch*).

Bawd, I. *s.* der Kuppler, die Kupplerin. II. *v.a.* kuppeln. **—ry**, *s.* die Kuppelei; die Unzüchtigkeit. **—y**, *adj.* unzüchtig.

Bawl, *v.a. & n.* schreien; laut ausrufen; (bellow) brüllen; plärren (*as children*); to — s.th. after a p., einem etwas nachschreien.

[1]**Bay**, *adj.* rötlichbraun; (light) — horse, der Fuchs. **—ard**, *s.* das rotbraune Pferd, der Rotbraune.

[2]**Bay**, *s.* (—-tree) der Lorbeerbaum (*Bot.*); rose —, der Oleander. *Comp.* **—-leaf**, *s.* das Lorbeerblatt. **—-rum**, *s.* der Pimentspiritus.

[3]**Bay**, *s.* die Bai, Bucht; der Meerbusen, der Busen; das Fach, die Abteilung (*Build.*); a barn of two —s, eine Scheune mit zwei Bansen; head —, das Oberhaupt (*Hydr.*). *Comp.* **—-salt**, *s.* das Seesalz. **—-window**, *s.* das viereckige Erkerfenster *or* viereckig ausgebaute Fenster.

[4]**Bay**, *s.*; to stand at —, sich widersetzen, sich zur Wehre setzen; to keep at —, hinhalten, abwehren; he kept her pursuers at — until . . ., er hielt ihre Verfolger so lange hin, bis . . .; to hold at —, in Schach halten; the stag at —, der sich zur Wehr setzende Hirsch.

[5]**Bay**, *v.n.* bellen; anschlagen.

Bayonet, I. *s.* das Bajonett; sword —, das Haubajonett; to carry a position at the point of the —, eine Stellung mit stürmender Hand nehmen; with fixed —s, mit aufgepflanztem Seitengewehr. II. *v.a.* mit dem Bajonett erstechen; he was —ted, er wurde niedergestochen.

Bazaar, *s.* der Bazar; die Verkaufshalle; der Warenmarkt; der Marktplatz; das Warenhaus.

Be, *ir.v.n.* sein; bleiben; vorhanden sein, existieren; there is, there are, es ist, es sind, es giebt; there is a man, es giebt einen Mann; letters to — answered, zu beantwortende Briefe; let him —! laß ihn in Ruhe! let it —! rührt es nicht an! — that as it may, dem sei, wie ihm wolle; it is with me as with you, es verhält sich mit mir wie mit Ihnen; to — well *or* ill, sich wohl *or* übel befinden; how are you to-day? wie geht es Ihnen *or* wie befinden Sie sich heute? what is that to you? was macht Ihnen das aus? what is she at? was hat sie vor? they are at it as soon as we leave them, so bald wir sie verlassen, zanken sie sich (*coll.*); so — it, so sei es; how much is it? wieviel kostet das? wieviel macht das? (*coll.*); the weather is very fine to-day, is it not? nicht wahr, das Wetter ist heute wunderschön? (*As aux. with present participle expressing incompleteness and continuity*) I am reading, ich lese; I was telling him a story when you came, als Sie kamen, erzählte ich ihm gerade eine Geschichte; I have just been drinking tea, ich habe eben Tee getrunken; I shall — writing whilst you are practising, ich werde beim Schreiben sein, während Sie üben; to — reading, beim Lesen sein, gerade lesen. (*As aux. with infinitive expressing necessity or condition*) he is to come to-day, er soll heute kommen; he is to die, er muß sterben; his wife that is to —, seine zukünftige Frau; if I were to die, wenn ich sterben sollte. (*As aux. of the passive*) werden; I shall — loved, ich werde geliebt werden; it is to — hoped, es steht zu hoffen. **—ing**, *see* Being. *Comp.* **—-all**, *s.*; the —-all and end-all, das Ein und Alles.

Beach, I. *s.* der Strand, das Gestade, (Meeres-) Ufer. II. *v.a.* auf den Strand ziehen.

Beacon, *s.* die Bake; der Leuchtturm, die Feuerwarte; der Leitstern (*fig.*); to mark by —s, abbaken. **—age**, *s.* das Bakengeld.

Bead, I. *s.* das Kügelchen, Perlchen (*of a rosary*); die Perle; der Tropfen (*on wine, etc., or of perspiration*). II. *attrib.*; — cuffs, Manschetten mit Perlenstickerei. **—s**, *pl.* Perlen, Korallen, der Rosenkranz; to tell one's —s, den Rosenkranz beten; to string —s, Perlen anreihen. **—ing**, *s.* die Perlenstickerei; das Leistenwerk, der Perlstab (*Arch.*). **—roll**, *s.* das Verzeichnis derjenigen, für die in Kirchen gebetet werden soll. **—sman**, *s.* der Fürbitter (*obs.*); Bewohner eines Armenhauses, Armenhäusler. **—swoman**, *s.* die Fürbitterin (*obs.*); Armenhäuslerin. **—-work**, *s.* die Perl(en)stickerei.

Beadle, *s.* der Kirchenvogt; der Gerichtsbote; der Pedell; (parish —) der Büttel (*Law*).

Beagle, *s.* der Spürhund; Spion; to run with the —s, mit der Meute (als Sport) laufen.

[1]**Beak**, *s.* der Schnabel (*of birds*); die Röhre (*of a still*); die Schnauze (*of vessels, etc.*); die Spitze; die obrigkeitliche Person (*sl.*); — of an anvil, das Amboßhorn; — of a prow, die Schiffsschnabelspitze. **—ed**, *adj.* (— -shaped) schnabelförmig; geschnäbelt.

[2]**Beak**, *see* Bask (*Scotch*).

Beaker, *s.* der Becher; das Becherglas (*Chem.*).

Beal, *v.n.* eitern, schwären (*prov.*).

Beam, I. *s.* der Balken; der (Haupt-)Balken (*Build.*); der (Deck-)Balken (*Shipb.*); der Lagerbalken, Brückenträger (*of a bridge*); der Hebebaum (*of a drawbridge*); der Weberbaum (*of a loom*); der Baum, die Deichsel (*of a plough*); der Wag(e)balken (*of a balance*); der Balancier (*of steam-engines*); die Breite (*of a ship*); der Strahl, Lichtstrahl; der Glanz (*of the eye*); the —s of the moon, die Mondstrahlen; draw —, der Wendelbaum; — of a windlass, der Haspelbaum; — of the roof, der Dachbalken; — of a bell, der Glockenbalken; right on the —, dwars ein (*Naut.*). II. *v.n.* strahlen; —ing countenance, strahlendes Gesicht. *Comp.* **—-compasses**, *pl.* der Stangenzirkel. **—-ends**, *pl.*; the ship is on her —-ends, das Schiff liegt ganz auf der Seite; he is on his —-ends, er sitzt in der Klemme (*sl.*). **—-engine**, *s.* Dampfmaschine mit Balancier.

Bean, *s.* die Bohne; broad —, Saubohne; haricot —, Stangenbohne; French —, grüne Bohne; new —s, junge Bohnen. *Comp.* **—-stalk**, *s.* die rankende Bohne, Bohnenranke.

[1]**Bear**, I. *s.* der Bär; der Baissier (*C.L.*); the — growls, der Bär brummt; the Great and Little —, der große und der kleine Bär; she —, die Bärin. II. *attrib.*; — fur, der Bärenpelz. **—ish**, *adj.* bärenhaft; plump, mürrisch. *Comp.* **—-baiting**, *s.* die Bärenhetze. **—-garden**, *s.* der Bärenzwinger; (*fig.*) lärmende Versammlung. **—-leader**, *s.* der Bärenführer. **—'s-ear**, *s.* das Bärenöhrchen, die Aurikel (*Bot.*). **—'s-grease**, *s.* das Bärenfett. **—skin**, *s.* der Bärenpelz, das Bärenfell; die Bärenmütze (*of a grenadier*).

[2]**Bear**, *ir.v.* I. *a.* tragen (*a burden*); (bring, give) bringen, überbringen; tragen (*fruit, etc.*); zur Welt bringen, gebären (*children*); hegen (*ill-will, love, etc.*); tragen, führen (*a name, etc.*); vertragen, ertragen, aushalten (*a p. etc.*); dulden, leiden (*pain, etc.*); to — a loss, einen Verlust tragen, leiden; I (will) — the blame, ich nehme es auf mich, ich trage die Schuld; to — o.s. well, sich gut betragen, sich gut halten; to — in mind, sich erinnern, im Gedächtnis behalten; sich (*dat.*) eine Sache hinters Ohr schreiben (*coll.*); — my warning in mind, vergessen Sie meine Warnung nicht; to — witness, Zeugnis ablegen; — a little to the right, wenden Sie sich ein wenig rechts; the tea could — a little more sugar, der Tee könnte noch ein wenig Zucker vertragen; this dress will not — turning, dieses Kleid läßt sich nicht kehren; the text will not — such an interpretation, die Stelle kann nicht so ausgelegt werden; to — s.o. a grudge, Groll gegen einen hegen; to — a p. goodwill, einem gewogen sein; I — no hatred, ich empfinde keinen Haß; this word does not — that sense, dies Wort hat jenen nicht Sinn, darf nicht in dem Sinne genommen werden; he —s a charmed life, sein Leben ist gefeit, er ist (stich- und kugel-)fest; it will be a disgrace, if they — it, es wird eine Schande sein, wenn sie es sich gefallen lassen; — a hand! faß an! greif zu! faß zu! to — a date, datiert sein; to — a resemblance to, Ähnlichkeit haben mit; — and forbear, leide und meide; capable of —ing arms, waffenfähig; to bring to —, in Schußweite bringen; geltend machen; I cannot — him, ich kann ihn nicht ausstehen; I will — you company, ich werde dir Gesellschaft leisten; the love he —s me, die Liebe, die er für mich hegt; it —s no relation at all to . . ., es steht in gar keinem Verhältnis zu . . .; born and bred, von Geburt und Erziehung; **— away**, fort *or* davon tragen; **— down**, niederdrücken; he —s down all before him, er überwindet alles, drückt alles vor sich nieder; **— off**, wegtragen, entführen; **— out**, unterstützen, verteidigen, bestätigen; you can — out my statement, Sie können meine Erzählung bekräftigen; **— up**, stützen, unterstützen; — up the helm! laß das Schiff mehr mit dem Winde gehen. II. *n.* tragen; fruchtbar werden, tragen; leiden, dulden; this tree will — next year, dieser Baum wird nächstes Jahr tragen; **— away**, das Schiff abfallen lassen, um vor dem Winde zu segeln; — away! Helm luvwärts! **— down** upon, stoßen auf (*acc.*); zu erreichen streben, alle Segel beisetzen um etwas einzuholen; **— to** the right, left, sich rechts, links halten; **— up**, Stand halten, Mut behalten, fest bleiben; to — up under adversity, im Unglück nicht verzagen; to — up against, widerstehen; to — up against misfortune, im Unglück den Mut nicht sinken lassen, dem Unglück Trotz bieten; to — up before the wind, vor dem Winde hinsegeln; to — up towards (*the coast*), auf (*acc.*) hinsegeln; that does not — **upon** the question, das hat keinen Bezug auf die Frage, das hat mit der Frage nichts zu tun; to bring to — upon (*or* on) . . ., etwas eine Sache (*or* Person) beeinflussen lassen; the guns were brought to — upon . . ., das Feuer wurde auf . . . gerichtet; **— with**, geduldig ertragen, Nachsicht haben mit. **—able**, *adj.*, **—ably**, *adv.* erträglich, zu ertragen. **—er**, *s.* der Träger; der Schildhalter (*Her.*); der (indische) Diener; der Überbringer (*of a letter*); der Inhaber (*of a bill*); —er of a despatch, Überbringer einer Depesche; the —ers, die Leichenträger. **—ing**, I. *p. see* Bear. II. *s.* das Tragen; das Betragen, die Haltung; die Beziehung, der Bezug; (relation) das Verhältnis; die Richtung, Lage (*Surv., etc.*); die Hauptfigur eines Wappens; die Spannweite, Tragweite (*Arch.*); das Lager (*Mach.*); I know him by his noble —ing, ich kenne ihn an seiner edeln Haltung; it has no —ing on this matter, es bezieht sich nicht auf diese Sache; to take the —ings, die Gegend aufsuchen, sich orientieren; there is no —ing with him, er ist unausstehlich; his arrogance is past —ing, sein Hochmut ist unerträglich, unausstehlich, nicht zu ertragen; armorial —ings, das Wappen. III. *adj.*; —ing spring, die Hängefeder, Tragfeder; —ing wall, die Mittelwand, Scheidemauer. *Comp.* **—ing-rein**, *s.* der Aufsatzzügel.

Beard, I. *s.* der Bart; to a p.'s —, einem ins Gesicht. II. *v.a.* bei dem Barte zupfen; trotzen; angreifen. **—ed**, *adj.* bärtig. **—less**, *adj.* bartlos, unbärtig.

Beast, I. *s.* das Tier, Vieh; das Labet (*game of cards*); die (das) Bete (*stake of the loser in the game*); brutaler, roher Mensch; (filthy —) das Schwein, die Sau (*vulg.*); — of burden, Lasttier. —s of prey, Raubtiere. II. *v.a.* labet machen.

III. *v.n.* labet werden. **—liness**, *s.* das viehische Wesen; die Schmutzigkeit, Schweinerei (*fig.*). **—ly**, *adj.* viehisch; ekelhaft, schauderhaft, scheußlich (*sl.*); —ly weather, Hundewetter, Sauwetter (*sl.*); —ly shame, Affenschande, Gemeinheit (*school-boys' sl.*).

Beat, I. *ir.v.a.* schlagen, prügeln; klopfen (*cotton*); schlagen, schmieden (*gold, etc.*); schwingen (*flax*); ausklopfen (*clothes, etc.*); rühren, quirlen (*eggs*); schlagen, rühren (*the drum*); abbamsen (*skins*); bahnen, betreten (*a path*); aufjagen (*game*); schlagen, besiegen (*an enemy*); übertreffen (*a rival*); we — the enemy, wir schlugen den Feind; the enemy was —en, der Feind wurde geschlagen; Tom was —, Tom wurde geprügelt (*obs.*); to — a parley, Chamade schlagen; to — a retreat, zum Rückzuge trommeln; (*fig.*) sich zurückziehn, fortgehn; to — to arms, zu den Waffen trommeln, die Lärmtrommel rühren; to — a tattoo, (den) Zapfenstreich schlagen; to — time, Takt schlagen; there is nothing to — it, darüber geht nichts; that altogether —s me, das geht über meine Begriffe; no one —s me, keiner tut es mir zuvor; to — the air, Lufthiebe tun, sich vergeblich bemühen, leere Worte machen; — **back**, zurückschlagen; — **down**, niederschlagen, niederdrücken; the wind and rain have —en down the corn, der Wind und der Regen haben das Korn gelegt; to — a p. down (in buying s.th.), (beim Kaufen) den Preis herabsetzen, feilschen; — **into**, hineintreiben; — **off**, abklopfen (*Typ.*); abschlagen; — **out**, ausschlagen; to — out iron, Eisen ausbreiten; to — out copper, Kupfer austiefen; they are —ing **up** recruits everywhere, es wird überall stark geworben; to — up the enemy's quarters, den Feind im Lager überfallen; to — hollow, besiegen, bei weitem übertreffen, vollständig ausstechen *or* in den Schatten stellen. II. *ir.v.n.* schlagen; the drum —s, es wird getrommelt; the general —s, der Generalmarsch wird geschlagen; to — about the bush, sondieren, auf den Busch klopfen; wie die Katze um den heißen Brei herumgehen; feel, how my heart —s, fühle, wie heftig mein Herz schlägt; to — about for a th., nach einer S. forschen. III. *s.* das Schlagen, der Schlag; der Taktschlag (*Mus.*); das Revier, die Runde (*of a policeman, etc.*); — of a drum, der Trommelschlag. **—en**, *p.p. & adj.;* —en gold, das Blütengold, geschlagene Gold; a —en path, ein gebahnter Weg; a —en track, ein viel begangener Weg; a weather- —en face, ein wettergebräuntes Gesicht. **—er**, *s.* der Schläger; der Treiber (*Sport.*). **—ing**, I. *p. & adj.* schlagend &c. *see* Beat. II. *s.* das Schlagen, Klopfen; die Schläge, die Züchtigung; das Treiben (*Sport.*); to get a sound —ing, tüchtige Schläge bekommen.

Beati—fic, *adj.*, **—fically**, *adv.* beseligend; selig machend. **—fication**, *s.* die Seligsprechung. **—fy**, *v.a.* selig machen; selig sprechen. **—tude**, *s.* die Seligkeit; the —tudes, die Seligpreisungen.

Beau, *s.* (*pl.* —x) der Stutzer; (admirer) der Anbeter. **—teous**, **—ty**, *etc. see under* Beaut—. *Comp.* **—ideal**, *s.* das Ideal, Vorbild, Urbild des Schönen. **—monde**, *s.* die feine Welt.

Beaut—eous, *adj.* sehr schön. **—eousness**, *s.* die Schönheit. **—ification**, *s.* die Verschönerung. **—ifier**, *s.* der Verschönerer; das Verschönernde. **—iful**, *adj.*, **—ifully**, *adv.* schön. **—ify**, *v.a.* verschöne(r)n; (deck) ausschmücken. **—y**, *s.* die Schönheit; the —y of it all is, das Schönste an der ganzen Sache ist; it is really a —y, es ist eine wahre Pracht; —y and the Beast, die Schöne und das Tier (*a fairy tale*); the Sleeping —y, Dornröschen; Camberwell —y, der Trauermantel (*Ent.*). *Comp.* **—y-spot**, *s.* das Schönpflästerchen.

Beaver, I. *s.* der Biber; das Visor (*of a helmet*); der Tüffel, Biber, schwerer Wollenstoff für Hüte, Überzieher, *etc.;* (— hat) er Kastorhut, Biberhut; —'s cods, die Bibergeilen. II. *attrib.;* — skin, das Biberfell. *Comp.* **—dam**, **—lodge**, *s.* der Biberbau.

Becalm, *v.a.* beruhigen; bekalmen; to be —ed, blind liegen, von einer Windstille überfallen sein *or* werden, aufgehalten werden.

Became, *imperf. of* Become.

Because, *conj.* weil, auf daß; (*in comp.* =*prep.*) — of, wegen; — of you, um Ihretwillen.

Bechamel, *s.* feine Rahmsauce, Zwiebelsauce.

Bechance, *v.a. & n.* begegnen, ergehen.

Becharm, *v.a.* bezaubern.

[1]**Beck**, *s.* der Wink, das Kopfnicken; to be at a p.'s — and call, einem vollständig zu Gebote stehen. **—on**, *v.n.* mit der Hand oder dem Kopfe winken.

[2]**Beck**, *s.* der Bottich, Kessel, die Kufe.

[3]**Beck**, *s.* der Bach (*dial., poet.*).

Becloud, *v.a.* umwölken.

Becom—e, *ir.v.* I. *n.* werden; what is to —e of her? was soll aus ihr werden? what has —e of him? was ist aus ihm geworden? they became friends, sie schlossen Freundschaft mit einander. II. *a.* geziemen; (einem) anstehen, ziemen, (einen) zieren; (sich) passen, sich schicken; his conduct —es his station, er benimmt sich seinem Stande gemäß; it ill —es you to say so, es steht Ihnen übel an, so etwas zu sagen; the bonnet —es you, der Hut steht Ihnen; everything —es a pretty face, einem hübschen Gesicht steht alles, hübsche Menschen können alles tragen. **—ing**, *adj.*, **—ingly**, *adv.* geziemend, passend; schicklich; wohlanstehend; he was treated with —ing respect, man behandelte ihn mit gehöriger Ehrerbietung, man erwies ihm alle geziemende Ehre; such conduct is not —ing, es schickt sich nicht, so etwas zu tun. **—ingness**, *s.* die Schicklichkeit; das Passende.

Bed, I. *s.* das Bett; (flower —) das Beet; das Lager, die Schicht; — of a river, Flußbett; — of the ocean, der Meeresgrund; — of a mountain torrent, der Graben; — of stone (*for receiving a railway*), die Steinbettung; — of a gun, die Laffettenwand; — of a mortar, das Zapfenlager; — of state, Paradebett; flower —, Blumenbeet; a — of clay, eine Tonschicht; double —, zweischläfriges Bett; to go to —, zu Bette gehen; — and board, Tisch und Bett; can I have a — for the night? haben Sie ein Schlafzimmer *or* Nachtquartier? can we offer you a —? wollen Sie nicht über Nacht hier bleiben? — of coal, das Kohlenlager; to take to one's —, sich legen; as one makes one's —, so one must lie, wie man sich bettet, so schläft man (*prov.*); early to — and early to rise, makes a man healthy, wealthy and wise, Morgenstunde hat Gold im Munde (*prov.*); a sick —, ein Krankenlager; to be brought to —, niederkommen, entbunden werden; to put to —, schlafen legen, zu Bett legen. II. *attrib.;* — curtains, Bettvorhänge; — lift, die Hebevorrichtung für das Krankenbett, um Schütteln des Patienten zu verhindern; — rest, das Gestell unter dem Kopfkissen eines Krankenbetts zur Unterstützung eines im Bett Sitzenden. III. *v.a.* betten (*beasts*); in die Erde legen, pflanzen (*plants, etc.*). IV. *v.n.;* to — with a person, mit einem zusammenschlafen. **—ding**, *s.* das Bettzeug; die Streu, Lagerstreu (*for cattle*); — and —ding, Bett und Zubehör. *Comp.* **—chamber**, *s.* das Schlafzimmer, Schlafgemach; Lord of the King's —chamber, königlicher Kammerherr; Lady of the (Queen's) — chamber, königliche Hofdame; —chamber woman, die Kammerfrau. **—clothes**, *pl.* das Bettzeug. **—fellow**, *s.* der Bettgenoß, die Bettgenossin, der Schlafkamerad; poverty makes one acquainted with strange —fellows, die Not bringt einen zu seltsamen Schlafstellen. **—linen**, die Bettwäsche. **—maker**, *s.* die Bettmacherin, die Bettfrau; die Aufwärterin der Studenten zu Cambridge. **—post**, *s.* die Bettsäule. **—quilt**, *s.* die Bettdecke. **—ridden,** *adj.* bettlägerig. **—-rock,** *s.* das feste Gebirge; die Grundlage, felsenfeste *or* unerschütterliche Unterlage. **—room,** *s.* das Schlafzimmer. **—side,** *s.* die Bettseite; by her —side, an ihrem Bette. **—-sore,** *s.;* the patient has —-sores, der Kranke hat sich wund gelegen. **—stead,** *s.* die Bettstelle; an iron —stead, ein eisernes Bett. **—tick,** *s.* die Bettzieche. **—time,** *s.* die Schlafenszeit, Zeit zu Bett zu gehen.

Bedaub, *v.a.* beschmieren, bemalen.

Bedeck, *v.a.* schmücken, zieren.

Bedell, *s.* der Universitätspedell; Esquire —, Graduierter der Universität, welcher dem Rektor in Universitätsfunktionen zur Seite steht (*2 esquire —s in Cambridge University*).

Bedevil, *v.a.* behexen. **—ment,** *s.* die Verhexung, Teufelei; Besessenheit; die teuflische Mißhandlung.

Bedew, *v.a.* betauen, benetzen; besprenger

Bedizen, *v.a.* herausputzen, ausstaffieren.

Bedlam, *s.* das Tollhaus, Irrenhaus. **—ite,** *s.* der Tollhäusler.

Bed(r)aggle, *v.a.* beschmutzen (*clothes*).

Bee, I. *s.* die Biene; the — hums, die Biene summt; (working party) das Arbeitskränzchen, eine Anzahl von Personen, die eine freiwillige unentgeltliche Arbeit zu Gunsten jemands leisten (*Amer.*); a swarm of —s, ein Bienenschwarm; —s of the bowsprit, Backen (Violinen) des Bugspriets; queen —, die Bienenkönigin. II. *attrib.;* — culture, die Bienenzucht; — management, die Bienenzucht. *Comp.* **—-bread,** *s.* das Bienenbrot. **—-eater,** *s.* der Bienenspecht. **—-glue,** *s.* das Stopfwachs. **—hive,** *s.* der Bienenstock. **—line,** *s.* der gerade Weg (*Amer.*). **—-master,** *s.* der Bienenvater. **—swax,** (**—s'wax,**) I. *s.* das Bienenwachs. II. *v.a.* (den Fußboden) bohnen, (Möbel) abreiben.

Beech, I. *s.* (—-tree) die Buche; common —, die Rotbuche. II. *attrib.;* — forest, der Buchenwald. **—en,** *adj.* buchen. *Comp.* **—-mast,** *s.* die Früchte der Buchen, die Buchmast. **—-nut,** *s.* die Buchecker. **—-oil,** *s.* das Buchöl. **—-tree,** *s.* die Buche.

Beef, *s.* das Rindfleisch; roast —, Rinderbraten; sirloin of —, das Lendenstück vom Rinde, der Lendenbraten; boiled —, gekochtes Rindfleisch; corned —, Büchsenfleisch; round of (salt) —, das große Stück Pökelfleisch; stewed —, geschmortes, gedünstetes Ochsenfleisch. **—y,** *adj.* fleischig. *Comp.* **—-eater,** *s.* der Rindfleischfresser; (yeoman of the guard) der (mittelalterlich gekleidete, mit Hellebarde bewehrte, englische) Leibgardist. **—-steak,** *s.* das Beefsteak, die Rindfleischschnitte. **—-tea,** *s.* die Fleischbrühe, Brühe.

Been, *p.p. see* Be.

Beer, *s.* das Bier. *Comp.* **—-barrel,** *s.* das Bierfaß. **—-house, —-shop,** *s.* das Bierhaus, die Kneipe, Schenke. **—-money,** das Biergeld (der zur Beförderung der technischen Erziehung den Grafschaftsräten überwiesene Überfluß der Steuer auf geistige Getränke) (*coll.*).

Beestings, *pl.* die Biestmilch.

Beet, *s.* die Bete, Runkelrübe; red —, rote Bete, rote Rübe. *Comp.* **—-root,** *s.* die Runkelrübe; —-root sugar, der Runkelrübenzucker.

[1]**Beetl—e,** I. *s.* der Schlägel, Bleuel (*for linen, etc.*); die Ramme (*for paving*); die Schwinge, der Schwingstock (*for hemp*); der Rammblock (*in a mill*). II. *v.a.* mit einem Schlägel schlagen, stampfen; kalandern. III. *v.n.* überhangen. *Comp.* **—e-browed,** *adj.* mit überhangenden Augenbrauen. **—ing-mill,** *s.* der Stampfkalander.

[2]**Beetle,** *s.* der Käfer (*Ent.*); black —, die Küchenschabe; the — hums *or* buzzes, der Käfer summt *or* brummt; as blind as a —, stockblind.

Beeves, *pl.* Rindvieh, Rinder; a drove of —, eine Herde Rinder.

Befall, *ir.v.a. & n.* befallen, begegnen, zustoßen, widerfahren; (happen) sich ereignen; Madam, all joy — your grace! es möge euch, gnädige Frau, alle Freude widerfahren; did any evil — him? ist ihm ein Unglück zugestoßen? how now, what hath —en? was ist denn vorgefallen?

Befit, *v.a.* sich schicken, sich geziemen, gebühren; he filled his station with —ting dignity, er hat sein Amt mit geziemender Würde bekleidet.

Befog, *v.a.* in Nebel hüllen; in Dunkelheit hüllen; (*fig.*) verwirren, irreführen.

Befool, *v.a.* betören, betrügen, foppen.

Before, I. *adv.* (in front) vorn; (on in front) voran; (previously) vorher, früher, ehemals; (sooner) eher; (already) bereits, schon; — and behind, vorn und hinten; that was never known —, ehemals wußte man das nicht; you tell me what I knew —, du sagst mir, was ich schon wußte; I told him —, that, ich sagte ihm vorher, daß; an hour —, eine Stunde vorher; he is gone on —, er ist vorausgegangen. II. *conj.* bevor; ehe; — the hills appeared, ehe die Hügel erschienen; he knew — I told him, bevor ich es ihm sagte, wußte er; I guessed it — he had told me, ich vermutete es, ehe er es mir noch gesagt hatte; I would die — I would behave so, lieber stürbe ich, als daß ich mich so aufführte; it will not be long — you repent of it, Sie werden es bald bereuen; look — you leap, Trau, Schau, wem (*prov.*); — he came, vor seiner Ankunft. III. *prep.* vor; he summoned him — the court, er lud ihn vor das Gericht; — the door, vor der Tür; — my very eyes, gerade vor meinen Augen; — his arrival, vor seiner Ankunft; the day — his death, der Tag vor seinem Tode; the day — yesterday, vorgestern; hang it — the fire, hänge es vor das Feuer; she went — him, sie ging vor ihm her; to preach — the king, vor dem Könige predigen; your favour is —us, Ihr Geehrtes liegt zur Beantwortung vor uns; to get — a p., einem zuvorkommen; to sail — the wind, vor dem Winde segeln. *Comp.* **—hand,** *adv.* vorher, im voraus; I think it necessary to observe —hand, ich halte es für notwendig, von vornherein zu bemerken; to be —hand with a p., einem zuvorkommen. **—-mentioned,** *adj.* vorhererwähnt. **—time,** *adv.* zu früh.

Befoul, *v.a.* besudeln, beschmutzen.

Befriend, *v.a.* als Freund behandeln, unterstützen, begünstigen; she —ed him, sie nahm sich seiner an.

Befurred, *adj.* bepelzt, im Pelz.

Beg, *v.* I. *a.* bitten, ersuchen; betteln; to — one's way to . . ., sich durchbetteln nach . . .; to — of a p., einen bitten *or* ersuchen um; I — to (say), ich erlaube mir zu (bemerken); I — to inform you, ich gestatte mir Ihnen mitzuteilen; I — your pardon, (ich bitte) um Verzeihung; wie beliebt? wie sagen Sie? was befehlen Sie? to — the question, einen unbewiesenen Satz zum Beweise brauchen. II. *n.* betteln; to —, to go a —ging, betteln gehen. **—gar,** I. *s.* der Bettler, die Bettlerin; der Bittsteller; —gars must not be choosers, arme Leute dürfen nicht wählerisch sein (*prov.*); set a —gar on horseback and he 'll ride to the devil, es giebt nichts Stolzeres, als einen reich gewordenen Bettler (*prov.*); a —gar's purse is always empty, der Bettelsack wird nie voll (*prov.*). II. *attrib.;* —gar boy, der Betteljunge; —gar maid, das Bettelmädchen, die Bettlerin; —gar man, der Bettelmann; —gar woman, das Bettelweib, die Bettlerin. III. *v.a.* zum Bettler machen, arm machen; erschöpfen (*fig.*). **—gardom,** *s.* die Bettlerschaft. **—gared,** *adj.* bettelarm. **—garliness,** *s.* die Bettelarmut, Armseligkeit; die Erbärmlichkeit. **—garly,** *adj.* bettelhaft, lumpig, armselig; erbärmlich. **—gary,** *s.* die Bettelarmut; to reduce to —gary, an den Bettelstab bringen. *Comp.* **—gar-my-neighbour,** *s.* ein Kinder-Kartenspiel.

Began, *imperf. of* Begin.

Begat, *obs. imperf. of* Beget.

Beget, *ir.v.a.* zeugen; hervorbringen, erzeugen; the only begotten Son of God, Gottes eingeborner Sohn. **—ter**, *s.* der Erzeuger, Vater. **—ting**, *s.* die Erzeugung, Zeugung.
Begin, *ir.v.a. & n.* anfangen, beginnen; to — a journey, eine Reise antreten; to — the world, als selbstständiger Mensch in die Welt treten, für sich anfangen; to — again, von neuem anfangen; he began to feel unwell, es ward ihm übel; I — to see (clearly), es geht mir ein Licht auf; well begun is half done, wohl begonnen ist halb gewonnen (*prov.*). **—ner**, *s.* der Anfänger; der Urheber. **—ning**, I. *p. see* Begin. II. *s.* der Anfang; der Ursprung; das Anfangen; in the —ning God created . . ., im Anfang schuf Gott . . . (*B.*); small —nings, ein kleiner Anfang; from —ning to end, von Anfang bis zu Ende.
Begird, *ir.v.a.* umgürten; umgeben, einschließen.
Begirt, *p.p.* eingeschlossen, umgeben.
Begone, *int.* fort! weg (mit dir)! packe dich!
Begonia, *s.* die Begonie, das Schiefblatt.
Begorra, *inter.* bei Gott! (*Irish*).
Begot, *imperf.*, **Begotten**, *p.p.*, *of* Beget.
Begrime, *v.a.* rußig machen, (ein)schwärzen.
Begrudge, *v.a.* mißgönnen, beneiden.
Beguil—e, *v.a.* täuschen, betrügen, bestricken; hinbringen, verkürzen (*time*); (lead astray) verführen. **—er**, *s.* der Betrüger; der Verführer. **—ing**, *adj.*, **—ingly**, *adv.* verführerisch, betrügerisch.
Begum, *s.* (in Ostindien eine) Prinzessin, Fürstin, *or* vornehme Dame.
Begun, *p.p. of* Begin.
Behalf, *s.* der Behuf, Vorteil, Nutzen; die Verteidigung; on — of a p., im Namen jemandes; on — of the poor, zum Besten der Armen; counsel appeared on — of the complainant, der Kläger wurde vor Gericht von einem Anwalt vertreten; I only speak on — of myself, ich spreche nur für mich; on — of your son, zu Gunsten Ihres Sohnes.
Behav—e, *v.* I. *n.* handeln, sich betragen; well —ed, wohlgesittet. II. *r.*; to —e o.s., sich gut betragen. **—iour**, *s.* das Betragen, das sittliche Verhalten, die Aufführung; he is on his good —iour, er nimmt sich in Acht, daß er sich gut aufführt; she was on her best —iour, sie benahm sich vorzüglich; sie war die Höflichkeit und Zuvorkommenheit selbst.
Behead, *v.a.* enthaupten. **—ing**, *s.* die Enthauptung.
Beheld, *imperf. & p.p. of* Behold.
Behest, *s.* das Geheiß, der Befehl.
Behind, I. *adv.* hinten, zurück; why did you leave me —? warum ließen Sie mich zurück? to get up —, hinten aufsteigen; to be —, zurück sein, im Rückstande sein. II. *prep.* hinter; — the house, hinter dem Hause; (to go, etc., gehen, 2c.) hinter das Haus; look — you, sehen Sie sich um, sehen Sie hinter sich; she is not — him in zeal, sie steht ihm an Eifer nicht nach; — the scenes, hinter den Kulissen; to be — one's time, sich verspätet haben; the groom rode — him, der Diener ritt hinter ihm her; — s.o.'s back, heimlich; to slander a p. — his back, einem hinter dem Rücken Böses nachsagen. *Comp.* **—hand**, *adv.* im Rückstande, zurück; (in arrears) rückständig.
Behold, I. *ir.v.a.* anschauen, ansehen, betrachten; sehen, schauen, erblicken. II. *int.* siehe (da)! **—en**, *adj.* verpflichtet, verbunden. **—er**, *s.* der Anschauer, Zuschauer.
Behoof, *s.* der Behuf, Bedarf; der Vorteil.
Behove, *v.a. & imp.* gebühren, frommen, sich ziemen; it —s me, es geziemt mir.
Beige, *s.* eine Art dünnes, wollenes Tuch.
Being, I. *pres. part. of* Be; — sick, indem ich krank bin *or* war; he came near to — killed, er war nahe daran, getötet zu werden. II. *adj.*; for the time —, für jetzt, für den Augenblick. III. *s.* das Sein, Dasein, die Existenz; das Wesen; a fleet in —, eine Manöverflotte; his troops are still in —, seine Truppen stehen noch tätig im Felde; to call into —, ins Leben rufen; the Supreme —, das höchste Wesen.
Bejewelled, *adj.* mit Juwelen geschmückt.
Belabour, *v.a.* tüchtig prügeln, durchprügeln.
Belated, *adj.* verspätet; von der Nacht überfallen.
Belaud, *v.a.* preisen, erheben.
Belay, *v.a.* belegen, festmachen (*Naut.*). *Comp.* **—ing-cleat**, *s.* das Belegholz (*Naut.*). **—ing-pin**, *s.* der Koveinnagel (*Naut.*).
Belch, *v.n.* ausstoßen; aufstoßen, rülpsen; to — out, ausstoßen, ausspeien.
Beldam(e), *s.* das alte Mütterchen, die alte Vettel; (witch) die alte Hexe.
Beleaguer, *v.a.* belagern. **—er**, *s.* der Belagerer.
Belemnite, *s.* der Belemnit.
Belfry, *s.* der Glockenturm; das Glockengerüst.
Belie, *v.a.* belügen, verleumden; verleugnen their trembling hearts — their boastful tongues, ihre zitternden Herzen strafen ihre prahlerischen Zungen Lügen.
Belief, *s.* der Glaube; das Glaubensbekenntnis; past all —, unglaublich; hard of —, schwergläubig. **—s**, *pl.* Glaubensanschauungen, Glaubensmeinungen.
Believ—able, *adj.* glaublich. **—e**, *v.a. & n.* glauben; to —e in God, an Gott glauben; to —e in the victory of truth, an den Sieg der Wahrheit glauben; he is not to be —ed, man darf ihm nicht glauben; I — him to be an honest man, ich halte ihn für einen ehrlichen Menschen; I —e so, ich glaube, ja, das glaub' ich; to make —e, vorgeben, vorschützen; to make a p. —e that black is white, einem ein X für ein U machen; to make a p. —e, einen glauben lassen, einem weis machen; making —e, indem er nur so tat. **—er**, *s.* der Gläubige; he was a strong —er in all . . ., er glaubte steif und fest an alle . . .; true —er, der Rechtgläubige. **—ingly**, *adv.* im Glauben, gläubig.
Belike, *adv.* wahrscheinlich, vermutlich.
Belittle, *v.a.* verkleinern, verächtlich machen.
Bell, I. *s.* die Glocke; die Schelle, Klingel; der Kelch (*of a flower*); die Glocke (*Arch.*); der Schalltrichter (*of a trumpet*); pealing chime of —s, das Geläut; a peal of —s, ein Glockenspiel; —s (*on harness*), die Schellen, Glöckchen, das Schellengeläut; curfew —, Abendglocke; to carry off the —, den Preis davon tragen, der Erste sein; cap and —s, die Schellenkappe; diving —, Taucherglocke; passing —, Totenglocke; das Armesünder-Glöcklein. II. *attrib.*; — clapper, der Glockenklöppel; — harness, das Schellengeschirr; — wire, der Glockendraht. III. *v.a.*; to — the cat, der Katze eine Schelle anhängen. **—ow**, I. *v.n.* brüllen; blöken; (*of a deer*) schreien, röhren; bellen. II. *s.* das Gebrüll; das Blöken; Bellen. *Comp.* **—-crank**, *s.* der Glockenarm; (*pl.*) das Winkeleisen. **—-founder**, *s.* der Glockengießer. **—-founding**, *s.* der Glockenguß. **—-foundry**, *s.* die Glockengießerei. **—-gable**, *s.* der Glockengiebel. **—-glass**, *s.* die Glasglocke. **—-hanger**, *s.* der Hausschlosser. **—-metal**, *s.* das Glockenmetall, die Glockenspeise. **—-mouth**, *s.* das glockenförmige Mundstück, der Schalltrichter (eines Sprachrohrs). **—-mouthed**, *adj.* trichterförmig. **—-pull**, *s.* der Schellenzug; (—-rope) die Klingelschnur, der Glockenstrang. **—-ringer**, *s.* der Glöckner. **—-ringing**, *adj.*; —-ringing machine, die Läutevorrichtung. **—-shaped**, *adj.* glockenförmig. **—-telegraph**, *s.* der Glockentelegraph. **—-wether**, *s.* der Leithammel.
Bell—adonna, *s.* die Belladonna. **—e**, *s.* die Schöne. **—es lettres**, *pl.* schöne Wissenschaften.
Bellied, *adj.* mit einem Bauche, bauchig; (*in cpds.*) -bäuchig; — out, aufgeblasen.
Belligerent, *adj.* kriegführend; kriegerisch.

Bell—ows, I. *pl.* der Blasebalg; das Gebläse; —ows (*in mines*), der Ventilator. II. *attrib.;* —ows blower, der Bälgetreter. **—y**, I. *s.* der Bauch (*of a harp*); die Decke (*of a violin*); (abdomen) der Schmerbauch, Unterleib; der Kasten (*of musical instruments*). II. *v.n.* bauchen, bauchig werden; the —ying canvas, die schwellenden Segel. *Comp.* **—y-ache**, *s.* die Kolik, die Leibschmerzen (*vulg.*). **—y-band**, *s.* der Bauchgurt (*for horses*).

Belong, *v.n.* gehören; angehören; betreffen; essays of Schiller which — to this period, Aufsätze Schillers, welche dieser Zeit angehören *or* welche in diese Zeit fallen; it —s to me, es gehört mir; this town —s to Prussia, diese Stadt gehört zu Preußen; whatever —s to him, was ihm auch gehört; whoever —s to him, wer ihm auch angehört, wer auch nur zu ihm gehört. **—ings**, *pl.* das Zubehör, die Habe, Habseligkeiten; with all his —ings, mit Hab und Gut, mit seiner ganzen Habe.

Beloved, *adj.* geliebt, teuer; dearly —! meine Lieben! my — brethren, meine Geliebten!

Below, I. *adv.* unten; hienieden; in der Hölle; in einem Untergericht (*Law*); it shall be noticed —, es soll unten bemerkt werden. II. *prep.* unter; — par, unter Pari; — stairs, unten; im Reich der Dienstboten, im Erdgeschoß.

Belt, I. *s.* der Gürtel; der Kranz (*Arch.*); der Riemen (*Mach.*); das Degengehenk, die Degenkuppel; der Belt (*Geog.*); die Bandage, das Bruchband (*Surg.*); —s of Jupiter, die Gürtel des Jupiter. II. *attrib.;* — maker, der Gürtler. **—ed**, *adj.* mit einem Gürtel (versehen).

Bemoan, *v.a.* betrauern, beklagen; to — one's fate, über sein Geschick wehklagen.

Bench, I. *s.* die Bank, die Werkbank; die Gerichtsbank (*Law*); das Gericht, die Richter; die Berme (*Railw., etc.*); carpenter's —, eines Tischlers Bank, Hobelbank; court of the King's —, das Oberhofgericht; the King's — division, der höchste Gerichtshof Englands in Strafsachen (Teil des High Court of Justice); the whole — was agreed as to the sentence, sämmtliche (Friedens-)Richter stimmten dem Ausspruche bei; the — and the bar, Richter und Sachwalter, alle Rechtsgelehrten. II. *v.a.* mit Bänken versehen. **—er**, *s.* Mitglied eines der großen Londoner Gerichtshöfe, Jurist; —ers of the Inns of Court, die ältern Mitglieder der Inns of Court (einer Rechtsschule). *Comp.* **—-plane**, *s.* der Bankhobel. **—-warrant**, *s.* der Verhaftbefehl, Befehl zur Festnahme.

Bend, I. *v.a.* beugen, biegen, krümmen; spannen (*a bow*); festmachen (*sails*); anschlagen (*a sail to a yard*); richten (*one's thoughts, etc.*); to — the knee, das Knie beugen; to — back, zurückbiegen; with bent brow, mit gerunzelter Stirn. II. *v.n.* sich beugen, sich biegen, sich neigen (to, vor); überhangen; to — forward, sich bücken, sich neigen; he —s under the heavy burden, er beugt sich unter der schweren Last; bent on mischief, zum Unheilstiften geneigt. III. *s.* die Biegung, Krümmung; der Schrägbalken (*Her.*); der Bruch (*Artil.*). **—able**, *adj.* biegsam.

Bene, *adj.* gut. **—diction**, *s.* der Segen; die Segnung, Einsegnung, der Segensspruch. **—faction**, *s.* die Wohltat. **—factor**, *s.* der Wohltäter. **—factress**, *s.* die Wohltäterin. **—fice**, *s.* die Pfründe. **—ficed**, *adj.* mit einer Pfründe bedacht, im Besitz einer Pfründe. **—ficence**, *s.* die Wohltätigkeit. **—ficent**, *adj.*, **—ficently**, *adv.* wohltätig. **—ficial**, *adj.*, **—ficially**, *adv.* heilsam, wohltätig, zuträglich; vorteilhaft, nutznießend. **—ficiary**, *s.* der, welcher etwas durch die Gunst eines andern besitzt; der Pfründner; der Almosenempfänger. **—fit**, I. *s.* die Wohltat; (advantage) der Vorteil, Nutzen, Gewinn; das Benefiz (*Theat.*); —fit of clergy, das Vorrecht der Geistlichen; for the —fit of his health, seiner Gesundheit wegen; to take the —fit of the act, den Schutz des Bankerottgesetzes beanspruchen. II. *attrib.;* —fit night, die Benefizvorstellung (*Theat.*). III. *v.a.* begünstigen, Nutzen bringen; nützen; heilsam sein; my friend's health has —fited greatly by the change of air, die Luftveränderung ist der Gesundheit meines Freundes außerordentlich vorteilhaft gewesen *or* zugute gekommen; exercise —fits the health, körperliche Bewegung fördert die Gesundheit. IV. *v.n.* Nutzen (von etwas) haben *or* gewinnen; I —fited by the mistake, der Irrtum hat mir zum Vorteil gereicht. **—volence**, *s.* das Wohlwollen; (kindness) die Güte; (kind act) die Wohltat; die allgemeine Menschenliebe; eine freiwillige Steuer (*Eng. Hist.*). **—volent**, *adj.*, **—volently**, *adv.* wohlwollend, gütig; —volent fund, der Unterstützungsfonds; —volent institution, der Hilfsverein, Unterstützungsverein. *Comp.* **—fit-society**, *s.* die Wohltätigkeitsgesellschaft.

Beneath, I. *adv.* unten. II. *prep.* unter; it would be — me to do such a thing, es würde unter meiner Würde sein, so etwas zu tun.

Benighted, *adj.* von der Nacht überfallen, durch den Einbruch der Nacht überrascht; unwissend.

Benign, *adj.*, **—ly**, *adv.* gütig, gutartig, mild; (beneficial) wohltuend, heilsam; (favourable) günstig. **—ant**, *adj.* gütig; holdselig; *see* Benign. **—ity**, *s.* (kindness) die Güte, Milde; (graciousness) die Holdseligkeit; der wohltätige Einfluß (*of the air, etc.*).

Bent, I. *p.p. & adj.* gebogen; (inclined) geneigt; (set) erpicht; *see* Bend; — on, geneigt, entschlossen zu, versessen auf (*acc.*). II. *s.* die Neigung, der Hang, Trieb; der Wille; die Richtung; the full —, the top of one's —, der höchste Grad, die höchste Kraftanstrengung (des Geistes); to the top of one's —, bis zum Äußersten. *Comp.* **—-grass**, *s.* das Straußgras (*Bot.*).

Benumb, *v.a.* erstarren; betäuben. **—ed**, *p.p. & adj.* erstarrt, starr; —ed with cold, vor Kälte erstarrt, starr vor Kälte. **—edness**, *s.* die Erstarrung; die Betäubung (*fig.*).

Benz—ine, *s.* das Benzin. **—oic**, *adj.;* —oic acid, die Benzoesäure. **—ole**, *s.* das Benzol, Benzin (*Chem.*). **—oline**, *s.* das Benzol. **—olize**, *v.a.* mit Benzol sättigen.

Bepaint, *v.a.* bemalen, übermalen.

Bepraise, *v.a.* beloben, sehr herausstreichen.

Bequeath, *v.a.* (letztwillig) vermachen; hinterlassen. **—er**, *s.* der Erblasser.

Bequest, *s.* das Vermächtnis.

Bereave, *v.a.* berauben; me have ye bereft of my children, mich habt ihr meiner Kinder beraubt (*B.*); to — a p. of a th., einem eine S. rauben, einen einer S. berauben. **—ment**, *s.* die Beraubung; der Verlust; your sad —ment, Ihr schmerzlicher *or* unersetzlicher Verlust; in their —ment, in ihrer Verlassenheit.

Bereft, *imperf. & p.p. of* Bereave.

Bergamot, *s.* (pear) die Bergamotte; die Bergamottenzitrone; essence of —, das Bergamottöl.

Berme, *s.* die Berme, der Böschungsabsatz (*Fort.*).

Berry, *s.* die Beere. *Comp.* **—-bearing**, *adj.* beerentragend. **—-shaped**, *adj.* beerenförmig.

Berth, *s.* das Schiffsbett, Kajütenbett, die Schlafstelle (*in a boat*); der Ankerplatz (*Naut.*); der Raum; die Stelle (*fig.*); I always give such people a wide —, ich gehe solchen Leuten immer weit aus dem Wege; the pilot gave the rock a wide —, der Lotse steuerte weit vom Felsen ab, ließ den Felsen weit zur Seite liegen; loading —, die Ladestelle.

Beryl, *s.* der Beryll (*Min.*); die Beryllfarbe, helles Meergrün.

Beseech, *ir.v.a.* dringend ersuchen, flehentlich bitten. **—ing**, *adj.*, **—ingly**, *adv.* flehend, dringend *or* eindringlich bittend, flehendlich.

Beseem, *v.a. & n.* geziemen, sich schicken.

Beset, *v.a.* (surround) besetzen, umringen; (be-

siege) umlagern; —ting sin, die Gewohnheitssünde, Lieblingssünde; she was hard —, sie war hart bedrängt; he was — with entreaties, man bestürmte ihn mit Bitten; — with difficulties, von Schwierigkeiten umgeben, äußerst schwierig.
Beshrew, *v.a.* verwünschen, verfluchen.
Beside, I. *adv. see* —s. II. *prep.* neben, an, bei, dicht bei; außer, über, nicht gemäß; he sat — me, er saß neben mir; sit down — me, setze dich neben mich *or* an meine Seite; nobody — me, niemand außer mir; — the purpose, nicht zweckdienlich; he is — himself with rage, er ist außer sich vor Wut. **—s,** I. *adv.* überdies, ohnedies, außerdem, zudem; nobody —s, sonst niemand. II. *prep.* außer; —s all this, außer allem diesem.
Besiege, *v.a.* belagern, umdrängen; bedrängen, bestürmen (*fig.*). **—r,** *s.* der Belagerer.
Beslaver, *v.a.* mit Geifer besudeln, begeifern.
Beslobber, *v.a.* besudeln (mit Geifer, 2c.).
Besmear, *v.a.* bestreichen, beschmieren, beschmutzen.
Besmirch, *v.a.* besudeln.
Besom, *s.* der Besen.
Besot, *v.a.* betören, dumm machen (durch den Trunk); betäuben; vernarrt machen. **—ted,** *adj.* vernarrt, betrunken; trunksüchtig.
Besought, *imperf. & p.p. of* Beseech.
Bespatter, *v.a.* bespritzen, beflecken.
Bespeak, *ir.v.a.* (order) sich (*dat.*) vorher bestellen; (address) anreden; (claim) in Anspruch nehmen; (betoken) ankündigen, anzeigen; (show) verraten; to — a room (*at an hotel*), sich (*dat.*) ein Zimmer voraus bestellen; a thousand copies are bespoken, tausend Exemplare sind bestellt; his manners — the gentleman, sein Benehmen verrät den Mann von Bildung; to — a p.'s favour, einen auf irgend eine Weise zu gewinnen suchen; bespoke work a specialty, Anfertigung auf Bestellung ist in diesem Geschäfte die Hauptsache. **—er,** *s.* der Besteller.
Bespoke, *imperf. & p.p. of* Bespeak.
Besprinkle, *v.a.* besprengen.
Best, I. *adj.* (*sup. of* good) best; —man, der Brautführer; the —part, der beste (größte) Teil; to put the — construction on a th., etwas aufs beste deuten; the — man in the world, der beste Mensch von der Welt. II. *adv.* am besten; am meisten; what had I — do? was sollte ich wohl tun? I think it — not to go, ich halte es für das Beste, nicht zu gehen. III. *s.* das Beste; der, die, das Beste; at the —, aufs beste, im besten Falle; for the —, zum Besten; he did it all for the —, er tat es in der Meinung, daß es das Beste sei, in der besten Absicht; to do one's —, sein Bestes tun, sein Möglichstes tun; to the — of my knowledge, nach bestem Wissen, so viel ich weiß; to the — of my recollection, so viel ich mich erinnere; to have the — of it, dabei am besten wegkommen; did he get the — of it? hat er gewonnen? to make the — of a bad job *or* bargain, sich so gut wie möglich aus einem schlimmen Handel ziehen, gute Miene zum bösen Spiele machen; to make the — of, aufs beste benutzen, tun was man kann (mit); the — (thing) you can do is to go away, das Beste, was Sie tun können, ist fortzugehen; I made the — of my way to . . ., ich ging so geschwind wie möglich *or* möglichst schnell nach . . .; do your — *or* your worst, machen Sie es wie Sie wollen; at —, im Grunde; life is at — very short, das Leben ist, wenn es auf das Höchste kommt, sehr kurz. *Comp.* **—-beloved,** *adj.* am meisten geliebt.
Bestial, *adj.* tierisch, viehisch. **—ity,** *s.* das viehische Wesen, die Unvernunft; die Bestialität. **—ize, —ise,** *v.a.* vertieren.
Bestir, *v.r.;* to — o.s., sich rühren; — yourself! mach schnell.
Bestow, *v.a.* (give) erteilen, geben, schenken; (stow) stellen, legen; (employ) anwenden, verwenden; to — kindness upon s.o., einem Gefälligkeiten erweisen; labour well —ed, gut angewandte Mühe; to — one's daughter upon s.o., seine Tochter an einen verheiraten. **—al,** *s.* die Schenkung, Verleihung.
Bestraddle, *v.a. see* Bestride.
Bestrew, *ir.v.a.* bestreuen.
Bestrid(den), *p.p. of* Bestride.
Bestride, *ir.v.a.* (rittlings) besteigen, reiten; beschreiten.
Bestrode, *imperf. of* Bestride.
Bet, I. *s.* die Wette. II. *v.a. & n.* wetten; (stake) setzen; what do you —? was gilt die Wette? I will — five to one, ich will fünf gegen eins wetten. **—ting,** *s.* das Wetten.
Betake, *ir.v.r.;* to — oneself to, (go to) sich begeben nach; (have recourse to) seine Zuflucht nehmen zu; (take to) ergreifen.
Beteem, *v.n.* erlauben, gewähren (*obs.*).
Bethink, *ir.v.r.* sich besinnen, sich bedenken, sich erinnern; I have bethought me of another fault, ich habe mich eines andern Fehlers besonnen (*obs.*).
Betide, *v.* I. *a.* befallen, zustoßen, begegnen; woe — him! wehe ihm! II. *n.* geschehen, stattfinden.
Betimes, *adv.* beizeiten, früh, zeitig.
Betoken, *v.a.* bezeichnen, andeuten; voraussagen, verkünden.
Betook, *imperf. of* Betake.
Betray, *v.a.* verraten, zum Verräter werden an (einem); (seduce) verführen, verleiten. **—al,** *s.* der Verrat. **—er,** *s.* der Verräter.
Betroth, *v.a.* verloben. **—al,** *s.* die Verlobung. **—ed,** *s.;* your —ed, Ihr Fräulein Braut, Ihr Herr Bräutigam *or* Verlobter.
Better, I. *adj. & adv.* (*comp. of* Good) besser, vorteilhafter; annehmlicher; gesünder, stärker; his — half, seine bessere Hälfte; the — the day, the — the deed, je heiliger der Tag, desto besser *or* heiliger die Tat; she is no — than she should be, man kann es nicht besser von ihr erwarten; upon — acquaintance, wenn wir uns (sie sich) besser kennen; looking very much — for his sojourn in the Vosges, der nach seinem Aufenthalt in den Vogesen viel wohler aussah *or* dem sein Aufenthalt in den Vogesen sehr gut bekommen war. II. *s.* das Bessere, der, die, das Bessere; my —s, meine Oberen, Vorgesetzten, Leute, die besser, vornehmer sind als ich; for —, for worse, auf *or* in Glück und Unglück; to get the — of a p. *or* a th., einen *or* etwas überwinden (*a dislike*), besiegen (*an enemy*), einem den Vorteil abgewinnen *or* den Rang ablaufen; to change for the —, sich bessern. III. *adv.* besser; mehr; in besserem Gesundheitszustande; to be — off, besser daran sein; so much the —, um so besser, desto besser; I like her — than him, ich liebe sie mehr, habe sie lieber als ihn; — and —, mehr und mehr; six foot and —, sechs Fuß und darüber (*coll.*); you had — not provoke me, Sie täten besser, mich nicht zu reizen; you had — go, es wäre besser, Sie gingen; — late than never, besser spät, als nie; I like it none the — for that, deswegen liebe ich es nicht mehr; I love him all the — for it, ich liebe ihn deswegen nur um so mehr; I thought — of it, ich habe mich eines Besseren besonnen; it shall be the — for you, es soll dir zum Vorteil gereichen; I am none the — for it, es hat mir nichts genützt; ich fühle mich deshalb nicht wohler. IV. *v.n.* besser werden. V. *v.a.* bessern, verbessern; befördern; to — o.s., sich *or* seine Verhältnisse verbessern, vorwärts kommen. **—ment,** *s.* die Verbesserung (*coll.*).
Between, I. *adv.* dazwischen; the space —, der dazwischen liegende Raum, der Zwischenraum. II. *prep.* zwischen; — London and Paris, zwischen London und Paris; — ourselves, unter uns; unter vier Augen; we bought it — us, wir kauften es gemeinschaftlich; — two and three o'clock, zwischen zwei und drei Uhr; it is — two and three years since we met, es sind etwa zwei bis drei Jahre her, seit wir uns trafen; — whiles, von Zeit zu Zeit, dann und wann; betwixt and —, zwischen beiden, in der Mitte; there is no-

thing — them, sie stehen in keinem besonderen Verhältnis zu einander. *Comp.* **—-decks**, *s.* das Mitteldeck.
Betwixt, *prep. see* Between.
Bevel, I. *adj.* schräg, schief; **—** (—led) wheel, das Kegelrad, konische Rad. **II.** *s.* der schiefe Winkel *or* die schräge Richtung von zwei Flächen; die Schiefe, Schräge, Gehrung; die Schmiege (*Carp.*); der Anschlagewinkel (*Mas.*); der Winkelpasser (*of locksmiths*); on a —, schräg, überquer. III. *v.a.* schrägab schneiden, abschrägen. IV. *v.n.* eine schräge, schiefe Richtung haben. **—led**, *p.p. & adj.* abgeschrägt, abgeschliffen, *see* Bevel; —led glass, schräg abgeschliffenes Glas.
Beverage, *s.* das Getränk, der Trank.
Bevy, *s.* der Flug (Vögel); der Haufen, die Schar; der Schwarm (of girls, junger Mädchen).
Bewail, *v.* I. *a.* beklagen, beweinen. II. *n.* wehklagen (um einen). **—ing**, I. *p. & adj. see* Bewail. II. *s.* das Wehklagen.
Beware, *v.a. & n.;* to — of **(a p.)**, sich hüten vor (einem); — ! nimm dich in acht! sieh dich vor! — of that! nehmt euch davor in acht! tut das ja nicht! — of imitations! vor Nachahmungen wird gewarnt! — of pickpockets! vor Taschendieben wird gewarnt! I shall —, ich werde mich hüten *or* mich in acht nehmen.
Bewilder, *v.a.* verirren, irre führen; verwirren, verwirrt machen. **—ing**, *p. & adj.*, **—ingly**, *adv.* verwirrend. **—ment**, *s.* die Verwirrung.
Bewitch, *v.a.* behexen, bezaubern. **—ery**, *s.* die Bezauberung, der Zauber. **—ing**, *adj.*, **—ingly**, *adv.* bezaubernd, reizend. **—ingness**, *s.* das Bezaubernde. **—ment**, *s.* die Bezauberung.
Bey, *s.* der Bey.
Beyond, I. *adv.* über (eine S.) hinaus; auf der andern Seite; to go —, über (eine S.) hinausgehen, überschreiten, (outdo) übertreffen. II. *prep.* jenseits, über; außer; a little — his house, etwas weiter als sein Haus; — endurance, unerträglich; to live — one's means, mehr ausgeben, als einem die Mittel erlauben; — all praise, über alles Lob erhaben; — the sea, jenseits des Meeres; — dispute, außer allem Zweifel, unstreitig; — measure, über die Maßen; — what is sufficient, mehr als genug; — expression, unaussprechlich, unsäglich, unbeschreiblich; — recovery, unrettbar; — retreat, bis dahin, wo Rückzug unmöglich ist; that is — me, das geht über meine Begriffe; — all price, unbezahlbar; to stay — one's time, über die Zeit *or* zu lange bleiben; to go — one's depth, festen Fuß verlieren, den Grund unter den Füßen verlieren; she has got — my control, sie ist mir über den Kopf gewachsen; that is — my reach, das kann ich nicht erreichen, das ist außer meinem Bereiche; — the —s, über alles Jenseits hinaus.
Bezel, *s.* der Kasten (*of a ring*).
Bhang, *s.* indisches berauschendes Getränk.
Biangular, **Biangulate**, *adj.* zweiwinkelig.
Bias, I. *adj. & adv.* schräg, überzwerch; to cut (on the) —, schräg schneiden. II. *s.* die Quere, Schräge; die beschwerte Seite, die Seite des Übergewichts (da wo in den Bowling Kugeln das Blei eingelassen ist); (fondness for) die Zuneigung; (inclination) die Neigung, der Hang; (prejudice) das Vorurteil; a strong — in favour of, eine starke Neigung zu; free from —, unparteiisch, unbefangen. III. *v.a.* neigen, richten, leiten, hinneigen, bestimmen; to be —sed by interest, durch Eigennutz geleitet sein; she was —sed in his favour, sie war für ihn eingenommen.
Bib, *s.* das (Geifer)=Lätzchen, der Pichel; in best — and tucker, im Sonntagsstaat (*coll.*). **—ber**, *s.* der Trinker (*sl.*); der Bezechte (*sl.*). **—ulous**, *adj.* schwammig, einsaugend.
Bibl—e, *s.* die Bibel; —e oath, der Schwur auf die Bibel. **—ical**, *adj.*, **—ically**, *adv.* biblisch. **—icist**, *s.* der Bibelkenner. **—io—**, *see* Biblio—. *Comp.* **—e-society**, *s.* die Bibelgesellschaft.
Biblio—grapher, *s.* der Bücherkenner, Bücherbeschreiber, Bibliograph. **—graphic**, *adj.*, **—graphically**, *adv.* die Bücherkenntnis betreffend, bibliographisch. **—graphy**, *s.* die Bücherkunde, Bibliographie. **—latry**, *s.* die übertriebene Büicherverehrung, Bibliolatrie. **—mania**, *s.* die Büchersucht, Bibliomanie; die Sucht alte und seltene Bücher zu sammeln. **—maniac**, *s.* der Büchernarr, Bücherliebhaber.
Bicarbonate, *s.;* — of soda, doppelt kohlensaures Natron.
Bice, *s.* blaßblaue Farbe aus Schmalte; green —, das Lasurgrün.
Biceps, *pl.* der zweiköpfige Armmuskel; der zweiköpfige Schenkelmuskel; die Armkraft.
Bichromate, *s.* doppelchromsaures Salz (*Chem.*); — of potash, doppelchromsaures Kali.
Bicker, *v.n.* zanken, streiten, hadern. **—ings**, *pl.* der Hader, das Gezänk.
Bickern, *s.* das Doppelhorn, der Zweispitzambos.
Bi-coloured, *adj.* zweifarbig; a — impression, ein zweifarbiger Druck (*stamps*).
Bicuspid, *adj.* zweispitzig.
Bicycl—e, I. *s.* das Zweirad, Fahrrad, Rad; to ride a —e, Zweirad fahren, radfahren, radeln. II. *attrib.;* —e shed, der Schuppen für Fahrräder; —e ride, die Spazierfahrt auf dem Fahrrad; will you come for a —e ride? wollen Sie mit mir ausradeln? III. *v.a.* radfahren, radeln. **—ist**, *s.* der (Zwei)radfahrer, die (Zwei)radfahrerin, der Radler, die Radlerin.
Bid, I. *ir.v.a.* (order, tell) befehlen, heißen, gebieten; bieten (*at auctions, etc.*); (announce) melden, ankündigen; (invite) bitten, einladen; to — up, in die Höhe treiben; to — a p. the time of the day, einen grüßen, einem die Tageszeit bieten; to — s.o. good morning, einem einen guten Morgen wünschen; to — farewell, Lebewohl sagen; to — defiance, Trotz bieten; to — fair, versprechen, Aussicht haben, zu Hoffnungen berechtigen; to — a p. welcome, einen willkommen heißen; do as you are —, tue was dir geheißen *or* was man dich heißt; to — the banns, Verlobte aufbieten; I was — to come for you, man hieß mich euch holen. II. *ir.v.n.;* to — for an article, auf einen Artikel bieten. III. *s.* das Gebot (*at auctions, etc.*). **—dable**, *adj.* folgsam, fügsam (*coll.*). **—der**, *s.* der Bieter; der Einlader (*to a feast*); highest —der, der Meistbietende. **—ding**, I. *p. see* Bid I. II. *s.* das Bieten (*at auctions*); das Aufgebot (*of banns*); das Geheiß, der Befehl; die Einladung; to do a p.'s —ding, jemandes Befehlen *or* Befehl gehorchen. *Comp.* **—ding-prayer**, *s.* das Bittgebet (für die Seelen verstorbener Wohltäter).
Bide, *ir.v.* I. *n.* blieben, wohnen. II. *a.* erwarten, abwarten; I — my time, ich warte meine Zeit ab, ich warte, bis sich mir eine gute Gelegenheit bietet.
Bidenta—l, **—te**, *adj.* zweizähnig; zackig.
Bidet, *s.* kleine Sitzwanne zum Waschen und für Einspritzungen.
Biennial, *adj.*, **—ly**, *adv.* von zwei Jahren, zweijährig; alle zwei Jahre stattfindend, zweijährlich, ein Jahr ums andere.
Bier, *s.* die Bahre, die Totenbahre.
Bifoliate, *adj.* zweiblätterig.
Bifurcat—e, I. *adj.* zweizackig, zweizinkig, zweiästig. II. *v.n.* sich gabeln, sich abzweigen (*of a way*). **—ion**, *s.* die gabelförmige Spaltung, Gabelung (*of a way*).
Big, *adj.*, **—ly**, *adv.* groß; (— with) schwanger, trächtig; stolz; (stout) dick (*also fig.*); a — man, ein großer stattlicher Mann; ein dicker Herr; a woman — with child, eine schwangere Frau; — with misfortune, unheilschwanger; — with fate, verhängnisvoll; his heart is —, sein Herz ist übervoll *or* schwer; to talk —, stolze Reden führen, aufschneiden, prahlen; to look —, eine hochfahrende Miene annehmen, die Nase hoch tragen. **—ness**, *s.* die Größe, Dicke, der Umfang. *Comp*

—**bellied**, *adj.* dickbäuchig. —**-boned**, *adj.* stark von Knochen, starkknochig, vierschrötig.
Bigam—ist, *s.* der Bigamist, der (die) in Doppelehe Lebende. —**y**, *s.* die Doppelehe.
Bigeminate, *adj.* doppelt gepaart (*Bot.*).
[1]**Biggin**, *s.* die Kindermütze; die Mütze des englischen Sachwalters.
[2]**Biggin**, *s.* der Kaffeesack, Kaffeetopf mit Filter, die Kaffeemaschine.
Bight, *s.* die Bucht (*Geog.*); die Bugt (*Naut.*).
Bigot, *s.* der Frömmler (*Rel.*); der blinde Anhänger (einer Partei, *rc.*). —**ed**, *adj.* frömmelnd; blind eingenommen (für). —**ry**, *s.* die Frömmelei, der blinde religiöse Eifer.
Bike, *coll. for* Bicycle (*as s. and v.a.*).
Bilabial, *adj.* mit beiden Lippen gesprochen, beidlippig, bilabial; a — sound, ein beidlippiger Laut (b, p, m).
Bilabiate, *adj.* zweilippig, zwei Lippen habend.
Bilateral, *adj.* zweiseitig.
Bilberry, *s.* die Heidelbeere, Blaubeere, der Besing; red —, die Preißelbeere, Kronsbeere.
Bilbo, *s.* die spanische Degenklinge, das Rapier; (*poet.*) das Schwert, die Klinge. —**es**, *pl.* die Fußfesseln.
Bil—e, *s.* die Galle. —**iary**, *adj.* zur Galle gehörig; —iary duct, *see* —e-duct. —**ious**, *adj.* gallig, gallicht; gall(en)süchtig; a —ious attack, ein Anfall von Gallenfieber; —ious fever, das Gallenfieber. *Comp.* —**e-duct**, *s.* der Gallengang.
Bilge, I. *s.* der Bauch (*of a cask, etc.*); die Weite eines Schiffsbodens, der Schiffsraum. II. *v.n.* leckwerden. *Comp.* —**-pump**, *s.* die Schlagpumpe. —**-water**, *s.* das Schlagwasser, Kimmwasser. —**-ways**, *pl.* die Schlittenbalken.
Bilingu—al, *adj.* in zwei Sprachen; zweisprachig, zwei Sprachen sprechend. —**ist**, *s.* einer der zwei Sprachen von Kindheit auf sprechen gelernt hat. —**ous**, *adj.* zweisprachig; doppelzüngig.
Bilk, *v.* I. *a.* betrügen, prellen, (einen um eine S.) bemogeln; im Stiche lassen. II. *n.* (einem) entwischen; durchbrennen, ausreißen (ohne zu bezahlen) (*coll.*).
[1]**Bill**, I. *s.* der Schnabel (*of a bird, etc.*); die Axt, Spitzhacke; die Hippe, das Gartenmesser (*Hort.*); die Spitze (*Naut.*). II. *v.n.;* to — and coo, (einander) schnäbeln und girren, sich verliebt benehmen, liebeln. *Comp.* —**-hook**, *s.* (hedging-—) die Hippe, das Gartenmesser; das Faschinenmesser (*Mil.*).
[2]**Bill**, I. *s.* die Schrift, Rechtsschrift (*Law*); (list) das Verzeichnis, die Liste; (— of sale, *etc.*) der Schein, Brief; (poster, *etc.*) der Zettel; der Gesetzentwurf, die Vorlage, die Bill (*Parl.*); der Wechsel (*C.L.*); die Rechnung (*C.L.*); — in chancery, die Rechtsklage bei dem Kanzleigerichte; — of costs, die Kostenrechnung; — of credit, der Kreditbrief; — of divorce, der Scheidebrief; — of entry, die Zolldeklaration; — of exceptions, die Einredeschrift; — of exchange, die Tratte, der Wechsel; — of exchequer, der Schatzkammerschein; — of fare, der Küchenzettel, die Speisekarte, die Karte; — of health, der Gesundheitspaß; — of indemnity, die Entschädigungsakte; — of indictment, die Anklageschrift; — of lading, der Frachtbrief, der Verladungsschein; — of mortality, die Sterbeliste; — of parcels, die Faktura; —s receivable book, das Rimessenbuch; —s payable book, das Trattenbuch; — of Rights, die Freiheitsurkunde (1689); — of sale, der Kaufbrief; the grand — of sale, der Beilbrief; the holder of a —, der Inhaber eines Wechsels; to bring in a true —, eine Anklage für gültig erklären; to find a true —, eine Anklage annehmen; a true — was found by a Grand Jury, die Anklagejury befand die Anklage für begründet (zur Überweisung) an die Geschworenen; the Grand Jury threw out *or* ignored the —, die Anklagejury verwarf die Anklage als unbegründet; to bring in a —, eine Bill einführen, einen Gesetzvorschlag *or* Gesetzentwurf vor das Parlament bringen; the — was committed, der Gesetzentwurf wurde einem Ausschuß zur Prüfung überwiesen; the — was rejected, der Gesetzentwurf wurde verworfen; a — was passed, enacting . . ., ein Gesetz ging durch, demzufolge . . .; the — was passed, der Gesetzentwurf wurde angenommen *or* zum Gesetz erhoben; to accept a —, einen Wechsel acceptieren; to draw a —, trassieren; to take up a —, einen Wechsel einlösen; he is the bearer of a — of exchange drawn on us, er hat einen Wechsel auf uns; this — of exchange drawn on you is endorsed to my order, dieser auf Sie gezogene Wechsel ist an meine Ordre giriert; first (—) of exchange, der Primawechsel; will you get these —s discounted for me? wollen Sie diese Wechsel für mich diskontieren lassen? the — has been protested, der Wechsel ist protestiert worden; to post —s, Zettel anschlagen; stick no —s! hier dürfen keine Plakate angeschlagen werden! to make out a —, eine Rechnung ausschreiben. II. *attrib.;* — brokerage, die Wechselcourtage; — business, das Wechselgeschäft; — discounter, der Geldverleiher, Wechseldiskontierer; — doer, der Wechselreiter; — jobber, der Wechselreiter; — poster, der Plakatanschläger; — posting, das Anschlagen von Plakaten; — stamp, der Wechselstempel. [1]—**et**, I. *s.* das Briefchen; der Quartierzettel; das Quartier; every bullet has its —et, jede Kugel hat ihre Bestimmung (*prov.*). II. *v.a.* einquartieren (on, bei). *Comp.* —**-book**, *s.* das Wechselbuch. —**-broker**, *s.* der Wechselmakler. —**-sticker**, *s.* der Zettelankleber, Plakatanschläger.
[2]**Billet**, *s.* das Scheit (*of wood*).
Billiard—s, *pl.* das Billard; a game of —s, eine Partie Billard; German —s, das Tivolispiel. *Comp.* —**-ball**, *s.* die Billardkugel. —**-cue**, *s.* der Billardstock, das Queue. —**-marker**, *s.* der (Billard-)Marqueur. —**-table**, *s.* das Billard.
Billion, *s.* die Billion.
Billow, *s.* die Woge. —**y**, *adj.* wogend, wogig.
Bimetallis—m, *s.* die Doppelwährung. —**t**, *s.* der Anhänger der Doppelwährung.
Bin, *s.* der Kasten, die Lade (*for corn, etc.*); wine —, der Weinbehälter, verschlossener Verschlag in Weinkellern; dust —, das Kehrichtfaß; street orderly —, der Straßenmüllkasten, Straßenkehrichtbehälter.
Bin—ary, *adj.* binär, binarisch, aus zwei Einheiten bestehend; —ary arithmetic, die Dyadik; —ary compound, binäre Verbindung (*Chem.*); —ary measure, der gerade Takt (*Mus.*); —ary number, die Zweizahl. —**ate**, *adj.* zweizählig (*Bot.*). —**ocle**, *s.* das Doppelfernrohr. —**ocular**, *adj.* zweiäugig. —**omial**, *adj.* binomisch; —omial quantity, das Binomium; —omial theorem, der binomische Lehrsatz.
Bind, *ir.v.* I. *a.* binden; binden, einbinden (*books*); verbinden; verpflichten; fest, gewiß machen; aufdingen (*apprentices, etc.*); fesseln (*with chains*); bordieren, einfassen (*a skirt, etc.*); beschlagen (*a wheel, etc.*); stopfen (*the bowels*); binden (*notes, Mus.*); to — together, zusammenbinden; to — up wounds, Wunden verbinden; bound in gratitude, aus Dankbarkeit verpflichtet; to — over, (einen) durch Bürgschaft verpflichten; he was bound over in two sureties to keep the peace, er wurde unter Gewährleistung von zwei Bürgen gerichtlich verpflichtet, sich friedfertig zu benehmen; am I bound by this promise? bindet mich dieses Versprechen? bin ich durch dies Versprechen gebunden? his interests are bound up with the interests of the others, seine Interessen sind mit denen der andern aufs engste verknüpft; to — apprentice, in die Lehre tun; I'll be bound, ich mache mich anheischig, ich bürge dafür; bound in calf, in Kalblederband, in Franzband. II. *n.* binden; dicht werden; eine Verstopfung verursachen; ver-

pflichten. —**er**, *s.* der Binder, Buchbinder; die Binde, das Band (*for a child, etc.*); der Garbenbinder (*Agr.*); der Hauptbalken (*Arch.*). —**ing**, I. *p. & adj.* bindend; *see* Bind. II. *s.* das Binden; der Einband (*of a book*); der Besatz, die Borte, Einfassung (*of a dress*). —**ingness**, *s.* die bindende Kraft. *Comp.* —**weed**, *s.* die Winde (*Bot.*).

Binnacle, *s.* das Kompaßhaus (*Naut.*).

Bio—graph, *s.* der lebende Bilder vorführende Apparat. —**grapher**, *s.* der Lebensbeschreiber, Biograph. —**graphic(al)**, *adj.*, —**graphically**, *adv.* biographisch. —**graphy**, *s.* die Lebensbeschreibung. —**logical**, *adj.* biologisch, zur Lebenskunde gehörig. —**logy**, *s.* die Lebenslehre, Lebenskunde. —**magnetism**, *s.* der tierische Magnetismus. —**metry**, *s.* die Lebensmessungslehre, Berechnung der wahrscheinlichen Lebensdauer. —**nomics**, *s.* die Lebensbedingungen. —**nomy**, *s.* Wissenschaft von den Gesetzen des Lebens. —**plastic**, *adj.* Keimzellen betreffend.

Biparous, *adj.* zwei Junge auf einmal gebärend; mit zwei Zweigen.

Bipartit—e, *adj.* zweiteilig. —**ion**, *s.* die Zweiteilung.

Biped, *s.* das zweifüßige Tier.

Bipetalous, *adj.* mit zwei Blumenblättern.

Biquadratic, I. *adj.* biquadratisch. II. *s.* das Biquadrat.

Birch, I. *s.* die Birke; — rod, das Birkenreis, die Rute. II. *v.a.* mit der Rute züchtigen. III. *adj.*, —**en**, *adj.* birken.

Bird, *s.* der Vogel; — of paradise, der Paradiesvogel; — of passage, der Zugvogel; to kill two —s with one stone, zwei Fliegen mit einer Klappe schlagen; —s of a feather flock together, Gleich und Gleich gesellt sich gern (*prov.*); a little — told me, ich habe ein Vögelchen singen hören; a — in the hand is worth two in the bush, ein Sperling in der Hand ist besser denn eine Taube auf dem Dache (*prov.*); the early — catches the worm, Morgenstunde hat Gold im Munde (*prov.*). *Comp.* —**-cage**, *s.* (der *and*) das Vogelbauer. —**-call**, *s.* der Vogelruf, die Lockspeise. —**-catcher**, *s.* der Vogelfänger, Vogelsteller. —**-fancier**, *s.* der Vogelliebhaber. —**-lime**, *s.* der Vogelleim. —**'s-eye**, *s.* das Vogelauge (*Bot.*); —'s-eye tobacco, feiner Tabak; —'s-eye view, Blick aus der Vogelschau. —**'s-nest**, I. *s.* das Vogelnest. II. *v.n.* Vogelnester ausnehmen; they went —('s)-nesting, sie gingen auf die Suche nach Vogelnestern.

Birth, *s.* die Geburt; (origin) der Ursprung; (rise) die Entstehung; (ancestry) die Herkunft, Abstammung; die Veranlassung (*fig.*); she has given — to a son, sie hat einen Sohn geboren; the new —, Wiedergeburt; an untimely —, eine Frühgeburt; to have two (children) at a —, Zwillinge gebären; of noble —, adelig von Geburt; she is by — a Scotchwoman, sie ist eine Schottin von Geburt; — is much, but breeding more, Erziehung gilt mehr als Geburt. *Comp.* —**day**, *s.* der Geburtstag. —**place**, *s.* der Geburtsort. —**right**, *s.* das Geburtsrecht.

Biscuit, I. *s.* hartes Gebäck, der Schiffszwieback; dog —, der Hundekuchen. II. *attrib.*; — china, das Biskuit; — kiln, der Verglühofen. —**s**, *pl.* Cakes, Knusperchen.

Bisect, *v.a.* halbieren. —**ion**, *s.* die Halbierung.

Bisexual, *adj.* zweigeschlechtig, hermaphroditisch.

Bishop, *s.* der Bischof; der Läufer (*at Chess*); (a drink) der Bischof. —**ric**, *s.* das Bistum.

Bismuth, *s.* der Wismut.

Bison, *s.* der Bison, der amerikanische Büffel; der Auerochs.

Bissextile, *s.* Schalt=; — day, der Schalttag; — year, das Schaltjahr.

Bistoury, *s.* das Ritzmesser, Bistouri (*Surg.*).

Bistre, I. *s.* der *and* das Bister, das Nußbraun. II. *adj.* braungelb.

Bisulph—ate, *s.*; —ate of potash, zweifach schwefelsaures Kali. —**ite**, *s.* doppelschwefligsaures Salz. —**uret**, *s.*; —uret of iron, das Doppel=Schwefeleisen.

Bit, I. *s.* der Bissen, das Stück; das bißchen; das Gebiß (*of a bridle*); das Bohreisen (*Mech.*); die Schülpe (*of an auger*); *see* Bitt; der Schieber (*of an umbrella*); — of a key, der Bart eines Schlüssels; not a —, nicht ein bißchen, nicht im Geringsten; a tiny little —, ein ganz klein bißchen; wait a —, warte einen Augenblick (*coll.*); every —, alles, das Ganze; by —s, — by —, in kleinen Stücken, stückweise; he does n't care a —, er macht sich gar nichts daraus, es ist ihm ganz einerlei; to champ the —, am Gebisse kauen; bars of a —, Stangen eines Gebisses. II. *imperf. see* Bite.

Bitch, *s.* die Hündin, Petze; die Metze (*fig.*).

Bite, I. *ir.v.a. & n.* beißen; stechen, schneiden, brennen (*as mustard, etc.*); verletzen, beißen (*as wit*); anbeißen (*as a fish*); to — in, ätzen (*as an acid*), eingreifen (*of a wheel*); a biting jest, ein beißender Scherz; a biting wind, ein scharfer, schneidend kalter Wind; to — the dust, ins Gras beißen; the anchor —s, der Anker greift zu; the —r bit, der betrogene Betrüger; wer andern eine Grube gräbt, fällt selbst hinein (*prov.*); to — one's nails, an den Nägeln kauen; to — one's lip, sich (*dat.*) auf die Lippe beißen; to — at, anbeißen; to — off, abbeißen. II. *s.* das Beißen, der Biß; das Anbeißen (*of fishes*); der Bissen; give me a —, laß mich einmal anbeißen. —**r**, *s.* der Beißer; *see* Bite I.

Biting, I. *p. & adj. of* Bite, —**ly**, *adv.* scharf, beißend, satirisch. II. *s.* das Beißen; — in, das Ätzen (*of acids, etc.*).

Bitten, *p.p. of* Bite.

Bitter, *adj.*, —**ly**, *adv.* bitter, scharf, herb; bitter, heftig; erbittert; schmerzhaft; streng, rauh; beißend; as — as gall, so bitter wie Galle; a — enemy, ein Todfeind; — principle, der Bitterstoff (*Chem.*); a — quarrel, ein heftiger, wütender Streit; — blast, schneidender Wind; — words, beißende Worte; — sorrow, herber Schmerz; to inveigh —ly against a p., heftig auf einen schmähen; to the — end, bis aufs letzte, bis aufs äußerste. —**ness**, *s.* die Bitterkeit; in the gall of —ness, voll bitterer Galle (*B.*). —**s**, *pl.* der Magenbitter, Bittere; tonisches Mittel (*Med.*); das Bitterbier (*coll.*). *Comp.* —**-gourd**, *s.* die Coloquinte. —**sweet**, I. *adj.* bittersüß. II. *s.* das Bittersüß (*Bot.*).

Bittern, *s.* die Rohrdommel (*Orn.*); the — booms *or* bellows, die Rohrdommel ruft *or* schreit.

Bitt—s, *pl.* die (große) Beting (*Naut.*); —s and brace, die Armdruve.

Bitum—en, *s.* das Bitumen, Bergpech, Erdharz. —**inous**, *adj.* erdharzig, erdpechartig, bituminös; —inous clay, harzhaltiger Ton.

Bivalv—e, I. *s.* die zweischalige Muschel; die zweiklappige Frucht. II. —**e**, —**ular**, *adj.* zweischalig; zweiklappig (*Bot.*).

Bivouac, I. *s.* das Biwak (*Mil.*). II. *v.n.* biwakieren, sein Feld(nacht)lager im Freien halten.

Blab, I. *s.* der Schwätzer, Ausplauderer (*vulg.*). II. *v.a. & n.* schwatzen; to — out, ausschwatzen, ausplaudern.

Black, I. *adj.*, —**ly**, *adv.* schwarz; dunkelfarbig; finster, düster, mürrisch; abscheulich (*as a crime*); to beat — and blue, einen durchbleuen, einen braun und blau schlagen; the — art, die schwarze Kunst; — squall, die schwere Bö; I have got into his — books, ich bin bei ihm schlecht angeschrieben; a — man, ein Schwarzer, Neger; a — sheep, ein räudiges Schaf, ein Taugenichts (*fig.*); to look — at a p., einen mit finstern Blicken ansehen. II. *s.* das Schwarz, die Schwärze; (— dress) der schwarze Anzug, das Trauerkleid; (negro) der Neger; shoe- —, der Schuhputzer; to wear —, schwarz gekleidet sein; to have s.th. in — and white, etwas Schwarz auf Weiß haben. III. *v.a. see* —en; wichsen (*boots, etc.*). —**en**, *v.* I. *a.* schwärzen; anschwärzen, verleumden (*fig.*); (cloud) bewölken. II. *n.* schwarz werden. —**ener**, *s.* einer der schwärzt. —**er**, *s.*; —er of shoes, der Schuhputzer. —**ing**, I. *s. see* — II.; die Schuhwichse. II. *attrib.*; —ing brush, die Wichsbürste. —**ish**, *adj.* schwärzlich. —**ness**, *s.* die Schwärze; die Abscheulichkeit (*fig.*). *Comp.* —**amoor**, *s.* der Neger, Mohr. —**ball**, I. *s.* die schwarze Wahlkugel; die gegnerische Stimme. II. *v.a.* durch eine schwarze Kugel einen bei einer Wahl durchfallen lassen, ausballotieren; he has been —balled, er ist bei der Kugelwahl durchgefallen, ist hinausballotiert. —**berry**, *s.* die Brombeere. —**bird**, *s.* die Amsel. —**board**, *s.* die schwarze Schultafel, die Schulwandtafel; das schwarze Brett (*Univ. and Coll.*). —-**book**, *s.* das Strafbuch. —-**cap**, *s.* der kleine Mönch (*Orn.*); die Tannenmeise (*Orn.*); die schwarzköpfige Möve. —**cock**, *s.* das Birkhuhn (*Orn.*). —-**eyed**, *adj.* schwarzäugig. —**guard**, *s. see* Blackguard. —**head**, *s.* der Mitesser. —-**hole**, *s.* das finstere Loch, Hundeloch. —**lead**, I. *s.* das Reißblei, Pottlot, der Graphit; —lead pencil, der Bleistift. II. *v.a.* schwärzen. —-**leg**, *s.* die Klauenseuche; der Gauner, Schwindler (*obs.*), Nichtmitglied eines der englischen Gewerkvereine; an einem allgemeinen Ausstand nicht teilnehmender Arbeiter (*coll.*). —-**letter**, I. *s.* die Fraktur, die gotische Schrift. II. *attrib.* mit gotischer Schrift gedruckt, in gotischer Schrift; —-letter day, unglücklicher Tag. —**mail**, I. *s.* der Räubersold; Erpressung (durch Drohung), Erpressungsgeld. II. *v.a.* durch Drohungen erpressen. —**mailing**, *s.* Erpressung. —-**mouthed**, *adj.* schwarzmäulig; lästermäulig, klatschsüchtig. —-**pudding**, *s.* die Blutwurst. —-**rod**, *s.*; Gentleman Usher of the —-Rod, der höchste Dienstbeamte des englischen Oberhauses; erster Zeremonienmeister bei Kapiteln des Hosenbandordens. —**smith**, *s.* der Grobschmied; der Hufschmied. —**thorn**, *s.* der Schwarzdorn, Schlehdorn. —-**visaged**, *adj.* mit düsterem Gesichte.

Blackguard, I. *s.* der Lumpenhund; der Spitzbube, Schuft; roher Kerl, gemeiner Patron. II. *adj.* & *adv.* gemein, pöbelhaft, niedrig; schuftig. III. *v.a.* gemeine Reden führen gegen, beschimpfen. —**ism**, *s.* die pöbelhafte Redeweise, die gemeine, schuftige Denkart oder Handlungsweise.

Bladder, *s.* die Blase; die Schwimmblase; die Urinblase (*Anat.*). *Comp.* —-**campion**, *s.* der klimmende Besen (*Bot.*); Taubenkropf (*Orn.*). —-**nut**, *s.* die gemeine Pimpernuß.

Blade, *s.* das Blatt, der Halm (*of grass, etc.*); die Klinge (*of a knife, etc.*); der Degen (*fig.*); shoulder- —, Schulterblatt; — of grass, der Grashalm; — of an oar, Blatt eines Riemens.

Blain, *s.* die Beule; chil—, Frostbeule.

Blam—**able**, *adj.*, —**ably**, *adv.* tadelnswert, tadelhaft. —**ableness**, *s.* die Tadelnswürdigkeit. —**e**, I. *s.* der Tadel; die Schuld; all the —e falls upon him, die ganze Schuld trifft ihn. II. *v.a.* tadeln; to be to —e, zu tadeln sein, Unrecht haben; you are to —e for having suffered it, Sie sind tadelnswert, daß Sie es duldeten; no one can —e you for it, das kann Ihnen niemand verargen. —**eless**, *adj.*, —**elessly**, *adv.* tadellos. —**elessness**, *s.* die Tadellosigkeit; die Unschuld. *Comp.* —**eworthiness**, *s.* die Tadelnswürdigkeit. —**eworthy**, *adj.* tadelnswert.

Blanch, *v.* I. *a.* weißen, bleichen; weiß sieden (*metals*); abhülsen, schälen (*almonds*); bleichen (*vegetables*); (*fig.*) bleich machen. II. *n.* erbleichen.

Blanc-mange, *s.* das Blancmanger, die weiße Gallerte, das Mandelgallert, Nußgallert.

Bland, *adj.*, —**ly**, *adv.* schmeichelnd; mild, sanft, freundlich. —**ish**, *v.a.* schmeicheln; liebkosen; sanft behandeln. —**ishment**, *s.* die Schmeichelei; die gewinnende Freundlichkeit. —**ness**, *s.* die Milde; das einschmeichelnde Wesen; die Höflichkeit; die große Freundlichkeit.

Blank, I. *adj.*, —**ly**, *adv.* blank, weiß; unbeschrieben, leer (*of paper, etc.*); reimlos (*of verse*); verwundert, bestürzt (*fig.*); — acceptance, der in Blanko Accept; — endorsement, die Indossierung in Blanko; — cartridge, die Platzpatrone; — form, unausgefülltes Formular; — cheque, unausgefüllter Wechsel; to leave —, in Blanko lassen; — space, der weiße leere Raum; — wall, türlose Mauer, eine Mauer ohne Tür und Fenster; in — astonishment, in starrem Erstaunen; he denied it point —, er hat es ganz und gar in Abrede gestellt; I told him point —, ich sagte es ihm frei heraus. II. *s.* das Weiße (*in a target, etc.*); der leere Raum (*in a book, etc.*); das unbeschriebene Papier, Blanquet; die Setzlinie (*Typ.*); die Niete (*in a lottery*); die Münzplatte, der Schrötling (*Mint*); his memory has become a —, er hat sein Gedächtnis gänzlich verloren; in —, in Blanko. —**et**, I. *s.* die wollene Decke, Schlafdecke; die Lagerdecke (*Mil.*); die Filzunterlage (*Typ.*); a wet —et, ein Dämpfer, kalter Wasserstrahl (*fig.*); ein Spielverderber (*fig.*); to put a wet —et on a th., etwas dämpfen, niederschlagen, ersticken; he threw a wet —et over all of us, er verdarb uns allen das Vergnügen; to toss in a —et, (*also* —**et**, *v.a.*,) in einer Bettdecke prellen. —**eting**, *s.* das Prellen in einer Bettdecke; das Zeug zu Bettdecken. —**ness**, *s.* die Weiße; the —ness of her look, ihr bestürztes Aussehen.

Blare, *v.n.* brüllen, plärren (*vulg.*); schmettern (*of trumpets; poet.*).

Blarney, *s.* die außerordentlich schmeichelhafte, verbindliche Sprache (*Irish*).

Blasphem—**e**, *v.a.* & *n.*; to —e (against) God, Gott lästern. —**er**, *s.* der Gotteslästerer. —**ous**, *adj.*, —**ously**, *adv.* (gottes)lästerlich. —**y**, *s.* die Gotteslästerung, Lästerung.

Blast, I. *s.* der Windstoß; der kalte *or* eisige Hauch; der Schall, Stoß (*of trumpets*); die Explosion (of gunpowder, etc., des Sprengpulvers, &c.); die Lufterschütterung (*by a cannon-shot*); (blight) der Pesthauch, Mehltau, Brand (im Getreide, an Bäumen, &c.); das Gebläse, die Gebläseluft (*Metall.*). II. *attrib.*; — apparatus, die Gebläsevorrichtung. III. *v.a.* sprengen; (blight) versengen, verdorren; (destroy) vernichten, schlagen; (curse) fluchen, verfluchen; to — a p.'s reputation, einen um seinen guten Namen bringen; —ed corn, verbranntes Getreide; —ed hopes, vereitelte Hoffnungen. —**ing**, I. *p.* & *adj. see* Blast; —ing agent, das Sprengmittel; —ing operation, die Sprengarbeit; —ing powder, das Sprengpulver. II. *s.* das Sprengen; das Versengen; das Verderben. *Comp.* —-**furnace**, *s.* der Hochofen. —-**hole**, *s.* das Sprengloch, Bohrloch. —-**pipe**, *s.* das Blasrohr.

Blatant, *adj.* blökend, lärmend; schreiend (*fig.*); the — Beast, die Verleumdung (*fig.*).

Blaz—**e**, I. *s.* der Lichtschein, das Lodern des Feuers; die Flamme; die Blesse (*on a horse's forehead*); die Aufregung (*fig.*). II. *v.n.* flammen, lodern, hell leuchten; glänzen; the fire was —ing away, das Feuer brannte lichterloh. III. *v.a.*; to —e abroad, ausposaunen; to —e a tree, einen Baum anschalmen. —**er**, *s.* leichte Flanell-Jacke von bunter Farbe; —er abroad, der Verbreiter von Gerüchten. —**on**, I. *s.* die Wappenkunst; die Wappenbeschreibung; das Wappen(schild); die Verkündigung; der Pomp. II. *v.a.* Wappen beschreiben (*Her.*); (emblazon) schildern; (deck) schmücken; (display) zur Schau auslegen; (—on forth) ausposaunen; —oned windows of a college hall, wappengeschmückte Fenster des Speisesaals eines College. —**oner**.

s. der Wappenerklärer; der Herold; (—oner abroad) der Verbreiter, Verkünder, Ausposauner; der Lobredner. **—onry,** *s.* die Wappenkunde.
Bleach, *v.a. & n.* bleichen. **—er,** *s.* der Bleicher. **—ing,** I. *p. & adj.* bleichend. II. *s.* das Bleichen. *Comp.* **—field, —green,** *s.* die Bleiche. **—ing-powder,** *s.* das Bleichpulver.
Bleak, I. *adj.,* **—ly,** *adv.* rauh, kalt und unfreundlich, öde, freudenlos; ungeschützt. II. *s.* der Weißfisch. **—ness,** *s.* die Kälte, Rauhheit; die Öde, Unfreundlichkeit; die Unbeschütztheit.
Blear-eyed, *adj.* triefäugig.
Bleat, I. *v.n.* blöken. II., **—ing,** *s.* das Blöken, Geblöke.
Bleb, *s.* kleine Blase.
Bled, *imperf. & p.p. of* Bleed.
Bleed, *ir.v.* I. *n.* bluten; to — to death, sich verbluten. II. *a.* bluten lassen; zur Ader lassen; (einen) sich verbluten lassen; einen schröpfen, rupfen, beschwindeln (*coll.*); —ing heart, blutendes Herz; tropfendes Herz (*Bot.*). **—ing,** I. *p. & adj.* blutend. II. *s.* der Blutfluß; der Aderlaß (*Surg.*); das Saftabzapfen (*of trees*); —ing at the nose, das Nasenbluten.
Blemish, I. *s.* der Mackel, Flecken (*also fig.*); (bodily —) das Gebrechen; der Schandfleck (*fig.*). II. *v.a.* verunstalten, entstellen; beschmutzen, beflecken, brandmarken.
Blench, *v.n.* zurückweichen, stutzen.
Blend, *v.* I. *a.* mischen, vermischen. II. *n.* sich vermischen. III. die Mischung, das Gemisch. **—er,** *s.* der Vermischer, Mischer.
Blende, *s.* die Blende (*Min.*).
Blenn—orrhœa, *s.* der Schleimfluß. **—y,** *s.* der Schleimfisch.
Blent, *imperf. & p.p. of* Blend.
Bless, *v.a.* segnen; einsegnen (*at confirmation, etc.*); beglücken, glücklich machen; (extol) selig preisen, loben; — me! O Himmel! God — you! Gott sei mit dir! (*after sneezing*) wohl bekomm's! **—ed,** *adj.,* **—edly,** *adv.* (happy) glücklich, selig; gesegnet; verwünscht, verflixt (*vulg.*); the —ed Virgin, die hochgelobte *or* (hoch)gebenedeite Jungfrau; of —ed memory, seligen Angedenkens, selig; King William of —ed memory, der hochselige König Wilhelm. **—edness,** *s.* die Glückseligkeit, Seligkeit; (salvation) das Heil; single-—edness, die Ehelosigkeit. **—er,** *s.* der Beglücker. **—ing,** *s.* das Segnen; der Segen; die Segnung; (benefit) die Wohltat; by the —ing of God, durch Gottes Segen *or* Huld; to ask a —ing, das Tischgebet sprechen.
Blest, I. *p.p. of* Bless. II. *adj.* glücklich, selig.
Blight, I. *s.* der Mehltau, Brand; die Schärfe; der durch Frost entstandene Schaden; der Gifthauch (*fig.*). II. *v.a.* durch Mehltau verderben, am Gedeihen hindern; vereiteln; —ed hopes, vereitelte, im Keime erstickte Hoffnungen.
Blind, I. *adj.* blind, blödsichtig; blind (to, gegen); unsichtbar, geheim (*of a staircase, etc.*); — alley, die Sackgasse; — man, der Blinde; Person mit verbundenen Augen; — of one eye, auf einem Auge blind; — to one's own failings, gegen die eigenen Fehler blind; a p.'s — side, jemandes schwache Seite; a — wall, eine blinde Mauer. II. *s.* die Decke, Blende, Hülle, der Vorsetzer, die kleine Verhüllung der unteren Fensterscheiben; (roller) die Fensterblende, der Rollvorhang, das Rouleau; (Venetian —) der Stabvorhang, die Jalousie; das Scheuleder (*Saddl.*); die Blende (*Fort.*); der Vorwand (*fig.*); die Bemäntelung (*fig.*). III. *v.a.* blind machen, blenden; verblenden (to, gegen); betrügen. **—s,** *pl.* das Blendwerk, Deckwerk, die Blendung; inside (outside) —s, Fensterblenden innerhalb (außerhalb) der Fenster. **—ly,** *adv.* blind, blindlings, unbesonnen, ins Blaue hinein. **—ness,** *s.* die Blindheit. *Comp.* **—fold,** I. *adj.* mit verbundenen Augen; blind (*fig.*). II. *v.a.* die Augen verbinden. **—man,** *s.*; **—man's buff,** die Blindekuh; —man's holiday, das Zwielicht, der Feierabend. **—-worm,** *s.* die Blindschleiche.
Blink, I. der flüchtige Blick; das Blinzeln; (ray) der Schimmer; (sparkle) der Strahl; (twinkling) der Augenblick (*dial.*); — of sunshine, ein Sonnenblick. II. *v.a.* aus den Augen lassen, absichtlich übersehen; nicht sehen wollen; nicht stellen (*Sport*); to — the facts, die Wahrheit nicht sehen wollen, absichtlich übersehen, nicht zugeben; there is no —ing the truth, man darf sich der Wahrheit nicht verschließen, man muß der Wahrheit fest ins Gesicht sehen. III. *v.n.* blinken; blinzeln. **—ard,** *s.* der Blinzler. **—er,** *s.* die Blende, das Scheuleder, die Scheuklappe. *Comp.* **—-beer,** *s.* Bier das einen Stich hat (*Amer.*). **—-eyed,** *adj.* fortwährend blinzelnd.
Bliss, *s.* die Seligkeit, Wonne. **—ful,** *adj.,* **—fully,** *adv.* selig, wonnig, wonnevoll. **—fulness,** *s.* die Glückseligkeit, Wonne. **—less,** (*obs.*) *adj.* unglückselig, freudeleer.
Blister, I. *s.* die Blase, Blatter; das Blasenpflaster, Zugpflaster (*Med.*); die Blase (*on metals*). II. *v.a.* Blasen ziehen *or* machen; Blasenpflaster auflegen; brennen machen *or* lassen (wie von Blasen) (*fig.*); —ing fluid, die brennende Flüssigkeit, Blasenflüssigkeit. III. *v.n.* Blasen bekommen. **—ed,** *adj.* voller Blasen. *Comp.* **—-steel,** *s.* der Blasenstahl.
Blithe, *adj.,* **—ly,** *adv.* munter, lustig, heiter, wohlgemut; (*obs.*) — to the people, leutselig. **—ness,** *s.* die Fröhlichkeit, Munterkeit. **—some,** *adj.* fröhlich, munter, vergnügt. **—someness,** *s. see* —ness.
Blizzard, *s.* das (orkanartige) Schneetreiben, der (nordamerikanische) schwere Schneesturm.
Bloat, *v.a.* aufblasen, aufschwellen; to — herrings, Häringe räuchern. **—ed,** *adj.* aufgedunsen. **—er,** *s.* der geräucherte Häring, Bück(l)ing.
Blob, I. *s.* die Blase; das Kügelchen, Klümpchen, der Klecks; die herabhängende Unterlippe (*fig.*). II. *v.a.* klecksen. III. *v.n.* Blasen werfen. **—ber,** *adj.* aufgeschwollen, vorstehend (*of lips*). *Comp.* **—ber-lipped,** *adj.* dicklippig.
Block, I. *s.* der Block, Klotz; der Block (*Mach., Artil., Naut.*); der Stock (*of the anvil*); die Hutform, der Hutstock; der Stein (*Typ.; Bookb.*); das Druckmodell (*of calico-printers*); das Lochholz (*of shoemakers*); der Richtblock (*of the executioner*); der Perrückenstock (*of wigmakers*); (stumbling-—) das Hindernis; der Tölpel, Klotz, Dummkopf (*fig.*); der Würfel (*Rail.*); — of marble, ein Marmorblock; a — of houses, der Häuser-Komplex; to put on the —, (auf dem Stock) formen; to come to the —, enthauptet werden. II. *v.a.* (— up) versperren, sperren; einschließen, blocken, blockieren; aus freier Hand bedrucken (*Typ.*); zurichten; to be no longer —ed, entblockt sein (*of a railway line*); to — out, zurichten; to — a hat, einen Hut über den Stock schlagen. **—ade,** I. *s.* die Blockade; to run the —ade, die Blockade brechen. II. *v.a.* blockieren. **—ing,** *s.* die Blockung (*of railway lines*). **—ish,** *adj.,* **—ishly,** *adv.* klotzig, dumm. **—ishness,** *s.* das tölpische Wesen. *Comp.* **—-books,** *pl.* mit Holztafeln gedruckte Bücher (*Typ.*). **—head,** *s.* der Dummkopf. **—-headed,** *adj.* dumm. **—house,** *s.* das Blockhaus (*Fort.*). **—-letters,** *pl.* Holztypen. **—-printing,** *s.* der Holzdruck, der Handdruck. **—-sheaves,** *pl.* die Blockscheiben (*Naut.*). **—-system,** *s.* das Blocksignalsystem. **—-telegraph,** *s.* der Signaltelegraph (*Railw.*). **—-trail,** *s.* der Lafettenschwanz (*Artil.*).
Bloke, *s.* der Mann, Kerl (*sl. contempt.*).
Blomary, *see* Bloomery.
Blond—e, I. *s.* die Blondine. II. *adj.* hell, blond. *Comp.* **—-lace,** *s.* die Blonde, seidene Spitze.
Blood, I. *s.* das Blut; (lineage) die Abstammung, Herkunft, das Geblüt; (kindred) die Blutsfreundschaft; (life) das Leben; die Rasse.

das Blut (*of horses*); (juice) der Saft; he has lost much —, er hat einen bedeutenden Blutverlust erlitten; princes of the —, Prinzen von königlichem Geblüt; a young —, ein feuriger, junger Mann; ein Hitzkopf; ein Stutzer; full —, das Vollblut(pferd); half —, (*of a horse*) das Halblut(pferd), (*of a person*) halbbürtige Geschwister; the whole — is preferred to the half, vollbürtige Kinder gehen den Stiefkindern vor; in cold —, mit kaltem Blute; to breed bad —, böses Blut machen, die Gemüter erbittern; his — is up, sein Blut ist in Wallung, er ist tief erregt; er ist entrüstet; with good — in his veins, von guter Herkunft; the deed was done in hot —, die Tat geschah (in einem Augenblicke des Zorns) im Zorne; avenger of —, der Bluträcher; it runs in the —, es steckt im Blute; true — will show itself, das Blut verleugnet sich nicht, Art läßt nicht von Art; — is thicker than water, Blutsverwandtschaft ist das stärkste Bindemittel. I. *v.a.* blutig machen. —**ily**, *adv.* blutig. —**iness**, *s.* das Blutigsein; das Blutige; die Blutgier. —**less**, *adj.*, —**lessly**, *adv.* blutlos, unblutig. —**y**, *adj.* blutig; (—thirsty) blutgierig; (—stained) blutbefleckt; sehr, verdammt (*vulg.*); (cruel) grausam; —y (piece of) work, grausame Handlung, Tat; —y sweat, der Blutschweiß; —y flux, der Blutfluß; a —y scoundrel, ein verfluchter Schuft (*vulg.*). *Comp.* —**-curdling**, *adj.* haarsträubend, grausig. —**-dyed**, *adj.* blutgefärbt. —**-guiltiness**, *s.* die Blutschuld. —**-heat**, *s.* die Blutwärme. —**-horse**, *s.* das Vollblutpferd. —**hound**, *s.* der Bluthund. —**letting**, *s.* das Aderlassen. —**-red**, *adj.* blutrot. —**-relation**, *s.* der *or* die Blutsverwandte. —**-relationship**, *s.* die Blutsverwandtschaft. —**shed**, *s.* das Blutvergießen. —**shot**, *adj.* blutunterlaufen. —**-spitting**, *s.* das Blutspeien. —**stained**, *adj.* blutbefleckt. —**stone**, *s.* der Blutstein. —**sucker**, *s.* der Blutsauger. —**thirstiness**, *s.* die Blutdürstigkeit, der Blutdurst. —**thirsty**, *adj.* blutdürstig. —**vessel**, *s.* das Blutgefäß. —**y-minded**, *adj.* blutgierig, mordsüchtig.

[1]**Bloom**, I. *s.* die Blüte (*also fig.*); der Flor; die Blume; das Blaue, der blaue Reif (*on plums, etc.*); der Flaum (*on peaches, etc.*); in full —, in vollem Blütenschmuck; — of youth, die Jugendblüte. II. *v.n.* blühen (*also fig.*). —**ing**, *p. & adj.* blühend.

[2]**Bloom**, *s.* die Luppe (*Metall.*). —**ery**, *s.* das Frischfeuer, Luppenfeuer; —ery hearth, der Rennherd.

[1]**Bloomer**, *s.* blühende Pflanze; entwickelte Knospe.

[2]**Bloomer**, *s.*, —**s**, *pl.* die Reformhose, Radfahr-Damenbeinkleider; Gegenstände der Bloomertracht; — costume, der Reformanzug.

Blossom, I. *s.* die Blüte. II. *v.n.* blühen, Blüte treiben. —**ing**, I. *p. & adj.* blühend; —ing time, die Blütezeit. II. *s.* das Blühen.

Blot, I. *v.a.* beflecken (*also fig.*); (daub) klecksen; löschen (*with blotting-paper*); to — out, ausstreichen, auslöschen, verwischen; to — out of the book of life, aus dem Buche des Lebens tilgen; to — out sins, Sünden vergeben. II. *s.* der Fleck, Klecks, Tintenfleck; der Makel. —**ch**, *s.* die Finne, Hitzblatter; der Klecks. —**chy**, *adj.* finnig. —**ter**, *s.* der Tintenlöscher; das Löschblatt, Löschpapier, Fließpapier. *Comp.* —**ting-book**, *s.* die Mappe, das Buch von Löschpapier. —**ting-pad**, *s.* die Schreibunterlage. —**ting-paper** *s.* das Löschpapier, Löschblatt, Fließpapier.

Blouse, *s.* die Bluse.

[1]**Blow**, *s.* der Schlag (*also fig.*); to come to —s, handgemein werden; without striking a —, ohne Schwertstreich; at a —, plötzlich, auf einmal.

[2]**Blow**, I. *v.n.* blühen; (*fig.*) erblühen. II. *s.* die Blüte.

[3]**Blow**, *ir.v.* I. *n.* blasen, wehen; (puff, gasp) keuchen, schnaufen; schallen, erschallen; to — hot and cold, aus einem Munde kalt und warm blasen, unzuverlässig (in seinen Äußerungen) sein; to — **on** one's fingers, sich (*dat.*) in die Hände blasen, um sie zu erwärmen; to — **over**, vorüberziehen (*as a storm*), ohne Wirkung vorüber gehen, verwehen; some of the enemy's magazines blew **up**, einige Vorratshäuser des Feindes flogen in die Luft; —**upon**, beschmeißen. II. *a.* blasen; wehen; treiben; anblasen, anfachen (*the fire, etc.*); aufblasen (*also fig.*); ausflammen (*guns*); to — one's nose, sich schnauben *or* schneuzen; — **away** *or* **off**, wegblasen, verjagen; —**down**, umwehen, umblasen; to — down fruit, Obst herunterwehen; to — **off** steam, Dampf auslassen, ausblasen; — **out**, ausblasen, auslöschen (*light*); to — one's brains out, sich (*dat.*) eine Kugel durch den Kopf jagen, to — **up**, aufblasen, anblasen, vernichten; to — up a rock, einen Felsen sprengen; to — up a mine, eine Mine springen lassen; to — a p. up, einen tüchtig ausschelten (*coll.*); to — up a bladder, eine Blase aufblasen; to — an egg, ein Ei ausblasen; what wind blew you hither? welcher (gute) Wind hat dich hierher geweht? this meat is fly—n, dieses Fleisch hat den Stich bekommen; 't is an ill wind that —s no one any good, es ist nichts so schlimm, es ist zu etwas gut (*prov.*) —**er**, *s.* der Bläser, das Schiebblech (in Kaminen, ꝛc.); der Zinnschmelzer; organ —er, der Bälgetreter; —er and spreader, Wattenmaschine. *Comp.* —**-hole**, *s.* das Luftloch, Zugloch. —**ing-apparatus**, *s.* der Schmelzapparat. —**-off**, *attrib.*; —-off cock, der Ausblashahn; —-off pipe, das Ausblasrohr. —**pipe**, *s.* das Blaserohr; das Lötrohr; die Pfeife (*of glass-blowers*).

Blowz—ed, *adj.* rotbäckig, pausbäckig, hochrot; bäurisch, roh. —**y**, *adj.* pausbäckig, hochrot; wirr, zerzaust, nachlässig.

Blubber, I. *s.* der Wallfischspeck; der Tran. II. *adj.*; —cheeks, dicke, fleischige Backen. III. *v.n.* plärren, heulen, weinen, schluchzen (*coll.*). —**-lipped**, *adj.* dicklippig, großmäulig.

Bludgeon, *s.* der Knüttel; die Schutzmannswaffe.

Blue, I. *adj.* blau; trübe, niedergeschlagen, schwermütig (*coll.*); — blood, blaues, aristokratisches Blut; true —, echt (blau), treu, unwandelbar; to look —, trüb, mißvergnügt aussehen. II. *s.* das Blau; die Bläue (*Laundry*); she is a bit of a — (*i.e.* blue-stocking), sie ist eine gelehrte Dame, etwas blaustrümpfig; to be a (University) —, ein hervorragender Athlet sein, der in den großen Wettkämpfen für seine Universität (Cambridge oder Oxford) gespielt hat; the —s, die englische Leibgarde zu Pferd; the light (dark) —s, die Studenten von Cambridge (Oxford); he is a true —, er ist gut konservativ; it gives me a fit of the —s, es macht mich ganz melancholisch; Prussian —, Berliner Blau. III. *v.a.* blau färben, bläuen. —**ish**, *adj.* bläulich. —**ness**, *s.* die Bläue. *Comp.* —**bell**, *s.* die (blaue) Glockenblume. —**book**, *s.* das Blaubuch, die staatliche Veröffentlichung (*in England*) (*Parl.*). —**bottle**, *s.* die blaue Schmeißfliege, die Fleischfliege (*Ent.*); die Kornblume (*Bot.*). —**-coat**, *attrib.*; —-coat boy, der blauröckige Schüler von Christ's Hospital; —-coat school, die Blaurockschule, Christ's Hospital; (eine höhere Stiftungsschule bei London). —**-devils**, *pl.* (*coll.*) der Trübsinn; der Säuferwahnsinn (*delirium tremens*). —**-eyed**, *adj.* blauäugig. —**-peter**, *s.* die Signalflagge zum Segeln. —**-pill**, *s.* die Merkurpille; die blaue Bohne, Kugel. —**-ribbon**, *s.*; he has got the —-ribbon (of the Garter), er ist ein Ritter des Hosenbandordens (geworden); he wears the —-ribbon (is a —-ribbonite), er ist ein Mitglied des Mäßigkeitsvereins, ein Temperänzler. —**-stocking**, *s.* der Blaustrumpf. —**-vitriol**, *s.* das Kupfervitriol.

Bluff, I. *adj.* stark, plump; breit, offen, gutmütig (of a face); kräftig; (abrupt) schroff, kurz; *see* Blustering. II. *s.* das steile Ufer, Felsenufer, das Scheuleder; die Täuschung, Irreführung;

die herausfordernde Haltung, prahlerische Rede, der Schreckschuß. —**ness**, *s.* die Schroffheit.
Blunder, I. *s.* der Schnitzer, Fehler. II. *v.a. & n.* sich gröblich irren; einen groben Fehler machen, einen Bock machen; stolpern; sich übereilen; to — about, blind zufahren, zutappen; — **out**, herausplatzen (mit etwas); mit der Tür ins Haus fallen; — **upon**, auf (eine S.) stolpern. —**er**, *s.* der Tölpel, Faseler, Faselhans.
Blunderbuss, *s.* die Donnerbüchse.
Blunt, I. *adj.*, —**ly**, *adv.* stumpf; plump, grob, derb (*fig.*); (stupid) dumm; (unpolished) ungeschliffen; (insensible) unempfindlich; to grow —, sich abstumpfen; — cone, der Stumpfkegel; to be — with a p., einen barsch behandeln. II. *v.a.* stumpf machen, abstumpfen (*also fig.*). III. *s.* das Geld (*sl.*); —s, der Ausschuß von Nähnadeln. —**ing**, I. *p. see* — II. II. *s.;* the —ing of the angles of a battalion, ein Manöver, das Quarree in ein Achteck zu verwandeln. —**ness**, *s.* die Stumpfheit; die Plumpheit, Derbheit. *Comp.* —**-edged**, *adj.* stumpfkantig. —**-witted**, *adj.* stumpfsinnig, dumm.
Blur, I. *s.* der Fleck; (*fig.*) der Schandfleck; die Verschwommenheit. II. *v.a.* beflecken; auslöschen.
Blurt, *v.a.;* to — out, unbesonnen heraussagen, (mit einer Sache) unüberlegt herausplatzen.
Blush, I. *s.* das Erröten; die Schamröte; to put s.o. to the —, einen schamrot machen, beschämen; at the first —, beim ersten flüchtigen Blick; im ersten Augenblick (*coll.*). II. *v.n.* erröten (at a th., über eine S.), rot werden. —**ing**, I. *p.adj.* errötend. II. *s.* das Erröten.
Bluster, I. *s.* das Brausen, Toben; das Getöse, Geräusch; die Prahlerei. II. *v.n.* brausen, lärmen, toben; (*swagger*) prahlen; *see* Bully. —**er**, *s.* der Polterer; der Prahlhans, Bramarbas. —**ing**, I. *adj. & adv.* tobend, lärmend; prahlend. II. *s.* das Poltern; das Prahlen.
Bo, *int.* buh! huh! he cannot say — to a goose, er kann keine Gans erschrecken, er kann nicht bis fünf zählen. *Comp.* —**-peep**, *int.* hutt, bäh; weg, guck; to play at —-peep, guck guck spielen.
Boa, *s.* die Boa; der Halspelz (in Schlangenform). *Comp.* —**-constrictor**, *s.* die Riesenschlange.
Boar, *s.* der Eber; wild —, wildes Schwein, Wildschwein; young wild —, der Frischling; —'s head, der Wildschweinskopf. *Comp.* —**-spear**, *s.* der Saufspieß.
Board, I. *s.* das Brett; die Diele; der Tisch, die Tafel; der Bord (*Naut.*); die Pappe (*Bookb.*); die Kost, der Unterhalt (*fig.*); das Kostgeld, die Pension; der Ausschuß; das Gericht, die Behörde; —s, Pappband (*books*); school- —, der Erziehungsrat für Elementarschulen; weather- —, der hohe Bord eines Schiffes, die Windseite, Luvseite; the —s, die Bühne (*Theat.*); — of agriculture, das Ministerium für Landwirtschaft; — of customs, das Zollamt; — of directors, das Direktorium; — of health, die Sanitätsbehörde; — of revenue, das Finanzbureau; the Special — for Modern Languages, der Ausschuß für Neuere Sprachen (*Univ.*); —s of study, (beratende und gesetzgebende) Fakultätsausschüsse; — of works, die Baukommission (zu London); — of trade, das Handelsgericht, Handelsministerium; — of control, der Aufsichtsrat; to act above- —, unverhehlt, offen handeln; to go on — ship, sich einschiffen, an Bord gehen; to go by the —, über Bord geworfen *or* aufgegeben werden; to put on —, an Bord bringen; to fall over—, über Bord fallen; to put to —, in die Kost geben; he has his — free, er hat freie Kost *or* Tafel; — and lodging, Kost und Logis, volle Pension. II. *v.a.* täfeln, dielen; entern (*Naut.*); in die Kost geben; beköstigen, verköstigen. III. *v.n.* in der Kost sein; to — up, zuschlagen mit Brettern. —**able**, *adj.* enterbar. —**er**, *s.* der Kostgänger, Pensionär; der Kostschüler (*in a school*). —**ing**, *s.* das Dielen, der Verschlag; die Kost, der Tisch; das Entern (*Naut.*). *Comp.* —**ing-house**, *s.* die Pension. —**ing-pike**, *s.* die Enterpike. —**ing-school**, *s.* das Internat; das Pensionat. —**-room**, *s.* das Sitzungszimmer eines Direktoriums. —**-school**, *s.* die Volksschule. —**-wages**, *pl.* das Kostgeld; servants on —-wages, Dienstboten, die sich (in Abwesenheit der Herrschaft) für ein bestimmtes Wochengeld selbst verköstigen.
Boast, I. *v.n.* sich rühmen (of a thing, einer Sache); prahlen. II. *v.a.* rühmen, erheben. III. *s.* die Prahlerei, der Ruhm; great —, small roast, viel Geschrei und wenig Wolle (*prov.*). —**er**, *s.* der Prahler, Prahlhans. —**ful**, *adj.*, —**fully**, *adv.* prahlerisch. —**fulness**, *s.* die Ruhmredigkeit.
Boat, I. *s.* das Boot, der Kahn; to be in the same —, in gleicher Lage sein. II. *attrib.;* — cleats, die Bootsklampen. III. *v.n.* in einem Boote fahren. —**ing**, I. *s.* das Bootfahren, die Bootfahrt; they went —ing, sie gingen zum Rudern, *or* um eine Wasserpartie zu machen. II. *attrib.;* —ing excursion, die Bootfahrt, Wasserfahrt; —ing party, die Wasserpartie. *Comp.* —**-building**, *s.* der Bootbau. —**-hook**, *s.* der Bootshaken. —**man**, *s.* der Bootsmann, Ruderer. —**-race**, *s.* das Wettrudern, die Wettfahrt. —**-shaped**, *adj.* bootförmig, nachenförmig. —**swain**, *s.* der Bootsmann; —swain's call, die Bootsmannspfeife; —swain's mate, der Bootsmannsmaat.
Bob, I. *s.* etwas Hängendes, Baumelndes; (pendant) das Gehänge, die Baumel; (jerk) der Stoß; die Linse (*Horol.*); (curtsy) der kurze Knix; der Schilling (*sl.*); eine besondere Art von Glockengeläute. II. *v.n.* baumeln, hängen; eine kurze Verbeugung, kleine Knixe machen; mit der Aalflöße angeln; to — up and down, auf und untertauchen. III. *v.a.* schlagen; to — the head, nicken. —**bin**, *s.* die Spule, der Klöppel. —**by**, *s.* der Polizist (*sl.*). *Comp.* —**bin-frame**, *s.* die Spindelbank, Spulmaschine. —**bin-lace**, *s.* geklöppelte Spitzen. —**bin-net**, *s.* der Spitzengrund, Bobbinet. —**tail**, *s.* zerlumpte Person, Lump; rag-tag and —tail, Krethi und Plethi. —**-wig**, *s.* die Stutzperrücke.
Bode, *v.a.* vorbedeuten, Anzeichen sein (von); vorhersagen, ankündigen; ahnen lassen.
Bodega, *s.* die spanische Weinstube, Bodega.
Bod—ice, *s.* das Leibchen (*of a dress*); das Mieder, Schnürleibchen. —**ied**, *adj.* (*in comp.*) big- —ied, dickleibig; strong- —ied, nervig; full- —ied, stark (*of wine*); able- —ied, gesund, stark, handfest (*as paupers*); dienstfähig (*of sailors*). —**iless**, *adj.* unkörperlich. —**ily**, *adj. & adv.* körperlich, leiblich; wirklich. —**y**, *see* Body.
Bodkin, I. *s.* die Schnürnadel; der Pfriem (*Bookb.*); die Ahle (*Typ.*); die Haarnadel; der Dolch (*obs.*). II. *adv.;* he sat —, er saß zwischen uns (ihnen) als dritter (wo eigentlich nur Platz für zwei war).
Body, *s.* der Körper, Leib; der Kasten (*of a coach*); (person) die Person, der Mensch; (torso, hulk) der Rumpf; (corpse) der Leichnam; (substance) die Substanz; (stuff) der Stoff, die Materie; (essence) das Wesentliche; (whole —) die Gesammtheit; der Körper (*Phys.*); die körperliche Figur (*Geom.*); das Schiff (*of a church*); das Hauptgebäude (*of a building*); das System, die Sammlung (*of laws*); der Körper, die Stärke (*of wine*); die Dichtigkeit, der Kern (*of cloth, etc.*); der Stoff, (Haupt-)Inhalt, Hauptbestandteil (*of a discourse, etc.*); die Masse, Gesammtheit, das Ganze (*of things*); die Dichtigkeit (*of a liquid*); heavenly —, der Himmelskörper; — corporate, die Körperschaft; solid —, fester Körper; — of a letter, der Schriftkegel; main — of an army, das Gros, der Hauptteil des Heeres; a — of troops, eine Abteilung Soldaten; the — of the clergy, die gesammte Geistlichkeit; what is a — to do, was soll man tun? in a —, zusammen; to come in a —, in einem Haufen

kommen; the Parliament in a —, das gesammte Parlament; the professors in a —, sämmtliche Professoren, das ganze Professorenkollegium; deeds done in the —, des Fleisches Geschäfte (*B.*), wirklich ausgeübte Missetaten; the legislative —, die gesetzgebende Körperschaft; the — of civil law, das Corpus Juris; the — politic, der Staatskörper; issue of the —, die Leibesfrucht; any—, irgend einer; every—, jedermann, ein jedermann. *Comp.* **—-colour**, *s.* die Deckfarbe. **—-guard**, *s.* die Leibwache. **—-snatcher**, *s.* der Leichendieb.

Bog, I. *s.* der Sumpf, Morast, das Bebemoor. II. *v.a.* im Kote herumwälzen. **—gy**, *adj.* sumpfig. *Comp.* **—-berry**, *s.* die Moorheidelbeere. **—-land**, *s.* das Marschland. **—-oak**, *s.* die (irische) Mooreiche. **—-ore**, *s.* der Sumpfeisenstein. **—-trotter**, *s.* der Sumpfbewohner; der Irländer (*hum.*).

Boggle, *v.n.* stutzen, zurückfahren; (demur) Anstand nehmen, unschlüssig sein; pfuschen, stümpern.

Bogie, I. *s.* das bewegliche Radgestell. II. *attrib.*; — wheel, das bewegliche Rad. *Comp.* **—-engine**, *s.* die Lokomotive mit beweglichem Radgestell.

Bogus, *adj.* nachgemacht, falsch, unecht; — bank, die Schwindelbank.

Bogy, Bogey, *s.* der Kobold, Popanz, das Schreckgespenst; — man, der Butzemann.

Bohea, *s.* der schwarze Tee.

Boil, I. *s.* die Beule, der Schwären. II. *v.a.* & *n.* sieden, kochen; erregt werden (*fig.*); to — away *or* down, einkochen; to — over, übersieden, überwallen; to — over with rage, rasend werden; the —ing waves, die brausenden, brandenden Wellen. **—er**, *s.* die Sieder; der Kessel; der Dampfkessel (*Locom. etc.*). **—ing**, I. *p.* & *adj.* *see* Boil; —ing hot, siedend heiß. II. *s.* das Kochen, Sieden; das (auf einmal) Gekochte; the whole —ing, die ganze Sippschaft (*vulg.*). *Comp.* **—ing-point**, *s.* der Siedepunkt.

Boisterous, *adj.*, **—ly**, *adv.* ungestüm, heftig, laut, rauh. **—ness**, *s.* der *and* das Ungestüm.

Bold, *adj.*, **—ly**, *adv.* (brave) kühn, mutig; keck, dreist; (impudent) frech; a — coast, eine steile Küste; a — outline, ein kühn entworfener Umriß; to make —, sich erkühnen *or* erdreisten; to make so — as to, sich (*dat.*) die Freiheit nehmen, sich (*dat.*) Freiheiten herausnehmen, sich erdreisten; if I may make so —, mit Erlaubnis; that is a — word, das ist viel gesagt. **—ness**, *s.* der Mut, die Kühnheit; die Dreistigkeit; die Frechheit, Unverschämtheit; die Steilheit; —ness of style, kühne Schreibart *or* Redeweise, kühner, großzügiger Stil.

[1]**Bole**, *s.* der Stamm (*of a tree*).

[2]**Bole**, *s.* der Bolus.

Boletus, *s.* der Hutpilz, Löcherschwamm (*Bot.*).

Boll, *s.* die Samenkapsel; der runde Knopf.

Bollard, *s.* aufrecht stehender Pfahl; der Poller.

Bolster, I. *s.* das Polster, Kissen; das Bäuschchen (*Surg.*). II. *v.a.* polstern, Kissenunterlegen; to — up, unterstützen; etwas künstlich zu halten suchen.

[1]**Bolt**, I. *s.* der Bolzen; der Riegel, Schließhaken; der Pfeil; thunder—, der Donnerkeil; spring —, Riegel mit einer Feder; to shoot the —, den Riegel vorschieben; to make a — (for), stürzen (nach), reißausnehmen (*coll.*); —s of the bitts, Letingsbolzen (*Naut.*); — upright, (*adv.*) pfeilgerade, kerzengerade. II. *attrib.*; — drawer, der Bolzenausheber. III. *v.a.* verbolzen; verriegeln, zuriegeln; Speisen ohne sie zu kauen hinunterschlingen; mit Bolzen befestigen. IV. *v.a.* durchgehen; davonlaufen; to — **out** with a th., mit etwas herausplatzen. **—er**, *s.* der Ausreißer, Durchgänger (*coll.*); ein Pferd, welches durchgeht. *Comp.* **—-head**, *s.* der Kolben.

[2]**Bolt**, *v.a.* beuteln, sichten. **—er**, *s.* der Beutel, das Beutelsieb; eine Art Netz. *Comp.* **—ing-cloth**, *s.* das Beuteltuch. **—ing-hutch**, *s.* der Beutelkasten. **—ing-tub**, *s.* das Beutelgefäß.

Bolus, *s.* die Arzneikugel, große Pille (*Med.*).

Bomb, *s.* die Bombe. **—ard**, *v.a.* bombardieren, beschießen. **—ardier**, *s.* der Bombardier; der Bombardierkäfer (*Ent.*). **—ardment**, *s.* die Beschießung. *Comp.* **—-proof**, *adj.* bombenfest. **—-shell**, *s.* die Bombe.

Bombast, *s.* der Schwulst. **—ic**, *adj.* schwülstig.

Bona fide, *adv.* in gutem Glauben; echt, zuverlässig, wirklich; — purchaser, Käufer auf Treu und Glauben, der den Verkäufer für den rechtmäßigen Besitzer hält; — student, wahrer Student.

Bond, I. *s.* (tie) das Band, der Strick; der (Mauer-) Verband, die Verbindung (*Mas.*); (obligation) die Verpflichtung; (signature) die Handschrift; Verschreibung; die Schuldverschreibung, Obligation (*Law*); —s, die Fesseln, die Gefangenschaft; gold —s, auf Gold lautende Schuldscheine; — of amity, Freundschaftsband; goods in —, Waren unter Zollverschluß; under —, unter Kaution; to enter into —, sich verpflichten, Kaution stellen; I must have your —, Sie müssen mir eine Schuldverschreibung ausstellen; an honest man's word is as good as his —, ein Mann, ein Wort (*prov.*). II. *adj.* gebunden; leibeigen; unter Zollverschluß (liegend). III. *v.a.* in Zollverschluß legen; to have goods —ed, Waren in die Zollniederlage bringen. **—age**, *s.* die Gefangenschaft; die Knechtschaft, Sklaverei. **—ed**, *p.p.* & *adj.*; —ed warehouse, der Zollspeicher, die Zollniederlage. *Comp.* **—-debts**, *pl.* Obligationsschulden. **—holder**, *s.* der Besitzer von Obligationen. **—ing-warehouse**, *s.* die Zollniederlage. **—maid**, *s.* die Leibeigene. **—man**, — **servant**, *s.* der Leibeigene. **—service**, *s.* die Leibeigenschaft. **—sman**, *s.* der Bürge.

Bone, I. *s.* der Knochen, das Bein; die Gräte (*of fish*); die beinerne Spindel (*Weav.*); — of contention, der Zankapfel; I have a — to pick with you, ich habe mit Ihnen ein Hühnchen zu pflücken; what is bred in the — will come out in the flesh, jung gewohnt, alt getan; Art läßt nicht von Art (*prov.*). II. *adj.* beinern. III. *v.a.* die Knochen nehmen, ausbeinen; Fischbein einsetzen (*in a dress, etc.*). **—d**, *adj.*; big-—d, großknochig. **—s**, *pl.* die Knochen, die Gebeine; das Gebein (*poet.*); die Kastagnetten (*Mus.*); to make no —s about, kein Bedenken tragen über (*acc.*). *Comp.* **—-dust**, *s.* das Knochenmehl. **—-earth**, *s.* die Beinasche. **—-lace**, *s.* geklöppelte Spitzen. **—-manure**, *s.* das Knochenmehl. **—setter**, *s.* der Heilgehilfe, Wundarzt, Knocheinrichter (*coll. hum.*). **—-shaker**, *s.* der Knochenrüttler, altes Fahrrad. **—-spavin**, *s.* der Huffpat.

Bonfire, *s.* das Freudenfeuer.

Bon-mot, *s.* das Witzwort, der sinnreiche Einfall.

Bonnet, *s.* der Damenhut, Fassonhut ohne Krempe; das Bonnet (*Fort.*, *Naut.*); die Mütze, Kappe (*for men*); Scotch —, schottische Mütze; he has a bee in his —, er hat einen Vogel, er hat einen Sparren zu viel.

Bonn—y, *adj.*, **—ily**, *adv.* hübsch, munter.

Bonus, *s.* die Prämie, Extradividende, der Profit; cash —, bar ausgezahlte Dividende.

Bony, *adj.* knöchern, beinern; (full of bones) sehr knochig; (big-boned) starkknochig, stark von Knochen; (thin) mager.

Booby, *s.* der Tölpel (*also Orn.*), der Narr.

Book, I. *s.* das Buch; die Abteilung, der Abschnitt (eines Buches); — of Books, Buch der Bücher, die Bibel; blue-—, staatliche Veröffentlichung (*in England*) (*Parl.*); music-—, Notenbuch; account-—, Rechnungsbuch; commonplace-—, das Konzeptbuch; — of reference, Nachschlagebuch, Hilfsbuch; — of sales, (Waren-)Verkaufsbuch; to swear upon the —, auf das Evangelium schwören; to make a —, die gemachten und angenommenen Wetten ins Notizbuch eintragen; to speak without —, ohne Autorität sprechen; to repeat, say without —, off —, auswendig hersagen; he is deep in our —s, er ist uns viel schuldig; to be in a p.'s good —s, in großer Gunst bei einem stehen, bei einem gut angeschrieben sein; to be in a p.'s bad —s, bei jemand schlecht angeschrieben sein; to keep —s, Bücher führen. II. *v.a.* einschreiben; in ein Buch eintragen, buchen; to — a place (*in a coach, etc.*), sich (auf der Post, 2c.) einschreiben lassen, sich (*dat.*) einen Platz nehmen; he —ed right through to Vienna, er nahm eine durchgehende Fahrkarte nach Wien; I wish to — for Hanover, ich bitte um eine Fahrkarte nach Hannover. **—ish,** *adj.*, **—ishly,** *adv.* den Büchern ergeben; pedantisch; I'm not —ish, ich bin kein (großer) Bücherfreund, kein Bücherkenner. **—ishness,** *s.* die Buchgelehrsamkeit. *Comp.* **—-account,** *s.* das Konto in einem Handlungsbuche. **—binder,** *s.* der Buchbinder. **—binding,** *s.* das Buchbinden; (*trade of —binding*) die Buchbinderei. **—case,** *s.* der Bücherbehälter, Bücherständer; open —case, das Bücherregal, Regal; revolving —case, drehbarer Bücherständer; —case with (glass) doors, der Bücherschrank. **—-debts,** *pl.* die Buchschulden. **—ing-office,** *s.* das Einschreibebüreau; der Schalter (zur Lösung von Fahrkarten) (*Rail.*). **—-keeper,** *s.* der Buchführer, Buchhalter. **—-keeping,** *s.* die Buchhaltung. **—-knowledge,** *s.* das Buchwissen. **—-learning,** *s.* die Büchergelehrsamkeit. **—-maker,** *s.* der Büchermacher, Bücherschmied; der Buchmacher (*Sport.*). **—man,** *s.* der Gelehrte. **—-muslin,** *s.* der feine, gesteifte Musselin. **—-plate,** *s.* das Bücher-Etikett, die Bibliothekmarke. **—-post,** *s.* die Expedition für Drucksachen; Gedrucktes, Drucksache (*on wrappers*). **—-rack,** *s.* das Bücherregal. **—seller,** *s.* der Buchhändler. **—selling,** *s.* der Buchhandel. **—-shelf,** *s.* das Bücherbrett. **—shop,** *s.* die Buchhandlung, der Bücherladen. **—stall,** *s.* der Bücherstand eines Antiquars *or* auf Bahnhöfen. **—stand,** *s.* das Büchergestell. **—-trade,** *s.* der Buchhandel. **—worm,** *s.* der Bücherwurm (*also fig.*).

[1]**Boom,** *s.* der Baum (*Fort., Naut., etc.*); (spar) die Stange, Spiere; (outrigger) der Ausleger, die Lut (*of smacks*); main —, der Großsegelsbaum; spanker —, der Giekbaum. *Comp.* **—-sails,** *pl.* die Baumsegel.

[2]**Boom,** *v.n.* fortbrausen, fortstürmen; dumpf schallen, dröhnen (*as a cannon or a mill*); schreien (*as a bittern*); to come —ing, mit vollen Segeln fahren (*Naut.*); a —ing sound, dumpfer, dröhnender Schall.

[3]**Boom,** I. *s.* der geschäftliche Aufschwung. II. *v.a.* etwas energisch in die Höhe bringen, für eine S. Reklame machen (*C. L.*).

Boomerang, *s.* eine Art australischer (in die Hand des Werfenden zurückkehrender) gekrümmter Schleuder, der Bumerang.

[1]**Boon,** *s.* (kindness) die Wohltat; (service) die Dienstleistung; a great —, eine wahre Wohltat.

[2]**Boon,** *adj.* freundlich; munter; a — companion, der gute, lustige Gesellschafter, der Zechbruder.

Boor, *s.* der Bauer; der Lümmel, der rohe, ungesittete Mensch. **—ish,** *adj.*, **—ishly,** *adv.* bäurisch; grob. **—ishness,** *s.* das bäurische Wesen; die Grobheit, Tölpelei.

[1]**Boot,** I. *s.* der Vorteil; der Nutzen; die Zugabe, Zubuße; to —, obendrein, noch dazu. II. *v.a.* nutzen, frommen; Vorteil bringen; what —s it? was hilft es? it —s little, es ist wenig daran gelegen. **—less,** *adj.* nutzlos. **—y,** *s.* die Beute.

[2]**Boot,** *s.* der Stiefel; der spanische Stiefel; der Kasten; fore —, der Kasten (in einem Wagen) unter dem Bocke; hind —, der Kasten im hinteren Teil des Wagens; das Hinterfach; to put on one's —s, seine Stiefel anziehen; to take off one's —s, sich (*dat.*) die Stiefel ausziehen; fishing —, Wasserstiefel. **—s,** *s.* der Hausknecht (*at an inn*). *Comp.* **—-jack,** *s.* der Stiefelknecht. **—-last, —-tree,** *s.* der Stiefelleisten. **—-lace,** *s.* das Schuhband, der Schnürsenkel. **—-maker,** *s.* der Stiefelmacher. **—-straps,** *pl.* Stiefelstrippen. **—-stretchers,** *pl.* die Stiefeldehner.

Booze, *v.n.* trinken, saufen.

Bo-peep, *s.* das Guckspiel.

Bora—cic, *adj.* boraxhaltig; —cic acid, die Boraxsäure. **—cite,** *s.* der Boracit. **—te,** *s.* das boraxsaure Salz; —te of magnesia, *see* —cite; —te of lime, der Kalkborax. **—x,** *s.* der Borax.

Bord—el, *s.* (*obs.*) öffentliches Haus Frauenhaus, Bordell; the inmate of a —el, das Freudenmädchen. **—er,** I. *s.* der Rand, Saum; die Rabatte (*Hort.*); (edging, edge) die Einfassung, Borte; der Rain (*of a wood, etc.*); die Grenze (*of a country*); (bank) das Ufer; (shore) das Gestade; die Buchdruckerleiste (*Typ.*); wallpaper —ers, Tapetenborten. II. *v.a.* einfassen, besetzen (*dresses, etc.*); rändeln (*coins*). III. *v.n.*; to —er **upon,** anstoßen, grenzen an. **—erer,** *s.* der Angrenzer; der Grenzbewohner. **—ure,** *s.* der Schildrand (*Her.*). *Comp.* **—er-plant,** *s.* Pflanze zur Einfassung von Beeten.

[1]**Bore,** I. *v.a.* bohren, ausbohren, aushöhlen; langweilen, belästigen; to — a way through a crowd, sich durchdrängen; he —s me continually with his company, er langweilt mich fortwährend mit seiner Gesellschaft. II. *s.* das Bohrloch; die Höhlung der Blasinstrumente; die Bohrung, Seele (*of a gun*); eine langweilige Person *or* Sache; eine Plage; smooth (rifle) —, glatte (gezogene) Bohrung; what a — this man is! wie langweilig ist dieser Mensch! **—dom,** *s.* das Langweilige; die Lästigkeit. **—r,** *s.* der Bohrer; der Bohrwurm. *Comp.* **—cole,** *s.* der Grünkohl.

[2]**Bore,** *imperf. of* Bear.

[3]**Bore,** *s.* die Springflut, außerordentlich hohe in ein enges Flußbett eindringende Flut.

Borea—l, *adj.* nördlich. **—s,** *s.* der Boreas, Nordwind.

Born, *p.p. & adj. see* Bear; a nobleman —, ein geborner Edelmann; Dante had been — and bred a Guelf, Dante war seiner Geburt und Erziehung nach ein Welf; I never saw such a thing in all my — days, mein Lebtag habe ich so etwas nie erlebt (*coll.*); to be — blind, blind geboren werden, blind auf die Welt kommen; to be — with a silver spoon in one's mouth, ein Glückskind, Sonntagskind sein; — to renown, zum Ruhme bestimmt. **—e,** *p.p. see* Bear; the charges to be —e jointly, die Kosten sollen gleichmäßig getragen werden.

Borough, *s.*, der Wahlflecken, Ort mit städtischer Verwaltung, welcher Vertreter ins Parlament sendet; municipal —, städtischer Wahlbezirk; —council, der Stadtrat; —councillor, der Stadtrat.

Borrow, *v.a.* borgen, erborgen, sich (*dat.*) leihen; he has —ed £10 of me, er hat mir 10 Pfund abgeborgt, er hat sich 10 Pfund von mir geliehen. **—er,** *s.* der Borger. **—ing,** *s.* das Borgen; he that goes a-—ing goes a-sorrowing, Borgen macht Sorgen (*prov.*).

Bos—cage, *s.* das Gebüsch, Gehölz; die Waldlandschaft (*Paint.*). **—ky,** *adj.* buschig, waldig.

Bosh, *s.* dummes Zeug, Blödsinn, Unsinn (*coll.*).

Bosom, I. *s.* der Busen; die Tiefe; die Brust, der Busen; das Herz; der Schoß (*of the church, etc.*); das Innere (*of the earth*); the — of the sea, die Tiefe des Meeres; come to my —, komm an mein Herz; the wife of his —, das Weib seines Herzens; in the — of his family, im Schoße seiner Familie; — friend, der Busenfreund, Herzensfreund. II. *v.a.* in das Herz schließen; geheim halten verbergen.

[1]**Boss,** I. *s.* die Beule, der Buckel, Auswuchs; der Knopf, Beschlag, Geschirrnagel (*on horses' trappings*). II. *v.a.* mit Buckeln, Knöpfen beschlagen bossieren, erhaben arbeiten. **—y,** *adj.* buckelig; mit Buckeln verziert. *Comp.* **—-hammer,** *s.* der Bunzenhammer.

[2]**Boss,** I. *s.* der Meister, Arbeitgeber (*Amer.*); der

tonangebende Mann (*Amer.*). II. *v.a.* veranstalten, einrichten; to — it, Meister sein; to — the show, den Herrn spielen, das entscheidende Wort sprechen (*Amer. sl.*).

Bot, *s.*, **—s**, *pl.* Pferdewürmer, Engerlinge; —s on it! zum Henker! *Comp.* **—-fly**, *s.* die Pferdebremse.

Botan—ic(al), *adj.*, **—ically**, *adv.* botanisch. **—ist**, *s.* der Botaniker. **—ize**, **—ise**, *v.n.* botanisieren; —izing case, die Botanisierbüchse. **—y**, *s.* die Botanik, Pflanzenkunde.

[1]**Botch**, *s.* die Beule, das Geschwür.

[2]**Botch**, I. *s.* der Flecken, Lappen; schlechte Arbeit, Pfuscherarbeit; das Flickwerk. II. *v.a.* hunzen, verderben; stümpern; flicken. **—er**, *s.* Flicker, Flick-Schneider, -Schuster. *Comp.* **—work**, *s.* das Flickwerk, die Pfuscherei.

Both, I. *adj. & pron.* beide, beides; I will take them —, ich will sie alle beide mitnehmen; — her sisters, ihre beiden Schwestern, ihre Schwestern . . . beide. II. *conj.;* — . . . and, sowohl . . . als (auch); — as to . . . and, sowohl in Rücksicht auf . . . als auch; — in word and deed, sowohl mit Worten als mit Taten.

Bother, I. *v.a.* plagen, quälen, belästigen; in Verlegenheit setzen. II. *v.n.* sich (ab)quälen (mit), sich beunruhigen (über eine S.), sich (*dat.*) Gedanken machen (über eine S.). III. *s.* die Plage, Belästigung (*coll.*); —! — take it! zum Henker damit (*vulg.*); — the boys! die verflixten Jungen! — the wasps! abscheuliche Wespen! — the music! laß mich mit der Musik in Frieden *or* ungeschoren! **—ation**, (*vulg.*) *see* — III.

Bottle, I. *s.* die Flasche; der Bund, das Bündel (*of hay*); leathern —, der Schlauch; to look for a needle in a — of hay, unnütz suchen. II. *attrib.;* — feeding, das Aufbringen von Kindern mit der Flasche; — label, die Flaschenetikette; — neck, der Flaschenhals; — washer, der Flaschenspüler; das Faktotum (*coll.*). III. *v.a.* auf Flaschen ziehen; to — up one's wrath, seinen Zorn unterdrücken, sich beherrschen; —d beer, Flaschenbier. *Comp.* **—-ale**, *s.* das Flaschenbier. **—-brush**, *s.* die Flaschenbürste. **—-case**, *s.* der Flaschenkeller, das Flaschenfutter. **—-friend**, *s.* der Zechbruder. **—-glass**, *s.* das grüne Flaschenglas, Buttelglas. **—-gourd**, *s.* der Flaschenkürbiß. **—-holder**, *s.* der Flaschenhalter; (beim Boxen) der Sekundant, Helfer (*sl.*). **—-jack**, *s.* der senkrechte Bratenwender. **—-nose**, *s.* die Branntweinnase, Kupfernase; der Entenwal (*Zool.*). **—-nosed**, *adj.* dicknasig, rotnasig. **—-rack**, *s.* das Flaschengestell (für leere Flaschen), Flaschenbrett.

Bottom, I. *s.* der Boden, Grund; die Tiefe; der Boden (*of a cask; of the sea, etc.*); das Schiff (*fig.*); der Bauch, das Flach (*of a ship*); das Ende (*of the street, etc.*); die Grundlage, der Grund (*of a building*); der Fuß (*of a hill, stairs, etc.*); der Bodensatz, die Hefe (*of beer, etc.*); der Knäuel (*of silk, etc.*); der Käse, Boden, Stuhl (*of an artichoke*); der Sitz (*of a chair*); der Hintere, das Hinterteil (*of men and animals*); der Ursprung (*fig.*); die Kraft, Stärke (*of a horse, etc., vulg.*); at the —, am untersten Ende, ganz unten, im Grunde; he is at the — of his class, er ist der Letzte *or* Unterste seiner Klasse; to get to the — of a th., etwas gründlich verstehen; to get to the — of a matter, einer Sache auf den Grund kommen; love is at the — of it, Liebe steckt dahinter; I thought you were at the — of it, ich dachte mir wohl, daß Sie der Urheber davon seien; from top to —, von oben bis unten; — upwards, Kiel oben, kielaufwärts; — row, die unterste, letzte Reihe. II. *v.a.* gründen (*arguments, etc.*); mit einem Boden *or* Sitz versehen; a flat-—ed boat, ein Prahm; full-—ed wig, eine Allongeperrücke; leather-—ed chairs, Lederstühle; rush-—ed chairs, Stühle mit Binsengeflechte zum Sitze. **—less**, *adj.* bodenlos; the —less pit, die tiefste Tiefe, die Hölle. **—ry**, I. *s.* die Bodmerei, Art von Schiffsverpfändung (*Naut.*). II. *attrib.;* —ry bond, der Schiffswechsel. III. *v.a.* ein Schiff verpfänden. *Comp.* **—-fishing**, *s.* das Grundangeln. **—-lands**, *pl.* das flache Uferland; reiche Ländereien in den Tälern.

Boudoir, *s.* das Boudoir, Damenzimmerchen.

Bough, *s.* der Zweig, Ast; *pl.* das Geäst, Astwerk.

[1]**Bought**, *imperf. & p.p. of* Buy.

[2]**Bought**, *s.* Biegung, Einbuchtung (*obs.*).

Bougie, *s.* die Wachskerze; der Katheter (*Surg.*).

Bouillon, *s.* die Fleischbrühe.

Boulder, *s.* der Rollstein, Felsblock; das Geröll; erratic —, der erratische Block.

Bounce, I. *v.n.* aufspringen, springen, prahlen; platzen; (talk big) aufschneiden; the ball —s high, der Ball springt hoch in die Luft; to — into a room, ins Zimmer herein platzen; a bouncing girl, ein frisches, stämmiges Mädchen. II. *s.* der plötzliche Sprung, Rücksprung, Rückprall; die Prahlerei (*sl.*); die freche Lüge (*sl.*). **—r**, *s.* (*sl.*) eine unverschämte Lüge; eine stämmige Person.

[1]**Bound**, I. *imperf. & p.p. of* Bind. II. *adj.* (obliged) verpflichtet; I will be — he is still there, ich bin fest überzeugt, daß er immer noch dort ist; the best horse is — to win, das beste Pferd muß sicher gewinnen; to be — apprentice, in die Lehre gegeben werden; to be — over to appear at the next assizes, durch Stellung von Bürgen sich anheischig machen, bei den nächsten Assisen sich zu stellen. **—en**, (*obs. p.p.*) *adj.;* it is your —en duty, es ist Ihre Pflicht und Schuldigkeit.

[2]**Bound**, *adj.* (*not connected with* '*to bind*') fertig; bestimmt; a ship — for London, ein nach London bestimmtes Schiff; whither are you —? wohin geht's? wo wollen Sie hin?

[3]**Bound**, I. *s.* der Sprung; der Aufsprung, Rücksprung, Prall, Anprall. II. *v.n.* springen, hüpfen, Sätze machen; zurückspringen, abspringen, aufprallen, abprallen; her —ing steed, ihr feuriges Roß.

[4]**Bound**, I. *s.;* **—s**, *pl.* die Grenze; die Schranke; der Markstein; within —s, mit Maßen, mäßig; to keep within the —s of propriety, sich in den Grenzen der Wohlerzogenheit halten; den Anstand nicht überschreiten; to set —s to one's desires, seine Wünsche in Schranken halten; beyond all —s, übermäßig; to overstep the —s, die Grenze überschreiten; to beat the —s, die (Kreis-)Grenzen bezeichnen; out of —s, außerhalb des Umkreises, in dem sich Schüler aufhalten dürfen, verboten. II. *v.a.* begrenzen, einschränken. **—ary**, I. *s.* die Grenze; the —aries of Germany, die Grenzen Deutschlands. II. *adj.;* —ary line, die Grenzlinie. **—less**, *adj.*, **—lessly**, *adv.* grenzenlos. **—lessness**, *s.* die Grenzenlosigkeit.

Bounder, *s.* einer, welche die Grenze festsetzt; holperiger Wagen (*sl.*); ungebildeter Gesell (*sl.*).

Bount—eous, *adj.*, **—eously**, *adv.* freigebig; a —eously spread board, ein reich besetzter Tisch. **—iful**, *see* —eous; —iful harvests, reiche Ernten. **—y**, *s.* (munificence) die Freigebigkeit, Wohltätigkeit; (gift) die Wohltat, Gabe; die Prämie (*C.L.*); das Handgeld, Werbegeld (*for recruits*); Queen Anne's —y, die Spende der K. A. (Teil der Jahreseinkünfte der engl. Hochkirche zur Unterstützung armer Geistlicher); the king's —y, das königliche Almosengeld. **—ies**, *pl.* Rückvergütungen, Prämien.

Bouquet, *s.* der Strauß; die Blume (*of wine*).

Bourgeois, I. *s.* eine Schriftgattung (*Typ.*); Bürger, Philister. II. *adj.* bürgerlich, philisterhaft.

Bourgeon, *v.n.* knospen, ausschlagen.

Bourne, *s.* die Grenze; das Ziel (*rare, poet.*).

Bout, *s.* das Mal; die Reihe, Wechselfolge; der Gang (*Fenc.*, *Weav.*); drinking —, das Zechgelage, der Schmaus; — of illness, ein Anfall von Krankheit; let us have a — at fencing, laßt uns fechten!

Bovine, *adj.* zum Rinde gehörig, Rind=; dumm; träge; — tuberculosis, die Rindertuberkulose.

Bovril, *s.* eine Art Fleischextrakt.

[1]**Bow**, *s.* der Bug (*of a ship*); der vorderste Mann im Boot, der dem Bug am nächsten sitzt; the —s of a ship, die Backen eines Schiffes; starboard —, der Bug am Steuerbord; port —, der Bug am Backbord. —**er**, *s.* der Buganker; best —er, der Steuerbordanker. *Comp.* —**line**, *s.* die Buline. —**sprit**, *s.* das Bugspriet (*Naut.*).

[2]**Bow**, I. *s.* der Bogen; der Fachbogen (*of hatmakers*); die Schleife (*of ribbon*); — of a key, der Schlüsselring; — of a violin, Geigenbogen; rain-—, der Regenbogen; cross-—, die Armbrust; saddle-—, der Sattelbogen; to draw the long—, aufschneiden (*coll.*); to have two strings to one's —, mehr als ein Mittel bereit haben. II. *v.a.* den Bogen führen (*Viol.*). —**ing**, *s.* die Bogenführung. *Comp.* —**-compasses**, *pl.* der Bogenzirkel. —**-drill**, *s.* der Treibbogen. —**-legged**, *adj.* krummbeinig. —**man**, *s.* der Bogenschütze. —**shot**, *s.* der Bogen=, Pfeil=schuß; within —shot, in Bogenschußweite. —**string**, *s.* die Bogensehne. —**-window**, *s.* das runde Bogenfenster, das vorspringende halbkreisförmige Fenster.

[3]**Bow**, *s.* die Verbeugung, Verneigung; to make one's —, sich verbeugen; von der Bühne abtreten. II. *v.a.* bücken, biegen, neigen (*the head*); unterdrücken, vernichten; to — the knee, die Knie beugen; to — and scrape, Kratzfüße machen; to — one's assent, seine Genehmigung zunicken; to — the ear to s.o., einem Gehör geben; einen anhören; to — a p. out, einen hinausbekomplimentieren. III. *v.n.* sich bücken, sich neigen; sich biegen; to — down, sich niederbücken, niedersinken; —ed down, niedergebeugt; to be on —ing terms, (mit einem) auf dem Grüßfuße stehen.

Bowdleriz—e, Bowdleris—e, *v.a.* zustutzen, erwässern, von anstößigen Stellen reinigen, verballhornen. —**ation**, *s.* die Zurechtstutzung, Verballhornung. —**m**, *s.* die Reinigungssucht.

Bowel, *s.*, —**s**, *pl.* das Eingeweide; das Innere (*fig.*); der Sitz des Mitleidens, das Herz; to have no —s (*of compassion or mercy*), gefühllos sein (*obs.*); action of the —s, der Stuhlgang; — complaint, die Diarrhöe.

Bower, *s.* die Laube, der schattige Gartenplatz; (*obs.*) die Kammer, das Gemach (der Burgfrau).

Bowie-knife, *s.* das lange Jagdmesser.

[1]**Bowl**, *s.* der Napf, die Schale; der Becher, Kopf (*of a pipe*); die Schale, Höhlung (*of a spoon*).

[2]**Bowl**, I. *s.* die Kugel. —**s**, *pl.* das Kegelspiel. II. *v.a.* rollen, kugeln; mit der Kugel werfen; den Ball werfen, kugeln (*at cricket*); to — **down**, umkegeln; to — **out**, mit dem Ball die Stäbe berühren, herauswerfen; well —ed, wohl getroffen. III. *v.n.* rollen, kegeln; to — **along**, dahin rollen. —**er**, *s.* der Kegler; der Roller (*Cricket*); —er (hat), niedriger steifer Filzhut. —**ing**, *s.* das Kugeln. *Comp.* —**ing-alley**, *s.* die Kegelbahn. —**ing-green**, —**ing-ground**, *s.* der Rasenplatz, Kugelspielplatz, Ballplatz.

Bow-wow, I. *int.* wau, wau! II. *s.* das Bellen. III. *v.a.* bellen, wau wau sagen.

[1]**Box**, I. *s.* der Buchsbaum (*Bot.*); die Büchse, Schachtel, Dose; der Kasten, das Kistchen; (trunk) der Koffer; der (Kutscher=)Bock; die Loge (*in a theatre*); das Fach des Schriftkastens (*Typ.*); das Häuschen; (compass-—) der Kompaßmörser; (hunting-—) das kleine Landhaus, Jagdhaus; loose —, vollständig eingeschlossener Pferdestand, in dem das Pferd frei steht; money-—, Sparbüchse; — of a wheel, Wagenbüchse; ballot-—, Kugelbüchse; dice-—, der Würfelbecher; Christmas-—, das Weihnachtsgeschenk; — of bricks, Baukasten; — of tricks, der Zauberkasten; to be in the wrong —, sich irren; to get into the wrong —, vor die unrechte Schmiede kommen. II. *v.a.* mit Büchsen versehen (*a wheel*); Bäume anzapfen; to — **up**, einschließen; to — **off**, in Fächer abteilen. III. *adj.* von Buchsbaum. *Comp.* —**-bed**, *s.* der Bettschrank. —**-drain**, *s.* der bedeckte, ausgemauerte Abzugskanal. —**ing day**, *s.* der zweite Weihnachtstag, an welchem an Briefträger, Laufburschen u. a. Geschenke (Christmas-—es) gegeben werden und der ein Bank holiday ist. —**-iron**, *s.* das Bügeleisen (mit einem Kasten). —**-keeper**, *s.* der (die) Logenschließer(in). —**-lobby**, *s.* der Vorraum zu den Logen (*Theat.*). —**-lock**, *s.* das Kastenschloß. —**-office**, *s.* die Theaterkasse (zur Lösung von Eintrittskarten) (*Theat.*). —**-room**, *s.* die Kofferkammer. —**-thorn**, *s.* der Buchsdorn. —**wood**, *s.* das Buchsbaumholz.

[2]**Box**, I. *s.* der Schlag (*obs.*); — on the ear, eine Ohrfeige. II. *v.n.* sich mit der Faust schlagen, sich boxen. III. *v.a.*; to — s.o.'s ears, einen ohrfeigen. —**er**, *s.* der Faustkämpfer, Boxer.

[3]**Box**, *v.a.* die Vorsegel backlegen (*Naut.*); to — the compass, die Striche des Kompasses in der Ordnung hersagen. *Comp.* —**haul**, *v.a.* halsen, auf schnelle Art vor dem Winde umwenden.

Boy, *s.* der Bube, Knabe, Junge; the —, der Junge; a —, ein Junge; an old —, ein früherer Schüler einer Lehranstalt; —s will be men, Kinder werden Leute (*prov.*). —**hood**, *s.* das Knabenalter. —**ish**, *adj.*, —**ishly**, *adv.* knabenhaft; in my —ish days, in meinem Knabenalter, in meiner Jugend. —**ishness**, *s.* das knabenhafte Wesen, das jugendliche Benehmen.

Boycott, *v.a.* boykottieren, in Verruf erklären.

Brace, I. *s.* das Band, die Binde, der Riemen; das Balkenband, Strebeband, der Bug (*Arch. Carp.*); der Schwungriemen (*of a carriage, etc.*); die Bohrdruve, die Brustleier, das Bohrwerkzeug (*Carp.*); das Achselband (*of a barrow, etc.*); die Spannschnur (*of a drum*); die Verbindungsklammer (*Mus., Typ.*); das Paar (*of partridges*) (tension) die Spannung; die Brasse (der Raaen *Naut.*); a pair of —s, ein Paar Hosenträger or Tragbänder, die Hosenträger; a — of pistols, ein Paar Pistolen; —s of a carriage, die Schwungriemen einer Kutsche. II. *attrib.*; — springs, die Hängeriemfedern an Kutschen. III. *v.a.* straff anziehen, spannen; zusammen schnüren; mit Ankern verstärken (*Arch.*); brassen (*Naut.*); (*fig.*) anspannen, stärken (*the mind, etc.*); —ed by the greatness of their object, angespornt durch die Größe ihres Zweckes; bracing air, erfrischende Luft; our climate is not bracing, unser Klima ist nicht stärkend, nicht erfrischend, ist erschlaffend; to — aback, backbrassen. —**let**, *s.* das Armband; die Armschiene.

Brach, *s.* die Petze; der Spürhund.

Brachia—l, *adj.* zum Arme gehörig, Arm=; — nerves, Armnerven. —**te**, *adj.* armförmig.

Bracket, I. *s.* der Kragstein, Träger (*Arch.*) das Wandbrettchen, Rippbrettchen; die Knagge (*Carp.*); corner —, das Eckbrett; gas- —, der an einer Wand angebrachte vorspringende Gasbrenner. —**s**, *pl.* die Klammer (*Typ.*); die Wände, Seitenstücke (der Blocklaffette). II. *v.a.* einklammern; to — together, zusammenklammern (*names in a class-list, etc.*); they were —ed together, sie wurden in eine Linie gestellt; sie wurden einander völlig gleich *or* gleich gut erklärt; he was —ed sixth in the class-list, in der Rangliste wurde er zusammen mit einem andern an sechster Stelle genannt.

Bracken, *s.* das Farnkraut. *See also* Brake.

Brackish, *adj.* (etwas) salzig; — water, das Brackwasser. —**ness**, *s.* das Salzige.

Bracte—ate, I. *adj.* mit Neben=, Deckblättern versehen; aus dünnem Metall geprägt. II. *s.* der Brakteat, die dünne nur auf einer Seite geprägte Münze. —**olate**, *adj.* mit einem Deckblättchen versehen.

Brad, *s.* der Spiekernagel, Fußbodennagel. *Comp.* **—awl**, *s.* der Spitzbohrer, die Bindahle.
Brag, I. *s.* die Prahlerei. II. *v.n.* prahlen, aufschneiden; to — of a thing, sich einer Sache rühmen. **—gadocio**, *s.* der Prahler. **—gart**, I. *s.* der Prahler. II. *adj.* prahlerisch. **—gartism**, *s.* die Prahlerei. **—ging**, I. *s.* die Prahlerei. II. *p. & adj.*, **—gingly**, *adv.* prahlend.
Braid, I. die Borte; die Flechte; die Litze, das Stoßband, die (Besatz=)Schnur; der Schnurenbesatz (*of a coat, etc.*); die Haarflechte. II. *v.a.* flechten (*the hair*); zusammenweben; Litze ꝛc. auf eine S. aufnähen, bordieren; —ed tresses, geflochtene Haare, das Haargeflecht. **—er**, *s.* der Schnuraufnäher (*Sew.-M.*). **—ing**, *s.* der Schnurenbesatz. *Comp.* **—ing-apparatus**, *see* —er. **—ing-machine**, *s.* die Schnurmaschine.
Brail, I. *s.* das Geitau. II. *v.a.;* to — up, aufgeien (*Naut.*).
Brain, I. *s.* (*gen'lly* **—s**, *pl.*) das Gehirn; der Verstand, Kopf (*fig.*); to blow a p.'s —s out, einem eine Kugel durch den Kopf jagen; to puzzle, rack one's —s, sich (*dat.*) den Kopf zerbrechen; to pick a p's —s, einen um allerlei Auskünfte bitten; to have s.th. on the —, einen Gedanken nicht loswerden können, fortwährend an eine S. denken müssen; he has not got much —s (*sl.*), er hat das Pulver nicht erfunden. II. *v.a.* (einem) den Kopf zerschmettern. **—ed**, *adj.;* hare—ed, scatter—ed, gedankenlos, verrückt. **—less**, *adj.* hirnlos; ohne Verstand. *Comp.* **—-fever**, *s.* die Gehirnentzündung. **—-pan**, *s.* die Hirnschale. **—sick**, *adj.* verrückt; geisteskrank.
Brake, *s.* das Farnkraut; das Farngebüsch; (thicket) das Dickicht, Dorngebüsch.
Brake, **Break**, *s.* die (Flachs=)Breche; die Brechbank (*Bak.*); die schwere Egge (*Agr.*); der Pumpenschwengel; der Geckstock (*Naut.*); der Hemmschuh, die Bremse (*Railw.*); die Bremsvorrichtung; das Break, der Wagen, vor welchen die einzufahrenden jungen Pferde zuerst gespannt werden; vierrädriger hoher schmaler Wagen mit Bremsvorrichtung; self-acting —, selbstwirkende Bremse; to put on the —, bremsen, (das Rad, ꝛc.) hemmen. *Comp.* **—(s)man**, *s.* der Bremser, Bremsenwärter. **—-spoon**, *s.* der Bremslöffel (*Cycl.*). **—-van**, *s.* der Bremswagen. **—-wheel**, *s.* das Hemmrad.
Brake, *obs. imperf. of* Break.
Brambl—e, *s.* der Brombeerstrauch; das Gestrüpp. **—ing**, *s.* der Bergfink (*Orn.*). *Comp.* **—e-bush**, *s.* der Brombeerbusch, die Brombeerstaude. **—e-finch**, *see* —ing.
Bran, *s.* die Kleie.
Branch, I. *s.* der Ast, Zweig, Schoß (*of a tree*); der Arm (*of a candlestick; of a river, etc.*); der Zweig (*of an artery; of a family; of science, business, etc.*); das Fach; die Linie (*in a genealogical tree*); der Abkömmling (*of a family*); der Schenkel (*of a spur*); der Teil (*of a whole*); die Rippen, der Bogen (*Arch.*); die Erzader (*Min.*); —es of a stag's head, Stangen eines Hirschgeweihes; a candlestick with seven —es, ein siebenarmiger Leuchter; charity is a — of Christian duty, die Wohltätigkeit ist ein Teil der Christenpflicht; — of a bank, die Zweigbank. II. *attrib.;* — establishment, das Nebengeschäft, Zweiggeschäft, die Filiale; — line, die Zweigbahn, Seitenlinie (*Railw.*); die Verzweigungslinie (*Math.*); — post-office, die Postexpedition. III. *v.n.;* **— out**, sich verzweigen; to — out into a long dissertation, sich weitläufig über einen Gegenstand verbreiten; **— off**, sich abzweigen, sich trennen. IV. *v.a.;* —ed with gold, goldgeblümt. **—less**, *adj.* zweiglos.
Brand, I. *s.* der (Feuer=)Brand; (stigma) das Brandmal, der Schandfleck; das (Waren=)Zeichen, die Marke (*C. L.*); die Sorte (*of cigars*); das Schwert (*poet.*). II. *v.a.* brandmarken; Zeichen einbrennen. **—er**, *s.* der Bratrost, Handrost; *see* —ing-iron. **—ish**, *see* Brandish. *Comp.* **—-goose**, *s. see* Brentgoose. **—(ing)-iron**, *s.* das Brenneisen; der Brandbock. **—-new**, *adj.* (*lit.*) frisch vom Feuer; (*fig.*) ganz neu, funkelnagelneu.
Brandish, *v.a.* schwingen. **—er**, *s.* der Schwinger.
Brandy, *s.* der Kognak, Schnap(p)s; cherry —, das Kirschwasser. *Comp.* **—-faced**, *adj.* rot im Gesicht.
Bran-new, *see* Brand-new.
Bras—en, **—ier**, *see* Brazen, Brazier.
Brass, I. *s.* das Messing; die Unverschämtheit (*sl.*); to have —, eine eherne Stirn haben (*sl.*). II. *adj.;* — instrument, das Blasinstrument; — wire, der Messingdraht. **—es**, *pl.* das Messinggeschirr, die Verzierungen von Messingwerk. **—y**, *adj.* ehern, erzartig. *Comp.* **—-band**, *s.* Truppe mit Blasinstrumenten. **—-founder**, *s.* der Gelbgießer.
Brat, *s.* der Balg, das Kind.
Brav—ado, *s.* die Prahlerei. **—e**, I. *v.a.* trotzen, herausfordern; mit Tapferkeit ertragen, (einer S.) mutig begegnen; to —e it out, etwas mit Dreistigkeit durchsetzen. II. *adj.*, **—ely**, *adv.* tapfer, kühn, mutig; brav; (excellent) herrlich; (goodly) stattlich. III. *s.* (chief) der Häuptling. **—ery**, *s.* der Mut, die Tapferkeit, der Heldenmut; (finery) der Putz, die Pracht. **—o**, *s.* I. der Bandit, Räuber, Meuchelmörder. II. *int.* bravo!
Brawl, I. *v.n.* laut zanken, lärmen, schreien; belfern; —ing brook, murmelnder Bach; —ing scold, belferndes, zänkisches Weib. II. *s.* der Lärm, Zank; der Aufruhr, Auflauf; street —, Straßenauflauf. **—er**, *s.* der Lärmer, Zänker. **—ing**, *see* Brawl II.
Brawn, *s.* das Eberfleisch; das Schweine=Pökelfleisch, die Sülze aus Schweinefleisch, der Schwartenmagen; das Muskelfleisch; die Muskelkraft. **—iness**, *s.* die Festigkeit des Fleisches; die Stärke. **—y**, *adj.* sehnig, muskulös, fest.
[1]**Bray**, I. *v.n.* ia(n)en, schreien wie ein Esel; dröhnen, schmettern; —ing trumpets, schmetternde Trompeten. II. *v.a.;* — out, laut verkünden. III. *s.* das Eselgeschrei; das Schmettern.
[2]**Bray**, *v.a.* zerstoßen, klein reiben.
Braz—en, I. *v.a.;* to —en it out, sich (*dat.*) durch Unverschämtheit helfen. II. *adj.* ehern; (—en-faced) mit eherner Stirn, unverschämt. **—enness**, *s.* das Erzartige; die Frechheit. **—ier**, *s.* der Kupferschmied; die Kohlenpfanne; —ier's ware, die Messingwaren.
Breach, *s.* der Bruch; der Riß, (Wall=)Bruch, die Bresche (*Fort.*); der Bruch, die Übertretung, Verletzung (*fig.*); (quarrel) die Uneinigkeit, der Zwist; to batter in a —, eine Bresche schießen *or* machen; — of a covenant, Bruch eines Vertrages; — of duty, Übertretung der Pflicht; — of honour, Verletzung der Ehre; — of the peace, Friedensbruch; — of promise (of marriage), die Wortbrüchigkeit in Bezug auf ein Eheversprechen; she sued him for — of promise, sie verklagte ihn wegen Nichteinhaltung seines Eheversprechens; — of trust, die Veruntreuung, Verletzung des Vertrauens. *Comp.* **—-battery**, *s.* die Breschbatterie (*Mil.*).
Bread, *s.* das Brot; home-made —, hausbackenes Brot; — and butter, Butterbrot; (*fig.*) des Lebens Notdurft und Nahrung; to quarrel with one's — and butter, sich (*dat.*) selbst im Lichte stehen; he knows on which side his — is buttered, er versteht sich auf seinen Vorteil; er weiß, wo Barthel Most holt (*prov.*); to break — with s.o., mit einem essen; —-and-butter miss, der Backfisch; to get, earn one's —, sein Brot verdienen; French —, französisches Brot, das Weißbrot; pulled —, Stückchen gerösteter Brotkrume. *Comp.* **—-basket**, *s.* der Brotkorb; der Magen (*sl.*). **—-stuffs**, *pl.* Stoffe (Früchte), aus denen Brot gewonnen werden kann, das Mehl. **—-winner**, *s.* der Brotverdiener, Ernährer, Hausvater.
Breadth, *s.* die Breite, Weite, Ausdehnung.

Break, I. *s.* der Bruch, die Lücke, Öffnung, der Zwischenraum; (pause) die Unterbrechung, Pause; (line) der Strich (*Typ.*); das Spatium, der Absatz (*Typ.*); der Gußzapfen (*Type-founding*); die Vertiefung (*Arch.*); der Neubruch (*Agr.*); die Lichtung, der Durchhau (*in woods*); der Anbruch (*of day*); der Abrichtwagen, *see* Brake; der Kremser, omnibusähnlicher offener Wagen für Landpartieen; die Bremse, *see* Brake. II. *ir.v.a.* brechen; zerbrechen, zerschlagen; erbrechen (*locks, doors, letters, etc.*); brechen (*laws, etc.*); zum Fallieren bringen, bankerott machen; sprengen (*a bank*); (einem Offizier) den Abschied geben, (ihn) verabschieden; a broken heart, ein gebrochenes Herz; the broken pitcher, der zerbrochene Krug; that will — his back, das wird ihm den Hals brechen, ihn zu Grunde richten; to — bulk, zu löschen anfangen, die Last brechen (*Naut.*); to — the commandments, die heiligen Gebote nicht halten; to — cover, aus dem Versteck herauskommen; to — **down**, niederbrechen, niederschlagen; to — a fall, den Fall aufhalten, schwächen; to — one's fast, frühstücken; to — ground, pflügen, die ersten Anfänge zu etwas machen; with broken health, mit zerstörter Gesundheit; to — a p.'s heart, einem das Herz brechen; to — hemp, Hanf brechen; the horse broke a blood-vessel, dem Pferde platzte ein Blutgefäß; to — the ice, Bahn brechen; eine Unterhaltung anfangen; to — **in**, einbrechen (*a door*); to — in a dog, einen Hund dressieren; to — in a horse, ein Pferd zureiten; to — (in) a horse to harness, ein Pferd einfahren; to — the laws of nature, die Naturgesetze übertreten; to — a matter to a p., einem etwas mitteilen, eröffnen; you must — this bad news to him, Sie müssen ihm diese schlimme Nachricht beibringen; to — **off**, abbrechen, aufhören lassen; to — off a match, eine Heirat rückgängig machen; to — o.s. of a habit, sich von einer Gewohnheit abbringen, sich (*dat.*) etwas abgewöhnen; to — **open**, aufbrechen, erbrechen; to — a promise, ein Versprechen nicht halten; to — a p.'s pride, jemandes Stolz demütigen; her sleep was broken, ihr Schlaf wurde gestört; to — small, in kleine Stücke brechen; they broke his windows, sie warfen ihm die Fenster ein; to — **up**, abbrechen (*a ship, etc.*); auseinander gehen lassen (*as an army*); auflösen (*a meeting, etc.*); schließen (*a school*); to — up one's establishment, die Haushaltung aufgeben; to — up land, das Land neubrechen, pflügen. III. *ir.v.n.* brechen, zerbrechen, zerspringen, in Stücke gehen; sich brechen, branden (*as waves*); (split) aufspringen; (— in two) entzwei gehen; (fail) bankerott werden; my heart is ready to —, mir will das Herz zerspringen; to — **away** from a p., sich von einem losreißen; day is —ing, der Tag bricht an; to — **down**, zusammenbrechen, Abnehmen sein; durchfallen (*at an examination*); umgeworfen werden (*of a carriage*); he broke down (in his speech), er blieb (in seiner Rede) stecken; her health is —ing down, ihre Gesundheit wird schlechter und schlechter; to — **forth**, hervorbrechen, ausbrechen; to — **in** upon a p., auf einen hereinplatzen; to — **out**, ausbrechen; to — out into praise of a p., sich in Lobeserhebungen einer Person ergießen; to — out into a fit of laughter, in Lachen ausbrechen; the waves broke **over** him, die Wogen schlugen über ihm zusammen; to — **up**, sich auflösen, aufbrechen, sich zerteilen; we broke up early, wir brachen zeitig auf; when does school — up? wann beginnen die Schulferien? to — **with** a p., mit einem brechen, einem die Freundschaft kündigen; the abscess has broken, das Geschwür ist aufgebrochen. —**able**, *adj.* zerbrechlich. —**age**, *s.* das Brechen; der Bruch; payment for —age, die Refaktie; free from —age, bruchfrei. —**er**, *s.* der Brecher; der Zerstörer; der Störer; der Bereiter; die Sturzsee (*Naut.*). —**ers**, *pl.* die Brandung; —ers ahead! Vorsicht, Gefahr droh (*fig.*). —**ing**, *s.* das Brechen; he has a —ing out all over his body, er hat einen Ausschlag am ganzen Leibe; —ing up of an establishment, das Eingehen einer Anstalt, Aufgeben eines Geschäfts. *Comp.* —**-down**, *s.* der Sturz, das Mißgeschick; die Zerrüttung (*of health*); eine Art Tanz. —**fast**, *see* Breakfast. —**-neck**, *adj.* gefährlich, halsbrecherisch; a —-neck rider, ein wilder Reiter. —**-up**, *s.* die Aufhebung, der Schluß; —-up of the constitution, die Zerrüttung der Gesundheit; die Brechung, Brisure (*Fort.*). —**water**, *s.* der Hafendamm; der Wellenbrecher.

Breakfast, I. *v.n.* frühstücken. II. *s.* das Frühstück. III. *attrib.*; — room, das Frühstückszimmer; — things, das Frühstücksgerät.

[1]**Bream**, *s.* der Brassen (*Icht.*).

[2]**Bream**, *v.a.* brennen, abflammen (*Naut.*).

Breast, I. *s.* die Brust; der Busen; das Herz; — of a hill, die Vorderseite eines Hügels; to make a clean — of it, sein Herz ausschütten. II. *v.a.* die Brust entgegen setzen, trotzen; to — a hill, einen Hügel hinauf steigen; to — the waves, gegen die Strömung schwimmen (*lit.*), (der Strömung) Trotz bieten (*fig.*); a double-—ed frock-coat, ein Gehrock mit zwei Reihen Knöpfe. *Comp.* —**bone**, *s.* das Brustbein, der Brustknochen. —**-cloth**, *s.* der Brustlatz. —**-harness** *s.* das Brustblattgeschirr. —**-high**, *adj.* brusthoch. —**knot**, *s.* die Brustschleife. —**plate**, *s.* der Brustharnisch (*of armour*); das Brustschil (*of priests*). —**work**, *s.* die Brustwehr (*Build. Fort.*); das Schott, die Bretterwand (*of ships*) —work of the quarterdeck, das Schott der Schanze.

Breath, I. *s.* der Atem; der Hauch; (drawing of —) der Atemzug; das Leben (*fig.*); — of air das Lüftchen; there is not the least — of wind es regt sich kein Lüftchen; above one's —, hörbar, laut; under one's —, leise; out of —, außer Atem; to take *or* draw —, Atem schöpfen o. holen; at a —, auf einmal; in the same —, in einem Atem; give me time to draw —, laß mi ein wenig zu Atem kommen; scant of —, kurzatmig; keep your — to cool your porridge behalte deinen Rat für dich (*vulg.*); the least — of suspicion, die leiseste Spur von Verdacht; a every —, bei jedem Atemzuge; to waste one's — in den Wind reden; with bated —, mit verhaltenem Atem. II. *attrib.*; — group, Lautgruppe, di in einem Atemzuge sprechbar ist. —**e**, *v.* I. *a* atmen, Atem holen lassen, verschnaufen lasse (*horses*) (*rare*); einatmen; to —e into, einhauchen; to —e out, aushauchen; to —e a wish, eine Wunsch äußern; —ing vengeance, Rache schnaubend; to —e one's last, die Seele aushauchen; yo must not —e a word of it to any one, lassen Si gegen niemand ein Wort davon verlauten; to — upon, anhauchen; to —e upon one's reputation jemandes Ruf verletzen; to —e a vein, eine Ade öffnen; Saul yet —ing out threatenings an slaughter, Saulus aber schnaubte noch mit Drohe und Morden (*B.*). II. *n.* atmen; leben (*fig.*) Atem holen; to —e on a p., einen anhauchen —**er**, I. *s.* der Atmende. —**ing**, I. *p. see* —e. I *adj.* lebenstreu, sprechend (*as a portrait*). II *s.* das Atmen, Hauchen. —**less**, *adj.*, —**lessly** *adv.* atemlos; außer Atem; —less with joy, vo Freude atemlos. —**lessness**, *s.* die Atemlosigkeit. *Comp.* —**ing-hole**, *s.* das Luftloch. —**ing space**, —**ing-time**, *s.* die Zeit zum Atemschöpfen; die Ruhezeit, Pause.

Breccia, *s.* die Breccia, das Trümmergestein —**ted**, *adj.* aus Trümmergestein bestehend.

Bred, *imperf. & p.p. of* Breed; well-—, wohl erzogen; born and —, von Geburt und Erziehung a well-— man, ein Mann von feiner Bildung; h has been — to it, er wurde dazu erzogen; he wa — a scholar, er wurde zum Gelehrten herangebildet; thorough-— (horse), (Pferd) von rein

Rasse, das Vollblut; cross-— dog, Hund gekreuzter Rasse.

Breech, I. *s.* der Hintere; der Boden, Stoß einer Kanone (*Art.*); die Schwanzschraube (*Gun.*); der äußere Winkel eines Krummholzes (*Shipb.*). II. *attrib.;* —end, die Pulverkammer (*of a gun-barrel*); — leather, das Fahrleder (*of miners*); — mouldings, die Zierraten (des Stoßes, des Mastes); — steam-pipe, die Seitendampfröhre. III. *v.a.* einem Jungen die ersten Hosen anziehen; behosen; (einem) die Hosen stramm ziehen, (einen) durchbleuen; einem Schießgewehr die Schwanzschraube einsetzen (*Gun.*); to — the guns, die Kanonen backsen; —ed with gore, mit Blut befleckt. **—es**, I. *pl.* die Reithosen; knee-—es, die Kniehosen; to wear the —es, die Hosen anhaben, die Herrschaft im Hause haben. II. *attrib.;* —es pocket, die Hosentasche. **—ing**, *s.* der hintere Teil; die Brok (*Naut.*); das Hinterzeug (*Saddl.*). *Comp.* **—-loader**, *s.* der Hinterlader. **—-loading**, *adj. & s.* die Hinterladung; —-loading rifle, der Hinterlader. **—-nail**, **—-pin**, **—-plug**, **—-screw**, *s.* die Kreuzschraube. **—-sight**, *s.* das hintere Visier (*Gun.*). **—-wrench**, *s.* das Windeeisen.

Breed, I. *ir.v.n.* sich erzeugen, sich vermehren; to — in and in, sich innerhalb der Art *or* durch Inzucht fortpflanzen. II. *ir.v.a.* erzeugen, hervorbringen, (auf)erziehen; aufziehen (*cattle*); ausbrüten, ersinnen (*fig.*); bred to the bar, eine juristische Erziehung genossen habend. III. *s.* die Brut, Zucht, Art, Rasse; das Geblüt (*of horses*); die Geburt, der Schlag. **—er**, *s.* der Erzeuger, die Erzeugerin; der Züchter (*of cattle*). **—ing**, I. *s.* die Erziehung; die Bildung; die Zucht (*of cattle, etc.*); —ing in and in, die Inzucht; a man of good —ing, ein Mann von feiner Lebensart, von guter Erziehung. II. *attrib.;* —ing pond, der Laichteich; —ing stone, der Puddingstein (*Min.*).

[1]**Breez—e**, *s.* die Brise, der leichte Wind, die Kühlte; der Lärm, Streit (*sl.*); land —e, der Landwind; sea —e, der Seewind; strong —e, steife Kühlte *or* Brise. **—y**, *adj.* windig, luftig, von einem frischen, kühlen Winde bestrichen.

[2]**Breeze**, *s.* die Bremse (*Ent.*).

[3]**Breeze**, *s.* der Kokesabfall, die Lösche.

Brehon, *s.* irischer Landrichter. *Comp.* **—-laws**, *pl.* die alten irischen Gesetze (*before 1650*).

Brent-goose, *s.* die Brandgans.

Brest, *s.* der Stab, Rundstab, Torus (*Arch.*).

Brethren, *pl. of* Brother (*B. & Eccl.*); my —, meine Geliebten, liebe Brüder, Geliebte im Herrn, andächtige Zuhörer.

Brev—e, *s.* die lange Note (*Mus.*); das Zeichen der Kürze (*over a vowel*). **—et**, *s.* das Patent (für Offiziere); —et rank, der Titularrang. **—iary**, *s.* das Brevier (*R. C.*). **—ier**, *s.* die Petitschrift (*Typ.*). **—ity**, *s.* die Kürze; —ity is the soul of wit, Kürze ist des Witzes Würze (*prov.*).

Brew, I. *v.a. & n.* brauen; (mix) mischen, vermischen; (prepare) zubereiten; brauen, schmieden, anzetteln (*mischief*); as you have —ed so you must drink, was man sich einbrockt muß man ausessen (*prov.*). II. *v.n.* im Anzuge sein, heranziehen (*as a storm, etc.*); a storm is —ing, ein Ungewitter zieht auf *or* ist im Anzuge. III. *s.* das Gebräu. **—er**, *s.* der Brauer, Bierbrauer. **—ery**, *s.* die Brauerei, das Brauhaus. **—ing**, *s.* das Brauen; das Gebräu, das auf einmal Gebraute; a —ing, im Brauen begriffen.

Briar, *see* Brier.

Bribe, I. *s.* das Geschenk (zur Bestechung), die Bestechung; to offer a p. a —, einen bestechen wollen; he is above taking a —, er ist unbestechlich. II. *v.a.* bestechen; to — a p. into . . ., einen durch Bestechung zu . . . vermögen. **—r**, *s.* der Bestecher. **—ry**, *s.* die Bestechung; attempt at —ry, der Bestechungsversuch.

Brick, I. *s.* der Ziegelstein, Backstein; —s for coping, die Decksteine; —s for drains, Abzugsziegel; Dutch —s, die Stallklinker; fire-—s, feuerfeste Ziegelsteine; paving —s, Pflasterziegel; he is a regular —, er ist ein ganz famoser Kerl, ein Prachtkerl (*sl.*). II. *attrib.;* — burner, der Ziegelbrenner. III. *adj.;* — colour, (— red,) das Ziegelrot; — facing, die Verblendung einer Mauer mit Backsteinen; — wall, die Backsteinmauer; he can see through a — wall, er hört das Gras wachsen; er kann alles. IV. *v.a.* mit Backsteinen mauern; mit Ziegeln ausfüllen; Ziegel imitieren (*in decoration*). *Comp.* **—bat**, *s.* der Ziegelbrocken. **—-clay**, *s.* der Ziegellehm, die Ziegelerde. **—-dust**, *s.* das Ziegelmehl. **—kiln**, *s.* der Ziegelofen, die Ziegelhütte. **—layer**, *s.* der (Ziegel-)Maurer. **—laying**, *s.* die Backstein- *or* Ziegel-Maurerei. **—-(making-)machine**, *s.* die Ziegelformmaschine. **—-mould**, *s.* die Ziegelform. **—work**, *s.* der Backsteinbau, das Backsteinmauerwerk. **—-works**, *pl.* die Ziegelhütte.

Brid—al, I. *adj.* bräutlich; —al dress, das Brautkleid; —al procession, der Brautzug, Hochzeitszug; —al day, der Hochzeitstag; —al array, der Hochzeitsputz, Brautschmuck; —al chamber, das Brautgemach; —al race, der Brautlauf (*obs.*); —al wreath, der Brautkranz, Jungfernkranz. II. *s.* die Hochzeit, das Hochzeitsfest. **—e**, *s.* die Neuvermählte, die junge Frau; die Braut (*rare*); die Verlobte (*poet.*); —e elect, die Braut (*before the wedding*); —e's veil, der Brautschleier; to give the —e away, Brautvater sein; he was on his wedding tour with his —e, er war mit seiner jungen Frau auf der Hochzeitsreise. *Comp.* **—e-cake**, *s.* der Hochzeitskuchen. **—e-chamber**, *s.* das Brautgemach. **—e-groom**, *s.* der Bräutigam; der junge Ehemann. **—esman**, *s.* der Begleiter des Bräutigams bei der Hochzeit. **—esmaid**, *s.* die Brautjungfer.

Bridewell, *s.* das Zuchthaus, Arbeitshaus.

Bridge, I. *s.* die Brücke; der Steg (*of string instruments*); der Rücken (*of the nose*), Nasenrücken; die (Kommando-)Brücke (*Naut.*); die Querhölzer einer Lafette (*Artil.*); — of an aqueduct, Wasserleitungsbrücke; — of boards, die Laufbrücke (*Naut.*); — of boats, Schiffbrücke, Pontonbrücke; cable-suspension —, Drahtkabelbrücke; chain —, Kettenbrücke; draw—, Zugbrücke; foot—, der Steg; floating *or* flying —, schwimmende Brücke; — of ropes, Seilbrücke; stone —, steinerne Brücke; suspension —, Hängebrücke; temporary —, Notbrücke; wooden —, Holzbrücke; tubular —, Röhrenbrücke; wire suspension —, Drahtseilbrücke; upper (under) —, Wegbrücke (die Wegunterführung) (*Railw.*). II. *v.a.* eine Brücke schlagen; to — over, überbrücken; to — a river, eine Brücke über einen Fluß schlagen. II. *attrib.;* — building, der Brückenbau; — pile, der Jochpfahl, Brückenpfahl; — railing, das Brückengeländer; — toll, der Brückenzoll.

Bridle, I. *s.* der Zaum, Zügel; das Querholz (*Artil.*); die Stange am Flintenschloß (*Gun.*); to give a horse the —, einem Pferde die Zügel schießen lassen. II. *v.a.* zäumen, aufzäumen; im Zaume halten, bändigen; to — one's tongue, seiner Zunge einen Zügel anlegen. III. *v.n.* sich brüsten; to — (up), den Kopf zurückwerfen. *Comp.* **—-hand**, *s.* die linke Hand. **—-path**, *s.* der Reitpfad. **—-rods**, *pl.* die Lenkstangen.

Bridoon, I. *s.* die Trense, der Knebel (*Saddl.*); snaffle —, Wassertrense. II. *attrib.;* — bit, das Trensengebiß.

Brief, I. *adj.*, **—ly**, *adv.* kurz, bündig, kurz gefaßt; (soon passing away) flüchtig; in —, in Kürze. II. *s.* das Breve (*of the Pope*); der offizielle, offene Brief; der schriftliche Befehl; das Rechtsdokument; to hold a —, eine Sache vor Gericht vertreten, — to counsel, die von dem nichtplaidierenden Anwalt dem plaidierenden erteilte schriftliche Instruktion. **—less**, *adj.* ohne Klageschrift, ohne Prozesse. **—ness**, *s.* die Kürze.

Brier, *s.* der Dornstrauch; der Brombeerstrauch;

der Hagebuttenstrauch, die wilde Rose; sweet-—, die Dünenrose, Riechrose.

Brig, *s.* die Brigg. **—ade**, *s.* die Brigade; —ade major, der Brigademajor. **—adier**, *s.* der Brigadier, Brigadekommandeur, Befehlshaber einer Brigade. **—and**, *s.* der Räuber, Freibeuter. **—andage**, *s.* die Straßenräuberei.

Bright, *adj.*, **—ly**, *adv.* hell, glänzend, klar; heiter (*of the spirits, etc.*); (clever) aufgeweckt; a — colour, eine helle Farbe; — eyes, helle, strahlende Augen; a — face, ein heiteres, fröhliches Gesicht; — pewter pots, blanke, zinnerne Töpfe; — prospects, glänzende Aussichten; a — day, ein sonniger Tag; —ly shining, hellscheinend. **—en**, *v.* I. *a.* glänzend machen; aufhellen (*fig.*); aufheitern (*a p.'s prospects, etc.*); abklären, avivieren (*Dye.*); to —en up, (etwas) polieren; to —en (a p.) up, (einen) aufgeweckt machen; (cheer) aufheitern. II. *n.* hell werden, sich aufhellen, sich aufklären (*fig.*); our prospects are —ening, unsere Aussichten werden günstiger; the sky is —ening up, der Himmel klärt sich auf. **—ness**, *s.* der Glanz; die Klarheit; die Heiterkeit (*of the countenance, the sky, etc.*); die Glätte (*as a polish, etc.*); die helle Farbe; die Aufgeklärtheit (*of the understanding*); der Scharfsinn. *Comp.* **—-eyed**, *adj.* helläugig. **—-haired**, *adj.* mit hell glänzendem Haar. **—-hued**, *adj.* von glänzender Farbe.

Brill, *s.* der Glattbutt (*Icht.*).

Brillian—cy, *s.* der Glanz; das Feuer (der edeln Steine). **—t**, I. *adj.*, **—tly**, *adv.* glänzend, funkelnd; herrlich, prächtig; —t exploits, glänzende Taten; a —t gem, ein funkelnder Edelstein; he is a —t talker, er ist ein höchst geistvoller Redner. II. *s.* der Brillant, der von allen Seiten geschliffene Diamant; der Brillantdruck (*Typ.*).

Brim, I. *s.* der Rand; die Krempe; to fill to the —, bis zum Rande voll schenken. II. *v.n.* gestrichen voll sein; — over, übervoll sein, überlaufen; —ming eyes, tränenvolle *or* überlaufende Augen. **—ful**, *adj.* bis zum Rande voll. **—less**, *adj.* randlos. **—med**, *p.p. & adj.;* a broad-—med hat, ein Hut mit einer breiten Krempe. **—mer**, *s.* das bis an den Rand gefüllte *or* gestrichen volle Glas.

Brimstone, *s.* der Schwefel; — in rolls, Stangenschwefel.

Brindled, *adj.* gefleckt, scheckig.

Brin—e, I. *s.* die Salzsole, das Salzwasser, die Lake; das Meer, die See (*fig.*). II. *attrib.;* —e gauge, —e prover, die Salzwage, Solspindel; —e tub, das Solfaß; —e valve, das Schnüffelventil (*Locom.*). **—y**, *adj.* salzig; the —y deep, die salzige Tiefe, das Meer.

Bring, *ir.v.a.* bringen; (carry) tragen, führen; to — **about**, zustande bringen; to — an action **against** a p., einen gerichtlich belangen; to — **away**, wegbringen, fortnehmen; to — **back**, zurückbringen *or* führen; to — **down**, hinunterbringen, herunter-bringen *or* -holen; to — s. o. (a p.'s pride) down, einen (jemandes Stolz) demütigen; to — down prices, die Preise niederdrücken; his illness has brought him down greatly, seine Krankheit hat ihn sehr geschwächt, heruntergebracht; to — down the house, die ganze Zuhörerschaft zu lauten Beifallsrufen hinreißen; to — **forth**, (produce) hervorbringen, darstellen; (disclose) ans Licht bringen; (cause) verursachen; gebären (*children*), werfen (*young, puppies*); to — **forward**, vorwärts bringen, fördern (*pupils, etc.*); voranrücken (*troops, etc.*); anführen (*a passage in a book, etc.*); übertragen (*C. L.*); to — forward evidence, Beweise beibringen; brought forward, Übertrag, Transport (*C. L.*); to — **home** to a p., einem ergreifend darstellen, einem eindringlich vorstellen; einen etwas fühlen lassen; to — **in**, hinein bringen, in die Gewohnheit bringen; to — in (*a fashion*), to — into fashion, in die Mode bringen; to — in, (yield) Gewinn bringen, einbringen; to — in goods, Waren einführen; to — in guilty (not guilty), für schuldig erklären (freisprechen); to — **into**, bringen in (*acc.*); to — into notice, einführen, bekannt machen; to — a p. into trouble, einen in Verlegenheit *or* Not bringen; to — **off**, fortbringen; to — **on**, herbeiführen (*war, etc.*); to — on (*the stage*), auf die Bühne bringen; aufführen lassen; to — **out**, herausbringen, in die Welt führen (*a young lady*); to — out a book, ein Buch herausgeben, veröffentlichen, verlegen; to — **over**, herüber bringen, *see* to — forward (*C.L.*); to — a p. over to one's own way of thinking, einen zu seiner eigenen Denkweise überreden *or* bekehren; to — **round**, vorfahren (*as a carriage*); zum erwünschten Ziele führen; the doctor thinks he can — him round, der Arzt meint, er werde ihn wieder herstellen können; to — s. o. round (to an opinion), einen (zu einer Ansicht) überreden; to — **to**, beidrehen (*Naut.*); to make a ship — to, ein Schiff beilegen; to — to account, in Rechnung stellen; to be brought to bed (of a son), (mit einem Sohne) in die Wochen kommen, (von einem Sohne) entbunden werden; I can never — myself to do it, ich kann es nie übers Herz bringen es zu tun; to — to an issue, zum Austrag bringen; to be brought to a fine pass, schön daran sein; to — a p. to (himself), einen wieder zu sich bringen; to — s. o. to justice, einen gerichtlich belangen; to — to nothing, vernichten; to — to bear, anbringen; anwenden auf (*acc.*), richten auf (*acc.*); to — to beggary, an den Bettelstab bringen; to — to a close, zum Abschluß bringen; to — to a head, zur Entscheidung bringen; to — to pass, bewerkstelligen; to — to one's remembrance, sich erinnern; to — to a p.'s remembrance, einen erinnern; to — to reason, zur Vernunft bringen; to — **together**, zusammenbringen, errichten, erbauen; to — **under**, bezwingen; to — **up**, heraufbringen; (*fig.*) aufziehen; I was brought up by him, er hat mich erzogen; to — up a child by hand, ein Kind ohne Muttermilch großziehen; to — up the rear, den Nachtrab bilden; to — up for the church, (einen) zum Geistlichen heranbilden, (einem) eine theologische Erziehung geben; to — up to date, bis auf den heutigen Tag *or* die Gegenwart fortführen; dem jetzigen Stande der Wissenschaft gemäß umgestalten.

Brink, *s.* der Rand; — of a river, das Ufer eines Flusses; he is on the — of the grave, er steht am Rande des Grabes *or* mit einem Fuß im Grabe; on the — of eternity, an den Pforten der Ewigkeit; on the — of discovery, am Vorabend der Entdeckung.

Brisk, I. *adj.*, **—ly**, *adv.* lebhaft; (active) flink; feurig (*as beer*); a — fire, ein gut brennendes Feuer; ein lebhaftes Feuergefecht (*Mil.*); a — gale of wind, ein frischer Wind; — sale, schneller Absatz. II. *v.n.;* to — up, sich aufmuntern (*coll.*). **—ness**, *s.* die Lebhaftigkeit (*also C. L.*).

Brisket, *s.* das Bruststück (*Butch.*).

Bristl—e, I. *s.* die Borste (*also Bot.*), die Schweinsborste; dressed —es, sortierte Borsten. II. *v.n.* sich sträuben; stief *or* starr dastehen, starren; —ing with jewels, vor Edelsteinen steif; —ing with bayonets, von Bajonetten starrend; to —e with difficulties, von Schwierigkeiten rings umgeben sein, von Schwierigkeiten strotzen; to —e up, auffahren. **—ed**, *adj.* struppig. **—y**, *adj.* borstig, borstenartig.

Brittle, *adj.* zerbrechlich, spröde, brüchig; leicht zerstörbar (*fig.*); — iron, sprödes Eisen. **—ness**, *s.* die Sprödigkeit, Brüchigkeit, Zerbrechlichkeit.

Broach, I. *s.* die Nadel, der Bratspieß; der Ausschroter (*Carp.*); der Spieß (*of chandlers*); der Weinstecher (*Coop.*); der Ausbohrstahl (*of dentists*); die Reibahle, Räumahle (*Gun.*); der

Dorn (eines Schlosses); der Aufräumer (*Horol.*). II. *v.a.* anspießen; anzapfen, anbohren (*a cask, etc.*); ausbohren, aufräumen (*a hole*); to — a conversation, ein Gespräch anknüpfen; to — a subject, das Gespräch auf eine S. bringen.

Broad, *adj.*, **—ly**, *adv.* breit, weit; offen, klar, hell (*as daylight, etc.*); laut, grob (*as laughter*); (coarse) frei, unanständig, grob; (comprehensive) umfassend, weit, allgemein; stark, grob (*as an accent*); a — stare, ein starres Angaffen, ein frecher Blick; in — daylight, am hellen lichten Tage; he is a —-Churchman, er gehört zu den Gemäßigt-Liberalen (nicht zu den Strenggläubigen) in der Kirche; — views on a subject, aufgeklärte, weitherzige Ansichten über einen Gegenstand; a — joke, ein grober Spaß; it's as — as it's long, es kommt auf eins hinaus. **—en**, *v.* I. *a.* breiter machen, verbreitern, erweitern. II. *n.* breiter werden, sich weiten *or* erweitern, sich ausbreiten. **—ish**, *adj.* etwas breit. **—ness**, *s.* die Gemeinheit, Roheit der Sprache, Grobheit; die Schlüpfrigkeit (*of a joke*). *Comp.* **—-axe**, *s.* die Zimmeraxt (*Carp.*); das Breitbeil (*Coop.*). **—-brimmed**, *adj.* mit weitem Rande; breitkrempig (*as a hat*). **—-bottomed**, *adj.* vollgebaut (*of a ship*). **—-built**, breitgebaut; breitschultrig. **—cast**, *adj.* aus der Hand gesäet, ausgestreut; weit verbreitet (*widely disseminated*); —cast sowing-machine, die Wurfsäemaschine (*Agr.*); to sow —cast, breitwürfig säen; to spread —cast, nach allen Richtungen hin verbreiten. **—-chested**, *adj.* breitbrüstig. **—cloth**, *s.* feines schwarzes Tuch. **—-gauge**, *s.* die Schienenweite von mehr als 56½ Zoll (*Railw.*). **—-minded**, *adj.* weitherzig, duldsam. **—-nosed**, *adj.* breitnäsig; —-nosed whale, der Butzkopf (*Icht.*). **—-pennant**, *s.* der Kommodore-Stander (*Naut.*). **—-ribbed**, *adj.* breitrippig. **—sheet**, *s.* das Flugblatt, das fliegende Blatt; der Anschlagezettel, das Plakat. **—-shouldered**, *adj.* breitschulterig. **—side**, *s.* die Abfeuerung aller Kanonen auf einer Seite eines Schiffes (*Artil.*); die (oberhalb des Wassers sich befindende) Seite eines Schiffes; der Mandatbogen (*Typ.*); das Querformat (*Typ.*); to give a —side, alle Kanonen auf einer Seite des Schiffes abfeuern; —side through the water, Dwars ab (*Naut.*). **—sword**, *s.* der Säbel, Pallasch, das Schwert; —sword exercise, das Säbelfechten, Hiebfechten. **—wise**, *adv.* nach der Breite.

Brocade, *s.* der Brokat. **—d**, *adj.* brokaten.

Broccoli, *s.* der Blumenkohl, Broccoli; sprouting —, der Rosenkohl.

Broché-goods, *pl.* die broschierten Stoffe.

Brochure, *s.* die Flugschrift, Broschüre.

Brock, *s.* der Dachs; (*fig.*) der Schmutzfink.

Brocket, *s.* der Spießer, zweijähriger Hirsch.

Brogue, *s.* der dicke, plumpe, mit großen Nägeln versehene Schuh; der irländische Akzent; die dialektische Aussprache.

1**Broil**, *s.* der Lärm, Tumult; der lärmende Streit, Zwist, Zank; domestic —s, häusliche Zwistigkeiten.

2**Broil**, I. *v.a.* auf dem Roste braten, rösten. II. *v.n.* in der Sonne braten. III. *s.* ein auf dem Roste gebratenes Stück (Fleisch, ꝛc.). **—ing**, *adj.* glühend heiß.

Broke, *imperf* (*& obs. & poet. p.p.*) *of* Break.

Broken, *p.p. of* Break (*& adj.*); to die of a — heart, an gebrochenem Herzen sterben; to speak — English, gebrochen Englisch sprechen; — glass, zerbrochenes Glas; — health, zerrüttete Gesundheit; — meat, die Überbleibsel von Mahlzeiten, die Brocken; — quarter, angefangenes Quartal; — sleep, unterbrochener Schlaf; a — spirit, ein niedergeschlagener Geist; — stones, der Steinschlag, Steinbeschläge; a — week, eine Woche, in welcher Feiertage vorkommen. **—ly**, *adv.* unterbrochen. *Comp.* **—-backed**, *adj.* krumm, gekrümmt; —-backed ship, Schiff, welches einen Katzenrücken hat. **—-down**, *adj.* gebrochen, niedergeschlagen; vereitelt. **—-hearted**, *adj.* mit gebrochenem zerknirschtem Herzen verzweifelt. **—-winded**, *adj.* kurzatmig, keuchend.

Broker, *s.* der Makler; der Trödler, Pfandleiher; the honest —, der ehrliche Makler; exchange-—, der Wechselmakler; insurance-—, Versicherungsmakler; stock-—, der Börsenmakler, Makler in Staatspapieren; —'s memorandum, der Schlußzettel des Maklers. **—age**, *s.* die Maklergebühr, Provision, das Maklergeld.

Brom—al, *s.* das Bromal (*Chem.*). **—ate**, *s.* das bromsaure Salz. **—hydric**, *adj.*; —hydric acid, die Bromwasserstoffsäure. **—ic**, *adj.*; —ic acid, die Bromsäure. **—ide**, *s.* das Bromid; —ide of potassium, das Bromkalium. **—ine**, *s.* das Brom.

Brome-grass, *s.* die Trespe.

Bronch—ial, *adj.* zur Luftröhre gehörig; —ial cold, der Bronchialkatarrh; —ial tube, die Luftröhre; —ial ways *or* passages, die Luftwege. **—itis**, *s.* die Luftröhrenentzündung. **—ocele**, *s.* der Kropf, Luftröhrenbruch.

Bronz—e, I. *s.* die Bronze; die bronzene Figur; das Bronzebraun; the age of —e, das eherne Zeitalter. II. *v.a.* bronzieren; his —ed countenance, sein (wetter)gebräuntes Gesicht. **—ing**, *s.* das Bronzieren; der Metallglanz.

Brooch, *s.* die Brosche, Busennadel.

Brood, I. *s.* die Brut (*also fig.*); der Flug (*of pigeons*). II. *v.n.* brüten; to — on a matter, über einer S. brüten, über eine S. lange nachdenken. *Comp.* **—-mare**, *s.* das Zuchtpferd.

1**Brook**, *s.* der Bach. **—let**, *s.* das Bächlein. *Comp.* **—side**, *s.* das Bachufer.

2**Brook**, *v.n.* ertragen, leiden, dulden, vertragen, sich (*dat.*) gefallen lassen.

Broom, *s.* der Besen; der Ginster (*Bot.*); common —, Besenginster; dyer's —, das Färbekraut; new —s sweep clean, neue Besen kehren gut (*prov.*). *Comp.* **—stick**, *s.* der Besenstiel.

Broth, *s.* die (Fleisch-)Brühe, Kraftbrühe, Bouillon; snow —, das Schneewasser.

Brothel, *s.* das Bordell. **—ry**, *s.* die Unzucht.

Brother, *s.* der Bruder; your —, Ihr (Herr) Bruder; —-in-law, der Schwager; — in arms, der Waffenbruder; — officer, der Mitoffizier, Kamerad; — Jonathan, Spitzname der Vereinigten Staaten von Nordamerika; —s in affliction, Leidensbrüder. **—hood**, *s.* die Brüderschaft. **—ly**, *adj.* brüderlich; —ly love, die Bruderliebe.

Brougham, *s.* der Brougham; vierrädriger geschlossener zweisitziger Wagen.

Brought, *imperf. & p.p. of* Bring.

Brow, *s.* (eyebrow) die Augenbraue; (forehead) die Stirne; (countenance) das Gesicht, Ansehen; to contract one's —, die Stirne runzeln; — of a hill, der Abhang eines Hügels; by the sweat of thy —, im Schweiß deines Angesichts; his — was clouded, seine Stirne war umwölkt. *Comp.* **—-antlers**, *pl.* die ersten Eissprießel (am Geweih). **—beat**, *v.a.* durch hochmütige Rede *or* finstere Blicke einschüchtern, entmutigen.

Brown, I. *adj.* braun, bräunlich; to be in a — study, in Gedanken versunken *or* in Nachsinnen verloren sein; — Bess, eines Soldaten Gewehr (*sl.*); — bread, das Schwarzbrot; — girl, die Brünette; — holland, ungebleichte, bräunliche Leinwand; — paper, das Packpapier; — sugar der braune Zucker, gelber Farinzucker. II. *v.a.* braun machen; brünieren. **—ie**, *s.* ein gutmütiger Hausgeist, Heinzelmännchen. **—ish**, *adj.* bräunlich. **—ness**, *s.* die braune Farbe.

Browse, *v.* I. *a.* abfressen, abweiden. II. *n.* weiden.

Bruis—e, I. *v.a.* zermalmen, (zer)quetschen, zerstoßen; wund (braun und blau) schlagen; to be —ed all over (from being jolted), zerschlagen sein; to —e the malt, Malz schroten; —ed malt, das Malzschrot; —ing mill, die Quetschmühle. II. *s.* die Quetschung. **—er**, *s.* die Schleifschale (*Opt.*); der Boxer (*sl.*).

Bruit, I. *s.* das Gerücht. II. *v.a.* verkünden, verbreiten, aussprengen.

Brunette, *s.* die Brünette.

Brunt, *s.* der Stoß, Angriff, Anfall; to bear the — of the battle, die Wucht des ersten Angriffs aushalten.

Brush, I. *s.* die Bürste; der Pinsel (*Paint.*); die Rute (*of a fox*); (skirmish) das Scharmützel; der Bestreichpinsel (*Bak.*); die Lunte (*Artil.*); das elektrische Strahlenbündel (*Phys.*); blacking —, Wichsbürste; clothes- —, Kleiderbürste; hair- —, Haarbürste; to have a — with a p., mit einem aneinander geraten; a sharp — with the enemy, ein hitziges Gefecht mit dem Feinde. II. *attrib.;* — bolter, die Mehlbürstmaschine; — maker, der Bürstenbinder; der Bürstenfabrikant; — proof, der Bürstenabzug. III. *v.a.* bürsten, abbürsten; to — **against**, streifen leicht berühren; to — **away**, — **off**, abbürsten, wegbürsten; to — **past** a p., einen im Vorbeieilen streifen; to — **up**, reinigen, wieder auffrischen; I must — up my German, ich muß mein Deutsch wieder auffrischen *or* (*coll.*) wieder auf den Damm bringen. III. *v.n.;* to — past, vorbeischnellen, vorbeieilen. *Comp.* **—wood**, *s.* das Dickicht, Gestrüpp.

Brusque, *adj.*, **—ly**, *adv.* barsch, derb, schroff, kurz angebunden; (downright) offen. **—ness**, *s.* die Barschheit, Schroffheit.

Brut—al, *adj.*, **—ally**, *adv.* tierisch, viehisch; (cruel) unmenschlich, grausam; (unrefined) grob, roh. **—ality**, *s.* die Unmenschlichkeit, Roheit, Brutalität. **—alize**, **—alise**, *v.a.* zum Vieh erniedrigen, unmenschlich machen. **—e**, I. *s.* das unvernünftige Vieh; der rohe, grausame Mensch; der Flegel, Grobian. II. *adj.* tierisch; unvernünftig; grob; (sensual) fleischlich; (insensate) gefühllos; sinnlos; —e passions, tierische Leidenschaften, —e violence, die rohe Gewalt. **—ish**, *adj.* tierisch, viehisch; fleischlich; unzüchtig; gefühllos; dumm; —ish pleasures, sinnliche Lüste. **—ishness**, *s.* das viehische Wesen; die Roheit; die Dummheit.

Bryony, *s.* die Zaunrübe (*Bot.*).

Bubble, I. *s.* die Blase; die wertlose Sache, der leere Schein; (*fig.*) die Seifenblase, der Schwindel; to rise in —s, wallen, aufsprudeln; South Sea —, der Südsee-Schwindel (*coll.*). II. *v.n.* aufwallen, Blasen aufwerfen. III. *v.a.;* to — iron, das Eisen aufwallen lassen.

Bubo, *s.* der Bubo, die Leistenbeule (*Med.*). **—nic**, *adj.;* —nic plague, die Beulenpest. **—nocele**, *s.* der Leistenbruch.

Buccaneer, I. *s.* der Seeräuber, Freibeuter. II. *v.a.* freibeutern, Seeräuberei treiben.

[1]**Buck**, I. *s.* der Bock; (roe—) der Rehbock; der Dambock (*of the fallow deer*); (he-goat) der Ziegenbock; das Männchen (*of various animals*); (dandy) der Stutzer (*vulg.*). II. *v.n.* einander belaufen, bespringen; bocken, stoßen (*as a horse*). **—ish**, *adj.*, **—ishly**, *adv.* stutzerhaft. *Comp.* **—hound**, *s.* der Hund zur Parforcejagd auf Rehböcke; Master of the —hounds, königlicher Oberjägermeister (*at the English court*). **—shot**, *s.* die Rehposten. **—skin**, *s.* das Buckskin, Bocksfell. **—thorn**, *s.* der Wegdorn, Faulbaum (*Bot.*).

[2]**Buck**, I. *s.* die Lauge, Beuche; die (auf einmal zu waschende) Wäsche. II. *attrib.;* — ashes, die ausgelaugte Asche. III. *v.a.* mit alkalischen Laugen behandeln; to — soiled linen, Wäsche einweichen, beuchen; to — ore, Erze zerkleinern. *Comp.* **—-basket**, *s.* der Waschkorb. **—washing**, *s.* das Waschen (in Lauge).

Buck—board, **—-cart**, **—-waggon**, *s.* vierrädriger Wagen, dessen Gestell aus einem Brett mit Sitz besteht (*Amer.*).

Bucket, *s.* der Eimer, Schöpfeimer; der Kühleimer (*Artil.*); die Pütze (*Naut.*); dredge —, Baggereimer; — of a paddle-wheel, die Radschaufel; to kick the —, ins Gras beißen, sterben (*vulg.*). *Comp.* **—-chain**, *s.* die Eimerkette. **—-wheel**, *s.* das Zellenrad.

Buckle, I. *s.* die Schnalle. II. *v.a.* schnallen; to — up, aufschnallen; to — on, anschnallen; to — on one's armour, die Rüstung anlegen, sich rüsten. III. *v.n.;* to — to a th. (*coll.*) sich eifrig auf eine S. legen. **—r**, *s.* der Schild.

Buckram, *s.* die Steifleinwand, der Buckram.

Buckwheat, *s.* der Buchweizen.

Bucolic, I. *adj.* bukolisch, hirtenmäßig; — poetry, die Hirtendichtung, Schäferdichtung. II. *s.* das Hirtengedicht.

Bud, I. *s.* die Knospe, das Auge; nipped in the —, im Keime erstickt. II. *v.n.* Knospen treiben, knospen; blühen (*fig.*); —ding love, junge, aufkeimende Liebe; —ding maiden, aufblühende Jungfrau; —ding scholar, angehender Gelehrter. III. *v.a.* okulieren, pfropfen (*of plants*). *Comp.* **—ding-knife**, *s.* das Okuliermesser.

Buddl—e, I. *s.* der Erzwaschtrog, Schlämmherd. II. *v.a.* Erze waschen, abslauen.

Budge, *v.n.* sich rühren, sich regen; don't —! nicht von der Stelle! rührt euch (rühr' dich) nicht!

Budget, *s.* die lederne Tasche, Satteltasche, der Reisesack (*obs.*); (stock) der Vorrat; das Budget, der Staatshaushaltsplan (*Pol.*); der Haushaltsplan, Voranschlag; — of news, der Vorrat, Sack voll (Tages-)Neuigkeiten; to open the —, das Budget vorlegen; debate on the —, die Budgetberatung; in accordance with the —, voranschlagsmäßig.

Buff, I. *s.* das Büffelleder, Sämischleder; (colour) die Lederfarbe; (skin) die bloße Haut; in one's —, nackt (*vulg.*). II. *adj.* ledergelb, rötlichgelb, sämisch; — coat, — jerkin, das lederne Wams; — gloves, hirschlederne Handschuhe. **—alo**, *s.* der Büffel. *Comp.* **—alo-grass**, *s.* das Elfengras. **—alo-hide**, *s.* die Büffelhaut. **—alo-robe**, *s.* zubereitete Büffelhaut.

Buffe—r, I. *s.* der Puffer, das Stoßkissen; (*sl.*) Kerl, Junge, Gottlieb; the old —r, der alte Kerl; India-rubber —r, der Kautschukpuffer. II. *attrib.;* —r state, der Pufferstaat (zwischen zwei Großmächten). **—t**, I. *s.* der Puff, Faustschlag. II. *v.a.* puffen, mit der Faust schlagen; to —t the waves, mit den Wellen kämpfen. **—tings**, *pl.* die Schläge, der Anprall. *Comp.* **—r-beam**, *s.* das Pufferholz. **—r-spring**, *s.* die Pufferfeder.

Buffet, *s.* der Schenktisch.

Buffoon, *s.* der Possenreißer; der Narr; to play the —, Possen reißen. **—ery**, *s.* die Possenreißerei; die Possen.

[1]**Bug**, *s.* das Gespenst (*obs.*). *Comp.* **—bear**, *s.* der Popanz.

[2]**Bug**, *s.* die Wanze. **—gy**, *adj.* voller Wanzen.

Buggy, *s.* ein leichtes, vierrädriges, einsitziges Gefährt (*Amer.*); der Kohlenwagen. *Comp.* **—-boat**, *s.* Boot das zur Landbeförderung mit Rädern versehen werden kann. **—-plough**, *s.* das Pfluggestell mit mehreren Pflugscharen und einem Sitz für den Pflügenden.

[1]**Bugle**, (**—-horn**,) I. *s.* das Jagdhorn, Hifthorn; das Signalhorn. II. *attrib.;* — call, das Hornsignal; military — call, militärisches Hornsignal. **—r**, *s.* der Hornbläser, Hornist.

[2]**Bugle**, *s.* die Schmelzperle, (schwarze) längliche Glasperle.

Bugloss, *s.* die Ochsenzunge (*Bot.*).

Buhl, *s.* Material zu eingelegter Arbeit (mattes Gold, Perlmutter, Schildpatt, 2c.). *Comp.* **—work**, *s.* die eingelegte Arbeit.

Build, I. *v.a.* bauen, erbauen; to — upon s. o., auf einen bauen; to — up (*v.a.*), aufmauern; zubauen (Fenster, 2c.); to — a nest, ein Nest bauen; nisten; horsten (*of eagles*). II. *s.* die Form;

die Gestalt. **—er**, *s.* der Bauende; der Baumeister; (he who builds a house for his own use *or* has a house built for his own use by an architect) der Bauherr. **—ing**, *s.* das Bauen; das Bauwesen; (thing built) das Gebäude; additional —ing, der Anbau; the art of —ing, die Baukunst; —ing above ground, der Tagbau; framed —ing, der Fachwerkbau; main —ing, der Hauptbau, das Hauptgebäude; ship —ing, der Schiffsbau. *Comp.* **—ing-contract**, *s.* der Baukontrakt; der Beilbrief (*Shipb.*). **—ing-ground**, *s.* der Bauplatz. **—ing-lease**, *s.* die Baupacht. **—ing-mortar**, *s.* der Mörtel. **—ing-site**, *s.* der Bauplatz. **—ing-stone**, *s.* der Baustein.

Built, *p.p. of* Build, gebaut; English —, von englischer Bauart; frigate- —, fregattenartig.

Bulb, *s.* der Knollen (*Bot.*); das Gefäß, die Kugel, Kapsel; die Zwiebel; die Kugel (*of a thermometer*); der Apfel (*of the eye*); incandescent (electric) light —, die (elektrische) Glühlampe. **—ous**, *adj.* zwiebelartig, knollig; —ous root, die Zwiebelwurzel.

Bulg—e, I. *v.n.* einen Bauch machen, vorragen; hervorstehen; to —e out, ausbauchen. II. *s.* die Ausbauchung (*Build.*); —e of a cask, der Bauch eines Fasses.

Bulk, *s.* der Umfang, die Größe (*of a man's body, etc.*); die Masse (*of a body*); (greater part) der größte Haufe, größte Teil, Hauptteil; der ganze innere Raum eines Schiffes; to break —, die Ladung zu löschen anfangen; in the —, im Durchschnitt, im Ganzen; purchase in the —, der Kauf im Ganzen, Bauschkauf, Ramschkauf; increase in — of barley, das Aufquellen der Gerstenkörner (zu Malz). **—iness**, *s.* der große Umfang; die Dickleibigkeit; that won't do because of its —iness, das geht nicht, wegen seines großen Umfangs. **—y**, *adj.* dick, von großem Umfange. *Comp.* **—head**, *s.* das Schott. **—headed**, *adj.* mit Schotten *or* wasserdichten Abteilungen versehen.

[1]**Bull**, *s.* der Stier, Bulle; the — bellows, der Stier brüllt; der Börsenmakler, Haussier (*C.L.*); to take the — by the horns, den Stier bei den Hörnern packen (*i.e.* to come straight to a difficulty). **—ace**, *s.* eine Art Pflaume *or* Schlehe. **—ock**, *s.* der junge Ochse, Farre. **—y**, *see* Bully. *Comp.* **—-baiting**, *s.* die Stierhetze. **—dog**, *s.* der Bullenbeißer; der Pedell; der Pudel (*Univ. sl.*). **—fight**, *s.* das Stiergefecht. **—finch**, *s.* der Dompfaff, Gimpel; the —finch pipes, der Dompfaff pfeift. **—-frog**, *s.* der Ochsenfrosch, Brüllfrosch. **—head**, *s.* der Ochsenkopf; der Dummkopf; die Flußgroppe, der Kaulbarsch. **—-necked**, *adj.* dickhalsig. **—ock-waggon**, *s.* der Ochsenwagen. **—'s-eye**, *s.* die Blendlaterne; das Ochsenauge, die Wettergalle (*Naut.*); die Rausche (*for securing ropes*); der Butzen (*Glassw.*); das Zentrum, Schwarze einer Schießscheibe (*Mil., etc.*); die Konzentrationslinse (*Opt.*); das Ochsenauge (eine Art Konfekt); —'s-eye glass, die Butzenscheibe; —'s-eye window, das Ochsenauge (*Build.*).

[2]**Bull**, *s.* die Bulle, päpstliche Urkunde. **—et**, I. *s.* die Kugel; explosive —et, die Sprengkugel. II. *attrib.;* —et bore, der Bohrer (*Gun.*); —et dividers, —et compasses, der Kolbenzirkel; —et extractor, die Kugelzange; —et hole, das Schußloch; —et iron, das schwedische Stangeneisen; —et shell, die Sprengkugel; —et shot, der Flintenschuß; —et valve, das Muschelventil (*Locom.*).

[3]**Bull**, *s.* der Widerspruch, Unsinn, die Ungereimtheit, Lächerlichkeit; to make a —, eine lächerliche Verkehrtheit begehen, einen Pudel machen, einen Bock schießen; an Irish —, ein fauler Witz, ein Kalauer.

Bulletin, *s.* das Bulletin, der Tagesbericht, die kurze (ärztliche *or* militärische) Bekanntmachung; Titel mancher Zeitschriften. *Comp.* **—-board**, *s.* das Anschlagsbrett.

Bullion, *s.* Gold oder Silber in Barren; das ungemünzte Gold oder Silber.

Bully, I. *s.* der Eisenfresser, Raufdegen, der herrisch auftretende große Feigling; he is a —, er ist ein Zänker, Händelsucher; the — and the bullied, der Einschüchterer und der Eingeschüchterte. II. *v.a.* einschüchtern, ins Bockshorn jagen; tyrannisieren; to — a p. into . . ., einen durch Einschüchtern zu . . . bringen; to — s.o. out of . . ., mit Drohungen einem etwas abdringen.

Bulrush, *s.* die (große, glatte) Binse, der Rohrkolben.

Bulwark, *s.* das Bollwerk, die Befestigung (*Fort.*); das Schanzkleid (*of a ship*); der Schutz, Halt, die Stütze (*fig.*).

[1]**Bum**, *v.n. see* Hum. *Comp.* **—bee, —ble-bee**, *see* Humble-bee.

[2]**Bum**, *interj.; (dial.)* to say neither ba nor —, gar nichts sagen, stockstill *or* mäuschenstill sein.

[3]**Bum**, *s.* der Hintere, Steiß (*vulg.*). *Comp.* **—bailiff**, *s.* der Büttel, Scherge.

[4]**Bum**, *v.a.* Provianthandel treiben. *Comp.* **—boat**, *s.* das Marktboot, Proviantboot.

Bump, I. *s.* der Schlag, Stoß; die Beule; der Höcker (*Phren.*); (*fig.*) Organ (für), Sinn (für); to have the — of a th., das Talent zu einer S. *or* die Begabung für eine S. haben. II. *v.a.* stoßen, schlagen; beim Bootrennen ein Boot überholen, mit dem Buge oder Ruder stoßen und dadurch besiegen; to make a —, ein Boot überholen, berühren, schlagen. **—y**, *adj.;* —y way, holperiger Weg.

Bumper, *s.* das volle Glas, der Humpen; der Eisbrecher (*Naut.*); der Puffer (*Railw.*).

Bumpkin, *s.* der Bauerntölpel; country —, der Tölpel vom Lande, die Landpomeranze.

Bumptious, *adj.* aufgeblasen, anmaßend (*vulg.*).

Bun, *s.* der süße Semmel (mit Korinthen); (hot) cross- —, der (gewärmte) Karfreitagssemmel.

Bunch, I. *s.* das Bund (*of keys, etc.*); das Bündel, Bund (*of straw, etc.*); der Büschel (*of hair, etc.*); die Beule (*obs.*); der Höcker, Buckel (*obs.*); — of radishes, das Bund Radieschen; — of hair, der Haarbüschel; — of grapes, die Weintraube; — of flowers, der Blumenstrauß; — of feathers, der Federbusch; — of fruit, die an einer Stange hängenden Fruchtbeeren. II. *v.n.* (to — out) aufschwellen. **—iness**, *s.* das bauschige Wesen; das Höckerige; das Traubenförmige. **—y**, *adj.* in Büscheln wachsend, büschelig; bauschig; büschelförmig.

Buncom(b)e, *s.* leeres Geschwätz (*fig.*); to speak for —, leere Worte machen (*really:* eine auf die Wähler von B. [in Nord Carolina] berechnete Rede halten), eine auf Scheinwirkung berechnete Rede halten (*Amer.*).

Bundl—e, I. *s.* das Bund, Bündel, Packet; die Rolle; —e of flax, das Bündel Flachs (60,000 Ellen); —e of hemp, die Loppe Hanf; —e of lace, die Rolle Spitzen; —e of paper, zwei Ries Papier; —e of wool, Bündel Wolle; he is a mere —e of nerves, er ist ein hochgradig nervöser Mensch. II. *attrib.;* —e press, die Garnpresse, Packmaschine. III. *v.a.;* —e **up**, einbündeln, in Bündel binden; —ing machine, die Bündelformmaschine. IV. *v.n.;* —e **off**, sich packen, aufpacken, weggehen; —e **out**, sich fortpacken.

Bung, I. *s.* der Spund, Spundzapfen; der Kapselstoß (*Pott.*); der Kohlenraum (*Naut.*). II. *v.a.* (zu)spunden; to — up, verspunden; zerschießen (*Milit.*). *Comp.* **—-hole**, *s.* das Spundloch. **—-vent**, *s.* das Luftloch am Spund.

Bungalow, *s.* leichtes langgestrecktes einstöckiges Sommerhaus; ostindisches Stationshaus.

Bungl—e, I. *s.* die Pfuscherei, Stümperei. II *v.a.* (ver)pfuschen, verhunzen. **—er**, *s.* der Stümper, Pfuscher. **—ing**, *adj.*, **—ingly**, *adv.* ungeschickt, stümperhaft; in a —ing way, auf ungeschickte, stümperhafte Weise; —ing work, die Stümperei, Pfuscherei, das Pfuschwerk.

Bunion, *s.* die Schwiele (an der großen Zehe).

Bunk, *s.* die Schlafbank; die Schlafstelle, das Schiffsbett. **—er**, *s.* der Kohlenraum auf einem Dampfschiffe; der Kasten, die Kiste; der Kasten, welcher als Bank gebraucht wird.
Bunkum, *s. see* Buncombe.
Bunny, *s.* das Kaninchen.
[1]**Bunting**, *s.* das Flaggentuch; die Flagge; the ships showed a great display of —, die Schiffe hatten alle Flaggen gehißt; there was plenty of — all over the town, die Stadt prangte überall im reichsten Flaggenschmuck.
[2]**Bunting**, *s.* die Ammer (*Orn.*).
[3]**Bunting**, *s.* das Balkenlager für Maschinen.
Bunt-lines, *pl.* die Bauchgordingen (*Naut.*).
Buoy, I. *s.* die Boje, Bake, Wahrtonne; beacon —, die Bakentonne; life-—, die Rettungsboje; wooden —, die Blakboje; das Flott (*of a net*); the — is floating in sight, die Ankerboje wacht. II. *v.a.;* to — up, flott erhalten, aufbojen; to be —ed up by the water, vom Wasser emporgehoben werden; to be —ed up with hope, von der Hoffnung aufrecht erhalten *or* getragen werden. **—ancy**, *s.* die Schwimmkraft, das Tragvermögen (*Phys.*, *etc.*); die Schwungkraft, Regsamkeit, Frische, Lebenskraft (*of the mind, etc.*). **—ant**, *adj.*, **—antly**, *adv.* schwimmend, leicht; sich leicht erhebend, elastisch, heiter (*as the spirits*).
Bur, *s.* die Klette (*Bot.*, *Manuf.*); to cling like a —, wie eine Klette an einer S. haften *or* festhalten; — of a cast bullet, der Ansatz einer Flintenkugel. **—dock**, *s.* die Klette (*Bot.*).
Burbot, *s.* die Aalraupe, Quappe (*Icht.*).
[1]**Burden**, I. *s.* die Bürde, Last; die Ladung (*of a ship*); (tonnage) die Tragkraft, der Tonnengehalt; beast of —, das Lasttier; a ship of —, ein Lastschiff; the ship's — is . . ., das Schiff trägt . . . II. *v.a.* aufbürden, belasten. **—some**, *adj.* drückend, lästig. **—someness**, *s.* die Lästigkeit; die Beschwerlichkeit.
[2]**Burden**, *s.* der Kehrreim, Refrain (*of a song*); der Hauptinhalt (*of a speech*).
Bureau, *s.* das Geschäftszimmer, Amtszimmer, Bureau; die Unterabteilung eines Regierungsdepartements (*Amer.*); das hochstehende verschließbare Schreibpult mit Auszügen, das Schreibbureau, Schreibpult. **—cracy**, *s.* die Beamtenherrschaft, Bureaukratie.
Burgeon, *s.* die Knospe, das Auge; der Keim.
Burgess, *s.* der Wahlbürger, Wähler; der Abgeordnete eines Wahlfleckens.
Burgh, *s.* die Stadt (*Scotch*). **—er**, *s.* der Bürger; halbholländischer Kolonist (*Ceylon, South Africa*); der Angehörige der konservativen religiösen Partei (*Scotl.*) (*obs.*). *Comp.* **—-mote**, *s.* das Gericht eines Wahlfleckens. **—-school**, *s.* schottische städtische Lateinschule.
Burgl—ar, *s.* der Einbrecher. **—e**, *v.a.* einbrechen (*hum.*); a gentleman of the —ing profession, ein Einbrecher (*hum.*). **—arious**, *adj.*, **—ariously**, *adv.* einbrecherisch. **—ary**, *s.* der nächtliche Diebstahl mit Einbruch; insurance against —ary, die Einbruchsversicherung. *Comp.* **—ar-proof**, *adj.* diebessicher.
Burgomaster, *s.* der Bürgermeister.
Burial, *s.* das Begräbnis, die Beerdigung, Leichenfeier. *Comp.* **—-ground**, *s.* der Begräbnisplatz, Kirchhof; der Gottesacker (*poet.*). **—-service**, *s.* der Leichengottesdienst, die Totenfeier.
Burk(e), *v.a.* heimlich, besonders für den anatomischen Bedarf, morden, ersticken, erwürgen; insgeheim abtun, vertuschen, beiseitigen, aus der Welt schaffen (*hum.*); to — enquiry, Nachforschungen leise vertuschen.
Burlesque, I. *adj.* burlesk, possierlich. II. *s.* das Burleske; die Burleske (*Mus.*); das Possenspiel, die Farce (*Theat.*). III. *attrib.;* — writer, der Travestierer; Verfasser einer Posse. IV. *v.a.* lächerlich machen, possierlich behandeln, travestieren; Virgil —d, der travestierte Vergil.

Burl—iness, *s.* die Stämmigkeit. **—y**, *adj.* stäm mig, stark, kräftig gebaut; a —y fellow, ein vier schrötiger Kerl.
[1]**Burn**, *s.* der Bach (*Scotch*).
[2]**Burn**, I. *v.a.* brennen lassen, verbrennen; an brennen (*meat, etc.*); brennen (*coals, tiles, etc.*) einbrennen (*a mark, colours, etc.*); verbrennen (*o the sun*); verzehren (*as passion, etc.*); röste (*Metal.*); to — one's fingers, sich (*dat.*) die Finge verbrennen; to — the candle at both ends, sic allzu sehr ausgeben, auf seine Gesundheit un bedacht losarbeiten; — **down**, niederbrennen; — **out**, ausbrennen; — **up**, gänzlich verbrennen. II. *v.n.* brennen; heftige Leidenschaft empfinde (*fig.*); to — away, abbrennen; the light — dim, das Licht brennt trübe. III. *s.* der Brand (schaden); (scar) das Brandmal. **—er**, *s.* de Brenner; bat's wing —er, der Fledermaus brenner; charcoal —er, der Kohlenbrenner; je —er, der Strahlbrenner. **—ed**, *p.p. see* —t —ed alive, lebendig verbrannt. **—ing**, I. *p.* & *adj.* brennend; heiß, glühend; leidenschaftlich the —ing bush, der feurige Busch (*B.*); the —in plains of India, die glühenden Ebenen Indiens a —ing shame, eine schreiende Ungerechtigkeit II. *s.* das Brennen, der Brand; das Rösten Brennen (*Metall.*, *etc.*); (batch) der Satz; to smel of —ing, nach Brand riechen. **—t**, *p.p.* (*see* Burn & *adj.;* —t up, von der Hitze ausgedörrt; hi —t letter, sein verbrannter Brief; a —t chil dreads the fire, gebrannte Kinder scheuen das Feuer (*prov.*); —t almonds, gebrannte Mandeln —t bricks, Backsteine; —t earthenware, di Terrakotta; —t steel, der übergare Stahl; — umber, die gebrannte Umber. *Comp.* **—ing glass**, *s.* das Brennglas (*Opt.*). **—t-offering** *s.* das Brandopfer.
Burnet, *s.* die Becherblume, Bibernelle.
Burnish, *v.a.* glätten, polieren, glänzend machen drücken (*Turn.*); bräunen; —ed gilding, da Vergolden mit Blattgold. **—er**, *s.* der Glätter der Polierstahl, das Poliereisen; der Polierstein **—ing**, *s.* das Glätten, Polieren; das Ausschlei fender Öhre (*of needles*); das Drücken (*Turn.*) **—ing**, *p.* & *adj.;* —ing lathe, die Druckdrehbank —ing stick, der Polierstahl; —ing stone, de Glättstein.
Burnoose, (**Burnouse**,) *s.* der Burnus.
Burr, *s.* die rauhe uvulare Aussprache des r, da Zäpfchen-r; the Northumbrian —, die Kehlkopf aussprache des r, das Zäpfchen-r.
Burrel-fly, *s.* die Bremse.
Burrow, I. *s.* der Bau (der Kaninchen), die Kanin chenhöhle. II. *v.n.* Löcher in die Erde graben; sic eingraben, in eine Erdhöhle verkriechen.
Bursar, *s.* der Schatzmeister, Zahlmeister, Seckel wart, Verwalter der gemeinschaftlichen Kasse; de Schaffner eines Klosters; der Stipendiat (*in Scotc universities*). **—y**, *s.* das Schatzamt (*of a con vent*); das Stipendium. **—ship**, *s.* das Schatz meisteramt, Rentamt, Kassenamt.
Burst, I. *v.n.* bersten, platzen (with envy, laugh ter, vor Neid, Lachen); aufspringen; (explode explodieren; krepieren (*Artil.*); the monsoo has —, der Monsun ist ausgebrochen; to — **fron** a p.'s arms, sich aus jemandes Armen los reißen; the spring —s from the earth, di Quelle sprudelt aus der Erde hervor; — **forth** hervorbrechen; to — **into** a room, in ei Zimmer hereinplatzen; to — into flame, auf flammen; to — into leaf, aufblühen; to — into tears, in Tränen ausbrechen; to — **in** upon a p. plötzlich, unbemerkt über einen hereinbrechen — **out**, hervorbrechen; he — out laughing, e brach in Gelächter aus; to — out into, aus brechen in; suddenly there — **upon** the ea . . ., plötzlich erklang . . .; to — upon the view sich dem Auge plötzlich eröffnen *or* darstellen. I *v.a.* sprengen, zersprengen, zerspringen machen the river —s its banks, der Fluß durchbricht sein

Dämme; I have — a blood-vessel, mir ist eine Ader geplatzt. III. *s.* das Bersten, der plötzliche Ausbruch; der Riß, Bruch; die Spalte; a — of applause, ein Ausbruch des Beifalls; — of tears, eine Tränenflut; — of thunder, der Donnerschlag. **—ing**, *s.* das Bersten; der Bruch; the —ing of a dam, der Dammbruch. *Comp.* **—ing-charge**, *s.* die Sprengladung.

Burthen, *see* Burden.

Bury, *v.a.* begraben, beerdigen; (hide) verbergen; (cover over) vergraben; to — the hatchet, die Streitaxt vergraben, Frieden schließen; to — in oblivion, der Vergessenheit weihen. *Comp.* **—ing-ground**, *s.* der Kirchhof; die Begräbnisstätte.

Bus, I. *s. coll. for* Omnibus. II. *v.a.* mit dem Omnibus fahren; to — it, den Omnibus benutzen, die Strecke im Omnibus fahren.

Bush, *s.* der Busch, Strauch; der Kranz (*of a tavern*); (copse) das Gebüsch; das Pfannenlager (*Mach.*); good wine needs no —, gute Ware lobt sich selbst; to beat about the —, auf den Busch klopfen, um den heißen Brei herum gehen. **—iness**, *s.* das Buschige. **—y**, *adj.* buschig; gebüschig; —y beard, buschiger Bart. *Comp.* **—man**, *s.* der Buschman. **—ranger**, *s.* der Buschklepper.

Bushel, *s.* der (englische) Scheffel; große Menge (*fig.*); die Wagenbüchse.

Busi—ed, *p.p. see* Busy. **—ly**, *adv.* geschäftig, emsig; eifrig. **—ness**, I. *s.* (calling) das Geschäft; (affair) die Angelegenheit, Sache; (trade) der Handel, das Getriebe; the —ness of a tailor, das Gewerbe *or* das Geschäft eines Schneiders; a line *or* branch of —ness, ein Geschäftszweig; to do —ness, Geschäfte machen; men of —ness, Geschäftsleute; on —, geschäftlich, in Angelegenheiten des Geschäftes; to set up —ness, ein Geschäft gründen; to put to a —ness, in ein(em) Geschäft einstellen; to carry on —ness on one's own account, ein Geschäft auf eigne Rechnung treiben; to be connected in —ness with . . ., in Geschäftsverbindung mit . . . stehen; it is the —ness of a clergyman to . . ., es ist die Pflicht eines Geistlichen zu . . .; I shall make it my —ness to see him to-morrow, ich werde es so einrichten, daß ich ihn morgen sehe; he makes this his —ness, er läßt sich dies angelegen sein; have you heard of this —ness? haben Sie von dieser Geschichte gehört? to have one's hands full of —ness, viel zu tun haben; that is not in my line of —ness, das liegt außer meinem Bereich, ich habe geschäftlich nichts damit zu tun; to go about one's —ness, sein Geschäft verrichten; to send a p. about his —ness, einen forttreiben, einem die Tür weisen; a pretty piece of —ness! eine schöne Geschichte! what —ness is that of yours? was geht das Sie an? that 's my —ness, das ist meine Sache; what —ness have you here? was habt Ihr hier zu schaffen? mind your own —ness! kümmere dich um deine Sachen *or* um das, was dich angeht! that did his —ness! das hat ihn geliefert, das hat ihm den Hals gebrochen! (*vulg.*) II. *attrib.;* —ness hand, die Kaufmannshand, kaufmännische Hand(schrift). *Comp.* **—ness-like**, *adj.* kaufmännisch, geschäftsmäßig; to do in a —ness-like way, auf geschäftsmäßige Weise tun, auf gut kaufmännische Art ausführen.

Busk, *s.* das Planchett, Blankscheit.

Busk, *v.r.* (*Scotch*) sich vorbereiten; sich ankleiden.

Buskin, *s.* der Halbstiefel; der Kothurn; — style, tragische Schreibart. **—ed**, *adj.* Halbstiefel tragend; im Kothurn; —ed hero, ein Theaterheld.

Buss, I. *s.* der Schmatz (*vulg.*). II. *v.a.* küssen.

Bust, *s.* die Büste; das Rundwerk.

Bustard, *s.* die gemeine Trappe (*Orn.*).

Bustl—e, I. *v.n.* (hurry) sich regen, sich rühren; to —e about, geschäftig, unruhig sein, geräuschvoll umherlaufen, mit Aufregung betreiben. II. *s.* der Lärm; das Getöse; das Aufsehen; what 's all this —e about? woher dieser Lärm? to be in a —e, in Unruhe sein; aufgeregt umherlaufen. **—ing**, I. *p. see* —e I. II. *adj.* rührig, geschäftig; lärmend, aufgeregt.

[2]**Bustle**, *s.* die Tournüre.

Busy, I. *adj.* beschäftigt; geschäftig, emsig, fleißig, tätig; the — bee, die geschäftige Biene; he is — at work, er ist fleißig an *or* bei der Arbeit; to be — with a th., mit einer Sache beschäftigt sein; a — day, ein Tag, an dem man viel zu tun hat; ein besetzter, voller Tag. II. *v.a.* beschäftigen; to — o.s. with . . ., to be busied with, sich mit . . . beschäftigen. *Comp.* **—body**, *s.* einer, der sich in alles mischt, seine Nase in alles stecken muß, die geschäftige Marthe (*coll.*)

But, I. *conj.* aber, allein, sondern; wenn nicht; dessen ungeachtet, indessen, nichts desto weniger; not only . . ., — also . . ., nicht nur . . ., sondern auch . . .; I will come if I can, — you must not expect me, kommen will ich, wenn ich kann, du darfst mich aber nicht fest erwarten; I not only saw him, — spoke to him, ich sah ihn nicht nur, sondern ich sprach ihn auch; I could do it, — that I fear, ich könnte es tun, wenn ich nicht fürchtete; who knows — he may be ill? wer weiß, ob er nicht vielleicht krank ist? she is not so old — she may learn, sie ist nicht zu alt, um noch lernen zu können; they seldom meet — they quarrel, sie kommen selten zusammen, ohne sich zu zanken; one cannot — hope, man muß nur hoffen, man kann nicht umhin zu hoffen; I cannot — wish, ich kann nur wünschen, ich kann nicht umhin zu wünschen; there is no doubt — she will come, es leidet keinen Zweifel, daß sie kommen wird; — that, wenn nicht, wo nicht; — that I love her, wenn ich sie nicht liebte; — though, doch, wiewohl; — yet, aber doch, dennoch; not — that, nicht daß, nicht als wenn; not — that I have often warned him, nicht als ob ich ihn nicht öfters gewarnt hätte. II. *prep. or with another part.* = *prep. & negation*, außer, ausgenommen; the last — one, der Vorletzte, Zweitletzte; the last line — one, die vorletzte Zeile; all — he, alle, bis auf ihn; — for, wenn nicht gewesen wäre; I should have told him my opinion — for you, ich würde ihm meine Meinung gesagt haben, wenn Sie nicht davon abgeraten hätten; — for me he would have been lost, es wäre um ihn geschehen gewesen, wenn ich es nicht verhindert hätte. III. = *rel. pron. & negation;* not a day passes — I tell it him, es vergeht kein Tag, an dem ich es ihm nicht sage; there is no one — knows, da ist keiner, der nicht weiß; there is nobody — has his fault, es giebt keinen, der nicht seinen Fehler hätte (*coll.*). IV. *adv.* nur; — just, soeben, eben erst; kaum noch; — now, erst jetzt, soeben; all —, fast, nahe daran; she all — told him, sie war nahe daran (es) ihm zu sagen; she is — a child, sie ist ja nur ein Kind; anything — (clever), nichts weniger als (klug); nothing —, nichts als. V. *s.* das Aber; — me no —s, mache mir keine Einwendungen!

Butcher, I. *s.* der Fleischer, Metzger, Schlächter; der Mörder (*fig.*); —'s cleaver, das Metzgerbeil; —'s steel, der Wetzstahl; —'s meat, das Schlachtfleisch. II. *v.a.* metzeln (*also fig.*); schlachten; (kill) ermorden. **—y**, *s.* die Metzgerei; die Metzelei; die Bluttat (*fig.*).

Butler, *s.* der Kellermeister, Haushofmeister; der oberste Diener (in vornehmen Familien); —'s pantry, der Aufbewahrungsraum für Glas und Porzellan.

[1]**Butt**, *s.* die Butte, das große Faß, das Stückfaß.

[2]**Butt**, I. *s.* der Stoß mit dem Kopfe; die Grenze, das Ziel, die Zielscheibe; das Stichblatt (*for ridicule, etc.*); he is the — of the company, er dient der ganzen Gesellschaft als Zielscheibe des Spottes; — and —, der Anstoß (*Carp. etc.*).

II. *v.n.* mit dem Kopfe stoßen; to — at, stoßen nach (*dat.*), auf (*acc.*). —**ress**, *see* Buttress. —**s**, *pl.* der Scheibenstand (*Artil.*). *Comp.* —**-bolt**, *s.* der Stoßbolzen (*Shipb.*). —**-end**, *s.* das dicke Ende; der Kolben, das Endstück (*Gun.*). —**-hinge**, *s.* das Fischband.

Butter, I. *s.* die Butter; das dickflüssige, mineralische Salz (*Chem.*); bread and —, Butterbrod; she looks as if — would not melt in her mouth, sie sieht so still aus als ob sie kein Wasser trüben könnte. II. *v.a.* mit Butter bestreichen; to — up, schmeicheln (*vulg.*); —ed toast, geröstete Brotschnitte mit Butter; to know on which side one's bread is —ed, seinen Vorteil kennen. —**y**, I. *adj.* butterig. II. *s.* die Speisekammer. *Comp.* —**-bur**, *s.* der großblätterige Huflattig. —**-cooler**, *s.* das Butterkühlgefäß, die Butterbüchse. —**-crock**, *s.* das irdene Buttergefäß. —**cup**, *s.* die Butterblume. —**-fingers**, *s.* einer, der nicht fest zufaßt (*coll.*). —**-fingered**, *adj.* mit schlüpfrigen *or* schwachen Fingern; ungeschickt im Gebrauch der Hände. —**fly**, *s.* der Schmetterling. —**man**, *s.* der Butterhändler. —**milk**, *s.* die Buttermilch. —**-print**, *s.* die Butterform, der Butterstempel. —**-scotch**, *s.* Art eine Stangenzucker (aus Butter und Zucker). —**tub**, *s.* das Butterfaß. —**woman**, *s.* die Butterfrau, Butterverkäuferin. —**y-hatch**, *s.* die Schenktür, Halbtüre, über welche hinweg die Speisen und Getränke verabfolgt werden.

Buttock, I. *s.* das Hinterteil, der Hintere; der Spiegel (*of a pontoon*). II. *attrib.*; — beef, das Fleisch vom Keulenstück des Ochsen. —**s**, *pl.* die Hinterbacken, der Hintere; —s of a ship, die Billen eines Schiffes.

Button, I. *s.* der Knopf; der Kleiderknopf; der Metallkönig, das Korn (*Metall.*); die Traube (*Artil.*); der Hode(n); — of a window, der Reiber, Wirbel am Fensterstocke; covered —, überzogener Knopf; it's not worth a —, es ist wertlos; a boy in —s, ein Diener in Livree. II. *v.a.* (— up) zuknöpfen. —**s**, *s.* der Page, kleine Diener. *Comp.* —**hole**, *s.* das Knopfloch; das Knopflochsträußchen. —**-hook**, *s.* der Knopfhaken. —**-mould**, *s.* die Knopfform. —**-shank**, *s.* die Knopföse.

Buttress, I. *s.* der Strebepfeiler, die Strebe (*Arch.*); flying-—, der Strebebogen, die fliegende Strebe. II. *v.a.* durch einen Strebepfeiler oder Schwibbogen stützen; stützen (*fig.*); unterstützen.

Butyri—c, *adj.* butterartig; —c acid, die Buttersäure. —**ne**, *s.* das Butterfett, Butyrin.

Buxom, *adj.* frisch und kräftig aussehend, gesundheitstrotzend, drall; biegsam, geschmeidig, schmiegsam (*obs.*); (brisk) flink; (lively) munter; a — lass, eine dralle Dirne.

Buy, *v.* I. *a.* kaufen, einkaufen; teuer zahlen, erkaufen (*experience, etc.*); to — s.th. of a p., etwas von einem kaufen, einem etwas abkaufen; — forward, auf Spekulation für späteren Gebrauch kaufen (*C. L.*); — **in**, einkaufen; zurückkaufen; to — in at auctions, Sachen in Auktionen zurückkaufen; — **off**, loskaufen (*as a soldier*), erkaufen; to — **on** commission, auf Kommission kaufen; to — on credit, auf Kredit kaufen; — **out**, auskaufen, abkaufen; ein Geschäft (von jemandem) käuflich übernehmen; — **up**, aufkaufen; to — a pig in a poke, die Katze im Sack kaufen. II. *n.* handeln; kaufen. —**er**, *s.* der Käufer; —er of a bill, der Wechselnehmer (*C.L.*); —ers, vom Käufer gebotene Preise (*C. L.*). —**ing**, *s.* das Kaufen, Handeln.

Buzz, I. *v.n.* summen, sumsen; the fly —es, die Fliege summt. II. *v.a.*; to — a th. about, etwas herumflüstern, ausplaudern. III. *s.* das Summen, Gesumse.

Buzzard, *s.* der Bussard (*Orn.*); der rachsüchtige Mensch (*Amer.*); der Dummkopf (*obs., dial.*).

By, I. *prep.* (beside) neben, an; (near) nahe; (about) bei; (before, by the time of) bei, gegen, um, in; (from, owing to) durch, von, nach, aus; (by the help of, with) durch, mit; loved — all, von jedermann geliebt; — the advice of, auf (den) Rat des; to be represented — attorney, sich durch einen Anwalt vertreten lassen; — birth, von Geburt; — break of day, mit Tagesanbruch; — the by(e), *see* By II.; — candle-light, bei Licht; — chance, durch Zufall, zufällig; day — day, tagtäglich, (daily) täglich; — your description, nach Ihrer Beschreibung; — degrees, allmählich; — your desire, auf Ihren Wunsch, Ihr Verlangen; — dint of, kraft, vermöge; do to others as you would be done —, handle gegen andere, wie du möchtest, daß andere gegen dich handelten; — experience, aus Erfahrung; — the favour of ..., begünstigt von ...; — force, mit Gewalt; — giving, durch Geben; — good luck, zum Glück; — heart, auswendig; — the hundred weight, zentnerweise; — hundreds, zu hunderten, hundertweise; — the hour, stundenweise; (for hours) stundenlang; — the dozen, dutzendweise; I don't think you will gain much — it, ich glaube nicht, daß du dabei weiterkommen wirst; — itself, für sich, an und für sich, allein; put it — itself, lege es bei Seite, tue es besonders; a chapter — itself, ein Kapitel für sich; — land, zu Lande; — sea, zur See, zu Wasser; — coach, mit der Kutsche, zu Wagen; — letter, brieflich; — the laws of nature it is permitted, es ist nach dem Naturrecht statthaft; — little and little, nach und nach; — his looks I perceived ..., ich sah an seinen Blicken ...; I have no money — me, ich habe kein Geld bei mir; — all means, (certainly) allerdings, freilich; gewiß; (positively) durchaus; — no means, keineswegs; — means of, mittelst, vermittelst; — so much more, um so mehr; — name, dem Namen nach; to know — name, dem Namen nach kennen; he goes — the name of, er führt den Namen ...; — his office, (kraft) seines Amtes; to live — o.s., für sich leben; to stand — a p., neben einem stehen, (support a p.) einem beistehen; — the pound, pfundweise; to come — Paris, über Paris kommen; to pass — the city of Paris, durch die Stadt Paris kommen; to take example — a p., sich (*dat.*) an einem ein Beispiel nehmen; point — point, Stück für Stück; — profession, seinem Beruf nach, von Beruf; to go — rail, mit der Eisenbahn reisen; to fall — the sword, durch das Schwert umkommen; — reason of, wegen; to live — rule, regelmäßig leben; — my soul, bei meiner Seele; younger — six years, um sechs Jahre jünger; — stealth, verstohlener Weise; — this time to-morrow, morgen um diese Zeit; he should be here — eleven o'clock, er sollte um elf Uhr hier sein; — this day fortnight, heute über 14 Tage; — this time, schon, (vor dieser Zeit,) jetzt schon, mittlerweile; he is — trade a shoemaker, er ist seinem Gewerbe nach *or* seines Zeichens ein Schuhmacher; — which train will you be going? mit welchem Zuge wirst du fahren? — turns, der Reihe nach, wechselweise; 3 feet — 10, drei Fuß lang und zehn Fuß breit; two — two, — twos, je zwei, zu zweien, zwei und zwei; — my watch, nach meiner Uhr; — way of a jest, scherzweise; — way of trial, versuchsweise; — word of mouth, mündlich; — the way, beiläufig, im Vorbeigehen; — what I have heard nach dem, was ich gehört habe; the house — th river, das Haus am Flusse; he walks — the river, er geht an dem Flusse hin *or* den Fluß entlang; put —, lay —, aufsparen. II. *adv.*; — and —, nächstens, bald, nachher; by the —, apropos, gelegentlich, im Vorbeigehen, nebenher; hard —, close —, dicht dabei; to go —, vorbeigehen, vorbei kommen; to stand —, dabei sein, in der Nähe, anwesend sein; the passers-—, die Vorübergehenden; those standing —, die Umstehenden. —**e**, *s.* das Spiel eines Einzelnen ohne Partner gegen zwei (*Tennis*); ein von den batsmen gemachter run wenn der Ball nicht schnell genug angehalten wird (*Cricket*). *Comp.* —-**election**, *s.* die Ergänzungswahl, Nachwahl. —**gone**, *adj.* vergangen, veraltet; —gone days, vergangene Tage. —-**law**, *s.* das Nebengesetz, das Lokalgesetz, Ortsstatut. —-**pass**, *s.* der Kleinsteller (*Gas*). —-**play**, *s.* das Zwischenspiel. —-**road**, —**way**, *s.* der Nebenweg. —-**stander**, *s.* der Zuschauer; (*pl.*) die Umstehenden. —-**street**, *s.* die Seitenstraße. —-**term**, *s.* das Extratrimester, Extraquartal, welches ein engl. Student oder Schüler bekommt, wenn er einen Termin vor dem Beginn der Jahreskurse kommt. —**word**, *s.* das Sprichwort; das Stichblatt.

Byre, *s.* der Kuhstall (*Scotch*).

Byrnie, *s.* die Brünne, der Brustharnisch.

C

C, c, C, c; C & C (*Mus.*); *as abbr.* C. = centum, Hundert (100)· c. = cent (*Amer.*). *For other abbreviations see Index at the end of the English-German part.*

Cab, I. *s.* die (einspännige) Droschke, der Fiaker; der verdeckte Stand des Lokomotivführers (*Railw.*). II. *attrib.*; — driver, der Droschkenkutscher; — fare, der Droschkentarif; das Fahrgeld; — proprietor, der Fuhrherr. III. *v.a.* in einer Droschke fahren (*coll.*); I shall have to — it, ich werde mir eine Droschke nehmen *or* mit einer Droschke hinfahren müssen (*coll.*). *Comp.* —**man**, *s.* der Droschkenkutscher. —-**stand**, *s.* der Droschkenhalteplatz.

Cabal, I. *s.* die Kabale. II. *v.n.* Ränke schmieden. —**a**, *s.* die Kabbala. —**ism**, *s.* die Geheimlehre der Kabbalisten. —**ist**, *s.* der Kabbalist. —**istic**, *adj.*, —**istically**, *adv.* kabbalistisch. —**ler**, *s.* der Ränkeschmied.

Cabbage, I. *s.* der Kohl; head of —, der Kohlkopf. II. *attrib.*; — lettuce, der Kopfsalat; — turnip, die Kohlrübe. *Comp.* —-**net**, *s.* Netz zum Kohlkochen. —-**tree**, *s.* die Kohlpalme.

Cabby (*famil. sl.*) *see* Cabman; das Kutscherchen; our —, unser Rosselenker (*hum.*).

Cabin, I. *s.* die Hütte, das Häuschen (*Build.*); die Kajüte (*Naut.*); quarter-deck —, obere Kajütte. II. *v.a.* in eine Hütte einsperren. —**et**, I. *s.* das Zimmerchen, das Kabinett; der Schubladenschrank; das Ministerium, die Regierung, das Kabinett (*Pol.*); —et of coins, Münzkabinett; —et of minerals, die Mineraliensammlung. II. *attrib.*; —et edition, die Kabinettausgabe; —et minister, der Kabinettsminister; —et organ, die Stubenorgel. *Comp.* —-**boy**, *s.* der Schiffsjunge. —**et-council**, *s.* der Ministerrat; die Kabinettssitzung. —**et-maker**, *s.* der Kunsttischler, Möbelschreiner. —**et-making**, *s.* die Kunsttischlerei, Möbelschreinerei. —**et-photograph**, *s.* die Kabinettphotographie. —**et-picture**, *s.* das Kabinettstück.

Cable, I. *s.* das Seil, Tau, Kabel; das Telegraphenkabel; a —'s length, eine Kabellänge; stream —, Wurfankertau; wire —, Drahtkabel. II. *attrib.*; — buoy, die Ankerboje; — core, der metallische Kabelkern; — room, das Kabelgatt; — serving, das Kabellied; — transfer, die Kabelrimesse. III. *v.a.* kabeln (*Tele.*). —**gram**, *s.* die Kabeldepesche. *Comp.* —**moulding**, *s.* die Schiffstauverzierung (*Arch.*).

Caboose, *s.* die Schiffsküche, Kombüse; der einem Güterzug angehängte Personenwagen (*Amer.*).

Cabriolet, *s.* *see* Cab (*its abbr'v'd form*).

Cacao, *s.* der Kakao.

Cache—xy, *s.* der ungesunde Zustand (*also fig.*); die Verdorbenheit der Säfte (*Med.*). —**ctic(al)**, *adj.* ungesund, voll verdorbener Säfte (*Med.*).

Cachinnat—ion, *s.* das Gelächter. —**ory**, *adj.* wiehernd, Lach-.

Cackle, I. *v.n.* gackern, gackeln (*as a hen*); schnattern (*as a goose*). II. *s.* das Gackeln, Gegacker; das Schnattern, Geschnatter; das Geschwätz. —**r**, *s.* das gackelnde *or* gackernde Huhn, die schnatternde Gans; der Schnatterer, Schwätzer.

Caco—demon, *s.* der böse Geist. —**ethes**, *s.* das bösartige Geschwür. —**phony**, *s.* der Mißklang.

Cactus, *s.* der Kaktus.

Cad, *s.* der niedriggesinnte gemeine Kerl. —**dish**, *adj.* ungeschliffen (*sl.*). —**dishness**, *s.* die Ungeschliffenheit (*sl.*). —**et**, *s.* der jüngere Bruder; der Kadett (*Mil.*). —**etship**, *s.* die Kadettenstelle.

Cadaverous, *adj.*, —**ly**, *adv.* leichenhaft; a — look, ein leichenartiges Aussehen.

Caddy, Catty, *s.* das Teekästchen.

Cade, *v.a.* zahm aufziehen. —-**lamb**, *s.* das mit der Hand aufgezogene zahme Lamm, Hauslamm.

Cadence, *s.* der Fall; der Schlußfall, der Tonfall; die Kadenz, die rhythmische Bewegung (*Rhet., Mus.*); der Takt (*Mil.*).

Cade-oil, *s.* das Kadeöl, Tonnenöl.

Cadg—e, *v.a.* eine Last tragen (*prov.*); betteln (*sl.*). —**er**, *s.* wandernder Höker, Hausierer; gemeiner Bettler. —**ing**, *s.* das Schmarotzerwesen.

Cadmia, *s.* der Galmei.

Caduc—ity, *s.* die Hinfälligkeit, Baufälligkeit; das Verfallensein (*Law*). —**ous**, *adj.* hinfällig.

Cæsura, *s.* der Verseinschnitt, die Zäsur.

Caffein, *s.* der Kaffeestoff, das Kaffein.

Cage, I. *s.* der Käfig, das Gehege (*for animals*); (bird-—) das (*also* der) Vogelbauer; das Gehäuse (*of a windmill*); das Treppenhaus (*of a staircase*); der Korb (*Mach., etc.*); (prison) das Gefängnis; osier —, der Weidenkorb; safety —, Sicherheitskorb (*Min.*). II. *v.a.* in ein Bauer *or* in einen Käfig tun; einsperren.

Caïque, *s.* der Kaik, die türkische Barke.

Cairn, *s.* der keltische Stein(grab)hügel; der Steinhaufen (als Signal oder Denkmal auf hohen Bergen). *Comp.* —**gorm**, *s.* der Rauchtopas.

Caisson, *s.* der Senkkasten, Versenkungskasten (*Hydr., etc.*); der Pulverwagen, Munitionswagen (*Mil.*); der Schwimmkasten (*Naut.*).

Caitiff, I. *s.* der Schurke, Elende, Schuft. II. *adj.* schurkisch, niederträchtig; elend, arm (*obs.*).

Cajole, *v.a.* schmeicheln, beschwatzen; durch Schmeicheleien zu verführen suchen. —**r**, *s.* der Schmeichler. —**ry**, *s.* die Schmeichelei, die süßen, verführerischen Worte.

Cake, I. *s.* der Kuchen; — of ice, eine Eisscholle; — of paint, die Tuschfarbe; — of soap, das Stück Seife; — of wax, die Wachsscheibe; land of —s, Schottland; to take the —, den Preis davontragen (*coll.*). II. *v.n.* hart werden; zusammenbacken; coal that —s, die Schmiedekohle; —d coal, die zusammengesinterte Steinkohle. *Comp.* —-**crusher**, *s.* die Quetschmühle für Ölkuchen.

Calabar-skin, *s.* das Grauwerk (*Furr.*).

Calabash, *s.* die Kalabasse, der Flaschenkürbis.

Calamanco, *s.* der Kalamank.

Calamine, *s.* der Galmei, das Zink-Erz (*Min.*).

Calamint, *s.* der Basilien-Quendel (*Bot.*).

Calamit—ous, *adj.*, —**ously**, *adv.* unheilvoll; elend, jammervoll. —**y**, *s.* das Elend, Unglück, Unheil.

Calamus, *s.* das Rohr, der Kalmus.

Calash, *s.* die Kalesche, der offene Reisewagen; das Kaleschendach; seidene Frauenkapuze (*obs.*).

Calc—areous, *adj.* kalkig, kalkhaltig; kalkartig; —areous earth, die Kalkerde; —areous limestone, der Kalkstein. —**areousness**, *s.* die Kalkartigkeit, Kalkhaltigkeit. —**ination**, *s.* die Verkalkung. —**inate**, —**ine**, *v.* I. *a.* kalzinieren; brennen, rösten (*Min.*); —ined alum, der geröstete Alaun; —ined bones, die Knochenasche. II. *n.* zu Kalk werden, verkalken. —**iner**, *s.* (—ining furnace) der Brennofen, Kalzinierofen.

Calceolaria, *s.* die Pantoffelblume, Kalzeolarie.

Calcul—able, *adj.* berechenbar. —**ate**, *v.* I. *a.* berechnen; erwarten, vermuten, denken (*Amer., coll.*); to —ate the expenses, die Unkosten berechnen: to be —ated, so beschaffen sein, dazu geeignet sein; religion is —ated to make men happy, die Religion bezweckt, die Menschen glücklich zu machen. II. *n.* rechnen; he —ates on preferment, er macht sich Rechnung auf Beförderung. **—ation**, *s.* die Rechenkunst; die Berechnung; to be out in one's —ation, sich verrechnet haben; at the lowest —ation, nach dem niedrigsten Anschlage. **—us**, *s.* der Blasenstein (*Med.*); das Rechnen, die Rechnungsart; differential —us, die Differentialrechnung; integral —us, die Integralrechnung; literal —us, die Buchstabenrechnung. *Comp.* **—ating-machine**, *s.* die Rechenmaschine.

Caldron. *s.* der (große) Kessel.

Calefaction, *s.* die Erhitzung, Erwärmung; das Heißschüren (*Glassw.*).

Calend—ar, I. *s.* der Kalender; die Liste; —ar month, der Kalendermonat. II. *v.a.* in einen Kalender schreiben. **—s**, *pl.* die Kalenden; at the Greek —s, auf Nimmermehrstag, niemals.

Calender, I. *s.* der Kalander, die Zylindermange; —s, (*pl.*) die Satiniermaschine (*Pap.*); glazing —s, die Glanzpresse. II. *v.a.* kalandern, mangen, rollen. **—er**, *s.* die Tuchbereiter-Walze. **—ing**, *s.* das Kalandern, Mangen, Plätten.

Calenture, *s.* das hitzige Klimafieber.

Calf, I. *s.* (*pl.* Calves) das Kalb; das junge Tier, das Junge; die Wade (*of the leg*); bound in —, in Ledereinband, Franzband; — binding, der Franzband, Einband in Kalbleder; half — (binding), der Halbfranzband; moon-—, das Mondkalb, der Tölpel; —'s foot (calves-foot) jelly, die von Kalbsfüßen bereitete Gallerte. *Comp.* **—-love**, *s.* die erste Jugendliebe, erste Neigung zwischen unreifen jungen Leuten. **—-skin**, *s.* das Kalbfell, Kalbleder. **—-skins**, *pl.* das Fahlleder.

Caliber, **Calibre**, *s.* das Kaliber, die Geschützweite (*Artil., etc.*); das Kugelmaß (*Gun., etc.*); die Beschaffenheit, der Wert, Schlag. *Comp.* **—-compasses**, *pl. see* Callipers.

Calico, *s.* der Kaliko, Kattun, Zitz; printed —, gedruckter Kattun; — for bookbinding, der Buchbinderkattun.

Calif, **Caliph**, *s.* der Kalif.

Calipers, *see* Callipers.

Calk, *see* Caulk.

Call, I. *v.a.* rufen, herbeirufen; (appeal to) anrufen, berufen; (— together) zusammenrufen, versammeln; (name) heißen, (be)nennen; (summon) kommen lassen, zitieren; please — me to-morrow at six o'clock, bitte, wecken Sie mich morgen um sechs Uhr; what do you — that? wie nennen Sie das? what are —ed, sogenannt (*to be inflected*), *e.g.* they were what are —ed sandwich-men, sie waren sogenannte wandelnde Plakate; Mr. What d'ye — him? Herr Dingskirchen! Herr wie heißt er doch? to — a meeting of one's creditors, die Gläubiger jemands berufen; to be —ed to the bar, in den Juristenstand aufgenommen werden; to — a p. names, einem Schimpfnamen geben; to — one's game, sein Spiel ansagen (*Whist*); — all the servants, laß alle Diener kommen; to — a p.'s attention to s.th., (einen) auf eine S. aufmerksam machen; I — God to *or* as witness, ich rufe Gott zum Zeugen an; to — **after**, einem nachschreien; to — **aside**, bei Seite rufen; to — **away**, abrufen; to — **down**, herunterrufen; to — down curses upon a p., Flüche auf einen herabflehen; to — **forth**, hervorrufen; to — forth all the faculties of the mind, alle Geistesfähigkeiten in Tätigkeit setzen, aufbieten; to — **from**, abrufen; to — **home**, zurückrufen; to — **in**, hereinrufen; to — in debts, Schulden einfordern; to — in clipped money, schlechtes Geld außer Kurs setzen; to — in question, in Frage stellen, bezweifeln; to — into play, in Tätigkeit setzen; to — **off**, abrufen; to — off the attention, die Aufmerksamkeit abziehen, ablenken; to — **out**, ausrufen, herausrufen; (challenge) herausfordern; (summon) unter die Waffen rufen, ausheben (*troops*); to — **over**, (eine Liste) überlesen, (die Namen) vorlesen; to — a p. over the coals, einem gehörig den Text lesen (*coll.*); to — **to** account, zur Rechenschaft ziehen; to — to the chair, als *or* zum Vorsitzer erwählen; to — to mind, ins Gedächtnis zurückrufen, sich erinnern; to — to order, zur Ordnung rufen; to — **up**, heraufrufen, erregen; to — up money, Geld einfordern, einziehen; to — up spirits, Geister beschwören, zitieren; to — up an idea in one's mind, einen Gedanken im Geiste erwecken. II. *v.n.* rufen; he —ed, but did not find me at home, er sprach vor, fand mich aber nicht zu Hause; may I — at your house to-morrow, darf ich morgen bei Ihnen vorkommen? tell the man to — **again**, sage dem Mann, er solle wiederkommen; to — at a port, einen Hafen anlaufen (*Naut.*); to — **for**, rufen nach (*help, etc.*), herausrufen (*Theat.*), fordern, verlangen (*something*), to — for a p., einen abholen, bei jemandem einsprechen, um einen oder etwas abzuholen; an article much —ed for, ein vielbegehrter Artikel; this is an abuse that —s loudly for redress, dies ist ein Mißbrauch, der dringend Abhilfe erheischt; the present time —s for a system of education, die Gegenwart erfordert ein Erziehungssystem; an un—ed-for remark, eine unberufene Bemerkung; to be —ed for, postlagernd (*on letters*); a letter to be —ed for, ein postlagernder Brief; he —ed **in** this morning, heute morgen sprach er vor; to — **on**, anrufen, auffordern; I — on you for aid, ich fordere Sie auf, mir Beistand zu leisten; I shall — on you at your brother's, ich werde Sie bei Ihrem Herrn Bruder besuchen; to — on the name of the Lord, den Herrn, Gott anbeten, des Herrn Namen anrufen (*B.*); he —ed **to** me, but I did not hear him, er rief mir zu, ich hörte ihn aber nicht; to — **upon** a p., sich an einen wenden; (visit) bei einem vorsprechen, einen besuchen *or* aufsuchen; I shall — upon my readers, ich will mich an meine Leser wenden, ich wende mich an meine Leser; to be —ed upon, berufen, genötigt sein; I feel myself —ed upon to refute these assertions, ich fühle mich genötigt, gedrungen, diese Behauptungen zu widerlegen. III. *s.* der Ruf, Schrei; (calling) die Berufung, der Ruf; (heavenly —) die göttliche Berufung, Eingebung von Gott; (claim) die Forderung; (visit) der kurze Besuch; (lure) der Lockruf; das Pfeifen des Bootsmanns (*Naut.*); (demand) die Nachfrage (*C.L.*); der Einschuß (*on shares*); die Einberufung, Aushebung (*of troops*); die Kapitaleinberufung (*C. L.*); die Nachzahlung an Aktionäre (*C. L.*); — for help, Ruf nach Hilfe, Hilferuf; to give a p. a —, einen besuchen; to obey the — of nature, seine Notdurft verrichten; to be ready at a p.'s —, stets bereit sein, einem zu dienen, auf jemands Ruf bereit sein; to be within —, in Rufweite, in der Nähe sein; a — upon a p.'s pocket, eine Forderung an die Tasche jemands; morning —, kurzer Besuch am Vormittage, kurzer Morgenbesuch; to make a —, einen kurzen Besuch abstatten. IV. *attrib.*; — fees, die Anrufgebühren (*Teleph.*); — money, tägliches Geld. **—ing**, *s.* der Beruf, das Gewerbe; die Berufung (*B.*); the —ing in, die Einforderung, Einziehung; the —ing of the plaintiff, das Vorrufen des abwesenden Klägers. *Comp.* **—-bird**, *s.* der Lockvogel.

Calligraph—ist, *s.* der Schönschreiber, Kalligraph. **—y**, *s.* die Schönschreibekunst.

Calliper—s, *pl.* der Greifzirkel, Tasterzirkel; sliding —s, der Stoßmesser (*Artil.*); —s for taking the thickness of barrels, der Rohrzirkel (*Artil.*). *Comp.* **—-scale**, *s.* der Kalibermaßstab. **—(-sliding)-square**, *s.* das verstellbare Winkelmaß.

Callisthenic, *adj.* Leibesübungen betreffend, turnerisch. **—s**, *pl.* Freiübungen (für Mädchen): das Mädchenturnen.

Callo—sity, *s.* die Schwiele, Härte, Verhärtung der Haut: die schwielige, knorrige Beschaffenheit

—us, *adj.* hart, verhärtet, knorrig; unempfindlich (*fig.*). **—usness**, *s.* die Härte, Verhärtung; die Unempfindlichkeit (*fig.*).
Callow, *adj.* kahl, nackt, federlos, unbefiedert, (*fig.*) unerfahren.
Calm, I. *adj.*, **—ly**, *adv.* ruhig, sanft, still; leidenschaftslos; a — day, ein windstiller Tag; to be —, ruhig, gelassen sein; to grow —, sich legen (*as a storm*); sich beruhigen (*as passion*). II. die Stille, Ruhe; die Windstille (*Naut., etc.*); a dead —, eine völlige Windstille; after a storm comes a —, auf Regen folgt Sonnenschein. III. *v.a.* stillen, beruhigen, besänftigen. **—ness**, *s.* die Stille, Ruhe (*of the wind, etc.*); die Gemütsruhe, Leidenschaftslosigkeit.
Calomel, *s.* das Kalomel, Quecksilberchlorür.
Calori—c, *s.* der Wärmestoff; conductor of —c, der Wärmeleiter; —c engine, die Heißluftmaschine. **—fic**, *adj.* Wärme erzeugend, erhitzend; —fic intensity *or* power, die Heizkraft. **—fere**, *s.* der Luftwärmeofen; (hot-water —fere) die Heißwasserheizung.
Calotype, *s.* das Papierbild (*Photo.*); — process, die Kalotypie.
Caltrop, *s.* die Fußangel (*Mil.*); das Wolfseisen (*Sport*); die Wegedistel (*Bot.*).
Calumn—iation, *s.* die Verleumdung. **—iator**, *s.* der Verleumder. **—iatory**, *adj.* verleumderisch. **—ious**, *adj.*, **—iously**, *adv.* verleumderisch. **—y**, *s.* die Verleumdung.
Calve, *v.n.* kalben, ein Kalb werfen. **—s**, *pl.* *see* Calf.
Calyx, *s.* der Kelch (*Bot.*).
Cam, *s.* der Hebezapfen (*Mach.*); das Herzrad (*Mach.*).
Camber, **—ing**, *s.* die Biegung, Krümmung, Wölbung (*Carp.*); der Katzenrücken des Kiels (*Shipb.*); —ing (of a piece of wood), die Aufbucht. **—ed**, *adj.* gekrümmt; —ed deck, das gekrümmte Verdeck mit hohem Mitteldeck.
Cambist, *s.* der Wechsler, Wechselmakler (*C.L.*).
Cambric, *s.* die feine Battistleinwand. *Comp.* **—-muslin**, *s.* der Battist-Musselin.
[1]**Came**, *imperf. of* Come.
[2]**Came**, *s.* das Fensterblei.
Camel, *s.* das Kameel (*also Naut.*); —'s hair, das Kameelhaar; —'s hair brush, der Kameelhaarpinsel. **—opard**, *s.* der Kameelpardel, die Giraffe. *Comp.* **—-driver**, *s.* der Kameeltreiber.
Camellia, *s.* die Kamelie (*Bot.*).
Cameo, *s.* die Kamee; die erhabene Arbeit. *Comp.* **—type**, *s.* die Medaillon-Vignette (*Typ.*).
Camera, *s.* die Camera (*Phot.*); die Kammer; das gewölbte Gemach, Gewölbe (*Arch.*); (the hearing of a case) in —, unter Ausschluß der Öffentlichkeit. *Comp.* **—-lucida**, *s.* die Lichtkammer. **—-obscura**, *s.* die Dunkelkammer.
Camisole, *s.* das Kamisol, Wams, die kurze Jacke mit Ärmeln.
Camlet, *s.* der Kamelott (*Manuf.*).
Camomile, *s.* die Kamille. *Comp.* **—-tea**, *s.* der Kamillentee.
Camp, I. *s.* das Lager, Feldlager; to pitch one's —, sein Lager aufschlagen; to strike *or* break up a —, ein Lager abbrechen. II. *v.n.* sich lagern; to — out, im Freien lagern. **—aign**, *see* Campaign. *Comp.* **—-bed**, *s.* das Feldbett. **—-ceiling**, *s.* die teilweise gewölbte Decke. **—-chair**, *s.* der Feldstuhl (mit Lehne). **—-dress**, *s.* die Feldmontur. **—-duty**, *s.* der Lagerdienst. **—-follower**, *s.* der Marketender; der Schlachtenbummler. **—-meeting**, *s.* der Feldgottesdienst (*Amer.*). **—-party**, *s.* die im Freien lagernde Gesellschaft. **—-quarters**, *pl.* das Quartier für europäische Kaufleute im Orient. **—-stool**, *s.* der Feldstuhl, Klappstuhl.
Campaign, I. *s.* die Ebene (*obs.*); der Feldzug. II. *v.n.* einen Feldzug mitmachen; —ing life, das Soldatenleben; —ing stories, Lager- *or* Soldaten-geschichten. **—er**, *s.* der ein Lagerleben führt; der alte, erprobte Soldat, der Veteran.
Campan—iform, *adj.* glockenförmig. **—ile**, *s.* der Glockenturm (*Arch.*). **—ula**, *s.* die Glockenblume.
Campeachy-wood, *s.* das Kampeche-Blauholz.
Camph—ine, *s.* das Kampfin (*Chem.*). **—or**, *s.* der Kampfer. **—orated**, *adj.* mit Kampfer gesättigt *or* versetzt; —orated spirit(s), der Kampferspiritus. **—oric**, *adj.* kampferhaltig; —oric acid, die Kampfersäure.
Campion, *s.* Lychnis; Feuernelke; meadow —, die Kuckucksblume.
Camwood, *s.* das Kambalholz, Rotholz.
[1]**Can**, *ir.v. 1 & 3 sing. & 1, 2 & 3 pl. of the pres. ind. of the old English infin.* cunnan (= können); I, he —, ich, er kann; we, you, they —, wir können, ihr könnt, sie können; I —not tell you, ich kann (es) dir nicht sagen; I —not but wish, ich kann nur wünschen.
[2]**Can**, *v.a.* in luftdichten Büchsen einmachen; —ned milk, die Büchsenmilch; —ned beef *or* meat, das Büchsenfleisch.
[3]**Can**, I. *s.* die Kanne; die Flasche (*Spin.*). II. *attrib.*; — roving frame, die Flaschenmaschine (*Spin.*). *Comp.* **—-buoy**, *s.* die Klappboje.
Canal, *s.* der Kanal, die Wasserleitung, der Kunstfluß; die Rinne, Röhre; der Gang (*Anat.*); — for navigation, der Schifffahrtskanal. **—iculate**, *adj.* rinnenförmig ausgehöhlt. **—ization**, *s.* der Kanalbau. *Comp.* **—-boat**, *s.* das Kanalboot. **—-lift**, *s.* die Hebemaschine zum Transport von Kanalbooten. **—-lock**, *s.* die Kanalschleuse. **—-navigation**, *s.* die Kanalschifffahrt.
Canary, *s.* (—-bird) der Kanarienvogel; (—wine) der Kanariensekt. *Comp.* **—-coloured**, *adj.* kanariengelb. **—-seed**, *s.* der Kanariensamen. **—-tree**, *s.* der gemeine Kanariennußbaum. **—-weed**, *s.* die Färberflechte.
Canaster, *s.* der Binsenkorb zur Verpackung des westindischen Tabaks; — tobacco, der Knaster.
Cancel, *v.a.* (run the pen through) durchstreichen; (annul) aufheben, annullieren, vernichten; kanzellieren, umgittern (*obs., Her.*); widerrufen (*an order*); to — a debt, einen Schuldposten austun; to — a will, ein Testament ungültig machen; to — equal factors, die Zahlen vereinfachen (*Math.*); —led, kanzelliert; durchstrichen; entwertet. **—late**, *adj.* gegittert (*Bot.*). **—lation**, *s.* die Entwertung (*of postage stamps*). *Comp.* **—ling-stamp**, *s.* der Entwertungsstempel (*for stamps*).
Cancer, I. *s.* der Krebs; das Krebsgeschwür (*Med.*). II. *v.a.* zerfressen. **—ous**, *adj.* krebsartig.
Cande—labrum, *s.* (*pl.* —labra) der Kandelaber, Armleuchter. **—scent**, *adj.* glühend, weißglühend, weiß vor Hitze.
Candid, *adj.*, **—ly**, *adv.* aufrichtig, redlich, offen; (*obs.*) glänzend weiß. **—ate**, *s.* der Kandidat, Bewerber um eine Stelle, Anwärter auf eine Stelle; der Prüfling, Examinand; a —ate for glory, ein Ruhmbegieriger; I was a —ate for the post, ich bewarb mich um die Stelle; —ate for the throne, der Kronprätendent; unsuccessful —ate, durchgefallener Bewerber *or* Prüfling; successful —ate, einer, welcher die Prüfung bestanden *or* die Stelle erhalten hat. **—ature**, *s.* die Kandidatur, Kandidatenschaft, Bewerbung. **—ness**, *see* Candour.
Candied, *adj.* überzuckert, kandiert.
Candle, *s.* das Licht, die Kerze; die Normalkerze; das Grubenlicht; dip —, gezogenes Licht; mould —, gegossenes Licht; wax —, Wachskerze; stearine —, Stearinlicht; rush —, Binsenlicht; tallow —, Talglicht; kerosene —, Erdwachskerze; medicated —, das Räucherkerzchen; composition —, Stearinkerze; to hide one's — under a bushel, sein Licht unter den Scheffel stellen (*B.*); the game is not worth the —, das Spiel ist den Einsatz nicht wert; he could'nt hold a — to him, er reicht ihm das Wasser nicht; to

burn the — at both ends, mit seinen Mitteln *or* seiner Kräften allzu verschwenderisch sein. *Comp.* **—-box**, *s.* die Lichtlade. **—-dipper**, *s.* die Lichtziehmaschine. **—-ends**, *pl.* Lichtstückchen; Brocken, Bruchstücke (*fig.*). **—-extinguisher**, *s.* das Lichthütchen. **—-holder**, *s.* der Lichthalter. **—-light**, *s.*; by —-light, bei (Kerzen=)Licht. **—mas**, *s.* Lichtmeß (*Feb. 2*). **—-shade**, *s.* der Lichtschirm. **—-snuffers**, *pl.* die Lichtputze. **—stick**, *s.* der Leuchter; branched —stick, der Armleuchter. **—-stuff**, *s.* der Talg. **—-wick**, *s.* der Lichtdocht. **—wood**, *s.* das Rosenholz, Zitronenholz. **—-works**, *pl.* die Lichterfabrik.

Candour, *s.* die Offenherzigkeit, Biederkeit, Redlichkeit, Aufrichtigkeit.

Candy, I. *s.* das Zuckerwerk; sugar —, der Kandiszucker. II. *v.a.* überzuckern, glasieren; mit Zucker einmachen. III. *v.n.* kristallieren. *Comp.* **—-man**, *s.* der Zuckerwarenhändler. **—-store**, *s.* die Konditorei (*Amer.*).

Can—e, I. *s.* das Rohr; der Rohrstock; der (Spazier=)Stock; (sugar —e) das Zuckerrohr; hydraulic —e, das Wasserhebungsrohr; the head of a —e, der Stockknopf. II. *v.a.* (einem) den Stock geben, (einen) prügeln. **—ing**, *s.*; a severe —ing, eine gehörige Tracht Prügel. *Comp.* **—e-blinds**, *pl.* die Rohrjalousien. **—e-brake**, *s.* das Geröhr. **—e-chair**, *s.* (—e-bottomed chair) der Rohrstuhl. **—e-harvester**, *s.* die Zuckerrohrschneidemaschine. **—e-juice**, *s.* der Zuckerrohrsaft. **—e-plaiting**, *s.* das Rohrgeflecht. **—e-sugar**, *s.* der Rohrzucker. **—e-straw**, **—e-trash**, *s.* das ausgepreßte Zuckerrohr. **—e-worker**, *s.* der Rohrflechter.

Cani—cula, **—cule**, *s.* der Hundsstern, Sirius (*Astr.*). **—cular**, *adj.* zum Hundsstern gehörig; —cular days, die Hundstage. **—ne**, *adj.* hündisch, Hunde=, Hunds=; —ne madness, die Hundswut; —ne teeth, die Hundszähne (*of dogs*), Augenzähne (*of men*); —ne varieties, Hundespielarten.

Canister, *s.* die Blechbüchse, Kaffeebüchse, Teebüchse; das Körbchen (*obs.*). *Comp.* **—-shot**, *s.* die Kartätsche, der Kartätschenschuß.

Canker, I. *s.* der Krebs, Rost, Brand (*on trees, etc.*); das Krebsgeschwür (*Med.*); eine Krankheit an den Füßen der Pferde, in den Ohren der Hunde, in der Kehle der Tauben; der Rost (*on iron*); der Wurm; grief is beauty's —, der Kummer ist der Schönheit Wurm. II. *v.n.* angefressen werden; rosten; angesteckt werden. **—ed**, *adj.* angefressen, verdorben; verkehrt; mürrisch. **—ous**, *adj.* fressend (wie der Krebs). *Comp.* **—-blossom**, *s.* der Blütenwurm. **—-worm**, *s.* die schädliche Raupe; (*fig.*) der nagende Wurm.

Cannel-coal, *s.* die Kannelkohle.

Cannibal, *s.* der Menschenfresser, Kannibale. **—ism**, *s.* der Kannibalismus, die Menschenfresserei.

Cannon, I. *s.* die Kanone, das Geschütz; die Karambolage (*Bill.*); die Krone einer Glocke (*Found.*); rifled —, gezogenes Geschütz. **—ade**, I. *s.* das Geschützfeuer, die Kanonade. II. *attrib.*; —borer, der Stückbohrer; — foundry, die Stückgießerei; — hole, die Stückpforte; — metal, das Stückmetall, Kanonengut. III. *v.a.* beschießen. IV. *v.n.* kanonieren. **—eer**, *s.* der Kanonier, Artillerist. *Comp.* **—-ball**, *s.* die Kanonenkugel. **—-bit**, *s.* das hohle Mundstück am Pferdegebiß. **—-pinion**, *s.* der Zapfen des Minutenzeigers (*Horol.*). **—-proof**, *s.* bombenfest, bombensicher. **—-shot**, *s.* der Kanonenschuß, die Kanonenkugel. **—-stove**, *s.* der Kanonenofen.

Cann—y, *adj.*, **—ily**, *adv.* klug, vorsichtig, schlau, ungefährlich; hübsch.

Canoe, *s.* der Baumkahn, leichte Nachen, das Kanu.

[1]Canon, *s.* (law) der Kanon, die Regel, Richtschnur; (ecclesiastical law) das Kirchengesetz, Ordensgesetz, der Kanon; das autorisierte Heiligenverzeichnis; the sacred —, die autorisierten Bücher der heiligen Schrift, die heilige Schrift; der Meßkanon, das Meßgebot; der Kanon (*Typ.*, *Mus.*) die Formel (*Math.*, *Pharm.*). **—ical**, *adj.* kanonisch; —ical books, die kanonischen Bücher, di Bibel; —ical hours, von der Kirche vorgeschriebene Gebetsstunden; Stunden zur Verrichtung geistlicher Amtshandlungen; —ical punishment die Kirchenstrafe. **—icity**, *s.* die Kirchengemäßheit, kanonische Gültigkeit. **—ist**, *s.* der Kanonist **—ization**, **—isation**, *s.* die Heiligsprechung **—ize**, **—ise**, *v.a.* heilig sprechen. *Comp.* **—-law**, *s.* das Kirchenrecht, kanonische Recht.

[2]Canon, *s.* der Kanoniker, Domherr, Stiftsherr regular —s, klösterlich beisammen lebende Dom *or* Stifts=herren; secular —s, zerstreut lebend Dom= *or* Stifts=herren. **—ess**, *s.* das Stiftsfräulein. **—icals**, *pl.* der Domherrenschmuck **—icate**, *s.* die Domherrnstelle, das Kanonikat **—ry**, *s.* die Stiftspfründe, das Kanonikat, di Stelle *or* das Amt eines Kanonikers.

Cañon, *s.* enge Bergschlucht; das Schluchtental.

Canop—ied, *adj.* mit einem Baldachin versehen (shaded) bedeckt. **—y**, I. *s.* (*pl.* —ies) de Baldachin, Betthimmel, Thronhimmel; (shade die Decke; portable —y, der Traghimmel; —y of an altar, der Altarhimmel; the —y of heaven das Himmelsgewölbe, das Himmelszelt; —y o clouds, das Wolkendach. II. *attrib.*; —y bed das Himmelbett. III. *v.a.* (mit einem Baldachin bedecken.

Can't, Cannot, = Can not.

[1]Cant, I. *s.* die Kante, ausspringende Ecke (*Build etc.*); das Umkehren, Kentern (*Carp. etc.*); de Stoß. II. *v.a.* stoßen; werfen, stürzen; auf di Seite legen. **—ed**, *adj.* eckig, kantig. **—een**. *see* Canteen. **—ilevers**, *pl.* die Sparrenköpf (*Arch.*). **—on**, *see* Canton. *Comp.* **—-chisel** *s.* der Kantbe(i)tel. **—-column**, *s.* die Säule mi eckigen Kannellierungen. **—-hook**, *s.* der Kanthaken (*Naut.*). **—-rib-bands**, *pl.* die Latten (*Naut.*). **—-spar**, *s.* die dünne Spiere. **—-timbers**, *pl.* die schrägen Spanten.

[2]Cant, I. *s.* die heuchlerische Redeweise, das scheinheilige Gewinsel; die Scheinheiligkeit; die Heuchelei; (— of a trade, *etc.*) die Kunstsprache, Zunftsprache; (slang) die Studenten=, Soldaten= Pöbelsprache, der Straßendialekt; das Kauderwelsch; a — phrase, Lieblingsphrase, stehende Redensart; — term, ein Kunstausdruck. II. *v.n* scheinheilig reden; sich scheinheilig benehmen; **—ing** fellow, —ing fellow, ein Andächtler, Scheinheiliger. **—ata**, *s.* die Kantate. **—er**, *s. see* —ing fellow **—icle**, *s.* der Gesang; der Lobgesang, ein Tei des Kirchengesanges der anglikanischen Kirche; die Abteilung eines Gesanges. **—icles**, *pl.* das hohe Lied Salomonis. **—o**, *s.* der Gesang; di Abteilung eines längeren epischen Gedichts; di Diskantstimme eines Gesanges (*Mus.*). **—or**, *s* der Sänger; der Vorsänger.

Cantaloup, *s.* die Beutelmelone.

Cantankerous, *adj.*, **—ly**, *adv.* mürrisch, leich reizbar, streitsüchtig, rechthaberisch (*coll.*).

Canteen, *s.* die Feldflasche; die Marketenderbude die Kantine, Kasernenwirtschaft.

Canter, I. *s.* der kurze Galopp. II. *v.n.* in kurzem, leichtem Galopp reiten.

Cantharides, *pl.* die spanischen Fliegen.

Canton, *s.* der Bezirk, Kanton; das Eckschildchen, Quartierchen (*Her.*); die Abteilung (*Paint.*) **—al**, *adj.* einem Bezirke gehörig; Kantons . . **—ment**, *s.* die Kantonierung, Einlagerung Unterbringung der Truppen.

Cantrap, Cantrip, *s.* (*Scotch*) der Zauber; das Blendwerk, der betrügerische Streich, Kniff.

Canvas, I. *s.* der Kanevas (*Manuf.*); das Segeltuch (*Naut.*); die Malerleinwand (*Paint.*); (sails die Segel; die Packleinwand (*for bales, etc.*) die Zeltleinwand; das Zelt (*fig.*); das Gemälde (*fig.*); — for wool-work, die Stickgaze, der Stramin; the ship has all her — spread das Schiff hat alle Segel ausgespannt; under —

biwakierend, in Zelten wohnend. II. *attrib.;* — blind, leinener Fenstervorhang ; — frame, ein Kasten mit einem Leinwandrahmen (*Calico-Print.*) ; — yarn, das Segelgarn. *Comp.* —**-covered**, *adj.* mit Leinwand überzogen.

Canvass, *s.* die gründliche Untersuchung, Erörterung, Ausforschung ; (solicitation of votes) die Bewerbung, Stimmenwerbung. II. *v.a.* (examine) prüfen, genau untersuchen ; sichten ; (solicit) sich um eine S. bewerben ; (to persuade freshmen to join a students' club) keilen ; (discuss) erörtern. III. *v.n.;* my mother was at that moment —ing for me, zu dieser Zeit bewarb sich meine Mutter um Wahlstimmen für mich ; Wanted : a man to — for subscribers, Gesucht ; ein Mann, um Abonnenten zu sammeln. —**er**, *s.* der Bewerber, Stimmenwerber. —**ing**, *s.* die Werbung um (Wahlstimmen, 2c.) ; die Erörterung ; die Untersuchung.

Caoutchouc, *s.* der Kautschuk.

Cap, I. *s.* die Kappe, Mütze (*for boys, etc.*); die Haube (*for women*) ; das Zündhütchen (*of a gun*) ; die Zünderplatte (*of a cannon*) ; der Aufsatz (*Carp.*); die Kappe, der Hut (*Chem.*) ; die Krone der Presse (*Typ.*) ; die Kronschwelle (*of a bridge*); das Eselshaupt (*Naut.*) ; die (viereckige) Mütze der Oxforder und Cambridger Studenten, mit Troddel ; — and gown, Barett und Talar, akademische Tracht (*in Oxford and Cambridge*); — of the mainmast, das große Eselshaupt ; — of the foremast, das Fockeselshaupt ; the black —, das schwarze Barett eines engl. Richters (beim Sprechen eines Todesurteils ; — and bells, die Narrenkappe ; — of maintenance, die Schirmhaube ; forage —, die Feldmütze ; that is a feather in his —, darauf darf er sich etwas einbilden ; to put on one's considering —, über eine S. nachdenken ; she sets her — at him, sie sucht ihn zu gewinnen ; let him whom the — fits, put it on, wen's juckt, der kratze sich (*prov.*). II. *v.a.* (oben) bedecken; bekleiden; (surpass) übertreffen (*vulg.*) ; bekappen (*shoes*) ; (vor einem) die Mütze ziehen ; wechselsweise, im Wettstreit hersagen; to — a professor, vor einem Professor die Mütze abnehmen; to — verses, Verse in die Wette hersagen, so daß jeder seinen Vers mit dem Buchstaben anfängt, womit der letzte hergesagte Vers geendet hat; cloud-—ped mountains, mit Wolken bedeckte *or* wolkenverhüllte Berge. —**-a-pie**, *s.* (armed —-a-pie) vom Scheitel bis zur Sohle. (gerüstet). —**ful**, *s.* eine Mütze voll; einwenig.

Capa—bility, *s.* die Fähigkeit. —**ble**, *adj.*, —**bly**, *adv.* fähig, vermögend imstande; a port — ble of containing 1000 ships, ein Hafen, der 1000 Schiffe fassen kann; he is not —ble of feeling the shame, er ist nicht imstande *or* fähig die Schande zu fühlen ; he is not —ble of receiving good instruction, er ist für gute Belehrungen unzugänglich *or* nicht empfänglich ; a man —ble of judging the merits of the work, ein Mann, der die Verdienste des Werkes zu beurteilen vermag. —**cious**, *adj.*, —**ciously**, *adv.* viel-, weitumfassend, geräumig ; a —cious mind, ein umfassender Verstand. —**ciousness**, *s.* die Geräumigkeit, Weite ; das Umfassende (*fig.*). —**citate**, *v.a.* fähig machen, befähigen. —**city**, *s.* die Weite, Geräumigkeit, der Raum, körperliche Inhalt ; der kubische Inhalt (*Geom.*) ; die Empfänglichkeit für die Aufnahme luftförmiger oder flüssiger Körper (*Chem.*); die Ladungsfähigkeit (*of a ship*) ; (ability) die Fassungskraft, Fähigkeit, Leistungsfähigkeit, Tüchtigkeit ; (character) der Charakter, (Zu-)Stand ; in his —city of clerk, in seiner Eigenschaft als Kommis ; in his ministerial —city, als Minister ; —city for heat, die Wärmekapazität ; —city for saturation, das Sättigungsvermögen.

Caparison, I. *s.* die Schabracke ; die Ausstaffierung. II. *v.a.* mit einer Schabracke bedecken, eine Schabracke auflegen; ausstaffieren.

[1]**Cape**, *s.* der Kragen, Mantelkragen (*Tail.*) ; der Kragenmantel (*Tail.*).

[2]**Cape**, *s.* das Vorgebirge, Kap ; — of Good Hope, das Kap der Guten Hoffnung.

[1]**Caper**, I. *s.* der Bocksprung, Luftsprung ; to cut —s, Kapriolen machen. II. *v.n.* Luftsprünge *or* Freudensprünge machen, springen, hüpfen.

[2]**Caper**, *s.* die Kaper. *Comp.* —**-bush**, *s.* der Kapernstrauch. —**-sauce**, *s.* die Kapernsauce.

Capercaillie, (**Capercalzie**,) *s.* der Auerhahn.

Capillar—y, *adj.* haarförmig ; haarfein; —y pyrites, der Haarkies. —**ity**, *s.* (—y attraction) die Haarröhrchenkraft, Kapillaranziehung.

[1]**Capit—al**, I. *adj.*, —**ally**, *adv.* Kopf- (*obs.*); Leib und Leben betreffend, auf den Tod (*as a penalty*), (chief) hauptsächlich, vorzüglich, Haupt- ; (excellent) vortrefflich, prächtig, famos ; a —al city, eine Hauptstadt ; —al crime, ein Todesverbrechen, todeswürdiges Verbrechen ; —al letters, große Anfangsbuchstaben (*Typ.*), Hauptbuchstaben. II. *s.* (city) die Hauptstadt ; großer Anfangsbuchstabe, Majuskel ; das Kapital (*C. L.*) ; circulating —al, umlaufendes Kapital ; —al uncalled, gezeichnetes, aber noch einzuzahlendes Aktienkapital ; —al of a firm, Gesellschaftskapital ; —al put or paid in, Einlagekapital ; circulating, working, trading —al, Betriebskapital, Umsatzkapital ; unproductive —al, totes Kapital ; invested —, Anlagekapital; authorized —al, das Stammkapital; fixed al, festes Kapital; small —als, die Kapitälchenschrift. —**alism**, *s.* der Kapitalbesitz ; die Macht des Großkapitals. —**alist**, *s.* der Kapitalist. —**alize**, —**alise**, *v.a.* kapitalisieren. —**ation**, *s.* die Kopfschätzung, Zählung nach den Köpfen ; —ation tax, die Kopfbesteuerung, Kopfsteuer; —ation fee, das Kopfgeld. —**ular**, I., —**ulary**, *adj.* stiftsmäßig. II. *s.* das Stiftsmitglied ; das Kapitulare. —**ulate**, *v.a.* sich vergleichen, einen Vergleich schließen ; kapitulieren ; sich auf Vertrag ergeben. —**ulation**, *s.* der Vertrag, Vergleich ; die Übergabe ; die Kapitulation (eines Unteroffiziers) ; terms of —ulation, die Vertragsbedingungen ; die Übergabebedingungen.

[2]**Capital**, I. *s.* das Kapitäl, der Säulenknauf (*Arch.*) ; der Destillierhelm. II. *v.a.* mit einem Kapitäl versehen.

Capitol, *s.* das Kongreßhaus (zu Washington) (*Amer.*) ; das Regierungsgebäude (eines einzelnen Staates) (*Amer.*) ; *see the Index of names.*

Capivi, *s.* der Kopaivabalsam.

Capon, *s.* der Kapaun; der Verschnittene (*vulg.*).

Capot, *s.* der Matsch (im Piket).

Capote, *s.* die Kapotte, Theaterkappe ; der Regenmantel mit Kapuze.

Capric—e, *s.* die Laune, Grille, der plötzliche Einfall. —**ious**, *adj.*, —**iously**, *adv.* launenhaft ; mutwillig. —**iousness**, *s.* das launische Wesen, die grillenhafte Gemütsart ; —iousness of fortune, die Launenhaftigkeit des Glücks.

Capricorn, *s.* der Steinbock.

Capsicum, *s.* der spanische Pfeffer.

Capsize, *v.* I. *a.* umwerfen. II. *n.* umfallen.

Capstan, *s.* die stehende Welle, die Erdwinde (*Mach.*) ; die Schachtwinde (*Min.*) ; das Gangspill, Spill (*Naut.*).

Capsul—ar(y), *adj.* kapselförmig ; —ar ligament, das Kapselband (*Anat.*). —**e**, *s.* die Kapsel (*Bot.*) ; der Schmelztiegel (*Metall.*) ; die Abdampfschale (*Chem.*); die Kapsel (einer Bombe).

Captain, *s.* der (Schiffs)Kapitän (*Naut.*) ; der Hauptmann (*Mil.*) ; — of foot, Hauptmann bei der Infanterie ; — in the navy, der Kapitän zur See ; — of a riverboat, der Stromschiffer ; — of the foretop, der Ausgucker auf dem Vormars ; — of a school, Primus omnium ; — of a football team, Anführer in einer Fußballpartie. —**cy**, *s.* die Hauptmannschaft ; die Führerstelle, Führerrolle.

Captious, *adj.*, **—ly**, *adv.* zänkisch; (insidious) verfänglich; a — argument, ein Trugschluß. **—ness**, *s.* die Zanksucht; die Tadelsucht; die Verfänglichkeit.

Captiv—ate, *v.a.* gefangen nehmen; fesseln, einnehmen (*fig.*); bestricken, bezaubern; to be —ated by a lady's beauty, von der Schönheit einer Dame eingenommen *or* bezaubert sein. **—ating**, *adj.* fesselnd, reizend. **—e**, I. *adj.* gefangen; gefesselt; —e state, die Gefangenschaft; to take the senses —e, die Sinne fesseln, gefangen nehmen; —e balloon, der Fesselballon. II. *s.* der Kriegsgefangene; der Gefangene (*lit. & fig.*). **—ity**, *s.* die Gefangenschaft; (bondage) die Knechtschaft; thou hast led —ity —e, Du hast das Gefängnis gefangen (*B.*).

Captor, *s.* der Fänger; der Kaper (*Naut.*).

Capture, I. *s.* das Fangen; das Erbeuten; der Fang, die Beute. II. *v.a.* fangen; erbeuten; to be —d, in Gefangenschaft geraten.

Capuchin, *s.* die Kapuze; (— monk) der Kapuziner.

Car, *s.* der Wagen, Karren; der Nachen (*of a balloon*); der Eisenbahnwagen, Personenwagen (*Amer.*); Wagen einer Trambahn; electric —, Wagen der elektrischen Straßenbahn; sleeping-—, der Schlafwagen (*Railw.*); triumphal —, der Triumphwagen; Irish jaunting —, ein zweiräderiger Wagen, auf dem die Sitze der Länge nach oder Rücken gegen Rücken angebracht sind; the —s, die Eisenbahnwagen (*Amer.*); die Straßenbahnwagen. *Comp.* **—-wheel**, *s.* das Wagenrad.

Car(a)bine, *s.* der Karabiner. **—er**, *s.* der Karabinier.

Caracole, I. *s.* die halbe Wendung (*of a horse*); die Wendeltreppe (*Arch.*). II. *v.n.* karakolieren.

Carafe, *s.* die gläserne Wasserflasche, Karaffe.

Caramel, *s.* der Karamel.

Carapace, *s.* der Rückenschild der Schildkröten.

Carat, *s.* das Karat.

Caravan, *s.* die Karawane; der Möbeltransportwagen; der Menageriewagen; großer Reisewagen. **—sary**, *s.* die Karawanserei.

Caraway, *s.* der Kümmel; essence of —, das Kümmelöl. *Comp.* **—-seed**, *s.* der Kümmelsamen; —-seeds, der Kümmel.

Carbolic-acid, *s.* die Karbolsäure (*Chem.*).

Carbon, I. *s.* der Kohlenstoff. II. *attrib.*; — dioxide, *see* —ic acid. **—aceous**, *adj.* kohlenstoffhaltig, Kohlen=; —aceous iron ore, der Kohleneisenstein. **—ate**, I. *v.a.* mit Kohlensäure sättigen (*Chem.*); karbonisieren (*Manuf.*); saturieren (*beet-sugar*). II. *s.* das Karbonat, kohlensaure Salz; das Sodasalz; —ate of lime, die Kreide, der Kalkstein; —ate of soda, das kohlensaure Natron. **—ic**, *adj.* kohlenartig; —ic acid, die Kohlensäure; —ic acid gas, kohlensaures Gas; —ic oxide, das Kohlenoxydgas. **—iferous**, *adj.* Kohlenstoff erzeugend; Kohlen enthaltend. **—ization**, **—isation**, *s.* die Verkohlung; die Karburation (*of gas*). **—ize**, **—ise**, *v.a.* verkohlen; mit Kohlensäure behandeln. **—izer**, *s.* der Apparat zur Karburation des Leuchtgases. **—hydrous**, *adj.* aus Kohlen= und Wasser=stoff bestehend. *Comp.* **—-black**, *s.* feiner Lampenruß. **—-light**, *s.* das elektrische Bogenlicht. **—-paper**, *s.* das Durchdruckpapier, Pauspapier. **—-photograph**, *s.* durch Kohle=Verfahren hergestellte Photographie. **—-printing**, *s.* der Kohlelichtdruck.

Carbo-sulphuret, *s.* der Kohlenschwefel.

Carboy, *s.* der Ballon (*Chem.*).

Carbuncle, *s.* der Karfunkel (*Min.*); der Karbunkel, Furunkel, das Blutgeschwür (*Med.*).

Carburet, *s.* die Kohlenstoffverbindung; — of iron, das Eisenkarburet. **—ted**, *adj.* mit Kohlenstoff verbunden; —ted hydrogen, das Sumpfgas.

Carcass, **Carcase**, *s.* der Körper; (corpse) der Leichnam; das Aas (*of beasts*); das Gerippe (*of a ship, a house, etc.*); die Brandkugel (*Mil.*); round —, die Brandbombe (*Mil.*); — of a roof, das Sparrwerk.

[1]**Card**, *s.* die Karte; der Pappdeckel; (playing-—) Spielkarte; (visiting-—) Visitenkarte; (compass —) die Windrose; (post-—) Postkarte; a pack of —s, ein Spiel Karten; to leave a — on a p. bei einem seine Karte abgeben; to pack the —s die Karten auf betrügerische Weise mischen; to speak by the —, es sehr genau mit seinen Worten nehmen; on the —s, an sich möglich — to view, Erlaubniskarte zur Besichtigung *Comp.* **—board**, *s.* der Pappdeckel, die (dünne) Pappe; perforated —board, der Papierstramin **—-case**, *s.* das (Visiten) Kartentäschchen. **—-counters**, *pl.* die Spielmarken; Zahlpfennige **—-party**, *s.* die Spielgesellschaft. **—-room** *s.* das Spielzimmer. **—-sharper**, *s.* falscher Spieler, Betrüger beim Kartenspiel. **—-table** *s.* der Spieltisch. **—-trick**, *s.* das Kartenkunststück.

[2]**Card**, I. *s.* die Karde, Kardätsche, Kratze (*for flax and cotton*); der Krempelkamm, die Wollkratze, der Wollkamm (*for wool*); die Wergkratzmaschine (*for tow*); das Band (*of wool, etc. as it comes from the card*). II. *v.a.* (Wolle) krempeln; (Baumwolle) kardätschen, krempeln; —ed wool, Streichwolle; — for waste silk, die Florettkratze. **—er**, *s.* der Krempler, Wollkämmer; der Kardätscher. **—ing**, I. *s.* das Kratzen, Streichen, Kardätschen (*Spin.*). II. *attrib.*; —ing-machine, *s.* die Streichmaschine, Kratzmaschine.

Cardi—ac, **—acal**, *adj.* zum Herzen gehörig; herzstärkend; —ac passion, das Herzweh. **—acs**, *pl.* herzstärkende Mittel (*Med.*). **—algia**, *s.* das Herzweh; das Sodbrennen (*Med.*). **—oid**, *s.* die Herzlinie, Kardioide (*Math.*). **—tis**, *s.* die Herzentzündung (*Med.*).

Cardinal, I. *adj.* vornehmlich, vornehmst, hauptsächlichst, Haupt=; Kardinal=; the — numbers, die Kardinalzahlen; the — points, die vier Punkte des Horizonts, Kardinalpunkte; the — virtues, die Kardinaltugenden. II. *s.* der Kardinal (*Eccl.*); der Kardinalfink; — cape, der Kardinalskragen; — red, tiefrot. **—ate**, *s.* die Kardinalswürde.

Cardoon, *s.* die Kardonen=Artischoke (*Bot.*).

Care, I. *s.* (anxiety) die Sorge, Besorgnis; (providence) die Fürsorge; (heed) die Achtsamkeit, Hut, Vorsicht; (sorrow) der Kummer, die Sorge; (carefulness) die Sorgfalt; (— of a patient) die Pflege; (object of —) der Gegenstand der Sorge *or* Pflege; — of (c/o) . . ., per Adresse, bei (b/) . . ., mit Briefen des Herrn . . .; my son's happiness was all my —, meines Sohnes Glück war meine einzige Sorge; he was under the — of Dr. . . ., er war in der Behandlung des Herrn Doktor . . .; to cast aside all —, sich jeder Sorge entschlagen; she nursed him with great —, sie pflegte ihn mit großer Sorgfalt, he was educated with great —, er wurde mit großer Sorgfalt erzogen; entrusted to my —, meiner Obhut anvertraut; to take —, sich in Acht nehmen; you must take good — not to offend him, du mußt dich sehr hüten, ihn zu beleidigen; have a —! take —! vorgesehen! Vorsicht! Achtung! take — of your purse, gieb Acht auf deinen Beutel, nimm dein Geld in Acht! to take great — of a p., einen auf das sorgfältigste pflegen; — will kill a cat, Kummer macht vor der Zeit alt; he is well taken — of, er wird gut gepflegt. II. *v.n.* sorgen, sich bekümmern; what do I —! was frage ich danach! was kümmert's mich? I don't — a straw, ich mache mir nichts *or* nicht das Geringste daraus, das ist mir höchst gleichgültig; for all (*or* aught) I —, meinetwegen; I don't — if I do, schön, meinetwegen; to — for nobody, sich um niemanden kümmern; to — for nothing, nach nichts fragen, sich um nichts bekümmern. —**ful**, *adj.*, —**fully**, *adv.* (anxious) sorgenvoll, besorgt; (provident) sorgsam, achtsam, vorsichtig; to be —ful of one's health, sorgfältig auf seine Gesundheit achten; be —ful what you do, geht vorsichtig zu Werke; be —ful of this, gehen Sie damit vorsichtig um; he was —ful of his honour, er war sehr besorgt um seine Ehre; thou art —ful and troubled about many things, Du hast viel Sorge und Mühe (*B.*); we are not —ful to answer thee in this matter, es ist nicht Not, daß wir Dir darauf antworten (*B.*). —**fulness**, *s.* (solicitude) die Sorgsamkeit, Sorgfalt; (providence) die Vorsicht, Wachsamkeit; (exactness) die Sorgfalt. —**less**, *adj.*, —**lessly**, *adv.* (without —) sorgenfrei, sorglos, unbekümmert; (negligent) nachlässig; (thoughtless) gedankenlos, unbedachtsam, unachtsam, unvorsichtig; (cheerful) heiter; (without art) einfach, schlicht, ungekünstelt; —less about, unbekümmert um; —less of, sorglos um, unachtsam auf (*acc.*), gleichgültig gegen; a —less, good-for-nothing fellow, ein liederlicher, nichtsnutziger Mensch. —**lessness**, *s.* die Sorglosigkeit; die Unachtsamkeit; die Nachlässigkeit. *Comp.* —-**taker**, *s.* der Hausmeister, Hausverwalter; Wärter, Pfleger; Verwalter. —-**worn**, *adj.* von Sorgen gedrückt, abgehärmt.

Careen, *v.a.* kielholen. —**age**, *s.* das Kielgeld. *Comp.* —**ing-block**, *s.* der Werftblock (*Naut.*). —**ing-wharf**, *s.* die Kielholwerft.

Career, I. *s.* (rapid course) voller Lauf; die Laufbahn, Bahn (*of life*); die Rennbahn (*obs.*); der Flug (*of a hawk*); Goethe's literary —, Goethes litterarische Laufbahn; in full —, in vollem Laufe, mit verhängtem Zügel, in der höchsten Eile. II. *v.n.* schnell laufen, eilen.

Caress, I. *s.* die Liebkosung; conjugal —es, die ehelichen Zärtlichkeiten. II. *v.a.* liebkosen; (embrace) umarmen; (pat) streicheln. —**ing**, I., *adj.*, —**ingly**, *adv.* liebkosend. II. *s.* das Liebkosen.

Caret, *s.* das Einschaltungszeichen, Auslassungszeichen, Zeichen, daß etwas fehlt (∧).

Cargo, I. *s.* die Fracht, Schiffsladung; — in packets, Stückgüter. II. *attrib.*; — vessel, das Frachtschiff; — port, die Luke, durch welche die Fracht eingeladen wird.

Caricatur—**e**, I. *s.* das Zerrbild, die Karikatur. II. *v.a.* verzerrt *or* im Zerrbilde darstellen, karikieren; (ridicule) lächerlich machen. —**ist**, *s.* der Karikaturenzeichner.

Cari—**es**, *s.* der Knochenfraß, die Beinfäule; die krebsartige Fäulnis. —**ous**, *adj.* angefressen.

Carillon, *s.* das Glockenspiel.

Cark, *v.n.* sich ängstigen; —ing care, kummervolle, bittre, herznagende Sorge.

Carl, *s.* der Kerl (*Scotch*).

[1]**Carlin**(**e**), *s.* (*dial.*) altes Weib; die Hexe.

[2]**Carline**, *s.* der Eberwurz, Judendorn.

Carminative, I. *adj.* Blähungen zerteilend, lösend. II. *s.* blähungtreibendes Mittel.

Carmine, *s.* der Karmin; — red, das Karminrot.

Carn—**age**, *s.* das Gemetzel, Blutbad, die Metzelei. —**al**, *adj.*, —**ally**, *adv.* fleischlich, sinnlich; —ally minded, fleischlich gesinnt; to have —al intercourse with, geschlechtlichen Umgang haben mit; —al delight, die Fleischeslust, Sinnenlust; —al desire, —al passion, sinnliche Leidenschaft. —**ality**, *s.* die Fleischeslust, Sinnlichkeit. —**ation**, *s.* die Fleischfarbe (*Dyer*); die Gartennelke (*Bot.*); die Fleischdarstellung, das Inkarnat (*Paint.*). —**elian**, *s.* der Karneol. —**ival**, *s.* der Karneval, der Fasching; —ival procession, der Faschingszug, Fastnachtsaufzug. —**ivora**, *pl.* fleischfressende Tiere. —**ivorous**, *adj.* fleischfressend. —**osity**, *s.* der Fleischauswuchs.

Carob, *s.* die Karobe (*C.L.*). *Comp.* —-**bean**, *s.* das Johannisbrot. —-**tree**, *s.* der Johannisbrotbaum.

Carol, I. *s.* der Gesang; der Lobgesang, Jubelgesang; Christmas —, das Weihnachtslied. II. *v.a.* besingen; lobpreisen. III. *v.n.* singen, jubeln.

Carotid, I. *s.* die Kopfschlagader, Halsschlagader. II. *adj.*; — arteries, die Halspuls-, Kopf- oder Haupt-schlagadern (*Anat.*).

Carous—**al**, *s.* das Zechen, Trinkgelage. —**e**, I. *s.* das Zechgelage. II. *v.n.* zechen, trinken.

[1]**Carp**, *s.* der Karpfen (*Icht.*).

[2]**Carp**, *v.n.*; to — at a th., etwas bekritteln, tadeln, auf eine S. sticheln; —ing criticism, kleinlich tadelnde, alles bekrittelnde Kritik. —**er**, *s.* der Krittler, Kritikaster.

Carpent—**er**, I. *s.* der Zimmermann; —er's bench, die Hobelbank; —er's chisel, der Stechmeißel; —er's rule, der Zollstock; —er's work, die Zimmerarbeit, Zimmermansarbeit. II. *v.n.* zimmern. —**ry**, *s.* das Zimmerhandwerk.

Carpet, I. *s.* die Fußdecke, der Teppich; stair- —, der Treppenläufer; Turkey —, der türkische Teppich; the grassy — of this plain, der grüne Teppich dieser Ebene. II. *v.a.* mit Teppichen belegen, bedecken. —**ing**, *s.* das Teppichzeug. *Comp.* —-**bag**, *s.* der Reisesack, Nachtsack; —-bag politician, politischer Abenteurer. —-**beater**, *s.* der Teppichausklopfer. —-**binding**, *s.* die Teppicheinfassung. —-**broom**, *s.* der Teppichbesen. —-**knight**, *s.* der Weichling; der Salonlöwe, Damenheld. —-**slippers**, *s.* gestickte Pantoffeln. —-**stretcher**, *s.* die Teppichbreitmaschine. —-**sweeper**, *s.* der mechanische Teppichbesen.

Carpolites, *pl.* Karpolithen, Fruchtsteine.

Carpus, *s.* das Handgelenk (*Anat.*).

Carrageen-moss, *s.* das Perlmoos (*Bot.*).

Carriage, I. *s.* der Wagen, das Fuhrwerk; (transport) die Verfrachtung; (cost of —) die Fracht, der Fuhrlohn; (deportment) die Haltung, der Gang; (conduct) das Benehmen, Betragen, die Aufführung; (act of conveying) das Führen, Fahren, Fortschaffen; (management) die Durchführung; der Wagen, das Gestell (*Mach.*); die Lafette, der Protzwagen (*Artil.*); der Karren, das Laufbrett an der Presse (*Typ.*); (railway —) der Eisenbahnwagen, Personenwagen; — of a mortar, die Bettung eines Mörsers; — of a sale, die Leitung eines Verkaufs; overland —, der Landtransport; — by sea, der Seetransport; goods sent by —, das Frachtgut; — of sounds, das Forttragen, Fortpflanzen der Töne; 1st, 2d, & 3d class —, Personenwagen erster, zweiter und dritter Klasse (*Railw.*); composite —, der aus mehreren Klassen gemischte Personenwagen (*Railw.*); one-horse —, der Einspänner. II. *attrib.*; — bar, der Lafettenriegel (*Artil.*); — beam, — pole, der Kutschbaum; — brake, der Brems, die Bremse; — builder, der Wagenbauer; — building, der Wagenbau; — coupling, die Wagenkuppelung (*Railw.*); — door, der Kutschenschlag; — drive, die Anfahrt vor einem Hause (*see* —way); — exercise, die Bewegung im Wagen; die Gelegenheit zum Ausfahren; — frame, das Wagengestell; — grease, die Wagenschmiere; — horse, das Wagenpferd; — road, der Fahrweg; — top, das Wagendach. *Comp.* —-**bridge**, *s.* die Wagen- *or* Rollbrücke. —-**spring**, *s.* die Wagenfeder. —**way**, *s.* der Fahrweg.

Carr—**ied**, *p.p. see* Carry. —**ier**, *s.* der Fuhrmann; (messenger) der Bote; der Träger; (shipper, *etc.*) der Spediteur, Beförderer; das Probierscheibchen (*Elect.*); common —ier, der Lohnfuhrmann; —ier and forwarding agent, der Spediteur. —**y**, *v.* I. *a.* tragen, fahren, führen, bringen (*to a place, etc.*); tragen, führen (*arms, etc.*); führen (*sail*); im Sinne behalten (*Arith.*); erobern (*outworks, etc., Mil.*); to —y all before one, alles mit sich fortreißen, alles bemeistern; to — coals to Newcastle, Wasser ins Meer, *or* Eulen nach Athen, tragen; to —y the day, den Sieg davontragen, siegen; to fetch and —y, apportieren (*of dogs*); den gehorsamen Diener spielen (*of people*); to —y it with a high hand, sich gebieterisch benehmen; to —y a high head, den Kopf hoch tragen; to —y a jest too far, einen Scherz zu weit treiben; to —y one's point, seinen Zweck erreichen, eine Sache durchsetzen; the motion was —ied, der Antrag ging durch; his motion was not —ied, sein Antrag fiel durch; the ship —ied too much sail, das Schiff hatte zu viele Segel aufgesetzt; to —y **away**, wegtragen, fortschaffen; fortreißen (*also fig.*); a mast was —ied away, ein Mast wurde abgesegelt; passion —ied him away, Leidenschaft verführte ihn; to be —ied away with . . ., von . . . fortgerissen werden; to —y **forth**, hinaustragen; to —y **forward**, übertragen, vortragen (*C.L.*), fortführen, fortsetzen; amount —ied forward, der Übertrag; to —y **off**, wegführen, wegnehmen, vertreiben; the plague —ied him off, die Seuche *or* Pestilenz hat ihn weggerafft; to —y off the ring, den Ring abstechen (*at tournaments*); to —y **on**, (conduct) anführen, (continue) fortführen; to —y on, sich betragen (*coll.*); to —y on business, ein Geschäft betreiben, führen; ein Geschäft weiterführen; to —y on a negotiation, eine Verhandlung pflegen; to —y on a conversation, ein Gespräch führen; to —y on a war, einen Krieg führen; to —y on the war, den Krieg fortsetzen; to —y **out**, durchsetzen; to —y out a plan, einen Plan durchführen; to —y **over**, hinüberführen, *see* —y forward (*C.L.*); amount —ied over, der Vortrag, Übertrag (*C.L.*); to —y **to** a new account, auf neue Rechnung stellen (*C.L.*); to —y **through**, durchsetzen, durchführen; to —y **with** it, (*fig.*) im Gefolge haben, mit sich bringen. II. *n.* tragen, schießen (*as a gun*); a pillar that —ies false, eine Säule, die nicht senkrecht auf der Basis steht. —**ying**, I. *s.* das Fuhrwesen (*C.L.*); das Fahren; —ying and forwarding (trade), das Speditionsgeschäft. II. *attrib.*; —ying business, das Speditionsgeschäft; —ying roller, die Laufrolle (*Mach.*); —ing traffic, der Güterverkehr (auf der Eisenbahn). *Comp.* —**ier-pigeon**, *s.* die Brieftaube. —**ying-trade**, *s.* das Frachtgeschäft, Speditionsgeschäft, die Reederei.

Carrion, *s.* das Aas. *Comp.* —**-crow**, *s.* die Aaskrähe. —**-vulture**, *s.* der Aasgeier.

Carronade, *s.* die Karronade, Schiffshaubitze.

Carrot, *s.* die Karotte, Mohrrübe, gelbe Rübe; die Karotte (*for smoking*); —s, der Rotkopf, rotes Haar (*vulg.*).

Carry, *see under* Carr—ied.

Cart, I. *s.* der Karren, Frachtwagen, die Karre; das Fuhrwerk; dog-—, das Jagdgig; hand-—, der Handkarren; spring-—, Lastwagen auf Federn; — for carrying ore, Laufkarren; to put the — before the horse, die Pferde hinter den Wagen spannen, das Pferd am Schwanze zäumen. II. *attrib.*; — house, der Wagenschuppen; — rack, die Wagenleiter; — rope, das Karrenseil; — rut, das Wagengeleise, die Radspur. III. *v.a.* auf dem Karren wegführen. —**age**, *s.* die Beförderung auf der Achse; (cost of —age) der Fuhrlohn, die Transportkosten. —**er**, *s.* der Fuhrmann, Kärrner. *Comp.* —**-horse**, *s.* das Zugpferd. —**-tail**, *s.* das *or* der Hinterteil eines Karrens. —**-wheel**, *s.* das Wagenrad. —**wright**, *s.* der Karrenmacher, Wagner.

[1]**Carte**, *s.* die Karte, Speisekarte. —**-blanche**, *s.* das Blankett; die unbeschränkte Vollmacht.

[2]**Carte**, *s.* die Quarte (*Fenc.*).

Cart—el, *s.* das Kartell; der Kartellvertrag, Auslieferungsvertrag; der Fehdebrief (*obs.*). —**eller**, *s.* der Herausforderer. *Comp.* —**el-ship**, *s.* das Parlamentärschiff.

Cartilag—e, *s.* der Knorpel. —**inous**, *adj.* knorpelig. *Comp.* —**e-bone**, *s.* der Knorpelknochen.

Cartoon, *s.* der Karton; die Musterzeichnung; das Vollbild.

Cartouch, *s.* (cartridge) die Patrone, Kartusche; (case) die Kartätschenpatrone (*obs.*); (—-box) die Patrontasche (*Mil.*); die Randverzierung, Umrahmung, Schönleiste, Kartusche (*Arch.*).

Cartridge, *s.* die Kartusche; die Patrone; (—-box) die Patrontasche; der Schwärmer (*Firew.*); blank —, die Platzpatrone; empty —, die Patronenhülse; ball —, scharfe Patrone. *Comp.* —**-belt**, *s.* der Patronengürtel, Munitionsgürtel. —**-box**, *s.* die Patrontasche. —**-gauge**, *s.* die Patronenlehre. —**-needle**, *s.* die Kartuschnadel. —**-paper**, *s.* das Kartuschpapier. —**-primer**, *s.* das Zündhütchen. —**-priming-machine**, *s.* die Patronenlademaschine —**-wire**, *s.* der Zünddraht.

Caruncle, *s.* die Karbunkel, Drüse, das Fleischwärzchen (*Anat.*); der Fleischauswuchs am Kopfe oder Halse von Vögeln (*Orn.*).

Carv—e, *v.* I. *a.* schneiden, vorschneiden, tranchieren (*a joint, etc.*); schnitzen, ausschneiden, meißeln (*Carp., Sculp., Engr.*); to —e in wood, in Holz schneiden *or* schnitzen; he —ed his way to wealth, er bahnte sich (*dat.*) den Weg zum Reichtum. II. *n.* vorschneiden (*at table*). —**ed**, *p.p. & adj.* geschnitzt, durchbrochen; —ed work, das Schnitzwerk (*Arch.*), die Schnitzarbeit. —**er**, *s.* der Vorschneider; der Schnitzer, Bildner (*Art.*); der Bildhauer (*Sculp.*); —er in wood, Holzschnitzer. —**ers**, *s.* das Tranchierbesteck. —**ing**, *s.* die Durchbrechung; das Schnitzen; das Schnitzwerk in Holz oder Stein, Maßwerk; die Bildhauerarbeit. *Comp.* —**ing-fork**, *s.* die Vorlegegabel. —**ing-knife**, *s.* das Vorlegemesser.

Caryatide, *s.* die Karyatide.

Cascade, *s.* der Wasserfall; — of sparks, der Feuerregen; — of lace, wellig herabfallender Busenstreif aus Spitzen.

[1]**Case**, I. *s.* das Futteral, Gehäuse, Etui, der Kasten; die Kiste; (sheath) die Scheide; der Überzug (*of a pillow, etc.*); das Besteck (*of instruments*); (outside) das Äußere; die Bekleidung (*of a boiler*); der Mantel, Bleimantel (*Artil.*); die Raketenhülse (*Firew.*); die Formkappe (*Found.*); der Mantel (*Mach.*); der Rahmen (*Min.*); — for pens, das Pennal, der Federkasten; — of a watch, das Uhrgehäuse; — of bottles, der Flaschenkeller; door-—, das Türgestell; letter-—, der Schriftkasten (*Typ.*); lower (upper) —, die untere (obere) Hälfte des Schriftkastens; pistol-—, die Pistolenhalfter; — of a violin, der Geigenkasten; — of a window, das Fensterfutter; — of mathematical instruments, das Reißzeug; surgical —, das Besteck; packing-—, die Packkiste. —**ment**, *s.* (window) der Fensterflügel, das Flügelfenster; das Fensterfutter; die Hohlkehle (*Build.*); double —ment, das Doppelfenster; English —ment, der Falzfutterrahmen; French —ment, die Fensterflügel. II. *v.a.* mit einem Überzug *or* Futteral versehen; two volumes —d, zwei Bände in (gelieferte) Pappdeckel eingebunden. *Comp.* —**harden**, *v.a.* von außen härten, durch Einsatz härten; verhärten (*fig.*). —**hardening**, *s.* der Hartguß (*Metall.*). —**-knife**, *s.* das große Tischmesser im Futteral. —**-man**, *s.* der Schriftsetzer (*Typ.*). —**-paper**, *s.* die äußeren Bogen eines Buches *or* Rieses Papier. —**-roasting**, *s.* das Rösten in Stadeln (*Metall.*). —**-shot**, —**-shrapnel**, *s.* die Kartätsche (*Mil.*).

[2]**Case**, *s.* (circumstance) der Fall, Umstand, die Sache; (event) der Vorfall; (accident) der Zufall; (condition) der Zustand; (law —) der Rechtsfall; der Kasus (*Gram.*); — of conscience, ein Gewissenspunkt; in —, im Falle; in any —, jedenfalls; auf jeden Fall; in no —, keinenfalls, in keinem Falle, auf keinen Fall; in your —, an Ihrer Stelle; there 's a lady in the —, es betrifft eine Dame, eine Dame ist dabei im Spiele; in — of need *or* emergency, im Notfalle; a — in point, ein zur Sache gehörendes Beispiel, ein (hier)hergehöriger Fall, ein solcher *or* derartiger Fall; a leading —, ein Präzedenzfall; for example, take the — of . . ., zum Beispiel, nehmen Sie der Fall von . . .; to

make out a —, (etwas) beweisen; as the — stands, wie die Sache (nun einmal) liegt, wie die Sachen stehen; the — is this, es hat folgende Bewandtnis.

Case—in(e), *s.* das Kasein, der Käsestoff; vegetable —ine, Pflanzenkasein. **—ous**, *adj.* käsig, käseartig.

Casemate, *s.* die Kasematte (*Fort.*); die Hohlkehle (*Arch.*). **—d**, *adj.* kasemattiert.

Cash, I. *s.* die Kasse; (money) das Geld; (ready —) das bare Geld; for —, gegen bar; in —, in Kassa, per Kassa; are you in —, sind Sie bei Gelde? the proceeds in —, der Kassenertrag; balance in —, der Kassenbestand; net — in advance, Netto Cassa im Voraus; payment in —, die Barzahlung; £15 in —, fünfzehn Pfund bar, in barer Münze, in barem Gelde; to keep the —, die Kasse führen; down with the —, her mit dem Gelde! (*vulg.*). II. *attrib.*; — advance, der Geldvorschuß; — purchases, die Bareinkäufe. III. *v.a.* zu Geld machen, einwechseln; to get —ed, sich (*dat.*) bar auszahlen lassen, einwechseln; to — a bill, einen Wechsel einlösen *or* einkassieren. **—ier**, I. *s.* der Kassierer (*C.L.*). II. *v.a.* ablöhnen, abdanken, entlassen. **—ierment**, *s.* die Entlassung. *Comp.* **—-account**, *s.* das Kassa-Konto. **—-book**, *s.* das Kassabuch, Kassenbuch; petty —-book, das kleine Kassabuch. **—-box**, *s.* der Geldkasten. **—-keeper**, *s.* der Kassierer.

Cashew, *s.* der Nierenbaum, Elefantenlausbaum.

Cashmere, I. *s.* der Kaschmir. II. *attrib.* Kaschmir-.

[1]**Casing**, *s.* der Überzug, die Umhüllung; die Verkleidung (*Build.*); das Simswerk (*Build.*); der Mantel (*Found.*); — of timber work, die Holzbekleidung; — of a wall, die Bekleidung einer Mauer; steam —, der Dampfkasten; — with stone, das Plackwerk.

[2]**Casing**, *adj.*; — paper, das Packpapier, Einschlagepapier.

Casino, *s.* das Gesellschaftshaus, das Kasino.

Cask, I. *s.* das Faß, die Tonne; cleansing —, das Klärfaß (*Brew.*). II. *v.a.* in ein Faß füllen; the wine is —ed, der Wein schmeckt nach dem Fasse. **—et**, *s.* das Kästchen; die Schatulle (*obs.*). *Comp.* **—-buoy**, *s.* die Tonnenboje.

Casque, *s.* der Helm, die Sturmhaube (*Mil.*). **—t**, *s.* leichter offener Helm (*obs.*).

Cassation, *s.* die Kassierung, Aufhebung, Vernichtung; die Absetzung; court of —, das Kassationsgericht, Hofgericht.

Cassava, *s.* der Kassawastrauch.

Cassia, *s.* die Kassia. *Comp.* **—-buds**, *pl.* Zimmetblüten. **—-sticks**, *pl.* die Rohrkassia.

Cassock, *s.* langer enganschließender Priesterrock; die Soutane (*R.C.*); der langer Überrock (*obs.*).

Cassonade, *s.* die Kassonade, der Farinzucker.

Cassoon, *s.* der Munitionskasten.

Cassowary, *s.* der (ostindische gehelmte) Kasuar.

Cast, I. *ir.v.a.* (*imperf. & p.p. also* —) werfen; wegwerfen; fallen lassen; gießen (*iron*); auswerfen, werfen (*the anchor*); werfen (*light, etc.*); verbreiten, auswerfen (*a glow of heat*); werfen (*young*); berechnen, ausrechnen (*accounts*); stellen (*a nativity*); trees — their leaves, die Bäume lassen ihre Blätter fallen, entblättern sich; to — a balance, den Saldo ziehen; to — blame on a p., einen tadeln; to — the defendant, den Beklagten den Prozeß verlieren lassen; to — one's eyes upon, seine Blicke auf (eine S.) richten; to — one's feathers, sich mausern; to — lots for, um (eine S.) losen; to — the parts of a play, die Rollen eines Stückes verteilen; to — seed, säen; to — the skin, sich häuten; to — teeth, die Zähne verlieren; to — (s.th.) in a p.'s teeth, einem (etwas) vorwerfen; to — a trench, einen Graben ziehen, bauen; to be — in a lawsuit, einen Prozeß verlieren; to — **about**, umwerfen; to — about (for means), (auf Mittel und Wege) sinnen; to — **aside**, bei Seite legen; to — **away**, verwerfen, wegwerfen; to be — away, verschlagen werden; to — away care, die Sorgen verbannen; to — **behind**, zurückwerfen; to — a look behind, zurückblicken; to — **down**, niederwerfen, niederschlagen (*the eyes*); to be — down, niedergeschlagen sein; to — **into** prison, ins Gefängnis werfen; to — into a sleep, einschläfern; to — **off**, abwerfen, abschütteln; to — off stitches, Maschen abwerfen; to — off the dogs, die Hunde loslassen (*Sport*); to — **on**, anschlagen (knitting); to — **out**, (hin-)auswerfen, vertreiben; to — **over** in one's mind (*dial.*), überlegen; to — **up**, in die Höhe werfen; (vomit) durch Erbrechen von sich geben; to — up accounts, zusammenrechnen; to — **upon**, darauf werfen; to — glory, splendour upon, Ehre, Glanz werfen auf (*acc.*); to — o.s. upon a p.'s kindness, sich bittend an einen wenden. II. *s.* (throw) der Wurf, das Werfen; (distance) die Wurfweite; (mould) die Gußform; der Guß, Gußabdruck (*Metall.*); das gegossene Bild (*Art*); (squint) das Schielen; (tinge) die Farbe, Hinneigung zu einer Farbe, Schimmer; it has a — of green, es spielt ins Grüne; (— of countenance) die Gesichtsbildung; das Auswerfen (*of the lead, a net, etc.*); (kind) die Art, Gattung; — at dice, Wurf mit den Würfeln; to have a — in one's eye, schielen; — of parts, die Rollenverteilung, Rollenbesetzung; with the original —, mit denen, welche die Rollen zuerst spielten, mit der ursprünglichen Besetzung; plaster —, der Gipsabdruck; — of balls, die Kugeltresse (*Mil.*); to take a —, prägen, abdrucken. III *adj.*; — steel, — iron, der Gußstahl, das Gußeisen. **—er**, *see* Caster. **—ing**, I. *p. see* — I.; den Ausschlag gebend; —ing vote, die ausschlaggebende *or* entscheidende Stimme. II. *s. see* Casting. *Comp.* **—away**, I. *adj.* weggeworfen, unnütz, wertlos. II. *s.* der Verunglückte; der Verworfene (*of God*). **—ing-ladle**, *s.* die Gießkelle. **—ing-net**, *s.* das Wurfnetz. **—-off**, *adj.* abgelegt; —-off clothes, alte Kleider, abgelegte Kleidungsstücke. **—-iron**, *see under* — II.

Castanets, *pl.* die Kastagnetten, Tanzklapper.

Caste, *s.* die Kaste; to lose —, seine Stellung in der Gesellschaft verlieren, auf eine gesellschaftlich niedere Stufe herabsinken.

Castella—n, *s.* der Kastellan, Burgvogt. **—ted**, *adj.* mit Zinnen *or* Türmen versehen.

Caster, *s.* der Werfer; der Berechner (*of accounts*); der Nativitätsteller (*Astrol.*); die Streubüchse (*for the table*); die Laufrolle (*on chairs*); set of —s, die Plattmenage.

Castigat—e, *v.a.* züchtigen. **—ion**, *s.* die Züchtigung. **—ory**, *adj.* züchtigend.

Casting, *s.* das Gießen; der Guß; (cast) der Abguß; chill —, der Hartguß; — in iron moulds, — in chills, der Schalenguß; — of plate glass, der Guß von Spiegelglas; rough —, das Tünchen mit Kalk. *Comp.* **—-box**, *s.* der Gießkasten (*Found.*). **—-mould**, *s.* der Einguß, die Gießform. **—-pattern**, *s.* das Gießmodell.

Castle, I. *s.* die Burg, das Schloß, Kastell; der Turm, Roche (*Chess*); —s in the air, Luftschlösser. II. *attrib.*; — hill, der Schloßberg; — moat, der Schloßgraben. III. *v.n.* rochieren (*Chess*). **—d**, *adj.* getürmt, mit Schlössern. *Comp.* **—-building**, *s.* das Luftschlösserbauen. **—-ward**, *s.* der Schloßvogt; die Burgvogtei; die Burgsteuer.

Castor, *s.* der Biber (*Zool.*); der Biberhut; das Bibergeil (*Pharm.*). **—eum**, das Bibergeil *Comp.* **—-oil**, *s.* das Rizinusöl.

Castrat—e, *v.a.* kastrieren, verschneiden; verstümmeln. **—ion**, *s.* die Kastration; die Verstümmelung.

Casu—al, *adj.*, **—ally**, *adv.* zufällig, unbestimmt, unsicher. **—alty**, I. *s.* der Zufall; (accident) der Unglücksfall; (fatal accident) der Todesfall. II. *attrib.*; —alty returns, die Verlustlisten; der Verlust (*in battle, etc.*). **—alties**, *s.* Unfälle, der Verlust (*in battle*). **—ist**, *s.* der Kasuist,

Gewissensrat. —**istical**, *adj.* kasuistisch. —**istry**, *s.* die Kasuistik.

Cat, I. *s.* die Katze; female —, die Katze; tom- —, der Kater; wild- —, die Wildkatze; domestic —, die Hauskatze; Manx —, die schwanzlose Katze; neuter —, verschnittener (zur Fortpflanzung unfähiger) Kater; —-o'-nine-tails, die neunschwänzige Katze; the — mews, die Katze miaut; the — purrs, die Katze schnurrt; to lead a — and dog life, wie Hund und Katze leben; when the —'s away the mice will play, wenn die Katze aus dem Hause ist, spielen die Mäuse auf Tischen und Bänken; to bell the —, der Katze die Schelle anhängen; a — may look at a king, sieht doch die Katz' den Kaiser an; to let the — out of the bag, ein Geheimnis ausplaudern; it was raining —s and dogs, es regnete Bindfaden. II. *v.a.;* to — the anchor, den Anker aufketten. —**erwaul**, *v.n.* schreien wie eine Katze. —**erwauling**, *s.* die Katzenmusik. —**kin**, *s.* das Kätzchen (*Bot.*). —**ling**, *s.* das Zergliederungsmesser; die Darmsaite. *Comp.* —**-block**, *s.* der Katblock. —**call**, *s.* die Schreipfeife. —**fish**, *s.* der getigerte Haifisch. —**gut**, *s.* die Darmsaite; der Seidenstramin (*Weav.*). —**-holes**, *pl.* die Kattlöcher (*Naut.*). —**-hook**, *s.* der Ankerhaken. —**-like**, *adj.* katzenhaft. —**-pipe**, *see* —call. —**'s-eye**, *s.* das Katzenauge (*Min.*). —**'s-paw**, *s.* die Katzenpfote; die als Werkzeug gebrauchte Person (*fig.*); die Brise, Kühlte (*Naut.*); to make a —'s-paw of a p., einen vorschieben (als Werkzeug für etwas gebrauchen, das man selbst nicht unternehmen will), sich (*dat.*) von einem andern die Kastanien aus dem Feuer holen lassen.

Cata—baptist, *s.* der Gegner der Taufe (*obs.*). —**caustic**, *adj.* katakaustisch; —caustic curve, die Brennlinie. —**clysm**, *s.* die Überschwemmung, Sündflut. —**comb**, *s.* die Katakombe. —**coustics**, *s.* die Lehre vom Zurückwerfen des Schalles. —**falco**, —**falque**, *s.* der Katafalk, das Leichengerüst. —**lectic**, *adj.* katalektisch; —lectic verses, unvollständige, zu früh abbrechende, im letzten Fuß verkürzte Verse. —**lepsy**, *s.* der Schlaganfall. —**leptic**, *adj.* starrsüchtig, kataleptisch. —**logue**, I. *s.* das Verzeichnis, der Katalog. II. *v.a.* in ein Verzeichnis aufnehmen *or* eintragen. —**menia**, *s.* der Monatsfluß (*Med.*). —**plasm**, *s.* der Breiumschlag. —**pult**, *s.* die Wurfmaschine, Katapulte (*Hist.*); die Wurfgabel, gabelförmige Knabenschleuder zum Fortschnellen von Steinchen. —**ract**, I. *s.* der große Wasserfall, Stromsturz; der graue *or* weiße Star (*of the eye*); der Katarakt (*of steam engines*); to couch the —ract, den Star stechen. II. *attrib.;* —ract needle, die Starnadel (*Surg.*). —**rrh**, *see* Catarrh. —**strophe**, *s.* die Katastrophe, entscheidende Wendung, Schicksalswendung (*in a drama*); der traurige Ausgang, das schreckliche Ende; (sudden calamity) plötzlich hereinbrechendes Unheil; —strophe of a tragedy, die Katastrophe, entscheidende Wendung zum Schlimmen, der erschütternde Ausgang eines Trauerspiels.

Catarrh, *s.* der Katarrh; (cold in the head) der Schnupfen. —**al**, *adj.* katarrhalisch, Schnupfen=; —al syringe, die Nasenspritze.

Catch, I. *ir.v.a.* fangen, fassen, ergreifen; (get) bekommen, erhalten; fangen (*fire*); bekommen, kriegen (*coll.*), sich (*dat.*) zuziehen, von etwas angesteckt werden (*a disease*); (hear) vernehmen, verstehen; to — a ball (*at cricket*), auffangen; (seize upon) überfallen; to — cold, sich erkälten; to — one's death (*fam.*), sich (*dat.*) den Tod holen; to — a p.'s eye, einem ins Auge fallen, jemandes Blick begegnen; to — the Speaker's eye, vom Vorsitzenden (im engl. Parlamente u. s. w.) das Wort erhalten; to — a glimpse of, erblicken; to — hold of, ergreifen, sich an eine S. anhalten; to — it (hot), derb ausgescholten *or* durchgeprügelt werden; to — s.o. **in** *or* **telling a lie**, einen auf einer Lüge ertappen; to — the scent, wittern (*Sport*); to — a crab, beim Rudern das Ruder zu hoch einsetzen (und dabei manchmal rücklings von der Ruderbank fallen); to — a Tartar (*of a wife*), eine böse Sieben heiraten; he caught a Tartar, er ist übel angekommen; to — a train, einen Zug erreichen; not to — a train, einen Zug versäumen *or* verpassen; to — a p. at s.th., einen über einer S. ertappen; — me! (*coll.*) das fällt mir nicht ein! — me ever telling him anything again! da kannst du lange warten, ehe ich ihm je wieder etwas sage! — me doing that again, ich werde mich hüten, das wieder zu tun; a —ing air, eine leicht faßliche *or* ins Ohr fallende Melodie; a —ing illness, eine ansteckende Krankheit. II. *v.n.* (in einander greifen, anhaken (*as hooks*); einspringen (*as a spring*); to be —ing, ansteckend sein; to — **at**, haschen, greifen nach; drowning men — at straws, um sich (*dat.*) aus der Not zu helfen, versucht man alles; to — **on**, hängen bleiben (*as a dress on a nail*); to — **up**, auffangen; (overtake) einholen. III. *s.* (seizure) das Fangen, der Fang; (gain) die Beute, der Vorteil, Nutzen; der Rundgesang, die Fuge (*Mus.*); der Haken, Griff, Schnäpper (*Mech.*); der Einfall (*of a latch*); der Schließhaken, Klinkhaken (*of locks*); die Fangschürze (*Min.*); (trick) die Attrappe; die Verzahnung, die Sperre (*Horol.*); der Kugelfang (*of a ball*); der Stützhaken (*Arch.*); der Tenakel (*Typ.*); — of a door, die Türklinke; — of a bolt, der Angriff eines Riegels; by —es, stückweise, abgesetzt, wechselweise; she was a great —, sie war ein guter Fang, eine reiche Partie (*sl.*). —**er**, *s.* der Fänger, Ergreifer; cow- —er, der Kuhfänger (*Locom.*); spark- —er, der Funkenfänger (*Locom.*). —**y**, *adj.* verfänglich, heikel. *Comp.* —**-fly**, *s.* die Pechnelke (*Bot.*); das Beinkraut (*Bot.*). —**-line**, *s.* die Schlußzeile (*Typ.*). —**penny**, *s.* die wertlose Ware, der Flitterkram, Schund, Plunder, wertloser Lappen, Wisch. —**poll**, *s.* der Häscher, Büttelknecht. —**-word**, *s.* das Stichwort (*Theat.*); der Kustos (*Typ.*); das Losungswort, Schlagwort, die Parteiparole (*of a party*).

Cate, *s.* der Leckerbissen.

Catech—etical, *adj.*, —**etically**, *adv.* katechetisch. —**ize**, —**ise**, *v.a.* katechisieren, durch Fragen belehren; im Katechismus unterrichten; ins Gebet nehmen, zurechtweisen, ausschelten. —**ist**, *s.* der Religionslehrer. —**umen**, *s.* der Katechumen, der Konfirmand; (*fig.*) der Neuling.

Catechu, *s.* das Katechu.

Categor—ical, *adj.*, —**ically**, *adv.* kategorisch; bestimmt, unbedingt, entscheidend; —ical imperative, der kategorische Imperativ, das unbedingte ,Du sollst', das Sittengesetz. —**y**, *s.* die Kategorie; die Gedankenform, das Begriffsfach, Gedankenfach; (class) die Klasse, Art, der Schlag.

Catenar—ian, *see* —y. —**y**, I. *adj.* Ketten=; —y curve, die Kettenlinie. II. *s.* die Kettenlinie.

Cater, *v.n.* (to — for) (für einen) Lebensmittel anschaffen, einkaufen; (*fig.*) für jemandes Bedürfnisse sorgen. —**er**, *s.* der Proviantmeister, Einkäufer von Lebensmitteln; der Lieferant.

Caterpillar, *s.* die Raupe.

Cathartic, I. *adj.* reinigend, ausleerend, abführend. II. *s.* das Abführungsmittel (*Med.*).

Cathedra, *s.* der Bischofsstuhl; der Lehrstuhl, die Lehrkanzel, der *and* das Katheder. —**l**, I. *s.* die Stiftskirche, Kathedrale, Domkirche, der Dom. II. *attrib.;* —l music, die (Dom=)Kirchen=Musik.

Catheter, *s.* der Katheter, die Harnröhrensonde (*Surg.*).

Catholic, I. *adj.* katholisch; rechtgläubig; allgemein, universal, unparteiisch. II. *s.* (Roman —) der Katholik. —**ism**, *s.* der Katholizismus; (— faith) der katholische Glaube; *see* —ity. —**ity**, *s.* die Katholizität; Allgemeinheit, Universalität; die Vorurteilslosigkeit.

Catopt—er, *s.* das Spiegelfernrohr (*Opt.*). **—ric**, *adj.* katoptrisch; —ric light, das Reflexionslicht. **—rics**, *pl.* die Katoptrik.

Cattle, *s. & pl.* das Vieh; das Hornvieh; horned —, black —, Hornvieh; breeding —, Zuchtvieh; 6 head of —, sechs Stück Vieh. *Comp.* **—-breeder**, *s.* der Viehzüchter. **—-breeding**, *s.* die Viehzucht. **—-drover**, *s.* der Viehtreiber. **—-fair**, *s.* der Viehmarkt. **—-feeder**, *s.* der Futterschütter, Fütterungsapparat. **—-market**, *s.* der Viehmarkt. **—-plague**, *s.* die Rinderpest. **—-range**, *s.* die Viehweide, Trift. **—-run**, *s.* der Weidegrund. **—-shed**, *s.* der Viehstall. **—-show**, *s.* die Viehausstellung. **—-stall**, *s.* der Viehständer. **—-truck**, *s.* der Viehwagen.

Caucus, I. *s.* die Bürgerversammlung, in welcher die Wahlliste besprochen und festgesetzt wird; politische Versammlung. II. *v.a.* durch eine Wählerversammlung bewirken. III. *v.n.* eine Besprechung der Wahlliste abhalten.

Cauda—l, *adj.* zu einem Schwanze gehörend; —l rhyme, der Schweifreim. **—te**, *adj.* geschwänzt.

Caudle, *s.* die Kraftsuppe, der Stärkungstrank.

Caught, *imperf. & p.p. of* Catch.

Caul, *s.* die Netzhaut (*Anat.*); (net) das Haarnetz; to be born with a —, ein Glückskind sein.

Cauldron, *s. see* Caldron.

Cauli—flower, *s.* der Blumenkohl. **—form**, *adj.* stengelförmig. **—ne**, *adj.* aus dem Stengel wachsend.

Caulk, Calk, *v.a.* kalfatern (*Naut.*); Pferde beschlagen (*Farr.*); to — a boiler, die Nähte eines Kessels verstemmen. **—er**, *s.* der Kalfaterer. **—ing**, *s.* das Kalfatern.

Caus—al, I. *adj.*, **—ally**, *adv.* ursächlich. II. *s.* das Kausalwort, die Kausalpartikel (*Gram.*). **—ality**, *s.* die Kausalität, Ursache *or* Veranlassung einer Sache, der ursächliche Zusammenhang. **—ation**, *s.* die Verursachung, Ursächlichkeit. **—ative**, *adj.* eine Ursache anzeigend *or* enthaltend, als Ursache bewirkend. **—e**, I. *s.* die Ursache, der Grund; die Sache; der Prozeß (*Law*); I have given you no —e to blame me, ich habe Ihnen keinen Grund gegeben, mich zu tadeln; to give —e for suspicion, Verdacht erregen; he worked hard for the —e, er arbeitete eifrig für die gute Sache *or* unsre Sache; to die in a good —e, für eine gute Sache sterben; to plead a —e, eine Rechtssache führen; small —e court, Gerichtshof für Bagatellsachen. II. *v.a.* verursachen, veranlassen, Anlaß geben, bewirken; he —ed me to be invited, er ließ mich einladen, veranlaßte meine Einladung; to —e grief, Kummer machen, verursachen. **—eless**, *adj.*, **—elessly**, *adv.* grundlos, unbegründet; ohne Ursache. **—elessness**, *s.* die Grundlosigkeit. **—er**, *s.* der Urheber.

Causeway, *s.* die Kunststraße; die Chaussee, *see* Pavement; der Fahrdamm (*Hydr.*); rubble —, das unregelmäßige Pflaster.

Caustic, I. *adj* kaustisch, ätzend, brennend; scharf, beißend (*fig.*); (satirical) satirisch; — curve, die Brennlinie; — lye, die Ätzkalilauge; — wit, beißender Witz. II. *s.* das Ätzmittel; (— soda) Ätznatron; lunar —, der Höllenstein; to remove by —s, abätzen. **—ity**, *s.* die Ätzkraft, die Beizkraft.

Cauter—ize, —ise, *v.a.* ausbrennen, fortätzen, wegbeizen. **—ization, —isation**, *s.* das Ausbrennen. **—y**, *s.* das Brenneisen.

Cautio—n, I. *s.* die Vorsicht, Behutsamkeit; die Warnung; by way of —n, als Warnung; —n! Vorsicht (beim Überschreiten der Gleise)! (*Railw.*); to be let off with a —n, mit einer Verwarnung davonkommen; ride with —n, vorsichtig fahren! (*Cycl.*). II. *v.a.* warnen (vor einer S., against a th.). **—nary**, *adj.* warnend. **—us**, *adj.*, **—usly**, *adv.* behutsam, vorsichtig. **—usness**, *s.* die Vorsicht, Behutsamkeit. *Comp.* **—n-money**, *s.* die Kaution, das Kautiongeld.

Caval—cade, *s.* der Reiterzug, die Reitgesellschaft; der Reiteraufzug. **—ier**, I. *s.* der Reiter; (knight) der Ritter, hochherzige Kriegsmann; der Kavalier, Anhänger Karls des Ersten (von England); der Kavalier, Reiter, die Katze (*Fort.*); —iers and Roundheads, Royalisten und Puritaner. II. *adj.*, **—ierly**, *adv.* ritterlich; (brave) tapfer; (presumptuous) anmaßend; (contemptuous) verächtlich. **—ry**, I. *s.* die Kavallerie, Reiterei. II. *attrib.*; —ry charge, der Reiterangriff; —ry sergeant, der Wachtmeister; —ry spur, der Anschraubsporn; —ry sword, der Schlepp-, Reiter-säbel (*Mil.*).

Cavatina, *s.* die Kavatine (*Mus.*).

Cave, I. *s.* die Höhle. II. *v.n.*; to — in, (sink) einstürzen; (yield) nachgeben. **—rn**, *see* Cavern. *Comp.* **—-dwellers** *or* **—-men**, *pl.* die Höhlenmenschen, Höhlenbewohner.

Caveat, *s.* der Einspruch (*Law*); die Anmeldung eines einzuholenden Patents (*Amer.*); (reminder) die Warnung; to enter a —, einen Einspruch erheben, einen Hemmungsspruch tun.

Cavern, *s.* die Höhle. **—ous**, *adj.* hohl; voller Höhlen, höhlenreich.

Caves(s)on, *s.* der Kappzaum.

Caviare, *s.* der Kaviar; — to the general, (*fig.*) Kaviar fürs Volk.

Cavil, I. *v.n.* (to — at) kritteln, bekritteln; tadeln; Spitzfindigkeiten vorbringen, Einwürfe machen. II. *s.* die Spitzfindingkeit; without —, fraglos, zweifellos. **—ler**, *s.* der Tadler, (Be)krittler; (sophist) der Rechtsverdreher. **—ling**, I. *p.* & *adj.* tadelnd, spitzfindig. II. *s.* die Spitzfindigkeit. **—lingly**, *adv.* auf tadelnde, spitzfindige Weise.

Cavity, *s.* die Höhlung, Vertiefung; die Mulde.

Caw, I. *v.n.* krächzen. II. *interj.* krah, krah!

Cayenne-pepper, *s.* der spanische Pfeffer, Cayennepfeffer.

Cayman, *s.* der Kaiman.

Cease, *v.* I. *n.* (— from) aufhören (mit); ablassen (von); (rest) ruhen; to — (from) work, mit der Arbeit aufhören; — from anger, stehe ab vom Zorn (*B.*). II. *a.* aufhören; einstellen; endigen; to — work, die Arbeit einstellen; — firing! Gewehr in Ruh'! **—less**, *adj.*, **—lessly**, *adv.* unaufhörlich, unablässig.

Cedar, *s.* die Zeder; red —, die virginische Zeder. *Comp.* **—-wood**, *s.* das Zedernholz.

Cede, *v.a.* abtreten, überlassen; to — one's whole property to one's creditors, sein ganzes Vermögen den Gläubigern überlassen. **—r**, *s.* der Abtreter.

Cedilla, *s.* die Cedille (ç).

Ceil, *v.a.* eine Decke verschalen, (ein Zimmer) gipsen. **—ing**, *s.* die Decke eines Zimmers; der Weger (*Shipb.*); vaulted —ing, die gewölbte Decke; boarded —ing, getäfelte Decke; coved —ing, Spiegeldecke; plaster —ing, Gipsdecke.

Celebr—ant, *s.* zelebrierende Priester. **—ate**, *v.a.* feiern (*a birthday, etc.*); (extol) erheben, preisen; den Gottesdienst abhalten; (das Abendmahl) feiern; (die Messe) lesen. **—ated**, *adj.* berühmt. **—ation**, *s.* die Feier, das Fest; das Feiern; (—ation of the Lord's supper), die Abendmahlsfeier. **—ator**, *s.* der Lobpreiser. **—ity**, *s.* die Berühmtheit; (person) die Zelebrität, berühmte Persönlichkeit.

Celerity, *s.* die Geschwindigkeit, Schnelligkeit.

Celery, *s.* der Sellerie (*Bot.*); a stick of —, ein Blattstiel des (roh gegessenen) Sellerie.

Celestial, *adj.*, **—ly**, *adv.* himmlisch; the — body, der Himmelskörper; the — empire, China; the — globe, die Himmelskugel; — harmony, himmlischer Wohlklang; — being, der Himmelsbürger, der Engel.

Celiba—cy, *s.* die Ehelosigkeit; der *and* das Zölibat (*of the clergy*). **—te**, I. *s.* der Ehelose. II. *adj.* ehelos, unverheiratet.

Cell, *s.* die Zelle, das kleine Gemach (*Build.*); die Zelle (*Bot.*, *Biol.*, *Zool.*), (dungeon) das Kerkerloch; das Fach im Schriftkasten (*Typ.*); die Einfassung der Linse (*Opt.*); galvanic —, das galvanische Element. —**ar**, *s.* der Keller; salt-—ar, das Salzfäßchen, die Salzbüchse. —**arage**, *s.* das Kellergeschoß; die Kellermiete, das Kellergeld. —**aret**, *s.* der Flaschenkeller. —**arer**, *s.* der Kellermeister (*in a monastery, etc.*). —**ular**, *adj.* zellig, aus Zellen bestehend; —ular tissue, das Zellengewebe. —**ule**, *s.* das Zellchen. —**ulose**, I. *adj.* aus Zellen bestehend. II. *s.* der Zellstoff, die Zellulose.

Cement, I. *s.* der *and* das Zement, der Wassermörtel; der Kitt, die Kalksteinmischung; calcareous —, der hydraulische Kalk; decorator's —, der Gipszement; diamond —, der Demantkitt; mastic —, der Steinkitt; Portland —, der Portlandzement; Roman —, der Romanzement. II. *v.a.* zementieren, verkitten; verbinden, vereinigen (*fig.*); —ed masonry, das Mauerwerk in Zement. III. *v.n.*; to — well, gut binden. —**er**, *s.* der Kitter; das Band, der Vereiniger (*fig.*). *Comp.* —**ing-furnace**, *s.* der Zementierofen. —**-stone**, *s.* der Zementmergel.

Cemetery, *s.* der Kirch-, Fried-hof, Gottesacker.

Cenobite, *s.* der Klostermönch, Zönobit.

Cenotaph, *s.* das leere Ehrengrabmal.

Censer, *s.* das Rauchfaß, Weihrauchfaß.

Cens—ion, *s.* die Schätzung. —**or**, *s.* der Zensor; (—or of morals) der Sittenrichter; der strenge Kritiker, der unnachsichtige Tadler. —**orial**, *adj.* den Zensor betreffend; tadelsüchtig, streng. —**orious**, *adj.*, —**oriously**, *adv.* streng, tadelsüchtig. —**oriousness**, *s.* die Tadelsucht. —**orlike**, *adj.* streng. —**orship**, *s.* das Zensoramt, die Zensorwürde; die Zensur. —**urable**, *adj.* tadelhaft, tadelnswert. —**ure**, I. *s.* (blame) der Tadel; (reproof) der Verweis; die Kirchenstrafe (*Eccl.*); (judgment) das (richterliche) Urteil. II. *v.a.* tadeln, rügen, (be)urteilen; verurteilen (*Law*). —**us**, *s.* die Volkszählung; der Zensus.

Cent, *s.* das Hundert; der Zent (*Amer.*); per —, Prozent, aufs Hundert; to pay interest at 5 per —, Zinsen zu fünf Prozent *or* vom Hundert bezahlen; loan at 5 per —, fünfprozentige Anleihe. —**age**, *s.*; per—age, der Zinsfuß, das Prozent; der Prozentsatz; at a high per—age, zu hohen Prozenten; at a fair per—age, zu mäßigen Zinsen. —**enarian**, *s.* der Hundertjährige. —**enary**, I. *adj.* Hundert enthaltend; hundertjährig. II. *s.* das Hundert; das Jahrhundert; die Hundertjahrfeier, die hundertjährige Feier. —**ennial**, *adj.* ein Jahrhundert betreffend; alle hundert Jahre wiederkehrend. —**esimal**, *adj.* hundertteilig. —**igrade**, *adj.* hundertgradig, hundertteilig; —igrade scale, die Zentesimaleinteilung; —igrade thermometer, das hundertgradige (Celsius'sche) Thermometer. —**igram**, *s.* das Zentigramm. —**inody**, *s.* der Wegerich (*Bot.*). —**iped**(**e**), *s.* der Tausendfuß. —**ipedal**, *adj.* zu den Tausendfüßern gehörig (*Zool.*). —**ner**, *s.* der Zentner (*50 kilograms*). —**o**, *s.* die Kompilation, das Flickwerk. —**uple**, I. *adj.* hundertfach, hundertfältig. II. *v.a.* verhundertfachen. —**uplicate**, *v.a.* verhundertfältigen. —**urion**, *s.* der Befehlshaber über 100 Mann (*Rom. Hist.*); der Hauptmann von Kapernaum (*B.*). —**ury**, *s.* das Jahrhundert; das Hundert (*Rom. Hist.*).

Centaur, *s.* der Centaur, Kentaur (*Myth.*). —**y**, *s.* die Flockenblume, das Tausendgüldenkraut.

Centering, *s.* der Lehrbogen, das Bogengerüst.

Central, *adj.* zentral, den Mittelpunkt bildend; — criminal court, Gerichtshof zur Untersuchung solcher Kriminalverbrechen, welche in der Nähe von London stattfinden; — point, der Mittelpunkt. —**ity**, *s.* die Zentralität. —**ization**, *s.* die Zentralisation. —**ize**, —**ise**, *v.a.* zentralisieren.

Centre, I. *s.* der Mittelpunkt, das Zentrum; das Bogengerüst; — of attraction, der Attraktionsmittelpunkt; dead —, der tote Punkt einer Kurve; — of an arch, der Lehrbogen; — of friction, der Reibungspunkt; — of gravity, der Schwerpunkt; — of motion, der Punkt, um welchen die andern Teile eines Körpers sich drehen: — of rotation, der Drehpunkt; — of vibration, der Schwingungspunkt. II. *attrib.*; — arch, der Mittelbogen; — transom, der Mittelriegel (*Artil.*). III. *v.a.* konzentrieren, auf einen Punkt *or* in einem Punkte vereinigen. IV. *v.n.* sich in einem Punkte vereinigen, ruhen (auf). *Comp.* —**bit**, *s.* der englische Zentrumbohrer; (expanding —bit) der Universalzentrumbohrer. —**-board**, *s.* das (Kiel-)schwert (*Naut.*); —-board vessel, das Schwertboot. —**piece**, *s.* der Tafelaufsatz. —**-rail**, *s.* die Mittelschiene (*Railw.*).

Centrifugal, *adj.* vom Mittelpunkte abstrebend, auseinanderstrebend; — force, die Zentrifugalkraft.

Centripetal, *adj.* nach dem Mittelpunkte hinstrebend; — force, die Zentripetalkraft.

Centurion, *s. see* Cent—.

Ceramic, *adj.* keramisch; — art, die Keramik, Töpferkunst. —**s**, *pl.* Tonwaren.

Cer—ate, *adj.* die Wachssalbe. —**ated**, *adj.* mit Wachs überzogen. —**e**, I. *s.* die Wachshaut der Raubvögel. II. *v.a.* mit Wachs bestreichen (*obs.*). —**ement**, *s.* die Wachsleinwand, in welche die einbalsamierten Körper eingewickelt wurden. *Comp.* —**ecloth**, *s.* die Wachsleinwand; das Leichentuch.

Cereal, *adj.* Getreide-; — crops, der Ertrag *or* die Früchte des Landbaus. —**s**, *pl.* das Getreide.

Cereb—ellum, *s.* das kleine Gehirn. —**ral**, *adj.* was sich auf das Gehirn bezieht; —ral affection, die Gehirnkrankheit. —**rum**, *s.* das Gehirn.

Ceremon—ial, I. *adj.* auf eine Zeremonie sich beziehend; feierlich; —ial laws, Zeremonialgesetze. II. *s.* das Zeremoniell, die hergebrachten Förmlichkeiten. —**ious**, *adj.*, —**iously**, *adv.* feierlich; zeremoniös; mit Gepränge; you are too —ious, Sie machen zu viele Umstände; to take a —ious leave, Abschied nehmen mit peinlicher Beobachtung aller Förmlichkeiten, sich umständlich verabschieden. —**iousness**, *s.* das Feierliche, die Feierlichkeit, das Umständliche; der Hang zu Förmlichkeiten. —**y**, *s.* die Zeremonie, Förmlichkeit; (rite) die Feier, geziemende Feierlichkeiten; (usage) der Gebrauch; church —y, Kirchengebrauch; court —y, Hofgebrauch; wedding —y, Hochzeitsfeier(lichkeit); to use no —y, keine Umstände machen; don't stand on —y with me! machen Sie mit mir (ja) keine Umstände! the master of —ies, der Zeremonienmeister.

Cerise, *adj.* kirschrot.

[1]**Certain**, *adj.* (sure) sicher, gewiß; (fixed) bestimmt; (indubitable) unzweifelhaft; (trustworthy) zuverlässig; (unchanging) unveränderlich; — of your brethren, gewisse Leute Ihres Schlages; a — man went down from Jerusalem, es war ein Mensch, der ging von Jerusalem hinab (*B.*); to my — knowledge, wie ich gewiß weiß; for —, gewiß; he will come for — (will —ly come), er wird sicherlich kommen. —**ly**, *adv.* gewiß, unbezweifelt; (of course) allerdings. —**ty**, *s.* die Gewißheit; das Gewisse; (reliability) die Zuverlässigkeit; to know for a —ty *or* of a —ty, ganz sicher wissen.

[2]**Cert—ain**, *see* Certain. —**ificate**, I. *s.* das Zeugnis, die Bescheinigung; (diploma) das Diplom; —ificate of health, das Gesundheitsattestat, -zeugnis; —ificate of the customhouse, die Zollquittung; —ificate of posting, die Postquittung, der Postempfangsschein; —ificate of character, das Dienstbotenzeugnis; to suspend a skipper's —ificate, einem Schiffskapitän die Ausübung seines Berufs zeitweilig untersagen. II. *v.a.* einem ein Zeugnis geben; —ificated, mit einem Zeugnis-Diplom, &c. versehen. —**ification**, *s.* die Bescheinigung; (notice) die Meldung. —**ifier**, *s.* der Bescheiniger; der Benachrichtiger (*of news*). —**ify**, *v.a.* bescheinigen, bezeugen;

(to —ify of) benachrichtigen, versichern. —**itude**, *s.* die Gewißheit.
Cerulean, *adj.* himmel(=blau).
Ceruse, *s.* das Bleiweiß.
Cervical, *adj.* Nacken=, Hals=.
Cervine, *adj.* Hirsch=.
Cess, I. *s.* die Grundsteuer. II. *v.a.* schätzen, einschätzen; besteuern.
Cess—ation, *s.* das Aufhören, die Einstellung; der Schluß, die Beendigung; —ation of hostilities, die Einstellung der Feindseligkeiten; der Waffenstillstand. —**ion**, *s.* (yielding) das Nachgeben, Weichen; (giving up) die Abtretung, Überlassung. —**ionary**, *adj.* abtretend.
Cesspool, *s.* die Senkgrube, Abtrittsgrube, Latrine.
Cetace—a, —**ans**, *pl.* Waltiere Walfische. —**an**, —**ous**, *adj.* walfischartig.
Cetate, *s.* das cetinsaure Salz.
Chaf—e, *v.* I. *a.* warm reiben; erhitzen, erzürnen; wund reiben (*the skin, etc.*). II. *n.* toben, wüten; sich entrüsten. *Comp.* —**ing-dish**, *s.* das Kohlenbecken.
Chafer, *s.* der Käfer; the — hums, buzzes, der Käfer summt.
Chaff, I. *s.* die Spreu; das Häckfel (*of straw, etc.*); die Neckerei (*sl.*). II. *v.a.* necken (*sl.*); he can't stand —ing, er versteht keinen Spaß; I —ed him about it, ich zog ihn damit auf. *Comp.* —-**cutter**, *s.* das Häckselmesser. —-**cutting**, *adj.*; —-cutting machine, die Häckselmaschine.
Chaffer, *v.n.* schachern, handeln; to — away, verhandeln, verschachern. —**er**, *s.* der Käufer; der Händler, Schacherer; Knickerer.
Chaffinch, *s.* der Buchfink.
Chagrin, I. *s.* der Ärger, Verdruß. II. *v.a.* ärgern, kränken.
Chain, I. *s.* die Kette; die Meßkette (*Surv.*); der Zettel (*Weav.*); —s, (*pl.*) die Püttingen (*Naut.*); to put s.o. in —s, einen in Ketten legen; Albert —, die kurze, im Knopfloch getragene Uhrkette; — of buckets, die Kettenkunst (*Hydr.*); catenary —, Kette, welche die Brückenbahn einer Kettenbrücke trägt; endless —, endlose, geschlossene Kette; a — of hills (mountains), eine Hügelkette (Bergkette, Gebirgskette). II. *v.a.* (— up) anketten, an die Kette legen; fesseln (*fig.*). *Comp.* —-**bridge**, *s.* die Kettenbrücke. —-**cable**. *s.* die Ankerkette. —-**coupling**, *s.* die Kettenkuppelung (*Rail.*). —-**moulding**, *s.* das kettenartige Gesimswerk. —-**pump**, *s.* die Kettenpumpe; die Kettenkunst (*Hydr.*). —-**rod**, *s.* die Kettenrute. —-**rule**, *s.* die Kettenregel (*Arith.*). —-**shot**, *s.* die Kettenkugel. —-**stay**, *s.* die Kettenstrebe. —-**stitch**, *s.* der Kettenstich. —-**wheel**, *s.* das Kettenrad.
Chair, I. *s.* der Stuhl, Sessel; (seat) der Sitz; das Schienenlager (*Railw.*); (presidency) der Vorsitz; sedan —, Tragsessel; easy —, Lehnstuhl; folding —, Klappstuhl; upholstered —, Polsterstuhl; professorial —, Lehrstuhl; a new — was founded, eine Professur *or* ein Lehrstuhl wurde gegründet; to be called to the —, zum Vorsitzenden (einer Versammlung) berufen werden; to take the —, den Vorsitz übernehmen; Dr. J. in the —, Dr. J. als Vorsitzer *or* Vorsitzender; with Dr. J. in the —, unter dem Vorsitz von Dr. J.; to address the —, den Vorsitzenden anreden; —! —! zur Ordnung! II. *attrib.*; — back, die Stuhllehne; — bottom, der Sitz des Stuhles; — caning, das Rohrflechten; — cover, der Stuhlüberzug. III. *v.a.* triumphierend umhertragen. *Comp.* —**man**, *s.* der Vorsitzende, Vorsitzer; der Sänftenträger (*for sedan —s*); —man of the board of directors, Vorsitzende des Verwaltungsrates; —man and committee, Vorsitzer und Beisitzer. —**manship**, *s.* der Vorsitz. —-**rail**, *s.* die Stuhlschiene.
Chaise, *s.* die Halbkutsche, Chaise.
Chalcedony, *s.* der Chalcedon (*Min.*).
Chalcograph—er, *s.* der Kupferstecher. —**y**, *s.* die Kupferstecherkunst.
Chaldron, *s.* ein Kohlenmaß von 36 Bushels.
Chalice, *s.* der Kelch; der Abendmahlskelch.
Chalk, I. *s.* die Kreide; der Kreidestift; —s, bunte Stifte; — formation, das Kreidegebirge; black —, Zeichenkreide; red —, der Rötel, der Rotstift; powdered —, das Kreidemehl; not by a long —, lange nicht (*sl.*). II. *attrib.*; — earth, die Kalkerde; — marl, der Kalkmergel. III. *v.a.* mit Kreide bezeichnen; to — out, entwerfen (*a plan, etc.*), vorzeichnen (*a way, etc.*); to — down (*or* up), ankreiden, auf Rechnung setzen. —**iness**, *s.* das kreidige Wesen. —**y**, *adj.* kreidig; —y clay, der Mergel. *Comp.* —-**cutter**, *s.* der Kreidegräber. —-**holder**, *s.* der Stifthalter (*Draw.*). —-**line**, *s.* die Schlagschnur. —-**pit**, *s.* die Kreidegrube.
Challenge, I. *s.* die Herausforderung (*to fight, etc.*); die Aufforderung (*to a contest*); die Anrufung (*of a sentry, etc.*); (claim) der Anspruch; die Einwendung, Verwerfung (*of jurymen, etc.*); der Anschlag (*Sport*). II. *v.a.* herausfordern; anrufen (*Mil.*); zur Verantwortung ziehen, vorfordern; (claim) beanspruchen; verwerfen, Einwendungen machen; (dispute) bestreiten; (invite) auffordern; — cup, der Preisbecher (um welchen bei jedem neuen Wettspiel aufs neue gekämpft wird), Wanderpreis; — plate, das als Kampfpreis ausgesetzte Silber, Preissilber(geschirr). —**r**, *s.* der Herausforderer; der Verwerfer (*Law*).
Chalybeate, *adj.* stahlhaltig; — water, das Stahlwasser.
Chamade, *s.* das Ergebungssignal, die Schamade (*Mil.*).
Chamber, I. *s.* die Kammer, das Zimmer, Gemach; (court) das Kammergericht, die Kammer; (council) die Kammer; das Kammerstück (*Mil.*); der Nachttopf; die Kammer (*of a gun*); exploding —, die Kammer einer Mine; — of a pump, der Stiefel; — of commerce, Handelskammer; — of a lock, Schleusenkammer (*Hydr.*). II. *v.n.* ein liederliches Leben führen (*obs.*). —**ed**, *adj.* mit Kammern versehen, =kammerig. —**lain**, *s.* der Kammerherr; der Kammerdiener; the Lord High —lain, der Lord Kämmerer; the Lord —lain, der Oberkammerherr. —**s**, *pl.* (vornehme) Junggesellenwohnung. *Comp.* —-**council**, *s.* die vertraute Beratung. —-**counsel**, *s.* der Rechtsfreund, Rechtskonsulent; der geheime Rat. —-**fellow**, *s.* der Stubengenosse. —-**maid**, *s.* das Zimmermädchen. —-**organ**, *s.* die Zimmerorgel. —(-**pot**), *s.* der Nachttopf. —-**practice**, *s.* die Rechtskonsulentenpraxis.
Chameleon, *s.* das Chamäleon. *Comp.* —-**like**, *adj.* veränderlich in der Farbe (wie ein Chamäleon), chamäleonartig.
Chamfer, I. *v.n.* auskehlen, kannelieren (*Arch.*); verstäben (*a column*); abschärfen (*a cornice*). II. *s.* die Auskehlung, Hohlrinne an einer Säule; die abgestoßene Kante, Schrägkante (*Carp.*). —**ing**, *s.* das Abkanten, die Abschrägung. *Comp.* —**ing-tool**, *s.* zweischneidiger Senkbohrer.
Chamois, *s.* die Gemse; (— leather) das Sämischleder.
Champ, *v.a.* kauen; to — the bit, am Gebiß kauen; in die Zügel schäumen (*poet.*).
Champagne, *s.* der Champagner; dry —, herber Ch.; sparkling —, moussierender Ch.; still —, nicht moussierender Ch.; iced —, Ch. in Eis *or* auf Eis.
Champ—aign, I. *adj.* flach, eben. II. *s.* die Ebene. —**ion**, I. *s.* der Kämpe, Verfechter, Vorkämpfer; (defender) der Verteidiger; (one who excels) der Meister; —ion boxer, der beste Boxer; —ion of the truth, Wahrheitskämpe; king's —ion, der Kämpe des Königs. II. *v.a.* herausfordern; beschützen, verteidigen. —**ionship**, *s.* die Verteidigung, Verfechtung, das Eintreten (für); die Meisterschaft.
Chance, I. *s.* der Zufall; (fate) das Schicksal, Los; (fortune) das Glück; (opportunity) die Gelegen-

heit; (— event) das Ereignis; (success) der Erfolg; (possibility) die Möglichkeit; (likelihood) die Wahrscheinlichkeit; the —s of war, das Kriegsglück; game of —, ein Glücksspiel; to run a bad —, schlechte Aussichten haben; not a ghost of a —, not the slightest —, nicht die geringste Aussicht; by —, von ungefähr, zufällig; to look to the main —, auf den persönlichen Vorteil sehen; a mere —, ein bloßer Zufall; an even —, eine gleiche Chance, Aussicht; there is no — that . . ., es ist nicht anzunehmen, daß . . .; the —s are in your favour, die Wahrscheinlichkeit ist auf eurer Seite; give him a —! gieb ihm freie Bahn! laß es ihn doch einmal versuchen! to take one's — of a th., es darauf *or* auf eine S. ankommen lassen, es wagen. II. *v.a.* wagen, versuchen (*coll.*). III. *v.n.* sich ereignen; it —d, es geschah, ereignete sich; I —d to meet him, ich traf ihn zufällig; if my letter should — to be lost, falls mein Brief verloren gegangen sein sollte; I —d to be there when she came, es traf sich gerade, daß ich dort war, als sie ankam; to — upon, auf (eine S.) stoßen. IV. *adj.* zufällig; the — comer, der zufällig Kommende; a — customer, ein zufälliger Kunde.

Chancel, *s.* der Altarplatz, die Chorschranke. —**lor**, *s.* der Kanzler; der Oberrichter; —lor of a cathedral, Kanzler eines Domstifts; —lor of a diocese, der Rechtskonsulent eines Bischofs; imperial —lor, der Reichskanzler; —lor of the Exchequer, der Schatzkanzler; Lord High —lor, der Kanzler (*highest legal authority in England*); —lor of a university, der Rektor einer Universität. —**lorship**, *s.* das Amt *or* die Würde eines Kanzlers *or* Rektors.

Chancery, *s.* das Kanzleigericht; court of —, der oberste Gerichtshof; — suit, ein Rechtsstreit im Kanzleigerichte; bill in —, die Rechtsklage bei dem Kanzleigerichte; masters in —, die Beisitzer, Referenten des Kanzleigerichts; a ward in —, vom Kanzleigericht unter Vormundschaft gehaltenes Kind; to get a p.'s head into —, (beim Ringkampf) den Kopf des Gegners unter den Arm bekommen (*also fig.*); to sit in —, Kanzleirichter sein.

Chancr—e, *s.* der Schanker. —**ous**, *adj.* mit dem Schanker behaftet.

Chand—elier, *s.* der Hängeleuchter, Kronleuchter; das Bockgestell (*Fort.*). —**ler**, *s.* der Lichtzieher; der Lichthändler; der Krämer; ship's —ler, der Schiffsproviantkrämer; corn- —ler, der Kornhändler. —**lery**, *s.* Fettwaren; das Krämergeschäft.

Change, I. *v.a.* (alter) ändern, verändern; (exchange) (ans)tauschen, vertauschen, wechseln; to — colour, sich entfärben, (grow red) rot werden; to — one's clothes, to — (*coll.*), sich umziehen, sich umkleiden; to — hands, in andere Hände übergehen; to — one's lodgings, eine andere Wohnung beziehen; to — one's mind, sich anders besinnen, andern Sinnes werden; to — money, Geld wechseln; to — for, vertauschen gegen; to — from . . . into . . ., verwandeln aus . . . in . . . II. *v.n.* sich ändern, anders werden; the moon —s, wir haben Mondwechsel; how the world —s! wie sich die Welt doch ändert! — for Cambridge, umsteigen nach Cambridge! (*Railw.*). III. *s.* die Änderung, Veränderung; der Wechsel; die Abwechselung; der Tausch (*C.L.*); (small money) das Kleingeld; (exchange) die Börse; (conversion) die Bekehrung; (improvement) die Besserung; —s of many sorts, mancherlei Veränderungen; I have no — about me, ich habe kein Kleingeld bei mir; give me —, please, bitte, geben Sie mir heraus; have you got — for a pound? können Sie mir ein Pfund wechseln? grammatical —, der grammatische Wechsel (*Gramm.*); — of air, die Luftveränderung; — of carriage, der Wagenwechsel (*Rail.*); a — of clothes, ein zweiter Anzug (zum Wechseln); — of life, die Übergangsperiode im Leben; — of the tide, die Widerzeit, der Wechsel von Ebbe und Flut; — of the moon, der Mondwechsel; a decided — for the better in the condition of, eine entscheidende Wendung zum Bessern im Befinden von; to ring the —s, eine Reihe Glocken melodisch läuten, wechselläuten (*lit.*); dieselbe Sache in immer neuen Formen behandeln, immer bei der alten Leier bleiben (*fig.*). —**ability**, *s.* die Veränderlichkeit. —**able**, *adj.*, —**ably**, *adv.* veränderlich, wandelbar; schillernd (*in colour*); wankelmütig (*of persons*); —able weather, unbeständiges Wetter. —**ableness**, *s.* die Veränderlichkeit, Unbeständigkeit; der Wankelmut, die Neigung zur Veränderung. —**ful**, *adj.* unbeständig; unzuverlässig; veränderlich; —ful as a child, wankelmütig wie ein Kind; —ful as the weather, veränderlich *or* wechselvoll wie das Wetter. —**less**, *adj.* unveränderlich; beständig. —**ling**, *s.* der Wechselbalg, das untergeschobene Kind. —**r**, *s.* der Veränderer; der Unbeständige; money- —r, der (Geld-)Wechsler.

Channel, I. *s.* der Kanal; das Flußbett; die Röhre, Rinne, Gosse; (furrow) die Furche; die Auskehlung, Kannelierung, Hohlrinne (*Arch.*); die Furche (*Mas.*); Mittel und Weg einer Mitteilung (*fig.*); —s of commerce, Handelswege; cross— services, Schiffsverkehr zwischen England und Frankreich. II. *v.a.* Rinnen machen, Furchen auskehlen; to — out, rinnenförmig aushöhlen.

Chant, I. *s.* der Gesang, die Weise; eine besondere Art des Kirchengesangs. II. *v.a.* besingen; (*also v.n.*) singen (die Psalmen, Liturgie, 2c., wie man sie in den englischen Kathedralen singt). —**er**, *s.* der Sänger; der Vorsänger in einer Domkirche, Kantor; die Diskantpfeife des Dudelsacks (*Mus.*). —**ry**, *s.* die Stiftung von Seelenmessen; Seelenmessen singende Priester; die kleine Kapelle in einer Kathedrale.

Chao—s, *s.* das Chaos, Urgemisch; der Wirrwarr (*fig.*). —**tic**, *adj.* chaotisch, wüst.

[1]**Chap**, I. *s.* der Spalt, Sprung, Riß. II. *v.a.* aufspringen, spalten; cold, dry winds — the hands and lips, von kalten, trockenen Winden springen die Hände und Lippen auf. —**ped**, *p.p. & adj.* gespalten, offen.

[2]**Chap**, *s.* der Kinnbacken. —**s**, *pl.* die Kinnbacken, der Rachen. *Comp.* —**fallen**, *adj.* mit herunterhängendem Maule; niedergeschlagen (*sl.*).

[3]**Chap**, *s.* der Bursche, Geselle, Kerl (*coll.*); old —, alter Junge (*sl.*). *Comp.* —**book**, *s.* das Volksbuch, das kleine billige Buch, welches kolportiert wird. —**man**, *s.* der Käufer, Kunde; der Verkäufer.

Chap—el, I. *s.* die Kapelle; das Gotteshaus (*of dissenters*); die Druckerei (*Print.*); to attend —el regularly, regelmäßig dem Gottesdienst beiwohnen; church versus —el, Hochkirche gegen Sekten; —el of ease, die Filialkirche. II. *v.a.*; to —el a ship, eine Eule fangen (*Naut.*). —**eron**, *s.* die Anstandsdame, Duenna; die Kappe (*obs.*); das Barrett der Ritter des Hosenbandordens; Kopfschmuck der Pferde (*obs.*). II. *v.a.* chaperonnieren, ein junges Mädchen begleiten, bemuttern. —**lain**, *s.* der Kaplan, der Hausprediger; acting chaplain to his Majesty's forces, Feldprediger, Feldgeistlicher; Schiffsgeistlicher. —**laincy**, *s.* die Kaplanstelle. —**let**, *s.* der Kranz; der Rosenkranz (*also Arch.*); (—elet) das Paternosterwerk (*Hydr.*); der Steigbügelriemen mit den Bügeln (*Saddl.*).

Chapt—er, I. *s.* das Kapitel (*also fig. & Eccl.*); and so on to the end of the —er, und so weiter bis ans Ende; to give —er and verse for a statement, eine Behauptung aufs genauste *or* bis in alle Einzelheiten begründen. II. *v.a.* in Kapitel teilen. —**rel**, *s.* der Knauf, Kämpfer. *Comp.* —**er-house**, *s.* das Kapitelhaus.

[1]**Char, Chare**, *v.n.* im Tagelohn arbeiten; allerlei Hausarbeit im fremden Hause tun; to go out

—ring, Tagearbeit außer seinem eigenen Hause verrichten, scheuern gehen. *Comp.* **—-woman**, *s.* die Tagelöhnerin für häusliche Arbeiten, Scheuerfrau, Arbeitsfrau.

²Char, *v.a.* verkohlen. *Comp.* **—coal**, *see* Charcoal. **—-oven**, *s.* der Torfkohlenofen.

Char-à-bancs, *s.* der Personenwagen (für größere Ausflüge), der Kremser.

Character, I. *s.* (sign) das Zeichen; (letter) das Schriftzeichen, der Buchstabe; (figure) die Ziffer, das Zahlzeichen; (moral character) der Charakter, die Gemütsart, persönliche Eigenschaft; die Rolle (*Theat.*); (written —) das Zeugnis; (reputation) der Ruf; (nature) die Art, Beschaffenheit; (—istic) das Merkmal, Kennzeichen; (strange person) das Original, der Sonderling; his intellectual —, seine geistige Begabung; his moral —, sein Charakter, seine Gemütsart; the — of the handwriting, die Beschaffenheit der Handschrift; strange —s, sonderbare Schriftzüge; she has not a good —, her — is not good, sie steht in keinem guten Rufe; she has a ten years' —, sie hat zehn Jahre bei derselben Herrschaft gedient; in — with, übereinstimmend mit, passend zu; to appear in —, einen Charakteranzug tragen, maskiert sein; out of all —, völlig unpassend; public —s, öffentliche Charaktere, Personen von öffentlicher Stellung *or* Berühmtheit; to give a p. a high —, eine vorteilhafte Schilderung von einem machen. II. *v.a.* einschreiben; eingraben. **—istic**, I. *adj.*, **—istically**, *adv.* charakteristisch; bezeichnend (für); this is —istic of the man, es ist bezeichnend für den Mann, dies charakterisiert den Mann; generosity is —istic of true bravery, Großmut ist ein Merkmal wahrer Tapferkeit; —istic shell, die Leitmuschel. II. *s.* das Merkmal, Kennzeichen; der Charakterbuchstabe (*of a word*); die Kennziffer, der Exponent (*of a logarithm*); the principal —istic, das Hauptkennzeichen, die hervorstechende Eigentümlichkeit; one of the chief —istics, eine der Haupteigentümlichkeiten, einer der wichtigsten Kennzüge. **—ization**, **—isation**, *s.* das Charakterisieren, die Charakteristik; die künstlerliche Darstellung von Charakteren. **—ize**, **—ise**, *v.a.* charakterisieren; kennzeichnen; eingehend schildern; (judge) beurteilen; (stamp) einprägen (*obs.*). **—less**, *adj.* ohne besonderes Kennzeichen; ohne Charakter, charakterlos. **—y**, *s.* das Schriftzeichen.

Charade, *s.* das Silbenrätsel, die Scharade.

Charcoal, I. *s.* die Holzkohle; bone —, Knochenkohle, Tierkohle. II. *attrib.*; — dust, der Kohlenstaub; — filter, der Kohlenfilter; — heap, der liegende Kohlenmeiler; — pile, der Kohlenmeiler; — point, die Kohlenspitze (*Elect.*). **—ing**, *s.* das Filtrieren durch Knochenkohle (*Sug. ref.*). *Comp.* **—-burner**, *s.* der Köhler, Kohlenbrenner. **—-burning**, *s.* die Kohlenbrennerei. **—-pencil**, *s.* die Reißkohle (*Art*); der Kohlenstift (*Elect.*).

Chard, *s.* innerer Blattstiel der Artischoke.

Charge, I. *s.* (load) die Ladung, Last; die Ladung (*of a gun, a mine, battery, etc.*); (care) die Verwahrung; (office) die Stelle, das Amt; (person under —) der Schützling, Mündel; (thing under —) die Hinterlage; (expense) die Kosten; (price) der Preis; die Anrede, Ermahnung (*of a bishop to his clergy, of a judge to the jury*); (command) der Befehl; das Zeichen zum Angriff, der Angriff (*Mil.*); (accusation) die Beschuldigung; die Beschickung, der Einsatz (*Metall.*); to give a th. in — of a p., eine Sache einem andern zur Aufbewahrung übergeben; to give a child in — to a p., ein Kind der Aufsicht eines andern anvertrauen; to give a p. in —, einen festnehmen lassen; to have in —, beauftragt sein mit, in Verwahrung haben; to take — of, übernehmen, sorgen für; to take a p. in —, einen festnehmen; free of —, kostenlos, unberechnet; no —! frei! unentgeltlich! no — for admission! der Eintritt frei! the pastor's —, die dem Pastor anvertrauten Pfarrkinder; the heads of the —, die Klagepunkte; to lay s.th. to a p.'s —, einen einer Sache beschuldigen, einem etwas zur Last legen; to give a p. strict — (to . . .), einem ernstlich empfehlen; — of bursting powder, die Sprengladung; to sound the —, das Signal zum Angriff geben. II. *attrib.*; —s book, das Spesenbuch. III. *v.a.* beladen, belasten (*also fig.*); laden (*a gun, an electric battery, etc.*); füllen (*glasses*); Auftrag erteilen, beauftragen (*with a duty, etc.*); (entrust) anvertrauen; (command) befehlen; (enjoin) anbefehlen; (inculcate) ans Herz legen, einschärfen; (warn) mahnen; (accuse) beschuldigen; (exhort) anreden, ermahnen; (demand) fordern; anschreiben (*in an account*); (attack) angreifen; to — a p. with theft, einen eines Diebstahls beschuldigen; he was —d with having picked the pockets of a lady, er wurde des Taschendiebstahls bei einer Dame angeklagt; the judge —d the jury, der Richter hielt eine (belehrende) Anrede an die Geschworenen; to — to a p.'s account, einen (mit etwas) debitieren, jemandes Konto belasten; to — o.s. with a matter, ein Geschäft selbst übernehmen; how much do you — for it? wie viel nehmen *or* rechnen Sie dafür? IV. *v.n.* einen Angriff machen; to — with fixed bayonets, mit gefälltem Seitengewehr angreifen; prepare to —! Gewehr zur Attacke rechts! —! fällt das Gewehr! **—able**, *adj.* (—able to) zuzuschreiben, zuzurechnen; (responsible) verantwortlich; to be —able to, (einem 2c.) zur Last fallen; this mistake is —able to you, Sie sind für diesen Fehler verantwortlich; his writings are —able with negligence, seinen Schriften wirft man mit Recht Nachlässigkeit vor; wine is —able with a duty, der Wein bezahlt eine Abgabe, der Wein ist versteuerbar (mit . . .). **—r**, *s.* die Ladevorrichtung (*Gun., Min.*); (horse) das Schlachtroß; (dish) die große Schale, Schüssel; der große Napf (*B.*); (accuser) der Kläger. **—s**, I. *pl.* die Belastung, die Kosten, Unkosten, Spesen (*C. L.*); —s to be deducted, ab an Unkosten; forwarding —s, Speditionskosten; incidental —s, darauf lastende Unkosten; all —s included, mit Einschluß aller Kosten.

Chargé-d'affaires, *s.* der Geschäftsträger.

Charging, *s.* die Beladung; die Beschickung (*Metall.*); der Bajonettangriff. *Comp.* **—-hole**, *s.* die Einsatztür.

Char—ily, *adv.* (cautiously) behutsam, vorsichtig; (sparingly) sparsam, spärlich, mäßig. **—iness**, *s.* die Behutsamkeit, Bedenklichkeit. **—y**, *see* Chary.

Chariot, *s.* der Wagen; die Halbkutsche; (war —) der Kriegswagen; (triumphal car) der Triumphwagen; (car of state) der Staatswagen. **—eer**, *s.* der Wagenlenker (*of a war —*); der Fuhrmann (*poet. or hum.*). *Comp.* **—-race**, *s.* das Wagenrennen.

Charit—able, *adj.*, **—ably**, *adv.* (liberal) wohltätig, mild, freigebig; (loving) liebreich; (kind) gütig; (favourable) günstig; a —able construction (*of a p.'s words, actions, etc.*), eine freundliche, günstige Auslegung; a —able institution, eine milde Stiftung; —able purpose, guter mild(tätig)er Zweck. **—ableness**, *s.* die Mildtätigkeit; Wohltätigkeit; die Nachsicht; die Günstigkeit. **—ies**, *pl.* milde Gaben, Almosen; milde Stiftungen. **—y**, *s.* (love) die (werktätige) Liebe (*B.*); die Mildtätigkeit; (liberality) die Freigebigkeit; (alms) die Almosen; (—able gift) die milde Gabe; (—able foundation) die milde Stiftung; (mercifulness) die Barmherzigkeit; —y begins at home, jeder ist sich selbst der Nächste (*prov.*); to be in —y with all men, eine wohlwollende Gesinnung gegen alle Menschen hegen; to do out of —y, for —y's sake, für Gotteslohn, umsonst tun; sister of —y, die barmherzige Schwester; —y to one's neighbour, das Liebeswerk; —y school, die Armenschule, Freischule; —y Commission, der Stiftungsrat, Aufsichtsrat über die milden Stiftungen (unter ihnen viele große englische Schulen); —y Organization Society, der Wohltätigkeitsverein, (*sometimes* =) Verein gegen Hausbettelei.

Charivari, *s.* die Katzenmusik.

Charlatan, *s.* (quack) der Quacksalber; der Charlatan. **—ry**, *s.* die Charlatanerie, Quacksalberei.

Charm, I. *s.* das Zaubermittel; der Zauber, Reiz (*fig.*); to break the —, den Zauber lösen. II. *v.a.* bezaubern, behexen; entzücken, reizen, fesseln (*fig.*); music the fiercest grief can —, Musik kann den tiefsten Kummer beschwören *or* lindern; to have *or* bear a —ed life, fest *or* gefeit sein; the —ed ring, der Zauberring; to — against (evil), durch Zaubermittel vor (einem Übel) schützen; to — away, wegzaubern; —ed with, bezaubert von, entzückt von. **—er**, *s.* der Zauberer, die Zaub(r)erin (*also fig.*); my —er, mein Schatz. **—ing**, *adj.*, **—ingly**, *adv.* bezaubernd, reizend. **—ingness**, *s.* der Reiz.

Charnel-house, *s.* das Beinhaus.

Chart, *s.* die Tabelle, Karte; die Seekarte; — of the metric system, die Maßgewichtstafel; Mercator's —, die reduzierte *or* Merkator'sche Karte. **—er**, I. *s.* (deed) die Urkunde (wodurch ein Privilegium bewilligt wird); (contract) der Vertrag, Kontrakt; (grant) der Gnadenbrief; (privilege) der Freibrief, das Privilegium; die Schiffsmiete (*Naut.*); (right) das Recht; —er of the forest, die Forstgesetze; —er of incorporation, der Schutzbrief, das Patent; —er of the constitution, die Verfassungsurkunde; a royal —er, ein königlicher Freibrief. II. privilegieren, mit Vorrechten ausstatten; mieten (*a ship*); befrachten, verfrachten (*a ship*); —ered accountant, geprüfter Rechnungsrevisor; —ered company, privilegierte, durch Freibrief geschützte Gesellschaft; —ered rights, Privilegien. **—ism**, *s.* der Chartismus (in England). **—ists**, *pl.* die Chartisten. *Comp.* **—erhouse**, *s.* die Kartause; —erhouse School, die ehemals in dem alten Londoner Kartäuserkloster befindliche, jetzt nach Godalming in Surrey verlegte höhere Knabenschule. **—er-party**, *s.* die Charterpartie, Certepartie, der Frachtkontrakt.

Chary, *adj.* sparsam, spärlich, knapp; (cautious) behutsam, vorsichtig.

Chasable, *adj.* jagdbar (*obs.*).

[1]**Chase**, I. *s.* die Jagd; das gejagte Wild; die Verfolgung (*of persons, etc.*); (hunting-ground) das Jagdrevier; a wild-goose —, eine planlose *or* erfolglose Verfolgung; I sent him on a wild-goose —, ich schickte ihn in den April; to follow the —, die Jagd verfolgen; to give —, Jagd machen (auf einen *or* eine S.). II. *v.a.* jagen, Jagd machen auf (*acc.*); (— away) verjagen, vertreiben; (pursue) nachsetzen, verfolgen. **—r**, *s.* der Jäger, Verfolger; jagdmachendes Schiff. *Comp.* **—-gun**, *s.* das Jagdstück. **—-port**, *s.* die Jagdpforte.

[2]**Chas—e**, I. *s.* der Formrahmen; der Kupferstecherrahmen. II. *v.a.* treiben, ziselieren, ausmeißeln; —ed work, getriebene Arbeit. **—er**, *s.* der Graveur (*Engr.*). **—ing**, *s.* das Treiben, Austiefen (*of metals*); das Ziselieren (*Engr.*); die ziselierte, getriebene Arbeit. *Comp.* **—ing-hammer**, *s.* der Treibhammer (*Metall.*). **—ing-tools**, *pl.* das Ziselierwerkzeug.

[3]**Chase**, *s.* langes Feld eines Geschützrohrs; der Einschnitt, die Rinne, Furche.

Chasm, *s.* die Kluft, Spalte, der Schlund.

Chast—e, *adj.*, **—ely**, *adv.* keusch, züchtig; rein (*as language*); a —e passion, eine reine Liebe. **—en**, *v.a.* züchtigen, strafen; durch auferlegte Strafe reinigen; (discipline) kasteien; (humble) demütigen. **—ened**, *adj.* geläutert (durch Trübsal gereinigt). **—ener**, *s.* der Züchtiger. **—ening**, *s.* die Züchtigung. **—isable**, *adj.* strafbar. **—ise**, *v.a.* züchtigen, strafen. **—isement**, *s.* die Züchtigung, Strafe. **—iser**, *s.* der Züchtiger. **—ity**, *s.* die Keuschheit, Züchtigkeit; die Reinheit (*of style*); to take the vow of —ity, das Gelübde der Keuschheit ablegen. *Comp.* **—e-eyed**, *adj.* keusch blickend.

Chasuble, *s.* das Meßgewand.

Chat, I. *v.n.* plaudern, schwatzen. II. *s.* das Geplauder. **—ter**, I. *v.n.* (gabble) schnattern; (twitter) zwitschern; (talk) schwatzen, plappern, plaudern; klappern; his teeth are —tering with cold, er klappert vor Kälte mit den Zähnen. II. *v.a.;* to —ter nonsense, dummes Zeug reden, Blödsinn schwatzen. III. *s.* das Geplapper, Geschwätz. **—terer**, *s.* der Schwätzer; der Seidenschwanz (*Orn.*). **—tering**, *s.* das Schnattern (der Gänse); das Zwitschern (der Vögel); das Geschwätz, Geplauder; —tering of the teeth, das Zähneklappern. **—ty**, *adj.* geschwätzig, plauderhaft. *Comp.* **—terbox**, *s.* die Plaudertasche (*coll.*).

Chauffeur, *m.* der Autolenker, Kraftwagenführer.

Chattel, *s.* das bewegliche und unbewegliche Gut, die Habe; —s personal, das bewegliche Gut, die fahrende Habe; goods and —s, Hab und Gut.

Cheap, *adj.*, **—ly**, *adv.* wohlfeil, billig; gering, gemein; to get off —ly, mit einem blauen Auge davonkommen; — for what it is, billig für das, was es ist, verhältnismäßig billig; a — pennyworth, ein billiger Einkauf; to make o. s. —, sich wegwerfen; to hold (a th.) —, gering schätzen; — beauty, leicht zu erkaufende Schönheit; dirt —, spottwohlfeil (*vulg.*); — jack, der Marktschreier. **—en**, *v.a.* handeln, dingen, feilschen; herabsetzen. **—ness**, *s.* die Wohlfeilheit.

Cheat, I. *s.* der Betrug; (person) der Betrüger, Schwindler. II. *v.a.* betrügen, anführen; to — a p. into a belief, einen mit List glauben machen; to — a p. out of a th., einen um eine S. betrügen. **—ing**, *s.* die Betrügerei.

Check, I. *s.* (reprimand) der Verweis, die Zurechtweisung; (hindrance) das Hindernis, der Einhalt, die Hemmung; (curb) der Zügel; der Unfall, die Schlappe (*Mil.*); das Gegenzeichen; der Kontrazettel (*C. L.*); (cheque) die Bankanweisung, der Scheck; die Kontramarke (*in the theatre*); die Marke, das Billet (*Railw., Amer.*); das karrierte Tuch; das Schach (*Chess*); der Verschlußlaut; hard —, tonloser Verschlußlaut (*P, T, K*), Tenuis; soft —, tönender Verschlußlaut (*B, D, G*), Media; Clerk of the —, der Oberkontrolleur; to keep a p. in —, einen im Zaume halten; the British Parliament is a — to the royal authority, das britische Parlament hält die Macht des Königtums im Zaum; —! Schach dem König! (*Chess*). II. *attrib.;* — account, das Gegenregister, die Kontrolle (*C. L.*); — braces, die Schwungriemen. III. *v.a.* Einhalt tun, einhalten, hemmen; zähmen, bändigen; verweisen; kontrollieren; Schriften, Rechnungen gegen einander vergleichen; prüfen, nachrechnen, untersuchen; to — one's anger, seinen Zorn zurückhalten; to — one's appetite, seine Begierden überwinden; to — an invoice, eine Faktura auf ihre Richtigkeit nachprüfen. III. *v.n.* Schach bieten. **—er, Chequer**, I. *s.* das gewürfelte Zeug. II. *v.a.* scheckig, würfelig, bunt machen, karrieren buntscheckig verzieren; mischen, untermischen; our life is —ered with good and evil, unser Leben ist mit Gutem und Bösem untermischt; —ed career, an Wechselfällen reiches Leben. *Comp.* **—-book**, *s.* das Kontrollbuch (*C. L.*); *see* Cheque-—. **—mate**, I. *s.* das Schachmatt. II. *v.a.* schachmatt machen. **—-rein**, *s.* kurzer Pferdezügel. **—-string**, *s.* die Zugschnur (*in carriages, etc.*). **—-taker**, *s.* der Kontramarkenabnehmer (*Theat.*).

Cheek, I. *s.* die Backe, Wange; die Dreistigkeit, Frechheit (*sl.*); der Klobenarm, die Scherwange (*of a balance*); door —, der Türpfosten; die Laffettenwand (*of a gun carriage*); — of a printing-press, die Preßwand; — of a block, a pulley, der Backen eines Blockes; none of your —! halte deinen Schnabel (*vulg.*). II. *attrib.*; — rail, die Backenschiene (*Railw.*). III. *v.a.*; to — a p., einen frech anreden *or* behandeln (*vulg.*). **—y**, *adj.* frech (*sl.*); —y fellow, frecher Dachs (*sl.*). *Comp.* **—-bone**, *s.* der Backenknochen. **—-piece**, *s.* der Kolbenbacken (*Gun.*).

Cheep, *v.n.* zirpen, piepen.

Cheer, I. *s.* der Freudenruf; (applause) der Beifallsruf; (food) die Bewirtung, Speise; (state of feeling) der Mut; (gaiety) die Fröhlichkeit; three —s for, ein dreifaches donnerndes Hoch auf! (*acc.*); the toast was given with three —s, die Gesundheit wurde mit dreimaligem Hoch ausgebracht; the sailors gave three —s, die Matrosen riefen dreimal hurra; to be of good —, guten, heitern Mutes sein; filled with good —, mit guter Speise (an)gefüllt; what —? was giebt's? wie geht's? II. *v.a.* freudig begrüßen; (— up) aufmuntern, ermuntern; good news —s the heart, gute Nachricht erfreut das Herz. III. *v.n.* Vivat rufen; they —ed lustily, sie riefen aus voller Kehle Lebehoch; — up! nur Mut! lustig! **—ful**, *adj.*, **—fully**, *adv.* heiter, munter, froh; to look —ful, ein frohes Gesicht machen; to do —fully, mit frohem Mute tun. **—fulness**, *s.* die Heiterkeit, der Frohsinn. **—ily**, *see* —y. **—iness**, *s.* der Frohsinn, die Fröhlichkeit. **—ing**, *adj.*, **—ingly**, *adv.* erfreuend, ermunternd, erheiternd. **—less**, *adj.*, **—lessly**, *adv.* freudlos; unerfreulich, traurig; mutlos; trostlos. **—lessness**, *s.* die Freud(en)losigkeit. **—y**, *adj.* heiter, froh; aufheiternd, erfreulich.

Chees—e, *s.* der Käse; cream —e, Rahmkäse; they are as unlike as chalk and —e, sie gleichen einander wie Tag und Nacht. **—y**, *adj.* käsig. *Comp.* **—e-cake**, *s.* der Quarkkuchen, eine Art Eierkuchen mit Käse. **—e-curd**, *s.* der Käsequark. **—e-maker**, *s.* der Senn, Senner, Älpler (*in the Alps*). **—e-mite**, *s.* die Käsemilbe. **—e-monger**, *s.* der Käsehändler. **—e-paring**, I. *s.* die Käserinde; die Knauserei, Knickerei. II. *adj.* sparsam, knickerig, knauserig. **—e-press**, *s.* die Käsepresse. **—e-scoop**, *s.* der Käsestecher, Käsehobel. **—e-stand**, *s.* der Käseteller. **—e-toaster**, *s.* der Käseröster.

Cheffonier, *s.* kleinerer Tisch mit mehreren Platten übereinander.

Cheiropter—a, *pl.* flatterfüßige Tiere. **—ous**, *adj.* flatterfüßig.

Chemi—cal, *adj.*, **—cally**, *adv.* chemisch; —cal colours, die Tafelfarben; —cal compound, chemische Verbindung; —cal products, chemische Präparate; —cal works, chemische Fabrik. **—cals**, *pl.* Chemikalien. **—st**, *s.* der Chemiker; analytical —st, der Chemiker; dispensing —st, der Apotheker; pharmaceutical —st and druggist, der Apotheker; practical —st, der technische Chemiker. **—stry**, *s.* die Chemie; (agricultural —) Agrikulturchemie; (animal —) Tierchemie; applied, practical —) angewandte Chemie.

Chemise, *s.* das Frauenhemd; der Mauermantel (*Fort.*); der Mantel (*Artil.*). **—tte**, *s.* das (Frauen-)Chemisett; das Vorhemdchen.

Chenille, *s.* die Chenille.

Cheque, Check, *s.* der Bankschein, die Bankanweisung, der Scheck, der Zahlschein. *Comp.* **—-book**, *s.* das Buch mit eingehefteten Bankanweisungen zum Ausreißen, das Scheckbuch. **—r**, *see* Checker.

Cherish, *v.a.* mit Liebe und Zärtlichkeit behandeln, hegen und pflegen; (take care of) pflegen, wohltun; aufbewahren, hegen; to — ill will, Groll hegen; to — a hope, eine Hoffnung hegen.

Cheroot, *s.* die Manillazigarre.

Cherry, I. *s.* die Kirsche. II. *adj.*; — lip, die rote Lippe. *Comp.* **—-brandy**, *s.* das Kirschwasser, der Kirsch(geist). **—-coloured**, *adj.* rot, kirschfarbig. **—-orchard**, *s.* der Kirschengarten. **—-stone**, *s.* der Kirschkern. **—-tree**, *s.* der Kirschbaum.

Chersonese, *s.* die Halbinsel.

Chert, *s.* der Feuer-, Horn-stein, der Quarz.

Cherub, *s.* (*pl.* —im & —s) der Cherub; der geflügelte Engelskopf. **—ic**, *adj.* engelhaft, himmlisch unschuldig. **—im**, *pl.* die Cherubim.

Chervil, *s.* der Kälberkropf, Kerbel (*Bot.*).

Chess, I. *s.* das Schach(spiel). II. *attrib.*; — problem, die Schachaufgabe; — tournament, das Schachturnier. *Comp.* **—-board**, *s.* das Schachbrett. **—-man**, *s.* die Schachfigur. **—-player**, *s.* der Schachspieler.

Chest, *s.* die Kiste, Lade, der Kasten; die Kasse; die Brust (*Anat.*); die Truhe (*Min.*); der Bauch (*of a violin*); — of drawers, die Kommode; slide —, Schieberkasten (*of steam-engines*); stuff —, die Zeugbütte (*Pap.*); to suffer from a disease of the —, brustkrank sein. **—ed**, *adj.*; broad-—ed, breitbrüstig; narrow-—ed, engbrüstig.

Chestnut, I. *s.* die Kastanie. II. *adj.* kastanienbraun; — horse, der Brauner, Fuchs. *Comp.* **—-brown**, *s.* (— colour) das Kastanienbraun. **—-tree**, *s.* der Kastanienbaum; horse-—(-tree), der gemeine Roßkastanienbaum.

Che(e)tah, *s.* der Jagdleopard (*Felis jubata*).

Cheval—ier, *s.* der Ritter (*obs.*); der Ritter eines (nicht englischen) Ordens; — of fortune, der Glücksritter, Hochstapler, Schwindler. *Comp.* **—-glass**, *s.* der große Drehspiegel.

Chev—eril, *s.* das Ziegenleder. **—ron**, *s.* der Sparren (*Her.*); der Chevron (*Mil.*); die Zickzackverzierung (*Arch.*). **—rotain**, *s.* das Moschustier.

Cheviot, *s.* dicker, rauher Tuchstoff.

Chew, *v.a.* kauen, käuen; auf eine S. sinnen (*fig.*); to — the cud, wiederkäuen; (etwas) überlegen (*fig.*).

Chiaroscuro, *s.* das Helldunkel.

Chibouque, *s.* lange türkische Pfeife, der Tschibuk.

Chicane, *v.n.* schikanieren. **—ry**, *s.* die Rechtsverdreherei; die Haarspalterei.

Chick, *s.* das Küchlein; —! —! put! put! **—en**, *s.* das Hühnchen, Küchlein; the —en peeps, das Küken *or* Küchlein piepst; no —en, nicht mehr jung; to count one's —ens before they are hatched, die Haut verkaufen ehe man den Bären getötet hat, zu früh krähen *or* triumphieren. *Comp.* **—en-hearted**, *adj.* feig, mutlos, zaghaft. **—en-pox**, *s.* die Windpocken (*Med.*).

Chickling, —-vetch, *s.* die Platterbse.

Chick—-pea, *s.* die Kicherebse. **—weed**, *s.* der Hühnerdarm (*Bot.*).

Chicory, *s.* die Zichorie, Wegwarte (*Bot.*).

Chid, *imperf. & p.p. of* —e. **—den**, *p.p. of* —e. **—e**, *v.a.* (aus)schelten, verweisen. **—er**, *s.* der Scheltende. **—ing**, *adj.*, **—ingly**, *adv.* scheltend.

Chief, I. *adj.*, **—ly**, *adv.* höchst, vornehmst, erst; (principal) hauptsächlich(st); — burgomaster, der Oberbürgermeister; — business, das Hauptgeschäft; — clerk, der erste Kommis; — command, der Oberbefehl; — Justice, der Oberrichter; — mourner, der Hauptleidtragende (*at funerals*); — points, Hauptpunkte; — town, die Hauptstadt. II. *s.* (head) das Haupt, Oberhaupt; der Häuptling (*of a clan*); (conductor) der Anführer; (principal) der Vorsteher, Eigentümer, Besitzer, Hauptinhaber, Chef; (— part) der Hauptteil; das Schildhaupt (*Her.*); commander in —, der Oberbefehlshaber; — engineer, der Oberingenieur; — officer, der Obersteuermann (*Naut.*); — partner, der Hauptteilhaber eines Handelshauses; — station, die Hauptstation. **—tain**, *s.* der Häuptling; der Anführer. **—taincy**, *s.* die Häuptlingsschaft.

Chiffchaff, *s.* kleiner Weidenzeisig.

Chiffonier, *s.* der kleine Schrank, das Kästchen für Schmucksachen.

Chignon, *s.* der Haarwulst der Damen.

Chilblain, *s.* die Frostbeule.

Child, I. *s.* das Kind; (*obs. often spelt* —e) der Junker, Ritter; from a —, von Kindheit auf; with

—, in andern Umständen, schwanger. II. *attrib.;* — murder, der Kindermord. —**hood**, *s.* die Kindheit. —**ish**, *adj.*, —**ishly**, *adv.* kindisch; —ish days, Tage der Kindheit. —**ishness**, *s.* das kindliche Wesen; die Kinderei (*of old people, etc.*). —**less**, *adj.* kinderlos. —**like**, *adj.* kindlich, wie ein Kind; —like obedience, kindlicher Gehorsam. —**ren**, *pl. see* Child. *Comp.* —**bearing**, *s.* das Gebären, die Niederkunft; to be past —bearing, keine Kinder mehr haben können. —**bed**, *s.* das Kindbett; to be in —bed, in den Wochen liegen; woman in —bed, die Wöchnerin. —**birth**, *s.* die Niederkunft, das Gebären; to die in —birth, bei der Niederkunft sterben. —**ermas**, *s.* (—ermas day) das Fest der unschuldigen Kindlein (*Dec. 28*) (*obs.*). —**'s-play**, *s.* das Kinderspiel.

Chiliarch, *s.* der Chiliarch, Befehlshaber über 1000 Mann.

Chill, I. *s.* (cold thrill) der Schauer; (feverish shiver) der Fieberfrost; (cold) die Erkältung; (coldness) die Kälte; die Schale (*Found.*); water with the — off, verschlagenes Wasser; to take the — off, verschlagen *or* überschlagen lassen, leicht anwärmen; water with just the — taken off, schwach lauwarmes Wasser. II. *adj.* kalt, frostig; her — reserve, ihre kühle Zurückhaltung; — casting, der Kapselguß, Schalenguß (*Found.*). III. *v.a.* kalt machen, durchkälten; mutlos machen; it —s my blood to think of it, mein Blut erstarrt, wenn ich nur daran denke; to — a p.'s courage, jemandes Mut niederschlagen; a —ing reception, ein niederschlagender *or* frostiger Empfang; —ed shot, das Hartblei. —**iness**, *s.* die Kälte. —**ing**, *p. & adj. see* Chill III. —**y**, *adj.* frostig, kalt; a —y day, ein kalter Tag

Chillies, *pl.* die Schoten des Cayennepfeffers.

[1]**Chime**, I. *s.* die Kimme. II. *attrib.;* — plane, der Kimmhobel.

[2]**Chime**, I. *s.* das Glockenspiel (*of bells*); der Einklang, die Harmonie (*also fig.*); the —s, das Glockenspiel, Glockengeläute. II. *v.a.* ertönen lassen; to — the hours, die Stunden schlagen. III. *v.n.* zusammenstimmen, im Einklange tönen; übereinstimmen; to — in, im Chor mitsingen, in den Chor einstimmen; to — in with a p.'s view, einem beistimmen; he —d in with a remark every now and then, er warf dann und wann eine Bemerkung ein.

Chimer—a, *s.* die Chimäre (*Myth.*); das Schreckbild (*fig.*); das Hirngespinnst, die Einbildung. —**ical**, *adj.*, —**ically**, *adv.* chimärisch, eingebildet.

Chimney, *s.* der Kamin, Schornstein; der Zylinder (*for lamps*); back of the —, die Kaminplatte; stack of —s, der Schornsteinbau; — on fire, der Schornsteinbrand. *Comp.* —**-corner**, *s.* die Kaminecke; in the —-corner, hinter dem warmen Ofen. —**-flue**, *s.* die Schornsteinröhre. —**-glass**, *s.* der Spiegel über dem Kaminaufsatz. —**-ornament**, *pl.* Nippsachen für das Kamingesims. —**-piece**, *s.* das Kaminsims, Kaminstück. —**-pot**, *s.* die Zugröhre, Kaminkappe; schwarzer Zylinderhut, die Angströhre (*hum.*). —**-swallow**, *s.* die Rauchschwalbe. —**-sweep**, *s.* der Schornsteinfeger. —**-top**, *s.* die Schornsteinkappe, der Schornsteinkranz.

Chimpanzee, *s.* der Schimpanse (*Zool.*).

Chin, I. *s.* das Kinn. II. *attrib.;* — rest, der Kinnhalter (*Viol.*).

China, I. *s.*, (—**-ware**, *s.*,) das Porzellan; English —, das englische feine Steingut. II. *attrib.;* — bark, die Chinarinde; — cabinet, der Porzellanschrank; — crape, der Schawlkrepp. *Comp.* —**-clay**, *s.* das Kaolin, die Porzellanerde. —**-rose**, *s.* die Sinarose. —**-shop**, *s.* der Porzellanladen.

Chinchilla, *s.* die Wollmaus.

Chine, *s.* der Rückgrat; das Rückenstück (*Butch.*); der Riß, der Spalt, Schlund, die zum Meere hinabführende Bergschlucht (*dial.*).

[1]**Chink**, *s.* die Ritze, Spalte, der Riß, Spalt.

[2]**Chink**, I. *s.* der Klang (*of keys, money, etc.*); (money) das Geld (*vulg.*). II. *v.a.* durch Schütteln klingen machen; to — a purse of money, mit einer Geldbörse klimpern.

Chintz, *s.* der Zitz, der Möbelkattun.

Chip, I. *s.* das Schnitzchen, Schnitzel, oer Span; a — of the old block, ganz wie der Vater, der leibhafte Vater. II. *v.a.* in kleine Stücke schneiden, schnitzeln, abschaben; (hack) zerhauen; from —ping come —s, wo man Holz haut, da fallen Späne (*prov.*). III. *v.n.;* to — off, sich (ab)blättern. —**s**, *pl.* der Abfall, die Späne, Splitter; —s of wood, Hobelspäne; —s of leather (*for heels*), der Absatzkuchen. *Comp.* —**-hat**, *s.* der Basthut.

Chir—agra, *s.* die Handgicht, das Chiragra. —**ograph**, *s.* eine doppelt geschriebene Urkunde (*obs.*); die Geldbuße (*obs.*); die Urkunde, päpstlicher Erlaß. —**ographer**, *s.* der (Ab)schreiber; der Gerichtsschreiber (*of fines*). —**ography**, *s.* die Schreibekunst, Handschrift. —**ographist**, *see* —ographer, —omancer. —**omancer**, *s.* der Chiromant. —**omancy**, *s.* die Handwahrsagerei, Handkunde. —**oplast**, *s.* der Chiroplast, Handbildner. —**opodist**, *s.* der Leichdornbeschneider.

Chirp, *v.n.* zirpen, zwitschern; crickets —, Heimchen zirpen; sparrows —, Sperlinge zwitschern. —**ing**, I. *s.* das Zirpen, Gezirpe. II. *attrib.;* —ping cup, der fröhlich stimmende Becher.

Chirrup, *v.n. see* Chirp; to — to horses, Pferde durch einen Zuruf ermuntern.

Chirurgeon, (*obs.*) *see* Surgeon.

Chisel, I. *s.* der Meißel; das Stemmeisen (*Carp.*); der Betel (*Carp.*, *Naut.*); der Steinmeißel (*Mas.*); graver's —, der Grabstichel; sculptor's —, der Bildhauermeißel. II. *v.a.* meißeln, ziselieren; übervorteilen, betrügen (*sl.*).

Chit, *s.* das kleine Geschöpf, Ding. —**terling**, *s.* die Krause (*of shirts*) (*obs.*); —terlings (*pl.*) die Kaldaunen, Gedärme. —**chat**, *s.* das Geplauder, die Plauderei.

Chivalr—ic, *adj.*, —**ous**, *adj.*, —**ously**, *adv.* ritterlich. —**y**, *s.* die Ritterschaft; (knighthood) die Ritterwürde, der Ritterstand; (institution of —y) das Rittertum; (order of —y) der Ritterorden; (body of knights) die Ritterschaft, die sämmtlichen Ritter; (—ousness) die Ritterlichkeit; (—ous act) die Rittertat; court of —y, das Rittergericht; romance of —y, der Ritterroman, der höfische Roman.

Chive, Cive, *s.* der Schnittlauch (*Bot.*).

Chlor—al, *s.* das Chloral (*Chem.*). —**ate**, *s.* das Chlorat; —ate of lime, der chlorsaure Kalk; —ate of potash, das chlorsaure Kali. —**ic**, *adj.;* —ic acid, die Chlorsäure. —**ide**, *s.* das Chlorid, die Chlorverbindung; —ide of lime, der Chlorkalk; —ide of potassium, das Chlorkalium. —**ine**, *s.* das Chlor, Chlorgas. —**oform**, I. *s.* das Chloroform. II. *v.a.* chloroformieren. —**ometer**, *s.* der Chlormesser. —**ophyll**, *s.* das Chlorophyll, Blattgrün. —**osis**, *s.* die Bleichsucht (*Med.*). —**otic**, *adj.* bleichsüchtig.

Chocolate, I. *s.* die Schokolade; die Schokoladenfarbe. II. *adj.* schokoladenfarbig; — cake, die Tafel Schokolade; der Schokoladenkuchen; — creams, gefüllte Schokoladebonbons, Pralinees; — drops, Schokoladeplätzchen; — powder, das Schokolademehl; — tablet, die Tafel Schokolade.

Chode, *obs. imperf. of* Chide.

Choice, I. *s.* die Wahl; die Auswahl; (object of —) das Ausgewählte; to have no —, keine Wahl haben, nicht wählen können; to have Hobson's —, das nehmen müssen, was man bekommen kann; there is great — of articles in his shop, er hat eine reiche Auswahl von Sachen in seinem Laden; if it depended upon me alone you should be my —, hinge es von mir allein ab, so würde ich Sie wählen; men of —, auserlesene Leute; to make a —, wählen, eine Wahl treffen; to take one's —, nach Belieben wählen. II. *adj.* auserlesen; vorzüglich; kostbar (*B.*); (difficult to please) wählerisch; to be — with regard to one's company, sorgfältig in der Auswahl seiner Bekannten sein; — commodities, vorzügliche Waren; — epithet, ausgesuchtes Beiwort; — fruit, erlesenes Obst, vorzügliche Früchte; — society, gewählte Gesellschaft; a — spirit, ein Mann von vorzüglicher Begabung, ein Bruder Lustig (*iron.*); the — spirits of the age, die großen Männer des Jahrhunderts. —**ly**, *adv.* mit Auswahl oder Sorgfalt. —**ness**, *s.* die Erlesenheit; der hohe Wert; die Feinheit (*of words, etc.*).

Choir, *s.* der Sängerchor; das Chor (*Arch.*). *Comp.* —-**boy**, *s.* der Chorknabe, Chorsänger. —-**organ**, *s.* die Chororgel. —-**school**, *s.* Schule für Chorknaben. —-**screen**, *s.* die Chorschranke.

Choke, *v.* I. *a.* ersticken; erwürgen; (— up) verstopfen; unterdrücken (*fig.*); hindern (*fig.*); to be —d up with mud, verschlammt sein; to be —d (*or* choking) with thirst, vor Durst verschmachten; to — a p. off, einen bei der Kehle fassen und so zum Loslassen zwingen, abschrecken; —d pump, unklar verstopfte Pumpe. II. *n.* sich würgen, ersticken (an einer S.). —**er**, *s.*; white —er, weißes Halstuch (*coll.*). *Comp.* —-**damp**, *s.* die Nachschwaden, Stickwetter (*Min.*). —-**pear**, *s.* (*obs.*) die Würgbirne.

Choler, *s.* die Galle; der Zorn (*fig.*); to engender —, böses Blut machen. —**a**, (—**a morbus**,) *s.* I. die Cholera. II. *attrib.*; —a belt, die (warme) Leibbinde. —**ic**, *adj.* cholerisch, gallensüchtig; zum Zorne geneigt; jähzornig, hitzig, zornsüchtig; a —ic word, ein im Zorne ausgestoßenes Wort; a —ic temperament, ein galliges, cholerisches Temperament.

Choose, *v.* I. *a.* wählen, auswählen; to — rather, (prefer) vorziehen, lieber wollen *or* mögen; take which you —, nehmen Sie, welches Ihnen beliebt. II. *n.* wählen; he cannot — but, er kann nicht umhin zu . . ., er muß . . .; there is nothing to —, es giebt keine Wahl; there is not much to — between them, es ist fast gar kein Unterschied zwischen ihnen, der eine ist ziemlich ebenso gut wie der andre. —**r**, *s.* der Wähler.

[1]**Chop**, I. *s.* das abgehauene Stück, die Schnitte; pork —, das Schweinsrippchen; mutton —, das Hammelkotelett, die Schöpskarbonade. II. *v.a.* hauen, klein schlagen, hacken, spalten; to — meat, Fleisch in kleine Stücke zerhauen; to — timber, ein Stück Holz behauen; to — off, abhauen; to — off the branches, abästen. —**per**, *s.* das Hackmesser, Hackbeil. —**ping**, *p.* & *adj.* hauend, rc. —**s**, *pl.* die Kinnbacken, das Maul (*of animals*); der Mund (*vulg.*). *Comp.* —-**house**, *s.* das Speisehaus, die Garküche. —**ping-block**, *s.* das Hackbrett, die Hackbank. —**ping-knife**, *s.* das Hackmesser. —-**stick**, *s.* das Eßstäbchen der Chinesen.

[2]**Chop**, I. *v.a.* tauschen, vertauschen (*obs.*); handeln (*rare*). II. *v.n.* wechseln; to — and change, fortwährend ändern; the wind —s about, der Wind springt um; to — logic, disputieren. III. *s.* der (Glücks)wechsel. —**ping**, I. *p.* & *adj.*; —ping sea, die hohle See. II. *s.* der Tausch, Handel. *Comp.* —-**logic**, *s.* der Disputant; der Weisheitskrämer.

Chopin, *s.* der Schoppen (*Scotch*).

Chopine, *s.* der Schuh mit sehr hoher Sohle (*obs.*).

Chor—al, *adj.* zum Chor gehörig; im Chor singend; chorartig; —al service, der Chorgesang. —**ally**, *adv.* im Chor, chorartig. —**ea**, *s.* der Veitstanz (*Med.*). —**episcopal**, *adj.* chorbischöflich. —**iamb(us)**, *s.* der Choriambus (´ ˘ ˘ ´). —**ister**, *s.* der Chorsänger, Chorist. —**us**, *s.* der Chor (*also Theat.*), Singchor; das von einem Musikchor vorgetragene Musikstück; to sing in —us, im Chor singen.

Chord, *s.* die Saite (*of a musical instrument*); der Akkord (*Mus.*); die Sehne (*Geom.*); common —, der Dreiklang; vocal —s, die Stimmbänder; — of an arch, die Kämpferlinie eines Bogens; length of the —, die Spannung (*Arch.*); major (minor) —, der Durakkord (Mollakkord).

Chor—ion, *s.* das Chorion (*Anat.*). —**oid**, *s.* die Gefäßhaut des Auges, Choroide.

Chorograph—er, *s.* der Landbeschreiber, Chorograph. —**y**, *s.* die Landbeschreibung.

Chose, *imperf. of* Choose. —**n**, I. *p.p. of* Choose. II. *adj.* erwählt, auserlesen; the —n few, die wenigen Auserwählten; —n troops, Kerntruppen; the —n people, das auserwählte Volk; a —n vessel, ein erlesenes Rüstzeug, ein auserwählter gottbegnadeter Mensch.

Chough, *s.* die Dohle; Cornish —, die Bergdohle.

Chowder, *s.* eine Art Fischgericht (*Amer.*).

Chris—m, *s.* das Chrisma, das feierlich geweihte Salböl. —**mal**, *adj.* das Chrisma betreffend. —**matory**, *s.* der Salbkrug. —**om**, *s.* das Taufkleid; —om-child, unschuldiges Kindchen (*fig.*); Kind, das im ersten Monat stirbt. —**ten**, *v.a.* taufen; (name) benennen. —**tendom**, *s.* die Christenheit. —**tening**, I. *attrib.* Tauf-. II. *s.* die Taufe. —**tian**, I. *adj.* christlich; —tian name, der Taufname, Vorname; they began to —tian-name each other, sie fingen an, einander bei ihren Vornamen zu nennen; —tian era, christliche Zeitrechnung; since the —tian era, seit Christi Geburt; in the year 1800 of the —tian era, im Jahre 1800 nach Christo. II. *s.* der Christ. —**tianity**, *s.* die christliche Religion, das Christentum. —**tianize**, —**tianise**, *v.a.* zum Christen machen, bekehren. —**tless**, *adj.* ohne Glauben an Christus.

Christmas, I. *s.* das Christfest, Weihnachtsfest, (*also* die) Weihnachten; Father —, der Weihnachtsmann. II. *attrib.*; — box, das Weihnachtsgeldgeschenk (an Diener und junge Leute aus Geschäften), Weihnachtstrinkgeld; — card, die Weihnachtskarte, der Weihnachtsglückwunsch; — carol, das Weihnachtslied; — day, der Christtag, der (erste) Weihnachtstag; — Eve, der Christabend, Heiligabend, Weihnachtsabend; — gift, — holidays, die Weihnachtsferien; — present, das Weihnachtsgeschenk; — pudding, der Plumpudding; — rose, die Weihnachtsrose.

Christy minstrels, *pl.* Gesellschaft(en) von (angeblichen) Negern, die besonders in den englischen Seebädern konzertieren.

Chrom—ate, *s.* das chromsaure Salz; —ate of iron, der Chromeisenstein; —ate of lead, das chromsaure Bleioxyd; —ate of potash, das chromsaure Kali. —**atic**, *adj.* chromatisch (*Mus.*, *Phys.*); —atic bugle, das Klapphorn; —atic instruments, Instrumente, auf welchen sich chromatische Töne und Tonreihen ausführen lassen; —atic printing, der Farbendruck. —**atics**, *pl.* die Farbenlehre. —**atogene**, *adj.* farbenerzeugend (*Chem.*). —**atrope**, *s.* das Chromatrop (*Opt.*). —**e**, *s.* das doppelt chromsaure Kali —**ium**, *s.* das Chrom. —**ic**, *adj.* Chrom . . . chromsauer. —**olithograph**, *s.* die Chromolithographie, das Karten(stein)druckbild. —**olithography**, *s.* die Chromolithographie. —**oxylograph**, *s.* das Öldruckbild. —**otype**, *s.* die Chromophotographie. *Comp.* —**e-yellow**, *s.* das Chromgelb, chromsaures Bleioxyd.

Chron—ic, *adj.* chronisch; langwierig, dauernd, bleibend, chronisch (*diseases*). —**icle**, I. *s.* die Chronik; die Zeitgeschichte, Ortsgeschichte, das Jahrbuch, Geschichtsbuch; der Bericht. II. *v.a.* in eine Chronik eintragen; aufzeichnen, verzeichnen. —**icler**, *s.* der Chronik(en)schreiber; der Geschichtschreiber. —**icles**, *pl.* die Chroniken, Jahrbücher; Bücher der Chronika (*B.*). —**ogram**, *s.* das Chronogramm. —**ographer**, *s.* der Chronograph. —**ologer**, —**ologist**, *s.* der Chronolog, Zeitkundige. —**ological**, *adj.*, —**ologically**, *adv.* chronologisch; in —ological order, in richtiger Zeitfolge, nach der Zeitfolge geordnet. —**ology**, *s.* die Chronologie, Zeitfolge; die Zeitbestimmung, Zeitrechnung. —**ometer**, *s.* der (das)

Chronometer, Zeitmesser. **—ometry**, *s.* die Zeitmeßkunst, Chronometrie.

Chrys—alid, I. *adj.* puppenhaft, puppenartig. II. *s.*, **—alis**, *s.* die Puppe. **—anthemum**, *s.* die Wucherblume. **—ocoma**, *s.* das Goldhaar (*Bot.*). **—ography**, *s.* die Goldschrift. **—olite**, *s.* der Chrysolith. **—oprase**, *s.* der Chrysopras.

Chub, *s.* der Döbel, Dickkopf (*Icht.*). **—by**, (**—by-faced**,) *adj.* pausbackig, rundwangig; plump.

[1]**Chuck**, I. *v.n.* glucken (*as a hen*). II. *s.* das Glucken; (darling) Täubchen. **—le**, *v.n.* kichern, in sich hinein lachen.

[2]**Chuck**, I. *v.a.* sanft schlagen; (throw) werfen; to — a p. under the chin, einen sanft unter das Kinn schlagen. II. *s.* der Kinngriff, die leichte Berührung unter dem Kinn. *Comp.* **—-farthing**, *s.* ein Knabenspiel, wobei eine kupferne Münze nach einem gewissen Ziel oder Grübchen geworfen wird, das Grübchenspiel. **—-lathe**, *s.* die Dockendrehbank.

Chum, I. *s.* der Stubenbursche; der Kamerad; they were great —s, sie waren unzertrennlich, Busenfreunde (*coll.*). II. *v.n.;* to — together, zusammenwohnen (*coll.*). **—my**, *adj.* gesellig; intim; to be very —my, auf sehr vertrautem Fuße stehen, sehr intim sein.

Chump, *s.* das kurze, dicke Stück Holz; — end of a sirloin, das dicke Ende eines Lendenbratens; — chop, das Kotelett aus dem dicken Ende der Hammelkeule.

Chunk, *s.* das kurze, dicke Stück (*coll.*), Priemchen.

Chupatty, *s.* ungesäuerter indischer Brotkuchen.

Church, I. *s.* die Kirche; (— service) der Gottesdienst; to go to —, in die Kirche *or* zur Kirche gehen; to go into the —, ein Geistlicher werden; to go to — with (*coll.*), mit . . . getraut werden; — is over, die Kirche ist aus; to be educated for the —, eine theologische Erziehung erhalten, sich zum Geistlichen ausbilden. II. *adj.;* — authority, die kirchliche Gewalt; — discipline, die Kirchenzucht; — history, die Kirchengeschichte; — law, das Kirchenrecht, kanonische Recht; — missionary society, die anglikanische Missionsgesellschaft; — porch, die Vorhalle einer Kirche; — preferment, die Pfründe; — school, nach den Grundsätzen der anglikanischen Kirche geleitete englische Volksschule; — time, die Kirchzeit. III. *v.a.* für eine (vom Kindbett genesene) Wöchnerin die vorgeschriebene Danksagung abhalten; to be —ed, Kirchgang gehalten haben. **—ing**, *s.* die Einsegnung einer Wöchnerin. **—ism**, *s.* die Kirchlichkeit. **—y**, *adj.* streng kirchlich. *Comp.* **—-burial**, *s.* das nach den kirchlichen Gebräuchen vollzogene Begräbnis. **—-goer**, *s.* der Kirchenbesucher, Kirchgänger. **—-lands**, *pl.* das Kirchengut. **—-man**, *s.* der Anhänger der anglikanischen Kirche. **—-membership**, *s.* die Kirchenmitgliedschaft, Kirchengemeinschaft, Gemeindezugehörigkeit. **—-mouse**, *s.;* as poor as a —-mouse, arm wie eine Kirchenmaus. **—-music**, *s.* die Kirchenmusik, geistliche Musik. **—-service**, *s.* der Gottesdienst; das Kirchenbuch. **—warden**, *s.* der Kirchenvorsteher. **—woman**, *s.* die streng (anglikanisch) kirchlich gesinnte Frau. **—yard**, *s.* der Kirchhof.

Churl, *s.* der rohe Mensch, Grobian; der mürrische, verdrießliche Mensch; der Bauer (*obs.*); (niggard) der Geizige. **—ish**, *adj.*, **—ishly**, *adv.* roh; karg; mürrisch; grob; geizig. **—ishness**, *s.* die Grobheit; das mürrische Wesen; die Härte; the —ishness of fortune, die Ungunst *or* Tücke des Geschicks.

Churn, I. *s.* das Butterfaß, der Butterstoßapparat. II. *v.a.* Butter stoßen, buttern; in heftige Bewegung versetzen, zu Schaum peitschen. **—ing**, *s.* das Buttern; how much butter do you get at a —ing? wie viel Butter machen Sie auf einmal? *Comp.* **—-staff**, *s.* der Butterstößel, Kolben eines Butterfasses.

Chyle, *s.* der Chylus, Milchsaft, Speisesaft.

Chyme, *s.* der Chymus, Speisebrei.

Chymist, *s.* *see* Chemist.

Ciborium, *s.* der Speisekelch; die Hostienkapsel, Monstranz; (*obs.*) der Altarüberhang (*Arch.*).

Cicada, *s.* die Heuschrecke, Zikade.

Cicatri—ce, *s.* die Narbe. **—zation**, *s.* die Vernarbung. **—ze**, **—se**, *v.a.* vernarben; zuheilen.

Cicerone, *s.* der Cicerone, Fremdenführer.

Cider, *s.* der Zider, der Apfelwein, Obstmost. **—-mill**, *s.* die Apfelquetschmühle; die Apfelweinfabrik.

Cigar, I. *s.* die Zigarre. II. *attrib.;* — tip, die abgeschnittene Zigarrenspitze, der Zigarrenabschnitt. **—ette**, *s.* die Papierzigarre, Zigarette. *Comp.* **—-case**, *s.* das Zigarrenetui. **—-cutter**, *s.* Zigarren(spitzen)abschneider. **—-end**, *s.* der Zigarrenstummel. **—ette-filler**, *s.* die Zigarrettenfüllmaschine. **—ette-paper**, *s.* das Zigarrettenpapier. **—-lighter**, *s.* der Zigarrenanzünder. **—-holder**, *s.* die Zigarrenspitze. **—-maker**, *s.* der Zigarrenarbeiter.

Cilia—ry, *adj.* die Augenwimpers betreffend, Wimper-; —ry processes, Ciliarfortsätze. **—te**, *adj.* bewimpert.

Cinchona, (**Chinchona**,) *s.* der Chinarindenbaum, Fieberrindenbaum.

Cincture, *s.* der Gürtel.

Cinder, *s.* die ausgebrannte Kohle; live —, die glühende Kohle; burnt to a —, zur Kohle verbrannt. **—ella**, *s.* (das) Aschenbrödel. *Comp.* **—-sifter**, *s.* das Aschensieb.

Cinematograph, *s.* der Kinematograph, lebende Photographien (*pl.*)

Cinerar—ia, *s.* die Aschenpflanze. **—y**, *adj.;* —y urn, die Totenurne, der Aschenkrug.

Cinnabar, *s.* der Zinnober.

Cinnamon, *s.* der Zimmt; die Zimmtfarbe.

Cinque, *s.* die Fünf (*at play*). *Comp.* **—foil**, *s.* das Fünffingerkraut; das Fünfblatt (*Arch.*). **—-ports**, *pl.* die Fünfhäfen (an Englands Südküste, von Wilhelm dem Eroberer befestigt); warden of the —-ports, der Lord-Aufseher der Fünfhäfen (noch jetzt bestehende Sinekure).

Cipher, I. *s.* die Ziffer; (nobody) die Null; die Chiffre, Geheimschrift; to be a mere —, eine reine Null sein; despatch in —, das Ziffertelegramm. II. *v.n.* rechnen. **—er**, *s.* der Rechner. **—ing**, *s.* das Rechnen.

Circ—le, I. *s.* der Zirkel (*also fig.*), Kreis; der Umkreis; (—le of acquaintance) der Bekanntenkreis; (diadem) das Diadem; (ring) der Ring, Reif; (vicious —le) der Zirkelschluß; —le of altitude, der Höhenkreis (*Astr.*); —le of amplitude, der Weitenzirkel; antarctic —le, der südliche Polarkreis; arctic —le, der nördliche Polarkreis; horary —le, Stundenkreis; —les of longitude, Längenkreise. II. *v.a.* umgehen; umgeben, einschließen. III. *v.n.* sich in einem Kreise bewegen, kreisen. **—let**, *s.* das Zirkelchen, der Ring. **—uit**, I. *s.* (the revolving around) die Kreisbewegung, der Kreislauf; (circle) der Umkreis, Umfang; (district) der Gerichtsbezirk, Distrikt (*Law*); die Rundreise der Richter zur Abhaltung der Assisen (*Law*); der Stromkreis (*Tele.*); die Leitung (*Tele.*); to make a —uit, einen Umgang machen; to go on —uit, die Assisen abhalten; within a —uit of 10 miles, im Umkreise von 10 Meilen; broken —uit, unterbrochener, offener Stromkreis; Morse's —uit, Morsesche Leitung. II. *v.n.* sich im Kreise bewegen. III. *v.a.* umherreisen. **—uitous**, *adj.*, **—uitously**, *adv.* weitläufig, weitschweifig; a —uitous way, ein Umweg; a —uitous way of treating a subject, eine weitschweifige Art einen Gegenstand zu behandeln; a —uitous path, ein weitläufiger Weg. **—uity**, *s.* die Bewegung im Kreise; (*fig.*) der Umschweif langwieriger Prozeß. **—ular**, I. *adj.* kreisförmig; im Zirkel herumgehend; —ular current, der kreisförmige elektrische Strom; —ular fortification, die Kreisbefestigung; —ular letter, *see* —ular II.; a —ular note, —ular letter of credit, ein Zirkularkreditbrief, ein Akkreditiv (*C. L.*); —ular motion, die Kreisbewegung; —ular numbers, Zirkularzahlen; —ular sailing, das Segeln in einem großen Bogen; —ular saw, die Kreissäge; —ular sector, der Kreisteil (*Geom.*); —ular style, der Rundbogenstil; —ular tour, die Rundreise; —ular track, der Schienenring (*Rail.*); —ular velocity, die Geschwindigkeit, mit der ein Planet sich um seine Achse dreht. II. *s.* das Kreisschreiben, Rundschreiben, Zirkularschreiben. —**ulate**, *v.* I. *n.* umlaufen, im Umlauf sein (*C. L.*); sich kreisförmig bewegen. II. *a.* in Umlauf bringen; to —ulate bills, Wechsel girieren; to —ulate a report, ein Gerücht verbreiten. —**ulating**, *p. & adj.* umlaufend; —ulating library, eine Leihbibliothek; —ulating decimal, der periodische Dezimalbruch; —ulating medium, das Umlaufmittel. —**ulation**, *s.* der Umlauf, Kreislauf; der (Geld)umlauf (*of money, etc.*); die Verbreitung (*of a report*); —ulation of the blood, der Blutumlauf; —ulation of the air in mines, die Wetterlosung; bank of —ulation, die Girobank; —ulation of bills, notes, der Wechselverkehr; to be in —ulation, im Umlauf sein, zirkulieren. —**um**, *see* Circum—. —**us**, *s.* der Zirkus. *Comp.* —**le-cutter**, *s.* die Rundschneidemaschine. —**uit-brake**, —**uit-breaker**, *s.* die Leitungsbremse (*Tele.*). —**uit-closer**, *s.* der Stromschließer. —**ular-instrument**, *s.* das graduierte Instrument (*Astr.*).

Circum—ambient, *adj.* umgebend, einschließend; the —ambient air, die uns umgebende Luft. —**ambulate**, *v.* I. *n.* herumgehen; (*fig.*) auf den Busch klopfen. II. *a.* umgehen. —**cise**, *v.a.* (die Vorhaut) beschneiden. —**cision**, *s.* die Beschneidung (der Vorhaut). —**ference**, *s.* der Kreisumfang, die Kreislinie, Peripherie; die Oberfläche eines runden Körpers. —**ferential**, *adj.* den Umfang eines Kreises betreffend; *see* Circuitous; —ferential velocity, die Umfangsgeschwindigkeit. —**ferentor**, *s.* der Winkelmesser, Hängekompaß (*Surv.*). —**flect**, *v.a.* zirkumflektieren. —**flex**, *s.* das Dehnungszeichen, der Zirkumflex (^). —**gyrate**, *v.n.* umkreisen. —**jacent**, *adj.* umliegend. —**locution**, *s.* die Umschreibung; der Umschweif. —**locutory**, *adj.* umschreibend. —**navigable**, *adj.* umschiffbar. —**navigate**, *v.a.* umschiffen. —**navigation**, *s.* die Umschiffung. —**navigator**, *s.* der Umsegler, (— of the globe) Weltumsegler. —**scribe**, *v.a.* umschreiben; begrenzen, beschränken. —**scription**, *s.* die Umschrift; die Begrenzung, Beschränkung. —**spect**, *adj.*, —**spectly**, *adv.* umsichtig, vorsichtig. —**spection**, *s.* die Umsicht, Vorsicht, Behutsamkeit. —**stance**, *s.* der Umstand; (occurrence) der Zufall; (circumlocution) der Umschweif; —stances, (*pl.*) die Umstände, Verhältnisse, die Sachlage, der Zustand; (details) das Nähere; to be in easy —stances, wohlhabend sein; our —stances are straitened, unsere Vermögensumstände sind sehr beschränkt; under existing —stances, unter den obwaltenden Umständen; —stances require it, die Verhältnisse bringen es so mit sich. —**stanced**, *adj.* gestellt; to be —stanced, sich in einer Lage befinden; —stanced as I was, in meiner Lage, unter den Umständen, in denen ich mich befand. —**stantial**, *adj.*, —**stantially**, *adv.* umständlich; den Umständen gemäß; (accidental) zufällig; —stantial evidence, das aus den Umständen geschöpfte Zeugnis. —**stantiality**, *s.* die Umständlichkeit. —**stantiate**, *v.a.* umständlich beschreiben; (prove by —stances) durch die (aus den) Umstände(n) beweisen. —**vallation**, *s.* die äußere Umwallung eines festen Platzes. —**vent**, *v.a.* überlisten, mit List hintergehen; umringen; umgehen. —**vention**, *s.* die Überlistung. —**volution**, *s.* die Umwälzung, Umdrehung; *see* —locution; die Wulst der Schnecke an der ionischen Säule.

Cirr—ipeds, *pl.* die Rankenfüßler, Cirripeden (*Mollusc.*). —**ous**, —**ose**, *adj.* rankig, rankenförmig. —**us**, I. *s.* (*also* —hus), die Ranke (*Bot.*). II. *attrib.*; —us cloud, die Federwolke (*Meteor.*).

Cistern, I. *s.* das Reservoir, der Behälter (*for any liquid*); der Wasserbehälter, Wasserfang, die Zisterne (*Arch.*); die Zisterne (*Locom.*); house —, das Reservewasserbassin in Häusern; railway —, das Bassin für das Kesselspeisewasser. II. *attrib.*; — barometer, der Gefäßbarometer.

Cistus, *s.* das Ciströschen (*Bot.*).

Cit, *s.* der Städter, Spießbürger, Philister (*coll.*). —**adel**, *s.* die Burg; die Zitadelle (*Fort.*). —**izen**, *s.* der Bürger; (inhabitant) der Einwohner, Bewohner; der Städter (*of a town, etc.*); —izen of the world, Weltbürger; fellow —izen, Mitbürger. —**izenship**, *s.* das Bürgerrecht, Bürgertum; die Staatsangehörigkeit. —**y**, I. *s.* die Stadt; inkorporierte Stadt (mit Bischofssitz und Kathedrale); die Altstadt und Geschäftsgegend (*especially the East Centre of London*); Mr. A. of this —y, Herr A. hiesigen Ortes; I refer to Messrs. A. B. of your —y, ich beziehe mich auf die dortigen Herrn A. B. II. *adj.* städtisch, zu einer Stadt gehörig; —y arab, das (Londoner) Straßenkind; the —y authorities, der Stadtrat, die Stadtbehörden; —y life, das Stadtleben; a —y man, ein Geschäftsmann; —y prices (*as opposed to West End*), billigere Preise; —y walls, die Stadtmauern; freedom of the —y, das (Ehren)bürgerrecht der Stadt; the —y of Berlin, die Stadt Berlin.

Cit—ation, *s.* die Vorladung, Zitation (*before a tribunal*); die Anführung (*of a passage, etc.*); (mention) die Erwähnung. —**atory**, *adj.* vorladend; letters —atory, die schriftliche Vorladung. —**e**, *v.a.* (summon) vorladen, vorfordern; vor Gericht laden; anführen, zitieren (*a passage*). —**er**, *s.* der Vorladende; der Zitierende.

Citharist, *s.* der Zitherspieler, die Zitherspielerin.

Cither(n), *s.* die Zither.

Citizen, —**ship**, *see* Cit.

Citr—ate, *s.* das Zitrat, die zitronensaure Verbindung; —ate of iron, zitronensaures Eisenoxyd. —**ic**, *adj.*; —ic acid, die Zitronensäure. —**on**, *s.* die Zitrone; candied —on, das Zitronat.

City, *see* Cit.

Civet-cat, *s.* die (afrikanische) Zibetkatze.

Civi—c, *adj.* bürgerlich, Bürger=; —c crown, die Bürgerkrone. —**l**, *adj.* bürgerlich, einem Bürger *or* dem Bürgerstande gemäß; (not criminal; not military) zivil; (courteous) artig, höflich; (mannerly) gesittet; (intestine) einheimisch, innerlich; —l commotion, der Bürgeraufstand; —l engineer, der Zivilingenieur; —l law, das bürgerliche (römische) Recht; —l life, der Zivilstand; (ways) die bürgerliche Lebensweise; —l list, die Zivilliste; —l rights, bürgerliche (Ehren) Rechte; —l service, der Zivildienst, Staatsdienst; —l service examination, Prüfung für den Staatsdienst; —l war, der Bürgerkrieg; a —l servant, ein Staatsbeamter; —l year, das bürgerliche Jahr. —**lian**, *s.* der Bürger; der Zivilist (*Law*); (official) der Zivilbeamte. —**lities**, *pl. of* —lity. —**lity**, *s.* die Artigkeit, Höflichkeit. —**lization**, *s.* die Zivilisation, Kultur, Gesittung; (process of —lization) die Sittenverfeinerung. —**lize**, —**lise**, *v.a.* zivilisieren, gesittet machen, bilden. —**lizer**, —**liser**, *s.* der Sittenbildner, Sittenverfeinerer. —**lly**, *adv.* höflich, artig; zivil (*Law*).

Clack, I. *v.n.* klappern; plappern (*coll.*); gackern (*of hens*). II. *s.* das Klappen, Geklapper; die Klapper; das Plappern (*coll.*); die Klappe (*of a pump*); — of a mill, das Mühlglöckchen. *Comp.* —**-valve**, *s.* das Klappenventil.

Clad, *imperf. & p.p. of* Clothe; ivy-—, mit Efeu bedeckt, efeuumrankt, efeuumsponnen.

Claim, I. *v.a.* in Anspruch nehmen, fordern. II. *s.* der Anspruch; (right) das Recht; to have a — upon a p. (a thing), Anspruch auf einen (eine Sache) haben; to lay — to, Anspruch auf (eine S.) machen *or* erheben; to give up all —, Verzicht (auf eine S.) leisten; —s, Ansprüche; einzuziehende Schulden. **—able**, *adj.* beanspruchbar, zu beanspruchen. **—ant**, *s.* der Anspruchmacher, Reklamant.

Clair—obscure, *s.* das Helldunkel. **—voyance**, *s.* das Hellsehen (*Med.*); (*fig.*) der Scharfsinn. **—voyant**, *s.* Hellseher.

[1]**Clam**, *s.* die amerikanische Venusmuschel. *Comp.* **—-shell**, *s.* die Schale der Venusmuschel.

[2]**Clam**, *v.* I. *a.* leimen, mit einem klebrigen Stoffe überziehen. II. *n.* naß, feucht sein. **—miness**, *s.* die Klebrigkeit. **—my**, *adj.*, **—mily**, *adv.* kaltfeucht, klebrig; —my sweat, klebrige Schweißtropfen.

Clamber, *v.a. & n.* klettern; to — up, hinaufklettern, emporklettern.

Clamor, *see* Clamour. **—ous**, *adj.*, **—ously**, *adv.* schreiend, lärmend; ungestüm.

Clamour, I. *s.* das Geschrei, Getöse; das lärmende, eindringliche Geschrei um eine S.; (complaining outcry) die überlaute, lärmende Klage. II. *v.n.* schreien (for a th., nach einer S.).

Clamp, I. *s.* die Klampe, Klammer, Klemmvorrichtung; wooden —, die Holzklammer; (— of a door) die Einschiebleiste (*Carp.*); die Kneifzange (*Gun.*); spring —, das Spannblech. II. *v.a.* unternageln (*Carp.*); mit Leisten einfassen; klammern, festklammern; to — bricks, Ziegelsteine zum Brennen *or* Trocknen in Meiler setzen. **—ing**, *s.* die Verklammerung; die Verbindung mit Hirnleisten. *Comp.* **—-irons**, *pl.* das Gatter auf dem Boden des Kamins. **—-screw**, *s.* die Preßschraube (*Mech.*); (*also* screw- —) die Schraubenzwinge (*Carp.*).

Clan, I. *s.* der Stamm; (clique) die Sippschaft. II. *v.n.*; to — together, sich zusammenrotten. **—nish**, *adj.* für die Mitglieder seines Stammes eingenommen, sehr anhänglich an seine Verwandten. **—nishness**, *s.* stammverwandtschaftliche Anhänglichkeit. **—ship**, *s.* die Stammverbindung; der freiwillige Lehnsverband unter einem Häuptling. *Comp.* **—sman**, *s.* der Stammverwandte. **—jamphrie**, *s.* (*Scotch*) die Sippschaft, Zunft, Horde, das Pack; der Unsinn.

Clandestine, *adj.*, **—ly**, *adv.* heimlich, verstohlen, insgeheim; — trade, der Schleichhandel. **—ness**, *s.* die Heimlichkeit.

Clang, I. *s.* der Klang, Schall, klingende Ton; the trumpet's —, der Trompetenschall; — of arms, das Waffengeklirr. II. *v.a.* schallen lassen. III. *v.n.* schallen; schreien (*of cranes*) (*poet.*). **—orous**, *adj.* scharf, schrill, gellend, tönend. **—our**, *s.* der Schall, das Geschmetter (*of trumpets, etc.*); der Klang, das Geläut (*of bells*).

Clank, I. *s.* das Gerassel, Geklirr, Klirren. II. *v.a.* rasseln mit. III. *v.n.* rasseln.

Clap, I. *v.a. & n.* klappen, klatschen; (*only v.a.*) klopfen, schlagen; to — to, zuschlagen (*as a door*); to — one's hands, mit den Händen klatschen; Beifall klatschen; to — an actor, a piece, einen Schauspieler, ein Stück beklatschen; to — a p. on the back, einen auf den Rücken klopfen, schlagen; to — spurs to a horse, einem Pferde die Sporen geben; to — a pistol to a p.'s breast, einem eine Pistole auf die Brust setzen; to — into prison, (ohne Weiteres) einstecken (*coll.*). II. *s.* der Klapp(s), Schlag; (noise made by a —) der Knall; (—ping) das Beifallklatschen; — of thunder, der Donnerschlag. **—per**, *s.* der Klöppel (of a bell, an einer Glocke); die Mühlklappen (*of a mill*); die Pumpenklappe (*of a pump*); der Klopfer (*on a door*); (applauder) der Beifallklatschende; die Zunge (*fig.*). *Comp.* **—board**, *s.* das Brett; die Dachschindel (*Build.*); die Faßdaube (*Coop.*). **—-dish**, *s.* hölzerne Schüssel (*obs.*). **—-net**, *s.* das Lerchennetz mit dem Spiegel. **—-sill**, *s.* die Schlagschwelle; (—-sills, *pl.*) das Schlaggeschwell. **—-trap**, I. *s.* der Kniff, Streich (*Theat.*); der Köder, die Lockspeise; (humbug) die Windbeutelei, Prellerei. II. *adj.* effektmachend; betrügerisch, täuschend.

Clar—et, *s.* der Rotwein, Bordeaux; das Weinrot; das Blut (*sl.*); —et cup, (gekühlte) Rotweinbowle; hot —et cup, der Glühwein. **—ification**, *s.* die Abklärung, Läuterung. **—ifier**, *s.* das, was abklärt, läutert, das Klärmittel; die Klärpfanne. **—ify**, *v.a.* abklären, läutern (*fluids*); klären (*sugar*); abklären, schönen (*wine*); —ified toothpicks, abgeputzte Federzahnstocher. **—ity**, *s.* die Klarheit; der Glanz. **—y**, *s.* das Scharlachkraut (*Bot.*).

Clari—(o)net, *s.* die Klarinette. **—(o)nettist**, *s.* der Klarinettenbläser. **—on**, I. *s.* die Zinke, das Klarin; das Klarino (*Org.*); der helle Ton, das Trompetengeschmetter. II. *adj.* laut, schmetternd. III. *v.a.* mit lauten Trompetenstößen verkünden, hervorschmettern.

Clash, I. *v.n.* zusammenschlagen; klirren, schmettern; (to — with) (einem *or* einer S.) entgegen, zuwider, hinderlich sein; in Widerspruch stehen (mit); ecclesiastical and temporal powers often —, oft steht die geistliche Gewalt mit der weltlichen in Widerspruch; to — with a p.'s interest, gegen jemandes Interesse sein, dem Interesse jemandes nachteilig sein. II. *v.a.* mit Geräusch an einander schlagen. III. *s.* (action) der Stoß, Schlag; (noise produced) das Gerassel, Geschmetter; der Streit, Widerspruch (*fig.*); — of arms, das Waffengeklirr. **—ing**, I. *p. & adj.*; —ing interests, (einander) widerstreitende Interessen. II. *s.* das Klirren; der Widerstreit.

Clasp, I. *v.a.* (hook together *or* in) zuhäkeln, einhaken, anhaken; anklemmen, festhalten; ranken (*as tendrils*); umfassen (*the knees, etc.*); to — in one's arms, umarmen; to — to one's bosom, ans Herz drücken; to — hands, die Hände gegenseitig fassen und drücken; to — one's hands (together), die Hände falten (*in prayer*), die Hände zusammenpressen (*in anguish*). II. *v.n.* festhalten. III. *s.* der Haken, Haspen, Heftel; (staple, cramp) die Klammer; die Schnalle (*of a belt*); die Spange, der Verschluß, das Schloß (*of a book*); (tendril) die Ranke; das Schließeisen (*of locks*); das Hakenblatt (*of locks*); die Presse (*Spin.*); adjusting —, der Stellhaken. *Comp.* **—-knife**, *s.* das Einlege- *or* Taschen-messer. **—-nail**, *s.* der Hakennagel, Schindelnagel.

Class, I. *s.* die Klasse; die Schulklasse; (rank) der Stand, die Gesellschaftsklasse; first- —, (*adj.*) erster Klasse; erstklassig, hervorragend; a first- — compartment, ein Abteil erster Klasse; a first- — battleship, ein Schlachtschiff erster Klasse, ein erstklassiges Schlachtschiff; a first- — performance, eine hervorragende Leistung. II. *attrib.*; — list, die Liste, in welcher die Namen derjenigen Schüler oder Studenten, welche eine Prüfung bestanden haben, nach Klassen geordnet veröffentlicht werden; his name does not appear in the — list, er ist in der Prüfung durchgefallen; — struggle, der Klassenkampf. III. *v.a.* nach *or* in Klassen ordnen; to — with, einer Klasse zuzählen, in eine Klasse stellen mit, gleichstellen mit. **—ic**, *see* Classic. **—ification**, *s.* die Einteilung (in Klassen), Anordnung. **—ify**, *v.a.* (in Klassen) einteilen. *Comp.* **—-mate**, **—-fellow**, *s.* Mitschüler derselben Klasse.

Classic, I., **—al**, *adj.*, **—ally**, *adv.* klassisch, mustergültig; klassisch, griechisch-römisch; berühmt. II. *s.* der klassische Schriftsteller, Klassiker; der alte klassische (griechisch-römische) Schriftsteller; der klassische Philolog, Kenner der alten Sprachen. **—ism**, *s.* der Klassizismus; die klassische Form; der klassische Stil; die klassische Bildung. **—ist**, *s.* ein Kenner und Verehrer des Klassischen und der klassischen Schriftsteller.

—s, *pl.* die alten Sprachen; alte *or* klassische Philologie; he is a student of the —s, er ist ein Altphilolog, er studiert alte Philologie; —s and modern languages, alte und neuere Sprachen; the —s, die alten Klassiker (Griechenlands und Roms); die klassischen Schriftsteller.

Clatter, I. *v.n.* klappern, rasseln, klirren; (chatter) klatschen, schwatzen (*vulg.*). II. *v.a.* klirren, rasseln lassen. III. *s.* das Gerassel, Getöse; das laute Geschwätz; das Geschnatter. **—er**, *s.* der Plapperer. **—ing**, *s.* das klirrende, rasselnde Geräusch; das Plappern; to keep up a continual —ing, fortwährend *or* unaufhörlich schwatzen.

Clause, *s.* der Redeteil, Teil eines Satzes, das Satzglied; ein kleiner Satz; (condition) die besondere Bedingung, Klausel; —s, Glieder einer Periode; principal —, der Hauptsatz; dependent —, der Nebensatz.

Claustral, *adj.* klösterlich.

Clave, *obs. imperf. of* Cleave.

Clav—ecin, *s.* das Spinett; das Klavezimbel (*hum.*). **—ichord**, *s.* das Klavichord, alte Art von Klavier. **—ier**, *s.* die Klaviatur, Tastatur.

Clavic—le, *s.* das Schlüsselbein (*Anat.*); die Ranke (*Bot.*). **—ular**, *adj.* Schlüsselbein=...

Claw, I. *s.* die Klaue, Kralle (*of birds*); die Pfote (*of dogs, cats, etc.*); die Schere (*of crabs, etc.*); — of a table, der Klaufuß; table with pillar and —, Tisch mit Säule und Klauenfüßen; — of a hammer, die Hammerklaue, gespaltene Finne. II. *v.a.* kratzen, zerkratzen; — me and I'll — thee, Wurst wider Wurst; wie du mir, so ich dir; to — off, abkratzen. **—ed**, *adj.* mit Klauen.

Clay, I. *s.* der Ton, die Tonerde, der Lehm; die Erde, Staub und Asche (*fig.*); potter's —, der Töpferton. II. *adj.*; — bottom, — land, — soil, der Lehmboden, die Tonerde; — brick, der Lehmstein; — hut, die Lehmhütte; — tile, der Tonziegel, Lehmziegel; — wall, die Bleichwand. III. *v.a.* mit Ton verschmieren, bedecken; decken, terrieren (*sugar*). **—ey**, *adj.* tonig, lehmig, tönern, Ton=, Lehm=. *Comp.* **—-marl**, *s.* (—ey marl) der Tonmergel; der Kleiber (*Build.*). **—-pit**, *s.* die Lehmgrube.

Claymore, *s.* altes schottisches Breitschwert; Fechter mit dem Breitschwert.

Clean, I. *adj.* rein, reinlich, sauber; blank; knotenfrei (*as wood*); rein, fehlerfrei (*B.*); geschickt, gewandt (*in doing things*); — bill of health, reiner Gesundheitspaß; to make a — breast of it, alles frei heraus gestehen; einem reinen Wein einschenken; — proof, frischer Abzug eines Korrekturbogens. II. *adv.* rein, gänzlich, ganz, völlig; geschickt; it went — through, es ging gerade hindurch, durch und durch; to leap — over, rein darüber springen. III. *v.a.* reinigen, säubern, blank machen, putzen; to — out a harbour, einen Hafen ausbaggern, von Schlamm reinigen; to — a gun, ein Gewehr putzen. **—liness**, *s.* die Reinlichkeit, Sauberkeit; die Reinheit (*fig.*). **—ly**, *adj. & adv.* reinlich, sauber, säuberlich; nett; geschickt, gewandt; rein (*fig.*). **—ness**, *s.* die Reinigkeit, Reinlichkeit, Sauberkeit; die Reinheit (*from infectious disease*); (moral —ness) die Reinheit; (innocence) die Unschuld. **—se**, *v.a.* reinigen, säubern; scheuern, putzen (*vessels, etc.*); abkreischen (*Typ.*); to —se from sin, von Sünden reinigen. **—ser**, *s.* der Reiniger, Ausputzer; das Reinigende; der Ausräumer (*of wells, etc.*). **—sings**, *pl.* die Ausfegsel. *Comp.* **—-handed**, *adj.* mit reinen Händen; ehrlich. **—-limbed**, *adj.* von ebenmäßigem Gliederbau. **—-shaped**, *adj.* wohlgebaut. **—-shaven**, *adj.* glattrasiert.

Clear, I. *adj.*, **—ly**, *adv.* (bright) klar, hell; rein, hell (*of sound*); klar, durchsichtig (*as glass*); (serene) heiter; (acute) scharfsichtig; (impartial) unparteiisch, unbefangen; (free from blame) schuldlos, unbefleckt; ohne Abzug, rein, netto (*C. L.*); (open) frei; (evident) deutlich; (indisputable) unleugbar; see that the coast is —, siehe zu, daß uns nichts im Wege steht; — amount, der Nettobelauf; a — case, eine klare Sache, unzweifelhaft, deutlich; — day, klarer, heiterer Tag; four — days, vier volle Tage; — discourse, verständliche Rede; — fire, hellbrennendes Feuer; — gain, reiner Gewinn; a — head, ein heller, offener Kopf; — judgment, reine helle Urteilskraft; — mind, reines, lauteres Gemüt; — reason, klarer Verstand; a — spot, eine lichte Stelle (*in the sky*); — style, klare Schreibart; — title, unbestrittenes Recht; — voice, reine, helle, unbelegte, volltönende, deutliche Stimme; in a — voice, mit heller Stimme; — water, offenes Wasser (*Naut.*), reines Wasser; — weather, helles Wetter; to keep — of, sich fern halten von, sich nicht hineinmischen, (einem) weit aus dem Wege gehen. II. *adv.* offenbar; gänzlich, völlig, ganz und gar; to get — (of), los werden, sich losmachen; to get — of a disagreeable companion, sich von einem unangenehmen Gefährten losmachen; to come off —, glücklich davon kommen, frei ausgehen; to leap — over, frei hinüberspringen; to stand —, aus dem Wege gehen. III. *s.* die Helle; der innere Raum (*Mach., Arch.*); in the —, im Lichten. IV. *v.a.* klar, hell machen, erhellen, aufklären; säubern; lichten, abholzen (*a wood, etc.*); (free) befreien, lösen; (— out) aufräumen, ausräumen, ausladen, entleeren; (— from blame) rechtfertigen; lossprechen (*Law*); (vault over) über eine Sache hinweg=springen, =setzen; als reinen Gewinn einziehen, ohne Abzug gewinnen (*C.L.*); to — accounts, Rechnungen ins Reine bringen, saldieren (*C.L.*); to — the coast, sich von der Küste entfernt halten (*Naut.*); reine Bahn machen (*fig.*); to — the course, die Rennbahn von Menschen reinigen; to — an estate, ein Gut entlasten; to — goods at the custom-house, Waren klarieren; to — the ground, eine Strecke Landes urbar machen; to — a hedge, über eine Hecke springen; to — liquors, Flüssigkeiten abklären; to — a port, aus einem Hafen absegeln, auslaufen; to — a room, ein Zimmer räumen; to — a ship for action, ein Schiff kampffertig *or* zum Gefechte klar machen; to — the table, (den Eßtisch) abdecken; to — £1000 a year, 1000 Pfund jährlich netto einnehmen; to — one's throat, sich räuspern; — the way! Platz da! aus dem Wege! to — **away** (*or* up) a difficulty, eine Schwierigkeit heben; to — away (*or* up) a doubt, einen Zweifel lösen; to — **off**, I. *v.a.* abschleifen. II. *v.n.* sich entfernen; to — **out**, I. *v.a.* ausräumen (*a cupboard*), ausleeren (*a box*). II. *v.n.* sich davon machen (*coll.*); his stock was quite —ed out, sein Lager wurde völlig ausverkauft; to — **up**, aufklären, enträtseln; to — up an affair, a matter, eine Sache ins Reine bringen. V. *v.n.* (— up) sich aufhellen, hell *or* klar werden; the weather is —ing up, das Wetter klärt sich auf *or* wird schön. **—ance**, I. *s.* (riddance) die Befreiung; das Reinigen; (—ing up) die Abräumung; die Ausräumung (eines Warenlagers); (clear space) der Zwischenraum, Spielraum; die Verzollung (*of ships*); (certificate) der Zollschein; —ance of the piston, der Kolbenspielraum. II. *attrib.*; —ance sale, der Ausverkauf (*C. L.*). **—ed**, *p.p. & adj.*; —ed out, am Zollhause klariert (*C.L.*), ganz ausverkauft, ausgeleert werden (*C.L.*). **—er**, *s.* die Wendewalze (*Spin.*); der Aufklärer. **—ing**, *s.* die Rechtfertigung (*B.*); das Reinmachen; die Lichtung (*in a wood*); das urbar gemachte Stück Land (*Agr.*); die Quittung (*C. L.*); the —ing of drafts, of cheques, die Ausgleichung der Rechnungen durch gegenseitige Bankanweisungen (*C.L.*). **—ness**, *s.* die Klarheit, Helle; die Klarheit, Deutlichkeit; die Unbescholtenheit; —ness of sound, die Klarheit des Tones; —ness of voice, die Deutlichkeit der Stimme. *Comp.* **—-eyed**, *adj.* helläugig. **—-headed**, *adj.* klardenkend, einsichtig, mit offnem

Kopf. —**ing-house**, *s.* das Abrechnungsbureau (*Railw.*); das (Londoner) Abrechnungshaus, wo die tägliche Verrechnung der gegenseitigen Bankanweisungen stattfindet. —**ing-sale**, *s.* der Ausverkauf (*C. L.*). —**-shining**, *adj.* hellscheinend, glänzend. —**-sighted**, *adj.* scharfsichtig; klarsehend, einsichtig (*fig.*); the most —-sighted, die hellsten Köpfe. —**-starch**, *v.a.* stärken (feine Wäsche). —**-story**, *s.* das lichte Stockwerk; das Fenstergeschoß des Hauptschiffs (*Arch.*). —**-toned**, *adj.* helltönig. —**-voiced**, *adj.* hellstimmig, mit heller Stimme.

Cleat, *s.* der Anguß für den Aufsatz am Geschützrohr (*Artil.*); der Schildzapfenflügel (*Artil.*); die Leiste (*Carp.*); die Klampe (*Naut.*); das Hufeisen auf Schuhsohlen; — of the gangway, die Fallrampsklampe.

Cleav—able, *adj.* spaltbar. —**age**, *s.* das Spalten; die Spaltung; die Spaltung, der Spalt; —age of crystals, die Spaltungsweise *or* Spaltbarkeit der Kristalle.

[1]**Cleav—e**, *ir.v.* I. *a.* spalten, zerspalten. II. *n.* sich spalten; the ground clave asunder under them, es zerriß die Erde unter ihnen (*B.*). —**er**, *s.* der Spalter; der Klöber (*Carp.*); das Hackmesser (*for wood*); butcher's —er, das Schlachtbeil, Metzgerbeil; wood —er, der Holzhacker. *Comp.* —**e-saw**, —**ing-saw**, *s.* die Klobsäge. —**ing-hammer**, *s.* der Schrothammer.

[2]**Cleave**, *ir.v.n.* kleben, ankleben, sich anhängen; my tongue —s to the roof of my mouth, meine Zunge klebt an meinem Gaumen (*B.*); — to that which is good, hanget dem Guten an (*B.*). —**rs**, *s.* kletterndes Labkraut.

Cleek, *s.* der Haken, Hakenstock (*dial.*); der Golfstock.

Clef, *s.* der Schlüssel (*Mus.*).

Cleft, I. *imperf. & p.p. of* [1]Cleave. II. *s.* die Spalte, Kluft. III. *adj.*; — palate, die Gaumenspalte. *Comp.* —**-footed**, *see* Cloven-footed. —**-graft**, *v.a.* in den Spalt pfropfen.

Cleg, *s.* die Pferdefliege, Bremse (*prov.*).

Clem, **Clam**, *v.* I. *n.* verdursten, verhungern (*dial.*). II. *a.* verschmachten lassen (*dial.*).

Clematis, *s.* die Waldrebe, Klematis (*Bot.*).

Clemen—cy, *s.* die Gnade, Milde; die Schonung; —cy of the air, milde *or* weiche Luft. —**t**, *adj.*, —**tly**, *adv.* (gracious) gnädig; (indulgent) nachsichtig; (mild, merciful) sanft, mild, gütig.

Clench, *v.a.* vernieten, festklammern; *see* Clinch; to — one's fist, die Faust ballen; with —ed teeth, mit zusammengebissenen Zähnen.

Clepsydra, *s.* die Wasseruhr.

Clerestory, *old spelling for* Clear-story.

Cler—gy, *s.* die Geistlichkeit, Klerisei, der Klerus. —**gyman**, *s.* der Geistliche der Staatskirche; a —gyman, ein Geistlicher. —**ic**, *s.* der Geistliche. —**ical**, *adj.* zum geistlichen Stande gehörig, den geistlichen Stand betreffend; einen Schreiber betreffend; —ical work, die Schreiberarbeit, Schreiberei. —**-icalism**, *s.* der Klerikalismus, klerikale Grundsätze, geistlicher Einfluß. —**k**, *see* Clerk.

Clerk, *s.* der Schreiber; der Kommis, Handlungsgehilfe, der Sekretär; der Geistliche (*obs.*); der Gelehrte (*obs.*); der Laie, der die Responsen in der anglikanischen Kirche liest; — of the assizes, der Gerichtsschreiber bei den Assisen; collecting —, Kommis für Inkasso; confidential —, erster Kommis; correspondence —, der Korrespondent; articled —, ein juristischer Student, der sich bei einem praktizierenden Advokaten in die Lehre giebt; bank(er's) —, der Bankschreiber; — of the market, der Marktschreiber; — of the weather, der Wettersekretär (*hum.*), der Direktor des meteorologischen Bureaus (*Amer. hum.*); ordnance —, der Sekretär des Generalzeugmeisteramtes; — of the House of Lords, der Sekretär des Oberhauses; — to the Senate, Senatssekretär; town —, der Stadtschreiber; — to the Board of Works, der Bauaufseher. —**ly**, *adj. & adv.* gelehrt; geschickt. —**ship**, *s.* die Schreiberstelle; die Kommisstelle; das Sekretariat.

Clever, *adj.*, —**ly**, *adv.* klug, gescheit; geistreich, witzig (*as an answer*); (skilful) geschickt, gewandt; (talented) begabt; wohlgebaut (*prov.*). —**ish**, *adj.* ziemlich geschickt, ziemlich gescheit. —**ness**, *s.* die Klugheit; die Geschicklichkeit; die Fähigkeit.

Clew, *s.* der Knaul, Knäuel (*dial.*); der Leitfaden; *see* Clue; das Schothorn (*Naut.*). *Comp.* —**-line**, *s.* das Geitau (der kleineren Segel).

Click, I. *s.* der kurze, scharfe Ton; der Schlag; der Tick-Tack; der Sperrhaken (*Mech.*); the — formed with the tip of the tongue, der Schnalzer, Schnalzlaut; — of a repeater, der Sperrkegel einer Repetieruhr. II. *v.n.* schlagen, ticken, klappern; to — one's tongue, mit der Zunge schnalzen. —**ing**, *s.* das Ticken.

Client, *s.* der Klient, die Klientin; der Schützling; der Gefolgsmann, Anhänger. —**age**, *s.* die Gefolgschaft; das Gefolge. —**èle**, *s.* die Kundschaft.

Cliff, *s.* die Klippe. *Comp.* —**head**, der Klippenvorsprung.

Clima—cteric, I. *adj.* klimakterisch; —cteric years, die kritischen Jahre. II. *s.* das Wechseljahr, kritische Jahr (im menschlichen Leben). —**x**, *s.* die Klimax; der höchste Grad, Gipfel; der Höhepunkt (*of a dramatic action*).

Clim—ate, *s.* das Klima, der Himmelsstrich. —**atic**, *adj.* klimatisch, Klima-. —**atize**, *v.a.* an ein Klima gewöhnen. —**atology**, *s.* die Klimatenlehre, Lehre von den Klimaten. —**e**, *s.* (*poet. for* —ate), der Himmelsstrich.

Climb, *v.* I. *a.* erklimmen (*a tree, etc.*); (mount) hinaufsteigen, besteigen. II. *n.* klettern, klimmen; —ing-irons, Steigeisen (*Mount.*). —**er**, *s.* der Steiger, Kletterer; (—ing plant) die Schlingpflanze; der Hinaufkletterer (*fig.*); das Zahnrad (*Locom.*). —**ers**, *pl.* mit Sporen versehene Kletterstiefel (*Tele.*); Klettervögel (*Orn.*).

Clinch, I. *v.a.* nieten, vernieten, verklinken; *see* Clench; klinkerweise legen (*tiles*); verstärken (*fig.*); to — a cable, ein Tau an den Ankerring stecken; to — a bolt, einen Bolzen umnieten, verklinken; to — the rail-foot, den Fuß der Schiene einkarten; to — an argument, einen Beweis verstärken, überwiegende Beweisgründe anführen; this —ed matters, das entschied *or* gab den Ausschlag. II. *v.n.* festhalten. III. *s.* die Klinke (*of a bolt, etc.*); der Ankerstrich (*of a cable*); das Nagelniet, die Vernietung (*of a nail*). —**er**, *s.* die Klampe, Klammer; der unumstößliche Beweis, Trumpf (*coll.*). —**ing**, *s.* das Verstopfen der Schießlöcher (*Naut.*); das Einkerben (*of the rails, Railw.*). *Comp.* —**er-built**, **Clinker-built**, *adj.* klinkerweise gebaut. —**er-nail**, *s.* der Schraubennagel. —**er-work**, *s.* das Klinkerwerk; die schindelartige Beplattung (*of an iron-clad*).

Cling, *ir.v.n.* sich festhalten, anhangen, sich klammern; anhangen, anschließen (*as a dress*); to — to a p., einem anhangen, sich fest an einen anschließen. —**ing**, *adj.* anhängend, anhänglich, sich anschließend; of a —ing disposition, von anhänglicher Natur, anhänglich. *Comp.* —**stone**, *s.* der Klingstein.

Clinical, *adj.*, —**ly**, *adv.* klinisch; bettlägerige Kranke betreffend; — lecture, Vorlesung im Klinikum, Vortrag am Krankenbett; — thermometer, das Bluthermometer.

Clink, I. *s.* der Klang, das Geklirr. II. *v.n.* grell klingen; rasseln, klirren; —ing of glasses, das Anstoßen der Gläser. III. *v.a.* rasseln, klirren lassen; to — glasses, (mit den Gläsern) anstoßen. —**er**, *s.* der Klinker, hartgebrannte Backstein (*Build.*); Dutch —er, der holländische Klinker. *Comp.* —**er-built**, *adj. see* Clincher-built.

Clinometer, *s.* die Bergwage, Böschungswage, der Neigungsmesser, das Klinometer (*Surv.*). —**ry**, *s.* die Neigungsmessung.

¹Clip, I. *v.a.* beſchneiden, abſchneiden (*hair, etc.*); ſcheren (*horses, sheep, etc.*); (ab)ſchroten (*needles, pins, etc.*); kippen (*coin*); ſtutzen (*a bird's wings, etc.*); abkneipen (*Artil.*); to — one's words, die Silben verſchlucken; to — s.o.'s wings, einem die Flügel beſchneiden. II. *s.* die Schafſchur; die Schur; (blow) der Klapps, Schlag (*sl.*). **—per**, *s.* der Beſchneider, Scherer; der Kipper (*of coin*); der Klipper, Schnellſegler (*Naut.*). **—pers**, *pl.* die Stutzſchere, Schafſchere. **—ping**, *s.* die Beſchneidung, Abſtutzung. **—pings**, *pl.* die Abfälle. *Comp.* **—per-built**, *adj.* ſcharfgebaut. **—ping-shears**, *pl.* die Pferdeſchere, Schafſchere.

²Clip, I. *v.a.* (*obs.*) umfaſſen, feſt umſchließen, umarmen. II. *s.* (*obs.*) die Umarmung; das Umfaſſende; die Zwecke; die Muſterklammer, der Klemmer (*for papers*); die Hoſenklammer (*Cycl.*).

Clique, *s.* die Bande; die Sippſchaft.

Cloak, I. *s.* der Mantel; der Deckmantel (*fig.*). II. *v.a.* mit einem Mantel bedecken; bemänteln (*fig.*). *Comp.* **—room**, *s.* die Garderobe, der Ablegeraum (*Theat.*); der Aufbewahrungsort für das Handgepäck, die Gepäckannahme und Gepäckausgabe (*Railw.*); **ladies'—room**, die Damentoilette. **—strap**, *s.* der Mantelriemen.

Clock, *s.* die Schlaguhr, Pendeluhr; der Bockkäfer (*Ent.*); der Zwickel (*in stockings*); alarm —, die Weck(er)uhr, der Wecker; — that chimes the hours, Uhr mit Glockenſpiel; musical —, Spieluhr; what o'— is it? wie viel Uhr iſt es? sidereal —, Uhr nach Sternzeit; — for a mantelpiece, Stutzuhr, Kaminuhr. **—ed**, *adj.* mit geblümtem Zwickel. *Comp.* **—dial**, **—face**, *s.* das Zifferblatt. **—hand**, *s.* der (Uhr=)zeiger. **—maker**, *s.* der Uhrmacher. **—movement**, **—work**, *s.* das Uhrwerk; like —work, ganz regelmäßig, pünktlich; automatiſch.

Clod, I. *s.* der (Erd=)Kloß, die Erdſcholle; der Klumpen; der Klotz, Tölpel (*fig.*). II. *v.a.* mit Erdſchollen bewerfen (*prov.*). *Comp.* **—crusher**, *s.* der Erdſchollenbrecher. **—hopper**, *s.* der Bauernlümmel, der Klutentreter (*dial.*).

Clog, I. *v.a.* mit einem Klotz verſehen, belaſten; (*fig.*) hindern, hemmen, aufhalten, verzögern; (— up) verſtopfen; —ged with dirt, durch Schmutz zum Stocken gebracht; this ink never —s the pen, dieſe Tinte bleibt immer flüſſig in der Feder. II. *v. n.* ſtocken, verkleben (vor Schmutz). III. *s.* der Klotz; der Klöppel, Bengel (*for beasts*); die Beſchwerde, Laſt, Feſſel, das Hindernis (*fig.*); der Holzſchuh; a pair of —s (Holz=) Pferde=Überſchuhe; —s, for garden horses, Hufbewickelung für Garten Raſenpferde.

Cloist—er, I. *s.* das Kloſter (*obs.*). II. *v.a.* in ein Kloſter einſchließen. **—ered**, *adj.* mit Kreuzgängen verſehen, kloſterartig; einſam abgeſchieden. **—ers**, *pl.* der Kloſtergang, Kreuzgang (*Arch.*). **—ral**, *adj.* zu einem Kloſter gehörig, klöſterlich, Kloſter=; (*fig.*) abgeſchloſſen, zurückgezogen.

Clomb, *obs. & poet. imperf. & p.p. of* Climb.

¹Close, I. *adj.* (shut) verſchloſſen, zugemacht; geſchloſſen (*of vowel sounds*); (retired) eingeſchloſſen, verſchloſſen; (hidden) verborgen; (reserved) zurückhaltend, verſchloſſen; (silent) verſchwiegen; (dense) dicht; (narrow) knapp, eng; (compressed) gedrängt, kurz; (closed up) verſtopft; (exact in quantity, length, *etc.*) genau, ſparſam, karg; (parsimonious) ſparſam; (niggardly) knickerig, filzig; (viscous) zäh; ſchwül, trüb (*as the air*); (near) eng, enganſchließend, anliegend; unabläſſig, ſorgſam, eifrig; (precise) genau; (to the point) direkt zugehend; (not open to all) geſchloſſen, verſchloſſen; (familiar) vertraut; (short) kurz; (alike, nearly equal) ziemlich gleich, ſehr gleich; dicht, feſt (*of stuffs*); — air, dumpfe *or* dumpfige Luft; — attention, volle *or* geſpannte Aufmerkſamkeit; a — ball, ein kollierter Ball (*Bill.*); — box, der Verſchlag; — cell, enge Zelle; to be in — conversation, in lebhaftem, eifrigem Geſpräche ſein; — correspondence, vertrauter Briefwechſel; — debate, ernſthafte, eifrige Diskuſſion; — fight, das Handgemenge; it was a — fight, lange war es unentſchieden, wer von den Kämpfern ſiegen würde; — fire, auf einen Punkt gerichtetes (Geſchütz= *or* Gewehr=)Feuer; a — friend, ein ſehr intimer Freund; — friendship, beſonders warme Freundſchaft; a — hand, eine ſparſam ausgebende, karge Hand; a — prisoner, einer, der in enger Gefangenſchaft ſitzt, einer der durch Krankheit, Geſchäfte ꝛc. an das Haus, das Zimmer gebunden iſt; — piece of cloth, ein dickes Stück Zeug; — quarters, das Treffen in der Nähe; to come to — quarters, handgemein werden; to live in — quarters with a p., dicht bei einem *or* mit einem zuſammen wohnen; — proximity, unmittelbare Nähe; — season, — time, die Schonzeit; — shaver, der Geizhals (*sl.*); a — shave, ein Entkommen mit genauer Not; — stool, der Nachtſtuhl; — study, eifriges Studium; — style, bündiger gedrängter, knapper Stil; — substance, dichte, zähe Subſtanz; — translation, eine ſich dem Original eng anſchließende genaue, wortgetreue Überſetzung; — weather, drückendes, ſchwüles Wetter. II. *adv.* nicht offen, verſchloſſen, zu; (near to) nahe daran, dicht an, dicht dabei, an einander; (exactly) genau; (secretly) verborgen, heimlich; to live —, knapp, ſparſam leben; to lie —, dicht daran ſein; to draw the curtains —, die Vorhänge dicht zuziehen; keep —! verbirg dich, halt dich zurückgezogen, ſchweig; halte dich dicht an mir, mir zur Seite! — to the ground, dicht am Boden; to sail — to the wind, (dicht) beim Winde ſegeln; to stick — to a p., ſich dicht an einen halten; to follow — upon a p., einem auf dem Fuße folgen; to sit — round the fire, dicht ums Feuer ſitzen; — by, dicht dabei, daneben. III. *s.* der Schluß; das Ende; der eingeſchloſſene Raum; das eingehegte, umzäunte, eingepferchte Feld, Gehege; die Einfriedigung; der Domhof, Hof einer Abtei; enge Straße; at the — of day, beim Anbruche der Nacht; at the — of the year, am Jahresſchluß, an der Jahreswende. IV. *v.a.* ſchließen, zuſchließen, zumachen, zutun; verſchließen; abſchließen, beſchließen; endigen; to — an account, eine Rechnung abſchließen; to — an affair (a concern), einer Sache ein Ende machen, eine S. beendigen, ein Geſchäft abmachen; to — a book, ein Buch zumachen; to — the books, die Bücher ſchließen (*C.L.*); to — a bargain, einen Kauf abſchließen; to — the current, den elektriſchen Strom ſchließen; to — the door against a p., die Tür vor einem ſchließen, einem die Tür verſchließen; to — the door upon a p., die Tür hinter einem zumachen (*lit.*), einen verſtoßen (*fig.*); to — the line (the ranks), die Schiffe dichter zuſammenrücken laſſen (die Reihen enger aufſchließen laſſen *Mil.*); to — a seam, einen Stoff zuſammennähen, eine Naht überwendlich nähen; to — a sentence, einen (Rede=)ſatz ſchließen; to — in, einſchließen; to — up, verſchließen; to — a wound, eine Wunde zuſchließen, zunähen. V. *v.n.* ſich ſchließen, zuheilen; zuſammengeraten; (ſich) endigen; to — with the enemy, mit dem Feinde handgemein werden; to — with an offer, ein Anerbieten annehmen **—ly**, *adv. see* Close II.; the election was —ly contested, es gab einen harten Wahlkampf; to attend —ly to a p.'s orders, ſich ſtreng an jemandes Befehle halten; he must be watched —ly, man muß ihm ſcharf auf die Finger ſehen. **—ness**, *s.* die Verſchloſſenheit, Eingeſchloſſenheit; die Dichtheit, Dichtigkeit (*of cloth, etc.*); die Heimlichkeit, Verſchwiegenheit; die Zurückhaltung; die Zurückgezogenheit; die Einſamkeit; die Enge, Knappheit (*of a dress*); die Dumpfheit (*of a room, etc.*); die Kargheit; der Geiz;

(nearness) die Nähe; die Genauigkeit (*of a translation*); die Dringlichkeit, Straffheit (*of an argument*); die Hitze (*of a debate*); the —ness of an enquiry, die Genauigkeit einer Nachfrage, Nachforschung. **—r**, *s.* der Beschließer, der Schließer; der Schlußstein (*Arch.*). **—t**, *see* Closet. *Comp.* **—-bodied**, *adj.* eng, knapp anliegend. **—-cropped**, *adj.* kurz geschoren. **—-fisted**, *adj.* geizig, karg (*fig.*); to be —-fisted, zugeknöpfte Taschen haben. **—-fitting**, *adj.* eng anschließend *or* anliegend. **—-hauled**, *adj.* dicht gebraßt; to sail —-hauled, dicht beim Winde segeln. **—-pent**, *adj.* eng verschlossen. **—-quarters**, *pl.* hölzerne Scheidewände, starke Schotten (zur Verteidigung beim Entern); (*fig.*) der Nahkampf; to come to —-quarters with a p., mit einem handgemein werden. **—-time**, *s.* die Schonzeit (des Wildes). **—-tongued**, *adj.* verschwiegen.

²Clos—e, *etc.*, *see* Close, *etc.* **—ing**, I. *p. & adj.;* —ing word, das Schlußwort; —ing needle, die Stemmnadel. II. *s.* das Schließen; sign of —ing up, das Vereinigungszeichen (*Typ.*). **—ure**, *s.* das Verschließen; das Zuschließen; der Schluß (der Debatte, *Pol.*); to apply the —ure, eine Debatte schließen.

Closet, I. *s.* das Geheimzimmer, Kabinett; der Wandschrank; (water-)— (W. C.), der Abort, Abtritt. II. *v.a.* in einen Wandschrank, ein Kabinett einschließen; to be —ed with a p., mit einem eine vertrauliche Unterredung *or* Beratung haben; the king and the queen remained for some time —ed together, der König und die Königin blieben einige Zeit in vertraulicher Besprechung zusammen.

Clot, I. *s.* der Klump, das Klümpchen; — of blood, der Blutklumpen. II. *v.n.* sich verdichten, klumpig werden, gerinnen; —ted cream, verdickter Rahm; —ted milk, geronnene Milch.

Cloth, I. *s.* das Tuch; (table-—) das Tischtuch; die geistliche Tracht, Kleidung (*fig.*); der Predigerstand (*fig.*); das Zeug, der Stoff; bolting-—, Siebtuch, Beuteltuch; broad—, feines Wollentuch; fancy —, das gemusterte Zeug; sail-—, Segeltuch; — of a sail, das Kleid eines Segels; stout —, starkes, grobes, schweres Tuch; twilled —, Köperzeug; — of gold, das Goldtuch; to lay the —, (den Tisch) decken; to remove the —, (den Tisch) abdecken. II. *attrib.;* — beam, der Weberbaum; — binding, der Leinenband; — board, der Leinwanddeckel; — cuttings, Tuchabfälle; — merchant, der Tuchhändler; — presser, der Stoffdrücker (*Sew.-m.*); — printing, der Zeugdruck; — weaver, der Tuchweber. **—e**, *see* Clothe. **—ler**, *s.* der Kleiderhändler, Tuchhändler. **—ing**, *s.* die Kleidung, der Anzug; under-—ing, das Unterzeug, die Leibwäsche. **—s**, *pl. see* Cloth; Zeug-, Tuch-arten. *Comp.* **—-plate**, *s.* die Nähplatte (*Sew.-m.*). **—-wheel**, *s.* das Zuführrad (*Sew.-m.*). **—worker**, *s.* der Tuchmacher, Tuchwirker; —workers' Company, die Tuchmacherinnung.

Clothe, *reg. & ir.v.a.* kleiden, ankleiden, bekleiden; einkleiden (*recruits*); kleiden, bekleiden (*fig.*); to — one's thoughts in words, seine Gedanken in Worte kleiden. **—s**, I. *pl.* die Kleider, die Kleidung; (bed-—s) das Bettzeug; baby —s, das Kinderzeug; cast-off —s, abgetragene Kleider, alte Kleider; under-—s, Unterzeug; soiled —s, schmutzige Wäsche; old —s, alte Kleider, abgetragene Kleider; small-—s, Beinkleider, Kniebeinkleider; a suit of —s, ein (vollständiger) Anzug; to put on *or* don one's —s, sich ankleiden *or* anziehen; to take off one's —s, sich auskleiden, ausziehen, entkleiden. II. *attrib.;* plain-—s officer, der Geheimpolizist, Spitzel. *Comp.* **—s-bag**, *s.* der Wäsch(e)beutel. **—s-basket**, *s.* der Wäsch(e)korb. **—s-brush**, *s.* die Kleiderbürste. **—s-horse**, *s.* der Wäschetrockenständer. **—s-line**, *s.* die Waschleine. **—s-man**, *s.;* old-—s-man, der Kleidertrödler. **—s-peg**, **—s-pin**, *s.* die Waschklammer. **—s-press**, *s.* der Kleiderschrank; die Presse für Kleidungsstücke. **—s-wringer**, *s.* die Wringmaschine.

Cloud, I. *s.* die Wolke; das Gedränge, Gewühl (*fig.*); (multitude) die Schar, dichte Menge; die Mohr (*in stuffs*); der dunkle Fleck, die Ader (*in guns, etc.*); der Umhang (*worn by ladies*); — of tobacco-smoke, der Tabaksqualm; to be in the —s, träumen; he is under a —, es hängt eine Wolke über ihm; to cast a — upon, trüben; — of dust, Staubwolke. II. *v.a.* bewölken, bedecken, trüben, verdunkeln; ädern, flammen (*wood, paper, etc.*); moirieren (*stuff*); abschmutzen (*Print.*). III. *v.n.* sich umwölken, trübe werden. **—ily**, *adv.* wolkig; dunkel. **—iness**, *s.* die Umwölkung, Dunkelheit; das Wolkige, Trübe, Dunkle; das Fleckige, Wässerige (*of stones and stuffs*); —iness of aspect, trübes Aussehen; —iness of the atmosphere, die trübe Luft; —iness of a diamond, die Feuerlosigkeit eines Diamanten. **—ing**, *s.* die Trübe (*of stones*); die Flammierung (*in stuffs*). **—less**, *adj.*, **—lessly**, *adv.* wolkenlos, unbewölkt, klar. **—let**, *s.* das Wölkchen. **—y**, *adj.* wolkig, bewölkt, trübe; wolkig (*of gems, etc.*); traurig (*fig.*); a —y brow, eine umwölkte Stirn; a —y night, eine finstere wolkendüstre Nacht; —y notions, unklare Begriffe. *Comp.* **—-capped**, *adj.* von Wolken umgeben, wolkenbedeckt, in die Wolken ragend. **—-compelling**, *adj.* Wolken sammelnd; —-compelling Jove (the —-compeller), der Wolkensammler Zeus. **—-covered**, *adj.* wolkenumhüllt, bewölkt. **—-girt**, *adj.* von Wolken umgeben. **—-wrapt**, *adj.* in Wolken eingehüllt, wolkenumzogen.

¹Clout, I. (*obs. & dial.*) *s.* der Lappen; (dish-—) der Wischlappen; der Fleck, das Flecken (*on shoes, etc.*); das Achsschenkelblech (*of wheels*); (iron —) die Anstoßschiene (*Artil.*); a — on the head, on the ear, eine Kopfnuß, Ohrfeige (*vulg.*). II. *v.a.* flicken; mit eisernen Scheiben *or* Schienen beschlagen.

²Clout, I. *s.*, **—-nail**, *s.* der kleine Nagel, Schuhnagel, Plattnagel. II. *v. a.* mit Nägeln versehen.

¹Clove, (*obs.*) *imperf. of* ¹Cleave. **—n**, *p.p. & adj.* gespalten; —n foot, der gespaltene Fuß; (*fig.*) Pferdefuß, der böse Feind, Teufel; to show the —n foot *or* hoof, den Pferdefuß zeigen, seinen wahren (bösen) Charakter zeigen. *Comp.* **—n-footed**, *adj.* spaltfüßig, zweihufig.

²Clove, *s.* die Gewürznelke; das Nägelein (*poet.*); oil of —s, das Gewürznelkenöl. *Comp.* **—-bark**, *s.* die Nelkenrinde. **—-cinnamon**, *s.* der Nelkenzimmt. **—-gillyflower**, **—-pink**, *s.* die Gartennelke.

Clover, *s.* der Klee; to live *or* be in —, im Überflusse leben, üppig leben; in der Wolle sitzen, leben wie Gott in Frankreich; lanceolated —, das spitze Kleeblatt (*Arch.*). *Comp.* **—-leaf**, *s.* das Kleeblatt. **—-seed**, *s.* die Kleesaat.

Clown, *s.* (lout) der Grobian, Tölpel; der Hanswurst, Possenreißer (*in a pantomime, etc.*). **—ish**, *adj.*, **—ishly**, *adv.* bäu(e)risch, roh, grob. **—ishness**, *s.* das bäurische Wesen, die Grobheit.

Cloy, *v.a.* übersättigen, überladen, anekeln (*fig.*).

Club, I. *s.* (thick, short stick) die Keule, der Knüttel, Stock; das Treff, das Kreuz (*Cards*); die geschlossene Gesellschaft, der Klub; das Kasino. II. *v.a.* (contribute to a common object) beisteuern, (Geld) zusammenschießen; mit einer Keule schlagen; to — a musket, ein Gewehr verkehrt nehmen. III. *v.n.* sich (zu gemeinschaftlichen Zwecken) versammeln; beisteuern; we all —bed together to . . ., wir steuerten alle bei zu . . . *or* wir schossen alle zusammen . . . *Comp.* **—-foot**, *s.* der Klumpfuß. **—-footed**, *adj.* klumpfüßig. **—-house**, *s.* das Klublokal, Klubhaus, Kasino. **—-law**, *s.* das Faustrecht; die Klubgesetze. **—-man**, *s.* der Klubbist; der Keulenträger. **—-**

moss, *s.* das Kolbenmoos. **—-room**, *s.* das Klubzimmer. **—-shaped**, *adj.* keulenförmig.

Cluck, *v.n.* glucken; —ing hen, die Gluckhenne.

Clue, *s.* der Knäuel (*of thread, etc.*); der Faden (*of a tale*); der Leitfaden, Anhaltspunkt, Schlüssel (to, zu, für) (*fig.*); Lebensfaden.

Clump, I. *s.* der Klotz, Klumpen (*of wood, etc.*); die Gruppe; — of trees, eine Baumgruppe. II. *v.a.* unternageln; mit Leisten einfassen. III. *v.n.* plumpsen, stampfend, *or* schwerfällig gehen (*vulg.*). **—s**, *s.* das Gruppenspiel.

Clums—ily, *adv. see* —y. **—iness**, *s.* die Plumpheit. **—y**, *adj.* plump, tölpisch, täppisch, unbeholfen, ungeschickt.

Clung, *imperf. & p.p. of* Cling.

Cluster, I. *s.* die Traube, der Büschel; der Haufe, die Gruppe (*of trees*); der Schwarm (*of bees*); der Büschel (*of cherries*); — of grapes, Weintraube; — of islands, Inselgruppe; — of trees, Baumgruppe; — of crystals, die Kristalldruse. II. *v.n.* in Büscheln *or* Trauben wachsen; sich sammeln; —ing trees, dicht bei einander stehende Bäume, gruppenweise wachsende Bäume, Baumgruppen.

Clutch, I. *s.* (seizing) der Griff; (claw) die Klaue; die Kuppelung (*Mach.*); das Schwungrad (*Naut.*); age hath clawed me in his —, das Alter hat mich gepackt. II. *v.a.* greifen, packen, ergreifen. **—es**, *pl.* die Klauen, Krallen; to fall into the —es of a cat, unter die Klauen einer Katze geraten; to keep out of s.o.'s —es, sich vor den Krallen *or* dem Griff eines anderen hüten.

Clutter, I. *s.* der verworrene Haufe, Wirrwarr, die Unordnung; das verworrene Geräusch; — —, anhaltender wirrer Lärm. II. *v.a.* durch einander werfen; in Verwirrung bringen; hastig und verwirrt sprechen. III. *v.n.* sich in Unordnung sammeln. **—er**, *s.* hastig und verwirrt redender Mensch.

Clype—ate, **—iform**, *adj.* schildförmig (*Bot.*).

Clyster, *s.* das Klistier, die Einspritzung. *Comp.* **—-pipe**, **—-pump**, *s.* die Klistierspritze.

Coach, I. *s.* die Kutsche, der Wagen; die Hütte (*Naut.*); (private tutor) der Privatlehrer; der Einpauker; — and four, vierspännige Kutsche; hackney- —, Mietkutsche; mail- —, Post- und Personen-kutsche; stage-—, Eilwagen. II. *v.a.* in einer Kutsche fahren; we —ed it as far as N., wir fuhren mit der Kutsche bis N. (*coll.*); to — a p. for an examination, einen auf ein Examen vorbereiten, für eine Prüfung einpauken; he —ed with me, er hatte bei mir Privatunterricht. **—ing**, I. *adj.;* the old —ing days, die (gute) alte Zeit, wo man noch in Kutschen fuhr. II. *s.* der Privatunterricht; die Einpaukerei. *Comp.* **—-box**, *s.* der Bock, Kutscherbock. **—-braces**, *pl.* die Schwungriemen. **—-builder**, *s.* der Wagenbauer. **—-fare**, *s.* der Fuhrlohn. **—-house**, *s.* die Wagenremise. **—ing fee**, *s.* das Honorar für Privatunterricht, Stundengeld. **—man**, *s.* der Kutscher. **—-office**, *s.* das Passagier-Einschreibebureau. **—-stand**, *s.* der Droschkenhalteplatz. **—-step**, *s.* der Wagentritt.

Co—action, *s.* das Zusammenwirken **—active**, *adj.* mitwirkend **—adjutor (—adjutrix)**, *s.* der Gehilfe, Beistand (die Gehilfin); der Koadjutor (*obs. title*). **—adjutorship**, *s.* die Mithilfe, Beihilfe; die Stelle eines Koadjutors. **—agulate**, *v.n.* gerinnen. **—agulation**, *s.* die Gerinnung; (result of —tion) das Geronnene. **—agulum**, *s.* das Gerinnsel (*Chem.*); das Käselab. **—alesce**, *v.n.* sich vereinigen; verschmelzen; zusammenfließen. **—alescence**, *s.* das Zusammenfließen; die Vereinigung, Verschmelzung; die Einheit, Einhelligkeit. **—alition**, *s.* die Verbindung (zu einem augenblicklichen Zweck, einem gemeinschaftlichen Feinde gegenüber); —alition ministry, *s.* das Koalitions-Ministerium. **—-editor**, der Mitherausgeber. **—education**, *s.* gemeinsame Unterrichtung und Ausbildung, *or* Zusammenerziehung beider Geschlechter. **—educational**, *adj.* die Zusammenerziehung der Geschlechter betreffend. **—efficient**, I. *adj.* mitwirkend. II. *s.* der Koeffizient (*Math.*); —efficient of linear expansion, der lineare Ausdehnungskoeffizient. **—equal**, *adj.* gleich mit. **—erce**, *v.a.* zwingen, nötigen; durch Zwang in Schranken halten; zurückhalten. **—ercible**, *adj.* einschränkbar, erzwingbar; zusammendrückbar (*Phys.*). **—ercion**, *s.* die Einschränkung, Beschränkung; der Zwang; —ercion act, das Zwangsgesetz. **—ercionist**, *s.* Anhänger der Zwangspolitik, Befürworter von Ausnahmegesetzen. **—ercive**, *adj.*, **—ercively**, *adv.* einschränkend; zwingend. **—essential**, *adj.* des gleichen Wesens. **—eternal**, *adj.* gleichewig. **—eval**, *adj.* gleichzeitig, gleichalt(e)rig. **—-executor**, (**—-executrix**,) *s.* der (die) Mit-Testamentsmitvollstrecker(in). **—exist**, *v.n.* zugleich vorhanden sein. **—existence**, *s.* das gleichzeitige Dasein (mit). **—existent**, *adj.* mit *or* gleichzeitig vorhanden. **—extend**, *v.n.* gleichen Umfang, gleiche Dauer haben, sich gleich weit erstrecken. **—extension**, *s.* die gleiche Dauer, Ausdehnung, der gleiche Umfang. **—extensive**, *adj.* von gleichem Umfange, sich gleich weit erstreckend. **—gent**, **—gitate**, **—gnate**, *etc. see* Cogent, Cogitate, Cognate, *etc.* **—habit**, *v.n.* beisammen *or* zusammen wohnen; beiwohnen (einer Frau, with a woman). **—habitation**, *s.* das Beisammenwohnen; die eheliche, fleischliche Beiwohnung, der Beischlaf. **—heir**, **—heiress**, *s.* der Miterbe, die Miterbin. **—here**, *v.n.* zusammenhängen. **—herence**, **—herency**, *s.* der Zusammenhang; das Zusammenhalten; die Folge. **—herent**, *adj.*, **—herently**, *adv.* zusammenhängend. **—hesibility**, *s.* die Kohärenz; die Kohäsionskraft. **—hesion**, *s.* die Kohäsion, Flächenanziehung, der Zusammenhalt; der Zusammenhang (*fig.*); absolute —hesion, die Zähigkeit. **—hesive**, *adj.* fest zusammenhängend. **—hesiveness**, *s.* die Anziehungskraft der Teile eines Körpers, die Kohäsion. **—incide**, *etc.*, *see* Coin—, *etc.* **—ition**, *s.* das Zusammentreffen; die Begattung, der Beischlaf. **—juror**, *s.* der Mitgeschwor(e)ne. **—l—**, **—m—**, **—n—**, *see* Col—, Com—, Con—, **—nominee**, *s.* der Miternannte. **—öperate**, *v.n.* mitwirken. **—öperation**, *s.* die Mitwirkung. **—öperative**, *adj.* mitwirkend; —öperative stores, das Warenlager eines Konsumvereins; —öperative societiés, Wirtschaftsgenossenschaften, Konsumvereine. **—öpt**, *v.a.* hinzuwählen. **—öptation**, *s.* die Zuwahl, Ergänzungswahl. **—ördinate**, *adj.* beigeordnet, gleichgestellt; —ördinate pillars, in gleichen Reihen stehende Pfeiler (*Arch.*). **—ördinates**, *pl.* die Koordinaten (*Geom.*). **—ördination**, *s.* die Gleichheit des Ranges, Gleichstellung im Range; das Zusammenwirken (*of causes, Phys.*). **—partner**, *s.* der Teilhaber, Associé. **—partnership**, *s.* die Teilhaberschaft. **—p—**, *see* Copious, Copula. **—r—**, *see* Cor—. **—secant**, *s.* die Kosekante. **—sine**, *s.* der Kosinus. **—s—**, *see* Cost, Costive. **—surety**, *s.* der Mitbürge. **—temporaneous**, *see* Contemporaneous. **—terminous**, *see* Conterminous. **—venant**, *see* Covenant

Coal, I. *s.* die Kohle (*Min.*); mineral —, Steinkohle; cannel —, Kannelkohle; small —, —dust, slacky —, die Kleinkohle, das Kohlengrus; slaty —, Schieferkohle; vegetable —, Pflanzenkohle; to call a p. over the —s, einen zur Rechenschaft ziehen, einem einen Verweis erteilen; to carry —s to Newcastle, Wasser in den Rhein *or* Eulen nach Athen tragen. II. *attrib.;* — fire, das Kohlenfeuer; — putter, der Fördermann; — seam, die Kohlenader; — shift, die Verwerfungskluft im Kohlengebirge; — shovel, die Kohlenschaufel; — tip, der Abladeplatz für Kohlen; — trolley, der Hunt; — vein, das Kohlenflötz; — waggon, der Kohlenwagen; —

wharf, der Kohlenabladeort; — whipper, der Kohlenmesser. III. *v.n.* Kohlen einnehmen (*Naut.*); —ing station, die Kohlenstation. *Comp.* **—-box**, *s.* der Kohlenbehälter, Kohlenkasten, das Kohlenbecken. **—-bunker**, *s.* der Kohlenraum (*in steamers*). **—-cellar**, *s.* der Kohlenkeller. **—-dust**, *s.* der Kohlenstaub; das Gestübte; *see* Coal I. **—-field**, *s.* das Kohlenfeld. **—-formation**, *s.* die Steinkohlenbildung. **—-gas**, *s.* das Leuchtgas, Steinkohlengas. **—-heaver**, *s.* der Kohlenträger. **—-hole**, *s.* der Kohlenraum. **—-measure**, *s.* das Kohlenmaß; das Kohlengebirge (*Geol.*). **—-merchant**, *s.* der Kohlenhändler. **—-mine**, *s.* das Kohlenbergwerk. **—-oil**, *s.* das Teeröl. **—-pit**, *s.* die Kohlengrube. **—-plants**, *pl.* Pflanzenabdrücke in Steinkohlenlagern. **—-screen**, *s.* das Kohlensieb. **—-scuttle**, *see* —-box. **—-ship**, *see* Collier. **—-stove**, *s.* der Steinkohlenofen. **—-tar**, *s.* der Steinkohlenteer.

Coarse, *adj.*, **—ly**, *adv.* grob; roh, plump, gemein (*fig.*); (not refined) ohne Bildung; — bread, grobes Brot; — language, gemeine, anstößige Sprache; — manners, rohe, ungeschliffene Manieren. **—ness**, *s.* die Grobheit; die Rohheit, Gemeinheit (*fig.*); das Anstößige (*of conversation*). *Comp.* **—-grained**, *adj.* grobkörnig.

Coast, I. *s.* die Küste, das Seeufer; das Küstenland, die Gegend am Seeufer; mit Schnee oder Eis bedeckter Abhang (*Amer.*); foul —, gefährliche Küste; clear —, fahrbare Küste; the — is clear, die Bahn ist frei, die Luft ist rein (*fig.*). II. *attrib.*; — scenery, die Uferlandschaft. III. *v.n.* (— along) längs der Küste hinsegeln, an der Küste hinfahren; auf einem Schlitten einen Abhang herabgleiten; das Rad (bergab) laufen lassen, die Füße von den Pedalen nehmen (*Cycl.*). **—er**, *s.* der Küstenfahrer. **—ing**, *s.* die Küstenfahrt, Küstenschiffahrt. *Comp.* **—-battery**, *s.* die Strandbatterie. **—-defence**, *s.* die Küstenverteidigung. **—-guard**, *s.* die Küstenwache (*Naut.*); (man) der Küstenwächter. **—ing-pilot**, *s.* der Küstenlotse. **—ing-tours**, Seefahrten an der Küste entlang. **—ing-trade**, *s.* der Küstenhandel. **—ing-vessel**, *see* —er. **—line**, *s.* die Küstenlinie. **—-survey**, *s.* die Küstenvermessung.

Coat, I. *s.* der Rock; das Oberkleid, Gewand (*prov.*); das Fell, der Pelz (*of beasts*); der Bewurf (*Build.*); der Anstrich, Überzug, die Schicht (*Build.*); die Teerung (*Naut.*); die Formkleidung (*Found.*); der Kragen (*of sailcloth*); — of arms, das Wappen(-schild), der Wappenrock; — of mail, das Panzerhemd; —s of the mast, die Kragen des Mastes; — of paint, der Anstrich; first — in oil painting, der erste Ölanstrich, die Gründung; — of paint *or* pitch, die Farbenlage, Pechlage (*Naut.*); — of plaster, der Gipsbewurf; double-breasted —, doppelreihiger Rock; great —, Überrock, Überzieher, Winterpaletot; dress —, der Frack; single-breasted —, einreihiger Rock; frock —, der Gehrock; morning —, der gewöhnliche Taillenrock, kurzer ausgeschnittener Rock; to cut one's — according to one's cloth, sich nach der Decke strecken; to turn one's —, den Mantel nach dem Winde hängen, abtrünnig werden; turn—, der Abtrünnige. II. *attrib.*; — pocket, die Rocktasche; — tail, der Rockschoß. III. *v.a.* überziehen, bekleiden; to — with lime, bekalken. **—ing**, *s.* der Überzug, die Bedeckung, der Anstrich; der Rockstoff.

Coax, *v.a.* streicheln, beschwatzen, durch Liebkosungen bewegen; to — a p. into (doing) a th., einen zu etwas beschwatzen, überreden; he —ed her out of her money, er schmeichelte ihr all ihr Geld ab. **—er**, *s.* (flatterer) der (die) Schmeichler(in); (persuader) der Beschwatzer; (caresser) der Liebkoser. **—ingly**, *adv.* schmeichelnd.

[1]**Cob**, *s.* ein kleines dickes Pferdchen, starker Pony; (top) der Kopf, die Spitze; (maize) der Maiskolben; (spider) die Spinne (*prov.*); der große Kieselstein; der ungebrannte Backstein; (lump, ball) der Klumpen, die Klumpe. *Comp.* **—nut**, *s.* die Haselnuß, große Zitternuß. **—wall**, *s.* die Mauer aus Luftziegeln; die Lehmwand. **—web** I. *s.* das Spinnengewebe, Spinnweb(e). II. *attrib.*; —web micrometer, das Spinnewebemikrometer. **—webbed, —webby**, *adj.* mit Spinnweb überzogen, voller Spinnweb. **—work**, *s.* der Lehmbau.

[2]**Cob**, *v.a.* schlagen, peitschen (*sailors, etc.*). **—ble**, *see* Cobble.

Cobalt, *s.* der Kobalt. **—ic**, *adj.*; —ic compounds, Kobaltoxydverbindungen. **—ine**, *s.* der Glanzkobalt. **—ous**, *adj.* Kobaltoxydul. *Comp.* **—-blue**, *s.* das Kobaltblau.

[1]**Cobble**, *v.a.* flicken (*shoes*), schlecht, stümperhaft ausbessern. **—r**, *s.* der Schuhflicker, Schuster; (botcher) der Pfuscher; Stümper; —r, stick to your last, Schuster, bleib bei deinem Leisten! (*prov.*); —r's wax, das Schusterpech.

[2]**Cobble**, *s.* (—stone) der Stromstein. **—s**, *pl.* Würfelkohlen, etwas größere Nußkohlen; kleine Stücke von Mineralien.

[3]**Cob(b)le**, *s.* die Häringsbüse, Büse (*Naut.*).

Cobra, *s.* die Brillenschlange.

Coca, *s.* die Koka (*Bot.*).

Cocaine, *s.* das Kokain.

Cocciferous, *adj.* beerentragend.

Coccyx, *s.* das Steißbein (*Anat.*).

Cochineal, *s.* die Cochenille; das Scharlachrot.

Cochleate, *adj.* schneckenförmig (*Bot.*).

[1]**Cock**, I. *s.* der Hahn; (male of birds) das Männchen; (vane) der Wetterhahn; (barrel —) der Hahn zum Abziehen des Getränkes; der Hahn, Krahn (*T.*); (hay—) der kleine Heuschober; der Hahn am Gewehr (*Gun.*); (steam —) Dampfhahn; der Unruhedeckel (*Horol.*); — crows, der Hahn kräht; black—, das Birkhuhn; blow-off —, Abblasehahn; box of the —, das Hahnengehäuse; cleansing —, Putzhahn; fighting —, der Kampfhahn; stop—, der Sperrhahn; wood—, die Waldschnepfe; — of the matchlock, der Luntenhahn; — of a percussion gun, der Perkussionshammer; at *or* on full —, mit gespanntem Hahn; at half —, mit Hahn in Ruh; to be — of the walk, der Hahn im Korbe sein; — of the roost, ein Mann, der sich vor allen auszeichnet; to tell a —-and-bull story, ein Wundermärchen erzählen, albernes Zeug schwatzen, à la Münchhausen lügen; to be —-a-hoop, frohlocken, stolz sein, sich brüsten, stolz tun; to live like fighting —s, wohlhabend leben, alles im Überfluß haben; sich (*dat.*) nichts abgehen lassen; that — won't fight, dieser Plan geht nicht durch (*coll.*); —-a-doodle-doo, das Kikeriki des Hahnes, der Kikeriki; —-a-leeky, —ie-leekie, die Hühnersuppe mit Lauch. II. *v.a.* (— up) in die Höhe richten; (set up) aufsetzen; schobern (*hay*); den Hahn spannen (*of a gun*); to — one's hat, den Hut schief setzen; to — the nose, die Nase hoch tragen; to — the ears, die Ohren spitzen; to — the eye, mit dem Auge winken. **—ade**, *s.* die Kokarde. **—atrice**, *s.* der Basilisk. **—ed**, *p.p. & adj.* gestülpt; ready —ed, mit gespanntem Hahne; —ed hat, der Stülphut. **—erel**, *s.* der junge Hahn. *Comp.* **—-bill**, *s.*; the anchor is a-—-bill, der Anker hängt vor dem Krahn, ist zum Fallen klar (*Naut.*). **—chafer**, *s.* der Maikäfer. **—-crow(ing)**, *s.* das Hahnengeschrei, der Hahnenschrei; der Tagesanbruch (*fig.*); at —-crow, beim ersten Hahnenschrei, in aller Frühe. **—-fight**, *s.* der Hahnenkampf. **—-horse**, *s.* das Steckenpferd; a-— -horse, *adv.* zu Pferde sitzend; hoch, triumphierend. **—-loft**, *s.* die Dachkammer; der Hahnenbalken. **—-pit**, *s.* der Kampfplatz bei Hahnenkämpfen; das Parterre (*Theat.*); das Raumdeck; der Verbandplatz auf Schiffen; fore —-pit, das Bootsmannsgatt. **—-scomb**, *s.* der Hahnenkamm; der gemeine Hahnenkamm (*Bot.*); *see* Coxcomb. **—-spur**, *s.* der Hahnensporn (*Bot.*); der Kapselständer (*Pott.*). **—-stride**, *s.* der

Hahnenschritt. —**-sure**, *adj.* des Erfolges ganz gewiß; ganz sicher (*coll.*). —**tail**, *s.* das Pferd mit gestutztem Schwanz; (beetle) Kurzflügler; amerikanischer Likör. —**-water**, *s.* (*obs.*) das Wasser zum Reinigen der Erze (*Min.*).

²**Cock**, (—**-boat**,) *s.* die Schaluppe, Jolle, das kleine Boot. *Comp.* —**-swain**, **Coxswain**, *s.* der Steuermann, Führer eines Bootes.

³**Cock**, *s.*; (*obs.*) by — and pye! zum Kuckuck!

Cockatoo, *s.* der Kakadu.

Cocker, *v.a.* hätscheln, verhätscheln.

Cocket, *s.* das Zollsiegel, der Zollstempel; die Ausfuhr-Deklaration.

¹**Cockle**, *s.* (corn- —) die Kornrade; das Unkraut (*fig.*); die Dornen (*B.*); der Schörl (*Min.*).

²**Cockle**, I. *s.* die Herzmuschel (*Mollusc.*); hot —s, die Handschmisse, das Zusaßspiel. II. *v.n.* sich runzeln; sich kräuseln. *Comp.* —**-stairs**, *pl.* die Wendeltreppe (*obs.*).

Cockney, I. *s.* das Londoner Stadtkind. II. *adj.*; — dialect, die Mundart der richtigen Londoner. —**ism**, *s.* die Mundart, Manier, ꝛc. eines Cockney. *Comp.* —**-bred**, *adj.* in London erzogen.

Cockroach, *s.* der Kakerlak, die Sch(w)abe.

¹**Cocoa**, I. *s.* der Kakao. —**tina**, *s.* raffinierter Kakao. II. *attrib.*; — bean, die Kakaobohne; — butter, — fat, die Kakaobutter, das Kakaonußöl; — paste, die Kakaomasse; — powder, das Kakaopulver; die Gesundheitsschokolade.

²**Cocoa**, *s.* (—-nut tree) die Kokospalme, der Kokosbaum. *Comp.* —**-nut**, I. *s.* die Kokosnuß. II. *attrib.*; —-nut fibre, der Kokosbast.

Cocoon, I. *s.* der Kokon, das Gespinst um die Puppe der Seidenraupe. II. *v.n.* einen Kokon bilden. —**ery**, *s.* der Raum *or* das Gebäude für Seidenzucht.

¹**Cod**, *s.* (pod) die Schote, Hülse; die Hode, der Hodensack; das Kissen (*Scotch*). —**ling**, *s.* eine Kochapfelsorte; hot —ling, der Bratapfel.

²**Cod**, (—**fish**,) *s.* der Kabeljau, Dorsch; dried —, der Stockfisch; salt —, der Labberdan. —**ling**, *s.* der junge Kabeljau. *Comp.* —**-liver**, *adj.*; —-liver oil, der Lebertran.

Coddle, *v.a.* gelinde kochen; verhätscheln; verpäppeln, verweichlichen.

Cod—e, I. *s.* der Kodex, die Gesetzsammlung, das Gesetzbuch; das konventionelle Alphabet oder Phrasenbuch für Telegraphie, Geheimschrift, ꝛc.; civil —e, die Zivilprozeßordnung; commercial —e, das Handelsgesetzbuch; criminal —e, penal —e, die Strafprozeßordnung; —e of signals, das Flaggensignalsystem. II. *attrib.*; —e telegram, das Ziffertelegram. —**ex**, *s.* die Handschrift, der Kodex; das Gesetzbuch. —**icil**, *s.* das Kodizill, der Zusatz (zu einer letztwilligen Verfügung). —**ification**, *s.* die Feststellung des Rechtszustandes, Kodifizierung. —**ify**, *v.a.* kodifizieren, (einen Rechtszustand) feststellen.

Codger, *s.* der Grobian; der Geizhals; der Sonderling.

Cœliac, *adj.* Unterleibs-; — passion, die Milchruhr, der Durchfall; — artery, die Baucharterie.

Coffee, I. *s.* der Kaffee; ground —, gemahlener Kaffee; raw —, ungebrannter Kaffee; roasted —, gebrannter Kaffee. II. *attrib.*; — bag, der Kaffeebeutel; — biggin, die Filtrierkanne; — grounds, der Kaffeesatz; — machine, die Kaffeemaschine, der Kaffeekocher; — service, das Kaffeegeschirr. *Comp.* —**-bean**, *s.* die Kaffeebohne. —**-berry**, *s.* die Kaffeebeere (mit zwei Bohnen). —**-cup**, *s.* die Kaffeetasse. —**-house**, *s.* das Kaffeehaus. —**-pot**, *s.* die Kaffeekanne. —**-roaster**, *s.* der Kaffeebrenner, die Kaffeetrommel. —**-room**, *s.* das Gastzimmer (*in a hotel, etc.*); das Kaffeelokal.

Coffeine, *s.* das Kaffein (*Chem.*).

Coff—er, *s.* der Koffer, Kasten; der vertiefte und bedeckte Gang; das Deckenfeld, die Kassette (*Arch.*); der Geldkasten; der bedeckte Gang durch einen trockenen Graben (*Fort.*); (—**ers**, *pl.*) die Schatzkammer, der Schatz. —**in**, I. *s.* der Sarg; as close as a —in, verschwiegen wie das Grab. II. *v.a.* in den Sarg legen, einsargen. *Comp.* —**er-dam**, *s.* der Fangdamm. —**er-work**, *s.* das Füllmauerwerk; —er-work of loam-earth, das Kastenwerk. —**in-bone**, *s.* das Hufbein.

¹**Cog**, I. *s.* der Kamm, Zahn. II. *v.a.* mit Zähnen versehen; verkämmen (*Carp.*). —**ged**, *adj.* gezahnt. *Comp.* —**-wheel**, I. *s.* das Kammrad, Zahnrad. II. *attrib.*; —-wheel railway, die Zahnradbahn.

²**Cog**, I. *s.* der Betrug; der Kniff (*obs.*). II. *v.a.* betrügen; to — the dice, die Würfel kneipen.

³**Cog**, *s.* das Fischerboot.

Cogen—cy, *s.* die Gewalt, zwingende Kraft; die Unwiderstehlichkeit (*of an argument*). —**t**, *adj.*, —**tly**, *adv.* zwingend; unwiderstehlich, schlagend.

Cogitat—e, *v.n.* denken; nachdenken; to —e upon a th., über eine S. nachdenken. —**ion**, *s.* das Denken; das Nachdenken, die Überlegung. —**ive**, *adj.* nachdenkend.

Cognac, *s.* der Kognak.

Cognate, *adj.* verwandt; blutsverwandt; urverwandt; — words, urverwandte Wörter.

Cogni—tion, *s.* die Kenntnis, Kunde. —**zable**, —**sable**, *adj.* erkennbar; zuständig (*by a judge*); zu gerichtlicher Untersuchung geeignet. —**zance**, —**sance**, *s.* die Kenntnis; die Erkenntnis; das gerichtliche Erkenntnis; die Gerichtsbarkeit (*Law*); (badge) das Abzeichen, Kennzeichen; to take —zance of a th., Notiz von (einer S.) nehmen, eine S. untersuchen; to fall under the —zance of a p., vor einen *or* in das Gebiet des . . . gehören. —**zant**, *adj.* wissend; to be —zant of a th., um eine Sache wissen.

Cognomen, *s.* der Zuname, Beiname.

Cohort, *s.* die Kohorte; die Kriegsschar, Schar (*poet.*).

Coif, I. *s.* die Kappe, Haube; die weiße Kappe der Sergeants-at-law (*obs.*); (*fig.*) der Juristenstand; brother of the —, der Jurist, Rechtsgelehrte. II. *v.a.* mit einer Kappe bedecken; zum Juristen machen. —**fure**, *s.* der Kopfputz; die Kopfbedeckung.

Coign, *s.* die Ecke (*obs.*); — of vantage, vorteilhafte Stellung, guter Beobachtungsposten.

Coil, I. *s.* die Windung, der Wickel, die Rolle; die Drahtrolle (*of wire*); die Spule, Spirale (*Tele.*); die Scheibe (*Naut.*); galvanometer —, Galvanometerspule; induction —, Induktionsrolle (*Elect.*, *Tele.*). II. *v.a.* ringförmig wickeln, aufwickeln; spiralförmig aufwinden (*springs, etc.*); to — a rope, ein Tau aufschießen, in einen Ring, ein Gewinde zusammenlegen. III. *v.n.* sich winden, sich in Windungen bewegen; to — o.s., sich zusammenrollen (*of snakes*).

Coin, I. *s.* das geprägte Geld, die Münze; base —, geringhaltige, schlechte Münze; counterfeit —, falsche Münze; small —, die Scheidemünze; worn-out —, blindes Geld; to pay a p. back in his own —, einem Gleiches mit Gleichem vergelten *or* in gleicher Münze heimzahlen. II. *v.a.* Münzen schlagen, prägen, stempeln; erwerben (*money*); schmieden, erdichten (*a tale, etc.*); to — false money, Falschmünzerei treiben; to — words, Wörter prägen; newly —ed words, neugeschmiedete Wörter. —**age**, *s.* das Münzen; die Münzkunst; das (gesetzlich gemünzte, zirkulierende) Geld; die Erdichtung, Erfindung (*fig.*). —**er**, *s.* der Münzer, Geldschläger; —er of words, der Wörterschmied.

Coincide, *v.n.* zusammentreffen; übereinstimmen (*fig.*); there I — with you, darin stimme ich mit Ihnen überein; we —d in opinion, wir waren gleicher Meinung. —**nce**, *s.* das Zusammentreffen; die Übereinstimmung (*fig.*). —**nt**, *adj.*, —**ntly**, *adv.* zusammentreffend; übereinstimmend.

Coir, *s.* der Kokosbast.

Coke, I. *s.* der Koks; — from gas-coal, der Gaskoks. II. *v.a.* (Steinkohlen) verkoken.

Colander, *s.* der Durchschlag, die Seihe.
Colchicum, *s.* die Zeitlose (*Bot.*).
Colcothar, *s.* der Totenkopf, das Englischrot.
Cold, I. *adj.*, —**ly**, *adv.* kalt (*also fig.*); (indifferent) gleichgültig; (unimpassioned) leidenschaftslos; (reserved) zurückhaltend; (chaste) keusch; (unsympathetic) teilnahmlos; to act in — blood, kaltblütig handeln; to do a th. in — blood, etw. mit vollem Bewußtsein *or* ganz ruhig tun; I am —, mich friert; — blast, die kalte Gebläsluft; — chisel, der Hartmeißel; — comfort, schlechter Trost; — meat, kalte Küche; a — look, ein kalter, unfreundlicher Blick; a — reception, ein frostiger Empfang; — scent, schwache Fährte (*Sport.*); to give a p. the — shoulder, einen kalt behandeln; — spectator, teilnahmloser Zuschauer. II. *s.* die Kälte; der Frost; (— in the head) der Schnupfen; die Erkältung (*Med.*); feverish —, das Schnupfenfieber; to catch —, sich erkälten, sich (*dat.*) eine Erkältung holen; I have caught a bad —, ich habe mich stark erkältet *or* mir eine schlimme Erkältung geholt. —**ish**, *adj.* kältlich, kühl, frisch. —**ness**, *s.* die Kälte (*also fig.*). *Comp.* —-**blooded**, *adj.* kaltblütig; gefühllos (*fig.*). —-**cream**, *s.* der Coldcream. —-**hearted**, *adj.* kaltherzig; gefühllos; leidenschaftslos. —-**heartedness**, *s.* die Kaltherzigkeit. —-**short**, *adj.* kaltbrüchig.
Cole, *s.* der Kohl. *Comp.* —-**rape**, *s.* die Rübe. —**wort**, *s.* der Grünkohl.
Coleopter—a, *pl.* die Deckflügler. —**ous**, *adj.* hornartige Flügeldecken habend.
Colic, *s.* die Kolik, das Bauchgrimmen; bilious —, die Gallenkolik; renal —, die Nierenkolik. —**ky**, *adj.* kolikkrank, Kolik=.
Coll—aborator, *s.* der Mitarbeiter. —**apse**, I. *s.* das Zusammenfallen; der Zusammenbruch, das schnelle Sinken der Kräfte (*at the approach of death*). II. *v.n.* zusammenfallen, einfallen; zusammenbrechen. —**apsible**, *adj.* dem Zusammenfallen ausgesetzt; zum Zusammenfallen eingerichtet; —apsible drinking-cup, zusammenklappbarer Taschenbecher. —**ate**, *v.a.* kollationieren, vergleichen; verleihen, erteilen (*a living*); to —ate a clergyman to a living, einen Geistlichen in eine Pfründe einsetzen. —**ateral**, *adj.* zur Seite; gleichlaufend; nebenseitig; zur Seitenlinie gehörig, seitenverwandt; nebenher laufend, gleichzeitig; —ateral acceptance, die Ehrenannahme (*C.L.*); —ateral circumstances, Nebenumstände; —ateral descent, die Abstammung von einer Seitenlinie; —ateral pressure, Druck von der Seite; —ateral relations, Seitenverwandte; —ateral security, die Nebensicherheit, gegenseitige Sicherheit. —**ation**, *s.* die Vergleichung, Gegeneinanderhaltung von Schriften; die Verleihung, Schenkung (*of a living*); (right of presentation) die Kollatur, das Besetzungsrecht einer erledigten Pfründe (*Eccl.*); die Zwischenmahlzeit; a cold —ation, ein kalter Imbiß. —**ative**, *adj.*; advowson —ative, Patronat, wobei der Patron und Bischof eine und dieselbe Person sind. —**ator**, *s.* der Kollationierende, der Schriften oder Handschriften vergleicht; der Patron. —**eague**, *s.* der Kollege, Amtsbruder. —**ect**, *etc.*, *see* Collect, *etc.* —**ege**, *s.* (council) das Kollegium; das College (*at Cambridge, Oxford, Dublin, e. g. Trinity College*, alles Internate); (school) die höhere Schule (*e.g. Eton College*); höhere (oft Universitätsunterricht erteilende) Bildungsanstalt (*e. g. University College, London*); die Universität (*Amer.*); die (gelehrte) Genossenschaft, Haus einer solchen Gesellschaft (*e. g. College of Physicians; College of Preceptors*); —ege of cardinals, Kardinalkollegium; —ege dues, Collegegebühren; —ege lecturer, Dozent an einem College; —ege tutor, Berater und Vertreter der Studenten eines College (*at Oxford and Cambridge*). —**egian**, *s.* der Student; der höhere Schüler. —**egiate**, *adj.* zu einem Kollegium gehörig; einem College eigentümlich; —egiate school, von einem Kollegium verwaltete Schule, Korporationsschule. —**ide**, *v.n.* zusammenstoßen, =schlagen. —**imation**, *s.* die Gesichtslinie, Sehlinie (*Opt.*); (levelling) das Zielen; (aim) das Ziel; line of —imation, die Sehlinie. —**imator**, *s.* das Fernrohr mit Apparat zur Korrektur von Irrtümern bei der Bestimmung der optischen Axe. —**ineation**, *s.* das Zielen. —**ision**, *s.* der Zusammenstoß; der Widerstreit; to come into —ision with a p., sich mit einem entzweien, mit einem in Meinungsverschiedenheit geraten. —**ocate**, *v.a.* stellen, ordnen; in Klassen einteilen. —**ocation**, *s.* die Stellung, Ordnung; die Einteilung in Klassen. —**ogue**, *v.* I. *a.* beschwatzen. II. *n.* eine vertrauliche Unterredung halten (*coll.*). —**oquial**, *adj.*, —**oquially**, *adv.* zur Umgangssprache gehörig, gesprächsweise. —**oquialism**, *s.* (—oquial expression) der Ausdruck der Umgangssprache, die Wendung aus der Sprache des täglichen Lebens. —**oquy**, *s.* die Unterredung, das Gespräch. —**ude**, *v.n.* sich verstehen, ein heimliches Einverständnis haben. —**usion**, *s.* das heimliche Einverständnis; die geheime, betrügliche Verabredung.
Collar, I. *s.* (necklace, dog-collar) das Halsband; der Kragen (*of a dress, etc.*); die Halskette (*of metal, etc.*); die Ordenskette (*Her.*); der Ring, Halsring, Astragal (*Arch.*); der Querbalken (*Carp.*); die Pfanne, das Zapfenlager (*Mach.*); stand-up —, der Stehkragen; turn-down —, der Umlegekragen; horse —, das Kummet. II. *attrib.*; — harness, das Kummetgeschirr. III. *v.a.* beim Kragen ergreifen, fassen, anpacken; Fleisch zusammenrollen und binden. —**et**, *s.* der kleine Damenkragen; die Halsrüstung, die Halsberge. *Comp.* —-**beam**, *s.* der Querbalken. —-**bone**, *s.* das Schlüsselbein (*Anat.*).
Collect, I. *v.a.* sammeln, zusammenbringen, einsammeln; versammeln, zusammenbringen (*of people*); to — outstanding debts, ausstehende Schulden einkassieren; to — o.s., sich sammeln, seine Gedanken zusammenfassen; to — gases, Gase auffangen. II. *v.n.* sich sammeln. III. *s.* das kurze Gebet, die Kollekte. —**ed**, *adj.*, —**edly**, *adv.* gesammelt, gefaßt, ruhig (*fig.*). —**edness**, *s.* die Fassung (*of the mind*). —**ion**, *s.* das Sammeln; die Einziehung von Geldern; das Gesammelte (*as money*); die Sammlung (*of coins, etc.*). —**ive**, *adj.* gesammelt, versammelt, gesammt, zusammengefaßt; a —ive noun, das Sammelwort, Kollektivum. —**ively**, *adv.* insgesammt, im Ganzen. —**or**, *s.* der Sammler; der Kassierer (*C. L.*); der Einnehmer (*of tolls, etc.*); tax- —or, Zolleinnehmer; —or of electricity, der Verdoppler. —**orship**, *s.* die Zolleinnehmerei.
Collie, *s.* der schottische Schäferhund.
Collier, *s.* der Kohlenarbeiter; das Kohlenschiff. —**y**, *s.* das Kohlenbergwerk; —y disaster, das Grubenunglück; —y explosion, der Grubenbrand.
Collodi—on, —**um**, *s.* das Kollodium (*Chem.*); sensitized —um, das präparierte Kollodium; —um process, das Kollodiumverfahren (*Phot.*).
Colly, *s.* der Ruß (*obs., dial.*).
Colocynth, *s.* die Koloquinte.
Colon, *s.* der Doppelpunkt, das Kolon; der Grimmdarm (*Anat.*).
Colonel, *s.* der Oberst; lieutenant- —, der Oberstleutnant. —**cy**, *s.* die Oberstenstelle; der Rang eines Obersten.
Colonnade, *s.* der Säulengang, die Säulenhalle.
Colon—ial, *adj.* Kolonial=; —ial department, das Kolonial=Ministerium; —ial office, das Kolonialamt; —ial produce, die Kolonialwaren; —ial secretary, der Kolonialminister; —ial trade, der Kolonialhandel. —**ist**, *s.* der Ansiedler. —**ization**, —**isation**, *s.* das Kolonisieren, die Besiedelung. —**ize**, —**ise**, *v.* I. *a.* kolonisieren, besiedeln. II. *n.* eine Kolonie gründen, sich ansiedeln. —**izer**, —**iser**, *s.* der Ansiedler. —**y**, *s.*

die Kolonie, Ansiedlung, Niederlassung; (—ists) die Kolonisten; die Schar, Menge (*of beasts, etc.*); —y hives, Magazinkörbe (*of bees*).
Colophon, *s.* der Kolophon (*Typ.*); from title page to —, vom Anfang bis zum Schluß; von Anfang bis zu Ende.
Colophony, *s.* das Kolophonium, Geigenharz.
Color—ation, *s.* das Färben; die Färbung; —ation test, die kolorimetrische Probe. —**ature**, *s.* die Koloratur (*Mus.*). —**ific**, *adj.* färbend.
Colour, I. *s.* die Farbe; (complexion) Gesichtsfarbe; (dye) die Färbung; die Färbebrühe (*of dyers*); (appearance) der Anstrich, Anschein; (pretence) der Deckmantel, Vorwand; the —s, die Fahne (*Mil.*); service with the —s, der Dienst bei der Fahne; to join the —s, zu den Fahnen eilen, zur Fahne einberufen werden; to desert one's —s, desertieren (*also fig.*); trooping (of) the —, Fahnenparade (*usually in celebration of the king's birthday on the Horse Guards parade, London*); body —, die Deckfarbe; composite —s, compound —s, die zusammengesetzten Farben; fast —, echte, haltbare Farbe; primary —s, die Grundfarben; glaring —s, schreiende Farben; moist —s, die Aquarellfarbe in Teigform; national —s, die Nationalflagge; oil —, Ölfarbe; pigment —s, Körperfarben; priming —, Grundierfarbe; primitive —s, einfachen, ursprüngliche Farben; secondary —s, zusammengesetzte Farben; the seven fundamental —s, die sieben Regenbogenfarben; to have a —, blühend aussehen; to change —, die Farbe wechseln; her — comes and goes, sie wird abwechselnd rot und blaß; to be in —s, ein farbiges Kleid anhaben; to give — to a th., einer S. den Anschein der *or* Anstrich von Wahrscheinlichkeit geben; to paint a p. in his true —s, einen nach dem Leben schildern; to come out in one's true —s, sich in seinem wahren Lichte zeigen; to come off with flying —s, den Sieg davontragen; play of —, das Farbenspiel, Schillern; theory of —s, die Farbenlehre. II. *v.a.* färben; kolorieren; einen Anstrich geben, beschönigen (*fig.*). III. *v.n.* erröten; she —ed up to the eyes, sie wurde über und über rot. —**able**, *adj.*, —**ably**, *adv.* scheinbar, plausibel, annehmbar; (fictitious) fingiert; mutmaßlich, proforma (*C.L.*). —**ed**, *adj.* gefärbt, koloriert; bunt, farbig; beschönigt; —ed glass, das gefärbte Glas; —ed impression, der Buntdruck (*Typ.*); —ed men, —ed people, Farbige, Neger; —ed pencil, bunter Bleistift; —ed plan, farbiger Plan; —ed ray, farbiger Strahl (*Phys.*). —**ing**, I. *adj.;* —ing body, der Farbenkörper; —ing matter, der Farbstoff. II. *s.* das Färben; die Färbung, Farbengebung, das Kolorit (*Paint.*); das Beschönigen (*fig.*); der Schein (*fig.*). —**ist**, *s.* der Farbengeber, Kolorist, Farbenkundige. —**less**, *adj.*, —**lessly**, *adv.* farblos. *Comp.* —**-blind**, *adj.* farbenblind. —**-box**, *s.* der Malkasten, Farbenkasten. —**-brush**, *s.* der Pinsel. —**-grinder**, *s.* der Farbenreiber. —**-photography**, *s.* die farbige Photographie, Farbenphotographie. —**-printing**, *s.* der Farbendruck. —**-saucer**, *s.* das Farbennäpfchen.
Coloss—al, *adj.* riesenhaft, ungeheuer, kolossal; massig. —**us**, *s.* das riesige Standbild, der Koloß.
Colport—age, *s.* der Hausierhandel (mit Büchern). —**eur**, *s.* der (Bibel=)Kolporteur.
Colt, *s.* das Füllen; das Hengstfüllen; der Lappe (*fig.*). —**ish**, *adj.* wie ein Füllen, mutwillig; ausgelassen. *Comp.* —**sfoot**, *s.* der Huflattig (*Bot.*). —**'s-tooth**, *s.* der Milchzahn (*Vet.*).
Colter, Coulter, *s.* das Pflugeisen, die Pflugschar.
Columb—ary, *s.* das Taubenhaus. —**ine**, *s.* der Ackelei (*Bot.*).
Column, *s.* die Säule (*Arch.*); die Kolonne (*Mil.*); die Kolumne, Spalte (*Typ.*); die Luftsäule (*Phys.*); der Dampfzylinder (*of steam engines*); commemorative —, Denksäule; — of mercury, Quecksilbersäule; a flying —, ein Streifkorps, eine Streifkolonne; twisted —, gewundene Säule; shaft of a —, der Stammschaft; — of water, Wassersäule; in —s, kolumnenweise; kolonnenweise. —**ar**, *adj.* säulenförmig.
Colza, *s.* der Winterreps; — oil, das Rüböl.
Coma, *s.* die anhaltende Bewußtlosigkeit, Schlafsucht (*Med.*). —**tose**, *adj.* schlafsüchtig. —**tosity**, *s.* die Schlafsucht (*also fig.*).
Comb, I. *s.* der Kamm; (flax —) die Hechel; horse-—, curry-—) der Striegel; (honey—) die Honigscheibe; (—for wool) der Wollkamm; der Hahnstift (*Gun.*); (*also* Combe, Coomb) das Tal, Tälchen; child's round —, Reifkamm; back —, Aufsteckkamm; pocket-—, Taschenkamm. II. *v.a.* kämmen; striegeln; krämpeln; hecheln; to — one's hair, sich kämmen. III. *v.n.* brechen (*of waves*). —**er**, *s.* der Kämmer. —**ings**, *pl.* ausgekämmte Haare. *Comp.* —**-brush**, *s.* die Kammbürste (*for cleaning combs*). —**-cutter**, *s.* der Kammmacher.
Com—bat, I. *s.* der Kampf, Streit; single —bat, der Zweikampf. II. *v.a.* bekämpfen, bestreiten (*an opinion, etc.*). III. *v.n.* sich streiten, kämpfen (with, mit). —**batant**, *s.* der Kämpfer; der Verfechter. —**bative**, *adj.* streitsüchtig. —**bativeness**, *s.* die Streitsucht; bump of —bativeness, das Organ der Rauflust (*Phren.*). —**binable**, *adj.* vereinbar. —**bination**, *s.* die Vereinigung; das Bündnis; das Hemdunterbeinkleid, die Hemdhosen; die Verbindung (*of qualities, etc.*), die Mischung (*of stuffs*); die Kombination (*Math.*); chemical —bination, chemische Verbindung; doctrine of —binations, die Kombinationslehre; —bination room, das Zimmer in einem (Cambridger) College, in dem Zeitungen ausliegen und von dem aus sich die älteren Collegemitglieder gemeinsam zum Essen begeben, der Versammlungssaal. —**bine**, *v.* I. *a.* vereinigen, zusammensetzen, verbinden; kombinieren. II. *n.* sich verbinden, sich vereinigen (*of persons & things*); sich verbünden, einen Bund schließen (*of persons*). —**bustible**, *adj.* brennbar. —**bustibles**, *pl.* das Brennmaterial. —**bustibility**, —**bustibleness**, *s.* die Brennbarkeit. —**bustion**, *s.* die Verbrennung; der Brand; entire —bustion, das Totbrennen; spontaneous —bustion, die Selbstentzündung. —**bustion-chamber**, *s.* die Verbrennungskammer, der Flammkasten (*Locom., etc.*). —**fit**, *s.* das Konfekt, der überzuckerte Koriander, Kümmel, Zimmt, 2c. —**fort**, I. *s.* die Behaglichkeit, Gemächlichkeit, Bequemlichkeit; der Trost; (help) die Hülfe; (support) der Beistand; das Labsal, die Labung, Erleichterung (*of mind & body*); soldiers' —forts, Liebesgaben für Soldaten im Felde; die Stütze (*of the aged, etc.*); pious children are the —fort of aged parents, fromme Kinder erheitern das Leben ihrer bejahrten Eltern; to be of good —fort, guten Mutes sein; to take —fort, sich trösten, Mut fassen. II. *v.a.* trösten; erquicken; erheitern; the sight of you always —forts me, dein Anblick erfreut mich stets; she was —forted, sie wurde getröstet; be —forted! sei getrost! —**fortable**, *adj.*, —**fortably**, *adv.* behaglich, angenehm, gemütlich, wohnlich, bequem; (well off) behäbig, wohlhabend; warm (*as a wrap*); erfreulich, erquicklich; to make o.s. —fortable, sich (*dat.*) es bequem machen; to feel more —fortable, Linderung, Erleichterung spüren (*as an invalid*). —**fortableness**, *s.* die Behaglichkeit. —**forter**, *s.* der Tröster (*also B.*); das wollene Halstuch. —**fortless**, *adj.*, —**fortlessly**, *adv.* (disconsolate) trostlos; (uncomfortable) unbehaglich; (not comforting) unerfreulich. —**fortlessness**, *s.* die Unbehaglichkeit —**itia**, *s.* die Volksversammlung der Römer. —**mand**, *see* Command, *etc.* —**measurable**, *see* —mensurable. —**memorable**, *adj.* denkwürdig. —**memorate**, *v.a.* feiern (das Andenken). —**memoration**, *s.* die

Gedächtnisfeier ; in —memoration of, zum Andenken an (*acc.*); —memoration (day), die Gedächtnisfeier (an einen Heiligen *or* an Wohltäter *or* ein wichtiges erfreuliches Ereignis); das große jährliche Wohltäterfest (*Oxford*). **—memorative,** *adj.* als Andenken *or* zur Erinnerung dienend ; erinnernd. **—mence,** *v.a. & n.* anfangen. **—mencement,** *s.* der Anfang. **—mend,** *etc., see* Commend, *etc.* **—mensal,** I. *adj.* an demselben Tische essend. II. *s.* der Tischgenoß. **—mensurability,** *s.* die Gleichmeßbarkeit, Kommensurabilität. **—mensurable,** *adj.,* **—mensurably,** *adv.* nach gleichem Maße meßbar ; —mensurable quantities, kommensurable Größen. **—mensurate,** *adj.,* **—mensurately,** *adv.* ausmeßbar (*Arith.*); verhältnismäßig; angemessen. **—mensurateness,** *s.* das Gleichmaß ; das gleiche Verhältnis. **—ment,** **—merce,** *see* Comment, *etc.,* Commerce, *etc.* **—mination,** *s.* die Bedrohung (*Eccles.*) ; die Vorlesung der göttlichen Drohungen gegen Sünden an bestimmten Tagen. **—minatory,** *adj.* drohend. **—mingle,** *v.n.* sich vermischen, sich vermengen. **—minute,** *v.a.* zerkleinern, pulvern. **—minution,** *s.* das Pulvern, Zerreiben, Pulverisieren. **—miserate,** *v.a.* bemitleiden ; bedauern. **—miseration,** *s.* das Mitleid, die Erbarmung ; das Bedauern. **—missariat,** *etc., see* Commiss—. **—mit,** *v.a.* begehen, verüben, ausüben (*a sin, etc.*); (consign) übergehen ; to —mit to prison, verhaften lassen; ins Gefängnis senden; the prisoner was —mitted for trial, der Angeklagte wurde dem Gerichte zur Aburteilung überwiesen ; to —mit o.s., sich bloßstellen, sich kompromittieren ; to —mit adultery, ehebrechen; to —mit outrages, Exzesse begehen; to —mit to memory, auswendig lernen ; to —mit to paper, zu Papier bringen. **—mitment,** *s.* die Verhaftung ; der Verhaftsbefehl ; die Übergabe, Anheimstellung an einen Ausschuß, 2c. **—mittal,** *s. see* —mitment ; die Begehung, Verübung, Ausübung (*of a crime, etc.*). **—mittee,** *s.* der Ausschuß ; member of a —mittee, der Beisitzer, das Ausschußmitglied ; —mittee of management, geschäftsleitender Ausschuß ; —mittee of supply, Ausschuß für Geldbewilligung ; standing *or* permanent —mittee, ständiger Ausschuß. **—mitter,** *s.* der Täter. **—mix,** *v.a.* vermischen. **—mixture,** *s.* die Mischung. **—mode,** *s.* der Nachtstuhl ; die Kommode. **—modious,** *adj.,* **—modiously,** *adv.* bequem ; gemächlich ; (suitable) passend (for, für). **—modiousness,** *s.* die Bequemlichkeit, Gemächlichkeit. **—modity,** *s.* die Ware ; manufactured —modities, Manufakturwaren. **—modore,** *s.* der Kommodore; der Geschwaderchef; der älteste Kapitän eines Geschwaders; das Kommodorschiff ; das voransegelnde Convoischiff, Hauptschiff einer Handelsflotte. **—mon,** *etc., see* Common, *etc.* **—motion,** *s.* die heftige Bewegung ; der Tumult, Aufruhr, Aufstand. **—munal,** *adj.* Kommunal=. **—mune,** I. *v.n.* sich mitteilen, sich unterhalten, sich unterreden (with, mit). II. *s.* die Gemeinde ; die Kommune (*in Paris, 1871*). **—municable,** *adj.* mitteilbar. **—municableness,** *s.* die Mitteilbarkeit. **—municant,** *s.* der Kommunikant, Teilnehmer(in, *f.*) am Abendmahl. **—municate,** *v.* I. *a.* mitteilen, benachrichtigen ; teilen. II. *n.* kommunizieren, gemeinschaftlich das Abendmahl genießen; (be connected) in Verbindung stehen ; Umgang haben. **—munication,** *s.* die Mitteilung, Bekanntmachung ; (news) die Kunde, Nachricht ; der Umgang, Verkehr ; die Verbindung ; der Korridor ; der Zusammenhang (*of roads, rivers, etc.*); der Verbindungsgang (*Fort.*); I have no —munication with him, ich habe keinen Verkehr mit ihm ; evil —munications corrupt good manners, schlechter Umgang verdirbt gute Sitten (*prov.*) ; —munication by rail, die Eisenbahnverbindung ; —munication of motion, die Fortpflanzung der Bewegung. **—municative,** *adj.* mitteilsam (talkative) gesprächig ; (frank) offenherzig. **—municativeness,** *s.* die Mitteilsamkeit ; di Gesprächigkeit ; die Offenherzigkeit. **—municator,** *s.* der Mitteiler ; der Zeichengebe (*Tele.*) ; die Notleine (*Railw.*). **—munion,** *s* die Gemeinschaft ; die Kirchengemeinschaft die Glaubensgemeinschaft; das heilige Abendmahl ; —munion cup, der Abendmalskelch **—munism,** *s.* der Kommunismus. **—munist** *s.* der Kommunist. **—munity,** *s.* die Gemeinschaft ; die Staatsgesellschaft ; der Staat, da Gemeinwesen ; —munity of goods, Gütergemeinschaft. **—mutability,** *s.* die Vertauschbarkeit **—mutable,** *adj.* vertauschbar. **—mutation,** *s* die Veränderung ; die Vertauschung ; der Tausch Austausch ; die Verwandlung einer Strafe in ein gelindere. **—mute,** *v.a.* austauschen, umtauschen, verändern ; to —mute a sentence, ein Strafe mildern ; the death sentence was —muted to penal servitude for life, die Todesstrafe wurde in lebenslängliche Zuchthausstraf umgewandelt. **—pact,** I. *adj.,* **—pactly,** *adv* dicht zusammengedrängt ; dicht, fest ; (succinct gedrungen, bündig. II. *v.a.* zusammenfügen verbinden ; (consolidate) verdichten. III. *s* der Vergleich, Vertrag. **—pactness,** *s.* di Dichtheit, Festigkeit. **—panion,** *s.* der Gesellschafter, die Gesellschafterin ; (playmate) de Gespiele, die Gespielin ; (comrade) der Kamerad, Genoß, Mitgenoß ; (escort) der Begleiter (fellow-traveller) der Gefährte, Mitarbeiter ; di schiebbare Kappe (*Naut.*) ; boon —panion, fidele Kneipbruder; —panion of the Bath (*C. B.*), de Ritter des Bath=Ordens. **—panionable,** *adj.,* **—panionably,** *adv.* gesellig. **—panionableness** *s.* die Geselligkeit. **—panionship,** *s.* die Gesellschaft, Genossenschaft. **—pany,** *s.* die Gesellschaft ; die Kompagnie (*Mil., C. L.*); die Handelsgesellschaft (*C. L.*) ; (guild) die Zunft (crowd) der Haufen; to be good —pany, ein gute Gesellschafter sein; to bear *or* keep a p. —pany einem Gesellschaft leisten ; to keep —pany with Umgang haben mit ; to receive —pany, Gesellschaft bei sich empfangen ; —pany's hall, da Zunfthaus, Gildehaus. **—parable,** *adj.* vergleichbar. **—parative,** *adj.,* **—paratively,** *adv* vergleichend, vergleichsweise ; in Vergleichung relativ, beziehlich ; —parative degree, der Komparativ (*Gram.*) ; —parative beauty, relativ Schönheit ; —parative philology, vergleichend Sprachwissenschaft. **—pare,** I. *v.a.* vergleiche (with, mit) ; gleichachten, gleichstellen (to, mi den Komparativ bilden (*Gram.*); kollationiere (*manuscripts, etc.*) ; Solon —pared the peopl to a sea, Solon verglich das Volk mit einen Meere ; he is not to be —pared with hi brother, er ist mit seinem Bruder nicht zu vergleichen. II. *v.n.* sich vergleichen. III. *s.* di Vergleichung, der Vergleich (*gen'lly poet.*) ; beyond —pare, ohne jeden Vergleich, unvergleichlic **—parer,** *s.* der, welcher vergleicht. **—parison** *s.* der Vergleich ; die Vergleichung ; (simile das Gleichnis ; die Steigerung, Komparatio (*Gram.*); to bear —parison with, den Vergleic aushalten mit, sich sehr wohl vergleichen lasse mit ; beyond —parison, unvergleichlich, übe jeden Vergleich ; in —parison with, im Vergleich zu. **—partment,** *s.* die Abteilung ; da Fach ; der Abteil (*Railw.*) ; smoking —partment Abteil für Raucher, das Rauchcoupé. **—pass,** I *s.* (circuit, range) der Umfang, Umkreis ; (pass of the voice) der Stimmumfang; (sphere range) der Bezirk, Bereich; (limit) die Grenz Schranke; (space of time) die Zeit, der Zeitraum mariner's —pass, der Seekompaß; point of th —pass, der Kompaßstrich; to keep within —pass sich mäßigen, die Schranken einhalten; to keep p. within —pass, einen in Schranken halten; t reduce in —pass, in engern Rahmen fassen.

attrib.; —pass variation, die Deklination der Magnetnadel; —pass box, *etc. see* —**pass-box**, *etc.* III. *v.a.* umgehen; (enclose) umfassen; (besiege) umlagern; (contrive) bewerkstelligen; (bring about) durchsetzen, zustande bringen; (plot) anstiften; to —pass a p.'s death, einem nach dem Leben trachten, seinen Tod bewerkstelligen. —**passes**, *pl.* der Zirkel; crooked —passes, Bauchzirkel; bow —passes, Bogenzirkel; to measure with the —passes, abzirkeln; —passes with shifting points, Stechzirkel; pencil —passes, Zirkel mit Reißfeder. —**passion**, *s.* das Mitleid, Erbarmen. —**passionate**, *adj.*, —**passionately**, *adv.* mitleidig, zum Mitleid geneigt; —passionate allowance, das Gnadengehalt, das Gnadenquartal (*for widows*). —**passionateness**, *s.* die mitleidige Stimmung. —**patibility**, *s.* die Verträglichkeit; die Vereinbarkeit; die Angemessenheit. —**patible**, *adj.*, —**patibly**, *adv.* verträglich; vereinbar; angemessen, schicklich, passend; verträglich (*Math.*); clemency towards offenders is not always —patible with the public safety, Milde gegen Verbrecher verträgt sich nicht immer mit der öffentlichen Sicherheit. —**patriot**, *s.* der Landsmann. —**peer**, *s.* der Gleiche; der Genoß, Kamerad. —**pel**, *v.a.* zwingen, nötigen. —**peller**, *s.* der Zwingende. —**pendium**, *s.* das Kompendium; das Handbuch, der Auszug. —**pendious**, *adj.*, —**pendiously**, *adv.* kurzgefaßt, abgekürzt, gedrängt. —**pendiousness**, *s.* die Kürze, Gedrängtheit. —**pensate**, *v.* I. *a.* ersetzen; ausgleichen. II. *n.* einen Ersatz geben (for, für). —**pensation**, *s.* (amends) der Ersatz; (reward) die Vergütung; (set-off) die Ausgleichung, Kompensation; (remuneration) der Lohn; —pensation damages, Schadenersatz; —pensation apparatus, der Ausgleichungsapparat (*Horol.*). —**pensatory**, *adj.* ausgleichend, vergütend, als Ersatz dienend; —pensatory vowel-lengthening, die Ersatzdehnung. —**pete**, *v.n.* sich mit bewerben (um); sich messen mit; konkurrieren (for, um); —pete for a scholarship, sich (vermittelst einer Konkurrenzprüfung) um ein Stipendium bewerben. —**petence**, —**petency**, *s.* (livelihood) das Auskommen; (capability) die Befähigung, Tüchtigkeit; die Befugnis, Kompetenz, der Amtskreis (*Law*); to enjoy a —petence, sein Auskommen haben. —**petent**, *adj.*, —**petently**, *adv.*, (sufficient) zulänglich, hinreichend, hinlänglich; angemessen, passend; entsprechend; kompetent (*as a judge*); befugt, gültig (*as a court*); a —petent person, ein Sachverständiger. —**petition**, *s.* die Mitbewerbung, Konkurrenz, der Wettbewerb; unfair —petition, unlauterer Wettbewerb; notice of —petition, das Preisausschreiben. —**petitive**, *adj.* konkurrierend; —petitive examination, die Konkurrenzprüfung. —**petitor**, *s.* der Mitbewerber, Konkurrent. —**pilation**, *s.* die Kompilation, Zusammentragung, Sammlung; das Sammelwerk. —**pile**, *v.a.* zusammentragen (from, aus); verfassen. —**piler**, *s.* der Sammler, Zusammensteller, Kompilator. —**placence**, —**placency**, *s.* das Wohlgefallen (das man selbst empfindet), das Behagen; (civility) die Gefälligkeit; self- —placency, die Zufriedenheit mit sich selbst, Selbstzufriedenheit. —**placent**, *adj.*, —**placently**, *adv.* behaglich, selbstzufrieden; (polite) höflich. —**plain**, *v.* I. *n.* klagen, sich beklagen; Klage führen (of a p., über einen) (*Law*); —plain of a th., über eine Sache klagen; sich über eine Sache beklagen; he —plained to me of him, er beklagte sich bei mir über ihn. II. *a.* beklagen (*poet. obs.*). —**plainant**, *s.* der Kläger, Klagende, die Klägerin. —**plainer**, *s.* der, die Klagende; der, die Unzufriedene. —**plaint**, *s.* die Klage (*also Law*); die Krankheit, das Übel (*Med.*). —**plaisance**, *s.* die Gefälligkeit, Willfährigkeit, Dienstwilligkeit; (politeness) die Höflichkeit; (courteousness) das gefällige höfliche Wesen. —**plaisant**, *adj.*, —**plaisantly**, *adv.* gefällig, verbindlich, artig; höflich. —**plement**, *s.* die Ergänzung; (full number) die vollständige Anzahl; (completeness) die Vollständigkeit, Vollzähligkeit; das Komplement (*Math.*); die Entfernung (*of a star*); die dekadische Ergänzung (*of a logarithm*); —plement of the curtain, der Rest der Defensionslinie an der Kurtine (*Fort.*). —**plementary**, *adj.* ergänzend, vollendend; —plementary colours, Komplementärfarben. —**plete**, I. *adj.*, —**pletely**, *adv.* vollzählig; (perfect) vollständig, vollkommen; (whole) ganz; (finished) vollendet. II. *v.a.* vollständig, vollzählig, vollkommen machen; vervollständigen; ergänzen; erfüllen; vollenden. —**pleteness**, *s.* die Vollständigkeit, Vollkommenheit. —**pletion**, *s.* (finishing) die Vollendung; (fulfilment) die Erfüllung; (supplement, finish) die Ergänzung; —pletion of the predicate, die Ergänzung des Prädikats. —**plex**, *adj.* zusammengesetzt (*also Arith.*); vielteilig; verwickelt (*fig.*). —**plexion**, *s.* die Hautfarbe, Gesichtsfarbe, der Teint; (temperament) das Temperament, die Natur; for the —plexion, für den Teint. —**plexity**, *s.* die Verwickelung, Verflechtung. —**pliance**, *s.* die Willfahrung, Einwilligung; in —pliance with your wishes, Ihren Wünschen gemäß, Ihren Wünschen entsprechend. —**pliancy**, *s.* die Willfährigkeit. —**pliant**, *adj.*, —**pliantly**, *adv.* nachgiebig, willfährig, gefällig. —**plicacy**, *s.* die Verwickelung. —**plicate**, I. *v.a.* verflechten, verwickeln. II. *adj.* dachziegelartig übereinander liegend (*Bot.*). —**plication**, *s.* die Verflechtung, Verschlingung, Verwickelung; komplizierte Krankheit (*Med.*); —plication of ideas, Verwickelung der Ideen; —plication of miseries, Anhäufung von Unglücksfällen, ein Gewebe von Elend. —**plicity**, *s.* die Mitschuld. —**plied**, *pret. & p.p. of* —ply. —**pliment**, I. *s.* die Empfehlung, das Kompliment; das Honorar; (*pl.*) Empfehlungen; in —pliment to . . ., aus Artigkeit gegen . . .; wishing you the —pliments of the season, mit den freundlichsten Empfehlungen *or* mit den besten Wünschen zu Weihnachten, zu Neujahr *or* zum neuen Jahre *or* zum Jahreswechsel, zu Ostern; give her my —pliments, grüßen Sie sie von mir, empfehlen Sie mich ihr bestens. II. *v.a.* komplimentieren, einem ein Kompliment machen; einem fein schmeicheln; (praise) loben; (einen) beglückwünschen; (einem) gratulieren. III. *v.n.* Komplimente machen. —**plimentary**, *adj.* höflich, bekomplimentierend; —plimentary dinner, das Festessen, Zweckessen; —plimentary ticket, die Freikarte, freie Eintrittskarte. —**plimenter**, *s.* der Komplimenten-macher *or* -drechsler. —**ply**, *v.n.* (—ply with) willfahren (einem), sich fügen in eine S., einwilligen in eine S., nachgeben (in einer S.); at last he —plied with her entreaties, endlich gab er ihren Bitten nach. —**ponent**, I. *adj.* einen Teil bildend; —ponent parts, Bestandteile. II. *s.* der Bestandteil. —**port**, *v.* I. *r.* sich betragen, sich benehmen. II. *n.* sich vertragen (*rare*). —**portment**, *s.* das Betragen. —**pose**, *v.a.* (put together) zusammensetzen; (form) bilden; verfassen, dichten (*a poem, etc.*); komponieren (*Mus.*); (Schrift) setzen (*Typ.*); zurechtlegen (*the limbs, etc.*); stillen, beruhigen (*the mind, etc.*); gütlich beilegen (*a quarrel*); a few things —pose all their possessions, wenige Sachen machen ihre ganze Habe aus; to be —posed of . . ., aus *or* in (*dat.*) . . . bestehen; to —pose o.s. (*calm o.s.*) sich beruhigen; (look grave) eine ernsthafte Miene annehmen; (collect o.s.) sich fassen; to —pose o.s. to sleep, sich zum Schlafe anschicken. —**posed**, *adj.*, —**posedly**, *adv.* gefaßt, gesetzt, ruhig. —**poser**, *s.* der Verfasser, Dichter (*of a poem*); der Komponist (*Mus.*). —**posing**, I. *adj.* beruhigend; —posing draught, der Schlaftrunk; —posing galley, *etc., see* —posing-galley, *etc.* II. *s.* das Bilden; das Komponieren; das Dichten; das

Schriftsetzen. —**posite**, *adj.* zusammengesetzt (*also Arch. & Bot.*); —posite candles, Kerzen aus einer Mischung von Talg und Stearinsäure; —posite sloop, eine Schaluppe, deren Spanten aus Stahl sind über den sich Holzlagen erstrecken. —**position**, *s.* die Zusammensetzung, Mischung; die Beschaffenheit, Art, Natur; die Zusammenstellung, Komposition (*of a picture*); das Verfassen; die Komposition, Tonsetzung (*Mus.*); die Komposition (*Chem., Metall.*); der Satz (*Typ.*); die Setzkunst (*Typ.*); die Übereinkunft, der Vergleich, Akkord (*C.L.*); Übersetzung aus der Muttersprache in die Fremdsprache; ordinary —position, die Hinübersetzung, Übertragung eines zusammenhängenden Textes in die Fremdsprache; free —position, original —position, der Aufsatz; German —position, die Übersetzung ins Deutsche; —position done in class, unprepared or class —position, das Extemporale; (writing) die Arbeit, das Werk; to have a —position with one's creditors, sich mit seinen Gläubigern wegen eines Akkords vergleichen. —**positor**, *s.* der Schriftsetzer, Setzer; —positor's board, das Setzbrett. —**post**, *s.* der Kompost, Mischdünger (*Agr.*); eine Komposition (*Build.*). —**posure**, *s.* die Gemütsruhe, Fassung, Gelassenheit, Gesetztheit; die Ausgleichung (*of a quarrel*). —**pound**, I. *adj.* zusammengesetzt (*also Bot.*); —pound interest, Zinseszinsen; —pound number, zusammengesetzte Zahl; —pound proportion, Regel de Quinque; —pound words, (—pounds, *pl.*) Komposita, zusammengesetzte Wörter; —pound pillar, der Bündelpfeiler; —pound engine, die Hoch- und-Niederdruck-maschine. II. *s.* das Kompositum; die Zusammensetzung, Mischung; das Gemisch; die Verbindung (*Chem.*); das Gehäge um das Haus (*in India*). III. *v.a.* zusammensetzen; beilegen, schlichten (*a quarrel*); to —pound a felony, ein Verbrechen (wegen erhaltener Entschädigung) nicht verfolgen (*Law*). IV. *v.n.* sich vertragen, sich vergleichen, akkordieren (for, wegen; with, mit); to —pound with one's creditors, ein Abkommen mit seinen Gläubigern treffen. —**pounder**, *s.* der Akkordierende; der Kombinator (*in gas-works*). —**prehend**, *v.a.* (include) in sich fassen; (understand) begreifen. —**prehensible**, *adj.*, —**prehensibly**, *adv.* faßlich, begreiflich. —**prehensibleness**, *s.* die Faßlichkeit. —**prehension**, *s.* die Fassungskraft; (inclusion) das Zusammenfassen, die Vereinigung; act of —prehension, der Parlamentsbeschluß für alle Parteien. —**prehensive**, *adj.*, —**prehensively**, *adv.* umfassend; —prehensive dictionary, das Handwörterbuch. —**prehensiveness**, *s.* das Umfassende; die Ausdehnung (*of a view, etc.*); die gedrängte, bündige Kürze (*of an essay, etc.*). —**press**, I. *v.a.* zusammendrücken, zusammendrängen; kondensieren; —pressed ball, gepreßte Bleikugel (*Mil.*); —pressed air, komprimierte Luft; —pressed brick, gepreßter Ziegel; to —press gunpowder, das Schießpulver verdichten. II. *s.* die Kompresse (*Surg.*). —**pressibility**, *s.* die Preßbarkeit. —**pressible**, *adj.* zusammendrückbar; preßbar, verdichtbar (*of elastic bodies*). —**pression**, *s.* das Zusammendrücken, Pressen; der Druck, die Zusammendrückung. —**prise**, *v.a.* in sich fassen, einschließen. —**promise**, I. *s.* die Übereinkunft, der Ausgleich, Kompromiß, der gütliche Vergleich; to make a —promise, einen Vergleich eingehen. II *v.a.* gütlich abmachen; kompromittieren, bloßstellen; in Ungelegenheiten bringen. —**pulsion**, *s.* der Zwang. —**pulsory**, *adj.* zwingend, durch Zwang; —pulsory instruction, allgemein verbindlicher Unterricht; —pulsory military service, allgemeine Wehrpflicht. —**punction**, *s.* das Stechen; die Zerknirschung des Herzens, die Gewissensbisse (*fig.*). —**putable**, *adj.* berechenbar, zählbar. —**putation**, *s.* die Berechnung, Rechnung; der Kostenüberschlag (*C.L.*). —**pute**, *v.a.* berechnen; überschlagen; den Preis bestimmen; —puted tax, die Durchschnittstaxe. —**puter**, *s.* der Rechner; der Kalkulator. *Comp.* —**munion-cup**, *s.* der Abendmahls-Kelch. —**munion-service**, *s.* der anglikanische Ritus bei der Austeilung des Abendmahls. —**munion-table**, *s.* der Altar, der Tisch des Herrn. —**panion-ladder**, *s.* die auf das Quarterdeck führende Treppe (*Naut.*). —**panion-stairs**, *pl.*, —**panion-way**, *s.* die Kajütenhütte. —**pass-box**, *s.* der Kompaßmörser. —**pass-card**, *s.* die Windrose. —**pass-needle**, die Magnetnadel. —**posing-galley**, *s.* das Setzerschiff (*Typ.*). —**posing-machine**, *s.* die Setzermaschine. —**posing-rule**, *s.* das Kolumnenmaß (*Typ.*). —**posing-stick**, *s.* der Winkelhaken (*Typ.*).

Come, *ir.v.n.* kommen; (arrive, reach) gelangen, ankommen; (approach) ankommen, näher kommen; (succeed) gelingen; (arise) entstehen; when I — to die, wenn es zum Sterben kommt, wenn ich sterben soll; the time to —, die Zukunft; the life to —, das künftige Leben; there is cheese to —, es kommt noch Käse; the malt —s, das Malz keimt; — life, — death, auf Leben und Sterben; first —, first served, wer zuerst kommt, mahlt zuerst; how —s it to be yours? wie seid Ihr dazu gekommen? he had — to speak German fluently, er hatte fließend deutsch sprechen gelernt; I have — to be a good cyclist, ich bin ein guter Radler geworden, ich habe gut radeln gelernt; he himself came to feel that he had done wisely, er selbst fühlte allmählich, daß er klug gehandelt hatte; to — and go, hin und her gehen; to — home, nach Hause kommen, (return) zurückkommen; (touch the feelings) (einem) nahe gehen, (einen) tief ergreifen; to — **about**, sich ereignen (*as events*); to — **across** a p., auf einen stoßen; to — **after**, (pursue) folgen, (seek) suchen, (follow) nachkommen, (woo) mit Liebesanträgen verfolgen (*vulg.*); to — **again**, wiederkommen, zurückkommen; to — **along**, (hasten) sich beeilen; (accompany) mitkommen; to — **amiss**, verkehrt kommen, zu ungelegener Zeit geschehen; to — **asunder**, in Stücke gehen; to — **at**, erlangen, gelangen zu (*vulg.*); to — **away**, sich weg begeben, aus . . . herauskommen; to — **back**, zurückkommen; to — **behind**, (follow) nachkommen, hinterherkommen; (not — up to) zurückbleiben, nicht erreichen; to — **between**, **betwixt**, dazwischenkommen; to — **by**, (pass) vorbeikommen; (get) erlangen, erwerben; (arrive at) dazukommen; to — by one's death, sich (*dat.*) den Tod holen; to — **down**, (descend) herunterkommen; (fall) fallen, einstürzen, zusammenfallen; (be humbled) sich demütigen; herunterreichen (*of a dress, etc.*); he came down handsomely, er bewies sich sehr freigebig, machte sich sehr nobel (*sl.*); to — down upon a p., einem auf den Kopf kommen, einen hart anlassen, einen tadeln, schelten; to — down with . . ., herausrücken mit . . .; to — **for**, (— to get) kommen für; (fetch) abholen; may I — for you? darf ich Sie abholen? to — **forth**, heraus-, hervor-kommen; to — **forward**, (advance) vorwärtskommen; (appear) sich zeigen, auftreten; to — **from**, (arise from) herkommen, herrühren von; where do you — from? wo kommen Sie her? to — **in**, (enter) hereinkommen, hereintreten; (somebody is knocking at the door) "— in!" (jemand klopft an die Tür) „Herein"! (— home, *etc.*) sich einstellen nach Haus kommen, (arrive) einlaufen, anlangen, (— into fashion) aufkommen, Mode werden; to — in for, Teil haben, Teil erhalten an (einer S.); to — in for an inheritance, eine Erbschaft machen; to — in for a good thrashing, tüchtig durchgeprügelt werden; to — into property, erben, zu Vermögen gelangen; to — into sight, in Sicht kommen; to — into the world, auf die Welt kommen; to — **near**, sich nähern; (resemble) ähnlich sein; (almost attain) beinahe erreichen; I came near breaking my neck, ich hätte mir beinahe den Hals gebrochen; to — **of**, (originate in) herkommen, abstammen von; (arise from) entstehen aus; — of it what will, es entstehe daraus, was mag; this —s of judging by the eye, das kommt davon, wenn man nach dem Augenschein urteilt; to — **off**, davon kommen, entkommen; to — off creditably, mit Ehren davonkommen *or* loskommen; to — off a loser, dabei verlieren; to — **on**, vorrücken, heranrücken; (proceed) fortkommen; (thrive) gedeihen, wachsen; (progress) Fortschritte machen; (— to one's turn) an die Reihe kommen; it will very likely — on to rain, es wird wohl Regen geben; — on! nur zu! komm nur an! night is coming on, die Nacht rückt heran; to — **out**, auskommen; (be published) herausgehen, veröffentlicht werden; (go out) ausgehen, herausgehen; (be made public) entdeckt werden, an den Tag kommen; (appear) erscheinen; ausschlagen (*as an eruption*); (make a debut) zum ersten Male in die große Welt *or* auf die Bühne treten; (fall out) ausfallen; (disappear) ausgehen (*as stains*); (appear, shine) hervorkommen; die Bälle besuchen (*of a girl*); she has — out, sie ist in die Gesellschaft eingeführt, sie geht auf Bälle; his teeth are coming out, ihm fallen die Zähne aus; when does the piece — out? wann wird das neue Stück (zum ersten Male) gespielt werden? to — out with s.th., mit etwas herausrücken; (blurt out) etwas vorbringen; to — **over**, herüberkommen; (go over) übertreten; (overreach) bemeistern, betrügen, überschleichen; to — **round**, (recover) sich erholen (*coll.*); (change in opinion) sich bedenken, sich anders *or* eines Bessern besinnen; (return, *as an anniversary, etc.*) wiederkehren; (return, *as a term*) fällig werden; (change, *as the wind*) sich drehen; to — **to**, zu, auf, in *or* an etwas kommen; (attain) gelangen; (approach) sich nähern; how came you to (know) this? wie habt Ihr dies erfahren? it has — to my knowledge, ich habe erfahren, mir ist zu Ohren gekommen; to — to an anchor, ankern; how much, what does it — to? wie viel macht es aus? to — to o.s., zu sich, zum Bewußtsein kommen; to — to blows, handgemein werden; to — to the crown, zur Krone gelangen; to — to an end, zu Ende kommen; ein Ende machen; to — to a bad end, ein schlechtes Ende nehmen; he will never — to any good, aus ihm wird nie etwas Rechtes werden; to — to a head, sich voll entwickeln; to — to nought, zu Nichts werden; to — to pass, sich ereignen; to — to the same (thing), auf eins herauskommen; what has — to you? was ist dir begegnet? (*coll.*); to — **up**, heraufkommen; (— up to the University; *Eng.*) als Student kommen, Student werden, (auf der Universität) ankommen; (turn up) herauskommen; (grow up) aufgehen, keimen; (become fashionable) modisch werden, eingeführt werden; to — up to, (reach) erreichen; (overtake) nachholen; (approach) auf einen zugehen; to — up to the mark, genügen, den Ansprüchen Genüge leisten; to — up to a p.'s expectations, jemandes Erwartungen entsprechen; to — up with, einholen; (equal) gleichkommen; to — upon, auf eine S. kommen; (surprise) überfallen, überraschen. —**liness**, *s.* die Schönheit, Anmut; (propriety) der Anstand. —**ly**, *adj.* (proper) geziemend, anständig; (suitable) passend; (pleasing) anmutig; (pretty) hübsch. —**r**, *s.* der, die, das Kommende; new —rs, neue Ankömmlinge. *Comp.* —**-at-able**, *adj.* zugänglich; erreichbar (*as a place*) (*coll.*).

Comed—ian, *s.* der Schauspieler; (writer) der Lustspieldichter. —**y**, *s.* das Lustspiel; farcical —y, der Schwank, die Posse.

Comet, *s.* der Komet. —**-like**, *adj.* kometenähnlich, kometenhaft.

Comfrey, *s.* der Beinwurz, Schwarzwurz (*Bot.*).

Comic, *adj.* komisch, Lustspiel-; a — actor, ein Komiker; a — paper, ein Witzblatt. —**al**, *adj.* komisch, lustig, drollig, spaßhaft. —**ality**, *s.* das komische Wesen; der komische Einfall; das Komische, die Komik. —**alness**, *s.* das Komische.

Coming, I. *p. of* Come; —, Sir! gleich, mein Herr! II. *adj.* (future) künftig. III. *s.* das Kommen; der Keim (*of malt*); — man, Mann der Zukunft; — of age, das Mündigwerden; — in, der Eintritt.

Comma, *s.* der Beistrich, das Komma; inverted —s, die Anführungszeichen, Gänsefüßchen.

Command, I. *v.a.* (einem) befehlen, gebieten; (be at the head of) befehligen; führen (*ships*); (overlook) beherrschen, bestreichen (*also Mil.*); (govern) beherrschen; kommandieren (*Mil.*); to — silence, Stillschweigen gebieten; — me, madam, gnädige Frau, verfügen Sie ganz über mich! these articles — a ready sale, diese Artikel verkaufen sich leicht, sind leicht abzusetzen (*C. L.*); her beauty —s love and admiration from all, ihre Schönheit flößt allen Liebe und Bewunderung ein; to — one's passions, seine Leidenschaften beherrschen. II. *v.n.* den Befehl führen, herrschen; kommandieren. III. *s.* die Herrschaft; (order) das Gebot, der Befehl; das Kommando (*Mil.*); das Beherrschen, Bestreichen (*Fort.*); to have in one's —, in seiner Gewalt haben; this window —s a fine view, von diesem Fenster hat man eine schöne Aussicht; he has his passions well under —, er kann seine Leidenschaften beherrschen, er hat große Selbstbeherrschung; to be at a p.'s —, zu jemandes Befehl stehen; word of —, das Kommandowort (*Mil.*); he has no — over himself, er hat keine Selbstbeherrschung. —**ant**, der Befehlshaber, Kommandant. —**atory**, *adj.* gebieterisch, befehlend. —**eer**, *v.a.* zum Kriegsdienst zwingen; für Militärzwecke in Beschlag nehmen. —**er**, *s.* der Gebieter; der Befehlshaber (*also Mil.*); der Kapitän (*Naut.*); das Formband (*of hats*); die Beinlade (*Surg.*); die Handramme (*Mech.*); —er in chief, der Oberbefehlshaber. —**ership**, *s.* die Führerstelle, der Oberbefehl. —(**e**)**ry**, *s.* die Komturei, Ordenspfründe. —**ing**, *adj.* gebietend Herrscher-; —ing ground, beherrschende Anhöhe. —**ingly**, *adv.* gebieterisch. —**ite**, *s.* die stille Teilhaberschaft, Kommandite (*C. L.*). —**ment**, *s.* das Gebot, Gesetz, die Vorschrift; the ten —ments, die zehn Gebote. —**o**, *s.* der Kriegsdienst; to be on —o, im Felde stehen.

Commend, *v.a.* (praise) rühmen, loben; (recommend) empfehlen; (entrust to) übergeben, anvertrauen. —**able**, *adj.* löblich, empfehlenswert. —**ableness**, *s.* der Wert, die Würdigkeit. —**am**, *s.* die Kommende, Kommendenpfründe (*Eccl.*); in —am, in Verwaltung. —**atary**, *s.* der Interimsverwalter einer erledigten Pfründe. —**ations**, *s.* die Empfehlung; das Lob. —**atory**, *adj.* empfehlend, lobend; —atory letter, das Empfehlungsschreiben; —atory bishop, ein Bischof, welcher eine Pfründe bis zur definitiven Besetzung derselben verwaltet.

Comment, I. *v.n.* Auslegungen, Anmerkungen, Bemerkungen machen (upon, über). II. *s.* (note) die Auslegung, Erklärung, Erläuterung; (remark) die Bemerkung, Anmerkung. —**ary**, *s.* der Kommentar, die Erläuterungsschrift; Cæsar's —aries, Cäsars Denkwürdigkeiten. —**ate**, *v.a.* mit Erläuterungen begleiten, mit Anmerkungen versehen, erläutern. —**ator**, *s.* der Ausleger, Erläuterer, Kommentator. —**er**, *s.* einer der Bemerkungen macht.

Commerc—e, *s.* der Handel; (intercourse) der Umgang, die Verbindung; Faculty of —e, die Handelsfakultät. —**ial**, *adj.* den Handel betreffend kommerziell; —ial academy, die Handelshochschule; —ial affairs, Handelsangelegenheiten;

—ial alliance, der Handelsvertrag; —ial crisis, der Krach; —ial directory, das Handelsadreßbuch; —ial education, kaufmännische Bildung, Vorbildung für den Handelsstand; —ial hotel, Gasthof für Geschäftsreisende; —ial law, das Handelsrecht; —ial manager, geschäftlicher Leiter; —ial school, die Handelsschule; —ial room, das Gastzimmer für Handelsreisende; —ial tariff, der Handelstarif; —ial traveller, der Handelsreisende, Geschäftsreisende; —ial Union of Germany, der deutsche Zollverein. **—ially**, *adv.* kaufmännisch.

Commiss—ariat, *s.* das Kommissariat; das Verpflegungswesen, die Intendantur; —ariat magazine, das Proviantmagazin, das Proviantamt; —ariat stores, Proviantvorräte für Militärverpflegung. **—ary**, *s.* der gesetzlich Bevollmächtigte; der Kommissär; —ary of stores, der Proviantmeister; —ary of horses, Beaufsichtiger der Militärpferde. **—ion**, I. *s.* (errand, order) der Auftrag; (act of committing) die Begehung; (percentage) die Kommissionsgebühr; (post) die Stelle, das Amt; das Offizierspatent (*Mil.*); (board) die Behörde, der Ausschuß; die Indienststellung (*of a man of war*); sins of —ion, Begehungssünden; —ion of bankruptcy, Konkursbehörde; a royal —ion, ein vom König berufener Ausschuß (zur Untersuchung irgend einer wichtigen Frage); a ship in —ion, ein auf den Kriegsfuß eingerichtetes Schiff; to put out of —ion, außer Dienst stellen; to receive one's —ion, das Offizierspatent erhalten; book of —ions, Warenbestellungsbuch; to sell on —ion, im Auftrag, für Rechnung eines andern verkaufen; to give a —ion for, bestellen (*a picture, etc.*); to be in the —ion of the peace, Friedensrichter sein. II. *attrib.*; —ion business, das Kommissionsgeschäft. III. *v.a.* beauftragen, bevollmächtigen; auftragen, einen Auftrag geben; anvertrauen; abordnen; dienstbereit machen, in Dienst stellen (*as a ship*); a —ioned officer, ein vom Könige angestellter Offizier, ein in Gehalt stehender Offizier; a non- —ioned officer, ein Unteroffizier; to be —ioned, den Auftrag haben. **—ionaire**, *s.* der Dienstmann (in der Londoner Geschäftsgegend). **—ioner**, *s.* der Beauftragte, Bevollmächtigte; der Kommissär (*of the navy*); town —ioner, der Ratmann; the king's high —ioner, des Königs Statthalter; —ioner for (the administration of) oaths, Eidabnehmer, beeidigter Notar. **—ure**, *s.* die Fuge (*Arch.*); die Kommissur (*Anat.*); die Verbindung (*Bot.*). *Comp.* **—ion-agent**, **—ion-merchant**, *s.* der Kommissionär (*C.L.*).

Common, I. *adj.*, **—ly**, *adv.* (usual) gewöhnlich, gemein; (general) allgemein; (— to many) gemeinschaftlich; (vulgar) gemein; (low) niedrig; (lowborn) unadelig; beiderlei Geschlechts (*Gram.*); to make — cause with, gemeinschaftliche Sache mit (einem) machen; — chord, der Dreiklang; — ground, der Gemeindeboden, die Allmende; to be on — ground, auf gleichen Voraussetzungen fußen; the — herd, das niedere Volk; Court of — Pleas, Gerichtshof für Zivilsachen (*obs.*); Book of — Prayer, das anglikanische Gebetbuch; — rights, Menschenrechte; — room, das gemeinsame Zimmer, die Gaststube (*in hotels*); das Zimmer in einem (Oxforder) College, in dem Zeitungen ausliegen und von dem aus sich die älteren (graduierten) Mitglieder des College gemeinsam zu den Mahlzeiten begeben; — talk, der Gegenstand der allgemeinen Unterhaltung, des Stadtgesprächs; — usage, ein weit verbreiteter Gebrauch; the — voice, die allgemeine Stimme; the — weal, das gemeine Wohl, Gemeinwohl. II. *s.* das Gemeindeland, die Gemeindeweide; — of pasture, das Weiderecht; to have in — gemeinschaftlich besitzen; to make — cause with, gemeinschaftliche Sache machen mit. **—al(i)ty**, *s.* das gemeine Volk. **—er**, *s.* einer der nicht adelig ist, der Bürgerliche; das Mitglied des englischen Unterhauses (*Parl.*). **—ness**, *s.* das häufige Vorkommen, die Gewöhnlichkeit; die Gemeinheit. **—s**, *pl.* die Gemeindeweiden, Gemeindeböden; die gemeinschaftliche Kost; the (House of) —s, das Haus der Gemeinen, Unterhaus des Parlaments; to be kept on short —s, nicht satt zu essen bekommen, schmale Kost haben. *Comp.* **—-council**, *s.* der Gemeinderat; (the members) die gesammte Bürgerschaft. **—-councilman**, *s.* das Ratsmitglied. **—-crier**, *s.* öffentlicher Ausrufer. **—-law**, *s.* das Gewohnheitsrecht, gemeine Recht. **—-measure**, *s.* gemeinsamer Teiler; gemeinschaftliches Maß. **—-minded**, *adj.* niedrig gesinnt, unedel. **—-noun**, *s.* der Sachname. **—place**, I. *adj.* alltäglich, gewöhnlich; (trite) abgedroschen; —place wit, der Alltagswitz. II. *s.* der Gemeinplatz; die täglich gehörte Behauptung; das Zitat. **—place-book**, I. *s.* das Notizbuch; das Kollektaneenbuch. II. *v.a.*; to —place a thing, etwas zum Gemeinplatz machen; etwas in ein Sammelheft eintragen. **—-sense**, *s.* der gesunde Menschenverstand. **—-time**, *s.* der Viervierteltakt (*Mus.*). **—wealth**, *s.* die bürgerliche Verfassung *or* Gesellschaft, der Staat; die Republik; the —wealth, die republikanische Regierungsform in England von 1649 bis 1660; the —wealth of learning, die Gelehrtenrepublik.

Comrade, *s.* der Kamerad, Genoß, Gefährte; she was his —, sie war seine Gefährtin. **—ship**, *s.* die Kameradschaft.

[1]Con-, *prefix* (*before l*, Col-; *before b, p, m*, Com-) together; with; against; *often* intensive *or* emphasizing.

[2]Con, *s.* (*abbr. of* Contra); pro and —, für und wider; pros and —s, Gründe für und wider

[3]Con, *v.a.* fleißig studieren, wiederholt lesen; —ning tower, der Kommandoturm eines Kriegsschiffes.

Concatenat—e, *v.a.* verketten, zusammenketten. **—ion**, *s.* die Verkettung (*fig.*); die Reihe von Kettengliedern.

Concav—e, *adj.* konkav, hohl, hohlrund, ausgehöhlt; double —e, bikonkav; —e glasses, Hohlgläser (*Opt.*); —e lens, die Hohllinse; —e mirror, der Hohlspiegel. **—ity**, *s.* die Hohlründung, Aushöhlung; die Bogenründung (eines Gewölbes, *of a vault*). **—o-concave**, *adj.* auf beiden Seiten konkav. **—o-convex**, *adj.* konkav-konvex.

Conceal, *v.a.* verhehlen, verbergen; to — s.th. from a p., einem (etwas) verheimlichen. **—able**, *adj.* verhehlbar, zu verheimlichen. **—ed**, *adj.*, **—edly**, *adv.* verborgen. **—er**, *s.* der Verhehler. **—ment**, *s.* die Verhehlung, Verheimlichung; (secrecy) die Heimlichkeit; (place of —ment) das Versteck; —ment of material facts and circumstances, Verhehlung von wesentlichen Tatsachen.

Concede, *v.* I. *a.* einräumen, zugestehen, gewähren, bewilligen. II. *n.* zugeben, einräumen.

Conceit, I. *s.* (idea) der Gedanke, die Idee, Einbildung (*obs.*); (opinion) die Meinung; (imagination) die Einbildung; (fancy) der Einfall; (quirk) der Witz; (vanity) die Eitelkeit; self- —, der Eigendünkel; idle —s, törichte Einfälle; to be out of — with a th., einer Sache überdrüssig sein; to be out of — with o.s., mit sich selbst unzufrieden sein; to put a p. out of — with, einem die Lust (zu einer Sache) benehmen; to take the — out of a p., einen demütigen. II. (*obs.*) *v.a. & n.* (fancy) sich (*dat.*) einbilden, sich (*dat.*) vorstellen; (believe) meinen, glauben (*obs.*). **—ed**, *adj.* (—ed of) eingebildet; (vain) dünkelhaft, eitel. **—edness**, *s.* der (Eigen)dünkel.

Conceiv—able, *adj.*, **—ably**, *adv.* denkbar; begreiflich, faßlich; the best relation —able, das denkbar beste Verhältnis. **—e**, *v.* I. *a.* in sich aufnehmen, fassen; (imagine) sich (*dat.*) denken, sich vorstellen; (understand) fassen, begreifen, verstehen; (think) meinen; (nourish a project) im Busen hegen, in sich nähren; to —e an affection for a p., eine Zuneigung zu einem fassen; to

—e a desire, einen Wunsch hegen; to —e a design against, einen Anschlag gegen (einen) fassen. II. *n.* empfangen, schwanger (*of women*) *or* (*dat.*) trächtig (*of beasts*) werden; begreifen, sich (*dat.*) einen Begriff machen.

Concelebrat—e, *v.a.* (*obs.*) gemeinschaftlich feiern. **—ion,** *s.* die gemeinsame Feier.

Concentr—e, *v.* I. *n.* sich in einem Mittelpunkte vereinigen. II. *a.* in einen Mittelpunkt vereinigen. **—ate,** *v.a. see* —e II; konzentrieren; (draw closer) zusammenziehen, vereinigen; (condense) verdichten. **—ation,** *s.* die Konzentration, Vereinigung in einen (Mittel-)Punkt; die Verdichtung. **—ativeness,** *s.* die Fähigkeit sich zu konzentrieren; der Beharrlichkeitssinn (*Phren.*). **—ic,** *adj.* konzentrisch. **—icity,** *s.* die Konzentrizität. *Comp.* **—ation-camp,** *s.* das Sammellager.

Concept, *s.* der Begriff; der Entwurf, das Konzept. **—acle,** *s.* das Behältnis; das Samenbehältnis (*Bot.*). **—ion,** *s.* das Erfassen; die Empfängnis; die Vorstellung, der Begriff; die Fassungskraft; der Entwurf, Plan, die Idee; false —ion, die Mißgeburt, Mole (*Med.*); immaculate —ion, unbefleckte Empfängnis; to form a —ion of, sich (*dat.*) einen Begriff von (einer Sache) machen; this passes all —ion, das geht über *or* übersteigt alle Begriffe.

Concern, I. *v.a.* (touch, affect) betreffen, angehen; Sorge, Kummer, Teilnahme erwecken; to be —ed about (a th.), for (a p.), betrübt, bekümmert über (eine Sache), um (eine Person) sein; that does not — you, das geht Sie nichts an; we need not — ourselves with (*or* about) the affairs of our neighbours, wir brauchen uns nicht um die Angelegenheiten unserer Nachbarn zu kümmern; he is said to be —ed in the robbery, er soll an dem Diebstahl beteiligt sein; we are —ed in these affairs, wir haben an diesen Dingen ein Interesse; the parties —ed, die Beteiligten. II. *s.* (affair) die Angelegenheit, Sache, das Geschäft; (interest) das Interesse, der Anteil, die Teilnahme; (matter, thing) das Ding; (importance) der Belang; (care) die Sorge, Kummer; (business) das Geschäft; a paying —, ein Geschäft, das sich bezahlt macht; a matter of the utmost —, eine Sache von der äußersten Wichtigkeit; to have no — with, mit (einer Sache, &c.) nichts zu tun haben; that's your own —, das ist eure Sache; we have a most practical — in what happens in Egypt, wir haben ein höchst unmittelbares Interesse an den Vorgängen in Ägypten; to mind one's own —s, sich um seine eignen Angelegenheiten bekümmern; to have no — for, sich nicht kümmern um. **—ed,** *p.p. & adj.*, **—edly,** *adv.* beteiligt, interessiert, Anteil habend (an einer S.); —ed in, verwickelt (in eine S.); —ed at *or* about *or* for, bekümmert, besorgt, in Unruhe, in Sorge, in Angst (um, für, wegen, in betreff); betroffen, betreten, verlegen; to be —ed, in Betracht kommen; the parties —ed, die Beteiligten, Interessenten, Teilhaber. **—ing,** *prep.* in Betreff, betreffend, betreffs, hinsichtlich; —ing my friend, betreffs meines Freundes, in Bezug auf meinen Freund; —ing him, was ihn betrifft *or* anbelangt; —ing it, mit Bezug darauf, hierüber, darüber, hinsichtlich dessen.

Concert, I. *v.a.* (heimlich) verabreden, abmachen; planen, sich (*dat.*) ausdenken, erdenken. II. *s.*; die Übereinstimmung, das Einverständnis; das Konzert (*Mus.*); the European —, das europäische Konzert, das Einverständnis der Großmächte Europas; to act in —, in Übereinstimmung, in gegenseitigem Einverständnisse handeln. **—ina,** *s.* die Konzertina (*Mus.*). **—ed,** *adj.*; —ed action, gemeinschaftliches Vorgehen; —ed music, die Konzertmusik. **—o,** *s.* das Konzertstück. *Comp.* **—-pitch,** *s.* der Kammerton. **—-room,** *s.* der Konzertsaal.

Concessi—on, *s.* (yielding) das Zugeben, Nachgeben; (permission) die Gestattung; (thing conceded) das Zugeständnis; (grant) die Einräumung. **—onist,** *s.* der Befürworter von Zugeständnissen. **—ve,** *adj.*, **—vely,** *adv.* einräumend, zugebend; —ve clauses, (*Gram.*) Konzessivsätze.

Conch, *s.* die Schneckenmuschel, große Seemuschel. **—oid,** *s.* die Schneckenlinie, Muschellinie, Konchoide (*Math.*); das Säulenprofil (*Arch.*). **—oidal,** *adj.* muschelig. **—ological,** *adj.* die Schaltierkunde betreffend, Muschel-. **—ologist,** *s.* der Konchyliolog, Schaltierkenner, Muschelkenner. **—ology,** *s.* die Konchyliologie, die Muschelkunde. **—ylia,** *pl.* die Schaltiere, Muscheltiere, Konchylien.

Conciliat—e, *v.a.* (reconcile) versöhnen, beschwichtigen; (gain over) gewinnen. **—ion,** *s.* die Versöhnung. **—or,** *s.* der Vermittler. **—ory,** *adj.* vermittelnd, gewinnend, zum Frieden dienlich.

Concise, *adj.*, **—ly,** *adv.* (brief) kurz, gedrängt, knapp; (pithy) bündig. **—ness,** *s.* die Kürze; die Bündigkeit.

Conclave, *s.* das Geheimzimmer; das Konklave (*electing a Pope*); die geheime Versammlung.

Conclu—de, *v.* I. *a.* (end) (be)schließen, endigen, zu Ende führen; (decide) eine S. beschließen, entscheiden; (accomplish) zustande bringen; (infer) schließen, folgern; (ab)schließen (*a business, peace, etc.*). II. *n.* endigen, zu Ende kommen, enden, ein Ende nehmen; to —de, schließlich. **—ding,** *p. & adj.* schließend; —ding stanzas, Schlußstrophen; —ding sentence, Schlußsatz. **—sion,** *s.* der Schluß, das Ende (*of a speech, etc.*); die Folge, Folgerung, der Schluß (*Log.*); (decision) die Entscheidung; (resolve) der Beschluß; —sion of peace, der Friedensschluß; to try —sions, Proben anstellen; in —sion, zum Beschluß, schließlich. **—sive,** *adj.*, **—sively,** *adv.* entscheidend; (convincing) überzeugend; (indubitable) zweifellos; (final) abschließend; —sive argument, entscheidender Beweis. **—siveness,** *s.* die Endgültigkeit; das Entscheidende.

Concoct, *v.a.* kochen, bereiten, anrichten (*Cook.*); (plot) aussinnen, schmieden. **—er,** *s.* der Koch, der Zubereiter; der Anstifter (*of mischief, etc.*) (*fig.*). **—ion,** *s.* die Bereitung, Anrichtung (*of food*); das Gebräu, die Köcherei (*hum. contempt.*).

Concomitan—ce, —cy, *s.* das Zusammenbestehen. **—t,** I. *adj.* mitwirkend; mitverbunden, begleitend. II. *s.* der Begleiter; begleitender Umstand. **—tly,** *adv.* in Begleitung.

Concord, *s.* (union) die Eintracht, Harmonie, Einigung; (agreement) die Übereinstimmung (*also Gram.*); der Zusammenklang, die Konsonanz (*Mus.*), der Vertrag (*Law*). **—ance,** *s.* die Übereinstimmung; die Konkordanz (*to the Bible, etc.*). **—ant,** *adj.*, **—antly,** *adv.* einstimmig, einhellig, übereinstimmend; harmonisch. **—at,** *s.* der Vergleich, Vertrag; das Konkordat.

Concourse, *s.* der Zusammenlauf (*of persons*); (crowd) die Versammlung, Menge, der Haufe.

Concret—e, I. *adj.*, **—ely,** *adv.* zusammengesetzt; (*opp. to* abstract) konkret; benannt (*as a number*); (solid) verdichtet, fest; —e noun, das Konkretum. II. *s.* der Steinmörtel, Konkretmörtel (*Build.*); das Pisé (*Build.*); das Konkrete (*Log.*); in the —e, im konkreten Falle, im besonderen Falle, in der Wirklichkeit. III. *v.a.* durch die Konkretion zu einer Masse machen. IV. *v.n.* zusammengerinnen; aufschießen (*of crystals*). **—eness,** *s.* die Verdichtung; das Konkrete. **—ion,** *s.* das Zusammenwachsen; die zusammengewachsene Masse; das Verhärten.

Concubin—age, *s.* die wilde Ehe, freie Liebe, das Konkubinat. **—e,** *s.* die Beischläferin, Konkubine.

Concupiscen—ce, *s.* die sinnliche, fleischliche Begierde, Sinnlichkeit, Fleischeslust. **—t,** *adj.* lüstern, sinnlich.

Concur, *v.n.* zusammentreffen; (agree) übereinstimmen, sich vereinigen; mitwirken (to, zu); I — with you in thinking that . . ., ich stimme Ihrer Meinung bei, daß . . .. ich denke wie Sie, daß . . . —**rence**, *s.* das Zusammentreffen; (agreement) die Übereinstimmung; (assent) die Zustimmung; (joint action) die Mitwirkung; in —rence with, gemeinschaftlich mit. —**rent**, *adj.*, —**rently**, *adv.* gemeinsam, begleitend, mitwirkend.

Concuss, *v.a.* erschüttern (with, durch); durch Drohung beeinflussen (into *or* to, *with infin.*). —**ion**, *s.* die Erschütterung; —ion of the brain, die Gehirnerschütterung.

Condemn, *v.a.* verdammen; (sentence) verurteilen; (disapprove of) mißbilligen, tadeln; (— as worthless) für untüchtig erklären; als untüchtig verwerfen, als wertlos beseitigen; to — a p. to pay a fine, einem eine Geldbuße auflegen; (the ship) was —ed, (das Schiff) wurde für seeuntüchtig erklärt. —**able**, *adj.* verwerflich; verdammlich, strafbar. —**ation**, *s.* die Verurteilung, Verdammung; die Verwerfung. —**atory**, *adj.* verurteilend. —**er**, *s.* der verurteilende Richter.

Condens—ation, *s.* die Verdichtung; die Eindickung (*of milk, etc.*); die Abkürzung. —**ability**, *s.* die Verdichtbarkeit. —**e**, *v.* I. *a.* verdichten, eindicken, kondensieren; (compress) abkürzen, zusammendrängen; —ed water, destilliertes Wasser; —ed milk, eingedickte Milch. II. *n.* sich verdichten. —**ed**, *p.p. & adj.* verdichtet; eingedickt, kondensiert; (*fig.*) zusammengedrängt. —**er**, *s.* der Kondensator (*Phys., etc.*), das Kühlrohr (*of a distillery*). —**ing**, *adj.* verdichtend; —ing engine, die Kondensatordampfmaschine; —ing lens, die Sammellinse.

Condescen—d, *v.n.* sich herablassen; (deign) geruhen; (yield) nachgeben; einwilligen (aus Güte). —**ding**, *adj.*, —**dingly**, *adv.* herablassend, gütig; (obliging) gefällig. —**sion**, *s.* die Herablassung; die Gefälligkeit.

Condign, *adj.* verdient; gehörig, angemessen; — punishment, wohlverdiente Strafe.

Condiment, *s.* die Würze; die Zutat.

Condition, I. *s.* (state) die äußere Stellung, Bewandtnis, Lage, der Zustand; (rank) der Rang, Stand; (circumstances) die Umstände; (temperament, character) die Gemütsbeschaffenheit, das Temperament (*obs.*); (stipulation) die Bedingung; (clause in a compact) die Klausel; (quality) die Eigenschaft; die Qualität, der Zustand (*C. L.*); die Gare (*of leather, copper, etc.*); implied —s, stillschweigende Bedingungen; in good —, in gutem Zustande; kräftig, gesund, üppig; on — that, mit *or* unter der Bedingung. II. *v.a. & n.* Bedingungen machen, bedingen. —**al**, *adj.* bedingt; bedingend; konditionell (*Gram.*); —al acceptance, bedingte Annahme; —al clause, der Bedingungssatz; —al promise, bedingtes Versprechen. —**ality**, *s.* das Bedingtsein. —**ally**, *adv.* unter (gewissen) Bedingungen. —**ed**, *adj.* beschaffen, geartet; (having —s) bedingt.

Condol—atory, *adj.* Beileid bezeigend, Beileids=. —**e**, *v.n.* (—e with) sein Beileid bezeigen, mittrauern, kondolieren; they came to —e with him on his loss, sie kamen um ihm über seinen Verlust ihr Beileid zu bezeigen. —**ence**, *s.* die Beileidsbezeigung, das Beileid, die Mittrauer; letter of —ence, der Beileidsbrief. —**er**, *s.* der Kondolierende.

Condon—ation, *s.* die Verzeihung. —**e**, *v.a.* verzeihen, erlassen, nachsehen (einem etwas).

Condor, *s.* der Kondor.

Condu—ce, *v.n.* beitragen, dienen, förderlich sein; (contribute to) mitwirken. —**cive**, *adj.* förderlich, dienlich, beitragend. —**ct**, I. *s.* (leading) die Führung, Leitung; (managing) die Verwaltung; (escort) die Begleitung, Bedeckung; die Leitung (*Elect.*); (behaviour) die Aufführung, das Betragen, Benehmen; die Führung (*Mil.*); —ct of war, die Kriegsführung; —ct of the state, die Staatsverwaltung; good —ct badge, Abzeichen für gute Führung im Dienst (*Mil.*); safe —ct, der Geleitsbrief. II. *v.a.* leiten, führen; begleiten, geleiten; verwalten; anordnen, leiten, führen (*a business*); leiten (*Elect.*); to —ct o.s., sich aufführen, benehmen; sich führen (*Mil.*); —cted tours, Gesellschaftsreisen (unter Begleitung eines Kuriers). —**ctibility**, *s.* die Leitungsfähigkeit (*Elect.*). —**cting**, I. *adj.*; —cting ray, der Leitstrahl; —cting wire, der Leitungsdraht (*Tele.*). II. *s.* das Leiten; capable of —cting, leitungsfähig. —**ction**, *s.* die Leitung; —ction of heat, die Wärmeleitung. —**ctivity**, *s.* das Leitungsvermögen. —**ctor**, *s.* der Führer, Anführer; der Leiter (*Phys.*); der Dirigent, Kapellmeister (*Mus.*); der Schaffner, Kondukteur (*Railw.*); das Leitinstrument (*Surg.*); non-—ctor, Nichtleiter; lightning —ctor, der Blitzableiter; —ctor's baton, der Dirigentenstock, Taktstock. —**it**, *s.* die Leitung (*gas, etc.*); die Röhre, das Gerinne; der Kanal; die Wasserleitung durch Röhren (*Hydr.*). II. *attrib.*; —it pipe, das Leitungsrohr; die Pochröhre (*Min.*).

Condyle, *s.* der Gelenkhügel (*Anat.*).

Cone, *s.* der Kegel (*Geom.*); der Tannenzapfen (*of firs*); das Krystallisiergefäß (*Sug.-ref., etc.*); — of rays, der Strahlenkegel, kegelförmiges Strahlenbüschel. *Comp.* —**-bit**, *s.* die Stollenfeile (*Artil.*). —**-pulley**, *s.* die konische Scheibe.

Coney, *see* Cony.

Confab, (*coll.*) *see* Confabulate.

Confabulat—e, *v.n.* vertraulich mit einander plaudern, schwatzen. —**ion**, *s.* das trauliche Gespräch, das gemütliche Geplauder.

Confect, I. *s.* das Konfekt. II. *v.a.* mit Zucker einmachen. —**ion**, *s.* die Zubereitung, Zusammensetzung, Mischung; das Gemisch; das Zuckerwerk, Eingemachte; der Modeartikel, Konfektionsartikel (*of ladies' dresses, hats, etc.*). —**ionary**, *s.* die Konditorei. —**ioner**, *s.* der Konditor, Zuckerbäcker. —**ionery**, *s.* das Zuckerwerk; (*shop, etc.*) die Konditorei.

Confedera—cy, *s.* das Bündnis, der Bund; die Verschwörung. —**te**, I. *adj.* verbündet, verbunden. II. *s.* der Verbündete, Bundesgenoß; (accomplice) der Mitschuldige. III. *v.a.* verbünden. IV. *v.n.* sich verbünden. —**tion**, *s.* die Verbündung, das Bündnis, der Bund; the North German —tion (1866–1871) der Norddeutsche Bund.

Confer, *v.* I. *a.* (bestow) geben, erteilen, zuteil werden lassen; to — a favour on a p., einem eine Gunst *or* Gefälligkeit erweisen; to — a living upon a clergyman, einem Geistlichen eine Pfründe erteilen. II. *n.* unterhandeln, sich besprechen; beratschlagen (with a p. about a th., mit einem über eine S.). —**ence**, *s.* die Verhandlung, Unterredung, Beratung; (meeting) die Sitzung, Konferenz; to hold a —ence, eine Sitzung (ab)halten. —**rer**, *s.* der Erteiler, Verleiher; der Beratende.

Conferva, *s.* der Wasserfaden (*Bot.*).

Confess, *v.* I. *a.* (acknowledge) zugestehen, einräumen; bekennen (*a debt, etc.*); (grant) eingestehen; beichten (*sins*); (make known) kund geben; (einem) Beichte hören (*as a priest*); it is —ed that, es wird eingeräumt, daß . . .; he —ed her, er nahm ihr die Beichte ab *or* hörte ihre Beichte. II. *n.* beichten. —**edly**, *adv.* unleugbar, offenbar; (by —ion) durch Geständnis. —**ion**, *s.* das Geständnis, Bekenntnis; (—ion of faith) das Glaubensbekenntnis; die Beichte; auricular —ion, die Ohrenbeichte. —**ional**, *s.* der Beichtstuhl. —**or**, *s.* der Glaubensbekenner; father —or, der Beichtvater; Edward the —or, Eduard der Bekenner.

Confid—ant, *s.* der Vertraute; der Mitwisser. —**ante**, *s.* die Vertraute. —**e**, *v.* I. *a.* anvertrauen (s.th. to a p., einem etwas). II. *n.* vertrauen, sich verlassen; may I —e in him? darf ich mich auf ihn verlassen? you —e too much in your own strength, Sie vertrauen zu sehr auf Ihre Kräfte. —**ence**, *s.* (trust) das Vertrauen

Zutrauen; (communication) die vertrauliche Mitteilung; (assurance) die Zuversicht; self—ence) das Selbstvertrauen; (forwardness) die Dreistigkeit; (boldness) die Kühnheit; —ence in a man, Vertrauen auf einen Mann, zu einem Manne; to place, repose —ence in a p., Vertrauen zu einem fassen, auf einen setzen. **—ent,** *adj.*, **—ently,** *adv.* vertrauend, voll Vertrauen; gewiß, zuversichtlich; mutig; keck, dreist; I feel —ent, ich bin fest (davon) überzeugt, ich glaube zuversichtlich; —ent of success, des Erfolges gewiß. **—ential,** *adj.*, **—entially,** *adv.* im Vertrauen, vertraulich; vertraut; private and —ential, vertraulich, im Vertrauen. **—er,** *s.* der Vertrauende. **—ing,** *adj.* vertrauend, vertrauensvoll; (too —ing) vertrauensselig. **—ingness,** *s.* die Zutraulichkeit.

Configuration, *s.* die Gestaltung, der Bau (*Phys.*); der Planetenaspekt.

Confin—able, *adj.* begrenzbar; beschränkbar. **—e,** I. *v.a.* begrenzen, einschränken; (shut up) einschließen, einsperren; beschränken (to, auf eine S.); to —e o.s. to, sich zurückziehen in, sich beschränken auf (sein Haus, one's house); to be —ed to bed, das Bett hüten müssen; to be —ed, entbunden werden, in den Wochen liegen; to be —ed of a son, eines Sohnes genesen sein, von einem Sohne entbunden werden, einen Sohn bekommen; —ed in an asylum, in einem Irrenhause eingesperrt. II. *s.* (*gen'lly* **—es,** *pl.*) die Grenze, der Bezirk; on the —es of death, am Rande des Grabes. **—ement,** *s.* (imprisonment) die Einsperrung, Haft, Gefangenschaft; die Entbindung; das Wochenbett; die Beschränkung (auf eine S.) Enthaltung (von einer S. *or genit.*).

Confirm, *v.a.* (strengthen) bekräftigen, bestärken; (establish) bestätigen; (corroborate) bestätigen; einsegnen, konfirmieren (*of Protestants*), firme(l)n (*of Roman Catholics*) (*Eccl.*); to — by oath, eidlich erhärten, bekräftigen. **—ation,** *s.* die Bestätigung, Bekräftigung; die Konfirmation, Einsegnung; Firm(el)ung (*R. Cath.*); in —ation of this, zur Bestätigung dieses. **—ative,** *adj.*, **—atively,** *adv.*, **—atory,** *adj.* bestätigend. **—ed,** *p.p. & adj.* fest, bestimmt; eingewurzelt, chronisch, unverbesserlich; a —ed drunkard, ein Gewohnheitstrinker, unverbesserlicher Trunkenbold; a —ed invalid, ein stets leidender Kranker; a —ed sceptic, ein Erzzweifler, unverbesserlicher Zweifler.

Confiscat—e, I. *v.a.* in Beschlag nehmen, mit Beschlag belegen, konfiszieren. II. *adj.* verfallen, konfisziert. **—ion,** *s.* die Einziehung, Beschlagnahme, Konfiszierung. **—or,** *s.* der Konfiszierende. **—ory,** *adj.* der Beschlagnahme *or* Konfiszierung übergebend.

Conflagration, *s.* der große Brand, die (gewaltige) Feuersbrunst.

Conflict, I. *s.* (collision) der Zusammenstoß; (fight) der Kampf, Streit; mental —, Seelenkampf. II. *v.n.* zusammenstoßen; streiten; (oppose) widerstreiten. **—ing,** *adj.* einander widerstreitend, entgegengesetzt (*as evidence, etc.*); —ing views, einander engegengesetzte Ansichten.

Conflu—ence, *s.* der Zusammenfluß (*of rivers*), der Zulauf (*of people*). **—ent,** *adj.* zusammenfließend. **—x,** *s.* der Zusammenfluß (*of rivers*); das Zusammenströmen (*of people*).

Conform, *v.* I. *a.* gleichförmig machen; (adapt) anpassen. II. *n.*; to — to, sich fügen, sich richten nach, sich bequemen, sich schicken in (*acc.*), sich anpassen (*dat. or* an eine S.). **—able,** *adj.*, **—ably,** *adv.* gleichförmig; gemäß, angemessen; (complaint) nachgiebig, fügsam. **—ation,** *s.* die Bildung, Gestaltung, Gestalt, der Bau; (act of —ing) die Übereinstimmung. **—ist,** *s.* der Angehörige der anglikanischen Staatskirche, Staatskirchler. **—ity,** *s.* die Gleichförmigkeit, Ähnlichkeit; die Übereinstimmung; in —ity with, gemäß (*dat.*); to live in —ity with the world, **gemäß** *or* **nach den Grundsätzen der Welt leben.**

Confound, *v.a.* (mix together) vermischen, vermengen; verwechseln (*one p. or th. with another*); (confuse) verwirren, konfus machen; beschämen (*B.*); (overthrow) vernichten, zu Grunde richten, zerstören; — him! zum Kuckuck mit ihm! — it! hol's der Teufel! **—ed,** *adj.* verwirrt; verflucht, verwünscht. **—er,** *s.* der Vernichter.

Confraternity, *s.* die Brüderschaft.

Confront, *v.a.* gegenüberstellen; (face) entgegentreten *or* die Stirn bieten (einem). **—ation,** *s.* die Gegeneinanderstellung, Gegenüberstellung (der Zeugen).

Confus—e, *v.a.* (mix) vermischen; vermengen (*fig.*); (disorder) verwirren; (confound) bestürzt machen, aus der Fassung bringen. **—ed,** *adj.*, **—edly,** *adv.* verwirrt, wirr, bestürzt. **—ion,** *s.* die Verwirrung, Unordnung; die Verlegenheit; die Vernichtung; (shame) die Beschämung.

Confut—able, *adj.* widerlegbar. **—ation,** *s.* die Widerlegung. **—e,** *v.a.* widerlegen, zum Schweigen bringen. **—er,** *s.* der Widerlegende.

Congé, *s.* der Abschied; der Urlaub; (curtsey, *etc.*) die Höflichkeitsbezeigung beim Weggehen; lower (upper) —, der Anlauf (Ablauf) (*Arch.*).

Congeal, *v.* I. *n.* (ge)frieren; dick werden; erstarren (*fig.*). II. *a.* gefrieren machen; erstarren. **-able,** *adj.* gefrierbar. **—ment,** *s.* das Gefrieren. **—ing, Congelation,** *s.* das Erstarren, Abkühlen, Gefrieren; rapid congelation, das plötzliche Erstarren.

Congen—er, *s.* die (das) gleichartige Person, (Ding). **—ial,** *adj.* gleichartig, ähnlich; (kindred) geistesverwandt; (suitable) zusagend, angemessen. **—iality,** *s.* die Gleichartigkeit; die Geistesverwandtschaft; die Angemessenheit. **—ital,** *adj.* angeboren. **—itally,** *adv.* von Geburt auf.

Conger, *s.* (— eel) der Meeraal.

Congeries, *s.* die Anhäufung, das Gemengsel.

Congest, *v.* I. *n.* sich ansammeln. II. *a.* (mit Blut) überfüllen (*Med.*); (*obs.*) anhäufen; our —ed cities, unsre überfüllten Städte. **—ion,** *s.* die Anhäufung; die (Blut-)Überfüllung (*Med.*); —ion of the brain, der Blutandrang nach dem Kopfe; —ion of the lungs, die Kongestion der Lungen; —ion of population, die Übervölkerung.

Conglob—ate, I. *v.a.* zusammenballen. II. *adj.* geballt, dicht. **—ation,** *s.* das Ballen, die Zusammenballung; der Ball. **—ulate,** *v.n.* eine kleine runde Masse bilden, sich zusammenballen.

Conglomerat—e, I. *adj.* zusammengeballt, zusammengeknäult; —e rocks, das Konglomeratgebirge. II. *s.* das Konglomerat. III. *v.a.* zusammen-ballen, -knäueln. **—ion,** *s.* die Anhäufung; das Konglomerat; die zusammengewürfelte Masse; die Mischung (*fig.*).

Conglutinat—e, *v.a.* zusammenleimen, zusammenfügen. **—ion,** *s.* das Zusammenleimen; (*fig.*) die Vereinigung.

Congratulat—e, *v.a.* beglückwünschen, Glück wünschen, gratulieren; to —e a p. upon an event, einem zu einem Ereignis Glück wünschen. **—or,** *s.* der Beglückwünschende, Gratulant. **—ory,** *adj.* glückwünschend, Glückwunsch-.

Congregat—e, *v.* I. *a.* versammeln, zusammenbringen. II. *n.* sich versammeln; to be —ed, sich sämtlich befinden. **—ion,** *s.* (the assembling) das Sammeln; (assembly) die Versammlung; die Ansammlung; (—ion of a church) die Gemeinde, Kirchenbesucher (*plur.*); die Versammlung des akademischen Senats (*Cambr. Oxf.*); tabernacle of the —ion, die Stiftshütte (*B.*). **—ional,** *adj.* kirchengemeindlich; independent (*Eccl.*). **—ionalism,** *s.* die Selbstregierung der Kirchengemeinde. **—ionalist,** *s.* der Independent.

Congress, *s.* die (politische *or* wissenschaftliche) Tagung; der Kongreß (*Amer.*). **—ional,** *adj.* eine Versammlung *or* einen Kongreß betreffend; —ional debates, Kongreßdebatten.

Congru—ence, —ency, *s.* die Übereinstimmung;

(suitableness) die Gemäßheit. —**ent**, *adj.* gemäß, passend; (agreeing) übereinstimmend. —**ity**, *s.* die Übereinstimmung; die Gemäßheit, Folgerichtigkeit, Schicklichkeit; die Kongruenz. —**ous**, *adj.* (in sich) übereinstimmend (to, with, mit), gemäß, entsprechend (*dat.*), geeignet, passend, schicklich (to, für).

Conic, —**al**, *adj.*, —**ally**, *adv.* kegelförmig, konisch; — frustrum, der Kegelstumpf; — section, der Kegelschnitt. —**s**, (—**-sections**,) *pl.* die Lehre von den Kegelschnitten.

Conifer, *s.* der Zapfenträger, die Konifere. —**æ**, *pl.* die Nadelhölzer. —**ous**, *adj.* zapfentragend.

Conirosters, *pl.* Kegelschnäbler (*Orn.*).

Conjectur—**able**, *adj.*, —**al**, *adj.*, —**ally**, *adv.* mutmaßlich. —**e**, I. *s.* die Mutmaßung, Vermutung, hingeworfene Meinung; (idea) die Idee; die Konjektur, vorgeschlagene Besserung einer verderbten Textstelle; to go upon —es, sich auf Vermutungen stützen. II. *v.a.* mutmaßen, vermuten.

Conjoin, *v.a.* verbinden. —**t**, *adj.* verbunden, gemeinschaftlich. —**tly**, *adv.* im Verein, gemeinschaftlich.

Conjuga—**l**, *adj.*, —**lly**, *adv.* ehelich, Ehe=; —l affection, eheliche Liebe; —l joys, Ehefreuden; —l life, das Eheleben, die Ehe, der Ehestand; —l love, die Gattenliebe. —**te**, I. *adj.* gepaart (*Bot.*); konjugiert (*Math.*); —te axis, konjugierte Achse. II. *v.a.* (ein Zeitwort) abwandeln, konjugieren (*a verb*). III. *v.n.* sich paaren (*Biol.*). —**tion**, *s.* die Abwandlung (der Zeitwörter), Konjugation.

Conjunct, *adj.* verbunden. —**ion**, *s.* (union) die Vereinigung, Verbindung; die Konjunktion (*Astr.*); das Bindewort (*Gram.*). —**iva**, *s.* die Bindehaut des Auges (*Anat.*). —**ive**, *adj.* verbindend; —ive mood, die Vorstellungsform, der Konjunktiv. —**ively**, *adv.* in Verbindung; taken —ively, zusammengenommen. —**ure**, *s.* die Konjunktur; das Zusammentreffen (von Umständen); (crisis) die Krise, Krisis, der Wendepunkt.

Conjur—**ation**, *s.* die (Geister=)Beschwörung; die feierliche Anrufung; die Zauberformel; die Zauberei. —**e**, *v.* I. *a.* beschwören; (implore) feierlich, ernst anflehen; (bind by oath) eidlich verbinden; to —e up, heraufbeschwören. II. *n.* Zauberei treiben; a name to —e with, ein Name von zauberhafter Gewalt; —ing trick, das Zauberkunststück, Taschenspielerstück(chen). —**er**, —**or**, *s.* der Beschwörer; der Zauberer; he is no —er, er ist kein Hexenmeister.

Connat—**e**, *adj.* mitgeboren; angeboren (notions, Begriffe); zusammengewachsen (*Bot.*). —**ural**, *adj.* gleicher Natur; verwandt; angeboren.

Connect, *v.a.* verknüpfen, verbinden; (unite) zusammenfügen; koppeln (*Mach.*). —**ed**, *adj.*, — —**edly**, *adv.* verbunden; zusammenhängend (*as a discourse*); to be —ed with a p., in Verbindung mit einem stehen; to be —ed with a th., bei *or* an einer Sache beteiligt sein. —**ing**, *adj.*; —ing curve, die Verbindungskurve (*Railw.*); —ing passage, der Durchgang. —**ion**, *s.* die Verbindung; (coherence) der Zusammenhang; (person —ed) der, die Verwandte; (relationship) die Verwandtschaft; —ions, einflußreiche Verbindungen, Konnexionen; business —ion(s), Handelsverbindungen; to be in —ion with, in Verbindung stehen mit; in this —ion, in diesem Zusammenhange; to run in —ion, (*of trains*) Anschluß haben (an einen andern Zug). —**ive**, I. *adj.* verbindend. II. *s.* das Verbindungswort. —**or**, *s.* der verbindende Teil; eine Art Klemmschraube (*Elect.*); die Wagenkuppelung (*Railw.*). *Comp.* —**ing-link**, *s.* die Kulisse (*Mach.*); das Bindeglied (*fig.*). —**ing-rod**, *s.* die Lenkstange (*Mach.*); —ing-rod of a switch, die Weichenstange.

Connexion, *see* Connection.

Conniv—**ance**, —**ence**, *s.* das Durch=die=Finger=Sehen, die Konnivenz; das Übersehen. —**e**, *v.n.* konnivieren; durch die Finger sehen, leiden; to —e at a p.'s escape, bei jemandes Entweichen ein Auge zudrücken. —**ent**, *adj.* gegen einander gebogen, konvergierend (*Bot.*); —ent valves, Darmzellen (*Anat.*). —**er**, *s.* einer, der einen Unfug nachsieht, der stillschweigend Teil daran nimmt.

Connoisseur, *s.* der Kenner, Kunstkenner.

Connot—**ate**, *v.a.* (*obs.*) *see* —e. —**ation**, *s.* die Mitbezeichnung, das Merkmal, die Bedeutung. —**e**, *v.a.* mit bezeichnen, in sich schließen.

Connubial, *adj.* ehelich, Ehe=; verheiratet.

Conoid, *s.* der Afterkegel, das Konoid. —**al**, *adj.* afterkegelförmig, konoidisch.

Conquer, *v.* I. *a.* erobern, besiegen, bezwingen, sich (*dat.*) erringen. II. *n.* siegen. —**able**, *adj.* besiegbar, überwindlich. —**ing**, *adj.*, —**ingly**, *adv.* siegend. —**or**, *s.* der Eroberer; der Sieger.

Conquest, *s.* die Eroberung, Besitzergreifung; (victory) der Sieg; (thing conquered) das Besiegte; (prize) die Errungenschaft; the (Norman) —, die normannische Eroberung.

Consanguin—**eous**, *adj.* blutsverwandt. —**ity**, *s.* die Blutsverwandtschaft.

Conscien—**ce**, *s.* (consciousness) das Bewußtsein (*obs.*); das Gewissen; to have the —ce to do a th., die Frechheit besitzen, etwas zu tun (*coll.*); a matter of —ce, eine Gewissenssache; to make it a matter of —ce, sich (*dat.*) ein Gewissen daraus machen; in all —ce, wahrhaftig; that's enough in all —ce, das ist billigerweise genug; upon my —ce, wahrhaftig, fürwahr; out of all —ce, unbillig, über alle Maßen; a good —ce is a soft pillow, ein gutes Gewissen, ein sanftes Ruhekissen (*prov.*). —**celess**, *adj.* gewissenlos. —**tious**, *adj.*, —**tiously**, *adv.* gewissenhaft; (just) mit gutem Gewissen. —**tiousness**, *s.* die Gewissenhaftigkeit. *Comp.* —**ce-clause**, *s.* Gesetzverfügung, welche Kinder von Sektirern vom Religionsunterricht in den Volksschulen befreit. —**ce-money**, *s.* das Gewissensgeld, die freiwillige direkte Nachzahlung an den Staat (besonders im Falle zu niedriger Selbsteinschätzung für direkte Steuern). —**ce-proof**, *adj.* unempfindlich gegen Gewissensbisse. —**ce-smitten**, —**ce-struck**, —**ce-stricken**, *adj.* vom Gewissen gerührt.

Conscionabl—**e**, *adj.*, —**y**, *adv.* gewissenhaft. —**eness**, *s.* die Gewissenhaftigkeit.

Conscious, *adj.*, —**ly**, *adv.* bewußt; — of a th., wissend um eine S., kundig (einer S.), Kenntnis habend (von einer S.); to be — of a th., um eine S. *or* von einer S. wissen; — of my innocence, meiner Unschuld (mir) bewußt; — lovers, die ihrer Liebe sich bewußten Liebenden. —**ness**, *s.* das Bewußtsein; die sichere Kenntnis.

Conscript, I. *adj.* zwangsweise ausgehoben. II. *s.* der Dienstpflichtige, der ausgehobene Rekrut (*Mil.*). —**ion**, *s.* die (Zwangs=)Aushebung.

Consecrat—**e**, I. *v.a.* weihen, einsegnen; (dedicate) widmen; (render holy) heiligen; (pronounce holy) heilig sprechen. II. *adj.*, —**ed**, *adj.* geweiht, heilig. —**ion**, *s.* die Weihung, Einweihung, Weihe; die Heiligsprechung (*at the mass*). —**or**, *s.* der Einsegnende.

Consecuti—**on**, *s.* die Aufeinanderfolge; die Schlußfolge. —**ve**, *adj.* aufeinanderfolgend; —ve narrative, zusammenhängende Erzählung. —**vely**, *adv.* nach einander, fortlaufend. —**veness**, *s.* die Aufeinanderfolge.

Consensus, *s.* die allgemeine Übereinstimmung; — of opinion, die allseitige Zustimmung.

Consent, I. *s.* die Einwilligung, Zustimmung, Genehmigung; die Sympathie (*Med.*); with one —, einstimmig; silence gives —, Stillschweigen gilt für Einwilligung; with the — of, mit Genehmhaltung von. II. *v.n.* (— to) einwilligen, genehmigen, beistimmen; he readily —ed, er gab bereitwillig seine Zustimmung, er willigte ohne weiteres ein; and Saul was —ing unto his death, Saulus aber hatte Wohlgefallen an seinem Tode (*B.*). —**aneous**, *adj.*, —**aneously**, *adv.* übereinstimmend; (consistent with) gemäß, passend (zu). —**ient**, *adj.* einstimmend.

Consequen—ce, *s.* die Folge, das Ergebnis; (effect) die Wirkung (einer Ursache); der Folgesatz, Schluß (*Log.*); (influence) der Einfluß; (importance) die Wichtigkeit; to take the —ces, die Folgen tragen *or* auf sich nehmen; of little —ce, von geringer Bedeutung; that 's of no —ce, das ist von keiner Bedeutung, das macht nichts aus, das tut nichts; in —ce, folglich; in —ce of which, weswegen; a man of —ce, ein angesehener Mann, Mann von Bedeutung; to give o.s. an air of —ce, sich (*dat.*) ein wichtiges Ansehen geben; to set up for a person of —ce, sich wichtig machen. —**t**, I. *adj.* folgend; folgerecht (*Log.*); this is —t on . . ., dies ist die Folge von. II. *s.* die Folge; die Wirkung; die Folgerung, Schlußfolgerung, der Schluß (*Log.*); —t of a ratio, das Hinterglied eines Verhältnisses (*Math.*). —**tial**, *adj.* folgend, erfolgend (as result); folgerichtig (*Log.*); (pretentious) wichtig tuend; (pompous) hochtrabend. —**tially**, *adv.* folgerichtig; auf wichtigtuerische Weise. —**tly**, *adv.* folglich, als Folge, davon.

Conserv—able, *adj.* erhaltbar. —**ancy**, *s.* das Stromgericht; Thames Court of —ancy, der (zur Erhaltung der Fischerei, 2c.) auf der Themse jährlich gehaltene Stromgerichtshof. —**ant**, *adj.* erhaltend. —**ation**, *s.* die Erhaltung, Bewahrung; —ation of energy, die Erhaltung der Kraft (*Phys.*). —**atism**, *s.* der Konservatismus. —**ative**, I. *adj.* erhaltend; konservativ (*Pol.*). II. *s.* der Konservative. —**ator**, *s.* der Erhalter; (official) der Konservator, Aufseher. —**atory**, I. *s.* das Treibhaus, Gewächshaus (*for plants*); die Hochschule für Musik, das Konservatorium. II. *adj.* erhaltend. —**e**, I. *v.a.* erhalten, (auf)bewahren; einmachen (*fruit*). II. *s.* das Eingemachte; die Konserve (*Pharm.*). —**er**, *s.* der Bewahrer, Erhalter.

Consider, *v.* I. *a.* (look at closely) sorgfältig ansehen, betrachten; (reflect on) reiflich überlegen, erwägen, bedenken, in Betracht ziehen; (take into account) in Anschlag bringen, berücksichtigen; (regard) schätzen, halten für, ansehen für; (reward) lohnen, vergüten; — the matter and let me know, erwägt die Sache und laßt mich wissen; I — him a clever person, ich halte ihn für einen klugen Mann; they wish to be —ed wise, sie möchten für weise gelten; — yourself at home, tun Sie, als wären Sie zu Hause; he may — himself lucky, er kann von Glück sagen. II. *n.* nachdenken, erwägen, überlegen. —**able**, *adj.*, —**ably**, *adv.* ansehnlich, bedeutend, wichtig. —**ate**, *adj.*, —**ately**, *adv.* rücksichtsvoll; bedächtig; überlegt; (prudent) vorsichtig (*obs.*). —**ateness**, *s.* die Rücksicht, das rücksichtsvolle Wesen. —**ation**, *s.* (act of —ing) die Betrachtung, Überlegung; (importance) die Beträchtlichkeit, Bedeutung, das Ansehen; (influence) der Einfluß; (—ateness) die Rücksicht; (compensation) die Vergeltung, Entschädigung; (payment) die Vergütung; (motive) der Beweggrund, die Ursache; die Gegenleistung; das Trinkgeld; the matter is under —ation, es wird über die Sache beratschlagt, sie ist noch nicht entschieden; to take into —ation, in Betracht ziehen; in —ation of, in Anbetracht, in Betreff (einer Sache); in —ation of the sum of . . ., für die Summe von . . .; want of —ation, die Rücksichtslosigkeit; der Mangel an Valuta (*C.L.*). —**ing**, I. *adj.;* to put on one's —ing cap, über eine S. mit sich zu Rate gehen. II. *p.* = *prep.;* —ing the weakness of our nature, in Anbetracht der Schwäche unserer Natur; that is very well done —ing, das ist im ganzen recht hübsch gemacht.

Consign, *v.a.* übergeben, überliefern, übertragen; (*entrust*) anvertrauen; übersenden, übermachen, konsignieren (*C.L.*); to — to writing, schriftlich aufsetzen; to — to oblivion, der Vergessenheit überliefern. —**ation**, *s.* die Überlieferung; die Konsignation (*C.L.*). —**ee**, *s.* der Warenempfänger, Konsignatär. —**er**, —**or**, *s.* der Warensender, Übersender. —**ment**, *s.* die Übersendung, Versendung, Zustellung, Konsignation; —ment of specie, die Barsendung; goods in —ment, Konsignationswaren; a fresh —ment of tea, eine neue Teesendung.

Consist, *v.a.* bestehen (of, aus; in, in einer S.); (coexist) mitexistieren; to — with, bestehen mit; by him all things —, und es bestehet alles in ihm (*B.*). —**ence**, —**ency**, *s.* (density) die Festigkeit, Dichtigheit, Konsistenz; (durability) die Dauer, der Bestand; (agreement) die Übereinstimmung, Gemäßheit, Folgerichtigkeit; —ency of paste, Teigkonsistenz. —**ent**, *adj.*, —**ently**, *adv.* fest, dicht; (not fluid) nicht flüssig; (—ent with) übereinstimmend, gemäß; (congruous) folgerecht, konsequent; to make —ent with, in Einklang bringen mit; his conduct is not —ent with prudence, sein Benehmen verträgt sich nicht mit der Klugheit; he is at least —ent, er ist wenigstens konsequent. —**orial**, *adj.* konsistorialisch, zu einem Konsistorium gehörig. —**ory**, *s.* das Konsistorium; die Versammlung der Kardinäle zu Rom.

Consol—able, *adj.* Trost zulassend, tröstbar, zu trösten. —**atory**, *adj.* tröstend, tröstlich, trostreich. —**e**, *v.a.* trösten. —**er**, *s.* der Tröster.

Console, *s.* der Kragstein, die Konsole (*Arch.*). *Comp.* —**-table**, *s.* das Pfeilertischchen.

Consolidat—e, *v.a.* fest machen, verdichten; (unite into one) vereinigen (*fig.*); fundieren (funds, eine Staatsschuld); zwei Pfründen in eine verwandeln (*Law*); zwei Parlamentsbills in eine verwandeln (*Parl.*); —ed annuities, stocks, *etc.*, *see* Consols. —**ion**, *s.* die Verdichtung; die Vereinigung; die Konsolidation (*of funds, etc.*).

Consols, *pl.* die konsolidierten *or* fundierten Staatsschulden, die englischen Staatsschuldscheine, Konsols; 3 per cent —, die konsolidierte dreiprozentige Rente.

Consonan—ce, *s.* die Konsonanz (*Mus.*); (agreement) die Übereinstimmung. —**t**, I. *adj.*, —**tly**, *adv.* konsonierend (*Mus.*); übereinstimmend, gemäß. II. *s.* der Geräuschlaut, Konsonant; back —t, der gutturale *or* velare Konsonant; dental —t, der Zahnlaut; front —t, der palatale Konsonant, Palatallaut; lingual —t, der Zungenlaut; lip —t, der Lippenlaut; stopped —t, der Verschlußlaut, die Muta; a surd —t, ein stimmloser Konsonant; a whispered —t, ein Flüsterkonsonant.

Consort, I. *s.* der Gefährte, Genoß; (spouse) der Gemahl, die Gemahlin; *see* Concert; (— ship) das Geleitschiff; Prince —, der Prinzgemahl. II. *v.n.* sich gesellen (with, zu), Umgang haben (with, mit).

Conspicuous, *adj.*, —**ly**, *adv.* (visible) sichtbar; auffallend; — by, hervorragend durch; — by one's absence, durch seine Abwesenheit glänzend.

Conspir—acy, *s.* die Verschwörung; (concurrence) das Zusammenwirken. —**ator**, *s.* der Verschwörer, Verschworene, Mitverschworene. —**e**, *v.n.* sich (zu einem bösen Zwecke) verbinden; sich verschwören; (work together) zusammentreffen, zusammenwirken; all things —e to make him happy, alles trifft zu seinem Glücke zusammen, alles vereinigt sich, ihn glücklich zu machen.

Constab—le, *s.* der Polizist, Schutzmann; der Konnetabel; Lord High —le of England, Großkonnetabel von England. —**ulary**, *s.* (—ulary force) die Schutzmannschaft, (*pl.*) die Polizisten, Schutzleute.

Constan—cy, *s.* die Standhaftigkeit; (stability) die Beständigkeit, Beharrlichkeit, Festigkeit; (permanency) die Dauer, der Bestand; (indestructibleness) die Unerschütterlichkeit; (unchangeableness) die Unveränderlichkeit; (fidelity) die Treue.

—t, I. *adj.*, **—tly**, *adv.* beständig, unverändert, unveränderlich; fortwährend; beständig, beharrlich (*fig.*); treu, getreu; konstant, fest, nicht flüssig (*Math. Phys.*); —t to one's purpose, seinem Vorsatze (ge)treu; to be —t to a friend, einem Freunde treu sein; a —t friend, ein treuer Freund; —t noise, beständiges, ewiges Geräusch; —t rain, anhaltender Regen; —t force, konstante Kraft; —t current, konstanter Strom (*Elect.*). II. *s.* die konstante Größe (*Math.*, *Mech.*, *Phys.*).

Constellation, *s.* die Konstellation, das Gestirn, Sternbild (*also fig.*).

Consternation, *s.* die Bestürzung.

Constipat—e, *v. a.* verstopfen, konstipieren. **—ion**, *s.* die (Leibes=)Verstopfung, Hartleibigkeit (*Med.*).

Constitu—ency, *s.* die Wählerschaft. **—ent**, I. *adj.* wesentlich, Ur=, Grund=; —ent parts, Bestandteile; —ent bodies, Wahlkörper, Wählerschaften. II. *s.* der Wähler, Wahlmann (*Pol.*); der wesentlichste Teil, Bestandteil; (appointer) der Vollmachtgeber. **—te**, *v.a.* (establish) festsetzen; (set up) errichten; (cause) herbeiführen; (compose) ausmachen; (appoint) ernennen, bestellen, einsetzen; this —utes a precedent, dies giebt einen Präzedenzfall; the —uted authorities, die verfassungsmäßigen Behörden. **—ter**, *s.* der Stifter. **—tion**, *s.* (act of —ting) das Festsetzen, die Anordnung, Errichtung; (nature) die Beschaffenheit; (condition of body) die Leibesbeschaffenheit; (mental —tion) die Gemütsart, das Temperament; (government) die Staatsverfassung; (particular law) die Satzung, Verordnung; by —tion, von Natur; worn-out —tion, zerrüttete Gesundheit; strong —tion, kräftiger Körperbau, gute Natur. **—tional**, I. *adj.*, **—tionally**, *adv.* in der Leibesbeschaffenheit begründet, ursprünglich; natürlich, temperamentsmäßig; verfassungsmäßig, konstitutionell; —tional charter, die Verfassungsurkunde; —tional disease, angeborenes Übel; —tional liberty, verfassungsmäßige Freiheit. II. *s.* der Verdauungsspaziergang (*coll.*). **—tionalist**, *s.* der Konstitutionelle, Anhänger verfassungsmäßiger Regierungsformen. **—tive**, *adj.* gesetzgebend; wesentlich.

Constrain, *v.a.* zwingen, nötigen. **—able**, *adj.* dem Zwange unterworfen, bezwingbar. **—ed**, *adj.*, **—edly**, *adv.* gezwungen. **—t**, *s.* der Zwang, die Nötigung; (confinement) die Haft.

Constrict, *v.a.* zusammenziehen. **—ion**, *s.* die Zusammenziehung, Zusammenpressung. **—or**, *s.* der Schließmuskel (*Anat.*); die Schlinger, Riesenschlange; boa- —or, die Abgottschlange, Königsschlange. **—ores**, *pl.* Riesenschlangen.

Constringent, I. *adj.* zusammenziehend. II. zusammenziehendes Mittel.

Construct, *v.a.* zusammensetzen (*a machine*); errichten, aufbauen (*a building*); konstruieren (*Math.*); bilden, erdenken, aufstellen (*fig.*); to — a fieldwork, eine Schanze aufwerfen. **—ion**, *s.* die Zusammensetzung; das Erbauen, Aufsetzen; (thing —ed) der Bau, das Gebäude; (manner of —ing) die Form, Bauart; (—ion of sentences) die Konstruktion, Wortfügung, der Satzbau; der Aufriß, die Konstruktion (*Geom.*); der Ansatz (*Alg.*); (interpretation) die Auslegung; (meaning) der Sinn, die Deutung; what —ion is to be put upon the conduct of such a man? wie ist das Betragen eines solchen Mannes zu erklären? to put the worst —ion on a th., eine Sache aufs schlimmste auslegen *or* deuten; cost of —ion, die Baukosten; —ion of bridges, der Brückenbau; —ion of roads, der Wegebau; —ion of vessels, Schiffsbau. **—ive**, *adj.* aufbauend, bildend; erfinderisch; Bau=, Konstruktions=; (inferred) gefolgert, hergeleitet. **—ively**, *adj.* durch Zusammensetzung; durch Auslegung, durch Folgerung. **—iveness**, *s.* der Bausinn (*Phren.*); die Verbindungsfähigkeit. **—or**, *s.* der Erbauer; —or of machines, der Maschinenbauer.

Construe, *v.a.* konstruieren (*Gram.*); (translate) übersetzen; (interpret) auslegen, deuten.

Consubstantia—l, *adj.* gleichen Wesens, gleicher Natur. **—te**, *v.a.* in demselben Wesen vereinigen. **—tion**, *s.* die Gegenwart des Leibes und Blutes Christi im heiligen Abendmahl.

Consuetud—e, *s.* die Gewohnheit (*rare*). **—inal**, **—inary**, *adj.* gewohnheitsmäßig, gebräuchlich.

Consul, *s.* der Konsul. **—ar**, *adj.* konsularisch. **—ate, —ship**, *s.* die Konsulwürde; **—ate**, *s.* das Konsulat (office and premises). **—t**, *see* Consult. *Comp.* **—-general**, der Generalkonsul.

Consult, *v.* I. *n.* sich beraten (with a p. about a th., mit einem über eine S.). II. *a.* zu Rate ziehen, um Rat fragen; (consider) Rücksicht nehmen auf (*acc.*), berücksichtigen; to — one's own advantage, seinen eignen Vorteil berücksichtigen; to — an author, in den Werken eines Schriftstellers nachschlagen; —ing physician, der Spezialist (welcher nur konsultiert wird). **—ation**, I. *s.* die Beratung, Konsultation; die beratschlagende Versammlung (*of doctors, lawyers, etc.*); writ of —ation, die Verweisung an den ursprünglichen Gerichtshof. II. *attrib.*; —ation (*or* —ing) room, das Sprechzimmer (eines Arztes). **—ative**, *adj.* beratend.

Consum—able, *adj.* verzehrbar. **—e**, *v.* I. *a.* verzehren, aufzehren; (use) verbrauchen; (waste) durchbringen; (destroy) vernichten. II. *n.* sich verzehren. **—edly**, *adv.* gewaltig, kolossal (*sl.*). **—er**, *s.* der Verzehrer, Verbraucher, Abnehmer, Kunde (*C. L.*); smoke —er, der Rauchverbrennungsapparat. **—ption**, *s.* (use) der Verbrauch; die Auszehrung, Schwindsucht (*Med.*); der Absatz, Konsum, Bedarf (*C. L.*). **—ptive**, *adj.* verzehrend; schwindsüchtig. **—ptiveness**, *s.* die Anlage zur Schwindsucht.

Consummat—e, I. *v.a.* vollziehen, vollenden. II. *adj.*, **—ely**, *adv.* vollendet; —e fool, ausgemachter Narr. **—ion**, *s.* die Vollziehung; die Vollendung; (close) das Ende; —ion of marriage, Vollziehung der ehelichen Verbindung.

Contact, I. *s.* die Berührung; point of —, der Berührungspunkt; to come in — with, in Berührung kommen mit. II. *attrib.*; — action, die Kontaktwirkung (*Phys.*).

Contagio—n, *s.* die Ansteckung; (—us matter) der Ansteckungsstoff; (—us disease) die Seuche, ansteckende Krankheit. **—us**, *adj.*, **—usly**, *adv.* ansteckend; seuchenartig. **—usness**, *s.* die Ansteckungskraft; die Pestartigkeit.

Contain, *v.* I. *a.* enthalten, in sich (*dat.*) halten; to — o.s., sich enthalten, sich mäßigen, sich in Schranken halten. II. *n.* keusch leben, enthaltsam sein (*B.*). **—able**, *adj.* enthaltbar.

Contaminat—e, *v. a.* beflecken, verunreinigen; (corrupt) verderben; (infect) anstecken, vergiften. **—ion**, *s.* die Befleckung, Verunreinigung. **—ive**, *adj.* befleckend.

Contemn, *v.a.* verachten, verschmähen. **—er**, *s.* der Verächter. **—ingly**, *adv.* geringschätzig.

Contemplat—e, *v.* I. *a.* betrachten; (intend) beabsichtigen; a result which I had not —ed, ein Ergebnis, welches nicht in meiner Absicht lag. II. *n.* (über eine S.) nachsinnen. **—ion**, *s.* die Betrachtung, geistige Beschauung; (meditation) das Nachsinnen; to have in —ion, vorhaben. **—ive**, *adj.*, **—ively**, *adv.* beschaulich, nachsinnend, tiefsinnig; nachdenklich; —ive faculty, die Denkkraft.

Contempora—neous, *adj.*, **—neously**, *adv.* gleichzeitig. **—neousness**, *s.* die Gleichzeitigkeit. **—ry**, I. *adj.* gleichzeitig; —ry historians, gleichzeitige Geschichtsschreiber; a —ry record, ein Bericht aus der Zeit der Handlung. II. *s.* der Zeitgenosse; zeitgenössisches Blatt, gegenwärtig erscheinende Zeitung, Zeitschrift.

Contempt, *s.* die Verachtung; (contumely) die

Schmähung; (— of court) die Mißachtung des Gerichtshofes; (non-appearance) das Nicht-Erscheinen vor Gericht, die Kontumaz; criminal —, vorsätzliches Ausbleiben; to hold in —, mit Verachtung ansehen; beneath —, ganz und gar verächtlich, völlig wertlos. **—ible**, *adj.*, **—ibly**, *adv.* verächtlich, verachtungswert. **—ibleness**, *s.* die Verächtlichkeit. **—uous**, *adj.*, **—uously**, *adv.* verachtend, höhnisch; (haughty) hochmütig; —uous air, verächtliche Miene; to speak —uously of s.o., von einem mit Verachtung reden. **—uousness**, *s.* das verachtende Wesen; die Verachtung; der Hohn.

Conten—d, *v.* I. *n.* streiten, kämpfen, ringen; to —d for mastery, um den Vorzug streiten; it is useless—ding with you, es ist nutzlos mit Ihnen zu streiten. II. *a.* bestreiten, behaupten; for the defence it was —ded, von Seiten der Verteidigung wurde geltend gemacht. **—der**, *s.* der Streiter. **—ding**, *pres. part. & adj.* streitend; widerstreitend, entgegenstehend. **—tion**, *s.* der Streit, Kampf; (emulation) der Wetteifer; (debate) der Wortstreit; (argument) die Beweisführung. **—tious**, *adj.*, **—tiously**, *adv.* streitig; streitsüchtig. **—tiousness**, *s.* die Streitsucht.

Content, I. *adj.* zufrieden, *see* —ed. II. *v.a.* befriedigen, zufrieden stellen; (set at rest) beruhigen; I can — myself with little, ich kann mich mit Wenigem begnügen. III. *s.* die Zufriedenheit, Genügsamkeit; (extent) der Umfang. **—ed**, *adj.*, **—edly**, *adv.* zufrieden, genügsam; (willing) willig; —(ed) with one's lot, mit seinem Lose zufrieden; I could be —(ed) to live here, ich könnte hier schon wohnen; you must be —(ed) to go along with us, Sie müssen sich's gefallen lassen mit uns zu gehen; to bear —edly, mit Geduld (er)tragen. **—edness**, *s.* die Zufriedenheit, Genügsamkeit. **—ment**, *s.* die Zufriedenheit. **—s**, *pl.* der Inhalt; der Rauminhalt, Gehalt (*of a vessel*); cubic —s, der Kubikinhalt; solid —s, das Volumen; solid —s of water, feste Bestandteile des Wassers; table of —s, das Inhaltsverzeichnis.

Contermin—al, —ous, *adj.* angrenzend; dieselbe Grenze habend mit.

Contest, I. *s.* der Streit, Kampf. II. *v.a.* bestreiten. III. *v.n.* streiten; to — a borough, sich um das Mandat eines Wahlkreises bewerben, als Parlamentskandidat für einen Wahlkreis auftreten; to — with a p. for a th., mit einem um eine S. wetteifern; —ed etymologies, angefochtene Etymologien; a —ed passage, eine bestrittene *or* vielumstrittene Stelle; —ed election, angefochtene Wahl. **—able**, *adj.* bestreitbar, anfechtbar.

Context, *s.* der Zusammenhang. **—ure**, *s.* das Gewebe; der Bau, das System.

Contigu—ity, *s.* das Aneinanderstoßen, Aneinanderliegen; das Angrenzen, die Grenznachbarschaft (*of countries*); (nearness) die Nähe. **—ous**, *adj.*, **—ously**, *adv.* anstoßend, angrenzend, nahe an. **—ousness**, *s. see* —ity.

Continen—ce, *s.* (abstinence) die Enthaltsamkeit; (moderation) die Mäßigung; (chastity) die geschlechtliche Enthaltsamkeit, die Keuschheit. **—t**, I. *s.* das Festland, der Kontinent. II. *adj.*, **—tly**, *adv.* enthaltsam; mäßig; keusch. **—tal**, *adj.* Kontinental-; —tal system, das Kontinentalsystem (*of Napoleon I.*), die Kontinentalsperre (gegen englische Waren).

Contingen—ce, —cy, *s.* der mögliche Fall, Zufall, die Zufälligkeit. **—cies**, *pl.* Möglichkeiten; —cies of war, Zufälligkeiten im Kriege, das Waffenglück. **—t**, I. *adj.*, **—tly**, *adv.* (accidental) zufällig; (uncertain) möglich, eventuell; an gewisse Bedingungen geknüpft; —t on, abhängig von. II. *s.* der Zufall; der Beitrag; das Kontingent (*of soldiers*).

Continu—al, *adj.*, **—ally**, *adv.* fortwährend, beständig, unablässig, fortdauernd, anhaltend; (uninterrupted) ununterbrochen, fortgesetzt; (unceasing) unaufhörlich, (*coll.*) ewig. **—ance**, *s.* die Fortdauer, Dauer; (perseverance) die Beharrlichkeit, Ausdauer; (stay) der Aufenthalt, das Verweilen; der Aufschub (*Law*); —ance of the species, die Fortpflanzung des Geschlechts, der Art. **—ant**, I. *adj.* verlängert, ausgehalten. II. *s.* der Reibelaut, Dauerlaut. **—ation**, *s.* (extension) die Fortsetzung; (uninterrupted succession) ununterbrochene Fortdauer; (transfer) die Übertragung (*C. L.*); die Prämie, welche für die Verlängerung des Termins eines Kontraktes ausgezahlt wird, die Prolongation (*C.L.*). **—ative**, *adj.* fortdauernd. **—e**, *v.* I. *a.* fortsetzen, weiterführen, fortführen; (retain) ferner erhalten, behalten; verlängern (*a line, etc.*). II. *n* verbleiben, verharren; anhalten, beharren; fortfahren; the town —es to be in a state of great excitement, die Stadt ist (befindet sich) noch immer in einem Zustande großer Erregung; to —e in sin, in der Sünde beharren; to —e (in) a business, (in einem Geschäfte bleiben), ein Geschäft fortsetzen; to be —ed (in our next), Fortsetzung folgt; he —ed his story, er setzte seine Erzählung fort, er fuhr in seiner Erzählung fort; after a short pause he —ed, nach einer kurzen Pause fuhr er fort; please —e! bitte fahren Sie fort! bitte setzen Sie Ihre Geschichte fort! —ed fraction, der Kettenbruch; —ed proportion, stetiges Verhältnis; —ed quantity, stetige Größe. **—er**, *s.* der Fortsetzer; der Fortdauernde. **—ity**, *s.* die Stetigkeit; (cohesion) der Zusammenhang; die ununterbrochene Fortdauer. **—ous**, *adj.*, **—ously**, *adv.* ununterbrochen; zusammenhängend; —ous force, dauernde Kraft; —ous brake, kontinuierliche Bremse (*Railw.*).

Contort, *v.a.* verdrehen; (twist) zusammendrehen, krümmen. **—ion**, *s.* die Krümmung (*also Geol.*); die Verdrehung; —ions of the face, die Verzierung(en) des Gesichts.

Contour, *s.* der Umriß, die Außenlinie, Kontur.

Contra—band, *adj.* verboten, gesetzwidrig; —band goods, verbotene Waren; —band trade, der Schleichhandel, Schmuggel. **—dict**, *v.a.* widersprechen (s.o., einem); das Gegenteil behaupten; he —dicted my report, er widersprach meinem Bericht; (be contrary to) im Widerspruch stehen mit. **—diction**, *s.* das Widersprechen, der Widerspruch, die Gegenrede; (inconsistency) die Unverträglichkeit, die Uneinigkeit mit sich selbst; (denial) die Leugnung; without —diction, ohne Widerrede. **—dictious**, *adj.* zum Widerspruch geneigt. **—dictor**, *s.* der Widersprecher, Widerspruchsgeist. **—dictoriness**, *s.* die Unverträglichkeit; das Widersprechende; der Widerspruchsgeist. **—dictory**, *adj.*, **—dictorily**, *adv.* sich *or* einander widersprechend, einander entgegengesetzt; (inclined to —dict) widersprecherisch, zum Widerspruch geneigt; (inconsistent) zuwiderlaufend, unvereinbar; —dictory reports, einander widersprechende Berichte. **—lto**, *s.* der zweite Alt; die tiefe Altstimme (*Mus.*). **—puntal**, *adj.* den Kontrapunkt betreffend. **—puntist**, *s.* der Kontrapunktist. **—ry**, *etc. see* Contrar—. **—st**, *see* Contrast. **—vallation**, *s.* die Gegenverschanzung. **—vene**, *v.a.* (conflict) im Widerspruch stehen mit, widerstreiten; (oppose) zuwiderhandeln; (violate) übertreten. **—vener**, *s.* der Zuwiderhandelnde, Übertreter. **—vention**, *s.* das Entgegenhandeln, Zuwiderhandeln; die Übertretung. *Comp.* **—-bass**, *s.* der Baß, Kontrabaß; der tiefe Baß. **—-bassist**, *s.* der Baßgeiger, Baßspieler, Kontrabassist. **—-dance**, *s.* der Reigen, der Gegentanz. **—distinction**, *s.* der Gegensatz; in —distinction to, im Gegensatze zu. **—-tenor**, *s.* der zweite Tenor (*Mus.*).

Contract, I. *v.a.* zusammenziehen; (narrow) verengen; (shorten) abkürzen, verkürzen; sich (*dat.*) zuziehen (*disease, etc.*); sich (*dat.*) aneignen (*habits,* *etc.*); schließen (*a marriage, a friendship, etc.*); runzeln (*the brow*); machen (*debts*); einengen, beengen (*the mind, spirit*); to — a word, ein Wort abkürzen; to — a debt, Schulden machen; where did you — this vicious habit? woher hast du diese schlechte Gewohnheit? II. *v.n.* sich zusammenziehen, einschrumpfen; (become less) enger, kürzer werden; (bargain) einen Handel eingehen, einen Vertrag schließen; to — for, für . . . kontrahieren; —ing parties, die Vertragschließenden. III. *s.* der Kontrakt, Vertrag; to have work done by —, eine Arbeit in Akkord geben; to undertake the — for a job, eine Arbeit im Akkord übernehmen; marriage —, Ehekontrakt; by private —, unter der Hand; simple —, Kontrakt ohne Siegel; special —, Kontrakt mittelst eines Instrumentes, unter Siegel. IV. *attrib.*; — work, die Akkordarbeit. **—ed,** *p.p. & adj. see* Contract I.; —ed syllable, zusammengezogene Silbe. **—ible,** *adj.* zusammenziehbar. **—ibility,** *s.* die Zusammenziehbarkeit. **—ile,** *adj.* sich zusammenziehend. **—ility,** *s.* die Fähigkeit sich zusammen zu ziehen (*of muscles*); die Kontraktilität der Muskeln. **—ion,** *s.* die Zusammenziehung (*also* zweier Silben rc. in eine (*Gram.*). **—or,** *s.* der Kontrahent; der Unternehmer, Akkordträger (*Build. etc.*); der Akkordant (*Min.*); der Reeder (*Naut.*); —or for a loan, der Unterhändler bei einer öffentlichen Anleihe; —or for provisions, der Lieferant.

Contrar—ies, *pl. see* —y; Sätze, die sich gegenseitig aufheben (*Log.*). **—iety,** *s.* der Widerspruch; die Widerwärtigkeit; (inconsistency) die Unverträglichkeit. **—ily,** *adv. see* **—y. —iness,** *s.* die entgegengesetzte Beschaffenheit; (opposition) der Widerspruch, Widerstand; (perverseness) die Widerspenstigkeit (*of persons*); die Widerwärtigkeit (*of things, coll.*). **—iwise,** *adv.* im Gegenteil; (conversely) umgekehrt. **—y,** I. *adj.* entgegengesetzt; (adverse) ungünstig, widrig; (perverse) widerwärtig; (*with* to = *prep.*) zuwider, entgegen, gegen, widersprechend, im Gegensatz zu; —y to my wish, gegen meinen Wunsch, meinem Wunsch entgegen; —y to good sense, dem gesunden Menschenverstand zuwider; he that believes it and yet acts —y to it, derjenige, der es glaubt und dennoch dawider *or* ihm zuwider handelt; in the —y case, widrigenfalls, im entgegengesetzten Falle. II. *s.* das Gegenteil, der Gegensatz; two —ies cannot exist together, zwei entgegengesetzte Eigenschaften können nicht neben einander bestehen; he could say nothing to the —y, er konnte nichts dagegen einwenden; on the —y, im Gegenteil.

Contrast, I. *v.a.* (zu einander) in Gegensatz bringen; einander entgegenstellen; (compare) (mit einander) vergleichen. II. *v.n.*; to — with, abstechen gegen, einen Gegensatz bilden zu *or* mit. III. *s.* der Gegensatz, Abstand; (—ing) die Entgegensetzung.

Contretemps, *s.* widriger Zufall.

Contribut—ary, *adj. see* —ory. **—e,** *v.* I. *a.* beitragen, beisteuern; zusammenschießen (towards, zu); he —ed much to my success, er trug viel zu meinem Erfolg bei. II. *n.* beitragen, mitwirken (to, towards, zu). **—ion,** *s.* (subscribing) das Beitragen; (aiding) die Mitwirkung; (subscription) der Beitrag, die Beisteuer, Beihilfe; die Brandschatzung (*Mil.*); to lay under —ion, zu einem Beitrage heranziehen; brandschatzen. **—ive,** *adj.* beitragend. **—or,** *s.* der Beisteuernde; (helper) der Beitragende, Helfer, Mitarbeiter; der Mitarbeiter (to a magazine, newspaper, an einer Zeitschrift, Zeitung), der Einsender, Korrespondent. **—ory,** beitragend *or* beisteuernd zu einer S., förderlich (einer S.).

Contrit—e, *adj.*, **—ely,** *adv.* zerknirscht, reuevoll. **—eness, —ion,** *s.* die Zerknirschung, Reue.

Contriv—able, *adj.* erfindbar. **—ance,** *s.* (invention) die Erfindung; (arrangement) die Vorrichtung; (plan) der Entwurf, Plan; (artifice) der Kniff, Pfiff, Kunstgriff; (—ing faculty) der Scharfsinn, erfinderische Sinn, die Findigkeit; full of —ances, erfinderisch, erfindungsreich, findig; (tricky) voller Kniffe. **—e,** *v.* I. *a.* erfinden, ersinnen, entwerfen; ausdenken, planen; (arrange) veranstalten; to —e means to do a th., Mittel ersinnen, um etwas zu tun; he —ed means for his escape, er ermöglichte es seine Flucht zu bewerkstelligen. II. *n.*; to —e to, (*with infin.*) es verstehen, es ermöglichen, es fertig bringen; es möglich machen; he —ed to escape his pursuers, es gelang ihm, seinen Verfolgern zu entschlüpfen; I will —e to see you this evening, ich will die Sache so einrichten, daß ich Sie diesen Abend sehe; to —e against, Anschläge machen gegen. **—er,** *s.* der Erfinder, Entwerfer; der Veranstalter (*of a party*); an excellent —er, ein erfinderischer Kopf.

Control, I. *s.* (check) der Einhalt, das Hemmnis, der Zwang; die Aufsicht; die Leitung; (authority) die Gewalt, der Befehl; (*obs.*) die Gegenrechnung; *see* —ler; to be under a p.'s —, unter jemandes Befehl stehen; he gets beyond my —, er wächst mir über den Kopf; without —, uneingeschränkt. II. *v.a.* gegenrechnen, durch Gegenrechnung prüfen; (overlook) beaufsichtigen, überwachen, leiten; (restrain) einschränken, beschränken, im Zaume halten; to — the sale, den Vertrieb besorgen; (govern) gebieten (über einen), beherrschen. **—lable,** *adj.* kontrollierbar, lenksam. **—ler,** *s.* der Aufseher, Überwacher; der Leiter, Geschäftsführer; der Rechnungsprüfer.

Controver—sial, *adj.*, **—sially,** *adv.* zum Streit gehörig; streitlustig, polemisch. **—sialist,** *s.* der Polemiker. **—sy,** *s.* der (*gen'lly* schriftlich geführte) Streit; (cause of —sy) die Streitsache, Streitfrage; without —sy, unstreitig. **—t,** *v.a.* bestreiten; (refute) widerlegen. **—tible,** *adj.*, **—tibly,** *adv.* bestreitbar, streitig.

Contum—acious, *adj.*, **—aciously,** *adv.* hartnäckig, trotzig, widerspenstig, unlenksam; ungehorsam (*Law*). **—aciousness,** *see* —acy. **—acy,** *s.* (stubbornness) die Halsstarrigkeit; (obstinacy) die Widerspenstigkeit; der absichtliche Ungehorsam; das vorsätzliche Nichterscheinen vor Gericht, die Kontumaz (*Law*). **—elious,** *adj.*, **—eliously,** *adv.* (contemptuous) schnöde, verächtlich; (insolent) frech; (abusive) schmähend, beschimpfend, beleidigend; schimpflich; —elious language, Schmähreden. **—ely,** *s.* die Beschimpfung, Verhöhnung, der Hohn; (disgrace) die Schmach.

Contus—e, *v.a.* quetschen. **—ion,** *s.* die Quetschung; slight —ion, leichte Quetschung.

Conundrum, *s.* das Scherzrätsel; die kaum lösbare Frage, Vexierfrage.

Convalesce, *v.n.* genesen. **—nce,** *s.* die Genesung. **—nt,** I. *adj.* genesend. II. *s.* der Genesende, in der Genesung Begriffene. III. *attrib.*; —nt home, das Genesungsheim.

Convect—ion, *s.* die Übertragung, Fortpflanzung (*Phys.*). **—ive,** *adj.* auf Fortpflanzung *or* Übertragung beruhend, Fortpflanzungs-.

Conven—e, *v.* I. *a.* zusammenberufen, versammeln. II. *n.* zusammenkommen, sich versammeln. **—er,** *s.* der Einberufer (einer Versammlung); der Vorsitzende (*Scotch*). **—ience,** *s.* (fitness) die Schicklichkeit; (suitableness) die Angemessenheit; (commodiousness) die Bequemlichkeit, Gemächlichkeit, bequeme Einrichtung; at your earliest —ience, baldmöglichst; to do at one's own —ience, etwas nach seiner Bequemlichkeit tun, etwas tun, wenn es einem paßt *or* gelegen ist; please suit your own —ience, bitte tun Sie das ganz nach Ihrem Belieben, halten Sie es damit ganz wie Sie wollen. **—ient,** *adj.*, **—iently,** *adv.* schicklich, passend; (useful) dienlich; bequem; (favourable) günstig, gelegen; this table is —ient for writing on, dieser Tisch ist sehr bequem zum Schreiben; it will not be —ient for me to see him to-day, es paßt mir schlecht, ihn heute zu sehen; —ient for the purpose, dem Zwecke dienlich, zweckdienlich; with all —ient speed, mit möglichster Eile. **—ing**, *s.* die Einberufung. **—t**, *s.* das Kloster. **—ticle**, *s.* (assembly) die Versammlung; das Konventikel (*of Nonconformists*); der Winkelverein. **—tion**, *s.* die Zusammenkunft; (assembly) die Versammlung; (coming together) das Zusammenkommen; (treaty) der Vertrag, Vergleich, Konvent; the national —tion, der National-Konvent; (tradition) das Herkommen, der Brauch, die Gewohnheitsregel. **—tional**, *adj.*, **—tionally**, *adv.* (agreed upon) verabredet; (founded on usage, etc.) üblich, herkömmlich; willkürlich festgesetzt; —tional treatment, die Behandlung nach der Schablone (*Paint.*). **—tionalism**, *s.* das Haften am Hergebrachten; das Schablonenwesen, die hergebrachte Form; die leere Redensart. **—tionality**, *s.* die Schablonenmäßigkeit. **—tual**, *adj.* klösterlich.

Converg—e, *v.n.* sich gegen einander neigen, konvergieren. **—ence, —ency**, *s.* die Annäherung, Neigung (*of two lines*); das Zusammenlaufen in einem Punkt. **—ent, —ing**, *adj.* zusammenlaufend, konvergierend; —ing rays, konvergente Lichtstrahlen; —ing lens, die Sammellinse.

Convers—able, *adj.* gesprächig; (sociable) umgänglich. **—ableness**, *s.* die Gesprächigkeit; die Umgänglichkeit, Leutseligkeit. **—ant**, *adj.* vertraut (mit), bewandert (in einer S.); —ant with, kundig (einer S.), erfahren (in einer S.). **—ation**, *s.* das Gespräch, die Unterredung; (intercourse) der Umgang; (conduct) das Betragen, der Lebenswandel; (intimate knowledge of) die vertraute Bekanntschaft (mit); criminal —ation (*abbr.* Crim. con.), der verbotene Umgang, Ehebruch; —ation picture, das Anschauungsbild für Sprechübungen. **—ational**, *adj.* die Unterhaltung betreffend, Unterhaltungs . . .; gesellig; possessed of great —ational powers, von großer Unterhaltungsgabe. **—ationalist**, *s.* gewandter Gesellschafter, guter Unterhalter. **—azione**, *s.* große Abendgesellschaft (meist) in einem öffentlichen Gebäude.—**e**, I. *v.n.* verkehren (with, mit); to —e with a p., sich mit einem unterhalten, mit einem reden. II. *s.* das Gespräch, die Unterredung; der Umgang; der Gegensatz, Kehrsatz, umgekehrte Satz (*Math., Log.*). **—ely**, *adv.* umgekehrt, auf entgegengesetze Weise. **—ion**, *s.* (change) die Umwandelung; der Umtausch, die Umsetzung (*C. L.*); die Konvertierung (*of a debt*); (reformation) die Bekehrung (*Theol.*); (change in opinion) die Meinungsänderung; (going over) der Übertritt; die Schwenkung (*Mil.*); die Aneignung fremden Besitztums zum eignen Gebrauch (*Law*); —ion of equations, die Umkehrung der Gleichungen; —ion of propositions, die Umkehrung der Sätze; —ion of paper into cash, die Umwandlung eines Papiers in bares Geld *or* in klingende Münze.

Convert, I. *v.a.* (change) umändern, umwandeln; umsetzen (*C. L.*); zum Übertritt veranlassen (*to a party, etc.*); bekehren (*Theol. etc.*); (apply to) zu (einem gewissen Gebrauche) verwenden; to — a proposition, einen Satz umkehren. II. *v.n.* sich umändern. III. *s.* der Bekehrte, Proselyt. **—er**, *s.* der Bekehrer, Proselytenmacher. **—ibility**, *s.* die Umwandelbarkeit, Umkehrbarkeit; die Umsetzbarkeit (einer Banknote, *C. L.*). **—ible**, *adj.* umwandelbar; (exchangeable) umwechselbar; umsetzbar, verkäuflich (*C.L.*); —ible terms, einander deckende Ausdrücke.

Convex, I. *adj.*, **—ly**, *adv.* konvex, rund erhaben; — mirror, der Konvexspiegel. II. *s.* der konvexe Körper. **—ity**, *s.* die Runderhabenheit, gewölbte Form, Ausbauschung; der Bogen, Bug (*Shipb.*). *Comp.* **—o-concave**, *adj.* konvex-konkav.

Convey, *v.a.* (fort)bringen, (fort)schaffen, hintragen, übersenden; mitteilen (*news, etc.*); beibringen (*comfort, etc.*); übertragen (*Law*); to — an idea, einen Begriff durch Worte übertragen, einen Begriff geben; to — one's meaning clearly, sich klar ausdrücken; to — by water, verschiffen; to — compliments, Grüße überbringen *or* bestellen; to — letters, Briefe übermachen. **—ance**, *s.* das Fortfahren, Forttragen, Fortschaffen; (transport) die Beförderung, der Transport; die Spedition (*C. L.*); (delivery) die Überlieferung, Überbringung; (carriage) das Fuhrwerk, Gefährt; (means of —ance) die Fahr- *or* Fuhrgelegenheit, das Fortschaffungsmittel; die Übertragung (*of estates, etc.*); die Leitung (*Elect.*); bill of —ance, die Speditionsrechnung; charges for —ance, Transportkosten; deed of —ance, die Übergabeurkunde; mode of —ance, die Versendungsart; —ance by land, by water, der Land-, der Wasser-transport. **—ancer**, *s.* der öffentliche Notar, welcher Übergabeurkunden abfaßt; —ancing clerk, der Notar, welcher Abtretungsurkunden verfaßt; der Schreiber in einem Geschäft, das Verkäufe von Häusern und Grundbesitz vermittelt.

Convict, I. *v.a.* überweisen, überführen (of a crime, eines Verbrechens); (prove) durch Beweise dartun (*obs.*); to — a p. of an error, einem einen Irrtum nachweisen; to be —ed of murder, des Mordes überführt werden. II. *s.* der überführte Missetäter, Sträfling. III. *attrib.*; — settlement, die Sträflingskolonie; — ship, das Transportschiff für Sträflinge. **—ion**, *s.* (act of —ing) die Überweisung, Überführung; die Schuldigerklärung (*by the jury*); (belief) die Überzeugung; strong —ion, feste Überzeugung.

Convinc—e, *v.a.* überzeugen. **—ible**, *adj.* überzeugbar, zu überzeugen. **—ing**, *adj.*, **—ingly**, *adv.* überzeugend; —ing proof, schlagender Beweis.

Convivial, *adj.* festlich; (social) gesellig; (jovial) lustig; — gathering, die fröhliche Zechgesellschaft, die frohe Tafelrunde. **—ity**, *s.* der Hang zur Schmauserei; die Gastlichkeit, Geselligkeit; die Lustbarkeit (bei Tafel).

Convo—cation, *s.* (calling together) die Zusammenberufung; (assembly) die Versammlung; die Kirchenversammlung (in England); die Versammlung des akademischen Senats (*in Oxford*). **—ke**, *v.a.* zusammenberufen, versammeln.

Convol—ute, *adj.* zusammen-gerollt, -gewickelt (*also Bot.*). **—ution**, *s.* die Zusammenwickelung; die Windung; zusammengerollte Ranke (*Bot.*). **—ve**, *v.a.* zusammen-, auf-rollen. **—vulus**, *s.* die Winde (*Bot.*).

Convoy, I. *v.a.* geleiten. II. *s.* das Geleit (*also Mil.*); die Bedeckung; das Geleitschiff; der Bremsklotz, Bremswagen (*Railw.*); — captured, der Militärtransport mit Bedeckung gefangen.

Convuls—e, *v.a.* Zuckungen verursachen; erschüttern (*fig.*); —ed with laughter, sich vor Lachen ausschüttend. **—ion**, *s.* die Zuckung, der Krampf; —ions of laughter, krampfhaftes Lachen. **—ions**, *pl.* konvulsivische Zufälle (*Med.*). **—ive**, *adj.*, **—ively**, *adv.* krampfhaft, zuckend.

Cony, Coney, *s.* das Kaninchen, der Dummkopf (*obs.*). *Comp.* **—-burrow**, *s.* der Kaninchenbau.

Coo, *v.n.* girren, gurren (*of doves*); to bill and —, sich schnäbeln, zärtlich tun. **—ing**, *s.* das Girren; billing and —ing, die Zärtlichtuerei.

Cook, I. *s.* der Koch; (female —) die Köchin. II. *v.a. & n.* kochen, Speisen für die Tafel zubereiten; to — up, aufwärmen; to — accounts (*fig.*), Rechnungen schminken (*coll.*); —ing range, der Kochherd; —ing stove, der Kochofen; gas —ing stove, der Gasherd. **—ery**, I. *s.* das Kochen; (art of —ery) die Kochkunst. II. *attrib.*; —ery book, das Kochbuch. *Comp.* **—room**, *s.* die Kombüse, Schiffsküche (*Naut.*). **—shop**, *s.* die Garküche.

Cool, I. *adj.*, **—ly**, *adv.* kühl, frisch; (indifferent) gleichgültig, teilnahmlos; (calm) ruhig, bedächtig; (cold) kalt; (impudent) frech. II. *s.* die Kühle, Frische. III. *v.a.* (ab)kühlen, mäßigen (*fig.*); to — the guns, die Kanonen (ab)kühlen; let him — his heels, laß ihn warten (*sl.*). IV. *v.n.* kühl werden; erkalten (*fig.*). **—er**, *s.* der Kühler (*also Brew., etc.*); das Kühlgefäß (*for butter, etc.*). **—ing**, *p. & adj.* kühlend, erfrischend. **—ish**, *adj.* ziemlich kühl. **—ness**, *s.* die Kühle; (want of zeal) der Kaltsinn; die Kälte, Kaltblütigkeit; die Gleichgültigkeit; die Frechheit; (estrangement) die Spannung. *Comp.* **—-cup**, *s.* kühlendes Getränk, der Kühltrank, die Limonade (*coll.*). **—-headed**, *adj.* besonnen, leidenschaftslos.

Coolie, *s.* der chinesische Lastträger, Kuli.

Coomb, Combe, *s.* das enge von hohen Bergen eingeschlossene Tal (*dial.*).

Coop, I. *v.a.* —up, einsperren. II. *s.* die Kufe, der Bottich; der Hühnerkäfig. **—er**, *s.* der Küfer, Böttcher. **—erage**, *s.* das Küferhandwerk; (cost) der Küferlohn.

Co—operate, —opt, —ordinate, *etc. see under* Co—.

Coot, *s.* das Wasserhuhn.

Cop, *s.* der Gipfel, die Kuppe; (crest) der Kamm, die Kuppe, der Büschel.

Copaiba, *s.* der Kopaiv(a)balsam (*Pharm.*).

Copar—cen(ar)y, *s.* gemeinsames Recht auf Erbschaft oder Erbfolge; die Miterbschaft. **—tner**, *s.* der Teilhaber; der Associé (*C.L.*). **—tnership**, *s.* die Genossenschaft; die Teilhaberschaft.

[1]**Cop—e**, I. *s.* (vestment) der Priesterrock, Chorrock; (top) der Gipfel; (dome) die Kuppel; der Gewölbebogen (*of a doorway, etc.*); das Dach (*of a house*); (sky) das Himmelsgewölbe; die Bekrönung, Überdachung (*Build.*); under the —e of heaven, unter der Sonne; *see* —ing. II. *v.a.* decken, abdachen. III. *v.n.* heraussstehen, hervorragen (*Arch.*). **—ing**, I. *s.* die Mauerkappe, Mauerabdeckung; (ridge) der First. II. *adj.;* —ing brick, der Kappenziegel; —ing stone, der Kappenstein; der Schlußstein, Abschluß, die Krönung, Krone (*fig.*). **—ped**, *adj.* zugespitzt.

[2]**Cope**, *v.* I. *n.* wetteifern, sich messen (mit), es mit (einem) aufnehmen, (einem) die Spitze bieten; I cannot — with this disaster, ich kann diesem Unglück nicht standhalten. II. *a.* kämpfen (mit).

[3]**Cope**, *v.a.* (*obs. dial.*) handeln, austauschen, kaufen. **—r**, *s.* der Händler; horse —r, der Pferdehändler, Roßtäuscher.

Copeck, *s.* die Kopeke (*a little over a farthing*).

Copi—ed, *p.p. of* Copy. **—er**, *s. see* Copyist; der Plagiator, Buchausschreiber. **—es**, *pl. of* Copy.

Copious, *adj.*, **—ly**, *adv.* reich, reichlich; (overflowing) überflüssig; (not concise) weitläufig; — tears, reichliche Tränen; — matter, inhaltschwerer Stoff (*Poet.*). **—ness**, *s.* die Fülle; der Überfluß; die Weitläufigkeit.

Copper, I. *s.* das Kupfer (*Min.*); die Kupfermünze (*Mint. & coll.*); die Kupferbronze; (boiler) der (kupferne) Kessel; (pan) die Pfanne; der Braukessel (*Brew.*); die Siedepfanne (*Sug. Ref.*). **—ing**, *s.* das Verkupfern. **—ish, —y**, *adj.* kupferig; kupferhaltig. **—s**, *pl.* Kupferkessel (*on board ship*); Kupfermünzen, Pfennige; he gave the boy a few —s, er gab dem Jungen einige Kupfermünzen *or* ein paar Pfennige; art of engraving on —, die Kupferstecherkunst; electrotype —, galvanisches Kupfer. II. *adj.* kupfern; — ashes, die Kupferasche, der Kupferhammerschlag; — bloom, die Kupferblüte; — kettle, der kupferne Kessel; der Talgkessel (*of chandlers*); — money, das Kupfergeld; — ore, das Kupfererz; — sheathing, der Kupferbeschlag (*Shipb.*); — sulphate, das Kupfersulphat, blaues Vitriol; — wire, der Kupferdraht. III. *v.a.* mit Kupfer beschlagen, verkupfern. **—y**, *adj.* kupferig, Kupfer-; kupferhaltig; kupferartig; kupferähnlich. *Comp.* **—-nose**, *s.* die rote Nase. **—plate**, I. *s.* die Kupferplatte, der Kupferstich (*Engr.*); —plate for roofing, das Dachkupfer; to write like —plate, schreiben wie gestochen. II. *attrib.;* —plate print, der Kupferdruck; —plate printing, die Kupferdruckerei (*Engr.*), die Plattendruckerei (*Calico-print.*); —plate printing machine, die Plattendruckmaschine. **—-pyrites**, *pl.* der Kupferkies. **—smith**, *s.* der Kupferschmied. **—-worm**, *s.* der Bohrwurm. **—-works**, *pl.* das Kupferwerk, die Kupferhütte, der Kupferhammer.

Coppice, Copse, *s.* das Schlagholz; (— wood) der Niederwald, das Unterholz, Dickicht.

Copula, *s.* die Kopula (*Gram.*). **—te**, *v.* I. *n.* sich begatten. II. *a.* verbinden, vereinigen. **—tion**, *s.* das Paaren, die Paarung, Begattung. **—tive**, *adj.* verbindend; —tive conjunction, das kopulative *or* erweiternde Bindewort (*Gram.*).

Copy, I. *s.* (duplicate) die Abschrift, Kopie; (machine —) der Abklatsch; (model) die Vorschrift, das Muster; das Nachbild, der Nachriß, Nachstich (*Paint. Sculpt.*); das Exemplar, der Abdruck (*of a book*); das druckfertige Manuskript (*Typ.*); rough —, die Kladde, das Unreine; fair —, die Reinschrift; — in use, das Handexemplar. II. *v.a.* abschreiben, kopieren; (imitate) nachbilden, nachahmen (*also fig.*); to — a p., einem nachahmen; to — fair, (make a fair — of) ins Reine schreiben. III. *v.n.* kopieren, nachahmen; to — from the life, nach der Natur, nach dem Leben zeichnen. **—ing**, *adj.;* —ing clerk, der Kopist; —ing telegraph, der Kopiertelegraph. **—ist**, *s.* der Abschreiber; der Kopist; der Nachdrucker. *Comp.* **—-book**, *s.* das Schreibheft; (—-book with copies) das Vorschriftenbuch, Schönschreibheft; das Briefkopierbuch (*C. L.*). **—hold**, *s.* (tenure) das Zinslehen; (estate) das Lehngut. **—holder**, *s.* der Erbpächter, Besitzer eines Lehnguts *or* Zinslehens. **—ing-ink**, *s.* die Kopiertinte. **—ing-machine, —ing-press**, *s.* die Kopiermaschine, Kopierpresse. **—ing-paper**, *s.* (dünnes) Kopierpapier. **—right**, *s.* das Verlagsrecht; law of —right, das Gesetz über literarisches Eigentumsrecht; the book is —right, Nachdruck ist verboten; alle Rechte vorbehalten; —right edition, verlagsrechtliche Ausgabe.

Coquet, *v.n.* kokettieren. **—ry**, *s.* die Gefallsucht, Koketterie. **—te**, *s.* die Kokette, gefallsüchtige Schöne, gefallsüchtiges Mädchen. **—tish**, *adj.*, **—tishly**, *adv.* gefallsüchtig, kokett.

Coracle, *s.* das mit Leder *or* Wachstuch überzogene Korbboot.

Corah, *s.* die ungefärbte Seide.

Coral, I. *s.* die Koralle. II. *adj.* korallen; — beads, Korallenkügelchen; das Korallenhalsband; — diver, der Korallenfischer; — polyp, das Korallentierchen. **—lin**, *s.* das Korallin (*Chem.*). **—line**, I. *adj.* korallenähnlich; Korallen enthaltend. II. *s.* das Korallenmoos. **—loid**, I. *adj.* korallenartig. II. *s.* die Korallenkruste. *Comp.* **—-island**, *s.* die Koralleninsel. **—-reef**, *s.* das Korallenriff.

Corbeil, *s.* kleiner Schanzkorb (*Mil.*); der Blumenkorb, Fruchtkorb (*as an ornament on the Corinthian capital*).

Corbel, *s.* der Kragstein, die Konsole, der Balkenkopf; *see* Corbeil. *Comp.* **—-steps**, *pl.* die Giebelstufen, Katzentreppe (*hum.*). **—-table**, *s.* auf Kragsteinen ruhender Mauervorsprung, der Bogenfries.

Corbie, *s.* der Rabe (*Scotch*).

Cord, I. *s.* der Strick, das Seil; (packing —) die Packschnur; die Meßschnur (*Surv.*); — of a drum, das Trommelseil; — of wood, eine Klafter Holz. II. *v.a.* mit Stricken binden, befestigen; to — wood, Holz zu Klaftern schlagen. **—age**, *s.* das Tauwerk. **—elier**, *s.* (französischer) Franziskanermönch. **—on**, *s.* die Truppenkette, Wehrlinie, der Kordon (*Mil.*); der Mauerkranz (*Arch.*); das Band, Ordenszeichen. **—s**, *pl.* die Fesseln; *see* Corduroy. **—uroy**, *s.* dickes, baumwollenes, geripptes Zeug; —uroys, Beinkleider aus Kord (für Arbeiter).

Cord—ate, *adj.* herzförmig. **—ial**, I. *adj.*, **—ly**, *adv.* herzlich, von Herzen; (sincere) aufrichtig. II. *s.* das herzstärkende Mittel, der Labetrank; das Labsal (*fig.*). **—iality**, *s.* die Herzlichkeit, Traulichkeit, Zutraulichkeit, Wärme.

Cordwain, (Cordovan,) *s.* der Korduan, das Korduanleder. **—er**, *s.* der Schuhmacher; —ers' company, die Londoner Schuhmacherinnung.

Core, *s.* das Innerste einer Sache, der Kern; das Kerngehäuse, der Griebs (*in fruit*); der Eiter eines Geschwürs; rotten at the —, im Herzen faul; the heart's —, der Herzensgrund; to the —, bis zum Grunde, bis auf den Grund. **—r**, *s.*; apple —r and slicer, ein Instrument zum Entkernen und Zerschneiden von Äpfeln.

Coriaceous, *adj.* aus Leder, ledern, lederartig.

Cork, I. *s.* der Kork, das Korkholz (*Bot.*); (stopper) der Stöpsel, der Kork; das Pantoffelholz (*Tan.*). II. *attrib.*; — bungs, große Korkspunden; — leg, das künstliche Bein; — sole, die Korksohle; — tumbler, der Stehauf, das Stehmännchen. III. *v.a.* (zu)korken; (blacken) mit angebranntem Kork schwärzen. **—age**, *s.* das Pfropfengeld (in Gasthäusern). **—ed**, *adj.*; the wine is —ed, der Wein schmeckt nach dem Korke. **—s**, *pl.* Korkflossen. **—y**, *adj.* korkig; aus Kork; korkartig; korkähnlich. *Comp.* **—ing-pins**, *pl.* große Stecknadeln. **—-jacket**, *s.* die Korkjacke. **—screw**, I. *s.* der Korkzieher, Pfropfenzieher. II. *attrib.*; —screw curls, Korkzieherlocken, Ringellocken; —screw staircase, die Wendeltreppe (*Build.*). II. *v.a.* wie einen Korkzieher sich winden lassen; allmählich herausziehen (*coll.*).

Cormorant, *s.* die Scharbe, der Wasserrabe (*Orn.*); der Vielfraß (*fig. obs.*).

Corn, I. *s.* das Getreide; (pickle, seed) das Korn; Indian —, der türkische Weizen; to give a horse a feed of —, einem Pferde Hafer zu fressen geben. II. *attrib.*; — campion, die Kornrade (*Bot.*). III. *v.a.* einsalzen, pökeln; körnen, granulieren; —ed beef, das Pökelfleisch. *Comp.* **—-bag**, *s.* der Futtersack (*Mil.*). **—-bin**, *s.* die Kornlade. **—-chandler**, *s.* der Getreidehändler. **—-cockle**, *see* — campion. **—-exchange**, *s.* die Getreidebörse, Produktenbörse. **—-factor**, *s.* der Korn-(Groß)Händler; der Kornmakler. **—field**, *s.* das Kornfeld. **—loft**, *s.* der Kornboden. **—-flour**, *s.* das Kornmehl. **—flower**, *s.* die Kornblume. **—-harvester**, *s.* die Kornschneidemaschine. **—-land**, *s.* das Getreideland. **—-laws**, *pl.* die Getreidegesetze, Getreideschutzzollgesetze; repeal of the —-laws, Aufhebung des Getreideschutzzolles. **—-merchant**, *s.* der Getreidehändler. **—-poppy**, *s.* die Klatschrose. **—-trade**, *s.* der Kornhandel, Getreidehandel.

[2]**Corn**, *s.* das Hühnerauge. **—ea**, *s.* die Hornhaut des Auges. **—el**, *s.* (—el cherry) die Kornelkirsche. **—elian**, *see* Cornelian. **—eous**, *adj.* hornig. **—er**, *see* Corner. **—et**, *see* Cornet. **—iculate**, *adj.* gehörnt, zackig, hornförmig. **—y**, *adj.* hornig. *Comp.* **—-plaster**, *s.* das Leichdornpflaster, Hühneraugenpflaster.

Cornelian, *s.* der Karneol (*Min.*).

Corner, I. *s.* der Winkel, die Ecke; to do in a hole and — way, im Verborgenen, heimlich tun (*coll.*); to turn the —, um die Ecke biegen; to be in a —, in der Klemme sitzen, in Verlegenheit sein (*fig.*); to drive a p. into a —, einen in die Enge treiben *or* in Verlegenheit setzen. II. *attrib.*; — bracket, — shelf, das Eckbrett; — cupboard, der Eckschrank; — house, das Eckhaus; — room, das Eckzimmer. III. *v.a.* in eine Ecke treiben; in die Enge treiben (*fig.*). **—ed**, *adj.* eckig; three-—ed, dreieckig. *Comp.* **—-stone**, *s.* der Eckstein. **—-wise**, *adv.* eckig; diagonal.

Cornet, I. *s.* die Zinke, das (Zinken)horn, Kornett (*Mus.*); der Kornett (*Mil.*); (paper —) die Düte; — à piston(s), das Klapp(en)horn. II. *attrib.*; — player, der Kornettbläser. **—cy**, *s.* die Kornettsstelle (*Mil.*).

Cornice, *s.* der Karnies, das (Kranz-)Gesims (*Arch.*); der Überhang (*of snow*).

Cornucopia, *s.* das Füllhorn.

Corolla, *s.* die Blumenkrone (*Bot.*). **—ry**, *s.* der Folgesatz (*Log. Math.*).

Coron—a, *s.* die Krone; die Kranzleiste (*Arch.*); die Krone (*of the teeth; also Bot.*); der Kirchenkronleuchter; der Hof um den Mond *or* um die Sonne. **—al**, I. *adj.* zum Wirbel des Kopfes gehörig; —al suture, die Kranznaht, Kronnaht. II. *s.* die Krone, der Kranz; die erste Schädelnaht. **—ary**, *adj.* Kronen-, Kranz- (*Anat.*); —ary arteries, Kranzarterien; —ary plants, Koronarien. **—ate**, *adj.* mit einem Kranze versehen. **—ation**, *s.* die Krönung; (festival) die Krönungsfeier; —ation oath, der Krönungseid. **—er**, *s.* der Leichenbeschauer; —oner's inquest, die Totenschau; —oner's jury, das Totenschau-Schwurgericht. **—et**, *s.* die kleine Krone (*also Her.*); —et of a count, Grafenkrone; —et of a horse, die Krone des Hufes. **—eted**, *adj.* mit einer Krone.

Coronach, *s.* die Totenklage, der Klagegesang (*Scotch*).

[1]**Corporal**, *s.* der Unteroffizier, Korporal (*Mil.*).

[2]**Corp—oral**, I. *adj.*, **—orally**, *adv.* körperlich, leiblich; *see* —oreal; —oral punishment, körperliche Strafe, Körperstrafe. II. *s.* das Korporale (*Eccl.*). **—orality**, *s.* die Körperlichkeit. **—orate**, *adj.*, **—orately**, *adv.* in eine Körperschaft verbunden; —orate body, *see* —oration; —orate effort, vereinte Bemühung; —orate towns, inkorporierte Städte. **—orateness**, *s.* die Körperschaft, Gemeinschaft, das Vereintsein. **—oration**, *s.* die Körperschaft; die Gemeindebehörde, Stadtverordnung; (trade-guild) die Gilde, Zunft, Innung; (paunch) der dicke Bauch; mayor and —oration, Bürgomeister und Rat. **—oreal**, *adj.*, **—oreally**, *adv.* körperlich; materiell; to be —oreally present, persönlich zugegen sein. **—oreity**, *s.* die Körperlichkeit; die Materialität. **—osant**, *s.* das St. Elmsfeuer (*Naut.*). **—s**, *s.* (*also pl.*) das Korps (*Mil.*); —s de garde, die Scharwache. **—so**, *s.* die Leiche, der Leichnam. **—ulence, —ulency**, *s.* die Dickleibigkeit, Fettleibigkeit. **—ulent**, *adj.* dickleibig, wohlbeleibt, fleischig. **—us**, *s.*; —us Christi Day, der Fronleichnamstag. **—uscle**, *s.* das Körperchen; blood —uscle, das Blutkügelchen. **—uscular**, *adj.* Körperchen betreffend; —uscular philosophy, die Urstofflehre, die Atomistik.

Corr—ect, etc., *see* Correct. **—elate**, I. *s.* das Korrelat. II. *v.n.* sich auf einander beziehen. III. *v.a.* etwas in Wechselbeziehung bringen, auf einander beziehen. **—elation**, *s.* die Wechselbeziehung. **—elative**, *adj.*, **—elatively**, *adv.* in Wechsel-beziehung, -wirkung stehend. **—espond**, *v.n.* (agree, answer) übereinstimmen, entsprechen, gemäß sein; (write) in Briefwechsel stehen; it does not —espond to my expectations, es entspricht meinen Erwartungen nicht; —esponding to, entsprechend, gemäß. **—espondence**, *s.* die Übereinstimmung, Gemäßheit, das Entsprechen; der Briefwechsel; die Verbindung (*C. L.*); to keep up a —espondence, einen Briefwechsel unterhalten; to be in —espondence with a p., mit einem Briefe wechseln *or* in Briefwechsel stehen. **—espondent**, I. *adj.* übereinstimmend, entsprechend, passend. II. *s.* der Korrespondent, Geschäftsfreund (*C. L.*); foreign —espondent, der Kommis, welcher die Korrespondenz mit dem Auslande besorgt; our —espondent abroad, unser auswärtiger Geschäftsfreund; our special —espondent, unser eigner Berichterstatter (*Newsp.*). **—espondently**, *adv.* demgemäß, in Übereinstimmung. **—igible**, *adj.* verbesserlich; strafbar; lenksam. **—oborate**, *v.a.*

stärken; bekräftigen, bestätigen, erhärten (*fig.*). **—oboration**, *s.* die Bekräftigung, Bestätigung. **—oborative**, *adj.* stärkend, bekräftigend. **—ode**, *v.a.* zerfressen, wegätzen, beizen. **—odent**, I. *adj.* zerfressend, ätzend. II. *s.* das Ätzmittel. **—odibility**, *s.* die Zerfreßbarkeit. **—osion**, *s.* das allmähliche Zerfressen, Einfressen, die Ätzung. **—osive**, I. *adj.* fressend, ätzend, zernagend; nagend (*fig.*); —osive liquor, ätzende Flüssigkeit; —osive ulcer, krebsartiges Geschwür; —osive cares, nagende Sorgen. II. *s.* das Ätzmittel. **—osiveness**, *s.* das Ätzende, die Ätzkraft. **—ugate**, I. *v.a.* runzeln; —ugated iron, geriestes *or* gewelltes Eisenblech, Eisenwellblech; —ugated roofing, das Wellblech für Dächer. II. *adj.* gerunzelt. **—ugation**, *s.* das Runzeln. **—upt**, I. *v.a.* verderben (*also fig.*); (bribe) bestechen, erkaufen; (poison) vergiften; fälschen (*writings, etc.*); (mislead) verführen; —upt practices at parliamentary elections, unlautere Beeinflussungen bei Parlamentswahlen. II. *v.n.* faulen, verderben. III. *adj.*, **—uptly**, *adv.* (putrid) faul, verdorben; (depraved) verderbt, unmoralisch, schlecht, lasterhaft; (venal) bestochen, bestechlich; (incorrect) verfälscht, unecht; —upt tree, fauler Baum (*B.*); the text is —upt, der Text ist verderbt, entstellt. **—upter**, *s.* der Verderber; der Verführer; der Bestecher. **—uptibility**, *s.* die Verderblichkeit, Verweslichkeit; die Bestechlichkeit. **—uptible**, *adj.*, **—uptibly**, *adv.* verderblich; verweslich; (perishable) vergänglich; bestechlich, käuflich. **—uption**, *s.* die Verwesung, Fäulnis; die Verderbtheit, Verderbnis (*of morals*); die Verdorbenheit; (deterioration) die Verschlechterung, die Entartung (*of a language, etc.*); die Verfälschung, Entstellung (*of a text, etc.*); die Verführung; die Bestechung; (ruin) die Zerstörung. **—uptive**, *adj.* verderbend, ansteckend. **—uptness**, *s.* die Verdorbenheit; die Bestechlichkeit; die Verderbtheit.

Correct, I. *adj.*, **—ly**, *adv.* richtig, fehlerfrei; (according to rule) regelrecht, kunstgemäß, sinngemäß, tadellos; in Ordnung, gemäß (*C. L.*); the accounts were found —, die Rechnungen fand man in Ordnung, die Rechnungen stimmten; — translation, richtige Übersetzung, genaue Übertragung; if found —, nach Rechtbefinden; a — ear, ein richtiges Gehör (*Mus.*); — manners, gute Sitten, tadellose Aufführung. II. *v.a.* (set right) berichtigen, verbessern; (reprove) tadeln, zurechtweisen; (punish) strafen; mäßigen, mildern (*acidity of the stomach, etc.*); abstellen (*abuses*); (— for the press) durchkorrigieren, Korrekturen lesen; I stand —ed, ich gestehe meinen Fehler ein. **—ion**, *n.* die Berichtigung, Verbesserung; die Druckberichtigung (*Print.*); der Tadel, Verweis; die Bestrafung, Züchtigung; die Milderung, Mäßigung (*Med.*); —ion (of exercises), Durchsicht (der Schulhefte); —ion of proofs, das Korrektur(en)lesen; house of —ion, das Zuchthaus; under —ion, mit Verlaub; I speak under —ion, ich sage es, ohne die Richtigkeit meiner Worte verbürgen zu wollen, dies ist meine unmaßgebliche Meinung; —ion for the curvature of the earth, die Erdkrümmungskorrektion (*Surv.*); marks of —ion, Korrekturzeichen. **—ional**, *adj.* Besserungs-. **—ive**, I. *adj.* verbessernd; durch Beimischung mildernd (*Med.*). II. *s.* das Milderungsmittel. **—ness**, *s.* die Fehlerfreiheit, Sicherheit, Richtigkeit; (accuracy) die Genauigkeit; (decorum) die Anständigkeit. **—or**, *s.* der Berichtigende; der Korrektor (*Print.*); das Milderungsmittel (*Med.*); das Verbesserungsmittel.

Corridor, I. *s.* der Korridor, Gang; der bedeckte Weg (*Fort.*). II. *attrib.*; — train, der Durchgangszug, D-Zug.

Corsair, *s.* der Seeräuber; das Raubschiff.

Cors—e, *see* Corpse. **—(e)let**, *s.* das Bruststück; der leichte *or* halbe Küraß; das Brustlätzchen; das Brustschildchen (*Ent.*). **—et**, *s.* das Schnürleibchen, Korsett.

Cortège, *s.* das Gefolge.

Cortes, *s.* die Kortes (*Spanish*).

Cortica—l, *adj.* rindig; Rinde tragend (*Bot.*); äußerlich (*fig.*). **—te(d)**, *adj.* rindenartig.

Coruscat—e, *v.n.* blitzen, funkeln, glänzen. **—ion**, *s.* das Schimmern, Funkeln, Blitzen; (electric flash) das Wetterleuchten; das plötzliche Aufflammen (*of wit, etc.*).

Corvette, *s.* die Korvette; armour-plated —, die Panzerkorvette.

Corvine, *adj.* rabenartig, krähenartig.

Corymb, *s.* die Doldentraube, der Blumenbüschel. **—iferous**, *adj.* Doldentrauben tragend.

Coryphæus, *s.* der Koryphäe, Chorführer; der Vornehmste, Hervorragendste (*fig.*); der Leiter.

Cos—iness, *s.* die Behaglichkeit, Traulichkeit. **—y**, I. *adj.* behaglich, traulich, gemütlich. II. *s.* der Kaffee- *or* Tee-wärmer.

Cosecant, *see* under Co—.

Cosher, *v.* I. *a.* mit Leckerbissen pflegen; liebkosen, verziehen, verhätscheln. II. *n.* sich umsonst bewirten lassen (*Irish*). **—er**, *s.* der Umherschmauser. **—ing**, *s.* die Sitte der irischen Lehnsherren, bei ihren Vasallen und Pächtern zu verweilen und sich von ihnen umsonst unterhalten zu lassen.

Cosine, *see* under Co—.

Cosmetic, I. *adj.* verschönernd. II. *s.* das Schönheitsmittel.

Cosm—ic(al), *adj.* kosmisch. **—o**, *see* Cosmo—.

Cosmo—gony, *s* die Weltentstehungslehre, Kosmogonie. **—grapher**, *s.* der Weltbeschreiber. **—graphic**, *adj.* kosmographisch. **—graphy**, *s.* die Weltbeschreibung. **—logical**, *adj.* kosmologisch. **—logy**, *s.* die Weltkunde, Kosmologie. **—politan** *or* **—polite**, I. *adj.* weltbürgerlich. II. *s.* der Weltbürger. **—politanism**, *s.* die Weltbürgerschaft. **—politism**, *s.* das Weltbürgertum. **—rama**, *s.* das Kosmorama. **—ramic**, *adj.* Kosmorama-. **—s**, *s.* der Kosmos, die Weltordnung, das Weltall.

Cossack, *s.* der Kosak.

Cosset, I. *s.* das ohne Mutter aufgezogene Lamm; der Liebling (*fig.*). II. *v.a.* verhätscheln.

Cost, I. *s.* die Kosten; der Preis; (loss) der Schaden, Nachteil; at prime *or* first —, zum Selbstkostenpreis, Einkaufspreis (*C. L.*); free of —, kostenfrei; to my —, zu meinem Schaden; that I know to my —, das weiß ich aus teuer erkaufter Erfahrung; it will not pay the —, es macht sich nicht bezahlt, es lohnt die Kosten nicht. II. *attrib.*; — price, der Selbstkostenpreis. III. *v.a. & n.* (*also pret. & p.p.*) kosten; it will — him much time and labour, es wird ihn viel Zeit und Mühe kosten. **—lier**, *comp. of* —ly. **—liest**, *superl. of* —ly. **—liness**, *s.* die Kostbarkeit, Kostspieligkeit. **—ly**, *adj.* kostspielig, teuer; (gorgeous) kostbar, prächtig, köstlich; travelling was —ly at that time, das Reisen war damals teuer. **—s**, *pl.* die Gerichtskosten; with —s, mit (Einschluß der) Prozeßkosten.

Costa—l, *adj.* zu den Rippen gehörig. **—te**, *adj.* gerippt (*Bot.*).

Costermonger, *s.* der umherziehende Obsthändler, der Höker.

Costive, *adj.*, **—ly**, *adv.* verstopft, hartleibig, trocken, steif (*fig.*). **—ness**, die Hartleibigkeit.

Costum—e, *s.* das Kostüm; die Tracht; der Damenanzug aus einem Stoff; tailor-made —e, vom Herrenschneider gemachtes Damenkleid. **—ier**, *s.* der Kostümschneider.

Cot, *s.* das kleine Bett; die Hängematte mit Rahmen (*Naut.*); *see* —tage; sheep—, der Schafstall. **—e**, *s.* die Schafhürde. **—tage**, I. *s.* das Häuschen; das Landhäuschen. II. *attrib.*; —tage oven, tragbarer Ofen; —tage (piano), das Pianino. **—tager**, *s.* der Häusler, Kossäte, Hüttenbewohner. **—ter**, **—tier**, *s. see* —tager

Coterie, *s.* die Koterie; die intriguierende Partei

Cothurnus, *s.* der Kothurn.
Cotillon, *s.* der Gabentanz, Kotillon.
Cotquean, *s.* (*obs.*) das Mannweib; der Topfgucker, weibische Mann.
Cotter, *s.* der Pflock, Vorsteckepflock, Schließbolzen.
Cotton, I. *s.* die Baumwolle; (— yarn, — thread) der Baumwollfaden; (calico) der Kattun; — in the seed, ungereinigte Baumwolle; treble-milled —, der Mol(le)ton; explosive —, Schießbaumwolle. II. *attrib.*; — bale, der Baumwollenballen; — reel, die Fadenrolle; — spinner, der Baumwollspinner; der Besitzer einer Baumwollspinnerei. III. *adj.* baumwollen; — binding, das Baumwollenband. IV. *v.* I. *n.*; to — to a p., sich eng an einen anschließen (*coll.*); to — to a th., sich zu einer S. bequemen (*coll.*). II. *a.* in Baumwolle einpacken (*also fig.*). **—y**, *adj.* flaumig, wollig. *Comp.* **—-gin**, *s.* die Egreniermaschine. **—-grower**, *s.* der Baumwollenpflanzer. **—-mill**, *s.* die Baumwoll-Spinnerei. **—-picker**, *s.* die Maschine zum Entnehmen der Baumwolle aus den Samenhülsen; die Maschine zum Auflockern der Baumwolle. **—-plant**, **—-shrub**, *s.* die Baumwollstaude. **—-waste**, *s.* der Baumwollenabfall. **—-wool**, *s.* die (Roh-)Baumwolle; die Watte.
Cotyledon, *s.* der Samenlappen (*Bot.*). **—ous**, *adj.* mit Samenlappen versehen.
Couch, I. *s.* das Ruhelager, Ruhebett, der Ruhesitz, das Halbsofa; (bed) das Bett, Lager; (lair) das Lager; (layer) die Schicht, Lage. II. *v.a.* (nieder)legen; (deposit, lay) einlegen; kautschen (*paper*); (hide away) verbergen; to — a cataract, den Star stechen; to — malt, Malz aufschütten; to — the lance, die Lanze einlegen; to — in writing, schriftlich aufsetzen; to — in careful terms, in sorgfältigen Ausdrücken abfassen. III. *v.n.* sich legen, sich lagern, sich niederlegen; versteckt liegen; (crouch) kauern; (bow down) sich bücken. **—ed**, *adj.* im Lager (*Sport.*). **—ing**, *s.* das Starstechen (*Surg.*). *Comp.* **—-grass**, *s.* das Queckengras. **—ing-needle**, *s.* die Starnadel.
Cougar, *s.* der Kuguar, Silberlöwe, das Puma.
Cough, I. *s.* der Husten; churchyard —, der trockene, schwindsüchtige Husten (*coll.*). II. *v.n.* husten. III. *v.a.*; — up, aushusten (*phlegm*); to — a p. down, einen durch Husten zum Schweigen bringen; to catch a —, den Husten bekommen, sich (*dat.*) den Husten holen. **—er**, *s.* der Hustende. **—ing**, *s.* das Husten.
Could, *imperf.* of Can; I — find it in my heart, ich hätte wohl *or* nicht übel Lust (*coll.*).
Coulisse, *s.* die Kulisse.
Coulter, Colter, *s.* das Kolter, Pflugeisen (*Agr.*).
Council, *s.* (assembly) die (Rats-)Versammlung, der Rat; der Senat (*in America*); (deliberation) die Beratung; *see* —-chamber; die Kirchenversammlung (*Eccl.*); clerk of the —, der Sekretär des geheimen Rats; aulic —, Hofrat; cabinet —, Kabinettsrat; common- —, Stadtrat, Gemeinderat; ecumenical —, das allgemeine Konzil; privy- —, der geheime Rat; — of education, der Oberschulrat; — of war, Kriegsrat; to summon a —, die Mitglieder des Rates zusammenberufen. **—lor**, *s.* der Ratgeber; (member of —) der Ratsherr; privy- —lor, Geheimrat. *Comp.* **—-board**, *s.* der Ratstisch; die Ratsversammlung (*fig.*). **—-chamber**, *s.* die Ratsstube. **—-man**, *see* —lor.
Counsel, I. *s.* die Beratung, Beratschlagung; (advice) der (erteilte) Rat; (design) das Vorhaben, der Plan, Anschlag (*B.*); (prudence) die Klugheit; (secret) das Geheimnis; der Rechtsanwalt (*Law*); God's —, Gottes Rat, der Ratschluß Gottes (*Theol.*); a — of perfection, ein allzu idealer, unausführbarer Rat; all . . . took — against Jesus to put him to death, alle . . . hielten einen Rat über Jesum, daß sie ihn töteten (*B.*); to take —, sich beraten; to take — of one's pillow, etwas beschlafen, über einer S. schlafen; to be the — in a case, eine Rechtssache führen; to keep one's —, seine Absicht geheim halten; to take — with one's own heart, mit sich selbst zu Rate gehen; King's —, geheimer Justizrat. II. *pl.* die (plaidierenden) Advokaten, Rechtskonsulenten (*Law*). III. *v.a.* raten, beraten, Rat geben; (warn) ermahnen; (urge) anraten. **—lor**, *s.* der Ratgeber; der Advokat; *see* Councillor. **—lorship**, *s.* die Ratsstelle. *Comp.* **—-keeper**, *s.* der Bewahrer eines Geheimnisses, der Vertraute.
1**Count**, *s.* der Graf. **—ess**, *s.* die Gräfin. **—y**, I. *s.* die Grafschaft. II. *attrib.*; —y council, der Grafschaftsrat; —y councillor, Mitglied des Grafschaftsrats; —y men, Leute aus derselben (englischen) Grafschaft. *Comp.* **—y-corporate**, *s.* eine Stadt, mit den Privilegien einer Grafschaft ausgestattet. **—y-court**, *s.* das Provinzial-, Amts-, Kreis-gericht. **—y-palatine**, *s.* die Pfalzgrafschaft. **—y-town**, *s.* die Kreisstadt, Hauptstadt einer Grafschaft.
2**Count**, I. *v.a.* zählen; rechnen, berechnen (*a sum, etc.*); (consider) meinen, dafür halten; (esteem) schätzen; (impute) zurechnen; to — one's chickens before they are hatched, die Rechnung ohne den Wirt machen; to — money **before** a p., einem Geld vorzählen; to — **over**, durchzählen, durchrechnen, nachzählen; to — **out**, auszählen (*money*). II. *v.n.* (to — on) rechnen, sich verlassen, zählen (auf). III. *s.* (reckoning) die Rechnung; (number) die Zahl; (charge) der Klagepunkt; out of all —, unzählbar; to lose —, sich verzählen; to — out, die Sitzung aufheben weil nicht genug Mitglieder anwesend sind (*Parl.*). **—er**, *s.* der Rechner; die Spielmarke (*Cards*); der Zähltisch, Zahltisch; der Ladentisch; der Zähler (*Mach.*). **—ing**, *s.* das Rechnen, Zählen. **—less**, *adj.* unzählig, zahllos. *Comp.* **—er-jumper**, *s.* der Ladenschwengel. **—er-men**, *pl.* die Ladendiener. **—ing-house**, *s.* das Kontor, Geschäftslokal.
Countenance, I. *s.* das Gesicht; (composure) die Fassung, Gemütsruhe; (support) die Unterstützung, Gunst; (patronage) der Schutz; (confirmation) die Beglaubigung, Bestätigung; this gives — to the report, dies bestätigt das Gerücht; to change —, die Gesichtsfarbe wechseln; to keep one's —, die *or* seine Fassung behalten; (keep grave) sich des Lachens enthalten; his — fell, sein Gesicht wurde sehr lang, er machte ein langes Gesicht; to keep a p. in —, einen (durch seine Gegenwart) ermutigen, unterstützen, einen vor Beschämung bewahren; to put a p. out of —, einen verblüffen; to stare a p. out of —, einen durch Anstarren ganz *or* völlig außer Fassung bringen; to give one's — to a th., etwas durch seinen Schutz befördern. II. *v.a.* (favour) begünstigen, unterstützen; (corroborate) beglaubigen; (allow) zulassen, erlauben. **—r**, *s.* der Unterstützer, Beschützer.
Count—er, *adv.* entgegen, zuwider, entgegengesetzt, Gegen-; to run —er, (to a th., einer S.) zuwiderlaufen *or* sein. **—eract**, *etc.*, *see* Counter—.
Counter—act, *v.a.* entgegenhandeln, entgegenwirken, zuwiderhandeln, hindern. **—action**, *s.* die Entgegenwirkung, der Widerstand. **—-approaches**, *pl.* die Gegenlaufgräben (*Fort.*). **—-attraction**, *s.* die entgegengesetzte Anziehungskraft. **—balance**, I. *s.* das Gegengewicht II. *v.a.* das Gegengewicht halten, aufwiegen; ausgleichen (*C.L.*); —balanced by, aufgewogen durch; durch Gegenrechnung saldierend (*C.L.*). **—check**, I. *s.* der Gegenstoß; (check) der Einhalt. II. *v.a.* aufhalten; verhindern; (einem) entgegenwirken. **—-claim**, *s.* die Gegenforderung. **—-current**, *s.* der Gegenstrom. **—draw**, *v.a.* kalkieren (*Draw.*). **—-effect**, *s.* die Gegenwirkung. **—-evidence**, *s.* der Gegenbeweis. **—feit**, *see* Counterfeit. **—foil**, *s.* das Kontrollblatt; der Abreißzettel. **—fort**, *s.* der Sterbepfeiler

(*Arch.*). —**-guard**, *s.* die Bollwerkswehr. —**-hatching**, *s.* die Kreuzschraffierung. —**-insurance**, *s.* die Rückversicherung. —**-irritant**, *s.* aufreizendes Gegenmittel. —**mand**, *see* Countermand. —**march**, I. *s.* der Rückmarsch; der Rückzug (*fig.*). II. *v.n.* zurückmarschieren. —**mark**, *s.* das Gegenzeichen. —**mine**, *s.* die Gegenmine (*Fort.*); die Gegenlist (*fig.*). —**-movement**, *s.* die Gegenbewegung, der Gegenzug. —**pane**, *see* Counterpane. —**part**, *s.* (duplicate) das Gegenstück, Duplikat, die Kopie; (facsimile) das Gegenbild; die Gegenstimme (*Mus.*). —**plea**, *s.* die Replik (*Law*). —**point**, *s.* der Kontrapunkt (*Mus.*). —**poise**, I. *s.* das Gegengewicht, Gleichgewicht. II. *v.a.* gegeneinander abwägen; das Gleichgewicht halten (*fig.*). —**proof**, *s.* der Gegenabdruck (*Typ.*). —**scarp**, *s.* die äußere Gegenböschung, Konter-Eskarpe (*Mil.*). —**-security**, *s.* die Rückbürgschaft; der Rückbürge. —**sign**, I. *s.* die Parole, Losung (*Mil.*); die Mitunterschrift. II. *v.a.* gegenzeichnen, mitunterschreiben. —**-signature**, *s.* die Gegenzeichnung. —**sink**, I. *v.a.* eine Versenkung austiefen (*Build.*, *etc.*); einlassen (*a rivet, etc.*). II. *s.* der Versenkbohrer. —**-statement**, *s.* der Gegenbericht, die Widerlegung. —**stroke**, *s.* der Gegenstoß, Rückschlag. —**-surety**, *s. see* —-security. —**tenor**, *s.* der Alt, die Altstimme. —**-ticket**, *s.* die Gegenmarke.

Counterfeit, I. *v.a.* (imitate) nachahmen; (forge) unterschieben, verfälschen; (feign) erheucheln, erdichten; to — illness, sich krank stellen. II. *v.n.* sich verstellen. III. *adj.* nachgeahmt, nachgemacht; falsch, unecht (*as a document*); (feigned) verstellt, erheuchelt; — kindness, erheuchelte Freundlichkeit; — goodness, die Gleißnerei. IV. *s.* das Nachgemachte, Verfälschte, Unechte; (*obs.*) das Konterfei, Porträt; (— coin) die falsche Münze. —**er**, *s.* der Nachahmer; der Fälscher, Verfälscher; der Falschmünzer; der Heuchler.

Countermand, I. *s.* der Gegenbefehl; die Widerrufung, Abbestellung. II. *v.a.* einen Gegenbefehl erteilen; widerrufen, abbestellen.

Counterpane, *s.* die Bett(stepp)decke.

Countervail, *v.a.* entgegenwirken, aufwiegen; (compensate) ersetzen.

Countri—es, *pl. see* Country. —**fied**, *adj.* ländlich; (unpolished) bäurisch; *see* Country II.

Country, I. *s.* das Land; (neighbourhood) die Gegend; (native —) das Vaterland; das Gelände (*Mil.*); das Land (*opp. to town*); (people of a —) die Einwohner (einer Gegend); to appeal to the —, an das Volk *or* die Wähler appellieren; to die for one's —, für sein Vaterland sterben, den Tod fürs Vaterland leiden; to go into the —, aufs Land gehen; to go up —, sich ins Innere des Landes begeben; to fly the —, land(es)flüchtig werden. II. *adj.* Land-, vom Lande, auf dem Lande; — bumpkin, der Bauernlümmel; — cousin, die Unschuld vom Lande (*hum.*); — gentleman, der Gutsbesitzer, der auf dem Lande wohnt, Landjunker; — house, das Landhaus, die Villa; — life, Landleben; — parson, der Landpfarrer; — road, die Landstraße; — squire, der Landjunker, Krautjunker; — town, die Landstadt. *Comp.* —**-dance**, *s.* der Reigen(tanz). —**man**, *s.* der Landsmann; (rustic) der Landmann, Bauer. —**-seat**, *s.* der Landsitz. —**woman**, *s.* die Landsmännin; (rustic) die Bäu(e)rin, Bauerfrau, Frau vom Lande.

Coup, *s.*; — d'état, der Staatsstreich; — de grace, der Gnadenstoß; — de main, die Überrumpelung, der plötzliche Überfall; — d'œil, der schnelle Überblick, der flüchtig hingeworfene Blick.

Coupé, *s.* das Coupé, zweisitziger geschlossener Wagen; die Vordersitze im (geteilten) Postwagen.

Coupl—e, *s.* das Paar; die Koppel (*Sport.*); a —e of pigeons, ein Paar Tauben, ein Taubenpaar; a —e of words, ein paar Worte; a married —e, ein Ehepaar; in —es, zu zweien; je zwei und zwei. II. *v.a.* koppeln; mit einander verbinden; (marry) ehelich verbinden; —ed engine, die Zwillingsmaschine (*Railw.*); —ed windows, die Fensterpaare; —ing reins, die Kreuzzügel; —ing rod, die Kuppelungsstange (*Locom.*). —**er**, *s.* der Schieber (*Mach.*). —**et**, *s.* das Verspaar; in riming —ets, in kurzen Reimpaaren. —**ing**, *s.* die Kuppelung; —ing of the shafts, das Ein- und Aus-rückzeug.

Coupon, *s.* der Zinsschein, Coupon; — sheet, der Couponbogen.

Courage, *s.* der Mut, die Tapferkeit. —**ous**, *adj.*, —**ously**, *adv.* mutig, herzhaft, beherzt, tapfer.

Cour—ier, *s.* der Eilbote, Kurier; der (bezahlte) Führer bei Gesellschaftsreisen.

Course, I. *s.* (a running) das Laufen, Rennen; (passage) die Fahrt, Reise, der Gang; (way, track) die Laufbahn, Rennbahn; (direction) der Lauf; (progress) der Fortgang, Fortschritt; (method of procedure) die Handlungsweise, das Verfahren; (way of life) die Lebensweise, der Wandel; der Lehrgang, Kursus (*of lectures, etc.*); (— of life) der Lebenslauf; (revolution) der Umlauf; (regular succession) die Reihenfolge, Reihe, Folge; der Gang (*of dishes*); der Kurs (*of a ship*); die Reihe, Schicht (*Mas. etc.*); der Kurs (*C. L.*); clear the —! macht den Rennplatz *or* die Bahn frei! direct —, Generalkurs (*Naut.*); — corrected for leeway, der behalfene Kurs; — of exchange, Wechselkurs; — of justice, der Lauf der Gerechtigkeit; — of law, Rechtsgang; — of dishes, die Speisenfolge; — of lectures (upon a subject), eine Reihe von Vorlesungen (über einen Gegenstand); to take a — of medicine, eine Kur gebrauchen; — of nature, der natürliche Lauf *or* Verlauf der Dinge; of —, natürlich, selbstredend, gewiß, versteht sich; matter of —, eine Sache, die sich von selbst versteht; words of —, leere Worte; in — of construction, im Bau begriffen; in the — of time, im Laufe der Zeit, mit der Zeit; in due —, zu seiner Zeit, zu rechter Zeit; to take one's —, seinen eignen Weg verfolgen; to let the world take its —, die Welt gehen lassen, wie sie geht; the last — (of dishes), der Nachtisch. II. *v.n.* laufen, rennen, jagen. III. *v.a.* jagen, mit Hunden verfolgen. —**r**, *s.* der Renner, das Rennpferd; (warhorse) das Schlachtroß; der Jäger; der Rennvogel. —**s**, *pl.* der Monatsfluß.

Coursing, *s.* die Hetzjagd.

Court, I. *s.* (—-yard) der Hof, Hofraum; der Vorhof (*B.*); der Hof (*of a prince*); (people of the —) der Hof, die Hofleute, Hofgesellschaft; (justice-room) der Gerichtshof; das Gericht (*of justice*); (justices) die Gerichtsbehörde; (attentions) der Hof, die Cour; die Sackgasse; der (Ball-)Spielplatz; to pay — to a p., einer Person den Hof machen *or* seine Aufwartung machen; — of bankruptcy, Fallitengericht; — of Common Pleas, der Zivilgerichtshof; — of High Commission, Obergerichtshof; — of directors, die Direktorenversammlung; — of equity, das Billigkeitsgericht; — of guard, (persons) die Scharwache, Wachtmannschaft; (guard-room) die Wachtstube; —s of Probate, Erbschaftsgericht (*Amer.*); — of King's Bench, das Oberhofgericht; to go into —, klagen; to bring into —, vor das Gericht bringen, (einen) verklagen. II. *v.a.* (einer Person) den Hof machen; sich (um etwas) bewerben; to — a p.'s favour, sich eifrig um jemandes Gunst (be)mühen, einem zu gefallen suchen; to — sleep, sich zu schlafen bemühen. —**eous**, *adj.*, —**eously**, *adv.* höflich, artig; (gracious) anmutig; —eous reader, geneigter Leser (*obs.*). —**eousness**, *s.* die Höflichkeit, Artigkeit, das liebenswürdige Entgegenkommen. —**er**, *s.* der Bewerber. —**esan**, —**ezan**, *s.* die Buhlerin. —**esy**, *s.* die Höflichkeit, Artigkeit; (favour) die

Vergünstigung; (—eous action) die Gunstbezeugung; (indulgence) die Gefälligkeit; a title by —esy, der Höflichkeitstitel; to hold by —esy, aus Gefälligkeit *or* Vergünstigung eines andern besitzen. **—ier,** *s.* der Höfling, Hofmann; der Bewerber. **—liness,** *s.* das höfliche, artige Betragen, der feine Ton. **—ly,** *adj.* & *adv.* höfisch; höflich, artig; Hof-. **—ship,** *s.* die Bewerbung, das Freien, die Freite. *Comp.* **—-bred,** *adj.* am Hofe erzogen, höfisch. **—-card,** *s.* die Figur (*Cards*). **—-chaplain,** *s.* der Hofprediger. **—-circular,** *s.* der Hofbericht, die Hofnachrichten. **—-dress,** *s.* die Hoftracht. **—-house,** *s.* das Gerichtshaus, der Justizpalast. **—-intrigue,** *s.* die Hofintrigue. **—-martial,** I. *s.* das Kriegsgericht. II. *v.a.;* to —-martial a p., einen vor ein Kriegsgericht stellen. **—-party,** *s.* die Hofpartei. **—-plaster,** *s.* das englische Pflaster. **—-promises,** *s.* leere Versprechungen. **—-yard,** *s.* der Hof.

Cousin, *s.* der Vetter; (female —) die Base, das Bäschen, die Cousine; first —, — german, der (die) leibliche Vetter (Base); —s german, Geschwisterkinder; second —s, Kinder der Geschwisterkinder, Vettern im zweiten Grade; (first) — once removed, der Vetter im Verhälinis zu den Kindern seines Vetters oder seiner Base. **—ly,** *adj.* vetterlich. **—ship,** *s.* die Vetterschaft.

[1]**Cov—e,** I. *s.* die kleine Bucht; kleines Tal (*dial.*); die Wölbung (*Arch.*). II. *v.a.* überwölben; —ed ceiling, die Spiegeldecke. **—ing,** *see* Coving.

[2]**Cove,** *s.* der Kerl, Bursche (*vulg.*).

Covenant, I. *s.* (compact) der Vertrag; (stipulation) die Bedingung; (league) der Bund, das Bündnis; der Bund (*Theol.*); — of marriage, das Ehebündnis; der Ehevertrag (*Law*); Scotch —, der Kovenant, das Bündnis der schottischen Protestanten; breaker of a —, der Bundesbrüchige. II. *v.n.* sich vergleichen, einen Vergleich machen, übereinkommen; they —ed with him for 30 pieces of silver, sie kamen mit ihm überein um dreißig Silberlinge. III. *v.a.* (promise) geloben; (stipulate) (aus)bedingen. **—er,** *s.* der Verbündete; das Mitglied des Bundes der schottischen Protestanten.

Cover, I. *v.a.* bedecken, decken; (put on a —) zudecken; decken (*C. L.*); (— over with, mit etwas) überziehen; (put on one's hat) sich bedecken; (conceal) verhehlen; (excuse) verdecken, verhüllen; (protect) bedecken, beschützen, decken; zurücklegen; bespringen, bedecken (*mares, etc.*); einschlagen (*with sand, etc.*); to — with leather, etc., mit Leder 2c. beschlagen; to — with lime, bekalken, (über)tünchen; to — a roof, ein Dach decken; the receipts do not — the outlay, die Einnahme deckt die Kosten nicht; they —ed 20 miles, sie legten 20 Meilen zurück; —ed with glory, ruhmbedeckt; pray sir, be —ed! bitte behalten Sie Ihren Hut auf! to be —ered, Deckung in Händen haben (*C. L.*). II. *s.* die Decke; *see* —let; (lid) der Deckel; (wrapping) der Umschlag; der Einband, Umschlag (*of a book*); (case) das Futteral; (shelter) das Obdach; (thicket) das Dickicht; das Gedeck, Kuvert (*at dinner, etc.*); (pretence) der Vorwand; (*also* —t) das Lager (*Sport.*); under —, eingeschlagen, im Briefumschlag (as letters), gedeckt (*Mil.*); unter dem Schutze (*of night*); under — of the guns, unter Deckung der Geschütze; to place under —, verdeckt aufstellen; to break —, ins Freie gehen; to draw a —, suchen, bis man das Wild auf der Spur hat; book in paper —s, broschiertes Buch. **—cle,** *s.* der Formdeckel (*Found.*). **—ing,** I. *adj.* deckend. II. *s.* die Decke; das Futteral; (material to —) das Deckmaterial; (clothes) die Bekleidung, Hülle; der Überzug, die Plattierung (for hats); die Bedachung, Dachdeckung (of roofs). **—let, —lid,** *s.* die (äußere) Bettdecke. **—t,** I. *adj.*, **—tly,** *adv.* bedeckt, gedeckt, geschützt; (private) geheim, heimlich; (disguised) versteckt; (insidious) hinterlistig; under —t baron, unter dem Schutze des Mannes stehend (*Law*); feme —t, verheiratete Frau. II. *s.* der bedeckte Ort, Zufluchtsort; der Schutz (*fig.*); (shady place) der schattige Platz; (thicket) das Wäldchen, Dickicht; (hiding-place) der Versteck, das Lager, der Wildpark (*for game*). **—tness,** *s.* die Heimlichkeit. **—ture,** *s.* (—ing) die Bedeckung; (roof) das Obdach; (defence) der Schutz; (—t) der Zufluchtsort; der Frauenstand (*Law*).

Covet, *v.* I. *a.* begehren, heftig wünschen, ersehnen, sich gelüsten lassen (nach einer S.). II. *n.* trachten nach, Gelüste haben nach. **—er,** *s.* der Begehrende. **—ous,** *adj.*, **—ously,** *adv.* begehrlich, gierig (of, nach); (avaricious) geizig, habsüchtig; —ous of glory, ruhmsüchtig; —ous of praise, lobgierig. **—ousness,** *s.* die Begierde; die Habgier, der Geiz.

Covey, *s.* die Brut, Hecke; — of partridges, eine Kette Rebhühner, ein Flug Rebhühner.

Coving, *s.* das Überhängen, der Vorsprung (*Arch.*); — of a chimney, die Seitenwand.

[1]**Cow,** *s.* die Kuh; das Weibchen (*of various beasts*); —s low, moo, Kühe brüllen, muhen. *Comp.* **—-bunting,** *s.* der Kuhstar. **—-boy, —-herd,** *s.* der Kuhhirt; der berittene amerikanische Rinderhirt. **—-catcher,** *s.* der Schienenräumer (*Locom.*). **—-hide,** I. *s.* die Kuhhaut; (whip) der Ochsenziemer. II. *v.a.* (einem) den Ochsenziemer geben. **—-house,** *s.* der Kuhstall. **—-itch,** *s.* die Kuhkrätze (*Bot.*). **—-keeper,** *s.* einer, der Kühe hält; der Kuhhirt. **—-lick,** *s.* geleckt aussehende Seitenlocke, Spucklocke (*sl.*). **—-like,** *adj.* kuhähnlich. **—-parsnip,** *s.* der Bärenklau (*Bot.*). **—-pox,** *s.* die Kuhpocken.

[2]**Cow,** *v.a.* einschüchtern, bange machen.

Coward, *s.* der Feigling, die Memme. **—ice,** *s.* die Feigheit. **—liness,** *s.* die Memmenhaftigkeit, Feigheit. **—ly,** *adj.* & *adv.* feig(e).

Cower, *v.n.* kauern; (squat) niederhocken.

Cowl, *s.* die Mönchskappe; die Schornsteinkappe (*Build.*); it is not the — that makes the monk, das Kleid macht den Mann nicht.

Cowry, *s.* die echte Kauri(muschel), Porzellanschnecke (*Mollusc.*); (—shell) das Muschelgeld.

Cowslip, *s.* die Schlüsselblume.

Coxcomb, *s. see* Cockscomb; der Geck, Stutzer; die Narrenkappe; der Hahnenkamm (*Bot.*). **—ry,** *s.* die Geckenhaftigkeit.

Coxswain, *see* Cockswain.

Coy, *adj.*, **—ly,** *adv.* blöde, scheu, spröde; sittsam, züchtig; zimperlich. **—ness,** *s.* die Sprödigkeit, Blödigkeit; die Sittsamkeit.

Coz, *abbr.* of Cousin.

Cozen, *v.a.* betrügen, prellen. **—age,** die Täuschung, der Betrug. **—er,** *s.* der Betrüger. **—ing,** *s.* die Betrügerei.

[1]**Crab,** *s.* der (gemeine) Taschenkrebs, die Krabbe; der Krebs (*Astr.*); die Erdspille, lose Spille (*Naut.*); to catch a —, das Ruder nicht genügend aus dem Wasser bringen *or* den Streich verfehlen.

[2]**Crab,** I. *adj. see* —bed. II. *s.* (—-apple) der Holzapfel; (—-stick) der Knotenstock. **—bed,** *adj.*, **—bedly,** *adv.* mürrisch, grämlich, sauer; —bed style, eine holperige, verworrene Schreibart. **—bedness,** *s.* das mürrische, finstere Wesen; das Holperige (*of style*). *Comp.* **—-apple (tree),** *s.* der Holzapfel(baum).

Crack, I. *v.a.* (burst) (zer)spalten, zersprengen; knallen (a whip, mit einer Peitsche); to — a bottle, eine Flasche ausstechen (*coll.*); to — a joke, einen Witz reißen; to — nuts, Nüsse knacken; to — up, prahlerisch anpreisen (*vulg.*). II. *v.n.* (burst, split) bersten, sich spalten; (break partially) Sprünge *or* Risse bekommen, zerspringen; krachen; knallen (mit der Peitsche); klatschen; (chat) plaudern (*sl.*); brechen, umschlagen (*of the voice*). III. *s.* der Krach, Knall; (clap) der

Schlag; (split) der Riß, Sprung, die Spalte; (chat) das Geplauder (*vulg.*); — of a whip, Peitschen-schlag, -knall; in a —, im Nu (*vulg.*); the — of doom, der jüngste Tag. IV. *adj.* vorzüglich, famos; geschickt; a — hand, ein Meister; — horse, das Hauptpferd (*Rac.*); — shot, der Meisterschütz(e); — regiment, patentes Regiment. V. *int.* klasch! platsch! patsch! **—ed,** *p.p. & adj.;* to be —ed, geborsten sein, einen Sprung haben; etwas verrückt sein (*coll.*); he is a little —ed, er ist nicht recht gescheit, er ist nicht ganz bei Troste (*coll.*); this cup is —ed, diese Tasse hat einen Sprung; his voice is —ed, seine Stimme wechselt; seine Stimme hat ihren Klang verloren. **—er,** *s.* das Knallbonbon (*Conf.*); der (das) hartgebackene Biskuit (*Bak.*); (fire-—er) der Schwärmer (*Firew.*); nut—er(s), der Nußknacker. **—ing,** *s.* das Umschlagen (*of the voice*). **—le,** *v.n.* knistern. **—ling,** I. *p. & adj. see* —le. II. *s.* das Geknatter, Geknister. **—nel,** *s.* das aus Pfeilwurzmehl gebackene Biskuit. *Comp.* **—brained,** *adj.* verrückt.

Cradle, I. *s.* die Wiege; die Kindheit (*fig.*); die Schiene (*Surg.*); (goldwashing —) die Röstkratze; der Schlotten (*Shipb.*); das Laufbrett (*Print.*); der Schienenstuhl (*Railw.*); das Reff (*Agr.*); to rock the —, wiegen; from his —, von Jugend auf. II. *v.a.* einwiegen. III. *v.n.* wie in einer Wiege liegen (*obs.*); eingeschlossen sein (*fig.*). *Comp.* **—-scythe,** *s.* die Reffsense. **—-song,** *s.* das Wiegenlied.

Craft, *s.* (trade) das Handwerk, Gewerbe; (skill) die Kunst, Fertigkeit, Geschicklichkeit; (cunning) die List, Verschlagenheit; (vessel) das Schiff; die Fahrzeuge, Schiffe (*pl.*); (guild) die Zunft; of the same —, gleichen Handwerks; small —, alle Arten kleiner Schiffe *or* Fahrzeuge. **—ily,** *adv.*, **—y,** *adj.* listig; (cleverly) geschickt. **—i-ness,** *s.* die List, Schlauheit; die Kunstfertigkeit. *Comp.* **—sman,** *s.* der Handwerker.

Crag, *s.* die Klippe, Felsenspitze. **—gy,** *adj.* schroff, uneben, felsig.

Crake, *s.* (corn—) die Landralle (*Orn.*).

Cram, I. *v.a.* vollstopfen (*a vessel, etc.*); stopfen, mästen, nudeln (*poultry*); mit Speisen überfüllen (*a child*); mit Kenntnissen vollpfropfen, pressen (*coll.*); to — s.th. down a p.'s throat, einem etwas mit aller Gewalt aufdrängen; to — a student for an examination, einen Studenten für eine Prüfung einpauken (*sl.*); to — into, hineinstopfen. II. *v.n.* sich vollpfropfen lassen, hastig sich allerlei Kenntnisse anlernen; to — for an examination, auf eine Prüfung ochsen *or* büffeln; sich auf eine Prüfung einpauken lassen. III. *s. see* —ming; eine Lüge (*sl.*). **—mer,** *s.* der Einpauker. **—ming,** *s.* das Einpauken, die Einpaukerei; —ming establishment, die Presse.

Crambo, *s.* das Reimspiel; das Reimwort.

Cramp, I. *s.* der Krampf; (restraint) die Fessel, das Hindernis; (holdfast) die Klammer; der Holzhaken (*Carp.*); (clamp) die Schraubzwinge; die Klammer (*of a lock*). II. *v.a.* krampfhaft verziehen (*Med.*); (hamper) beengen; (narrow down) einschränken; (hinder) hemmen; (fasten with —-irons) einklammern. **—ed,** *adj.* krampfig, steif; beengt; a —ed hand, eine steife Handschrift. **—onee,** *s.; (Her.)* cross —onee, das Stollenkreuz. **—o(o)ns,** *pl.* die Eissporen (*for glacier-climbing*); die Steigeisen beim Stürmen (*Mil.*). *Comp.* **—-iron,** *s.* die eiserne Klammer; der Enterhaken (*Naut.*); der eiserne Winkel (*Print.*).

Cran—age, *s.* die Krangerechtigkeit; das Krangeld. **—e,** I. *s.* der Kranich (*Orn.*); der Kran (*Mach.*); hoisting —e, Hebekran; travelling —e, Laufkran; feeding —, Speisungskran (*Railw.*); the — trumpets, clangs, der Kranich trompetet (*poet.*). II. *v.a.;* to — (one's neck), den Hals vorstrecken, einen langen Hals machen. III. *v.n.* sich ausrecken (nach). *Comp.* **—esbill,** *s.* der Storchschnabel, das Geranium (*Bot.*); die Kranichschnabelzange (*Surg.*).

Cranberry, *s.* die Kronsbeere, Preiselbeere.

Crani—ology, *s.* die Schädellehre. **—um,** *s.* der Schädel, die Hirnschale.

Crank, I. *s.* (turn) die Windung; (pun) das Wortspiel; die Schnurre; die Laune; die Kurbel (*Mech.*); der Schwengel; der Leitarm (*Min.*); grillenhafter *or* grilliger Mensch; (— of a pump) Brunnenschwengel; — chain-wheel, großes Kettenrad (*Cycl.*); bell-—, Glockenschwengel; quips and —s, Possen und Schnurren. II. *adj.* flink, lustig; in Gefahr umzukippen (*of a ship*). *Comp* **—-axle,** *s.* (—ed axle) die Kurbelachse. **—-engine,** *s.* die Kurbeldampfmaschine. **—-shaft,** *s.* die Kurbelwelle. **—-wheel,** *s.* das Seilerrad.

Crank—iness, *s.* die Launen- *or* Grillen-haftigkeit. **—y,** *adj.* reizbar, launisch; verschroben.

Crann—ied, *adj.* voller Spalten, rissig. **—ies,** *pl. see* —y. **—y,** *s.* (crevice) der Riß, Spalt; (corner) der Versteck, Winkel.

Crap—e, I. *s.* der Flor, Krepp (*C.L.*); double —e, Doppelkrepp. II. *v.a.* krausen, kräuseln; mit Krepp versehen; —ing iron, das Kräuseleisen.

Crapulence, *s.* der Rausch; der Katzenjammer.

[1]**Crash,** I. *s.* (noise) das Gekrach, Krachen, Getöse; (failure) der Bankrott; (fall) der Zusammensturz (*fig.*). II. *v.n.* krachen, platzen.

[2]**Crash,** *s.* grober Drillich (*Manuf.*).

Crasis, *s.* die Zusammenziehung, Krasis (*Gram.*).

Crass, *adj.* dick, grob, derb; — ignorance, grobe *or* krasse Unwissenheit. **—ness,** *s.* die Grobheit.

Crate, *s.* großer geflochtener Korb zum Tragen von Porzellan- und Ton-waren.

Crater, *s.* der Krater; der Kelch (*Astr.*). **—iform,** *adj.* kraterförmig.

Craunch, *v.* I. *a. see* Crunch.

Cravat, *s.* die Halsbinde, Krawatte.

Crav—e, *v.* I. *a.* flehen dringend bitten um eine S.; the stomach —es food, der Magen verlangt (nach) Nahrung. II. *n.;* he —es for mercy, er fleht um Gnade. **—ing,** *s.* das heftige Verlangen, die heftige Begier, Sehnsucht (nach einer S.).

Craven, I. *adj.* feig(herzig). II. *s.* die Memme.

Craw, *s.* der Kropf (*of fowls*).

Crawfish, *s.* die Languste; der Bachkrebs.

Crawl, *v.n.* kriechen; schleichen; to — **about,** umherschleichen; to — **forth,** hervorkriechen, auskriechen; to be —ing **with** vermin, von Ungeziefer wimmeln; a —ing sensation, ein krabbelndes, juckendes Gefühl, ein Krabbeln. **—er,** *s.* der Kriecher. **—ing,** I. *p. & adj.*, **—ingly,** *adv.* kriechend. II. *s.* das Kriechen.

Crayfish, *s.* der Bachkrebs, Flußkrebs, Krebs.

Crayon, I. *s.* der Zeichenstift; black —, red —, der Bleistift, Rotstift; coloured —s, Pastell-Farben. II. *attrib.;* — drawing, die Kreidezeichnung.

Craz—e, I. *s.* die Verrücktheit; die Manie (für eine S.). II. *v.a.* zerrütten, verwirrt machen. **—ed,** *adj.* verrückt. **—edness, —iness,** *s.* die Geistesschwäche; die Geisteszerrüttung, Verrücktheit. **—y,** *adj.*, **—ily,** *adv.* (broken down) hinfällig, gebrechlich; baufällig (*as a building*); gebrechlich, schwach, seeuntüchtig (*of a ship*); verrückt (*of the mind*).

Creak, *v.* I. *n.* knarren. II. *a.* knarren (mit einer S.). III. *s.* das Knarren.

Cream, I. *s.* der Rahm, die Sahne; das Beste, Vorzüglichste (*fig.*); (quintessence) der Kern; die Creme, das Schaumgericht (*Conf.*); whipped —, die Schlagsahne (*Cook.*); almond —, Mandelcreme (*for the skin*); — of the joke, der Witz des Spaßes; — of tartar, der gereinigte Weinstein. II. *v.a.* abrahmen. **—y,** *adj.* voller Sahne, sahnig, süß wie Sahne; fein. *Comp.* **—-bowl,** *s.* der Rahmnapf. **—-cheese,** *s.* der Rahmkäse. **—-coloured,** *adj.* rahmfarbig; gelblichweiß. **—-laid, —-wove,** *adj.;* —-laid, —-wove, paper, dickes, weißgelbliches Schreibpapier. **—-tart,** *s.* die Rahmtorte.

Creas—e, I. *s.* die (falsche) Falte, Runzel; das Ohr (*in a book*); der Umschlag, die Falte (*in cloth*); der Kreidestrich (*Cricket*). II. *v.a.* falten, kniffen, umbiegen. III. *v.n.* Falten werfen. **—er**, *s.* der Falter (*Sew.-m.*).

Creat—e, *v.a.* schaffen, erschaffen, hervorbringen; (call forth) hervorrufen, verursachen; (beget) erzeugen; ernennen, machen (zum Minister, *etc.*). **—ion**, *s.* (act of —ion, what is —ed, the universe) die Schöpfung; (causing) die Verursachung; (—ion of the imagination) die Erschaffung; (calling forth) die Hervorbringung; die Ernennung (zu einer Würde). **—ive**, *adj.* schaffend, erschaffend; schöpferisch, fruchtbar (*as genius*). **—iveness**, *s.* (—ive power) die schöpferische Kraft, Schaffenskraft, Produktivität. **—or**, *s.* der Schöpfer; der Verursacher. **—ure**, I. *s.* das Geschöpf, die Kreatur; the dumb —ures, das liebe Vieh, die Tiere; sweet —ure! süßes Geschöpf(-chen)! herziges Wesen! I hadn't a —ure to help me, ich hatte niemand, der mir helfen konnte. II. *attrib.*; —ure comforts, die materiellen Annehmlichkeiten des Lebens.

Crèche, *s.* die Kleinkinderbewahranstalt.

Cred—ence, *s.* der Glaube; to give —ence to a story, einer Geschichte Glauben schenken. **—enda**, *pl.* die Glaubensartikel. **—ential**, I. *adj.* beglaubigend. II. *s.* die Beglaubigung. **—entials**, *pl.* das Beglaubigungsschreiben, Empfehlungsschreiben; die Kreditive (*diplomatic lang.*). **—ibility**, *s.* die Glaubwürdigkeit; (probability) die Glaublichkeit. **—ible**, *adj.*, **—ibly**, *adv.* glaublich (*of things*); glaubwürdig (*of persons*); to be —ibly informed, glaubwürdige Nachricht haben. **—ibleness**, *s.* die Glaubwürdigkeit. **—it**, I. *s.* (belief) der Glaube; (reputation) der (gute) Ruf, Kredit, gute Name, das Ansehen; (testimony) das Zeugnis; (honour) die Ehre; (trust reposed) das Zutrauen; (balance in a p.'s favour) das Guthaben; der Kredit (*C.L.*); (trust) der Borg (*C.L.*); (influence) der Einfluß; on —it, auf Borg, auf Kredit; leihweise; at 3 months' —it, auf drei Monate Ziel; to put to a p.'s —it, einem gutschreiben; to give —it, Kredit geben; letter of —it, der Kreditbrief; public —it, der Kredit eines Staates; transactions on —it, Zeitgeschäfte; to get, take on —it, auf Kredit bekommen, nehmen; place it to the —it of my account, schreiben Sie es mir gut, setzen Sie es auf mein Guthaben; worthy of —it, glaubwürdig; to give —it (*to a story, etc.*), (einer Geschichte) Glauben beimessen; he is a —it to his family, er macht seiner Familie Ehre; to do —it to a p., einem Ehre machen; you do me no —it, mit dir lege ich keine Ehre ein; to give a p. (the) —it for, einem (die Ehre von etwas) zuschreiben, (etwas) zutrauen; to take —it to o.s. for a th., sich (*dat.*) eine S. zur Ehre anrechnen, sich (*dat.*) etwas zuschreiben *or* das Verdienst an einer S. zurechnen; —it side, die Kreditseite (*C. L.*). II. *v. a.* (believe) Glauben beimessen, glauben; (trust) trauen; kreditieren (*C. L.*); (honour) Ansehen, Kredit verschaffen; to stand —ited with, kreditiert sein mit. **—itable**, *adj.*, **—itably**, *adv.* ehrenvoll, mit Ehren, (estimable) achtbar; (honourable) ehrbar, ehrenwert, anständig; (reputable) ehrsam, unbescholten; it is very —itable to him, es macht ihm alle Ehre; they supported themselves —itably, sie brachten sich anständig durch. **—itor**, *s.* der Gläubiger (*C.L.*); —itor in trust, der Direktor einer Fallitmasse; —itor's side, die Kreditseite; to be a —itor on the bank-books, ein Bankkonto haben. **—ulity**, *s.* die Leichtgläubigkeit. **—ulous**, *adj.*, **—ulously**, *adv.* leichtgläubig. **—ulousness**, *see* —ulity. *Comp.* **—ence-cup**, *s.* der Kredenzbecher. **—ence-table**, *s.* der Kredenztisch (beim Altar).

Creed, *s.* das Glaubensbekenntnis; (belief) der Glaube; die Ansicht, Überzeugung; the Apostles' **—**, das apostolische Glaubensbekenntnis.

Creek, *s.* die Bucht, Bai, der Schlupfhafen; der kleine Fluß, Bach (*Amer.*). **—y**, *adj.* buchtig, voller Biegungen.

Creel, *s.* der Weidenkorb, Fischkorb.

Creep, I. *v.n.* kriechen; schleichen, kriechen (*fig.*); einschmeicheln (into favour); I felt my flesh begin to —, es überlief mich *or* durchschauerte mich eiskalt, mich überlief eine Gänsehaut; old age —s on apace, das Alter naht sich schnell. II. *s.;* the —s *or* cold —s, die Gänsehaut (*coll.*), der kalte Schauer, das Gruseln (*coll.*). **—er**, *s.* der Kriecher; (vermin) das Ungeziefer; die Schlingpflanze (*Bot.*); der Baumläufer (*Orn.*); Virginia(n) —er, wilder Wein. **—y**, I. *adj.* kriechend; fröstelnd, frostig; I feel —y, es gruselt mir (*coll.*). II. *s.* eine Art Schemel (*Scotch*).

Creese, *s.* der Malaiendolch.

Cremat—e, *v.a.* einäschern; Leichen verbrennen. **—ion**, *s.* die Einäscherung; die Leichenverbrennung. **—ory**, **—orium**, *s.* die Einäscherungshalle, Leichenverbrennungshalle.

Crenat—e, I. *v.a.* einkerben. II. *adj.* zackig, gekerbt. **—ure**, *s.* die Kerbung, Auszahnung (*Bot.*).

Crenel, **—le**, *s.* die Zinnenlücke, Schießscharte. **—late**, *v.a.* mit Schießscharten versehen.

Crenulate, *adj.* gekerbt, gezackt (*Bot.*, *Zool.*).

Creosote, I. *s.* das Kreosot. II. *v.a.* mit Kreosot durchtränken.

Crepitat—e, *v.n.* knistern, prasseln. **—ion**, *s.* das Knistern, Prasseln.

Crept, *imperf. & p.p. of* Creep.

Crepuscular, *adj.* dämmernd, dämmerig; im Zwielicht *or* in der Dämmerung erscheinend, Dämmerungs-.

Crescen—do, I. *adv.* zunehmend, steigend an Stärke, crescendo (*Mus.*). II. *s.* das Crescendo. **—t**, I. *adj.* wachsend, zunehmend. II. *s.* der zunehmende Mond, Halbmond; die halbmondförmig gebaute Häuserreihe; das Hörnchen (*Bak.*). *Comp.* **—t-shaped**, *adj.* halbmondförmig.

Cress, *s.* die Kresse (*Bot.*).

Cresset, *s.* brennender Pechkranz, das Leuchtfeuer.

Crest, *s.* der Kamm (*of a cock*); der Schopf, Strauß (*on birds, etc.*); der Helmbusch (*of a helmet*); der Helmschmuck (*Her.*); (helmet) der Helm; (ridge) der Rücken, Gipfel, die Spitze; (— of a hill) der Bergrücken; — of a wave, der Kamm einer Welle. **—ed**, *adj.* geschopft, gehaubt; mit einem Helmschmucke; —ed lark, die Haubenlerche (*Orn.*). *Comp.* **—-fallen**, *adj.* niedergeschlagen; mutlos; (abashed) beschämt.

Cretaceous, *adj.* kreidig, kreideartig; kreidehaltig; kreideweiß (*Bot.*); — group, die Kreidegruppe.

Cretin, *s.* der Kretin, Kretine. **—ism**, *s.* der Kretinismus, die Kropfsucht, Trottelkrankheit.

Cretonne, *s.* die Cretonne.

Crev—asse, *s.* die Gletscherspalte, der Bergschrund, Spalt, die Spalte; der Dammbruch (*Amer.*). **—ice**, *s.* der Riß, die Spalte, enge Öffnung.

[1]**Crew**, *s.* die Schar; (gang) die Bande, Rotte; (ship's —) die Schiffsmannschaft; merry —, lustiges Völkchen, lustige Gesellschaft.

[2]**Crew**, *obs. imperf. of* Crow.

Crewel, *s.* die Crewelwolle, feinste Stickwolle. *Comp.* **—-work**, *s.* die Plattstickerei.

Crib, I. *s.* die Krippe; (stall) der Ochsenstall, Stand; (hut) die Hütte; (bed) das Kinderbett, die Kinderbettstelle; die Eselsbrücke (*school sl.*). II. *v.a.* einsperren; (steal) stehlen; stibitzen; sich einer Eselsbrücke bedienen (*at school*). **—bage**, *s.* die Cribbage. *Comp.* **—-biter**, *s.* der Krippenbeißer.

Cribble, *s.* das grobe Sieb.

Crick, *s.* der Krampf; — in the neck, der steife Hals.

[1]**Cricket**, *s.* die Grille, das Heimchen (*Ent.*); the — chirps, das Heimchen zirpt; merry as a —, vergnügt wie ein Lämmerschwänzchen.

²Cricket, I. *s.* das Kricketspiel, Schlagballspiel, der Schlagball. II. *v.n.* Kricket spielen. **—er**, *s.* der Kricketspieler. *Comp.* **—-ball**, *s.* der Schlagball. **—-bat**, *s.* das Schlagholz. **—-field**, *s.* der Kricketspielplatz. **—-match**, *s.* die Kricketpartie.
Cricoid, *adj.* ringförmig; — cartilage, der Ringknorpel.
Crie—d, *imperf. & p.p. see* Cry. **—r**, *s.* der Schreier; (public —r) der Ausrufer; town—er, der Stadtausrufer, öffentliche Ausrufer. **—s**, *pl. see* Cry.
Crim—e, *s.* das Verbrechen, der Frevel; (sin) die Sünde; capital —e, Kapital-Verbrechen; to commit a —e, ein Verbrechen begehen. **—inal**, I. *adj.*, **—inally**, *adv.* verbrecherisch (*of persons*), strafbar; (sinful) sündlich; kriminal, Straf- (*opp. to* Civil); —inal code, das Kriminal-Gesetzbuch; —inal conversation, der Ehebruch; —inal law, das Strafrecht. II. *s.* der Verbrecher; (accused) der Angeklagte. **—inality**, *s.* das Verbrecherische; (guilt) die Schuld. **—inate**, *v.a.* eines Verbrechens beschuldigen, anklagen. **—ination**, *s.* die Beschuldigung, Anklage.
Crimp, I. *v.a.* kräuseln; (gewaltsam, listig) werben (*sailors, etc.*); (seize) packen, ergreifen; (Fische) aufschlitzen und in Brunnenwasser legen (*Cook.*). II. *s.* der Werber, Matrosenmakler; der Werber. **—er**, *s.* die Kräuselmaschine. *Comp.* **—ing-house**, *s.* das Werbehaus. **—ing-machine**, *s.* die Kerbmaschine.
Crimson, I. *s.* das Karmesin, Karmin, das Hochrot. II. *adj.* hochrot, karmesin, karmin. — dyes, Karmesinfarben. III. *v.n.* erröten.
Cring—e, *v.n.* sich krümmen, sich schmiegen, kriechen (to, vor); bowing and —ing, viele Bücklinge machend. **—er**, *s.* der Kriecher. **—ing**, I. *adj.* kriechend, kriecherisch. II. *s.* die Kriecherei.
Crinkle, I. *s.* die Biegung, Windung; Falte, Runzel. II. *v.a.* faltig machen; kräuseln. III. *v.n.* Falten werfen.
Crinoline, *s.* der Reifrock, die Krinoline.
Cripple, I. *s.* der Krüppel. II. *adj.* lahm. III. *v.a.* verkrüppeln; entkräften, lähmen (*fig.*).
Crisis, *s.* (*pl.* Crises) die Krisis, Krise (*Med.*); der Entscheidungspunkt, Wendepunkt (*fig.*).
Crisp, I. *adj.*, **—ly**, *adv.* kraus (*of hair*); bröckelig, knusperig (*of cakes*); gebogen, gekräuselt (*of waves*); frisch (*of air*); knorpelig, kruspelig (*as meat*). II. *v.a.* kräuseln; braun rösten, braten (*meat, etc.*). **—ate**, *adj.* gekräuselt. **—ness**, *s.* das Bröckelige, Knusprige; die Krausheit.
Criss-cross, I. *s.* das Kreuzzeichen (statt der Unterschrift). II. *adj. & adv.* gekreuzt. III. *v.a.* kreuzen, durchkreuzen.
Crit—erion, *s.* das Kennzeichen, der Prüfstein; die Norm. **—ic**, *s.* der Kritiker; (censurer) der Tadler; (art —ic) der Kunstrichter; (reviewer) der Rezensent, Kritiker. **—ical**, *adj.*, **—ically**, *adv.* (discriminating) kunstrichterlich, kritisch; kritisch, entscheidend; (captious) tadelsüchtig; kritelnd, krittelig; (grave) bedenklich; (dangerous) gefährlich; (accurate) genau, fein, scharf (*obs.*); the —ical moment, der entscheidende Augenblick; —ical times, bedenkliche Zeiten; a —ical position, eine kitzliche Lage. **—icalness**, *s.* die kritische Lage, Bedenklichkeit. **—icize**, *v.a.* kritisieren, beurteilen; rezensieren; tadeln. **—icism**, *s.* die Kritik; die Kunstbeurteilung; die Rezension; —icism lesson, die Probelektion; open to —icism, anfechtbar. **—ique**, *s.* die Kritik.
Croak, I. *v.n.* krächzen (*as a raven*); quaken (*of frogs*); knurren (*also fig.*); Schlechtes prophezeien. II. *s.*, **—ing**, *s.* das Quaken, Gequake; das Krächzen. **—er**, *s.* der Unglücksprophet.
Crochet, I. *s.* die Häkelei. II. *v.a. & n.* häkeln. **—ed**, *adj.* gehäkelt. **—ing**, *s.* das Häkeln. *Comp.* **—-cotton**, *s.* das Garn zum Häkeln. **—-needle**, *s.* die Häkelnadel. **—-stitch**, *s.* der Häkelstich. **—-work**, *s.* die Häkelarbeit.
Crock, I. *s.* der irdene Topf; unbrauchbarer Invalide (*sl.*). II. *attrib.*; — butter, die Topf-, gesalzene Winterbutter. **—ery**, *s.* das Steingut, die Töpferware.
Crocket, *s.* die Kriechblume (*Arch.*).
Crocodile, I. *s.* das Krokodil; (*abbrev.* croc.) das Mädchenpensionat zu zwei und zwei (auf dem Schulwege oder Spaziergang) (*sl.*). II. *attrib.*; — tears, Krokodilstränen.
Crocus, *s.* der Krokus, Safran (*Bot.*).
Croft, *s.* das kleine umzäunte, nahe am Hause liegende Feldstück; das kleine Pachtgut. **—er**, *s.* der Kleinbauer, kleine Landpächter (*dial.*).
Cromlech, *s.* der Kromlech, druidischer Steinbau.
Cron—e, *s.* das alte Weib. **—y**, *s.* (old —y) vertrauter (alter) Freund; der Kamerad.
Crook, I. *s.* die Krümmung; (hook) der Haken; der Schürhaken (*Found.*); (shepherd's —) der Schäferstab; (crosier) der Hirtenstab; (unpleasantness) die Widerwärtigkeit; by hook or by —, mit Recht oder Unrecht. II. *v.a.* krümmen, krumm biegen. **—ed**, *adj.*, **—edly**, *adv.* krumm; (not straight) schief; (perverse) verschroben; —ed mind, verschrobener Kopf; —ed ways, krumme Wege. **—edness**, *s.* die Krummheit, Krümme; (deformity) das Verwachsensein. **—s**, *pl.* die Klammern (*obs.*). *Comp.* **—(ed)-backed**, *adj.* buckelig.
Croon, *v.n.* leise singen, vor sich hin summen; wimmern, wehklagen.
Crop, I. *s.* der Kropf (*of a fowl*); die Ernte, das Getreide; das kurz abgeschnittene Haar, der Stutz. II. *v.a.* kurz abschneiden, abstutzen; abfressen (*grass*). III. *v.n.*; to — out, up, zu Tage streichen. **—ped**, *p.p. & adj.* kurz (ab)geschnitten. **—per**, *s.* der Abschneider, Abmäher; der Tuchbereiter; die Appretiermaschine; die Kropftaube; der Fall, Sturz (*sl.*); to come a —per, einen schweren Sturz tun; Mißerfolg haben (*sl.*). *Comp.* **—-ear**, *s.* das Stutzohr. **—-eared**, *adj.* stutzohrig, mit gestutzten Ohren.
Croquet, *s.* das Croquet-, Krocket-Spiel.
Crosier, *s.* der Bischofsstab, Krummstab.
Cross, I. *s.* das Kreuz; (sorrow) das Leiden; (trial) die Trübsal, Widerwärtigkeit, das Kreuz; (crucifix) das Kruzifix; das Kreuz (*Theol.*); das Kreuzzeichen (*as signature*); die Aversseite (*of a coin*); der Kreuzsteg (*Typ.*); die Kreuzung (*of races*); (hybrid) der Bastard; to cut on the —, schräg schneiden; to take up one's —, sein Kreuz auf sich nehmen. II. *adj.* kreuzweise, schräg, schief; (contrary) entgegengesetzt; (contradictory) widerwärtig; (perverse) widerspenstig; (ill humoured) übelgelaunt, mürrisch; — battery, die Kreuzbatterie; — street, die Quergasse; as — as two sticks, äußerst ärgerlich (*coll.*); to be at — purposes, sich gegenseitig mißverstehen; sich unabsichtlich bekämpfen. III. *adv.* quer, schief, überzwerch; verkehrt, unglücklich (*fig.*). IV. *v.a.* kreuzen, kreuzweise legen; unterschlagen (*the arms*); (step across) hinübergehen, überschreiten; kreuzen, mischen (*races, plants*); (come across a p.) (einem) in den Weg kommen; (pass over) überfahren, sich übersetzen lassen, setzen über (*acc.*); (— out) ausstreichen, durchstreichen; (thwart) hindern, zuwider sein, durchkreuzen, widerstreben; to — the bar, die vor dem Hafeneingang liegende Sandbank hinter sich lassen und ins offne Meer hinaus fahren; to — the frontier, die Grenze überschreiten; to — o.s., sich bekreuzen; to have one's plans, wishes, etc. —ed, von Widerwärtigkeiten heimgesucht werden; he shall never — my threshold again, er soll mir nie wieder über die Schwelle kommen; to be —ed in love, unglücklich in der Liebe sein; to — a p.'s hand (with money), einem Geld in die Hand legen; to — a cheque, einen Scheck *or* Zahlschein querschreiben. V. *v.n.* sich kreuzen (*as letters*). **—ing**, *s.* der Übergang, die Überfahrt; die Durchquerung (*of Africa, etc.*); (street —ing) der Straßenübergang; der Kreuzweg; die Kreuzung (*of races*;

also Railw.); level —ing, der Niveauübergang (*Railw.*); —ing sweeper, der (Trinkgelder erwartende freiwillige) Feger von Straßenübergängen (bei schlechtem Wetter). —**ly**, *adv.* mürrisch, verdrießlich, ärgerlich. —**ness**, *s.* die Quere; die schlechte Laune, das mürrische Wesen; (perverseness) die Verkehrtheit. —**wise**, *adv.* kreuzweise. *Comp.* —**-aisle**, *s.* der Seitenflügel einer Kreuzkirche. —**bar**, *s.* die Querstange; die Querstange, Querleine (beim Fußballspiel); —-bars of a window, das Fensterkreuz. —**bill**, *s.* der Kreuzschnabel (*Orn.*) —**beam**, *s.* der Querbalken. —**birth**, *s.* schwere Geburt. —**bones**, *pl.* Kreuzknochen. —**bow**, *s.* die Armbrust. —**breed**, *s.* die durch Kreuzung gewonnene Rasse. —**bun**, *s.*; (hot) —-bun, (gewärmter) Karfreitagsemmel —**cut**, *s.* der Querschnitt. —**-examination**, *s.* das Kreuzverhör (*Law*). —**-examine**, *v.a.* im Kreuzverhör vernehmen; die Kreuz und die Quere fragen. —**-eyed**, *adj.* schielend. —**fire**, *s.* das Kreuzfeuer (*Mil.*). —**grained**, *adj.* wider den Strich geschnitten; störrisch, widersinnig, widerspenstig (*fig.*). —**legged**, *adj.* mit übereinander geschlagenen Beinen. —**marriage**, —**match**, *s.* die Wechselheirat. —**multiplication**, die kreuzweise Multiplikation im Duodezimalsystem. —**patch**, *s.* der Murrkopf. —**piece**, *s.* der Querbalken; das Querholz (*of timber*). —**purpose**, die Gegenabsicht, das Mißverständnis; —-purposes, das Rätselspiel, Frage- und Antwortspiel. —**question**, *see* —-examine. —**references**, wechselseitige Verweisungen, Verweisungen von einer Stelle auf die andere. —**road**, *s.* der Kreuzweg, die Wegscheide. —**stitch**, *s.* der Kreuzstich. —**trees**, *s.* die Dwarsschlingen (*Naut.*). —**wind**, *s.* der senkrecht zum Kurse wehende Wind.

Crotch, I. *s.* der Haken; der Stieper (*Naut.*).

Crotchet, *s.* (whim) die Grille; die gabelförmige Stütze (*Artil.*); der Einschnitt in einer bedeckten Wegfahrt (*Fort.*); die Viertelnote (*Mus.*); die eckige Klammer ([ ] *Typ.*). —**y**, *adj.* grillenhaft, wunderlich, launenhaft.

Croton, *s.* der Kroton (*Bot.*); — oil, das Krotonöl. —**ic**, *adj.*; —ic acid, die Krotonsäure.

[1]**Crouch**, *v.n.* sich ducken, sich schmiegen (to, vor; *of dogs, etc.*); schmeicheln, kriechen (*fig.*).

[2]**Crouch**, *v.n.* bekreuzen, mit einem Kreuz versehen (*obs.*); —ed friars, Kreuzbrüder.

[1]**Croup**, *s.* die häutige Bräune, der Krupp.

[2]**Croup**, *s.* der Bürzel (*of birds*); das Kreuz, die Kruppe (*of horses*).

Croupier, *s.* der Croupier.

Crow, I. *s.* die gemeine Krähe (*Orn.*); das Krähen (*of a cock*); *see* —bar; to have a — to pluck with a p., ein Hühnchen mit einem zu rupfen haben; to be as hoarse as a —, heiser wie ein Rabe sein; —'s feet, Runzeln unter den Augen; as the — flies, in gerader Linie, in der Luftlinie; —'s nest, der Mastkorb (*Naut.*). II. *v.n.* krähen; triumphieren; to — over a p., sich stolz über einen erheben, einen andern seine Überlegenheit empfinden lassen. *Comp.* —**bar**, *s.* das Brecheisen. —**foot**, *s.* der Hahnenfuß, die Ranunkel (*Bot.*). —**-quill**, *s.* die Krähenfeder.

Crowd, I. *s.* (throng) das Gedränge; der Haufe, die Menge (*of people*); (mob) das gemeine Volk, der Pöbel. II. *v.a.* (fill) anfüllen, überfüllen; (throng) drängen, pressen; (press close) zusammendrängen; to — all sail, alle Segel beisetzen; to — **in**, sich eindrängen; his article was —ed **out**, sein Artikel wurde wegen Mangel an Raum nicht eingerückt. III. *v.n.* sich drängen; to — **in**(**to**), sich hineindrängen; these things came —ing **upon** his memory, diese Sachen stürmten auf sein Gedächtnis ein. —**ed**, *p.p.*; —ed to suffocation, zum Ersticken voll; —ed with, angefüllt mit, wimmelnd von.

Crown, I. *s.* (wreath) der Kranz; die Krone (*of kings, etc.*); (honour) die Ehre, der Ruhm; (ornament) der Schmuck; (top) der Gipfel, die Spitze; (completion) die Krone, Vollendung; das Fünfschillingstück, die Krone (*Mint.*); der Wirbel (des Kopfes, of the head); der Kopf (*fig.*); der Kranz (*Hatm.*); das Kreuz (*of an anchor*); der Schlußstein (*of an arch*); the half-— packet, das Paket zum Preise von 2.50 M.; from the — of the head to the sole of the foot, von Kopf zu Fuß; — of a bell, die Platte eines Glockenhutes. II. *attrib.*; — colony, die Kronkolonie, Reichskolonie; — octavo, das Klein-Oktav; — surveyor, königlicher Ingenieur. III. *v.a.* krönen; bekränzen (*fig.*); (adorn) schmücken, zieren, Ehre bringen; the evening —s the day, es ist noch nicht aller Tage Abend; (reward) belohnen; (perfect) vervollkommen; —ed heads, gekrönte Häupter; to — a man, einen Stein aufdamen, aufsetzen (*Draughts*); to — a tooth, einem Zahne eine künstliche Krönung aufsetzen. —**er**, *s. see* Coroner; der, welcher krönt. *Comp.* —(**-demesne**)**-lands**, *pl.* Krongüter. —**escapement**, *s.* die Spindelhemmung (*Horol.*). —**-glass**, *s.* das Kronglas. —**-jewels**, *pl.* die Reichskleinodien. —**-lease**, *s.* der Pachtvertrag einer Domäne. —**-moulding**, *s.* das Oberglied (*of a cornice*). —**-office**, *s.* das Krongericht, Kriminalgericht der King's Bench. —**post**, *s.* (king-post) die Giebelsäule; die obere Hängesäule (*Arch.*). —**-prince**, *s.* der Kronprinz. —**-solicitor**, *s.* der Staatsanwalt. —**work**, *s.* das Kronwerk (*Fort.*).

Cruci—**al**, *adj.* maßgebend, entscheidend; to put to a —al test, auf eine entscheidende Probe stellen. —**feræ**, *pl.* Kreuzblütler (*Bot.*). —**fix**, *s.* das Kruzifix. —**fixion**, *s.* die Kreuzigung. —**form**, *adj.* kreuzförmig. —**fy**, *v.a.* kreuzigen, ans Kreuz schlagen.

Crucian, *s.* die Karausche.

Crucible, *s.* der Schmelztiegel; der Probiertiegel. *Comp.* —**steel**, *s.* der Tiegelgußstahl.

Crud—**e**, *adj.*, —**ely**, *adv.* roh (*also fig.*); (unripe) unreif (*also fig.*); grell, hart (*Paint.*); —e material, der Rohstoff; —e thoughts, unreife Gedanken. —**eness**, *s.* das Rohe; die Rohheit, das Unreife; —eness of a theory, das Unverdaute einer Theorie. —**ity**, *s.* die Rohheit; unüberlegter, unreifer Gedanke.

Cruel, *adj.*, —**ly**, *adv.* grausam; (hard) hart, unbarmherzig; (inhuman) unmenschlich; (painful) peinlich, grausam; (extreme, great) sehr, äußerst (*prov.*). —**ty**, *s.* die Grausamkeit; die Härte; society for the prevention of —ty to animals, der Tierschutzverein.

Cruet, *s.* das (Essig- 2c.) Fläschchen. *Comp.* —**stand**, *s.* die Plattmenage, der Essig- und Öl-ständer.

[1]**Cruise**, *see* Cruse.

[2]**Cruise**, I. *s.* die Vergnügungsfahrt zur See, Kreuztour. II. *v.n.* kreuzen (*Naut.*); to — along a coast, an einer Küste kreuzen. —**r**, *s.* der Kreuzer; armoured —r, der Panzerkreuzer.

Crumb, I. *s.* die Krume, Brosame; die Krume (*opp. to* Crust). II. *v.a.* krümeln. —**le**, *v.* I. *a.* krümeln, zerbröckeln. II. *n.* sich krümeln, zerbröckeln; to —le into dust, in Staub zerfallen. —**ling**, *adj.* hinfällig. —**ly**, *adj.* krumig, bröckelig. *Comp.* —**brush**, *s.* die Krumen-, Tafelbürste. —**cloth**, *s.* eine über den Teppich (unter dem Tisch) ausgebreitete Decke. —**tray**, *s.* die Krumenschaufel.

Crumpet, *s.* weicher, schwach gebackener Kuchen.

Crumple, *v.a.* zerknüllen, zerknittern; a —d piece of paper, ein zerknittertes Stück Papier. II. *v.n.* faltig werden; — up, einschrumpfen.

Crunch, *v.* I. *n.* mit den Zähnen knirschen. II. *a.* zerknirschen, mit den Zähnen zermalmen.

Crupper, *s.* der Schwanzriemen; die Kruppe, das Kreuz (*of a horse*).

Crural, *adj.*; — artery, — vein, die Schenkelpulsader, Schenkelblutader.

Crusade, *s.* der Kreuzzug, die Kreuzfahrt. **—r**, *s.* der Kreuzfahrer; —rs' song, das Kreuzlied.
Cruse, *s.* kleiner Krug; — of honey, Honigkrug.
Crush, I. *v.a.* drücken, drängen (*people, etc.*); (zer)quetschen, zerdrücken, zermalmen; (oppress) unterdrücken; (ruin) vernichten; (overthrow) überwältigen; to — out, auspressen. II. *v.n.* zusammengedrückt werden; zerknittern (*as a dress*); —ed sugar, der Brosamen-, Staub-Zucker. III. *s.* das Gedränge. **—er**, *s.* der Quetschende; der Stoßer, die Quetschmaschine. *Comp.* **—-hat**, *s.* der Quetschhut. **—ing-machine**, *s.* die Quetschmaschine.
Crust, I. *s.* die Kruste, Rinde; der Blätterteig (*of a tart*); — of bread, die Brodkruste, Brotrinde; earth's —, feste Erdrinde; — of a boiler, der Kesselstein; kissing —, der Anstoß am Brote. II. *v.a.* mit Kruste, Rinde überziehen. III. *v.n.* eine Kruste, einen Schorf bilden. **—acea**, *pl.* Krustentiere. **—aceous**, *adj.* gelenkschalig, krustenartig. **—ily**, *adv.* grämlich. **—iness**, *s.* das Krustige, Schalige; das mürrische Wesen. **—y**, *adj.* krustig, schalig; (surly) grämlich, mürrisch; —y fellow, der Sauertopf, sauertöpfische Gesell.
Crutch, *s.* die Krücke; to go on —es, an Krücken gehen. **—ed**, *adj.* auf Krücken gestützt.
Crux, *s.* das Kreuz; die Schwierigkeit, harte Nuß (*fig.*); das Verzwickte.
Cry, I. *v.n.* schreien, rufen; (weep) weinen (for, vor; at, über eine S.); öffentlich ausrufen (*wares, etc. in the streets*); to — **down**, verschreien; to — **for** a thing, etwas weinend verlangen; to — **off**, eine S. plötzlich aufgeben; to — **out**, laut schreien; to — **out** against, sich laut beschweren über (*acc.*); to — one's eyes out, sich (*dat.*) die Augen ausweinen; to — **to**, zurufen, anrufen; to — **up**, rühmen, erheben, (bid up) in die Höhe treiben. II. *s.* der Schrei, Ruf; das Geschrei (*of children, beasts*); das Bellen (*of dogs*); der Ausruf; das Weinen, Klagen; the (popular) —, die Volk(e)sstimme; war —, der Kriegsruf; in full —, laut bellend, in voller Jagd; the cries of London, die Ausrufe der Londoner Straßenverkäufer; to have a good —, sich recht ausweinen. III. *attrib.*; — baby, der kleine Schreihals. **—er**, *see* Crier; der Geierfalk. **—ing**, *adj.* schreiend; himmelschreiend (*sin*); dringend (*need*).
Crypt, *s.* die Krypte, Gruft. **—ical**, *adj.* verborgen, geheim. **—ogam**, *s.* kryptogamische Pflanze. **—ogamia**, *pl.* die Kryptogamen. **—ographer**, *s.* der Geheimschriftschreiber. **—ography**, *s.* die Geheimschrift. **—ology**, *s.* die Geheimsprache.
Crystal, I. *s.* der Kristall; (— glass) das Kristallglas; das Uhrglas (*Horol.*); double refracting —, (Iceland spar) der Doppelspat. II. *adj.* kristallen; kristallklar, hell, durchsichtig. **—line**, *adj.* kristallen; Kristall- (*Anat., etc.*); —line rock, der Bergkristall. **—lization**, **—lisation**, *s.* die Kristallisation, Kristallbildung. **—lize**, **—lise**, *v.* I. *a.* umkristallisieren. II. *n.* sich kristallisieren, in Kristallen anschießen. **—lography**, *s.* die Kristallographie. **—lotype**, *s.* die Photographie auf Glas.
Cub, *s.* das Junge (eines Bären, Löwen, Fuchses 2c.); junges unerzogenes Ding, ungeschlachter Junge; unlicked —, der rohe Bengel, Grünschnabel (*contempt.*).
Cub—ature, *s.* die Kubierung (*Math.*); der kubische Inhalt. **—e**, I. *s.* der Kubus, Würfel (*Geom.*); die Kubikzahl, Würfelzahl (*Arith.*). II. *attrib.*; —e sugar, der Würfelzucker. III. *v.a.* kubieren, auf die dritte Potenz erheben (*Arith.*); das Volumen bestimmen. **—ic(al)**, *adj.* kubisch; —ic contents, der Kubikinhalt; —ic foot, der Kubikfuß; —ic equation, kubische Gleichung. **—iform**, *adj.* würfelförmig. **—oid(al)**, *adj.* kubusähnlich. *Comp.* **—e-root**, *s.* die Kubikwurzel.
Cubeb, *s.* die Kubebe.
Cubicle, *s.* der abgeschorene kleine Schlafraum für je einen Schüler in den Schlafsälen (dormitories) größerer Internatsschulen.
Cubit, *s.* der Kubitus. **—al**, *adj.* Ellbogen-.
Cucking-stool, *s.* der Schandstuhl.
Cucko—ld, *s.* der Hahnrei. II. *v.a.* zum Hahnrei machen. **—ldom**, *s.* die Hahnreischaft. **—o**, *s.* der Kuckuck; the —o calls, der Kuckuck ruft. *Comp.* **—o-clock**, *s.* die (Schwarzwälder) Kuckucksuhr. **—o-flower**, *s.* die Kuckucksblume. **—o-pint**, *s.* gefleckter Aron (*Bot.*).
Cucumber, *s.* die Gurke; as cool as a —, kalt; (calm) ruhig; pickled —, Pfeffergurke.
Cucurbit, *s.* der Destillierkolben (*Chem.*). **—aceous**, *adj.* kürbißähnlich.
Cud, *s.* das Futter im Vormagen; to chew the —, wiederkäuen; überlegen, nachdenken (*fig.*).
Cud-bear, *s.* der rote Indigo (*Scotch*).
Cuddle, *v.* I. *a.* warm halten, verhätscheln. II. *n.* warm liegen, sich zusammenkauern, sich warm anschmiegen; to lie —d up, in ein Knäuel gehüllt liegen. III. *s.* die Umarmung, Liebkosung (*coll.*).
[1]**Cuddy**, *s.* die Kajüte; die Vorratskammer; die Pflicht.
[2]**Cuddy, Cudden, Cuddin**, *s.* der Kohlfisch.
Cudgel, I. *s.* der Knüttel; to take up the —s for a p., jemands Sache verfechten. II. *v.a.* prügeln, schlagen; to — one's brains about a th., sich (*dat.*) den Kopf über eine S. zerbrechen. *Comp.* **—-play**, *s.* das Prügelfechten.
Cue, *s.* der Schwanz; (tail of hair) der Haarzopf; das Stichwort (*Theat.*); (hint) der Wink; (part) die Rolle; (humour) die Laune; der Billardstock, das Queue (*Bill.*); to give a p. his —, einem die Worte in den Mund legen; to take one's — from s.o., sich (*dat.*) einen zur Richtschnur nehmen.
[1]**Cuff**, I. *s.* der Schlag; to be at fisti—s, sich balgen. II. *v.a.* (mit Fäusten) schlagen, knuffen.
[2]**Cuff**, *s.* die Manschette; der Aufschlag (*of a sleeve*).
Cuirass, *s.* der Küraß, Brustharnisch. **—ier**, *s.* der Küraßier.
Cul-de-sac, I. *s.* die Sackgasse. II. *attrib.*; — station, die Kopfstation.
Culinary, *adj.* Küchen-, Koch-; — art, die Kochkunst; — herbs, Küchenkräuter.
Cull, *v.a.* auslesen; (pluck) pflücken; (seek out) aussuchen. **—ing**, *s.* das Auslesen; die Auslese.
Cullender, Colander, *s.* das Sieb, der Durchlauf.
Cullet, *s.* das Bruchglas; der Boden.
[1]**Culm**, *s.* der Halm, Stengel (der Gräser); dürre Halme, Stroh (*collect.*); der Destillierkolben.
[2]**Culm**, *s.* der Kohlenstaub, Kohlengrus, die Staubkohle; die unreine grusartige Anthrazitkohle; der Kulm.
Culminat—e, *v.n.* den Höhepunkt erreichen, kulminieren, gipfeln. **—ion**, *s.* die Kulmination (*Astr.*); der Gipfel, die Spitze, der Höhepunkt (*fig.*).
Culp—ability, *s.* die Strafbarkeit, Schuld. **—able**, *adj.*, **—ably**, *adv.* strafbar; (blamable) strafwürdig, tadelnswert; (guilty) schuldig. **—ableness**, *see* —ability. **—rit**, *s.* der Schuldige; der Angeklagte; der Verbrecher.
Cult, *s.* der Kultus. **—ivable**, **—ivatable**, *adj.* anbaufähig. **—ivate**, *v.a.* anbauen, bebauen, bearbeiten (*land*); kultivieren, erbauen (*crops*); ziehen (*flowers, etc.*); bilden, ausbilden (*the mind, science, etc.*); üben. vervollkommnen (*talents*); pflegen, hegen (*the affections, the taste, etc.*); unterhalten (*an acquaintance, etc.*); verfeinern, gesittet machen (*a people, etc.*). **—ivation**, *s.* der Bau, Anbau, Feldbau; die Bebauung; das Ziehen; die Bildung, Ausbildung; die Gesittung, Verfeinerung, Veredlung; die Übung, Schärfung (*of the intellect*). **—ivator**, *s.* der Anbauer, Landwirt; der Veredelnde, Verbesserer. **—ure**, I. *s.* die Kultur (*also fig.*). II. *v.a.* kultivieren, ausbilden.
Culver, *s.* die Taube (*obs.*).
Culverin, *s.* die Feldschlange (*Artil.*) (*obs.*).
Cumb—er, *v.a.* beschweren, überladen; (obstruct)

hindern; Martha was —ered about much serving, Martha machte sich viel zu schaffen, ihm zu dienen (*B.*). —**ersome**, *adj.* beschwerlich, lästig; (unwieldy) schwer zu handhaben. —**ersomeness**, *s.* die Beschwerlichkeit; (unwieldiness) die Schwerfälligkeit. —**rous**, *adj.*, —**rously**, *adv.* lästig, beschwerlich; (obstructive) hinderlich; (heavy) schwerfällig.

Cumulative, *adj.* (auf)häufend; hinzugefügt (*Law*); anhäufend (*as a drug*).

Cum(m)in *s.* der Kümmel, Kreuzkümmel (*Bot.*).

Cun—eal, —**eated**, —**eiform**, —**iform**, *adj.* keilförmig; —eiform characters, die Keilschrift.

Cunning, I. *adj.*, —**ly**, *adv.* listig, schlau, verschlagen; (skilful) geschickt, kundig, kunstreich; —fellow, der Schlaukopf. II. *s.* die Geschicklichkeit, Kunst; die Erfahrenheit (*B.*); (craftiness) die List, Verschlagenheit, Verschmitztheit.

Cup, I. *s.* die (Trink=)Schale, der Becher; die Tasse (*for tea, etc.*); der Kelch (*at communion; of a flower, etc.*); der Trunk; die (kalte) Bowle; —and ball, das Fangbecher(spiel); —and saucer, Ober= und Untertasse; claret —, die Rotweinbowle; loving —, die Erinnerungsbowle, Becher, der im Kreise herum geht; to be in one's —s, betrunken sein; there's many a slip 'twixt the cup and the lip, zwischen Lipp' und Kelches Rand schwebt der finstern Mächte Hand (*prov.*). II. *v.a.* schröpfen (*Surg.*). —**el**, —**ola**, *see* Cupel, Cupola. *Comp.* —**bearer**, *s.* der Mundschenk. —**board**, *s.* der Schrank; der Speiseschrank. —**board-love**, *s.* eigennützige Liebe (*fig.*). —**ping-glass**, *s.* der Schröpfkopf. —**-shaped**, *adj.* becherförmig.

Cupel, I. *s.* die Kapelle. II. *v.a.* (ab)treiben, läutern (*metals*). —**lation**, *s.* die Kapellenprobe (*Chem.*); das Abtreiben (*Metall.*). —**ling**, *s.* das Abtreiben (auf dem Treibherd), die Läuterung; —ling furnace, der Treibherd.

Cupidity, *s.* die (sinnliche) Begierde.

Cupola, *s.* die Kuppel; —furnace, der Kuppelofen. *Comp.* —**-ship**, *s.* das (Panzer=)Turmschiff.

Cupr—eous, *adj.* kupfern. —**ic**, *adj.*; —ic oxide, das Kupferoxid. —**ous**, *adj.*; —ous oxide, das Kupferoxydul. —**iferous**, *adj.* kupferhaltig.

Cur, *s.* der (schlechte) Hund, Köter; der Hund, Schurke, Halunke (*fig.*). —**rish**, *adj.*, —**rishly**, *adv.* hündisch, beißig, mürrisch.

Cur—able, *adj.* heilbar. —**ability**, —**ableness**, *s.* die Heilbarkeit. —**acy**, *s.* die Pfarr(verweser)=stelle, die Unterpfarre. —**ate**, *s.* der Hilfsgeistliche, Unterpfarrer. —**ative**, *adj.* heilend, Heil=. —**ator**, *s.* der Kurator (*Law*); der Aufseher; Vorsteher (*of a museum*). —**atorship**, *s.* das Amt eines Kurators; die Vormundschaft. —**e**, I. *s.* die Heilung, Kur; (remedy) das Heilmittel; die Seelsorge (eines Geistlichen); die Pfarre; to undergo a —e, in der Kur sein, sich einer Kur unterziehen; past —e, unheilbar. II. *v.a.* heilen; einsalzen, einpökeln, räuchern (*meat*); beizen (*tobacco*); trocknen (*hay, etc.*); what can't be —ed must be endured, was man nicht kann meiden, muß man willig leiden; was muß sein, da schick dich drein (*prov.*). —**ing**, *s.* das Einmachen, Einpökeln.

Curassow, *s.* der Hokko (*Orn.*).

Curb, I. *s.* die Kinnkette; der Prellstein; der Zaum (*fig.*); — of a well, die Brunneneinfassung, der Brunnenrand. II. *v.a.* zäumen; zügeln, im Zaume halten; einfassen. *Comp.* —**-bit**, *s.* die Kinnkettenstange. —**-chain**, *s.* die Kinnkette; die Panzerkette (*Horol.*). —**less**, *adj.* zügellos. —**-roof**, *s.* das Mansardendach. —**-stone**, *s.* der Prellstein.

Curd, I. *s.* die geronnene Milch, der Käsequark; dicke Milch; to turn to —s, gerinnen. II. *attrib.*; — soap, weiße, feste Kernseife. —**le**, *v.n.* (*& a.*) gerinnen (machen); erstarren (machen) (*fig.*). —**ler**, *s.* das Gerinnmittel. —**ling**, *adj.*; blood-—ling, das Blut in den Adern erstarren machend, grauenvoll, entsetzlich.

Curfew, *s.* das Läuten der Abendglocke; (— bell) die Abendglocke, Vesperglocke.

Curio, *s.* die Rarität, Kuriosität. —**sity**, *s.* die Neugier(de); (desire to know) die Wißbegierde; (object of —sity) die Rarität, Kuriosität, Seltenheit; der Sonderling (*coll.*); old —sity shop, der Antiquitätenladen; cabinet of —sities, das Varietätenkabinett. —**so**, *s.* der Kunstkenner, Raritätenkenner; der Sonderling. —**us**, *adj.*, —**usly**, *adv.* neugierig; wißbegierig; genau; (strange) sonderbar, seltsam; (nice) zart, fein, zierlich; (made with care) künstlich. —**usness**, *s.* die Sorgfalt; die Genauigkeit; die Zierlichkeit; *see* —sity.

Curl, I. *s.* der (Haar=)Ringel, die Locke; (wave) die Kräuselung, Wallung; her lip assumed a haughty —, sie warf die Lippen hochmütig auf. II. *v.a.* kräuseln, locken, ringeln, frisieren (*the hair*); kräuseln (*waves*); aufwerfen, rümpfen (*the lip*). III. *v.n.* sich kräuseln, sich locken; wogen (*as waves*); sich winden (*as smoke*); sich schlängeln (*as a serpent*). —**iness**, *s.* das Lockige, Krause. —**ing**, I. *adj.*, —**ingly**, *adv.* kräuselnd. II. *s.* eine Art Spiel auf dem Eise (Schottisch). —**y**, *adj.* lockig, gekräuselt. *Comp.* —**ing-stone**, *s.* der schwere beim —ing=Spiel gebrauchte Stein. —**ing-irons**, —**ing-tongs**, *pl.* das Kräuseleisen; das Brenneisen (*Shipb.*). —**ing-pin**, *s.* die Toupiernadel. —**-paper**, *s.* das Papillotenpapier. —**-papers**, *pl.* Haarwickel, Papierwickel. —**y-haired**, —**y-headed**, *adj.* lockenköpfig.

Curlew, *s.* der Brachvogel; stone —, der Dickfuß.

Curmudgeon, *s.* der Geizhals, Filz; (surly fellow) mürrischer *or* sauertöpfischer Mensch.

Currant, *s.* die Johannisbeere; (dried —) die Korinthe; black —, schwarze Johannisbeere.

Curr—ent, *etc.*, *see* Curren—. —**icle**, *s.* das Kabriolet, Karriol. —**iculum**, *s.* der Kursus; der Lehrplan.

Curren—cy, *s.* die Gangbarkeit, allgemeine Annahme (*of a report, etc.*); der Umlauf, die Gangbarkeit (*of coin, paper, etc.*); der Kurs, die Währung (*C. L.*); (circulating medium) das Umlaufsmittel; —cy of a country, die Landesvaluta; to give —cy to a th., etwas in Umlauf setzen. —**t**, I. *adj.*, —**tly**, *adv.* laufend (*of time*); umlaufend, zirkulierend, gangbar, gültig (*C. L.*); allgemein bekannt, umlaufend (*as a report*); marktgängig (*of prices*); fließend (*as water*); (usual) gang und gäbe, allgemein; (contemporary) gleichzeitig; the —t year, das laufende Jahr; at the —t exchange, zum jetzigen Kurse; —t hand(-writing), die Kurrentschrift; to sell for —t payment, gegen Bar verkaufen; to pass —t, für gültig (voll) angenommen werden; it passes for —t that . . ., es wird allgemein angenommen, daß . . .; this money is not —t, dies Geld ist nicht gangbar; —t price, —t value, der gangbare Wert, laufende Preis; —t opinions, allgemein angenommene Ansichten. II. *s.* der Strom (*of water, air, etc.*); die Strömung (*in the sea*); der Lauf, Gang (*of events, etc.*); —t of air, die Luftströmung; —t of a river, die Strömung eines Flusses; electric —t, elektrischer Strom; secondary —t, der Polarisationsstrom (*Elet.*); — of modern opinion, der Strom moderner Anschauungen.

Curr—ier, *s.* der Lederbereiter, Gerber. —**y**, *v.a.* Leder zurichten; striegeln (*a horse*); to —y a p.'s hide, einem das Fell durchprügeln, durchgerben (*vulg.*); to —y favour with a p., sich bei einem einschmeicheln. *Comp.* —**y-comb**, *s.* der Striegel.

Curr—y, *s.* ein mit —y-powder bereitetes Reisragout. —**ies**, *pl.* mit scharfen indischen Gewürzen eingemachte Fleischkonserven (*C. L.*). *Comp.* —**y-powder**, *s.* ostindisches Ragoutpulver.

Curs—e, I. *v.a.* verfluchen, verwünschen; to —e

a p., einem fluchen, einen zum Teufel wünschen. II. *v.n.* fluchen. III. *s.* der Fluch, die Verwünschung; (evil) das Unglück; intemperance is the —e of this land, die Trunksucht ist der Fluch dieses Landes. **—ed**, **—t**, *adj.*, **—edly**, *adv.* verflucht. **—edness**, *s.* das Verfluchtsein.

Curs—ive, *adj.* laufend; kursiv (*as handwriting*). **—or**, *s.* der Läufer (*Mech.*, *Math.*). **—ory**, *adj.*, **—orily**, *adv.* eilfertig, flüchtig; —ory glance, der flüchtige Blick; der schnelle Überblick. **—oriness**, *s.* die Flüchtigkeit.

Curt, *adj.*, **—ly**, *adv.* kurz, kurzgefaßt, trocken, barsch. **—ail**, *v.a.* abkürzen; beschränken; schmähen, herabsetzen; to —ail a privilege, ein Vorrecht beschränken; to be —ailed (of a th.), (in einer S.) beeinträchtigt werden. **—ailment**, *s.* die Abkürzung.

Curtain, I. *s.* der Vorhang, die Gardine; die Kurtine, der Mittelwall (*Fort.*); das Gezelt (*B.*); to draw the —, den Vorhang vorziehen; to draw up the —, den Vorhang aufziehen; — behind the stage, Schlußgardine; the — rises, der Vorhang geht auf; under the — of night, unter dem Schleier der Nacht. II. *v.a.* mit Vorhängen umhängen. *Comp.* **—-lecture**, *s.* die Gardinenpredigt. **—-pole**, **—-rod**, *s.* die Vorhangstange.

Curtilage, *s.* die Maklergebühr, Courtage.

Curts(e)y, *s.* die Verbeugung, der Knicks; to drop a —, knicksen.

Curv—ated, *adj.* gekrümmt. **—ature**, *s.* die Krümmung; —ature of the spine, die Rückgratsverkrümmung. **—e**, I. *s.* die Krümmung, etwas Krummes *or* Gebogenes; (—ed line) die Krummlinie; die Bogenlinie (*Draw.*); der Bogen (*Shipb.*); caustic —e, Brennlinie; circular —e, Kreislinie. II. *v.a.* krümmen, biegen; —ed, geschweift. **—et**, I. *s.* die Kurbette (*of a horse*). II. *v.a.* Bogensprünge machen, kurbettieren; vor Freude tanzen und springen. **—ilinear**, *adj.* krummlinig.

Cushat, *s.* die Ringeltaube.

Cushion, I. *s.* das Kissen, Polster; die Bande (*Bill.*); das Polsterkapital (*Arch.*); *see* Bobbin; — of a carriage, Sitzkissen. II. *attrib.*; — tire, der Polsterreifen (*Cycl.*). III. *v.a.* mit Kissen versehen; polstern; to — a ball, einen Ball dublieren (*Bill.*); —ed seat, die Polsterbank.

Cusp, *s.* die Spitze (*Arch.*, *Geom.*); das Horn (*of the moon*); — of an arch, die Nase eines Bogens. **—idate(d)**, *adj.* feingespitzt.

Custard, I. *s.* der Eierrahm, die Eiercreme. II. *attrib.*; — powder, ein als Ersatz für Eier dienendes Pulver. *Comp.* **—-apple**, *s.* die Frucht des Flaschenbaums.

Custo—dial, *adj.* vormundschaftlich; die Haft betreffend. **—dian**, *s.* der Hüter; der Kustos. **—dy**, *s.* der Gewahrsam, die Haft; (care) die Aufsicht, Sorge, Hut, Verwahrung; (protection) der Schutz, die Beschützung, Bedeckung. **—s**, *s.* der Bewahrer; —s rotulorum, der Archivar.

Custom, *s.* (habit) die Gewohnheit, der Gebrauch; (usage) die Sitte; every land has its —s, ländlich, sittlich (*prov.*); das Gewohnheitsrecht (*Law*); die Kundschaft (*C. L.*); trade —, die Usance, der Handelsbrauch. **—arily**, *adv. see* —ary. **—ariness**, *s.* die Gebräuchlichkeit, Gewöhnlichkeit. **—ary**, *adj.* (usual) gebräuchlich, üblich, gewöhnlich; (conformable to usage) der Gewohnheit gemäß, herkömmlich; durch das Gewohnheitsrecht besitzend. **—ed**, *see* Accustomed. **—er**, *s.* der Kunde, Käufer; regular —er (of a restaurant, inn), der Stammgast. **—s**, *pl.* die Zölle, der Zoll; board of —s, die Zollbehörde; —s inwards, (outwards) Eingangs-, (Ausfuhr-) zoll; —s policy, die Zollpolitik. *Comp.* **—-house**, I. *s.* das Zollamt, Zollhaus. II. *attrib.*; —-house charges, die Zollspesen; —-house entry, —-house clearance, die Klarierung beim Zollamte; —-house officer, der Zollbeamte.

Cut, I. *v.a.* (*also imperf. & p.p.*) schneiden, hauen, abschneiden; kappen (*the cable*); anschneiden (*bread*); (split) aufspalten; (carve) hauen, schnitzen (*stone, wood*); aufschneiden (*cloth, the leaves of a book, etc.*); (— through) durchschneiden; (— up) zerschneiden; bekommen (*teeth*); mähen (*corn, etc.*); ziehen, stechen (*a ditch*); anhauen (*bricks*); schneiden, schleifen (*gems*); bohren (a tunnel, einen Tunnel); aufspringen machen (*the wind*); beschneiden (*corns, etc.*); beschneiden, abkürzen (*a play, etc.*); to — the knot, den Knoten durchhauen; this is — and come again, hier ist Vorrat in Hülle und Fülle (*coll.*); to — a p., einen (beim Begegnen) ignorieren, nicht sehen wollen, schneiden; to — the beard, den Bart scheren *or* schneiden; to — capers, Kapriolen schneiden; to — a deplorable figure, sich jämmerlich anstellen; eine jämmerliche Figur machen, eine traurige Rolle spielen; to — cards, die Karten abheben; finely — features, feingeschnittene Züge; to — one's own throat, sich (*dat.*) den Hals abschneiden (*fig.*); to — a lecture, eine Vorlesung *or* ein Kolleg schwänzen (*coll.*); to — one's teeth, zahnen, Zähne bekommen; a —ting remark, eine beißende Bemerkung; —ting wind, ein (das Gesicht) schneidender Wind; to — a dash, groß tun; to — (s.o.) short, (einen) plötzlich unterbrechen; he — me short, er fiel mir ins Wort; to — the matter short . . ., um es kurz zu machen . . .; to — one's stick, sich eilig davon machen (*vulg.*); — your coat according to your cloth, strecke dich nach der Decke (*prov.*); to — **asunder**, durchschneiden, von einander schneiden; to — **away**, abschneiden, verschneiden; to — **down**, niederhauen, fällen, (Getreide) abmähen, (Holz) stemmen, (Preise) herabsetzen; verkürzen, verringern, vermindern (*fig.*); to — **in** stone, in Stein hauen; to — in two, entzwei hauen, durchschneiden; to — **off**, abschneiden, beschneiden; umstoßen (*the entail*); to — off the enemy's retreat, dem Feinde den Rückzug abschneiden; to — off with a shilling, to — off an heir, den rechtmäßigen Erben von der Erbschaft ausschließen; to — off hopes, Hoffnungen vernichten; to — off supplies, die Zufuhr abschneiden; to — off a connection, eine Verbindung abbrechen; to be — off, sterben (*sl.*); to — **out**, aus-, zu-schneiden (*dresses, etc.*); to — a p. out, einen ausstechen; to be — out for . . ., zu . . . gemacht *or* geboren sein, das Zeug zu einer S. haben; to — out work for a p., einem viel zu schaffen machen; to — one's way **through**, sich durchhauen; to — **to** the quick, bis ins Leben schneiden, aufs tiefste verwunden; to — to the heart, ins Herz treffen, aufs bitterste kränken; to — to pieces, in Stücke hauen; to — **up**, aufschneiden, zerschneiden, zerlegen; to — a p. up, einen schlecht machen, heruntermachen; to — up a book, ein Buch herunterreißen, sehr streng kritisieren; his conduct — me up greatly, sein Betragen betrübte *or* ergriff mich aufs Höchste. II. *v.n.* schneiden, hauen; sich schneiden lassen; to — and run, sich eiligst davon machen (*sl.*); to — **across** (*country, etc.*), einen kürzeren Weg (durchs Feld) einschlagen; to — **for** deal, (cards) um das Geben abheben; to — for the stone, den Stein schneiden; to — **in**, ziehen, um die Mitspielenden zu bestimmen (*Cards*); to — **up** rough, böse, aufgebracht sein; to — **under**, unter dem Preise verkaufen (*vulg.*). III. *s.* der Schnitt, Hieb; die Wunde; (— with a whip) der Peitschenhieb; der Durchschnitt (*Draw.*); der Kupferstich (*Engr.*); (wood-—) der Holzschnitt; der Kleiderschnitt (*Tail., etc.*); (piece) der Schnitt, das Stückchen; das Schnitt (*Typ.*); das Ignorieren, Nichtsehenwollen (*fig.*); to draw —s, losen, Hölzchen ziehen; short —, Richtweg; whose — is it? wer muß abheben? direct —, das direkte Ignorieren; — and thrust, das Hieb- und Stoß-fechten; —-and-thrust sword, der Pallasch; that 's **a** — above me, so weit reichen meine Kräfte nicht, das ist mir zu hoch (*vulg.*). IV. *p.p. & adj.* geschnitten, abgeschnitten; geschliffen (*glass*); —and dry *or* dried, fertig zum Gebrauch, fix und fertig; im voraus fertig; schablonenhaft, abgedroschen; — stone, der behauene Stein. **—ter**, *s.* der Schneidende; der Zuschneider (*Tail.*); der Kutter (*Naut.*); das Schneidezeug (*Mach.*); die Schneid(e)maschine (*for fodder*); der Grabstichel (*Engr.*); hair —ter, der Haarschneider, Friseur; revenue —ter, das Zollwachtschiff. **—ting**, I. *adj.* scharf, schneidend, beißend; *see* Cut I.; —ting edge, die Schneide; —ting out, das Zuschneiden (*Tail.*); das Prisenmachen in den Häfen (*Naut.*). II. *s.* das Schneiden; der Einschnitt, Durchstich (*Railw., etc.*); der Steckling, Setzling (*Bot.*); (felled wood) der Abtrieb. **—tings**, *pl.* Schnitzel, Späne, Abfälle; newspaper —tings, Ausschnitte aus Zeitungen; *see* —ting. *Comp.* **—away**, *adj.*; —away coat, vorn abgeschnittener Rock. **—-glass**, *s.* das geschliffene Glas. **—purse**, I. *s.* der Beutelschneider. II. *adj.* spitzbübisch. **—throat**, I. *s.* der Halsabschneider. II. *adj.* meuchelmörderisch. **—ting-(out-)board**, *s.* der Zuschneidetisch (*Tail.*). **—ting-line**, *s.* die Schnittlinie (*Typ.*). **—water**, *s.* das Brustholz des Gallions (*Naut.*). **—-work**, *s.* die durchbrochene Arbeit, Stickerei.

Cut—aneous, *adj.* zur Haut gehörig; —aneous diseases, Hautkrankheiten; —aneous eruption, der Hautausschlag. **—icle**, *s.* das Oberhäutchen, die Epidermis (*Bot., Anat.*). **—icular**, *adj.* die Oberhaut betreffend.

Cute, *adj.* (*coll.*) *see* Acute.

Cutl—ass, *s.* der Stutzsäbel; das Entermesser (*Naut.*). **—er**, *s.* der Messerschmied. **—ery**, *s.* die Messerschmiedewaren; das Messerschmiedehandwerk.

Cutlet, *s.* das Kotelett, die Kotelette.

Cuttle—-bone, *s.* das weiße Fischbein. **—-fish**, *s.* der Tintenfisch, Blackfisch.

Cutty, I. (*dial.*) *adj.* kurz. II. *s.* stämmiges, untersetztes Mädchen; kleine Dirne; (—-pipe) kurze Tabakspfeife. *Comp.* **—-stool**, *s.* der niedrige Schemel; der Armesünderstuhl.

Cyan—ate, I. *adj.* cyansauer. II. *s.* das cyansaure Salz. **—ic**, *adj.*; —ic acid, die Cyansäure. **—ide**, *s.* das Cyanid (*Chem.*). **—ite**, *s.* der Cyanit (*Min.*).

Cyclamen, *s.* das Alpenveilchen (*Bot.*).

Cycl—e, I. *s.* (bi—e, tri—e) das Fahrrad; (circle) der Zirkel, Kreis; (—e of time) der Zyklus, Zeitkreis; der Cyklus (*of legends, etc.*); recurring in —es, periodisch wiederkehrend; —e of the moon (sun), der Mond=(Sonnen=)zyklus; —e of indiction, der Indiktionszyklus. II. *v.n.*; to —e, radfahren, radeln. **—ic**, *adj.*; —ic poets, die Zykliker. **—ing**, *adj.*; Radfahr=, Radler=; —ing club, der Radfahr(er)verein, Radlerverein; —ing costume, der Radleranzug, das Radfahrkostüm; —ing knickers, die Radfahrkniehose. **—ist**, *s.* Radfahrer, Radler; lady —ist, die Radlerin; —ists' touring club, der Radfahr(er)verein, Radlerklub; accommodation for —ists, Unterkunft für Radfahrer. **—oid**, *s.* die Zykloide, Radlinie (*Geom.*). **—one**, *s.* der Zyklon, Wirbelsturm. **—opædia, —opedia**, *s.* die Enzyklopädie, das Konversationslexikon. **—opædic, —pedic**, *adj.* enzyklopädisch. **—opean**, *adj.* zyklopisch; ungeheuer. **—ops**, *s.* der Zyklop.

Cygnet, *s.* der junge Schwan.

Cylind—er, I. *s.* der Zylinder, die Walze (*Geom.*); die Bohrung, Seele (*of a gun*); die Walze, Druckwalze (*Typ.*); der Dampfzylinder (*Locom. etc.*); der Aufwinder (*Spin.*). II. *attrib.*; —er jacket, der Zylindermantel (*Locom., etc.*); —er printing, der Walzendruck; —er watch, die Zylinderuhr. **—ric(al)**, *adj.* zylindrisch, walzenförmig; kugelgleich gebohrt (*Artil.*).

Cymbal, *s.* die Zimbel (*Mus.*).

Cyme, *s.* die Afterdolde (*Bot.*).

Cyn—ic, I. *adj.*, **—ical**, *adj.*. **—ically**, *adv.* zynisch; menschenfeindlich; spöttisch, satirisch. II. *s.* der Zyniker. **—osure**, *s.* der kleine Bär; der Polarstern im kleinen Bären (*Astr.*); der Leitstern (*fig.*); der Anziehungspunkt.

Cypher, *see* Cipher.

Cypress, *s.* die Zypresse.

Cyprian, I. *adj.* zyprisch. II. *s.* die Buhldirne.

Cyst, *s.* der Eitersack. **—ic**, *adj.* Blasen=; —ic arteries, Gallenblasenarterien; —ic tumour, die Balggeschwulst. **—otomy**, *s.* der Blasenschnitt.

Czar, *s.* der Zar. **—ina**, *s.* die Zarin, Zariza. **—owitch**, *s.* der Zarewitsch.

D

D, d, 𝔇, 𝔡, D (*Mus.*); D = 500. *For abbreviations see the index at the end of the English-German part.*

Dab, I. *v.a.* mit der flachen Hand leicht schlagen, antippen (*coll.*); mit etwas Weichem oder Feuchtem leise berühren, betupfen; abklatschen, klischieren; *see* Daub. II. *s.* der Klecks, Spritzfleck; (soft blow) der Klaps, sanfte Schlag; das Klümpchen; to be a — at a th., sich auf eine S. verstehen (*coll.*). **—ber**, *s.* der Tupfballen; das Bällchen (*Engr.*). **—ble**, *v.* I. *a.* netzen, bespritzen. II. *n.* plätschern; to —ble in a science, in eine Wissenschaft (hinein) pfuschen. **—bler**, *s.* der Plätscherer; der Stümper, Pfuscher. **—blingly**, *adv.* stümperhaft. *Comp.* **—chick**, *s.* (eben ausgekrochenes) Küchlein; der Steißfuß, Haubentaucher (*Orn.*).

Da capo, noch einmal (*Mus.*).

Dace, *s.* der Weißfisch, der Häsling.

Dactyl, *s.* der Daktylus. **—ic**, *adj.* daktylisch. **—ioglyphy**, *s.* die Ring= *or* Stein=schneidekunst. **—iology**, *s.* die Lehre von den geschnittenen Fingerringen, Gemmenkunde. **—ology**, *s.* die Fingersprache.

Dad, —a, —dy, *s.* Papa, Väterchen (*coll.*). *Comp.* **—dy-long-legs**, *s.* die langbeinige Mücke (*Ent.*).

Dado, *s.* die Bekleidung der untern Zimmerwand, die Täfelung; der obere Tapetenabschluß nach der Decke zu; Tapete, die ein Zimmergetäfel nachahmt; der Würfel einer Säule, Postamentwürfel (*Arch.*).

Daffodil, *s.* die gelbe Narzisse (*Bot.*).

Daft, *adj.* einfältig, verdreht, närrisch (*Scotch*). **—ness**, *s.* die Einfältigkeit, Verrücktheit.

Dagger, *s.* der Dolch; der Rappierdolch (*Fenc.*) (*obs.*); das Kreuzzeichen (*Typ.*); to look —s at a p., einen mit den Augen erdolchen; to be at —s drawn, sich (*dat.*) *or* einander feindlich gegenüberstehen, Todfeinde sein.

Daggle, *v.* I. *a.* durch den Kot hinschleppen, besudeln. II. *n.* durch den Kot gehen; im Schmutz *or* feuchtem Grase wühlen. *Comp.* **—-tail**, I. *s.* die Schlumpliese (*obs.*). II. *adj.*, **—(d-)tail**, *adj.* mit unten beschmutztem Kleide; beschmutzt.

Daguerreotype, *s.* das Daguerreotyp, Lichtbild.

Dahl—ia, *s.* die Georgine (*Bot.*). **—ine**, *s.* das Dahlin (*Chem.*).

Daily, I. *adj. & adv.* täglich; (usual) üblich; — task, das Tag(e)werk; — paper, die täglich erscheinende Zeitung, Tageszeitung, das Tag(e)=blatt; — governess, die Halbgouvernante (welche nicht im Hause der Zöglinge wohnt); — routine, die Tageseinteilung; — experience, tagtägliche Erfahrung; event of — occurrence, alltägliches Ereignis; — wages, der Tag(e)lohn. II. *s.* = daily paper; the dailies, die Tagesblätter, die Tagespresse.

Daint—ies, *pl.* das Naschwerk. **—ily**, *adv.* lecker, zierlich, niedlich; to fare —ily, lecker leben. **—iness**, *s.* die Leckerhaftigkeit (*in eating*); die Leckerei (*of food*); (fastidiousness) die Feinheit, Zierlichkeit; (sauciness) der Hochmut. **—y**, I. *adj.* lecker, delikat, köstlich (*of food*); lecker(haft) (*of persons*); (nice) zart, zartgeformt, fein, zierlich; (neat) sauber, nett; (scrupulous) geziert, umständlich; —y bit, *see* —y II. II. *s.* der Leckerbissen.

Dairy, *s.* die Milchkammer (*in a house*); die Molkerei; Käserei, Milchwirtschaft. *Comp.* **—-cart**, *s.* der Milchwagen. **—-farm**, *s.* die Meierei, Milchwirtschaft. **—-keeper**, *s.* der Molkereibesitzer. **—-maid**, *s.* das Milchmädchen. **—-man**, *s.* der Milchmann. **—-room**, *s.* die Milchkammer.

Dais, *s.* der erhöhte Platz in einem Saale, die Estrade; der Thronsitz, Thronhimmel, Baldachin.

Dais—ied, *adj.* mit Maßlieben übersäet, geschmückt. **—y**, *s.* das Marienblümchen, Gänseblümchen; dog —y, die Hundekamille; ox-eye —y, die Wucherblume.

Dakoit, *s.* der ostindische Bandit.

Dale, *s.* das Tal. *Comp.* **—sman**, *s.* der Talbewohner.

Dall—iance, *s.* das Schäkern, der Liebeshandel; das Liebkosen, die Liebkosung; (delay) die Verzögerung, der Aufschub (*obs.*); der Scherz; (trifling) die Tändelei. **—y**, *v.n.* schäkern, tändeln; liebeln; (waste time) die Zeit vertändeln.

Daltonism, *s.* die Farbenblindheit.

[1]**Dam**, I. *s.* der Deich, Damm, Wasserbrecher, das Wehr. II. *v.a.* (— in, — up) abdämmen, eindämmen, zudämmen; stauchen (*Mill.*).

[2]**Dam**, *s.* die Mutter (der vierfüßigen Tiere). **—e**, *s.* die Frau, ältliche *or* vornehme Dame; die Lehrerin einer ländlichen Elementarschule. *Comp.* **—e('s)-school**, *s.* die Elementarschule.

Damage, I. *s.* der Schaden, Nachteil; (loss) der Verlust; — by sea, die Havarie; to do a p. —, einem Schaden zufügen; what 's the —? was kostet es? was habe ich zu bezahlen? (*vulg.*). II. *v.a.* beschädigen, Schaden zufügen. **—able**, *adj.* leichtverderbend; zerbrechlich; zart, heikel. **—d**, *p.p. & adj.* beschädigt; in a —d state, in schadhaftem Zustande. **—s**, *pl.* der Schadenersatz; to make good the —s, (einen) für den Verlust entschädigen, einem den Verlust vergüten; to recover —s, entschädigt werden, Entschädigung erhalten.

Damas—k, I. *s.* der Damast; linen —k, Leinendamast; silk —k, Seidendamast; woollen —k, worsted —k, der Woll(en)damast. II. *attrib.*; —k loom, der Damastwebstuhl. III. *adj.* damasten; —k carpet, der Damastteppich. IV. *v.a.* damaszieren (*steel*); damassieren, mit Bildern oder Blumen weben; verzieren (*fig.*). **—keen**, **—cene**, *v.a.* damaszieren. **—king**, *s.* die Bildweberei. **—sin**, *s.* der Gold- oder Silber-damast. *Comp.* **—k-rose**, *s.* die Damaszenerrose.

Damn, *v.a.* verdammen; (condemn) verschreien, verwerfen; (curse) verwünschen; auszischen (*a play*); — it! verwünscht! hol's der Henker! the —ed, die Verdammten. **—able**, *adj.*, **—ably**, *adv.* verdammlich, verdammungswürdig, verdammenswert; verdammt, abscheulich. **—ableness**, *s.* die Verdammlichkeit. **—ation**, I. *s.* die Verdammnis, Verdammung. II. *int.* Donnerwetter! verwünscht! **—atory**, *adj.* verdammend. **—ing**, *p. & adj.* verdammend.

Damp, I. *adj.* feucht; — rot, nasse Fäulnis. II. *s.* die Feuchtigkeit; his presence casts a — upon the conversation, seine Gegenwart wirkt lähmend auf die Unterhaltung *or* setzt der U. einen Dämpfer auf. III. *v.a.* (be)feuchten, anfeuchten, niederschlagen (*fig.*); entkräften (*zeal*); to — a p.'s spirits, einem den Mut benehmen, einen niederschlagen. **—er**, *s.* der Schieber, die Zugklappe (*of an oven*); die Klappe (*Locom.*); der Dämpfer (*Mus. & fig.*); —er of a chimney, die Klappe, das Register. **—ish**, *adj.* ein wenig feucht. **—ness**, *s.* die Feuchtigkeit. **—s**, *pl.* Nebeldünste; das böse schlagende Wetter (*Min.*). *Comp.* **—-proof**, *adj.* vor Nässe schützend, gegen Nässe geschützt.

Damsel, *s.* junges Mädchen, das Fräulein, die Jungfrau (*poet. B.*); kleines, unerwachsenes Mädchen; das Edelfräulein (*obs.*).

Damson, *s.* die Damaszener Pflaume.

Danc—e, I. *v.a.* tanzen; tanzen lassen; kochen, heiß aufwallen; it makes one's blood —e, es bringt einem das Blut in Wallung; to —e attendance on a p., einem häufig seine Aufwartung machen, (einer Dame) sehr den Hof machen. II. *v.n.* tanzen. III. *s.* der Tanz; die Tanzmusik, Tanzweise; die Tanzpartie, der Ball. **—er**, *s.* der (die) Tänzer(in). **—ing**, *s.* das Tanzen. *Comp.* **—ing-girl**, *s.* die Tänzerin. **—ing-lesson**, *s.* die Tanzstunde. **—ing-master**, *s.* der Tanzlehrer. **—ing-room**, *s.* der Tanzsaal. **—ing-school**, *s.* die Tanzschule.

Dandelion, *s.* der Löwenzahn (*Bot.*).

[1]**Dand—er**, *v.n.* umherschweifen (*prov.*). **—ified**, *adj.* stutzerhaft. **—le**, *v.a.* auf dem Schoße, auf den Knien oder Armen schaukeln, wiegen, hüpfen lassen; liebkosen (*obs.*); tändeln mit (*obs.*). **—y**, *s.* der Stutzer, Modenarr; eine Art Kutter (*Naut.*). **—yish**, *adj.* stutzerhaft. **—yism**, *s.* das stutzerhafte Wesen.

[2]**Dand—er**, *see* —ruff; der Zorn (*fig.*); to feel one's —er rise, sein Blut kochen fühlen (*sl.*). **—ruff**, *s.* der (Kopf-)Schorf, Kopfgrind, die Schuppen auf dem Kopfe.

Dang; — it! *see* Damn it!

Danger, *s.* die Gefahr; in case of —, im Falle von Gefahr, falls Gefahr droht *or* drohen sollte; the nation is in — of war, dem Volke droht ein Krieg. **—ous**, *adj.*, **—ously**, *adv.* gefährlich. **—ousness**, *s.* die Gefährlichkeit. *Comp.* **—-signal**, **—-whistle**, *s.* das Notsignal.

Dangle, *v.n.* hängen, baumeln, hin und her flattern; to — about *or* after girls, die Mädchen umflattern, ihnen die Cour machen. **—r**, *s.* der Schürzenjäger, Mädchenjäger, Damenheld.

Dank, *adj.* dunstig, feucht, naßkalt.

Daphne, *s.* der Lorbeerbaum.

Dapper, *adj.*, **—ly**, *adv.* niedlich, schmuck, nett; (brisk) behend, gewandt.

Dapple, I. *adj.* getupft, fleckig; — gray, apfelgrau; — gray (horse), der Apfelschimmel. II. *v.a.* sprenkeln, tüpfeln, scheckig machen.

Dar—e, I. *v.n.* dürfen, wagen, sich erkühnen, sich getrauen; I —e not tell him, ich getraue mich *or* mir nicht, es ihm zu sagen; I —e not do it, ich wage nicht *or* ich getraue mich nicht es zu tun: if I may —e to say so, wenn ich so sagen darf; I —e say, das glaube ich wohl; ohne Zweifel, gewiß; how —e you . . . ? wie können Sie es wagen . . . ? II. *v.a.* herausfordern, trotzen. **—ing**, I. *adj.*, **—ingly**, *adv.* kühn, tapfer, mutig; (rash) verwegen; (audacious) keck, dreist; (presumptuous) anmaßend. II. *s.* die Kühnheit, der Mut; die Keckheit; deed of —ing, die kühne Tat, Heldentat. **—ingness**, *s. see* —ing II.

Dark, I. *adj.*, **—ly**, *adv.* dunkel, finster; (opaque) undurchsichtig; schwärzlich, dunkel (*in colour*); (obscure) dunkel; (mysterious) geheimnisvoll, dunkel; (ignorant) unwissend, unaufgeklärt; (gloomy) finster, düster; (blind) blind; (concealed) verborgen; — hued, schwarzfarbig; — lantern, die Blendlaterne; — saying, ein dunkler, rätselhafter Ausspruch, ein Rätsel; the — ages, die dunkeln Zeiten, das Mittelalter. II. *s.* das Dunkel, die Dunkelheit; after —, nach Eintritt der Dunkelheit; to leave a p. in the —, einen in Unwissenheit lassen, nicht aufklären (*fig.*). **—en**, *v.* I. *a.* verdunkeln, verfinstern; verdüstern, verdunkeln, trübe machen (*fig.*); (perplex) verwirren; (sadden) trüben; verschmelzen (shades, Lichttöne); I shall never —en his doors again, ich werde seine Schwelle nie wieder betreten. II. *n.* dunkel werden. **—ish**, *adj.* schwärzlich (*of colour*); etwas dunkel, trübe; dämmerig. **—ling**, I. *adv.* im Dunkeln. II. *adj.* dunkel; düster (*fig.*); verdunkelnd; geblendet. **—ness**, *s.* die Finsternis, Dunkelheit; die Dunkelheit, Unwissenheit (*fig.*); acts of —ness, schlechte, lasterhafte Taten; powers of —ness, die Mächte der

Finsternis, Höllenmächte. —**some**, *adj.* dunkel, trübe. —**y**, *s.* der Neger (*coll.*). *Comp.* —**browed**, *adj.* finster. —-**eyed**, *adj.* dunkeläugig. —-**room**, *s.* die Dunkelkammer (*Photogr.*).

Darling, I. *adj.* teuer, lieb; Lieblings- . . .; my own — boy, mein einzig geliebter Junge, Herzensjunge; — love, Herzensschatz, Herzgeliebte(r). II. *s.* der Liebling, das Herzblatt, Herzblättchen.

Darn, I. *v.a.* stopfen. II. *s.* das Gestopfte, der Stopffleck, die Stopfnaht (*in cloth*). —**er**, *s.* die Stopferin. —**ing**, *s.* das Stopfen. *Comp.* —**ing-cotton**, *s.* das Stopfgarn. —**ing-needle**, *s.* die Stopfnadel. —**ing-wool**, —**ing-yarn**, *s.* das Stopfgarn.

Darnel, *s.* der Lolch (*Bot.*).

Dart, I. *s.* der Wurfspieß, Pfeil; die abgenähte Falte, der Abnäher (*in skirts*); plötzliche Bewegung, der Sprung. II. *v.a.* (Pfeile, Geschosse) schleudern, werfen; to — a look at a p., einem einen schnellen Blick zuwerfen. III. *v.n.* fliegen, davonschießen, sich schnell und plötzlich bewegen; sich stürzen (at, on a p., auf einen); to — forth, hervorbrechen (from, aus).

Dash, I. *v.a.* (strike) schlagen, schmeißen; (— to pieces) zerschmettern; (— out) ausschlagen, zerschmeißen; (shatter) zerschmettern; (—over) übergießen; (mix) vermischen, vermengen; (bespatter) bespritzen; ausschütten (*water*); to — the pen through (a line, eine Zeile) ausstreichen; to — off, schnell entwerfen, aufs Papier hinwerfen; to — a p.'s spirits, einen niederschlagen; to — a p.'s hopes, einem die Hoffnung benehmen; to — a p.'s brains out, einem den Schädel einschlagen. II. *v.n.* stoßen, schlagen; stürzen; (splash) platschen; to — **against**, schlagen, stoßen, rennen (an eine S.); scheitern (an einer S.); to — **down**, niederstürzen (*as a waterfall*); to — **into**, hineinstürzen in, einbrechen in; to — **off**, (drive) schnell abfahren, (ride) dahinsprengen, (run) fortlaufen, ausreißen; the horses —ed off at full gallop, die Pferde sprengten in gestrecktem Galopp davon; to — **over**, überlaufen; the water —ed over the ship's side, das Wasser stürzte über die Seiten des Schiffes; to — **through**, durchbrechen, durchpatschen. III. *s.* der Schlag, Schmiß, Streich; (collision) das Zusammenstoßen, der Zusammenstoß; (clash) der Klatsch; (rush) der Sturz, Anlauf; (— of the pen) der Federstrich; der Strich (*Mus.*, *Tele.*, *Typ.*); (mixture) die Beimischung; der Anflug (*fig.*); a — of eccentricity, ein Anflug von Überspanntheit; to cut a —, eine Figur machen; at first —, auf das erste Mal. —**er**, *s.* flotter, schneidiger Kerl; die Radschaufel. —**ing**, *adj.* auffallend gekleidet; prunkend; platschend, rauschend; flott, fesch (*coll.*); the —ing exploit of Lieut. H., die kühne Wagetat des Lieutenants H.; —ing fellow, flotter, verwegener Bursche; —ing officer, schneidiger Offizier. *Comp.* —-**board**, *s.* das Schmutzleder (*of carriages*); die Schaufel (*of a paddle-wheel*).

Dastard, I. *s.* die Memme. II. —**ly**, *adj. & adv.* feig; abscheulich, fluchwürdig, heimtückisch. —**liness**, *s.* die Feigheit.

Dat—a, *pl.* Data; Angaben, Tatsachen, die besonderen Einzelheiten. —**e**, I. *s.* das Datum, die Zeitangabe; die Jahreszahl (*on coins*); (time) die Zeit; die Verfallzeit eines Wechsels (*C. L.*); up to —e, heutig, zeitgemäß, modern; to bring a book up to —e, ein Buch zeitgemäß umarbeiten *or* ausstatten; out of —e, veraltet; your letter bearing —e the 9th inst., Ihr vom 9ten dieses datierter Brief; of this —e, vom heutigen Tage; two months after —e, zwei Monat nach d. Datum; long —e, lange Sicht (*C. L.*). II. *v.a.* datieren. III. *v.n.*; to —e (from), sich herschreiben (von). —**eless**, *adj.* ohne Datum. —**ive**, *s.* (—ive case) der Wemfall, Dativ. —**um**, *s.* die gegebene Tatsache; die gegebene Größe (*Math.*); die Grundlage.

Date, *s.* die Dattel. *Comp.* —-**palm**, —-**tree**, *s.* die Dattelpalme.

Daub, I. *v.a.* beschmieren, besudeln; schmieren, sudeln (in painting, im Malen). II. *v.n.* schmieren, sudeln (*Paint.*). III. *s.* der Klecks; das Sudelgemälde (*Paint.*); der Lehm; wattle and —, mit Lehm beworfenes Flechtwerk. —**er**, *s.* der Sudler, Schmierer, Farbenkleckser.

Daughter, *s.* die Tochter; —-in-law, Schwiegertochter; step-—, Stieftochter. —**liness**, *s.* das töchterliche Betragen. —**ly**, *adj.* töchterlich.

Daunt, *v.a.* entmutigen. —**less**, *adj.*, —**lessly**, *adv.* furchtlos, kühn; (undaunted) unerschrocken.

Dauphin, *s.* der Dauphin. —**ess**, *s.* die Dauphine.

Davenport, *s.* das (Schreibtisch-) Schränkchen.

Davit, *s.* die Jütte, der Davit (*Naut.*).

Davy, *s.* (*coll. corrupted from* Affidavit) der Eid; on my —, auf mein Wort! (*coll.*).

Davy-lamp, *s.* (Davy's) Sicherheitslampe.

Daw, *s.* die Dohle (*Orn.*).

Dawdle, I. *v.n.* tändeln, dahlen; to — one's time away, die Zeit vergeuden *or* vertrödeln. II. *s.*, —**r**, *s.* der müßige Arbeiter, Trödler; der Tagedieb; die Schlafmütze.

[1]**Dawk**, *s.* die Fahrpost (in Ostindien).

[2]**Dawk**, *s.* (*dial.*) der Kerb, Einschnitt, Schlitz (*Carp.*).

Dawn, I. *s.* die Dämmerung, Morgendämmerung; (beginning) der Anfang, Anbeginn; (first ray) der erste Lichtstrahl; der Morgen (*of life*); — of intelligence, das Erwachen des Verstandes. II. *v.n.* dämmern, tagen; it —ed upon me, mir ging plötzlich auf. —**ing**, I. *s. see* Dawn. II. *adj.* dämmernd, sich erschließend, beginnend.

Day, I. *s.* der Tag; (—light) das Tageslicht; (time) die Lebenszeit, Zeit; (term) die Frist, der bestimmte Tag; to win the —, den Sieg *or* die Schlacht gewinnen; the — was his, ihm fiel der Sieg zu; he was a good workman in his —, er war seiner Zeit ein tüchtiger Arbeiter; they have had their —, sie haben ihre Zeit gehabt, ihre Zeit ist jetzt vorüber; in the —s of our forefathers, zur Zeit *or* in den Zeiten unserer Väter; as clear as —, so klar wie die Sonne; to-—, heute; one of these —s, in diesen Tagen, dieser Tage, bald; the other —, vor einigen Tagen; for ever and a —, für immer und ewig; to have a (fine) — of it, einen (schönen) Tag haben; to this —, bis auf den heutigen Tag; to a —, (genau) auf den Tag; from this — forward, von heute an; the — before yesterday, vorgestern; the — after to-morrow, übermorgen; every other —, einen Tag um den andern, alle zwei Tage; this — week, heute über acht Tage; this — month, heute in *or* über vier Wochen; — after —, — by —, Tag für Tag, (daily) täglich; from — to —, von Tag zu Tag, von einem Tag zum andern; —-to- — money, tägliches Geld (*C. L.*); in these —s, now-a-—s, heutzutage; twice a —, täglich zweimal, zweimal des Tages; what's the time of —? wie viel Uhr ist es? every dog has his —, alles hat seine Zeit (*prov.*); — of grace, die Gnadenzeit (*Theol.*); —s of grace, Verzugstage (*Law*), Respekttage, Respittage (*C. L.*); intercalary —, Schalttag; pay-—, Zahltag, Verfalltag; settling —, Abrechnungstag. II. *attrib.*; — training college, Lehrer(innen)seminar, welches ein Externat ist. *Comp.* —**book**, *s.* das Tagebuch, Journal (*C. L.*). —-**boy**, *see* —-scholar. —**break**, *s.* der Tagesanbruch. —**dream**, *s.* die Träumerei; —dreams, Phantasiegebilde. —-**labour**, *s.* das Tagewerk. —-**labourer**, *s.* der Tag(e)löhner. —**light**, *s.* das Tageslicht; der Zwischenraum zwischen wettfahrenden Booten; in broad —light, am hellen lichten Tage. —-**scholar**, *s.* der Tagschüler, Extern-Schüler, Externe. —-**school**, *s.* das Externat. —-**shaft**, *s.* der Lichtschacht. —**spring**, *s.* der Tagesanbruch. —**star**, *s.* der Morgenstern. —'**s-work**, *s.* die Tagesarbeit; das Etmal (*Naut.*). —**time**, *s.* der Tag.

Daz—e, *v.a.* (dazzle) blenden; (stupefy) betäuben. **—zle**, *v.a.* blenden. **—zling**, *p. & adj.*, **—zlingly**, *adv.* blendend (*also fig.*).

Deacon, *s.* der Diakonus. **—ess**, *s.* die Diakonissin. **—ry**, *s.* das Diakonat.

Dead, I. *adj.* tot; (— to) unempfindlich, abgestorben (für); tot, leer, öde (*of a neighbourhood*); abständig (*of timber*); abgestorben, dürr (*as plants*); tot, still, flau (*C. L.*); glanzlos, matt, tot (*of colour*); schal, flau, matt (*of beer, etc.*); verloschen, verlöscht, tot (*as a fire*); erloschen, glanzlos (*of eyes*); tief (*of sleep*); (unemployed) unbenutzt, totliegend; bürgerlich tot (*Law*); — as a doornail, mausetot; to be a — man, ein Kind des Todes sein; he shot her —, er schoß sie tot; to wait for — men's shoes, auf eine Erbschaft lauern; to make a — set at a th., einen entschlossenen Angriff machen auf (*acc.*); to come to a — stop, plötzlich anhalten; —-and-alive, halbtot; — against, gerade entgegen; — angle, toter Winkel; — bargain, der Spottpreis; — born, totgeboren; — calm, tote Stille, völlige Windstille; — centre, *see* — point; — certainty, zuverlässige, völlige Gewißheit; to a — certainty, völlig sicher; — colouring, das Grundieren, Untermalen (*Paint.*); — flesh, abgestorbenes, totes, faules Fleisch; — gold, mattes Gold; — heat, der unentschiedene Wettlauf; — letters, unbestellbare Briefe; a — level, eine einförmige Ebene; die Eintönigkeit (*fig.*); literature sank to a — level, die Litteratur sank zu höchster Eintönigkeit und Interesselosigkeit herab; — meat, frisches Schlachtfleisch; — point, der tote Punkt; — reckoning, die Gissung; — Sea apples *or* fruit, vergebliche Sache, Täuschung (*fig.*); — season, stille, geschäftslose Zeit; a — shot, ein nie fehlender Schütze; — silence, die Totenstille; — steam, der Abgangsdampf; — walls, tote Mauern; a — weight, eine schwere drückende Last. II. *adv.*; — beat, gänzlich erschöpft; — drunk, im höchsten Grade betrunken; — slow, ganz langsam (*Naut. & sl.*); — tired, totmüde; he cut me —, er ignorierte mich vollständig (*sl.*). III. *s.* die Tiefe, Stille (of the night, der Nacht); in the — of winter, mitten im Winter; the —, die Toten; risen from the —, von den Toten (*or* vom Tode) auferstanden. **—en**, *v.a.* abstumpfen, schwächen, dämpfen (*sounds, feelings, etc.*); matt machen (*gold, etc.*); to —en a ship's way, die Fahrt eines Schiffes hemmen. **—liness**, *s.* die Tödlichkeit, das Tödliche. **—ly**, *adj. & adv.* tödlich, todbringend, totenähnlich; (mortal, implacable) unversöhnlich; —ly pale, totenblaß; —ly enemy, der Todfeind; —ly hate, tödlicher Haß; —ly sin, die Todsünde. **—ness**, *s.* der Mangel an Lebenskraft, Zustand des Todes; (frigidity) die Erstarrung; (weakness) die Mattigkeit, Schwäche; (indifference) die Gleichgültigkeit; (apathy) die Empfindungslosigkeit, Abgestumpftheit; (flatness) die Schalheit; die Flauheit (*of trade*). *Comp.* **—-eye**, *s.* der Jungferblock (*Naut.*). **—head**, *s.* blinder Passagier, Nassauer. **—-letter**, *attrib.*; —-letter office, das Postamt für unbestellbare Briefe. **—-light**, *s.* der Lukendeckel, Laden für Kajütenfenster (*Naut.*). **—-lock**, *s.* der Stillstand, die völlige Stockung, Klemme; to come to a —-lock, ins Stocken geraten, stecken bleiben; to be at a —-lock, in der Klemme sitzen, völlig festgefahren *or* verfahren sein, nicht vom Fleck kommen *or* können, nicht aus noch ein wissen. **—ly-nightshade**, *s.* die Belladonna, Tollkirsche (*Bot.*). **—-nettle**, *s.* die Taubnessel, der Bienensaug.

Deaf, *adj.* taub; — to, taub gegen (*or* für); as — as a post, stocktaub; to turn a — ear to a th., auf eine S. nicht hören wollen; — and dumb, taubstumm; — and dumb asylum, die Taubstummenanstalt. **—en**, *v.a.* taub machen; betäuben (with, von, durch). **—ness**, *s.* die Taubheit; das Taubsein (to, für, gegen). *Comp.* **—-mute**, *s.* der Taubstumme.

[1]**Deal**, I. *v.a.* (divide) teilen; (distribute) austeilen; geben (*cards*); to — a p. a blow, einem eins versetzen. II. *v.n.* handeln, Handel treiben (*in goods, etc.*); verfahren (*fig.*); Karten geben; to — in politics, sich mit der Politik abgeben; to — honestly with s.o., sich redlich gegen einen betragen; he does n't know how to — with him, er weiß ihn nicht zu behandeln; to — with difficulties, mit Schwierigkeiten kämpfen. III. *s.* der Teil; (quantity) die Menge; das Kartengeben (*Cards*); a good —, viel, sehr; to make a great — of a p., viel aus einem machen; to think a great — of a p., einen hochschätzen; it's my —, ich muß geben. **—er**, *s.* der Handelsmann, Händler; der Kartengeber; hardware —er, Eisenwarenhändler; —er in old clothes, der Altkleiderhändler, Trödler; —er in old books, der Antiquar; —er in antiquities, der Antiquitätenhändler; plain —er, redlicher, offener Mann; double —er, der falsche Mensch, Achselträger. **—ing**, *s.* das Teilen; (*gen'lly* **—ings**, *pl.*) das Verfahren, die Behandlung; (intercourse) der Umgang, Verkehr; der Geschäftsverkehr, Handel (*C. L.*); mode of —ing, die Handlungsweise; I have no —ings with him, ich habe nichts mit ihm zu tun *or* zu schaffen; we have no —ings with that house, wir haben keinen geschäftlichen Verkehr mit dem Hause; there 's no —ing with this fellow, man kann mit diesem Menschen nicht auskommen, nicht fertig werden. **—t**, *pret. & p.p. of* Deal; questions to be —t with, Fragen welche zur Verhandlung kommen werden; the following questions were —t with, folgende Fragen wurden vorgenommen (erledigt).

[2]**Deal**, I. *s.* das dünne Brett, die Diele, Planke, Bohle; das Tannenholz, Fichtenholz, Kiefernholz. II. *attrib.*; — boards, Dielen, Tannenbretter; — box, die Spanschachtel; — door, die Brettertür.

Dealt, *imperf. of* Deal.

Dean, *s.* der Dechant, Dekan; der Dekan (*Univ.*); der Vorsteher eines Domkapitels. **—ery**, *s.* (house, *etc.*, jurisdiction) die Dekanei; (office, dignity) das Dekanat.

[1]**Dear**, I. *adj. & adv.*, **—ly**, *adv.* teuer; (beloved) lieb, teuer, wert; — Lizzie, das gute Lieschen; Lizzie —! — Lizzie! liebes Lieschen! there's a — child, sei lieb! sei artig! (*coll.*); — Sir, geehrter Herr! — Doctor! sehr geehrter Herr Doktor! — friend, lieber *or* liebster Freund! werter Freund! — madam! gnädige Frau! hochgeehrte Frau . . .! sehr geehrte Frau (Professor, Doktor . . .); — Mrs. Ransom, liebe Frau Ransom! geehrte *or* sehr geehrte *or* hochverehrte Frau Ransom; to be —, to cost —, teuer sein; it cost him —, es kam ihm teuer zu stehen; a — year, ein Jahr der Teuerung; —ly bought, teuer erkauft; to pay — for, (etwas) teuer bezahlen; —ly beloved, innig geliebt. II. *s.* der Liebling; my —, mein Schatz, Liebe(r), Teure(r); Lizzie is a —, Lieschen ist doch ein gutes Kind *or* ein liebes Herz. **—ness**, *s.* die Teuerung; der Wert; die Wertschätzung; her —ness to me, ihr Wert für mich; meine große Liebe für sie. **—th**, *s.* die Teurung; (scarcity) der Mangel.

[2]**Dear**, *int.*; O —! verflixt! das hole doch dieser und jener! — me! ach (herr)je! verwünscht!

Death, *s.* der Tod; civil —, der bürgerliche Tod; —s, Todesfälle; to die a natural —, eines natürlichen Todes sterben; it will be the — of me, es wird mein Tod sein (*coll.*); to put to —, hinrichten; to catch one's —, sich (*dat.*) den Tod holen (*vulg.*); to die the —, sterben; to die the — of a hero, den Heldentod sterben; hour of —, die Todesstunde; house of —, das Trauerhaus. **—less**, *adj.* unsterblich. **—like**, *adj.* totenähnlich. *Comp.* **—-agony**, *s.* der Todeskampf. **—-bed**, *s.* das Sterbebett, Totenbett. **—-blow**, *s.* der Todesstoß; to give the —-blow to a theory, einer Ansicht den Todesstoß versetzen. **—-dealing**, *adj.*

tötend, tödlich. **—-knell**, *s.* das Totengeläut(e). **—-rate**, *s.* die Sterblichkeitsziffer. **—-rattle**, *s.* das Todesröcheln, letzte Röcheln. **—'s-door**, *s.* die Todespforte; to be at —'s door, in den letzten Zügen liegen. **—'s-head**, *s.* der Totenkopf. **—-warrant**, *s.* das Todesurteil; der Befehl zur Vollstreckung eines Todesurteils. **—-watch**, *s.* der Klopfkäfer, die Totenuhr.

Debar, *v.a.*; to — from, ausschließen von, hindern an (*dat.*); he is —red the liberty . . ., ihm ist die Freiheit . . . versagt; to — o.s. of a pleasure, sich (*dat.*) ein Vergnügen versagen. **—ment**, *s.* die Ausschließung (from, von).

Debark, *see* Disembark.

Debas—e, *v.a.* erniedrigen, herabwürdigen, verschlechtern, verschlimmern, verringern; verfälschen (coin, Münzen); verderben (*a language*); —ed coin, geringhaltige Münze. **—ement**, *s.* die Erniedrigung, Entwürdigung. **—ing**, *adj.*, **—ingly**, *adv.* erniedrigend, entwürdigend.

Debat—able, *adj.* bestreitbar, streitig, fraglich; —able land, streitiges Gebiet; —able claims, bestreitbare Ansprüche. **—e**, I. *s.* der Wortstreit, Redekampf, die Debatte; (quarrel) der Streit; (formal —e) die Debatte. II. *v.a.* *see* —e III.; (dispute) streitig machen. III. *v.n.* erörtern; debattieren; to —e with o.s., bei sich überlegen. **—er**, *s.* der Wortkämpfer, Disputant, Debattierende. **—ing**, *p.* & *adj.* debattierend. *Comp.* **—ing-society**, *s.* der Debattierverein, Debattierklub.

Debauch, I. *v.a.* (lead astray) verführen, verleiten; (seduce) verführen; (corrupt) verderben, liederlich machen; abtrünnig, abspenstig machen (*soldiers, etc.*). II. *v.n.* ausschweifen or liederlich leben. III. *s.* die Schwelgerei, Ausschweifung. **—ed**, *adj.* verdorben, liederlich, unzüchtig. **—ee**, *s.* der Wüstling, Schwelger. **—er**, *s.* der Verführer. **—ery**, *s.* die Schwelgerei, Liederlichkeit; (act of —ing) die Verführung.

Deb—enture, *s.* der Schuldschein, die Prioritätsobligation; der Rückzollschein (*Customs*); redeeming of —entures, Einlösung von Schuldscheinen. **—entured**, *adj.*; —entured goods, Waren, auf welche der Rückzoll bezahlt worden ist. **—it**, I. *s.* das Soll, der Schuldposten, die Schuld, das Debet; (—it side) die Debetseite des Hauptbuches. II. *v.a.* in das Soll eintragen, debitieren, belasten; we shall —it you with the amount, wir werden Ihre Rechnung dafür belasten; —it and credit, Soll und Haben; the —its exceed the credits, die Schuldposten übersteigen die Guthaben. **—t**, *see* Debt.

Debilit—ate, *v.a.* schwächen, entkräften. **—ation**, *s.* die Schwächung. **—y**, *s.* die Schwäche.

Debonair, *adj.* artig; freundlich, gutherzig.

Debouch, *v.n.* sich aus einem Engpasse entwickeln, aus einem Engpaß herausmarschieren (*Mil.*); debouchieren. **—ment**, *s.* das Herausmarschieren or Hervorbrechen aus einem Engpaß (*Mil.*); die Mündung (einer Schlucht). **—ure, Débouchure**, *s.* die Ausmündung eines Flusses oder einer Meerenge.

Débris, *s.* die Überbleibsel; die Trümmer (*also Geol.*).

Debt, *s.* die Schuld (*also fig.*); to contract —s, Schulden machen; to run into —, sich in Schulden stürzen; to be in a p.'s —, einem schuldig sein; I shall always consider myself in your —, ich werde mich immer als Ihren Schuldner betrachten; in —, verschuldet; to pay the — of nature, der Natur den schuldigen Tribut bezahlen; —s active and passive, Aktiva und Passiva; national —, die Staatsschuld; — of gratitude, die Dankesschuld; he owes her a great — of gratitude, er ist ihr vielen Dank schuldig or ist ihr zu großem Danke verpflichtet; —s of honour, Ehrenschuld(en); active —, die ausstehende Forderung; outstanding —s, die Außenstände; bad —s, nicht einzubringende Schulden. **—or**, *s.* der Schuldner; der Verpflichtete; —or and creditor, Schuldner und Gläubiger (*C. L.*); to be on the —or side, im Debet stehen. *Comp.* **—-book**, *s.* das Schuldbuch.

Début, *s.* das erste or erstmalige Auftreten, Debüt (*of an actor, etc.*). **—ant, —ante**, *s.* der (die) zum ersten Male Auftretende, Debütant(in).

Deca—de, *s.* die Zehnzahl, das Zehnt, der Zehner, die Anzahl von zehn Stück. **—gon**, *s.* das Zehneck, Dekagon. **—hedron**, *s.* der Zehnflächner, die zehnseitige Figur. **—logue**, *s.* der Dekalog, die zehn Gebote (Mosis). **—ndrian, —ndrous**, *adj.* zehnmännerig (*Bot.*). **—style**, I. *s.* das Dekastilon (*Arch.*). II. *adj.* zehnsäulig. **—syllabic**, *adj.* zehnsilbig; —syllabic verse, der Zehnsilbler.

Decaden—ce, *s.* der Verfall, Zerfall, das Sinken; die Dekadenz. **—t**, *adj.* verfallend, im Verfall begriffen; dekadent.

Decamp, *v.n.* aus dem Lager aufbrechen; sich fortmachen, sich aus dem Staube machen, sich davon machen. **—ment**, *s.* der Aufbruch aus dem Lager, das Abmarschieren.

Decant, *v.a.* umfüllen; dekantieren, klar abgießen (*of fluids*); to — wine, Wein in Karaffen füllen. **—ation**, *s.* das Abgießen, Umfüllen. **—er**, *s.* die Karaffe; das Abklärgefäß (*Chem.*).

Decapitat—e, *v.a.* enthaupten, köpfen. **—ion**, *s.* die Enthauptung, das Köpfen.

Decarbonize, *v.a.* entkohlen, von Kohlenstoff befreien.

Decay, I. *v.n.* verfallen, in Verfall geraten, verwelken; abnehmen, sinken (*fig.*); (die) ab-, aussterben, verfaulen (*of wood, etc.*); verwesen (*Chem.*); —ed with age, altersschwach (*of living beings*), verfallen (*of buildings*); —ed teeth, hohle or schlechte Zähne; a —ed beauty, eine verblühte Schönheit; —ed families, heruntergekommene, (extinct) ausgestorbene Familien. II. *s.* der Verfall, die Abnahme (*of health, strength, happiness, wealth*); das Verblühen (*of beauty*); to fall into —, in Verfall geraten, verfallen, zu Grunde gehen.

Decease, I. *s.* das Hinscheiden, der Tod. II. *v.n.* sterben, verscheiden; the —d, der (die) Verstorbene.

Deceit, *s.* die Täuschung, der Trug; *see* —fulness; (fraud) der Betrug, die Betrügerei; (stratagem) die Hinterlist. **—ful**, *adj.*, **—fully**, *adv.* (illusive) täuschend; trügerisch, betrügerisch, listig, falsch. **—fulness**, *s.* die Betrüglichkeit, Falschheit; die Betrügerei.

Deceiv—able, *adj.* leicht zu betrügen; täuschend. **—e**, *v.a.* betrügen; (mislead) verleiten; (disappoint) täuschen; to be —ed, sich täuschen, sich irren (in a p., in einem); he has —ed me, er hat mich hinters Licht geführt. **—er**, *s.* der Betrüger.

Decem—ber, *s.* der Dezember. **—vir**, *s.* der Dezemvir. **—virate**, *s.* das Dezemvirat.

Decen—cy, *s.* die Schicklichkeit, der Anstand; (modesty) die Sittsamkeit, Bescheidenheit; sense of —cy, das Schicklichkeitsgefühl; for —cy's sake, anstandshalber. **—t**, *adj.*, **—tly**, *adv.* schicklich, anständig; züchtig, sittsam; bescheiden; (sufficient) ziemlich gut, ganz nett (*schoolboys' sl.*); (generous) freigebig (*sl.*); —t behaviour, anständiges Betragen; a —t fellow, ein ganz netter Mensch.

Decenn—ial, *adj.* zehnjährig. **—ium, —ary**, *s.* das Jahrzehnt.

Decentraliz—ation, *s.* die Verstreuung, Dezentralisation. **—e**, *v.* auseinanderlegen, in verschiedene Orte legen, verstreuen, dezentralisieren.

Decepti—on, *s.* der Betrug, die Betrügerei; (stratagem) der Betrug, Irrtum; (illusion) die Täuschung. **—ve**, *adj.* betrüglich. **—veness**, *s.* die Betrüglichkeit.

Decern, *v.a.* unterscheiden (*obs. see* Discern); richten, zuerkennen (*Scotch Law*).

Decide, *v.* I. *a.* entscheiden; to — a case, eine Rechtssache entscheiden. II. *n.* (sich) entscheiden;

to — upon a th., entscheiden über eine S.; he —d to go out, on going out, er entschied sich auszugehen. —**d**, *adj.*, —**dly**, *adv.* entschieden, bestimmt, gewiß. —**r**, *s.* der Entscheider.

Deciduous, *adj.* (im Herbst)abfallend; jedes Jahr das Laub verlierend. —**ness**, *s.* die Eigenschaft des Abfallens (*of leaves*); die Hinfälligkeit.

Decim—al, I. *adj.* zehnteilig, dezimal, zehn Einheiten enthaltend; —al system, das Zehnersystem, Dezimalsystem. II. *s.* (—al fraction) das Zehntel, der Zehnerbruch. —**ally**, *adv.* nach zehn *or* Zehnern gerechnet. —**ate**, *v.a.* den Zehnten nehmen; dezimieren. —**ated**, *adj.* dezimiert, stark zusammengeschmolzen. —**ation**, *s.* die Verzehntung; die Dezimierung. —**o-sexto**, *s.* das Sedezformat.

Decipher, *v.a.* entziffern; enträtseln (*fig.*). —**able**, *adj.* entzifferbar.

Decisi—on, *s.* die Entscheidung (*also Law*); der Ausspruch (*Law*); (resoluteness) die Entschlossenheit, Entschiedenheit; to come to a —on, zu einer Entscheidung kommen über (*acc.*); we came to the —on, wir entschieden uns dahin, beschlossen endlich; a man with —on of character, ein fester, entschlossener Charakter. —**ve**, *adj.*, —**vely**, *adv.* entscheidend, bestimmt, ausschlaggebend; entschieden (*of persons*). —**veness**, *s.* die Entschiedenheit.

Deck, I. *v.a.* bekleiden; schmücken; mit einem Deck versehen (*Naut.*); —ed, bedeckt, geschmückt; —ed vessel, Fahrzeug mit einem Deck. II. *s.* das Deck, Verdeck; berth —, Banjerdeck, Zwischendeck; entire —, durchgehendes Verdeck; flush —, Glattdeck; gun —, Batteriedeck, Geschützdeck; main —, Hauptdeck; the between —s, Zwischendeck; hurricane —, die Kommandobrücke; we went on —, wir gingen aufs Verdeck; we were on —, wir waren auf dem Verdeck; to clear the —s, ein Schiff zum Gefecht klar machen; to sweep the —s, alles vom Deck hinwegfegen (*of a wave*); das Deck bestreichen (*of guns*); all hands on —, alle Mann auf Deck! III. *attrib.*; —cabin, Kajüte auf dem Verdeck; — carriage, die Schiffslafette; — guns, die Schiffsbatterie. —**er**, *s.*; a three-—er, der Dreidecker.

Declaim, *v.* I. *a.* laut vortragen, kunstmäßig vortragen, deklamieren. II. *n.* deklamieren; to — against, losziehen gegen. —**er**, *s.* der Deklamator, Vortragskünstler; der Eiferer (gegen).

Declamat—ion, *s.* die öffentliche Ansprache; die Deklamation, der schwungvolle Vortrag; die pomphafte Redeweise. —**ory**, *adj.* rednerisch, deklamatorisch; (bombastic) schwülstig, lärmend.

Declar—ant, *s.* der Komparent (*Law*). —**ation**, *s.* die Erklärung; die Angabe (*Customs*); —ation of Independence, Unabhängigkeitserklärung; —ation of love, Liebeserklärung. —**atory**, *adj.* erklärend; ausdrücklich. —**e**, *v.* I. *a.* erklären; (make known) kund tun; (announce) verkündigen; (assert) behaupten; ausbieten (for sale, zum Verkauf); angeben (at the custom-house, beim Zollamte); to —e o.s., sich erklären; I —e, you are a model of a husband, ich muß sagen, Sie sind ein Mustergatte! I —e! wahrhaftig! fürwahr! II. *n.*; to —e (for, against), sich erklären (für, gegen). —**ed**, *adj.* offen.

Declension, *s.* die Abweichung (*also fig.*); (decline) der Verfall, die Abnahme; die Biegung *or* Abwandlung der Hauptwörter (Eigenschaftswörter und Fürwörter), Deklination (*Gram.*).

Declin—able, *adj.* veränderlich, deklinierbar. —**ation**, *s.* die Neigung, Abschüssigkeit; das Sinken, die Abnahme, der Niedergang, Verfall (*fig.*); die Abweichung, Deklination (*Phys.*, *Astr.*). —**ator**, *s.* der Deklinator (*Phys.*). —**atory**, *adj.*; —atory plea, die Ablehnungserklärung. —**e**, I. *v.a.* (bend down) neigen, biegen; deklinieren, abwandeln (*Gram.*); (refuse) ablehnen, ausweichen, abweisen; he —ed to go with me, er lehnte es ab, mit mir zu gehen. II. *v.n.* sich niederbeugen; abweichen (from, von); (draw to an end) sich neigen, zu Ende gehen; (refuse) sich weigern; fallen (*as prices*); abnehmen (*as strength*); the day is —ing, der Tag neigt sich; sugar has very much —ed, die Zuckerpreise sind bedeutend gefallen. III. *s.* die Beugung; die Abweichung, Abnahme, Verminderung; der Niedergang, Verfall; die Auszehrung (*Med.*); to be on the —e, auf die Neige gehen; herunter gehen, fallen (*of prices*); —e of learning, der Verfall der Gelehrsamkeit; —e of life, das vorgerückte Alter. —**ometer**, *s.* der Abweichungsmesser.

Decliv—ity, *s.* der Abhang; (fall) die Abschüssigkeit. —**itous**, —**ous**, *adj.* abhängig, abschüssig.

Decoct, *v.a.* (aus)kochen; (heat) in Wallung bringen. —**ion**, *s.* das Absieden; das Dekokt, der Absud.

Decode, *v.a.* entziffern; the despatch must first be —d, die Depesche muß erst entziffert werden.

Decolorant, I. *adj.* bleichend. II. *s.* das Bleichmittel.

Decompos—e, *v.* I. *a.* zersetzen; zerlegen (*Phys.*). II. *n.* verwesen. —**ition**, *s.* die Zersetzung, Auflösung (*Chem.*); die Zerlegung (*Phys.*, *Mech.*).

Decor—ate, *v.a.* schmücken, zieren; —ated style, die Spätgotik (*Engl. Arch.*). —**ation**, *s.* die Verzierung; der Schmuck, Zierrat; —ations, die Dekoration(en) (*in a theatre, etc.*). —**ative**, *adj.* zierend, schmückend, verschönernd; —ative painting, die Dekorationsmalerei; —ative plants, Zierpflanzen. —**ator**, *s.* der Verzierer; der Dekorateur, Dekorationsmaler, Anstreicher und Tapezierer; der Gipser (*in stucco*); —ator's cement, der Stuck. —**ous**, *adj.*, —**ously**, *adv.* schicklich, anständig, geziemend, gebührlich. —**um**, *s.* der Anstand, die Schicklichkeit.

Decorticat—e, *v.a.* abrinden, schälen (*trees, etc.*); aushülsen (*shell-fruit, barley, peas, etc.*). —**ion**, *s.* das Schälen; das Enthülsen.

Decoy, I. *v.a.* locken, ködern; verleiten, (ver-) locken (*fig.*). II. *s.* die Lockung; die Lockspeise, der Köder. *Comp.* —**bird**, *s.* der Lockvogel.

Decre—ase, I. *v.n.* abnehmen, sich vermindern, schwinden. II. *v.a.* verringern, vermindern. III. *s.* die Abnahme, Verminderung; das Abnehmen (*of the moon, etc.*). —**scent**, *adj.* abnehmend; —scent moon, der abnehmende Mond.

Decree, I. *s.* die Verordnung, Vorschrift, das Dekret; (judgment) der Bescheid, Erlaß; der Ratschluß (of God, Gottes); — nisi, der bedingte Bescheid, Richterspruch (*in divorce cases*); — nisi with costs, bedingtes Scheidungserkenntnis unter Erlegung der Prozeßkosten. II. *v.a.* (einen Beschluß) erlassen; verordnen.

Decre—e, *see* Decree. —**tal**, I. *adj.* Dekretal-. II. *s.* (—tal epistle) der Dekretalbrief; das die Dekretale enthaltende Gesetzbuch. —**tals**, *pl.* die Dekretalien. —**tory**, *adj.* dekretorisch; entscheidend, kritisch (*Med.*).

Decrepit, *adj.* altersschwach, abgelebt. —**ate** *v.* I. *n.* abknistern. II. *a.* abknistern lassen; dekrepitieren (*Chem.*). —**ation**, *s.* das Abknistern. —**ude**, *s.* die Altersschwäche, Abgelebtheit.

Decri—al, *s.* die üble Nachrede, Verleumdung, der Verruf. —**er**, *s.* der Verschreier, Verleumder.

Decry, *v.a.* verschreien, verrufen; laut und tadelnd sich aussprechen gegen; tadeln, heruntermachen.

Decrustation, *s.* das Abkrusten.

Decuple, I. *adj.* zehnfach. II. *s.* das Zehnfache. III. *v.a.* verzehnfachen.

Decurrent, *adj.* herablaufend (*Bot.*).

Decussate, *adj.* sich kreuzend, gekreuzt; kreuzständig (*Bot.*).

Dedicat—e, I. *v.a.* weihen; widmen. II. *adj.*, —**ed**, *adj.* geweiht; gewidmet. —**ion**, *s.* die Widmung; die Zueignung, Widmung (*of a book, etc.*); die Zueignungsschrift. —**or**, *s.* der, welcher widmet, *rc.* —**ory**, *adj.* widmend, zueignend; —ory epistle, die Zueignungsschrift.

Deduc—e, *v.a.* (conclude) schließen; (derive) ableiten, herleiten (from, von), folgern (aus). —**ible**, *adj.* herzuleiten; zu schließen. —**t**, *v.a.* abziehen; after —ting . . ., nach Abzug (von) . . .; —ting expenses, abzüglich der Kosten —**tion**, *s.* das Abziehen; der Abzug; der Nachlaß (*C.L.*); der Schluß (*Log.*). —**tive**, *adj.* durch Folgerung.

Deed, *s.* die Tat, Handlung; (exploit) die Großtat; (reality, fact) die Tat; (document) die Urkunde; — of gift, Schenkungsurkunde; — of partnership, der Teilhabervertrag; in very —, wahrhaftig; taken in the very —, auf der Tat, *or* auf frischer Tat, ertappt. *Comp.* —**-box**, *s.* die Kassette zur Aufbewahrung von Urkunden.

Deem, *v.* I. *a.* (judge) beurteilen (*obs.*). II. *n.* dafür halten, denken, urteilen, vermuten. —**ster**, *s.* der Richter (auf der Insel Man).

Deep, I. *adj.*, —**ly**, *adv.* tief; (low down) niedrig gelegen; (abstruse) schwer zu begreifen, tief verborgen, dunkel; (dark) dunkel; (secret) geheim, verborgen; (sly, cunning) schlau, listig, verschlagen; (penetrating) durchdringend, eindringlich; (sharp, sagacious) scharfsinnig; (solemn) feierlich; (intense) stark, innig empfunden, inbrünstig; (low-sounding) tieftönend; (profound) tief, gründlich; —ly affected, tief ergriffen; three —, drei Mann hoch; troops in ranks of two —, Truppen in zwei Gliedern aufgestellt; —(ly) in debt, tief verschuldet; — designs, versteckte Absichten, geheimnisvolle Pläne; a — fellow, ein Schlauberger, Schlaumeier; —(ly) in love, sehr verliebt; — mourning, tiefe Trauer; he has —ly offended his friends, er hat seinen Freunden großen Anstoß gegeben; —ly read, sehr *or* außerordentlich belesen; — scholar, der große Gelehrte; a — sense of guilt, ein tiefes Schuldgefühl; a — sense of gratitude, ein starkes *or* warmes Dankgefühl; — silence, tiefes Schweigen, das feierliche Stillschweigen. II. *s.* die Tiefe; die See, das Meer. —**en**, *v.* I. *a.* tiefer machen, vertiefen; (ver)dunkeln, dunkler machen (*colours*), steigern, vergrößern (*sorrow, etc.*); tiefer stimmen (*tones*). II. *n.* tiefer werden; sich vertiefen; sich dunkler färben; stärker werden. —**ness**, *s.* die Tiefe. *Comp.* —**-drawn**, *adj.* aus der Tiefe geholt. —**-felt**, *adj.* tiefempfunden. —**-laid**, *adj.*; —-laid schemes, schlau angelegte Pläne. —**-mouthed**, *adj.* von starker Stimme. —**-rooted**, *adj.* tief eingewurzelt. —**-sea**, I. *s.* die Tiefsee. II. *attrib.* Tiefsee-; —-sea lead, das schwere Lot, Tiefseelot; —-sea line, die große Lotleine. —**-seated**, *adj.* tiefsitzig. —**-toned**, *adj.* tieftönend.

Deer, I. *s.* das Rotwild, Hochwild, Hirsch, Reh, Wild; fallow —, der Damhirsch, das Damwild; red —, Edelhirsch, Rothirsch; the — whistles, der Hirsch röhrt. II. *pl. see* Deer I *Comp.* —**-hound**, *s.* der Jagdhund für Rotwild, Hetzhund. —**-shot**, *s.* die Rehposten. —**-skin**, *s.* die Hirschhaut, das Rehfell; das Hirschleder, Rehleder (*C. L.*). —**-stalker**, *s.* der Pirscher auf Rotwild. —**-stalking**, *s.* das Pirschen auf Rotwild. —**-stealer**, *s.* der Wilddieb. —**-stealing**, *s.* die Wilddieberei.

Deface, *v.a.* entstellen, verunstalten; Geschriebenes ausstreichen; (mar) verderben. —**ment**, *s.* die Entstellung, Verunstaltung; das Entstellende. —**r**, *s.* der Verunstalter, Verderber.

Defalcation, *s.* die Kassenveruntreuung, Unterschlagung, der Unterschleif; (sum embezzled) das unterschlagene Geld.

Defam—ation, *s.* die Verleumdung. —**atory**, *adj.* verleumderisch, ehrenrührig, schmähend; —atory libel, die Schmähschrift. —**e**, *v.a.* verschreien, verleumden, schmähen, verunglimpfen. —**er**, *s.* der Verleumder, Lästerer.

Default, I. *s.* (omission) die Unterlassung, Vernachlässigung; (fault) der Fehler; das Nichterscheinen (*Law*); *see* Defalcation; in — of, in Ermangelung von; to make —, nicht erscheinen, nicht nachkommen, nicht bezahlen; to suffer judgment by —, wegen Nichterscheinens den Prozeß verlieren; the dogs are at a —, die Hunde haben die Spur verloren (*obs.*). II. *v.n.* wortbrüchig sein. III. *v.a.* zu erfüllen unterlassen, nicht erfüllen; wegen Nichterscheinens verurteilen. —**er**, *s.* der Pflichtvergessene; derjenige, der seinen Verbindlichkeiten nicht nachkommt (*C.L.*); a declared —er, ein für zahlungsunfähig erklärtes Börsenmitglied; der nicht vor Gericht Erscheinende (*Law*).

Defea—sance, *s.* die Aufhebung, Annullierung; die Annullierungsurkunde. —**t**, I. *s.* die Niederlage; das Zurückschlagen (*of persons attacking*); (frustration) die Vernichtung, Vereitelung; to suffer —t, eine Niederlage erleiden, geschlagen werden. II. *v.a.* schlagen, überwinden (*an army*); vereiteln (*hopes, one's own object*); the enemy has been totally —ted, der Feind ist vollständig aufs Haupt geschlagen.

Defect, *s.* der Fehler; (blemish) der Makel, Flecken; (want) das Gebrechen; (imperfection) die Unvollkommenheit. —**ion**, *s.* der Abfall, die Abtrünnigkeit; die Pflichtvergessenheit; (revolt) die Empörung. —**ive**, *adj.* mangelhaft, unvollkommen, unvollständig; defekt, schadhaft (*C.L.*), fehlerhaft, tadelnswert; mangelhaft, defektiv (*Gram.*); —ive in, mangelhaft an (*dat.*), fehlend an (*dat.*); —ive currency, schadhafte Münze; —ive fifth, die kleine Quinte (*Mus.*). —**ively**, *adv.* mangelhafterweise. —**iveness**, *s.* die Mangelhaftigkeit, Fehlerhaftigkeit.

Defen—ce, *s.* die Verteidigung; die Einrede (*Law*), (protection) der Schirm, Schutz; (resistance) der Widerstand; (vindication) die Rechtfertigung; ein Festungswerk, das andere flankiert (*Fort.*); —ces, Verteidigungswerke; to plead in one's own —ce, zu seiner eignen Rechtfertigung (etwas) vorbringen. —**celess**, *adj.* schutzlos, wehrlos, ohne Verteidigung; (unfortified) unbefestigt; (weak) schwach. —**celessness**, *s.* die Schutzlosigkeit. —**d**, *v.a.* schützen, verteidigen; sichern (against, gegen); bewahren (from, vor); verteidigen, aufrecht erhalten (rights, *etc.*, Rechte, 2c.); befestigen (*as a city*). —**dable**, *adj.* verteidigungsfähig, zu verteidigen, zu halten. —**dant**, *s.* der Verteidiger; der (die) Angeklagte (*Law*). —**der**, *s.* der Verteidiger; der Beschützer, Verfechter. —**sible**, *adj.* der Verteidigung fähig, haltbar; recht. —**sibleness**, *s.* die Haltbarkeit. —**sive**, I. *adj.*, —**sively**, *adv.* verteidigend, schützend; —sive arms, Schutzwaffen; —sive war, der Verteidigungskrieg. II. *s.* das Verteidigungsmittel; die Defensive, der Verteidigungszustand; to act *or* stand on the —sive, verteidigungsweise verfahren, sich verteidigen.

[1]**Defer**, *v.* I. *a.* aufschieben, verschieben; —red annuity, eine Leibrente, deren Abzahlung erst nach Ablauf einer gewissen Zeit begonnen wird; —red payment, der Zahlungsaufschub. II. *n.* zögern, warten. —**ment**, *s.* der Aufschub, die Verschiebung.

[2]**Defer**, *v.a.* dem Urteile eines andern überlassen *or* anheimstellen; to — to another's opinion, der Meinung eines andern unterwerfen. —**ence**, *s.* (respect) die Achtung, Ehrerbietung; (courteous submission) die Nachgiebigkeit, Gefälligkeit; (yielding of judgment, *etc.*) das Nachgeben, die Unterwerfung; in —ence to, aus Rücksicht gegen *or* auf. —**ential**, *adj.*, —**entially**, *adv.* ehrerbietig.

Defi—ance, *s.* (challenge) die Herausforderung; (contemptuous disregard) der Trotz, Hohn; to bid —ance to, set at —ance, (einem 2c.) Trotz bieten, Hohn sprechen; to bid —ance to common sense, wider den gesunden Verstand handeln; in —ance of a p., einem zum Trotze; in —ance of my command, trotz meines Befehls, meinem Befehl zuwider. —**ant**, *adj.*, —**antly**, *adv.* trotzend, herausfordernd. —**er**, *s.* der Trotzende; der Herausforderer.

Defici—ency, *s.* die Mangelhaftigkeit, Unvollständigkeit, Unzulänglichkeit, der Mangel; (defect) der Fehler; das Defizit (in weight, am Gewichte) (*C. L.*); to make up for a —ency, das Fehlende ergänzen. **—ent**, *adj.*, **—ently**, *adv.* (imperfect) mangelhaft, unvollkommen, unzulänglich; (insufficient) ungenügend (in a th., an einer S.); to be —ent in, Mangel haben an (*dat.*), es fehlen lassen an (*dat.*), to be —ent, verfehlen, ermangeln, fehlen (in weight, am Gewichte). **—t**, *s.* das Defizit.

Defil—ade, *v.a.* defilieren, (Schanzen) sicher stellen (*Fort.*). [1]**—e**, I. *v.n.* defilieren (*Mil.*). II. *s.* der Engpaß, enge Weg.

[2]**Defile**, *v.a.* beflecken, besudeln; trüben (*fluids*); (violate) schänden, entehren; (corrupt) verderben; verunreinigen (*B.*). **—ment**, *s.* die Befleckung; die Schändung. **—r**, *s.* der Entweiher, Besudler; der Verunglimpfer, Schänder.

Defin—able, *adj.* bestimmbar; erklärbar. **—e**, *v.a.* (fix bounds) begrenzen, (die Grenze) genau bezeichnen; (determine) genau bestimmen, festsetzen; erklären (*words*); bestimmen, definieren (*ideas, etc.*). **—er**, *s.* der Beschreibende, Ausleger, Erklärer; der Bestimmende. **—ite**, *adj.*, **—itely**, *adv.* bestimmt (*as an outline, etc., also Gram., Log.*); fertig, in sich abgeschlossen; (clear) ausdrücklich, deutlich; (exact, precise) genau; —ite article, bestimmter Artikel. **—iteness**, *s.* die Bestimmtheit. **—ition**, *s.* die Begriffsbestimmung, Erklärung, Definition. **—itive**, I. *adj.*, **—itively**, *adv.* (positive) bestimmt, entschieden, ausdrücklich; entscheidend; (final) abschließend, endgültig; —itive treaty, der definitive Traktat. II. *s.* das Bestimmungswort. **—itiveness**, *s.* die Bestimmtheit, das Entscheidende.

Deflect, *v.* I. *a.* ablenken, umbiegen. II. *n.* abweichen. **—ion**, *see* Deflexion.

Deflexion, *s.* die Abbiegung, Abweichung.

Deflorate, *adj.* abgeblüht, verblüht.

Deflour, Deflower, *v.a.* der Blumen berauben; des Reizes berauben (*fig.*); entehren, entjungfern, schänden. **—er**, *s.* der Jungfernschänder.

Defluxion, *s.* der Abfluß.

Deform, I. *v.a.* entstellen, verunstalten. II. *adj.*, **—ed**, *adj.* entstellt, verunstaltet, mißgestaltet. **—ity**, die Ungestaltheit, Mißgestalt; die Unregelmäßigkeit, der Fehler (*fig.*).

Defraud, *v.a.* betrügen, übervorteilen (of, um); defraudieren (*C.L.*); einen Unterschleif begehen. **—ation**, *s.* der Betrug; die Unterschlagung, Hinterziehung; der Unterschleif (*of taxes*). **—er**, *s.* der Betrüger, Defraudant.

Defray, *v.a.*; to — expenses, die Kosten tragen *or* bestreiten, bezahlen; **to — a p.'s** expenses, einen frei halten.

Deft, *adj.*, **—ly**, *adv.* nett; (dexterous) geschickt, gewandt. **—ness**, *s.* die Gewandtheit.

Defunct, I. *adj.* verstorben. II. *s.* der Verstorbene.

Defy, *v.a.* (challenge) herausfordern; (brave) (einem) Trotz bieten, trotzen.

Degenera—cy, *s.* die Entartung; die Verkommenheit. **—te**, I. *v.n.* aus der Art schlagen, entarten, ausarten; wit may easily —te into indecency, der Witz kann leicht in Unanständigkeit ausarten. II. *adj.*, **—tely**, *adv.* entartet; (depraved) verkommen. **—teness**, *s.* die Entartung; *see* —cy. **—tion**, *s.* die Entartung.

Deglutition, *s.* das Schlucken.

Degrad—ation, *s.* (removal from office, *etc.*) die Absetzung, Entsetzung; (lowering) die Herabsetzung; (lessening) die Verringerung; (debasement) die Erniedrigung, Herabwürdigung, Entwürdigung; die Abstufung (*Paint., Geol.*); die Degradation (*Mil.*). **—e**, *v.a.* absetzen, entsetzen; heruntersetzen, verkleinern; verringern; herabwürdigen, entehren, erniedrigen; abstufen (*Geol.*). **—ed**, *adj.* abgesetzt, erniedrigt; heruntergekommen (*fig.*). **—ing**, *adj.* entehrend.

Degree, *s.* die Stufe, der Grad; (rank) der Rang, Stand; der Grad (*Geog., Math., Phys.*); das Intervall (*Mus.*); (extent) der Grad, das Maß; men of high —, Männer von hohem Stande; — of relationship, der Verwandtschaftsgrad; by —s, allmählich, nach und nach; to a —, in hohem Grade, äußerst, außerordentlich; to a certain —, bis zu einem gewissen Grade, gewissermaßen; in some —, einigermaßen; — of latitude, der Breitengrad; — of longitude, der Längengrad; —s of comparison, die Komparationsgrade (*Gram.*); pass —, ordinary —, gewöhnlicher Universitätsgrad; an honours —, der Grad eines . . . mit Auszeichnung; a university —, ein akademischer Grad; to take one's —, sich (*dat.*) einen akademischen Grad erringen, zum (Baccalaureus, Magister, Doktor) promoviert werden; he took his first —, er wurde zum Baccalaureus promoviert; he obtained the doctor's —, er errang die Doktorwürde, holte sich den Doktorhut, er doktorierte.

Dehortatory, *adj.* abmahnend.

Dehumanize, *v.a* entmenschlichen.

Dei—fication, *s.* die Vergötterung. **—fier**, *s.* der Vergötterer; der, welcher vergöttert. **—form**, *adj.* göttlicher Gestalt. **—fy**, *v.a.* vergöttern (*also fig.*). **—sm**, *s.* der Deismus. **—st**, *s.* der Deist. **—stic(al)**, *adj.* deistisch. **—ty**, *s.* die Gottheit; der Gott.

Deign, *v.* I. *n.* geruhen, sich herablassen. II. *a.* (grant) gewähren; (think worthy of) würdigen.

Deject—ed, *adj.*, **—edly**, *adv.* niedergeschlagen, betrübt, gebeugt. **—edness**, *s.* die Niedergeschlagenheit. **—ion**, *s.* die Niedergeschlagenheit, der Trübsinn, die Schwermut.

Delaine, *s.* halbwollener bunter Damenkleiderstoff.

Delat—e, *v.a.* anklagen, denunzieren (*Scotch*). **—ion**, *s.* die kirchliche Anklage (*Scotch*).

Delay, I. *v.a.* verzögern, auf-, ver-schieben; (keep back) hindern, hinhalten; to — payment, mit der Zahlung hinhalten. II. *v.n.* zögern, zaudern, anhalten. III. *s.* die Verzögerung; der Aufschub, Verzug; this matter admits of no —, diese Sache leidet keinen Aufschub; without —, ohne Aufschub, unverzüglich, unverweilt; — of payment, die Fristung (*C.L.*). **—er**, *s.* der, welcher zögert, Zauderer.

Del credere, Del Credere, *s.*; to stand —, Bürgschaft leisten, Delcredere stehen (*C.L.*).

Dele, I. *imper. of Latin verb.* streich aus, tilge. II. *s.* das Deleatur (*Typ.*).

Delecta—ble, *adj.*, **—bly**, *adv.* erfreulich, ergötzlich, angenehm. **—bleness**, *s.* die Ergötzlichkeit. **—tion**, *s.* die Ergötzung.

Delegat—e, I. *v.a.* überweisen, übertragen; (of persons) mit Vollmacht versehen und absenden; to —e to a p., einem anvertrauen, übertragen. II. *adj.* abgeordnet. III. *s.* der Beauftragte, Abgeordnete, das Ausschußmitglied; the —es, der Ausschuß, das Komitee. **—ion**, *s.* die Überweisung, Übertragung (*of a duty, etc.*); (—es) die Abgeordneten, der Ausschuß.

Deleterious, *adj.* schädlich, verderblich, giftig.

Delf(t), *s.* (— ware) das Delfter Porzellan.

Deliberat—e, I. *v.a. & n.* reiflich überlegen, erwägen, bedenken. II. *v.n.* (hesitate) sich bedenken. III. *adj.*, **—ely**, *adv.* (slow) langsam, bedächtig; (wary, cool) besonnen; (circumspect) umsichtig; (fully considered) wohl überlegt *or* erwogen; the —e intention, die vorgefaßte *or* wohl erwogene Absicht. **—eness**, *s.* die Bedächtigkeit, Langsamkeit. **—ion**, *s.* die Überlegung; die Berat(schlag)ung. **—ive**, *adj.* überlegend, beratschlagend; —ive body, beratschlagende Körperschaft.

Delic—acy, *s.* die Köstlichkeit; der Leckerbissen, die Delikatesse; die Leckerhaftigkeit; die Feinheit, Zartheit; die Zierlichkeit; die Genauigkeit, Sorgfalt; das Feine, Zarte (*of expression*); (politeness) die Höflichkeit; die Schwächlichkeit zarte Leibesbeschaffenheit; die Niedlichkeit, Zartheit (*of ornaments, etc.*); die Empfindlichkeit (*of a balance, etc.*); (considerateness) die Nachsicht, zarte Rücksicht; —acy of feeling, das Zartgefühl; —acy of behaviour, die Feinheit des Betragens, die Rücksicht; —acy of taste, der feine, zarte Geschmack. **—ate**, *adj.*, **—ately**, *adv.* (pleasing to the taste) schmackhaft, köstlich; (luxurious, dainty) lecker; (fastidious) wählerisch; (choice) ausgewählt; zart, sanft (*in colour*); fein (*in texture*); zart (*as a hand*); (refined) fein, zart; (—ate in feeling) zartfühlend; (elegant) zierlich, niedlich; (nice in conduct) artig, feinfühlig (im Betragen); (sickly, weak) schwächlich, schwach; (difficult, nice) kitzlich, bedenklich; (sensitive) empfindlich; in a —ate state of health, von zarter Gesundheit, sehr schwächlich; a —ate question, eine kitzliche *or* heikelige Frage; —ately bred, weichlich erzogen. **—ious**, *etc.*, *see* Delicious.

Delicious, *adj.*, **—ly**, *adv.* köstlich, äußerst wohlschmeckend; lieblich, herrlich. **—ness**, *s.* die Köstlichkeit.

Delight, I. *s.* (pleasure) die Lust, das Vergnügen; die hohe Freude, Wonne; to take — in a thing, Vergnügen an einer S. finden. II. *v.a.* ergötzen, erfreuen. III. *v.n.* sich erfreuen, sich ergötzen (in, an); to — in flowers, große Freude an Blumen haben; to — in mischief, schadenfroh sein. **—ed**, *adj.* höchst erfreut, entzückt; —ed with, entzückt von, sehr froh *or* glücklich über (*acc.*); I am —ed at the idea of (meeting him), ich freue mich sehr bei dem Gedanken, daß ich (ihn treffen werde). **—ful**, *adj.*, **—fully**, *adv.* höchst angenehm, höchst erfreulich, entzückend; a —ful book, ein köstliches Buch; a —ful prospect, eine reizende Aussicht; a —ful excursion, ein herrlicher Ausflug. **—fulness**, *s.* die Ergötzlichkeit; die Annehmlichkeit; die Wonne.

Delineat—e, *v.a.* entwerfen, skizzieren, zeichnen, im Abriß darstellen; (paint) malen; (depict) schildern, beschreiben. **—ion**, *s.* der Umriß, die Skizze; die Schilderung. **—or**, *s.* der Maler; der Schilderer.

Delinquen—cy, *s.* die Pflichtvergessenheit; (misdeed) das Vergehen, Verbrechen, die Missetat. **—t**, I. *adj.* pflichtvergessen. II. *s.* der Missetäter, Verbrecher.

Deliquesce, *v.n.* zergehen, schmelzen, zerfließen (*Chem.*). **—nt**, *adj.* zerfließend; vergehend (*fig.*).

Deliri—ous, *adj.*, **—ously**, *adv.* irre, wahnsinnig; to be —ous, phantasieren, irre reden; to become —ous, in Fieberphantasien verfallen. **—ousness**, *s.* der Wahnsinn. **—um**, *s.* der Wahnsinn, Irrsinn; das Phantasieren, Irrereden; (rapture) die Verzückung; —um tremens, der Säuferwahnsinn.

Deliver, *v.a.* (set free) befreien; (rescue) erretten, erlösen, befreien; (— up) übergeben, überreichen, überlassen; (hand over, give) ausliefern, abliefern, einhändigen, zustellen; abgeben (*letters*); einreichen (*a petition, etc.*); ausrichten, überbringen (*a message*); äußern (*an opinion*); vortragen, halten (*a speech, etc.*); entbinden (*Med.*); abgeben, liefern (*goods, etc.*); to — in trust, in Verwahrung geben; to be —ed in eight days, mit 8-tägiger Lieferungsfrist; to — into a p.'s hands, einem eigenhändig übergeben; to be —ed, auszuliefern; to — free on board, frei an Bord liefern; she was —ed of a boy, sie wurde von einem Knaben entbunden. **—able**, *adj.* zu liefern. **—ance**, *s.* die Befreiung, Erlösung, Errettung; die Aussage, Ausführung; *see* **—y**. **—er**, *s.* der Befreier; der Erretter, Erlöser. **—y**, *s.* die Befreiung, Erlösung, Errettung; die Entbindung, Niederkunft (*Med.*); die Übergabe (*of a deed*); die Ablieferung, Lieferung, Abgabe (*of goods*); die Austragung, Ablieferung, Abgabe (*of letters*); (address) der Vortrag; das Werfen (*of a cricketball*); —y of a pump, die Leistung einer Pumpe; bill of —y, der Liefer(ungs)schein; to sell on —y, auf Lieferung verkaufen. *Comp.* **—y-cock**, *s.* der Ablaßhahn. **—y-pipe**, *s.* das Ausströmrohr (*Railw.*); das Druckrohr. **—y-roller**, *s.* die Ableg-, Abzugs-walze (*Pap.*).

Dell, *s.* das enge, stark gesenkte Tal, die Schlucht.

Delphine, *adj.* zum Delphin gehörig; dem französischen Dauphin gehörig; — edition of the classics, die Ausgabe der (lateinischen) Klassiker zum Gebrauch des Dauphin.

Delt—a, *s.* das Delta (*Geog.*). **—afication**, *s.* die Deltabildung. **—oid**, *adj.* deltaförmig.

Delude, *v.a.* betrügen, anführen; vereiteln, täuschen, zunichte machen (*hopes, etc.*); to — a p. into, einen verleiten zu. **—r**, *s.* der Betrüger.

Deluge, I. *s.* die Überschwemmung; (the —) die Sündflut (*B.*); die Flut (*fig.*). II. *v.a.* überfluten.

Delus—ion, *s.* die Täuschung, Verblendung, der Trug; (error) der Irrtum, Wahn. **—ive**, *adj.*, **—ively**, *adv.* (be)trügerisch, täuschend. **—iveness**, *s.* das Trügerische; das betrügerische Wesen. **—ory**, *see* —ive.

Delve, *v.n.* graben. **—r**, *s.* der Gräber.

Demagnetize, *v.a.* entmagnetisieren.

Demagog—ic(al), *adj.* demagogisch, volksverführerisch, aufwieglerisch. **—ue**, *s.* der Demagoge, Volksführer; Volksverführer, Aufwiegler.

Demand, I. *v.a.* verlangen, fordern, begehren (of, von); (require) erfordern, nötig machen; beanspruchen, einfordern (*Law*); (ask) fragen. II. *s.* das Verlangen, Begehren; das Fordern (*of a price*); der Bedarf (*for water, etc.*); die Einforderung (*C.L.*); die Nachfrage (for, nach); der Rechtsanspruch (*Law*); in —, begehrt; in less —, bei geringerer Nachfrage; this article is in great —, dieser Artikel wird sehr gesucht; on —, auf Verlangen; payable on —, bei Sicht, auf Verlangen zahlbar; bill payable on —, der Sichtwechsel; supply and —, Angebot und Nachfrage. III. *attrib.*; — note, der Zahlungsauftrag (*taxes*). **—er**, *s.* der Forderer.

Demarcation, *s.* die Abgrenzung; line of —, die Grenzlinie, Abgrenzungslinie, Scheidelinie.

Demean, *v.r.* sich benehmen; (degrade) sich erniedrigen. **—our**, *s.* das Benehmen.

Demented, *adj.* wahnsinnig, toll.

Demerit, *s.* das Verschulden; der Unwert, Fehler.

Demesne, *s.* das freie Erbgut, die Domäne; das Landgut, Domänengut.

Demi— (*in comp.* =) halb. **—-bastion**, *s.* das halbe Bollwerk. **—-brigade**, *s.* die Halbbrigade. **—-god**, *s.* der Halbgott. **—-lance**, *s.* die kurze Lanze; der Leichtbewaffnete. **—-octavo**, *s.* das Medianoktav. **—-relievo**, I. *adj.* halb erhaben. II. *s.* das Halbrelief. **—-semiquaver**, *s.* die Zweiunddreißigstelnote.

Demijohn, *s.* die große Korbflasche, der Ballon.

Demise, I. *s.* das Ableben, der Tod; die Landesübertragung (by lease or will, durch Pacht oder Testament); — and redemise, die Pachtung und Afterpachtung. II. *v.a.* übertragen; — by will, testamentarisch vermachen.

Demiurge, *s.* der Demiurg (*Platonic Philos.*).

Democra—cy, *s.* die Demokratie. **—t**, *s.* der Demokrat. **—tic(al)**, *adj.*, **—tically**, *adv.* demokratisch; the growth of —tic Socialism, das Umsichgreifen der Sozialdemokratie.

Demoli—sh, *v.a.* niederreißen, einreißen, demolieren; vernichten, zerstören (*fig.*). **—sher**, *s.* der Zerstörer. **—tion**, *s.* das Niederreißen, die Zerstörung, Vernichtung.

Demon, *s.* der böse Geist, Dämon, Teufel. **—iac**, I. *adj.*, **—iacal**, *adj.* dämonisch. II. *s.* der vom Teufel Besessene. **—ism**, *s.* der Glaube an Dämonen. **—ology**, *s.* die Dämonenlehre.

Demonstra—ble, *adj.*, **—bly**, *adv.* beweisbar, erweislich, nachweislich. **—bleness**, *s.* die Erweislichkeit, Nachweisbarkeit. **—te**, *v.* I. *a.* anschaulich dartun, zeigen, beweisen (from, aus); beweisen (*Math.*). II. *a. & n.* durch Vorzeigen erklären; demonstrieren (*Anat.*). **—tion**, *s.*

(proving) das Beweisen, die Beweisführung; (proof) der Beweis, Erweis; die Äußerung, Kundgebung, Bezeigung (*of joy*); der Beweis (*Log.*, *Math.*); der anatomische Vortrag mit praktischen Erläuterungen (*Anat.*); der Scheinangriff; die Demonstration (*Mil.*). **—tive**, *adj.*, **—tively**, *adv.* beweiskräftig; (convincing) überzeugend; bündig; die Gefühle an den Tag legend, ausdrucksvoll; —tive pronoun, das hinweisende Fürwort. **—tiveness**, *s.* die überzeugende Eigenschaft; der Hang zu starken Gefühlsäußerungen. **—tor**, *s.* der Beweisführer, Erklärer; der Demonstrator (*Anat.*).

Demoraliz—ation, *s.* die Entsittlichung, Sittenverschlechterung. **—e**, *v.a.* entsittlichen, moralisch verschlechtern; demoralisieren (*Mil.*).

Demur, I. *v.n.* Anstand nehmen, zweifeln, unschlüssig sein; (object) Einreden, Ausflüchte vorbringen, Einwendungen (gegen eine S.) erheben. II. *s.* der Zweifel, Skrupel. **—rage**, *s.* das Liegegeld; die Überliegezeit (von Schiffen oder Eisenbahnfrachten); days of —rage, die Liegetage; die Liegezeit der Schiffer. **—rer**, *s.* der Unschlüssige, Zauderer; der Rechtseinwand (*Law*).

Demure, *adj.*, **—ly**, *adv.* ernsthaft, ernst, gesetzt; (prim) zimperlich, spröde. **—ness**, *s.* die Gesetztheit; die Sprödigkeit.

Demy, *s.* eine Art von kleinem Druck- oder Packpapier (meist etwa 22 × 17 Zoll); der Halbkollegiat (zu Magdalen-College, Oxford). **—ship**, *s.* die Stelle eines Halbkollegiaten (im Genuß eines College-Stipendiums).

[1]**Den**, *s.* die Höhle, Grube; die Bude (*stud. sl.*); das Lager (eines wilden Tieres); — of thieves, Räuberhöhle, Mördergrube (*B.*); robbers' —, das Raubnest; student's —, die Bude.

[2]**Den**, *s.*; (*from* [goo]d e'en) good —, guten Abend.

Denationalize, *v.a.* entnationalisieren, des Nationalcharakters berauben.

Denaturalize, *v.a.* unnatürlich machen, der Natur entfremden, denaturalisieren.

Dendr—iform, *adj.* baumförmig. **—ite**, *s.* der Baumstein. **—itic**, *adj.* dendritisch. **—oid**, *adj.* baumähnlich. **—olite**, *s.* die Baumversteinerung. **—ology**, *s.* die Baumkunde.

Deni—able, *adj.* verneinbar, zu verneinen. **—al**, *s.* (negation) die Verneinung; (refusal) die abschlägige Antwort, Verweigerung; (disavowal) das Leugnen, die Verleugnung; **self-—al**, die Selbstverleugnung. **—er**, *s.* der Leugner.

Denizen, *s.* der Bewohner; der Eingebürgerte. **—ship**, *s.* das Heimatsrecht, Bürgerrecht.

Denominat—e, *v.a.* (be)nennen. **—ion**, *s.* die Benennung; (sect) die Sekte, Klasse. **—ional**, *adj.* zu einer Sekte gehörig, sektirerisch, Sekten-, konfessionell; —ional school, konfessionelle Schule. **—ive**, *adj.* benennend. **—or**, *s.* der Benenner; der Nenner (*Arith.*); the common —or, der Generalnenner.

Denot—ative, *adj.* bezeichnend. **—e**, *v.a.* bezeichnen, andeuten; (signify) bedeuten.

Dénouement, *s.* die Entwickelung, Lösung.

Denounce, *v.a.* anzeigen, denunzieren; (inveigh against) rügen, brandmarken; to — a treaty, einen Vertrag kündigen. **—ment**, *s.* die Denunziation, das Angeben, die Anklage.

Dens—e, *adj.*, **—ely**, *adv.* dicht, fest; dick (*as a fog*); beschränkt, dumm, schwer von Begriffen (*coll.*); —ely packed together, dicht zusammengedrängt. **—eness**, *s.* die Dichtigkeit; die geistige Schwerfälligkeit, Beschränktheit. **—ity**, *s.* die Dichtheit; die Undurchsichtigkeit; das spezifische Gewicht (*Phys.*).

Dent, I. *s.* der Einschnitt, die Kerbe. II. *v.a.* (aus)kerben, zacken.

Dent—al, I. *adj.* zu den Zähnen gehörig, Zahn- . . .; zahnärztlich; —al sounds, die Zahnlaute; —al surgeon, der Zahnarzt; —al surgery, die Zahnheilkunde. II. *s.* der Zahnlaut. **—ate**, *adj.* gezähnt (*Bot.*). **—icle**, *s.* das Zähnchen; *see* —il. **—iculate(d)**, *adj.* gezahnt, gezähnelt; mit Zahnschnitten versehen (*Arch.*). **—iform**, *adj.* zahnförmig. **—ifrice**, *s.* das Zahnpulver. **—il**, *s.* der Zahnschnitt, der Kälberzahn. **—irostres**, *pl.* Zahnschnäbler (*Orn.*). **—ist**, *s.* der Zahnarzt; —ist's professional attendance, zahnärztliche Behandlung. **—istry**, *s.* die Zahnheilkunde, der Beruf *or* das Geschäft des Zahnarztes. **—ition**, *s.* das Zahnen.

Denud—e, *v.a.* entblößen; berauben (*fig.*). **—ed**, *p.p.* & *adj.* entblößt, (—ed of leaves) entblättert. **—ation**, *s.* die Entblößung (*also Geol.*); die Beraubung.

Denunciat—e, *see* Denounce. **—ion**, *s.* das Angeben, die Angabe; die (öffentliche) Rüge; der Tadel. **—or**, *s.* der Angeber, Denunziant. **—ory**, *adj.* tadelnd, rügend.

Deny, *v.a.* verneinen; (disavow) leugnen; (refuse) verweigern, abschlagen; (disown) verleugnen; to — on oath, eidlich ableugnen; to — o.s. a pleasure, einem Vergnügen entsagen, sich (*dat.*) ein Vergnügen versagen; it cannot be denied, es läßt sich nicht leugnen *or* in Abrede stellen; to — o.s. (to a visitor), sich verleugnen lassen; I have been denied this pleasure, dies Vergnügen ist mir versagt gewesen; the Volunteers led on the left flank and would not be denied, die Freiwilligen hatten die Führung auf der linken Flanke und ließen sich nicht abweisen.

Deodand, *s.* das verfallene Gut, der Gottverfall.

Deodorize, *v.a.* von Gerüchen befreien. **—r**, *s.* geruchvertilgendes Mittel, die Räucherkerze.

Deoxid—ate, **—ize**, *v.a.* desoxydieren. **—ation**, *s.* die Desoxydation.

Depart, *v.* I. *n.* abreisen, abfahren (for, nach); (sail) absegeln, auslaufen; scheiden, sich trennen (from, von); (swerve) abstehen, (ab)weichen, abgehen; (die) sterben, verscheiden, abscheiden, aus der Welt gehen; the —ed, (*pl.*) die Verschiedenen; his glory has —ed, sein Ruhm ist verschwunden *or* dahin; we cannot — from our rules, wir können von unsern Regeln nicht abweichen *or* abgehen. II. *a.* verlassen; to — this life, sterben; he has —ed this life, er ist verschieden. **—ment**, *s.* der Bezirk; der Geschäftskreis, das Fach; die Abteilung; das Departement; education —ment, das Unterrichtsministerium. **—mental**, *adj.* Abteilungs-, Fach-; —mental chief, der Abteilungsvorsteher. **—ure**, *s.* das Weggehen, die Abreise, Abfahrt; der Tod; das Verscheiden, Abscheiden (*from this world*); das Abstehen, Ablassen (from, von); das Aufgeben (*from a plan*). *Comp.* **—ure-station**, *s.* die Abgangsstation, Absendestation (*Railw.*, *Tele.*).

Depend, *v.n.* (hang down) herabhängen; (ab)hängen, abhängig sein (on, von); (rely on) sich verlassen, sich stützen (upon a p., auf einen); we have nothing to — upon, wir können auf nichts bauen *or* uns auf nichts verlassen; people to be —ed upon, zuverlässige Leute; that —s (on circumstances), je nachdem, je nach den Umständen, das kommt darauf an; that —s upon circumstances, das kommt darauf an. **—able**, *adj.* zuverlässig. **—ant**, *s.* der Abhängige, der Diener; der Vasall; der Anhänger. **—ence**, **—ency**, *s.* das Herabhängen; (connection) die Verkettung; der Zusammenhang; die Abhängigkeit (*upon*, von); (reliance) das Vertrauen (on, auf); the —ency, das schutzherrliche Gebiet, die Kolonie; our —ence upon God, unsere Abhängigkeit von Gott. **—encies**, *pl.* die Pertinenzien; die Kolonien. **—ent**, I. *adj.*, **—ently**, *adv.* herabhängend; abhängig (on, von); bauend (on, auf). II. *s. see* —ant.

Depeople, *v.a.* entvölkern (*obs.*).

Depict, *v.a.* (ab)malen; schildern, beschreiben (*fig.*).

Depilatory, I. *adj.* enthaarend. II. *s.* das Enthaarungsmittel.

Deplet—e, *v.a.* entleeren; erschöpfen (*fig.*). —

ion, *s.* die (Blut)entleerung (*Med.*); die Erschöpfung (*fig.*). **—ory**, *adj.* die Entleerung befördernd.

Deplor—able, *adj.*, **—ably**, *adv.* beweinenswert, bedauernswürdig, jammervoll, kläglich; —able stupidity, erbärmliche Dummheit. **—ableness**, **—ability**, *s.* das Elend, die Kläglichkeit, Jämmerlichkeit, das Jämmerliche. **—e**, *v.a.* beweinen, betrauern, bejammern. **—er**, *s.* der Beweinende, Bejammernde.

Deploy, *v.a. & n.* deployieren, (sich) entfalten; aufmarschieren, (sich) in Schlachtordnung stellen (*Mil.*). **—ment**, *s.* das Deployieren, Deploiement.

Depolariz—ation, *s.* die Aufhebung der Polarität. **—e**, *v.a.* depolarisieren.

Depone, *v.a.* eidlich aussagen, deponieren. **—nt**, I. *adj.* deponierend; —nt verb, das Deponens (*Gram.*). II. *s.* der Deponent.

Depopulat—e, *v.a.* entvölkern. **—ion**, *s.* die Entvölkerung, Verheerung.

Deport, *v.a.* forttragen, aus dem Lande verbannen, deportieren; to — o.s., sich benehmen, sich betragen, sich verhalten. **—ation**, *s.* die Verbannung, Landesverweisung. **—ment**, *s.* das Benehmen, Betragen; (carriage) die Haltung.

Depos—able, *adj.* absetzbar. **—e**, *v.a.* absetzen, entsetzen (*fig.*); entthronen (*a king, etc.*); vor Gericht aussagen *or* bezeugen; —e on oath, eidlich erhärten. **—it**, I. *s.* das Niedergelegte, der Niederschlag (*Geol.*, *Phys.*, *Chem.*); das Depositum, der Einschuß, die Einlage (*C.L.*); (pledge) das Unterpfand; —it in a bank, das Bankdepositum, die Einzahlung in die Bank, das Bankguthaben; fixed —its, auf bestimmte Zeit eingezahlte Gelder; net —its, Wert der in den Banken niedergelegten Kapitalien nach Abzug der Zinsen (*C.L.*); —its in a boiler, der Kesselstein. II. *v.a.* legen (*eggs*); absetzen, niederlegen; anschwemmen (*land*); einlegen, einzahlen (*money*); in Verwahrung geben, hinterlegen; (entrust to) anvertrauen; to —it the amount, den Betrag deponieren; to —it as pledge, als Unterpfand geben, hinterlegen. **—itary**, *s.* der Verwahrer, Depositar. **—ition**, *s.* die eidliche Zeugenaussage; die beglaubigte, schriftliche Aussage; die Absetzung, Entsetzung (*from an office, etc.*); die Entthronung; die Anschwemmung (*of mud, etc.*). **—itor**, *s.* der Depositor, Einleger; —itor's book, das Einlagebuch. **—itory**, *s.* der Verwahrungsort, Niederlageort, Speditionsplatz. *Comp.* **-it-account**, *s.* das Depositen-Konto, Guthaben. **-it-book**, *s.* das Einlagebuch. **—it-receipt**, *s.* der Depositenschein.

Depot, *s.* die Niederlage (*C.L.*); (magazine) das Lagerhaus; der Bahnhof (*obs. Amer.*).

Deprav—ation, *s.* die Verschlechterung; die Verderbtheit, Entartung; die Lasterhaftigkeit, Entsittlichung. **—e**, *v.a.* verführen, verschlechtern, verderben. **—ed**, *adj.* moralisch verdorben. **—ity**, *s.* die Verderbtheit, Verdorbenheit; die Verworfenheit.

Deprecat—e, *v.a.* durch Bitten abzuwenden suchen, abbitten; (regret) bedauern; (condemn) tadeln, weit von sich abweisen, ausdrücklich mißbilligen, seine Mißbilligung einer S. offen äußern. **—ingly**, *adv.* durch Bitten abwendend. **—ion**, *s.* die flehentliche Bitte, das bittende Abwehren; die Abbitte. **—ory**, *adj.* abbittend; —ory letter, Abbitte-Brief.

Depreciat—e, *v.* I. *a.* herabsetzen (*prices*); herabwürdigen, geringschätzen (*fig.*); —ed coinage, herabgesetzte Münze. II. *n.* im Werte sinken. **—ion**, *s.* die Verringerung (*of the value, etc.*); die Entwertung; die Geringschätzung, abfällige Kritik. **—ive**, *adj.* den Preis herabsetzend; unterschätzend, geringschätzig. **—ory**, *adj.* geringschätzig.

Depredat—e, *v.a.* plündern; verwüsten. **—ion**, *s.* das Rauben, Plündern, die Räuberei. **—or**, *s.* der Räuber, Plünderer, Verwüster. **—ory**, *adj.* raubend, plündernd, verheerend.

Depress, *v.a.* niederdrücken, senken; niederdrücken, einschränken (*trade, etc.*); herabsetzen (*prices*); niederschlagen (*one's spirits*); to — the pole, den Pol für das Auge dem Horizonte näher bringen; trade is very much —ed, der Handel liegt sehr darnieder, das Geschäft ist sehr flau; to be —ed, sinken (*of fluids, etc.*). **—ed**, *p.p. & adj.* niedergeschlagen, gedrückt; flau (*C.L.*). **—ion**, *s.* die Niederdrückung, der Druck, die Senkung; die gedrückte Stimmung, Niedergeschlagenheit; (physical —ion) die (Körper-)Schwäche; die Flauheit (*of trade, etc.*); die Depression (*of the pole, of a star*); das Stechen (*of cataract*); die Depression, das Sinken (*of the barometer*); agricultural —ion, die Notlage der Landwirtschaft. **—or**, *s.* der Niederziehmuskel (*Anat.*).

Depriv—ation, *s.* die Beraubung; die Entsetzung, Absetzung (*Eccl.*); (loss) die Entbehrung, der Verlust. **—ative**, *adj.* beraubend. **—e**, *v.a.* (—e a p. of a th., einen einer S.) berauben, (einem etwas) benehmen, entziehen; (shut out from a th., von einer S.) ausschließen; (divest of an office, eines Amtes) entsetzen; this —es us of the pleasure, dies beraubt uns des Vergnügens *or* raubt uns das Vernügen; I must —e myself of that pleasure. ich muß mir dieses Vergnügen versagen.

Depth, *s.* die Tiefe (*also fig.*); (sea) das Meer; das Hohl (*of a ship*); die Teufe (*Min.*); — of misery, der Abgrund des Elends; in the — of night, in tiefster Nacht *or* mitten in der Nacht; — of winter, mitten im Winter; to go beyond one's —, to get out of one's —, den (sichern) Grund unter den Füßen verlieren (*also fig.*).

Depurat—e, *v.a.* reinigen, läutern. **—ion**, *s.* die Reinigung, Läuterung. **—ive**, *adj.* reinigend.

Deput—ation, *s.* die Abordnung; (person(s) sent) der (die) Abgeordnete(n). **—e**, *v.a.* abordnen, bevollmächtigen, absenden. **—y**, I. *s.* der Abgeordnete, Abgesandte, der Stellvertreter (*Law*); der Vollmachtinhaber (*C. L.*); by —y, durch Stellvertretung; chamber of —ies, das Abgeordnetenhaus. II. *attrib.*; —y chairman, der stellvertretende Vorsitzer, Vizepräsident; —y governor, der Unterstatthalter.

Deracinat—e, *v.a.* entwurzeln, ausraufen, ausrotten. **—ion**, *s.* das Entwurzeln, die Entwurzelung, Ausrottung.

Derail, *v.* I. *a.* entgleisen lassen, zum Entgleisen bringen; —ing of a train, absichtliches Entgleisenlassen eines Zuges. II. *n.* entgleisen. **—ment**, *s.* die Entgleisung (*Railw.*).

Derange, *v.a.* (disorder) in Unordnung bringen, verwirren, stören; (disorder the mind) den Geist zerrütten. **—ment**, *s.* die Unordnung, Verwirrung, Störung; die Geistes-Störung.

Derelict, I. *adj.* verlassen; — goods, herrenlose Güter. II. *s.* herrenloses Gut; treibendes Wrack; vom Meere verlassener trocken gelegter Strich Landes. **—ion**, *s.* die Aufgabe, das Verlassen, Imstichelassen; —ion of duty, die Pflichtversäumnis, Pflichtvernachlässigung. **—s**, *pl.* Wrackgüter; die vom Meere trocken gelegten Ländereien.

Deri—de, *v.a.* verlachen, verhöhnen, verspotten. **—der**, *s.* der Spötter, Verhöhner. **—dingly**, *adj.* spöttisch, höhnisch. **—sion**, *s.* die Verspottung; der Hohn, Spott; (object of —sion) der Spott, das Gespött. **—sive**, *adj.*, **—sively**, *adv.* spöttisch, höhnisch.

Deriv—able, *adj.* ableitbar; an argument —able from facts, ein aus Tatsachen herzuleitender Beweis. **—ation**, *s.* die Ableitung, Herleitung; die (Wort-)Ableitung (*Gram.*). **—ative**, I. *adj.*, **—atively**, *adv.* abgeleitet, hergeleitet, durch Ableitung; —ative chord, der vom Grundton abgeleitete Akkord. II. *s.* das abgeleitete Wort, Derivatum (*Gram.*); das Abgeleitete (*Math.*); das Derivat (*Chem.*). **—e**, *v.a.* ableiten, herleiten (from, von); (receive by transmission) durch Übergabe, Abstammung erhalten haben; (owe to) verdanken; to —e profit from (a th.), Nutzen aus (einer Sache) ziehen; to —e one's birth, seine Geburt ableiten *or* herleiten

Derma—l, *adj.* die Haut betreffend, Haut=; auf die Haut wirkend (*Surg.*). **—tology**, *s.* die Hautlehre.

Derogat—e, *v.n.* & *a.* vermindern, schmälern, Abbruch tun; to —e from o.s., sich erniedrigen, seiner Würde etwas vergeben; I will not —e from his merits, ich will seinen Verdiensten nicht zu nahe treten *or* seine Verdienste nicht schmälern; to —e from rules, von den Regeln abgehen (*Law*). **—ion**, *s.* die Herabwürdigung, Entwürdigung. **—ory**, *adj.* Eintrag tuend, schmälernd, beeinträchtigend; —ory to his honour, seiner Ehre schadend; —ory to truth, die Wahrheit beeinträchtigend; to act in a manner —ory to o.s., seiner unwürdig handeln; there was nothing —ory in that, es lag nichts Verletzendes darin; so etwas war nicht unter seiner Würde.

Derrick, *s.* der Dirk, Piekfall (*Naut.*); der Arm, bewegliche Auslieger (*of a crane*).

Derry, *int.* heißa! juchhe! —down! heißa, lustig!

Dervish, *s.* der Derwisch.

Descant, I. *v.n.* Diskant singen; trillern, variieren (*Mus.*); to — upon a th., sich weitläufig auslassen über eine S. II. *s.* (treble) der Diskant, Sopran; mehrstimmiger, kunstvoller Gesang; die Variation eines Liedes; der Läufer; die längere Auslassung (über eine S.).

Descend, *v.n.* (get down from) herab=, herunter=steigen, =kommen (von); (fall) fallen, sinken; (invade) in ein Land einfallen *or* einbrechen; tiefer werden, fallen (*Mus.*); (spring) abstammen, herkommen; (fall to) durch Erbschaft zufallen, anheimfallen; (abase o.s.) sich herablassen, sich erniedrigen; the rain —ed, der Regen fiel herab; as well —ed as thyself, von ebenso guter Herkunft wie Du (selbst); it —s to his son, es geht auf seinen Sohn über, es fällt an seinen Sohn; to be —ed (from), abstammen *or* herstammen (von); I cannot — to acts of meanness, ich kann mich nicht zu Handlungen der Niederträchtigkeit erniedrigen; —ing rhythm, absteigender Rhythmus; —ing series, fallende Reihe (*Math.*). —**ant**, *s.* der Abkömmling, Nachkomme.

Descen—sion, *s.* das Herabsteigen; die Absteigung, Deszension (*Astr.*). **—t**, *s.* das Herabsteigen, Heruntergehen, das Fallen; der Hang, Fall, die Neigung (*Surv.*, *Build.*); der Niedergang in den Graben (*Fort.*); die Einfahrt (*into a mine*); der Fall (*of bodies*, *Phys.*); (birth, ancestry) die Abstammung, Herkunft, Geburt; (race) das Geschlecht; (slope) der Abhang; (degree, step) der Grad, die (niedere) Rangstufe; das Herabgehen zu einem tieferen Ton (*Mus.*); (invasion) der (feindliche) Einfall, die Landung; (attack) der Anfall; der Heimfall, die Übertragung (*of property, etc.*); (fall) der Fall, die Erniedrigung; —t from the Cross, die Kreuzabnahme; —t into Hell, die Höllenfahrt; —t upon an island, Einfall in eine Insel; collateral —t, Seitenabstammung; lineal —t, Abstammung in gerader Linie.

Describ—able, *adj.* beschreiblich. **—e**, *v.a.* beschreiben; schildern, darstellen; to —e a curve, eine krumme Linie *or* Kurve beschreiben.

Descrier, *s.* der Entdecker, Erspäher.

Descripti—on, *s.* die Beschreibung; die Schilderung, Darstellung; (sort) die Art, Gattung; you should have no intercourse with persons of this —on, mit Leuten dieser Art darfst du keinen Umgang haben; the view beggars all —on, die Aussicht übersteigt alle Beschreibung; past all —on, ganz unbeschreiblich. **—ve**, *adj.* beschreibend, schildernd; a story —ve of the times, eine die damaligen Zeiten schildernde Erzählung; —ve power, die Darstellungskunst.

Descry, *v.a.* ausspähen, entdecken; (perceive) gewahren, wahrnehmen; to — land in the distance, Land in der Ferne erblicken.

Desecrat—e, *v.a.* entweihen, entheiligen. **—ion**, *s.* die Entweihung, Entheiligung.

[1]**Desert**, I. *adj.* wüst, öde; (—ed) unbewohnt. II. *s.* die Wüste, Einöde. III. *v.a.* verlassen; im Stiche lassen (*a friend*); to — a cause, a party, einer Sache, einer Partei abtrünnig, untreu werden. IV. *v.n.* fahnenflüchtig werden, desertieren. **—er**, *s.* der Ausreißer, Fahnenflüchtige (*Mil.*); der Abtrünnige. **—ion**, *s.* das Verlassen (*of a place, etc.*); das Im=Stich=Lassen (*of a friend*); die Fahnenflucht, Desertion.

[2]**Desert**, *s.* (*also* —s) das Verdiente, der verdiente Lohn, die wohlverdiente Strafe; you have got your —s, Sie haben bekommen was Sie verdienen.

Deserv—e, *v.* I. *a.* verdienen; he —es (is —ing of) esteem, er verdient Achtung. II. *n.* Belohnung verdienen; he has —ed well of his country, er hat sich um sein Vaterland verdient gemacht. **—ed**, *adj.* verdient. **—edly**, *adv.* verdienter Weise, nach Verdienst, mit Recht. **—ing**, *adj.* verdient; a —ing man, ein verdienter Mann, ein Mann von Verdienst.

Deshabille, *s.* das Morgenkleid, der Hausrock.

Desiccat—e, *v.* I. *a.* austrocknen. II. *n.* trocken werden. **—ion**, *s.* die Austrocknung; das Trockenwerden. **—ive**, *adj.* austrocknend.

Desiderat—e, *v.a.* bedürfen; vermissen, zurückwünschen. **—ive**, *adj.* ein Verlangen anzeigend. **—um**, *s.* (*pl.* —a) das Gewünschte, Wünschenswerte, Erfordernis; a great —um, etwas höchst Wünschenswertes, ein dringendes Erfordernis.

Design, I. *v.a.* (sketch) zeichnen, entwerfen; (intend, plan) beabsichtigen, vorhaben, sich (*dat.*) vornehmen, mit (einer S.) umgehen; his father —ed him for the bar, sein Vater bestimmte ihn zum Rechtsanwalt. II. *s.* (intention) das Vorhaben, die Absicht; (project) der Anschlag, Plan, das Projekt; die Anordnung, Einteilung (*of a work*); (drawing) die Zeichnung; der Aufriß, Entwurf, (*Arch., etc.*); (pattern) das Muster, die Musterzeichnung, der Musterriß; der Endzweck; altered —, neue Zeichnung, die Umzeichnung; with the — to injure us, in der Absicht, uns zu schaden; to have some —, etwas in Schilde führen; school of —, die (Muster=)Zeichenschule. **—ed**, *adj.*, **—edly**, *adv.* absichtlich. **—er**, *s.* der Erfinder (*of a machine, etc.*); der Zeichner; der Musterzeichner; (planner) der Projektenmacher; (plotter) der Ränkeschmied, Intrigant. **—ing**, *adj.* hinterlistig, ränkevoll.

Designat—e, I. *v.a.* (denote) bezeichnen; ernennen, bestimmen (for, zu). II. *adj.* ernannt, bestimmt; bezeichnet. **—ion**, *s.* die Bezeichnung; die Bestimmung, Ernennung.

Desilverize, *v.a.* entsilbern.

Desir—able, *adj.*, **—ably**, *adv.* wünschenswert; (pleasing) erwünscht, angenehm; a —able acquaintance, eine wünschenswerte Bekanntschaft; a —able residence, eine angenehme freundliche Wohnung. **—ability**, **—ableness**, *s.* die Erwünschtheit, das Wünschenswerte. **—e**, I. *v.a.* wünschen, verlangen, begehren; (beg) bitten, ersuchen; (bid) befehlen, heißen; to leave much (nothing) to be —ed, viel (nichts) zu wünschen übrig lassen. II. *s.* das Verlangen, die Sehnsucht, große Lust, der lebhafte Wunsch. **—ous**, *adj.* begierig (of, nach); I am —ous to, ich möchte gern; —ous of glory, ruhmbegierig.

Desist, *v.n.* abstehen, ablassen; to — from one's purpose, von seinem Vorhaben abstehen.

Desk, *s.* das Pult; reading-—, das Lesepult writing-—, das Schreibepult; Oxford —, stellbares Schreibepult; prayer —, Betpult; roll-top —, das Zylinderbureau.

Desolat—e, I. *adj.*, **—ely**, *adv.* einsam; (waste) wüst, öde; (afflicted) tief betrübt, trostlos; (sad)

traurig; (uninhabited) unbewohnt; she is now quite —e, sie ist jetzt ganz verlassen. II. *v.a.* verwüsten, verheeren. **—er**, *s.* der Verwüster. **—ion**, *s.* die Verödung, Verwüstung; die Einöde; das Elend; to bring to —ion, zu Grunde richten.

Despair, I. *s.* die Hoffnungslosigkeit, Verzweiflung; to drive to —, zur Verzweiflung bringen. II. *v.n.*; to — of, verzweifeln an (*dat.*); his life is —ed of by the doctors, die Ärzte geben ihn auf. **—ing**, *adj.*, **—ingly**, *adv.* verzweifelnd, hoffnungslos.

Despatch, *see* Dispatch.

Despera—do, *s.* der Wagehals, Tollkopf. **—te**, *adj.*, **—tely**, *adv.* hoffnungslos, verzweifelt; (reckless) verwegen, toll; (very great) arg, schrecklich, ungeheuer (*coll.*); in a —te condition, in einer verzweifelten Lage; a —te remedy, ein äußerstes Heilmittel; rendered —te by (driven to —tion by) . . ., zur Verzweiflung gebracht durch . . .; —te fool, großer Narr; —te smoker, arger *or* unverbesserlicher Tabackraucher (*coll.*). **—tion**, *s.* die Verzweiflung; die Hoffnungslosigkeit; (fury) die Raserei.

Despicabl—e, *adj.*, **—y**, *adv.* verächtlich; jämmerlich. **—eness**, *s.* die Verächtlichkeit.

Despise, *v.a.* verachten, geringschätzen; verschmähen.

Despite, I. *s.* (contempt) die Verachtung; (contemptuous defiance) der Trotz, die Widersetzlichkeit; in — of you, euch zum Trotze; in his own —, wider seinen Willen, sich selbst zum Trotze. II. *prep.* (*or comp. prep.* — of) trotz; — his protestations, trotz seiner Beteuerungen. **—ful**, *adj.* boshaft, tückisch. **—fully**, *adv.* aus Bosheit.

Despoil, *v.a.* plündern, berauben; —ed of her innocence, ihrer Unschuld beraubt. **—er**, *s.* der Plünderer, Räuber. **—ing**, *see* Spoliation.

Despond, *v.n.* verzagen, verzweifeln (of a th., an einer S.); die Hoffnung aufgeben. **—ency**, *s.* die Verzagtheit, Mutlosigkeit, der Kleinmut. **—ent**, **—ing**, *adj.*, **—ently**, **—ingly**, *adv.* ganz verzagt, ganz mutlos *or* kleinmütig.

Despot, *s.* der Gewaltherrscher, Zwingherr, Despot; (tyrant) der Tyrann; (lord) der Souverän. **—ic**, *adj.*, **—ically**, *adv.* unumschränkt, despotisch; (imperious) gebieterisch. **—ism**, *s.* die Gewaltherrschaft, der Despotismus.

Despumat—e, *v.n.* abschäumen. **—ion**, *s.* das Abschäumen.

Desquamation, *s.* das Abschuppen (der Haut, rc.).

Dessert, *s.* der Nachtisch, das Dessert. *Comp.* **—-knife**, *s.* das Dessertmesser, Obstmesser. **—-service**, *s.* das Dessertservice, Obstgerät. **—-spoon**, *s.* der Dessertlöffel, kleine Löffel.

Destin—ation, *s.* die Bestimmung; (place of —ation) der Bestimmungsort; der Abladeplatz (*C. L.*); I fear the letter never reached its —ation, der Brief, befürchte ich, ist nie an seine Adresse gelangt. **—e**, *v.a.* bestimmen; (choose out) ausersehen; that is the purpose for which it was —ed, es war zu diesem Zwecke bestimmt; —ed to an early death, einem frühen Tode verfallen. **—ies**, *pl.* die Schicksalsgöttinnen, Parzen. **—y**, *s.* das Schicksal, Geschick, Verhängnis; to read a p.'s —y, einem seine *or* jemandes Zukunft vorhersagen.

Destitut—e, *adj.* verlassen, hülflos; (deprived of) bar, entblößt; —e of comfort, jeder Behaglichkeit ermangelnd; a land —e of inhabitants, ein entvölkertes Land; the —e poor, die hülfsbedürftigen Armen, die hülflose Armut. **—ion**, *s.* (want) der Mangel (an, *dat.*); die bittere Not.

Destroy, *v.a.* zerstören, vernichten; (pull down) niederreißen; (demolish) demolieren; (ravage) verheeren; (kill) töten; (extirpate) ausrotten, vertilgen; zersetzen, auflösen (*Chem.*); to — one's health, seine Gesundheit zerrütten; to — s.o.'s hopes, jemandes Hoffnungen zunichte machen. **—able**, *adj.* zerstörbar. **—er**, *s.* der Zerstörer, Verwüster; der Mörder. **—ing**, I. *p.* & *adj.* vernichtend, verheerend; —ing angel, Würgengel. II. *s.* die Zerstörung, Vernichtung.

Destructi—bility, *s.* die Zerstörbarkeit. **—ble**, *adj.* zerstörbar. **—on**, *s.* die Zerstörung, Vernichtung, Verwüstung; das Zugrunderichten; die Tötung, der Mord; (ruin) das Verderben, der Untergang; to work one's own —on, seinen eignen Untergang herbeiführen. **—ve**, *adj.*, **—vely**, *adv.* zerstörend; (ruinous) verderblich, schädlich; intemperance is —ve of health, Unmäßigkeit untergräbt *or* zerstört die Gesundheit; —ve to the morals, sittenverderblich. **—veness**, *s.* die zerstörende Gewalt; der Zerstörungssinn.

Desuetude, *s.* das Abkommen eines Gebrauches; die Entwöhnung; lost by —, in Folge der Nichtgeltendmachung verloren gegangen.

Desulphurate, **Desulphurize**, *v.a.* entschwefeln.

Desultor—ily, *adv.* flüchtig, eilig, obenhin. **—iness**, *s.* die Flüchtigkeit, Oberflächlichkeit; die Flatterhaftigkeit, der Unbestand. **—y**, *adj.* (rambling) desultorisch, abspringend; (unconnected) unzusammenhängend; (superficial) oberflächlich; (hasty) flüchtig; —y attack, zerstreuter Angriff; a —y conversation, ein unzusammenhängendes Gespräch; —y fighting, das Geplänkel; —y firing, planloses, unregelmäßiges Feuern; —y reading, oberflächliche, planlose Lektüre; —y remark, beiläufige Bemerkung.

Detach, *v.a.* losmachen, ablösen, trennen, absondern; detachieren, absenden (*Mil.*); abspenstig machen (*fig.*). **—able**, *adj.* abnehmbar, abtrennbar, ablöslich. **—ed**, *v.a.* alleinstehend (*Arch.*); —ed family residence, freistehendes Wohnhaus; —ed pieces, einzelne Stücke; —ed work, das Außenwerk (*Fort.*). **—ment**, *s.* die Absonderung, Trennung, das Losmachen; die Abteilung (*Mil.*).

Detail, I. *v.a.* ausführlich *or* umständlich darstellen, erzählen; abkommandieren (*Mil.*). II. *s.* das Einzelne, die Einzelheit; —s, die Nebenumstände, Besonderheiten; in —, umständlich, in allen Einzelnheiten; to go into the —s of a subject, ins Einzelne einer Sache eingehen, eine Sache umständlich *or* eingehend erörtern. **—ed**, *p.p.* & *adj.* eingehend, umständlich, ausführlich.

Detain, *v.a.* (keep) zurückhalten, abhalten, verhindern; anhalten, festhalten (*in prison*); I was —ed longer than I expected to be, ich wurde länger aufgehalten, als ich erwartete. **—er**, *s.* der Zurückhaltende, Vorenthaltende; widerrechtliche Vorenthaltung; to lodge a —er against a p., einen verhaften lassen, Beschlag auf jemandes Gut legen lassen (*Law*).

Detect, *v.a.* aufdecken, ertappen, entdecken. **—able**, *adj.* entdeckbar. **—ion**, *s.* die Entdeckung. **—ive**, *s.* der Geheimpolizist, Spitzel; —ive force, die Geheimpolizei.

Detent, *s.* der Vorfall (*Horol.*); der (Spring=) Kegel (*Gun.*); der Sperrkegel (*Mech.*). **—ion**, *s.* die Zurückhaltung, Vorenthaltung; (delay) die Abhaltung, der Verzug; (confinement) der Verhaft; (taking possession of) die Beschlagnahme; house of —ion, das Haftlokal; unlawful —ion, die Freiheitsberaubung.

Deter, *v.a.* abschrecken; (hinder) abhalten, verhindern. **—ment**, *s.* das Hindernis. **—rent**, I. *s.* das Abschreckende, Abschreckungsmittel. II. *adj.* abschreckend; —rent principle, das Abschreckungsprinzip.

Deter—gent, I. *adj.* reinigend. II. *s.*, *also* **—sive**, *s.* das Reinigungsmittel.

Deteriorat—e, *v.* I. *a.* verschlechtern, verschlimmern. II. *n.* sich verschlimmern, schlechter werden; entarten. **—ion**, *s.* die Verschlimmerung, Verschlechterung; die Entartung.

Determin—able, *adj.* bestimmbar. **—ant**, I. *adj.* bestimmend. II. *s.* das Bestimmende; die Determinante (*Math.*). **—ate**, *adj.*, **—ately**, *adv.* (ascertained) festgesetzt; (—ed upon) beschlossen; (certain) gewiß; (definite, settled) bestimmt;

(resolute) entſchloſſen. **—ateness**, *s.* die Beſtimmtheit; (resolution) die Entſchloſſenheit. **—ation**, *s.* die Entſchloſſenheit, Entſchiedenheit; (decision) die Entſcheidung, der Beſchluß; (resolve) der feſte Vorſatz, Entſchluß; die Beſtimmung (*of the will*). **—ative**, *adj.* beſtimmend; beſchränkend; einſchränkend (*of words, etc.*); entſcheidend. **—e**, *v.* I. *a.* (limit) beſchränken; (influence) beſtimmen, eine Richtung geben; (decide) beſtimmen, feſtſetzen, entſcheiden; (ascertain) ausfindig machen, ausmitteln, beſtimmen; (settle) zur Entſcheidung bringen, entſcheiden; before you —e whether . . ., ehe Sie ſich entſcheiden ob . . .; this circumstance —ed him to the study of the law, dieſer Umſtand beſtimmte ihn zum Rechtsſtudium; to —e s.o. in favour of a p., einen für jemand günſtig ſtimmen; I am —ed to pursue my course, ich bin entſchloſſen, meinen Weg fortzuſetzen. II. *n.* (ſich) endigen (*obs.*); zu einem Schluß kommen, einen Entſchluß faſſen. **—ed**, *adj.* entſchloſſen.

Detest, *v.a.* verabſcheuen, haſſen. **—able**, *adj.*, **—ably**, *adv.* verabſcheuungswürdig, abſcheulich. **—ableness**, *s.* die Abſcheulichkeit. **—ation**, *s.* die Verabſcheuung, der Abſcheu (of, vor); to hold in —ation, verabſcheuen.

Dethrone, *v.a.* entthronen, vom Throne ſtoßen, abſetzen. **—ment**, *s.* die Entthronung.

Detonat—e, *v.* I. *n.* verpuffen, explodieren. II. *a.* verpuffen laſſen, verpuffen, losknallen; —ing cap, das Zündhütchen; —ing composition, der Perkuſſionsſatz; —ing (fog-)signal, das Knallſignal (*Railw.*); —ing powder, das Knallpulver. **—ion**, *s.* die Verpuffung, Exploſion der Knall; loud —ions, laute Exploſionen. **—or**, *s.* der Puffer.

Detour, *s.* der Umweg.

Detract, *v.a.* abziehen, entziehen; (— from a th.) (einer S.) Eintrag tun; — from a p.'s reputation, einen herabſetzen, jemandes Ruf ſchmälern; to — from the merit of an action, das Verdienſt einer Handlung beeinträchtigen *or* herabſetzen. **—ion**, *s.* die Herabſetzung, Schmälerung, Beeinträchtigung. **—ive**, *adj.* verleumderiſch. **—or**, *s.* der Verleumder; der Abziehmuskel (*Anat.*).

Detrain, *v.* I. *a.* ausſchiffen (auf der Bahn), ausſteigen laſſen (*Mil.*). II. *n.* ausſteigen, den Zug verlaſſen. **—ment**, *s.* Ausſchiffung (*of troops*) (*Mil.*).

Detriment, *s.* der Abbruch, Schaden, Nachteil. **—s**, *pl.* jährlicher Beitrag zur baulichen Unterhaltung eines College (*Eng.*) **—al**, *adj.*, **—ally**, *adv.* ſchädlich, nachteilig.

Detritus, *s.* das Geröll(e) (*Geol.*).

[1]**Deuce**, *s.* die Zwei (im Würfel und Kartenſpiel), das Daus; —ace, das Zwei-Aß, Zwei und Ein.

[2]**Deuce**, *s.* der Teufel; what the — do you mean? was zum Teufel wollen Sie damit ſagen? **—d**, *adj.*, **—dly**, *adv.* verteufelt.

Deuteronomy, *s.* das fünfte Buch Moſis.

Deutoxide, *s.* das Deutoxyd (*Chem.*).

Devastat—e, *v.a.* verwüſten. **—ion**, *s.* die Verwüſtung, Verheerung. **—or**, *s.* der Verwüſter.

Develop, *v.* I. *a.* entwickeln, entfalten; hervorrufen (*a photograph*). II. *n.* ſich entwickeln; ſich herausmachen. **—er**, *s.* das Entwickelungsmittel (*Photo.*). **—ing**, *s.* das Hervorrufen des photographiſchen Bildes. **—ment**, *s.* die Entwickelung, Entfaltung.

Deviat—e, *v.n.* abweichen (from, von). **—ion**, *s.* die Abweichung; die Verſegelung, der Wahnkurs (*Naut.*); angle of —ion, der Ablenkungswinkel; —ion of a balance, der Ausſchlag einer Wage.

Device, *s.* (invention) die Erfindung; (contrivance) der Plan, Entwurf, Einfall; (plot) der Anſchlag; der Wappenſpruch, das Sinnbild (*Her.*); (motto) der Denkſpruch; a man full of —s, ein anſchlägiger, erfinderiſcher Kopf; an excellent —! ein vortrefflicher Plan.

Devil, I. *s.* der Teufel; (printer's —) der Laufburſche (aus der Druckerei); eine ſtark gewürzte (auf dem Roſte) gebratene Geflügelkeule (*Cook.*); der Wolf, Teufel (*Mach.*); a — of a fellow, ein verteufelter Kerl; speak of the — and he appears, male den Teufel nicht an die Wand (*prov.*); the —! alle Teufel! das wäre der Kuckuck! the —'s in it, if . . ., das muß mit dem Teufel zugehen, wenn . . .; the — a bit, nicht das Allergeringſte (*sl.*); how the — came you here? wie zum Teufel kamſt du hierher? (*sl.*); to give the — his due, jedem das Seinige einräumen; to go to the —, zu Grunde gehen, verkommen; the — of a go! eine verteufelte Geſchichte! (*sl.*); to play the — with, arg mitſpielen; the blue —s, der Katzenjammer (*sl.*). II. *v.a.* ſtark pfeffern und auf dem Roſte (zum zweiten Male) röſten; wolfen (*Mach.*); —ing machine, der Wolf. **—ish**, *adj.*, **—ishly**, *adv.* teufliſch; verteufelt, ungeheuer (*sl.*). **—ishness**, *s.* das Teufliſche, die Teufelei. **—ment**, *s.* die Schelmerei, Teufelei, die Poſſen. **—ry**, *s.* die Teufelei; teufliſche Handlung. *Comp.* **—-may-care**, *adj.* dreiſt, verwegen, ſorglos, burſchikos. **—-worship**, *s.* der Teufelsdienſt.

Devious, *adj.*, **—ly**, *adv.* (vom gewöhnlichen Wege) abweichend; (wandering) herumirrend, wandernd, herumſchweifend; (erring) vom Rechten abweichend, irrig, falſch; — paths, Abwege. **—ness**, *s.* das Umherſchweifen; die Abweichung.

Devis—able, *adj.* erdenkbar, erfindbar. **—e**, I. *v.n.* erſinnen, erdenken, erfinden; (bequeath) vermachen; we must —e means to . . ., wir müſſen Mittel ausfindig machen zu . . . II. *s.* das Vermachen; (will) das Teſtament; (bequest) das Vermächtnis. **—er**, *s.* der Erfinder. **—or**, *s.* der Erblaſſer.

Devitalize, *v.a.* der Lebenskraft berauben.

Devitrif—ication, *s.* die Entglaſung. **—y**, *v.a.* entglaſen.

Devoid, *adj.* ohne (*acc.*), bar (*gen.*), leer (an einer S.), -los; — of pity, mitleidslos; — of fear, furchtlos; — of understanding, ohne Verſtändnis, verſtändnislos; — of all feelings of humanity, aller menſchlichen Gefühle bar, ohne jedes menſchliche Gefühl.

Devoir, *s.* (*obs.*) die Höflichkeitsbezeigung; to pay one's —s, (einem) ſeine Aufwartung machen, (einer Dame) Höflichkeit erweiſen (*obs.*).

Devol—ution, *s.* die Abwälzung, das Herabrollen; der Heimfall (*Law*). **—ve**, *v.* I. *a.* abwälzen; (transfer) übertragen. II. *n.* anheimfallen, zufallen; the crown —ves on his eldest son, die Krone fällt an ſeinen älteſten Sohn; it now —ves upon me to tell him the state of the case, es liegt mir jetzt ob, ihm die Sachlage auseinander zuſetzen.

Devot—e, *v.a.* (dedicate) widmen, weihen; zum Untergange verurteilen, dem Untergange weihen (*B.*); (give up wholly) übergeben, ergeben; (offer up) aufopfern; (doom) zum Opfer auserſehen, beſtimmen. **—ed**, *adj.* ergeben; —ed to him, ihm ganz *or* herzlich ergeben; zärtlich; (given over to) übergeben, hingegeben; (dem Tode, Verderben ꝛc.) geweiht, verurteilt; a —ed husband, father, ein zärtlicher Gatte, Vater; the —ed city, die dem Untergang geweihte Stadt; —ed to the pursuit of learning, dem Studium ergeben. **—edly**, *adv.* ergeben. **—ee**, *s.* der Verehrer; der (der Religion ꝛc) Geweihte; (bigot) der Andächtler. **—ion**, *s.* die Widmung, Weihung; das Gewidmetſein; (piety) die Frömmigkeit; (prayer) die Andacht, Gottesdienſt; (affection) die innige Liebe, Ergebenheit; (ardour) der Eifer; —ion to him, Ergebenheit für ihn; —tion to duty, Eifer in der Erfüllung ſeiner Pflicht; to be at one's —ions, ſeine Andacht verrichten, im Gebet begriffen ſein. **—ional**, *adj.*, **—ionally**, *adv.* andächtig, fromm; —ional exercises, (**—ions**,) Andachtsübungen; —ional book, Erbauungsbuch; —ional frame of mind, fromme Gemütsart.

Devour, *v.a.* verschlingen, auffressen, verzehren; to — (the contents of) a book, den Inhalt eines Buches (begierig) verschlingen. **—er**, *s.* der Verschlinger; der Verschwender, Verschlinger (*fig.*). **—ingly**, *adv.* verschlingend; gierig.

Devout, *adj.*, **—ly**, *adv.* andächtig, fromm; (earnest) ernstlich, innig, inbrünstig; a consummation —ly to be wished, eine aufs innigste zu wünschende Vollendung. **—ness**, *s.* die Frömmigkeit; die Andächtigkeit.

Dew, *s.* der Tau; the — is falling, es taut, der Tau fällt. **—iness**, *s.* die Taufeuchtigkeit. **—y**, *adj.* tauig, taufeucht; tauähnlich. *Comp.* **—-berry**, *s.* die Ackerbeere, kriechende Brombeere. **—-drop**, *s.* der Tautropfen. **—lap**, *s.* die Wamme.

Dexter, I. *adj.* recht, rechtsseitig (*Her.*). II. *s.* die rechte Seite. **—ity**, *s.* (agility) die Behendigkeit; (adroitness) die Gewandtheit; (cleverness) die Geschicklichkeit. **—ous**, *adj.*, **—ously**, *adv.* behende, hurtig; gewandt; geschickt.

Dia—betes, *s.* die Harnruhr, Zuckerkrankheit. **—caustic**, I. *adj.* diakaustisch; —caustic curve, krumme Refraktionslinie. II. *s.* die Brennlinie (*Opt.*, *Math.*). **—coustic**, *adj.* diakustisch, die Schallbrechungslehre betreffend. **—dem**, *s.* das Stirnband, Diadem. **—gnosis**, *s.* die Diagnose. **—gnostic**, I. *adj.* diagnostisch. II. *s.* das Erkennungszeichen. **—gonal**, I. *adj.*, **—gonally**, *adv.* diagonal, schräg, querlaufend, überzwerch; —gonal cut, der Schrägschnitt. II. *s.* die Diagonale. **—gram**, *s.* die Figur, das Diagramm; (illustration) die Illustration; der Riß (*Mach.*). **—graph**, *s.* der Diagraph, das Zeicheninstrument. **—lect**, *s.* die Mundart, der Dialekt; study of —lects, die Mundartenforschung, Dialektkunde. **—lectic(al)**, *adj.* mundartlich, dialektisch. **—lectician**, *s.* der Dialektiker. **—lectics**, *pl.* die Dialektik. **—logue**, *s.* das Zwiegespräch, die Wechselrede. **—lysis**, *s. see* Diæresis; das Trennungszeichen; die Dialysis. **—meter**, *s.* der Durchmesser. **—metrical**, *adj.*, **—metrically**, *adv.* diametrisch, gerade durch, mitten durch; —metrically opposed, gerade entgegengesetzt. **—mond**, *see* Diamond. **—ndrian**, *adj.* zweimännig, diandrisch (*Bot.*). **—pason**, *s.* die Oktave (*Mus.*); die Mensur (*of organs*); der Einklang (*Poet.*); der Umfang einer Singstimme *or* eines Instrumentes. **—phaneity**, *s.* die Durchsichtigkeit. **—phanous**, *adj.* durchsichtig; diaphan. **—phonics**, *pl.* die Schallbrechlehre. **—phoretic**, I. *adj.* schweißtreibend. II. *s.* das schweißtreibende Mittel. **—phragm**, *s.* das Zwerchfell (*Anat.*); die Scheidewand, das Diaphragma. **—rrhœa**, *s.* der Durchfall, die Diarrhöe. **—stole**, *s.* die Diastole (*Pros.*, *Med.*). **—style**, *s.* das weitsäulige Gebäude; das Diastylon (*Arch.*). **—thermal**, *adj.* Wärme durchlassend. **—thesis**, *s.* die Körperbeschaffenheit. **—tonic**, *adj.* diatonisch, stufentönig (*Mus.*). **—tribe**, *s.* die Diatribe; (abusive harangue) die anzügliche Rede, Schmährede; der Ausfall.

Diab—lerie, *s.* die Teufelei, Hexerei. **—olic(al)**, *adj.*, **—olically**, *adv.* teuflisch. **—olicalness**, *s.* das Teuflische.

Diacona—l, *adj.* einen Diakonus betreffend. **—te**, *s.* das Diakonat.

Diæresis, Dieresis, *s.* die Diäresis, getrennte Aussprache (zweier zusammenstehender Vokale); das Trennungszeichen.

Dial, *s.* die Sonnenuhr; das Zifferblatt (*of a clock, etc.*). **—ist**, *s.* der Verfertiger von Sonnenuhren; der in der Gnomonik Erfahrene. **—ling**, *s.* die Sonnenuhrkunst; art of —ling, die Gnomonik. *Comp.* **—-plate**, *s.* das Zifferblatt. **—-telegraph**, *s.* der Zeigertelegraph.

Diamond, I. *s.* der Diamant; der Demant (*poet.*); der Rhombus, die Raute (*Geom.*); das Carreau, Karo (*Cards*); die Diamantschrift (*Typ.*); facetted —, der Rautenbrillant; rose —, die Rosette, Raute; a rough —, ein ungeschliffener Diamant (*fig.*); it was — cut —, da stand List gegen List. II. *attrib.*; —cement, der Diamantkitt; — edition, die Ausgabe in Diamantschrift; —mine, die Diamantengrube; —point, die Diamantspitze. *Comp.* **—-cutter**, *s.* der Diamantschleifer. **—-dust**, *s.* der Diamantstaub. **—-shaped**, *adj.* rautenförmig. **—-work**, *s.* der Netzverband (*Arch.*).

Diaper, I. *s.* die geblümte, gemusterte Leinwand (*Weav.*); die Windel. II. *v.a.* mustern, blümen; ein Kind in Windeln wickeln. *Comp.* **—-work**, *s.* das wiederkehrend geblümte Getäfel.

Diary, *s.* das Tagebuch; der Schreibkalender; das Fristbuch (*Min.*); to keep a —, Tagebuch führen.

Dibbl—e, I. *s.* der Pflanzstock, Setzstock (*Hort.*). II. *v.a.* mit dem Pflanzstock pflanzen. **—er**, *s.* (—ing machine), die Setzmaschine.

Dic—e, I. *s. pl.* (*see* Die) die Würfel; to play at —e, Würfel spielen, würfeln; to cog the —e, die Würfel kneipen; game at —e, das Würfelspiel. II. *v.a.* würfeln, Würfel spielen. *Comp.* **—e-box**, *s.* der Würfelbecher. **—e-player, (—er,)** *s.* der Würfler, Würfelspieler.

Dicentra, *s.* tropfendes Herz (*Bot.*).

Dicephalous, *adj.* zweiköpfig.

Dickens, *s.* der Teufel (*sl.*); what the — are you about? was zum Teufel *or* zum Kuckuck machen Sie da *or* haben Sie vor? (*sl.*).

Dicker, *s.* die Zahl von 10, der Decher (*obs.*); a — of gloves, 10 Dutzend Paar Handschuhe.

Dick(e)y, *s.* der Dienersitz, Sitz hinten am Wagen; (front) das Vorhemdchen.

Dicky-bird, *s.* das Vögelchen, der Piepmatz (*coll.*).

Dicotyledon, *s.* eine zweisamenlappige Pflanze. **—ous**, *adj.* zwei Samenlappen habend.

Dict—ate, I. *v.a.* vorschreiben, befehlen; (impose) vorschreiben, auferlegen; diktieren, in die Feder diktieren, sagen (*for a p. to write down*); vorsagen, in den Mund legen, eingeben (*fig.*); he will not suffer to be —ated to, er läßt sich (*dat.*) nichts vorschreiben *or* sich (*dat.*) keine Vorschriften machen. II. *v.n.* in die Feder diktieren; befehlen; vorschreiben. III. *s.* die Vorschrift; die Richtschnur; *see* —ates. **—ates**, *pl.* die Eingebungen (*fig.*); to obey the —ates of conscience, den Eingebungen des Gewissens folgen. **—ation**, *s.* das Diktieren; das Diktatschreiben, das Schreiben nach Diktat; to write from —ation, nach Diktat schreiben; (what is —ed) das Diktat; der Befehl, das Geheiß; das Befehlen. **—ator**, *s.* der Diktator; der unumschränkte Machthaber *or* Gebieter. **—atorial**, *adj.*, **—atorially**, *adv.* gebieterisch. **—atorship**, *s.* die Diktatur; die angemaßte, unumschränkte Gewalt. **—ion**, *s.* die Ausdrucksweise, der Stil; (language) die Sprache. **—ionary**, *s.* das Wörterbuch. **—um**, *s.* (*pl.* —a), der Spruch, Ausspruch; der Machtspruch.

Did, *imperf. of* Do.

Didactic, *adj.*, **—ally**, *adv.* lehrend, belehrend, lehrhaft, didaktisch; — disposition, die Lehrhaftigkeit; — poem, das Lehrgedicht.

Diddle, *v.a.* betrügen, prellen (*vulg.*); you were nicely —d there, man hat dich da schön zum Besten gehabt; to — out of, um (etwas) prellen.

[1]**Die**, *v.n.* sterben (of, an (*dat.*); from, vor); absterben, verwelken (*as a plant*); untergehen, vernichtet werden; to — of an illness, an einer Krankheit sterben; to — of hunger, Hungers sterben; to — a . . . death, eines . . . Todes sterben; to — a natural death, eines natürlichen Todes sterben; to — to sin, der Sünde absterben; cowards — many times before their death, die Feigen erleiden die Todesschmerzen vielmals vor ihrem Tode; his heart —d within him, sein Herz erstarb in ihm; to — away, allmählich abnehmen, schwächer und schwächer werden (*as the wind*), sich verlieren, verhallen, ersterben (*as sounds*), sich verlieren (*as colours*), verlöschen (*as light*), hinsinken (*as a person*); to — game, bis

zum letzten Augenblick standhalten; to — hard, nicht leicht sterben, furchtlos sterben (*fam.*); old customs — hard, alte Gebräuche halten sich lange, haben ein zähes Leben (*fig.*); to — by the sword, durch das Schwert umkommen; to — for love, vor Liebe sterben; that I will say, though I were to — for it, das will ich sagen, und wenn es mir auch das Leben kosten sollte; to — out, aussterben; to — with laughing, vor Lachen sterben; to — with shame, vor Scham vergehen; never say —! ergebt euch nie! haltet aus bis zum Äußersten! *Comp.* **—-hard**, *s.* tapferer Krieger (der lieber stirbt als sich ergibt) (*sl.*).

[2]**Die**, *s.* der Würfel; (stamp) der (Münz=)Stempel; der Würfel am Säulenstuhl (*Arch.*); die Stanze, der Grabstichel (*Engr.*); der Kubus; (*obs.*: lot, chance) der Zufall, das Schicksal; the — is cast, der Würfel *or* das Los ist gefallen. *Comp.* **—-sinker**, *s.* der Münzstecher. **—-stamp**, *s.* der Prägestempel. **—-stock**, *s.* die Kluppe.

Dielytra, *s. see* Dicentra.

Diem, *s.*; per —, täglich.

Diet, I. *s.* die Lebensweise, Kostregel, Diät (*Med.*); (food) die Speise; (provisions) die Kost; (public assembly) der Landtag, Reichstag; spare —, schmale Kost; to observe a strict —, strenge Diät beobachten; meat is a nourishing —, das Fleisch ist eine nahrhafte Speise. II. *v.a.* (einem) Diät vorschreiben, (einen) auf schmale Kost setzen; (feed) speisen, ernähren, beköstigen. III. *v.n.* Diät halten. **—ary**, I. *adj.* diätetisch. II. *s.* die Diätsregel; die Ration. **—etic**, *adj.* diätetisch. **—etics**, *pl.* die Diätetik.

Differ, *v.n.* (be different) sich unterscheiden, verschieden sein; andrer Meinung sein, abweichen (*from a p.*); (not agree) nicht übereinstimmen (with, mit); I am sorry to — from you in opinion, es tut mir leid anderer Meinung zu sein, als Sie; we — very much in opinion, wir sind sehr verschiedener Meinung; I — with you in this respect, in dieser Hinsicht stimme ich mit Ihnen nicht überein; I beg to — from you in this respect, ich bedaure in diesem Punkte mich Ihrer Meinung nicht anschließen zu können; they are always —ing, sie geraten beständig in Streit. **—ence**, *s.* der Unterschied, die Verschiedenheit, der Zwiespalt, Streit (*Naut.*, *Math.*, *Log.*); (disproportion) das Mißverhältnis; (distinction) die Unterscheidung; (distinguishing mark) das Unterscheidungszeichen, Merkmal; (cause of —ence) die Streitfrage; that makes all the —ence, das macht einen himmelweiten Unterschied, das giebt der Sache einen ganz andern Anstrich; to have a —ence with a p., mit einem uneinig sein; to make up the —ence, das Fehlende ersetzen. **—ent**, *adj.*, **—ently**, *adv.* verschieden; as —ent as black from white, so verschieden *or* unähnlich wie Tag und Nacht; he has done it in a —ent way, er hat es anders gemacht; you will soon think —ently, Sie werden bald anders denken; the same thing affects men —ently, dieselbe Sache berührt verschiedene Menschen verschieden, den einen so, den andern anders. **—ential**, *adj.* differential; —ential calculus, die Differentialrechnung; —ential character, das Unterscheidungsmerkmal; —ential duties, der Differentialzoll (*C. L.*); postal differential rates, Verschiedenheit der Portosätze. **—entiate**, *v.* I. *a.* einen Unterschied machen, unterscheiden; differenzieren (*Math.*). II. *n.* sich unterscheiden, unterschieden sein. **—entiation**, *s.* die Unterscheidung; die Veränderung (*Biol.*); das Differenzieren (*Math.*).

Difficult, *adj.* schwer, schwierig; (laborious) mühsam; schwer zu befahren (*as a river*); I did not think it was so —, ich glaubte nicht, daß es so schwer wäre, hielt es nicht für so schwierig. **—y**, *s.* die Schwierigkeit; die Beschwerlichkeit; die Verlegenheit; in pecuniary —ies, in (Geld=)Not, Geldverlegenheit; to throw —ies in a p.'s way, einem Schwierigkeiten in den Weg legen; to experience a —y, auf eine Schwierigkeit stoßen; to find —y in doing a th., es schwierig finden etwas zu tun.

Diffiden—ce, *s.* der Mangel an Selbstvertrauen, die Schüchternheit. **—t**, *adj.*, **—tly**, *adv.* schüchtern, bescheiden.

Difform, *adj.* unregelmäßig (in der Form), ungleichförmig; unförmig, ungestalt; ungleich.

Diffract, *v.a.* brechen, beugen. **—ion**, *s.* die Beugung des Lichts, die Brechung der Strahlen.

Diffus—e, I. *adj.*, **—ely**, *adv.* weit verbreitet, zerstreut; (not concise) weitschweifig, weitläufig. II. *v.a.* ausschütten, ausgießen; ergießen, verbreiten (*fig.*). **—ed**, *adj.* verbreitet, zerstreut; (confused) verwirrt; (*poet.*: loose, flowing) lose. **—eness**, *s.* die Weitläufigkeit, Weitschweifigkeit; die Zerstreuung. **—ibility**, *s.* die Verbreitbarkeit, Ergießbarkeit. **—ible**, *adj.* ergießbar. **—ion**, *s.* die Verbreitung; die Diffusion (*Chem.*, *Opt.*). **—ive**, *adj.*, **—ively**, *adv.* sich weit verbreitend; (widely spread) ausgebreitet; (copious) weitschweifig; (extensive) ausgedehnt, verbreitet; —ive charity, ausgebreitete Mildtätigkeit. **—iveness**, *s.* die Fähigkeit des Verbreitens; die Ausdehnung; die Weitschweifigkeit.

Dig, I. *ir.v.a.* graben; (excavate) ausgraben (*a well, a pit, potatoes, etc.*); to — the ground, den Boden umgraben; to — **down**, untergraben; to — **out**, ausgraben. II. *ir.v.n.* graben; to — **for** (a th.), (einer S.) nachgraben; to — **in**, (in eine S.) hineingraben; to — **through**, (durch eine S.) durchgraben. III. *s.* der Stoß (*vulg.*); to give a p. a — in the ribs, einem einen Rippenstoß versetzen. **—ger**, *s.* der Grabende, Gräber; grave- —ger, Totengräber. **—ging**, *s.* das Graben. **—gings**, *pl.* die Örtlichkeit (*sl.*); (lodgings, *etc.*) die Wohnung, Bude (*sl.*); gold- —gings, die Goldminen.

Digamma, *s.* das Digamma.

Digest, I. *v.a.* verdauen (*food*); auflösen, zersetzen (*Chem.*); (classify) ordnen, einteilen, klassifizieren; (settle) ordnen; (ruminate upon) durchdenken; (put up with) erdulden; to — a plan, einen Plan durchdenken; to — an affront, eine Beleidigung sich (*dat.*) ruhig gefallen lassen; to — one's anger, seinen Ärger verbeißen; I have read the book, but have not yet properly —ed it, ich habe das Buch gelesen, aber seinen Inhalt noch nicht gehörig verarbeitet *or* in mich aufgenommen. II. *v.n.* digerieren; eitern (*Med.*). III. *s.* (*Law*) die Sammlung von Gesetzen und Urteilssprüchen; die Pandekten; die Sammlung, der Auszug, Abriß. **—er**, *s.* der Ordner; der Verdauer; das Verdauungsmittel; der Digestor, der Papinsche Topf. **—ible**, *adj.* verdaulich. **—ibility**, *s.* die Verdaulichkeit. **—ion**, *s.* die Verdauung; die Digestion (*Chem.*); das methodische Anordnen und Durcharbeiten (*obs.*). **—ive**, I. *adj.* die Verdauung befördernd; —ive organs, Verdauungsorgane. II. *s.* das Verdauungsmittel.

Dight, *v.a.* ordnen, herrichten; schmücken, putzen (*obs.*).

Digit, *s.* die Fingerbreite (¾ Zoll); die Ziffer; der astronomische Zoll. **—al**, *adj.* die Finger betreffend. **—alis**, *s.* der Fingerhut (*Bot.*). **—ate**, *adj.* gefingert, fingerförmig (*Bot.*). **—ation**, *s.* die fingerförmige Ausbreitung. **—igrade**, *s.* der Zehengänger (*Zool.*).

Digni—fied, *adj.* würdevoll; (exalted) erhaben; —fied conduct, edles, würdiges Betragen. **—fy**, *v.a.* mit Würde bekleiden; (exalt) erhöhen, veredeln, verherrlichen, ehren. **—tary**, *s.* der Würdenträger; der Prälat; —taries of the church, hohe Geistliche, kirchliche Würdenträger, Kirchenfürsten. **—ty**, *s.* die Würde (*in conduct or appearance*); (high office) die Ehrenstelle, Würde; (exaltedness) die Erhabenheit, der Adel; (exalted rank) der hohe Stand, Rang; die Würdenpfründe (*Eccl.*);—ty of soul, die Seelengröße, der Seelenadel.

Digraph, *s.* der Digraph, die Ligatur (*Gram.*).

Digress, *v.n.* abschweifen; you — too much, Sie schweifen zu sehr von der Frage ab. **—ion**, *s.* die Abschweifung. **—ive**, *adj.*, **—ively**, *adv.* abschweifend.

Dike, I. *s.* der Deich, Damm; (ditch) der Graben; die Felsenader (*Geol.*); stone —, Steindamm. II. *v.a.* eindeichen, eindämmen.

Dilapidat—e, *v.* I. *a.* zerstören; in Verfall geraten lassen. II. *n.* verfallen. **—ed**, *adj.* baufällig. **—ion**, *s.* die Zerstörung, der Verfall; das Verfallenlassen der Gebäude (*Eccl.*).

Dilat—able, *adj.* dehnbar. **—ation**, **—ion**, *s.* die Ausdehnung, Erweiterung; —ion of the pupils, die Pupillenerweiterung. **—e**, *v.* I. *a.* ausdehnen, erweitern. II. *n.* sich ausdehnen, erweitern; to —e upon a th., weitläufig über (eine S.) sprechen, sich über (eine S.) auslassen. **—er**, *s.* das Erweiternde. **—ibility**, *s.* die Ausdehnbarkeit (*Phys.*). **—or**, *s.* der Dilator (*Surg.*). **—orily**, *adv.*, **—ory**, *adj.* (procrastinating) aufschiebend, verzögernd; (tardy) zaudernd, saumselig; (lazy) träge, untätig; (slow) langsam; —ory measures, hinhaltende Maßregeln; —ory pleas, verzögerliche Einreden (*Law*); he is very —ory in all he does, er ist sehr saumselig in allem, was er tut. **—oriness**, *s.* die Saumseligkeit.

Dilemma, *s.* das Dilemma (*Log.*); die Klemme (*fig.*); to be in (*or* on the horns of) **a —**, in Verlegenheit sein, in der Klemme stecken *or* sitzen

Dilettant—e, *s.* (*pl.* —i) der Dilettant, Kunstliebhaber. **—(e)ism**, *s.* der Dilettantismus.

Diligen—ce, *s.* die Emsigkeit, der Fleiß, Eifer; (care) die Sorgfalt; der Eilwagen. **—t**, *adj.*, **—tly**, *adv.* fleißig, emsig; sorgfältig.

Dilly-dally, *v.n.* die Zeit vertrödeln.

Dilu—ent, *adj.* verdünnend. **—te**, I. *v.a.* verdünnen, entkräften; schwächen (*fig.*). II. *adj.*, **—ted**, *adj.* verdünnt; geschwächt. **—tion**, *s.* das Verdünnen; die Verdünnung. **—vial**, **—vian**, *adj.* diluvianisch, Diluvial=. **—vialist**, *s.* der Erklärer der Erdbildung aus der Sündflut. **—vium**, *s.* das aufgeschwemmte Land; (flood) die Überschwemmung.

Dim, I. *adj.*, **—ly**, *adv.* trübe, düster, dunkel; (not clear) undeutlich; matt (*of colours*); trübe (*as the eyes*); to remember —ly, eine schwache *or* dunkle Erinnerung (von etwas) haben; the lights burn faint and —, die Lichter brennen schwach und trübe; —ly lighted, matt erleuchtet. II. *v.a.* verdunkeln; trüben (*fig.*); to — the sight, das Gesicht verdunkeln. **—ness**, *s.* die Dunkelheit, Düsterheit; die Blödsichtigkeit; die Mattheit. *Comp.* **—sighted**, *adj.* blödsichtig.

Dime, *s.* das Zehncentstück ($\frac{1}{10}$ *Dollar*).

Dimension, *s.* die Ausdehnung (*also Geom.*); (measure) das Maß; (size) der Umfang, die Größe; die Dimension (*Math.*); superficial —, Flächenausdehnung; linear —, Längenausdehnung.

Dimeter, *s.* der Vers von zwei Takten oder Versfüßen, Dimeter.

Dimin—ish, *v.* I. *a.* vermindern, verringern; verkleinern; verjüngen (*Arch.*); schwächen (*fig.*); —ished interval, vermindertes Intervall (*Mus.*); to —ish the value of coins, Münzen herabsetzen; —ished image, verkleinertes Bild (*Phot.*). II. *n.* sich vermindern; to —ish in weight, an Gewicht verlieren. **—uendo**, *adv.* (an Tonstärke) abnehmend, diminuendo (*Mus.*). **—ution**, *s.* die Verkleinerung, Verminderung; die Abnahme (*in size, etc.*); die Verjüngung (*Arch.*); die Herabsetzung (*of value*); die Abnahme der Tonstärke, das Diminuendo (*Mus.*). **—utive**, I. *adj.*, **—utively**, *adv.* klein, winzig. II. *s.* das Diminutiv, Verkleinerungswort (*Gram.*). **—utiveness**, *s.* die Kleinheit, Geringheit, Geringfügigkeit.

Dimissary, *adj.* entlassend; letter —, das Entlassungsschreiben.

Dimity, *s.* der Dimity, geköperte Barchent.

Dimple, I. *s.* das Grübchen. II. *v.n.* Grübchen bekommen. III. *v.a.* Grübchen machen, kräuseln; the stone —d the surface of the water, der Stein ließ die Oberfläche des Wassers sich kräuseln. **—d**, *p.p. & adj.* mit Grübchen versehen; —d face, das Gesicht mit Grübchen.

Din, I. *s.* das Getöse, betäubende Geräusch; das Geklirr (*of arms*); das Gerassel (*of carriages, etc.*). II. *v.a.* durch Lärm betäuben; to — into a p.'s ears, einem in die Ohren schreien immer dieselben Wörter, vorpredigen.

Din—e, *v.* I. *n.* zu Mittag essen, speisen, dinieren; to —e with Duke Humphrey, mit den Bildern speisen, nichts zu essen bekommen (*sl.*); to —e out, außer dem Hause *or* nicht zu Hause speisen. II. *a.* zu Mittag bewirten; to —e 20 people, zwanzig Menschen speisen; room capable of —ing 300 people, Saal, in dem 300 Personen speisen können, Speisesaal für 300 Personen. **—er**, *s.* der Speisende; a —er out, einer, der (oft) außer dem Hause speist; (sponger) der Schmarotzer. **—ner**, *s.* das Mittagessen, Mittagsmahl; das Festmahl, großes Essen; late —ner, späte Hauptmahlzeit (zwischen 6 und ½ 9 Uhr); early —ner, Mittagessen vor 6 Uhr nachmittags; to —ner, zum Mittagessen; after —ner, nach dem Essen, nach Tisch(e); I expect a friend to —ner, ich erwarte einen Freund zu Tische *or* zum Essen; public —ner, das Zweckessen; I made a good —ner, ich ließ es mir schmecken; I have not made much of a —ner, ich habe nur wenig zu Mittag gespeist; to take —ner with a p., bei einem speisen; to stay for —ner, zu Mittag bleiben; to serve up —ner, das Mittagessen auftragen; —ner is ready *or* waiting, das Essen ist bereit, or steht auf dem Tische; what are we to have for —ner? was bekommen wir (zu essen)? **—nerless**, *adj.* ohne Mittagessen. *Comp.* **—ing-car**, *s.* der Speisewagen. **—ing-room**, *s.* das Speisezimmer. **—ing-table**, *s.* der Eßtisch. **—ner-bell**, *s.* die Tischglocke, Essensglocke. **—ner-hour**, *s.* die Essensstunde. **—ner-jacket**, *s.* der Smoking, Frack ohne Schöße. **—ner-party**, *s.* die (große) Tischgesellschaft, Abendgesellschaft. **—ner-service**, *s.* das Tafelgeschirr, Tafelservice. **—ner-time**, *s.* die Tischzeit, Essenszeit.

Ding, *v.a.*; to — s.th. into a p.('s ears), einem (mit etwas) in den Ohren liegen. **—dong**, I. *int.* bimbam. II. *s.* der Klingklang.

Dingle, *s.* die Talschlucht.

Ding—ily, *adv.*, **—y**, *adj.* schwärzlich, dunkel; (dirty) schmutzig; (dull) trübe. **—iness**, *s.* die düstere Farbe, das Dunkelbraune; der Schmutz; das schmutzige Äußere, ein schmutziges Äußeres.

Dint, I. *s.* der Schlag; der Eindruck; die Strieme; (force) die Gewalt, Kraft; by — of, kraft (*gen.*), vermöge (*gen.*), durch (*acc.*). II. *v.a.* einschneiden, eindrücken, eingraben.

Dioces—an, I. *adj.* zu einem Sprengel gehörig, Diözesan=. II. *s.* der Diözesan(=Bischof). **—e**, *s.* der Kirchensprengel, die Diözese.

Diœcian, Diœcious, *adj.* zweihäusig (*Bot.*).

Dioptric—al, *adj.* dioptrisch. **—s**, *pl.* die Dioptrik, Lichtbrechungslehre.

Dioram—a, *s.* das Diorama, der große Guckkasten. **—ic**, *adj.* dioramisch.

Dip, I. *v.a.* (ein)tauchen, eintunken (in, into, in); (baptize) durch Untertauchen taufen; anfeuchten (*a hide*); to — out of *or* from, aus . . . schöpfen. II. *v.n.* (unter)tauchen; (incline downwards) sich neigen (*Magnet.*); streichen, einfallen (*Min.*); unter=gehen, =tauchen (untersinken) (*as the sun*); (dip into) sich nur obenhin (auf eine S.) einlassen; to — into a book, ein Buch oberflächlich durchblättern. III. *s.* (—ping) das Eintauchen; die Neigung; (slope) der Abhang; die Senkung (*in a landscape, or in a race-course*); das Bad

(*Dyer.*); (bath) das Eintauchen, kurzes Bad; das Einfallen des Ganges (*Min.*); die magnetische Deklination (*Magnet.*); gezogenes Licht; — of the horizon, der Depressionswinkel, die Düking, der Kimm; — of the parapet, Kronenfall; — in the sea, (kurzes) Seebad. —**per**, *s.* der Taucher; der Tauchende; der gemeine Wasserstar (*Orn.*). —**ping**, *s.* das Eintauchen. *Comp.* —**-chick**, *see* Dabchick. —**ping-needle**, *s.* die Neigungsnadel, Deklinationsnadel.

Dipetalous, *adj.* zweiblätterig (*Bot.*).

Diphtheri—a, *s.* die Diphtheritis, brandige Bräune. —**c**, *adj.* diphtheritisch.

Diphthong, *s.* der Diphthong, Doppellauter. —**al**, *adj.* diphthongisch. —**ation**, —**ization**, *s.* die diphthongische Aussprache.

Diploma, *s.* das Diplom. —**cy**, *s.* die Diplomatie; diplomatische Geschicklichkeit *or* Feinheit. —**tic**, *adj.*, —**tically**, *adv.* diplomatisch; —tic body, das diplomatische Korps, die fremden Gesandten. —**tics**, *pl.* die Diplomatik. —**tist**, *s.* der Diplomat.

Dipsas, *s.* die Durstschlange, Durstnatter.

Dipsomania, *s.* die Trunksucht. —**c**, *s.* der Trunksüchtige.

Diptera, *pl.* Zweiflügler. —**l**, *adj.* zweiflügelig. —**n**, *s. see* Diptera.

Diptote, *s.* das Diptoton (*Gram.*).

Diptych, *s.* (doppelt zusammenlegbare) Schreibtafel der Alten; zusammenlegbares Altargemälde.

Dire, *adj.* schrecklich, grausam, gräßlich, fürchterlich; (dismal) höchst traurig. —**ful**, *see* Dire. —**fulness**, *s.* die Schrecklichkeit, Gräßlichkeit.

Direct, I. *adj.* gerade, direkt; unmittelbar, direkt (*C. L.*); durchgehend (*of trains*); rechtläufig (*Astr.*); (straightforward) gerade, offen; (plain) klar, deutlich; a descendant in the — line, ein Abkömmling in gerader Linie; he acted in — opposition to my command, er handelte in geradem *or* ausdrücklichem Widerspruche mit meinem Befehl; — taxes, direkte Steuern; — train, durchgehender Zug; — way, der gerade *or* nächste Weg. II. *v.a.* richten (*one's course, etc.*); (aim) zielen; (point out, show) hinweisen, (an)weisen, auf (*acc.*) . . . richten, zeigen; (conduct) einrichten, anordnen, leiten, führen; (manage) verfügen, disponieren; (order) anordnen, bestimmen; (instruct) beauftragen; adressieren (*a letter*); pray, — me how to do this, zeigen Sie mir gefälligst, wie ich dies machen soll; Mr. A. has —ed me to you, Herr A. hat mich an Sie gewiesen; as —ed, nach Vorschrift *or* Angabe; laut Verfügung; —ing engineer, der Oberingenieur; —ing line, die Richtungslinie; —ing mark, das Richtungszeichen. —**ion**, I. *s.* die Richtung (*also fig.*); der Lauf (*of a ball, etc.*); die Bestimmung, Anordnung; die Leitung, Führung; (address) die Adresse, Aufschrift; (command) die Anweisung, Vorschrift, Verfügung; (guidance) die Leitung; —ions, die Gebrauchsanweisung; to await further —ions, weitere Verfügungen abwarten; the noise seemed to come from that —ion, das Geräusch schien aus jener Richtung zu kommen; in the —ion of, in der Richtung nach, nach . . . hin, nach . . . zu. II. *attrib.*; —ion cosines, die Richtungs-Kosinusse einer Linie (*Math.*). —ion line, die Richtungslinie (*Railw.*); die Normzeile (*Print.*). —**ly**, I. *adv.* gerade; gleich, unmittelbar; (promptly) ohne Verzug; geradezu; offenbar; deutlich, klar; I shall come —ly, ich komme gleich *or* sofort; —ly opposed, gerade entgegengesetzt. II. *used colloquially as conj.* gleich, wenn, sobald als, sowie; —ly the children have arrived safely they will wire to us, sowie die Kinder glücklich angelangt sind, werden sie uns Drahtnachricht senden. —**ness**, *s.* die gerade Richtung; (decisiveness) die Bestimmtheit; die Geradheit, Unumwundenheit, Aufrichtigkeit. —**or**, *s.* der Direktor, Dirigent, Leiter, Führer, Aufseher, Vorsteher; Board of —ors, der Aufsichtsrat, Verwaltungsrat, das Direktorium. —**orate**, *s.* das Direktorat; das Direktorium, der Vorstand. —**orial**, *adj.* leitend; Direktorial-. —**orship**, *s.* die Direktorstelle. —**ory**, *s.* das Adreßbuch, der Wohnungsanzeiger; (confessional —ory) der Kirchenkalender; (—orate) der Vorstand; das Direktorium (*in France*); die abgefaßte Verordnung für den Gottesdienst (*in England*). —**ress**, *s.* die Vorsteherin. —**rix**, *s.* die Leitlinie (*Math.*).

Dirge, *s.* das Klagelied, der Grabgesang.

Dirk, *s.* der kurze Dolch der Bergschotten.

Dirt, *s.* der Schmutz, Kot; to trample in the —, in den Schmutz treten; to throw — at a p., einen in den Kot ziehen, verleumden (*fig.*); spot of —, der Schmutzfleck; — cheap, spottwohlfeil (*vulg.*). —**ied**, *pret. & p.p. of* —y. —**ily**, *adv. see* —y. —**iness**, *s.* der Schmutz; die Gemeinheit, Niederträchtigkeit (*fig.*). —**y**, I. *adj.* schmutzig, kotig, unflätig; gemein, schmutzig, niederträchtig (*fig.*); —y fellow, gemeiner Kerl, Lumpenkerl; —y red, das Schmutzrot; —y trick, gemeiner Streich. II. *v.a.* beschmutzen, besudeln. *Comp.* —**-scraper**, *s.* die Straßenkehrmaschine.

Disab—ility, *s.* das Unvermögen, die Machtlosigkeit; (incapacity) die Unfähigkeit, Untüchtigkeit; die (Rechts-)Unfähigkeit (*Law*). —**le**, *v.a.* (incapacitate, disqualify) unfähig, untüchtig, unbrauchbar machen, außerstand setzen; (weaken) entkräften, schwächen; rechtsunfähig machen (*Law*); to —le a battery, eine Batterie zum Schweigen bringen, zusammenschießen; to —le a gun, ein Geschütz demontieren, untauglich machen, außer Gefecht setzen; to —le a ship, ein Schiff dienstunfähig machen; —**led**, *adj.* unfähig, untauglich; (crippled) verkrüppelt; dienstunfähig (*Mil.*, *Naut.*); —led soldier, der Invalide. —**lement**, *s.* die Entkräftung; das gesetzliche Hindernis.

Disabuse, *v.a.* enttäuschen, aus dem Irrtum reißen, eines Bessern belehren; to — one's mind of prejudices, (seine) Vorurteile ablegen.

Disaccord, *v.n.* nicht übereinstimmen.

Disaccustom, *v.a.* abgewöhnen.

Disadvantage, *s.* der Nachteil; (injury) der Schaden; die nachteilige Lage; he labours under the — of being . . ., er hat den Nachteil . . . zu sein; to sell to —, mit Verlust verkaufen. —**ous**, *adj.*, —**ously**, *adv.* nachteilig, schädlich, abträglich, (unfavourable) ungünstig; —ous to her interest, ihrem Interesse schädlich *or* Abbruch tuend. —**ousness**, *s.* die Nachteiligkeit, Schädlichkeit; das Ungünstige; der Schaden.

Disaffect, *v.a.* mißvergnügt, unzufrieden machen; abgeneigt, abspenstig machen; (cause to desert) abtrünnig machen. —**ed**, *adj.* unzufrieden; —ed towards the king, dem Könige abgeneigt, dem Könige nicht ergeben; the —ed, die Mißvergnügten. —**edness**, *s.* die Abgeneigtheit, Unzufriedenheit. —**ion**, *s.* (discontentment) die Unzufriedenheit, das Mißvergnügen; (ill will) der Widerwille, die Abgeneigtheit, Feindseligkeit; (unfriendliness) die Unfreundlichkeit; —ion towards the government, die Unzufriedenheit mit der Regierung.

Disafforest, *v.a.* (einem Walde) das Forstrecht nehmen.

Disagree, *v.n.* nicht übereinstimmen, uneinig sein; (differ in opinion) verschiedener Meinung sein; (quarrel) streiten; (contradict) widersprechen; nicht zuträglich sein, schlecht bekommen (*as food*). —**able**, *adj.*, —**ably**, *adv.* unangenehm; (offensive) widrig; (annoying) verdrießlich. —**ableness**, *s.* das Unangenehme, Widrige. —**ables**, *pl.* die Unannehmlichkeiten. —**ment**, *s.* die Verschiedenheit (*in form, etc.*); die Mißhelligkeit, der Streit; (incongruity) die Unangemessenheit; —ment in opinion, die Verschiedenheit der Meinungen, Meinungsverschiedenheit.

Disallow, *v.a.* (not admit) nicht zugeben, nicht einräumen; nicht gelten lassen; (reject) verwerfen; to — a claim, einen Anspruch zurückweisen.

Disannul, *v.a.* aufheben, abschaffen.

Disappear, *v.n.* verschwinden; the epidemic has —ed, die Epidemie hat aufgehört; to — from circulation, außer Umlauf kommen (*C. L.*). **—ance**, *s.* das Verschwinden.

Disappoint, *v.a.* täuschen, vereiteln (*hopes etc.*); enttäuschen (a p.); to —of, um . bringen; he —ed me (failed to come) ich wartete vergeblich auf ihn; they —ed our designs, sie vereitelten unsere Anschläge; don't — me! halten Sie mir gewiß Wort! lassen Sie mich nicht sitzen! —ed, getäuscht; to be —ed in one's expectations, sich in seinen Erwartungen getäuscht *or* betrogen finden; he is sadly —ing, er bereitet uns eine große Enttäuschung, wir hatten uns mehr unter ihm vorgestellt. **—ment**, *s.* die getäuschte Hoffnung, Täuschung; (frustration) die Vereitelung; (miscarriage) das Mißlingen, der Unfall; (balk) der Strich durch die Rechnung; —ments, Enttäuschungen; —ment in love, getäuschte unglückliche Liebe; to meet with a —ment, seine Erwartungen nicht erfüllt finden, enttäuscht werden.

Disapprobat—ion, *s.* die Mißbilligung. **—ory**, *adj.* mißbilligend.

Disapprov—al, *s.* die Mißbilligung. **—e**, *v.* I. *a.* mißbilligen, tadeln; (reject) verwerfen. II. *n.*; —e of a th., eine S. mißbilligen; I —e of his conduct altogether, ich mißbillige sein Betragen durchaus *or* in jeder Hinsicht.

Disarm, *v.* I. *a.* entwaffnen; unschädlich machen; (calm) entkräften, besänftigen; my words —ed his rage, meine Worte besänftigten seine Wut; religion —s death of its terror, die Religion beraubt den Tod seines Schreckens. II. *n.* abrüsten. **—ament**, *s.* die Entwaffnung; die Abrüstung.

Disarrange, *v.a.* in Unordnung bringen. **—ment**, *s.* die Unordnung, Verwirrung.

Disarray, I. *s.* die Unordnung, Verwirrung; die nachlässige Kleidung. II. *v.a.* (disorder) verwirren, in Verwirrung bringen; entkleiden; entwaffnen (*a knight*).

Disassociate, *v.a.* trennen; to — o. s. from a th., sich von einer S. lossagen, nichts damit *or* mit ihr zu tun haben wollen.

Disast—er, *s.* das Unglück, Mißgeschick, der Unfall; to bring —er, Unheil bringen. **—rous**, *adj.*, **—rously**, *adv.* unglücklich, unheilvoll, unselig. **—rousness**, *s.* die Un(glück)seligkeit.

Disavow, *v.a.* nicht anerkennen, (ab)leugnen; he —s his signature, er erkennt seine Unterschrift nicht an. **—al**, *s.* die Nichtanerkennung, das Ableugnen.

Disband, *v.* I. *a.* abdanken, verabschieden, entlassen (*troops*); a —ed officer, ein abgedankter Offizier. II. *n.* sich trennen, auseinandergehen.

Disbelie—f, *s.* der Unglaube. **—ve**, *v.a.* nicht glauben, für unwahr halten, bezweifeln. **—ver**, *s.* der Ungläubige, Zweifelsüchtige, Zweifler.

Disburden, *v.a.* entbürden, entlasten; to — one's heart, one's feelings, sein Herz ausschütten.

Disburse, *v.a.* auszahlen, ausgeben; money —d, der Geldvorschuß, die Auslage (*C. L.*). **—ment**, *s.* die Ausgabe, Auszahlung; die Auslage, der Vorschuß. **—r**, *s.* der Auszahler; der Ausleger.

Disc, *see* Disk.

Discard, *v.* I. *a.* aus der Hand werfen (*cards*); entlassen, verabschieden (*men*); ablegen (*prejudices, etc.*); to — a companion, den Umgang mit einem Bekannten aufgeben. II. *n.* die unnützen Karten aus der Hand werfen.

Discern, *v.* I. *a.* (discriminate) unterscheiden; (recognize) erkennen; (see) sehen; (judge) beurteilen. II. *n.* unterscheiden. **—ible**, *adj.*, **—ibly**, *adv.* unterscheidbar; erkennbar, sichtbar, merklich. **—ing**, I. *adj.*, **—ingly**, *adv.* scharfsinnig, scharfsichtig, verständig. II. *s.* das Unterscheiden; der Scharfsinn, die Scharfsicht. **—ment**, *s.* das Unterscheiden; (power of —ing) die Einsicht, Beurteilungskraft; (judgment) der Scharfsinn.

Discharg—e, I. *v.a.* entladen, abladen, ausladen, ausschiffen (*a load, goods, etc.*); löschen (a cargo, eine Ladung); abfeuern, losschießen; abmachen, bezahlen (*debts, etc.*); quittieren (*a bill of exchange*); befriedigen (*one's creditors*); verabschieden entlassen (*servants*); abdanken (*soldiers, sailors*); entlassen (*a jury, etc.*); loslassen, freisprechen (*a prisoner*); erfüllen (one's duty, seine Pflicht, seine Verbindlichkeiten); (emit) ausbrechen lassen; auslassen (*anger*); entledigen, überheben (einen einer S.), entbinden (einen eines Versprechens *or* von einem Versprechen); verwalten, versehen, verrichten (*an office*); ausfließen *or* auslaufen lassen (*as water from a pipe*); to —e a volley, eine Salve geben; to —e a bond, einen Schuldschein einlösen; to —e the debt of nature, der Natur ihren Tribut bezahlen; he has —ed his duty well, er hat seine Pflicht gut erfüllt; he —ed his office to the satisfaction of all, er versah sein Amt zur Zufriedenheit aller Parteien; the ulcer —es matter, das Geschwür eitert; this river —es itself into . . ., dieser Fluß mündet in . . .; to —e one's conscience, sein Gewissen entladen, erleichtern. II. *v.n.* eitern; (—e itself) sich entladen. III. *s.* das Ab-, Aus-laden, die Ausladung, Löschung; das Losschießen (*of fire-arms*); (charge) die Ladung; der Ausfluß, das Ausströmen (*of water, etc.*); (that which is —ed) der Ausfluß; der Betrag der ausgeflossenen Flüssigkeit; die Eiterung, der Ausfluß, Eiterauswurf; die Bezahlung, Entrichtung (*C. L. etc.*); (receipt) die Quittung; die (Dienst-)Entlassung, Verabschiedung; die Entlassungsschrift; die Freisprechung; die Verwaltung, Verrichtung; die Leistung (*of a duty*); (execution) die Vollziehung; port of —e, der Löschplatz; he has got his —e, er hat seinen Abschied bekommen; in the —e of his duties (one's office), in der Erfüllung seiner Pflichten; —e in full, vollständige Quittung. **—r**, *s.* der Ablader; der Entlader (*Phys.*). **—ing**, *adj.*; —ing arch, der Entlastungsbogen (*Arch.*); —ing cock (—e-cock), der Ablaßhahn; —ing rod, der Entlader.

Discipl—e, *s.* der Schüler, Jünger; der Anhänger (*of Plato, etc.*); Christ's —es, die Jünger Christi; —eship, die Jüngerschaft. **—inable**, *adj.* gelehrig, folgsam. **—inarian**, I. *adj.* disziplinarisch. II. *s.* einer, der strenge auf Zucht und Ordnung hält, Zuchtmeister; he is a good —inarian, er hält seine Schüler *or* Untergebenen in guter Ordnung, in strenger Zucht. **—inary**, *adj.* disziplinarisch, zur Zucht und Ordnung gehörig. **—ine**, I. *s.* die Zucht; (training) die Erziehung; (education) die Bildung; (order) die Ordnung; (punishment) die Züchtigung, Strafe, Bestrafung; military —ine, soldatische Zucht, Mannszucht, Kriegszucht; by way of —ine, zur Disziplin. II. *v.a.* erziehen, bilden; in (die) Zucht nehmen; züchtigen, bestrafen; geißeln, kasteien (*Eccles.*); der Kirchenzucht unterwerfen.

Disclaim, *v.a.* nicht anerkennen, verleugnen; (renounce) entsagen (einer S.), Verzicht leisten (auf eine S.), nicht beanspruchen; he —s all pretension to eloquence, er mißt sich keine Beredsamkeit bei. **—er**, *s.* der Verleugner; der Entsagende; (renunciation) die Verzichtleistung; (refusal to acknowledge) die Verleugnung (*Law*); der (öffentliche) Widerruf, das Dementi.

Disclos—e, *v.a.* enthüllen; entdecken, offenbaren, an den Tag bringen (*designs, etc.*); (betray) verraten, enthüllen. **—er**, *s.* der Entdecker. **—ure**, *s.* die Enthüllung, Offenbarung (*of a secret*); (communication) die Mitteilung; (that which is —ed) das Entdeckte, das Mitgeteilte.

Discolo—ration, *s.* die Entfärbung, Verfärbung; der Fleck (*of the skin, etc.*). **—ur**, *v.a.* die Farbe ändern; entstellen (*fig.*); —uring of the skin, braune und blaue Flecken auf der Haut.

Discomfit, *v.a.* (defeat) schlagen, in die Flucht jagen; (disconcert) entmutigen, verwirren, aus der Fassung bringen, verwirren; (disappoint) vereiteln. **—ure**, *s.* die Niederlage; (confusion) die Verwirrung, Beschämung; die Vereitelung.

Discomfort, *s.* das Mißbehagen, die Unbehaglichkeit.

Discommon, *v.a.* Gemeindeland absondern und einfriedigen, des Gemeinderechts berauben; einem ein Recht *or* Privilegium entziehen; vom geschäftlichen Verkehr mit den Studenten ausschließen (*Univ.*); —ed tradesman, in Verruf erklärter Geschäftsmann.

Discompos—e, *v.a.* in Unordnung bringen; (disturb) aufregen, beunruhigen; this intelligence has quite —ed me, diese Nachricht hat mich ganz aus der Fassung gebracht. **—ure**, *s.* die Unruhe; —ure of mind, Gemütsunruhe.

Disconcert, *v.a.* (frustrate) vereiteln; (disturb) beunruhigen; (embarrass) aus der Fassung bringen, verlegen machen.

Disconnect, *v.a.* trennen; entkuppeln (*Mach.*).

Disconsolate, *adj.*, **—ly**, *adv.* trostlos, untröstlich. **—ness**, *s.* die Trostlosigkeit.

Discontent, *s.* die Unzufriedenheit, das Mißvergnügen. **—ed**, *adj.*, **—edly**, *adv.* unzufrieden, mißvergnügt; the —ed party, die Mißvergnügten; to be —ed with a p.'s conduct, mit jemandes Betragen unzufrieden sein. **—edness**, *s.* die Unzufriedenheit. **—ment**, *s.* die Unzufriedenheit.

Discontinu—ance, *s.* (interruption) die Unterbrechung; (cessation) das Aufhören, die Aufgabe; without —ance, ohne Aufhören, ohne Unterlaß; —ance of a suit, die Nichtverfolgung einer Klage. **—e**, *v.* I. *a.* (stop) unterbrechen, nicht fortsetzen, einstellen; (leave off) liegen lassen, unterlassen; to —e (taking in) a newspaper, eine Zeitung abbestellen *or* zu halten aufhören. II. *n.* aufhören, nachlassen.

Discord, *s.* die Zwietracht, Uneinigkeit, der Streit; die Dissonanz, der Mißklang, Mißton (*Mus.*). **—ance**, *s.* der Mangel an Übereinstimmung, die Uneinigkeit; die Mißhelligkeit. **—ant**, *adj.*, **—antly**, *adv.* mißhellig, uneinig; (contrary) widersprechend; (inconsistent) unverträglich, nicht gemäß; (jarring) mißtönend, mißklingend; nicht zusammenstimmend (*Mus.*).

Discount, I. *s.* der Abzug, Rabatt (*C.L.*); der Diskonto (*on bills*); the — was 3 per cent, der Diskonto war drei Prozent; the goods are at a —, die Waren sind nicht beliebt; — off, hievon geht ab an Rabatt. II. *v.a.* diskontieren; to get a bill —ed, einen Wechsel diskontieren lassen; what do you charge for —ing the bills? wie viel Diskonto nehmen Sie? —ing business, das Diskontogeschäft. **—able**, *adj.* diskontierbar. **—er**, *s.* der Diskontierer.

Discountenance, *v.a.* offen mißbilligen, nicht billigen, nicht unterstützen.

Discourag—e, *v.a.* entmutigen; abschrecken (*from doing*); (advise against) abraten. **—ement**, *s.* das Entmutigen, Abschrecken; die Entmutigung; (—ing fact) das Hindernis, die Schwierigkeit; (want of courage) die Mutlosigkeit.

Discourse, I. *s.* das Gespräch; die Rede; (treatise) die Abhandlung; (sermon) die Predigt. II. *v.n.* (treat of) abhandeln, einen Vortrag halten (über einen Gegenstand); (talk) reden, sprechen, sich unterhalten; predigen (über einen Text).

Discourte—ous, *adj.*, **—ously**, *adv.* unhöflich, unmanierlich, ungefällig, unartig. **—sy**, *s.* die Unhöflichkeit, Grobheit, das rohe Benehmen.

Discover, *v.a.* entdecken, enthüllen; (show) zeigen, sehen lassen; (reveal) offenbaren, mitteilen; (find out) auskundschaften, ermitteln, ausfindig machen; (perceive) gewahr werden; (detect) (einen) ertappen; findig machen (*Min.*); to — o.s. to a p., sich einem gegenüber frei und offen aussprechen, sich einem entdecken. **—able**, *adj.* entdeckbar; sichtbar. **—er**, *s.* der Entdecker. **—y**, *s.* die Entdeckung, Enthüllung (*of a plot*); die Offenbarung (*of a secret*); die Auffindung (*of something hidden, unknown, etc.*); (what is —ed) das Entdeckte, die Entdeckung.

Discredit, I. *s.* der schlechte Ruf; (dishonour) die Unehre, Schande; to bring a p. into —, einem einen schlechten Namen machen, einen in Mißkredit bringen; to the — of their family, zur Schande ihrer Familie. II. *v.a.* nicht glauben; in übeln Ruf bringen; (dishonour) verunglimpfen. **—able**, *adj.* entehrend, ehrwidrig, ehrenrührig.

Discreet, *adj.*, **—ly**, *adv.* verständig, umsichtig, klug; (modest) bescheiden, taktvoll; verschwiegen. **—ness**, *see* Discretion.

Discrepan—cy, *s.* die Verschiedenheit, der Widerspruch in Ansichten und Handlungen. **—t**, *adj.*, **—tly**, *adv.* verschieden; widerstreitend.

Discret—e, *adj.* getrennt, abgesondert; diskret, nicht stetig (*Math.*); disjunktiv (*Log.*). **—ion**, *s.* die Klugheit, Verständigkeit, Besonnenheit; der feine Takt; (pleasure) das Belieben, Gutdünken, die Willkür; to act with —ion, mit Einsicht *or* taktvoll handeln; years of —ion, die Jahre der Vernunft, mündiges Alter; to surrender at —ion, auf Gnade und Ungnade sich ergeben; I shall use my own —ion, ich werde nach eignem Ermessen handeln; I leave the matter to your —ion, ich überlasse die Sache Ihrem (besten) Gutdünken, ich stelle Ihnen die Sache völlig anheim. **—ionary**, *adj.* willkürlich, unumschränkt, beliebig; —ionary powers, richterliche Machtvollkommenheit, unumschränkte Vollmacht. **—ive**, *adj.* getrennt; disjunktiv (*Log.*, *Gram.*).

Discriminat—e, *v.* I. *a.* unterscheiden; (select) auswählen. II. *n.* unterscheiden. **—ing**, *adj.* unterscheidend, charakteristisch; scharfsichtig. **—ion**, *s.* die Unterscheidung; (difference) der Unterschied; (discernment) der Scharfsinn. **—ive**, *adj.*, **—ively**, *adv.* unterscheidend, charakteristisch; den Unterschied beobachtend; —ive Providence, die unterscheidende Vorsehung. **—or**, *s.* der Beurteiler.

Discursive, *adj.*, **—ly**, *adv.* rasch von einem Gegenstand auf einen andern übergehend; (desultory) unstet, flüchtig, unzusammenhängend; einen Schluß ziehend, folgernd, Urteils- (*Philos.*); the — faculty, die Urteilskraft, Denkkraft.

Discus, *s.* die Wurfscheibe, der Diskus; die Scheibe (*Astr.*, *Bot.*).

Discuss, *v.a.* erörtern, besprechen, erläutern; (debate upon) abhandeln, verhandeln; zerlegen, gemütlich genießen (*wine, fowls, etc.*); to — a bottle, eine Flasche ausstechen (*coll.*). **—ion**, *s.* die Erörterung; the lecture was followed by a lively —ion, auf den Vortrag folgte eine lebhafte Erörterung *or* ein lebhafter Gedankenaustausch.

Disdain, I. *s.* die Verachtung, Verschmähung, Geringschätzung das Schmähen; to hold in —, gering schätzen; lady —, Fräulein Spöttlich. II. *v.a.* verachten, verschmähen. **—ful**, *adj.*, **—fully**, *adv.* voll Verachtung, voll(er) Geringschätzung, verächtlich, verachtend; (haughty) hochmütig; (scornful) höhnisch; a —ful glance, ein verächtlicher Blick. **—fulness**, *s.* die Verächtlichkeit; (scorn) die Verachtung.

Disease, *s.* die Krankheit. **—d**, *adj.* krank.

Disembark, *v.a. & n.* ausschiffen, landen. **—ation**, *s.* das Ausschiffen, die Landung.

Disembarrass, *v.a.* aus der Klemme ziehen; losmachen.

Disembod—ied, *adj.* entkörpert; aufgelöst (*Mil.*). **—y**, *v.a.* entkörpern; des Kriegsdienstes entlassen (*Mil.*).

Disembogue, *v.* I. *a.* ergießen, ausgießen. II. *n.* sich ergießen.

Disembowel, *v.a.* ausweiden, ausnehmen; den Bauch aufschlitzen. **—ler**, *s.* der Bauchaufschlitzer.

Disenchant, *v.a.* entzaubern; he —ed her of her

illusions, er riß sie aus allen ihren Himmeln. —**er**, *s.* der Entzauberer. —**ment**, *s.* die Entzauberung.

Disencumber, *v.a.* entlasten, entbürden; von . . . befreien, frei-, los-machen (*fig.*).

Disendow, *v.a.* einer Stiftung ihre Pfründen *or* ihr Einkommen entziehen. —**ment**, *s.* die Einziehung der Pfründen.

Disengage, *v.a.* befreien, von . . . losmachen; entbinden (*Phys.*); to — the gear, die Maschinerie ausrücken. —**d**, *adj.* frei, unbeschäftigt; are you —d just now? sind Sie gerade nicht beschäftigt? haben Sie eben jetzt nichts vor? I shall be —d at 10 o'clock, um zehn Uhr werde ich frei sein; driver, are you —d? Kutscher, sind Sie frei? —**ment**, *s.* das Losmachen, die Befreiung; die Entbindung (*from obligation, etc., also Phys.*); (leisure) die Muße

Disentangle, *v.a.* auseinanderwickeln, entwirren (*knots, etc.*); befreien (*fig.*); to — o.s. (from difficulties), sich (von Schwierigkeiten) befreien. —**ment**, *s.* die Entwirrung.

Disenthrall, *v.a.* von Knechtschaft befreien.

Disestablish, *v.a.* eine (staatliche) Einrichtung aufheben; to — the church, die Kirche entstaatlichen. —**ment**, *s* die Trennung vom Staate; —ment of the Church, die Entstaatlichung der Kirche.

Disesteem, *s.* die Mißachtung, Geringschätzung.

Disfavour, *s.* die Ungunst, Ungnade; das Mißfallen.

Disfigur—ation, *s.* die Entstellung, Verunstaltung. —**e**, *v.a.* entstellen, verunstalten. —**ement**, *see* —ation.

Disfranchise, *v.a.* (einem) das Wahlrecht nehmen; (eine Stadt) der bürgerlichen Freiheiten berauben. —**ment**, *s.* die Entziehung des Wahlrechts *or* Bürgerrechts.

Disgorge, *v.a.* auswerfen, ausspeien; ausstoßen, ausgießen. —**ment**, *s.* das Ausspeien, Ausstoßen.

Disgrace, I. *s.* die Ungnade; (dishonour) die Unehre, Schande; he retired from court in —, er zog sich in Ungnade vom Hofe zurück; he is a — to his family, er ist der Schandfleck seiner Familie. II. *v.a.* in Ungnade bringen; entehren, schänden, (einem) zur Schande gereichen. —**d**, *p.p.* & *adj.* in Ungnade (gefallen). —**ful**, *adj.*, —**fully**, *adv.* entehrend, schändlich; intemperance is —ful, die Unmäßigkeit gereicht zur Schande.

Disguise, I. *v.a.* verkleiden, vermummen, maskieren; verstellen (*fig.*); to — one's feelings, seine Gefühle verstellen; to — the truth from a p., einem die Wahrheit verhehlen. II. *s.* die Verkleidung; (mask) die Maske; (false appearance) der (falsche) Schein; (pretence) der Vorwand; under the — of friendship, unter dem Scheine *or* der Maske der Freundschaft.

Disgust, I. *s.* der Ekel, Widerwille; der Widerwille, die Abneigung (*fig.*); to take a — to . . ., Ekel empfinden vor . . . II. *v.a.* anekeln, Ekel verursachen; Widerwillen (gegen) erregen, verleiden (einem etwas) (*fig.*); he is —ed with him for not . . ., er ist höchst ärgerlich über ihn, weil er nicht . . .; it —s me to have any connection with such people, es ekelt mir, mit solchen Leuten in irgend einer Verbindung zu stehen; he has become —ed with life, das Leben ist ihm zum Ekel geworden, er ist des Lebens überdrüssig. —**ing**, *adj.*, —**ingly**, *adv.* ekelhaft, widerlich; (annoying) verdrießlich, schauderhaft, abscheulich.

Dish, I. *s.* die Schüssel, Platte; das Gericht, die Speise; this — does not agree with me, dies Gericht bekommt mir nicht (gut). II. *v.a.*; to — up, anrichten, auftragen; schlecht behandeln, betrügen (*coll.*); he was (nicely) —ed, er wurde auf den Leim geführt (*sl.*). *Comp.* —**-cloth**, —**-clout**, *s.* das Schüsseltuch, der Wischlappen. —**-cover**, *s.* die Schüsselstürze, der Schüsseldeckel. —**-mat**, *s.* die Schüsselmatte. —**-stand**, *s.* der Untersatz. —**-warmer**, *s.* der Schüsselwärmer. —**-water**, *s.* das Spülicht.

Dishearten, *v.a.* entmutigen, niederschlagen; (frighten from a th.) abschrecken (von einer S.).

Dishevel, *v.a.* auflösen (*hair*), in Unordnung bringen; —led hair, aufgelöstes Haar, fliegende Haare.

Dishonest, *adj.*, —**ly**, *adv.* unehrlich, unredlich. —**y**, *s.* die Unredlichkeit, Unehrlichkeit.

Dishonour, I. *s.* die Unehre, Schmach, Schande. II. *v.a.* verunehren, entehren, schänden; (seduce) schänden, verführen; to — a bill, einen Wechsel nicht honorieren; to — a signature, eine Unterschrift Not leiden lassen; to return a bill —ed, einen Wechsel mit Protest zurückschicken. —**able**, *adj.*, —**ably**, *adv.* entehrend, schändlich; a — able man, ein Ehrloser. —**ableness**, *s.* die Ehrlosigkeit, Schande.

Disillusion, —**ize**, *v.a.* enttäuschen, ernüchtern, aus einem Wahn reißen.

Disinclin—ation, *s.* die Abneigung. —**e**, *v.a.* abgeneigt machen. —**ed**, *adj.* abgeneigt.

Disinfect, *v.a.* von Ansteckungsstoff befreien, desinfizieren. —**ant**, *s.* das Desinfektionsmittel. —**ing**, —**ion**, *s.* die Desinfektion.

Disingenuous, *adj.*, —**ly**, *adv.* unaufrichtig, falsch; (crafty) hinterlistig; — conduct, unredliches Benehmen. —**ness**, *s.* die Falschheit, Unredlichkeit; (want of frankness) der Mangel an Offenheit.

Disinherit, *v.a.* enterben. —**ance**, *s.* die Enterbung.

Disintegrat—e, *v.a.* auflösen, zerteilen. —**ion**, *s.* die Auflösung, Verwitterung; die Zerstückelung (*of an empire*). —**or**, *s.* die Pulverisiermaschine.

Disinter, *v.a.* ausgraben. —**ment**, *s.* das Ausgraben (*especially of a dead body*).

Disinterested, *adj.*, —**ly**, *adv.* uneigennützig; (impartial) unparteiisch. —**ness**, *s.* die Uneigennützigkeit; die Unparteilichkeit.

Disjoin, *v.a.* trennen. —**t**, *v.a.* verrenken, ausrenken; zerlegen, zerschneiden (*a fowl*); auseinander nehmen (*Carp.*). —**ted**, *adj.* abgebrochen, unzusammenhängend; a —ted discourse, eine unzusammenhängende *or* zusammenhangslose Rede. —**tedness**, *s.* der Mangel an Zusammenhang.

Disjunct, *adj.* getrennt. —**ive**, *adj.*, —**ively**, *adv.* trennend; disjunktiv (*Gram.*); —ive propositions, Disjunktivsätze (*Log.*).

Disk, I. *s.* die Scheibe. II. *attrib.*; — engine, die Scheibenmaschine.

Dislike, I. *s.* die Abneigung; (disapproval) die Mißbilligung; my — to him arises from . . ., mein Widerwille gegen ihn kommt her von . . .; — to a th., Abneigung gegen eine S. II. *v.a.* mißbilligen; (not like) nicht mögen, nicht lieben, nicht leiden mögen *or* können; (feel unpleasant) unangenehm, widrig finden; I — it, ich mag es nicht (leiden), es mißfällt mir.

Dislocat—e, *v.a.* verrenken, ausrenken; to —e one's shoulder, sich (*dat.*) die Schulter verrenken. —**ion**, *s.* die Verrenkung; die Verrückung (*Geol.*); die Verwerfung (*Min.*).

Dislodge, *v.a.* verjagen, vertreiben; aufjagen (*game*); verlegen, versetzen (*troops*); to — the enemy, den Feind aus seiner Stellung vertreiben.

Disloyal, *adj.*, —**ly**, *adv.* treulos, pflichtvergessen; (treacherous) falsch, verräterisch; (faithless) ungetreu. —**ty**, *s.* die Untreue.

Dismal, I. *adj.*, —**ly**, *adv.* trübe, düster; (sad) traurig; (horrible) schrecklich, grausig. II. *s.*; in the —s, niedergeschlagen (*coll.*). —**ness**, *s.* die Traurigkeit, Niedergeschlagenheit; die Schrecklichkeit.

Dismantle, *v.a.* entkleiden, entblößen; niederreißen (*Build.*); abtakeln (*a ship*); to — a fortress, die Befestigungswerke schleifen.

Dismast, *v.a.* entmasten.

Dismay, I. *s.* der Schreck(en), die Bestürzung. II. *v.a.* bange machen, in Schrecken setzen, erschrecken; to be —ed, bestürzt sein, bange sein.

Dismember, *v.a.* zergliedern, zerstücke(l)n. —**ment**, *s.* die Zergliederung, Zerstückelung.
Dismiss, *v.a.* fortschicken, verabschieden entlassen; abdanken (*sailors*); to — a maid-servant, eine Magd fortschicken; to — a case, eine Sache bei Gericht abweisen; to — a p. from office, einen seines Amtes entlassen; he was —ed the service, er wurde aus dem Dienst entlassen, seines Dienstes *or* Amtes enthoben; I —ed him without ceremony, ich fertigte ihn ohne Umstände ab; to — a th. quickly, lightly, from one's mind, sich (*dat.*) eine S. schnell aus dem Sinn *or* aus den Gedanken schlagen, leicht über eine S. fortkommen. —**al**, *s.* die Entlassung; die Abweisung (*Law*).
Dismount, *v.* I. *n.* vom Pferde steigen, absteigen; absitzen (*Mil.*); —! abgesessen! (*Mil.*). II. *a.* vom Pferde abwerfen, aus dem Sattel heben; demontieren (*Mil.*); demontieren, von der Lafette nehmen (*a gun*).
Disobe—dience, *s.* der Ungehorsam. —**dient**, *adj.*, —**diently**, *adv.* ungehorsam (to, gegen). —**y**, *v.a.* (einem) nicht gehorchen, (einem) ungehorsam sein; mißachten (*commands*); I will not be —yed, ich dulde keinen Ungehorsam.
Disoblig—e, *v.a.* (gegen einen) ungefällig sein; (offend) (einen) kränken. —**ing**, *adj.*, —**ingly**, *adv.* unfreundlich, ungefällig, unverbindlich, unartig. —**ingness**, *s.* die Ungefälligkeit, das unverbindliche Wesen.
Disorder, I. *s.* die Unordnung, Verwirrung; (tumult) der Aufruhr; (illness) die Unpäßlichkeit; (disease) die Krankheit; the army retired in —, das Heer zog sich in Unordnung zurück; what is his —? was ist sein Übel? mental —, die Geistesstörung. II. *v.a.* in Unordnung bringen, verwirren; zerrütten (*body or mind*); my stomach is —ed, ich habe mir den Magen verdorben. —**liness**, *s.* die Unordnung. —**ly**, I. *adj.* unordentlich; (lawless) regellos, gesetzlos; (riotous) aufrührerisch, stürmisch; (irregular) ausschweifend, liederlich; —ly behaviour, liederliches Benehmen; —ly doings, Ausschweifungen; —ly house, das Bordell. II. *adv.* in Unordnung.
Disordinate, *adj.* unordentlich, regellos.
Disorganiz—ation, *s.* die Zerstörung (des organischen Zusammenhangs), Auflösung, Zerrüttung (*fig.*). —**e**, *v.a.* (Organisches) auflösen, zerrütten; in Unordnung *or* Verwirrung bringen. —**er**, *s.* der Zerrütter, Zerstörer.
Disown, *v.a.* nicht (als sein eigen) anerkennen; verstoßen; (deny) verleugnen, ableugnen; nicht zugestehen, nicht zugeben.
Dispar—age, *v.a.* herabsetzen, verringern, schmälern, verkleinern. —**agement**, *s.* die Schmälerung, Beeinträchtigung, Verkleinerung; no —agement to you! ohne Ihnen zu nahe treten zu wollen! —**aging**, *adj.*, —**agingly**, *adv.* geringschätzend, geringschätzig. —**ate**, *adj.* ungleichartig, unvereinbar, disparat. —**ates**, *pl.* unvergleichbare Dinge. —**ity**, *s.* die Ungleichheit, Verschiedenheit.
Dispart, I. *v.a.* trennen; spalten, zerreißen; (ein Geschütz) vergleichen, ein Visier anbringen (*Gun.*). II. *v.n.* sich spalten. III. *s.* der Durchmesser einer Geschützmündung; das Visier, Absehen. *Comp.* —**-sight**, *s.* das Richtkorn, Visier (*Artil.*).
Dispassionate, *adj.*, —**ly**, *adv.* leidenschaftslos; (calm) ruhig, gelassen; (impartial) unparteiisch.
Dispatch, I. *v.a.* (send off) abfertigen, absenden, abgehen lassen; (do speedily) schnell abmachen, erledigen; (expedite) eilig abfertigen; (kill) töten, in die andere Welt schicken; to — a piece of business, ein Geschäft (schnell) abmachen. II. *s.* (prompt execution) die schnelle Ausführung, Erledigung; (sending away) die (schnelle) Absendung, Abfertigung; (haste) die Eile; (killing) das Töten; die Drahtung, Depesche, das Telegramm (*Amer.*); with —, sobald als möglich; wenn segelfertig (*C. L.*). —**er**, *s.* der Absender. —**es**, *pl.* die Depeschen; bearer of —es, der Eilbote, Depeschenträger, Kurier. *Comp.* —**-boat**, *s.* das Depeschenschiff. —**-box**, *s.* die Aktenkapsel.
Dispel, *v.a.* vertreiben; zerstreuen (*vapours, etc.*); verbannen (*doubt, care, etc.*).
Dispensable, *adj.* erläßlich; verteilbar.
Dispens—ary, *s.* die Armenapotheke; die Poliklinik für Arme; —ary committee, der Ausschuß für das Armenmedizinalwesen; —ary doctor, der Armenarzt. —**ation**, *s.* (dealing out) die Austeilung, Ausspendung; die Dispensation, Erlassung einer Verbindlichkeit, Erlaubnis (*R. C.*); die Dispensation, Erteilung der göttlichen Offenbarung (*in the Old and New Testaments*); the —ations of providence, die Fügungen der Vorsehung. —**atory**, I. *adj.* dispensierend. II. *s.* das Apothekerbuch, die Pharmakopöe (*Med.*). —**e**, *v.* I. *a.* austeilen, verteilen, spenden; (administer) verwalten; nach Vorschrift fertigen, bereiten (*medicines*); —ing chemist, der Apotheker. II. *n.;* to —e with a th., etwas nicht verlangen; (einem) etwas erlassen; (do without) verzichten auf (*acc.*), fertig werden ohne; the court will —e with your attendance, das Gericht wird Sie vom Erscheinen entbinden; we can —e with your company, wir können Ihre Gesellschaft entbehren. —**er**, *s.* der Austeiler, Ausspender; der Verwalter (*of justice, etc.*); der Dispensierende (*Med.*).
Dispers—e, *v.* I. *a.* zerstreuen, verbreiten, ausbreiten (*fig.*); —ing lens, die Zerstreuungslinse (*Opt.*). II. *n.* sich zerstreuen; auseinandergehen, auseinanderlaufen. —**ion**, *s.* die Zerstreuung.
Dispirit, *v.a.* entmutigen, niederschlagen. —**ed**, *adj.*, —**edly**, *adv.* entmutigt, niedergeschlagen.
Displace, *v.a.* verlegen, versetzen, verrücken; (remove from office) absetzen, eines Amtes entsetzen. —**ment**, *s.* das Verlegen, Verschiebung, die Versetzung; die anderweitige Verwendung (*of funds*); die Absetzung; das Deplacement (*of ships*).
Display, I. *v.a.* (unfold) entfalten, entwickeln; fliegen lassen (*a flag*); (exhibit) ausstellen, auslegen, zur Schau stellen, auskramen; to — one's courage, seinen Mut zeigen; to — one's wit, seinen Witz spielen lassen. II. *s.* das Auslegen zur Schau, die Schaustellung; (show) der Pomp; there was a great — of plate on the sideboard, auf dem Buffet prunkte viel Silbergeschirr; grand — of fireworks, großes Feuerwerk.
Displeas—e, *v.a.* mißfallen, kränken; to —e the eye, das Auge beleidigen. —**ed**, *adj.* mißvergnügt; (angry) ungehalten (über eine S.), unbefriedigt (von), unzufrieden (mit); to go away —ed, verdrießlich fortgehen. —**ing**, *adj.* mißfällig, unangenehm. —**ure**, *s.* das Mißfallen; anger) der Ärger, to incur a p.'s —ure, jemandes Mißfallen erregen *or* auf sich (*acc.*) ziehen; he expressed his —ure at . . ., er gab sein Mißfallen über (*acc.*) . . . zu erkennen.
Disport, I. *v.n.* sich belustigen, sich ergötzen, scherzen. II. *s.* die Belustigung, Lustbarkeit, Kurzweil.
Dispos—able, *adj.* verfügbar, disponibel. —**al**, *s.* die Anordnung, Einrichtung; (management) die Leitung, Führung; (control) die Verfügung, Disposition; (discretion) die Willkür, Macht; (use) die Bestimmung, der Gebrauch; (giving away) die Übergabe, Vergebung; I am at your —al, ich stehe zu Ihrer Verfügung *or* Ihnen zur Verfügung; I am not at your —al, Sie haben über mich nicht zu verfügen; I leave these things to your —al, ich überlasse diese Sachen Ihrer Bestimmung; I have no funds at my own —al, ich habe keine disponibeln Fonds; my time is at my own —al, ich kann frei über meine Zeit verfügen. —**e**, *v.* I. *a.* (an)ordnen, einrichten, gliedern, verteilen; (incline) geneigt machen, stimmen, lenken. II. *n.;* to —e of, verfügen, gebieten (über eine S.), (employ) verwenden, anwenden, (use) brauchen, (sell) verkaufen, (get rid of) abschaffen, weg-

schaffen, (place) unterbringen (*goods*), anstellen (*persons*); to —e of a matter, eine S. abmachen, sich einer S. entledigen; über eine S. verfügen; to —e of a th. by will, eine S. (testamentarisch) vermachen; to —e of in marriage, durch Heirat versorgen, verheiraten; the goods have been —ed of, über die Waren ist verfügt worden; he cannot —e of his goods, er kann seine Waren nicht an den Mann bringen; how will you —e of yourself this evening? was wollen Sie heute abend anfangen? man proposes, God —es, der Mensch denkt und Gott lenkt (*prov.*). **—ed**, *adj.* geneigt, gesonnen; —ed to mirth, zur Fröhlichkeit aufgelegt; ill —ed, übel gelaunt, (not —ed) abgeneigt; you are —ed to be merry, Sie sind fröhlichen Gemüts. **—er**, *s.* der Erteiler, Geber; der Anordner, Lenker; der Herrscher; the —er of all events, der Lenker aller Dinge. **—ing**, *s.* die Anordnung; die Verfügung. **—ition**, *s.* (arrangement) die Anordnung, Einrichtung, die Gliederung, der Plan; (control) die Disposition, Verfügung; (giving away) die Verteilung; (inclination) die Neigung, Gesinnung, Stimmung; (temperament) die Gemütsart; a good —ition, ein gutes Herz; an unamiable —ition, eine unliebenswürdige Gemütsart.

Dispossess, *v.a.* aus dem Besitze treiben, entsetzen (*gen.*), berauben (*gen.*). **—ion**, *s.* die Entsetzung.

Dispraise, I. *v.a.* tadeln. II. *s.* der Tadel.

Dispr—oof, *s.* die Widerlegung. **—ove**, *v.a* widerlegen.

Disproportion, *s.* das Mißverhältnis. **—able**, *adj.*, **—ably**, *adv.* unverhältnißmäßig. **—al**, *adj.* unverhältnismäßig, disproportioniert; (unsuitable) unpassend, ungeeignet. **—ate**, *adj.* ohne Verhältnis, unverhältnismäßig. **—ateness**, *s.* die Unverhältnismäßigkeit.

Disput—able, *adj.* bestreitbar. **—ant**, *s.* der Streiter, Disputant. **—ation**, *s.* die Disputation, der gelehrte Streit, Kampf der Meinungen; (debate) die Streitübung. **—atious**, *adj.* streitsüchtig. **—e**, I. *s.* der Streit; beyond all —e, unstreitig, ohne jede Frage; in —e, streitig, strittig, umstritten. II. *v.a.* bestreiten; streitig machen, (einem etwas) abstreiten; (question) Zweifel setzen (in eine S.), bezweifeln (eine S.); to —e every inch, jeden Zoll streitig machen. III. *v.n.* streiten; to —e about trifles, um Kleinigkeiten streiten; to —e about nothing, um des Kaisers Bart streiten. **—er**, *s.* der Wortfechter; *see* —ant.

Disqualif—ication, *s.* die Unfähigmachung; (unfitness) die Unfähigkeit, Untauglichkeit; —ication for an office, die Unfähigkeit zu einem Amte; this constitutes a —ication, dies macht untauglich (zu) *or* ungeeignet (für). **—y**, *v.a.* unfähig, untauglich machen; für unfähig erklären (*Law*).

Disquiet, I. *v.a.* beunruhigen, stören. II. *s. see* —ude. **—ing**, *adj.* beunruhigend. **—ude**, *s.* die Unruhe; (trouble) der Kummer, die Sorge.

Disquisition, *s.* die Untersuchung, Erörterung; (discourse) die Rede, Abhandlung.

Disregard, I. *s.* die Nichtachtung, Mißachtung. II. *v.a.* nicht achten, mißachten; (neglect) vernachlässigen.

Disrelish, I. *s.* der Ekel (vor), Widerwille (gegen); (aversion) die Abneigung (gegen), der Widerwille (to, gegen). II. *v.a.* keinen Geschmack finden (an einer S.), widrig finden.

Disrepair, *s.* der schlechte Zustand

Disreput—able, *adj.*, **—ably**, *adv.* verrufen, gemein, nicht respektabel; (discreditable) ehrwidrig, schimpflich; —able inn, gemeines Wirtshaus, niedrige Kneipe; —able society, gemeine, schlechte Gesellschaft. **—e**, *s.* der üble Ruf; to bring a th. (a p.) into —e, etwas (einen) in Verruf bringen, einem einen bösen Namen machen.

Disrespect, *s.* der Mangel an Ehrerbietung; (disregard) die Nichtachtung, Mißachtung; (scorn) die Geringschätzung; (contempt) die Verachtung; (incivility) die Unhöflichkeit; die Unehrerbietigkeit (gegen einen); to show — (act —fully) towards a p., sich unehrerbietig gegen einen benehmen, einen unehrerbietig behandeln. **—ful**, *adj.*, **—fully**, *adv.* unehrerbietig; (rude) unhöflich; —ful behaviour, unehrerbietiges Benehmen.

Disrobe, *v.a.* ...

Disruption, *s.* das Abreißen, die Zerreißung; (breach) der Bruch, die Zerspaltung, der Zerfall; the — of the Liberal party, der Zerfall *or* die Zersetzung der liberalen Partei.

Dissatisf—action, *s.* die Unzufriedenheit (mit), Unbefriedigtheit (von). **—actory**, *adj.* unbefriedigend. **—ied**, *adj.* unzufrieden, mißvergnügt. **—y**, *v.a.* nicht befriedigen; (make —ied) unzufrieden machen; (displease) mißfallen.

Dissect, *v.a.* zerlegen, zergliedern, zerschneiden; sezieren (*Anat.*); zergliedern (*fig.*); —ing knife, das Seziermesser. **—ion**, *s.* die Zerlegung; die Sektion (*Anat.*); die Zergliederung (*fig.*).

Disseiz—e, *v.a.* widerrechtlich aus dem Besitze setzen. **—in**, *s.* die widerrechtliche Besitzentsetzung.

Dissemble, *v.* I. *a.* unter einem falschen Vorwande verbergen, verhehlen, verdecken; (simulate) heucheln. II. *n.* (to play the hypocrite) heucheln; sich verstellen. **—r**, *s.* (hypocrite) der Gleißner, Heuchler; der Verhehler.

Disseminat—e, *v.a.* aussäen, ausstreuen, zerstreuen; (disperse) verbreiten; to —e news, Nachrichten aussprengen *or* verbreiten. **—ed**, *adj.* eingesprengt (*Min.*). **—ion**, *s.* das Ausstreuen; die Ausstreuung, Verbreitung. **—or**, *s.* der Ausbreiter, Verbreiter.

Dissen—sion, *s.* die Mißhelligkeit, Zwietracht; (strife) der Streit; die Uneinigkeit (in opinion, der Meinungen); to sow —sion amongst friends, Zwietracht unter Freunden stiften. **—t**, I. *s.* die Meinungsverschiedenheit; die Abweichung (*in the church*). II. *v.n.* nicht übereinstimmen; (von der anglikanischen Kirche) abweichen; I am sorry to be obliged to —t from you, es tut mir leid, anders als Sie denken zu müssen. **—ter**, *s.* der Andersdenkende; der Dissenter, Nonkonformist, von der anglikanischen Kirche abweichender Protestant. **—tient**, I. *adj.* andersdenkend; (disapproving) mißbilligend; without a —tient vote, einstimmig. II. *s.* der Andersdenkende.

Dissertation, *s.* die Auseinandersetzung; die (gelehrte) Abhandlung (on a subject, über einen Gegenstand); die Dissertation (for a doctor's degree, Doktordissertation).

Disservice, *s.* der Nachteil; der schlechte Dienst.

Dissever, *v.a.* trennen; (divide) zerteilen.

Dissiden—ce, *s.* die Uneinigkeit. **—t**, I. *adj.* nicht übereinstimmend, anders denkend. II. *s.* der Dissident; der Dissenter.

Dissilien—ce, *s.* das Zerspringen, Zerplatzen. **—t**, *adj.* zerspringend, aufplatzend (*Bot.*).

Dissimilar, *adj.* unähnlich, ungleich, verschiedenartig. **—ity**, *s.* die Unähnlichkeit, Verschiedenartigkeit.

Dissimulat—e, *v.a.* verhehlen, verdecken, verstellen. **—ion**, *s.* die Verstellung, Heuchelei.

Dissipat—e, *v.* I. *a.* zerstreuen, zerteilen (*fog*); zerstreuen, verscheuchen, verbannen (*care*); (squander) vergeuden, verschwenden. II. *n.* sich zerstreuen; (disappear) verschwinden. **—ed**, *adj.* ausschweifend, liederlich; a —ed life, ein wüstes, ausschweifendes Leben; a —ed person, ein Wüstling. **—ion**, *s.* die Zerstreuung (*also fig.*); die Verflüchtigung (*Phys.*); die Verschwendung; (disorderliness) die Liederlichkeit; *see* —ed life.

Dissociat—e, *v.a.* trennen; to —e o.s. from a th., sich von einer S. lossagen, nichts mit einer S. zu tun haben wollen. **—ion**, *s.* die Trennung; die Zersetzung (*Chem.*).

Dissol—ubility, *s.* die Auflösbarkeit, Löslichkeit; die Trennbarkeit. **—uble**, *adj.* (auf)löslich; (separable) trennbar, teilbar. **—ute**, *adj.*, **—utely**, *adv.* ausschweifend, liederlich; a —ute life, ein wüstes Leben; a —ute character, ein liederlicher Mensch. —**uteness**, *s.* die Liederlichkeit, das ausschweifende Wesen. —**ution**, *s.* die Auflösung (*also Chem., C. L.*); (liquefaction) die Schmelzung, das Flüssigmachen; (destruction) die Zerstörung; (death) der Tod; (separation) die Tren[illegible]ution of parliament, Auflösung des Parlaments; —ution of an assembly, die Aufhebung einer Versammlung; the —ution of the body, die Zersetzung, der Zerfall des Körpers; —ution of the blood, die Blutzersetzung. —**vable**, *adj.* auf=lösbar, =löslich. —**ve**, *v.* I. *a.* auflösen, schmelzen; trennen, teilen; auflösen, lösen (*fig.*); (abolish) aufheben; to —ve a marriage, eine Ehe (auf)lösen; to —ve partnership, eine Handelsgenossenschaft auflösen; to —ve into tears, in Tränen ausbrechen. II. *n.* sich auflösen; vergehen (*fig.*); sich zerteilen (*Med.*). —**vent**, I. *adj.* auflösend. II. *s.* auflösendes Mittel. —**ver**, *s.* das Auflösungsmittel. —**ving**, *adj.* auflösend; —ving views, Nebelbilder.

Dissonan—ce, *s.* der Mißklang, die Dissonanz (*also Mus.*); (disagreement) die Uneinigkeit, Mißhelligkeit. —**t**, *adj.* dissonierend; mißhellig

Dissua—de, *v.a.* (einem von einer S.) abraten, (einem eine S.) widerraten; I —ded him from the step, ich riet ihm von dem Schritte ab *or* widerriet ihm den Schritt. —**der**, *s.* der Abratende, Widerratende. —**sion**, *s.* die Abratung. —**sive**, *adj.*, —**sively**, *adv.* abratend.

Dissyllab—ic, *see* Disyllabic.

Distaff, *s.* der Spinnrocken, die Spindel, Kunkel; das weibliche Geschlecht (*fig.*).

Distan—ce, I. *s.* der Abstand, die Entfernung, Weite; (remoteness) die Entfernung, Ferne; die Distanz (*in races, fencing, etc.*); (—ce of time) der Zeitraum; der Zwischenraum, das Intervall (*Mus.*); die Entfernung (*Paint.*); der Abstand, die Entfernung (*fig.*); (reserve) die Zurückhaltung, Kälte; to keep one's —ce, sich zurückhaltend benehmen, (maintain one's dignity) seine Würde behaupten; to keep a p. at a —ce, einen fern halten, einen sich (*dat.*) vom Leibe halten (*coll.*), sich nicht gemein mit einem machen; at a —ce, von weitem; action at a —ce, die Wirkung in die Ferne; in the —ce, in der Ferne, von fern; keep at a —ce! bleib mir vom Leibe! within driving —ce, zu Wagen erreichbar; corrected *or* true —ce, der rechte, verbesserte Abstand (*Naut.*); focal —ce, die Brennweite (*Opt.*); visual —ce, die Sehweite; to cover a —ce, eine Strecke zurücklegen. II. *v.a.* hinter sich zurücklassen (*also fig.*); übertreffen (*fig.*). —**t**, *adj.* fern, entfernt (*in time or space*); entfernt (*in relationship, feeling, etc.*); zurückhaltend; a —t relation, ein weitläufiger Verwandter; —tly related to, weitläufig verwandt mit; not the most —t idea, nicht die leiseste Ahnung; a —t allusion, eine leichte Anspielung; a —t prospect, eine entfernte *or* schwache Hoffnung; I found him very —t, ich fand sein Betragen sehr zurückhaltend. *Comp.* —**ce-line**, *s.* der Hauptstrahl, die Sehachse (*Opt.*). —**ce-post**, *s.* der Distanzpfahl. —**ce-recorder**, *s.* der Entfernungsmesser, Taxameter (*in cabs*). —**ce-signal**, *s.* das Distanzsignal.

Distaste, *s.* (disrelish) der Ekel (vor); die Abneigung (gegen), der Widerwille (gegen), der Abscheu (vor), das Mißfallen (an) (*fig.*); to have a —[illegible] einen Widerwillen gegen (eine S.) haben. —**ful**, *adj.* Ekel erregend, ekelhaft; (dem Geschmacke) widrig; mißfällig, unangenehm, widerwärtig (*fig.*). —**fulness**, *s.* die Mißfälligkeit, Widrigkeit.

[1]**Distemper**, *s.* die Krankheit, Unpäßlichkeit; — of dogs) die Hundestaupe; (— of horses) der Rotz, die Pferdeinfluenza; (discontent) die Unruhe. —**ed**, *adj.* krank, unpäßlich; (immoderate) übertrieben; a mind —ed by interest, eine durch Eigennutz beeinflußte Gesinnung.

[2]**Distemper**, I. *s.* die Wasserfarbe, Mattfarbe; (painting in —) die Temperamalerei, Wasser(farben)malerei; gilding in —, die Leimvergoldung. II. *attrib.*; — colour, die Temperafarbe; — painting, die Temperamalerei. III. *v.a.* (Farben) zur Temperamalerei mischen; mit Wasserfarben streichen, in Temperamanier malen.

Disten—d, *v.a.* ausdehnen (*a bladder, the lungs*); spreizen (*the legs*). —**sible**, *adj.* ausdehnbar. —**tion**, *s.* die Ausdehnung; das Strecken, Spreizen; die Ausdehnung, Weite.

Distich, *s.* das Distichon. —**s**, *pl.* Distichen.

Distil, *v.* I. *a.* herabtropfen; abziehen, destillieren (*Chem.*); brennen (*spirits*); —led perfumes, ätherische Öle; —led waters, aromatische Wasser. II. *n.* tröpfeln; (flow) rinnen, fließen; destillieren. —**lation**, *s.* die Destillierung, Destillation; das Destillierte; —lation of spirits, die Branntweinbrennerei. —**ler**, *s.* der Destillateur, Destillierer; der Branntweinbrenner. —**lery**, *s.* die Branntweinbrennerei.

Distinct, I. *adj.*, —**ly**, *adv.* (separate) abgesondert, getrennt; (distinguished) unterschieden; (different) verschieden; (clear) klar, deutlich, vernehmlich; (decided) bestimmt. II. *adv.* klar, deutlich. —**ion**, *s.* die Unterscheidung; (difference) der Unterschied; (separation) die Absonderung, Einteilung; (eminence) die Auszeichnung; (that which confers —ion) das Auszeichnende, die Würde. —**ive**, *adj.* unterscheidend. —**ively**, *adv.* klar, deutlich. —**iveness**, *s.* das Unterscheidende. —**ness**, *s.* die Deutlichkeit, Bestimmtheit; die Klarheit, Genauigkeit.

Distinguish, *v.* I. *a.* unterscheiden; auszeichnen; to — o.s., sich auszeichnen; to be —ed by, sich unterscheiden durch. II. *n.* unterscheiden; einen Unterschied machen. —**able**, *adj.* unterscheidbar. —**ed**, *adj.* ausgezeichnet, vorzüglich; —ed by, kenntlich an (*dat.*). —**ing**, *adj.* unterscheidend; (characteristic) eigentümlich, bezeichnend.

Distort, *v.a.* verzerren, verdrehen; verrenken (*the limbs*); verziehen, verzerren (*the features*); verdrehen, entstellen (*the meaning of a passage*). —**ion**, *s.* die Verdrehung, Verziehung, Verrenkung; die Verdrehung, Sinnentstellung (*fig.*); die Verzerrung (*of the face or body*).

Distract, *v.a.* abziehen, ablenken; (disturb) beunruhigen, stören; (confuse) verwirren; (craze) den Verstand zerrütten, verrückt machen; to — the attention, die Aufmerksamkeit von einem besonderen Gegenstande abziehen, ablenken. —**ed**, *adj.* zerstreut, wahnsinnig, verrückt; to be —ed with pain, vor Schmerz außer sich sein. —**ion**, *s.* die Zerstreuung (*of mind*); (confusion) die Verwirrung; (madness) der Wahnsinn, die Raserei; (diversion) die Zerstreuung; to love to —ion, bis zum Wahnsinn lieben. —**ing**, *adj.* abziehend; wahnsinnig machend; —ing pain, wahnsinniger *or* rasender Schmerz.

Distrain, *v.* I. *a.* in Beschlag nehmen, mit Beschlag belegen; to — goods for rent, Hausgeräte wegen schuldiger Hausmiete auspfänden. II. *n.*; to — upon a th., sich schadlos halten (an einer S.). —**able**, *adj.* was mit Beschlag belegt werden kann, pfändbar. —**er**, *s.* der Beschlagnehmer, Auspfänder. —**t**, *s.* die Beschlagnahme; die Pfändung, Exekution.

Distraught, (*p.p.*) *see* Distracted.

Distress, I. *s.* (trouble) die Not, Trübsal, das Elend; die Qual, Pein, Angst, der Kummer, Schmerz (*of mind or body*); (calamity) das Unglück; (distraint) die Beschlagnahme, Auspfändung, der Beschlag; (chattels seized) das weggenommene Pfand; to be in great — for money, Geldnot haben; signal of —, das Notsignal; warrant of —, das Exekutionsmandat (*Law*); ship in —, Schiff in Not *or* Gefahr. II. *v.a.* in Not, Elend bringen, betrüben, quälen; *see* Distrain. —**ed**, *adj.* unglücklich; (in difficulties) in großer Not, bedrängt; (troubled) bekümmert, beängstigt;

I am —ed for her, ich bin um sie bekümmert; your —ed parents, deine tiefbetrübten Eltern. **—ful**, *adj.*, **—fully**, *adv.* unglücklich, kummervoll, unselig, elend; —ful cries, jämmerliches Geschrei. **—ing**, *adj.*, **—ingly**, *adv.* peinlich, qualvoll.

Distribut—able, *adj.* verteilbar. **—e**, *v.* I. *a.* verteilen, austeilen (among, unter, to, an, *acc.*); (arrange, classify) in Klassen einteilen, abteilen; (administer) handhaben; verallgemeinern (*a term*); to —e the type, die Schrift wieder in den Schriftkasten ablegen. II. *n.* (Almosen) geben (*B.*). **—er**, *s.* der Austeiler. **—ing**, *p. see* —e; —ing box, der Dampfkasten (*Locom.*); —ing rule, der Ablegespan (*Print.*). **—ion**, *s.* die Verteilung, Austeilung; die Abteilung, Einteilung (*into classes*). die Anordnung der Teile; die Verbreitung (*of plants, etc.*); die Auflösung eines Begriffes in seine Teile (*Log.*, *Rhet.*); das Ablegen der Druckschrift (*Print.*); die Einteilung, Anordnung (*Arch.*); die Intestat-Erbfolge (*Law*); —ion of alms, die Almosenspende, die Verabfolgung der milden Gaben; —ion of justice, die Handhabung der Gerechtigkeit. **—ive**, I. *adj.* austeilend, verteilend; (allotting) erteilend; einteilend (*Log.*, *Gram.*); distributiv (*Gram.*). II. *s.* das Distributivum (*Gram.*). **—ively**, *adv.* im Einzelnen, besonders.

District, I. *s.* der Bezirk, Kreis; (region) der Landstrich; (jurisdiction) der Gerichtsbezirk; das Gelände (*Mil.*); mountainous —, die Gebirgsgegend. II. *attrib.*; — rate, die Kommunalsteuer, die Gemeindesteuer. *Comp.* **—-court**, *s.* das Bezirksgericht. **—-nursing**, *s.* die Armen-Krankenpflege, freiwillige Krankenpflege. **—-rate**, *s.* die Kreissteuer, Kommunalsteuer. **—-visitor**, *s.* Besucher(in) der Armen und Kranken eines Bezirks.

Distrust, I. *v.a.* mißtrauen, Mißtrauen gegen jemand hegen. II. *s.* das Mißtrauen, der Argwohn, Zweifel. **—ful**, *adj.*, **—fully**, *adv.* mißtrauisch; —ful of o. s., schüchtern, ängstlich, ohne Selbstvertrauen, mißtrauisch. **—fulness**, *s.* das Mißtrauen.

Disturb, *v.a.* (disarrange) in Unordnung bringen; (trouble) stören; (disquiet) beunruhigen; (excite) aufregen; aufrühren (*sediment, etc.*); to — a train of thought, einen Gedankengang unterbrechen; I have given orders not to be —ed, ich habe Befehl gegeben, daß niemand mich stört. **—ance**, *s.* die Störung, Beunruhigung; die Aufregung, der Aufruhr; the —ances in Ireland, die Unruhen in Irland; to raise a —ance, sich lärmend benehmen, den Frieden stören; einen Aufruhr erregen. **—er**, *s.* der Störer; —er of the peace, der Friedensstörer.

Disuni—on, *s.* die Trennung; die Uneinigkeit, Entzweiung, Spaltung (*fig.*). **—te**, *v.* I. *a.* entzweien, trennen. II. *n.* sich trennen.

Disuse, I. *s.* der Nichtgebrauch; (desuetude) das Abkommen eines Gebrauches; to fall into —, außer Gebrauch kommen, abkommen, ungebräuchlich werden. II. *v.a.* nicht mehr gebrauchen, nicht üben.

Disyllab—ic, *adj.* zweisilbig, aus zwei Silben bestehend. **—le**, *s.* zweisilbiges Wort.

Ditch, I. *s.* der Graben (*Hydr.*, *Arch.*, *Fort.*); (drain) der Drainiergraben; draining —, der Entwässerungsgraben; foundation —, die Grundgrube; to dig a —, einen Graben ziehen. II. *v.n.* graben. III. *v.a.* mit einem Graben umgeben; durch Gräben trocken legen. **—er**, *s.* der Gräber, Grabenschneider.

Dither, I. *v.n.* zittern, schaudern (*with cold, wet*). II. *s.* das Zittern, Vibrieren.

Dithyramb, *s.* der Dithyrambus. **—ic**, I. *adj.* dithyrambisch. II. *s.* der Dithyrambus.

Dittany, *s.* der Diptam (*Bot.*).

Ditt—o, *adv.* desgleichen, ditto. **—y**, *s.* das (kleine) Lied, Liedchen; popular —y, das Volkslied.

Diuretic, I. *adj.* harntreibend. II. *s.* das harntreibende Mittel.

Diurnal, I. *adj.*, **—ly**, *adv.* täglich. II. *s.* das katholische Gebetbuch.

Divagation, *s.* die Abschweifung.

Divan, *s.* der Divan.

Divaricat—e, I. *v.n.* sich spreizen; (branch off) sich trennen, sich abzweigen, gabeln. II. *adj.* ausgespreitet (*Bot.*). **—ion**, *s.* das Auseinanderklaffen, die Trennung, Gabelung; die Meinungsverschiedenheit (*fig.*, *obs.*); die Durchkreuzung (*Anat.*).

Div—e, I. *v.n.* tauchen; (—e down) untertauchen; to —e into, in (eine S.) tief eindringen. II. *s.*; to make a —e at, langen nach. **—er**, *s.* der Taucher (*also Orn.*); (—er into) der Erforscher. *Comp.* **—ing-bell**, *s.* die Taucherglocke. **—ing-dress**, *s.* der Taucheranzug.

Diverg—e, *v.n.* auseinandergehen, divergieren; (turn off) abweichen. **—ence**, *s.* das Auseinanderlaufen; die Divergenz (*Geom.*); circle of —ence, der Zerstreuungskreis. **—ent**, **—ing**, *adj.* divergierend; —ing lens, die Zerstreuungslinse.

Divers, *adj. see* —e; *pl.* etliche, verschiedene, mehrere, mancherlei (*obs.*). **—e**, *adj.* verschieden; (various) mannigfaltig; eine verschiedene *or* abweichende Richtung habend. **—ely**, *adv.* verschieden. **—ification**, *s.* die Veränderung, Abwechselung; (variety) die Verschiedenheit, Mannigfaltigkeit (*obs.*). **—ified**, *adj.* voller Abwechslung, abwechslungsreich, mannigfaltig; a —ified landscape, eine viele Abwechslung darbietende Landschaft. **—ify**, *v.a.* (make different) verschieden machen; (vary) Mannigfaltigkeit, Abwechselung bringen in. **—ion**, *s.* die Abwendung, Ablenkung (*of a stream, etc.*); die Diversion (*Mil.*); (amusement) die Zerstreuung, der Zeitvertreib. **—ity**, *s.* die Verschiedenheit, Ungleichheit; (variety) die Mannigfaltigkeit.

Divert, *v.a.* abwenden, ablenken, abziehen; (amuse) belustigen, zerstreuen, ergötzen; zu einem andern Zwecke verwenden; to — a p. from his purpose, (einen) von seinem Vorhaben abbringen.

Dives, *s.* der reiche Mann (im Evangelium).

Divest, *v.a.* entkleiden; berauben (*of rights, etc.*); to — o. s. of a th., einer S. entsagen, auf eine S. verzichten; to — o. s. of a right, sich eines Rechtes begeben.

Divid—e, *v.* I. *a.* teilen; (separate) absondern, trennen; (partition) abteilen; (cut through) durchschneiden, zerteilen; (set at variance) entzweien, uneinig machen; (part among) austeilen, verteilen; einteilen (*one's time, etc.*); dividieren (*Arith.*); the equator —es the earth into two hemispheres, der Äquator scheidet die Erde in zwei Halbkugeln; to —e the House, das Haus abstimmen lassen (*Parl.*). II. *n.* sich trennen, sich spalten; sich entzweien; durch Teilung (namentlich) abstimmen (*Parl.*); —e! zur Abstimmung! **—end**, *s.* die Dividende, der Gewinnanteil (*C. L.*); der Dividendus (*Arith.*); they give a —end of 10 per cent, sie werfen eine Dividende von 10 vom Hundert ab. **—ing**, *adj.* teilend; —ing line, die Trennungslinie; —ing ridge, die Wasserscheide.

Divin—ation, *s.* die Weissagung, Wahrsagung; (foreboding) die Ahnung. **—ator**, *s.* der Wahrsager, Weissagende. **—atory**, *adj.* weissagend; vorahnend. **—e**, I. *adj.*, **—ely**, *adv.* göttlich; (excellent) herrlich, vortrefflich; himmlisch; —e right of kings, das Königtum von Gottes Gnaden, Gottesgnadentum; king by —e right, König von Gottes Gnaden; —e songs, geistliche Lieder, Kirchenlieder; the —e nature, die göttliche Natur; —e grace, göttliche Gnade; —e service, —e worship, der Gottesdienst; —ely inspired, gottbegeistert. II. *v.a. & n.* weissagen, wahrsagen, vorhersagen; (have a presentiment of) ahnen; (conjecture) mutmaßen, erraten. III. *s.* der

Geistliche; der Theolog(e). **—eness**, *s.* die Göttlichkeit; die Vortrefflichkeit, Göttlichkeit. **—er**, *s.* der Weissager; der Errater. **—ity**, *s.* die Gottheit; (—e creature) das himmlische Wesen; (theology, *etc.*) die Gottesgelehrtheit, Theologie; professor of —ity, Professor der Theologie. *Comp.* **—ing-rod**, *s.* die Wünschelrute.

Divis—ibility, *s.* die Teilbarkeit. **—ible**, *adj.* teilbar. **—ibleness**, *s.* die Teilbarkeit. **—ion**, *s.* die Teilung; die Scheidewand (*Build.*); die Abteilung, Einteilung (*of time, etc.*); (partition) die Abteilung; (that which divides) das Teilende, Trennende; (body of men) die Abteilung; die Division (*Mil.*); (section, head) der Teil; (disagreement) die Spaltung, Zwietracht; die Division (*Arith.*); der Lauf, Läufer (*Mus.*); die namentliche Abstimmung, der Hammelsprung (*Parl.*); —ion of a word, die Abteilung, Trennung, das Absetzen eines Wortes (*Print.*); upon a —ion, als man abstimmte, bei der Abstimmung; the motion passed without a division, der Antrag ging glatt durch; to cause a —ion between friends, Freunde entzweien; general of —ion, Divisionsgeneral. **—ional**, *adj.* Teilungs-, Divisions-. **—or**, *s.* der Divisor (*Arith.*).

Divorce, I. *s.* die Scheidung, Ehescheidung; die Trennung, Spaltung (*fig.*); (sentence of —) der Ehescheidungsspruch; to obtain a — from, sich von . . . scheiden lassen. II. *v.a.* scheiden; (put away) verstoßen; trennen, entfernen, wegnehmen (*fig.*); he is —d from her, er hat sich von ihr scheiden lassen, er ist von ihr (gerichtlich) geschieden. **—able**, *adj.* scheidbar, trennbar. **—ment**, *see* Divorce I. **—r**, *s.* der die Scheidung veranlassende Teil. *Comp.* **—-court**, *s.* der Gerichtshof für Ehescheidungen.

Divulge, *v.a.* bekannt machen, entdecken, ausschwatzen. **—r**, *s.* der Verbreiter, Aussprenger.

Divulsion, *s.* die Abreißung, Trennung.

Dizz—iness, *s.* der Schwindel; to be seized with a —iness, einen Schwindelanfall bekommen. **—y**, I. *adj.* schwind(e)lig, betäubt; (causing —iness) Schwindel erregend; (giddy) gedankenlos, unbesonnen; a —y height, eine schwindelnde Höhe. II. *v.a.* schwindlig machen; (confuse) betäuben, verwirren.

¹Do, I. *ir.v.a.* tun, machen, verrichten; (effect) bewirken; (accomplish) ausführen, vollenden, vollbringen, zustande bringen; (transact) verrichten; (execute) ausrichten; (cook) bereiten, kochen; (hoax) prellen, hinters Licht führen, betrügen (*sl.*); (finish) machen, verfertigen, beendigen; erweisen, erzeigen (*kindness*); — your best, handle nach bestem Wissen, tun Sie Ihr Bestes, Möglichstes; to — a p.'s bidding, jemandes Geheiß ausführen; to — business with s.o., mit einem Geschäfte machen; he is said to be —ing a fine business, er soll bedeutende Geschäfte machen; I'll soon — his business for him, ich will ihn bald abfertigen (*vulg.*); to — a p. credit, einem Ehre machen; to — to death, töten; to — good (evil), Gutes, (Böses) tun; it —es one's heart good to see them so happy, es tut dem Herzen wohl, sie so glücklich zu sehen; this medicine —es me no good, diese Arzenei hilft mir nicht; to — 8 miles an hour, 8 Meilen in einer Stunde zurücklegen; your letter will — much . . ., ihr Brief wird viel ausrichten . . .; to — right, recht tun; to — London, sich (*dat.*) London besehen (*sl.*); to — the continent, den Kontinent schnell abmachen (*sl.*); to — a p. a good turn, to — well by a p., einem etwas Gutes antun; — what he would . . ., er mochte anfangen was er wollte . . .; (used instead of a preceding verb, statt eines vorhergehenden Zeitworts) he loves not games as you —, er liebt die Spiele nicht, wie du; you play much better than you did, Sie spielen viel besser als früher; — you like the German language? I —, gefällt Ihnen die deutsche Sprache? ja! to **— again** *or* over again, noch einmal machen; to **— into**, übersetzen *or* übertragen (into English, ins Englische); to — into German, verdeutschen; to **— over**, überstreichen, überziehen; to **— up**, zusammenlegen; wieder instandsetzen, in Ordnung bringen (*a dress*), reparieren (*a house*); to — up goods, Waren einpacken; to — a p. up, einen gänzlich ermüden; to **— with**, anfangen *or* tun mit; what am I to — with it? was soll ich damit anfangen? I did not know what to — with myself, ich wußte nicht, was ich anfangen *or* wie ich die Zeit hinbringen sollte. II. *ir.v.n.* tun, handeln; (behave) sich benehmen; (manage) fertig werden, zustande kommen; (be in a state) sich befinden; (answer) dem Zwecke entsprechen; (suit) angehen, tauglich sein, passen; (succeed) gelingen; that won't —, das geht nicht (an), damit ist es nicht getan, das reicht nicht zu; that will —, das genügt, das wird hinreichend sein, so ist es recht; will common paper —? ist gewöhnliches Papier gut genug? it will — to-morrow, das hat Zeit bis morgen; it will — for the present, es ist für jetzt gut genug; it did perfectly, es paßte vortrefflich, es ging vorzüglich; a little won't — for him, wenig ist ihm nicht genug, wenig hilft ihm nichts; how do you —? wie befinden Sie sich? Guten Morgen! Guten Tag! (*as a form of address*); he —es well to come, er tut wohl daran, daß er kommt; — as you would be done by, was du nicht willst, das man dir tu', das füg' auch keinem andern zu; was du nicht willst, das dir geschicht, das tu auch deinem Nächsten nicht (*prov.*); — as I —, mach's so wie ich; one must — at Rome as the Romans —, mit den Wölfen muß heulen (*prov.*); to — badly, schlechte Geschäfte machen, schlecht daran sein; to — well, sich gut machen, gut weiterkommen; have —ne! genug davon! to **— away** (with), beseitigen, abschaffen; to **— for**, passen für, richtig *or* genug sein für, (ruin) verderben, zu Grunde richten; that will — for him, das paßt für ihn; das wird ihn zur Ruhe bringen; to **— with**, tun, anfangen mit; what am I to — with it? was soll ich damit anfangen? to have to — with, zu tun *or* schaffen haben mit; I have —ne with him, ich will mit ihm nichts mehr zu schaffen haben, ich habe ihn aufgegeben, ich bin mit ihm fertig; that won't — with me, das geht bei mir nicht; to **— without**, entbehren. III. *aux.v.* **1.** (in interrogations, bei einer Frage) — you learn English? lernen Sie Englisch; did you see him? sahen Sie ihn? who —es not know . . .? wer kennt nicht . . .? wer weiß nicht? **2.** (in negative sentences, bei einer Verneinung) I — not know him, ich kenne ihn nicht; we did not — it, wir taten es nicht; did you not see him? sahen Sie ihn nicht? **3.** (emphatic, verstärkend) send it, —! schicke es doch! — make haste! beeile dich doch! I did see him, ich sah ihn auch wirklich. **4.** (*for yes*) — you see him? I —, sehen Sie ihn? Jawohl. IV. *s.* das Tun, Geschäft; (bustle) der Lärm (*obs. or dial.*); (swindle) der Schwindel (*sl.*). **—able**, *adj.* tunlich, ausführbar. **—-all**, *s.* das Faktotum (*rare*). **—er**, *s.* der Täter; der Verrichter; —ers of the law, die Beobachter des Gesetzes; evil —er, der Übeltäter. **—es**, *3rd sing. of the pres. ind. of* Do. **—ing —ne**, *etc., see* Doing, Done, *etc.* *Comp.* **—-nothing**, *adj.*; —-nothing policy, die Politik der Untätigkeit, des Nichtstuns.

²Do, *s.* das C (*Mus.*).

Docil—e, *adj.* gelehrig, lenksam, lenkbar. **—ity**, *s.* die Gelehrigkeit, Lenksamkeit, Lenkbarkeit.

Docimasy, *s.* die Probierkunst (*Chem.*).

¹Dock, *s.* das Ampferkraut (*Bot.*).

²Dock, I. *v.a.* stutzen (*dogs' or horses' tails, etc.*); kürzen, vermindern (*fig.*); beschneiden (*a bill*); aufheben (an entail, eine Erbfolge); abschneiden (*fig.*); to — horses, Pferde anglisieren; to — an account, eine Rechnung kürzen. II. *s.* der Stummel, Stutzschwanz; der dicke, festere Teil des Schwanzes. **—et**, I. *s.* die kurze Inhaltsangabe (*C. L.*); die Bescheinigung eines Patentes; (—et on goods, *etc.*) der Warenadreßzettel; (label) der Zettel; (summary) der Abriß, kurze Inhalt einer größeren Schrift; die Liste der anhängigen Rechtsfälle (*Law*); to strike a —et, die Zahlungsunfähigkeit eines Schuldners gerichtlich anzeigen. II. *v.a.* kurz angeben, ausziehen; (Akten, Schriften, 2c.) überschreiben; mit Adreßzetteln versehen.

[3]**Dock**, I. *s.* das Dock (*Naut.*); die Anklagebank (*Law*); dry- —, graving- —, Trockendock; floating- —, Schwimmdock; sectional —, Sektionsdock; wet- —, das Hafenbassin. **—age**, *s.* die Dockgebühren. *Comp.* **—-dues**, *see* —age. **—-gate**, *s.* das Docktor, die Dockschleuse. **—-master**, *s.* der Dockmeister. **—yard**, *s.* die Werft, der Schiffsbauhof.

Doct—or, I. *s.* der Doktor (*of Laws, Literature, etc.*); der Kirchenvater (*Theol.*); (medical man) der Arzt, Doktor; der Ausbesserer, Zustutzer (*fig., coll.*); das Abstreichmesser (*for calico*); der Papiermaschinenschaber (*Pap.*); die Farbenzuführungswalze (*Print.*); —or of laws, of medicine, Doktor der Rechte, der Medizin; to take one's —or's degree, promovieren, sich (*dat.*) den Doktorgrad erringen, doktorieren; —or's stuff, die Arznei; —or and Mrs. Skeat, Herr und Frau Dr. Skeat, (Herr) Dr. Skeat und Frau; dear —or, Lieber Herr Doktor! Hochgeehrter Herr Doktor! II. *v.a.* kurieren; (adulterate) vermischen; (patch up) (für einen bestimmten Zweck) ändern, zurechtmachen, zustutzen. **—orate**, *s.* die Doktorwürde. **—rinaire**, I. *s.* der Doktrinär. II. *adj.* doktrinär. **—rinal**, *adj.* zur Lehre gehörig; —rinal theology, die Dogmatik. **—rinally**, *adv.* als Lehre. **—rine**, *s.* die Lehre; die christliche Lehre; secret —rine, die Geheimlehre.

Document, *s.* die Urkunde, Beweisschrift, das Beweisstück. **—ary**, *adj.* urkundlich, dokumentarisch; —ary evidence, das Beweisstück.

[1]**Dodder**, *s.* die Flachsseide (*Bot.*).

[2]**Dodder**, *v.n.* schwanken, zittern.

Dodeca—gon, *s.* das Zwölfeck. **—hedral**, *adj.* zwölfflächig. **—hedron**, *s.* das Zwölfflach.

Dodge, I. *v.a.* (einem, einem Schlag, 2c.) durch eine Seitenbewegung ausweichen; (evade) entschlüpfen; (follow) nachlaufen (a p., einem); (cheat) betrüglich behandeln, zum besten haben (*sl.*). II. *v.n.* einen Seitensprung machen; (*fig., coll.*) ausweichen (a p., einem); (quibble) Ausflüchte, Kniffe gebrauchen. III. *s.* der Seitensprung; (trick) der Kniff (*sl.*). **—r**, *s.* der ausweichende, unzuverlässige Mensch; Ränkeschmied; artful —r, geriebener Bursche.

Dodo, *s.* der Dudu (*Orn.*).

Doe, *s.* das Reh, die Hindin; das Weibchen (*of rabbits*). *Comp.* **—skin**, *s.* der Doeskin (*Manuf.*); (*pl.*) Rehfelle.

Doff, *v.a.* abtun, abnehmen, ablegen (*clothes, etc.*); to — one's hat, den Hut abnehmen.

Dog, I. *s.* der Hund; (male animal) das Männchen; der Bock, das Gestell (*Mech.*); (andiron) der Feuerbock; (hook) die Klammer, der Klammerhaken; der Hundsstern (*Astr.*); (fellow) der Kerl; the — barks, howls, whines, der Hund bellt, heult, winselt; jolly —, lustiger Bursche; a — in-the-manger disposition, eine neidische Gemütsart; to be *or* to play the — in the manger, den Neidhammel machen; it is hard to teach an old — new tricks, was Hänschen nicht lernt, lernt Hans nimmermehr; every — has his day, jeder hat einmal seinen guten Tag, alles hat seine Zeit; to go to the —s, auf den Hund kommen, zu Grunde gehen; to throw to the —s, wegwerfen, verprassen; he has a —'s life of it, er führt ein Hundeleben. II. *v.a.* (einem) auf dem Fuße nachfolgen, (einen) unablässig verfolgen; the peril which —s the steps of royalty, die Gefahr, welche den Königen auf Schritt und Tritt folgt. **—ged**, *adj.*, **—gedly**, *adv.* mürrisch, starrköpfig; störrisch; unverdrossen, zäh; (obstinate) eigensinnig; —ged determination, zähe Entschlossenheit; —ged resistance, hartnäckiger Widerstand. **—gedness**, *s.* das störrische, eigensinnige Wesen; die Zähigkeit; (surliness) das mürrische Wesen. **—gerel**, I. *adj.* ärmlich; —gerel rhymes, Knittelverse. II. *s.* das Gedicht in Knittelversen. **—gish**, *adj.*, **—gishly**, *adv.* hündisch. *Comp.* **—bane**, **—'s-bane**, *s.* der Hundskohl. **—berry**, *s.* die Hundsbeere. **—-cart**, *s.* der Hundewagen; der leichte zweirädrige Jagdwagen, das Jagdgig. **—-days**, *pl.* die Hundstage. **—-fancier**, *s.* der Hundezüchter, Hundehändler. **—-fight**, *s.* der Hundekampf. **—fish**, *s.* der Dornhai. **—-kennel**, *s.* das Hundehaus, der Hundestall. **—-Latin**, *s.* das Küchenlatein, Krämerlatein. **—-licence**, *s.* der auf Grund bezahlter Hundesteuer ausgestellte Erlaubnisschein, einen Hund zu halten, der Hundesteuerschein. **—rose**, *s.* die Hagerose. **—'s-ear**, *s.* das Eselsohr (in a book, in einem Buche). **—(s')-eared**, *adj.* mit Eselsohren; zerknittert, zerknüllt. **—skin**, *adj.* von Hundsleder gemacht. **—-sleep**, *s.* der verstellte Schlaf. **—'s-meat**, *s.* das Hundefutter. **—-star**, *s.* Sirius, der Hundsstern. **—-tired**, *adj.* (*coll.*) hundemüde. **—tooth**, *s.* der Hundszahn, Augenzahn; (—tooth-ornament) der Zahnzierrat (*Arch.*). **—watch**, *s.* der Plattfuß (*Naut.*); the first —watch, die Wache von vier bis sechs. **—-weary**, *adj.* hundemüde. **—-whistle**, *s.* die Hundspfeife.

Doge, *s.* (of Venice) der Doge.

Dogger, *s.* das Dogboot, Doggerboot. **—man**, *s.* der Matrose eines Doggerboots.

Dogma, *s.* das Dogma, der Glaubenssatz. **—tic(al)**, *adj.*, **—tically**, *adv.* dogmatisch; (positive) ausdrücklich, bestimmt; (authoritative) gebieterisch; (arrogant) anmaßend. **—tics**, *pl.* die Glaubenslehre, Dogmatik. **—tism**, *s.* der Dogmatismus; die Bestimmtheit der Meinungen, Entschiedenheit; das anmaßende Wesen. **—tist**, *s.* der Dogmatist; der dreiste Behaupter, Absprecher, Rechthaber. **—tize**, *v.n.* (alles) mit Bestimmtheit behaupten, (über jede Sache entschieden) absprechen, dogmatisieren.

Doily, *see* D'oyley.

Doing, I. *p. of* Do; there is little — at present, augenblicklich wird wenig gemacht. II. *s.* das Tun; die Tat; that was your —, da hattet ihr die Schuld, da waret ihr die Veranlassung. **—s**, *pl.* Taten, Verrichtungen; fine —s these! schöne Geschichten, das! das sind (mir ja) schöne Dinge!

Doit, *s.* der Deut, Heller, Pfifferling.

[1]**Dole**, I. *s.* (share) der Teil, Anteil; (alms) die milde Gabe, das Almosen; (small portion) der kleine Teil. II. *v.a.* verteilen; to —e out, (zögernd) austeilen, langsam herausrücken (mit einer S.).

[2]**Dol—e**, *s.* der Kummer, das Leid (*obs.*). **—eful**, *adj.*, **—efully**, *adv.* kummervoll, traurig; —eful accent, der Klageton; —eful hymn, das Trauerlied; —eful days, elende Tage. **—efulness**, *s.* die Traurigkeit, der Kummer. **—orous**, *adj.*, **—orously**, *adv.* schmerzhaft, schmerzlich; Schmerz ausdrückend; —orous sighs, Schmerzensseufzer. **—our**, *s.* der Schmerz, das Weh, die Pein; (lamentation) der Jammer.

Doll, *s.* die Puppe. **—y**, *s. see* Doll; der Aufzug (*Mech.*); der Rührstock (*for washing*). *Comp.* **—y-tub**, *s.* die Waschbutte; das Schlämmfaß (*Metall.*).

Dollar, *s.* der Dollar.

Dolman, *s.* der Dolman (*also for ladies*).

Dolomite, *s.* der Dolomit, Bitterspat.

Dolphin, *s.* der Delphin (*also Artil.*).

Dolt, *s.* der Tölpel, Einfaltspinsel. **—ish**, *adj.*, **—ishly**, *adv.* dumm, tölpelhaft. **—ishness**, *s.* die Tölpelhaftigkeit.

Domain, *s.* die Herrschaft; das Gebiet; (estate)

das Gut, freie Grundeigentum; das Kammergut. die Domäne; das Gebiet (*fig.*); in the — of science, auf dem Gebiete der Naturwissenschaften; that is not within his —, das liegt außerhalb seines Faches.

Dome, *s.* die Kuppel, der Dom (*Arch.*); (lid) der gewölbte Deckel; die Haube (*Chem.*); der Dom, die Dampfhaube (*Railw.*); pointed —, das Kegelgewölbe; steam —, der Dampfdom. *Comp.* **—-cover**, *s.* das Domhemd. **—-shaped**, *adj.* domförmig.

Domesday, *obs. spelling for* Doomsday. *Comp.* **—-book**, *s.* das große (auf Befehl Wilhelms des Eroberers angelegte) Grundbuch Englands.

Domestic, I. *adj.*, **—ally**, *adv.* zum Hause, zur Familie gehörig, häuslich; Haus-, Familien-; zur Haushaltung gehörig, Haus-; inländisch, einheimisch, Landes-; — appliances, Haushaltungsgeräte; — affairs, häusliche Angelegenheiten; — drama, bürgerliches Drama; — duties, häusliche Pflichten; — dissensions, Familienzwistigkeiten; — animal, das Haustier; — consumption, der inländische Verbrauch; — drudge, der Packesel, das Aschenbrödel; — servants, Dienstboten; — servants' agency, Gesinde- *or* Dienstboten-vermittlungsbureau. II. *s.* der Diener, die Dienerin. **—ate**, *v.a.* häuslich machen; zum Familiengliede machen; zähmen (*beasts*); to become —ated, häuslich, heimisch, zahm werden; thoroughly —ated, durchaus häuslich (gesinnt). **—ation**, *s.* das Zahmmachen, Zähmen. **—ity**, *s.* die Häuslichkeit. **—s**, *pl.* das Gesinde, die Dienstboten.

Domicil—e, I. *s.* die Wohnung; der Wohnort. II. *v.a.* wohnhaft, ansässig machen; —ed bill, der domizilierte, auf ein Zahlungsdomizil angewiesene Wechsel (*C.L.*). **—ed**, *adj.* wohnhaft, ansässig; häuslich, Wohnungs-. **—iary**, *adj.* Haus-; —iary visit, die gerichtliche Haussuchung.

Domin—ant, I. *adj.* herrschend; —ant chord, der Dominantenakkord. II. *s.* die Dominante (*Mus.*). **—ate**, *v.a.* beherrschen. **—ation**, *s.* die Herrschaft. **—ator**, *s.* der Herrscher, das herrschende Gestirn (*Astr.*). **—eer**, *v.n.* den Herrn spielen; despotisch herrschen, tyrannisieren; (hector) prahlen; to —eer over, gebieten über (*acc.*), beherrschen. **—eering**, *adj.*, **—eeringly**, *adv.* herrisch, gebieterisch; (insolent) anmaßend, übermütig. **—ical**, *adj.* den Sonntag bezeichnend; —ical prayer, das Vater-Unser; —ical letter, der Sonntagsbuchstabe. **—ican**, *s.* (—ican friar) der Dominikaner. **—ie**, *s.* der Volksschullehrer (*Scotch*). **—ion**, *s.* (sovereign —ion) die Oberherrschaft; (rule) die Herrschaft, Gewalt; die Herrschaft (*fig.*); (district governed) das Gebiet, Land, der Bezirk, Staat. **—o**, *s.* (mask) der Domino. **—oes**, *pl.* das Dominospiel; to play —oes, Domino spielen.

[1]**Don**, *s.* der Don (*Spanish title*); (*Engl. Univ. sl.*); (= dominum, dominam) Graduirter (Graduirte) einer Universität, der später am College angestellt ist, meist fellow eines College; die (akademische) Respektsperson; —nish, wie ein Don, gravitätisch, steif, überlegen.

[2]**Don**, *v.a.* antun, anlegen, anziehen; to — a hat, einen Hut aufsetzen.

Don—ate, *v.a.* schenken, geben, verleihen. **—ation**, *s.* (giving) das Schenken; (gift) die Schenkung, Gabe; die Schenkungsurkunde (*Law*). **—ative**, I. *adj.* durch Schenkung übertragend. II. *s.* die Schenkung, das Geschenk; die ohne Beobachtung der gebräuchlichen Förmlichkeiten übertragene Pfründe (*Eccl.*). **—ee**, *s.* der Geschenknehmer, Beschenkte; der Belehnte (*Law*). **—or**, *s.* der Geschenkgeber, Schenker, Schenkende; der Belohner.

Done, *p.p. of* Do; well —, gut gekocht, gut gebraten, durchgebraten; under —, nicht gar; when I have —, then you may speak, wenn ich zu Ende bin, dann könnt ihr sprechen; have — with this nonsense! höre doch mit diesem Unsinn auf! he may go where he pleases, I have — with him, er kann gehen, wohin es ihm gefällt, ich habe nichts mehr mit ihm zu schaffen; when all is —, schließlich, am Ende; what is to be — now? was ist jetzt zu tun? what's to be — with it? was soll man daraus machen? I am utterly — (up), ich bin ganz erschöpft, ich bin ganz ab (*coll.*); he was completely —, er wurde gehörig betrogen *or* gemeiert (*sl.*); your errand —, come back to me, wenn Sie Ihre Botschaft ausgerichtet haben, kommen Sie zu mir zurück; to get s.th. —, (etwas) machen lassen; they have long been — away with, sie sind längst abgeschafft, beseitigt; he is — for, es ist aus mit ihm, er ist geliefert (*coll.*); —! es gilt! topp! well —! Bravo! no sooner said than —, gesagt, getan.

Donjon, *s.* das Burgverließ.

Donkey, *s.* der Esel; the — brays, der Esel iaht. *Comp.* **—-engine**, *s.* die Hilfsmaschine. **—-pump**, *s.* die Wasserpumpe an Dampfmaschinen, Hilfspumpe.

Don't, *abbr. of* Do not. I. *interj.*; —! laß das! laß (es) doch! II *s.* das Anstandsregelbuch.

Dooly, *s.* eine Art Sänfte oder verdeckte Tragbahre (in Indien).

Doom, I. *v.a.* (sentence) verurteilen (to death, etc., zum Tode, 2c.); (destine) bestimmen; (judge) urteilen, richten; he is —ed, er ist des Todes. II. *s.* das Urteil, der Spruch; die Verurteilung; (lot) das Schicksal, Los; (ruin) der Untergang, das Verderben; (final —) das jüngste Gericht. *Comp.* **—sday**, *s.* der Tag des jüngsten Gerichts; you may wait till —sday, da könnt Ihr lange warten. **—sday-book**, *s. see* Domesday.

Door, *s.* die Tür(e); der Eingang (*fig.*); (house) das Haus; back —, Hintertür; double —, Doppeltür; entry —, front —, street —, Haustür; folding —, Flügeltür; sliding —, Schiebetür; my house is the first — from the corner, meine Wohnung ist das erste Haus von der Ecke an; to show a p. the —, einem die Tür(e) weisen; to turn out of —s, aus dem Hause werfen; out of —s, außer dem Hause; out-of-— life, das Leben im Freien, Leben, bei dem man viel draußen ist; out-— work, die Arbeit außer dem Hause; in-— work, Hausarbeit, Stubenarbeit; within —s, im Hause; to keep within —s, zu Hause bleiben; he shall never darken my —s again, er soll mir nie wieder über die Schwelle kommen; the blame lies wholly at your —, es ist ganz Ihre Schuld, die Schuld trifft Sie allein; to lay at the — of . . ., (einem) Schuld geben; next — to, nebenan, nicht weit von; next — to a fool, nahezu verrückt (*coll.*); to be at death's —, am Rande des Grabes sein. *Comp.* **—-bell**, *s.* die Türklingel, Türschelle. **—-case**, *s.* das Türfutter. **—-cheek**, *s.* der Türpfosten. **—-handle**, *s.* der Türgriff. **—-keeper**, *s.* der Türhüter, Pförtner. **—-knocker**, *s.* der Türklopfer. **—-latch**, *s.* die Türklinke. **—-nail**, *s.* der Türnagel; dead as a —-nail, mausetot. **—-plate**, *s.* das Türschildchen. **—-post**, *s.* der Türpfosten. **—-sill**, *s.* die Türschwelle. **—-step**, *s.* die Stufe vor der Haustür. **—-way**, *s.* der Torweg; der Haustüreingang.

[1]**Dor**, *s.* der Roßkäfer; der Maikäfer (*dial.*); die Drohne (*obs.*).

[2]**Dor**, I. *s.* der Narrenstreich (*obs.*); der Narr (*obs.*). II. *v.a.* narren, zum besten haben.

Dori—an, *see* —c; —an mode, die dorische Tonart. **—c**, I. *adj.* dorisch; —c order, die dorische Säulenordnung (*Arch.*); —c mode, *see* —an. II. *s.* der dorische (breite) Dialekt.

Dorm—ancy, *s.* die Ruhe; die Betäubung. **—ant**, I. *adj.* schlafend, ruhend; ungebraucht, unbenutzt, tot (*fig.*); unbeweglich (*Mech.*); lion —ant, schlafender Löwe (*Her.*); —ant title, ungebrauchter Titel; —ant passions, schlummernde Leidenschaften; —ant partnership, stille

Teilhaberschaft. II. *s.* der Grundbalken (*Carp.*). **—itory**, *s.* der Schlafsaal (in Internatsschulen). *Comp.* **—er-window**, *s.* das Dachfenster, Bodenfenster.

Dormouse, *s.* die Haselmaus.

Dorsal, *adj.* den Rücken betreffend, Rücken= . . .; mit dem Zungenrücken gebildet, dorsal (*Phonet.*).

[1]**Dory**, *s.*; John —, der Petersfisch, Häringskönig.

[2]**Dory**, *s.* kleines Fischerboot.

Dose, I. *s.* die Dosis, die Portion (Arznei); (bitter —) das Unangenehme, die bittere Pille (*fig.*). II. *v.a.* die gehörige Dosis verschreiben; Arznei (in Dosen) eingeben, beibringen; Unangenehmes geben; the more dosing and nursing he underwent, je mehr er einnahm und gepflegt wurde.

[1]**Dot**, I. *s.* der kleine Punkt; der Punkt (*Mus.*, *Tele.*); der Knirps, Zwerg. II. *v.a.* tüpfeln (*also Bot.*); punktieren; sprenkeln; to — accounts, Konti punktieren. **—ted**, *p.p. & adj.* tüpfelig, punktiert; a —ted quaver, punktiertes Achtel; a landscape —ted with trees, eine mit Bäumen reich besetzte Landschaft. *Comp.* **—ting-needle**, *s.* die Punktiernadel.

[2]**Dot**, *see* Dowry. **—al**, *adj.* zum Heiratsgut *or* zur Mitgift gehörig (*Law*).

Dot—age, *s.* die geistige Altersschwäche; die Faselei; die übermäßige Zärtlichkeit, Affenliebe, Vernarrtheit; he is in his —age, er ist wieder zum Kind geworden. **—ard**, *s.* der kindische Greis; der alte Geck, verliebte Narr (*fig.*). **—e**, *v.n.* kindisch sein, faseln; schwärmerisch lieben; to —e on, vernarrt, verliebt sein in (*acc.*), zärtlich lieben; he —es on you, er hat nur Augen für Sie. **—ing**, *adj.*, **—ingly**, *adv.* faselnd, kindisch; innig verliebt, ganz vernarrt (on a p., in einen).

Dott(e)rel, *s.* der Regenpfeifer (*Orn.*).

Double, I. *adj.* doppelt, zwiefach; (in pairs) paarweise, zu Zweien; (bent) gebückt; (ambiguous) zweideutig; (treacherous) falsch, betrüglich; (intensified) vermehrt, vergrößert; — chin, das Doppelkinn; — flowers, gefüllte Blumen; a — game, das falsche, doppelte Spiel; — heart, das falsche Herz; — house, das Doppelhaus (welches Zimmer auf beiden Seiten des Eingangs hat); — letters, die Geminaten; die Ligaturen; — line, das Doppelgeleise (*Railw.*); — movement, der Doppelschlag (*Mus.*); — pica, die Tertschrift (*Print.*); — receipt, der doppelte Schein (*C. L.*); a — row, Doppelreihe; — rule of three, die Regel Duplex; — tooth, der Zweizahn; — track, das Doppelgeleise (*Railw.*); — usance, die doppelte Wechselfrist (*C. L.*). II. *s.* das Doppelte, Zweifache; (fold) die Falte; der Kreuzsprung (*of a hare*); (second self) das Ebenbild, der Doppelgänger; (duplicate) die Abschrift; (—-quick) der Geschwindschritt; at the —, im Geschwindschritt *or* Sturmschritt; to play —s or quits, doppelt oder quitt spielen. III. *v.a.* (ver)doppeln; (fold) zusammenlegen, umschlagen; ballen (*the fist*); umschiffen (a cape, ein Kap); doublieren (*Bill.*; *silk, etc.*); doppelt setzen (*Typ.*); (repeat) wiederholen; im Geschwindschritt marschieren; in Doppelreihen aufmarschieren (*Mil.*); — (the pace)! Marsch! Marsch! (*Mil.*); to — **down**, einschlagen (*a leaf in a book*); to — **up**, zusammenkrümmen; to — and twist, zwirnen. IV. *v.n.* sich verdoppeln; Kreuzsprünge machen (*of hares*); doppelt setzen (*Typ.*); den Einsatz verdoppeln; to — back, auf demselben Wege umkehren, die Spur verschlagen; to — upon, zwischen zwei Feuer bringen (*Mil.*, *Naut.*). V. *adv. see* Doubly. **—ness**, *s.* das Doppelte, Zweifache; die Zweideutigkeit (*fig.*); die Falschheit (*fig.*). **—t**, *s.* das (*or* der) Wams, Kamisol; die Doppelform, Nebenform; der Doppelsatz (*Typ.*); das Doublet (*Opt.*). *Comp.* **—-acting**, *adj.* doppeltwirkend. **—-barrel**, *s.* der Doppellauf. **—-barrelled**, *adj.* doppelläufig; a —-barrelled gun, eine Doppelflinte. **—-bass**, *s.* die Baßgeige; der Kontrabaß. **—-bedded**, *adj.*; a —-bedded room, ein Schlafzimmer mit zwei Betten. **—-breasted**, *adj.* doppelreihig, mit zwei Reihen Knöpfen. **—-dealer**, *s.* der Betrüger. **—-dealing**, *s.* die Falschheit, Achselträgerei. **—-dyed**, *adj.* zweimal gefärbt; —-dyed villain, der Erzschurke. **—-edged**, *adj.* zweischneidig. **—-entendre**, *s.* der Doppelsinn (*French*). **—-entry**, *s.* der doppelte Eintrag; bookkeeping by —-entry, die doppelte Buchführung (*C. L.*). **—-faced**, *adj.* doppelzüngig. **—-lock**, *v.a.* doppelt schließen. **—-meaning**, *s.* der Doppelsinn. **—-minded**, *adj.* wankelmütig. **—-octave**, *s.* die Doppeloktave. **—-quick**, *s.* der Geschwindschritt, Sturmschritt. **—-riveting**, *s.* die doppelte Vernietung. **—-threaded-screw**, *s.* die Doppelschraube. **—-tongued**, *adj* doppelzüngig, falsch.

Doubling, I. *p. see* Double. II. *s.* die Verdoppelung; die Falte; das Umsegeln (*of a cape*).

Doubloon, *s.* die Dublone (*old Spanish coin, worth about a guinea*).

Doubly, *adj.* doppelt, zwiefach, zweifach.

Doubt, I. *v.n.* zweifeln, zweifelhaft *or* im Zweifel sein; (waver) zögern, unentschlossen sein; I — not but he will come, ich zweifle nicht, daß er kommen wird; I — whether it is proper to do this, ich zweifle *or* bin im Zweifel, ob es richtig ist, dies zu tun. II. *v.a.* bezweifeln, in Zweifel ziehen; (suspect) mißtrauen; (fear) befürchten; I — his coming, ich zweifle an seinem Kommen. ich bezweifle, daß er kommen wird; I have heard the story, but I — the truth of it, ich habe die Geschichte gehört, bezweifle aber ihre Wahrheit; I — his ability to discharge the duties of this office, ich zweifle, ob er die Fähigkeit besitzt, dieses Amt zu verwalten; you make me — your love, Sie lassen mich an Ihrer Liebe zweifeln; I begin to — his honesty, ich fange an, an seiner Ehrlichkeit irre zu werden. III. *s.* der Zweifel; (uncertainty) die Ungewißheit; (scruple) das Bedenken; (dubiousness) die Bedenklichkeit; (objection) der Einwurf; to clear up all —s, alle Zweifel heben; I have my —s about the matter, ich habe meine Bedenken über diesen Punkt; there is no — but he will come, es ist kein Zweifel, daß er kommen wird; no —, ohne Zweifel; I have no — of it, ich zweifle nicht daran; to give a p. the benefit of the —, in zweifelhaftem Falle die günstigere Auslegung annehmen. **—er**, *s.* der Zweifler. **—ful**, *adj.* (in —) zweifelnd, unschlüssig, bedenklich; (dubious) zweifelhaft; verdächtig; (suspicious) argwöhnisch; unbestimmt (*as a colour*); zweideutig (*as an expression*); to be —ful of, an (*dat.*) . . . zweifeln. **—fully**, *adv.* auf zweifelnde *or* zweifelhafte Weise; *see* —ful. **—fulness**, *s.* die Zweifelhaftigkeit; die Ungewißheit, Unschlüssigkeit; die Zweideutigkeit (*of meaning*). **—ingly**, *adv.* zweifelnd, mißtrauisch. **—less**, *adv.* ohne Zweifel.

Douce (Douse), *adj.* gesetzt, ehrbar (*Scotch*).

Douche, I. *s.* die Dusche (mit einem Strahl); das Duschbad, Gußbad, Sturzbad. II. *v.a.* abbrausen.

Dough, *s.* der Teig; the — is rising, der Teig geht auf. **—y**, *adj.* teigig; (unbaked) ungar, unreif. *Comp.* **—nuts**, *pl.* runde Schmalzkuchen, Krapfen, (Berliner) Pfannkuchen.

Dought—ily, *adv.*, **—y**, *adj.*, tapfer, mannhaft, tüchtig. **—iness**, *s.* die Tapferkeit.

Dour, *adj.* hart(näckig); (sullen) starrköpfig, düster (*Scotch*).

Douse, *v.a. see* Souse; laufen lassen (*Naut.*).

Dove, *s.* die kleine, feine Taube; die wilde Taube; Liebchen, Täubchen (*fig.*). *Comp.* **—-colour**, *s.* die Lachtaubenfarbe. **—-cote**, *s.* der Taubenschlag. **—-like**, *adj.* taubengleich. **—tail**, I. *s.* der Schwalbenschwanz (*Carp.*); der Taubenschwanz (*Arch.*). II. *v.a.* mit dem Schwalbenschwanz verbinden, einschwalben; verbinden (*fig.*) III. *v.n.* genau in einander passen; sich innig verbinden *or* anschließen, mit einander verschmelzen (*fig.*). IV. *attrib.*; —tail saw, die Zinkensäge. **—tailing**, *s.* die Verzinkung.

Dow—ager, *s.* die Wittwe (von Stand); the queen —, die Königin-Wittwe; the —ager Lady C., die verwitwete Lady C. **—er**, I. *s. see* —ry; das Leibgedinge, Wittum; die Begabung (*fig.*). II. *v.a.* begaben; ausstatten. **—erless**, *adj.* ohne Mitgift. **—ry**, *s.* die Mitgift, der Brautschatz; *see* —er.

Dowdy, I. *s.* eine altmodisch gekleidete Frauensperson. II. *adj.* altmodisch angezogen; unelegant; schlumpig.

Dowlas, *s.* die grobe Lederleinwand.

[1]**Down**, *s.* der Flaum (*also fig.*); die Daunen; bed of —, das Daunenbett. **—y**, *adj.* flaumig; sanft, weich.

[2]**Down**, *s.* die Düne, der Sandhügel; die Erderhöhung, der Hügel (*obs. poet.*); unbewaldetes Hügelland, Hochebene; the —s, das dürre Hügelland für Schaftrift; *see* [3]Down.

[3]**Down**, I. *adv.* nieder, herunter *or* hinunter, unten, herab *or* hinab; that will not go — with me, das kann ich nicht verdauen (*sl.*); to be —, unten sein, herunter gekommen sein; he has come — in the world, er ist sehr heruntergekommen; the sun is —, die Sonne ist untergegangen; the wind has gone —, der Wind hat sich gelegt; I shall be — at 8 o'clock, um 8 Uhr werde ich auf sein und herunterkommen; to boil —, einkochen; —-calving cows, trächtige Kühe; get —! komm herunter! hold him —! haltet ihn nieder! upside —, das Oberste zu unterst; to turn upside —, auf den Kopf stellen; to be — upon a p., streng sein gegen einen, über einen herfallen (*coll.*); up and —, auf und nieder. II. *prep.* herab, herunter, hinab, hinunter; — stream, — the river, stromabwärts; to go — the river, den Fluß hinabfahren; to go — the hill, den Hügel hinabgehen; to fall — a precipice, in einen Abgrund fallen; — in the country, auf dem Lande; — the wind, unter dem Winde (*Naut.*). III. *int.* nieder! hinab! — with him! nieder mit ihm! —, (dog,) lege dich hin, kusch dich, kusch! IV. *s.*; the ups and —s of life, die Wechselfälle des Lebens. **—ward**, I. *adj.* sich senkend, herabkommend, abschüssig; his is a —ward course, er geht, eilt seinem Untergang entgegen. II. *adv.* (—wards) niederwärts, hinab, abwärts. *Comp.* **—cast**, *adj.* niedergeschlagen; —cast shaft, der Wettereinzug (*Min.*). **—fall**, *s.* der Sturz, Fall: der Verfall, Untergang (*fig.*). **—-hearted**, *adj.* niedergeschlagen. **—hill**, I. *adj.* abschüssig. II. *adv.* den Hügel hinab, bergab; he is fast going —hill, es geht mit ihm bergab; seine Kräfte nehmen zusehends ab. **—-platform**, *s.* der Bahnsteig für von der Hauptstation abgehende Züge. **—pour**, *s.* das Niederströmen (of rain, des Regens), der Regenguß. **—right**, I. *adj.* offen, offenherzig, redlich, unverstellt; (unceremonious) ohne Umstände; —right atheism, positiver Atheismus; —right nonsense (madness), barer Unsinn (Wahnsinn); a —right fool, ein völliger Narr; a —right rascal, ein Erzschurke; in a —right way, gerade heraus. II. *adv.* (right down) senkrecht; geradezu, offen, frei; (thoroughly) tüchtig, völlig; famos, brillant, auf ein Haar (*coll.*). **—rightness**, *s.* die Offenheit, Geradheit. **—-sitting**, *s.* das Niedersetzen; thou knowest my —-sitting and my uprising, ich sitze oder stehe auf, so weißt Du es (*B.*). **—-stairs**, *adj.*, *adv.* treppab, die Treppe hinab *or* hinunter; he is —-stairs, er ist unten. **—-stroke**, *s.* der Grundstrich (*in writing*); der Herunterstrich (*in fiddling*); —-stroke of a piston, der Kolbenniedergang. **—-toner**, *s.* abschwächendes Wort, abschwächende Partikel. **—-train**, *s.* der Zug von der Hauptstation (*Railw.*). **—trodden**, *adj.* niedergetreten; zertreten, zerstampft.

Doxology, *s.* die Doxologie, (die Hymne *or* der Psalm zur) Lobpreisung Gottes.

D'oyley, *s.* die kleine Dessert-Serviette.

Doze, I. *v.a.*; to — away one's time, etc., seine Zeit 2c. verduseln, verträumen. II. *v.n.* schlummern, duseln; to — over work, bei der Arbeit schlafen. III. *s. see* Nap.

Dozen, *s.* das Dutzend; to talk thirteen to the —, das Blaue vom Himmel schwatzen; a baker's —, dreizehn aufs Dutzend, dreizehn Stück; to give a p. a baker's —, einen gehörig verhauen (*sl.*).

[1]**Drab**, *adj.* mausgrau, mattbraun, schmutzfarben.

[2]**Drab**, *s.* das schmutzige, unordentliche Weib; die Hure. **—ble**, *v.a.* beschmutzen.

Drachm(a), *s.* die Drachme.

Draft, I. *s.* die Tratte; die Aushebung; die Abteilung, das Detachement (*Mil.*); die erste Skizze, Kladde, der Umriß, erste Entwurf, *see* Draught; — report, der Entwurf *or* die erste Fassung eines Berichtes; I have made the — payable to you, ich habe die Tratte auf Sie ausgestellt; — at sight on London, Sichttratte auf London. II. *v.a.* (Zeichnungen, Risse) entwerfen; schriftlich entwerfen, aufsetzen (*a lease, etc.*); auswählen und absenden, detachieren (*soldiers*).

Drag, I. *v.a.* schleppen, auf dem Boden hinziehen, schleifen; ziehen (*a fishing net*); (dredge) dreggen; eggen (*Agr.*); hemmen (*a wheel*); to — the anchor, vor Anker treiben; to — along, mit Gewalt hinschleppen, fortschleppen; to — out (on) a lingering life, ein elendes Leben hinschleppen. II. *v.n.* schleifen; dreggen, fischen; mit einem Schleppnetz fischen (for, nach); the business —s, das Geschäft geht flau. III. *s.* die Schleife (*for dragging burdens*); der Klotzwagen (*for wood, etc.*); die Erdkratze, Bodenscharre (*Agr.*); (carriage) eine Art Jagdwagen; (—net) das Schleppnetz; (brake) der Hemmschuh; (grapnel) der Dreghaken; (dredge) das Baggernetz; der Bagger (*Hydr.*); das Hemmende; he is a great — on his family, er fällt seiner Familie sehr zur Last. **—gle**, *see* Draggle. *Comp.* **—boat**, *s.* der Sandräumer. **—-bolt**, *s.* der Kuppelbolzen (*Locom.*). **—-chain**, *s.* die Hemmkette. **—-hook**, *s.* der Kuppelhaken. **—net**, *s.* das Schleppnetz. **—-wheel**, *s.* das Schlepprad.

Draggle, *v.* I. *a.* (im Schmutze) schleppen, beschmutzen. II. *n.* sich beschmutzen. *Comp.* **—tail**, *s.* die Schlumpe, Schmutzliese.

Dragoman, *s.* der (orientalische) Dolmetscher.

Dragon, *s.* der Drache (*also fig. & Astr.*); (*poet.*) der Lindwurm; der Teufel (*B.*). **—et**, *s.* der kleine Spinnenfisch (*Icht.*). *Comp.* **—-fly**, *s.* die See- *or* Wasser-jungfer, Libelle (*Ent.*). **—'s-blood**, *s.* das Drachenblut (*Bot.*). **—-tree**, *s.* der Drachenbaum.

Dragonade, *s.* die Verfolgung und Drangsalierung (durch Dragoner-Einquartierung).

Dragoon, I. *s.* der Dragoner. II. *v.a.* (durch Dragoner *or* Einquartierung) peinigen lassen; zwingen. *Comp.* **—guard**, *s.* der Gardedragoner.

Drain, I. *v.a.* Flüssigkeiten abtropfen lassen; entwässern, trocken legen, drainieren (*ground*); (draw off) abziehen, ableiten; (empty) ausleeren; (exhaust) verzehren; to — a pond, einen Teich abschützen; to — a p.'s purse, jemands Beutel leeren; to — off, ablassen. II. *v.n.* ablaufen, abfließen. III. *s.* der Abzug, Ableitungs-, Entwässerungs-graben; (gutter) die Gosse; die Senkgrube (*Build.*); that is a — on my purse, das nimmt meinen Geldbeutel (zu) stark in Anspruch. **—able**, *adj.* trockenlegbar. **—age**, *s.* das Ablaufen, Abfließen; die Entwässerung, Kanalisation; der Abzugskanal (*Build.*). **—er**, *s.* der Ableiter, Grabenzieher; (plate —er) das Tropfbrett. **—ing**, I. *p. & adj.* abziehend (*in cpds.*). II. *s.* die Entwässerung, Trockenlegung Drainage. **—s**, *pl.* die Abzugsröhren. *Comp.* **—-pipe**, *s.* das Abzugsrohr, die Abzugsröhre.

—**-tiles**, *pl.* die Rinnziegel, Abzugsziegel. —**-trap**, *s.* der Wasserschluß.

Drake, *s.* der Enterich; to play at ducks and —s, Jungfern *or* Hüpfsteine werfen; verschwenden (*fig.*).

Dram, *s.* der Trunk, Schluck; der Schnaps; *see* Drachma. *Comp.* —**-bottle**, *s.* die Schnapsflasche. —**-drinker**, *s.* der Schnapssäufer.

Drama, *s.* das Schauspiel, Drama. —**tic(al)**, *adj.*, —**tically**, *adv.* dramatisch; —tic art, die Schauspielkunst; —tic performance, die Aufführung. —**tis personæ**, *pl.* die Personen (im Schauspiel). —**tist**, *s.* der Dramatiker, Schauspieldichter, dramatische Dichter. —**tize**, *v.a.* als Schauspiel *or* dramatisch behandeln, dramatisieren. —**turgy**, *s.* die Dramaturgie.

Drank, *imperf. of* Drink.

Drape, *v.a.* drapieren, behängen. —**r**, *s.* der Tuchhändler; (*in comp.*) der -Händler; linen—r, der Leinwandhändler; —rs' company, die (Londoner) Tuchhändlerinnung. —**ry**, *s.* der Tuchhandel; (cloths) das Tuch, wollene Zeug; *see* Hangings; die Gewänder, der Faltenwurf (*Paint. etc.*). *Comp.* —**ry-goods**, *pl.* Leinen- und Baumwoll-waren; *see* Dry goods.

Drastic, *adj.* derb, kräftig, drastisch.

Drat, *v.a.*; — it! zum Henker damit! (*vulg.*); — the boys! die verflixten Buben!

Draught, *s.* (drawing) das Ziehen, der Zug; der Ahm (*Naut.*); der Wasserzug, Tiefgang (*of a ship*); (drink) der Zug, Schluck; der Zug (*of air, of fishes*); die Zeichnung, der Abriß (*Draw.*); (sketch) das Konzept, der Entwurf, schriftliche Aufsatz; die Aushebung (*of soldiers*); *see* Draft; das Gutgewicht (*C. L.*); wharf with good — of water, Werft mit guter Tiefe des Wassers; to drink off at one —, auf einen Zug austrinken; you are sitting in the *or* a —, Sie sitzen im Zuge; beer on —, Bier frisch vom Fasse. II. *v.a. see* Draft II. —**s**, *pl.* das Damenspiel; (—smen) die Steine; to play at —s, das Damenspiel spielen; let us play at —s, wir wollen Dame spielen. —**y**, *adj.* zugig. *Comp.* —**-board**, *s.* das Damenbrett, Dambrett; das Brettspiel. —**-horse**, *s.* das Zugpferd. —**sman**, *s.* der Zeichner; der Stein (*in draughts*). —**smanship**, *s.* die Kunst *or* Leistung eines Zeichners; die Kunst der Abfassung.

Draw, *ir.v.a.* (pull) ziehen; (drag) schleppen, schleifen; (attract) anziehen, an sich ziehen; abziehen (*beer, wine, etc.*); ablassen (*blood*); ausfischen (*a pond*); zuziehen (*the curtain*); saugen (*the breast, etc.*); losen (*cuts, lots*); ausdärmen (*a fowl, etc.*); zeichnen (*Draw.*); schildern (*a picture*); gewinnen, ziehen (*a prize, etc.*); ausstellen (*a bill*); anweisen (*C. L.*); to be —n, sich hinters Licht führen lassen (*sl.*); to — blood, Blut abzapfen, (bleed) zur Ader lassen; to — fresh courage from s.th., neuen Mut aus einer S. schöpfen; to — the bow, den Bogen spannen; to — the long bow, mit dem großen Messer schneiden, aufschneiden, prahlen; to — breath, Luft schöpfen; to — comparisons, Vergleiche anstellen; to — consolation from . . ., Trost schöpfen aus, sich mit . . . trösten; to — a cover, Wild ausspüren; good actors — full houses, gute Schauspieler füllen das Haus; to — one's pen through a passage, eine Stelle in einem Schreiben ausstreichen; to — profit, Vorteil ziehen (from, von, aus); to — a sigh, einen Seufzer ausstoßen; to — the sword, das Schwert ziehen; to — **after**, nach sich ziehen; to — **along**, fortziehen; to — **aside**, bei Seite nehmen *or* ziehen; to — **away**, wegziehen, wegnehmen, entwenden; to — **back**, zurückziehen; to — **forth**, herausziehen; to — **from**, (elicit) entlocken, herauslocken, (deduce) herleiten, hernehmen; to — **in**, einziehen; to — in one's horns, die Hörner einziehen, sich mäßigen, gelindere Saiten aufziehen; to — **into**, in (eine S.) hineinziehen; to — **off**, abziehen (*fluids*), ablenken (*the attention, etc.*); to — **on**, anziehen (*boots, etc.*), zuziehen (*blame, etc.*), herbeiführen (*war, etc.*), (allure) anlocken, (cause) veranlassen; to — **out**, herausziehen, (stretch) ausdehnen, in die Länge ziehen (*fig.*); to — out troops, Truppen detachieren; to — out into wire, zu Draht ausziehen; to — a p. out about a th., einen über eine Sache ausholen; to — **over**, herüberziehen, hinüberziehen (*fig.*); to — **up**, (her)aufziehen, in die Höhe ziehen; to — up boats, Boote ans Land ziehen; to — up a petition, eine Bittschrift aufsetzen; to — up a report, einen Bericht abfassen; to — up in order of battle, in Schlachtordnung aufstellen; they were —n up before his door, sie waren vor seiner Tür aufgestellt; to — (a bill) **upon** (a person), (einen Wechsel auf einen) ausstellen. II. *ir.v.n.* ziehen (upon, auf); eine Karte ziehen; das Schwert ziehen; ziehen (*of tea, a plaster, etc.*); zeichnen (*Draw.*); we must let the tea —, der Tee muß (einige Zeit) ziehen; to — for the move, um den Zug losen; to — to a head, to a close, zu Ende gehen, sich dem Ende nähern; to — at long (at short) date, auf lange (auf kurze) Zeit ziehen *or* ausstellen (*bills*); to — **back**, sich zurückziehen, (fall away) abfallen, abtrünnig werden; to — **in**, sich neigen (*as the days*); to — **nigh**, **near**, sich nähern, heranrücken; my (last) hour —s nigh, meine letzte Stunde naht; harvest is —ing near, es geht gegen die Ernte; the time is —ing near, die Zeit rückt heran; to — **off**, sich zurückziehen; to — **on**, herannahen, anrücken; the night —s on apace, die Nacht rückt schnell heran; to — **together**, zusammenziehen; to — **towards**, sich neigen; to — **up**, vorfahren, anhalten (*as a carriage*); sich aufstellen (*as troops*). III. *s.* das Ziehen, der Zug das Los; die unentschiedene Partie; the game ended in a —, das Spiel blieb unentschieden. —**able**, *adj.* ziehbar. —**ee**, *s.* der Trassat (*C. L.*). —**er**, *s.* der Zieher; der Zapfer (*in an inn*); der Zeichner; der Trassant (*C. L.*); die Schublade; —er of a bird-cage, der Trog im Vogelbauer. —**ers**, *pl.* die Unterhosen; a chest, set of —ers, die Kommode. —**ing**, *s.* das Ziehen; das Zeichnen; die Zeichnung, Skizze; die Ausstellung (eines Wechsels, Trassierung; die Ziehung (*in a lottery*); der Riß (*Arch.*); crayon —ing, das Pastellzeichnen; die Pastellzeichnung; water-colour —ing, das Wasserfarbengemälde; working —ing, die Konstruktionszeichnung. —**ings**, *pl.* die Einnahmen (*C.L.*). —**n**, *adj.*; a —n battle, game, eine unentschiedene Schlacht, ein unentschiedenes Spiel; —n sword, das bloße Schwert; —n butter, zerlassene Butter. *Comp.* —**back**, *s.* der Rückzoll (*at the custom-house*); (recoil) der Zurücklauf; (disadvantage) der Nachteil, die Schattenseite, der Fehler, das Unangenehme, Störende. —**beam**, *s.* der Schwengel (*of a well*). —**bridge**, *s.* die Zugbrücke. —**ing-board**, *s.* das Zeichenbrett, Reißbrett. —**ing-chalk**, *s.* die Zeichenkreide. —**ing-compasses**, *pl.* der Reißzirkel. —**ing-master**, *s.* der Zeichenlehrer. —**ing-office**, *s.* das Büreau des Planzeichners (*Surv., etc.*). —**ing-paper**, *s.* das Zeichenpapier. —**ing-pen**, *s.* die Reißfeder. —**ing-pin**, *s.* der Reißnagel. —**ing-room**, *s.* das Gesellschaftszimmer, der Salon; the King holds a —ing-room to-day, heute hat der König großen Empfangstag. —**well**, *s.* der Ziehbrunnen.

Drawl, I. *v.a.* dehnen (die Worte). II. *v.n.* im Sprechen ziehen, dehnen. III. *s.* das Ziehen der Worte im Sprechen; die schleppende Sprechweise; a long —, eine lange schleppende und einförmige Rede.

Drawn, *p.p. of* Draw.

Dray, *s.* der niedrige Karren; der Förderungskarren (*Min.*). *Comp.* —**-cart**, *see* Dray. —**-horse**, *s.* der Karrengaul. —**-man**, *s.* der Kärrner. —**-plough**, *s.* der Schleppflug.

Dread, I. *s.* die Furcht; (terror) der Schrecken; (awe) die Ehrfurcht; to have a — of something, ein Grauen vor einer S. empfinden. II. *adj.* schrecklich, furchtbar; gefürchtet, erhaben, hehr, ehrwürdig; — liege, — lord, gestrenger Herr; God, a — judge, Gott, ein gestrenger Richter. III. *v.a.* fürchten, ein Grauen empfinden (vor). **—ful**, I. *adj.*, **—fully**, *adv.* schrecklich, furchtbar. II. *s.;* penny —ful, das billige Sensationsblatt; shilling —ful, der billige Schauerroman. **—fulness**, *s.* die Schrecklichkeit. *Comp.* **—nought**, *s.* der Wagehals, Unerschrockene(r), Unverzagte(r); der Oberrock von dickem Fries.

Dream, I. *s.* der Traum. II. *v.a.* träumen; to — away life, sein Leben verträumen. III. *v.n.* träumen; (be —y) müßig gehen, träumerisch sein; I never —t of such a thing, so etwas ist mir nie im Traume eingefallen *or* habe ich mir nie träumen lassen. **—er**, *s.* der Träumer. **—ily**, *adv.*, **—y**, *adj.* träumerisch; Träumereien ergeben; —y ways, träumerisches Wesen. **—ing**, *s.* die Träumerei. **—less**, *adj.* traumlos.

Drear, *adj.*, *see* —y. **—ily**, *adv.*, **—y**, *adj.*, traurig, öde; (tiresome) langweilig. **—iness**, *s.* die Traurigkeit, Öde.

[1]**Dredg—e**, I. *s.* das Schleppnetz; *see* —ing-machine. II. *v.a.* ausbaggern (*Hydr.*), draggen (*Naut.*); mit dem Schleppnetze fangen. **—er**, *s.* der Fischer mit dem Schleppnetze, Austernfischer; der Bagger, die Baggermaschine; steam —er, der Dampfbagger. **—ing**, *in comp.* Bagger=.

[2]**Dredge**, *v.a.* (mit Mehl, ꝛc.) bestreuen (*Cook.*). **—r**, *s.* die Streubüchse.

Dregs, *pl.* die Hefe, der Bodensatz; der Schund, Auswurf, Abschaum, die Hefe (*fig.*); — of wine, die Weinhefe.

Drench, I. *s.* der Trunk; der Trank (*Vet.*). II. *v.a.* (soak) durchnässen; (overflow) überschwemmen; (water) gehörig wässern; Arznei einzwingen; —ed in blood, blutdurchtränkt, in Blut getränkt; —ed with rain, vom Regen (bis auf die Haut) durchnäßt; —ed in tears, in Tränen gebadet.

Dress, I. *v.a.* kleiden; (adorn) schmücken; bearbeiten, bauen (*Agr.*); anrichten (*food*); behauen (*stones*); appretieren (*stuffs*); zubereiten (*leather*); rauhen (*cloth*); bestoßen (*type*); hecheln (*flax*); brechen (*hemp*); pöhlen (*a skin*): to — the ranks, sich richten; to — o.s., sich (an)kleiden; to — a wound, eine Wunde verbinden; the wound was —ed with a little oil, die Wunde wurde mit etwas Öl behandelt; to — a lady's hair, eine Dame frisieren; to — the vine, den Weinstock beschneiden; to — a ship, ein Schiff mit Flaggen und Wimpeln schmücken; to — a p. up, einen herausputzen. II. *v.n.* sich (an)kleiden; sich putzen; sich richten (*Mil.*); to — elegantly, sich geschmackvoll kleiden; to — for a ball, ein Ballkleid anlegen; to — up, sich fein *or* zierlich kleiden, putzen; (Waren) akkomodieren (*C.L.*). III. *s.* der Anzug, die Kleidung; das Kleid; full —, das Galakleid; in full —, in Gala, in vollem Staate. IV. *attrib.;* — ball, der Galaball; — boxes, die Logen; — shirt, das (Herren=)Oberhemd; — suit, der Frackanzug; — sword, der Staatsdegen. **—er**, *s.* der Ankleider; die Ankleiderin; der Anrichter; (kitchen —er) der Anrichtetisch. **—ing**, *s.* das Ankleiden; das Behandeln (*of a wound*); der Verband, Umschlag (*Surg.*); die Zubereitung, Appretur; top —ing, der auf dem Acker ausgestreute Dünger (*Agr.*); preliminary —ing (of a wound), der Notverband; —ing of linen, die Glänzung; salad- —ing, die Salatzubereitung. **—y**, *adj.* prunkhaft, auffallend gekleidet; fein, modisch; dem Putze ergeben. *Comp.* **—-circle**, *s.* der erste Rang (*Theat.*). **—-coat**, *s.* der Frack. **—-guard**, *s.* der Rockschützer (*Cycl.*). **—ing-apparatus**, *s.* die Sichtmaschine, der Zylinder. **—ing-bag**, *s.* die Toiletten=Handtasche. **—ing-case**, *s.* das Toilettenkästchen. **—ing-glass**, *s.* der Toilettenspiegel. **—ing-gown**, *s.* der Schlafrock. **—ing-jacket**, *s.* der Frisiermantel. **—ing-room**, *s.* das Ankleidezimmer. **—ing-table**, *s.* die Toilette, der Toilettentisch. **—-jacket**, *s.* der Smoking. **—maker**, *s.* die Kleidermacherin, Damenschneiderin. **—-rehearsal**, *s.* die Generalprobe.

Drew, *imperf. of* Draw.

Drib—ble, I. *v.n.* tröpfeln, in Tropfen herabfallen; geifern (*as a child*). II. *v.a.* in Tropfen fallen lassen; in leichten kurzen Tritten (den Ball) vor sich hertreiben (*Footb.*). **—blet**, **—let**, *s.* das Bischen, die kleine Summe, Kleinigkeit, Lappalie.

Drie—d, *p.p.* (*see* Dry) *& adj.* getrocknet, trocken. **—r**, *s.* der Trocknende; das Trockenmittel.

Drift, I. *s.* das Getriebene; (impulse) der Trieb; (aim) der Zweck, das Ziel; das erratische Geschiebe; der horizontale Druck (*Arch.*); die Furt (*South Africa*); snow- —, die Schneewehe; — of a discourse, der Gedankengang; (aim) der Endzweck einer Rede. II. *v.a.* zusammen=treiben, =wehen. III. *v.n.* vorwärts getrieben werden; dahin treiben, sich von der Strömung tragen lassen; sich aufhäufen; triftig sein (*Naut.*); the snow —s, der Schnee häuft sich. **—ing**, *adj.* triftig. **—y**, *adj.* voller Wehen, leicht Schneewehen bildend. *Comp.* **—-ice**, *s.* das Treibeis. **—-sand**, *s.* der Treibsand. **—-way**, *s.* der Treibweg, die Trift (*for cattle*); die Strecke (*Min.*). **—-wood**, *s.* das Treibholz.

[1]**Drill**, I. *v.a.* bohren, drillen (*holes, etc.*); exerzieren, einexerzieren, drillen (*Mil.*); in Rillen *or* Furchen säen; to — a thing into a p., einem etwas einpauken. II. *s.* *see* — bore; der Versenkbohrer (*Horol.*); das Exerzieren (*Mil.*); (furrow) die Furche, Rille; phonetic —, gründliche phonetische Schulung; extra —, das Nachexerzieren. III. *attrib.;* —bore, der Drillbohrer; —ground, der Exerzierplatz. **—ing**, *s.* das Bohren; das Exerzieren. *Comp.* **—-hall**, *s.* das Exerzierhaus. **—-harrow**, *s.* die Bohregge. **—-master**, *s.* der Exerzierlehrer. **—-plough**, *s.* die Säemaschine. **—-sergeant**, *s.* der einexerzierende Unteroffizier; der Rekruten=Unteroffizier.

[2]**Drill**, **Drilling**, *s.* der Drillich.

Drink, I. *ir.v.a.* trinken; saufen (*of beasts*); to — o.s. into an illness, sich durch Trinken eine Krankheit zuziehen, sich (*dat.*) eine Krankheit antrinken (*coll.*); to — (to) the health of s.o., auf jemandes Gesundheit trinken; to — **away**, vertrinken; to — **in**, einziehen, einsaugen, einatmen (*fig.*); to — in a piece of news, eine Nachricht verschlingen; to — in the spirit of liberty, den Geist der Freiheit in sich aufnehmen; to — **off**, — **up**, austrinken, ausleeren; to — **out**, austrinken. II. *v.n.* trinken; übermäßig trinken, zechen; to — hard, deep, stark trinken; to — **to**, (einem) zutrinken, trinken auf (*acc.*). III. *s.* der Trank, Trunk; (strong —) das geistige Getränk; a — of water, ein Trunk Wasser. **—able**, *adj.* trinkbar. **—ables**, *pl.* Getränke (*vulg.*). **—er**, *s.* der Trinker; der Zecher; (drunkard) der Trunkenbold, Säufer. **—ing**, *s.* das Trinken; given to —ing, dem Trunk(e) ergeben. *Comp.* **—ing-bout**, *s.* das Trinkgelag(e). **—ing-cup**, *s.* der Becher. **—ing-fountain**, *s.* der Brunnen mit fließendem Trinkwasser; der Trinknapf am Vogelbauer. **—ing-horn**, *s.* das Trinkhorn. **—ing-song**, *s.* das Trinklied **—ing-water**, *s.* das Trinkwasser. **—-offering**, *s.* das Trankopfer.

Drip, I. *v.n.* tröpfeln, herunter tropfen *or* tröpfeln. II. *s.* das Herabtröpfeln; (drops) die Traufe; das Traufdach (*Arch.*). **—ping**, I. *p. & adj.* tröpfelnd. II. *s.* das Bratenfett, Schmalz. *Comp.* **—ping-eaves**, *pl.* die Dachrinne, Traufe. **—ping-pan**, *s.* die Tröpfelpfanne; (roasting pan) die Bratpfanne. **—-stone**, *s.* der Filtrierstein; die Kranzleiste (*Arch.*).

Drive, I. *ir.v.a.* treiben (*away, etc.*); (forced

zwingen; treiben, hetzen (*Sport.*); fahren (*a carriage*); treiben, führen (*a business*); führen (*an engine*); to — a coach, kutschieren; to — a bargain, einen Handel, einen Kauf bewerkstelligen; to — a hoop, einen Reifen schlagen; to — all before one, alles überwinden; to — home, nach Hause fahren; (einem etwas) eindringlich zu Gemüte führen; do not — me mad, mache mich nicht verrückt; it was enough to — one mad, es war zum Rasendwerden; to be within —ing distance, zu Wagen leicht erreichbar (*or* zu erreichen) sein; to — **away**, vertreiben; to — **back**, zurück treiben; to be —n back on one's own resources, auf seine eignen Hilfsmittel angewiesen, beschränkt werden; to — **from**, von . . . abbringen, treiben; to — **in**, zurücktreiben (*Mil.*), eintreiben, einschlagen (*as nails, etc.*); to — in a pile, einen Pfahl einrammen; to — **into**, hineintreiben; to — a th. into a p., einem etwas einremsen; to — a p. into a rage, einen in Wut bringen; to — **off**, wegtreiben; to — an actor off the stage, einen Schauspieler auspfeifen; to — **on**, vorwärts treiben, (— on with) eifrig betreiben; to — **out**, hinaustreiben, forttreiben; to — a p. out of the house, einen aus dem Hause jagen; to — **to**, zu . . . bringen, treiben; to — a p. to despair, einen zur Verzweiflung bringen; to — **up**, in die Höhe treiben (*prices*); to — up against, rennen gegen. II. *ir.v.n.* treiben (*also Naut.*); fahren; the ship —s before the wind, das Schiff treibt vor dem Winde; to — to leeward, abtreiben; to — upon a coast, (mit dem Schiffe) auf die Küste zutreiben; he —s uncommonly well, er fährt ganz vorzüglich; to — up to a house, vor einem Hause vorfahren; to — off, wegfahren; — on, coachman! fahren Sie zu, Kutscher! I know what he's driving at, ich weiß, wo er hinaus will. III. *s.* die Spazierfahrt; (way) der Fahrweg; (carriage —) die Auffahrt vor einem Hause; to take a —, ausfahren; a pleasant —, eine angenehme Fahrt. —**n**, I. *p.p. see* Drive. II. *adj.;* white as the —n snow, weiß wie frischgefallener Schnee. —**r**, *s.* der Treiber (*of oxen, etc.*); der Fuhrmann, Kutscher; der Rammblock (*Build.*); slave-—r, der Sklavenaufseher; engine-—r, Lokomotivführer; pile-—r, die Ramme; —r's seat, der Kutschersitz, Kutschbock.

Drivel, I. *v.n.* geifern (*as infants*); faseln (*fig.*); —(l)ing imbecility, faselnde Geistesschwäche. II. *s.* der Geifer; die Faselei. —(**l**)**er**, *s.* der Geiferer; der Faselhans.

Driving, I. *p. see* Drive. II. *s.* das Treiben. *Comp.* —**-anchor**, *s.* der Treibanker. —**-box**, *s.* der Kutsch(er)bock. —**-cushion**, *s.* das Kutscherkissen. —**-gear**, *s.* das Getriebe. —**-reins**, *s.* die Leitriemen. —**-shaft**, *s.* die Treibachse (*Locom., etc.*). —**-wheel**, *s.* das Treibrad (*Locom.*). —**-whip**, *s.* die Fuhrmanns- *or* Kutscher-Peitsche.

Drizzl—**e**, I. *s.* der feine Nebel, Sprühregen. II. *v.n.* rieseln, fein regnen. —**ing**, I. *adj.*, —**y**, *adj.* rieselnd. II. *s. see* —e I.

Droll, *adj.* drollig; — fellow, der drollige Kerl, Hanswurst. —**ery**, *s.* die Posse, Schnurre, Spaßhaftigkeit, der Spaß, das Drollige.

Dromedary, *s.* das Dromedar.

[1]**Dron**—**e**, I. *s.* das Gesumme, Gebrumme; der einförmige Ton im Lesen oder Sprechen; die Baßpfeife (*of the bagpipes*). II. *v.n.* summen, brummen. III. *v.a.;* to —e out, hersummen, herbrummen. —**ing**, I. *p. & adj. see* —e. II. *s.* das Summen; die einförmige, summende, unverständliche Sprechart.

[2]**Drone**, I. *s.* die Drohne, männliche Biene; der Faulenzer, Müßiggänger (*fig.*). II. *v.n.* müßig gehen, faulenzen. III. *v.a.;* to — away, müßig verbringen.

Droop, I. *v.a.* sinken lassen. II. *n.* verwelken, niederhangen (*as flowers*); hinsinken, zusammenfallen; verschmachten; den Kopf hängen lassen (*fig.*); (decline) abnehmen. —**ing**, *adj.*, —**ingly**, *adv.* matt, hinfällig, schmachtend, mutlos.

Drop, I. *s.* der Tropfen; das Fallbrett (of gallows, am Schnellgalgen); das Plätzchen (*Conf.*); der Vorhang (*Theat.*). —**s**, *pl.* Tropfen (*Med., Arch.*); Zuckerplätzchen, Fruchtbonbons (*Conf.*); the — serene, die Amaurosis (*Med.*); he has not drunk a —, er hat keinen Tropfen getrunken; he has had a — (too much), er ist bespitzt, angesäuselt, hat zu tief ins Glas geguckt. II. *v.a.* tropfen, tröpfeln; sprenkeln (*fig.*); (lower) senken; auswerfen (*the anchor*); fallen lassen (*also a thing, a matter, a word, etc.*); werfen (in the letter-box, in den Briefkasten); gebären, setzen (*the young of beasts*); to — a person, an acquaintance, eine Bekanntschaft aufgeben, nichts mehr mit einem zu tun haben wollen; to — a hint, einen Wink fallen lassen *or* hinwerfen; — me a line as soon as you can, schreiben Sie mir, eine Zeile sobald Sie nur können; to — a curtesy, einen Knicks machen, knicksen (*of girls*); to — a p. on the way, einen Passagier unterwegs absetzen; to — the pilot, den Lotsen entlassen; to — a subject, einen Gegenstand fallen lassen, nicht weiter berühren; let us — that subject! lassen Sie uns von etwas anderm sprechen! the bill was —ped, der Antrag fiel durch; to — a tear, eine Träne vergießen. III. *v.n.* tröpfeln, triefen; fallen (*as leaves*); (herab) fallen, sinken; hinsinken, sterben (*as a p. shot*); aufgegeben, nicht weiter berührt werden; to be ready to —, so ermattet sein, daß man umfallen möchte *or* dem Hinsinken nahe ist; to — **asleep**, einschlafen; to — **astern**, zurückbleiben; to — **away**, allmählich abfallen; to — **down** a river, stromabwärts segeln, rudern; to — **in**, unerwartet kommen, vorsprechen (bei); I shall — in at your brother's on the way, unterwegs werde ich bei deinem Bruder vorsprechen; several orders have —ped in within the last week, in der letzten Woche sind mehrere Aufträge eingelaufen; to — **off**, abtropfen, (go away) allmählich fortgehen, (die) hinsterben, (— asleep) einschlafen, (desert) abfallen; to — **out**, tropfen, (slip away) entwischen. IV. *attrib.;* — earrings, die Ohrringe mit Gehänge. —**per**, *s.* die Augenspritze. —**ping**, I. *p. & adj. see* Drop; a —ping fire, das Rottenfeuer (*Mil.*). II. *s.* das Tröpfeln; das Tropfende; der Mist (*especially of birds, hens*); constant —ping wears the stone, stetes Tropfen höhlt den Stein. *Comp.* —**-scene**, *s.* der Vorhang (*Theat.*).

Drops—**ical**, *adj.* wassersüchtig. —**ied**, *adj.* wassersüchtig. —**y**, *s.* die Wassersucht.

Dros(h)ky, *s.* die Droschke.

Drosometer, *s.* der Taumesser.

Dross, *s.* das Gekrätz, die Krätze, Schlacke (*Metall.*); (refuse) der Auswurf, Unrat; — of iron, der Hammerschlag.

Drought, *s.* die Dürre, Trockenheit; (thirst) der Durst. —**iness**, *s.* die Dürre, Trockenheit. —**y**, *adj.* dürr, trocken; durstig.

Drove, I. *imperf. of* Drive. II. *s.* die Viehherde, Trift (Vieh). —**r**, *s.* der Viehtreiber.

Drown, *v.* I. *a.* ertränken, ersäufen; (inundate) überschwemmen; übertäuben, betäuben (*fig.*); dämpfen (*one's voice*); (stifle) ersticken; the woman was —ed, die Frau wurde ertränkt; the cat was —ed, die Katze wurde ersäuft; his voice was —ed by the noise, seine Stimme wurde vom Lärm übertönt; to — care in wine, sich (*dat.*) die Grillen vertrinken. II. *n.* ertrinken, ersaufen; the girl was —ed, das Mädchen ertrank; they have all been —ed, sie sind alle ertrunken; she is —ing, sie ertrinkt (eben). —**ing**, I. *p. & adj. see* Drown; a —ing man catches at a straw, der Ertrinkende greift nach einem Strohhalm (*prov.*). II. *s.* das Ertrinken.

Drows—**e**, *v.* I. *n.* schlummern, (unterbrochen) schlafen; schläfrig sein. II. *a.* schläfrig machen (*obs.*). —**ily**, *adv.* schläfrig. —**iness**, *s.* die Schläfrigkeit, Schlafsucht. —**y**, *adj.* schläfrig; einschläfernd. *Comp.* —**y-headed**, *adj.* schläfrig.

Drub, I. *v.a.* schlagen, prügeln; trommeln; to — s.th. into a p., einem etwas einpauken. II. *s.* der Schlag, Puff. —**bing**, *s.*; to give a p. a good —bing, einen tüchtig durchprügeln.

Drudge, I. *s.* der Packesel, Knecht, Sklave, das Aschenbrödel. II. *v.n.* sich (ab)placken; schwere, langweilige Arbeit verrichten. —**ry**, *s.* die langweilige Arbeit, Plackerei, Langweilerei.

Drug, I. *s.* die Apothekerware, Arzneiware, Drogue; die abgestandene, unverkäufliche Ware, der Ladenhüter (*coll.*); these articles have become a — in the market, diese Waren sind gar nicht mehr zu verkaufen, sind wenig begehrt; —s for dyeing, Färbestoffe. II. *v.a.* mit Zutaten vermischen; viel Arznei eingeben; (stupefy) durch ein Schlafmittel betäuben; to — wine, den Wein verfälschen, etwas Betäubendes in den Wein tun. —**gist**, *s.* der Droguist; chemist and —gist, der Apotheker; der Materialien= und Chemikalien=Händler; —gist's shop, die Droguenhandlung.

Drugget, *s.* der Droget(t).

Druid, *s.* der Druide. —**ic(al)**, *adj.* druidisch; Druiden=; —ical circles, Druidenkreise. —**ism**, *s.* das Druidentum.

Drum, I. *s.* die Trommel (*Mil.*, *Mech.*, *Anat.*); der Korb (*for figs*); die große Abendgesellschaft (mit Kartenspiel) (*obs.*); (kettle-—) der Nachmittagstee (*coll.*); der Kapitälkelch, die Glocke (*Arch.*); to beat the —, die Trommel rühren *or* schlagen, trommeln. II. *v.n.* trommeln; klopfen (on a table, mit den Fingern auf einen Tisch). III. *v.a.*; to — out, unter Trommelschlag fortjagen; to — into a p.'s head, einem (etwas) einpauken. —**mer**, I. *s.* der Trommler, Trommelschläger. II. *attrib.*; —mer boy, der kleine Trommelschläger. —**ming**, *s.* das Trommeln. *Comp.* —**-case**, *s.* der Trommelsarg. —**-head**, *s.* das obere Fell der Trommel; —-head court-martial, plötzlich zusammenberufenes Kriegsgericht, das Standrecht (*Mil.*). —**-major**, *s.* der Tambour=Major. —**-stick**, *s.* der Trommelstock, Trommelschlägel.

Drunk, I. *p.p. of* Drink. II. *adj.* betrunken, trunken; berauscht (*fig.*); dead —, im höchsten Grade betrunken; to get —, sich betrinken. —**ard**, *s.* der Trunkenbold. —**en**, I. *p.p. see* — I. (*poet.*). II. *adj.* dem Trunke ergeben, Säufer=. —**enness**, *s.* die Trunkenheit; (intemperance) die Trunksucht.

Drup—aceous, *adj.* steinfruchtartig. —**e**, *s.* die Steinfrucht.

Dry, I. *adj.* (not wet) trocken; (sapless) dürr; (thirsty) durstig (*vulg.*); trocken (*fig.*); (jejune) schmucklos, nüchtern; (uninteresting) karg, abgeschmackt; trocken, derb, sarkastisch (*as wit*); (cold) teilnahmlos, kalt, zurückhaltend; (— -eyed) tränenlos; milchlos (*as a cow*); — champagne, herber Champagner; — cough, trockener Husten; a — crust, ein Stück trocknen Brotes. II. *v.a.* trocknen, abtrocknen; austrocknen, dörren; (empty) ausleeren; to — a meadow, eine Wiese trocken legen; to — up, austrocknen, vertrocknen lassen (*of plants*); to — (up) one's tears, seine Tränen trocknen. III. *v.n.* trocknen, trocken werden; (— up) eintrocknen, vertrocknen, verdorren; and his hand dried up, und seine Hand verdorrete (*B.*). —**ing**, I. *adj.* trocknend; —ing ground, der Trockenplatz; —ing kiln, der Trockenofen; —ing loft, der Trockenboden; —ing oil, der Ölfirnis; —ing room, die Darrstube. —**ly**, *adv.* trocken. —**ness**, *s.* die Trockenheit, Dürre (*fig.*). *Comp.* —**-dock**, *s.* das Trockendock. —**-eyed**, *adj.* trocknen Auges. —**-goods**, I. *s.* Schnittwaren, Leinen= und Baumwoll=waren (*Amer.*). II. *attrib.*; —-goods merchant, der Schnitt(waren)händler. —**-measure**, *s.* trockenes Maß. —**-nurse**, *s.* das Kindermädchen. —**-plate**, *attrib.*; —-plate photography, das trockene Kollodium=Verfahren. —**-rot**, *s.* der Löcherschwamm (*Bot.*); die trockne Fäulnis (*in wood*); die Milbigkeit (*in cheese*); die Lungenfäule (*in sheep*). —**-rub**, *v.a.* trocken (ab)reiben; (den Fußboden) bohnen. —**-salter**, *s.* der Material= und Korbwaren=händler. —**-shod**, *adj.* trocknen Fußes.

Dryad, *s.* die Dryade, Baumnymphe.

Dual, I. *s.* der Dual(is) (*Gram.*). II. *adj.* di Zahl zwei ausdrückend; — alliance, der Zweibund; — number, die Zweizahl. —**ism**, *s.* de. Dualismus. —**ist**, *s.* der Dualist. —**ity**, *s.* die Zweiheit.

Dub, *v.a.* zum Ritter schlagen; (name) betiteln; ernennen. —**bing**, *s.* der Ritterschlag.

Dubi—ous, *adj.*, —**ously**, *adv.* zweifelhaft; (undecided) unbestimmt, unsicher. —**ousness**, *s.* die Zweifelhaftigkeit, Ungewißheit. —**tate**, *v.n.* zweifeln, zögern (*obs.*). —**tation**, *s.* das Zweifeln, Zögern.

Du—cal, *adj.* herzoglich; —cal coronet, der Herzogshut. —**cat**, *s.* der Dukaten. —**chess**, *s.* die Herzogin. —**chy**, *s.* das Herzogtum.

[1]**Duck**, *s.* die Ente; a lame —, ein beschädigtes Kriegsschiff (*coll.*); to play at —s and drakes, Jungfern werfen, flache Steine auf dem Wasser aufprallen lassen; to make —s and drakes of one's money, sein Geld verschleudern. —**ing**, *s.* die Entenjagd. —**ling**, *s.* das Entchen. *Comp.* —**bill**, *s.* das Schnabeltier (*Zool.*). —**-gun**, *s.* die Entenflinte. —**-shooting**, *s.* die Entenjagd. —**-weed**, *s.* die Entengrütze (*Bot.*).

[2]**Duck**, *s.* das Püppchen, der Liebling; my little —, mein kleines Herzblatt; she is a little —, sie ist ganz allerliebst; a — of a bonnet, ein reizender Hut (*coll.*).

[3]**Duck**, I. *s.* die Verbeugung, Neigung des Kopfes. II. *v.n.* (unter=)tauchen; sich bücken. III. *v.a.* tauchen. —**ing**, *s.* das (Unter=)Tauchen; die Taufe (*Naut.*); to get a good —ing, tüchtig naß werden. —**ing-stool**, *s.* der Tauchschemel (für zänkische Weiber).

[4]**Duck**, *s.* das Schiertuch; die Zeltleinwand.

Duct, *s.* der Gang, die Röhre. —**ile**, *adj.* dehnbar, streckbar; lenksam, biegsam. —**ility**, *s.* die Dehnbarkeit, Streckbarkeit.

Dud, *s.* der Lappen, Lumpen. —**s**, *pl.* alte Kleider, Lumpen (*coll.*).

Dude, *s.* der Stutzer, Geck, Gigerl (*coll. Amer.*). —**ss**, *s.* die Modenärrin, Zierpuppe (*coll. Amer.*).

[1]**Dudgeon**, *s.* der Groll, Zorn; to be in high —, sehr böse sein (*coll.*); to take a th. in great —, etwas sehr übel nehmen (*coll.*).

[2]**Dudgeon**, *s.* kleiner Dolch, Dolch(griff) (*obs.*)

Due, I. *adj.* gebührend, geziemend, schuldig, angemessen; fällig (*C. L.*); (direct) gerade; — respect, schuldige Achtung; he has met with his — reward, der ihm gebührende Lohn ist ihm (zu Teil) geworden; to come in — time, zur rechten Zeit kommen; to be —, to fall —, fällig sein, fällig werden; the train is — at 8 o'clock, der Zug kommt um 8 Uhr an; die Ankunftszeit des Zuges ist um 8 Uhr; this is — to carelessness, dies ist eine Folge der Nachlässigkeit; honour to whom honour is —, Ehre wem Ehre gebührt; when —, bei Verfallzeit; debts — and owing, Aktiva und Passiva; with — course, in gradem Laufe (steuernd); in — course, (zu) seiner Zeit; to take — note, gehörig notieren (*C.L.*); over —, überfällig; the steamer is over —, der Dampfer hat Verspätung, sollte längst angelangt sein. II. *adv.* gerade; — east, grade östlich, genau nach Osten. III. *s.* die Gebühr, Schuld, das Recht; (reward) der Lohn; (tax) die Abgabe; (debt) die Schuld; to give every one his —, jedem das Seinige geben; to give the Devil his —, dem Teufel Gerechtigkeit widerfahren lassen.

Duel, *s.* der Zweikampf, das Duell; students' —, die Mensur; to fight a —, sich duellieren, ein Duell ausfechten; auf die Mensur gehen (*stud. sl.*). **—ling**, *s.* das Duellieren; —ling bout, die Mensur. **—list**, *s.* der Duellant, Zweikämpfer; student —list, der Paukant.

Duenna, *s.* die Anstandsdame, Duenna.

Duet, *s.* das Duett; piano —, vierhändiges Klavierstück.

Duffel, Duffle, *s.* der Düffel, dickes Wolltuch.

[1]**Dug**, *s.* die Zitze (*of cows, etc.*); die Brustwarze.

[2]**Dug**, *imperf. & p.p. of* Dig.

Duke, *s.* der Herzog. **—dom**, *s.* das Herzogtum; (—'s rank) die Herzogswürde. **—ry**, *s.* der Herzogssitz; the —ries, die alten Herzogssitze (*in Nottinghamshire*); der alte Adel.

Dulc—et, *adj.* wohlklingend. **—ify**, *v.a.* versüßen. **—imer**, *s.* das Hackbrett.

Dull, I. *adj.* (stupid) dumm, schwer von Begriffen; (sluggish) träge, schwerfällig, untätig; (obtuse) unempfindlich, stumpfsinnig; (blunt) stumpf; (dry) geistlos, platt, schal, abgeschmackt; (cheerless) unerfreulich; (uninteresting) langweilig; (gloomy) trübsinnig, niedergeschlagen; glanzlos, leblos, matt (*as eyes*); schwach (*as the fire*); matt (*as colours or metals*); trübe (*as weather*); dumpf (*of sounds*); flau, stockend (*as trade*); windstill (*Naut.*); — of understanding, schwer von Begriffen *or* begreifend; a — discourse, eine langweilige Rede; — of hearing, harthörig; the — season, die stille Zeit; he feels —, er hat Langeweile, langweilt sich. II. *v.a.* stumpf machen, abstumpfen; to — one's senses, sich betäuben. **—ard**, *s.* der Dummkopf. **—ness, Dulness**, *s.* die Stumpfheit; die Stumpfsinnigkeit; die Schwerfälligkeit; die Schwäche (*of the hearing, etc.*); die Mattheit (*of the colour, etc.*); die Glanzlosigkeit; (darkness) die Dunkelheit; die Flauheit, Stille (*C. L.*); (—ness of spirits) der Mißmut; die Niedergeschlagenheit. **—y**, *adv. see* Dull I. *Comp.* **—-eyed**, *adj.* trübblickend. **—-head**, *s.* der Dummkopf; der stumpfsinnige, langweilige Mensch.

Duly, *adv. see* Due I; we have — received . . ., wir haben . . . seiner Zeit richtig erhalten.

Dumb, *adj.*, **—ly**, *adv.* stumm; to strike —, verstummen machen, betäuben; deaf and —, taubstumm; — brutes *or* creatures, unvernünftige, sprachlose Tiere; — show, die Pantomime. **—ness**, *s.* die Stummheit. *Comp.* **—-bell**, *s.* die Hantel (*Gymn.*). **—-waiter**, *s.* der stumme Diener, Drehtisch.

Dumfound, *v. a.* verstummen machen, zum Schweigen bringen, betäuben. **—ed**, *p.p. & adj.* wie vom Donner gerührt, sprachlos vor Erstaunen.

Dumm—y, *s.* der Statist (*Theat.*); der Strohmann (*fig.*); die Kleider-Puppe; etwas das zum Schein *or* zur Täuschung dient; Schein-, Schwindel-.

Dump, I. *s.* der dumpfe Aufschlag, Plumps, Bums. II. *v.a.* heftig hinwerfen, umstürzen, umkippen. **—er**, *s.* der Karrenkipper. **—ling**, *s.* der Kloß. **—y**, *adj.* kurz und dick. *Comp.* **—-cart**, *s.* der Kippkarren. **—ing-ground**, *s.* der Abladeplatz.

Dump, *s.* (*usually in the plural* —s) trübe *or* verdrießliche Stimmung, schlechte Laune; to be in the —s, schlecht gelaunt, verdrießlich *or* nicht aufgelegt sein (*coll.*).

Dump, *s.* der tiefe Wassertümpel (*dial.*).

Dun, *adj.* schwarzbraun; dunkel, trübe, finster; — clouds, düstre Wolken; —-coloured horse, der Braune.

Dun, I. *s.* der drängende Gläubiger. II. *v.a.* ungestüm (wegen einer Schuldforderung) mahnen, treten (*sl.*); belästigen, plagen (with entreaties, mit Bitten); —ning letter, der Mahnbrief; to keep —ning a th. into a p.'s ears, einem mit etwas immer in den Ohren liegen.

Dunce, *s.* der Dummkopf, Pappschädel.

Dunder, *s.* der Bodensatz des Zuckers.

Dunderhead, *s.* der Dummkopf (*coll.*). **—ed**, *adj.* dumm (*coll.*).

Dune, *s.* die Düne.

[1]**Dung**, I. *s.* der Dünger, Mist; der Kot, Dreck der Tiere. II. *v.a.* düngen. *Comp.* **—-beetle**, *s.* der Mistkäfer. **—-fly**, *s.* die Mistfliege. **—-heap, —hill**, I. *s.* der Misthaufen; to lift a p. from the —hill, einen aus dem Staube erheben. II. *attrib.*; —hill cock, der Haushahn.

[2]**Dung**, *imperf. of* Ding.

Dungeon, *s.* der Bergfried; das Burgverließ.

Duo, *s.* das Duett. **—decimal**, *adj.* duodezimal. **—decimo**, *s.* das Duodez(format). **—decimos**, *pl.* Bücher im Duodezformat. **—denum**, *s.* der Zwölffingerdarm (*Anat.*). **—logue**, *s.* ein von zwei Personen gespieltes kleines Theaterstück.

Dup—able, *adj.* leicht anzuführen, zu hintergehen. **—e**, I. *s.* der Betrogene; der Gimpel; to be a p.'s —e, sich von einem anführen *or* hinters Licht führen lassen. II. *v.a.* betrügen, anführen, prellen. **—ery**, *s.* die Prellerei.

Dupl—ex, *adj.* doppelt, zweifach; —ex burner, (lamp) der Doppelbrenner; —ex telegraphy, das Gegensprechen. **—icate**, I. *adj.* doppelt; in —icate, zweimal ausgestellt; —icate copy, das Duplikat; —icate (stamp), die Doublette, Tauschmarke. II. *s.* das Duplikat, die Kopie; —icates of a bill, die Duplikate eines Wechsels. III. *v.a.* verdoppeln. **—ication**, *s.* die Verdoppelung. **—icator**, *s.* die Kopiermaschine. **—icity**, *s.* die Zweiheit; die Falschheit, Doppelzüngigkeit.

Dur—ability, *s.* die Dauerhaftigkeit. **—able**, *adj.*, **—ably**, *adv.* dauerhaft. **—ableness**, *s.* die Dauerhaftigkeit, Dauer. **—ance**, *s.* der Gewahrsam, das Gefängnis (*poet.*); to keep in —ance, gefangen halten. **—ation**, *s.* die Dauer, Fortdauer. **—ess**, *s.* der Zwang; (imprisonment) die Haft; der (unrechtmäßige) Verhaft (*Law*); under —ess, in Not; in Haft. **—ing**, *prep.* während; —ing this day, während dieses Tages.

Durst, *old imperf. of* Dare.

Dusk, I. *adj.* düster, dunkel. II. *s.* die Dämmerung; — of the evening, Abenddämmerung; after —, nach Einbruch der Dämmerung. **—iness**, *s.* die Dunkelheit. **—y**, *adj.*, **—ily**, *adv.* (dark) schwärzlich; (gloomy) düster, trüb.

Dust, I. *s.* der Staub; (money) das Geld (*sl.*); (row) der Lärm (*sl.*); clouds of —, Staubwolken; to gather —, staubig werden; to lay the —, den Staub dämpfen; to throw — in a p.'s eyes, einem Sand in die Augen streuen, einem ein X für ein U machen; to bite the —, ins Gras beißen; down with the —! heraus mit dem Mammon! (*vulg.*). II. *v.a.* aus-, ab-stäuben; (sprinkle with —) bestäuben; (sprinkle) bestreuen. **—er**, *s.* der Wischlappen; (feather brush) der Federbesen. **—iness**, *s.* die Staubigkeit. **—y**, *adj.* staubig, voll(er) Staub; schmutzig (*in colour*). *Comp.* **—-bin**, *s.* der Kehrichtbehälter, Schmutzkasten. **—-cart**, *s.* der Kehrichtwagen. **—-cloak**, *s.* der Staubmantel. **—-heap**, *s.* der Kehrichthaufen. **—-hole**, *s.* die Kehrichtgrube. **—-man**, *s.* der Kehricht- und Aschen-Kärrner. **—-sieve**, *s.* das Staubsieb.

Dut—eous, *adj.*, **—eously**, *adv.* pflichtgetreu; (obedient) gehorsam; (deferential) ehrerbietig. **—iable**, *adj.* zollpflichtig. **—iful**, *adj.*, **—ifully**, *adv.* pflichtgetreu, gehorsam; (deferential) ehrerbietig. **—ifulness**, *s.* der Gehorsam; die Ehrerbietigkeit, Ehrerbietung. **—y**, *s.* (obligation) die Pflicht, Schuldigkeit; (act of homage) die Ehrerbietung; das Amt; die Dienstpflicht (*of an office*); der Dienst, Kriegsdienst (*of an officer, etc.*); (impost) die Abgabe, Auflage, der Zoll; on —y, diensttuend; he is on —y to-day, er hat heute Dienst; to be off —y, nicht im Dienste sein; to pay the —y on goods, Waren versteuern *or* verzollen; —y upon exportation, der Ausfuhrzoll; —y upon importation, der Einfuhrzoll; —y off, unverzollt; —y paid, nach Errichtung der Zollgebühr; prohibitive (protective) —y, Schutzzoll; —y on value, Advalorenzoll; in —y bound, pflichtgemäß; I have done my —y by him, ich habe meine Schuldigkeit an ihm getan. *Comp.* **—y-free**, *adj.* zollfrei, steuerfrei.

Duumvir, *s.* der Duumvir. **—ate**, *s.* das Duumvirat, der Zweimännerbund.

Dwale, *s.* die schwarze *or* dunkle Farbe (*Her.*).

Dwarf, I. *s.* der Zwerg. II. *adj.* Zwerg=; — elder, der Zwerghollunder; — poppy, der Feldmohn; — rose, wurzelechte Rose; standards and — roses, hochstämmige und wurzelechte Rosen. III. *v.a.* im Wachstume hindern. **—ed**, *p.p. & adj.* verbuttet; verkümmert, nicht ausgewachsen. **—ish**, *adj.*, **—ishly**, *adv.* zwergig, zwergwüchsig, zwerghaft, winzig. **—ishness**, *s.* die Zwergartigkeit.

Dwell, *v.n.* wohnen; verweilen, sich aufhalten; to — on, verweilen bei, (insist on) bestehen auf (*dat.*), (gaze on with delight) mit Vergnügen hängen an; to — upon a subject, bei einem Gegenstande verweilen; to — upon a syllable, eine Silbe betonen, aushalten, dehnen. **—er**, *s.* der Bewohner. **—ing**, *s.* die Wohnung. *Comp.* **—ing-house**, *s.* das Wohnhaus. **—ing-place**, *s.* der Wohnort.

Dwelt, *imperf. & p.p. of* Dwell.

Dwindl—e, *v.v.* abnehmen, kleiner werden, (hin=) schwinden; (degenerate) ausarten (into a th., in eine S.); (sink) werden zu; our days have —ed down to naught, unsere Tage sind in ein Nichts dahingeschwunden.

Dye, I. *v.a.* färben; to — in the grain, in der Wolle färben; —d in the grain, von echtem Schrot und Korn (*fig.*); to — afresh, wieder auffärben. II. *v.n.* sich färben lassen. III. *s.* die Farbe, Färbung, der Farbstoff; die Art (*fig.*); vegetable —, Pflanzenfarbe; fast —, echte, beständige Farbe; crimes of the deepest —, schwarze Freveltaten. **—ing**, *s.* das Färben; die Färbekunst; piece —ing, das Färben im Stücke. **—r**, der Färber; —r's broom, der Färberginster; —r's weed, das Gelbkraut, der Wau. *Comp.* **—(ing)-house**, *s.* die Färberei. **—(ing)-vat**, *s.* das Färberfaß. **—stuffs**, *pl.* Farbstoffe, Farbestoffe. **—works**, *pl.* die Färberei.

Dying, I. *p. see* Die. II. *adj.* sterbend; verglimmend (*as the fire*); verhallend (*of a voice, sound*); to be in a — condition, auf den Tod krank liegen; to be (a-)—, im Sterben liegen; — bed, das Sterbebett; — day, der Sterbetag; — words, die letzten Worte eines Sterbenden; — numbers, schmelzende Harmonien (*poet.*). III. *s.* das Sterben; the —, die Sterbenden; the — away of the wind, das Verwehen des Windes.

Dyke, *see* Dike.

Dynam—eter, *s.* der Dynameter (*Opt.*). **—ic(al)**, *adj.* dynamisch; —ic accent, dynamischer Akzent, die Tonstärke; —ic theory, das dynamische System; —ic unity, die Arbeitseinheit. **—ics**, *pl.* die Dynamik. **—ite**, *s.* der Dynamit. **—o**, *s.* die Dynamomaschine. **—ometer**, *s.* der (traction-, Zug=)Dynamometer.

Dynast—ic, *adj.* dynastisch, auf das Herrscherhaus bezüglich. **—y**, *s.* die Dynastie, das Herrschergeschlecht.

Dys—entery, *s.* die Ruhr. **—pepsia**, **—pepsy**, *s.* die Dyspepsie, Schwerverdaulichkeit. **—peptic**, I. *adj.* magenschwach; gallig, schwermütig (*fig.*); —peptic views, pessimistische Anschauungen. II. *s.* der Dyspeptiker. **—phagia**, *s.* die Schluckbeschwerde, Schlingbeschwerde. **—phonia**, *s.* erschwertes fehlerhaftes Sprechen in Folge eines Zungenfehlers. **—pnœa**, *s.* die Atembeschwerde, Atemnot. **—teleological**, *adj.* nicht teleologisch, zwecklos (*Philos.*). **—trophy**, *s.* gestörte *or* schlechte Ernährung.

E

E, e, *s.* E, e (*also Mus.*); E-flat, Es; E-minor, E-moll; E-sharp, Eis; *for abbreviations see the Index at the end of this part.*

Each, I. *adj.* jed(=er, 2c.); — one, jeder, ein jeder; — other, einander, sich; they see — other every day, sie sehen einander jeden Tag. II. *pron.* jeder, jede, jedes, ein jeder, eine jede, ein jedes; they cost a shilling —, sie kosten einen Schilling das Stück.

[1]**Eager**, *adj.*, **—ly**, *adv.* eifrig, hitzig; (desirous) begierig; the soldiers were — to attack the enemy, die Soldaten waren begierig *or* brannten darauf, den Feind anzugreifen; men pursue wealth —ly, die Menschen bemühen sich eifrig um den Besitz von Reichtum; — for revenge, dürstend nach Rache, rachedurstig; —ly bent upon, eifrig bemüht um, erpicht auf (*acc.*). **—ness**, *s.* die Hitze, Heftigkeit; die Begierde, das heftige Verlangen.

[2]**Eager, Eagre**, *s.* die Sturmflut, Springflut.

Eagle, *s.* der Adler (*also Mint., Astr., Her.*); the — screams, der Adler kreischt. **—t**, *s.* der junge Adler. *Comp.* (*gen'lly*, Adler=) **—-eyed**, *adj.* adleräugig, scharfsichtig (*also fig.*).

[1]**Ear**, I. *s.* die Ähre. II. *v.n.* in Ähren schießen; —ed, mit Ähren versehen.

[2]**Ear**, *s.* das Ohr; das Gehör (*Mus.*); (handle) der Henkel, das Öhr; das Öhr, der Haken (*of shells*); he has no — for music, er hat kein musikalisches Gehör; by —, nach dem Gehör (spielen); — of a porringer, das Öhr, der Henkel eines Napfes; to lend (a p.) an —, (einem) das Ohr leihen, (einem) Gehör schenken, (einem) zuhören; to be all —(s), ganz Ohr sein; to turn a deaf — to, nicht hören auf (*acc.*), taub sein gegen; to have the — of, in Gunst stehen bei; to meet the —, zu Ohren kommen; to give —, Gehör geben; in at one — and out at the other, zu einem Ohre hinein und zum andern wieder hinaus; over head and —s, über Hals und Kopf; to be over head and —s in love, sterblich verliebt sein; up to the —s, bis über die Ohren; to set by the —s, an einander hetzen; dog's-—s, Eselsohren (*in books*). **—ed**, *adj.* beohrt; öhrig. **—less**, *adj.* ohrenlos; ohne Gehör; ohne Ohre. **—wig**, *s.* der Ohrwurm (*Ent.*). *Comp.* **—ache**, *s.* der Ohrenschmerz, das Ohrenreißen. **—-deafening**, *adj.* ohrbetäubend. **—-mark**, I. *s.* das Ohrenzeichen (*on sheep*); das Eigentumszeichen (*fig.*). II. *v.a.* an den Ohren zeichnen (*sheep*); mit einem Kennzeichen versehen (*fig.*); sich (*dat.*) ausschließlich vorbehalten. **—-marking**, *s.* die ausschließliche Vorbehaltung. **—-pick**, *s.* die Ohrschaufel, der Ohrlöffel (*Surg.*). **—-piercing**, *adj.* ohrdurchdringend, ohrzerreißend. **—-ring**, *s.* der Ohrring, das Ohrgehänge. **—-shot**, *s.* die Hörweite; to sit within —shot, in Hörweite sitzen; to stand out of —shot, etwas nicht mehr hören können. **—-trumpet**, *s.* das Hörrohr. **—-wax**, *s.* das Ohrenschmalz. **—-witness**, *s.* der Ohrenzeuge.

[1]**Earing**, *s.* das Ährensetzen; das Pflügen (*obs.*).

[2]**Earing**, *s.* der Nockbändsel (*Naut.*).

Earl, *s.* der Graf. **—dom**, *s.* die Grafschaft; die Grafenwürde. *Comp.* **—-marshal**, *s.* der Lordmarschall von England.

Earl—iness, *s.* die Frühzeitigkeit. **—y**, *adj. & adv.* früh, (früh)zeitig; (soon) bald; —y in the morning, frühmorgens, am frühen Morgen; —y to bed and —y to rise makes a man healthy, wealthy and wise, Morgenstunde hat Gold im Munde (*prov.*); in —y life, in der Jugendzeit; in —ier times, in früheren Zeiten.

Earn, *v.a.* erwerben, verdienen. **—ings**, *pl.* der Erwerb, der Arbeitslohn, der Verdienst; gross —ings, Bruttoeinnahmen.

[1]**Earnest**, I. *adj.*, **—ly**, *adv.* (serious) ernst,

ernsthaft, wichtig; (eager) eifrig, emsig; (importunate) ernstlich, dringend; (sincere) im Ernst; — prayers, inbrünstige Gebete. II. *s.* der Ernst; in good —, in völligem Ernste; you are not in —, surely? das ist wohl nicht Ihr Ernst? are you in —? ist das Ihr Ernst? ist es Ihnen Ernst damit? are you in — or joking, soll das Ernst oder Scherz sein? I am in bitter —, es ist mir bitterer Ernst. **—ness**, *s.* der Ernst, die Ernstlichkeit; der Eifer; die Wärme.

Earnest, *s.* das D(a)raufgeld, Handgeld; die Bürgschaft; der Vorgeschmack (*fig.*).

Earth, I. *s.* die Erde; (land) das Land; (ground) der Boden; (people of the —) die Welt; der Bau (*of a fox, etc.*); potter's —, der Töpferton; —s, die Erdarten; fuller's —, die Walkererde; —'s axis, die Erdachse; —'s rotation, die Umdrehung der Erde. II. *v.a.*; to — up, anhäufeln, anackern. III. *v.n.* sich einscharren. **—en**, *adj.* irden; —en floor, der Lehmstrich; —en pot, der irdene Topf; —en vessel, das irdene Geschirr. **—iness**, *s.* das Erdige, die Erdigkeit. **—liness**, *s.* das Irdische, Körperliche; irdisches Wesen; die Weltlichkeit, der weltliche Sinn. **—ling**, *s.* der Erdenbürger; das Weltkind. **—ly**, *adj.* erdig; (unspiritual) irdisch, körperlich, sinnlich; (low) gemein; (conceivable) denkbar (*coll.*); Erden= (*in compds.*); —ly bliss, das Erdenglück; not an —ly word, kein Sterbenswort; no —ly reason, kein erdenklicher Grund, nicht der geringste Grund. **—ward**, *adj.* der Erde zugewandt; irdisch. **—y**, *adj.* erdig; erdfarben; irdisch, sinnlich, roh; to have an —y smell, einen Erdgeruch haben. *Comp.* **—-apple**, *s.* das Saubrot; der Erdapfel, die Kartoffel. **—bags**, *pl.* die Erdsäcke (*Fort.*). **—-bank**, *s.* der Erdwall. **—-barrel**, *s.* der Schanzkorb. **—born**, *adj.* erdgeboren; irdisch. **—bound**, *adj.* an die Erde gebunden, am Staube klebend. **—-engendered**, *adj.* erdgeboren, erderzeugt (*poet.*). **—enware**, *s.* die Töpferware, das irdene Geschirr; das Steingut. **—flax**, *s.* der Erdflachs (*Min.*). **—ly-minded**, *adj.* irdisch gesinnt. **—ly-mindedness**, *s.* der Erden=, Welt=sinn; die Sinnlichkeit. **—quake**, *s.* das Erdbeben. **—-shaking**, *adj.* erderschütternd. **—work**, *s.* der Erdbau. **—worm**, *s.* der Regenwurm.

Eas—e, I. *s.* die Gemächlichkeit, Bequemlichkeit, Behaglichkeit, das Behagen; (rest) die Ruhe; (relief) die Linderung; (freedom from constraint) die Ungezwungenheit, Freiheit; (readiness) die Leichtigkeit; (comfort) das Wohlsein; (freedom) die Freiheit; at —e, gemächlich; stand at ease! rührt euch! (*Mil.*); to be *or* feel at —e, sich behaglich fühlen; ill at —e, unbehaglich, unruhig; to live at one's —e, in guten Umständen sein; to take one's —e, es sich (*dat.*) bequem machen, der Ruhe pflegen; bed of —e, das Faulbett; chapel of —e, die Filialkirche. II. *v.a.* erleichtern, lindern; (calm) beruhigen; (make looser) auslassen (*a seam*), ausschneiden (*an armhole*), bequemer machen; (relieve) befreien (von); den Spielraum vergrößern (*Mach.*); to —e off, —e away, losgeben, abvieren, (ein Tau) abschricken; to —e the ship, anluven; —e the helm! fall ab! **—ement**, *s.* die Erleichterung; die Bequemlichkeit. **—ily**, *adv.* leicht, ohne Schwierigkeit. **—iness**, *s.* die Bequemlichkeit, Gemächlichkeit; die Leichtigkeit; die Ungezwungenheit; —iness of belief, die Leichtgläubigkeit. **—y**, I. *adj.* leicht; bequem, behaglich; frei von Beschwerden (*as a patient*); unbesorgt; ruhig; (content) zufrieden; sanft; ungezwungen, frei, leicht, natürlich (*in manners*); (ready) bereitwillig; (credulous) leichtgläubig; the work is —y, die Arbeit ist leicht; to make o.s. —y, es sich (*dat.*) bequem machen; make your mind —y! beruhige dich! in —y circumstances, in guten Verhältnissen, wohlhabend; I am quite —y about the future, um die Zukunft bin ich ganz unbesorgt; an —y style (of writing), eine leichte, natürliche Schreibart; a woman of —y virtue, ein gefälliges Weib; free and —y way of, bequeme Art zu; —y to be borne, erträglich; it is —y for you to talk, Sie haben gut reden. II. *adv.* leicht; to take things —y, die Sachen leicht nehmen; take it —y! nur ruhig! bleibe ruhig! *Comp.* **—y-chair**, *s.* der Lehnstuhl. **—y-going**, *adj.* gutmütig, gemütlich; an —y-going fellow, ein Mann, der die Sachen auf die leichte Achsel *or* leicht nimmt. **—y-tempered**, *adj.* gutmütig.

Easel, *s.* die Staffelei.

East, I. *s.* der Osten, Ost (*poet.*); der Orient, das Morgenland; — by south, Ost zum Süden; the far —, Ostasien; the three kings from the —, die Weisen aus dem Morgenlande. II. *adj.* & *adv.* ost=, östlich; — variation, die Nordostering (*Phys.*, *Naut.*); the — end of London, der Osten Londons, der östliche Teil von London. **—er**, *see* Easter. **—erly**, I. *adj.* östlich. II. *adv.*, **—ward**, *adv.* ostwärts. **—ern**, *adj.* östlich, morgenländisch; nach Osten; Great —ern railway, die (englische) Ostbahn; far —ern questions, ostasiatische Fragen. **—ing**, *s.* zurückgelegter östlicher Kurs; östliche Entfernung von einem bestimmten Meridian; die Annäherung an östliche Richtung; das Umschlagen nach Osten (*of wind*). *Comp.* **—-bound**, *adj.* nach Osten fahrend.

Easter, *s.* die Ostern (*pl.*), das Osterfest; Oster=; at —, zu Ostern; — greetings, Ostergrüße.

Eat, *ir.v.* I. *a.* essen; fressen (*of beasts*); (corrode) zerfressen, ätzen; (consume) verzehren; (gnaw) zernagen; (devour, swallow up) verschlingen; to — up, aufessen, auffressen; to — one's words, (das Gesagte) widerrufen; —en up with passion, von Leidenschaft verzehrt; to — up one's ambitious heart, sich vor Ehrgeiz verzehren; to — a p. out of house and home, einem Haus und Hof verzehren. II. *n.* essen; (taste) schmecken; to — in(to), ein=fressen, =dringen; rust —s into iron, der Rost frißt das Eisen an. **—able**, *adj.* eßbar. **—ables**, *pl.* die Eßwaren, Lebensmittel. **—er**, *s.* der Esser; you are a poor —er, Sie essen nur wenig. **—ing**, *s.* das Essen; —ing apple, der Eßapfel. *Comp.* **—ing-house**, *s.* das Speisehaus.

Eaten, *p.p.* of Eat.

Eau-de-Cologne, *s.* Kölnisches Wasser.

Eaves, *pl.* die Traufe, Dachrinne. **—drop**, *v.n.* lauschen. **—dropper**, *s.* der Lauscher, Horcher. **—dropping**, *s.* das Lauschen, Horchen.

Ebb, I. *s.* die Ebbe; die Ebbe, Abnahme, Neige (*fig.*); the beginning of the —, die erste *or* Vorebbe; at a low —, gedrückt (*of prices*); matters are at a low — with him, die Sachen stehen bei ihm sehr traurig. II. *v.a.* ebben; abnehmen (*fig.*); —ing tide, die Ebbe. *Comp.* **—-anchor**, *s.* der Ebbeanker. **—-tide**, *s.* die Ebbe.

Ebon, *adj.* aus Ebenholz; schwarz (wie Ebenholz). **—ist**, *s.* der Kunsttischler, Ebenist. **—ize**, *v.a.* schwarz wie Ebenholz färben *or* polieren. **—y**, I. *s.* das Ebenholz. II. *attrib.*; —y tree, der Ebenbaum.

Ebri—ate, *adj.* berauscht. **—ety**, *s.* die Trunkenheit.

Ebulli—ent, *adj.* aufwallend. **—tion**, *s.* die Aufwallung; die heftige Aufwallung (*fig.*).

Eburn—ean, **—ine**, *adj.* elfenbeinern.

Écarté, *s.* das Ecarté (Kartenspiel).

Eccentric, I. *adj.*, **—ally**, *adv.* exzentrisch (*also fig.*), wunderlich, überspannt. II. *s.* der exzentrische Kreis; (— person) der Sonderling. **—ity**, *s.* die Überspanntheit, Exzentrizität.

Ecclesia—rch, *s.* der Kirchenvorsteher (*in the old Greek church*). **—stes**, *s.* der Prediger Salomo. **—stic**, I. *see* —stical. II. *s.* der Geistliche. **—stical**, *adj.*, **—stically**, *adv.* kirchlich, geistlich; —stical courts, geistliche Gerichtshöfe; —stical history, die Kirchengeschichte. **—sticism**, die Kirchlichkeit, das Kirchentum. **—sticus**, *s.* das Buch Jesus Sirach.

Echelon, I. *s.* die stufenförmige Aufstellung, Staffel (*Mil.*); in —, staffelförmig, staffelweise. II. *v.a.* staffelweise aufstellen; —ed troops, längs . . . aufgestellte Truppen. *Comp.* —-**lens**, *s.* die Zonenlinse.

Echidna, *s.* der Ameisenigel (*Zool.*).

Echin—ite, *s.* versteinerter Seeigel. —**us**, *s.* (*pl.* —i) der Seeigel; stacheliger Samenkopf (*Bot.*) (*obs.*); die eirunde Verzierung der ionischen Säulenordnung, der Pfühl, die Wulst (*Arch.*).

Echo, I. *s.* das Echo, der Widerhall. II. *v.a.* widerhallen; nachsprechen (*fig.*). III. *v.n.* wider=hallen, =schallen. —**less**, *adj.* ohne Echo.

Éclaircissement, *s.* die Aufklärung.

Eclat, *s.* das Aufsehen; die Auszeichnung, der Ruhm; allgemeiner Beifall, die Zustimmung, der Glanz, Effekt.

Eclectic, I. *adj.* eklektisch, wählerisch, auswählend. II. *s.* der Eklektiker. —**ism**, *s.* der Eklektizismus.

Eclip—se, I. *s.* die Verfinsterung, Finsternis; —se of the sun, die Sonnenfinsternis; —se of the moon, die Mondfinsternis. II. *v.a.* ver=finstern; verdunkeln (*also fig.*). —**tic**, *s.* die Ekliptik, Sonnenbahn; obliquity of the —tic, die Achsenneigung, die Schiefe der Ekliptik.

Eclogue, *s.* das Hirtengedicht, die Ekloge.

Econom—ic, *adj.*, —**ical**, *adj.*, —**ically**, *adv.* ökonomisch; haushälterisch, wirtschaftlich; (frugal) sparsam. —**ics**, *pl.* die Haushaltungs=kunst; die Staatshaushaltslehre, Volkswirt=schaft(slehre), Staatswirtschaft, Nationalökono=mie; rural —ics, die Landwirtschaftslehre. —**ist**, *s.* der sparsame Ausnutzer, gute Wirtschafter; political —ist, der Staatswirtschaftslehrer, Nationalökonom. —**ize**, —**ise**, *v.* I. *n.* sparen (in, an, with, mit). II. *a.* sparsam umgehen mit. —**y**, *s.* die Haushaltung, Wirtschaft; die Wirtschaftlichkeit, Sparsamkeit; die Organisa=tion (*of plants & animals*), Einrichtung; die Anordnung (*of a poem*); political —y, die Volkswirtschaft(slehre), Staatswirtschaft(slehre), Nationalökonomie.

Ecsta—sy, *s.* das Außersichsein (vor Erstaunen, Entsetzen, Wonne, *etc.*), die übergroße Erregung; das Entzücken, die Wonne; (religious rapture) die Verzückung; (enthusiasm) die Begeisterung. —**tic**, *adj.*, —**tically**, *adv.* entzückend; (enraptured) entzückt, hingerissen; —tic fit, Verzückung.

Ecumenic(al), *adj.* ökumenisch, allgemein.

Eczema, *s.* das Hautbläschen. —**tous**, *adj.* ekzematisch, Hautbläschen habend *or* betreffend.

Eddy, I. *s.* der Wirbel, Wirbelstrom; (back current) die Gegenströmung. II. *v.n.* wirbeln.

Edentat—a, *pl.* zahnlose Tiere; Tiere ohne Vorderzähne. —**e(d)**, *adj.* zahnlos.

Edge, I. *s.* die Schärfe, Schneide (*of a knife, etc.*); (ledge) die scharfe Kante; (brink) der Rand; (border) der Rand, Saum; die Ecke (*of a table*); der Schnitt (*of a book*); (keenness) die Schärfe, Stärke, Heftigkeit; die Feinheit (*of wit, etc.*); the — of the appetite, die Schärfe des Appetits; to blunt the —, die Schärfe ab=stumpfen; to take the — off, abstumpfen; to put to the — of the sword, über die Klinge springen lassen (*B.*); to put an — on, schärfen; to lay, set on —, hochkantig legen, stellen; to set the teeth on —, die Zähne stumpf machen; — of the water, der Rand des Wassers, das Ufer, Gestade; bound in calf with gilt —s, in Kalb=leder gebunden mit Goldschnitt. II. *v.a.* säumen, besetzen, umgeben; to — in, hineinschieben; he could not manage to — a word in, es wollte ihm nicht gelingen, ein Wort anzubringen. III. *v.n.* sich seitwärts (heran)bewegen; to — forward, vorwärtsrücken; to — off, von . . . abhalten (*Naut.*), wegrücken, wegrutschen. —**ed**, *adj.* scharf; two-—ed, zweischneidig; —ed with lace, mit Spitzen eingefaßt; to play with —(d) tools, leichtsinnig mit gefährlichen Dingen um=gehen, mit Schießgewehr spielen (*coll.*). —**less**, *adj.* stumpf. —**wise**, (—**wavs**,) *adv.* seitwärts, von der Seite, hochkantig. *Comp.* —-**rail**, *s.* di Kantenschiene. —-**tool**, *s.* das Schneidewerkzeug

Edging, I. *p. see* Edge. II. *s.* die Einfassun (*Hort.*, *Semp.*, *etc.*); (lace —) die Kantenspitzen

Edible, *adj.* eßbar. —**ness**, *s.* die Eßbarkeit.

Edict, *s.* das Edikt, die Verordnung.

Edif—ication, *s.* die Erbauung (*fig.*). —**ice** *s.* das Gebäude. —**ier**, *s.* der Erbauer. —**y** *v.a.* erbauen. —**ying**, *adj.*, —**yingly**, *adv* erbaulich; belehrend.

Edile, *s.* der Ädil (*Rom. Hist.*).

Edit, *v.a.* herausgeben, edieren. —**ion**, *s.* di Auflage, Ausgabe; second —ion, zweite Aus gabe (*of a paper*); third —ion, dritte Auflag (*of a book*). —**or**, *s.* der Herausgeber (*of book*); der Schriftleiter, Redakteur (*of a journa etc.*). —**orial**, I. *adj.* vom Herausgeber, Redak tions=; —orial labours, die Mühen eines Heraus gebers. II. *s.* vom Herausgeber einer Zeitun verfaßter oder veranlaßter Zeitungsartikel, Leit artikel. —**orship**, *s.* die Schriftleitung, Redak tion; das Amt eines Herausgebers.

Educat—e, *v.a.* erziehen, bilden. —**ion**, *s.* die Er ziehung, Bildung; das Erziehungswesen, Schul wesen; primary (*or* elementary) —ion, das Volks schulwesen; secondary (*or* intermediate) —ion das höhere Schulwesen; university —ion, di Universitätsbildung, das Hochschulwesen; libera —ion, höhere Schulbildung, gelehrte Bildung gute Allgemeinbildung; —ion department, da Unterrichtsministerium; minister of —ion, de Unterrichtsminister; journal of —ion, die Mo natsschrift für Erziehungswissenschaft *or* Un terrichtswesen. —**ional**, *adj.* die Erziehun betreffend, erziehlich, Unterrichts=, Erziehungs= —ional council, der Oberschulrat; —ional estab lishment, die Erziehungsanstalt. —**ion(al)ist** *s.* einer, der sich mit Erziehungsfragen beschäftig der Schulmann, Pädagoge. —**ive**, *adj.* erzieh lich. —**or**, *s.* der Erzieher.

Educ—e, *v.a.* heraus=, hervor=ziehen. —**ible** *adj.* hervorziehbar. —**t**, *s.* das Ausgezogen Edukt (*rare*). —**tion**, *s.* die Hervorziehung —**tor**, *s.* das Hervorziehende. *Comp.* —**tion pipe**, *s.* die Abzugsröhre (*Locom.*, *etc.*).

Edulcorat—e, *v.a.* aussüßen; (purify) rei waschen. —**ion**, *s.* das Aussüßen.

Eel, *s.* der Aal; bed of —s, das Aallager; ne for —s, die Aalwate. *Comp.* —-**backed**, *ad* mit einem Aalstreif. —-**dam**, *s.* das Aalweh —-**fishing**, *s.* der Aalfang. —**pot**, *s.* die Aa reuse. —-**pout**, *s.* die Aalraupe. —**spear**, die Aalgabel.

Een (*Scotch*) *for* Eyes.

E'en (*abbrev.*) *for* Even. **E'er** (*abbrev.*) *for* Ever

Eerie, *adj.* (*dial.*) furchtsam; unheimlich.

Efface, *v.n.* auswischen, auslöschen; vertilge verwischen (*fig.*); völlig in Schatten stellen; t — o.s., freiwillig zurückstehen *or* in den Hinte grund treten. —**able**, *adj.* verwischbar, ve tilgbar. —**d**, verwischt. —**ment**, *s.* die Aus löschung; (destruction) die Vertilgung.

Effect, I. *s.* die Wirkung; (result) die Folg Wirkung, das Ergebnis; (reality) die Wirklic keit, Wahrheit; (power) die Kraft, Gültigkeit (purport) der Inhalt; (purpose) der Zweck, di Absicht; (use) der Nutzen; (impression) d Eindruck, Effekt, die Wirkung; die Wirkun (*Mech.*); for —, auf den Effekt berechnet; in — in der Tat, in Wirklichkeit; to this —, zu de Ende, in der Absicht, deshalb; a message to th —that . . ., eine Botschaft, welche besagt(e), da . . .; the law is now of no —, das Gesetz hat je keine Gültigkeit mehr; to no —, vergeblich, um sonst; to the same —, desselben Inhalts; t carry into —, ausführen; to take —, wirke Eindruck machen (on a p., auf einen), die e wünschte Wirkung haben, anschlagen. II. *v.* bewirken, bewerkstelligen, ausführen; to — junction with the army, sich dem Heere anschli zen; the insurance is —ed on . . ., die Versicherung validiert auf . . . —**ive**, I. *adj.* (operative) wirkend; (powerful) wirksam, kräftig, effektvoll; (causing) —ive of, bewirkend (*obs.*); (available) dienstfähig, kampffähig; —ive horsepower, wirkliche Pferdekräfte. II. *s.* der Bestand, die Präsenzstärke; das Bargeld. —**ively**, *adv.* (forcibly) mit Nachdruck; (efficaciously) mit Wirkung, wirkungsvoll. —**iveness**, *s.* die Wirksamkeit. —**s**, *pl.* die Barvorräte (*C. L.*), Effekten, Güter, Vermögensstücke, die Habe. —**ual**, *adj.*, —**ually**, *adv.* wirksam; kräftig. —**uate**, *v.a.* bewerkstelligen, bewirken, ausführen.

Effemina—cy, *s.* die Verweichlichung, Weichlichkeit, das weibische Wesen. —**te**, I. *v.a.* verweichlichen, weibisch machen (*obs.*). II. *adj.*, —**tely**, *adv.* weibisch, weichlich, verzärtelt. —**teness**, *see* —cy.

Effendi, *s.* der Efendi.

Effervesc—e, *v.n.* (auf)brausen, gähren. —**ence**, *s.* das Aufbrausen, Schäumen. —**ent**, —**ing**, *adj.* (auf)brausend; —ent powder, das Brausepulver.

Effete, *adj.* abgenutzt; (exhausted) erschöpft, kraftlos, entkräftet; (decrepit) altersschwach. —**ness**, *s.* die Erschöpftheit, Kraftlosigkeit.

Effic—acious, *adj.*, —**aciously**, *adv.* wirksam, kräftig. —**aciousness**, *s.* die Wirksamkeit. —**acy**, *s.* die Wirksamkeit, Kraft. —**iency**, *s.* der Nutzungswert, die Kraft; die Leistungsfähigkeit, Tüchtigkeit. —**ient**, I. *adj.*, —**iently**, *adv.* wirksam, wirkend. II. *s.* die Ursache; der Urheber; (—ient volunteer) der ausgebildete Freiwillige.

Effigy, *s.* das Bild(nis), Abbild; to burn in —, im Bildnisse *or* in Effigie verbrennen.

Effloresc—e, *v.n.* aufblühen; beschlagen, auswittern; Kristalle ansetzen. —**nce**, *s.* die Blüte (*Bot.*); der Beschlag (*Chem.*). —**nt**, *adj.* efflorescierend, beschlagend, auswitternd.

Efflu—ence, *s.* der Ausfluß, das Ausströmen. —**ent**, I. *adj.* ausströmend. II. *s.* der Ausfluß. —**vium**, *s.* (—**via**, *pl.*) die Ausdünstung. —**x**, *s.* das Ausfließen, Ausströmen.

Effort, *s.* die Anstrengung, das Bestreben; to make an —, sich anstrengen; to make every —, alles aufbieten, alle Kräfte anspannen. —**less**, *adj.* ohne Anstrengung, mühelos.

Effrontery, *s.* die Frechheit, Unverschämtheit.

Effulgen—ce, *s.* das (Aus=)Strahlen, der Glanz. —**t**, *adj.*, —**tly**, *adv.* strahlend, glänzend.

Effus—e, *adj.* ausgebreitet (*Bot.*). —**ion**, *s.* die Ausgießung, Vergießung; (outpouring) die Ergießung, der Erguß (*fig.*); the —ion of the Holy Spirit, die Ausgießung des heiligen Geistes. —**ive**, *adj.*, —**ively**, *adv.* ausgießend, vergießend, verschüttend; übertrieben, überschwenglich (*fig.*). —**iveness**, *s.* die Überschwenglichkeit.

Eft, *s.* der Wassermolch.

Eftsoon(s), *adv.* bald nachher; von neuem, wiederum; sofort, sogleich (*obs. poet.*).

Egad, *int.* wahrhaftig! meiner Treu!

Egg, *s.* das Ei; white, yolk of (an) —, das Eiweiß, der Eidotter; fried —s, Spiegeleier, Setzeier; buttered —s, scrambled —s, Rühreier; poached —s, verlorene Eier; addled —, das Windei; rotten —s, faule Eier; hard (soft) boiled —, hart (weich) gekochtes Ei. *Comp.* —-**beater**, —-**whisk**, *s.* der Schlagbesen. —-**cup**, *s.* der Eierbecher. —-**frame**, *s.* das Eiergestell. —-**glass**, *s.* der Eierbecher; kleine Sanduhr zum Eierkochen. —-**moulding**, *s.* der Eierstab (*Arch.*). —-**nog**, *s.* der Eierpunsch. —-**plant**, *s.* die Eierpflanze. —-**sauce**, *s.* die Eiersauce. —-**shell**, *s.* die Eierschale.

Egg, *v.a.*; — on, hetzen, anreizen.

Eglantine, *s.* die wilde Rose.

Ego, *s.* das Ich. —**ism**, *s.* der Egoismus, die Selbstsucht. —**ist**, *s.* der Egoist. —**tism**, *s.* das zu häufige Reden von sich selbst; *see* —ism. —**tist**, *s.* der immer von sich selbst Redende; *see* —ist. —**tistic(al)**, *adj.* alles auf sich beziehend, zu viel von sich redend, selbstsüchtig, selbstisch, egoistisch.

Egregious, *adj.*, —**ly**, *adv.* (extraordinary) ausgezeichnet; (monstrous) ungeheuer, unerhört. —**ness**, *s.* die Vortrefflichkeit.

Egress, *s.* der Ausgang; der Ausfluß (*of water*).

Egression, *s.* das Weggehen, Abgehen, der Austritt; der Auszug der Israeliten (*from Egypt*).

Egret, *s. see* Aigrette.

Eh, *interj.* he? nicht wahr? wie? ei! sieh da!

Eight, I. *num. adj.* acht; — times, achtmal; — score, achtmal zwanzig. II. *s.* die Acht; der Achter; die Ruderer eines Achters. —**een**, *num. adj.* achtzehn. —**eenth**, *num. adj.* achtzehnt. —**fold**, *adj.* achtfach. —**h**, I. *num. adj.* (der, die, das) acht(e). II. *s.* das Achtel (*Mus.*). —**hly**, *adv.* achtens. —**ieth**, *num. adj.* (der, die, das) achtzigst(e). —**y**, *num. adj.* achtzig.

Eikon, *s.* das Bild, Heiligenbild.

Eisteddfod, *s.* das wallisische Nationalfest, Sänger= und Musik=fest, die Bardenversammlung.

Either, I. *adj. & pron.* einer, eine, eins; (both) beide; (each) jeder, jede, jedes (*of two or more*); he is stronger than — of you, er ist stärker als irgend einer von euch beiden; — of these masters will answer your purpose, jeder dieser Lehrer wird Ihrem Zwecke entsprechen; in — case, in beiden Fällen; on — side, auf jeder Seite, beiden Seiten; I did not see — of them, ich sah keinen von ihnen. II. *conj.* entweder; I did not see — him or his son, ich sah weder ihn noch seinen Sohn.

Ejaculat—e, *v.a.* ausstoßen. —**ion**, *s.* der Ausruf; (prayer) das Stoßgebet. —**ory**, *adj.* ausstoßend; —ory prayer, das Stoßgebet.

Eject, *v.a.* ausstoßen; (drive out) hinauswerfen, verstoßen, vertreiben; (dispossess) aus dem Besitze treiben; entsetzen (from office, eines Amtes). —**ion**, *s.* das Ausstoßen; die Ausleerung (*Mech.*); die Absetzung (*from office*); die Vertreibung (*from possession*). —**ment**, *s.* die Vertreibung; gerichtliche Aussetzung. —**or**, *s.* einer, der einen andern austreibt; der Ejektor (*Mach.*).

Ek—e, *v.a.*; to —e out, ergänzen, verlängern; (—e out cloth, etc.) ansetzen, anstücken, durch ein Ansetzstück verlängern; to —e out a miserable existence, sich kümmerlich durchschlagen. *Comp.* —**ing-piece**, *s.* das Ansetzstück, der Anstoß (*Tail. etc.*); das Verlängerungsstück (*Carp.*).

Elaborat—e, I. *v.a.* (sorgsam) ausarbeiten. II. *adj.*, —**ely**, *adv.* sorgfältig ausgearbeitet; (exact) mit Genauigkeit ausgeführt; (finished) gekünstelt. —**eness**, *s.* die sorgfältige Bearbeitung. —**ion**, *s.* die sorgfältige Ausarbeitung; (perfecting) die Verfeinerung, Vervollkommnung. —**or**, *s.* der Ausarbeiter.

Elapse, *v.n.* entgleiten, verfließen, verlaufen.

Elastic, I. *adj.* elastisch, spannkräftig; leicht nachgebend, schmiegsam, elastisch (*fig.*); — band, der (dünne) Gummiring. II. *s.* das Gummiband, der Gummizug; round —, die Gummikordel. —**ity**, *s.* die Elastizität, Feder=, Spann=kraft; die Schwungkraft, Elastizität (*of spirits, etc.*).

Elat—e, I. *v.a.* aufblähen, stolz machen. II. *adj.*, —**ed**, *adj.*, —**edly**, *adv.* aufgeblasen, stolz (at a th., über eine S., with, von); froh erregt (über). —**er**, *s.* der Springkäfer (*Ent.*); der Springfaden (*Bot.*). —**ion**, *s.* die Aufgeblasenheit, der Hochmut; die frohe Erregung (über eine S.).

Elbow, I. *s.* der Ellbogen; (bend) die Krümme, der Bug, die Biegung; das Knie, der Winkel (*Mach.*); — of a chair, die Armlehne; to be at a p.'s—, einem sehr nahe sein, einem auf dem Halse liegen; he is out at —s, der Ellbogen guckt ihm zum Rocke heraus, er lebt in schlechten Verhältnissen; to shake the —, würfeln (*sl.*). II. *v.a.* mit dem Ellbogen stoßen, wegstoßen; he was —ed, er wurde angerempelt; to — one's way through a crowd, sich durch einen

Haufen hindurchdrängen; to — out, verdrängen. *Comp.* —**-chair**, *s.* der Armstuhl, Lehnsessel. —**-room**, *s.* der Spielraum.

Eld, *s.* das Greisenalter; (old people) alte Leute; das Altertum, alte Zeiten (*obs. poet.*); *see* Old. —**er**, I. *adj.* (*comp. of* Old) älter. II. *s.* der Ältere; der Älteste (*in a church, etc.*); der Alte (*B.*); my —ers, Leute, welche älter sind als ich. —**erly**, *adj.* ältlich. —**ership**, *s.* das Amt eines Kirchenältesten. —**est**, *adj.* (*sup. of* Old) ältest; the —est, der, die, das älteste; the —est born, der Erstgeborene.

Elder, *s.* der Holunder, Flieder. *Comp.* —**berry**, *s.* die Holunderbeere. —**-blossoms**, *pl.* Flieder-blüten, blühender Flieder. —**-bush**, *s.* der Fliederbusch, Holunderstrauch.

El Dorado, *s.* das Eldorado.

Elect, I. *v.a.* (aus)wählen (*out of several*); (er)-wählen (to *or* into, zu); auserwählen (*Theol.*); (prefer) vorziehen. II. *adj.* (aus) gewählt; aus-erwählt, -erlesen (*Theol.*); designiert; the —, die Auserwählten; the bishop —, der designierte Bischof. —**icism**, *s.* der Eklektizismus. —**ion**, *s.* die Erwählung, Wahl; die Gnaden-wahl (*Theol.*); day of —ion, der Wahltag; right of —ion, das Wahlrecht. —**ioneer**, *v.n.* um Wahlstimmen werben. —**ioneerer**, *s.* der Stimmen-werber, -sammler. —**ioneering**, *s.* die Wahlumtriebe, der Wahlkampf. —**ive**, *adj* wählend, Wahl . . .; —ive affinity, die Wahlver-wandtschaft; —ive office, das Wahlamt. —**ive-ly**, *adv.* durch Wahl. —**or**, *s.* der Wähler, Wahl-mann; (prince) der Kurfürst; —or Palatine, der Kurfürst von der Pfalz. —**oral**, *adj.* sich auf eine Wahl beziehend; kurfürstlich; —oral committee, der Wählerausschuß. —**orate**, *s.* die Kurwürde; (territory of an —or) das Kurfürstentum. —**ress**, *s.* die Kurfürstin.

Electre, *s.* der Bernstein; das Elektrum, aus Gold und Silber gemischtes Metall (*obs.*).

Electr—ic(al), *adj.*, —**ically**, *adv.* elektrisch; —ic alarm, elektrisches Schlagwerk; —ic battery, elektrische Batterie; —ic charge, elektrische La-dung; —ic current, galvanischer Strom; —ic eel, der Zitteraal (*Icht.*); —ical engineer, der Elektrotechniker; —ical engineering, die Elektro-technik; —ic fluid, der Blitzstoff; —ic jar, die Ladungsflasche; —ic light, elektrisches Licht; —ic machine, die Elektrisiermaschine; —ic rail-way, elektrische Eisenbahn; —ic ray, der Zitter-roche (*Icht.*); —ic shock, elektrischer Schlag. —**ician**, *s.* der Elektrizitätskundige. —**icity**, *s.* die Elektrizität. —**ifiable**, *adj.* elektrisierbar. —**ification**, *s.* die Elektrisierung. —**ify**, *v.a.* elektrisieren, elektrisch machen; entflammen, in Begeisterung versetzen, durchschauern (*fig.*). —**ocute**, *v.a.* durch elektrischen Strom töten. —**ocution**, *s.* die Hinrichtung durch Elektrizität. —**ode**, *s.* die Elektrode. —**olysis**, *s.* die Elektro-lyse (*Chem.*). —**olyte**, *s.* der Elektrolyt. —**ometer**, *s.* der Elektrometer, Elektrizitätsmesser. —**omotor**, *s.* der Elektromotor. —**oscope**, *s.* das Elektroskop. —**otype**, I. *s.* der galvanische Niederschlag, die galvano-graphische Abbildung. II. *adj.* galvanoplastisch. —**otypist**, *s.* der Galvanoplast. —**otypy**, *s.* die Galvanoplastik.

Electro— (*in comp.*) —**-chemical**, *adj.* elek-trochemisch. —**-chemistry**, *s.* die Elektro-chemie. —**-dynamics**, *s.* die Elektrodynamik. —**-etching**, *s.* galvanische Ätzung. —**-gilding**, *s.* galvanische Vergoldung. —**magnetic**, *adj.* elektromagnetisch; —magnetic bell-appa-ratus, das elektrische Läutewerk; —magnetic telegraph, der elektromagnetische Telegraph. —**magnetism**, *s.* der Elektromagnetismus. —**metallurgy**, *s.* die Galvanoplastik, Elektro-metallurgie. —**plate**, *s.* galvanisch versilberte Ware. —**plating**, *s.* galvanische Versilberung; galvanische Vergoldung.

Electron, der Bernstein; *see* Electre.

Electrum, *see* Electre.

Electuary, *s.* die Latwerge (*Pharm.*).

Eleemosynary, I. *adj.* als Almosen gegeben; (alms-receiving) von Almosen lebend; — cor-poration, milde Stiftung. II. *s.* der Almosen-empfänger.

Elegan—ce, —**cy**, *s.* die Zierlichkeit, Eleganz, ge-schmackvolle Erscheinung, Feinheit; die Schönheit, Feinheit (*of language, etc.*); (symmetry) die Anmut der Formen. —**t**, *adj.*, —**ly**, *adv.* fein, zierlich, elegant; —t manners, feines Benehmen; an —t speaker, ein geschmackvoller Redner.

Eleg—iac, I. *adj.* elegisch. II. *s.* der elegische Vers, das Distichon. —**iast**, —**ist**, *s.* der Ele-giendichter. —**ize**, *v.a.* in Elegien besingen. —**y**, *s.* die Elegie, das Gedicht in elegischem Vers-maß *or* in Distichen; die Elegie, das Klagelied, Trauerlied.

Element, *s.* der Urstoff; (ingredient) der (Grund-) Bestandteil; das Element, Atom (*Chem.*); (nat-ural sphere) das Element; water is the — of fishes, das Wasser ist das Element der Fische; he is in his —, er ist in seinem Elemente. —**al**, *adj.* (innate) natürlich, angeboren. —**ariness**, *s.* die Einfachheit. —**ary**, *adj.* zu den Elementen gehörig, elementar; (simple) urstofflich, unbe-arbeitet; (rudimentary) anfangsmäßig, nach den Anfangsgründen; —ary education, der Elemen-tarunterricht, das Volksschulwesen; —ary school, die Volksschule; —ary teacher, der Volks-schullehrer. —**s**, *pl.* die Grundzüge, Anfangs-gründe, Elemente (*of a science, art, etc.*); Bro[t] und Wein im Abendmahl.

Elench, *s.* der Gegenbeweis; der Trugschluß (*obs.*).

Elephant, I. *s.* der Elefant; —'s tusk, der roh[e] Elefantenzahn; the — trumpets, der Elefan[t] trompetet. II. *attrib.*; — octavo, eine Art großes und breites Oktav. —**iasis**, *s.* die Elefantiasis, Dickhäutigkeit (*Med.*). —**ine**, *adj.* Elefanten-, elefantenhaft, riesenhaft, unbeholfen (*fig.*) *Comp.* —**-beetle**, *s.* der Elefantenkäfer.

Elevat—e, *v.a.* in die Höhe heben, erhöhen, em-porheben; die Höhenrichtung geben (*Artil.*) erheben (*to a dignity etc.*); erheben, veredel[n] (*the mind, etc.*); aufmuntern, beleben (*the spirits etc.*); to —e the voice, die Stimme erheben —**ed**, *p.p. & adj.* hoch; —ed with, erhoben aufgeblasen von; to be —ed with wine, wein-selig sein. —**ing**, *adj.* erhebend. —**ion**, *s* (raising) die Erhebung, Erhöhung (*also fig.*) (—ed place) die Anhöhe; (height) die Höhe; di[e] Erhabenheit, der Aufschwung (*of mind, th[e] thoughts, ideas, etc.*); die Erhabenheit (*of char-acter*); (high station, dignity) die Hoheit Würde, der Rang; die Erhebung (*of the voice etc.*); der Aufriß (*Arch., etc.*); die Höhe (*Astr.*) (angle of the line of fire) der Erhöhungswinkel die Elevation (*Artil.*); die Elevation, Empor-hebung (*of the host*); der Seitenriß (*Shipb.*) —ion of the pole, die Polhöhe; sectional —ion der Längen- *or* Quer-schnitt; side —ion, di[e] Seitenansicht. —**or**, *s.* der, die, das Empor-hebende; der Hebemuskel (*Anat.*); das Hebeeisen (*Surg.*); der Personen-Aufzug, Fahrstuhl (*Amer.*); die Winde (*Mach.*). —**ory**, I. *adj* zum Heben geeignet, Hebe-. II. *s.* das Hebe-eisen; der Hebemuskel.

Eleven, *num.* I. *adj.* elf. II. *s.* die Elf, Elfzahl die elf Spieler auf der einen Seite einer Cricket Partie; the Cambridge —, die Cambridge Cricket-Partie (gegen Oxford u.s.w.). —**th** *num. adj.* elft. —**thly**, *adv.* elftens.

Elf, *s.* (*pl.* —s, Elves) der Elfe, Kobold; (dwarf) der Zwerg. —**in**, *adj.* elfisch, Elfen-. —**ish** —(**in-**)**like**, *adj.* elfengleich; tückisch, boshaf[t] hinterhaltig. *Comp.* —**-king**, *s.* der Elfen-könig. —**-locks**, *pl.* das verfilzte Haar. —**shot**, *adj.* behext.

Elicit, *v.a.* entlocken, herauslocken; to — truth b[y] discussion, durch Erörterung die Wahrheit a[...]

das Licht bringen. **—ation,** *s.* die Hervorbringung, das Herauslocken.
Elide, *v.a.* elidieren, (einen Vokal) ausfallen lassen; annullieren (*dial.*).
Eligib—ility, *s.* die Wählbarkeit, Wahlfähigkeit; (desirableness) die Vorzüglichkeit. **—le,** *adj.*, **—ly,** *adv.* wahlwürdig, den Vorzug verdienend; (suitable) passend, angemessen; (desirable) wünschenswert; wählbar (*for an office*); heiratsfähig (*coll.*); —le for re-election, wieder wählbar.
Eliminat—e, *v.a.* ausstoßen, ausmerzen; entfernen, eliminieren, ausscheiden (*Chem.*); ausziehen (*Metall.*); eliminieren, fortschaffen (*Alg.*). **—ion,** *s.* die Ausstoßung, Ausmerzung, Wegschaffung; das Fortschaffen (einer Größe).
Elision, *s.* die Ausstoßung *or* Unterdrückung eines unbetonten Vokals, Elision.
Élite, *s.* der Kern, Ausbund.
Elixir, *s.* das Elixir, der Heiltrank (*Med.*); (quintessence) die Quintessenz, der Kern; (cordial) das Labsal; der Stein der Weisen (*Alchem.*).
Elk, *s.* der Elch, das Elentier.
Ell, *s.* die Elle.
Ellip—se, *s.* die Ellipse. **—sis,** *s.* die Ellipsis, Weglassung, Auslassung eines Wortes, &c. (*Gram.*); der Ergänzungsstrich (*Typ.*). **—sograph,** *s.* der Ellipsograph. **—soid,** *s.* das Ellipsoid. **—tic(al),** *adj.*, **—tically,** *adv.* elliptisch. **—ticity,** *s.* die Elliptizität.
Elm, —tree, *s.* die Ulme, Rüster.
Elmo, *s.;* St. —'s fire, das St. Elmsfeuer.
Elocution, I. *s.* der Vortrag. II. *attrib.;* —classes, Vortragsübungen. **—ary,** *adj.* den Vortrag betreffend. **—ist,** *s.* der Redekünstler.
Elongat—e, *v.a.* verlängern, ausdehnen. **—ion,** *s.* die Verlängerung, Ausdehnung; die Ausweichung (*Astr.*); die unvollkommene Verrenkung durch Ausdehnung der Gelenkbänder (*Surg.*); angle of —ion, der Abstandswinkel.
Elope, *v.n.* von Hause (mit dem Geliebten) entfliehen, sich entführen lassen; he —d with her, er entführte sie. **—ment,** *s.* das Entlaufen **—r,** *s.* die entlaufende Person.
Eloquen—ce, *s.* die Beredsamkeit, Beredtheit. **—t,** *adj.*, **—tly,** *adv.* beredtsam, beredt; —t eyes, ausdrucksvolle *or* sprechende Augen.
Else, I. *adv.* sonst, weiter; any one —, irgend ein anderer; anything —, irgend etwas anderes; no one —, niemand anders, sonst niemand, kein anderer; nowhere —, nirgend anders; somewhere —, anderswo, sonst irgendwo, irgendwo anders; what —, was sonst noch? was anders? who —? wer anders? wer sonst? II. *conj.* sonst, wo nicht; repent, or — I will . . ., tue Buße, sonst werde ich . . . *Comp.* **—where,** *adv.* sonstwo, anderswo; anderswohin.
Elucidat—e, *v.a.* aufhellen, aufklären, erläutern. **—ion,** *s.* die Erläuterung, Beleuchtung; die Klarstellung, Aufklärung. **—ory,** *adj.* aufklärend.
Elude, *v.a.* ausweichen, entschlüpfen, entwischen; entgehen, sich entziehen; lucky for you that you succeeded in eluding the blow, ein Glück für Sie, daß es Ihnen gelang, dem Schlage auszuweichen.
Elus—ion, *s.* listige Ausflucht; *see* Evasion; (trickery) die List. **—ive,** *adj.* (mit List) ausweichend. **—oriness,** *s.* das Trügliche. **—ory,** *adj.* trügerisch, betrüglich.
Elzevir, *s.* die Perlschrift (*Typ.*).
Emaciat—e, *v.* I. *a.* abzehren, ausmergeln. II. *n.* abmagern, mager werden. **—ion,** *s.* die Abmagerung, Abzehrung, Auszehrung.
Emana—te, *v.n.* ausfließen; (arise) herrühren (from, von). **—tion,** *s.* der Ausfluß; die Ausströmung; die Ausdünstung. **—nt,** *adj.* ausfließend; herrührend (*fig.*).
Emancipat—e, *v.a.* für mündig erklären (*Rom. Hist.*); freigeben, freilassen (*a slave*); (set free) befreien. **—ion,** *s.* die Aufhebung des Abhängigkeitsverhältnisses, die Freilassung; die Befreiung, Emanzipation, bürgerliche Gleichberechtigung. **—ionist,** *s.* der Verteidiger der Sklavenbefreiung (in Amerika). **—or,** *s.* der Befreier.
Emasculat—e, I. *adj.* entmannt; weibisch (*fig.*). II. *v.a.* entmannen. **—ion,** *s.* die Entmannung.
Embalm, *v.a.* einbalsamieren, salben; sorgsam bewahren (*fig.*); to be —ed in, fortleben in (*dat.*). **—ment,** *s.* das Einbalsamierung.
Embank, *v.a.* ein-deichen, -dämmen; aufschütten.
[1]**Embankment,** *s.* die Ein-dämmung, -deichung; der (Erd-)Damm, Eisenbahndamm (*Railw.*); die Einfassung eines Ufers; Thames —, der Themsekai (*in London*).
[2]**Embankment,** *s.* die Wechselspekulation (*C.L.*); das Bankkonto (*C.L.*).
Embargo, *s.* der Beschlag auf Schiffe, die Handelssperre; to lay an — on, Beschlag auf (a ship, ein Schiff) legen (*lit.*), sperren (*fig.*).
Embark, *v.* I. *a.* einschiffen; (Geld) anlegen; (the yacht) is to — the king, soll den König an Bord nehmen; he has —ed all his property in this speculation, er hat sein ganzes Vermögen zu dieser *or* auf diese Spekulation verwendet *or* bei dieser Spekulation aufs Spiel gesetzt. II. *n.* sich einschiffen, in See stechen; (engage) sich einlassen (in, auf, in); sich verwickeln (in eine S.); to — in an enterprise, sich auf eine Unternehmung einlassen. **—ation, Embarcation,** *s.* die Einschiffung; die Verladung; (cargo) die Ladung (*obs.*).
Embarrass, *v.a.* (perplex) verwirren; (confuse) in Verlegenheit setzen; (entangle) verwickeln; (obstruct) hindern, belästigen. **—ed,** *adj.* verlegen; in Geldverlegenheit. **—ment,** *s.* die Verwickelung; die Verwirrung, Verlegenheit, Klemme; (pecuniary —ment) die Geldverlegenheit; das Hindernis.
Embassy, *s.* die Botschaft (*in the larger capitals*); die Gesandtschaft.
Embattle, *v.a.* in Schlachtordnung aufstellen; mit Zinnen versehen.
Embed, *v.a.* betten, einbetten, lagern, legen; to — in sand, in Sand vergraben.
Embellish, *v.a.* verschöne(r)n, schmücken, zieren. **—er,** *s.* der Verschönerer. **—ment,** *s.* die Verschönerung, Verzierung, Zierde, der Schmuck.
[1]**Ember—** (*in comp.*) **—days,** *pl.* Quatember. **—goose,** *s.* die Embergans, der Eisseetaucher. **—week,** *s.* die Quatemberwoche.
[2]**Ember,** *s.* (*usually pl.* —s) glimmende Kohle, heiße glühende Asche; life's last —s, der letzte Lebensfunken (*fig.*).
Embezzle, *v.a.* veruntreuen, unterschlagen. **—ment,** *s.* die Veruntreuung, Unterschlagung, der Unterschleif. **—r,** *s.* der Veruntreuende, Unterschlagende.
Embitter, *v.a.* verbittern; to — a p.'s life, einem das Leben sauer machen. **—ment,** *s.* das Verbittern; die Verbitterung.
Emblazon, *v.a.* mit Wappenbildern schmücken, blasonieren; pomphaft verkünden, erheben (*fig.*). **—er,** *s.* der Wappenmaler; der Herold. **—ment,** *s.* das Bemalen mit Wappenbildern; der Wappenschmuck. **—ry,** *s.* das Wappengemälde.
Emblem, *s.* das Sinnbild, Emblem; (inlaid work) die eingelegte Arbeit (*obs.*). **—atic(al),** *adj.*, **—atically,** *adv.* emblematisch, sinnbildlich. **—atize,** *v.a.* sinnbildlich darstellen.
Embod—iment, *s.* die Verkörperung. **—y,** *v.a.* verkörpern; (incorporate) einverleiben (concentrate) vereinigen; to —y laws, Gesetze sammeln; to —y troops, Truppen zusammenziehen.
Embolden, *v.a.* kühn machen, ermutigen.
Embolism, *s.* die Einschaltung (eines Monats); (intercalated time) eingeschaltete Zeit, der Schalttag, das Schaltjahr; die Verstopfung (eines Blutgefäßes); die Fürbitte (nach dem Vaterunser).
Embosom, *v.a.* ins Herz schließen, im Herzen tragen, lieben; einschließen; umgeben.
Emboss, *v.a.* (mit dem Hammer) auftreiben,

bosseln, bossieren; mit erhabener Arbeit bedecken; in getriebener Arbeit anfertigen; austreiben, ausnieten (*Metall.*); pressen (*paper*), gaufrieren (*linen*). **—ed**, *adj.* gebosselt, getrieben, erhaben gearbeitet (*Sculpt.*); gaufriert; —ed leather, das Körnerleder, genarbte Leder; —ed printing, erhabener Druck; —ed work, Bossieren; die Bildtreiberei; das Pressen, Gaufrieren. **—ing**, *s.* die Bossierarbeit. *Comp.* **—ing-stick**, *s.* das Bossierholz.

Embouchure, *s.* die Mündung; das Mundstück, der Ansatz (*Mus.*).

Embowel, *v.a.* ausweiden. **—ment**, *s.* die Ausweidung.

Embower, *v.a.* (mit einer Laube) decken, umgeben, umhüllen.

Embrace, I. *v.a.* umarmen, umfassen; (accept) (willig) annehmen; (seize) ergreifen; (include) in sich begreifen, enthalten, einschließen; to — the Christian religion, die christliche Religion annehmen. II. *v.n.* sich *or* einander umarmen. III. *s.* die Umarmung.

Embrasure, *s.* die Fenster-, Tür-Vertiefung; die Schießscharte (*Fort.*).

Embrocat—e, *v.a.* einreiben. **—ion**, *s.* die Einreibung; das Einreibemittel (*Pharm.*).

Embroider, *v.a.* sticken; verschönern, ausschmücken (*fig.*). **—ing**, *s.* das Sticken. **—er**, *s.* der (die) Sticker(in). **—y**, *s.* die Stickerei; flat-stitch —y, Plattstichstickerei; gold thread —y, Goldstickerei; open-work —y, durchbrochene Stickerei; raised —y, erhabene Stickerei. *Comp.* **—ing-machine**, *s.* die Stickmaschine. **—y-cotton**, *s.* das Stickgarn. **—y-frame**, *s.* der Stickrahmen. **—y-needle**, *s.* die Sticknadel.

Embroil, *v.a.* verwickeln (in a quarrel, in einen Streit); (confuse) verwirren. **—ment**, *s.* die Verwickelung, Verwirrung.

Embryo, *s.* der Fruchtkeim, die unentwickelte Leibesfrucht, der Embryo; der Keimling (*Bot.*); der Keim, erste Anfang (*fig.*); in —, im Keim, im Werden, unentwickelt. **—logy**, *s.* die Lehre vom Embryo. **—nic**, *adj.* embryonisch; unentwickelt, im Keime vorhanden. **—tomy**, *s.* die Embryotomie (*Surg.*).

Emend, *v.a.* (Texte) verbessern *or* berichtigen. **—ation**, *s.* die Verbesserung, Textbesserung. **—ator**, *s.* der Textverbesserer, Textberichtiger. **—atory**, *adj.* verbessernd.

Emerald, I. *s.* der Smaragd. II. *adj.* smaragdfarbig, smaragdgrün, smaragden; the — isle, die Smaragdinsel (Irland).

Emer—ge, *v.n.* auftauchen, emporkommen; (come forth) hervorgehen, entstehen; (arise) sich erheben; (reappear) hervorragen, herauskommen; the rays —ge, die Strahlen brechen heraus. **—gence**, *s.* das Auftauchen, Sichtbarwerden. **—gency**, *s.* unerwartetes Ereignis, dringende Not; in case of —gency, im Notfalle; a great —gency, ein großer Moment, ein kritischer Augenblick; —gency exit, der Notausgang (*in theatres*); —gency men, Männer zur Aushilfe. **—gent**, *adj.* auftauchend, hervorkommend. **—sion**, *s.* das Auftauchen; der Austritt, die Emersion (*Astr.*).

Emeritus, *adj.* ehrenvoll verabschiedet, in den Ruhestand getreten; he is an — professor, er ist ein emeritierter Professor, ein Professor, der sich zur Ruhe gesetzt hat.

Emery, *s.* der Schmirgel; to rub with —, schmirgeln. *Comp.* **—ball**, *s.* die Schmirgelkugel. **—paper**, *s* das Schmirgelpapier.

Emetic, I. *adj.* Erbrechen bewirkend; tartar —, der Brechweinstein. II. *s.* das Brechmittel.

Emigra—nt, I. *adj.* auswandernd. II. *s.* der Auswanderer. **—te**, *v.n.* auswandern. **—tion**, *s.* die Auswanderung.

Eminen—ce, *s.* (hill, *etc.*) die Erhöhung, Höhe, Anhöhe; (elevation) die Höhe, Erhabenheit; (distinction) die Auszeichnung, der Vorrang, Vorzug, Ruhm; (high station) der hohe Rang; (title) die Eminenz. **—t**, *adj.*, **—tly**, *adv.* hoch, erhaben; ausgezeichnet, vorzüglich (*fig.*); —tly fitted, ganz besonders *or* vorzugsweise geeignet; —t in learning, ausgezeichnet durch Gelehrsamkeit; he was —t for his piety, er zeichnete sich durch seine Frömmigkeit aus.

Emir, *s.* der Emir.

Emiss—ary, I. *s.* der Sendling, Abgesandte. II. *adj.* herausgeschickt, sich abzweigend. **—ion**, *s.* das Aussenden; die Ausströmung (*Phys.*); (the circulating) der Ausfluß, das In-Umlaufsetzen; die Serie (*of paper money, etc.*).

Emit, *v.a.* ausströmen (*rays, etc.*); (throw out) auswerfen; (issue) in Umlauf setzen; abschießen (*an arrow, etc.*); ergehen lassen (an order).

Emmenagogue, *s.* das die Menstruation befördernde Mittel.

Emmet, *s.* die Ameise.

Emollient, I. *adj.* erweichend. II. *s.* das erweichende Mittel.

Emolument, *s.* das Gehalt; der Nutzen, Vorteil. **—s**, *pl.* die Einkünfte; die Nebeneinkünfte.

Emotion, *s.* die Gemütsbewegung, Aufregung, Rührung. **—al**, *adj.* Gefühls-, Gemüts-; (easily moved) leicht aufgeregt *or* gerührt; rührselig; —al person, der Gefühlsmensch.

Empale, *see* Impale.

Empanel, **Impanel**, I. *s.* die Geschwornenliste. II. *v.a.* in die Geschwornenliste einschreiben.

Emperor, *s.* der Kaiser. **—ship**, *s.* die Kaiserwürde.

Empha—sis, *s.* der Nachdruck, die Emphase. **—size**, *v.a.* betonen, mit Nachdruck aussprechen; nachdrücklich hervorheben. **—tic(al)**, *adj.*, **—tically**, *adv.* nachdrücklich, nachdrucksvoll, emphatisch.

Emphysema, *s.* die Windgeschwulst (*Med.*).

Empire, *s.* das Reich, Kaiserreich; (sovereignty) die Oberherrschaft; for emperor and —, für Kaiser und Reich; the British —, Großbritannien und seine Kolonien; the — of the sea, die Seeherrschaft; the middle —, das Reich der Mitte.

Empiric, I., **—al**, *adj.*, **—ally**, *adv.* auf (bloße) Erfahrung gegründet, erfahrungsmäßig, empirisch; quacksalberisch; —al remedies, Hausmittel. II., **—ist**, *s.* der Empiriker; der Empirist (*Philos.*); der Quacksalber, Pfuscher. **—ism**, *s.* der Empirismus; die Quacksalberei (*Med.*).

Employ, I. *v.a.* (use) brauchen, anwenden, verwenden; (occupy) beschäftigen; (engage in service) anstellen; to — funds, Geld(er) anlegen; to — o.s., sich beschäftigen; to be —ed in, sich beschäftigen mit, arbeiten an, angestellt sein bei; to — one's life in . . ., sein Leben zubringen mit . . . II. *s.* das Geschäft, die Beschäftigung. **—é**, *s.* der Angestellte. **—ee**, *s.* der Arbeitnehmer, der Arbeiter. **—er**, *s.* der Anwender; der Auftraggeber, Kommittent (*C.L.*); der Arbeitgeber, Dienstherr. **—ment**, *s.* die Beschäftigung; (business) das Geschäft; (office) das Amt, die Anstellung; (service) der Dienst; die Anlegung (*of capital*); to be in a p.'s —ment, bei einem arbeiten, in jemandes Geschäft tätig sein.

Emporium, *s.* der Stapelplatz, Handelsplatz; die Niederlage, das Magazin; der Vorrat (*fig.*).

Empower, *v.a.* ermächtigen, bevollmächtigen. **—ment**, *s.* die Vollmacht.

Empress, *s.* die Kaiserin; the — Dowager, die Kaiserin-Witwe.

Emprise, I. *s.* das Unternehmen, Wagnis. II. *v.a.* unternehmen.

Empt—ier, *s.* der Ausleerer. **—iness**, *s.* die Leere, Leerheit; die Eitelkeit, Nichtigkeit (of human things, etc., der menschlichen Dinge, 2c.).

Emption, *s.* der Kauf; bill of —, der Kaufbrief.

Empty, I. *adj.* leer, ledig; (—ied) ausgeleert; eitel, nichtig (*fig.*); ohne Ladung (*C. L.*); an — room, ein leeres, unmöbliertes Zimmer; — cartridge, die Patronenhülse; — coxcomb, ein eitler Geck. II. *v.a.* leeren, entleeren, ausleeren. III.

s. leeres Faß; pl. Empties, leere Fässer. *Comp.* **—-handed**, *adj.* mit leeren Händen. **—-headed**, *adj.* gedankenarm, hohlköpfig.

Empurple, *v.a.* purpurrot *or* purpurn färben.

Empyrea—l, *adj.* empyreisch, das Empyreum, den Feuerhimmel betreffend. **—n**, I. *s.* der Feuerhimmel, höchste Himmel; das Firmament. II. *adj. see* —l.

Empyreumatic, *adj.* brenzlich.

Emu, *s.* der australische Kasuar (*Orn.*).

Emul—ate, *v.a.* wetteifern (mit einem), nacheifern (einem). **—ation**, *s.* der Wetteifer, die Nacheiferung; (jealousy) die Eifersucht. **—ous**, *adj.* (mit einem) wetteifernd, (einem) nacheifernd; eifersüchtig (of a p., auf einen).

Emulsion, *s.* die Mandelmilch, Emulsion (*Pharm.*).

Emunctory, *s.* das Aussonderungsorgan.

Enable, *v.a.* befähigen, instand setzen; this —d me, dies machte mich fähig, machte es mir möglich.

Enact, *v.a.* (decree) verordnen, verfügen, beschließen; (establish as a law) Gesetzeskraft geben *or* verleihen. **—ive**, *adj.* verordnend. **—ment**, *s.* (decree) die gesetzliche Verfügung, Verordnung; die Erhebung zum Gesetz. **—or**, *s.* der Verordner, Gesetzgeber.

Enamel, I. *s.* der Schmelz, das Email; die Glasur (*of the teeth*). II. *v.a.* emaillieren, mit Schmelz *or* Email überziehen; in Email arbeiten *or* malen; bunt machen, schmücken (*fig.*); —led work, die Schmelzarbeit. **—ler**, *s.* der Emailleur; —ler's lamp, die Blaselampe. **—ling**, *s.* das Emaillieren. *Comp.* **—-painting**, *s.* die Emailmalerei.

Enamo—ur, —r, *v.a.* verliebt machen; to be —ured of, in (eine Person *or* Sache) verliebt sein.

Encaenia, *s.* die Jahresfeier einer Tempel- oder Kirchen-Einweihung; das jährliche Wohltäterfest (*in Oxford*).

Encage, *v.a.* in (*or* wie in) einen Käfig einsperren.

Encamp, *v.* I. *a.* lagern. II. *n.* sich lagern; to be —ed, lagern; — against the city, belagert die Stadt (*B.*). **—ment**, *s.* das Lagern, die Lagerung; (camp) das Lager.

Encaustic, I. *adj.* enkaustisch; — tiles, glasierte Ziegel. II. *s.* die eingebrannte Wachsmalerei.

Enceinte, I. *adj.* schwanger. II. *s.* die Enceinte, Umwallung, Umfassung (*Fort.*).

Enchain, *v.a.* anketten; fesseln, verketten (*fig.*).

Enchant, *v.a.* bezaubern, behexen; bezaubern, hinreißen, entzücken (*with*, von) (*fig.*); —ed castle, das Zauberschloß. **—er**, *s.* der Zauberer. **—ing**, *adj.*, **—ingly**, *adv.* bezaubernd. **—ment**, *s.* die Bezauberung, Zauberei; der Zauber; distance lends —ment to the view, in der Ferne macht sich die Sache besser. **—ress**, *s.* die Zauberin.

Enchas—e, *v.a.* ziselieren (*Engr.*); einfassen (*guns, etc.*); einlassen, einlegen (*Carp.*); schmücken (*fig.*); —ed work, getriebene Arbeit. *Comp.* **—ing-hammer**, *s.* der Treibhammer.

Encircle, *v.a.* umringen; umfassen (*fig.*).

Enclitic, I. *adj.* enklitisch. II. *s.* das Anhängewort.

Enclos—e, *v.a.* (fence in) einzäunen, einfriedigen; (surround) einschließen, umgeben; einschließen, beifügen (*a letter, etc.*); (comprise) in sich halten, fassen; the —ed (letter, *etc.*), der Einschluß, Beischluß, die Einlage; —ed card, beigeschlossene *or* einliegende Karte. **—ing**, *s.* die Einzäunung. **—ure**, *s.* die Einzäunung, Einfriedigung, der Zaun; das Gehege (*in a wood*); der Bezirk; die Einlage, der Einschluß (*in a letter*).

Encomi—ast, *s.* der Lobredner. **—astic**, *adj.*, **—astically**, *adv.* preisend, lobpreisend. **—um**, *s.* die Lobrede.

Encompass, *v.a.* (surround) umringen, umschließen, einschließen; umzingeln (*an enemy*); (go round) umfahren, umgehen, umsegeln (*obs.*).

Encore, I. *int.* noch einmal! da capo! (*Theat., etc.*). II. *v.a.* da capo rufen, nochmals verlangen; Patti was repeatedly —d, die Patti wurde wiederholt gerufen. III. *s.* die Wiederholung; der Dacaporuf; to receive an —, zur Wiederholung aufgefordert werden, gerufen werden.

Encounter, I. *s.* das zufällige Begegnen, Zusammentreffen; (fight) das Gefecht, Treffen; (duel) der Zweikampf; (contest) das lebhafte Gespräch, der Wortkampf, Streit. II. *v.a.* begegnen, treffen; (oppose) widerstehen, entgegentreten; (meet unexpectedly) unvermutet, plötzlich begegnen, stoßen auf (*acc.*); (strive with) sich zanken mit, sich schlagen mit; (assail) anfallen; bestehen (*an adventure*); stoßen auf (*difficulties*). III. *v.n.* zusammentreffen; to — a storm, von einem Sturm überfallen werden.

Encourag—e, *v.a.* ermutigen, ermuntern, aufmuntern, antreiben, beleben (*trade*); befördern (*the arts, etc.*). **—ement**, *s.* die Aufmunterung, Ermutigung; die Beförderung, Unterstützung, der Antrieb (*fig.*). **—er**, *s.* der Aufmunterer; der Beförderer, Unterstützende, Gönner. **—ing**, *adj.*, **—ingly**, *adv.* ermutigend, aufmunternd.

Encroach, *v.n.* Eingriffe machen, eingreifen (upon, in, *acc.*); Land abspülen, abreißen (*as the sea*); eingreifen, in (*acc.*), beeinträchtigen; to — upon a p.'s kindness, jemandes Güte mißbrauchen. **—er**, *s.* einer, der Eingriffe tut. **—ment**, *s.* der Eingriff (on rights, in Rechte).

Encrust, *v.a.* bekrusten, inkrustieren.

Encumb—er, *v.a.* belasten, beladen, beschweren; to —er an estate, ein Gut mit Schulden belasten. **—rance**, *s.* (burden) die Last; die Beschwerde, Beschwerlichkeit, das Hindernis (*fig.*); (useless addition) das Unnütze; die Hypothekenschuld, Schuldenlast (*Law*). **—rancer**, *s.* der Pfandgläubiger.

Encycl—ical, *adj.* umlaufend, Kreis-; —ical epistle, das Rundschreiben, Zirkular; die päpstliche Enzyklika. **—opædia, —opedia**, *s.* die Enzyklopädie, das Sachwörterbuch, das Konversationslexikon; Wörterbuch des allgemeinen Wissens. **—opædian, —opedic**, *adj.* enzyklopädisch. **—opædist, —opedist**, *s.* der Mitarbeiter an einer Enzyklopädie; the —opedists, die Enzyklopädisten (*Lit. Hist.*).

Encyst, *v.a.* einkapseln. **—ed**, *adj.* eingekapselt, eingebalgt, in eine Blase eingeschlossen.

End, I. *s.* das Ende; (aim) das Ziel, Ende; (purpose) der Zweck, Endzweck; (issue) die Folge; (fragment) das Endchen, Stück, der Rest; (point) die Spitze; der Kopf, das Kopfende (*Carp.*); the — of study, das Ziel des Studiums; to be mindful of one's latter —, seines Todes eingedenk sein; candle —, Lichtendchen; odds and —s, verschiedenartige Dinge, allerhand Kleinigkeiten; to be at an —, zu Ende sein, aufhören; to be at one's wits' —, sich (*dat.*) nicht mehr zu helfen und zu raten wissen; to bring to an —, zu Ende führen; to come to an —, enden, zu Ende kommen; to make an — of, beendigen; (kill) umbringen; on —, aufrecht; ununterbrochen; his hair stood on —, die Haare standen ihm zu Berge; for many years on —, auf viele Jahre ohne Unterbrechung; my patience is now at an —, jetzt reißt mir die Geduld; it comes to very much the same thing in the —, es kommt schließlich auf eins hinaus; to have at one's fingers' —s, am Schnürchen haben; . . . and there 's an —, . . . und damit gut; to what —? wozu? to no —, vergebens; ohne jeden Zweck; to the — that, damit; in the —, am Ende; to gain one's —s, seine Zwecke erreichen; for one's own (private) —s, für seine persönlichen Zwecke; (to fight) to the bitter —, bis aufs äußerste *or* zum letzten Blutstropfen; to make both —s meet, (mit der jährlichen Einnahme) auskommen, sich nach der Decke strecken; without —, unendlich; world without —, immer und ewiglich; the West — of London, der Westen Londons, der westliche Teil von London. II. *v.a.* endigen, zu Ende bringen *or* führen. beendigen,

III. *v.n.* sich endigen; all 's well that —s well, Ende gut, Alles gut (*prov.*); all his fine plans —ed in nothing, alle seine schönen Pläne wurden zu Wasser. **—ing**, *s.* das Ende, der Schluß, Abschluß; die Endung (*Gram.*). **—less**, *adj.*, **—lessly**, *adv.* endlos, unendlich, fortdauernd; unendlich (*Math.*); ohne Ende, geschlossen (*Mech.*). **—lessness**, *s.* die Endlosigkeit, Unendlichkeit. **—way(s)**, **—wise**, *adv.* aufrecht, gerade. *Comp.* **—-all**, *s.* der Schluß; the be-all and —-all, das Ein und Alles.

Endanger, *v.a.* gefährden, in Gefahr bringen. **—ing**, *s.* die Gefährdung.

Endear, *v.a.* lieb, wert, teuer machen. **—ing**, *adj.* lieb *or* teuer machend, zärtlich, lockend. **—ment**, *s.* die Liebkosung, Zärtlichkeit; (charm) die Lockung; (state of being —ed) die Beliebtheit.

Endeavour, I. *s.* die Bemühung, Bestrebung; with one's utmost —s, angelegentlichst, aufs eifrigste. II. *v.n.* sich bemühen, sich bestreben; to — to obtain . . ., sich bemühen, (um) . . . zu erhalten.

Endecagon, *s.* das Elfeck (*Geom.*).

Endemic, I. *adj.*, **—al**, *adj.*, **—ally**, *adv.* endemisch; (local) örtlich, einheimisch. II. *s.* endemische, an bestimmten Orten auftretende Krankheit.

Endive, *s.* die Endivie.

Endo—carp, *s.* die innere Fruchthülle, Fruchthaut. **—gen**, *s.* das Endogen.

Endorse, *v. a.* auf der Rückseite überschreiben; indossieren, girieren, überweisen, übertragen (*C.L.*); mit Rücken(=Einband) versehen (*Bookb.*); (ratify) gut heißen; to — a view, einer Ansicht (völlig) beipflichten, eine Ansicht annehmen. **—ment**, *s.* die Aufschrift, Überschrift; das Indossement, Giro (*C.L.*); die Bestätigung. **—r**, *s.* der Indossant, Girant.

Endow, *v.a.* begaben, ausstatten; aussteuern (*Law*); ausschmücken, zieren (*fig.*); subventionieren, dotieren (*a church, school*); —ed school, die Stiftungsschule. **—ment**, *s.* die Begabung, Ausstattung; die Aussteuer, Dotation (*of a bride*); (talent) die Gabe, Begabung; die Dotation, Ausstattung, das stiftungsmäßige Einkommen, die milde Stiftung. **—ments**, *pl.* die Stiftungsgelder, das Stiftungsvermögen.

Endue, *v.a.* anziehen (Kleider); kleiden, bekleiden; ausstatten, begaben.

Endur—able, *adj.* erträglich, leidlich. **—ance**, *s.* die Dauer, Fortdauer; (the bearing) das Ertragen, Aushalten; (power of —ing) die Ausdauer, Geduld, Beharrlichkeit; past —ance, unerträglich. **—e**, *v.* I. *a.* aushalten, ausdauern; ertragen, erdulden, leiden; not to be —ed, nicht auszuhalten, unerträglich. II. *n.* (continue) fortdauern; aushalten; leiden, dulden. **—ing**, *adj.* dauernd; duldend, duldsam.

Enema, *s.* das Klystier.

Enemy, *s.* der Feind, Gegner; der Teufel, der alte böse Feind (*Theol.*); how goes the —? wie viel ist die Uhr? (*sl.*).

Energ—etic, *adj.*, **—etically**, *adv.* tatkräftig, energisch; (active) tätig, wirksam; (forcible) kraftvoll. **—y**, *s.* die Tatkraft, Energie, der Nachdruck; die Wirksamkeit, Tätigkeit; das Feuer (*of expression, etc.*); die Energie, Spannkraft; (actual —y) lebendige Kraft (*Phys., Mech.*); potential —y, die potentielle, mögliche Energie; conservation of —y, die Erhaltung der Kraft.

Enervat—e, I. *adj.* kraftlos, entnervt. II. *v.a.* entkräften, kraftlos machen, schwächen, entnerven, *see* Enfeeble; die Nerven durchschneiden (*Vet.*) (*obs.*). **—ing**, *adj.* entkräftend, schwächend. **—ion**, *s.* die Entkräftigung, Entnervung, Schwächung; (weakness) die Schwäche.

Enfeeble, *v.a.* schwächen, entkräften. **—ment**, *s.* die Schwächung.

Enfeoff, *v.a.* zum Lehensmann machen, belehnen. **—ment**, *s.* die Belehnung; (deed of —ment) der Lehensbrief.

Enfilad—e, I. *s.* die gerade Linie; die Bestreichung in gerader Linie, das Längen=, Seiten=Feuer (*Artil.*). II. *v.a.* der Länge nach bestreichen; they found themselves —ed by the English, sie befanden sich unter dem Enfilierfeuer *or* Seitenfeuer der Engländer. **—ing**, *adj.*; —ing battery, die Flankenbatterie; —ing fire, *see* —e.

Enfold, Infold, *v.a.* einhüllen, einschlagen; umschließen; falten, in Falten legen.

Enforce, *v.a.* (ratify) (ver)stärken, kräftigen; (force) erzwingen; (urge upon) mit Nachdruck hervorheben, nachdrücklich geltend machen (*an argument, etc.*); zur Geltung bringen (*the law, etc.*); to — payment, die Zahlung mit Gewalt eintreiben; the law will be strictly —d against . . ., das Gesetz wird gegen . . . streng gehandhabt werden. **—ment**, *s.* die Verstärkung; (compulsion) die Gewalttätigkeit, Aufnötigung, der Zwang; die Einschärfung, Anwendung der Strenge des Gesetzes, Vollziehung (*of the law*); (that which gives force) die Bekräftigung.

Enfranchise, *v.a.* befreien, frei geben; (invest with a freeman's rights) für politisch frei erklären; (give the franchise) das Bürgerrecht *or* Wahlrecht erteilen. **—ment**, *s.* die Freilassung; (naturalization) die Einbürgerung; das Erteilen des Bürgerrechts und Stimmrechts.

Engag—e, *v.* I. *a.* (pledge) verpfänden, versetzen; (bind) verpflichten, verbinden; (wager) daran setzen; (gain over) einnehmen, gewinnen; (attract) auf sich (*acc.*) ziehen; (employ) beschäftigen; (appoint) anstellen; dingen. in Dienst nehmen (*a servant, etc.*); mieten (*a house, etc.*): lösen (*seats, etc.*); (enlist, involve) verwickeln (in), beteiligen (an), hineinbringen (in); angreifen, handgemein werden mit (*the enemy*); engagieren (*C. L.*); he at once —ed the enemy, er griff den Feind unverzüglich an; he —ed him as tutor, er engagierte ihn als Hauslehrer; to —e a lady to dance, eine Dame zum Tanze auffordern, engagieren; to be —ed (for a dance), für einen Tanz versagt sein, einen Tanz schon versprochen haben; to get —ed (to be married), sich verloben; to be —ed to be married, verlobt sein, Braut *or* Bräutigam sein; you were so deeply —ed in conversation, that . . ., Sie waren so sehr in die Unterhaltung vertieft, daß . . .; to —e in conversation, ein Gespräch (mit einem) anknüpfen, sich mit einem auf ein Gespräch einlassen; tell him I am —ed, sage ihm, ich sei anderweitig beschäftigt. II. *n.* sich verpflichten *or* verbindlich machen (to, zu); sich einlassen (in a th., auf eine S.), unternehmen; (fight) sich schlagen, in Kampf geraten; to —e in wild speculations, sich auf unbesonnene Spekulationen einlassen. **—ement**, *s.* die Verpflichtung; die Verlobung (*of lovers*); die Stellung, Beschäftigung; die Einladung (*to dinner, etc.*); (appointment) die Verabredung; (fight) das Gefecht, Handgemenge; an —ement was fought, ein Treffen wurde geliefert, ein Zusammenstoß erfolgte; the —ement is broken off, die Verlobung ist rückgängig gemacht *or* aufgehoben; to meet one's —ements, seinen Verpflichtungen nachkommen; my numerous —ements will . . ., meine zahlreichen Beschäftigungen werden . . .; owing to a previous —ement, infolge einer früheren Verabredung; da ich mich bereits anderweit gebunden habe, da ich schon eine andere Einladung angenommen habe. **—ing**, *adj.*, **—ingly**, *adv.* einnehmend, gewinnend, anmutig, reizend. **—ingness**, *s.* das einnehmende Wesen.

Engender, *v.a.* (er)zeugen; erzeugen, verursachen (*fig.*). **—er**, *s.* der Erzeuger; die Ursache.

Engine, *s.* die Maschine; (steam —) die Dampfmaschine; die Lokomotive (*Railw.*); die Kunst (*Min.*); der Holländer (*Pap.*); (fire —) die Feuerspritze; hydraulic —, Wasserkunst; marine —, Schiffsmaschine; traction —, die Zuglokomobile; vertical —, stehende Dampfmaschine.

—er, *s.* der Ingenieur, Techniker; *see* —-builder; royal —er, military —er, Militäringenieur, Genieoffizier, Kriegsbaumeister; marine —er, Schiffsingenieur; naval —er, der Schiffbautechniker; mining —er, Bergwerksingenieur; civil —er, Zivilingenieur; assistant —er, Unteringenieur; chief —er, Oberingenieur; electrical —er, Elektrotechniker. **—ering**, I. *attrib.*; —ering drawing, die Maschinenzeichnung; —ering laboratory, Lehrsaal für Maschinenbaukunst. II. *s.*; civil —ering, die Ingenieurkunst; electrical —ering, die Elektrotechnik; military —ering, das Genie, die Kriegsbaukunst; mechanical —ering, die Maschinenbaukunst. *Comp.* **—-builder**, *s.* der Maschinenbauer. **—-driver**, *s.* der Lokomotivführer (*Railw.*); der Maschinenführer. **—-fitter**, *s.* der Monteur. **—-house**, *s.* der Lokomotivschuppen (*Railw.*); das Maschinengestell. **—-man**, *s.* der Maschinenwärter.

Engird, *v.a.* umgürten, umschließen, umgeben.

Engirt, *p.p. see* Engird; umgürtet, umgeben.

Engraft, *see* Ingraft.

Engrail, *v.a.* auszacken (*Her.*).

Engrain, Ingrain, *v.a.* in der Wolle färben, tief färben; unauslöschlich einprägen (einem etwas) (*fig.*).

Engrav—e, *v.a.* (*p.p. also* —en) gravieren, stechen, ziselieren; einprägen (*fig.*); to —e upon brass, in Erz graben. **—ed**, *p.p. & adj.* gestochen. **—er**, *s.* der Graveur, Bildstecher; —er on copper, of music, on metal, of stamps, in steel, on stone, der Kupferstecher, Notenstecher, Metallstecher, Stempelschneider, Stahlstecher, Steinschneider; wood- —er, der Holzschneider. **—ing**, *s.* das Gravieren, Bildstechen; die Metallstecherkunst; (picture) der Kupferstich, Holzschnitt; —ing on copper, die Kupferstecherei; copper-plate —ing, der Kupferstich; steel —ing, die Stahlstecherei, (picture) der Stahlstich; —ing on stone, Steinschneidekunst, (lithograph) der Stein(ab)druck; wood- —ing, Holzschneidekunst, (wood-cut) Holzschnitt.

Engross, *v.a.* an sich ziehen, ganz in Anspruch nehmen; mundieren, mit großen Buchstaben (ab)schreiben (*Law*); to — the conversation, das Gespräch völlig an sich reißen *or* monopolisieren, das große Wort führen; —ed by, eingenommen von, den Kopf voll habend von; —ed in, with, vertieft in (*acc.*); his attention was —ed, seine Aufmerksamkeit war völlig in Anspruch genommen. **—er**, *s.* (forestaller) der Auf-, Vor-käufer (*obs.*); der Monopolisierer; der Urkundenabschreiber. **—ing**, *adj.* fesselnd, völlig in Anspruch nehmend; —ing hand, die Kanzlei-, Fraktur-schrift. **—ment**, *s.* der Aufkauf; das Abschreiben *or* die Abschrift einer Urkunde; das völlige In-Anspruch-genommen-sein; die Mundierung (von Urkunden).

Engulf, *v.a.* verschlingen.

Enhance, *v.a.* erhöhen; (increase) vergrößern. **—ment**, *s.* die Erhöhung; die Vergrößerung.

Enharmonic, *adj.* enharmonisch.

Enigma, *s.* das Rätsel. **—tic(al)**, *adj.*, **—tically**, *adv.* rätselhaft; (obscure) zweideutig, dunkel.

Enjambement, *s.* das Enjambement.

Enjoin, *v.a.* (— upon a p., einem) auferlegen, anbefehlen, einschärfen, zur Pflicht machen.

Enjoy, *v.a.* genießen, besitzen, sich erfreuen (einer S. *or* an einer S.); (like) genußreich finden; (have pleasure in) Freude (an einer S.) haben; to — good health, sich einer guten Gesundheit erfreuen; I — the coffee, der Kaffee schmeckt mir; we —ed Sassnitz, wir genossen den Aufenthalt in Saßnitz; to — o.s., sich gut unterhalten; how did you — yourself? wie hast du dich unterhalten *or* amüsiert? wie hat es dir gefallen? we —ed ourselves immensely, wir amüsierten uns köstlich. **—able**, *adj.* genießbar (of food); genußreich, erfreulich; —able trip, genußreicher Ausflug; it was most —able, es war höchst erfreulich (gelungen, angenehm). **—er**, *s.* der Genießende; der Besitzer. **—ment**, *s.* der Genuß, die Freude.

Enkindle, *v.a.* entzünden, entflammen.

Enlarg—e, *v.* I. *a.* erweitern, ausdehnen, vergrößern; erweitern (*the mind, etc.*); (set free) freilassen; laufen lassen (*a stag*). II. *n.* sich vergrößern, sich ausdehnen; to —e upon, sich weitläufig verbreiten über (*acc.*). **—ed**, *p.p. & adj.*; —ed ideas, erweiterte Begriffe; —ed scale, der vergrößerte Maßstab (*Draw.*). **—ement**, *s.* die Vergrößerung, Erweiterung, Ausdehnung; die Erweiterung (*of the mind, etc.*); die Verbreitung (upon, über); die Loslassung. **—ing**, *adj.*; —ing process, das Vergrößern (*Phot.*).

Enlighten, *v.a.* erleuchten; aufklären, belehren (*a person*), erleuchten (*the mind*). **—ed**, *s.*; —ed views, aufgeklärte Ansichten; the —ed, die Aufgeklärten. **—ment**, *s.* die Aufklärung.

Enlist, *v.* I. *a.* anwerben (*soldiers*); (enrol) einschreiben; (gain over) gewinnen (für). II. *n.* sich anwerben lassen, Soldat werden.

Enliven, *v.a.* beleben, beseelen, ermuntern. **—er**, *s.* der, welcher belebt, ermuntert; das Ermunterungsmittel, die Belebung. **—ment**, *s.* die Belebung.

Enmity, *s.* die Feindschaft; die Feindseligkeit; to be at — with, in Feindschaft leben mit.

Enneagon, *s.* das Neuneck (*Geom.*).

Ennoble, *v.a.* adeln, in den Adelstand erheben; veredeln, erheben (*fig.*). **—ment**, *s.* das Adeln, die Erhebung in den Adelstand; die Veredlung.

Ennui, *s.* die Langeweile.

Enorm—ity, *s.* (atrociousness) die Ungeheuerlichkeit; (atrocity) die Abscheulichkeit; (monstrous thing) das Ungeheure. **—ous**, *adj.*, **—ously**, *adv.* ungeheuer; (atrocious) abscheulich, unerhört; (excessive) übermäßig, ungeheuer. **—ousness**, *s.* die Ungeheuerlichkeit.

Enough, I. *adv.* genug; well —, so leidlich, ziemlich gut; natural —, ganz natürlich; sure —, he was there, (und) richtig, da war er; true —, nur zu wahr; like —, höchst wahrscheinlich. II. *adj.* genug, hinlänglich; I have had — of it, ich habe genug davon, ich habe es *or* die Geschichte satt; we have time —, wir haben hinlängliche Zeit; it is — for me to know . . ., es genügt mir, zu wissen . . . III. *s.* das Genügende, die Genüge.

Enquire, *see* Inquire.

Enrage, *v.a.* wütend machen, aufbringen; —d at, aufgebracht *or* entrüstet über (*acc.*).

Enrapt, *adj.* verzückt. **—ure**, *v.a.* entzücken.

Enrich, *v.a.* bereichern; fruchtbar machen, befruchten (*the land*); bereichern (*the mind, etc.*); (adorn) ausschmücken, ausstatten. **—ment**, *s.* die Bereicherung; (adornment) die Verzierung.

Enrol, *v.a.* einschreiben, (in ein Verzeichnis) eintragen; (register) protokollieren; to — o. s., sich anwerben lassen. **—ment**, *s.* das Eintragen, die Einschreibung; (register) das Verzeichnis.

Ensample, *s. poet. for* Example.

Ensconce, *v.a.* verschanzen, verstecken; (cover) decken; to — o.s., sich verbergen; sich niederlassen, sich setzen (*coll.*).

Ensemble, *s.* das Ganze; das Zusammenspiel, Ensemble (*Theat.*); der Einklang (*Mus.*); die Gesammtwirkung.

Enshrine, *v.a.* einschließen, als Heiligtum verwahren; einhüllen.

Enshroud, *v.a.* umhüllen, einhüllen.

Ensign, *s.* (flag) die Fahne, Standarte; das Abzeichen, Kennzeichen; der Fähnrich (*Mil.*); naval —, die National-, Schiffs-flagge; the blue —, die (englische) Kriegsflagge. **—cy**, *s.* die Fähnrichsstelle. *Comp.* **—-bearer**, *s.* der Fähnrich, Fahnenträger. **—-halliards**, *pl.* der Flaggenfall (*Naut.*). **—-staff**, *s.* der Flaggenstock.

Ensilage, *s.* das Aufbewahren des Grünfutters in unterirdischen Gruben *or* Silos; das ungepreßte Grünfutter.

Enslave, *v.a.* zum Sklaven machen, unterjochen.

—**ment**, *s.* die Knechtung. —**r**, *s.* der Unterjocher, die Unterjocherin.
Ensnare, *v.a.* (in einer Schlinge) fangen, (in einem Netz) verstricken; verführen (*fig.*).
Ensu—e, *v.* I. *n.* (result) folgen, erfolgen, sich ergeben; (succeed, follow) nachfolgen, erfolgen. II. *a.* verfolgen (*B.*). —**ing**, *adj.*; —ing ages, die Nachwelt.
Ensure, *v.a.* sichern, befestigen; *see* Insure; to — success, um sich des Erfolges zu versichern.
Entablature, *s.* das Hauptgesims, Säulengebälk.
Entail, I. *s.* (inalienable possession) die unveräußerliche Erbschaft, das Fideikommiß; die bestimmte Erbfolge im Besitze von Gütern; to cut off the —, die bestimmte Erbfolge, das Fideikommiß umstoßen; in strict —, als unveräußerliches Erblehen. II. *v.a.* die Erbfolge bestimmen; — on, (einen) als Nacherben einsetzen (*of an estate, etc.*), vererben (diseases, Krankheiten) auf (*acc.*);—ed upon, zugefallen, angeerbt. —**ment**, *s.* die Übertragung als Erblehen.
Entangle, *v.a.* verwickeln (in); (catch) fangen; (embarrass) verlegen machen; to be —d in, verstrickt sein in (*dat. & acc.*). —**ment**, *s.* die Verwickelung, Verwirrung; die Liebschaft (*coll.*).
Enter, *v.* I. *a.* hineingehen, eintreten, gehen, ziehen, treten, kommen in; (penetrate) hineindringen, hineingehen; (begin) antreten, treten in; (join) treten in; (enrol, write down) einschreiben, eintragen; to — in a book, in ein Buch schreiben; to — an action, eine Klage einschreiben (*Law*); to — one's appearance, sich zu Protokoll nehmen lassen; to — the German army, in das deutsche Heer eintreten, deutscher Soldat werden; to — the University, die Hochschule beziehen, Student werden; to — goods (at the customhouse), Waren klarieren, (beim Zollamte) angeben; to — a harbour, in einen Hafen einlaufen; to — a horse (for a race), den Namen eines Pferdes (als Mitrenner) einschreiben lassen; I will never — your house again, ich will Ihr Haus nie wieder betreten; to — in the ledger, in das Hauptbuch eintragen; to — the lists, in die Schranken treten; it never —ed (into) my mind, es ist mir nie in den Sinn gekommen; to — one's name, sich einschreiben; to have one's name —ed, sich einschreiben lassen; to — a protest, Verwahrung einlegen, protestieren (gegen); to — a room, in ein Zimmer treten, ein Zimmer betreten; he has —ed my service, er ist in meine Dienste getreten; the river —s the sea, der Fluß ergießt sich ins Meer; to be —ed as a student, sich immatrikulieren lassen; he was —ed a student of . . ., er wurde in . . . immatrikuliert. II. *n.*; to — **into**, hinein-, herein-kommen, hineingehen, eintreten (in), (share) teilen (*one's feelings, etc.*), (join) Teil nehmen an (*dat.*), sich aufnehmen lassen in (*acc.*); to — into an arrangement, einen Vergleich eingehen; to — into the joke, auf den Scherz eingehen; to — into partnership, sich (mit einem) geschäftlich verbinden; to — into the spirit of an author, in den Geist eines Schriftstellers eindringen; to — into a p.'s views, auf jemandes Ideen eingehen; that does not — into my plan, das gehört nicht in meinen Plan, das paßt mir nicht in den Kram (*coll.*); to — **on, upon**, vornehmen, sich einlassen in *or* auf (eine S.), eintreten in (an office, ein Amt), antreten (one's duties, sein Amt), in Besitz nehmen, antreten (an estate, ein Gut), beginnen (a conversation, business, etc., ein Gespräch, Geschäft, 2c.); she has just —ed (upon) her 18th year, sie ist soeben in ihr 18tes Jahr getreten, sie ist eben 17 Jahr alt geworden. —**ing**, I. *p. see* Enter. II. *s.* der Eintritt; das Einreihen (*Weav.*); *in cpds.* Eingangs-, Eintritts-. —**prise**, —**tain**, etc. *see* Enterprise, Entertain, etc. *Comp.* —**ing-gouge**, *s.* das aufgeworfene Hohleisen. —**ing-ladder**, *s.* die Fallrangstreppe (*Naut.*). —**ing-port**, *s.* die Fallrangsluke.
Enter—ic, *adj.* die Eingeweide betreffend, Darm-; —ic fever, der Unterleibstyphus. —**itis**, *s.* die Darmentzündung. —**ocele**, *s.* der Darmbruch.
Enterpris—e, *s.* die Unternehmung, das Wagstück; die Unternehmung, Spekulation (*C. L.*); der Unternehmungsgeist. —**ing**, *adj.* unternehmend, unternehmungslustig; (daring) kühn.
Entertain, *v.a.* unterhalten; (treat as guest) gastlich bewirten, gastfreundlich aufnehmen; hegen (*an opinion, resentment*); annehmen (*a proposal*); (amuse) unterhalten, ergötzen; he —ed them at dinner, er gab ihnen ein Mittagsessen; he did not — the proposal for a moment, er verwarf den Vorschlag ohne Weiteres; to — thoughts of revenge, Rachegedanken Raum geben. —**er**, *s.* der Wirt, Gastherr. —**ing**, *adj.*, —**ingly**, *adv.* unterhaltend, ergötzlich. —**ment**, *s.* die Unterhaltung; (hospitality) die Bewirtung; (banquet) das Gastmahl; (amusement) die Unterhaltung, Belustigung, der Zeitvertreib; (admission) die Aufnahme, Zulassung; dramatic —ment, die Aufführung (eines Stückes), das Schauspiel; musical —ment, musikalische Gesellschaft.
Enthral, *v.a.* unterjochen; einnehmen, bezaubern (*fig.*).
Enthrone, *v.a.* auf den Thron setzen; to be —d, auf dem Throne sitzen; thronen (*fig.*). —**ment**, *s.* die Thronerhebung.
Enthuse, *v.n.* schwärmen, in Entzücken geraten (*coll.*).
Enthusias—m, *s.* die Begeisterung, Schwärmerei, der Enthusiasmus. —**t**, *s.* der Begeisterte, Schwärmer; der leidenschaftliche Verehrer (*in art, etc.*). —**tic**, *adj.*, —**tically**, *adv.* enthusiastisch, begeistert; (about, für) schwärmerisch (*in religion, etc.*); leidenschaftlich eingenommen (für).
Entic—e, *v.a.* (an)locken, anziehen, reizen; (lead astray) verführen; to —e away, (einem etwas) abspenstig machen. —**ement**, *s.* die Lockung; die Anreizung (*to evil*); die Verführung. —**er**, *s.* der Anlocker, Verlocker; der Verführer. —**ing**, *adj.*, —**ingly**, *adv.* verführerisch, reizend.
Entire, *adj.*, —**ly**, *adv.* ganz, unversehrt, unverletzt, ungeschmälert; (complete) völlig, vollständig; (unmixed) unvermischt, echt (*as beer*); ungeteilt (*B.*); unverschnitten (*of horses*); my — affection, meine ungeteilte Liebe. —**ness**, *s.* die Ganzheit, Vollständigkeit; die Ungeteiltheit. —**s**, *pl.* (envelopes, postcards, *etc.*) Ganzsachen. —**ty**, *s.* die Ganzheit; (whole) das Ganze.
Entitle, *v.a.* betiteln (*books & persons*); to — to, berechtigen zu, ein Recht geben auf (*acc.*); to be —d to, berechtigt sein zu, ein Anrecht haben auf.
Entity, *s.* die Wesenheit, das Wesen.
Entomb, *v.a.* begraben; to be —ed, (lebendig) begraben werden. —**ment**, *s.* das Begräbnis.
Entomolog—ical, *adj.*, —**ically**, *adv.* entomologisch, Insekten betreffend, Insekten-. —**ist**, *s.* der Insektenkenner. —**y**, *s.* die Insektenkunde.
Entozo—on (*pl.* —**a**), *s.* der Eingeweidewurm.
Entr'acte, *s.* der Zwischenakt, die Pause; das Zwischenspiel (*Theatre*).
Entrails, *pl.* die Eingeweide; das Innere (*fig.*).
Entrain, *v.* I. *a.* in einen Eisenbahnzug verladen, einschiffen, verschiffen (auf der Eisenbahn); the —ing of the troops, die Verschiffung der Truppen auf der Bahn. II. *n.* sich in einen Zug begeben (*of troops*); at eleven the King will — for London, um elf Uhr wird der König (mit der Bahn) nach London fahren.
[1]**Entrance**, *s.* (entry) der Eintritt, Einzug, das Eintreten; (door, etc.) der Eingang, die Tür; (the entering upon) der Anfang, Auftritt; (— upon office) Amtsantritt; (taking possession of) Antritt (eines Besitztums); (— hall) die Hausflur, Eintrittshalle; (passage) der Eingang; to give — to, (einem) den Eintritt gestatten; they have their exits and their —s, sie treten auf und gehen wieder ab. *Comp.* —-**duty**, *s.* der Einfuhrzoll, Eingangszoll. —-**examination**, *s.* die Aufnahmeprüfung. —-**exhibition**, —-**scholarship**, *s.*

das Stipendium beim Eintritt in eine Schule oder ein College; —-scholarship examination, die (Konkurrenz)prüfung zur Erlangung dieser Stipendien. —-money, s. das Eintrittsgeld.
²**Entrance**, *v.a.* entzücken, hinreißen.
Entrap, *v.a.* fangen, verstricken.
Entreat, *v.a.* ersuchen, ernstlich bitten (for, um); (treat) behandeln (*obs.*). —**ingly**, *adv.* flehendlich. —**y**, *s.* die ernstliche *or* dringende Bitte.
Entrée, *s.* der Zutritt; der Eintritt, das Auftreten (*into the world, etc.*); (course) das Mittelgericht, Zwischengericht, die Vorspeise.
Entremets, *s.* die Zwischenschüssel, Zwischenspeise.
Entrench, *v.* I. *a.* einschneiden, eingraben (*obs.*); mit Graben versehen (*Mil.*). II. *n.* (— upon) sich (*dat.*) etwas aneignen, Grenzen überschreiten. —**ment**, *s.* die Verschanzung.
Entrust, *v.a.* anvertrauen (s.th. to a p., einem eine S.), betrauen (a p. with s.th., einen mit einer S.); I — it to you, ich vertraue es dir an.
Entry, *s.* der Eingang (*to a house, etc.*); der Eingang, Eintritt (*fig.*), der feierliche Einzug; die Besitznahme, der Antritt (upon an estate, eines Gutes); das Eintragen, Einschreiben (in a book, in ein Buch); (note) das Eingetragene; der Posten (*C. L.*); die Einfuhr (*of goods*); die Zoll-angabe, -deklaration (*at the custom house*); die Nennung, Anmeldung (*for games*); to make one's —, seinen Einzug halten; to make an — of a th., eine Sache buchen, (einen Posten in die Handelsbücher) eintragen; bookkeeping by double —, die doppelte Buchführung; bill of entries, das Eingangszollverzeichnis.
Entwine, *v.* I. *a.* herumwickeln, verflechten. II. *n.* sich um eine S. winden; umwunden, umschlungen *or* verflochten werden.
Entwist, *v.a.* verflechten.
Enumerat—e, *v.a.* aufzählen. —**ion**, *s.* die Aufzählung.
Enunciat—e, *v.a.* aussagen; (utter) hervorbringen; (pronounce) aussprechen. —**ion**, *s.* das Aussprechen; die Aussage; die Aussprache; der Vortrag (*Rhet.*); die Aufstellung (*of a proposition*). —**ory**, *adj.* aussagend, lautend.
Envelop, *v.a.* einwickeln, einhüllen; (surround) umhüllen, umgeben. —**e**, *s.* der Briefumschlag; der Vorwall (*Fort.*); die Umhüllungs-Kurve (*Math.*). —**ment**, *s.* die Einwickelung, Einhüllung.
Envenom, *v.a.* vergiften; vergiften, erbittern (*fig.*).
Env—iable, *adj.* beneidenswert. —**ier**, *s.* der Neider. —**ious**, *adj.*, —**iously**, *adv.* neidisch (of a p., auf einen); mißgünstig; the —ious, die Mißgünstigen, Neider; to be —ious of a p. because of . . ., einen um . . . beneiden. —**iousness**, *s.* die Mißgunst. —**y**, I. *s.* der Neid, die Mißgunst; (malice) die Bosheit, der Haß. II. *v.a.* (be)neiden; (grudge) (einem etwas) mißgönnen; better be —ied than pitied, besser beneidet als bemitleidet.
Environ, *v.a.* umgeben, umringen; (besiege) belagern; —ed by, umgeben von. —**ment**, *s.* die Umschließung; (surroundings) die Umgebung(en). —**s**, *pl.* die Umgegend, die Umgebung(en); London and its —s, London und seine Umgebung.
Envisage, *v.a.* (einer Gefahr, *etc.*) ins Auge blicken; (etwas) ins Auge fassen, betrachten, in Betracht ziehen; anschauen (*fig.*).
Envoy, *s.* der Gesandte; der Bevollmächtigte.
Enwrap, *v.a.* einwickeln.
Enzone, *v.a.* einschließen, umgeben.
Eocene, *adj.* das Eozän betreffend.
Epact, *s.* die Epakte (*Astr.*).
Epaule, *s.* die Schulter (einer Bastei). —**ment**, *s.* die Schulterwehr (*Fort.*). —**tte**, *s.* das Achselband, die Achselschnur, Achseltroddel.
Epenthe—sis, *s.* die Einschaltung *or* Einschiebung eines Buchstabens, Epenthese (*Gram.*). —**tic**, *adj.* eingeschaltet, eingeschoben.
Epergne, *s.* der Tafelaufsatz.
Ephemer—a, *s.* die Eintagsfliege; eintägiges Fieber (*obs.*). —**al**, *adj.* eintägig; (short-lived) schnell vorübergehend. —**is**, *s.* (*pl.* —ides) (diary) das Tagebuch; (almanac) astronomische Tabelle über die täglichen Bewegungen der Planeten (*Astr.*); —ides, Tagesblätter, Zeitungen; das Tagebuch. —**ist**, *s.* der Tagebuchführer; der Astronom, Planetenberechner. —**on**, *s.* die Eintagsfliege.
Ephod, *s.* der Leibrock (des Hohenpriesters).
Epic, I. *adj.* episch. II. *s.* (— poem) das Heldengedicht, das Epos; heroic —, das (volkstümliche) Heldengedicht; national —, das Volksepos.
Epi—carp, *s.* die Fruchtdecke. —**cene**, *adj.* beidgeschlechtig (*Gram.*). —**cycle**, *s.* der Epizykel, Nebenkreis. —**cycloid**, *s.* die Epizykloide, Radlinie (*Geom.*). —**demic**, I. *adj.* epidemisch, in einem Lande herrschend, seuchenartig. II. *s.* die epidemische Krankheit, herrschende ansteckende Krankheit, Seuche, Epidemie. —**dermis**, *s.* die Oberhaut. —**gastric**, *adj.* epigastrisch, Bauch-. —**glottis**, *s.* der Kehldeckel. —**gram**, *s.* das Sinngedicht, Epigramm; das Spottgedicht. —**grammatic**, *adj.* epigrammatisch, nach Art eines Epigramms, kurz und treffend. —**grammatist**, *s.* der Epigrammatiker, Verfasser von Sinngedichten. —**graph**, *s.* die Überschrift; (motto) das Motto, der Denkspruch. —**graphist**, *s.* der Inschriftenkundige. —**lepsy**, *s.* die Fallsucht. —**leptic**, I. *adj.* fallsüchtig. II. *s.* der Fallsüchtige. —**logue**, *s.* die Schlußrede, der Epilog. —**phany**, *s.* das Drei-Königsfest. —**phora**, *s.* das Tränenauge. —**sode**, *s.* die Abschweifung vom Hauptgegenstande, die Neben-, Zwischenhandlung; (incident) der Zwischenfall, Vorfall. —**sodic(al)**, *adj.* eingeschaltet, dazwischenkommend, episodisch. —**stle**, *see* Epist—. —**style**, *s.* der Architrav (*Arch.*). —**taph**, *s.* die Grabschrift. —**thalamium**, *s.* das Hochzeitsgedicht. —**therm**, *s.* der nasse Umschlag (*Med.*). —**thet**, *s.* (adjective) das (schmückende) Beiwort, der Beiname; (designation) die Benennung, der Titel. —**thetic**, *adj.* epithetisch. —**tome**, *s.* der kurze Auszug, Abriß. —**tomist**, *s.* der Verfasser eines Auszugs. —**tomize**, *v.a.* einen Auszug machen (aus einem Buche), (ein Buch) ausziehen; (abridge) abkürzen. —**tomizer**, *see* —tomist.
Epicur—e, *s.* der Feinschmecker, das Leckermaul. —**ean**, I. *adj.* epikureisch; schwelgerisch, sinnlich. II. *s.* der Epikuräer, der Lebemann. —**eanism**, *s.* die Lehre des Epikur, der Epikureismus. —**ism**, *s.* der Hang zum Wohlleben.
Episcopa—cy, *s.* die bischöfliche Verfassung. —**l**, *adj.* bischöflich. —**lian**, I. *adj.* bischöflich; —lian church, die Episkopal-Kirche. II. *s.* der Anhänger der bischöflichen Kirche. —**lianism**, *s.* das Episkopalsystem. —**te**, *s.* die Bischofswürde, das Episkopat; die Gesammtheit der Bischöfe.
Epist—le, *s.* das Sendschreiben, der Brief; langweiliger, weitschweifiger Brief; die Epistel (*Poet.*); the gospels and the —les, die Evangelien und die Episteln; the —le to the Romans, der Römerbrief. —**olary**, *adj.* brieflich; Brief-; —olary intercourse, der Briefwechsel.
Epoch, *s.* die Epoche.
Epode, *s.* die Epode, der Abgesang.
Eponym, *s.* das bezeichnende Beiwort.
Epo—pee, *s.* das Heldengedicht, die Epopöe. —**s**, *s.* das Heldengedicht, Epos.
Epsom-salts, *pl.* das (Epsomer) Bittersalz.
Equa—bility, *s.* die Gleichheit, Gleichförmigkeit; der Gleichmut (*of temper, etc.*). —**ble**, *adj.*, —**bly**, *adv.* gleichförmig, gleich. —**bleness**, *s.* die Gleichförmigkeit. —**l**, I. *adj.*, —**lly**, *adv.* gleich; (uniform) gleichmäßig; (fit) gewachsen, fähig, imstande; death makes all men —l, der Tod macht alle Menschen gleich; he was not —l to the task, er war der Aufgabe nicht gewachsen; —lly good, ebenso gut, gleich gut; —l to the

demand, der Nachfrage angemessen (*C. L.*). II. *s.* der Gleiche; he has not his —l, er hat seines-gleichen nicht; between —ls, unter Gleichstehenden. III. *v.n.* gleichen, gleich machen; (einem) gleich kommen, gleichen. **—lity**, *s.* die Gleichheit; sign of —lity, das Gleichheitszeichen (*Math.*). **—lization**, *s.* die Gleichmachung, Gleichstellung. **—lize**, *v.a.* gleichmachen. **—lness**, *s.* die Gleichheit, Gleichmäßigkeit. **—nimity**, *s.* der Gleichmut. **—te**, *v.a.* gleichmachen, ausgleichen; auf ein Durchschnittsmaß bringen. **—tion**, *s.* die Gleichung. **—tor**, *see* Equator.

Equator, *s.* der Äquator, Gleicher; die Linie (*Naut.*). **—ial**, I. *adj.* äquatorial. II. *s.* das Äquatorial.

Eque—rry, *s.* der Stallmeister. **—strian**, I. *adj.* die Reitkunst betreffend; reitend, beritten; —strian exercise, die Reitübung, der Spazierritt; —strian order, der Ritterstand (*Rom. Hist.*); —strian statue, das Reiterstandbild. II. *s.* der Reiter; (—strian performer) der Kunstreiter.

Equi—angular, *adj.* gleichwinkelig. **—distant**, *adj.* gleichweit entfernt. **—lateral**, I. *adj.* gleichseitig. II. *s.* die gleichseitige Figur. **—librium**, *s.* das Gleichgewicht; to be in —librium, sich (*dat.*) *or* einander das Gleichgewicht halten. **—noctial**, I. *adj.* äquinoktial, zur Zeit der Tag- und Nachtgleiche eintretend; —noctial gales, Äquinoktialstürme. II. *s.* die Äquinoktiallinie, der Himmels-Äquator. **—nox**, *s.* die Tag- und Nachtgleiche; vernal —nox, die Frühlings-Tag- und Nacht-gleiche. **—poise**, *s.* das Gleichgewicht. **—table**, etc., *see* Equit—. **—valence**, *s.* die Gleichwertigkeit. **—valent**, I. *adj.* gleichwertig, entsprechend; gleichbedeutend; to be —valent to, gleichen Wert haben mit, ebensoviel gelten wie; so viel heißen wie. II. *s.* der gleiche Wert, gleiche Betrag, Gleichwert, Gegenwert, der Wert-Ersatz; das Äquivalent (*Chem.*, *Mech.*). **—vocal**, *adj.*, **—vocally**, *adv.* doppelsinnig; (ambiguous) zweideutig, unbestimmt; —vocal generation, die Urzeugung, Selbstentstehung von Organismen aus unorganischen Stoffen (*Physiol.*). **—vocalness**, *s.* die Zweideutigkeit. **—vocate**, *v.a.* zweideutig reden; (prevaricate) (in der Rede) Ausflüchte gebrauchen, um die Wahrheit herumgehen. **—vocation**, *s.* die Zweideutigkeit; die Ausflucht. **—vocator**, *s.* einer der zweideutig redet, Wortverdreher.

Equi—ne, *adj.* pferdeartig, Pferde-. **—tation**, *s.* das Reiten; die Reitkunst.

Equip, *v.a.* ausrüsten (*also Mil.*, *Naut.*), ausstatten; mit dem Nötigen versehen; kleiden, ausstaffieren; well —ped, mit allem Nötigen reichlich versehen. **—age**, *s.* die Equipage. **—ment**, *s.* die Ausrüstung (*also Mil.*); der Betriebsbedarf (*Railw.*).

Equiset—iform, *adj.* schachtelhalmförmig. **—um**, *s.* der Schachtelhalm (*Bot.*).

Equit—able, *adj.*, **—ably**, *adv.* (fair) billig; (impartial) unparteiisch; (just) gerecht. **—ableness**, *s.* die Billigkeit; die Unparteilichkeit. **—y**, *s.* die Billigkeit; die Gerechtigkeit; (—able claim) die billige Forderung; die billige Gesetzesauslegung, das Billigkeitsrecht (*Law*); court of —y, das Billigkeitsgericht.

Era, *s.* die Ära; four years before the Christian —, vier Jahre vor Christi Geburt *or* vor Christo; in the year 350 of the Christian —, im Jahre 350 nach Christo, im Jahre des Herrn 350.

Eradica—ble, *adj.* ausrottbar; not —ble, nicht auszurotten. **—te**, *v.a.* entwurzeln, ausrotten. **—tion**, *s.* die Entwurzelung, Ausrottung.

Eras—able, *adj.* vertilgbar, auslöschlich. **—e**, *v.a.* auskratzen, auslöschen, ausstreichen; to —e from the memory, aus dem Gedächtnisse vertilgen. **—ement**, *s.* das Auskratzen. **—er**, *s.* das Radiermesser; (ink- —er) das Radiergummi. **—ure**, *s.* das Auskratzen; die ausgekratzte Stelle, das ausgekratzte Wort.

Ere, I. *conj.* ehe, bevor. II. *prep.* vor; — this, schon vorher; — long, in kurzem, bald; — now, vor diesem, vormals.

Erect, I. *adj.* aufrecht, aufgerichtet, gerade. II. *v.a.* aufrichten; erbauen, errichten (*a monument, etc.*); (found) (be)gründen; (set up) aufstellen; (exalt) erheben. **—er**, *s.* der Errichtende, Erbauer. **—ile**, *adj.* aufrichtbar (*Anat.*). **—ion**, *s.* das Aufrichten; die Errichtung; die Gründung; (building) der Bau, das Gebäude; die Erektion (*Med.*). **—ly**, *adv.* in aufrechter Stellung, aufrecht. **—ness**, *s.* die Geradheit, aufrechte Haltung. **—or**, *s.* der Aufrichtemuskel.

Eremite, *s.* der Einsiedler, Eremit.

Ergo, *adv. & conj.* also, folglich, daher.

Ergot, *s.* der Brand, das Mutterkorn (*Agr.*); die Flußgalle (*Vet.*). **—ism**, *s.* das Mutterkorn.

Eric, *s.* das Wergeld, die Buße für Totschlag.

Ermine, I. *s.* das Hermelin (*Zool.*); der Hermelinpelz; das Richteramt, die Richterwürde (*fig.*). II. *attrib.*; — tips, die Hermelinschwänze.

Erne, *s.* der Seeadler, Fischgeier.

Ero—de, *v.a.* zerfressen, wegfressen. **—se**, *adj.* ausgebissen, unregelmäßig gezackt (*Bot. Zool.*). **—sion**, *s.* die Zerfressung, Erosion; der Krebs (*Med.*).

Erotic, I. *adj.* erotisch, die Liebe betreffend; sinnlich. II. *s.* das erotische Gedicht.

Err, *v.n.* herumirren; sich irren (*fig.*); sich verirren; (— from) abweichen (*fig.*); umherwandern, umherziehen (*obs.*). **—ant**, *adj.* irrend; abweichend (from, von); knight —ant, der fahrende Ritter. **—antry**, *s.* das Umherschweifen; die Irrfahrt (*of a knight*); knight —antry, fahrendes Rittertum. **—ata**, *pl. see* —atum; das Druckfehlerverzeichnis. **—atic**, *adj.*, **—atically**, *adv.* wandernd; regellos, wandelbar, unordentlich; —atic blocks, (**—atics**, *pl.*) erratische Blöcke, Findlinge (*Geol.*). **—atum**, *s.* der Druckfehler. **—oneous**, *adj.*, **—oneously**, *adv.* irrig, unrichtig. **—or**, *s.* der Irrtum, Fehler, Schnitzer; Fehldruck; die Abweichung (*of the compass*); der Formfehler (*Law*); —or of policy, politischer Fehler; writ of —or, Befehl zur Revision eines Urteils; —ors excepted, Irrtümer vorbehalten (*C. L.*).

Errand, *s.* die Botschaft, der Auftrag; to go —s, Botschaften ausrichten, Aufträge ausführen. *Comp.* **—boy**, *s.* der Laufbursche, Ausläufer.

Erst, *adv.* ehedem, einst, bisher; (at first) zuerst (*obs.*).

Eructat—e, *v.n.* rülpsen, aufstoßen. **—ion**, *s.* das Aufstoßen, der Rülps.

Erudit—e, *adj.*, **—ely**, *adv.* gelehrt; kenntnisreich. **—ion**, *s.* die Gelehrsamkeit.

Erupti—on, *s.* der Ausbruch (*of lava, etc.*); der Ausfall (*of hostile troops*) (*obs.*); der Ausschlag (*Med.*). **—ve**, *adj.* ausbrechend; mit Ausschlag begleitet (*Med.*).

Eryngo, *s.* die Mannstreu (*Bot.*).

Erysipela—s, *s.* die Rose, der Rotlauf (*Med.*). **—tous**, *adj.* rosenartig, rotlaufartig.

Escalade, I. *s.* die Ersteigung der Festungswälle mit Sturmleitern, Erstürmung; by —, mit Sturmleitern, im Sturm. II. *v.a.* mit Sturmleitern ersteigen, erstürmen.

Escallop, *see* Scallop.

Escap—ade, *s.* der mutwillige Streich, Jugendstreich. **—e**, I. *v.a.* entschlüpfen, entwischen, entkommen, entgehen; (evade) umgehen; it has —ed my recollection, es ist mir entfallen; it —ed my notice, ich bemerkte es nicht, ich übersah es; the word —ed me, das Wort entging mir; he narrowly —ed being taken prisoner, er entging mit genauer Not der Gefangenschaft. II. *v.n.* entkommen, entrinnen; to —e from one's creditors, seinen Gläubigern entwischen. III. *s.* das Entrinnen, die Flucht; das Entkommen (*of a danger, etc.*); der Anlauf, Ablauf (*of a column*);

die Entweichung (*of gas*); —e of steam, die Dampfentweichung; fire —e, die Rettungsleiter; to have a narrow —e, mit genauer Not davonkommen; they had a narrow —e from drowning, sie wären ums Haar ertrunken; to make one's —e, sich aus dem Staube machen; to make good one's —e, glücklich davonkommen. **—ement**, *s.* die Hemmung (*Horol.*). *Comp.* **—e-pipe**, *s.* das Abflußrohr. **—e-valve**, *s.* das Auslaßventil.

Escarp, I. *v.a.* böschen, abdachen. II. *s.* die Böschung, Abdachung. **—ment**, *s.* die steile Böschung, Abdachung.

Eschalot, *s.* die Schalotte, kleine Zwiebel.

Eschar, *s.* der Grind, Schorf, die Kruste.

Eschatology, *s.* die Lehre von den letzten Dingen (des Menschen), Eschatologie (*Theol.*).

Escheat, I. *s.* der Heimfall (an den Lehnsherrn oder an den Staat); (—ed lands) das heimgefallene Gut. II. *v.n.* (an)heimfallen.

Eschew, *v.a.* vermeiden, scheuen, unterlassen.

Escort, I. *s.* die Begleitung (*also Mil.*), das Geleit, die Begleitmannschaft, Bedeckung, Bedeckungsmannschaft, Eskorte (*also Mil., Naut.*). II. *v.a.* geleiten, bedecken, decken, eskortieren.

Escritoire, *s.* das Schreibpult.

Esculapian, *adj.* ärztlich.

Esculent, I. *adj.* eßbar. II. *s.* das Lebensmittel.

Escutcheon, *s.* der *and* das Wappenschild; a blot on a p.'s —, ein Flecken auf jemandes Ruf.

Esoteric, *adj.* esoterisch, geheim.

Espalier, *s.* das Spalier.

Especial, *adj.* vorzüglich, besonder. **—ly**, *adv.* (ganz) besonders, hauptsächlich.

Espial, *s.* das Spähen, Spionieren, Auskundschaften.

Espionage, *s.* das Spionieren.

Esplanade, *s.* die Esplanade (*also Fort.*); der Grasplatz (*Hort.*).

Espous—al, *s.* die Verlobung (*obs.*); die Annahme, Verteidigung (*of a cause, etc.*). **—als**, *pl.* die Verlobung; (marriage) die Vermählung. **—e**, *v.a.* verloben (to, mit); vermählen, verheiraten (to, an (*acc.*)); sich einer S. annehmen, eintreten für eine S.; he —ed his friend's quarrel, er nahm sich des Streites seines Freundes an.

Esprit, *s.* der Geist, Witz; — de corps, der Korpsgeist, das Gefühl der Zusammengehörigkeit.

Espy, *v.a.* erspähen, entdecken, erblicken.

Esquire, *s.* der Schildknappe; der Ritter (einer Dame); der Landedelmann, Gutsbesitzer, Esquire; (*as a general title given to gentlemen on letters abbr. to* Esq(re). =) Wohlgeboren, Hochwohlgeboren; J. C. Smith, —, Herrn J. C. Smith, Hochwohlgeboren.

Essay, I. *v.a.* versuchen, probieren; *see* Assay. II. *s.* der Versuch; der Aufsatz, die kurze literarische Abhandlung; (trial) die Probe; (postage stamp) der Probedruck; — on the writings of Milton, Aufsatz über die Schriften Miltons. **—ist**, *s.* der Essayist, Feuilletonist, Verfasser von Aufsätzen, litterarischen Abhandlungen.

Essen—ce, *s.* das Wesen, Sein (*obs*); der Geist, das Wesen einer S.; (—tial principle) die Substanz, der wesentliche Teil; (extract) das Extrakt; (perfume) die (wohlriechende) Essenz, das Parfüm. **—tial**, I. *adj.*, **—tially**, *adv.* wesentlich; rein (*Chem.*); (important) wichtig, durchaus notwendig; —tial oils, ätherische Öle; —tial salts, wesentliche Pflanzensalze. II. *s.* das Wesentliche; das Wichtigste, die Hauptsache. **—tiality**, **—tialness**, *s.* die Wesentlichkeit.

Establish, *v.a.* festsetzen; (found) errichten, gründen; (institute) verordnen, einrichten; aufrichten (*a covenant, B.*); verordnen, festsetzen (*laws, rules, etc.*); (confirm) bestätigen; anlegen (*a colony*); unterbringen, versorgen (*one's children, etc.*); anlegen (*a battery*); etablieren (*C.L.*); to — o.s., sich (wohnhaft) niederlassen; to — the church, die Kirche zur Staatskirche machen; —ed church, die Staatskirche; —ed laws, bestehende Gesetze; to — a connection, eine Verbindung herstellen. **—er**, *s.* der Stifter; der Verordner. **—ment**, *s.* die Festsetzung, Gründung, Errichtung; die Bestätigung; die Verordnung; die Einrichtung; (residence) der Wohnsitz; (servants, *etc.*) der Haushalt; (institution) die Anstalt; das Etablissement (*C.L.*); (military —ment) das stehende Heer, die Kriegsmacht; (—ed religion) die Staatsreligion; peace (war) —ment, Friedensfuß, (Kriegsfuß); to keep up a large —ment, ein großes Haus machen; to break up one's —ment, seinen Haushalt auflösen.

Estacade, *s.* die Verpfählung (*Mil.*).

Estafette, *s.* der außerordentliche reitende Eilbote.

Estate, *s.* (state) der Zustand; (position) der Rang, Stand; (fortune) das Besitztum; (property) das Gut, die Güter; die (Konkurs-)Masse; das Besitzrecht an einem Gut; der Nachlaß; —s of inheritance, die Erbgüter; — for life, das Besitzrecht auf Lebenszeit; freehold —s, die Freisassenrechte; —s for a term of years, Besitzrechte auf eine gewisse Anzahl von Jahren; man's —, das männliche Alter; to come to man's —, mannbar werden; —s of the realm, Reichsstände; the three —s of the realm, die drei Stände des (britischen) Reiches (= die hohe Geistlichkeit, der Adel, die Gemeinen); the fourth —, der vierte Stand, die Arbeiter; personal —, bewegliche Habe, Mobilien; real —, Immobilien; residuary —, Nachlaß eines Verstorbenen nach Abzug der Legate. *Comp.* **—agent**, *s.* Landverkäufer, Agent für Grundstücke.

Esteem, I. *v.a.* schätzen, hochschätzen, achten; (deem) erachten, dafür halten. II. *s.* die Hochachtung, Hochschätzung, Achtung; to be in great — with, in großem Ansehen stehen bei.

Estima—ble, *adj.* (that can be —ted) schätzbar, taxierbar; (valuable) schätzbar, kostbar, wertvoll; (worthy of esteem) wertvoll, achtungswert, schätzbar. **—bleness**, *s.* die Schätzbarkeit. **—te**, I. *v.a.* schätzen, würdigen; (reckon) schätzen, taxieren, rechnen; to —te at its true value, nach seinem wahren Werte schätzen, richtig einschätzen. II. *s.* die Schätzung; der (Vor)anschlag, Überschlag; der Bauanschlag (*Build.*); rough —te, der ungefähre Überschlag, der Überschlag in Bausch und Bogen. **—tion**, *s.* die Schätzung; (computation) die Schätzung, Berechnung; (opinion) die Meinung; (esteem) die Achtung. **—tor**, *s.* der Schätzer, Taxator.

Estival, *adj.* sommerlich, Sommer-.

Estrade, *s.* erhöhter Tritt, die Estrade (*Build.*).

Estrange, *v.a.* entfremden (from a p., einem); abwenden, abwendig machen; zurückziehen (von); to — the affections of a p., sich (*dat.*) einen abgeneigt machen. **—ment**, *s.* die Entfremdung.

Estuary, *s.* der Meeresarm; die (in einen Meeresarm übergehende, der Ebbe und Flut unterliegende) Flußmündung.

Et cetera = und so weiter, und so fort.

Etch, *v.a.* ätzen, radieren; mit der Feder (nach der Ätzmanier) zeichnen, radieren. **—er**, *s.* der Radierer, Ätzer; der Zeichner. **—ing**, *s.* das Ätzen; (pen & ink drawing) die Radierung; (—ed impression) der Ätzdruck. *Comp.* **—ing-ground**, *s.* der Ätzgrund. **—ing-needle**, *s.* die Radiernadel. **—ing-point**, *s.* die Spitze der Radiernadel.

Etern—al, I. *adj.*, **—ally**, *adv.* ewig; (perpetual) immerwährend; (unchangeable) unveränderlich. II. *s.* das Ewige; the —al, der Ewige. **—alize**, *v.a.* verewigen. **—ity**, *s.* die Ewigkeit. **—ize**, *v.a.* ewig machen, unendlich ausdehnen; verewigen, unsterblich machen.

Etheling, *s.* der Edeling.

Ether, *s.* der Äther; acetic —, Essigäther; nitric —, Salpeteräther. **—eal**, *adj.*, **—eally**, *adv.* ätherisch (*also fig.*); himmlisch, zart (*fig.*). —

ialize, *v.a.* ätherisch machen, verflüchtigen; vergeistigen.
Ethic—al, *adj.*, **—ally**, *adv.* sittlich, moralisch, ethisch. **—s**, *s.* die Sittenlehre, Ethik, Moralphilosophie.
Ethmoid, *adj.*; — bone, das Siebbein.
Ethn—ic(al), *adj.* heidnisch. **—ographer**, **—ologist**, *s.* der Völkerbeschreiber, Völkerkundige. **—ographic**, **—ological**, *adj.*, **—ologically**, *adv.* ethnographisch, die Völkerkunde betreffend. **—ography**, *s.* die Völkerbeschreibung, Völkerkunde. **—ology**, *s.* die Völkerkunde.
Ethyl, *s.* das Äthyl.
Etiolat—e, *v.* I. *a.* (durch Ausschließen des Lichts) weiß machen, bleichen. II. *n.* dünn und farblos aufschießen. **—ion**, *s.* das Entfärben; die Bleichsucht (*Hort.*).
Etiquette, *s.* gesellschaftliche Umgangsformen, die (Hof-)Sitte, Etikette.
Etui, *s.* der Behälter, das Etui, Futteral.
Etymo—logical, *adj.*, **—logically**, *adv.* etymologisch, die Wortableitung betreffend. **—logist**, *s.* der Etymolog(e). **—logy**, *s.* die Wortableitung, Etymologie, Lehre vom Ursprung der Wörter. **—n**, *s.* das Stammwort.
Eu—calyptus, *s.* der Eukalyptus. **—charist**, *s.* das heilige Abendmahl. **—charistic**, *adj.* Abendmahls-. **—diometer**, *s.* der Eudiometer, Luftgütemesser. **—logist**, *s.* der Lobredner. **—logistic**, *adj.*, **—logistically**, *adv.* lobend, hochpreisend, lobrednerisch. **—logium**, *s.*, **—logy**, *s.* die Lobrede; (praise) das Lob. **—logize**, *v.s.* loben, preisen. **—pepsia**, **—pepsy**, *s.* die gute *or* leichte Verdauung. **—peptic**, *adj.* leicht verdaulich; (of good digestion) gut verdauend. **—phemism**, *s.* der Milderungsausdruck, das Beschönigungswort. **—phemistic**, *adj.* mildernd; beschönigend. **—phonious**, *adj.*, **—phoniously**, *adv.* wohlklingend, wohllautend. **—phony**, *s.* der Wohlklang, Wohllaut. **—phuism**, *s.* der Euphuismus, gezierte, überladene Ausdrucksweise, der Schwulst. **—phuist**, *s.* gezierter Redner. **—phuistic**, *adj.* geziert, gespreizt. **—thanasia**, *s.* sanfter Tod.
Euchre, **Eucre**, *s.* ein Kartenspiel.
Eunuch, *s.* der Verschnittene, Entmannte, Eunuch.
Evacuat—e, *v.a.* (empty) leeren, ausleeren; abführen (*Med.*); räumen (*Mil.*). **—ion**, *s.* die Ausleerung; die Abführung; die Räumung.
Evade, *v.a.* (geschickt) ausweichen (einer S.); entwischen, entrinnen (einem).
Evanesce, *v.n.* dahinschwinden, vergehen. **—nce**, *s.* das (Dahin-)Schwinden. **—nt**, *adj.*, **—ntly**, *adv.* (ver)schwindend; the joys of life are —nt, die Freuden des Lebens schwinden schnell dahin.
Evangel, *s.* das Evangelium. **—ic(al)**, *adj.*, **—ically**, *adv.* evangelisch; the —ical party, die Evangelisch-Gesinnten in der Anglikanischen Kirche. **—icalism**, *s.* die Anhänglichkeit an die evangelischen Lehren. **—ist**, *s.* der Evangelist; der Prediger des Evangeliums. **—ization**, *s.* der Unterricht in dem Evangelium; die Bekehrung zur christlichen Religion. **—ize**, *v.a.* in dem Evangelium unterrichten; (convert) zur christlichen Religion bekehren.
Evaporable, *adj.* verdunstbar, verdampfbar.
Evaporat—e, *v.* I. *n.* verdunsten, verdampfen (*also fig.*). II. *a.* abdampfen lassen. **—ion**, *s.* die Ausdünstung; das Abdampfen (*Chem.*). **—ive**, *adj.* Dampf-; —ive power, das Verdampfungsvermögen. **—or**, *s.* der Verdampfapparat. *Comp.* **—ing-vessel**, *s.* das Abdampfungsgefäß.
Evasi—on, *s.* die Ausflucht, Ausrede. **—ve**, *adj.*, **—vely**, *adv.* ausweichend. **—veness**, *s.* das Ausweichende, das ausweichende Benehmen.
Eve, *s.* der Abend; (— of a festival) der Vorabend; Christmas —, der Weihnachtsabend, heilige Abend, Heiligabend; on the — of, am Vorabend von (*or gen.*), nahe an (*dat.*). **—n**, *see* —ning I. **—ning**, I. *s.* der Abend; one fine —ning, eines schönen Abends. II. *adj.* Abend-; —ning dress, der Gesellschaftsanzug (*for gentlemen*), Frackanzug; —ning party, die Abendgesellschaft; —ning prayer, das Abendgebet; der Abendgottesdienst, Nachmittagsgottesdienst; —ning star, der Abendstern. *Comp.* **—n-song**, *s.* der Abendgesang; der Nachmittagsgottesdienst, die Vesper. **—ntide**, *s.* die Abendzeit.
Even, I. *adj.*, **—ly**, *adv.* eben, gerade, gleich; (uniform) gleich-mäßig, -förmig; (calm) gelassen, ruhig; (fair) unparteiisch; (balanced) quitt, rein, richtig; (smooth) glatt; gleich, flach (*Surv.*, *Build.*); gerade (*as a number*); to make — with the ground, dem Boden gleich machen; to be — with a p., einem nichts schuldig bleiben, mit einem quitt sein; to go an — gallop, gleichförmig galoppieren; — number, gerade Zahl; — sum, runde Summe; — or odd, gerade oder ungerade. II. *adv.* (just) gerade, eben; nämlich (*B.*); selbst, sogar, ja auch; I knew the facts, — when I wrote to you, ich kannte die Tatsachen, selbst als ich an Sie schrieb; these discoveries were new — to the learned, diese Entdeckungen waren selbst den Gelehrten neu; whither the tribes go up, — the tribes of the Lord, da die Stämme hinauf gehen, nämlich die Stämme des Herrn (*B.*); not —, nicht einmal; — now, noch eben, eben jetzt; — though, wenn auch, selbst wenn. III. *v.a.* gleich machen; (put on a level) gleich stellen (*coll.*). **—ness**, *s.* die Ebenheit, Geradheit, Gleichheit; die Ebenmäßigkeit, Gleichförmigkeit; die Unparteilichkeit; —ness of temper, die Gleichmütigkeit, der Gleichmut. *Comp.* **—-Christian**, *s.* der Mitchrist, der christliche Bruder. **—-handed**, *adj.*; —-handed justice, die unparteiische Gerechtigkeit. **—-tempered**, *adj.* gleichmütig, gelassen.
Event, *s.* (incident), die Begebenheit, das Ereignis, Vorkommnis, der Vorfall; (result) der Ausgang, Erfolg; einzelner Teil eines Festprogramms; das einzelne Preisspiel (*at tennis tournaments*); athletic —s, Spiel- und Turn-Aufführungen; table of —s, das Festprogramm (*e.g. of a school speech-day*); at all —s, auf alle Fälle, jedenfalls. **—ful**, *adj.* ereignisvoll. **—ual**, *adj.* (resultant) erfolgend; (final) schließlich, endlich; (contingent) etwaig, möglich. **—ually**, *adv.* am Ende. **—uate**, *v.n.* auslaufen, endigen.
Ever, *adv.* (always) immer; (continually) stets, beständig; (at any time) je, jemals, zu irgend einer Zeit; (in any degree) noch, irgend; did you — see the like? hast du je so etwas gesehen? let him be — so rich, er mag noch so reich sein; as soon as — he had done, sobald er es irgend fertig hatte; as soon as — I can, sobald ich nur irgend kann; — since, von der Zeit an; scarcely —, fast nie; — and anon, von Zeit zu Zeit; for — (and —), immer und ewig; (continually) immerfort; for — and a day, immer und ewig; — after, seit der Zeit, von da an; or —, ehe; — so long, Jahr und Tag; liberty for —, es lebe die Freiheit; I would not offend him for — so much, ich möchte ihn um alles in der Welt nicht beleidigen. **—y**, *adj.* jed(-er, -e, -es); alle; — one, ein jeder, jeder(mann); —y one of them, alle insgesamt, die ganze Sippschaft; —y one present, jeder Anwesende, alle Anwesenden; —y other day, jeden zweiten Tag, einen Tag um den andern; —y twenty years, alle zwanzig Jahre; on —y side, von allen Seiten; my —y thought, jeder meiner Gedanken; —y whit, gänzlich, ganz und gar. *Comp.* **—green**, I. *s.* das Immergrün. II. *adj.* immergrün. **—lasting**, *adj.*, **—lastingly**, *adv.* immerdauernd, immerwährend, ewig; (continual) unaufhörlich (*coll.*). **—-living**, *adj.* ewig, unsterblich **—more**, *adv.* immerfort, immerdar, ewig; (continually) stets; now and — more, jetzt und immerdar, auf immer und ewig. **—ybody**, *pron.* jeder(mann), ein jeder. **—yday**, *adj.* alltäglich

tagtäglich. —**ything**, *pron.* alles. —**ywhere,** *adv.* allenthalben, überall.

Ever—sion, *s.* der Umsturz (*obs.*); die Auswärtskehrung (der Augenlider). —**t,** *v.a.* nach außen kehren, wenden.

Evict, *v.a.* gerichtlich aus dem Besitze vertreiben; —ed farm, ein Gut, dessen (zahlungsunfähiger) Pächter gerichtlich vertrieben ist. —**ion,** *s.* die gerichtliche Ausstoßung aus dem Besitze.

Eviden—ce, I. *s.* (proof) der Beweis; das Zeugnis (*in a court of law, etc.*); (witness) der Zeuge; (documentary —ce) das Beweisstück; to furnish —ce of, etwas dartun, beweisen; to turn King's —ce, Staatszeuge werden, gegen seine Mitschuldigen zeugen; piece of —ce, das Beweisstück, der Beleg. II. *v.a.* augenscheinlich machen; (prove) beweisen, dartun. —**t,** *adj.*, —**tly,** *adv.* (visible) augenscheinlich, einleuchtend; (obvious) offenbar, deutlich, unstreitig.

Evil, I. *adj.* übel, böse, schlimm; (wicked) schlecht; — communications, schlechte Gesellschaft; the — eye, der böse Blick; the — one, der böse Feind, der Böse, Teufel; to look with an — eye upon a p., einen scheel ansehen. II. *adv.* übel; to be — spoken of, verlästert werden (*B.*). III. *s.* das Übel, Böse; (malady) die Krankheit; (calamity) das Unglück, Elend; (wickedness) die Sünde; full of —, voll Arges (*B.*); king's —, Skrofeln. —**ly,** *adv.* übel. —**ness,** *s.* die Bösartigkeit, Schlechtigkeit, das Böse. *Comp.* —**-disposed,** *adj.* boshaft. —**doer,** *s.* der Übeltäter, Missetäter. —**-minded,** *adj.* übelgesinnt, boshaft. —**speaking,** *s.* die Verleumdung, üble Nachrede.

Evince, *v.a.* dartun, erweisen, zeigen.

Eviscerat—e, *v.a.* ausweiden. —**ion,** *s.* die Ausweidung.

Evo—cate, *see* —ke. —**cation,** *s.* die Hervorrufung, die Geisterbeschwörung —**ke,** *v.a.* hervorrufen; beschwören (*spirits*).

Evol—ution, *s.* die Entwickelung, Entfaltung (*also Phys.*); (—ved series) die Reihe; die Evolution (*Geom.*); das Wurzelausziehen (*Math.*); die Evolution, Schwenkung; doctrine of —ution, die Entwickelungslehre, Evolutionstheorie. —**utionary,** *adj.* Evolutions-. —**ve,** *v.* I. *a.* entwickeln, entfalten. II. *n.* sich entfalten.

Ewe, I. *s.* das Mutterschaf. II. *attrib.*; — lamb, das Schaflamm.

Ewer, *s.* der Ausguß, die Wasserkanne; die Waschwasserkanne; claret —, die Glaskanne für Bordeauxwein.

Ex, I. *prep.* = out (of), aus; — officio, von Amtswegen (*especially in certain legal and commercial phrases*); — post facto, hintennach, nach geschehener Tat; —-post-facto law, rückwirkendes Gesetz. II. *pref.* = out of, out, formerly, ehemalig, früher; —-chancellor of the Exchequer, der ehemalige Finanzminister.

Exacerbation, *s.* die Erbitterung; die (Krankheits-)Steigerung (*Med.*).

Exact, I. *adj.*, —**ly,** *adv.* genau, pünktlich; (careful) sorgfältig; (strictly correct) ganz richtig; the — amount, der genaue Betrag. II. *v.a.* eintreiben (*payment*); erpressen (*money*); (demand) fordern, verlangen; the laws of God — obedience from all men, Gottes Gesetze fordern Gehorsam von allen Menschen. —**er,** *see* —or. —**ing,** *adj.* anspruchsvoll; he was very —ing, er stellte sehr hohe Anforderungen, er war sehr genau. —**ion,** *s.* die Beitreibung, Eintreibung (*of money, debts, etc.*); (claiming) die Forderung; (tribute, *etc.*) die erpreßte Abgabe. —**itude,** *s.* die Genauigkeit, Pünktlichkeit. —**ness,** *s. see* —itude; (care) die Sorgfalt; (accuracy) die Richtigkeit. —**or,** *s.* der Beitreiber, Eintreiber; der Placker, Leuteschinder, Erpresser; einer, der hohe Anforderungen stellt, der viel *or* zu viel fordert.

Exaggerat—e, *v.a.* übertreiben (*also Paint.*). —**ion,** *s.* die Übertreibung.

Exalt, *v.a.* (raise) erhöhen, erheben; (ennoble) erheben, veredeln; (extol) preisen, erheben; (elate) erfreuen. —**ation,** *s.* die Erhebung, Erhöhung; (—ed rank) die Höhe; der höchste Stand der Planeten (*Astrol.*). —**ed,** *adj.* erhaben, hoch; (exalté) exaltiert, begeistert. —**er,** *s.* der Erhöhende.

Examin—ation, *s.* die Prüfung, das Examen, die Untersuchung; das Verhör, die Vernehmung (*Law*); die (Zoll-)Revision (*in the custom-house*); cross- —ation, Kreuzverhör; to take *or* go in for an —ation, sich prüfen lassen; sich einer Prüfung unterziehen; to pass an —ation, to get through an —ation, eine Prüfung bestehen, in einer Prüfung durchkommen; to be ploughed (*or* plucked *or* rejected) in an —ation, in einer Prüfung durchfallen; he failed in his —ation, er fiel in seiner Prüfung durch; to be distinguished in an —ation, eine Prüfung mit Auszeichnung bestehen; the board of —ation(s), der Prüfungsausschuß, die Prüfungskommission; —ation marks, in einer Prüfung erhaltene Points; —ation paper, der (gedruckte) Fragebogen (in einer schriftlichen Prüfung); to set an —ation paper, einen Prüfungsfragebogen aufstellen; to look over —ation papers, schriftliche Prüfungsaufgaben durchsehen und beurteilen. —**ational,** *adj.* eine Prüfung betreffend. —**e,** *v.a.* (prove, try) untersuchen; prüfen; vernehmen, verhören (*Law*); (question closely) ausfragen; (look into) genau ansehen, betrachten; examinieren, ein (Schul-, 2c) Examen halten; eine Prüfung abhalten; to —e accounts, Rechnungen prüfen, examinieren; to —e o.s., sich selbst prüfen; if one —es it closely, wenn man es bei Licht besieht; to —e (*also v.n.* —e into) the merits of the case, die Verdienste der Sache erforschen; —ing committee, der Untersuchungsausschuß; der Prüfungsausschuß, die Prüfungskommission. —**ee,** *s.* der Prüfling, der (die) Kandidat(in). —**er,** *s.* der Prüfende, Untersuchende; der Examinator; der Verhörrichter (*Law*); —er to the University of London, das Mitglied der wissenschaftlichen Prüfungskommission der Universität London.

Example, *s.* das Beispiel, Vorbild; (pattern) das Muster; die Folgerung (*Log.*); to set an —, ein Beispiel geben; to set a good —, mit gutem *or* einem guten Beispiele vorangehen; to take — by, (sich (*dat.*)) ein Beispiel nehmen an (einem); to make an — of a p., ein Exempel an einem statuieren; for —, zum Beispiel.

Exarch, *s.* der Exarch.

Exasperat—e, *v.a.* aufreizen, aufs höchste erbittern; —ed, aufs äußerste erbittert, aufgebracht (at, über). —**ion,** *s.* die Erbitterung, Reizung zum Zorne; (state of —ion) das Erbittertsein, die Erbitterung; (irritation) die Entrüstung.

Excavat—e, *v.a.* aushöhlen, ausgraben. —**ion,** *s.* die Aushöhlung; die Ausgrabung (*Railw.*); die Grundgrube (*Build.*); (cavity) die Höhle, Vertiefung. —**or,** *s.* die Ausgrabungsmaschine, (navvy) der Erdarbeiter.

Exceed, *v.* I. *a.* (go beyond) überschreiten, übersteigen, hinausgehen über (*acc.*); (surpass) übertreffen (in a th., an einer S.); überschreiten (credit, limits, das Guthaben, die Grenzen); he —s all his contemporaries in . . ., er übertrifft alle seine Zeitgenossen an (*dat.*) . . . II. *n.* zu weit gehen. —**ing,** *adj.* übersteigend, mehr als; übermäßig. III. *adv.*, —**ingly,** *adv.* außerordentlich, übermäßig, äußerst.

Excel, *v.* I. *n.* sich auszeichnen; (be excellent) vorzüglich sein; he —s in mathematics, er zeichnet sich in der Mathematik aus. II. *a.* übertreffen. —**lence,** —**lency,** *s.* die Vortrefflichkeit, Vorzüglichkeit; (dignity) die Erhabenheit; (title) die Exzellenz; your —lency, Ew. (= Eure) Exzellenz. —**lent,** *adj.*, —**lently,** *adv.* vortrefflich, vorzüglich.

Except, I. *v.a.* ausnehmen, ausschließen. vorbe

halten. II. *conj.* außer, es sei denn daß, wenn nicht; — the Lord build the house, wo der Herr nicht das Haus bauet (*B.*); — he repent, es sei denn, daß er bereut, falls er nicht bereut. III. *prep.* mit Ausnahme von, ausgenommen; all — one, alle bis auf einen, mit Ausnahme von einem. **—ing**, *prep. see* — III. **—ion**, *s.* die Ausnahme; (objection) die Einwendung, der Einwurf; an —ion to the general rule, eine Ausnahme von der allgemeinen Regel; to take —ion to, sich aufhalten über (*acc.*), Einwand erheben gegen, (be offended) übel nehmen. **—ionable**, *adj.* anfechtbar, tadelnswert, anstößig. — **ional**, *adj.* außergewöhnlich. **—ionally**, *adv.* ausnahmsweise, außerordentlich.

Excerpt, I. *v.a.* ausziehen. II. *s.* der Auszug.

Excess, I. *s.* das Übermaß; (intemperance) die Unmäßigkeit; der Überschuß, Unterschied (*Arith.*, *Geom.*); das Auslaufen (*Typ.*); —es, Ausschweifungen, Ausschreitungen; — of goodness, zu viel Güte; to carry to —, (etwas) übertreiben. II. *attrib.*; — luggage, die Überfracht. **—ive**, *adj.*, **—ively**, *adv.* übermäßig, übertrieben; ungemein. **—iveness**, *s.* die Übermäßigkeit.

Exchange, I. *v.a.* (aus-, ein-, um-, ver-)tauschen, (ver-, aus-)wechseln (for, gegen); to — books, Bücher umtauschen; to — compliments, greetings, ideas, Gedanken, Grüße, Komplimente austauschen; to — money, Geld wechseln; to — prisoners, Gefangene auswechseln; to — shots, Schüsse wechseln. II. *s.* der Tausch, Austausch (*also of thoughts, etc.*), die Auswechselung; (equivalent, fair —) der Gegenwert; der Wechsel, Umsatz (*of money*); (rate of —) der (Wechsel-)Kurs; (place of —) die Börse; — of prisoners, die Auswechselung von Gefangenen; on —, an *or* auf der Börse; in —, im Tausch, dafür, dagegen; in — for, als Gegensatz für, dagegen; to make an —, tauschen; — of money, der Geldwechsel; par of —, das Wechselpari; under the quoted —, unter dem Kurse; account of —, das Wechselkonto; arbitration of —, die Wechselarbitrage; bill of —, der Wechsel, die Tratte; inland bill of —, inländischer Wechsel; fluctuating —, der unbeständige Kurs. III. *attrib.*; — advice, der Kursbericht; — business, das Wechselgeschäft; — circulation, der Wechselumlauf; — list, der Kurszettel; — operations, Wechseloperationen; — regulations, Börsenordnungen, Wechselordnungen. **—ability**, *s.* die Austauschbarkeit. — **able**, *adj.* austauschbar, auswechselbar. **—r**, *s.* der Tauscher; (money —r) der Wechsler. *Comp.* **—-broker**, *s.* der Wechselmakler.

Exchequer, I. *s.* das Finanzamt, die Staatskasse; das Schatzkammergericht; die Schatzkammer; Chancellor of the —, der (englische) Finanzminister. II. *attrib.*; — bill, der Schatzkammerschein.

Excis—able, *adj.* steuerbar. **—e**, I. *s.* die (indirekte) Steuer, Akzise, Maut. II. *attrib.*; —e duties, Abgaben von (Spirituosen, etc.). III. *v.a.* besteuern. *Comp.* **—eman**, **—e-officer**, *s.* der Akziseeinnehmer, Mautner.

Excise, *v.a.* (her)ausschneiden.

Excision, *s.* die Ausschneidung (*Surg.*); (extirpation) die Ausrottung, Zerstörung; die Ausschließung (*Theol.*).

Excit—ability, *s.* die Erregbarkeit. **—able**, *adj.* erregbar, reizbar. **—ant**, *s.* das Reizmittel. — **ation**, *s.* die Reizung, Aufmunterung, der Antrieb. **—e**, *v.a.* erregen, wachrufen, aufregen (*also Med.*), aufreizen; (incite) anreizen. **—ed**, *adj.*, **—edly**, *adv.* aufgeregt. **—ement**, *s.* die Erregung, Aufregung; (incitement) die Anreizung, der Antrieb; die Reizung, Erregung (*Med.*); popular —ement, die Volksbewegung. **—er**, *s.* der Erreger, Antreiber, Aufwiegler. **—ing**, *adj.* aufregend; —ing cause, unmittelbare Ursache.

Exclaim, *v.* I. *n.* ausrufen, schreien; to — against, eifern, schreien über (*acc.*); to — with astonishment, voll Verwunderung ausrufen. II. *a.* ausrufen. **—er**, *s.* der Schreier; der Eiferer.

Exclamat—ion, *s.* der Ausruf, die Ausrufung; der Ausruf (*Rhet.*); note of —ion, das Ausrufungszeichen; —ions, das Geschrei. **—ory**, *adj.* ausrufend; —ory words, Ausrufsworte.

Exclude, *v.a.* ausschließen (aus einer Gesellschaf von Vorrechten).

Exclusi—on, *s.* die Ausschließung, der Ausschluß; (separation) die Aussonderung. **—ve**, *adj.*, **—vely**, *adv.* ausschließend; ausschließlich (*as privileges, etc.*); (select) wählerisch, exklusiv; —ive of, mit Ausschluß von (*or gen.*), abgesehen von, ohne Rücksicht auf (*acc.*); —ive of other charges, andere Kosten ungerechnet. **—veness**, *s.* die Ausschließlichkeit; die Exklusivität, das Wählerische (*of a company*).

Excogitat—e, *v.a.* ausdenken, aussinnen, ersinnen. **—ion**, *s.* die Ersinnung; (invention) die Erfindung; (thought) der Gedanke.

Excommunicat—e, I. *v.a.* in den Kirchenbann tun; von der Kirchengemeinschaft ausschließen, exkommunizieren. II. *adj.*, **—ed**, *adj.* im Kirchenbann, gebannt; to be —ed, exkommuniziert sein *or* werden. **—ion**, *s.* der Kirchenbann, die Exkommunikation.

Excoriat—e, *v.a.* (die Haut) abziehen; (die Haut) aufschürfen. **—ion**, *s.* das Aufschürfen.

Excrement, *s.* das Extrement, der Kot (*Physiol.*), der Auswurf (*fig.*). **—al**, *adj.* Kot-.

Excrescen—ce, *s.* der Auswuchs. **—t**, *adj.* auswachsend; überflüssig, unpassend.

Excret—ion, *s.* die Aussonderung, Absonderung; (excrement) der Auswurf. **—ive**, *adj.* absondernd, abführend. **—ory**, *adj. see* —ive; Aussonderungs-.

Excruciat—e, *v.a.* martern, quälen, foltern. — **ing**, *adj.*, **—ingly**, *adv.* peinigend, höchst peinlich; —ing pain, folternder Schmerz. **—ion**, *s.* das Martern; (pain) die Pein, Qual.

Exculpat—e, *v.a.* entschuldigen; (justify) rechtfertigen. **—ion**, *s.* die Entschuldigung; die Rechtfertigung. **—ory**, *adj.* entschuldigend.

Excursion, *s.* der Ausflug, Abstecher; die Abschweifung (*from a subject*); (inroad) der Streifzug; to undertake an — (to), einen Ausflug (nach) . . . machen *or* unternehmen. **—ist**, *s.* der Ausflügler. *Comp.* **—-train**, *s.* der Vergnügungszug.

Excurs—ive, *adj.*, **—ively**, *adv.* umherstreifend, umherschweifend; umherirrend. **—us**, *s.* die Abschweifung; der Exkurs.

Excus—able, *adj.*, **—ably**, *adv.* entschuldbar, verzeihlich; —able homicide, der unvorsätzliche Totschlag. **—ableness**, *s.* die Entschuldbarkeit. **—e**, I. *v.a.* entschuldigen; (serve as —e) rechtfertigen, zur *or* als Entschuldigung dienen; (overlook) Nachsicht haben mit; —e haste, entschuldigen Sie die Eile; I desire to be —ed, ich bitte mich zu entschuldigen. II. *s.* die Entschuldigung, Rechtfertigung; die Ausflucht; to make —es, Entschuldigungen vorbringen.

Exeat, *s.* der Urlaub (für Studenten), Urlaubsschein zum Verlassen der Universitätsstadt; bischöflicher Urlaub zum Verlassen der Diözese.

Execra—ble, *adj.*, **—bly**, *adv.* fluchwürdig, abscheulich. **—bleness**, *s.* die Abscheulichkeit. **—te**, *v.a.* (curse) verfluchen; (abhor) verabscheuen. **—tion**, *s.* die Verwünschung; to hold a p. in —tion, einen verabscheuen.

Execut—e, *v.a.* ausführen, vollführen, vollziehen, verrichten, ausrichten; vollziehen, ausführen (*orders*); ausfertigen (*a deed, a will*); (put to death) hinrichten; (complete) vollziehen (*Law*); vortragen (*Mus.*); (make valid) (durch Namensunterschrift und Siegel) rechtsgültig machen (*a deed, etc.*). **—er**, *s.* der Vollzieher, Vollstrecker. **—ion**, *s.* die Ausführung, Vollstreckung, Vollziehung, Ausübung; der Vortrag, die Ausführung, das Spiel (*Mus.*); die (Finger=) Fertigkeit, Technik (*Mus.*); die Hinrichtung; die Vollstreckung, Vollziehung (*of a sentence*); die Ausfertigung (*of a deed*); die Auspfändung, Exekution (*for debt; of criminals*); (writ of —ion) der Vollziehungsbefehl; to take out an —ion against a p., einen auspfänden lassen; to take goods in —ion, Güter exekutieren; place of —ion, der Richtplatz; to do —ion, Wirkung tun; to do great —ion upon the enemy, dem Feinde großen Schaden tun; to carry into, put in —ion, ausführen, zur Ausführung bringen. **—ioner,** *s.* der Scharfrichter, Henker. **—ive,** I. *adj.* vollziehend, ausübend; —ive council, der Ministerrat (*Amer.*); —ive power, die vollziehende, ausübende Gewalt. II. *s.* die ausübende Gewalt (im Staate); die Obrigkeit. **—or,** *s.* der (Testaments=)Vollstrecker. **—orship,** *s.* das Amt eines Testamentsvollziehers. **—ory,** *adj.* vollziehend; exekutorisch. **—rix,** *s.* die Testamentsvollstreckerin.

Exege—sis, *s.* die Bibelauslegung, Bibelerklärung, Exegese. **—te,** *s.* der Bibelerklärer, Exeget. **—tical,** *adj.*, **—tically,** *adv.* exegetisch.

Exemplar, *s.* das Muster, Vorbild. **—iness,** *s.* die Musterhaftigkeit. **—y,** *adj.* musterhaft, zum Beispiel dienend; (deterrent) abschreckend.

Exemplif—ication, *s.* die Beispielgebung, Erläuterung durch Beispiele; (example) das Beispiel, Muster. **—y,** *v.a.* durch Beispiele erweisen, erläutern; (illustrate) für eine S. zum Beispiele *or* Beleg dienen; eine rechtsgültige Abschrift nehmen (von).

Exempt, I. *v.a.* ausschließen (from, von), befreien (from, von), verschonen (from, mit). II. *adj.* befreit, verschont, frei (from, von). III. *s.* der Bevorrechtigte. **—ion,** *s.* die Befreiung, Freiheit; —ion from taxation, Steuerfreiheit.

Exequies, *pl.* das Leichenbegängnis, die Totenfeier.

Exercis—able, *adj.* ausführbar, anwendbar, anzuwenden. **—e,** I. *v.a.* üben (*the body or mind*); ausüben (*power, sway, a profession, an art*); (practise) einüben; exerziereren, drillen (*soldiers*); bewegen, in Übung halten (*a horse*); üben (*patience, etc.*); verwalten (*an office*); to —e great cruelty, Grausamkeit ausüben; to —e discipline, Disziplin handhaben; to —e one's mind, sich geistig beschäftigen. II. *v.n.* exerzieren (*Mil.*); sich (*dat.*) Bewegung machen. III. *s.* die Übung; die Ausübung (*of an art, etc.*); bodily —e, die körperliche Bewegung, Leibesübung; written —e, die schriftliche Aufgabe *or* Arbeit; religious —e(s), die Andachtsübung, der Gottesdienst; to take —e, sich (*dat.*) im Freien Bewegung machen, spazieren gehen (reiten, radeln, *rc.*); you do not take enough —, du machst dir nicht genug Bewegung. *Comp.* **—ing-ground,** *s.* der Exerzierplatz (*Mil.*).

Exergue, *s.* der untere Münzabschnitt.

Exert, *v.a.* (employ) anwenden; äußern, zeigen; to — o.s., sich anstrengen, sich bemühen; to — one's influence (in favour of a p.), seinen Einfluß geltend machen (zugunsten jemandes). **—ion,** *s.* die Anstrengung; die Äußerung; die Anwendung.

Exeunt, (sie gehen) ab (*Theat.*).

Exfoliat—e, *v.n.* sich abblättern (*Min., Surg.*). **—ion,** *s.* die Abblätterung, Abschieferung.

Exhal—ation, *s.* die Ausdünstung; (vapour, *etc.*) der Dunst, Dampf; der Brodem (*Min.*); —ations, Dunstgebilde. **—e,** *v.a.* ausdünsten; verdunsten; aushauchen; (draw out in vapour) herauspressen, =ziehen; flowers —e perfume, Blumen hauchen Duft *or* Wohlgeruch aus. II. *n.* verdunsten.

Exhaust, *v.a.* erschöpfen; to — the air in . . ., . . . luftleer pumpen. **—ed,** *p.p. & adj.* erschöpft, abgemattet (*fig.*); to be —ed, vergriffen sein (*as the edition of a book, etc.*). **—ible,** *adj.* erschöpflich. **—ing,** *adj.* anstrengend, mühselig; —ing chamber, der Dampfraum (*in a boiler*). **—ion,** *s.* die Erschöpfung; die Exhaustion (*Math.*). **—ive,** *adj.*, **—ively,** *adv. see* —ing; erschöpfend. **—less,** *adj.* unerschöpflich.

Exhibit, I. *v.a.* sehen lassen, zeigen; ausstellen (*for inspection, etc.*); (display) zeigen, darlegen, an den Tag legen; anbringen (*a charge, etc., Law*); verordnen (*Med.*). II. *s.* das Exhibitum, die schriftliche Eingabe (*Law*); das ausgestellte Muster, der Ausstellungsgegenstand. **—er,** *s.* der Aussteller. **—ion,** *s.* die Ausstellung; (manifestation) die Darlegung, Äußerung; (display) die Zurschaustellung; die Einreichung (*Law*); die Eingebung (*Med.*); das (kleine) Stipendium (*Univ.*); universal *or* international —ion, Weltausstellung; to make an —ion of o.s., sich lächerlich machen. **—ioner,** *s.* der Stipendiat.

Exhilarat—e, *v.a.* erheitern, aufheitern. **—ing,** *adj.*, **—ingly,** *adv.* erheiternd. **—ion,** *s.* die Erheiterung; die Heiterkeit. **—ive,** *adj.* erheiternd.

Exhort, *v.a.* ermahnen, ermuntern (to, zu); (advise) (einem) dringend raten. **—ation,** *s.* die Ermahnung, Mahnung. **—atory,** *adj.* ermahnend, mahnend. **—er,** *s.* der Ermahner.

Exhum—ation, *s.* die Ausgrabung (*of buried bodies*). **—e,** *v.a.* ausgraben.

Exigen—ce, **—cy,** *s.* (necessity) das Bedürfnis, der Bedarf; (emergency) der Notfall, dringende Fall. **—t,** *adj.* dringend.

Exigu—ity, *s.* die Kleinheit, Winzigkeit; die Unzulänglichkeit. **—ous,** *adj.* klein, winzig, dürftig.

Exile, I. *s.* die Verbannung, das Exil; (seclusion) die Abgeschiedenheit; (—d person) der Verbannte, Vertriebene. II. *v.a.* verbannen.

Exist, *v.n.* sein, da sein; (live) leben; (continue) bestehen. **—ence,** *s.* das Dasein, Vorhandensein; das Leben; —ence of God, Dasein Gottes; —ence of proofs, Vorhandensein von Beweisen; the most miserable being in —ence, das elendste Geschöpf unter der Sonne. **—ent,** **—ing,** *adj.* vorhanden, bestehend; seiend.

Exit, I. = (geht) ab (*Theat.*). II. *s.* der Abgang; (final —) der Tod; (way out) der Ausgang; to make one's —, abtreten, (finally) verscheiden.

Exodus, *s.* der Auszug (*esp'lly* der Kinder Israels aus Ägypten); das zweite Buch Mosis.

Ex officio, *adj. & adv.* amtlich, von Amtswegen.

Exogen, *s.* dikotyledonische, nach außen wachsende Pflanze. **—ous,** *adj.* nach außen hin wachsend.

Exonerat—e, *v.a.* entlasten, entbinden, befreien; to —e a p. from a charge, einen von einer Beschuldigung freisprechen. **—ion,** *s.* die Entlassung, Befreiung. **—ive,** *adj.* entlastend.

Exophthalmia, *s.* der Augapfel=Vorfall.

Exorbitan—ce, **—cy,** *s.* die Abschweifung, Unregelmäßigkeit (*obs.*); das Abweichen vom rechten Wege; die Ausschweifung, grenzenlose Verdorbenheit; (enormity) das Übermaß, die Maßlosigkeit. **—t,** *adj.*, **—tly,** *adv.* maßlos, übermäßig.

Exorcis—e, *v.a.* (Geister, *rc.*) beschwören. **—er,** **—t,** *s.* der Geisterbeschwörer. **—m,** *s.* die Geisterbeschwörung; (charm) die Beschwörungsformel.

Exordium, *s.* der Eingang einer Rede.

Exoteric, *adj.* öffentlich, exoterisch.

Exotic, I. *adj.* ausländisch, exotisch. II. *s.* das ausländische Gewächs; das Fremdwort.

Expan—d, *v.* I. *a.* (spread out) ausspannen, ausbreiten; (distend) ausdehnen; (enlarge) erweitern. II. *n.* sich ausbreiten, sich ausspannen, sich auftun; sich ausdehnen; sich erweitern; his heart —ds with joy, sein Herz schwillt vor Freude. **—se,** *s.* die Ausdehnung; (open space) der weite Raum, die Fläche; the —se of heaven, die Himmelswölbung. **—sibility,** *s.* die Ausdehnbarkeit. **—sible,** *adj.* (aus) dehnbar. **—sion,** *s.* die Ausdehnung, Ausbreitung; (the —ding) das Ausdehnen; die Erweiterung; (—se) der Umfang, Raum; —sion of England, die Ausdehnung Englands (über die Erde, durch festen Zusammenschluß mit seinen Kolonien). —**sive**, *adj.* (—ding) ausdehnend; (—sible) ausdehnungsfähig; gefühlsüberströmend, gefühlvoll; (—ded) ausgedehnt, breit; —sive force, die Spannkraft. —**siveness**, *s.* die Ausdehnungsfähigkeit; die Breite.

Expatiat—e, *v.n.* frei umher wandern; weitläufig sprechen, sich weitläufig verbreiten *or* auslassen (upon, über eine S.) (*fig.*). —**ion**, *s.* die weitläufige Auslassung. —**ory**, *adj.* weitläufig.

Expatriat—e, *v.a.* (aus dem Vaterlande) verbannen; to —e o. s., sein Vaterland verlassen, auswandern. —**ion**, *s.* die Verbannung; die Auswanderung aus dem Vaterlande.

Expect, *v.a.* erwarten; warten auf (*acc.*); (look forward to) entgegensehen (*dat.*); (reckon on) zählen auf (*acc.*). —**ancy**, *s.* die Erwartung; die Anwartschaft (auf, *acc.*) (*Law*). —**ant**, I. *adj.* erwartend; heir —ant, Anwärter auf ein Erbe. II. *s.* der Anwärter (auf, *acc.*). —**ation**, *s.* die Erwartung; (hope) die Hoffnung; (what is —ed) die Erwartung, Aussicht; —ation of life, mutmaßliche Lebensdauer (*C. L.*).

Expectora—nt, I. *adj.* brustreinigend. II. *s.* das Brustmittel. —**te**, *v.* I. *a.* aus-werfen, -husten, -speien. II. *n.* Schleim ausspeien, aushusten. —**tion**, *s.* der (Schleim)auswurf.

Expedi—ence, —**ency**, *s.* die Schicklichkeit, Füglichkeit; die Ratsamkeit, Zweckmäßigkeit. —**ent**, I. *adj.*, —**ently**, *adv.* (fitting) schicklich, füglich; (advisable) ratsam; (advantageous) zuträglich. II. *s.* das Mittel; (shift) der Notbehelf, Ausweg; to be fruitful in —ents, einen erfinderischen Kopf haben. —**te**, *v.a.* beschleunigen, befördern; (facilitate) erleichtern; (despatch) absenden. —**tion**, *s.* (haste) die Eile, Geschwindigkeit; (hostile march) der Zug, Feldzug; (journey, etc.) die Reise, Fahrt, Expedition; punitive —tion, die Strafexpedition. —**tionary**, *adj.* Expeditions-. —**tious**, *adj.*, —**tiously**, *adv.* schnell, hurtig, geschwind, eilig; most —tiously, aufs förderlichste.

Expel, *v.a.* vertreiben, wegtreiben, (from, von, aus); fortschicken (*school*); relegieren (*Univ.*).

Expen—d, *v.a.* ausgeben (*money*); aufwenden, verwenden (*labour*)(on a th., auf eine S.); (use up) verbrauchen. —**diture**, *s.* die Ausgabe; die Kosten. —**se**, *s.* die Ausgabe, Auslage, die Kosten; der Aufwand (*of time, etc.*); at my —se, auf meine Kosten; to be at the —se of, die Ausgaben bestreiten müssen; at little —se, mit geringen Kosten, um ein Geringes; to put a p. to great —se, einen in große Kosten stürzen; einem große Kosten machen *or* verursachen; to go to great —se, sich (*dat.*) große Kosten machen; he went to great —se for it, er ließ es sich (*dat.*) viel kosten; incidental —ses, Nebenausgaben, unvorhergesehene Ausgaben; travelling —ses, Reisekosten; Reisespesen (*C. L.*); working —ses, Betriebskosten; to cover —ses, die Auslagen decken. —**sive**, *adj.*, —**sively**, *adv.* kostspielig, teuer; (extravagant) verschwenderisch; you will find this an —sive hobby, Sie werden finden, daß diese Liebhaberei Ihnen teuer zu stehen kommen wird. —**siveness**, *s.* die Kostspieligkeit.

Exper—ience, I. *s.* die Erfahrung; a man of —ience, ein erfahrener Mann; to know by —ience, aus Erfahrung wissen, ein Liedchen davon singen können; great —ience in business, große Geschäftserfahrung. II. *v.a.* erfahren; erleiden (*a loss*); to —ience a difficulty, auf eine Schwierigkeit stoßen. —**ienced**, *adj.* erfahren, erprobt; —ienced in business, geschäftskundig. —**iment**, I. *s.* der Versuch, das Experiment, die Probe; to demonstrate by —iment, experimentell *or* durch ein Experiment erläutern. II. *v.n.* Versuche anstellen (upon, mit), experimentieren. —**imental**, *adj.*, —**imentally**, *adv.* auf Erfahrung gegründet; Versuche betreffend; —imental philosophy, die praktische Philosophie. —**imentalist**, —**imenter**, *s.* der Experimentierende. —**imentalize**, *v.n.* Versuche anstellen, Experimente machen. —**t**, I. *adj.*, —**tly**, *adv.* (—ienced) erfahren, kundig; (skilful) geschickt, gewandt. II. *s.* der Sachverständige, Fachmann; to be an —t at s.th., sich auf eine S. verstehen, in einem Fache beschlagen sein. —**tness**, *s.* die Gewandtheit.

Expia—ble, *adj.* sühnbar. —**te**, *v.a.* (ab)büßen, sühnen; (avert) abwenden. —**tion**, *s.* die Büßung, Sühne, Entsühnung; *see* —tory sacrifice. —**tory**, *adj.* sühnend, aussöhnend; —tory sacrifice, das Sühnopfer.

Expir—ation, *s.* (breathing out) das Ausatmen; (termination) der Ablauf, Verlauf, das Ende; at the —ation of a certain time, nach Verlauf einer gewissen Zeit; —ation of a treaty (lease), Ablauf eines Vertrages (Mietkontraktes); at the time of —ation, zur Verfallzeit (*C.L.*). —**atory**, *adj.;* ausatmend, Ausatmungs-; —atory accent, dynamischer Akzent, die Tonstärke. —**e**, *v.n.* aushauchen; (die) sterben, verscheiden; zu Ende gehen, ablaufen, verfließen, erlöschen (*as time, a contract, etc.*).

Explain, *v.* I. *a.* erklären, auslegen, verständlich machen; auseinandersetzen (*motives, reasons*); to — away, wegerklären, beseitigen. II. *n.* Erklärungen geben, sich erklären. —**able**, *adj.* erklärbar. —**er**, *s.* der Erklärer.

Explanat—ion, *s.* die Erklärung, Auslegung; die Verständigung; to have an —ion with a p., mit einem eine Auseinandersetzung haben, sich mit einem auseinandersetzen. —**ory**, *adj.* erklärend.

Expletive, I. *adj.* ausfüllend. II. *s.* das Füllwort; (oath) der Fluch; (stop-gap) der Lückenbüßer.

Explic—able, *adj.* erklärlich. —**ative**, —**atory**, *adj.* erklärend. —**it**, *adj.*, —**itly**, *adv.* ausdrücklich, deutlich, klar; (decided) bestimmt; (outspoken) offen. —**itness**, *s.* die Deutlichkeit, Bestimmtheit.

Explod—e, *v.* I. *a.* explodieren lassen; this theory is now —ed, diese Theorie ist jetzt veraltet, aufgegeben. II. *n.* explodieren, in die Luft fliegen; ausbrechen, hervorbrechen (*of passion*), zerplatzen. *Comp.* —**ing-chamber**, *s.* die Kammer (am Flintenschloß).

Exploit, I. *s.* die Großtat, Heldentat. II. *v.a.* ausnutzen, ausbeuten. —**able**, *adj.* ausnutzbar. —**ation**, *s.* die Ausbeutung.

Explor—ation, *s.* die Erforschung, Untersuchung. —**e**, *v.a.* er-, aus-forschen, untersuchen; to —e a country, ein Land erforschen. —**er**, *s.* der Erforscher, Forschungsreisende. —**ing**, *p.;* an —ing expedition, eine Entdeckungs-, Forschungsreise.

Explosi—on, *s.* die Explosion, Losplatzung, Zersprengung; (burst) der Ausbruch; —on of a boiler, die Kesselexplosion; colliery —on, die Explosion in einem Bergwerk. —**ve**, I. *adj.*, —**vely**, *adv.* mit Knall ausbrechend, losknallend, explodierend, Explosions-; —ve air, das Knallgas; —ve bullet, die Explodierkugel, Sprengkugel; —ve cotton, die Schießbaumwolle; —ve power, die Explosionskraft, Brisanz; —ve shells, Granaten mit Knalloxyd, Sprenggranaten. II. *s.* der Sprengstoff; der Verschlußlaut (*Gram.*). —**veness**, *s.* die Explodierbarkeit.

Exponent, *s.* der Exponent (*Math.*); (expounder) der Erklärer, Ausleger; — of a view, der Vertreter einer Ansicht. —**ial**, *adj.* Exponential-; —ial equation, die Exponentialgleichung.

Export, I. *v.a.* ausführen, (ins Ausland) versenden, exportieren. II. *s.* die Ausfuhr; (—ed article) der Ausfuhrartikel; — duty, der Ausfuhrzoll; — trade, der Ausfuhr-, Export-handel. —**able**, *adj.* ausführbar. —**ation**, *s.* die Ausfuhr; for —ation, zur Ausfuhr bestimmt. —**er**, *s.* der Exporthändler, Warenversender.

Expos—e, *v.a.* aussetzen, ausstellen; belichten (*Photogr.*); (disclose) an den Tag legen, darlegen; (subject) aussetzen, bloßstellen; (—e to danger) der Gefahr aussetzen, preisgeben; to —e to censure, dem Tadel aussetzen; to —e for sale, zum Verkauf auslegen; to —e o.s., sich (*dat.*) eine Blöße geben; she —ed herself to ridicule, sie setzte sich dem Spotte aus, machte sich lächerlich; to —e one's plans, seine Pläne darlegen; to —e a p.'s weakness, jemandes Schwäche aufdecken. **—er**, *s.* einer, der andere auf irgend eine Weise bloßstellt. **—ition**, *s.* (interpretation) die Erklärung, Auslegung; (commentary) die Auslegung, der Kommentar; (exhibition) die Ausstellung; the —ition of a passage, die Erklärung einer Stelle. **—itor**, *s.* der Ausleger, Erklärer. **—itory**, *adj.* erklärend. **—ure**, *s.* die Ausstellung; das Bloßgestelltsein, die Bloßstellung (*to danger, to ridicule*); die ungeschützte Lage; das Aussetzen, die Belichtung (*Phot.*); a southern —ure, eine südliche Lage.

Expostulat—e, *v.n.* fragen (*obs.*); to —e with a p. upon, on *or* for, einem ernste Vorstellungen machen über (*acc.*). **—ion**, *s.* das Rechten; der Streit, Wortwechsel; (remonstrance) die ernste Vorstellung, Vorhaltung, der Verweis. **—ory**, *adj.* Vorstellungen machend; —ory letter, eine Beschwerdeschrift.

Expound, *v.a.* auslegen, erklären; to — the meaning of a passage, den Sinn einer Stelle deuten. **—er**, *s.* der Erklärer, Ausleger.

Express, I. *v.a.* äußern, sagen, ausdrücken, aussprechen (*one's thoughts, opinions, etc.*); (squeeze out) ausdrücken, auspressen; (show, exhibit) bezeigen, zu erkennen geben (*love, etc.*), darstellen (*in art, poetry*); to — one's opinion, seine Meinung aussprechen; he —ed himself greatly pleased, er erklärte sich für sehr befriedigt. II. *adj.* (plain, clear) ausdrücklich, klar, deutlich, bestimmt; (special) eigen, expreß; — engine, die Eilzugmaschine; — train, der Eilzug, Kurierzug, D. Zug. III. *adv.*; to send a messenger —, einen Eilboten abschicken. IV. *s.* der Eil-, Eigenbote, die Stafette; *see* — train, etc. **—ible**, *adj.* ausdrückbar. **—ion**, *s.* der Ausdruck; das Auspressen, Ausdrücken; die Formel (*Math.*); an odd —ion, ein seltsamer Ausdruck. **—ionless**, *adj.* ausdruckslos. **—ive**, *adj.*, **—ively**, *adv.* ausdrückend; ausdrucksvoll (*as the countenance*); (powerful) nachdrücklich, kräftig; a letter —ive of gratitude, ein Dankbarkeit ausdrückender Brief. **—iveness**, *s.* das Ausdrucksvolle; die Ausdrücklichkeit, Energie, der Nachdruck. **—ly**, *adv.* ausdrücklich, bestimmt, ganz besonders; (specially) eigens.

Expropriat—e, *v.a.* enteignen, des Eigentums berauben. **—ion**, *s.* die Enteignung, gerichtliche Eigentumsentäußerung.

Expulsi—on, *s.* die Vertreibung. **—ve**, *adj.* vertreibend, austreibend.

Expunge, *v.a.* ausstreichen, auslöschen; (destroy) vertilgen. **—r**, *s.* der Tilger, Ausstreicher.

Expurgat—e, *v.a.* (Bücher von Anstößigem) reinigen, säubern, berichtigen; —ed classic, klassischer Schriftsteller für den Schulgebrauch von anstößigen Stellen gereinigt. **—ion**, *s.* die Reinigung. **—or**, *s.* der Reiniger. **—ory**, *adj.* reinigend, säubernd; —ory index, das Verzeichnis der vom Papste verbotenen Bücher.

Exquisite, I. *adj.*, **—ly**, *adv.* (choice) (aus)erlesen, vortrefflich, vorzüglich; fein (*as the ear, the taste, etc.*); (of delicate perception) höchst empfindlich; (extreme) hochgradig; — pain, höchst empfindlicher Schmerz; — pleasure, lebhaft empfundenes Vergnügen; an — ear, ein äußerst feines Gehör; — sensibility, ungemeine Empfindlichkeit; — torments, die ausgesuchtesten, grausamsten Martern; — workmanship, vorzügliche Arbeit. II. *s.* der Stutzer (*abs.*). **—ness**, *s.* die Vorzüglichkeit, Vortrefflichkeit, Auserlesenheit; die Schärfe, Feinfühligkeit (*of judgment, etc.*).

Extant, *adj.* hervorstehend (over, über); (noch) vorhanden.

Extasy, *see* Ecstasy.

Extempor—aneous, *adj.*, **—aneously**, *adv.* *see* —e. **—ary**, *adj. see* —e; —ary prayer, ein Gebet aus dem Stegreife. **—e**, *adj. & adv.* aus dem Stegreife, unvorbereitet. **—ize**, *v.a. & n.* aus dem Stegreife reden, spielen, dichten, extemporieren. **—izer**, *s.* der Stegreif-redner, -spieler, -dichter, Improvisator.

Exten—d, *v.* I. *a.* ausdehnen (*limits, etc.*); ausstrecken (*the hand, etc.*); erweitern, vergrößern (*one's dominions, etc.*); verlängern (*time*); (offer) erteilen, anbieten; to —d a line, eine Linie ziehen. II. *n.* sich erstrecken, reichen (to, bis); his urbanity —ded to everybody, seine Höflichkeit erstreckte sich auf jedermann. **—der**, *s.* der Ausdehnende. **—sibility**, *s.* die Dehnbarkeit. **—sible**, *adj.* dehnbar, streckbar. **—sion**, *s.* die Ausdehnung (*also of a railway, etc. & Phys.*); (compass) der Umfang, die Ausdehnung; —sion of the term of payment, die Verlängerung des Zahlungstermins; —sion of university teaching, university —sion, die Volkshochschule; —sion lecturer, der Wanderredner; —sion lectures, Volkshochschulvorträge. **—sive**, *adj.*, **—sively**, *adv.* weit ausgedehnt; (comprehensive) umfassend; an —sive business, ein ausgebreitetes Geschäft. **—siveness**, *s.* die Ausdehnung, Weite, Größe, der Umfang. **—sor**, *s.* der Streckmuskel (*Anat.*). **—t**, *s.* die Ausdehnung, Weite, der Umfang (*of a p.'s power, authority, etc.*); die Größe, Länge, Strecke (*of country, etc.*); (space) der Raum; (degree) der Grad; to a certain the —t of, bis zum Betrage von; to a certain —t, gewissermaßen, bis zu einem gewissen Grade.

Extenuat—e, *v.a.* verringern, verkleinern, mildern, (palliate) verringern, bemänteln; —ing circumstances, mildernde Umstände. **—ion**, *s.* die Milderung, Verringerung, Beschönigung.

Exter—ior, I. *adj.* äußerlich; (foreign) auswärtig; —ior angle, der äußere Winkel. II. *s.* das Äußere. **—nal**, I. *adj.*, **—nally**, *adv.* äußerlich, äußer; (not intrinsic) äußerlich; (visible) sichtbar; (bodily) körperlich; (foreign) auswärtig. II. *s.*, **—nals**, *pl.* das Äußere, Äußerliche; (outward forms) die Zeremonien, die äußeren Formen, das Äußerliche.

Exterminat—e, *v.a.* ausrotten, vertilgen, vernichten. **—ion**, *s.* die Vertilgung, Vernichtung, Ausrottung. **—or**, *s.* der Vertilger, Ausrotter.

Exterritorial, *adj.* der Gerichtsbarkeit des Wohnsitzes nicht unterworfen (*of ambassadors*).

Extinct, *adj.* erloschen, ausgestorben; (at an end) geendigt, zu Ende, aus; (abolished) aufgehoben; — species, ausgestorbene Gattung (*of animals*); — volcano, ausgebrannter Vulkan. **—ion**, *s.* das Auslöschen, Erlöschen; das Aussterben, der Untergang (*fig.*); die Erlöschung, Tilgung; (destruction) die Vernichtung.

Extinguish, *v.a.* auslöschen (*fire, etc.*); (stifle) dämpfen, ersticken; (destroy) vertilgen, zerstören; tilgen (*claims*). **—er**, *s.* das Löschhütchen, der Lichtdämpfer (*for a candle*); der Auslöschende. **—ment**, *s. see* Extinction.

Extirpat—e, *v.a.* ausrotten; ausschneiden (*Surg.*). **—ion**, *s.* die Ausrottung, gänzliche Zerstörung; die Ausschneidung. **—ive**, *adj.* ausrottend. **—or**, *s.* der Ausrotter, Zerstörer. **—ory**, *adj.* ausrottend.

Extol, *v.a.* erheben, preisen, loben. **—ler**, *s.* der Lobpreiser.

Extort, *v.a.* erpressen, (einem etwas) abdringen, abzwingen. **—er**, *s.* der Erpresser. **—ion**, *s.* (exaction) die Erpressung; (overcharge) die Beutelschneiderei. **—ionate**, *adj.* erpressend; (oppressive) drückend. **—ioner**, *s.* der Leuteschinder, Wucherer.

Extra, I. *adj.* nachträglich; — charges, Nebenspesen, außerordentliche Unkosten; — freight, die Extrafracht; — pay, die Extrabezahlung; — work, die Nebenarbeit. II. *s.* das Außergewöhnliche, das in den gewöhnlichen Preis nicht mit Eingeschlossene; das Extra-Gericht (*in a restaurant, etc.*). —**dos**, *s.* der Bogenrücken, Oberbogen (*Arch.*). —**s**, *pl.* die Neben-Ausgaben. *Comp.* —**judicial**, *adj.* außergerichtlich. —**mundane**, *adj.* außerweltlich. —**mural**, *adj.* außerhalb der Mauern einer Stadt liegend *or* vorgehend; — mural work of the University, Volkshochschulkurse. —**parochial**, *adj.* nicht zum Kirchspiele gehörig; —parochial land, zehentfreie Ländereien.

Extract, I. *v.a.* ausziehen (*a tooth, etc.*); einen Auszug machen (*from books*); ausscheiden (*Chem.*); ausgraben (*Min.*); ausziehen (*Math.*). II. *s.* der Auszug (*from a book, etc.*); der Auszug, Extrakt (*Chem., etc.*); Liebig's — of meat, der Liebigsche Fleischextrakt. —**ion**, *s.* das Heraus-, Aus-ziehen; die Ausziehung, Ausscheidung (*Chem.*); das Ausziehen (*Math.*); (descent) die Abkunft, Abstammung; die Gewinnung (*Min., Metall.*). —**or**, *s.* der Auszieher; die Geburtszange (*Surg.*).

Extradit—able, *adj.* auslieferbar, auszuliefern. —**e**, *v.a.* ausliefern. —**ion**, *s.* die Auslieferung.

Extraneous, *adj.* nicht zu einer Sache gehörig; (foreign) fremd; (non-essential) nicht wesentlich.

Extraordinar—ily, *adv.* außerordentlich. —**iness**, *s.* das Außerordentliche. —**y**, *adj.* außerordentlich, außergewöhnlich; (remarkable) merkwürdig; ambassador —y, der außerordentliche Gesandte; —y charges, Extrakosten.

Extravagan—ce, —**cy**, *s.* (excess) die Ausschweifung; (prodigality) die (törichte) Verschwendung; (wildness) die Schwärmerei, Extravaganz, Überspanntheit; (vehemence) die übertriebene Heftigkeit; die Übertriebenheit (*of language*); to commit —ces, törichte Streiche begehen. —**t**, *adj.*, —**tly**, *adv.* verschwenderisch; ausschweifend; übertrieben, übermäßig, überspannt (*of ideas, etc.*); (excessive) übermäßig, unsinnig; —t demands, übertriebene Ansprüche; we are very —t, wir lassen viel darauf gehen. —**za**, *s.* die Operette, Zauberposse (*Mus.*).

Extravasat—e, *v.* I. *a.* austreten lassen; —ed blood, ausgetretenes Blut. II. *n.* ausfließen, austreten. —**ion**, *s.* das Austreten (des Blutes aus seinen Gefäßen).

Extrem—e, I. *adj.*, —**ely**, *adv.* äußerst; äußerst, außerordentlich, höchst (*fig.*); (last) letzt; (ultra) übertrieben; an —e case, ein Notfall; to an —e degree, im höchsten Grade; —e measures, die äußersten Mittel; —e necessity, die dringendste Not; —e unction, die letzte Ölung. II. *s.* das Äußerste, das äußerste Ende; das Äußerste, Extrem; der höchste Grad; die Übertreibung; das äußerste Glied (*Math.*); —es meet, die Extreme berühren sich; the —es of a syllogism, das Prädikat und Subjekt eines Schlusses; —es of a proportion, die äußeren Glieder einer Proportion. —**ist**, *s.* der Anhänger extremer Anschauungen, der Ultra; der (Ultra-)Radikale (*Pol.*). —**ities**, *pl.* die Endglieder, Extremitäten, Gliedmaßen; to proceed to —ities, zum Äußersten schreiten; to be reduced to —ities, aufs Äußerste gebracht sein; ganz heruntergekommen *or* in höchster Not sein; to carry to —ities, übertreiben, zu weit treiben, auf die Spitze treiben. —**ity**, *s.* das Äußerste, äußerste Ende, die äußerste Grenze; (point) die Spitze; (verge) der Rand, die Grenze; (straits) äußerste Verlegenheit; verzweiflungsvolle Lage; (—e need) die äußerste Not; what is to be done in this —ity? was ist in diesem Notfalle zu tun? last —ity, äußerster Notfall.

Extrica—ble, *adj.* herausziehbar. —**te**, *v.a.* heraus-wickeln, -winden (*from a difficulty, etc.*); freimachen. —**tion**, *s.* die Heraus-wickelung, -windung, das Losmachen; die Entwickelung.

Extrinsic, *adj.*, —**ally**, *adv.* äußerlich, von außen.

Exuberan—ce, —**cy**, *s.* der Überfluß, das Übermaß (*of zeal, etc.*); der Schwall (*of language*); die Überschwänglichkeit; die Fülle, Üppigkeit; (luxuriant growth) der üppig Wuchs, das üppige Wachrtum. —**t**, *adj.*, —**tly**, *adv.* überflüssig; reich, üppig, wuchernd, überschwenglich.

Exud—ation, *s.* die Ausschwitzung. —**e**, *v.a. & n.* ausschwitzen.

Exult, *v.n.* frohlocken (at, over, über); to — over a fallen enemy, über einen gefallenen Gegner triumphieren. —**ant**, *adj.* frohlockend; triumphierend. —**ation**, *s.* das Frohlocken.

Eye, I. *s.* das Auge (*also fig.*); (glance) der Blick; (oversight) die Aufsicht, Leitung; (opinion) die Meinung, das Urteil; (view) der Augenschein; das Öhr (*of a needle*), die Öse (*for a dress*); das Auge, die Knospe (*of a plant*); der Nabel (*of seeds*); das Auge (*of a peacock's feather; in a strap, of an anchor, of a bolt, also Typ., Arch.*); the evil —, der böse Blick; an — for an —, Auge um Auge; shade for the —s, der Augenschirm; to look with an evil — at a p., einen scheel ansehen; up to the —s in work, bis über die Ohren in der Arbeit; to be wise in one's own —s, sich klug dünken; hooks and —s, Haken und Ösen; it's all my —! dummes Zeug! Windbeutelei! (*sl.*); to catch a p.'s —, jemandes Blick treffen, seine Aufmerksamkeit fesseln; to catch the Speaker's —, zu Worte kommen (*Parl.*); to have a cast in one's —, schielen; in the twinkling of an —, im Augenblick, im Nu; to be all —s, große Augen machen; to go right in the — of the wind, gerade in den Wind segeln; to have an — for beauty, ein gutes Auge für Schönheit haben; to have an — to one's own advantage, seinen eigenen Vorteil im Auge haben *or* behalten; to have in one's —, im Auge haben; to have one's —s about one, auf alles merken; to find favour in a p.'s —s, jemandes Gunst gewinnen; to keep a strict — upon s.o., ein wachsames Auge auf einen richten; to open a p.'s —s, einem die Augen (er)öffnen; to shut one's —s to, ein Auge (bei etwas) zudrücken; to set —s upon, (etwas, einen) zu Gesicht bekommen; to show, turn up the whites of one's —s, die Augen verdrehen; with an — to . . ., mit Rücksicht auf (eine Sache), mit der Absicht . . . II. *v.a.* ansehen, betrachten, ins Auge fassen; (ogle) beäugeln; to — over from head to foot, mit den Augen mustern; he —d me from top to toe, er maß mich vom Scheitel bis zur Sohle; to — needles, Nadeln öhren; to be born with one's —s open, Haare auf den Zähnen haben. —**d**, *adj.;* black- —d, schwarzäugig; blear- —d, triefäugig. *Comp.* —**ball**, *s.* der Augapfel. —**bright**, *s.* der Augentrost (*Bot.*). —**brow**, *s.* die Augenbraue. —**-doctor**, *s.* der Augenarzt. —**-glass**, *s.* der Kneifer, Zwicker, Klemmer; das Augenglas, Okular (*of a telescope*); double —-glass, die Lorgnette. —**lash**, *s.* die Augenwimper. —**let**, —**let-hole**, *s.* das Schnürloch; das Reefgatt (*Naut.*). —**lid**, *s.* das Augenlid. —**-lotion**, *s.* das Augenwasser. —**-piece**, *s.* das Okular (*of a microscope*); das Absehen (*of a spirit level*). —**-salve**, *s.* die Augensalbe. —**-servant**, *s.* der Augendiener. —**-service**, *s.* der Augendienst, die Augendienerei. —**sight**, *s.* das Augenlicht, Gesicht; (power of vision) die Sehkraft. —**sore**, *s.* der Dorn im Auge. —**-tooth**, *s.* der Augenzahn. —**-wash**, *s.* das Augenwasser. —**-witness**, *s.* der Augenzeuge. II. *v.a.* als Augenzeuge beobachten.

Eyot, *s.* die kleine Insel, der Werder.

Eyre, *s.* das wandernde Gericht (*obs.*); justices in —, herumreisende Richter.

Eyrie, *s.* der (Adler-)Horst, das Nest (eines Raubvogels).

F

F, f, *s.* F, f; das F (*Mus.*); *for abbreviations see the Index of abbreviations at the end of the English-German part;* — sharp, das Fis; — flat, das Fes; — major, F-Dur; — minor, F-Moll; scale in — major, die F-Dur Tonleiter; — clef, der F-Schlüssel.

Fab—le, I. *s.* die Fabel; das Märchen; (story) die Lüge; it is a mere —le, es ist völlig aus der Luft gegriffen; the world of —le, die Fabelwelt; die Märchenwelt. II. *v.a.* erdichten, fabeln, zusammenlügen; —led, in Fabeln erzählt. —**ulist,** *s.* der Fabeldichter. —**ulous,** *adj.*, —**ulously,** *adv.* (fictitious) fabelhaft, erdichtet; (told of in —les) in Fabeln berühmt; a —ulous sum, eine fabelhafte *or* fabelhaft große Summe.

Fabric, *s.* (edifice) das Gebäude, der Bau; (cloth, *etc.*) das Zeug, Fabrikat, Gewebe, der Stoff; social —, die menschliche Gesellschaft. —**ate,** *v.a.* (build) bauen, errichten; (manufacture) verfertigen, anfertigen, herstellen, fabrizieren; (invent) schmieden, erfinden. —**ation,** *s.* der Bau; die Herstellung, Fabrikation (*of cloth, etc.*); die Erdichtung; the story is doubtless a —ation, die Geschichte ist ohne Zweifel eine Erfindung. —**ator,** *s.* der Verfertiger; der Lügenerfinder.

Fa—çade, *s.* die Fassade, Vorderseite (*Build.*). —**ce,** *see* Face. —**cer,** *s.* ein Schlag ins Gesicht (*sl.*). —**cet,** *s.* die Facette, Rautenfläche (*of stones*); die Kante (*Carp.*). —**cial,** *adj.* zum Gesichte gehörig; —cial angle, der Gesichtswinkel. —**cing,** *s.* die Bekleidung, Verblendung (*Build.*); der Aufschlag (*Tail.*).

Face, I. *s.* das Gesicht, das Angesicht; Antlitz (*high style*); (expression of —) der Ausdruck, die Miene; die Gesichtslinie (eines Festungswerkes); (surface) die Oberfläche, Fläche, Seite; die Vorderseite (*of a building, a coin, etc.*); (look) der Anblick; (effrontery) die Stirn, Dreistigkeit, Keckheit, Unverschämtheit; die Front, Fassade (*Arch.*); die Schneide (*of a knife*); das Zifferblatt (*Horol.*); rechte Seite (*of cloth*); to draw a long —, ein langes Gesicht machen; — to —, von Angesicht zu Angesicht; gegenüber; before a p.'s —, vor jemands Augen; to a p.'s —, einem ins Gesicht; to fly in a p.'s —, einem zu Leibe gehen; to fly in the — of Providence, sich gegen die Vorsehung auflehnen; in the — of heavy odds, bedeutender Übermacht zum Trotz; ruin stared them in the —, der Untergang starrte ihnen entgegen; on the — of it, auf den ersten Blick, augenscheinlich; to have the — to . . ., die Unverschämtheit haben, zu . . .; to look a p. in the —, einem ins Gesicht sehen; to make —s, Gesichter schneiden; to put a bold — on the matter, sich (*dat.*) ein Herz fassen; to put the best — on things, gute Miene zum bösen Spiel machen; to run one's — for a th., etwas leichtsinnig auf Borg kaufen (*Amer.*); to set one's — against, (etwas) entschieden mißbilligen, sich gegen (etwas) stemmen; to show one's —, sich sehen lassen; to shut the door in a p.'s —, einem die Tür vor der Nase zuschlagen. II. *v.a.* (einem) ins Gesicht sehen; (be opposite) gegenüber liegen *or* stehen; (look on) gehen auf (*acc.*); (brave) keck begegnen, trotzen; (coat) überkleiden, bekleiden; aufschlagen, verbrämen, besetzen (*a dress, etc.*); verblenden, verkleiden (*a wall*); a house facing the sea, ein der See unmittelbar gegenüberliegendes Haus; this window —s the garden, dieses Fenster geht auf den Garten; I can — him, ich kann ihm die Stirne bieten; to — death, dem Tode ins Angesicht sehen; to — out a lie, eine Lüge fest behaupten. III. *v.n.*; to — about, sich (um)drehen, sich wenden; right-about —! kehrt euch! —**d,** *adj.*; full-—d, mit rundem, vollem Gesichte; two-—d, falsch; honest-—d, mit einem ehrlichen Gesichte; —d card, eine bunte Karte. *Comp.* —**-ache,** *s.* der Gesichtsschmerz. —**-cloth,** *s.* das Gesichtstuch (eines Toten). —**-guard,** *s.* der Schirm, die Maske für das Gesicht.

Facetious, *adj.*, —**ly,** *adv.* (merry) lustig; (witty) drollig, witzig; (joking) scherzhaft; you are pleased to be —, Sie belieben zu scherzen. —**ness,** *s.* die Drolligkeit, Scherzhaftigkeit.

Facil—e, *adj.* leicht; (affable) gefällig, umgänglich, gutmütig; (pliant) leicht zu überreden, nachgiebig; (ready) leicht, gewandt. —**itate,** *v.a.* erleichtern. —**itation,** *s.* die Erleichterung. —**ity,** *s.* die Leichtigkeit, Gewandtheit; die Gefälligkeit, Leutseligkeit; (pliancy) die Nachgiebigkeit; (opportunity) die günstige Gelegenheit.

Facsimile, *s.* das Faksimile.

Fact, *s.* (deed) die Tat, Handlung; (reality) die Wirklichkeit; (matter of —) die Tatsache; that's a —, das ist tatsächlich so; in —, in der Tat; ja sogar; in point of —, wirklich. —**ion,** *s.* die Partei, Faktion; (dissension) die Zwietracht, Unruhe, der Parteistreit. —**ionist,** *s.* der Parteigänger. —**ious,** *adj.*, —**iously,** *adv.* parteieifrig; (turbulent) aufrührerisch; (disloyal) ungehorsam, treulos. —**iousness,** *s.* der Parteigeist; der aufrührerische Sinn. —**itious,** *adj.*, —**itiously,** *adv.* nachgemacht, künstlich, unecht. —**or,** *s.* der Faktor, Agent (*C. L.*); der Faktor (*Arith.*). —**ory,** I. *s.* die Faktorei, Handelsniederlassung (*in foreign countries*); die Fabrik, das Fabrikgebäude. II. *attrib.*; —ory operative, der Fabrikarbeiter; —ory system, das Fabrikwesen. —**otum,** *s.* das Faktotum; der Packesel (*fig.*).

Facult—y, *s.* die Fähigkeit, Kraft, das Vermögen; (talent) die Gabe, das Talent; das Vorrecht, die Dispensation (*Law*); die Fakultät (*Univ.*); die Befugnis (*R. C.*); —y of divinity, die theologische Fakultät.

Fad, *s.* die Grille, Laune, das Steckenpferd (*fig.*); *see* —dist. —**dist,** *s.* der Grillenfänger, Sonderling, schrullenhafter Mensch, einer der irgend ein Steckenpferd hat. —**dy,** *adj.* grillenhaft, launisch.

Fad—e, *v.n.* (ver)welken; (lose colour) verbleichen, verschießen; to —e away, vergehen. —**ing,** *adj.*, —**ingly,** *adv.* vergänglich. —**ingness,** *s.* die Vergänglichkeit.

Fæces, *pl.* (sediment) die Hefe, der Bodensatz; der Auswurf, die Exkremente.

Faery, *obs. spelling for* Fairy.

Fag, I. *v.n.* schwer arbeiten, sich abmühen, schinden, plagen; als Fag dienen (in Schulen); to —, ochsen (*school sl.*). II. *v.a.* zu niedriger Arbeit zwingen. III. *s.* der Büffler, Ochser; der Schüler, der einem älteren Dienste leisten muß (*in public schools*); der Packesel (*fig.*). IV. *attrib.*; — master, älterer Schüler, dem ein jüngerer als Fag kleine Dienste verrichten muß. —**ged,** *adj.* erschöpft, ermüdet; quite —ged out, gänzlich ermüdet, ganz ab *or* fertig. —**ging,** I. *s.* die Plackerei; die Dienstleistung jüngerer Schüler an ältere. II. *attrib.*; —ging system, die Einrichtung, daß jüngere Schüler einem Primaner kleine Dienste leisten müssen. *Comp.* —**-end,** *s.* die Sahlleiste (*of cloth*); das aufgedrehte Tauende (*Naut.*); (letztes, schlechtes) Ende (*coll.*).

Fa(g)got, *s.* das Holzbündel, die Welle, Faschine.

Faience, *s.* die Fayence, weißes Steingut, unechtes Porzellan.

Fail, I. *v.n.* (be wanting) fehlen, mangeln; (miss) fehlschlagen, mißlingen; versiegen (*as springs*); nicht aufgehen (*as seed*); stocken, versagen (*voice*); schwächer werden, ermatten, nachlassen (*strength*); ermangeln (*in a duty*); zahlungsunfähig werden, Bankerott machen (*C.L.*); he will not — to . . ., er wird nicht ermangeln zu . . .; they will not — to win, sie werden unfehlbar (sicher) gewinnen; they never —ed to be present, sie waren regelmäßig zugegen; they never —ed to assure me, sie verfehlten nie mir zu versichern; he cannot — to notice, er kann nicht umhin zu bemerken; he cannot — to see that . . ., er kann nicht anders als einsehen, daß . . .; his strength begins to —

seine Kräfte fangen an nachzulassen; his voice —ed, seine Stimme versagte; in which attempt he —ed, welcher Versuch ihm mißlang. II. *v.a.* im Stiche lassen, verlassen; verfehlen, versäumen; my heart —s me, mich verläßt der Mut; that will — him, das wird ihn durchfallen lassen. III. *s.*; without —, unfehlbar, ganz gewiß. **—ing**, I. *p.*; —ing health, immer schwächer *or* schlechter werdende Gesundheit; —ing an heir, in Ermangelung eines Erben. II. *s.* der Fehler, die Schwäche. **—ure**, *s.* das Fehlen, Ausbleiben (of crops, springs, etc., der Ernte, der Quellen, 2c.); die Ermangelung; die Abnahme, das Hinsinken; das Fehlschlagen, Mißlingen (*of an enterprise, etc.*); das Falissement, der Bank(e)rott (*C. L.*); that man is a —ure, aus dem Manne wird nichts, der Mann ist untüchtig; it is doomed to —ure, es hat keine Aussicht auf Erfolg; the paper proved a —ure, das Blatt hatte keinen Erfolg.

Fain, I. *adj.* froh, geneigt; nicht ungern, genötigt. II. *adv.* gern; I would — assist you, gern würde ich Ihnen beistehen.

Faint, I. *adj.*, **—ly**, *adv.* schwach, kraftlos, ohnmächtig; schwach, matt, leise (*as sounds*); blaß (*as a colour*); — recollection, dunkle *or* schwache Erinnerung; — heart ne'er won fair lady, wer nicht wagt, gewinnt nicht, das Glück ist dem Kühnen hold (*prov.*). II. *v.n.* ohnmächtig werden, in Ohnmacht fallen (*with*, vor); (grow weak) ermatten, schwach, matt werden; (lose courage) verzagen. III. *s.* (—ing fit) die Ohnmacht, ein Ohnmachtsanfall. **—ish**, *adj.* etwas schwach. **—ness**, *s.* die Schwäche, Mattigkeit; die Schwachheit (*fig.*); (—ness of heart) der Kleinmut, die Verzagtheit. *Comp.* **—hearted**, *adj.* schwachherzig, kleinmütig, zaghaft. — **heartedness**, *s.* der Kleinmut.

[1]**Fair**, I. *adj.* (beautiful) schön, hübsch; (blonde) hellfarbig, blond; (pure) unbefleckt, unbescholten; (clear) hell, rein; (serene) heiter. II. *adj. & adv.* günstig (*as wind*); (legible) sauber, rein, leserlich; schön, gut (*as a prospect*); (equitable) ehrlich, redlich; (just) billig, unparteiisch, gerecht; (pure) unbefleckt, unbescholten; (civil) freundlich; (average) gewöhnlich, Mittel=; — catch, der Freifang (*Footb.*); — copy, die Reinschrift; — dealing, die Redlichkeit; a — face, ein schönes Gesicht (*lit.*), ein freundliches Gesicht (*fig.*); by — means, durch Güte, auf gutem Wege; auf ehrliche Weise; — play, ehrliches Spiel, redliches Verfahren, die Rechtlichkeit; to give a p. — play, einen ehrlich behandeln; — promises, schöne Versprechungen; the — sex, das schöne Geschlecht; — and softly, sachte; — trade, Handel unter billigen Bedingungen, billiger Wettbewerb (*as opposed to free trade*); — trial, unparteiische Untersuchung; to give a p. — warning, einen zeitig und ernstlich warnen; to be in a — way, gute Aussichten haben; to bid —, sich gut anlassen, (promise) versprechen; to promise —, viel versprechen; to speak a p. —, einem gute Worte geben; the wind sits —, der Wind ist günstig. III. *s.* die Schöne; the —, das schöne Geschlecht. **—ly**, *adv.* (passably) erträglich, leidlich; (justly) ehrlich, billig; (legibly) leserlich; (completely) vollständig, ganz, gänzlich; —ly held, festgehalten (*Footb.*). **—ness**, *s.* die Schönheit (*of a form*); die Hellfarbigkeit (*of complexion*); die Unbescholtenheit; die Redlichkeit, Billigkeit; in —ness to a p., um einem Gerechtigkeit widerfahren zu lassen. *Comp.* **—-complexioned**, *adj.* hellfarbig. **—-faced**, *adj.* schön von Gesicht; dem äußern Scheine nach schön (*fig.*). **—-haired**, *adj.* mit blondem Haar. **—-minded**, *adj.* aufrichtig, ehrlich. **—-spoken**, *adj.* höflich, artig. **—-weather**, *adj.* bei günstigem Wetter stattfindend; a —-weather friend, ein Freund im Glück *or* solange die Sonne scheint.

[2]**Fair**, *s.* die Messe, der Jahrmarkt; to come a day after the —, einen Postag zu spät kommen. **—ing**, *s.* das Meßgeschenk, Jahrmarktsgeschenk, die Kirmeß. *Comp.* **—-day**, *s.* der Jahrmarktstag.

Fairy, I. *adj.* feenhaft, zauberisch, Feen=, Zauber=; — kingdom, das Feenreich, Elfenreich; — queen, die Feenkönigin, Elfenkönigin. II. *s.* die Fee, der Elf; — of the water, die Wassernixe. *Comp.* **—-dance**, *s.* der Feenreigen. **—-fingers**, *s.* roter Fingerhut. **—-land**, *s.* das Feenland, Elfenreich; das Märchenland, Zauberland (*fig.*). **—-like**, *adj.* feenartig; feenhaft. **—-rings**, *s.* die Feenkreise. **—-stone**, *s.* der Alpstein, Alpschoß. **—-tale**, *s.* das Märchen, Feenmärchen.

Faith, *s.* (trust) das Vertrauen; (belief) der Glaube (*also Theol.*); (creed) das Glaubensbekenntnis; (honesty, veracity) die Treue, Redlichkeit, Ehrlichkeit; (promise, pledge) das Wort; —! fürwahr! i' —! (bei) meiner Treu! in good —, auf Treu' und Glauben, ehrlich; in — whereof, und zur Bewahrheitung dieses; to put — in . . ., an (*acc.*) . . . glauben. **—ful**, I. *adj.*, **—fully**, *adv.* treu, getreu; wahrhaft, ehrlich; (ge)treu (*to one's promises*); (conscientious) gewissenhaft, wahrhaft; (believing) gläubig; rechtgläubig; beständig (*in love, etc.*); wahr (*as a narrative*); treu (*as a translation*); a —ful account, ein wahrheitsgetreuer Bericht; a —ful servant, ein (ge)treuer Diener; to carry out —fully, (ge)treulich, genau, gewissenhaft ausführen. II. *s.*; the —ful, die Rechtgläubigen. **—fulness**, *s.* die Treue, Ehrlichkeit; die Pflichttreue (*of servants*); die Wahrhaftigkeit (*of God*); die Beständigkeit. **—less**, *adj.*, **—lessly**, *adv.* treulos. **—lessness**, *s.* die Treulosigkeit. *Comp.* **—-cure**, **—-healing**, *s.* die Heilung durch den Glauben, das Gesundbeten.

Fake, I. *v.a.* zu betrügerischen Zwecken herrichten, aufputzen, zurecht machen; betrügen; stehlen, (be)rauben; fälschen; a —d rhyme, ein ad hoc gemachter Reim. II. *s.* der Betrug; der Schwindler; das wertlose Ding. **—ment**, *s.* der Betrug, die Schwindelei.

Fakir, *s.* der Fakir.

Falchion, *s.* der Pallasch; das Schwert (*poet.*).

Falcon, *s.* der Falke. **—er**, *s.* der Falkner. **—ry**, *s.* die Falknerei; die Falkenbeize, Falkenjagd.

Fall, I. *ir.v.n.* fallen, sich ergießen (*as rivers*); (— down) fallen, (nieder=)stürzen; einfallen (*as houses*); verwelken (*as flowers*); (— off) abfallen; fallen, abnehmen, heruntergehen (*as prices*); fallen, herabstürzen (*from a high position, etc.*); sich legen, fallen (*as the wind*); (begin) anfangen; (become) werden; (light) fallen, geraten, stoßen, treffen (on a p., auf einen); (attack a p.) herfallen über (einen); fallen, eintreffen (*as a point of time*); he fell ill, er wurde krank; his countenance fell, sein Gesicht verfinsterte sich; to — a weeping, anfangen zu weinen; to — **asleep**, einschlafen; to — **away**, abfallen, (desert) abtrünnig werden, (grow thin) abmagern, mager werden; to — **back**, zurückfallen, zurücktreten; the troops fell back, die Truppen wichen *or* zogen sich zurück; to — back upon a th., auf eine S. zurückgreifen *or* zurückkommen; to — **down**, niederfallen, (tumble down) einfallen, einstürzen; to — (down) at a p.'s feet, einem zu Füßen fallen; to — **due**, fällig, zahlbar werden; to — **foul of**, sich reiben an (*dat.*), verwickeln mit; to — foul of, ungestüm über (*acc.*) herfallen (*fig.*); to — **from**, abfallen; an exclamation of displeasure fell from him, ihm entfuhr ein Ausruf des Mißfallens; to — **in**, einfallen, einstürzen (*as houses*); einfallen (*as the cheeks*), sich in Reihen formieren; — in! angetreten! (*Mil.*); to — in for calling roll, zum Appell antreten; to — in love, sich verlieben; to — in with a p.'s views, mit jemandes Ansichten übereinstimmen, im Einklang sein; where did you — in with him? wo trafen Sie ihn? to — in with the enemy, mit dem Feinde zusammenstoßen; it does not — in my way, es schlägt nicht in mein Fach; to — **into** a passion, in Wut geraten; the river —s into the sea, der Fluß ergießt sich ins Meer; to — into difficulties, in Schwierigkeiten geraten; to — into error, in Irrtum verfallen; to — **off**, herab=, herunter=fallen; abfallen (von einem), (einem) abtrünnig werden (*fig.*); my pupil has lately —en off greatly, mein Schüler hat in der letzten Zeit sehr nachgelassen; to — **on**, herabfallen auf (*acc.*); (attack) herfallen über (*acc.*); fear fell on them, Furcht bemächtigte sich ihrer; to — on one's feet, Glück haben; to — on a Sunday, auf einen Sonntag fallen; to — **out**, ausfallen, ausfällig werden, zanken; (chance) vorfallen, sich ereignen; he has —en out with him, er hat sich mit ihm überworfen (*coll.*); to — out well, gut ausfallen; gut rentieren (*C. L.*); to — out of one's hands, den Händen entfallen; to — **short of**, nicht zureichen, fehlen; to — short of the mark, das Ziel nicht treffen; this fell short of our expectations, dies entsprach unsern Erwartungen nicht; this did not — short of a miracle, dies war geradezu ein Wunder; we fell short of provisions, es fehlte uns an Lebensmitteln, die Lebensmittel gingen uns aus; to — **to**, anfangen, sich an (*acc.*) machen (*work*), herfallen über (eine Speise, *coll.*); to — to a p.('s lot), einem zufallen; it —s to me (to . . .), es liegt mir ob (zu . . .); to — to pieces, verfallen, zerfallen; to — to ruin, in Verfall geraten; to — **under**, unter (eine S.) fallen, dazu gerechnet werden; it —s under that class of poetry, es gehört unter jene Klasse von Dichtung; to — under censure, sich dem Tadel aussetzen; to — **upon**, auf (eine S.) fallen, (einen) anfallen, befallen; to — upon a p.'s neck, einem um den Hals fallen; to — upon an expedient, auf ein (Auskunfts=)Mittel verfallen. II. *s.* das Fallen, der Fall, Sturz; der Fall, Untergang, Sturz, die Vernichtung (*fig.*); das Fallen, Sinken, der Abschlag (*in prices*); die Senkung (*of the voice*); die Kadenz (*Mus.*); (water—) der Wasserfall; der Überfluß (*of dikes*); das Abfallen (*of the leaf*); (declivity) der Fall, Abhang; der Verfall (*of an empire*); (defeat) die Niederlage; der Fall (*Phys.*); ein kurzer Schleier (für Damen); — (of man), der Sündenfall; — of a river, das Stromgefälle; — in wages, das Herabgehen der Löhne; operator for the —, der Baissier (*C.L.*); — of rain (snow), der Regenguß (Schneesturz); to have *or* sustain a —, fallen, stürzen; the —, der Herbst (*Amer.*). III. *attrib.*; — trade, das Herbstgeschäft (*Amer.*). —**ing**, *s.* das Fallen; —ing away, die Abmagerung, Abzehrung; a —ing away, from, off, der Abfall; die Verminderung; a —ing out, eine Mißhelligkeit. *Comp.* —**ing-star**, *s.* die Sternschnuppe. —**ing-stone**, *s.* der Meteorstein. —**ing-sickness**, *s.* die Fallsucht.

Fallac—ious, *adj.*, —**iously**, *adv.* trügerisch (*as hopes*); betrüglich; —ious argument, trügerische Beweisführung, sophistisches Argument. —**iousness**, *s.* die Trüglichkeit; die Sophisterei. —**y**, *s.* der Betrug, die Täuschung; der Trugschluß (*Log.*).

Fallib—ility, *s.* die Fehlbarkeit. —**le**, *adj.*, —**ly**, *adv.* fehlbar.

Fallopian, *adj.* fallopisch; — tubes, die Muttertrompeten (*Anat.*).

Fallow, I. *adj.* fahl, falb; brach (*Agr.*). II. *s.* das Brachfeld. III. *v.a.* brachen. —**ness**, *s.* das Brachliegen; die Unfruchtbarkeit (*fig. obs.*). *Comp.* —**-deer**, *s.* das Damwild.

Fals—e, I. *adj. & adv.*, —**ely**, *adv.*, falsch, unwahr; unrichtig; treulos, unehrlich (to, gegen); unecht, Schein=; —e bottom, der falsche, blinde Boden; —e imprisonment, unrechtmäßige Verhaftung; —e keel, der Gegenkiel; —e key, der Nachschlüssel; —e note, die falsche, unrichtige Note; —e step, der Fehltritt; to play a p. —e, einen betrügen, ein falsches Spiel mit einem treiben. II. *s.* das Falsche, Unwahre. —**ehood**, *s.* die Lüge, Unwahrheit; die Falschheit, Treulosigkeit; die Lügenhaftigkeit (*of a report*); to tell a —ehood, eine Unwahrheit sagen. —**eness**, *s.* die Falschheit. —**etto**, *s.* das Falsett (*Mus.*). —**ification**, *s.* die Verfälschung; die Fälschung. —**ifier**, *s.* der Verfälscher; der Fälscher. —**ify**, *v.a.* fälschen (*coin*); verfälschen (*writings, etc.*); als falsch erweisen, widerlegen. —**ity**, *s.* die Falschheit. *Comp.* —**e-faced**, *adj.* heuchlerisch. —**e-hearted**, *adj.* treulos.

Falter, *v.* I. *a.* stammeln; to — out, herausstottern. II. *n.* stottern, stammeln (*in speaking*); wanken, schwanken (*in walking*); stocken, stecken bleiben (*in a speech or answer*).

Fam—e, *s.* der Ruhm, der (gute) Ruf; (report) das Gerücht, der Ruf; desire of —e, die Ruhmbegier. —**ed**, *adj.* berühmt (for, wegen). —**ous**, *adj.*, —**ously**, *adv.* berühmt; (remarkable) ausgezeichnet; famos (*coll.*). —**ousness**, *s.* die Berühmtheit.

Famil—iar, I. *adj.*, —**iarly**, *adv.* vertraut, vertraulich, intim; wohlbekannt (with, mit); (affable) leutselig, umgänglich; (habitual) gewohnt, gewöhnlich; (unceremonious) zu vertraut, frei; —iar friend, vertrauter Freund; —iar quotation, das geflügelte Wort, das beliebte *or* oft gehörte Zitat; —iar style, leichte Schreibart. II. *s.* der Vertraute; (—iar spirit) der Hausgeist, Kobold; der Diener, Familiar der Inquisition. —**iarity**, *s.* die Vertraulichkeit; die Leutseligkeit, Zugänglichkeit; (freedom) die Ungezwungenheit; —iarity breeds contempt, allzugroße Vertraulichkeit erzeugt Verachtung. —**iarize**, *v.a.* vertraut machen; to —iarize o.s. with, sich gewöhnen an (*acc.*), sich bekannt machen mit. —**y**, I. *s.* die Familie; (race) die Familie, der Stamm; die Familie, Gattung (*of plants and animals*); father of a —y, der Familienvater; of good —y, von guter Herkunft. II. *adj.* zur Familie gehörig; —y doctor, der Hausarzt; —y vault, die Familiengruft; in the —y way, in andern Umständen, guter Hoffnung (*coll.*).

Fami—ne, *s.* die Hungersnot; der Mangel (an einer S.). —**sh**, *v.* I. *a.* aushungern, verhungern lassen; (exhaust) verschmachten lassen. II. *n.* Hunger *or* Durst leiden; Hungers sterben, verhungern; verschmachten (*fig.*).

Fan, I. *s.* der Fächer; die Wanne, Schwinge (*for corn, etc.*); die Anregung, der Antrieb (*fig.*); der Ventilator (*Mach.*). II. *v.a.* schwingen (*corn*); fächeln, wedeln; anfachen (*a flame*); entfachen, entflammen (*fig.*). —**ner**, *s.* die Kornschwinge; der Worfler. *Comp.* —**-light**, *s.* das Fächerfenster, halbkreisförmige Fenster, die Lünette. —**ning-machine**, *s.* die Kornschwinge. —**-palm**, *s.* die Fächerpalme. —**-shaped**, *adj.* fächerförmig. —**-tail**, *s.* (—-tail pigeon) die Pfauentaube. —**-tracery**, *s.* das Fächermaßwerk (*Arch.*); —-(tracery-)vaulting, das Fächergewölbe.

Fanatic, I. *adj.*, —**al**, *adj.*, —**ally**, *adv.* fanatisch, schwärmerisch. II. *s.* der Fanatiker, (Religions=) Schwärmer, Eiferer, Schwarmgeist. —**ize**, *v.* I. *a.* fanatisieren, in blinden Eifer *or* blinde Wut, Begeisterung versetzen. II. *n.* den Glaubensschwärmer spielen. —**ism**, *s.* die (religiöse) Schwärmerei.

Fanc—ier, *s.* der Liebhaber; dog-—ier, der Hundeliebhaber, Hundezüchter, Hundehändler. —**iful**, *adj.*, —**ifully**, *adv.* phantastisch, schwärmerisch; wunderlich, grillenhaft. —**ifulness**, *s.* das phantastische *or* grillenhafte Wesen; das Wunderliche. —**y**, I. *s.* die Phantasie, Einbildungskraft; (idea) der Begriff, die Idee; (whim) die Grille; (notion) der Einfall; (taste) der Geschmack; (liking) die Neigung (zu), Vorliebe (für); (caprice) die Willkür; where is —y bred? wo wird die Liebeslust erzeugt? to take a —y to, (einen *or* eine S.) lieb gewinnen; it strikes my —y, es gefällt mir. II. *v.a.* sich (*dat.*) einbilden, sich (*dat.*) vorstellen, sich (*dat.*) denken; (regard as) halten für; (like) Gefallen haben an (*dat.*) lieben. III. *v.n.* sich (*dat.*) einbilden, sich (*dat.*) vorstellen. IV. *adj.*; —y articles, Modeartikel, Mode-, Luxus-artikel; — cakes, Torten, feines Gebäck; —y cloth, der Modestoff; —y costume, das Maskenkostüm, der kostümierte Anzug; —y needlework, feinere Handarbeit(en), Stickerei; —y trade, der Modewarenhandel, das Galanteriewarengeschäft. *Comp.* —**y-(dress-)ball**, *s.* der Maskenball, Kostümball. —**y-fair**, *s.* der Wohltätigkeitsbasar. —**y-free**, *adj.* liebefrei. —**y-goods**, *pl.* Galanteriewaren. —**y-price**, *s.* der Liebhaberpreis, übertrieben hoher Preis; he gave a —y-price for it, er bezahlte einen unverhältnismäßigen Preis. —**y-stocks**, *pl.* unsichere Spekulationspapiere (*Amer.*). —**y-work**, *s.* feine (weibliche) Handarbeit; der Luxusartikel, die Luxusarbeit.

Fandango, *s.* der Fandango, spanische Tanz.

Fane, *s.* der Tempel.

Fanfar—e, *s.* der Trompetentusch, Tusch, die Fanfare. —**onade**, *s.* die Prahlerei.

Fang, *s.* der Fang, die Klaue; (tusk) der Hauzahn; der Fangzahn. —**ed**, *adj.* mit Fängern, Hauern versehen *or* bewaffnet. —**led**, *see* New—led.

Fantas—ia, *s.* die Phantasie (*Mus.*). —**tic(al)**, *adj.*, —**tically**, *adv.* phantastisch, eingebildet; (odd) grillenhaft, närrisch, seltsam, wunderlich. —**ticalness**, *s.* das Phantastische; die Grillenfängerei. —**y**, *see* Fancy I.

Far, I. *adj.* fern, entfernt, weit; the — East, Ostasien; on the — side, auf der andern Seite, jenseits; — be it from me, fern sei es von mir; — from God, weit von Gott entfernt, Gott ganz entfremdet. II. *adv.* fern, weit; (greatly) zum großen Teil, sehr viel; as — as, so weit als, bis dahin; by —, bei weitem; from —, von weitem; — away, weit entfernt; — from being offended . . ., weit (davon) entfernt, beleidigt zu sein . . .; — and near *or* wide, weit und breit; this goes — to justify their conduct, dies rechtfertigt ihr Benehmen in hohem Grade; this went — to convince us, dies trug wesentlich dazu bei, uns zu überzeugen; — and away better, sehr viel besser; — gone in consumption, schwindsüchtig in hohem Grade; — gone (in drink), stark benebelt; — off, weit weg, entlegen; — on in the day, spät (am Tage); the day was — spent, es war spät am Tage (*B.*); to carry (a th.) too —, (eine Sache) zu weit treiben *or* übertreiben; thus —, bis dahin, soweit. —**ness**, *s.* die Entfernung. *Comp.* —**-famed**, *adj.* weitberühmt. —**-fetched**, *adj.* weit hergeholt, gesucht, gezwungen, bei den Haaren herbeigezogen. —**-reaching**, *adj.* weitreichend, weittragend. —**-sighted**, *adj.* weitsichtig.

Farc—e, I. *s.* der Schwank (*Theat.*); die Posse (*also Theat.*); a mere *or* complete —e, eine wahre oder rechte Posse. II. *v.a.* füllen, farzieren. —**ical**, *adj.* possenhaft, drollig; —cical comedy, die Posse, der Schwank.

Fardel, *s.* das Bündel; die Bürde, Last (*fig.*).

Fare, I. *v.n.* (get on) ergehen, sich befinden, daran sein; (feed) essen; (be) leben; you may go further and — worse, man kann lange suchen, ohne etwas Besseres zu finden; to — well *or* ill (in a matter), (bei einer Sache) gut *or* schlimm fahren *or* wegkommen; I —d badly there, es ist mir dort schlecht gegangen; — thee well, gehab' dich wohl, lebe wohl; —well, leben Sie wohl; lebewohl. II. *s.* der Fuhrlohn, das Fahrgeld; (passenger) der Passagier, Reisende, Fahrgast; (food) die Speise; bill of —, der Speisezettel, die Speisekarte; indifferent —, schlechte Verpflegung *or* Kost; is the — good? ist die Kost gut? there is poor — to-day, heute giebt's schmale Kost; what is the —? was habe ich zu bezahlen? was kostet die Fahrt? wieviel kostet die Fahrkarte? *Comp.* —**well**, I. *adj.* Abschieds-; —well letter, der Abschiedsbrief; —well message, eine Abschiedsbotschaft. II. *s.* das Lebewohl, der Abschied; to bid —well to, (einem) Lebewohl sagen, (von einem) Abschied nehmen. III. *interj.* lebewohl!

Farina, *s.* der Sonnenstaub (*Bot.*); das Mehl; das Satzmehl (*Chem.*). —**ceous**, *adj.* mehlig; mehlhaltig; —ceous food, mehlhaltige Speisen, Mehlspeisen; —ceous substances, Mehlstoffe.

Farm, I. *s.* der Pachthof, die Meierei; (— land) das Gut; (lease) die Pacht; mixed —, Gut, auf dem Milch- und Ackerwirtschaft betrieben wird; model —, die Musterwirtschaft. II. *v.a.* bauen; (— out) verpachten; to — the revenue, die Staatseinkünfte in Pacht geben; to — a school, eine (kleine, meist ländliche) Schule an den Direktor verpachten. III. *attrib.*; — bailiff, der Verwalter; — offices, die Wirtschaftsgebäude; — servant, der Bauernknecht, die Bauernmagd. —**er**, *s.* der Pächter, Meier; (landed proprietor) der Landwirt; der Pächter (*of the revenues, etc.*); —er's boy, der Bauernknecht. —**ery**, *s.* Gutsgebäude und Stallungen. —**ing**, I. *adj.* zum Ackerbau gehörig; —ing implements *or* utensils, Ackergeräte, das Ackergeschirr; —ing purposes, landwirtschaftliche Zwecke; —ing stock, landwirtschaftliche Haustiere. II. *s.* die Landwirtschaft, der Ackerbau. *Comp.* —**-horse**, *s.* das Arbeitspferd. —**-house**, *s.* der Meierhof, die Meierei, Gehöft. —**stead**, *s.* der Bauernhof, das Gehöft. —**-yard**, *s.* der (Wirtschafts-)Hof.

Faro, *s.* das Pharo(spiel); — table, der Pharotisch.

Farrago, *s.* das Gemisch, Gemengsel, der Mischmasch.

Farrier, *s.* der Hufschmied; (horse doctor) der Roßarzt; —'s tools, das Beschlagzeug. —**y**, *s.* die Roßarzneikunde; das Hufschmiedehandwerk.

Farrow, I. *s.* der Wurf (Ferkel), das Ferkel; with —, trächtig (*of sows*). II. *v.a. & n.* ferkeln, werfen.

Farthe—r, *adj. & adv.* (*comp. of* Far) ferner, weiter. —**st**, I. *adj.* (*sup. of* Far) fernst, weitest, entferntest. II. *adv.*; at —st, am fernsten, am weitesten.

Farthing, *s.* der Heller, Farthing (¼ Penny).

Farthingale, *s.* der Reifrock.

Fasc—es, *pl.* die Liktorenstäbe. —**ia**, *s.* das Band; der Streif (*Arch.*); der Gürtel (*Astr.*); die Sehnenbinde (*Anat.*). —**icle**, *s.* der Büschel (*Bot.*). —**icular**, *adj.* büschelförmig. —**ine**, *s.* die Faschine (*Fort.*).

Fascinat—e, *v.a.* bezaubern. —**ion**, *s.* die Bezauberung; (charm) der Zauber, Reiz; dumb —ion, regungslose Spannung.

Fash, *v.* (*dial.*) I. *a.* plagen, ärgern. II. *n.* übellaunig sein, sich ärgern.

Fashion, I. *s.* die Mode; (form) die Gestalt; (äußere) Form; (cut) der Schnitt; (— in dress) die herrschende Tracht, Mode; (custom) die Sitte, der Gebrauch; (manner) die Art und Weise, Manier; die feine Lebensart, gute Manieren; rank and —, die vornehme Welt; people of —, modische Leute, Leute von gutem Tone, Tonangebende; man of —, modisch gekleideter Mann, Mann von feinem Benehmen, feiner Mann; to be in (out of) —, in (aus der) Mode sein; after the — of, nach der Art von; to set the —, den Ton angeben; in Mode bringen, die Mode aufbringen *or* angeben. II. *v.a.* bilden, gestalten, formen, modeln; fassonieren, verfertigen (*a dress*). —**able**, I. *adj.*, —**ably**, *adv.* modisch, Mode-; (elegant) fein, elegant; (new) modern; it is —able, es ist Mode; —able hours, das Spätspeisen, Spätaufstehen; —able woman, eine feine Dame, Modedame; —able party, feine Gesellschaft; —able resort, ein Vergnügungsort für die feine Welt; to dress —ably, sich nach der Mode kleiden. II. *s.* der Modeherr. —**ableness**, *s.* das Beliebtsein, Modesein; das Modische, Moderne, die modische Eleganz. —**er**, *s.* der Former, Gestalter (*also fig.*); der Zuschneider, Verfertiger; the King's —er, der königliche Leibschneider. *Comp.* —**-monger**, der Modenarr.

[1]**Fast**, *adj. & adv.* fest; fest, tief (*as sleep*); schnell; flott, fesch (*coll.*); — friends, vertraute, innige, beständige Freunde; to play — and loose, unzuverlässig *or* unredlich handeln; — colours, echte Farben; — liver, der Wüstling; — girl, emanzipiertes, freies Mädchen; to be — asleep, fest schlafen; it is raining —, es regnet stark; as — as I can, so schnell ich nur kann; to hold —, festhalten; to make —, zumachen; to make (*a ship*) —, meeren, mit Tauen festmachen; — train, der Schnellzug, Eilzug; my watch is —, meine Uhr geht vor. **—en**, *v.* I. *a.* fest machen, befestigen (to, an); fest zumachen (*doors*); (—en together) verbinden, festhalten, verkitten, zusammenfügen; his eyes were —ened upon her, seine Augen hefteten sich auf sie. II. *n.* sich festhalten, sich ansetzen (upon, an, *acc.*). **—ener**, *s.* der Befestiger. **—ening**, das Befestigungsmittel, Band; der Riegel, Haken, das Schloß; die Verschlußvorrichtung. **—ness**, *s.* die Festigkeit; der feste Platz, die Festung, die Schnelligkeit. *Comp.* **—-sailing**, *adj.*; —-sailing ship, der Schnellsegler.

[2]**Fast**, I. *v.n.* fasten. II. *s.*, **—ing**, *s.* das Fasten; to break one's —, frühstücken. *Comp.* **—-day**, *s.* der Fasttag.

Fastidious, *adj.*, **—ly**, *adv.* eigen, ekel (*in eating*), wählerisch; schwer zu befriedigen. **—ness**, *s.* das wählerische Wesen; die Mäkelei.

Fat, I. *adj.* fett (*also fig.*); dick, fleischig, plump; fruchtbar (*as soil*); to grow —, fett werden. II. *s.* das Fett. **—ling**, *s.* junges Mastvieh. **—ness**, *s.* die Fettigkeit, Fettheit, das Fett; die Wohlbeleibtheit, Fettleibigkeit; die Fruchtbarkeit (*of the soil*). **—ten**, *etc.*, *see* Fatten.

Fat—al, *adj.*, **—ally**, *adv.* verhängnisvoll, unglücklich, unheilbringend; tödlich, gefährlich (*as wounds, etc.*); —al stroke, der Todesstreich; tidings — to their hopes, für ihre Hoffnungen verhängnisvolle Nachrichten. **—alism**, *s.* der Fatalismus, Glaube an Vorherbestimmung, die Verhängnislehre. **—alist**, *s.* der Fatalist. **—alistic**, *adj.* fatalistisch, an Vorherbestimmung glaubend. **—ality**, *s.* das Verhängnis; das Mißgeschick (*fig.*); (disastrousness) die Verderblichkeit, das Verhängnisvolle; (deadliness) die Tödlichkeit. **—e**, *s.* das Schicksal, Verhängnis, Geschick; (doom) der Tod, Untergang, das Verderben; the —es, die Parzen. **—ed**, *adj.* vom Schicksal verhängt, bestimmt; (doomed) dem Verderben geweiht. **—eful**, *adj.*, **—efully**, *adv.* verhängnisvoll.

Fata-Morgana, *s.* die Fata Morgana, Luftspiegelung.

Father, I. *s.* der Vater; der Pater (*R.C.*); your —, Ihr (Herr) Vater; — Christmas, der Weihnachtsmann; the child is — of the man, aus Kindern werden Leute (*prov.*); the early —s, die Kirchenväter; to be gathered to one's —s, zu seinen Vätern versammelt werden, sterben. II. *v.a.* (er)zeugen; adoptieren; to — a child upon a p., einen als Vater eines Kindes angeben; to — s.th. upon a p., einem etwas zuschreiben, beimessen. **—hood**, *s.* die Vaterschaft. **—less**, *adj.* vaterlos. **—liness**, *s.* die väterliche Zärtlichkeit, Väterlichkeit. **—ly**, *adj.* väterlich. *Comp.* **—-in-law**, *s.* der Schwiegervater. **—land**, *s.* das Vaterland; the —land (Fatherland), das (deutsche) Vaterland, Deutschland.

Fathom, I. *s.* die Klafter, der Faden (1829 Meter). II. *v.a.* umklaftern (*obs.*); ergründen, abmessen, sondieren; ergründen, eindringen in (*a design*). **—able**, *adj.* meßbar; ergründlich. **—less**, *adj.* unergründlich, bodenlos. *Comp.* **—-line**, *s.* die Lotleine.

Fatigue, I. *s.* die Ermüdung; die Erschöpfung; die ermüdende Arbeit, Strapaze; our great —s, unsere großen Strapazen; spent with —, ganz müde und matt. II. *v.a.* ermüden, abmatten. *Comp.* **—-duty**, *s.* der Arbeitsdienst (*Mil.*). **—-party**, *s.* zur Arbeit abkommandierte Abteilung (*Mil.*).

Fatt—en, *v.* I. *a.* fett machen, mästen. II. *n.* fett werden. **—ener**, *s.* der Mäster. **—ening**, *s.* das Mästen. **—ish**, *adj.* etwas fett. **—y**, I. *adj.* fettig. II. *s.* Dicker, Dick(er)chen (*coll.*).

Fatu—ity, *s.* die Albernheit. **—ous**, *adj.* albern, dumm; (impotent) kraftlos; (illusory) nichtig.

Faucal, *adj.* Kehl=, Rachen=; — stop, Verschlußlaut mit velarer Öffnung, mit Senkung des Gaumensegels (*with breath through the nose*).

Faucet, *s.* der Zapfen, Hahn, Faßspund.

Faugh, *int.* pfui!

Fault, *s.* der Fehler, das Vergehen, Versehen; die Flözkluft (*Min.*); (want) der Mangel; it is my —, es ist meine Schuld; to find — with a th., etwas tadeln *or* bemängeln, an einer S. etwas auszusetzen haben; to be at —, Schuld haben, die Schuld tragen; auf falscher Fährte sein; in Verlegenheit sein; —! Fehler! falsch (*L.T.*). **—ily**, *adv. see* —y. **—iness**, *s.* die Fehlerhaftigkeit. **—less**, *adj.*, **—lessly**, *adv*, fehlerfrei, tadellos. **—lessness**, *s.* die Fehlerlosigkeit. **—y**, *adj.* fehlerhaft, mangelhaft.

Faun, *s.* der Faun. **—a**, *pl.* die Tierwelt einer Gegend, Fauna.

Faux-pas, *s.* der Fehltritt, Mißgriff.

Favo(u)r, I. *s.* die Gunst, Güte, Gewogenheit; (kind act) der Gefallen; (patronage) der Schutz; (knot) die (Band)schleife; white —s, weiße Rosetten, Bandschleifen; do me the — to . . ., tun Sie mir den Gefallen und . . .; the — of an early answer is requested, um gefällige baldige Antwort wird gebeten; in (a p.'s) —, in — of, zum Besten (jemandes); to be in — of, für (einen, eine Sache) sein; to be in — with a p., bei einem in Gunst stehen; they are at present in great —, sie sind gegenwärtig sehr begehrt (*C.L.*); to curry — with a p., sich bei einem einschmeicheln; balance in your —, Saldo zu Ihren Gunsten; by — of, under the — of, begünstigt durch; your — of the 20th ult., Ihr Geehrtes vom 20sten v. M. (*C.L.*). II. *v.a.* begünstigen, (einem) geneigt sein; (encourage) unterstützen; gleichen, ähnlich sehen; the child —s his father, das Kind ähnelt seinem Vater; to —, be —ably disposed towards a p., einem günstig gesinnt sein; — us with a song, singen Sie uns gütigst ein Lied, geben Sie uns ein Lied zum besten; — us with your visit, beehren Sie uns mit ihrem Besuche; — me with an answer, antworten Sie mir gefälligst; —ed by, begünstigt von; überreicht von. **—able**, *adj.*, **—ably**, *adv.* günstig; begünstigend (to, zu); (opportune) gelegen (for, zu); (advantageous) vorteilhaft, günstig. **—ableness**, *s.* das Günstige; das Vorteilhafte; the —ableness of the times for . . ., die dem (Unternehmen, 2c.) günstigen Zeiten. **—ed**, *adj.* begünstigt; gestaltet (*of features*); the —ed few, die wenigen Auserwählten; ill —ed, schlecht aussehend, häßlich; well —ed, schön. **—er**, *s.* der Gönner, Freund. **—ite**, I. *s.* der Günstling; der mutmaßliche Sieger (*of race-horses*). II. *adj.* Lieblings=. **—itism**, *s.* die Günstlingswirtschaft (*at courts*); die unberechtigte Bevorzugung *or* Begünstigung.

[1]**Fawn**, I. *s.* das Rehkalb. II. *v.a.* (Rehe) setzen. III. *s.* die Rehfarbe. *Comp.* **—-coloured**, *adj.* rehfarben.

[2]**Fawn**, *v.n.* schwänzeln (*as a dog*); schweifwedeln (upon, vor); to — upon a p., sich vor einem schmiegen, vor einem kriechen, ihm kriechend schmeicheln. **—er**, *s.* der Kriecher. **—ing**, I. *adj.*, **—ingly**, *adv.* kriecherisch. II. *s.* das Kriechen.

Fay, *s.* die Fee.

Fealty, *s.* die Lehenstreue, Huldigung.

Fear, I. *s.* die Furcht; (anxiety) die Besorgnis; (awe) die Ehrfurcht, Scheu; —s, die Befürchtungen, die Furcht; — of the Lord, die Furcht Gottes, Furcht vor dem Herrn; to stand in —

of, sich fürchten vor; for — of, aus Furcht (vor); there is no — of . . ., . . . steht nicht zu befürchten. II. *v.a.* fürchten; fürchten, verehren (*fig.*); I — his revenge, ich fürchte seine Rache, ich fürchte mich vor seiner Rache; no need to —, there is nothing to —, da ist nichts zu befürchten; — me not, sei unbesorgt um mich (*obs.*). III. *v.n.* sich fürchten, Furcht haben *or* empfinden; never — ! seien Sie ganz unbesorgt! **—ful**, *adj.*, **—fully**, *adv.* (timid) furchtsam; (dreadful) furchtbar, fürchterlich; (dread) Ehrfurcht gebietend; to be —ful of a th., eine S. fürchten, vor einer S. Furcht haben. **—fulness**, *s.* die Furchtbarkeit, Fürchterlichkeit; die Furchtsamkeit, Furcht. **—less**, *adj.*, **—lessly**, *adv.* furchtlos, unbesorgt. **—lessness**, *s.* die Furchtlosigkeit.

Feasib—ility, *s.* die Tunlichkeit. **—le**, *adj.*, **—ly**, *adv.* tunlich, möglich, ausführbar; what is —le, das Tunliche. **—leness**, *see* —ility.

Feast, I. *s.* das Fest; (rich repast) das Gastmahl, der Schmaus; enough is as good as a —, genug ist ein Fest wert. II. *v.a.* (einem) einen guten Schmaus geben, (einen) festlich bewirten, speisen. III. *v.n.* (gut) schmausen (on, von); sich gütlich tun; sich weiden, sich ergötzen (upon a th., an einer S.). **—er**, *s.* der Schmauser; der Festgeber. **—ing**, *s.* die festliche Bewirtung, der Schmaus.

Feat, *s.* die Heldentat; (— of arms) die Waffentat; (— of agility, *etc.*) das Kunststück, Kraftstück. **—ure**, *s.* der Gesichtszug, Zug; (characteristic) der Hauptzug, Zug; —ures, die Züge, die Gesichtsbildung; —ures of a landscape, der Charakter einer Landschaft. **—ureless**, *adj.* ohne bestimmte Züge.

Feather, I. *s.* die Feder; (bunch of —s) der Federbusch; fine —s make fine birds, Kleider machen Leute (*prov.*); birds of a — flock together, gleich und gleich gesellt sich gern (*prov.*); — in one's cap, das Ehrenzeichen (*coll.*); that is a — in his cap, er kann sich etwas darauf zu Gute tun (*coll.*); light as a —, federleicht; to show the white —, sich feige zeigen; in high —, munter und wohl, höchst erfreut. II. *v.a.* befiedern; bereichern (*fig.*); to — one's nest, sich warm betten, sein Schäfchen scheren *or* ins Trockne bringen; to — the oars, die Ruder platt werfen. III. *attrib.*; —quilt, die Federbettdecke; — screw, die Nußschraube. **—ed**, *adj.* befiedert, gefiedert; —ed game, das Federwild; the —ed tribe, die Vogelwelt. **—y**, *adj.* federartig; gefiedert. *Comp.* **—-bed**, *s.* das Federbett. **—-brain**, *s.* die unbesonnene *or* unbeständige Person. **—-brained**, *adj.* unbesonnen, töricht. **—-broom**, **—-duster**, *s.* der Federwisch. **—-edge**, *s.* die scharfe Kante. **—-grass**, *s.* das Federgras. **—-moss**, *s.* das Astmoos. **—-spring**, *s.* die (Pfann-)Deckelfeder.

Feaze, *v.a.* aufdrehen (ropes, Taue).

Febri—fuge, *s.* das Fiebermittel. **—le**, *adj.* fieberhaft, fieb(e)risch.

February, *s.* der Februar.

Fec—es, *see* Fæces. **—ulence**, *s.* das Hefige, Trübe; (dregs) die Hefen, der Bodensatz. **—ulent**, *adj.* hefig, trübe, schlammig, unrein.

Feckless, *adj.*, **—ly**, *adv.* schwach befähigt, in allem unfähig, unbeholfen.

Fecund, *adj.* fruchtbar. **—ate**, *v.a.* befruchten. **—ation**, *s.* die Befruchtung. **—ity**, *s.* die Fruchtbarkeit.

Fed, *imperf. & p.p. of* Feed.

Federa—cy, *s.* die Verbündung, der Bund. **—l**, I. *adj.* bundesmäßig, Bundes-; —l council, der Bundesrat; —l states, Bundesstaaten; —l government, die Bundesregierung. II. *s.*, **—list**, *s.* der Föderalist. **—lism**, *s.* der Föderalismus. **—te**, *adj.* verbündet. **—tion**, *s.* die Verbündung; *see* —l government. **—tive**, *adj.* föderativ.

Fee, I. *s.* die Gebühr, der Lohn; das Honorar (*of a doctor, lawyer, professor, etc.*); das Trinkgeld; (possession) das Besitztum, Eigentum; das Lehen (*Law*); — simple *or* absolute, das Eigengut, Allodialgut; — base *or* qualified, das bedingte Lehen; retaining —, vorläufiges Honorar an bedeutende Rechtsanwälte, oder gelehrte Mitglieder einer Prüfungskommission, um sich ihre Dienste zu sichern; estate in — tail, Lehen, das nur auf bestimmte Erben übergeht. II. *v.a.* bezahlen, belohnen; honorieren; (hire) mieten. *Comp.* **—-farm**, *s.* von allen Lasten freie Pacht, Erbpacht, Erbzinslehen; to hold in —-farm, zu Lehen haben.

Feebl—e, *adj.*, **—y**, *adv.* schwach. **—e-minded** *adj.* geistesschwach. **—eness**, *s.* die Schwäche.

[1]**Feed**, *imperf. & p.p. of* Fee.

[2]**Feed**, I. *ir.v.a.* füttern (*cattle*); speisen, ernähren (*people*); unterhalten (*a fire*); füllen (*a pen*); weiden (*God's flock*); to — hope, die Hoffnung nähren; to — the eye with, upon s. th., die Augen weiden an einer S. II. *ir.v.n.* essen (*as men*); fressen, weiden (*as beasts*); leben, sich nähren (upon herbs, etc., von Kräutern, &c.). III. *s.* das Futter; die Mahlzeit (*coll.*); a — of oats, eine Metze Hafer. **—er**, *s.* der Fütterer; der Speiseapparat; der Speisegraben, Zuflußgraben (*Hydr.*); der Pichel, Latz (*for infants*); der Anreizer (*fig.*). **—ing**, I. *s.* die Weide, Nahrung; die Fütterung (*of cattle*); high —ing, das Wohlleben. II. *attrib.*; —ing crane, der Wasserkrahn (*Railw.*). *Comp.* **—-bag**, *s.* der Futtersack. **—-cock**, *s.* der Speisehahn. **—ing-bottle**, *s.* die Saugflasche. **—-pipe**, *s.* die Speiseröhre.

Feel, I. *ir.v.a.* fühlen, befühlen, betasten; (be sensible of) empfinden; to — a p.'s pulse, einem den Puls fühlen, (sound a p.) einem auf den Zahn fühlen, einen sondieren; I felt it deeply, es schmerzte mich tief, ich empfand es tief (schmerzlich); to — one's way, vorsichtig vorgehen (*fig.*). II. *ir.v.n.* fühlen, empfinden; sich fühlen; it —s soft, es fühlt sich weich an; to — inclined, sich geneigt fühlen, geneigt sein; to — for, teilnehmen an (*dat.*); we — for them, sie dauern uns, sie tun uns leid; we felt refreshed, wir fühlten uns erquickt; how do you — to-day? wie befinden Sie sich heute? I — better, ich fühle mich wohler, es geht mir besser; I — queer, mir ist sonderbar zu Mute; I felt as if, ich hatte das Gefühl als ob; to — sure of a th., überzeugt sein von einer S.; to — hurt at, sich beleidigt *or* verletzt fühlen durch. III. *s.* das Fühlen; der Gefühlssinn; das Gefühl, die Empfindung (*fig.*). **—er**, *s.* der Fühlende; der Fühler, die sondierende Äußerung; das Fühlhorn (*Ent.*); to throw out a —er, sondieren. **—ing**, I. *adj.*, **—ingly**, *adv.* fühlend; gefühlvoll; voller Gefühl, tief empfunden. II. *s.* das Fühlen; das Gefühl, die Empfindung; die Stimmung; man of —ing, Mann von Gefühl; to hurt a p.'s —ings, einen kränken *or* verletzen, einem weh tun, jemands Gefühle verletzen.

Feet, *pl. see* Foot.

Feign, *v.* I. *a.* (invent) erdichten; (pretend) heucheln; to — sickness, sich krank stellen; to — friendship, Freundschaft heucheln. II. *n.* heucheln, sich verstellen. **—ed**, *adj.* falsch, verstellt; Schein-; —ed treble, die Fistel. **—edly**, *adv.* vorgeblich, zum Schein. **—er**, *s.* der Erdichter; der Heuchler. **—ing**, *s.* die Heuchelei.

Feint, *s.* die Verstellung; die Finte (*fig. & Fenc.*); der Scheinangriff (*Mil.*); to make a — of . . ., sich stellen als ob . .

Feldspar, *etc.*, *see* Felspar, *etc.*

Felicit—ate, *v.a.* beglückwünschen (upon, zu); beglücken (*obs.*). **—ation**, *s.* die Beglückwünschung. **—ous**, *adj.*, **—ously**, *adv.* glücklich; gut gewählt (*expressions*). **—y**, *s.* das Glück, die Glückseligkeit.

Feline, *adj.* katzenartig, Katzen-.

[1]**Fell**, I. *pret. of* Fall. II. *v.a.* fällen; hinstrecken; einsäumen, einnähen. **—er**, *s.* der Holzfäller.

[2]**Fell**, *adj.* grausam, grimmig (*poet.*); (bloody) blutgierig.

[3]**Fell**, *s.* der steinige Hügel, steile Berg (*dial.*).

[4]**Fell**, *s.* das Fell, die Haut (*obs.*).

Fellah, *s.* (*pl.* **—een**) der Fellah (*pl.* die Fellah(s)).
Fellow, I. *s.* der Gefährte, Genosse, Kamerad; Mit= (*in compounds*); (equal) der, die, das Gleiche von einem Paar (*e.g. stockings, gloves*); das Mitglied eines Kollegiums, einer Körperschaft; der Kerl, Gesell, Bursche (*coll.*); two shoes that are not —s, zwei ungleiche Schuhe; where is the — of this glove? wo ist der andere Handschuh? to be —s, zusammengehören; this man has not his —, dieser Mann hat seinesgleichen nicht; this — of a barber, dieser Kerl von (einem) Barbier; good —, guter Kerl. II. *v.a.* gleichstellen (mit). **—ship**, *s.* die Genossenschaft; die Mitgliedschaft; das Einkommen und die Stelle eines Fellow (*Univ.*); his —ship is worth £250, er bezieht von seinem College ein Jahreseinkommen von £250; he was elected to a —ship at King's College, er wurde zum Fellow von King's College erwählt; good —ship, die Geselligkeit, Herzensbrüderschaft; rule of —ship, die Gesellschaftsregel. *Comp.* **—-citizen**, *s.* der Mitbürger. **—-commoner**, *s.* der adlige, ältere, oder sonst privilegierte Student, Tischgenoß der Fellows eines College (*Univ.*). **—-countryman**, *s.* der Landsmann. **—-creature**, *s.* der Mitmensch. **—-feeling**, *s.* das Mitgefühl, die Sympathie. **—-labourer**, *s.* der Mitarbeiter. **—-lodger**, *s.* der Stubennachbar, Hausgenoß. **—-passenger**, *s.* der Reisegefährte. **—-prisoner**, *s.* der Mitgefangene. **—-servant**, *s.* der Dienstgenoß. **—-soldier**, *s.* der Mitsoldat, Kamerad. **—-student**, *s.* der Mitstudent; we were —-students at Berlin, wir studierten zusammen in Berlin. **—-sufferer**, *s.* der Leidensgefährte. **—-teacher**, der Kollege. **—-traveller**, *s.* der Reisegefährte.
Felly, *s.* die (Rad=)Felge.
Felo-de-se, *s.* der Selbstmörder.
Felon, I. *s.* der Verbrecher, Missetäter; das Nagelgeschwür (*Surg.*). II. *adj.* grausam (*obs.*). **—ious**, *adj.*, **—iously**, *adv.* verbrecherisch; treulos; (deliberate) böslich, mit böser Absicht. **—y**, *s.* Staatsverbrechen, schweres Verbrechen.
Felspa—r, **—th**, *s.* der Feldspat. **—those**, *adj.* feldspatig.
[1]**Felt**, *imperf. & p.p. of* Feel.
[2]**Felt**, I. *s.* der Filz. II. *attrib.*; — carpet, der Filzteppich; — hat, der Filzhut; — roofing, (roofing —) der Asphaltfilz, die Dachpappe. III. *v.a.* (ver)filzen; —ed cloth, das Filztuch.
Fem—ale, I. *adj.* weiblich; —ale child, das Mädchen; —ale friend, die Freundin; —ale screw, die Schraubenmutter; —ale servant, die Magd, das Dienstmädchen; —ale student, die Studentin. II. *s.* das Weib; das Weibchen (*of beasts, etc.*). **—inine**, *adj.* weiblich (*also Gram.*); (soft) zart; (unmanly) weibisch, unmännlich; —inine gender, das weibliche Geschlecht, Femininum. **—ininity**, *s.* die Weiblichkeit, das weibliche Wesen. **—(m)e**, *s.*; —(m)e covert, die Verheiratete, Ehefrau; —(m)e sole, die Unverheiratete.
Femoral, *adj.* zu den Schenkeln gehörig, Schenkel=.
Fen, *s.* der Sumpf, das Moor, Marschland. **—ny**, *adj.* moorig, marschig, sumpfig. *Comp.* **—land**, *s.* das Marschland. **—-shooting**, *s.* die Jagd auf Sumpfgeflügel.
Fenc—e, I. *s.* die Einfriedigung, Umzäunung, der Zaun, das Gehege; (paling) die Pallisaden, die Umpfählung; die Schutzwehr (*fig.*); (—ing) das Fechten; der Diebeshehler (*sl.*). II. *v.a.* einfriedigen, einhegen, umzäunen; (protect) befestigen; (defend) verteidigen, schützen; to —e off, abwehren; all other fish are —ed, alle andern Fische sind gesetzlich geschützt, dürfen nicht gefangen werden. III. *v.n.* fechten, kämpfen; abwehren, ausweichen (*fig.*); he was merely —ing, es war nur Spiegelfechterei bei ihm. **—eless**, *adj.* offen. **—er**, *s.* der Fechter. **—ible**, *adj.* verteidigungsfähig; zur Landwehr gehörig (*Mil.*). **—ibles**, *pl.* die Landwehr. **—ing**, *s.* das Fechten; die Fechtkunst. *Comp.* **—ing-foil**, *s.* der Stoßdegen, das Rapier. **—ing-gloves**, *pl.* die Fechthandschuhe. **—ing-master**, *s.* der Fechtmeister. **—ing-school**, *s.* die Fechtschule.
Fend, *v.* I. *a.*; to — off, abwehren. II. *n.*; to — for . . ., für . . . sorgen (*Scotch*). **—er**, *s.* der Kaminvorsatz, das Kamingitter.
Fenestral, *adj.* Fenster=.
Fenian, I. *adj.* fenisch. II. *s.* der Fenier. **—ism**, *s.* der Fen(ian)ismus.
Fennel, *s.* der Fenchel. *Comp.* **—-bush**, *s.* die Fenchelstaude. **—-flower**, *s.* die Fenchelblume.
Feod, *see* Feud.
Feoff, *see* Fief. **—ee**, *s.* der Belehnte.
Ferment, I. *s.* die Gärung; to put in a —, in Gärung *or* Wallung bringen. II. *v.a.* gären lassen; erregen (*fig.*). III. *v.n.* gären, in Gärung geraten. **—ability**, *s.* die Gärungsfähigkeit. **—able**, *adj.* gärungsfähig. **—ation**, *s.* die Gärung. **—ing**, I. *adj.* gärend. II. *attrib.*; —ing trough, die Faulbütte (*Pap.*). III. *s.* das Gären.
Fern, *s.* das Far(re)nkraut. **—y**, *adj.* mit Farnkraut überwachsen. **—ery**, *s.* die Farnkrautpflanzung. *Comp.* **—-seed**, *s.* der Farnsamen.
Feroci—ous, *adj.*, **—ously**, *adv.* wild, grimmig, grausam; —ous animals, Raubtiere. **—ty**, *s.* die Wildheit, Grausamkeit, Grimmigkeit.
Ferr—eous, *adj.* eisern. **—iferous**, **—uginous**, *adj.* eisenhaltig.
[1]**Ferret**, I. *s.* das Frett(chen). II. *v.a.*; to — out, aus dem Verstecke treiben; (find out) aus=forschen, =spüren. **—er**, *s.* der Frettjäger; der Spürhund.
[2]**Ferret**, *s.* das Florettband (*obs.*).
Ferrule, *s.* die Zwinge, der Beschlag (*on a walking stick, etc.*).
Ferry, I. *s.* (— boat) die Fähre; horse —, Pferdefähre; railway —, das Trajektboot. II. *v.a. & n.* fahren. *Comp.* **—man**, *s.* der Fährmann.
Fertil—e, *adj.*, **—ely**, *adv.* fruchtbar, reich, ergiebig (in a th., an einer S.); fruchtbar, erfinderisch (*fig.*). **—ity**, *s.* die Fruchtbarkeit (*also fig.*), Ergiebigkeit. **—ization**, *s.* die Befruchtung, Fruchtbarmachung. **—ize**, *v.a.* befruchten, fruchtbar machen. **—izer**, *s.* das Düngmittel.
Ferule, I. *s.* der Stock, die Rute, das Lineal. II. *v.a.* mit dem Stocke züchtigen, mit dem Lineal schlagen.
Ferv—ency, *s.* die Glut; die Inbrunst; to pray with —ency, inbrünstig beten. **—ent**, *adj.*, **—ently**, *adv.* heiß; heftig, eifrig, inbrünstig, glühend; —ent piety, inbrünstige Frömmigkeit; —ent prayer, inbrünstiges *or* inniges Gebet; —ent zeal, glühender Eifer; —ent in spirit, eifrigen Geistes. **—id**, *adj.*, **—idly**, *adv.* heiß, brennend, glühend; (fiery) feurig, hitzig; (ardent) eifrig. **—idness**, *s.* die Glühhitze; die Hitze, der Eifer, das Feuer (*fig.*). **—our**, *s.* die Hitze; die Inbrunst, der Eifer; —our of love, die Liebesglut.
Fesse, *s.* die Binde, der Balkenstreif (*Her.*).
Fest—al, *adj.*, **—ally**, *adv.* festlich. **—ival**, *s.* der Festtag, das Fest. **—ive**, *adj.*, **—ively**, *adv.* festlich, fröhlich. **—ivity**, *s.* die Festlichkeit, Fröhlichkeit. **—oon**, I. *s.* die Guirlande; das Blumengewinde, Frucht= *or* Blumen=gehänge; die Frucht= *or* Blumen=schnur (*Arch.*). II. *v.a.* mit Guirlanden behängen.
Fester, I. *v.n.* schwären, eitern; verfaulen, vermodern. II. *v.a.* zum Schwären bringen.
Fet—al, **Fœt—al**, *adj.* zum Fötus gehörig. **—us**, der Fötus, die Leibesfrucht.
Fetch, *v.* I. *a.* holen, bringen; (bring in) einbringen, eintragen; (call for) abholen; to — a sigh, seufzen; to — a high price, einen hohen Preis einbringen *or* erzielen; — and carry, apportieren (*as dogs*); to — **away**, wegholen, forttragen; to — **down**, herunterholen; to — **from**, herholen aus; to — **in**, herein=holen, =bringen; to — **out**, zum Vorschein bringen; to

— **up**, heraufholen. —**er**, *s.* der Holende. —**ing**, *adj.* bezaubernd, verführerisch (*sl.*).
Fête, I. *s.* das Fest. II. *v.a.* feiern, fetieren.
Fetid, *adj.* stinkend.
Fetish, *s.* der Fetisch. —**ism**, *s.* der Fetischdienst.
Fetlock, I. *s.* das Hufhaar, Kötenhaar; die Fessel (für weidende Pferde). II. *attrib.*; — joint, das Kötengelenk. —**ed**, *adj.* mit Hufhaar; gefesselt (*of horses*).
Fetter, I. *v.a.* fesseln. II. *s.* die Fessel; —s for horses, Spannstricke. —**less**, *adj.* fessellos.
Fettle, *s.*; in good —, ganz auf dem Damm (*coll.*).
[1]**Feud**, *s.* die Fehde, der Streit.
[2]**Feud**, *s.* das Leh(e)n. —**al**, *adj.* lehnbar, Lehn(s)=; —al system, das Lehnsystem. —**alism**, *s.* das Lehnswesen, der Feudalismus. —**ality**, *s.* die Lehnbarkeit; (—al constitution) die Lehnsverfassung. —**alization**, *s.* die Lehnbarmachung. —**alize**, *v.a.* in Lehn verwandeln. —**atory**, *s.* der Lehnsmann.
Feuillemort, Filemot, *s.* das Braungelb.
Fever, *s.* das Fieber. —**ed**, *adj.* vom Fieber erhitzt, fieberisch. —**ish**, *adj.* fieberhaft, fieberisch; fieberkrank (*Med.*); heiß, glühend (*fig.*); —ish cold, das Schnupfenfieber. —**ishness**, *s.* die Fieberhaftigkeit, Fieberglut.
Few, I. *adj.* wenig, wenige; a —, some —, einige wenige. II. *s.*; a —, some —, einige wenige. —**ness**, *s.* die geringe Anzahl.
Fez, *s.* der Fez.
Fiancé, *s.* der Verlobte, Bräutigam; my —, mein Bräutigam; thy —, dein Bräutigam, dein Verlobter; your —, Ihr Herr Verlobter, Ihr Herr Bräutigam. —**e**, die Braut, Verlobte; my —e, meine Braut; your —e, Ihr Fräulein Braut.
Fiasco, *s.* der Mißerfolg, das Fiasko.
Fiat, *s.* der Machtspruch, unbedingte Befehl.
Fib, I. *s.* die (kleine) Lüge, Flunkerei; to tell a —, *see* — II. II. *v.n.* lügen, flunkern. —**ber**, *s.* der Flunkerer.
Fibr—e, *s.* die Fiber, Faser. —**eless**, *adj.* ohne Fibern. —**in(e)**, *s.* der Faserstoff. —**ous**, *adj.* fiberig, faserig.
Fickle, *adj.* wankelmütig; veränderlich, unbeständig. —**ness**, *s.* der Wankelmut, Unbestand.
Fictile, *adj.* formbar, plastisch; tönern, irden; — art, die Töpferkunst, Keramik; — ivory, imitiertes Elfenbein; — ware, das Steingut, die Tonware(n). —**ness**, *s.* die Formbarkeit (*of clay*).
Ficti—on, *s.* die Erdichtung; (romances, *etc.*) die Dichtung; Prosadichtung, Romandichtung; work of —on, der Roman. —**tious**, *adj.*, —**tiously**, *adv.* erdichtet; (false) unecht, nachgemacht. —**tiousness**, *s.* das Erdichtete.
Fid, *s.* das Schloßholz (*Naut.*).
Fiddle, I. *s.* die Fiedel, Geige, Violine; to play first (second) —, die erste (zweite) Geige spielen (*also fig.*); die Hauptrolle (Nebenrolle) spielen (*fig.*). II. *v.n.* geigen; (trifle) tändeln, spielen; zwecklos geschäftig sein, immer in Bewegung sein ohne rechten Zweck. III. *v.a.* fiedeln, (auf der) Geige spielen. —**de-dee**, I. *s.* der Unsinn (*prov.*). II. *int.* Unsinn! —**r**, *s.* der Geiger; Fiedler; der Spielmann; —r's rosin, das Geigenharz. *Comp.* —**-back**, *s.* der Bauch einer Geige. —**-bridge**, *s.* der Geigensteg. —**-case**, *s.* der Geigenkasten. —**-faddle**, *s.* die Lappalie, Lapperei. —**-peg**, *s.* der Geigenwirbel. —**-stick**, *s.* der Geigenbogen. —**sticks**! *interj.* Unsinn! Possen! —**-string**, *s.* die Geigensaite, Violinsaite.
Fidelity, *s.* (honesty) die Redlichkeit, Ehrlichkeit; (faithfulness) die Pflichttreue; conjugal —, die eheliche Treue; (veracity) die Wahrhaftigkeit.
Fidget, I. *v.n.* unruhig sein, sich beständig bewegen. II. *v.a.* nervös machen, quälen. III. *s.* die Unruhe, nervöse Aufregung; eine Unruhe, unruhige Person; to have the —s, nicht ruhig sein können (*coll.*). —**iness**, *s.* die Aufgeregtheit. —**y**, *adj.* unruhig, ruhelos; nervös aufgeregt.

Fiducia—l, *adj.* zuversichtlich. —**ry**, I. *adj.* (confident) zuversichtlich; (undoubted) unzweifelhaft; (entrusted) anvertraut. II. *s.* der (mit einer S.) Betraute, Fiduziarius.
Fie, *int.* pfui!
Fief, *s.* das Lehen.
Field, I. *s.* das Feld (*also fig.*); (— of battle) das Schlachtfeld; das Spielfeld, der Spielplatz; der Grund (*Paint.*); das Feld (*Her.*); die Gesamtheit der Spieler in einem Wettspiel; die Gesamtheit der auf dem Rennplatz erschienenen Pferde; die Anzahl der Wettbewerber (*fig.*); in the —, im Wettbewerb (*fig.*); im Gefechte (*Mil.*); to take the —, ins Feld rücken; to keep the —, auf dem Felde kampieren, im Felde bleiben; das Feld behaupten; he backed my horse against the —, er wettete auf mein Pferd gegen alle andern Renner; — of vision *or* view, das Sehfeld, Gesichtsfeld (*Opt.*); — of ice, das Eisfeld. II. *v.n.* im Spielfeld stehen (um den Ball zu fangen), den Ball auf(zu)halten (suchen) (*Cricket*); im Ausfeld spielen (*Baseball*). —**er**, *s.* der Cricketspieler, der den Ball fängt (*opp. to* Batter & Bowler), Fänger; der Spieler, der im Ausfeld spielt (*Baseball*). —**fare**, *s.* der Krammetsvogel. *Comp.* —**-artillery**, *s.* die Feldartillerie. —**-book**, *s.* das Notizbuch (*Surv.*). —**-colours**, *pl.* das Richtfähnchen (*Surv.*); die Quartierfahne (*Mil.*). —**-cornet**, *s.* der Hauptmann im Burenheere, Feldkornett. —**-day**, *s.* die Felddienstübung; to hold a —-day, eine Felddienstübung abhalten. —**-glass**, *s.* der Krimstecher, das kleine Fernrohr. —**-gun**, *see* —-piece. —**-lark**, *s.* die Ackerlerche. —**-marshal**, *s.* der Feldmarschall. —**-mouse**, *s.* die Feldmaus. —**-officer**, *s.* der Stabsoffizier. —**-piece**, *s.* das Feldstück, Geschütz. —**-preaching**, *s.* die Feldpredigt. —**-sports**, *pl.* die Wettkämpfe im Freien *or* auf dem Spielplatz. —**-work**, *s.* die Feldschanze.
Fiend, *s.* der Unhold; (devil) der böse Feind, Teufel. —**ish**, *adj.*, —**ishly**, *adv.* teuflisch; boshaft. —**ishness**, *s.* die Bosheit.
Fierce, *adj.*, —**ly**, *adv.* wild, grimmig, wütend; (cruel) grausam; (vehement) heftig, hitzig, ungestüm. —**ness**, *s.* die Wildheit, Wut, der Grimm; das Ungestüm, die Heftigkeit; (ferocity) die Grausamkeit, Grimmigkeit.
Fier—iness, *s.* die Hitze, das Feuer. —**y**, *adj.*, —**ily**, *adv.* feurig, glühend (*also fig.*), Feuer=; —y red, feuerrot, glührot.
Fife, I. *s.* die (Quer=)Pfeife. II. *v.n.* auf der Querpfeife blasen. —**r**, *s.* der (Quer=)Pfeifer.
Fift—een, I. *num. adj.* fünfzehn; —een-all! fünfzehn gleich! fünfzehn beide! (*L.T.*); —een-love! fünfzehn (zu) nichts! (*L.T.*). II. *s.* die Fünfzehnzahl; die fünfzehn Spieler einer Fußballpartie; the captain of the Rugby —een, der Hauptmann der Rugbyer Fußballpartie. —**eenth**, I. *num. adj.* (der, die, das) fünfzehnt(e). II. *s.* das Fünfzehntel. —**h**, I. *num. adj.* (der, die, das) fünft(e); —h-monarchy men, die Fünfmonarchisten. II. *s.* das Fünftel; die Quinte (*Mus.*). —**hly**, *adv.* fünftens. —**ieth**, I. *num. adj.* (der, die, das) fünfzigst(e). II. *s.* das Fünfzigstel. —**y**, *num. adj.* fünfzig; by —ies, zu fünfzigen, fünfzigerweise; —y fold, fünfzigfach.
[1]**Fig** (*familiar abbrev. of* Figure), *s.* der Putz, die Gala; in full —, in vollem Wichs (*sl.*).
[2]**Fig**, *s.* die Feige; (—-tree) der Feigenbaum; die Feigwarze; etwas ganz Wertloses (*fig.*); a — for it, was frage ich danach? I don't care a — for him, ich frage nichts nach ihm. *Comp.* —**-leaf**, *s.* das Feigenblatt. —**-wort**, *s.* die Feigwurz, Braunwurz.
Fight, I. *ir.v.n.* fechten, kämpfen, streiten; sich schlagen, duellieren; — against (a th.), sich (einer S.) widersetzen, (etwas) bestreiten; to — for, (etwas) verfechten; to — shy of a p., einen vermeiden, einem aus dem Wege gehen. II. *ir.v.a.* fechten,

kämpfen (mit *or* gegen), schlagen (*a battle*); bekämpfen, sich schlagen mit; (dispute) verfechten; to — a duel, sich duellieren; to — a p., einen bekämpfen, gegen einen kämpfen, mit einem den Kampf aufnehmen; to — one's way, sich durchschlagen; to — it out, es ausfechten. III. *s.* das Gefecht, der Kampf; die Schlägerei; hand to hand —, das Handgemenge; to show —, kampflustig *or* zum Kampfe bereit sein. **—er**, *s.* der Fechter, Streiter, Kämpfer, Krieger; der Duellant; —er against, der Verfechter. **—ing**, I. *adj.* streitbar, kampffähig; Kampf=; —ing men, Kämpfer; way of —ing, die Kampfesart, Kampf(es)weise; —ing cock, der Kampfhahn; —ing force, Kriegstruppe, schlagfertige Truppe. II. *s.* das Gefecht, der Kampf.

Figment, *s.* die Erdichtung.

Figur—ability, *s.* die Bildsamkeit. **—able**, *adj.* bildsam. **—ant(e)**, *s.* der (die) Ballettänzer(in); der (die) Figurant(in), Statist(in) (*Theat.*). **—ate**, *adj.* eine bestimmte Gestalt habend, Bild=; figuriert, (mit Tonfiguren) verziert (*Mus.*); figuriert (*Math.*); —ate descant, der Figuralgesang (*Mus.*). **—ation**, *s.* die Gestaltung; die Figuration (*Mus.*). **—ative**, *adj.*, **—atively**, *adv.* (typical) bildlich, vorbildlich, sinnbildlich; (not literal) bildlich, figürlich; (flowery) bilderreich. **—ativeness**, *s.* das Bildliche, die Sinnbildlichkeit. **—e**, I. *s.* die Figur, Gestalt, Form; (character) der Charakter, die Figur; die menschliche Figur (*Draw. etc.*); (representation) die Abbildung; die Figur (*Geom.*); die Ziffer (*Arith.*); das Muster (*Weav., etc.*); das Choroskop (*Astr.*); die Notenziffer (*Mus.*); die Figur (*Danc.*); das Vorbild (*Theol.*); die Redefigur (*Rhet.*); die Schlußfigur, syllogistische Figur (*Log.*); to cut a —e, eine Figur machen (*vulg.*); to make a —e (in the world), eine glänzende Rolle spielen; what a —e you are! wie Sie aussehen! it runs into six —es, es geht in die Hunderttausende; what's the —e? was ist der Preis? (*vulg.*); lay —, die Gliederpuppe, der Gliedermann; Roman —es, römische Zahlbuchstaben. II. *v.a.* bilden, gestalten, formen; (represent) darstellen; (ab)formen (*Sculpt.*); broschieren, blümen (*stuffs*); figurieren (*Mus.*); to —e to o.s., sich (*dat.*) denken, sich (*dat.*) vorstellen. III. *v.n.* eine Rolle spielen. **—ed**, *adj.* figuriert, gemustert, fassonniert; —ed bass, der bezifferte Baß (*Mus.*); —ed counterpoint, der verzierte Kontrapunkt. *Comp.* **—e-head**, *s.* die Bugfigur (*Naut.*); die Dekorationsfigur, der Repräsentant (*fig.*).

Fil—aceous, *adj.* aus Fäden. **—ament**, *s.* die Faser. **—amentous**, *adj.* faserig. **—e**, I. *s.* der Aufreihfaden, (Aufreih=); Draht; der Stoß (of papers, Papiere); (list) die Rolle, Liste; die Reihe, das Glied (*Mil.*); rank and —, die Gemeinen, die Mannschaft; in rank and —, in Reih' und Glied; left —e! in Rotten, Gliedern links! to go in single —e, einer hinter dem andern gehen *or* marschieren; im Gänsemarsch gehen (*coll.*); in double —, zu zweien hintereinander. II. *v.a.* anreihen, aufreihen; to —e a bill, dem Gerichte eine Klage vorlegen. III. *v.n.* (—e past) defilieren, in Reihen vorbeiziehen. **—iform**, *adj.* faserförmig. **—igree**, *s.* das Filigran. **—let**, *see* Fillet. **—ose**, *adj.* fadenförmig (*Zool.*). *Comp.* **—e-leader**, *s.* der Vordermann, Flügelmann.

Filbert, *s.* die Lambertsnuß.

Filch, *v.a.* stehlen, mausen. **—er**, *s.* der Dieb.

[1]**File**, *see under* Filaceous.

[2]**Fil—e**, I. *s.* die Feile. II. *v.a.* feilen; to —e away, wegfeilen; to open by —ing, auffeilen. **—ings**, *pl.* das Feilicht, der Feilstaub. *Comp.* **—e-cutter**, *s.* der Feilenhauer. **—e-dust**, *s.* der Feilstaub.

Filemot, *s.* das Braungelb.

Filia—l, *adj.* kindlich. **—tion**, *s.* die Kindschaft; (adoption) die Adoption; die Legitimierung eines außerehelichen Kindes; —tion of languages, das Verwandtschaftsverhältnis der Sprachen; —tion of manuscripts, das Abhängigkeitsverhältnis der Handschriften.

Filibuster, *s.* der Freibeuter.

Fill, I. *v.a.* (an)füllen; (stuff) stopfen; (supply) reichlich versehen; einschenken (*one's glass*); ausfüllen (*a post*); besetzen, bekleiden (*an office*); einnehmen (*a throne*); (satisfy) sättigen (*vulg.*); vollbrassen (*Naut.*); erfüllen; he —ed my glass, er füllte mein Glas; er schenkte mir ein; courage —ed their hearts, Mut erfüllte ihre Herzen; to — a p.'s place, jemandes Stelle einnehmen; jemandes Stelle ausfüllen, einen ersetzen; to — **in**, einsetzen, einschalten; to — **out**, ausfüllen, ausdehnen; to — **up**, voll machen, auf=, aus=füllen; to — up a grave, ein Grab mit Erde auffüllen; to — up the time, die Zeit ausfüllen; to — up the measure of sin, das Maß der Sünde voll machen. II. *v.n.* sich füllen, voll werden; to — out, stärker *or* stark werden. III. *s.* die Fülle, Genüge; I have had my —, ich habe vollauf daran gehabt; to (gaze) drink one's —, sich satt (sehen) trinken (an einer S.). **—er**, *s.* der Füller, Auffüller; der Trichter (*for wine, etc.*). **—ing**, *s.* die Füllung; das Füllsel, die Farce (*Cook.*); die Plombe (*Dent.*); die Ergänzung, Zutat (*fig.*).

Fillet, I. *s.* die Kopfbinde; das Filet, der Lendenbraten (*Butch.*); die Leiste, das Band, der Reif (*Arch.*); der Goldstreif (*Paint.*); der schmale Papierstreifen zur Aufnahme von Telegrammen (*Tele.*); die Leiste (*Print.*). II. *v.a.* mit einer Leiste, &c. zieren (*Arch.*); mit Goldstreifen zieren (*Bookb.*); Fische von Gräten befreien und in Schnitten braten (*Cook.*); Fleisch zu Roulade herrichten (*Cook.*).

Fil(l)ibeg, *s.* das kurze Röckchen der Bergschotten.

Fillip, I. *s.* der Schneller, Nasenstüber; die Anregung (*fig.*). II. *v.a.* (mit dem Finger) schnellen, nasenstübern.

Filly, *s.* das Stutenfüllen; (girl) das (leichtfertige) Mädchen (*sl.*).

Film, I. *s.* das dünne Häutchen, die Membrane; das feine Gewebe (*fig.*); der Film (*Photogr.*); der Schleier vor den Augen (*Med.*). II. *v.n.* sich überhäuten, sich mit einem Häutchen bedecken. **—y**, *adj.* häutig, aus Häutchen bestehend.

Filoselle, *s.* die Filoselle=, Florett=seide.

Filt—er, I. *s.* das Filter, Seihtuch, der Durchseiher; bag —er, das Beutelfilter. II. *v.a.* durchseihen, filtrieren. III. *v.n.* durchsickern, durchlaufen. **—rate**, I. *s.* das Filtrat, die filtrierte Flüssigkeit. II. *v.a. see* —er II. **—ration**, *s.* das Durchseihen. *Comp.* **—ering-paper**, *s.* das Filtrierpapier.

Filth, *s.* der Schmutz, Kot, Unflat. **—ily**, *adv.* schmutzig, kotig. **—iness**, *s.* die Unreinlichkeit, Unflätigkeit; (moral —iness) die Unsittlichkeit, Unfläterei. **—y**, *adj.* unflätig (*also fig.*), schmutzig; zotig (*as conversation*).

Fin, *s.* die Finne, Flosse, Floßfeder. **—ned**, *adj.* mit Flossen. **—ny**, *adj.* mit Flossen; the —ny tribe, die Fische, die Fischwelt (*Poet.*).

Fin—al, *adj.* endlich, schließlich, End=, Schluß=; (decisive) entscheidend, definitiv; —al cause, die Endursache; —al aim, das Endziel; —al consonant, auslautender Konsonant. **—ale**, *s.* das Finale (*also Mus.*). **—ality**, *s.* die Finalität; die Zwecklehre. **—ally**, *adv.* zuletzt, zum Schluß; am Wortende. **—e**, *see* [1]Fine. **—is**, *s.* das Ende. **—ish, —ite**, *see* Finish, Finite.

Fin—ance, I. *s.* das Finanzwesen; science of —ance, die Finanzwissenschaft. II. *v.a.* finanziell unterstützen; the undertaking was —anced by . . ., die Geldmittel für das Unternehmen wurden von . . . beschafft. **—ances**, *pl.* die Finanzen, (Staats=)Einkünfte; his —ances are low, er ist nicht sehr bei Gelde. **—ancial**, *adj.*, **—ancially**, *adv.* finanziell, Finanz=; —ancial position, die Finanzlage, Vermögensverhältnisse (*pl.*). **—ancier**, *s.* der Finanzmann; der Staatswirt,

Kameralist; der Finanzpächter (*in France*). —**e**, *see* ²Fine.

Finary, *s.* der Frischofen, Frischherd (*Metall.*).

Finch, *s.* der Fink; the — warbles, der Fink schlägt.

Find, I. *ir.v.a.* finden; (meet with) (an)treffen; (— by experience) finden, befinden, erfahren; (discover) entdecken; (think out) erfinden, ersinnen; (perceive) gewahr werden; befinden, erklären (*Law*); finden, erreichen (*means, etc.*); (supply with) versehen; (get) suchen, holen; to — pleasure in, Freude an (einer S.) haben; to be found (out) in *or* telling a lie, auf einer Lüge ertappt werden; to — a (true) bill, die Anklagepunkte für gültig erklären; — me a cab! suchen *or* holen Sie mir einen Wagen! I will not — you in pocket-money, ich werde dich nicht mit Taschengeld versehen; who will — the money for . . ., wer wird das Geld für . . . be-, verschaffen; I found myself surrounded by strangers, ich fand mich von Fremden umgeben; I found myself in a strange house, ich befand mich in einem fremden Hause; to — o.s., sich befinden, sich selbst beköstigen; I will give you so much for the work, but you must — everything, ich will Ihnen so viel für die Arbeit geben, Sie müssen aber alles Material liefern *or* selbst anschaffen; all found, alles frei, volle Beköstigung (*in situations for domestic servants*); my footman —s himself in boots, mein Bedienter muß selbst für seine Stiefel sorgen; I did not — it so very much amiss, ich fand es keineswegs so übel; **to** — fault with a p., einen tadeln; to make a p. — his legs (his tongue), einem Beine machen (die Zunge lösen); I could not — it in my heart to punish him, ich konnte es nicht übers Herz bringen, ihn zu bestrafen; to — out (by pondering over a th.), etwas herausbekommen, herausfinden, herausbringen; to — out (by experience), erfahren, finden; to — out (an invention), erfinden; we could not — out the meaning of this passage, wir konnten den Sinn dieser Stelle nicht herausbekommen *or* herausbringen; to — out an enigma, ein Rätsel lösen; to — for, entscheiden zu Gunsten von (*Law*). II. *s.* der Fund. —**er**, *s.* der Finder, Entdecker. —**ing**, *s.* die Entdeckung; der Ausspruch, das Erkenntnis, das Ergebnis einer Untersuchung; the —ing of the committee, das Erkenntnis des Ausschusses; the —ing of the jury, der Ausspruch *or* Beschluß der Geschworenen.

¹**Fine**, *adj.*, —**ly**, *adv.* schön, fein; fein, dünn (*as hair, silk, etc.*); scharf (*as an edge*); spitz (*as a point*); fein, rein (*as gold*); fein, verfeinert (*as taste*); schön, zierlich (*in appearance*); fein, gebildet (*of manners*); (delicate) fein, zart; (cunning) listig, schlau; (excellent) vortrefflich; (subtile) subtil; (— in dress) geputzt; (nice) fein; the — arts, die schönen Künste (*usually: painting and sculpture*); a — scholar, ein großer Gelehrter; a — mind, ein vortrefflicher Verstand; these are — doings, indeed! das sind wahrhaftig schöne Geschichten! you are a — fellow, du bist mir (aber) ein netter Kerl! you have a — time of it now! Sie führen jetzt ein herrliches Leben! that is all very —, but . . ., das ist alles recht gut und schön, aber . . . —**ness**, *s.* die Feinheit; die Zartheit (*of feelings, etc.*); die Reinheit (*of wine, etc.*); die Schärfe; die Schönheit; die Schlauheit. —**r**, *see* Refiner. —**ry**, *s.* (splendour) der Glanz; (— clothes) der Putz, Staat; *see* Finary (*Metall.*). —**sse**, I. *s.* die Schlauheit, List; die Finesse, Finte (*at cards*). II. *v.n.* Kunstgriffe anwenden. III. *v.a.* (eine Karte) nicht übernehmen. *Comp.* —**draw**, *v.a.* feinstopfen, zustopfen. —**drawing**, *s.* das Zunähen mit verborgenen Stichen. —**-spoken**, *adj.* schönredend, glattzüngig. —**-spun**, *adj.* fein gesponnen, dünn; subtil (*fig.*).

²**Fine**, I. *s.* die Geldstrafe, Geldbuße; a — not exceeding 40 shillings, eine Geldstrafe bis zu 4[illegible] Mark. II. *v.a.* zu einer Geldstrafe verurteile[n], um Geld strafen.

³**Fine**, *s.* das Ende (*obs.*); in —, endlich.

Finger, I. *s.* der Finger (*also fig.*); the — [of] God, Gottes Finger (*B.*); to have a — in th[e] pie, (bei einer S.) die Hand im Spiele haben; [to] have at one's —s' ends, an den Fingern he[r]sagen können, am Schnürchen haben. II. *v.a.* [be]tasten, befühlen; den Fingersatz angeben (*Mus.*) (play) spielen. III. *v.n.* fingern, die Finge[r] richtig setzen (*Mus.*). —**ed**, *adj.* gefingert, fin[]gerförmig (*Bot.*); light-—ed, langfingerig, die[]bisch. —**ing**, *s.* die leichte Berührung; d[er] Fingersatz (*Mus.*). *Comp.* —**-basin**, *see* — glass. —**-board**, *s.* das Griffbrett (*of the vi[o]lin*), die Klaviatur (*of a piano*). —**-bowl**, — **glass**, *s.* das Glasgefäß zum Abspülen d[er] Finger nach dem Essen. —**-plate**, *s.* die Fi[n]gerplatte (*on doors*). —**-post**, *s.* der Wegweise[r]. —**-stall**, *s.* der Däumling, Fingerling.

Finical, *adj.*, —**ly**, *adv.* geckenhaft; geziert; über[]trieben eigen in Kleinigkeiten. —**ness**, *s.* d[ie] Geziertheit; die Geckenhaftigkeit.

Fini(c)kin(g), *adj. see* Finical.

Finish, I. *v.a.* endigen, beendigen, vollenden; (u[se] up) verbrauchen, aufbrauchen; (eat, drink u[p]) aufessen, austrinken; (stop) aufhören; glätt[en] (*paper*); zurichten, appretieren (*cloth*); to — composing, aussetzen (*Typ.*); to — a p., eine[m] den Rest geben (*coll.*); to — off (a dish), ei[ne] Speise aufessen, sich (*dat.*) das letzte Stück ne[h]men. II. *v.n.* aufhören; enden; (cease) aufhöre[n]; to have —ed with, fertig sein mit. III. *s.* d[ie] Vollendung, letzte Hand; (end) der Schluß; fig[ht] to the —, Kampf bis zur Entscheidung; die A[p]pretur (*on cloth*). —**er**, *s.* der Appretierer; d[ie] Auskarde, Feinkratze (*Spin.*). —**ing**, *adj.*; [to] give the —ing touch to, die letzte Hand an (ei[ne]) S.) legen; —ing card, die Feinkratze (*Mach.*) —ing governess, Erzieherin, welche den letzte[n] feinen Schliff geben soll; to put the —ing han[d] to a th., die letzte Hand an eine S. legen; —i[ng] stroke, der Gnadenstoß; —ing school, ei[ne] Schule, wo an die Erziehung die letzte Han[d] gelegt wird.

Finite, *adj.*, —**ly**, *adv.* endlich, begrenzt; — verb, das Verbum finitum, regierende Zeitwo[rt]. —**ness**, *s.* die Eingeschränktheit, Endlichkeit.

Fiord, **Fjord**, *s.* der Fjord.

Fir, *s.* (—-tree) die Tanne, Fichte, der Tanne[n]baum; Scots —, die Föhre, Kiefer (*pinus sy[l]vestris*); silver —, die Tanne (*abies*), Edeltann[e], Weißtanne; spruce —, Tanne, Fichte, Rottann[e] (*picea*). *Comp.* —**-cone**, *s.* der Tannenzapfe[n].

Fire, I. *s.* das Feuer (*also fig.*); (conflagratio[n]) das Feuer, der Brand, die Feuersbrunst; (hea[t]) die Hitze, Glut; das Feuer, die Glut, Leidenscha[ft] (*fig.*); (lustre) das Feuer; das (Geschütz-)Feu[er] (*Mil.*); wild-—, das Lauffeuer; to spread li[ke] wild-—, sich wie ein Lauffeuer verbreiten; [to] open —, das Feuer eröffnen, Feuer geben (*Mil.*) withering, decimating —, vernichtendes Feuer; [to] hang —, sich verzögern; to be on —, in Bran[d] stehen, brennen; to miss —, nicht losgehen, ver[]sagen; to set — to, in Brand stecken, anzünden he will never set the Thames on —, er hat da[s] Pulver nicht erfunden (*prov.*); to catch, take — Feuer fangen; to take — at, in Hitze, in W[ut] geraten über (*acc.*). II. *v.a.* in Brand stecke[n], anzünden; anfeuern, entflammen (*fig.*); to — o[ff] abfeuern. III. *v.n.* Feuer geben, feuern, schieße[n] (at, upon, auf); to — up at, in Feuer un[d] Flammen geraten über (eine S.), auffahre[n]. *Comp.* —**-alarm**, *s.* der Feuerlärm; der Feue[r]alarmapparat. —**arms**, *pl.* Feuerwaffe[n], Schießgewehre; breechloading —arms, Hinter[]lader. —**ball**, *s.* die Granate. —**box**, *s.* d[er] Feuerraum, die Feuerbüchse (*Locom., etc.*) —**brand**, *s.* der Feuerbrand; der Unheilstifte[r].

Aufwiegler (*fig.*). —**brigade**, *s.* die Feuerwehr. —**bucket**, *s.* der Feuereimer. —**damp**, *s.* das Grubengas; das schlagende Wetter. —-**dogs**, *pl.* die Feuerböcke. —-**engine**, *s.* die Feuerspritze. —-**escape**, *s.* die Feuerleiter, der Rettungsapparat. —-**extinguisher**, *s.* der chemische Löschapparat, Extinkteur. —**fly**, *s.* der Leuchtkäfer, Glühwurm. —-**gilt**, *adj.* feuervergoldet. —-**grate**, *s.* der Feuerrost. —-**guard**, *s.* das Kamingitter. —-**insurance**, *s.* die Feuerversicherung, Brandschadenversicherung, Versicherung gegen Brandschaden; —-insurance company, die Feuerversicherungs-Gesellschaft. —-**irons**, *pl.* die Schüreisen, das Kamingerät. —-**lighter**, *s.* der Feueranzünder. —**lock**, *s.* das Schloß am Gewehre; (gun) das Schießgewehr. —**man**, *s.* der Heizer, Schürer (*Locom.*, *etc.*); der Feuerwehrmann; —men, *pl.* die Feuerleute, die Feuerwehr. —**master**, *s.* der Oberfeuerwerker (*Mil.*); der Anführer der Löschmannschaft, Branddirektor. —**place**, *s.* der Kamin; (hearth) der Herd. —**plug**, *s.* der Feuerhahn, Feuerstöpsel an Wasserröhren. —-**proof**, *adj.* feuerfest, feuersicher; —-proof safe, der feuerfeste Geldschrank. —-**screen**, *s.* der Feuerschirm. —**ship**, *s.* der Brander. —**shovel**, *s.* die Feuer-Kohlenschaufel. —**side**, I. *s.* der Herd, Kamin; das häusliche Leben, der Familienkreis (*fig.*). II. *adj.* häuslich; —side joys, die im Familienkreise genossenen, häuslichen Freuden; —side tale, die Familiengeschichte, Erzählung am häuslichen Herde. —**stone**, *s.* der Feuerstein (*Min.*); der Schwefelkies. —-**tongs**, *pl.* die Feuerzange. —**wood**, *s.* das Brennholz; wheel —wood, der Feueranzünder in runder Form. —**works**, *pl.* das Feuerwerk. —-**worship**, *s.* die Feueranbetung. —-**worshipper**, *s.* der Feueranbeter.

Firing, I. *p. see* Fire. II. *s.* das Feuern, Schießen (*Mil.*); individual —ing (in quick time), das Schnellfeuer; (setting on fire) das Anzünden; (heating) die Heizung; (fuel) das Brennmaterial; to cease —, das Gefecht abbrechen; cease —! Gewehr in Ruh!

Firkin, *s.* das Viertelfaß; ein Fäßchen (of butter, Butter); ein (Getränke-)Maß (*B.*).

Firm, I. *adj.*, —**ly**, *adv.* fest, hart; standhaft (*fig.*); prices remain — at . . ., Preise stehen fest auf . . . ; he remained —, er blieb fest (bei seinem Beschluß). II. *s.* die (Handels-)Firma (*C. L.*). —**ament**, *s.* das Firmament, Himmelsgewölbe. —**ness**, *s.* die Festigkeit, Stärke; (resoluteness) die Standhaftigkeit; die Festigkeit (*fig.*); (durability) die Dauer.

Firman, *s.* der Ferman, der großherrliche Befehl.

First, I. *adj.* erst; in the — place, — of all, zuerst, erstens, erstlich, an erster Stelle; — and foremost, vor allen Dingen, zuvörderst, erstlich; — book, das Elementarbuch; — cost, der Einkaufspreis; — quality, Prima-Sorte; — cousin, das Geschwisterkind; — mate, der Obersteuermann. II. *adv.* erst (*in time*), zuerst (*in time, rank, order*); erstlich, erstens, fürs erste; (previously) erst; at —, erst, anfangs, anfänglich; — come, — served, wer zuerst kommt, mahlt zuerst; to go —, vorangehen. III. *s.* der, die, das Erste; die erste Klasse (*Railw.*); — of exchange, der Primawechsel; — not paid, Prima nicht; to go —, erster Klasse fahren (*Railw.*). —**ling**, *s.* der Erstling, die Erstgeburt. —**ly**, *adv.* erstlich, erstens, zum Ersten, zuerst. *Comp.* —-**begotten**, *adj.* erstgeboren, erstererzeugt. —-**born**, I. *adj.* erstgeboren, ältest. II. *s.* der Erstgeborene. —-**class**, *adj.* erstklassig; —-class article, erstklassiges Fabrikat. —-**fruits**, *pl.* Erstlinge. —-**hand**, I. *s.*; at —-hand, unmittelbar, aus erster Hand, direkt. II. *adj.*; —-hand bills, Briefe von der Hand (*C. L.*). —-**rate**, *adj.* best, ausgezeichnet, vorzüglich, tadellos, vortrefflich, famos.

Firth, *see* Frith.

Fiscal, I. *adj.* fiskalisch; — year, das Finanzjahr. II. *s.* der Fiskal.

Fish, I. *s.* der Fisch; Fische, der Fisch (*collectively*); (counter) die Spielmarke; freshwater —, Flußfisch; odd —, queer —, wunderlicher Kauz (*coll.*); the — rises, der Fisch beißt an; to land (*or* grass) a —, den Fisch aus dem Wasser ziehen; to have other — to fry, andere Dinge zu tun haben; a pretty kettle of —, eine nette Bescherung; he is like a — out of water, er ist wie ein Fisch auf trockenem Sand, er ist nicht in seinem Elemente; neither flesh nor —, weder Fleisch noch Fisch, nicht gehauen noch gestochen. II. *v.a.* fischen, fangen; to — up, auffischen; to — out, ausforschen; to — a river, in einem Flusse angeln *or* Netze auslegen. III. *v.n.* fischen; to — in troubled waters, im Trüben fischen; to — for, haschen nach (*fig.*); to — for compliments, nach Komplimenten haschen; to — for pikes, nach Hechten angeln *or* fischen. —**er**, *s.* der Fischer. —**ery**, *s.* die Fischerei; das Gebiet einer Fischerei. —**ing**, I. *pr.p.*; to go —ing, auf den Fischfang ausgehen; to go trout- —ing, Forellen fangen wollen, auf den Forellenfang gehen. II. *s.* das Fischen, der Fischfang. III. *adj.* fischend; fischerähnlich; Fischer-; —ing boots, Wasserstiefel. —**y**, *adj.* fischartig (*of a taste*); fischreich (*as the sea*); verdächtig, faul, unsicher (*coll.*). *Comp.* —-**bone**, *s.* die Gräte. —**erman**, *s.* der Fischer. —-**hook**, *s.* die Fischangel; der Kenterhaken (*Naut.*). —**ing-boat**, *s.* das Fischerboot. —**ing-fly**, *s.* die künstliche Fliege zum Angeln. —**ing-ground**, *s.* der Fischergrund. —**ing-line**, *s.* die Angelschnur. —**ing-rod**, *s.* die Angelrute. —**ing-smack**, *s.* das Fischerboot. —**ing-tackle**, *s.* das Angelgerät. —**ing-village**, *s.* das Fischerdorf. —**kettle**, *s.* der Fischkessel. —-**knife**, *s.* das Fischmesser. —**like**, *adj.* fischähnlich. —**market**, *s.* der Fischmarkt. —**monger**, *s.* der Fischhändler. —**pond**, *s.* der Fischteich. —**wife**, *s.* die Fischverkäuferin, das Fischweib.

Fiss—**ion**, *s.* die Spaltung; die spontane Teilung (der Zellen). —**irostral**, *adj.* spaltschnäbelig. —**ure**, I. *s.* der Spalt, Riß, die Spalte, Ritze. II. *v.a.* spalten, sprengen.

Fist, *s.* die Faust; to clench one's —, die Faust ballen. —**ed**, *adj.* eine Faust habend; close- —ed, light- —ed, die Faust geschlossen haltend; knauserig, geizig (*fig.*). —**icuffs**, *pl.* Faustschläge.

Fistul—**a**, *s.* die Fistel. —**ar**, *adj.* rohrartig. —**ous**, *adj. see* —ar; fistelartig.

[1]**Fit**, I. *adj.*, —**ly**, *adv.* (appropriate) tauglich, passend, gut; (qualified) fähig; (proper) angemessen, schicklich; wohlauf, auf dem Damm (*coll.*); in guter Form (*Sport*); it is not —, es ziemt sich nicht; to be — for, taugen (zu); to think —, für gut halten; as — as a fiddle, in bester Verfassung, famos zu Wege (*coll.*); he is — for Bedlam, er ist reif fürs Irrenhaus; — for service, dienstfähig, diensttauglich; more than is —, über die Gebühr. II. *s.* das genaue Passen, Anschließen; it is a bad —, es paßt schlecht; to be a tight — in, nur eben mit genauer Not hineingehen in (*acc.*). III. *v.a.* (einem) maß nehmen; (einem einen Anzug) anprobieren, anpassen (*Tail.*, *etc.*); einrichten; (answer) passen für *or* zu, angemessen sein; a —ting dressmaker, eine Schneiderin zum Maßnehmen *or* Anprobieren; every shoe —s not every foot, man kann nicht alle Leute über einen Leisten schlagen; to — with, versorgen mit; this coat does n't — me, dieser Rock paßt *or* sitzt mir nicht; to — **out**, ausrüsten, ausstatten; to — **up**, einrichten, ausstatten; ausmöblieren; montieren. IV. *v.n.* sich schicken; anschließen, passen; the dress —s nicely, das Kleid paßt gut, sitzt ausgezeichnet *or* wie angegossen. —**ness**, *s.* die Füglichkeit, Schicklichkeit, Tauglichkeit. —**ted**, *p.p.* & *adj.*;

ausgeſtattet ; montiert ; a tube was —ted to it, eine Röhre wurde daran angebracht; she came to be —ted, ſie kam zum Anprobieren *or* zur Anprobe. —**ter**, *s.* der welcher anprobiert ; gas-—ter, der Gaseinrichter, Inſtallateur. —**ting**, *adj.*, —**tingly**, *adv.* ſchicklich, paſſend ; geeignet. —**tings**, *pl.* die Einrichtung *or* Ausſtattung eines Hauſes oder Geſchäftes (ohne die eigentlichen Möbel).

[2]**Fit**, *s.* der Anfall, Zufall; epileptic —s, die Fallſucht; (mood) die Laune, Anwandlung, der Einfall; a drunken —, ein Rauſch; — of hysterics, hyſteriſcher Zufall ; — of jealousy, Anfall von Eiferſucht ; by —s and starts, ſtoßweiſe, ruckweiſe; dann und wann; if the — takes me, wenn mich die Laune anwandelt. —**ful**, *adj.*, —**fully**, *adv.* abwechſelnd, unterbrochen ; (inconstant) unbeſtändig; launiſch. —**fulness**, *s.* die Unbeſtändigkeit, Launenhaftigkeit.

[3]**Fit, Fytte**, *s.* der Abſchnitt eines altgermaniſchen epiſchen Gedichtes ; der Teil eines längeren Gedichtes, der auf einmal geſungen wurde (*obs.*).

Five, *num. adj.* fünf ; — score, hundert, das Hundert. —**fold**, *adj.* fünffach. —**s**, *pl.* eine Art Ballſpiel. *Comp.* —**-barred**, *adj.* ; — -barred gate, Schlagbaum mit fünf Barren. —**s-court**, *s.* der Platz, wo das Ballſpiel Fives geſpielt wird.

Fix, I. *v.a.* befeſtigen, feſtmachen, anheften; beſtimmen, feſtſetzen (*a time, a price, etc.*) ; aufſchlagen (one's abode in a place, ſeine Wohnung an einem Orte) ; verdichten (*a gaseous body*) ; to — the eyes upon, die Augen auf (*acc.*). . . heften; to — in, einpaſſen; to — the attention, die Aufmerkſamkeit feſſeln ; to — the attention upon a th., die Aufmerkſamkeit auf eine S. richten ; — swords (*or* bayonets), das Seitengewehr pflanzt auf ! (*Mil.*). II. *v.n.;* to — on, ſich entſchließen für, wählen. III. *s.* die üble Lage, Klemme (*coll.*) ; to be in a nice —, ſchön in der Klemme ſitzen. —**ed**, *adj.* feſt; fix (*Chem.*) ; beſtimmt; —ed air, fixe Luft ; —ed prices, feſte Preiſe ; —ed salts, feuerbeſtändige Salze; —ed star, der Fixſtern ; —ed salary, feſtes *or* beſtimmtes Gehalt. —**edly**, *adv.* feſt; unverwandt; ſtandhaft. —**edness**, *s.* die Feſtigkeit; die Feuerbeſtändigkeit (*of gold, etc.*); die Standhaftigkeit, Beharrlichkeit (*fig.*). —**ing**, *s.* das Aufſtellen, Einbringen (*Mech., etc.*) ; die Fixierung (*Chem.*). —**ings**, *pl.* das Zubehör, die Einrichtungen (*Amer.*). —**ity**, *s.* die Feſtigkeit; —ity of tenure, die Feſtigkeit des Lehens, feſtes Lehen. —**ture**, *s.* die Feſtſetzung, Abmachung, feſte Verabredung; die feſte Stellung; die angeſeſſene Perſon (*fig.*); niet- und nagel-feſter Gegenſtand (in einem Gebäude), das Pertinenzſtück. —**tures**, *pl.* die Ausſtattung eines Hauſes (ohne die eigentlichen Möbel), feſte Anlage; feſt getroffene Verabredungen für Verſammlungen, Wettſpiele, *etc.*).

Fizz, I. *v.n.* ziſchen. II. *s.* das Geziſch. —**le**, *v.n.* ziſchen, brauſen ; ſummen ; erlöſchen, ſchwächer werden (*Amer.*) ; ſtecken bleiben (*Amer. sl.*).

Flabbergast, *v.a.* verblüffen (*coll.*) ; to be quite —ed, vollſtändig *or* ganz paff ſein (*coll.*).

Flabb—iness, *s.* die Schlaffheit, das Welkſein. —**y**, *adj.* ſchlaff, weich; kraftlos, gehaltlos (*fig.*).

Flaccid, *adj.* welk, ſchlaff, ſchlotterig. —**ity**, *s.* die Schlaffheit.

[1]**Flag**, *s.* die Flagge (*Naut.*) ; die Fahne (*Mil.*) ; — of truce, Friedensflagge, Parlamentärflagge; the black —, die Seeräuberflagge; to hang out the red —, die rote Flagge aufziehen, zum Kampfe herausfordern ; to keep the — flying, die Fahne hoch halten ; to strike or lower the —, die Flagge niederholen ; all their —s were struck, alle ihre Fahnen wurden eingezogen, wurden geſtrichen, alle erklärten ſich für beſiegt. *Comp.* —**-officer**, *s.* der Flaggenoffizier. —**-ship**, *s.* das Flagg(en)ſchiff. —**-staff**, *s.* die Flaggenſtange, der Flaggenſtock.

[2]**Flag**, *v. n.* ermatten, erſchlaffen, nachlaſſen ; (grow spiritless) mutlos werden ; his —ging courage, ſein ſinkender Mut.

[3]**Flag**, I. *s.*, —**stone**, *s.* die Flieſe, Platte, der Fliesſtein. II. *v.a.* mit Flieſen belegen, platten; —ged pavement, das Flieſenpflaſter. —**ging**, *s.* das Pflaſtern mit Flieſen. *Comp.* —**ging-stone**, *s.* die Steinplatte, Flieſe.

[4]**Flag**, *s.* die Schwertlilie.

Flagella—nt, *s.* der Geißelbruder, Geißler. —**te**, *v.a.* geißeln. —**tion**, *s.* die Geißelung.

Flageolet, *s.* das Flageolett.

Flagitious, *adj.*, —**ly**, *adv.* abſcheulich, ſchändlich, boshaft ; (guilty) ſchuldbeladen, laſterhaft. —**ness**, *s.* die Abſcheulichkeit, Verruchtheit.

Flagon, *s.* das Fläſchchen.

Flagran—cy, *s. see* Flagitiousness; die offenkundige Begehung ; die Schändlichkeit, Abſcheulichkeit. —**t**, *adj.*, —**tly**, *adv.* abſcheulich, entſetzlich; (notorious) berüchtigt ; —t outrage, empörende Verletzung (der Sittlichkeit).

Flail, *s.* der Dreſchflegel.

Flak—e, I. *s.* die Flocke (*of snow ; wool, etc.*) ; (—e of fire) der Feuerfunke; (layer) die Schichte, Lage, Platte. II. *v.a.* zu Flocken machen ; in Platten brechen. III. *v.n.* zu Flocken werden; in Platten brechen, ſich ſchichten ; to —e off, ſchichtweiſe abblättern. —**iness**, *s.* das Flockige ; das Schieferige. —**y**, *adj.* flockig ; blätterig (*as pie-crust*) ; geſchichtet, ſchieferig, in Schichten. *Comp.* —**e-white**, *s.* das Wismut-, Schmink-weiß.

Flam—beau, I. *s.* die Fackel. —**boyant**, *adj.* flammend ; —boyant style, der Flammenſtil (*Arch.*). —**e**, *s.* die Flamme ; (fire) das Feuer; (ardour) die Hitze, Heftigkeit des Gemüts, Leidenſchaft; (love) die Liebesglut ; (sweetheart) der, die Geliebte ; an old —e, eine alte Flamme (Liebſchaft). II. *v.n.* flammen, lodern; to — up, auffahren, in Zorn geraten (*fig.*). —**eless**, *adj.* flammenlos. —**ing**, *adj.*, —**ingly**, *adv.* flammend ; feurig ; glühend, hitzig (*fig.*). *Comp.* —**e-coloured**, *adj.* feuerfarbig, feuerfarben.

Flamingo, *s.* der Flamingo.

Flange, *s.* die Flantſche, der Flantſch (*of a pipe, a girder, etc.*); — of a wheel, der Spurkranz ; outside —, der äußere Rand (*Railw.*). *Comp* —**-rail**, *s.* die Randſchiene (*Railw.*).

Flank, I. *s.* die Seite, Weiche (*of animals*) ; die Flanke (*Mil.*) ; die Flanke, Streichlinie (*Fort.*) ; to take the enemy in the —, den Feind in der Flanke faſſen, dem Feinde in die Flanke fallen ; in the —, ſeitwärts. II. *attrib.* ; — guard, die Seitendeckung. III. *v.a.* flankieren, ſeitwärts decken; (einen) in der Flanke bedrohen, (einem) in die Flanke fallen ; (den Feind in der Flanke) umgehen. IV. *v.n.* angrenzen. —**ing**, *adj.* ; —ing angle, der Streichwinkel ; —ing fire, das Flanken-, Beſtreich-feuer ; —ing movement, die Seitenbewegung, Umgehung ; —ing scouts, die Seitenpatrouille.

Flannel, *s.* der Flanell ; in —s, im Flanellanzug; hygienic —, Geſundheitsflanell.

Flap, I. *s.* der Klaps ; die Klappe ; das Läppchen (*of the ear*) ; die Krempe (*of a hat*); die Klappe, das Blatt (*of a table*) ; der Flügelſchlag, Schlag (*of wings*) ; (—ping movement) das Baumeln, Schlagen (eines lockern Körpers); der Rockſchoß (*Tail.*). II. *v.a. & n.* klappen, ſchlagen. III. *v.n.* loſe herabhängen. —**per**, I. *s.* der Klappſer Fächer ; der Mahner (*fig.*) ; der Backfiſch (*sl.*). *Comp.* —**-eared**, *adj.* ſchlappohrig, mit langen Hängeohren.

Flar—e, I. *v.n.* flackern, lodern, ſchimmern, flammen; to —e in a p.'s eyes, einem die Augen blenden ; to —e up, aufflackern, aufflammen ; aufbrauſen, in Hitze geraten (*fig.*). II. *s.* das flackernde Licht ; das zur Schau Tragen (*fig.*) —**ing**, *adj.* aufflackernd ; ſchimmernd, blendend , auffallend (*of dress*).

Flash, I. *s.* das plötzliche Licht, der Blitz (*of lightning*) ; das Aufblitzen, Auflodern (*fig.*) ; der plötzliche Ausbruch (*of wit, mirth, etc.*); — of the eye, das Blitzen des Auges; — of fire, die blitzähnliche Flamme; — of wit, witziger Einfall; —es of wit, Witz(es)funken; — in the pan, das Abblitzen, Versagen des Gewehrs (*lit.*), der mißlungene Versuch (*fig.*). II. *adj.* (gaudy) bunt, prunkend, flimmernd (*sl.*); (false) falsch; — language, das Rotwelsch. III. *v.n.* auflodern, funkeln, blitzen; (— forth) ausbrechen, hervorbrechen (*fig.*); to — in the pan, versagen; the thought —ed across my mind, der Gedanke fuhr mir durch den Kopf. IV. *v.a.* auflodern *or* glänzen lassen; to — a light, ein Licht aufblitzen lassen, ein Licht werfen (auf eine S.); his eyes —ed fire, seine Augen schossen Blitze *or* loderten, sein Blick sprühte Flammen. **—ily**, *adv.*, **—y**, *adj.* bunt, durch buntes Äußere in die Augen fallend, prunkend; oberflächlich. **—iness**, *s.* das Schimmernde, Prunkende; das Oberflächliche. *Comp.* **—(ing)-light**, *s.* das Blickfeuer (*Naut.*); taken by —-light, durch Blitzlichtphotographie.

Flask, *s.* die (überflochtene) Flasche, Feldflasche; powder-—, die Pulverflasche.

Flat, I. *adj.* platt, flach; schal, matt, unschmackhaft; geschmacklos, platt, gemein (*as a speech, book, etc.*) (*fig.*); (positive) ausdrücklich, unbedingt, absolut; moll (*Mus.*); tief, weich (*Gram.*); flau (*C.L.*); that 's —, das ist klar (*coll.*); I won't, that 's —, rund heraus gesprochen, ich tue es nicht! a — refusal, eine unbedingte Verweigerung; I gave a — denial to it, ich habe es rundweg abgeleugnet; — on the ground, auf dem Boden ausgestreckt, platt auf der Erde; to lay —, dem Boden gleich machen; - seam, die flache Naht. II. *adv.*; to sing —, zu tief, falsch singen; to fall —, keinen Eindruck machen (*fig.*). III. *s.* die Fläche, Ebene; die Untiefe; das Be, ♭ (*Mus.*); das Stockwerk, die Etage (*of a house*); die Fläche, breite, flache Seite (*of a sword*); der Einfaltspinsel (*sl.*). **—ly**, *adv. see* — I.; platt; geradezu, rundweg. **—ness**, *s.* die Fläche; die Flauheit (*C. L.*); die Flachheit; die Tiefe (*of a note*). **—ten**, *v.a.* platt, flach machen, breit schlagen, strecken; herunterstimmen (*Mus.*). **—tener**, *s.* der Setzhammer; der Strecker (*Glassw.*); der Pflöcker (*for needles, etc.*). **—tening**, *s.* das Plattmachen; das Strecken; das Pflöcken; —tening of the earth, die Abplattung der Erde. **—ter**, I. *s.* der Streckhammer. II. *v. see* [2]Flatter. **—tish**, *adj.* ein wenig flach. *Comp.* **—-bottomed**, *adj.* mit plattem Boden; —-bottomed boat, der Prahm. **—-chested**, *adj.* plattbrüstig. **—-fish**, *s.* der Flachfisch. **—-footed**, *adj.* plattfüßig. **—-iron**, *s.* das Plätteisen, Bügeleisen. **—-nosed**, *adj.* plattnasig. **—-race**, *s.* das Rennen ohne Hindernisse. **—-roofed**, *adj.* mit flachem Dache. **—wise**, *adv.* platt nieder, flach.

[1]**Flatter**, *see under* Flat.

[2]**Flatter**, *v.a.* schmeicheln; falsche, ungegründete Hoffnungen erwecken; he —s her, er schmeichelt ihr; she was —ed, es schmeichelte ihr; she felt —ed by this remark, sie fühlte sich durch diese Bemerkung geschmeichelt; to — a p. out of a th., einem etwas abschmeicheln. **—er**, *s.* der Schmeichler. **—ing**, *adj.*, **—ingly**, *adv.* schmeichelhaft, schmeichlerisch. **—y**, *s.* die Schmeichelei.

Flatu—lence, —lency, *s.* die Blähung; die Blähsucht (*Med.*); die Windigkeit (*fig.*). **—lent**, *adj.* voll Blähungen, blähend; Blähungen verursachend (*as food*); (empty) windig; aufgebläht, schwülstig (*fig.*). **—s**, *s.* die Blähung.

Flaunt, *v.* I. *a.* mit etwas paradieren. II. *n.* prangen, prunken, aufgeputzt stolzieren.

Flavo(u)r, I. *s.* der (würzige) Geschmack; (smell) der Wohlgeruch, Duft, das Aroma (*of a rose, a cigar*); die Blume (*of wine*); die Würze (*fig.*). II. *v.a.* (einer Speise) einen Geschmack *or* Duft geben, (eine Speise *etc.*) würzen. **—ed**, *adj.*; well —ed, wohlschmeckend, schmackhaft, würzig; wohlriechend. **—less**, *adj.* geschmacklos.

Flaw, *s.* der Fehler; (crack) der Sprung, Riß, Bruch; die Blase (*in gems, cast metal, etc.*); der Schaden, die Platte (*in cloth*); der Fehler, Schaden, Flecken (*fig.*). **—less**, *adj.* fleckenlos; fehlerfrei.

Flax, *s.* der Flachs, Lein. **—en**, *adj.* flächsen; flachsartig; flachsfarben, Flachs= (*hair*). **—y**, *adj.* flachsartig; flachsfarben, hellgelb. *Comp.* **—-dresser**, *s.* der Flachshechler. **—en-haired**, *adj.* flachshaarig; —en-haired child, ein kleiner Flachskopf. **—-yarn**, *s.* das Leinengarn.

Flay, *v.a.* schinden, die Haut abziehen. **—er**, *s.* der Schinder. **—ing**, *s.* das Schinden, die Schinderei.

Flea, *s.* der Floh; to put a — in a p.'s ear, einem einen Floh ins Ohr setzen. *Comp.* **—bane**, *s.* das Flohkraut (*Bot.*). **—bite**, *s.* der Flohstich; eine unbedeutende Wunde, ein Nichts (*fig.*). **—bitten**, *adj.* von Flöhen gestochen *or* zerstochen; rötlich getupft (*fig.*); —bitten gray horse, der Mückenschimmel.

Fleam, *s.* die Lanzette (*Surg.*); die Fliete (*Vet.*).

Fleck, I. *v.a.* flecken, sprenkeln. II. *s.* der kleine Fleck(en). **—less**, *adj.* fleckenlos, unschuldig.

Fled, *imperf. & p.p. of* Flee.

Fledge, I. *adj.* flügge (*obs. poet.*). II. *v.a.* befiedern. III. *v.n.* flügge werden. **—d**, *p.p. & adj.* flügge, mit Federn versehen; befiedert, beschwingt. **—ling**, *s.* der eben flügge gewordene Vogel.

Flee, *v.a. & n.* fliehen; to — from a th., eine S. meiden; to — one's country, aus seinem Vaterlande fliehen, sein Vaterland verlassen.

Fleec—e, I. *s.* das Vlies; the golden —e, das goldene Vlies. II. *v.a.* scheren; scheren, rupfen (*fig.*). **—er**, *s.* der Plünderer, Bauernfänger. **—y**, *adj.* wollig; wollähnlich, flockig; —y snow, flockiger Schnee; —y clouds, Schäfchen.

Fleer, I. *v.n.* höhnisch lächeln, hohnlächeln; spotten (at s.th., über eine S.). II. *s.* der Spott, das Hohnlachen.

Fleet, I. *adj.*, **—ly**, *adv.* schnell, flink, flüchtig; — of foot, schnellfüßig. II. *v.n.* dahin eilen *or* fliehen, flüchtig sein. III. *s.* die Flotte; die Kriegsflotte; a — in being, eine Manöverflotte. **—ing**, *adj.* flüchtig, vergänglich. **—ness**, *s.* die Schnelligkeit; die Flüchtigkeit.

Flesh, I. *s.* das Fleisch (*also fig.*); to be made —, Mensch werden (*B.*); to pick up *or* put on —, Fleisch ansetzen; it makes my — creep to think of it, beim Gedanken daran überläuft mich eine Gänsehaut. II. *attrib.*; — diet, die Fleischkost. III. *v.a.* mit Fleisch füttern; (initiate) einweihen, abrichten; ausfleischen (*skins*); to — one's sword, das Schwert üben. **—iness**, *s.* die Fleischigkeit. **—less**, *adj.* fleischlos, mager. **—liness**, *s.* die Fleischlichkeit, Sinnlichkeit. **—ly**, *adj.* fleischlich, körperlich; (sensual) sinnlich, fleischlich; (earthly) irdisch, menschlich. **—y**, *adj.* fleischig, fett; (corporeal) leiblich; (pulpy) fleischig (*also Bot.*). *Comp.* **—brush**, *s.* die Frottierbürste. **—-colour**, *s.* die Fleischfarbe. **—-coloured**, *adj.* fleischfarben, fleischrot. **—-hook**, *s.* der Fleischhaken. **—ing-knife**, *s.* das Ausfleischmesser. **—pot**, *s.* der Fleischtopf.

Fleur-de-lis, *s.* die Lilie (*Her.*); die Schwertlilie (*Bot.*).

Flex—ibility, *s.* die Biegsamkeit (*also fig.*). **—ible**, *adj.*, **—ibly**, *adv.* biegsam; biegsam, lenksam, fügsam, nachgiebig (*fig.*); the —ible minds of youth, die lenksamen Gemüter der Jugend. **—ile**, *see* —ible. **—ion**, *see* das Biegen; die Biegung, Beugung. **—or**, *s.* der Beugemuskel (*Anat.*). **—ure**, *s.* das Biegen; die Biegung, Beugung, Krümmung; (bent part) der Bug; *see* Joint; kriechende Verbeugung.

Flibbertigibbet, *s.* der Kobold; der unsinnige, leichtsinnige Mensch.

Flick, I. *s.* der leichte (Peitschen=)Schlag. II. *v.a.* leicht schlagen, schnellen (at, nach).

Flicker, I. *v.n.* flackern. II. *s.* das Flackern, Flattern.

Flier, Flyer, *s.* der Fliegende, Fliehende; das schnellfüßige Pferd, vorzügliche Rennpferd (*Sport*); der Flüchtling; das Schwungrad; die Freitreppe, Doppeltreppe.

Flight, *s.* die Flucht; (flying) das Fliegen, der Flug; (flock) der Flug; der Flug (*of time, etc.*); — of stairs, — of steps, der Treppenlauf, die Stufen (*between two landings*); (outside —) die Freitreppe; — of fancy, der Flug der Phantasie; to put to —, in die Flucht schlagen; to take to —, die Flucht ergreifen. **—iness**, *s.* die Flüchtigkeit (*also fig.*); die Geistesabwesenheit (*coll.*). **—y**, *adj.*, **—ily**, *adv.* flüchtig; leichtsinnig, unbeständig; geistesabwesend, zerstreut, faselnd.

Flims—ily, *adv. see* —y. **—iness**, *s.* das Lockere, die Dünnheit; die Geringfügigkeit, Nichtigkeit (*fig.*). **—y**, I. *adj.* locker, lose, dünn; schwach, nichtig, schal; —y excuse, nichtige Entschuldigung. II. *s.* dünnes Kopierpapier.

Flinch, *v.n.* (zurück=)weichen, wanken; (recoil) zurückschaudern; don't —! bleibe standhaft! wanke und weiche nicht!

Fling, I. *ir.v.a.* werfen, schleudern; to — **about**, umherwerfen; to — **away**, wegwerfen, (squander) verschleudern, (let slip) fahren lassen; to — **down**, niederwerfen; to — **in**, hineinwerfen; to — **off**, abwerfen; to — **open**, aufreißen; to — **out**, I. *v.a.* auswerfen. II. *v.n.* (kick out as a horse) hinten ausschlagen, (show restiveness) unbändig werden; to — **up**, in die Höhe werfen. II. *s.* (throw) der Wurf; der Schlag (*of a horse*); die volle Freiheit; der tolle Ausbruch (*fig.*); to have a — at, nach (etwas) werfen, (etwas) versuchen; let him have his —, laß ihn gewähren, austoben; to have a — at a p., einen Stein auf einen werfen; einem Eins anhängen (*fig.*); Highland —, lebhafter schottischer Tanz. **—er**, *s.* der Werfende, Schleuderer.

Flint, *s.* der Kiesel, Feuerstein; — and steel, das Feuerzeug; skin—, der Geizhals; heart of —, das Felsenherz. **—y**, *adj.* kieselig, steinicht; hart (*fig.*). *Comp.* **—-glass** *s.* das Flintglas. **—-lock**, *s.* das Steinschloß.

Flip, I. *v.a.* leicht schlagen, klapsen, schnellen. II. *s.* der leichte Schlag; egg —, der Eierpunsch.

Flippan—cy, *s.* die Leichtigkeit (im Sprechen), Geschwätzigkeit; die Leichtfertigkeit (im Reden), der Leichtsinn; (pertness) die Keckheit, das naseweise Wesen. **—t**, *adj.*, **—tly**, *adv.* geläufig (im Sprechen); vorlaut; leichtsinnig, keck; —t tongue, das Plappermaul.

Flirt, I. *v.n.* kokettieren; sich (*dat.*) gern die Kur machen lassen, liebeln; to — with a girl, mit einem Mädchen kokettieren. II. *v.a.*; to — a fan, mit einem Fächer kokettieren. III. *s.* die Kokette, das gefallsüchtige Mädchen; (male —) der Courschneider, Schäker. **—ation**, *s.* das Kokettieren.

Flit, *v.n.* huschen, flitzen, hin und her flattern; ausziehen (*Scotch*); the thought —ted across my mind, der Gedanke schoß mir durch den Kopf; to — **along**, dahinflattern, fortziehen; to — **away**, wegflattern; to — **by** *or* **past**, vorübergleiten, vorüberfliegen, vorbeiflattern. **—ting**, *s.* das Vorüberfliegen; das Ausziehen (aus einer Wohnung), der Umzug (*Scotch*); two —tings are as bad as a fire, zwei Umzüge sind so schlimm wie einmal abbrennen.

Flitch, *s.*; — of bacon, die (eingesalzene) Speckseite.

¹Flitter, *v.n.* flattern. *Comp.* **—mouse**, *s.* die Fledermaus (*obs. dial.*).

²Flitter, *s.* das Metallplättchen; der Lappen, Fetzen; worn to —s, abgetragen, schäbig.

Flittern, *s.* die junge Eiche.

Float, I. *s.* das Schwimmende; (raft) das Floß; der Kork, die Flöße (*of anglers*). II. *v.n.* obenauf schwimmen, vom Wasser getragen werden, (dahin)treiben; (— in the air) in der Luft flattern, schweben, wehen; (glide) gleiten, sich leicht und anmutig bewegen; she —ed past, sie schwebte vorüber; the buoy is (not) —ing in sight, die Ankerboje wacht (die Boje steht blind). III. *v.a.* flößen; flott machen (*a ship, etc.*); flott machen, in Gang bringen (*C.L.*). **—ing**, *adj.* zirkulierend, im Umlaufe; unsicher, vag; —ing battery, schwimmende Batterie; —ing bridge, die Schiffbrücke; —ing buoy, wachende Boje; —ing capital, das Umlaufskapital; —ing debt, schwebende Schuld; —ing dock, schwimmendes Dock; —ing ice, das Treibeis; —ing light, das Leuchtschiff; —ing pier, schwimmende Landungsbrücke; —ing population, schwankende Bevölkerung; —ing recollections, dunkle Erinnerungen; —ing rumours, umlaufende Gerüchte; —ing security, unsichere Bürgschaft; —ing stage, das Kalfatfloß; —ing tables, schwimmende Tische (*in mud baths*).

Floc—cillation, *s.* das Flockenlesen (*Med.*). **—cose**, *adj.* flockig (*Bot.*). **—k**, *s.* die Flocke, Locke (*of wool*). *Comp.* **—k-mattress**, *s.* eine Wollmatratze. **—k-paper**, *s.* das Flockpapier, velutierte Papier.

¹Flock, *see under* Floccillation.

²Flock, I. *s.* die Herde (*of sheep, also fig.*); die Gemeinde (*fig.*); der Haufe, die Menge, Schar; der Flug (*of birds*). II. *v.n.* sich haufenweise sammeln, (— together) sich gesellen; zusammenströmen; birds of a feather — together, gleich und gleich gesellt sich gern (*prov.*); to — to a p., einem zuströmen; the people — to the theatre, das Volk strömt in das *or* zu dem Theater.

Floe, *s.* das schwimmende Eisfeld; das Tafeleis.

Flog, *v.a.* peitschen, stäupen, züchtigen. **—ging**, *s.* das Prügeln; die Rutenstrafe, Prügelstrafe; to get a —ging, geprügelt werden, die Rute bekommen.

Flood, I. *s.* die Flut, Überschwemmung (*also fig.*); der Strom (*Poet.*); die Sündflut (*B.*); (—-tide) die Flut; by — and field, zur See und zu Lande; — of tears, Tränenflut, Tränenstrom. II. *v.a.* überfluten, überschwemmen. **—ing**, *s.* das Überfluten; die starke Verblutung aus dem Uterus. *Comp.* **—-gate**, *s.* das Fluttor; (sluice) die Schleuse. **—-mark**, *s.* die Flutmarke, das Hochwasserstandszeichen. **—-tide**, *s.* die Flut.

Floor, *s.* der Fußboden, Flur, Estrich; das Geschoß, Stockwerk (*Build.*); die Flur (*Poet.*); die Tenne (*of a barn*); ground-—, das Parterre, Erdgeschoß; second —, zweiter Stock; earthen —, der Lehmstrich; wooden —, boarded —, der gedielte Fußboden; inlaid —, das Parkett, der getäfelte Fußboden; — of a boat, die Lanen. II. *v.a.* Dielen, Fußboden legen; (strike down) zu Boden schlagen; zum Schweigen bringen (*fig.*). **—ing**, *s.* die Dielung, der Fußboden; die Dielung, 2c., das Material zum Belegen des Fußbodens. *Comp.* **—-cloth**, *s.* die Fußbodendecke (von Wachstuch). **—-timbers**, *pl.* die Dielenträger (*Carp.*); die Bauchstücke (*Shipb.*).

Flop, I. *v.a. see* Flap. II. *v.n.* mit den Flügeln schlagen; hinplumpsen (*coll.*). II. *s.* das Hinplumpsen; plötzlicher Zusammenbruch (*coll.*). III. *interj.* plumps!

Flor—a, *s.* die Blumenwelt, Flora. **—al**, *adj.* Blüten=, Blumen=. **—iculture**, *s.* die Blumenzucht. **—id**, *adj.* blühend, hochrot, von lebhafter Farbe; blühend (*fig.*); —id countenance, hochrote Gesichtsfarbe; —id style, blumenreicher Stil, *see* Flamboyant. **—idness**, *s.* lebhafte Farbe; das Blumige (*of style*). **—in**, *s.* der Gulden. **—ist**, *s.* der Blumenhändler, Kunstgärtner; der Blumenkundige; der Blumenliebhaber.

Floret, *s.* der Stoßdegen, das Florett.

¹Floss, *s.* die Samenwolle; ungezwirnte Seidenfäden. **—y**, *adj.* feinseiden. *Comp.* **—-silk**, *s.* die Flock=, Florett=seide.

²Floss, *s.* kleiner Bach.

Flot—illa, *s.* die Flotille, das kleine Geschwader. **—sam**, *s.* das Strandgut, Wrackgut.

¹Flounce, *v.n.* platschen, umherschlagen; to — out

of the room, trotzig, ungehalten aus dem Zimmer stürzen.

²Flounce, I. *s.* die Falbel, der lose Besatz, Volant. II. *v.a.* mit Falbeln, Volants besetzen; —d and furbelowed, mit vielen Volants besetzt.

¹Flounder, *v.n.* sich abarbeiten, zappeln, hin und her taumeln; umhertappen (*fig.*).

²Flounder, *s.* der Flunder, die Scholle (*Icht.*); flat as a —, platt wie eine Scholle.

Flour, I. *s.* das feine (Weizen=)Mehl. II. *v.a.* mit Mehl bestreuen. **—ish**, *see* Flourish. *Comp.* **—-bag**, *s.* der Mehlbeutel. **—-box**, *s.* die Mehl=Streumaschine. **—ing-mill**, *s.* die Mahlmühle (*Amer.*).

Flourish, I. *v.n.* blühen, gedeihen; Schnörkel machen (*in writing*), sich blumenreich ausdrücken; schmettern (*of trumpets*); präludieren (*Mus.*). II. *v.a.* schwingen (*a sword*); schwenken (*a flag*). III. *s.* der Schnörkel (*in writing, also Arch.*); die Leiste, Vignette (*Typ.*); das Vorspiel (*Mus.*); rhetorical —, rednerische Blumen; to write (one's name) with a —, (seinen Namen) zierlich verschnörkeln; to do with a —, mit einem gewissen Stolze, mit einer prunkhaften Schwenkung (der Hand, 2c.) tun; — of trumpets, die Trompetenfanfare, der Tusch. **—ing**, *adj.*, **—ingly**, *adv.* blühend; gedeihend; a —ing business, ein blühendes *or* schwunghaftes Geschäft; we are all —ing, wir befinden uns alle vorzüglich.

Flout, I. *v.a.* verhöhnen. II. *v.n.* spotten; to — at fortune, dem Glücke Hohn sprechen.

Flow, I. *v.n.* fließen; sich ergießen; strömen (*as air, light*); (over—) (über)fließen; leicht, anmutig herabhängen, herabwallen; to — from, (result) herrühren von, herkommen von, entspringen aus; it has —n, es ist geflossen (from, aus); to — from, fließen aus, entfließen *or* entströmen (*dat. poet.*). II. *s.* der Fluß, Zufluß (*of water, blood, etc.*); der Fluß, Strom, Schwall (*of words*); (abundance) der Überfluß; die Flut (*of tides*); a — of spirits, eine heitere Laune. **—ers**, *pl.* der Monatsfluß. **—ing**, *adj.* fließend; —ing beard, langer, herabhängender, wallender Bart; —ing cups, volle *or* überschäumende Becher; —ing garments, wallende Gewänder; —ing locks, wallende Locken; —ing period, fließende(r Satz), gewandte Satzbildung.

Flower, I. *s.* die Blume; die Blüte (*also fig.*); (the best of anything) der Kern, die Auswahl; (ornament) die Zierde, der Schmuck; die Vignette, Leiste (*Typ.*); cut —s, Schnittblumen, frische Blumen; artificial —s, künstliche Blumen; —s dried and cut, getrocknete und frische Blumen; —s of rhetoric, Rednerblumen; —s of sulphur, Schwefelblumen; —-de-luce, *see* Fleur-de-lis; the — of the troops, der Kern der Truppen; as welcome as —s in May, höchst willkommen. II. *v.n.* blühen (*also fig.*). **—iness**, *s.* das Blumige; das Blumenreiche, der Schmuck (of speech, der Rede). **—ing**, I. *adj.* blühend, blumig. II. *s.* das Blühen; die Blütezeit. **—y**, *adj.* blumenreich; mit Blumen geschmückt; geblümt (*of cloth*); blumenreich (*of style*). *Comp.* **—-bed**, *s.* das Blumenbeet. **—-dust**, *s.* der Blütenstaub. **—ing-ash**, *s.* die Manna=Esche. **—ing-rush**, *s.* die Blumenbinse. **—-leaf**, *s.* das Blumenblatt. **—-pot**, *s.* der Blumentopf. **—-show**, *s.* die Blumenausstellung. **—-stalk**, *s.* der Blumenstiel. **—-stand**, *s.* das Blumengestell. **—-vase**, *s.* das Blumengefäß, die Blumenvase. *Comp.* **—-de-luce**, *s.* die Lilie (*Her.*); die Schwertlilie (*Bot.*).

Fluctuat—e, *v.n.* schwanken, wogen, schaukeln; steigen und fallen (*as prices*); schwanken, schweben (*between different opinions*); (be irresolute) unschlüssig sein. **—ing**, *adj.* veränderlich; —ing prices, schwankende, unbeständige Preise. **—ion**, *s.* das Schwanken, Wogen, Wallen; das Schwanken (*fig., Phys., Math.*); die Unschlüssigkeit; —ions of the market, die Schwankungen des Marktes.

¹Flue, *s.* der Rauchfang, die Rauchröhre; der Zugkanal; der Feuerzug (*Locom., etc.*); der Fuchs (*Found.*); die Wärmeröhre (*for hot air*).

²Flu—e, *s.* der Flaum; die Staubflocke. **—ff**, *s.* leichte Staubflocke, Federflocke. **—ffy**, *adj.* mit leichtem Flaum bedecke, flaumig; leicht verstäubend.

Flu—ency, *s.* der Fluß (*of speech*, der Rede); (volubility) die Geläufigkeit (im Sprechen). **—ent**, *adj.*, **—ently**, *adv.* fließend; geläufig (sprechend). **—id**, I. *s.* die Flüssigkeit; electric (magnetic) —id, das elektrische (magnetische) Fluidum. II. *adj.* flüssig. **—idity**, *s.* die Flüssigkeit, Fluidität.

¹Fluke, *see* Flounder (*Icht.*).

²Fluke, *s.* die Ankerhand.

³Fluke, *s.* der glückliche Zufall, Schlump (*coll.*); der Fuchs (*Bill.*); a mere —, der reine Schlump.

Flummery, *s.* der Haferbrei; leere Komplimente, dummes Zeug, leeres Gewäsch (*fig. coll.*).

Flung, *imperf. & p.p. of* Fling.

Flunkey, *s.* der Livreebediente; (toady) der niedrige Schmeichler, Speichellecker. **—dom**, *s.* Livreebedienten (*coll.*). **—ism**, *s.* die Speichelleckerei, der Knechtssinn.

Fluor-spar, *s.* der Flußspat.

Flurr—ied, *see* —y II. **—y**, I. *s.* die Verwirrung, ängstliche Eile; die nervöse Aufregung *or* Bewegung; der Windstoß; —y of snow, das Schneegestöber; —y of arrows, der Pfeilregen, Hagel von Pfeilen; —y of birds, der Vogelschwarm; to be in a —y, (be —ied) ganz verwirrt sein. II. *v.a.* aufregen, verwirren, bestürzt machen; he easily gets —ied, er gerät leicht außer Fassung; don't —y yourself, rege dich nicht auf!

Flush, I. *v.n.* plötzlich erröten. II. *v.a.* plötzlich erröten machen; (elate) erregen, erheben, stolz machen; aufjagen (*ducks*); to — the sewers, die Schleusen ausspülen; to — the joints, die Fugen mit der Kelle ausstreichen; —ed with victory, siegestrunken; —ed with wine, vom Wein erhitzt. III. *s.* das plötzliche Erröten; die Aufwallung (*of joy*); die Flut (*of passion*); (abundance) die Fülle; der Fluß (*Cards*). IV. *adj.* gleich (*Carp.*); — of money, mit Geld gut versehen, gut bei Kasse (*sl.*).

Fluster, I. *s.* die Hitze; die Verwirrung; all in a —, ganz verwirrt. II. *v.a.* erhitzen, verwirren.

Flut—e, I. *s.* die Flöte (*Mus.*); die Rinne, Riefe (*Arch.*); die Fliete, runde Falte (*in curtains, etc.*); die gaufrierte, geglockte Falte (*Laundry*). II. *v.a.* kannelieren, ausriefeln; gaufrieren, fälteln. III. *v.n.* auf der Flöte spielen, flöten. **—ed**, *adj.* kanneliert, ausgekehlt, gerieft. **—ing**, *s.* die Kannelierung (*of a column*); das Gaufrieren, Stellen (*of clothes*); das Gaufrierte. *Comp.* **—e-player**, *s.* der Flötenspieler, Flötenbläser, Flötist. **—e-stop**, *s.* das Flötenregister.

Flutter, I. *v.n.* flattern, die Flügel bewegen; flattern, wehen (*as flags*); zucken (*as the heart*); to — about, umherflattern, sich hin und her bewegen. II. *v.a.* beunruhigen. III. *s.* das Geflatter, die Schwingung, schnelle, heftige Bewegung; die Unruhe (*fig.*); (agitation) die Angst, (confusion) die Verwirrung; to be all in a —, in größter Aufregung und Verwirrung sein.

Fluvial, *adj.* Fluß=, zu den Flüssen gehörig.

Flux, *s.* der Fluß; das Ausströmen; (circulation) der Umlauf; der Ausfluß (*Med.*); der Fluß (*Metall., Chem.*); — and re—, die Flut und Ebbe; bloody —, die Rotruhr. **—ion**, *s.* der Fluß (*Med.*); —ions, die Differential=Rechnung, Fluxion (*Math.*). **—ionary**, *adj.* Fluxions=, die Fluxionsrechnung.

Fly, I. *ir.v.n.* fliegen; eilen, entfliehen (*as time*); (hasten) eilen, sich stürzen; (flee) fliehen; to — from justice, sich der Gerechtigkeit entziehen; to let —, losschießen; to pay a —ing visit, einen kurzen Besuch machen; to — about, umherfliegen;

(circulate) sich verbreiten; to — **asunder**, auseinanderfliegen; to — **at**, anfahren, herfallen über (*acc.*); to — **in** a p.'s face, einen anfahren; (— in pieces) zerspringen; to — **into** a passion, in Zorn geraten; to — **off**, wegfliehen; to — **open**, auffliegen; to — **out**, herausfliegen; (— out at a p.) (gegen einen) aufbrausen. II. *ir.v.a.* fliegen lassen (*hawks, a kite, etc.*); the ship was —ing the royal standard, am Mast des Schiffs wehte die Königsstandarte. III. *s.* die Fliege; der Einspänner, die leichte Droschke; die künstliche Fliege (*Sport*); das Flugblatt (*coll.*); the — buzzes, die Fliege summt; to break flies on a wheel, Mücken seihen. **—er**, *s.* der Fliehende; *see* Flier. **—ing**, *p. & adj.* fliegend; eilig; a —ing column, ein Streifkorps; —ing visit, kurzer Besuch; eine Stippvisite (*coll.*). *Comp.* **—blow**, I. *v.a.* beschmeißen; —blown, von Fliegen beschmutzt. II. *s.* der Fliegenschmeiß. **—boat**, *s.* das Flieboot. **—catcher**, *s.* der Fliegenfänger; der Fliegenschnäpper (*Orn.*). **—fisher**, *s.* der (mit Fliegen) Angelnde. **—flap**, *s.* der Fliegenwedel. **—ing-artillery**, *s.* leichte Artillerie. **—ing-buttress**, *s.* der Strebebogen. **—ing-fish**, *s.* der fliegende Fisch. **—ing-jib**, *s.* der Außen- *or* Buten-klüver. **—ing-jibboom**, *s.* der Außenklüverbaum. **—ing-machine**, *s.* die Flugmaschine. **—ing-squirrel**, *s.* das fliegende Eichhörnchen. **—leaf**, *s.* das Vorsetzblatt (*Typ.*). **—net**, *s.* das Fliegennetz. **—paper**, *s.* das Fliegenpapier. **—press**, *s.* das Stoßwerk (*also Mint.*). **—sheet**, *s.* das Flugblatt. **—trap**, *s.* die Fliegenfalle. **—wheel**, *s.* das Schwungrad (*Mach.*).

Foal, I. *s.* das Fohlen, Füllen; with —, trächtig. II. *v.a. & n.* fohlen, (ein Füllen) werfen.

Foam, I. *s.* der Schaum. II. *v.n.* schäumen; he —ed at the mouth, sein Mund schäumte. **—ing**, *adj.*, **—ingly**, *adv.* schäumend. **—y**, *adj.* schaumig.

Fob, *s.* die Uhrtasche (in der Hose); das Uhrband, Anhängsel, die Berlocke (*Amer.*).

Foc—al, *adj.* den Brennpunkt betreffend; —al distance, die Brennweite. **—us**, I. *s.* der Brennpunkt; conjugated —i, (*pl.*) die konjugierten Brennpunkte. II. *v.a.* (das Instrument) einstellen, fixieren, den Fokus suchen.

Fodder, I. *s.* das (trockene) Futter. II. *v.a.* füttern.

Foe, *s.* der Feind, die Feindin, der Gegner, die Gegnerin. *Comp.* **—man**, *s.* der Feind (*poet.*).

Fœtus, *s.* die Leibesfrucht, der Fötus.

Fog, I. *s.* der (dicke) Nebel; die Umnebelung, Verwirrung, Unsicherheit (*fig.*); we have got into a — here, wir sind auf einen Holzweg geraten (*fig.*). II. *v.a.* (die Sinne) umnebeln, benebeln; in Verlegenheit setzen. **—giness**, *s.* die Nebligkeit. **—gy**, *adj.* nebelig, dicht; mistig (*Naut.*); unklar, unsicher (*fig.*). *Comp.* **—bank**, *s.* die Nebelschicht. **—bound**, *adj.* durch Nebel zurückgehalten (*of ships*); —bound London, das in Nebel gehüllte London. **—horn**, *s.* das Nebelhorn.

Fogey, *s.*; old —, der verschrobene, altmodische, wunderliche Mensch, konservativer Stockphilister; komischer Kauz (*coll.*).

Foible, *s.* die Schwäche, schwache Seite.

[1]**Foil**, *s.* die Folie (*for gems, mirrors*); to be a — for, act as — to, (einem) zur Folie dienen (*fig.*).

[2]**Foil**, I. *v.a.* vereiteln, vernichten (*efforts, plans, etc.*). II. *s.* die Niederlage, der Schläger, Fechtdegen, das Rapier.

Foist, *v.a.* unterschieben, einschieben; to — spurious articles upon the public, das Publikum mit falschen Artikeln betrügen.

[1]**Fold**, I. *s.* die Falte (*in cloth, etc.*); der Falz (*Bookb.*); (*in comp.* =) -fach, -fältig. II. *v.a.* einpferchen (*sheep, etc.*); falten; falzen; übereinanderlegen (*the arms, etc.*); with —ed arms, mit untergeschlagenen Armen; to — **down** (a leaf, ein Blatt) einschlagen; to — **in**, einhüllen; to — in one's arms, umarmen, in die Arme schließen; he —ed her in his arms, er schloß sie in seine Arme; to — **up** (letters, Briefe) zusammenlegen. III. *v.n.* schließen; in- *or* auf-einander schließen (*as doors*); sich zusammenlegen lassen, zusammenklappen. **—er**, *s.* der Faltende; der Falzer (*Bookb.*); (bone —er) das Falzbein; das Heft, die Broschüre (*Amer.*). **—ers**, *pl.* der Kneifer, Zwicker. **—ing**, *adj.* zusammenlegbar, Klapp-; —ing stand for music, zusammenlegbares Notenpult. *Comp.* **—ing-chair**, *s.* der Klappstuhl. **—ing-door**, *s.* die zweiflügelige Tür, Flügeltür. **—ing-hat**, *s.* der Klapphut. **—ing-machine**, *s.* die Falzmaschine. **—ing-screen**, *s.* die spanische Wand. **—ing-table**, *s.* der Klapptisch.

[2]**Fold**, *s.* die (Schaf-)Hürde, der Pferch, Schafstall (*for sheep, etc.*); (flock) die Herde (*also fig.*).

Foli—aceous, *adj.* blätterig; Blätter-. **—age**, *s.* das Laub(werk). **—ated**, *adj.* mit Folie belegt; (lamellar) blätterig, Blatt-. **—ation**, *s.* die Blattentwickelung, Blätterbildung, der Baumschlag; das Blätterwerk (*Arch.*); die Belegung (*of a mirror, etc.*); das Schlagen zu Blättern (*Metall.*). **—o**, *s.* das Folio (*also Bookkeeping*); das (Folio-)Blatt (*Typ.*); book in —o, der Foliant; large square —o, das Atlasformat; — oblong, das Querfolio.

Folk, *s.* die Leute, das Volk. *Comp.* **—lore**, *s.* die Volkskunde; die Märchen- und Sagen-kunde. **—lorist**, *s.* der Kenner der Volkskunde; der Märchen- und Sagen-forscher, Erforscher der Volks-gebräuche und -überlieferungen.

Follicle, *s.* die Balgkapsel (*Bot.*); die Blase, der Balg (*Anat.*); (gland) die Drüse.

Follow, *v.* I. *a.* (einem) folgen (*also fig.*); (pursue) (einen) verfolgen; auf eine S. folgen, einer S. (nach-)folgen; (accompany) begleiten; (imitate) nachahmen, folgen; (obey) befolgen, beobachten; (— with the eyes) nachschauen; sich halten an (*acc.*) (*a rule, etc.*); sich bekennen zu (*a doctrine, etc.*); (result from) die Folge sein von; (adhere to) nachfolgen; treiben, ausüben (*a business*); nachhängen (*one's fancies*); intemperance is generally —ed by poverty, auf Unmäßigkeit folgt meistens Armut; to — the fashion, sich nach der Mode richten, alle Moden mitmachen; he —s me, er folgt mir; I shall — his advice, ich werde seinem Rat folgen; he was —ed by a large crowd, eine große Menge folgte ihm; I am —ed, man folgt mir, mir folgt jemand; to — suit, nachfolgen, Farbe bekennen (*cards & fig.*); to — one's nose, geradeaus gehen; to — one's pleasure, seinem Vergnügen nachgehen; to — a profession, einen Beruf ausüben, einem Berufe nachgehen; . . . to (*or* if we) — the teachings of St. Paul, der Lehre des Paulus gemäß . . .; to — **out**, durchführen; to — **up**, verfolgen; (— up by) auf eine S. etwas anderes folgen lassen. II. *n.* folgen; it —s from this, daraus folgt; to — in a p.'s footsteps, in jemandes Fußstapfen treten; he spoke as —s, er sprach wie folgt *or* folgendermaßen. **—er**, *s.* der Nachfolger (*also fig.*); (adherent) der Anhänger; (disciple) der Schüler. **—ers**, *pl.* das Gefolge; (adherents) der Anhang; no —ers allowed, Besuch von Schätzen nicht gestattet (*coll.*). **—ing**, I. *adj.* folgend, kommend; on the —ing day, am Tage darauf. II. *s.* das Folgen; (what —s) das Folgende, Folgendes; *see* —ers.

Folly, *s.* die Torheit, Narrheit; to turn to —, leichtsinnig werden, schlecht werden; a piece of —, eine Torheit, ein dummer Streich, Narrenstreich.

Foment, *v.a.* warm baden, bähen; erregen, anreizen, anregen (*sedition, etc.*). **—ation**, *s.* die Bähung, das Baden; das Bähmittel; die Anreizung. **—er**, *s.* der Bähende; der Anreizer.

Fond, *adj.*, **—ly**, *adv.* (loving) liebevoll, zärtlich; (doting) übertrieben zärtlich; to be — of (a p. *or* a th.), (einen oder eine S.) gern haben, (etwas) gern essen, trinken (*food, etc.*), sehr lieben (*peo-*

ple); he is (very) — of music, er ist ein (großer) Freund von Musik; he is — of jesting, er macht gern Scherz. —**le**, *v.a.* liebkosen; verzärteln. —**ler**, *s.* der Liebkosende. —**ness**, *s.* die Liebe (for, zu), Vorliebe (für), Zärtlichkeit (für), der Hang (zu).

Font, *s.* der Taufstein; *see* Fount (*Typ.*). —**anel**, *s.* das Fontanell (*obs. Surg.*); die Fontanelle (*Anat.*).

Food, *s.* die Speise, Nahrung; die Beköstigung, Verpflegung; das Futter (*of beasts*); die Nahrung (*fig.*); animal —, tierische Nahrung. *Comp.* —**stuffs**, *pl.* Nahrungsmittel (im Rohzustande).

[1]**Fool**, I. *s.* der Narr, Tor; (female —) die Närrin, Törin; der Hanswurst, Possenreißer (*at courts*); (court —) der Hofnarr; (—ish person) der törichte Mensch; der Blödsinnige; der Lasterhafte, Gottlose (*B.*); — of fortune, das Spielwerk des Geschicks; to play the —, den Narren spielen, sich lächerlich machen; to make a — of o.s., eine Torheit begehen, närrisch handeln; to make a — of a p., einen zum Besten haben; he 's no —, er läßt sich nicht hinters Licht führen; to make an April — of a p., einen in den April schicken; —'s paradise, das Schlaraffenland; —'s errand, das vergebliche Bemühen; —'s cap, die Narrenkappe; all —s' day, der erste April. II. *v.a.* zum Narren haben; to — away, vergeuden (*coll.*); he has —ed me out of my money, er hat mir mein Geld abgeschwindelt. III. *v.n.* den Narren machen, tändeln; to — about, Narrenspossen treiben, Unsinn machen (*coll.*). —**ery**, *s.* die Torheit. —**ing**, *s.* das Narrentreiben; Narrenwesen. —**ish**, *adj.*, —**ishly**, *adv.* närrisch, töricht, albern; (unwise) unklug; (ridiculous) lächerlich; sündhaft, gottlos (*B.*). —**ishness**, *s.* die Torheit, Narrheit; (—ish nonsense) die Narrespposse; die Torheit (*B.*). *Comp.* —**hardiness**, *s.* die Tollkühnheit. —**hardy**, *adj.* tollkühn. —**scap**, *s.* die Narrenkappe; (—scap paper) das Kanzleiformat, Propatriapapier.

[2]**Fool**, *s.* die Creme, das Mus (*Cook.*).

Foot, I. *s.* der Fuß (*also Arch.; of a page; of a stocking; of a mountain, etc.*); (lowest place) das untere Ende, Fußende, der Fuß; der Schuh (*of a boot*); das Fußvolk, die Infanterie (*Mil.*); der Fuß (= 12 Zoll); der Versfuß (*Pros.*); der Bodensatz (*of oil, etc.*); he has one — in the grave, er steht mit einem Fuß im Grabe; to be on —, auf den Beinen sein; at his feet, ihm zu Füßen; at their feet, ihnen zu Füßen; I refer you to the price list at —, ich verweise Sie auf die am Fuße dieses befindliche Preisliste; the 125th (regiment of) —, das 125. Infanterieregiment; to put one's best — foremost, sich nach Kräften anstrengen; to put one's — in it, sich in eine Verlegenheit *or* Klemme bringen; I have put my — into it, da bin ich schön hereingefallen (*coll.*); to put down one's —, fest bei einer Sache *or* Absage bleiben; from head to —, von Kopf zu Fuß; on —, zu Fuß(e); to set on —, in Gang bringen, ins Werk setzen; to fall on one's feet, Glück haben; Schwein haben (*coll. & stud. sl.*); to tread under —, mit Füßen treten; I know the length of his —, ich kenne ihn ganz genau (*coll.*). II. *v.a.* Füße anstricken; (eine Rechnung) summieren. III. *v.n.;* to — it, tanzen, springen; (walk) zu Fuße gehen. —**ed**, *adj.* (*in comp.* =) -füßig; flat- —ed, plattfüßig. —**ing**, *s.* (basis) der Grund, Halt, die Basis; (—hold) der feste Fuß, feste Besitz, Einstand; (place for the —) der Raum für den Fuß; der Stützpunkt (*fig.*); (state, position) die Lage, der Zustand; to get, gain a —ing, festen Fuß fassen; upon the same —ing as, auf gleichem Fuße mit; he is not on a —ing with us, er steht uns nicht gleich, ist uns nicht ebenbürtig; to lose one's —ing, ausgleiten, -glitschen; to pay one's —ing, seinen Einstand bezahlen. *Comp.* —**ball**, *s.* der Fußball; das Fußballspiel. —**-board**, *s.* das Fußbrett. —**boy**, *s.* der Laufbursche. —**bridge**, *s.* der Steg. —**fall**, *s.* der Tritt; das Stolpern, der Fehltritt. —**-fault**, (*s.*) *interj.* Stellung! (*L. T.*) —**guard**, *s.* der Fußschutz. —**guards**, *pl.* das Garderegiment zu Fuß, die Gardeinfanterie. —**hold**, *s.* der Raum für die Füße. —**lights**, *pl.* die Lampen an der Rampe; der Name für einen Dilettantenklub für dramatische Aufführungen. —**man**, *s.* der Lakei, (Livree-)Bediente. —**mark**, *see* —print. —**-note**, *s.* die Fußnote, Anmerkung zum Text. —**pace**, *s.* der Spazierschritt. —**pad**, *s.* der Straßenräuber zu Fuß. —**-passenger**, *s.* der Fußgänger. —**path**, *s.* der Fußweg, Fußpfad. —**-pound**, *s.* das Fußpfund (*Mech.*). —**prints**, *pl.* Fußstapfen. —**-race**, *s.* der Wettlauf. —**-rest**, *s.* das Fußbänkchen; die Fußrast, die Rast (*Cycl.*). —**rot**, *s.* die Fußfäule. —**-rule**, *s.* der Fußstock, Maßstock von 12 Zoll. —**soldier**, *s.* der Fußsoldat, Infanterist. —**soldiers**, *pl.* das Fußvolk. —**sore**, *adj.* fußwund. —**stalk**, *s.* der Stengel, Stiel. —**step**, *s.* die Fußstapfe, (Fuß-)Spur. —**stool**, *s.* der Schemel, die Fußbank. —**-warmer**, *s.* der Fußwärmer (im Wagen und Eisenbahnwagen). —**way**, *s.* der Fußpfad; der Bürgersteig (*in towns, etc.*). —**wear**, *s.* das Schuhwerk, Schuhzeug; for —wear, als Schuhwerk.

Fop, *s.* der Geck, Stutzer. —**pery**, *s.* der leere Prunk; (folly) die Narrheit; die Ziererei. —**pish**, *adj.*, —**pishly**, *adv.* geckenhaft, stutzerhaft; (affected) geziert. —**pishness**, *s.* die Geckenhaftigkeit; das gezierte Wesen.

For, I. *prep.* (in place of) für, anstatt; (in exchange —) für, um; (as) als, für; (— the sake of) um (einer Sache) willen; will you take this letter — me to the post? wollen Sie diesen Brief für mich zur Post bringen? he gave up law — the church, er gab das Rechtsstudium auf um Theolog zu werden; word — word, Wort für Wort; line — line, Zeile um *or* für Zeile; I hear — certain, ich erfahre als gewiß; to leave — the continent, nach dem Kontinente reisen; I am off — . . ., ich reise nach . . . ab; it is — art to express, es ist Sache *or* die Aufgabe der Kunst auszudrücken; it is — your interest to . . ., es liegt im Ihrem Interesse *or* kann Ihnen nur zum Vorteil gereichen, zu . . .; we depend on . . . — success, hinsichtlich des Erfolges hängen wir von . . . ab; — ever, für immer, auf ewig *or* immer; — life, lebenslänglich; — a while, auf einige Zeit; — some days, einige Tage lang, auf einige Tage; — the next 3 weeks, während der nächsten 3 Wochen; to write — money, — fame, für Geld, des Ruhmes halber schreiben; good —, gut zu *or* für; to be good — nothing, nichts taugen; tall — his age, groß für sein Alter; — how much? wie teuer; — all that, bei alledem, trotz alledem; at a loss —, verlegen um; he could not speak — laughing, er konnte vor Lachen nicht sprechen; I don't believe you — all your swearing! ich glaube euch trotz allen Schwörens nicht! — all he is so rich . . ., obgleich er so reich ist . . .; he did not do it, — all that, er tat es dessen ungeachtet nicht; — God's sake! um Gottes willen! all — nothing, alles umsonst; he gave orders — the charge to be made, er gab Befehl, den Angriff zu machen *or* daß der Angriff gemacht werden solle; you may — me, meinetwegen tun Sie es nur (*coll.*); but — you, should . . ., wäre es nicht um Ihretwegen geschehen, so würde ich . . .; what —? warum? weswegen? — what? wofür? whom are you —? für wen stimmen Sie? — his money, seines Geldes halber; to leave the country — good, das Land auf immer verlassen; once — all, ein für alle Mal; Bismarck — ever! Bismarck soll leben! Vivat Bismarck! that 's the man — me! so einen Menschen lobe ich mir! das ist mein Mann! there 's a man — you! das ist dir einmal ein Kerl! there 's a shower — you! das nenne ich einen Guß!; (*to be translated by the dative of the person interested*) let me hold the stick — you, lassen Sie mich Ihnen den Stock halten; take that — your pains! nimm das für deine Mühe! now — it! jetzt ans Werk! jetzt gilt's! — example, — instance, zum Beispiel; it is not — me to . . ., es ziemt mir nicht zu . . ., es geziemt sich nicht für mich zu . . .; as — me, was mich anbetrifft; a curse upon thee — a traitor! fluch dir, Verräter! — shame! pfui! schäme dich! Oh, — ! hätte ich nur . . . ! II. *conj.* denn; (because) weil, da; — if you do, you will . . ., denn wenn Sie es tun, werden Sie . . .; — it gives great pleasure, denn es macht viel Vergnügen, weil es viel Vergnügen macht. **—e**, **—mer**, **—th**, **—ward**, *see* Fore, Former, Forth, Forward. *Comp.* **—asmuch**, *adv.* weil, da, insofern. **—ever**, *adv. see* — ever.

Forag—e, I. *s.* das Futter, die Furage; (food) das Lebensmittel; (act of —ing) das Furagieren. II. *v.n.* Futter holen, furagieren; sich weiden (*fig.*); to go —ing, on a —ing expedition, furagieren. **—er**, *s.* der Furier. **—ing**, *s.* das Furagieren. *Comp.* **—(ing)-cap**, *s.* die Feldmütze, Stallmütze, leichte Soldatenmütze. **—ing-party**, *s.* der Furagierzug.

Foramen, *s.* das Loch, die Pore (*Anat.*).

Foray, I. *s.* der räuberische Einfall. II. *v.a.* einen Raubzug unternehmen, plündern.

Forbear, I. *ir.v.a.* Geduld haben mit; I cannot — smiling, ich kann nicht umhin zu lächeln; I could scarcely — laughing, ich konnte mich kaum des Lachens enthalten. II. *ir.v.n.* sich enthalten, unterlassen; (desist from) ablassen; (restrain o.s.) sich enthalten; (be patient) sich gedulden; shall I go up against Ramoth Gilead or shall I —? soll ich gen Ramoth in Gilead ziehen zu streiten oder soll ich's lassen anstehen? (*B.*); — ! laß das! **—ance**, *s.* die Geduld, Nachsicht; die Unterlassung; die Enthaltsamkeit; —ance is no acquittance, aufgeschoben ist nicht aufgehoben (*prov.*). **—ing**, *adj.*, **—ingly**, *adv.* geduldig, langmütig.

Forbid, *ir.v.a.* verbieten; (prevent) hindern; I forbade him (to enter) my house, ich verbot ihm das Haus; he was —den the use of his arms, der Gebrauch seiner Waffen wurde ihm verboten; God — ! Gott bewahre! **—den**, *adj.* verboten; the —den city, die nicht zu betretende Stadt. **—ding**, *adj.*, **—dingly**, *adv.* abstoßend, widerwärtig, abschreckend; a —ding appearance, ein widerwärtiges Aussehen; he is cold and —ding, er ist kalt und abstoßend.

[1]**Force**, I. *s.* die Kraft, Macht, Stärke, Gewalt (*in things moral, physical and mechanical*); (validity) die Gültigkeit, Kraft; (violence) der Zwang; (necessity) die Not; (emphasis) der Nachdruck; die Stärke, das Gewicht (*of an argument, etc.*); die Kraft (*of a word, etc.*); (military —) die Kriegsmacht; the local police —, die Ortspolizei; this law is still in —, dies Gesetz ist noch in Kraft; of no —, nicht bindend; in full —, in voller Kraft; by main —, mit aller Kraft, gewaltsam. II. *v.a.* zwingen, nötigen; erstürmen, durch Sturm einnehmen (*a city, etc.*); durchbrechen, erbrechen (*a door, lock, etc.*); erkünsteln, erzwingen (*smiles*); (violate) notzüchtigen; (im Gewächshause) treiben, zeitigen (*Hort.*); to — the meaning of a phrase, einer Redensart eine gezwungene Deutung geben; to — **along**, vorwärts treiben; to — along with, mit sich fortreißen; to — **away**, wegreißen; to — **back**, zurücktreiben; to — **down**, hinunterdrücken; to — **forward**, vorwärts treiben; to — **from**, vertreiben aus, (einem etwas) abdringen, abpressen; you have —d the secret from me, Sie haben mir das Geheimnis abgedrungen; to — **in**, **into**, hineintreiben; to — **off**, zu jedem Preise losschlagen, verschleudern (*C.L.*); to — **on**, antreiben; **to — open**, mit Gewalt aufbrechen; the door was —d open, die Tür wurde gesprengt, gewaltsam geöffnet, aufgebrochen; to — **out**, heraustreiben; to — out of, vertreiben; to — a way **through**, durchbrechen, sich (*dat.*) einen Weg öffnen; to — **upon** a p., einem (etwas) aufdringen. **—d**, *adj.* erzwungen; (unnatural) gezwungen, erkünstelt; —d loan, die Zwangsanleihe; —d marches, Eilmärsche; —d smile, gezwungenes Lächeln; —d style, gekünstelter Stil. **—s**, *pl.* **Truppen**. *Comp.* **—ful**, *adj.* kräftig, wirkungsvoll.

[2]**Force**, *s.* der Wasserfall (*dial.*).

[3]**Force**, *v.a.* füllen, farcieren. *Comp.* **—meat**, I. *s.* gehacktes Füllfleisch. II. *attrib.*; —meat ball, das Fleischklößchen.

Forceps, *s.* die Zange (*Surg.*).

Forcibl—e, *adj.*, **—y**, *adv.* kräftig, mächtig; (efficacious) wirksam; (impetuous) heftig, ungestüm; (violent) gewaltsam; (impressive) eindringlich, überwiegend; —e abduction, gewaltsame Entführung (eines Kindes, &c.); —e detainer, gewaltsame Entziehung von Ländereien. **—eness**, *s.* die Gewalt; die Gewaltsamkeit.

Forcing, *s.* das Zwingen; das Treiben, Zeitigen (*Hort.*); *see* Force. *Comp.* **—-house**, *s.* das Treibhaus. **—-pump**, *s.* die Druckpumpe.

Ford, I. *s.* die Furt. II. *v.a.* durchwaten. **—able**, *adj.* durchwatbar, zu durchwaten, seicht. **—ableness**, *s.* die Durchwatbarkeit, Seichtigkeit.

Fore, I. *adv.* vorn; — and aft, vorn und hinten, die ganze Schiffslänge; to the —, vorn, voran; vorhanden; is he still to the —? ist er noch am Ruder? II. *adj.* vorder. *Comp.* **—arm**, I. *s.* der Vorderarm. II. *v.a.* im Voraus bewaffnen. **—bear**, *s.* der Vorfahr, Ahne, die Ahne, Ahnfrau. **—bode**, *v.a.* vorbedeuten; (feel before) ahnen. **—boder**, *s.* der Ahnende. **—boding**, *s.* die Vorbedeutung; die Ahnung. **—-cabin**, *s.* die vordere Kajüte. **—cast**, I. *s.* die Vorhersagung; —cast of the weather, die Wetter-Vorhersage; der Wetterbericht; —cast of the future, die Ausdeutung der Zukunft, der Ausblick in die Zukunft. II. *v.a.* vorbedeuten, vorhersehen. **—castle**, I. *s.* das Vorderkastell. II. *attrib.*; —castle crew *or* men, die Backsposten. **—close**, *v.a.* ausschließen, präkludieren; to — close a mortgage, eine Hypothek für verfallen erklären. **—closure**, *s.* die Ausschließung, Präklusion. **—-court**, *s.* der Vorhof. **—-deck**, *s.* das Vorderdeck. **—doom**, *v.a.* vorher bestimmen, im Voraus verurteilen. **—fathers**, *pl.* die Vorfahren, Ahnen. **—fend**, *see* Forfend. **—finger**, *s.* der Zeigefinger. **—foot**, *s.* der Vorderfuß. **—front**, *s.* die Vorderseite; die erste, vorderste Reihe; — front of the battle, die vorderste Schlachtlinie. **—go**, **—gone**, *see* Forgo. **—ground**, *s.* der Vordergrund. **—hand**, I. *s.* die Vorhand. II. *attrib.* mit Vorhand gespielt (*L. T.*). **—head**, *s.* die Stirn. **—know**, *ir.v.a.* vorherwissen. **—knowledge**, *s.* das Vorherwissen. **—land**, *s.* das Vorland, Vorgebirge. **—lock**, *s.* die Vorderlocke, das Stirnhaar; to take time by the —lock, die Gelegenheit (beim Schopf) ergreifen. **—man**, *s.* der Obmann (*of a jury*); der Faktor (*also Typ.*); der Werkführer, Vormann, Werkmeister, Vorsteher, Aufseher (*Manuf.*). **—mast**, *s.* der Fockmast. **—mentioned**, *adj.* vorher erwähnt. **—most**, I. *adj.* vorderst, erst (*in place*); erst (*in rank, etc.*). II. *adv.* zuerst; voran; first and —most, zu allererst. **—noon**, *s.* der Vormittag. **—ordain**, *v.a.* vorher-bestimmen, -verordnen. **—ordination**, *s.* die Vorherbestimmung. **—part**, *s.* der erste Teil (*of the day, etc.*); das Vorderteil (*of a ship, etc.*). **—runner**, *s.* der Vorläufer, Vorgänger; das Vorzeichen. **—sail**, *s.* das Focksegel. **—see**, *ir.v.a.* vorher-sehen, -wissen. **—shadow**, *v.a.* vorher andeuten, ahnen lassen. **—shadowings**, *pl.* Vorahnungen. **—shore**, *s.* das Uferland, Land am Wasser. **—shorten**, *v.a.* in der Verkürzung zeichnen. **—shortening**, *s.* die Verkürzung. **—show**, *v.a.* vorher anzeigen. —**sight**, *s.* die Voraussicht; die Vorsorge, Vorsicht, der Vorbedacht, das Vorwärtsvisieren (*Surveying*); das Standvisier (*Mil.*). —**skin**, *s.* die Vorhaut. —**stall**, *v.a.* vorbauen, (einem) zuvorkommen, (einem etwas) vorwegnehmen; vorweg kaufen, im Voraus aufkaufen (*C.L.*). —**staller**, *s.* der Vorkäufer, Aufkäufer. —**taste**, *s.* der Vorgeschmack. —**tell**, *ir.v.a.* vorhersagen; vorbedeuten (*fig.*). —**thought**, *s.* der Vorbedacht. —**top**, *s.* der Fockmars, Vormars (*Naut.*); —topsail, das Vormarssegel; —topgallant-sail, Vorbramsegel; —topgallant royal, Voroberbramsegel. —**warn**, *v.a.* vorher warnen; vorhersagen; —warned, —armed, vorhergewarnt heißt vorhergerüstet, gewarnter Mann gegen zwei sich wahren kann (*prov.*). —**woman**, *s.* die Vorsteherin, Aufseherin.

Foreign, *adj.* ausländisch, auswärtig, fremd, ungehörig (*fig.*); — attachment, die Beschlagnahme des Eigentums eines Fremden; — bills, auf Auswärtige gezogene Wechsel; — country, — parts, das Ausland; — office, das Ministerium des Äußeren, das auswärtige Amt; the Secretary of State, — department, der Minister des Äußeren; — post-card, die Weltpostkarte; — to my purpose, liegt meinem Zwecke fern; this remark is — to the subject, diese Bemerkung gehört nicht hierher *or* zur Sache. —**er**, *s.* der Ausländer, Fremde. —**ness**, *s.* die Fremdheit; das Ungehörige (*fig.*).

Forensic, *adj.* gerichtlich, Gerichts=; — medicine, gerichtliche Medizin.

Forest, I. *s.* der Forst, Wald. II. *attrib.* Wald=, Forst=. III. *v.a.* mit Wald bedecken, beforsten. —**er**, *s.* der Förster; der Forstbewohner. —**ers**, *pl.* Mitglieder eines Vereins zur Pflege der Geselligkeit und Wohltätigkeit. —**ry**, *s.* die Forstkultur, Forstwirtschaft, das Forstwesen. *Comp.* —**-laws**, *pl.* die Forstgesetze.

Forfeit, I. *v.a.* verwirken, sich einer Sache verlustig machen, (einer Sache) verlustig gehen *or* werden. II. *adj.* verwirkt, verfallen. III. *s.* das Verlustigwerden; (penalty) die Buße, Strafe; das verwirkte Pfand; das Reugeld (*in horse races*). —**able**, *adj.* verlierbar, verwirkbar. —**s**, *pl.* das Pfänderspiel. —**ure**, *s.* die Verwirkung; die Geldstrafe.

Forfend, *v.a.* verwehren, abwehren; bewahren; Heaven —! verhüte es der Himmel!

Forg—e, I. *v.a.* schmieden; schmieden, erdichten (*fig.*); fälschen, nachmachen (*a document*); to —e coin, Geld fälschen, falschmünzen. II. *s.* die Schmiede, der Schmelzofen, der Herd (*Metall.*). —**er**, *s.* der Schmiedende; der Fälscher, Verfälscher; —er of coin, der Falschmünzer; —er of documents, der Urkundenfälscher. —**ery**, *s.* die Verfälschung, Fälschung; (invention) die Erdichtung, Lüge. *Comp.* —**e-bellows**, *pl.* das Schmiedegebläse. —**e-iron**, *s.* das Schmiedeeisen.

Forget, *ir.v.* I. *a.* vergessen; he forgot himself so far as to, er vergaß sich so weit, daß er; (neglect) vernachlässigen; he does not — his own interest, er läßt seinen Vorteil nicht außer acht; never to be forgotten, unvergeßlich. II. *n.* vergessen; I —, ich habe vergessen, ich kann mich nicht (mehr) erinnern *or* entsinnen, ich weiß nicht mehr. —**ful**, *adj.* vergeßlich; unachtsam. —**fulness**, *s.* die Vergeßlichkeit; (oblivion) die Vergessenheit; die Vernachlässigung. *Comp.* —**-me-not**, *s.* das Vergißmeinnicht.

Forgiv—able, *adj.* verzeihlich, vergebbar. —**e**, *ir.v.a.* vergeben, verzeihen; (remit) erlassen; I forgave him, ich verzieh *or* vergab ihm; not to be —en, unverzeihlich; —e us our trespasses, vergieb uns unsre Schuld. —**eness**, *s.* die Vergebung, Verzeihung; *see* —ingness. —**er**, *s.* der Vergebende. —**ing**, *adj.* zum Vergeben geneigt, versöhnlich, mild. —**ingness**, *s.* die Geneigtheit zum Vergeben, Versöhnlichkeit.

Forgo, *v.a.* verzichten auf (*acc.*); aufgeben; I will — my advantage, ich begebe mich meines Vorteils. —**ne**, *adj.* vorherbestimmt; —ne conclusion, eine bestimmte Voraussetzung.

Fork, I. *s.* die Gabel; gabelförmige Spitze, (— in a road) die Wegscheide; der Teilungspunkt, die Gabelung (*of a road, two rivers, etc.*). II. *v.a.* gabeln, aufgabeln; to — out money, Geld *or* mit dem Gelde herausrücken (*sl.*). III. *v.n.* sich spalten, sich gabeln; schossen (*as corn*). IV. *attrib.*; — blades, die Gabelscheiden (*Cycl.*). —**ed**, *adj.* gabelig, Gabel=; —ed lightning, der zickzackförmige Blitz.

Forlorn, *adj.* verloren; verlassen; (helpless) hülflos; (solitary) einsam; (wretched) unglücklich; all —, ganz verlassen, mutterseelenallein; — hope, der verlorne Posten; to lead a — hope, auf ein aussichtsloses Unternehmen ausgehen. —**ness**, *s.* die Verlassenheit, Einsamkeit, Hülflosigkeit.

Form, I. *s.* die Gestalt, Form (*of a body*); die Form, Anordnung (*of words, etc.*); (system) die Methode; (model) das Muster, Modell; (formula) die Formel; (appearance) der Schein, das äußere Ansehen; (state) der Zustand, die Verfassung; (ceremony) die Zeremonie, Formalität; die (gesetzte) Form (*Typ.*); (bench) die Schulbank; die (Schul)klasse; die Sasse, das Lager (*of a hare*); die Form (*Cook.*); die Formalität (*C. L.*); to be in —, tüchtig sein (*Sport*); she is not good —, sie hat keinen guten Ton; that is bad —, das verstößt gegen den guten Ton, ist nicht fein; the excellent mountain air will put me in good —, die köstliche Bergluft wird mich frisch und munter machen (*coll.*); to be in good —, gut zu Wege sein, sich vorzüglich befinden (*coll.*); he was in the same — with me, er war in derselben Klasse mit mir; a mere (matter of) —, eine leere Form, eine bloße Formsache; —s of a court, gerichtliche Formalitäten; — of prayer, of worship, die Gebetsformel, der vorgeschriebene Gottesdienst; in due —, in gehöriger Form, vorschriftsmäßig; for —'s sake, der Form wegen, um der Form *or* Vorschrift zu genügen; to bring into, reduce to —, gestalten, zustutzen, formieren. II. *attrib.*; — master, der Klassenlehrer. III. *v.a.* formen, bilden, gestalten; bilden (*the mind, etc.*); heranbilden (to, zu); entwerfen, erdenken (*a plan, etc.*); aufstellen, formieren (*a line of battle*); vereinigen (into, in, zu); to — a body of laws, eine Gesetzsammlung veranstalten; to — an alliance, eine Verbindung eingehen, ein Bündnis schließen; to — an estimate of a th., etwas (ab)schätzen; to — an opinion, sich (*dat.*) eine Meinung (über eine S.) bilden. IV. *v.n.* sich bilden, Gestalt gewinnen. —**al**, *adj.*, —**ally**, *adv.* förmlich; (exact) pünktlich; (ceremonious) formell, umständlich, steif; *see* Conventional; (external) äußerlich, scheinbar; formal (*Philos.*). —**alism**, *s.* der Formalismus. —**alist**, *s.* der Formalist, Formenmensch. —**ality**, *s.* die Förmlichkeit, Formalität; (ceremonial) die Förmlichkeit; —alities, die Zeremonie, Umständlichkeit; without —alities, ohne Umstände; —alities of law, die gesetzlichen Förmlichkeiten. —**ation**, *s.* das Bilden; die Bildung; die Formation (*Geol.*); der Verband (*Milit.*). —**ative**, *adj.* bildend, plastisch; bildend, zur Ableitung dienend (*Gram.*). —**er**, *s.* der Bildner, Bildende; der Urheber (*fig.*). —**less**, *adj.* formlos. —**ula**, *s.* die Formel (*also Math., Chem., Theol.*); das Rezept (*Med.*). —**ulary**, I. *s.* das Formular, Formelbuch. II. *adj.* vorgeschrieben, vorschriftsmäßig. —**ulate**, *v.a.* formulieren, formelmäßig abfassen.

Former, *adj.* vorig, früher; (late) ehemalig; vorder (*in place*); (aforementioned) vorher erwähnt; ersterer, dieser (*opp. to* letzterer, jener, *latter*); in — times, *see* —ly. —**ly**, *adj.* ehemals, früher.

Formic, *adj.*; — acid, die Ameisensäure; — ether, der Ameisenäther. —**ation**, *s.* das Ameisenkriechen (*Med.*).

Formidabl—e, *adj.*, **—y,** *adv.* furchtbar, fürchterlich, schrecklich.
[1]**Fornicate,** *adj.* gewölbt, gebogen.
[2]**Fornicat—e,** *v.a.* Unzucht treiben, huren. **—ion,** *s.* die Unzucht, Hurerei. **—or,** *s.* der Hurer.
Forsake, *ir.v.a.* aufgeben; (einer S.) entsagen, (auf eine S.) verzichten, (eine S.) aufgeben; verlassen (*a country*); treulos verlassen, preisgeben (*friends*); (fall away from) abtrünnig werden (von). **—n,** *adj.* verlassen.
Forsooth, *adv.* fürwahr, traun, in der Tat.
Forswear, *ir.v.a.* verschwören, abschwören; to — a p.'s company, jemandes Umgang abschwören; to — o.s., meineidig werden. **—er,** *s.* der (die) Abschwörende; der (die) Meineidige.
Fort, *s.* das Fort, das Festungswerk; die Schanze; star —, die Sternschanze. **—alice,** *s.* das kleine Außenwerk. **—e,** I. *adv.* forte, laut (*Mus.*). II. *s.* die Stärke (*of a sword-blade*); die starke Seite (*fig.*). **—ification,** *s.* (—ifying) die Befestigung; (science of —ifying) die Befestigungskunst, Befestigungslehre; (work) das Befestigungswerk, die Befestigung; *see* Fort; subterraneous —ification, die Minierkunst. **—ified,** *adj.* befestigt, verschanzt; —ified place, fester Platz, die Festung. **—ifier,** *s.* der Befestiger; der Festungsbaumeister; der Unterstützer (*fig.*). **—ify,** *v.a.* befestigen (*also fig.*); (encourage) stärken, ermutigen; (confirm) bekräftigen. **—issimo,** *adv.* sehr stark, sehr laut. **—itude,** *s.* die Seelenstärke, Tapferkeit, der Mut. **—ress,** *s.* die Festung.
Forth, *adv.* fort, weiter; vorwärts (*of time*); her, vor, hervor (*of place and rank*); (out) heraus, hinaus; (abroad, out) draußen, außer dem Hause; from this day —, von heute an; from this time —, künftighin; and so —, und so fort, weiter; another parable put he —, er legte ihnen ein anderes Gleichnis vor; to set —, eine Reise antreten; to set — s.th., etwas aufzeigen, darlegen, eingehend zeigen. *Comp.* **—coming,** *adj.* bereit zu erscheinen, bevorstehend; bereit; to be —coming, zum Vorschein kommen, sich zeigen, vorhanden sein; as the money was not —coming, da das Geld nicht bezahlt wurde. **—with,** *adv.* sogleich, sofort, ohne Weiteres.
Fort—ieth, *adj.* vierzigst. **—y,** *num. adj.* vierzig.
Fortnight, *s.* vierzehn Tage; this day —, heute über 14 Tage; a — ago, heute vor 14 Tagen; this —, seit 14 Tagen. **—ly,** *adj.* alle vierzehn Tage; —ly (review), die Halbmonatsschrift.
Fortu—itous, *adj.*, **—itously,** *adv.* zufällig. **—itousness,** *s.* die Zufälligkeit. **—ity,** *s.* der Zufall. **—nate,** *adj.* glücklich. **—nately,** *adv.* glücklicherweise. **—nateness,** *s.* die Glücklichkeit, das Glück. **—ne,** *see* Fortune.
Fortune, *s.* das Glück; (fate) das Geschick, Schicksal; (chance) der Zufall, das Ungefähr; (wealth) das Vermögen, der Reichtum; (dowry) das Heiratsgut, die Mitgift; Fortuna, die Glücksgöttin (*Myth.*); good —, das Glück; to marry a —, eine reiche Partie machen; ill —, das Unglück; the wheel of —, das Glücksrad; to have one's — told, sich (*dat.*) wahrsagen lassen; to make (seek) one's —, sein Glück machen (suchen); he has inherited a large —, er hat ein großes Vermögen geerbt; — favours the bold, dem Mutigen ist das Glück hold; by good —, glücklicherweise. **—less,** *adj.* arm; ohne Mitgift. *Comp.* **—book,** *s.* das Wahrsagebuch. **—hunter,** *s.* der Glücksjäger; der Geldfreier, Goldfischjäger. **—hunting,** *s.* die Jagd nach dem Glück; die Jagd nach einer reichen Heirat. **—teller,** *s.* der (die) Wahrsager(in). **—telling,** *s.* die Wahrsagerei.
Forum, *s.* das Forum, der öffentliche (Versammlungs-)Platz; das Tribunal, Gericht (*fig.*).
Forward, I. *adj.* (fore) vorn (befindlich); (ready) bereitwillig, fertig; (over ready) voreilig; (bold) vorlaut, keck, naseweis; (willing) geneigt; (early) frühreif, frühzeitig; (advanced) vorgerückt. II. *adv.* vorwärts; from this (that) time —, von jetzt (von der Zeit) an; brought —, Übertrag *or* Transport auf der folgenden Seite; balance carried —, Saldo vorgetragen. III. *v.a.* (be)fördern, beschleunigen; (favour) begünstigen; (despatch) befördern, absenden, spedieren; (send) zuschicken; to be —ed, nachzuschicken (*on letters*); zu befördern (*on parcels*); please —, bitte nachzuschicken; not to be —ed, nicht nachzuschicken; goods to be —ed, Speditionsgüter. IV. *s.* der Stürmer (*Footb.*). **—ing,** *s.* die Versendung, Spedition. **—ly,** *adj.* vorschnell. **—ness,** *s.* die Bereitwilligkeit; die Voreiligkeit; die Keckheit, das vorlaute Wesen, die Unbescheidenheit; die Frühzeitigkeit; die Fortschritte (*in knowledge*). **—s,** *adv. see* —; backwards and —s, hin und her. *Comp.* **—ing-agent,** *s.* der Spediteur. **—ing-house,** *s.* das Speditionsgeschäft. **—ing-note,** *s.* der Frachtbrief. **—ing-office,** *s.* das Speditionsbureau.
Foss—e, *s.* der Graben. **—il,** I. *adj.* aus der Erde gegraben, fossil, versteinert; verknöchert (*fig.*). II. *s.* das Fossil. **—iliferous,** *adj.* fossilienhaltig. **—ilist,** *s.* der Fossilienkenner. **—ilization,** *s.* die Versteinerung; die Verknöcherung (*fig.*). **—ilize,** *v.* I. *a.* versteinern. II. *n.* sich versteinern; verknöchern (*fig.*). **—orial,** *adj.* grabend.
Foster, *v.a.* nähren, pflegen, aufziehen; hegen, pflegen, begünstigen (*fig.*). **—er,** *s.* der Pflegevater; (nurse) die Amme. **—ing,** I. *adj.* befördernd. II. *s.* das Ernähren, Aufziehen, die Pflege. **—ling,** *s.* das Pflegekind, der Pflegling. *Comp.* **—brother,** *s.* der Milchbruder; der Pflegebruder. **—child,** *s.* das Pflegekind. **—father,** *s.* der Pflegevater. **—mother,** *s.* die Nährmutter; die Pflegemutter. **—nurse,** *s.* die Säugamme.
Fought, *imperf. & p.p. of* Fight.
Foul, I. *adj.* schmutzig; schädlich (*fig.*); garstig (*as words*); unzüchtig, zotig, schmutzig (*as language*); (unfair) ungehörig, unehrlich; voll Druckfehler (*Typ.*); unklar (*Naut.*); to fall — of a p., ungestüm über einen herfallen, einen derb ausschelten; to run — of a ship, ein Schiff ansegeln, übersegeln; the ship is — of a rock, das Schiff ist gegen einen Felsen gefahren; the anchor is —, der Anker ist unklar; — bottom, schlechter Ankergrund; — breath, übelriechender Atem; — chimney, verrußter Schornstein; — coast, faule Küste; — copy, das Unreine, die Kladde; — deeds, ruchlose Taten; — fiend, der böse Feind, Teufel; — impression, der Fehldruck (*Typ.*); — means, Gewaltstreiche; — play, falsches Spiel, Unredlichkeit; unredliche Mittel; there was — play in that business, es ging bei dem Geschäft *or* bei der Sache unsauber zu; — practices, unsaubere Geschichten, Unredlichkeiten; — pump, unklare Pumpe; — spirit, böser Geist; — stream, schlammiger Fluß; — tongue, belegte Zunge, (evil-speaking) böse Zunge, loses Maul; — water, trübes Wasser; — weather, schlechtes Wetter; — wrong, ruchlose Ungerechtigkeit; — work, Schlechtigkeiten. II. *v.a.* beschmutzen; anstoßen (an eine S.), anrennen (gegen *or* an) (*of ships*). III. *s.* der Zusammenstoß, das Anfahren (von Schiffen). **—ness,** *s.* die Unreinigkeit (*also fig.*); die Schändlichkeit; die Unredlichkeit, Falschheit (*of intentions*). **—ly,** *adv.* schändlich; unredlich. *Comp.* **—mouthed,** *adj.* ein loses Maul habend; (—spoken) schmutzige Reden führend.
[1]**Found,** *imperf. & p.p. of* Find. **—ling,** *s.* der Findling. *Comp.* **—ling-hospital,** *s.* das Findelhaus.
[2]**Found,** *v.a.* gründen; (endow) stiften; errichten, einrichten (*fig.*); stützen (*a theory*). **—ation,** *s.* die Gründung, Grundlegung; der Grund, Grundbau (*of a building*); die Grundlage, das Fundament; die Grundfeste (*poet.*); der Ursprung, Anbeginn (*fig.*); die Stiftung, das Stipendium;

a pious —ation, eine milde Stiftung; to be on the —ation of . . ., ein Stipendiat von . . . sein. —**ationer**, *s.* der Stipendiat. —**er**, *s.* der Gründer, Begründer, Stifter. —**ress**, *s.* die Stifterin, Begründerin. *Comp.* —**ation-plate**, *s.* die Grundplatte. —**ation-school**, *s.* die Stiftsschule. —**ation-stone**, *s.* der Grundstein.

[2]**Found**, *v.a.* gießen. —**er**, *s.* der Schmelzer, Gießer. —**ry**, I. die Gießerei; iron- —ry, Eisengießerei.

Founder, *v.n.* scheitern (*Naut. fig.*); sinken, untergehn (*fig.*); steif werden, lahmen; a —ed horse, ein steifes Pferd.

Fount, *s.* die Quelle, der Quell; der Ursprung (*fig.*); der Guß (*Typ.*). —**ain**, *s.* die Quelle (*also fig.*); der Springbrunnen. *Comp.* —**ain-head**, *s.* der Urquell; die wahre Quelle, erste Hand (*fig.*). —**ain-pen**, *s.* die Füllfeder.

Four, *num. adj.* vier; on all —s, auf allen Vieren; — double, vierfach zusammengelegt (*coll.*). —**fold**, *adj.* vierfach. —**teen**, *num. adj.* vierzehn. —**teenth**, I. *num. adj.* vierzehnt. II. *s.* das Vierzehntel. —**th**, I. *num. adj.* viert. II. *s.* das Viertel; die Quarte (*Mus.*, *also C.L.*). —**thly**, *adv.* viertens, zum vierten. *Comp.* —**-cornered**, *adj.* viereckig. —**-edged**, *adj.* vierkantig. —**-footed**, *adj.* vierfüßig. —**-handed**, *adj.* mit vier Händen; —-handed game, Spiel zu vieren (*L. T.*). —**-in-hand**, I. *s.* der Vierspänner, das Viergespann; der Viererzug. II. *adv.*; to drive —-in-hand, vierspännig fahren. —**-leaved**, *adj.* vierblätterig. —**-post**, *adj.*; —-post bedstead, (—**-poster**, *s.*), die vierpfostige Bettstelle. —**score**, *adj.* achtzig; a man of —score, ein Achtziger. —**square**, *adj.* viereckig. —**-wheeled**, *adj.* vierräderig. —**-wheeler**, *s.* der vierrädrige Wagen, die Droschke.

Fowl, I. *s.* der Vogel (*rare*); das Huhn; (—s) das Geflügel, Federvieh. II. *v.n.* Vogelstellerei treiben, Vögel stellen *or* schießen. —**er**, *s.* der Vogler, Vogelsteller. —**ing**, *s.* der Vogelfang, die Vogeljagd. *Comp.* —**ing-piece**, *s.* die Vogelflinte. —**run**, *s.* der Auslauf (für Hühner).

Fox, *s.* der Fuchs (*also fig.*); the — barks, der Fuchs bellt; she —, die Füchsin; to set the — to keep the geese, den Bock zum Gärtner machen; with —es one must play the —, man muß mit den Wölfen heulen (*prov.*). —**y**, *adj.* fuchsartig, Fuchs-; schlau, verschmitzt; fuchsrot; verschossen, schäbig. *Comp.* —**-brush**, *s.* der Fuchsschwanz. —**glove**, *s.* der Fingerhut (*Bot.*). —**-earth**, *s* der Fuchsbau. —**hound**, *s.* der Fuchsjagdhund. —**hunt**, *s.* die Fuchsjagd, Fuchshetze. —**hunter**, *s.* der Fuchsjäger. —**hunting**, *s.* die Fuchsjagd. —**tail**, *s.* der Fuchsschwanz (*also Bot.*). —**tailed**, *adj.*; —tailed monkey, der Fuchsaffe. —**trap**, *s.* die Fuchsfalle.

Fracas, *s.* der lärmende Streit, Aufruhr.

Fract—ion, *s.* das Bruchstück; der Bruch (*Arith.*). —**ional**, *adj.* gebrochen; —ional part, der Bruch, Bruchteil. —**ious**, *adj.*, —**iously**, *adv.* ärgerlich, reizbar; (quarrelsome) zänkisch; (snappish) bissig. —**iousness**, *s.* die Reizbarkeit; die Zanksucht; das auffahrende *or* mürrische Wesen. —**ure**, I. *s.* der Knochenbruch. II. *v.a.* (zer)brechen.

Fragil—e, *adj.* zerbrechlich; gebrechlich, schwach (*fig.*). —**ity**, *s.* die Zerbrechlichkeit; die Schwachheit, Gebrechlichkeit, Hinfälligkeit (*fig.*).

Fragment, *s.* das Bruchstück; —s, die Bruchstücke, Überbleibsel; —s of time, Zeitteilchen. —**ary**, *adj.* abgebrochen, zerstückt, fragmentarisch, bruchstückartig.

Fragran—ce, *s.* der Wohlgeruch, süße Duft. —**t**, *adj.*, —**tly**, *adv.* wohlriechend, duftig.

Frail, *adj.* gebrechlich, schwach (*also fig.*), leicht zerbrechlich, zart, hinfällig. —**ness**, *s.* die Gebrechlichkeit, Schwäche, Schwachheit. —**ty**, *s.* die Gebrechlichkeit, Schwäche (*also fig.*); (failing) die Schwachheitssünde, der Fehltritt.

Frail, *s.* der Binsenkorb.

Fram—e, I. *v. a.* bilden, bauen; ineinander fügen, einfügen, verbinden, einfassen (*Carp.*); einrahmen (*a picture, etc.*); aufpflanzen (*guns*); bilden, verfertigen, entwerfen, machen, verfassen (*fig.*); (adjust) einrichten, nach (einer S.) richten; entwerfen (plans); (invent) erfinden, ersinnen; ersinnen, schmieden (*an excuse, etc.*); den Satz einfassen (*Typ.*). II. *s.* das Gebälk (*of a house, etc.*); (structure) der Bau, das Gebäude; das Gestell, Gerüste (*Mach.*); (—e that encloses) die Einfassung, Einrahmung; der Rahmen (*of a picture, of a window, for needlework, also Locom.*); das Spant (*Shipb.*); das Regal (*Typ.*); das Rahmwerk, Rahmholz (*Carp.*); das Stuhlgestell (*Weav.*); die Maschine (*Spin.*); —e of spectacles, die Brilleneinfassung; forcing —e, der Treibkasten (*Hort.*); iron —, der Eisenrahmen; lady of a delicate —e, zartgebaute Dame; passion shakes your very —e, Leidenschaft durchschüttert euern Körper; —e of mind, der Gemütszustand, die Stimmung. —**er**, *s.* der Bildner; der Rahmenmacher; der Erfinder. —**ing**, *s.* die Einrahmung, Einfassung. *Comp.* —**e-house**, *s.* das hölzerne Haus. —**ework**, *s.* das Fachwerk, Riegelwerk (*Carp.*); das Gestell (*Locom.*); (structure) der Bau, das Gebäude (*fig.*).

Franchise, *s.* das Vorrecht, die Gerechtsame; das bürgerliche Wahlrecht, Bürgerrecht.

Frangib—ility, *s.* die Zerbrechlichkeit. —**le**, *adj.* zerbrechlich.

Frank, I. *adj.*, —**ly**, *adv.* frei, offen; offenherzig. II. *s.* der portofreie Brief mit Frankovermerk, frankierte Brief. III. *v.a.* frankieren, postfrei machen. —**ed**, *adj.* postfrei, frankiert. —**incense**, *s.* der Weihrauch. —**lin**, *s.* der Freisasse, Gutseigentümer (*obs.*). —**ness**, *s.* die Offenheit; die Offenherzigkeit.

Frantic, *adj.*, —**ally**, *adv.* rasend, wahnsinnig; — with rage, außer sich vor Wut.

Frat—ernal, *adj.*, —**ernally**, *adv.* brüderlich. —**ernity**, *s.* die Brüderlichkeit; (society) die Brüderschaft; (academic club) die Verbindung, Genossenschaft, der Verein (*Amer.*). —**ernization**, *s.* die Verbrüderung. —**ernize**, *v.n.* sich verbrüdern. —**ricidal**, *adj.* brudermörderisch. —**ricide**, *s.* der Bruder-, Schwester-mord; der Bruder-, Schwester-mörder.

Fraud, *s.* der Trug, Betrug; (deceit) die List, Falschheit; der Schwindler, Betrüger; he is a —, er ist nicht das, wofür er gilt *or* sich ausgiebt. —**ulence**, *s.* die Betrüglichkeit; (fraud) der Betrug, die Betrügerei. —**ulent**, *adj.*, —**ulently**, *adv.* betrügerisch, betrüglich.

Fraught, *adj.* beladen, voll; — with meaning, bedeutungsvoll, bedeutungsschwer; — with mischief, unheilschwanger.

[1]**Fray**, *s. see* Affray; der Straßentumult.

[2]**Fray**, I. *v.a.* reiben, abreiben; abschlagen (the horns, das Gehörn). II. *v.n.* sich ausfasern.

Freak, *s.* das Sonderbare, die Sehenswürdigkeit; die Laune, Grille; der drollige Einfall *or* Streich. —**ish**, *adj.*, —**ishly**, *adv.* launenhaft, wunderlich, grillenhaft. —**ishness**, *s.* die Grillenhaftigkeit.

Freckl—e, I. *s.* die Sommersprosse; kleiner Fleck. II. *v.n.* sich sprenkeln. —**ed**, *adj.* (—e-faced) sommersprossig. —**y**, *adj.* sommersprossig.

Free, I. *adj.* frei; (independent) frei, unabhängig; (— of charges) kosten-los, -frei, unentgeltlich; (permitted) erlaubt, frei; (unforced) ungezwungen, frei; leicht, ungezwungen (*in manner*); (frank) offenherzig; (unrestrained) zügellos; (liberal) freigebig; — library, die Volksbücherei, öffentliche Lesehalle, Volkshalle; — passage, freier Lauf; unentgeltliche, freie Überfahrt; post —, postfrei, franko; — gift, freiwillige Gabe; — from business, geschäftsfrei; — from care, sorgenfrei; — from damage, unbeschädigt; — of debt, schuldenfrei; — from error, fehlerfrei; — from fear, furchtlos; — of income-tax, frei von Einkommensteuer; — liver, der Schlemmer; —

port, der Freihafen; — school, die Freischule; he **is** — to do it, es steht ihm frei, es zu tun; to have — scope, freie Hand haben; — wheel, das Rad mit Freilauf; to make — with a p., sich (*dat.*) Freiheiten erlauben gegen einen; to make — with a th., mit etwas schalten und walten; to make — with one's constitution, seine Gesundheit leichtsinnig aufs Spiel setzen; to make a p. — of a city, einen zum Ehrenbürger machen; to make a p. — of a corporation, einen in eine Zunft aufnehmen; to set —, frei geben; to have — quarters, Freiquartier *or* freies Quartier haben. II. *v.a.* befreien; frei lassen. **—booter**, *s.* der Freibeuter. **—dom**, *s.* die Freiheit; das Befreitsein; die Ungezwungenheit (*in speaking, etc.*); —dom of a city, das (Ehren-)Bürgerrecht; —dom of a company, das Meisterrecht; —dom from passion, die Leidenschaftslosigkeit. **—ly**, *adv.* frei; ohne Zwang; reichlich, im Überflusse; vertraulich; freimütig; to drink —ly, stark trinken; to bleed —ly, reichlich, stark bluten. **—ness**, *s.* die Freiheit; die Offenheit; (generosity) die Freigebigkeit;—ness of divine grace, die freie Erteilung der göttlichen Gnade. *Comp.* **—-chapel**, *s.* die Privatkapelle. **—-church**, *s.* die von Patronatsrechten unabhängige Freikirche (*obs.*). **—dman**, *s.* der Freigelassene. **—-fooder**, *s.* der Gegner einer Steuer auf Nahrungsmittel (*coll.*). **—hand**, *adj.*; —hand drawing, das Freihandzeichnen. **—-handed**, *adj.* mit freien Händen, ungehindert; freigebig. **—hold**, *s.* (—hold property) das Freigut, Freilehen; der freie Grundbesitz; unbeschränkter Besitz (*fig.*); —hold building land, ein Bauplatz, der Grundeigentum ist; —hold property, freier Grundbesitz; a —hold residence, ein Haus auf eigenem Grund und Boden. **—holder**, *s.* der Freisasse; der (unabhängige) Grundbesitzer. **—-lance**, *s.* der Söldner auf eigne Hand, Söldneranführer (*in olden times*); der Freibeuter; der durch keine Partei gebundene rücksichtslose Gegner. **—man**, *s.* der Freimann; (— citizen) der Bürger; der Wahlberechtigte (*Pol.*); der Meister (of a guild, einer Zunft). **—mason**, *s.* der Freimaurer. **—masonry**, *s.* die Freimaurerei. **—spoken**, *adj.* frei im Reden; leutselig (*prov.*). **—stone**, *s.* der Sandstein. **—thinker**, *s.* der Freidenker, Freigeist. **—thinking**, *s.* die Freidenkerei; das Freidenken. **—-trade**, *s.* der Freihandel. **—-trader**, *s.* der Freihändler. **—-will**, *s.* der freie Wille.

Freez—e, *v.* I. *a.* gefrieren machen (*water*); erfrieren machen (*living beings*); erstarren machen (*fig.*). II. *n.* (ge)frieren; erstarren (*fig.*); to —e to death, erfrieren. **—ing**, I. *adj.* gefrierend. II. *s.* das Gefrieren. *Comp.* **—ing-machine**, *s.* die Eismaschine. **—ing-mixture**, *s.* die Kältemischung. **—ing-point**, *s.* der Gefrierpunkt.

Freight, I. *s.* die Fracht (*C. L.*); die Befrachtung, Ladung (*Naut.*); (— cost) das Frachtgeld, der Frachtlohn; bill of —, der Frachtbrief; terms of —, Frachtbedingungen; to take in — for . . ., Ladung einnehmen nach . . .; — out, — home, Hin-, Rück-fracht. II. *v.a.* befrachten, beladen (*a ship*). **—age**, *s.* die Schiffsladung, Fracht; das Frachtgeld; der Transport, die Fracht. **—er**, *s.* (giver in —) der Verfrachter; der Befrachter. *Comp.* **—-car**, *s.* der Güterwagen (*Amer.*).

Fren—etic, *adj.*, **—etical**, *adj.* wahnsinnig. **—zied**, *adj.* wahnsinnig; (frantic) rasend. **—zy**, *s.* der Wahnsinn; die Raserei.

Frequen—cy, *s.* die Häufigkeit, die häufige Wiederholung. **—t**, I. *adj.*, **—tly**, *adv.* häufig; I see him —tly, ich sehe ihn öfters. II. *v.a.* häufig, öfters besuchen; to —t a house, in einem Hause aus- und ein-gehen. **—tative**, *adj.* frequentativ; —tative verb, das Frequentativum. **—ter**, *s.* der fleißige Besucher. **—tness**, *s. see* **—cy**.

Fresco, *s.* (— painting) die Freskomalerei; (— picture) das Freskogemälde, Fresko; to paint in — *or* al —, in Fresko malen.

Fresh, I. *adj.*, **—ly**, *adv.* frisch; (not salt) ungesalzen, frisch, süß; (not stale, new) neu, frisch; munter, lustig (*as a horse*); (active, strong) frisch; (blooming) frisch; — air, frische Luft; — water, süßes Wasser; — butter, frische Butter; — arrivals, neue Ankömmlinge (*of people*); frische Zufuhren (*of goods*); I feel quite —, ich fühle mich frisch und gesund. II. *s.* das süße Wasser; (*also* —es) das Oberwasser, Brackwasser (an Flußmündungen); *see* —et. **—en**, *v.* I. *a.* frisch machen, erfrischen. II. *n.* frisch werden; the wind —ens, der Wind wird stärker (*Naut.*). **—er**, *s.* der Fuchs, Student(in) im ersten Semester (*sl.*). **—et**, *s.* die Überschwemmung, das Austreten des Flußwassers (*Amer.*); der Bach (*obs.*). **—ness**, *s.* die Frische; die Neuheit, Unerfahrenheit. *Comp.* **—-looking**, *adj.* frisch aussehend. **—man**, *s.* der Fuchs (*Univ. sl.*). **—-water**, *adj.* Süßwasser-, Fluß-, Landsee-; unerfahren, unversucht (*coll.*); —-water fish, der Süßwasserfisch, Flußfisch.

[1]**Fret**, I. *v.a.* abreiben, aufreiben; (corrode) zerfressen, einfressen; (hollow out) aushöhlen; (vex) ärgern, kränken; (agitate) aufregen. II. *v.n.* sich verzehren; (fray) sich abreiben; (grieve) sich ärgern, sich quälen, sich grämen; (chafe) sich erzürnen; don't —! grämt euch nicht! seid nicht böse! III. *s.* die Aufregung, Gemütsbewegung; (vexation) der Ärger, Verdruß; to keep a p. in a continual —, einen in beständiger Aufregung erhalten. **—ful**, *adj.*, **—fully**, *adv.* ärgerlich, mürrisch, verdrießlich. **—fulness**, *s.* der Unmut, das mürrische, verdrießliche Wesen.

[2]**Fret**, *v.a.* eingraben, erhaben arbeiten (*Arch., etc.*); mit der Laubsäge arbeiten; (variegate) bunt machen, Abwechslung geben; yon gray lines, that — the clouds, jene grauen Streifen, die das Gewölk durchziehen. *Comp.* **—-saw**, *s.* die Laub-, Loch-säge. **—work**, *s.* das geflochtene Gitterwerk; die Laubsägearbeit; durchbrochene Arbeit.

[3]**Fret**, I. *v.a.* mit Griffen, mit Bunden versehen. II. *s.* der Bund (*of a guitar*).

[4]**Fret**, *s.* der griechische, gebrochene Stab, Zinnenfries (*Arch.*).

Friab—ility, **—leness**, *s.* die Zerreiblichkeit. **—le**, *adj.* zerreiblich, bröck(e)lig.

Friar, *s.* der Mönch (*also Typ.*); **—'s cowl**, die Mönchskutte, das Mönchsgewand.

Fricassee, I. *s.* das Schnittfleisch, Frikassee. II. *v.a.* frikassieren, Fleisch klein hacken, einhacken; —d chicken, Hühnerfrikassee; —d veal, Kalbsfrikassee.

Friction, *s.* die Reibung; das Frottieren (*Med.*). **—al**, *adj.*; —al electricity, die Reibungselektrizität. *Comp.* **—-primer**, *s.* der Friktionszünder (*Artil.*). **—-wheel**, *s.* das Friktionsrad.

Friday, *s.* der Freitag; good —, Karfreitag.

Fried, *imperf. & p.p. of* Fry.

Friend, *s.* der Freund, (female —) die Freundin; der Quäker; the Society of Friends, die Quäker; to make a —, sich (*dat.*) einen Freund gewinnen; to make —s, Freundschaft schließen, (become reconciled) sich versöhnen; to be —s with, (jemandes) Freund sein; a — in need, ein Freund in der Not; a — in need is a — indeed, die Not prüft Freunde; a — to, ein Freund von (charities, milden Stiftungen); — at court, einflußreicher Freund. **—less**, *adj.* ohne Freunde, freundlos. **—lessness**, *s.* die Freundlosigkeit; die Verlassenheit. **—lies**, *pl.* verbündete Stämme (der Eingeborenen fremder Weltteile). **—liness**, *s.* die Freundlichkeit, das freundliche, liebenswürdige Wesen. **—ly**, *adj.* freundlich, freundschaftlich; (favourable) günstig; befreundet (*as a prince*); a —ly state, ein Freundesland; a —ly nation, ein uns wohlgesinntes Land; a —ly turn, ein Freundschaftsstück(chen); to be on —ly terms with, auf freundschaftlichem Fuße mit . . . stehen; —ly society, der (Arbeiter-)Unterstützungsverein. **—s**, *pl.* Freunde; die Quäkersekte. **—ship**, *s.* die Freundschaft.

[1]**Frieze**, *s.* der Fries (*Manuf.*).

[2]**Frieze**, *s.* der Fries (*Arch.*).

Frigate, *s.* die Fregatte. *Comp.* **—-built**, *adj.* auf Fregattenart gebaut.

Fright, I. *s.* der Schrecken; die Fratze, das Schreckbild, Scheusal (*fig.*); to get a —, plötzlich erschreckt werden (*coll.*); to take —, (sich) erschrecken, in Schrecken geraten (*coll.*); the horse took — at it, das Pferd wurde davor scheu; to make a — of o.s., sich auffallend häßlich machen; what a —! welche Fratze! II. —, **—en**, *v.a.* erschrecken, in Furcht setzen; to —en away, verscheuchen; to —en a p. out of his wits, einen vor Furcht außer sich bringen. **—ful**, *adj.*, **—fully**, *adv.* schrecklich, fürchterlich. **—fulness**, *s.* die Schrecklichkeit.

Frig—id, *adj.*, **—idly**, *adv.* kalt, frostig; (frozen) erstarrt; (cool) kalt, gefühllos; (dull) stumpf, geistlos; steif, frostig (*in manner, etc.*); the —id zones, die kalten Zonen. **—idity**, *s.* die Kälte, Frostigkeit. **—orific**, *adj.* Kälte erzeugend.

Frill, I. *s.* die Hals- *or* Hand-krause; der gefaltete Busenstreif. II. *v.a.* fälteln, kräuseln. III. *v.n.* sich kräuseln (*Phot.*). **—ing**, *s.* das Kräuseln; die Krausen, der Krausenstoff.

Fringe, I. *s.* die Franse, der Besatz; der durchbrochene Zierrat (*fig.*); der fransenähnliche Rand, Saum, die Einfassung; (*pl.* —s) das in die Stirne gekämmte Haar, die Ponyfrisur; the —s of a cloud, die Ränder einer Wolke; twisted —, Spiralfranse, gewundene Franse; idiot —s, Simpelfransen. II. *v.a.* befransen, mit Fransen besetzen.

Frippery, I. *s.* die Trödelware; der Trödel; (piece of —) der Flitterkram, die Lumperei (*fig.*). II. *adj.* geringfügig, verächtlich.

Frisk, I. *v.n.* hüpfen und springen, umherhüpfen. II. *s.* das Hüpfen und Springen, der Freudensprung. **—iness**, *s.* die Munterkeit, Lebendigkeit. **—y**, *adj.*, **—ily**, *adv.* munter, lustig, lebhaft; springend, hüpfend; unruhig (*of a horse*).

Frit, I. *s.* die Fritte. II. *v.a.* (den Glassatz) fritten. **—ter**, I. *s.* das Schnittchen, der kleine Pfannkuchen; (fragment) das Stückchen. II. *v.a.* in kleine Stücke schneiden; zerstückeln; to —ter away, verzetteln, verschwenden (one's money, sein Geld), vertändeln (one's time, seine Zeit). **—ters**, *pl.* arme Ritter; apple —ters, Äpfelschnittchen.

Frith, *s.* der Meeresarm; die Mündung (*of a river*).

Fritillary, *s.* die Kaiserkrone (*Bot.*); der Perlmutterfalter (*Ent.*).

Frivol—ity, *s.* die Leichtfertigkeit; die Geringfügigkeit, Nichtigkeit. **—ous**, *adj.*, **—ously**, *adv.* (trifling) nichtig, wertlos, unbedeutend; (given to —ity) leichtfertig, leichtsinnig.

Frizz, *see* —le I. **—le**, *v.* I. *a.* kräuseln, frisieren (*hair, cloth, etc.*). II. *n.* sich kräuseln. **—ly**, *adj.* kraus, gekräuselt. *Comp.* **—ling-irons**, *s.* das Kräuseleisen.

Fro, *adv.*; to and —, hin und her, auf und ab

Frock, *s.* das Kleid (*for women*); das Kinderröckchen; (smock —) der Kittel, das Staubhemd, die Kutte. *Comp.* **—-coat**, *s.* der (meist zweireihige) Gehrock, Überrock.

Frog, I. *s.* der Frosch; der Schnurbesatz (eines Mantels); das Kreuzungsstück, Herzstück einer Schiene (*Railw.*); die Gabel, der Strahl (*Vet.*); the — croaks, der Frosch quakt. II. *v.a.* mit Schnüren besetzen *or* befestigen. **—ged**, *adj.*; —ged coat, ein mit Schnüren besetzter Rock. **—s**, *pl.* der Schnurbesatz; die Verschnürung. **—gy**, I. *adj.* froschartig. II. *s.* der Froschesser; *see* —-eater, 2. *Comp.* **—-eater**, *s.* der Froschesser; Spitzname für einen Franzosen.

Frolic, I. *s.* der lustige Streich, die Posse, das Spiel; (merrymaking) die Lustbarkeit. II. *v.n.* lustige Streiche spielen, Possen treiben, spielen. **—some**, *adj.* lustig, ausgelassen, vergnügt. **—someness**, *s.* die Lustigkeit, Ausgelassenheit; (pranks) lustige Streiche.

From, *prep.* von; (out of) aus; (because of) aus; (judging from) nach; vor; — year's end to year's end, jahraus, jahrein; — a child, von Kindheit an; to defend —, schützen vor; — his dress, I should say . . ., nach seinem Anzuge würde ich sagen . . .; — what you have told me, nach dem, was Sie mir gesagt haben; to keep a p. — doing s.th., einen abhalten, hindern, etwas zu tun; — **above**, von oben herab; — **afar**, von weitem, aus der Ferne; — **before**, — von vorn; away — before me, von mir weg; — **behind**, von hinten; — **below**, — **beneath**, von unten; — **between**, aus, dazwischen hervor; — **beyond**, von jenseits; — **on high**, aus der Höhe, vom Himmel; — **out**, aus, aus . . . heraus; — **under**, unter . . . hervor; — **within**, von innen, aus dem Innern (des Hauses, 2c.); — **without**, von außen.

Frond, *s.* der (Farnkraut-)Wedel (*Bot.*). **—escence**, *s.* die (Zeit der) Belaubung. **—iferous**, *adj.* wedeltragend.

Front, I. *s.* die Vorderseite, Stirnseite; (brow) die Stirn; (face) das Antlitz; (false —) der falsche Scheitel; die Front (*of a battalion, etc.*); (shirt—) das Vorhemd(chen); in — of, vorne an; in — of me, vor mir; to the —, nach vorne, voraus, voran; to come to the —, hervortreten, sich (*dat.*) einen Namen machen; to be ordered to the —, zur Front kommandiert werden; to show a bold —, die Stirne bieten. II. *attrib.* Vorder-; — box, die Vorderloge; — door, die Haustür; — driver, der Vorderradtreiber das übersetzte Hochrad (*Cycl.*); — driving safety, das Niederrad mit Vorderantrieb (*Cycl.*); — elevation, die Vorderansicht (*Arch.*); — gate, das Vordertor; — room, das Vorderzimmer, Zimmer nach vorn hinaus; — row, die Vorderreihe, erste Reihe; — view, die Vorderansicht; — wheel, das Vorderrad (*Cycl.*). III. *v.a.* gegenüberstehen (*dat.*). **—age**, *s.* die Vorderfront (*Arch.*). **—al**, I. *adj.* von vorn kommend; Stirn-, Vorder-; —al attack, der Frontangriff, Angriff in der Front. II. *s.* die Stirnbinde; kleines Tür- *or* Fenster-giebeldach (*Arch.*); der Stirnumschlag (*Med.*). **—ier**, I. *s.* die Grenze. II. *adj.* Grenz-, angrenzend. **—ispiece**, *s.* das Frontispiz, die Vorderseite (*Arch.*); das Titelbild (*Typ.*). **—let**, *s.* das Stirnband; das Stirnblatt (*of the Jews*); der Kopfrand (*Orn.*).

Frost, I. *s.* der Frost; das Flitterglas (*Glassw.*); der Mißerfolg, Hereinfall (*sl.*); black —, trockener Frost; hoar —, der Reif, Rauhreif; slippery —, das Glatteis; white —, der Reif. II. *v.a.* mit Zuckerstaub bestreuen, mit Zuckerguß bedecken (*Cook.*); mit etwas Reifartigem bedecken. — **—ed**, *adj.*; —ed cake, Kuchen mit Zuckerguß. — **ily**, *adv. see* —y. **—iness**, *s.* das frostige Wesen, die (Eis-)Kälte (*also fig.*). **—ing**, *s.* der Zuckerschaum. **—y**, *adj.* frostig, eiskalt; kalt(-sinnig); (white) eisgrau. *Comp.* **—bite**, *s.* das Erfrieren. **—bitten**, *adj.* vom Frost beschädigt, erfroren. **—bound**, *adj.* vom Frost gehindert *or* gefesselt; zugefroren. **—nail**, I. *s.* der Eisnagel. II. *v.a.* mit Eisnägeln beschlagen. **—work**, *s.* Eisblumen; Arbeit mit rauher Oberfläche.

Froth, I. *s.* der Schaum; das leere Gepränge; die Blume (*of beer*). II. *v.a.* schäumen machen. III. *v.n.* schäumen. **—iness**, *s.* das Schäumige; die Nichtigkeit, Leerheit (*fig.*). **—y**, *adj.* schäumig; leer, nichtig.

Frousy, Frowzy, *adj.* muffig, stinkend, ranzig; schmutzig, schlumpig, unsauber.

Froward, *adj.*, **—ly**, *adv.* widerspenstig, eigensinnig, hartnäckig, unlenksam; (morose) mürrisch; (undutiful) ungehorsam; (adverse) ungünstig. **—ness**, *s.* der Eigensinn, die Widerspenstigkeit.

Frown, I. *s.* das Stirnrunzeln, die Runzel; (scowl) der finstere, unzufriedene Blick; —s of fortune, die Widerwärtigkeiten des Geschicks. II. *v.a.*

durch finstere Blicke zurückweisen, abstoßen; to — a p. into silence, durch finsteres Ansehen einen zum Stillschweigen bringen. III. *v.n.* die Stirne runzeln, finster, mürrisch *or* drohend aussehen; to — at, upon, (einen) finster anblicken; fortune seems still to — on him, das Glück scheint ihm noch abhold zu sein. **—ingly**, *adv.* finster, mürrisch, tadelnd.

Frozen, *p.p. of* Freeze; — up *or* over, zugefroren; — ocean, Eismeer; — zones, kalte Zonen.

Fruct—escence, *s.* die Fruchtzeit. **—ification**, *s.* (fertilization) die Befruchtung; (fertility) die Fruchtbarkeit; die Befruchtungsteile (*Bot.*) **—ify**, *v.* I. *a.* befruchten. II. *n.* Früchte tragen; fruchten, frommen (*fig.*).

Frug—al, *adj.*, **—ally**, *adv.* genügsam, mäßig, sparsam. **—ality**, *s.* die Mäßigkeit, Sparsamkeit. **—ivorous**, *adj.* von Früchten lebend, frucht(fr)essend.

Fruit, *s.* die Frucht (*also fig.*); die Früchte, das Obst (*collect.*); (result) die Folge; (dessert) der Nachtisch; —s of the earth, die Früchte, Erzeugnisse der Erde; first-—s, die Erstlinge; will you take some —? ist Ihnen etwas Obst gefällig? that is the — of all my endeavours, das sind die Früchte aller meiner Bemühungen; stewed —, gekochtes Obst, das Kompott; to bear —, Frucht bringen, Früchte tragen. **—age**, *s.* das Obst. **—erer**, *s.* der Obsthändler. **—ful**, *adj.*, **—fully**, *adv.* fruchtbar, reich; ergebnisreich, ergiebig (*fig.*). **—fulness**, *s.* die Fruchtbarkeit. **—ion**, *see* Fruition. **—less**, *adj.*, **—lessly**, *adv.* fruchtlos, vergeblich, unnütz. **—lessness**, *s.* die Fruchtlosigkeit (*fig.*). **—y**, *adj.* fruchtartig; würzhaft (*as wine*). *Comp.* **—-basket**, *s.* der Obstkorb. **—bearing**, *adj.* fruchttragend. **—-drop**, *s.* das Fruchtbonbon. **—-knife**, *s.* das Obstmesser. **—-market**, *s.* der Obstmarkt. **—-stalk**, *s.* der Fruchtstiel. **—-time**, *s.* die Obstzeit. **—-tree**, *s.* der Obstbaum.

Fruition, *s.* der Genuß, Vollgenuß.

Frument—aceous, *adj.* weizenartig; aus Weizen *or* Korn bestehend. **—y**, *s.* der Weizenbrei.

Frump, *s.* das wunderliche, altmodisch gekleidete Frauenzimmer; old —, alte Schachtel.

Frustrat—e, *v.a.* vereiteln, zu nichte *or* zu Schanden machen; to —e a p.'s hopes, einen in seinen Erwartungen täuschen; to be —ed, zu nichte werden (*of hopes*). **—ion**, *s.* die Vereitelung. **—ive**, *adj.* vereitelnd.

[1]**Fry**, I. *v.a.* in der Pfanne braten *or* schmoren; fried eggs, Spiegeleier, Setzeier; fried potatoes, Bratkartoffeln. II. *v.n.* braten, rösten. III. *s.* das Gebratene; die Aufregung (*fig.*). *Comp.* **—ing-pan**, *s.* die Bratpfanne; out of the —ing-pan into the fire, aus dem Regen in die Traufe.

[2]**Fry**, *s.* die Fischbrut; (swarm) die Brut, der Haufen; the whole —, die ganze Sippschaft (*coll.*).

Fuchsia, *s.* die Fuchsie.

Fuddle, *v.* I. *a.* berauschen. II. *n.* sich betrinken. **—d**, *adj.* angeheitert, angesäuselt (*coll.*).

Fudge, I. *s.* die Aufschneiderei. II. *int.* dummes Zeug! Unsinn! III. *v.a. & n.* pfuschen, schwindeln; *v.a.* ersinnen; *v.n.* aufschneiden, windbeuteln.

Fuel, *s.* die Feuerung, das Brennmaterial; to add — to the fire, Öl ins Feuer gießen.

Fug—acious, *adj.* flüchtig; vergänglich (*fig.*). **—itive**, I. *adj.* flüchtig (*also fig.*); —itive writings *or* compositions, flüchtige Kompositionen, Flugschriften; —itive colour, empfindliche Farbe. II. *s.* der Flüchtling; der Ausreißer, Deserteur. **—itiveness**, *s.* die Flüchtigkeit.

Fugleman, *s.* der Flügelmann (*Mil.*); der Führer (*fig.*).

Fugue, *s.* die Fuge (*Mus.*).

Fulcrum, *s.* die Stütze; der Stütz-, Ruhe-punkt (*Mech.*).

Fulfil, *v. a.* erfüllen, vollziehen, vollbringen. **—ler**, *s.* der Erfüller, Vollbringer. **—ment**, *s.* die Erfüllung, Vollführung.

Fulgen—cy, *s.* der Glanz. **—t**, *adj.* glänzend.

[1]**Full**, I. *adj.* voll; (filled) besetzt; (fat) voll, plump, dick; (sated) gesättigt; satt (*vulg.*); sättigend (*as a meal*); (complete) vollständig, unverkürzt, völlig, vollkommen; voll, stark (*as the voice*); (mature) voll, reif; unumschränkt (*as power*); (copious) ausführlich, weitläufig; of — age, volljährig, mündig; — allowance, reichliche Ration, das Vollgeld; — amount, der ganze Betrag; — band, volles Orchester; to be — of oneself, von sich eingenommen sein; the whole town is — of it, die ganze Stadt ist voll davon, spricht nur davon; — consent, völlige Einwilligung; — chorus, voller Chor; — costs (costs in —), sämmtliche Kosten; in — cry, in eifriger Verfolgung; — description, ausführliche Beschreibung; (at) — gallop, in gestrecktem Galopp, mit verhängtem Zügel; to have one's hands —, vollauf zu tun haben; — intent, feste Absicht; at — length, ausführlich; — moon, der Vollmond; — of business, mit Geschäften überhäuft; — pay, der ganze, volle Arbeitslohn; — powers, unumschränkte Vollmacht; (at) — speed, spornstreichs; mit voller Geschwindigkeit (*Naut.*); — statement, genaue Darstellung; — steam ahead, Volldampf voraus; — stop, der Punkt (*Gramm.*); der Ruhepunkt, Stillstand (*fig.*); to come to a — stop, plötzlich stillstehen *or* zum Stillstand kommen; — swing, gestreckten Laufs; to be — up, ganz besetzt sein (*of a carriage, compartment*); in — view (of), gerade gegenüber; of — weight, vollwichtig. II. *adv.* völlig, ganz; genau, gerade; recht, sehr; to look a p. — in the face, einem gerade ins Gesicht sehen; — oft, sehr oft (*poet.*); — many a flower, gar manche Blume (*poet.*); — well, gar wohl; to the —, reichlich; to pay in —, voll bezahlen; acquittance in —, die Generalquittung. III. *s.* die Fülle, Genüge; die Sättigung; das Ganze (*fig.*); — of the moon, Vollmond; at — of the tide (at — tide), beim höchsten Stande der Flut. **—y**, *adv.* voll, völlig, gänzlich; (in detail) ausführlich. *Comp.* **—-blown**, *adj.* in voller Blüte, voll aufgeblüht. **—-bodied**, *adj.* dick, stark; schwer (*as wines*). **—-bottomed**, *adj.* breit; —-bottomed wig, Allongeperücke; mit großem Ladungsraum (*of ships*). **—-breasted**, *adj.* vollbrüstig. **—-dress**, I. *s.* der Gesellschaftsanzug, die Galauniform. II. *attrib.*; —-dress rehearsal, die Generalprobe (im Kostüm). **—-eared**, *adj.* vollährig. **—-faced**, *adj.* ein volles Gesicht habend, mit rundem Gesicht. **—-fledged**, *adj.* flügge (*also fig.*). **—-grown**, *adj.* ausgewachsen, völlig erwachsen. **—-length**, *adj.* in Lebensgröße. **—-mouthed**, *adj.* starktönend. **—-orbed**, *adj.* ganz rund; —-orbed moon, Vollmond. **—-rigged**, *adj.* völlig aufgetakelt. **—-size**, *adj.* lebensgroß, in Lebensgröße.

[2]**Full**, *v.a.* walken. **—er**, *s.* der Walker, Walkmüller. *Comp.* **—er's-earth**, *s.* die Walkererde. **—er's-weed**, *s.* die Weberkarde. **—ing-mill**, *s.* die Walkmühle.

Fulmar, *s.* der Fulmar, die Eismöve (*Orn.*).

Fulmin—ate, I. *v.n.* donnern, krachen; schelten, wettern; verpuffen. II. *v.a.* verpuffen; ausdonnern, ausschleudern (*curses*). III. *s.* die knallsaure Salzverbindung (*Chem.*); das Knallpulver; —ate of mercury, das Knallquecksilber. **—ating**, *adj.*; —ating gold, das Knallgold; —ating powder, das Knallpulver; —ating substances, feuersprühende Stoffe. **—ation**, *s.* das Donnern; das Schleudern des Bannstrahls; das Verpuffen (*Chem.*). **—atory**, *adj.* donnernd. **—ic**, *adj.* verpuffend.

Fulness, *s.* die Fülle, der Reichtum; (extent) die Ausdehnung; (completeness) die Vollständigkeit; — of the heart, Fülle des Herzens; in the — of time, da die Zeit erfüllet war (*B.*).

Fulsome, *adj.*, **—ly**, *adv.* widrig, ekelhaft; — praise, widerliches Lob. **—ness**, *s.* die Ekelhaftigkeit; die Widerlichkeit, Plumpheit (*of praise, etc.*).

Fumbl—e, *v. n.* herumfühlen, umhertappen. **—ing**, *adj.*, **—ingly**, *adv.* tappend; (awkward) täppisch.

Fum—e, I. *s.* der Rauch (*obs.*); (exhalation) der Dunst, Dampf; (agitation) die Aufwallung, Hitze; to be in a —e, zornig, aufgebracht sein. II. *v.n.* dampfen, dunsten; (—e away) verdunsten, sich auflösen; toben, aufgebracht sein (*fig.*); aufgeregt sein. **—igate**, *v.a.* räuchern. **—igation**, *s.* die Räucherung. **—igatory**, *adj.* durch Rauch reinigend. **—ing**, *adj.*, **—ingly**, *adv.* aufgebracht; a —ing little man, ein aufgeregter kleiner Mensch. **—itory**, *s.* der Erdrauch (*Bot.*).

Fun, *s.* der Scherz, Spaß, die Kurzweil; to make —, Kurzweil treiben, spaßen, scherzen; to poke — at a p., seinen Spott mit einem treiben; to make — of a p., einen zum besten haben; for —, zum Spaß. **—nily**, *adv.*, **—ny**, *adj.* komisch; drollig; —ny bone, der Ellenbogenknochen, kleine Ellbogen, Musikantenknochen (*coll.*).

Function, *s.* die Amtsverrichtung, Funktion; (employment) die (Amts)tätigkeit, Wirksamkeit; (calling) der Beruf; die Verrichtung, Funktion (*Physiol.*); die Funktion (*Math.*). **—al**, *adj.* funktionell, Funktions=. **—ary**, *s.* der Beamte.

Fund, I. *s.* der Fonds, das Grundvermögen; (store) der Vorrat, Schatz, die Fülle; —s, der Geldvorrat; (public —s) die fundierten Papiere, Fonds, Staatsschulden, Aktien; sinking —, Schuldentilgungs=fonds *or* =kasse; — of wit, Fülle von Witz. II. *v.a.* Geld in Staatspapieren anlegen; kapitalisieren; —ed debts, fundierte Staatsschulden. **—ament**, *s.* der Grund; das Gesäß, der Steiß (*fig.*). **—amental**, *adj.* die Grundlage bildend, zu Grunde liegend, Grund=; —amental tone, der Grundton; —amental truths, Grundwahrheiten. **—amentally**, *adv.* im Grunde, wesentlich. **—amentals**, *pl.* die Grundlage, Grundlehre; die Grundwahrheiten; (essentials) Hauptsachen. *Comp.* **—holder**, *s.* der Inhaber von englischen Staatspapieren, Kapitalist, Fondsbesitzer.

Funer—al, I. *s.* das Leichenbegängnis; die Beerdigung, das Begräbnis. II. *adj.* bei Leichenbegängnissen üblich, Leichen=, Trauer=; —al pile, der Scheiterhaufen; —al oration, —al sermon, die Leichenpredigt. **—eal**, *adj.*, **—eally**, *adv.* leichenmäßig; wehklagend, traurig; —eal wailings, das Trauergeheul, Leichenklagen (*pl.*).

Fung—i, *pl. see* Fungus. **—oid**, *adj.* pilzähnlich. **—osity**, *s.* die Schwammigkeit, der schwammige Auswuchs. **—ous**, *adj.* schwammartig. **—us**, *s.* der Schwamm; der Pilz, das schwammartige Gewächs.

Funicular, *adj.* faserig; Seil=; — curve, die Stricklinie; — railway, die Drahtseilbahn.

Funk, I. *v.n.* in Angst und Furcht geraten (*sl.*). II. *s.* der Gestank; die große Angst; der Feigling; he got into a —, ihm wurde angst und bange, kolossal angst (*sl.*). **—y**, *adj.* feige, bange.

Funnel, *s.* der Trichter; (— of a chimney) die Röhre; der (große) Schornstein; die Esse (*on ships*); a large steamer with two —s, ein großer Dampfer mit zwei Schornsteinen. *Comp.* **—shaped**, *adj.* trichterförmig.

Fur, I. *s.* der Pelz, das Fell; (muffs, boas, *etc.*) das Pelzwerk; der Belag (*Med.*); der (Kessel= 2c.) Stein. II. *adj.*; — cap, die Pelzmütze; — cloak, der Pelzmantel. **—red**, *adj.* mit Pelz gefüttert, überzogen *or* besetzt; —red gown, das Pelzkleid; —red tongue, belegte Zunge. **—rier**, *s.* der Kürschner; der Pelzhändler. **—riery**, *s.* das Pelzwerk, der Pelzwarenhandel. **—ry**, *adj.* mit Pelz bedeckt; aus Pelz bestehend; pelzartig.

Furbelow, I. *s.* die Falbel, der Vorstoß. II. *v.a.* befalbeln, mit einem Vorstoß versehen.

Furbish, *v.a.* polieren, putzen; to — up, aufputzen. **—er**, *s.* der Polierer; der Schwertfeger.

Furcat—e(d), *adj.* gabelförmig. **—ion**, *s.* die Ausgabelung.

Furious, *adj.*, **—ly**, *adv.* wütend, rasend; wild, ungestüm (*fig.*). **—ness**, *s.* die Wut, Raserei.

Furl, *v.a.* aufrollen (*a flag*), festmachen, beschlagen (*sails*); —ing line, die Beschlagleine, der Beschlagbindsel.

Furlong, *s.* die Achtelmeile (= ⅛ englische Meile *or* 201.164 Meter).

Furlough, I. *s.* der Urlaub; on —, auf Urlaub; soldier on —, der Urlauber. II. *v.a.* (einen) beurlauben; einem Soldaten Urlaub geben.

Furnace, *s.* der Ofen, Schmelzofen; the fiery —, der feurige Ofen.

Furnish, *v.a.* versehen, versorgen (with, mit); möblieren (*rooms*), ausmöblieren (*houses*); (adorn) schmücken, zieren; (get) verschaffen, liefern; to — with teeth, zähneln; —ed rooms, apartment(s), möblierte Zimmer. **—er**, *s.* der Lieferant; (house- —er) der Möblierer. **—ing**, I. *s.* die Einrichtung (eines Hauses *or* Zimmers). II. *attrib.*; —ing house, das Geschäft für Hauseinrichtungen.

Furniture, I. *s.* das Hausgerät, der Hausrat, die Möbel (*pl.*), das Mobiliar; stuffed —, Polstermöbel. II. *attrib.*; — binding, englischer Einband; — damask, der Möbeldamast; — polish, die Möbelpolitur; — van, der Möbelwagen.

Furore, *s.* das Furore, der rasende *or* rauschende Beifall.

Furrow, I. *s.* die Furche (*also fig.*). II. *v.a.* furchen, Furchen ziehen; aushöhlen.

Further, I. *adj.* weiter, ferner, entfernter; the — side, jenseits; till — orders, bis auf weiteren Befehl, bis auf weiteres; — particulars, nähere Umstände. II. *adv.* weiter, ferner; (besides) überdies; what —? was sonst noch? nothing —? weiter nichts? to go — and fare worse, weiter gehen und schlechter fahren. III. *v.a.* (be=)fördern. **—ance**, *s.* die Förderung, Unterstützung. **—er**, *s.* der Förderer, Gönner. **—more**, *adv.* ferner, überdies, außerdem. **—most**, I. *adj.* weitest, fernst. II. *adv.* am weitesten.

Furthest, *see* Furthermost; at —, spätestens.

Furtive, *adj.* verstohlen. **—ly**, *adv.* verstohlener Weise, heimlich.

Fury, *s.* die Raserei, Wut; (heat) die Heftigkeit; die Furie (*Myth.*).

Furz—e, *s.* der Stechginster. **—y**, *adj.* voll Stechginster, ginsterig.

[1]**Fus—e**, *v.a.* & *n.* schmelzen. **—ee**, *s.* die Schnecke (*Horol.*). **—ibility**, *s.* die Schmelzbarkeit. **—ible**, *adj.* schmelzbar. **—ion**, *s.* das Schmelzen; die Verschmelzung.

[2]**Fus—e**, *s.* der Zünder, Brander. **—ee**, *s.* der Zigarrenzünder; das Windfeuerzeug, Räucherzündhölzchen. **—ilier**, **—ileer**, *s.* der Füsilier. **—illade**, I. *v.a.* erschießen. II. *s.* die Erschießung.

Fuss, *s.* I. (noise) der Lärm; das Wesen, Getue (*fig.*). II. *v.n.* (to make much — about a th.) viel Aufhebens machen (von einer S.). **—iness**, *s.* übertriebene Umständlichkeit. **—y**, *adj.*, **—ily**, *adv.* viel Wesens *or* Aufhebens um nichts machend.

Fustian, I. *s.* der Barchent; der Schwulst, Bombast (*fig.*). II. *adj.* barchent; schwülstig.

Fustigat—e, *v.a.* prügeln. **—ion**, *s.* das Prügeln.

Fust—iness, *s.* der muffige Geruch; das Muffige. **—y**, *adj.* muffig.

Futil—e, *adj.*, **—ely**, *adv.* (trifling) nichtig, eitel, unnütz; (vain) wirkungslos. **—ity**, *s.* die Nichtigkeit; (inadequacy) die Unzulänglichkeit.

Futtock, *s.* der Auflanger.

Futur—e, I. *adj.* künftig, zukünftig; —e tense, das Futurum. II. *s.* die Zukunft; das Futurum (*Gram.*); in *or* for the —e, in Zukunft, künftig. **—es**, *pl.* Lieferungen auf später (*C.L.*). **—ity**, *s.* die Zukunft, das Zukünftige.

Fuzz, I. *v.n.* sich fasern *or* auflösen. II. *s.* feine, lose Teilchen (*pl.*). **—y**, *adj.* lose, zottig, struppig.

Fy, *int.* pfui! to cry — upon a p., pfui rufen über einen.
Fytte, *s.* die Abteilung, der Abschnitt (eines alten epischen Gedichtes) (*obs.*).

G

G, g, *s.* g, G (*also Mus.*); der Altschlüssel (*Mus.*); G sharp, das Gis; G flat, das Ges; key of G, G-Schlüssel. *For abbreviations see the Index at the end of the English-German part.*
Gab, *s.* das Geplauder (*coll.*); gift of the —, die Redefertigkeit; he has the gift of the —, er ist ein großer Redeheld, er schwadroniert (*coll.*). **—ble**, I. *v.n.* schnattern (*as geese, also fig.*); (chatter) schwatzen. II. *s.* das Geschnatter; das Geschwätz. **—bler**, *s.* der Schwätzer. **—bling**, I. *adj.* schnatternd. II. *s. see* —ble II.
Gab—ardine, **—erdine**, *s.* der grobe Oberrock, Bauernkittel; der lange Oberrock, Kaftan (der Juden).
Gaberlunzie, *s.* der Brotsack; (— man) der Bettler; der arme Reisende (*dial.*); der Hausierer (*Scotch*).
Gabion, *s.* der Schanzkorb. **—nade**, *s.* die Brustwehr von Schanzkörben.
Gable, *s.* der Giebel. **—d**, *adj.* gegiebelt, Giebel-; —d window, das Fenster mit Spitzverdachung. *Comp.* **—-window**, *s.* das Giebelfenster.
Gad, *v. n.*; to — about, umherlaufen, herumstreichen. **—der**, *s.* (—der about) der Herumschweifer *or* -läufer. **—ding**, I. *adj.*; —ding gossip, die Stadtklatsche. II. *s.* das Umherlaufen. *Comp.* **—fly**, *s.* die Viehfliege.
Gaff, *s.* (— hook) die Harpune, der Haken; die Gaffel (*Naut.*); das Volkstheater.
Gaffer, *s.* der Gevatter, Großvater; (foreman) der Vormann; der Gedingnehmer (*Min.*).
Gag, I. *v.a.* den Mund knebeln; den Mund verschließen; extemporieren (*Theat.*); the —ging of the press, die Preßknebelung. II. *s.* der Knebel, die Mundsperre; extemporierte Einschaltungen (*Theat.*); to put in —, extemporieren.
Gage, *s.* das Pfand; die Bürgschaft (*also fig.*).
Gai—ly, *adv. see* Gay. **—ety**, *s.* die Heiterkeit, Fröhlichkeit; (finery) der Putz; (pleasure) die Vergnügung; *see* Gayness.
Gain, I. *s.* der Gewinn. II. *v.a.* gewinnen; (get) bekommen; (reach) erlangen, erreichen; he will not — much by it, er wird dabei keine Seide spinnen; to — one's bread, sein Brod verdienen; to — the day, den Sieg davontragen; to — ground, Boden gewinnen; um sich greifen; to — one's ends, seinen Zweck erreichen; to — over, gewinnen für, an sich ziehen, bewegen zu; to — possession, Besitz ergreifen. III. *v.n.* gewinnen; vorgehen (*Horol.*); to — on (a p., einem) den Vorteil abgewinnen, näher kommen (*in a race, etc.*), Eingriffe machen in (*land, etc.*). **—er**, *s.* der Gewinner, Gewinnende; to be a —er by, bei . . . gewinnen. **—s**, *pl.* der Gewinnst.
Gainsay, *v.a.* widersprechen; bestreiten; (deny) (ab)leugnen.
Gait, *s.* der Gang, die Gangart; (way) der Weg.
Gaiter, *s.* die Gamasche.
Gala, *s.* die Gala; — days, Gala-Tage.
Galactometer, *s.* die Milchwage.
Galaxy, *s.* die Milchstraße; glänzende Versammlung (*fig.*).
Galban(um), *s.* das Galban.
[1]**Gale**, *s.* der heftige Wind, der Sturm(wind); it is blowing a —, es stürmt, der Wind ist stürmisch; a terrific — was raging, ein schrecklicher Sturm wütete.
[2]**Gale**, *s.* die periodische Renten- *or* Steuer-Zahlung; hanging —, rückständiger Zins. *Comp.* **—-day**, *s.* der Rentenzahl(ungs)tag.
Galeated, *adj.* behelmt; gehelmt (*Bot.*).
Galena, *s.* der Bleiglanz.
Galilee, *s.* innere (Büßer-)Vorhalle (*Arch.*).
Gal(l)iot, *s.* die Galliote.
[1]**Gall**, *s.* die Galle (*also fig.*); — of glass, die Glasgalle. *Comp.* **—-bladder**, *s.* die Gallenblase. **—-duct**, *s.* der Gallengang. **—-stone**, *s.* der Gallenstein.
[2]**Gall**, *s.* (—-nut) der Gallusapfel. II. *v.a.* gallieren. **—ic**, *adj.*; —ic acid, die Gallussäure. *Comp.* **—-insect**, *s.* die Gallwespe.
[3]**Gall**, I. *s.* das Wundreiben, der Wolf. II. *v.a.* wundreiben; quälen, ärgern, reizen (*fig.*); belästigen, bestreichen (*Mil.*). **—ing**, I. *adj.* ärgerlich, verletzend, bitter. II. *s.* das Aufreiben.
Gallant, I. *adj.*, **—ly**, *adv.* tapfer, brav; (fine) schön, herrlich, glänzend, stattlich; (noble) edel; (courtly) höflich, artig, aufmerksam gegen Damen; the — member (for), der Herr Abgeordnete (für) (*in case of a military or naval member*) (*Eng. Parl.*). II. *s.* der tapfere Mann (*obs.*); der Galan, Liebhaber. III. *v.a.* den Hof machen; mit Grazie handhaben (*a fan, etc.*). **—ry**, *s.* die Tapferkeit; der Edelmut; die Galanterie, Artigkeit (gegen Frauen); die Buhlerei.
Galleon, *s.* die Gallione.
Gallery, *s.* die Galerie, Säulenhalle (*Arch.*); die Emporkirche, Empore (*of a church*); (passage) der Gang, Korridor; die Galerie (*Min., Fort.*); painted —, Galerie mit Wandmalereien; picture —, Gemäldegalerie; to play to the —, für die Galerie spielen, nach Effekt haschen.
Galley, *s.* die Galeere; offenes Ruderboot (*on the Thames*); die Schiffsküche (*Shipb.*); das Setzschiff (*Typ.*). *Comp.* **—-proof**, *s.* der Fahnenabzug. **—-slave**, *s.* der Galeerensklave.
Gallimaufr(e)y, *s.* das Ragout; der Mischmasch (*fig.*).
Galliot, *see* Galiot.
Gallipot, *s.* der Apothekertopf.
Gallivant, *v.n.* umherlaufen, herumschwärmen; auf Liebesabenteuer ausgehen; to go —ing round the world, die ganze Welt durchstreifen.
Gallon, *s.* die Gallone (4.54 Liter enthaltend).
Galloon, *s.* (lace) die Tresse, Borte, Litze, der Galon.
Gallop, I. *s.* der Galopp (*also Mus., Danc.*); full (hand) —, gestreckter (kurzer) Galopp; the horse artillery rode at a —, die Feldartillerie fuhr im Galopp auf. II. *v.n.* galoppieren; to — at the enemy's squares, auf die feindlichen Vierecke lossprengen. **—ade**, *s.* die Galoppade.
Gallows, I. *s. & pl.* der Galgen (*also Typ.*); (*pl., also* **—es**) die Hosenträger (*coll.*). II. *attrib.*; — bird, der Galgenvogel, Galgenschwengel, Galgenstrick. **—-tree**, *s.* der Galgen.
Galop, *s.* der Galopp (*Mus., Danc.*).
Galore, I. *s.* die Fülle (*Irish*). II. *adv.* im Überflusse, in Menge, viel (*Irish*).
Galosh, *s.* der Holzschuh; der Überschuh, Gummischuh, die Galosche.
Galvan—ic, *adj.* galvanisch. **—ism**, *s.* der Galvanismus. **—ize**, *v.a.* galvanisieren. **—ometer**, *s.* der Galvanometer. **—oplastic**, *adj.* galvanoplastisch.
Gambit, *s.* das Gambit.
Gam—ble, *v.* I. *n.* (hoch) spielen, um hohen Einsatz spielen. II. *a.*; to —ble away, verspielen. **—bler**, *s.* der Spieler. **—bling**, *s.* das Spielen (um Geld). **—e**, I. *s.* das Spiel (*also fig.*); der Scherz, die Belustigung; jagdbare Tiere, das Wild; to die —e, furchtlos in den Tod gehen; to have a hard —e to play, eine schwierige Rolle durchzuführen haben; to play —es, Spiele *or* Gesellschaftsspiele spielen; to make —e of a p., einen zum Besten haben; —es of chance, Glücksspiele, Hasardspiele; outdoor —es, Bewegungsspiele im Freien. II. *v.n.* spielen. III. *adj.* mutig, bereit, entschlossen (*coll.*). **—ester**, *s.* der Spieler. **—ing**, *s.* das Spielen. **—mon**, I. *s.* das Puffspiel; (hoax) der Trug; —mon! dummes Zeug! Flausen! II. *v.a.* matsch machen; (hoax) betrügen, anführen. *Comp.* **—bling-hell**, *s.* die Spielhölle, das Spielhaus. **—e-bag**, *s.*

die Jagdtasche. **—e-cock**, *s.* der Kampfhahn. **—e-covers**, *pl.* Wildgehege. **—e-keeper**, *s.* der Förster; der Wildhüter. **—e-license**, *s.* der Jagdschein, die Jagdkarte. **—ing-table**, *s.* der Spieltisch.

Gamboge, *s.* das Gummigutt.

Gambol, I. *s.* der Luftsprung. II. *v.n.* lustige Sprünge machen, fröhlich hüpfen.

[1]Gammon, *see under* Gamble.

[2]Gammon, *s.;* — of bacon, der (geräucherte) Schinken.

Gamut, *s.* die Tonleiter.

Gander, *s.* der Gänserich.

Gang, *s.* die Horde, Bande, Rotte; der Gang (*Min.*); die Abteilung (of workmen, Arbeiter). **—way**, *s.* der Durchgang, Quergang; die Laufplanke, der Steg (*Naut.*); schmaler Quergang im englischen Unterhause, welcher den Mittelgang und die rechts und links von diesem aufgestellten Bänke rechtwinklig durchschneidet; below the —way (vom Speaker aus jenseits) sind die Plätze für unabhängige Parlamentsmitglieder; the members below the —way, die Wilden (*Parl. lang.*).

Ganglion (*pl.* —s *and* Ganglia), *s.* der Nervenknoten.

Gangren—e, I. *s.* der (heiße) Brand. II. *v.a.* anfressen. III. *v.n.* angefressen werden. **—ous**, *adj.* brandig.

Gantlet, *s.* das Gassenlaufen, Spießrutenlaufen; to pass *or* run the — (*also* gauntlet), Spießruten laufen.

Gaol, **—er**, *etc. see* Jail.

Gap, *s.* die Öffnung, Kluft, der Riß, das Loch; (breach) die Bresche; der Hiatus (*Gram.*); die Lücke (*fig.*); to stop a —, ein Loch zustopfen. **—e**, I. *v. n.* den Mund aufsperren; (yawn) gähnen; (open) sich spalten, sich öffnen, klaffen; to —e at, angaffen; to stand —ing in the air, Maulaffen feil halten. **—er**, *s.* der Gähner; der Gaffer. **—ing**, I. *adj.* weit offen. II. *s.* das Gähnen; das Gaffen.

Garb, *s.* die Tracht, Kleidung, das Gewand.

Garb—age, *s.* der Abfall, Auswurf. **—le**, *v.a.* verstümmeln, zustutzen; a —led account, ein parteiisch aufgefaßter *or* zugestutzter Bericht.

Garden, I. *s.* der Garten; nursery —, die Baumschule; hanging —, hängender *or* schwebender Garten. II. *attrib.;* — grounds, parkartiger Garten. III. *v.n.* sich mit Gartenbau beschäftigen; im Garten arbeiten. **—er**, *s.* der Gärtner. **—ia**, *s.* die Gardenie. **—ing**, *s.* der Gartenbau, die Gartenpflege; die Gartenarbeit. *Comp.* **—-roller**, *s.* die Gartenwalze. **—-shears**, *pl.* die Heckenschere. **—-stuff**, *s.* Gartengewächse. **—-tools**, *pl.* Gartenwerkzeuge.

Garg—le, I. *s.* das Gurgelwasser. II. *v.a.* gurgeln. III. *v.n.* sich gurgeln. **—oyle**, *s.* der Wasserspeier, die Schnauze der Dachrinne.

Garish, *adj.*, **—ly**, *adv.*, grell, prunkend.

Garland, I. *s.* der (Blumen-)Kranz; das Blumengewinde (*Arch.*); die Blumenlese (*fig.*). II. *v.a.* bekränzen.

Garlic, *s.* der Knoblauch.

Garment, *s.* das Kleidungsstück, Gewand.

Garner, I. *s.* der Kornboden. II. *v.a.* aufspeichern.

Garnet, *s.* der Granat.

Garni—sh, *v.a.* zieren, schmücken; (Gerichte, Schüssel) mit Gemüsen rc. berändern, belegen. **—shing**, *s.* das Garnieren; die Garnierung. **—shment**, *s.* der Zierat, Schmuck, die Verzierung. **—ture**, *s.* der Schmuck; der Zubehör.

Garret, *s.* die Dachstube, das Dachstübchen.

Garrison, I. *s.* die Garnison, Besatzung; der Standort; in —, garnisonierend, in Garnison. II. *v.a.* mit einer Besatzung versehen, Besatzung legen in; durch besetzte Festungen verteidigen; the regiment is —ed at . . ., das Regiment steht in . . .

Garrot—e, **—te**, I. *s.* die Garotte; die Erdrosselung. II. *v.a.* garottieren. **—er**, *s.* der Garotteur. **—ing**, *s.* das Garottieren.

Garrul—ity, *s.* die Schwatzhaftigkeit Geschwätzigkeit. **—ous**, *adj.*, **—ously**, *adv.* geschwätzig.

Garter, I. *s.* das Strumpfband; das Hosenband; order of the —, der Hosenband-Orden; knight of the —, der Ritter des Hosenbandordens. II. *v.a.* (auf)binden.

Garth, *s.* die Einzäunung (*dial.*).

Gas, *s.* das Gas (*also Chem.*, *Phys.*). **—elier**, *s.* die Gaskrone, der (Gas-)Kronleuchter. **—eous**, *adj.* gas-artig, -förmig. **—ification**, *s.* die Verwandlung in Gas. **—ify**, *v.a.* in Gas verwandeln. **—ometer**, *s.* der Gasmesser, die Gasuhr. *Comp.* **—-bracket**, *s.* der Gasarm. **—-burner**, *s.* der Gasbrenner. **—-fittings**, *pl.* die Gaseinrichtung. **—-lamp**, *s.* die Gaslampe. **—-light**, I. *s.* das Gaslicht. II. *attrib.;* —-light company, die Gasgesellschaft. **—-main**, *s.* die Hauptgasleitungsröhre. **—-pipe**, *s.* die Gasröhre. **—-stove**, *s.* der Gasofen. **—-supply**, *s.* die Gasversorgung, Versorgung mit Gas. **—-works**, *pl.* die Gas(bereitungs)anstalt.

Gasconade, I. *v.n.* prahlen, aufschneiden. II. *s.* die Prahlerei, Aufschneiderei. **—r**, *s.* der Prahler.

Gash, I. *v.a.* tief ins Fleisch schneiden. II. *s.* die klaffende Wunde, Schnittwunde, der Schmiß.

Gasp, I. *s.* das schwere Atmen; der schwere Atemzug; to be at the last —, in den letzten Zügen liegen. II. *v.a.;* to — out, ausatmen, aushauchen. III. *v.n.* schwer atmen; to — for breath, nach Luft schnappen.

Gastr—ic, *adj.* gastrisch; —ic juice, der Magensaft. **—itis**, *s.* die Magenentzündung. **—ocele**, *s.* der Magenbruch. **—onomer**, **—onomist**, *s.* der Feinschmecker, Gastronom. **—onomy**, *s.* die Speisekunde; die Kochkunst; die Feinschmeckerei. **—otomy**, *s.* der Bauchschnitt.

Gat, *obs. imperf. of* Get.

Gate, I. *s.* das Tor; die Pforte (*also fig.*); die Barriere (*Railw.*) der Verschluß (*canal*). II. *v.a.* (einem) das Tor schließen (*Eng. Univ. sl.*); he was —d, ihm wurde verboten das College zu verlassen (*Eng. Univ. sl.*). *Comp.* **—-keeper**, **—man**, *s.* der Barrierenwärter (*Railw.*). **—way**, *s.* der Torweg, die Einfahrt.

Gather, I. *v.a.* sammeln (*also fig.*); (— in) ernten; (pick) pflücken, lesen; (— from) schließen (from, aus); (learn) erfahren; (gain) gewinnen; aufreihen, -fassen, kräuseln (*a dress*, *etc.*); to — strength, zu Kräften kommen; rolling stones — no moss, ein unstäter Mensch kommt zu nichts; to — **together**, versammeln; to — oneself together, sich sammeln, sich zusammennehmen; to — **up**, aufnehmen (*clothes*, *etc.*), (ein)sammeln (*rays*, *etc.*), auftuchen (*sails*). II. *v.n.* sich sammeln; sich versammeln (*as people*); (increase) sich vergrößern; to — to a head, eitern; zur Reife kommen (*fig.*); to be —ed to one's fathers, zu seinen Vätern versammelt werden. III. *s.* die Kräusel, Falte. **—er**, *s.* der Sammler; der Kräuselapparat (*Sew.-m.*); tax—er, der Steuererheber. **—ing**, I. *s.* die Versammlung; die Lage (*Print.*); das Kräuseln, Aufreihen (*Semp.*); das Eitern. II. *adj.* (stets) zunehmend.

Gatling, *attrib.;* — gun, die Revolverkanone, Mitrailleuse.

Gaud—ily, *adv. see* —y. **—iness**, *s.* prunkhafter Aufputz, geschmacklose Geputztheit. **—y**, I. *adj.* prunkhaft, prächtig, aufgedonnert, aufgeputzt. II. *s.;* the —y, großes Festmahl (*Eng. Univ.*).

Gauffer, *v.a.* glöckeln, gaufrieren. **—ing**, I. *s.* das Glöckeln. II. *attrib.;* —ing machine, die Gaufriermaschine, das Glockeisen.

Gauge, I. *v.a.* abmessen, ausmessen; eichen; abschätzen (*fig.*). II. *s.* das Maß, Normalmaß, der Maßstab; die Spurweite, Spurbreite; weather —, der Wettermesser; — for strings, der Saitenmesser. **—er**, *s.* der Eichmeister

Gaunt, *adj.*, **—ly**, *adv.* mager, hager, dürr. **—ness**, *s.* die Hagerkeit.
Gauntlet, *s.* der Panzerhandschuh, Fehdehandschuh; to throw down the —, (einem) den Handschuh hinwerfen, (einem) Fehde ansagen, (einen) herausfordern; *see* Gantlet.
Gauz—e, *s.* die Gaze; silk —e, Seidengaze; wire —e, das Drahtgeflecht. **—y**, *adj.* gazeartig.
Gave, *imperf. of* Give.
Gavot(te), *s.* die Gavotte.
Gawk, *s.* der Tölpel; (simpleton) der Einfaltspinsel; (cuckoo) der Kuckuk. **—y**, *adj.* tölpisch, linkisch; dumm.
Gay, *adj.* heiter, lustig, fröhlich; bunt, glänzend (*as colours*); (overdressed) sehr geputzt; lebenslustig, flott; (dissolute) ausschweifend. **—ety**, **—ness**, *see* Gaiety; die Buntfarbigkeit.
Gaze, I. *v.a.* anstarren. II. *v.n.* starren, starr blicken; to — fixedly at a th., fest auf eine S. blicken. III. *s.* der feste, starre Blick; das Anstarren. **—r**, *s.* der Anstaunende.
Gazelle, *s.* die Gazelle.
Gazette, I. *s.* die Zeitung; das Amtsblatt. II. *v.a.* in die Zeitung setzen, amtlich bekannt geben *or* machen; he has been —d captain, seine Ernennung zum Hauptmann ist im Staatsanzeiger veröffentlicht; he has been —d colonel, er ist zum Oberst ernannt, ist Oberst geworden. **—er**, *s.* der (offizielle) Zeitungsschreiber; (directory, *etc.*) geographisch-statistisches Nachschlagebuch.
Gear, *s.* die Kleidung; (harness, *etc.*) das (Pferde-)Geschirr; das Zeug (*Mil.*); (property) die Habe, das Gut; das Triebwerk (*Mach.*); das Zubehör, Geschirr (*Naut.*); night —, der Nachtbedarf; running —, das gehende Getriebe; to throw out of —, (den Mechanismus) in Unordnung bringen (*lit.*); zerstören, verwirren (*fig.*). **—ing**, *s.* das Triebwerk, Getriebe (*Mach.*); das Geschirr; die Übersetzung, Übertragung (*Cycl.*). *Comp.* **—-case**, *s.* der Kasten mit Triebwerk, Kettenkasten (*Cycl.*).
Gee, **—-ho**, **—-up**, *int.* hott! hotthü! hottehü!
Geese, *pl. see* Goose.
Geisha, *s.* die (japanische) Geisha.
Gelatin—ate, *v.* I. *a.* zu Gallerte machen. II. *n.* sich in Gallerte verwandeln. **—ation**, *s.* die Verwandlung in Gallerte. **—e**, I. *s.* die (tierische) Gallerte. II. *adj. see* —ous; —e process, der Gelatineprozeß (*Phot.*). **—ous**, *adj.* gallertartig.
Gelid, *adj.* sehr kalt, eiskalt.
Geld, *v.a.* verschneiden. **—ed**, **Gelt**, *p.p.* verschnitten. **—ing**, *s.* das Verschneiden; (horse) der Wallach.
Gem, I. *s.* der Edelstein; die Knospe. II. *v.a.* mit Edelsteinen besetzen; verzieren (*fig.*). **—mate**, *adj.* knospig. **—mation**, *s.* das Knospen. **—miferous**, *adj.* knospend. **—miparous**, *adj.* Knospen tragend *or* treibend.
Gemin—ation, *s.* die Verdoppelung. **—i**, *pl.* die Zwillinge, Kastor und Pollux (*Astr.*).
Gendarme, *s.* der Gendarm, Polizeisoldat.
Gender, *s.* die Gattung; das Geschlecht (*also Gram.*).
Genealog—ical, *adj.* genealogisch; —ical tree, der Stammbaum. **—ist**, *s.* der Genealog. **—y**, *s.* die Genealogie; der Stammbaum.
Gener—al, I. *adj.* allgemein; (joint, common) gemeinschaftlich; (public) öffentlich; (usual) gewöhnlich; Haupt-, General-; —al election, allgemeine Wahlen; —al order, der Tagesbefehl; to have a —al invitation, ein für allemal eingeladen sein; —al Post Office (G. P. O.), das Hauptpostamt. II. *s.* das Allgemeine, das große Ganze; das Volk; der General, der Feldherr (*Mil.*); der Generalmarsch (*Mil.*); *see* Particular; caviare to the —al, Kaviar fürs Volk; in —al, gewöhnlich, im allgemeinen; in —al terms, in ganz allgemeinen Ausdrücken, ganz im allgemeinen; brigadier —al, der Brigadegeneral, Generalmajor; Lieutenant —al, der Generalleutnant. **—alissimo**, *s.* der Oberbefehlshaber. **—ality**, *s.* die Allgemeinheit; der größte Teil; —ality of mankind, die meisten Menschen. **—alization**, *s.* die Verallgemeinerung; to indulge in —alizations, immer gern verallgemeinern. **—alize**, *v.a.* verallgemeinern. **—ally**, *adv.* im Ganzen, im allgemeinen; (in —al) überhaupt; meistens, gewöhnlich; —ally speaking, im allgemeinen, im Ganzen genommen. **—alness**, *s.* die Allgemeinheit, das Gewöhnliche. **—alship**, *s.* der Generalsrang, die Feldherrnwürde; (strategy) die Feldherrnkunst; die Leitung (*fig.*). **—ate**, *v.a.* zeugen; erzeugen (*fig.*); (cause) verursachen. **—ation**, *s.* das Zeugen; die Erzeugung, Hervorbringung; die Bildung; die Geschlechtsfolge, Generation, das Geschlecht; (people of one's —ation) die Altersgenossen; (period) das Zeitalter. **—ative**, *adj.* zeugend, Zeugungs-; fruchtbar; —ative power, das Zeugungsvermögen, die Zeugungskraft. **—ator**, *s.* der Erzeuger; der Grundton (*Mus.*). **—ic**, *adj.*, **—ically**, *adv.* generisch, Gattungs-. **—osity**, *s.* der Edelmut, die Großmut; die Freigebigkeit. **—ous**, *adj.*, **—ously**, *adv.* großmütig, edelmütig; (liberal) freigebig; kühn, feurig (*as horses*); edel (*as wine*). **—ousness**, *see* —osity.
Genesis, *s.* die Zeugung; das Entstehen (*Geom.*); die Entstehung; Entstehungsgeschichte; das erste Buch Mosis.
[1]**Genet**, *s.* der Zelter, spanische Klepper.
[2]**Genet**, *s.* die Ginsterkatze.
Genial, *adj.*, **—ly**, *adv.* leutselig; (enlivening) belebend; (cheering) aufheiternd, ermunternd; gemütlich; wohltuend; in — company, in gemütlicher Gesellschaft. **—ity**, *s.* die Leutseligkeit; die Herzlichkeit; das gemütliche, freundliche Wesen, die Gemütlichkeit.
Genit—al, *adj.* Zeugungs-; —al organs, die Geschlechtsteile. **—als**, *pl.* Zeugungsglieder, Geschlechtsteile. **—ive**, *s.* der Wesfall, zweite Fall, Genetiv.
Geni—us, *s.* (*pl.* —uses) (person) das Genie, der Genius, geniale Mensch; die Anlage, Naturgabe, besondere Geistesfähigkeit; (characteristic) das Eigentümliche, Charakterische; (*pl.* —i) der Genius; the good —us, der gute Genius, der Schutzgeist; his evil —us, sein böser Geist *or* Genius; men of —us, die Genies; his —us does not lie in that direction, dazu hat er keine Anlage; —us of the times, der Zeitgeist, das Eigentümliche *or* der Geist der Zeiten; the —i, die Genien.
Genre, I. *s.* das Genre, die Art und Weise; der Stil. II. *attrib.*; —painting, die Genremalerei.
Gent, *s. coll. abbrev. see* —leman. **—eel**, *adj*, **—eelly**, *adv.* fein, vornehm, anständig (*obs.*); elegant (*as dress*). **—ile**, I. *s.* der Heide. II. *adj.* heidnisch. **—ility**, *s.* die edle Abkunft; der vornehme Stand, die feine Lebensart. **—le**, *adj.*, **—ly**, *adv.* mild, sanft; gelind (*as a breeze*); fromm, zahm (*as beasts*); ruhig, sanft dahinfließend (*as rivers*); of —le birth *or* blood, von vornehmer Abkunft; —le reader, geneigter Leser; —le and simple, Vornehm und Gering. **—lemanly**, *see* —lemanlike. **—leness**, *s.* die Milde, Güte; die Sanftmut. **—ry**, *s.* der niedere Adel; light-fingered —ry, die Herren Langfinger (*sl.*); nobility and —ry, der Adel und die Vornehmen. *Comp.* **—lefolk**, **—lefolks**, *pl.* vornehme Leute. **—leman**, I. der Herr, der Mann von Stand, vornehme Mann; der Mann von Bildung und Lebensart; der feine, gebildete, gesellschaftsfähige Mann; a —leman of private means, ein Rentner; country —leman, Landedelmann, gesellschaftsfähiger Gutsbesitzer; he is too much of a —leman to do that, er ist zu sehr Ehrenmann, als daß er so handeln könnte; he is no —leman, er hat keine Lebensart, er ist kein feiner Mensch *or* ein Mann ohne Gefühl und Manieren, ohne Bildung und Lebensart; —leman of the bedchamber, der königliche Kammerjunker; —leman of the long robe, der Jurist;

—leman's —leman, der Kammerdiener (*sl.*); —lemen's gloves, Herrenhandschuhe; for —lemen, für Männer. **—leman-commoner,** *s.* vornehmer Student zu Oxford (*obs.*). **—leman-like, —lemanly,** *adj.* vornehm; fein, gebildet; ritterlich, anständig, ehrenhaft; anständig, wohlgesittet, fein; —lemanly manners, feine Sitten. **—lemen-at-arms,** *pl.* die königliche Leibwache. **—lewoman,** *s.* vornehme, gebildete Dame; die Kammerfrau (*at court*).

Gentian, *s.* der Enzian, die Gentiane.

Genufle—ction, —xion, *s.* die Kniebeugung.

Genuine, *adj.*, **—ly,** *adv.* echt, wahr; the — article, die echte Ware, das Richtige. **—ness,** *s.* die Echtheit.

Gen—us, *s.* (*pl.* —era) die Gattung.

Geo—centric, *adj.* geozentrisch. **—desy,** *s.* die Geodäsie, Feldmeßkunst, Vermessungskunde. **—detic,** *adj.* geodätisch, die Vermessungskunst betreffend. **—gnosy,** *s.* die Geognosie, Erdschichtenkunde. **—grapher,** *s.* der Geograph. **—graphical,** *adj.*, **—graphically,** *adv.* erdkundlich, geographisch. **—graphy,** *s.* die Geographie, die Erdbeschreibung, Erdkunde. **—logical,** *adj.* erdgeschichtlich, geologisch. **—logist,** *s.* der Geolog. **—logize,** *v.n.* geologische Studien machen. **—logy,** *s.* die Geologie, Lehre von der Erdgeschichte und Erdbeschaffenheit. **—mancer,** *s.* der Erdwahrsager, Wahrsager aus Sandfiguren. **—mancy,** *s.* die Geomantie; die Punktierkunst. **—meter, —metrician,** *s.* der Geometer, Erdmesser, Landmesser. **—metric(al),** *adj.*, **—metrically,** *adv.* geometrisch. **—metry,** *s.* die Erdmeßkunst, Geometrie; die Raumlehre, Geometrie; plane —metry, die Geometrie der Ebene, Planimetrie; solid —, die Stereometrie. **—physics,** *s.* (*also pl.*) die Geophysik, Lehre von den physischen Vorgängen im Erdinneren.

Georgic, I. *adj.* ländlich, Ackerbau-. II. *s.* das Gedicht über den Ackerbau *or* vom Lande. **—s,** *pl.* Georgika.

Geranium, *s.* der Storchschnabel, das Geranium.

Gerfalcon, *s.* der Geierfalke, Gierfalke.

Germ, *s.* der Keim (*also fig.*). **—an, —ane,** *adj.* (der Sache) zugehörig; verwandt; cousin —an, der leibliche Vetter; a —ane subject, ein ansprechender *or* anziehender Gegenstand. **—icide,** *s.* das keimtötende Mittel. **—inal,** *adj.* zum Keim gehörig. **—inant,** *adj.* sprossend. **—inate,** *v.n.* keimen, sprossen, ausschlagen. **—ination,** *s.* das Keimen, die Ausschlagung.

[1]**German,** *see under* Germ.

[2]**German,** *see the Index of Names.*

Germanism, *s.* der deutsche Ausdruck, Germanismus.

Gerund, *s.* das Gerundium. **—ial,** *adj.* Gerundial-. **—ive,** *s.* das Gerundiv(um). *Comp.* **—-grinding,** *s.* der mechanische Unterricht in formaler Grammatik, grammatische Einpaukerei (*iron. coll.*).

Gest—ation, *s.* die Trächtigkeit (*of beasts*); die Schwangerschaft (*of women*). **—atory,** *adj.* tragbar; die Schwangerschaft, rc. betreffend. **—iculate,** *v.n.* Gebärden machen. **—iculation,** *s.* das Gebärdenspiel. **—iculator,** *s.* der Gebärdenmacher. **—iculatory,** *adj.* durch Gebärden darstellend. **—ure,** *s.* die Gebärde; (movement) die Körperbewegung.

Get, *ir.v.* I. *a.* erhalten, bekommen; erlangen, sich (*dat.*) verschaffen; (earn) erwerben; (buy) sich (*dat.*) kaufen; (merit) verdienen; (have) haben; (beget) zeugen, erzeugen; (induce) bewegen, überreden, vermögen; (seize) ergreifen; nehmen (*a wife*); annehmen (*habits*); (cause, have) lassen; to have got, haben, besitzen; to — one's hair cut, sich (*dat.*) das Haar schneiden lassen; I got him to do it, ich bewog ihn es zu tun; I got my suit mended, ich ließ meinen Anzug ausbessern; — me the book, besorge mir das Buch; he will soon — to be useful to me, er wird mir bald nützlich werden; he has got to do it, er muß es tun; to — the better of . . ., (einen, rc.) überwinden, den Vorzug vor . . . erhalten; to have got, haben; where is my book? Lizzie has got it, wo ist mein Buch? Lieschen hat es; to — dinner, *etc.* ready, das Essen bereiten; to — information of, Nachricht einziehen über; to — a place, ein Amt, eine Stelle bekommen; to — possession of, sich (einer S.) bemächtigen, in den Besitz von . . . gelangen; to — the start of a p., einem den Vorsprung abgewinnen; to — teeth, Zähne bekommen; to — with child, schwängern; ill gotten goods never thrive, unrecht Gut gedeiht nicht (*prov.*); to — **away,** wegbringen; I could not — him away, ich konnte ihn nicht fortbringen; to — **back,** zurückerhalten; to — **down,** hinunterbringen, (swallow) hinunterschlucken; to — **in,** hinein-, herein-bringen, einschieben, (*of crops*) einbringen; to — **off,** ausziehen (*clothes*), unterbringen (*goods*), wegtun; to — **on,** anziehen; to — **out,** heraus-bringen, -locken; to — **over,** hinüberbringen; to — rid of, sich frei *or* losmachen von; to — **through,** durchbringen; to — **up,** aufbringen, einrichten; the book is beautifully got up, das Buch ist prächtig ausgestattet; to — up a play, ein Schauspiel für die Bühne vorbereiten; to — up linen, Wäsche waschen und plätten; to — up steam, den Dampf im Kessel ansammeln lassen (*Locom.*), den Mut anfeuern (*sl.*); I have to — it up for my examination, ich muß mir das für meine Prüfung einstudieren, einlernen, einpauken. II. *r.*; — thee out from this land, ziehe aus diesem Lande (*B.*). III. *n.* (arrive) gelangen, geraten, kommen, ankommen, anlangen; (go) sich begeben, gehen; (become) werden; we got there early, wir kamen früh dorthin, langten früh dort an; to — cold, late, hungry, sleepy, *etc.*, kalt, spät, hungrig, schläfrig, rc. werden; to — **abroad,** bekannt werden, unter die Leute kommen; to — **along,** weiterkommen; — along with you! mach', daß du wegkommst! (*vulg.*); to — **among,** fallen unter (*acc.*); to — **at,** an (*acc.*) . . . kommen, (*acc.*) erreichen; to — **back,** zurückkommen; to — **before,** zuvorkommen; to — **clear,** frei werden; to — **down,** hinunterkommen; hinabsteigen, absteigen; to — **forward,** vorwärtskommen, weiterkommen; to — **home,** nach Hause kommen *or* gelangen; to — **in,** eindringen, ins Haus gehen; ins Parlament kommen; to — **into,** hineinkommen; to — into debt, in Schulden geraten, Schulden machen; to — **near,** nahe kommen; to — **off,** davonkommen, (escape) entwischen, freigesprochen werden (*as a prisoner*); to — off cheaply, mit einem blauen Auge davonkommen; to — off from, absteigen von (*a horse, cycle, etc.*); to — **on,** gelangen auf (*acc.*), (progress) Fortschritte machen, vorwärtskommen; (go on) fortrücken; aufsteigen (*Cycl.*); — on! nur weiter! to — on one's legs *or* feet, aufstehen; to — on in life, im Leben weiter- *or* vorwärts kommen; to — on with a p., mit einem auskommen; not to — on in the world, auf keinen grünen Zweig kommen; to — **out,** hinauskommen; aussteigen; — out of the house! mache, daß du aus dem Hause kommst! to — out of one's depth, den Grund unter den Füßen verlieren; von Sachen sprechen, die man nicht versteht (*fig.*); to — **over,** hinwegkommen über, überwinden (*difficulties*); sich erholen von (*a loss, an illness*); to — **round,** durchkommen, sich erholen; to — round a p., einen (durch Schmeichelei) für sich gewinnen; to — **through,** durch-gehen, -kommen; to — **to,** erreichen; to — **together,** zusammenkommen; to — **up,** aufsteigen, (rise) aufstehen; to — up to, erreichen, (overtake) einholen. **—ter,** *s.* der Zeuger; der Erlanger; der Gewinner. **—ting,** *s.* der Gewinn(st). *Comp.* **—-at-able,** *adj.* erreichbar. **—-up,** *s.* der Anzug, Putz, die Ausstaffierung

(*coll.*); (of a book, drama) die Ausstattung (eines Buches), die Inszenierung (eines Stückes).
Gewgaw, *s.* der Tand.
Geyser, *s.* der Geyser; der Badeofen.
Ghastl—iness, *s.* das geisterhafte Aussehen; die Totenblässe; das Grausen. **—y**, *adj.* geisterhaft, totenbleich; (dreadful) gräßlich.
Ghee, *s.* zu Öl eingekochte Butter.
Gherkin, *s.* die Pfeffer-, Essig-gurke.
Ghost, I. *s.* der Geist, das Gespenst; Holy —, der heilige Geist; to give up the —, den Geist aufgeben; he looked as if he had seen a —, er sah aus als ob er ein Gespenst gesehen hätte; not the — of a chance, nicht die geringste *or* entfernteste Aussicht. II. *attrib.;* — word, das Unwort (*rare*). **—ly**, *adj. see* —like; geistlich; —ly father, der Beichtvater. *Comp.* **—like**, *adj.* geisterhaft. **—story**, *s.* die Gespenstergeschichte, Geistergeschichte.
Ghoul, *s.* der leichenverzehrende Dämon; die Larve.
Giant, I. *s.* der Riese; —'s grave, das Hünengrab. II. *adj.* riesenhaft, riesig. **—ess**, *s.* die Riesin.
Giaour, *s.* der Nicht-Mohammedaner Ungläubige, Christ.
Gibber, *v.n.* undeutlich sprechen, schnattern. **—ish**, *s.* das Geschnatter, Kauderwelsch.
Gibbet, I. *s.* der Galgen; das Querholz (*Carp.*); der Krahnbalken (*Mach.*). II. *v.a.* (auf)hängen.
Gibbo—sity, *s.* die Wölbung; das Buckelige, Höckerige. **—us**, *adj.* gewölbt; buckelig; the moon is —us, der Mond ist im zweiten oder letzten Viertel.
Gib—e, I. *s.* der Spott, die Stichelei. II. *v.a.* höhnen, bespötteln, aufziehen. **—er**, *s.* der Spötter. **—ing**, *adj.*, **—ingly**, *adv.* spöttisch.
Giblet, *s.*, **—s**, *pl.* das Gänseklein.
Gidd—ily, *adv. see* —y. **—iness**, *s.* der Schwindel (*in the head*); die Drehkrankheit (*of sheep*); (folly) die Unbesonnenheit, der Leichtsinn; (fickleness) die Unbeständigkeit. **—y**, *adj.* schwindelig; taumelnd, wankend; unbeständig; unbesonnen, leichtsinnig; —y height, schwindelnde Höhe. *Comp.* **—y-headed**, *adj.* unbesonnen, gedankenlos.
Gift, *s.* die Gabe, das Geschenk; (giving) das Geben; (right of giving) das Verleihungsrecht, Patronatsrecht; (talent) die (Natur-)Gabe, das Talent; the living is in his —, er hat die Pfründe zu verleihen; deed of —, die Schenkungsurkunde. **—ed**, *adj.* begabt. *Comp.* **—-horse**, *s.;* to look a —-horse in the mouth, einem geschenkten Gaul ins Maul sehen.
Gig, *s.* der offene, einspännige, zweirädrige Wagen, das Kabriolett; der Schiffsnachen (*Naut.*); das lange leichte Ruderboot.
Gigantic, *adj.* riesenhaft, gigantisch; ungeheuer.
Giggle, I. *v.n.* kichern. II. *s.* das Gekicher. **—r**, *s.* der, die Kichernde.
Gild, *ir.v.a.* vergolden; (adorn) zieren; mit schönen Redensarten verbergen (*fig.*); to — the (bitter) pill, die Pille vergolden, die bittre Pille versüßen. **—er**, *s.* der Vergolder. **—ing**, *s.* die Vergoldung; rough —ing, schraffierte Vergoldung. *Comp.* **—ing-brush**, *s.* der Vergolderpinsel. **—ing-size**, *s.* das Koliment.
[1]**Gill**, *s.* die Kieme (*Icht.*); der Bartlappen (*Orn.*); das Fleisch unter dem Kinne.
[2]**Gill**, *s.* die Viertelpinte.
[3]**Gill**, *s.* das Mädchen, Schätzchen; das leichtfertige Mädchen, die Dirne; der Erdefeu; das Kräuterbier.
[4]**Gill**, *s.* die Bergschlucht (*dial.*).
Gillie, *s.* der Bursche, Diener (*Scotch*).
Gillyflower, *s.* der Goldlack; die Nelke (*rare*).
Gilpy, Gilpey, *s.* der übermütige Bursche, das lustige Mädchen (*Scotch*).
Gilt, I. *imperf. & p.p. of* Gild. II. *s.* die Vergoldung. *Comp.* **—-edged**, *adj.* mit Goldschnitt; hochfein (*C.L. sl.*).
Gimbals, *pl.* die Bügel.
Gimcrack, *s.* der wertlose Kram, Tand; das Spielzeug.
Gimlet, I. *s.* der (Zwick)bohrer. II. *attrib.;* — eye, scharfspähendes Auge, Luchsauge (*coll.*).
Gimp, *s.* der Gimp(f), die Gimpe.
[1]**Gin**, I. *s.* der Wachholderbranntwein. II. *attrib.;* — palace, feiner Branntweinladen, großes Destillationsgeschäft, der Schnapspalast.
[2]**Gin**, I. *s.* der Bock, das Hebezeug (*Mach.*); cotton-—, die Egreniermaschine. III. *v.a.* egrenieren.
[3]**Gin**, *s.* der Fallstrick, die Schlinge.
Ginger, *s.* der Ingwer; das Gelblich-Braun; der Rotkopf (*sl.*). **—ly**, *adv.* behutsam, sachte; to walk —ly, mit vorsichtigen Schritten, zimperlich gehen. *Comp.* **—-beer**, *s.* das Ingwerbier. **—bread**, *s.* der Pfefferkuchen. **—-nut**, *s.* die Pfeffernuß.
Gingham, *s.* der Gingan(g), im Garn gefärbtes Zeug, der Regenschirm (*sl.*).
Gipsy, I. *s.* der (die) Zigeuner(in). II. *adj.* zigeunerartig, Zigeuner-. *Comp.* **—-ring**, *s.* der Ring mit drei einzelnen Steinen (*e.g. two rubies and one diamond*).
Giraffe, *s.* die Giraffe.
Girandole, *s.* großer Armleuchter; die Feuergarbe, das Feuerrad.
[1]**Gird**, *ir.v.a.* gürten; (surround) umgeben; to — on, umgürten; to — up the loins, sich zur Reise anschicken. **—er**, *s.* der Binde-, Trag-balken, das Verbindungsstück (*Build.*); der Brückenträger (*of bridges*). **—le**, *s.* der Gurt, Gürtel.
[2]**Gird**, I. *v.a.* verhöhnen. II. *v.n.* sticheln, spotten (at a p., über einen). III. *s.* der Stich, Spott.
Girdle, *see under* [1]Gird.
Girl, *s.* das Mädchen. **—hood**, *s.* das Mädchentum; die Mädchenjahre. **—ish**, *adj.*, **—ishly**, *adv.* mädchenhaft, jugendlich. **—ishness**, *s.* das Mädchenhafte, das mädchenhafte Wesen.
Girt, *imperf. & p.p. of* Gird.
Girth, *s.* der Gurt; (width) der Umfang.
Gist, *s.* der Hauptpunkt, Kernpunkt, das Wesentliche.
Give, *ir.v.* I. *a.* geben; hergeben, hingeben; (deliver up) abgeben, preisgeben; (bestow upon) verleihen, schenken, erteilen; (grant) gewähren, gestatten; (permit) erlauben; (yield) überlassen; (quit) räumen, verlassen; (cause) verursachen; von sich geben (*a groan, etc.*); zum besten geben (*a song, etc.*); to — attention to, Acht geben auf (*acc.*); to — battle, eine Schlacht liefern; to — chase, Jagd machen auf (*acc.*); to — credit to a report, einem Bericht Glauben schenken *or* beimessen; to — a p. his due, einem das Seinige zukommen lassen; to — ear to, horchen auf (*acc.*); to — an edge to the appetite, den Appetit reizen; to — it to a p., einen durchprügeln, einem tüchtig die Meinung sagen (*sl.*); to — lectures on, Vorlesungen halten über (*acc.*); to — a p. a look, einem einen Blick zuwerfen, einen Blick auf einen werfen, einen anblicken; to — one's mind to, sich auf (eine S.) legen, sich (einer Sache) hingeben; to — offence (pain), beleidigen, Anstoß geben (Schmerz verursachen, weh tun); to — trouble, Mühe machen; to — way, nachgeben; — me the English, ich lobe mir die Engländer! to — **again**, wieder-, zurück-geben; to — **away**, weggeben, überlassen; to — away the bride, die Braut dem Bräutigam übergeben, Brautvater sein; don't — me away, stelle mich nicht bloß! (*coll.*); to — **back**, zurückgeben; to — **forth**, herausgeben, bekannt machen, von sich geben; to — **in**, eingeben, einreichen (*a petition, etc.*); zugeben, dreingeben (*in measuring, etc.*); to — in one's finding (as a juror, als Geschworener) seine Stimme abgeben, stimmen; to — in one's name, sich einschreiben lassen; to — a p. in charge, einen verhaften lassen; to — a th. **into** s.o.'s charge, einem etwas anvertrauen; to — **out**, ausgeben (*money, etc.*); (distribute) austeilen, von sich

geben (*perfume, etc.*), entwickeln (*Chem.*), vorbringen (*a theory, etc.*), bekannt machen, aussprengen (*a report*); to — out (a psalm), zum Singen vorsagen; to — o.s. out as *or* for, sich für (einen Prinzen, &c.) ausgeben; to — **over**, aufgeben (*patients, etc.*), abtreten (*rights*), (surrender) übergeben, überlassen; to — o.s. over (*or* up) to, sich hingeben, sich ergeben; to — **up**, aufgeben (*the ghost, rights, business*); to — o.s. up, sich als Gefangenen stellen, sich ergeben; (— o.s. up for lost), sich für verloren halten; the doctors have —n him up, die Ärzte haben ihn aufgegeben; this ticket must be —n up on demand, dies Billet muß auf Verlangen abgegeben werden; to — o.s. up to a th., sich einer S. hingeben *or* widmen; I — it up, ich gebe es auf, ich kann es nicht raten; to — way, nachgeben. II. *n.* geben; (— way) nachgeben, weichen; to — **in**, nachgeben, weichen; (— in to) einwilligen; to — in to a p.'s opinion, jemandes Meinung beitreten; to — **on**, **upon**, führen in, auf, hinausgehen nach; to — **over**, aufhören. —**n**, *p.p. of* —, & *adj.*; —n to, zu . . . geneigt; to be carnally —n, sinnlich beanlagt sein; a —n time, sum, eine bestimmte Zeit, Summe; I am —n to understand, man hat mir zu verstehen gegeben *or* gesagt, wie ich höre. —**r**, *s.* der Geber; —r of a bill, der Wechselaussteller.

Gizzard, *s.* der Magen (des Vogels).

Glaci—al, *adj.* eisig, Gletscher-. —**er**, *s.* der Gletscher. —**s**, *s.* der Abhang (*Geol.*); das Glacis (*Fort.*).

Glad, *adj.* froh, erfreut (of, at a th., über eine S.); (joyous) heiter, fröhlich, vergnügt; (joyful) freudig, erfreulich; I am — of it, ich freue mich darüber, das freut mich; to be — of heart, frohen Herzens sein; I am — to say, zu meiner Freude. —**den**, *v.a.* froh machen, erfreuen. —**ly**, *adj.* gern, mit Freuden. —**ness**, *s.* die Freude, Fröhlichkeit. —**some**, *adj.* freudig, fröhlich.

Glade, *s.* die Lichtung (im Walde).

Gladi—ator, *s.* der Gladiator. —**atorial**, *adj.* gladiatorisch; —atorial fights, Gladiatorenkämpfe. —**ole**, —**olus**, *s.* der Schwertel, die Siegwurz.

Glair, *s.* das Eiweiß; eiweißartiger Stoff.

Glaive, *s.* das Schwert (*obs. poet.*).

Glamour, *s.* die Augentäuschung; der Zauber.

Glance, I. *s.* (flash) der Blitz, Schimmer; (quick look) der flüchtige Blick; at a —, mit einem *or* auf einen Blick, auf den ersten Blick; to cast a — at, (einen) anblicken; to recognize at first —, auf den ersten Blick erkennen. II. *v.n.* (flash) strahlen, glänzen, schimmern; to — **aside**, anstreifen, abgleiten, leicht berühren; to — **at**, Blicke werfen auf (*acc.*), anblicken, (hint) anspielen, sticheln, *see* — over; to — **off**, abprallen; to — **over**, flüchtig überblicken, mit dem Augen durchlaufen.

Gland, *s.* die Drüse (*Anat.*, *Bot.*). —**ered**, *adj.* rotzig, rotzkrank (*of horses*). —**ers**, *s.* die Druse (*of horses*). —**ular**, *adj.* drüsig.

Glar—e, I. *s.* das Funkeln, der blendende Glanz, Schimmer; der wilde, durchbohrende Blick. II. *v.n.* funkeln, glänzen, blenden; (stare) starren; to —e at *or* upon a p., einen anstarren, anstieren, anglotzen; he —ed at him, er betrachtete ihn mit durchbohrenden Blicken. —**ing**, *adj.*, —**ingly**, *adv.* funkelnd, blendend, grell brennend; (notorious) auffallend, offenkundig; schreiend (*as a crime*); auffallend, grell (*as colours*); starrend; —ing sun, pralle Sonne.

Glass, I. *s.* das Glas; (tumbler) Trinkglas, Wasserglas; (looking-—) der Spiegel; (hour-—) Stundenglas; (weather-—) das (der) Barometer; sheet —, gewöhnliches Fensterglas; plate —, dickes Ladenfensterglas; a — of, ein Glas (voll); broken —, Glasscherben. II. *adj.* gläsern, Glas-; — bottle, die Glasflasche; — bubble, Kolbenglas; — beads, Glaskorallen; — case, das Glasgehäuse; der Glaskasten, Schaukasten; — cover, der Glassturz, die Glasstürze, Glasglocke (*for cheese*); — house, gläsernes Haus; — jar, der Glaszylinder; — shade, die Glasglocke, der Glasschirm. —**es**, *pl.* die Brille, der Kneifer. —**iness**, *s.* das Glasige; die Spiegelglätte (*of roads*). —**y**, *adj.* gläsern; glasig, glasartig; —y stream, durchsichtiger, klarer Bach. *Comp.* —**-blower**, *s.* der Glasbläser. —**works**, *pl.* die Glashütte.

Glaucoma, *s.* grüner Star, das Glaukom(a).

Glaz—e, I. *v.a.* mit Glasscheiben versehen; glasieren (*a cake, etc.; also Paint., Pott.*); glätten (*cloth, paper, etc.*); to —e a window, ein Fenster verglasen; —ed paper, das Glanzpapier. II. *s.* die Glasur; die Glätte; der Glanz (*Photo.*). —**ier**, *s.* der Glaser; —ier's diamond, der Glaserdiamant; —ier's putty, der Glaserkitt. —**ing**, *s.* das Glasieren, die Verglasung; (gloss) die Glasur (*on china, etc.*); das Glätten.

Gleam, I. *s.* der Lichtstrahl, Strahl, Schimmer, Glanz; — of hope, der Hoffnungsstrahl, der Schimmer von Hoffnung. II. *v.n.* strahlen, funkeln, schimmern; (shine) leuchten, scheinen.

Glean, *v.* I. *a.* nachlesen; auflesen (*fig.*); to — from, schließen aus. II. *n.* Ähren lesen. —**er**, *s.* der Ährenleser; der Sammler (*fig.*). —**ing**, *s.* das Nachstoppeln. —**ings**, *pl.* die Nachlese.

Glebe, I. *s.* der Boden; der Pfarracker. II. *attrib.*; — lands, die Pfarräcker und Wiesen.

Glede, *s.* die Gabelweihe (*Orn.*).

Glee, *s.* die Freude, Fröhlichkeit; das Tafellied, der Rund-, Wechsel-gesang. —**ful**, *adj.* fröhlich, vergnügt. —**fulness**, *s.* die Fröhlichkeit. *Comp.* —**-club**, *s.* der Männergesangverein, Quartettverein, die Liedertafel. —**man**, *s.* der Sänger, Musikant; a wandering —man, ein fahrender Spielmann.

Gleed, *s.* die glühende Kohle; (spark) der Funken.

Gleet, *s.* der dünne Eiter.

Gleg, *adj.* klug, schlau, gewitzigt (*Scotch*).

Glen, *s.* nicht bewaldetes, enges, von einem Bergbach durchströmtes Felsental, die Bergschlucht.

Glib, *adj.*, —**ly**, *adv.* glatt, fließend; (voluble) zungenfertig; — tongue, geläufige Zunge. —**ness**, *s.* die Zungenfertigkeit, Geläufigkeit in Reden. *Comp.* —**-tongued**, *adj.* glattzüngig.

Glide, I. *v.n.* sanft fließen; (— along) dahingleiten; (move) gleiten. II. *s.* das Gleiten.

Glim—mer, I. *v.n.* flimmern, glimme(r)n; (shine faintly) schimmern, dämmern. II. *s.* der Schimmer, Glimmer; der Glimmer (*Min.*). —**mering**, *s.* der Schimmer; a faint —mering (*of the truth, etc.*), eine schwache Ahnung. —**pse**, *s.* der Flimmer; (flash) der Lichtblick, Schimmer; (glance) der flüchtige Blick *or* Anblick; to catch a —pse of a p., einen auf einen Augenblick zu sehen bekommen.

Glint, I. *v. n.* glänzen, schimmern. II. *s.* der Schimmer, Glanz, Lichtschein durch eine Ritze.

Glissade, *s.* das Gleiten auf dem Eise (*Mount.*).

Glisten, *v.n.* glänzen, glitzern, schimmern.

Glitter, *v.n.* glitzern, glänzen, funkeln (*also fig.*); all is not gold that —s, nicht alles ist Gold, was glänzt (*prov.*). —**ing**, *adj.*, —**ingly**, *adv.* glänzend, glitzernd.

Gloaming, *s.* die Dämmerung.

Gloat, *v.n.* glotzen, stieren; to — over, sich weiden an (*dat.*).

Glob—ate, *adj.* kugelförmig. —**e**, I. *s.* die Kugel; (earth) die Erdkugel; der Globus (*Geogr.*); the habitable —e, der bewohnbare Erdkreis; —e for a lamp, die Lampenglocke, Lampenkuppel. II. *v.a.* kugelförmig bilden. —**ose**, *see* —ular. —**osity**, *s.* die Kugelgestalt. —**ulous**, —**ular**, *adj.* kugelförmig, rund; —ular chart, der Planiglob. —**ule**, *s.* das Kügelchen. *Comp.* —**e-flower**, *s.* die Kugelblume. —**e-trotter**, *s.* der Weltbummler, Weltdurchstreifer. vielgereister und vielreisender Mann (*coll.*).

Glomerat—e, *adj.* knäuelförmig, geballt. —**ion**, *s.* das Zusammenballen; der geballte Körper.

Gloom, *s.* die Dunkelheit, Düsterkeit; der Trübsinn (*fig.*). —**ily**, *adv. see* —y. —**iness**, *s.* die Düsterheit; die Schwermut (*fig.*). —**y**, *adj.* düster, dunkel; schwermütig, trübsinnig, verdrießlich; —y silence, düsteres Schweigen.

Glor—ification, *s.* die Verherrlichung. —**ified**, *p.p. & adj. see* —ify. —**ify**, *v.a.* verherrlichen; (extol) preisen; (transfigure) verklären; (make blessed) verherrlichen, herrlich machen. —**ious**, *adj.*, —**iously**, *adv.* (worthy of —y) glorreich, erhaben; (illustrious) ruhmvoll; (excellent) herrlich, prächtig. —**iousness**, *s.* die Herrlichkeit. —**y**, I. *s.* die Herrlichkeit; (honour) der Ruhm, die Ehre; (heavenly —y) die himmlische Herrlichkeit, Seligkeit; die Verklärung; die Glorie, der Strahlenhof, Heiligenschein (*Paint.*); love of —y, die Ruhmliebe. II. *v.n.* (rejoice) sich freuen (in a th., über eine S.); stolz sein (in a th., auf eine S.); (boast) sich (einer Sache) rühmen.

[1]**Gloss**, I. *s.* die Glosse, erklärende Bemerkung. II. *v.a. & n.* erklären, auslegen, Bemerkungen machen. —**ary**, *s.* das Wörterverzeichnis, Glossar. —**ographer**, *s.* der Glossator, Kommentator. —**ography**, *s.* das Glossenschreiben. —**ologist**, *s.* der Glossator, der Glossolog. —**ology**, *s.* die Glossologie; die Erläuterung dunkler Wörter.

[2]**Gloss**, I. *s.* der Glanz (*also fig.*); (polish) die Politur, der Firnis; die Glasur (*Pott.*); der äußere Schein (*fig.*). II. *v.a.* glänzend machen; glasieren; *see* Glaze; to — over, beschönigen, bemänteln (*fig.*). —**iness**, *s.* der Glanz, die Glätte, Politur. —**ing**, *s.* das Pressen, die Appretur. —**y**, *adj.* glänzend, glatt, poliert.

Glott—al, *adj.* die Stimmritze betreffend; —al stop, der Kehlkopfsverschlußlaut. —**ic**, *adj.* die Zunge betreffend; sprachwissenschaftlich. —**is**, *s.* die Stimmritze.

Glove, *s.* der Handschuh; a pair of —s, ein Paar Handschuhe; to be hand and —, enge Freunde sein; fencing —s, boxing —s, Fechthandschuhe; furred —s, Pelzhandschuhe; to throw down the —, den Fehdehandschuh hinwerfen; she has won a pair of —s, sie hat Anrecht auf ein Paar Handschuhe (eine Dame, die einen schlafenden Herrn küßt). —**r**, *s.* der Handschuhmacher. *Comp.* —**-box**, *s.* der Handschuhkasten. —**-stretcher**, *s.* der Handschuh(aus)weiter.

Glow, I. *s.* die Glut, das Glühen. II. *v.n.* glühen. —**ing**, *adj.*, —**ingly**, *adv.* glühend. *Comp.* —**-worm**, *s.* der Glühwurm, Leuchtkäfer.

Gloze, I. *v.a.;* to — over, einen Anstrich geben, bemänteln. II. *v.n.* schmeicheln, sanft reden (*obs.*); (on, upon a th., eine S.) falsch deuten. III. *s.* die Schmeichelei; (specious show) der falsche Schein.

Glue, I. *s.* der Leim. II. *v.a.* leimen (*Carp.*); kleben. —**y**, *adj.* klebrig, leimig. *Comp.* —**-pot**, *s.* der Leimtiegel. —**-water**, *s.* der Farbenleim.

Glum, *adj.* mürrisch, sauer, finster.

Glum—aceous, *adj.* spelzig (*Bot.*). —**e**, *s.* die Spelze, der Balg.

Glut, I. *v.a.* verschlingen; (sate) über-sättigen, -füllen; sättigen (*fig. & Chem.*); to — the market, den Markt überfüllen; to — one's revenge, sein Mütchen kühlen. II. *s.* (overmuch) die Über-fülle, -sättigung; (stoppage) die Verstopfung; they are a — in the market, der Markt ist damit überfüllt. —**ton**, *s.* der Schwelger, Schlemmer; der Unersättliche (*fig.*); der Vielfraß (*Zool.*). —**tonous**, *adj.*, —**tonously**, *adv.* gefräßig, gierig, Schwelger-. —**tony**, *s.* die Gefräßigkeit, Schwelgerei.

Glut—en, *s.* der Kleber, das Gluten. —**inous**, *adj.* leimig; leimartig, leimhaltig.

Glycerine, *s.* das Glyzerin.

Glyp—h, *s.* der Glyph, Schlitz. —**hography**, *s.* die Glyphographie. —**tic**, *adj.* mit Bildern (*Min.*); die Steinschneidekunst betreffend.

Gnarl, *v. n.* knurren, brummen. —**ed**, *adj.* knurrig

Gnash, *v.a.* knirschen. —**ing**, *s.;* —ing of teeth, das Zähneknirschen; das Zähneklappern.

Gnat, *s.* die Mücke; mückenartiges Insekt.

Gnaw, *v.a.* nagen. —**er**, *s.* der Nagende; das Nagetier.

Gneiss, *s.* der Gneiß.

Gnom—e, *s.* der Erdgeist, Gnom; die Gnome, der Sinnspruch. —**ic**, *adj.* gnomisch, Spruch-; —ic poetry, die Spruchdichtung. —**on**, *s.* der Sonnenzeiger, das Gnomon. —**onical**, *adj.*, —**onically**, *adv.*, gnomonisch. —**onics**, *s.* die Gnomonik.

Gnostic, I. *adj.* gnostisch. II. *s.* der Gnostiker. —**ism**, *s.* der Gnostizismus.

Go, *ir.v.n.* gehen; (— on) fortgehen; (pass on) dahingehen (to, nach), (— away) abgehen; (move) sich bewegen; (travel) reisen, reiten, fahren (to, nach); (become) werden, in einen Zustand geraten; (be current) gelten; verfließen, vergehen, verstreichen (*as time*); (reach) sich erstrecken, reichen; (fall out) ausfallen; (fare) gehen; gehen, in Gang sein (*Mach.*); to let —, fahren lassen, loslassen; by which train do you —, mit welchem Zuge fahren Sie? to — for a walk (drive), spazieren gehen (fahren); how —es the time? wie spät ist es? ten years had —ne, zehn Jahre waren vergangen *or* verstrichen; be —ne! get you —ne! packt euch! (*vulg.*); I must be —ne *or* —ing, it is getting late, ich muß fort, es wird spät; to — begging, betteln gehen; he went fishing, er ging fischen; he was —ne, er war fort, verschwunden; she went to Germany, to Switzerland, sie reiste nach Deutschland, nach der Schweiz; when I am dead and —ne, wenn ich tot und dahin bin; —ne is —ne, hin ist hin; it shall — hard but . . ., es müßte mit dem Henker zugehen, wenn . . . nicht . . .; to — it strong, entschlossen auftreten, aufschneiden (*sl.*); to — mad, toll werden; to — shares, teilen; to — halves with, Halbpart machen, Gewinn und Verlust teilen; to — wrong, fehl *or* schief gehen, sich irren, auf Abwege geraten; to — a long way, weit *or* lange reichen; to — a great way, weit gehen; — ! los! — it, los damit, vorwärts! to — **aboard** (on board), sich einschiffen; to — **about**, wenden (*Naut.*), umhergehen, gehen um; (attempt) an (eine S.) gehen, etwas vornehmen; to — **abroad**, ins Ausland gehen *or* reisen; (be published) ruchbar werden; to — **after**, nachgehen, nachlaufen; to — **against**, ziehen wider (*an enemy*), (oppose) widerstehen, (disgust) anwidern; to — against the grain, (einem) gegen den Strich gehen; to — **ahead**, vorwärtsgehen; — ahead! vorwärts! weiter! to — **along**, fortgehen, dahingehen; to — along with, begleiten; — along! fort mit dir! (*coll.*); to — **asunder**, auseinander gehen; to — **away**, weggehen, davonkommen; to — **back**, zurückgehen, (retract) zurücknehmen; I have had to — back on my promise, ich habe mein Versprechen zurücknehmen müssen; to — **before**, vorhergehen, (take precedence) den Vorrang haben, vorgehen; to — **behind**, hinterhergehen, folgen; to — **between**, dazwischen gehen (*lit.*), vermitteln zwischen, den Vermittler spielen (*fig.*); to — **by**, vorbei-, vorüber-gehen, (pass) verfließen, (judge by) sich richten nach; to — by the name of . . ., den Namen . . . führen; years —ne by, verflossene, vergangene, entschwundene (*poet.*) Jahre; to — **contrary to**, gehen, handeln gegen; to — **down**, hinuntergehen, sich lagern (*as wind*), (sink) untergehen; die Universität verlassen, sich exmatrikulieren lassen; to — down in the world, in Verfall kommen; his name will — down to posterity, sein Name wird auf die Nachwelt kommen; that won't — down with me, das kann ich nicht glauben; ich lasse mir so etwas nicht gefallen (*sl.*); to — **far**, weitgehen, (effect much) großen Einfluß haben (with, bei); to — **for**, gehen nach, holen, (pass for) gehalten werden für, gelten; **to — for a p.,**

auf einen losgehen (*sl.*); to — **forth**, hervorgehen, (be published) sich verbreiten; to — **forward**, vorwärts gehen, vorrücken, (progress) fortschreiten, (— on) vor sich gehen; to — **from**, weggehen, verlassen, (one's word, sein Wort) nicht halten; to — **in**, hineingehen, gehen in; to — in for, sich eifrig befassen mit, sich legen auf (*acc.*); he —es in for mathematics, er spezialisiert in der Mathematik, er will Mathematiker werden; to — in for rowing, sich viel mit Rudern abgeben; he —es in for being a philosopher, er will für einen Philosophen gelten; to — **into**, gehen in, gehen nach; to — into mourning, trauern, Trauerkleider anlegen; to — into partnership, sich mit einem assoziieren; to — into a matter, eine Sache genau untersuchen; to — **near**, sich nahen; it will — near to . . ., es wird nicht viel daran fehlen, daß . . .; to — **off**, weggehen, abgehen (*as people, trains, etc.*), Abgang finden (*as goods*), vonstatten gehen, ablaufen (*as a ball*); losgehen (*as a gun*); to — **on**, vorwärts gehen, weitergehen; (scold) losfahren, schelten (*vulg.*); (be) sich befinden; (behave) handeln, verfahren, sich benehmen; (progress) fortfahren, Fortgang haben; to — on an embassy, als Gesandter gehen; to — on an expedition, eine Expedition unternehmen; the coat will not — on, ich kann den Rock nicht anziehen; he is —ing on very well, sein Befinden bessert sich, er macht ganz gute Fortschritte, es steht mit seiner Gesundheit ganz gut; to — on horseback, reiten; pray — on, bitte fahren Sie fort! she went on with her story, sie setzte ihre Geschichte fort, sie fuhr in ihrer Geschichte fort; to — **out**, ausgehen (*also of a fire*); aus dem Ministerium scheiden (*Pol.*); to — **over**, gehen über, übersetzen über (*a river*), übergehen (*to a party*), durchgehen (*a paper*), untersuchen, prüfen (*an account*); to — **through**, durchgehen; (experience) bestehen; to — through with, durchsetzen, zustande kommen mit; to — **to**, zu (etwas) gehen; 16 ounces — to a pound, 16 Unzen gehen auf das Pfund; the property —es to his brother, das Besitztum fällt an seinen Bruder; to — to law, einen Prozeß anfangen; to — to work, an die Arbeit *or* ans Werk gehen; to — to sea, in See stechen, zur See gehen; to — to war, Krieg anfangen, Krieg führen; to — **together**, zusammengehen, (suit) zusammenpassen; this will — far **towards** . . ., dies wird zu . . . viel beitragen; to — **under**, gehen unter (the name, dem Namen); to — **up**, hinauf-gehen, -steigen; prices are —ing up, die Preise steigen; to — up to town, nach der Hauptstadt reisen; to — up to the University, (*or simply*) to — up, die Universität beziehen; to — **upon**, gehen auf (*lit.*), sich gründen *or* stützen auf (*fig.*); to — **with**, gehen mit, begleiten, (agree with) es halten mit, (suit) passen zu; to — well (ill) with a p., einem gut (schlecht) ergehen; to — **without**, sich behelfen ohne; entbehren; that —es without saying, das versteht sich von selbst. II. *s.* (*vulg. or sl.*) der Gang; (fashion) die Mode; die Prüfung (*sl.*); Great —, die Hauptprüfung; Little —, die Aufnahmeprüfung (in die Universität Cambridge) (*stud. sl.*); to have a — at, einen Versuch machen mit, probieren (*vulg.*); to be all the —, Furore machen, Mode sein; there is plenty of — in that ballad, es ist viel Schwung in dieser Ballade; it's no —! das geht nicht! always on the —, immer in *or* in fortwährender Bewegung. **—er**, *s.* der Gehende, Läufer (*also of horses*). **—ing**, **—ne**, *see* Going, Gone. *Comp.* **—-ahead**, *adj.* (rasch) fortschreitend, rührig, energisch, tätig. **—-aheadativeness**, *s.* das Vorwärtsstreben, die Rührigkeit, Unternehmungslust, Tatkraft (*Amer.*). **—between**, *s.* der Vermittler. **—by**, *s.*; to give a p. the —-by, einen unbeachtet lassen, ignorieren. **—-cart**, *s.* der Gängelwagen, das Laufgestell für kleine Kinder.

Goad, I. *s.* der Stachelstock. II. *v.a.* anstacheln, anregen (*fig.*).

Goal, *s.* der Pfahl; das Ziel; das Mal, Tor (*Sport.*); der Zweck, das Ziel (*fig.*); das Treiben des Balles durch oder über das Mal (*Football*); to get a —, ein Spiel gewinnen. *Comp.* **—-keeper**, *s.* der Malwächter, Torwächter (*Football*). **—-post**, *s.* die Malstange.

Goat, *s.* die Ziege; he —, der Ziegenbock; the — bleats, die Ziege meckert. **—ish**, *adj.* bockig; geil (*fig.*). *Comp.* **—herd**, *s.* der Ziegenhirt. **—skin**, *s.* das Ziegenfell. **—sucker**, *s.* der Ziegenmelker, die Nachtschwalbe (*Ornith.*).

Gobble, *v.* I. *a.* (— up) hastig verschlingen. II. *n.* kollern (*as a turkey*). **—r**, *s.* der Schlinger; der Truthahn.

Gobelin, *s.* (— tapestry) die Gobelintapete.

Goblet, *s.* der Becher, Pokal.

Goblin, *s.* der Kobold, Gnom, Erdgeist; der Elf.

God, *s.* der Gott; (idol) der Abgott, Götze; der Abgott (*fig.*); would to —, wollte Gott! — be with you, Gott (sei) mit euch! Gott steh' euch bei! **—dess**, *s.* die Göttin. **—head**, *s.* die Gottheit. **—less**, *adj.*, **—lessly**, *adv.* gottlos. **—liness**, *s.* die Frömmigkeit, Gottesfurcht. **—ly**, *adj.* fromm, gottesfürchtig. *Comp.* **—child**, *s.* das Patenkind, Patchen. **—daughter**, *s.* das (weibliche) Patenkind. **—father**, *s.* der Taufpate, Gevatter; to stand —father, Gevatter stehen. **—-fearing**, *adj.* gottesfürchtig. **—-given**, *adj.* von Gott gegeben. **—like**, *adj.* Gott ähnlich; göttlich, erhaben. **—mother**, *s.* die Pate, Patin, Gevatterin. **—send**, *s.* guter, unverhoffter Fund, eine unerwartete Wohltat (Gottes), ein wahrer Segen. **—son**, *s.* das (männliche) Patenkind. **—-speed**, *s.* der Scheidegruß, das Lebewohl; to bid —-speed, glückliche Reise wünschen.

Goggle, *v.n.* die Augen verdrehen *or* rollen (*obs.*). **—s**, *pl.* die Schutzbrille. *Comp.* **—-eye**, *s.* das Glotzauge. **—-eyed**, *adj.* starr-, glotz-äugig.

Going, I. *p. of* Go; gehend; gut gehend, im Gange, im Schwange; vorkommend, vorhanden (*coll.*); to be —, (eben) gehen, reisen; (*before an inf.*) im Begriff sein, gedenken; I was just — to tell you, ich wollte dir eben sagen; he thought he was — to die, er glaubte, er stürbe; we are — to have company to-morrow, morgen werden wir Gesellschaft haben; to keep —, im Gange erhalten; to set a-—, in Gang bringen; a — concern, ein Geschäft in vollem Betrieb, ein schwunghaftes Geschäft; the greatest scoundrel —, der größte Schurke, den es nur giebt; —, —, gone! zum ersten, zum zweiten, zum dritten und letzten) Mal! II. *s.* das Gehen, der Gang; das Angehen (*of meat*); — **back**, das Zurückgehen; there is no — back, das Zurückziehen ist unmöglich, das Los ist gefallen; — **down**, der Untergang (*of the sun*), das Hinabgehen. *Comp.* **—s-on**, *s.* das Verfahren, Treiben, die Handlungsweise; pretty —s-on these! schöne Geschichten wahrhaftig! there were strange —s-on, es ging da bunt her.

Goitr—e, *s.* der Kropf. **—ous**, *adj.* kropfartig.

Gold, I. *s.* das Gold; die Goldmünze; das Geld (*fig.*); all is not — that glitters, es ist nicht alles Gold, was glänzt (*prov.*). II. *adj.* golden, Gold-. **—en**, *adj.* golden; —en number, rule, age, goldene Zahl, Regel, Zeit; —en opinions, gute Meinung (anderer); a —en key opens every lock, mit Gold kommt man überall durch; —en pudding, Sirup-Pudding. *Comp.* **—beater**, *s.* der Goldschläger. **—beater's-skin**, *s.* das Goldschlägerhäutchen. **—-dust**, *s.* der Goldstaub. **—en-crested**, *adj.*; —en-crested wren, das Goldhähnchen. **—en-pheasant**, *s.* der Goldfasan. **—finch**, *s.* der Stieglitz, Distelfink. **—fish**, *s.* der Goldfisch. **—lace**, *s.* die Goldtresse. **—leaf**, *s.* das Goldblatt. **—-mounted**, *adj.* in Gold gefaßt. **—smith**, *s.* der Goldschmied. **—stick**, *s.*; —stick in waiting, der Oberst der königlichen Leibgarde im Dienste. **—ylocks**, *s.*

das Goldhaar (*Bot.*); goldhaariger Hahnenfuß (*Bot.*).

Golf, *s.* das Golfspiel, Lochballspiel. **—er**, *s.* der Golfspieler. **—ing**, I. *s.* das Golfspielen. II. *attrib.;* —ing suit, der Golfanzug. *Comp.* **—-links**, *pl.* der Golfspielplatz.

Golosh, *s. see* Galoche.

Gondol—a, *s.* die Gondel, das venetianische Ruderboot. **—ier**, der Gondelführer, Gondolier.

Gone, I. *p.p. of* Go. II. *adj.* tot; verloren; fort; he is a — coon, es ist aus mit ihm (*Amer. sl.*).

Gonfalon, *s.* der Gonfalon, die Schlachtfahne.

Gong, *s.* der Gong, das flache Metallbecken.

Goniomet—er, *s.* der Winkelmesser. **—ry**, *s.* die Winkelmeßkunst.

Gonorrhea, *s.* der Samenfluß.

Good, I. (Better, Best) *adj.* gut; (kind) gütig, freundlich; gangbar (*as coins*); gültig (*Law*); gut, sicher, zahlungsfähig (*C. L.*); (just) gerecht; (virtuous) tugendhaft, fromm, gut; (fit) passend, gut, schicklich; (beneficial) heilsam; gut, frisch (*as meat*); unverdorben (*as fruit*); vollständig, völlig (*as a number*); (useful) nützlich, schätzbar; a — old age, ein hohes Alter; as — as, ebenso gut wie; to be as — as one's word, sein Wort halten; — at, geschickt in (*dat.*); on — authority, aus guter Quelle; — creature, herzensgute Person; a — deal, viel; in — earnest, in vollem Ernste; — for, gut gegen (*disease, etc.*) *or* für; what is it — for? wozu nützt es? a — half, reichlich die Hälfte; — health, das Wohlbefinden; to hold —, gelten (für), Anwendung finden (auf, *acc.*); — luck! viel Glück! you make — the proverb, Sie machen das Sprichwort wahr; to make — (a loss to a p.), (einen) entschädigen (für eine S.); to make — one's escape, seine Entweichung *or* Flucht glücklich bewerkstelligen; a — many, viele; I have a — mind, ich hätte wohl Lust; — news, erfreuliche Nachricht; to stand —, giltig bleiben; to think, see —, für gut *or* passend halten; in — time, zu rechter Zeit; (early) bei Zeiten; a — turn, eine glückliche Wendung, (kindness) eine Gefälligkeit; to do a p. a — turn, einem eine Gefälligkeit erweisen; a — while, eine gute Weile. II. *adv.* gut; as — as, so gut wie; as —, eben so gut *or* wohl; he has as — as . . ., es ist so gut als hätte er . . . III. *s.* (benefit) das Gute, Wohl, Beste; a strong influence for —, ein starker Einfluß zum Guten; the —, (*pl.*) die Gerechten, Frommen; —s, Güter, Waren; dry-—s, Kurzwaren, Schnittwaren; soft —s, Tuchwaren; white —s, Weißwaren; —s and chattels, Hab und Gut; the — of the state, das Wohl des Staates; for the — of one's health, seiner Gesundheit wegen; much — may it do you! wohl bekomm' es Ihnen! for —, auf immer; he is gone for —, er ist fort auf Nimmerwiedersehn; what — will it do you? was wird es Ihnen helfen? I can do no — here, ich kann hier nichts nützen; it does me — to see you, es macht mir Freude, Sie zu sehen. IV. *int.* gut; sehr recht! very —, sir, zu Befehl, Herr (Leutnant, Oberst usw.); —, said my aunt, schön, sagte meine Tante. **—ish**, *adj.;* —ish deal, ziemlich viel (*coll.*). **—liness**, *s.* die Anmut. **—ly**, *adj.* schön, anmutig; (pleasant) angenehm; (fine) stattlich; a —ly number, viele. **—ness**, *s.* die Güte (*also of meat*); (excellence) die Vortrefflichkeit; (piety) die Frömmigkeit; (kindness) die Güte, Gütigkeit; (soundness) die Frische; for —ness' sake! um's Himmelswillen; my —ness! ach je! —ness gracious! du meine Güte! ach du liebe Zeit! *Comp.* **—-breeding**, *s.* die gute Erziehung, Bildung, feine Lebensart. **—bye**, I. *s.* das Lebewohl; to wish —bye, (einem) lebewohl sagen. II. *int.* lebewohl! adieu! **—-day**, *int.* guten Tag. **—-fellowship**, *s.* die (gute) Kameradschaft; lustige Gesellschaft. **—-Friday**, *s.* der Karfreitag. **—-humour**, *s.* gute Laune. **—-humoured**, *adj.*, **—-humouredly**, *adv.* bei guter Laune, fröhlich gestimmt; gutmütig. **—-living**, *s.* die Feinschmeckerei, Schwelgerei. **—man**, *s.* der Ehemann. **—-nature**, *s.* die Gutmütigkeit. **—-natured**, *adj.* gutmütig. **—-night**, I. *s.* der Nachtgruß. II. *adv.* gute Nacht. **—-sense**, *s.* der gesunde Menschenverstand. **—-speed**, *s.* (—-luck) das Glück; (success) der Erfolg. **—s-train**, *s.* der Güterzug. **—s-traffic**, *s.* der Güterverkehr. **—-temper**, *s.* (—-humour) die gute Laune; die Sanftmut, Gleichmütigkeit. **—-tempered**, *adj.* gut gelaunt; sanft-, gutmütig. **—wife**, *s.* die Hausfrau. **—will**, *s.* das Wohlwollen, die Gunst, Zuneigung; die Kundschaft (*C. L.*); to buy the —will of a house, die Kundschaft mit der Firma zugleich kaufen.

[1]**Goody**, *adj.* frömmelnd, zimperlich; — —, süßlich.

[2]**Goody** (*from* Goodwife), *s.* gute Frau, Frau Gevatterin.

[3]**Goody**, *s.* das Zuckerwerk, Bonbon (*coll.*).

Goosander, *s.* der Sägetaucher.

Goose, *s.* (*pl.* Geese) die Gans; das Bügeleisen (*Tail.*); all his geese are swans, bei ihm ist immer alles besser als bei andern; what is sauce to the — is sauce to the gander, was dem einen recht ist, ist dem andern billig; the — cackles, gaggles, die Gans schnattert; wild-— chase, unnütze, planlose Verfolgung, törichte abenteuerliche Unternehmung. **—y**, *s.* das Gänschen. *Comp.* **—-egg**, *s.* das Gänseei; der Mißerfolg (*fig.*). **—-flesh**, *s.* die Gänsehaut (*fig.*). **—grass**, *s.* das Klebekraut. **—quill**, *s.* der Gänsekiel. **—-skin**, *s.* die Gänsehaut. **—winged**, *adj.* mit in der Mitte festgemachtem Untersegel.

Gooseberry, *s.* die Stachelbeere. *Comp.* **—-fool**, *s.* das Stachelbeer(en)mus; Stachelbeer-Crême. **—-wine**, *s.* der Stachelbeerwein.

Gopher-wood, *s.* das Holz, aus dem Noah seine Arche baute.

Gordian, *adj.;* — knot, der gordische Knoten; to cut the — knot, den gordischen Knoten zerhauen.

[1]**Gore**, I. *s.* die Gehre, der Zwickel (*Semp.*); das dreieckige Stückchen. II. *v.a.* vergehren, in Zwickel schneiden (*Semp.*); durch-bohren, -stechen (*as bulls*).

[2]**Gor—e**, *s.* geronnenes Blut. **—y**, *adj.* blutig.

Gorge, I. *s.* die Gurgel, Kehle, der Schlund; (pass) die (Berg-)Schlucht, der (Gebirgs-)Paß; der Säulenhals (*Arch.*); (hollow moulding) die Hohlleiste; die Kehle (*Fort.*); (what is —d) das Verschluckte, das zu Verschlingende, Futter; my — rises, es wird mir übel. II. *v.a.* verschlingen; (sate) vollpfropfen. III. *v.n.* fressen. **—ous**, *adj.*, **—ously**, *adv.* prächtig, glänzend, prunkhaft, Prunk-. **—ousness**, *s.* die Pracht, der Prunk. **—t**, *s.* die Halsberge (*obs.*); das Halstuch (*of women*) (*obs.*); der Halskragen (*of officers*).

Gorgonzola, *s.* der Gorgonzola-Käse.

Gorilla, *s.* der Gorill(a).

Gormand, I. *s.* der Fresser. II. *adj.* gefräßig. **—ize**, *v.n.* fressen, schlemmen. **—izing**, *s.* die Schlemmerei.

Gorse, *s.* der Stechginster.

Gosha, *adj.* abgeschlossen, sich nicht öffentlich zeigend.

Gos—hawk, *s.* der Hühnerhabicht. **—ling**, *s.* das Gänschen.

Gospel, I. *s.* das Evangelium; all he says is not to be taken for —, nicht alles ist wahr, was er spricht. II. *attrib.;* — truth, buchstäbliche Wahrheit; to take a th. as — truth, etwas auf Treu und Glauben hinnehmen. **—ler**, *s.* der Vorleser des Evangeliums am Altar.

Gossamer, *s.* die dünne Gaze, die Sommerfäden, der Altweibersommer (*coll.*).

Gossip, I. *s.* (tattler) die Schwätzerin, Klatschbase; (male —) Klatsche; (crony) die Frau Base; (sponsor) der (die) Gevatter(in); (tattle) der Klatsch; die Klatschgeschichte, das Geschwätz. II. *v.n.* schwatzen. **—ing**, *s.* das Geklatsch. **—y**, *adj.* geschwätzig; gemütlich schwatzend *or* plaudernd.

Gossoon, *s.* der Bursche (*Irish*).
Got, *imperf. & p.p.*, **—ten**, *p.p. of* Get.
Gouge, I. *s.* der Hohlmeißel, das Hohleisen; die Güdse (*Naut.*); das Flachhohleisen (*Sculpt.*); der Hohlstichel (*Engr.*). II. *v.a.* ausmeißeln.
Gourd, *s.* der Kürbiß; die Kürbisflasche.
Gourmet, *s.* der Feinschmecker; *see* Gormand.
Gout, *s.* die Gicht; (foot —) das Podagra. **—iness**, das Gichtische. **—y**, *adj.* gichtisch; he is rather —y, er hat Anlage zur Gicht.
Govern, *v.* I. *a.* regieren, beherrschen, verwalten; regieren (*Gram.*). II. *n.* regieren, herrschen. **—able**, *adj.* lenksam, folgsam. **—ess**, *s.* die Gouvernante, Erzieherin. **—ing**, *adj.* herrschend; leitend; —ing body, das Kuratorium. **—ment**, I. *s.* (conduct) die Regierung, Führung, Leitung; die Beherrschung, Herrschaft (of, über); die Regierung (*of a state*); (system of —ment) die Regierungsform, Verfassung; (council) das Ministerium; (province) der Regierungsbezirk; (guidance) die Richtschnur; das Regieren (*Gram.*); British —ment, die britische Regierung; military —ment, die Militärverwaltung; petticoat —ment, das Weiberregiment; self-—ment, die Selbstbeherrschung. II. *attrib.;* —ment grant, die Staatsunterstützung; —ment loan, die Staatsanleihe; —ment office, die Regierungskanzlei; —ment official, der Staatsbeamte; —ment securities, die (*pl.*) Staatspapiere. **—mental**, *adj.* Regierungs-. **—or**, *s.* (ruler) der (Be-)Herrscher, Regent; der Statthalter (*of a province, etc.*); (administrator) der Verwalter; (tutor) der Hofmeister; (father) der Vater, Alte (*sl.*); (principal) der Prinzipal (*sl.*); der Regulator (*Mach.*); —ors (of a school), der leitende Ausschuß *or* das Kuratorium (einer Schule). **—orship**, *s.* die Statthalterschaft. *Comp.* **—or-general**, *s.* der Generalgouverneur, Vizekönig.
Gown, *s.* das Frauenkleid; das Amtsgewand, der Talar (*of university teachers and students*); cap and —, Barett und Talar; town and —, Philister und Bursche, Philister und Studenten, Bürgerschaft und Universität. *Comp.* **—sman**, *s.* der Student, das Mitglied der Universität (zu Oxford und Cambridge).
Graal, *s. see* Grail.
Grab, I. *v.a.* ergrapsen. II. *v.n.* haschen, greifen (at, nach). III. *s.* **der Graps.** **—ber**, *s.* der Habsüchtige, **Geizhals; land-—ber, der Landgierige; money-—ber, der Geldgierige, Geldmensch.**
Grace, I. *s.* (favour) die Gunst, Gnade, das Wohlwollen; (mercy) die Gnade, Verzeihung; (pleasingness) die Anmut, der Reiz; (—fulness) die Grazie; (accomplishment, etc.) die Zier(de); (indulgence) die Nachsicht; die Gnade (of God, Gottes); with a good —, mit guter Manier, freundlich, bereitwillig; with a bad —, mit Widerstreben, widerwillig; by the — of God, von Gottes Gnaden; (kindness) die Gunstbezeugung; to say —, das Tischgebet sprechen; your —, Euer Gnaden; day of —, der Gnadentag; days of —, die Gnadenfrist (*C.L.*); — of the Senate, der dem Senat zur Billigung vorgelegte Gesetzentwurf (*in Cambridge*); by — of the Senate, durch Senatsbeschluß; the — has been rejected, der Senat hat den Entwurf abgelehnt. II. *v.a.* schmücken, zieren; (honour) beehren, begünstigen. **—ful**, *adj.*, **—fully**, *adv.* anmutig, hold, graziös; (appropriate) passend; a —ful remark, eine hübsche, artige, freundliche Bemerkung. **—fulness**, *s.* die Anmut, Grazie, Zierlichkeit. **—less**, *adj.* reizlos; gottlos; (depraved) verworfen. **—s**, *pl.* Verzierungen (*Mus.*), Grazien (*Myth.*); to get into a p.'s good —s, jemandes Gunst erlangen.
Gracious, *adj.*, **—ly**, *adv.* (affable) gütig, huldreich, wohlwollend; (kind) freundlich; (merciful) gnädig, gnadenvoll; (graceful) anmutig; — goodness! du meine Güte! good —! lieber Himmel! **—ness**, *s.* die Gnade (*also* of God), Huld, Freundlichkeit; die Anmut.
Grad—ate, *v.a.* abstufen, allmählich in einander übergehen lassen. **—ation**, *s.* der Stufengang, die Stufenfolge; die Reihenfolge; die Abstufung (*Paint.*); die Steigerung (*Rhet.*); die Folgenreihe (*Log.*); der Ablaut (*of vowels*) (*Gram.*). **—e**, *s.* der Grad, Rang; (step) die Stufe; die Neigung (*Railw.*); high —e, die Hochstufe (*of accent*); higher —e school, höhere Volksschule; various —es of tea, verschiedene Sorten Tee. **—ient**, *s.* (ascending) die Steigung; (descending) die Neigung, das Gefälle. **—ual**, I. *adj.*, **—ually**, *adv.*, stufenweise fortschreitend; allmählich. II. *s.* das Graduale. **—uate**, I. *v.a* in Grade abteilen, abstufen; (advance) allmählich steigern; gradieren (*Chem.*); mit einer Skala versehen (*Phys.*); fein abstufen, schattieren (*fig.*); —uated measures, Mensuren (*Chem., Pharm.*). II. *v.n.* sich abstufen; graduieren, einen akademischen Grad erlangen, promovieren (*Univ.*). III. *adj.;* —uate student, der Graduierte, welcher nach Ablegung seiner Prüfungen seine Studien an der Universität noch weiter verfolgt; to —uate in classics, sich (*dat.*) einen Universitätsgrad in der klassischen Philologie erringen; to —uate with A. B., seinen B. A. machen (*Amer.*). IV. *s.* der, welcher den ersten Universitätsgrad errungen hat, der Graduierte; girl —uate, junges Mädchen, welches einen Universitätsgrad errungen hat. **—uation**, *s.* der Stufengang; die Gradierung (*Chem.*); der Abteilung in Grade (*Phys.*); die Promovierung (*Univ.*). **—uator**, *s.* der Gradmesser (*Math.*).
Graft, I. *v.a.* pfropfen, impfen; (insert) einfügen; einimpfen (*fig.*). II. *s.* das Propfreis. **—er**, *s.* der Pfropfende. *Comp.* **—ing-knife**, *s.* das Propfmesser.
Grain, I. *s.* das Korn, Getreide (*coll.*); das Korn, Körnchen (*of sand, sugar, salt, powder, truth*); der Gran (*apothecaries' measure*); das Grän, Aß (*of gold, etc.*); die Lagerung, Struktur (*of a stone*); die Längenrichtung, die Längenfasern (*in wood*); die Adern, Narben, das Korn, der Strich (*in leather*); dyed in the —, in der Wolle gefärbt; against the —, wider den Strich, widerwillig (*fig.*); it goes against the — (with me), es geht mir gegen den Strich, ist mir sehr zuwider. II. *attrib.;* — crop, der Kornwuchs, die Getreideernte. III. *v.a.* adern, marmorieren (*wood*), abnarben (*leather*).
Gramary(e), *s.* die Zauberkunst.
Gramin—eal, **—eous**, *adj.* grasartig. **—ivorous**, *adj.* Gras fressend.
Gramma—logue, *s.* die Sigle. **—r**, *s.* die Grammatik; that is good (bad) —ar, das ist grammatisch richtig (falsch). **—rian**, *s.* der Grammatiker. **—tical**, *adj.*, **—tically**, *adv.* grammatisch. *Comp.* **—r-school**, *s.* die lateinische Schule, Gelehrtenschule; die Mittelschule (*Amer.*).
Grammophone, *s.* das Grammophon.
Grampus, *s.* der Butzkopf.
Granary, *s.* der Speicher.
Grand, *adj.*, **—ly**, *adv.* (great) groß; (noble, great) groß, vornehm; (lofty) hoch, großartig, erhaben, sublim; (splendid) herrlich, prächtig, stattlich; — piano(forte), der Flügel; short — (piano), kleiner Flügel; oblique —, Konzertflügel. **—am**, *s.* die Großmutter; altes Mütterchen. **—ee**, *s.* der Grande (*in Spain*); der Große, Magnat. **—eur**, *s.* die Größe, Pracht, Hoheit, Würde, Herrlichkeit; die Erhabenheit (*of thought, expressions, sentiments, etc.*). **—iloquence**, *s.* die Schwülstigkeit der Rede, der Redeprunk. **—iloquent**, *adj.*, **—iloquently**, *adv.* hochtrabend, schwülstig. **—iose**, *adj.* erhaben grandios; imponierend, (pompous) hochtrabend, prunkvoll. **—ness**, *s.* die Erhabenheit; *see* —eur. *Comp.* **—child**, *s.* der Enkel, die Enkelin, das Großkind. **—dad**, *s.* der Großvater (*coll.*). **—**

daughter, *s.* die Enkelin, Großtochter. **—-duchess**, *s.* die Großherzogin. **—-duchy**, *s.* das Großherzogtum. **—-duke**, *s.* der Großherzog. **—father**, *s.* der Großvater; —father's clock, die hohe Standuhr. **—-juror**, *s.* das Mitglied der Anklagejury. **—-jury**, *s.* die Anklagejury. **—-Master**, *s.* der Großmeister (*also Free-m.*). **—mother**, *s.* die Großmutter. **—nephew**, *s.* der Großneffe. **—niece**, *s.* die Großnichte. **—parent**, *s.* der Großvater, die Großmutter; (*pl.*) Großeltern. **—sire**, *s.* der Großvater; (forefather) der Ahnherr. **—son**, *s.* der Enkel, Großsohn. **—-stand**, *s.* die Tribüne (bei Wettrennen). **—-vizier**, *s.* der Großvezier.

Grange, *s.* der (abgelegene) Meierhof; die Loge des Ordens der 'patrons of husbandry' (*Amer.*)

Gran—iferous, *adj.* körnertragend. **—ite**, I. *s.* der Granit. II. *adj.* granitartig, Granit-. **—itic**, *adj. see* —ite II.; zum Granit gehörig. **—ular**, *adj.* körnig, gekörnt; (like grain) körnicht; —ular limestone, der Roggenstein; —ular ore, natürliches Graupenerz. **—ulate**, *v.a.* granulieren, körnen; (roughen) mit einer rauhen Oberfläche versehen. **—ulated**, *adj.* feinkörnig. **—ulation**, *s.* das Granulieren (*also Chem.*); das Körnen (*of powder*); die Granulation (*Med.*). **—ule**, *s.* das Körnchen. **—ulous**, *adj.* körnig.

Granny, *s.* das Großmütterchen (*coll.*).

Grant, I. *v.a.* bewilligen, gewähren, gestatten, zulassen; (admit) zugeben, zugestehen, einräumen; verwilligen (*lands*); to take for —ed, für ausgemacht, als erwiesen annehmen; it is taken for —ed, es wird vorausgesetzt *or* angenommen; —ing this be true, angenommen, dies wäre wahr; God — . . .! Gott gebe! II. *s.* die Bewilligung, Gewährung, Erteilung; (gift, *etc.*) die (schriftliche) Schenkung, überwiesene Sache; (money —) bewilligte pekuniäre Unterstützung (von Schulen, 2c). **—ee**, *s.* der Begünstigte. **—er**, *s.* der Bewilliger.

Grape, *s.* die (Wein-)Traube, Weinbeere. **—ry**, *s.* das Weintreibhaus. *Comp.* **—-crusher**, *s.* die Traubenquetsche. **—shot**, *s.* (Trauben-) Kartätschen. **—stone**, *s.* der Traubenkern. **—-vine**, *s.* der Weinstock.

Graph—ic, *adj.*, **—ically**, *adv.* graphisch (*also fig.*); schildernd, malerisch; anschaulich, lebhaft (*description*); deutlich, bildlich, getreu. **—ite**, *s.* der Graphit, das Reißblei. **—itic**, *adj.* graphitisch. **—ology**, *s.* die Beurteilung des Charakters aus der Handschrift, Graphologie. **—ometer**, *s.* der Graphometer. **—ophone**, *s.* das Graphophon.

Grap—nel, *s.* (anchor) der Dreganker; der Enterhaken (*Naut.*). **—ple**, I. *v.a.* verklammern (*Build.*); anhaken (*Naut.*). II. *v.n.* ringen, handgemein werden; to —ple with, eine S. ernstlich in Angriff nehmen *or* anfassen, sich ernstlich an eine S. machen. III. *s.* der Schiffshaken, Enterhaken. *Comp.* **—pling-hook**, **—pling-iron**, *see* —ple III.

Grasp, I. *v.a.* greifen; ergreifen, sich (*dat.*) anmaßen (*fig.*); begreifen (*an idea, etc.*); — all, lose all, wer zuviel unternimmt, beendet wenig. II. *v.n.;* to — at, nach einer S. greifen, streben (*fig.*). III. *s.* der Griff; die Gewalt; die Fassungskraft; in s. o.'s —, in jemandes Gewalt; within the — of, im Bereiche von. **—ing**, *adj.* habgierig, geizig.

Grass, *s.* das Gras, der Rasen; to put, turn out to —, auf die Weide treiben, schicken; meadow —, Rispen-, Vieh-gras. **—iness**, *s.* das Grasige, die Fülle von Gras. **—y**, *adj.* grasig, grasreich; grün (wie Gras). *Comp.* **—-cloth**, *s.* das Grasleinen. **—-green**, *adj.* grasgrün. **—hopper**, *s.* der Grashüpfer. **—land**, *s.* das Grasland, Weideland. **—-plot**, *s.* der Rasenplatz. **—-widow**, *s.* die Strohwittwe; das Mädchen, das ein uneheliches Kind hat (*dial.*).

[1]**Grat—e**, *s.* der (Feuer-)Rost; (—ing) das Gitter. **—ed**, *adj.* mit einem Gitter versehen. **—ing**, *s.* das Gitter, Gatter, die Vergitterung.

[2]**Grat—e**, *v.* I. *a.* kratzen, raspeln; reiben (*to powder, etc.*); (offend) beleidigen, verletzen; to —e the teeth, mit den Zähnen knirschen. II. *n.* kratzen, knarren, knirschen, schwirren; to —e upon the nerves, die Nerven verletzen, auf die Nerven gehen, den Nerven wehe tun (*fig.*). **—er**, *s.* das Reibeisen. **—ing**, *adj.* knirschend, mißtönig, grell, schrill; widrig; unangenehm, aufreizend.

Grat—eful, *adj.*, **—efully**, *adv.* dankbar, erkenntlich; (pleasing) angenehm, zusagend, wohltätig; —eful to me (you), dankbar gegen mich (dich). **—efulness**, *s.* die Dankbarkeit, Erkenntlichkeit. **—ification**, *s.* die Befriedigung (*of the palate, senses, taste, mind, etc.*); (satisfaction) die Freude, das Vergnügen, der Genuß; (—uity) das Geschenk. **—ify**, *v.a.* befriedigen, (einem) willfahren, gefällig sein; (please) erfreuen; to —ify a wish, einen Wunsch erfüllen *or* befriedigen. **—ifying**, *adj.* erfreulich. **—is**, *adv.* unentgeltlich, umsonst. **—itude**, *s.* die Dankbarkeit, Erkenntlichkeit. **—uitous**, *adj.*, **—uitously**, *adv.* unentgeltlich, umsonst; freiwillig; (unmerited) unverdient, grundlos, willkürlich. **—uity**, *s.* das kleine Geldgeschenk, das Trinkgeld. **—ulatory**, *see* Congratulatory.

Grav—amen, *s.* der Beschwerde- *or* Klage-punkt. **—e**, *adj.*, **—ely**, *adv.* ernst(haft), gesetzt; feierlich; (weighty) wichtig; prunklos, dunkelfarben (*as dress*); —e accent, der Gravis, das Graviszeichen; —e writer, ernsthafter Schriftsteller. **—imeter**, *s.* das Gravimeter, der Dichtigkeitsmesser, der Schweremesser. **—itate**, *v.n.* gravitieren. **—itation**, *s.* die Schwerkraft, Gravitation; law of —itation, das Gesetz der Schwere. **—ity**, *s.* die Schwere (*Phys.*); die Wichtigkeit, Größe, Bedenklichkeit (*of a fact, crime, etc.*); (solemnity) der Ernst, die Ernsthaftigkeit, Gesetztheit; die Feierlichkeit, Würde; force of —ity, die Schwerkraft; centre of —ity, der Schwerpunkt; specific —ity, das spezifische Gewicht.

[1]**Grave**, *see under* Grav—amen.

[2]**Grave**, I. *v.a. & n.* (*p.p.* —d & —n) graben, eingraben (*also fig.*); stechen, schnitzen. II. *s.* das Grab; to have one foot in the —, mit einem Fuß im Grabe stehen. **—n**, *adj.;* —n image, das Götzenbild. **—r**, *s.* der Bildstecher; (tool) der Grabstichel. *Comp.* **—-clothes**, *pl.* Sterbekleider. **—-digger**, *s.* der Totengräber. **—-side**, *s.* das offene Grab. **—-yard**, *s.* der Friedhof (*Amer.*)

[3]**Grav—e**, *v.a.* kalfatern (*Naut.*). **—y**, *s.* der Fleischsaft, Bratensaft, das Bratenfett. *Comp.* **—ing-dock**, *s.* das Trockendock, Kalfaterdock. **—y-boat**, *s.* die Schale für Bratenfett. **—y-soup**, *s.* die Kraftbrühe, Fleischbrühe.

Gravel, I. *s.* der Kies, Gries; der (Nieren-, Blasen-, 2c.) Gries (*Med.*). II. *attrib.;* —walk, der Kiesweg. III. *v.a.* bekiesen, mit Kies bedecken, bestreuen. **—ly**, *adj.* kiesig, Kies-. *Comp.* **—-pit**, *s.* die Kiesgrube.

Gray, I. *adj.* grau; — friar, der Kapuziner; the friar of orders —, der Bruder Graurock, Kapuziner; the — mare is the better horse, die Frau führt das Regiment. II. *s.* das Grau; — of the morning, die Morgendämmerung. **—ish**, *adj.* ziemlich grau. **—ness**, *s.* die Äsche; das Graue. *Comp.* **—-beard**, *s.* der Graubart. **—-haired**, *adj.* grauhaarig. **—-headed**, *adj.* grauköpfig. **—hound**, *see* Greyhound.

[1]**Graz—e**, *v.* I. *a.* abgrasen, weiden. II. *n.* grasen, weiden. **—er**, *s.* der Grasende. **—ier**, *s.* der Viehzüchter, Viehmäster. **—ing**, I. *attrib.;* —ing land, das Wiesenland, Weideland. II. *s.* das Weiden; die Weide, Trift.

[2]**Graze**, I. *v.a.* streifen, leicht berühren; grazing fire, bestreichendes Feuer (*Artil.*). II. *s.* die Schramme; der Aufschlag (*Artil.*).

Greas—e, I. *s.* das Fett, (der) Schmer; die

Schmiere; die Mauke (*Vet.*). II. *v.a.* schmieren; (soil) beschmieren, beflecken; to —e a cake-tin *or* mould, eine Form zum Backen ausstreichen. **—iness**, *s.* das Schmierige, die Fettheit, Fettigkeit. **—y**, *adj.* schmierig, fettig; (oily) fettartig, ölartig; (dirty) schmutzig, garstig. *Comp.* **—e-box**, *s.* die Schmierbüchse. **—e-chamber**, *s.* die Schmierkammer; der Schmierbehälter (*Locom.*). **—e-spot**, *s.* der Fettfleck, Schmierfleck.

Great, I. *adj.* groß (*as a house, number, distance, time, etc.*); (important) wichtig; (exalted) erhaben; (mighty) mächtig; (venerable) ehrwürdig; (eminent) ruhmvoll, berühmt; (remarkable) wunderbar; (magnificent) prächtig, prachtvoll; (noble) hochherzig, großmütig; — Britain, Großbritannien; —er Britain, Großbritannien und seine Kolonieen; a — friend, ein vertrauter *or* intimer Freund; — with young, trächtig; a — deal, sehr viel; a — many, sehr viele; a — way, ein weiter Weg; a — while, eine lange Zeit, lange; in — favour, in hoher Gunst (with a p., bei einem); — circles, die Gleicher (*Astr.*); the — powers, die Großmächte; the — seal, das große Staatssiegel; it is no — matter, es macht nicht viel aus; she is — on the piano, sie spielt famos Klavier (*coll.*). II. *pl.* die Großen, Vornehmen. **—ly**, *adv.* in hohem Grade, beträchtlich. **—ness**, *s.* die Größe, die Bedeutung, Wichtigkeit; die Würde, Gewalt, Herrschaft, der hohe Rang; die Erhabenheit, Größe (*of the mind, etc.*); (gloriousness) die Herrlichkeit; die Kraft, Stärke (*of heat, sounds, passions, etc.*). *Comp.* **—coat**, *s.* der Überrock. **—-grandchild**, *s.* der (die) Urenkel(in). **—-grandfather**, *s.* der Urgroßvater. **—-—-grandfather**, *s.* der Ururgroßvater. **—-hearted**, **—-minded**, *adj.* hochherzig.

[1]**Greaves**, *pl.* die Beinschienen.

[2]**Greaves, Graves**, *pl.* die Talggrieben.

Grebe, *s.* der Steißfuß.

Greed—iness, *s.* die Gierigkeit (*also fig.*), Gefräßigkeit. **—y**, *adj.*, **—ily**, *adv.* gierig (*also fig.*), gefräßig; —y of gain, geldgierig, gewinnsüchtig.

Green, I. *adj.* grün; (fresh) neu, frisch; grün, frisch (*as wood, etc.*); unreif (*as fruit*); unerfahren, einfältig (*sl.*); — in one's memory, noch in frischem Andenken; — old age, frisches Greisenalter. II. *s.* das Grün, die grüne Farbe; der Grasplatz, Anger; (leaves, *etc.*) das Laub; —s, (*pl.*) das Gemüse; der Grünkohl; bunch —s, Küchenkräuter (auf dem Gemüsemarkt). **—ery**, *s. see* —house; grüne Pflanzen. **—ish**, *adj.* grünlich. **—ness**, *s.* das Grün(e); die Frische (*fig.*); die Unreife; die Unerfahrenheit, Einfalt (*sl.*). *Comp.* **—back**, *s.* der Schatzkammerschein (*Amer.*). **—-crop**, *s.* die noch auf dem Halme stehende Ernte von frischen Gartengewächsen. **—-eyed**, *adj.* grünäugig; argwöhnisch (*fig.*). **—finch**, *s.* der Grünfink. **—-fly**, *s.* die Blattlaus. **—gage**, *s.* die Reine-Claude (plum, Pflaume). **—-goods**, *pl.* falsche Banknoten (*Amer.*). **—-goose**, *s.* das Gänschen; die dumme Person (*fig.*). **—grocer**, *s.* der Obst-, Gemüse-, Grünkram-händler. **—groceries**, *pl.* die Obstwaren, Gemüsewaren, der Grünkram. **—horn**, *s.* der Grünschnabel, unerfahrene Junge, Neuling. **—house**, *s.* das Gewächshaus. **—-room**, *s.* das Versammlungszimmer (*Theat.*). **—shank**, *s.* das Grünbein; die Regenschnepfe. **—-sickness**, *s.* die Bleichsucht. **—sward**, *s.* der Rasen. **—wood**, I. *s.* der grün belaubte Wald. II. *attrib.*; —wood shade, der Waldesschatten.

Greet, *v.a.* (be)grüßen; (accost) grüßend anreden. **—ing**, *s.* die Begrüßung; der Gruß; with —ings from all of us, mit (herzlichen) Grüßen von uns allen.

Gregarious, *adj.*, **—ly**, *adv.* in Herden, Scharen gehend *or* lebend, sich zusammenhaltend, gesellig. **—ness**, *s.* das Zusammenleben.

Grenad—e, *s.* die Granate. **—ier**, *s.* der Grenadier.

Grenadine, *s.* die Grenadine.

Grew, *imperf. of* Grow.

Grey, *see* Gray. **—hound**, *s.* das Windspiel.

Grid—dle, *s.* das Blech zum Kuchenbacken (*prov.*). *Comp.* **—iron**, *s.* der Bratrost.

Grief, *s.* der Kummer, Gram, das Weh; (cause of —) die Beschwerde; to come to —, sich (*dat.*) ein Unglück zuziehen, zu Schaden kommen, verderben, zerbrechen.

Griev—ance, *s.* die Beschwerde, der Verdruß, Grund zur Klage, Mißstand; one of my —ances, eine meiner Nöte, ein Grund zur Beschwerde für mich. **—e**, *v.* I. *a.* kränken, betrüben, (einem) wehe tun; (offend) ärgern, beleidigen; it —es me to the heart, es tut mir in der Seele weh; I was much —ed to hear, es tat sehr mir leid, zu erfahren, ich hörte *or* vernahm mit großem Bedauern. II. *n.* sich grämen, trauern. **—ous**, *adj.*, **—ously**, *adv.* schmerzlich, empfindlich, verdrießlich, unangenehm, kränkend; (oppressive) schwer, drückend; (piteous) erbärmlich; (heinous) abscheulich; a —ous fault, ein schweres Versehen. **—ousness**, *s.* das Drückende, der Druck; (affliction) der Kummer, das Betrübende; (misery) das Elend; die Abscheulichkeit (*of sin, etc.*).

Griff—in, *s.* der (Vogel)Greif; der Neuling (in Ostindien); die Anstandsdame (*coll.*); bearded —in, der Lämmergeier (*Orn.*).

Grig, *s.* das Heimchen; (eel) der Sandaal.

[1]**Grill**, I. *v.a.* auf dem Roste braten, rösten. II. *v.n.* braten, schmoren. III. *s.* das geröstete Fleisch. **—ade**, *s.* das Braten auf dem Rost *Comp.* **—-room**, *s.* der Eßsaal in einem Speisehaus, wo das bestellte Stück Fleisch vor den Augen der Gäste auf dem Rost gebraten wird.

[2]**Grill**, *v.a.* quälen, ärgern, reizen (*obs.*).

Grim, *adj.*, **—ly**, *adv.* (fierce) grimmig; (stern) finster, abschreckend; (hideous) abscheulich, scheußlich, gräßlich. **—ness**, *s.* das Finstere; die Scheußlichkeit; das grimmige Wesen. *Comp.* **—-faced**, **—-visaged**, *adj.* böse, mürrisch aussehend.

Grim—ace, *s.* die Grimasse, Fratze. **—e**, I. *s.* der tiefe Schmutz. II. *v.a.* beschmutzen, berußen. **—y**, *adj.* schmutzig, rußig.

Grimalkin, *s.* die (alte) Katze.

Grin, I. *v.n.* grinsen, den Mund verziehen; to — and bear it, gute Miene zum bösen Spiel machen. II. *s.* das Grinsen, Fletschen.

Grind, I. *ir.v.a.* (comminute) reiben, zerreiben, zermalmen; mahlen (*corn, coffee, etc.*); (whet) schleifen, wetzen; schleifen (*glass, etc.*); polieren (*needles*); quälen, (unter-)drücken (*fig.*); to — a barrel-organ, eine Orgel drehen, orgeln; to — the teeth, mit den Zähnen knirschen; to — colours, Farben reiben. II. *ir.v.n.* sich mahlen lassen; sich schräfen, glätten; büffeln, ochsen (*sl.*). III. *s.* (drudgery) die Plackerei; das Ochsen, Büffeln (*sl.*). **—er**, *s.* der Schleifer; der Backenzahn; der Einpauker (*sl.*); der Farbenreiber (*Paint.*). **—ing**, *s.* das Mahlen, Schleifen; —ing institution, die Presse. *Comp.* **—ing-mill**, *s.* die Mahlmühle. **—stone**, *s.* der Mühlstein; der Schleif-, Wetz-stein; to keep a p.'s nose to the —stone, einen zu fortwährender Arbeit anhalten; to be kept with one's nose to the —stone, schuften müssen, büffeln müssen (*coll.*).

Grip, I. *s.* der Griff; *see* Hold; der Händedruck (*Freem.*). II. *v.a.* ergreifen, fassen, packen; festhalten, kneipen. **—e**, I. *v.a. see* — II.; zusammenpressen; schließen (*one's hand*); (oppress) drücken, peinigen; Bauchgrimmen verursachen (*Med.*). II. *v.n.* zugreifen; die Kolik haben (*Med.*); luvgierig sein (*Naut.*). III. *s. see* — I.; (clutches) die Klauen; der Besitz, die Gewalt (*fig.*); (hardship) die Not, Bedrückung; —e of poverty, der Druck der Armut. **—es**, *pl.* die Kolik (*Med.*). **—ing**, I. *adj.* kneipend, nagend;

geizig; luvgierig (*Naut.*). II. *s.* das Kneipen; die Kolik. **—per**, *s.* einer, der zugreift. *Comp.* **—sack**, *s.* die Handtasche, Reisetasche (*Amer.*).

Griskin, *s.* das Rückgratsstück des Schweins.

Grisly, *adj.* scheußlich, entsetzlich, grausig.

Grist, *s.* das Gemahlene, Mehl; zum Mahlen zugerichtetes Korn; das Lebensmittel (*fig.*); that's — to his mill, das ist Wasser auf seine Mühle; to bring — to the mill, Nutzen bringen.

Gristl—e, *s.* der Knorpel. **—y**, *adj.* knorpelig.

Grit, *s.* das Schrot; (coarse meal) das Schrotmehl; (gravel, *etc.*) der Kies, Gries, grobe Sand; grobkörniger Sandstein (*Min.*); (pluck) der Mut. **—s**, *pl.* Grütze. **—tiness**, *s.* das Griesige, Sandige. **—ty**, *adj.* griesig, kiesig, sandig.

Grizzl—e, I. *s.* das Grau, die graue Farbe. II. *v.n.* grau werden. **—ed**, *adj.* grausprenklich. **—y**, *adj.* grau, graulich; —y bear, der graue Bär.

Groan, I. *v.n.* stöhnen, ächzen; to — for, nach (*dat.*) . . . verlangen, sich sehnen; to — away, sich ausstöhnen. II. *v.a.*; to — down, durch mißfälliges Stöhnen *or* Grunzen zum Schweigen bringen. III. *s.* das Stöhnen, Seufzen, Ächzen; das Grunzen des Mißfallens, Murren; —s for . . ., ein Pereat dem . . . ! **—ing**, *s.* das Gestöhn, Stöhnen.

Groat, *s.* der Grot (= 4 Pence) (*obs.*); not worth a —, keinen Heller wert.

Groats, *pl.* die Hafergrütze.

Grocer, *s.* der Materialwarenhändler, (Gewürz)-krämer; —'s shop, die Materialwarenhandlung. **—ies**, *pl.* die Materialwaren. **—y**, *s.* (—y business) der Kolonialwarenhandel.

Grog, *s.* der Grog, Branntwein mit heißem Wasser. **—gy**, *adj.* betrunken; steif, abgejagt (*as horses*). **—ram**, *s.* (kind of coarse stuff) der Grogram.

Groin, I. *s.* der Schambug (*Anat.*); der Grat, die Rippe (*Arch.*). II. *attrib.*; — rib, die Gratrippe (*Arch.*). III. *v.a.* mit Rippen *or* Gurten versehen (*Arch.*); —ed ceiling, gerippte Decke; —ed vaulting, das Rippen-, Kreuz-gewölbe.

Groom, I. *s.* der Stallknecht, Reitknecht; (bride—) der Bräutigam; — of the chamber, königlicher Kammerdiener; — in waiting, diensttuender Kammerjunker. II. *v.a.* (Pferde) putzen, besorgen. *Comp.* **—s-man**, *s.* der Brautführer.

Groov—e, I. *s.* die Rinne, Auskehlung, Furche; die Hohlkehle (*Arch.*); die Furche, Nut, der Falz (*Carp.*); die Nut (*Mach.*); die Kerbe, Rinne (*in needles*); die Gewohnheit, Schablone, das alte ausgefahrene Gleis (*fig.*); to run in a —e, immer in demselben Geleise fortleben *or* bleiben. II. *v.a.* auskehlen, furchen; nuten; falzen, fugen. **—es**, *pl.* Züge (*Gun.*). **—ing**, I. *s.* die Auskehlung; das Nuten 2c. II. *attrib.*; —ing plane, der Nut-, Spund-hobel.

Grope, *v.* I. *a.* (be)tasten; to — one's way, seinen Weg tastend suchen, im Finstern (fort-)tappen. II. *n.* tappen, tastend fühlen (for, nach); to — about, umherirren. **—r**, *s.* der Tappende.

Grosbeak, Grossbeak, *s.* der Kernbeißer.

Gross, I. *adj.*, **—ly**, *adv.* (fat) dick, fett, feist; (coarse) grob, roh; (dull) dumm, schwerfällig; (indelicate) unanständig, schmutzig; (sensual) grobsinnlich; (enormous) sehr groß, ungeheuer; Brutto- (*C. L.*); — amount, der Bruttobetrag; — earnings, Bruttoeinnahmen; — error, grober Irrtum; — produce, der Rohertrag; — weight, das Bruttogewicht; —ly vulgar, höchst gemein. II. *s.* die Masse, der Hauptteil (*of an army, etc.*); das Groß (= 12 Dutzend); in (the) —, im Ganzen, in Bausch und Bogen, ungerechnet. **—ness**, *s.* die Dichtheit (*of vapours*); die Grobheit; die Grobheit, Roheit, Gemeinheit (*of wit, etc.*); die Abscheulichkeit (*of a crime*). *Comp.* **—beak**, *see* Grosbeak.

Grot, —to, *s.* die Felsenhöhle, Grotte.

Grotesque, *adj.*, **—ly**, *adv.* grotesk, wunderlich, lächerlich. **—ness**, *s.* das Groteske.

[1]**Ground**, I. *s.* der Grund, Boden; (region) die Gegend, das Gebiet; (property) das Grundstück; (battle-—) das Schlachtfeld, der Kampfplatz; (play-—) der Spielplatz; der Grund (*Paint., Manuf., Engr.*); (*also* —s) der (Beweis-)Grund, die Grundlage (*of an argument, etc.*); das Thema (*Mus.*); on the — that, aus dem Grunde, weil; on German —, auf deutschem Grund und Boden, auf deutschem Gebiet; under —, unter der Erde; building under —, der Tiefbau; to dispute every inch of —, sich tapfer verteidigen; to the —, zu Boden, zur Erde; to fall to the —, zu nichts kommen (*fig.*); to gain —, vorwärts kommen, Boden gewinnen, um sich greifen; to gain — upon a p., einem Boden abgewinnen; to hold one's —, sich *or* seinen Platz behaupten; to lose —, weichen, Boden verlieren; rising —, die Anhöhe. II. *v.a.* auf den Grund setzen; niedersetzen (*arms*); den Grund machen zu; begründen (auf eine S.) (*fig.*); in den Anfangsgründen unterrichten. III. *v.n.* an den Grund raken. **—age**, *s.* das Hafen-, Anker-geld. **—ing**, *s.* der Anfangsunterricht, erste Unterricht. **—less**, *adj.*, **—lessly**, *adv.* grundlos; unbegründet. **—ling**, *s.* der Gründling. **—s**, *pl.* (dregs) der Bodensatz, die Hefen; (rudiments, elements) die Anfangsgründe, Grundsätze. **—sel**, *s.* das Kreuzkraut. *Comp.* **—-angling**, *s.* das Grundangeln. **—-floor**, *s.* das Erdgeschoß, Parterre; on the —-floor, zu ebener Erde, im Erdgeschoß. **—-ice**, *s.* das Grundeis. **—-ivy**, *s.* der Erdefeu. **—-line**, *s.* das Bauniveau (*Build., Fort.*); die Grundlinie (*Draw.*). **—-plan**, *s.* der Grundriß. **—-plate**, *s.* die Schwelle, Sohle (*Build.*); die Unterlagsplatte (*Railw.*); die Erdplatte (*Tele.*). **—-rent**, *s.* der Grundzins. **—-sill**, *s.* die Grundschwelle. **—-story**, *see* —-floor. **—-swell**, *s.* die Dünung (*Naut.*). **—-tier**, *s.* die Parkettlogen(reihe) (*Theat.*). **—work**, *s.* die Erdarbeiten; der Unterbau, das Fundament (*Build.*); die Grundierung (*Paint.*); die Grundlage, der Grund (*also fig.*).

[2]**Ground**, *imperf. & p.p. of* Grind; — glass, matt geschliffenes Glas.

Group, I. *s.* die Gruppe. II. *v.a.* gruppieren. **—ing**, *s.* das Gruppieren, die Gruppierung.

Grouse, *s.* das Waldhuhn; black —, das Birkhuhn; red —, schottisches Schneehuhn.

Grout, I. *s.* das Schrotmehl (*obs.*); (lees) der Bodensatz; der dünne Mörtel; die feine Tünche. II. *v.a.* mit Mörtel bestreichen *or* überziehen.

Grove, *s.* das Gehölz, Wäldchen; der Hain (*poet.*); (avenue) die Baumallee.

Grovel, *v.n.* auf dem Bauche liegen; auf der Erde kriechen. **—ler**, *s.* der Kriecher. **—ling**, I. *adj.* kriechend; niedrig, gemein, unwürdig. II. *s.* die Kriecherei, das unwürdige Benehmen.

Grow, *ir.v.* I. *n.* wachsen; (become) werden; (increase) zunehmen; Fortschritte machen, weiter kommen; to — angry, böse werden; to — better, sich bessern; to — dark, dunkel werden; to — in favour, an Gunst zunehmen; to — into a habit, zur Gewohnheit werden; to — less, sich vermindern; it —s colder, es wird kälter; to — light, sich erhellen, aufklären; to — obsolete, veralten; to — old, altern, alt werden; to — poor, verarmen; to — worse, sich verschlimmern; to — out, herauswachsen; to — out of, herauswachsen aus, entwachsen (*dat.*; *fig.*); erwachsen, entstehen aus; (outgrow) mit dem Altern verlieren, auswachsen (*clothes*); to — **to**, anwachsen; to — to a brawl, zum Zank werden; to — **together**, zusammenwachsen; to — **up**, aufwachsen; it —s **upon** me, es wird mir immer lieber *or* vertrauter; this habit will — upon you, diese Gewohnheit wird bei dir immer stärker werden. II. *ir.v.a.* bauen, ziehen (*Agr.*); to — a beard, sich (*dat.*) einen Bart stehen *or* wachsen lassen. **—er**, *s.* der, die, das Wachsende; der Pflanzer, Bauer (*Agr.*). **—ing**, I. *adj.*; —ing weather, fruchtbares Wetter; —ing pains,

Schmerzen vom Wachstum. II. *s.* das Wachsen; der Bau. **—n**, *p.p. & adj.* (—n up) erwachsen; —n over, over—n, überwachsen. **—th**, *s.* der Wuchs, das Wachstum; (increase) die Zunahme, der Anwuchs; (progress) die Fortschritte (*pl.*); (product) das Erzeugnis, Produkt; das Gewächs (*of wine, etc.*); fine —th of wood, schöner (Holz-) Schlag; native —ths, Landesprodukte; it is not of your own —th, Sie haben es nicht selbst gezogen, es ist kein eignes Gewächs.

Growl, I. *s.* das Knurren, Brummen; das Geknurre; das dumpfe Getöse (*of thunder*). II. *v.n.* knurren, brummen; to — at a p., einen anknurren. III. *v.a.* herausbrummen. **—er**, *s.* der knurrige Hund; (person) der Brummbart.

Grub, I. *v.n.* graben, wühlen; essen (*vulg.*). II. *v.a.*; to — up, ausjäten, ausreuten. III. *s.* der Wurm, Engerling; (maggot) die Made; das Futter (*vulg.*). **—ber**, *s.* der Gräber; der Ausroder. *Comp.* **—(bing)-axe**, *s.* die Jäthacke. **—bing-hoe**, *s.* die Rodehacke. **—-saw**, *s.* die Handsäge für Marmor. **—-street**, *see the Index of names.*

Grudg—e, I. *v.a.* mißgönnen (a p. a thing, einem etwas); ungern geben; mit Widerwillen tun *or* leiden; to —e no pains, sich keine Mühe verdrießen lassen; to —e the time, die Zeit nicht gern hergeben. II. *v.n.* (feel reluctant to) unwillig sein, ungern sehen; (be envious) neidisch, mißgünstig sein. III. *s.* (enmity) der Groll, Haß, die Mißgunst; (reluctance) der Widerwille; to bear a —e against a p., Groll hegen gegen einen. **—er**, *s.* der Neider, Mißgünstige. **—ingly**, *adv.* grollend, ungern.

Gruel, *s.* der Haferschleim.

Gruesome, *adj.* schauerlich, grausig, greulich.

Gruff, *adj.*, **—ly**, *adv.* mürrisch; (surly) barsch, schroff. **—ness**, *s.* das mürrische Wesen; die Barschheit.

Grumble, I. *v.n.* murren, brummen (at, über eine S.); rollen, murmeln (*as thunder*). II. *s.* das Murren. **—r**, *s.* der Murrende, Mißvergnügte.

Grumous, *adj.* geronnen, klümperig, klumpig.

Grumpy, *adj.* mürrisch, verdrießlich (*coll.*).

Grunt, I. *v.n.* grunzen. II. *s.* das Grunzen. **—er**, *s.* der, die, das Grunzende; das Schwein.

Guaiacum, *s.* der Guajak, das Guajakholz.

Guanaco, *s.* (kind of llama) der Guanako.

Guano, *s.* der Guano, Vogeldünger.

Guarant—ee, I. *s.* der Bürge, Gewährsmann; (pledge) die Bürgschaft. II. *v.a.* Gewähr leisten (für), bürgen (für), garantieren; —eed pure, für Reinheit wird gebürgt. **—or**, *s.* der Bürge, Zeichner einer Garantiesumme. **—y**, *s.* die Gewährleistung, Bürgschaft.

Guard, I. *v.a.* (be)hüten, bewahren, (be)schützen, bewachen (from, vor); (escort) Schutzgeleit geben. II. *v.n.* auf der Hut sein; to — (o.s.) against, sich hüten, sich in Acht nehmen vor. III. *s.* die Wache, Bewachung, Hut; (caution) die Vorsicht; (that which —s) das Beschützende; die Wache, Wachmannschaft (*Mil.*); der Schaffner (*Railw.*); der Bahnwärter (*Amer.*); die Auslage, Deckung, Parade (*Fenc.*); der Bügel (*Gun.*); das Stichblatt (*of a sword*); der Falz (*Bookb.*); *see* Fire; (watch-—) die Uhrkette; the advanced — *or* van—, die Vorhut; —'s brake, die Schaffnerbremse; chief —, der Zugführer; —'s van, der Wagen des Zugführers; life-—s, Leibwache; on —, auf Wache; to go on —, auf (die) Wache ziehen; to be, stand on one's —, auf seiner Hut sein; to put a p. on his —, einen warnen, einem einen Wink geben; to come off —, von der Wache kommen; to be off one's —, unachtsam, unbedacht sein; to throw, put off one's —, überraschen. **—ed**, *adj.*, **—edly**, *adv.* vorsichtig, behutsam, zurückhaltend; —ed in one's expressions, vorsichtig in seinen Ausdrücken. **—er**, *s.* der Hüter, Wächter. **—ian**, I. *s. see* —er; der Vormund (*Law*); board of —ians (of the poor), das Armenamt. II. *adj.* schützend, Schutz-. **—ianship**, *s.* die Obhut, der Schutz; die Vormundschaft. **—s**, *pl.* die Garde(truppen). *Comp.* **—-house**, *s.* die Wache, das Wachthaus (*Mil.*). **—ian-angel**, *s.* der Schutzengel. **—-rail**, *s.* die Sicherheitsschiene, Gegenschiene (*Rail.*). **—-room**, *s.* die Wachtstube. **—-ship**, *s.* das Wachtschiff. **—sman**, *s.* der Gardist.

Guava, *s.* die Gujava; der Gujavabaum.

Gudgeon, *s.* der Gründling; der Einfaltspinsel (*fig.*).

Guelder-rose, *s.* der Schneeball.

Guerdon, I. *s.* der Lohn. II. *v.a.* belohnen.

Guer(r)illa, *s.* (— war) der unregelmäßige Kleinkrieg, Guerillakrieg; der Kleinkrieger (*Amer.*).

Guess, I. *v.a.* (conjecture) mutmaßen, vermuten; erraten (*a riddle*); glauben, denken, meinen (*Amer.*). II. *v.n.* (— at) mutmaßen, raten. III. *s.* die Mutmaßung, Vermutung; to give a —, *see* — II. **—er**, *s.* der Mutmaßende. **—ingly**, *adv.* mutmaßlich. *Comp.* **—work**, *s.* das aufs Geratewohl getane Werk, die Mutmaßung, Raterei.

Guest, *s.* der Gast; der Fremde (*in an inn*); paying —, der Kostgänger, Pensionär. *Comp.* **—-chamber**, **—-room**, *s.* das Fremdenzimmer (*in a private house*); das Gastzimmer (*at an inn*).

Guffaw, *s.* lautes, schallendes Gelächter, das Gewieher.

Guid—able, *adj.* lenksam, lenkbar. **—ance**, *s.* die Führung, Leitung. **—e**, I. *s.* der Führer (*also fig.*), Wegweiser; der Führer, das Lineal (*Sew.-m.*); der Führer, die Leitung (*Mach.*); die Sicherheitsschiene (*Railw.*); *see* —e-book. II. *v.a.* führen, leiten (*also fig.*). **—ing**, *p.p. & adj.*; —ing star, der Leitstern. *Comp.* **—e-book**, *s.* das Reisehandbuch, der Reiseführer Wegweiser, Führer; —e-book to Switzerland, Führer durch die Schweiz. **—e-post**, *s.* der Wegweiser.

Guidon, *s.* die Standarte (*of cavalry*); die Signalflagge.

Guild, *s.* die Gilde, Zunft, Innung; member of a —, — brother, das Gildenmitglied. *Comp.* **—hall**, *s.* das Innungshaus; das Rathaus.

[1]**Guile**, *s.* die List, Arglist; das Falsche (*B.*). **—ful**, *adj.*, **—fully**, *adv.* arglistig, trügerisch. **—less**, *adj.*, **—lessly**, *adv.* arglos, ohne Falsch. **—lessness**, *s.* die Arglosigkeit, Unschuld.

[2]**Guile**, *s.* der Gärbottich, die Kufe.

Guillemot, *s.* die Lumme (*Ornith.*).

Guillotine, I. *s.* das Fallbeil, die Guillotine. II. *v.a.* guillotinieren, mit dem Fallbeil hinrichten.

Guilt, *s.* die Schuld; die Strafbarkeit. **—ily**, *adv.* schuldig; *see* —y. **—iness**, *s.* die Schuld; die Strafbarkeit. **—less**, *adj.*, **—lessly**, *adv.* schuldlos, unschuldig; (ignorant) unkundig. **—y**, *adj.* schuldig; (punishable) strafbar, verbrecherisch; (conscious of —) schuldbewußt; to plead —y, sein Verbrechen eingestehen, die Klage anerkennen; to find —y, für schuldig erklären; —y conscience, böses Gewissen.

Guinea, *s.* die Guinee.

Guise, *s.* (appearance) das äußere Ansehen, die Gestalt; (garb) der Anzug; (cloak) die Maske, der Vorwand; under the — of religion, unter der Maske der Religion.

Guitar, *s.* die Guitarre.

Gulch, *s.* tiefe Schlucht (*Amer.*).

Gules, I. *s.* das Rot (*Her.*). II. *adj.* rot.

Gulf, *s.* der Meerbusen, Golf, die Bucht; (abyss) der Abgrund, Schlund; (eddy) der Strudel. *Comp.* **—-stream**, *s.* der Golfstrom.

[1]**Gull**, *s.* die Möve.

[2]**Gull**, *s.* das Gänschen.

[3]**Gull**, I. *s.* der Einfaltspinsel, Tor, Narr, Gimpel. II. *v.a.* betrügen, zum besten haben; verleiten (into, zu). **—ibility**, *s.* die Leichtgläubigkeit. **—ible**, *adj.* leicht anzuführen, einfältig.

Gull—et, *s.* die Gurgel, der Schlund. **—y**, *s.* die Wasserrinne, Wasserfurche; die Eisrinne

(*Mount.*). *Comp.* **—y-hole**, *s.* das Abflußloch, die Mündung eines Abzugskanals.

Gulp, I. *v.a.* gierig (ver=)schlucken; to — down, hinunterschlucken, schnell hinunterschlingen. II. *s.* der Schluck, das Schlucken.

[1]**Gum**, I. *s.* das Gummi; der Pflanzenschleim; das Klebegummi; die Gummierung; —s, die Gummi(über)schuhe (*Amer.*). II. *v.a.* gummieren; (close) zukleben. **—my**, *adj.* gummiartig, klebrig. *Comp.* **—-arabic**, *s.* das Gummiarabicum, der arabische Gummi. **—-lac**, *s.* der Gummilack. **—-resin**, *s.* das Gummiharz. **—-tree**, *s.* die starke Schönmütze (*Bot.*).

[2]**Gum**, *s.* das Zahnfleisch. *Comp.* **—-boil**, *s.* das Zahngeschwür.

Gumption, *s.* der Verstand, Mutterwitz (*vulg.*).

Gun, I. *s.* (firearm) das Feuergewehr; (musket, *etc.*) die Flinte, Büchse; (cannon) das Geschütz; a big —, eine Kanone (*lit.*), ein Berühmter (*fig. coll.*); rifled —, ein gezogenes Geschütz; machine —, das Maschinengeschütz; as sure as a —, ganz gewiß; the artillerymen stood to their —s, die Artilleristen blieben bei den Geschützen; the promoters of this reform have stuck to their —s, die Verfechter dieser Reform sind ihren Grundsätzen treu geblieben. II. *v.a.*; to —, *or* to go —ning, auf die Jagd gehen (*Amer.*). **—nage**, *s.* die Anzahl Geschütze auf Kriegsschiffen (*rare*). **—ner**, *s.* der Kanonier, Artillerist; der Geschützmeister; —ner's quadrant, der Stückquadrant. **—nery**, *s.* die Geschützkunst, Artillerie(wissenschaft). *Comp.* **—-barrel**, *s.* der Flintenlauf. **—boat**, *s.* das Kanonenboot. **—-carriage**, *s.* die Lafette. **—-cotton**, *s.* die Schießbaumwolle. **—-deck**, *s.* das Batteriedeck. **—-jacket**, *s.* der Kanonenmantel. **—-ladle**, *s.* die Ladeschaufel. **—-metal**, *s.* das Kanonenmetall, Stückmetall. **—-picker**, *s.* die Raumnadel. **—-ports**, *pl.* die Stückpforten. **—powder**, I. *s.* das Schießpulver. II. *attrib.*; —powder tea, der Kugeltee; —powder plot, die Pulververschwörung. **—-rack**, *s.* das Flintengestell. **—room**, *s.* die Kadettenmesse (*Naut.*). **—shot**, I. *s.* der Schuß; die Schußweite; within —-shot, in Schußweite. II. *adj.*; Schuß=; —shot wound, die Schußwunde. **—smith**, *s.* der Büchsenmacher. **—-stock**, *s.* der Kolben. **—-tackle**, *s.* das Ruckseil. **—-wale**, *s.* das Schandeck; das Dollbord (*on row-boats*).

Gurgl—e, I. *v.n.* murmelnd rieseln; glucksen. II. *s.*, **—ing**, *s.* das Gemurmel, Gurgeln.

Gush, I. *v.n.* hervorströmen, sich ergießen (from, aus), entströmen (from the eyes, den Augen); schwärmen, sich überschwenglich ausdrücken (*fig.*); to — out, ausströmen. II. *s.* der Guß, Strom; überspanntes Reden, der Erguß. **—ing**, *adj.*, **—ingly**, *adv.* sich ergießend; überschwenglich, überspannt, sich gern in überschwenglichen Ausdrücken ergehend.

Gusset, I. *s.* der Zwickel. II. *v.a.* mit einem Zwickel versehen.

[1]**Gust**, *s.* der Windstoß; — of passion, der Ausbruch der Leidenschaft. **—y**, *adj.* stürmisch, ungestüm.

[2]**Gust**, *s.* der Genuß, Geschmack (*obs.*). **—atory**, *adj.* Geschmacks=. **—o**, *s.* der Geschmack; (pleasure) der Genuß, das Vergnügen; with —o, mit großem Behagen.

Gut, I. *s.* der Darm; (passage) der enge Durchweg. II. *v.a.* ausweiden; ausleeren (*fig.*); the warehouse was —ted, das Lagerhaus wurde völlig ausgeplündert. **—s**, *pl.* das Eingeweide, Gedärm; (stomach) der Magen.

Gutta-percha, I. *s.* die Guttapercha. II. *attrib.*; — tubing, die Röhren aus Guttapercha.

Gutter, I. *s.* die Wasserrinne, der Rinnstein, die Gosse; die Dach=, Trauf=rinne (*Build.*); he picked him up in the —, er las ihn von der Straße auf. II. *attrib.*; — tile, der Kehlziegel. III. *v.a.* aushöhlen. IV. *v.n.* ausgehöhlt werden; (drop) rinnen, triefen; ablaufen (*as a candle*). *Comp.* **—-snipe** *s.* das Straßenkind.

Guttural, I. *adj.* zur Kehle gehörig; Kehl=. II. *s.* (— sound) der Kehllaut, Guttural.

[1]**Guy**, *s.* der Achterholer (*Naut.*).

[2]**Guy**, *s.* die Vogelscheuche, seltsam aussehende Person.

Guzzle, *v.n.* unmäßig *or* gierig trinken, zechen.

Gymn—asium, *s.* die Turnhalle, der Turnplatz; (school) das Gymnasium. **—ast**, *s.* der Gymnast (*Hist.*); der Turner. **—astic**, *adj.*, **—astically**, *adv.* gymnastisch, Turn=. **—astics**, *pl.* die Turnkunst, das Turnen, die Freiübungen (*pl.*); die Gymnastik; intellectual —astics, die Geistesgymnastik, formale Bildung. **—osophist**, *s.* der Gymnosophist. **—osperm**, *s.* nacktsamige Pflanze. **—ospermous**, *adj.* nacktsamig. **—otus**, *s.* der Finn=, Zitter=aal.

Gyn—andria, *pl.* weibermännige Pflanzen. **—andrian**, **—androus**, *adj.* weibermännig. **—archy**, **—ocracy**, *s.* die Weiberherrschaft.

Gyp, *s.* der Studenten=Aufwärter, Stiefelfuchs (*Camb.*).

Gyps—ine, *adj.* gipsartig. **—um**, *s.* der Gips.

Gypsy, *see* Gipsy.

Gyr—ate, *v.n.* wirbeln. **—ation**, *s.* die Kreisbewegung, das Drehen. **—omancy**, *s.* die Gyromantie, Kreiswahrsagerei.

Gyrfalcon, *s.* *see* Gerfalcon.

Gyves, *pl.* Fesseln, Fußbande.

H

H, h, *s.* H, h. *For abbreviations see the Index at the end of the English-German part.*

Ha, *int.* ha! wie? was? —, —! ha, ha!

Habeas-Corpus, *s.* die Habeas=Korpus=Akte.

Haberdasher, *s.* der Schnitt=, Kurzwaren=händler, Posamentier. **—y**, *s.* Kurzwaren; der Kurzwarenhandel.

Habergeon, *s.* das Panzerhemd.

Habiliment, *s.* das Kleidungsstück. **—s**, *pl.* die Gewänder (*pl.*), die Kleidung.

Habit, I. *s.* die Beschaffenheit (*of body*); (custom) der Gebrauch, die Gewohnheit; (dress) der Anzug, die Kleidung; die Lebensweise (*Bot. & Zool.*); of a full (spare) —, vollblütig (mager); low — of body, die Schwäche; to have fallen into bad —s, schlechten Gewohnheiten *or* in schlechte Gewohnheiten verfallen sein; to be in the — of, gewohnt sein zu, pflegen zu; to get (into) the — of, sich (*dat.*) eine S. angewöhnen; to get out of the — of, sich (*dat.*) eine S. abgewöhnen; to do a thing from —, etwas aus Gewohnheit *or* gewohnheitsmäßig tun. II. *v.a.* (an)kleiden. **—able**, *adj.* bewohnbar. **—ableness**, *s.* die Bewohnbarkeit, Wohnlichkeit. **—ant**, *s.* *see* Inhabitant. **—at**, *s.* der Wohnort, Aufenthaltsort, die Heimat (eines Tiers, einer Pflanze). **—ation**, *s.* das Wohnen; (abode) der Wohnort, die Wohnung. **—ual**, *adj.*, **—ually**, *adv.* gewohnt, gewöhnlich, Gewohnheits=; —ual drunkard, der Gewohnheitssäufer, Trunkenbold. **—uate**, *v.a.* (an)gewöhnen; to —uate o.s. to a thing, sich gewöhnen an eine S. **—ude**, *s.* die Gewohnheit, der Brauch. *Comp.* **—-shirt**, *s.* das Vorhemdchen.

[1]**Hack**, I. *v.a.* (zer)hacken, klein hauen. II. *v.n.* (einem) einen Fußtritt versetzen (at football, beim Fußballspiel). III. *s.* die Kerbe, der Einschnitt; (cut, blow) der Hieb; der Fußtritt (*at football*). **—ing**, *adj.*; —ing cough, kurzer, trockener Husten.

[2]**Hack**, I. *s.* das gewöhnliche Reitpferd, der abgetriebene Gaul, Klepper; das Mietpferd; der schwer Arbeitende (*fig.*); (hireling) der Mietling; (— cab, *etc.*) der Mietwagen; literary —, der (gemeine) Lohnschreiber, Zeilenreißer, literarische Packesel. II. *adj.* zum Mieten, zu jedermanns Gebrauch gemietet; abgenutzt; gemein. **—ney**, I. *s.* das gewöhnliche Reitpferd, der Gaul; das Droschkenpferd; der Mietling; (prostitute) die

Dirne. II. *adj. see* — IV.; —ney carriage, die Droschke, der Mietwagen. —**neyed**, *adj.* abgenutzt; (trite) alltäglich, platt, gemein; —neyed expression, der abgenutzte Ausdruck, die abgedroschene Redensart; —neyed remark, der Gemeinplatz.
Hackle, I. *v.a.* hecheln. II. *s.* rohe Seide, ungesponnene Fäden; lange Rückenfeder eines Hahns.
Had, *pret. & p.p. of* Have; — we not better ...? täten wir nicht besser (zu) ...? to be —, zu haben; — I wist! hätte ich nur gewußt! (*obs.*).
Haddock, *s.* der Schellfisch.
Hæm—atite, *etc. see* Hem—atite.
Haft, *s.* die Handhabe; der Griff.
Hag, *s.* (witch) die (alte) Hexe, Unholdin; das häßliche alte Weib, das Scheusal. —**gard**, *adj.* wild, ungezähmt; hager (und bleich), abgemagert, dürr; abgehärmt; entstellt. —**gish**, *adj.* hexenhaft, scheußlich.
[1]**Haggard**, *see under* Hag.
[2]**Haggard**, *s.* die Schober-Einfriedigung.
Haggis, *s.* eine Art Wurst (*Scotch*).
[1]**Haggl—e**, *v.n.* feilschen, knickern. —**er**, *s.* der Feilscher, Knicker. —**ing**, *s.* das Feilschen.
[2]**Haggle**, *v.a.* (zer)hacken (*obs.*).
Hagio—cracy, *s.* die Herrschaft der Heiligen; die Priesterherrschaft. —**grapha**, *pl.* die Hagiographa; die Lebensgeschichten der Heiligen, Heiligenlegenden; das Hagiograph, die Heiligen-Schrift. —**graph**, *s.* der Verfasser von Heiligenlegenden.
Haha, *s.* künstlich nachgeahmte Schlucht, das Aha, Haha, auf welches man (in einem Garten) unvermutet stößt.
[1]**Hail**, I. der Hagel. II. *v.n.* hageln. III. *v.a.;* to — down, niederhageln lassen, ausschütten. *Comp.* —**stone**, *s.* das Hagelkorn, die Schloße. —**storm**, I. *s.* das Hagelwetter.
[2]**Hail**, *int.* Heil! Glück zu! all —, Macbeth! Heil dir, Macbeth!
[3]**Hail**, I. *v.a.* (call to) anrufen; (salute) beglückwünschen, begrüßen; (einem Schiffe) zurufen, (ein Schiff) preien, anrufen (*Naut.*); to — from, kommen aus; he —s from Hanover, er stammt aus Hannover. II. *s.* der Anruf; die Rufweite; within —, im Bereich der Stimme. *Comp.* —-**fellow**, *s.* der Genoß; to be —-fellow well met, mit einem vertraut umgehen, (with every one) ein Allerweltsfreund sein.
Hair, I. *s.* das Haar; die Haare; a fine head of —, ein schöner Haarwuchs; to a —, auf ein Haar, aufs Haar, ganz genau; a —'s breadth, eine Haarbreite; — for stuffing, das Polsterhaar. II. *attrib.;* — mattress, die Roßhaarmatratze; — sieve, das Haarsieb; — tonic, — wash, das Haarwasser. —**ed**, *adj.* haarig. —**iness**, *s.* die Haarigkeit, Behaartheit. —**less**, *adj.* ohne Haare, unbehaart, kahl. —**y**, *adj.* haarig, behaart. *Comp.* —**breadth**, I. *s.;* within a —breadth, —'s-breadth, um ein Haar, ums Haar, beinah. II. *adj.;* it was a —breadth escape, er ist mit genauer Not entkommen. —-**broom**, *s.* der Borstwisch. —-**brush**, *s.* die Haarbürste. —**cloth**, *s.* das (Roß-) Haartuch. —**dresser**, *s.* der Haarschneider, Friseur. —-**dressing**, *s.* die Haarschneidekunst. —-**dye**, *s.* das Haarfärbemittel. —-**oil**, *s.* das Haaröl. —**pencil**, *s.* der Haarpinsel. —-**pin**, *s.* die Haarnadel. —-**powder**, *s.* der (Haar-)Puder. —**shirt**, *s.* das härene Hemd. —-**splitting**, I. *adj.* haarspaltend. II. *s.* die Haarspalterei, Wortklauberei. —-**spring**, *s.* die Haar-, Schnecken-, Spiral-feder. —-**stroke**, *s.* der Haarstrich. —**trigger**, *s.* der Stecher an der Büchse. —**worker**, *s.* der Haar-künstler, -arbeiter.
Hake, *s.* der Hechtdorsch (*Ichth.*).
Halberd, (**Halbert**,) *s.* die Hellebarde. —**ier**, *s.* der Hellebardier.
Halcyon, I. *s.* der Eisvogel, Königsfischer. II. *adj.* friedlich, ruhig.
[1]**Hale**, *adj.* frisch und gesund, ungeschwächt; — and hearty, frisch und gesund.
[2]**Hale**, *v.a.* (haul) gewaltsam ziehen, einholen; schleppen (*archaic*).
Half, I. *s.* die Hälfte, das (Universitäts-)Semester; his better —, seine bessere Hälfte, seine Gattin *or* Eheliebste; to do (a thing *or* things) by halves, nicht gründlich *or* nicht vollständig tun; he does nothing by halves, er besorgt *or* tut alles aufs gründlichste; to go halves with a p., mit einem halbpart machen. II. *adj.* halb; — a pound, ein halbes Pfund; a pound and a —, anderthalb Pfund; two pounds and a —, drittehalb Pfund, zwei und ein halbes Pfund; — the amount, halb so viel, der halbe Betrag, die Hälfte; at — the price, zum halben Preise; — a crown, eine halbe Krone (*i.e. two shillings and sixpence, a little more than 2.50 mark*); a — crown (piece), ein Halbkronenstück; — past two (four), halb drei (fünf); not —, eigentlich nicht, gar nicht (*coll.*); he is not — bad, er ist gar nicht übel, er ist sehr nett; I don't — like him (it), ich mag ihn (es) gar nicht leiden, er (es) ist mir sehr unangenehm *or* herzlich zuwider. III. *v.a. see* Halve. *Comp.* —-**and-half**, *s.* eine Mischung von gleichen Quantitäten von Porter und Bier, Branntwein und Wasser 2c. (*sl.*). —-**back**, *s.* der Halbspieler, Markmann (*Footb.*). —-**blood**, I. *s.* das Halbblut. II. *adj.*, (*also* —-**bred**, *adj.*) halbbürtig, Halbblut-. —-**breed**, *s.* der Mischling. —-**brother**, *s.* der Halb-, Stiefbruder. —-**calf**, *adj.;* —-calf binding, der Halbfranzband. —-**caste**, I. *adj.* halbbürtig. II. *s.* das Kind von Eingebornen und Europäern. —-**cock**, *s.* die Vorderruhe, Mittelrast (eines Gewehres); to be at —-cock, in Ruhe stehen. —-**court**, *adj.;* —-court line, die Mittellinie (*L.T.*). —-**dead**, *adj.* halbtot. —-**deck**, *s.* das Halbdeck. —-**drunk**, *adj.* angesäuselt, benebelt. —-**hearted**, *adj.* mattherzig, lau, gleichgültig; knauserig. —-**holiday**, *s.* der freie Nachmittag. —-**hourly**, *adv.* halbstündlich, jede halbe Stunde. —-**landing**, *s.* der Treppenabsatz. —-**length**, *adj.;* —-length portrait, das Kniestück. —-**measure**, *s.* die halbe Maßregel. —-**moon**, *s.* der Halbmond (*also Fort.*). —-**mourning**, *s.* die Halbtrauer. —-**pay**, I. *s.* der halbe Sold. II. *adj.* auf halbem Solde stehend. —**penny**, I. *s.* der halbe Penny (etwa 5 Pfennige). II. *adj.* einen halben Penny kostend. —**pennyworth**, *s.* (Ha'porth, *vulg.*) der Wert eines halben Penny, für einen halben Penny. —-**pint**, *s.* der Schoppen, die halbe Pinte. —-**price**, *s.;* at —-price, zu halbem Preise. —-**seas-over**, *adj.* angesäuselt. —-**sheet**, *s.* das Duodezformat (*Typ.*). —-**sister**, *s.* die Halb-, Stief-schwester. —-**sovereign**, *s.* das Zehnschillingsstück. —-**speed**, *s.* halbe Geschwindigkeit. —-**starved**, *adj.* halbverhungert. —-**time**, *s.* die Pause, Halbzeit (*Footb.*). —-**volley**, *s.* der Sprungschlag (*L. T.*). —-**way**, I. *adv.* halbwegs; to meet a p. —-way, einem auf halbem Wege entgegenkommen. II. *adj.* auf halbem Wege liegend, in der Mitte; —-way house, die Schenke an der Landstraße; die Zwischenstation, Etappe (*fig.*). —-**witted**, *adj.* töricht, albern, nicht recht gescheit. —-**yearly**, *adv.* halbjährlich.
Halibut, *s.* die Heilbutte, eine Art Steinbutte.
Hall, I. *s.* (room) die Halle, der Saal; (entrance —) der Hausflur, Vorsaal, Vorplatz; (— of justice) Gerichtssaal; (country-seat) das Herrenhaus, Gutshaus, Schloß, der Landsitz; (college) das Studienhaus (Name einiger Colleges in Cambridge und Oxford); der Speisesaal (in den Colleges zu Cambridge und Oxford); Versammlungssaal wissenschaftlicher Vereine (*Amer.*); wissenschaftlicher Verein (*Amer.*); servants' —, die Bedientenstube; Apothecaries' —, die Londoner Apotheker-Innung; I shall not go to — to-night, ich werde heute abend nicht im Speisesaal (des College) essen. II. *attrib.;* — clock, die Vorplatzuhr; — lamp, die Flurlampe.

Comp. **—-mark,** *s.* der Feingehaltsstempel der Goldschmiedeinnung für Gold- und Silber-waren, Stempel der Echtheit. **—-marked,** *adj.* gestempelt; vollwertig, echt. **—-stand,** *s.* der Flurstän; der.

Hallelujah, *s.* & *int.* (das) Hallelujah *Comp.* **—-lass,** *s.* weiblicher Soldat der Heilsarmee. (*coll.*).

Halliard, *see* Halyard.

Halloo, I. *v.n.* Hallo rufen; nach den Hunden rufen. II. *int.* Hallo! III. *s.* der Ruf.

Hallow, *v.a.* heiligen, weihen; —ed be thy name, geheiliget werde Dein Name. **—eve, —e'en,** *s.* der Allerheiligen-Abend. **—mas,** *s.* das Allerheiligen(fest).

Hallucination, *s.* (mistake) der Irrtum; die Sinnestäuschung, der Sinnentrug (*also Med.*).

Halo, *s.* der Hof (*round the moon, etc.*); der Heiligenschein (*Paint.*).

Halt, I. *v.n.* Halt machen; (limp) lahmen, hinken (*also fig.*); (hesitate) schwanken, zögern; —ing verses, hinkende Verse. II. *v.a.* Halt machen lassen (*troops, etc.*). III. *s.* der Halt; to make a —, Halt machen; to come to a —, zum Stehen *or* Stillstand kommen, stille stehen, halten. IV. *adj.* lahm, hinkend; the —, die Lahmen (*B.*). **—ingly,** *adv.* hinkend; langsam.

Halter, *s.* die Halfter (*for a horse, etc.*); (rope) der Strick.

Halve, *v.a.* halbieren, zur Hälfte teilen. **—s,** *pl. see* Half; to do by —s, nur halb tun, obenhin verrichten; to cry —s, halbpart rufen; to go —s with, teilen *or* gemeinschaftlich unternehmen mit.

Halyard, *s.* das Fall; topsail —s, die Marsfallen; ensign —, das Flaggenfall.

Ham, *s.* der Schinken; die Lende, der Schenkel (*Anat.*). *Comp.* **—-sandwich,** *s.* das Schinkenbrötchen. **—string,** I. *s.* die Kniefleehsen. II. *v.a.* die Kniefleehsen zerschneiden.

Hamadryad, *s.* die Hamadryade, Baumnymphe.

Hame, *s.* das Kummet. **—s,** *pl.* Kummetfedern.

Hamlet, *s.* der Weiler, das Dörfchen.

Hammer, I. *s.* der Hammer; der Pfannendeckel (*Gun.*); der Hahn (*of a percussion-lock*); to come *or* go to the —, öffentlich versteigert *or* meistbietend verkauft werden; to bring to the —, versteigern lassen; they went at it — and tongs, sie zankten sich gewaltig; claw- —, Klauenhammer. II. *v.a.* hämmern, schlagen; to — out, aushämmern (*lit.*), mühsam ausarbeiten (*fig.*). III. *v.n.* hämmern; to — at, lange und anhaltend arbeiten an (einer S.). **—er,** *s.* der Hämmerer. *Comp.* **—-cloth,** *s.* die Kutschbockdecke. **—-dressed,** *adj.* mit dem Hammer behauen. **—-head, —-fish,** *s.* (—-headed shark) der Hammer(fisch).

Hammock, *s.* die Hängematte.

[1]Hamper, *s.* der Packkorb, Marktkorb; der Korb mit Eßwaren; (— for bottles) der Flaschenkorb.

[2]Hamper, *v.a.* verstricken, verwickeln; hemmen, belästigen (*fig.*).

Hamster, *s.* der Hamster.

Hanaper, *s. see* [1]Hamper; der Behälter für Kostbarkeiten.

Hand, I. *s.* die Hand; (—writing) die Handschrift; (signature) die Unterschrift; (measure) die Handbreite (= 4 Zoll); (workman, *etc.*) der Arbeiter; (sailor) der Mann, Matrose; (side) die Seite; (helping —) die Hilfe; die Karten (die man in der Hand hat); der Zeiger (*Horol.*); by show of —s, durch Aufheben der Hände; to be — and glove with a p., mit einem ein Herz und eine Seele sein; on the one —, auf der einen Seite, einerseits; on the other —, andererseits; all —s on deck! alle Mann auf Deck! the ship was lost with all —s, das Schiff ging mit Mann und Maus unter; to ask the — of Miss E. S., um Fräulein E. S. anhalten, sich um Fräulein E. S.'s Hand bewerben; to bear a —, Hilfe leisten; bear a —! greift zu! by the — of, vermittelst, durch; to bring up by —, ohne Muttermilch aufziehen; to change —s, in andere Hände übergehn *or* kommen, den Besitzer wechseln; at —, zur Hand, bei der Hand, nah(e); near at —, nah(e), nahebei; at first —, aus erster Hand; he deserves well at our —s, er hat sich um uns verdient gemacht; to be a good — at . . ., in (*dat.*) . . . geschickt sein; to fall into s.o.'s —s, in jemandes *or* einem in die Hände fallen; from — to —, von einer Hand zur andern; (to fight) — to —, Leib an Leib (fechten); to give one's — upon a th., (einem) die Hand darauf geben; to have a — in, die Hand im Spiele haben bei, bei (etwas) tätig sein; you had a — in the business, Sie waren auch dabei beteiligt; to have one's —s full, die Hände voll haben; I have my —s full, ich habe alle Hände voll (zu tun); — in —, Hand in Hand; the matter in —, die vorliegende Sache; to take in —, in die Hand nehmen, übernehmen; now in —, eben unter der *or* in Arbeit; my — is in, ich habe schon angefangen, bin im Zuge; to keep a firm — over, streng im Zaume halten; to lay —s upon a th., etwas ergreifen; eine Sache angreifen; to lay —s upon o.s., Hand an sich selbst legen; to lend a —, Handreichung tun, helfen; light —, leichte Hand; to live from — to mouth, vor der Hand in den Mund leben; note of —, der Handwechsel, Handschuldschein; —s off! weg da! Hände weg! off- —, ohne Zögern, aus dem Stegreif; geläufig; to be off —, etwas kurz angebunden sein; to take off s.o.'s —s, einem etwas abkaufen; to wash one's —s of a p., sich von einem losmachen, nichts mehr mit einem zu tun haben wollen; to wash one's —s of a th., sich wegen einer Sache die Hände in Unschuld waschen, eine Sache gehen lassen wie sie geht; on —, in Händen, (in stock) vorrätig; I have him on my —s, ich bin für ihn verantwortlich, er liegt mir auf der Tasche; on the one (other) —, auf der einen (anderen) Seite; on all —s, von allen Seiten; out of —, auf der Stelle, sogleich; to get out of —, unlenkbar werden; to buy second- —, antiquarisch *or* aus zweiter Hand kaufen; to shake —s, einander die Hände drücken; to shake a p. by the — *or* to shake —s with a p., einem die Hand schütteln; to take a — at a game, in einem Spiele mitspielen; to one's —, bereit; to come to —, einlaufen; in the turn of a —, im Handumdrehen; not a —'s turn, nichts, nicht das Geringste; to take by the —, bei der Hand nehmen (*lit.*), unter seinen Schutz nehmen (*fig.*); to try one's — at a th., etwas versuchen; under — and seal, unterschrieben und besiegelt; the upper —, die Oberhand; with one's own —, mit eigner Hand; with a strong —, mit Gewalt; with a high —, hochfahrend, gewalttätig; busy —s make happy minds, Arbeit macht das Leben süß (*prov.*). II. *v.a.* einhändigen, geben, überreichen; to — **about,** herumgeben; to — **down,** herunterlangen, herunterreichen; to — down to posterity, der Nachwelt überliefern; to — **in,** eingeben, einreichen (*a letter, petition*); (help in) hineinhelfen; to — **out,** aushelfen; to — out of a difficulty, aus einer Schwierigkeit heraushelfen; to — **over** (to s.o.), überliefern, einhändigen (an einen); to — **round,** herumreichen. **—ed,** *adj.* (*in comp.* =) mit Händen; empty- —ed, mit leeren Händen. **—ful,** *s.* eine Handvoll (*also fig.*); the merest —ful, das kleinste Häufchen, eine bloße Handvoll; a heavy —ful, ein tüchtiges *or* schweres Stück Arbeit. **—icap,** I. *s.* ein Wettrennen, wobei die Pferde durch Gewichte gleich schwer gemacht, oder sonstige Ungleichheiten der Pferde ausgeglichen werden, Wettrennen mit Vorgabe, das Handicap(rennen); das Ausgleichs-Preisspiel (*Lawn Tennis*). II. *v.a.* ein Pferd zum Wettrennen durch Gewichte den andern Rennern gleich schwer machen; Beschränkungen auferlegen, hemmen, behindern (*fig.*); he was —icapped in the race of life, auf seinem Flug durchs Leben sind ihm viel Gewichte an die Flügel gehängt, in seinem Lebenslauf sind ihm viel Steine in den Weg geworfen. —**icapper**, *s.* der, welcher bei Rennen die Gewichtsauflage bestimmt; der Ausgleicher. —**icraft**, *s.* das Handwerk, Gewerbe. —**icraftsman**, *s.* der Handwerker. —**ily**, *adv. see* —y. —**iness**, *s.* die Behendigkeit, Gewandtheit; (convenient size) die Handlichkeit; (convenience) die Bequemlichkeit. —**iwork**, *s.* die Handarbeit, das Kunstwerk, die Schöpfung. —**le**, *see* Handle. —**sel**, I. *s.* das Handgeld; der erste Gebrauch; der Vorgeschmack. II. *v.a.* zum ersten Male gebrauchen *or* tun; das Handgeld geben. —**some**, *see* Handsome. —**y**, *adj.* gewandt, geschickt; handlich, bequem; zur Hand, leicht erreichbar, nah. *Comp.* —**barrow**, *s.* der Schiebkarren; (litter) die Trage. —-**basket**, *s.* der Handkorb. —**bell**, *s.* die Tischglocke, Schelle. —**bill**, *s.* der (gedruckte) Zettel, Reklamezettel. —**book**, *s.* das Handbuch. —**breadth**, *s.* die Handbreite. —-**cart**, der Handkarren. —**cuff**, I. *s.* die Handschelle. II. *v.a.* (einem) Handschellen anlegen, (einen) fesseln. —-**gallop**, *s.* der kurze Gallop. —-**glass**, *s.* der Handspiegel; das Vergrößerungsglas mit Stiel zum Lesen, Leseglas; die Glasglocke (*Hort.*). —-**grenade**, *s.* die Handgranate. —-**hold**, der Griff. —-**kerchief**, *s.* das Taschentuch; das dünne Halstuch. —-**loom**, I. *s.* der Hand(webe)stuhl. II. *attrib.*; —-loom weaver, der Handstuhlweber. —-**machine**, *s.* die Handnähmaschine. —-**made**, *adj.* mit der Hand gemacht. —**maid**(**en**), *s.* die Magd. —-**mill**, *s.* die Handmühle. —-**post**, *s.* der Wegweiser. —-**power**, *s.* der Handgebrauch. —-**rail**, *s.* die Geländerstange. —**saw**, *s.* die Handsäge. —**shaking**, *s.* der Händedruck. —**spike**, *s.* die Hebestange, Handspake. —-**spun**, *adj.*; —-spun yarn, das Handgarn. —-**to**-—, *adj.*; a —-to-— fight, das Handgemenge. —**writing**, *s.* die Handschrift.

Handle, I. *v. a.* anfassen; angreifen, mit der Hand berühren; (manage) handhaben; behandeln (*a subject*). II. *s.* die Handhabe, der Griff; das Heft (*of a knife, sword, etc.*); die Kurbel (*of a telephone*); der Henkel (*of a vessel*); der Tragring, Handgriff (*on a trunk*); — of a plough, die Pflugsterze; — of a door, der Türgriff; pump-—, der Pumpenschwengel; to give a — to, eine Handhabe bieten, eine günstige Gelegenheit geben (*fig.*); a — to a name, ein Titel vor einem Namen (*coll.*). *Comp.* —-**bar**, *s.* die Lenkstange (*Cycl.*).

Handsome, *adj.*, —**ly**, *adv.* hübsch, schön; (elegant) zierlich; (noble) groß-, edel-mütig; a — fortune, ein hübsches Vermögen; — is that — does, edel ist, wer Edles tut (*prov.*). —**ness**, *s.* die Schönheit; die Anmut, Artigkeit.

Hang, I. *reg.* (*& ir.*) *v.a.* (auf)hängen; (droop) hängen lassen; einhängen (*doors*); tapezieren (*rooms*); to — o.s., sich erhängen; — it! zum Henker (damit)! I'll be —ed if I . . ., ich will mich hängen lassen, wenn ich . . .; to — fire, nachbrennen, nicht zustande kommen wollen, auf sich warten lassen; to — the lip, die Lippe hängen lassen, schmollen; one must not — a man for his looks, man muß den Menschen nicht nach dem Äußern beurteilen (*prov.*); to — **out**, aushängen (*clothes, etc.*); to — **up**, aufhängen. II. *ir.v.n.* hangen; hängen, schweben (over a th., über einer S.); (be —ed) gehängt (*obs.* gehenkt) werden; (dangle) baumeln; schweben, flattern (*as a flag*); (incline) sich neigen; (cling to) anhangen, ankleben; to — **about**, faulenzen, müßig umherschlendern; a feeling of illness still —s about me, ein Gefühl des Krankseins empfinde ich noch immer; to — about a p., sich an einen schmiegen, sich immer in jemandes Nähe halten; to — **back**, zurückhalten (*also C. L.*), nicht daran wollen; to — **down**, herabhängen; to — **loose**, flattern, schwebend herabhängen; to — **on**, sich anklammern an (*acc.*), hangen an (*dat.*), (rest on) ruhen auf (*dat.*), (depend on) abhängen von; to — **out**, aushangen; wohnen (*sl.*); to — **over**, überhangen, schweben über (*dat.*); to — **to**, sich anklammern an (*acc.*); to — **together**, zusammenhalten, zusammenhängen; to — **upon**, hängen an (*dat.*); time —s heavy upon my hands, mir wird die Zeit lang; to — upon the rear of the enemy, dem Feind dicht auf der Ferse bleiben. III. *s.* der Abhang; (bent) die Neigung. —**er**, *s.* das Gehenk; (cutlass) der Stutzsäbel, das Waidmesser; der w...bige Abhang; der Aufhänger. —**ing**, I. *adj.*, hängendswert, Galgen-; —ing bridge, die Hängebrücke; a —ing business, eine ...ssache. II. *s.* das Hangen, Hängen. —**ings**, *pl.* die Tapete, der Behang; (curtains) die Vorhänge; paper-—ings, die Papiertapete. *Comp.* —**er-on**, *s.* der Anhänger; (parasite) der Schmarotzer. —**ing-garden**, *s.* hängender Garten. —**man**, *s.* der Henker.

Hank, *s.* die Docke, Strähne, der Knäuel.

Hanker, *v.n.*; to — after a th., sich nach einer S. sehnen; nach einer S. verlangen. —**ing**, I. *adj.*, —**ingly**, *adv.* sehnsüchtig. II. *s.* das starke Verlangen, die Sehnsucht.

Hansom, *s.* die schnellfahrende leichte einspännige Droschke, mit Kutscherbock hinter am Wagendeck.

[1]**Hap**, *v.a.* einhüllen, bedecken (*prov.*).

[2]**Hap**, I. *v.n.* sich zutragen, sich ereignen. II. *s.* der Zufall; (luck) das Glück; (fate) das Schicksal; by good —, glücklicherweise. —**less**, *adj.* unglücklich. —**ly**, *adv.* vielleicht; zufällig, von ungefähr; möglicherweise. —**pen**, *v.n.* sich ereignen, (zufällig) geschehen; passieren (*coll.*); I —pened to read, ich las zufällig; we —pened to be looking out of the window, wir sahen gerade aus dem Fenster; to —pen on, zufällig auf (eine S.) stoßen, mit (einem) zusammentreffen. —**pier**, *comp. of* —py, glücklicher. —**piest**, *sup. of* —py, glücklichst. —**pily**, *adv.* glücklicherweise; glücklich; (skilfully) geschickt, gewandt. —**piness**, *s.* die Glückseligkeit; (good luck) das Glück; (gracefulness, *etc.*) die Gefälligkeit, Gewandtheit. —**py**, *adj.* (lucky) glücklich; (contented, *etc.*) glückselig; (favourable) günstig; (skilful) geschickt; I am very —py to learn, ich freue mich sehr, zu erfahren; to be —py in expressing oneself, sich gut, treffend ausdrücken *or* auszudrücken wissen; he is —py in his replies, er versteht es (gut), passende Antworten zu geben, ist in seinen Antworten glücklich; in a —py hour, zu glücklicher Stunde. *Comp.* —-**hazard**, *s.* der Zufall, das Geratewohl; at —-hazard, aufs Geratewohl. —**py-go-lucky**, *adj.* unbekümmert, sorglos.

Ha'porth = Halfpenny worth; to be not a — of good to anyone, keinem auch nur für einen Pfennig nutzen.

Haptics, *s.* die Tastlehre, Tastkunde.

Harangue, I. *v.a.* feierlich anreden. II. *v.n.* eine feierliche Ansprache halten; das große Wort führen. III. *s.* die (An-)Rede; empty —, die bombastisch Rede. —**r**, *s.* der Redner.

Harass, *v.a.* fortwährend belästigen, quälen, plagen, beunruhigen.

Harbinger, I. *s.* der Vorbote, Vorläufer; der Quartiermacher (*obs.*). II. *v.a.* vorhergehen, einführen; ankündigen.

Harbour, I. *s.* der Hafen; der Zufluchtsort, das Asyl (*fig.*); — of refuge, der Zufluchtshafen (*Naut.*); mouth of the —, die Einfahrt in den Hafen. II. *v.a.* beherbergen; (protect) schützen, (einem) Schutz geben; hegen (*revenge, etc.*). III. *v.n.* herbergen. —**age**, *s.* die Herberge, Zuflucht, das Unterkommen. —**er**, *s.* der Beherberger, Wirt; der Schützer. —**less**, *adj.* ohne Hafen; ohne Herberge *or* Schutz. *Comp.* —-**dues**, *pl.* Hafengebühren. —-**master**, *s.* der Hafenmeister. —-**pilot**, *s.* der Hafenlotse.

Hard, I. *adj.* hart; (difficult) schwer (zu verstehen,

auszuführen, &c.), mühsam, hart; (stern) streng, hart; (oppressive) drückend; (cruel) grausam; hart, streng (*as frost, winter, etc.*); (unfeeling) gefühllos, unbarmherzig, hart; (unkind) unfreundlich, hart; (unfair) unbillig, ungerecht; herb, sauer (*to the taste*); (stingy) karg, geizig; (forcible) kräftig; tüchtig, fleißig (*as a worker*); (inflexible) unbeugsam; hart, grob (*as features*); unschmackhaft, mager, schlecht (*as fare*); schlecht, schlimm (*as times*); — bargain, schwerer Kauf; he is — to please, er ist schwer zu befriedigen; — to digest, schwer zu verdauen; — of hearing, schwerhörig; — to deal with, schwer auszukommen mit; — drinker, der Säufer; a — student, ein fleißiger Student; ein Büffler (*coll.*); a — case, eine harte Fügung, ein schlimmer, harter Fall; a — death, ein schwerer Tod; a — and fast rule, eine unabänderliche *or* ausnahmslose Regel; — work, schwere Arbeit; to be — upon a p., hart gegen einen verfahren *or* sein. II. *adv.* (forcibly) heftig, stark, mit Kraftanstrengung; (diligently) fleißig, tüchtig; (with difficulty) mit Mühe; — by, neben an, dicht dabei, gleich nebenan; to blow, drink, rain, freeze —, stark wehen, trinken, regnen, frieren; to ride —, schnell reiten; — -a-port! das Ruder ganz beim Steuerbord! it will go — with me, but I . . ., da müßte es schon schlimm kommen, wenn ich nicht . . .; they are — pressed, sie sind schwer bedrängt *or* in großer Bedrängnis; he is — put to it, er muß es sich sauer werden lassen; — at work, fleißig bei *or* an der Arbeit; to bear — upon, streng behandeln, drücken; to press — for, ernstlich dringen auf (*acc.*); to work —, angestrengt *or* fleißig arbeiten; — up, in großer Not, sehr arm; to be — up for, schlimm daran sein in Beziehung auf (*acc.*) . . .; to die —, einen harten Todeskampf haben, ein zähes Leben haben (*lit.*), sein Leben teuer verkaufen (*fig.*); the principle is dying —, der Grundsatz stirbt nur langsam aus. **—en**, *v.* I. *a.* härten; (inure) abhärten, gewöhnen an (eine S.); (confirm) verhärten, bestärken (*in sin, etc.*); (strengthen) stärken; (make callous) gefühllos, hart machen. II. *n.* hart werden, sich verhärten; hart, unempfindlich werden (*fig.*); the money-market is —ening, Geld zieht an. **—ihood**, *s.* die Kühnheit, Tapferkeit, Unerschrockenheit; (effrontery) die Dreistigkeit. **—ily**, *adv.* kühn, dreist. **—iness**, *s.* die Kühnheit; (strength, *etc.*) die Rüstigkeit, Ausdauer, Festigkeit; die Dreistigkeit. **—ly**, *adv.* mit Mühe, mühsam; (harshly) hart, streng; (scarcely) kaum, schwerlich; (unwelcomely) unwillkommen, unangenehm; to think —ly of, eine ungünstige Meinung von . . . haben; to be —ly dealt with, übel behandelt werden. **—ness**, *s.* die Härte; (firmness) die Festigkeit; (difficulty) die Schwierigkeit; die Härte, der Druck (*of the times*); die Grausamkeit; die Grobheit, Strenge, Härte; (penuriousness) die Kargheit; die Strenge (of the weather, der Witterung); —ness of heart, die Hartherzigkeit; die Verstocktheit, Unbußfertigkeit. **—ship**, *s.* die Beschwerde, Mühseligkeit, das Ungemach; (injury) die Bedrückung, das Unrecht. **—y**, *adj.* stark; abgehärtet; a —y plant, eine abgehärtete Pflanze. *Comp.* **—-beset**, *adj.* hart bedrängt. **—-earned**, *adj.* sauer erworben, schwer verdient. **—-featured**, *adj.* mit harten Gesichtszügen. **—-fisted**, *adj.* geizig. **—-headed**, *adj.* verständig, klug, schlau; festen Sinnes. **—-hearted**, *adj.* hartherzig. **—-heartedness**, *s.* die Hartherzigkeit. **—-mouthed**, *adj.* hartmäulig. **—-set**, *adj.* starr (*of a glance*); gezwungen (*of smiles*); unbeugsam, hart. **—ware**, *s.* die Eisenwaren, Metallwaren. **—working**, *adj.* fleißig.

Har—e, *s.* der Hase. **—rier**, *s.* der Hasenhund. *Comp.* **—ebell**, *s.* die rundblätterige Glockenblüte. **—ebrained**, *adj.* gedankenlos, faselig. **—elip**, *s.* die Hasenscharte.

Harem, *s.* der Harem, das Serail.

Haricot, I. *s.* das Ragout von Hammelfleisch und Gemüse. II. *attrib.*; — bean, welsche Bohne.

Hark, I. *v.n.* horchen. II. *int.* horch!

Harlequin, *s.* der Hanswurst, Possenreißer, Harlekin. **—ade**, *s.* das Possenspiel, Possenstück, die Posse.

Harlot, *s.* die Hure, Dirne; gemeiner Kerl (*obs.*). **—ry**, *s.* die Hurerei, gemeine Buhlerei.

Harm, I. *s.* (hurt) der Schaden, Nachteil; (evil) das Böse, Unrecht, der Frevel; to do a p. —, einem Schaden tun *or* zufügen; it will do you no —, es wird dir nicht(s) schaden; no — done, (das) hat nichts zu sagen; I don't mean any —, ich führe nichts Böses im Schilde, meine es nicht böse; to keep out of —'s way, die Gefahr meiden, sich vorsehen. II. *v.a.* beschädigen, verletzen; (einem) schaden, Leid zufügen. **—ful**, *adj.*, **—fully**, *adv.* nachteilig, schädlich, verderblich. **—fulness**, *s.* die Schädlichkeit. **—less**, *adj.*, **—lessly**, *adv.* harmlos, unschädlich; (innocent) schuldlos; to hold a p. —less, einen schadlos halten. **—lessness**, *s.* die Harmlosigkeit; die Unschädlichkeit; die Unschuld.

Harmon—ic, *adj.* wohlklingend, harmonisch (*Mus.*); übereinstimmend, harmonisch (*Math.*); —ic proportion, harmonisches Verhältnis; —ic triad, harmonischer Dreiklang. **—ica**, *s.* die Harmonika. **—ical**, *see* —ic. **—ics**, *pl.* die Lehre vom musikalischen Wohlklang, die Harmonik. **—ious**, *adj.*, **—iously**, *adv.* wohlklingend, harmonisch; (concordant) zusammenstimmend; (symmetrical) symmetrisch; (agreeing) übereinstimmend, friedlich. **—iousness**, *s.* der Einklang; die Übereinstimmung; das Ebenmaß. **—ist**, *s.* der Harmonist; (writer) der Harmoniker. **—ium**, *s.* die Hausorgel, das Harmonium. **—ize**, *v.* I. *n.* überein-, zusammen-stimmen, einmütig *or* einig sein. II. *a.* harmonisch machen, in Einklang bringen; ein Tonstück mehrstimmig setzen. **—izer**, *s.* der Harmonist, Tonsetzer; einer, der in Übereinstimmung bringt. **—y**, *s.* die Harmonie, Übereinstimmung (*Mus., Paint.*); das Ebenmaß (*Arch.*); die Übereinstimmung, Eintracht, Friedlichkeit (*fig.*); to be in —y with, im Einklang stehen mit, stimmen zu.

Harness, I. *s.* (armour) der Harnisch, die Rüstung; das Geschirr; to be in —, mitten in der Arbeit stehen (*fig.*); to go in —, ziehen; to die in —, in Ausübung seines Berufes sterben (*fig.*). II. *v.a.* anschirren. *Comp.* **—-maker**, *s.* der Geschirrmacher, Sattler. **—-room**, *s.* die Geschirrkammer.

Harp, I. *s.* die Harfe (*Mus.*); Jews'- —, die Maultrommel. II. *v.n.* harfen; to — on a subject, stets auf dasselbe Thema zurückkommen, ein Thema immer wieder vorbringen; to be always —ing on the same string, immer bei der alten Leier bleiben. **—er**, **—ist**, *s.* der Harfner, die Harfnerin, Harfenspielerin. **—ing**, *s.* das Harfenspielen. **—oon**, I. *s.* die Harpune. II. *v.a.* harpunieren. **—sichord**, *s.* das Spinett, altmodisches Klavier. **—y**, *s.* die Harpye; die habsüchtige, raubgierige Person (*fig.*).

Harridan, *s.* die alte Vettel, alte Hexe.

Harrow, I. *s.* die Egge; die Sturmegge (*Fort.*). II. *v.a.* eggen; (— up) quälen, martern. **—ing**, *adj.* herzzerreißend, qualvoll, schrecklich.

Harrier, *s.* der Hasenhund; (—-kite) der Weih.

Harry, *v.* I. *a.* verheeren, plündern (*a land*); (torment) quälen, plagen; berauben (*a nest*); to — out of, verjagen von *or* aus. II. *n.* Raubzüge unternehmen.

Harsh, *adj.*, **—ly**, *adv.* rauh (*to the touch*); herb, streng (*to the taste*); hart, rauh, harsch, barsch, grell, mißklingend (*to the ear*); (severe) streng, barsch, unsanft, hart, unfreundlich; (morose) mürrisch. **—ness**, *s.* die Rauheit; die Härte, Rauheit, Barschheit (*fig.*).

Hart, *s.* der Hirsch; — of ten, der Zehnender; —

royal, der vom König vergebens gejagte und deshalb für unverletzlich geltende Hirsch (*obs.*). *Comp.* —**shorn**, *s.* das Hirschhorn; spirits of —shorn, der Hirschhorngeist. —**'s-tongue**, *s.* die Hirschzunge (*Bot.*).

Harum-scarum, I. *adv.* Hals über Kopf. II. *adj.* hastig, wild, flüchtig, gedankenlos, leichtsinnig, zerstreut.

Harvest, I. *s.* die Ernte; der Erfolg, Ertrag (*fig.*); *see* —-time. II. *v.a.* ernten; einheimsen. III. *attrib.*; — thanksgivings, das Erntedankfest. —**er**, *s.* der Erntende, Schnitter; (—ing machine) die Mähmaschine. *Comp.* —-**home**, *s.* das Erntefest. —-**moon**, *s.* der Vollmond zu Anfang des Herbstes. —-**mouse**, *s.* die Feldmaus, Zwergmaus. —-**time**, *s.* die Erntezeit.

Has, —**t**, *2 & 3 sing. pres. ind. of* Have.

Hash, I. *s.* gehacktes Fleisch; das Gehackte, der Mischmasch, das Ragout (*fig.*); to make a — of a th., etwas verderben *or* verbruddeln, eine S. festfahren. II. *v.a.* klein hacken, zu Brei schlagen.

Hasp, I. *s.* die Haspe, Klampe, das Schließband, der Schließhaken; (spindle) der, die Haspel. II. *v.a.* mit einer Haspe schließen, zuriegeln.

Hassock, *s.* das Kniekissen, Betkissen (*in church*).

Hast—e, I. *s.* die Hast, Eile; (passion) die Hitze, Hastigkeit; to make —e, eilen, sich beeilen; post-—e, in aller Eile; in —e, in Eile, eilig; more —e less speed, Eile mit Weile (*prov.*). II. —**e**, —**en**, *v.a.* beschleunigen; to —en on, antreiben. III. —**e**, —**en**, *v.n. & r.* eilen, sich beeilen, sich sputen; to —e away, forteilen. —**ener**, *s.* der, die Eilende; der Beschleuniger. —**ily**, *adv.* eilig, in Eile; (rashly) voreilig, übereilt; (hotly) hitzig, ungeduldig. —**iness**, *s.* die Hast, Eilfertigkeit; die Übereilung; die Hitze, Heftigkeit. —**y**, *adj.* hastig, eilig, eilfertig; voreilig, überschnell; hitzig, hastig, jähzornig; a —y line, in Eile ein paar Worte. *Comp.* —**y-pudding**, *s.* der Mehlpudding.

Hat, *s.* der Hut; silk —, der Seidenhut; top —, der Zylinder; to touch one's — to a p., einen grüßen, indem man den Hut mit der Hand berührt. —**ter**, *s.* der Hutmacher. *Comp.* —-**band**, *s.* das Hutband. —-**box**, —-**case**, *s.* die Hutschachtel. —-**brush**, *s.* die Hutbürste. —-**rack**, *s.* der Hutkaken. —-**string**, *s.* die Hutschnur.

[1]**Hatch**, I. *v.a.* aushecken, ausbrüten (*also fig.*); to count one's chickens before they are —ed, die Rechnung ohne den Wirt machen. II. *v.n.* brüten; sich entwickeln. III. *s.* die Hecke, Brut; (half-door) die halbe Tür; die Luke (*Naut.*); die Einfahrt (*Min.*); under —es, eingesperrt. *Comp.* —**way**, *s.* die (Treppen-)Luke.

[2]**Hatch**, *v.a.* schraffieren; gründen (*silver and gold*). —**et**, *see* Hatchet. —**ing**, *s.* die Schraffierung (*Draw.*, *Engr.*); die Aufkratzung (*with gilders*); counter —ing, Kreuzschraffierung. *Comp.* —**ing-knife**, *s.* der Ritzer.

Hatchet, *s.* das Beil, die kleine Axt; to bury the —, die Streitaxt vergraben, Frieden schließen (*fig.*); to send the helve after the —, die Flinte ins Korn werfen, alles verloren geben. *Comp.* —-**face**, *s.* das Gesicht mit scharfgeschnittenen Zügen. —-**shaped**, *adj.* beilförmig.

Hatchment, *s.* das Totenschild, Wappenschild eines Verstorbenen.

Hat—e, I. *s.* der Haß (to, towards, gegen, wider, auf einen). II. *v.a.* hassen; I —e . . ., . . . hasse ich, ist mir höchst zuwider, finde ich schauderhaft, kann ich nicht ausstehen. —**eful**, *adj.*, —**efully**, *adv.* (—ed) verhaßt; gehässig. —**efulness**, *s.* die Gehässigkeit. —**er**, *s.* der Hasser. —**red**, *s.* der Haß, Groll, Abscheu, die Feindseligkeit.

Haught—ily, *adv.* hochmütig. —**iness**, *s.* der Hochmut, Stolz. —**y**, *adj.* hochmütig, stolz.

Haul, I. *s.* der kräftige Zug; der Fischzug; at a —, auf einen Zug. II. *v.a.* ziehen, schleppen (*also Naut.*); to — **ashore**, ans Land ziehen; to — **down**, niederholen, streichen (the flag, die Flagge, *Naut.*), niederziehen (*fig.*); to — a p. **over** the coals, einen tüchtig ausschelten; to — **tight**, straff anholen; to — **up**, aufholen; to — the wind, beim Winde brassen.

Haulm, *s.* der Halm, der (trockene) Pflanzenstengel.

Haunch, I. *s.* die Hüfte; die Keule; die Hüfte, Hanke, der Schenkel (*of a horse*); der Schenkel (*Arch.*); — of venison, Wildpretkeule. II. *attrib.*; —bone, der Hüftknochen, das Lendenstück. —**ed**, *adj.* mit (starken, *etc.*) Hüften.

Haunt, I. *v.a.* häufig besuchen, heimsuchen; durch häufige Besuche plagen; (wie ein Gespenst) verfolgen; to — a spot, sich oft an einem Ort herumtreiben; to — a house, in einem Hause spuken; (the) mind-—ing presence of the sea, dem Geist stets fühlbare Gegenwart des Meeres. II. *s.* der häufig besuchte Ort, gewohnte Aufenthalt; die Höhle, das Lager, Nest, der Gang (*of beasts*); s.o.'s —s, der Ort, wo einer sich meist *or* gern aufhält. —**ed**, *p.p. & adj.*; —ed man, ein von Geistern verfolgter Mensch; the —ed castle, das verwunschene Schloß; the —ed house, das gespenstige Haus, Spukhaus; this house is —ed, in diesem Hause spukt es *or* geht es um. —**er**, *s.* der (die) fleißige Besucher(in).

Hause, *s.* die Paßhöhe, Höhe eines Bergpasses (*dial.*).

Hautboy, *s.* die Hoboe, Oboe.

Have, I. *ir.v.a.* (possess) haben, besitzen; (contain) enthalten; (get) erhalten, bekommen; (learn) haben, hören; (cause) lassen; (be obliged) müssen; (enjoy) genießen; tickets may be had of the conductor, Fahrscheine kann man beim Schaffner bekommen; we shall — rain, wir werden Regen bekommen; they will — many presents, sie werden viele Geschenke erhalten *or* bekommen; you — but to speak the truth, Sie brauchen nur die Wahrheit zu sagen; he had to confess, er mußte gestehen, er war genötigt zu gestehen; you — my word for it that . . ., ich gebe Ihnen mein Wort (darauf), daß . . .; I would — all men workers, ich wünschte, daß alle Menschen Arbeiter wären; I would not — you do this, ich möchte nicht, daß ihr dies tätet, ich wollte euch nicht raten dies zu tun; you must — these trees cut down, Sie müssen diese Bäume abhauen lassen; I would — you know, Sie müssen wissen; he had three horses killed under him, ihm wurden drei Pferde unter dem Leibe erschossen; you — it! Sie haben es getroffen! the ayes — it, die Mehrheit ist für den Antrag; — a care! vorgesehen; to — one's say, seine Meinung ausdrücken; — done! laß das! höre auf! there I had him! da hatte ich ihn, konnte ich ihn fassen! as good luck would — it, glücklicherweise; to — a mind, Lust haben; to let a p. — a th., einem etwas zukommen lassen; to — rather, lieber haben, vorziehen; to — advice, (den Arzt, Anwalt) zu Rate ziehen; I had as good, es wäre ebenso gut, daß ich . . .; I had better, es wäre besser, daß ich . . .; I had best, das Beste wäre wohl, daß ich . . . *or* wenn ich . . .; to — **about** one, bei sich haben; I — no money about me, ich habe kein Geld bei mir; — **at** you! es gilt dir! nimm dich in Acht! he has your happiness at heart, dein Glück liegt ihm am Herzen; to — **back**, zurückkommen lassen; to — **in** derision (honour), verachten (achten); to — in keeping, zum Aufbewahren haben, verwahren, aufbewahren; God — you in his keeping! Gott halte dich in seiner Hut! to — **on**, anhaben, aufhaben, tragen; he has a new hat on, er hat einen neuen Hut auf; what dress has she on? was für ein Kleid hat sie an, trägt sie? II. *ir.v.aux.* haben; sein; we — seen, wir haben gesehen; he has come, er ist gekommen; they — **fallen**, sie sind gefallen: —

you seen it? I —, haben Sie es gesehen? ja; you — done what I told you, — you not? nicht wahr, Sie haben getan, was ich Ihnen sagte?

Haven, *s.* der Hafen (*also fig.*); die Freistätte (*fig.*).

Haversack, *s.* der Brotbeutel, Futterbeutel (*Mil.*); (gunner's case) der Lederbeutel (für die Munition); der Rucksack.

Having, I. *p. see* Have. II. *s.* das Eigentum, die Habe, der Besitz. III. *adj.* habgierig (*obs., dial.*).

Havoc, *s.* die Verwüstung; —! Mord! to make — of a th., etwas verwüsten, zerstören; (waste) vergeuden.

[1]**Haw**, *s.* der Hag; die Hagebutte (*Bot.*). **—haw**, *s. see* Haha. *Comp.* **—finch**, *s.* der Kernbeißer. **—thorn**, *s.* der Hagedorn, Weißdorn.

[2]**Haw**, I. *s.* das Räuspern. II. *v.n.* stottern. **—haw**, *v.n.* laut *or* herzlich lachen.

[1]**Hawk**, I. *s.* der Habicht, Falke; (cheat) der Gauner. II. *v.n.* mit Falken beizen, jagen. **—er**, *s.* der Falkenjäger. **—ing**, *s.* die Falkenbeize. *Comp.* **—-eyed**, *adj.* scharfsichtig, falkenäugig. **—moth**, *s.* der Habichtskäfer. **—-nosed**, mit einer Habichtsnase. **—weed**, *s.* das Habichtskraut.

[2]**Hawk**, *v.n.* sich räuspern; to — **up**, ausräuspern.

[3]**Hawk**, *v.a.* hökern, hausieren. **—er**, *s.* der Höker, Hausierer; —er of books, der fliegende Buchhändler. **—ing**, *s.* das Hausieren.

Hawse, *s.* die Lage der Ankertaue vor den Klüsen. **—r**, I. *s.* das Kabeltau. II. *attrib.*; steel —r wire, das Schlepptau von Draht. *Comp.* **—-holes**, *pl.* die Klüsen. **—-pieces**, *pl.* die Klüsenhölzer.

Hay, *s.* das Heu; to make (into) —, (zu) Heu machen; to make — while the sun shines, das Eisen schmieden, solange es noch heiß ist; to make — in a p.'s rooms, in jemandes Zimmer alles durcheinander werfen (*sl.*). *Comp.* **—cock**, *s.* der Heuhaufen, kleiner Heuschober. **—-fever**, *s.* das Heufieber. **—-harvest**, *s.* die Heuernte. **—-loft**, *s.* der Heuboden. **—maker**, *s.* der Heumacher. **—making**, *s.* das Heumachen. **—mow**, *s.* aufgeschichtetes Heu. **—rick**, **—stack**, *s.* der Heuschober.

Hazard, I. *s.* (danger) die Gefahr, das Wagestück, Wagnis; (chance) der Zufall; das Hasardspiel (*Cards*); to play the losing —, sich verlaufen (*Bill.*); at all —s, auf alle Fälle; at the — of one's life, auf Gefahr seines Lebens. II. *v.a.* dem Zufall aussetzen, wagen, aufs Spiel setzen, in die Schanze schlagen. **—ous**, *adj.* gewagt, gefährlich.

Haz—e, *s.* der leichte Nebel, Höhenrauch, Dunst. **—iness**, *s.* die Nebeligkeit; die Unbestimmtheit (*fig.*). **—y**, *adj.* nebelig, dunstig.

Hazel, I. *s.* die Hasel(=staude). II. *adj.*, nußbraun; — eyes, nußbraune Augen. **—ine**, *s.* das Haselin (*Med.*). *Comp.* **—-nut**, *s.* die Haselnuß. **—-wood**, *s.* das Haselgebüsch.

He, I. *pers. pron.* er; der, derjenige; — who, derjenige, welcher. II. *in comp.* = das männliche Tier, Männchen; — goat, der Ziegenbock.

Head, I. *s.* der Kopf; das Haupt (*high style*); (individual) der Mann, das Stück; (chief) der Häuptling, Führer, das Oberhaupt; (principal) der Vorsteher, Verwalter; (chief place) das Haupt, die Spitze; (understanding) der Kopf, Verstand; (prow) der Schiffsschnabel; (source) die Quelle; die Höhe, Krisis (*of an illness*); (division) der Punkt, Hauptpunkt, Abschnitt; der Posten (*in accounts*); das obere Ende (*of a bay, etc.*); der Gipfel, Wipfel, die Krone (*of a tree*); die Spitze (*of a column, an army, an arrow, a violin bow, etc.*); die Schnecke (*of a violin*); der Vorsteher (*of a college*); der Griff (of a corkscrew, an einem Korkzieher); der Kopf (*of a nail, a hatchet, a pin, a bed, a poppy, a cabbage, etc.*); der Avers (*of a coin*); my — spins round, es schwindelt mir; he has a fine — of hair, er hat einen schönen Haarwuchs; per —, auf den Kopf, für jeden Einzelnen; 40 — of cattle, 40 Stück Rindvieh; 20 — of oxen, 20 Stück Ochsen; to be at the — of (an army, ein Heer) anführen, (an establishment, einer Anstalt) vorstehen; to come to a —, eitern (*as an ulcer*); reifen (*fig. of plans*); crowned —s, gekrönte Häupter; from — to foot, von Kopf (bis) zu Fuß, von oben bis unten; to gather —, überhand nehmen, zu Kräften kommen; to get (up) into one's —, in den Kopf bekommen, (in den Kopf steigen); to give a horse his —, einem Pferde die Zügel schießen lassen; to make neither — nor tail of a th., aus einer Sache nicht klug werden können; —(s) or tail(s)? Kopf oder Schrift? (over) — and ears, bis über die Ohren, vollständig, völlig; by the — and shoulders, durchaus, mit aller Gewalt; no hair of your — shall be harmed, es soll dir kein Haar gekrümmt werden; you cannot put old —s on young shoulders, Jugend hat nicht Tugend (*prov.*); too much by the —, vorlastig (*Naut.*); — over heels, Hals über Kopf, köpflings; a — of celery, ein Stück Sellerie; —s of the charges, die Klagepunkte; — of the Catholic church, das Oberhaupt der katholischen Kirche; —s of departments, Abteilungsvorstände; —s of a discourse, die Hauptpunkte einer Abhandlung; — of the galley, die Zunge am Setzschiff; — of the house *or* family, der Hausvater, das Oberhaupt der Familie; — of a (business-) house, der Geschäftsinhaber, Geschäftsleiter, Besitzer; — of the stairs, der oberste Teil einer Treppe; — of the table, der obere Teil des Tisches; she sat at the — of the table, sie saß oben am Tische; to carry a high —, den Kopf hoch tragen; to make — against a th., einem die Spitze bieten; they put their —s together, sie berieten sich, beratschlagen; to lose one's —, den Kopf verlieren; on this —, hierüber; out of one's —, aus dem Kopfe; to put into s.o.'s —, einem (etwas) in den Kopf setzen; to puzzle one's — at *or* over a th., sich (*dat.*) über eine S. den Kopf zerbrechen; his — runs on nothing but, er denkt an nichts als (an); to set a price upon a p.'s —, einen Preis auf jemands Kopf setzen; to take the —, den Vorrang abgewinnen; to take s.th. into one's —, sich (*dat.*) etwas in den Kopf setzen. II. *adj.* (*in comp.*) der, die, das vordere, erste, vorzüglichste, Haupt=, Ober=; — porter, der erste Portier; — waiter, der Oberkellner. III. *v.a.* (an)führen, befehligen (*an army, etc.*); (be at the — of) an der Spitze stehen; (go before) vorausgehen; (furnish with a —) mit einem Kopfe, Knopfe, einer Spitze, einer Überschrift versehen; (oppose) entgegenkommen; anköpfen (*pins*); verbodmen (*a cask*); the wind —s us, der Wind ist uns entgegen. IV. *v.n.* how does she —? wie läuft das Schiff? der Kurs? wie liegen wir? **—ed**, I. *p.p. see* — III.; —ed by, angeführt von; —ed with, beschlagen mit. II. *adj.*; cool-—ed, kaltblütig; giddy-—ed, schwindelköpfig; hot-—ed, tollköpfig; long-—ed, gescheit, schlau. **—er**, *s.* der Anköpfer (*of pins, nails, etc.*); (plunge) der Kopfsprung. **—iness**, *s.* das Berauschende (*of wine, etc.*). **—ing**, *s.* der Kolumnentitel, Titelkopf (*Typ.*); das Anköpfen (*of a pin*); (inscription) die Überschrift; das Fortstoßen des Balles mit dem Kopfe (*Association football*). **—less**, *adj.* ohne Kopf, kopflos (*also fig.*); (leaderless) ohne Führer. **—long**, I. *adj.* jäh, abschüssig; (rushing violently) ungestüm; (rash) unbesonnen, unüberlegt, voreilig. II. *adv.* (head-foremost) köpflings=; kopfüber, mit dem Kopfe voran; (precipitately) Hals über Kopf; unbedachtsam, eilig, hastig, plötzlich. **—most**, *adj.* vorderst (*of ships*). **—ship**, *s.* die höchste Gewalt; die leitende Rolle oder Stelle, die Führerschaft, der Oberbefehl, die Oberleitung, das Direktorat. **—y**, *adj.* berauschend. *Comp.*

—**ache**, *s.* der Kopfschmerz, das Kopfweh. —**band**, *s.* die Kopfbinde; das Kapitälchen (*Bookb.*). —**-clerk**, *s.* der erste Kommis; der erste Schreiber. —**-dress**, *s.*, —**-gear**, *s.* der Kopfputz. —**land**, *s.* das Vorgebirge, die Landspitze; die Anwand (*Agr.*). —**line**, *s.* die Hauptzeile (*Typ.*). —**man**, *s.* der Vorsteher, das Haupt. —**-master**, *s.* der Direktor, Schulvorsteher, Vorsteher (einer Schule). —**-mastership**, *s.* die Direktorstelle, die Stelle eines Schulvorstehers; he has been appointed to the —-mastership of the Perse School, er ist zum Vorsteher der Perse Schule ernannt worden. —**-miner**, *s.* der Obersteiger. —**-mistress**, *s.* die Schulvorsteherin, Vorsteherin (einer Schule). —**-money**, *s.* das Kopfgeld. —**-piece**, *s.* der Helm; die Titelvignette (*of a book*); der Stirnriemen (*Saddl.*); a good —-piece, ein fähiger Kopf (*fam.*). —**quarters**, *pl.* das Hauptquartier; der Haupt-Aufenthaltsort; der Mittelpunkt, Sammelpunkt; at —quarters, im Hauptquartier; an der Quelle (*fig.*). —**s-man**, *s.* der Scharfrichter. —**stall**, *s.* das Kopfstück (*of a bridle*); die Halfter. —**stone**, *s.* der Grabstein; der Kopfstein (*Arch.*); der Schlußstein. —**strong**, *adj.* (rash) hitzig, ungestüm; (obstinate) starrköpfig, halsstarrig, eigensinnig. —**way**, *s.* die Vorwärtsbewegung, der Fortschritt, Erfolg (*fig.*); to make —way, vorankommen, Fortschritte machen; to be under —way, im Schusse sein. —**-wind**, *s.* der Gegenwind. —**-work**, *s.* die Kopfarbeit. —**-workman**, *s.* der erste unter den Arbeitern, der Obermann, Vorarbeiter.

Heal, *v.a. & n.* heilen, versöhnen (*fig.*); to — up, zuheilen. —**er**, *s.* der Heilende, Heiler. —**ing**, I. *adj.* heilend, heilsam; versöhnend (*fig.*); —ing art, die Heilkunst, Heilkunde. II. *s.* das Heilen. —**thy**, *see* Health.

Health, I. *s.* die Gesundheit (*also in drinking*); good (bad) —, das Wohlbefinden (die Kränklichkeit); the soul's —, das Seelenheil; certificate, bill of —, das Gesundheitsattest; board of —, der Gesundheitsrat; in the best of —, in bestem Wohl sein; here's to the — of . . ., . . . soll leben! es lebe . . .! your good —! auf Ihr Wohl(sein)! II. *attrib.*; — resort, der Kurort. —**ful**, *adj.*, —**fully**, *adv.* gesund; gesund, heilsam, der Gesundheit zuträglich (*as a climate*). —**fulness**, *s.* die Gesundheit, Heilkraft. —**iness**, *s.* die Gesundheit. —**less**, *adj.* ungesund, kränklich. —**y**, *adj.* gesund.

Heap, I. *s.* der Haufe(n), die Masse; die Menge (*of people etc., vulg.*); der Steinhaufe(n) (*B.*); der Haufe(n) (*Typ.*); to be struck all of a —, ganz verblüfft sein (*vulg.*); in —s, haufenweise. II. *v.a.* häufen; to — **on**, hinzutun; to — **up**, aufhäufen, ansammeln.

Hear, I. *ir.v.a.* hören; anhören; (— and grant) erhören; (listen to) zuhören; (attend to) gehorchen; abhören (*a case, a witness, reading, a fact*); (learn) vernehmen, erfahren; überhören (lessons, Aufgaben); let me — how you are getting on, laßt mich wissen, was ihr macht; let us — from you, laß von dir hören! to — out, bis zu Ende hören; if I have —d that once, I have —d it fifty times, ich habe das gewiß fünfzigmal gehört. II. *ir.v.n.* hören; horchen; erfahren; I —d from him last week, vorige Woche bekam ich Nachricht von ihm; to — say *or* tell, sagen hören. III. *int.* horch! hört! —! —! sehr wahr! sehr richtig! (*Parl.*). —**er**, *s.* der Hörer; der Zuhörer (*of a preacher, etc.*). —**ing**, *s.* das Hören; (sense of —ing) das Gehör; (audience) die Audienz; das Verhör (*Law*); die Hörweite, Schallweite; within —ing, im Bereich der Stimme; in my —ing, vor meinen Ohren, wie ich selbst hörte; to give a p. a —ing, einen anhören, einem Gehör schenken; the —ing of witnesses, das Zeugenverhör. *Comp.* —**ing-trumpet**, *s.* das Hörrohr. —**say**, I. *s.* das Hörensagen; by —say, von Hörensagen. II. *adj.*; —say evidence, der Beweis durch Hörensagen.

Hearken, *v.* I. *n.* horchen, lauschen. II. *a.* erhorchen, erlauschen (*poet.*).

Hearse, *s.* der Leichenwagen, Totenwagen; die Bahre. *Comp.* —**cloth**, *s.* das Bahrtuch.

Heart, *s.* das Herz (*also fig.*); (inner part) das Innere; das Herz (*of a country, etc.*); (essence) das Wesentlichste, Leben, die Seele; dear —! geliebtes Herz! mein Herzchen! sweet—! mein Schatz *or* Schätzchen! enlargement of the —, die Herzerweiterung; to have at —, auf dem Herzen haben; by —, auswendig; with hand and —, mit Herz und Hand; that did my — good, das tat meinem Herzen wohl; my — fails me, mich verläßt der Mut; I could not find it in my —, ich konnte es nicht übers Herz bringen; in good —, in gutem Zustande, fruchtbar (*of land*); wohlgemut (*prov.*); — of iron, Felsenherz; in the — of, im Herzen, im Innern *or* Innersten von; in my — of —s, tiefsten Herzen *or* im Innersten meines Herzens; king of —s, der Herzenskönig (*Cards*); to lay, take s.th. to —, sich (*dat.*) etwas zu Herzen nehmen; my — misgives me, der Mut verläßt mich; searching of —(s), das Insichgehen; to open one's — to a p., einem sein Herz ausschütten; out of —, mutlos; to set a p.'s — at rest, einen beruhigen; to set one's — on, sein Herz hängen an (*acc.*); I have set my — on going, ich habe es mir in den Kopf gesetzt, zu gehen; to speak from one's —, frei *or* frisch von der Leber weg sprechen; to take the — out of s.o., einen mutlos machen; to take — of grace, sich (*dat.*) ein Herz fassen; to wear one's — upon one's sleeve, allzu offenherzig sein; his — sank, da sank ihm der Mut; with all my —, herzlich gern; (I watched them) with my — in my mouth, in atemloser Spannung; to (his) —'s content, nach Herzenslust; what the — thinketh the mouth speaketh, wes das Herz voll ist des fließet der Mund über (*B.*); his — is ready to leap into his mouth, er weiß seine Freude kaum zu verschweigen; his — went down to his heels, das Herz entfiel ihm, er verlor den Mut. —**en**, *v.a.* aufmuntern; bessern (*land*). —**ily**, *adv.* herzlich, von (ganzem) Herzen; (vigorously) tüchtig. —**iness**, *s.* die Herzlichkeit, Innigkeit; die Stärke (*of appetite*). —**less**, *adj.*, —**lessly**, *adv.* herzlos; (spiritless) zaghaft, feig; (dispiriting) entmutigend. —**lessness**, *s.* die Herzlosigkeit. —**some**, *adj.* aufmunternd; erheiternd; herzensfroh, munter. —**y**, I. *adj.* herzlich, innig, warm; (healthy) gesund, frisch, munter; (sincere) aufrichtig; (sound) fest, kernig; stark, tüchtig; —y appetite, starker, tüchtiger Appetit; to make a —y meal, tüchtig essen und trinken, fleißig zulangen; to be —y in, ernst sein um; —iest greetings, herzlichste Grüße. II. *s.*; my —ies! meine Herzensjungen! (*coll.*). *Comp.* —**-ache**, *s.* das Herzweh. —**-beat**, *s.* der Herzschlag. —**-break**, *s.* der Herzenskummer. —**-breaking**, *adj.* herzbrechend. —**-broken**, *adj.* gebrochenen Herzens; she is —-broken, sie ist tief traurig, zum Tode betrübt. —**-burn**, *s.* das Sodbrennen. —**-burning**, *s.* das Sodbrennen; die Unzufriedenheit, der Neid, die Eifersucht (*fig.*). —**-complaint**, *s.* das Herzleiden. —**-disease**, *s.* die Herzkrankheit. —**-felt**, *adj.* tief empfunden, herzlich. —**-piercing**, *adj.* herzergreifend. —**-rending**, *adj.* herzzerreißend. —**'s-blood**, *s.* das Herzblut. —**-searching**, *adj.* herzerforschend, herzergründend. —**'s-ease**, *s.* die Gemütsruhe; die Herzstärkung (*coll. of a* Likör); das Stiefmütterchen. —**-shaped**, *adj.* herzförmig. —**-sick**, *adj.* herzkrank; tief betrübt (*fig.*). —**-sore**, *adj.* herzenswund. —**-sorrow**, *s.* der Herzensschmerz. —**-stirring**, *adj.* herzergreifend. —**-strings**, *pl.* Herzfibern; innigste Hingebung (*fig.*). —**-whole**, *adj.* frei von Liebe *or* Leidenschaft; frischen Mutes; aufrichtig.

Hearth, *s.* der Herd (*also fig.*). *Comp.* **—-brush**, *s.* der Herdbesen. **—-rug**, *s.* der Kaminteppich, die Kaminvorlage. **—stone**, *s.* der Herdstein.

Heat, I. *s.* die Hitze; die Wärme, Glut (*Phys.*); die Hitze, Heftigkeit, der Zorn (*fig.*); das Feuer, der Eifer (*of argument, etc.*); der Gang, die Partie, das Rennen, der einzelne Lauf (*Sport.*); dead —, unentschiedenes Rennen, unentschiedener Wettkampf; final —, Schluß-, Entscheidungs-Rennen, letzter Gang; degree of —, der Wärmegrad; mechanical equivalent of —, das mechanische Wärmeäquivalent; to be in —, läufig sein (*of dogs*). II. *v.a.* heiß machen, heizen; erhitzen (*also fig.*). III. *v.n.* heiß, warm werden. **—er**, *s.* der Heizer, Heizende; der Bügel-, Plättstahl (*of an iron*). **—ing**, *s.* die Heizung; die Erhitzung (*Mach.*); die Anheizung (*of a furnace, etc.*); —ing by gas, by hot air, Gas-, Luft-heizung. *Comp.* **—ing-apparatus**, *s.* der Heizapparat. **—ing-power**, *s.* die Heizkraft. **—ing-tube**, *s.* das Wärmrohr, Heizungsrohr.

Heath, *s.* die Heide; (the flower) die Heide, das Heidekraut (*Bot.*). **—er**, I. *s.* die Heide, das Heidekraut. II. *attrib.*; —er bells, Heideblumen. **—y**, *adj.* voller Heide. *Comp.* **—cock**, *s.* der Birkhahn. **—-hen**, *s.* das Birkhuhn.

Heathen, I. *s.* der Heide; she was a —, sie war eine Heidin; the —(s), die Heiden. II. *adj.* heidnisch. **—dom**, *s.* das Heidentum. **—ish**, *adj.* heidnisch; roh, wild (*fig.*); (cruel) grausam. **—ishness**, *s.* das heidnische Wesen. **—ism**, *s.* das Heidentum; die Barbarei.

Heav—e, I. *v.a.* (auf-, er-)heben; (swell) schwellen; ausstoßen (*a sigh*); to —e the anchor, den Anker lichten; to —e the lead, das Lot auswerfen; to —e overboard, über Bord werfen; to —e out, auswerfen; to —e up, aufheben. II. *v.n.* sich heben, (auf)schwellen, sich emporbrängen; (retch) sich übergeben wollen; schwellen (*as the sea*); to —e astern, von hinten auf den Anker treiben; to —e in sight, auftauchen, sichtbar werden; to —e to, backbrassen; beidrehen; the ship hove to, das Schiff drehte bei. III. *s.* das Heben, Aufheben der Hub; das Schwellen (*of the breast*); die Übelkeit; (throw) der Aufwärtsstoß. **—en**, *see* Heaven. **—er**, *s.* der Heber. **—ily**, *adv. see* —y. **—iness**, *s.* die Schwere, das Gewicht (*of a body*); (—iness of spirit) die Schwermut, der Trübsinn; (drowsiness) die Schläfrigkeit, Mattigkeit; (cumbrousness, sluggishness) die Schwerfälligkeit; der Druck (*of taxes*); die Schwere, Dichtheit (*of the air*); die Schwere, Fettigkeit (*of the soil*). **—ing**, I. *adj.* schwellend (*as the sea, the breast, etc.*). II. *s.* das Schwellen (*of the breast*); das Keuchen. **—y**, I. *adj.* schwer; traurig, schwermütig; schwerfällig; (torpid) schläfrig, matt; schwer, unverdaulich (*as food*); fett, feucht; heftig, stark (*as rain, etc.*); (dull) trüb, finster; a —y book, ein schwerfällig geschriebenes Buch; —y bread, pappiges, nicht aufgegangenes Brot; —y cloud, dicke Wolke; —y cavalry, schwere Reiterei; —y expenses, schwere *or* bedeutende Kosten; —y eyes, matte Augen; —y face, plumpes Gesicht; —y fire, starkes Geschützfeuer. II. **—y**, **—ily**, *adv.* schwer; drückend, lästig. *Comp.* **—e-offering**, *s.* das Hebeopfer. **—y-armed**, *adj.* schwer bewaffnet. **—y-gaited**, *adj.* schwerfälligen Gangs. **—y-handed**, *adj.* plump. **—y-headed**, *adj.* (sleepy) schläfrig; dumm (*fig.*). **—y-hearted**, I. *adj.* tief bekümmert. II. *adv.* schweren Herzens. **—y-laden**, *adj.* schwerbeladen.

Heaven, *s.* der Himmel; O —s! o, Himmel! du lieber Himmel! **—liness**, *s.* das himmlische Wesen, das Himmlische. **—ly**, *adj.* himmlisch; göttlich; erhaben. **—ward**, I. *adv.* himmelwärts. II. *adj.* gen Himmel strebend; —ward flight, der Aufschwung zum Himmel. *Comp.* **—-born**, *adj.* vom Himmel stammend; himmelentsprossen; himmlisch. **—-directed**, *adj.* zum Himmel gerichtet (*as one's gaze*); (—-guided) vom Himmel geleitet. **—-high**, *adj.* himmelhoch. **—-inspired**, *adj.* gottbegeistert. **—ly-minded**, *adj.* himmlisch gesinnt, fromm. **—ly-mindedness**, *s.* die Frömmigkeit.

Hebdomada—l, **—ry**, *adj.* wöchentlich; —l Council, der wöchentlich zusammentretende Rat (der Oberstudienrat der Universität Oxford).

Hebet—ate, *v.a.* stumpf machen. **—ation**, *s.* das Abstumpfen; die Stumpfheit. **—ude**, *s.* die Stumpfheit; die Blödigkeit, Dummheit.

Hecatomb, *s.* die Hekatombe.

Heckl—e, I. *v.a.* hecheln. II. *s.* die Hechel. **—er**, *s.* der Hechler. *Comp.* **—ing-machine**, *s.* die Hechelmaschine.

Hectic, I. *adj.* auszehrend; hektisch; schwindsüchtig, brustleidend, Schwindsuchts-. II. *s.* die Auszehrung; der Schwindsüchtige. *Comp.* **—-fever**, *s.* das Zehrfieber.

Hectogram(me), *s.* das Hektogramm.

Hector, I. *s.* der Prahler, anmaßende Mensch; (bully) der Eisenfresser; der Bramarbas. II. *v.a.* bedrohen, anmaßend behandeln. III. *v.n.* den Eisenfresser spielen; bramarbasieren.

Heddle, *s.* die Litze. *Comp.* **—-eye**, *s.* das Litzenhäuschen. **—-hook**, *s.* die Einziehnadel.

Hederaceous, *adj.* efeuartig.

Hedge, *s.* die Hecke, der Zaun; over — and ditch. über Stock und Stein; to make a —, *see* — III. II. *v.a.* einzäunen, einfriedigen; (encircle) umgeben einfassen; to — **in**, einzäunen, einschließen; einhegen (*fig.*); to — **out**, ausschließen; to — **up**, sperren. III. *v.n.* auf beiden Seiten (für und wider) wetten. **—r**, *s.* der Zaunmacher; der Heckenbeschneider. *Comp.* **—-bill**, *s.* das Hage-, Garten-messer. **—hog**, *s.* der Igel. **—-priest**, *s.* der Winkelprediger, Bettelpfaffe. **—row**, *s.* die Hecke, der Zaun. **—-school**, *s.* die im Freien gehaltene (irische) Schule (*obs.*); gemeine Schule (*fig.*). **—-shears**, *pl.* die Heckenschere. **—-sparrow**, **—-warbler**, *s.* die braungefleckte Grasmücke.

Hedging, *s.* das Zaunmachen. *Comp.* **—-bill**, *see* Hedge-bill.

Hedoni—c, *adj.* das Vergnügen betreffend, hedonisch. **—sm**, *s.* die Lustphilosophie, der Hedonismus. **—st**, *s.* der Lustphilosoph, Hedoniker.

Heed, I. *v.a.* (be)achten, Acht geben auf (*acc.*). II. *v.n.* achten. III. *s.* die Achtung; to give *or* pay — to a th., Acht geben auf eine Sache, einer Sache Beachtung schenken; to take —, sich in Acht nehmen, sich vorsehen (of, vor). **—ful**, *adj.*, **—fully**, *adv.* achtsam, aufmerksam; (wary) wachsam, vorsichtig. **—fulness**, *s.* die Achtsamkeit; die Wachsamkeit. **—less**, *adj.*, **—lessly**, *adv.* achtlos; (negligent) sorglos; (thoughtless) unbesonnen, gedankenlos. **—lessness**, *s.* die Unachtsamkeit, Achtlosigkeit; die Sorglosigkeit; die Rücksichtslosigkeit.

[1]**Heel**, I. *s.* die Ferse; der Absatz (*on shoes, etc.*); das Hiel (*of a mast, the keel, etc., Naut.*); (end) der letzte Teil, das Ende; to be out at —s, Löcher im Strumpfe haben (*lit.*), in erbärmlichen Umständen sein (*fig.*); to be at the —s of a p., einem dicht auf den Fersen sein *or* folgen; to cool one's —s, müßig einen erwarten (*coll.*); to follow close at —, dicht auf dem Fuße folgen; to kick up one's —s, hinten ausschlagen; to lay by the —s, fesseln; my heart sank into my —s, das Herz fiel mir in die Hosen (*vulg.*); to show a pair of —s, ausreißen (*vulg.*); to take to one's —s, die Flucht ergreifen, Fersengeld geben, das Hasenpanier ergreifen; to tread upon the —s of (a p.), (einen, 2c.) ereilen; to tumble head over —s, kopfüber fallen. II. *v.a.* mit einem Absatze versehen; bespornen (*cocks*); to — out, hinausfersen (*Footb.*). **—ing**, *s.* das Erneuern der Absätze. *Comp.* **—-piece**, *s.* der Absatzfleck. **—-tap**, *s.* die Absatzplatte (*Shoem.*); die Neige (*in a glass*); no —-taps! ausgetrunken!

[2]**Heel**, *v.n.* sich neigen, krengen (*Naut.*).

Hegemony, *s.* die Hegemonie, Oberherrschaft; die Vormachtstellung, politische Führung; unification of Germany under the — of Prussia, Deutschlands Einigung unter Preußens Führung.
Hegira, *s.* die Hedschra, Flucht Mohammeds (622).
Heifer, *s.* die Färse, junge Kuh; to plough with another man's —, mit fremdem Kalbe pflügen (*B.*).
Heigh, *int.* he! **—-ho**, *int.* ach! o weh!
Height, *s.* die Höhe (*also fig.*); (size) die Größe; (rising ground) die Anhöhe, der Hügel; (summit) der Gipfel, höchste Grad; — of folly, der Gipfel der Torheit, die ärgste Torheit; — between decks, Tiefe des Zwischendecks. **—en**, *v.a.* erhöhen; (increase) vergrößern, vermehren; (elevate) erheben; heben, steigern (*the effect, etc.*).
Heinous, *adj.*, **—ly**, *adv.* abscheulich, verrucht. **—ness**, *s.* die Abscheulichkeit, Verruchtheit.
Heir, *s.* der Erbe (*also fig.*); — to the throne, der Thronerbe; to be — to a th., etwas erben; he was left — to the professor's library, er erbte des Professors Bücherei; — apparent, rechtmäßiger, gesetzmäßiger Erbe, Thronfolger; — aspirant, — expectant, möglicher Erbe; — at law, rechtmäßiger Erbe; — presumptive, mutmaßlicher Erbe. **—ess**, *s.* die Erbin, die reiche Erbin, die Erbtochter. **—less**, *adj.* ohne Erben. **—loom**, *s.* das Erbstück. **—ship**, *s.* die Erbschaft.
Held, *imperf. & p.p. of* Hold.
Heli—ac(al), *adj.* heliakisch, zur Sonne gehörig. **—anthus**, *s.* die Sonnenblume. **—ocentric**, *adj.* heliozentrisch, auf den Mittelpunkt der Sonne bezüglich. **—ochromic**, *adj.* heliochromisch. **—ochromy**, *s.* die Farbenphotographie. **—ograph**, *s.* der Heliograph, Spiegel-Telegraph. **—ographic**, *adj.* heliographisch; —ographic chart, die Sonnenkarte; —ographic communication, heliographische Verbindung (mit); die Mitteilung durch den Sonnentelegraphen, Heliographen. **—ography**, *s.* die Heliographie, Spiegeltelegraphie, das Telegraphieren mit dem Sonnenspiegel. **—ogravure**, *s.* der Kupferlichtdruck, die Lichtkupferätzung. **—oscope**, *s.* das Helioskop, Sonnenfernrohr. **—otrope**, *s.* das Heliotrop (*Astr.*, *Bot.*, *Surv.*, *Min.*); bläulichrote Farbe. **—otype**, *s.* der Lichtdruck.
Heli—cal, *adj.* schneckenförmig; —cal curve, Spiral-, Schnecken-linie. **—x**, *s.* die Schneckenlinie, Schnecke; äußere Ohrleiste (*Anat.*).
Hell, *s.* die Hölle; die Unterwelt; der Platz, wo man Abfälle (vom Tuche, &c.) hintut; (gambling —) die Spielhölle. **—ish**, *adj.* höllisch; abscheulich. **—ishness**, *s.* das Höllische; das Abscheuliche. *Comp.* **—fire**, *s.* das Höllenfeuer; — fire! Sapperment! **—-hound**, *s.* der Höllenhund.
Hellebore, *s.* der Nieswurz.
[1]**Helm**, *s. see* —et; der Helm (*Her.*, *Chem.*). **—et**, *s.* der Helm; die Sturmhaube; der Helm (*Bot.*); spiked —et, die Pickelhaube. **—eted**, *adj.* behelmt. **—et-shaped**, *adj.* helmförmig.
[2]**Helm**, *s.* das Steuer(ruder); das Ruder (*fig.*); to be at the —, am Ruder sein *or* sitzen, (das Schiff) lenken; — a-lee! das Ruder in Lee! starboard the —! Steuerbord, das Ruder! *Comp.* **—sman**, *s.* der Steuermann, Lenker (des Schiffes).
Helminth, *s.* der Eingeweidewurm. **—ic**, *adj.* zu den Würmern gehörig; wurmtreibend. **—ics**, *pl.* wurmtreibende Mittel. **—ology**, *s.* die Wurmkunde, Lehre von den Eingeweidewürmern.
Helot, *s.* der Helote. **—ism**, *s.* das Helotentum, die rechtlose Sklaverei, sklavische Abhängigkeit.
Help, I. *v.a.* (einem) helfen, beistehen, Hülfe leisten; (support) (einen) unterstützen; (remedy) abhelfen (einer S.); (forbear) unterlassen; reichen, geben, bedienen (*at table*); I —ed him, ich half ihm, ich unterstützte ihn; I could not — going there, ich konnte nicht umhin *or* vermeiden hinzugehn; I cannot — laughing, ich kann nicht umhin zu lachen, ich muß lachen; I —ed the lady to a chair, ich verhalf der Dame zu einem Stuhl, verschaffte *or* brachte ihr einen Stuhl; she —ed me to the salt, sie reichte mir das Salz (*at table*); allow me to — you to a little sauce, lassen Sie mich Ihnen etwas Soße geben; — yourself, bitte bedienen Sie sich, langen Sie zu; so — me God! so wahr mir Gott helfe; I cannot — it, ich kann nichts dafür, ich kann es nicht ändern; how could he — it? wie hätte er es vermeiden können? it cannot be —ed, es läßt sich nicht ändern, man kann nichts (dagegen) tun; I cannot — my nature, ich kann nichts für meine Natur; to — **down**, (einem) hinunterhelfen; to — **forward**, (einem) forthelfen; to — **in**, (einem) hineinhelfen; to — **off**, (einem) ablegen helfen (*one's coat, etc.*); (einem) davonhelfen, durchhelfen; to — **out**, (einem) aushelfen; to — a p. out of a difficulty, einem aus einer Schwierigkeit heraushelfen; to — a p. **over** a difficulty, einem über eine Schwierigkeit hinweghelfen; to — **through**, (einem) durchhelfen; to —**up**, (einem) (hin)aufhelfen. II. *v.n.* helfen, dienen (to, zu). III. *s.* die Hilfe(leistung), der Beistand; (that which, one who —s) das Hilfsmittel; der, die Hilfeleistende; (servant) der Bediente, die Magd (*Amer.*); (remedy) das Mittel; lady's —, die Stütze (der Hausfrau); by the — of, mit Hilfe von, vermittelst; there is no — for it, es läßt sich nicht ändern, es ist nicht zu ändern; *see* —er, —ing. **—er**, *s.* der Helfer, Beistand; der, die Helfende; (assistant) der Gehilfe; die Stütze (der Hausfrau). **—ful**, *adj.*, **—fully**, *adv.* hilfreich, behilflich, dienlich, nützlich; (salutary) heilsam. **—fulness**, *s.* die Dienlichkeit, Nützlichkeit. **—ing**, *s.* das Hilfeleisten; die Hilfeleistung; (portion) die Portion, der Anteil; two large —ings of meat, zwei gehörige Portionen Fleisch. **—less**, *adj.*, **—lessly**, *adv.* hülflos. **—lessness**, *s.* die Hilflosigkeit. **—mate**, **—meet**, *s.* die Helferin, Gehilfin, Gattin; (assistant) der Gefährte, Gehilfe.
Helter-skelter, *adv.* holterdipolter, Hals über Kopf, wirr, durcheinander.
Helve, I. *s.* der Stiel, Helm, Griff. II. *v.a.* bestielen, anschäften. *Comp.* **—-hammer**, *s.* schwerer Schmiedehammer.
[1]**Hem**, I. *s.* der Saum; open-work —, durchbrochener Saum. II. *v.a.* säumen; to — in, einschließen, umgeben. *Comp.* **—stitch**, *s.* der Hohlsaum. **—stitched**, *adj.*; —stitched handkerchief, das mit Hohlsaum genähte Taschentuch.
[2]**Hem**, I. *s.* das Räuspern. II. *v.n.* sich räuspern, mit einem hm! anrufen. III. *int.* hm!
Hem—atite, *s.* der Blutstein, Roteisenstein. **—atocele**, *s.* der Blutbruch. **—atology**, *s.* die Blutlehre. **—atosis**, *s.* die Blutbildung. **—aturia**, *s.* das Blutharnen. **—orrhage**, *s.* der Blutfluß, die Blutung. **—orrhagic**, *adj.* blutflüssig. **—orrhoidal**, *adj.* hämorrhoidalisch. **—orrhoids**, *pl.* die Hämorrhoiden.
Hemi—circle, *s.* der Halbkreis. **—cycle**, *s.* der Halbkreis; die Bogenrundung (*Arch.*). **—ptera**, *pl.* Halbflügler. **—sphere**, *s.* die Halbkugel, Erdhalbkugel, Hemisphäre; (map) die Himmelskarte. **—spherical**, *adj.* halbkugelig. **—stich**, *s.* der Halbvers, die Halbzeile.
Hemlock, *s.* der Schierling. *Comp.* **—-spruce**, **—-tree**, *s.* die Schierlingstanne, der Tannenbaum.
Hemp, *s.* der Hanf. **—en**, *adj.* hanfen, hänfen, Hanf-; —en rope, das Hanfseil. *Comp.* **—-comb**, *s.* die Hanfhechel. **—-dresser**, *s.* der Hanfbrecher. **—-seed**, *s.* der Hanfsame(n).
Hen, I. *s.* die Henne; (female) das Weibchen; the — clucks, das Huhn gluckt. II. *attrib.*; the — pheasant, das Fasanenhuhn; the — bird, das (Vogel)weibchen. **—nery**, *s.* der Hühnerstall, der Hühnerhof. *Comp.* **—bane**, *s.* das Bilsenkraut, Gift (*fig.*). **—bit**, *s.* die Todnessel. **—-coop**, *s.* der Hühnerkorb. **—-driver**, **—-harrier**, *s.* die Kornweihe. **—-house**, *s.* das Hühnerhaus, der Hühnerstall. **—-peck**, *v.a.* (den Ehemann)

beherrschen *or* unter dem Pantoffel haben. — **pecked**, *adj.* unter dem Pantoffel stehend; — pecked husband, der Pantoffelheld. —**-roost**, *s.* die Hühnerstange.

Hence, I. *adv.* (away) von hinnen, weg, hinweg, fort; (from this) hieraus, daraus, von da; daher, deshalb, deswegen. folglich; (from now) von nun an, von jetzt an; (off) von hier entfernt; — it comes, daher kommt es; a week —, in einer Woche. II. *int.* fort! hinweg! —**forth**, —**forward**, *adv.* hinfort, von nun an.

Henchman, *s.* der Leibdiener, Knappe (*obs.*); feiler Anhänger (*fig.*).

Hendeca—gon, *s.* das Elfeck. —**syllable**, *s.* der elfsilbige Vers, der Elfsilbler.

Hendiadys, *s.* das Hendiadys, die Darstellung eines Begriffs durch zwei sinnverwandte Wörter.

Henna, *s.* der (Al)hennastrauch; das (Haar)färbemittel.

Hepa—r, *s.* die Leber; die Schwefelleber (*obs. Chem.*). —**tic(al)**, *adj.* hepatisch, Leber-. — **tica**, *s.* (anemone —tica) die Leberblume, das Leberblümchen. —**tite**, *s.* der Hepatit. —**titis**, *s.* die Leberentzündung.

Hepta—gon, *s.* das Siebeneck. —**gonal**, *adj.* siebeneckig. —**hedron**, *s.* der Siebenflächner. — **ndrous**, *adj.* siebenmännerig. —**ngular**, *adj.* siebenwinklig. —**rchy**, *s.* die ehemaligen sieben angelsächsischen Reiche in England, die Heptarchie. —**teuch**, *s.* der Heptateuch.

Her, I. *pers. pron.* (*acc. and dat. of* She) sie; ihr; we saw —, wir sahen sie; we gave — the book, wir gaben ihr das Buch. II. *poss. adj.* ihr; (*referring to masc. & neuter nouns:*) sein; — family disapproved of it, ihre Familie mißbilligte es; how Great Britain keeps — colonies, wie Großbritannien seine Kolonien festhält. —**s**, —**self**, *see* Her—s, *etc.*

Herald, I. *s.* der Herold; der Wappenherold (*Her.*); der Verkündiger, Vorbote (*fig.*). II. *v.a.* feierlich einführen; (proclaim) anmelden. —**ic**, *adj.* heraldisch; —ic emblems, heraldische Sinnbilder. —**ry**, *s.* die Heraldik, Wappenkunde; (—'s office) das Heroldsamt.

Herb, *s.* das Kraut, die Pflanze. —**aceous**, *adj.* krautartig. —**age**, *s.* Futterkräuter, das Gras, die Weide. —**al**, *s.* die Pflanzensammlung; das Pflanzen-, Kräuter-buch. —**alist**, *s.* der Kräuterkenner; der Kräutersammler. —**arium**, *s.* die (Preß-)Pflanzensammlung, das Pflanzenbuch, Herbarium. —**ary**, *s.* der Kräutergarten. —**escent**, *adj.* krautartig, Kraut-. —**ivora**, *pl.* pflanzenfressende Tiere, Pflanzenfresser. — **ivorous**, *adj.* gras-, kräuter-fressend. *Comp.* —**-bennet**, *s.* das Benediktenkraut. —**-robert**, *s.* das Roberts-, Ruprechts-kraut.

Herd, I. *s.* die Herde; der große Haufe; — of deer, das Rudel Hochwild; — of oxen, der Trieb Ochsen; the common —, die große Menge; one of the common —, ein Herdenmensch, ein ganz gewöhnlicher Mensch. II. *v.a.* eine Herde hüten. III. *v.n.* in Herden gehen; to — with, sich gesellen *or* scharen zu. —**sman**, *s.* der Hirt, Älpler, Senn(er), Sennhirt. *Comp.* —**-book**, *s.* der Stammbaum (*of cattle*).

Here, *adv.* hier, hiesigen Orts; (— below) hienieden, in diesem Leben; (*with verbs of motion:*) hierher, her; she lives —, sie lebt hier; she came — for sixteen days, sie kam auf sechzehn Tage hierher; come —, komm her! — and there, hier und dort, hier und da, hin und wieder; neither — nor there, weder hier noch dort, nirgends; that's neither — nor there, das gehört nicht zur Sache; it was Lady B. —, Lady B. there, es hieß Lady B. hinten und vorn; —'s to . . . ! auf das Wohl *or* die Gesundheit von . . . ! —'s to you! auf euer Wohl! *Comp.* —**about(s)**, *adv.* hier herum. —**after**, I. *adv.* hernach, künftighin, in Zukunft; im künftigen Leben. II. *s.* die Zukunft, das künftige Leben. —**at**, *adv.* hierbei, hierüber. —**by**, *adv.* (by this) hierdurch; (close by) nebenbei, nebenan; beigefügt, hiemit (*C.L.*) —**in**, *adv.* hierin. —**of**, *adv.* hiervon. —**on**, *adv.* hierauf, hierüber. —**to**, *adv.* hierzu. — **tofore**, *adv.* vormals, vor diesem. —**upon**, *adv.* hierauf, darauf. —**with**, *adv.* hiermit; you receive —with, beifolgend erhalten Sie.

Heredit—ament, *s.* das Erbgut. —**ary**, *adj.* erblich; —ary prince, der Erbprinz; —ary taint, die erbliche Belastung. —**y**, *s.* die Erblichkeit; der Forterbungstrieb.

Heres—iarch, *s.* der Erzketzer. —**y**, *s.* die Ketzerei.

Heretic, *s.* der Ketzer. —**al**, *adj.* ketzerisch.

Heriot, *s.* der Hauptfall (*obs. Law*).

Herisson, *s.* der spanische Reiter, Sperrbaum (*Fortif.*); (instrument of torture) der Stachelbock.

Herita—ble, *adj.* erbfähig; (inheritable) erblich. —**ge**, *s.* die Erbschaft, das Erbgut.

Hermaphrodit—e, I. *s.* der Zwitter; die Zwitterpflanze (*Bot.*). II. *adj.* zwitterartig. —**ic**, *adj.* zwitterhaft. —**ism**, *s.* die Zwitterbildung, der Zwitterzustand.

Hermeneutic, *adj.* auslegend, hermeneutisch. —**s**, *pl.* die Auslegungskunst, Hermeneutik.

Hermetic, *adj.*, —**ally**, luftdicht, hermetisch; — closure, luftdichter Verschluß; —ally sealed, luftdicht verschlossen.

Hermit, *s.* der Einsiedler, Eremit, Klausner; (beadsman) der Betbruder. —**age**, *s.* die Einsiedelei. *Comp.* —**-crab**, *s.* der Einsiedlerkrebs. —**-crow**, *s.* der Alpenrabe.

Hernia, *s.* der Bruch. —**l**, *adj.* Bruch-.

Hero, I. *s.* der Held; der Heros (*Myth.*). II. *attrib.*; — cycle, — saga, die Heldensage. —**ic**, —**ical**, *adj.*, —**ically**, *adv.* heldenmäßig; (brave) tapfer, heldenmütig; —ic race, das Heldengeschlecht; —ic metre, das epische Versmaß; —ic poem, das Heldengedicht; mock —ic, komisches Epos; —ic remedy, heroisches Mittel; —ic saga, die Heldensage. —**ics**, *pl.* das epische Versmaß; to go into —ics, schwärmen; begeistert sprechen. —**ine**, *s.* die Heldin. —**ism**, *s.* der Heldenmut, Heldensinn, Heroismus. *Comp.* —**-worship**, *s.* die Heldenverehrung.

Heron, *s.* der Reiher. —**ry**, *s.* der Reiherstand.

Herpe—s, *s.* die Flechte. —**tic**, *adj.* flechtenartig. —**tology**, *s.* die Reptilienkunde.

Herring, *s.* der Hering; kippered —, gespaltener, gesalzener und geräucherter Hering; pickled —, marinierter Hering; rolled —, (Berliner) Rollmops; red —, der Bückling; king of the —s, der Heringskönig. *Comp.* —**bone**, I. *s.* die Heringsgräte; der Hexenstich (*Semp.*); (—bone work) der Fischgrätenverband, Heringsgrätenbau (*Mas.*). II. *v.a.* mit Hexenstich nähen. —**-fishery**, *s.* die Heringsfischerei. —**-net**, *s.* das Heringsnetz. —**-pond**, *s.* das (atlantische) Meer (*coll.*). —**-smack**, *s.* das Heringsboot.

Her—s, *poss. pron.* ihr, der, die, das ihrige; this bonnet is —s, dieser Hut ist der ihrige, gehört ihr; a friend of —s, eine ihrer Freundinnen. —**self**, *pron.* selbst, sie selbst; ihr selbst; sich (selbst); she —self did not approve of it, sie selbst billigte es nicht; she thought —self unhappy, sie hielt sich für unglücklich; I gave it to — —self, ich gab es ihr selbst, in ihre eignen Hände; by —self, von selbst; allein; she has come to —self, sie ist (wieder) zu sich gekommen.

Herse, *s.* das Schutz-, Fall-gatter (*Fort.*); die Sturmegge (*Mil.*); *see* Hearse.

Hesita—ncy, *s.* die Unschlüssigkeit, das Zögern. —**te**, *v.n.* zögern, zaudern, anstehen, unschlüssig sein, Bedenken tragen; stocken, anstoßen (in speaking, im Reden). —**ting**, *adj.*, —**tingly**, *adv.* unschlüssig, zögernd; stockend, anstoßend. —**tion**, *s.* das Zaudern, die Unschlüssigkeit, Bedenklichkeit; das Stocken; without any —tion, sogleich, ohne jedes Bedenken.

Hest, *s.* (*poet.*) *see* Behest.

Hetero—clite, *s.* unregelmäßig gebeugtes Wort;

der Sonderling, (die, das) von der Regel Abweichende (*fig.*). **—clitic(al)**, *adj.* anders abwandelnd (*Gram.*); abweichend, eigentümlich. **—dox**, *adj.* irrlehrig, heterodox; irrgläubig. **—doxy**, *s.* die Irrlehre, Heterodoxie; der Irrglaube. **—geneity**, **—geneousness**, *s.* die Ungleichartigkeit, Fremdartigkeit. **—geneous**, *adj.*, **—geneously**, *adv.* ungleich=, verschiedenartig.

Hetman, *s.* der Kosakenhauptmann, Hetman.

Heuristic, *adj.*, auf eignes Finden angelegt, heuristisch; — method, zum eigenen Finden, zur Selbsttätigkeit anleitende Lehrweise.

Hew, *v.a.* (*p.p.* —n) hauen, hacken; (dress) be=, zu=hauen; to — **down**, niederhauen, fällen; to — **off**, abhauen; to — **out**, aushauen, bilden; to — **up**, — in pieces, zerhauen. **—er**, *s.* der Holz=, Stein=hauer; der Häuer (*of coal*). **—ing**, *s.* das Abhauen; das Behauen (*of stone*).

Hewn, *p.p. of* Hew.

Hexa—chord, *s.* das Hexachord, sechssaitiges Tonwerkzeug. **—gon**, *s.* das Sechseck. **—gonal**, *adj.* sechseckig. **—hedral**, *adj.* sechsflächig. **—hedron**, *s.* der Würfel, der Sechsflächner. **—meter**, *s.* der Hexameter, sechsfüßige (abgleitende) Vers. **—metric(al)**, *adj.* hexametrisch. **—ngular**, *adj.* sechswinkelig. **—stich**, *s.* sechszeiliges Gedicht. **—style**, *s.* das sechssäulige Gebäude.

Hey, *int.* he! hei! auf! **—day**, *see* Heyday.

Heyday, I. *int.* he! was giebt's! heisa! II. *s.* die Lustigkeit, Munterkeit; der Höhepunkt, die Höhe, Hochflut; der Aufruhr, Sturm (*of passion*).

Hiatus, *s.* die Lücke, Kluft; der Gähnlaut (*Gram.*); das Gesperr, der Hiatus (*Gram.*).

Hibernat—e, *v.n.* (den) Winterschlaf halten. **—ion**, *s.* der Winterschlaf.

Hiccough, Hiccup, I. *s.* der Schlucken, Schluckauf. II. *v.n.* den Schlucken *or* Schluckauf haben.

Hickory, *s.* weißer, nordamerikanischer Wallnußbaum.

Hid, *pret. & p.p. of* —e. **—den**, I. *p.p. of* —e. II. *adj.* heimlich. **—e**, *ir.v.* I. *a.* verbergen, verstecken; verbergen, verheimlichen (*fig.*); to —e a th. from a p., einem (*or* vor einem) eine S. verheimlichen *or* verbergen; to play at —e and seek, Verstecken(s) spielen. II. *n.* sich verbergen. **—ing**, *s.* das Verbergen; der (das) Versteck; die Verborgenheit. *Comp.* **—ing-place**, *s.* der, das Versteck; der Schlupfwinkel.

[1]**Hide**, *see under* Hid.

[2]**Hide**, *s.* die Hufe Landes.

[3]**Hid—e**, I. *s.* die (Tier)haut, das Fell; to cury a p.'s —e, einen tüchtig durchprügeln. II. *v.a.* prügeln (*coll.*). **—ing**, *s.* die Tracht Prügel (*vulg.*). *Comp.* **—ebound**, *adj.* angewachsen; steif engherzig (*fig.*); to be —ebound by tradition, im Bann der Überleiferung stecken.

Hideous, *adj.*, **—ly**, *adv.* schrecklich, scheußlich. **—ness**, *s.* die Scheußlichkeit.

Hie, *v.n. & r.* eilen.

Hiema—l, *adj.* winterlich. **—tion**, *s.* die Überwinterung.

Hier—arch, *s.* der Anhänger der Priesterherrschaft, Hierarch. **—arch(ic)al**, *adj.*, **—archically**, *adv.* der (geistlichen) Rangordnung entsprechend, hierarchisch. **—archy**, *s.* die Priesterherrschaft, Kirchenverfassung; die (geistliche) Rangordnung, Beamtenfolge. **—atic(al)**, *adj.* priesterlich. **—oglyph**, *s.* die Hieroglyphe, das heilige Bildzeichen. **—oglyphic**, *adj.* in Bilderschrift, hieroglyphisch; geheimnisvoll, rätselhaft; unleserlich. **—oglyphics**, *pl.* die Hieroglyphen, (altägyptische) Bilderschrift; undeutliche, rätselhafte Schrift. **—oglyphist**, *s.* der Kenner der altägyptischen Bilderschrift, Hieroglyphenkundiger. **—oglyphy**, *s.* die Bilderschriftkunde. **—ogrammatist**, *s.* der Bilderschrift=Schreiber *or* =Kundige; der altägyptische Tempelschreiber. **—ology**, *s.* die Beschreibung heiliger Dinge; die Bilderschriftkunde. **—omancy**, *s.* die Weissagung aus Opfern, Opferschau, Hieromantie. **—ophant**, *s.* der (Ober)priester, Hierophant.

Higgle, *v.n.* (hawk) hausieren; (chaffer) knickern, feilschen. **—dy-piggledy**, *adv.* alles durcheinander (*fam.*). **—r**, *s.* der Feilscher, Knicker.

High, I. *adj.* hoch; (noble) edel, vornehm; (exalted) hoch, erhaben; (proud) stolz; (arrogant) anmaßend; (—-flown) hochtrabend; (abstruse, difficult) schwer, schwierig, dunkel; angegangen, pikant, Hautgout habend (*as meat*); (dear) teuer, hoch; (great) groß, stark, heftig; hoch; laut, stark (*voice, tone*); — birth, hohe Abstammung; to have a — colour, viel Farbe haben; — commendation, großes Lob; — courage, hoher Mut; — feeding, — living, die üppige Kost; — forehead, hohe Stirne; with a — hand, mit starker Hand; to carry matters with a — hand, sich bei einer Sache hochfahrend, *or* rücksichtslos, benehmen; — hat, der Hut mit hohem Kopfe; to mount the, *or* one's, — horse, sich aufs hohe Pferd setzen; — interest, hohe Zinsen; — opinion, eine hohe Meinung; a — pitch, hohe Stimmung (*lit.*); eine bedeutende Höhe (*fig.*); — school, die höhere Schule; — school for girls, höhere Mädchenschule, höhere Töchterschule; — school for boys, höhere Knabenschule; — seas, hochgehende Seen; on the — sea(s), auf offenem Meere; — spirits, muntere, ausgelassene Laune; — tea, Tee mit Fleischspeisen; to dine at the — table, am Tisch der Graduirten speisen; — time, hohe Zeit; — wind, starker Wind; — words, stolze, heftige Worte; at last it came to — words, endlich kam es zu gereizten Worten; on —, in die Höhe, hinauf; in der Höhe, oben; from on —, von oben, aus der Höhe; glory be to God on —, Ehre sei Gott in der Höhe; — and dry, gestrandet; — and mighty, großmächtig. II. *adv.* hoch; stark, mächtig; (in a great measure) in hohem Grade; to run —, hoch gehen (*of waves*); heftig werden (*of temper*); to run mountains —, berghoch gehen; to stand —, in gutem Rufe stehen. **—er**, *comp. of* — I. & II. höher; to bid —er, mehr bieten. **—est**, *sup. of* —, höchst; —est bidder, Meistbietende(r). **—ly**, *adv.* hoch, höchlich, sehr; —ly finished, bis ins Kleinste ausgearbeitet; stark appretiert; —ly coloured, lebhaft; übertrieben (*fig.*); —ly gifted, hochbegabt; a —ly strung nature, eine hochgespannte Natur; to think —ly of, viel (von einem *or* auf einen) halten. **—ness**, *s.* die Höhe; die Hoheit (*fig.*); His (Your) Royal —ness, Seine (Eure, Ew.) Königliche Hoheit. *Comp.* **—-altar**, *s.* der Hochaltar. **—-backed**, *adj.* mit hoher Lehne. **—-bailiff**, *s.* der Oberamtmann. **—-born**, *adj.* hochgeboren. **—-bred**, *adj.* vornehm erzogen. **—-Church**, *s.* die (anglikanische) Hochkirche. **—-coloured**, *adj.* von lebhafter Farbe. **—-day**, *s.* hoher Festtag; it is —-day, es ist hoch am Tage. **—-flavoured**, **—-seasoned**, **—-spiced**, *adj.* hochgewürzt, pikant. **—-flier**, *s.* der Schwärmer; der Vornehmtuer. **—-flown**, *adj.* hochtrabend, schwülstig. **—-flying**, *adj.* hochstrebend; hochfliegend; hochtuerisch. **—-handed**, *adj.* anmaßend, hochfahrend, willkürlich, gewaltsam. **—-heeled**, *adj.* mit hohen Absätzen. **—-land**, *s.* das Hochland; Scotch —lands, das schottische Hochland. **—-lander**, *s.* der Hochländer, der Bergschotte. **—-life**, *s.* das vornehme Leben; die vornehme Welt; —-life below stairs, vornehmes Leben in der Bedientenstube. **—-master**, *s.* der Schulvorsteher, Direktor (*rare*). **—-minded**, *adj.* hochgesinnt. **—-mindedness**, *s.* die Hochherzigkeit, der Hochsinn. **—-placed**, *adj.* hochgestellt. **—-pressure**, *s.* der Hochdruck. **—-priest**, *s.* der Hohepriester; der Oberpriester. **—-principled** *adj.* von hohen, edeln Grundsätzen. **—-relief**, *s.* die hoch erhabene Arbeit. **—-road**, *s.* die (große) Landstraße; die breite Heerstraße; to be on the —road to success, auf dem besten Wege sein sein Glück zu machen. **—-sheriff**, *s.* der

Oberrichter. —**-souled**, *adj.* hochherzig. —**-sounding**, *adj.* hochtönend. —**-spirited**, *adj.* hochsinnig; munter, lustig, ausgelassen; stolz, kühn; reizbar. —**-stepping**, *adj.* hochtrabend; ausgreifend (*of a horse*). —**-street**, *s.* die Hauptstraße. —**-tide**, *s.* hohe Flut. —**-treason**, *s.* der Hochverrat. —**-water**, *s.* das Hochwasser, die Fluthöhe, der höchste Wasserstand; —-water mark, das Hochwasserstandzeichen, das Flutzeichen. —**way**, I. *s.* die Heerstraße, Landstraße. II. *attrib.*; —way robbery, der Straßenraub. —**wayman**, *s.* der Straßenräuber. —**-wrought**, *adj.* von vollendeter Arbeit; tief, heftig bewegt (*fig.*).

Hight, *obs. imperf.* hieß.

Hilari—ous, *adj.*, —**ously**, *adv.* lustig, vergnügt. —**ty**, *s.* die Heiterkeit, Fröhlichkeit.

Hilary term, *s.* die Periode vom 11 Januar bis 8 April (*Law Sittings*).

Hill, *s.* der Hügel; (ant-—) der (Ameisen) Haufen; down-(up-)—, bergab (bergan *or* bergauf); up— and down— (*or* up — and down dale), bergauf, bergab; up— work, (äußerst anstrengende) Arbeit, langsame und mühselige Arbeit; as old as the —s, so alt wie die Berge, steinalt. —**iness**, *s.* die Hügeligkeit. —**ock**, *s.* der kleine Hügel. —**y**, *adj.* hügelig. *Comp.* —**side**, *s.* der Hügelabhang. —**-site**, *s.* erhöhte Lage. —**top**, *s.* die Bergspitze.

Hilt, *s.* das Heft, (Degen=)Gefäß; up to the —, bis ans Heft, durch und durch, ganz. —**ed**, *adj.* mit einem Hefte, Gefäße.

Him, *pers. pron.* (*acc. of* He) ihn; (*dat. of* He, to —) ihm; den, dem(=jenigen); *see* —self. —**self**, selbst, (er, sich) selbst, sich; he flatters —self, er schmeichelt sich; he did it —self, er tat es selbst; of —self, von selbst; by —self, allein, für sich; for —self, für sich; to —self, zu sich; für sich; he makes much of —self, er macht viel aus sich (*coll.*); he is not —self, er ist nicht bei sich, ist nicht wie sonst, ist nicht ganz wohl (*fam.*).

[1]**Hind**, *s.* die Hindin, Hirschkuh; das Tier (*Hunt.*). *Comp.* —**-calf**, *s.* das Hirschkalb.

[2]**Hind**, *s.* der Knecht, Bauer.

[3]**Hind**, *adj.* (*especially in compounds*) hinter, Hinter=; — leg, das Hinterbein; — part, der hintere Teil, das Hinterschiff (*Shipb.*); — quarter, das Hinterviertel; — quarters, die Hüften (*of a horse*). —**er**, I. *adj.* (*comp. of* —) hinter. II. *v.a.* hindern (from, an einer S.), aufhalten, stören; (keep back) zurückhalten. —(**e**)**rance**, *s.* das Hindernis, die Verhinderung; (injury) der Nachteil; the main —rance to, das Haupthindernis für (*acc.*). —**erer**, *s.* der Hindernde. —**most**, *adj.* hinterst, letzt; the devil take the —most, der Teufel hole den Letzten. *Comp.* —**-hand**, *s.* die Hinterhand (*of a horse*). —**-head**, *s.* der Hinterkopf.

Hinge, I. *s.* die Angel, Haspe (*of a door, window*); das Scharnier (*of a box, etc.*); die Angel, der Angelpunkt (*fig.*). II. *v.n.*; to — upon, sich drehen um, ankommen auf (*acc.*) (*fig.*).

Hint, I. *v.a. & n.* andeuten, einen Wink geben; to — at, auf (*acc.*) . . . anspielen. II. *s.* der Wink; die Anspielung; a broad —, ein deutlicher Wink, Wink mit dem Zaunpfahl; he threw out (some) —s, er gab zu verstehen, er ließ merken; to take a —, einen Wink verstehen, sich (*dat.*) es *or* eine S. gesagt sein lassen.

Hinterland, *s.* das Hinterland.

[1]**Hip**, *s.* die Hüfte; der Gratanfall (*Build.*); (— corner) der Grat; I had him on the — there, da habe ich ihn recht gepackt; to smite — and thigh, hart an Schultern und Lenden schlagen, völlig besiegen. II. *v.a.* lendenlahm machen; mit einem Grat versehen. —**ped**, *p.p. & adj.* lendenlahm. *Comp.* —**-bath**, *s.* das Sitzbad. —**-bone**, *s.* das Hüftbein. —**-joint**, *s.* das Hüftgelenk. —**-rafter**, *s.* der Gratsparren. —**-roof**, —**ped-roof**, *s.* das Walmdach. —**-shot**, *adj.* lendenlahm.

[2]**Hip**, *s.* die Hagebutte (*Bot.*).

[3]**Hip**, *v.a.* melancholisch machen. —**ped**, *p.p. & adj.* milzsüchtig, melancholisch (*fam.*).

[4]**Hip**, *int.* hip! — —, hurra! Hurra! Hurra!

Hippo—camp(**us**), *s.* das Seepferdchen. —**drome**, *s.* die Rennbahn, der Rennplatz. —**griff**, —**gryph**, *s.* der Roßgreif, das Flügelpferd, Musenroß. —**phagy**, *s.* das Essen von Pferdefleisch. —**potamus**, *s.* das Flußpferd.

Hircine, I. *adj.* bockig, Bocks=; stinkend (*fig.*). II. *s.* das Hirzin.

Hire, I. *v.a.* mieten (*a horse, house, etc.*); dingen, mieten (*a servant, etc.*); heuern (*Naut.*); (bribe) bestechen; to — out, vermieten; to — o.s. (out) to, sich (um Lohn) vermieten bei. II. *s.* das Mieten; (cost of —) die Miete; der (Arbeits) Lohn; pianos on —, Pianos zu vermieten. —**ling**, I. *s.* der Mietling, Lohnarbeiter. II. *adj.* um Lohn dienend; feil. —**r**, *s.* der Mieter; —r out, der Vermieter. *Comp.* —**-purchase**, *adj.*; —-purchase system, das Abzahlungssystem, der Kauf mit Ratenzahlung.

Hirsute, *adj.* haarig (*also Bot.*).

His, I. *poss. pron.* sein, seine, seines; der, die, das seinige; a book of —, eins seiner Bücher. II. *poss. adj.* sein, seine, sein; he has hurt — finger, er hat sich den Finger verletzt.

Hispid, *adj.* borstig, steifhaarig, rauh.

Hiss, I. *v.a.* auszischen. II. *v.n.* zischen. III. *s.* das Zischen (*of a serpent, etc.*); das Gezisch. —**ing**, I. *adj.*, —**ingly**, *adv.* zischend; —ing sound, der Zischlaut. II. *s.* das Zischen, Gezisch.

Hist, *int.* pst! psch! still!

Histor—ian, *s.* der Geschichtschreiber; der Geschichtskundige. —**ic**(**al**), *adj.*, —**ically**, *adv.* geschichtlich, Geschichts=; —ical painter, Geschichtsmaler. —**iographer**, *s.* der Geschichtschreiber, Historiograph. —**iography**, *s.* die Geschichtschreibung. —**y**, *s.* die Geschichte; (narrative) die Geschichte, Erzählung; universal —y, die Weltgeschichte; pertaining to universal —y, weltgeschichtlich; this is now ancient —, das ist jetzt eine alte Geschichte; das ist jetzt längst vergessen *or* ein überwundener Standpunkt.

Histrionic, *adj.* schauspielerisch; theatralisch. —**s**, *pl.* die Schauspielkunst.

Hit, I. *ir.v.a. & n.* schlagen; stoßen; treffen (*the mark, the note, an expression, etc.*); you have — it, (du hast es) getroffen; — or miss, es geht wohl oder übel; aufs Geratewohl; to — home, einem einen Schlag versetzen (*fig.*); to — the nail on the head, den Nagel auf den Kopf treffen; to — **off**, richtig darstellen, schildern, treffen (*coll.*); to — **out**, ausschlagen; to — **upon**, zufällig auf (eine S.) kommen, stoßen, verfallen. II. *s.* der Schlag, Stoß; (happy —) der glückliche Zufall, Treffer, Glücksfall; der Treff (*in a speech, etc.*); he made a great — in Hamlet, er erzielte großen Erfolg durch seinen Hamlet.

Hitch, I. *s.* der Haken; der Knoten (*Naut.*); there is a — in the business, das Ding hat einen Haken; the party went off without a —, die Gesellschaft verlief ohne die geringste Störung. II. *v.a.* (an)haken; festknüpfen, festmachen; fangen (*the buoy*); to — up, hinaufziehen. III. *v.n.* (hobble) hinken; (fidget) unruhig sein; (be entangled) sich verwickelt haben, angehakt sein.

Hither, I. *adv.* hierher; — and thither, hierher und dorthin. II. *adj.* diesseitig. —**to**, *adv.* bisher, bisjetzt. —**ward**, *adv.* hierher.

Hive, I. *s.* der Bienenkorb, Bienenstock; (— of bees) der Bienenschwarm; der Schwarm (*fig.*) II. *v.a.* (Bienen) in einen Stock tun. III. *v.n.* sich zusammengesellen. —**s**, *pl.* die Wasserbläschen auf der Haut, die Bräune. *Comp.* —**-bee**, *s.* die Honigbiene.

Ho, *int.* ho! — there! holla! wer da?

Hoar, I. *adj.* weiß; weißgrau; grau (*with age*) ehrwürdig (*fig.*). II. *s.* die Grauheit des Alters

—iness, *s.* das Weißgrau, die Grauheit; (mouldiness) das Schimmelige. **—y**, *adj.* weiß; (alters=)grau, eisgrau. *Comp.* **—-frost**, *s.* der (Rauh=)Reif. **—y-headed**, *adj.* weißköpfig.

Hoard, I. *s.* der Vorrat, Schatz; der Hort (*poet.*). II. *v.a.* aufhäufen, sammeln; to — up, aufhäufen, sparen, zurücklegen. III. *v.n.* Schätze, Vorräte sammeln, aufhäufen. **—er**, *s.* der Sammler.

[1]**Hoarding**, *s.* das Schätzesammeln, Schätzeaufhäufen, die Ersparnis. **—s**, *pl.* die Ersparnisse.

[2]**Hoarding**, *s.* der Bauzaun.

Hoarse, *adj.*, **—ly**, *adv.* heiser, rauh. **—ness**, *s.* die Heiserkeit.

Hoax, I. *s.* die Täuschung, der Betrug; der Schwank, Streich, die Fopperei. II. *v.a.* foppen, zum besten haben, anführen.

Hob, *s.* der Kaminvorsprung, die Kaminseite; die Nabe (*of a wheel*). **—ble**, I. *v.n.* humpeln; hinken (*also fig.*) II. *v.a.* fesseln (die Füße); to — a horse, ein Pferd fesseln. III. *s.* das Hinken, der humpelnde Gang; (difficulty) die Verlegenheit, Patsche (*coll.*). **—bler**, *s.* der Humpler. **—bling**, *adj.*, **—blingly**, *adv.* humpelnd. **—by**, *s.* das Steckenpferd (*also fig.*). *Comp.* **—by-horse**, *s.* das Steckenpferd. **—nail**, *s.* der Hufnagel. **—nailed**, *adj.* mit Hufnägeln beschlagen.

Hob—bledehoy, *s.* junger (linkischer) Mensch, junges Bürschchen. **—goblin**, *s.* der Kobold.

Hobnob, *v.n.* anstoßen (beim Trinken); vertraulich zusammen=trinken *or* =plaudern (*fam.*).

[1]**Hock**, I. *s.* die Kniekehle (*of horses*); die Knieflechse. II. *v.a.* die Knieflechsen zerschneiden.

[2]**Hock**, *s.* der Hochheimer, weißer Rheinwein.

Hockey, *s.* das Schlagballspiel mit Hakenstöcken.

Hocus, I. *s.* der Betrüger. II. *v.a.* betrügen; fälschen (*wine, etc.*); Opium mit geistigen Getränken vermischen. **—-pocus**, *s.* der Hokuspokus, die Gaukelei.

Hod, *s.* der Mörteltrog. *Comp.* **—man**, *s.* der Handlanger.

Hodegetics, *s.* die wissenschaftliche Einführung, Anweisung zum methodischen Studium der Wissenschaften, Hodegetik.

Hodge, *s.* der Bauer, unwissende Mann.

Hodgepodge, *s.* der Mischmasch; das Gericht aus allerlei Gemengsel.

Hodometer, *s.* der Wegmesser.

Hoe, I. *s.* die Gartenhacke, Haue; die Keilhaue. II. *v.a.* behacken, um=, auf=hacken.

Hog, *s.* das Schwein (*also fig.*); verschnittenes Schwein; (sheep) einjähriges Schaf; einjähriges Bullenkalb; der Schiffsbesen (*Naut.*); gemeiner Kerl; to go the whole —, etwas ganz und gar verfechten *or* annehmen, keine halbe Maßregel ergreifen (*vulg.*). **—ged**, *adj.* gekrümmt; Enden habend, die tiefer stehen als die Mitte. **—get**, *s.* das einjährige Schaf. **—gish**, *adj.*, **—gishly**, *adv.* schweinisch; schmutzig (*fig.*). **—gishness**, *s.* das schweinische Wesen; die Gefräßigkeit; die Schmutzigkeit. *Comp.* **—-maned**, *adj.* mit kurz geschnittener Mähne. **—'s-back**, *s.* der niedrige Bergrücken. **—-skin**, *s.* das Schweinsleder. **—'s-lard**, *s.* das Schweinefett. **—wash**, *s.* das Spülicht.

Hogshead, *s.* das Oxhoft (in England about 50 gallons = 250 Liter); großes Packfaß (*Amer.*).

Hoiden, *s.* ausgelassenes Mädchen, die Range. **—ish**, *adj.* ausgelassen, wild; bäurisch, unverschämt.

Hoist, I. *v.a.* in die Höhe ziehen, aufwinden; hissen (*flags, sails, boats*); to — out a boat, ein Boot aussetzen; to — up, aufhissen; to — the flag of truce, die weiße Fahne hissen. II. *s.* der Aufzug, Personenaufzug; die Tiefe (*of a flag*). **—ing**, *s.* das Aufziehen; das Hissen. *Comp.* **—ing-engine**, *s.* der Aufzug; die Fördermaschine (*Min.*).

Hoity-toity, I. *adj.* lustig, mutwillig. II. *int.* potztausend! sieh mal einer! alle Wetter!

Hold, I. *ir.v.a.* halten, festhalten; (contain) enthalten, in sich halten; (keep) anhalten; (believe) glauben, der Meinung sein; (maintain) behaupten; (consider) halten für, ansehen; (possess) inne haben, besitzen; the professor —s, der Professor ist der Ansicht, vertritt die Überzeugung; to — an argument, disputieren; to — back, zurückhalten; to — one's breath, den Atem anhalten; to — counsel, sich beraten; to — dear, lieben, wert halten; to — a conversation, reden; to — down, niederhalten; to — s. o. in esteem, einen achten; to — excused, entschuldigen; to — a farm of *or* under Lord . . ., einen Hof von Lord . . . in Pacht haben; to — a feast, ein Fest veranstalten; to — as fief, zu Lehen tragen; to — in, einhalten; to — in bondage, in Knechtschaft halten; to — an office, ein Amt bekleiden, eine Stelle inne haben; to — a meeting, eine Versammlung abhalten; to — an opinion, eine Meinung haben; to — off, abhalten, entfernt halten; to — of no *or* little account, geringschätzen; to — one's own, sich behaupten, Stand halten; nicht weichen (*as combatants*); dieselbe Entfernung behaupten (*in a race, etc.*); nicht schlimmer werden (*as a patient*); to — one's own against a p., sich behaupten gegen einen, einem gewachsen sein; to — one's peace *or* one's tongue, schweigen; to — out, ausstrecken; (offer) darbieten; to — a p. to his promise, einen beim Wort halten; to — shares, Aktien haben *or* besitzen; to — up, in die Höhe halten, (support) stützen, aufrechthalten; to — a p. up to ridicule, einen dem Spotte aussetzen; to — a wager, eine Wette halten; to — water, wasserdicht sein (*lit.*), gelten, Stich halten, stichhaltig sein (*fig.*). II. *ir.v.n.* halten; (— on) festhalten; (— good for) gelten, sich bewähren (für), anwendbar sein (auf eine S.); (— out) Stand halten, sich halten; to — **back**, sich zurückhalten, sich fernhalten (from, von); to — **forth**, öffentlich reden, sich verbreiten (on, über *acc.*); predigen; to — **good**, gelten, richtig sein; sich bestätigen; to — **in**, innehalten, einhalten; (restrain oneself) sich enthalten; to — **off**, sich fernhalten, spröde tun; to — **on**, (last) fortdauern, anhalten; aushalten; manage to — on for a few days, halte noch einige Tagen aus! (cling) sich fest halten (an); — on! warte einen Augenblick! (*fam.*); to — **out**, (continue) aushalten, ausdauern; (not yield) standhaft bleiben, sich halten; (keep up) sich erhalten; (endure) dauern; (last) dauern, reichen; to — out against, widerstehen; to — out hopes, (einem) Hoffnung machen, (in einem) Hoffnung erregen *or* erwecken (of a th., auf eine S.); to — **to**, sich halten an (eine S.); to — **together**, zusammenhalten (*also fig.*); to — **under**, (jemandes) Lehnsmann sein; to — **up**, sich aufrecht halten; (keep from) sich halten. III. *s.* der Halt, Griff; das Halten; (authority) die Macht, Gewalt; (support) der Halt, Widerhalt; (claim) der Anspruch; (influence) der Einfluß; der Laderaum (*Naut.*); (custody) der Gewahrsam; (retreat) der Zufluchtsort; das Lager (*of a beast*); after —, der hintere Teil des Laderaums (*in ships*); to get — of a th., eine S. erfassen; to have a — of, in seinem Griffe haben, bemeistern; to let go one's —, loslassen; to keep —, festhalten; to lay — of a th., eine S. ergreifen; to miss one's —, fehlgreifen; to take — of a th., eine S. anfassen; it took a strong — upon his mind, es gewann einen starken Einfluß auf seinen Geist. IV. *int.* halt! halt ein! laß ab! genug! **—er**, *s.* der, die, das Haltende; (tenant) der Pächter, Lehnsmann; der Inhaber (*of a bill, stock, etc.*); der Halter, Griff (*of a pen, etc.*); —er of shares, der Aktienbesitzer, Aktionär; —er forth, der Redner. **—ing**, *s.* die Haltung; das Pachtgut, Zinsgut; small —ings, der kleine Grundbesitz; cash —ings in the banks, Barbestände in den Banken. *Comp.* **—-all**, *s.* die Plaidhülle. **—-fast**, I. *s.* die Klam=

mer; der Klammerhaken, die Zwinge. II. *adj.* fest, solide (*e. g. safes*).

Holden, (*obs.*) *p.p. of* Hold.

Hole, I. *s.* das Loch; (cavity) die Höhle, Grube; (hiding-place) der Schlupfwinkel; das Bohrloch (*Min.*); die Kammer (*of a gun*); full of —s, durchlöchert; to pick a — in s.o.'s coat, einem etwas am Zeuge flicken; to pick —s in s.th., etwas bekritteln, an einer S. Ausstellungen machen. II. *v.a.* aushöhlen; machen (*Bill.*). *Comp.* —**-and-corner,** *adj.* heimlich, versteckt.

Hol—iday, —yday, I. *s.* (festival) der Festtag, Feiertag; der freie Tag; we have a —iday today, wir haben heute frei; half —iday, der (schul)freie Nachmittag; (*pl.*) die Ferien; to leave for one's —idays, in die Ferien gehen. II. *adj.* festtäglich, Fest-; —iday course, der Ferien-kurs, -kursus. —**iness,** *s.* die Heiligkeit; His —iness, Seine Heiligkeit. —**y,** *see* Holy. *Comp.* —**iday-makers,** *s.* der Ausflügler.

Holla, Hollo, I. *int. & s.* (das) Hallo. II. *v.n.* halloen, hallo *or* holla rufen; (— to) laut anrufen; to — out, ausschreien.

Hollow, I. *adj.* hohl; (sunken) tiefliegend, vertieft; hohl, dumpf (*as a sound*); (sham) falsch, verstellt, leer; — adze, die Hohldeißel. II. *adv.* gänzlich; to beat —, vollständig überwinden (*coll.*). III. *s.* die Höhle, Höhlung, Tiefe; (cavity) das Loch, die Grube, Öffnung, Erdhöhle; (groove) die Nut, Rinne; (channel) der Durchgang, Kanal; — of the hand, die hohle Hand. IV. *v.a.* (aus-)höhlen; auskehlen (*Carp.*); austiefen (*a spoon, etc.*); to — out, ausbauchen (Glasgefäße, *zc.*). —**ness,** *s.* das Hohlsein, die Hohlheit; die Leerheit, Falschheit (*fig.*). *Comp.* —**-cheeked, —-eyed,** *adj.* hohl-wangig, -äugig. —**-hearted,** *adj.* falschherzig. —**-square,** *s.* das Viereck, offene Karree.

Holly, *s.* die Stechpalme. *Comp.* —**-oak,** *s.* die Steineiche.

Hollyhock, *s.* die Rosenpappel, Rosenmalve.

[1]**Holm,** *s.* (island) der Werder, die Flußinsel (*dial.*); der Landstrich am Wasser (*dial.*).

[2]**Holm,** *see* Holly. *Comp.* —**-oak,** *see* Holly-oak.

Holo—caust, *s.* das Brandopfer; große Zerstörung (*fig.*). —**graph,** I. *s.* die eigenhändige Urkunde. II. *adj.* eigenhändig geschrieben.

Holp, —en, (*obs.*) *pret. & p.p. of* Help.

Holster, *s.* die (Pistolen-)Halfter. —**ed,** *adj.* mit Halftern.

Holt, *s.* das Gebüsch, der Hain.

Holy, I. *adj.* heilig; — cross, *see* —-rood; — Ghost, der heilige Geist; — Land, das heilige Land; — Thursday, der Himmelfahrtstag; der Grün-Donnerstag (*R. C.*); — war, heiliger Krieg, Kreuzzug; — Week, die Karwoche; — Writ, die heilige Schrift. II. *s.*; — of holies, der Allerheiligste. *Comp.* —**-orders,** *s.* das Priesteramt, der geistliche Stand; to be in —-orders, dem geistlichen Stande angehören, Geistlicher sein; to take —-orders, ordiniert werden, in den geistlichen Stand eintreten. —**-rood,** I. *s.* das Kruzifix. II. *attrib.*; —-rood Day, das Kreuz-Erhöhungsfest. —**stone,** I. *s.* der Scheuerstein. II. *v.a.* scheuern. —**-water,** *s.* das Weihwasser.

Homage, *s.* die Huldigung (*also fig.*); to do, pay, render —, huldigen (a p., einem).

Home, I. *s.* das Heim; (dwelling) das Haus, die Wohnung; (native place) die Heimat; the original — of the Aryans, die Urheimat *or* der ursprüngliche Wohnsitz der Indogermanen; our —s, unsere Heimstätten, Heimwesen, Heimatsorte; unsere Heimat; —s for servant girls, Mädchenheime; at —, zu Hause, bei sich, (in one's country) in der Heimat; Mrs. B. is at — on ..., Frau B. empfängt (Gesellschaft) am ..., hat am ... ihren Empfangstag; at — to no one, für niemand zu Hause; to be at — in a subject, in einem Gegenstand völlig zu Hause *or* wohl bewandert sein; to make o.s. at —, tun als ob man zu Hause wäre; from —, abwesend, verreist; away from —, von Hause fort, nicht zu Hause; to go to one's long —, heimgehen; — is —, be it ever so humble, there is no place like —, eigner Herd ist Goldes wert (*prov.*); charity begins at —, ein jeder ist sich selbst der Nächste. II. *adj.* (domestic) heimisch, häuslich, inländisch; (direct, to the point) derb, treffend; — affairs, innere Angelegenheiten; — circle, der Familienkreis; — Department, das Ministerium des Innern; — journey die Rückreise, Rückfahrt, Heimkehr; — lessons, häusliche Arbeiten, die Hausarbeit (*School*); — Office, das Ministerium *or* Reichsamt des Innern; — Secretary, S. for the — Department, der Minister des Innern (*Engl.*); — service, der Dienst im Lande selbst; — thrust, der Treffer; that is a — thrust, das sitzt; — trade, der Binnenhandel, inländische Handel; — work, die Hausarbeit, häusliche Arbeit; the National — Reading Union, der Verein zur Beförderung häuslicher Fortbildung (durch Lesen ausgewählter Bücher). III. *adv.* heim, nach Hause; (back) zurück; (pointedly) zur Sache, treffend; (thoroughly) gänzlich; to bring s.th. — to a p., einem etwas ordentlich geben *or* deutlich sagen, einem etwas tüchtig unter die Nase reiben (*coll.*); to come —, heim, nach Hause kommen (*lit.*); nahe berühren (*fig.*); that comes — to you, das geht auf Sie; it will come — to him, er wird es schon empfinden; the anchor comes —, der Anker ist triftig; to haul the guns —, die Kanonen einholen; to hit, strike —, den rechten Fleck treffen, (einem) eins versetzen, (einen) in die Enge treiben; welcome —! willkommen zu Hause! —**less,** *adj.* heimatlos; ohne Wohnung. —**liness,** *s.* die Häuslichkeit; die Einfachheit, Schlichtheit (*in dress, etc.*); der Mangel an Schönheit; (want of polish) das ungebildete Benehmen. —**ly,** *adj.* heimisch; einfach, schlicht; nicht hübsch; gewöhnlich, ungebildet. —**stead,** *s.* die Heimstätte; (seat) der Ursitz; das Gehöft. —**ward(s),** *adv.* heimwärts. *Comp.* —**-baked,** *adj.* hausbacken. —**-bound,** *see* —ward-bound. —**-brewed,** *adj.* zu Hause gebraut. —**-cured,** *adj.*; —-cured ham, zu Hause geräucherter Schinken. —**-felt,** *adj.* tief empfunden. —**like,** *adj.* heimatlich. —**-made,** *adj.* zu Hause gemacht, gebacken; im Lande gemacht. —**-rule,** *s.* die Selbstverwaltung; die Selbstverwaltung Irlands mit Parlament in Dublin. —**-ruler,** *s.* der Befürworter der Gewährung irischer Selbstverwaltung. —**-sick,** *adj.* heimwehkrank; an Heimweh leidend; he is —-sick, er hat Heimweh. —**-sickness,** *s.* das Heimweh. —**-spun,** I. *adj.* zu Hause, im Lande gesponnen *or* verfertigt; (—ly) schlicht, einfach. II. *s.* grober lose gewebter Wollstoff; hausbackner Mensch (*fig.*). —**ward-bound,** *adj.* nach Hause bestimmt, auf der Rückreise begriffen.

Homeopath, *see* Homœopath.

Homicid—al, *adj.* mörderisch. —**e,** *s.* der Totschlag, Mord; der Totschläger.

Homil—etic, *adj.* kanzelrednerisch, homiletisch. —**etics,** *pl.* die Kanzelberedsamkeit, Homiletik. —**ist,** *s.* der Kanzelredner, Homiletiker. —**y,** *s.* die Homilie; die (bibelerklärende) Predigt.

Homing, I. *adj.* wieder nach Hause zurück kehrend (*of carrier-pigeons*); — instinct, die Fähigkeit, den Heimatsort wiederzufinden. II. *s.* das richtige Heimkehren (der Brieftauben).

Hominy, *s.* das Maismehl; der Maisbrei.

Homœopath, *see* —ist. —**ic,** *adj.*, —**ically,** *adv.* homöopathisch. —**ist,** *s.* der Homöopath. —**y,** *s.* die Homöopathie.

Homo—geneous, *adj.* gleichartig; homogen (*Phys.*). —**geneousness,** *s.* die Gleichartigkeit. —**genesis,** *s.* die Erzeugung von Wesen, welche den Stammeltern gleichen (*Biol.*). —**logate,** *v.a.* autheißen, bestätigen. —**logous,**

adj. homolog. **—logy,** *s.* die vom Bau abhängige Affinität. **—nym,** *s.* das gleichlautende Wort. **—nymous,** *adj.* gleichlautend. **—pterous,** *adj.* gleichflügelig. **—sexual.** *adj.* gleichgeschlechtlich, das gleiche Geschlecht liebend.

Homunculus. *s.* der Homunkulus; das Menschlein, der Knirps.

Hone, *s.* der Wetzstein.

Honest, *adj.*, **—ly,** *adv.* redlich, ehrbar, rechtschaffen, aufrichtig; (just) billig, gerecht; (virtuous) ehrbar, sittsam, tugendhaft; he has made an — woman of her, er hat ihr die Ehre wiedergegeben, hat sie geheiratet. **—y,** *s.* die Ehrlichkeit, Redlichkeit, Aufrichtigkeit; die Sittsamkeit; —y is the best policy, ehrlich währt am längsten.

Honey, *s.* der Honig; die Süßigkeit (*fig.*); (my) —! mein Herzchen! Süßchen! **—ed,** *adj.* honigreich; honigsüß (*fig.*). *Comp.* **—-bag,** *s.* die Honigblase, der Honigmagen. **—-bee,** *s.* die Honigbiene. **—-buzzard,** *s.* der Bienenfresser. **—comb,** *s.* die Honigwabe, Honigscheibe, die Galle, (Guß=)Blase. **—combed,** *adj.* zellig; durchzogen; löcherig, blasig (*of metal*). **—dew,** *s.* der Honigtau; mit Melasse angefeuchteter Tabak. **—moon,** *s.* der Honigmond, die Flitterwochen; they went to Switzerland for their — moon, sie machten ihre Hochzeitsreise in die Schweiz. **—mooners,** *pl.* Hochzeitsreisende (*coll.*). **—-mouthed,** *adj.* süßschmeichelnd. **—suckle,** *s.* das Geißblatt, der Jelängerjelieber. **—-tongued,** *adj.* glattzüngig.

Honied, *see* Honeyed.

Honor, *s. see* Honour. **—arium,** *s.* das Honorar, die Gebühren. **—ary,** *adj.* Ehren bringend, ehrend; Ehren=; —ary degree, member, der Ehrengrad, das Ehrenmitglied; —ary secretary, der (unbezahlte) Schriftführer.

Honour, I. *s.* die Ehre; (rank) die Würde; (distinction) die Auszeichnung, Ehrenbezeigung; (glory) der Ruhm; (respect) die Achtung, Ehrerbietung; (reputation) der gute Name, Ruf; (sense of —) das Ehrgefühl, die Ehrbarkeit; (chastity) die Ehre, Reinheit, Keuschheit, der gute Ruf; die Figur, das Bild (*Cards*); a banquet given in his —, ein ihm zu Ehren gegebenes Festmahl; he is an — to his profession, er gereicht seinem Berufe zur Zierde; your —, Euer Gnaden; affair of —, die Ehrensache; bound in —, durch Ehrenpflicht gebunden; debts of —, Ehrenschulden; to do — to a p., einem Ehre erweisen; to gain — by, Ehre einlegen mit; I have the — to be, ich habe die Ehre zu sein; man of —, der Ehrenmann; maid of —, das Hoffräulein, die Hofdame; — bright! upon (my) —! auf Ehre! point of —, der Ehrenpunkt; with —, glorreich, ehrenvoll; word of —, das Ehrenwort; — to whom — is due, Ehre, wem Ehre gebührt (*prov.*). II. *v.a.* ehren, Ehre erweisen; beehren (with, mit); (dignify) verherrlichen; honorieren, akzeptieren (*C. L.*). **—able,** *adj.*, **—ably,** *adv.* ehrenvoll, rühmlich, glorreich; ehrenhaft, ehrenvoll; (upright) ehrlich, redlich, rechtschaffen; ehrbar (*as conduct*); ehrenwert (*as title, abbrev.* Hon.); Right —able, Sehr Ehrenwert. **—ableness,** *s.* das Ehrenvolle, Ehrenhafte; der Edelmut; die Würde. **—less,** *adj.* ehrlos, nicht geehrt. **—s,** I. *pl.* die Ehrenstellen, Standesvorrechte; (distinctions) die Ehrenbezeigungen; die Honneurs (*also Cards*); two by —s, zwei Honneurs; to do the —s, die Honneurs machen, Gäste empfangen; —s of war, kriegerische Ehren *or* Ehrenbezeugungen. II. *attrib.;* —(s) man, der Student, welcher sich (im Gegensatz zu einem pass man) einer schwierigeren Universitätsprüfung unterzieht oder unterzogen hat.

Hood, *s.* die Kapuze; die Haube, Kappe (*of falcons*); die Kappe (*of a pump, a chimney, also Shipb.*); kapuzenartiger Überwurf über den Talar (*Univ.*). **—ed,** *adj.* mit einer Kapuze *or* Kappe versehen; verkappt; verhüllt (*fig.*); —ed crow, die Nebelkrähe. *Comp.* **—wink,** *v.a.* die Augen verbinden; (blind) verblenden; (deceive) täuschen.

Hoof, *s.* der Huf, die Klaue. **—ed,** *adj.* hufig, gehuft. **—less,** *adj.* huflos. *Comp.* **—bound,** *adj.* hufzwängig.

Hook, I. *s.* der Haken; die Sichel (*Agr.*); (fish-—) die Fischangel, der Angelhaken; Tiegelhaken (*Typ.*); der Klamm(er)haken (*Carp.*); —s and eyes, Haken und Ösen; safety —, Sicherheitshaken; to take one's —, sich aus dem Staube machen (*coll.*); by — or by crook, auf irgend eine Weise; on one's own —, auf eigene Faust (*coll.*). II. *v.a.* haken; fangen (*also fig.*); to — one's dress, sich (*dat.*) das Kleid haken; to — it, weglaufen (*sl.*); he has become —ed by the girl, das Mädchen hat ihn geangelt, er hat sich von ihr fangen lassen; to — **off,** loshaken; to — on, anhaken. III. *v.n.* sich festhaken. **—ed,** *adj.* krumm, hakig, hakenförmig; —(ed) nose, eine Habichtsnase.

Hooka(h), *s.* die Huka, orientalische Wasserpfeife.

Hooker, *s.* der Huker (*Naut.*).

Hooligan, *s.* der brutale rauflustige Straßenlümmel. **—ism,** *s.* das rauflustige Wesen, brutale Benehmen von Straßenlümmeln, die Brutalität auf der Straße.

[1]**Hoop,** I. *s.* der Reif(en), Faßreif(en); (ring) der Ring, Reif; (—-petticoat) der Reifrock; to drive a —, einen Reifen schlagen. II. *v.a.* (ein Faß) binden, mit Reifen belegen. **—er,** *s.* der Faßbinder, Böttcher.

[2]**Hoop,** *s. see* Whoop. **—er,** *s.* der wilde Schwan. **—oe, —oo,** *s.* der gemeine Wiedehopf. *Comp.* **—ing-cough,** *s.* der Keuchhusten, Stickhusten.

Hoot, *v.* I. *n.* schreien (*of owls*), gröhlen; to — **after,** nachschreien; to — **at,** auspfeifen (*a person, etc.*), verspotten (*an idea, etc.*). II. *a.* durch Geschrei vertreiben, auszischen. III. *s.* der Schrei; höhnisches Geschrei; tiefe Dampfpfeife.

[1]**Hop,** I. *s.* der Hopfen. II. *v.a.* hopfen. **—per,** *see* —-picker. *Comp.* **—-bine,** *s.* die Hopfenranke. **—-garden, —-ground,** *s.* der Hopfengarten, das Hopfenfeld. **—-grower,** *s.* der Hopfenbauer. **—-kiln,** *s.* die Hopfendarre. **—pole,** *s.* die Hopfenstange.

[2]**Hop,** I. *s.* der Hupf, Sprung; das Tänzchen (*coll.*). II. *v.n.* hüpfen, springen; to — about, herumhüpfen. **—per,** *s.* das Becken eines Wasserverschlusses; die Käsemade (*Ent.*); der Trichter (*Mach.*); *see* —scotch. *Comp.* **—-o'-my-thumb,** *s.* der Dreikäsehoch, Knirps, Däumling. **—scotch,** *s.* das Hüpfspiel.

[1]**Hope,** I. *s.* die Hoffnung; (trust) das Vertrauen; (expectation) die Erwartung; there is no — for him, für ihn giebt es keine Hoffnung mehr, es ist aus mit ihm. II. *v.a. & n.* hoffen; erwarten; to — for, auf (eine S.) hoffen; I — this will find you all well, hoffentlich werden diese Zeilen Sie alle wohl antreffen; I —, doch. **—ful,** I. *adj.*, **—fully,** *adv.* hoffnungsvoll; hoffnungsreich; (promising) hoffnungerweckend, vielversprechend. II. *s.* der junge Kerl, die hoffnungsvolle Pflanze; young —ful, kleiner Tunichtgut (*coll.*). **—fulness,** *s.* das Hoffnungsvolle; die zur Hoffnung geneigte Natur. **—less,** *adj.*, **—lessly,** *adv.* hoffnungslos. **—lessness,** *s.* die Hoffnungslosigkeit. **—r,** *s.* der Hoffende.

[2]**Hope,** *in* Forlorn —, *see* Forlorn.

Horary, *adj.* Stunden=, eine Stunde betreffend.

Horde, *s.* die Horde.

Horizon, *s.* der Gesichtskreis, Horizont; rational —, wahrer Gesichtskreis; sensible —, scheinbarer Horizont. **—tal,** *adj.*, **—tally,** *adv.* zum Horizonte gehörig; wagerecht, horizontal; wasserrecht (*Naut.*); —tal bar, das Reck (*Gymn.*); **—tal** watch, die Zylinderuhr.

Horn, *s.* das Horn (*of beasts, the moon, etc., also Mus.*); das Fühlhorn (*Ent.*); (beaker) das Trinkhorn; stag's —s, das Geweih; — of plenty, Füllhorn; to draw in one's —s, die Hörner einziehen (*fig.*). —**ed**, *adj.* gehörnt; —ed cattle, das Hornvieh; —ed owl, die Horneule; —ed snake, die Hornschlange. —**et**, *s.* die Hornisse. —**less**, *adj.* hornlos. —**y**, *adj.* hornig, hörnern. *Comp.* —**beam**, *s.* die Hainbuche. —**bill**, *s.* der Hornrabe; der Nashornvogel. —**blende**, *s.* die Hornblende. —**blower**, *s.* der Hornbläser, Hornist. —**book**, *s.* eine Art A. B. C.=Buch (*obs.*). —**pipe**, *s.* die Hornpfeife; schneller Einzeltanz zur Musik der Hornpfeife, Matrosentanz.

Horo—graphy, *s.* die Horographie. —**loge**, *s.* der Stundenzeiger. —**logical**, *adj.* Uhren betreffend; zum Uhrmachen gehörig. —**logy**, *s.* die Uhrmacherei; die Stundenmessungskunst. —**scope**, *s.* das Horoskop. —**scopy**, *s.* das Horoskopstellen.

Horr—ent, *adj.* borstig, starrend (*poet.*). —**ible**, *adj.*, —**ibly**, *adv.* entsetzlich, schrecklich, fürchterlich; scheußlich. —**ibleness**, *s.* die Entsetzlichkeit. —**id**, *adj.*, —**idly**, *adv.* schrecklich, entsetzlich; höchst widrig; (hideous) scheußlich. —**ify**, *v.a.* erschrecken, entsetzen, schaudern machen; I was —ified at the idea, ich war entsetzt bei dem Gedanken. —**or**, *s.* das Entsetzen, Grausen, Grauen, der Greuel; (—ible thing) das Grauenvolle, der Greuel; —ors of war, die Greuel des Krieges; to give a p. the —s, einem ein Grauen verursachen (*coll.*). *Comp.* —**or-stricken**, *adj.* von Entsetzen ergriffen *or* erfaßt.

Horse, I. *s.* das Pferd, Roß; (cavalry) die Reiterei, Kavallerie; (stand) das Gestell, der Bock; (*pl.*) die Paarden (*Naut.*); shire —, der Hengst; heavy —, schwere Kavallerie; master of the —, der Stallmeister; stalking-—, Schutzpferd; the — neighs, das Pferd wiehert; single harness —, das einzeln gehende Pferd; to sound to —, zum Aufsitzen blasen! to —! zu Pferde! aufgesessen! aufsitzen! to take —, sich zu Pferde setzen, aufsitzen; I took — to, ich ritt nach; he got on his high — with me, er setzte sich gegen mich aufs hohe Pferd; to give a — its head, einem Pferde die Zügel schießen lassen. II. *v.a.* auf dem Rücken tragen; belegen, beschälen. —**y**, *adj.* Pferde liebend; wie ein Jockey *or* Stallknecht. *Comp.* —-**artillery**, *s.* reitende Artillerie. —**back**, *s.;* on —back, zu Pferde, beritten; to be on —back, reiten; to get on —back, aufsitzen, zu Pferde steigen; to go on —back, reiten. —-**block**, *s.* der Aufsteigeblock. —-**boat**, *s.* die Zugfähre; die Pferdefähre. —-**box**, *s.* der Pferdetransportwagen. —-**breaker**, *s.* der Bereiter. —-**car**, *s.* der Pferdebahnwagen (*Amer.*); to get on a —-car, mit der Pferdebahn fahren. —-**chestnut**, *s.* die (rote) Roßkastanie. —-**cloth**, *s.* die Pferdedecke. —-**collar**, *s.* das Kummet. —-**comb**, *s.* der Striegel. —-**dealer**, *s.* der Pferdehändler. —-**doctor**, *s.* der Roßarzt. —-**droppings**, *s.* die Pferdepillen, der Pferdemist. —**flesh**, *s.* das Pferdefleisch; die Pferde (*collect. fig. slang*). —-**fly**, *s.* die Pferdefliege. —-**gear**, *s.* der Göpelbaum. —-**guards**, *pl.* englisches Garde=Kavallerie Regiment. —**hair**, I. *s.* das Roßhaar. II. *attrib.;* —hair cloth, das Roßhaarzeug. —-**jockey**, *s.* der Reitknecht, Jockey. —-**laugh**, *s.* das wiehernde Gelächter. —-**load**, *s.* die Pferdelast. —**man**, *s.* der Reiter. —**manship**, *s.* die Reitkunst. —-**marine**, *s.* der berittene Seesoldat. —**mint**, *s.* die Roßminze. —-**play**, *s.* der grobe, plumpe Scherz. —-**pond**, *s.* die Pferdeschwemme. —-**power**, *s.* die Pferdekraft, Pferdestärke (*abbrev.:* P.S.); 10,000 —-power, 10000 Pferdekräfte. —-**race**, *s.* das Pferderennen, Rennen. —-**radish**, *s.* der Meerrettig. —-**rug**, *s.* die Pferdedecke. —**shoe**, I. *s.* das Hufeisen. II. *attrib.;* —shoe arch, der hufeisenförmige Bogen. —-**tail**, *s.* der Pferdeschwanz; der Schachtelhalm. —-**trappings**, *pl.* das Pferdegeschirr. —**whip**, I. *s.* die Reitgerte. II. *v.a.* mit der Reitpeitsche schlagen. —**woman**, *s.* die Reiterin.

Hortatory, *adj.* ermahnend, Ermahnungs=.

Hort—icultural, *adj.* den Gartenbau betreffend, Garten=. —**iculture**, *s.* der Gartenbau. —**iculturist**, *s.* der Gartenkünstler.

Hosanna, *s.* das Hosianna.

Hos—e, *s.* (tubing) der Schlauch; der Spritzenschlauch; die Dille (*of a spade*); (langer) Strumpf; die Kniehose (*obs.*); garden —e, der Gartenschlauch. —**ier**, *s.* der Strumpfwarenhändler, Wollwarenhändler. —**iery**, *s.* die Strumpfwaren.

Hospi—ce, *s.* das Herbergskloster, Hospiz. —**table**, *adj.*, —**tably**, *adv.* gastfreundlich, gastfrei; —table house, gastliches Haus; —table roof, wirtliches Dach. —**tableness**, *s.* die Gastfreiheit, Gastfreundlichkeit. —**tal**, I. *s.* das Krankenhaus, Hospital, Spital. II. *attrib.;* —tal nurse, die berufsmäßige Krankenpflegerin, Schwester; —tal Sunday, der Sonntag, an welchem zum Besten der Krankenhäuser in den Kirchen gesammelt wird; —tal train, der Lazarettzug. —**tal(l)er, knight-—tal(l)er**, *s.* der Johanniter(ritter), Hospitaliter, Ritter des Spitals (St. Johannis des Täufers). —**tality**, *s.* die Gastfreiheit, Gastfreundschaft; to show —tality, gastfrei sein.

[1]**Host**, *s.* der Wirt; der Gastgeber; der Gast; to reckon without one's —, die Rechnung ohne den Wirt machen. —**el**, *s.* das Pensionshaus für Schüler *or* Studenten unter Leitung eines Vorstehers. —**el(ry)**, *s.* das Gasthaus. —**ess**, *s.* die Wirtin. —**ler**, *s.* der Hausknecht.

[2]**Host**, *s.* das Heer, die Schar; die große Menge, Anzahl, der Schwarm; Lord of —s, der Herr der Heerscharen; the heavenly —s, die himmlischen Heer(es)scharen; — of questions, eine Menge Fragen; he is a — in himself, er kann so viel wie hundert andere. —**age**, *s.* der Geisel, Leibbürge. —**ile**, *adj.*, —**ilely**, *adv.* feindlich; feindselig, abhold; —ile country, Feindesland; —ile to a plan, einem Plane abgeneigt. —**ility**, *s.* die Feindseligkeit (to, gegen).

[3]**Host**, *s.* die (geweihte) Hostie (*R. C.*).

Hot, *adj.*, —**ly**, *adv.* heiß; hitzig, feurig (*fig.*); (spicy) beißend, stark, gewürzt; a — fight, ein hitziges Gefecht; — shot, die glühende Kugel; the place became too — for him, es wurde ihm dort zu schwül; there is — work there, da geht es heiß her. —**ness**, *s.* die Hitze. —**ter**, —**test**, *comp. & sup. of* —. *Comp.* —-**air**, *adj.;* —-air bath, das heiße Luftbad. —**bed**, I. *s.* das Mistbeet; die Brutstätte (*fig.*). II. *attrib.;* —bed frame, der Mistbeetrahmen. —-**blast**, *s.* die heiße Gebläseluft. —-**blooded**, *adj.* hitzig; heißblütig, leidenschaftlich (*fig.*). —-**brained**, —**headed**, *adj.* hitzköpfig, ungestüm, unbesonnen. —**house**, *s.* das Treibhaus. —-**press**, *v.a.* dekatieren (*cloth*), heißpressen (*paper*). —**spur**, *s.* der Heißsporn, Hitzkopf. —-**tempered**, *adj.* heftig, heißblütig. —-**water**, *adj.;* —-water bottle, die Wärmflasche.

Hotchpotch, *s.* der Mischmasch.

Hotel, *s.* der Gasthof, das Hotel; — de Russie, Russischer Hof; family —, private —, die Familienpension, Hotelpension; commercial —, der Gasthof für Handlungsreisende.

Hough, see [1]Hock.

Hound, I. *s.* der Jagdhund, Hund (*fig.*). II. *v.a.* [illegible]n; jagen; to — on, anhetzen auf (*acc.*).

Hour, *s.* die Stunde; die Zeit, Uhr; the last —, die Todesstunde; das letzte Stündlein (*high style*); book of —s, das Gebetbuch; the —s (Hours), die Horen; what — is it? wieviel Uhr ist es? a quarter of an —, eine Viertelstunde; three quarters of an —, dreiviertel Stunde(n); the working —s, die Arbeitszeit; during the small —s of the night, die frühen Morgenstunden; to keep early —s, früh zu Bette gehen; to keep late —s, bis spät aufsitzen; it's past the —, die Stunde ist vorüber, die Zeit ist vorbei; to keep good —s, abends zu rechter Zeit nach Haus kommen, zeitig schlafen gehen. —**ly**, *adj. & adv.* stündlich. *Comp.* —**-glass**, *s.* das Stundenglas, die Sanduhr. —**-hand**, *s.* der Stundenzeiger.

Houri, *s.* die Huri (*a nymph of Mohammed's Paradise*).

House, I. *s.* das Haus; die Wohnung; das Geschlecht, Haus, der Stamm (*fig.*); das Geschäft, die Firma (*C.L.*); (—hold affairs) das Hauswesen, die Haushaltung; (table) der Tisch, die Tafel; das Parlament, Versammlungshaus; das College (*Univ.*); das Pensionshaus für Schüler einer Internatsschule; das Ha[illegible] *Astr.*); — of Assembly, die Repräsentanten[illegible]kammer (*Amer.*); commercial —, Handelshaus; — of Commons, of Lords, Unter-, Ober-haus; — of call, die Herberge, das Arbeitsnachweislokal; — of correction, die Besserungsanstalt, das Zuchthaus; — of God, das Gotteshaus; — of ill repute, liederliches Haus, Dirnenhaus; — of mourning, das Trauerhaus; — of refuge, das Rettungshaus, die Besserungsanstalt; — of Representatives, das Unterhaus des Kongresses; to be in the —, im Parlamente sitzen; to bring down the —, mit größtem Beifall von der Versammlung aufgenommen werden; die Zuhörerschaft zum Beifall hinreißen; to constitute a —, ein verfassungsmäßiges Haus bilden; to keep the —, das Haus hüten; to keep —, die Haushaltung führen, haushalten; to keep open —, offenes Haus halten, offne Tafel führen; neither — nor home, weder Dach noch Fach; my — is my castle, ich bin Herr in meinem Hause. II. *v.a.* unter Dach, in Sicherheit bringen, einbringen (*corn*) *or* unterbringen, beherbergen (*people*); stallen (*cattle*); unterbringen; provision is made for housing bicycles, die Fahrräder können an einem geeigneten Orte untergebracht werden. III. *v.n.* hausen, wohnen. —**less**, *adj.* ohne Haus; obdachlos. *Comp.* —**-agent**, *s.* der Häuser-Agent, -Makler. —**-bell**, *s.* die Hausglocke. —**-boat**, *s.* das bedeckte, hausähnliche Boot, das Hausschiff (in dem Familien im Sommer auf Flüssen leben). —**-breaker**, *s.* der Einbrecher. —**-breaking**, *s.* der Einbruch. —**-decorator**, *s.* der Zimmermaler. —**-fly**, *s.* die Stubenfliege. —**-hold**, I. *s.* die Haushaltung, der Haushalt; die Familie; (servants, *etc.*) die Dienerschaft; king's —hold, königliche Hofhaltung. II. *adj.* häuslich, Haus-, Familien-; —hold bread, gewöhnliches Bäckerbrot; —hold expenses, Haushaltungskosten; —hold gods, die Hausgötter; —hold suffrage, das Wahlrecht eines Hausbesitzers; —hold troops, Gardetruppen; —hold words, Alltagsworte. —**holder**, *s.* der Hausvater, Hausherr. —**-keeper**, *s.* die Hausmutter; die Haushälterin, Wirtschafterin. —**-keeping**, I. *adj.* häuslich. II. *s.* das Haushalten. —**-linen**, *s.* das Weißzeug. —**maid**, *s.* die Hausmagd, das Stubenmädchen; —maid's knee, die Knieentzündung. —**-master**, *s.* der Lehrer an einer Internatsschule, welcher die Aufsicht über die in dem Schulhause oder in seinem eignen Pensionshause wohnenden Schüler führt. —**-painter**, *s.* der Anstreicher; *see* —decorator. —**-parlourmaid**, *s.* das Mädchen für Hausarbeit und Aufwartung in den Zimmern. —**-physician**, *s.* der Anstaltsarzt, im Krankenhause selbst wohnende Arzt. —**-rent**, *s.* die Hausmiete. —**-room**, *s.* das Gelaß im Hause; to give —-room to, ins Haus nehmen. —**-servants**, *pl.* die Dienerschaft, die Domestiken. —**-surgeon**, *s.* der Anstalts-Wundarzt (in einem Krankenhause). —**-top**, *s.* der Hausgiebel, das Dach. —**-warming**, *s.* die Gesellschaft zur Einweihung eines neu bezogenen Hauses, der Einzugsschmaus in einer neuen Wohnung. —**-wife**, *s.* die Hausfrau, die Wirtschafterin; (case) das Nähtäschchen. —**-wifely**, *adj. & adv.* häuslich, haushälterisch. —**-wifery**, *s.* die Hauswirtlichkeit; das Hauswesen, die Hauswirtschaft.

[1]**Housing**, *s.* die Behausung, Herberge; das Lagern (*C. L.*); die Nische (*Arch.*); die Überdachung (*Shipb.*); der Einschnitt (*Carp.*, *Artil.*); the — of the poor, die Unterbringung der Armen, die Besorgung der Armenwohnungen.

[2]**Housing**, *s.* die Schabracke; der Kummetdeckel (*Saddl.*).

Hove, *pret. of* Heave.

Hovel, *s.* armseliges Häuschen, elende Hütte.

Hover, *v.n.* schweben; (waver) schwanken; to — **about**, umherwandern, umschweben; to — **round**, umschwärmen.

[1]**How**, *adv. & int.* wie; — do you do? — are you? wie geht es Ihnen? — many soever, so viele (ihrer) auch sind; — now? nun? warum das? — much is it? was *or* wieviel kostet es? wieviel macht das? (*coll.*); he knows — to ride, er kann reiten; he does not know — to say it, er weiß nicht, wie er es sagen soll. *Comp.* —**beit**, I. *adv.* wie dem auch sei, jedoch, dennoch. II. *conj.* wenngleich (*B.*). —**ever**, I. *adv.* wie sehr auch, auf welche Art auch; (at least) wenigstens; (at all events) jedenfalls, auf alle Fälle; —ever it may be, wie es auch sein *or* wie es sich damit auch verhalten mag; he will not be able to do it, —ever he may try, er wird es nicht zu stande bringen, so viel er es auch versuchen mag. II. *conj.* doch, dennoch, gleichwohl. —**soever**, *adv.* wie auch immer.

[2]**How**, *s.* die sanfte runde Erhebung, der Hügel (*dial.*).

Howda(h), *s.* der zeltartig überdachte Sitz auf einem Elefanten.

Howitzer, I. *s.* die Haubitze. II. *attrib.*; —shell, *s.* die Haubitz-Granate.

Howl, I. *v.n.* heulen (*also fig.*). II. *v.a.*; to — out, herausheulen, losheulen. III. *s.* das Geheul. —**er**, *s.* grober Fehler (*sl.*). —**ing**, I. *adj.* heulend; furchtbar (*sl.*); —ing wilderness entsetzliche Einöde. II. *s.* das Geheul.

Howlet, *s.* die Nachteule.

[1]**Hoy**, *s.* der Lichter (*Naut.*).

[2]**Hoy**, *int.* holla! he! halt!

Hub, *s.* die Nabe (*of a wheel*); die Patrize (*Mint.*); (hilt) der Griff, das Heft; up to the —, so weit wie möglich; the — of the universe, das Zentrum, der Mittelpunkt des Weltalls.

Hubbub, *s.* der Lärm, Tumult, das Getöse.

Huckaback, *s.* der Drell.

Huckle, *s.* die Hüfte. *Comp.* —**berry**, *s.* die (amerikanische) Heidelbeere. —**bone**, *s.* der Fußknöchel; der Hüftknochen.

Huckst—er, I. *s.* der Höker. II. *v.n.* höke(r)n. —**ress**, *s.* die Hökerin, Hökerfrau, das Hökerweib.

Huddle, *v.* I. *n.* sich drängen; to — **together**, zusammenkauern. II. *a.* hudeln; (— together) unordentlich durcheinander werfen; to — **in**, eilig bedecken; to — **on**, geschwind und unordentlich überwerfen, anziehen.

[1]**Hue**, *s.* die Farbe, Färbung, der Farbenton. —**d**, *adj.* gefärbt.

[2]**Hue**, *s.* das Geschrei; — and cry, Zetergeschrei, die Hetze; to raise a — and cry after a p., einen mit lautem Geschrei *or* Halloh verfolgen, über einen Zeter schreien.

Huff, I. *s.* üble Laune; to take — at a th., etwas übel nehmen; to be in a —, schmollen. II. *v.a.* beleidigen, kränken; blasen (*Draughts*). III. *v.n.* in üble Laune geraten, schmollen; easily —ed, (—**ish**, *adj.*,) prahlend, trotzig; übelnehmerisch. —**iness**, —**ishness**, *s.* die Prahlerei, Anmaßung, Aufgeblasenheit. —**y**, *adj. see* —ish.

Hug, I. *v.a.* umarmen; umfassen; (— fast) festhalten, fassen; hätscheln, liebkosen; to — o.s., sich (*dat.*) schmeicheln. II. *v.n.*; to — the wind (land), dicht bei dem Winde (an der Küste hin-) segeln. III. *s.* die Umarmung, Umfassung; die Liebkosung; der Griff (*in wrestling*); a good —, eine tüchtige Liebkosung.

Huge, *adj.*, **—ly**, *adv.* sehr groß; gewaltig, ungeheuer, kolossal. **—ness**, *s.* ungeheure Größe.
Hugger-mugger, *adv.* unordentlich; (secretly) insgeheim.
Hulk, *s.* der Rumpf; der alte Schiffsrumpf, Hulk (*Naut.*). **—ing**, *adj.* schwerfällig, plump.
Hull, I. *s.* (husk) die Hülse, Schale; der Rumpf (*Naut.*). II. *v.a.* schälen, (ab=)hülsen; in den Rumpf schießen.
Hullabaloo, *s.* der Wirrwarr.
Hullo! *int.* holla! he!
Hum, I. *v.n.* summen, sumsen; (murmur) murmeln; to — and haw, stottern. II. *v.a.* summen (*an air, etc.*); to — **over**, herbrummen. III. *s.* das Summen, Gesumse, Gesumme (*of insects, etc.*); der Schwindel; it's all a —, es ist nichts daran! dummes Zeug! IV. *interj.* hm! hum! **—bug**, I. *s.* der Humbug, Betrug, die Prellerei, Windbeutelei; der Unsinn, Mumpitz (*coll.*); der Schwindler, Windbeutel, Aufschneider, Betrüger. II. *v.a.* betrügen, durch Aufschneiderei prellen, täuschen; (hoax) zum Besten haben, foppen. **—drum**, *adj.* alltäglich, langweilig. *Comp.* **—ming-bird**, *s.* der Kolibri.
Human, I. *adj.*, **—ly**, *adv.* menschlich; —ly speaking, menschlich zu reden, nach menschlichen Begriffen. II. *s.* der Mensch (*coll.*). **—e**, *adj.*, **—ely**, *adv.* menschenfreundlich, leutselig, liebreich, human; humanistisch; (merciful) barmherzig, mild; —e learning, Humaniora; —e society, die Gesellschaft zur Rettung im Wasser Verunglückter. **—ism**, *s.* der Humanismus; die Humanität, das Weltbürgertum. **—ist**, *s.* der Humanist. **—istic**, *adj.* humanistisch. **—itarian**, I. *s.* der Menschenfreund. II. *adj.* die Wohlfahrt der Menschen betreffend, menschenfreundlich; Humanitäts=; humanitarisch (*Theol.*). **—ities**, *pl.* die Humaniora, die Philologie. **—ity**, *s.* (— nature) die Menschheit, Humanität; (man) das Menschengeschlecht; die Menschenliebe, Humanität, Menschlichkeit (*fig.*). **—ization**, **—isation**, *s.* die Sittigung. **—ize**, **—ise**, *v.a.* vermenschlichen, menschlich, mild, gesittet machen. *Comp.* **—kind**, *s.* das Menschengeschlecht.
Humbl—e, I. *adj.*, **—y**, *adv.* (modest) bescheiden, demütig; (not lofty) niedrig, gering; (low) niedrig, nieder; my —e self, meine Wenigkeit; your —e servant, Ihr ergebenster Diener; to eat —e pie, Abbitte tun, sich demütigen. II. *v.a.* erniedrigen, demütigen; (crush) niederbeugen; (degrade) herabwürdigen; to —e o.s., sich demütigen, sich erniedrigen, sich herablassen. **—eness**, *s.* die Niedrigkeit (*of birth, etc.*); die Demut. **—ing**, *adj.* demütigend, kränkend. *Comp.* **—e-bee**, *s.* die Hummel.
Humectation, *s.* die Anfeuchtung.
Humer—al, *adj.* Schulter=. **—us**, *s.* das Schulterbein.
Humid, *adj.* feucht, naß. **—ness**, **—ity**, *s.* die Feuchtigkeit.
Humili—ate, *see* Humble II. **—ating**, *adj. see* Humbling. **—ation**, *s.* die Demütigung, Erniedrigung. **—ty**, *s.* die Demut, Bescheidenheit.
Humor, *see* Humour. **—al**, *adj.* die Körpersäfte betreffend, humoral. **—ist**, *s.* der Humorist; a great —ist, ein sehr humorvoller Schriftsteller. **—ous**, *adj.*, **—ously**, *adv.* launig, spaßhaft, humoristisch; launisch, wunderlich. **—ousness**, *s.* das launige, humorvolle Wesen; das launische, eigensinnige Wesen.
Humour, I. *s.* die Feuchtigkeit, der Saft (*Physiol.*); das Temperament, die Gemütsart (*fig.*); (temper) die Laune, Stimmung; (whim) die Grille; (humorousness) der Humor; (inclination) die Neigung; in a good, bad —, gut, schlecht aufgelegt *or* gelaunt; in the — for, aufgelegt zu; while the — lasts, so lange die Lust dauert; it put me out of —, es hat mich um meine gute Laune gebracht. II. *v.a.* (einem) willfahren, gefällig sein; Nachsicht (gegen einen) üben; we must not — children too much, Kindern darf man nicht zu viel ihren Willen lassen; — him a little, gieb ihm ein wenig nach. **—some**, *adj.* launisch, wunderlich (*prov.*).
Hump, *s.* der Höcker, Buckel; to have the —, verdrießlich sein (*coll.*). **—y**, *adj.* buckelig. *Comp.* **—back**, **—backed**, *see* Hunchback.
Humph, *int.* h'm! hum!
Humus, *s.* der Humus, die Fruchterde.
Hunch, I. *s. see* Hump; — of bread, dickes Stück Brod. II. *v.a.* krümmen; puffen, stoßen. *Comp.* **—back**, *s.* der Buck(e)lige; *see* Hump. **—backed**, *adj.* buckelig.
Hundred, I. *num. adj.* hundert; a — people, hundert Leute; several — steps, mehrere hundert Schritt(e). II. *s.* das Hundert; (district) der Bezirk, Cent, Gau; five in the —, fünf vom Hundert, fünf Prozent. **—fold**, *adj.* hundertfältig, hundertfach. **—th**, *num. adj.* hundertst. *Comp.* **—-court**, *s.* das Gau=, Cent=gericht. **—weight**, *s.* der Zentner.
Hung, *pret. & p.p. of* Hang; — beef, das Rauchfleisch.
Hung—er, I. *s.* der Hunger; —er is the best sauce, Hunger ist der beste Koch (*prov.*). II. *v.n.* hungern; to —er after, heftig begehren nach, dürsten nach. **—(e)red**, *adj.*; an —ered, ausgehungert, hungrig. **—rily**, *adv.* hungrig, gierig. **—ry**, *adj.* hungrig; begierig, dürstend (*fig.*); unfruchtbar, mager (*as soil*).
Hunk, *s.* dickes Stück (*prov.*).
Hunt, I. *v.a.* jagen, hetzen; (pursue) verfolgen; (— through) durchjagen, durchlaufen; (use in —ing) auf der Jagd gebrauchen; to — **down**, zu Tode hetzen; to — **from**, wegjagen; to — **out**, ausspüren, ausforschen; to — **up**, aufjagen. II. *v.n.* der Jagd folgen; jagen, Jagd machen (for wolves, auf Wölfe); (nach einer S.) forschen; to — **for**, jagen nach; to — for s.th., emsig nach einer S. suchen, einer S. eifrig nachforschen *or* nachspüren; to — **through** all the shops, alle Läden durchlaufen *or* durchstöbern; to — **up** and **down**, allenthalben suchen. III. *s.* die Jagd, Hetzjagd (*in England*); das Nachsetzen, die Verfolgung; das Suchen; the — is up, die Jagd hat begonnen; to have a — for, eine Jagd nach (einer S.) anstellen. **—er**, *s.* der Jäger, Fuchsjäger; das Jagdpferd. **—ing**, *s.* das Jagen, Fuchsjagen (*in England*); die Verfolgung (*fig.*). **—ress**, *s.* die Jägerin. **—sman**, *s.* der Jäger, Weidmann; der Aufseher der Koppel Jagdhunde. **—smanship**, *s.* die Jagdkunst; (—ing) die Jägerei; das Weidwerk (*poet.*). *Comp.* **—ing-box**, **—ing-lodge**, *s.* der Jagdsitz, das Jagdhaus. **—ing-coat**, *s.* der Jagdrock. **—ing-ground**, *s.* das Jagdrevier. **—ing-horn**, *s.* das Jagdhorn, das Jägerhorn. **—ing-party**, *s.* die Jagdpartie. **—-the-slipper**, *s.* die Pantoffeljagd.
Hurdle, I. *s.* die Hürde, das Weidengeflecht; das Hindernis aus Reisig und Flechtwerk; der Schanzkorb (*Fort.*). II. *v.a.* umhürden. *Comp.* **—-race**, *s.* das Hürdenrennen.
Hurdy-gurdy, *s.* die Drehleier, der Leierkasten.
Hurl, I. *v.a.* werfen, schleudern; ausstoßen, heftig äußern (*fig.*); strudeln; to — defiance at a p., einem den Fehdehandschuh hinwerfen. II. *v.r. & n.* sich schnell bewegen. III. *s.* das Schleudern. **—er**, *s.* der Werfende, Schleuderer. **—ing**, *s.* das Schleudern; eine Art Treibballspiel.
Hurly-burly, *s.* der Tumult, das Getümmel.
Hurrah, *int.* Hurra!
Hurricane, I. *s.* der Sturmwind, heftige Sturm, Orkan. II. *attrib.*; — deck, das Sturmdeck.
Hurr—ied, *adj.*, **—iedly**, *adv.* in größter Eile; übereilt. **—y**, I. *v.a.* (an)treiben zu größerer Geschwindigkeit, jagen; (do —iedly) eilig verrichten; (hasten) beschleunigen; (precipitate) übereilen, überstürzen; to —y **away**, eiligst fortschicken *or* wegbringen; to —y **back**, eiligst

zurückschicken; to —y **in**, eiligst hineinbringen; to —y **into**, drängen in (*acc.*); he —ied them into a boat, er drängte sie eilig in ein Boot; to —y **on**, treiben, drängen; to —y **up** (a p.), (einen) antreiben sich zu beeilen (*coll.*). II. *v.n.* eilen, sich beeilen; (he warned them) not to —y, (er warnte sie) sich nicht zu übereilen *or* zu überstürzen, es nicht zu eilig zu haben; to —y on to one's ruin, seinem Verderben zueilen; —y up! beeilt euch! macht schnell! to —y **back**, zurückeilen; to —y **in**, hereinlaufen, eilig hereinkommen; to —y **off**, forteilen; to —y **on**, weiter eilen; to —y **over** a th., schnell über eine S. hinweggehen, etwas schnell abfertigen. III. *s.* die große Eile; die Übereilung; das Drängen; (bustle) der Tumult, die Unruhe; to be in a —y, große Eile haben; in the —y of business, im Drange der Geschäfte. —**y-scurry**, I. *s.* der Wirbel (von Vergnügungen). II. *adv.* auf übereilte Weise, in der Verwirrung; durcheinander.

Hurt, I. *ir.v.a.* (*also pret. & p.p.*) verletzen; (vex) (einem) wehe tun; (injure) (einem) schaden *or* Schaden zufügen, (einen) beschädigen; to — s.o.'s feelings, jemandes Gefühle verletzen; he has — my honour, er hat mich an meiner Ehre angegriffen; to be — at, sich verletzt fühlen über (*acc.*). II. *ir.v.n.* wehe tun. III. *s.* die Verletzung, Wunde; der Nachteil, Schade; das Übel. —**ful**, *adj.*, —**fully**, *adv.* schädlich, nachteilig. —**fulness**, *s.* die Schädlichkeit. —**le**, *v.n.* (an)stoßen, anrennen; (clash) klirren; wirbeln, sausen.

Husband, I. *s.* der Ehemann, Mann, Gatte; ship's —, der dirigierende Reeder. II. *v.a.* sparen, haushälterisch *or* sparsam umgehen mit, haushälterisch verwalten; to — one's time, mit seiner Zeit geizen. —**less**, *adj.* gattenlos. —**ry**, *s.* der Ackerbau, die Landwirtschaft. *Comp.* —**man**, *s.* der Ackerbauer; der Landwirt.

Hush, I. *int.* still. II. *s.* die Stille. III. *v.a.* stillen, zum Schweigen bringen; (calm) beruhigen; to — up, vertuschen; —ing sound, labialer Zischlaut (sh, sch). IV. *v.n.* still sein. —**aby**, *int.* still, still! —**ed**, *adj.* still. *Comp.* —**-money**, *s.* das Schweigegeld.

Husk, I. *s.* die Hülse, Schale; die Schote (*of peas*); die Schale (*fig.*). II. *v.a.* enthülsen. —**y**, *adj.* hülsig, schalig. —**s**, *pl.* Träber (*B.*).

Husk—ily, *adv. see* —y. —**iness**, *s.* die Rauheit, Heiserkeit. —**y**, *adj.* rauh, heiser.

Hussar, *s.* der Husar.

Hus—sif, *s.* das Nähtäschchen. —**sy**, *s.* die Haushälterin (*obs.*); die Dirne; das Weibsbild; little —sy! kleine Hexe! —**tings**, —**wife**, —**band**, *etc.*, *see* Hustings, Housewife, Husband, *etc.*

Hustings, *pl.* die Rednerbühne, Wahlbühne.

Hustle, *v.* I. *a.* drängen, (zusammen=)stoßen; to — off, fortstoßen. II. *n.* sich drängen.

Hut, *s.* die Hütte; die Feldhütte (*Mil.*); shelter —, die Schutzhütte, Alpenhütte (*Mount.*).

Hutch, *s.* der Kasten; (kneading trough) der Backtrog; rabbit —, Kaninchenkasten.

Hux, *v.a.* (Hechte) mit Angeln und Schnüren an schwimmenden Blasen fangen.

Huzza, I. *interj.* hussa! hoch! II. *s.* das Hussa, Jauchzen. III. *v.n.* hussa rufen, jauchzen. IV. *v.a.* (einem) zujauchzen.

Hyacinth, *s.* die Hyazinthe. —**ine**, *adj.* Hyazinthen=.

Hyæna, *s.* die Hyäne.

Hyal—ine, *adj.* glasartig, durchsichtig, Glas=. —**ite**, *s.* der Hyalit. —**oid**, *adj.* glasartig, Glas=; —oid membrane, die Glashaut (*Anat.*).

Hybrid, I. *adj.* unecht, zwitterhaft, Bastard=; —word, das Mischwort. II. *s.* der Zwitter, Mischling, das Bastardtier, die Bastardpflanze. —**ism**, *s.* das Bastardartige.

Hydra, *s.* die Hydra (*Myth. & fig.*); die Wasserschlange (*Astr.*); der Armpolyp (*Zool.*). —**gogue**, *s.* wassertreibendes Mittel (*Med.*). —**ngea**, *s.* die Hortensie. —**nt**, *s.* der Hydrant. —**te**, *s.* das Hydrat. —**ted**, *adj.* mit Wasser verbunden; —ted acid, das Säurehydrat; —ted oxide, das Oxydhydrat. *Comp.* —**-headed**, *adj.* hydraköpfig.

Hydraulic, *adj.* durch Wasserdruck bewegt, hydraulisch; — architecture, die Wasserbaukunst; — belt, der wollene, endlose Riemen zum Wasserheben; — blower, das Wasserdruckgebläse; — dock, das Schwimmdock; — engine, die Wasserhebmaschine; — engineer, der Wasserbaumeister; — engineering, die Wasserbaukunst; — friction, die Flüssigkeitsreibung; — gauge, der Wasserdruckmesser; — main, die Vorlage; — motor, der Wassermotor; — power, die Wasserdruckkraft; — ram, der Stoßheber; — screw, die Wasserschraube. —**s**, *s.* die Wasserkraftlehre, Mechanik der flüssigen Körper, Hydraulik.

Hydri—c, *adj.* mit Wasserstoff verbunden. —**te**, *s.* die Wasserstoffverbindung. —**odic**, *adj.*; —odic acid, die Jodwasserstoffsäure.

Hydro-, (*in comp.* =) Wasser=. —**carbon**, *s.* der Kohlenwasserstoff. —**cele**, *s.* der Wasserbruch. —**cephalus**, *s.* der Wasserkopf, die Gehirnwassersucht. —**chloric**, *adj.* salzsauer; —chloric acid, der Chlorwasserstoff, die Salzsäure. —**cyanic**, *adj.*; —cyanic acid, die Blausäure. —**dynamic**, *adj.* hydrodynamisch. —**dynamics**, *s.* die Wasserkraftlehre, Hydrodynamik. —**gen**, *s.* der Wasserstoff. —**genous**, *adj.* Wasserstoff enthaltend. —**grapher**, *s.* der Hydrograph. —**graphy**, *s.* die Gewässerbeschreibung, Hydrographie. —**logy**, *s.* die Wasserkunde, Gewässerlehre. —**mancy**, *s.* die Wasserwahrsagung. —**mel**, *s.* das Honigwasser. —**meter**, *s.* der Wassermesser, das (der) Hydrometer. —**metric**, *adj.* hydrometrisch. —**pathic**, *adj.* wasserheilkundlich, hydropathisch; —pathic establishment, die Kaltwasser=Heilanstalt. —**pathist**, *s.* der Wasserarzt; der Hydropath. —**pathy**, *s.* die Wasserheilkunde, Wasserkur. —**phobia**, *s.* die Wasserscheu, Hundswut. —**phobic**, *adj.* wasserscheu, hydrophobisch. —**phyte**, *s.* die Wasserpflanze. —**pneumatic**, *adj.* hydropneumatisch. —**scope**, *s.* die Wasseruhr; das Hydrometer (*Phys.*). —**static**, *adj.* hydrostatisch. —**statics**, *pl.* die Lehre vom Gleichgewicht der Flüssigkeiten, Hydrostatik.

Hyena, *see* Hyæna.

Hygien—e, *s.* die Gesundheitslehre. —**ic**, *adj.* der Gesundheitslehre entsprechend, der Gesundheit zuträglich, gesundheitlich, Gesundheits=.

Hygro—meter, *s.* der Feuchtigkeitsmesser, das (der) Hygrometer. —**metric**, *adj.* hygrometrisch. —**scope**, *see* —meter.

Hymen, *s.* der Hymen (*Myth.*); die Ehe, das Eheband (*poet.*); das Jungfernhäutchen (*Anat.*); das Knospenhäutchen (*Bot.*). —**eal**, I. *adj.* hochzeitlich. II. *s.* das Hochzeitslied. —**opter**, *s.* der Hautflügler.

Hymn, I. *s.* das Kirchenlied, Loblied, der Gesang, Choral. II. *v.a.* in Hymnen preisen, lobpreisen. —**al**, *adj.* hymnenartig. —**ic**, *adj.* hymnisch, lobpreisend. —**ody**, *s.* das Hymnensingen; die Kirchenliedersammlung. —**ology**, *s.* die Hymnenkunde, Hymnologie; die Hymnensammlung (*obs.*). *Comp.* —**-book**, *s.* das Gesangbuch.

Hyper (*prep.* = über). —**bola**, *s.* die Hyperbe (*Math.*). —**bole**, *s.* die Übertreibung, Hyperbel. —**bolical**, *adj.*, —**bolically**, *adv.* übertreibend, hyperbolisch. —**bolism**, *s.* der Gebrauch der Hyperbel. —**boloid**, *s.* die Hyperboloide. —**borean**, *adj.* hyperboräisch, nördlich. —**critic**, *s.* der Hyperkritiker, Splitterrichter, Nörgler. —**critical**, *adj.* überkritisch, allzu kritisch. —**criticism**, *s.* überstrenge Kritik. —**oxyd**, *s.* das Hyperoxyd. —**sarcosis**, *s.* das wilde Fleisch. —**trophy**, *s.* übermäßiges Wachstum, die Hypertrophie.

Hyphen, *s.* das Teilungszeichen, der Bindestrich.
Hypnoti—c, *adj.* einschläfernd, hypnotisch. **—ze**, *v.a.* einschläfern, in Schlaf versetzen, hypnotisieren. **—zer**, *s.* Einschläferer, Hypnotiseur. **—sm**, *s.* magnetischer Schlaf, Hypnotismus.
Hypo (*prep.* = unter). **—chondria(sis)**, *s.* die Schwermut, Trübseligkeit, Grillenfängerei, Hypochondrie. **—chondriac**, I. *adj.* schwermütig, grillenfängerisch, hypochondrisch. II. *s.* der Grillenfänger, der Schwermütige, Hypochonder. **—crisy**, *s.* die Heuchelei. **—crite**, *s.* der Heuchler; (religious —crite) der Scheinheilige. **—critical**, *adj.*, **—critically**, *adv.* heuchlerisch. **—gastric**, *adj.* Unterbauchs=. **—gastrocele**, *s.* der Bauchbruch. **—gynous**, *adj.* unterweibig. **—phosphate**, *s.* unterschwefelsaures Salz. **—stasis**, **—stasy**, *s.* die Grundlage, Hypostase. **—tenuse**, *s.* die Hypotenuse. **—thecary**, *adj.* pfandrechtlich. **—thecate**, *v.a.* verpfänden, hypothekieren. **—thesis**, *s.* die Vermutung, Hypothese. **—thetic(al)**, *adj.* vermeintlich, vermutlich, vorausgesetzt, angenommen.
Hyssop, *s.* der Ysop (*Bot.*); der Weihwedel.
Hyster—ia, *s.* das Unterleibsleiden (bei Frauen), die Hysterie. **—ical**, *adj.* hysterisch; —ical sobs, heftiges Schluchzen mit hysterischen Krämpfen. **—icalness**, *s.* das Hysterische. **—ics**, *pl.*; fit of —ics, hysterischer Anfall. **—ocele**, *s.* der Gebärmutterbruch. **—ology**, *s.* die Hysterologie. **—omania**, *s.* die Mutterwut, Mannstollheit. **—otomy**, *s.* der Kaiserschnitt (*Med.*).

I

[1]**I, i**, *s.* J, i; i' = in, in. *For abbreviations see the Index at the end of the English-German part.*
[2]**I**, *pers. pron.* ich; it is —, ich bin es.
Iamb—ic, I. *adj.* jambisch, iambisch. II. *s.* iambischer Vers, Jambus. **—us**, *s.* der Jambus; der aufsteigende Vers.
Ibex, *s.* der Steinbock.
Ibidem, *adv.* ebendaselbst, ebenda.
Ibis, *s.* der Ibis.
Ice, I. *s.* das Eis; das Gefrorene (*Conf.*); field (of) —, zusammengetriebenes Eis; floating —, Treibeis; to break the —, das Eis aufhauen, brechen (*lit.*), das Eis brechen (*fig.*); to skate over very thin —, auf des Messers Schneide tanzen (*fig.*). II. *v.a.* in Eis verwandeln, gefrieren machen; überzuckern (*Conf.*); kühlen (*wine*). *Comp.* **—-axe**, *s.* das Eisbeil, der Pickel (*Mount.*). **—berg**, *s.* der (schwimmende) Eisberg. **—-blink**, *s.* der Eisblink. **—-boat**, *s.* das Eisboot, der Eisbrecher; der Segelschlitten. **—-bound**, *adj.* eingefroren. **—-breaker**, *s.* der Eisbrecher. **—-cream**, *s.* das Eiscreme, Gefrorene. **—-field**, *s.* das Eisfeld. **—-floe**, *s.* die große Scholle Treibeis. **—-house**, *s.* der Eiskeller. **—-pail**, *s.* der Eiskübel, Weinkühler. **—-plant**, *s.* das Eiskraut. **—-plough**, *s.* der Eispflug. **—-safe**, *s.* der Eisschrank.
Ichneumon, *s.* das (der) Ichneumon.
Ichnograph, *s.* der Grundriß. **—er**, *s.* der Grundrißzeichner.
Ichor, *s.* der Ichor, das Götterblut; die Jauche (*Med.*). **—ous**, *adj.* eiterig.
Ichthyo—graphy, *s.* die Fischbeschreibung, Fischkunde. **—lite**, *s.* der versteinerte Fisch; der Fischabdruck. **—logist**, *s.* der Fischkundige. **—logy**, *s.* die Fischlehre. **—phagist**, *s.* der Fischesser. **—phagous**, *adj.* Fisch essend. **—saurus**, *s.* die Fischeidechse.
Ici—cle, *s.* der Eiszapfen. **—ly**, *adv. see* Icy. **—ness**, *s.* die Eisigkeit. **—ng**, *s.* der Zuckerguß, die Überzuckerung.
Icon, *s.* das Bild, Christusbild, Heiligenbild. **—oclasm**, *s.* die Bilderstürmerei. **—oclast**, *s.* der Bilderstürmer. **—oclastic**, *adj.* Bilder stürmend *or* zerstörend. **—ography**, *s.* die Bilderbeschreibung. **—olatry**, *s.* die Bilderanbetung. **—ology**, *s.* die Bilderkunde.
Icosahedron, *s.* der Zwanzigflächner.
Icteric, *adj.* gelbsüchtig; gut gegen die Gelbsucht.
Ictus, *s.* rhythmischer Akzent, Iktus.
Icy, *adj.* eisig; kalt, frostig (*fig.*); — cold, eiskalt.
Idea, *s.* die Idee, der Begriff; die Vorstellung; (purpose) die Absicht (*coll.*); (opinion) der Gedanke; I have an — that he . . ., ich denke, er . . .; to form an —, sich (*dat.*) vorstellen; I can't form any — of it, ich kann mir keinen Begriff davon machen. **—l**, I. *adj.*, **—lly**, *adv.* ideal, vorbildlich; (fanciful) nicht wirklich, eingebildet; gedanklich, ideell; Gedanken=, Ideen=; (beyond reality) ideal, hoch vollendet. II. *s.* das Musterbild, Ideal. **—lism**, *s.* der Idealismus. **—list**, *s.* der Idealist. **—listic**, *adj.* idealistisch. **—lity**, *s.* die Idealität; die höchste Vollkommenheit. **—lize**, *v.* I. *a.* idealisieren, über die Wirklichkeit emporheben, veredeln. II. *n.* Ideale bilden.
Idem, *adj.* derselbe, dasselbe.
Identi—cal, *adj.*, **—cally**, *adv.* (ganz) übereinstimmend, gleichgeltend, gleichlautend, einerlei, identisch. **—calness**, *s.* die Übereinstimmung, Einerleiheit. **—fiable**, *adj.* identifizierbar, als gleich nachweislich. **—fication**, *s.* die Identifikation. **—fy**, *v.a.* identifizieren, die Gleichartigkeit *or* die Persönlichkeit feststellen; I —fy myself with my school, ich betrachte mich als völlig eins mit meiner Schule. **—ty**, *s.* die Identität, Wesenseinheit; *see* —calness; mistaken —ty, die Personenverwechselung.
Ideology, *s.* die Begriffslehre.
Ides, *pl.* die Iden.
Idio—cy, *s.* der Blödsinn, Irrsinn, die Blödsinnigkeit, Geistesschwäche, Dummheit. **—m**, *s.* die Spracheigenheit, Sprechweise, Mundart; die sprichwörtliche Redensart, der idiomatische Ausdruck. **—matical**, *adj.*, **—matically**, *adv.* idiomatisch. **—pathic**, *adj.* idiopathisch. **—pathy**, *s.* die selbständig entstandene Krankheit, Idiopathie. **—syncrasy**, *s.* die Natureigentümlichkeit, Eigenart, Vorliebe (für), natürlicher Widerwille (gegen), persönliche Empfänglichkeit (für). **—t**, *s.* der Geistesschwache, Schwachsinnige; (stupid person) der Dummkopf, Tropf; asylum for —ts, die Irrenanstalt, Idiotenanstalt. **—tcy**, *see* **—cy**. **—tic**, *adj.* schwachsinnig, idiotisch, blödsinnig; dumm. **—tism**, *s.* die (mundartliche) Spracheigenheit; der Stumpfsinn.
Idle, I. *adj.*, **Idly**, *adv.* (unoccupied) müßig; (indolent) träge, faul; (empty) eitel, leer; (futile) vergeblich, unnütz, fruchtlos; — hour, müßige, freie Stunde; — boys, faule Knaben; — talk, eitles Geschwätz; — wheel, das Zwischenrad; das Spannungsrad; — words, unnütze Worte. II. *v.n.* faulenzen. III. *v.a.*; to — away one's time, seine Zeit mit Nichtstun hinbringen. **—ness**, *s.* der Müßiggang, die Untätigkeit; (leisure) die Muße; die Faulheit, Trägheit; die Nichtigkeit, Eitelkeit; die Unfruchtbarkeit; —ness is the parent of vice, Müßiggang ist aller Laster Anfang (*prov.*). **—r**, *s.* der Faulenzer, Müßiggänger.
Idol, *s.* das Götzenbild; der Abgott, Gegenstand übermäßiger Verehrung (*fig.*). **—ater**, *s.* der Götzendiener. **—atress**, *s.* die Götzendienerin. **—atrize**, *v.* I. *n.* Abgötterei treiben. II. *a.* abgöttisch verehren. **—atrous**, *adj.*, **—atrously**, *adv.* abgöttisch. **—atry**, *s.* der Götzendienst; die Vergötterung. **—ize**, *v.* I. *a.* vergöttern, anbeten. II. *n.* Abgötterei treiben. **—on**, (*pl.* —a) das Bild; das Trugbild.
Idyl, *s.* die Idylle; das Schäfergedicht, Hirtengedicht, Idyll, die Idylle. **—lic**, *adj.* idyllisch, ländlich; —lic poetry, die Idyllendichtung.
If, I. *conj.* wenn, falls, wofern; ob; — he should write, wenn er schreiben sollte; I don't know — I can do it, ich weiß nicht, ob ich es tun kann; I will do it, — I die for it, ich tue es und sollte es

mir das Leben kosten; as —, als wenn, als ob; — not, wo nicht; — so, in dem Falle; — so be that, gesetzt, es wäre. II. *s.* das Wenn; without —s or ands, ohne viele Ausflüchte.

Ign—eous, *adj.* feurig; durch Feuer gebildet. **—is-fatuus**, *s.* das Irrlicht. **—ite**, *v.* I. *a.* anzünden, entzünden, in Brand setzen. II. *n.* sich entzünden, Feuer fangen. **—itible**, *adj.* entzündbar. **—ition**, *s.* das Anzünden; in a state of —ition, im Brand.

Ignobl—e, *adj.*, **—y**, *adv.* unedel, gering; gemein, unedel, niedrig (*as birth*). **—eness**, *s.* die Gemeinheit; die Niedrigkeit (*of birth*).

Ignomin—ious, *adj.*, **—iously**, *adv.* schmählich, schimpflich, entehrend. **—y**, *s.* die Schmach, Schande, der Schimpf.

Ignor—amus, *s.* der Unwissende, Ignorant. **—ance**, *s.* die Unwissenheit. **—ant**, *adj.* unwissend, ununterrichtet, unkundig; to be —ant of, unbekannt sein mit, nichts wissen von; —ant of the world, ohne Weltkenntnis. **—antly**, *adv. see* —ant; aus Unwissenheit. **—e**, *v.a.* nicht wissen; (not notice) nicht beachten; für unbewiesen erklären (*Law*).

Iguana, *s.* die Kammeidechse.

Ileac, Iliac, *adj.* iliisch, darmgichtig, Krummdarm=; — passion, die Darmgicht.

Ilex, *s.* die Stecheiche, Stechpalme.

Iliad, *s.* die Ilias, Iliade.

[1]**Ilk**, *adj.* jeder, jede, jedes (*dial.*).

[2]**Ilk**, *adj.;* of that —, desselben Namens; Grahame of that —, Grahame von Grahame (*Scotch*).

Ill, I. *adj. & adv.* übel, böse; schlimm, schlecht; (sick) krank; — humour, schlechte Laune; an — turn, schlimmer Streich; — at ease, unbehaglich; — weeds grow apace, Unkraut verdirbt nicht (*prov.*); to take —, übel nehmen; to be taken, to fall —, krank werden. II. *adv.* schwerlich, mit Mühe, nicht gut; he can — bear it, er kann es schwerlich ertragen. III. *s.* das Übel, Böse; (misfortune) das Unglück. **—ness**, *s.* das Unwohlsein, die Krankheit. *Comp.* **—-advised**, *adj.* übel beraten; unbesonnen. **—-affected**, *adj.* übelgesinnt. **—-arranged**, *adj.* schlecht eingerichtet. **—-assorted**, *adj.* nicht zu einander passend, unpassend. **—-behaved**, *adj.* unartig, unhöflich. **—-bred**, *adj.* ungebildet. **—-conditioned**, *adj.* schlecht beschaffen. **—-disposed**, *adj.* übel gesinnt, unfreundlich; boshaft. **—-fated**, *adj.* unglücklich. **—-favoured**, *adj.* häßlich. **—-feeling**, *s.* die Verstimmung, Abneigung, der Unwille. **—-gotten**, *adj.* mit Unrecht erworben; —-gotten wealth never prospers, unrecht Gut gedeiht nicht (*prov.*); — got, — spent, wie gewonnen, so zerronnen (*prov.*). **—-judged**, *adj.* schlecht bedacht, unbesonnen, verkehrt. **—-luck**, *s.* das Unglück; as — -luck would have it, unglücklicherweise. **—-matched**, *adj.* schlecht zusammenpassend. **—-merited**, *adj.* unverdient. **—-nature**, *s.* die Bösartigkeit, Böswilligkeit. **—-natured**, *adj.* boshaft, bösartig; —-natured attempts, remarks, böswillige Versuche, Bemerkungen. **—-omened**, *adj.* von schlimmer Vorbedeutung. **—-pleased**, *adj.* unzufrieden (mit), unbefriedigt (von). **—-starred**, *adj.* unglücklich. **—-tempered**, *adj.* übellaunig. **—-timed**, *adj.* ungelegen. **—-treat**, **—-use**, *v.a.* mißhandeln. **—-usage**, *s.* schlechte Behandlung. **—-will**, *s.* das Übelwollen; to bear s.o. —-will, einem übel gesinnt *or* gram sein.

Illati—on, *s.* das Folgern, der Schluß. **—ve**, I. *adj.* folgernd. II. *s.* (—ve particle) die Schlußpartikel.

Illegal, *adj.*, **—ly**, *adv.* ungesetzlich, gesetzwidrig, rechtsungültig. **—ity**, *s.* die Ungesetzlichkeit, Gesetzwidrigkeit.

Illegib—ility, **—leness**, *s.* die Unleserlichkeit. **—le**, *adj.*, **—ly**, *adv.* unleserlich.

Illegitima—cy, *s.* die Unehelichkeit; (illegality) die Unrechtmäßigkeit, Ungültigkeit; die Unechtheit (*of a document, etc.*). **—te**, *adj.*, **—tely**, *adv.* unehelich; unrechtmäßig, widerrechtlich; (unjustified) unberechtigt.

Illiberal, *adj.*, **—ly**, *adv.* unfreigebig, karg; unfreisinnig, engherzig. **—ity**, *s.* die Kargheit; die Ungroßmütigkeit, Engherzigkeit.

Illicit, *adj.* unerlaubt, verboten, unzulässig.

Illimitabl—e, *adj.*, **—y**, *adv.* unbegrenzbar, grenzenlos.

Illitera—cy, *s.* die Ungelehrtheit, Unwissenheit. **—te**, *adj.*, **—tely**, *adv.* ungelehrt, unwissend, des Schreibens und Lesens unkundig.

Illogical, *adj.*, **—ly**, *adv.* unlogisch; (reasonable) vernunftwidrig. **—ness**, *s.* das Unlogische.

Illu—de, *v.a.* täuschen; verblenden. **—sion**, *s.* die Täuschung, Verblendung; (delusion) das Wahnbild. **—sive**, *adj.* täuschend, verführerisch, Schein=. **—siveness**, *s.* die Täuschung, Trüglichkeit, der Schein. **—sory**, *see* —ive.

Illum—e, *v.a.* erleuchten. **—inate**, *v.a.* beleuchten, erhellen; aufklären, erleuchten (*fig.*); festlich erleuchten, illuminieren (*streets, etc.*); illustrieren, bunt ausmalen (*a manuscript*); —inated manuscript, die Bilderhandschrift; the text is —inated by a series of views, der Text wird durch eine Anzahl von Ansichten illustriert *or* veranschaulicht. **—inati**, *pl.* die Illuminaten, Lichtbrüder. **—ination**, *s.* die Illumination; die Beleuchtung; die Illuminierung, Verzierung durch Bilder, der Bilderschmuck. **—inator**, *s.* der Erleuchter; der Illuminierer (*Art.*). **—ine**, *v.a. see* —inate; verherrlichen.

Illustr—ate, *v.a.* klar, hell, glänzend machen; (durch Bilder, &c.) klar machen; erläutern, erklären; mit Abbildung versehen, illustrieren (*a book*). **—ation**, *s.* (elucidation) die Erläuterung, Erklärung, die Illustration, erläuternde Abbildung. **—ator**, *s.* der Illustrierer, Bilderzeichner; der Erläuterer. **—ious**, *adj.*, **—iously**, *adv.* berühmt, ausgezeichnet, erhaben; (august) erlaucht, durchlauchtig(st). **—iousness**, *s.* die Erlauchtheit; die Berühmtheit.

Image, I. *s.* das Bild (*also Rhet. & Opt.*); (statue) das Standbild, die Statue; (idol) das Götzenbild; (of saints) das Heiligenbild; (copy) das Abbild, Ebenbild; (idea) die Vorstellung, Idee. II. *v.a.* abbilden, vorstellen. **—ry**, *s.* (—s) das Bildwerk, die Figuren; die Bilder, Tropen, anschauliche Schilderung (*Rhet.*); die Vorstellungskraft, Fähigheit, anschauliche Vorstellungen zu bilden. *Comp.* **—-breaker**, *s.* der Bilderstürmer. **—-maker**, *s.* der Bildner; der Bildschnitzer, Herrgottschnitzer. **—-worship**, *s.* der Bilderdienst.

Imagin—able, *adj.*, **—ably**, *adv.* vorstellbar, erdenklich, denkbar; all the means —able, alle erdenkbaren Mittel. **—ary**, *adj.* eingebildet; Schein=, imaginär (*also Math. & C. L.*). **—ation**, *s.* die Einbildung, Vorstellung; (power of —ation) die Einbildungskraft, Phantasie. **—ative**, *adj.* erfinderisch; phantastisch; —ative faculty, (**—ativeness**, *s.*) die Einbildungs=, Erfindungs=kraft. **—e**, *v.* I. *a.* sich (*dat.*) einbilden, sich (*dat.*) vorstellen, sich (*dat.*) denken; (think) sich (*dat.*) denken, dafürhalten, glauben; (devise) er=, aus=sinnen. II. *n.* sich vorstellen; —e! denke dir! denkt euch! he —es, er bildet sich ein, er glaubt, er denkt sich. **—ing**, *s.* die Einbildung.

Imbecil—e, *adj.* blödsinnig. **—ity**, *s.* der Blödsinn; die Geistesschwäche.

Imbibe, *v.a.* einsaugen. **—r**, *s.* der, die Einsaugende.

Imbricate, *adj.* dachziegelförmig; dachziegelartig, übereinanderliegend.

Imbroglio, *s.* die Verwicklung; (plot) die verwickelte Handlung.

Imbrue, *v.a.* benetzen, beflecken; eintauchen (one's hands in blood, seine Hände in Blut).

Imbue, *v.a.* tränken; tief färben; durchtränken,

erfüllen; einprägen (*fig.*); —d with an idea, von einem Gedanken erfüllt, eines Gedankens voll.
Imita—ble, *adj.*, —**bly**, *adv.* nachahmbar. —**te**, *v.a.* nachahmen; (copy) nach=machen, =bilden; not to be —ated, nicht nachzuahmen; (inimitable) unnachahmbar, unnachahmlich; —ate him! ahmt ihm nach! —**tion**, I. *s.* die Nachahmung; (copy) das Nachgeahmte, Nachgemachte; die Nachbildung; in —tion of, zur Nachahmung, nach dem Muster von. II. *attrib.* unecht, nachgemacht. —**tive**, *adj.* nachahmend; nachgeahmt (of a th., einer S.); —tive arts, die bildenden Künste. —**tor**, *s.* der Nachahmer.
Immaculate, *adj.*, —**ly**, *adv.* unbefleckt, makellos, rein; — conception, unbefleckte Empfängnis. —**ness**, *s.* die Unbeflecktheit, Reinheit.
Immanat—e, *v.n.* (hin)einfließen. —**ion**, *s.* das Einströmen.
Immanent, *adj.* einwohnend, in(ne)wohnend; immanent (*Philos.*).
Immaterial, *adj.*, —**ly**, *adv.* (incorporeal) unkörperlich; (non-essential) unwesentlich; unbedeutend.
Immatur—e, *adj.*, —**ely**, *adv.* unreif, unzeitig; (premature) vorzeitig, verfrüht. —**eness**, —**ity**, *s.* die Unreife, Unreifheit.
Immeasurabl—e, *adj.*, —**y**, *adv.*, unermeßlich. —**eness**, *s.* die Unermeßlichkeit.
Immedia—cy, *s.* die Unmittelbarkeit. —**te**, *adj.* (direct) unmittelbar; (at once) augenblicklich, unverzüglich, sofortig. —**tely**, *adv.* unmittelbar; sogleich, auf der Stelle.
Immemorial, *adj.*, —**ly**, *adv.* undenklich; from time —, seit undenklichen Zeiten.
Immens—e, *adj.*, —**ely**, *adv.* unermeßlich, unendlich; (enormous) ungeheuer; to be —ely rich, steinreich sein. —**ity**, *s.* die Unermeßlichkeit, Unmeßbarkeit, Unendlichkeit; ungeheure Größe. —**urability**, *s.* die Unermeßlichkeit. —**urable**, *adj.* unmeßbar, unermeßlich.
Immerge, *v.n.* eintauchen; immergieren (*Astr.*).
Immers—e, *v.a.* unter=, ein=tauchen; versenken (in, in), überhäufen (in, mit); —ed in business, in Geschäfte vertieft, mit Geschäften überhäuft. —**ion**, *s.* das Ein=, Unter=tauchen; die Eintauchung (*Med.*); die Versenkung, Versunkenheit (*fig.*); die Immersion (*Astr.*).
Immigra—nt, *s.* der Einwanderer. —**te**, *v.n.* einwandern. —**tion**, *s.* die Einwanderung.
Imminen—ce, *s.* das Bevorstehen. —**t**, *adj.*, —**tly**, *adv.* bevorstehend, drohend, nah.
Immiscible, *adj.* unvermischbar.
Immitigabl—e, *adj.*, —**y**, *adv.* nicht zu besänftigen.
Immobil—e, *adj.* unbeweglich. —**ity**, *s.* die Unbeweglichkeit.
Immoderate, *adj.*, —**ly**, *adv.* unmäßig, übermäßig, maßlos. —**ness**, *s.* die Unmäßigkeit.
Immodest, *adj.*, —**ly**, *adv.* unbescheiden; unsittlich, unkeusch, unzüchtig; — thought, unreiner Gedanke. —**y**, *s.* die Unbescheidenheit; die Unsittlichkeit, Unzüchtigkeit.
Immolat—e, *v.a.* opfern, als Opfer darbringen; aufopfern (*fig.*). —**ion**, *s.* die Opferung; die Aufopferung (*fig.*). —**or**, *s.* der Opfernde.
Immoral, *adj.*, —**ly**, *adv.* unmoralisch, unsittlich, sittenlos. —**ity**, *s.* die Unsittlichkeit.
Immortal, *adj.*, —**ly**, *adv.* unsterblich; ewig, unvergänglich; an —, ein Unsterblicher. —**ity**, *s.* die Unsterblichkeit. —**ize**, *v.a.* unsterblich machen, verewigen.
Immortelle, *s.* die Immortelle.
Immovab—ility, *s.* die Unbewegbarkeit. —**le**, *adj.*, —**ly**, *adv.* unbewegbar, unentwegbar; (firm) fest, unerschütterlich; (unchanging) unabänderlich, unveränderlich; (unfeeling) unempfindlich. —**leness**, *s.* die Unbewegbarkeit; die Festigkeit.
Immuni—fy, —**se**. *v.a.* immunisieren (*Med.*). —**ty**, *s.* die Freiheit, Befreiung von Dienstpflichten; die Steuerfreiheit; das Ausgenommensein, Verschontsein; das Verschontbleiben von Ansteckung, die Immunität (*Med.*).
Immure, *v.a.* einmauern; einkerkern.
Immutab—ility, *s.* die Unveränderlichkeit, Unwandelbarkeit. —**le**, *adj.*, —**ly**, *adv.* unveränderlich, unwandelbar, beständig.
Imp, *s.* das Teufelchen; (child) der kleine Teufel, die Unart, Range, der Schelm. —**ish**, *adj.*, —**ishly**, *adv.* see Impish.
Impact, *s.* der (Zusammen=)Stoß.
Impair, *v.a.* schwächen (*health, etc.*); (lessen) vermindern; (injure) (eine S.) beeinträchtigen, (einer S.) schaden; entkräften, schwächen (*the force of evidence, etc.*).
Impale, *v.a.* pfählen, spießen; einpfählen, umpfählen; umschließen, einschließen (*fig.*); (zwei Wappen) pfahlweise mit einander verbinden (*Her.*). —**ment**, *s.* das Pfählen, Spießen, die Pfählung; die Umpfählung; der eingeschlossene Raum; die Abteilung eines Schildwappens (*Her.*).
Impalpabl—e, *adj.*, —**y**, *adv.* unfühlbar, sehr fein; unfaßbar (*fig.*).
Impan(n)el, *v.a.* einschreiben (*a jury*).
Imparity, *s.* die Ungleichheit, das Mißverhältnis.
Impart, *v.a.* geben, mitteilen; verleihen, erteilen; erweisen; (disclose) kund tun, eröffnen. —**ial**, *adj.*, —**ially**, *adv.* unparteiisch. —**iality**, *s.* die Unparteilichkeit.
Impassable, *adj.* ungangbar, unfahrbar; — mountains, unübersteigbare Gebirge.
Impasse, *s.* das Stocken, der völlige Stillstand (*newspaper sl.*).
Impassi—ble, *adj.* leidensunfähig, unempfindlich. —**on**, *v.a.* leidenschaftlich bewegen, tief erregen —**oned**, *adj.* leidenschaftlich, voller Leidenschaft. —**ve**, *adj.* unempfindlich. —**veness**, *s.* die Unempfindlichkeit.
Impatien—ce, *s.* die Ungeduld; die Unduldsamkeit. —**t**, *adj.*, —**tly**, *adv.* ungeduldig; unduldsam; heftig, ungestüm; —t of, ungeduldig über (*acc.*); —t for, begierig *or* sich sehnend nach; to be —t under troubles, Widerwärtigkeiten schwer ertragen; he is —t of contradiction, er duldet keinen Widerspruch.
Impawn, *v.a.* verpfänden.
Impeach, *v.a.* (einen einer S.) beschuldigen, anklagen (*of high treason, etc.*); (call to account) zur Verantwortung ziehen; in Zweifel ziehen. —**able**, *adj.* anfechtbar; anklagbar; zur Verantwortung zu ziehen; tadelnswert. —**ment**, *s.* die Anklage; gerichtliches Verfahren in Folge einer Anklage; (charge) die Beschuldigung; (reproach) der Tadel, Vorwurf; die Anfechtung, das In-Zweifel=Ziehen (*of one's motives, etc.*).
Impeccab—ility, *s.* die Sündlosigkeit; die Unfehlbarkeit. —**le**, *adj.* unfehlbar, sündlos.
Impecunio—sity, *s.* die Geldbedürftigkeit, der Geldmangel. —**us**, *adj.* mittellos, geldlos.
Imped—e, *v.a.* (ver)hindern. —**iment**, *s.* das Hindernis (to, für); —iment in a p.'s speech, schwere Zunge; you will find this an —iment to your further progress, Sie werden finden, daß dies Ihrem weiteren Fortkommen hinderlich sein wird. —**imenta**, *pl.* das Gepäck.
Impel, *v.a.* (an)treiben; anregen (to, zu).
Impend, *v.n.* überhangen, schweben (over, über einem); nahe bevorstehen, drohen. —**ent**, —**ing**, *adj.* überhangend; bevorstehend, drohend.
Impenetrab—ility, *s.* die Undurchdringlichkeit; die Unerforschlichkeit (*fig.*); (dulness) die Unempfindlichkeit. —**le**, *adj.*, —**ly**, *adv.* undurchdringlich; unerforschlich; unempfindlich. —**leness**, see —ility.
Impeniten—ce, *s.* die Unbußfertigkeit. —**t**, *adj.*, —**tly**, *adv.* unbußfertig, reuelos, verstockt.
Imperative, I. *adj.*, —**ly**, *adv.* befehlend, gebietend; (obligatory) verpflichtend, zwingend. II. *s.* (— mood) der Imperativ, die Befehlsform.
Imperceptib—le, *adj.*, —**ly**, *adv.* unmerklich,

unwahrnehmbar. —**leness**, —**ility**, *s.* die Unmerklichkeit.
Imperfect, *adj.*, —**ly**, *adv.* unvollkommen; (unfinished) unvollendet; (defective) mangelhaft; schwach, unvollkommen (*fig.*); — sheets, Defektbogen; — tense, das Imperfektum. —**ion**, *s.* die Unvollkommenheit; der Mangel, Fehler, das Gebrechen, die Schwäche (*fig.*); der Defekt (*Typ.*). —**ness**, *s.* die Unvollkommenheit, Unvollständigkeit.
Imperforate, *adj.* undurchbohrt; ohne Öffnung (*Surg.*); ungezähnt (*postage stamps*).
Imperi—al, I. *adj.*, —**ally**, *adv.* kaiserlich, Reichs=; (sovereign) oberherrlich, gebietend; (majestic) staatlich; —al chamber, das Reichskammergericht; —al city, die Reichsstadt; —al diet, deutscher Reichstag; —al measure, gesetzliches Flüssigkeitshohlmaß (wonach eine Gallone Wasser 10 Pfund wiegt und 8 Pinten enthält); —al policy, kaiserliche Politik; Großbritannische Politik, die nach festem Zusammenschluß des Mutterlandes mit den Kolonien strebt; —al roof, das Kaiserdach. II. *s.* (baggage-case) der Gepäckbehälter; das Wagenverdeck mit Sitzen, die Imperiale (*of a coach*); (—al paper) das Imperialpapier; kleiner Knebelbart, Napoleonsbart. —**alism**, *s.* der Imperialismus; die Reichsfreundlichkeit (*Pol.*); das Streben nach festem Zusammenschluß Großbritanniens mit seinen Kolonien (*Eng.*); die Politik, Land zu annektieren, dessen Bewohner jedoch nicht als vollberechtigte Bürger zu behandeln (*Amer.*). —**alist**, *s.* der Imperialist, Kaiserlich=Gesinnte. —**ous**, *adj.*, —**ously**, *adv.* gebieterisch, herrisch, anmaßend, stolz; (urgent) dringend. —**ousness**, *s.* gebieterisches Wesen.
Imperil, *v.a.* gefährden, in Gefahr bringen.
Imperishabl—e, *adj.*, —**y**, *adv.* unvergänglich.
Impermeabl—e, *adj.*, —**y**, *adv.* undurchdringlich, wasserdicht. —**eness**, *s.* die Undurchdringlichkeit.
Impermutable, *adj.* unvertauschbar.
Impersonal, *adj.*, —**ly**, *adv.* unpersönlich (*also Gram.*). —**ity**, *s.* die Unpersönlichkeit.
Impersonat—e, *v.a.* verkörpern, personifizieren. —**ion**, *s.* die Verkörperung; die Darstellung einer Person auf der Bühne, Personifikation. —**or**, *s.* der Verkörperer; der Darsteller (auf der Bühne).
Impertinen—ce, —**cy**, *s.* die Ungehörigkeit, Ungereimtheit; die Frechheit, Unverschämtheit, Ungebührlichkeit. —**t**, *adj.*, —**tly**, *adv.* (irrelevant) ungehörig, ungelegen; (trifling) unnötig, unbedeutend, unnütz; (rude) frech, grob; (officious) unbescheiden, zudringlich, unverschämt; —t to the matter in hand, in keiner Beziehung zur vorliegenden Sache.
Imperturbab—ility, *s.* die Seelenruhe, Unerschütterlichkeit; die Gelassenheit. —**le**, *adj.*, —**ly**, *adv.* unstörbar; unerschütterlich, gleichmütig, gelassen.
Impervious, *adj.*, —**ly**, *adv.* unzugänglich, undurchdringlich, unwegsam; — to water, wasserdicht. —**ness**, *s.* die Unzugänglichkeit, Unwegsamkeit, Undurchdringlichkeit.
Impetu—osity, *s.* das Ungestüm, die Heftigkeit. —**ous**, *adj.*, —**ously**, *adv.* ungestüm, heftig, stürmisch, hitzig. —**s**, *s.* der Trieb, Antrieb (*also fig.*), Stoß (vorwärts); die Bewegungskraft (*Phys.*); die Geschwindigkeitshöhe (*Artil.*); der Antrieb, Impuls (*fig.*); that gave an —s to all of us, das gab uns allen einen neuen Antrieb.
Impi—ety, *s.* die Gottlosigkeit; (act of —ety) ruchlose Handlung; der Mangel an kindlicher Ehrfurcht *or* Liebe. —**ous**, *adj.*, —**ously**, *adv.* gottlos, ruchlos, pietätlos.
Impinge, *v.a.* anstoßen, verstoßen (upon, against, gegen); einwirken (auf eine S.) (*fig.*).
Implacab—ility, —**leness**, *s.* die Unversöhnlichkeit. —**le**, *adj.*, —**ly**, *adv.* unversöhnlich, unerbittlich; (immitigable) nicht zu mildern or besänftigen; —le hatred, tief eingewurzelter unversöhnlicher Haß.
Implant, *v.a.* einpflanzen.
Implement, *s.* das Gerät; (tool) das Werkzeug; agricultural —s, Ackerbaugerät(schaften).
Implicat—e, *v.a.* (in) verwickeln, hineinziehen; (include) (in) mit einbegreifen, umfassen. —**ion**, *s.* die Ein=, Ver=wicklung; (inference) die Folgerung; by —ion, als Folgerung, mitverstanden.
Implicit, *adj.*, —**ly**, *adv.* unbeschränkt; (unhesitating) unbedenklich; *see* Implied II.; — faith, blinder Glaube; — obedience, confidence, unbedingter Gehorsam, volles Vertrauen. —**ness**, *s.* die Unbeschränktheit, Unbedenklichkeit.
Implied, I. *pret. & p.p.* of Imply. II. *adj.* mit einbegriffen, stillschweigend verstanden.
Implor—e, *v.a.* (einen) anflehen, flehenlich bitten; (zu einem) flehen; he —ed his friends for help, er flehte seine Freunde um Hülfe an; er flehte zu seinen Freunden um Hülfe; I —e you, ich beschwöre dich. —**er**, *s.* der Flehende, Bittende. —**ing**, *adj.*, —**ingly**, *adv.* flehend.
Imply, *v.a.* enthalten, in sich schließen, andeuten.
Impoli—cy, *s.* die Unklugheit. —**tic**, *adj.* unpolitisch, unklug.
Impolite, *adj.*, —**ly**, *adv.* unhöflich, ungesittet, grob. —**ness**, *s.* die Unhöflichkeit, Grobheit.
Imponderab—ility, *s.* die Unwägbarkeit. —**le**, *adj.* unwägbar, gewichtlos. —**les**, *pl.* Imponderabilien (*Phys.*); unwägbare Dinge, Dinge, welche sich unsrer Berechnung entziehen (*fig.*).
Import, I. *v.a.* ein=, zu=führen, importieren (*C.L.*); (denote) bedeuten; (imply) mit sich bringen. II. *v. imp.* einem daran liegen, ihn angehen. III. *s.* die Einfuhr; (purport) der Inhalt, Sinn, die Bedeutung; (weight) der Belang. IV. *attrib.*; — duty, der Einfuhrzoll. —**ance**, *s.* die Wichtigkeit; die Bedeutsamkeit; das Gewicht: die Anmaßung, Wichtigtuerei (*fig.*); (authority) der Einfluß; do not attach so much —ance to it, nehmen Sie es nicht so hoch auf, legen Sie nicht so viel Gewicht darauf; man of —ance, der Mann von der Bedeutung, ein einflußreicher Mann. —**ant**, *adj.*, —**antly**, *adv.* wichtig, folgenreich; (influential) einflußreich, bedeutend; (considerable) erheblich. —**ation**, *s.* die Wareneinfuhr; (import) die Einfuhr, der Einfuhrartikel. —**er**, *s.* einer, der Waren einführt. —**s**, *pl.* Einfuhrwaren.
Importun—ate, *adj.*, —**ately**, *adv.* lästig, beschwerlich (fallend), zudringlich. —**ateness**, *s.* die Zudringlichkeit. —**e**, *v.a.* (einen) belästigen, (einem) lästig fallen, (in einen) dringen, (einen) bestürmen; without being —ed, ohne genötigt zu sein, ohne Nötigung. —**ity**, *s.* dringendes Anliegen, die Zudringlichkeit, Belästigung.
Impos—e, *v.* I. *a.* auflegen, erheben (*a tax; the hands*); vorschreiben, auflegen (*a duty*); auferlegen (*a punishment, terms*); zur Last legen, aufbürden (*a task, burden*); ausschießen (*Typ.*); to —e a fine upon a p., einem eine Geldbuße auferlegen. II. *n.*; to —e upon (a p.), (einen) betrügen, täuschen, hintergehen; (einem) eine Nase drehen; your good-nature has been —ed upon, man hat Ihre Gutherzigkeit mißbraucht. —**ing**, *adj.* Achtung fordernd *or* gebietend, imponierend, eindrucksvoll. —**ition**, *s.* die Auflegung (*of hands, of taxes*); die Beilegung, Erteilung (*of a name*); die Auferlegung; (tax) die Auflage, Steuer; (burden) die Bürde; die Strafarbeit (*in schools*); (deceit) die Betrügerei; (fraud) der Betrug. —**t**, *s.* die Auflage, Steuer; der Kämpfer (*Arch.*). *Comp.* —**tor**, *s.* der Betrüger. —**ture**, *s.* der Betrug, die Betrügerei.
Impossib—ility, *s.* die Unmöglichkeit. —**le**, *adj.*, —**ly**, *adv.* unmöglich.
Imposthume, *s.* das Geschwür.
Impot, *s.* (*schoolboys' sl.*) *for* Imposition.
Impoten—ce, —**cy**, *s.* das Unvermögen, die

Schwäche, Hinfälligkeit, Unfähigkeit; die männliche Schwäche *or* Untüchtigkeit, Zeugungsunfähigkeit, Impotenz. **—t**, *adj.*, **—tly**, *adv.* unvermögend, schwach; zeugungsunfähig.

Impound, *v.a.* einpferchen, einsperren, einschließen; (take possession of) in Beschlag nehmen.

Impoverish, *v.a.* arm machen; aussaugen (*land*). **—ment**, *s.* die Verarmung; das Aussaugen.

Impracticab—ility, **—leness**, *s.* die Untunlichkeit, Unausführbarkeit; die Unlenksamkeit, Unfügsamkeit. **—le**, *adj.*, **—ly**, *adv.* untunlich, unausführbar; (stubborn) unfügsam, hartnäckig; unfahrbar, ungangbar (*as roads*).

Imprecat—e, *v.a.* verwünschen, verfluchen. **—ion**, *s.* die Verwünschung; (curse) der Fluch. **—ory**, *adj.* einen Fluch enthaltend, Verwünschungs=.

Impregnab—ility, *s.* die Unüberwindlichkeit; die Unerschütterlichkeit (*fig.*). **—le**, *adj.*, **—ly**, *adv.* uneinnehmbar, unbezwinglich; unerschütterlich (*fig.*).

Impregnat—e, *v.a.* schwängern (*also Chem.*); befruchten (*Bot.*); durchtränken, sättigen (*Chem.*); —ed with, getränkt mit, voll von. **—ion**, *s.* die Schwängerung; die Befruchtung; die Durchtränkung, Sättigung; die Füllung (*fig.*).

Imprescriptibl—e, *adj.*, **—y**, *adv.* unverjährbar; (self-evidencing) klar an sich; the —e laws of reason, die ewigen Gesetze der Vernunft.

Impress, I. *v.a.* ein=, auf=drücken, prägen (on, auf); drucken, abklopfen (*Print.*); (enjoin) einprägen; Eindruck machen (on, auf); to — s.o. with, einen durchdringen mit, ihm (eine S.) einflößen; to — seamen, Matrosen zum Seedienst pressen; —ed with the idea, unter dem Eindrucke (of his own importance, etc., seiner eigenen Wichtigkeit, &c.); he was —ed with the necessity, er war von der Notwendigkeit durchdrungen; he was deeply —ed by these words, diese Worte machten (einen) tiefen Eindruck auf ihn. II. *s.* der Eindruck, Abdruck, das Abbild; (distinguishing mark) das Zeichen, Merkmal, der Stempel; (device) die Devise, das Motto. **—ible**, *adj. see* —ionable. **—ion**, *s.* (mental and physical —ion) der Eindruck, die Spur; das Gepräge, der Stempel; (effect) die Wirkung, der Eindruck; (notion) dunkle Erinnerung; der Druck, Abdruck, Abzug (*Print.*); (edition) die Auflage; to make a favourable —ion upon a p., einen günstigen Eindruck auf einen machen; I have an —ion that . . ., es schwebt mir dunkel vor, daß . . . **—ionable**, *adj.* für Eindrücke empfänglich, leicht bestimmbar. **—ionism**, *s.* die Anschauungen und Lehren der Impressionisten (*Paint.*). **—ionist**, *s.* der Impressionist (*Paint.*). **—ionistic**, *adj.* impressionistisch. **—ive**, *adj.*, **—ively**, *adv.* eindringlich, ergreifend, nachdrucksvoll. **—iveness**, *s.* das Eindringliche, Ergreifende. **—ment**, *s.* das Pressen, die gewaltsame Anwerbung.

Imprimatur, *s.* die Druckbewilligung, die Druckerlaubnis, das Imprimatur.

Imprimis, *adv.* zuerst, erstens.

Imprint, I. *v.a.* aufdrücken, eindrücken, prägen (on a th., auf eine S.); drucken (*Print.*); einprägen (*fig.*). II. *s.* der Druckort.

Imprison, *v.a.* einkerkern, verhaften, ins Gefängnis setzen *or* werfen. **—ment**, *s.* die Haft, Gefangenschaft; (—ing) die Einkerkerung; false —ment, ungesetzliche Haft *or* Verhaftung.

Improbab—ility, *s.* die Unwahrscheinlichkeit. **—le**, *adj.*, **—ly**, *adv.* unwahrscheinlich.

Impromptu, I. *adj. & adv.* aus dem Stegreif. II. *s.* die Rede aus dem Stegreif, das Stegreifgedicht, das Impromptu; der witzige Einfall.

Improp—er, *adj.*, **—erly**, *adv.* (unsuitable) unpassend, untauglich; (indecent) unschicklich, unanständig; (incorrect) unrichtig; uneigentlich (*Arith.*). **—riety**, *s.* die Unschicklichkeit, Ungehörigkeit; die Unrichtigkeit.

Impropriat—e, *v.a.* zueignen; Kirchengut an Weltliche übertragen (*Eccl.*). **—ion**, *s.* das Übertragen einer Pfründe an einen Weltlichen; (—ed property) die (so übertragene) Pfründe. **—or**, *s.* der weltliche Pfründenbesitzer.

Improv—able, *adj.* verbesserlich, verbesserungsfähig, bildsam; (useful) nützlich; anbau=fähig, =bar (*as lands*). **—e**, *v.* I. *a.* verbessern, vervollkommnen; veredeln, ausbilden, verfeinern (*the mind, manners*); (utilize) benutzen, sich (*dat.*) zunutze machen; anbauen, bebauen, kultivieren (*lands*); (add to) vermehren, vergrößern, weiter treiben. II. *n.* sich verbessern; Fortschritte machen; sich vervollkommnen (in a th., an einer S.); sich bessern (*in health*); to —e on a th., etwas verbessern, überbieten. **—ement**, *s.* die Verbesserung, Vervollkommnung; die Anwendung, Benutzung, Nutzanwendung; die Veredlung (*of the race, etc.*); die Veredlung, Ausbildung (*of the mind, etc.*); die Besserung; (progress) der Fortschritt; —ements, Verbesserungen. **—er**, *s.* der Verbesserer; die Volontärin, die sich Ausbildende (*Semp.*). **—ing**, *adj.* verbessernd, gedeihlich (*as a business, etc.*); it had an —ing effect on his character, es machte einen wohltätigen Eindruck auf seinen Charakter.

Improviden—ce, *s.* die Unvorsichtigkeit, Unklugheit. **—t**, *adj.*, **—tly**, *adv.* unvorsichtig, unklug.

Improvis—ation, *s.* die Stegreifdichtung; die Phantasie (*Mus.*). **—ator**, *s.* der Improvisator. **—atrice**, *s.* die Stegreifdichterin. **—e**, *v.a. & n.* improvisieren, aus dem Stegreif machen.

Impruden—ce, *s.* die Unklugheit, Unvorsichtigkeit. **—t**, *adj.*, **—tly**, *adv.* unklug, unbedachtsam.

Impuden—ce, *s.* die Unverschämtheit. **—t**, *adj.*, **—tly**, *adv.* unverschämt, schamlos, frech.

Impugn, *v.a.* anfechten, bestreiten. **—able**, *adj.* bestreitbar, anfechtbar. **—er**, *s.* der Anfechter, Bestreiter. **—ment**, *s.* der Einwand (to, gegen).

Impuls—e, *s.* (—ion) der Anstoß, Stoß, Trieb; die Anregung; der Antrieb, Impuls, die Regung (*fig.*). **—ive**, *adj.*, **—ively**, *adv.* erregbar, leidenschaftlich; (impellent) (an)treibend, Trieb=. **—ion**, *s.* der Stoß, Anstoß; (—e) der Antrieb, die Anregung. **—iveness**, *s.* die Erregbarkeit, Leidenschaftlichkeit.

Impunity, *s.* die Straflosigkeit; with —, ungestraft, ohne Nachteil, ruhig.

Impur—e, *adj.*, **—ely**, *adv.* unrein (*also fig.*), unsauber; (sexually —e) unkeusch, unzüchtig; (unholy) unheilig. **—ity**, *s.* die Unreinheit, Unreinlichkeit; (adulteration) die Verfälschung; die Unreinheit (*of language*); die Verdorbenheit, Unkeuschheit; (—e thing) das Unreine; (obscenity) die Unfläterei, Zote; (that which defiles) das Verunreinigende.

Imput—able, *adj.* zuzuschreiben, beizumessen. **—ation**, *s.* die Zurechnung, Beimessung; (accusation) die Anschuldigung, Beschuldigung. **—e**, *v.a.* zurechnen, beimessen, zuschreiben, zur Last legen. **—er**, *s.* einer, der etwas beimißt.

In, I. *prep.* in; an; auf; bei; aus; nach; unter; zu; von; über; mit; durch; — adversity, im Unglücke; — the morning, am Morgen, morgens; — the afternoon, nachmittags; — 1870, im Jahre 1870; — answer to, als Antwort auf; — appearance, dem Anschein, seinem Äußern nach; — arms, unter den Waffen; infant — arms, Kind, welches noch nicht gehen kann; — comparison, im Vergleich; — contempt, aus Verachtung; — conclusion, schließlich; — the country, auf dem Lande; — due course, zu rechter Zeit, seiner Zeit; — the daytime, bei Tage; — debt, verschuldet, (tief) in Schulden; — s.o.'s defence, zu jemands Verteidigung; — a few words, in *or* mit wenigen Worten, in aller Kürze, kurz, kurzum; to find a friend — s.o., einen Freund an einem finden; — former times, ehemals, in früheren Zeiten; — general, im allgemeinen; — heaven, im Himmel; to glory —, sich rühmen mit; — haste, in Eile; — health, gesund; — hopes, in der Hoffnung; I am — hopes, ich hoffe sehr; — a hurry, eilig; — honour of, zu Ehren von; there is nothing — it, es ist nichts daran, es ist ganz aus der Luft gegriffen; my father- — -law, mein Schwiegervater; — life, bei Lebzeiten; — all likelihood, aller Wahrscheinlichkeit nach; — my opinion, meiner Meinung nach; — this manner, auf diese Weise, in dieser Weise; — obedience, aus Gehorsam; one — ten, einer von zehn; not one — ten, nicht der Zehnte; — particular, im besonderen; — peace and war, in Krieg und Frieden; — pieces, in Stücken; (asunder) auseinander; a shilling — the pound, ein Schilling aufs Pfund; — praise of, zum Lobe von; — the press, im Druck, unter der Presse; — print, im Druck, gedruckt; — pup, foal, *etc.*, trächtig; — the reign, unter der Regierung; — respect to, was anlangt, betrifft; — short, kurz; — sickness and health, in kranken und gesunden Tagen; — his sleep, während er schlief; — store, vorrätig; — tears, in Tränen; — time, zu rechter Zeit, rechtzeitig; — trouble, in Not; — truth, wahrhaftig; — turn, der Reihe nach; — no way, auf keine Weise, durchaus nicht; — writing, schriftlich. II. *adv.* hinein; herein; (with —) drinnen; to be —, zu Hause sein; (of the party) dabei, im Spiele; (within) drinnen; (in office) im Ministerium sein; to be — for, zu erwarten haben; he is — for it, er sitzt fest, er hat keinen Ausweg mehr, er muß es ausessen; I am — for that examination, ich habe mich für die Prüfung gemeldet; come —! herein! to get —, eindringen; to go —, hineingehen, eingehen; to go — for a th., sich mit einer S. beschäftigen; to keep —, nachsitzen lassen (*in school*); to keep — with s.o., sich mit einem vertragen, in seiner Gunst bleiben; to keep one's hand —, die Hand im Spiele behalten. III. *s.*; the —s, die Regierenden, Minister (*Pol.*); the —s and outs, die Winkel und Ecken, alle Einzelheiten, die Vorteile und Nachteile; die herrschende politische Partei und ihre Gegner (*coll.*). **—ly**, **—ner**, *etc.*, *see* Inly, *etc.* IV. *pref. see* Income, *etc.* *Comp.* **—asmuch**, *etc.*, *see* Inasmuch, *etc.*

Inability, *s.* die Unfähigkeit, das Unvermögen.

Inaccessib—ility, *s.* die Unzugänglichkeit. **—le**, *adj.*, **—ly**, *adv.* unzugänglich, unnahbar (*also fig.*); unerreichbar (*for the understanding*); nicht beizubringen, nicht zu erlangen (*as documents*).

Inaccura—cy, *s.* die Ungenauigkeit; (mistake) der Fehler; die Unrichtigkeit (*of an expression*); die Nachlässigkeit. **—ate**, *adj.*, **—ately**, *adv.* ungenau; unrichtig (*as an expression, a copy, etc.*); nachlässig (*as a person*).

Inacti—on, *s.* die Untätigkeit. **—ve**, *adj.*, **—vely**, *adv.* untätig; (indolent) träge; (inoperative) nicht aktiv. **—vity**, *s.* die Untätigkeit.

Inadequa—cy, **—teness**, *s.* die Unzulänglichkeit, Unangemessenheit. **—te**, *adj.*, **—tely**, *adv.* unzulänglich, unangemessen, nicht hinreichend.

Inadmissib—ility, *s.* die Unzulässigkeit. **—le**, *adj.*, **—ly**, *adv.* unzulässig.

Inadverten—ce, **—cy**, *s.* die Unachtsamkeit; (oversight) das Versehen. **—t**, *adj.* unachtsam; (careless) nachlässig. **—tly**, *adv.* aus Versehen.

Inalienab—le, *adj.*, **—ly**, *adv.* unveräußerlich. **—leness**, **—ility**, *s.* die Unveräußerlichkeit.

Inalterabl—e, *adj.*, **—y**, *adv.*, unveränderlich. **—eness**, *s.* die Unveränderlichkeit.

Inamorat—a, *s.* die Verliebte; (love) das Liebchen. **—o**, *s.* der Verliebte, Liebhaber.

Inan—e, *adj.*, **—ely**, *adv.* leer, nichtig (*fig.*); geistlos, albern. **—ition**, *s.* (emptiness) die Leere; die Schwäche, Entkräftung (aus Mangel an Nahrung, *Med.*). **—ity**, *s.* (void space) die Leerheit; die Nichtigkeit, (geistige) Leere, Albernheit (*fig.*).

Inanimate, *adj.* leblos, unbeseelt; unbelebt (*fig.*).

Inapplicab—ility, *s.* die Unanwendbarkeit. **—le**, *adj.* unanwendbar; (unsuitable) unpassend.

Inapposite, *adj.* unangemessen, unpassend.

Inappreciable, *adj.* unberechenbar; geringwertig

Inapproach—able, *adj.* unnahbar, unzugänglich, unerreichbar.

Inappropriate, *adj.*, **—ly**, *adv.* ungeeignet, unpassend, unangemessen. **—ness**, *s.* die Ungeeignetheit, Unangemessenheit.

Inapt, *adj.*, **—ly**, *adv.* unpassend; ungeschickt. **—ness**, **—itude**, *s.* die Untauglichkeit; die Untüchtigkeit (for, zu); (awkwardness) die Ungeschicklichkeit.

Inarch, *v.a.* absäugen, ablaktieren (*Hort.*).

Inarticulate, *adj.*, **—ly**, *adv.* undeutlich, unvernehmlich; (not jointed) ungegliedert. **—ness**, *s.* die Unvernehmlichkeit, Undeutlichkeit.

Inasmuch, *adv.*; — as, da, weil, in so fern als.

Inattenti—on, *s.* die Unaufmerksamkeit, Unachtsamkeit; (negligence) die Nachlässigkeit. **—ve**, *adj.*, **—vely**, *adv.* unaufmerksam, unachtsam, nachlässig, achtlos.

Inaudibl—e, *adj.*, **—y**, *adv.* unhörbar. **—eness**, *s.* die Unhörbarkeit.

Inaugura—l, *adj.* Einweihungs=, Antritts=; —l lecture, die Antrittsvorlesung. **—te**, *v.a.* einweihen, feierlich eröffnen; (induct) feierlich einführen; beginnen. **—tion**, *s.* die Einweihung, feierliche Eröffnung; die feierliche Einführung, Einsetzung; der glückliche Anfang. **—tor**, *s.* der Einführende, Einweihende. **—tory**, *adj.* Einweihungs=, Einführungs=, Antritts=.

Inauspicious, *adj.*, **—ly**, *adv.* ungünstig, unglücklich, von böser Vorbedeutung. **—ness**, *s.* üble Vorbedeutung.

Inboard, *adj.* & *adv.* binnen bords; — cargo, innere Schiffsladung, die Fracht im Raum.

Inborn, **Inbred**, *adj.* angeboren; natürlich; — vices, Naturfehler.

Inbreathe, *v.a.* einhauchen.

Inca, *s.* der Inka.

Incalculab—ility, **—leness**, *s.* die Unberechenbarkeit. **—le**, *adj.*, **—ly**, *adv.* unberechenbar, unmeß=bar, =lich.

Incandescen—ce, *s.* das Weißglühen. **—t**, *adj.* weißglühend; —t light, das (Gas=)Glühlicht.

Incantation, *s.* die Beschwörung(sformel); der Zauberspruch.

Incapa—bility, *s.* die Unfähigkeit, Untüchtigkeit; (unfitness) die Untauglichkeit. **—ble**, *adj.*, **—bly**, *adv.* unfähig (zu), ungeeignet (für); (not admitting of) nicht zulassend; (incompetent) untüchtig; (useless) untauglich; —ble of telling a lie, keiner Lüge fähig; drunk and —ble, betrunken und hilflos. **—citate**, *v.a.* unfähig machen. **—citation**, *s.* die Unfähigmachung; *see* —city. **—city**, *s.* die Unfähigkeit (*also Law & fig.*), Untüchtigkeit; (weakness) die (Geistes=)Schwäche.

Incarcerat—e, *v.a.* einkerkern, einsperren, festsetzen, hinter Schloß und Riegel setzen. **—ion**, *s.* die Einkerkerung.

Incarnadine, *v.a.* fleischrot färben.

Incarnat—e, *adj.* Fleisch geworden; fleischfarben; eingefleischt (*fig.*); devil —e, leibhaftiger Teufel; God —e, der Gottmensch. **—ion**, *s.* die Fleischwerdung; die Menschwerdung Christi (*Theol.*); der Fleischwuchs (*Surg.*); die Fleischfarbe; das Inkarnat; die Verkörperung (*fig.*).

Incase, *v.a.* (in einen Behälter) einschließen; umschließen, umhüllen.

Incautious, *adj.*, **—ly**, *adv.* unvorsichtig, unbehutsam. **—ness**, *s.* die Unvorsichtigkeit.

Incendiar—ism, *s.* die Brandstiftung. **—y**, I. *adj.* brandstifterisch, mordbrennerisch; (seditious) aufrührerisch; —y fires, Brandstiftungen. II. *s.* der Brandstifter; der Aufruhrstifter.

[1]**Incense**, I. *s.* der Weihrauch. II. *v.a.* beräuchern.

[2]**Incense**, *v.a.* entrüsten, erzürnen; aufreizen; (incite) antreiben. **—ment**, *s.* die Wut, Entrüstung.

Incentive, I. *adj.* anreizend. II. *s.* der Antrieb, Beweggrund, die Anreizung.

Inceptive, *adj.* anfangend; — magnitudes, Größen, welche, wenn auch an sich ohne Ausdehnung,

dennoch Ausdehnung bewirken können; —verbs, Inchoativverba, Zeitwörter, welche den Anfang einer Handlung ausdrücken.
Incertitude, *s.* die Ungewißheit.
Incessant, *adj.*, **—ly**, *adv.* unaufhörlich, stets.
Incest, *s.* die Blutschande. **—uous**, *adj.* blutschänderisch; —uous person, der Blutschänder.
Inch, *s.* der Zoll (2.54 Cm.); die Kleinigkeit (*fig.*); — by —, Zoll für Zoll, allmählich; every —, jeder Zoll; by —es, zollweise; (gradually) nach und nach; (slowly) langsam; he would not move an —, er wollte sich gar nicht rühren, er wollte keinen Zollbreit weichen; give him an — and he'll take an ell, gieb ihm den kleinen Finger, so nimmt er die ganze Hand (*prov.*). **—ed**, *adj.* (*in comp.* =) =zöllig. *Comp.* **—meal**, *adv.* zollweise, allmählich.
Inchoat—e, *adj.* angefangen, begonnen. **—ive**, *adj.* einen Anfang bezeichnend; —ive verb, das Inchoativum, den Anfang einer Handlung bezeichnendes Zeitwort.
Inciden—ce, *s.* der Einfall, die Inzidenz (*Phys.*); angle of —ce, der Einfallswinkel. **—t**, I. *adj.* einfallend (*Phys.*); (by the way) beiläufig; (accidental) zufällig; (peculiar) gewöhnlich, eigen; —t to human nature, der menschlichen Natur eigen; —t proposition, der Nebensatz, Zwischensatz. II. *s.* der Zufall, Vorfall, Zwischenfall; (minor circumstance) der Nebenumstand; *see* Episode; der Nebenpunkt (*Law*). **—tal**, *adj.*, **—tally** *adv.* zufällig, gelegentlich; (subordinate) beiläufig, Neben=, Zwischen=; it is —tal to, es gehört zu.
Incinerate, *v.a.* zu Asche verbrennen.
Incipien—cy, *s.* der Anfang. **—t**, *adj.* anfangend, im Entstehen begriffen; einleitend.
Incis—ion, *s.* der Einschnitt, Schnitt. **—ive**, *adj.*, **—ively**, *adv.* schneidend, scharf (*fig.*); einschneidend. **—ors**, *pl.* die Schneidezähne.
Incit—ation, *s.* die Anreizung, Anregung, das Antreiben. **—e**, *v.a.* anreizen, anspornen, aufstacheln. **—ement**, *s. see* —ation; (motive) der Antrieb. **—er**, *s.* der Aufhetzer.
Incivil, *adj.* unhöflich. **—ity**, *s.* die Unhöflichkeit.
Inclemen—cy, *s.* die Härte, Strenge; die Rauheit, Unfreundlichkeit (*of the weather*). **—t**, *adj.* hart, streng; unfreundlich, rauh.
Inclin—ation, *s.* die Neigung (*also fig.*); der Hang (*fig.*); an —ation for a th., ein Hang zu einer S. **—atory**, *adj.*; —atory needle, die Inklinationsnadel. **—e**, I. *v.n.* sich neigen (*also fig.*); geneigt sein; (have a propensity) einen Hang, eine Neigung haben; I don't feel —ed to go, ich habe keine Lust, fühle mich nicht geneigt, zu gehen; —ing to red, ins Rötliche spielend. II. *v.a.* neigen, beugen; (dispose) richten, lenken, geneigt machen; to —e the head, das Haupt senken, den Kopf neigen; this circumstance —es me to doubt, dieser Umstand läßt mich zweifeln. III. *s.* die Neigung; der Abhang. **—ed**, *adj.* geneigt, abschüssig; —ed to evil, zum Bösen geneigt; —ed plane, schiefe Ebene.
Inclos—e, *see* Enclos—.
Include, *v.a.* einschließen, enthalten, in sich begreifen, umfassen (*fig.*).
Inclusi—on, *s.* die Einschließung. **—ve**, *adj.*, **—vely**, *adv.* einschließend; in sich begreifend, einschließlich, mit Einschluß von (*fig.*); (comprehended in) mitgerechnet; alles eingeschlossen, keine Extras (*in advertisements*); from Monday to Wednesday —ve, von Montag bis Mittwoch, den Mittwoch inbegriffen; to be —ve of a th., eine S. in sich schließen; terms —ve, Bedienung und Licht sind im Zimmerpreise mit einbegriffen; an —ve stipend, Gehalt *or* Honorar mit Einschluß der Reisekosten.
Incogni—to, I. *adv.* unerkannt, inkognito, unter fremdem Namen. II. *s.* das Inkognito. **—zance**, *s.* das Nichterkennen, Nichtwissen. **—zant**, *adj.* nicht erkennend, nicht begreifend, unbekannt (mit).
Incoheren—ce, **—cy**, *s.* die Zusammenhangslosigkeit, das Unzusammenhängende; die Unvereinbarkeit, der Widerspruch. **—t**, *adj.*, **—tly**, *adv.* unzusammenhängend, folgewidrig, inkonsequent; to speak —tly, faseln.
Incombustible, *adj.* unverbrennbar.
Incom—e, *s.* das Einkommen, die Einkünfte. **—er**, *s.* der Hereinkommende. **—ing**, *s.* das Eintreten, der Eintritt. *Comp.* **—e-tax**, *s.* die Einkommensteuer.
Incommensura—bility, *s.* der Mangel einer gemeinschaftlichen Masseneinheit; die Un(aus)meßbarkeit (*Math.*); die Unermeßlichkeit (*fig.*). **—ble**, *adj.*, **—bly**, *adv.* durch gleiches Maß nicht meßbar (*Math.*). **—te**, *adj.*, **—tely**, *adv.* unmeßbar; (inadequate) nicht angemessen.
Incommod—e, *v.a.* beschweren, belästigen, (einem) lästig fallen. **—ious**, *adj.* unbequem, lästig.
Incommunica—bility, **—bleness**, *s.* die Unmitteilbarkeit. **—ble**, *adj.* unmitteilbar; *see* —tive. **—tive**, *adj.* nicht mitteilsam; (reserved) verschlossen, zurückhaltend.
Incommutable, *adj.* unentziehbar, unvertauschbar.
Incomparabl—e, *adj.*, **—y**, *adv.* unvergleichlich. **—eness**, *s.* die Unvergleichlichkeit.
Incompatib—ility, *s.* die Unvereinbarkeit, Unverträglichkeit. **—le**, *adj.*, **—ly**, *adv.* unverträglich (*as tempers*); (inconsistent) unvereinbar; (unsuitable) unpassend.
Incompeten—ce, **—cy**, *s.* (inadequacy) die Unzulänglichkeit; (incapacity) die Unfähigkeit, Untüchtigkeit; das Unvermögen, die Unfähigkeit (*of body*); die Inkompetenz (*of a judge, etc.*). **—t**, *adj.*, **—tly**, *adv.* unzulänglich; unfähig, untüchtig; unvermögend; inkompetent, unzuständig, unbefugt; (disqualified) ungültig.
Incomplete, *adj.*, **—ly**, *adv.* unvollendet, unvollständig; mangelhaft, unvollkommen; unvollständig (*Bot.*). **—ness**, *s.* die Unvollständigkeit.
Incomprehensib—ility, *s.* die Unbegreiflichkeit. **—le**, *adj.*, **—ly**, *adv.* unbegreiflich.
Incompressib—ility, *s.* die Unzusammendrückbarkeit. **—le**, *adj.* nicht zusammendrückbar.
Inconceivabl—e, *adj.*, **—y**, *adv.* unbegreiflich. **—eness**, *s.* die Unbegreiflichkeit.
Inconclusive, *adj.*, **—ly**, *adv.* keine Beweiskraft habend, nicht überzeugend, nicht entscheidend. **—ness**, *s.* der Mangel an Beweiskraft.
Incongru—ity, *s.* die Unangemessenheit, Ungehörigkeit; (want of symmetry) das Mißverhältnis; die Widersinnigkeit, Vernunftwidrigkeit; (—ous thing) das Unangemessene; —ity of speech) die Sprachwidrigkeit, der Sprachfehler. **—ous**, *adj.*, **—ously**, *adv.* unangemessen, unpassend, ungereimt.
Inconsequen—ce, *s.* die Folgewidrigkeit. **—t**, **—tial**, *adj.* folgewidrig, inkonsequent.
Inconsidera—ble, *adj.* unbedeutend, unbeträchtlich, gering. **—te**, *adj.*, **—tely**, *adv.* (thoughtless) unbedachtsam, unbesonnen, unüberlegt; rücksichtslos (towards others, gegen andere). **—teness**, *s.* die Gedankenlosigkeit, Unbesonnenheit; die Rücksichtslosigkeit.
Inconsisten—cy, *s.* die Unverträglichkeit; (self-contradiction) der Widerspruch mit sich selbst; die Inkonsequenz (*of a p.*); (absurdity) die Ungereimtheit; (unsteadiness) die Veränderlichkeit, Unbeständigkeit. **—t**, *adj.*, **—tly**, *adv.*, unverträglich, nicht übereinstimmend; (contradictory) widersprechend; ungereimt, absurd; to be —t, inkonsequent sein; that is —t with his views, das verträgt sich nicht mit seinen Anschauungen.
Inconsolabl—e, *adj.*, **—y**, *adv.* untröstlich, trostlos. **—eness**, *s.* die Trostlosigkeit, Untröstlichkeit.
Inconspicuous, *adj.*, **—ly**, *adv.* unmerklich; unbemerkbar.
Inconstan—cy, *s.* die Unbeständigkeit, Veränder-

lichkeit; der Wankelmut. **—t**, *adj.* unbeständig, wankelmütig, unstet; (changing) wandelbar.
Incontestabl—e, *adj.*, **—y**, *adv.* unstreitig, unwidersprechlich.
Incontinen—ce, *s.* die Unenthaltsamkeit, Unmäßigkeit; (lewdness) die Unkeuschheit; der Fluß (*of urine, etc.*); das Bettnässen. **—t**, *adj.*, **—tly**, *adv.* unenthaltsam; unkeusch; sofort, unverzüglich.
Incontrovertibl—e, *adj.*, **—y**, *adv.* unbestreitbar, unstreitig.
Inconvenien—ce, I. *s.* die Unannehmlichkeit, Lästigkeit, Unbequemlichkeit; (hindrance) das Hindernis. II. *v.a.* belästigen, (einem) beschwerlich fallen. **—t**, *adj.*, **—tly**, *adv.* unbequem, lästig, beschwerlich; (unseasonable) ungelegen; (unsuitable) unschicklich, unpassend; it will be —t for me to pay you to-morrow, es wird mir sehr ungelegen sein, Sie morgen zu bezahlen.
Inconvertib—le, *adj.*, **—ly**, *adv.* unverwandelbar; nicht umsetzbar, unkonvertierbar (*C. L.*). **—ility**, *s.* die Unverwandelbarkeit; die Unkonvertierbarkeit.
Inconvincible, *adj.* unüberzeugbar, nicht zu überzeugen.
Incorpor—ate, I. *adj.* (embodied) einverleibt; (united) vereinigt; —ate body, die Korporation. II. *v.a.* zu einem Körper vereinigen; (unite) vereinigen; (embody) einverleiben; eingemeinden in eine Körperschaft verbinden (*trades, towns, etc.*); Holland was —ated with France, Holland wurde mit Frankreich vereinigt; —ated by Royal Charter, durch königlichen Freibrief anerkannt und mit Rechten und Pflichten versehen. III. *v.n.* sich vermischen; sich einverleiben (*fig.*). **—ation**, *s.* die Einverleibung; die Vermischung; (close union) die innige Verbindung; die Bildung eines gesellschaftlichen Körpers, Inkorporation, Eingemeindung. **—eal**, *adj.*, **—eally**, *adv.* unkörperlich, immateriell, geistig. **—eity**, *s.* die Unkörperlichkeit, Immaterialität.
Incorrect, *adj.*, **—ly**, *adv.* unrichtig, fehlerhaft, ungenau; (untrue) unwahr, irrtümlich. **—ness**, *s.* die Unrichtigkeit, Fehlerhaftigkeit; die Ungenauigkeit.
Incorrigib—le, *adj.*, **—ly**, *adv.* unverbesserlich. **—leness**, **—ility**, *s.* die Unverbesserlichkeit.
Incorrupt, *adj.* (unspoiled) unverdorben; unverderbt (*fig.*). **—ibility**, **—ibleness**, *s.* die Unverderblichkeit, Unverweslichkeit; die Unbestechlichkeit. **—ible**, *adj.*, **—ibly**, *adv.* unverderblich; redlich, unbestechlich (*fig.*). **—ion**, *s.* die Unverdorbenheit; die Unverweslichkeit (*of the body, etc.*); das Unverwesliche (*B.*).
Increas—e, I. *v.n.* wachsen, zunehmen; (be fruitful) sich vermehren; stärker, heftiger werden (*as a storm, heat, fever, pain*); (swell) schwellen, anwachsen; auflaufen (*as debt*); they have —ed in, sie haben zugenommen an (*dat.*), sie sind gewachsen an (*dat.*); his misery —ed with his sins, sein Elend nahm mit seinen Lastern zu. II. *v.a.* vermehren, vergrößern, verstärken; (make worse) verschlimmern. III. *s.* das Zunehmen, die Zunahme, das Wachstum, die Vergrößerung; (increment) der Zuwachs; der Ertrag (of the soil, des Bodens); (production) das Erzeugnis; das Zunehmen (*of the moon*); —e of trade, das Aufblühen des Handels. **—ing**, I. *adj.*, **—ingly**, *adv.* zunehmend.
Incredib—ility, *s.* die Unglaublichkeit. **—le**, *adj.*, **—ly**, *adv.* unglaublich.
Incredul—ity, *s.* die Ungläubigkeit, der Unglaube. **—ous**, *adj.*, **—ously**, *adv.* ungläubig.
Increment, *s.* das Wachstum, die Zunahme; (increase) der Ertrag, Zuwachs; das Differenzial.
Incriminate, *v.a.* anschuldigen, eines Vergehens beschuldigen.
Incrust, *v.a.* überkrusten, bekrusten. **—ation**, *s.* die Überkrustung, Rinde; der Überzug (*Build.*); die Furnierung (*Carp.*); der Kesselstein (*Locom. etc.*); die Kruste, Inkrustation (*Chem.*).
Incub—ate, *v.n.* brüten. **—ation**, *s.* das Brüten; to produce by —ation, ausbrüten. **—ator**, *s.* der Brütofen, Brütapparat. **—us**, *s.* der Alp, das Alpdrücken, der Incubus; die Beschwerde (*fig.*); (bore) der wahre Alp.
Inculcat—e, *v.a.* einschärfen, einprägen. **—ion**, *s.* das Einschärfen; die Einprägung.
Inculpat—e, *v.a.* beschuldigen; anklagen. **—ion**, *s.* die Beschuldigung, der Vorwurf. **—ory**, *adj.* tadelnd, vorwerfend; Anklage=.
Incumben—cy, *v.a.* der Besitz einer Pfründe; die Obliegenheit (*fig.*). **—t**, I. *adj.*, **—tly**, *adv.* aufliegend (*also Bot.*); obliegend (*fig.*); I feel it —t on me, ich halte es für meine Pflicht; it is —t upon me, es liegt mir ob. II. *s.* der Pfründeninhaber, Amtsinhaber.
Incunabula, *pl.* die Erstlingsdrucke, (books printed before 1500) Wiegendrucke, Inkunabeln; die Brutstätte eines Vogels (*Ornith.*).
Incur, *v.a.* sich (*dat.*) zuziehen; sich aussetzen (*danger*); to — debts, Schulden machen. **—sion**, *s.* der (feindliche) Einfall, Streifzug.
Incurab—ility, **—leness**, *s.* die Unheilbarkeit. **—le**, *adj.*, **—ly**, *adv.* unheilbar, nicht zu heilen. **—les**, *pl.* die Unheilbaren.
Incurve, *v.a.* krümmen, biegen, beugen.
Indebted, *adj.* (in debt) verschuldet, schuldig; verpflichtet (*fig.*); he is — to you for all he knows, er verdankt Ihnen alles, was er weiß. **—ness**, *s.* das Verschuldetsein, die Verschuldung; das Verpflichtetsein, die Verpflichtung.
Indecen—cy, *s.* die Unanständigkeit. **—t**, *adj.*, **—tly**, *adv.* unanständig; unschicklich, ungebührlich.
Indecipherable, *adj.* unentzifferbar.
Indecisi—on, *s.* die Unentschlossenheit, Unentschiedenheit. **—ve**, *adj.*, **—vely**, *adv.* nicht entscheidend (*as a battle*); (undecided) unentschieden; (irresolute) schwankend.
Indeclinable, *adj.* undeklinierbar.
Indecomposable, *adj.* unzerlegbar, unzersetzbar.
Indecor—ous, *adj.*, **—ously**, *adv.* unanständig, unschicklich. **—ousness**, *s.* die Unanständigkeit, Unschicklichkeit. **—um**, *s. see* —ousness.
Indeed, I. *adv.* in der Tat, wirklich; (certainly) wahrlich, fürwahr; did you tell him so? — I did, sagten Sie es ihm? Gewiß! II. *part. of concession;* allerdings, freilich, zwar. III. *int.* wirklich! ist es möglich?
Indefatigab—ility, *s.* die Unermüdlichkeit, Unverdrossenheit. **—le**, *adj.*, **—ly**, *adv.* unermüdlich, unverdrossen.
Indefeasib—ility, *s.* die Unverletzbarkeit (*of a title*); die Unveräußerlichkeit (*of property*). **—le**, *adj.* unverletzlich, unveräußerlich, unwiderruflich.
Indefensib—ility, *s.* die Unhaltbarkeit. **—le**, *adj.*, **—ly**, *adv.* nicht zu verteidigen, unhaltbar.
Indefin—able, *adj.*, **—ably**, *adv.* unbestimmbar; (inexplicable) unerklärlich. **—ite**, *adj.*, **—itely**, *adv.* unbestimmt (*also Gram.*); (boundless) unbeschränkt, unbegrenzt. **—iteness**, *s.* die Unbestimmtheit.
Indelib—ility, *s.* die Unvertilgbarkeit, Unzerstörbarkeit. **—le**, *adj.*, **—ly**, *adv.* unvertilgbar; unauslöschlich; unvergänglich (*as ink*).
Indelica—cy, *s.* der Mangel an Zartgefühl, die Unzartheit, das Unfeine; die Grobheit. **—te**, *adj.*, **—tely**, *adv.* unzart, unfein; (coarse) roh, grob.
Indemni—fication, *s.* die Schadloshaltung, Entschädigung. **—fy**, *v.a.* schadlos halten, entschädigen. **—ty**, *s. see* —fication; die Straflosigkeit; (compensation) der Schadenersatz, die Entschädigung; act of —ty, die Amnestie, der Indemnitätsbeschluß.
Indent, I. *v.a.* (notch) einzähnen, einschneiden; eine Zeile einrücken (*Typ.*); einen Vertrag abschließen (*Law*); *see* —ure. II. *s.* der Einschnitt, die

Kerbe; die Einrückung einer Zeile. **—ation**, *s.* der zackige Einschnitt; der Zahnschnitt (*Arch.*); das Einrücken (*Typ.*). **—ed**, *adj.* ausgezackt; (winding) wellenförmig; —ed line, das Sägewerk (*Fort.*). **—ure**, I. die Vertragsurkunde, der Kontrakt; der Lehrbrief (*of an apprentice*); to draw up an —ure, einen Kontrakt aufsetzen. II. *v.a.* aufdingen, in die Lehre geben.

Independen—ce, *s.* die Unabhängigkeit; (income, etc.) das Vermögen; der Independentismus (*Theol.*). **—t**, *adj.*, **—tly**, *adv.* unabhängig, selbstständig; —t firing (*in quick time*), das Schnellfeuer; —t means, eignes Vermögen; to be —t, auf eignen Füßen stehen; to act —tly of others, eigenmächtig, auf eigne Faust handeln. **—ts**, *pl.* die Independenten.

Indescribabl—e, *adj.*, **—y**, *adv.* unbeschreiblich.

Indestructib—ility, *s.* die Unzerstörbarkeit. **—le**, *adj.*, **—ly**, *adv.* unzerstörbar.

Indetermina—ble, *adj.*, **—bly**, *adv.* unbestimmbar; nicht erklärbar. **—te**, *adj.*, **—tely**, *adv.* unbestimmt, unentschieden. **—teness**, *s.* die Unbestimmtheit.

Index, I. *s.* (*pl.* —es, Indices) der Anzeiger, Nachweiser, der Zeiger (*Horol.*); der Zeigefinger; (fingerpost) der Wegweiser; das Inhaltsverzeichnis (*of a book*); das Diopterlineal (*Surv.*); die Hand (*Typ.*); der Zeiger, Exponent (*Math.*); die Kennziffer (*of a logarithm*); expurgatory —, der Reinigungs-Katalog; — of refraction, der Brechungsopponent. II. *v.a.* mit einem Inhaltsverzeichnis versehen. **—er**, *s.* der Anfertiger eines Inhaltsverzeichnisses. *Comp.* **—finger**, *s.* der Zeigefinger.

Indicat—e, *v.a.* anzeigen, andeuten, ankündigen; —ed horse-power (*abbrev.* I. H. P.), indizierte Pferdekraft. **—ion**, *s.* die Anzeige; das Anzeichen; (sign) das Merkmal, Kennzeichen. **—ive**, *adj.*, **—ively**, *adv.* anzeigend; —ive mood, der Indikativ; this change of wind is —ive of frost, dies Umspringen des Windes deutet auf Frost. **—or**, *s.* der Anzeiger; der Indikator (*Locom. etc.*); der Zeigerapparat (*Tele.*). **—ory**, *adj.* anzeigend, dartuend.

Indices, *pl. see* Index.

Indict, *v.a.* (schriftlich) anklagen, belangen. **—able**, *adj.* anklagbar; (actionable) klagbar; a transfer of the ticket is an —able fraud, eine Übertragung des Fahrscheins ist ein klagbarer Betrug. **—er**, *s.* der Ankläger. **—ment**, *s.* (schriftliche) Anklage; die schriftliche, vor einer großen Jury vorgebrachte Anklage.

Indifferen—ce, *s.* die Gleichgültigkeit; (impartiality) die Unparteilichkeit; (mediocrity) die Mittelmäßigkeit. **—t**, *adj.*, **—tly**, *adv.* gleichgültig; unparteiisch, teilnahmlos; leidlich, mittelmäßig; schlecht (*of health*); her reputation is very —t, sie steht in keinem sonderlichen Rufe; he is in very —t health, mit seiner Gesundheit steht es recht schlecht.

Indigen—ce, *s.* die Dürftigkeit, Armut; Not. **—t**, *adj.*, **—tly**, *adv.* dürftig, arm.

Indigen—e, *s.* (native) der Eingeborne; einheimisches Tier (*Zool.*); einheimische Pflanze (*Bot.*). **—ous**, *adj.* eingeboren, einheimisch.

Indigesti—ble, *adj.* unverdaulich. **—bleness**, *s.* die Unverdaulichkeit. **—on**, *s.* die Verdauungsstörung, Magenverstimmung; to suffer from —on, an Magenverstimmung *or* schlechter Verdauung leiden.

Indign—ant, *adj.* entrüstet, aufgebracht, verletzt (at a th., über eine S.); unwillig, indigniert (*as a reply*); I felt —ant at his letter, sein Brief empörte mich. **—antly**, *adv.* mit Entrüstung. **—ation**, I. *s.* die Entrüstung, der Zorn. II. *attrib.*; —ation meeting, die Versammlung behufs Kundgebung der allgemeinen Unzufriedenheit mit Zuständen oder Vorschlägen. **—ity**, *s.* die Beleidigung, schimpfliche Behandlung; (insult) der Schimpf.

Indigo, I. *s.* der Indigo. II. *attrib.*; — blue, das Indigblau; — plant, die Indigpflanze.

Indirect, *adj.*, **—ly**, *adv.* indirekt, nicht gerade; (crooked) schief, krumm; (remote) mittelbar; (not fair) unredlich; by — means, auf indirekte Weise; — taxes, indirekte Steuern; — way, der Umweg. **—ness**, *s.* die Schiefheit (*also fig.*).

Indiscernible, *adj.* nicht wahrnehmbar, unbemerkbar, unmerklich.

Indiscreet, *adj.*, **—ly**, *adv.* unbedachtsam, unbesonnen; (foolish) unklug; (reckless) rücksichtslos; leichtsinnig, leichtfertig, schwatzhaft, indiskret.

Indiscretion, *s.* die Unklugheit, Unbedachtsamkeit; (frivolity) der Leichtsinn, die Leichtfertigkeit; (error) das Vergehen.

Indiscriminat—e, *adj.*, **—ely**, *adv.* ununterschieden, unterschiedslos; *see* —ing; (promiscuous) ohne Unterschied, allgemein. **—ing**, **—ive**, *adj.* keinen Unterschied machend. **—ion**, *s.* der Mangel an Unterscheidung, die Unterschiedslosigkeit.

Indispensabl—e, *adj.*, **—y**, *adv.* unentbehrlich, unumgänglich nötig; (essential) unerläßlich; he is —e to us, er ist uns unentbehrlich. **—eness**, *s.* die Unerläßlichkeit, Unentbehrlichkeit.

Indispos—e, *v.a.* abgeneigt, unlustig machen; (unfit) untauglich machen. **—ed**, *adj.* unpäßlich, unwohl; (averse) abgeneigt, unwillig; I was —ed for . . ., ich war zu . . . nicht aufgelegt. **—ition**, *s.* die Unpäßlichkeit, das Unwohlsein; die Abneigung, der Widerwille.

Indisputab—le, *adj.*, **—ly**, *adv.* unbestreitbar, unstreitig. **—ility**, *s.* die Unbestreitbarkeit.

Indissol—ubility, *s.* die Unauflöslichkeit; die Unzertrennbarkeit (*fig.*). **—uble**, *adj.*, **—ubly**, *adv.* unauflöslich; unzertrennlich (*fig.*). **—ubleness**, *s.* die Unauflöslichkeit. **—vable**, *adj.* unauflöslich.

Indistinct, *adj.*, **—ly**, *adv.* ununterscheidlich, unklar (*to the eye*); undeutlich (*of sounds*); trübe (*as vision*); verworren, unklar, undeutlich (*as ideas*). **—ness**, *s.* die Undeutlichkeit; (confusion) die Verworrenheit, Unklarheit.

Indistinguishabl—e, *adj.*, **—y**, *adv.* ununterscheidbar, nicht zu unterscheiden.

Indite, *v.a.* schreiben, abfassen. **—r**, *s.* der Schreiber, Abfasser.

Individual, I. *adj.* persönlich, nur auf einen passend; besonder, eigentümlich, individuell; (single) einzeln; (inseparable) untrennbar, ungeteilt. II. *s.* das Einzelwesen, Individuum; (person) die Person, das Individuum; every —, jeder insbesondere; a private —, ein Privatmann, eine Privatperson. **—ism**, *s.* der Individualismus; die Besonderheit, Einzelwesenheit; (self-interest) das Sonderinteresse. **—ity**, *s.* die Individualität; (idiosyncrasy) die (Natur-)Eigentümlichkeit, Persönlichkeit, Individualität; die Auffassung materieller Objekte als Einheiten (*Phren.*). **—ization**, *s.* die Vereinzelung, Individualisierung. **—ize**, *v.a.* als Einzelwesen darstellen, individualisieren, kennzeichnen. **—ly**, *adv.* einzeln genommen, für sich; —ly and collectively, einzeln und insgesamt.

Indivisib—ility, **—leness**, *s.* die Unteilbarkeit. **—le**, *adj.*, **—ly**, *adv.* unteilbar.

Indocil—e, *adj.* ungelehrig, unlenksam. **—ity**, *s.* die Ungelehrigkeit.

Indoctrinat—e, *v.a.* unterrichten, unterweisen. **—ion**, *s.* der Unterricht, die Belehrung.

Indolen—ce, *s.* die Trägheit, Indolenz. **—t**, *adj.*, **—tly**, *adv.* träge, lässig, stumpfsinnig, indolent; schmerzlos, nicht schmerzhaft (*as a tumour*).

Indomitabl—e, *adj.*, **—y**, *adv.* unbezwinglich, unbezähmbar. **—eness**, *s.* die Unbezähmbarkeit.

Indoor, *adj.*, **—s**, *adv.* im Hause, zu Hause; — footman, der Diener, welcher nur im Hause bedient, die Herrschaft bei Ausfahrten nicht begleitet; — game, das Zimmerspiel.

Indorse, **—e**, *etc.*, *see* Endorse.

Indubitabl—e, *adj.*, **—y**, *adv.* unzweifelhaft, ohne Zweifel, gewiß. **—eness**, *s.* die Zweifellosigkeit, Gewißheit.

Induc—e, *v.a.* herbeiführen, verursachen; (prevail on) bewegen, dahinbringen, verleiten, überreden; nothing could —e him to agree to the proposal, nichts konnte ihn bewegen, auf den Vorschlag einzugehen; a fever —ed by fatigue, ein durch Ermüdung herbeigeführtes Fieber; —ed current, der Induktionsstrom; —ed magnetism, der Induktionsmagnetismus. **—ement**, *s.* die Veranlassung, der Anlaß, Beweggrund. **—ible**, *adj.* herbeizuführen(d); herzuleiten(d).

Induct, *v.a.* einsetzen, einführen (*Eccl.*). **—ion**, *s.* die Einleitung; die Einführung, Einsetzung (in den Besitz einer Pfründe, in ein Amt); die Induktion (*Phys.*, *Log.*); (conclusion) der Schluß (vom Einzelnen auf das Ganze). **—ive**, *adj.*, **—ively**, *adv.* (leading) bewegend, leitend (to, zu); (productive) hervorbringend; induktiv (*Log.*, *Phys.*); —ive circuit, der Induktionsstrom. **—or**, *s.* der Einführende; der Induktionsapparat.— *Comp.* **—ion-current**, *s.* der Induktionsstrom.

Indue, *v.a.* ausrüsten, begaben.

Indulge, *v.* I. *a.* (yield) nachgeben, mit Nachsicht behandeln; einem gefällig sein *or* willfahren; (grant) gestatten, erlauben; (pamper) verzärteln, zu zärtlich behandeln, verwöhnen; (gratify desires) nachgeben, sich ergeben; (foster) hegen; to — one's desires, passions, seinen Wünschen, Leidenschaften fröhnen, nachhängen; he —s his children too much, er verwöhnt, verhätschelt seine Kinder zu sehr, er läßt ihnen zu Vieles hingehen; to — o.s., zu nachsichtig gegen sich sein; (allow) sich (*dat.*) gestatten *or* erlauben; to — a p. in his fancies, einem seine Liebhabereien nachsehen. II. *n.* sich (*dat.*) erlauben; he —s in smoking, er ergiebt sich *or* frönt dem Rauchen; he —ed in a glass of wine, er tat sich mit einem Gläschen Wein gütlich. **—nce**, *s.* die Nachsicht, Milde, Schonung; die Verzärtelung (*of children*); die Befriedigung (*of appetites*); (favour) die Gunst; (liberality) die Toleranz; der Ablaß (*R. C.*); —nce in vice, das dem Laster Fröhnen. **—nt**, *adj.*, **—tly**, *adv.* mild, nachsichtig, nachgiebig.

Induplicate, *adj.* eingefaltet (*Bot.*).

Indurat—e, I. *v.a.* hart machen; verhärten (*fig.*). II. *v.n.* hart werden. III. *adj.* verhärtet, verstockt. **—ion**, *s.* die Verhärtung (*also Med.*).

Industr—ial, *adj.* zum Gewerbfleiß gehörig; gewerbtreibend, industriell; —ial exhibition, die Gewerbeausstellung; —ial school, die Gewerbeschule; —ial war, industrieller Wettbewerb, Wettkampf auf dem Gebiete des Gewerbes. **—ious**, *adj.*, **—iously**, *adv.* fleißig, arbeitsam; (diligent) eifrig, emsig. **—y**, *s.* der Fleiß, die Tätigkeit, Betriebsamkeit, Erwerbsamkeit; der Eifer; das Gewerbe; (—ial arts) die Industrie; product of —y, das Industrieerzeugnis; branch of —y, der Industriezweig; art —, das Kunstgewerbe.

Indwelling, I. *adj.* einwohnend. II. *s.* das Einwohnen.

Inebriat—e, I. *adj.*, (**—ed**, *adj.*) betrunken, berauscht. II. *s.* der Trunkenbold. III. *v.a.* betrunken *or* berauscht machen. **—ety**, *s.*, **—ion**, *s.* die Trunkenheit, der Rausch.

Ineffabl—e, *adj.*, **—y**, *adv.* unaussprechlich. **—eness**, *s.* die Unaussprechlichkeit.

Ineffaceable, *adj.* unauslöschlich, unvertilgbar.

Ineffect—ive, **—ual**, *adj.*, **—ively**, **—ually**, *adv.* wirkungslos, ohne Wirkung, fruchtlos; (impotent) machtlos. **—iveness**, *s.* die Unwirksamkeit, Fruchtlosigkeit.

Ineffic—acious, *adj.*, **—aciously**, *adv.* unwirksam, fruchtlos, erfolglos. **—acy**, *s.* die Unwirksamkeit, Fruchtlosigkeit. **—iency**, *s.* die Ungeschicklichkeit, Unfähigkeit; die Kraftlosigkeit, Erfolglosigkeit. **—ient**, *adj.*, **—iently**, *adv.* *see* —acious; (powerless) kraftlos, machtlos; nicht tatkräftig, ungeschickt; unfähig.

Inelegan—ce, **—cy**, *s.* die Unzierlichkeit, Geschmacklosigkeit. **—t**, *adj.*, **—tly**, *adv.* unzierlich, geschmacklos, unelegant.

Ineligib—ility, *s.* die Unwählbarkeit, Ungeeignetheit für eine Wahl; die Wahlunwürdigkeit. **—le**, *adj.*, **—ly**, *adv.* (not eligible) nicht wählbar; (unworthy, unsuitable) nicht würdig gewählt zu werden, unpassend, unratsam, unrätlich.

Inept, *adj.*, **—ly**, *adv.* (unfit, useless) untüchtig, untauglich; (foolish) albern, abgeschmackt. **—itude**, **—ness**, *s.* die Untüchtigkeit; die Albernheit, Abgeschmacktheit.

Inequality, *s.* die Ungleichheit (*in degree, quality, length, size, amount, distance, motion*); das Mißverhältnis; (unevenness) die Unebenheit; *see* Inadequacy; die Verschiedenheit (of rank, des Standes).

Inequilateral, *adj.* ungleichseitig.

Inequit—able, *adj.* ungerecht, unbillig. **—y**, *s.* die Ungerechtigkeit, Unbilligkeit.

Ineradicab—le, *adj.*, **—ly**, *adv.* unausrottbar.

Inert, *adj.*, **—ly**, *adv.* träge, untätig, stumpf, schlaff. **—ia**, *s.* die Trägheit, das Beharrungsvermögen; die Schlaffheit, Untätigkeit (*Med.*). **—ness**, *s.* die Trägheit.

Inestimabl—e, *adj.*, **—y**, *adv.* unschätzbar.

Inevitabl—e, *adj.*, **—y**, *adv.* unvermeidlich. **—eness**, *s.* die Unvermeidlichkeit.

Inexact, *adj.*, **—ly**, *adv.* ungenau. **—ness**, *s.* die Ungenauigkeit.

Inexcusabl—e, *adj.*, **—y**, *adv.* unentschuldbar, unverzeihlich; unverantwortlich (*as actions*). **—eness**, *s.* die Unverzeihlichkeit; die Unverantwortlichkeit.

Inexhausti—bility, *s.* die Unerschöpflichkeit. **—ble**, **—ve**, *adj.*, **—bly**, *adv.* unerschöpflich.

Inexorab—ility, **—leness**, *s.* die Unerbittlichkeit. **—le**, *adj.*, **—ly**, *adv.* unerbittlich.

Inexpedien—cy, *s.* das Unpassende, die Unschicklichkeit; die Untunlichkeit, Unrätlichkeit. **—t**, *adj.*, **—tly**, *adv.* unangemessen, unpassend, unschicklich, unrätlich, nicht ratsam.

Inexpensive, *adj.*, **—ly**, *adv.* nicht teuer, billig.

Inexperience, *s.* die Unerfahrenheit. **—d**, *adj.* unerfahren; unbefahren (*Naut.*).

Inexpert, *adj.* unerfahren, ungeübt. **—ness**, *s.* die Unerfahrenheit, Ungeübtheit.

Inexpiable, *adj.* unsühnbar, nicht zu sühnen.

Inexplicabl—e, *adj.*, **—y**, *adv.* unerklärlich.

Inexpressi—ble, *adj.*, **—bly**, *adv.* unaussprechlich, unsäglich. **—bles**, *pl.* die Unaussprechlichen, die Unflüsterbaren, Beinkleider (*sl.*). **—ve**, *adj.* ausdruckslos. **—veness**, *s.* die Ausdruckslosigkeit.

Inextinguishabl—e, *adj.*, **—y**, *adv.* unauslöschbar.

Inextricabl—e, *adj.*, **—y**, *adv.* unentwirrbar. **—eness**, *s.* die Unentwirrbarkeit.

Infallib—ility, *s.* die Unfehlbarkeit, Untrüglichkeit; the —ility of the Pope, die Unfehlbarkeit des Papstes; doctrine of the —ility, die Unfehlbarkeitslehre. **—le**, *adj.*, **—ly**, *adv.* unfehlbar, untrüglich; sicher.

Infam—ous, *adj.*, **—ously**, *adv.* ehrlos; (base) niederträchtig; (odious) abscheulich; (scandalous) schmachvoll, schändlich; (of ill fame) verrufen, berüchtigt. **—y**, *s.* die Ehrlosigkeit; die Schande; der üble Ruf; die Schändlichkeit; die Niederträchtigkeit; die Abscheulichkeit.

Infan—cy, *s.* die Kindheit; die Unmündigkeit (*Law*). **—t**, I. *s.* das kleine Kind; der, die Unmündige. II. *adj.* kindlich, die erste Kindheit betreffend; zart, jugendlich (*fig.*); unmündig, unter 21 Jahren (*Law*); —t baptism, die Kindertaufe. **—ta**, *s.* die Infantin. **—te**, *s.* der Infant. **—ticide**, *s.* der Kindermord. **—tile**, *adj.* kindisch. **—tine**, *adv.* kindlich, jugendlich.

—**try**, I. *s.* das Fußvolk, die Fußtruppen, die Infantrie. II. *attrib.;* —try charge, der Infanterieangriff; —try manual, das Infantrie-Exerzier-Reglement. *Comp.* —**t-school**, *s.* die Kleinkinder-schule.

Infatuat—**e**, *v.a.* betören, verblenden. —**ed**, *adj.* betört; töricht; von törichter Leidenschaft erfüllt, verliebt. —**ion**, *s.* die Betörung, Verblendung.

Infect, *v.a.* anstecken (*also fig.*); verpesten (*rooms, etc.*); he has been —ed by the bad example, das schlechte Beispiel hat ihn angesteckt. —**ion**, *s.* die Ansteckung; die Vergiftung (*fig.*); (virus) das Gift; to catch the —ion, angesteckt werden. —**ious**, *adj.* ansteckend. —**iousness**, *s.* die ansteckende Beschaffenheit.

Infelicit—**ous**, *adj.* unglücklich; wenig glücklich (gewählt), unpassend. —**y**, *s.* (unhappiness) die Unglückseligkeit; unglückliche Wahl (*of an expression*); (inauspiciousness) das Ungünstige.

Infer, *v.a.* schließen, folgern, ableiten (from, aus). —**able**, *adj.* zu folgern, ableitbar. —**ence**, *s.* der Schluß, die Folgerung; to draw an —ence, einen Schluß ziehen (from, aus). —**ential**, *adj.* herzuleiten, zu schließen; (deduced) gefolgert. —**entially**, *adv.* durch Folgerung.

Infer—**ior**, I. *adj.* (lower) unter, niedriger; minderwertig (*in quality*); geringer, Unter-, untergeordnet (*in rank*); schwächer (*in number*); he is —ior to none, er steht keinem nach, giebt niemand etwas nach; —ior letters, Lettern, welche unter der Schriftlinie stehen; —ior officer, Subalternoffizier; —ior quality, geringere Güte; —ior person, unbedeutender Mensch; —ior considerations, unerhebliche Sachen; —ior leaves, die untern Blätter; —ior courts, Gerichtshöfe mit beschränkter Gerichtsbarkeit. II. *s.* der Untere, Geringere, Niedere; der Untergeordnete (*in office, etc.*). —**iority**, *s.* niedrigere Lage; (—ior rank) der geringere Stand, die Niedrigkeit (*fig.*); die Untergeordnetheit; (lower value) der geringere Wert, die schlechtere Beschaffenheit; (—ior number) geringere Zahl. —**nal**, *adj.*, —**nally**, *adv.* Höllen-, höllisch; —nal machine, die Höllenmaschine; —nal regions, die Unterwelt, Hölle.

Infest, *v.a.* (worry) plagen, quälen, belästigen; (ravage) verheeren; überschwemmen (*as vermin, etc.*); the forest is —ed with wolves, der Wald wird von Wölfen unsicher gemacht.

Infidel, I. *adj.* ungläubig. II. *s.* der Ungläubige. —**ity**, *s.* der Unglaube; die Treulosigkeit (*of lovers, wives, etc.*); der Verrat, Treubruch (*of friends, servants, etc.*).

Infiltration, *s.* das Ein-, Durch-sickern.

Infinit—**e**, I. *adj.*, —**ely**, *adv.* unendlich, endlos; (countless) unzählig; (unlimited) unbegrenzt; (great) ungeheuer; —ely obliged, außerordentlich verbunden. II. *s.* das Unendliche. —**eness**, *s.* die Unendlichkeit. —**esimal**, I. *adj.*, —**esimally**, *adv.* unendlich klein. II. *s.* die Infinitesimalgröße. —**ive**, *adj.;* —ive mood, (—**ive**, *s.*) die Nennform, der Infinitiv. —**ude**, *s.* die Unendlichkeit; (immensity) die Unermeßlichkeit; (countlessness) die unzählige Menge; (eternity) die Ewigkeit. —**y**, *s.* die Unbegrenztheit, Unendlichkeit, Endlosigkeit; (—e number, quantity) unendlich große Menge *or* Anzahl; —y of goodness, unendliche Güte.

Infirm, *adj.* kraftlos; (weak) schwach; unsicher; (— of purpose) unentschlossen. —**ary**, *s.* das Krankenhaus; die Krankenstube (*in schools, etc.*). —**ity**, *s.* die Schwäche; (disease) das Gebrechen, die Krankheit; die Unentschlossenheit; (foible) die Schwäche, der Fehler.

Infix, I. *v.a.* hineintreiben; befestigen; tief einprägen (*fig.*). II. *s.* das Eingefügte, Eingeprägte; das Infix (*Gram.*).

Inflam—**e**, *v.a.* anzünden; entzünden, entflammen (*love, desire, anger, etc.*); (heat) erhitzen; entzünden (*Med.*). —**mability**, —**mableness**, *s.* die Entzündlichkeit, Entzündbarkeit. —**mable**, *adj.*, —**mably**, *adv.* entzündbar. —**mables**, *pl.* leicht entzündliche Stoffe. —**mation**, *s.* die Entzündung (*also Med.*). —**matory**, *adj.* entzündlich; aufhetzend, aufstachelnd, aufrührerisch (*fig.*), —matory fever, Entzündungsfieber.

Inflat—**e**, *v.a.* aufblasen, aufblähen (*also fig.*), aufpumpen (*tires*). —**ion**, *s.* die Aufblähung; die Aufgeblasenheit (*fig.*).

Inflect, *v.a.* beugen, biegen (*also Gram.*). —**ion**, *s.* die Biegung; die Beugung, Wendung (*Math., Phys.*); die Modulation (*of the voice*); der Stimmfall; die Abwandlung, Wortbeugung, Flexion (*Gram.*); point of —ion, der Wendepunkt einer Kurve.

Inflex—**ible**, *adj.*, —**ibly**, *adv.* unbiegsam, unbeugsam; (inexorable) unerbittlich; (firm) unbeweglich; (obstinate) hartnäckig, starrköpfig. —**ibleness**, —**ibility**, *s.* die Unbiegsamkeit, Sprödigkeit (*Phys.*); die Unbeugsamkeit, Unerbittlichkeit; die Strenge, Härte. —**ion**, *see* Inflection.

Inflict, *v.a.* auferlegen; to — o.s. upon a p., sich einem aufbürden; to — a defeat upon the enemy, dem Feinde eine Niederlage beibringen. —**ion**, *s.* die Auferlegung (einer Strafe); (punishment) die Bestrafung; die Heimsuchung.

Inflorescence, *s.* die Blütenentfaltung; der Blütenstand.

Influen—**ce**, I. *s.* der Einfluß, die Einwirkung; I thought you had great —ce with her, ich glaubte, Sie vermöchten viel bei ihr, Sie hätten großen Einfluß auf sie. II. *v.a.* Einfluß ausüben auf (*acc.*), beeinflussen, bestimmen; —ced by . . ., durch . . . veranlaßt, beeinflußt. —**tial**, *adj.*, —**tially**, *adv.* einflußreich. —**za**, *s.* die Influenza, Grippe, das Schnupfenfieber.

Influx, *s.* das Einfließen, Einströmen (*of a fluid*); (flowing in) das Zuströmen; der Zufluß (*of people, also of a river*).

Infold, *v.a.* (inwrap) einhüllen; (clasp) einschließen.

Inform, *v.* I. *a.* benachrichtigen, unterrichten, belehren; I am —ed . . ., es ist mir mitgeteilt worden . . ., ich habe vernommen. II. *n.* die Nachricht geben; den Angeber spielen, petzen; to — against, (einen) angeben, denunzieren. —**al**, *adj.*, —**ally**, *adv.* formlos; (unceremonious) zwanglos, ohne Förmlichkeit; (not in official form) nicht der amtlichen Form gemäß; (irregular) unregelmäßig; (not in good form) formwidrig. —**ality**, *s.* die Formlosigkeit; die Ungezwungenheit; die Formwidrigkeit (*Law*); (breach of formality) der Formfehler. —**ant**, *s.* der Berichterstatter; my —ant, mein Gewährsmann; *see* —er. —**ation**, I. *s.* die Erkundigung; (knowledge) die Kenntnis; (intelligence) die Kunde, Nachricht, Auskunft; (instruction) die Belehrung; die Anklage (*Law*); to gather —ation upon a subject, Erkundigung über eine Sache einziehen; he possesses all-round information, er ist überall gut beschlagen. II. *attrib.;* —ation office, die Auskunftsstelle. —**er**, *s.* der Berichterstatter; (queen's evidence) der Angeber. *Comp.* —**ation-bureau**, —**ation-office**, *s.* die Auskunftei, das Auskunftsamt.

Infraction, *s.* der Bruch, die Verletzung.

Infrequen—**cy**, *s.* die Ungewöhnlichkeit, Seltenheit. —**t**, *adj.*, —**tly**, *adv.* selten, nicht häufig.

Infringe, *v.* I. *a.* brechen, übertreten, verletzen (*contracts, etc.*). II. *n.;* to — upon, beeinträchtigen. —**ment**, *s.* die Übertretung, Verletzung (*of a patent, contract, etc.*).

Infundibular, *adj.* trichterförmig (*Bot.*).

Infuriate, *v.a.* wütend machen, erzürnen, aufbringen.

Infus—**e**, *v.a.* (diffuse) erfüllen, ergießen; (instil) einflößen, eingeben; aufgießen (*tea, etc.*), einweichen (*Chem., Pharm.*). —**er**, *s.* der Einflößer. —**ible**, *adj.* einflößbar. —**ion**, *s.* (—ing) das Aufgießen; (decoction) der Aufguß,

Tee; (inculcation) die Einflößung; die Einmischung (*fig.*). **—oria**, *pl.* die Infusionstierchen, Infusorien. **—orial**, *adj.* infusorisch, Infusions-. **—orium**, *s.* das Aufgußtierchen.
Ingathering, *s.* das Einernten.
Ingen—ious, *adj.*, **—iously**, *adv.* (clever) sinnreich, geistreich; (inventive) erfinderisch; sinnreich (ersonnen *or* angelegt), künstlich, kunstvoll (*as a machine*). **—uity**, *s.* der Geist, Scharfsinn, die Erfindungskraft; das Sinnreiche, die Kunst. **—uous**, *adj.*, **—uously**, *adv.* aufrichtig, bieder, treu- *or* offen-herzig, freimütig, unbefangen. **—uousness**, *s.* der Freimut, die Offenherzigkeit, Treuherzigkeit, Unbefangenheit.
Inglorious, *adj.*, **—ly**, *adv.* unrühmlich; (obscure) ruhmlos; (shameful) ehrlos.
Ingoing, I. *s.* das Hineingehen; der Antritt. II. *adj.* eintretend (in ein Amt *or* eine Pacht), antretend (ein Amt, eine Pacht).
Ingot, *s.* der Barren; —s of gold or silver, Gold- *or* Silber-barren, -stangen. *Comp.* **—-mould**, *s.* die Gießform.
Ingraft, *v.a.* an-, auf-, ein-pfropfen; (implant) einpflanzen; tief einprägen (*fig.*).
Ingrain, I. *v.a.* in der Wolle färben. II. **—ed**, *adj.* in der Wolle gefärbt; eingewurzelt (*fig.*).
Ingrat—e, *s.* der Undankbare. **—itude**, *s.* die Undankbarkeit, der Undank.
Ingratiate, *v.a.*; to — o.s., sich beliebt machen, sich einschmeicheln; he sought to — himself with me, er suchte sich bei mir in Gunst zu setzen.
Ingredient, *s.* der Bestandteil, die Ingredienz.
Ingress, *s.* der Eintritt (*also Astr.*).
Inguinal, *adj.* Leisten-.
Ingurgitate, *v.a.* hinunterschlucken, schlürfen.
Inhabit, *v.* I. *a.* bewohnen. II. *n.* wohnen. **—able**, *adj.* bewohnbar. **—ableness**, *s.* die Bewohnbarkeit. **—ant**, *s.* der Bewohner, Einwohner. **—ation**, *s.* das Bewohnen; (the being —ed) das Bewohntsein.
Inhal—ation, *s.* das Einatmen, die Einatmung, Einsaugung; (what is —ed) das Eingesaugte, die Inhalation. **—e**, *v.a.* einatmen, inhalieren. **—er**, *s.* der Einatmer; (respirator) der Respirator; der Inhalationsapparat (*for miners, etc.*).
Inharmonious, *adj.*, **—ly**, *adv.* unharmonisch. **—ness**, *s.* der Mangel an Harmonie.
Inhere, *v.n.* (einem *or* einer S.) anhaften, eigen sein, inwohnen. **—nce**, **—ncy**, *s.* die innewohnende Eigenschaft, Inhärenz. **—nt**, *adj.*, **—ntly**, *adv.* inhärierend; anhangend, anhaftend; (innate) angeboren, eigen, innewohnend.
Inherit, *v.* I. *a.* (be)erben; (receive) in Besitz nehmen, gewinnen. II. *n.* erben, geerbt haben; he —ed from his forefathers all their pride, er hatte von seinen Vorfahren ihren ganzen Stolz geerbt. **—able**, *adj.* erblich. **—ance**, *s.* das Erbgut, Erbe, Erbteil; (—ing) die Erbschaft. **—or**, *s.* der Erbe. **—ress** *or* **—rix**, *s.* die Erbin.
Inhibit, *v.a.* (restrain) hemmen, hindern; (forbid) verbieten, (einer S.) Einhalt tun. **—ion**, *s.* die Hemmung; die Untersagung, das Verbot, der Einhalt. **—ory**, *adj.* verbietend; hemmend.
Inhospita—ble, *adj.*, **—bly**, *adv* unwirtlich ungastlich. **—lity**, *s.* die Ungastlichkeit.
Inhuman, *adj.*, **—ly**, *adv.* unmenschlich. **—ity**, *s.* die Unmenschlichkeit.
Inhum—ation, *s.* die Beerdigung. **—e**, *v.a.* beerdigen, begraben.
Inimical, *adj.*, **—ly**, *adv.* feindlich, feindselig.
Inimitab—ility, **—leness**, *s.* die Unnachahmbarkeit. **—le**, *adj.*, **—ly**, *adv.* unnachahmlich.
Iniquit—ous, *adj.*, **—ously**, *adv.* höchst unbillig, widerrechtlich; (wicked) frevelhaft, lasterhaft. **—y**, *s.* die Ungerechtigkeit; (—ous act) die Missetat; (evil) die Schlechtigkeit, Sittenverderbnis.
Initia—l, I. *adj.* anfänglich, Anfangs-; (incipient) beginnend; —l consonant, anlautender Konsonant. II. *s.* der Anfangsbuchstabe. III. *v.a.* mit dem *or* den Anfangsbuchstaben unterschreiben **—te**, *v.a.* (enter upon) anfangen, beginnen; den ersten Vorschlag machen, eine Sache als Erster beantragen; (introduce) einführen, einweihen (*into a society, etc.*); (instruct) in den Anfangsgründen unterrichten, bekannt machen mit; (prepare) einleiten. **—tion**, *s.* die Einweihung; Einführung in die Anfangsgründe; der Unterricht in den Anfangsgründen. **—tive**, I. *adj.* einweihend. II. *s.* erste Einleitung zu etwas; (first step) die Initiative; die Fähigkeit etwas zu beginnen; to take the —tive, die ersten Schritte tun. **—tory**, *adj.* einleitend, einweihend; als Einleitung dienend (*as a rite*).
Inject, *v.a.* hineinwerfen; einspritzen (*Med.*). **—ion**, *s.* die Einspritzung (*Med., Locom., etc.*); die Ausspritzung (*Anat.*); das Eingespritzte; (*in comp.*) Einspritz-. **—or**, *s.* der Injektor.
Injudicious, *adj.*, **—ly**, *adv.* unverständig, unsinnig, unklug. **—ness**, *s.* die Unverständigkeit.
Injunction, *s.* die Einschärfung; (order) ausdrücklicher Befehl; gerichtliche Aufforderung, gerichtliches Gebot *or* Verbot; to give strict —s to a p., einem etwas dringend einschärfen *or* auf die Seele binden; interim —, vorläufiger Spruch (*Law*).
Injur—e, *v.a.* beschädigen (*things*); beeinträchtigen, schaden (*people*); schwächen, schädigen, (*health*); (wound) verletzen; (wrong) (einem) Unrecht tun. **—er**, *s.* der Beeinträchtigende. **—ious**, *adj.*, **—iously**, *adv.* schädlich, nachteilig; this assertion might prove —ious to my reputation, diese Behauptung könnte meinem guten Rufe Abbruch tun. **—iousness**, *s.* das Schädliche. **—y**, *s.* das Unrecht; der Schade, Nachteil, die Verletzung; die Kränkung, Beleidigung.
Injustice, *s.* die Ungerechtigkeit, das Unrecht.
Ink, I. *s.* die Tinte; copying —, Kopiertinte; printer's —, die Druckerschwärze; marking —, unauslöschliche Tinte; blot of —, der Tintenfleck, der Klecks; as black as —, pechschwarz, kohlschwarz. II. *attrib.*; — lead-pencil, der Tintenstift. III. *v.a.* mit Tinte schwärzen; (spot) beklecksen; to — the form, die Schwärze auf die Druckwalze auftragen **—iness**, *s.* die Schwärze. **—y**, *adj.* tintig; (black) tintenschwarz. *Comp.* **—-bottle**, *s.* die Tintenflasche. **—horn**, *s.* das Tintenfaß, der Tintenstecher. **—ing-roller**, *s.* die Farbewalze. **—-spiller**, *s.* der Tintenkleckser. **—stand**, *s.* das Tintenfaß, Schreibzeug. **—-stone**, *s.* der Tintenstein; das Tuschreibeplättchen.
Inkling, *s.* das unbestimmte Gerücht, Gemunkel; (hint) der Wink; (slight knowledge) oberflächliche Kenntnis; (slight foreknowledge) eine Ahnung, leise Idee; to have an — of a th., eine Ahnung von etwas haben, etwas wittern.
Inlaid, *adj.* eingelegt, Mosaik-; — floor, der Parkettfußboden; — woodwork, die Holzmosaik.
Inland, I. *adj.* inländisch, binnenländisch; (domestic) einheimisch, Landes-, Binnen-; — bill, der auf einen im Lande Wohnenden gezogene Wechsel, Inlandswechsel; — duty, der Binnenzoll; — produce, Landesprodukte; — revenue, die Steuereinnahmen; — sea, der Binnensee; — town, die Binnen-, Land-stadt; — trade, der Binnenhandel. II. *adv.* landeinwärts; im Inlande. III. *s.* das Innere des Landes, Binnenland. **—er**, *s.* der In-, Binnen-länder.
Inlay, *v.a.* einlegen; täfeln, parkettieren (*a floor*). **—ing**, *s.* das Einlegen; die Täfelung, Einlegung, Parkettierung (*of floors*).
Inlet, *s.* der Einlaß, Eingang, Zugang; die Einfahrt; (creek) die Bucht.
Inly, *adj. & adv.* innerlich, geheim.
Inmate, *s.* der Insasse, Mitbewohner; —s of the same house, Hausgenossen.
Inmost, *adj.* innerst; — thoughts, geheimste *or* verborgenste Gedanken.
Inn, *s.* der Gasthof, das Wirtshaus; —s of Court, die alten Advokaten-Innungen, (alte, noch blü-

hende) Rechtsschulen (*in London*). *Comp.* —**keeper**, *s.* der Wirtshausbesitzer, Gastwirt.

Innate, *adj.*, —**ly**, *adv.* angeboren, natürlich.

Inner, *adj.* inner, inwendig; (secret) geheim, verborgen; innerlich (*fig.*). *Comp.* —**most**, *adj.* innerst, geheimst.

Innings, *pl.* der Gang, das Dransein (*Cricket*); now you have your —, Sie sind jetzt an der Reihe (das Schlagholz zu führen).

Innocen—ce, *s.* die Unschuld; die Schuldlosigkeit (*of a crime, etc.*); (harmlessness) die Harmlosigkeit; (simplicity) die Einfalt. —**t**, I. *adj.*, —**tly**, *adv.* unschädlich (*as drugs, etc.*); schuldlos; unschuldig; harmlos; (silly) einfältig, dumm. II. *s.* der Unschuldige; *see* Imbecile; the murder of the —ts, der Bethlehemitische Kindermord; —ts' Day, das Fest der unschuldigen Kinder (Dec. 28).

Innocuous, *adj.*, —**ly**, *adv.* unschädlich; (harmless) harmlos.

Innominate, *adj.* namenlos, unbenannt.

Innovat—e, *v.n.* Neuerungen machen, einführen. —**ion**, *s.* die Neuerung, Veränderung. —**or**, *s.* der Neuerungstifter.

Innoxious, *see* Innocuous.

Innuendo, *s.* die Andeutung, Anspielung, der (zarte) Wink.

Innumerabl—e, *adj.*, —**y**, *adv.* unzählig, unzählbar, zahllos.

Innutritious, *adj.* nicht nahrhaft, nicht nährend.

Inobservant, *adj.* nicht beobachtend; nicht befolgend.

Inoculat—e, *v.a.* einimpfen, inokulieren; impfen (*also fig.*), okulieren (*Hort.*). —**ion**, *s.* die Einimpfung, Impfung (*Surg.*); das Okulieren. —**or**, *s.* der Impfarzt; der Okulierende.

Inodorous, *adj.* geruchlos.

Inoffensive, *adj.*, —**ly**, *adv.* harmlos, arglos, gutartig. —**ness**, *s.* die Harmlosigkeit.

Inoperative, *adj.* unwirksam. —**ness**, *s.* die Unwirksamkeit.

Inopportune, *adj.*, —**ly**, *adv.* ungelegen, unzeitig.

Inordina—cy, *s.* die Regellosigkeit, Unordnung; die Unmäßigkeit. —**te**, *adj.*, —**tely**, *adv.* regellos; unmäßig, ausschweifend; an —te desire of fame, eine allzu große Ruhmbegierde; —te love of the world, unmäßige Weltliebe. —**teness**, *s.* die Unmäßigkeit.

Inorgani—c, —**zed**, *adj.* unorganisch.

Inosculat—e, *v.* I. *a.* verbinden, einfügen. II. *n.* einmünden. —**ion**, *s.* die Zusammenmündung der Gefäße.

In ovo, in der Entstehung, im Anfange.

In-patient, *s.* der (die) Anstaltskranke, Spitalkranke, in der Klinik verpflegter Patient.

In perpetuum, auf immer.

In propria persona, in eigner Person.

In puris naturalibus, splitternackt.

Inquest, *s.* die gerichtliche Untersuchung; coroner's —, die Totenschau, Leichenschau.

Inquietude, *s.* die Unruhe.

Inquir—e, *v.* I. *n.* (nach einer S.) fragen, (einer S.) nachfragen, sich (nach einer S.) erkundigen; —e within, Näheres im Hause; to —e about, after, for, nach einer S. fragen, sich erkundigen; Mrs. N. has sent to —e after your sister's health, Frau N. hat sich nach dem Befinden deiner Schwester erkundigen lassen; to —e into a th., eine Sache untersuchen, erforschen; the matter will certainly be —ed into, die Sache wird sicherlich untersucht werden. II. *a.* erfragen, erforschen; sich erkundigen nach (*dat.*); to —e the way, nach dem Wege fragen. —**er**, *s.* der Fragende, Frager; der Untersucher. —**ing**, *adj.*, —**ingly**, *adv.* forschend. —**y**, *s.* die Nachfrage, Frage, Erkundigung; (—y into) die Untersuchung, Forschung, Prüfung; die Untersuchung (*Law*); writ of —y, der richterliche Befehl zur Zusammenberufung einer Jury; to make —ies, sich erkundigen, fragen (for, nach); with kind —ies, in freundlicher Erkundigung, mit den besten Wünschen für gute Besserung (*on visiting cards left at the house of friends who are ill*); with thanks for kind —ies, mit herzlichem Dank für gütige Nachfrage (*on visiting cards sent on recovery to friends who have made —ies*).

Inquisit—ion, *s.* die Untersuchung (*also Law*); das Ketzergericht, die Inquisition (*R.C.*). —**ive**, *adj.*, —**ively**, *adv.* neugierig; (seeking to know) wißbegierig; to be —ive about, etwas gern wissen mögen. —**iveness**, *s.* die Neugier; die Wißbegierde. —**or**, *s.* der Untersucher; der Inquisitor (*R.C.*). —**orial**, *adj.* inquisitorisch.

Inroad, *s.* der (feindliche) Einfall; der unberechtigte Eingriff (*fig.*).

Insalubrious, *adj.* ungesund.

Insan—e, I. *adj.*, —**ely**, *adv.* wahnsinnig, unsinnig, toll. II. *pl.* die Wahnsinnigen, Irrsinnigen; hospital for the —e, die Irrenanstalt. —**ity**, *s.* der Wahnsinn, Irrsinn.

Insatia—bility, *s.* die Unersättlichkeit. —**ble**, *adj.*, —**bly**, *adv.* unersättlich. —**te**, *adj.* unersättlich.

Inscribe, *v.a.* (enter) einschreiben; (dedicate) zuschreiben, widmen; (write an inscription) überschreiben; ein-, be-schreiben (*Geom.*); einprägen (*fig.*); to — one's name, seinen Namen schreiben. —**r**, *s.* der Einschreiber; der Dedizierende.

Inscription, *s.* die Inschrift, Aufschrift, Überschrift; (entering) die Einschreibung; (dedication) die Zuschrift, Widmung, Zueignungsschrift; (titular line) die Überschrift.

Inscrutab—ility, —**leness**, *s.* die Unerforschlichkeit. —**le**, *adj.*, —**ly**, *adv.* unerforschlich, unergründlich.

Insect, *s.* das Kerbtier, Insekt; —s buzz (chirp, as grasshoppers), Insekten summen, surren (zirpen, z. B. Grashüpfer).

Insecti—cide, *s.* das Insektenvertilgungsmittel. —**vora**, *pl.* Insektenfresser. —**vorous**, *adj.* insektenfressend.

Insecur—e, *adj.*, —**ely**, *adv.* unsicher; (precarious) ungewiß, der Gefahr, dem Verluste ausgesetzt. —**ity**, *s.* die Unsicherheit; die Ungewißheit.

Insens—ate, *adj.* unverständig; sinnlos; (insensible) unempfindlich, gefühllos. —**ibility**, *s.* die Unempfindlichkeit, Gefühllosigkeit; (dulness) der Stumpfsinn; state of —ibility, die Bewußtlosigkeit. —**ible**, *adj.*, —**ibly**, *adv.* unempfindlich, gefühllos (of, to, für); (unconscious) bewußtlos; (imperceptible) unmerklich; (indifferent) gleichgiltig; he was —ible to the danger, er war sich der Gefahr nicht bewußt; —ible decay, langsames Dahinschwinden.

Insentient, *adj.* gefühllos.

Inseparabl—e, *adj.*, —**y**, *adv.* untrennbar, unzertrennlich. —**eness**, *s.* die Untrennbarkeit.

Insert, *v.a.* einsetzen, einschalten, einfügen (*a letter, word, passage*); einrücken (*an advertisement*). —**ion**, *s.* die Einsetzung; die Einrückung; die eingerückte Anzeige, das Inserat; der Einsatz(-streifen) (*Semp.*); die Einfügung (*Bot., Anat.*).

Insessor—es, *pl.* die Nesthocker (*pl.*). —**ial**, *adj.* hockend, Hock-.

Inshore, I. *adv.* an *or* nahe der Küste. II. *adj.* an der Küste befindlich, Küsten-.

Inside, I. *adj.* inner, inwendig; — passenger, der im Wagen sitzende Passagier; — shutter, innerer Fensterladen. II. *adv.* im innern, drinnen; hinein. III. *prep.* innerhalb, im Innern; — (of) the circle, innerhalb des Kreises. IV. *s.* innere Seite, das Innere; (entrails) das Eingeweide.

Insidious, *adj.*, —**ly**, *adv.* (treacherous) hinterlistig, ränkevoll; (crafty) verfänglich, heimtückisch, trügerisch. —**ness**, *s.* die Hinterlist.

Insight, *s.* die Einsicht (into a th., in eine S.).

Insignia, *pl.* die Abzeichen, Amtszeichen, Insignien; — of the Empire, die Reichskleinodien.

Insignifican—ce, **—cy**, *s.* die Bedeutungslosigkeit, Geringfügigkeit, Unwichtigkeit. **—t**, *adj.*, **—tly**, *adv.* unbedeutend, unwichtig, geringfügig; (mean) verächtlich.
Insincer—e, *adj.*, **—ely**, *adv.* unaufrichtig, verstellt; (false) falsch. **—ity**, *s.* die Unaufrichtigkeit; (hypocrisy) die Heuchelei; die Falschheit.
Insinuat—e, *v.* I. *a.* sanft hineinbringen, hineinwinden; (hint) zu verstehen geben, gewandt beibringen, merken lassen, auf (eine S.) anspielen; to —e o.s. into a p.'s good graces, sich in jemandes Gunst einschmeicheln. II. *n.* unvermerkt eindringen; auf eine S. anspielen, etwas zu verstehen geben. **—ing**, *adj.*, **—ingly**, *adv.* einschmeichelnd; (calculated to please) einnehmend. **—ion**, *s.* das allmähliche, unvermerkte Eindringen; die Einschmeichelung; die Einflüsterung, feine Anspielung, der Wink; (—ing ways) einschmeichelndes Wesen.
Insipid, *adj.*, **—ly**, *adv.* unschmackhaft; geschmacklos; fade, schal, abgeschmackt (*fig.*). **—ity**, *s.* die Unschmackhaftigkeit; die Abgeschmacktheit, Fadheit.
Insist, *v.n.;* to — upon, bestehen auf (*dat.*); beharren auf (*dat.*); (dwell, lay stress on) Gewicht legen auf (*acc.*), hervorheben, betonen, nicht nachlassen, (etwas zu tun) verweilen bei; you must — on immediate payment, Sie müssen auf sofortiger Bezahlung bestehen. **—ence**, *s.* die Beharrlichkeit, das Bestehen auf (*dat.*). **—ent**, *adj.* beharrlich, auf einer S. bestehend; eindringlich.
Insnare, *v.a.* in einer Schlinge fangen; verführen, berücken, bestricken (*fig.*).
Insobriety, *s.* die Unmäßigkeit, Trunkenheit.
Insolen—ce, *s.* die Unverschämtheit, Frechheit; (haughtiness) der Übermut. **—t**, *adj.*, **—tly**, *adv.* unverschämt, frech, vermessen; übermütig.
Insolub—ility, *s.* die Unauflöslichkeit. **—le**, *adj.* unauflöslich; unerklärbar (*fig.*).
Insolven—cy, *s.* die Zahlungsunfähigkeit. **—t**, *adj.* zahlungsunfähig; —t debtors' court, das Fallitengericht, die Gantbehörde.
Insomnia, *s.* die Schlaflosigkeit.
Insomuch, *adv.* so, dergestalt.
Inspect, *v.a.* besichtigen, (genau) besehen, untersuchen (*goods, etc.*); (oversee) beaufsichtigen. **—ion**, *s.* die Besichtigung, Beschauung, Untersuchung, die Aufsicht; der Appell (*Mil.*); boot —ion, der Stiefelappell (*Mil.*); for —ion, zur Ansicht (*C. L.*). **—or**, *s.* der Inspektor, Aufseher; official —or, amtlicher Besichtiger; customs —or, der Zollinspektor; —or of works, der Bauaufseher; —or of mines, der Berginspektor; —or of schools, der Schulinspektor. **—orship**, *s.* das Inspektor-, Aufseher-amt.
Inspir—ation, *s.* das Einatmen, Einhauchen; die Inspiration, Begeisterung; divine —ation, göttliche Eingebung. **—e**, *v.a.* einhauchen (*life*); (blow into) hineinblasen; einatmen (*air*); begeistern (*fig.*); eingeben, einhauchen, einflößen (*thoughts*); the —ed word, das von Gott eingegebene, inspirierte Wort; an article evidently —ed, ein (von der Regierung 2c.) augenscheinlich eingegebener *or* veranlaßter Artikel; to —e a p. with awe, einem Ehrfurcht einflößen. **—er**, *s.* der Eingebende; der heilige Geist. **—ing**, *adj.* begeisternd, belebend. **—it**, *v.a.* anfeuern, beseelen, beleben, ermutigen.
Inspissat—e, I. *v.a.* ein-, ver-dicken. II. *adj.* eingedickt, verdickt. **—ion**, *s.* die Ein-, Ver-dickung.
Instability, *s.* die Unbeständigkeit, Wandelbarkeit, der Unbestand.
Instal, *see* Install. **—ment**, *s.* die Rate; by —ments, terminweise, ratenweise; stückweise; payment by —ments, die Teilzahlung, Ratenzahlung; das Teilzahlungssystem.
Install, *v.a.* einsetzen, einführen (in ein Amt), bestallen; installieren; duly —ed, wohlbestallt. **—ation**, *s.* die Bestallung, Einführung; die (technische) Anlage (*e.g. of electricity*).
Instan—ce, I. *s.* die dringende, inständige Bitte, das Ansuchen, Anhalten; (example) das Beispiel, der Fall; for —ce, zum Beispiel; in the first —ce, beim ersten Vorkommen, das erste Mal, zuerst; to produce another —ce, einen zweiten Fall *or* Beweis anführen; at the —ce of our friend Mr. G., I . . ., auf Ansuchen *or* Veranlassung unseres Freundes Herrn G., . . . ich. II. *v.a.* als Beispiel anführen. **—t**, I. *adj.* (urgent) inständig, dringend; anhaltend (*in prayer*); (current) gegenwärtig, laufend; on the 10th —t, am zehnten dieses (Monats) *or* d. m. II. *s.* der Augenblick, der jetzige Moment; in an —t, in einem Nu, augenblicklich. **—ly**, *adv.* sogleich. **—taneous**, *adj.*, **—taneously**, *adv.* augenblicklich, in einem Augenblicke geschehend; —taneous photography, die Augenblicksphotographie, Momentphotographie. **—taneousness**, *s.* die Augenblicklichkeit. **—ter**, *adv.* sogleich, unverzüglich.
Instate, *v.a.* einsetzen.
In statu pupillari, der akademischen Zucht und Gerichtsbarkeit unterworfen (*Camb. Oxf.*).
Instead, *adv.* dafür; — of, anstatt, statt; — of me, statt meiner; — of my brother, anstatt meines Bruders; — of writing, (an)statt zu schreiben; to be — of, eintreten *or* gelten für.
Instep, *s.* der Spann, Rist, die Fußbiege; to be high in the —, die Nase hoch tragen (*coll.*).
Instigat—e, *v.a.* anreizen, aufhetzen; to —e a p. to crime, einen zum Verbrechen antreiben. **—ion**, *s.* der Antrieb, die Anreizung, Aufhetzung; die Verführung (*to evil*); at the —ion of, auf Antrieb von. **—or**, *s.* der (die) Anreizer(in), Aufhetzer(in), Verführer(in).
Instil, *v.a.* (drop in) eintröpfeln; einflößen, beibringen, eingeben (*fig.*). **—lation**, **—ment**, *s.* das Eintröpfeln; die Einflößung.
Instinct, I. *adj.* bewegt, belebt (with, durch), voll. II. *s.* der Naturtrieb, Instinkt. **—ive**, *adj.*, **—ively**, *adv.* instinktmäßig, unwillkürlich, ahnend, Ahnungs-.
Institut—e, I. *v.a.* einsetzen, stiften, einrichten; verordnen, ins Werk setzen; (found) gründen, errichten; in den geistlichen Teil einer Pfründe einsetzen (*Eccl.*); to —e an inquiry, a comparison, eine Nachforschung, Vergleichung anstellen. II. *s.* die (gelehrte) Gesellschaft, das Institut; (building) das Institut; Justinian's —es, Justinians Institutionen *or* Gesetzsammlung. **—ion**, *s.* das Einsetzen; (establishment) die Einsetzung, Einrichtung, Stiftung; (regulation) die Anordnung; die Anstellung (of an inquiry); (—e) das Institut, die Anstalt; (law, etc.) das Gesetz, die Satzung, Einrichtung; die Einführung Geistlicher (*Theol.*); educational —ion, Erziehungsanstalt; benevolent —ion, milde Stiftung. **—or**, *s.* der Stifter; der Anordner; (—or of laws) der Gesetzgeber; der einführende Geistliche.
Instruct, *v.a.* (teach) (be)lehren, unterweisen, unterrichten; (direct) mit Verhaltungsbefehlen versehen; einleiten, instruieren (*Law*); to — s. o. in s. th., einem in einer S. Unterweisung geben, einen in einer S. unterrichten. **—ion**, *s.* die Vorschrift, Weisung; (directions) der Verhaltungsbefehl; (information) der Unterricht, die Belehrung, Unterweisung; der Dienstunterricht, die Instruktion (*Mil.*); (order) der Auftrag; die Instruktion (*Law*); course of —ion, der Lehrplan; contrary to —ions, gegen ausdrückliche Weisung. **—ive**, *adj.*, **—ively**, *adv.* belehrend, lehrreich, unterrichtend. **—iveness**, *s.* das Belehrende. **—or**, *s.* der Lehrer; —or at an American college, der Dozent an einer amerikanischen Universität. **—ress**, *s.* die Lehrerin.
Instrument, *s.* das Werkzeug, Instrument; das Instrument (*Mus.*); das Werkzeug, Mittel (*fig.*); (creature) der Handlanger, die Kreatur; the chosen —, das auserwählte Rüstzeug (*B.*). **—al**, *adj.* als Werkzeug dienend, dienlich; förderlich, behilflich; —al music, Instrumentalmusik; to be

—al in, beitragen zu; he was —al in bringing about great changes, er war das Werkzeug, um große Veränderungen hervorzubringen. —alist, s. der Musiker, welcher ein Instrument spielt, Instrumentspieler. —ality, s. die Mitwirkung, Vermittlung, das Mittel. —ation, s. die Instrumentierung.

Insubordinat—e, *adj.* widersetzlich, widerspenstig. —**ion**, *s.* die Widersetzlichkeit, der Ungehorsam, die Auflehnung (gegen Vorgesetzte), Meuterei.

Insufferabl—e, *adj.*, —**y**, *adv.* unerträglich, unleidlich; (detestable) abscheulich.

Insufficien—cy, *s.* die Unzulänglichkeit, Ungenügsamkeit; (incapacity) die Unfähigkeit. —**t**, *adj.*, —**tly**, *adv.* unzulänglich, unzureichend, ungenügend; unfähig.

Insufflation, *s.* das Anhauchen (*R. C.*); das Einblasen, die Einblasung (*Med.*).

Insula—r, *adj.* insular(isch), Insular=. —**rity**, *s.* insulare Beschaffenheit; die (insulare) Beschränktheit (*fig.*). —**te**, *v.a.* zur Insel machen; (isolate) isolieren (*also Elect.*), absondern. —**tion**, *s.* die Absonderung; die Isolierung (*Elect.*). —**tor**, *s.* der Isolator.

Insult, I. *s.* die Beleidigung, der Schimpf. II. *v.a.* beleidigen, beschimpfen, verächtlich behandeln. III. *v.n.* übermütig sein. —**ing**, *adj.*, —**ingly**, *adv.* beschimpfend; —ing language, Grobheiten, Schmähreden, beschimpfende Worte.

Insuperab—le, *adj.*, —**ly**, *adv.* unüberwindlich; unübersteigbar (*as a barrier*). —**leness**, —**ility**, *s.* die Unüberwindlichkeit, Unübersteiglichkeit.

Insupportable, *adj.* unerträglich, unausstehlich.

Insuppressibl—e, *adj.*, —**y**, *adv.* ununterdrückbar; unbezwinglich.

Insur—ance, *s.* die Versicherung, Assekuranz; —ance against fire, Feuerversicherung; general —ance, allgemeine Versicherung; life —ance, Lebensversicherung; to effect the —ance of the goods at a high premium, die Waren zu hoher Prämie versichern (lassen). —**e**, *v.a.* sichern, gewiß machen; (guarantee) verbürgen, stehen für; versichern (*C. L.*); to —e at 5 per cent, zu 5 Procent versichern. —**ed**, *adj.;* the —ed party, der Versicherte. —**er**, *s.* der Versicherer. *Comp.* —**ance-agent**, *s.* der Versicherungsagent. —**ance-broker**, *s.* der Assekuranzmakler. —**ance-company**, *s.* die Versicherungsgesellschaft. —**ance-office**, *s.* das Versicherungskontor. —**ance-policy**, *s.* die Police.

Insurgent, I. *adj.* aufrührerisch. II. *s.* der Aufrührer, Empörer.

Insurmountable, *adj.* unübersteigbar; unüberwindlich (*fig.*).

Insurrection, *s.* die Empörung, der Aufruhr, Aufstand; the Polish —, der Polenaufstand.

Insusceptib—ility, *s.* die Unempfänglichkeit. —**le**, *adj.* unempfänglich (of, für); unfähig (einer S.); gefühllos (für eine S.) (*fig.*); a heart —le of pity, ein mitleidsloses Herz.

Intact, *adj.* unberührt; unversehrt, unverletzt.

Intaglio, *s.* der Intaglio, geschnittene Stein.

Intake, *s.* das Einnehmen; (narrowing) die Verengerung (*of a pipe*); die Einlaßöffnung (*of a pipe*).

Intangib—le, *adj.*, —**ly**, *adv.* unberührbar; unbetastbar. —**leness**, —**ility**, *s.* die Unberührbarkeit.

Integ—er, *s.* die ganze Zahl, das Ganze. —**ral**, I. *adj.* ganz, vollständig; integral (*Arith.*); —ral calculus, die Integral=Rechnung; wesentlich; —ral parts, die ergänzenden Teile. II. *s.* das Integral (*Math.*); (whole) das Ganze. —**rant**, *adj.* zu einem Ganzen gehörend, integrierend; —rant particles, Integralbestandteile. —**rate**, *v.a.* ergänzen, vervollständigen, integrieren; integrieren, das Integral aufsuchen (*Math.*). —**ration**, *s.* die Ergänzung, Vervollständigung. —**rity**, *s.* (entireness) der Vollbestand, die Unverletztheit, Vollständigkeit; die Integrität (*of the empire*); (uprightness) die Redlichkeit, Biederkeit; die Echtheit.

Integument, *s.* die Decke (*also Anat. & Bot.*).

Intellect, *s.* der Verstand, die Verstandeskräfte; die Urteilskraft; (—ual people) die Aufgeklärten, Gebildeten. —**ual**, *adj.*, —**ually**, *adv.* den Verstand betreffend; (—ually endowed) verständig, einsichtsvoll; (ideal) geistig, intellektuell, vernünftig; —ual gymnastics, die Geistesgymnastik, die formale Bildung; —ual powers, Geisteskräfte, geistige Kraft; an —ual being, ein mit Verstand begabtes Wesen. —**uality**, *s.* die Begabung mit Verstand, Intellektualität.

Intellig—ence, *s.* der Verstand, das Erkenntnisvermögen; die Einsicht, das Verständnis; (news) die Nachricht, Mitteilung, Kunde; —ence has been received, die Nachricht ist eingelaufen; we have received no —ence of the matter, wir haben nichts von der Sache gehört; shipping —ence, Schiffahrtsnachrichten; racing —ence, der Rennbericht. —**encer**, *s.* einer der Nachrichten giebt, über wichtige Verhandlungen berichtet, Korrespondent; (title of newspaper) der Anzeiger (*obs.*). —**ent**, *adj.*, —**ently**, *adv.* mit Verstand begabt, verständig, intelligent; (sharp, bright) scharfsinnig, aufgeweckt; klug (*as an answer*). —**ible**, *adj.*, —**ibly**, *adv.* verständlich, klar. —**ibility**, —**ibleness**, *s.* die Verständlichkeit. *Comp.* —**ence-department**, *s.* das Nachrichtenamt (*of a state*); das Aufklärungsamt, das Meldeamt (*Mil.*). —**ence-office**, *s.* das Auskunftsbureau, Anzeigebureau.

Intempera—nce, *s.* die Unmäßigkeit; die Trunksucht, Völlerei. —**te**, *adj.*, —**tely**, *adv.* unmäßig, maßlos; (drunken) trunksüchtig; (violent) ungestüm; hitzig, leidenschaftlich (*as language*).

Intend, *v.a.* meinen, beabsichtigen, wollen, willens sein, vorhaben; what was this —ed for? welchen Zweck hatte das? I cannot conceive what he —s by it, ich begreife gar nicht, was er dabei für eine Absicht hat; —ed for, bestimmt zu (*the church, the public good, etc.*), gemeint als (*a joke, etc.*); —ing subscribers, alle, welche vorauszubestellen wünschen. —**ant**, *s.* der Verwalter, Vorsteher; der Intendant (*of a theatre*); —ant of mines, der Berghauptmann. —**ed**, I. *adj.* beabsichtigt, geplant; absichtlich; bestimmt (für *or* zu); zukünftig; verlobt; —ed husband, der Verlobte, Bräutigam, zukünftige Gatte. II. *s.* der (die) Zukünftige, der Bräutigam, die Braut. —**ing**, *adj.* angehend.

Intens—e, *adj.* aufs Höchste gespannt, angestrengt (*as study, application, etc.*); (extreme) stark, groß, heftig; (deep) tief; —e desire, sehnlichster Wunsch; an —e pleasure, eine Herzensfreude. —**ely**, *adv. see* —e; sehr. —**eness**, *s.* die Anstrengung, Anspannung, Heftigkeit. —**ification**, *s.* die Verstärkung. —**ify**, *v.a.* stärken, verstärken, verschärfen, vergrößern, steigern. —**ity**, *s.* die Heftigkeit, Stärke, Größe, das Übermaß; die Intensität, Stärke (*Phys.*); —ity of light, die Lichtstärke. —**ive**, I. *adj.* Spannung zulassend; Verstärkungs=; angespannt, angestrengt, stark; unablässig, fleißig; verstärkend, krafterregend, bedeutungverstärkend. II. *s.* das Verstärkungswort, die Verstärkungspartikel (*Gram.*); —ives and down-toners, verstärkende und abschwächende Wörter *or* Partikeln (*Gram.*).

Intent, I. *adj.*, —**ly**, *adv.* (— on) gespannt, aufmerksam auf (*acc.*); eifrig, beschäftigt mit, bedacht auf (*acc.*). II. *s.* die Absicht; (plan) der Plan, das Vorhaben; to the — that, damit, in der Absicht, um; to all —s and purposes, so gut wie, im Grunde, der praktischen Wirkung nach. —**ion**, *s.* die Absicht, das Vorhaben; (meaning) die Willensmeinung; (aim) der Zweck. —**ional**, *adj.*, —**ionally**, *adv.* absichtlich, vorsätzlich, geflissentlich, mit Fleiß. —**ioned**, *adj.;* well —ed gut gesinnt. **—ness,** *s.* die Angestrengtheit *or* (An)spannung (des Geistes), der Eifer, Fleiß.

Inter, *v.a.* beerdigen, begraben. **—ment,** *s.* die Beerdigung, das Begräbnis.

Interact, I. *s.* das Zwischenspiel. II. *v.n.* auf einander einwirken, sich gegenseitig beeinflussen. **—ion,** *s.* die Wechselwirkung, gegenseitige Beeinflussung; die Zwischenhandlung.

Interbreed, *v.* I. *a.* kreuzen, sich kreuzen lassen; durch Kreuzung erziehn. II. *n.* sich kreuzen.

Intercala—ry, *adj.* eingeschaltet; —ry day, Schalttag; Zwischentag, fieberfreier Tag. **—te,** *v.a.* einschalten. **—tion,** *s.* die Einschaltung.

Intercede, *v.a.* dazwischen treten, sich (für einen) verwenden, bitten, (für einen) *or* Fürbitte einlegen; he —d with his father in my behalf, er verwendete sich bei seinem Vater für mich. **—r,** *s.* der Vermittler, Fürsprecher.

Intercellular, *adj.* zwischen den Zellen (befindlich).

Intercept, *v.a.* auffangen (*a person*), auffangen, unterschlagen (*letters*); (obstruct) hemmen; aufhalten, auffangen (*rays of light, a current*); unterbrechen, abschneiden (communication); to — the trade, dem Handel Abbruch tun; to — the sky, den Himmel verdunkeln. **—er,** *s.* einer der auffängt, unterschlägt &c.

Intercess—ion, *s.* die Fürbitte, Fürsprache, Verwendung; to make —ion for, Fürbitte einlegen für. **—or,** *s.* der Fürsprecher. **—ory,** *adj.* fürbittend, eine Fürbitte enthaltend.

Interchange, I. *v.a.* gegenseitig austauschen, auswechseln; (alternate) abwechseln lassen. II. *v.n.* abwechseln, auf einander folgen. III. *s.* der Tausch, Austausch; (alternation) die Abwechslung, wechselnde Folge; der Tauschhandel (*C. L.*); — of civilities, Austausch von Artigkeiten; — of ideas, der Gedankenaustausch; — of kind offices, gegenseitige Gefälligkeiten. **—able,** *adj.*, **—ably,** *adv.* austauschbar; abwechselnd. **—ability, —ableness,** *s.* die Austauschbarkeit, Vertauschbarkeit.

Intercollegiate, *adj.* unter den Colleges; — lectures, (— examinations), Vorlesungen (Prüfungen), an welchen Angehörige verschiedener Colleges sich gemeinsam beteiligen.

Intercolonial, *adj.* zwischen Kolonieen, von Kolonie zu Kolonie.

Intercolumniation, *s.* die Säulenweite, der Säulenabstand.

Intercommunicat—e, *v.* I. *n.* mit einander Gemeinschaft haben, unter einander verkehren. II. *a.* einander mitteilen, auf einander übertragen. **—ion,** *s.* das mit einander in Verbindung Stehen; der gegenseitige Verkehr.

Intercommunion, *s.* vertrauter Verkehr.

Interconnect, *v.a.* gegenseitig eng verbinden. **—ion,** *s.* gegenseitige innige Verbindung.

Intercostal, *adj.* zwischen den Rippen liegend.

Intercourse, *s.* der Verkehr, Umgang; die Verbindung; commercial —, der Geschäftsverkehr; sexual —, geschlechtlicher Umgang *or* Verkehr.

Intercross, *v.* I. *n.* sich (gegenseitig) kreuzen. II. *a.* kreuzen; geschlechtlich kreuzen.

Intercurrent, *adj.* dazwischen laufend; zwischenlaufend (*Med.*).

Intercutaneous, *adj.* subkutan, unter der Haut.

Interdental, *adj.* zwischen den Zähnen gebildet.

Interdependen—ce, *s.* wechselseitige Abhängigkeit. **—t,** *adj.* wechselseitig *or* gegenseitig von einander abhängig.

Interdict, I. *v.a.* untersagen, verbieten; mit dem Interdikte belegen (*R. C.*). II. *s.* das Verbot, die Untersagung; das Interdikt (*R.C.*). **—ion,** *s.* *see* — II. **—ory,** *adj.* untersagend, verbietend.

Interdigital, *adj.* zwischen den Fingern *or* Zehen.

Interest, I. *v.a.* interessieren; (concern) (einen) angehen, wichtig sein für; (excite sympathy) Teilnahme einflößen; (move) bewegen, rühren; (excite in favour of) anziehen, einnehmen; (give a share in) einen Anteil geben (an); I am not —ed in it, ich bin nicht dabei beteiligt (*C.L.*), (feel no —) es hat für mich kein Interesse; I am —ed to know . . ., es interessiert mich zu wissen . . .; his story —ed me greatly, seine Erzählung zog mich sehr an; to — o.s. (take an —) in Anteil nehmen an (*dat.*), sich interessieren für; t — s.o. in our favour, einen für uns gewinnen. II. *s.* (sympathy) die Teilnahme (in a th., für eine S.), der Anteil (an einer S.); (good, profit) der Vorteil, Nutzen (von einer S.); (influence) der Einfluß, die moralische Macht; (share) der Anteil (*in a business, etc.*); der Zins, die Zinsen (*C.L.*); (charm) die Anziehungskraft, der Reiz; self-—, der Eigennutz; to use one's — for a p., seinen Einfluß zu jemandes Gunsten anwenden; he has no — in the county, er hat keinen Einfluß in der Grafschaft; they have lost their — at court, sie haben allen Kredit bei Hofe verloren; — in a question, der Anteil an einer Frage, das Interesse für eine Frage; he takes no — in music, er hat kein Interesse (*or* interessiert sich nicht) für Musik; he showed much — in this boy, er zeigte großen Anteil an diesem Knaben; she takes a great — in this matter, sie nimmt großes Interesse an dieser *or* zeigt große Teilnahme für diese Sache; to have an — in a speculation, bei einem Unternehmen (finanziell) beteiligt sein; to lend on —, Geld auf Zinsen leihen; I can't pay the — on the capital, ich kann das Kapital nicht verzinsen; compound —, Zinseszinsen; vested —s (in a th.), feste Rechte, fest begründetes Anrecht (auf eine S.); contingent life —, an gewisse Bedingungen gebundener lebenslänglicher Zinsgenuß. **—ed,** *adj.* angeregt; beteiligt; (selfish) eigennützig; the parties —ed, die Beteiligten. **—ing,** *adj.*, **—ingly,** *adv.* fesselnd, anziehend, unterhaltend, interessant.

Interfere, *v.n.* sich (in eine S.) einmischen *or* einmengen, dazwischen treten, sich ins Mittel schlagen; (clash) einander widerstreiten, einander entgegen sein; störend einwirken; sich streichen (*Vet.*); there's no need for you to —, Sie brauchen sich nicht einzumischen; private interest ought never to — with duty, Privatrücksichten sollten nie störend auf die (Amts-)Pflicht einwirken. **—nce,** *s.* die Einmischung, Dazwischenkunft, Vermittelung; die Interferenz (*Phys.*); der Eintrag, Abbruch (*fig.*).

Interfoliaceous, *adj.* zwischenblätterig.

Interfus—e, *v.a.* dazwischen gießen; mit einander mischen. **—ion,** *s.* das Dazwischengießen; die gegenseitige Vermischung.

Interim, I. *s.* die Zwischenzeit; das Interim (*Hist.*); ad — *or* in the —, unterdessen, mittlerweile, vorläufig. II. *adj. & adv.* einstweilig, vorläufig; — report, vorläufiger Bericht.

Interior, I. *adj.* inner, innerlich; inwendig; (inland) binnenländisch. II. *s.* das Innere (*of a thing*); das Innere, Binnenland (*of a country*).

Interjection, *s.* die Interjektion, der Ausruf. **—al,** *adj.*, dazwischen geschoben, eingerückt.

Interlac—e, *v.a.* durchflechten, verschlingen, verflechten; —ing arches, Kreuzungsbögen.

Interlard, *v.a.* (durch)spicken; untermischen, vermengen (*fig.*).

Interleave, *v.a.* durchschießen.

Interlin—e, *v.a.* zwischen die Zeilen schreiben; durchschießen (*Typ.*). **—ear,** *adj.* zwischenzeilig; —ear translation, —ear method, die Interlinear-Übersetzung, -Methode. **—eation,** *s.* die Zwischenschreibung, das Dazwischenschreiben; (words, etc., —ed) das Zwischengeschriebene.

Interlock, *v.a.* in einander greifen, schließen.

Interlocut—ion, *s.* die Unterredung, das Zwiegespräch; die Zwischenrede; das Zwischenurteil (*Law*). **—or,** *s.* der Zwischenredner, die redend eingeführte Person; my —or, die Person, mit welcher ich spreche (*or* sprach). **—y,** *adj.* in Gesprächsform; interlokutorisch (*Law*).

Interlope, *v.n.* sich unbefugt eindrängen; den Markt aufkaufen, Waren verteuern. **—r**, *s.* der Eindringling; der Schleichhändler, Schmuggler.

Interlude, *s.* das Zwischenspiel.

Interlunar, *adj.* die Zeit des Neumondes betreffend.

Intermarr—iage, *s.* die Wechselheirat. **—y**, *v.n.* wechselheiraten schließen; unter einander heiraten; other tribes will not —y with them, andere Stämme wollen mit ihnen keine Heiraten eingehen.

Intermeddle, *v.n.* sich (unberufen) einmengen in. **—r**, *s.* unberufener Vermittler.

Intermedia—ry, I. *adj.* dazwischen befindlich. II. *s.* der Vermittler. **—te**, *adj.* in der Mitte liegend, Verbindungs-, Mittel-, Zwischen-; —te education, das höhere Schulwesen, Mittelschulwesen; —te examination, die Zwischenprüfung; die mittlere Universitätsprüfung (zwischen Aufnahmeprüfung und Schlußprüfung für den Grad) (*e.g. at London University*); die Prüfung von Schülern aus höheren Schulen (Mittelschulen) (*in Ireland and Wales*); —te examination board, Aufsichtsrat über Mittelschulprüfungen, über Prüfungen höherer Schulen (*in Ireland*); —te school, die höhere Schule, Sekundärschule; die Mittelschule (*Amer.*, *Austria*); —te station, die Zwischenstation.

Intermezzo, *s.* das Intermezzo, Zwischenspiel; der lustige Zwischenfall.

Intermina—ble, *adj.*, **—bly**, *adv.* endlos, unendlich. **—bleness**, *s.* die Unendlichkeit. **—te**, *adj.* unbegrenzt, endlos.

Intermingle, *v.* I. *a.* vermischen, untermischen. II. *n.* sich vermischen.

Intermission, *s.* das Aussetzen, Unterlassen (*of a work*, *etc.*); (interruption) die Unterbrechung, Unterlassung; (pause) die Zwischenzeit, Pause; without —, ohne Unterlaß, unablässig.

Intermit, *v.* I. *a.* aussetzen, unterbrechen, einstellen. II. *n.* nachlassen, zeitweise aussetzen, wechseln (*as fever*). **—tent**, *adj.* nachlassend, aussetzend, unterbrochen; an —tent fever, ein Wechselfieber; —tent pulse, intermittierender Puls; short —tent pain, kurze, unterbrochene Schmerzen; —tent light, unterbrochenes Licht, das Blinkfeuer (*of lighthouses*). **—ting**, *adj.*, **—tingly**, *adv. see* —tent; in Absätzen.

Intermix, *v.* I. *a.* untermischen. II. *n.* sich mischen. **—ture**, *s.* das Untermischen; (—ed mass) die Mischung, das Gemisch; *see* Admixture.

Intermundane, *adj.* zwischenweltlich.

Intermural, *adj.* zwischen Mauern.

Intern, *v.a.* internieren. **—al**, *adj.*, **—ally**, *adv.* inner(-lich); (domestic) einheimisch; —al evidence, der in dem Dinge selbst befindliche Beweis; —al peace, innerer Friede. **—ment**, *s.* die Internierung.

International, *adj.* zwischen Völkern, International-; — exhibition, die Weltausstellung; — law, das Völkerrecht; — law of copyright, das internationale Verlagsrecht; — relations, völkerrechtliche Beziehungen.

Internecine, *adj.* gegenseitige Zerstörung bezweckend, Vernichtungs-; (deadly) tötlich, mörderisch.

Internode, *s.* das Zwischenknotenstück, Stengelglied (zwischen zwei Knoten) (*Bot.*).

Interoceanic, *adj.* zwischen zwei Weltmeeren befindlich, zwei Weltmeere verbindend (*canal*).

Interpellat—e, *v.a.* interpellieren, um Aufschluß ersuchen. **—ion**, *s.* der Einspruch; die Anfrage, Interpellation (*Parl.*).

Interpenetrat—e, *v.n.* sich wechselseitig völlig durchdringen. **—ion**, *s.* die gegenseitige Durchdringung.

Interpolat—e, *v.a.* einschalten, unter-, ein-schieben; interpolieren (*also Math.*). **—ion**, *s.* die Einschiebung, Interpolation; die Einschaltung, Interpolierung (*also Math. & Phys.*); unterschobene Stelle; die Textfälschung; text with numerous —ions, Text mit zahlreichen (späteren) Einschiebungen *or* Einschiebseln. **—or**, *s.* der Einschalter, Textfälscher.

Interpos—e, *v.* I. *a.* dazwischen stellen, legen, setzen; einschieben (*a remark*, *etc.*); to —e one's authority, mit seinem Ansehen ins Mittel treten. II. *n.* sich ins Mittel legen, vermitteln; (intervene) dazwischentreten, liegen; (interrupt) im Reden unterbrechen, einfallen. **—ition**, *s.* das Dazwischentreten; (placing among) die Zwischenstellung; die Dazwischenkunft (*also of Providence*), die Vermittlung (*fig.*); by the —ition of (providence) a friend, durch die Vermittlung (der göttlichen Vorsehung) eines Freundes.

Interpret, *v.a.* auslegen, erklären, deuten (*dreams*, *etc.*); übersetzen, verdolmetschen; (render) darstellen, geben; vortragen (*Mus.*). **—ation**, *s.* die Auslegung, Erklärung, Deutung; die Darstellung, der Vortrag. **—er**, *s.* der Ausleger; der Übersetzer; der Dolmetscher; der Darsteller.

Interregnum, *s.* die Zwischenregierung.

Interrelation, *s.* gegenseitige(n) Beziehung(en).

Interrogat—e, *v.* I. *a.* fragen, befragen; verhören (*witnesses*). II. *n.* (einem) Fragen stellen. **—ion**, *s.* das Befragen; (question) die Frage; das Verhör; das Verhören; note of —ion, das Fragezeichen. **—ive**, I. *adj.* fragend, Frage-. II. *s.* das Fragewort. **—ively**, *adv.* frageweise. **—ory**, I. *adj.* eine Frage enthaltend, fragend. II. *s.* die Frage; die gerichtliche Befragung, das Verhör.

Interrupt, *v.a.* unterbrechen; aufhalten (*in work*); (disturb) stören; (divide) trennen, teilen; to — a p., einem in die Rede fallen; don't let me — you, lassen Sie sich durch mich nicht stören. **—ed**, *adj.* unterbrochen, gestört. **—edly**, *adv.* mit Unterbrechungen. **—er**, *s.* der Unterbrecher, Störer. **—ion**, *s.* die Unterbrechung; die Störung; without —ion, ohne Unterbrechung, ununterbrochen, in einem fort.

Intersect, *v.* I. *a.* durchschneiden. II. *n.* sich durchschneiden, kreuzen. **—ion**, *s.* das Durchschneiden; der Durchschnitt (*Geom.*), die Kreuzung.

Interspace, *s.* der Zwischenraum.

Intersperse, *v.a.* einstreuen, einmischen, vermischen, sprenkeln.

Interstellar, *adj.* zwischen den Sternen.

Intersti—ce, *s.* der Zwischenraum; die Lücke. **—tial**, *adj.* mit Zwischenräumen; —tial absorption, allmähliche Absorption.

Interstratified, *adj.* dazwischen geschichtet.

Intertwine, *v.* I. *a.* verflechten, ineinanderschlingen. II. *n.* sich ineinander verflechten.

Inter-University, *adj.*; — sports, Kampfspiele zwischen Studenten verschiedener Universitäten (*in England: Oxford and Cambridge*).

Interval, *s.* (space) der Abstand, Zwischenraum; (space of time) die Zwischenzeit, Pause; das Intervall, der Tonabstand (*Mus.*); at —s, dann und wann; lucid —s, lichte Augenblicke.

Interven—e, *v.n.* dazwischenkommen, dazwischentreten; (lie between) dazwischen liegen (*also of time*); (occur) hinzu-, ein-treten, sich ereignen; (hinder) dazwischenkommen; (interpose) sich ins Mittelschlagen, vermitteln. **—tion**, *s.* das Dazwischenliegen; die Dazwischenkunft (*fig.*); die Vermittelung.

Interview, I. *s.* die Zusammkunft, Unterredung, Besprechung; der Besuch eines Zeitungsberichterstatters, der Ausfragebesuch, das Interview. II. *v.a.* einen besuchen, um dessen Ansichten zu erfahren und zu veröffentlichen, einen bei einem Besuche ausholen *or* ausfragen. **—er**, *s.* der ausfragende Zeitungsberichterstatter.

Intervocalic, *adj.* zwischenvokalisch.

Interweave, *ir.v.a.* ineinanderweben, verweben; einweben, einmischen, untermischen (*fig.*).

Interwove, *pret.*, **—n**, *p.p. see* Interweave.

Intesta—cy, *s.* die Abwesenheit *or* das Fehlen eines Testaments. **—te**, I. *adj.* ohne Testament;

an —te estate, Besitztum, über welches keine letztwilligen Verfügungen getroffen worden sind. II. *s.* der Intestatus, Person, die ohne ein (rechtskräftiges) Testament gestorben ist.

Intestin—al, *adj.* die Darm-, Ein-geweide betreffend; —al canal, der Darmgang. —**e**, I. *adj.* inner, einheimisch; —e war, der Bürgerkrieg. II. *s.* (*usually pl.* —s) das Gedärm, Eingeweide.

Intima—cy, *s.* die Vertrautheit, der vertraute Umgang. —**te**, I. *adj.*, —**tely**, *adv.* innig, vertraut, intim. II. *s.* der, die Vertraute. III. *v.n. see* Intimat—.

Intimat—e, *v.n.* andeuten, zu verstehen geben, anzeigen. —**ion**, *s.* die Andeutung; (hint) der Wink; (notice) die Anzeige, Meldung.

Intimidat—e, *v.a.* einschüchtern. —**ion**, *s.* die Einschüchterung. —**ory**, *adj.* einschüchternd.

Into, *prep.* in (*with acc.*); to bribe — secrecy, durch Bestechung zum Schweigen bringen; to cheat s.o. — accepting . . ., einen listig zur Annahme (von etwas) bewegen; to dip —, flüchtig durchlesen (*a book*); to get — trouble, in Unannehmlichkeiten geraten; to go — a house, in ein Haus gehen; to grow —, werden zu; to be led — error, zum Irrtum veranlaßt werden; his house looks — my garden, sein Haus hat die Aussicht auf meinen Garten; to put — a harbour, in einen Hafen einlaufen; to put — execution, ausführen; to resolve —, auflösen in (*acc.*); to surprise — an avowal, (einem) durch Überraschung ein Geständnis entlocken.

Intolera—ble, *adj.*, —**bly**, *adv.* unerträglich, unausstehlich. —**bleness**, *s.* die Unerträglichkeit. —**nce**, *s.* die Unduldsamkeit; die Intoleranz (*Theol.*). —**nt**, *adj.*, —**ntly**, *adv.* unduldsam; intolerant.

Inton—ation, *s.* das Tonangeben (*Mus.*); die Intonation (*in churches*); der Tonfall, die Betonung, Modulation. —**e**, *v.a.* & *n.* anstimmen, intonieren, den Ton angeben.

Intoxica—nt, *s.* berauschendes Getränk. —**te**, *v.a.* berauschen (*also fig.*); —ted with love, liebetrunken; —ted with the idea, von dem Gedanken berauscht. —**tion**, *s.* die Berauschung (*also fig.*); (state of —tion) der Rausch.

Intractab—ility, —**leness**, *s.* die Unlenksamkeit, Störrigkeit, Starrsinnigkeit; die Unbändigkeit. —**le**, *adj.*, —**ly**, *adv.* unlenksam, widerspenstig, störrig; unbändig (*as beasts*).

Intrados, *s.* innere Kurve eines Bogens.

Intramural, *adj.* innerhalb der Mauern (einer Stadt, Universität, Anstalt) vorkommend, inner; innerhalb der Gebärmutterwand (*Anat.*).

Intransigent, *adj.* intransigent, unversöhnlich, unnachgiebig. —**s**, *pl.* die Unversöhnlichen, Intransigenten.

Intransitive, I. *adj.*, —**ly**, *adv.* intransitiv. II. *s.* (— verb) das Intransitivum.

Intransmissible, *adj.* unübertragbar.

Intrench, *v.a.* einen Graben machen um verschanzen (*Fort.*). —**ment**, *s.* die Verschanzung, Schanze.

Intrepid, *adj.*, —**ly**, *adv.* unerschrocken, herzhaft, furchtlos. —**ity**, *s.* die Unerschrockenheit, Furchtlosigkeit, Herzhaftigkeit, der Mut.

Intrica—cy, *s.* die Verwicklung; (difficulty) die Schwierigkeit. —**te**, *adj.*, —**tely**, *adv.* verwickelt, verworren, schwierig; verwebt (*Bot.*).

Intrigu—e, I. *s.* das Ränkespiel, die Intrigue, die Schliche (*pl.*); das Truggewebe; (drama) die Verwickelung, Knotenschürzung; (liaison) der Liebeshandel. II. *v.n.* Ränke schmieden, Zettelungen anstiften, intrigieren. —**er**, *s.* der Ränkeschmied, Intrigant. —**ing**, *adj.* ränkevoll, verschmitzt, arglistig.

Intrinsic(al), *adj.*, —**ly**, *adv.* inner(lich); wahr, wirklich, wesentlich, eigentlich (*fig.*).

Introduc—e, *v.a.* einführen (*also to a club, etc.*); bekannt machen, vorstellen (*people*); (*insert*) einführen (*Med.*); einschieben; einführen, aufbringen (*fashions, etc.*); einleiten (*a book, etc.*); zur Sprache bringen, vorbringen (*a topic*); he —ed me to her, er stellte mich ihr vor; let me —e Mr. Z. to you, erlauben Sie mir, Ihnen Herrn Z. vorzustellen; to —e changes, Veränderungen vornehmen. —**er**, *s.* der Einführer. —**tion**, *s.* die Einführung; die Vorstellung, das Bekanntmachen; die Einleitung, Vorrede; die Introduktion (*Mus.*); die Anleitung (*to a study*); der Leitfaden, das Lehrbuch; das Einführen (*of a probe, etc.*); letter of —tion, der Einführungsbrief, das Empfehlungsschreiben. —**tory**, *adj.* einleitend, vorausgeschickt; —tory discourse, eine Einleitungsrede; —**tory remarks**, die Vorbemerkungen.

Introit, *s.* der Introitus, Eingang der Messe.

Intromit, *v.n.* sich in fremdes Eigentum mischen (*Scotch Law*).

Introrse, *adj.* einwärts gekehrt (*Bot.*).

Introspecti—on, *s.* das Hineinsehen; (self- —on) die Selbstschau, Selbstbeobachtung. —**ve**, *adj.* hineinblickend; beschaulich, zur Selbstbeschauung neigend *or* geneigt.

Introvert, *v.a.* einwärts kehren.

Intru—de, *v.* I. *n.* sich eindrängen, sich aufdrängen, stören, ungelegen kommen; I hope I don't —de, hoffentlich störe ich nicht; don't let me —de upon you, bitte lassen Sie sich gar nicht stören! these thoughts will —de upon us, diese Gedanken drängen sich uns (unwiderstehlich) auf. II. *a.* eindrängen. —**der**, *s.* der Eindringling; der ungebetene Gast; (disturber) der Störer. —**sion**, *s.* die Eindrängung, das Aufdringen; gesetzwidrige Besitznahme (*Law*). —**sive**, *adj.*, —**sively**, *adv.* zudringlich, lästig, sich eindrängend. —**siveness**, *s.* die Zudringlichkeit.

Intrust, *v.a.* anvertrauen, (a th. to a p., einem etwas, s.o. with the care of a th., etwas der Sorgfalt einer Person, einen mit der Sorge für eine S.) betrauen.

Intuiti—on, *s.* die (geistige) Anschauung; unmittelbare (nicht durch Beweis herbeigeführte) Erkenntnis. —**ve**, *adj.*, —**vely**, *adv.* anschauend, anschaulich, durch unmittelbare Anschauung erfaßt, intuitiv; —ve knowledge, faculty, intuitives Wissen; das Intuitions-, Anschauungsvermögen.

Inundat—e, *v.a.*, überschwemmen (*also fig.*) —**ion**, *s.* die Überschwemmung.

Inure, *v.a.* gewöhnen (to, an eine S.), abhärten (gegen eine S.).

Inutility, *s.* die Nutzlosigkeit.

Invade, *v.a.* einfallen in (ein Land), (ein Land) überfallen, feindlich eindringen in (ein Land); to be —d by fears, von Furcht ergriffen sein —**r**, *s.* der Angreifer; (intruder) der Eindringling.

Invalid, I. (*pron.* inval'id) (of no force) schwach, kraftlos; haltlos, hinfällig (*of arguments*); rechtsungültig (*Law*); (*pron.* in'valid) (ill) schwach, gebrechlich; dienstuntauglich; (*in comp.*) Kranken-. II. *s.* (*pron.* in'valid) der Kranke; der Dienstunfähige (*Mil., Naut.*); he is a confirmed —, er ist unheilbar krank. III. *v.a.* auf die Invalidenliste setzen. —**ate**, *v.a.* schwächen, entkräften; ungültig machen, umstoßen (*Law*). —**ation**, *s.* das Entkräften, Schwächen; das Ungültigmachen. —**ity**, *s.* die Kraftlosigkeit; die Nichtigkeit, Hinfälligkeit.

Invaluabl—e, *adj.*, —**y**, *adv.* unschätzbar. —**eness**, *s.* die Unschätzbarkeit.

Invariabl—e, I. *adj.*, —**y**, *adv.* unveränderlich, beständig. II. *s.* die Konstante, invariable Größe (*Math.*). —**eness**, *s.* die Unveränderlichkeit, Beständigkeit.

Invasi—on, *s.* der (feindliche) Einfall, Überfall, Angriff; (encroachment) der Eingriff; der Anfall (*of the plague, etc.*). —**ve**, *adj.* anfallend, angreifend, Angriffs-.

Invective, I. *s.* heftiger Ausfall (gegen), Schmähung, Schimpfrede; to break out into —s against s.o., in Schimpfworte gegen einen ausbrechen. II. *adj.* anzüglich, schimpfend, ausfällig.
Inveigh, *v.n.* schimpfen, schmähen auf (*acc.*); to — against, zu Feld ziehen, losziehen gegen, heftig schelten auf (*acc.*).
Inveigle, *v.a.* verlocken, verleiten, verführen. —**ment**, *s.* das Verlocken, Verführen.
Invent, *v.a.* erfinden; (devise) erdichten, erdenken, ersinnen; (concoct) aussinnen, schmieden. —**ion**, *s.* die Erfindung; (discovery) das Erfundene, die Entdeckung; (fabrication) die Erdichtung, Lüge; (—ive faculty) der Erfindungsgeist, die Erfindungsgabe; —ion of the cross, Kreuzfindung. —**ive**, *adj.*, —**ively**, *adv.* erfinderisch, erfindungsreich, erfindsam; —ive genius, der erfinderische Kopf. —**iveness**, *s.* die Erfindungsgabe. —**or**, *s.* der Erfinder; der Erdichter. —**ory**, I. *s.* das Inventar(ium), Verzeichnis; die Inventur (*C.L.*); to take an —ory, *see* —ory II. II. *v.a.* ein Inventar(ium) aufnehmen von einer S., eine S. invent(arif)ieren.
Inver—se, *adj.*, —**sely**, *adv.* umgekehrt; in the —se ratio, —sely, umgekehrt; —se proportion, umgekehrtes Verhältnis. —**sion**, *s.* die Umkehrung (*also Math., Mus., Log., Gram.*). —**t**, *v.a.* umkehren; umwandeln. —**ted**, *adj.* umgekehrt (*also Her.*); kopfstehend; —ted arch, umgekehrter Bogen (*Arch.*); —ted commas, Anführungszeichen, Gänsefüßchen; —ted interval, umgekehrtes Intervall.
Invertebrat—a, *pl.* wirbellose Tiere. —**e**, I. *adj.* wirbellos, ohne Rückgrat; schwankend, haltlos (*fig.*). II. *s.* (*pl.* —es) *see* —a.
Invest, *v.a.* bekleiden (with, mit); belehnen (mit), einsetzen (in), bestallen (*fig.*); anlegen (*money*); einschließen, blockieren (*Mil.*); to — money in land, Geld in Ländereien anlegen; to — s.o. with full power, einen mit Vollmacht bekleiden *or* ausrüsten. —**iture**, *s.* die Investitur, Einsetzung (in den Besitz einer Würde, Pfründe &c.). —**ment**, I. *s.* die Blockade, das Berennen (*Mil.*); das Anlegen (*of money*); die Geldanlage; to make an —ment, Geld anlegen. II. *attrib.*; —ment clause, die Testamentsverfügung, welche sich auf die Anlage des Kapitals bezieht. —**or**, *s.* einer, der Geld anlegt.
Investigat—e, *v.a.* erforschen, untersuchen. —**ion**, *s.* die Erforschung, Untersuchung. —**or**, *s.* der Forscher, Untersucher.
Invetera—cy, *s.* das Eingewurzeltsein, die Hartnäckigkeit (*of disease*). —**te**, *adj.*, —**tely**, *adv.* eingewurzelt (*as hatred*); eingefleischt (*gambler*).
Invidious, *adj.*, —**ly**, *adv.* gehässig; (envious) neidisch, bösartig. —**ness**, *s.* die Gehässigkeit.
Invigilat—e, *v.n.* bei einer schriftlichen Prüfung die Aufsicht führen. —**ion**, *s.* die Aufsicht bei einer Klausurarbeit *or* schriftlichen Prüfung.
Invigorat—e, *v.a.* kräftigen, stärken, Leben einflößen, Lebenskraft geben. —**ing**, *adj.* belebend. —**ion**, *s.* die Kräftigung, Stärkung.
Invincib—le, *adj.* unüberwindlich, unbezwinglich, unbesiegbar. —**ility**, —**leness**, *s.* die Unbezwinglichkeit, Unbesiegbarkeit.
Inviola—bility, *s.* die Unverletzbarkeit; die Unverbrüchlichkeit (*of an oath, etc.*). —**ble**, *adj.*, —**bly**, *adv.* unverletzlich; unverbrüchlich (*of a contract, promise, etc.*); (sacred) heilig. —**te**, *adj.* unverletzt; unversehrt; unentweiht.
Invisib—ility, *s.* die Unsichtbarkeit. —**le**, *adj.*, —**ly**, *adv.* unsichtbar.
Invit—ation, *s.* die Einladung; cards of —ation, Einladungskarten; your kind —ation (for), Ihre gütige Einladung (auf *or* zu). —**e**, *v.a.* einladen; auffordern (zu einer S.), herausfordern (*criticism*). —**ing**, *adj.*, —**ingly**, *adv.* einladend, lockend.
Invocat—e, *v.a.* anrufen. —**ion**, *s.* das Anrufen; die Anrufung; —ion of saints, die Anrufung der Heiligen.
Invoice, I. *s.* die Faktur(a), Warenrechnung; das Verzeichnis steuerbarer Waren (*Amer.*); as per —, laut Faktura, wie fakturiert; — continued, Faktur-Transport; simulated —, der Konto finto. II. *v.a.* fakturieren; the goods are —d at a price . . ., die Waren sind zu einem Betrage fakturiert . . .
Invoke, *v.a.* anrufen, anflehen, flehen zu.
Involu—cral, *adj.* hüllenständig. —**cre**, *s.* die Hülle (*Bot.*). —**te**, I. *adj.* eingerollt (*Bot.*). II. *s.* die Involute, Evolvente (*Geom.*). —**tion**, *s.* die Potenzierung, Erhebung zu einer Potenz (*Math.*); die Einschiebung (*Gram.*).
Involuntar—ily, *adv. see* —y. —**iness**, *s.* die Unfreiwilligkeit; die Unwillkürlichkeit. —**y**, *adv.* unfreiwillig; (spontaneous) unwillkürlich.
Involve, *v.a.* (envelop) einwickeln, einhüllen; (include) in sich schließen, einschließen; verwickeln (*in difficulties, etc.*); (connect) verbinden; (complicate) verwickeln; potenzieren (*Math.*); —ed sentence, der verwickelte Satz, Satz mit vielen Einschachtelungen; to — o.s. in trouble, sich in Ungelegenheiten versetzen; —d in debt, verschuldet.
Invulnerab—ility, —**leness**, *s.* die Unverletzbarkeit, Unverwundbarkeit. —**le**, *adj.* unverwundbar, unverletzlich; unanfechtbar (*fig.*).
Inward, I. *adj.* inner, inwendig. II. *adv.* einwärts, nach innen; (within) im Inneren; (into the mind, etc.) in das Innere. III. *s.* das Innere (*fig.*). —**ly**, *adv.* innerlich, im Innern (*also fig.*); (turned —) einwärts; to mourn —ly, sich heimlich grämen. —**ness**, *s.* die innere Beschaffenheit, der innere Zustand; die Innigkeit. —**s**, *pl.* die Eingeweide.
Inweave, *v.a.* einweben; verschlingen (*fig.*).
Inwrap, *v.a.* einwickeln, einhüllen.
Inwreathe, *v.a.* umkränzen.
Iodi—c, *adj.* jodsauer; —c acid, die Jodsäure. —**de**, *s.* das Jodid; —de of iron, das Jodeisen. —**ne**, *s.* das Jod. —**sm**, *s.* die Jodkrankheit. —**ze**, *v.d.* iodieren.
Iota, *s.* das Jota; die Kleinigkeit, das Tüttelchen; not an —, kein Tüttelchen.
Ipecacuanha, *s.* die Ipekakuanha, Brechwurzel.
Ipse dixit, *s.* die Behauptung (ohne Beweis).
Ipsissima verba, *s.* die eigenen Worte.
Ipso facto, *adv.* durch die Tat selbst, so wie so.
Irascib—ility, *s.* die Reizbarkeit, der Jähzorn. —**le**, *adj.*, —**ly**, *adv.* reizbar, jähzornig.
Irate, *adj.* erzürnt, zornig, ärgerlich.
Ire, *s.* der Zorn, die Wut. —**ful**, *adj.*, —**fully**, *adv.* zornig, wutentbrannt.
Iridescen—ce, *s.* das Schillern in den Regenbogenfarben. —**t**, *adj.* regenbogenfarbig.
Iris, *s.* der Regenbogen; die Regenbogenhaut (*Anat.*); die Schwertlilie (*Bot.*).
Irk, *v.a.* (*usually impers.*) ermüden, ärgern, verdrießen; schmerzen. —**some**, *adj.*, —**ly**, *adv.* lästig, beschwerlich, ermüdend, verdrießlich. —**someness**, *s.* die Beschwerlichkeit, das Ermüdende, Ärgerliche.
Iron, I. *s.* das Eisen (*also fig.*); (smoothing —) Bügeleisen, Plätteisen; rod of —, eiserne Rute; cast —, das Gußeisen, der Eisenguß; citrate of —, zitronensaures Eisenoxyd; scrap —, Ramaßeisen; sheet —, dünne Eisenplatten; pig —, Roheisen; wrought —, Schmiedeeisen; to have too many —s in the fire, zu vielerlei Geschäfte haben, sich mit zu vielen Dingen zugleich befassen, sich *or* seine Kräfte zersplittern; strike the — while it is hot, man muß das Eisen schmieden, solange es heiß ist (*prov.*). II. *adj.* eisern (*also fig.*); hart, fest, unerschütterlich (*fig.*); the — age, eisernes Zeitalter; the — Chancellor, der eiserne Kanzler, Bismarck; — frame, eisenfester Körperbau. III. *v.a.* plätten, ausbügeln. —**er**, *s.* der (die) Plätter(in). —**s**, *pl.* Fesseln; to put into —s, in Fesseln schlagen *or* legen. *Comp.* —**bound**, *adj.* eisenbeschlagen; felsig, von Felsen

umgeben (*as a coast*). **—clad**, I. *adj.* gepanzert. II. *s.* das Panzerschiff, der Panzer. **—-clay**, *s.* der Eisenton. **—-dust**, *s.* der Eisenfeilstaub. **—-foundry**, *s.* die Eisengießerei. **—-gray**, *adj.* eisengrau. **—-hearted**, *adj.* hartherzig. **—ing-blanket**, *s.* der Bügelteppich. **—ing-board**, *s.* das Plättbrett, Bügelbrett. **—ing-table**, *s.* der Plätt-, Bügel-tisch. **—master**, *s.* der Eisenhüttenbesitzer. **—monger**, *s.* der Eisenhändler; —monger's shop, die Eisenhandlung. **—mongery**, *s.* der Eisenhandel; (— wares) Eisenwaren. **—-mould**, *s.* der Eisenrost, Rostfleck. **—-moulded**, *adj.* rostfleckig. **—-ore**, *s.* das Eisenerz. **—-pyrites**, *s.* der Schwefelkies. **—-scales**, *pl.* der Hammerschlag. **—sides**, *pl.* die Reiterei Cromwells. **—smith**, *s.* der Eisenarbeiter. **—stone**, I. *s.* der Eisenstein. II. *attrib.*; —stone china, feines Steingut. **—-trade**, *s.* der Eisenhandel. **—ware**, *s.* die Eisenwaren. **—work**, *s.* das Eisenwerk. **—-works**, *pl.* die Eisenhütte.

Iron—ical, *adj.* spöttelnd, ironisch. **—y**, *s.* der feine, versteckte Spott, die Spötterei, Ironie.

Irradia—nce, **—ncy**, *s.* das Strahlenwerfen, Ausstrahlen, Bestrahlen; der Strahlenschein, Glanz. **—te**, *v.* I. *a.* bestrahlen; erleuchten (*the mind*). II. *n.* Strahlen werfen. **—tion**, *s.* das Strahlenwerfen; die Bestrahlung (*Phys.*); die Erleuchtung (*fig.*).

Irrational, *adj.*, **—ly**, *adv.* unvernünftig, vernunftwidrig; irrational (*Math.*). **—ity**, *s.* die Unvernunft, Vernunftlosigkeit, Vernunftwidrigkeit.

Irreclaimabl—e, *adj.*, **—y**, *adv.* unwieder-ruflich, -bringlich; (incorrigible) unverbesserlich.

Irrecogni—zable, *adj.* nicht erkennbar; nicht wiederzuerkennen. **—tion**, *s.* die Nichtanerkennung; das Beiseitelassen.

Irreconcilabl—e, *adj.*, **—y**, *adv.* unversöhnlich; unvereinbar (mit); it is —e with, es verträgt sich nicht mit. **—eness**, *s.* die Unversöhnlichkeit; die Unvereinbarkeit.

Irrecoverabl—e, *adj.*, **—y**, *adv.* unersetzlich, unrettbar, unwiederbringlich (verloren). **—eness**, *s.* die Unersetzlichkeit, Unwiederbringlichkeit.

Irredeemabl—e, *adj.* nicht loszukaufen; unablöslich; nicht zu vollem Werte einlösbar (*as a paper currency*). **—y**, *adv. see* —e; (irreparably) unwiederbringlich.

Irreducible, *adj.* nicht zu vermindern, nicht (weiter) reduzierbar; nicht verwandelbar (into, in eine S., to, zu einer S.); the — minimum, das Allergeringste, das wovon nichts mehr abgehen kann, was durchaus bleiben muß.

Irrefragab—ility, *s.* die Unwiderleglichkeit, Unumstößlichkeit. **—le**, *adj.*, **—ly**, *adv.* unwiderleglich, unumstößlich.

Irrefutab—ility, *s.* die Unwiderlegbarkeit. **—le**, *adj.*, **—ly**, *adv.* unwiderleglich, unwiderlegbar.

Irregular, *adj.*, **—ly**, *adv.* unregelmäßig, regellos, regelwidrig; irregulär (*Mil.*); (not right) unrichtig; unordentlich (*as one's ways*). **—ity**, *s.* die Unregelmäßigkeit, Ungleichmäßigkeit; (lawlessness) die Regellosigkeit, Abweichung; (want of order) die Unordentlichkeit, Unordnung; (wrong action) der Fehler; die Ausschweifung(en), Exzesse. **—s**, *pl.* irreguläre Truppen.

Irrelevan—cy, *s.* die Unanwendbarkeit. **—t**, *adj.*, **—tly**, *adv.* unanwendbar, nicht gehörig *or* ohne Beziehung (zu); belanglos, ohne Belang, unerheblich; these considerations are —t, diese Betrachtungen sind belanglos, stehen zu der Frage in keiner Beziehung.

Irreligio—n, *s.* die Irreligiosität; (unbelief) der Unglaube; (godlessness) die Gottlosigkeit. **—us**, *adj.*, **—usly**, *adv.* irreligiös; gottlos. **—usness**, *s. see* —n.

Irremediabl—e, *adj.*, **—y**, *adv.* unheilbar; nicht wieder gut zu machen(d), dem sich nicht abhelfen läßt; unabänderlich; unersetzlich. **—eness**, *s.* die Unheilbarkeit; die Unabänderlichkeit.

Irremovabl—e, *adj.*, **—y**, *adv.* unbeweglich; unabsetzbar (*from office, etc.*).

Irreparab—ility, **—leness**, *s.* die Unersetzlichkeit. **—le**, *adj.*, **—ly**, *adv.* nicht wieder gut zu machen, unersetzlich.

Irreprehensibl—e, *adj.*, **—y**, *adv.* untadelhaft, tadellos. **—eness**, *s.* die Tadellosigkeit.

Irrepressibl—e, *adj.*, **—y**, *adv.* ununterdrückbar, nicht zu unterdrücken, unbezähmbar.

Irreproachabl—e, *adj.*, **—y**, *adv.* untadelhaft, tadellos, unbescholten, vorwurfsfrei. **—eness**, *s.* die Tadellosigkeit.

Irreprovabl—e, **—y**, *see* Irreproachable, *etc.*

Irresistib—ility, *s.* die Unwiderstehlichkeit. **—le**, *adj.*, **—ly**, *adv.* unwiderstehlich.

Irresolut—e, *adj.*, **—ely**, *adv.* unschlüssig, unentschlossen, schwankend. **—eness**, **—ion**, *s.* die Unentschlossenheit, Unschlüssigkeit.

Irresolvable, *adj.* unauflösbar, unlöslich.

Irrespective, *adj.*, **—ly**, *adv.* ohne Rücksicht; — of, ohne Rücksicht auf (*acc.*), abgesehen von.

Irresponsib—ility, *s.* die Unverantwortlichkeit. — **—le**, *adj.*, **—ly**, *adv.* unverantwortlich; nicht verfügungsfähig, unzurechnungsfähig (*Law*).

Irretentive, *adj.* nicht festhaltend, nicht behaltend, schwach (*of memory*).

Irretrievabl—e, *adj.*, **—y**, *adv.* unersetzlich, unwiederbringlich, rettungslos. **—eness**, *s.* die Unersetzlichkeit.

Irreveren—ce, *s.* die Unehrerbietigkeit, Mißachtung. **—t**, *adj.*, **—tly**, *adv.* unehrerbietig.

Irreversibl—e, *adj.*, **—y**, *adv.* unumstößlich, unwiderruflich.

Irrevocabl—e, *adj.*, **—y**, *adv.* unwiderruflich; unabänderlich (*as a doom*). **—eness**, *s.* die Unwiderruflichkeit.

Irrigat—e, *v.a.* bewässern. **—ion**, *s.* die Bewässerung.

Irrita—bility, *s.* die Reizbarkeit. **—ble**, *adj.*, **—bly**, *adv.* reizbar. **—bleness**, *see* —bility. **—nt**, I. *adj.* aufreizend. II. *s.* das Reizmittel. **—te**, *v.a.* (an)reizen; (make angry) reizen, erzürnen, ärgern (at a th., über eine S.); entzünden (*a wound*). **—tion**, *s.* die Reizung; die Entzündung (*of a wound*); die Reizung, Aufregung, Erbitterung (*fig.*).

Irrupti—on, *s.* der Einbruch, Einfall. **—ve**, *adj.* (her)einbrechend.

Is, *3d sing. of* Be, ist; wird; it — I, ich bin es; it — not for me to . . ., es geziemt mir nicht, zu . . .; there — no man who . . ., es giebt keinen Menschen, welcher . . .; that — to say, das heißt; how — it that . . .? woher kommt es, daß? how — she? wie geht es ihr? wie befindet sie sich?

Isinglass, *s.* der Fischleim, die Hausenblase.

Isl—and, *s.* die Insel, das Eiland. **—ander**, *s.* der Inselbewohner. **—e**, *s.* das Eiland, die Insel (*poet.*). **—et**, *s.* das Inselchen.

Iso—bar, *s.* die Isobare, Linie des gleichen Luftdruckes. **—chromatic**, *adj.* gleichfarbig. **—chronal**, **—chronous**, *adj.* gleichzeitig, isochronisch. **—chronism**, *s.* die Gleichzeitigkeit. **—clinic**, *adj.* isoklinisch (*Magnet.*). **—dynamic**, *adj.* gleichkräftig. **—meric**, *adj.* gleichgeteilt gleichteilig, isomerisch. **—merism**, *s.* die Isomerie. **—metric(al)**, *adj.* isometrisch. **—morphism**, *s.* die Gleichgestaltigkeit. **—morphous**, *adj.* gleichgestaltet. **—perimetrical**, *adj.* gleichen Umfang habend. **—perimetry**, *s.* die Umfangsgleichheit. **—sceles**, *adj.* gleichschenkelig. **—therm**, *s.* die Isotherme, Linie gleicher mittlerer Jahreswärme. **—thermal**, *adj.* von gleichem Wärmegrade; —thermal lines, Linien von gleicher mittlerer Jahreswärme, Isothermen.

Isolat—e, *v.a.* vereinzeln, vereinsamen, absondern; isolieren (*Phys.*). **—ion**, *s.* die Abgesondertheit; die Absonderung, Vereinsamung.

Issue, I. *s.* das Heraus-gehen, -kommen, -strömen (*of water, etc.*); der Fluß, Abfluß, Abgang (*of blood*); (passage out) der Ausgang, Ausweg die Erlassung, der Erlaß (*of orders*); (publication) die Verkündigung; die Ausgabe, das Herausgeben (*of shares, notes, a loan, a newspaper, books, etc.*); (progeny) Kinder, die Nachkommenschaft; das Austeilen (*of provisions, powder, etc.*); (result) der Ausgang, Erfolg, die Folge, das Ende, Ergebnis; die Schlußverhandlung (*Law*); der Ausspruch (*of a jury*); das Fontanell (*Surg.*); to die without —, kinderlos *or* ohne Leibeserben *or* Nachkommenschaft sterben; to join — with a p., jemandes Meinung bestreiten, das Gegenteil von einem behaupten; here we must join — with him, hier müssen wir von ihm abweichen; at —, streitig, strittig; im Widerspruch, uneinig; point at —, der strittige Punkt, Gegenstand des Streites; that is the question at —, das ist die streitige Frage; the matter lies at —, die Sache ist in der Schwebe; side —s, nebensächliche Punkte. II. *v.a.* aus-, er-lassen, ergehen lassen (*an order, writ, proclamation, decree*); ausgeben, emittieren (*bills, money, etc.*); (her)ausgeben, austeilen (*provisions, etc.*). III. *v.n.* heraus-kommen, -fließen, -gehen; (rush out) hervorbrechen, ausfallen; (spring) herkommen, entspringen; abstammen (*as offspring*); (end) ausgehen, sich endigen; auslaufen (*Law*). —**less**, *adj.* ohne Nachkommenschaft. —**r**, *s.* der Aussteller (*of bills*); Erlasser (*of orders*). *Comp.* —-**department**, *s.* die Abteilung für Banknoten-Ausgabe. —-**pea**, *s.* die Fontanellerbse (*Med.*).

Isthmus, *s.* die Landenge, der Isthmus.

It, *pron.* es; **1.** (*as nom.*) — is not your fault, Ihre Schuld ist es nicht; — is I, ich bin es. **2.** (*as acc.*) give — to me, gieb es mir; I remember —, ich erinnere mich dessen; we can walk —, wir können die Strecke *or* den Weg zu Fuß zurücklegen; from, of —, davon; for —, dafür; do you know any remedy for —? wissen Sie ein Mittel da-für, -gegen? **3.** (*as subject of imp. verb*) — rains, snows, es regnet, schneit. **4.** (*as grammatical subject to introduce a sentence*) — is glorious to see a great man, es ist herrlich, einen großen Mann zu sehen. **5.** (*in emphatic statements*) — is the men of Uri who . . ., die Urner sind es, die . . .; — is on that account that he was praised by all, eben deshalb (*or* aus eben diesem Grunde) wurde er von allen gepriesen. **6.** how is — with your headache? wie steht's mit deinem Kopfweh? what a night I've had of —! was habe ich für eine erbärmliche Nacht gehabt! we will make a night of —, wir wollen uns eine lustige Nacht machen! **7.** (*pleonastically after v.n.*) to lord — over a p., den Herrn spielen gegen einen; to foot —, tanzen (*coll.*); to go —, es wagen (*coll.*); go —! nur Mut! drauf los! —**s**, I. *poss. pron. 3 sing. neuter*, sein, dessen. *Comp.* —**self**, *pron.* es selbst, selbst, sich; of —self, von selbst; in —self, in sich, an sich; by —self, für sich allein, ohne Hilfe; (apart) besonders.

Itch, I. *s.* das (Haut-)Jucken; die Krätze (*Med.*); *see* —ing. II. *v.n.* jucken; to — after, gelüsten nach; my fingers — to be at him, ich habe große Lust, ihn durchzuprügeln. —**ing**, I. *adj.*; an —ing palm, eine hohle Hand. II. *s.* das Jucken; das Gelüste (*fig.*). —**y**, *adj.* krätzig.

Item, I. *adv.* desgleichen, ferner auch. II. *s.* die Einzelheit, der Gegenstand; der Artikel, Posten; —s of interest, interessante Punkte. III. *v.a.* notieren (*obs.*).

Iterat—e, *v.a.* wiederholen, von neuem vorbringen. —**ion**, *s.* die Wiederholung.

Itinera—ncy, *s.* das Umherwandern. —**nt**, I. *adj.* wandernd, (herum)reisend; —nt judges, herumziehende Richter; —nt gleemen, fahrende Sänger. II. *s.* der Reisende; (—nt preacher) der Wanderprediger. —**ry**, I. *s.* das Reisebuch, die Reisebeschreibung; das Reisegebet (*R. C.*). II. *adj.* die Reise betreffend.

Iv—ied, *adj.* mit Efeu bedeckt. —**y**, *s.* der Efeu; ground —y, Erdefeu; overrun with —y, efeuumsponnen, efeuumwoben. *Comp.* —**y-clad**, *adj.* efeubekränzt. —**y-mantled**, *adj.* von Efeu umschlungen, efeuumwoben, efeuumrankt.

Ivory, I. *s.* das Elfenbein. II. *adj.* elfenbeinern.

J

J, j, *s.* das J, j; *abbr.* J. C. = Jesus Christ, Jesus Christus.

Jabber, I. *v.a.* undeutlich sprechen. II. *v.a. & n.* schnattern, plappern. III. *s.* das Geschnatter, Geplapper, Gewäsch.

Jackal, *s.* der Schakal; der Handlanger (*fig.*).

Jackdaw, *s.* die Dohle. —'s nest, Dohlennest.

Jacket, *s.* die Jacke; steam —, der Dampf-, Zylinder-mantel; potatoes in their —s, Kartoffeln mit den Schalen, Pellkartoffeln.

Jact—ation, *s.* das Werfen, Schleudern; das Durchschütteln des Körpers. —**itation**, *s.* das Herumwerfen des Körpers, die heftige Bewegung, Unruhe; die Großsprecherei.

[1]**Jade**, I. *s.* die (Schind-)Mähre; (wench) das Weibsbild; (girl) wildes Mädchen, die Dirne. II. *v.a.* abmatten, ermüden.

[2]**Jade**, *s.* der Nierenstein, Nephrit.

Jag, I. *s.* die Zacke, Kerbe; (prick) der Stich (*dial.*). II. *v.a.* kerben, (aus-)zacken; stechen; —ged leaves, gezähnelte Blätter. —**gedness**, *s.* das Ausgezackte; die Unebenheit. —**gy**, *adj.* zackig, gekerbt; uneben.

Jaguar, *s.* der Jaguar.

Jail, *s.* der Kerker, das Gefängnis. —**er**, —**or**, *s.* der Gefängniswärter, Kerkermeister; —er's fees, das Schließgeld. *Comp.* —**bird**, *s.* der Zuchthäusler, der vorbestrafte Verbrecher. —-**delivery**, *s.* die Gefängnis-Ausleerung. —-**fever**, *s.* das Kerkerfieber.

Jalap, *s.* die Jalapen-, Purgier-wurzel.

[1]**Jam**, *s.* das Eingemachte, (süße) Fruchtgelee, die Obstkonserve, (süße) Marmelade.

[2]**Jam**, *v.* I. *a.* hinein-zwängen, -klammern, einkeilen; festtreten (*Agr.*); bekneifen (*Naut.*). II. *s.* das Quetschen, die Einzwängung; das Gedränge, Volksgewühl.

Jamb, *s.* der Pfosten (*of a door*); *pl.* die Einfassung.

Jangl—e, I. *v.n.* zanken; (sound discordantly) mißtönen, rasseln, kreischen. II. *v.a.* unharmonisch klingen lassen. III. *s.* der Mißklang; (wrangling) das Gezänk. —**ing**, I. *adj.* mißtönend, schrill, rauh. II. *s. see* —e, III.

Janitor, *s.* der Pförtner; der Pedell, Pudel (*students' sl.*).

Janizary, **Janissary**, *pl.* der Janitschar.

Jansenis—m, *s.* der Jansenismus. —**t**, *s.* der Jansenist.

January, *s.* der Januar.

Japan, I. *s.* Japan (*see Index of Names*); (varnish) der Lackfirnis; (—ned work) lackierte Arbeit. II. *v.a.* lackieren; —ned goods, lackierte Sachen; —ned tin ware, lackiertes Weißblech. —**ner**, *s.* der Lackierer. —**ning**, *s.* das Lackieren.

[1]**Jar**, I. *v.n.* schnarren, klappern, knarren, rasseln; schwirren (*as a violin-string*); streiten; to — **upon** the ear, das Ohr unangenehm berühren, mißtönig klingen; to — **with**, widerstreiten, in scharfem Gegensatz stehen (zu). II. *v.a.* rütteln unangenehm berühren. III. *s.* das Schwirren, Knarren; der Mißton; (strife) der Streit, die Mißhelligkeit.

[2]**Jar**, *s.* der Krug; der Topf (*of pickles, etc.*) Leyden —, die Leydener Flasche.

[3]**Jar**, *s.*; a—, on the —, angelehnt, halb offen.

[1]**Jargon**, *s.* das Kauderwelsch; die Kunstsprache (*of professions*); der Jargon.

[2]**Jargon**, *s.* der Zirkon, grauer Hyazinth (*Min.*) —**elle**, *s.* die Jargonelle, Frühbirne.

Jasmine, *s.* der Jasmin.

Jasper, *s.* der Jaspis.
Jaundice, *s.* die Gelbsucht. **—d**, *adj.* gelbsüchtig; scheelsüchtig, neidisch; (prejudiced) vorher, zuvor eingenommen; with a —d eye, mit befangenem Auge, durch gefärbte Brillen; (enviously) mit scheelen Blicken.
Jaunt, I. *v.n.* herumstreifen, umher-laufen, -fahren, bummeln (*coll.*). II. *s.* der Ausflug, die Wanderung; to take a —, spazieren fahren, eine Fahrt *or* Tour machen. **—ily**, *adv. see* —y. **—iness**, *s.* die Schmuckheit; die Lustigkeit; die Leichtigkeit im Auftreten und Bewegen. **—y**, *adj.* munter; lebhaft; flott; (smart) schmuck; elegant.
Javelin, *s.* der Wurfspieß, der Ger.
Jaw, I. *s.* der Kinnbacken, Kiefer; das Maul; (talk) das Reden, Schimpfen, Geträtsch (*vulg.*). II. *v.a.* ausschimpfen, anschnauzen (*vulg.*). III. *v.n.* (chatter) schwatzen; schwadronieren; Schimpfreden ausstoßen. **—ed**, *adj.* (*in comp.* =) mit Kinnbacken. **—ing**, *s.* das Geschelte, Anfahren. **—s**, *pl.* der Rachen, Schlund; —s of death, hell, der Todesrachen, Höllenschlund. *Comp.* **—-bone**, *s.* der Kinnbacken.
[1]**Jay**, *s.* der (Eichel-)Häher; schlechter Schauspieler, Stümper (*Theat. sl.*); liederliches Frauenzimmer (*obs.*).
[2]**Jay**, *s.* der Buchstabe Jot (*obs.*).
Jealous, *adj.*, **—ly**, *adv.* eifersüchtig (of a p., auf einen); (suspicious) argwöhnisch, mißtrauisch; besorgt; to be — **of** one's honour, viel auf seine Ehre halten; to be — **for** a th., eifern um eine S. (*B.*); I am — **over** you, ich eifere über euch (*B.*). **—y**, *s.* die Eifersucht; der Argwohn, das Mißtrauen; der Eifer (for, für); (anxiety) die Besorgnis (um), ängstliche Furcht (vor); **petty** —y, Eifersüchtelei.
Jean, *s.* eine Art Barchent.
Jeer, I. *v.a. & n.* höhnen, spotten (über einen), sticheln (auf einen); he did not see that they were —ing at him, er merkte nicht, daß man seiner spottete *or* ihn verhöhnte, verspottete. II. *s.* der Spott, die Spötterei, Stichelei. **—er**, *s.* der Spötter. **—ing**, *s.* die Spötterei. **—ingly**, *adv.* spöttisch, auf höhnische Weise.
Jejune, *adj.*, **—ly**, *adv.* nüchtern, trocken, fade. **—ness**, *s.* die Nüchternheit, Trockenheit.
Jelly, I. *s.* die Gallerte, das Gelee. II. *v.n.* zu Gallerte werden, sich verdicken. **—graph**, *s.* die Gelee-Kopiermaschine. *Comp.* **—-bag**, *s.* der Geleebeutel. **—-fish**, *s.* die Qualle, Seenessel.
[1]**Jemmy**, *adj.* nett, sauber, schmuck (*sl.*).
[2]**Jemmy**, *s. see Index of names;* (tool) das Brecheisen.
Jennet, *s.* der Zelter.
Jenny, *s.* Hannchen (*see Names*); (spinning —) die Jennyspinnmaschine, der Feinspinnstuhl.
Jeopard—ize, *v.a.* gefährden, aufs Spiel setzen. **—ous**, *adj.* gewagt, gefährlich. **—y**, *s.* die Gefahr; to be, stand in —y, in Gefahr sein, stehen.
Jerboa, *s.* die Springmaus.
[1]**Jerk**, I. *s.* der plötzliche Stoß, Wurf, Ruck; (leap) der Satz; with a —, plötzlich; by —s, stoßweise, ruckweise. II. *v.a.* stoßen; (throw) fortschnellen. III. *v.n.* zusammenzucken, auffahren. **—y**, *adj.* stoßweise, ruckweise, krampfhaft; launisch.
[2]**Jerk**, *v.a.* dünn schneiden und an der Sonne trocknen (beef, Rindfleisch).
Jerkin, *s.* der Wams; (jacket) die Jacke; leather —, das Koller.
Jerry-built, *adj.* unsolide gebaut.
Jessamine, *see* Jasmine.
Jesses, *pl.* Fußbänder des Falken.
Jest, I. *s.* der Scherz, Spaß; (laughing-stock) die Zielscheibe des Scherzes; to make a —, scherzen; in —, im Spaß, scherzweise; to make a — of, über (eine S.) scherzen. II. *v.n.* scherzen, spaßen, spotten. **—er**, *s.* der Spaßvogel, Possenreißer; king's —er, der Hofnarr. **—ing**, I. *adj.* spaßhaft, zum Spaße dienend: this is no —ing matter, dies ist keine Sache zum Spaßen. II. *s.* das Scherzen, Spaßen; der Schwank. **—ingly**, *adv.* scherzweise.
[1]**Jet**, *s.* der Gagat, Jet, die Pechkohle. *Comp.* **—-black**, *adj.* pechschwarz.
[2]**Jet**, I. *v.n.* hervorragen, vorspringen. II. *v.a.* herausspeien, herausschießen, heraussprühen; der Erguß, Wurf; der Strahl; (tube) die Röhre; — of water, Wasserstrahl; — of gas, Gasstrahl. **—sam**, **—tison**, *s.* das Überbordwerfen der Güter; (goods thrown overboard) das Strand-, Wrack-gut. **—ty**, *s.* der Hafendamm, die Mole (*Hydr.*); der Vorsprung (*Arch.*).
Jewel, I. *s.* die Juwele, das (der) Juwel, das Kleinod, der Edelstein. II. *v.a.* mit Juwelen schmücken *or* versehen. **—ler**, *s.* der Juwelenhändler, Juwelier. **—ry**, **—lery**, *s.* Juwelen, Schmucksachen (*pl.*), der Schmuck, das Geschmeide. **—s**, *pl.* das Geschmeide, der Schmuck.
[1]**Jib**, *s.* der Klüver (*Naut.*).
[2]**Jib**, **Jibe**, *v.a.* die Segel umlegen (*Naut.*).
[3]**Jib**, *v.n.* scheuen; störrisch sein. **—ber**, *s.* widerspenstiges, scheues Pferd.
Jibe, *see* Gibe.
Jiffy, *s.* der Augenblick (*coll.*); in a —, in Nu (*coll.*); wait a —, wart' ein bischen! (*coll.*).
Jig, I. *s.* die Gigue (*Mus.*); lustiger Tanz (*Irish*); (trick) der Streich. II. *v.n.* eine Gigue tanzen, herumhüpfen. **—ger**, *s.* der Hüpfer, Tänzer; das Setzsieb (*Min.*); der Steertblock (*Naut.*).
Jigjog, I. *s.* der Ruck, die stoßweise Bewegung. II. *adv.* ruckweise.
Jilt, I. *s.* die Kokette. II. *v.a.* den Liebhaber *or* die Geliebte narren, mit Hoffnungen hinhalten, und ihn *or* sie nachher verabschieden, (einem) den Laufpaß geben, (ein Mädchen) sitzen lassen. III. *v.n.* kokettieren.
Jingle, I. *v.n.* klingeln, klimpern, rasseln. II. *v.a.* klingeln lassen. III. das Geklingel, Gerassel; das Reimgeklingel (*of verses*).
Jink, *v.n.* sich schnell *or* leicht bewegen. **—s**, *pl.* ausgelassene Lustigkeit; in high —s, in übermütiger Laune, ganz aus dem Häuschen (*coll.*)
Job, I. *s.* die kleine (Lohn-)Arbeit; (work done by the —) die Akkordarbeit, Stückarbeit; (piece of business) die Verrichtung, Sache, das Geschäft; (undertaking) aufgegebene Arbeit, das Pensum; his being put into that office was a —, er erlangte den Posten durch besondere Privatvergünstigung; that was a —, das war ein schweres Stück Arbeit (*coll.*); to work by the —, akkordweise arbeiten; this — has brought me in a good sum, dies Geschäft hat mir viel Geld eingebracht; to make a good — of it, etwas ordentlich machen; it is a good — that, es ist ein wahres Glück, daß (*coll.*); it is a bad —! es ist eine schlimme Sache, es ist nichts damit zu machen; to do odd —s, gelegentliche Stückarbeiten, mancherlei Geschäfte verrichten; horses let on —, Pferde (auf längere Zeit) ausgeliehen. II. *adj.;* — lot, die Ramschware; — horses, Mietpferde; — printer, der Akzidenzdrucker; — work, Akkordarbeit. III. *v.a.* (hire) mieten; (hire out) vermieten; im Ramsch kaufen. IV. *v.n.* Arbeit in Akkord nehmen; mit Staatspapieren handeln, mäkeln (*C. L.*); Pferde 2c. vermieten; Pferde 2c. mieten; to — in bills, Wechselreiterei treiben. **—ber**, *s.* der Stückarbeiter, Handlanger, Lohn- *or* Akkord-arbeiter; *see* —-master; der Makler, Zwischenhändler, Aktienhändler (*C.L.*). **—bery**, *s.* das Maklertum, Maklerwesen; a piece of —bery, eine abgekartete Geschichte. **—bing**, I. *s.* das Akkordarbeiten; —bings, kleine gelegentliche Arbeiten. II. *adj.;* —bing politician, politischer Intrigant. *Comp.* **—bing-business**, *s.* das Maklergeschäft. **—cobbler**, *s.* der Flickschuster. **—-horse**, *s.* das Mietpferd. **—-master**, *s.* der Pferdevermieter, der Mietwagenbesitzer.
Jockey, I. *s.* der Jockei, Reitknecht; (cheat) der Betrüger. II. *v.a.* betrügen, prellen; (jostle) anrennen (beim Reiten); hereinlegen (*sl.*); the

minister had been thoroughly —ed, der Minister war gründlich hereingelegt (*sl.*).

Joc—ose, *adj.*, **—osely**, *adv.* scherzhaft, heiter; (given to jokes) scherzlustig; (facetious) drollig, spaßhaft; scherzhaft (*of style*). **—oseness**, **—ularity**, *s.* die Scherzhaftigkeit, Lustigkeit. **—ular**, *adj.*, **—ularly**, *adv.* spaßhaft, scherzhaft, lustig. **—und**, *adj.*, **—undly**, *adv.* fröhlich, munter, lustig.

Joe, *s.* der Geliebte, Schatz (*Scotch*).

Jog, I. *v.a.* (mit dem Ellenbogen) stoßen, rütteln; to — a p.'s memory, dem Gedächtnis nachhelfen. II. *v.n.;* to — along, on, sich langsam fortbewegen, dahinschlendern; I must be —ging, ich muß weg (*coll.*). III. *s.* der leichte Stoß; das Stoßen (*of a carriage*). *Comp.* **—-trot**, I. *s.* der langsame Schaukeltrab; der Schlendrian. II. *adj.* schlendernd; einförmig, schlafmützig (*fig.*); in a —-trot way, in behaglich schlenderndem Gang.

Joggle, I. *v.a.* leicht schütteln, rütteln; verschränken, verzahnen. II. *v.n.* sich schütteln. III. *s.* die Treppenfuge (*Build.*); der Falz, die Nut (*in stone*). *Comp.* **—-beam**, *s.* der verzahnte Balken. **—-joint**, *s.* feste Fuge. **—-piece**, *s.* die Dachstuhlsäule. **—-work**, *s.* das Mauerwerk mit verzahnten Fugen.

Join, I. *v.a.* verbinden, vereinigen, zusammenfügen (one th. to another, eine Sache mit einer andern); (attach o.s. to s.o.) sich einem zugesellen, beitreten (a society, einem Vereine); to — in marriage, ehelich verbinden, vermählen; to — the army, in die Armee eintreten; to — battle, den Kampf beginnen; to — company (with), sich anschließen; to — issue with a p., jemandes Meinung bekämpfen, von einem in seiner Ansicht abweichen; —ed masonry, verbundene Mauerarbeit; to — one's regiment, zu seinem Regiment stoßen; to — by forging, anschmieden; to — a ship, ein Schiff einholen, zu einem Schiffe stoßen; — swords! bindet die Klingen! (*students' duel*). II. *v.n.* sich verbinden, sich vereinigen; (adjoin) anstoßen, angrenzen; to — **in**, sich (einer S.) anschließen, sich beteiligen an (einer S.), eine S. mitmachen; to — in praise of s.o., in jemands Lob einstimmen; to — in an undertaking, sich zu einem Unternehmen verbinden; I — **with** you in thinking that . . ., ich teile (völlig) Ihre Ansicht, daß . . . III. *s.* die Verbindungsstelle, Fuge; die Verbindungslinie (*Math.*); der Durchschnittspunkt (*Math.*). **—der**, *s.* die Vereinigung zweier Sachen in einem Prozeß; —der in demurrer, die Vereinigung beider Parteien über die Zulässigkeit eines Rechtseinwandes. **—er**, *s.* der Tischler, Schreiner. **—ery**, *s.* die Tischlerei; die Tischlerarbeit. **—t**, I. *s.* die Verbindung, Fuge; der Stoß (*Carp.*); der Schienenstoß (*Railw.*); die Naht (*in tins*); das Scharnier (*Mech.*); das Gelenk (*Anat.*); der Knoten (*Bot.*); das Fleischstück, die Bratenkeule (*Butch.*); —ts, die Deckelbänder (*Bookb.*); ball and socket —t, das Kugelgelenk; to put out of —t, aus den Fugen bringen, (one's arm, sich (*dat.*) den Arm) verrenken; out of —, aus Rand und Band (*fig.*); to put a p.'s nose out of —, einen aus dem Sattel heben. III. *v.a.* zusammenfügen; (divide) nach den Gelenken zerschneiden, zergliedern. III. *adj.* vereint, verbunden; zusammengesetzt; (united in interest) gemeinschaftlich, Mit-; —t authorship, gemeinsame Verfasserschaft; —t editorship, die Mitherausgeberschaft. **—ted**, *adj.* gegliedert; knotig (*Bot.*); (divided) zergliedert; —ted doll, die Gliederpuppe. **—tly**, *adv.* gemeinschaftlich, vereint, mit einander, sämmtlich. **—ture**, *s.* das Wittum, Leibgedinge. *Comp.* **—t-account**, *s.* die gemeinschaftliche Rechnung. **—t-Board**, *s.* der von den Universitäten Oxford und Cambridge gemeinsam ernannte und aus Mitgliedern beider Universitäten zusammengesetzte Ausschuß zur Abhaltung (freiwilliger) Prüfungen an den besten höheren Knaben- und Mädchen-schulen Englands (joint board examinations). **—t-chair**, *s.* der Stoßstuhl (*Railw.*). **—t-heir**, *s.* der Miterbe. **—t-heiress**, *s.* die Miterbin. **—t(ing)-rule**, *s.* die Schmiege. **—t-labourer**, *s.* der Mitarbeiter. **—t-owner**, *s.* der Mitbesitzer, Miteigentümer. **—t-proprietor**, *s.* der Miteigentümer. **—t-ring**, *s.* der Doppelring. **—t-stock**, I. *s.* zusammengeschossenes Kapital. II. *attrib.;* —t-stock bank, die Bankgesellschaft auf Aktien; —t-stock company, die Aktiengesellschaft (mit unbeschränkter Haftpflicht). **—t-stool**, *s.* der Klappstuhl. **—t-tenancy**, *s.* der Mitbesitz. **—t-tenant**, *s.* der Mitbesitzer.

Joist, I. *s.* der Querbalken; binding —, der Hauptbalken. II. *v.a.* mit Querbalken belegen.

Jok—e, I. *s.* der Scherz, Spaß; in —e, im Scherze, aus Spaß; it 's all a —e, es ist nur Spaß; to crack —es, Scherze machen; to see *or* take a —e, Spaß verstehen; he cannot take a —e, er versteht keinen Spaß, läßt nicht mit sich spaßen; to play a practical —e upon a p., einem einen Schabernack antun *or* einen Streich spielen. II. *v.a.* aufziehen, necken (a p. about a thing, einen über etwas). III. *v.n.* scherzen, spaßen; to —e with a p., mit einem spaßen. **—er**, *s.* der Witzbold, Spaßvogel. **—ing**, I. *adj.*, **—ingly**, *adv.* scherzend, spaßhaft. II. *s.;* —ing apart! Scherz beseite!

Jole, *see* Jowl; der Fischkopf.

Joll—ification, *s.* die Lustbarkeit; (carouse) das Trinkgelage. **—ily**, *adv. see* —y. **—iness**, **—ity**, *s.* die Lustigkeit, Munterkeit, Fröhlichkeit. **—y**, I. *adj.* lustig, munter, fidel; (fine, nice) schön, hübsch (*obs.*); (pleasant) famos (*sl.*). II. *adv.* sehr, riesig, außerordentlich (*sl.*).

Jolly-boat, *s.* die Jolle, kleinstes Ruderboot.

Jolt, I. *v.a. & n.* schütteln, stoßen, rütteln. II. *s.* der plötzliche Stoß. **—ing**, I. *adj.* stoßend, rüttelnd, holperig. II. *s.* das Stoßen.

Jonquil, *s.* die Jonquille.

Jorum, *s.* großer Topf, großes Trinkgefäß und dessen Inhalt, die Bowle.

Joss, *s.* chinesischer Götze. *Comp.* **—-house**, *s.* der chinesische Tempel. **—-stick**, *s.* das Räucherrohr in chinesischen Tempeln.

Jostl—e, *v.a. & n.* anstoßen, anrennen; to —e out, off, hinaus-, weg-stoßen, verdrängen; to —e (against) a p., einen anrempeln (*students' sl.*).

Jot, I. *s.* das Jota, Pünktchen; not a —, nicht das Geringste, kein Tüttelchen *or* Bischen. II. *v.a.* (— down) flüchtig hinwerfen, kurz skizzieren. **—ting**, *s.* die Bemerkung, kurze Notiz; university —tings, kurze Universitätsnachrichten.

Journ—al, I. *s.* (diary) das Tagebuch, Journal; (periodical) die Zeitschrift; das Tageblatt; das Journal (*C.L.*, *also Naut.*); der Zapfen (*Mach.*). **—alese**, *s.* die Sprache der Zeitungsschreiber, Zeitungs-(Englisch, *etc.*). **—alism**, *s.* das Zeitungswesen, Zeitschriftenwesen; (—alist's profession) die (Tages-)Schriftstellerei, das Schriftstellertum. **—alist**, *s.* der Zeitungsschreiber, Tagesschriftsteller, Journalist. **—alistic**, *adj.* journalistisch. **—ey**, I. *s.* die Reise; the double —ey, die Hin- und Rück-Reise; a day's —ey, eine Tagereise. II. *v.n.* reisen, wandern. **—eying**, *s.* das Reisen. *Comp.* **—eyman**, I. *s.* der Tagelöhner (*obs.*); (workman) der (Handwerks-) Geselle, der wandernde Handwerksbursche; (mechanic) der Handwerker. II. *attrib.:* —eyman printer, der Buchdruckergehülfe.

Joust, I. *s.* das Turnier, Turnierspiel. II. *v.n.* turnieren. **—ing**, *adj.* Turnier-.

Jovial, *adj.*, **—ly**, *adv.* frohsinnig, heiter, jovial. **—ity**, *s.* die Lustigkeit, Jovialität, der Frohsinn.

Jowl, *s.* der Backen; cheek by —, dicht neben einander. **—er**, *s.* der Spürhund.

Joy, I. *s.* die Freude; (gaiety) die Fröhlichkeit, Lustbarkeit; it gives me great —, es freut mich sehr; to wish s.o. — of, einem Glück wünschen, gratulieren zu; to leap for —, vor Freude hüpfen. II. *v.n.* sich freuen, entzückt sein (*poet.*). III. *v.a.* erfreuen, erheitern (*obs.*). **—ful**, *adj.*, **—fully**, *adv.* freudvoll, freudig; (rejoicing) sich freuend. **—fulness**, *s.* die Fröhlichkeit. **—less**, *adj.*, **—lessly**, *adv.* freudlos, freudenleer; (dispiriting) unerfreulich. **—lessness**, *s.* die Freudlosigkeit. **—ous**, *adj.*, **—ously**, *adv.* freudevoll, froh, erfreulich. **—ousness**, *s.* die Freudigkeit.

Jubil—ant, *adj.* jubelnd, frohlockend. **—ate**, I. *s.* (der Sonntag *or* der Psalm) Jubilate. II. *v.n.* jubeln. **—ation**, *s.* das Jubeln. **—ee**, *s.* das Jubelfest, die Jubelfeier (*50th, etc. anniversary*) das Jubiläum; das Halljahr (*of the Jews*); das Jubeljahr (*R.C.*).

Judge, I. *s.* der Richter (*Law*); (one who —s) der Schiedsrichter, der Beurteiler; (connoisseur) der Kenner, Kunstverständige; (expert) der Sachverständige; to be a — of, sich auf (eine Sache) verstehen; the Book of —s, das Buch der Richter (*B.*); I am no — of these things, ich habe kein Urteil über diese Sachen; you shall be — of this affair, Sie sollen selbst darüber entscheiden; as God is my —! so wahr Gott mich richten soll! — in criminal cases, Kriminalrichter. II. *v.n.* urteilen (from, nach); to — of one man by another, von einem Manne auf den andern schließen; to — of a p. from his conduct, über eine Person nach ihrem Benehmen urteilen. III. *v.a.* richten; beurteilen, (über einen) urteilen; (regard) ansehen (für), halten für. **—ship**, *s.* das Richteramt. **—ment**, *see* Judgment.

Judg(e)ment, *s.* das Urteil (*also Log.*); (sentence) der Urteilsspruch; (right of —) die Gerichtsbarkeit, das Gericht; (faculty of —) die Beurteilungskraft, Urteilskraft, der Verstand; (punishment) die (göttliche) Bestrafung; (opinion) die Beurteilung, Meinung; a man of great —, ein scharfsinniger Mann; he acted with great —, er handelte sehr vernünftig *or* mit großer Einsicht; to give —, das Urteil sprechen; to pass — upon, seine Ansicht über (einen, rc.) sagen, das Urteil über (*acc.*) aussprechen; to sit in —, zu Gericht sitzen; day of —, the last —, das jüngste Gericht; according to my —, meiner Meinung nach; his — will decide how I shall act, seine Entscheidung wird meine Handlungsweise bestimmen. *Comp.* **—-day**, *s.* der jüngste Tag. **—-hall**, *s.* die Gerichtshalle. **—-seat**, *s.* der Richterstuhl.

Judic—ature, *s.* (court of justice) der Gerichtshof; (jurisdiction) die Gerichtsbarkeit; (administration of justice) die Rechtspflege; the High Court of —ature, das Oberlandesgericht. **—ial**, *adj.*, **—ially**, *adv.* gerichtlich, richterlich; —ial acts, Aktenstücke; —ial proceedings, Gerichtsverhandlungen; —ial procedure, richterliches Verfahren; —ial sale, gerichtlicher Verkauf. **—iary**, I. *adj.* gerichtlich, richterlich. II. *s.* das Gerichtswesen. **—ious**, *adj.*, **—iously**, *adv.* verständig, vernünftig, klug, einsichtsvoll, gescheit. **—iousness**, *s.* die Klugheit, die Einsicht.

Jug, I. *s.* der Krug. II. *v.a.* dämpfen, in der eignen Brühe schmoren (*Cook.*); —ged hare, der Hasenpfeffer (*Cook.*).

Juggernaut, *s.* etwas (Brauch, Gedanke), dem einer sich blind opfert oder dem einer geopfert wird.

Juggl—e, I. *v.n.* gaukeln, Kunststücke machen; (cheat) hinterlistig verfahren. II. *s.* die Gaukelei; der Betrug. **—er**, *s.* der Gaukler, Taschenspieler; der Betrüger. **—ery**, *s.* die Gaukelei; die Betrügerei. **—ing**, I. *s.* das Gaukelspiel; die Betrügerei. II. *adj.*, **—ingly**, *adv.* betrügerisch, täuschend; gauklerisch.

Jugular, *adj.* zur Gurgel gehörig, Gurgel=; — vein, die Gurgelader.

Juic—e, *s.* der Saft; lemon —e, Zitronensaft. **—iness**, *s.* die Saftigkeit. **—y**, *adj.* saftig.

Jujube, *s.* die Brustbeere (*Bot.*); die Brustbeeren-Paste, das Bonbon (*Conf.*).

Julep, *s.* der Kühltrank, Julep(p).

July, *s.* der Juli; the month of —, der Monat Juli.

Jumbl—e, I. *v.a.* unordentlich unter einander werfen, vermengen. II. *v.n.* unordentlich gemengt sein; zusammengerüttelt werden (into a th., in eine S.). III. *s.* der Wirrwarr, Mischmasch; der Ring (*Conf.*). IV. *attrib.*; a —e sale, ein Verkauf im Ramsch. **—er**, *s.* der Verwirrer. **—ingly**, *adv.* auf eine unordentliche, ungeschickte Weise.

Jump, I. *v.n.* springen, hüpfen; (jolt) stoßen; (agree) übereinstimmen, einerlei Meinung sein; to — **at** an offer, ein Anerbieten freudig annehmen *or* mit beiden Händen ergreifen; to — at a conclusion, eine vorschnelle Schlußfolgerung ziehen, vorschnell folgern *or* schließen; to — **down**, abspringen; hinunterspringen; to — **out** of one's skin, aus der Haut fahren; to — **over**, *see* — II.; to — **up**, aufspringen. II. *v.a.* hin-über-springen, -setzen; (skip) überspringen; the train —ed the metals, der Zug kam aus dem Geleise *or* entgleiste. III. *s.* der Sprung, Satz; das Wagnis (*poet.*); to give a —, einen Satz machen, einen Sprung tun; the horse would not take the —, das Pferd wollte nicht springen *or* über (den Graben, Zaun, *etc.*) setzen. **—er**, *s.* der Springer; eine Art Methodist; der Steinbohrer (*Quarrying*); die Käsemade (*Ent.*). *Comp.* **—ing-hare**, *s.* der Springhase. **—ing-pole**, *s.* die Springstange.

Junct—ion, *s.* die Verbindung, Vereinigung; die Berührung (*Surv.*, *Geom.*); (place of —ion) der Vereinigungspunkt, Knotenpunkt (*Railw.*). **—ure**, *s.* der Verbindungspunkt; die Vereinigung, Fuge; kritischer Augenblick; der Zeitpunkt; —ures of time, Zeitumstände. *Comp.* **—ion-line**, *s.* die Verbindungsbahn (*Railw.*).

June, *s.* der Juni; the month of —, der Monat Juni.

Jungle, *s.* das Dschungel, Sumpfdickicht, Schilfrohrdickicht, der Sumpfwald.

Junior, I. *adj.* jünger; — class, — year, die dritte Klasse, das dritte Jahr (*Amer. Univ.*); — department (of a school), Vorschule, nebst Unterklassen (II–IV) der Hauptschule, Unterstufe einer größeren Schule (*Eng.*); — partner, jüngerer Teilhaber, Associe; — securities, später ausgegebene Aktien. II. *s.* der (die) Jüngere; der tiefer Stehende; der Student im dritten Jahre (*Amer. Univ.*); he is my — (in office), er ist nach mir ins Amt gekommen; he is my — by some years, er ist einige Jahre jünger als ich; my —s, Leute die jünger sind als ich.

Juniper, *s.* der Wachholder.

[1]**Junk**, *s.*; Chinese —, die Dschunke, großes chinesisches Boot.

[2]**Junk**, *s.* altes zerhacktes Tauwerk (*Naut.*); Kehricht, Überbleibsel; zähes Pökelfleisch (*in ships*).

[3]**Junk**, *s.* der Klumpen, das dicke Stück; *see* Chunk.

Junket, I. *s.* die dicke, geronnene Milch; (dainty) der Leckerbissen (*obs.*). II. *v.n.* schmausen, ein Fest feiern; —ing party, das Picknick (*coll.*).

Junt—a, *s.* die Ratsversammlung, (spanische) Junta. **—o**, *s.* die geheime Verbindung, Kabale.

Jurassic, *adj.* jurassisch, den Jura(kalk) betreffend.

Juris—diction, *s.* die Rechtsprechung; die Gerichtsbarkeit; (extent of —diction) der Gerichtsbezirk. **—prudence**, *s.* die Rechts-wissenschaft, -gelehrsamkeit, Jurisprudenz. **—prudential**, *adj.* rechtswissenschaftlich. **—t**, *s.* der Rechtsgelehrte Jurist.

Jur—or, *s.* der Geschwor(e)ne. **—y**, *s.* das Schwurgericht, Geschworenengericht, die Geschworenen; die Preisrichter (bei Ausstellungen); das Preisrichterkollegium, Preisgericht; grand (petty) —y, große (kleine) Jury. *Comp.* **—y-box**, *s.* die Geschworenenbank. **—yman**, *see* —or.

Jury-mast, *s.* der Notmast.

Just, I. *adj.* gerecht, rechtschaffen; (fair) billig; (pious) fromm; (impartial) gerecht, unparteiisch; (faithful) getreu; (true) der Wahrheit gemäß, wahr; (accurate) genau; (due) gehörig, recht, passend; that is perfectly —, das ist ganz recht; my — right, mein volles Recht; — distance, richtige Entfernung; to be — towards s.o., gerecht gegen einen handeln; the —, die Gerechten. II. *adv.* (exactly) gerade, genau; eben (*of time*); (nearly) fast, beinahe; (barely) mit genauer Not; — as, eben, gerade als; — as I do, eben so *or* genau so wie ich; I met him — as I . . ., ich traf ihn gerade, als ich . . .; — as large, ebenso groß; — now, eben jetzt, gerade; I spoke to him — now, soeben habe ich mit ihm gesprochen; these articles won't sell — now, gerade jetzt *or* augenblicklich lassen sich diese Artikel nicht verkaufen; — enough, eben genug; but —, eben erst; — tell me, sage mir einmal; — let me see, laß 'mal sehen, zeig' einmal her! **—ice**, *s.* die Gerechtigkeit (*of people and things*); die Billigkeit (*of a claim*); (judge) der Richter; das Recht; (deserts) gerechte, verdiente Strafe; (rectitude) die Redlichkeit; —ice of the peace (*abbrev.* J. P.), der Friedensrichter; to administer —ice, die Gerichtsbarkeit handhaben; to bring to —ice, gerichtlich belangen; to see —ice done to a p., einem Recht verschaffen; to do s.o. —ice, einem Recht *or* Gerechtigkeit widerfahren lassen; to do —ice to a dish, einer Speise tüchtig zusprechen, einem Gericht Ehre antun; in —ice, von Rechtswegen. **—iceship**, *s.* das Richteramt. **—ifiable**, *adj.*, **—ifiably**, *adv.* zu rechtfertigen; (lawful) rechtmäßig; —ifiable homicide, zu rechtfertigende Tötung. **—ifiableness**, *s.* die Rechtmäßigkeit; die Entschuldbarkeit. **—ification**, *s.* die Rechtfertigung (*also Theol.*, *Law*); die Ausschließung, Justierung (*Typ.*). **—ificatory**, *adj.* rechtfertigend, verteidigend. **—ifier**, *s.* der Rechtfertiger, Verteidiger; der Justierer, Zurichter (*Mech.*). **—ify**, *v.a.* rechtfertigen; (absolve) lossprechen; justieren (*Typ.*); the end —ifies the means, der Zweck heiligt die Mittel. **—ly**, *adv.* mit Recht; *see* — I. **—ness**, *s.* die Gerechtigkeit, Billigkeit; (accuracy) die Richtigkeit, Genauigkeit.

Jut, *v.n.* (— out) hervorstehen, hinausragen, vorspringen. *Comp.* **—-window**, *s.* das Erkerfenster, vorspringende Fenster.

Jute, *s.* die Jute, Jutefaser, der Jutehanf.

Juven—escence, *s.* das Jungwerden; the well of —escence, der Jungbrunnen. **—escent**, *adj.* sich verjüngend; unreif, unentwickelt. **—ile**, I. *adj.* jung, jugendlich; Kinder-; —ile warehouse, das Konfektionsgeschäft für Kinder. II. *s.* der junge Mensch. **—ility**, *s.* die Jugendlichkeit; das jugendliche Feuer, der jugendliche Leichtsinn.

Juxtaposition, *s.* die Nebeneinanderstellung.

K

K, k, *s.* K, k; *for abbreviations see the Index at the end of the English and German part.*

Kafir, Kaffir, *s.* der Kaffer.

Kaftan, *s.* der Kaftan.

Kail, Kale, *s.* der Kohl (*Scotch*); (curly —) Krauskohl. *Comp.* **—-pot**, *s.* der Suppentopf.

Kaleidoscop—e, *s.* das Kaleidoskop. **—ic**, *adj.* kaleidoskopisch; bunt durcheinander gewürfelt.

Kali, *s.* gemeines Salzkraut; das Kali (*Chem.*).

Kalifa, *s.* der Kalif.

Kangaroo, *s.* das Känguruh.

Kaolin, *s.* das Kaolin.

Kedge, I. *s.*; (— anchor) der Wurfanker, Warpanker. II. *v.a.* (ein Schiff) warpen, es mit einem an einem kleinen Anker befestigten Tau flußaufwärts ziehen.

Keel, I. *s.* der Kiel (*Naut.*, *Bot.*); (ship) das Schiff; false —, falscher Kiel; length in — . . ., auf dem Kiel . . . lang; on an even —, hinten und vorn gleich schwer beladen. II. *v.n.*; to — over, umschlagen, kieloben liegen. **—age**, *s.* das Kielgeld. **—ed**, *adj.* kielförmig (*Bot.*) **—haul**, *v.a.* kielholen. **—son**, *s.* das Kielschwein (*Naut.*).

Keen, *adj.*, **—ly**, *adv.* scharf (*as an edge*); (eager) eifrig, erpicht (for a th., auf eine S.); durchdringend, streng, scharf (*as cold*); stark, groß (*as appetite*); (subtle) fein, subtil, spitzfindig; (acute) scharfsinnig; beißend (*as wit*); to give a razor a — edge, ein Rasiermesser abziehen; — competition, starker Wettbewerb; — perception of, feines Gefühl für. **—ness**, *s.* die Schärfe; die Heftigkeit; die Strenge; (mental —ness) der Scharfsinn; das Schneidende (*of satire, etc.*); die Feinheit; —ness of sight, die Scharfsichtigkeit. *Comp.* **—-edged**, *adj.* scharf geschliffen, schneidig. **—-eyed**, *adj.* scharfsichtig. **—-witted**, *adj.* scharfsinnig.

Keep, I. *ir.v.a.* halten; (hold) (in seinem Besitze) behalten, haben; behaupten (*the field*); (guard) (auf)bewahren, bewachen, beschützen; (preserve from) abhalten (von), hindern (an); (support) erhalten, ernähren, unterhalten; (observe) beobachten (*festivals, silence*), feiern (*a festival*); erfüllen, halten (*a promise, etc.*); verfolgen (*a path*); hüten (*one's bed or room, the house*); befolgen (*rules*); unterhalten (*a mistress, an army*); feilhalten, auf Lager haben, führen (*books*); führen (*accounts, the cash, a good table, etc.*); to — a p. advised, einen regelmäßig benachrichtigen; to — o.s. clean, sich reinlich halten; to — (a th.) close, (etwas) verschweigen; to — company, (einem) Gesellschaft leisten; to — one's countenance, seine Fassung bewahren; sein Lachen verbeißen; — your distance! bleib mir vom Leibe! zehn Schritt vom Leibe! to — one's ground, Stand halten; to — guard, Wache halten (over a p., über einem); to — a guard over one's tongue, seine Zunge im Zaume halten; to — a house, eigne Wirtschaft haben; *see* House; to — the peace, den Frieden aufrecht erhalten; Ruhe halten; to — secret, verschweigen, geheim halten; to — silence, still sein; to — a stiff upper lip, die Ohren steif halten (*sl.*); don't — me in suspense, lassen Sie mich nicht in Ungewißheit; to — a term, die erforderliche Anzahl von Tagen während des Semesters anwesend sein (*Univ.*); to — a tight rein over a p., einen streng halten; to — one's temper, an sich halten, sich beherrschen; to — time, richtig gehen (*of watches*); Takt, Schritt, halten (*Mus.*, *Mil.*); to — a p. waiting, einen warten lassen; to — watch, Wache stehen; to — **asunder**, getrennt halten; to — **at** a distance, von sich entfernt halten; to — s.o. (constantly) at work, einen beständig beschäftigen, bei der Arbeit haben; to — **away**, abhalten, fernhalten; to — **back**, zurückhalten; (withhold) (einem etwas) vorenthalten; (not disclose) (einem etwas) verschweigen; to — **down**, niederdrücken (*prices, etc.*); (— under) niederhalten; (humble) erniedrigen; to — down the steam, den Dampf unter der Spannung halten; to — **from**, abhalten, zurückhalten, (hinder) verhindern (from coming, zu kommen), (preserve from) bewahren, schützen (vor); to — a th. from s.o., einem etwas verschweigen; (not give) einem etwas vorenthalten; to — **in**, innehalten, zurückhalten; (hold in) an sich halten (*as one's breath*); (restrain) bändigen; *see* In; to — in one's own hands, selbst verwalten; to — in mind, im Gedächtnis behalten; I shall — it in mind, ich will daran denken; to — in money, mit Geld versehen; to — in temper, bei guter Laune erhalten; to — in repair, in gutem Zustande erhalten; to — o.s. in clothes, seine Kleider mit eignem Gelde anschaffen; to — in view, im Auge behalten; to — **off**, abhalten, abwehren; to — **on**, anbehalten (*clothes*), aufbehalten (*hat*), weiter behalten (*a* *servant*); (feed on) ernähren, füttern (mit); to — **out**, nicht hereinlassen, ausschließen, (withhold) vorenthalten (einem etwas); to — out of sight, (etwas) verbergen; to — a p. **to** his promise, einen anhalten, sein Versprechen zu erfüllen; to — a p. to a th., einen zu etwas anhalten; to — a th. to o.s., etwas für sich behalten; to — **under**, niederhalten (*lit.*); im Zaume halten (*fig.*); to — **up**, (hold up) in die Höhe halten, aufrecht halten; (— from falling) hoch *or* auf der (ihrer) Höhe erhalten (*as prices*); behalten (*one's reputation*); unterhalten (*a conversation, correspondence, etc.*); aufbehalten (*from bed*); — it up! immer zu! how long did you — it up last night? wie lange habt ihr gestern abend noch ausgehalten (*of dancing, etc.*); to — up a heavy fire, ein regelmäßiges Feuer unterhalten (*Mil.*); to — up appearances, den Schein wahren; to — up a great show, großen Staat führen; to — up one's spirits, frisch und vergnügt bleiben. II. *ir v.n.* sich halten; (stay) sich aufhalten, bleiben; fortwährend tun; sich halten (*as fruit, meat, etc.*); to — **abreast** with the times, mit der *or* seiner Zeit fortschreiten *or* Schritt halten; to — **aloof**, sich entfernt halten; to — aloof from s.o., mit einem nichts zu tun haben wollen; to — **away**, sich fernhalten (einer S. *or* von einer S.), fernbleiben (einer S.); to — **back**, zurückbleiben; to — **clear** of a th., sich von einer S. frei *or* fern halten; the pilot kept clear of the rock, der Lotse steuerte weit vom Felsen ab; to — **close**, sich eingezogen halten; to — **from**, sich enthalten; to — **in** with, in Gunst bleiben bei; to — **off**, davon bleiben; — off! bleib mir vom Leibe! zehn Schritt vom Leibe! to — **on**, fortfahren; (proceed) vorwärtsschreiten; she kept on singing, sie fuhr fort zu singen, sie sang weiter; it kept on raining, es regnete (immer) weiter *or* fortwährend; the fine weather will — on longer, das schöne Wetter wird sich noch halten; to — **out**, draußen bleiben; to — out of debt, sich schuldenfrei erhalten; to — out of reach, aus dem Bereiche bleiben; to — out of sight, sich nicht blicken lassen, sich verbergen; you have long kept out of sight, Sie haben sich lange nicht sehen lassen; to — **to**, (sich) halten an; I have said it and will — to it, gesagt habe ich es und will dabei bleiben; to — to one's word, sein Wort halten; to — (o.s.) to o.s., für sich bleiben (*coll.*); to — to the rule, sich an die Regel halten; — to the left! links fahren! links ausweichen! halten Sie sich links! to — **up**, sich erhalten; (— up one's spirits) den Mut nicht sinken lassen; (— out of bed) aufbleiben; prices are —ing up, die Preise behaupten sich; to — up with, Schritt halten mit. III. *s.* die Kost, der Unterhalt (*coll.*); die Weide (*of cattle*); (donjon) das Burgverließ. **—er**, *s.* der Verwahrer; der Inhaber, Besitzer (*of a hotel, etc.*); (overseer) der Wächter, Aufseher; (jailer) der Gefängniswärter; (maintainer) der Unterhalter; (ring) der Schutzring; —er of the great seal, der Großsiegelbewahrer; —er of the privy purse, der Intendant der königlichen Zivilliste; —er of the privy seal, der Geheimsiegelbewahrer; am I my brother's —er? soll ich meines Bruders Hüter sein? (*B.*); a —er at home, *see* Stay-at-home. **—ing**, *s.* (care) die Verwahrung, Aufsicht, Pflege; (custody) der Gewahrsam; (support) der Unterhalt; die Haltung (*Paint.*); to be in —ing with, übereinstimmen mit, dazu stimmen *or* passen; in —ing with the spirit of our language, dem Geiste unserer Sprache angemessen; to have in —ing, in Händen haben; to entrust to s.o.'s —ing, (etwas) der Verwahrung eines andern anvertrauen. **—sake**, *s.* das (Geschenk zum) Andenken; das Freundschaftszeichen; (book) der Almanach; as a —sake, zum Andenken.

Keg, *s.* das Fäßchen.

Keld, *s.* die Quelle (*dial.*).

Kelp, *s.* das Salzkraut (*Bot.*); der Kelp (*Chem.*).

Kelpie, *s.* der Wassergeist (in der Gestalt eines Pferdes) (*Scotch*).

Ken, I. *s.* der Gesichtskreis, die Sehweite, beyond his —, über seinen Gesichtskreis hinaus; außerhalb des Kreises, der ihm vertraut ist (*fig.*), out of —, außer Sehweite; within —, sichtbar. II. *v.a.* wissen (*dial.*); (recognize) erkennen (*dial.*).

[1]**Kennel**, I. *s.* der Hundestall, das Hundehaus. II. *v.n.* im Loche liegen. III. *v.a.* in einem Hundestalle halten; —, sir! kusch dich!

[2]**Kennel**, *s.* die Gosse, Rinne (*obs.*).

Kept, I. *p.p. see* Keep. II. *adj.*; — mistress, die Maitresse.

Kerb, *s.* (— stone) der Randstein; *see* Curbstone.

Kerchief, *s.* das Kopftuch (*for the head*); das Halstuch (*for the neck*); *see* Handkerchief. **—ed**, *adj.* verschleiert.

Kermes, *s.* der Kermes; (*pl.*) die Kermeskörner.

Kernel, *s.* der Kern (*of nuts, etc.*); das Samenkorn (*of oats, etc.*); die Drüse (*in flesh*); das Innerste, der Kern (*fig.*).

Kerosene, *s.* das Kerosen, raffiniertes Petroleum.

Kersey, *s.* der Kersei, grobes Wollzeug.

Kestrel, *s.* der Turmfalke.

Ketch, *s.* die Kits, kleines starkes zweimastiges Schiff.

Ketchup, *s.* pikante, aus Champignons bereitete Soße, die kalt zugegossen wird.

Kettle, *s.* der Kessel; a pretty — of fish! eine schöne Geschichte! *Comp.* **—-drum**, *s.* die (Kessel-)Pauke; die Nachmittagstee-Gesellschaft (*coll.*). **—-drummer**, *s.* der Paukenschläger. **—-holder**, *s.* der Kesselanfasser, Kesselhalter.

Key, *s.* der Schlüssel (*of a door, watch, bed; of a position; also Tele.*); die Taste (*of a piano, etc.*); die Klappe (*of a flute, etc.*); die Tonart (*Mus.*); der Ton (*fig.*); der Keil, das Band (*Carp.*); (solution) Schlüssel; to keep under lock and —, unter Schloß und Riegel halten; to turn the —, abschließen; to speak in a high —, in hohem Tone sprechen. **—ed**, *adj.* mit Tasten *or* Klappen versehen; —ed instrument, Tasteninstrument; six-—ed flute, Flöte mit sechs Klappen. *Comp.* **—-basket**, *s.* der Schlüsselkorb. **—-board**, *s.* die Tastatur. **—-bugle**, *s.* das Klappenhorn. **—hole**, *s.* das Schlüsselloch. **—less**, *adj.* ohne Schlüssel; —less watch, die Remontoiruhr. **—-map**, *s.* die Übersichtskarte. **—-note**, *s.* der Grundton. **—stone**, *s.* der Schlußstein.

Khaki, I. *adj.* staubfarben. II. *s.* staubfarbenes grüngelbliches Uniformtuch, das Khaki.

[1]**Khan**, *s.* der Chan, Tatarenfürst. **—ate**, *s.* das Chanat, die Herrschaft oder Würde eines Chan.

[2]**Khan**, *s.* die Karawanserei.

Khedive, *s.* der Chedive, Khedive.

Kibe, *s.* aufgebrochene eiternde Frostbeule.

Kick, I. *v.a.* mit dem Fuße stoßen, ausschlagen (*as horses*); (einem) einen Fußtritt geben; to — the ball, den Fußball stoßen; to — the bucket, in Gras beißen (*vulg.*); to — s.o. down stairs, einen die Treppe hinunterwerfen; to — up one's heels, ausschlagen; to — up a row, Radau *or* Spektakel machen (*vulg.*). II. *v.n.* mit den Füßen ausschlagen; stoßen (*as fire-arms*); to — against, sich auflehnen gegen. III. *s.* der Fußstoß, Fußtritt; to get more —s than halfpence, mehr Prügel als zu essen bekommen. **—er**, *s.* das Pferd, welches hinten ausschlägt. *Comp.* **—-off**, *s.* der Anstoß, Anfang (des Fußballspiels).

Kickshaw, *s.* die Nippsache, Delikatesse.

Kid, I. *s.* junge Ziege, das Zicklein; (child) das Kind (*sl.*); *see* — leather. II. *v.n.* zickeln. III. *adj.*; — gloves, ziegenlederne Handschuhe, Glacéhandschuhe; — leather, das Ziegenleder, Bockleder. **—nap**, *v.a.* (Kinder, Menschen) stehlen, entführen, rauben; für das Heer oder die Flotte pressen, mit List zum Dienst werben. **—napper**, *s.* der Kinderdieb; Menschenräuber, Seelenverkäufer. —**napping**, *s.* der Kinderraub; Menschenraub.

Kidney, *s.* die Niere; die Art, Sorte, der Schlag (*coll.*). *Comp.* —**-bean**, *s.* türkische Bohne, Schminkbohne. —**-shaped**, *adj.* nierenförmig.

Kilderkin, *s.* das Fäßchen (= 18 Gallonen *or* 80 L.).

Kill, *v.a.* töten (*also fig.*), umbringen; schlachten (*cattle*); to — time, die Zeit totschlagen *or* vertreiben; to — two birds with one stone, zwei Fliegen mit einer Klappe schlagen. —**er**, *s.* der Totschläger. —**ing**, I. *adj.* mörderisch; unwiderstehlich, reizend. II. *s.* das Töten. *Comp.* —**-joy**, *s.* der Freudenstörer, Störenfried, Spielverderber.

Kiln, *s.* der Brennofen, die Darre; lime-—, der Kalkofen. *Comp.* —**-dry**, *v.a.* darren, dörren; —-dried malt, das Darrmalz.

[1]**Kilt**, I. *s.* das kurze Röckchen der Bergschotten. II. *v.a.* in Falten legen (*Semp.*); (— up) aufschürzen (*one's skirts, etc.*). —**ed**, *adj.* in kurzem Röckchen, (dem Kilt) der Bergschotten. —**ing**, *s.* das Fältern.

[2]**Kilt**, (*prov.*) *p.p. see* Kill.

Kimbo, *adv.*; a—, in die Seite gestemmt.

Kin, *s.* die (Bluts-)Verwandtschaft; (relation) der, die Verwandte; (—dred) die Verwandten; (sort) *see* —d; next of —, die nächsten Verwandten. —**d**, *see* Kind. —**dred**, I. *s.* die Verwandtschaft; (relations) die Verwandten. II. *adj.* verwandt, gleichartig; —dred minds, souls, spirits, gleichgesinnte, gleichgestimmte, geistesverwandte Seelen. —**g**, *see* King. *Comp.* —**sfolk**, *pl.* die Verwandten, die Verwandtschaft. —**sman**, —**s-woman**, *s.* der, die Verwandte.

Kind, I. *adj.* gut, gütig, freundlich; — to me, gütig, (freundlich) gegen mich; be — enough, be so — as to . . ., haben Sie die Güte zu . . .; — regards, freundliche *or* beste Grüße (an, *acc.*); to send one's — regards to a p., einen freundlich grüßen lassen. II. *s.* (sort) die Art, Gattung, das Geschlecht; (way) die Beschaffenheit, Art und Weise; to pay in —, in Produkten bezahlen; taxes paid in —, Natural-Abgaben; a queer — of fellow, ein merkwürdiger Mensch; an affair of this —, eine Sache dieser Art; flowers of all —s, Blumen jeder Art *or* aller Arten; there are many —s of style, es giebt viele Stilarten; every — of . . ., allerlei; nothing of the —, bewahre! mit nichten! nichts dergleichen. —**liness**, *s.* die Freundlichkeit. —**ly**, *adj. & adv.* gütig, freundlich; (benevolent) wohlwollend; wohltätig (*as rain*); to take it —ly of a p., (einem für eine S.) Dank wissen, (etwas) gut aufnehmen (von einem); to take —ly (to), (einen *or* etwas) gern haben, lieben; remember me most —ly to, empfehlen Sie mich . . . (*dat.*) aufs freundlichste. —**ness**, *s.* die Güte, die Gütigkeit, Freundlichkeit; (act of —ness) die Gunstbezeugung, Gefälligkeit; to have a —ness for, (einen) gern haben. *Comp.* —**hearted**, *adj.* gutherzig, wohlwollend.

Kindl—e, *v.* I. *a.* anzünden; entzünden, entflammen (*fig.*). II. *n.* sich entzünden, Feuer fangen; entbrennen (*fig.*). —**er**, *s.* der Apparat zum Feueranzünden; (inflamer) der Aufwiegler. —**ing**, *s.* das Anbrennholz.

Kine, *pl. see* Cow (*Scotch*).

Kine—matics, *s.* die Bewegungslehre, Getriebelehre, Kinematik. —**matography**, *s.* die Vorführung von Bewegungsbildern. —**tic**, *adj.* bewegend, Bewegung erzeugend, kinetisch. —**tics**, *s.* die Kinetik.

King, *s.* der König (*also Cards & Chess*); die Dame (*Draughts*); the —'s Own, das 4te Infanterie-Regiment (*Eng.*); —'s counsel, der Justizrat; —'s evidence, der Kronzeuge; to give (turn) —'s evidence, Kronzeuge sein (werden); —'s evil, die Skrofeln. —**dom**, *s.* das Königreich; (sovereignty) die Regierung; (region) das Gebiet; das Reich (*Nat. Hist.*); the animal —dom, das Tierreich; the vegetable —dom, das Pflanzenreich; the —dom of God, das Reich Gottes, Gottesreich. —**let**, *s.* das Königlein, der Heckenkönig, schwache König. —**liness**, *s.* das Königliche. —**ly**, *adj. & adv.* königlich; (monarchical) monarchisch. —**ship**, *s.* die Königswürde, das Königtum. —**s**, *pl.* Bücher der Könige (*B.*). *Comp.* —**craft**, *s.* die Herrscherkunst. —**cup**, *s.* der Hahnenfuß. —**fisher**, *s.* der Eisvogel. —**like**, *adj.* königlich, erhaben. —**-post**, —**-piece**, *s.* die Giebelspitze, Dachspitze.

Kink, I. *s.* der Kink, die Schleife im Tau (*Naut.*); der närrische Einfall, Vogel, Sparren (*fig. coll.*). II. *v.n.* sich bekneifen.

Kino, *s.* das Kino-(gummi).

Kiosk, *s.* der Kiosk, Sommerpavillon; die Zeitungsverkaufsbude, Straßenbude.

Kipper, I. *s.* der Lachs nach der Laichzeit; der leicht gesalzene und geräucherte Hering. II. *v.a.* (Fisch) leicht räuchern und einsalzen; —ed herring, der halb (auf schottische Art) geräucherte Häring.

Kirk, *s.* die Kirche (*Scotch*).

Kirtle, *s.* das Wams, die kurze Jacke; der Unterrock, Weiberrock; der Ballen (of flax, Flachs, = etwa 100 Pfund). —**d**, *adj.* mit einem Röckchen, Unterrock bekleidet.

Kiss, I. *v.a.* küssen; to — one's hand to, (einem) einen Kuß *or* eine Kußhand zuwerfen; to — hands (of the king, etc.), (dem König ꝛc.) einen Handkuß geben; to — the rod, sich ergeben, sich fügen; to — the Pope's toe, dem Papst den Pantoffel küssen; to — and be friends, sich wieder vertragen. II. *s.* der Kuß; das Zuckerwerk; hearty—, schallender Kuß. *Comp.* —**ing-crust**, *s.* der Anstoß am Brote (wo zwei Brote beim Backen einander berührten).

[1]**Kit**, *s.* die kleine dreisaitige Fiedel.

[2]**Kit**, *s.* (bottle) große Flasche; (pail) der Milcheimer, Zuber; das Kistchen, die Habe; das Handwerksgerät, Nähzeug; die feldmarschmäßige Ausrüstung (*of a soldier, etc.*). *Comp.* —**-bag**, *s.* der Tornister.

[3]**Kit**, *s.* die Familie, Sippe, Brut; all the —, the whole —, die ganze Sippschaft *or* Gesellschaft.

Kitcat, *adj.*; — portrait, das Brustbild.

Kitchen, *s.* die Küche; die Zukost (*dial.*). —**er**, *s.* der Spar-Kochofen; der Oberkoch, Küchenmeister (*obs.*). *Comp.* —**-garden**, *s.* der Gemüsegarten, Küchengarten. —**-maid**, *s.* die Küchenmagd. —**-midden**, *s.* vorhistorischer Hügel aus Küchenabfällen (*especially on the Danish coast*). —**-range**, *s.* der Kochofen. —**-salt**, *s.* das Kochsalz. —**-stuff**, *s.* das für die Küche Erforderliche; der Küchenabfall. —**-work**, *s.* die Küchenarbeit.

Kite, *s.* die Gabelweihe; (paper —) der Drache; der Geier (*fig.*); der Proformawechsel, Kellerwechsel (*sl.*); to fly a —, einen Drachen steigen lassen; Proformawechsel ausstellen, Wechselreiterei treiben (*sl.*). *Comp.* —**-flying**, *s.* das Drachensteigenlassen; die Wechselreiterei (*sl.*).

Kith, *s.*; — and kin, die Sippschaft; he has neither — nor kin, er hat weder Kind noch Kegel.

Kitten, I. *s.* das Kätzchen. II. *v.n.* kätzeln. —**ish**, *adj.* kätzchenhaft.

Kittiwake, *s.* dreizehige Möve.

Kittl—e, (*dial.*) *adj.* kitzlich; schwer zu behandeln: (unsafe) unsicher. —**ish**, *adj.* kitzlich.

Kleptomania, *s.* die Diebssucht, Kleptomanie. —**c**, *s.* der Diebssüchtige, Kleptomane.

Knack, *s.* der Kunstgriff, Kniff; die Fertigkeit, Kunst (at, of, in, in (*dat.*)); to have the — (of it), den Rummel kennen (*sl.*).

Knacker, *s.* der Abdecker, Schlächter alter Pferde.

Knag, *s.* der Knorren, Knoten (*in wood*); (peg) der hölzerne Pflock (*dial.*); der Zacken am Geweih (*Sport.*); die Erhöhung; die Quaste. —**gy**, *adj.* knorrig, knotig; höckerig, zackig; grob (*fig.*).

Knapsack, *s.* der Tornister; der Rucksack.

Knarl, *s.* der Knorren (*wood*). **—ed**, *adj.* knorrig.

Knav—e, *s.* der Schelm, Schalk; der Bube (*Cards*); der Bursche; arrant —e, Erzspitzbube. **—ery**, *s.* die Schurkerei, Büberei, der Schurkenstreich; lose Streiche (*obs.*). **—ish**, *adj.*, **—ishly**, *adv.* spitzbübisch, schurkisch; schelmisch, schalkhaft (*obs.*); a —ish trick, ein Bubenstück, schurkischer Streich. **—ishness**, *s.* die Schurkerei.

Knead, *v.a.* kneten; to — clay, Ton abtreten. *Comp.* **—ing-trough**, *s.* der Backtrog.

Knee, *s.* das Knie (*also Shipb.*); to go on one's —s, sich auf die Kniee niederlassen, auf die Kniee fallen, niederknieen. **—l**, *ir.v.n.* knieen; to —l to . . ., vor (*dat.*) . . . niederknieen. **—ler**, *s.* der Knieende. *Comp.* **—-breeches**, *pl.* kurze Kniehosen. **—-buckle**, *s.* die Knieschnalle. **—-cap**, *s.* die Kniebinde (*Surg.*); das Knieleder (*Saddl.*). **—-deep**, *adj.* knietief. **—-joint**, *s.* das Kniegelenk. **—-pan**, *s.* die Kniescheibe. **—-string**, die Kniesflechse (*Anat.*). **—-timber**, *s.* das Krummholz, Knieholz.

Knell, I. *s.* die Totenglocke, das Totengeläut, Grabgeläute; to ring the — of s.th., etwas zu Grabe läuten, eine S. für abgetan erklären. II. *v.a.* zu Grabe läuten.

Knelt, *imperf. & p.p. of* Kneel.

Knew, *imperf. of* Know.

Knickerbocker, *s.* die weite Kniehose; —s (*abbr.* Knickers), Kniehosen (mit Wadenstrümpfen).

Knick-knack, *s.* das Spielzeug, die Kleinigkeit, der Tand, die Nippsache. **—ery**, *s.* der Tand, Trödelkram. **—s**, *pl.* Nippsachen, Spielereien.

Knife, *s.* das Messer; clasp —, Schnappmesser, Einschlagemesser; carving —, Vorlegemesser; pocket —, das Taschenmesser; war to the —, der Krieg bis aufs Messer. *Comp.* **—-board**, *s.* das Schleifbrett. **—-cleaner**, *s.* die Messerputzmaschine. **—-edge**, *s.* die Schneide (eines Wagebalkens). **—-grinder**, *s.* der Schleifer. **—-handle**, *s.* das Heft, der Griff. **—-polish**, *s.* das Mittel zum Messerputzen. **—-rest**, *s.* das Messerbänkchen, -böckchen. **—-tray**, *s.* der Messerkorb.

Knight, I. *s.* der Ritter; (champion) der Kämpe, Ritter, Held; der Springer (*Chess*); —'s tour, der Rösselsprung (*Chess*); — of the Garter (K. G.), Ritter des Hosenband-Ordens; — of the rueful countenance, Ritter von der traurigen Gestalt (Don Quijote); — of the shears, der Ritter von der Schere; — of the shire, das Parlamentsglied für eine Grafschaft. II. *v.a.* zum Ritter schlagen. **—age**, *s.* die Ritterschaft; das Register der Ritter. **—hood**, *s.* die Ritterwürde; (knights) die Ritterschaft. **—liness**, *s.* die Ritterlichkeit. **—ly**, *adj.* ritterlich. *Comp.* **—-errant**, *s.* der fahrende Ritter. **—errantry**, *s.* fahrende Ritterschaft. **—-service**, *s.* der Ritterdienst; lands held by —-service, (—'s-fee, *s.*) das Ritterlehen.

Knit, *ir.v.* I. *a.* stricken (*stockings*); verbinden, vereinigen (*as a bone*); to — the brows, die Stirn runzeln; a well- — frame, ein gutgebauter Körper. II. *n.* sich verbinden; stricken. **—ter**, *s.* der (die) Stricker(in). **—ting**, *s.* das Strickzeug. *Comp.* **—ting-cotton**, *s.* das Strickgarn. **—ting-machine**, *s.* die Strickmaschine. **—ting-needle**, *s.* die Stricknadel. **—ting-yarn**, *s.* das Strickgarn.

Knob, *s.* der Knopf; (knag) der Knorren, Knoten. **—bed**, *adj.* mit einem Knopfe versehen. **—by**, *adj. see* —bed; knorrig, knotig.

Knock, I. *v.n.* klopfen; pochen; stoßen, schlagen; — and ring, Bitte mit dem Türklopfer anzuklopfen und zugleich zu klingeln! to — **about**, sich umhertreiben, herumbummeln; to — **at** the door, an die Tür klopfen; to **on**, vorschlagen (*Football*); to — **together**, an einander stoßen; to — **under**, sich gefangen geben, sich vorschlagen. II. *v.a.* klopfen, stoßen, schlagen; to — **about**, von allen Seiten schlagen, umherstoßen; to — one's head **against** the table, mit dem Kopfe an den Tisch stoßen; to — **down**, niederschlagen; to — down to the highest bidder, (einen Artikel) dem Meistbietenden zuschlagen; to — **in**, einschlagen; to — **off**, abbrechen (*also Typ.*); to — **out**, (her)ausschlagen; to — **on** the head, auf den Kopf schlagen, totschlagen (*a p.*); vereiteln (*a plan*); abmachen, fertig bringen (*a task*); to — **over**, zu Boden schlagen, über den Haufen werfen; to — **up**, aufklopfen; (exhaust) erschöpfen; I am quite —ed up, ich kann nicht mehr, ich bin völlig erschöpft, ganz ab *or* fertig. III. *s.* der Schlag, Stoß; das Anklopfen, Pochen (*at the door*); single —, einmaliges Anpochen. **—er**, *s.* der Klopfende; der (Haustür-)Klopfer. *Comp.* **—-kneed**, *adj.* X-beinig (*of persons*), kuhhessig (*of horses*); hinkend, lahm (*of arguments*). **—-about**, *s.* der kleine weiche Filzhut.

[1]**Knoll**, *s.* der kleine Hügel; (hilltop) die Spitze eines Hügels.

[2]**Knoll**, I. *s.* das Grabgeläut(e). II. *v.a.* zu Grabe läuten.

Knop, *s.* die Knospe, der Knopf (*Bot.*).

Knot, I. *s.* der Knoten; der Knoten, Knorren (*in wood*); der Knoten, die Seemeile ($\frac{1}{60}$ of a degree of latitude, der 60te Teil eines Grades); das Auge, die Knospe (*Bot.*); (bond) die Verbindung, das Band; die Schleife (*of ribbon, etc.*); (shoulder —) das Achselstück, die Epaulette; (perplexity) die Verwicklung; (group) der Haufe, Klumpen; die felsige Erhöhung auf Bergen (*dial.*); sailor's —, der Matrosenknoten (der Halsbinde); true lovers' —, der Liebesknoten; to cut the —, den Knoten durchhauen; to tie a —, einen Knoten schlagen. II. *v.a.* verknüpfen; verbinden (*fig.*). III. *v.n.* Knoten bekommen, schossen (*Bot.*); sich verschlingen. **—ted**, *adj.* knotig, knorrig; (intricate) verwickelt, verflochten. **—tiness**, *s.* das Knotige, Knorrige; (difficulty) die Schwierigkeit. **—ty**, *adj.* knotig, knorrig; schwierig, verwickelt. *Comp.* **—grass**, *s.* der Knöterich. **—hole**, *s.* das Astloch.

Knout, I. *s.* die Knute. II. *v.a.* (einem) die Knute geben, (einen) mit der Knute peitschen.

Know, *ir.v.* I. *a.* wissen; (be acquainted) kennen; (recognize) erkennen; unterscheiden (*one th. or p. from another*); (experience) erleben, erfahren; erkennen (*B.*); he —s it, er weiß es; to — a man, einen Mann kennen; to — a poem, ein Gedicht kennen; to — the way, den Weg kennen *or* wissen; to — one's way about a house, sich in einem Hause zurechtfinden; he —s him, er kennt ihn; I have —n him for sixteen years, ich kenne ihn seit sechzehn Jahren; I have —n snow fall in May, ich habe es erlebt, daß im Mai Schnee gefallen ist; I — him to be a fool, ich weiß, daß er ein Narr ist; to let a p. —, einen wissen lassen, ihm Bescheid geben; to — o.s., sich selbst kennen; — thyself! erkenne dich selbst! II. *n.* wissen; I would have you — that . . ., ich möchte Sie wissen lassen, daß . . .; I — that she will come here, ich weiß, daß sie hierher kommen wird; to — by heart, auswendig wissen, auswendig können; to — by sight, von Ansehn kennen; to come to —, erfahren; to come to be —n, bekannt werden; to — how to do a th., (Bescheid) wissen, wie etwas zu tun ist; I don't — how to begin, ich weiß nicht, wie ich es anfangen soll; he —s how to speak, er versteht es zu reden, versteht sich aufs Reden, kann gut reden; — all men by these presents, kund und zu wissen sei hiemit jedermann; I — better than that! so dumm bin ich nicht! it's not worth —ing, es ist nicht des Wissens wert; to make —n, bekannt machen; to make o.s. —n, sich (einem) vorstellen; sich (*dat.*) einen Namen machen. **—able**, *adj.* (er)kennbar. **—ing**, I. *adj.* (skilful) geschickt; (cunning) schlau, durchtrieben; (intelligent) verständig; a —ing look, ein verständnisvoller Blick; a —ing one, ein schlauer Fuchs (*vulg.*). II. *s.* das Wissen. —

ingly, *adv.* (purposely) wissentlich, vorsätzlich; geschickt. —**ingness**, *s.* die Schlauheit, Durchtriebenheit. —**ledge**, *s.* das Wissen; (information) die Kenntnis, Kunde; (learning, *etc.*) die Wissenschaft; die Kenntnis (*of an art, etc.*); die Bekanntschaft (of a p., mit einem); an extensive —ledge, ausgebreitete Kenntnisse; the tree of —ledge, der Baum der Erkenntnis; to my —ledge, soviel ich weiß; to the best of my —ledge, nach bestem Wissen, so viel ich irgend weiß; his —ledge of chemistry is superficial, seine Kenntnisse in der Chemie sind oberflächlich; without my —ledge, ohne mein Wissen; how came it to your —ledge, wie kam es zu Ihrer Kenntnis *or* Ihnen zu Ohren? to come to the —ledge of a th., eine S. erfahren; to have carnal —ledge of, fleischlich erkennen. —**n**, *adj.* gewußt; bekannt; anerkannt; well—n, wohl bekannt. *Comp.* —**-all**, *s.* der Alleswisser (*iron.*). —**-nothing**, *s.* der Nichtswisser, Unwissende, Ignorant.

Knuckle, I. *s.* der Knöchel, das Gelenk; das Kniestück (*of veal, etc.*). II. *v.n.;* to — down, sich bücken; (yield) sich unterwerfen, nachgeben; to — under, nachgeben. *Comp.* —**-bones**, *s.* das Knöchelspiel.

Knurl, *see* Knarl.

Koorbash, *s.* die Karbatsche.

Kopeck, *s.* die Kopeke (*less than a farthing*).

Koran, *s.* der Koran.

Kraal, *s.* das Hottentottendorf, der Kra(a)l.

Kreosote, *s.* das Kreosot.

Kreutzer, *s.* der Kreuzer (*less than a farthing*).

Kudos, *s.* der Ruhm, das Ansehen.

Kumiss, *s.* der Kumys (gegorene Stutenmilch).

L

L, l, *s.* L, l; (*for abbreviations see the Index at the end of the English-German part*).

[1]**La**, *s.* das A (*Mus.*).

[2]**La**, *int.* sieh! sieh da! da seh' mal einer! pah! ach! wahrhaftig! —, —! na, na!

Laager, I. *s.* das Burenlager, die Wagenburg. II. *v.a. & n.* sich lagern, lagern; the Boers were —ed to the east, die Buren lagerten östlich.

Labarum, *s.* die Kreuzesfahne, Prozessionsfahne.

Label, I. *s.* die Etikette, der Zettel, das Schildchen, die Etikette (*on medicine bottles*); (tie-on —) der an das Gepäckstück angehängte Kofferzettel, Kollianhänger, Gepäckzettel; (stick-on —) der Gepäckbeklebezettel; der Paketbeklebezettel; (codicil) das Kodizill; die Kranzleiste (*Arch.*). II. *v.a.* mit einem Zettel versehen, etikettieren; bekleben; I had my luggage —led to Hanover, ich ließ mein Gepäck nach Hannover bekleben.

Labi—al, I. *adj.* Lippen=. II. *s.* der Lippenlaut; der Lippenbuchstabe, Labial. —**alize**, *v.n.* labialisieren, ründen, mit Lippenründung sprechen. —**ate**, *adj.* lippenförmig (*Bot.*). —**o-dental**, I. *adj.* labiodental (*sound*). II. *s.* Lippenzahnlaut, durch Pressen der Oberzähne auf die Unterlippe hervorgebrachter Reibelaut (f, v).

Labor—atory, *s.* das Laboratorium (*Chem.*); (workshop) die Werkstatt. —**ious**, *adj.*, —**iously**, *adv.* mühsam, mühevoll; (diligent) arbeitsam, fleißig. —**iousness**, *s.* die Mühsamkeit; die Arbeitsamkeit.

Labour, I. *s.* (work) die Arbeit, das Werk; (toil) die Mühe, Anstrengung, Arbeit, Beschwerde; (travail) die Wehen; to lose one's —, sich umsonst abmühen; in —, in Kindesnöten; hard —, Zuchthausarbeit; sentenced to 9 months' hard —, zu 9 Monaten Zuchthaus verurteilt; manual —, Handarbeit. II. *attrib.;* — bureau, das Arbeitsnachweisbureau. III. *v.n.* arbeiten; (toil) sich anstrengen, sich bemühen; (take trouble) sich abmühen, sich (*dat.*) Mühe geben; (move with difficulty) sich mühsam bewegen; arbeiten (*Naut.*); (travail) in Kindesnöten sein, in Wehen liegen, kreisen; to — tooth and nail, es sich (*dat.*) blutsauer werden lassen; to — at a th., an einer Sache arbeiten, sich anstrengen etwas zu begreifen *or* auszuführen; to — under difficulties, mit Schwierigkeiten zu kämpfen haben; to — under bad health, disadvantages, an schlechter Gesundheit, unter ungünstigen Verhältnissen leiden; to — under a mistake, sich im Irrtum befinden; all ye that — and are heavy laden, Alle, die ihr mühselig und beladen seid (*B.*). III. *v.a.* mit Mühe ausarbeiten; (till) bauen; (fabricate) verfertigen, bearbeiten. —**ed**, *adj.;* a —ed composition, ein mühsam ausgearbeiteter *or* schwerfälliger Aufsatz; —ed style, steife, gezwungene Schreibart. —**er**, *s.* der Arbeitsmann, Handarbeiter, Handlanger; day-—er, der Tagelöhner. —**ing**, *adj.;* —ing breath, schwerer Atem; —ing classes, Arbeitsleute, die Arbeiterbevölkerung; —ing force, mechanische Leistung. *Comp.* —**-saving**, *adj.* arbeitsparend.

Laburnum, *s.* der Goldregen, Bohnenbaum.

Labyrinth, *s.* das Labyrinth; der Irrgang, Irrgarten, Irrbau; das Wirrsal, Gewirr (*fig.*). —**ian**, —**ine**, *adj.* labyrinthisch; vielverschlungen, gewunden, verwickelt, verworren (*fig.*).

[1]**Lac**, *s.* der Gummilack; shell —, der Schellack; stick —, der Holzlack. —**quer**, *see* Lacquer. *Comp.* —**-varnish**, *s.* der Lackfirnis.

[2]**Lac, Lack**, *s.* das Hunderttausend; a — of rupees, 100,000 Rupien (*in India*).

Lace, I. *s.* die Spitze(n); (gold, etc., —) die Tresse; (cord) die Schnur; (boot—) das (Stiefel=)Schnürband, Schuhband, der Schnürsenkel; machine-made —, Maschinenspitzen; point —, genähte Spitzen; stay-—, das Korsettschnürband. II. *v.a.* (zu=)schnüren, (fest)schnüren, (ein)schnüren; mit Tressen, rc. besetzen (*as a coat*); mit Spirituosen vermischen (*arch.*); to — o.s., sich schnüren; to — a p.'s coat for him, einen gehörig durchprügeln (*coll.*). —**d**, *adj.;* —d boots, Schnürstiefel. *Comp.* —**-bobbins**, *pl.* Spitzenklöppel. —**-maker**, *s.* der (die) Spitzenklöppler(in). —**-pillow**, *s.* das Klöppelkissen.

Lacerat—e, I. *v.a.* zerreißen. II. *adj.* zerrissen; zerfetzt (*Bot.*). —**ion**, *s.* die Zerreißung; (wound) der Riß; die Verletzung.

Lacert—a, *s.* die Eidechse. —**ine**, *adj.* eidechsenartig, Eidechsen=.

Lachrym—al, *adj.* Tränen=; —al glands, Tränendrüsen. —**atory**, *s.* der Tränenkrug. —**ose**, *adj.* tränenreich, weinerlich, traurig.

[1]**Lack**, I. *v.a.* ermangeln (einer S.), bedürfen, entbehren, Mangel leiden an (*dat.*). II. *v.n.* (be in want) Mangel leiden; (be wanting) fehlen; his works are —ing in humour, es fehlt seinen Büchern an Humor. III. *s.* der Mangel; there was no — of . . ., es fehlte nicht an . . . *Comp.* —**-lustre**, *adj.* glanzlos, matt.

[2]**Lack**, *see* Lac.

Lackada—isical, *adj.*, —**isically**, *adv.* sehnsuchtsvoll, schmachtend; (affected) geziert; a —isical tone of voice, schmachtender Ton. —**isy**, —**y**, *int.* ach! leider!

Lackey, Lacquey, *s.* der Lakai.

Laconi—c, *adj.*, —**cally**, *adv.* lakonisch, markig, gedrängt; einsilbig, kurz angebunden, wortkarg. —**cism**, —**sm**, *s.* die gedrängte Kürze, treffende Kürze, knappe Redeweise, der Lakonismus.

Lacquer, I. *v.a.* lackieren. II. *s.* der Lack, Lackfirnis; —ed work, lackierte Arbeit, Lackarbeit.

Lacrosse, *s.* eine Art Ballspiel (mit gekrümmten geflochtenen langen Ballkellen).

Lact—ation, *s.* das Säugen; period of —ation, die Säugezeit. —**eal**, —**ean**, *adj.* milchig; Milch führend (*Anat.*); Milch=. —**eals**, *pl.* (—eal vessels) Milchgefäße. —**ic**, *adj.* milchig; —ic acid, die Milchsäure. —**ometer**, *s.* der Laktometer. —**ose**, *s.* der Milchzucker.

Lacun—a, *s.* die Lücke. —**ar**, I. *s.* (ceiling) die Decke mit vertieften Feldern; (panel) das Feld. —**ose**, *adj.* vertieft, grubig (*Bot.*).

Lad, *s.* der Junge, Bursch(e); Jüngling; a — and his lass, ein Bursch und sein Mädchen (*Scotch*).

Ladder, *s.* die Leiter; die Stufenleiter (*fig.*); — of rope, Strickleiter, das Fallreepstau; educational —, das von der Volksschule bis zur Hochschule stufenweise aufsteigende Erziehungssystem.

Lad—e, *v.a.* laden; beladen, befrachten; ausschöpfen (*water, etc.*). **—en**, *p.p. & adj.*; heavy —en, schwer beladen. **—ing**, *s.* die Ladung; bill of —ing, der Verladungsschein.

Ladies, *pl. see* Lady; —! meine geehrten Damen; — and gentlemen, meine verehrten Damen und Herrn! hochgeehrte Versammlung!

Ladle, I. *s.* der Schöpf-Löffel; (kitchen —) der Kochlöffel; die Ladeschaufel (*Artil.*); punch —, soup —, der Punsch-, Suppen-löffel. II. *v.a.*; to — out, ausschöpfen (*water out of a boat*); auslöffeln, mit dem großen Löffel ausschöpfen.

Lady, *s.* die Dame, Frau von Bildung und Stand; (title) die Edelfrau, Freifrau, Lady, Frau von . . .; (ruler, mistress) die Herrin; (wife) die Gattin, Gemahlin; she is a (thorough) —, sie ist eine echte Dame; she is no —, sie ist keine feine Frau; my —, gnädige Frau; Our (blessed) —, unsere liebe Frau; Church of Our —, die Marienkirche, Frauenkirche; — in waiting (to the Queen, etc.), Hofdame (der Königin). **—ship**, *s.*; her —ship, die gnädige Frau, das gnädige Fräulein; your —ship, gnädige Frau, Euer Gnaden, gnädiges Fräulein. *Comp.* **—-bird**, *s.* der Marienkäfer; das Marienwürmchen. **—-day**, *s.* Mariä Verkündigung (der 25ste März). **—-killer**, *s.* (ladies' man) der Damenheld, Mädchenjäger. **—like**, *adj.* damenhaft, mit den Manieren einer feinen Dame, wie eine Dame, wohlerzogen; frauenzimmerlich. **—-love**, *s.* die Geliebte, Herz(aller)liebste. **—'s-bedstraw**, *s.* das echte Labkraut (*Bot.*). **—'s-help**, *s.* die Stütze (der Hausfrau). **—'s-maid**, *s.* das Kammermädchen; die Kammerjungfer, Zofe. **—'s-slipper**, *s.* der Frauenschuh. **—'s-smock**, *s.* das Schaumkraut (*Bot.*).

Lag, *v.n.* zaudern; (— behind) zurückbleiben. **—gard**, I. *adj.* zaudernd, saumselig, träge. II. *s.* der Zauderer, Schlenderer. **—ging**, *adj.* langsam, zaudernd, zurückbleibend.

Lagoon, Lagune, *s.* die Lagune.

Lai—c, I. *s.* der Laie. II. *adj.* weltlich, laienhaft. **—ty**, *s.* die Laien, der Laienstand, die Laienwelt.

Laid, *imperf. & p.p. of* Lay; — paper, geripptes Papier; to be — up, krank darniederliegen (with, an, *dat.*); garden tastefully — out, geschmackvoll angelegter Garten; money well — out, gut angewandtes Geld.

Lain, *p.p. of* Lie.

Lair, *s.* das Lager.

Laird, *s.* der Herr, Gutsherr (*Scotch*).

[1]**Lake**, I. *s.* der See. II. *attrib.*; — district, der Seekreis, die Seeengegend; — poet, der Dichter aus der englischen Seeschule; the lady of the —, das Fräulein vom See. *Comp.* **—-dwellers**, *pl.* die Pfahlbaubewohner. **—-dwellings**, *pl.* Pfahlbauten.

[2]**Lake**, *s.* der Lack; Lackfarbe; crimson —, Karmesinlack; dull —, matter Lack.

Lama, *s.* der Lama. **—ism**, *s.* der Lamaismus.

Lamb, I. *s.* das Lamm; the — bleats, das Lamm blökt. II. *v.n.* lammen. **—kin**, *s.* das Lämmchen. *Comp.* **—like**, *adj.* lammgleich; lammfromm. **—skin**, *s.* das Lammfell, Lämmerfell. **—'s-wool**, *s.* die Lämmerwolle.

Lambent, *adj.* leckend, schleckend; darüber hinspielend, züngelnd, umspielend (*of flames*); funkelnd.

Lam(b)doidal, *adj.* lambdaförmig.

Lame, I. *adj.*, **—ly**, *adv.* lahm, hinkend; (unsatisfactory) mangelhaft, faul; hinkend, holperig (*as verses*); — of, lahm an (*dat.*); to walk —, hinken; — excuse, schlechte Entschuldigung, faule Ausrede. II. *v.a.* lähmen, lahm machen; (disable) verkrüppeln; entkräften, lähmen (*fig.*). **—ness**, *s.* die Lahmheit, Lähmung; die Schwäche.

Lamell—a, *s.* das Plättchen, Blättchen. **—ar**, *adj.* blätterartig, blätterig. **—ate(d)**, *adj.* blätterig, in Plättchenform. **—iform**, *adj.* blättchenartig.

Lament, I. *v.a.* beklagen, bejammern. II. *v.n.* (weh)klagen; trauern (for, um). III. *s.* die (Weh-)Klage; das Klagelied. **—able**, *adj.*, **—ably**, *adv.* beklagenswert; (mournful) kläglich; (pitiful) jämmerlich. **—ation**, *s.* die Wehklage. **—ations**, *s.* Klagelieder Jeremiä (*B.*). **—ing**, *s.* das Wehklagen, die Wehklage.

Lamina, *s.* das Plättchen, die Schuppe; die Platte (*Bot.*). **—r**, *adj.* in Plättchen. **—te(d)**, *adj.* blätterig. **—tion**, *s.* das Plätten.

Lammas—day, —tide, *s.* die Kettenfeier Petri, der erste August.

Lammergeier, *s.* der Lämmergeier.

Lamp, *s.* die Lampe; die Leuchte, das Licht (*fig.*); reading —, die Studierlampe; safety —, Sicherheitslampe; (street —), die (Straßen)laterne. *Comp.* **—black**, *s.* der Lampenruß. **—-chimney, —-glass**, *s.* der Lampenzylinder. **—light**, *s.* das Lampenlicht. **—lighter**, *s.* der Laternenanzünder. **—-lit**, *adj.* durch Laternen *or* Lampen erleuchtet. **—-oil**, *s.* das Brennöl. **—-post**, *s.* der Laternenpfahl. **—-shade**, *s.* die Lampenglocke. **—-wick**, *s.* der Lampendocht.

Lampoon, I. *s.* die Schmähschrift, das Spottgedicht (on a p., auf einen). II. *v.a.* eine Schmähschrift machen auf *or* gegen einen. **—er**, *s.* der Verfasser einer Schmähschrift.

Lamprey, *s.* die Lamprete, das Neunauge.

Lanate, *adj.* wollig.

Lance, I. *s.* die Lanze, der Wurfspieß; *see* —r; free —, der Soldat auf eigne Hand, Parteigänger; der Freibeuter; rücksichtsloser Gegner; to couch a —, eine Lanze einlegen. II. *v.a.* aufschneiden; mit einer Lanzette öffnen (*Surg.*). **—olate**, *adj.* lanzenförmig. **—r**, *s.* der Lanzenreiter, Ulan. **—rs**, *pl.* die Ulanen; die Lanziers, englische Quadrille. **—t**, *s.* die Lanzette; Name einer medizinischen Zeitschrift. *Comp.* **—-corporal**, *s.* der Gefreite. **—t-arch**, *s.* der Spitzbogen. **—t-window**, *s.* das Spitzbogenfenster.

Land, I. *s.* das feste Land; (country) das Land; (ground) der Boden, die Erde, das Land; (property) das Grundstück, Gut, die Ländereien; — of the living, das Reich der Lebendigen; ploughed —, bebauter Ackerboden; to lay the —, das Land aus dem Gesicht verlieren (*Naut.*); to make (the) —, Land zu Gesicht bekommen (*Naut.*); to see how the — lies, sehen, wie das Land liegt (*lit.*), wie die Sache steht (*fig.*). II. *v.a.* landen; löschen (*of a ship's cargo*); (set down) absetzen; goods safely —ed, Waren glücklich gelöscht; to — a p. in a difficulty, einen in eine Klemme geraten lassen; to — a fish, einen Fisch ans Land bringen *or* ziehen. III. *v.n.* landen; (arrive) ankommen. **—ed**, *adj.*; —ed interest, das Interesse des Grundbesitzers; —ed property, der Landbesitz, das Grundeigentum, die Ländereien; —ed proprietor, der Grundbesitzer. **—grave**, *s.* der Landgraf. **—gravine**, *s.* die Landgräfin. **—ing**, *s.* die Landung; der Treppenabsatz (*of stairs*); *see* —ing-place. **—loper**, *s.* der Landstreicher. **—scape**, *s.* die Landschaft; das Landschaftsstück (*Paint.*). **—ward**, *adv.* landwärts. *Comp.* **—-agent**, *s.* der Vermittler bei Güterverkäufen (*C.L.*); der Gutsverwalter. **—-breeze**, *s.* der Landwind. **—-forces**, *pl.* die Landmacht, das Landheer. **—-grabber**, *s.* der Landschnapper. **—-holder**, *s.* der Gutsbesitzer. **—ing-charges**, *pl.* Löschungsspesen. **—ing-net**, *s.* der Hamen. **—ing-place**, *s.* der Landungsplatz, die Landestelle; der Treppen-Absatz (*Arch.*). **—ing-stage**, *s.* die schwimmende Landungsstelle. **—-jobber**, *s.* der Gütermakler. **—lady**, *s.* die Gutsbesitzerin; die Wirtin (*of an inn*); my —lady, meine Hauswirtin. **—-league**, *s.* die Landliga (in Irland). **—-leaguer**, *s.* der Landligist. **—locked**, *adj.* vom Lande eingeschlossen. **—lord**, *s.* der Gutsherr; der Wirt (*of an inn, etc.*); my —lord, mein Hauswirt. **—lubber,** *s.* die Landratte. —**man,** *s.* der Landbewohner. **—mark,** *s.* der Grenzstein; (mark) das Merkmal (*fig.*); die Landmarke (*Naut.*). **—-measure,** *s.* die Landmessung; das Landmaß. **—-owner,** *s.* der Gutsbesitzer. **—-rail,** *s.* der Wiesenläufer (*Ornith.*). **—-rent,** *s.* der Bodenzins, die Grundrente. **—scape-gardening,** *s.* die Landschaftsgärtnerei. **—scape-painter,** *s.* der Landschaftsmaler, Landschafter (*coll.*). **—-shark,** *s.* der Betrüger (*sailors' sl.*). **—slide, —slip,** *s.* der Bergsturz. **—sman,** *s.* der Landbewohner; die Landratte. **—-steward,** *s.* der Gutsverwalter. **—-surveying,** *s.* die Land(ver)messung; (mapping) die Landaufnahme. **—-surveyor,** *s.* der Landmesser. **—-tax,** *s.* die Grundsteuer. **—-valuer,** *s.* der Landtaxator.

Landau, *s.* der Landauer.

Lane, *s.* der schmale (zwischen Hecken laufende) Weg; die Gasse, das Gäßchen (*in towns*); to form a —, eine Gasse bilden, Spalier machen; it is a long — that has no turning, alles hat sein Ziel.

Lang-syne, *adv.* lange her; auld —, die längst vergangne Zeit; die frohe Jugendzeit.

Language, *s.* die Sprache; (expressions) die Worte, Reden; (style) die Sprache, Ausdrucksweise, der Stil; bad —, grobe Reden, Schimpfreden, gemeine Ausdrücke; teacher of —s, der Sprachlehrer; Modern — Association, der Verein für Neuere Sprachen, Neuphilologenverein; Modern — Quarterly, Vierteljahrschrift für neuere Sprachen. **—d,** *adj.* eine Sprache habend; mit einer Sprache vertraut.

Langu—id, *adj.*, **—idly,** *adv.* schlaff, erschlafft, matt, schwach; (spiritless) mutlos; flau (*C.L.*). **—idness,** *s.* die Mattigkeit, Schlaffheit. **—ish,** *v.n.* (grow —id) matt, schwach, schlaff werden; (pine away) dahinschmachten; (droop) verschmachten; schmachten (for, nach); erschlaffen, stocken (*as war*); darniederliegen (*as trade*). **—ishing,** *adj.*, **—ishingly,** *adv.* schmachtend; matt; flau (*C.L.*); —ishing with disease, siech. **—or,** *s.* die Schwäche, Entkräftung, Mattigkeit, Schlaffheit; (dulness) die Stumpfheit.

Laniar—y, *adj.* zerreißend. **—ies,** *pl.* (—y teeth) Hundszähne.

Lank, *adj.*, **—ly,** *adv.* dünn, mager, schmächtig; — hair, schlichte Haare; — purse, schlaffe Börse. **—ness,** *s.* die Dünnleibigkeit, Magerkeit. **—y,** *adv.* mager, dünnleibig, hochaufgeschossen.

Lanner, *s.* das Weibchen des Würgfalken; der Würgfalk. **—et,** *s.* der Würger, Wachtelfalk.

Lanoline, *s.* das Lanolin.

Lansquenet, *s.* der Landsknecht.

Lantern, *s.* die Laterne (*also Naut.*); durchbrochenes Türmchen (*Arch.*); poop —, Achterlaterne; dark —, Blendlaterne. *Comp.* **—-jawed,** *adj.* hohlwangig, schmalbackig. **—-jaws,** *pl.* hageres Gesicht.

Lanyard, *s.* das Taljereep.

[1]**Lap,** *s.* der Schoß (*of a coat, of a person, also fig.*); der Vorstoß (*of tiles, etc.*); das Band (*Spin.*); — of the ear, das Ohrläppchen. **—el,** *s.* der Aufschlag (am Rocke). **—ful,** *s.* ein Schoßvoll. **—pet,** *s.* der Zipfel (*of a coat*); der Flügel (*of a cap*). *Comp.* **—dog,** *s.* der Schoßhund.

[2]**Lap,** *v.a.* umschlagen; (fold) einschlagen; übereinanderlegen (*boards, etc.*). **—per,** *s.* der Einwickelnde, Aufwickler. *Comp.* **—ping-machine,** *s.* die Lapping-, Doublier-maschine.

[3]**Lap,** I. *s.* das Lecken; das Geräusch anschlagenden Wassers. II. *v.a.* auflecken, aufschlappen; aufschlagen (der Wellen auf einen Felsen).

Lapi—dary, I. *adj.* Stein-, Lapidar-, lapidarisch; —dary style, der kurzgefaßte Stil, Lapidarstil. II. *s.* der Steinschneider; (dealer) der Steinhändler, Juwelier. **—s-lazuli,** *s.* der Lasurstein.

Lapse, I. *s.* das Gleiten; der Lauf (*of a stream*); der Verlauf (*of time*); das Verfallen (*into indolence, etc.*); der Heimfall (*Eccl., Law*); (fault) der Fehler, Fehltritt, das Versehen; der Fall (Adams) (*Theol.*); after the — of a considerable time, nachdem eine beträchtliche Zeit verstrichen war. II. *v.n.* fallen, gleiten; verlaufen, verstreichen, verfließen (*as time*); straucheln, Fehltritte begehen; (slip) verfallen, geraten (into, in); (fail) fehlen, irren; abfallen (from, von); heimfallen (*Law*); —d legacy, verfallenes Vermächtnis.

Lapwing, *s.* der Kibitz.

Larboard, *s.* das Backbord, die linke Seite des Schiffes; pull to —! streich Backbord!

Larceny, *s.* der Diebstahl; simple (compound) —, der Diebstahl ohne erschwerende Umstände (mit verschlimmernden Umständen).

Larch, *s.* die Lärche, Lärchentanne.

Lard, I. *s.* das Schweineschmalz. II. *v.a.* spicken. **—aceous,** *adj.* schmalzartig. **—er,** *s.* die Speisekammer. *Comp.* **—ing-needle,** *s.* die Spicknadel.

Lares, *pl.* die Hausgötter, Laren.

Large, *adj.* groß (*in number and size*); (plentiful) reichlich; (extensive) groß, weit, ausgedehnt; (big) dick, stark; to be (set) at —, frei sein (aus der Haft entlassen sein); a gentleman at —, einer, der nicht mehr zu arbeiten nötig hat; still at —, noch in Freiheit, noch nicht eingefangen (*of criminals*); to talk at —, in den Tag hineinreden; to treat of (a th.) at —, (eine S.) ausführlich besprechen; as — as life, in Lebensgröße. **—ly,** *adv.* reichlich; (greatly) großenteils, größtenteils. **—ness,** *s.* die Größe, Dicke, Stärke; (width) die Weite, Ausdehnung; die Größe (*of mind, etc.*). *Comp.* **—-boned,** *adj.* starkknochig. **—-hearted,** *adj.* großherzig. **—-limbed,** *adj.* starkgliederig. **—-minded,** *adj.* großherzig, weitherzig, hochgesinnt. **—-sized,** *adj.* von großem Format; (large) groß.

Largess, *s.* die Freigebigkeit; die Gabe, Schenkung.

[1]**Lark,** *s.* die Lerche; the — sings, trills, carols, warbles, die Lerche singt, tiriliert, schmettert, wirbelt. *Comp.* **—spur,** *s.* der Rittersporn.

[2]**Lark,** I. *s.* der lustige Streich, Spaß, Schabernack (*sl.*). II. *v.n.* tolle Streiche ausführen, necken (*sl.*).

Larmier, *s.* die Traufplatte, Kranzleiste (*Arch.*).

Larva, I. *s.* die Larve, Puppe (*Entom.*). II. *pl.* Larven, Gespenster. **—l,** *adj.* larvenartig. **—te(d),** *adj.* verlarvt.

Laryn—gitis, *s.* die Luftröhrenentzündung, Kehlkopfentzündung. **—gotomy,** *s.* der Luftröhrenschnitt. **—x,** *s.* der Kehlkopf.

Lascar, *s.* der indische Diener; indische Matrose.

Lascivious, *adj.*, **—ly,** *adv.* wollüstig, geil, unzüchtig, lüstern, unkeusch. **—ness,** *s.* die Geilheit, Lüsternheit; die Unkeuschheit.

Lash, I. *s.* die Schmitze (*of a whip*); (stroke) der Hieb, Streich; (whip) die Peitsche; die Geißel, Rute; to be under the —, unter der Rute stehen. II. *v.a.* peitschen, hauen, geißeln; geißeln (*fig.*); waves — the shore, Wellen schlagen (wütend) an das Ufer; to — **to,** anbinden; to — **up,** aufforren (*hammocks*). III. *v.n.* die Geißel schwingen; to — **out,** hinten ausschlagen (*as a horse*), ausschweifen (*fig.*). **—ing,** *s.* das Peitschen; der Bändsel, Sorrtau (*Naut.*).

Lass, *s.* das Mädchen; die Liebste, der Schatz. **—ie,** *s.* das kleine Mädchen; das Liebchen.

Lassitude, *s.* die Müdigkeit, Mattigkeit.

Lasso, I. *s.* die Wurfschlinge, der Lasso. II. *v.a.* mit dem Lasso fangen.

[1]**Last,** I. *adj.* letzt; (next before) vorig, vergangen; (extreme) äußerst, höchst; (lowest) geringst, niedrigst; the —, der, die, das Letzte (*in time*), Letzte, Hinterste (*in order*); we have not seen the — of it yet, die Sache ist noch nicht zu Ende; es ist noch nicht aller Tage Abend (*prov.*); we shall never hear the — of it, davon werden wir ewig hören; — but one, vorletzt; — of all, (der)allerletzt(e); zu allerletzt; to the —, bis ans Ende; of the — importance, von der

größten Wichtigkeit; — night, gestern abend; to breathe one's —, den letzten Atemzug tun, den Geist aufgeben; at —, schließlich, am Ende; —, not least, zuletzt, aber nicht zumindest. II. *adv.* zuletzt; am Letzten; (—ly) zum Schlusse; when did I see you —? wann habe ich Sie zuletzt gesehen? —**ly**, *adv.* zum Letzten, schließlich.

[2]**Last**, I. *v.n.* dauern, bleiben, bestehen, währen; halten (*as colour*); hinreichen, ausreichen (*as provisions*); ausdauern (*at races*). —**ing**, *adj.*, —**ingly**, *adv.* dauerhaft; (permanent) immerwährend, beständig; —ing colour, echte, haltbare Farbe. —**ingness**, *s.* die Dauerhaftigkeit.

[3]**Last**, *s.* der Leisten; to put on the —, auf *or* über den Leisten schlagen.

[4]**Last**, *s.* die Schiffslast; a — of herrings, 12 Fässer Häringe.

Latch, I. *s.* die Klinke, der Drücker, Schnapper (*on doors*). II. *v.a.* (zu)klinken, zuschließen. *Comp.* —**-key**, *s.* der Haus(tür)schlüssel, der Drücker.

Latchet, *s.* der Schuhriemen.

Late, I. *adj.* (not early) spät; (tardy) zu spät, verspätet; (advanced) vorgerückt; (dead) jüngst verstorben, selig; (former) ehemalig, vormalig; (recent) jüngst; the — owner, der frühere Besitzer; my — brother, mein seliger Bruder; her — husband, ihr verstorbener Mann; the — emperor, der hochselige Kaiser; of —, letzthin, seit einiger Zeit; of — years, seit einigen Jahren; at a — hour, zu später Stunde, sehr spät; to keep — hours, bis tief in die Nacht aufbleiben; you are —, du kommst spät, du kommst zu spät, hast dich verspätet; the train is —, der Zug hat Verspätung. II. *adv.* spät, *see* —ly; of —e, neulich, seit einiger Zeit. —**ly**, *adv.* kürzlich, vor kurzem. —**ness**, *s.* die Verspätung; (— t me) die späte Zeit; die Neuheit (*of a discovery, etc.*); späte Entwicklung (*Hort.*); the —ness of the hour, die späte Stunde.

Lateen-sail, *s.* das Lateinsegel.

Laten—cy, *s.* die Verborgenheit. —**t**, *adj.*, —**tly**, *adv.* verborgen; gebunden, latent (*Phys.*).

Lateral, *adj.* zur Seite gehörig, seitlich, Seiten=; von der Seite kommend, Seiten=, Neben=; seitenständig (*Bot.*).

Lath, I. *s.* die Latte; das Brett (*of a bed*). II. *attrib.*; — partition, der Lattenverschlag. III. *v.a.* latten.

Lathe, *s.* die Drechselbank. *Comp.* —**-band**, *s.* die Treibschnur.

Lather, I. *s.* der (Seifen=)Schaum. II. *v.a.* einseifen; prügeln (*vulg.*). III. *v.n.* schäumen.

Latish, *adj.* etwas spät, ziemlich *or* einigermaßen spät.

Latitud—e, *s.* die Breite, Weite; die Breite, Polhöhe (*Geog., Astr.*); (comprehensiveness) der Umfang, die Ausdehnung; (scope) der Spielraum; (laxity) die Freiheit; in 43° north —e, unter dem dreiundvierzigsten Grade nördlicher Breite; to allow o.s. great —e, sich (*dat.*) große Freiheiten erlauben. —**inal**, *adj.* zur Breite gehörig, Breiten=. —**inarian**, I. *adj.* uneingeschränkt, ungebunden, frei; freigeisterisch, frei denkend *or* handelnd, liberal gesinnt (*Theol.*). II. *s.* der Freidenker. —**inarianism**, *s.* die Freigeisterei, Duldsamkeit.

Latten, I. *s.* das (der) Messing, das Messingblech. II. *adj.* Messing=. *Comp.* —**-wire**, *s.* der Messingdraht.

Latter, *adj.* (*also comp. of* Late) später; (modern) neuer, modern; dieser, dieses, Letzterer, Letztere(s) (*of two*); the — end, der Schluß; — end of the week, das Ende der Woche; — day, der jüngste Tag (*obs.*). —**ly**, *adv.* neuerdings, in der letzten Zeit. *Comp.* —**-day**, *adj.* aus neuster Zeit stammend; —-day Saints, die Mormonen.

Lattice, I. *s.* das Gitter, Gitterwerk; (— window) das Gitterfenster. II. *v.a.* gittern; — (up), übergittern, vergittern. *Comp.* —**-blind**, *s.* der Rolladen, die Jalousie. —**-window**, *s.* das Gitterfenster. —**-work**, *s.* das Gitterwerk.

Laud, *v.a.* loben, preisen; to — a p. up to the skies, einen bis in den Himmel erheben. —**able**, *adj.*, —**ably**, *adv.* lobenswert, löblich, empfehlenswert. —**ableness**, —**ability**, *s.* die Löblichkeit. —**ation**, *s.* das Lob. —**atory**, *adj.* lobend, preisend.

Laudanum, *s.* die Opiumtinktur.

Laugh, I. *v.n.* lachen (*also Poet., fig.*); to — **at**, lachen über (eine S.), (eine S.) belachen; to — at a p. to his face, einem ins Gesicht lachen; — **away!** lache nur zu! to — **down**, durch Lachen verscheuchen; to — **off**, sich lachend (darüber) wegsetzen; to — **out**(**right**), laut lachen; to — out of, durch Lachen abbringen von; to — to scorn, als verächtlich verlachen; to — on the wrong side of the mouth, weinen (*fam.*); to — in one's sleeve, sich (*dat.*) ins Fäustchen lachen. II. *s.* das Lachen, Gelächter; to burst into a tremendous —, eine gewaltige Lache aufschlagen. —**able**, *adj.*, —**ably**, *adv.* lächerlich. —**ableness**, *s.* die Lächerlichkeit. —**er**, *s.* der Lacher. —**ing**, I. *adj.*, —**ingly**, *adv.* lachend; it is no —ing matter, es ist nichts *or* nicht zum Lachen. II. *s.* das Lachen. —**ter**, *s.* das Gelächter; roars of —ter, schallendes Gelächter. *Comp.* —**ing-gas**, *s.* das Lachgas. —**ing-stock**, *s.* Gegenstand des Gelächters, das Stichblatt *or* die Zielscheibe des Spottes. —**ter-loving**, *adj.* vergnügt.

Launch, I. *v.a.* (hurl) schleudern, werfen; vom Stapel laufen lassen (*a ship*); aussetzen (*a boat*); hinaussenden; in Gang setzen (*fig.*); to — into eternity, in die Ewigkeit schicken. II. *v.n.* sich in (eine S.) hineinbegeben; in See gehen (*Naut.*); to — forth, fortgehen (into the world, in die weite Welt), sich verbreiten (*into praises, etc.*), ausschweifen (*into extravagance*). III. *s.* der Stapellauf; (boat) das große Boot (eines Schiffes); steam —, die Dampfpinasse.

Laundr—ess, *s.* die Wäscherin. —**y**, *s.* die Waschanstalt, das Waschhaus; (washing) die Wäsche. *Comp.* —**y-maid**, *s.* das Waschmädchen, Wäschermädchen, die Waschfrau, Wäscherin.

Laur—eate, I. *adj.* mit Lorbeer geschmückt. II. *s.* (poet —eate) der gekrönte Dichter; (court poet) der Hofdichter. —**eateship**, *s.* die Hofpoetenstelle, Stelle *or* der Rang eines Hofdichters. —**el**, *s.* der Lorbeer; crown of —el, der Lorbeerkranz. —**elled**, *adj.* mit Lorbeer geschmückt. —**ustinus**, *s.* der wilde Lorbeerbaum, Laurustinus.

Lava, *s.* die Lava.

Lav—atory, *s.* der Waschraum (oft mit Klosett); der Waschplatz; die Wäsche (*Min.*); public —, die Bedürfnisanstalt. —**e**, *v.* I. *a.* waschen, baden; benetzen, bespülen (*as waves*). II. *n.* sich baden. —**er**, *s.* das Waschbecken.

Lavender, *s.* der Lavendel; to lay up in —, sorgfältig aufbewahren (*fig.*). *Comp.* —**-water**, *s.* das Lavendelwasser, Lavendelöl.

Lavish, I. *adj.*, —**ly**, *adv.* (of, in) freigebig (mit), verschwenderisch (mit); (wild) zügellos; to be — of one's promises, mit Versprechungen um sich werfen. II. *v.a.* verschwenden; to — favours on a p., einen mit Gunstbezeugungen überhäufen. —**ishness**, *s.* die Verschwendung.

Law, *s.* (rule) das Gesetz, die Vorschrift, Regel; die Gesetze, das Recht (*Law*); (— proceedings) das gerichtliche Verfahren, der Prozeß; (science of —) die Rechtswissenschaft, Rechtskunde, Rechtsgelehrsamkeit, (—**s**, *pl.*) die Rechte; das Gesetz (*B.*); die Regel (*of a game, etc.*); —s of the game, Spielregeln; custom-—s, die Zollgesetze; — of nature, das Naturgesetz; — of the land, das (allgemeine) Landrecht; — of reprisals, das Repressalienrecht; canon —, das kanonische Recht; civil —, das bürgerliche Recht; commercial —, das Handelsrecht; common —, das gemeine Recht, Gewohnheitsrecht, Herkommen; criminal —, das Strafrecht; divine —, das göttliche Gesetz; ecclesiastical —, das Kirchenrecht; international —, das Völkerrecht; lynch —, die Lynchjustiz; marine —, das Seerecht; martial —, das Kriegsrecht; moral —, das Sittengesetz; municipal —, das Stadtgesetz; (—**s**, *pl.*) die Stadtrechte, Statuten; physical —, das physikalische Gesetz; statute —, das Verordnungsrecht, das geschriebene Recht; unwritten —, das Gewohnheitsrecht, Herkommen; to study —, die Rechte *or* Jura studieren; to go to —, den Rechtsweg beschreiten; to go to — with s.o., sue a p. at —, einen gerichtlich belangen; to become —, pass into —, zum Gesetze werden; to take the — into one's own hands, sich (*dat.*) selbst Recht verschaffen, eigenmächtig richten; to lay down the —, das Gesetz eigenmächtig diktieren, selbstherrlich verfahren; at —, gerichtlich; good in —, rechtsgültig; in —, Schwieger-; brother *etc.* in —, Schwiegerbruder *etc.*; doctor of —(s) (LL.D.), Doktor der Rechte (Dr jur.); to give a hare good —, einem Hasen einen Vorsprung gewähren. —**ful**, *adj.*, —**fully**, *adv.* gesetzlich, gesetzmäßig; (rightful) rechtmäßig; (legally of force) gültig; (permitted) erlaubt; —ful children, eheliche, rechtmäßige Kinder. —**fulness**, *s.* die Gesetzlichkeit, Rechtmäßigkeit. —**less**, *adj.*, —**lessly**, *adv.* gesetzlos; (illegal) gesetzwidrig, unrechtmäßig; (licentious) zügellos. —**lessness**, *s.* die Gesetzlosigkeit; die Zügellosigkeit. —**yer**, *s.* der Rechtsgelehrte, Rechtsanwalt, Jurist, Advokat. *Comp.* —**-abiding**, *adj.* den Gesetzen gehorchend; —-abiding citizens, friedliche *or* ruhige Bürger. —**-breaker**, *s.* der Gesetzesübertreter. —**-breaking**, *s.* die Gesetzesüberschreitung. —**-court**, *s.* der Gerichtshof. —**giver**, —**maker**, *s.* der Gesetzgeber. —**-Lords**, *pl.* rechtsgelehrte Lords. —**-report**, *s.* die Gerichtszeitung. —**suit**, *s.* der Prozeß, Rechtshandel, die Klage; to carry on a —suit, einen Prozeß führen. —**yer-like**, *adj.* wie ein Jurist.

[1]**Lawn**, *s.* der Rasenplatz, die Rasenfläche. *Comp.* —**-mower**, *s.* die Rasenmähmaschine. —**-roller**, *s.* die Rasenwalze. —**-tennis**, I. *s.* das Netzballspiel, Tennis; to play —-tennis, Netzball *or* Tennis spielen. II. *attrib.*; —-tennis club, der Netzballverein, Tennisklub.

[2]**Lawn**, *s.* die Schleierleinwand, der Battist; French —, der Linon. *Comp.* —**-sleeves**, *pl* die Batistärmel der anglikanischen Bischöfe.

Lax, *adj.* schlaff (*as a cord*); lose, locker (*also fig.*) (not exact) unbestimmt, nicht genau; schlaff (*as discipline*); am Durchfall leidend (*Med.*). —**ative**, I. *adj.* abführend, laxierend. II. *s.* das Abführmittel. —**ity**, —**ness**, *s.* die Ungenauigkeit, Unbestimmtheit; die Schlaffheit (*of morals, etc.*); offener Leib (*Med.*).

[1]**Lay**, *adj.* weltlich, Laien-; (non-professional) nicht fachmännisch, laienhaft, Laien-; — brother, der Laienbruder; — habit, weltliche Kleidung; — clerk, der Laie, welcher die Responsen in der Kirche liest; — preacher, der Laienprediger; — sermons, weltliche Reden, Laienpredigten. *Comp.* —**man**, *s.* der Laie. —**men**, *pl.* die Laien, die Laienwelt.

[2]**Lay**, *s.* das Lied, der (Ge)sang; der Lai; — of Roland, das Rolandslied; — of the Last Minstrel, des letzten Sängers Lied.

[3]**Lay**, I. *s.* das Unternehmen (*sl.*); die Lade (*Weav.*); die Richtung (*in ropemaking*).

[4]**Lay**, *imperf. of* Lie.

[5]**Lay**, *ir.v.a.* legen (*eggs; a cable, etc.*); (— down) niederlegen; umlegen (*corn, etc.*); legen (*dust, etc.*); bannen (*ghosts*); mäßigen, legen (*wind*); (place) legen, (hin)stellen, setzen; (allay) lindern, beruhigen; (present) vorlegen, darlegen; (bet) wetten; how much will you —? was gilt die Wette? (*coll.*); to — bare, entblößen, bloßlegen; to — the cloth, den Tisch decken; to — hold of, (etwas) ergreifen (*lit.*); (einem etwas) anhaben (*fig.*); to — hands on a th., eine S. in Besitz nehmen, ergreifen; they laid their heads together, sie beratschlagten (mit einander); to — low, zu Falle bringen, stürzen; to — open, enthüllen; to — o.s. open to s. th., sich einer S. aussetzen; to — a plot, ein Komplott machen; to — to rest, zur letzten Ruhe bestatten; to — siege to, belagern; to — a tax on, (a th., etwas) besteuern, (a people, einem Volke) eine Steuer auflegen; to — a wager, eine Wette machen, wetten; to — wait for a p., (einem) auflauern; to — waste, verheeren, verwüsten; to — **apart, aside**, bei Seite legen; to — **away**, weglegen; (store) aufheben; to — **by**, beilegen, zurücklegen (*money, etc.*); ablegen (*clothes*); bei Seite legen (*a matter*); to — **down**, niederlegen (*weapons, an office*); bar bezahlen (*money*); einlegen (*wine*); hingeben (*one's life*); aufstellen (*principles*); vorschreiben (*rules*); to — down the law, Gesetze vorschreiben (*lit.*); seine Meinung rücksichtslos zur Geltung bringen (*fig.*); you must — down the (stakes) money, Sie müssen den Einsatz bar erlegen; to — o.s. down, sich niederlegen; to — down in grass, (Land) zu Weideland machen; to — **in**, einlegen, einkaufen, anschaffen; to — **off**, ablegen; to — **on**, auflegen (*colours*); aufzählen (blows, Schläge); anlassen (water, Wasserleitung); to — it on thick, fürchterlich übertreiben, mit dem großen Messer schneiden (*vulg.*); to — the blame upon s.o., einem die Schuld zuschreiben; to — a command on, einschärfen; to — **out**, auslegen, zur Schau stellen (*for show*); ausstellen (*goods, a corpse*); auslegen, ausgeben (*money*); anlegen (*a garden*); aufreißen (*Draw.*); tragieren (*a railway*); entwerfen (*a road*); to — o.s. out (for), sich einrichten für; to — o.s. out to please, sich (*dat.*) Mühe geben (um) zu gefallen; to — **over**, belegen; to — **to**, beilegen (*Naut.*); to — to a p.'s charge, einem (etwas) zur Last legen; to — claim to, Anspruch (auf eine S.) machen *or* erheben; to — to heart, sich (*dat.*) zu Herzen nehmen; to — **together**, zusammenlegen; to — **under**, unterwerfen; to — under an obligation, verbindlich machen, verbinden; to — **up**, (a th., etwas) hinlegen, aufbewahren; (knowledge, money, Kenntnisse, Geld) sammeln; (land, Land) brach liegen lassen, (s.o., einen) krank machen; (a vessel, ein Schiff) abdanken, auflegen; he has been laid up with the gout, er hat einen Anfall von Gicht, Podagra gehabt; she has been laid up with influenza, sie hat infolge von Influenza das Bett *or* das Zimmer hüten müssen. II. *ir.v.n.* Eier legen; to — **about** one, um sich schlagen; to — **on**, zuschlagen (*vulg.*). —**er**, *s.* der Legende; (stratum) die Schicht, Lage, das Lager; der Ableger, Setzling (*Hort.*); plate —er, der Schienenleger (*Railw.*). —**ering**, *s.* das Niederbinden der Steckreiser. —**ing**, *s.* das Legen; das Bewerfen mit Mörtel (*Mas.*); hens past —ing, Hennen, welche nicht mehr legen; —ing out, das Abschnüren (*Surv.*); the —ing out of a garden, die Anlage eines Gartens.

Lay-figure, *s.* die Gliederpuppe, der Gliedermann.

Lazar—et(to), *s.* (—**-house**, *s.*) das Siechenhaus, Krankenhaus, Lazarett, die Heilanstalt.

Laz—ily, *adv. see* —y. —**iness**, *s.* die Faulheit, Trägheit. —**y**, *adj.* faul, träge; (tardy) langsam, träge. —**y-bones**, *s.* der Faulenzer (*coll.*).

Lea, *s.* die Wiese(nfläche), Aue, Flur.

Leach, Letch, I. *s.* die Holzasche zur Lauge. II. *v.a.* (Holzasche) auslaugen. *Comp.* —**-tub**, —**ing-vat**, *s.* das Laugenfaß.

[1]**Lead**, I. *s.* das Blei (*Min., Metall., Chem.*); das Bleilot (*Naut.*); der Bleistift (*Draw.*); der Durchschuß (*Typ.*); citrate of —, salpetersaures Bleioxyd (*Pharm.*); to seal with —, plombieren; to heave the —, loten; phosphate of —, phosphorsaures Blei; sugar of —, der Bleizucker; —white, das Schieferweiß. II. *v.a.* verbleien, mit

Blei überziehen; durchschießen (the lines, die Schriftzeilen). **—ed,** *adj.* durchschossen (*Typ.*). **—en** *adj.* bleiern; bleifarben; (dull, heavy) schwerfällig; —en eyes, tote, glanzlose Augen. **—s,** *pl.* Bleidächer, das glatte Bleidach (*Build.*); die Durchschußlinien (*Typ.*). *Comp.* **—-ashes,** *pl.* Bleiasche. **—-ball,** *s.* die Bleikugel. **—-glance,** *s.* der gemeine Bleiglanz. **—-line,** *s.* die Lotleine. **—-mine,** *s.* die Bleigrube. **—-ore,** *s.* das Bleierz. **—-pencil,** *s.* der Bleistift; ink —-pencil, der Tintenstift. **—-pipe,** *s.* die Bleiröhre.

[2]**Lead,** I. *ir.v.a.* leiten, führen; anführen (*a party, an army*); (— the way) vorangehen; (induce) bewegen, veranlassen, vermögen; anspielen, ausspielen (*a card*); vorspielen, vorsingen (*Mus.*); to — captive, in Gefangenschaft führen; to — a dance, vortanzen; to — s.o. a dance, einen gehörig springen lassen, einem alle Hände voll zu tun geben; to — the fashion, die Mode angeben; to — a sedentary life, eine sitzende Lebensweise führen; to — s.o. a sad life (of it), einen ein Hundeleben führen lassen; to — the way, vorausgehen, vorangehen; den Weg weisen; to — **astray,** verleiten, verführen; to — **into,** (hin)einführen; to — into trouble, in Unglück stürzen; (einem) Kummer verursachen; to — **off,** ableiten, (begin) anfangen; to — off the ball, vortanzen, aufführen; to — **out,** hinausführen; this road —s **to** N, dieser Weg führt nach N. II. *ir.v.n.* (go before) voraus-, vorangehen; (conduct) anführen; die Vorhand haben, anspielen (*Cards*); führen; vorsingen, vorspielen (*Mus.*); to — **off,** vorangehen, beginnen. III. *s.* die Führung, Leitung, die Vorhand (*Cards*); (first throw) der erste Wurf; der Aussatz (*Bill.*); (leash) die Leine; to have the —, den Ton angeben; ausspielen, die Vorhand haben, anwerfen; to take the —, die Führung übernehmen, (of a p., einem) zuvorkommen. **—er,** *s.* der (An-)Führer, Leiter; der Führer (*of a party*); der Vormann, Direktor (*Mus.*); der Vorgeiger (*of an orchestra*); der Tonangeber (*in a choir*); der Leitartikel (*in a newspaper*); (horse) das Riempferd; der Führer, Leiter (*of the House of Commons*). **—ership,** *s.* die Führerschaft; (guidance) die Leitung. **—ing,** I. *adj.* leitend; (chief) hervorragend, erst; —ing article, der Leitartikel (*in a newspaper*); gangbare Ware (*C. L.*); —ing card, erste angespielte Karte; —ing fashion, herrschende Mode; —ing men, führende Geister; Häupter von Parteien; —ing note, große Septime; —ing question, die Suggestivfrage; —ing rein, der Leitzügel. II. *s.* die Leitung, Führung. *Comp* **—ing-strings,** *pl.* das Gängelband, Laufband; to be in —ing-strings, der Leitung anderer unterworfen sein.

Leaf, *s.* (*pl.* Leaves) das Blatt (*of a tree or book, of a table*); der Flügel (*of a door, gate, window, drawbridge*); der Schaft (*Weav.*); der Schleusenflügel (*Hydr.*); das Blättchen (*of gold*); over —, auf dem nächsten Blatte; to turn over a new —, sich bessern, einen neuen Menschen anziehen; to take a — out of a p.'s book, einem nachahmen; to put forth leaves, burst *or* come into —, ausschlagen. **—age,** *s.* das Laub. **—iness,** *s.* die Belaubtheit. **—less,** *adj.* blattlos, entblättert, unbelaubt. **—let,** *s.* das Blättchen. **—y,** *adj.* blätterig, blattreich, belaubt; (tea) gutblättrig. *Comp.* **—-bud,** *s.* die Blätterknospe. **—-gilding,** *s.* die Vergoldung mit Blattgold. **—-gold,** *s.* das Blattgold. **—-stalk,** *s.* der Blattstiel. **—-tobacco,** *s.* der Blättertabak.

[1]**League,** I. *s.* das Bündnis, der Bund; der Verein; die Liga; national —, die National-Liga; naval *or* navy —, der Flottenverein. II. *v.n.* sich verbünden, sich verbinden. **—r,** *s.* der Verbündete.

[2]**League,** *s.* die Seemeile, Meile (= 3 englische Meilen).

[1]**Leaguer,** *s.* das Lager; die Belagerung (*obs.*)

[2]**Leaguer,** *s. see* [1]League.

Leak, I. *s.* die Spalte, das (*and* der) Leck; to spring a —, ein Leck bekommen. II. *v.n.* lecken, laufen, leck werden, leck sein; to — out, auslaufen (*lit.*); allmählich bekannt werden (*fig.*). **—age,** *s.* das (*and* der) Leck; (—ing) Auslecken, Auslaufen; die Leckage (*C.L.*). **—y,** *adj.* leck.

Leal, *adj.* treu (*Scotch*).

[1]**Lean,** *ir.v.* I. *n.* lehnen (against a th., an einer S.), sich lehnen (against a th., an eine S.); sich neigen (to one side, auf eine Seite); (depend) sich verlassen (on a p., auf einen); to — over, überhängen; to — to an opinion, sich zu einer Meinung hinneigen; he —s to old habits, er hängt an alten Gebräuchen. II. *a.* stützen. **—t,** *imperf. & p.p. of* Lean. *Comp.* **—-to,** I. *s.* der Anbau mit Pultdach (*Build.*). II. *a.* anlehnbar.

[2]**Lean,** I. *adj.* mager. II. *s.* das Magere. **—ness,** *s.* die Magerkeit, Dürre; die Leere (*of the purse*). *Comp.* **—-faced. —-visaged,** *adj.* hager im Gesicht.

Leap, I. *v.a.* springen, hüpfen; (dart) hervorschießen; to — for joy, vor Freude hüpfen; to — on . . ., auf (*acc.*) . . . losspringen; to be ready to — out of one's skin, vor Freude aus der Haut fahren mögen (*coll.*); by —s, sprungweise; by —s and bounds, in großen Sätzen, gewaltig schnell; look before you —, trau schau wem! erst besinn's, dann beginn's! (*prov.*); my heart —t to my mouth, beinahe wäre ich herausgeplatzt. II. *v.n.* (cause to —) springen lassen; überspringen, setzen über (*a stream, etc.*). III. *s.* der Sprung, Satz; (space —ed) die Sprungweite; to take a —, einen Sprung tun; einen Satz machen. **—er,** *s.* der Springer. *Comp.* **—-frog,** *s.* das Bockspringen. **—-year,** *s.* das Schaltjahr.

Learn, *v.a.* (*pret. & p.p.* —ed *or* —t) lernen; erfahren; he —s German, er lernt Deutsch; here I —ed the death of my teacher, hier erfuhr ich den Tod meines Lehrers; to — from, ersehen aus; to — of, von . . . lernen; to — how to do a th., erfahren, wie eine S. sich bewerkstelligen läßt; to — wisdom by experience, durch Erfahrung klüger werden; to — by heart, auswendig lernen; to — by rote, mechanisch auswendig lernen. **—ed,** *adj.*, **—edly,** *adv.* gelehrt; erfahren (in einer S.), kundig (einer S.); kenntnisreich; the —ed, die Gelehrten. **—er,** *s.* der Lernende. **—ing,** *s.* (knowledge) die Gelehrsamkeit, der Kenntnisse (*pl.*); (act of —ing) das Lernen, die Erlernung.

Lease, I. *s.* (letting) die Verpachtung, Pacht, Miete; (deed) der Pacht-brief, -vertrag; (time of —) die Pachtzeit; — of life, die Lebensfrist, Lebensdauer; to take a new — of life, neues Leben schöpfen; to have a — of a th., eine S. in Pacht haben; to let (out) on —, verpachten; to take a — of, pachten. II. *v.a.* verpachten; (rent) pachten. *Comp.* **—hold,** I. *s.* die Pachtung; (farm) das Pachtgut. II. *adj.* gepachtet; —hold estate, das Pachtgut; das Mietgrundstück. **—holder,** *s.* der Pächter.

Leash, I. *s.* die Koppelleine (*for dogs*); die Koppel (= 3 Stück); (—-band) das Band. II. *v.a.* koppeln; (bind) zusammenbinden.

Leasing, *s.* das Lügen, die Lüge (*obs.*).

Least, I. *adj.* geringst, kleinst, mindest. II. *adv.* am wenigsten; at (the) —, wenigstens; not in the —, nicht im geringsten, durchaus nicht, keineswegs; — of all, am (aller-)wenigsten; to say the — of it, gelinde gesagt.

Leather, I. *s.* das Leder; upper —s, Oberleder. II. *adj.* ledern, Leder-; — bottle, lederner Schlauch. **—n,** *adj.* ledern. **—y,** *adj.* lederartig. *Comp.* **—-cutter,** *s.* der Riemer. **—-dresser,** *s.* der Lederbereiter.

[1]**Leave,** *s.* die Erlaubnis, Einwilligung; (farewell) der Abschied; (— of absence) der Urlaub; he asked (for) —, er bat um Erlaubnis; he asked for — of absence, er bat um Urlaub, kam um Urlaub ein; by your —, mit Ihrer Erlaubnis;

to go on —, Urlaub nehmen, auf Urlaub gehen; to take —, Abschied nehmen, sich empfehlen; to take French —, sich wegstehlen (aus einer Gesellschaft), weggehen, ohne Abschied zu nehmen; ticket of —, das Entlassungszeugnis. *Comp.* **—-taking**, *s.* das Abschiednehmen.

[2]**Leav—e**, *ir.v.* I. *a.* verlassen; lassen; (bequeath) hinterlassen, vermachen; (entrust, refer) überlassen; (suffer to remain) bestehen lassen; (—e alone) zufrieden, in Ruhe lassen; we left the house, him, wir verließen das Haus, ihn; we left him there, wir ließen (*or* verließen) ihn dort; the Emperor left Kiel for Berlin yesterday afternoon, der Kaiser reiste gestern nachmittag von Kiel nach Berlin ab; he will shortly —e London for the country, er wird bald von London aufs Land reisen; we have left all and have followed thee, wir haben alles aufgegeben und sind Dir gefolgt (*B.*); I —e it to you to arrange the matter, ich überlasse es Ihnen, die Sache zu ordnen; I —e (it) entirely to you (your discretion), ich gebe Ihnen (hierin) völlig freie Hand; —e me alone, laß mich in Ruhe *or* zufrieden; laß mich ungeschoren (*sl.*); —e off crying, laß das Weinen; to —e a p. in the lurch, einen im Stich lassen; to —e one's card, seine Visitenkarte abgeben; to —e a p. word, einem sagen lassen; where have I left my hat? wo habe ich meinen Hut liegen lassen? to — go, fahren lassen, loslassen; to —e **behind**, zurücklassen, hinterlassen; hinter sich lassen; to —e **off**, aufhören (*speaking, etc.*); einstellen (*work*); ablegen (*clothes*); aufgeben (*habits*); to —e **open**, offen lassen (*a door, etc.*); unentschieden lassen (*a question*); to —e **out**, auslassen, fortlassen, weglassen; to —e **over**, übrig lassen; left over, bleibt (übrig) (*Arith.*). II. *n.* ablassen; (depart) abreisen, weggehen. —**ing**, I. *pr. & adj.*; —ing certificate, das Abiturientenzeugnis, das Maturitätszeugnis (*in German secondary schools*); —ing examination, die Abiturientenprüfung. II. *s.* das Verlassen. —**ings**, *pl.* die Überbleibsel, Reste.

Leave—d, *adj.* blätterig; two- —d gate, das Tor mit zwei Flügeln. —**s**, *pl. see* Leaf; das Laub.

Leaven, I. *s.* der Sauerteig (*also fig.*), die Hefe. II. *v.a.* säuern; (taint) anstecken, vergiften; geheimnisvoll und mächtig beeinflussen.

Lecher, *s.* der Wüstling. —**ous**, *adj.*, —**ously**, *adv.* wollüstig, unzüchtig, geil. —**y**, *s.* die Unzucht, Wollüstigkeit; die Geilheit.

Lect—ern, *s.* das Lesepult, Chorpult (*Eccl.*). —**ionary**, *s.* das Kollektenbuch (*Eccl.*). —**ure**, I. *s.* die Vorlesung (on, über, *acc.*); (reproof) die Strafpredigt, der Verweis; to give a —ure, eine Vorlesung halten; curtain —ure, die Gardinenpredigt; to attend a —ure, ein Kolleg besuchen *or* hören; to cut *or* shirk a —ure, eine Vorlesung *or* ein Kolleg schwänzen; University —ures, Universitätsvorlesungen, Vorlesungen an der Universität; University extension —ures, Volkshochschulkurse; to give a course of —ures on, Vorlesungen halten *or* Kolleg lesen über (*acc.*). II. *v.n.* Vorlesungen, ein Vorlesung, einen Vortrag halten (on, über); he is —uring on the Minnesingers, er liest über die Minnesänger. III. *v.a.* (einem) den Text lesen; don't —ure me! halte mir keine Moralpredigt! —**urer**, *s.* der Vortragende, Vorleser; der Hilfsprediger (*Eccl.*); University —urer, der (außerordentliche) Professor; to be appointed —urer, einen Lehrauftrag erhalten. —**ureship**, *s.* das Vorleseramt; die Professur (*Univ.*); das Hilfspredigeramt. *Comp.* —**ure-dues**, *pl.* Kolleg(ien)gelder. —**ure-list**, *s.* das Vorlesungsverzeichnis. —**ure-notes**, *pl.* das Kollegheft, Heft; to take down —ure-notes, ein Kolleg nachschreiben. —**ure-room**, *s.* der Saal für Vorlesungen; der Hörsaal, das Auditorium (*Univ.*).

Led, *imperf. & p.p. see* Lead; — horse, das Handpferd.

Ledge, *s.* der Sims; der hervorragende Rand, Vorsprung; die Tragleiste; der Vorstoß, Anschlag (*Carp.*); (layer) das Lager, die Schicht; die Riffkette, Klippenreihe; die Leiste (*Print.*); — of rocks, das Felsenriff. —**r**, I. *s.* das Hauptbuch (*C. L.*). II. *attrib.*; he has a —r account with, er steht in laufender Rechnung mit.

Ledger-line, *s.* die Nebenlinie (*Mus.*).

[1]**Lee**, *s.* der Schutz; die (Lee)seite; under the —, unter dem Winde, windsicher; under the — of the shore, im Schutz der Küste. —**ward**, I. *adj. & adv.* leewärts, unter dem Winde; to fall to —ward, vom Winde abkommen. *Comp.* —**way**, *s.* die Abtrift; der Rückgang, das Zurückbleiben (*fig.*); to make —way, stark abtreiben; zurückkommen (in einer S.) (*fig.*).

[2]**Lee**, *s.*, —**s**, *pl.* die Hefen.

Leech, I. *s.* der Blutegel (*Zool.*); der Arzt (*obs.*). II. *v.a.* (einem) Blutegel setzen. *Comp.* —**craft**, *s.* die Heilkunde (*obs.*).

Leek, *s.* der Lauch.

Leer, I. der schiefe (boshafte, verliebte) Blick. II. *v.n.* von der Seite sehen, schielen, blinzeln, Seitenblicke werfen (at, nach).

Leet, *s.* das adelige Lehngericht. —**man**, *s.* der Lehngerichtsuntertan.

[1]**Left**, I. *adj.* link; — hand, linke Hand. II. *s.* die Linke; on the —, to the —, links, linkerhand; the second turn to the —, die zweite Querstraße links; keep to the —! links fahren! links ausweichen! links halten! III. *adv.* links; right and —, rechts und links; — turn! linksum! *Comp.* —**-handed**, *adj.* linkhändig; a —-handed person, ein Linkser, Linkhändiger; (awkward) linkisch, ungeschickt; unaufrichtig, boshaft (as a compliment); —-handed marriage, morganatische Ehe. —**-handedness**, *s.* die Linkhändigkeit.

[2]**Left**, *imperf. & p.p. of* Leave.

Leg, *s.* das Bein; die Keule (*of mutton, etc.*); das Bein (*of a chair, etc.*); der Schenkel (*of compasses*); der Schaft (*of boots*); turned-in —s X-Beine; bandy —s, O-Beine; wooden —, der Stelzfuß; to have not a — to stand on, völlig erschöpft sein (*lit.*); keinen Grund zur Entschuldigung haben (*fig.*); to set a p. on his —s, einem (wieder) auf die Beine helfen; to be on one's last —s, aus dem letzten Loche pfeifen (*coll.*). —**ged**, *adj.* (*in comp.*) beinig, mit Beinen; bandy- —ged, O-beinig. —**gings**, *pl.* Gamaschen. *Comp.* —**-bail**, *n.*; to give —-bail, Reißaus nehmen, Fersengeld geben (*coll.*).

Lega—cy, *s.* das Vermächtnis, Legat. —**tee**, *s.* der (Vermächtnis)erbe. —**tor**, *s.* der Erblasser. *Comp.* —**cy-duty**, *s.* die Erbschaftsteuer. —**cy-hunter**, *s.* der Erbschleicher. —**cy-hunting**, *s.* die Erbschleicherei.

Legal, *adj.*, —**ly**, *adv.* gesetzlich, gesetzmäßig; (of — force) rechtsgiltig; — adviser, der Rechtsbeistand, Rechtsfreund; — debt, rechtsgiltige Schuld; — decision, rechtskräftiges Urteil; — documents, Aktenstücke; — proceedings, das Rechtsverfahren; to take — proceedings, den Rechtsweg beschreiten, (einen) vor Gericht verklagen; — profession, die Rechtsgelehrsamkeit; der Beruf eines Rechtsgelehrten; (lawyers) die Rechtsgelehrten; — remedy, das Rechtsmittel; — tender, (als) gesetzliches Zahlungsmittel (dienend). —**ity**, *s.* die Gesetzlichkeit, Gesetzmäßigkeit. —**ization**, *s.* die gerichtliche Beglaubigung; die gesetzliche Bestätigung; die Erhebung zum Gesetz; die Anerkennung einer S. als gesetzlich. —**ize**, *v.a.* rechtskräftig machen; gerichtlich beglaubigen; gerichtlich abfassen; (justify) für rechtmäßig erklären; als gesetzlich anerkennen.

Legat—e, *s.* der Gesandte; der (päpstliche) Legat. —**ion**, *s.* die Gesandtschaft.

Legato, *adv.* gezogen, gebunden (*Mus.*).

Legend, *s.* die (Heiligen)legende (*R.C.*); die Sage; (fable) das Märchen; (inscription) die Umschrift; heroic —, die Heldensage; popular —s, volks-

tümliche Sagen, Volkssagen; the Arthurian —, die Artursage; the — of the Holy Grail, die Gralsage. **—ary**, I. *adj.* sagenhaft; märchenhaft; fabelhaft; —ary tales, Volkssagen. II. *s.* das Legendenbuch.
Legerdemain, *s.* die Gaukelei; (trick) das Kunststück, Taschenspielerstück.
Legib—ility, *s.* die Lesbarkeit, Leserlichkeit. **—le**, *adj.*, **—ly**, *adv.* leserlich, lesbar; (clear) deutlich. **—leness**, *s. see* —ility.
Legion, *s.* die Legion; (great many) große Menge; die Schar; — of Honour, Ehrenlegion. **—ary**, *s.* der Legionssoldat.
Legislat—e, *v.n.* Gesetze geben *or* machen. **—ion**, *s.* die Gesetzgebung. **—ive**, *adj.* gesetzgebend; —ive body, gesetzgebender Körper. **—or**, *s.* der Gesetzgeber. **—ure**, *s.* die Legislatur, gesetzgebende Versammlung.
Legitim—acy, *s.* die Gesetzmäßigkeit; die Berechtigung (*of conclusions, etc.*): (—acy of birth) eheliche Geburt. **—ate**, *adj.*, **—ately**, *adv.* gesetzmäßig; rechtmäßig, wohlbegründet, berechtigt (*as arguments*); ehelich geboren. **—ation**, *s.* der Ausweis, die Berechtigung; die Legitimierung. **—ize**, *v.a.* für gesetzlich erklären; für ehelich (geboren) erklären. **—ist**, *s.* der Legitimist.
Legum—e, *s.* die Hülse. **—es**, *pl.* die Hülsenfrüchte. **—inous**, *adj.*; —inous plants, Hülsenpflanzen.
Leisure, I. *s.* die Muße; to be at —, Muße haben; von Geschäften frei sein; at your —, wann es Ihnen paßt, bei passender Gelegenheit, gelegentlich. II. *adj.* müßig; — hours, Mußestunden; — time, Muße. **—d**, *adj.*, frei, unbeschäftigt; the —d classes, die Vornehmen. **—ly**, *adj. & adv.* mit Muße, gemächlich, behaglich.
Leman, *s.* der (die) Geliebte; der Buhle (*obs.*).
Lemma, *s.* das Lemma; der Hilfssatz.
Lemon, *s.* die Zitrone. **—ade**, *s.* die Limonade. *Comp.* **—-coloured**, *adj.* zitronengelb. **—-ice**, *s.* Gefrorenes mit Zitrone. **—-juice**, *s.* der Zitronensaft. **—-peel**, *s.* die Zitronenschale; candied —-peel, das Zitronat. **—-scoop**, *s.* der Zitronenstecher. **—-squash**, *s.* das Getränk aus Zitronensaft, Sodawasser (und Eis). **—-squeezer**, *s.* die Zitronenpresse.
Lend, *ir.v.a.* (ver=)leihen; gewähren, leisten (*aid*); leihen (*an ear*); reichen, geben (*a hand*); hergeben (*one's name to*); ausleihen (*money on interest*); to — o.s. to, sich hergeben zu. **—er**, *s.* der (Aus=)Leiher, Verleiher.
Length, *s.* die Länge; (extent) die Strecke; die Zeitdauer, Dauer (*of time*); at —, ausführlich; (at last) endlich, zuletzt; at full —, at one's —, der Länge nach; at great —, sehr ausführlich; full —, in voller Länge *or* Ausdehnung; in Lebensgröße; to go to great —s, sehr weit gehen; to carry to great —s, sehr weit treiben; he went the — of saying . . ., er ging so weit, zu sagen . . . **—en**, *v.* I. *a.* verlängern, ausdehnen; dehnen (*syllables*); ausdehnen (*a discourse*); to —en one's stay, seinen Besuch verlängern. II. *n.* sich verlängern, sich ausdehnen. **—ening**, *s.* die Verlängerung. **—ily**, *adv. see* —y. **—iness**, *s.* die Länge; die Langwierigkeit. **—wise**, *adv.* der Länge nach, längelang. **—y**, *adj.* lang; (spun out) langwierig, gedehnt.
Leni—ency, *s. see* Lenity. **—ent**, *adj.*, **—ently**, *adv.* mild, gelind. **—tive**, I. *adj.* lindernd. II. *s.* das Linderungsmittel. **—ty**, *s.* die Milde, Gelindigkeit.
Lens, *s.* das Linsenglas, die Linse.
[1]**Lent**, *imperf. & p.p. of* Lend.
[2]**Lent**, I. *s.* die Fasten (*pl.*), Fastenzeit. II. *attrib.*; — lily, gelbe Narzisse; — sermon, die Fastenpredigt; — term, der zweite Universitätsterm des akademischen Jahres, das Quartal von Neujahr bis Ostern (*Cambridge Univ.*). **—en**, *adj.* Fasten=, fastenmäßig; —en fare, die Fastenspeise, magere Kost.
Lenti—cular, *adj.* linsenartig; (**—form**, *adj.*) linsenförmig. **—l**, *s.* die Linse. *Comp.* **—l-soup**, *s.* die Linsensuppe.
Leonine, *adj.* löwenartig; — strength, die Löwenstärke; — verses, leoninische Verse.
Leopard, *s.* der Leopard.
Lep—er, *s.* der Aussätzige. **—rosy**, *s.* der Aussatz. **—rous**, *adj.* aussätzig.
Lepidopter—a, *pl.* Schuppenflügler, Schmetterlinge. **—ous**, *adj.* zu den Schuppenflüglern gehörig.
Leporine, *adj.* hasenartig, hasenmäßig.
Lesion, *s.* die Beschädigung, Verletzung.
Less, I. *adj. & adv.* kleiner, geringer, weniger; weniger, minus (*Mathem.*); more or —, mehr oder minder; what he said was little — than treason, was er sagte war schon fast Hochverrat; I could not write, much — could I come, schreiben konnte ich nicht, kommen noch viel weniger; it was no — a person than . . ., es war kein Geringerer als . . .; I am a loser no — than you, ich verliere ebenso gut wie Sie; I cannot sell it for —, ich kann es nicht billiger abgeben; the — one praises o.s., the more . . ., je weniger man sich selber lobt, desto mehr . . .; neverthe—, nichtsdestoweniger. II. *s.* der, die, das Geringere, Wenigere; (inferior) der Geringere. **—en**, *v.* I. *a.* kleiner, geringer machen, verkleinern, verringern; schmälern (*one's reputation, etc.*); (degrade) herabsetzen; demütigen (*pride*); ermäßigen (*prices*); mildern (*pain*). II. *n.* kleiner, geringer werden, abnehmen. **—er**, *adj. & adv.* kleiner, geringer, weniger; the —er light, das kleinere Licht.
Less—ee, *s.* der Mieter, Pächter. **—or**, *s.* der Vermieter, Verpachtende.
Lesson, *s.* das Vorlesestück, der vorgeschriebene Bibeltext (*Eccl.*); (task) die Aufgabe, Lektion; (instruction) der Unterricht, die (Schul)stunde, (precept) die Lehre, Vorschrift; (warning) die Warnung, der Denkzettel; let this be a — to you, lassen Sie sich das zur Warnung dienen; to give **s.o.** a —, einem den Text lesen; to hear —s, Aufgaben abhören; home —s, häusliche Arbeiten.
Lest, *conj.* damit nicht, daß nicht; (for fear) aus Furcht daß; but — you should not understand me well, aber damit ihr mich recht verstehen möget; — he repent, damit er es nicht bereut.
[1]**Let**, *ir.v.* I. *a.* lassen; (permit) zulassen, gestatten, erlauben; vermieten, verpachten (*a house, etc.*); — him come, laß ihn kommen; to — alone, in Ruhe lassen, nicht anrühren; — me alone for that, laß mich nur machen; — well alone, was dich nicht brennt, das blase nicht (*prov.*); — alone anyone else, geschweige denn ein andrer; to — be, fahren lassen; — it be! rühre es nicht an! — me be! laß mich zufrieden; to — blood, zur Ader lassen; — come what may, es mag daraus entstehen, was da will; to — fly, fliegen lassen, abdrücken; to — go, (allow to depart) abgehen lassen; (set free) in Freiheit setzen; (— loose) fahren lassen, loslassen; (part with) verkaufen lassen; — us go, laßt uns gehen; to — a p. know, einen wissen lassen, einem zu wissen tun; she lives by —ting lodgings, sie lebt vom Zimmervermieten; to — pass, — slip, fahren lassen, entschlüpfen lassen; to — see, zeigen; to — **down**, niederlassen, herunterlassen, herablassen (*a curtain, etc.*); (lower) herablassen, erniedrigen; to — **in**, einlassen, (admit) hineinlassen, Zutritt gestatten; with red silk — in, mit roter Seide ausgeschlagen; to — **into**, einweihen in, wissen lassen (*a secret, etc.*); to — **off**, abschießen (*a gun, etc.*); to — a p. off, einem eine Strafe erlassen; (from a promise, an oath, etc., einen seines Versprechens, seines Eides, ꝛc.) entbinden; to — a p. off too easily, einem die Strafe zu leicht schenken; to — **on**, sich (*dat.*) merken lassen (*vulg.*); to — **out**, herauslassen; (widen) auslassen; (disclose) ausplaudern (*a secret*); (hire

out) vermieten; to — the cat out of the bag, das Geheimnis verraten, sich verplaudern. II. *n.* sich vermieten (at, for, für); a house to (be) —, ein Haus zu vermieten; this house —s well, dieses Haus vermietet sich gut.

[2]**Let**, *s.* das Hindernis; without —, ohne Widerstand; without — or hindrance, ohne irgend welchen Widerstand.

[3]**Let!** *interj.* gestreift! ungültig! (*Lawn Tenn.*).

Letch, *see* Leach.

Letharg—ic, *adj.*, **—ically**, *adv.* schlafsüchtig, lethargisch; träge (*fig.*). **—y**, *s.* die Schlafsucht, der todähnliche Schlaf, die Lethargie (*Med.*); die Trägheit, Schläfrigkeit, Stumpfheit (*fig.*).

Leth—e, *s.* die Lethe; die Vergessenheit (*fig.*). **—al**, *adj.* tödlich; —al chamber, die Vorrichtung zur Tötung herrenloser Hunde und Katzen.

Letter, I. *s.* der Buchstabe; die Letter, Schrift (*Typ.*); (epistle) der Brief; (literal meaning) der buchstäbliche Sinn, der Buchstabe; black-—, gotische Schrift; by —, brieflich; to the —, buchstäblich; dead —, toter Buchstabe (*fig.*); unbestellbarer Brief; dead-—office, Abteilung für unbestellbare Briefe; —of advice, Avisbrief; — of attorney, die Vollmacht; — of conveyance, Frachtbrief; — of credit, Kreditbrief; — of grace, Aufschubsbrief; Begnadigungsbrief; — of introduction, — of recommendation, Empfehlungsbrief; — of marque, Kaperbrief (*Naut.*); — of safe conduct, Geleitsbrief, Freipaß; —s patent, offene königliche Briefe, Patentbriefe, das Patent; registered —, eingeschriebener Brief; — exempt from postage, der portofreie Brief. II. *v.a.* mit Buchstaben versehen, zeichnen; (ein Buch) betiteln (*Bookb.*). **—ed**, *adj.* gelehrt, gebildet; wissenschaftlich, litterarisch; betitelt (*Bookb.*). **—ing**, *s.* die Bezeichnung mit Buchstaben; die Betitelung auf dem Einbande (*of a book*). **—s**, *pl.* die Literatur(=Wissenschaft); man of —s, der Literat, Gelehrte. *Comp.* **—-bag**, *s.* der Briefbeutel. **—-balance**, *s.* die Briefwage. **—-book**, *s.* das Briefbuch. **—-box**, *s.* der Briefkasten; der Briefschalter (*in post-offices*). **—-card**, *s.* die Briefkarte, der Kartenbrief. **—-carrier**, *s.* der Briefträger. **—-case**, *s.* die Brieftasche. **—-cover**, *s.* der Briefumschlag. **—-founder**, *s.* der Schriftgießer. **—-mark**, *s.* das Postzeichen. **—-packet**, *s.*, **—-package**, *s.* (bundle of —s) das Briefbund, Briefpaket. **—press**, I. *s.* der Druck, Text. II. *attrib.*; Pressen=. **—-press**, *s.* die Briefpresse, Kopierpresse. **—-shoot**, *s.* der Briefeinwurf. **—-weight**, *s.* der Briefbeschwerer. **—-writer**, *s.* der Briefschreiber.

Lettuce, *s.* der Lattich; cultivated —, garden —, der Salat; round-headed garden —, der Kopfsalat.

Leuco—ma, *s.* die Hornhauttrübung. **—rrhœa**, *s.* der weiße Fluß.

Levant, *v.n.* durchbrennen (*coll.*). **—er**, *s.* der Ausreißer, Durchbrenner (*coll.*).

[1]**Levee**, I. *s.* der Uferdamm, Schutzdamm eines Flusses (*Amer.*). II. *v.a.* einen Fluß eindämmen.

[2]**Levee**, *s.* das Lever, der Morgenempfang (eines Fürsten).

Level, I. *s.* die ebene Fläche; (equal height) gleiche Höhe, Gleichheit; (direction) die Richtung, Schußlinie, das Ziel; (carpenter's, etc. —) die Setz=, Wasser=, Blei=wage; die Richtschnur, der Maßstab (*fig.*); das Nivellierinstrument, die Libelle, Wage (*Surv.*); on a — with, in gleicher Höhe mit (*lit.*); auf gleicher Höhe, Stufe mit (*fig.*); — of the sea, der Meeresspiegel; spirit —, Wasserwage mit Libelle; true —, wahrer Horizont; water —, der Wasserspiegel. II. *v.a.* gleich, gerade, eben, wasserrecht machen; abwägen, nivellieren (*Surv.*); einebnen (*roads, etc.*); wagerecht machen (*Min.*); gleich machen (*fig.*); (point) zielen, richten, (at, auf, nach); to — with the ground, dem Boden gleich machen; to — up, auf die gleiche Höhe *or* den gleichen Rang erheben; to — down, herabdrücken, auf gleiche Höhe mit andern hinunterdrücken, ausgleichen. III. *v.n.* zielen, gerichtet sein. IV. *adj.* eben, gleich, flach, gerade, wagerecht; to make —, ebnen, gleich machen; — crossing, die Kreuzung im Niveau, der Niveauübergang; — plain, die wagerechte Fläche, Ebene; — range, der Kernschuß; — stress, die schwebende Betonung. **—ler**, *s.* der Gleichmacher (*also Pol.*); der Nivellierer (*Surv.*); (earth scraper) die Nivellierschaufel. **—ling**, I. *adj.* gleich machend; Nivellier=. II *s.* das Nivellieren; die Gleichmachung; der Formenausgleich, Systemzwang (*Gramm.*). **—ness**, *s.* die gleiche Höhe, Gleichheit; die Ebenheit.

Lev—er, *s.* der Hebel, das Hebeleisen; die Abgleichstange (*Horol.*). **—erage**, *s.* die Hebekraft. *Comp.* **—er-watch**, *s.* die Zylinderuhr.

Leveret, *s.* junger Hase im ersten Jahre.

Leviathan, *s.* der Leviathan.

Levigat—e, *v.a.* zu Staub zerreiben, pulverisieren. **—ion**, *s.* die Zerreibung zu Staub.

Levity, *s.* die Leichtfertigkeit, der Leichtsinn; die Sorglosigkeit, Flüchtigkeit; to treat with —, auf die leichte Achsel nehmen, leichtfertig behandeln.

Levy, I. *v.a.* erheben (*taxes*); ausheben (*troops*); anfangen (*war*); to — a fine, einen Prozeß um Landbesitz führen. II. *s.* die Erhebung; die Aushebung; (levied troops) ausgehobene Truppen; raw levies, nicht ausgebildete Rekruten; — en masse, das Massen=Aufgebot, der Landsturm.

Lewd, *adj.*, **—ly**, *adv.* ausschweifend, liederlich, unzüchtig. **—ness**, *s.* die Unzucht, Liederlichkeit.

Lewis, *s.* der Zwingkeil.

Lexico—grapher, *s.* der Wörterbuchschreiber, Verfasser eines Wörterbuches. **—graphic**, *adj.* lexikographisch. **—graphy**, *s.* die Abfassung eines Wörterbuchs. **—n**, *s.* das Wörterbuch.

Leze-Majesty, *s.* die Majestätsbeleidigung; der Hochverrat; crime of —, das Majestätsverbrechen.

Liab—ility, *s.* (responsibility) die Verantwortlichkeit; die Verbindlichkeit, Haftpflicht (*C. L.*); (exposedness) das Ausgesetztsein; (tendency) der Hang; limited —ility company, (Ltd.,) die Gesellschaft *or* Genossenschaft mit beschränkter Haftung (G. m. b. H.). **—le**, *adj.* ausgesetzt, geneigt; —le to duty, zollpflichtig, versteuerbar; this price is —le to discount, von diesem Preise geht ein Rabatt ab; —le for, verantwortlich für, verbindlich; to be —le to a th., einer Sache ausgesetzt sein; —le to be overlooked, in Gefahr übersehen *or* nicht gesehen zu werden.

Liaison, *s.* das (Liebes=)Verhältnis, die Liebschaft.

Liar, *s.* der Lügner, die Lügnerin; show me a — and I'll show you a thief, wer lügt, der stiehlt auch (*prov.*).

Lias, *s.* der Lias (*Geol.*).

Libation, *s.* das Trankopfer.

Libel, I. *s.* die Schmähschrift, Verunglimpfung, Verleumdung; das Libell, die Klageschrift (*Law*); der Klagegrund (*Scotch Law*); action for —, die Verleumdungsklage. II. *v.a.* schmähen, beschimpfen; schriftlich klagen gegen. III. *v.n.* Schmähschriften schreiben, Verunglimpfungen verbreiten. **—ler**, *s.* der Schmähschriftschreiber, der Verleumder. **—lous**, *adj.*, **—lously**, *adv.* schmähend, Schmäh=, verleumderisch.

Libella, *s.* die Wasserjungfer, Libelle (*Ent.*); die Wasserwage; die Wage (*Astron.*).

Liber, *s.* der Bast.

Liber—al, I. *adj.*; **—ally**, *adv.* freigebig; (noble) edel, großmütig; reichlich, nicht beschränkt (*as an allowance*), frei(sinnig), weitherzig, aufgeklärt (*as education, views*); (free) frei, offen; liberal, nicht streng (*as an interpretation*); liberal (*as politics*); he received a —al education, er erhielt eine tüchtige allgemeine Bildung *or* eine höhere Bildung; —al professions, die höheren Berufe, gelehrte Berufe; —al Unionist, ein

Liberaler, welcher an der Vereinigung Irlands mit England unter einem Parlament festhält. II. *s.* der Liberale, Freisinnige. **—alism**, *s.* der Liberalismus, Freisinn. **—ality**, *s.* die Großmut, Liberalität; die Freigebigkeit; (freedom from bigotry) die Freisinnigkeit, Unparteilichkeit, Vorurteilslosigkeit. **—ate**, *v.a.* befreien (from, von); frei geben *or* machen (*slaves*). **—ation**, *s.* die Befreiung (von); die Freilassung (aus). **—ator**, *s.* der Befreier. **—tine**, *s.* der Freigelassene (*Rom. Hist.*); der Wüstling. **—tinism**, *s.* die Liederlichkeit, Ausschweifung. **—ty**, *s.* die Freiheit; (privilege) das Recht, Vorrecht, Privilegium; (leave) die Erlaubnis; der Freibezirk; (breach of decorum) die Ungebührlichkeit, Frechheit; to take —ties, sich (*dat.*) Freiheiten erlauben; to be at —ty, frei sein; I am not at —ty to disclose ..., ... ich darf nicht enthüllen; to set at —ty, befreien; —ty of the press, Preßfreiheit.

Libidinous, *adj.*, **—ly**, *adv.* unzüchtig, wollüstig.

Libra, *s.* die Wage (*Ast.*). **—tion**, *s.* das Schwanken, Schweben.

Librar—ian, *s.* der Bibliothekar. **—ianship**, *s.* das Amt eines Bibliothekars. **—y**, *s.* die Bibliothek, Büchersammlung, Bücherei; circulating —y, Leihbibliothek; free —y, die Volksbücherhalle; reference —y, die Handbibliothek.

Librett—ist, *s.* der Librettoschreiber, Textdichter. **—o**, *s.* das Libretto, (Opern-)Textbuch.

Lice, *pl. see* Louse.

Licen—ce, *s.* (leave) die Erlaubnis, Freiheit, Genehmigung; die Vollmacht, Konzession; die Konzessionsabgabe; (—sing document) der Erlaubnisschein; (excess) die Zügellosigkeit, Ausschweifung; poetical —ce, dichterische Freiheit; —ce to print a book, die Druckerlaubnis; dog —ce, der Hundeschein; to take out a —ce, (sich, *dat.*) eine Konzession beschaffen *or* erwerben. **—se**, I. *s. see* —ce. II. *v.a.* mit einem Erlaubnisschein versehen, (einem) erlauben (*to sell, etc.*); (empower) obrigkeitlich bewilligen, konzessionieren, ermächtigen; zensieren (*a play, etc.*); —sed victualler, konzessionierter Gastwirt. **—ser**, *s.* der Aussteller einer Konzession, eines Erlaubnisscheins; der Zensor. **—sing**, *adj.*; —sing act, das Zensuredikt. **—tiate**, *s.* der Lizenziat. **—tious**, *adj.*, **—tiously**, *adv.* zügellos, ausschweifend; (dissolute) liederlich. **—tiousness**, *s.* die Ausschweifung, Liederlichkeit.

Lichen, *s.* die (Knötchen)flechte.

Lich-gate, *s.* das Friedhoftor (mit Seitenkapelle).

Lick, I. *v.a.* lecken; (beat) prügeln, durchwichsen (*vulg.*); to — the dust, ins Gras beißen; to — into shape, zurecht lecken; in die gehörige Form bringen (*fig.*); to — up, auflecken. II. *s.* das Lecken; (smear) die Schmiere, der oberflächliche Anstrich; (blow) der Schlag (*sl.*); salt —, die Salzlecke. **—er**, *s.* der Lecker. **—erish**, *adj.* leckerhaft; begierig, lüstern (after, nach); den Appetit reizend, lecker; verlockend (*fig.*). **—ing**, *s.*; to give s.o. a good —ing, einen gehörig durchwichsen *or* durchprügeln (*sl.*). *Comp.* **—spittle**, *s.* der Speichellecker, niedrige Schmeichler.

Lictor, der Liktor.

Lid, *s.* der Deckel; eye—, das Augenlid.

[1]**Lie**, I. *s.* die Lüge; to tell —s, lügen; to give the — (to a p.), (einen) Lügen strafen; white —, Notlüge. II. *v.n.* lügen; he —s like a book, er lügt wie gedruckt.

[2]**Lie**, I. *s.* die Lage. II. *ir.v.n.* liegen; (rest) liegen, ruhen; (be) sein, liegen; (consist) bestehen; (lean) sich stützen, sich lehnen (on, auf (*acc.*), against, an (*acc.*)); (remain) liegen bleiben; (— encamped) sich lagern; to — in prison, gefangen liegen; to — idle, müßig, tot liegen; her talents do not — that way, dafür ist sie nicht begabt, dazu hat sie keine Anlagen; to — **about**, umherliegen, herumliegen; to — **along**, schief liegen (*Naut.*); to — **at** full length, ausgestreckt daliegen; to — at the root of a matter, einer Sache zu Grunde liegen, etwas verursachen; this —s at his door, das ist ihm zuzuschreiben; to — **by**, still *or* unbenutzt liegen; (— near) neben liegen; to — **down**, sich niederlegen, schlafen gehen, ruhen; to — **in**, in Wochen liegen; as much as in me —s, so viel an mir liegt; to — in state, auf dem Paradebette liegen; to — in wait for a p., einem auflauern; to — **on**, obliegen; it —s on me now, es liegt mir jetzt ob; to — on hand, liegen bleiben; to — **over**, nicht zur Verfallzeit bezahlt werden (*C.L.*), aufgeschoben werden; to — **to**, beilegen; the way lay **through** a wood, der Weg führte durch ein Holz; to — **under**, unterliegen; to — under cover, von Batterien gedeckt sein; to — under a p.'s displeasure, bei einem in Ungnade stehen; to — under an imputation, angeschuldigt *or* beschuldigt sein (einer S.); to — under the necessity, genötigt sein; to — under obligations, Verpflichtungen haben; to — **with**, liegen bei ...; schlafen bei; (einem Frauenzimmer) beiwohnen; it —s with him, er muß, es ist an ihm, es steht bei ihm. **—r**, *s.*; —r in wait, der Auflaurer.

Lief, *adv.* gern; I had as — go as not, ich ginge eben so gern als nicht; I had as — die as do ..., ich würde lieber sterben als ... tun.

Liege, I. *adj.* lehenspflichtig; — lord, der Lehensherr, Souverän. II. *s.* der Lehensmann, Vasall; der Lehensherr.

Lien, *s.* das Retentions-, Pfand-recht (auf eine S.).

Lieu, *s.*; in — of, anstatt. **—tenancy**, *s.* die Leutnantsstelle; (—tenants) das Korps der Leutnants. **—tenant**, *s.* der Leutnant; Lord —tenant, der Vizekönig (von Irland); erster Friedensrichter (einer Grafschaft). **—tenantship**, *s.* die Leutnantsstelle. *Comp.* **—tenant-colonel**, *s.* der Oberstleutnant. **—tenant-colonelcy**, *s.* Oberstleutnantsstelle. **—tenant-general**, *s.* der Generalleutnant.

Life, *s.* das Leben; (vigour) das Leben, die Lebenskraft; (way of living) der Lebenswandel; (—time) die Lebenszeit; (biography) der Lebenslauf, die Lebensbeschreibung; (liveliness) die Lebendigkeit, Lebhaftigkeit; das Leben, Original (*Paint.*); (rank) der Stand; (living thing) das Menschenleben; das lebende Wesen, die Person; (*pl.*) Menschen(leben); through —, durch mein (sein *etc.*) ganzes Leben; they lost their lives, sie verloren ihr Leben, sie kamen ums Leben; many lives were saved, viele Menschen wurden gerettet *or* retteten ihr Leben, kamen mit dem Leben davon; drawn from —, nach dem Leben gezeichnet; high (low) —, das vornehme Leben, (die niederen Klassen); as large as —, in Lebensgröße; to come to — again, wieder aufleben; for —, auf Lebenszeit; for the — of me, und sollte es mir das Leben kosten; to enter upon —, in die Welt eintreten; to flee for one's —, sein Leben durch schleunige Flucht zu retten suchen, aus Leibeskräften rennen *or* davonlaufen; hold on for your lives, haltet fest, wenn euch euer Leben lieb ist! to give — to, put — into, beleben; still —, das Stilleben (*Paint.*); to have (*or* bear) a charmed —, kugelfest sein, unverwundbar sein; to the —, nach dem Leben, nach der Natur; — and death struggle, Kampf auf Leben und Tod; — to come, das zukünftige Leben, Leben nach dem Tode; — everlasting, das ewige Leben; there is — in it, die Sache ist noch nicht verloren (*coll.*). **—less**, *adj.*, **—lessly**, *adv.* leblos; unbelebt, tot; unwirksam (*fig.*); (dull) matt, schlaff. **—lessness**, *s.* die Leblosigkeit. *Comp.* **—-annuitant**, *s.* der Leibrentner. **—-annuity**, *s.* die Leibrente. **—-belt**, *s.* der Rettungsgürtel. **—-blood**, *s.* das Lebensblut. **—-boat**, *s.* das Rettungsboot. **—-buoy**, *s.* die Rettungsboje. **—-giving**, *adj.* belebend. **—-guard**, *s.* die Leibwache. **—-guardsman**, *s.* der Leibgardist. **—-insurance**, I. *s.* die Lebensversicherung. II. *attrib.*; —-insurance company, die Lebensversicherungsgesellschaft. —**like**, *adj.* lebenswahr, treu nach dem Leben. —**long**, *adj.* lebenslänglich. —-**membership**, *s.* die Mitgliedschaft auf Lebenszeit. —-**preserver**, *s.* der Schwimmgürtel, Rettungsgürtel; (stick) der Knüttel mit Bleiknopf, Totschläger. —-**size**, I. *s.* die Lebensgröße. II. *attrib.*; —-size picture, das Bild in Lebensgröße. —-**subscription**, *s.* einmaliger Beitrag auf Lebenszeit. —**time**, *s.* die Lebenszeit; in his —time, bei (*or* zu) seinen Lebzeiten.

Lift, I. *v.a.* (auf)heben; erheben (*fig.*); aufschlagen, erheben (*the eyes*), aufrichten (*the mind, one's head*), erheben (*the voice*); to — up one's eyes, die Augen erheben; to — (up) one's hand against a p., einen schlagen; (rebel) sich gegen einen auflehnen. II. *s.* das (Auf-)Heben; der Hub (*also Mech.*); das Hebewerkzeug, der Hebebaum (*Mach.*); der Toppenant (*Naut.*); hydraulic —, hydraulischer Aufzug; passenger —, der Fahrstuhl, Aufzug für Personen; to give a p. a —, einem helfen; einem einen Sitz im Wagen anbieten. —**er**, *s.* der, die, das Hebende. —**ing**, *s.* das Heben; machine for —ing, der Hebebock; —ing up, das Aufheben, Erheben.

Lig—**ament**, *s.* das Band, die Flechse. —**ation**, *s.* das Binden. —**ature**, *s.* das Band, die Binde; die Ligatur (*Surg.*); die Bindung (*Mus.*); der Doppelbuchstabe, die Ligatur (*Typ.*). —**ula**, —**ule**, *s.* das Blatthäutchen (*Bot.*).

[1]**Light**, I. *s.* das Licht (*also fig. & Paint.*); (day) der Tag, die Helligkeit, das Tageslicht; die Beleuchtung; (point of view) das Licht, der Gesichtspunkt; will you give me a — for my cigar, darf ich Sie um Feuer für meine Zigarre bitten? to throw — upon a subject, einen Gegenstand ins rechte Licht setzen, erklären, erläutern; to bring to —, an das Tageslicht bringen; to come to —, an den Tag kommen; to stand in one's own —, sich (*dat.*) selbst im Lichte stehen; according to his —s, nach bester Einsicht *or* besten Kräften. II. *adj.* licht, hell; leuchtend (*fig.*); (fair) blond; — blue, hellblau; the — Blues, die Cambridger Studenten (*coll.*). III. *ir.v.a.* anzünden; to — up, erleuchten; to — a p., einem leuchten; to — a fire, ein Feuer anmachen; to — a cigar, sich (*dat.*) eine Zigarre anzünden. IV. *v.n.*; his countenance —ed up, sein Gesicht wurde strahlend. —**en**, *v.n.* blitzen; (brighten) sich aufhellen. —**er**, *s.* der Leuchtende, Anzünder; lamp-—er, der Lampenanzünder; der Laternenanzünder (*of street lamps*). —**ning**, *see* Lightning. —**s**, *pl.* lungs (*of animals*). *Comp.* —-**ball**, *s.* die Feuerkugel. —**house**, *s.* der Leuchtturm. —-**ship**, *s.* das Feuer-, Leucht-schiff.

[2]**Light**, I. *adj. & adv.* leicht (*also of troops, food, money, rain, gait, character, etc.*); to make — of a th., eine S. nicht achten, gering schätzen, leicht nehmen; a — matter, eine Kleinigkeit; — of foot, leichtfüßig. II. *v.n.*; to — on, (fall) fallen auf, sich niederlassen auf (*as birds*); stoßen, geraten auf (eine Sache, eine Stelle); zufällig begegnen (a person, einem); *see* Alight; to — on one's feet, auf die Füße fallen. —**en**, *v.a.* leichter machen; lichten, löschen (*Naut.*); erleichtern (*fig.*). —**er**, *s.* der Lichter, das Lichterfahrzeug. —**erage**, *s.* das Lichtergeld. —**ly**, *adv.* leicht; (superficially) oberflächlich, obenhin; (thoughtlessly) gedankenlos, unbesonnen; (frivolously) leichtsinnig; (wantonly) leichtfertig, unsittlich; schnell; —ly come, —ly go, wie gewonnen, so zerronnen (*prov.*); to treat —ly, als unerheblich behandeln; to take —ly, auf die leichte Achsel nehmen. —**ness**, *s.* die Leichtigkeit; der Leichtsinn; die Leichtfertigkeit; (nimbleness) die Flinkheit, Gewandtheit; —ness of the head, der Schwindel. —**some**, *adj.* fröhlich, heiter. *Comp.* —-**armed**, *adj.* leicht bewaffnet. —-**bodied**, *adj.* leicht, schwach (*as wine*). —-**fingered**, *adj.* langfingerig, diebisch. —-**footed**, —-**heeled**, *adj.* leichtfüßig, schnellfüßig. —-**headed**, *adj.* wirr im Kopf; irr(e). —-**hearted**, *adj.* leichten Herzens, lustig, wohlgemut, fröhlich. —-**heartedness**, *s.* der Frohsinn. —-**horse**, *s.* die leichte Reiterei. —-**minded**, *adj.* leichtsinnig.

Lightning, *s.* der Blitz; forked (sheet) —, der Zickzack-Blitz, (das Wetterleuchten); —s flash, Blitze zucken; flash of —, der Blitzstrahl, Blitz. *Comp.* —-**conductor**, —-**rod**, *s.* der Blitzableiter. —-**discharge**, *s.* der Blitzschlag.

Lign—**eous**, *adj.* hölzern; (woody) holzig. —**ine**, *s.* die Holzfaser. —**ite**, *s.* der Lignit. —**um**, *s.* das Holz. —**um-vitæ**, das Guajakholz.

Lik—**able**, *adj.* liebenswürdig. —**e**, I. *adj. & adv.* gleich, ähnlich; (equal) gleich; in —e manner, in gleicher *or* der gleichen Weise, auf gleiche Weise, ebenso; —e a man, wie ein Mann; that's just —e him, das sieht ihm ähnlich; of —e extent, von gleicher Ausdehnung, eben so groß; he is —e to die, er wird wahrscheinlich sterben; it is nothing —e so large, es ist bei weitem nicht so groß; 'tis —e enough! es ist wohl glaublich! —e a gentleman, auf feine Weise; such —e, dergleichen; there's nothing —e travelling, nichts geht über das Reisen; that's something —e! das lass' ich mir wohl gefallen! (*coll.*); —e master, —e man, wie der Herr, so der Knecht (*prov.*); —e father, —e son, der Apfel fällt nicht weit vom Stamm (*prov.*); quit you —e men! benehmt euch wie Männer! seid Männer! I did not feel —e going, ich fühlte mich nicht geneigt zu gehen. II. *s.* das Gleiche, das Ähnliche; der Gleiche; *see* —ing; to look upon one's —e, auf seinesgleichen blicken. III. *v.a.* leiden, mögen, gern haben, gern sehen; I —e her, ich mag sie gern (leiden), sie gefällt mir (gut); to — well (better), gern (lieber) mögen; how did you — our town, wie gefiel Ihnen unsre Stadt? I —e potatoes, ich esse gern Kartoffeln; she —es to drive out, sie fährt gern aus, sie fährt mit Vorliebe spazieren; I should —e to know, ich möchte gern wissen; to make o. s. —ed, sich beliebt machen (bei); they are not such as you —e, sie sind nicht nach Ihrem Geschmacke. IV. *v.n.* belieben, wollen, Lust haben; as you —e, wie es Ihnen beliebt; as you —e it, wie es euch gefällt. V. *impers.*; his countenance —es me not, sein Gesicht gefällt mir nicht (*obs.*). —**elihood**, *s.* der Anschein, die Wahrscheinlichkeit; there is but little —elihood of his returning to-day, es ist kaum wahrscheinlich, daß er heute zurückkommt; in all —elihood, aller Wahrscheinlichkeit nach, allem Anschein nach. —**eliness**, *s. see* —elihood; (suitability) die Annehmlichkeit. —**ely**, I. *adj.* wahrscheinlich, anscheinend, vermutlich; (suitable) geeignet. II. *adv.* wahrscheinlich; it is very —ely that he will come, höchst wahrscheinlich wird er kommen. —**en**, *v.a.* vergleichen (to, mit). —**e-minded**, *adj.* gleichgesinnt. —**eness**, *s.* die Ähnlichkeit, Gleichheit; (portrait) das Bild, Porträt; (form) die Gestalt, das Äußere; to have one's —eness taken, sich malen lassen, sich photographieren lassen. —**ewise**, *adv.* ebenso, gleichfalls, auch. —**ing**, *s.* das Gefallen, die Lust, Neigung; (pleasure) das Vergnügen, die Freude; to take a —ing to a th., Gefallen an einer S. finden; to do to a person's —ing, (etwas) nach dem Geschmack *or* Wunsch eines andern tun; to have a —ing for a th., Gefallen, Geschmack an einer S. haben.

Lil—**ac**, I. *s.* der (spanische) Flieder. II. *adj.* lila. —**iaceous**, *adj.* lilienartig. —**y**, *s.* die Lilie; —y of the valley, das Maiglöckchen, die Maiblume. *Comp.* —-**y-handed**, *adj.* mit Lilienhänden. —-**y-livered**, *adj.* hasenherzig, feige. —-**y-white**, *adj.* lilienweiß.

Lilt, I. *s.* muntere Arie, heiteres Lied; der rhythmische Schwung. II. *v.n.* singen, trällern; hüpfen.

[1]**Limb**, *s.* das Glied; der Ast (*of a tree*); das Glied, Stück, der Teil (*fig.*); — of the devil, das Teufelskind (*sl.*); — of the law, der Advokat (*sl.*).

—ed, *adj.* -gliederig; strong- —ed, starkgliederig, stark gebaut. **—er**, *see* ²Limber.

²**Limb**, *s.* der Rand (*Astr.*, *Bot.*). **—er**, *see* ¹Limber. **—o**, *s.* die Vorhölle, der Höllenrand; die Höllenqual (*fig.*); das Gefängnis (*sl.*); die Rumpelkammer (*coll.*).

¹**Limber**, *adj.* biegsam, geschmeidig.

²**Limber**, I. *s.* die (Wagen)deichsel; der Protzwagen, Geschützwagen, die Protze (*Artill.*). II. *v.a.* (— up) aufprotzen. **—s**, *pl.* der Wasserlauf. *Comp.* **—-chain**, *s.* die Protzkette. **—-chest**, *s.* der Protzkasten.

¹**Lime**, I. *s.* der Leim (*for birds*, *etc.*); der Kalk (*Chem.*, *Min.*, *etc.*); chloride of —, Chlorkalk, Bleichkalk; quick- —, ungelöschter Kalk. II. *v.a.* mit Kalk düngen (*Agr.*); leimen. *Comp.* **—-burner**, *s.* der Kalkbrenner. **—-kiln**, *s.* der Kalkofen. **—-light**, I. *s.* das (Drummondsche) Kalklicht; das Spektroskop (*obs.*). II. *attrib.*; —-light view, das Lichtbild. **—-pit**, *s.* die Kalkgrube. **—-rod**, **—-twig**, *s.* die Leimrute. **—-stone**, *s.* der Kalkstein. **—-wash**, *s.* die Kalktünche. **—-water**, *s.* das Kalkwasser.

²**Lime**, *s.* die Linde; (—-tree) der Lindenbaum.

³**Lime**, *s.* der Limonen-, Zitronen-baum; die Limette. *Comp.* **—-juice**, *s.* der Limonensaft.

Limit, I. die Grenze, Schranke; das Ziel; die Frist; to set —s to a th., einer S. Grenzen setzen, eine S. beschränken; —s of a prison, das Gebiet eine Gefängnisses. II. *v.a.* begrenzen, beschränken; (define) bestimmen, vorschreiben; to — the meaning of a word, den Sinn eines Wortes einschränken. **—ation**, *s.* die Beschränkung, Begrenzung, Einschränkung; der engere beschränktere Sinn (*of a word*). **—ed**, *adj.* (*abbrev.* Ltd.) beschränkt (to, auf, *acc.*); —ed liability, begrenzte Haftpflicht; —ed liability company, Aktien-Gesellschaft mit beschränkter Haftpflicht (*or* Haftung); —ed monarchy, beschränkte Monarchie. **—er**, *s.* der, die, das Begrenzende, Beschränkende. **—less**, *adj.* grenzenlos, schrankenlos.

Limn, *v.a.* abmalen, zeichnen (*poet.*). **—er**, *s.* der Maler; der Portraitmaler.

¹**Limp**, I. *v.n.* hinken (*also fig.*), lahm gehen, lahmen. II. *s.* das Hinken. **—ing**, *adj.*, **—ingly**, *adv.* hinkend.

²**Limp**, *adj.* weich, welk, schlaff; biegsam.

Limpet, *s.* die Napf-muschel, -schnecke.

Limpid, *adj.* rein, klar, hell, durchsichtig. **—ity**, **—ness**, *s.* die Klarheit, Durchsichtigkeit (*of water*).

Limy, *adj.* leimig; kalkig (*as soil*).

Lin(n), *s.* der Sturzbach; das Wasserbecken.

Linch-pin, *s.* die Lünse.

Linden, *s.* die Linde; (—-tree) der Lindenbaum.

¹**Lin—e**, *v.a.* füttern, einfassen, besetzen (*of clothes*); spicken (*one's purse*). **—eage**, *s.* die Familie, Abkunft, das Geschlecht. **—eal**, *adj.*, **—eally**, *adv.* (composed of —es) aus *or* in Linien bestehend; in gerader Linie (abstammend); —eal descent, die Abstammung in gerader Linie; a —eal descendant, ein direkter Abkömmling; —eal measure, das Längenmaß; —eal succession, die Nachfolge in gerader Linie. **—eament**, *s.* der (Gesichts-)Zug. **—ear**, *adj.* Linien-, Linear-; linienförmig (*Bot.*); —ear equations, lineare Gleichungen; —ear numbers, Linear-Zahlen; —ear perspective, die Linear-Perspektive. **—ing**, *s.* das Futter, die Fütterung (*of dresses*, *etc.*); der Besatz; die Bekleidung (*arch.*); silver —ing (of a cloud), die Silberverbrämung (einer Wolke).

²**Line**, I. *s.* die Linie; die Richtschnur, Regel (*fig.*); die Leine, Lien (*Naut.*); (row) die Reihe; die Zeile (*Print.*); der Vers (*of a poet*); die Schnur (*Carp.*); der Entwurf (*of a building*); (note) das Briefchen; (12th of an inch) der Strich, die Linie; (lineage) die Familie, Geschlechtslinie, das Geschlecht; (lineament) der Zug; die Linie, der Strich (*Tenn.*); the —, der Äquator (*Geog.*); das Fußvolk (*Mil.*); der Schienenweg, das Geleise (*Railw.*); — of argument, der Gang der Beweisführung; — of battle, die Schlachtreihe, Schlachtlinie; that is not in my —, das schlägt nicht in mein Fach; to drop s.o. a —, einem schreiben; — of beauty, die Schönheitslinie; — of business, der Geschäftszweig; das Fach; — of conduct, das Verfahren, Verhalten; die Lebensweise; — of defence, Verteidigungslinie; — of demarcation, Abgrenzungslinie; — of no dip, der magnetische Äquator; — of direction, die Richtungslinie, Visierlinie (*Surv.*); double —, die doppelgleisige Bahnlinie (*Railw.*); fishing —, die Angelschnur; ground —, Grundlinie; horizontal —, Horizontallinie; to keep in —, Schritt halten; to bring into — with, auf gleiche Stufe stellen mit; to lay out by the —, nach der Schnur abstecken; — of life, Lebenslinie; — of light, der Lichtstrahl; main —, die Hauptlinie; das Hauptgeleise (*Railw.*); — of march, Marschlinie; — of operation, Operations-Linie; — of policy, die Richtung der Politik; railway —, der Schienenweg, die Bahnlinie; a train was thrown off the —, ein Zug entgleiste, wurde zum Entgleisen gebracht; tram —, das Straßenbahngeleise; the tramcar ran off the —, der Straßenbahnwagen entgleiste; — of resistance, Widerstandslinie; ship of the —, ein Linienschiff; — of sight, Visier-, Stand-linie; — of steamers, Dampfschiffahrts-Linie; telegraphic —, Telegraphenlinie; visual —, Gesichtslinie. II. *v.a.* (Land) abgrenzen; in eine Linie formieren; the streets were —d with troops, die Straßen waren in ihrer ganzen Länge (militärisch) besetzt. **—r**, *s.* das regelmäßige Packetboot *or* Passagierboot; der Zeilenschreiber, schlecht bezahlte Zeitungsschreiber; penny-a- —r, unbedeutender Zeitungsschreiber. **—s**, *pl.* Zeilen, Verse, das Gedicht, das Los, Geschick (*fig.*); hard —s, hartes Los; (marriage —s) der Trauschein (*coll.*); (drying —s) Aufhängeleinen, Trockenseile; (lineaments) die (Gesichts-)Züge; die Strafarbeit (*school sl.*).

Linen, I. *s.* die Leinwand, das Leinen, Linnen; (underclothing) die Wäsche; brown —, unbleached —, ungebleichte Leinwand; soiled —, schmutzige Wäsche; change of —, Wäsche zum Wechseln; to change one's —, reine Wäsche anziehen. II. *adj.* leinen, aus Leinwand. *Comp.* **—-damask**, *s.* der Leinendamast. **—-draper**, *s.* der Leinwandhändler. **—-prover**, **—-counter**, *s.* der Fadenzähler. **—-weaver**, *s.* der Leinweber. **—-yarn**, *s.* das Leinengarn.

¹**Ling**, *s.* der Leng (*Ichth.*).

²**Ling**, *s.* gemeine Besenheide.

Linger, *v.n.* (delay) zögern, zaudern, säumen; (tarry) weilen, harren; dahinschmachten. **—ing**, *adj.*, **—ingly**, *adv.* sich in die Länge ziehend, langwierig (*as diseases*); (slow) langsam; allmählich verschwindend, verblassend, verhallend; —ing fever, das schleichende Fieber; —ing sound, lange nachklingender Laut, langsam verhallender Ton; —ing poison, schleichendes Gift.

Ling—o, *s.* die (unverständliche, fremde) Sprache, das Kauderwelsch (*coll.*). **—uadental**, I. *adj.* mit Zunge und (Ober)Zähnen hervorgebracht. II. *s.* der Zungenzahnlaut. **—ual**, I. *adj.* Zungen-; —ual r, das Zungen(spitzen)-r. II. *s.* der Zungenlaut. **—uist**, *s.* der Sprachkenner, Linguist; Sprachenkundige; he is a good —uist, er spricht fremde Sprachen leicht und gewandt; I am not a good —uist, ich bin nicht sehr sprachgewandt. **—uister**, *s.* der Sprachpfuscher, Schwätzer. **—uistic(al)**, *adj.* sprachwissenschaftlich, linguistisch; —uistic faculty, das Sprachvermögen, die Anlage zum Sprechen; die Sprachfertigkeit; —uistic method, die Art Sprachen zu lehren; —uistic study, das Sprachstudium. **—uistics**, *pl.* die (vergleichende) Sprachwissenschaft, Sprachenkunde.

Liniment, *s.* die Einreibung, flüssige Salbe.

[1]**Link**, I. *s.* das Gelenk, Glied (*of a chain*); (bond, tie) das Band; connecting —, das Bindeglied, verbindender Ring (in der Kette); missing —, fehlendes Glied *or* Ringchen. II. *v.a.* verketten, verbinden; —ed in friendship, befreundet, in Freundschaft eng verbunden. **—s**, *pl.* (chain) die Kette; (studs) doppelte Hemdknöpfe (mit Kette).
[2]**Link**, *s.* die Pechfackel, Fackel. *Comp.* **—man**, **—boy**, *s.* der Fackelträger.
[3]**Links**, *pl.* Sandhügel; golf- —, der Golfspielplatz.
Linnet, *s.* der Hänfling, Flachsfink.
Linoleum, *s.* das Linoleum, der Korkteppich(stoff).
Linseed, *s.* der Leinsamen. *Comp.* **—-cake**, *s.* der Leinkuchen. **—-oil**, *s.* das Leinöl.
Linsey-wolsey, *s.* das halbwollene Zeug.
Linstock, *s.* der Luntenstock.
Lint, *s.* zubereiteter Flachs; die Charpie (*Surg.*).
Lintel, *s.* der Sturz, die Oberschwelle (*Arch.*).
Lion, *s.* der Löwe (*also Astr.*); der Löwe, Held (*fig.*); she —, die Löwin; the — roars, der Löwe brüllt; —s of a place, die Ortsmerkwürdigkeiten; literary —s, Modeschriftsteller, führende Geister; —'s share, der Löwenanteil. **—ess**, *s.* die Löwin. **—ize**, *v.a.* (die Ortsmerkwürdigkeiten) besehen; zum Löwen des Tages machen. *Comp.* **—-ant**, *s.* der Ameisenlöwe. **—-hearted**, *adj.* löwenherzig, mutig. **—-like**, *adj.* löwenartig. **—s'-den**, *s.* die Löwengrube. **—'s-mouth**, *s.* das Löwenmaul (*Bot.*).
Lip, I. *s.* die Lippe (*also Bot.*), Lefze; der Rand (*of a vessel*, *of a wound*); (mouth) der Mund; (speech) die Sprache; I heard it from his own —s, ich hörte es aus seinem eignen Munde; it has never passed my —s, es ist mir nie über die Lippen gekommen; to bite one's —, sich (*dat. or acc.*) auf die Lippe beißen. II. *v.a.* mit den Lippen berühren. **—ped**, *adj.* lippig; lippenförmig (*Bot.*). *Comp.* **—-articulation**, *s.* die Lippenartikulation. **—-salve**, *s.* die Lippenpomade. **—-service**, *s.* der Lippendienst.
Liqu—ation, *s.* das Schmelzen. **—efaction**, *s.* die Schmelzung; (—efied state) das Geschmolzensein. **—efiable**, *adj.* schmelzbar. **—efy**, *v.* I. *a.* schmelzen, flüssig machen. II. *n.* flüssig werden. **—id**, I. *adj.* flüssig, fließend; sanft (*Mus.*); liquid (*Gram.*); —id amber, flüssiger Amber. II. *s.* die Flüssigkeit; der flüssige Laut, Schmelzlaut, die Liquida (*Gram.*). **—idate**, *v.a.* liquidieren, saldieren (*debts*); (das Geschäft *or* die Geschäfte) abwickeln, liquidieren (*C.L.*). **—idation**, *s.* die Abwickelung, Liquidation (of debts, von Schulden; of a business, eines Geschäfts). **—idator**, *s.* der Liquidant. **—or**, *s.* die Flüssigkeit; (spirits) das geistige Getränk; to be in —or, betrunken sein.
Liquorice, *s.* das Süßholz, die Lakritze; der Lakritzensaft; bastard —, das falsche Süßholz.
Lisp, I. *v.a. & n.* lispeln, mit der Zunge anstoßen. II. *s.* das Lispeln. **—ing**, *adj.*, **—ingly**, *adv.* lispelnd. *Comp.* **—ing-sound**, *s.* der Lispellaut.
Lissom(e), *adj.* geschmeidig, biegsam. **—-ness**, *s.* die Biegsamkeit, Geschmeidigkeit.
[1]**List**, I. *s.* die Liste, das Verzeichnis (*of names*); *see* Selvage; die Leiste, der Streif (*Arch.*); — of subscribers, Subskriptionsliste. II. *v.a.* einschreiben; *see* Enlist; to — a door, eine Tür mit Sahlleiste versehen.
[2]**List**, I. *s.* die Lust (*obs.*); die Schlagseite (*Naut.*). II. *v.n. & v. imp.* gelüsten; as they —, nach ihrem Gutdünken. **—less**, *adj.*, **—lessly**, *adv.* ohne Lust (*obs.*); (careless) achtlos; (languid) gleichgültig, träge, apathisch. **—lessness**, *s.* die Achtlosigkeit; die Schlaffheit, Trägheit.
[3]**List**, *v.a. & n. see* —en; —! horch! **—en**, *v.n.* horchen, lauschen (to, auf (*acc.*)); to —en to s.o., einen anhören, einem zuhören, auf einen hören; (attend) einem Gehör schenken, Gehör geben, gehorchen; (follow) folgen. **—ener**, *s.* der Horcher, Lauscher; —eners never hear any good of themselves, ein Horcher an der Wand hört seine eigne Schand' (*prov.*).
Lists, *pl.* die Schranken; to enter the — against s. o., gegen einen in die Schranken treten, gegen einen auftreten, es mit einem aufnehmen.
Lit, *imperf. & p.p. of* [1]Light.
Litany, *s.* der Bittgesang, die Litanei.
Litera—l, *adj.*, **—lly**, *adv.* buchstäblich, wörtlich; (expressed by letters) Buchstaben-. **—lness**, *s.* die Wörtlichkeit, Buchstäblichkeit. **—ry**, *adj.* literaturfreundlich; schriftstellerisch, literarisch; —ry activity, schriftstellerische Tätigkeit; —ry education, gelehrte Bildung; —ry man, der Literat; —ry property, das geistige Eigentum; Goethe's —ry career, die schriftstellerische Laufbahn Goethes. **—te**, I. *adj.* gelehrt, von gelehrter Bildung. II. *s.* der Schriftsteller, Gelehrte. **—ati**, *pl.* Literaten, Gelehrte. **—ture**, *s.* das Schrifttum; die Literatur; (learning) die Gelehrsamkeit; history of —ature, die Literaturgeschichte.
Lith—arge, *s.* die Bleiglätte. **—ia**, *s.* das Lithion. **—ic**, *adj.* Stein-; den Blasenstein betreffend. **—oglyph**, *s.*, der Steinschnitt. **—oglyptics**, *pl.* die Steinschneidekunst. **—ograph**, I. *s.* der Stein-druck, -abdruck. II. *v.a. & n.* lithographieren. **—ographer**, *s.* der Steindrucker, Lithograph. **—ographic**, *adj.* in Steindruck, lithographisch; —ographic crayon, lithographische Kreide; —ographic print, die Lithographie, der Steindruck. **—ography**, *s.* die Steindruckerkunst, die Lithographie. **—ological**, *adj.* die Steinkunde betreffend; steinartig. **—ology**, *s.* die Steinkunde. **—otomy**, *s.* der Steinschnitt. **—otripsy**, **—otrity**, *s.* die Steinzermalmung. **—o(n)triptor**, **—otritor**, *s.* der Steinzermalmer.
Lithe, *adj.* geschmeidig, biegsam, gelenkig, schlank, graziös; sanft, mild (*obs.*). **—ness**, *s.* die Geschmeidigkeit, Gelenkigkeit. **—some**, *adj.* schmiegsam, biegsam, geschmeidig.
Lither, *adj.* schlecht, träge, ungesund (*obs.*).
Litig—ant, I. *adj.* streitend; —ant parties, die streitenden Teile, Parteien. II. *s.* der Prozessierende. **—ate**, *v.n.* prozessieren. **—ation**, *s.* der Rechtsstreit, Prozeß. **—ious**, *adj.*, **—iously**, *adv.* prozeßsüchtig, streitsüchtig; streitig (*Law*). **—iousness**, *s.* die Streitsucht, Prozeßsucht.
Litmus, *s.* der Lackmus.
Litotes, *s.* die Litotes (*Rhet.*).
Litre, Liter, *s.* das (*or* der) Liter.
[1]**Litter**, I. *s.* die Sänfte, Tragbahre; (straw) die Streu; (shreds) zerstreut auf der Erde umherliegende Dinge, Papierschnitzel; (disorder) die Unordnung; in a —, in Unordnung. II. *v.a.* eine Streu aufschütten (zum Lager), mit Streu versehen (*beasts*); (mit Stroh) bestreuen (*a stable*); to — a room, ein Zimmer in Unordnung bringen.
[2]**Litter**, I. *s.* die Brut, Tracht, der Wurf, Satz (*of animals, especially of pigs*); a — of pigs, eine Tracht Ferkel; at a —, auf einen Wurf. II. *v.a.* (Junge) werfen.
Little, I. *adj.* klein, gering; kurz (*of time, sleep, etc.*); (insignificant) geringfügig; (inconsiderable, small in amount) wenig; a — one, ein Kleines, ein Kind; my — ones, meine Kleinen, meine Kinder. II. *adv.* wenig; a — red, ein wenig rot, etwas rot; — less, beinah so (viel, gut, ꝛc.); in — less than a year, in nicht viel weniger als einem Jahre; be it ever so —, sei es auch noch so wenig. III. *s.* das Wenige, die Kleinigkeit; — or nothing, Wenig oder Nichts; by — and —, allmählich, nach und nach; ever so —, auch noch so wenig. **—ness**, *s.* die Kleinheit; die Geringfügigkeit; (meanness) die Niedrigkeit. *Comp.* **—-Englander**, *s.* der Gegner der imperialistischen Politik Englands. **—-go**, *s.* (die kleine Prüfung =) die Aufnahmeprüfung an der Universität Cambridge (*academic sl. for the official term* '*Previous Examination*').
Littoral, I. *adj.* zum Ufer gehörig, Ufer-. II. *s.* das Littorale, Küstenland.

Liturg—ic(al), *adj.* auf den Gottesdienst bezüglich, liturgisch. **—y**, *s.* die gottesdienstlichen Gebräuche, die gottesdienstliche Vorschrift, Liturgie.

[1]**Liv—e**, I. *v.n.* leben (dwell); wohnen, sich aufhalten; (continue) fortdauern; (subsist) leben, sich nähren; to —e a bachelor, als Junggesell leben; to —e to see, erleben; God grant I may never —e to see it! Gott gebe, daß ich es nie erlebe! you may —e to repent it, die Zeit kann kommen, wo du es bereust; the boats could not —e in the heavy sea, in der aufgeregten See konnten die Schiffe es nicht aushalten; to —e **by**, leben von; to —e by one's wits, von seinem Witze leben, Industrieritter sein; to —e **in** luxury, ein üppiges Leben führen; to —e in clover, in der Wolle sitzen, leben wie Gott in Frankreich; to —e **on** one's income, von seinem Einkommen leben; they —ed on bread, sie lebten von Brot; to —e on nothing, von der Luft leben; they —e on bad terms, sie vertragen sich schlecht; to —e **up** to, nach . . . leben, gemäß (*with gen.*) leben; to —e **upon** vegetables, sich von Gemüse nähren; to —e **with**, (zusammen) leben, wohnen bei; (cohabit) mit jemand in wilder Ehe leben. II. *v.a.* leben, durchleben, ein Leben führen; (put into practice) verwirklichen; to —e **down**, durch sein Leben widerlegen, überwinden. III. *adj. see* Live. **—elong**, *adj.* lange dauernd; the —elong night, die ganze Nacht hindurch; the —long day, den ganzen geschlagenen Tag, den lieben langen Tag. **—er**, *s.* der Lebende; a fast —er, ein Lebemann; loose —er, der Liederliche. **—ing**, I. *adj.* lebendig, lebend; (burning) brennend, glühend; the —ing, die Lebendigen; to be still in the land of the —ing, noch im Reiche der Lebendigen weilen, noch am Leben sein; no man —ing, kein Sterblicher. II. *s.* (life) das Leben; (—elihood) der (Lebens-)Unterhalt, das Auskommen; (food) die Kost, Speise; die Pfründe (*Eccl.*); (manner of life) die Lebensweise; to get one's —ing, sich (*dat.*) seinen Unterhalt *or* sein Brot verdienen; there is no —ing with him, mit ihm ist nicht auszukommen. III. *attrib.;* —ing room, das Wohnzimmer.

[2]**Live**, *adj.* lebendig; (burning) glühend; —animals, — stock, der Viehstand. **—d**, *adj.;* short-—d, von kurzer Dauer; long-—d, langlebig. **—lihood**, *s.* der Unterhalt, das Auskommen; to earn one's —lihood, sein Brod verdienen. **—liness**, *s.* die Lebhaftigkeit, Munterkeit; das Leben (*Paint.*). **—ly**, *adj.* lebhaft, munter, heiter, fröhlich; (vigorous) lebhaft, kräftig; stark, eifrig, heftig (*as faith, hope*); a —ly image, ein lebhaftes Bild. **—s**, *pl. see* Life.

[1]**Liver**, *see* under Liv—.

[2]**Liver**, *s.* die Leber. **—ed**, *adj.* leberig, mit . . . Leber (*only in compounds*); fat-—ed, mit fetter Leber; milk-—ed, white-—ed, feige. *Comp.* **—-coloured**, *adj.* leberbraun, leberfarbig. **—-complaint**, *s.* die Leberkrankheit. **—wort**, *s.* das Leberkraut.

Livery, I. *s.* die Livree, Diensttracht, Dienertracht; (dress) die Kleidung; das Gewand (*poet.*); die Wahlbürgerschaft (*of the city of London*); die Übergabe (*Law*); — of seizin, Übergabe von Ländereien; to keep horses at —, Pferde in Futter halten *or* nehmen; Pferde verleihen. II. *v.a.* mit einer Dienstkleidung versehen; kleiden (in). *Comp.* **—man**, *s.* der Livreebediente; das Zunftglied (in London). **—-servant**, *s.* der Livreebediente. **—-stable**, I. *s.* der Mietstall, Stall zur Verpflegung und Vermietung von Pferden. II. *attrib.;* —-stable keeper, der Pferdevermieter; der Pferdeverpfleger; der Lohnkutscher.

Livid, *adj.* bleifarbig, schwarzblau; leichenfarben, fahl. **—ness**, *s.* die Bleifarbe; die Totenblässe.

Lixivi—al, *adj.* laugenartig; (obtained by —ation) ausgelaugt; —al salts, Laugensalze. **—ate**, *v.a.* auslaugen. **—ation**, *s.* die Auslaugung. **—um**, *s.* die Lauge.

Lizard, *s.* die Eidechse.

Llama, *s.* das Lama.

Lo, *int.* siehe! seht! schau! schaut her *or* hin!

Loach, *s.* die Schmerle.

[1]**Load**, I. *s.* die Last, Ladung, Bürde; die Bürde, Last, Schwere (*fig.*); höchste Leistungsfähigkeit (*Mach.*); cart —, waggon —, das Fuder, die Fuhre, Wagenladung; —s, ungeheuer viel, massenhaft (*vulg.*). II. *v.a.* laden (*also guns*), beladen, belasten; beschweren (*the memory, etc.*); überhäufen (*with reproaches, etc.*); überfüllen (*the stomach*); to — dice, Würfel auf einer Seite mit Blei beschweren. **—er**, *s.* der Lader, Verlader. **—ing**, I. *adj.;* —ing berth, die Ladestelle (*Naut.*); —ing funnel, der Ladetrichter; —ing needle, die Räumnadel (*Artil.*). II. *s.* das Laden; (load) die Ladung, Fracht. *Comp.* **—(water-)line**, *s.* die Ladewasserlinie.

[2]**Load—star** (**Lodestar**), *s.* der Leitstern; (polar star) der Polarstern. **—stone**, *s.* der Magnet.

[1]**Loaf**, *s.* der Laib (Brot); — of sugar, der Zuckerhut; half a — is better than no bread, etwas ist besser als nichts; to cut a —, ein Brot anschneiden. *Comp.* **—-sugar**, *s.* der Hutzucker.

[2]**Loaf**, *v.n.* müssig umherlaufen, umherbummeln. **—er**, *s.* der Müssiggänger, Taugenichts.

Loam, I. *s.* der Lehm. II. *v.a.* mit Lehm bestreichen, überstreichen. **—y**, *adj.* lehmig. *Comp.* **—-work**, *s.* der Lehmguß.

[1]**Loan**, *s.* die Anleihe, das Darlehen; (lending) das Leihen; — of credit, die Erlaubnis jemandes Kredit benutzen zu dürfen; to put out to —, verleihen; government —, die Staatsanleihe; may I have the — of this book? würden Sie mir wohl dieses Buch leihen? public —, öffentliche Anleihe. *Comp.* **—-office**, *s.* die Leihbank, das Leihhaus. **—-society**, *s.* die Darlehnsgesellschaft. **—-word**, *s.* das Lehnwort.

[2]**Loan**, **—ing**, *s.* (*Scotch*) *same as* Lane.

Loath (**Loth**), *adj.* abgeneigt, widerwillig; I am — to do it, ich tue es ungern *or* mit Widerwillen. **—e**, *v.a.* mit Ekel ansehen, Ekel vor (einer S.) empfinden; (hate) hassen, verabscheuen; I —e the sight of him, sein Anblick ist mir zum Ekel, widert mich an. **—ing**, *s.* der Ekel, Widerwille, Abscheu. **—ingly**, *adv.* mit Ekel, mit Widerwillen. **—ly**, *adj.* gehässig, ekelhaft. **—ness**, *s.* der Widerwille. **—some**, *adj.* ekelhaft, widerlich; (odious) gehässig, abscheulich. **—someness**, *s.* die Ekelhaftigkeit; die Verhaßtheit.

Loaves, *pl. of* [1]Loaf.

Lob, *s.* der Lümmel, Flegel; (lump) große, dicke Masse; der Hochschlag (*Tenn.*). *Comp.* **—worm**, *s.* der Köderwurm.

Lob—ate, *adj.* lappig, gelappt (*Bot.*). **—e**, *s.* der Lappen, Flügel (*Anat.*); der Lappen (*Bot.*); —e of the ear, das Ohrläppchen. **—ule**, *s.* das Läppchen.

Lobby, I. *s.* die Vorhalle, Vorplatz (*Arch.*); der Vorsaal, Wandelgang (*of the Houses of Parliament*); das Foyer (*Theat.*). II. *attrib.;* — member, *see* —ist. **—ist**, *s.* einer, der in den Vorzimmern 2c. des Kongresses intriguiert (*Amer.*).

Lobelia, *s.* die Lobelie.

Lobster, *s.* der Hummer; spiny —, die Languste.

Loc—al, *adj.*, **—ally**, *adv.* örtlich, Orts-; —al affection, örtliches Übel; —al attraction, die Ablenkung; —al authorities, die Bezirksbehörde, der Ortsvorstand; —al branch, der Ortsverband; —al examinations, jährliche von den Universitäten Oxford oder Cambridge abgehaltene schriftliche Prüfungen, welchen sich viele höhere Schulen Englands und der Kolonien freiwillig unterziehen; —al option, Entscheidung der Ortsgemeinde (bezüglich der Schankgerechtigkeit); —al preacher, der Prediger, der neben dem Predigen einen andern Beruf ausübt; —al school, die Schule, welche ausschließlich die Bedürfnisse einer gewissen Örtlichkeit befriedigen will, meist Externat; —al traffic, der Ortsverkehr, Lokal-Verkehr;

—al self-government, die Lokal=Selbstregierung; —al tax, die Gemeindesteuer. —**alism**, *s.* ein irgend einem Orte eigentümlicher Ausdruck. —**ality**, *s.* der Ort, die Örtlichkeit; (position) die Lage; der Ortssinn (*Phren.*). —**alize**, *v.a.* örtlich beschränken, örtlich bestimmen, lokalisieren. —**ate**, *v.a.* (an einen Ort) versetzen, verlegen; die Grenzen von Ländereien abstecken (*Amer.*); einen Platz für etwas bestimmen (*Amer.*); to be —ated, gelegen sein, liegen; ansässig sein. —**ation**, *s.* das Stellen; (situation) die Lage, Stellung; (settling) die Niederlassung; die Vermietung, Verpachtung (*Law*); das Ausmessen und Bestimmen der Grenzen eines Landstriches (*Amer.*); (tract marked out) das vermessene und abgesteckte Stück Land (*Amer.*). —**ative**, *adj.;* —ative case, der Lokativ. —**c**—, *etc.*, —**um**—, *see* Loco—, Locum—.

Loch, *s.* der Landsee, See; die Bucht (*Scotch*).

[1]**Lock**, I. *s.* das Schloß; die Schleuse; (*in a canal*) der Verschluß; (weir) das Wehr; das Umfassen, der Kunstgriff (*wrestling*); dead-—, vollständige Stockung, gänzlicher Stillstand; to come to a dead-—, völlig ins Stocken geraten; nicht mehr wissen, wo aus und ein; to be under — and key, unter Schloß und Riegel sein. II. *v.a.* (zu=)schließen (*a door, etc.*); verschließen (*a secret, etc.*); hemmen (*a wheel*); (— up) ein=, verschließen; (embrace) schließen, fest umfassen; mit Schleusen versehen (*a canal*); to — **in**, einschließen; to — **out**, ausschließen, aussperren; to — **up**, verschließen, einschließen; (close up) sperren (*as frost a river*); to — up one's capital in . . ., sein Kapital in . . . festlegen. III. *v.n.* (sich) schließen; in einander eingreifen (*as wheels*). —**age**, *s.* (— works) die Schleusenwerke; (— toll) der Schleusenzoll; (rise and fall) die Schleusenhöhe. —**er**, *s.* der verschließbare Schrank; der Back (*Naut.*); Davy Jones's —er, der Ozean (*sl.*). —**et**, *s.* das Medaillon; (catch) das Schlößchen, Häkchen (*obs.*). *Comp.* —**-chamber**, *s.* die Schleusenkammer. —**-gates**, *pl.* die Schleusentore. —**jaw**, (—**ed-jaw**,) *s.* der Kinnbackenkrampf. —**-keeper**, *s.* der Schleusenwärter. —**-nut**, *s.* die Nuß am Gewehrschloß; die Gegenmutter (*Cycl.*). —**-out**, *s.* die Aussperrung der Arbeiter, Arbeitseinstellung (seitens der Arbeitgeber). —**smith**, *s.* der Schlosser. —**-stitch**, *s.* der Steppstich (*Sew-mach.*). —**-up**, *s.* der Polizeigewahrsam; University —-up, der Karzer.

[2]**Lock**, *s.* die Locke; die (Woll=)Flocke.

Locomot—ion, *s.* die Ortsveränderung; (motive power) die Ortsveränderungsfähigkeit; aerial —ion, die Luftschiffahrt. —**ive**, I. *adj.* der Ortsveränderung fähig, beweglich; —ive engine, *see* —ive II.; —ive power, fortbewegende Kraft. II. *s.* die Lokomotive; —ive for gradients, Berglokomotive. III. *attrib.;* —ive boiler, der Dampfwagenkessel; —ive engineer, der Lokomotivenbauer; —ive superintendent, der Obermaschinenmeister (*Railw.*). —**or**, I. *s.* der, die, das in Bewegung Setzende. II. *adj.* fortbewegend; —or ataxy, die Rückenmarksdarre.

Locum-tenens, *s.* der Stellvertreter.

Locust, *s.* die Heuschrecke. *Comp.* —**-tree**, *s.* der gemeine Erbsenbaum.

Locution, *s.* das Sprechen; der Ausdruck, die Redensart.

Lode, *s.* die Ader (*Min.*), Erzader (*Min.*); der Graben, Abzugsgraben. *Comp.* —**star**, *see* Loadstar. —**stone**, *s.* der Magnet.

Lodg—e, I. *v.a.* (place) niederlegen, in Verwahrung geben; (harbour) beherbergen, aufnehmen, unterbringen; einquartieren (*troops*); einstellen (*deer*); umlegen (*corn*); einzahlen, übergeben (*money*); hinein=treiben, =pflanzen, =senden (*an arrow, spear, etc.*); to —e a complaint against s.o., einen verklagen, eine Klage gegen einen vorbringen. II. *v.n.* wohnen, logieren; (pass the night) einkehren, sein Nachtlager nehmen; liegen, einquartiert sein (*Mil.*); sich lagern (*as corn*); (fest=)bleiben (*as a stone in falling*). III. *s.* (cottage) die Hütte, das Häuschen; Forst=, Park=, Pförtner=Haus; (dwelling) die Wohnung; (country house) die kleine Villa; Master's —e *or* The —e, die Amtswohnung eines College=Vorstehers (*Eng. Univ.*); porter's —e, die Pförtnerwohnung am Eingangstor; Free-Mason's —e, die Freimaurer=Loge. —**ed**, *adj.* gelagert (*Her.*). —**e-keeper**, *s.* der Pförtner. —**er**, *s.* der Mieter; (fellow-—er) der Hausgenosse. —**ing**, *s.* das Logieren; (abode) die Wohnung, das Logis; a night's —ing, ein Nachtquartier, Nachtlager. —**ings**, *pl.* die (Miets=)Wohnung; to look out for —ings, sich (*dat.*) eine Wohnung suchen; to move into —ings, sich einmieten, eine Wohnung beziehen; to leave one's —ings, ausziehen; board and —ing, Wohnung und Beköstigung. —**ment**, *s.* die Einzahlung (*of money in banks*); das Festbleiben; (accumulation) die Aufhäufung; die Verschanzung eines eroberten Postens (*Fort.*); das Logement (*Mil.*). *Comp.* —**ing-house**, I. *s.* das Mietshaus. II. *attrib.;* —ing-house keeper, der Besitzer eines Mietshauses.

Loft, *s.* der Boden, Speicher, Dachboden; die Bühne (*in churches*); (floor) das Stockwerk. —**ily**, *adv. see* —y. —**iness**, *s.* (height) die Höhe; (pride) der Stolz, Hochmut; (grandeur) die Erhabenheit; —iness of sentiment, die großherzige, edle Denkweise. —**y**, *adj.* hoch; stolz, hochmütig; erhaben; (stately) stattlich; —y style, erhabene Schreibweise.

Log, *s.* der (Holz=)Klotz; (diary) das Tagebuch; das Log, die Logge (*Naut.*); der Klotz (*fig.*); *see* —-book; to heave the —, loggen. —**ged**, *adj. see* Water—ged. —**gerhead**, *s.* der Dummkopf; at —gerheads, im Streite, im Widerstreit; to come to —gerheads, handgemein werden, sich balgen. *Comp.* —**-book**, *s.* das Logbuch, Schiffsjournal. —**-cabin**, —**-hut**, *s.* das Blockhaus. —**-line**, *s.* die Logleine. —**-roll**, *v.n.* sich gegenseitig helfen (*Amer.*). —**-rolling**, *s.* gemeinsames Handeln, gegenseitige Unterstützung (*Pol. sl.*). —**wood**, *s.* das Kampescheholz, Blauholz.

Logarithm, *s.* der Logarithmus; hyberbolic —s, hyperbolische, natürliche Logarithmen. —**ic**, *adj.* logarithmisch; —ic spirals, logarithmische Spirallinien; —ic tables, Logarithmentafeln.

Logic, *s.* die Logik; deductive —, deduktive Logik, Deduktionsmethode. —**al**, *adj.*, —**ally**, *adv.* logisch, folgerichtig. —**alness**, *s.* die Folgerichtigkeit im Denken. —**ian**, *s.* der Logiker.

Logistic, *adj.* logistisch (*Math.*).

Logo—graphic, *adj.* logographisch. —**graphy**, *s.* der Druck mit Worttypen, Logotypendruck. —**machist**, *s.* der Wortklauber, Silbenstecher. —**machy**, *s.* der Wortstreit, die Wortklauberei.

Loin, *s.* die Lende; das Lendenstück (*of meat*); roast —, der Lendenbraten; — of mutton, der Hammelbraten mit dem Nierenstück; — of veal, der Kalbsnierenbraten.

Loiter, *v.* I. *n.* zaudern, zögern, bummeln, tändeln. II. *a.;* to — away, vertrödeln. —**er**, *s.* der Zauderer, Zögerer; (idler) der Müßiggänger, Faulenzer. —**ing**, *adj.*, —**ingly**, *adv.* zaudernd, zögernd.

Loll, *v.n.* sich träge *or* bequem lehnen, nach Bequemlichkeit sich hinstrecken; heraushängen (*as the tongue*); to — about, umherlungern; to — upon, sich nachlässig lehnen auf (*acc.*).

Lollipop, *s.* das Zuckerwerk, Naschwerk.

Lone, *adj.* einsam. —**liness**, *s.* die Einsamkeit, Verlassenheit. —**ly**, —**some**, *adj.* einsam.

[1]**Long**, I. *adj.* lang; lang, gedehnt (*as tones*); (dilatory) langsam; bills drawn at — dates, langsichtige Wechsel; a — figure *or* sum, ein großer *or* hoher Preis; — measure, das Längenmaß; to draw *or* pull the — bow, aufschneiden, prahlen, übertreiben; one's — home, die Ewigkeit; the — vacation, die großen Ferien

die Sommerferien; the — hundred, das Großhundert, hundertundzwanzig (*obs.*); it's a — lane that has no turning, das Unglück dauert nicht ewig; in the — run, am Ende, zuletzt; (by) a — way, viel; a — way round, ein großer Umweg; a — time, lange; it is as broad as it is —, es kommt auf eins heraus. II. *adv.* lang; lange (*of time*); — ago, — since, vor langer Zeit; how — since is it? wie lange ist es her? not — before, nicht lange vorher, kurz vorher; it was not — before, es dauerte nicht lange bis; as — as, so lange als; ere —, in Kurzem, bald; don't be —! mach schnell! halte dich nicht lange auf! bleibe nicht lange fort! he was not — in recovering from . . ., er erholte sich bald von . . .; all night —, die ganze Nacht hindurch. III. *s.* die Länge, das Lange; die großen Ferien (*coll.*); die lange Note; die lange Silbe, (Silben)länge; the — and the short of a matter, die ganze Geschichte, das Ganze. **—er**, *adj. compar.* länger; mehr; this is no —er valid, dies gilt nicht mehr; I will not disturb you any —er, ich will nicht länger stören; she is no —er young, sie ist nicht mehr jung; the noise is not heard any —er, das Geräusch ist nicht mehr zu hören; no —er ago than yesterday, erst gestern. **—evity**, *s.* die Langlebigkeit; Lebensdauer. **—ipennate**, *adj.* langflügelig. **—irostral**, *adj.* langschnäbelig. **—ish**, *adj.* (etwas) länglich, ziemlich lang. **—itude**, *s.* die Länge; degree of —itude, der Längengrad. **—itudinal**, *adj.* die Länge betreffend; —itudinal section, der Längendurchschnitt. *Comp.* **—-boat**, *s.* das große Schiffsboot, die Pinasse. **—-bow**, *s.* der Langbogen. **—-continued**, *adj.* lange dauernd *or* fortgesetzt. **—-delayed**, *adj.* lange verzögert. **—hand**, *s.* die Kurrentschrift, gewöhnliche Schreibschrift. **—-headed**, *adj.* langköpfig; schlau, gescheut (*fig.*). **—-horned**, *adj.* langhörnig; mit langen Fühlern (*Ent.*). **—-legged**, *adj.* langbeinig. **—-legs**, *s.* das Langbein (*coll.*). **—-lived**, *adj.* lange lebend, langlebig. **—-primer**, *s.* die Korpus(schrift) (*Typ.*). **—shoreman**, *s.* der Werft- *or* Hafen-arbeiter. **—-sighted**, *adj.* weitsichtig, fernsichtig. **—-sightedness**, *s.* die Fernsichtigkeit; (shrewdness) der Scharfsinn. **—-suffering**, *adj.* langmütig. **—-tailed**, *adj.* langschwänzig, mit langem Schwanz; a —-tailed coat, langschößiger Rock. **—-tongued**, *adj.* geschwätzig. **—-waisted**, *adj.* langleibig. **—-winded**, *adj.* langatmig; weitschweifig, langweilig (*fig.*). **—wise**, **—ways**, *adv.* der Länge nach.

[2]**Long**, *v.n.* verlangen, sich sehnen (for, after, nach); I — for him, ich sehne mich nach ihm, mich verlangt nach ihm; I very much — to see you, es verlangt mich sehr, Sie zu sehen; the —ed-for rest, die ersehnte Ruhe. **—ing**, I. *adj.*, **—ingly**, *adv.* sehnsüchtig, sehnsuchtsvoll, sehnlich. II. *s.* die Sehnsucht, das Verlangen; das Gelüst (*Med.*).

Loo, I. *s.* das Lu (*a game of cards*). II. *v.a.* beim Luspiel alle Stiche machen. *Comp.* **—-table**, *s.* runder Spieltisch.

Looby, *s.* der Tölpel.

Loof, *s. see* Luff.

Look, I. *v.n.* schauen, blicken, sehen (at, on, auf (*acc.*), nach (*dat.*)); (consider) betrachten, erwägen; (take care) darauf sehen, dafür sorgen; (appear) scheinen; to — much better for one's stay in the Vosges, in Folge seines Aufenthalts in den Vogesen viel besser aussehen, ein viel besseres Aussehn haben; — before you leap! erst wäg's! dann wag's! erst besinn's, dann beginn's! trau, schau, wem! (*prov.*); he —s like my brother, er sieht aus, wie mein Bruder, er sieht meinem Bruder ähnlich; it —s smart, es sieht schneidig *or* flott aus; he —ed very much astonished, er sah höchst erstaunt aus, er machte große Augen; to — **about**, sich umsehen (for, nach); to — about one, sich vorsehen; to — **after**, sehen nach; (wait for) warten (*B.*); he is a boy that must be well —ed after, er ist ein Knabe, auf den man besonders achten muß; to — after the luggage, auf das Gepäck achten, nach dem Gepäck sehen; to — **at**, ansehen; — at me, sieh mich an; — at this action, erwägen Sie diese Handlung; to — **back**, zurücksehen, sich umsehen; to — back upon, auf (*acc.*) . . . zurückblicken; to — **down**, niedersehen, die Augen niederschlagen; to — down upon s. o., auf einen verächtlich herabblicken; to — **for** (a th.) (expect), (eine S.) erwarten; (seek) (nach einer S.) suchen; to — for a p., sich nach einem umsehn, nach einem ausschauen; to — **forward**, vor sich sehen, (expect) erwarten; to — forward to (s.th.), hoffen *or* sich freuen auf (eine S.); to — **in** upon s. o., einem einen (kurzen) Besuch machen; to — **into**, sehen in (*acc.*); (examine) untersuchen, erwägen; my windows — into the garden, meine Fenster gehen auf den Garten; to — into a matter, eine S. gründlich untersuchen; if you — closely into it, bei Lichte betrachtet; to — **on**, to — **upon**, ansehen, sehen auf (*acc.*); (consider) betrachten (als), halten (für); I — on him as my dearest friend, ich betrachte ihn als meinen besten Freund; I — upon it as a great honour, ich sehe es für eine große Ehre an; to — **out**, ausgucken (*Naut.*), hinaussehen; (— on) die Aussicht haben; to — out for, sich umsehen nach; I have been —ing out for you, ich habe nach Ihnen ausgeschaut; ich habe Sie erwartet; to — out for squalls, sich vor bösem Wetter (*lit.*), *or* Unannehmlichkeiten (*fig.*), in Acht nehmen; to — out at *or* of the window, zum Fenster hinaussehen; to — **over**, durchsehen, durchgehen; (overlook) übersehen, die Augen zudrücken bei; to — **through**, sehen durch; to — **to**, zusehen, sehen auf, Acht auf (*acc.*) . . . geben; — to it, geben Sie darauf Acht; — to it that you don't forget his orders, nehmen Sie sich in Acht, daß Sie seine Befehle nicht vergessen; to — to o.s., für sich selbst sorgen; I shall — to you for . . ., für . . . werde ich auf Sie rechnen *or* mich an Sie wenden; to — **up**, aufsehen, aufblicken, in die Höhe sehen; (rise) aufschlagen, steigen (*C. L.*); to — up to s. o., einen als Muster ansehen, sehr schätzen. II. *v.a.*; to — s. o. in the face, einem ins Gesicht sehen; she —ed daggers at me, mit ihren Blicken schien sie mich erdolchen zu wollen; to — out *or* up a word, ein Wort (im Wörterbuche) nachschlagen; to — a p. out of countenance, einen durch Blicke aus der Fassung bringen; to — up, suchen nach, aufsuchen; I have been —ing up an old friend, ich habe einen alten Freund wieder aufgesucht. III. *s.* der Blick; das Ansehen, Aussehen; he gave me a piteous —, er warf mir einen traurigen Blick zu. **—er**, *s.* der Schauer, Beschauer. *Comp.* **—er-on**, *s.* der Zuschauer. **—ing-glass**, *s.* der Spiegel. **—-out**, I. *s.*; on the —-out, auf der Lauer; to keep a good —-out, ein wachsames Auge haben (auf eine S.), sich wohl vorsehen; that's your own —-out, das ist deine Sache, da hast du zuzusehen. II. *attrib.*; the —-out man, der Ausgucker.

[1]**Loom**, *s.* der Webstuhl, Stuhl.

[2]**Loom**, *v.n.* sichtbar werden, undeutlich aufragen, erscheinen, sich in der Ferne auftun; the land —s high, das Land zeigt sich hoch. **—ing**, *s.* das Sichtbarwerden; die Kimmung.

[1]**Loon**, *s.* der Bengel, Taugenichts, Lümmel.

[2]**Loon**, *s.* großer Eistaucher (*Orn.*).

Loop, I. *s.* die Schlinge, Schleife; (ring) die Öse; die Krümmung; der Ring (*Gun.*); *see* —-line. II. *v.a.* schlingen; to — up, aufnehmen. III. *v.n.* sich winden. *Comp.* **—hole**, I. *s.* das Schlupfloch, Loch; die Schießscharte (*Fort.*); die Ausflucht (*fig.*). II. *v.a.* mit Schießscharten versehen. **—-line**, *s.* die Verbindungsbahn (*Railw.*).

Loose, I. *v.a.* (auf-)lösen, aufbinden; (undo) auftun, losbinden; (set free) loslassen, befreien; to — one's hold (on a th.), (eine S.) loslassen, fahren lassen. II. *v.n.* die Anker lichten (*Bibl.*). III. *adj.*, **—ly**, *adv.* los; locker, lose; schlaff; lose, weit (*as a dress, a bodice, etc.*); lose, fliegend (*as hair*); (scattered) zerstreut; (free) frei; ledig (from, of, von); (unconnected) unzusammenhängend; (untied) lose; (not concise) weitschweifig; (wanton) lose, liederlich; to get —, sich losmachen; to hang —, schlaff hängen; to let —, loslassen; — articles, lose, nicht eingepackte Waren; — box, der Stallabteil, in dem ein Pferd frei laufen darf; a — fish, — liver, ein lockerer Patron *or* Zeisig; — ice, offenes Eis; — money, kleines Geld. **—n**, *v.* I. *a.* losmachen, losbinden (*a string, etc.*); (auf)lockern (*earth*); öffnen (*the bowels*); befreien (*the hands, etc.*). II. *n.* losgehen, sich lösen. **—ness**, *s.* die Lockerheit, Schlaffheit; (levity) der Leichtsinn, die Leichtfertigkeit; (lewdness) die Liederlichkeit, Lockerheit; der Durchfall (*Med.*); der lose Zusammenhang; (inexactness) die Ungenauigkeit, Unbestimmtheit. *Comp.* **—-jointed**, **—-limbed**, **—-made**, *adj.* gelenkig.

Loot, I. *v.n.* plündern. II. *v.a.* erbeuten. III. *s.* die Kriegsbeute, Beute, das Raubgut.

¹Lop, I. *v.a.* beschneiden, behauen; stutzen, kappen; (*trees*); beschneiden (*fig.*). II. *s.* abgeschnittene Äste; — and top, Äste und Krone (*of trees*). **—pings**, *pl.* die abgeschnittenen Baumzweige. *Comp.* **—ing-shears**, *s.* die Baumschere, Heckenschere.

²Lop, *v.* I. *a.* herabfallen lassen. II. *n.* herabfallen. *Comp.* **—-eared**, *adj.* mit herabhängenden Ohren, mit Hängeohren. **—sided**, *adj.* nach einer Seite überhängend, schief; einseitig (*fig.*).

Loquaci—ous, *adj.* geschwätzig, schwatzhaft. **—ty**, *s.* die Geschwätzigkeit.

Lord, I. *s.* der Herr, Gebieter; (God) der Herr; (Christ) der Herr, Christus; (husband) der Gatte; (noble) der Edelmann, Pair; der Lord (*as title*); the —'s House, das Gotteshaus; the day of the —, das jüngste Gericht; the —'s Day (Prayer), der Tag des Herrn (das Vaterunser); the —'s Supper, das heilige Abendmahl; the — of Hosts, der Herr der Heerscharen, Herr Zebaoth; in the year of Our —, im Jahre des Herrn (anno domini); — advocate, der Generalanwalt (höchster richterlicher Beamter in Schottland); — chamberlain, Oberkammerherr; — chancellor, der Lordkanzler; — chief justice, der Lord-Oberrichter; — lieutenant, der Vizekönig (von Irland); — Mayor, der Oberbürgermeister; — of the manor, der Grundherr, Lehens-, Zinsherr; —s temporal, die weltlichen Mitglieder des (englischen) Oberhauses; —s spiritual, die geistlichen Mitglieder des (englischen) Oberhauses; my —, gnädiger Herr; — paramount, Oberlehnsherr; the (House of) —s, das Oberhaus, Herrenhaus. II. *v.a.;* to — it, den großen Herrn spielen; to — it over, herrschen über (*acc.*). **—liness**, *s.* die Hoheit, Stattlichkeit, Würde; (pride) der Hochmut. **—ling**, *s.* das Herrchen. **—ly**, *adj.* wie ein Lord, edel, großmütig; (*also adv.*) (proud) stolz, vornehm; (haughty) herrisch, gebieterisch, hochmütig. **—ship**, *s.* (*also* —'s domain) die Herrschaft; your —ship, Euer Gnaden; it was taken to his —ship, es wurde dem Lord gebracht.

Lore, *s.* die Lehre; die Wissenschaft, Kunde.

Lorgnette, *s.* die Lorgnette, Handbrille, das Augenglas.

Loricate, *v.a.* bepanzern; mit Ton umgeben, beschlagen (*vases, etc.*).

Lorn, *adj. see* Forlorn; (forsaken) verlassen

Lorrie, *s.* die Lori (*Railw.*).

Los—e, *ir.v.* I. *a.* verlieren; (forfeit) (eine S.) einbüßen, um (eine S.) kommen; (mislay) verlegen; (squander) vergeuden (*one's fortune*), vertändeln (*one's time*), unnütz anwenden (*one's labour*); verliegen (*the wind*); to —e sight of a p., einen aus dem Gesichte verlieren; (overlook) aus den Augen lassen; to —e ground, Boden verlieren, weichen; to —e in people's estimation, an Achtung verlieren; to —e one's way, sich verirren; he seldom —es an opportunity, er läßt selten eine Gelegenheit vorbeigehen. II. *n.* verlieren, den Kürzeren ziehen; nachgehen (*as a watch*). **—er**, *s.* der Verlierende, Verlierer; to come off a —er, den Kürzeren ziehen. **—ing**, *adj.;* —ing business, ein Geschäft, welches mit Verlust verbunden ist *or* bei dem zugesetzt wird; —ing game, die Fuchspartie (*Bill. & fig.*). **—s, —t**, *see* Loss, Lost.

Loss, *s.* der Verlust, die Einbuße; (injury) der Nachteil, Schaden; (waste) der Verlust; at a —, in Verlegenheit; he was at a — how to . . ., er wußte nicht wie er . . .; — of appetite, die Appetitlosigkeit; — of time, der Zeitverlust; to suffer a —, Verlust erleiden.

Lost, *prep. & p.p. see* Lose; verloren, (da)hin; to be — to all sense of shame, alles Schamgefühls bar sein; ten lives were —, zehn Leben gingen verloren; there is not much love — between them, sie haben nichts für einander übrig.

Lot, I. *s.* das Los; das Los, Geschick, Schicksal, die Lage (*fig.*); (share) der Teil, Anteil; die Partie, der Posten (*C. L.*); das Stück, die Parzelle (*of land*); (— of building ground) der Bauplatz, die Bauparzelle; eine Menge, Masse, Gesellschaft, ein Haufe, Pack (*coll.*); to cast in one's — with *or* among, sein Schicksal knüpfen an das (eines andern); to cast —s, das Los werfen (über eine S.); to draw —s, das Los ziehen, losen (for, um); it is —s to blanks, es ist zehn gegen eins; by —s, nach dem Lose; it fell to my —, es fiel mir zu, es wurde mir zuteil; to pay scot and —, Steuern nach Vermögen bezahlen; to sell in *or* by small —s, in kleinen Posten verkaufen *or* losschlagen (*C. L.*); to have —s of money, Geld wie Heu haben (*coll.*); a — of money, eine Masse Geld, ein Haufen Geld (*coll.*); (strawberries) give me the —, (Erdbeeren) gieb sie mir alle; is that the —? sind das alle? II. *v.a.* in Partieen abteilen, verlosen; ein Los, einen Anteil geben. **—tery**, *s.* die Lotterie, das Glücksspiel; (chance) das Los.

Lot—e, **—us**, *s.* der Lotos, Lotus. *Comp.* **—us-eater**, *s.* der Lotusesser, Lotophag.

Loth, *see* Loath.

Lotion, *s.* das Waschmittel, die Medizin zum Waschen und Einreiben; (washing) die Abwaschung; — for the eyes, das Augenwasser.

Loto, Lotto, *s.* das Lottospiel.

Loud, *adj.*, **—ly**, *adv.* laut; (noisy) lärmend, geräuschvoll; (showy) schreiend, grell (*coll.*). **—ness**, *s.* der laute Schall, Ton; der Lärm, das laute Geräusch; das Schreiende, Auffallende.

Lough, (*Irish*) *see* Loch.

Lounge, I. *v.n.* müßig gehen, faulenzen; ruhen (*on a sofa, etc.*); to — about, herumlungern. II. *s.* (lounging place) der Ort des müßigen Ruhens; (couch) die Chaiselongue, das Sofa. **—r**, *s.* der Faulenzer. *Comp.* **—-suit**, *s.* der bequeme Hausanzug.

Lour, *v.n. see* Lower.

Lous—e, *s.* die Laus; *pl.* **lice**, die Läuse. **—y**, *adj.* lausig; (low) gemein, verächtlich (*vulg.*).

Lout, *s.* der Tölpel, Lümmel. **—ish**, *adj.*, **—ishly**, *adv.* tölpisch, lümmelhaft, flegelhaft. **—ishness**, *s.* die Tölpelhaftigkeit.

Louver, Louvre, *s.* das Türmchen (auf dem Dache). **—s**, *pl.* die Jalousieläden. *Comp.* **—-window**, *s.* das Schalloch, das offene Fenster in Kirchtürmen.

Lovable, *adj.* liebenswürdig, liebenswert. **—ness**, *s.* die Liebenswürdigkeit.

Love, I. *v.a.* lieben; (like) lieb haben, gern mögen; (be inclined) geneigt sein; (to find pleasure in) Vergnügen finden an (einer S.); to — to do, gern tun; mit Vorliebe tun; to — better, lieber tun, es mehr lieben, vorziehen. II. *v.n.* lieben. III. *s.* die Liebe; (liking) die Anhänglichkeit; (sweetheart) das Liebchen, Herzblatt; (Cupid) der Liebesgott; Null (*L. T.*) (— affair) die Liebschaft; my —, mein Lieb, Liebling

Herzblatt; — of approbation, der Beifallstrieb; — of one's country, Vaterlandsliebe, Liebe zum Vaterlande; — of a p., Liebe zu einem *or* für einen; for — of, aus Liebe zu; for the — of God, um Gottes willen; for — or money, für Geld oder gute Worte; to be out of — with a th., einer Sache überdrüssig sein; to be in — with, in (eine Person) verliebt sein; to fall in — with, sich in (eine Person) verlieben; to be head and ears in —, bis über die Ohren verliebt sein; to make — (to a p.), mit (einem) liebeln, (einer Person) den Hof machen; to send one's — to a p., einen herzlich grüßen lassen; —'s labour lost, verlorne Liebesmüh; to play for —, um nichts spielen; four (to) —, vier gegen nichts (*Bill.*). **—less**, *adj.* lieblos. **—liness**, *s.* die Lieblichkeit, der Reiz. **—ly**, *adj.* lieblich, hold, reizend, liebreizend; (amiable) liebenswürdig. **—r**, *s.* der Liebende, Verliebte; der Liebhaber, Freund (*of flowers, etc.*); —rs, Liebende, ein Liebespaar. *Comp.* **—-affair**, *s.* die Liebschaft, der Liebeshandel. **—-apple**, *s.* der Liebesapfel. **—-bird**, *s.* der Sperlingspapagei. **—-charm**, *s.* der Liebeszauber. **—-child**, *s.* das Kind der Liebe, uneheliches Kind (*prov.*). **—-feast**, *s.* das Liebesmahl. **—-game**, *s.* das Nullspiel (*Tenn.*). **—-in-idleness**, *s.* das Stiefmütterchen. **—-knot**, *s.* der Liebesknoten. **—-letter**, *s.* der Liebesbrief. **—-lies-bleeding**, *s.* der Fuchsschwanz. **—-lock**, *s.* die (lange) Schmachtlocke. **—-longing**, *s.* die Liebessehnsucht. **—-lorn**, *adj.* liebeverlassen; sich in Liebe verzehrend. **—-making**, *s.* das Courmachen, Hofmachen, die Courschneiderei. **—-match**, *s.* die Liebesheirat, Heirat aus Liebe. **—-potion**, *s.* der Liebestrank. **—-set**, *s.* die Nullpartie (*Tenn.*). **—-sick**, *adj.* liebeskrank, liebesiech. **—-song**, *s.* das Liebeslied. **—-suit**, *s.* die Liebeswerbung. **—-tale**, *s.* die Liebesgeschichte. **—-token**, *s.* das Liebeszeichen.

Loving, I. *adj.*, **—ly**, *adv.* liebend; (affectionate) liebevoll; zärtlich; verliebt; your — mother, deine dich liebende Mutter; let us drink a — cup, wir wollen den Becher kreisen lassen. II. *s.* das Lieben. **—-kindness**, *s.* die göttliche Gnade; die Herzensgüte.

[1]**Low**, *adj. & adv.* niedrig; (deep) tief, leise (*as a voice*); kärglich, knapp (*as diet*); schwach (*as a pulse*); niedergeschlagen, gedrückt (*as the spirits*); niedrig, mäßig (*as a charge*); niedrig, wohlfeil (*in price*); (mean) gemein, niederträchtig, erbärmlich; tief am Horizonte (*as the sun*); to bring —, herunterbringen; (humble) demütigen; — bow, tiefe Verneigung; — Church, die Niederkirchlichen (derjenige Teil der Gläubigen in der englischen Kirche, welcher bei einfachem Gottesdienst die paulinischen Glaubenssätze stark vertritt); the — Countries, die Niederlande; a — fever, ein schleichendes Fieber; — language, gemeine Ausdrucksweise, unanständige Redensarten; — spirits, die Niedergeschlagenheit; — Sunday, Sonntag Quasimodo; — temperature, niedrige, mäßige Temperatur; — tide, — water, die niedrigste Ebbe. **—er**, I. *adj.* (*comp. of* Low); the —er House, das Unterhaus; the —er classes, die niederen Volksklassen, die untern Stände. II. *v.a.* nieder=, herab=, hinablassen; (let down) senken, sinken lassen; niederschlagen (*the eyes*); to —er one's voice, leise(r) sprechen; erniedrigen, demütigen (*pride*); herab=, herunter=setzen (*prices*); verringern (*one's reputation*); streichen (*flags, etc.*). **—ering**, *adj.* niederschlagend, beruhigend; drückend. **—ermost**, I. *adj.* niedrigst. II. *adv.* am niedrigsten. **—est**, *adj.* (*sup. of* —); the —est bidder, der Mindestbietende. **—liness**, *s.* die Demut; (— state) die Niedrigkeit; —liness of fortune, die geringen Vermögensumstände. **—ly**, I. *adj.* niedrig, tief; (humble) demütig; (modest) bescheiden. II. *adv.*; —ly born, von niedriger Abkunft. **—ness**, *s.* die Niedrigkeit (*of birth, mind, style, etc.*); —ness of price, die Wohlfeilheit; —ness of spirits, die Niedergeschlagenheit. *Comp.* **—-born**, *adj.* niedrig geboren. **—-bred**, *adj.* niedrig erzogen, ungebildet, roh, gemein. **—land**, *s.* das niedere Land, die Niederung. **—-minded**, *adj.* niedrig *or* gemein gesinnt. **—-necked**, *adj.* ausgeschnitten (*dress*). **—-pressure**, *s.* der Niederdruck. **—-priced**, *adj* wohlfeil, billig. **—-spirited**, *adj.* gedrückt, niedergeschlagen.

[2]**Low**, I. *v.n.* brüllen, muhen. II. *s.* das Gebrüll, Gemuh, Muhen.

[1]**Lower**, *see under* [1]Low.

[2]**Lower**, *v.n.* trübe, finster aussehen, sich verfinstern; (frown) die Stirne runzeln; finster aussehen. **—ing**, *adj.*, **—ingly**, *adv.* trübe, düster, finster.

Loyal, *adj.*, **—ly**, *adv.* treu, getreu, pflichttreu; — demonstrations, patriotische Kundgebungen, Ergebenheitsbezeugungen; — toasts, Gesundheiten auf den König, die Königin und das königliche Haus. **—ist**, *s.* der Treugesinnte. **—ty**, *s.* die Treue, Ergebenheit.

Lozenge, *s.* die Raute (*Geom.*, *Her.*); das rautenförmige Täfelchen (*Med.*); das Zuckerplätzchen, Brustbonbon (*Conf.*). *Comp.* **—-shaped**, *s.* rautenförmig.

Lubber, *s.* der Lümmel, Schlingel, Flegel, ungeschickte, tölpelhafte Mensch. **—ly**, *adj. & adv.* unbeholfen, tölpisch, plump.

Lubric—ant, *s.* das Schmiermittel. **—ate**, *v.a.* glätten, schlüpfrig machen; schmieren (*Mach.*). **—ation**, *s.* das Einschmieren; —ator, der Öler (*Cycl.*). **—ity**, *s.* die Schlüpfrigkeit; die Unbeständigkeit (*of fortune*); (lewdness) die Liederlichkeit, Geilheit.

Luce, *s.* der ausgewachsene Hecht.

Lucerne, *s.* die Luzerne (*Bot.*).

Lucid, *adj.*, **—ly**, *adv.* hell, leuchtend, glänzend; (pellucid) klar, durchsichtig; (plain) klar, deutlich; — intervals, lichte Augenblicke. **—ity**, **—ness**, *s.* die Helle; die Klarheit, Deutlichkeit.

Luck, *s.* das Glück, der Glücksfall; (hap) das Schicksal, Geschick; good —, das Glück; ill —, das Unglück; worse —, unglücklicherweise; as good — would have it, by good —, glücklicherweise; to have a run of good —, immerwährendes Glück haben. **—ily**, *adv.* zum Glücke, glücklicherweise; —ily for me, zu meinem Glücke. **—iness**, *s.* das Glück; (the being —y) die glückliche Beschaffenheit. **—less**, *adj.* unglücklich; a —less beggar, ein armer Teufel. **—y**, *adj.* glücklich; günstig; you are a —y fellow, Sie sind ein Glückspilz, Sie können nicht verderben; three is a —y number, aller guten Dinge sind drei; a —y hit, ein Glücksfall; to be —y, Glück haben.

Lucr—ative, *adj.*, **—atively**, *adv.* einträglich, gewinnbringend. **—e**, *s.* der Gewinn; filthy —e, schmutziger Gewinn.

Lucubrat—e, *v.* I. *n.* bei Nacht arbeiten. II. *a.* ausarbeiten. **—ion**, *s.* das Nachtarbeiten; (result of —) das bei Nacht Gearbeitete, die gelehrte Arbeit.

Ludicrous, *adj.*, **—ly**, *adv.* lächerlich; (funny) drollig, possierlich. **—ness**, *s.* das Possierliche, Drollige; das Lächerliche.

Luff, I. das (der) Luv, die Luvseite (*Naut.*). II. *v.n.* luven.

Lug, I. *v.a.* (— out, heraus=, — in, herein=) =schleppen, =zerren. II. *s.* der Henkel, das Öhr; (ear) das Ohr. **—gage**, *s.* das Gepäck; free —gage, das Freigepäck; heavy —gage, das große Gepäck; light —gage, das Handgepäck; to book the —gage, das Gepäck aufgeben; to register the —gage, das Gepäck einschreiben lassen. *Comp.* **—gage-label**, *s.* der Gepäckzettel. **—gage-office**, *s.* die Gepäckannahme, Gepäckausgabe. **—gage-rack**, *s.* die Leiste (*or* das Netz) für Handgepäck. **—gage-train**, *s.* der Güterzug. **—gage-van**, *s.* der Gepäckwagen. **—-sail**, *s.* das Luggersegel.

Lugger, *s.* der Lugger, Logger (*Naut.*).
Lugubrious, *adj.*, **—ly**, *adv.* traurig, kläglich, kummervoll. **—ness**, *s.* die Traurigkeit.
Lukewarm, *adj.* lau, lauwarm; lau, gleichgültig (*fig.*). **—ness**, *s.* die Lauigkeit; die Lauheit (*fig.*).
Lull, I. *v.a.* einlullen, einsingen (*to sleep*); (calm) beruhigen. II. die zeitweilige Ruhepause, Windstille. **—aby**, *s.* das Wiegenlied.
Lumba—go, *s.* das rheumatische Lendenweh, der Hexenschuß. **—r**, *adj.* zu den Lenden gehörig.
Lumber, I. *s.* das Gerumpel, Gerümpel, der Polterkram; (timber) das Bauholz, Stabholz. II. *v.a.* mit Gerumpel rc. vollpacken. III. *v.n.* poltern, rumpeln; sich schwerfällig fortbewegen. **—ing**, *adj.* schwerfällig, schleppend. *Comp.* **—-room**, *s.* die Rumpelkammer.
Lumin—ary, *s.* das Licht, der leuchtende Körper, Lichtkörper; das Himmelslicht (*poet.*); das Licht, Lumen (*fig.*). **—ous**, *adj.*, **—ously**, *adv.* leuchtend; (bright) hell, licht; (clear) klar (*fig.*); —ous matter, der Lichtstoff; —ous pencil, das Strahlenbündel; —ous paint, die Leuchtfarbe; —ous ray, der Lichtstrahl.
Lump, I. *s.* der Klumpen, die Masse, das Stück; der Deul, die Luppe (*Metall.*); — of gold, der Goldklumpen; two —s of sugar, zwei Stück Zucker; by the —, in the —, im Ganzen, in Bausch und Bogen. II. *v.a.* zusammennehmen, zu einer Gesammtmasse schlagen. **—ish**, *adj.* schwerfällig; (lazy) träge; (dull) dumm. **—y**, *adj.* klumpig, klümperig. *Comp.* **—fish**, *s.* der Seehase, Lump. **—-sugar**, *s.* der Lumpenzucker; der Würfelzucker.
Lun—acy, *s.* die Mondsucht; (madness) der Wahnsinn. **—ar**, *adj.* Mond=, Monds=; —ar caustic, der Höllenstein; —ar month, der Mondmonat; —ar tables, Mondtafeln; —ar year, das Mondjahr. **—atic**, I. *adj.* mondsüchtig; wahnsinnig, verrückt; —atic asylum, das Irrenhaus. II. *s.* der Mondsüchtige; der Wahnsinnige. **—ation**, *s.* der Mondwechsel, Mondlauf. **—e**, *s.* der Mond (*Geom.*). **—ette**, *s.* der kleine Halbmond; die Brillenschanze (*Fort.*); die Brille (*Opt.*).
Lunch, I. *s.* das Gabelfrühstück, das frühe Mittagsessen (*usually about one o'clock*). II. *v.n.* zu Mittag essen. **—eon**, I. *s. see* —I. II. *attrib.;* —eon basket, der Speisekorb.
Lung, *s.* die Lunge; to have a good pair of —s, ein gutes Paar Lungen haben. *Comp.* **—wort**, *s.* das Lungenkraut.
Lunge, I. *s.* der plötzliche Stoß, Ausfall; plötzlicher Angriff. II. *v.n.* ausfallen, stoßen; losfahren, losschlagen (at a p., auf einen).
Lunt, *s.* die Lunte.
Lupine, *s.* die Lupine (*Bot.*).
Lupus, *s.* bösartige Hautkrankheit.
[1]**Lurch**, *s.;* to leave in the —, im Stiche lassen.
[2]**Lurch**, I. *s.* das (plötzliche) Rollen oder Schlingern (*of a ship*). II. *v.n.* schlingern; taumeln.
Lurcher, *s.* der Spürhund.
Lure, I. *s.* der Köder, die Lockspeise. II. *v.a.* ködern, anlocken; to — out of, herauslocken.
Lurid, *adj.* (gloomy) düster, finster; schwarzgelb.
Lurk, *v.n.* lauern; (auf einen) lauern, (einem) auflauern; lauschen (*fig.*); (hide) sich verstecken. *Comp.* **—ing-place**, *s.* das Versteck.
Luscious, *adj.*, **—ly**, *adv.* übersüß; saftig; (delicious) lecker, köstlich. **—ness**, *s.* die (allzu große) Süßigkeit; die Saftigkeit.
Lush, *adj.* frisch, saftig, üppig (*of plants*); biegsam, schlaff (*obs.*).
Lust, I. *s.* die sinnliche Begierde, Gier; die Brunst, Wollust; — of gain, die Gewinnsucht. II. *v.n.* (ge)lüsten (after, nach), begehren. **—ful**, *adj.* wollüstig; (—-provoking) zur Wollust anreizend. **—fulness**, *s.* die Wollust, Geilheit. **—ily**, *adv.* munter, rüstig. **—iness**, *s.* die Rüstigkeit, Stärke. **—y**, *adj.* munter, stark, rüstig, stämmig; dick (*coll.*); —y cheers, schallende Beifallsrufe.
Lust—re, *s.* der Glanz, Schimmer (*of the sun, of silk, etc.*); der Glanz, Ruhm (*of deeds, birth, etc.*); (chandelier) der Kronleuchter; der Lüster (*Weav.*). **—reless**, *adj.* glanzlos, matt. **—ring**, *s.* der Glanztaffet. **—rous**, *adj.* glänzend.
Lustr—ation, *s.* die Reinigung; das Reinigungsopfer (*Rel.*). **—um**, *s.* das Lustrum, Jahrfünft; das Reinigungsopfer.
Lut—(an)ist, *s.* der Lautenspieler, Lautenschläger. **—e**, *s.* die Laute; to play the —, die Laute spielen *or* schlagen. *Comp.* **—e-string**, *s.* die Lauten=, Darm=seite; *see* Lustring.
[1]**Lute**, I. *s.* der Kitt, Beschlag; (packing-ring) der Dichtungsring. II. *v.a.* verkitten.
[2]**Lute**, *see under* Lutanist.
Luthern, *s.* das Dachfenster.
Luxur—iance, **—iancy**, *s.* die Üppigkeit. **—iant**, *adj.*, **—iantly**, *adv.* üppig; —iant health, eine Überfülle von Gesundheit. **—iate**, *v.n.* wuchern; (live —iously) üppig leben; (revel) sich weit ergehen, schwelgen (in a th., in einer S.). **—ious**, *adj.*, **—iously**, *adv.* schwelgerisch; (—iant) üppig; a —ious table, ein üppig besetzter Tisch. **—iousness**, **—y**, *s.* der Luxus, das Wohlleben, die Üppigkeit; die Prachtliebe; (extravagance) die Schwelgerei; —ies, Luxusartikel.
Lycanthrop—e, **—ist**, *s.* der Werwolf (*Myth.*); der Wolfswahnsinnige. **—y**, *s.* die Lykanthropie.
Lyceum, *s.* das Lyceum; (school) die Gelehrtenschule, das Gymnasium.
Lycopodium, *s.* der Bärlapp.
Lye, *s.* die Lauge.
Lying, I. *p. see* Lie. II. *s.;* — in state, das Liegen auf dem Paradebett, die Ausstellung einer fürstlichen Leiche. *Comp.* **—-in**, I. *s.* das Wochenbett. II. *attrib.;* —-in hospital, die Entbindungsanstalt. **—-to**, *s.* das Beilegen vor der Fock (*Naut.*).
Lymph, *s.* die Lymphe, das Blutwasser; der Impfstoff; das klare Quellwasser (*poet.*). **—atic**, *adj.* lymphatisch.
Lynch, *v.a.* Volksjustiz (an einem) üben, (einen) lynchen. *Comp.* **—-law**, *s.* das Lynchgesetz, die Volksjustiz.
Lynx, *s.* der Luchs. *Comp.* **—-eyed**, *adj.* luchsäugig.
Lyr—a, *s.* die Leier (*Astr.*). **—e**, *s.* die Leier, Lyra **—ic**, I. *adj.* lyrisch. II. *s.* lyrisches Gedicht. **—ist**, *s.* lyrischer Dichter.

M

M, m, *s.* M, m; M = 1000; *for abbreviations see the Index at the end of the English-German part*
Ma, *see* Mamma.
Ma'am, *see* Madam.
Macadamize, *v.a.* makadamisieren, beschottern.
Macaroni (*pl.* —s *or* —es), die Hohlnudel, Röhrnudel, italienische Nudel, Makkaroni (*pl.*); der Stutzer, Geck (*obs.*); das Gemisch (*fig.*). **—c**, *adj.* makkaronisch (*verses, poetry*); —c poetry, die Mischdichtung, makkaronische Dichtung.
Macaroon, *s.* die Makrone.
Macassar, *attrib.;* — oil, das Makassaröl.
Macaw, *s.* der Makao (Art roter Papagei). *Comp.* **—-tree**, *s.* der Makaobaum, die Fächerpalme.
[1]**Mace**, *s.* der Amtsstab, das Zepter; die Keule; die Masse (*Bill.*). *Comp.* **—-bearer**, *s.* der Stab=, Zepter=träger.
[2]**Mace**, *s.* die Muskatblüte. *Comp.* **—-ale**, *s.* das gewürzte Bier.
Macerat—e, *v.a.* beizen, einweichen. **—ion**, *s.* die Einweichung; die Ausmergelung; (mortifying) die Abhärmung, Kasteiung.
Machicolation, *s.* die Pechnasenreihe, der Verteidigungserker; das Herabwerfen von Steinen und heißem Pech auf die Angreifer einer Burg (*Fort.*).
Machination, *s.* die Machenschaft, Anzettelung, Machination. **—s**, *pl.* Schliche, Umtriebe, Ränke.

Machin—e, I. *s.* die Maschine, das Kunstgetriebe; die Maschine (*fig.*); das Fahrrad (*Cycl.*). II. *attrib.;* —e gun, das Schnellfeuergeschütz, Repetiergeschütz. **—ery,** *s.* die Maschinerie, der Mechanismus; by —ery, durch Maschinenkraft. **—ist,** *s.* der Maschinist; (—e-maker) der Maschinenbauer.

Mac(k)intosh, *s.* der wasserdichte Überzieher, Regenmantel, Gummimantel.

Mackerel, *s.* die Makrele. *Comp.* **—-(back-) sky,** *s.* der gestreifte Himmel, die Schäfchen.

Macro—biote, *s.* der Langlebige. **—biotic,** *adj.* langlebig. **—cosm,** *s.* das Weltall, Weltgebäude, der Makrokosmos. **—cosmic,** *adj.* umfassend, unermeßlich. **—meter,** *s.* der, das Makrometer. **—n,** *s.* das Längezeichen über Vokalen.

Macula, *s.* der Flecken. **—ture,** *s.* das Ausschußpapier, der Auswurfbogen, die Makulatur (*Print.*); das Löschpapier.

Mad, *adj.,* **—ly,** *adv.* verrückt, wahnsinnig, toll; (frantic) rasend, wütend; toll (*as a dog*); — after *or* for, erpicht *or* versessen auf (eine S.); to drive a p. —, einen um den Verstand bringen; to be — with joy, vor Freude außer sich (*dat.*) sein; as — as a hatter *or* March hare, völlig verrückt, ganz übergeschnappt (*coll.*); to go —, verrückt werden, überschnappen; to run like —, wie ein Verrückter dahinlaufen (*coll.*). **—den,** *v.a.* toll *or* verrückt machen. **—dening,** *adj.* wütend, rasend, wild; toll *or* verrückt machend. **—ness,** *s.* der Wahnsinn, die Tollheit. *Comp.* **—cap,** I. *s.* der Tollkopf; (—cap girl) der Wildfang, die Ausgelassene, kleine Närrin. II. *adj.* tollköpfig, wild; ausgelassen, freudig. **—house,** *s.* das Tollhaus, Irrenhaus. **—man,** *s.* der Tolle, Verrückte, Wahnsinnige.

Madam, *s.* gnädige Frau! gnädiges Fräulein! —? wie beliebt? was ist gefällig, gnädige Frau?

Madder, *s.* der Krapp, die Färberwurzel.

Made, *pret. & p.p. of* Make; — man, gemachter Mann; — dishes, Gerichte, zu deren Zubereitung mehrere Bestandteile gehören; — up, fertig (*as clothes*); (invented) erfunden, ausgedacht; — up of, bestehend aus.

Madrepore, *s.* die Löcherkoralle.

Madrigal, *s.* das Madrigal.

Magazine, *s.* das Warenhaus, Warenlager, die Niederlage; powder —, das Pulvermagazin; (literary —) die Zeitschrift.

Mage, *s.* (*rare for*) Magician.

Magenta, *s.* das Magenta-Rot.

Maggot, *s.* die Made, Larve; (whim) die Grille (*fam.*). **—y,** *adj.* madenartig; grillenhaft, grillig.

Mag—i, *pl.* die Magier. **—ic,** I. *s.* die Magie, Zauberei. II. *adj.,* **—ical,** *adj.,* **—ically,** *adv.* magisch, zauberisch, zauberhaft; —ic lantern, die Zauberlaterne, Laterna magica. **—ician, —us,** *s.* der Zauberer, Magier.

Magist—erial, *adj.* gebieterisch, herrisch; obrigkeitlich (*as authority, etc.*); (proud) stolz, hochmütig. **—racy,** *s.* die Magistratur; (—rates) die Obrigkeit, obrigkeitliche Behörde. **—rate,** *s.* obrigkeitlicher *or* richterlicher Beamter; (justice of the peace) der Friedensrichter.

Magnan—imity, *s.* die Großmut, Hochherzigkeit. **—imous,** *adj.,* **—imously,** *adv.* groß-, hochherzig.

Magnate, *s.* der Magnat, vornehme Adlige.

Magnesi—a, *s.* die Magnesia. **—an,** *adj.* magnesisch; —an limestone, der Bitterkalk. **—um,** *s.* das Magnesium.

Magnet, *s.* der Magnet. **—ic,** *adj.,* **—ically,** *adv.* magnetisch; anziehend (*fig.*); to be —ic of a th., etwas anziehen; —ic needle, die Magnetnadel; —ic influence, die magnetische Induktion; —ic iron ore, das Magneteisen; —ic telegraph, der magneto-elektrische Telegraph. **—ics,** *pl.* die Lehre von Magnetismus. **—ism,** *s.* der Magnetismus; animal —ism, tierischer Magnetismus. **—ization,** *s.* das Magnetisieren. **—ize,** *v.a.* magnetisieren. *Comp.* **—o-electricity,** *s.* der Elektromagnetismus.

Magnif—icat, *s.* das Magnifikat, der Lobgesang (Mariens). **—icence,** *s.* die Herrlichkeit, Pracht, Großartigkeit; Großwürden (*in titles*). **—icent,** *adj.,* **—icently,** *adv.* herrlich, prächtig, großartig, glänzend. **—ico,** *s.* der venetianische Edelmann. **—ier,** *s.* der Verherrlicher, Lobpreiser; *see* —ying-glass. **—y,** *v.a.* vergrößern; (extol) preisen, verherrlichen; —ying glass, das Vergrößerungsglas.

Magniloquen—ce, *s.* die Großsprecherei; der Bombast (*in writing*). **—t,** *adj.,* **—tly,** *adv.* großsprecherisch, prahlerisch; bombastisch.

Magnitude, *s.* die Größe; affairs of —, hochbedeutende *or* hochwichtige Angelegenheiten; star of the first —, Stern erster Größe.

Magnolia, *s.* die Magnolie.

Magnum, *s.* die Zweiquartflasche (*of wine*).

Magpie, *s.* die Elster.

Maharaja, *s.* der Maharadscha.

Mahlstick, *s.* der Malerstock.

Mahogany, *s.* der Mahagoni; (table) der (Mahagoni-)Tisch; to have one's feet under a person's —, bei einem zu Mittag essen; an eines andern Tische sitzen (*fig.*); über fremde Hilfsquellen verfügen (*fig.*).

Maid, I. *s.* das Mädchen; (virgin) die Jungfrau; (servant) die Dienstmagd, Magd, das Dienstmädchen; — of honour, die Hofdame; — of all work, das Mädchen für alles. **—en,** I. *s. see* Maid. II. *adj.* jungfräulich, mädchenhaft; (unmarried) unverheiratet; neu, frisch; Erstlings-, der (die, das) erste; uneingenommen (*as a fortress*); his —en aunt, seine unverheiratete Tante; —en name, der Mädchenname; her —en name was Smith, sie ist eine geborene Smith; —en sessions, Assisen ohne Kriminalfall; —en speech, die Jungfernrede, Erstlingsrede. **—enhead, —enhood,** *s.* die Jungfernschaft, Jungfräulichkeit. **—enliness,** *s.* die Mädchenhaftigkeit. **—enly,** *adj. & adv.* jungfräulich, mädchenhaft. *Comp.* **—enhair,** *s.* das Frauenhaar, Adiantum (*Bot.*). **—en-like,** *adj.* jungfräulich. **—servant,** *s.* die Dienstmagd, das Dienstmädchen, die Magd, das Mädchen.

[1]**Mail,** *s.* der Panzerring; der Panzer; (chain —) der Kettenpanzer; der Ringel (*Weav.*); coat of —, das Panzerhemd, der Harnisch; die Brünne (*poet.*). **—ed,** *adj.* gepanzert; (spotted) gefleckt (*obs.*); —ed fist, gepanzerte Faust, eiserne Faust. *Comp.* **—-clad,** *adj.* gepanzert, bepanzert.

[2]**Mail,** I. *s.* der Sack, Ranzen, das Felleisen (*obs.*); der Briefsack, das Postfelleisen; die Briefpost; die Postbriefschaften; die Postdampfschiffahrt; *see* —-bag; by return of —, mit wendender Post, umgehend; by this day's —, mit heutiger Post. II. *v.a.* mit der Post verschicken. *Comp.* **—-bag,** *s.* der Briefbeutel. **—-boat,** *s.* das Paketboot. **—-cart, —-coach,** *s.* die Postkutsche. **—-steamer,** *s.* der Postdampfer, das Paketboot. **—-train,** *s.* der Postzug.

Maim, *v.a.* verstümmeln, lähmen. **—ed,** *adj.* verstümmelt; the —ed, die Krüppel (*pl.*).

Main, I. *adj.* hauptsächlich, wichtigst, größt, Haupt-; voll, ganz (*obs.*); the — body, das Hauptkorps, Haupttreffen; the — business, das Hauptgeschäft; to have an eye to the — chance, auf die Hauptsache sehen, sein eigenes Interesse nicht aus dem Auge verlieren. II. *s.* der Hauptteil, das Ganze; (ocean) das Meer, die offene See; (pipe) das Hauptrohr einer Gas- oder Wasser-leitung; die Gewalt (*obs.*); in the —, im Ganzen, überhaupt, hauptsächlich; with might and —, mit voller Macht. **—ly,** *adj.* hauptsächlich. *Comp.* **—land,** *s.* das Festland. **—-line,** *s.* die Haupt(bahn)linie. **—mast,** *s.* der Großmast. **—spring,** *s.* die Hauptfeder; die Haupttriebfeder (*fig.*). —**stay**, *s.* das Großstag; die Hauptstütze (*fig.*). —**-top**, *s.* der Großmars. —**top-gallant-mast**, *s.* die große Bramstenge. —**top-gallant-sail**, *s.* das große Marssegel.

Maint—ain, *v.a.* erhalten; unterhalten (*a conversation*); (keep) fortsetzen; (sustain) aufrecht erhalten; (support) ernähren, unterhalten, alimentieren; behaupten (*one's ground*); behaupten, verteidigen (*an opinion*). —**ainable**, *adj.* haltbar; gerechtfertigt. —**ainer**, *s.* der Unterhalter; der Behauptende. —**enance**, *s.* die Erhaltung, Unterhaltung; (sustenance) die Beköstigung, der Unterhalt; (support) die Aufrecht(er)haltung; die Behauptung, Verfechtung; die Einmischung in fremde Prozesse durch Vorstrecken von Geld ꝛc.

Maize, *s.* der Mais.

Majest—ic, *adj.*, —**ically**, *adv.* majestätisch, würdevoll. —**y**, *s.* die Majestät; (dignity) die Würde, Hoheit; (might) die Macht, höchste Gewalt; His —y, Seine Majestät.

Majolica, *s.* die Majolika.

Major, I. *adj.* größer; der ältere (Bruder); Smith —, der große Smith, Smith der ältere; — third, die große Terz (*Mus.*); — key, die Dur-Tonart (*Mus.*); — part, der größte Teil. II. *s.* der Major (*Mil.*); der Obersatz (*Log.*); drum —, der Regimentstambour; brigade —, der Brigade-major; sergeant —, der Oberfeldwebel. —**ity**, *s.* die Mehrheit, Mehrzahl; die Mündigwerdung; die Mündigkeit (*Law*); die Majorsstelle (*Mil.*); —ity of votes, die Majorität, Stimmenmehrheit; vast —ity, überwiegende Mehrzahl; to attain one's —ity, die Volljährigkeit erlangen, volljährig, großjährig *or* majorenn werden; to go over to *or* to join the —ity, sterben. *Comp.* —**-domo**, *s.* der Haushofmeister. —**-general**, *s.* der Generalmajor.

Make, I. *ir.v.a.* machen; (fabricate) verfertigen, anfertigen, machen; (produce) hervorbringen; (create) schaffen; (form) bilden; (raise to a dignity, *etc.*) machen zu, ernennen zu; (gain) machen, gewinnen, zusammenbringen; (cause) bewirken, verursachen, lassen; leiden (*losses*); führen (*a complaint*); schließen (*peace, friendship*); verfassen, dichten (*poems*); halten (*a speech*); schneiden (*pens*); treffen (*arrangements, a choice*); machen (*beds*); aufsetzen, machen (*one's will*); he was made colonel, er wurde zum Obersten gemacht *or* ernannt; to — angry, ärgern; to — answer, antworten, erwidern; to — it one's boast, sich einer Sache rühmen; — the case your own, versetzen Sie sich in die Lage; they made him their chief, sie machten ihn zu ihrem Anführer; she made me do this, sie zwang mich dazu sie ließ *or* hieß mich das tun; he —s us feel, er läßt uns fühlen; I made him run, ich ließ ihn laufen; if he can be made to confess it *or* to see the truth, wenn man ihn dazu bringen kann, es zu gestehen, wenn ihm die Wahrheit beigebracht werden kann; to — a hearty (poor) meal, tüchtig (wenig) essen; to — no doubt, gar nicht bezweifeln; to — inquiries, sich erkundigen; to — good, wieder gutmachen (*some wrong done*); (einem Versprechen) nachkommen (*a promise*); erweisen (*a claim*); erfüllen (*a prophecy*); bewerkstelligen *or* glücklich ins Werk setzen (*one's escape*); to — hay while the sun shines, das Eisen schmieden so lange es heiß ist; to — haste, sich beeilen; to — the land, des Landes ansichtig werden (*Naut.*); to — little of, geringschätzen, wenig achten; to — the most of a th., so viel wie möglich aus einer S. machen; to — a match, eine Heirat zustande bringen; to — moan, klagen; I can — nothing of it, ich kann nicht klug daraus werden; to — one, sich dabei beteiligen; mittanzen (*in dancing*); mitspielen (*in cardplaying*); to — one's peace, sich aussöhnen (with, mit); all this —s for peace, alles dies befördert den Frieden *or* ist dem Frieden günstig; to — a port, einen Hafen anlaufen; to — preparations, Vorbereitungen treffen; to — provision, sorgen (for, für), Vorkehrungen treffen (against, gegen); to — ready, (sich) fertig machen; to — reply, erwidern; to — room, Platz machen; to — room for, einem (einer Sache) ausweichen; to — o.s. scarce, sich nicht blicken lassen, wegbleiben; to — shift, sich behelfen; to — shift to live, sich kümmerlich ernähren; to — a show, ein großes Gepränge (mit einer S.) machen, sich (*dat.*) den Schein geben (als ob . . .); (seem) den Schein an sich haben; to — a stand, Halt machen; feststehen, sich entschieden widersetzen; to — a stay, sich aufhalten; to — a stranger of a p., einen als Fremden behandeln; to — sure of (a th.), (etwas) als gewiß betrachten; (ascertain) sich vergewissern (einer S.); (seize) sich (einer Sache) versichern, bemächtigen; to — trial of, versuchen, probieren; they — good teachers, sie geben gute Lehrer ab; to — s.o. sit down, einen zum Sitzen nötigen; to — a vow, geloben; to — war (upon), bekriegen, Krieg anfangen (mit *or* gegen); to — water, leck werden (*Naut.*); sein Wasser abschlagen; to — way for (einem, einer Sache) den Durchgang verstatten; vor einem zurücktreten, sich (einem ꝛc.) unterwerfen; to — **out**, (discover) herausbekommen, entziffern, verstehen; (prove) beweisen, dartun; I cannot — him out yet, ich bin über ihn noch nicht im reinen; to — out an account, eine Rechnung ausfertigen, ausziehen; to — **over**, übergeben, übertragen; to — **up**, (finish) vollenden; (— **good**) ersetzen; (complete) vervollständigen; (compose) zusammensetzen; bilden (*a whole, etc.*); ausgleichen, abschließen (*accounts*); beilegen (*a quarrel*); machen, verfertigen (*dresses, etc.*); schmieden (*a story*); the story is made up, die Geschichte ist erfunden, aus der Luft gegriffen; to — up one's mind, sich (zu etwas) entschließen; to — up one's mind to do a thing, beschließen, *or* sich entschließen, etwas zu tun; I shall soon be able to — it up, bald werde ich es nachholen können; what the conversation wanted in wit was made up by . . ., was der Unterhaltung an Witz abging, wurde durch . . . ergänzt; to — it up to a p., einem etwas ersetzen; to — it up with, sich aussöhnen mit; these countries — up the great empire, diese Länder bilden das große Reich. II. *ir.v.n.* tätig sein, dabei zu tun haben; to — as if, sich stellen als ob; the tide —s, die Flut tritt ein; to — **after** s.o., einem folgen, nachjagen; to — **against**, (einem) schaden, sprechen gegen; to — **at**, auf (einen) losgehen; to — **away with**, etwas durchbringen; (kill) einen umbringen; to — **for**, zugehen wollen, eilen, gehen nach (a place, einem Orte); (tend to) dienen, beitragen; (serve) nützen; to — merry, sich belustigen, sich (*dat.*) gütlich tun; to — **of**, machen aus; to — **off**, sich fortmachen *or* aus dem Staube machen; to — **towards**, zugehen auf (*acc.*); to — **up for**, ersetzen; wieder gut machen; to — up for lost time, die verloren gegangene Zeit wieder nachholen; to be made **up of**, aus etwas zusammengesetzt sein, bestehen aus; to — **up to**, sich nähern; (pay court) die Cour machen (*vulg.*). III. *s.* die Form, Fasson; der Schnitt (*Tail.*); der Bau (*of the body, etc.*). —**r**, *s.* der Macher; (creator) der Schöpfer; der Fabrikant (*C. L.*); boiler- —er, der Kesselschmied; peace- —er, der Friedenstifter. *Comp.* —**-believe**, I. *s.* die Verstellung, der Vorwand. II. *adj.* verstellt. —**shift**, I. *s.* der Notbehelf. II. *adj.* als Notbehelf dienend. —**-up**, *s.* das Ausstaffieren, Schminken, der Aufputz. —**weight**, *s.* die Zulage, Zugabe.

Making, I. *p. see* Make. II. *s.* das Machen; (creation) die Schöpfung; it is of my own —, ich habe es selbst gemacht; that was the — of him, das hat ihn zu einem Manne gemacht; das hat sein Glück gemacht; he has the — of . . ., er hat das Zeug zu . . . — ready (*Typ.*), die Zurichtung.

Malachite, *s.* der Malachit.

Mal—ady, *s.* die Krankheit. —**a-fide**, *adj.* & *adv.* in böser Absicht trügerisch, treulos. —**aria**, *s.* die Sumpfluft; das Sumpffieber. **—arial, —arian, —arious,** *adj.* durch Sumpfluft erzeugt; Malaria *or* Sumpffieber erzeugend; — arial fever, das Sumpffieber, die Malaria. — **ediction,** *s.* die Verwünschung, der Fluch. — **efactor,** *s.* der Übeltäter, Verbrecher. **—evolence,** *s.* die Bosheit, das Übelwollen. **—evolent,** *adj.*, **—evolently,** *adv.* übelwollend, böswillig, feindselig. **—ice,** *s.* die Bosheit, Arglist; (hatred) der Haß, Groll; with —ice prepense, mit bösem Vorbedacht (*Law*); to bear —ice, Groll hegen (against, to, gegen). **—icious,** *adj.*, — **iciously,** *adv.* boshaft, schadenfroh, heimtückisch. **—iciousness,** *s.* die Boshaftigkeit, Schadenfreude. **—ign,** I. *adj.* schädlich. II. *v.a.* verleumden, verlästern. **—ignancy,** *s.* die Bosheit; die Bösartigkeit (*of an ulcer*); die Ungunst (*of fate*). **—ignant,** I. *adj.*, **—ignantly,** *adv.* boshaft; ungünstig; bösartig (*Med.*). II. *s.* der, die Übelgesinnte. **—igner,** *s.* der Verleumder. **—ignity,** *s.* die Bosheit, Feindseligkeit, Schadenfreude; die Bösartigkeit; die Gehässigkeit (*of sin, etc.*). **—inger,** *v.n.* Krankheit heucheln, sich krank stellen. **—ingerer,** *s.* der sich krank Stellende, der Simulant. **—ison,** *s.* der Fluch (*obs. poet.*). **—versation,** *s.* die ungetreue Verwaltung, der Unterschleif. *Comp.* **—adjustment,** *s.* die schlechte Anordnung. **—administration,** *s.* die schlechte Verwaltung. **—adroit,** *adj.* ungeschickt, linkisch. **—adroitness,** *s.* die Ungeschicklichkeit. **—adventure,** *s.* das Mißgeschick, der Unfall. **—apert,** *adj.* ungezogen, naseweis. — **apropos,** *adv.* zur Unzeit, ungelegen. **—conformation,** *s.* die Mißbildung. **—content,** I. *adj.* mißvergnügt. II. *s.* der Mißvergnügte. — **feasance,** *s.* die Übeltat, Missetat. **—formation,** *s.* die Verbildung, schlechte Bildung. — **odorous,** *adj.* übelriechend. **—practice,** *s.* die schlechte Behandlung (*Med.*). **—practices,** *pl.* gesetzwidrige Handlungen. **—treat,** *v.a.* schlecht behandeln, mißhandeln. **—treatment,** *s.* schlechte Behandlung, die Mißhandlung.

Malanders, *s.* die Rappe, Struppe (*Vet.*).

Malar, *adj.* die Backen betreffend, Backenbein-.

Male, I. *s.* der Mann; das Männchen (*of birds, etc.*). II. *adj.* männlich; — child, der Knabe; — issue, der Mannesstamm. *Comp.* **—-fern,** *s.* der Schildfarn. **—-screw,** *s.* die Schraubenspindel.

Malic, *adj.*; — acid, die Äpfelsäure.

Malkin, *s.* der Ofenwisch; (scarecrow) die Vogelscheuche; die gemeine, schmutzige Magd.

Mall, I. *s.* der Schlägel; ein gehegter, schattiger Spaziergang. II. *v.a.* durchhauen, durchbläuen.

Mallard, *s.* der wilde Enterich.

Malleability, *s.* die Hämmerbarkeit, Streckbarkeit. **—eable,** *adj.* hämmerbar, streckbar. **—eableness,** *s.* die Dehnbarkeit. **—et,** *s.* der Schlägel.

Mallow, *s.* die Malve.

Malmsey, *s.* der Malvasier(wein).

Malt, I. *s.* das Malz; — liquor, der Malztrank, das Bier. II. *v.a.* malzen. III. *v.n.* Malz werden. **—er, —ster,** *s.* der Mälzer, Malzer. *Comp.* **—-barn, -floor,** *s.* die Malztenne. **—-house,** *s.* das Malzhaus. **—-kiln,** *s.* die Malzdarre. **—ing,** *see* —-kiln.

Mamm—a (Mama), *s.* die Mamma. **—al,** *s.* das Säugetier. **—alian,** *adj.* Säugetier-. — **alogy,** *s.* die Lehre von den Säugetieren, Säugetierkunde. **—ary,** *adj.* Brust-, zu der weiblichen Brust gehörig. **—ifer,** *s.* das Säugetier. **—iferous,** *adj.* zu den Säugetieren gehörig, säugend. **—iform,** *adj.* brustförmig, zitzenförmig. **—illary,** *adj.* (brust)warzenähnlich; zu den Brustwarzen gehörig (*Anat.*). **—y,** *s.* (mamsie) Mütterchen! Muttchen! (*coll.*).

Mammon, I. *s.* der Mammon. II. *attrib.*; — worship, der Mammonsdienst.

Mammoth, I. *s.* das Mammut. II. *adj.* mammutähnlich, ungeheuer. III. *attrib.* Riesen-. *Comp.* **—-tree,** *s.* die kalifornische Riesentanne.

Man, I. *s.* (*pl.* Men, *see* Men) der Mann; (human creature) der Mensch; (—kind) die Menschen, das Menschengeschlecht; (—servant) der Diener, Knecht; (subject) der Untertan, Vasall; der Stein (*Draughts*); die Figur (*Chess*); (male) der Mann; a —, man, einer, ein Mensch; show yourself a —! zeige, daß du ein Mann bist! the good—, der Ehemann; her young —, ihr Schatz; oil- —, der Ölhändler; he is a science —, er ist ein Naturwissenschaft(l)er; he is a mathematical —, er studiert Mathematik *or* ist ein Mathematiker; he is our medical —, er ist unser Hausarzt; a Cambridge —, einer der in C. studiert *or* studiert hat; — of conscience, der gewissenhafte Mann *or* Mensch; — of letters, der Gelehrte; — of many parts, ein vielseitiger Mensch; — of many words, der Vielsprecher, Schwätzer; to crown a —, aufdamen (*Draughts*); — of the world, der Weltmann; to a —, bis auf den letzten Mann; no —, niemand; merchant—, das Kauffahrteischiff. II. *v.a.* bemannen, besetzen (*with troops*); ausrüsten, equipieren (*a ship*); to — the yards, die Rahen besetzen lassen; — the boat! fall ins Boot! **—akin, —ikin,** *see* —ikin; der Manakin (*Orn.*). **—ful,** *adj.*, — **fully,** *adv.* mannhaft, tapfer, herzhaft. **—fulness,** *s.* die Mannhaftigkeit. **—hood,** *s.* die Mannheit; (—liness) die Männlichkeit, Mannhaftigkeit, Mannheit; (—'s estate) die Männlichkeit, das Mannesalter; (human nature) die Menschheit. **—ikin,** *s.* das Männchen, der Zwerg; die Gliederpuppe. **—kind,** *s.* das Menschengeschlecht; (*opp. to* Womankind) das männliche Geschlecht; die Männerwelt; (men) Leute. — **liness,** *s.* die Männlichkeit, Mannhaftigkeit. — **ly,** *adj. & adv.* männlich, mannhaft, tapfer, kühn. **—nish,** *adj.* männisch. *Comp.* **—-at-arms,** *s.* der Bewaffnete. **—-cook,** *s.* der Koch. **—-eater,** *s.* der Menschenfresser; (tiger, *etc.*) das menschenfressende Raubtier. **—-hater,** *s.* der Menschenfeind. **—-hole,** *s.* das Fahrloch, Arbeitsloch, Reparierungsloch. **—-like,** *adj.* männlich. **—-milliner,** *s.* der Putzhändler, Modist. **—-of-war,** *s.* das Kriegsschiff. **—-rope,** *s.* das Fallreep (*Naut.*). **—-servant,** *s.* der Bediente. **—slaughter,** *s.* der Menschenmord; der (unvorsätzliche) Totschlag. **—slayer,** *s.* der Totschläger. **—stealing,** *s.* der Menschenraub.

Manacle, I. *s.* die Handfessel, Handschelle. II. *v.a.* Handschellen anlegen, fesseln; to — together, zusammenfesseln, zusammenschließen.

Manage, *v.* I. *a.* handhaben (*a sword, etc.*); führen, leiten, verwalten (*a business, etc.*); vorstehen (a matter, einer Sache); (direct) leiten, dirigieren; (contrive) einrichten, einleiten, einfädeln; abrichten, zureiten, dressieren (*horses*); (tame) bändigen; (husband) schonen, zu Rate halten; (treat cautiously) behutsam behandeln; verwalten, wirtschaften (*one's income, etc.*); leiten, lenken, stimmen (*a person*); he —d to creep up the sides, es gelang ihm (mit Mühe), die Seiten hinaufzuklettern; he just —d to get through, er kam noch eben durch; I can't — to live upon so small a sum, es ist mir nicht möglich, mit einer so kleinen Summe auszukommen. II. *n.* die Geschäfte führen, die Führung übernehmen; (contrive) es einrichten, zustande bringen. **—able,** *adj.* handlich, leicht zu handhaben; (tractable) lenksam, leicht zu behandeln. **—ment,** *s.* die Handhabung, Führung, Leitung, Verwaltung; (—rs) die Verwaltung, der Verwaltungsrat; (mode of —ment) die Handlungsweise; (wise conduct) das kluge Betragen, Verfahren; (contrivance) die Kunst; die Wirtschaft (*of forests*); die Behandlung (*of the voice*); —ment of a theatre, die Spielleitung, Oberleitung eines Schauspielhauses; by good —ment she contrived to make both ends meet, durch gutes

Haushalten ist es ihr gelungen auszukommen. —**r**, *s.* der Verwalter, Leiter, Vorsteher, Direktor (*of a business, etc.*); der Direktor (*of a theatre, a railway, etc.*); (economist) der (gute) Wirt, Verwalter, die (gute) Wirtin, Haushälterin, Verwalterin; (contriver) der Planmacher; goods —r, freight —r, der Güterverwalter (*of a railway*); board of —rs, der Verwaltungsrat. —**ress**, *s.* die Vorsteherin. —**rial**, *adj.* Verwaltungs=.

Managing, I. *p. & adj. see* Manage; — director, der geschäftsführende Vorsteher *or* Leiter einer Aktiengesellschaft; — directors, der Verwaltungsrat. II. *s.* die Verwaltung, Führung, Handhabung.

Manciple, *s.* der Ökonom, Verwalter, Wirtschafter (*especially in colleges; obs.*).

Manda—mus, *s.* der Befehl eines höheren Gerichtes an ein niederes, richterliche Befehl. —**tary**, —**tory**, *s.* der Mandatar, Auftraggeber (*Law*); der vom Papste zu einer Pfründe Empfohlene. —**te**, *s.* der Befehl, Erlaß, das Mandat; der Auftrag (*Law*). —**tor**, *s.* der Auftraggeber, Vollmachterteiler. —**tory**, I. *adj.* befehlend, vorschreibend, einen Befehl enthaltend. II. *s. see* —tory.

Mandarin, *s.* der Mandarin. *Comp.* —**-duck**, *s.* die Federkappe (*Orn.*). —**-orange**, *s.* die Mandarine.

Mandible, *s.* der Kinnbacken, Kiefer, die Kinnlade.

Mandolin(e), *s.* die Mandoline.

Mandragora, **Mandrake**, *s.* der Alraun; (potion) der Alraun, Schlafapfel, das Hexenkraut.

Mandrel, **Mandril**, *s.* der Dorn (*Found., Glassw., Gun.*); der Dorn, die Spindel, die Docke (*of a lathe*). *Comp.* —**-lathe**, *s.* die Dockendrehbank.

Mandrill, *s.* der Mandrill, Waldteufel (*Zool.*).

Manduca—ble, *adj.* kaubar, eßbar. —**te**, *v.a.* kauen, essen. —**tion**, *s.* das Kauen, Essen.

Mane, die Mähne. —**d**, *adj.* gemähnt, eine Mähne habend, mit einer Mähne. *Comp.* —**-comb**, *s.* der Striegel.

Manège, *s.* die Reitbahn, Reitschule; (horse-breaking) die Abrichtung, die Zureitung eines Pferdes; (horsemanship) die Reitkunst.

Manes, *pl.* die Manen, Geister der Abgeschiedenen.

Manet, *v.* er *or* sie bleibt (auf der Bühne) (*Theat.*).

Mangan—ate, *s.* das mangansaure Salz. —**ese**, *s.* das Mangan.

Mang—e, *s.* die Räude. —**iness**, *s.* die Räudigkeit. —**y**, *adj.* räudig; (mean) schäbig.

Mangel-wurzel, *s.* die Mangoldwurzel.

Manger, *s.* die Krippe; to live at rack and —, verschwenderisch leben (*coll.*); to be the dog in the —, ein Neidhammel sein.

[1]**Mangl—e**, I. *s.* die Mange, Mangel, Rolle, der Kalander. II. *v.a.* mangen, rollen (*clothes*). —**er**, *s.* der Manger. —**ing**, *s.* das Mangeln, Rollen, Kalandern.

[2]**Mangle**, *v.a.* zerreißen, zerhauen, zerstücken, verstümmeln; verstümmeln, entstellen (*fig.*).

Mango, *s.* der Mangobaum; die Mangobeere.

Mangolds, *see* Mangel-wurzel.

Mangrove, *s.* der Mangelbaum; der Paradiesfisch.

Mania, *s.* (madness) der Wahnsinn, Wahnwitz; die Manie, Sucht (*for gambling, etc.*). —**c**, I. *s.* der Wahnsinnige, Tolle. II. *adj.*, —**cal**, *adj.* wahnsinnig, wahnwitzig, verrückt, toll.

Manicure, I. *s.* die Hand= und Nägel=Pflege. II. *v.a.* Hände und Nägel pflegen.

Manifest, I. *adj.*, —**ly**, *adv.* offenbar, augenscheinlich, zweifellos; to make —, offenbaren, klar legen *or* stellen. II. *v.a.* offenbaren, bekannt machen; (display) an den Tag legen, darlegen. III. *s.*; ship's —, das Ladungsmanifest. —**ation**, *s.* die Offenbarung, Bekanntmachung, die Darlegung. —**o**, *s.* die öffentliche Kundmachung *or* Kundgebung, das Manifest.

Manifold, *adj.* mannigfaltig, mannigfach *Comp.* —**-writer**, *s.* der Vervielfältiger, Vervielfältigungs=Apparat.

Manil(l)a, *s.* die Manila=Zigarre. *Comp.* —**-cane**, *s.* das Manilarohr. —**-rope**, *s.* das Seil aus Manilahanf.

Manip—le, *s.* der Manipel; breite Armbinde des Meßpriesters (*R. C.*). —**ulate**, *v.a.* mit den Händen bearbeiten, behandeln; mit Verständnis handhaben. —**ulation**, *s.* die Behandlung, Bearbeitung, das Verfahren. —**ulative**, *adj.* Behandlungs=. —**ulator**, *s.* der Bearbeiter; die Absendevorrichtung am Zeigertelegraphe: (*Tele.*).

Manna, *s.* das Manna, die Himmelsspeise.

Manner, *s.* die Art, Weise; (custom) die Gewohnheit; die Manier, der Stil (*Paint., etc.*); in a —, gewissermaßen, gleichsam; in this —, in dieser *or* auf diese Weise; in like —, ebenso; in such a — that, so daß; as to the — born, als ob es (ihm) angeboren wäre; no — of, gar kein; no — of doubt, nicht der geringste *or* leiseste Zweifel; there is no — of doubt, da kann kein Zweifel obwalten; in the best — possible, aufs beste, bestens. —**ed**, *adj.* (*in comp.* =) gesittet. —**ism**, *s.* die Manier, Manieriertheit. —**ist**, *s.* der Manierist. —**liness**, *s.* die Manierlichkeit, das gesittete Betragen. —**ly**, *adj.* gesittet, höflich, artig. —**s**, *pl.* die Manieren, Sitten, die Lebensart; bad —s, schlechte, keine Lebensart; leave that for (Colonel) —s, laß das letzte Stück in der Schüssel und sei kein Gierlaps (*coll.*).

Manœuvre, I. *s.* (*also* —s) das Manöver (*Mil.*); das Manöver, der Kunstgriff (*fig.*). II. *v.n.* manövrieren; geschickt *or* listig zu Werke gehen (*fig.*). III. *v.a.* manövrieren lassen. —**r**, *s.* einer der manövriert.

Manometer, *s.* der Manometer, Luftdichtigkeitsmesser; der Dampfdruckmesser.

Man—or, *s.* das Rittergut; lord of the —or, der Gutsherr, adlige Grundherr. —**orial**, *adj.* zu einem Rittergut gehörig, Ritterguts=; —orial lord, der Gutsherr, Grundherr. —**se**, *s.* das Pfarrhaus (in Schottland rc.). —**sion**, *s.* das Wohnhaus; das Herrenhaus; family —sion, das Familienhaus. *Comp.* —**or-house**, *s.* das Herrschaftshaus, der Herrensitz; das Schloß.

Mansard-roof, *s.* das Mansardendach.

Mantel, *s.* die Kamineinfassung, der Kaminmantel. *Comp.* —**-piece**, *s.* der Kaminsims. —**-shelf**, *s.* die Platte des Kaminsimses.

Mant—illa, *s.* die Mantille. —**le**, I. *s.* der Mantel; der Deckmantel, Schleier (*fig.*); der Glühstrumpf (*in incandescent gaslight*); on these minstrels the —le of the Minnesingers seems to have fallen, in diesen Sängern scheint die Kunst der Minnesinger wieder lebendig geworden zu sein. II. *v.a.* verhüllen. III. *v.n.* sich (mit Röte rc.) bedecken. —**ua**, *s.* der Frauenmantel. *Comp.* —**le-maker**, —**ua-maker**, *s.* der Damenschneider; (dressmaker) die Schneiderin.

Manu—al, I. *adj.* mit der Hand verrichtet, Hand=, eigenhändig; —al aid, die tätige Beihilfe, Handreichung; —al exercise, die Kriegswaffen=Übung der Infanterie; —al instruction, der Handfertigkeitsunterricht; —al labour, die Handarbeit; sign —al, eigenhändige Unterschrift. II. *s.* das Handbuch, der Leitfaden; das Manual (*Eccl., Org.*). —**factory**, *s.* die Fabrik. —**facture**, I. *s.* die Fabrikation; (—factured stuff) das Fabrikat. II. *v.a.* fabrizieren; verarbeiten, bearbeiten. —**facturer**, *s.* der Verfertiger; der Fabrikant, Fabrikbesitzer (*C. L.*). —**facturing**, *adj.* Fabrik=; a —facturing town, eine Fabrikstadt, ein Industrieort; the —facturing population, die Arbeiterbevölkerung. —**mission**, *s.* die Freilassung. —**mit**, *v.a.* freilassen. —**script**, I. *s.* die Handschrift, das Manuskript, der Kodex; die Druckvorlage. II. *adj.* handschriftlich.

Manure, I. *v.a.* düngen. II. *s.* der Dünger.

Many, I. *adj.* viel(e); (— a) mancher, manche,

manches; — a time, oft; he is too — for me, er ist mir zu stark; in — ways, auf vielerlei Arten; — a man, mancher (Mann); — men, — minds, so viel Köpfe, so viel Sinne (*prov.*); — is the day, mancher Tag ist verstrichen. II. *s.* die große Masse, der große Haufe; a good —, viele; a great —, sehr viele. *Comp.* —**-cornered**, *adj.* vieleckig. —**-sided**, *adj.* vielseitig.

Map, I. *s.* die Karte, Landkarte. II. *v.a.* eintragen, aufzeichnen.

Maple, *s.* der Ahorn; — sugar, der Ahornzucker.

Mar, *v.a.* verderben, zerstören; (disfigure) entstellen; stören (*pleasure*). *Comp.* —**plot**, *s.* einer, der alle Anschläge vereitelt, der Störenfried, Unheilstifter.

Marabou, *s.* der Marabu (*Orn.*).

Maraschino, *s.* der Maraskino.

Marasmus, *s.* die Abzehrung, Auszehrung.

Maraud, *v.n.* auf Raub *or* Plünderung ausgehen, plündernd umherschweifen, marodieren. —**er**, *s.* der Plünderer, plündernde Nachzügler, Marodeur. —**ing**, *adj.*; —ing party, die Räuberhorde, Bande von Plünderern.

Marble, I. *s.* der Marmor; das Marmorkunstwerk, die Statue; der Farbenreibstein (*Paint.*); der Schusser, die Murmel, Schnellkugel (*of boys*); der Marmorstein (*Typ.*); to play at —s, Murmel spielen; Carrara —, karrarischer Marmor. II. *adj.* marmorn; marmorhart; steinern, hart (*fig.*); — slab, die Marmorplatte. III. *v.a.* marmorieren. *Comp.* —**-edged**, *adj.* mit buntem, marmoriertem Schnitt. —**-paper**, *s.* marmoriertes Papier.

Marbling, *s.* das Marmorieren.

[1]**March**, I. *v.n.* grenzen; *see* [2]—. II. *s.* die Grenze, Mark; das Grenzgebiet.

[2]**March**, I. *s.* der Marsch (*also Mus.*); der Marsch, Zug (*of soldiers*); der Fortschritt (*of intellect*); to steal a — upon a p., einem zuvorkommen; to strike up a —, einen Marsch anfangen *or* spielen; — past, der Vorbeimarsch im Paradeschritt, Parademarsch; funeral —, Trauermarsch; wedding —, Hochzeitsmarsch. II. *v.n.* marschieren, ziehen (*Mil.*); gehen, schreiten; —! marsch! to — **off**, abmarschieren; to — **on**, anmarschieren; weiterziehen; to — **out**, ausmarschieren; to — **past**, vorbeimarschieren (*Mil.*). III. *v.a.* marschieren lassen; to be —ed off, abgeführt werden. —**ing**, *p. & adj.*; —ing orders, der Marschbefehl; to be under —ing orders, Marschbefehl haben; —ing regiment, das (Infanterie)regiment.

[3]**March**, *s.* der März; — hare, der Märzhase.

Marchioness, *s.* die Marquise.

Marchpane, *s.* der Marzipan.

Mare, *s.* die Stute; to go on Shank's —, auf Schusters Rappen reiten (*coll.*). *Comp.* —**'s-nest**, *s.*; to have found a —'s-nest, sich einbilden, eine wichtige Entdeckung gemacht zu haben, welche sich als nichtig herausstellt. —**'s-tail**, *s.* der Tannenwedel (*Bot.*); (clouds) Schäfchen (*pl.*).

Margarine, *s.* das Margarin.

Marge, (*poet.*) *for* Margin.

Margin, *s.* der Rand; (latitude) der Spielraum; der Überschuß, Gewinn; named in the —, nebenstehend genannt; to leave a —, Spielraum lassen *or* geben (*fig.*). —**al**, *adj.* am Rande, Rand-; —al note, die Randglosse.

Margrav—**e**, *s.* der Markgraf. —**iate**, *s.* die Markgrafschaft. —**ine**, *s.* die Markgräfin.

Marigold, *s.* die Ringelblume.

Mari—**ne**, I. *adj.* zur See gehörig; (naval) zum Seewesen gehörig, See-; —ne affairs, das Seewesen; —ne insurance, die Seeassekuranz; —ne engineer, der Schiffsmaschinist; —ne parade, die Strandpromenade, Hauptstraße eines Badeortes am Strande entlang; —ne store, der Vorrat von Schiffsutensilien; —ne trade, der Seehandel. II. *s.* der Seesoldat; (naval affairs) die Marine, das Seewesen; das Seegemälde, Seestück (*Paint.*); —**nes**, Seetruppen; tell that to the —nes! das machen Sie andern weis! —**ner**, *s.* der Seefahrer, Seemann, Matrose; —ner's compass, der Seekompaß. —**time**, *adj.* zur See gehörig; (near the sea) an der See gelegen, wohnend; zur See ausgeführt; Seehandel treibend; —time affairs, das Seewesen; —time courts, Assekuranzgerichte; —time law, das Seerecht; —time powers, Seemächte; —time state, der Seestaat.

Mariolatry, *s.* die Marienanbetung, der Madonnenkultus.

Marionette, *s.* die Drahtpuppe, Marionette.

Marital, *adj.* ehelich; — rights, Gattenrechte.

Marjoram, *s.* der Dosten, Majoran, Meiran.

[1]**Mark**, *s.* die Mark (*worth about one shilling*).

[2]**Mark**, I. *s.* die Marke, das (Kenn-)Zeichen, Merkmal; (price) der Preiszettel, die Etikette; (trade-—) das Fabrikzeichen, die Fabrik-, Schutz-marke; (brand) das Brandmal; (scar) die Narbe, das Mal; (aim) das Ziel; das Handzeichen, Kreuz (*as signature*); das Zeichen (*on sheep*); die Kerbe (*Footb.*); (—s, *pl.*) points (*Exam.*); to obtain full —s (half —s) in an examination, alle Fragen (die Hälfte der Fragen) in einer Prüfung zufriedenstellend beantworten; — of respect, Zeichen der Achtung; a man of —, ein Mann von Bedeutung, hervorragender Mensch; to leave one's — upon a th., einer Sache seinen Stempel aufdrücken; to be up to the —, einer Sache gewachsen sein; to have made one's —, es zu etwas gebracht haben I am not up to the — to-day, ich bin heute nicht recht auf dem Damm (*coll.*); to be quite beside the —, fehlgeschossen haben, sich gewaltig irren; that is beside the —, das gehört nicht hierher; to miss one's —, sein Ziel verfehlen, fehlschießen; to hit the —, treffen; you have hit the —! Sie haben es getroffen! getroffen! ganz recht! speaking within the —, wenigstens, mindestens; we are within the — in saying that . . ., wir sind zu der Behauptung berechtigt, daß . . . II. *v.a.* (be-)zeichnen; (observe) beachten, sich (*dat.*) merken; andeuten (*the time, etc.*); (denote) bezeichnen; (note) anmerken; (single out) auszeichnen; auszeichnen (*goods*); zeichnen (*linen*); to — with a hot iron, brandmarken; to — time, auf der Stelle treten (*Mil.*); nicht vom Fleck kommen (*fig.*); — me! höre mich! —ed coin, abgestempelte Münze; —ed attention, besondere Aufmerksamkeit; —ed progress, deutlicher *or* merklicher Fortschritt. III. *v.n.* auf (*acc.*) . . . Acht geben; —! Achtung! —**ed**, *adj.*, —**edly**, *adv.* auffallend; (express) ausdrücklich; (visible) bemerklich. —**er**, *s.* der Marqueur (*Bill.*); (book- —) das (Buch-)Zeichen. —**ing**, *s.* die Markierung. *Comp.* —**ing-ink**, *s.* die (unauslöschliche) Zeichentinte. —**ing-iron**, *s.* das Brenneisen. —**ing-thread**, *s.* das Zeichengarn. —**sman**, *s.* der Schütze.

Market, I. *s.* der Markt; der Marktplatz; der Absatz; (trade) der Handelsverkehr; to meet with a ready —, schnellen Absatz finden; to glut the —, den Markt überschwemmen; a drug in the —, eine Ware, die keine Absatz findet; the best book in the —, das beste der vorhandenen Bücher; to find a — (for), die Ware an den Mann bringen. II. *v.n.* auf den Markt gehen; einkaufen. —**able**, *adj.* verkäuflich, gangbar —**ableness**, *s.* die Verkäuflichkeit, Gangbarkeit. —**ing**, *s.* das Besuchen des Marktes; to do one's —ing, seine Einkäufe besorgen. *Comp.* —**-basket**, *s.* der Marktkorb. —**-day**, *s.* der Markttag. —**-garden**, *s.* der Handelsgarten. —**-gardener**, *s.* der Handelsgärtner. —**-hall**, *s.* die Markthalle. —**-house**, *s.* das Kaufhaus. —**-place**, *s.* der Marktplatz. —**-price**, *s.* der Marktpreis. —**-town**, *s.* der Marktflecken, die Marktstadt.

Marl, I. *s.* der Mergel. II. *v.a.* mergeln. —**aceous**, *adj.* mergelartig. —**y**, *adj.* mergelig. *Comp.* —**pit**, *s.* die Mergelgrube.

Marline, Marling, *s.* die Marlleine, Marling.

Marmalade, *s.* die (bittere) Marmelade.

Marmoration, *s.* das Belegen mit Marmor.

marmose, *s.* die Beutelratte.
Marmoset, *s.* das Seidenäffchen.
Marmot, *s.* das Murmeltier; German —, der Hamster.
Marone, Maroon, *adj.* karmesinbraun, kastanienbraun, dunkelrot.
Maroon, *s.* der Maronneger, Negersklave.
Marque, *s.*; letters of —, der Kaperbrief.
Marqu—ee, *s.* die Zeltdecke, das Zelt. **—is**, *s.* der Marquis. **—isate**, *s.* das Marquisat.
Marquetry, *s.* eingelegte Arbeit, Marketerie.
Marr—iage, *s.* die Heirat, Eheschließung, Ehe; der Ehestand; (wedding) die Hochzeit; to ask in —iage, anhalten um. **—iageable**, *adj.* heiratsfähig, mannbar. **—iageableness**, *s.* die Heiratsfähigkeit. **—ied**, *adj.* ehelich; (wedded) verheiratet; —ied state, der Ehestand. **—y**, *v.* I. *a.* heiraten; nehmen (zur Frau); verheiraten, vermählen (*a daughter, etc.*); trauen (*as the clergyman*); (unite) verbinden; he —ied the girl, er heiratete das Mädchen *or* verheiratete sich mit dem Mädchen; she —ied him, sie heiratete ihn; the father —ied his daughter, der Vater verheiratete seine Tochter; the clergyman —ied the lovers, der Geistliche verheiratete *or* traute die Liebenden. II. *n.* heiraten, sich verheiraten; to —y beneath one *or* below one's position, eine Mißheirat schließen; we shall be —ied from his house, wir werden uns von seinem Hause zur Trauung in die Kirche begeben; she has got —ied at last, sie ist endlich unter die Haube gekommen; —y in haste and repent at leisure, schnell gefreit wird meist bereut (*prov.*). *Comp.* **—iage-articles**, *pl.*, **—iage-contract**, *s.* der Heiratsvertrag, Ehevertrag. **—iage-bed**, *s.* das Brautbett, Ehebett. **—iage-ceremony**, *s.* die Trauung. **—iage-chamber**, *s.* die Brautkammer. **—iage-customs**, *pl.* Hochzeitsgebräuche. **—iage-day**, *s.* der Hochzeitstag. **—iage-hater**, *s.* der Ehefeind. **—iage-lines**, *s.* der Trauschein (*fam.*). **—iage-portion**, *s.* das Heiratsgut, das (von der Frau) Eingebrachte; die Mitgift. **—iage-rites**, *pl.* Hochzeitsgebräuche. **—iage-settlement**, *s.* der Ehevertrag. **—iage-song**, *s.* das Hochzeitslied. **—iage-tie**, *s.* das Eheband. **—iage-vow**, *s.* das Ehegelübde, Ehegelöbnis.
Marrow, *s.* das Mark; (pith) das Mark, der Kern; vegetable —, der eiförmige längliche Kürbis. **—y**, *adj.* markig. *Comp.* **—-bone**, *s.* der Markknochen; (knee) das Knie; to bring a p. down on his —-bones, einen zwingen, fußfällig um Verzeihung zu bitten (*coll.*).
[1]**Marry**, *see under* Marriage.
[2]**Marry**, (*obs.*) *int.* wahrlich! fürwahr! ei freilich!
Marsh, *s.* der Morast, Sumpf, (—y land) die Marsch. **—iness**, *s.* die Sumpfigkeit. **—y**, *adj.* sumpfig; —y ground, der Sumpfboden. *Comp.* **—-fever**, *s.* das Sumpffieber, Wechselfieber. **—-gas**, *s.* das Sumpfgas. **—-land**, *s.* das Marschland. **—-mallow**, *s.* die Sammetpappel. **—-marigold**, *s.* die Dotterblume.
Marshal, I. *s.* der Marschall; (regulator of ceremonies) der Zeremonienmeister; der Zivilbeamte in einem Gerichtsbezirk, Landrat (*Amer.*); Earl — of England, Oberhofmarschall. II. *v.a.* ordnen, führen; in Ordnung stellen (*troops*). **—ler**, *s.* der Ordner. **—ship**, *s.* das Marschallamt.
Marsupial, I. *adj.* Beuteltiere betreffend. II. *s.* das Beuteltier.
Mart, *s.* der Markt.
Martagon, *s.* die Berglilie, der Türkenbund.
Martello-tower, *s.* der Martelloturm, Wartturm.
Marten, *s.* der Marder.
Martial, *adj.*, **—ly**, *adv.* kriegerisch, Kriegs=; — law, das Kriegsrecht; — law has been proclaimed in the town, die Stadt ist unter Kriegsrecht gestellt, der Belagerungszustand ist über die Stadt verhängt worden; — music, die Militärmusik; court- —, das Kriegsgericht.
Mart—in, *s.* die Mauerschwalbe. **—let**, *s.* der Vogel ohne Füße oder Schnabel (*Her.*).
Martinet, *s.* der strenge Offizier.
Martingale, *s.* der Sprungriemen (*Saddl.*); das Stampfstag (*Naut.*).
Martinmas, *s.* der Martinstag (11th November).
Martyr, I. *s.* der Märtyrer; der Dulder, das Opfer; to die a — (to one's principles), als Opfer (seiner Grundsätze) sterben, sein Leben aufopfern (für seine Grundsätze); to be a — to gout, beständig an Gicht leiden. II. *v.a.* zum Märtyrer machen; peinigen, quälen; (kill) hinrichten; —ed with, gequält von. **—dom**, *s.* das Märtyrertum, der Märtyrertod. **—ize**, *v.a.* als Opfer darbringen, opfern. **—ologist**, *s.* der Martyrolog. **—ology**, *s.* das Märtyrerbuch.
Marvel, I. *s.* das Wunder. II. *v.n.* sich wundern (at a th., über eine S.). **—lous**, I. *adj.*, **—lously**, *adv.* wunderbar, erstaunlich; (incredible) unglaublich. II. *s.* das Übernatürliche. **—lousness**, *s.* das Wunderbare.
Masculin—e, I. *adj.* männlich; mannhaft, kühn; männlich, grob (*of women's features*). II. *s.* das Maskulinum, das männliche Geschlecht. **—ity**, *s.* die Männlichkeit.
Mash, I. *s.* das Gemisch; das Mengfutter (*for horses*); der Maisch. II. *v.a.* mischen; (bruise) zerstoßen, zerquetschen; maischen (*Brew.*); to — a girl, einem Mädchen den Hof machen (*sl.*); —ed potatoes, der Kartoffelbrei. *Comp.* **—ing-tub**, *s.* das Maischfaß.
Masher, *s.* der Stutzer, Gigerl (*sl.*).
[1]**Mask**, I. *s.* die Maske, Larve; der Vorwand, Schein, die Ausflucht (*fig.*); die Larve, Fratze (*Arch.*); (masque) das Maskenspiel (*Theat.*, *Mus.*); die Blendung, Maske (*Fort.*); (mummery) das Mummenspiel; *see* Masquerade; to throw off the —, die Maske ablegen *or* fallen lassen. II. *v.a.* maskieren, vermummen; verbergen, verdecken (*fig.*); in Schach halten, maskieren (*Mil.*); —ed ball, der Maskenball; —ed battery, maskierte, verdeckte Batterie. III. *v.n.* sich maskieren, sich verlarven; sich verstellen (*fig.*). **—er**, *s.* (player) der Maskenspieler.
[2]**Mask**, *v.a.* aufgießen (*Scotch*).
Mason, *s.* der Maurer, Steinmetz; *see* Free—; —'s level, die Setzwage. **—ic**, *adj.* freimaurerisch. **—ry**, *s.* die Steinmetzarbeit, Maurerei; (—'s work) das Mauerwerk, Gemäuer; die Gebäude, Baulichkeiten; bound —ry, das Quaderwerk; solid —ry, massives Mauerwerk.
Masque, *see* Mask. **—rade**, I. *s.* der Maskenball; (disguise) die Verkleidung. II. *v.n.* maskiert gehen; auf einen Maskenball gehen. **—rader**, *see* Masker.
[1]**Mass**, *s.* die Messe; high —, das Hochamt; low —, stille Messe; — for the dead, die Seelenmesse; to say —, die Messe lesen; to attend —, in die Messe gehen. *Comp.* **—-book**, *s.* das Meßbuch. **—-priest**, *s.* der Meßpriester.
[2]**Mass**, I. *s.* die Masse; die große Menge, der große Haufe, die Volksmenge, Masse (*of the people*); der Hauptteil, Hauptkörper; the —es, die Massen, die große Masse des Volkes, die unteren Volksschichten; der Pöbel; — of fire, ein Feuermeer. II. *v.a.* (an)häufen; in Massen aufstellen (*troops*). III. *v.n.* sich in Massen vereinigen. **—ive**, *adj.*, **—ively**, *adv.*, **—y**, *adj.* massiv, dicht, schwer, gediegen. **—iveness**, *s.* das Massive, Dichte; (solidity) die Gediegenheit. *Comp.* **—-meeting**, *s.* die Massen=Versammlung.
Massacre, I. *s.* das Gemetzel, Blutbad. II. *v.a.* niedermetzeln.
Mass—age, I. *s.* das Massieren, die Massage. II. *v.a.* massieren. **—agist, —eur**, *s.* der Masseur.
[1]**Mast**, I. *s.* der Mast. II. *v.a.* bemasten. **—ed**, *adj.* (*in comp.*) =gemastet. *Comp.* **—-head**, *s* der Masttop.
[2]**Mast**, I. *s.* die Mast. II. *v.a.* mästen.
[1]**Master**, *s.*; three- —er, der Dreimaster.

Master, I. *s.* der Meister; (owner) der Herr, Eigentümer; (ruler) der Herrscher, Gebieter; der Lehrer (*of a school*); der Vorsteher (*of a college*); der Kapitän (*of a merchant-vessel*); der Schiffer (*in the navy*); der Meister, Lehrer, Virtuose (*in an art, etc.*); der Meister (*of a trade*); der Meister (*as title*); junger Herr, Herr (*in addressing a lad*); (— of the house) der Hausherr; the old —s, die alten Meister (*Art*); — and servant, Herr und Diener; — at arms, Exerziermeister (*Nav.*); — of Arts, der Magister (der freien Künste); — of the hounds, Oberjägermeister; — in chancery, der Beisitzer des Kanzleigerichts; — of the horse, Oberstallmeister; — of the mint, der Obermünzwardein; — of the rolls, der Oberkanzleidirektor; — of the robes, Garderobenmeister; Grand —, der Großmeister (*Free-m. etc.*); to be — of, Herr über (eine S.) sein; to be one's own —, sein eigner Herr sein; like — like man, wie der Herr, so der Knecht (*prov.*); want has no —, Not hat kein Gebot (*prov.*). II. *v.a.* (be)meistern, überwältigen; to — a language, einer Sprache mächtig werden. **—ful,** *adj.* herrisch, gewaltsam, gewalttätig; meisterhaft, gewaltig, großartig. **—fulness,** *s.* herrisches Wesen. **—less,** *adj.* herrenlos; zügellos, unbändig. **—liness,** *s.* das Meisterhafte, die Meisterschaft. **—ly,** *adj.* meisterhaft, meisterlich; (imperious) gebieterisch. **—ship,** *s.* die Meisterschaft, Meisterwürde; das Vorsteheramt, Direktorat, der Rang oder die Würde eines Vorstehers, Lehrers; to take a —ship, eine Lehrerstelle übernehmen. **—y,** *s.* die Herrschaft, Gewalt; (preeminence) der Vorrang, Vorzug, die Meisterschaft; to obtain the —y over, bemeistern, in seine Gewalt bekommen, die Oberhand über eine S. erlangen. *Comp.* **—-attendant,** *s.* der Hafenmeister (*Naut.*). **—-builder,** *s.* der Baumeister. **—-hand,** *s.* die Meisterhand, geschickte Person. **—-joiner,** *s.* der Tischlermeister. **—-key,** *s.* der Hauptschlüssel. **—-lode,** *s.* die Haupt(erz)ader. **—-mason,** *s.* der Maurermeister. **—-mind,** *s.* der Geist ersten Ranges, führender Geist. **—-passion,** *s.* herrschende Leidenschaft. **—-piece,** *s.* das Meisterstück. **—-song,** *s.* der Meistergesang (*Lit.*). **—-stroke,** *s.* der Meisterstreich, Meisterzug.

Mast-head, *s.* der Topp des Mastbaumes

Mastic, Mastich, *s.* der Mastix. **—ate,** *v.a.* kauen. **—ation,** *s.* das Kauen. **—atory,** *adj.* kauend, Kau-.

Mastiff, *s.* der Bullenbeißer, Kettenhund.

Mastodon, *s.* das Mastodon, fossiler Elefant.

Mat, I. *s.* die Matte. II. *v.a.* mit Matten bedecken, belegen; ineinander flechten, verflechten, verfilzen. III. *v.n.* sich ineinander flechten. **—ting,** *s.* der Stoff zu Matten, Decken; die Matte; die Matten, Decken; —ted hair, wirres Haar.

Matador(e), *s.* der Stiertöter; der Haupttrumpf (*Cards*).

[1]**Match,** I. *s.* das Zünd-, Streich-hölzchen, die Lunte, der Zündstock (*Artil.*); lucifer —, das Streichhölzchen; safety —, das Sicherheitszündhölzchen; slow- —, der Zündstrick. *Comp.* **—-box,** *s.* die Zündhölzchenschachtel; die Luntenkiste (*Artil., Min.*). **-lock,** *s.* das Luntenschloß (*Gun.*).

[2]**Match,** I. *s.* der, das Gleiche, Passende; (marriage) die Heirat; (consort) die Partie; (competition) die Partie, das Spiel, Wettspiel; to be (quite) a — for s. o., einem gewachsen sein; she was a — for him, sie blieb ihm keine Antwort schuldig; he 's more than a — for you, er ist dir überlegen; an ill-assorted —, ein schlecht zusammenpassendes Ehepaar; a good —, eine gute Partie; gut zusammen passende Sachen; the — is broken off, die Heirat ist rückgängig gemacht geworden; to meet one's —, seinen Mann finden. II. *v.a.* gleich kommen, gleichen; (put forward as —) ein Gleiches aufweisen, zeigen, finden; (suit) zusammenpassen; (compare) vergleichen; (oppose) es aufnehmen mit, (einem) die Spitze bieten, sich messen mit; (unite) verbinden; note paper and envelopes to —, Briefpapier mit den dazu gehörigen Umschlägen; this colour is hard to —, es ist schwer etwas zu dieser Farbe Passendes zu finden; I know nothing to — it, ich kenne seinesgleichen nicht; I 'll — this horse against the field, ich halte auf dies Pferd gegen alle Mit-Renner; a well- —ed couple, ein gut zusammenpassendes Paar. III. *v.n.* zusammenpassen. **—less,** *adj.* unvergleichlich, ohnegleichen; unübertrefflich. **—lessness,** *s.* die Unvergleichlichkeit. *Comp.* **—maker,** *s.* der (die) Ehestifter(in). **—making,** I. *adj.* ehestiftend; —making mother, eine Mutter, die gern Heiraten stiftet. II. *s.* das Ehestiften.

[1]**Mate,** I. *s.* der Gefährte, Genosse, Kamerad; (spouse) der Gatte, die Gattin; das Männchen, Weibchen (*of birds*); der Maat (*Naut.*); second —, der zweite *or* Unter-Maat. II. *v.a.* heiraten; paaren; es aufnehmen mit (*obs.*). III. *v.n.* sich paaren, sich gatten. **—less,** *adj.* ohne Gefährten.

[2]**Mate,** I. *adj.* matt. II. *v.a.* matt machen.

[3]**Mate,** *s.* der Matebaum.

Materia—medica, *s.* die Arzeneistoffe (*pl.*); die Arzeneimittellehre. **—l,** I. *s.* das Material, der Stoff, Bestandteil. II. *adj.*, **—lly,** *adv.* materiell (*also Log.*); (essential) wesentlich, wichtig (to, für); (corporeal) stofflich, materiell. **—lism,** *s.* der Materialismus. **—list,** *s.* der Materialist. **—listic,** *adj.* materialistisch. **—lize,** *v.n.* verkörpern, materiell machen.

Mat—ernal, *adj.*, **—ernally,** *adv.* mütterlich; von mütterlicher Seite; —ernal love, die Mutterliebe; —ernal uncle, der Onkel von mütterlicher Seite *or* mütterlicherseits. **—ernity,** *s.* die Mutterschaft; (— hospital) die Entbindungsanstalt. **—ricidal,** *adj.* muttermörderisch. **—ricide,** *s.* der Muttermord; (person) der Muttermörder. **—riculate,** *v.* I. *a.* immatrikulieren; —riculated student, der immatrikulierte Student. II. *n.* sich immatrikulieren lassen. **—riculation,** *s.* die Immatrikulation. **—rimonial,** *adj.*, **—rimonially,** *adv.* ehelich; —rimonial agency, das Heiratsbureau. **—rimony,** *s.* die Ehe; ein Spiel mit Karten. **—rix,** *s.* die Gebärmutter (*Anat.*); die Matrize (*Found.*); die Gangart (*Min.*); die Gießmutter (*Typ.*); die Haupt-, Urfarbe (*Dyer*); —rix of a screw, Schraubenmutter. **—ron,** *s.* die Matrone, verheiratete Frau; (chaperone) die Anstands-, Ehren-dame; die Hausmutter, Vorsteherin (*of a hospital or of the household of a boarding school*). **—ronize,** *v.a.* bemuttern; chaperonnieren. **—ronly,** *adj.* matronenhaft; gesetzt (*fig.*).

Mathematic—al, *adj.*, **—ally,** *adv.* mathematisch; —al man, der Mathematiker; der Student der Mathematik. **—ian,** *s.* der Mathematiker. **—s,** *s.* die Mathematik; pure —s, reine Mathematik; applied —s, angewandte Mathematik.

Matin, *adj.* Morgen-, früh. **—s,** *pl.* die Mette (*R. C.*); der Frühgottesdienst.

Matter, I. *s.* die Materie, der Stoff; der Eiter (*Surg.*); (materials) der Stoff; (contents) der Inhalt; (subject) der Gegenstand; (ground) die Ursache; (affair) die Sache, Angelegenheit, das Geschäft; der Satz (*Typ.*); that 's what the — is, da liegt der Hund begraben (*coll.*); — of fact, Tatsache; — of astonishment, Gegenstand der Verwunderung, eine Sache, worüber man sich wundert; it is a — for congratulation, es ist mit Freude und Dank zu begrüßen; — in hand, vorliegende Sache; — of consequence or moment, wichtige Angelegenheit; a — for keen regret, etwas höchst Bedauerliches; what 's the —? was ist's? was giebt's? what 's the — with you? was fehlt dir? something 's the —, or else . . ., es muß etwas vorgefallen sein, sonst . . .; (it makes) no —, es tut nichts, schadet nichts; it 's a — of indifference to me, es ist mir ganz einerlei *or* völlig gleichgültig; no — which, es ist mir einerlei, welches (welchen 2c.); it will be a — of £7, es wird etwa auf sieben Pfund kommen; for that —, was das anlangt *or* betrifft. II. *v.n.* von Bedeutung sein, daran gelegen sein; it —s little what he does, es ist wenig daran gelegen *or* ziemlich einerlei, was er tut. *Comp.* **—-of-course**, *adj.* (*only predic.*) selbstverständlich. **—-of-fact**, *adj.* tatsächlich; (prosaic) prosaisch; a —-of-fact person, ein nüchterner Tatsachenmensch.

Mattock, *s.* die Haue, Hacke; der Schrämhammer.

Mattress, *s.* die Matratze; hair —, Roßhaarmatratze.

Matur—ative, *adj.* zeitigend, reifend; die Zeitigung *or* Reife befördernd (*Med.*). **—e**, I. *adj.*, **—ely**, *adv.* reif. II. *v.a.* reifen; zur Reife bringen (*fig.*). III. *v.n.* reifen; verfallen (*as a bill*). **—ed**, *adj.* ausgereift (*plan*); fällig (*bill*). **—eness**, *s.* die Reife. **—ity**, *s.* die Reife; (manhood) die Volljährigkeit; die Verfallzeit (*of a bill*); at —ity, zur Verfallzeit (*of a bill*).

Matutinal, *adj.* morgendlich, Morgen=.

Maudlin, *adj.* halb bezecht, benebelt; (sentimental) süßlich, sentimental, überempfindlich. **—ism**, *s.* die Weinerlichkeit, Überempfindlichkeit.

[1]**Maul**, *v.a.* der Schlägel. II. *v.a.* schlagen, durchprügeln; (pull about) zerzausen, beschädigen.

[2]**Maul**, *adj.*, *see* Mahl-stick.

Maunder, *v.n.* leise und albern für sich sprechen.

Maundy—-Thursday, *s.* Gründonnerstag; the Royal — (gifts), am Gründonnerstag verabreichte Almosen (*in the Royal Chapel at Whitehall*).

Mausoleum, *s.* das Mausoleum.

Mauve, I. *s.* das Anilinviolett, die Malvenfarbe. II. *adj.* hellviolett, malven.

Mavis, *s.* die Singdrossel.

Maw, *s.* der Magen; (crop) der Kropf; der Rachen, Schlund (*fig.*). *Comp.* **—worm**, *s.* der Spülwurm.

Mawkish, *adj.*, **—ly**, *adv.* ekelhaft; (tasteless) geschmacklos. **—ness**, *s.* das Ekelhafte; die Geschmacklosigkeit.

Maxilla, *s.* die Kinnlade. **—ry**, *adj.* zu den Kinnbacken gehörig; —ry bone, der Backenknochen.

Maxim, *s.* die Maxime, der Grundsatz; das Axiom. **—um**, I. *s.* das Maximum. II. *adj.* höchst, größt; —um thermometer, das Maximalthermometer; —um weight, das Höchstgewicht, Maximalgewicht.

[1]**May**, I. *s.* der Mai(monat); der Lenz (*poet.*, *fig.*); (hawthorn) die Blüte des Weißdorns; welcome as the flowers in —, so willkommen wie Blüten im Mai. II. *v.n.*; to go a —ing, maien gehen, auf das Blumenpflücken am Maimorgen ausgehen. *Comp.* **—-bush**, *s.* der Weißdorn, Hagedorn. **—-day**, *s.* der erste Mai. **—-dew**, *s.* der Maitau. **—-flower**, *s.* *see* — I.; (Epigœa repens) die Maiblume. **—-morn**, *s.* der Maimorgen. **—-pole**, *s.* der Maibaum; die Hopfenstange (*fig.*). **—-queen**, *s.* die Maikönigin. **—-time**, *s.* die Maienzeit.

[2]**May**, *aux. v.* können, dürfen; mögen; you — well ask, du kannst mit gutem Grunde fragen; I — not tell you, ich darf Ihnen nicht sagen; happen what —, geschehe was da wolle; come what —, komme was da kommen mag; — we take a walk? dürfen wir spazieren gehen? — it please your Majesty, möge Euer Majestät geruhen, wenn es Eurer Majestät gefällt; — be, vielleicht. *Comp.* **—hap**, *adv.* vielleicht, möglicherweise.

Mayor, *s.* der Bürgermeister; Lord —'s day, der Einführungstag des neugewählten Oberbürgermeisters von London (Nov. 9). **—alty**, *s.* die Mayorwürde. **—ess**, *s.* die Frau Bürgermeisterin; Lady —ess, die Frau Oberbürgermeisterin.

Mazarine, *adj.* dunkelblau.

Maz—e, *s.* der Irrgang, das Labyrinth; die Verwirrung (*of thought, etc.*); to be in a —e, bestürzt, verlegen sein. **—ily**, *adv.*, **—y**, *adj.* labyrinthisch, verwickelt, sich schlängelnd; (confused) wirr, verwirrt.

Maz(o)urka, *s.* die Masurka.

Me, *s. pers. pron.* mich; (to —) mir; he was ashamed of —, er schämte sich meiner. *Comp.* **—thinks**, *imp. v.* mich dünkt. **—thought**, *imperf. of* —thinks, mich däuchte.

[1]**Mead**, *s.* der Met.

[2]**Mead**, **—ow**, *s.* die Wiese, der Anger. **—owy**, *adj.* wiesenreich. *Comp.* **—ow-grass**, *s.* das Rispengras. **—ow-lark**, *s.* die Feldlerche. **—ow-rue**, *s.* die Wiesenraute. **—ow-saffron**, *s.* die Herbstzeitlose.

Meagre, *adj.*, **—ly**, *adv.* mager, dürr; unfruchtbar (*as soil*); mager, arm (*as food*). **—ness**, *s.* die Magerkeit; die Unfruchtbarkeit; die Armseligkeit.

[1]**Meal**, *s.* das Mahl, die Mahlzeit; *see* Piece—. *Comp.* **—-time**, *s.* die Essenszeit.

[2]**Meal**, *s.* das grob gemahlene Mehl; whole —, ungebeuteltes Mehl; fossil —, Bergmehl. **—ies**, *pl.* eine Art von Maisgrütze. **—iness**, *s.* die Mehlartigkeit, Mehlhaltigkeit, Mehlähnlichkeit. **—y**, *adj.* mehlig; (like —) mehlähnlich. *Comp.* **—-worm**, *s.* der Mehlwurm. **—y-mouthed**, *adj.* blöde, mildernd im Reden, mit der Sprache zurückhaltend. **—y-mouthedness**, *s.* die Zurückhaltung, Abneigung mit der Sprache herauszurücken.

[1]**Mean**, *adj.*, **—ly**, *adv.* gemein, niedrig, gering (*as birth*); gemein, niedrig (*as thoughts*); (poor) gering, armselig; (abject) niederträchtig, verächtlich; no — achievement, keine geringe Leistung. **—ness**, *s.* die Gemeinheit, Niedrigkeit; die Ärmlichkeit (*of dress, etc.*); (miserliness) die Filzigkeit. *Comp.* **—-spirited**, *adj.* niederträchtig, von gemeinem Sinne *or* niedrer Denkart.

[2]**Mean**, I. *adj.* mittel, mittler, mittelmäßig; durchschnittlich (*Math.*); — proportion, das Durchschnittsverhältniß; — time, mittlere Zeit (*Astron.*); in the — time, (**—time**, **—while**) mittlerweile, unterdessen, indessen, inzwischen, einstweilen. II. *s.* die Mitte, der Mittelpunkt; (moderation) die Mittelmäßigkeit; die Durchschnittszahl (*Arith.*); golden —, goldene Mittelstraße; geometrical —, das geometrische Mittel. **—s**, *pl.* (income) die Mittel, Vermögensumstände; (*also sing.*) das Mittel, der Weg (*to an end*); to find the —s, Mittel und Wege finden; by this —s, hierdurch, dadurch; by —s of, mittels, vermittelst; by all —s, auf jeden Fall, jedenfalls; sicherlich, ganz gewiß; by no (manner of) —s, auf keine Weise, keineswegs, durchaus nicht; by fair —s, im guten, mit Güte; by foul —s, im bösen, mit Gewalt; by some —s or (an-)other, auf die eine oder andere Art; to live beyond one's —s, über seine Mittel *or* Verhältnisse leben; the —s of his ruin, die Ursache zu seinem Verderben; ways and —s, Mittel und Wege; independent —s, das Privatvermögen.

[3]**Mean**, *ir.v.a.* (intend) meinen, denken, gesinnt sein, vorhaben, beabsichtigen; (signify) bedeuten; what do you — by this? was wollen Sie damit sagen? he —s it for our good, er meint es gut mit uns, er will damit unser Bestes; I — you no ill, ich meine es nicht böse mit Ihnen; what I — to say is . . ., was ich sagen wollte, ist . . .; I did not — to . . ., ich hatte nicht die Absicht . . .; you don't — it, das ist nicht Ihr Ernst, das kann nicht dein Ernst sein, das meinst du nicht wirklich *or* im Ernst, Sie scherzen wohl; whether he —t it or no, ob es nun sein Ernst war oder nicht. **—ing**, I. *adj.*, **—ingly**, *adv.* bedeutsam, bedeutungsvoll; well —ing, wohlwollend. II. *s.* die Meinung, Absicht, Gesinnung, das Vorhaben; (significance) der Sinn, die Bedeutung; full of

—ing, bedeutungsvoll; what's the —ing of all this? was soll dies alles bedeuten? **—ingless,** *adj.* bedeutungslos; ausdruckslos (*as a face*). **—t,** *pret. & p.p. see* ³Mean.

Meander, I. *v.n.* sich winden, sich schlängeln. II. *s.* die Windung, der Schlängelweg.

Measl—ed, *adj.* finnig (*as pigs*). **—es,** *s.* die Masern (*also in wood*); die Finnen; German —es, die Röteln. **—y,** *adj.* maserig; finnig; niederträchtig, erbärmlich (*sl.*).

Measur—able, *adj.,* **—ably,** *adv.* meßbar; (moderate) mäßig; within —able distance, in absehbarer Entfernung. **—e,** I. *s.* das Maß (*also fig.*); (proportion) das Verhältnis, Maß; (standard) das Maß, der Maßstab; das Maß (*of wine, etc.*); das Zeitmaß, der Takt (*Mus.*); das Silbenmaß (*Poet.*); (means) die Maßregel, Verfahrungsweise; cubic —e, das Körpermaß; dry —e, das Maß für trockene Gegenstände; in some —e, gewissermaßen; in a great —e, großenteils; to take a p.'s —e, einem das Maß (for a suit of clothes, zu einem Anzug) nehmen; einen einschätzen (*fig.*); to take legal —es against s.o., einen gerichtlich belangen; to take —es accordingly, sich danach richten, seine Maßregeln danach nehmen; —e for —e, Maß für Maß, Gleiches mit Gleichem. II. *v.a.* messen, abmessen; ausmessen, vermessen (*Surv.*); abschienen (*a nine*); to —e by, abmessen nach; to —e a p. for, einem anmessen zu; to get —ed for a pair of shoes, sich (*dat.*) ein Paar Schuhe anmessen lassen. III. *v.n.* messen; the room —es 10 feet in length, das Zimmer ist 10 Fuß lang. **—ed,** *adj.;* with —ed steps, gemessenen Schrittes. **—eless,** *adj* unermeßlich. **—ement,** *s.* das Maß, die Messung; der Tonneninhalt (*of a ship*); superficial —ement, verlorene Schnur. **—ing,** *s.* das Messen, Vermessen; —ing of heights, die Höhenmessung. II. *adj.;* —ing chain, die Meßkette; —ing tape, die Meßschnur, das Meßband.

Meat, I. *s.* das Fleisch; (food) die Speise; fresh-killed —, frisch Geschlachtetes; minced —, gehacktes Fleisch; pickled —, Pökelfleisch; potted —, in Töpfchen eingemachtes Fleisch; preserved —, die Fleischkonserve; red, underdone —, halbgares Fleisch; roast —, der Braten; white —, Weißfleisch (von Geflügel); that's — for your master, das ist zu gut für dich; it is — and drink to him, er lebt ganz davon; what is one man's — is another man's poison, der Geschmack ist verschieden (*prov.*). II. *attrib.;* — pie, die Fleischpastete; — tea, Nachmittagstee mit Eiern und Fleischspeisen. *Comp.* **—-biscuit,** *s.* der Fleischzwieback. **—-chopper,** *s.* das Hackmesser. **—-cover,** *s.* die Metallstürze über einer Fleischschüssel. **—-extract,** *s.* der Fleischextrakt. **—-jack,** *s.* der Bratenwender. **—-market,** *s.* der Fleischmarkt. **—-offering,** *s.* das Speiseopfer. **—-safe,** *s.* der Speiseschrank, Fliegenschrank.

Mechani—c, I. *adj.,* **—cal,** *adj.,* **—cally,** *adv.* mechanisch; —cal equivalent of heat, das mechanische Wärme-Äquivalent. II. *s.* der Handwerker, (—cian) der Mechaniker; —cs' institute, der Handwerker-(Bildungs-)Verein; die Handwerkerschule. **—calness,** *s.* das Mechanische. **—cian,** *s.* der Mechaniker. **—cs,** *s.* die Mechanik. **—sm,** *s.* der Mechanismus, das Getriebe. **—st,** *s.* der Mechaniker, Maschinenbauer, Maschinentechniker; der mechanistische Philosoph.

Meconi—c, *adj.;* —c acid, die Mekonsäure. **—um,** *s.* das Kindespech (*Med.*).

Medal, *s.* die Denkmünze. **—lion,** *s.* die Kapsel, Schmuckkapsel, das Medaillon; (coin) große antike Münze. **—list,** *s.* der Medaillenschneider; (student of —s) der Münzenkenner; (prize-man) der Inhaber einer Preismedaille.

Meddl—e, *v.n.* sich (unberufen ein)mengen (in, in); sich abgeben (with, mit), sich einlassen (with, in (*acc.*)); to —e with things that don't concern one, sich mit Sachen abgeben, die einen nichts angehen; I will neither —e nor make, ich will mich nicht hineinmischen. **—er,** *s.* einer, der sich in fremde Dinge mischt. **—esome,** *adj.* sich gern in fremde Sachen mischend, lästig, aufdringlich. **—esomeness,** *s.* die Sucht, sich unberufen in fremde Angelegenheiten einzumengen. **—ing,** *p. & adj.;* —ing person, *see* —er; you must always be —ing, du mußt doch immer die Nase in alles stecken.

Medi—æval, *see* —eval. **—al,** *adj.* mittler(er); a —al consonant, ein inlautender Konsonant. **—ally,** *adv.* im Inlaut, im Wortinnern, in der Mitte eines Wortes. **—an,** *adj.* in der Mitte, Mittel-. **—ant,** *s.* die Mediante (*Mus.*). **—ate,** I. *adj.* in der Mitte befindlich, mittler; (indirect) mittelbar; —ate cause, mittelbare Ursache. II. *v.n.* sich ins Mittel schlagen, vermitteln (between, zwischen (*dat.*)). **—ation,** *s.* die Vermittelung, Dazwischenkunft; die Durchteilung (*Mus.*); (intercession) die Fürbitte. **—atization,** *s.* die Mediatisierung. **—atize,** *v.a.* mediatisieren. **—ator,** *s.* der Vermittler; (intercessor) der Fürbitter; der Mittler (*Theol.*). **—atorial,** *adj.,* **—atorially,** *adv.* fürbittend, Mittler-, als Mittler; —atorial office of Christ, das Mittleramt Christi. **—atorship,** *s.* das Mittleramt. **—atrix,** *s.* die Vermittlerin; die Fürbittende. **—ety,** *s.* das Mittel, die Hälfte; der Mittelstand, Durchschnitt. **—eval,** *adj.* mittelalterlich. **—evalism,** *s.* die Mittelalterlichkeit: mittelalterliche Zustände; die Vorliebe für das Mittelalter und mittelalterliches Wesen. **—ocre,** *adj.* mittelmäßig. **—ocrity,** *s.* die Mittelmäßigkeit. **—terranean,** *s.* (—terranean Sea) das mittelländische Meer, Mittelmeer. **—um,** I. *adj.* mittel, mittler; —um price, der Mittelpreis, (average) Durchschnittspreis; —um size, die Mittelgröße; of —um size, von mittlerer Größe, Durchschnittsgröße. II. *s.* die Mitte, der Mittelweg; (agency) das Mittel; das Medium, Mittel (*Phys.*); das Bindemittel (*Paint.*); das Mittelglied (*Math.*); der Mittelsatz (*Log.*); das Medium (*Spirit-rapping*); through the —um of, durch die Vermittlung von.

Medic—al, *adj.,* **—ally,** *adv.* ärztlich, medizinisch; Heil-; —al board, die Sanitätsbehörde; —al man, der Arzt, Mediziner; our —al man, unser Hausarzt; —al officer of health, der Bezirksarzt, Medizinalrat; officer in the —al department, der Militärarzt, Stabsarzt; —al practitioner, praktischer Arzt; —al properties, Heilkräfte; —al staff, das Sanitätskorps; the —al staff service, der Sanitätsdienst. **—ament,** *s.* das Heilmittel. **—ate,** *v.a.* mit Arznei ꝛc. vermischen, versetzen; —ated herbs, Heilkräuter; —ated waters, Gesundbrunnen. **—ation,** *s.* das Vermischen, Versetzen (mit etwas Medizinischen); die medizinische Behandlung. **—ative,** *adj.* heilend. **—inal,** *adj.,* **—inally,** *adv.* medizinisch, heilkräftig, heilsam; —inal drugs, Medizinalwaren; —inal springs, Heilquellen; —inal wine, der Krankenwein. **—ine,** *s.* die Arznei, Medizin, das Heilmittel, Mittel; (science of —ine) die Heilkunde, Medizin; student of —ine, der Student der Medizin, Mediziner; doctor of —ine, der Doktor der Medizin. *Comp.* **—ine-chest,** *s.* das Arzneischränkchen, die Hausapotheke.

Meditat—e, *v.* I. *n.* (—e on) nachdenken, nachsinnen (über eine S.), überlegen. II. *a.* im Sinne haben, beabsichtigen. **—ion,** *s.* das Nachdenken, Nachsinnen, Überdenken; (pious —ion) die Andacht. **—ive,** *adj.,* **—ively,** *adv.* nachdenklich, ernst. **—iveness,** *s.* die Nachdenklichkeit; der Tiefsinn.

Medlar, *s.* die Mispel; der Mispelbaum.

Medley, *s.* das Gemisch, Gemengsel.

Medull—a, *s.* das Mark. **—ary,** *adj.* das Mark betreffend; markig; —ary substance, markige Substanz. **—in,** *s.* das Medullin, der Markstoff

Meed, *s.* die Belohnung, der Lohn.

Meek, *adj.,* **—ly,** *adv.* sanft(mütig); (humble)

demütig, bescheiden. —**ness**, *s.* die Sanftmut; die Demut. *Comp.* —**eyed**, *adj.* mit sanften Augen, sanftäugig. —**-spirited**, *see* Meek.

Meerschaum, *s.* der Meerschaum.

[1]**Meet**, *adj.* paßlich, schicklich, tauglich, gelegen.

[2]**Meet**, I. *ir.v.a.* begegnen; (fall in with) (be)treffen, finden, stoßen (auf einen *or* eine S.), zusammentreffen (mit); (join battle with) feindlich zusammentreffen (mit); entgegenkommen (*views, opinions, etc.*); (oppose) die Stirne bieten, begegnen; (receive) finden, erhalten, erleiden; sich stellen vor (parliament, etc., dem Parlamente &c.); I met him, ich traf ihn, ich begegnete ihm; I have met him, ich bin ihm begegnet, ich habe ihn getroffen; he was met at the station by his brother, sein Bruder erwartete ihn am Bahnhof; the Emperor was met by all the high officers of state, der Kaiser wurde von allen hohen Staatsbeamten empfangen; to come to —, to go to —, entgegen-kommen, -gehen; well met! gut, daß wir uns treffen! to — half way, auf halbem Wege (einander) entgegenkommen (*also fig.*); to — an objection, einem Einwurf begegnen; to — the eye, dem Auge begegnen; (einem) ins Auge fallen; to — the ear, zu Gehör kommen, das Ohr treffen, hörbar werden; in order to — your demands (the exigencies of the case), um Ihrem Verlangen (den Umständen) gerecht zu werden; to — one's engagements, seinen Verpflichtungen nachkommen. II. *ir.v.n.* sich *or* einander begegnen, sich treffen, zusammentreffen, zusammenkommen; (unite) sich vereinigen; (feindlich) zusammentreffen (*as enemies*); (assemble) sich versammeln; the two armies met on the plain, die beiden Armeen wurden handgemein, kämpften in der Ebene; to — with a refusal, abgewiesen werden, eine abschlägige Antwort (einen Korb) bekommen; to — with one's match, seinen Mann finden; prepare to — with . . ., mach dich gefaßt auf . . .; to — with a good reception, gut empfangen werden; to — with an accident, verunglücken, von einem Unfall betroffen werden; this statement met with a flat denial, dieser Angabe wurde geradezu widersprochen; they are well met, sie passen zu einander; to make ends —, mit seinen Einkünften auskommen. to — with a loss, Verlust erleiden. III. *s.* die Jagdzusammenkunft. —**ing**, *s.* die Versammlung; (coming together) die Zusammenkunft; die Sitzung (*of a council, etc.*); die Tagung (*of a popular assembly*); das Zusammentreffen (*of two lines*); der Zusammenfluß (*of rivers*); (rendezvous) das Stelldichein, Rendezvous; to call a —ing of one's creditors, seine Gläubiger versammeln, zusammenberufen; go-to-—ing, der (die, das) beste, Sonntags- (*of dress*) (*vulg.*). *Comp.* —**ing-house**, *s.* das Bethaus der Dissidenten. —**ing-room**, *s.* der Sitzungssaal. —**ing-place**, *s.* der Sammelplatz.

Mega—lomania, *s.* der Größenwahnsinn. —**losaurus**, *s.* die Rieseneidechse. —**therium**, *s.* das Riesenfaultier.

Megrim, *s.* die Migräne. —**s**, *pl.* Grillen.

Melanchol—ia, *s.* die Schwermut, der Trübsinn, die Melancholie. —**ic**, *adj.* schwermütig, melancholisch; (sad) traurig; (gloomy) düster. —**iness**, *s.* die Melancholie; (depression) die Anlage zur Schwermut. —**y**, I. *s.* die Schwermut (*also Med.*), der Trübsinn. II. *adj.* schwermütig; (gloomy) düster; (calamitous) unselig.

Mêlée, *s.* das Handgemenge, Kampfgetümmel.

Meliorat—e, *see* Ameliorate. —**ion**, *s.* die Verbesserung.

Melliflu—ence, *s.* der Honigfluß. —**ous**, —**ent**, *adj.* honigfließend; honigsüß (*as a voice*). —**ousness**, *s.* der Honigfluß; die Lieblichkeit.

Mellow, I. *adj.* (ripe) reif; sanft (*in tone*); reif, mürbe, saftig (*as fruit*); mild, sanft, weich, wohltätig (*to the ear, eye, taste, etc.*). II. *v.a.* mild, weich machen; (ripen) reifen. III. *v.n.* mild, weich, mürbe, reif werden. —**ness**, *s.* die Reife, Mürbigkeit (*of fruit*); die Milde (*of wine*); die Sanftheit, Weichheit (*of tone*).

Melod—ious, *adj.*, —**iously**, *adv.* melodisch, wohlklingend. —**iousness**, *s.* der Wohlklang. —**ist**, *s.* der Tonkünstler, der Melodien schreibt oder singt. —**y**, *s.* die Melodie; die Tonart.

Melodrama, *s.* das Melodram(a); das Volksstück. —**tic**, *adj.* melodramatisch. —**tist**, *s.* der Melodramatiker.

Melon, *s.* die Melone.

Melt, *v.* I. *a.* schmelzen; to — **down**, einschmelzen. II. *n.* schmelzen; to — **away**, verschmelzen, zerschmelzen; to — into tears, in Tränen zerfließen. —**er**, *s.* der Schmelzer. —**ing**, I. *p. see* Melt. II. *adj.*, —**ingly**, *adv.* rührend; —ing mood, weiche *or* rührselige Stimmung; to be in the —ing pot, in völliger Umgestaltung begriffen sein. III. *s.* das Schmelzen; das Rühren (*fig.*).

Member, *s.* das Glied; der Teil; das Mitglied (*of Parliament, Congress*); der Abgeordnete; the sitting —, der gegenwärtige Abgeordnete; our —, unser Vertreter im Abgeordnetenhause; das Satzglied (*of a discourse, etc.*). —**ship**, *s.* die Mitgliedschaft; die Gemeinschaft.

Membran—e, *s.* das Häutchen; die Samen-, Pergament-haut (*Bot.*). —(**e**)**ous**, *adj.* häutig.

Mem—ento, *s.* das Gedächtniszeichen, Denkzeichen, Erinnerungszeichen, Andenken; —ento mori, die Todes-Mahnung. —**oir**, *s.* die Denkschrift; —oirs, Memoiren. —**orabilia**, *pl.* die Denkwürdigkeiten. —**orable**, *adj.*, —**orably**, *adv.* denkwürdig. —**orableness**, *s.* die Denkwürdigkeit. —**orandum**, *s.* das Memorandum, die Note. —**orative**, *adj.* geeignet das Andenken an eine S. zu erhalten, Erinnerungs-; —orative power, das Erinnerungsvermögen. —**orial**, I. *adj.* zum Andenken dienend. II. *s.* das Denkmal; die Denkschrift; (petition) die Bittschrift; to give as a —orial, zum Andenken schenken. —**orialist**, *s.* der Unterzeichner einer Denkschrift; der Bittschriftenschreiber. —**orialize**, *v.a.* ein schriftliches Gesuch einreichen bei, ersuchen. —**orize**, *v.a.* zur Erinnerung aufzeichnen; auswendig lernen. —**ory**, *s.* das Gedächtnis, Erinnerungsvermögen; das Andenken, die Erinnerung; if my —ory serves me right, wenn ich mich recht entsinne; to commit to —ory, auswendig lernen (*acc.*); matter to be committed to —ory, der Lernstoff, Stoff zum Auswendiglernen; in —ory of, zum Andenken an (*acc.*); that has escaped my —ory, das ist mir entfallen; beyond (within) the —ory of man, über (bei) Menschengedenken; it is within living —ory, es leben noch viele, die sich (der Sache) erinnern; William the First of blessed —ory, Wilhelm der Erste, seligen Andenkens. *Comp.* —**orandum-book**, *s.* das Taschenbuch, Notizbuch.

Men, *pl. see* Man; Robert Bruce and his —, R. B. und seine Männer *or* seine Leute; Moltke with 20,000 —, M. mit 20,000 Mann; with the — of the second army corps, mit den Mannschaften des zweiten Armeekorps; — and women, Männer und Frauen; we are all —, wir sind alle Menschen; — and women students, Studenten und Studentinnen; — of Kent, Bewohner von Kent. *Comp.* —**folk**, *s.* das Mannsvolk, die Mannsleute, Mannsbilder (*coll.*).

Menac—e, I. *s.* die Drohung. II. *v.a.* (be)drohen. —**ing**, I. *adj.*, —**ingly**, *adv.* drohend. II. *s.* das Drohen.

Menage, *s.* der Haushalt.

Menagerie, *s.* die Menagerie.

Mend, *v.* I. *a.* (ver)bessern; (patch) flicken, ausbessern; besser machen (*matters*); never too late to —, zum Bessern *or* zur Besserung ist 's nie zu spät; to — one's life, one's ways, sich bessern; to — one's pace, seine Schritte beschleunigen, schneller gehen; to — a pen, eine Feder zuschneiden. II. *v.n.* besser werden, genesen; she is —ing, sie

ist auf dem Wege der Besserung. III. *s.* die Besserung, der Weg der Besserung; she is on the —, sie befindet sich auf (dem Wege der) Besserung. —**er**, *s.* der Flicker, Ausbesserer.
Mendaci—ous, *adj.* lügnerisch, verlogen. —**ty**, *s.* die Lügenhaftigkeit, Verlogenheit.
Mendic—ancy, *s.* der Bettel, die Bettelei. —**ant**, I. *adj.* bettelnd; —ant friars, Bettelmönche. II. *s.* der Bettler; der Bettelmönch (*R. C.*). —**ity**, *s.* der Bettelstand; *see* —ancy; to reduce a p. to —ity, einen an den Bettelstab bringen. *Comp.* —**ity-society**, *s.* der Verein für Abschaffung der Bettelei, Verein gegen Hausbettelei.
Menial, I. *adj.* zum Gesinde gehörig; (servile) gemein, niedrig, knechtisch; — work, gemeine häusliche Arbeit. II. *s.* der Diener, Knecht; —s, die Dienerschaft, das Gesinde.
Meningitis, *s.* die Hirnhautentzündung.
Meniscus, *s.* die auf der einen Seite konvexe, auf der andern konkave Linse; der Meniskus.
Menopause, *s.* das Aufhören des Monatsflusses.
Mense, *s.* das feine Benehmen, die gute Lebensart (*Scotch*). —**ful**, *adj.* artig.
Mens—es, *pl.* die monatliche Reinigung. —**trual**, *adj.* monatlich; einen Monat dauernd (*Bot.*). —**truate**, *v.n.* menstruieren. —**truation**, *s.* die Menstruation.
Mensura—bility, —**bleness**, *s.* die Meßbarkeit. —**ble**, *adj.* meßbar. —**tion**, *s.* das Messen, die Abmessung; (science) die Meßkunst.
Ment—al, *adj.*, —**ally**, *adv.* geistig, Geistes-; —al alienation, die Geistesabwesenheit; —al arithmetic, das Kopfrechnen; —al disease *or* disorder, die Geisteskrankheit *or* Geistesstörung; —al gymnastics, die Geistesübung; —al power, die Geisteskraft; —al reservation, der geheime *or* stille Vorbehalt; —al state, die Gemütsverfassung; —al training, die Geistesbildung. —**ion**, *s. see* Mention.
Menthol, *s.* das Menthol.
Mention, I. *s.* die Erwähnung; to make — of a th., einer Sache Erwähnung tun, eine S. erwähnen. II. *v.a.* erwähnen; not to — their avarice, geschweige ihres Geizes; don't — it, bitte sehr, das hat nichts zu bedeuten, gern geschehen. —**able**, *adj.* erwähnbar.
Mentor, *s.* der weise, treue Ratgeber, Mentor.
Menu, *s.* die Speisenfolge; die Speisekarte.
Mephiti—c, *adj.* Stickluft enthaltend, erstickend, verpestet; —c air, mefitische Luft, Stickluft. —**s**, *s.* die Stickluft, verpestete Ausdünstung; das Stinktier (*Zool.*).
Merc—antile, *adj.* den Handel betreffend, Handels-; —antile reports, Handelsberichte; —antile classes, Handelsleute, der Handelsstand; —antile enterprise, die Handelsunternehmung; —antile fleet, die Handelsflotte; —antile letters, Handelsbriefe; —antile pursuits, der Handelsbetrieb; —antile spirit, der Handelsgeist; —antile town, die Handelsstadt. —**enary**, —**er**, —**hant**, *see* Mercenar—, Mercer, Merchan—.
Mercenar—iness, *s.* die Feilheit, Verkäuflichkeit. —**y**, I. *adj.*, —**ily**, *adv.* feil, käuflich; (hired) Lohn-, gedungen; gewinnsüchtig (*disposition*); —y marriage, die Geldheirat; —y soldiers, gedunge Soldaten, Mietstruppen. II. *s.* der Söldner, Mietling; army of —ies, das Söldnerheer.
Mercer, *s.* der Schnitt(waren)-, Ellenwaren-, Seidenhändler. —**y**, *s.* (—'s goods) Seiden-Ausschnitt-waren; (trade) der Schnitthandel.
Merchan—dise, *s.* die Ware; die Waren (*pl.*); der Handel. —**t**, I. *s.* der Kaufmann (im Großen), Großkaufmann, Handelsmann; (shopkeeper) der Kaufmann, Krämer; the —ts (of the place), die Kaufmannschaft; —t's clerk, der Kaufmannsdiener, Kommis. II. *adj. see* Mercantile. *Comp.* —**t-fleet**, —**t-navy**, *s.* die Handelsflotte. —**t-like**, *adj.* kaufmännisch. —**t-prince**, *s.* der Handelsfürst, Großkaufmann. —**t-service**, *s.* die Handelsmarine. —**t-tailor**, *s.* der Kleiderhändler. —**t-vessel**, —**tman**, *s.* das Kauffahrteischiff.
Merc—iful, *adj.*, —**fully**, *adv.* barmherzig, mitleidsvoll; gnädig (*as God*). —**ifulness**, *s.* die Barmherzigkeit; die Gnade. —**iless**, *adj.* —**ilessly**, *adv.* unbarmherzig, mitleidslos, hartherzig; (cruel) grausam. —**ilessness**, *s.* die Erbarmungslosigkeit, Mitleidlosigkeit. —**y**, *s.* die Barmherzigkeit, das Mitleid; (*also* act of —y) die Gnade; to be at s. o.'s —y, in jemandes Gewalt sein; to leave a p. to the tender —cies of . . ., einen schutzlos den Händen von . . . überlassen; at the —y of the waves, den Wellen preisgegeben; Sisters of —y, barmherzige Schwestern; —y on us! Gott sei uns gnädig! Lord have —y upon us! Herr, erbarme Dich unser! Gott sei uns gnädig! it is a —y that . . ., es ist eine wahre Wohltat, daß . . .; it is a —y that they escaped, es ist eine Gnade Gottes, daß sie der Gefahr entgingen. *Comp.* —**y-seat**, *s.* der Gnadenstuhl.
Mercur—ial, *adj.* von Quecksilber, merkurialisch; lebhaft, munter, flüchtig (*fig.*); —ial barometer, das Quecksilberbarometer; —ial gauge, das Quecksilbermanometer; —ial level, die Quecksilberwage. —**ialize**, *v.a.* mit Quecksilber behandeln. —**ic**, *adj.* Quecksilber-. —**y**, *s.* der Merkur (*Myth.*, *Astr.*); das Quecksilber (*Chem.*); der Nachrichtbringer, Bote (*fig.*).
[1]**Mere**, *adj.* rein, bloß, lauter, nichts als; (entire) völlig, rein, ganz, unvermischt. —**ly**, *adv.* allein, nur, bloß. —**st** (*sup. of* Mere); the —st chance, der reine Zufall, der größte Zufall von der Welt.
[2]**Mere**, *s.* der Teich, Weiher, der kleine See.
Meretricious, *adj.*, —**ly**, *adv.* buhlerisch; verführerisch; (false) unecht und prunkhaft.
Merganser, *s.* die Tauchente, der Taucher.
Merge, *v.* I. *a.* verschmelzen, versenken (in, mit); she —s her interests in those of her family, sie läßt ihre Interessen in denen ihrer Familie aufgehen. II. *n.* (sich) verschmelzen (in, mit), aufgehen (in, in (*dat.*)).
Meridian, I. *s.* der Meridian, die Mittagslinie; (noon) der Mittag; der Höhepunkt, Gipfel (*fig.*); the — of glory, der Gipfel des Ruhmes. II. *adj.* Mittags-, mittägig; — altitude, die Mittagshöhe. —**al**, *adj.* mittäglich, südlich; —al distance, die Entfernung vom Meridian.
Merino, *s.* der Merino; (— sheep) das Merinoschaf. *Comp.* —**-wool**, *s.* die Merino-Wolle.
Merit, I. *s.* das Verdienst; das Verdienstliche, Wertvolle (einer Sache); (—s, *pl.*) die Hauptpunkte, die Beschaffenheit (einer S.); the —s of a case, das Wesen, die Beschaffenheit einer Sache; to enquire into the —s of a cause, einer S. auf den Grund gehen; on the —s of the case, aus materiellen Gründen; to make a — of, sich (*dat.*) etwas zu Gute tun auf (*acc.*); to arrange in order of —, nach dem Verdienste *or* den Leistungen ordnen. II. *v.a.* verdienen. —**ed**, *adj* verdient, wohlverdient. —**orious**, *adj.*, —**oriously**, *adv.* verdienstlich. —**oriousness**, *s.* die Verdienstlichkeit.
Merl—e, *s.* die Amsel. —**in**, *s.* der Zwergfalk.
Merlon, *s.* die Schartenzeile, Mauerzacke.
Mer—maid, *s.* die Seejungfer, Nixe, das Wasserweib. —**man**, *s.* der Nix, Wassermann; der Triton (*Class. Mythol.*).
Merops, *s.* der Bienenfresser, Bienenfänger (*Orn.*).
Merr—ily, *adv.* lustig, vergnügt, guten Mutes, fröhlich. —**iment**, *s.* die Fröhlichkeit, Lustigkeit, Belustigung. —**iness**, *see* Mirth. —**y**, *adj.* lustig, vergnügt, fröhlich; (laughable) ergötzlich, spaßhaft; to live a —y life, ein vergnügtes Leben führen; —y jest, der Erzspaß; as —y as a cricket, kreuzfidel, lustig und guter Dinge. *Comp.* —**y-Andrew**, *s.* der Hanswurst. —**y-go-round**, *s.* das Karussell. —**y-making**, *s.* die Lustbarkeit; (feast) der lustige

Schmaus, das Fest. **—y-thought,** *s.* das Gabelbein *or* Brustbein eines Huhns.
Mésalliance, *s.* die Mißheirat.
Mesenteric, *adj.* zum Gekröse gehörig, Gekrös=; — glands, Gekrösdrüsen.
Mesh, I. *s.* die Masche; (net) das Netz. II. *v.a.* bestricken, umgarnen. *Comp.* **—-work,** *s.* das Netzwerk, Gespinnst.
Mesmeri—c, *adj.* mesmerisch. **—sm,** *s.* der Mesmerismus, tierische Magnetismus. **—st,** *s.* der Anhänger des Mesmerismus; *see* —zer. **—zation,** *s.* die Versetzung in den tierischen Magnetismus. **—ze,** *v.a.* magnetisieren. **—zer,** *s.* der Magnetiseur.
Mesne, *adj.* dazwischend kommend, mittel (*Law*); — lord, Afterlehnsherr; — process, der Nebenprozeß.
Mesothorax, *s.* mittelstes Bruststück der Insekten.
[1]**Mess,** I. *s.* das Gericht, die Portion; das Futter (*for cattle*); die Offizierstafel (*Mil., etc.*); die Back (*Naut.*); we are four at —, es essen unser vier zusammen. II. *v.n.* (an einem gemeinschaftlichen Tische) speisen, zusammenspeisen; to — together, Tischgenossen sein; to — with a p., jemandes Tischgenoß sein. **—age,** *s.* die Botschaft, Sendung; die Botschaft (*Pol.*); to go *or* take —ages, Botschaften ausrichten; to send s.o. a —age, einem eine Botschaft schicken, einen etwas wissen lassen. **—enger,** *s.* der Bote (*official*); der Botschafter, Gesandte; der Vorbote (*fig.*); die Kabelaar (*Naut.*); special —enger, der Expreßbote, Eilbote. *Comp.* **—enger-boy,** *s.* der Ausläufer. **—enger-pigeon,** *s.* die Brieftaube. **—mate,** *s.* der Tischgenoß.
[2]**Mess,** *s.* das Gemisch, Gemengsel; die Verwirrung, Unordnung; (state of dirt) der Schmutz; to be in a —, in der Patsche sitzen; to make a —, Schmutz machen; to make a — of o. s., sich beschmutzen; you've made a pretty — of it! ihr habt eine schöne Geschichte daraus gemacht!
Messuage, *s.* das Wohnhaus; — and outbuildings, das Wohnhaus und Anbauten.
Meta—bolic, *adj.* veränderlich, wandelbar — **bolism,** *s.* die Umwandlung, Umsetzung. — **carpus,** *s.* die Mittelhand. **—morphic,** *adj.* umgestaltet. **—morphism,** *s.* die Umwandlungsfähigkeit (*Geol.*). **—morphose,** *v.a.* um=, verwandeln, umgestalten. **—morphosis,** *s.* die Um=, Ver=wandlung, Umgestaltung, Metamorphose. **—phor,** *s.* der bildliche *or* übertragene Ausdruck, die Metapher. **—phoric,** *adj.*, **—phorical,** *adj.*, **—phorically,** *adv.* bildlich, übertragen, metaphorisch. **—physical,** *adj.*, **—physically,** *adv.* metaphysisch. **—physics,** *s.* die Metaphysik, Wissenschaft vom Übersinnlichen. **—physician,** *s.* der Metaphysiker. **—plasm,** *s.* die Wortveränderung, Wortumbildung. **—tarsal,** *adj.* Mittelfuß=. **—tarsus,** *s.* der Mittelfuß. **—thesis,** *s.* die Buchstabenversetzung; die Versetzung des Krankheitsstoffs auf einen unschädlichen Teil (*Med.*).
Metal, *s.* das Metall; die Kiesfüllung (*Surv.*); Chausseesteine zu makadamisierten Straßen, die Beschotterung, *see* Mettle; Britannia —, Britanniametall; road —, der Straßenbewurf; waste —, die Krätze; the —s, die Schienen, das Geleise (*Railw.*); to run off the —s, entgleisen. — **lic,** *adj.* metallisch, metallen, Metall=; —lic pencil, der Metallstift. **—liferous,** *adj.* metallhaltig; —liferous veins, Erzadern. **—liform,** *adj.* metallartig. **—line,** *adj.* metallen; *see* —liferous, —lic. **—list,** *s.* der Metallarbeiter. **—lize,** *v.a.* in Metall verwandeln. **—loid,** *s.* das Metalloid. **—lurgic,** *adj.* metallurgisch. **—lurgist,** *s.* der Metallurg. **—lurgy,** *s.* die Hüttenkunde, Erzscheidekunst.
Mete, *v.a.* (ab)messen; to — out, ausmessen, (einem etwas) zumessen. **—r,** *s.* der Messer; (gas —r) die Gasuhr; dry (wet) —r, trockene (nasse) Gasuhr.
Metempsychosis, *s.* die Seelenwanderung.
Meteor, *s.* die Lufterscheinung; die Feuerkugel, der Feuerball, das Meteor; die Lichterscheinung, Wundererscheinung (*fig.*); luminous —, Lichtmeteor. **—ic,** *adj.* Meteor=; —ic iron, das Meteoreisen; —ic shower, der Sternschnuppenschwarm; —ic stones, Meteorsteine, Meteorolithen. **—ite,** *s.* der Meteorstein. **—ological,** *adj.* meteorologisch, Wetter=; —ological report, der Witterungsbericht; —ological bureau, die Wetterwarte. **—ology,** *s.* die Witterungskunde.
Method, *s.* die Methode; die Lehrweise (*of teaching*); (— of proceeding) die Art des Verfahrens; die Schule (*Mus.*); die Ordnung, das System; das (Heil=)Verfahren (*Med.*); master of —, der Methodenlehrer, Lehrer der Pädagogik. **—ical,** *adj.*, **—ically,** *adv.* ordnungsmäßig, planmäßig, methodisch. **—ism,** *s.* der Methodismus (*Eccl.*). **—ist,** *s.* der Methodist (*Eccl.*); der Methodiker (*Philos., Med.*); der Pietist (*fig.*). **—istic(al),** *adj.* methodistisch. **—ize,** *v.a.* planmäßig (nach Gesichtspunkten) ordnen.
Methyl—ated, *adj.;* —ated spirits, der denaturierte Spiritus, der Fusel. **—ene,** *s.* das Methylen. **—ic,** *adj.* Methyl=.
Meticulous, *adj.* übergenau, ängstlich eigen; zaghaft.
Metonymy, *s.* die Namenvertauschung, Wortverwechselung, der Begriffsvertauschung, Metonymie.
Metope, *s.* das Zwischenfeld, die Metope.
Met—re, *s.* das Versmaß, Metrum; (measure) das Meter; cubic (square) —re, Kubik=, (Quadrat=)meter. **—ric,** *adj.;* —ric system, das Metermaß. **—rical,** *adj.*, **—rically,** *adv.* metrisch; das Versmaß betreffend, Vers=; —rical rule, die Versregel. **—ronome,** *s.* der Taktmesser, das Metronom. **—ronomy,** *s.* die Taktmessung, Metronomie.
Metropoli—s, *s.* die Hauptstadt. **—tan,** I. *adj.* hauptstädtisch; erzbischöflich (*Eccl.*); —tan railway, die hauptstädische unterirdische Eisenbahn; —tan Board of Works, das hauptstädische Oberbauamt; —tan church, die Metropolitankirche. II. *s.* (—tan bishop) der Erzbischof, Metropolitan; der Metropolit (*Greek Church*).
Mettle, *s.* der (Grund)stoff; die Naturanlage; der Mut, Eifer, das Feuer; to put a p. on his —, einen anspornen, sein Möglichstes zu leisten; horse of —, feuriges Pferd. **—d, —some,** *adj.* feurig, mutig **—someness,** *s.* das Feuer, der Mut.
[1]**Mew,** *s.* (sea—) die Möwe.
[2]**Mew,** I. *s.* das Miau. II. *v.n.* miauen. **—l,** *v.n.* heulen, schreien.
[3]**Mew,** I. *s.* das Gehege, der Käfig; (prison) das Gefängnis. II. *v.n.* sich mause(r)n; (change) sich erneuern. III. *v.a.* (die Federn, 2c.) abwerfen; (— up) einsperren; —ed up from the world, von der Welt abgeschlossen. **—s,** I. *pl.* der (königliche) Marstall. II. *sing.* das Gäßchen, in dem ein Marstall ist, in dem sich Ställe von Mietkutschern befinden.
Mezereon, *s.* der Seidelbast (*Bot.*).
Mezzo—-relievo, *s.* die halberhabene Arbeit. **—-soprano,** *s.* der Mezzo=Sopran; (singer) die Mittelsopranistin. **—tint(o),** *s.* die Stechkunst in geschabter Manier *or* Schabmanier.
Miasma, *s.* das Miasma, der Ansteckungsstoff. **—tic,** *adj.* miasmatisch, ansteckend.
Mica, I. *s.* der Glimmer. II. *attrib.;* — schist, — slate, der Glimmerschiefer. **—ceous,** *adj.* glimmerartig, Glimmer=.
Mice, *pl. see* Mouse.
Michaelmas, *s.* das Michaelsfest; at —, zu, auf Michaeli(s). *Comp.* **—-daisy,** *s.* die großblätterige Sternblume. **—-day,** *s.* der Michaelistag.
Mickle, I. *adj.* groß, ausgedehnt; zahlreich (*Scotch*). II. *s.* die Menge (*Scotch*).
Microb—e, *s.* die Mikrobe, Bakterie, der Bazillus. **—ial,** *adj.* durch Mikroben veranlaßt. **—icide,** *s.* der Mikroben tötende Stoff.
Micro—cosm, *s.* der Mikrokosmus, die kleine

Welt, die Welt im Kleinen. **—cosmical**, *adj.* mikrokosmisch. **—graphy**, *s.* die Mikrographie. **—meter**, *s.* der Mikrometer. **—phone**, *s.* das Mikrophon. **—scope**, *s.* das Mikroskop. **—scopic**, mikroskopisch. **—scopist**, *s.* der Mikroskopiker. **—scopy**, *s.* die Mikroskopie.
Micturition, *s.* der Drang zum Harnlassen.
Mid, **—st**, I. *prep. see* Amid. II. *adj.* mitten, in der Mitte befindlich; from — May to — July, von Mitte Mai bis Mitte Juli. **—den**, *s.* der Misthaufen, die Müllgrube. **—dle**, I. *s.* die Mitte, das Mittelstück; die Mitte, Zwischenzeit (*of time*), der Mittelpunkt; the —dle of the month, die Mitte des Monats; the —dle Empire, das Reich der Mitte. II. *adj.* mittel, mittler, in der Mitte; —dle age, das mittlere Alter; —dle Ages, *see* —dle-Ages; —dle aisle, das Mittel-, Haupt-schiff; —dle course, der Mittelweg; —dle term, das Mittelglied (*Log.*). **—dling**, I. *adj.* mittelmäßig, leidlich, Durchschnitts-. II. *adv.* ziemlich, leidlich, soso. **—dy**, *see* —shipman. **—st**, I. *s.* die Mitte; in the —st of, mitten in, mitten unter; in our —st, in unsrer Mitte, mitten unter uns; from the —st, aus der Mitte. II. *adv.* in der Mitte. III. *prep. see* Amidst. *Comp.* **—-air**, *s.*; in —-air, mitten in der Luft. **—-day**, I. *s.* der Mittag. II. *adj.* mittäglich; —-day meal, das Mittag(s)essen; das Mittagsmahl. **—dle-aged**, *adj.* in mittlerem Alter; —dle-aged person, eine Person in mittleren Jahren. **—dle-Ages**, *pl.* das Mittelalter. **—dle-class**, I. *s.* der Mittelstand. II. *adj.* zum Mittelstand gehörig, aus dem Mittelstand. **—dle-finger**, *s.* der Mittelfinger. **—dleman**, *s.* der Mittelsmann, Zwischenhändler; die Mittelsperson (*C. L.*). **—(dle)most**, *adj.* mittelst. **—dle-sized**, *adj.* von mittlerer Größe. **—-heaven**, *s.* die Mitte des Himmels. **—land**, *adj.* binnenländisch, mittelländisch; —land town, die Binnenstadt. **—-Lent**, *s.* die Mitte der Fasten. **—night**, I. *adj.* mitternächtig; —night revels, Nachtschwärmereien; —night sun, die Mitternachtssonne; to burn the —night oil, bis tief in die Nacht hinein aufsitzen, noch spät nachts arbeiten (*fam.*). II. *s.* die Mitternacht. **—-ocean**, *s.* die Mitte des Ozeans. **—rib**, *s.* die Mittelrippe (*Bot.*). **—riff**, *s.* das Zwerchfell. **—ship**, *adj.* zum mittleren Teil des Schiffes gehörig. **—shipman**, *s.* der Seekadett. **—ships**, *adv.* mitschiffs. **—stream**, die Mitte des Flusses. **—summer**, I. *s.* die Mitte des Sommers, der Hochsommer. II. *attrib.*; —summer day, der Johannistag; —summer holidays, die Sommerferien, die großen Ferien; —summer night, die Johannisnacht. **—way**, I. *s.* die Mittelstraße (*fig.*). II. *adj.* in der Mitte (zweier Sachen) befindlich. III. *adj.* auf halbem Wege, unterwegs. **—winter**, *s.* die Mitte des Winters.
Midge, *s.* die Mücke, Schnake. **—t**, *s.* die kleine Mücke; etwas ganz Kleines.
Midwife, *s.* die Hebamme. **—ry**, *s.* die Hebammenkunst, Geburtshülfe.
Mien, *s.* die Miene, Haltung, der Gesichtsausdruck.
Might, I. *pret. see* May. II. *s.* die Macht, Gewalt, Kraft; with all one's —, aus Leibeskräften; with — and main, mit aller Gewalt, aus Leibeskräften; — is right, der Stärkste hat Recht *or* Macht geht vor Recht (*prov.*). **—ily**, *adv.* (strongly) gewaltig, heftig, stark; (greatly) sehr. **—iness**, *s.* die Macht, Gewalt. **—y**, I. *adj.* mächtig, gewaltig, stark; (important) wichtig; (—y in number) zahlreich, groß; (violent) heftig, gewaltsam; (great) groß; (efficacious) wirksam; schrecklich, sehr drückend (*as a famine*); (huge) ungeheuer, gewaltig. II. *adv.* (exceedingly) sehr, mächtig (*coll.*).
Mignonette, *s.* die Reseda.
Migrat—e, *v.n.* (aus-)wandern, fortziehen (to, nach). **—ion**, *s.* die Wanderung, das Fortziehen, der Zug; —ion of nations, die Völkerwanderung. **—ory**, *adj.* (aus)wandernd, umherziehend; (roving) nomadisch; Zug-; —ory animals, Wandertiere; —ory birds, Zugvögel.
Mikado, *s.* der Mikado, Kaiser von Japan.
Milch, *adj.* Milch gebend; — cow, die Milchkuh.
Mild, *adj.*, **—ly**, *adv.* mild, gelind(e), sanft; gelinde wirkend (*as medicine*); ruhig, sanft. **—ness**, *s.* die Milde, Gelindigkeit (*of the climate, of medicine*); die Sanftheit (*of temper*). *Comp.* **—-tempered**, *adj.* sanftmütig.
Mildew, I. *s.* der Mehltau; der Brand (*in grain*); Moderflecke (*in paper*); Stockflecke (*in cloth*). II. *v.a.* mit Mehltau überziehen, brandig machen; to become —ed, brandig werden.
Mile, *s.* die Meile; English *or* statute —, die englische Meile (1760 Yards *or* 1609,315 Meter); geographical —, Seemeile (= 1855 Meter); for —s, auf Meilen hinaus, meilenweit. **—age**, *s.* die Meilen-länge, -zahl; das Meilengeld, der Fuhrlohn. *Comp.* **—stone**, *s.* der Meilen-stein, -zeiger.
Milfoil, *s.* die Schafgarbe.
Miliary, *adj.* hirseförmig, hirsen-; — fever, der Friesel; — glands, Hirsedrüsen.
Milit—ancy, *s.* der Kriegsstand. **—ant**, *adj.* kriegführend; streitend. **—ary**, I. *adj.* militärisch, kriegerisch; Kriegs-; —ary chest, die Kriegskasse; —ary man, der Soldat, Militär; —ary officer, der Offizier; —ary oath, der Fahneneid; —ary rifle, das Infanteriegewehr; —ary service, der Militärdienst; der Dienst; universal compulsory —ary service, die allgemeine Wehrpflicht, die Dienstpflicht; —ary stores, Kriegsbedürfnisse. II. *s.* das Militär, die Soldaten. **—ate**, *v.n.* (—ate against a th.) wider-sprechen, -streiten (*dat.*). **—ia**, *s.* die Miliz, der Landsturm. *Comp.* **—iaman**, *s.* der Landwehrmann.
Milk, I. *s.* die Milch; unskimmed —, die Vollmilch; skimmed —, die Magermilch. II. *v.a.* melken. **—er**, *s.* der Melker; (— cow) die Milchkuh. **—iness**, *s.* die Milchartigkeit; die Weichheit, Sanftheit (*fig.*). **—y**, *adj.* milchig, Milch-; (white) milchweiß; (—-like) milchartig; —y blue, milchblau; —y Way, die Milchstraße. *Comp.* **—-bill**, *s.* die Milchrechnung. **—-can**, *s.* die Milchkanne. **—-diet**, *s.* die Milchkost. **—-ewer**, **—-jug**, *s.* der Milchgießer, Milchtopf. **—-fever**, *s.* das Milchfieber. **—-gauge**, *s.* der Milchmesser. **—maid**, *s.* das Milchmädchen. **—man**, *s.* der Milch-verkäufer, -mann. **—-pail**, *s.* der Milcheimer. **—-pan**, *s.* die Milchschüssel. **—-pap**, *s.* die Zitze. **—-rice**, *s.* der Milchreis. **—sop**, *s.* der Weichling, das Muttersöhnchen. **—-tooth**, *s.* der Milchzahn. **—-vessels**, *pl.* Milchsaftgefäße (*Anat.*). **—-white**, *adj.* milchweiß. **—-woman**, *s.* die Milchfrau, Milchverkäuferin.
[1]**Mill**, I. *s.* die Mühle; (spinning-—) die Fabrik; das Prägewerk (*Mint.*); Barker's —, das Reaktionsrad; that is grist to his —, das ist Wasser auf seine Mühle (*prov.*); no — no meal, wer nicht arbeitet, soll auch nicht essen (*prov.*); to go through the —, durch Erfahrungen gewitzigt werden. II. *v.a.* mahlen, quirlen (*chocolate*); prägen (*money*); rändeln (*the edge of coins*); walken (*cloth*); durchwalken (*fig.*); —ed edge, die Rändelung. **—er**, *s.* der Müller (*also Ent.*). *Comp.* **—board**, *s.* starke Art Pappe. **—cake**, *s.* der Pulverkuchen; (oilcake) der Ölkuchen. **—-dam**, *s.* das Mühlwehr. **—-hopper**, *s.* der Mühl-trichter, -rumpf. **—-owner**, *s.* der Mühlenbesitzer; der Fabrikbesitzer. **—-pond**, *s.* der Mühlteich. **—-race**, *s.* das Mühlgerinne. **—stone**, *s.* der Mühlstein; to see through a —stone, das Gras wachsen hören, die dunkelsten Sachen zu durchschauen glauben. **—-stream**, *s.* der Mühlbach. **—-wheel**, *s.* das Mühlrad.
[2]**Mill**, *s.* das Mille (*Amer.* = $\frac{1}{10}$ Cent). **—enarian**, I. *adj.* tausendjährig; zum tausendjährigen Reiche gehörig. II. *s.* der Chiliast. **—enarianism**, *s.* der Chiliasmus. **—enary**,

I. *adj.* aus Tausend bestehend. II. *s.* die tausendjährige Wiederkehr des (Geburts-, Todes-) Tages; King Alfred's —, die Feier von König Alfreds tausendjährigem Geburtstag. **—ennial**, *adj. see* —enarian. **—ennium**, *s.* das tausendjährige Reich. **—eped**, **—iped**, *s.* der Tausendfuß. **—esimal**, *adj.* tausendst; (thousandfold) tausendfach. **—et**, *s.* die Hirse; —et-grass, das Flattergras. **—iard**, *s.* die Milliarde. **—iary**, *adj.* Meilen andeutend. **—igram**, *s.* das Milligramm. **—imetre**, *s.* das Millimeter. **—ion**, *s.* die Million; the —, die große Masse, der große Haufe, das Volk. **—ionaire**, *s.* der Millionär. **—ionth**, *adj.* millionst.

Milliner, *s.* die Putzmacherin, Putzhändlerin, Modistin; *see* Man—. **—y**, *s.* die Modewaren, Putzwaren; (business) die Modewarenhandlung.

[1]**Milt**, I. *s.* der Same, die Milch. II. *v.n.* den Rogen befruchten. **—er**, *s.* der Milchner, Milcher.

[2]**Milt**, *s.* die Milz.

Mim—e, *s.* der Mime. **—esis**, *s.* die Nachahmung (*Rhet.*). **—etic**, *adj.* nachahmend. **—ic**, I. *adj.* nachahmend, mimisch; (counterfeit) nachgemacht, nachgeahmt; —ic art, die Gebärdenkunst, Mimik. II. *s.* der Mimiker; der Gebärdenspieler, Possenreißer; der Schauspieler, Mime; (imitator) der Nachäffer. III. *v.a.* nachahmen, nachäffen. **—icker**, *see* —ic II. **—ic(k)ry**, *s.* possenhafte Nachahmung, die Nachäfferei; die Anähnlichung (*Zool.*); he is good at —icry, is a good —ic, er hat viel Nachahmungstalent. **—osa**, *s.* die Sinnpflanze.

Minaret, *s.* das Minaret.

Minatory, *adj.* drohend.

Minc—e, I. *v.a.* (kurz und klein) hacken (*meat*); mildern, beschönigen (*fig.*); to —e matters, verblümt sprechen, die Sache beschönigen, bemänteln, nur halb aussprechen (*one's words*); don't —e the matter, mache keine Umstände; he does not —e matters, er nimmt kein Blatt vor den Mund; to —e one's words, geziert sprechen. II. *v.n.* fein tun; zimperlich gehen; —ing steps, zimperliche Tritte. III. *s.* gehacktes Fleisch. **—ing**, *adj.*, **—ingly**, *adv.* geziert, affektiert; geziert; in kleinen Stücken; oberflächlich. *Comp.* **—e-meat**, *s.* gehacktes Fleisch. **—e-pie**, *s.* die Fleischpastete. **—ing-knife**, *s.* das Hackmesser. **—ing-machine**, *s.* die Hackmaschine.

Mind, I. *s.* (disposition) das Gemüt, der Sinn; (intention) die Absicht, das Vorhaben; (inclination) die Neigung, Lust, der Wille; (opinion) die Meinung, Ansicht; (memory) das Gedächtnis, die Erinnerung, Gedanken; (understanding) der Verstand, Geist; (soul) die Seele, der Geist; the working of a p.'s —, der Gedankenvorgang, die Vorstellungsweise; after my —, nach meinem Sinne; in his right —, bei vollem Verstande; out of his —, nicht bei Verstande, verrückt; to bear (a th.) in —, eingedenk sein (einer S.); to call to —, ins Gedächtnis zurückrufen; to change one's —, andern Sinnes werden, sich anders besinnen; I gave him a piece of my —, ich sagte ihm gründlich die Wahrheit, ich hielt mit meiner Ansicht nicht hinter dem Berge; to enter, come into one's —, einem in den Sinn fallen; to follow one's —, seinem Kopfe folgen; many men, many —s, viele Köpfe, viele Sinne (*prov.*); to speak one's —, seine Gedanken ausdrücken, frei herausreden; to put out of one's —, sich (*dat.*) aus dem Sinn schlagen; the —'s eye, der Geist; to have a great — to do a th., große Lust haben, etwas zu tun; I have half a — to . . ., ich hätte beinahe Lust . . .; to have it off one's —, an eine S. nicht mehr zu denken brauchen; I have made up my —, ich habe mich *or* ich bin entschlossen, ich habe beschlossen; to make up one's — to s.th. disagreeable, in den sauern Apfel beißen; to know one's own —, wissen, was man will; my — misgives me, es schwant mir (Böses); to put in — of, an (eine S.) erinnern; time out of —, seit undenklichen Zeiten; out of sight, out of —, aus den Augen, aus dem Sinn (*prov.*). II. *v.a.* achten, merken (auf, *acc.*), beobachten; (take care of) sich beschäftigen mit, sich bekümmern um; never —! es tut nichts! laß (es) gut sein! to — one's book, aufs Buch achtgeben, ins Buch sehen, to — the door, auf die Türe achtgeben; he doesn't — it, er macht sich nichts daraus; — your own business! bekümmere dich um deine Sachen! I don't — giving something towards . . ., ich habe nichts dagegen zu . . . beizutragen; I don't — saying, ich möchte wohl behaupten. III. *v.n.* achtgeben (auf, *acc.*); (remember) sich erinnern an, gedenken (*Scotch*). **—ed**, *adj.* geneigt, gesinnt, willens. **—ful**, *adj.* (einer Sache) eingedenk; (attentive) aufmerksam, achtsam. **—fulness**, *s.* die Achtsamkeit. **—less**, *adj.* achtlos; (stupid) ohne Verstand, dumm, geistlos; (unmindful) uneingedenk.

[1]**Mine**, I. *poss. adj. see* My; — host, der Herr Wirt. II. *poss. pron.* mein, meiner; der, die, das Meinige; a book of —, eins meiner Bücher, ein Buch von mir; this boy of —, mein Sohn hier; he sacrificed his life to save —, er opferte sein Leben auf, um das meinige zu retten; this moment is —, dieser Augenblick ist mein, gehört mir.

[2]**Min—e**, I. *s.* das Bergwerk, die Grube (*Min.*); die Mine (*Fort.*); —e worked in common, die Gemeinzeche; school of —es, die Bergakademie. II. *v.a. see* Under—. III. *v.n.* minieren, Gruben graben; (burrow) Höhlen in die Erde machen; Ränke schmieden (*fig.*). **—er**, *s.* der Bergmann; der Minierer (*Fort.*). **—eral**, I. *s.* das Mineral, Berggut. II. *adj.* mineralisch, Mineral-; —eral kingdom, das Mineralreich, Steinreich; —eral spring, der Gesundbrunnen, die Mineralquelle; —eral tar, der Bergteer; —eral waters, Mineralwasser. **—eralization**, *s.* die Vererzung; die Versteinerung. **—eralize**, *v.a.* vererzen; (impregnate with —eral) versteinern. **—eralogical**, *adj.* mineralogisch. **—eralogist**, *s.* der Mineralog. **—eralogy**, *s.* die Mineralogie. **—ing**, I. *adj.* Bergbau-, Berg-, Montan-; —ing academy (college, school), die Bergakademie; —ing district, der Bergbezirk; —ing engineer, der Bergingenieur; —ing operations, der Minenbau. II. *s.* der Bergbau. *Comp.* **—ing-ant**, *s.* die Minierameise.

Mingle, *v.* I. *a.* (ver)mischen, mengen. II. *n.* sich mengen (in (*acc.*)), sich mischen (unter (*acc.*)); to — in society, in Gesellschaft gehen.

Miniature, *s.* die Miniatur; das Miniaturbild; in —, im kleinen.

Minikin, I. *adj.* klein, winzig. II. *s.* die Jungfernnadel, kleine Stecknadel.

Minim, *s.* die halbe Note (*Mus.*); der Tropfen. **—ize**, *v.a.* verringern. **—um**, *s.* das Kleinste, Minimum; —um weight, das Mindestgewicht. **—us**, *s.* der Jüngste (von drei Brüdern) (*school sl.*).

Minion, *s.* der Günstling; die Kolonelschrift (*Typ.*).

Minist—er, I. *s.* der Diener; das Werkzeug; der Geistliche (der Dissenters), Priester (*Rel.*); der (Staats-)Minister (*Pol.*), (delegate) der Gesandte; —er of the Word, der Diener des Wortes; acting —er for Foreign Affairs in Russia, der russische Minister des Äußern. II. *v.n.* dienen, aufwarten; behilflich sein; den Gottesdienst, das Amt halten; —er to (a th.) (einer Sache) dienlich sein. III. *v.a.* geben, darreichen, verschaffen. **—erial**, *adj.*, **—erially**, *adv.* (serving) dienend, aufwartend; kirchlich, geistlich, priesterlich; ministeriell, Ministerial-; the —erial benches, die Ministerbänke; die Ministerial-Partei (*fig.*). **—erialist**, *s.* der Anhänger der Regierungspartei. **—rant**, *adj.* dienend. **—ration**, *s.* der Dienst, das Amt; (agency) Dienste (*pl.*), die Vermittlung, Mitwirkung, Hilfe; das (kirchliche) Amt. **—ry**, *s.* das Amt, der Dienst; (means) die Mitwirkung, Vermittlung; das geistliche Amt, Predigeramt; das Ministerium

(*Pol.*); (government) die Staatsverwaltung; (time of —ry) die Amtsdauer.

Minium, *s.* der Mennig, die Mennige.

Miniver, *s.* das Grauwerk; das russische Eichhörnchen.

Mink, *s.* der Mink, Nörz.

Minne—singers, *pl.* die Minnesänger. **—song**, *s.* der Minnesang (*Lit.*).

Minnow, *s.* die Elritze.

Minor, I. *adj.* kleiner, geringer; (unimportant) klein, unbedeutend; (under age) minderjährig, unmündig; moll, weich (*Mus.*); jünger; — canon, der untergeordnete Kanonikus; — third, kleine Terz; Asia —, Kleinasien; — point, der Nebenpunkt, die Nebensache; — premise, der Untersatz; — prophets, kleine Propheten; Hobson —, der jüngere *or* der kleine Hobson. II. *s.* der, die Minderjährige, Unmündige (*Law*); der Untersatz (*Log.*); das Moll (*Mus.*). **—ite**, *s.* der Minorit. **—ity**, *s.* die Minderjährigkeit, Unmündigkeit (*Law*); die Minderzahl, Minderheit; to be in the —ity, in der Minderheit sein. II. *attrib.*; —ity report, der Bericht der Minderheit (eines Ausschusses).

Minster, *s.* das Münster, die Kathedralkirche.

Minstrel, *s.* der Sänger, (fahrende) Spielmann; der Gassensänger, der umherziehende Musikant. **—sy**, *s.* die Spielmannsdichtung; die Musik; (—s) die Sängerschaft, der Sängerchor, die Spielleute; die volkstümliche Dichtung, der Bardengesang (*of Scotland, etc.*).

[1]**Mint**, *s.* die Minze (*Bot.*). *Comp.* **—sauce**, *s.* die saure Minzsoße (*served with lamb*).

[2]**Mint**, I. *s.* die Münze, Münzstätte; (source) die Quelle des Zuflusses, Fundgrube; he has a — of money, er ist steinreich, er ist ein Krösus; master of the —, der Obermünzmeister. II. *v.a.* münzen, Geld prägen. **—age**, *s.* das Münzen; (—ed coin) geprägtes Geld; (— fee) die Münzgebühr. **—er**, *s.* der Münzer.

Minu—end, *s.* der Minuendus. **—et**, *s.* das Menuett. **—s**, *adv.* weniger; to be —s a sum of money, eine Summe weniger haben, um eine Summe kommen. **—te**, I. *adj.*, **—tely**, *adv.* sehr klein, winzig; umständlich (*as details*); *see* Petty. II. *s.* die Minute; ein Augenblick (*fig.*); (note) kurzer Entwurf, das Konzept; to make a —te of, (etwas) zu Protokoll nehmen, notieren, aufschreiben. III. *v. a.* notieren; zu Protokoll nehmen. **—teness**, *s.* die Kleinheit; die Kleinlichkeit; die Umständlichkeit, Genauigkeit. **—tes**, *pl.* das Protokoll; —tes of a meeting, das Sitzungsprotokoll; the —tes of the last meeting were read and approved, das Protokoll der vorherigen Versammlung wurde vorgelesen und angenommen. **—tiæ**, *pl.* Einzelnheiten. *Comp.* **—te-book**, *s.* das Notizbuch; das Protokollbuch. **—te-glass**, *s.* die Minutensanduhr. **—te-gun**, *s.* das Minutengeschütz. **—te-guns**, *pl.*, Signalschüsse (die jede Minute abgefeuert werden). **—te-hand**, *s.* der Minutenzeiger.

Minx, *s.* das kecke, ausgelassene, naseweise Mädchen.

Miocene, *adj.* miozän; Miozän-.

Mira—cle, *s.* das Wunder; das Wunderwerk (*Theol.*); to work —cles, Wunder tun; next door to a —cle, an das Wunderbare grenzend (*coll.*). **—culous**, *adj.*, **—culously**, *adv.* wunderbar; (supernatural) übernatürlich. **—culousness**, *s.* das Wunderbare; das Übernatürliche. **—ge**, *s.* die Luftspiegelung, Kimmung, Fata Morgana. *Comp.* **—cle-working**, *adj.* wundertätig, wunderwirkend.

Mir—e, *s.* der Schlamm, Kot; to be deep in the —e, tief in der Tinte sitzen (*coll.*); to drag into the —, verunglimpfen, in den Kot ziehen (*fig.*). **—iness**, *s.* das Kotige. **—y**, *adj.* kotig.

Mirky, *see* Murky.

Mirror, I. *s.* der Spiegel (*also fig.*); das ovale Feld (*Arch.*). II. *v.n.* abspiegeln; darstellen (*fig.*).

Mirth, *s.* der Frohsinn, die Fröhlichkeit, Heiterkeit. **—ful**, *adj.*, **—fully**, *adv.* fröhlich, heiter, lustig. **—fulness**, *s.* die Fröhlichkeit, Lustigkeit.

Misadventure, *s.* das Unglück, Mißgeschick; homicide by —, der unvorsätzliche Totschlag.

Misalliance, *s.* die Mißheirat.

Misanthrop—e, **—ist**, *s.* der Menschenfeind. **—ic(al)**, *adj.*, **—ically**, *adv.* menschenfeindlich, misanthropisch. **—y**, *s.* der Menschenhaß, die Menschenscheu.

Misappl—ication, *s.* die falsche, verkehrte Anwendung; (wrong use) der Mißbrauch, verkehrte Gebrauch; the —ication of the funds, die Mißverwaltung der Gelder. **—y**, *v.a.* falsch, verkehrt anwenden; (use wrongly) mißbrauchen, zu unerlaubten Zwecken verwenden.

Misapprehen—d, *v.n.* mißverstehen. **—sion**, *s.* das Mißverstehen; das Mißverständnis; you are labouring under a —sion, Sie befinden sich sehr in Irrtum, Sie haben die Sache nicht richtig erfaßt *or* aufgefaßt.

Misappropriat—e, *v.a.* sich (*dat.*) mit Unrecht aneignen; (misapply) mißbrauchen; widerrechtlich verwenden. **—ion**, *s.* die unrechtmäßige Aneignung, der Mißbrauch; die Unterschlagung.

Misarrange, *v.a.* falsch *or* schlecht ordnen.

Misbecom—e, *v.a.* sich nicht schicken (für), sich nicht geziemen. **—ing**, *adj.* unziemend, unschicklich.

Misbegotten, *adj.* unrechtmäßig erzeugt; mißgeboren.

Misbehav—e, *v.n.* & *r.* sich schlecht betragen. **—iour**, *s.* das schlechte Betragen, die Unart.

Misbelie—f, *s.* der falsche Glaube, Irrglaube. **—ve**, *v.a.* falsch *or* irrig glauben.

Miscalculat—e, *v.* I. *a.* falsch berechnen. II. *n.* sich verrechnen. **—ion**, *s.* die falsche Berechnung; der Rechnungsfehler (*in an account, etc.*).

Miscall, *v.a.* falsch benennen; schimpfen (*prov.*).

Miscarr—iage, *s.* das Mißlingen, Fehlschlagen, Mißglücken (*of an undertaking, etc.*); (ill-luck) das Unglück; das Irrelaufen, Verlorengehen (*of a letter, etc.*); *see* Misconduct; (abortion) die Fehlgeburt; —iage of justice, der gerichtliche Fehlgriff *or* Verstoß. **—y**, *v.n.* mißlingen, fehlschlagen, mißglücken (*of plans*); fehl *or* verloren gehen; fehlgebären.

Miscellan—eous, *adj.*, **—eously**, *adv.* gemischt, vermischt; vielseitig. **—eousness**, *s.* die Gemischtheit; (variety) die Verschiedenheit, Mannigfaltigkeit, Vielseitigkeit. **—y**, *s.* das Gemisch; vermischte Schriften *or* Miszellaneen. **—ies**, *pl.* Miszell(ane)en.

Mischance, *s.* das Mißgeschick, der Unfall.

Mischarge, *v.a.* unrichtig berechnen *or* eintragen.

Mischie—f, *s.* der Unfug, das Unheil, Böse; (hurt) der Schaden; (pranks) Possen; young —f, kleiner Unhold; —fs come by the pound and go away by the ounce, Böses kommt geritten, geht aber weg mit Schritten; to get into —f, in Unglück geraten; to make —, Unheil stiften. **—vous**, *adj.*, **—vously**, *adv.* schädlich, nachteilig; (causing —f) unheilbringend; (wicked) boshaft, schadenfroh; (fond of pranks) mutwillig. **—vousness**, *s.* die Schädlichkeit, Nachteiligkeit, Verderblichkeit; die Bosheit; das mutwillige Wesen; die Heillosigkeit. *Comp.* **—f-loving**, *adj.* mutwillig; (wicked) schadenfroh. **—f-maker**, *s.* der Unheilstifter. **—f-making**, *adj.* unheilstiftend.

Misconce—ive, I. *v.a.* falsch auffassen. II. *v.n.* eine irrige Meinung hegen. **—ption**, *s.* das Mißverständnis, die falsche Auffassung.

Misconduct, I. *s.* schlechtes Benehmen, schlechte Aufführung; der Fehltritt, der unerlaubte geschlechtliche Verkehr, der Ehebruch (*Law*); (mismanagement) die schlechte Führung *or* Verwaltung. II. *v.a.* schlecht führen *or* verwalten. III. *v.r.* sich schlecht aufführen; sich vergehen, einen Fehltritt begehen.

Misconstru—ction, *s.* die irrige Auslegung, Mißdeutung. **—e**, *v.a.* mißdeuten, falsch auslegen, unrichtig deuten.

Miscount, I. *v.a.* falsch rechnen. II. *v.n.* sich verrechnen. III. *s.* die Verrechnung.
Miscreant, I. *s.* der Ungläubige; der Bösewicht. II. *adj.* ungläubig; abscheulich.
Misdate, I. *s.* falsches Datum. II. *v.a.* falsch datieren.
Misdeal, I. *ir.v.n.* die Karten vergeben. II. *s.* das Vergeben der Karten.
Misdeed, *s.* die Missetat, das Vergehen.
Misdeem, *v.a.* mißkennen.
Misdemean, *v.n.*; to — oneself, sich schlecht betragen. **—our**, *s.* die Missetat; das Vergehen (*also Law*).
Misdirect, *v.a.* irre leiten (*a traveller, etc.*); falsch adressieren, verkehrt überschreiben (*a letter*); mißleiten, schlecht anwenden (*fig.*); —ed energies, übel angewandte Energie. **—ion**, *s.* die Mißleitung; die falsche Adresse.
Misdo—er, *s.* der Missetäter, Übeltäter. **—ing**, *s.* die Missetat, das Vergehen; (wrong-doing) das Unrechttun.
Misdoubt, *v.* I. *a.* beargwohnen. II. *n.* zweifeln (an einem); Verdacht hegen (gegen einen).
Misemploy, *v.a.* schlecht anwenden, mißbrauchen. **—ment**, *s.* die Anwendung zu schlechten Zwecken, der Mißbrauch.
Mise-en-scène, *s.* die Inszenierung.
Miser, *s.* der Geizhals, Filz, Knicker. **—able**, *adj.*, **—ably**, *adv.* elend, jämmerlich; unglücklich; armselig, schlecht (*as a meal*); (mean) karg, geizig, filzig. **—ableness**, *s.* das Elend. **—ere**, *s.* das Miserere (*Arch.*, *Mus.*). **—liness**, *s.* die Knickerei, Knauserei, der Geiz. **—ly**, *adv.* filzig, geizig. **—y**, *s.* das Elend, der Jammer, die Not; (trouble) die Trübsal.
Misfeasance, *s.* das Vergehen, die Übertretung.
Misfit, *s.* das Nichtpassen; nicht passender Gegenstand.
Misfortune, *s.* das Unglück; der Unglücksfall; das Mißgeschick.
Misgiv—e, *ir.v.a.* mit Zweifel erfüllen, Böses bedeuten; my mind —es me with regard to . . ., es scheint mir bedenklich, daß; my heart misgave me, mir schwante Böses, ich hatte ein banges Vorgefühl; *see* Mind. **—ing**, *s.* die böse Ahnung, Befürchtung.
Misgovern, *v.a.* übel *or* schlecht regieren *or* verwalten. **—ment**, *s.* die schlechte Verwaltung, Regierung, Leitung *or* Behandlung; (misconduct) das üble Verhalten, die Unordnung.
Misguid—ance, *s.* die Mißleitung, Verleitung. **—e**, *v.a.* mißleiten, verleiten.
Mishap, *s.* der Unfall, das Unglück.
Mish-mash, *s.* der Mischmasch.
Mishna, *s.* die Mischna.
Misinform, *v.a.* falsch berichten. **—ation**, *s.* der falsche Bericht.
Misinterpret, *v.a.* mißdeuten, falsch *or* irrig auslegen. **—ation**, *s.* die Mißdeutung, falsche Auslegung.
Misjoin, *v.a.* unpassend verbinden. **—der**, *s.* die ungehörige Verbindung verschiedener Klagepunkte.
Misjudge, *v.* I. *a.* falsch beurteilen; don't — me! beurteilen Sie mich nicht falsch! II. *n.* falsch urteilen. **—ment**, *s.* das unrichtige Urteil.
Mislay, *v.a.* verlegen.
Misle, *v.n. see* Mizzle.
Mislead, *ir.v.a.* irre leiten, verleiten; he has been misled, er hat sich verleiten lassen; misled by, verleitet von. **—ing**, *p.* & *adj.* irreführend.
Mismanage, *v.a.* schlecht leiten, führen, schlecht verwalten *or* einrichten. **—ment**, *s.* die schlechte Verwaltung *or* Handhabung.
Misname, *v.a.* falsch benennen.
Misnomer, *s.* der Namensirrtum, die falsche Benennung.
Misog—amist, *s.* der Ehe-feind, -hasser. **—amy**, *s.* der Ehehaß. **—ynist**, *s.* der Weiberfeind, Misogyn. **—yny**, *s.* der Weiberhaß.
Misplace, *v.a.* unrecht *or* verkehrt stellen; versetzen; übel anbringen (*confidence*). **—ment**, *s.* das Versetzen; der Fehldruck (*postage stamps*).
Misprint, I. *v.a.* verdrucken, falsch drucken. II. *s.* der Druckfehler.
Misprision, *s.* das Vergehen, Versäumnis; die Hehlerei, Unterlassung (einer Anzeige); — of felony, die Vertuschung eines Verbrechens.
Mispron—ounce, *v.a.* & *n.* falsch aussprechen. **—unciation**, *s.* die falsche Aussprache.
Misquot—ation, *s.* die falsche Anführung, das falsche Zitat. **—e**, *v.a.* unrichtig anführen.
Misrepresent, *v.a.* falsch darstellen, verdrehen. **—ation**, *s.* die falsche Darstellung, Verdrehung.
Misrule, *s.* die unordentliche *or* schlechte Regierung; (disorder) die Unordnung, Verwirrung; Lord of —, der Anführer der Weihnachtsbelustigungen (*obs.*).
[1]**Miss**, *s.* das Fräulein; gnädiges Fräulein; yes, —, jawohl, gnädiges Fräulein; tell me, — L., sagen Sie mir doch, Fräulein L. *or* gnädiges Fräulein; bread and butter —, der Backfisch, das halbwüchsige junge Mädchen; the —es Bell, die Fräulein *or* Schwestern Bell. **—y**, *s.* kleines Fräulein.
[2]**Miss**, I. *v.a.* missen; (feel want) vermissen; verfehlen (*the way*); verfehlen, nicht treffen (*a mark, an object*); (not get) verfehlen, nicht bekommen; verlustig gehen (einer S., a thing, *one's dinner, etc.*); überspringen, auslassen (*a page, etc.*); to — fire, versagen; to — one's footing, ausgleiten; to — a train, einen Zug versäumen; to — one's opportunity, die günstige Gelegenheit verpassen; I shall — no opportunity, ich werde keine Gelegenheit unbenutzt vorübergehen lassen; we — him very much, er fehlt uns sehr. II. *v.n.* fehlgehen, verfehlen; nicht treffen. III. *s.* der Fehler, Irrtum; der Fehlstoß (*Bill.*). **—ing**, *adj.* abwesend; there are many books —ing, es fehlen viele Bücher; he was long —ing, er wurde lange vermißt *or* blieb lange aus; the —ing link, das fehlende Glied (der Kette).
Missal, *s.* das Meßbuch.
Missel, *s. see* Mistlethrush.
Missend, *ir.v.a.* unrichtig versenden, an die falsche Adresse schicken.
Misshapen, *adj.* ungestalt, mißgestalt, unförmlich.
Missi—le, *s.* das Wurfgeschoß. **—on**, *s.* die Sendung; (embassy) die Gesandtschaft; (errand, commission) der Auftrag; der Beruf, die Bestimmung (*in life*); die Mission (*Rel.*). **—onary**, I. *adj.* eine Mission betreffend, Missions-; —onary society, die Missionsgesellschaft. II. *s.* der Missionär, Missionar, Glaubensbote, Heidenbekehrer. **—ve**, *s.* das Sendschreiben.
Misspell, *v.a.* falsch buchstabieren; unrichtig schreiben (*a letter*). **—ing**, *s.* das falsche Buchstabieren *or* Schreiben.
Misspend, *v.a.* übel *or* schlecht anwenden (*time, etc.*); vertun, vergeuden (*money, etc.*).
Misstate, *v.a.* falsch darstellen, unrichtig angeben. **—ment**, *s.* falsche Angabe, unrichtige Darstellung.
Mist, *s.* der Nebel; Scotch —, der dicke, feuchte Nebel, Sprühregen; in a —, irre, verdutzt (*fig.*); to cast a — before a p.'s eyes, einem einen blauen Dunst vormachen. **—ily**, *adv.* nebelig, trüb; unklar, dunkel (*fig.*). **—iness**, *s.* die Trübheit, Nebeligkeit; die Unklarheit (*fig.*). **—y**, *adj.* nebelig; dunkel, unklar (*fig.*).
Mistak—(e)able, *adj.*, **—(e)ably**, *adv.* verkennbar. **—e**, I. *ir.v.a.* verwechseln, verkennen (*a person*); mißverstehen; to —e a p.'s character, to be —en in s. o., sich in einem irren; to —e one person for another, einen für einen andern halten; to —e one's way, sich verirren; to be —en, sich im Irrtum befinden. II. *ir.v.n.* sich irren, sich verrechnen. III. *s.* der Irrtum, Fehler; (misunderstanding) das Versehen, Mißverständnis; by —e, aus Versehen; to make a —e, sich versehen, sich irren. **—en**, *adj.*, **—enly**, *adv.* irrig; —en ideas, falsche Ideen, irrige Begriffe.

Mist—er, *s.* (*abbr.* Mr.) Herr. **—ress**, *s.* die Herrin, Gebieterin; (—ress of the house) die Hausfrau, Frau (vom Hause); (school- —ress) die Lehrerin; (love) die Geliebte; (kept —ress) die Maitresse; die Meisterin (*of a language, etc.*); —ress (*abbr.* Mrs.) gnädige Frau; head —ress, die Schulvorsteherin, Direktrice; assistant —ress, die Lehrerin an einer Schule; form —ress, die Klassenlehrerin; —ress of the robes, oberste Kammerfrau; she remained —ress of herself, sie wußte sich zu beherrschen. **—ress-ship**, *s.* die Stelle einer Lehrerin.
Mistime, *v.a.* zur Unzeit tun. **—d**, *adj.* unzeitig.
Mistlethrush, *s.* die Misteldrossel.
Mistletoe, *s.* die Mistel; to kiss a p. under the —, einen unter dem Mistelzweig küssen.
Mistral, *s.* der Mistral.
Mistranslat—e, *v.a.* falsch übersetzen. **—ion**, *s.* falsche Übersetzung.
Mistrust, I. *v.a.* (einem) mißtrauen, nicht trauen. II. *s.* das Mißtrauen, der Argwohn. **—ful**, *adj.*, **—fully**, *adv.* mißtrauisch.
Misunderstand, *ir.v.a.* mißverstehen; sich irren in (*a person's character*). **—ing**, *s.* das Mißverständnis, der Irrtum; (quarrel) das Mißverständnis, die Uneinigkeit.
Misuse, I. *v.a.* mißbrauchen. II. *s.* der Mißbrauch.
[1]**Mite**, *s.* die Milbe, Made.
[2]**Mite**, *s.* der Heller, das Scherflein; das kleine Kind; the widow's —, das Scherflein der Witwe; poor little —, armes kleines Ding.
Mitigat—e, *v.a.* mildern, lindern (*pain, grief, punishment, etc.*); besänftigen, beruhigen (*anger, etc.*); mäßigen (*cold, trouble, pride, etc.*). **—ion**, *s.* die Milderung, Linderung, Beschwichtigung.
Mitrailleuse, *s.* die Kugelspritze, Mitrailleuse.
Mit—re, I. *s.* die Bischofsmütze, Inful; die Bischofswürde (*fig.*); die Gehrung (*Carp.*). II. *v.a.* mit der Inful zieren; in einen halben rechten Winkel zusammenfügen. **—riform**, *adj.* mützenförmig (*Bot.*); am Rande gleichmäßig gezähnt.
Mitt—en, *s.* der Halbhandschuh, Handschuh ohne Finger; der Pulswärmer; der Fäustling; *see* —s; she gave him the —en, sie gab ihm einen Korb. **—s**, *pl.* Pulswärmer.
Mittimus, *s.* der Verhaftsbefehl; (writ to remove records) der Befehl zur Abschickung von Akten an einen andern Gerichtshof.
Mix, *v.* I. *a.* mischen, mengen. II. *n.* sich (ver-) mischen; to — in good society, feinen Umgang haben, in der guten Gesellschaft verkehren; he —es in no society, er läßt sich nie in Gesellschaft sehen; to — o.s. up with, sich mit einer S. befassen; to be —ed up with, in einer S. verwickelt sein. **—ed**, *adj.* gemischt, meliert (*of hair, cloth*); —ed company, bunte, gemischte Gesellschaft; —ed pickles, eingemachte pikante Gemüse von verschiedenen Sorten; —ed marriages, Mischehen. **—ture**, *s.* die Mischung; der Mischtrank, die Mixtur; das Gemisch (*fig.*).
Mizzen, I. *s.* das Besansegel. II. *attrib.*; — mast, der Besanmast; — topsail, das Kreuzsegel.
Mizzle, I. *v.n.* fein regnen, rieseln. II. *s.* der Staubregen, Sprühregen.
Mnemonic, *adj.* die Gedächtniskunst betreffend, Gedächtnis-, mnemonisch. **—s**, *pl.* die Gedächtniskunst.
Moan, I. *s.* das Stöhnen, Jammern, die Wehklage; to make —, wehklagen. II. *v.n.* wehklagen, jammern. **—ing**, *adj.* wehklagend, kläglich.
Moat, *s.* der Burggraben, Schloßgraben, große Wassergraben vor einer Burg. **—ed**, *adj.* mit einem Wassergraben umgeben.
Mob, I. *s.* das Gesindel, der Pöbel; (disorderly —) der (lärmende) Pöbelhaufe. II. *v.a.* lärmend anfallen; (illtreat) mißhandeln. **—bish**, *adj.* pöbelhaft, gemein, lärmend, aufrührerisch. **—bishness**, *s.* die Pöbelhaftigkeit, Roheit. **—ility**, *s.* die Beweglichkeit. **—ilization**, *s.* die Mobilmachung, das Aufgebot. **—ilize**, *v.a.* mobil machen, das Heer aufbieten. **—ocracy**, *s.* die Pöbelherrschaft. *Comp.* **—-courting**, *adj.* nach Volksgunst haschend. **—law**, *s.* die Volksjustiz, das Lynchgesetz.
Mob-cap, *s.* die Morgenhaube.
Moccasin, *s.* der Mokassin, Indianerschuh.
Mocha-stone, *s.* der Mochastein.
Mock, I. *v.a.* (deride) verspotten, verlachen, höhnen; (make game of) necken, aufziehen; *see* Mimic; (disappoint) täuschen, vereiteln. II. *v.n.*; to — at, spotten, spötteln über (*acc.*). III. *s.* der Spott, Hohn; die Nachahmung. IV. *adj.* nachgemacht, falsch, Schein-. **—er**, *s.* der Spötter, Spottvogel; (deceiver) der Betrüger. **—ery**, *s.* das Gespött, die Spötterei, der Spott; (counterfeit) das Blendwerk, Scheinbild; a —ery, ein Possenspiel; to make a —ery (of a th.), (etwas) verhöhnen, lächerlich machen; to turn a th. into —ery, mit einer S. sein Gespött treiben. **—ing**, *s.* das Gespött, der Hohn. **—ingly**, *adv.* zum Spotte, spottweise. *Comp.* **—-fight**, *s.* das Scheingefecht. **—-heroic**, *adj.* komisch-heroisch; —-heroic poem, komisches Heldengedicht. **—ing-bird**, *s.* die Spottdrossel. **—ing-song**, *s.* das Spottgedicht. **—-king**, *s.* der Schattenkönig. **—-modesty**, *s.* die Scheinsittsamkeit. **—-song**, *s.* die Travestie, das travestierte Gedicht. **—-style**, *s.* die burleske Schreibart. **—-trial**, *s.* das Scheinverhör. **—-turtle**, *attrib.*; —-turtle soup, nachgemachte Schildkrötensuppe.
Mod—al, *adj.* (ausschließlich) die Form betreffend, bedingt, zufällig, modal (*Log.*). **—ality**, *s.* die Modalität, Bedingtheit, Bestimmtheit, der zufällige Unterschied. **—e**, *s.* die Art (und) Weise; (fashion) die Sitte, Mode; die Tonart (*Mus.*); der Modus (*Gram.*); die zufällige Eigenschaft, Erscheinungsweise (*Philos.*). **—el**, I. *s.* das Modell (*Sculpt. etc.*); (pattern) das Muster; das Muster, Vorbild (*fig.*); der Gliedermann, das Modell (*Paint. etc.*); to act as —el, (einem) Modell stehen. II. *v.a. & n.* modeln, modellieren, abbilden; modeln (*fig.*). III. *adj.* vorbildlich, Muster-; —el drawing, das Zeichnen nach Vorlagen; —el farm, die Muster-meierei, -wirtschaft; —el school, die Musterschule. **—eller**, *s.* der Modellierer. **—elling**, *s.* das Modellieren. **—ish**, *adj.* modisch.
Moderat—e, I. *adj.*, **—ely**, *adv.* mäßig (*in eating, etc.*); gemäßigt, nicht heftig (*in temper, etc.*); mäßig, mild (*as a climate*); billig, mäßig, bescheiden (*as prices*); mäßig (*as the pace*); (middling) mittelmäßig. II. *v.a.* mäßigen (*heat etc.*); beruhigen, im Zaume halten, einschränken (*passions, etc.*). **—eness**, *s.* die Mäßigkeit, die Mittelmäßigkeit. **—ion**, *s.* die Mäßigung; (frugality) die Mäßigkeit; —ions, die zweite Universitätsprüfung (die erste für den Grad eines B. A.) (*Oxford*). **—or**, *s.* der, die Mäßigende; der Vorsitzende; das Mitglied der Prüfungskommission für die höchsten mathematischen Prüfungen (*Cambridge*); der Konsistorialpräsident (*Scotch*). *Comp.* **—or-lamp**, *s.* die Moderateurlampe.
Modern, I. *adj.* jetzig, heutig, neu, in lebendigem Gebrauch, modern; — languages, die neueren Sprachen; study of — languages, das neusprachliche Studium; — language association, der Verein für neuere Sprachen, Neuphilologenverein; — language student, der Neusprachler, Neuphilologe; — side, die Realabteilung (einer höheren Schule, of a secondary school); — times, die Neuzeit. II. *s.*; the —s, die Neuern. **—ize**, *v.a.* modernisieren. **—ness**, *s.* die Neuheit.
Modest, *adj.*, **—ly**, *adv.* (not forward) bescheiden, anspruchslos; (chaste) sittsam, ehrbar, keusch; (moderate) bescheiden. **—y**, *s.* die Bescheidenheit; die Anspruchslosigkeit; die Sittsamkeit, Keuschheit.
Modi—cum, *s.* das geringe Maß, das Wenige. **—fiable**, *adj.* abänderlich, veränderlich. **—fi-**

cation, *s.* die Abänderung, Abminderung; (limitation) die Einschränkung; (change) die Veränderung; —fication of a vowel, der Umlaut. —**fied**, *p.p. & adj.;* —fied vowels, umgelautete Vokale, Umlaute. —**fy**, *v.a.* modifizieren, abändern, anders *or* näher bestimmen; einschränken; (moderate) mäßigen; umlauten (*Gram.*).

Modillion, *s.* der Sparrenkopf (*obs.*).

Modul—ate, *v.a.* modulieren, harmonisch anpassen; in eine andere Tonart überleiten. —**ation**, *s.* die Modulation (*also Mus.*). —**ator**, *s.* der, die, das Modulierende; der Stimmleiter. —**e**, *s.* der Model (*Arch.*).

Moe, Mo, (*obs. & poet.*) *adj. & adv.* meh(r).

Mogul, *s.* der Mogul.

Mohair, *s.* das Angoraziegenhaar; (— **stuff**) das Mohairzeug.

Moiety, *s.* der Teil; (half) die Hälfte.

Moil, *v.n.* sich abmühen, abarbeiten, placken; to toil and —, sich placken und plagen.

Moire, *s.* der Mohr, Wasserglanz (auf Stoffen); der Moiréstoff.

Moist, *adj.* feucht; — sugar, klarer Zucker, der Streuzucker; die Kassonade; — colours, Aquarellfarben in Teigform. —**en**, *v.a.* (an)feuchten, befeuchten. —**ener**, *s.* der Befeuchter, Anfeuchter. —**ness**, —**ure**, *s.* die Feuchtheit, Feuchtigkeit, Nässe. *Comp.* —**-eyed**, *adj.* mit tränenfeuchten Augen.

Molar, *s.* (— tooth) der Backenzahn.

Molasses, *s.* die Melasse, der Zuckerdicksaft.

[1]**Mole**, *s.* das (Mutter=)Mal.

[2]**Mole**, *s.* der Maulwurf (*Zool.*). *Comp.* —**-catcher**, *s.* der Maulwurfsfänger. —**-cricket**, *s.* die Maulwurfsgrille. —**-eyed**, *adj.* maulwurfsäugig. —**hill**, *s.* der Maulwurfshügel; to make mountains of —hills, aus einer Mücke einen Elefanten machen. —**skin**, *s.* das Maulwurfsfell; der Moleskin, Beinkleiderstoff (Art Plüsch).

[3]**Mole**, *s.* der Hafendamm, Molo, Schutzdamm; die Mole; das Mausoleum, Grabmal (*Arch.*); der Flußdamm (*on a river*).

[4]**Mole**, *s.* das Mondkalb (*Med.*).

Molecul—ar, *adj.* die Molekülen betreffend, Molekular=; —ar volume, das Molekularvolum. —**e**, *s.* das kleinste Teilchen, Massenteilchen, Stoffteilchen, Molekül.

Molest, *v.a.* belästigen, beunruhigen, beschwerlich fallen. —**ation**, *s.* die Belästigung, Plage, Störung. —**er**, *s.* der Belästiger, Störer.

Mollif—ication, *s.* die Erweichung; (pacification) die Besänftigung. —**y**, *v.a.* lindern, erleichtern (*pain, etc.*); (pacify) besänftigen; die Härte mildern (*of a remark, etc.*).

Mollus—ca, —ks, *pl.* Weichtiere, Mollusken.

Mollycoddle, *s.* der Weichling (*coll.*).

Moloch, *s.* der Moloch.

Molossus, *s.* ein Versfuß von drei Längen.

Molten, *adj.* geschmolzen, zerschmolzen, gegossen; flüssig; — **calf**, das (gegossene) goldene Kalb.

Molybd—ate, *s.* das molybdänsaure Salz. —**enous**, —**ic**, *adj.* Molybdän=. —**enum**, *s.* das Molybdänmetall.

Moment, *s.* der Augenblick, Moment; (importance) die Wichtigkeit; *see* —um; it is of no great —, es ist von keiner großen Bedeutung. —**arily**, *adv. see* —ary. —**ariness**, *s.* die Vergänglichkeit. —**ary**, *adj.* augenblicklich; einen Augenblick dauernd, flüchtig, vergänglich; fliegend (*of a fever*); jeden Augenblick stattfindend *or* sich wiederholend; —ary sound, der Augenblickslaut. —**ous**, *adj.*, —**ously**, *adv.* wichtig; folgenschwer, kritisch. —**ousness**, *s.* die Wichtigkeit, Bedeutung. —**um**, *s.* das Moment, der Bewegungstrieb; die Triebkraft, der Antrieb; —um of inertia, das Trägheitsmoment; —um of resistance, das Widerstandsmoment; —um of a force, das statische Moment einer Kraft.

Mona—chism, *s.* das Mönchtum; (monkishness) das Mönchswesen. —**d**, *s.* die Monade; (atom) das Atom; das Pünktchen (*Zool.*); das einwertige Element (*Phys.*). —**delphian**, —**delphous**, *adj.* einbrüderig. —**ndrian**, *adj.* einmännig. —**rch**, I. *s.* der Herrscher, Fürst, Monarch; (king) der König. II. *adj.* königlich. —**rchic(al)**, *adj.* monarchisch. —**rchist**, *s.* der Monarchist. —**rchy**, *s.* die Königsherrschaft, Monarchie; (realm) das Königreich; absolute (limited) —rchy, die unumschränkte (beschränkte) Monarchie, Alleinherrschaft. —**stery**, I. *s.* das Kloster. II. *attrib.;* —stery school, die Klosterschule. —**stic(al)**, *adj.*, —**stically**, *adv.* monastisch, Mönchs=. —**sticism**, *s.* das Mönchtum, Mönchsleben, Klosterleben. *See* Monk, Mono—.

Monday, *s.* der Montag.

Mone—tary, *adj.* Geld=; —tary unit, die Münzeinheit. —**y**, das Geld; — Bill, das Steuerauflagegesetz (*Parl.*); —y down, ready —y, bar(es) Geld; to be out of —y by, verlieren an (*dat.*); to keep a p. out of his —y, einen mit der Zahlung hinhalten; to make —y, Geld verdienen; to make —y by, verdienen an (*dat.*) *or* bei. —**yed, Monied**, *adj.* vermögend, reich; —yed classes, die besitzenden Klassen, Kapitalisten. *Comp.* —**y-bag**, *s.* der Geldbeutel. —**y-box**, *s.* die Sparbüchse. —**y-changer**, *s.* der Geldwechsler. —**y-grubber**, *s.* der Geizhals (*fam.*). —**y-jobber**, *s.* der Geldhändler. —**y-lender**, *s.* der Geldverleiher. —**y-making**, I. *adj.* gelderwerbend. II. *s.* der Gelderwerb. —**y-market**, *s.* der Geldmarkt. —**y-matter**, *s.* die Geldsache; —y-matters, Geldangelegenheiten (*pl.*). —**y-monger**, *s.* der Wucherer. —**y-order**, *s.* die Posteinzahlung, Postanweisung. —**y-order-office**, *s.* das Geldpostamt. —**y-transactions**, *pl.* Geldgeschäfte. —**y's-worth**, *s.* der Geld(es)wert; he wanted his —y's-worth, er wollte für sein Geld etwas Entsprechendes haben; I did not get my full —y's-worth, ich erhielt nicht genug für mein Geld, ich habe die Sache zu teuer bezahlt.

Mong—er, *s.* der Krämer, Händler. —**rel**, I. *s.* der Mischling, Bastard. II. *adj.* von gemischtem Geschlecht, Bastard=; —rel breed, die Bastardrasse; —rel cur, der Blendling; —rel dialect, der Mischdialekt; —rel pup, der Bastardhund, Hund unreiner Rasse.

Mongoose, *s.* der Mongoz; indischer Halbaffe.

Monit—ion, *s.* die Mahnung, Warnung. —**or**, *s.* der (Er=)Mahner; der Lehrgehülfe, Schüler der höchsten Klasse vieler höherer Schulen mit gewissen Aufsichts= und Strafrechten über kleinern Schüler (*in schools*); der Monitor (*Shipb.*). —**orial**, *adj.* ermahnend, warnend; —orial schools, durch Lehrgehülfen versorgte Volksschulen (nach dem Lankaster'schen System); —orial system, das System, nach dem (in Volksschulen) ältere Schüler als Lehrgehülfen zum Unterricht der jüngeren herangezogen werden; das System, nach dem (in höheren Knabenschulen) die Primaner (*as* monitors *or* prefects) zur Aufrechterhaltung der Schulzucht herangezogen und mit gewissen Disziplinarrechten betraut werden. —**ory**, *adj.* ermahnend, warnend; —ory letters, Ermahnungsschreiben. —**ress**, *s.* die Aufseherin, Schul=Helferin.

Monk, *s.* der Mönch. —**ery**, *s.* das Mönchswesen, Mönchtum. —**ish**, *adj.* mönchisch, Mönchs=. *Comp.* —**'s-hood**, *s.* der Eisenhut (*Bot.*).

Monkey, *s.* der Affe (*also fig.*); fünfhundert Pfund (*sl.*); der Rammblock; little —, kleines Äffchen! —'s allowance, mehr Schläge als Brot (*vulg.*). *Comp.* —**-block**, *s.* der Grenadierblock. —**-engine**, *s.* die Rammmaschine. —**-flower**, *s.* die Gauklerblume. —**-house**, *s.* das Affenhaus. —**-jacket**, *s.* die enganschließende Matrosenjacke. —**-puzzle(-tree)**, *s.* die Schuppentanne. —**-tricks**, *pl.* Narrenspossen.

Mono—carpous, *adj.* einfrüchtig. —**chlamydeous**, *adj.* einblütdeckig. —**chord**, *s.* das Monochord. —**chrome**, I. *s.* das einfarbige Gemälde. II. *adj.* einfarbig. —**cle**, *s.* das Ein=

glas, Monokel. —**cotyledon**, *s.* einsamenlappige Pflanze; —cotyledons, Monokotyledonen. —**cular**, *adj.* einäugig; —cular microscope, das Mikroskop für ein Auge. —**dactylous**, *adj.* einzehig. —**don**, *s.* der Narwal. —**dy**, *s.* die Monodie, der Einzelgesang; die Eintönigkeit. —**gamist**, *s.* der Anhänger der Einehe, Monogamist. —**gamy**, *s.* die Einehe, Ehe mit einer Frau, Monogamie. —**gram**, *s.* der verschlungene Namenszug, das Monogramm. —**graph**, *s.* die Schrift über einen einzelnen wissenschaftlichen Gegenstand, Monographie. —**gyn**, *s.* die einweibige Pflanze. —**gynous**, *adj.* einweibig. —**lith**, *s.* der Meteorstein, Findlingsblock, erratische Block, Monolith. —**logue**, *s.* der Monolog, das Selbstgespräch. —**mania**, *s.* die fixe Idee, Monomanie. —**maniac**, *s.* der mit einer fixen Idee Behaftete, Monomane. —**mial**, *adj.* aus einer einzelnen Größe bestehend. —**petalous**, *adj.* ein(blum)blätterig. —**polist**, *s.* der Monopolist. —**polize**, —**polise**, *v.a.* monopolisieren; (engross) allein in Anspruch nehmen. —**poly**, *s.* der Alleinhandel, Alleinverkauf, das Monopol; ausschließliches Recht (of, auf (*acc.*)) (*fig.*). —**sperm**, *s.* einsamige Pflanze. —**stich(on)**, *s.* das Monostichon. —**syllabic(al)**, *adj.* einsilbig. —**syllable**, *s.* einsilbiges Wort. —**theism**, *s.* der Monotheismus, die Verehrung eines Gottes. —**theist**, *s.* der Monotheist. —**theistic**, *adj.* monotheistisch. —**tone**, *s.* das Eintönige. —**tonous**, *adj.* eintönig; (tiresome) einförmig, langweilig. —**tony**, *s.* die Eintönigkeit; die Einförmigkeit.

Monsoon, *s.* der Monsun (*in the Indian Ocean*).

Monst—er, I. *s.* das Ungeheuer (*also fig.*); die Mißgeburt, das Monstrum (*Physiol.*); das Wundertier (*fig.*); —er of ugliness, ein Ausbund von Häßlichkeit, wahres Scheusal. II. *adj.* ungeheuer groß, Riesen=; —er meetings, Massen-Volksversammlungen. —**rance**, *s.* die Monstranz. —**rosity**, die Ungeheuerlichkeit, das Ungeheuerliche, Scheußliche; (—er) die Mißgestalt. —**rous**, *adj.*, —**rously**, *adv.* widernatürlich, ungeheuer, ungeschlacht, ungestalt; (huge) ungeheuer groß, kolossal; (horrible) scheußlich, abscheulich. —**rousness**, *s.* die Ungeheuerlichkeit, Entsetzlichkeit, die Abscheulichkeit.

Month, *s.* der Monat; lunar (calendar) —, astronomischer *or* Mond= (Kalender=) Monat; solar —, der Sonnenmonat, bürgerliche Monat. —**ly**, I. *adj. & adv.* monatlich; — nurse, die Pflegerin (für Wöchnerinnen). II. *s.* die Monatsschrift.

Monument, *s.* das Denkmal, Grabmal, der Gedenkstein, das Monument. —**al**, *adj.* zum Denkmal gehörig; (as a memorial) zum Andenken dienend, Denkmal=, Denk=. —**ally**, *adv.* als Denkmal, zum Andenken.

Moo, I. *v.n.* muhen. II. *s.* das Muhen, Gemuh *or* Gebrüll einer Kuh. *Comp.* —**-cow**, *s.* die Muhkuh.

[1]**Mood**, *s* der Modus (*Gram.*); die Form (*Log.*); die Tonart (*Mus.*); *verb of* —, das Modalzeitwort.

[2]**Mood**, *s.* die Stimmung, Laune; the —s of nature, die Launen der Natur; in a melancholy —, niedergeschlagen; to be in the —, aufgelegt sein (zu). —**ily**, *adv.*, —**y**, *adj.* launisch; (gloomy) schwermütig, düster; (sullen) mürrisch, verstimmt. —**iness**, *s.* das mürrische *or* düstere Wesen, die üble Laune.

[1]**Moon**, I. *s.* der Mond; der Monat (*fig.*); full —, der Vollmond; new —, der Neumond; the — waxes, der Mond nimmt zu; the — wanes, der Mond nimmt ab; to cry for the —, das Unmögliche verlangen. II. *v.n.;* to — about, ziellos herumschweifen (*fam.*). —**ed**, *adj.* (*in compounds*) mondähnlich; mit einem Monde. —**et**, *s.* der kleine Mond. —**ish**, *adj.* wie der Mond, wandelbar. —**less**, *adj.* mondlos, ohne Mond. —**y**, *adj.* den Mond bezeichnend; mondartig; mondförmig; mondhell; mondsüchtig; unklar, verwirrt. *Comp.* —**beam**, *s.* der Mondenstrahl —**-calf**, *s.* das Mondkalb, der Tölpel. —**-eyed**, *adj.* mondblind; schwachsichtig (*as a horse*); blödsichtig (*fig.*). —**flower**, —**daisy**, *s.* die Wucherblume, große Maßliebe. —**light**, I. *adj* mondhell; —light flitting, das heimliche Ausziehen bei Nacht und Nebel (*coll.*). II. *s.* das Mondlicht, der Mondschein. —**-lighter**, *s.* der Mondscheinler, Verüber von nächtlichen Agrarverbrechen in Irland. —**-lit**, *adj.* vom Mond erleuchtet; mondhell. —**shine**, *s.* der Mondschein; der leere Schein, Schwindel, Unsinn; all —shine! Blödsinn! dummes Zeug! —**shiny**, *adj.* mondhell; unsinnig (*fig.*). —**struck**, *adj.* mondsüchtig. —**wort**, *s.* die Mondraute.

[2]**Moon**, *v.n.* (*obs.*) *see* Moan.

Moonshee, *s.* der Sprachlehrer (in Ostindien).

[1]**Moor**, *s.* das Moor, der Sumpf; (heath) die Hochlandsheide; the Yorkshire —s, das baumlose Bergheideland von Yorkshire. *Comp.* —**-cock**, *s.* der Hahn des Moorhuhns. —**-hen**, *s.* das Moorhuhn. —**-game**, *s.* Moorvögel. —**-grass**, *s.* das Elfengras.

[2]**Moor**, *s. see the Index of Names.*

[3]**Moor**, *v.* I. *a.* vor Anker legen, (ein Schiff) anbinden, verteien. II. *n.* vor Anker liegen. —**age**, *s.* der Ankerplatz. —**ing**, *s.* das Ankern. —**ings**, *pl.* die Hafenanker; (—age) der Ankerplatz, Liegeplatz; the vessel cast off her —ings, das Schiff lichtete die Anker. *Comp.* —**ing-buoy**, *s.* die Ankerboje. —**ing-post**, *s.* der Anbindepfahl.

Moose, *s.* (—-deer) das Elen(tier).

[1]**Moot**, I. *v.a.* anregen, zur Sprache bringen, diskutieren. II. *adj.;* — point, — case, die Streitfrage, der Streitfall, Streitpunkt, der strittige Punkt.

[2]**Moot**, *s.* die Volksversammlung (*obs.*). *Comp.* —**-hall**, *s.* das Versammlungshaus, die Gerichtshalle (*obs.*).

[1]**Mop**, I. *s.* der Scheuer=lappen, =wisch; (fair) der Gesindemarkt (*prov.*). II. *v.a.* abscheuern, abwischen; to — up, aufwischen. —**pet**, *s.* das Püppchen; (girl) das Püppchen, kleine artige Mädchen.

[2]**Mop**, I. *s.* die Grimasse. II. *v.n.* Gesichter schneiden; to — at, ein schiefes Gesicht machen zu.

Mop—e, I. *v.n.* mutlos, niedergeschlagen sein; schmollen. II. *s.* der betrübte, untätige Mensch. —**ed**, *adj.* entmutigt; (dull) gelangweilt; (sad) niedergeschlagen. —**ing**, *p.;* to sit —ing, betrübt, in tiefen Gedanken sitzen; schmollen. —**ingly**, *adv.* träumerisch und niedergeschlagen, mutlos; schmollend. —**ish**, *adj.* schmollend. —**ishness**, *s.* die Abgestumpftheit, Mutlosigkeit, Niedergeschlagenheit.

Moraine, *s.* die Moräne.

Moral, I. *adj.* moralisch, sittlich; (mental) geistig; innerlich; moralisch (*as evidence, etc.*); Moral=, Sitten=; the — character, der Charakter; the — law, das Sittengesetz; — philosopher, der Moralphilosoph, Ethiker; — philosophy, die Sittenlehre; — play, die Moralität (*Mediev. Theat.*); — sense, das Sittlichkeitsgefühl; — support, moralische Unterstützung; — temper, die Gemütsverfassung; that would lessen the — effect of the victory, das würde die moralische Wirkung des Sieges verringern. II. *s.* die Moral, Lehre, Nutzanwenoung (*of a story, etc.*); (intent) der geheime Zweck, die Bedeutung. —**ist**, *s.* der Sittenlehrer. —**ity**, *s.* die Sittenlehre, Moral; (observance of right and wrong) die Moralität, Sittlichkeit (*of a person*); die sittliche Reinheit (*of an action*); die Moralität (*Mediev. Theat.*). —**ization**, *s.* die moralische Betrachtung. —**ize**, *v.n.* moralisieren (upon, über eine S.). —**izer**, *s.* der Sittenprediger. —**izing**, *s.* das Moralisieren, Predigen. —**ly**, *adv.* moralisch, in moralischem Sinne; (virtuously) sittlich, tugendhaft; moralisch; —ly impossible, moralisch unmöglich. **—s,** *pl.* die Sittenlehre, Moralität, Moral; (— conduct) sittlicher Lebenswandel, die Sitten.

Morass, *s.* der Morast, Sumpf.

Morbid, *adj.*, **—ly**, *adv.* krankhaft, ungesund; — anatomy, pathologische Anatomie; — view, krankhafte Anschauung. **—ness,** *s.* krankhaftes Wesen.

Mordant, I. *adj.* beißend, ätzend, scharf. II. *s.* die Beize, das Beizmittel (*Dyer.*); der Klebestoff (*of gilders*).

More, I. *adj.* mehr; größer (*in number*); the — part, der mehrere (größere) Teil (*B.*); six miles —, noch sechs Meilen; not a word —! kein Wort mehr! one — song, noch ein Lied; only one —, nur noch eins; a few — people, noch einige Leute. II. *adv.* mehr; (in addition) noch (dazu); (again) wieder(um); — agreeable, angenehmer; — to the purpose, zweckmäßiger; no —, nicht mehr; (dead) gestorben; once —, noch einmal; the — he has the — he wishes to have, je mehr er hat, desto mehr wünscht er zu haben; so much the —, um so viel mehr; it will — than repay the trouble, es wird die Mühe überreichlich bezahlen; and — than that, und was noch mehr ist; to make — of a thing than it is, eine Sache übertreiben (*coll.*). III. *s.* das Mehr. **—over,** *adv.* überdies, außerdem, weiter, ferner, noch dazu, auch.

Moreen, *s.* der Moiré, wollene Mohr.

[1]**Morel,** *s.* gemeine Morchel.

[2]**Morel,** *s.* die Morelle, saure Kirsche.

[3]**Morel,** I. *adj.* dunkelfarbig. II. *s.* der Nachtschatten.

Moresque, *adj.* maurisch, moresk, arabeskisch. **—s,** *pl.* Arabesken.

Morganatic, *adj.* morganatisch; — marriage, die morganatische Ehe, Ehe zur linken Hand.

Morgay, *s.* der Hundshai.

Moribund, *adj.* im Sterben (liegend), sterbend.

Morilliform, *adj.* morchel=artig, =förmig.

Morion, *s.* die Sturmhaube, der Helm.

Morisco, *s.* der Maure, Morisko; die maurische Sprache; der Mohrentanz (mit Kastagnetten).

Morling, *s.* das an Krankheit verendete Tier; die Wolle von einem gefallenen Schafe.

Morn, *s.* der Morgen (*poet.*). **—ing,** I. *s.* der Morgen (*also fig.*); in the —ing, des Morgens; one fine —ing, eines schönen Morgens; to-morrow —ing, morgen früh. II. *adj.* früh, morgendlich, Morgen=; —ing gun, der Reveilleschuß; —ing paper, die Morgenzeitung; —ing performance, die Nachmittagsvorstellung; —ing prayers, das Morgen=Gebet; *see* Matins; —ing suit, der Ausgehanzug, Besuchsanzug; —ing watch, die Tag= *or* Morgen=Wache. *Comp.* **—ing-coat,** *s.* (einreihiger) Taillenrock. **—ing-gown,** *s*, das Morgenkleid (einer Dame). **—ing-room,** *s.* das Frühstückszimmer.

Morone, *s. see* Maroon.

Morose, *adj.*, **—ly,** *adv.* mürrisch, grämlich, verdrießlich. **—ness,** *s.* die Grämlichkeit, das mürrische Wesen.

Morph—ia, —ine, *s.* das Morphin. **—inism,** *s.* die Morphiumvergiftung. **—iomania,** *s.* die Morphiumsucht. **—ologic(al),** *adj.* morphologisch, die Gestaltungslehre betreffend; die Wortlehre betreffend (*Gram.*). **—ologist,** *s.* der Morpholog(e). **—ology,** *s.* die Gestaltungslehre, Morphologie; die Wortlehre (*Gram.*).

Morrice, Morris, *s.* der Mohrentanz; nine men's —, eine Art Mühlenspiel im Freien.

Morrow, *s.* der Morgen; (to-—) morgen; to-— morning (evening), morgen früh (morgen abend); the day after to-—, übermorgen; on the —, morgen, am nächsten Tage.

Morse, *s.* das Walroß (*obs.*).

Morsel, *s.* der Bissen; (piece) das Stück, Bischen.

Mort, *s.* der Jagdruf bei Erlegung des Wildes, das Halali, der Fiefstoß (*obs.*). **—al,** *adj.*, **—ally,** *adv.* sterblich; (human) menschlich; (deadly) tödlich; (extreme) gewaltig (*vulg.*); —al combat, der Kampf auf Leben und Tod; in all my —al days, mein lebelang (*vulg.*); —al foe, der Todfeind; —al fright, die Todesangst; two —al hours, zwei ausgeschlagene Stunden (*coll.*); —al wound, tödliche Verletzung, die Todwunde; —al sin, die Todsünde. **—ality,** *s.* die Sterblichkeit; (deaths) die Sterblichkeit, das (Ab=)Sterben; (humanity) die Menschheit; bills of —ality, die Sterbeliste. **—gage,** I. *s.* das Pfandgut; die Hypothek; (—gage deed) der Pfand=, Hypotheken=brief; to give in —gage, verpfänden. II. *v.a.* verpfänden, auf Hypothek geben, mit Hypotheken belasten. **—gagee,** *s.* der Hypothekengläubiger, Hypothekar. **—gager,** *s.* der Pfandgeber. **—ification,** *s.* der kalte Brand; (penance) die Kasteiung, Kreuzigung des Fleisches; (humiliation) die Demütigung, Erniedrigung; (chagrin) der Ärger, Verdruß; (that which —ifies) die Kränkung. **—ify,** *v.* I. *a.* die wirkende Kraft zerstören, abtöten; auflösen (*metals, etc.*); abtöten, kasteien, kreuzigen (*the flesh*); unterdrücken, zähmen (*lusts*); demütigen (*one's pride*); ärgern, kränken; he was deeply —ified at this decision, er war über diese Entscheidung tief gekränkt. II. *n.* absterben, brandig werden. **—main,** *s.* die tote Hand; unveräußerliches Gut; alienation in —main, die Veräußerung an die tote Hand (eine geistliche *or* weltliche Körperschaft). **—uary,** I. *adj.* Toten=, Leichen=; —uary chapel, die Begräbniskapelle. II. *s.* das Trauerhaus; (morgue) die Leichenschaustätte.

Mortar, *s.* der Mörser (*Artil.*, *Chem.*); der Mörtel, die Mauerspeise (*Build.*); prepared —, angemachter Mörtel.

Mortis—e, I. *s.* das Zapfenloch; —e and tenon, Nut und Zapfen. II. *v.a.* mit einem Zapfenloche versehen; (join by a —e) verzapfen. **—ing,** *s.* (—e-joints) die Verzapfung. *Comp.* **—e-chisel,** *s.* der Lochbeutel, das Locheisen. **—e-gauge,** *s.* das Zapfenstreichmaß. **—e-lock,** *s.* das Eisensteckschloß. **—ing-machine,** *s.* die Zapfenlochmaschine.

[1]**Mosaic,** I. *adj.* musivisch, Mosaik=; — floor, — pavement, der Mosaikfußboden; — gold, das Musivgold; — painting, die Mosaikmalerei. II. *s.* die Mosaik, musivische Kunst.

[2]**Mosaic,** *see the Index of names.*

Moschatel, *s.* das Bisamkraut.

Mosque, *s.* die Moschee.

Mosquito, *s.* der Moskito. *Comp.* **—-bite,** *s.* der Moskitostich. **—-net,** *s.* das Moskitonetz.

Moss, *s.* das Moos (*Bot.*); (bog) das Torfmoos; a rolling stone gathers no —, ein unsteter Mensch bringt es zu nichts (*prov.*). **—iness,** *s.* das Moosige; (—y growth) die Moosbedeckung, der Moosüberzug. **—y,** *adj.* moosig, bemoost; (—like) wollig, moosartig. *Comp.* **—-clad,** *adj.* moos=bedeckt, =bewachsen. **—-grown,** *adj.* bemoost, moosüberwachsen. **—-rose,** *s.* die Moosrose. **—-troopers,** *pl.* berittene Straßenräuber.

Most, I. *adj.* (*sup. of* Much) meist; größt; for the — part, größten=, meisten=teils; — men, die meisten Menschen. II. *adv.* meist(ens), am meisten; äußerst, außerordentlich; — probably, höchst wahrscheinlich; — happy, außerordentlich glücklich; — of all, am meisten; at (the) —, höchstens. III. *s.* das Meiste; (in number) die Meisten; (utmost) das Höchste, Äußerste; that's the — I'll give, das ist das Höchste, was ich dafür geben werde; to make the — of a th. etwas trefflich benutzen; (exaggerate) sehr *or* möglichst viel machen (aus einer S.). **—ly,** *adv.* meistens, größtenteils, hauptsächlich.

Mote, *s.* das Sonnenstäubchen, Atom; der Splitter (*B.*).

Mot—et, *s.* die Motette. **—to,** *see* Motto.

Moth, *s.* die Motte; der Nachtfalter. **—y,** *adj.* voll von Motten. *Comp.* **—-eaten**, *adj.* von Motten zerfressen.

[1]**Mother**, *s.* die Mutter; your —, deine Mutter, Ihre Frau Mutter; little —, Mütterchen; — of a family, Hausmutter; —'s help, die Stütze (der Hausfrau); —s' meeting, die Sitzung eines Hausfrauenvereins; —s' union, der Hausfrauenverein; every —'s son, jeder, jedes Mutterkind; — Carey's chickens, die Sturmschwalben. **—hood**, *s.* die Mutterschaft. **—less**, *adj.* mutterlos. **—lessness**, *s.* die Mutterlosigkeit. **—liness**, *s.* die Mütterlichkeit. **—ly**, *adj.* mütterlich. *Comp.* **—-church**, *s.* die Mutterkirche. **—-country**, *s.* das Vaterland, Heimatland. **—-in-law**, *s.* die Schwiegermutter. **—-of-pearl**, *s.* die Perlmutter. **—-tongue**, *s.* die Muttersprache. **—-wit**, *s.* der Mutterwitz.

[2]**Mother**, *s.* die (Essig- zc.) Mutter. **—y**, *adj.* dick, hefig. *Comp.* **—-water**, *s.* die Mutterlauge.

Mot—if, *s.* das Leitmotiv (*Mus.*). **—ility**, *s.* die Bewegungsfähigkeit. **—ion**, I. *s.* die Bewegung, der Gang (*also Mach.*); (manner of moving) die Bewegung, Haltung; (impulse) der Antrieb, die Regung (*also fig.*); (proposal) der Vorschlag, Antrag; die Bewegung (*Mech.*); das Triebwerk (*Locom.*); der Stuhlgang (*Med.*); to set in —ion, in Gang bringen; to bring forward a —ion, einen Antrag stellen (auf eine S.), beantragen; the —ion was put to the meeting, der Antrag wurde der Versammlung zur Abstimmung vorgelegt; the —ion was carried, der Antrag ging durch; circular, link, parallel, perpetual, retrograde —ion, die Kreisbewegung, Koulissensteuerung, Parallelführung; das Perpetuum mobile, der Rückgang. II. *v.a.* hin-, an-weisen; to —ion s.o. to a seat, einem durch eine Handbewegung einen Sitz anweisen. III. *v.n.* zuwinken, ein Zeichen mit der Hand geben. **—ionless**, *adj.* bewegungslos, regungslos, unbeweglich. **—ive**, I. *s.* der Beweggrund, Antrieb; (intent) die Absicht. II. *adj.*; —ive power, bewegende Kraft, Triebkraft. III. *v.a.* begründen, motivieren. **—iveless**, *adj.* grundlos. **—ivity**, *s.* die Bewegungsfähigkeit. **—or**, I. *s.* die Kraftmaschine, der Motor (*Mech.*); der, die, das Bewegende. II. *attrib.*; —or (—ory) nerves, die Beweger. III. *v.n.* (im) Automobil fahren, auteln. **—orial**, *adj.* bewegend, bewegungs-, motorisch. **—oring**, *s.* das Automobilfahren. **—orist**, *s.* der Automobilfahrer **—orities**, (*pl.*) Automobil-Artikel. *Comp.* **—ion-bars**, (*pl.*) die Leitstangen. **—or-bicycle**, *s.* das Motorrad. **—or-'bus**, *s.* der Motor-Omnibus. **—or-car**, *s* der Kraftwagen, das Auto(mobil). **—or-garage**, *s.* der Automobil-schuppen; die Autoleihstelle.

Mot—ley, *adj.* buntscheckig, bunt. **—tled**, *adj.* gefleckt, gesprenkelt, marmoriert.

Motto, *s.* der Spruch, Wahlspruch, das Motto.

[1]**Mould**, I. *s.* die Damm-, Garten-erde; (composition) der Stoff, das Wesen; der Schimmel (*on dry substances*); der Moder, Kahm (*on fluids*); iron —, der Rostflecken. II. *v.n.* (to contract —) schimmelig *or* kahmig werden, schimmeln. III. *v.a.* schimmelig werden lassen, verschimmeln lassen. **—er**, *v.* I. *a.* in Staub verwandeln, zerstören. II. *n.* (ver)modern, zerstäuben; to —er away, wegfaulen. **—iness**, *s.* das Schimmelige. **—y**, *adj.* schimmelig.

[2]**Mould**, I. *s.* die Form, Bildung; der Körperbau; das Vorbild; die Form (*Found., Cook.*); (pattern) die Schablone; das Mall (*Shipb.*); die Hirnschädelnaht (*Anat.*); bullet —, Kugelform; shot —, Schrotform. II. *v.a.* bilden, gestalten; gießen (*candles*); kneten (*dough, etc.*). **—er**, *s.* der Former, Bildner; der Lichtgießer; (modelmaker) der Modellmacher. **—ing**, *s.* die Formung, das Modellieren, die Formerei; das Gesims (*Arch.*); die Kehlung (*Carp.*); (—ing of bricks) das Ziegelstreichen; —ings, das Simswerk, Verzierungen; crown —ing, der Bekrönungsfries; —ing over a door, die Türbekönung; egg —ing, der Eierstab (*Arch.*); —ings of a gun, die Zieraten einer Kanone; breech —ings, Bodenfriesen. *Comp.* **—-candles**, *pl.* gegossene Lichter. **—ing-board**, *s.* das Formbrett. **—ing-frame**, *s.* die Gußlehre. **—ing-loam**, *s.* der Formlehm. **—ing-machine**, *s.* die Formmaschine; die Kehlmaschine (*for wood*). **—ing-wax**, *s.* das Modellierwachs.

Moult, *v.n.* sich mausern. **—ing**, I. *s.* das Mausern. II. *adj.*; —ing season, die Mauser(zeit).

[1]**Mound**, *s.* der Erdhügel; (rampart) der Damm, Wall.

[2]**Mound**, *s.* der Reichsapfel.

Mount, I. *s.* der Berg; (fence) der Wall, die Brustwehr; die Katze (*Fort.*); die Ein-rahmung, -fassung (*pictures, etc.*); das Reitpferd; can you give me a —? können Sie mir ein Reitpferd leihen? II. *v.a.* besteigen, reiten (*horses*); besteigen, ersteigen (*mountains*); (supply with a horse) beritten machen, mit Pferden versehen; besteigen (*a bicycle*); montieren, auf die Lafette setzen (*a gun*); besetzen, belegen, beschlagen (*with metal ornaments*); einrahmen (*pictures*); (auf Pappe) aufziehen (*photographs, drawings*); fassen (*jewels*); the frigate was —ed with 100 guns, die Fregatte führte 100 Kanonen; to — guard, auf Wache ziehen; to — the breach, die Bresche stürmen; —! aufgesessen! (*Mil.*); the cavalry is well —ed, die Reiterei ist gut beritten; —ed infantry (police), berittene Infanterie (Schutzmannschaft); —ed photograph, aufgezogene Photographie. **—ain**, *see* Mountain. **—ant**, *adj.* steigend (*Her.*). **—ebank**, *s.* der Marktschreier, Quacksalber. **—er**, *s.* der Steiger; der Einfasser. **—ing**, I. *adj.* steigend; zum Aufsitzen (*as a block*). II. *s.* das Aufsteigen; das Beschläge (*of bags, etc.*); die Einfassung (*of jewels*); der Beschlag (*Mach.*); —ing of a picture, das Bildereinrahmen; —ing of photographs, das Aufziehen von Photographieen; —ings, die Metallbeschläge, (trappings) Montierungsstücke.

Mountain, *s.* der Berg (*also fig.*); —s, Gebirge (*pl.*); to make a — of a molehill, aus einer Mücke einen Elefanten machen. **—eer**, *s.* der Bergbewohner. **—ous**, *adj.* gebirgig, bergig, Berg-, Gebirgs-. *Comp.* **—-air**, *s.* die Bergluft. **—-ash**, *s.* die Vogelbeere. **—-cock**, *s.* der Auerhahn. **—-cork**, *s.* der Bergkork. **—-pasture**, *s.* die Alp(e), Alpentrift. **—-railway**, *s.* die Gebirgsbahn. **—-scenery**, *s.* die Gebirgslandschaft. **—side**, *s.* der Bergabhang. **—-sprite**, *s.* der Bergschrat, Berggeist; der Bergesalte (*poet.*); Rübezahl (*in the Riesengebirge*). **—-top**, *s.* die Bergspitze. **—-valley**, *s.* das Gebirgstal.

Mourn, *v.* I. *a.* trauern (um einen), betrauern; Trauer tragen (um einen); I —ed for him, ich trauerte um ihn, betrauerte ihn. II. *n.* traurig sein, trauern. **—er**, *s.* der Trauernde; der Leidtragende (*at funerals*); chief —er, der erste Leidtragende, Anführer eines Leichenzuges. **—ful**, *adj.*, **—fully**, *adv.* traurig, Trauer-; klagend (*as a ditty*); beklagenswert. **—fulness**, *s.* die Traurigkeit, Trauer. **—ing**, I. *adj.* trauernd, Trauer-; —ing carriage, die Trauerkutsche; —ing pin, die schwarze Stecknadel; —ing warehouse, das Trauerkleidungsmagazin. II. *s.* das Trauern; die Trauer(kleidung); to go into —ing, trauern, Trauer anlegen (for, um); to go out of —ing, Trauer ablegen; court. half. second —ing, die Halbtrauer.

Mouse, I. *s.* die Maus (*Zool., Naut.*); (*pl.* Mice) Mäuse; the — squeaks, die Maus piept *or* pfeift. II. *v.n.* mausen. *Comp.* **—-buttock**, *s.* das Lendenstück. **—-colour**, *s.* die Mausefarbe. **—-coloured**, mausefarben. **—-deer**, *s.* malayischer Halbaffe. **—-ear**, *s.* das Habichtskraut;

das Vergißmeinnicht. **—-hawk,** *s.* der Mäusefalk. **—-hole,** *s.* das Mauseloch. **—-trap,** *s.* die Mausefalle.

Mouser, *s.* der Mauser, Mäusefänger.

Mousie, *s.* das Mäuschen, Mäuslein.

Moustache, I. *s.* der Schnurrbart. II. *attrib.;* —trainer, die Bartbinde.

Mouth, I. *s.* der Mund; das Maul, der Rachen (*of beasts*); die Mündung (*of a river, a cannon*); die Öffnung (*of a bag*); das Loch (*of a well, a furnace, etc.*); das Mundstück (*of wind instruments*); (grimace) die Gesichtsverzerrung; with a tender —, weichmäulig; passage through the —, der Mundkanal; to have one's name in everybody's —, Gegenstand des allgemeinen Gesprächs sein; by word of —, mündlich; down in the —, niedergeschlagen (*sl.*); to live from hand to —, von der Hand in den Mund leben; I watched them with my heart in my —, ich beobachtete sie während mir die Kehle wie zugeschnürt war; to stop a p.'s —, einen am Sprechen hindern; to laugh on the wrong side of the —, weinen (*sl.*); to make a — at, ein schiefes Maul machen über (*acc.*). II. *v.a. & n.* in den Mund nehmen; mit vollem Munde laut und affektiert aussprechen. **—ful,** *s.* der Mundvoll; das Bißchen (*fig.*). *Comp.* **—piece,** *s.* das Mundstück (*Mus., Saddl.*); der Ansatz (*Mus.*); das Sprachrohr, der Wortführer (*fig.*).

Mov—able, *adj.,* **—ably,** *adv.* beweglich; —able rail, die Weichenschiene (*Railw.*). **—ableness,** *s.* die Beweglichkeit. **—ables,** *pl.* fahrende Habe, bewegliche Güter, Mobilien. **—e,** I. *v.a.* bewegen; fortbewegen (*from a place*); rücken (*a chair, etc.*); ziehen (*a piece in Draughts, etc.*); (incite) antreiben, bewegen, anreizen; (set in motion) in Gang bringen, in Bewegung setzen; vorschlagen, vorbringen (*a resolution*); beantragen (*in Parliament*); anregen, antreiben, reizen (*the passions*); abführen (*Med.*); ergreifen, rühren (*the feelings*); (make angry) aufbringen, erzürnen, reizen, aufhetzen; erregen, erwecken (*mirth, etc.*); to —e s.o. to do a th., einen vermögen, bewegen, anregen etwas zu tun; to —e to tears, (einen) zu Tränen rühren; to be —ed at, von (etwas) gerührt sein *or* werden; to be —ed to pity, sich zum Mitleiden hinreißen lassen. II. *v.n.* sich bewegen, sich in Bewegung setzen; (stir) sich regen, sich rühren; (walk) gehen; (—e off) marschieren, abziehen; ziehen (*Chess, etc.*); ausziehen (*from rooms*); to —e in the best society, sich in den besten Kreisen bewegen; to —e **away,** fortziehen, sich fortbegeben, sich entfernen; to —e **in,** hineingehen, einziehen; to —e **into** new rooms, eine neue Wohnung beziehen; to —e **off,** sich davon machen; to —e **on,** weiter gehen, fortrücken, fortziehen; to —e **to,** ziehen nach; to —e **up** and **down,** auf- und ab-gehen. III. *s.* die Bewegung, das Ziehen; der Zug (*at Chess, etc.*); der Schritt (*fig.*), die Maßregel; on the —e, in Bewegung, auf dem Marsche; whose —e is it? wer hat zu ziehen? wer ist am Ziehen? **—ement,** *s.* die Bewegung (*also Mech., Mil.*); der Satz (*Mus.*); das Gehwerk (*of a watch*); to watch a p.'s —ements, einem auflauern. **—er,** *s.* der, die, das (sich) Bewegende; (stirrer up) der Bewegende, Anstifter, Anreger, Urheber; der Antragsteller (*Parl., etc.*); prime —er, der Motor (*Mech.*). **—ing,** *adj.,* **—ingly,** *adv.* bewegend; sich bewegend, beweglich (*as clouds*); rührend (*fig.*); —ing force, bewegende Kraft, Triebkraft; —ing spirit, anregender Geist, der Führer.

¹Mow, *s.* der Haufen Heu oder Korn, Heu-, Kornmasse; (barn) die Scheune.

²Mow, *v.* I. *a.* (ab)mähen; to — down, niedermähen; niedermachen (*fig.*). II. *n.* mähen. **—er,** *s.* der Mäher. **—ing,** *s.* das Mähen, die Mahd; —ed land) das Mähfeld, abgemähte Land. **—n,** *p.p. see* Mow. *Comp.* **—ing-machine,** *s.* die Mähmaschine.

Much, I. *adj.* viel; — happiness, viel Glück! he is too — for me, ich bin ihm nicht gewachsen. II. *adv.* sehr, weit, bei weitem; (almost) fast, beinahe; — obliged, sehr verbunden; as — more *or* again, noch einmal so viel; as — as, so viel wie; not so — as one, nicht einmal einer; it was not so — as heard of then, damals hatte man noch nicht einmal davon gehört; so — for the present, genug für diesmal, das genügt; I thought as —, das habe ich mir (gleich) gedacht; he said as —, der Sinn seiner Rede war etwa; — less . . ., geschweige denn . . .; he is not — of a scholar, er ist kein großer Gelehrter; to make — of, viel Wesens aus (*a circumstance, etc.*) machen, mit besonderer Aufmerksamkeit behandeln (*a person*); — good may it do you! wohl bekomme es Ihnen! wohl bekomm's! III. *s.* das Viel, ein großer Teil. **—ness,** *s.;* — of a —ness, so ziemlich von derselben Art (*vulg.*).

Muc—ic, *adj.;* —ic acid, die Schleimsäure. **—ilage,** *s.* der Pflanzenschleim; animal —ilage, *see* —us. **—ilaginous,** *adj.* schleimig; —ilaginous glands, Schleimdrüsen. **—ous,** *adj.* schleimig; —ous membrane, die Schleimhaut. **—us,** *s.* der Schleim.

Muck, I. *s.* der Mist, Kot, Unrat, Dreck (*also fig.*). II. *v.a.* düngen. **—y,** *adj.* schmutzig, dreckig. *Comp.* **—-heap,** *s.* der Misthaufen. **—-worm,** *s.* der Mistwurm.

Mud, *s.* der Schlamm, Schmutz; to stick in the —, im Schlamme stecken bleiben (*lit.*); in der Tinte sitzen (*fig.*). **—dily,** *adv. see* —dy. **—diness,** *s.* die Schlammigkeit. **—dle,** I. *v.a.* verwirren; in Verwirrung bringen; (fuddle) benebeln; to —dle away one's money, sein Geld verschleudern. II. *v.n.* im Schlamme wühlen; wühlen (*fig.*); to —dle about, zwecklos herumstöbern, sich zwecklos beschäftigen. III. *s.* die Verwirrung, Unordnung. **—dy,** I. *adj.* schlammig; trüb (*as water*); (dirty) schmutzig; (—like) erdfarbig, unklar, konfus (*fig.*). II. *v.a.* trüben, beschmutzen. *Comp.* **—-bath,** *s.* das Schlammbad. **—-floor,** *s.* der Lehmfußboden. **—-guard,** *s.* das Sch(m)utzblech (*Cycl.*). **—-house,** *s.* die Lehmhütte. **—-lark,** *s.* einer der im Schlamm, Kot *ɪc.* nach allerlei verkäuflichen Sachen sucht (*sl.*). **—-wall,** *s.* die Lehmwand.

¹Muff, I. *s.* der Muff. **—etee,** *s.* der Pulswärmer. **—in,** *s.* ein aus leichtem Teig gebackener Kuchen. **—ineer,** *s.* die Salz- *or* Zucker-büchse. **—le,** I. *v.a.* bedecken; (—le up) einhüllen, verhüllen; (stifle) dämpfen (*a drum*); bewickeln (*oars*); to —le a bell, den Klopfer einer (Tür)Glocke umwickeln, umbinden. II. *s.* die Muffel (*Chem., Metall.*). **—ler,** *s.* die wollene Halsbinde, das Halstuch; der Handschuh (*for boxing*).

²Muff, I. *s.* der Tropf, Dummkopf (*sl.*). II. *v.a. see* Muddle (*sl.*).

Mufti, *s.* der Mufti, Zivilanzug; in —, in Zivil.

¹Mug, *s.* der Krug, die Kanne; der Becher.

²Mug, *s.* der Mund; (face) das Gesicht (*sl.*).

Muggy, *adj.* dumpfig; (damp) naß, feucht.

Mugwort, *s.* der Beifuß (*Bot.*).

Mugwump, *s.* (*Amer.*) der zu keiner politischen Partei gehörige, der Wilde (*Parl.*).

Mulatto, *s.* der Mulatte, die Mulattin.

Mulberry, *s.* die Maulbeere; (—-tree) der Maulbeerbaum.

Mulct, I. *s.* die Geldstrafe. II. *v.a.* strafen (of, um), mit einer Geldstrafe belegen.

Mul—e, *s.* das Maultier, der Maulesel; der Bastard (*Bot., Zool.*); die Mulemaschine (*Spin.*). **—eteer,** *s.* der Mauleseltreiber. **—ish,** *adj.,* **—ishly,** *adv.* wie ein Maultier; (stubborn) eigensinnig, störrisch. **—ishness,** *s.* die Halsstarrigkeit.

Mulier, *s.* die (rechtmäßige) Ehefrau (*Law*); der ehelich geborene Sohn (*Law*). **—ose,** *adj.* weibersüchtig. **—osity,** *s.* die Weibertollheit. **—ty,** *s.* die eheliche Geburt (*Law*).

[1]**Mull**, *s.* das Vorgebirge, Kap.
[2]**Mull**, I. *v.a.* wärmen, glühen und mit Zucker und Gewürz versetzen (*wine, etc.*); *see* Muddle. **—ed**, *adj.*; —ed beer, gewürztes Warmbier; —ed wine, der Glühwein, Würzwein.
Mulle(l)n, *s.* das Wollkraut.
[1]**Mullet**, *s.* die Meeräsche.
[2]**Mullet**, *s.* das Spornrädchen (*Her.*).
Mulligatawny, *s.* eine scharf (mit curry) gewürzte (indische) Suppe.
Mullion, I. *s.* der Fensterpfosten, Mönch (*of a window*); der aufrechte Mittelfries (*of a door-frame*). II. *v.a.* wie Fensterpfosten einteilen.
Mult—angular, *adj.* vielwinkelig, vieleckig. **—ifarious**, *adj.*, **—ifariously**, *adv.* mannigfaltig. **—ifariousness**, *s.* die Mannigfaltigkeit. **—iform**, *adj.* vielgestaltig. **—ilateral**, *adj.* vielseitig. **—ilineal**, *adj.* viellinig. **—imillionaire**, *s.* der vielfache Millionär. **—inomial**, *adj.* vielnamig. **—ipartite**, *adj.* vielteilig. **—iple**, *s.* das Vielfache. **—iplex**, *adj.* vielfach. **—iplicand**, *s.* der Multiplikandus. **—iplicate**, *see* —iplex. **—iplication**, *s.* die Vervielfältigung, Vermehrung; die Multiplikation; the —iplication table, das Einmaleins. **—iplicity**, *s.* die Mannigfaltigkeit, Vielheit. **—iplier**, *s.* der Multiplikator (*Arith.*, *Elect.*); der Vermehrer. **—iply**, *v.* I. *a.* vermehren; vervielfachen, multiplizieren (*Arith.*). II. *n.* sich vermehren; be fruitful and —iply, seid fruchtbar und mehret Euch (*B.*); —iplying glass, das Vervielfältigungsglas. **—itude**, *s.* die Vielheit, Menge; (crowd) der große Haufe; (populace) der Pöbel. **—itudinous**, *adj.*, **—itudinously**, *adv.* zahlreich. **—ivalve**, I. *adj.* vielschalig. II. *s.* vielschalige Muschel.
Multure, *s.* das Mahlen; (grist) das gemahlene Korn; (fee) das Mahlgeld.
Mum, I. *adj.* stumm, ganz still; —'s the word! nichts gesagt! II. *int.* st! still! **—ble**, *v.* I. *n.* brummeln, murmeln, undeutlich *or* unvernehmlich sprechen. II. *a.* unvernehmlich hervorbringen, hermurmeln; (chew) mit verschlossenem Munde kauen; muffeln, mit zahnlosen Kiefern kauen. **—bling**, I. *adj.*, **—blingly**, *adv.* murmelnd. II. *s.* das Gemurmel. *Comp.* **—-chance**, *s.* der blöde, schweigsame Mensch; (silence) die Schweigsamkeit; to sit like —-chance, stumm da sitzen. **—p**, *v.a. & n.* mummeln; (chew) *see* —ble; (chatter) schnattern; (beg) betteln; (whine) greinen. **—pish**, *adj.* verdrießlich, grämlich, übellaunig. **—ps**, *s.* der Ziegenpeter (*Med.*); in the —ps, übel gelaunt, in verdrießlicher Stimmung.
Mummer, *s.* der Vermummte; (buffoon) der Possenreißer. **—y**, *s.* die Vermummung, Verkleidung; der Mummenschanz (*obs. poet.*); die Verstellung.
Mumm—ification, *s.* die Einbalsamierung (als Mumie). **—ify**, *v.* einbalsamieren, als Mumie aufbewahren. **—y**, *s.* die Mumie; to beat to a —y, breiweich schlagen (*fam.*); vegetable —y, der Mumiensaft.
Munch, *v.a. & n.* (geräuschvoll) kauen.
Mundane, *adj.* weltlich, Welt=.
Municipal, *adj.* zu einer Gemeinde *or* Stadt gehörig; Stadt=, Gemeinde=; — borough, der Stadtbezirk; — constitution, die städtische Verfassung; — council, der Gemeinderat; — laws, Gemeindegesetze; — officer, der städtische Beamte; — school, die städtische Schule, Stadtschule. **—ity**, *s.* der Gemeindebezirk.
Municifcen—ce, *s.* die Freigebigkeit. **—t**, *adj.*, **—tly**, *adv.* freigebig.
Muni—ment, I. *s.* die Urkunde. II. *attrib.*; —ment house, das Archiv. **—tion**, *s.* der Kriegsvorrat.
Mur—al, *adj.* Mauer=; —al painting, das Wandgemälde. **—e**, *see* Immure.
Murder, I. *s.* der Mord, die Mordtat; to commit —, Mord begehen; the —'s out, nun ist die Wahrheit heraus. II. *int.* Mordio! III. *v.a.* (er)morden; verhunzen (*a song*); radebrechen (*a language*); he —ed the King's (Queen's) English, er radebrechte englisch. **—er**, *s.* der Mörder. **—ess**, *s.* die Mörderin. **—ous**, *adj.*, **—ously**, *adv.* mörderisch; (bloody) blutig.
Murex, *s.* die Stachelschnecke; die Purpurschnecke.
Muriat—e, *s.* das salzsaure Salz; —e of lime, salzsaurer Kalk. **—ic**, *adj.* salzsauer; —ic acid, die Salzsäure.
Murk—y, *adj.*, **—ily**, *adv.* finster, trüb.
Murmur, I. *s.* das Gemurmel, Murmeln; das Murren; das Rauschen (*of a stream*). II. *v.a. & n.* murmeln; leise rauschen; murren (against, at a th., wider *or* über eine S.). **—er**, *s.* der Murrkopf. **—ing**, I. *adj.* murmelnd; murrend. II. *s.* das Murmeln; das Gemurr(e) (über), die Unzufriedenheit (mit).
Murrain, *s.* die Viehseuche, Maul= und Klauenseuche.
Musca—del, **—t**, **—tel**, *s.* der Muskateller(wein); die Muskateller=traube *or* =birne. **—dine**, I. *s.* der Muskatellerwein. II. *adj.* muskatellerfarbig.
Musc—le, *s.* der Muskel. **—ular**, *adj.*, **—ularly**, *adv.* muskelig, Muskel=; (brawny) muskelstark; —ular Christianity, das Kraft=Christentum. **—ularity**, *s.* die Muskelstärke, Muskelkraft.
Muscoid, *adj.* moosartig.
Muscovado, *s.* der Rohzucker, die Muskovade.
[1]**Mus—e**, *s.* die Muse. **—eum**, *s.* das Museum. **—ic**, *s.* die Musik, Tonkunst; die Musik (*fig.*); (written —ic) die Noten; have you brought any —ic? haben Sie Noten mitgebracht? —ic of the spheres, Sphärenmusik, Harmonie der Sphären; incidental —ic, zugehörige Musik; sacred —ic, Kirchenmusik; to copy —ic, Noten schreiben; to set to —ic, in Musik setzen, komponieren. **—ical**, *adj.*, **—ically**, *adv.* musikalisch; (melodious) wohlklingend; —ical box, die Spieldose; —ical chairs, ein Spiel; —ical clock, die Spieluhr; —ical festival, das Musikfest; —ical glasses, Glasharmonika; —ical instrument, das Tonwerkzeug, Instrument; —ical pitch, die Tonhöhe. **—icalness**, *s.* der Wohlklang. **—ician**, *s.* der Musiker, Tonkünstler; der Spielmann, Musikant; she is a good —ician, sie ist sehr musikalisch; sie spielt (*or* singt) vortrefflich. *Comp.* **—ic-book**, *s.* das Notenbuch. **—ic-hall**, *s.* das Variété=Theater. **—ic-loft**, *s.* die Musikerbühne. **—ic-master**, *s.* der Musiklehrer. **—ic-paper**, *s.* das Notenpapier. **—ic-pen**, *s.* das Rostral, der Notenlinienzieher. **—ic-room**, *s.* das Musikzimmer. **—ic-shop**, *s.* die Musikalienhandlung. **—ic-stand**, *s.* das Noten=gestell, =pult. **—ic-stool**, *s.* der Klavierstuhl.
[2]**Mus—e**, I. *s.*; to be in a —e, *see* —e II. II. *v.n.* (nach)sinnen, nachgrübeln (on a th., über eine S.), in Gedanken vertieft sein; to —e at, sich wundern über (*acc.*). **—er**, *s.* der Nachsinnende; der Träumer. **—ing**, I. *adj.*, **—ingly**, *adv.* nachsinnend. II. *s.* das Grübeln, Nachsinnen.
Mush, I. *s.* das Maismehlbrei (*Amer.*); das Mus niederschlagen. II. *v.a.* zu Brei stampfen (*prov.*).
Mushroom, I. *s.* der Pilz, Erdschwamm, Champignon; der Glückspilz (*fig.*). II. *attrib.*; —ketchup, *see* Ketchup. III. *adj.* neu, eben aufgetaucht, plötzlich entstanden (*fig.*).
Musk, *s.* der Moschus, Bisam; die Moschuspflanze (*Bot.*); *see* —-deer. **—y**, *adj.* nach Moschus riechend, wohlriechend. *Comp.* **—-beaver**, **—-rat**, *s.* die Bisamratte. **—-deer**, *s.* das Moschustier. **—-pear**, *s.* die Muskatellerbirne.
Musket, *s.* die Flinte, Muskete. **—eer**, *s.* der Musketier. **—ry**, *s.* das Musketenfeuer. *Comp.* **—-ball**, *s.* die Flintenkugel. **—-proof**, *adj.* kugelfest. **—ry-fire**, *s.* das Kleingewehrfeuer. **—ry-instructor**, *s.* der Schieß=Offizier, =Instruktor. **—-shot**, *s.* die Flintenschußweite; (discharge) der Flintenschuß.

Muslin, *s.* der Musselin; Indian —, der Mull; — de laine, der Wollmusselin.
Musrol(e), *s.* das Nasenband (am Pferdegeschirr).
Mussel, *s.* die Muschel.
[1]**Must**, *v.aux.* müssen; I —, ich muß (ich mußte); I — not . . ., ich darf nicht . . .; he — have lost his way, otherwise . . ., er muß sich verirrt haben *or* gewiß hat er sich verirrt, sonst . . .
[2]**Must**, *s.* der Most; (wine —) der Weinmost; *see* —iness. **—iness**, *s.* die Dumpfigkeit, Muffigkeit; (mould) der Schimmel. **—y**, *adj.* muffig.
Mustach—e, *see* Moustache. **—ioed**, *adj.* schnurrbärtig.
Mustang, *s.* das halbwilde Pferd in den Prairien, der Mustang.
Mustard, *s.* der Senf. *Comp.* **—-plaster, —-poultice**, *s.* das Senfpflaster. **—-seed**, *s.* der Senfsame.
Muster, I. *s.* die Musterung (*Mil.*), Heerschau, Parade; (— roll) die Musterrolle; (levy) das Aufgebot; (assembly) der Haufe; ein Geheck (peacocks, Pfauen); to pass —, hingehen, geduldet werden; such excuses will not pass — with him, solche Entschuldigungen läßt er nicht durchgehen *or* hingehen. II. *v.a.* mustern (*Mil.*); (collect) aufbringen, versammeln, zusammenbringen; (— up) zusammenraffen (*courage*); to — troops into (out of) service, Soldaten zum Dienst einstellen (entlassen). III. *v.n.* sich versammeln *or* ansammeln.
Muta—bility, *s.* die Veränderlichkeit; (changeableness) der Wankelmut. **—ble**, *adj.*, **—bly**, *adv.* veränderlich; wankelmütig, unbeständig. **—te**, *v.* I. *a.* verändern. II. *n.* umlauten (*Gram.*). **—tion**, *s.* die Veränderung; vowel —tion, der Umlaut (*Gram.*). **—tis —ndis**, *adv.* mit den nötigen Abänderungen.
Mutch, *s.* die Frauenhaube (*obs.*).
[1]**Mute**, I. *adj.*, **—ly**, *adv.* stumm, lautlos; — sorrow, stiller Kummer; — e, stummes e. II. *s.* der, die Stumme; die stumme Person, der stumme Zuschauer; der Dämpfer, die Sordine (*Mus.*); der Leichenwärter (*at funerals*); (— consonant) der Verschlußlaut, die Muta; voiced dental —, der stimmhafte dentale Verschlußlaut, die Dentalmedia. **—ness**, *s.* die Stummheit.
[2]**Mute**, *v.n.* den Kot von sich geben (*of birds*).
Mutilat—e, *v.a.* verstümmeln (*also fig.*). **—ion**, *s.* die Verstümmelung. **—or**, *s.* der Verstümmler.
Mutin—eer, *s.* der Meuterer, Aufrührer. **—ous**, *adj.*, **—ously**, *adv.* meuterisch, aufrührerisch. **—y**, I. *s.* die Meuterei; der Aufruhr; the Indian —y, der indische Aufstand. II. *v.n.* Meuterei anstiften, Aufruhr stiften, sich auflehnen, meutern.
Mutter, I. *v.a. & n.* murmeln, murren. II. *s.* das Murren. **—ing**, I. *adj.*, **—ingly**, *adv.* murmelnd. II. *s.* das Gemurmel; das Gemurr.
Mutton, *s.* das Hammelfleisch. *Comp.* **—-chop**, *s.* das Hammelrippchen. **—-pie**, *s.* die Hammelfleischpastete. **—-suet**, *s.* das Hammelfett.
Mutual, *adj.*, **—ly**, *adv.* gegenseitig, wechselseitig, beiderseitig; (common) gemeinschaftlich; our — friend, unser gemeinsamer Freund; by — consent, durch gegenseitige Übereinkunft. **—ity**, *s.* die Gegenseitigkeit.
Mutule, *s.* der Sparrenkopf.
Muzzl—e, I. *s.* (snout, *etc.*) das Maul, die Schnauze; die Mündung (*of a gun, pistol, bellows, etc.*); der Maulkorb (*for a dog*). II. *v.a.* das Maul verbinden, einen Maulkorb anlegen; (einem) den Mund stopfen (*fig.*); to —e the press, die Presse knebeln; a law —ing the press, das Preßknebelungsgesetz, Maulkorbgesetz. III. *v.n.* schnüffeln, schnuppern, schnobern.
Muzzy, *adj.* verwirrt (in Kopfe), duselig (*coll.*).
My, *poss. adj.* mein(e); — head is aching, mir tut der Kopf weh; oh — ! du meine Güte! (*coll.*). *Comp.* **—self**, *pron.* ich selbst, mich, mir; I have hurt —self, ich habe mich verletzt *or* mir weh getan.
Myo—graphy, *s.* die Muskelbeschreibung. **—logy**, *s.* die Muskellehre. **—tomy**, *s.* die Muskelzerlegung.
Myop—e, I. *s.* der Kurzsichtige. II. *adj.* kurzsichtig. **—ia, —y**, *s.* die Kurzsichtigkeit.
Myri—ad, *s.* die Myriade, Unzahl. *Comp.* **—ad-minded**, *adj.* vieltausendsinnig, viel tausendfach gelaunt, mit dem Geist vieler Tausend begabt. **—apod**, *s.* der Tausendfüßler. **—orama**, *s.* das Myriorama.
Myrmidon, *s.* der Myrmidone; der Scherge, Häscher (*sl.*).
Myr—rh, *s.* die Myrrhe, Balsamstaude, der Balsam. **—tle**, *s.* die Myrte. *Comp.* **—tle-grove**, *s.* der Myrtenhain.
Myst—erious, *adj.*, **—eriously**, *adv.* geheimnisvoll, rätselhaft, geheim, dunkel; (incomprehensible) unerklärbar, rätselhaft. **—eriousness**, *s.* das Geheimnisvolle, Dunkel; das Rätselhafte. **—eries**, *pl.* Religionsgeheimnisse; (secret rites) Geheimnislehren. **—ery**, *s.* das Geheimnis; (puzzle) das Rätsel; (secret art) die Geheimkunst. **—ic(al)**, I. *adj.*, **—ically**, *adv.* geheimnisvoll, dunkel, mystisch; (allegorical) dunkelsinnig. II. *s.* der Mystiker. **—icism**, *s.* die Glaubensschwärmerei, der Mystizismus. **—ification**, *s.* die Schrauberei, Fopperei, absichtliche Täuschung. **—ifier**, *s.* der Mystifizierer. **—ify**, *v.a.* anführen, foppen, zum besten haben, betrügen, mystifizieren (*a person*).
[1]**Mystery**, *see* under Myst—.
[2]**Mystery**, *s.* das Handwerk, der Beruf; das Mysteriendrama, das mittelalterliche geistliche Schauspiel; geistliche dramatische Vorstellung.
Myth, *s.* die Göttersage, Sage, Mythe; der Mythus; (invention) die Erdichtung; her husband's a —, ihr Ehemann ist wohl eine Mythe. **—ic(al)**, *adj.* mythisch, sagenhaft; (not true) erdichtet. **—ological**, *adj.*, **—ologically**, *adv.* mythologisch; sagenhaft, erdichtet (*fig.*); mythologisch. **—ologist**, *s.* der Mytholog(e). **—ology**, *s.* die Götterlehre, Mythologie. **—opœic, —opoetic**, *adj.* mythenbildend.

N

N, n, *s.* N, n; *for Abbreviations see the end of the English-German part.*
[1]**Nab**, *v.a.* erhaschen, erschnappen, erwischen (*vulg.*).
[2]**Nab**, *s.* der Felsvorsprung (*dial.*).
Nabob, *s.* der Nabob, Krösus, sehr reiche Mann.
Nacre, *s.* die Perlmutter. **—ous**, *adj.* perlmutterartig, Perlmutter-.
Nadir, *s.* der Nadir, Fußpunkt; der tiefste Stand, Tiefstand (*fig.*).
Naevus, *s.* das Mal; — maternus, Muttermal.
[1]**Nag**, *s.* das Pferdchen; (horse) der Klepper; Shank's —, *see* Mare.
[2]**Nag**, *v.* I. *a.* (mit einem) keifen; to — to death, (einen) mit Keifen zu Tode quälen. II. *n.* nörgeln, mäkeln, quengeln. **—ging**, *s.* die Nörgelei, das Mäkeln, Quengeln.
Naiad, *s.* die Najade, Wassernymphe, Flußgöttin.
Nail, I. *s.* der Nagel (*on fingers, etc. also of metal*); (ein Längenmaß von) 2½ Zoll; der Spiker (*Naut.*); clinch —, der Nietnagel mit umgebogener Spitze; scupper —, flacher Tapeziernagel; square —s, Absatzstifte (*Shoem.*); tree —, hölzerner Nagel; as dead as a door —, mausetot; to take out a —, einen Nagel herausziehen; on the —, auf der Stelle, bar (*fam.*); tooth and —, mit aller Gewalt; with tooth and —, mit Händen und Füßen; to work tooth and —, es sich blutsauer werden lassen; to hit the — on the head, den Nagel auf den Kopf treffen; one — drives out another, ein Keil treibt den andern (*prov.*). II. *v.a.* (an)nageln; (stud with —s) mit Nägeln beschlagen; festhalten, beim Worte nehmen (*fig.*); (catch) festnehmen (*sl.*); to — **down**, zunageln (*a box, etc.*); to — a p. down, einen (auf eine S.) festnageln; to — **to** the

cross, ans Kreuz schlagen, kreuzigen; to — to the ground, an den Boden spießen; to — **up**, aufnageln, *see* — down. —**er**, *s.* der Nagelschmied; famoser Kerl (*sl.*). *Comp.* —**-brush**, *s.* die Nagelbürste. — **-headed**, *adj.*; — -headed characters, die Keilschrift. —**-nippers**, *pl.* die Nagelzange. —**-scissors**, *pl.* die Nagelscheere.

Naissant, *adj.* emporsteigend (*Her.*).

Naïve, *adj.*, —**ly**, *adv.* naiv, ungekünstelt, natürlich, unbefangen. —**té**, —**ty**, *s.* die Naivität, Natürlichkeit, Unbefangenheit, natürliche Einfalt.

Naked, *adj.*, —**ly**, *adv.* nackt, bloß, unbedeckt, kahl (*also fig. & Bot.*): (undefended) wehrlos, unbewaffnet; (exposed) ausgesetzt; unverhüllt; (plain) deutlich; the — truth, die nackte, unverblümte Wahrheit; to strip —, ganz ausziehen; with the — eye, mit bloßem Auge, mit unbewaffnetem Auge; the — sword, das bloße Schwert. —**ness**, *s.* die Nacktheit, Blöße.

Namby-pamby, *adj.* albern, geziert, schal, abgeschmackt, verweichlicht.

Name, I. *s.* der Name, die Benennung; (title) der Titel; (reputation) der gute Name, Ruf; (renown) die Berühmtheit; (authority) der Auftrag; das Nennwort (*Gram.*); Christian —, der Taufname, Vorname; family —, der Familienname; don't mention —s! werden Sie nicht persönlich! to call a p. —s, einem Schimpfnamen geben; by —, mit Namen; to know by —, dem Namen nach kennen; in — only, dem bloßen Namen nach; in the — of . . ., im Namen des . . .; what is your —? wie heißen Sie? he has a bad — with me, er ist übel bei mir angeschrieben; he called me by —, er rief mich bei Namen. II. *v.a.* (be)nennen; (mention) erwähnen, namhaft machen; (appoint) ernennen; to — a member of Parliament, einen Abgeordneten zur Ordnung rufen (*Parl.*); zeitweilig von der Sitzung ausschließen (ein Parlamentsmitglied); to — a day, einen Tag bestimmen. —**able**, *adj.* nennbar. —**d**, *p.p.* genannt, namens; the above —d author, der oben angeführte Schriftsteller. —**less**, *adj.* namenlos; (unknown) unbekannt, nicht berühmt; (inexpressible) unaussprechlich; a gentleman who shall be —less, ein Herr, den ich nicht nennen will. —**lessness**, die Namenlosigkeit. —**ly**, *adv.* nämlich. —**sake**, *s.* der Namensvetter, die Namensschwester. *Comp.* —**-plate**, *s.* das Türschild.

Nankeen, *s.* der Nankin(g). —**s**, *pl.* Nankinhosen.

[1]**Nap**, I. *s.* das Schläfchen; to take a —, ein (Mittags-)Schläfchen halten. II. *v.n.* nicken; to catch a p. —ping, einen unversehens überfallen, ihn (auf Fehlern 2c.) ertappen.

[2]**Nap**, I. *s.* die Noppe, Pohle, der Flor (*of cloth*). II. *v.a.* noppen, aufreißen; —ped cloth, rauhes Tuch, Tuch mit Knötchen auf der rechten Seite. —**e**, *s.* der Nacken, das Genick. —**less**, *adj.* kahl, fadenscheinig.

[3]**Nap** = Napoleon; ein Kartenspiel.

Nap—ery, *s.* das Tisch-, Weiß-zeug, die Wäsche. —**kin**, *s.* das Tellertuch, die Serviette. *Comp.* —**kin-ring**, *s.* der Serviettenring.

Naphtha, *s.* das Bergöl, Steinöl, Naphtha. —**lene**, —**line**, —**lin**, *s.* das Naphthalin. —**lize**, *v.a.* mit Naphtha sättigen.

Nar—cissus, *s.* die Narzisse (*Bot.*). —**cotic**, I. *adj.* einschläfernd; narkotisch. II. *s.* das Schlafmittel.

Nard, *s.* die Narde (*Bot.*); die Nardensalbe. —**ine**, *adj.* nardenartig.

Narrat—e, *v.a.* erzählen. —**ion**, *s.* die Erzählung. —**ive**, I. *adj.* erzählend. II. *s.* die Erzählung, Geschichte. —**or**, *s.* der Erzähler.

Narrow, I. *adj.* eng, schmal; klein, kurz, knapp (*of space, time, circumstances*); (illiberal) engherzig, kleindenkend, beschränkt; the gate is strait and the way —, die Pforte ist enge und der Weg ist schmal (*B.*); to have a — escape, mit genauer Not entkommen; to bring into a — compass, kurz zusammenziehen. II. *v.a.* einengen, enger, schmäler machen; (limit) beschränken; (contract) einengen, beengen; einnehmen (*a stocking, etc.*). III. *v.n.* sich verengen, enger werden; einnehmen. IV. *s.* der Engpaß. —**ing**, I. *adj.* einengend II. *s.* die Einengung; der eingenommene Teil (*of a stocking, etc.*). —**ly**, *adv.* eng, schmal; (closely) genau, sorgfältig; (by a little) mit Mühe, kaum; to search into —ly, genau untersuchen. —**ness**, *s.* die Enge, Schmalheit; die Beschränktheit (*of capacity, circumstances, etc.*); (meanness) die Filzigkeit; —ness of mind, *see* — - mindedness. —**s**, *pl.* die Meerenge. *Comp.* —**-brimmed**, *adj.* schmal-randig, -krämpig. —**-chested**, *adj.* engbrüstig. —**-gauge**, I. *s.* die Schmalspur. II. *attrib.* schmalspurig. —**-minded**, *adj.* engherzig. —**-mindedness**, *s.* die Engherzigkeit.

Narwhal(e), **Narwal**, *s.* der Narwal, das See-Einhorn.

Nas—al, I. *adj.* Nasen-; —al tone, ein durch die Nase gesprochener Ton; —al twang, das Näseln. II. *s.* der Nasenlaut, Nasal; guttural —al, der Gutturalnasal (ng). —**ality**, *s.* die nasale Beschaffenheit, Nasalität. —**alization**, *s.* die Nasalierung. —**alize**, *v.a.* durch die Nase aussprechen, näseln. —**icorn**, *adj.* mit einem Horn auf der Nase, rhinozerosartig.

Nascent, *adj.* entstehend, wachsend, werdend.

Nast—ily, *adv. see* —**y**. —**iness**, *s.* der Schmutz, Unflat; die Unflätigkeit, Zotigkeit (*fig.*); die Ekelhaftigkeit. —**y**, *adj.* unflätig, schmutzig (*also fig.*); (disagreeable) mürrisch, unartig (*prov.*); ekelhaft; unangenehm; (serious) bedenklich, schwer; he has met with a —y accident, ein schwerer Unfall hat ihn betroffen (*coll.*).

Nasturtium, *s.* die große Kresse.

Nat—al, *adj.* zur Geburt gehörig, Geburts-; —al day, der Geburtstag. —**ion**, *s.* die Nation, das Volk. —**ional**, *adj.* volkstümlich, national, Staats-, National-; (patriotic) vaterländisch; volklich; (public) allgemein, öffentlich; —ional debt, die Staatsschuld; —ional air, das Volkslied, die Volksmelodie; —ional character, der Volksgeist; —ional costume, die Volkstracht, Landestracht; —ional schools, Kommunalschulen (für die ärmeren Klassen) (*especially in Ireland*); —ional assembly, die Nationalversammlung; —ional characteristics, die Volkseigentümlichkeiten; —ional festival, das Volksfest. —**ionalism**, *s. see* —icnality; der Nationalcharakter; das Verlangen nach nationaler Einheit; der irische Nationalismus (welcher sich hauptsächlich durch Feindseligkeit gegen England äußert). —**ionalist**, *s.* der Anhänger derjenigen irischen Partei, welche die Home Rule wünscht. —**ionality**, *s.* die Stammesangehörigkeit, Volksart, Nationalität. —**ionalize**, *v.a.* einbürgern, nationalisieren, in einen Staatsverband aufnehmen (*a person*); an das Volk bringen (*land*). —**ionalization**, *s.* die Einbürgerung, Nationalisierung.

Nata—nt, *adj.* schwimmend. —**tion**, *s.* das Schwimmen. —**tores**, *pl.* Schwimmvögel. —**tory**, *adj.* Schwimm-.

Nathless, *adv.* nichtsdestoweniger, dennoch (*obs.*).

Nativ—e, I. *adj.* gebürtig (of, aus), heimisch (of, in); (natural) natürlich, angeboren; (kindred) verwandt; gediegen (*as metals*); —e country, das Vaterland; —e gold, gediegenes Gold, Jungferngold; —e forests, Urwälder; —e tongue, die Muttersprache; —e troops, einheimische Truppen. II. *s.* der Eingeborene, das Landeskind; die (das) einheimische Pflanze (Tier); die künstlich gezüchtete Auster. —**ity**, *s.* die Geburt; die Nativität (*Astrol.*); to calculate *or* cast s. o.'s —ity, einem die Nativität stellen.

Natron, *s.* das Natron, die natürliche Soda.

Natterjack, *s.* die Kreuzkröte.

Natt—ily, *adv.*, —**y**, *adj.* nett, schmuck, gewandt. —**iness**, *s.* die Schmuckheit, Sauberkeit.

Natur—al, I. *adj.* natürlich, Natur= ; (uncultivated) wild; (innate) angeboren; (unaffected) ungezwungen, natürlich ; unehelich (*as a child*) ; to die a —al death, eines natürlichen Todes sterben ; —al disposition, die Eigentümlichkeit (des Charakters), das Naturell; —al history, die Naturgeschichte; —al philosophy, die Naturphilosophie; —al selection, natürliche Zuchtwahl. II. *s.* der Narr, Blödsinnige; das Auflösungszeichen, Wiederherstellungszeichen (*Mus.*). **—alism**, *s.* der Naturalismus (*Rel. & Lit.*) ; (state of —e) der Naturzustand. **—alist**, *s.* der Naturaliensammler; der Naturalienverkäufer; der Naturgläubige (*Rel.*). **—alization**, *s.* die Naturalisierung, Einbürgerung. **—alize**, *v.a.* einbürgern, (einem) das Heimatsrecht erteilen, naturalisieren; in eine Sprache aufnehmen; (make —al) zur andern Natur machen; (acclimatize) akklimatisieren; he has become —alized, er hat sich naturalisieren lassen. **—ally**, *adv.* natürlich; (by —e) von Natur ; (according to —e) naturgemäß, ungekünstelt; von selbst, wild; natürlicherweise. **—alness**, *s.* die Natürlichkeit ; die Ungezwungenheit; die Naturgemäßheit. **—e**, *s.* die Natur; das Wesen, die Art, Beschaffenheit, das Naturell; good —e, die Gutmütigkeit, Gefälligkeit; ill —e, die Bösartigkeit, Ungefälligkeit; of this —e, dieser Art ; in a state of —e, im Naturzustande, nackt; to draw from —e, nach der Natur zeichnen. **—ed**, *adj.* (*in comp.*) =geartet, =artig.

Naught, I. *adj.* nichtig. II. *adv.* keineswegs. III. *s. & pron.* das Nichts, Nichtsnutzige ; die Null; to come to —, zu nichte werden; to set at —, nicht achten, in den Wind schlagen; his hope came to —, seine Hoffnung wurde zu Wasser. **—ily**, *adv.*, **—y**, *adj.* unartig, ungezogen. **—iness**, *s.* die Ungezogenheit, Unartigkeit.

Nau—machy, *s.* die Seeschlacht; (sham fight) das Luftgefecht zu Schiff. **—sea**, *s.* die Seekrankheit, Übelkeit; der Ekel (*fig.*). **—seate**, *v.* I. *n.* Ekel empfinden (at, vor). II. *a.* verabscheuen; to be —seated, sich ekeln. **—seous**, *adj.*, **—seously**, *adv.* ekelhaft, widrig. **—seousness**, *s.* die Widerlichkeit. **—tical**, *adj.*, **—tically**, *adv.* nautisch, See=, Schiffahrts= ; —tical almanac, der Seealmanach; —tical chart, die Seekarte. **—tilus**, *s.* der Nautilus, die Schiffschnecke.

Nav—al, *adj.* zu Schiffen, zur See gehörig, See=, Schiff=, Schiffs= ; —al architect, der Schiffsbaumeister; —al cadet, der Seekadett; —al cadetship, die Stelle eines Seekadetten; —al college, die Seekadettenschule ; —al constructor, der Marine=, Schiffbau=Ingenieur ; —al engagement, das Seegefecht; —al forces, Seetruppen; —al league, der Flottenverein ; —al officers, Seeoffiziere ; —al power, die Seemacht ; —al stores, Schiffsvorräte; —al tactics, die Seetaktik. **—e**, *s.* das Schiff (*of a church*) **—icular**, *adj.* schiff=, nachen=förmig ; —icular bone, das Schiffbein. **—igable**, *adj.* schiffbar, fahrbar; —igable balloon, lenkbares Luftschiff. **—igability**, *s.* die Fahrbarkeit, Schiffbarkeit. **—igate**, *v.* I. *a.* beschiffen, befahren (*seas*); durchschiffen (*the air*); steuern, führen (*a ship*). II. *n.* segeln. **—igation**, I. *s.* das Fahren, die Schiffahrt, Seefahrt; (art of —igation) die Steuermannskunst, Schiffahrtskunde; act of — igation, die Navigationsakte ; aerial —igation, die Luftschiffahrt. II. *attrib.* ; —igation laws, Schiffahrtsgesetze. **—igator**, *s.* der Seefahrer; der Steuermann. **—y**, *s.* die Marine, Seemacht; (ships) die Flotte; (warships) die Kriegsflotte. *Comp.* **—y-bill**, *s.* die Schiffsnote. **—y-league**, *s.* der Flottenverein.

[1]**Nave**, *see under* Nav—.

[2]**Nave**, *s.* die Nabe. **—l**, *s.* der Nabel; die Mitte (*fig.*). *Comp.* **—l-string**, *s.* die Nabelschnur.

Navvy, *s.* der Erdarbeiter, E[illegible]bahnarbeiter.

Nawab, *see* Nabob.

Nay, I. *adv.* nein; (not only so) ja, sogar, vielmehr. II. *s.* die abschlägige Antwort; (voting) das Nein.

Naze, *s.* die Landspitze, Klippe.

Neap, *adj.* niedrig, abnehmend; — tide, das tote Wasser, die Nippflut. **—ed**, *adj.* benept (*Naut.*).

Near, I. *adj.* nahe (*in time, space or degree*) ; (closely related) nahe verwandt; gerade (*as a way*) ; (intimate) vertraut; genau, treu (*as a translation*) ; (miserly) geizig, karg; (left) link; — at hand, dicht dabei ; — the mouth of . . ., nahe der Mündung, bei der Mündung; to draw —, sich (einem 2c.) nähern; — horse, das Handpferd. II. *adv.* ; he was — being killed, er wäre beinahe ums Leben gekommen (*coll.*) ; far and —, weit und breit ; to come — to . . ., sich fast auf (*acc.*) . . . belaufen; this will go — to ruin him, dies wird ihn fast zu Grunde richten ; the ship sailed — the wind, das Schiff segelte hart am Winde. III. *prep.* (— to) nahe, nahe an *or* bei, bei. **—ly**, *adv.* nahe; fast, ungefähr; they are —ly related, sie sind nahe verwandt; I had —ly . . ., ich war nahe daran . . .; it —ly concerns me, es geht mich nahe an ; is the dinner —ly ready ? ist das Mittagsessen bald fertig ? **—ness**, *s.* die Nähe ; nahe Verwandtschaft ; die Kargheit. *Comp.* **—-sighted**, *adj.* kurzsichtig.

[1]**Neat**, *adj.*, **—ly**, *adv.* nett, sauber, rein, reinlich ; (tidy) ordentlich, gut aufgeräumt; (pretty) zierlich, niedlich; (pure) unvermischt. **—ness**, *s.* die Nettigkeit, Sauberkeit, Niedlichkeit ; die Zierlichkeit. *Comp.* **—-handed**, *adj.* geschickt. **—-handedness**, *s.* die Geschicklichkeit.

[2]**Neat**, *s.* das Rindvieh (*obs.*). *Comp.* **—herd**, *s.* der Rinderhirt (*obs.*). **—'s-foot-oil**, *s.* das Klauenfett.

Neb, *s.* der Schnabel (*prov.*).

Nebul—a, *s.* (*pl.* —æ) der Nebel=fleck, =stern (*Astr.*) ; der Nebel im Auge (*Surg.*). **—ar**, *adj.* Nebel=. **—osity**, *s.* die Nebelhaftigkeit. **—ous**, *adj.* bewölkt, nebelig.

Necess—aries, *pl. see* —ary II. ; —aries of life, Lebensbedürfnisse. **—arily**, *adv.* notwendig, durchaus. **—ariness**, *s.* die Notwendigkeit. **—ary**, I. *adj.* notwendig, unentbehrlich; unvermeidlich; unumstößlich (*as arguments*); (not free) gezwungen; it is —ary to . . ., man muß . . . ; absolutely —ary, unumgänglich notwendig. II. *s.* das Bedürfnis; (closet) der Abtritt. **—itarian**, *s.* der Fatalist. **—itate**, *v.a.* erfordern, notwendig machen ; (force) zwingen. **—itous**, *adj.* dürftig, notleidend. **—itousness**, *s.* (—itous circumstances) die Dürftigkeit, Not (*obs.*). **—ity**, *s.* die Notwendigkeit ; (inevitableness) die Unumgänglichkeit, Unvermeidlichkeit ; (constraint) der Zwang; (want) die Armut, Dürftigkeit, Not ; der Fatalismus, die Verhängnislehre; of —ity, notwendigerweise ; to make a virtue of —ity, aus der Not eine Tugend machen; —ity knows no law, Not bricht Eisen, Not kennt kein Gebot (*prov.*) ; —ity is the mother of invention, die Not macht erfinderisch.

Neck, *s.* der Hals, Nacken ; das Halsstück (*of mutton*) ; (bosom) der Busen ; das Leben, der Kopf (*fig.*) ; der Hals (*of a bottle, column, capital, embrasure, gun, guitar*) ; — of land, die Landzunge ; — and —, zusammen, zu gleicher Zeit ; — and crop, gänzlich, mit Haut und Haaren ; to break the — of, einer Sache die Spitze abbrechen (*fig.*) ; — or nothing, auf jede Gefahr hin; verzweifelt. **—ed**, *adj.* (*in comp.* =) =halsig. *Comp.* **—-band**, *s.* der Halsband am Hemde, Hemdkragen. **—-cloth**, *s.* das Halstuch. **—erchief**, *s.* das Halstuch (für Frauen). **—lace**, *s.* das Halsband, die Halskette, das Collier. **—-tie**, *s.* die Halsbinde, Kravatte.

Necro—logy, *s.* der Lebensabriß eines Verstorbenen, Nachruf auf einen Verstorbenen, Nekrolog. **—mancer**, *s.* der Schwarzkünstler, Zauberer. **—mancy**, *s.* die Schwarzkunst, Zauberei. **—phagous**, *adj.* aasfressend. **—polis**, *s.* die Totenstadt. **—sis**, *s.* der trockene Brand ; der Brand (*Bot.*).

Nectar, *s.* der Nektar. **—ine**, *s.* der Nektarinen-Pfirsich. **—y**, *s.* das Honiggefäß (*Bot.*).

Née, *adj.* geborene (*Fr.*); Mrs. Smith, — Miller, Frau Smith, geb. Miller.

Need, I. *s.* die Not, der Bedarf, das Bedürfnis; (poverty) die Not, Notdurft, Armut; in case of —, im Notfalle; a friend in —, ein Freund in der Not; a friend in — is a friend indeed, Freunde erkennt man in der Not (*prov.*); to be (stand) in — of a th., etwas nötig haben *or* brauchen; if — be, nötigenfalls; there's no — for . . ., es ist nicht nötig, daß . . .; that is more than is —ed, das ist mehr als nötig ist. II. *v.a.* nötig haben, brauchen, bedürfen. III. *v.n.* & *aux.* nötig sein; what — I care? was brauche ich darnach zu fragen? **—ful**, *adj.*, **—fully**, *adv.* notwendig, nötig, bedürftig. II. *s.* das Nötige, das nötige Geld (*sl.*). **—ily**, *adv.* in Not, arm. **—iness**, *s.* die Armut, Dürftigkeit. **—less**, *adj.*, **—lessly**, *adv.* unnötig, vergeblich. **—lessness**, *s.* die Unnötigkeit. **—s**, *adv.* notwendigerweise, durchaus. **—y**, *adj.* hülfsbedürftig, arm, dürftig.

Needle, *s.* die Nadel; darning, knitting, sewing —, Stopf-, Strick-, Näh-nadel; — of the compass, Magnetnadel; —'s eye, das Nadelöhr. **—ful**, *s.* die Nadelvoll. *Comp.* **—-alphabet**, *s.* das Alphabet des Zeigerapparats. **—-book**, *s.* das Nadelbuch. **—-case**, *s. see* —-book; die Nadelbüchse, das Nadelbuch, das Nadelfutteral. **—-gun**, *s.* das Zündnadelgewehr. **—-lock**, *s.* das Zündnadelschloß. **—-maker**, *s.* der Nadler. **—-plate**, *s.* die Stichplatte (*Sew-mach.*). **—-telegraph**, *s.* der Zeigertelegraph. **—-threader**, *s.* der Einfädelapparat. **—-woman**, *s.* die Näherin; she is a good —-woman, sie ist sehr geschickt mit der Nadel, sie näht gut. **—-work**, *s.* die Näharbeit; die Handarbeit.

Ne'er, *see* Never. *Comp.* **—-do-weel**, *s.* (*Scotch*) der Taugenichts, Tunichtgut.

Nefarious, *adj.*, **—ly**, *adv.* gottlos, frevelhaft, verrucht. **—ness**, *s.* die Ruchlosigkeit.

Negat—ion, *s.* die Verneinung. **—ive**, I. *adj.*, **—ively**, *adv.* verneinend; negativ (*opp. to* Positive); mit dem Minuszeichen (*Alg.*). II. *s.* die Negative, Verneinung; das Verneinungswort (*Gram.*); (—ive proposition) der Verneinungssatz; (veto) verneinende Stimme, das Veto; das Negativ (*Phot.*); to answer in the —ive, mit Nein antworten; verneinen. III. *v.a.* verneinen; ablehnen; (disprove) widerlegen.

Neglect, I. *s.* die Vernachlässigung (*of duty, etc.*); die Hintansetzung, achtungslose Behandlung, Mißachtung; (carelessness) die Nachlässigkeit; (omission to do) die Versäumnis; (—ed state) die Vernachlässigung, das Vernachlässigtwerden, Verwahrlosung. II. *v.a.* vernachlässigen, versäumen; vernachlässigen (*a person*); verfehlen (*an opportunity, etc.*); to — o.s., sich vernachlässigen. **—ed**, *adj.* verwahrlost. **—ful**, *adj.*, **—fully**, *adv.* achtlos (of, auf (*acc.*)); *see* Negligent.

Neglig—ee, *s.* das nachlässige, ungezwungene Gewand, die bequeme Haustracht, das Negligé (einer Frau). **—ence**, *s.* die Nachlässigkeit, Achtlosigkeit. **—ent**, *adj.*, **—ently**, *adv.* nachlässig, unachtsam; —ent of, gleichgültig gegen *or* in Bezug auf (*acc.*), unachtsam auf (*acc.*).

Nego—tiable, *adj.* verhandelbar, übertragbar; zu begeben (*as bills*); —tiable bills, Wechsel von soliden Häusern. **—tiate**, (**—ciate**,) *v.* I. *a.* verhandeln, abschließen (*a treaty, etc.*); unterhandeln (*also a peace, etc.*); vermitteln; to —tiate a bill, einen Wechsel ab-, be-geben. II. *n.* handeln; unterhandeln. **—tiation**, (**—ciation**,) *s.* das Ver-, Unter-handeln; der Handel; das Verhandeln, die Verwechselung (*of a bill*); die Vermittelung; der Abschluß (*of a treaty*); —tiation for time, der Zeitkauf; to enter into —tiations, in Unterhandlung treten **—tiator**, *s.* der Unterhändler, Vermittler

Negr—ess, *s.* die Negerin. **—o**, I. *s.* der Neger. II. *attrib.*; —o land, das Negerland. **—o(lo)id**, *adj.* negerartig.

[1]**Negus**, *s.* der Negus, König von Abessinien.

[2]**Negus**, *s.* der Glühwein.

Neigh, I. *v.n.* wiehern. II. *s.* das Wiehern.

Neighbour, I. *s.* der (die) Nachbar(in); (friend) der Freund, Vertraute; der Nächste, Mitmensch (*B.*). II. *adj.* benachbart, naheliegend, angrenzend. III. *v.a.* angrenzen. **—hood**, *s.* die Nachbarschaft, die Nähe. **—ing**, *adj. see* — II.; —ing parts, die Umgebung; —ing village, das Nachbardorf. **—liness**, *s.* die Nachbarlichkeit, das gute nachbarliche Verhältnis. **—ly**, *adj.* nachbarlich; (friendly) gesellig, freundschaftlich.

Neither, I. *pron.* keiner von beiden, keiner; — of them, keiner von ihnen *or* beiden. II. *adj.* kein(e); I shall take — part, ich werde neutral bleiben. III. *conj.* weder; — . . . nor, weder . . . noch; nor . . . —, auch nicht; he has — money nor friends, er hat weder Geld noch Freunde; ye shall not eat of it — shall ye touch it, esset nicht davon, rührt's auch nicht an; nor that —, und das auch nicht (*coll.*).

Neo—logian, *see* —logist. **—logism**, *s. see* —logy; das neugebildete Wort; die Neubildung, Sprachneuerung; der Neologismus. **—logist**, *s.* der Sprachneuerer; der Rationalist (*Rel.*). **—logy**, *s.* (—logism) die Sprachneuerung, Neubildung, Neologie; die Neulehre (*Rel.*). **—phyte**, *s.* der Neu-bekehrte, -geweihte; (novice) die Novize; (beginner) der Neuling, Anfänger. **—teric**, *adj.* neu, modern.

Nepenthes, *s.* der Nepenthes, Zaubertrank (*poet.*).

Ne—phew, *s.* der Neffe; der Vetter (*obs.*). **—potism**, *s.* der Nepotismus, die Neffengunst; die Vetternwirtschaft, Bevorzugung von Verwandten; die Gönnerwirtschaft, das Gönnertum. **—potist**, *s.* der Neffenbegünstiger.

Nephr—algia, *s.* der Nierenschmerz. **—ite**, *s.* der Nierenstein, Nephrit. **—itic**, I. *adj.* Nieren-; —itic disease, die Nierenkrankheit; —itic patient, der Nierenkranke. II. *s.* das Nierenmittel. **—itis**, *s.* die Nierenentzündung. **—otomy**, *s.* der Nierenschnitt.

Nereid, *s.* die Nereïde, Meernymphe.

Nerv—e, I. *s.* der Nerv; (sinew) die Sehne; die Geisteskraft, Selbstherrschaft, Seelenstärke, der Mut (*fig.*); die Rippe (*Bot.*); of great —e, starknervig. **—ed**, *adj.* nervig. **—eless**, *adj.* kraftlos. **—ine**, I. *adj.* nervenstärkend. II. *s.* nervenstärkendes Mittel. **—ous**, *adj.*, **—ously**, *adv.* Nerven-, nervös; (muscular) sehnig, kräftig, nervig; (vigorous) nervig, kräftig, gediegen, kraftvoll; (weak —ed) nervös, nervenschwach, reizbar; (timid) schüchtern, befangen; he is suffering from a —ous disease, er leidet an den Nerven, ist nervenkrank; the singer was —ous, der Sänger war ängstlich *or* befangen. **—ousness**, *s.* die Nervigkeit; die Stärke, Kraft (*fig.*); die Nervenschwäche; die Schüchternheit, Befangenheit.

Ness, *s.* das Vorgebirge, die Landzunge.

Nest, I. *s.* das Nest (*also fig.*); der Einsatz (*of boxes, etc.*); der Satz (*of hares*); crow's —, der Mastkorb; eagle's —, das Adlernest, der Horst; — of drawers, kleiner Schrank mit Schubladen; to build *or* make one's —, nisten; to feather one's —, sich bereichern. II. *v.n.* nisten, horsten. **—le**, *v.n.* (nest) nisten; sich einnisten (*also fig.*); to —le into, sich schmiegen in; to —le close to a p., sich eng an einen anschmiegen. **—ling**, *s.* der Nestling. *Comp.* **—-egg**, *s.* das Nestei; der Heck(e)pfennig (*fig.*).

[1]**Net**, I. *s.* das Netz, Garn, die Schlinge; das Netz, die Falle, der Fallstrick (*fig.*); der Spitzengrund, Tüll (*for millinery, etc.*); —! Netz! gestreift! (*Tenn.*); —-play, das Netzspiel. II. *v.a.* mit einem Netze fangen (*fish, etc.*); verstricken (*fig.*). III. *v.a.* & *n.* Filet stricken, Netzarbeit machen. **—ter**, *s.* der (die) Netzstricker(in). **—ting**, *s.* die

Filetarbeit; (net) das Netz, Netzwerk; wire —ting, das Drahtnetz. *Comp.* **—ting-needle,** *s.* die Filetnadel. **—ting-stitch,** *s.* der Netzstich. **—ting-pin,** *s.* der Filetstock. **—-work,** *s.* die Netzarbeit; das Netzwerk; —-work of railways, das Eisenbahnnetz.

[2]**Net(t),** I. *adj.* netto, rein; — amount, der Nettobetrag; —profit, der Reingewinn; — receipts, die Nettoeinnahme; — weight, das Nettogewicht. II. *v.a.* rein einbringen.

Nether, *adj.* nieder, unter, Unter-; — lip, die Unterlippe; — regions, — world, die Unterwelt. *Comp.* **—most,** I. *adj.* niedrigst, unterst. II. *adv.* zu unterst.

Nettle, I. *s.* die Nessel. II. *v.a.* mit Nesseln brennen; ärgern; to be —d at, geärgert werden durch. *Comp.* **—-rash,** *s.* der Nesselausschlag.

Neur—algia, *s.* der Nervenschmerz, die Neuralgie. **—algic,** *adj.* neuralgisch. **—itis,** *s.* die Nervenentzündung. **—ology,** *s.* die Nervenlehre. **—opter,** *s.* der Netzflügler. **—osis,** *s.* die Nervenkrankheit. **—otic,** I. *adj.* Nerven-. II. *s.* die Nervenkrankheit; (nervine) das Nervenmittel. **—otomist,** *s.* der Nervenzergliederer. **—otomy,** *s.* die Nervenzergliederung, der Nervenschnitt.

Neut—er, I. *adj.* geschlechtslos (*Gram.*); sächlich (*as nouns*); intransitiv (*of verbs*); —er cat, verschnittener Kater; —er gender, das sächliche Geschlecht; —er verb, das Intransitivum. II. *s.* das Geschlechtslose; das Neutrum (*Gram.*). **—ral,** I. *adj.*, **—rally,** *adv.* unbeteiligt, parteilos, neutral; (indifferent) gleichgültig; reizlos, neutral (*Chem.*); —ral point of a magnet, der Indifferenzpunkt; —ral tint, eine Farbe, die zu jeder andern paßt. II. *s.* der Unparteiische, Neutrale. **—rality,** *s.* die Neutralität, Parteilosigkeit; armed —rality, bewaffnete Neutralität. **—ralization,** *s.* die Neutralisierung; die Neutralisation (*Chem.*). **—ralize,** *v.a.* neutralisieren (*also Chem.*); neutral machen; (render null) unwirksam machen; to —ralize each other, sich gegenseitig aufheben.

Never, *adv.* nie, niemals, nimmer; (in no degree) auf keine Weise, ganz und gar nicht; — so, auch noch so, so sehr auch; be he — so bad, sei er auch noch so schlecht; — more, nimmermehr; — fear! nur nicht ängstlich! — to be mistaken, unverkennbar. **—theless,** *conj.* nichtsdestoweniger. *Comp.* **—-ceasing,** *adj.* unaufhörlich. **—-dying,** *adj.* unsterblich. **—-ending,** *adj.* unendlich. **—-fading,** *adj.* unverwelklich. **—-failing,** *adj.* unfehlbar; (sure) untrüglich; nie versiegend.

New, I. *v.a.* neu; frisch; neu erschienen (*book*); (modern) neu, modern; (inexperienced) unerfahren, ungeübt; to turn over a — leaf, sich bessern, ein neues Leben anfangen; — to the work, in der Arbeit ungeübt; to carry to a — account, aufs neue vortragen, übertragen; this is something — to me, dies ist mir etwas Neues; — bread, frisches Brot; — style, neue Zeitrechnung; — woman, emanzipierte Frau; die emanzipierte Frauenwelt. II. *adv.* (*gen'lly in comp.*) soeben. **—ly,** *adv.* neulich, jüngst, neu. **—ness,** *s.* die Neuheit; die Unerfahrenheit; —ness of life, ein neues Leben (*B.*). **—s,** *s.* die Nachricht, Neuigkeit(en); (something —) das Neue; what 's the —s? was giebt's Neues? a piece of —s, eine Neuigkeit; good —s, erfreuliche Nachricht(en); we have had —s that . . ., wir haben erfahren *or* gehört, daß . . . *Comp.* **—-born,** *adj.* neu geboren. **—-comer,** *s.* der Ankömmling. **—fangled,** *adj.* neuerungssüchtig; (novel) neugebacken; neumodisch; —fangled notions, nagelneue Ideen. **—-found,** *adj.* neu erfunden. **—-laid,** *adj.*; —-laid eggs, frische Eier. **—-model,** *v.a.* umformen. **—-mown,** *adj.* frisch gemäht. **—s-agent,** *s.* der Zeitungsverkäufer. **—s-boy,** *s.* der Zeitungsausträger; (seller) der Zeitungsverkäufer. **—smonger,** *s.* der Neuigkeitskrämer. **—spaper,** I. *s.* die Zeitung. II *attrib.*; —spaper German, das Zeitungsdeutsch; —spaper report, der Zeitungsbericht, die Zeitungsnachricht. **—s-room,** *s.* das Lesezimmer. **—s-vender,** *s.* der Zeitungsverkäufer. **—s-writer,** *s.* der Zeitungsschreiber. **—-Year's,** *attrib.*; —-Year's Day, der Neujahrstag; —-Year's eve, der Sylvesterabend; —-Year's gift, das Neujahrsgeschenk.

Newel, *s.* der Wendelbaum, die Spille, Spindel.

Newt, *s.* der Molch, die Sumpfeidechse.

Next, I. *adj.* nächst; the — day, den Tag darauf; the week after —, die übernächste Woche; — to, nächst, erst nach; (approaching) dicht an (*dat.*), nahe bei, grenzend an (*acc.*); — door, neben an; — door to, nahe bei; (almost) fast; — to nothing, fast (gar) nichts; — of kin, der nächste Verwandte; — time, ein andermal; better luck — time, mehr Glück das nächste Mal! II. *adv.* (zu)nächst, gleich darauf; what —? und dann? hernach? weiter? III. *prep.* nächst, bei, an.

Nib, *s.* der Schnabel (*of birds*) (*obs.*); die Spitze (*of a pen*); die Schreibfeder, (Stahl-)Feder (*coll.*); der Griff (*of a scythe*); cocoa —s, das grobe Pulver aus enthülsten Kakaobohnen. **—bed,** *adj.* mit einer Spitze.

Nibble, I. *v.a.* (be)nagen, beknabbern, beknappern; (eat in little bits) langsam essen; (in kleinen Bissen) fressen, abweiden (*as sheep*); anbeißen (*as fish*); erhaschen (*sl.*). II. *v.n.* weiden; nagen, knabbern. III. *s.* das Anbeißen, Nagen. **—r,** *s.* der Benager, Anbeißende.

Nice, *adj.*, **—ly,** *adv.* niedlich, hübsch, nett, artig, einnehmend (*in appearance*); wohlschmeckend, köstlich (*as food*); lecker; (fastidious) wählerisch, heikel; genau, regelrecht (*as proportions, workmanship*); (difficult) schwierig, kitzelig; (exact) genau, pünktlich; (delicate) geläutert, fein, scharf; (subtile) subtil, scharf beurteilend, spitzfindig; (scrupulous) skrupulös, bedenklich; he is more — than wise, er übertreibt die Vorsicht; he is very — in his food, er ist sehr eigen *or* lecker im Essen; a — point, ein kitzliger Punkt; — eye (for), scharfes Auge; a person of — taste, eine Person von feinem, geläutertem Geschmack; — discernment, scharfes Beurteilungsvermögen. **—ness,** *s.* die Feinheit, Zartheit (*of taste*); die Schärfe (*of judgment*); die Genauigkeit, Pünktlichkeit; (overfastidiousness) die Ziererei; die Niedlichkeit, Annehmlichkeit, Anmut. **—ty,** *s.* die Feinheit, Schärfe; (exactness) die Genauigkeit, Pünktlichkeit; (— distinction) die Subtilität, Spitzfindigkeit; to a —ty, bis aufs Haar; not to stand upon —ties, fünf gerade sein lassen, es nicht so genau nehmen

Niche, *s.* die Nische, Wandvertiefung.

[1]**Nick,** *s.* der Nix; Old —, der Böse, Teufel.

[2]**Nick,** I. *s.* der Einschnitt, die Kerbe; der höchste Wurf (*at dice*); der Unterschnitt (*Typ.*); der Einschnitt (*in the head of a screw*); in the — of time, gerade zur rechten Zeit, gerade recht, wie gerufen. II. *v.a.* (ein)kerben, einschneiden; anglisieren (*a horse*); betrügen um (*sl.*). **—-nack,** *s.* die Nippsache, der wertlose Tand. **—-stick,** *s.* das Kerbholz.

Nickel, I. *s.* das Nickel. II. *attrib.* aus Nickel bestehend, vernickelt. III. *v.a.* vernickeln. *Comp.* **—-plating,** *s.* die Vernickelung. **—-silver,** *s.* das Neusilber.

Nickname, I. *s.* der Spitzname. II. *v.a.* einen Spitznamen geben; fälschlich benennen; **—d** by us, der bei uns den Spitznamen führte.

Nicoti—an, *adj.* Tabak betreffend. **—ne,** *s.* das Nikotin.

Nict(it)—ate, *s.* blinzeln, die Augen auf- und zumachen; —(it)ating membrane, die Blinzhaut.

Niece, *s.* die Nichte; die Enkelin (*obs.*).

Niggard, I. *s.* der Geizhals, Knicker; be a — of advice! sei sparsam mit Ratschlägen! II. *adj.*, **—ly,** *adj. & adv.* geizig (of, in, mit); (sparing) karg; —ly doings, die Knauserei, Filzigkeit. **—liness,** *s.* die Kargheit, Knauserei, Filzigkeit.

Nigger, *s.* der Neger, Schwarze; to work like a —, arbeiten wie ein Pferd.

Nigh, I. *adj.* (—er, next) nah; sick — unto death, totkrank. II. *adv.* nahe; (well- —) beinahe, fast; to draw —, sich nähern. III. *prep.* neben.

Night, *s.* die Nacht, der Abend; die Nacht, Dunkelheit (*fig.*); to- —, heute abend; by —, in the —, nachts, bei Nacht, des Nachts; — after —, jeden Abend, jede Nacht; good- —, guten Abend; gute Nacht; to make a — of it, die ganze Nacht durchschwelgen, durchtoben; to stay all — in a place, an einem Orte die ganze Nacht bleiben *or* übernachten. **—ingale**, *s.* die Nachtigall; Invalidenbettjacke; the —ingale sings, die Nachtigall schlägt. **—less**, *adj.* nachtlos. **—ly**, I. *adj.* nächtlich, Nacht-; —ly revels, Nachtvergnügungen. II. *adv.* jede Nacht, alle Nächte. **—mare**, *s.* der Alp; das Schreckbild im Traum. *Comp.* **—-bell**, *s.* die Nachtglocke. **—-bolt**, *s.* der Nachtriegel. **—-cap**, *s.* die Nachtmütze; der Schlaftrunk (*sl.*). **—-clothes**, *s.* das Nachtzeug. **—-dress**, **—-gown**, das Nachtkleid, Nachthemd (einer Frau). **—-express**, *s.* der Nachtschnellzug. **—fall**, *s.* der Einbruch der Nacht. **—-jar**, *s.* der Ziegenmelker. **—-light**, *s.* das Nachtlicht. **—-long**, I. *adj.* eine Nacht dauernd, nachtlang. II. *adv.* die Nacht hindurch. **—-porter**, *s.* der Nachtpförtner (eines Gasthauses). **—-school**, *s.* die Abendschule. **—-shade**, *s.* der Nachtschatten (*Bot.*). **—-shirt**, *s.* das Nachthemd (eines Mannes). **—-soil**, *s.* der Inhalt der Abtritte. **—-stool**, *s.* der Nachtstuhl. **—-time**, *s.* die Nachtzeit. **—-watch**, *s.* die Nachtwache. **—-watchman**, *s.* der Nachtwächter. **—-work**, *s.* die Nachtarbeit.

Nihili—sm, *s.* der Nihilismus. **—st**, *s.* der Nihilist. **—stic**, *adj.* nihilistisch, umstürzlerisch. **—ty**, *s.* die Nichtigkeit, das Nichtssein.

Nil, *pron. & s.* nichts; leer, vakat (*C. L.*).

Nill, *v.a. & n.* nicht wollen, abschlagen (*obs.*); willy- —y, er mag wollen oder nicht.

Nimbl—e, *adj.*, **—y**, *adv.* flink, gewandt, hurtig, flüchtig. **—eness**, *s.* die Behendigkeit, Gewandtheit. *Comp.* **—e-footed**, *adj.* schnellfüßig.

Nimbus, *s.* die Strahlenkrone, der Heiligenschein, Nimbus; (cloud) die Regenwolke.

Nincompoop, *s.* der Tropf, Einfaltspinsel (*fam.*).

Nin—e, I. *num. adj.* neun; —e days' wonder, ein Hauptereignis. II. *s.;* the (sacred) —e, die neun Schwestern, die neun Musen. **—eteen**, *num. adj.* neunzehn. **—etieth**, *adj.* neunzigst. **—ety**, *num. adj.* neunzig. **—th**, I. *adj.* neunt. II. *s.* die None (*Mus.*). **—thly**, *adv.* neuntens. *Comp.* **—efold**, *adj.* neunfach. **—e-pins**, *s.* die Kegel (*pl.*); das Kegelspiel; to play at —e-pins, Kegel schieben, kegeln. **—e-score**, *adj.* neunmal 20.

Ninny, *s.* der Tropf, Pinsel, Einfaltspinsel (*fam.*).

[1]**Nip**, I. *v.a.* kneipen, zwicken, klemmen; durch Frost beschädigen, töten; schneiden (*as a wind*); to — off, abkneipen; to — in the bud, im Keime ersticken; —ped by the ice, vom Eise eingeschlossen. II. *s.* der Knipp, Zwick, Biß; der Frostbrand. **—per**, *s.* der Spötter (*obs.*); junger Bursch (*coll.*); der Vorderzahn (*of a horse*); die Kralle, Klaue (*of a bird*); die Schere (*of a crab*); der Zeising (*Naut.*); —per of the cable, Kabelarzeising. **—ping**, *adj.* **—pingly**, *adv.* beißend, schneidend. **—s**, *pl.* die Beißzange.

[2]**Nip**, *s.* das Schlückchen, das Nippen, der Nipp.

Nipple, *s.* die Brustwarze; der Zündstift, Piston (*Gun.*); das Saughütchen (*of a baby's bottle*). *Comp.* **—-bore**, *s.* der (Zünd-)Kanal. **—-shield**, *s.* der Brustwarzendeckel.

Nipt, *obs. pret. of* [1]Nip.

Nisi prius, *s.* die Vorladung der Geschworenen nach Westminster, falls die Richter nicht vorher die Assisen in der Grafschaft selbst halten; court of —, das Gericht für Zivilklagen, das Grafschaftsgericht.

Nit, *s.* die Niß, Nisse, das Lausei.

Nit—rate, I. *adj.* salpetersauer. II. *s.* salpetersaures Salz; —rate of silver, salpetersaures Silber; —rate of soda, salpetersaures Natron. **—re**, *s.* der (Natron-)Salpeter; spirits of —re, der Salpetergeist. **—ric**, *adj.* salpetersauer; —ric acid, die Salpetersäure. **—rification**, *s.* die Umwandlung in Salpeter. **—rify**, *v.a.* zu Salpeter bilden. **—rite**, *s.* das salpetrigsaure Salz. **—rogen**, I. *s.* der Stickstoff. II. *attrib.;* —rogen gas, das Stick(stoff)gas. **—rogenous**, *adj.* stickstoffhaltig. **—ro-muriatic**, *adj.;* —ro-muriatic acid, die Salpetersalzsäure. **—rous**, *adj.* salpeterig, Salpeter-; —rous oxide, das Stick(stoff)oxydul.

[1]**No.**, *abbr. of* Number.

[2]**No**, I. *adj.* kein; — good books, keine guten Bücher; — man, niemand; — one, keiner, nicht einer; that is — concern of yours, es geht Sie nichts an; by — means, auf keine Weise, keineswegs; — such thing, nichts dergleichen, nichts davon; in — time, in sehr kurzer Zeit. II. *adv.* nein; (not any) nicht; — more, nicht mehr. III. *s.* das Nein; the Ayes and the —es, die Stimmen für und gegen einen Vorschlag; the —es have it, die Mehrheit ist gegen den Vorschlag; der Antrag ist abgelehnt (*Parl.*). **—ne**, *see* None. *Comp.* **—body**, *s.* niemand; der unbedeutende Mensch, Mensch ohne Stand, Herr von Istnichts und Habenichts, die Null. **—way(s)**, *adv.* keineswegs. **—where**, *adv.* nirgend(s), nirgendwo. **—wise**, *adv.* in keiner Weise, auf keine Weise. **—whither**, *adv.* nirgendhin.

[1]**Nob**, *s.* der Kopf (*sl.*).

[2]**Nob**, *s.* der vornehme Herr (*sl.*). **—by**, *adj.* fein; (well dressed) elegant (*sl.*).

Nob—ility, *s.* der Adel; (—le rank) der Adelstand; die Größe, das Edle, Erhabene (*fig.*); —ility of birth, der Geburtsadel; —ility of soul, der Seelenadel. **—le**, *adj.*, **—ly**, *adv.* adelig; vornehm, erlaucht; edel, groß, erhaben (*fig.*); (magnanimous) großmütig; (splendid) prächtig; (excellent) vortrefflich, herrlich; a —le deed, eine edle Tat. II. *s.* der Adelige, Edle; (coin) der (Rose-)Nobel; —s, der Adel (*collect.*). **—leness**, *s.* der Adel, die hohe Geburt, Würde; der Edelsinn, Edelmut (*fig.*); (grandeur) die Erhabenheit, Größe, Würde; —leness of soul, die Seelengröße, Seelenhoheit. **—lesse**, *s.* der Adel; die Adeligen (*of a country*). *Comp.* **—leman**, *s.* der Edelmann, Adelige. **—le-minded**, *adj.* edelgesinnt, von edler, vornehmer Gesinnung. **—lewoman**, *s.* die Edelfrau.

Nocturn, *s.* die Nachtmette; das Notturno (*Mus.*). **—al**, *adj.*, **—ally**, *adv.* nächtlich, Nacht-.

Nod, I. *v.a. & n.* nicken; sich neigen, wogen; to — to s.o., einem zuwinken, einen durch Kopfnicken begrüßen; to — assent, durch Kopfnicken seine Einwilligung zu erkennen geben; to — off, einnicken, einschlafen. II. *s.* das Kopfnicken; (sign) der Wink; to go to the Land of —, schlafen gehen, in Morpheus Arme sinken (*coll.*). **—ding**, I. *adj.* nickend. II. *s.* das Nicken, Schwenken. **—dy**, *s.* der Tropf; die dumme Seeschwalbe (*Orn.*).

Nod—dle, *s.* der Kopf (*in contempt*). **—e**, *s.* der Knoten (*also Surg. & Astr.*); (—al line) die Knotenlinie (*Acoust.*); das Loch (*of a dial*); ascending (descending) —e, auf- (nieder-)steigender Knoten. **—osity**, *s.* das Knotige. **—ular**, *adj.* knotig, Knoten-. **—ule**, *s.* das Knötchen; die Niere (*Geol.*).

Noel, Nowel, I. *s.* die Weihnachten (*pl.*), das Weihnachtsfest; (carol) der Weihnachtsgesang, das Weihnachtslied. II. *interj.* —, —! Weihnacht! Weihnacht!

Nog, I. *v.a.* mit einem Holznagel befestigen; mit Ziegeln aussetzen (*Build.*). II. *s.* der Holznagel; der eingemauerte Holzblock; der Fußbolzen eines Strebers (*Shipb.*). **—gin**, *s.* der kleine (hölzerne) Krug, ein Flüssigkeitsmaß (= ¼ Pint). *Comp.* **—ging-piece**, *s.* der Riegel.

Nois—e, I. *s.* der Lärm, das Geräusch, Getöse;

(humming) das Summen; (roar) das Brausen, Donnern; (outcry) das Geschrei, Aufsehen (*fig.*); he will make a —e in the world, er wird Aufsehen in der Welt erregen. II. *v.a.;* to —e abroad, ausschreien; to be —ed abroad, ruchbar werden. **—eless**, *adj.*, **—elessly**, *adv.* geräuschlos. **—elessness**, *s.* die Geräuschlosigkeit. **—ily**, *adv.* mit Geräusch. **—iness**, *s.* das Geräusch, Getöse, der Lärm; das lärmende Geschrei. **—y**, *adj.* geräuschvoll, lärmend.

Noisome, *adj.* schädlich, ungesund; (disgusting) widerlich. **—ness**, *s.* die Schädlichkeit; die Widrigkeit.

Noli-me-tangere, *s.* das Springkraut, Rührmichnichtan, die gelbe Balsamine.

Nomad, I. *adj.* umherziehend, ohne festen Wohnsitz, unstet, nomadisch. II. *s.* der Nomade. **—ic**, *adj.;* —ic tribe, das Wandervolk, der Nomadenstamm. **—ism**, *s.* der Nomadenzustand.

Nombril, *s.* der Nabel, Schildnabel (*Her.*).

Nomenclat—or, *s.* der Namengeber; der Namenkundige; das Namenverzeichnis. **—ure**, *s.* die Namengebung, das Namenverzeichnis, die Zusammenstellung von Fachausdrücken, die Fachsprache, Nomenklatur.

Nomin—al, *adj.* (titular) Titular-, Nominal-, angeblich, namentlich; (containing names) Namen-; —al value, der Nennwert; —al sum, die Nominalsumme. **—alism**, *s.* der Nominalismus. **—ally**, *adv.* dem Namen nach, angeblich. **—ate**, *v.a.* nennen; (vorläufig) ernennen (*to an office*); (propose) zur Wahl vorschlagen; he was —ated professor, er wurde zum Professor ernannt. **—ation**, *s.* die vorläufige (der Bestätigung bedürftige) Ernennung, die Vorwahl; (right of —ation) das Ernennungsrecht; to be in —ation for, als Kandidat vorgeschlagen sein zu; his —ation to the headmastership, seine Ernennung zum Direktor. **—ative**, I. *adj.;* —ative case, der Nominativ. II. *s.* der Nominativ (*Gram.*). **—ator**, *s.* der Ernenner. **—ee**, *s.* der zur Wahl Vorgeschlagene, der zu einer Stelle (in der Vorwahl) Ernannte; die Person, auf deren Leben eine Rente festgesetzt ist (*C.L.*); die Person, an die ein Gut abgetreten wird (*Law*).

Non— (*in comp.*) **—-acceptance**, *s.* die Nichtannahme (*of a bill*). **—age**, *s.* die Minderjährigkeit. **—-appearance**, *s.* das Nichterscheinen. **—-arrival**, *s.* das Ausbleiben, Nichteintreffen. **—-attendance**, *s.* das Ausbleiben. **—-collegiate**, *adj.* keinem College angehörig. **—-combatant**, *s.* der Nichtkämpfer. **—-commissioned**, *adj.* nicht bevollmächtigt; ohne Bestallung; —-commissioned officer, der Unteroffizier. **—-committal**, I. *adj.* nicht bindend. II. *s.* freie Hand. **—-communicant**, *s.* eine Person, die noch nie kommuniziert hat. **—-compliance**, *s.* die Nichterfüllung; (refusal) die Weigerung. **—-comp(os-mentis)**, *adj.* nicht bei gesundem Verstande, unzurechnungsfähig. **—-conducting**, *adj.* nicht leitend. **—-conductor**, *s.* der Nichtleiter. **—conformist**, *s.* der englische Dissident. **—conformity**, *s.* die Ungleichförmigkeit; die Abweichung von der anglikanischen Kirche (*Rel.*). **—-contagious**, *adj.* nicht ansteckend. **—-content**, *s.* der mit Nein Stimmende. **—-delivery**, *s.* die Nichtabgabe. **—descript**, *adj.* unbeschrieben, nicht leicht zu beschreiben; unbestimmt; seltsam. **—entity**, *s.* das Nichtige, Eingebildete, Nichtding; (nobody) der unbedeutende Mensch. **—-essential**, I. *adj.* unwesentlich, nicht unbedingt notwendig. II. *s.* das nicht wesentliche Ding. **—-established**, *adj.* nicht vom Staate unterstützt. **—-existence**, *s.* das Nicht(da)sein. **—-existent**, *adj.* nicht vorhanden, nicht existierend. **—-feasance**, *s.* pflichtwidrige Unterlassung (*Law*). **—-fulfilment**, *s.* die Nichterfüllung. **—-interference**, *s.* die Nichteinmischung. **—juring**, *adj.* eidverweigernd, eidablehnend; —juring party, die Eidverweigerer, englische Jakobiten. **—juror**, *s.* der Eidverweigerer. **—-observance**, *s.* die Nicht-beobachtung, -erfüllung. **—pareil**, *s.* das Unvergleichliche, Muster; die Perlschrift (*Typ.*). **—-payment**, *s.* die Nichtzahlung. **—-performance**, *s.* die Nichtvollziehung. **—plus**, *v.a.* verblüffen, in Verlegenheit setzen, in die Enge treiben (*coll.*). **—-poisonous**, *adj.* giftfrei; unschädlich. **—-resident**, *adj.* abwesend (von dem amtlichen Wohnorte, von seinen Gütern); —-resident member (of a club or society), auswärtiges Mitglied. **—sense**, *see* Nonsense. **—-smoking**, *adj.;* —-smoking compartment, die Abteilung für Nichtraucher. **—such**, *see* None. **—suit**, I. *s.* die Aufhebung, Zurückweisung einer Klage. II. *v.a.* wegen eines Mangels in der Prozedur einem Rechtsgange entziehen, zur Aufhebung einer Klage verurteilen, vor Gericht abweisen.

Non—agenarian, I. *adj.* neunzigjährig. II. *s.* der Neunzigjährige. **—agesimal**, *adj.* neunzigster Grad der Ekliptik. **—agon**, *s.* das Neuneck. **—es**, *pl.* die Nonen.

Nonce, *s.;* for the —, dies Mal, für dies eine Mal, für den Fall, für den Augenblick.

Nonchalan—ce, *s.* die Fahrlässigkeit, Saumseligkeit; (indifference) die Gleichgültigkeit; die Leichtlebigkeit. **—t**, *adj.*, **—tly**, *adv.* nachlässig, saumselig; gleichgültig; (easy-going) leichtlebig.

None, I. *adj.* kein. II. *pron.* keiner, keine, keines; it 's — of your business, es geht Sie nichts an; — of them, keiner von ihnen; it 's — of the best, es ist keines von den besten. III. *adv.* nicht im Geringsten; — the less, nichtsdestoweniger. *Comp.* **—such**, *s.* das Unvergleichliche; (apple) der Nonpareilapfel.

Non liquet, *v. imp.* es ist nicht klar (*Law*).

Nonsens—e, I. *s.* der Unsinn, das dumme Zeug. II. *attrib.;* —e verses, sinnlose, aber in Bezug auf Versmaß korrekte Verse. **—ical**, *adj.*, **—ically**, *adv.* unsinnig, sinnlos; (silly) albern.

Noodle, *s.* der Tropf, Einfaltspinsel (*coll.*).

Nook, *s.* der Winkel, die Ecke.

Noon, *s.* der Mittag. *Comp.* **—day**, **—tide**, I. *s.* der Mittag. II. *adj.* mittägig; clear as the —, klar wie der Tag, sonnenklar.

Noose, *s.* die Schleife, Schlinge, der Laufknoten; der Fallstrick (*fig.*).

Nor, *conj.* noch; auch nicht; neither . . . —, weder . . . noch; — I either, ich auch nicht; — . . . —. . ., weder . . . noch . . .

Norm, *s.* das Muster, die Regel, Richtschnur, Norm. **—al**, *adj.*, **—ally**, *adv.* normal, vorschriftsmäßig, regelrecht; senkrecht (*Geom.*); —al day, der Normaltag, normale Arbeitstag; —al school, das Lehrerseminar; —al time, die Einheitszeit. **—alize**, *v.a.* regeln, gleichmachen, normalisieren.

North, I. *s.* der Norden, der Nord (*poet.*); — by east, Nord zum Osten. II. *adj. & adv.* nördlich; — Pole, der Nordpol; — star, der Nordstern; — wind, der Nordwind. **—erly**, *adj. & adv.* nördlich. **—ern**, *adj.* nordisch, nördlich; —ern China, Nordchina; —ern lights, das Nordlicht. **—erner**, *s.* der nördlich Wohnende. **—ernmost**, *adj.* am nördlichsten gelegen. **—ing**, *s.* die Bewegung, der Abstand von dem Äquator nordwärts (*Astr.*); die nördliche Richtung, der Weg nach Nord(en) (*Naut.*). **—ward**, I. *adj.* nördlich. II. *adv.* (*also* —wards) nordwärts. *Comp.* **—-east**, I. *s.* der Nordost(en). II. *adj. & adv.*, **—-eastern**, *adj.*, **—-easterly**, *adj. & adv.* nordöstlich; —-east by —, Nordost zum Norden. **—-easter**, *s.* der Nordostwind. **—man**, *s.* der Skandinavier. **—-west**, I. *s.* der Nordwest. II. *adj. & adv.*, **—-western**, *adj.*, **—-westerly**, *adj. & adv.* nordwestlich.

Nose, *s.* die Nase; (point) das Ende, die Spitze; (nozzle) die Röhre; under a p.'s very —, einem vor der Nase; a flat —, eine Stumpfnase; to follow one's —, immer der Nase nach gehen, gerade ausgehen; to cut off one's — to spite one's face, sich die Rache allzu viel kosten lassen (*coll.*); to lead by the —, bei der Nase herumführen; to put a p.'s — out of joint, einen ausstechen; to thrust one's — into, seine Nase stecken in (*acc.*); to turn up one's — at, die Nase über (eine S.) rümpfen. **—d**, *adj.* nasig. *Comp.* **—-bag**, *s.* der Futterbeutel für Pferde. **—-band**, *s.* der Nasenriemen (*Saddl.*). **—gay**, *s.* der Blumenstrauß, das Sträußchen.

Nos—e, *see* Nose. **—ing**, *s.* die Nase, der hervorstehende Teil (*Build.*); der Sims (of stairs). **—tril**, *s.* das Nasenloch, die Nüster.

Nosology, *s.* die Krankheitslehre.

Nostalgi—a, *s.* das Heimweh. **—c**, *adj.* Heimweh=; —c pains, der Heimwehschmerz.

Nostrum, *s.* das Geheimmittel.

Not, *adv.* nicht; I could — but, ich konnte nicht umhin (zu); — that I am — satisfied, nicht als ob ich nicht zufrieden wäre. **—withstanding**, I. *prep.* ungeachtet (*gen.*), trotz (*gen. dat.*). II. *conj.* dessen ungeachtet, trotzdem.

Not—able, I. *adj.*, **—ably**, *adv.* bemerkenswert, merklich, merkwürdig; (important) ansehnlich, wichtig, ausgezeichnet, hervorragend; —able housewife, fleißige, sorgsame Hausfrau. II. *s.* die angesehene, vornehme Person; die Standesperson, Notabilität; der Notabel (*of France*). **—ableness**, *s.* die Merkwürdigkeit, Wichtigkeit; (industry) der Fleiß, die Emsigkeit. **—arial**, *adj.* notarisch, Notariats=; (done by a —ary) von einem Notar ausgefertigt, beglaubigt; —arial seal, das Notariatssiegel. **—ary**, *s.* der Notar(ius); —ary public, öffentlicher Notar. **—ation**, *s.* die Aufzeichnung; die Bezeichnung (*Arith.*, *Geom.*); die Bezifferung (*Mus.*); die Zeichensprache, Terminologie (*Chem.*); arithmetical —ation, das Zahlensystem. **—e**, I. *s.* (notice) die Notiz; (memorandum) die Anmerkung, Note; (marginal —e) die Randglosse; (letter) das Briefchen, Billet; die Note (*Dipl.*, *Mus.*); (information) die Kunde, Nachricht; (bill) die Rechnung; der Ton, Gesang (*of birds*); —es, die Notizen; biographical —es, biographische Mitteilungen; lecture —es, Kollegheft; to take good —es of a lecture, eine Vorlesung gut nachschreiben; —e of interrogation, das Fragezeichen; —e of the course of exchange, der Geldkurszettel; —e of hand, promissory —e, der eigene (trockene) Wechsel, Handschuldschein; to take —e of, sich (*dat.*) (etwas) merken; to compare —es on a subject, über eine S. seine Ansichten austauschen, sich über eine S. beraten. II. *v.a.* bezeichnen; (—e down) aufschreiben, anmerken, notieren; (—ice) Notiz nehmen von, merken auf (*acc.*), bemerken; notieren (*a bill*); a bill —ed for protest, ein protestierter Wechsel. **—ed**, *adj.* berühmt, ausgezeichnet; (bad) berüchtigt. **—edly**, *adv. see* —ed; besonders; deutlich. **—er**, *s.* der Anmerker, Aufschreiber. *Comp.* **—e-book**, *s.* das Merkbuch, Taschenbuch, Notizbuch; (sketchbook) das Skizzenbuch. **—e-forger**, *s.* der Banknotenfälscher. **—e-paper**, *s.* das dicke Briefpapier. **—e-worthy**, *adj.* bemerkenswert, merkwürdig.

Notch, I. *s.* die Kerbe, der Einschnitt, Ausschnitt. II. *v.a.* kerben, einschneiden; —ed leaves, ausgezackte Blätter. *Comp.* **—weed**, *s.* die Melde.

Nothing, I. *pron.* & *s.* nichts; das Nichts, die Kleinigkeit; to come to —, zu nichte *or* zu Wasser werden; to make — of, sich (*dat.*) nichts aus (einer Sache) machen; mit (einer S.) nichts anfangen können; good for —, untauglich; for —, umsonst; he does — but . . ., er tut nichts als . . .; it will come to —, daraus wird nichts; — venture, — have, frisch gewagt ist halb gewonnen (*prov.*); — of a gentleman, keineswegs ein feiner, gebildeter Herr; — to what . . ., nichts im Vergleich zu . . .; — short of, geradezu, wirklich; Greek art was — short of a miracle, die griechische Kunst war geradezu ein Wunder; that is — to me, das ist mir ganz gleichgültig. II. *adv.* keineswegs; — like so . . ., bei weitem nicht so . . . **—ness**, *s.* (nihility) das Nichts, Nichtdasein; die Nichtigkeit.

Not—ice, I. *s.* (observation) die Beobachtung, Bemerkung; (intimation) die Notiz, Nachricht, Kunde, Anzeige; (—ice to leave) die Kündigung; (warning) die Warnung; (report) der Bericht, die Berichterstattung; (attention) die Aufmerksamkeit, höfliche Behandlung; at a moment's —ice, zu jeder Minute, jeden Augenblick; to avoid —ice, um Aufsehen zu vermeiden; to give s. o. —ice, einem kündigen, den Dienst aufkündigen; —ice to quit, die Aufkündigungsanzeige, Kündigung; she gave me —ice for Easter, sie hat mir auf Ostern gekündigt; Mr. X. has given —ice of a bill, Herr X. hat die Einbringung eines Gesetzentwurfs angekündigt; to receive —ice, Nachricht bekommen; to take —ice of a th. (a p.), etwas bemerken, Notiz von einer Sache (einer Person) nehmen, (eine Person beachten); take no —ice of it, beachte es nicht, laß dir nichts merken; take —ice that, kund und zu wissen sei hiermit; until further —ice, bis auf Weiteres. II. *v.a.* wahrnehmen, bemerken; sehen; (mention) bemerken, erwähnen; mit Aufmerksamkeit behandeln (*a person*). **—iceable**, *adj.*, **—iceably**, *adv.* merklich, zu bemerken; bemerkenswert. **—ification**, *s.* die Anzeige, Bekanntmachung, Bekanntgebung, Meldung; (sign) der Wink; die eine Anzeige enthaltende Schrift. **—ify**, *v.a.* anzeigen, kund tun, bekannt geben, melden. **—ion**, *see* Notion. *Comp.* **—ice-board**, *s.* das schwarze Brett, die Anschlagetafel.

Notion, *s.* der Begriff, die Vorstellung, Idee; (opinion) die Meinung, Idee; (intention) das Vorhaben, die Absicht; airy —s, leere Einfälle; I have a — that . . ., ich denke mir, bilde mir ein, daß . . .; I had no — that . . ., ich hatte keine Ahnung, daß . . . **—al**, *adj.* Begriffs=, Verstandes=; eingebildet, imaginär.

Notori—ety, *s.* die Offenkundigkeit, Kundbarkeit; die weitbekannte Sache *or* Persönlichkeit; an unenviabl —ety, eine nicht beneidenswerte Berühmtheit. **—ous**, *adj.*, **—ously**, *adv.* allgemein bekannt, weltbekannt, notorisch; (infamous) berüchtigt. **—ousness**, *s.* die Offenkundigkeit.

Nought, *s. see* Naught; die Null (*Arith.*); to set at —, in den Wind schlagen.

Noun, *s.* das Nomen, Nennwort; common, proper —, der Gattungs=, Eigen=name.

Nourish, *v.a.* nähren; ernähren, erhalten (*fig.*); (support) unterhalten; (cherish) pflegen, hegen; (bring up) aufziehen, erziehen; (strengthen) kräftigen, stärken. **—er**, *s.* der, die, das Ernährende, der Besorger. **—ing**, I. *adj.* nahrhaft. **—ment**, *s.* die Nahrung, das Nahrungsmittel.

Nous, *s.* der Verstand (*Philos.*); der Mutterwitz.

Nov—el, I. *adj.* neu; (strange) ungewöhnlich. II. *s.* der Roman; short —el, die Novelle; very short —el, die Novellette. —el with a purpose, Tendenzroman; idyllic —el, die Dorfgeschichte; psychological —el, Bildungsroman. **—elist**, *s.* der Romanschriftsteller; der Novellenschreiber; **—elty**, *s.* die Neuheit. **—ice**, *s.* der Neuling, Lehrling, Anfänger; der Noviz(e), die Novize (*in a convent, etc.*); der Neubekehrte (*B.*). **—iciate**, *s.* die Prüfungs=, Probe=zeit, das Noviziat; (apprenticeship) der Lehrlingsstand.

Nove—mber, *s.* der November. **—nary**, *adj.* zur Zahl neun gehörig. **—nnial**, *adj.* neunjährig.

Now, *adv.* nun, jetzt, gegenwärtig; eben; bald; — I am happy, jetzt bin ich glücklich; — let us go! nun wollen wir gehen! just —, soeben; — this — that, bald dies, bald jenes; — and then, dann und wann, hie und da, gelegentlich; — at length, jetzt endlich; — for them! jetzt mögen sie kommen! before —, schon einmal; — that, jetzt da, jetzt wo; — that the day has come, nun, da der Tag gekommen ist; — that I have money, jetzt, wo ich Geld habe; — then, nun! wohlan! **—adays**, *adv.* heutzutage.

Nowel, *see* Noel.
Noxious, *adj.*, **—ly**, *adv.* schädlich, verderblich. **—ness**, *s.* die Schädlichkeit.
Nozzle, *s.* die Schnauze, Nase, der Rüssel.
Nuance, *s.* die Farbenabstufung, Nuance, der Anflug (von), Stich (ins).
Nubil—e, *adj.* mannbar. **—ity**, *s.* die Mannbarkeit, die Heiratsfähigkeit.
Nucleoplasm, *s.* der Zell-Kernsaft.
Nucleus, *s.* der Kern.
Nud—e, *adj.* nackt, bloß; nichtig, ungültig (*Law*); the —e, die nackte menschliche Gestalt (*Paint.*); from the —e, nach einem Modell. **—ities**, *pl.* nackte Körperteile; nackte Figuren (*Paint.*). **—ity**, *s.* die Nacktheit, Blöße.
Nudge, I. *s.* leichter Stoß mit dem Ellbogen, der Rippenstoß. II. *v.a.* leicht mit dem Ellbogen anstoßen, einen Rippenstoß geben.
Nugatory, *adj.* albern, kindisch, nichtig; (ineffectual) ungültig, unwirksam.
Nugget, *s.* der Goldklumpen.
Nuisance, *s.* etwas Lästiges, Anstößiges, Nachteiliges; der Skandal; die Pest; a public —, ein öffentliches Ärgernis, ein öffentlicher Skandal; commit no —, vor Verunreinigung dieses Platzes wird gewarnt; to be indicted for a —, wegen eines dem öffentlichen oder Privat-Wohl schädlichen Vergehens angeklagt werden; this man is a — to society, dieser Mann ist eine Pest der Gesellschaft.
Null, *adj.* nichtig; to declare — and void, für null und nichtig, für ungültig erklären. **—ification**, *s.* die Aufhebung, Vernichtung, das Ungültigmachen; die Nichtigkeitserklärung (*Amer.*). **—ifier**, *s.* der Aufheber, Vernichter. **—ify**, *v.a.* vernichten, aufheben; für nichtig erklären. **—ity**, *s.* die Nichtigkeit, Ungültigkeit.
Numb, I. *adj.* erstarrt, starr, empfindungslos; — with cold, starr vor Kälte. II. *v.a.* erstarren. **—ness**, *s.* die Erstarrung, Betäubung.
Number, I. *s.* die Zahl (*also Gram.*); (multitude) die Menge, Schar; (numerousness) die Menge, Anzahl; das Heft, die Lieferung (*of a work*); die Nummer (*of a ticket*); even (odd) —, gerade (ungerade) Zahl; singular (plural) —, Einzahl (Mehrzahl); — of seats, die Anzahl der Plätze; a — of, mehrere; a great — of, eine große Anzahl von, viele. II. *v.a.* zählen, rechnen; numerieren (*houses, etc.*); to — with, rechnen zu, unter. **—less**, *adj.* zahllos. **—s**, *pl.* der Rhythmus (*Poet.*); die Verse (*fig.*); Numeri, das vierte Buch Mosis (*B.*); published in —s, in Lieferungen, heftweise erscheinend; in large —s, in großen Mengen, in Scharen.
Numbles, *pl.* das Hirsch-Gescheide.
Numer—able, *adj.* zählbar. **—al**, I. *adj.* eine Zahl anzeigend, bezeichnend, Zahl-. II. *s.* das Zahlzeichen, die Ziffer; (—al word) das Zahlwort. **—ation**, *s.* das Zählen; das Zahlenschreiben, -aussprechen, -lesen (*Arith.*). **—ator**, *s.* der Zähler (*of a fraction*). **—ical**, *adj.* numerisch, Zahlen-, Zahl-; to have the —ical superiority, (einem) an Zahl überlegen sein. **—ically**, *adv.* der Zahl nach. **—ous**, *adj.*, **—ously**, *adv.* zahlreich; meeting —ously attended, zahlreich besuchte Versammlung. **—ousness**, *s.* die Menge, Anzahl, große Zahl.
Numismat—ic, *adj.* numismatisch, Münzen betreffend, Münz-. **—ics**, *s.* die Münzkunde. **—ology**, *s.* die Münzwissenschaft, Münzkunde.
Nummulite, *s.* der Linsenstein, Nummulit.
Numskull, *s.* der Dummkopf (*fam.*).
Nun, *s.* die Nonne, Klosterfrau; die Blaumeise (*Orn.*). **—nery**, *s.* das Nonnenkloster.
Nunci—ature, *s.* die päpstliche Gesandtschaft, Nuntiatur. **—o**, *s.* der päpstliche Gesandte, der Nuntius.
Nuncupat—ive, **—ory**, *adj.* mündlich nennend, erklärend; —ory will, mündliche letztwillige Verfügung *or* Verordnung.
Nuptial, *adj.* hochzeitlich, Hochzeits-, ehelich: — bed, das Brautbett; — benediction, die Einsegnung der Ehe, die Trauung; — ceremony, die Trauung, die Trauungsfeierlichkeit; — repast, der Hochzeitsschmaus; — rites, die Trauungsgebräuche. **—s**, *pl.* die Hochzeit.
Nurs—e, I. *s.* die Kinderwärterin, Kindsmagd, das Kindermädchen; (wet —) die Amme; (foster mother) die Pflegemutter; sick —e, die Krankenwärterin; trained —e, die gelernte Krankenwärterin, die Schwester; monthly —e, eine Sechswochenfrau; male —, der Krankenwärter. II. *v.a.* säugen, stillen (*an infant*); (rear) aufziehen; pflegen (*the sick, etc.*); (take on the lap) auf den Schoß nehmen; klug, sparsam verwalten (*one's resources, etc.*); to —e a cold, wegen einer Erkältung das Zimmer hüten; to —e one's leg, das eine Bein über das andere schlagen; to put out to —, in die Pflege geben, zur Amme tun; (an estate, ein Gut) sequestrieren lassen; to be at —, in Pflege sein; verpfändet sein. **—er**, *s.* der Pfleger. **—ery** I. *s.* die Kinderstube; die Pflanz-, Baum-schule (*Hort.*); die Pflegeanstalt, Pflanzschule (*fig.*). II. *attrib.*; —ery rhyme, der Kinderreim; —ery rhymes, Kinderlieder, Kinderliedchen. **—ing**, I. *s.* die Pflege; Krankenpflege; district —ing, —ing of the sick poor, die Armen-Krankenpflege. II. *adj.*; —ing bottle, die Saugflasche; a —ing mother of heroes, eine Nährmutter von Helden. **—ling**, *s.* der Säugling, Pflegling; (pet) der Liebling. *Comp.* **—e-maid**, *s.* das Kindermädchen. **—ery-governess**, *s.* die Erzieherin für kleine Kinder, das Kinderfräulein. **—ery-man**, *s.* der Kunstgärtner; der Blumenzüchter.
Nurture, I. *s.* die Nahrung; die Erziehung, Bildung (*fig.*). II. *v.a.* nähren; er-, auf-ziehen; —d in the belief . . ., in dem Glauben auferzogen.
Nut, I. *s.* die Nuß (*also Mech., Naut., Gun.*); (screw —) die Schraubenmutter; die Schraubenhülse (*Print.*); der Frosch (*on a violin-bow*); axle —, Achsbüchsenschraubenmutter; to give s.o. a — to crack, einem eine harte Nuß zu knacken geben. II. *v.a.* Nüsse sammeln, suchen. **—s**, *pl.* Nußkohlen (*Min.*); Muttern; to crack —s, Nüsse knacken; this news will be —s to him, diese Nachricht wird ihm recht behagen (*sl.*); to be —s upon a p., auf einem versessen sein (*sl.*). **—ting**, I. *s.* das Nüssesammeln. II. *p.*; to go —ting, in die Nüsse gehen. **—ty**, *adj.* nußreich; nußartig. *Comp.* **—brown**, *adj.* nußbraun. **—cracker**, *s.* die Nußkrähe (*Orn.*); (pair of) —crackers, der Nußknacker. **—gall**, *s.* der Gallapfel. **—hatch**, **—pecker**, *s.* die Spechtmeise. **—shell**, *s.* die Nußschale; in a —shell, in sehr kleinem Raum; in knappster Form, in aller Kürze (*fig.*). **—tree**, *s.* der Nußbaum. **—wood**, *s.* das Nußbaumholz.
Nutation, *s.* das Wanken, Schwanken der Erdaxe; das Steigen der Pflanzen zur Sonne.
Nutmeg, I. *s.* die Muskatnuß. II. *attrib.*; —meg grater, das Muskatnußreibeisen, die Muskatnußraspel; —meg tree, der Muskatnußbaum.
Nutri—ment, *s.* die Nahrung, das Futter. **—tion**, *s.* die Ernährung; (aliment) die Nahrung. **—tious**, **—tive**, *adj.* nahrhaft, nährend. **—tiousness**, **—tiveness**, *s.* die Nahrhaftigkeit.
Nux vomica, *s.* die Brechnuß; der Brechnußbaum.
Nylghau, *s.* das Nylgau.
Nymph, *s.* die Nymphe; das Mädchen (*fig.*). **—omania**, *s.* die Mannstollheit, Nymphomanie. *Comp.* **—like**, *adj.* nymphenhaft.

O

[1]**O, o**, I. *s.* O, o; die Null (*Arith.*); das Ach; *for abbreviations see the Index at the end of the English-German part.* II. *int.* O! ach! O me! O weh! wehe mir!
[2]**O'**, *abbr. of* Of; Bezeichnung der Abkunft vor irischen Eigennamen, z. B. O'Connor, Connors Sohn *or* Abkömmling.

Oaf, *s.* see Changeling· der Dummkopf, Einfaltspinsel. **—ish**, *adj.* dumm, tölpelhaft.
Oak, *s.* die Eiche, der Eichbaum; common *or* British —, evergreen —, Steineiche; hearts of —, eichenfeste Herzen (*British sailors*); to sport one's —, die äußere Türe seiner Wohnung verschlossen halten (*Univ. sl.*). **—en**, *adj.* eichen. **—ling**, *s.* junge Eiche. *Comp.* **—-bark**, *s.* die Eichenrinde. **—-tree**, *s.* der Eichenbaum.
Oakum, *s.* das Werg; to pick —, Werg zupfen.
Oar, I. *s.* das Ruder; der Riemen (*Naut.*); die Malzkrücke (*Brew.*); bank of —s, die Ruderbank; to ship (unship) the —s, die Riemen klar machen (sie aus den Dollen nehmen); to lie on the —s, aufhören zu rudern; to rest on one's —s, feiern, müßig sein (*fig.*); to put one's — in, sich unberufen einmengen (*fig.*). II. *v.a.* & *n.* rudern. **—ed**, *adj.* mit Rudern; eight-—ed, achtruderig; eight-—ed boat, der Achtriemer. *Comp.* **—-footed**, *adj.* ruderfüßig. **—-lock**, **—-swivel**, *s.* die Rudergabel, Dolle. **—sman**, *s.* der Ruderer.
Oasis, *s.* (*pl.* Oases) die Oase.
Oast, *s.* die Hopfendarre.
Oat, *s.* der Hafer (*Agr.*); (pipe) das Haferrohr. **—en**, *adj.* von Hafer, aus Hafermehl; —en bread, das Haferbrot; —en pipe, die Pfeife aus Haferrohr. **—s**, *pl.* der Hafer; Quaker —s, das Hafermehl; to sow one's wild —s, sich (*dat.*) die Hörner ablaufen. *Comp.* **—-cake**, *s.* der Haferkuchen. **—meal**, *s.* das Hafermehl, die Hafergrütze.
Oath, *s.* der (Eid)Schwur; (blasphemous —) der (gotteslästerliche) Schwur, Fluch; — of supremacy, Supremats-Eid (Anerkennung der Obergewalt des Königs in Kirchensachen); — of allegiance, (*orig.*) der Lehnseid; (*now*) der Huldigungseid, Untertaneneid; to depose on —, eidlich erhärten; by, upon, with an —, eidlich; to administer, tender an — to a p., einem einen Eid zuschieben; to put a p. on his —, einen schwören lassen; to be under an — to, sich eidlich verpflichtet haben; to take an —, einen Eid leisten, einen Schwur ablegen (on *or* to, auf (*acc.*)); to make —, eidlich erhärten; I will take my — that . . ., ich will darauf schwören, daß . . .; military —, der Fahneneid. *Comp.* **—-breaker**, *s.* der Eidbrüchige, Meineidige. **—-breaking**, *s.* der Meineid, Eidbruch. **—-taking**, *s.* die Eidesleistung.
Obdura—cy, *s.* die Verhärtung, Verstocktheit; die Halsstarrigkeit. **—te**, *adj.*, **—tely**, *adv.* verhärtet, verstockt; hartherzig, unbeugsam; (obstinate) halsstarrig; (impenitent) unbußfertig. **—teness**, *s.* die Verstocktheit, Halsstarrigkeit.
Obe—dience, *s.* der Gehorsam. **—dient**, *adj.*, **—diently**, *adv.* gehorsam, folgsam. **—isance**, *s.* die Ehrerbietung; die Verbeugung. **—y**, *v.a.* gehorchen (a p., einem); befolgen (instructions, Vorschriften), Folge leisten (orders, Befehlen); he will be —yed, er verlangt unbedingten Gehorsam.
Obel—isk, *s.* die Spitzsäule, der Obelisk; das Kreuz († *Print.*). **—us**, *s.* das Verweisungszeichen, der Obelus (*Print.*).
Obes—e, *adj.* fettleibig. **—ity**, **—eness**, *s.* die Fettleibigkeit, Feistheit; die Fettsucht.
Obfuscat—e, *v.a.* verdunkeln. **—ion**, *s.* die Verdunkelung, Verfinsterung; die Benebelung (*fig.*).
Obit, *s.* der Tod, das Hinscheiden; das Leichenbegängnis; (service) die Hingangsmesse, Seelenmesse (*obs.*). **—uary**, I. *s.* das Totenverzeichnis, die Totenliste. II. *adj.* Toten-, Todes-; —uary notice, die Todesanzeige.
Object, I. *s.* der Gegenstand, das Objekt; (end) der Zweck, das Ziel; das Objekt (*Gram.*); he has made it his — to deceive me, er hat es darauf angelegt mich zu betrügen; salary no —, auf Gehalt wird nicht gesehen. II. *v.a.* & *n.* entgegenstellen, einwenden, vorbringen, Einwendungen machen, sich aussprechen (gegen). **—ion**, *s.* (—ing) die Einwendung, der Einwand, Einwurf; to raise, start —ions, Einwendungen machen *or* erheben (to, gegen); right of —ion, das Einspruchsrecht; I have no —ion to your . . ., ich habe nichts dagegen, daß Sie . . .; no —ion to a married man, ein verheirateter Kandidat nicht ausgeschlossen. **—ionable**, *adj.*, **—ionably**, *adv.* nicht einwandfrei, tadelnswert; (inadmissible) unzulässig. **—ive**, I. *adj.*, **—ively**, *adv.* objektiv. II. *s.* (—ive case) der Objektsfall (*dat.* & *acc.*); das Ziel, Endziel; das Operationsziel (*Mil.*). **—iveness**, **—ivity**, *s.* die Objektivität. **—less**, *adj.* zwecklos. **—or**, *s.* der Gegenredner. *Comp.* **—-glass**, *s.* das Objektiv(glas). **—-lesson**, *s.* die Anschauungs-Lehrstunde, der Anschauungsunterricht; die Lehre (*fig.*).
Objuration, *s.* die eidliche Verpflichtung.
Objurgat—e, *v.a.* (einen) schelten, (einem etwas) verweisen. **—ory**, *adj.* Tadel enthaltend.
[1]Oblat—e, *see* [2]Oblate. **—es**, *pl.* die Oblaten. **—ion**, *s.* die Opferdarbringung, Opferung; (offering) das Opfer, die Opfergabe.
[2]Oblate, *adj.* abgeplattet, flachgedrückt **—ness**, *s.* die Abplattung.
Oblig—ation, *s.* die Verbindlichkeit, Verpflichtung; die Schuldverschreibung, Obligation (*C. L.*); to be under an —ation (to a p.), (einem) verbunden sein; (owe gratitude) zu Dank verpflichtet sein; to lay s. o. under fresh —ations, sich (*dat.*) einen aufs neue verpflichten. **—atory**, *adj.* verbindend, verpflichtend; to be —atory on (einen) verpflichten, verbindlich sein (für); —atory on all, allgemein verbindlich; —atory education, die Schulpflicht; —atory military service, die Wehrpflicht; **—e**, *v.a.* verbinden, verpflichten; (constrain) nötigen, zwingen; to —e a p., einen verbinden, einem einen Gefallen tun; —e me by asking him, wollen Sie die Güte haben, ihn zu fragen? I am much —ed to you for . . ., ich bin Ihnen für . . . sehr verbunden; I am —ed to you for this, Ihnen habe ich dies zu verdanken; anything to —e you, alles, um Ihnen eine Gefälligkeit zu erweisen; I was —ed to do it, ich mußte es tun. **—ed**, *p.p.* genötigt, gezwungen; much —ed, sehr verbunden, danke bestens. **—ing**, *adj.*, **—ingly**, *adv.* verbindlich, gefällig, dienstfertig, zuvorkommend. **—ingness**, *s.* die Gefälligkeit.
Obliqu—e, *adj.*, **—ely**, *adv.* schief, schräg; mittelbar, versteckt (*fig.*); unaufrichtig; abhängig (*Gram.*); —e case, der Beugefall; —e speech *or* oration, indirekte Rede (*Gram.*); —e sailing, der Schräglauf. **—eness**, **—ity**, *s.* die Schiefheit, Schrägheit, schräge Richtung; die Unredlichkeit (*fig.*); (irregularity) die Unregelmäßigkeit.
Obliterat—e, *v.a.* auslöschen, ausstreichen, vertilgen; zerstören, vernichten (*fig.*). **—ed**, *p.p.* gestempelt (*stamps*). **—ion**, *s.* die Auslöschung, das Verwischen; die Vernichtung, Vertilgung.
Oblivio—n, *s.* die Vergeßlichkeit; (being forgotten) die Vergessenheit; act of —n, der allgemeine Gnadenerlaß, die Amnestie. **—us**, *adj.*, **—usly**, *adv.* vergeßlich; —us of a th., etwas vergessend; Vergessenheit bringend (*as sleep*).
Oblong, I. *adj.* länglich; eirund. II. *s.* das Rechteck, längliche Viereck.
Obloquy, *s.* der Vorwurf, Tadel, die Schmähung (shame) die Schande; to cast — upon a person (einem) Schlechtes nachreden.
Obnoxious, *adj.*, **—ly**, *adv.* berüchtigt, verrufen; (— to) verhaßt; I am — to him, ich bin ihm ein Dorn im Auge. **—ness**, *s.* die Gehässigkeit, Anstößigkeit.
Oboe, *s.* die Oboe.
Obole, *s.* der halbe Skrupel (*Pharm.*); der Obolus, Heller, das Scherflein.
Obscen—e, *adj.*, **—ely**, *adv.* schmutzig, unanständig, schlüpfrig, unzüchtig. **—ity**, *s.* die Schlüpfrigkeit, Unzüchtigkeit.
Obscur—ation, *s.* das Verdunkeln; (being dark) die Verdunkelung. **—e**, I. *adj.*, **—ely**, *adv.* düster, dunkel; dunkel, unklar, undeutlich, ver-

strict, unverständlich (*fig.*); (unknown) im Schatten stehend, unbekannt, unberühmt; (retired) verborgen, einsam; —e birth, geringe Herkunft; to lead an —e life, in der Stille *or* ganz zurückgezogen leben. II. *v.a.* verfinstern; verdunkeln (*also fig.*); (degrade) verkleinern. **—ity**, *s.* die Dunkelheit; die Undeutlichkeit, Unverständlichkeit; die Verborgenheit; die Niedrigkeit (*of birth*); to retire into —ity, sich vom öffentlichen Leben zurückziehen.

Obsequi—es, *pl.* das Leichenbegängnis, die Totenfeier. **—ous**, *adj.*, **—ously**, *adv.* unterwürfig, nachgiebig, willfährig; (cringing) kriechend, knechtisch. **—ousness**, *s.* die Willfährigkeit; die knechtische Unterwürfigkeit.

Observ—able, *adj.*, **—ably**, *adv.* bemerkbar; (remarkable) bemerkenswert. **—ance**, *s.* die Beobachtung, Haltung (*of rules, laws, ceremonies*); (attention) die Aufmerksamkeit; die Ehrerbietung; (rule) die Regel; (rite) die Observanz, der Ritus. **—ant**, *adj.*, **—antly**, *adv.* beobachtend, aufmerksam, achtsam (of a th., auf eine S.); rücksichtsvoll (towards, gegen); to be —ant of a th., etwas beachten, befolgen; an —ant child, ein Kind, das auf alles achtet, alles bemerkt; he was very —ant of forms, er hielt sehr auf Formen; she is very —ant, sie hat eine große Beobachtungsgabe. **—ation**, *s.* die Beobachtung (*of phenomena*); die Beobachtung, Befolgung, Haltung, Observanz (*of customs, a rule*); (remark) die Bemerkung; to fall under a p.'s —ation, von einem bemerkt werden. **—atory**, *s.* die Sternwarte, das Observatorium. **—e**, *v.* I. *a.* (notice) beobachten, merken (auf eine S.), bemerken, wahrnehmen; bemerken, sagen, äußern; halten, feiern (*holidays*); beobachten, folgen, halten (*rules*); (practise) (aus)üben; what I was going to —e, was ich sagen wollte. II. *n.* aufmerksam sein, aufmerken; bemerken, eine Bemerkung machen. **—er**, *s.* der Beobachter (*also of rites, etc.*); der Befolger (*of rules*).

Obsess, *v.a.* plagen, quälen, heimsuchen.

Obsidian, *s.* der Obsidian (*Min.*).

Obsidional, *adj.* Belagerungs-.

Obsole—scence, *s.* der Zustand des Veraltens, das Veralten. **—scent**, *adj.* veraltend, im Veralten *or* Aussterben begriffen. **—te**, *adj.* veraltet; außer Gebrauch, Kurs; undeutlich, wenig sichtbar (*Zool., Bot.*). **—teness**, *s.* die Ungebräuchlichkeit, das Veraltetsein; die Undeutlichkeit.

Obstacle, *s.* das Hindernis.

Obstetric, *adj.* geburtshülflich, Entbindungs- (-instruments, *etc.*, -zeug rc.); — art, *see* **—s**. **—ian**, *s.* der Geburtshelfer. **—s**, *s.* die Entbindungskunst, Geburtshilfe.

Obstina—cy, *s.* die Halsstarrigkeit, Hartnäckigkeit, Unbeugsamkeit, der Eigensinn. **—te**, *adj.*, **—tely**, *adv.* halsstarrig, eigensinnig; hartnäckig (*as a disease*).

Obstreperous, *adj.* lärmend, geräuschvoll, überlaut. **—ness**, *s.* das Lärmen, laute Wesen.

Obstruct, *v.a.* versperren (*the way, etc.*); (impede) hemmen, hindern; (stop up) verstopfen; aufhalten, nicht durchlassen (*a stream, etc.*); to — a p.'s passage, einem den Weg vertreten. **—er**, **—or**, *s.* der Verhinderer, Hindernde. **—ion**, *s.* die Verstopfung; die Hemmung, Hinderung; (obstacle) das Hindernis; parliamentary —ion, die systematische Hemmung des parlamentarischen Geschäftsganges. **—ionist**, *s.* der Hemmungspolitiker, der Obstruktionist. **—ive**, I. *adj.* hindernd, hinderlich, Hindernisse darbietend. II. *s.* das Hindernis; *see* —er.

Obtain, *v.* I. *a.* erlangen, erhalten, erreichen, bekommen; to — by flattery, (sich, *dat.*) erschmeicheln; to — by entreaty, erbitten; to — the victory, den Sieg davontragen. II. *n.* fortdauern, sich behaupten (*as a custom*); durchdringen (*as a view*); *see* Prevail. **—able**, *adj.* erreichbar, zu erlangen. **—ment**, *s.* die Erlangung.

Obtru—de, *v.* I. *a.* aufdringen; (force) aufzwingen. II. *n.* sich aufdrängen, zudringlich sein. **—der**, *s.* der Aufdringliche. **—sion**, *s.* das Aufdringen, die Aufnötigung. **—sive**, *adj.* aufdringlich. **—sively**, *adv.* aufdringlicher Weise **—siveness**, *s.* die Aufdringlichkeit.

Obturat—e, *v.a.* verstopfen, verschließen **—or**. *s.* der Schließmuskel (*Anat.*).

Obtuse, *adj.*, **—ly**, *adv.* stumpf (*also Bot.*); dumm (*fig.*); — angle, der stumpfe Winkel. **—ness**, *s.* die Stumpfheit; die Dummheit. *Comp.* **—-angled**, *adj.* stumpfwinkelig.

Obverse, I. *adj.* umgekehrt. II. *s.* die Vorderseite, Bildseite, der Avers (einer Münze *or* Medaille); die andre Seite (einer Sache).

Obvi—ate, *v.a.* (einer Sache) zuvorkommen, vorbeugen, abhelfen, (sie) verhindern; beseitigen (*difficulties*). **—ous**, *adj.*, **—ously**, *adv.* klar, deutlich, unverkennbar, augenscheinlich; that is —ous, das springt in die Augen, leuchtet ein, ist klar *or* selbstredend. **—ousness**, *s.* die Augenscheinlichkeit, Unverkennbarkeit.

Occasion, I. *s.* (cause) die zufällige Ursache, Veranlassung, der Anlaß; (opportunity) die Gelegenheit; (exigency) das Bedürfnis; (juncture) die Lage, die Umstände; to be the — of a th., eine S. veranlassen; there is no — for you to . . ., es ist kein Grund vorhanden, weshalb Sie . . ., es ist nicht nötig, daß Sie . . ., Sie brauchen nicht . . .; as — serves, wenn sich die Gelegenheit darbietet; to give —, Anlaß, Gelegenheit geben; to have — for, (etwas) nötig haben, bedürfen; he was equal to the —, er war der Sache *or* den Umständen gewachsen. II. *v.a.* veranlassen, Anlaß *or* Gelegenheit geben, verursachen. **—al**, *adj.*, **—ally**, *adv.* zufällig, gelegentlich, von Zeit zu Zeit; —al poems, Gelegenheitsgedichte; —al table, kleiner Tisch; —ally, bei Gelegenheit; dann und wann.

Occident, *s.* der Abend, Westen; das Abendland **—al**, *adj.* abendlich, westlich.

Occip—ital, *adj.* Hinterhaupt-. **—ut**, *s.* das Hinterhaupt, der Hinterkopf.

Occult, *adj.* verborgen, geheim; magisch; — disease, die unerforschte Krankheit; — line, die blinde Hülfslinie; — sciences, die geheimen Wissenschaften **—ation**, *s.* die Verbergung; die Bedeckung (*Astr.*). **—ism**, *s.* die Geheimlehre der Theosophisten.

Occup—ancy, *s. see* —ation; die Besitznahme; die Besitzergreifung (*Law*); during his —ancy of the house, solange er das Haus im Besitz hatte *or* bewohnte. **—ant**, *s.* der Besitzer, Inhaber; der Bewohner, Insasse (*of a house*); der Besitzergreifer. **—ation**, *s.* (—ancy) der Besitz; (seizing) die Besitznahme; die Besetzung, Einnahme (*Mil.*); (calling) der Beruf, das Geschäft, Handwerk; (employment) die Beschäftigung; army of —ation, das Besetzungsheer, die Okkupationsarmee. **—ier**, *s.* der Besitzer, Inhaber; der Insasse, Bewohner (*of a house*). **—y**, *v.* I. *a.* in Besitz nehmen; besetzen (*Mil.*); (possess) innehaben, besitzen; (fill) bekleiden, innehaben; einnehmen (*a space*); bewohnen (*a house, etc.*), bewirtschaften (*an estate, land*); beschäftigen (*workmen, etc.*); to —y a post, eine Stelle bekleiden, einnehmen; to —y o.s., be —ied with (in), sich mit (etwas) beschäftigen, arbeiten an (einer S.). II. *n.* innehaben; handeln (*B.*).

Occur, *v.n.* vorkommen, sich ereignen, vorfallen; (be met with) vorkommen, sich finden; einfallen, in die Gedanken kommen (*as an idea, word*); it —s to me, es fällt mir ein; it has actually —red, es ist wirklich vorgekommen. **—rence**, *s.* (—ring) das Vorkommen; der Vorfall; das zufällige Ereignis, der Zufall; to be of frequent —rence, oft vorkommen.

Ocean, I. *s.* das große Meer, Weltmeer, der Ozean. II. *adj.* Meeres-; — greyhound, (*fig for*) der Schnelldampfer; — steamer, der Seedampfer. **—ic,** *adj.* Meeres=, ozeanisch. — **ography,** *s.* die Meerbeschreibung. **—ology,** *s.* die Tiefseekunde.

Ocellate(d), *adj.* äugicht; augenfleckig (*Zool.*).

Ocelot, *s.* die kleine Unze, Pantherkatze, der Ozelot.

Ochre, *s.* der Ocher; red —, der Rötel; yellow —, das Berggelb. **—ous,** *adj.* ockerhaltig; (—-like) ockerartig.

O'clock, *see* Clock.

Oct—achord, *s.* ein Instrument von acht Saiten; (system) das System von 8 Tönen. **—agon,** I. *s.* das Achteck (*Geom.*); das Oktagon (*Fort.*). II. *adj.*, **—agonal,** *adj.* achteckig, achtseitig. — **ahedral,** *adj.* achtflächich. **—ahedron,** *s.* das Achtflach, der Oktaeder. **—andrian, —androus,** *s.* achtmännig (*of a plant*). **—angular,** *adj.* achteckig. **—ant,** *s.* der Oktant; der Oktilschein (*Astrol.*). **—astyle,** *s.* der achtsäulige Bau. **—ave,** *s.* die Oktave (*Mus.*, *Org.*, *Eccl.*); die (achtzeilige) Stanze (*Poet.*). **—avo,** I. *s.* das Oktav(=Format); demi- —avo, Median=Oktav=format; crown —avo, Kleinoktav; royal —avo, Großoktav. II. *adj.* Oktav=. **—ile,** *see* —ant. **—illion,** *s.* die Oktillion. **—ober,** *s.* der Oktober. **—odecimal,** *adj.* achtzehnflächich, oktodezimal. **—odecimo,** *s.* das Oktodez(=Format). **—odentate,** *adj.* achtzähnig. **—ogenarian,** *s.* I. der (die) Achtzigjährige. II. *adj.* achtzigjährig. **—opod, —opus,** *s.* der Achtfüßler, Seepolyp. **—osyllabic,** I. *adj.* achtsilbig. II. *s.* der Achtsilbler, achtsilbige Vers (*Metre*). — **osyllable,** *s.* das achtsilbige Wort.

Ocul—ar, *adj.* Augen=; —ar demonstration, der augenscheinliche Beweis; I had —ar demonstration of it, ich war selbst Zeuge davon. **—ate,** *adj.* Augen habend; (spotted) augenfleckig. — **ist,** *s.* der Augenarzt.

Odd, *adj.*, **—ly,** *adv.* (uneven) ungerade; (single) einzeln, vereinzelt; einige, etliche darüber; (not included) ungerechnet, nicht eingerechnet, unberücksichtigt; (strange) seltsam, wunderbar, wunderlich, ungewöhnlich; there is still some — money, es ist noch etwas Geld übrig; four score and —, etliche achtzig; £40 —, etwa 40 Pfund, an die 40 Pfund; the — 15 pence, die 15 Pence darüber, mehr; about the — shillings . . ., in Betreff der übrigen Schillinge . . .; 900 and — years, etwas über 900 Jahre; 3 pair and one — one, 3 Paar und Eins darüber; — fellow, *see* —ity; an — way of doing things, eine seltsame, ungewöhnliche Art und Weise zu handeln; it's — if . . ., es wäre ein Wunder, wenn . . .; to do at — times, (etwas) dann und wann tun, gelegentlich tun; to play at — and even, gerade und ungerade spielen; an — glove, ein einzelner Handschuh; three — volumes, 3 vereinzelte Bände (of a set, eines Werkes); — number, ungerade Zahl; — trick, der Trick. **—ity,** *s.* der seltsame Mensch, wunderliche Kauz, Sonderling; (—ness) die Seltsamkeit. **—ly,** *adv.* seltsam, wunderlich. **—ments,** *pl.* die Ladenreste. **—ness,** *s.* die Ungeradheit (*of a number*); die Seltsamkeit, Wunderlichkeit. **—s,** *s.* & *pl.* (inequality) die Ungleichheit, Verschiedenheit, der Unterschied; (advantage) die Überlegenheit, Übermacht, der Vorteil, das Übergewicht; die Wahrscheinlichkeit; der Streit, Hader, die Uneinigkeit; against tremendous —s, gegen große Überzahl, gegen riesige Vorteile; to bear up against —s, einer Überzahl Widerstand leisten; at —s, uneinig; they are always at —s, sie haben immer Händel; to set at —s, uneinig machen, veruneinigen; —s and ends, allerlei Reste, Stückchen, verschiedene Dinge; there's not much —s between them, sie sind einander so ziemlich gleich (*vulg.*); the —s are on his side, die Wahrscheinlichkeit ist für ihn; to give s.o. —s, (im Spiele) einem etwas vorgeben; owed —s, Minus=Vorgaben (*pl.*) (*Tenn.*); to take —s, sich (*dat.*) vorgeben lassen; to take the —s, eine ungleiche Wette eingehen; to have the —s against one, es mit einem Stärkeren zu tun haben. *Comp.* **—-Fellows,** *s.* (order of — Fellows) (ein großer amerikanischer) Unterstützungsverein, Wohltätigkeitsorden. — **looking,** *adj.* seltsam aussehend.

Ode, I. *s.* die Ode. II. *attrib.*; — poetry, die Odendichtung.

Odi—ous, *adj.*, **—ously,** *adv.* verhaßt, gehässig, (detestable) hassenswert, abscheulich; (repulsive) widrig, widerlich. **—ousness,** *s.* die Gehässigkeit, Verhaßtheit; die Hassenswürdigkeit; die Abscheulichkeit; die Widrigkeit. **—um,** *s.* (hatred) der Haß; die Gehässigkeit, das Gehässige; der Vorwurf, Tadel; to bring —um upon a p., einen verhaßt *or* unbeliebt machen.

Odol, *s.* ein Zahnwasser, das Odol.

Odometer, *s.* der Wegmesser, das Wegmaß.

Odont—algy, *s.* das Zahnweh. **—o,** *s.* ein Bewahrungsmittel für die Zähne. **—oid,** *adj.* zahnähnlich. **—ology,** *s.* die Zahnkunde.

Odor, *s. see* Odour. **—iferous,** *adj.*, **—iferously,** *adv.* wohlriechend; (balmy) Wohlgeruch verbreitend, duftend. **—ous,** *adj.*, **—ously,** *adv.* wohlriechend, duftend. **—ousness,** *s.* der Wohlgeruch, süße Duft.

Odour, *s.* der Duft, Geruch; (fragrance) der Wohlgeruch; — of sanctity, Geruch der Heiligkeit; to be in bad —, in schlechtem Rufe stehen. — **less,** *adj.* geruchlos.

Œdema, *s.* das Ödem(a). **—tous, —tose,** *adj.* (wasser=)schwülstig.

Œil-de-bœuf, *s.* rundes Dachfenster.

Œn—anthe, *s.* die Rebendolde. **—ometer,** *s.* der Weinmesser. **—othera,** *s.* die Nachtkerze (*Bot.*).

O'er, *see* Over.

Œsophagus, *s.* die Speiseröhre.

Of, *prep.* von; aus, unter, durch, über, für, auf, an, um, in, zu (*see phrases*); — age, mündig; 6 years — age, 6 Jahre alt; he awoke — himself, er wachte von selber auf; — a serious turn of mind, ernstgesinnt; to be — opinion, der Meinung sein; to be — a party, zu einer Gesellschaft gehören; to be ignorant —, (etwas) nicht wissen, nicht gehört haben; to be proud — a th., auf eine S. stolz sein; to be in need —, (einer Sache) bedürfen; the battle — Waterloo, die Schlacht bei Waterloo; the best — all, das, der Beste von allen *or* unter allen; all — them, sie alle; an angel — a child, ein Engel von einem Kinde; the city — Hanover, die Stadt Hannover; to complain —, klagen über (*acc.*); to deprive —, (einer Sache) berauben; to die —, sterben an (*dat.*); that's none — my doing, das habe ich nicht getan; the fear — death, die Furcht vor dem Tode, Todesfurcht; a glass — wine, ein Glas Wein; a man — rare endowments, ein mit seltenen Gaben ausgestatteter Mann; made — gold, von *or* aus Gold gemacht; a friend — mine, einer meiner Freunde (*or* eine meiner Freundinnen), ein Freund (*or* eine Freundin) von mir; a man — genius, — letters, ein Genie, ein Gelehrter; a man — wealth, ein wohlhabender Mann; the month — May, der Monat Mai; — one's own accord, aus eignem Antriebe; — all things, vor allen Dingen; — an afternoon, an einem Nachmittag, am Nachmittag, (an den Nachmittagen); — an ancient family, von altem Stamme; — late, neulich; — the name — . . ., mit Namen . . .; — necessity, notwendigerweise; — his great mercy, nach seiner großen Barmherzigkeit; — old, vor Alters, weiland; — set purpose, absichtlich; to think —, denken an (*acc.*); to treat —, handeln von; the university — Cambridge, die Universität Cambridge, die Cambridger Hochschule; — no value, von keinem Werte, wertlos; this world — ours, diese unsre Welt; — yore, ehemals, vor Alters; a pair — . . ., ein Paar . . .; plenty —, Überfluß an (*dat.*), viel; to remind —, erinnern an (eine S.); to repent —, (etwas) bereuen; south —

London, südlich von London; to wish s.o. joy —, einem zu (einer Sache) Glück wünschen.

Off, I. *adv.* (removed, distant) weg, davon, weit, bis dorthin, von hier; (*opp to* on, an) aus; (away, from) weg, hinweg; (*with verbs denoting separation* =) ab, weg, los; far —, weit entfernt; a great way —, sehr weit von hier; he had his coat —, er hatte seinen Rock ausgezogen, hatte keinen Rock an; the affair is —, die Sache ist aus, ist rückgängig geworden; — and on, ab und an, ab und zu, hin und her, bald so, bald anders; to put a th. —, etwas aufschieben, verschieben; how is he — for . . .? wie ist er daran in Beziehung auf . . .? well —, wohlhabend, in guten Vermögensumständen, gut daran; I am —, jetzt gehe ich fort; how did the play go —? wie verlief das Stück, wie gefiel das Schauspiel? my gun wouldn't go —, meine Flinte versagte; to learn — by heart, auswendig lernen; to turn a servant —, einen Diener, eine Magd aus dem Dienste schicken; to get —, davon kommen; to take — one's hat, den Hut abnehmen; to take —, einen nachahmen, kopieren (*coll.*). II. *prep.* (away from) von; auf der Höhe von (*Naut.*); I was never — my legs the whole day, ich war den ganzen Tag auf den Beinen; please keep — the grass, das Betreten des Rasens ist verboten; — hand, aus dem Stegreife, (readily) auf der Stelle, (easy) leicht, ungezwungen, frei; — duty, außer, nicht im Dienst; two miles — the road, zwei Meilen von der Straße ab; a street — Cheapside, eine Straße, die von Cheapside ausgeht; — Portsmouth, auf der Höhe von Portsmouth; —ff side, abseits (*Footb.*). III. *adj.* entferntest; recht; the — side, die rechte Seite (*of a horse, etc.*). IV. *int.* weg! hinweg! fort! hands —! Hände weg! **—al**, *s.* der Abfall, Abhub; (rubbish) der Auswurf, Ausschuß. **—chance**, *s.* letzte Möglichkeit *or* Chance. **—ing**, *s.* die (See=)Räumte, hohe, offene See; in the —ing, draußen, auf hoher See; the sea runs high in the —ing, die See geht draußen sehr hohe; to stand for the —ing, seewärts anliegen. *Comp.* **—glide**, *s.* der Nachschlag (*in long vowels*). **—hand**, *adj. see under* —; —hand manner, ein ganz ungezwungenes Benehmen. **—print**, *s.* der Sonderabzug, Sonderabdruck. **—scouring, —scum**, *s.* das Kehricht; der Auswurf, Unrat, Abschaum (*fig.*). **—set**, *s.* die Gegenforderung, Gegenrechnung (*C.L.*); das Absetzen, der Absatz einer Mauer (*Build.*); der Absenker (*Hort.*); die Ordinatee, Perpendikulare; (set-—) die Zierde (*prov.*); der Ausläufer (*of bills*); method of —sets, die Ordinatenmethode. **—shoot**, *s.* der Sprößling, Ableger; die Abzweigung: die Kolonie. **—spring**, *s.* der Nachkömmling, Abkömmling; (posterity) die Nachkommenschaft; (production) das Erzeugnis. **—time**, *s.* freie Zeit.

Offen—ce, *s.* (cause of —ce) der Anstoß, das Ärgernis, die Beleidigung; (wrong, trespass) das Vergehen, die Sünde, Missetat; (attack) der Angriff; (displeasure) der Verdruß; no —ce! nichts für ungut! to give —ce, Anstoß geben; to take —ce (at a th.), (etwas) übel nehmen; without —ce to his memory, ohne seinem Andenken zu nahe zu treten; weapons of —ce, Angriffswaffen. **—d**, *v.* I. *a.* angreifen, unangenehm berühren, beleidigen, verletzen (*the eye, ear, etc.*); (displease) beleidigen, Anstoß geben, verletzen, kränken; I was not aware of having done anything to —d you, ich wußte nicht, daß ich Ihnen irgend wie zu nahe getreten war *or* Ihnen etwas zuleide getan hatte; —ded at, über eine S. aufgebracht; —ded with a person, einem zürnen. II. *n.* (give —ce) Anstoß geben; (violate) sich vergehen, sündigen (against, gegen). **—der**, *s.* der Beleidiger; (transgressor) der Sünder, Missetäter. **—se**, *see* —ce. **—sive**, I. *adj.*, **—sively**, *adv.* anstößig, mißfällig; (disgusting) widrig, ekelhaft; (aggressive) angreifend, Angriffs=; (insulting) beleidigend, anstößig; —sive alliance, das Angriffs=Bündnis; —sive and defensive alliance, das Schutz= und Trutz=Bündnis; —sive breath, übelriechender Atem; —sive smell, schlechter, widerlicher Geruch. II. *s.* die Offensive; to assume, act on the —sive, die Offensive ergreifen. **—siveness**, *s.* das Anstößige, Beleidigende; die Widrigkeit, Ekelhaftigkeit.

Offer, I. *v.a.* (dar)bieten, darbringen; (— up) aufopfern, darbringen; (dedicate) weihen; bieten (*a sum*); (propose) anbieten, antragen; angeben, vorbringen, vortragen (*a reason*); ausbieten (*goods for sale*); he —ed to strike me, er machte Miene mich zu schlagen; to — s.o. help, — one's services to a p., einem seine Dienste anbieten; to — for a p.'s consideration, einem (etwas) zu bedenken geben; to — violence to a p., einem Gewalt antun. II. *v.n.* (— itself) sich darbieten, sich zeigen; (proffer) sich erbieten; (attempt) versuchen, den Versuch machen. III. *s.* das Erbieten, Anerbieten, der Antrag; das Angebot, Gebot (*at auctions, etc.*); (price) der gebotene Preis; (attempt) der Versuch; to make a girl an —, einem Mädchen einen Antrag machen, um ein Mädchen anhalten. **—er**, *s.* der Darbietende; der Anbieter. **—ing**, *s.* (sacrifice) das Opfer; das Anerbieten, der Antrag; burnt, sin, thank —ing, Brand=, Schuld=, Dank=opfer; —ings, dem Geistlichen zu entrichtende Gebühren (*Eccl.*). **—tory**, *s.* die Opfergabe; das Offertorium (*R. C.*); (—tory sentences) gewisse Sprüche, welche während der Almosensammlung vorgelesen werden (*in the English Church*); (collection) das Opfer.

Offic—e, I. *s.* das Amt, die Stelle; (occupation) das Geschäft; (duty) die Pflicht; (employment) der Dienst, das Geschäft, der Beruf; (function) der Dienst, die Funktion; (service) der Dienst, die Dienstleistung; der (Gottes=)Dienst (*Eccl.*); (divine —e) das Meßamt; (room, *etc.*) die Amt=, Geschäft=stube, das Geschäftslokal, Kontor, Büreau; (benefice) die Pfründe ohne Gerichtsbarkeit; Home —e, das Reichsamt des Innern; Foreign —e, das Reichsamt des Äußern; (persons in an —e) Beamten; —es, die Bedienten=, Gesinde=stuben, Speisekammer, Küchen, &c.; (outhouses) Nebengebäude, Stallungen, Wirtschaftsgebäude; it is the —e of a king, es kommt einem Könige zu; in —e, angestellt; to hold *or* fill an —e, ein Amt bekleiden, eine Stelle inne haben; to be in —e, ein öffentliches Amt bekleiden; im Ministerium sein; an der Regierung sein, regieren (*of a cabinet*); kind —es, gute Dienste; to come into —e, ins Ministerium treten (*Pol.*); die Regierungsgeschäfte eines Landes übernehmen (*of a body of ministers*) (*Pol.*); sein Amt antreten; to do the —e of, den Dienst, die Stelle versehen von; printing —e, die Druckerei; booking —e, ticket —e, der Schalter für die Ausgabe von Fahrscheinen (*Rail.*), das Einschreibebureau; drawing —e, das Zeichenbureau. II. *attrib.*; —e holder, der Amtsinhaber; —e hours, Geschäftsstunden; —e clerk, der Kontorist. **—er**, I. *s.* der Beamte; der Offizier (*Mil.*); (police —er) der Polizei=diener, =beamte; medical —er of health, der Sanitätsrat; military —er, der Offizier; petty —er, der Unteroffizier; plain clothes —er, der Geheimpolizist; returning —er, der Wahlkommissär; warrant —er, der vom Gemeinen zum Offizier (ohne Patent) Emporgestiegene, Feldwebelleutnant (*Mil.*), Deckoffizier (*Nav.*). II. *v.a.* mit Offizieren versehen. **—ial**, I. *adj.*, **—ially**, *adv.* amtlich, Amts=, offiziell; —ial duties, Amtspflichten; Amtshandlungen; —ial reports, amtliche Berichte; —ial stamp, die Dienstmarke; der Dienststempel. II. *s.* der Beamte. **—ialdom**, *s.* die Beamtenwelt, die Beamten. **—ialism**, *s.* das Beamtentum; der Bureaukratismus; das

Geschäftsmäßige. **—iate**, *v.n.* funktionieren, ein Amt versehen; den Gottesdienst abhalten, gottesdienstliche Handlungen verrichten; the —iating clergy, die diensttuenden Geistlichen; to —iate for another, bei Amtsverrichtungen die Stelle eines andern vertreten. **—inal**, *adj.* offizinell, Arznei-. **—ious**, *adj.*, **—iously**, *adv.* zudringlich, übertrieben eifrig *or* dienstfertig. **—iousness**, *s.* die übertriebene Dienstfertigkeit, Zudringlichkeit. *Comp.* **—e-bearer**, *s.* der Beamte. **—e-boy**, *s.* der Laufbursche.

Oft, I. *adj.* häufig. II. *adv.*, **—en**, *adv.* oft, öfters; (frequently) häufig; ever so —en, sehr oft; auch noch so oft; I have told him ever so —en, ich habe es ihm unzählige Male *or* außerordentlich oft gesagt; in spite of my telling him ever so —en, wenn ich es ihm auch noch so oft sagte, (hat er doch . . .) so oft ich es ihm auch sagte . . . *Comp.* —(**en**)**times**, *adv.* oft(mals). **—-tried**, *adj.* viel geprüft.

Og—ee, *s.* der (verkehrt steigende) Karnies (*Arch.*); das Metallband, der Rundstab (*on guns*). —**ival**, *adj.* Spitzbogen-, gotisch.

Ogle, *v.a.* beäugeln. **—r**, *s.* der Beäugler.

Ogre, *s.* der Oger. **—ss**, *s.* die Ogerin.

Oh, *int.* ach! wehe mir! **—o**, *int.* ei, ha!

Oil, I. *s.* das Öl; essential, volatile —s, flüchtige, ätherische Öle; (English) — of vitriol, Vitriolöl, Schwefelsäure; sweet —, Olivenöl; to strike —, Petrolöl in der Erde finden; auf etwas sehr Vorteilhaftes stoßen (*fig.*). II. *v.a.* (ein)ölen, beschmieren; —ed silk, der Wachstaffet; to have a well —ed tongue, eine geläufige *or* glatte Zunge haben (*fam.*). **—iness**, *s.* die ölige Beschaffenheit, Fettigkeit; das glatte Wesen (*fig.*). **—y**, *adj.* ölig; (—-like) ölicht; (greasy) fett, schmierig; —y tongue, glatte Zunge, schmeichlerische Zunge. *Comp.* **—-cake**, *s.* der Ölkuchen. **—-cloth**, *s.* das Wachstuch, die Wachsleinwand. **—-colour**, *s.* die Ölfarbe. **—man**, *s.* der Ölhändler. —**-mill**, *s.* die Ölmühle. **—-painting**, *s.* die Ölmalerei; (picture) das Ölgemälde. **—-press**, *s.* die Ölpresse. **—-shop**, *s.* der Olladen, Ölfarbenladen. **—skin**, *s.* der Wachstaffet; der Rock aus geölter Leinwand. **—-stone**, *s.* der Ölstein, feine Schleifstein.

Ointment, *s.* die Salbe.

Old, *adj.* alt; (worn) abgenutzt, verbraucht; (antiquated) veraltet; to grow —, altern; to have grown — in vice, im Laster ergraut sein; of —, in — times, vor Alters, vor Zeiten; a friend of —, ein alter Freund; as — as the hills, uralt; — age, das (hohe) Alter; an — boy, ein früherer *or* alter Schüler einer Anstalt; an — hand at, ein alter Praktikus in; the — woman, die Alte; three years —, drei Jahre alt; — fellow! Alter! —**en**, *adj.* alt. **—er**, *adj. comp. of* Old. **—ish**, *adj.* ältlich. **—ness**, *s.* das Alter. *Comp.* —**-fashioned**, *adj.* altmodisch; *see* Precocious. **—-fashionedness**, *s.* das altmodische Wesen. **—-maidish**, *adj.* altjungfernhaft, altjüngferlich. **—-maidishness**, *s.* das altjüngferliche Wesen, die Altejungfernart, das Altjungfertum. —**-womanish**, *adj.* altfrauenhaft.

Ole—aginous, *adj.* ölig, ölhaltig; salbungsvoll. **—ine**, *s.* das Olein. **—ograph**, *s.* das Öl-Druckbild. **—omargarine**, *s.* die Kunstbutter. **—ose**, *adj.* ölig, ölhaltig.

Oleander, *s.* der Oleander.

Olfactory, *adj.* zum Geruch dienend, Geruchs-.

Oligarch, *s.* der Oligarch. **—ical**, *adj.* oligarchisch. **—y**, *s.* die Oligarchie.

Olive, I. *s.* die Olive; (fruit) die Ölbeere; (—-tree) der Ölbaum. II. *adj.* (—-coloured) olivenfarbig; Mount of —s, der Ölberg. *Comp.* —**-branch**, *s.* der Ölzweig; das Friedenszeichen (*fig.*). **—-colour**, *s.* die Olivenfarbe, das Olivengrün. **—-green**, *adj.* olivengrün. **—-grove**, *s.* das Olivenwäldchen. **—-husks**, *pl.* die Öltrester. **—-oil**, *s.* das Olivenöl.

Olla-podrida, *s.* die Olla-podrida; der Mischmasch (*fig.*).

Olympi—ad, *s.* die Olympiade. **—an**, **—c**, I. *adj.* olympisch. II. *s.* der Olympier.

Omega, *s.* das Omega.

Omelet, *s.* der Eierkuchen; die Omelette.

Om—en, *s.* das Anzeichen, Vorzeichen, Omen, die Vorbedeutung. **—ened**, *adj.* vorbedeutend, von . . . Vorbedeutung. **—inous**, *adj.*, **—inously**, *adv.* bedeutungsvoll, von übler Vorbedeutung. **—inousness**, *s.* das Ominöse.

Omentum, *s.* das Netz (*Anat.*).

Omi—ssible, *adj.* auslaßbar, auszulassen. —**ssion**, *s.* die Unterlassung, Versäumnis; (leaving out) die Aus-, Weg-lassung; (what is —itted) das Ausgelassene. **—t**, *v.a.* unterlassen, versäumen; auslassen, übergehen.

Omni—bus, *s.* (*abbrev.* 'bus) der Omnibus; hotel —bus, der Gasthofswagen. **—potence**, *s.* die Allmacht. **—potent**, *adj.*, **—potently**, *adv.* allmächtig. **—presence**, *s.* die Allgegenwart. —**present**, *adj.* allgegenwärtig. **—science**, *s.* die Allwissenheit. **—scient**, *adj.*, **—sciently**, *adv.* allwissend. **—um**, *s.* das Omnium (*C. L.*). **—um-gatherum**, *s.* das Sammelsurium, der Mischmasch. **—vorous**, *adj.* alles verschlingend *or* fressend.

Omoplate, *s.* das Schulterblatt.

Omphal—ic, *adj.* zum Nabel gehörig, Nabel-. **—ocele**, *s.* der Nabelbruch. **—otomy**, *s.* das Abschneiden der Nabelschnur.

On, I. *prep.* an, auf, bei, zu, in, über, nach, von, um; (to pay) — account, à conto; — account of, wegen; — the alert, auf der Hut; with a lady — his arm, eine Dame am Arm(e führend); to bestow favours —, (einem) Freundlichkeit erweisen; to call — s.o., einen anrufen; (visit) einen besuchen; — these conditions, unter diesen Bedingungen; — the contrary, im Gegenteil; — delivery, auf Lieferung; bei Lieferung; — entering, beim Eintritt *or* Eintreten; — fire, in Brand, in Flammen; — the first of April, am ersten April; — foot, zu Fuß; to set — foot, in Gang bringen; — hand, auf Lager; — high, droben, hinauf; from — high, von oben herab; — my honour, auf Ehre; — horseback, zu Pferde; to lean — s.o.'s arm, sich auf jemands Arm lehnen; to lean — one's elbow, sich auf den Ellbogen stützen; — the left, zur Linken; my book lies — the desk, mein Buch liegt auf dem Pult; loss — loss, Verlust auf Verlust, Verlust über Verlust, ein Verlust nach dem andern; — pain of death, bei Todesstrafe; he talked — novels, er sprach über Romane; — our part, unsererseits, was uns anbetrifft; to have pity — a p., einen bemitleiden; — purpose, absichtlich, mit Fleiß; put it — the table, legen Sie es auf den Tisch; — receipt of this, nach *or* bei Empfang des Gegenwärtigen; — side, im Spiele (*Footb.*); — shore, am, ans Ufer; — the stroke of ten, Schlag zehn (Uhr); — a sudden, plötzlich, auf einmal; — the wing, im Fluge (*lit.*); in Bewegung, im Schwinden (*fig.*). II. *adv.* (forward) fort, weiter, ferner, hin, zu; (not off) an, auf; (further) vorwärts, weiter, hin; he went — whistling, er pfiff weiter; far — in the season, weit vorgerückt in der Jahreszeit; and so —, und so weiter; he had a blue coat —, er hatte einen blauen Rock an; he kept his hat —, er behielt seinen Hut auf; I can't get my boots —, ich kann meine Stiefel nicht anziehen *or* anbekommen; go —! weiter! fahren Sie fort! to sing —, fortsingen, weiter singen. III. *int.* voran! vorwärts! daran! — then! frisch drauf los! —**slaught**, *s.* der Angriff, Anfall, Sturm. —**ward**, I. *adv.* vorwärts, weiter. II. *adj.* vorwärtsschreitend, fortschreitend. **—Wards**, *see* —ward I. *Comp.* **—looker**, *s.* der Zuschauer.

—**set**, *s.* der Angriff, Anfall; to make an —set upon, einen Angriff machen auf (*acc.*).

Once, *adv.* ein Mal, einmal; (one time) ein einziges Mal; (formerly) einst, vormals, ehedem; (sometime) dereinst; — more, noch einmal; more than —, mehrmals, mehrere Male; at —, sogleich, gleich, sofort; all at —, auf einmal, plötzlich; — for all, ein für alle Mal; — upon a time there was . . ., es war einmal . . .; this —, dieses eine Mal; for —, für ein Mal; — in a while *or* way, gelegentlich, zuweilen, dann und wann; — there, we shall . . ., sind wir einmal da, so werden wir . . .

One, I. *adj.* ein; (single) einzig; there's not — of them, es ist kein einziger von ihnen; on the — hand, einerseits; as — man, einstimmig, einmütig; it is all —, es ist alles eins, einerlei; his — care, seine einzige Sorge; — with another, eins ins andere gerechnet, im Durchschnitt; — and the same, ein und derselbe; — by —, — after another, einzeln, einer nach dem andern; — and all, alle zusammen, sammt und sonders; my — and all, mein Ein und Alles; to be — and all with a person, alles bei einem gelten; — day, eines Tages; (once) eines Tages, einst; only — more, nur noch eins! — more song, noch ein Lied; — of these days, dieser Tage; — another, einander; — time, einmal; — thing or another, eine oder die andere Sache; we must love — another, wir müssen einander lieben; there was — John Smith present, es war ein gewisser John Smith gegenwärtig. II. *pron.* einer, eine, ein, eins; man; — knows, man weiß; any —, irgend einer, irgend jemand; such a —, so einer, der und der; every —, ein jeder; no —, keiner, niemand; — or other, einer oder der andere; I am not — to . . ., ich bin kein Mann, der . . .; to be — of a party, dabei sein; —('s) self, selbst, sich; to picture to —('s) self, sich (*dat.*) vorstellen; to cry —'s eyes out, sich (*dat.*) die Augen ausweinen; to take —'s walk, seinen Spaziergang machen; as — would have it, nach Wunsch; your breakfast will be a disturbed —, Ihr Frühstück wird gestört werden. III. *s.* Einer; Eins (*Arith.*); to take care of number —, für sich selbst sorgen; the great —s of the earth, die Großen der Erde; my little —s, meine Kleinen, meine Kinder; at —, einig. —**ness**, *s.* die Einheit, Nämlichkeit, Identität; —ness of purpose, ungeteilte Hingabe an einen einzigen Zweck. *Comp.* —**-edged**, *adj.* einkantig; einschneidig. —**-eyed**, *adj.* einäugig. —**-handed**, *adj.* einhändig. —**-horse**, *adj.*; a —-horse vehicle, ein Einspänner. —**-sided**, *adj.* einseitig. —**-sidedness**, *s.* die Einseitigkeit. —**-storied**, *adj.* einstöckig.

On—erous, *adj.* lästig, beschwerlich. —**us**, *s.* die Last, Beschwerde; —us probandi, die Beweislast.

Onion, *s.* die Zwiebel.

Only, I. *adj.* einzig. II. *adv.* (nothing but, not more than) nur, bloß; (not before, not further) erst; if I had — heard it before, wenn ich es nur (bloß) früher gehört hätte; he has — 4 marks left, er hat nur (bloß) 4 Mark übrig; I heard it — yesterday, ich hörte es erst gestern. III. *prep. see* Except. IV. *conj.* allein. *Comp.* —**-begotten**, *adj.* eingeboren. —**-beloved**, *adj.* einzig geliebt.

Onomatop—œia, *s.* die Klangnachahmung, Schallnachahmung, Tonmalerei. —**œic**, —**oetic**, *adj.* klangnachahmend, onomatopoëtisch.

Ontology, *s.* die Wesenlehre, Ontologie.

Onyx, *s.* der Onyx.

Oolit—e, *s.* der Oolith, Erbsenstein. —**ic**, *adj.* oolithenförmig, oolithisch.

Ooz—e, I. *v.n.* langsam ablaufen, wegsickern, träufeln; to —e out, allmählich bekannt werden (*fig.*). II. *s.* der Schlamm, Schlick; die Lohbrühe (*Tann.*). —**y**, *adj.* schlammig; —y bottom, der Schlickgrund.

Opa—city, *s.* die Undurchsichtigkeit; (darkness) die Dunkelheit (*also fig.*). —**que**, *adj.* undurchsichtig. —**queness**, *see* —city.

Opal, *s.* der Opal. —**esce**, *v.n.* in Opalfarben spielen, opalisieren, bunt schillern. —**escence**, *s.* das Opalisieren. —**escent**, *adj.* bunt schillernd. —**ine**, *adj.* Opal-, opalartig.

Ope, (*poet.*) *see* —n II. —**n**, I. *adj.*, —**nly**, *adv.* offen; (uncovered) unbedeckt, bloß, offen; (public) öffentlich; gelind, mild (*as weather*); (evident) offenbar, klar, augenscheinlich; (generous) offen(herzig), freimütig; freigebig; (well known) offen(kundig), allgemein bekannt; offen, frei, unbeschützt (*as a country, a port, etc.*); offen, laufend (*as accounts*); — to conviction, bereit sich (mich, dich, *etc.*) überzeugen *or* eines Bessern belehren zu lassen; an —n question, eine offene Frage; in —n arms *or* war, in offenem Kriege; with —n arms, mit offenen Armen; an —n verdict, ein richterlicher Ausspruch über einen unermittelt gelassenen Fall; in the —n (air), unter freiem Himmel, in freier Luft; in the —n street, auf offner Straße; in —n court, öffentlich, vor Gericht; a little —n, klaffend (*as a door*); with —n doors, bei offenen Türen; to break —, aufbrechen; to keep — house (table), offenes Haus (offene Tafel) halten; to keep one's eyes —n, die Augen offen halten; to lay —n, bloß legen, aussetzen; to lie —n, ausgesetzt, offen sein; to set, throw —n, öffnen; he did it —nly, er tat es vor aller Augen, er machte kein Geheimnis daraus. II. *v.a.* öffnen, aufmachen; entrollen, entfalten; (begin) anfangen; aufschließen (*one's heart*); ziehen (*floodgates*); eröffnen (*a campaign, a railway, fire*); to —n one's heart, seinem Herzen Luft machen; to —n negotiations, Verhandlungen beginnen *or* anknüpfen; to —n a case, einen Prozeß eröffnen; to —n up a country, ein Land erschließen, eröffnen; Livingstone —ned up Africa for us, Livingstone hat uns die Bahn gebrochen ins Innere von Afrika; to —n a line of railway, eine Bahn dem Verkehr übergeben. III. *v.n.* sich öffnen, sich auftun, aufgehen; aufblühen, sich öffnen (*as flowers*); anfangen; sich zeigen (*to one's view*). IV. *s.* freie Luft; freies Feld; in the —n, im Freien. —**ner**, *s.* der Öffner (*also Spin.*); der Eröffner (*of a debate*). —**ning**, I. *adj.*; —ning speech, die Eröffnungsrede. II. *s.* das Öffnen; die Eröffnung; die Lichtung (*in a wood*); (aperture) die Öffnung; (breach) die Bresche; (market) der Absatzweg, Markt; die Gelegenheit (for enterprise, zu Unternehmungen); die Eröffnung (*Railw. etc.*); der Anfang (*of a story, etc.*); there is an —ning for a doctor in this place, dieser Ort bietet einem Arzte gute Aussichten; the —ning of the Soudan to trade, die Erschließung des Sudans für den Handel. —**nness**, *s.* die Offenheit; die Aufrichtigkeit, Offenheit, Offenherzigkeit; die Klarheit, Deutlichkeit; die Gelindigkeit (*of weather*). *Comp.* —**n-eyed**, *adj.* die Augen offen haltend, mit offnen Augen, wachsam. —**n-handed**, *adj.* freigebig. —**n-hearted**, *adj.* offenherzig, aufrichtig. —**n-mouthed**, *adj.* mit aufgesperrtem Munde, gaffend; schreiend, lärmend. —**nwork**, *s.* durchbrochene Arbeit.

Oper—a, *s.* die Oper. —**ameter**, *s.* der Zählapparat. —**ate**, *v.n.* wirken (upon, auf ein S.; *also Med.*); operieren (*Surg.*). —**atic**, *adj.* opernhaft; —atic-stage, die Opernbühne. —**ation**, *s.* die Wirkung, das Verfahren, der Prozeß; die Operation, Unternehmung (*Mil., C. L.*); der (ärztliche) Eingriff, die Operation (*Surg.*); to put in —ation, in Wirksamkeit setzen. —**ative**, I. *adj.* wirksam, wirkend, tätig; (practical) praktisch; —ative arts, die Gewerke; to make —ative, (etwas) wirksam werden lassen, einführen, (etwas) in Wirksamkeit treten lassen. II. *s.* der Hand-, Fabrik-arbeiter. —**ator**, *s.* der, die, das Wirkende; der Operateur (*Surg.*); —ator for the fall, der Baissier (*C. L.*). —**ose**, *adj.*

mühsam. *Comp.* **—a-cloak**, *s.* der Theater=Umhang (einer Dame). **—a-dancer**, *s.* der (die) Ballettänzer(in). **—a-glass**, *s.* das Opernglas, der Operngucker. **—a-hat**, *s.* der Klapphut.

Operculum, *s.* der Deckel.

Ophicleide, *s.* die Ophikleide (*Mus.*).

Ophidia, *pl.* die Schlangen. **—n**, I. *adj.* schlangenartig, Schlangen=. II. *s.* die Schlange.

Ophthalmi—a, *s.* die Augenentzündung. **—c**, *adj.* die Augen betreffend, Augen=; —ic hospital, die Augen=Heilanstalt, Augenklinik.

Op—iate, I. *s.* das Opiat; das Einschläferungsmittel (*also fig.*). II. *adj.* einschläfernd. **—ium**, *s.* das Opium. **—odeldoc**, *s.* das Opodeldok.

Opin—e, *v.n.* meinen, der Meinung sein. **—ion**, *s.* die Meinung, Ansicht, das Urteil; legal —ion, das Rechtsgutachten, das Gutachten eines Advokaten; to win golden —ions, sich beliebt machen, die (allgemeine) Achtung gewinnen; to have a great —ion of o.s., eine (zu) hohe Meinung von sich haben; to hold an —ion, eine Meinung haben *or* hegen, der Ansicht sein; medical —ion, ärztliche Meinung; public —ion, die öffentliche Meinung; settled —ion, feste Meinung; to be of —ion, der Meinung sein; in my —ion, meiner Meinung nach, meines Erachtens (m. E.); to have a poor *or* low —ion of, nicht viel halten von; what is your —ion? was meinen Sie? was halten Sie davon? **—ionated, —ionative**, *adj.* (self- —ionated) hartnäckig, starrsinnig (in der Verteidigung seiner Meinung). **—ionativeness**, *s.* der Starrsinn, Eigensinn.

Opossum, *s.* die (nordamerikanische) Beutelratte.

Oppidan, *s.* der Externe (nicht im College selbst wohnende Schüler) (*at Eton*).

Oppo—nent, I. *adj.* entgegenstehend (*obs.*). II. *s.* der Gegner; der Opponent (*in a debate*). **—se**, *v.a.* entgegen=setzen, =stellen, gegenüberstellen; (object) einwenden, entgegensetzen, widerstehen, Widerstand leisten, sich entgegenstellen (*a person or thing*); (be —sed to) entgegen, zuwider sein; (combat) bestreiten, bekämpfen; (obstruct) hemmen, (einer Sache) Einhalt tun; durchkreuzen (*s. o.'s plans*); to —se a measure, eine Maßregel bekämpfen. **—ser**, *s.* der Gegner, Widersacher; der Opponent (*in debates*). **—site**, I. *adj.* gegenüberstehend, =liegend, entgegengesetzt; (—sed) widerstreitend, feindlich; gegenständig (*Bot.*); —site to (a house, etc., einem Hause &c.) gegenüber; —site angles, Scheitel=, Vertikal=winkel; —site cones, Gegen=Kegel; an effect —site to what was expected, eine ganz andere Wirkung, als die, welche man erwartet hatte. II. *s.* das Entgegengesetzte, Gegenteil. **—sition**, I. *s.* das Gegenüber=stehen, =liegen; (resistance) der Widerstand (to, gegen); (obstacle) das Hindernis; (contrast) der Gegensatz, die Verschiedenheit; (contradiction) der Widerspruch, Einspruch, Widerstreit; (competition) die Konkurrenz; die Gegenpartei; die der Regierungspolitik gegenüberstehende Partei, die Opposition (*Parl.*); der Widerspruch, Gegensatz (*Rhet.*); der Gegenschein (*Astr.*); in —sition to, im Widerspruch mit, im Gegensatz zu. II. *adj.* Oppositions=.

Opportun—e, *adj.*, **—ely**, *adv.* gelegen, günstig, passend, zeitgemäß, angebracht. **—ity**, *s.*, **—eness**, *s.* die rechte, gelegene Zeit, Zeitgemäßheit, das Gelegene. **—ity**, *s.* die günstige Gelegenheit; glückliche Umstände; to take the —ity of . . ., die Gelegenheit benutzen, ergreifen; —ity makes the thief, Gelegenheit macht Diebe (*prov.*).

Oppress, *v.a.* (be)drücken, unter=, nieder=drücken. **—ion**, *s.* die Be=, Unter=drückung, der Druck; (misery) das Elend, die Bedrängnis; (hardship, *etc.*) die Bedrückung; (depression) die Niedergeschlagenheit; die Beängstigung, Beklemmung (*Med.*). **—ive**, *adj.*, **—ively**, *adv.* (be=)drückend, niederschlagend; unterdrückend, tyrannisch (*as a government*); (overpowering) überwältigend. —ive heat, drückende Hitze. **—iveness**, *s.* das Drückende, der Druck; die Beklemmung, die Schwüle (*of the air*). **—or**, *s.* der Bedrücker.

Opprobri—ous, *adj.*, **—ously**, *adv.* schimpflich, beschimpfend, Schmäh=. **—ousness**, *s.* die Schimpflichkeit. **—um**, *s.* (abuse) der Schimpf; (disgrace) die Schmach.

Oppugn, *v.a.* bekämpfen, bestreiten (*fig.*).

Opt—ative, I. *adj.* wünschend. II. *s.* der Optativ (*Gram.*). **—ion**, *s.* die Wahl; at —ion, nach Belieben; what —s are allowed? welche Fächer sind wahlfrei? **—ional**, *adj.*, **—ionally**, *adv.* wahlfrei, freistehend, der Wahl überlassen, fakultativ; —ional subjects, wahlfreie Fächer; to leave it —ional, es (einem) frei stellen; to be —ional, (einem) frei stehen.

Optic, I. *adj.*, **—al**, *adj.*, **—ally**, *adv.* optisch; Seh=; — angle, der Seh=, Gesichts=winkel; — nerves, Sehnerven; —al delusion, die Augentäuschung, Gesichtstäuschung. II. *s.* das Sehwerkzeug; das Auge (*sl.*). **—ian**, *s.* der Optiker. **—s**, *s.* die Lichtlehre, die Optik.

Optim—e, *s.* Cambridger Student, welcher in der höchsten mathematischen Prüfung eine zweite (Senior **—e**) oder dritte Klasse (Junior —e) erlangt hat. **—ism**, *s.* der Optimismus, die Geneigtheit, die Dinge im rosigen Lichte zu sehen. **—ist**, *s.* der Optimist. **—istic**, *adj.* optimistisch.

Opulen—ce, **—cy**, *s.* der Reichtum, Wohlstand Überfluß. **—t**, *adj.*, **—tly**, *adv.* sehr reich, wohlhabend; reichlich, im Überfluß.

[1]**Or**, *conj.* oder.

[2]**Or**, *adv.* (— ever) ehe, bevor (*obs. dial.*).

Orac—le, *s.* das Orakel (*also fig.*); die Weissagung; to work the —le, andere zu seinem Vorteile benutzen (*fam.*); he speaks like an —le, er spricht wie gedruckt. **—ular**, *adj.*, **—ularly**, *adv.* orakelmäßig, orakelhaft; (obscure) dunkel, geheimnisvoll.

Oral, *adj.*, **—ly**, *adv.* mündlich; — examination, — test, die mündliche Prüfung.

[1]**Orange**, I. *s.* die Orange; (sweet —) die Apfelsine, Pomeranze, Orange; (— tree) der Orangenbaum. II. *adj.* orange(=gelb, =farbig). **—ade**, *s.* die (süße) Orangelimonade. **—ry**, *s.* die Orangerie. *Comp.* **—-blossom**, *s.* die Orangenblüte; wreath of —-blossoms, der Orangenblütenkranz, Brautkranz. **—-colour**, *s.* das Orangegelb. **—-lily**, *s.* die Feuerlilie. **—-man**, *s.* der Apfelsinenhändler. **—-marmalade**, *s.* die (bittre) Marmelade (aus Apfelsinenschale). **—-peel**, *s.* die Orangenschale, Pomeranzenschale.

[2]**Orange**, *s. see the Index of Names.*

Orang—-outang, **—-utan**, *s.* der Orang=Utang.

Orat—ion, *s.* die (öffentliche) Rede; to deliver an —ion, eine (große) Rede halten. **—or**, *s.* der Redner; the public —or, der offizielle Universitätsredner (*in Oxford and Cambridge*). **—orical**, *adj.*, **—orically**, *adv.* rednerisch. **—orio**, *s.* das Oratorium (*Mus.*). **—ory**, *s.* die Redekunst; (eloquence) die Beredsamkeit; (chapel) das Betzimmer, die Betkapelle.

Orb, *s.* der Kreis; der Himmelskörper (*fig.*); das Rad (*of a chariot*); der Reichsapfel (*Her.*); das Auge (*Poet.*); *see* —it (*Astr.*). **—ed**, *adj.* rund, kreisförmig; (encircled) umringt. **—icular**, *adj.* rundförmig, rund. **—iculate**, *adj.* kreisrund. **—it**, *s.* die Bahn (*Astr.*); die Augenhöhle (*Anat.*); die Augenhaut (*Orn.*).

Orchard, *s.* der Obstgarten, Baumgarten. *Comp.* **—-house**, *s.* das Treibhaus für Obst (ohne künstliche Wärme).

Orchestra, *s.* das Orchester. **—l**, *adj.* Orchester=; —l concert, das Orchester=Konzert.

Orchi—d, *s.* die Orchidee. **—s**, *s.* das Knabenkraut.

Ordain, *v.a.* (arrange) (an)ordnen, einrichten; (establish) festsetzen; ordinieren (*clergymen*); (appoint) bestimmen, verordnen (to, for, zu); machen, geben (*laws*); (order) verordnen, befehlen. **—er**, *s.* der Anordner; der Ordinierende. **—ment**, *s.* das Anordnen; die Ordinierung (*Eccles.*).

Ordeal, *s.* das Gottesurteil; die (Unschulds=)Probe; die schwere Prüfung, harte Probe (*also fig.*).

Ord—er, I. *s.* die Ordnung; die (öffentliche) Ruhe; (mandate) die Anordnung, Verordnung, der Befehl, das Gebot, Geheiß; (precept) die Regel, Vorschrift; (rule) die Maßregel; der Auftrag, die Bestellung (*C. L.*); das Einlaßschreiben, Freibillet (*for a theatre, etc.*); (custom) die Sitte, Gewohnheit; (rank) die Reihenfolge, Klasse, der Rang, Stand; die (Säulen=) Ordnung (*Arch.*); der Orden (*of the Garter, etc., also Rel.*); in good —er, in guter Ordnung (*Mil.*); wohlbehalten; in skirmishing —er, in Schützenketten; in extended —er, in ausgeschwärmter Schützenkette; the lower —ers, die unteren Klassen; to take (holy) —ers, in den geistlichen Stand treten, die (Priester=) Weihe erhalten; to be in —ers, Geistlicher sein; —er of merit, Rangordnung (auf Grund der Prüfungsergebnisse); —er of sailing, der Befehl, unter Segel zu gehen; marching —er, der Marschbefehl; he has given him marching —ers, er hat ihn den Laufpaß gegeben (*coll.*); —er of battle, Schlachtordnung; —er of the day (of proceedings), Tages=(Geschäfts=)ordnung; to pass to the —er of the day, zur Tagesordnung übergehen; —er of succession, die Nummerfolge; —er in council, der Regierungsbefehl; —er of the Sovereign, der Kabinettsbefehl; to take an —er for, einen Auftrag erhalten, eine Bestellung annehmen auf; in close —er, in dichten Reihen, enggeschlossen (*Mil.*); in —er to . . ., um, zu . . .; to make to —er, nach Bestellung anfertigen; in —er, in (der) Ordnung; the honourable member is not in —er, das ehrenwerte Mitglied bleibt nicht bei der Frage *or* Sache; the motion is not in —er, der Antrag ist ordnungswidrig; call to —er, der Ordnungsruf; —er! —er! zur Sache *or* Ordnung! (*Parl.*); he rose to —er, er sprach zur Geschäftsordnung; to give —ers, Aufträge geben; Befehle erteilen; by —er of Mr. S., im Auftrage von Herrn S.; by —er of the king, auf Befehl des Königs; to keep —er, Ordnung halten; to keep a p. in —er, einen in Ordnung halten; to put out of —er, in Unordnung bringen; to pay to s.o.'s —er, an jemandes Ordre bezahlen; money —er, die Postanweisung; postal —er, der Postbon; standing —ers, die regelmäßige *or* feststehende Geschäftsordnung; rather a big (tall) —er, eine etwas starke Zumutung (*sl.*). II. *v.a.* (an)ordnen, einrichten; befehlen; (prescribe) verordnen; bestellen (*C.L.*); (manage) leiten, regieren, in Ordnung halten; (put in order) in Ordnung bringen; —er the carriage to come round, laß vorfahren; to —er a suit of clothes, einen Anzug (bei einem Schneider) bestellen; we were —ed, wir erhielten Befehl; —er arms! Gewehr ab! to —er (a p.) **about**, (einem) fortwährend Befehle erteilen; to —er **out**, einberufen (*militia, etc.*); to —er out of, ausweisen aus; to —er **up**, heraufkommen lassen, herkommen lassen. **—erer**, *s.* der Befehlende, Anordner. **—ering**, *s.* das Ordnen; das Befehlgeben. **—erless**, *adj.* ohne Ordnung. **—erliness**, *s.* die Regelmäßigkeit; die Ordnungsliebe. **—erly**, I. *adj.* ordentlich (*of rooms etc. and people*); ruhig, sittsam; (regular) regelmäßig, regelrecht; (methodical) Ordnung beobachtend, methodisch; (well ordered) wohlgeordnet; —erly sergeant, die Ordonnanz; —erly book, das Befehlbuch; —erly room, das Regiments=, Bataillons=bureau. II. *s.* die Ordonnanz (*Mil.*); der (Offiziers)bursche (*of an officer*). **—inal**, I. *adj.* Ordnungs=; —inal numbers, Ordinalzahlen. II. *s.* das Ordnungszahlwort; das Ritual (*Eccl.*). **—inance**, *s.* die Ordnung, Verordnung; (rule) die Regel; (usage) der vorgeschriebene Gebrauch. **—inarily**, *adv. see* —inary. **—inary**, I. *adj.* (customary) gewöhnlich, herkömmlich; (commonplace) gebräuchlich, alltäglich; —inary seaman, der Leichtmatrose. II. *s.* das Gewöhnliche; (table d'hôte) der Wirtstisch, das Mahl im Speisehause; (inn) das Speisehaus; der ordentliche, kompetente Richter (*Law*); in —inary, Leib=, Hof=; chaplain in —inary to the king, Haus= *or* Hof=kaplan des Königs; ambassador in —inary, residierender Gesandter; physician in —inary, der Leibarzt. **—inate**, I. *adj.*; —inate figure, regelmäßige Figur. II. *s.* die Ordinate (*Geom.*). **—ination**, *s.* die Ordination, Einsetzung, Amtseinführung (eines Geistlichen). **—nance**, *s.* das schwere *or* grobe Geschütz, die Artillerie; piece of —nance, die Kanone; board of —nance, die Artillerie= und Zeug=Abteilung; master-general of the —nance, der Generalfeldzeugmeister. *Comp.* **—er-book**, *s.* das Bestellungsbuch; das Befehlbuch, Parolebuch (*Mil.*). **—er-form**, — **er-sheet**, *s.* der Bestellzettel. **—nance-survey**, I. *s.* die amtliche Landesvermessung (von Großbritannien und Irland). II. *attrib.*; —nance-survey map, die Generalstabskarte.

Ordure, *s.* der Unflat, Schmutz.

Ore, *s.* das Erz, Metall.

Oread, *s.* die Bergnymphe, Oreade.

Organ, *s.* das Organ, Werkzeug; (voice) das Organ, die Stimme; die Orgel (*Mus.*); das Sprachrohr der öffentlichen Meinung, die Zeitung (*fig.*); to grind an —, eine (Straßen=)Orgel drehen; the — peals, die Orgel braust. **—ic**, *adj.*, **—ically**, *adv.* organisch; —ic chemistry, organische Chemie. **—ism**, *s.* der Organismus. **—ist**, *s.* der Organist. **—ization**, *s.* der Bau, die Körperbildung; die Organisation, Bildung, Einrichtung (*also fig.*); student —izations, studentische Vereinigungen *or* Verbindungen. — **ize**, *v.a.* organisieren, einrichten. **—izer**, *s.* der Organisator, Anordner. *Comp.* **—-bellows**, *pl.* der Orgelbalg. **—-blower**, *s.* der Bälgetreter. **—-builder**, *s.* der Orgelbauer. **—-case**, *s.* das Orgelgehäuse. **—-grinder**, *s.* der Orgeldreher. **—-loft**, *s.* das, der Orgelchor. **—-stop**, *s.* der Orgelzug, das Register.

Organon, *s.* gedankliches Werkzeug (*Phil.*).

Orgasm, *s.* die Aufwallung, Erregung.

Org—ies, *pl.* Orgien. **—y**, *s.* nächtliche Schwelgerei, zügelloses Gelage, das Sauf=Gelage.

Orgue, *s.* das Sturmgatter, Fallgatter (*Fort.*); das Orgelgeschütz (*Artil.*).

Oriel, *s.* der Erker; der Nebensaal, die Galerie (*obs.*). *Comp.* **—-window**, *s.* das Erkerfenster.

Orient, I. *adj.* (rising) aufgehend; (eastern) östlich; (bright) glänzend. II. *s.* der Osten, Morgen; das Morgenland, der Orient. III. *v.a.* orientieren. **—al**, I. *adj.* östlich; morgenländisch. II. *s.* der Morgenländer, Orientale. **—alist**, *s. see* —al II.; der Orientalist (*Philol.*). **—ation**, *s.* die Ostung (*of a church*).

Orifice, *s.* die Mündung, Öffnung; der Magenmund (*of the stomach*).

Oriflamme, *s.* die Oriflamme, Flammenfahne.

Origin, *s.* der Ursprung, die Quelle; (beginning) der Anfang; (descent) die Herkunft, Abstammung. **—al**, I. *adj.*, **—ally**, *adv.* ursprünglich, urwüchsig, bodenständig, echt, Original=; (peculiar) eigentümlich; originell; (first) erst; —al conception, originelle Idee; —al thinker, selbständiger, eigenartiger, originaler Denker; —al manuscript, die Urhandschrift; —al sin, die Erbsünde; —al source, der Urquell; —al text, der Urtext; —al cause, die Grundursache. II. *s.* das Original; der Sonderling, das Original (*fam.*). **—ality**, *s.* die Ursprünglichkeit, Eigenart, Originalität. **—ate**, *v.* I. *a.* hervorrufen, ins Leben rufen. II. *n.* entstehen (in, aus; with, bei); the scheme —ated with her, sie faßte den ersten Gedanken des Planes. **—ation**, *s.* die Hervorbringung, Erzeugung; (source) der Ursprung; die Abstammung (*fig.*). **—ator**, *s.* der Urheber.

Orillon, *s.* das Orillon, Bollwerksohr.

Oriole, *s.* der Pirol (*Orn.*).

Orison, *s.* das Gebet (*poet.*).

Orle, —t, *s.* der Saum (*Arch.*).
Orlop, *s.* das Plattformdeck.
Ormolu, *s.* das Malergold.
Orna—ment, I. *s.* (*also* —ments) der Schmuck; die Verzierung, der Zierat (*also Arch.*); die Zierde (*fig.*). II. *v.a.* (ver)zieren, (aus)schmücken. **—mental,** *adj.*, **—mentally,** *adv.* zierend, Zier=; to be —mental, zieren, zur Zierde gereichen. **—mentation,** *s.* die Verzierung; die Ornamentierung (*Zool.*). **—te,** *adj.*, **—tely,** *adv.* geziert, geschmückt; (fine) schön, zierlich.
Ornitho—lites, *pl.* versteinerte Vögel, Ornitholithen. **—logical,** *adj.* die Vogelkunde betreffend, ornithologisch. **—logist,** *s.* der Vogelkundige, Ornitholog. **—logy,** *s.* die Ornithologie, Vogelkunde. **—rhynchus,** *s.* das Schnabeltier.
Oro—graphy, —logy, *s.* die Gebirgsbeschreibung, Gebirgskunde.
Orphan, I. *s.* der, die Waise. II. *adj.* verwaist; — child, das Waisenkind. III. *v.a.* zur Waise machen. **—age,** *s.* die Verwaistheit, der Waisenstand; (—s' home) das Waisenhaus. **—ed,** *p.p. & a.* verwaist.
Orpiment, *s.* das Rauschgelb, Auripigment.
Orrery, *s.* das Orrerium, Planetarium.
Orris, I. *s.* der Schwertel. II. *attrib.*; — root, die Veilchenwurzel.
Ortho—dox, *adj.* rechtgläubig; strenggläubig. **—doxy,** *s.* die Rechtgläubigkeit, Orthodoxie; die Strenggläubigkeit, strenge Kirchlichkeit. **—dromic,** *adj.* geradläufig. **—dromics,** *s.* die Kunst, im Bogen eines großen Zirkels zu segeln. **—dromy,** *s.* das Segeln in gerader Richtung; *see* —dromics. **—epic,** *adj.* die richtige Aussprache betreffend. **—epist,** *s.* der Kenner der Reinheit und Richtigkeit der Aussprache. **—epy,** *s.* die richtige Aussprache; die Orthoepie. **—graphic(al),** *adj.* schreibrichtig, orthographisch, den Regeln der Rechtschreibung gemäß; —graphic projection, der Aufriß, die Vertikalprojektion; —graphic reform, die Neugestaltung der Rechtschreibung. **—graphy,** *s.* die Rechtschreibung; die Lehre von der Rechtschreibung; der Aufriß (*Geom.*). **—logy,** *s.* die Sprachrichtigkeit. **—pædic,** *adj.* orthopädisch. **—pædy,** *s.* die Heilung der Körperverkrümmungen, Orthopädie. **—ptera,** *pl.* Geradflügler (*Ent.*).
Ortolan, *s.* die Fettammer, Gartenammer.
Oscillat—e, *v. n.* sich schwingen, Schwingungen machen, oszillieren; schwanken (*fig.*). **—ing,** *adj.* oszillierend, in schwingender Bewegung. **—ion,** *s.* die Schwingung, schwingende Bewegung; axis of —ion, die Schwingungsachse. **—ory,** *adj.* schwingend.
Osculat—e, *v.n.* küssen (*rare*); in höherer Ordnung berühren (*Geom.*). **—ion,** *s.* die Oskulation (*Geom.*). **—ory,** *s.* das Oskulatorium.
Osier, *s.* die Korbweide. *Comp.* **—-bed, —-ground, —-holt,** *s.* das Weidenpflanzung.
Osprey, *s.* der Flußadler, Fischadler.
Oss—elet, *s.* das Beingewächs (am Pferdefuß) (*Vet.*). **—eous,** *adj.* knöchern, Knochen=, beinartig. **—icle,** *s.* das Beinchen, Knöchelchen. **—iferous,** *adj.* Knochen tragend, aufweisend (*Geol.*). **—ification,** *s.* die Verknöcherung, Knochenbildung. **—ifrage,** *see* Osprey. **—ify,** I. *v.a.* verknöchern. II. *v.n.* sich verknöchern.
Osten—sible, *adj.*, **—sibly,** *adv.* vorgeblich, angeblich (*as motives*); (apparent) scheinbar. **—tation,** *s.* die Schaustellung; (parade) die Prahlerei, das Gepränge. **—tatious,** *adj.*, **—tatiously,** *adv.* prangend, prahlend; —tatious display, prunkhafte Schaustellung. **—tatiousness,** *s.* die Prahlsucht, Prahlerei.
Osteo—colla, *s.* der Knochenleim. **—logy,** *s.* die Knochenlehre. **—metry,** *s.* die Knochenmessung. **—sarcoma,** *s.* die Knochenerweichung.
Ostler (*usually* Hostler), *s.* der Stallknecht.
Ostracean, *s.* das austernartige Muscheltier.
Ostra—cize, —cise, *v.a.* durch das Scherbengericht verbannen (*Hist.*); in den Bann tun (*fig.*). **—cism,** *s.* der Ostrazismus, das alte athenische Scherbengericht, die Verbannung, der Verruf (*fig.*).
Ostrich, *s.* der Strauß. *Comp.* **—-egg,** *s.* das Straußenei. **—-farming,** *s.* die Straußenzüchterei, =züchtung. **—-hunting,** *s.* die Straußenjagd, Jagd auf Strauße.
Other, I. *adj.* ander; the — day, vor einigen Tagen, neulich; the — morning, neulich morgens; an— way of thinking, eine verschiedene Denkungsweise; on the — hand, dahingegen, andrerseits; on the — side, auf der umstehenden Seite; every — day, einen Tag um den andern, alle zwei Tage, jeden zweiten Tag. II. *pron.* der, die, das andere; each —, einander, sich gegenseitig; somebody or —, irgend einer, jemand, einer oder der andere. **—s,** *pl.* andere. *Comp.* **—wise,** I. *adv.* anders, auf andere Weise; rather pleased than —wise, eher zufrieden als nicht; unless you are —wise engaged, falls Sie nicht anders wie gebunden sind, falls Sie nichts anderes vorhaben. II. *conj.* sonst.
Otios—e, *adj.* müßig, untätig, faul; unnütz. **—ity,** *s.* der Müßiggang; die Zwecklosigkeit.
Otter, *s.* die Otter.
[1]**Ought,** *v.aux.* sollte; I — to do it, ich sollte es eigentlich tun; he — to have known better, er hätte es besser wissen sollen; she — not to have said it, sie hätte es nicht sagen sollen; if she had done as she —, wenn sie gehandelt hätte, wie sie hätte handeln sollen; it — to be so, so sollte es sein.
[2]**Ought,** I. *see* Aught. II. *adv.* im geringsten.
[1]**Ounce,** *s.* die Unze; by the —, nach (dem) Gewicht; half an —, ein Lot; (*in comp.*) =unzig.
[2]**Ounce,** *s.* der Irbis, Jaguar.
Our, *poss. adj.* unser. **—s,** *poss. pron.* unser(e), der, die, das Unserige *or* Unsere; a friend of —s, ein Freund von uns, einer unserer Freunde; in this world of —s, in dieser unserer Welt. **—self,** *pron.*; we —self, Wir Höchstselbst. **—selves,** *pl.* wir selbst, uns (selbst); we —selves, wir selbst; we asked —selves, wir fragten uns.
Ousel, *s.* die Amsel, Schwarzdrossel; die Ringdrossel.
Oust, *v.a.* ausstoßen, stoßen (from, von); entsetzen (einer Würde).
Out, I. *adv.* (not in) aus; (*with verbs of motion*) hinaus, heraus; (not at home) nicht zu Hause, ausgegangen; (outside) draußen; im Felde (*Mil.*); (open) aufgeblüht, in Blüte; (dislocated) verrenkt; (— of office) amtlos, nicht (mehr) im Ministerium, nicht mehr am Ruder; (at a loss) im Irrtum, verlegen, verwirrt; (extinct) aus, verloschen; (let —) verpachtet; (loudly) heraus, laut, offen; (openly) ohne Zurückhaltung *or* Scheu; (to the end) bis zu Ende; his time is —, seine Lehrzeit ist aus *or* vorüber; murder will —, der Mord kommt an den Tag; the secret is — das Geheimnis ist entdeckt; to have it — with s.o., die Sache mit einem ausreden *or* ausfechten; to be (quite) —, auf dem Holzwege sein, sich im Irrtum befinden; keinen Ausweg wissen; to be — in one's calculation, sich in der Rechnung irren; my hand is —, ich bin nicht mehr in der Übung; — at elbows, mit einem Loche am Ellbogen (*lit.*); in schlechten Umständen (*fig.*); I am —, ich bin (aus dem) nicht mehr im Spiele; she went —, sie ging hinaus; I came —, ich kam heraus; to come —, in die Gesellschaft eingeführt werden, ballfähig werden (*of a young girl*); we shall find the rascal —, wir werden den Spitzbuben ausfindig machen; — and home, hin und zurück (*C. L.*); to cry —, laut schreien; speak — ! heraus damit! (read —) lies laut! — and —, von Grund aus, völlig, ganz und gar, durchaus; way —, der Ausgang; way — of a difficulty, der Ausweg aus einer Schwierigkeit; — upon him! pfui über ihn! he is — of the business, er ist aus dem Geschäfte ausgetreten. —, aus! außen! (*Tenn. & Footb.*). II. *s.* die Aus=

lassung, Leiche (*Typ.*); the —s, Oppositions=mitglieder (*Parl.*); the ins and —s of the matter, die Sache in allen ihren Beziehungen; an — and —er, ein Haupt=, Mords=kerl (*sl.*), eine famose Sache (*sl.*). III. (— **of**) *prep.* aus, aus . . . heraus; (beyond) außer; (not in) außer, nicht in; (from) aus, von; (not in keeping) nicht gemäß, zuwider; to be — of, nicht haben, sein ohne; — of date, veraltet; — of humour, schlecht=gelaunt; — of money, nicht bei Kasse; to cheat — of, betrügen um; to laugh a p. — of, einem etwas (lachend) wegspotten; to manufacture — of, fertigen aus, von; — of doors, — of the house, außer dem Hause; — of breath, außer Atem; — of hand, auf der Stelle; the horses got — of hand, die Pferde gingen durch; — of health, ungesund; — of temper, schlecht gelaunt, in übler Laune; — of love, aus Liebe; to be — of love with, nicht mehr leiden mögen; — of sight, — of mind, aus den Augen, aus dem Sinn (*prov.*); — of play, aus dem Spiele, tot (*Footb.*); to be — of pocket by, verlieren an (*dat.*); — of print, nicht mehr im Druck vorhanden, (im Buchhandel *or* beim Verleger) vergriffen; — of time, aus dem Takte (gekommen); — of tune, verstimmt (*also fig.*), unrein; to play — of tune, unrein spielen; — of the way, (secluded) abgelegen, entlegen, (strange) wunderlich, (excessive) außerordentlich, übermäßig; to be — of the run, nicht mehr in Frage kommen; — of sorts, unwohl, matt (*coll.*); verstimmt (*coll.*); get — of my way! geh mir aus dem Wege! I shan't go — of my way to . . ., ich werde mir keine besondere Mühe geben zu . . .; — of the frying-pan into the fire, aus dem Regen in die Traufe. —**er**, *adj.* äußer, äußerst, fernst, außen=. —**ermost**, *adj.* äußerst. —**ing**, *s.* der Ausflug; der Spaziergang; die Landpartie; to have an —ing, einen Ausflug machen. —**ward**, *see* Outward. *Comp.* —**bid**, *ir.v.a.* überbieten. —**-board**, *adj.* außer dem Schiffe befindlich. —**brave**, *v.a.* übertrotzen; an Tapferkeit übertreffen. —**break**, *s.* der Ausbruch. —**building**, *s.* das Nebengebäude. —**burst**, *s.* der Ausbruch. —**cast**, I. *adj.* verstoßen, verworfen. II. *s.* der Auswurf; (person) der Verstoßene, Verbannte. —**classed**, *adj.* geschlagen, besiegt. —**come**, *s.* die Folge, das Ergebnis; it is the —come of . . ., es fließt, entspringt aus . . ., es schreibt sich her von . . . —**cry**, *s.* das laute Geschrei; der Ausbruch von Unzufriedenheit (*fig.*). —**do**, *ir.v.a.* übertreffen; to —do o.s., sich selbst überbieten. —**door**, *adj.* außer dem Hause; —door relief, Unterstützung der nicht im Armenhause befindlichen Armen; —door sports, Spiele im Freien; —door work, Arbeit außer dem Hause. —**doors**, *adv.* aus; hinaus, heraus. —**fall**, *s.* der Ausfluß (*Hydr.*). —**fit**, *s.* die Ausrüstung; die Ausredung (*of a ship*). —**fitter**, *s.* der Besitzer eines Herren=garderobegeschäfts. —**-flank**, *v.a.* überflügeln, umgehen; —-flanking movement, die Umgehung. —**flow**, *s.* der Ausfluß. —**go**, I. *v.a.* schneller gehen als; (einem) zuvorkommen; (einen) übertreffen, überbieten (*fig.*) II. *s.* die Ausgabe. —**going**, I. *s.* das Ausgehen. II. *adj.*; —going tenant, ausziehender Mieter. —**goings**, *pl.* die Auslagen, Ausgaben. —**grow**, *ir.v.a.* überwachsen; verwachsen (*a scar, etc.*); to —grow one's strength, durch zu rasches Wachsen die Kräfte erschöpfen, sich überwachsen. —**house**, *s.* das Hinter=, Neben=gebäude, der Anbau. —**landish**, *adj.* ausländisch; (strange) fremdartig. —**last**, *v.a.* überdauern, länger halten. —**law**, I. *s.* der Geächtete, Vogelfreie. II. *v.a.* ächten. —**lawry**, *s.* die Acht, Ächtung. —**lay**, *s.* die Auslage(n). —**leap**, *v.a.* überspringen. —**let**, *s.* der Ausgang, Ausfluß (*also fig.*); to find an —let, sich (*dat.*) Bahn brechen, sich (*dat.*) Luft machen (*fig.*). —**line**, I. *s.* der Umriß; der Entwurf (*fig.*). II. *v.a.* skizzieren. —**live**, *v.a.* überleben. —**look**, *s.* die Aussicht; der Ausblick in die Zukunft (*fig.*). —**lying**, *adj.* fern liegend (*as a district*), (foreign) auswärtig; (on the border) an der Grenze liegend. —**-march**, *v.a.* schneller marschieren als, (einem) zuvorkommen. —**most**, *adj.* äußerst. —**number**, *v.a.* an Zahl übertreffen. —**-pace**, *v.a.* einen (hinter sich) zurücklassen. —**-parish**, *s.* das äußere Kirchspiel. —**-patient**, *s.* der Haus=kranke (nicht im Hospital). —**post**, *s.* der Vorposten. —**pour**, *v.a.* ausgießen. —**pouring**, *s.* der Erguß. —**put**, *s.* die Produktion; das Förderquantum (*Min.*). —**rage**, I. *v.a.* schmählich behandeln; (violate) schänden, entehren. II. *s.* die Gewalttätigkeit, der Exzeß; das Vergehen (gegen die Sittlichkeit). —**rageous**, *adj.*, —**rageously**, *adv.* (violent) wütend, heftig; (atrocious) abscheulich; (excessive) übertrieben. —**rageousness**, *s.* das Unerhörte; die Abscheulichkeit. —**ride**, *ir.v.a.* im Reiten überholen. —**rider**, *s.* der Vorreiter. —**rigger**, *s.* der Ausleger (*Build.*); der Luvbaum (*Naut.*); (boat) der Ausleger. —**right**, *adv.* gänzlich, völlig; to laugh —right, laut auflachen. —**run**, *ir.v.a.* schneller laufen als (einem); zuvorlaufen; (exceed) übersteigen. —**set**, *s.* der Aufbruch, Anfang, Beginn; from the —set, von Anfang an. —**shine**, *ir.v.a.* überstrahlen. —**side**, I. *adj.* äußer; außensitzend (*as passengers*); äußerst (*as a price*). II. *adv.* (in the open air, without) draußen; I found them standing —side, ich fand sie draußen stehen. III. *s.* (exterior) das Äußere; die Außenseite; (surface) die Oberfläche; (uttermost) das Äußerste; on the —side, auf der Außenseite, außen; at the —side, höchstens, äußerstens; from the —side, von außen. IV. *prep.* außer, außen vor. —**sider**, *s.* der Uneingeweihte, Fernstehende. —**skirts**, *pl.* die Umgebungen; die Vorstädte (*of towns*); der Saum (*of a wood*). —**spoken**, *adj.* freimütig, offen; aufrichtig, offen redend. —**standing**, *adj.* ausstehend (*as debts*). —**-stay**, *v.a.* länger bleiben als; to —stay one's welcome, länger bleiben als dem Wirte lieb ist. —**stretch**, *v.a.* ausstrecken. —**strip**, *v.a.* *see* —run; übertreffen (*fig.*). —**vote**, *v.a.* überstimmen. —**weigh**, *v.a.* überwiegen. —**wit**, *v.a.* überlisten. —**work**, *s.* das Außenwerk (*Fort.*).

Outward, I. *adj.* (external) außer, äußerlich; (visible) sichtbar; (—s) nach außen; menschlich, fleischlich (*Theol.*). II. *adv.* (—s) auswärts, nach außen; (—ly) im Äußerlichen, äußerlich. —**ly**, *see* — II. —**s**, *see* — II. *Comp.* —**-bound**, *adj.*; —-bound ship, ein in See gehendes Schiff.

Ov-al, I. *adj.* eirund. II. *s.* das Eirund, Oval. —**arian**, *adj.* Eierstock=. —**ary**, *s.* der Eierstock; der Fruchtknoten (*Bot.*). —**ate**, *adj.* eiförmig.

Ovation, *s.* die öffentliche Ehrenbezeugung *or* Ehrung, die Huldigung, die Ovation; der kleine Triumph, die Ovation (*Rom. Hist.*).

Oven, I. *s.* der Backofen; Dutch —, der an den Feuerrost angehängte kleine Eisenofen. II. *attrib.*; — door, das Ofenschiebeblech.

Over, I. *adv.* über; (to this side) herüber; (to that side) hinüber; (on the other side) drüben; (on the top) darüber, darauf; (—flowing) (über=)fließend; (in excess) übrig, darüber; (too) allzu; (past) vorüber; (through) durch; — and above, überdies, noch dazu; — again, noch einmal; — and — again, wieder und wieder, immer wieder. — against, gegenüber; all —, überall, allenthalben; — and —, ein Mal über das andere; to tremble all —, am ganzen Leibe zittern; it is all — between us, zwischen uns ist alles aus *or* vorbei; fifty times —, fünfzig mal hinter einander; all the world —, durch die ganze Welt, to deliver —, ausliefern; he will never get — it, er wird nie darüber weg kommen, sich nie darüber hinweg setzen können; to give —, aufgeben, verloren geben; to make —, übertragen, vermachen; to pass — in silence, mit Stillschweigen übergehen; to read —, durchlesen; to run —, überfließen; the opera is —, die Oper ist aus. II. *prep.* über; — our heads, über unsern Häuptern; to walk — a field, über ein Feld hin gehen; all — the world, durch die ganze Welt; all — Europe, durch ganz Europa; — night, während der Nacht, über Nacht; (through the night) die Nacht hindurch; to stay — night, übernacht bleiben, übernachten; — a glass of wine, bei einem Glase Wein; he lives — the way, er wohnt gerade gegenüber; to brood, mourn, prevail, rule, think, triumph —, sinnen, trauern, obsiegen, herrschen, denken, triumphieren über (eine S.). *Comp.* **—act,** *v.a.* übertreiben. **—all,** *s.* der Überrock. **—alls,** *pl.* Überziehhosen. **—-anxious,** *adj.* allzuängstlich. **—arch,** *v.a.* überwölben. **—awe,** *v.a.* einschüchtern, in Furcht halten, setzen. **—balance,** I. *v.a.* überwiegen, aufwiegen; (tip up) umkippen. II. *v.n.* das Übergewicht bekommen. III. *s.* das Übergewicht. **—bear,** *ir.v.a.* (durch Unverschämtheit ꝛc.) überwinden. **—bearing,** *adj.* hochfahrend, herrisch, anmaßend. **—board,** *adv.* über Bord. **—bold,** *adj.*, **—boldly,** *adv.* überdreist. **—build,** *ir.v.a.* überbauen. **—burden,** *v.a.* überladen. **—careful,** *adj.* allzuängstlich *or* behutsam. **—cast,** I. *ir.v.a.* überziehen, bedecken; übernähen, *see* —sew. II. *adj.* bedeckt (*sky*); überwendlich (*seam*). **—charge,** I. *v.a.* überladen (*also of guns*); überfordern, überteuern; (exaggerate) übertreiben; you are —charging me, Sie verlangen mir zu viel ab, Sie machen mir einen zu hohen Preis. II. *s.* die Überladung; die Überteuerung. **—cloud,** *v.a.* überwölken, trüben. **—coat,** *s.* der Überrock, Überzieher. **—come,** *ir.v.a.* überwinden, überwältigen; to be —come with rage, von Wut hingerissen werden. **—-confidence,** *s.* das allzu große (Selbst-)Vertrauen. **—-confident,** *adj.*, **—-confidently,** *adv.* allzu vertrauend; (bold) vermessen. **—-credulous,** *adj.* zu leichtgläubig. **—crowd,** *v.a.* überfüllen. **—crowding,** *s.* die Überfüllung (*of learned professions, of railway trains*). **—-curious,** *adj.* gar zu neugierig. **—do,** *ir.v.a.* zu viel tun; übertreiben (*fig.*); zu sehr kochen, braten (*meat etc.*). **—done,** *adj.* übertrieben; übergar, zu stark gebraten, gesotten (*Cook.*). **—dose,** I. *s.* eine zu starke Dosis. II. *v.a.* eine zu starke Dosis geben. **—draw,** *ir.v.a.* übertreiben; to —draw one's account, über den Belauf des Saldo trassieren. **—dress,** *v.a.* (sich) übertrieben putzen, schmücken. **—drive,** *ir.v.a.* übertreiben, überjagen. **—due,** *adj.* überfällig (*C. L.*); the train was (much) —due, der Zug hatte (starke) Verspätung. **—-eager,** *adj.*, **—-eagerly,** *adv.* allzu eifrig. **—eat,** *v.n. & r.* sich überessen. **—estimate,** *v.a.* überschätzen. **—excitement,** *s.* übergroße Aufregung. **—-exert,** *v.a.* sich zu sehr anstrengen. **—-fatigue,** I. *s.* die zu große Ermüdung, Übermüdung. II. *v.a.* übermüden. **—feed,** *v.a.* überfuttern, überfüttern. **—flow,** I. *s.* der Überfluß; (flood) die Überschwemmung; das Enjambement (*Metre*). II. *v.a.* überfließen. III. *attrib.*; —flow meeting, eine Versammlung, die sich aus dem Überschuß einer größeren bildet. **—-fond,** *adj.* allzu verliebt, vernarrt. **—freight,** *s.* die Überfracht. **—grow,** *ir.v.a. & n.* überwachsen, bewachsen; an —grown boy, ein übermäßig großer Junge. **—hand,** I. *adv.* die äußere Handfläche nach oben gekehrt. II. *adj.* nach oben gekehrt; —hand (twist) service, der Hochaufschlag (mit Drehball) (*Tenn.*). III. *s.* die Oberhand, Übermacht. **—hang,** *ir. v.* I. *a.* überhängen. II. *n.* überhängen; überhangen (*obs. poet.*). **—haul,** *v.a.* gründlich durchstöbern; von neuem durchsehen (*accounts*); überholen, einholen (*a ship*). **—head,** I. *adv.* zu Häupten, oben. II. *adj.*; —head railway, die Hochbahn; —head traveller, der Laufkrahn auf Baugerüsten. **—hear,** *ir.v.a.* zufällig hören. **—hours,** *pl. see* —time. **—indulge,** *v.a.* zu nachsichtig behandeln. **—issue,** *v.a.* zu viel ausgeben (*notes, etc.*). **—joy,** *v.a.* entzücken. **—land,** *adj.* über Land, Überland-. **—lap,** *v.n.* übereinander greifen (*as slates*), übereinanderliegen. **—lay,** *v.a.* überziehen, bedecken. **—leap,** *v.a.* überspringen. **—load,** *v.a.* überladen. **—look,** *v.a.* hinausragen über (*as hills, etc.*); (look —) überblicken; (—see) die Aufsicht führen über (*acc.*), beaufsichtigen; übersehen (*a fault, etc.*); (neglect) vernachlässigen. **—lord,** *s.* der Ober(lehns)herr. **—lordship,** *s.* die Ober(lehns)herrlichkeit. **—mantel,** *s.* der Übermantel über dem Kamingesims, Kaminaufsatz. **—master,** *v.a.* bemeistern, überwältigen. **—much,** *adj. & adv.* allzu viel, zu sehr, übermäßig. **—pay,** *v.a.* zu gut bezahlen, überreichlich belohnen. **—-persuade,** *v.a.* durch Überredung bewegen, überreden. **—plus,** *s.* der Überschuß. **—power,** *v.a.* überwältigen. **—powering,** *adj.*, **—poweringly,** *adv.* überwältigend, gewaltig. **—pressure,** *s.* die Überbürdung (*in schools*). **—rate,** *v.a.* überschätzen. **—reach,** *v.* I. *a.* überlisten, übervorteilen. II. *n. see* —reach I.; in das Eisen hauen (*of horses*). **—-readiness,** *s.* die zu große Bereitwilligkeit. **—ride,** *ir.v.a.* überreiten; über den Haufen werfen, umstoßen (*fig.*); unterdrücken, tyrannisieren (*a minority, etc.*). **—ripe,** *adj.* überreif. **—rule,** *v.a.* übermeistern, überwältigen; (persuade) überreden; als ungültig verwerfen; his wishes were again —ruled, seine Wünsche wurden wieder beiseite gesetzt. **—ruling,** *adj.* regierend, alles lenkend. **—run,** *ir.v.a.* überrennen, überschwemmen; überwachsen, ganz bedecken (*as weeds*); umbrechen (*Typ.*); —run with ivy, efeuumrankt, efeuumsponnen. **—-scrupulous,** *adj.* allzu gewissenhaft. **—see,** *ir.v.a.* beaufsichtigen. **—seer,** *s.* der Aufseher; parish —seer, der Armenpfleger; board of —seers, der Aufsichtsrat. **—-sensitive,** *adj.* zu empfindlich. **—sew,** *v.a.* überwend-lich *or* -lings nähen. **—shadow,** *v.a.* überschatten verdunkeln. **—shoe,** *s.* der Überschuh. **—shoot,** *ir.v.a.* übers Ziel hinausschießen; to —shoot o.s. *or* the mark, sich verrechnen, zu weit gehen. **—shot,** *adj.* oberschlächtig. **—sight,** *s.* die Aufsicht; (mistake) der Irrtum, das Versehen. **—spread,** *ir. v. a.* überbreiten, überdecken; überziehen (*a country*). **—state,** *v.a.* zu hoch angeben, übertreiben. **—step,** *v.a.* überschreiten. **—stock,** *v.a.* überreichlich versehen, überfüllen. **—strain,** *v.* I. *a.* übermäßig anstrengen. II. *n.* sich verrenken. **—string,** *v.a.* (ein Klavier) kreuzweise besaiten. **—supply,** *s.* der Überfluß. **—take,** *ir.v.a.* einholen, ereilen, erreichen; (surprise) überfallen, überraschen. **—task,** *v.a.* (einem) eine zu schwere Aufgabe stellen, (einen) überbürden, überlasten. **—tax,** *v.a.* mit Steuern überladen; über-bürden, -laden (*fig.*). **—throw,** I. *ir.v.a.* umwerfen, umstürzen (*a religion, etc.*); (defeat) stürzen, vernichten; gänzlich besiegen (*an army, etc.*). II. *s.* der Umsturz (*also fig.*); die Niederlage (*Mil.*); der Untergang, die Vernichtung. **—time,** *adv.*; to work —time, in den Feierstunden arbeiten. **—tire,** *v.a.* zu sehr ermüden. **—top,** *v.a.* überragen. **—ture,** *see* Overt—. **—turn,** *v.a.* umkehren, umwerfen. **—valuation,** *s.* die allzu hohe Einschätzung; die Überschätzung. **—value,** *v.a.* zu hoch einschätzen *or* taxieren; überschätzen. **—weening,** *adj.* eingebildet, anmaßlich. **—weight,** *s.* das Übergewicht; die Überfracht. **—whelm,** *v.a.* überhäufen, überwältigen, niederdrücken. **—whelming,** *adj.*, **—whelmingly,** *adv.* überwältigend, niederdrückend. **—wise,** *adj.* überklug. **—work,** *v.* I. *a.* überarbeiten. II. *n.* sich überarbeiten. **—wrought,** *p.p. see* —work; übermäßig erregt (*of feelings*).

Overt, *adj.* offen; aufgeschlagen (*Her.*); — act, öffentliche, offenkundige Handlung. **—ure**, *s.* die Ouvertüre, Einleitung (*Mus.*); der Vorschlag, Antrag; to make —ures, Anträge stellen, Vorschläge machen, einleitende Schritte tun.
Ovi—duct, *s.* die Muttertrompete. **—parous**, *adj.* eierlegend. **—posit**, *v.n.* Eier legen. **—positor**, *s.* der Eierleger.
Ovo—lo, *s.* der Viertelstab (*Arch.*). **—viviparous**, *adj.* aus Eiern lebendig gebärend.
Ovu—le, *s.* das Eichen (*Bot.*). **—lite**, *s.* versteinertes Ei. **—m**, *s.* das Ei.
Ow—e, *v.a. & n.* schuldig sein, schulden; (thank) verdanken; —ing, schuldig; —ing to, zufolge, infolge von, dank (*dat.*); what is the account —ing? wie viel beträgt die Schuld? to be —ing to, herrühren, herkommen von; it is —ing to you that . . ., Ihnen verdankt man es, daß . . . **—ed**, *pret. & p.p. of* —e. **—n**, *see* [1]Own.
Owl, *s.* die Eule; the — hoots, screeches, die Eule schreit. **—et**, *s.* kleine Eule. **—ish**, **—like**, *adj.* eulenhaft.
[1]**Own**, I. *adj.* eigen; wirklich, richtig; innig geliebt; my — self, ich selbst; he has nothing of his —, er hat nichts Eigenes; it is his — fault, es ist seine eigne Schuld; he has his — troubles, er hat sein eigenes *or* auch sein Kreuz; for her — worth, ihrer persönlichen Eigenschaften wegen; you may have it at your — price, geben Sie mir, was Sie wollen; my — darling, mein Liebling; my — dear boy, mein einzig geliebter Junge. II. *s.*; to hold one's —, standhalten; sich behaupten; (*also fig.*) he is holding his —, es geht nicht schlimmer bei ihm. III. *v.a.* eignen, zu eigen haben, besitzen; (claim) für das Seinige anerkennen; who —s this house? wem gehört dieses Haus? **—er**, *s.* der (die) Eigentümer(in); ship —er, der Schiffsreder. **—ership**, *s.* das Eigentumsrecht; (possession) der Besitz.
[2]**Own**, *v.a. & n.* anerkennen; (acknowledge) bestätigen; (confess, — to) bekennen, gestehen; (grant) zugestehen, einräumen; to — to a name, sich zu einem Namen bekennen, einen Namen führen; please — receipt of this letter, bitte bestätigen Sie mir den Empfang dieses Briefes.
Ox, *s.* (*pl.* —en) der Ochs, das Rind; the — lows, der Ochse brüllt; the black — has trodden on his foot, ihm ist ein Unglück zugestoßen (*coll.*). *Comp.* **—-eyed**, *adj.* ochsenäugig. **—-hide**, *s.* die Ochsenhaut. **—-tail**, *s.* der Ochsenschwanz. **—-waggon**, *s.* der Ochsenwagen.
Oxal—ate, *s.* kleesaures Salz. **—ic**, *adj.* kleesauer, Klee-; —ic acid, die Sauerkleesäure; —ic ether, der Oxaläther.
Oxid—ate, *v.a. & n.* anrosten, oxydieren. **—ation**, *s.* die Oxydierung. **—e**, *s.* das Oxyd. **—ize**, *v.a. see* —ate.
Oxy—chloride, *s.* das Oxychlorid. **—gen**, *s.* der Sauerstoff. **—genate**, **—genize**, *v.a. see* Oxidate. **—gon**, *s.* spitzwinkeliges Dreieck. **—hydrogen**, *adj.*; —hydrogen blowpipe, das Knallgasgebläse; —hydrogen gas, das Knallgas, Hydrooxygengas; —hydrogen light, Drummonds Kalklicht. **—mel**, *s.* der Sauerhonig. **—tone**, I. *adj.* auf der letzten Silbe betont, oxytoniert. II. *s.* das auf der betonte Wort Endsilbe.
Oye—r, *s.* das Verhör, Abhören; —r of a bond, etc., die Mitteilung des Inhalts einer Obligation ꝛc. seitens des Klägers an den Beklagten. **—z**, *int.* hört! (*obs.*).
Oyster, *s.* die Auster. *Comp.* **—-bed**, *s.* die Austernbank. **—-knife**, *s.* das Austermesser. **—man**, *s.* der Austernhändler. **—-patty**, *s.* das Austerpastetchen.
Ozone, *s.* das Ozon.

P

P, p, *s.* P, p; *for abbreviations see the Index of abbreviations at end of English-German part.*

Pa, *coll. for* Papa.
Pabul—ar, *adj.* zum Futter gehörig, Futter-, nahrhaft, nährend. **—um**, *s.* die Nahrung.
Paca, *s.* das Paka.
Paca—ble, *adj.* versöhnlich, friedlich. **—tion**, *s.* das Versöhnen, Beruhigen.
Pace, I. *s.* der Schritt (*also Mil. & as measure*); (gait) der Gang; (amble) der Paßgang; die Herde (*of asses*); to keep — with, mit (einem) (gleichen) Schritt halten; at a great —, mit starken Schritten; to put a horse through his —s, ein Pferd alle Schulen machen lassen. II. *v.n.* (einher)schreiten; (amble) den Paß gehen. III. *v.a.* abschreiten, mit Schritten abmessen, begehen; im Schritte halten, (im Gehen) leiten. **—d**, *adj.*; slow-—d, langsam schreitend; a thorough-—d scoundrel, ein ganz durchtriebener Schurke. **—r**, *s.* der Schreitende· der Zeltgänger, Paßgänger.
Pacha, *s. see* Pasha.
Pachyd—actyl(e), *s.* der dickklauige Vogel. **—ermata**, *pl.* Dickhäuter. **—ermatous**, *adj.* dickhäutig.
Pacif—ic, *adj.*, **—ically**, *adv.* friedlich. **—ication**, *s.* die Friedensstiftung; die Besänftigung, Beruhigung (*fig.*). **—ier**, *s.* der Beruhiger, Friedensstifter. **—y**, *v.a.* beruhigen, besänftigen, zum Frieden bringen.
Pack, I. *s.* (bundle) der Pack, das Bündel, Paket; (burden) die Bürde, Last; die Rotte (*of thieves*); die Koppel (*of hounds*); das Spiel (*of cards*); ein Sack (*of wool*); *see* — ice; — of nonsense, lauter Unsinn; the whole —, die ganze Sippschaft; wet —, das Wickeln (in der Wasserkur). II. *v.a.* (zusammen)packen (*goods*); vollstopfen; wickeln (*Med.*); (— up) einpacken, packen (*cards*); (— off) fortschicken; parteiisch zusammensetzen (*members of Parliament*); to — a jury, parteiische Geschworne anstellen. III. *v.n.* sich packen (lassen) (*as goods*); seine Sachen einpacken; to send a p. —ing, einen fortjagen (*fam.*). **—age**, *s.* der Pack, das Bündel, Paket. **—ages**, *pl.* Verpackungen, Kolli (*C. L.*). **—er**, *s.* der Packer, Auflader. **—et**, *s.* das Paket, Päckchen; das Paketboot (*Naut.*); der Brief (of needles, Nadeln). **—ing**, *s.* das Packen, die Verpackung; (stuffing) die Packung. *Comp.* **—-cloth**, *s.* die Packleinwand. **—-ice**, *s.* das Packeis. **—-horse**, *s.* das Packpferd; das Saumtier; das Lasttier (*fig.*). **—ing-box**, *s.* die Stopfbüchse (*Locom.*). **—ing-case**, *s.* die Packkiste. **—ing-needle**, *s.* die Packnadel. **—ing-paper**, *s.* das Packpapier. **—-saddle**, *s.* der Packsattel. **—-thread**, *s.* der Bindfaden, Packzwirn.
Pact, *s.* der Vertrag, Pakt. **—ion**, *s.* die Abmachung (*rare*). **—ional**, *adj.* vertragsmäßig.
[1]**Pad**, *s.* der Steig, Fußweg (*obs.*); (foot—) der Straßenräuber.
[2]**Pad**, I. *s.* das Kissen, Polster, der Bausch. II. *v.a.* auspolstern; wattieren (*a coat*); durch leere Zutaten ausfüllen; beizen (*Dyer*). **—ding**, *s.* das Auspolstern; die Wattierung (*of a coat*); die Watte; der Farbstoff (*Dyer*); literary —ding, die Ausfüllung der Spalten, leere Füllsel. *Comp.* **—lock**, I. *s.* das Vorlegeschloß. II. *v.a.* mit einem Vorlegeschloß verschließen.
[3]**Pad**, *s.* (—-nag) das Reitpferd, der Gaul.
Paddle, I. *v.n.* (mit kurzen Schlägen) rudern, paddeln (*Naut.*); plätschern, patschen (*in water*); tätscheln. II. *s.* das Ruder; *see* —-board; (blade) die Fläche, das Blatt; das Rührholz (*Manuf.*). **—r**, *s.* der Ruderer; der Plätscherer. *Comp.* **—-board**, *s.* die Schaufel. **—-box**, *s.* der Radkasten. **—-steamer**, *s.* der Raddampfer. **—-wheel**, *s.* das Schaufelrad.
[1]**Paddock**, *s.* die Kröte, der Frosch. *Comp.* **—-stool**, *s.* der Pfifferling.
[2]**Paddock**, *s.* das eingehegte Grasland, Gehege (am Hause, für Pferde).
Paduasoy, *s.* ein schwerer Seidenstoff.

Pæan, *s.* das (altgriechische) Siegeslied, der Päan.
Pædo—, *see* Pedo—.
Pagan, I. *adj.* heidnisch. II. *s.* der Heide, die Heidin. **—ism**, *s.* das Heidentum.
[1]**Pag—e**, I. *s.* die Seite, das Blatt; die Schrift, das Buch; —es of history, die Tafeln der Geschichte. II. *v.a.* die Seiten zählen, paginieren. **—ination**, *s.* die Seitenzählung, Paginierung. **—ing**, I. *s. see* —ination. II. *attrib.*; —ing machine, die Paginiermaschine.
[2]**Page**, *s.* der Edelknabe, Edelknecht, Page; der junge Bediente; der Amtsdiener (*Amer.*); ladies' —, der Aufschürzer, Page.
Pageant, *s.* der Triumphwagen (*obs.*); der Festaufzug, Prunkaufzug; (—ry) der Prunk, das Gepränge; (vain show) das Flitterwerk. **—ry**, *s.* das Gepränge, der Prunk.
Pagoda, *s.* die Pagode; das Pagodenbild (*obs.*).
Paid, *imperf. & p.p. see* Pay; — up capital, eingezahltes Kapital.
Pail, *s.* der Eimer. **—ful**, *s.* der Eimervoll.
Paillasse, *s. see* Palliasse.
Pain, I. *s.* der Schmerz, das Weh; (anguish) die Pein; (sorrow) das Leid, der Kummer; (penalty) die Strafe; to be in —, leiden; upon — of, bei Strafe von . . .; upon — of my displeasure, bei Verlust meines Wohlwollens; to put to —, quälen. II. *v.a.* (einem) Schmerz verursachen, (einen) peinigen; (hurt) (einem) weh tun. **—ful**, *adj.*, **—fully**, *adv.* schmerzlich (*of mental pain*), schmerzhaft (*of bodily pain*); (embarrassing) peinlich. **—fulness**, *s.* die Schmerzlichkeit; die Schmerzhaftigkeit (*of physical pain*); die Peinlichkeit. **—less**, *adj.*, **—lessly**, *adv.* schmerzlos. **—lessness**, *s.* die Schmerzlosigkeit. **—s**, *pl.* die Schmerzen; (trouble) die Mühe; (labour —s) die Wehen; to take —s, sich (*dat.*) Mühe geben; to have one's labour for one's —s, sich umsonst abmühen; to be at —s (to) . . ., sich bemühen (mit) . . ., sich kümmern (um) . . . *Comp.* **—s-taking**, I. *adj.* arbeitsam, fleißig, sorgfältig. II. *s.* die Arbeitsamkeit, Sorgfalt.
Paint, I. *v.a.* malen; anstreichen, bemalen (*a wall, etc.*); malen (s.o.'s portrait, einen) (*coll. & vulg.*); schminken (*the face*); malen, schildern (*fig.*); to — from nature, nach der Natur malen; to — the lily, das Gewürz würzen. II. *v.n.* malen; sich schminken. III. *s.* die Farbe; der Anstrich; die Schminke. [1]**—er**, *s.* der (die) Maler(in); —er in water-colours, der Aquarellist, Aquarellmaler; —er in oils, der Ölmaler. **—ing**, *s.* das Malen, die Malerei; (picture) das Gemälde, Porträt; das Schminken; —ing on glass, Glasmalerei. *Comp.* **—-box**, *s.* der Malkasten, Farbenkasten. **—er's-colic**, *s.* die Malerkolik.
[2]**Painter**, *s.* die Fangleine eines Bootes; das Bootsseil, Bootstau; to cut the —, sich aus dem Staube machen (*fam.*).
Pair, I. *s.* das Paar; a carriage and —, zweispänniger Wagen, die Equipage; — of boots, ein Paar Stiefel; — of drawers, eine Unterhose; a — of scissors, eine Schere; a — of spectacles, eine Brille; up three — of stairs, drei Treppen hoch; a two- — back (room), ein Hinterzimmer, zwei Treppen hoch. II. *v.a.* paaren. III. *v.n.* sich paaren, sich gatten; to —, to — off, zu zweien gehen; sich abpaaren, mit einem Mitglied der Gegenpartei verabreden, sich beiderseitig einer Abstimmung zu enthalten (*in parliament or similar bodies*); —ing time, die Paarzeit.
Pal, *s.* der Kamerad, Genosse (*sl.*).
Pala—ce, *s.* der Palast, das Schloß. **—din**, *s.* der Paladin. **—tial**, *adj.* palastartig, prächtig, Palast=. *Comp.* **—ce-car**, *s.* der Salon=, Palastwagen. **—ce-yard**, *s.* der Schloßhof.
Palæo—graphy, *s.* die Altschriftkunde, Lehre von den alten Schriftarten, Paläographie. **—logy**, *s.* die Paläologie. **—ntologist**, *s.* der Paläontolog. **—ntology**, *s.* die Lehre von den vorweltlichen Wesen, die Paläontologie. **—zoic**, *adj.* paläozoisch.
Palanquin, *s.* der Palankin, Tragsessel, die Sänfte.
Palat—able, *adj.* schmackhaft; angenehm (*fig.*). **—ableness**, *s.* die Schmackhaftigkeit. **—al**, I. *adj.* Gaumen=. II. *s.* der Gaumenlaut. **—alization**, *s.* die Palatalisierung. **—e**, *s.* der Gaumen; der Geschmack (*also fig.*); the soft —e, der weiche Gaumen, das Gaumensegel; to please the —e, den Gaumen kitzeln.
Palaver, I. *s.* (parley) das Gespräch; (chatter) das Geschwätz; (flattery) die Schmeichelei. II. *v.n.* schwatzen, klatschen. III. *v.a.* (einen) beschwatzen, (einem) schmeicheln (*coll.*).
[1]**Pale**, I. *adj.* blaß, bleich, entfärbt; to grow —, *see* —II. II. *v.n.* erblassen, bleich *or* blaß werden. **—ness**, *s.* die Blässe, Farblosigkeit. *Comp.* **—-face**, *s.* das Bleichgesicht. **—-faced**, *adj.* blaß von Gesicht, mit bleichem Gesicht.
[2]**Pal—e**, I. *s.* der Pfahl; (—ing) das Pfahlwerk, der Zaun; (limits) die Grenze; der Umfang (*of society, etc.*); English —e, der englische Bezirk (*in Ireland*); within the —e of the church, im Schoß der Kirche. II. *v.a.* pfählen. **—ing**, *s.* das Pfählen; der Zaun von Pfählen. **—isade**, I. *s.* das Pfahlwerk; der Schanzpfahl; der Zaun, das Staket. II. *v.a.* verpfählen.
Paletot, *s.* der weite Überrock, Paletot.
Palette, *s.* das Farbenbrett, die Malerscheibe, Palette. *Comp.* **—-knife**, *s.* das Streichmesser.
Palfrey, *s.* der Zelter (*for ladies*).
Palimpsest, *s.* das Palimpsest.
Palin—drome, *s.* das Palindrom. **—genesis**, *s.* die Wiedergeburt; die Verpuppung (*Ent.*). **—ode**, *s.* die Palinodie (*Poet., Law*); der (poetische) Widerruf (eines Spottgedichtes).
[1]**Pall**, I. *s.* das Leichen=, Bahr=tuch; die Gabel (*Her.*); the supporters of the —, die Träger des Leichentuchs. II. *v.a.* einhüllen. **—ial**, *adj.* Mantel=. **—iate**, *v.a.* bemänteln; beschönigen; (mitigate) lindern; oberflächlich heilen, auf kurze Zeit lindern (*Med.*). **—iation**, *s.* die Bemäntelung; Beschönigung; die Linderung; in —iation of, als Entschuldigung für. **—iative**, I. *adj.* bemäntelnd; beschönigend; lindernd. II. *s.* die Bemäntelung; das Linderungsmittel. **—ium**, *s.* das Pallium. *Comp.* **—-bearer**, *s* der Bahrtuchhalter (bei Leichenfeiern).
[2]**Pall**, *v.* I. *n.* schal, matt werden (upon a p., einem), reizlos sein (upon, für). II. *a.* sättigen, überfüllen; kalt lassen, anwidern.
Palladium, *s.* das Palladium; (*fig.*) der Schutz, Hort.
[1]**Pallet**, *s.* das Strohbett.
[2]**Pallet**, *s. see* Palette; die Drehscheibe; der Vergoldstempel (*Bookb.*); die Pallette (*Gild., Pott.*); der Spindellappen (*Horol.*).
Palliasse, *s.* der Strohsack.
Pall—id, *adj.* bleich, blaß. **—idness**, **—or**, *s.* die Blässe, bleiche Farbe, Farblosigkeit.
Pall-mall, *s.* das Mailspiel.
Palm, I. *s.* die Palme, der Palmbaum; (—branch) der Palmzweig; (— of the hand) die flache Hand; die Handbreite (*as measure*); die Schaufel (*of antlers*); der Sieg (*fig.*); (*in comp.* =) Palm=. II. *v.a.* in der Hand verbergen, wegpraktizieren; to — off upon a p., einem (etwas) aufheften. **—a Christi**, *s.* die Christpalme, der Wunderbaum. **—ar**, *adj.* was auf die flache Hand Bezug hat. **—ate**, *adj.* handförmig (*Bot.*); schwimmfüßig (*Zool.*). **—er**, I. *s.* der Wallfahrer, Pilger. II. *attrib.*; —er worm, die Wanderraupe. **—iped**, *adj.* schwimmfüßig. **—istry**, *s.* die Handwahrsagerei; die Handgeschicklichkeit (*coll.*). **—itic**, *adj.*; —itic acid, die Palmatinsäure. **—y**, *adj.* palmenreich; siegesreich, glücklich, blühend (*fig.*). *Comp.* **—-Sunday**, *s.* der Palmsonntag. **—-wine**, *s.* der Palmwein.
Palp, *s.* (*pl.* —i) das Fühlhorn, der Taster.

—**ability**, *s.* die Fühlbarkeit; die Handgreiflichkeit (*fig.*). —**able**, *adj.*, —**ably**, *adv.* fühlbar; handgreiflich, offenbar (*fig.*). —**ableness**, *see* —ability. —**ation**, *s.* das Fühlen, Tasten (*Med.*). —**itate**, *v.n.* klopfen, schlagen; (tremble) zittern. —**itation**, *s.* das Klopfen; das Herzklopfen (*Med.*); die Aufregung (*fig.*).
Palpebral, *adj.* Augenlid=.
Pals—ied, *adj.* gichtbrüchig, vom Schlage gelähmt. —**y**, I. *s.* der Schlagfluß; das von einer Lähmung herrührende Zittern der Glieder. II. *v.a.* lähmen.
Palt—er, *v.n.* unredlich handeln. —**riness**, *s.* die Erbärmlichkeit. —**ry**, *adj*, —**rily**, *adv.* armselig, erbärmlich, lumpig; —**ry** excuse, armselige *or* lahme Entschuldigung.
Palu—dal, —**dine**, —**stral**, *adj.* sumpfig, Sumpf=.
Pampas, *pl.* die Pampas, südamerikanische Grasebenen *or* Steppen.
Pamper, *v.a.* gütlich tun, reichlich füttern; to — o.s., sich (*dat.*) gütlich tun; verzärteln, *see* Overindulge. —**ed**, *adj.* verzärtelt, verwöhnt.
Pamphlet, *s.* die Flugschrift, Broschüre; controversial —, die Streitschrift. —**eer**, I. *s.* der Flugschriftenschreiber. II. *v.n.* Flugschriften schreiben.
Pampre, *s.* Weinguirlande (*Arch.*).
[1]**Pan**, *s.* die Pfanne (*Cook.*, *Print.*, *Saltw.*, *etc.*); die Zündpfanne (*Gun*); brain-—, die Hirnschale; knee-—, die Kniescheibe. *Comp.* —**cake**, *s.* der Pfannkuchen, Fladen.
[2]**Pan**, *see the Index of names.*
Pan—acea, *s.* das Universalheilmittel, die Panacee. —**cratic**, *adj.* sehr stark; athletisch; pankratisch. —**creas** *s.* die Bauchspeicheldrüse. —**dects**, *pl.* Pandekten. —**demic**, *adj.* das ganze Volk ergreifend, pandemisch; *see* Epidemic. —**demonium**, *s.* die Hölle; das Pandämonium; lärmende Versammlung; der Höllenlärm. —**egyric**, *s.* die Lobrede. —**egyrist**, *s.* der Lobredner. —**egyrize**, *v.a. & n.* lobpreisen. —**hellenism**, *s.* das Allhellenentum, der Panhellenismus. —**oplied**, *adj.* völlig gerüstet. —**oply**, *s.* die völlige Rüstung. —**orama**, *s.* das Rundgemälde, Rundbild, Panorama. —**oramic**, *adj.* panoramisch. —**slavism**, *s.* der Panslavismus. —**stereorama**, *s.* die Reliefdarstellung. —**technicon**, *s.* die Gewerbehalle. —**theism**, *s.* der Pantheismus. —**theist**, *s.* der Pantheist. —**theistic**, *adj.* pantheistisch. —**theon**, *s.* die Ruhmeshalle; das Pantheon. —**tisocracy**, *s.* der Staatskommunismus. —**tograph**, *s.* der Storchschnabel. —**tomime**, *s.* das Gebärdenspiel, die Pantomime; (player) der Gebärdenspieler, Pantomime; ein zur Weihnachtszeit für Kinder aufgeführtes Theaterstück (meist dramatisiertes Märchen); das Ausstattungsstück. —**tomimic**, *adj.* pantomimisch.
Pan—ada, *s.* das Brodmus. —**nier**, —**try**, *see* Pannier, Pantry.
Pand—ar, *s. see* —er. —**er**, I. *s.* der Kuppler. II. *v.a.* verkuppeln (*obs.*). III. *v.n.* kuppeln; fröhnen (to one's passions, seinen Lüsten); (einem) Vorschub leisten.
Pan—e, *s.* die Fensterscheibe (*of glass*); die zugerichtete Fläche (*of a stone*). —**el**, I. *s.* das viereckige Stück, Feld, die Füllung (*of a door, of wainscoting, etc.*); die Tafel (*Arch.*); das Fach, Feld (*Mas.*); die Geschworenenliste (*of a jury*); (jury) die Geschwornen. II. *v.a.* täfeln; in Felder einteilen; —elled ceiling, getäfelte Decke. *Comp.* —**el-picture**, *s.* das Holzgemälde. —**el-work**, *s.* das Fachwerk, Täfelwerk.
Pang, *s.* der plötzliche Schmerz, das Weh, der Stich; die Qual, Angst (*fig.*); —s of conscience, Gewissensbisse; —s of death, Todesangst.
Pangolin, *s.* das kurzgeschwänzte Schuppentier.
Panic, *s.* der (panische) Schrecken, die Bestürzung, Panik; — price, niedriger Kurs (*C. L.*). —**le**, *s.* die Rispe. —**led**, *adj.* mit Rispen versehen.
Pannage, *s.* die Mast; das Mastgeld.
Pannier, *s.* der Tragkorb; der Aufwärter (*in the Inns of Court*); *see* Corbel (*Arch.*).
Pannikin, *s.* die kleine Pfanne *or* Kanne.
Pansy, *s.* das Stiefmütterchen (*Bot.*).
Pant, *v.n.* schwer atmen, keuchen (*also fig.*); to — for, after, verlangen, streben, lechzen nach; to — for breath, nach Luft *or* Atem schnappen.
Pant—aloon, *s.* der Pantalone, Hanswurst. —**aloons**, *pl.* lange Beinkleider. —**s**, (*short for* Pantaloons) *pl.* Herren=Unterbeinkleider.
Panther, *s.* der Panther.
Pantile, *s.* die Dachpfanne, der Breitziegel.
Pantry, *s.* die Speisekammer, Vorratskammer; housemaid's —, die Spülküche.
[1]**Pap**, *s.* die Brust, die Brustwarze.
[2]**Pap**, *s.* der Brei; das Fleisch (*of fruit*). —**py**, *adj.* weich, breiig, breiartig.
Pap—a, *s.* der Papa. —**acy**, *s.* das Papsttum; die päpstliche Würde *or* Gewalt. —**al**, *adj.* päpstlich. —**ist**, *s.* der Papist. —**istic(al)**, *adj.* päpstlich gesinnt, papistisch. —**istry**, *s.* das Papsttum, der Papismus.
Papaver, *s.* der Mohn. —**aceous**, —**ous**, *adj.* mohnartig.
Paper, I. *s.* das Papier; (news—) das (Zeitungs=)Blatt, die Zeitung; (writing, document) das Papier; (essay) der Aufsatz, die Abhandlung, der Vortrag; der Wechsel, die Aktie, die Anweisung (*C. L.*); (— money) das Papiergeld; (wall-—) die Tapete; der Brief (*of pins, etc.*); —s, Papiere, Briefschaften (*C. L.*); — at a short date, kurzsichtiges Papier; curl-—s, Haarwickeln; brown —, (braunes) Packpapier; daily —, die Tageszeitung, das Tageblatt; weekly —, das Wochenblatt; morning —, die Morgenzeitung; note —, Briefpapier; foreign note —, dünnes Briefpapier; stamped —, Stempelpapier; tissue —, Seidenpapier; tracing —, Pauspapier; writing —, Schreibpapier; — of patterns, das Musterbuch, die Musterkarte; hand-laid —, hand-made —, Handpapier; on —, auf dem Papier; schriftlich; to commit to —, (schriftlich) aufzeichnen; to put pen to —, die Feder ansetzen; to take in a —, sich (*dat.*) eine Zeitung halten. II. *adj.* von *or* aus Papier, papieren, Papier=; (slight) sehr dünn; gebrechlich (*fig.*); — army, ein Heer auf dem Papier; — bag, die Tüte; — credit, der Kredit auf Schuldscheine; (I. O. U.'s, *etc.*) Schuldverschreibungen; — kite, der Papierdrache. III. *v.a.* tapezieren (*a room*); to — up, in Papier verpacken. *Comp.* —**-chase**, *s.* die Schnitzeljagd. —**-clip**, *s.* der Briefhalter, Papierhalter; die Zeitungsklemme. —**-currency**, *s.* das (im Umlauf befindliche) Papiergeld. —**-cutter**, *s.* (—-knife) das Papiermesser; die Papierschneidemaschine (*Bookb.*). —**-folder**, *s.* das Falzbein. —**-hanger**, *s.* der Tapezierer. —**-hangings**, *pl.* Tapeten. —**-mill**, *s.* die Papiermühle. —**-money**, *s.* das Papiergeld. —**-stainer**, *s.* der Papierdrucker, Tapetenfabrikant. —**-weight**, *s.* der Papierbeschwerer.
Papier-maché, *s.* das Papiermaché, die Pappe.
Papilionaceous, *adj.* schmetterlingsförmig, Schmetterlings= (*Bot.*).
Papill—a, *pl.* Wärzchen. —**ary**, *adj. see* —ose; warzenartig, Papillar=. —**ate**, —**ose**, *adj.* warzig.
Papoose, *s.* das kleine Kind (bei den nord=amerikanischen Indianern).
Pappus, *s.* die Samenkrone, Wolle (*Bot.*).
Papyrus, *s.* der Papyrus.
Par, *s.* die Gleichheit; das Pari (*C. L.*); at —, vollwertig, auf Pari (*C. L.*); above, below —, über, unter Pari *or* dem Nennwert; — of exchange, Wechselpari; to be on a — with, (einem) gleich, ebenbürtig sein (an Wert, Rang, Wissen rc.); to put on a — with, gleichstellen mit.
Para—ble, *s.* die Gleichnisrede, Parabel; the —bles of Christ, die Gleichnisse Christi. —**bola**,

s. die Parabel (*Geom.*). **—bole**, *s.* das Gleichnis. **—bolic**, *adj.*, **—bolical**, *adj.*, **—bolically**, *adv.* in Gleichnissen; kegellinig, parabolisch (*Geom.*); —bolic curve, die Parabelkurve. **—boloid**, *s.* das Paraboloid. **—clete**, *s.* der Tröster (*Theol.*). **—digm**, *s.* das Musterbeispiel, Paradigma. **—dox**, *s.* (scheinbar) widersinnige Behauptung, das Paradox(on). **—doxical**, *adj.*, **—doxically**, *adv.* widersinnig, wunderlich, paradox. **—gon**, *s.* das Muster, Vorbild. **—graph**, I. *s.* der Absatz, Abschnitt; das Paragraphzeichen (§). II. *attrib.*; —graph advertisement, die Reklame. **—graphic**, *adj.* paragraphisch. **—graphist**, *s.* der Schreiber kleiner Zeitungsartikel. **—lipomena**, *pl.* nachgelassene Schriften; Nachträge. **—llax**, *s.* die Parallaxe, Abweichung. **—llel**, *see* Parallel. **—logism**, *s.* der Trugschluß. **—lysis**, *s.* die Gliederlähmung; —lysis of the heart, der Herzschlag. **—lytic**, I. *adj.* gelähmt, paralytisch. II. *s.* der Gelähmte; der Gichtbrüchige (*B.*). **—lyze**, **—lyse**, *v.a.* lähmen, unwirksam machen. **—meter**, *s.* der Parameter. **—nymph**, *s.* der Brautführer; (abettor) der Beistand. **—ph**, *s.* der Namenszug. **—phernalia**, *pl.* das Sondervermögen der Ehefrau, die Paraphernalgüter (*Law*); (things) Ausstaffierungen, Sachen, das Gerät. **—phrase**, I. *s.* die Umschreibung, Paraphrase. II. *v.a. & n.* umschreiben, paraphrasieren. **—phrastic**, *adj.*, **—phrastically**, *adv.* umschreibend, paraphrastisch. **—plegia**, *s.* die Gliederlähmung. **—site**, *s.* der Schmarotzer; die Schmarotzerpflanze (*Bot.*); das Schmarotzertier (*Ent.*). **—sitic**, *adj.*, **—sitically**, *adv.* schmarotzerisch, Schmarotzer-; —sitic plant, die Schmarotzerpflanze; —sitic vowel, der Sproßvokal, unorganische Vokal. **—taxis**, *s.* die Nebenordnung, Beiordnung, Parataxe.

Parachute, *s.* der Fallschirm.

Parade, I. *s.* der Prunk, Staat; das Gepränge; die Parade (*Mil.*); (—-ground) der Paradeplatz; (walk) der breite Spazierweg, die Promenade; das Parieren (*Fenc.*). II. *v.a.* in Parade aufziehen lassen, zur Parade versammeln, paradieren lassen (*troops*); (make a — of) prunken mit, zur Schau tragen; they —d the streets, sie durchzogen stolz die Straßen. III. *v.n.* in Parade aufziehen (*Mil.*); einherstolzieren.

Paradis—e, *s.* das Paradies; in —e, im Paradiese. **—aical**, *adj.* paradiesisch.

Paraffin(e), I. *s.* das Paraffin. II. *attrib.*; —candle, die Paraffinkerze.

Parallel, I. *adj.* gleichlaufend, parallel; entsprechend, dieselbe Tendenz *or* Richtung habend (*fig.*); (like) gleich, ähnlich; — bars, der Barren (*Gymn.*); — ruler, das Parallellineal; — passages, Parallelstellen; to run — to, gleichlaufen mit; — motion, die Parallelbewegung. II. *s.* die Parallele, Parallellinie; (— circle) der Parallelkreis; (— direction) gleiche Richtung; (similarity) die Gleichheit; (comparison) die Vergleichung, der Vergleich; (counterpart) das Gleiche, Gegenstück, die Parallele; der Laufgraben (*Fort.*); —s of latitude, Breitenkreise (*Geog.*); to find one's —, seinesgleichen finden; to draw a — between . . ., mit einander vergleichen, einen Vergleich anstellen zwischen. III. *v.a.* gleich sein (mit), gleich kommen (einer Sache); (correspond to) entsprechen; vergleichen. **—ism**, *s.* der Parallelismus. **—ogram**, *s.* das Parallelogram. **—opiped(on)**, *s.* das Parallelopipedon.

Par(r)amatta, *s.* ein baumwollartiger Stoff.

Paramount, I. *adj.* höchst, oberst, oberherrlich, unumschränkt; (preeminent) ausgezeichnet; to be — to, höher stehen als. II. *s.* (lord —t) der Oberlehnsherr.

Paramour, *s.* der Buhle(r); die Buhle, Geliebte.

Parapet, *s.* die Brustwehr (*also Fort.*); das Geländer.

Parasol, *s.* der Sonnenschirm.

Parboil, *v.a.* halb kochen, eben aufkochen lassen, abbrühen; Hitzblattern verursachen.

Parbuckle, I. *s.* das Schrottau. II. *v.a.* aufschroten.

Parcel, I. *s.* das Paket, Bündel; (piece) der Teil, das Stück; (lot) die Anzahl, Menge; der Haufe; die Menge (*of fools, etc.*). II. *v.a.* in Stücke teilen; (— out) austeilen; Schmarting legen über (*Naut.*). **—ling**, *s.* die Schmarting. *Comp.* **—post**, *s.* die Paketpost. **—s-delivery**, *s.* die Packetbeförderung.

Parcen—ary, *s.* der Mitbesitz (durch Erbschaft), gemeinschaftliche Besitz. **—er**, *s.* der Miterbe.

Parch, *v.* I. *a.* (aus)dörren, vertrocknen; (scorch) versengen; —ed with thirst, vor Durst verschmachtend; —ed lips, trockne *or* aufgesprungene Lippen. II. *n.* ausgedörrt werden, austrocknen, vertrocknen. **—edness**, *s.* die Dürre. **—ing**, *adj.* sengend.

Parchment, *s.* das Pergament.

Pard, *s.* der Parder, Leopard, Panther.

Pardon, I. *s.* die Verzeihung, Vergebung; (official —) die Begnadigung; der Ablaß (*Eccles.*); to sue for —, um Gnade bitten; to beg —, um Verzeihung bitten; —! Verzeihung! I beg your —, ich bitte um Entschuldigung; wie beliebt? wie meinen Sie? general —, *see* Amnesty. II. *v.a.* vergeben (*dat.*), verzeihen (*dat.*) (*a person*); verzeihen, übersehen (*faults, etc.*); begnadigen; — me! verzeihen, entschuldigen Sie! to — s.th. in a p., einem etwas zu gute halten. **—able**, *adj.*, **—ably**, *adv.* verzeihlich. **—ableness**, *s.* die Verzeihlichkeit. **—er**, *s.* der Verzeihende; der Ablaßkrämer (*obs.*; *Hist.*).

Par—e, *v.a.* (be)schneiden (*nails, etc.*); schälen (*apples, etc.*); abschärfen (*Bookb.*); beschneiden (*fig.*). **—ing**, *s.* das (Ab-)Schnitzel, Schabsel. **—ings**, *pl.* Spähne, Schnitzel. *Comp.* **—ing-knife**, *s.* das Abschärfmesser (*Bookb.*); das Schabeisen (*Tan.*); das Schustermesser (*Shoem.*)

Paregoric, I. *adj.* schmerzstillend. II. *s.* das Linderungsmittel; die Opiumtinktur.

Parent, I. *s.* der Vater, die Mutter (*also fig.*); die Ursache (*fig.*). II. *adj.* Mutter-, elterlich, Ur-. **—age**, *s.* die Abkunft, Abstammung, Familie; der Ursprung; die Urheberschaft (*fig.*). **—al**, *adj.*, **—ally**, *adv.* elterlich, väterlich, mütterlich; —al roof, das väterliche Dach, Elternhaus. **—less**, *adj.* elternlos. **—s**, *pl.* Eltern.

Parenthe—sis, *s.* die Parenthese; die Klammer (*Typ.*). **—tic(al)**, *adj.*, **—tically**, *adv.* beiläufig, eingeschaltet; eingeklammert (*Typ.*).

Parget, I. *s.* die Tünche, der Bewurf. II. *v.a.* tünchen, bewerfen. **—ing**, *s.* das Tünchen.

Parhelion, *s.* die Nebensonne.

Pariah, *s.* der Paria; der Ausgestoßene (*fig.*).

Parietal, I. *adj.* Wand-. II. *s.* das Scheitelbein.

Pari passu, *adv.* im Gleichschritt; gleichmäßig.

Parish, I. *s.* das Kirchspiel, die Pfarrei (*Eccl.*); die Gemeinde; to come upon the —, dem Kirchspiel (als Gemeinde-Armer) zur Last fallen. II. *adj.* zum Kirchspiele gehörig; Pfarr-; von der Gemeinde erhalten; — church, die Pfarrkirche; — clerk, der Küster; — duty, geistliche Amtspflicht; — poor, die Gemeindearmen; — priest, der Ortspfarrer; der Priester (*in Ireland*); — rates, der Kirchspiel-(Armen-)Steuer; — relief, die Gemeindeunterstützung; — schools, die Kirchspielschulen, Gemeindeschulen. **—ioner**, *s.* das Pfarrkind, Gemeindemitglied.

Pari—syllabic, *adj.* gleichsilbig. **—ty**, *s.* die Gleichheit, Parität.

Park, I. *s.* der Park (*also Mil.*), Lustwald, die Anlagen. II. *v.a.* zusammen aufstellen (*artillery*). *Comp.* **—keeper**, *s.* der Parkaufseher.

Parl—ance, *s.* die Rede(weise); das Gespräch; in common —ance, wie man sich im gewöhnlichen Leben ausdrückt. **—ey**, I. *v.n.* sich besprechen, unterhandeln; parlamentieren (*Mil.*). II. *s.* die Unterhandlung; to beat *or* sound a —ey, Schamade schlagen. **—lament**, *s.* das Parlament; in —iament, im Parlament, im Abgeordnetenhause. —**iamentarian**, *s.* der Parlamentsanhänger. —**iamentary**, *adj.* Parlaments-, parlamentarisch (*as acts, debates, papers, etc.*); —iamentary grant, die Parlamentsbewilligung von Staatsgeldern (*for educational, etc., purposes*); —iamentary train, der gewöhnliche Personenzug, Bummelzug; member of —iament, das Parlamentsmitglied, der Abgeordnete. —**our**, *s.* das Sprechzimmer (*in convents*); das Wohn-, Empfangs-zimmer. *Comp.* —**our-boarder**, *s.* der Pensionär in einer Kostschule. —**our-maid**, *s.* das (feinere) Hausmädchen; house-—our-maid, das Hausmädchen, Stubenmädchen.

Parochial, *adj.* zum Kirchspiel gehörig, Kirchspiel-; — officers, Kirchspielbeamte; — register, das Pfarr-, Kirchen-buch; — school, (schottische) Kirchspielschule; — tax, die Gemeindesteuer.

Parody, I. *s.* die Parodie. II. *v.a.* parodieren, scherzhaft nachbilden.

Parole, *s.* das Ehrenwort; die Parole, das Losungswort (*Mil.*); on —, auf Ehrenwort.

Paronym, *s.* das gleichlautende Wort. —**ous**, *adj.* gleichlautend.

Parotid, *adj.*; — gland, die Ohrendrüse.

Paroxysm, *s.* der Anfall. —**al**, *adj.* zum Paroxysmus gehörig. —**ic**, *adj.* krampfartig.

Paroxytone, *s.* das Paroxytonon, das auf der vorletzten Silbe betonte Wort.

Parquet, I. *s.* der Sperrsitz, das Parterre (*Theat.*). II. *attrib.*; — floor, getäfelter Fußboden, der Täfelboden. —**ry**, *s.* das Täfelwerk.

Parr, *s.* der junge Lachs.

Parr—al, —**el**, *s.* das Rack einer Raa (*Naut.*).

Par—rakeet, —**oquet**, —**aquet**, *s.* kleiner Papagei. —**rot**, I. *s.* der Papagei. II. *v.a.* geistlos nachplappern. III. *v.n.* wie ein Papagei sprechen.

Parricid—al, *adj.* vater-, mutter-mörderisch. —**e**, *s.* der Vater-, Mutter-mörder; (murder) der Vater-, Mutter-mord.

Parry, I. *s.* die Parade (beim Fechten). II. *v.a.* (einen Hieb, Stoß) parieren, abwehren, ablenken. III. *v.n.* parieren, fechten.

Pars—e, *v.a.* grammatikalisch analysieren, konstruieren. —**ing**, *s.* das Analysieren.

Parsimon—ious, *adj.*, —**iously**, *adv.* sparsam, knapp; (niggard) karg. —**iousness**, —**y**, *s.* die Sparsamkeit; die Kargheit.

Parsley, *s.* die Petersilie.

Parsnip, *s.* die Weißrübe, Pastinake.

Parson, *s.* der Pfarrer, Geistliche; der Pfaff(e) (*contempt.*). —**age**, *s.* die Pfarre, Pfarrstelle; das Pfarrhaus.

Part, I. *s.* der Teil; (piece) das Stück, der Teil; (number, quantity) die Anzahl, der Teil, Anteil; der Teil, das Glied (*of the body*); (—y) die Partei, Seite; die Rolle (*Theat. & fig.*); der Teil, das Heft, die Lieferung (*of a book*); die Stimme (*Mus.*); (duty) die Obliegenheit, Pflicht, das Amt; for my —, was mich betrifft; the most —, die meisten; for the most —, meistens; in —, auf Abschlag (*C.L.*), teilweise, zum Teil; on the — of, von seiten; to take — in, an (einer S.) teilnehmen; to take s.o.'s —, take — with a p., jemands Partei ergreifen; to take in good (bad) —, gut (schlecht) aufnehmen; she has chosen the better —, sie hat das bessere Teil erwählt (*B.*); — and parcel, wesentlicher Bestandteil; to do one's —, das Seinige tun. II. *adv.* teils, zum Teile. III. *v.a.* teilen; (distribute) ein-, austeilen; (break up) brechen; (divide) trennen, scheiden (*also Chem.*); to — company, sich trennen (with, von); the ship —ed her cables, das Schiff ist triftig gegangen. IV. *v.n.* sich trennen; scheiden, auseinandergehen; to — with, sich trennen, scheiden von, (etwas) aufgeben. —**ake**, —**ial**, —**icipate**, *etc.*, *see* Partake, Partial, Particip—, Particle, *etc.* —**ing**, I. *adj.* scheidend, Scheide-, Abschieds-; —ing breath, letzter Atemzug *or* Lebenshauch; —ing cup, der Abschiedstrunk; —ing gift, das Abschiedsgeschenk; —ing shot, der letzte Schuß (vor dem Fliehen), ein letztes bittres *or* boshaftes Wort (*fig.*). II. *s.* das Teilen; das Scheiden, der Abschied; die Scheidung (*Chem.*); der Scheitel (*of hair*); at —ing, beim Scheiden, Weggehen. —**isan**, —**ite**, —**ner**, —**y**, *see* Partisan, Partit—, Partner, Party. —**ly**, *adv. see* — II. —**s**, *pl.* die Gegend, (gifts) geistige Gaben, Anlagen; from all —s, von allen Ecken und Enden; man of (many) —s, talentvoller Mann; in these —s, hier zu Lande, in dieser Gegend; in foreign —s, im Auslande; —s of speech, Redeteile; component —s, Bestandteile. *Comp.* —-**music**, *s.* mehrstimmige Musik. —-**owner**, *s.* der Miteigentümer; der Mitreeder. —-**payment**, *s.* die Abschlagszahlung. —-**song**, *s.* mehrstimmiges Gesangsstück.

Partake, *ir.v.n.* teil-nehmen, -haben (of, in, an einer S.), (have in common) gemein haben (mit), etwas an sich haben (von); to — of, genießen, essen, zu sich nehmen. —**r**, *s.* der Teilnehmer, Teilhaber.

Parterre, *s.* das Blumenbeet (*Hort.*); das Parterre (*Theat.*).

Partial, *adj.*, —**ly**, *adv.* Teil-, teilweise, partiell; besonder, einfach (*Bot.*); parteiisch, eingenommen (to, für); to be — to, eingenommen sein, eine besondere Vorliebe haben für; — acceptance, bedingte Annahme; — bond, der Teilschuldschein; — success, der Halberfolg. —**ity**, *s.* die Parteilichkeit; (predilection) die Vorliebe (to, for, für).

Particip—ant, *s.* der Teilnehmer. —**ate**, *v.n.* teil haben *or* nehmen (in a th., an einer S.). —**ation**, *s.* die Teilnahme an (*dat.*); (share) der Anteil an (*dat.*). —**ative**, *adj.* teilnahmfähig. —**ator**, *s.* der Teilnehmer. —**ial**, *adj.*, —**ially**, *adv.* partizipial. —**le**, *s.* das Partizipium.

Particle, *s.* das Teilchen, Stückchen; das Atom (*Phys.*); die Partikel (*Gram.*); not a — of, kein Fünkchen von.

Particular, I. *adj.* besonder, einzeln; (individual) besonder; (peculiar) eigen, seltsam; (noteworthy) besonder, außerordentlich; (circumstantial) ausführlich, umständlich; (fastidious) wählerisch; to be very — in, about, in Bezug auf . . . heikel sein; you must not be too —, Sie dürfen es nicht zu genau nehmen; you must be — not to . . ., Sie müssen ja vorsichtig sein, daß Sie . . . nicht . . .; he is not — to a day, es kommt ihm auf einen Tag nicht an; — friend, vertrauter Freund. II. *s.* der einzelne Punkt, Umstand, die Einzelheit; in —, insbesondere; to argue from the general to the —, vom Allgemeinen auf das Besondere schließen. —**ism**, *s.* der Partikularismus. —**ist**, *s.* der Partikularist. —**ity**, *s.* (exactness) die Genauigkeit, Sorgfalt, Pünktlichkeit; die Umständlichkeit; die Besonderheit, Seltsamkeit. —**ize**, *v.a.* einzeln *or* umständlich angeben. —**ly**, *adv.* besonders, vorzüglich, insbesondere. —**s**, *pl.* nähere, besondere Umstände, das Nähere; for —s apply to . . ., das Nähere erfährt man bei . . ., wegen des Näheren wende man sich gefälligst an . . .; to enter into —s, ins Einzelne gehen.

[1]**Partisan**, *s.* der Anhänger, Parteigänger. —**ship**, *s.* die Parteianhänglichkeit; der Parteigeist.

[2]**Partisan**, *s.* die Partisane.

Partit—e, *adj.* geteilt. —**ion**, I. *s.* die Teilung, Absonderung; (part separated) die Abteilung; (—ion wall) die Scheidewand (*also Bot.*); (boarded —ion) der (Bretter-)Verschlag; das Fach (*in a cupboard, in a shop, etc.*). II. *v.a.* (ver)teilen. —**ive**, I. *adj.*, —**ively**, *adv.* partitiv. II. *s.* das Partitivum.

Partner, *s.* der Teilhaber, Teilnehmer, (Mit-)Genoß; der Kompagnon, Associé, Teilnehmer (*C.L.*); der Mitspieler (*Cards*); (dancing —) der (die) Tänzer(in); (spouse) der Gatte, die Gattin; chief —, managing —, der Chef, Prinzipal, Hauptteilhaber; sleeping —, stiller Teilnehmer; senior —, älterer Associé; to be a — in, Teil haben an (*dat.*). —**s**, *pl.* die Fischung (*Naut.*); to be —s, zusammen *or* in Kompagnie spielen. —**ship**, *s.* die Genossenschaft, Teilhaberschaft, Handelsgesellschaft; to enter into —ship with, sich mit (einem) geschäftlich verbinden *or* assoziieren; in eine Handelsgesellschaft eintreten; deed of —ship, der Gesellschaftsvertrag; dissolution of —ship, die Auflösung einer Handelsgesellschaft.

Partridge, *s.* das Rebhuhn; a brace of —s, ein Paar Rebhühner; a covey of —s, ein Volk Rebhühner.

Parturi—ent, *adj.* gebärend. —**tion**, *s.* das Gebären.

Party, I. *s.* die Partei (*Pol., etc.*); der streitende Teil, Kläger, Beklagte (*Law*); (interested —) der Teilhaber, Beteiligte; die Person (*referred to, etc.*); (man, *etc.*) der Mann, die Person (*vulg.*); (company) die Gesellschaft, Partie; das Streifkorps (*Mil.*); the parties concerned, die Beteiligten; offended —, beleidigter Teil; — in contempt, ausbleibender, ungehorsamer Teil; contracting —, der Kontrahent; to be a — to, teilhaben an (*dat.*), beteiligt sein bei; to go to a —, eine Gesellschaft besuchen, in eine Gesellschaft gehen. II. *adj.* Partei-; geteilt (*Her.*); — disputes, Parteikämpfe. *Comp.* —**-coloured, parti-coloured**, *adj.* bunt. —**-jury**, *s.* gemischte Jury. —**-man**, *s.* der Parteimann. —**-spirit**, *s.* der Parteigeist. —**-wall**, *s.* die Zwischenmauer, Scheidewand.

Parvenu, *s.* der Emporkömmling, Parvenu.

Parvis, *s.* die Vorhalle, der Vorhof (*Arch.*).

Pas—chal, *adj.* Passah-, Oster-; *see* Passover. *Comp.* —**que-flower**, *s.* die Osterblume.

Pasqui—n(ade), —**l**, *s.* die Schmähschrift, das Pasquill.

Pass, I. *v.n.* sich fortbewegen, fortgehen (*from one place to another*), ziehen, reisen, gehen, fahren; (occur) vorgehen, geschehen; (vanish) vergehen, verschwinden; verfließen (*as time*); übergehen (from . . . to . . ., von . . . zu); durchgehen (*as a bill*); (— over, end) vorübergehen, vorübersein; durchkommen (*in an examination*); (be tolerable) noch hingehen, angehen; (— current) gangbar sein, gelten; (— for) angesehen werden (für), gelten (für); abgehen (*Med.*); ausfallen, ausstoßen (*Fenc.*); passen, nicht spielen (*Cards, etc.*); to let —, (vorüber)gehen lassen; those who have —ed, die (in einer Prüfung) Bestandenen; to let — unpunished, unbestraft lassen; let that —, reden wir nicht mehr davon; it came to —, es geschah; whence it comes to —, woher es kommt; to — into law, zum Gesetze werden, in Kraft treten; to — **along**, vorbeigehen, dahingehen; to — **away**, fortgehen, weggehen, (vanish) vergehen; to — **by**, vorübergehen; to — **for**, gelten für; to — **into**, übergehen in (*acc.*); to — **off**, vorübergehen; to — **on**, fortgehen, fortrücken; to — **out**, hinausgehen; to — **over**, gehen, setzen &c. über; to — over to the other side, auf die andere Seite hinübergehen; to — **through**, durch-gehen, -reisen; to — through trials, Prüfungen durchmachen; to — **under**, erleiden, sich unterziehen. II. *v.a.* gehen, fahren, reisen, reiten, setzen &c. über, durch, an, an . . . vorbei, über . . . hinaus; kommen über (*one's lips*); (overstep) überschreiten; zubringen, hinbringen, verbringen (*the time*); (spend) verleben; (cause to —) fortschaffen, in Umlauf *or* in Bewegung setzen; fahren (one's hand over, mit der Hand über); (circulate) herumreichen, weiter geben; (strain) durchseihen; (let through, in) vorbeilassen, durchlassen; bestehen (*an examination*); (surpass) übertreffen; zurücklegen (*a year*); zulassen, gelten lassen, genehmigen (*bills, etc.*), ergehen lassen (*a law*); sprechen (*a judgment*); stoßen (*Fenc.*); that —es my comprehension, das geht über meinen Horizont; that —es all comprehension, das übersteigt alle Begriffe; to — o.s. off for, sich ausgeben für; he has —ed an uneasy night, er hat eine unruhige Nacht gehabt; the bill has not yet —ed (the house), der Gesetzentwurf ist im Parlamente noch nicht durchgegangen; the bill was —ed, das Gesetz wurde angenommen; to — an act, ein Gesetz machen; to — the bounds of moderation, die Grenzen der Mäßigung überschreiten; to — one's opinion upon, seine Meinung über (eine S.) äußern; — the butter, please, bitte reichen Sie mir die Butter; to — bad money, schlechte Münze unterschieben; to — to account, in Rechnung bringen (*C.L.*); to — a vote of thanks, einen Dank votieren; to — one's word, sein Wort geben (for, für); to — **by**, übergehen, (not notice) übersehen, unbeachtet lassen; to — **on**, weiterschicken, weitergeben; to — **over** in silence, stillschweigend übergehen. III. *s.* der Paß; (narrow —) der Engpaß; das Joch, der Sattel (*Mount.*); das Streichen (*of a mesmerizer*); (—port) der (Reise)paß; (free —) die Freikarte, das Freibillet; der Freipaß (*Railw.*); (state) der Zustand, die (üble) Lage; der Stoß, Ausfall (*Fenc.*); das Durchkommen, das Bestehen eines Examens; der gewöhnliche Grad (*Univ.*); he only tries for a —, er will nur die gewöhnliche Prüfung machen; things have come to such a — that . . ., die Lage der Dinge ist jetzt der Art, daß . . . —**able**, *adj.* gangbar, fahrbar, zu passieren; gangbar, gültig (*as money*); (—**ably**, *adv.*) erträglich, leidlich. —**ade**, *s.* die Passade; der Stoß, Ausfall (*Fenc.*). —**age**, *s.* das Durch-gehen, -ziehen; (transit) die Durchfahrt, Überfahrt; (sea —age) die Seereise, Überfahrt; der Durchzug (*of birds*); das Durchgehen (*of a bill*); der Korridor, Gang (*Build.*); (way) der Weg; die Stelle (*in a book*); der Lauf, die Passage (*Mus.*); connecting —age, der Verbindungsgang; air —age, der Luftkanal; —age out (in), der Ausgang (Eingang); —age at *or* of arms, der Waffengang; —age home, die Rückfahrt; to take one's —age, sich einschiffen, seine Überfahrt bezahlen; to work one's —age (out), die Überfahrt durch Arbeit abverdienen; birds of —age, Zugvögel. —**ant**, *adj.* schreitend (*Her.*). —**enger**, *s.* der Fahrgast, Reisende, Passagier (*in boat or carriage*); (—er-by) der Vorübergehende. —**er-by**, *s.* der Vorübergehende. —**ing**, I. *adj.* vorübergehend, flüchtig. II. *adj. & adv.* vorzüglich, außerordentlich (*obs.*); —ing strange, sehr sonderbar. III. *s.* der Durchgang; das Durchgehen (*of a bill*); das Ausgeben (*of money*); the —ing of Arthur, das Hinscheiden des Königs Artus; in —ing, im Vorbeigehen, beiläufig. —**over**, *s.* das Passahfest; (paschal lamb) das Osterlamm. *Comp.* —**age-boat**, *s.* das Boot zur Passagierbeförderung. —**age-money**, *s.* das Überfahrtsgeld. —**-bill**, *s.* der Passierschein. —**-book**, *s.* das Lagerbuch (über kreditierte Waren); das Privatkontobuch. —**enger-falcon**, *s.* der Wanderfalke. —**enger-pigeon**, *s.* die Wandertaube. —**enger-traffic**, *s.* der Personenverkehr. —**enger-train**, *s.* der Personenzug. —**-examination**, *s.* gewöhnliche, einfache Prüfung. —**ing-bell**, *s.* die Totenglocke. —**ing-note**, *s.* die Durchgangsnote. —**-key**, *s.* der Hauptschlüssel. —**-man**, *s.* der Student, der das einfache Examen macht. —**port**, *s.* der Paß; (safe-conduct) der Geleitsbrief (*also fig.*). —**-word**, *s.* das Losungswort, die Parole.

Passerine, *adj.* zu den Sperlingen gehörig.

Passim, *adv.* hie und da, an verschiedenen Orten.

Passion, *s.* das Leiden (*of Christ*); die Gemütsbewegung, Leidenschaft; heiße Liebe; (anger) der Zorn; leidender Zustand (*Phil.*); to have a — for, eine Vorliebe haben für; to be in a —, zornig sein; to fly into a —, plötzlich in Zorn geraten; to put in a —, aufbringen; — for gambling, die

Spiel=Wut. **—ate**, *adj.*,**— ately**, *adv.* leidenschaftlich; (vehement) heftig, hitzig; (warm) lebhaft, warm; (hot-tempered) zornig. **—ateness**, *s.* die Leidenschaftlichkeit, Hitze, das Ungestüm. **—less**, *adj.* leidenschaftslos, kalt. *Comp.* **—-flower**, *s.* die Passionsblume. **—-week**, *s.* die stille Woche, Charwoche.

Passiv—e, *adj.*, **—ely**, *adv.* leidend, duldend, passiv; —e verb, leidendes Zeitwort; —e voice, die Leideform (des Zeitworts), das Passiv(um). **—eness**, *s.* der leidende Zustand; (patience) die Geduld, Ruhe, Ergebung. **—ity**, *see* —eness; die Trägheit (*Phys.*).

Past, I. *p.p. see* Pass. II. *adj.* vergangen, ehemalig (*as misery, suffering, etc.*); a — master, ein vollkommener Meister; — participle, das Partizipium der Vergangenheit (*Gram.*). III. *s.* die Vergangenheit. IV. *adv.* vorbei, vorüber; to rush —, vorbeieilen; when the danger was —, als die Gefahr vorüber war. V. *prep.* (after) nach, über; (further than) über, mehr als; half — two, halb Drei; a quarter — twelve, ein Viertel auf Eins; it is — comprehension, es geht über alle Begriffe; — cure, help, recovery, unheilbar, rettungslos; — hope, hoffnungslos; — saving, unrettbar verloren; to be — all shame, alle Scham verloren haben.

Past—e, I. *s.* der Teig; der Kleister, die Pappe (*Bookb. etc.*); die Glaspaste, der Glasfluß (*Glassw.*); die Verdickung (*Cal.-Print.*); die Paste, der imitierte Edelstein (*Jewel.*). II. *v.a.* kleistern, pappen; to —e **on**, ankleistern, aufkleben; to —e **up**, aufkleistern. **—eboard**, I. *s.* der Pappdeckel, Karton, die Pappe. II. *attrib.;* aus Pappe gefertigt, pappen; —eboard binding, der Pappband; —eboard box, die Pappschachtel. **—el**, *s.* der Pastellstift; der Waid (*Dyer.*); (—drawing) das Pastellgemälde. **—il**, *s. see* —el; das Räucherkerzchen. **—ry**, *s.* das feine Backwerk; die Kruste von Backwerk; Pasteten, Konditorwaren (*collect.*). **—y**, I. *adj.* teigig. II. *s.* die (Fleisch=) Pastete. *Comp.* **—e-cutter**, *s.* das Teigrädchen (*Cook.*). **—e-pot**, *s.* der Kleistertopf. **—e-roller**, *s.* die Teigrolle. **—ry-cook**, *s.* der Pastetenbäcker, Konditor; —ry-cook's shop, die Konditorei.

Pastern, I. *s.* die Fessel. II. *attrib.;* — joint, das Fesselgelenk.

Pastime, *s.* der Zeitvertreib, die Kurzweil; as a —, zum Zeitvertreib.

Pastor, *s.* der Seelsorger, Pastor (*fig.*); der Hirte (*obs.*). **—al**, I. *adj.* Hirten=, Schäfer=; geistlich, Pastoral=; —al play, das Schäferspiel; —al poet, der Idyllendichter; —al poetry, die Hirtendichtung, Schäferdichtung; —al letter, der Hirtenbrief (*of a bishop, etc.*); —al duties, geistliche Pflichten; —al staff, der Hirtenstab (*Eccl.*). II. *s.* das Pastoral, Hirtengedicht; *see* —al letter; das Pastorale (*Mus.*). **—ate**, *s.* das Pfarramt, Pastorat. **—ship**, *s.* das Pfarramt, Pastorat.

Pastur—age, *s.* das Weiden; (—e land *or* grass) das Weideland, die Weide. **—e**, I. *s.* die Weide; *see* —e-land; common of —e, das Weiderecht (*Law*). II. *v.a. & n.* weiden. *Comp.* **—e-land**, *s.* das Weideland.

[1]**Pat**, *adj. & adv.* passend, treffend, tauglich; very —, gerade recht; he had it quite —, er hatte es am Schnürchen (*fam.*). **—ness**, *s.* die Paßlichkeit.

[2]**Pat**, I. *s.* der Patsch, Klapps; das Stück (*of butter*). II. *v.a.* gelinde schlagen, klopfen, tätscheln. **—ter**, *see* [1]Patter.

Patch, I. *s.* der Fleck, Lappen, Flicken; das Stück (of land, Land); das Schönpflästerchen (*for the face*); das Kugelpflaster (*Mil.*); cross- —, der Murrkopf (*vulg.*). II. *v.a.* (zusammen)flicken, ausbessern; verpfuschen (*fig.*); to — up, zusammenflicken; (arrange hastily) eilig abmachen; obenhin heilen (*a disease*); übertünchen (*a matter*). **—er**, *s.* der Flicker; der Pfuscher, Stümper (*fig.*). **—y**, *adj.* voller Flicken, zusammengestoppelt (*fig.*). *Comp.* **—work**, *s.* das Flickwerk.

Patchouli, *s.* das Patschuli, Patchouli.

Pate, *s.* der Kopf, Schädel (*fam.*); die Haut eines Kalbskopfs. **—d**, *adj.* =köpfig.

Pate—lla, *s.* die Kniescheibe (*Anat.*); die Schüsselschnecke (*Mollusc.*). **—lliform**, *adj.* schüsselförmig. **—n**, *s.* der Napf; die Patene, das Kelchschüsselchen (*Eccl.*). **—nt**, I. *adj.* offen (kundig), offenbar; (—nted) patentiert; —nt flue, die Preßkohlen; —nt leather, das Glanzleder; —nt (leather) boot, der Lackstiefel. II. *s.* das Patent, Privilegium; to take out a —nt for, ein Patent nehmen auf (*acc.*); the —nt is expired, das Patent ist erloschen, abgelaufen. III. *v.a.* patentieren. **—ntability**, *s.* die Patentierbarkeit. **—ntable**, *adj.* patentierbar. **—ntee**, *s.* der Patentinhaber. *Comp.* **—nt-office**, *s.* das Patentamt.

Pater—nal, *adj.*, **—nally**, *adv.* väterlich; —nal government, väterliche (oder übertriebene) Fürsorge der Regierung. **—nity**, *s.* die Vaterschaft. **—noster**, *s.* das Vaterunser; der Perlstab (*Arch.*); (rosary) der Rosenkranz. *Comp.* **—noster-pump**, *s.* das Paternosterwerk.

Path, *s.* der Pfad, Weg. **—less**, *adj.* pfadlos. *Comp.* **—way**, *s.* der Pfad (*also fig.*), Fußweg, Bürgersteig.

Path—etic, *adj.*, **—etically**, *adv.* rührend, ergreifend, erschütternd, pathetisch. **—ognomy**, *s.* die Krankheitszeichenlehre. **—ological**, *adj.*, **—ologically**, *adv.* pathologisch. **—ologist**, *s.* der Patholog. **—ology**, *s.* die Krankheitslehre. **—os**, *s.* die tiefe Gefühlserregung, das Pathos.

Patien—ce, *s.* die Geduld; die Duldung, Nachsicht; die Ausdauer; (forbearance) die Langmut; die Patience (*Cards*); to lose all —ce with, ungehalten werden über (*acc.*); to be out of —ce with, aufgebracht sein gegen *or* über (*acc.*). **—t**, I. *adj.*, **—tly**, *adv.* geduldig, langmütig; ausdauernd; (—t of) erduldend, geduldig ertragend. II. *s.* der, die Kranke; der, die Patient(in).

Patina, *s.* der Edelrost (auf Antiken).

Patonce, *s.* das Kleeblattkreuz (*Her.*).

Patri—arch, *s.* der Patriarch, Erzvater. **—archal**, *adj.* patriarchalisch. **—archate**, *s.* das Patriarchat. **—cian**, I. *adj.* patrizisch; adelig (*fig.*). II. *s.* der Patrizier. **—monial**, *adj.* ererbt, Erb=. **—mony**, *s.* das Erbgut, väterliche Erbteil, das Erbvermögen; —mony of St. Peter, das Patrimonium Petri. **—ot**, *s.* der Vaterlandsfreund, Patriot. **—otic**, *adj.* vaterlandsliebend, patriotisch. **—otism**, *s.* die Vaterlandsliebe, der Patriotismus. **—stic**, *adj.* patristisch, die Kirchenväter betreffend. **—stics**, *s.* die Patristik.

Patrol, I. *s.* die Runde (*Mil.*); (men) die Patrouille, Streifwache. II. *v.n.* die Runde machen, patrouillieren. III. *v.a.* durchschreiten, begehen; to — the streets, durch die Straßen die Runde machen, die Straßen abpatrouillieren (*Mil.*).

Patron, *s.* der Schutzherr, Patron; (protector) der Beschützer, Gönner; der Patron (*Eccl.*); (—saint) der Schutzheilige. **—age**, *s.* die Beschützung, Gönnerschaft; der Schutz; das Patronatsrecht (*Eccl.*). **—ess**, *s.* die Schutzherrin, Patronin; die Gönnerin. **—ize**, *v.a.* in Schutz nehmen, begünstigen; he is fond of —izing people, er mag gern patronisieren; the sale was —ized by, es interessierten sich für den Verkauf. **—izer**, *s.* der Beschützer, Gönner. **—izing**, *adj.*, **—izingly**, *adv.* beschützend; gönnerhaft; —izing air, die Gönnermiene. **—ymic**, *s.* der Geschlechtsname.

Patten, *s.* der Holzschuh; die Unterlage des Säulenstuhls, der Sockel (*Arch.*).

[1]**Patter**, *v.n.* platschend aufschlagen, niederplatschen; to — **along**, trippeln; to — **down**, platschend herabfallen.

[2]**Patter**, I. *v.a.* (her)plappern; to — flash, die Gaunersprache sprechen (*sl.*). II. *s.* das Kauderwelsch (*of a class, etc.*); (chatter) das Plappern,

Geplapper. *Comp.* **—-song**, *s.* das Lied, bei dem die Worte äußerst schnell gesprochen werden.

Pattern, I. *s.* das Muster (*also fig.*); needlework —, Stickmuster; book of —s, das Musterbuch; according to —, nach Muster; to take — by, sich (*dat.*) ein Beispiel nehmen an (*dat.*). II. *attrib.*; — pupil, der Musterschüler. *Comp.* **—-post**, *s.* die Warenproben-Post; to send by —-post, als Muster ohne Wert senden.

Patty, *s.* das Pastetchen.

Patulous, *adj.* offen ausgebreitet, abstehend (*Bot.*).

Paucity, *s.* die Wenigkeit, geringe Anzahl *or* Menge.

Paunch, *s.* der Wanst. **—y**, *adj.* dickbauchig.

Pauper, I. *s.* der Arme, Almosenempfänger, auf Gemeindekosten Erhaltene. II. *attrib.*; — children, Armenkinder; — school, die Armenschule. **—ism**, *s.* die Armut; das Armenwesen, der Pauperismus. **—ization**, *s.* die Verarmung. **—ize**, *v.a.* zum Armen machen, in Armut bringen. **—s**, *pl.* die Armen (*coll.*).

Paus—e, I. *s.* die Unterbrechung, Pause, das Innehalten, der Stillstand, Absatz; der Gedankenstrich (*Typ.*); die Fermate (𝄐 *Mus.*); to give —e, zum Stillstehen bringen; to make a —e, *see* —e II. II. *v.n.* innehalten, pausieren; (wait) warten; (hesitate) zögern. **—er**, *s.* der Pausierende. **—ingly**, *adv.* in Absätzen.

Pav—e, *v.a.* pflastern; bahnen (*the way, fig.*); —ed floor, gepflasterter Fußboden. **—ement**, *s.* das Pflaster, Straßenpflaster; (footway) der Bürgersteig; mosaic *or* tesselated, asphalt, flagged —ement, Mosaik-, Asphalt-, Fliesenpflaster; on the —ement, auf der Straße. **—er**, **—ier**, *s.* der Pflasterer. **—ing**, I. *adj.* Pflaster-. II. *s.* die Pflasterung; (—ement) das Pflaster-. *Comp.* **—ing-beetle**, *s.* die Handramme. **—ing-stone**, *s.* der Pflasterstein.

Pavilion, *s.* das Zelt; das Wappenzelt (*Her.*); das Häuschen, Gartenhäuschen, die Schutzhütte, der Pavillon (*Arch., in a garden, etc.*); die Flagge (*Mil.*); (— roof) das Zeltdach.

Pavonine, *adj.* pfauenartig.

Paw, I. *s.* die Pfote, Tatze; cat's —, das Katzenpfötchen. II. *v.a. & n.* scharren, kratzen. III. *v.a.* (fawn on) streicheln; tölpisch angreifen (*things*). **—ed**, *adj.* mit Pfoten (versehen); breitfüßig.

Pawk—iness, *s.* die Pfiffigkeit. **—y**, *adj.* pfiffig.

Pawl, *s.* der Sperrhaken. *Comp.* **—-press**, *s.* die Hebelpresse.

[1]**Pawn**, I. *s.* das Pfand, Unterpfand; in —, verpfändet, versetzt. II. *v.a.* verpfänden, versetzen. **—er**, *s.* der Verpfänder, Pfandschuldner. *Comp.* **—broker**, *s.* der Pfandleiher; —(broker's) shop, das Leihhaus. **—broking**, *s.* das (Pfand-) Leihgeschäft. **—-ticket**, *s.* der Pfandschein.

[2]**Pawn**, *s.* der Bauer (*Chess*).

Pay, I. *ir.v.a.* (be)zahlen, Zahlung leisten; (re—) (be)lohnen, vergelten; erweisen, bezeugen (*attention, etc.*); abstatten (*a visit*); to — an account, eine Rechnung bezahlen; to get paid, sich bezahlt machen; to — attention to . . ., Acht geben auf (*acc.*) . . .; he had to — dearly for it, es kam ihm teuer zu stehen; to — the reckoning, die Zeche bezahlen; to — **away**, ausgeben, auszahlen (*money*), ausstecken (*cable*); to — **back**, zurückzahlen, wiedergeben; to — a p. back in his own coin, einen mit gleicher Münze bezahlen; to — **down**, hinzahlen, bar bezahlen; to — **for**, *see* — II.; to — **in**, einschießen; to — **off**, abzahlen, abtragen (*capital, etc.*), abdanken (*a crew*); to — **out**, ausstechen (*Naut.*); to — s.o. out, es einen bitter vergelten lassen; to — **up**, vollständig einzahlen (*shares*). II. *ir.v.n.* sich bezahlt machen, sich lohnen; it does not —, es lohnt sich nicht; a —ing subject, ein Gegenstand, dessen Studium *or* Lehren sich bezahlt macht; a —ing concern, ein einträgliches Geschäft; a —ing guest, ein Pensionär; to — **for**, bezahlen für; (atone for) büßen für; (reward) lohnen. III. *s.* die Bezahlung; (wages) der Lohn; der Sold (*of a soldier, etc.*); die Belohnung (*fig.*). **—able**, *adj.* zahlbar; fällig, abgelaufen (*as bills*); to make —able (to), zahlbar machen (an). **—ee**, *s.* der Inhaber, der Vorzeiger eines Wechsels. **—er**, *s.* der (Be-)Zahler; der Trassat (*C. L.*). **—ment**, *s.* die (Be-)Zahlung; (wages, *etc.*) der Lohn; der Sold, die Löhnung (*Mil.*); die Belohnung (*fig.*); der Eingang (*of a draft, etc.*); —ment by results, Unterstützung von Schulen aus öffentlichen Mitteln je nach Ausfall der Prüfungen; —ment on account, eine a Contozahlung; as —ment for, als Gegensatz für; received —ment, dankend erhalten; —ment in kind, die Naturalbezahlung; —ment by instalments, die Teilzahlung; deferred —ment (arrangement), die Abschlagszahlung, Ratenzahlung. *Comp.* **—-bill**, *s.* die Auszahlungsliste (*Mil.*). **—-day**, *s.* der Zahltag; der Löhnungstag (*Mil.*). **—master**, *s.* der Zahlmeister; der Zahler. **—-office**, *s.* das Zahlamt.

Paynim, *s.* das Heidentum; der Heide (*obs.*).

Pea, *s.* die Erbse; sweet —s, wohlriechende Wicken. **—se**, *s.* Erbsen (*collectively*). *Comp.* **—-pod**, *s.* die Erbsenschote. **—-shooter**, *s.* das Pustrohr. **—-soup**, *s.* die Erbsensuppe.

Peace, I. *s.* der Friede; die Ruhe (*of mind, etc.*); to keep the —, sich ruhig verhalten; to hold one's —, schweigen; treaty of —, der Friedensvertrag; to make one's — with, sich mit (einem) aussöhnen; to make — between, (Personen) versöhnen; to be (live) at — with all men, in Eintracht mit allen Menschen leben; — of mind, die Seelenruhe. II. *attrib.*; — footing, — establishment, der Friedensfuß (*Mil.*). III. *int.* still! ruhig! **—able**, *adj.*, **—ably**, *adv.* fried-lich, -sam, -fertig; (quiet) ruhig, ungestört. **—ableness**, *s.* die Friedlichkeit, stille Ruhe. **—ful**, *adj.*, **—fully**, *adv.* *see* —able; sanft, mild. **—fulness**, *s.* *see* —ableness. *Comp.* **—maker**, *s.* der Friedensstifter. **—-offering**, *s.* das Sühnopfer. **—-officer**, *s.* der Sicherheitsbeamte, Polizeibeamte; der Schutzmann. **—-party**, *s.* die Friedenspartei.

[1]**Peach**, *s.* der Pfirsich. *Comp.* **—-colour**, *s.* die Pfirsichfarbe. **—-tree**, *s.* der Pfirsichbaum.

[2]**Peach**, *v.n.* angeben (*sl.*). **—er**, *s.* der Angeber.

Pea—chick, *s.* der junge Pfau. **—cock**, *s.* der (männliche) Pfau, Pfauhahn; the —cock screams, der Pfau schreit. **—fowl**, *s.* der Pfau. **—hen**, *s.* die Pfauhenne.

Pea-jacket, *s.* die schwere Tuchjacke.

Peak, I. *s.* die Spitze; der Gipfel, die Spitze (*of a hill, etc.*); das Horn, die Zinne (*Mount.*); — of a cap, der Mützenschirm. II. *v.n.* spitz aussehn, kränkeln. **—ed**, *adj.* spitz; —ed beard, der Spitzbart. **—ing**, **—ish**, **—y**, *adj.* kränklich aussehend.

Peal, I. *s.* der Schall; das Geläute (*of bells*); (bells) das Glockenspiel; das Getöse, Gekrach, Rollen (*of thunder, cannon, etc.*); organ —, das Orgelgebraus; —s of applause, der Beifallssturm; —s of laughter, schallendes Gelächter. II. *v.n.* krachen, donnern (*of cannon*); brausen (*of organs*). III. *v.a.* läuten; laut ausrufen.

Pear, *s.* die Birne; winter —, die Spätbirne. *Comp.* **—-shaped**, *adj.* birnenförmig. **—-tree**, der Birnbaum.

Pearl, I. *s.* die Perle (*also fig.*); die Perlschrift (*Typ.*); der Fleck im Auge (*Med.*); die Glattbutte (*Icht.*); string of —s, die Perlenschnur. II. *adj.* von Perlen; — necklace, Perlenhalsband. **—y**, *adj.* perlenreich; (—-like) perlenartig; perlend (*Mus.*). **—aceous**, *adj.* perlmutterartig. *Comp.* **—ash**, *s.* die Perlasche **—-barley**, *s.* die Perlgraupen. **—-diver**, *s.* der Perlfischer. **—-eye**, *s.* der weiße Fleck im Auge, der Star. **—-eyed**, *adj.* einen weißen

Fleck im Auge habend. **—-fishery**, *s.* die Perlenfischerei. **—-gray**, *adj.* perlengrau. **—-oyster**, *s.* indische Perlmuschel. **—-powder**, **—-white**, *s.* das Perlweiß.

Peasant, I. *s.* der Bauer, Landmann. II. *adj.* bäuerlich, ländlich; — proprietor, bäuerlicher Grundbesitzer; — woman, die Bäuerin. **—ry**, *s.* die Bauernschaft, das Landvolk.

Peat, *s.* der (Brenn=)Torf; to make —, Torf stechen. **—y**, *adj.* Torf=, torfähnlich. *Comp.* **—-bog**, *s.* das Torfmoor **—-stack**, *s.* der Torfstoß.

Pebbl—e, *s.* der Kieselstein. **—es**, *pl.* grober Kies; Scotch —es, bunte schottische Achatsteine. **—y**, *adj.* kieselig, Kiesel=.

Pecca—bility, *s.* die Sündhaftigkeit. **—ble**, *adj.* sündig, sündhaft. **—dillo**, *s.* kleine, leichte Sünde. **—nt**, *adj.* sündig; (bad) böse. **—vi**, *v.n.*; to cry —vi, um Vergebung bitten, seine Fehler bekennen.

Peccary, *s.* das Nabelschwein, Pekari.

¹Peck, *s.* ein Viertel Buschel; die Portion (*fig.*); die Menge (*of trouble, etc.*).

²Peck, I. *s.* der Pick. II. *v.a.* & *n.* picken (*as a bird*); hacken (*with an axe*); to — up, aufpicken. **—er**, *s.* der Pickende; *see* Wood—er; *see* Pick; das Relais (*Tele.*). **—ish**, *adj.* hungrig (*coll.*).

Pect—en, *s.* der Kamm (*Anat.*); die Kammuschel. **—inate**, *adj.* kammförmig. **—inite**, versteinerte Kammuschel.

Pectic, *adj.*; — acid, die Gallertsäure.

Pectoral, I. *adj.* zur Brust gehörig; Brust=. II. *s.* das Brustmittel; das Pektorale (*of Jewish priests*); das Brustschild (*R. C.*); (— fin) die Brustflosse.

Peculat—e, *v.a.* unterschlagen (*public money*); (steal) stehlen. **—ion**, *s.* der Unterschleif, die Veruntreuung öffentlicher Gelder; die Dieberei. **—or**, *s.* der Kassendieb.

Peculiar, *adj.*, **—ly**, *adv.* eigen(tümlich); (special) besonder; (strange) seltsam; vertraut (*as a friend*). **—ity**, *s.* die Eigenheit, Eigentümlichkeit, Seltsamkeit, Absonderlichkeit.

Pecuniary, *adj.* Geld betreffend, Geld=; from a — point of view, vom pekuniären Standpunkte aus; — aid, die Geldunterstützung; — demands, Geldforderungen; — trouble, die Geldverlegenheit.

Pedagog—ic, *adj.* erzieherisch, pädagogisch; —ic skill, das Lehrgeschick. **—ics**, *s.* die Erziehungslehre, Erziehungskunst, Pädagogik. **—ism**, *s.* das Erziehungswesen. **—ue**, *s.* der Erzieher, Schulmann, Pädagog; der Schulfuchs (*in contempt*). **—y**, *s. see* —ism, —ics.

Ped—al, I. *s.* das Pedal (*Piano, Organ*); der Treter (*Cycl.*). II. *v.a.* treten (*Cycl.*). **—ate**, *adj.* fußförmig; gefußt. **—estal**, *s.* das Fußgestell, der Ständer; der Säulenfuß. **—estrian**, I. *adj.* zu Fuß gehend; zu Fuß, Fuß=. II. *s.* der Fuß=gänger, =reisende. **—estrianism**, *s.* das Fußreisen. **—icel, —icle**, *s.* das Stielchen. **—icellate**, *adj.* gestielt. **—iment**, *s.* der (Zier=, Vorder=)Giebel, das Frontispiz. **—ometer**, *s.* der Schrittmesser. **—uncle**, *s.* der Stiel. **—uncular**, *adj.* Stiel=. **—unculate**, *adj.* gestielt.

Pedant, *s.* der Kleinigkeitskrämer, Silbenstecher, Pedant, die Pedantin. **—ic**, *adj.* pedantisch, kleinlich, schulmeisterlich, peinlich eigen. **—ry**, *s.* die Pedanterie.

Peddl—e, *v.n.* hausieren gehen; (trifle) sich mit Kleinigkeiten abgeben. **—er**, *see* Pedlar. **—ing**, *adj.* geringfügig; —ing commerce, ein Krämerhandel.

Pedicul—ar, —ous, *adj.* lausig.

Pedigree, *s.* der Stammbaum; die Abkunft, Herkunft.

Pedlar, *s.* der Hausierer. **—ism**, *s.* das Hausierwesen.

Pedobaptis—m, *s.* die Kindertaufe. **—t**, *s.* der Anhänger der Kindertaufe.

¹Peel, I. *v.a.* (ab)schälen. II. *v.n.* sich ausziehen (*sl.*); to — off, sich schälen, sich schiefern, abschiefern, abschilbern. III. *s.* die Schale, Rinde.

²Peel, *s.* die Back=, Brot=schaufel; das Kreuz (*Typ.*).

¹Peep, I. *v.n.* piepen. II. *s.* das Piepen.

²Peep, I. *v.n.* gucken, neugierig *or* verstohlen blicken; hervor=gucken *or* =ragen; sichtbar werden, zum Vorschein kommen; to — **at**, begucken; to — **in** (**out**), mühsam hinsehen, (hinaus=, heraus=) gucken; —ing Tom, der Neugierige. II. *s.* das Gucken; to take a — at, einen flüchtigen Blick werfen auf (*acc.*); — of day, der Anbruch des Tages. **—er**, *s.* der Laurer, Gucker; das Auge (*sl.*). *Comp.* **—-show**, *s.* der Guckkasten.

Peer, *s.* der Gleiche, Ebenbürtige; (mate) der Kamerad, Gefährte; (noble) der Pair; creation of —s, der Pairsschub; by his —s, von seines Gleichen. **—age**, *s.* die Pairswürde; (nobility) der Reichsadel; (book) das Adels=buch, =register. **—ess**, *s.* die Gemahlin eines Pairs. **—less**, *adj.*, **—lessly**, *adv.* unvergleichlich, einzigartig. **—lessness**, *s.* die Unvergleichlichkeit.

²Peer, *v.a.* scharf blicken, gucken (*for*, nach).

Peevish, *adj.*, **—ly**, *adv.* verdrießlich, mürrisch, übellaunig, empfindlich, grämlich. **—ness**, *s.* die Grämlichkeit, das verdrießliche Wesen.

Pe(e)wit, *s.* der Kiebitz; die Lachmöve.

Peg, I. *s.* der Pflock, Dübel; das Absatzpflöckchen (*Surv.*); (step) der Grad; der Wirbel (*Mus.*); (clothes-—) hölzerner Nagel; washing —, die Klammer; to take a p. down a —, einen demütigen; to come down a —, sich demütigen; gelindere Saiten aufziehen. II. *v.a.* fest=, an=pflöcken. III. *v.n.*; to — away, darauf los arbeiten; (eat) tüchtig drauflosessen (*vulg.*). *Comp.* **—ging-awl**, *s.* die Pflockahle. **—-ladder**, *s.* die Stangenleiter. **—-top**, *s.* der Kreisel.

Pekoe, *s.* der Pek(k)otee.

Pelargonium, *s.* das Pelargonium.

Pelerine, *s.* der Überwurfkragen, die Pelerine.

Pelf, *s.* das Geld, der Reichtum.

Pelican, *s.* der Pelikan (*Orn., Chem.*).

Pelisse, *s.* der Frauenüberrock, die Pelisse.

Pell, *s.* die Haut; (parchment) die Pergamentrolle. **—icle**, *s.* das Häutchen.

Pellet, *s.* das Kügelchen.

Pellitory, *s.* das Mauerkraut.

Pell-mell, *adj.* & *adv.* verworren, durcheinander.

Pellucid, *adj.*, **—ly**, *adv.* durchsichtig, hell, klar. **—ness**, *s.* die Durchsichtigkeit.

¹Pelt, *s.* der Pelz, das Fell; *see* Skin; zerrissener Raub des Falken (*Sport.*). **—er**, *s.* der Pelz(waren)händler. **—ry**, *s.* das Pelzwerk. *Comp.* **—-monger**, *s.* der Rauch(waren)händler, Kürschner. **—-wool**, *s.* die Sterblingswolle.

²Pelt, *v.* I. *a.* werfen (nach), bewerfen; to — a p. with stones, einen mit einem Steinhagel überschütten; to — s.o. with libels, einen mit Schmähschriften bombardieren. II. *n.* heftig zur Erde fallen, niederstürzen, niederplatzen; —ing rain, der Platzregen; the rain —ed down, der Regen fiel in Strömen, ein Platzregen goß herab.

Pelv—ic, *adj.* Becken=. **—is**, *s.* das Becken (*Med.*).

¹Pen, I. *s.* die (Schreib=)Feder; steel —, Stahlfeder. II. *v.a.* schreiben; (compose) abfassen. **—ner**, *s.* der Aufzeichner, Schreiber. *Comp.* **—-and-ink**, *adj.* Feder=. **—-case**, *s.* die Federbüchse, der Schreibkasten. **—craft**, *s.* die Schönschreibekunst. **—holder**, *s.* der Federhalter. **—knife**, *s.* das Federmesser. **—man**, *s.* der (Schön=)Schreiber; (author) der Schriftsteller. **—manship**, *s.* die Schreibkunst; (authorship) die Schriftstellerei. **—-marked**, *adj.* durch Federzug entwertet (*of postage stamps*). **—wiper**, *s.* der Federwischer.

²Pen, I. *s.* die Hürde; der Hühnerkorb. II. *v.a.* einpferchen, einschließen (*sheep*). **—t**, *see* Pent. *Comp.* **—-stock**, *s.* der Spannschütze (*Hydr.*).

Pena—l, *adj.* Straf=; (criminal) strafbar; —l code, das Strafgesetzbuch; —l settlement, die Strafkolonie; —l sum, das Strafgeld; he was sentenced to 4 years —l servitude, er

wurde zu 4 Jahren Zuchthaus verurteilt. **—lize,** *v.a.* einer Strafe unterwerfen, mit etw. bestrafen. **—lty,** *s.* die Strafe, Buße; under —lty of, bei Strafe von (*or gen.*); the extreme —lty, die Todesstrafe. **—nce,** *s.* die Buße, Büßung.
Penates, *pl.* die Penaten, Hausgötter.
Pence, *pl. see* Penny.
Pencil, I. *s.* der Pinsel (*Paint.*); (lead —) der Bleistift; (red —) der Rotstift, Rötel; (coloured —) bunter Bleistift, der Buntstift; der Strahlenbüschel (*Opt.*); der Stift (*Tele.*, *Draw.*, *etc.*); die Malerkunst (*fig.*). II. *v.a.* zeichnen, entwerfen; mit einem Bleistift anzeichnen *or* anstreichen. **—led,** *adj.* gezeichnet, gemalt; strahlend, büschelig (*Opt.*); —led eyebrows, schön gezeichnete Augenbrauen. *Comp.* **—-case,** *s.* das Bleistiftrohr, der Bleistifthalter; der Pinselköcher. **—-shaped,** *adj.* pinselförmig.
Pend—ant, *s.* das Gehänge; (ear —ant) das Ohrgehänge; der Bügel, das Gehänge (*Horol.*); (chandelier) der Hängeleuchter; der Hängezierat, Abhängling (*Arch.*); das Gegenstück Pendant (*Paint. etc.*). **—ent,** I. *adj.* hängend, schwebend. II. *s.* etwas (über)hängendes. **—ing,** I. *adj.* unentschieden, schwebend, in der Schwebe. II. *prep.* während; (until) bis (zu); —ing these arrangements, während diese Verhandlungen schweben *or* schwebten. **—ule,** *s.* die Pendeluhr, Standuhr, Stutzuhr. **—ulous,** *adj.* hängend; herabhängend. **—ulum,** *s.* das Pendel; (der *or*) das Perpendikel (*Horol.*). *Comp.* **—ant-lamp,** *s.* die Hängelampe. **—ulum-bob,** *s.* die Pendellinse. **—ulum-clock,** *s.* die Stand=, Pendeluhr. **—ulum-level,** *s.* die Pendel=,Setz=wage. **—ulum-rod,** *s.* der Pendelarm.
Penetra—bility, *s.* die Durchdringlichkeit, Durchdringbarkeit. **—ble,** *adj.* durchdringlich. **—lia,** *pl.* das Innerste; geheime, verborgene Dinge. **—te,** *v.a. & n.* durchdringen, eindringen in (*acc.*); (see into) erforschen, ergründen, durchschauen; —ted with, durchdrungen von; —ting mind, durchdringender Verstand. **—tion,** *s.* das Durchdringen, Eindringen; die Durchdringung (*Phys.*); (discernment) der Scharfsinn, die Einsicht; die Ergründung (*of a matter*). **—tive,** *adj.*, **—tively,** *adv.* eindringlich; durchdringend; scharfsinnig, fein. **—tiveness,** *s.* das Durchdringende, die Schärfe.
Penguin, *s.* die Fettgans, der Pinguin.
Peninsula, *s.* die Halbinsel. **—r,** *adj.* halbinselförmig; Halbinsel=; —r War, Krieg der Engländer auf der pyrenäischen Halbinsel (1808–14).
Penis, *s.* das männliche Glied, der Penis.
Peniten—ce, *s.* die Reue, Buße. **—t,** I. *adj.*, **—tly,** *adv.* reuig, bußfertig. II. *s.* der Bußfertige; der Büßer; das Beichtkind (*R. C.*). **—tial,** I. *adj.*, **—tially,** *adv.* reuevoll, bußfertig; als Buße auferlegt, Buß=. II. *s.* das Bußbuch, Pönitentiale (*R. C.*). **—tiary,** *s.* das Besserungshaus, Zuchthaus; der Bußpriester.
Penn—ant, *see* —on; der Wimpel. **—ate,** *adj.* geflügelt, gefiedert (*Zool.*); *same as* Pinnate (*Bot.*). **—iform,** *adj.* kielförmig. **—on,** *s.* das Fähnchen (*Mil.*).
Penn—iless, *adj.* ohne Geld, ganz arm; he is —iless, er hat keinen roten Heller. **—ilessness,** *s.* der völlige Geldmangel. **—y,** I. *s.* (*pl.* —ies, Pence) der (englische) Penny (= etwa 8½ Pfennig); das Geld (*fig.*); die Kleinigkeit (*fig.*); in for a —y, in for a pound, wer A sagt, muß auch B sagen (*prov.*); to turn an honest —y, sich (*dat.*) einen Groschen verdienen; no —y, no paternoster, umsonst ist der Tod. II. *attrib.*; —y post-card, die Weltpostkarte. *Comp.* **—y-a-liner,** *s.* der Zeitungsschreiber, Zeilenschreiber, Skribent. **—y-dreadful,** *s.* das (gemeine) Pfennigmagazin, das Schauerblatt (*sl.*); der Schauerroman (in Lieferungen) (*sl.*). **—y-postage,** *s.* das Pennyporto. **—yroyal,** *s.* die Polei=Minze (*Bot.*). **—yweight,** *s.* das englische Pfennig=gewicht (24 Gramm Troy=Gewicht). **—y-wise,** *adj.* sparsam in Kleinigkeiten; übergenau, knauserig, knickerig am unrechten Orte; he is —y-wise and pound-foolish, er spart Pfennige und wirft Taler weg, er spart am unrechten Ende. **—yworth,** *s.* der Pfennigwert, was man für einen Penny kaufen kann; (bargain) der (wohlfeile) Kauf; a —yworth of, für einen Penny.
Pensile, *adj.* hängend, schwebend.
Pension, I. *s.* das Jahrgeld, Ruhegehalt; das Kostgeld; die Pension; old age —, die Altersversorgung; retiring —, das Ruhegehalt. II. *v.a.* (einem) ein Jahrgeld geben; (—off) pensionieren. **—ary, —er,** *s.* der Empfänger eines Jahrgeldes *or* Ruhegehaltes; der Kostgänger, Pensionär; der Student, der für Kost 2c. im College bezahlt (*at Cambridge*); (dependant) der Abhängige.
Pensive, *adj.*, **—ly,** *adv.* gedankenvoll, nachdenklich; tiefsinnig; (grave) ernst. **—ness,** *s.* die Nachdenklichkeit; die Tiefsinnigkeit; die Schwermut.
Pent, *p.p. see* Pen; —-up wrath, verhaltener Grimm; —-up excitement, verhaltene Erregung. *Comp.* **—house,** *s.* das Wetter=, Schutzdach. **—-roof,** *s.* einhängendes Dach.
Pent—achord, *s.* das Pentachord(ium), fünfsaitiges Tonwerkzeug. **—acle,** *s.* der Drudenfuß, das Pentagramm. **—adactylous,** *adj.* fünffingerig. **—agon,** *s.* das Fünfeck. **—agonal,** *adj.* fünfeckig. **—ahedron,** *s.* das Fünfflach. **—ameter,** *s.* der Pentameter, Fünffuß (*Metr.*). **—andrian,** *adj.* fünfmännerig. **—angular,** *adj.* fünfwinkelig. **—aphyllous,** *adj.* fünfblätterig. **—astyle,** *s.* der Bau mit fünf Säulenreihen. **—ateuch,** *s.* der Pentateuch, die fünf Bücher Mosis. **—ecost,** *s.* das Pfingstfest, die Pfingsten. **—ecostal,** *adj.* Pfingst=.
Penult, *s.* vorletzte Silbe. **—imate,** I. *adj.* vorletzt. II. *s.* vorletzte Silbe.
Penumbra, *s.* der Halbschatten. **—l,** *adj.* halbdunkel.
Penur—ious, *adj.*, **—iously,** *adv.* dürftig; (niggard) karg, geizig. **—iousness,** *s.* die Dürftigkeit; die Kargheit, der Geiz. **—y,** *s.* die Dürftigkeit, Armut; der Mangel (an einer S.); die Kargheit.
Peony, *s.* die Päonie, Pfingstrose.
People, I. *s.* das Volk, die Leute; (nation) das Volk; (common —) das gemeine Volk; (subjects) die Untertanen; (servants) die Dienerschaft, Leute; (relatives) Verwandte; (one) man; country —, Landleute; many —, viele Leute; what will — say? was werden die Leute, was wird die Welt sagen? II. *v.a.* bevölkern. **—s,** *pl.* die Völkerschaften, Volksstämme; the —s of the world, die Völker der Erde.
Pepper, I. *s.* der Pfeffer. II. *v.a.* pfeffern; durchprügeln; anschießen (aus Versehen) (*fig.*). **—y,** *adj.* stark gepfeffert; hitzig (*fig.*). *Comp.* **—-box, —-caster,** *s.* die Pfefferbüchse. **—corn,** *s.* das Pfefferkorn. **—mint,** *s.* die Pfefferminze; der Pfefferminzplätzchen.
Pep—sin, *s.* das Pepsin. **—tic,** *adj.* die Verdauung betreffend, Verdauungs=.
Per, *prep.* durch, für 2c.; as — account, laut Rechnung; — annum, für das Jahr, jährlich; — bearer, durch den Überbringer; — cent, prozent, vom Hundert, auf das Hundert; — pound, (auf) das Pfund; — diem, täglich; — se, für sich.
Peradventure, *adv.* von ungefähr, vielleicht; — ten shall be found there, man möchte vielleicht 10 darinnen finden (*B.*).
Perambulat—e, *v.a.* durchwandern, durchschreiten; begehen, besichtigen (*boundaries, etc.*). **—ion,** *s.* das Durchwandern; das Besichtigen; die Grenzbegehung. **—or,** *s.* der Kinderwagen; der Wegmesser.
Perceiv—able, *adj.* wahrnehmbar. **—e,** *v.a.* wahrnehmen, sehen, (be)merken, gewahr werden; (feel) spüren, empfinden.

Percentage, *s.* der Prozentsatz; (commission) die Provision, Kommission (*C. L.*); die Tantieme (*of authors; Theat.*); der Prozentgehalt, die Prozentigkeit (*Chem.*).

Percepti—ble, *adj.*, **—bly**, *adv.* wahrnehmbar, merklich, vernehmlich, fühlbar. **—on**, *s.* die Wahrnehmung, Vorstellung; (sensation) die Empfindung; die Anschauung, Auffassung; (*also* —ve power) das Empfindungsvermögen (*Phil.*). **—ve**, *adj.* wahrnehmend, empfindend. **—vity**, *s.* das Wahrnehmungsvermögen.

[1]**Per—ch**, *s.* der Barsch (*Icht.*). **—cine**, **—coid**, *adj.* barschartig.

[2]**Perch**, I. *s.* die (Auffitz=)Stange (*for birds*), Hühnerstange (*for hens*); die Rute (= 5½ Yard *or* 5.03 Meter); der Langbaum (*Carr.*). II. *v.n.* sich setzen, aufsitzen; hoch sitzen (*fig.*). III. *v.a.* setzen. **—er**, *s.* der Sitzvogel.

Perchance, *adv.* von ungefähr; vielleicht.

Perchlor—ate, *s.* überchlorsaures Salz. **—ic**, *adj.*; —ic acid, die Überchlorsäure.

Percipient, I. *adj.* wahrnehmend, empfindend. II. *s.* das wahrnehmende 2c. Wesen.

Percolat—e, *v.n.* durch=sickern, =seihen. **—ion**, *s.* das Durchsickern, die Durchseihung. **—or**, *s.* der Spitzbeutel, Filtriertrichter.

Percussi—on, *s.* der Schlag, Stoß, die Perkussion; (resonance) der Widerhall; (shock) die Erschütterung. **—ve**, *adj. see* Percutient. *Comp.* **—on-cap**, *s.* das Zündhütchen. **—on-fuse**, *s.* der Stoßzünder. **—on-lock**, *s.* das Perkussionsschloß.

Percutient, I. *adj.* schlagend. II. *s.* der eine Erschütterung hervorrufende Gegenstand.

Perd—ition, *s.* der (völlige) Untergang, das Verderben; die Verdammnis (*Rel.*). **—u**, I. *adj.* & *adv.* auf der Lauer; (hidden) versteckt. II. *s.* der verlorene Posten; der moralisch Verkommene.

Peregrin—ate, *v.n.* wandern, herumreisen. **—ation**, *s.* die Wanderschaft, das Herumreisen; (sojourn) der Aufenthalt in der Fremde. **—ator**, *s.* der Wanderer, Reisende. **—e**, *s.* (—e falcon) der Wanderfalke.

Peremptor—ily, *adv. see* —y; geradezu; durchaus; ein für allemal. **—iness**, *s.* das Entscheidende, Peremptorische, Absprechende; (dogmatism) der Dogmatismus; das hartnäckige Beharren (auf einer Behauptung, of an assertion); die Bestimmtheit (*of a refusal, etc.*). **—y**, *adj.* bestimmt, entschieden, absprechend, unbedingt, peremptorisch; —y refusal, unbedingt abschlägige Antwort; a —y manner, etwas allzu Bestimmtes im Wesen, ein allzu bestimmtes Auftreten.

Perennial, I. *adj.*, **—ly**, *adv.* das ganze Jahr dauernd; perennierend (*Bot.*); (perpetual) fortdauernd, beständig. II. *s.* perennierende Pflanze.

Perfect, I. *adj.* vollkommen, fehlerlos; (complete) vollendet; (full) vollständig; (blameless) rein, schuldlos, lauter; — specimens, tadellose Exemplare; a — picture of a child, ein bildschönes Kind. II. *s.* (— tense) die (Zeitform der) Vergangenheit, das Perfektum. III. *v.a.* vervollkommnen, vollenden; (instruct fully) ausbilden. **—er**, *s.* der Vervollkommner, Ausbilder, Vollender. **—ible**, *adj.* vervollkommnungsfähig. **—ibility**, *s.* die Vervollkommnungsfähigkeit, Möglichkeit der Vervollkomnung. **—ion**, *s.* die Vollkommenheit, Vollendung; (excellence) die Trefflichkeit; to —ion, vollkommen, vortrefflich; to bring to —ion, vollenden; counsel of —ion, unausführbarer Rat(schlag). **—ly**, *adv. see* —I.; gänzlich, völlig. **—ness**, *s.* die Vollkommenheit; (dexterity) die Geschicklichkeit.

Perfervid, *adj.* sehr glühend, glutvoll.

Perfidious, *adj.*, **—ly**, *adv.* treulos, verräterisch, hinterlistig. **—ness**, **Perfidy**, *s.* die Treulosigkeit, der Verrat, Treubruch, die Hinterlist.

Perfoliate, *adj.* durchwachsen (*Bot.*).

Perforat—e, I. *v.a.* durchbohren, durchlochen; durchlöchern. II. *adj.*, **—ed**, *adj.* durchstochen, durchlöchert. **—ion**, *s.* die Durchbohrung, Durchlochung; Durchlöcherung; (hole) die Öffnung, das Loch. **—or**, *s.* der (Schädel=)Bohrer.

Perforce, *adv.* mit Gewalt, notgedrungen.

Perform, *v.* I. *a.* machen, tun, leisten, verrichten; (carry out) ausführen, vollziehen; (play) spielen, aufführen. II. *n.* spielen (*Theat., etc.*). **—ance**, *s.* die Ausführung, Verrichtung, Vollziehung; die Aufführung, Vorstellung, das Spiel (*Theat.*); die Erfüllung (*of a duty*); (work) das Werk; (feat) die (Helden=)Tat; promises without —ance, Versprechen ohne Erfüllung; —ances on horseback, Reiterkünste. **—er**, *s.* der Ausübende, Täter, Ausführende; der Schauspieler (*Theat.*); der Virtuos, (Ton)Künstler (*Mus.*); he is an excellent —er, er spielt ausgezeichnet. **—ing**, *adj.* ausübend; dressiert; —ing dogs, abgerichtete Hunde.

Perfume, I. *s.* der Wohlgeruch, Duft; (—d water, *etc.*) das Parfüm. II. *v.a.* durchdüften, parfümieren. **—r**, *s.* der Parfümeriewarenhändler. **—ry**, *s.* die Parfümerie.

Perfunctor—y, *adj.*, **—ily**, *adv.* nachlässig, obenhin, oberflächlich. **—iness**, *s.* die Nachlässigkeit.

Perhaps, *adv.* vielleicht, möglicherweise, etwa.

Peri, *s.* die Peri, persische Elfe.

Peri—anth, *s.* die Blumenhülle **—carditis**, *s.* die Herzbeutelentzündung. **—cardium**, *s.* der Herzbeutel. **—carp**, *s.* die Fruchthülle. **—cranium**, *s.* die Knochenhaut des Schädels; *see* Skull. **—gee**, *s.* die Erdnähe. **—helion**, *s.* die Sonnennähe. **—meter**, *s.* der Umfang. **—od**, *see* Period. **—osteum**, *s.* die Knochenhaut. **—patetic**, I. *adj.* peripatetisch. II. *s.* der Peripatetiker. **—phery**, *s.* der Umfang, Umkreis. **—phrasis**, *s.* die Umschreibung, Periprase (*Rhet.*). **—phrastic**, *adj.* umschreibend, periphrastisch. **—pteral**, *adj.* von Säulen umgeben. **—ptery**, *s.* von Säulen umgebenes Gebäude. **—sperm**, *s.* die Samenhülle. **—staltic**, *adj.* wurmförmig, peristaltisch. **—style**, *s.* das Peristyl, die ringsum mit Säulen umgebene Halle. **—toneal**, *adj.* Bauchfell=. **—toneum**, *s.* das Bauchfell. **—tonitis**, *s.* die Bauchfellentzündung. **—typhlitis**, *s.* die Blinddarm= und Bauchfell=entzündung.

Peril, *s.* die Gefahr; die Verantwortung; the yellow —, die Gefahr der gelben Rasse. **—ous**, *adj.*, **—ously**, *adv.* gefährlich. **—ousness**, *s.* die Gefährlichkeit.

Period, *s.* die Periode (*also Astr.*); (space of time) der Zeitraum, die Zeit; der Kreislauf (*of a planet, etc.*); (pause) die Pause, der Absatz; die Periode, der Redesatz, das Satzgefüge; der Punkt (*Typ.*); — of office, die Amtsdauer, Amtszeit. **—ic**, *adj.*, **—ically**, *adv.* regelmäßig wiederkehrend, periodisch. **—ical**, *s.* die Zeitschrift, das in regelmäßigen Zwischenräumen erscheinende Blatt. **—icity**, *s.* die regelmäßige Wiederkehr oder Erscheinung.

Perish, *v.n.* umkommen, sterben, untergehen; (be lost) vergehen; zunichte werden; (decay) hinschwinden, absterben; verdammt sein (*Theol.*); verunglücken (*at sea*); to — with hunger, Hungers sterben, verhungern; to be —ed with cold, vor Kälte umkommen, frieren, erfrieren. **—ability**, *s.* die Verderblichkeit; die Hinfälligkeit, Vergänglichkeit. **—able**, *adj.* vergänglich; leicht verderbend, nicht haltbar (*as fruit, goods, etc.*). **—ableness**, *s. see* —ability.

Periwig, *s.* die Perücke.

[1]**Periwinkle**, *s.* die Uferschnecke (*Mollusc.*).

[2]**Periwinkle**, *s.* das Immergrün, Sinngrün.

Perjur—e, *v.* I. *n.* falsch schwören, einen Meineid schwören, meineidig werden. II. *a.*; to —e o.s., falsch schwören, eidbrüchig werden. **—ed**, *adj.* eidbrüchig, meineidig. **—er**, *s.* der Eidbrüchige, Meineidige. **—y**, *s.* der Eidbruch, Meineid.

Perk, *v.* I. *n.* sich brüsten, die Nase hoch tragen; to — up, sich wieder erholen. II. *a.* putzen, schmücken;

to — up, aufrichten; to — up one's ears, die Ohren spitzen. III. *adj.* hoch hinaus, keck; geschniegelt, geputzt. —**iness**, *s.* keckes, übermütiges Wesen. —**ing**, *adj.* scharf ausspähend, neugierig. —**y**, *adj.* hoch emporstehend, keck aufragend; keck, übermütig; schnippisch, frech.

Permanen—ce, —**cy**, *s.* die Fortdauer, Permanenz; die Dauerhaftigkeit (of colours, *etc.*). —**t**, *adj.*, —**tly**, *adv.* (be)ständig, fortdauernd, bleibend; dauerhaft; —t abode, bleibender *or* dauernder Wohnsitz; —t appointment, ständige Anstellung; —t committee, ständiger Ausschuß; —t way, der Bahnoberbau, der Schienenstrang nebst Brücken und Übergängen.

Permea—bility, *s.* die Durchdringbarkeit. —**ble**, *adj.* durchdring=bar, =lich, durchlässig. —**te**, *v.a.* durchdringen. —**tion**, *s.* das Durchdringen.

Permiss—ible, *adj.* zulässig, statthaft. —**ion**, *s.* die Erlaubnis, Bewilligung. —**ive**, *adj.*, —**ively**, *adv.* zulassend, verstattend; verstattet, zugelassen.

Permit, I. *v.a.* erlauben, zulassen, gestatten; he was —ted to go, ihm wurde gestattet *or* erlaubt zu gehen, man erlaubte ihm zu gehen, er durfte gehen. II. *s.* die Erlaubnis; (written —) der Erlaubnisschein, Passierzettel. —**ter**, *s.* der Erlaubende.

Permuta—ble, *adj.* vertauschbar. —**tion**, *s.* die Um=, Ver=setzung; die Permutation (*Alg.*).

Pernicious, *adj.* schädlich, verderblich, nachteilig.

Peroration, *s.* der Redeschluß, Schluß, die Schlußerörterung; die bombastische Rede, Tirade.

Peroxide, *s.* das Super=, Hyper=oxyd.

Perpend, I. *v.a.* & *n.* erwägen (*rare*). II. *s.*, —**er**, *s.* der Durchbinder, Streckstein. —**icular**, I. *adj.*, —**icularly**, *adv.* senkrecht (to, auf, mit), perpendikulär; —icular style, die Spätgotik (in England im 15. u. 16. Jahrhundert), der Tudorstil. II. *s.* die Senkrechte, der, das Perpendikel. —**icularity**, *s.* senkrechte Richtung.

Perpetrat—e, *v.a.* verüben, begehen (*a crime*, *etc.*). —**ion**, *s.* die Verübung, Begehung. —**or**, *s.* der Begeher, Täter.

Perpetu—al, *adj.*, —**ally**, *adv.* unaufhörlich, fortwährend, beständig, stets, ewig; unkündbar (*C.L.*); —al motion, das Perpetuum mobile; —al curacy, lebenslängliche Pfründe *or* Pfarrstelle; —al three-per-cents, unkündbare dreiprozentige Rente. —**ate**, *v.a.* verewigen, immerwährend erhalten *or* fortsetzen. —**ation**, *s.* die Verewigung, immerwährende Dauer, stete Fortsetzung. —**ity**, *s.* die ununterbrochene Fortdauer, Beständigkeit, Ewigkeit; (—al annuity) lebenslängliche Rente; in —ity, auf immer.

Perplex, *v.a.* verwirren, bestürzt machen. —**ed**, *adj.*, —**edly**, *adv.* verwirrt, verlegen. —**ing**, *adj.* verwirrend. —**ity**, *s.* die Verwirrung, Verlegenheit; (confusion) die Verworrenheit.

Perquisite, *s.* die Akzidenz; der Erwerb, die Errungenschaft (*Law*). —**s**, *pl.* Akzidenzien, Nebeneinkünfte, Nebenbezüge.

Perron, *s.* die Freitreppe.

Persecut—e, *v.a.* verfolgen; (worry) belästigen, plagen; überlaufen (*with visits*, *etc.*). —**ion**, *s.* die Verfolgung. —**or**, *s.* der Verfolger, Bedränger. —**rix**, *s.* die Verfolgerin, Bedrängerin.

Persever—ance, *s.* die Beharrlichkeit, Standhaftigkeit, Ausdauer. —**e**, *v.n.* beharren, ausdauern, standhaft fortfahren. —**ing**, *adj.*, —**ingly**, *adv.* beharrlich, standhaft.

Persist, *v.a.*; to — in, bestehen auf (*dat.*), beharren in (*dat.*) *or* bei. —**ence**, —**ency**, *s.* das Beharren (in, in), die Beharrlichkeit; die Fortdauer (*Phys.*). —**ent**, *adj.*, —**ently**, *adv.* beharrlich, standhaft, fest, hartnäckig.

Person, *s.* die Person; (character) der Charakter (*obs.*); die Rolle, Person (*Theat.*); (body) der Körper; (appearance) das Äußere, die Person; **a** —, ein Mensch, jemand, einer; in —, in eigner Person, selbst; no —, niemand; the — who, derjenige, welcher; to have respect of —s, die Person ansehen. —**able**, *adj.* von angenehmer Erscheinung, von angenehmem Äußeren, wohlgestalt(et), anmutig; (to be seen) körperlich sichtbar; rechtsfähig (*Law*). —**age**, *s.* die hervorragende, vornehme, berühmte Person, Persönlichkeit, Standesperson. —**al**, *adj.*, —**ally**, *adv.* persönlich (*also Gram.*); Personal=; beweglich, Mobiliar= (*Law*); to become —al, persönlich *or* anzüglich werden, persönliche Anspielungen machen. —**ality**, *s.* die Persönlichkeit; (—al remark) die Anzüglichkeit; die Personalität (*Philos.*); *see* —alty. —**alty**, *s.* persönliches Eigentum. —**ate**, *v.a.* vorstellen; (represent) darstellen; repräsentieren (*another*). —**ation**, *s.* die Vorstellung, Nachbildung; false —ation, das betrügliche sich für einen andern Ausgeben. —**ator**, *s.* der Darstellende. —**ification**, *s.* die Verkörperung, Verwirklichung, dichterische Belebung, Personifikation. —**ify**, *v.a.* verkörpern, lebendig darstellen; versinnbildlichen. —**nel**, *s.* das Personal.

Perspective, I. *adj.* perspektivisch, Perspektiv=. II. die Perspektive, das (Gesamt=)Bild, die (Gesamt=)Ansicht; (science of —) die Perspektivlehre; (vista) der Fernblick, Ausblick, die Fernsicht; (— drawing) perspektivische Zeichnung; aerial, linear, oblique, parallel —, Luft=, Linear=, Akzidental=, Parallel=perspektive.

Perspic—acious, *adj.* scharfsichtig. —**acity**, *s.* der Scharfblick, die Scharfsichtigkeit. —**uity**, *s.* die Deutlichkeit, Klarheit, Verständlichkeit; *see* —acity. —**uous**, *adj.*, —**uously**, *adv.* klar, deutlich, verständlich, augenfällig.

Perspir—ation, *s.* der Schweiß, die Transpiration. —**e**, *v.n.* schwitzen, ausdünsten, transpirieren.

Persua—de, *v.a.* überreden, bereden (of, to, zu); be —ded, lassen Sie sich überreden; to be —ded of, von (etwas) überzeugt sein; to —de not to, (einem) abreden von. —**der**, *s.* der Überredende. —**sion**, *s.* die Überredung; (conviction) die Überzeugung; (belief) die Meinung, der Glaube. —**sive**, *adj.*, —**sively**, *adv.* über=redend, =zeugend. —**siveness**, *s.* überzeugende Kraft, Überredungsgabe.

Persulphate, *s.* das Übersulfat (*Chem.*).

Pert, *adj.*, —**ly**, *adv.* keck, naseweis, schnippisch, dreist, frech. —**ness**, *s.* die Keckheit, der Vorwitz.

Pert—ain, *v.n.* (an)gehören (*to a p. or th.*); betreffen (*a matter*). —**inacious**, *adj.*, —**inaciously**, *adv.* hartnäckig; (resolute) beharrlich, standhaft, anhaltend. —**inacity**, —**inaciousness**, *s.* die Hartnäckigkeit; die Standhaftigkeit, Beharrlichkeit. —**inence**, —**inency**, *s.* die Angemessenheit, Gemäßheit, Schicklichkeit. —**inent**, *adj.*, —**inently**, *adv.* gehörig, passend, schicklich, angemessen; treffend (*of a remark*).

Perturb, *v.a.* beunruhigen, in Unruhe setzen. —**ation**, *s.* die Störung (*also Magnet.*); die Unruhe; die Abweichung (*Astr.*).

Peruke, *s.* die Perücke.

Perus—al, *s.* das Durchlesen, die Durchsicht. —**e**, *v.a.* (durch)lesen. —**er**, *s.* der Leser.

Perva—de, *v.a.* durchdringen. —**sive**, *adj.* durchdringend. —**sion**, *s.* das Durchdringen.

Perver—se, *adj.*, —**sely**, *adv.* verkehrt; (obstinate) störrig, eigensinnig; *see* Petulant, Untoward. —**seness**, —**sity**, *s.* die Verkehrtheit, der Eigensinn; die Störrigkeit, das störrische Wesen. —**sion**, *s.* die Verkehrung, Verdrehung, der Abfall (von einem religiösen Glauben). —**sive**, *adj.* verderbend (of morals, die Sitten). —**t**, I. *v.a.* verkehren, verdrehen (*the laws*, *a meaning*, *etc.*); (mislead) verführen. II. *s.* der Abtrünnige (in Religionssachen). —**ter**, *s.* der Verdreher; der Verführer.

Pervious, *adj.* zugänglich (to, für), den Durchgang gestattend. —**ness**, *s.* die Durchdringlichkeit, Durchlässigkeit.

Pessary, *s.* der Mutterring; der Schutzring.

Pessimis—m, *s.* die Schwarzseherei, Schwarzfärberei, (zu) düstre Lebensanschauung, der Pessimismus. **—t**, I. *s.* der Schwarzseher, Schwarzfärber, Pessimist. II. *adj.*, **—tic**, *adj.* schwarzseherisch, schwarzfärberisch, pessimistisch.

Pest, *s.* die Pest, Seuche; die Plage (*fig.*). **—er**, *v.a.* plagen, quälen, belästigen; beängstigen. **—iferous**, *adj.* verpestend; pestartig; giftig; schädlich (*fig.*). **—ilence**, *s.* die Pestilenz, Pest. **—ilent**, *see* —iferous; boshaft. **—ilential**, *adj.* ansteckend; *see* —iferous; bösartig (*fig.*). *Comp.* **—-house**, *s.* das Haus für Pestkranke.

Pestle, *s.* die Mörserkeule, der Stößel.

[1]**Pet**, I. *s.* zahmes Tier; (— child, *etc.*) der Liebling, das Schoßkind; — dog, der Schoßhund. II. *attrib.* Lieblings-. III. *v.a.* hätscheln, verhätscheln, streicheln, zärteln, tätscheln.

[2]**Pet**, *s.* üble Laune; to be in a —, übellaunig *or* schlechter Laune sein; to take (the) —, sich wie ein verzogenes Kind benehmen; to do s.th. in a —, etwas in verdrießlicher Stimmung tun. **—tish**, *adj.*, **—tishly**, *adv.* empfindlich, launisch, übellaunig. **—tishness**, *s.* das launische Wesen, die Verdrießlichkeit.

Petal, *s.* das Blumenblatt. **—(l)ed**, **—ous**, *adj.* mit Blumenblättern. **—ism**, *s.* der Petalismus.

Petard, *s.* die Petarde; to be hoist with one's own —, in die Grube stürzen, die man andern gegraben hat.

Petiol—ate, *adj.* gestielt. **—e**, *s.* der Blattstiel.

Petition, I. *s.* die Bitte; (entreaty) das Gesuch; (written —) die Bittschrift; die Anspruchsklage (*Law*); — of right, die Bittschrift um Herstellung des Rechts; to put up a —, eine Bittschrift einreichen. II. *v.a.* bitten, ansuchen, anhalten (for, um); eine Bittschrift *or* ein Gesuch einreichen. **—er**, *s.* der Bittsteller, Ansucher.

Petrel, *s.* der Sturmvogel; stormy —, der Petersvogel, die Sturmschwalbe.

Petr—ifaction, *s.* die Versteinerung. **—ify**, *v.* I. *a.* versteinern; —ified with astonishment, vor Erstaunen starr. II. *n.* zu Stein werden. **—ol**, **—oleum**, *s.* das Steinöl, Erdöl, Petroleum. **—ology**, *s.* die Steinkunde. **—ous**, *adj.* steinhart, steinartig, steinig.

Pett—icoat, I. *s.* der Unterrock; das Unterkleid; das Weib (*fig.*). II. *attrib.*; —icoat affair, der Liebeshandel (*coll.*); —icoat government, das Weiberregiment; —icoat hold, das Kunkellehen (*Law*). **—ifogger**, *s.* der Winkeladvokat. **—ifogging**, *adj.* armselig, lumpig. **—iness**, *s.* die Kleinheit, Geringfügigkeit. **—itoes**, *pl.* Ferkelfüße; die Pfoten (*fig.*). **—o**, *s.* die Brust; in —o, geheim, für sich. **—y**, *adj.* klein, geringfügig, unbedeutend, kleinlich; —y cash, kleine Summen, geringe Beträge; —y cash book, kleines Kassabuch; —y jury, kleine (Zwölfmänner) Jury; —y larceny, kleiner Diebstahl; —y officer, der Unteroffizier; —y prince, unbedeutender Fürst; —y wares, Kurzwaren. *Comp.* **—icoat-bodice**, *s.* die Untertaille.

Petulan—ce, **—cy**, *s.* der Mutwille; *see* Peevishness. **—t**, *adj.*, **—tly**, *adv.* mutwillig; (capricious) launisch; (saucy) keck; *see* Peevish; (perverse) eigensinnig.

Pew, *s.* der Kirchen-stuhl, -sitz. *Comp.* **—-opener**, *s.* der Kirchendiener.

Pewit, *s.* der Kiebitz; die Lachmöve.

Pewter, I. *s.* das Hartzinn, Schüsselzinn; (— vessel) das zinnerne Gerät, Zinn. II. *adj.* zinnern. **—er**, *s.* der Zinngießer.

Phaeton, *s.* der offne vierrädrige Wagen.

Phageden—a, *s.* fressendes Geschwür. **—ic**, I. *adj.*, **—ous**, *adv.* um sich fressend. II. *s.* das Ätzmittel.

Phalan—g(e)al, *adj.* Finger- und Zehen-. **—ger**, *s.* der Kusu (*Zool.*). **—ges**, *pl.* Finger- und Zehen-knochen. **—x**, *s.* die Phalanx; die geschlossene Reihe; *see* —ges.

Phant—asm, *s.* das Wahngebild, Trugbild; die Erscheinung, das Phantom; (fancy) das Hirngespinnst. **—asmagoria**, *s.* das Gaukelbild, Blendwerk; die Phantasmagorie; *see* Medley; (apparatus) die Zauberlaterne. **—asmagoric**, **—asmagorial**, *adj.* gaukelhaft, traumhaft. **—asmal**, *adj.* geisterhaft, gespensterhaft, Phantom-. **—om**, *s.* das Trugbild, Scheinbild, Schattenbild, Phantom; (spectre) das Gespenst.

Pharmac—eutical, *adj.* pharmazeutisch. **—eutics**, *pl.* die Apothekerkunst. **—eutist**, *s.* (—eutical chemist) der Apotheker. **—ist**, *s.* der Apotheker. **—ology**, *s.* die Apothekerwissenschaft, Arzeneimittellehre. **—opœia**, *s.* das Arzenei(bereitungs)buch. **—y**, *s.* die Apothekerkunst, Arzeneibereitungskunst.

Pharos, *s.* der Leuchtturm.

Pharyn—geal, *adj.* Schlundkopf-. **—gotomy**, *s.* der Schlundkopfschnitt. **—x**, *s.* der Schlundkopf, die Rachenhöhle.

Phase, *s.* die Phase (*Astr. & fig.*).

Pheasant, *s.* der Fasan. **—ry**, *s.* die Fasanerie. *Comp.* **—-shooting**, *s.* die Fasanenjagd, Jagd auf Fasanen.

Phenomen—al, *adj.*, **—ally**, *adv.* phänomenal; höchst wunderbar, außerordentlich; äußerlich, Erscheinungs- (*Phil.*). **—on**, *s.* (*pl.* —a) das Phänomen, die Erscheinung; das Wunder (*fig.*).

Phial, *s.* das Fläschchen, die Phiole.

Phil—ander, *v.n.* den Liebhaber machen, liebeln. **—anthropic(al)**, *adj.*, **—anthropically**, *adv.* menschenfreundlich. **—anthropist**, *s.* der Menschenfreund. **—anthropy**, *s.* die Menschenliebe. **—atelic**, *adj.* die Briefmarkenkunde betreffend. **—atelist**, *s.* der Briefmarkenfreund, Markensammler. **—harmonic**, *adj.* Musik liebend. **—hellenic**, *adj.* griechenfreundlich. **—ological**, *adj.* sprachwissenschaftlich, philologisch. **—ologist**, *s.* der Sprachforscher, Philolog. **—ology**, *s.* die Sprachwissenschaft, Philologie. **—oprogenitiveness**, *s.* die Liebe zur Nachkommenschaft. **—osopher**, *s.* der Philosoph, Weltweise, Weisheitsfreund; natural —osopher, der Naturforscher, -philosoph; —osopher's stone, der Stein der Weisen. **—osophical**, *adj.*, **—osophically**, *adv.* philosophisch; (frugal) mäßig. **—osophize**, *v.n.* philosophieren. **—osophy**, *s.* die Philosophie, Weltweisheit; (mental) die Metaphysik, (moral) Ethik, Moralwissenschaft, (natural) Naturwissenschaft, Physik; die Gelassenheit, der Gleichmut (*fig.*); die Lebensweisheit (*fig.*). **—tre**, **—ter**, *s.* der Liebestrank.

Philippic, *s.* die Philippika; heftige Strafrede, Scheltrede, Strafpredigt, Standrede.

Philistin—e, I. *s.* der Philister; der Spießbürger. II. *adj.* philisterhaft, philiströs. **—ism**, *s.* die Philisterei.

Phiz, *s.* das Gesicht, die Visage (*hum.*).

Phlebotom—ist, *s.* der Aderlasser. **—ize**. *v.a.* (einem) zur Ader lassen. **—y**, *s.* der Aderlaß.

Phlegm, *s.* der Schleim; das Phlegma (*Chem. & fig.*). **—atic**, *adj.*, **—atically**, *adv.* schleimblütig, phlegmatisch; träge, gleichgültig.

Phlogiston, *s.* der Brennstoff, das Phlogiston.

Phlox, *s.* die Flammenblume.

Phon—etic, *adj.*, **—etically**, *adv.* lautlich, phonetisch; —etic script, die lauttreue Schreibung, die Lautschrift; —etic spelling, die Lautschrift. **—etics**, *s.* die (beschreibende) Lautlehre, Phonetik, Sprachphysiologie. **—ics**, *s.* die Phonetik; die Tonverbindungskunst. **—ograph**, I. *s.* der Phonograph. II. *v.a.* mit dem Phonographen aufzeichnen. **—ographic**, *adj.* phonographisch, den Phonographen betreffend, mit dem Phonographen gemacht; —ographic record, etwas in den Phonographen Gesprochenes oder Gesungenes. **—olite**, *s.* der Klingstein. **—ology**, *s.* die Schall-, Ton-lehre; die (geschichtliche) Lautlehre (*Gram.*). **—otypy**, *s.* die Lautdarstellung durch den Druck.

Phosph—ate, *s.* das Phosphat. **—or**, *see* —orus. **—orescence**, *s.* die Phosphoreszenz, das

Leuchten im Dunkeln; —orescence of the sea, das Meerleuchten. —**orescent**, *adj.* im Dunkeln leuchtend, phosphoreszierend. —**oric**, *adj.* phosphorisch, Phosphor-. —**orous**, *adj.* phosphorig, phosphorhaltig. —**orus**, *s.* der Phosphor (*Chem.*); der Morgenstern. —**uretted**, *adj.* mit Phosphor verbunden, Phosphor-.

Phot—ics, *s.* die Lehre von der Beleuchtung. —**o**, *see* —ograph. —**ochrome**, *s.* die Aufnahme in natürlichen Farben. —**ochromy**, *s.* die Farbenphotographie. —**o-collotype**, —**o-electrotypy**, —**o-engraving**, *s.* photographischer Stahlstich. —**ogen**, *s.* das Photogen. —**ograph**, *s.* die Photographie; chromo- —ograph, farbige Photographie, Farbenphotographie. —**ographer**, *s.* der Photograph. —**ographic**, *adj.* photographisch. —**ography**, *s.* die Photographie. —**ogravure**, *s.* der Kupfer(platten)lichtdruck, die Lichtkupferätzung, Photogravüre. —**olithograph**, *s.* das Steinlichtdruckbild. —**olithography**, *s.* der Steinlichtdruck, die Photolithographie. —**ology**, *s.* die Lichtlehre. —**ometer**, *s.* der Lichtstärkemesser. —**o-plastic**, *adj.* lichtbildnerisch. —**opsy**, *s.* das Funkensehen. —**otypy**, *s.* der Glaslichtdruck. —**ophone**, *s.* das Photophon.

Phrase, I. *s.* die Phrase; (idiom) die Redensart, der Ausdruck; der (kurze) Satz; der Tonsatz (*Mus.*). II. *v.a.* ausdrücken, nennen. III. *v.n.* Tonsätze bilden. —**ology**, *s.* die Redeweise, Ausdrucksweise, Phraseologie; (—-book) die Phrasensammlung.

Phren—etic, *adj.* wahnsinnig, unsinnig, rasend, wütend, toll, verrückt. —**itis**, *s.* die Tobsucht, Raserei; die Hirnentzündung (*Med.*). —**ological**, *adj.* phrenologisch. —**ologist**, *s.* der Phrenolog. —**ology**, *s.* die Schädellehre.

Phthisi—c, I. *adj.* schwindsüchtig. II. *s.* der Schwindsüchtige. —**s**, *s.* die Schwindsucht.

Phylactery, *s.* das Zauberzeichen; (charm) das Amulet; der Reliquienkasten; der Gebetriemen.

Phylloxera, *s.* die Reblaus; die Reblauskrankheit.

Physi—c, I. *s.* die Arzneikunde; (medicine) die Arznei; (purge) das Abführmittel; to take —c, einnehmen. II. *v.a.* Arznei eingeben; purgieren (*vulg.*). —**cal**, *adj.*, —**cally**, *adv.* physisch, natürlich; (bodily) körperlich; physikalisch (*as a science*); —cal impossibility, physische Unmöglichkeit; —cal training, körperliche Ausbildung. —**cian**, *s.* der Arzt (für innere Krankheiten). —**cs**, *s.* die Physik. —**cist**, *s.* der Physiker. —**ognomist**, *s.* der Mienenkenner, Physiognom. —**ognomy**, *s.* die Physiognomie; (art) die Mienenforschung, Physiognomik. —**ography**, *s.* die Naturbeschreibung. —**ologist**, *s.* der Physiolog. —**ology**, *s.* die Lebenslehre, Physiologie; —ology of plants, die Pflanzenphysiologie. —**que**, *s.* der Körperbau, die Körperbeschaffenheit.

Phyto—graphy, *s.* die Pflanzenbeschreibung. —**logy**, *s.* die Pflanzenlehre. —**phagous**, *adj.* pflanzenfressend. —**zoa**, *pl.* Pflanzentiere.

Pian—ist, *s.* der (die) Klavierspieler(in), Pianist(in). —**o**, I. *adv.* piano. II. *s.*, —**oforte**, *s.* das Pianoforte, Klavier; grand —o, der Flügel; semi-grand —o, kleiner Zimmerflügel; upright —o, cottage —o, (Wand)Piano, Pianino. —**ola**, *s.* das Pianola.

Piazza, *s.* der Platz; der Säulengang, die Arkade (*Arch.*); (balcony) der Altan (*Arch.*).

Pibroch, *s.* die wilde, aufreizende Musik Schlachtmusik der Bergschotten (für die Sackpfeife).

Pica, *s.* die Ciceroschrift; krankhafter Appetit.

Picar—esque, *adj.* spitzbübisch; —esque novel, der Schelmenroman. —**oon**, *s.* der (See-)Räuber; der Abenteurer, Spitzbube.

Piccolo, *s.* die Piccolo-, Oktav-flöte.

Pick, I. *v.a.* (peck) picken, hacken; stochern (*the teeth*); (be)nagen, (ab)knaupeln, klauben an (*a bone*); lesen (*vegetables, etc.*); pflücken (*fruit*); zupfen (*wool, oakum*); (auf)suchen, vom Zaun brechen (*a quarrel*); mit einem Dietrich öffnen (*a lock*); auswählen, aussuchen (*one's way*); bestehlen, leeren (*a p.'s pocket*); scheiden (*ore*); to — holes in s.o.'s coat, einem etwas am Zeuge flicken (*fig.*), etwas an einem auszusetzen haben; to give s.o. a bone to —, einem zu schaffen machen; to — a p.'s brains, einen gründlich ausfragen; to — **off**, ab-picken, -pflücken; to — **out**, herausheben (*Typ.*), ausstechen, hervorheben (*a pattern*), herauslesen, aussuchen; to — out one colour with another, eine Farbe durch eine andere hervorheben; to — **up**, sammeln (*information*), auf-picken, -heben; to — up a language, eine Sprache aufschnappen; to — up a living, sich mühsam durchschlagen. II. *v.n.* sorgfältig tun; (nibble) knaupeln; to — and steal, *see* Pilfer; to — and choose, auswählen, allzu wählerisch sein; to — up again, sich wieder erholen. III. *s.* der Spitzhammer, die Haue, Hacke; (choice) die Auswahl, Auslese, die Besten. —**ed**, *adj.* auserlesen; —ed troops, auserlesene Mannschaften, Kerntruppen. —**er**, *s.* der Pflücker, Leser, Zupfer; die Räumnadel (*Gun.*). —**et**, I. *s.* der Pfahl; der Kettenstab, Absteckpfahl (*Surv.*); das Pikett, die Feldwache (*Mil.*). II. *v.a.* mit Pfählen befestigen; (fence) einpfählen; (tether) an einen Pfahl binden; ein Pikett ausstellen (*Mil., etc.*). —**ing**, *s.* das Picken, Pflücken &c.; das Bestehlen (*of pockets*); der Gewinn. —**ings**, *s.* das Gestohlene, der Raub. *Comp.* —**axe**, *s.* die Pickhacke. —**lock**, *s.* der Dietrich; (thief, *etc.*) der Dieb, Einbrecher. —**-me-up**, *s.* eine Magenstärkung (*sl.*). —**pocket**, *s.* der Taschendieb; beware of —pockets, vor Taschendieben wird gewarnt. —**purse**, *s.* der Beutelschneider.

Pickaback, *adv.* huckepack.

Pickerel, *s.* der Grashecht, kleine Hecht.

Pickl—e, I. *s.* der Pökel, Salzbrühe; (—ed substance) das Eingepökelte; der Trotzkopf, Wildfang (*coll.*); —es, in Essig und Salz eingemachte Gemüse, das Eingemachte; mixed —es, gemischte (englische) Essigfrüchte; to be in a pretty —e, in der Patsche stecken (*coll.*); to have a rod in —e for a p., einem eine Rute binden. II. *v.a.* einpökeln; —ed cucumbers, Essiggurken; —ed herrings, Pökelhäringe. —**ing**, *s.* das Einpökeln.

Picnic, *s.* das Picknick; die Landpartie.

Pict—orial, *adj.*, —**orially**, *adv.* Maler-, malerisch; illustriert, Bilder- (*as an edition*). —**ure**, I. *s.* das Gemälde, Bild; (image) das Ebenbild; *see* Portrait; to draw a —ure of a th., etwas malen, schildern. II. *attrib.*; —ure postcard, die Ansichtspostkarte. III. *v.a.* (ab)malen; schildern (*fig.*); just —ure to yourself, stellen Sie sich einmal vor. —**uresque**, *adj.*, —**uresquely**, *adv.* malerisch. —**uresqueness**, *s.* das Malerische. *Comp.* —**ure-book**, *s.* das Bilderbuch. —**ure-cleaner**, *s.* der Bilderreiniger. —**ure-dealer**, *s.* der Bilderhändler. —**ure-frame**, *s.* der Bilderrahmen. —**ure-gallery**, *s.* die Bildergallerie, Gemäldegallerie.

Pidgin-English, *s.* das in chinesischen Seestädten gesprochene gebrochene Englisch. ('Pidgin' is the Chinese pronunciation of 'business.')

[1]**Pie**, *s.* die Pastete; (fruit —) die Torte; he has a finger in every —, er mischt sich in alle fremden Angelegenheiten; to eat humble —, sich demütigen. *Comp.* —**-crust**, *s.* die Pastetenkruste.

[2]**Pie**, *s.* die Elster (*Orn.*); die Ciceroschrift (*Typ.*). —**bald**, *adj.* bunt, scheckig; —bald horse, der Schecke. —**d**, *adj.* bunt, scheckig.

Piece, I. *s.* das Stück; (shred) der Fetzen; die Flinte (*Gun.*); das (Theater)stück; das Stück Geschütz (*Artil.*); die Figur (*Chess, etc.*); 2-mark —, Zwei-Mark-Stück; — of advice, der Ratschlag, gute Rat; — of bread and butter, das Butterbrod; — of folly, der Narrenstreich, eine Torheit; — of music, das Musikstück; — of news, die Neuigkeit, Nachricht; — of poetry, das Gedicht; a — of work, ein Stück Arbeit; by the —, stückweise; all of a —, (alle) aus einem Stücke, eins (with, mit); to break, cut, fall to —s, zerbrechen, zerschneiden, in Stücke gehen; to take to —s, auseinandernehmen; to tear in —s, zerreißen; — of cloth, das Stück Zeug; I gave him a good — of my mind, ich sagte ihm (gründlich) meine Meinung. II. *v.a.* anstücken, flicken, ansetzen; to — **out**, verlängern, ergänzen, zusammen-setzen, -stellen; to — **up**, ausflicken. III. *v.n.* sich verbinden. —**meal**, *adj. & adv.* stückweise, in Stücken, einzeln. *Comp.* —**-goods**, *pl.* die Stückgüter. —**-work**, *s.* die Akkordarbeit. —**-worker**, *s.* der Stückarbeiter.

Pied, *see* ^{2}Pie.

Pier, *s.* der (Strebe-)Pfeiler; der (Wehr-)Damm, die Mole, der Deich (*Hydr.*); der Lösch-, Landeplatz, Landungssteg (*Naut.*); das Widerlager (*of a bridge*). —**age**, *s.* (— dues) das Dammgeld. *Comp.* —**-glass**, *s.* der Pfeilerspiegel. —**-table**, *s.* der Pfeilertisch.

Pierc—e, *v.* I. *a.* durch-stechen, -bohren; durchdringen (*the ear*) (*fig.*); durchschneiden (*the heart*) (*fig.*); eindringen in (*acc.*) (*a secret, etc.*). II. *n. see* Penetrate. —**er**, *s.* der Durch-stechende, -bohrende; der (die) Pfriem(e) (*Shoem., etc.*); die Durchbrechnadel (*Semp.*); der Bohrer. —**ing**, *adj.*, —**ingly**, *adv.* schneidend, scharf, durchdringend (*also fig.*); rührend, eindringlich (*fig.*); —ing cold, schneidende Kälte; —ing cry, durchdringender Schrei; —ing look, durchbohrender Blick.

Piet—ism, *s.* der Pietismus. —**ist**, *s.* der Pietist. —**y**, *s.* die Frömmigkeit; die Pietät; filial —y, kindliche Liebe.

Pig, I. *s.* das Schwein; (young —) das Ferkel; die Gans, (kleine) Mulde (*Metall.*); the — grunts, das Schwein grunzt; the little — squeaks, das Ferkel quiekt; to buy a — in a poke, die Katze im Sacke kaufen. II. *v.n.* (— together) zusammenliegen, zusammengepfercht leben (*fam.*). —**gery**, *s.* der Schweinehof; *see* —sty. *Comp.* —**-headed**, *adj.* störrisch, eigensinnig; dumm. —**-iron**, *s.* das Roheisen. —**-lead**, *s.* das Muldenblei. —**-metal**, *s.* das Rohmetall. —**nut**, *s.* die Erdnuß; die Nuß des braunen Walnußbaums (*Amer.*). —**-skin**, *s.* das Schweinsleder. —**-sticking**, *s.* das Schweineschlachten. —**sty**, *s.* der Schweinestall. —**tail**, *s.* der Zopf; der Tabak in Rollen.

Pigeon, *s.* die (gewöhnliche) Taube; the — coos, die Taube girrt; carrier —, die Brieftaube; cock —, der Täuberich. *Comp.* —**-breasted**, *adj.* mit einer Hühnerbrust. —**-fancier**, *s.* der Taubenliebhaber; der Taubenzüchter. —**hole**, I. *s.* das Taubenloch. II. *v.a.* in ein Zettelfach legen; aufheben; vernachlässigen. —**holes**, *pl.* kleine Fächer in Schreibtischen für Papiere; set of —holes, der Bureaukasten, Bureauschrank. —**-house**, *s.* der Taubenschlag. —**-livered**, *adj.* sanftmütig; *see* Timid. —**-pie**, *s.* die Taubenpastete.

Piggin, *s.* die Schöpfgelte, der Schöpfeimer.

Pigm—ean, —**y**, *s. see* Pygmean, Pygmy.

Pigment, *s.* der Farb(e)stoff, Färbstoff, die Farbe, das Pigment.

Pigwidgeon, I. *s.* die Fee; winziges Ding (*fig.*). II. *adj.* winzig.

Pike, *s.* die Pike (*Mil.*); *see* Peak; die Heugabel (*Agr.*); *see* Turn—; der Hecht (*Icht.*). —**d**, *adj.* spitzig. *Comp.* —**man**, *s.* der Pikenträger, Pikenier. —**staff**, *s.* der Pik(en)schaft; der Stab mit Eisenspitze; as plain as a —staff, sonnenklar.

Pilaster, *s.* der Pilaster, viereckige Wandpfeiler.

^{1}**Pile**, I. *s.* (heap) der Haufe(n); der Stoß (*of wood*); das große Gebäude, eine Masse von Gebäuden (*Arch.*); die Pyramide (*Mil.*); die Säule (*Elec.*); *see* Pyre. II. *v.a.* (— up) in Haufen setzen, aufhäufen, aufschichten; zusammensetzen (*arms*).

Pile, I. *s.* der Pfahl; der Spitzpfahl (*Her.*) II. *v.a.* pfählen, rammen. *Comp.* —**-driver**, —**-engine**, *s.* die Ramme, der Rammklotz. —**-dwelling**, *see* Lake dwelling.

^{3}**Pile**, *s.* das Haar, die Fiber; der Flor, die Pole (*of velvet*); das Rauhe, Haarige (*of cloth*). —**ate**, *adj.* hutförmig.

^{4}**Piles**, *pl.* die Hämorrhoiden.

Pilfer, *v.a.* stehlen, mausen. —**er**, *s.* der Mauser, Entwender. —**ing**, *s.* das Mausen.

Pilgrim, *s.* der (die) Pilger(in); der Pilgrim, Wallfahrer, Waller (*high style*). —**age**, *s.* die Wall-, Pilger-fahrt (to, nach).

Pill, I. *s.* die Pille; to swallow the bitter —, in den sauern Apfel beißen (*coll.*). *Comp.* —**-box**, *s.* die Pillenschachtel.

Pillage, I. *s.* der Raub, die Plünderung. II. *v.a. & n.* plündern, rauben. —**r**, *s.* der Plünderer.

Pill—ar, *s.* der Pfeiler, Ständer, die Säule; to be driven from —ar to post, von Pontius zu Pilatus geschickt werden. —**ared**, *adj.* von Pfeilern unterstützt, mit Pfeilern versehen; (—ar-like) säulenförmig. —**ory**, I. *s.* der Pranger. II. *v.a.* an den Pranger stellen. *Comp.* —**ar-box**, *s.* der (in der Straße aufgestellte große) Briefkasten.

Pillion, *s.* das Sattelkissen, der Hintersattel.

Pillow, I. *s.* das Kopfkissen, der Pfühl; das Klöppelkissen. II. *v.a.* legen auf (*acc.*); to advise (*or* take counsel) with one's —, eine S. im Bett überlegen *or* beschlafen. *Comp.* —**-case**, *s.* der Kopfkissenüberzug. —**-lace**, *s.* geklöppelte Spitzen. —**-slip**, *s.* der Kissenbezug.

Pilose, Pilous, *adj.* haarig; behaart (*Bot.*).

Pilot, I. *s.* der Lotse, Steuermann; der Führer (*fig.*); dickes grobes Tuch; to drop the —, den Lotsen aussetzen. II. *v.a.* lotsen, steuern; führen. —**age**, *s.* das Lotsen; das Lotsengeld. *Comp.* —**-boat**, *s.* das Lotsenboot. —**-cloth**, *s.* dunkelblaues Friestuch. —**-engine**, *s.* der Vorläufer, die Warnlokomotive. —**-fish**, *s.* der Lotsenfisch. —**-flag**, *s.* die Lotsenflagge.

Piment—a, —**o**, *s.* der Jamaikapfeffer.

Pimp, I. *s.* der Kuppler. II. *v.n.* kuppeln.

Pimpernel, *s.* die Bibernell, Pimpinell.

Pimpl—e, *s.* die Blatter, Finne, Pustel, das Bläschen. —**ed**, —**y**, *adj.* finnig, voll(er) Pusteln.

Pin, I. *s.* die Stecknadel; (wooden —) der Nagel, Pflock; der Bolzen (*of metal*); der Stift (*Horol.*); der Wirbel (*Mus.*); der Kegel (*at ninepins*); (breast- —) Busennadel; hölzerne Rolle, Walze (*Cook.*); —s, die Beine (*sl.*); I don't care a —, es ist mir ganz gleichgültig (*fam.*). II. *v.a.* (an-)heften; (fasten) befestigen; (seize) fassen (*sl.*); festhalten; to — one's faith to, sein ganzes Vertrauen setzen auf; to — a p. down to, einen festhalten bei; to — up, auf-stecken, -schürzen. —**afore**, *s.* das Lätzchen, die Schürze. —**ion**, I. *s.* die Schwinge, der Flügel; das Getriebe (*Mach.*). II. *v.a.* die Arme festbinden, fesseln. —**ioned**, *adj.* gefesselt. —**nate**, *see* Pinn—. —**tle**, *s.* kleine Pinne, der Bolzen, Nagel; der Protznagel (*Artil.*); der Ruderhaken (*Naut.*). *Comp.* —**-cushion**, *s.* das Nadelkissen. —**feathers**, *pl.* Stoppelfeder. —**-head**, *s.* der Stecknadelkopf. —**hole**, *s.* der Nadelstich. —**-maker**, *s.* der Nadler. —**-money**, *s.* das Nadelgeld. —**-point**, *s.* die Nadelspitze; die Kleinigkeit (*fig.*); der Rapportstift. —**-prick**, *s.* der Nadelstich. —**tail**, *s.* die Spieß-, Spitz-ente. —**-wire**, *s.* der Nadeldraht.

Pincers, *pl.* die (Kneip-, Beiß-)Zange; die (Krebs-)Scheren; die Fühlhörner (*Ent., etc.*).

Pinch, I. *v.a.* kneifen, kneipen; (squeeze) klemmen, drücken; drücken (*fig.*); to be —ed, darben, in Not *or* in sehr beschränkten Verhältnissen sein; to — o.s., sich (*dat.*) etwas abdarben; to — off, abzwicken, abkneifen; to know where the shoe —es, wissen, wo der Schuh drückt. II. *v.n.* drücken; darben, sparen. III. *s.* das Kneipen, Zwicken; der Druck, die Klemme (*fig.*); die Prise (*of snuff*); at a —, zur Not. —**ed**, *adj.* zusammengedrückt, lang und schmal; —ed face, langes, hageres Gesicht. —**ers**, *s. see* Pincers.

Pinchbeck, I. *s.* das Prinzmetall, der Tombak. II. *adj.* unecht nachgemacht.

[1]**Pin—e,** *s.* die Kiefer, Föhre; (—eapple) die Ananas. **—eal,** *adj.;* —eal gland, die Zirbeldrüse. **—ery,** *s.* das Ananashaus; die Fichtenpflanzung. **—etum,** *s.* die Kiefernpflanzung, Nadelholzschonung. **—ic,** *adj.;* —ic acid, die Pininsäure. **—nace,** *see* Pinnace. *Comp.* **—eapple,** *s.* die Ananas; (cone) der Tannzapfen (*rare*). **—eclad,** *adj.* mit Kiefern bestanden *or* bewachsen. **—e-marten,** *s.* der Kiefer(n)marder. **—e-wood,** *s.* der Kiefernwald, das Kieferngehölz.

[2]**Pin—e,** *v.n.;* to —e **away,** sich abzehrern, vor Gram vergehen; to —e **for,** schmachten nach. **—ing,** I. *adj.* sich grämend. II. *s.* das Härmen.

Pinfold, I. *s.* der Pfandstall; die Viehhürde. II. *v.a.* einpferchen.

Ping-pong, *s.* das Zimmernetzballspiel, Tafelnetzball(spiel).

[1]**Pink,** I. *s.* die Nelke (*Bot.*); das Rosenrot, Rosa; *see* Minnow; der Jagdrock (*Sport.*); der Gipfel, höchste Grad (*fig.*); the very — of perfection, das Muster der Vollkommenheit; — of politeness, die Krone der Höflichkeit; — of propriety, personifizierter Anstand. II. *adj.* blaßrot, rosa.

[2]**Pink,** *s.* die Pinke (*Naut.*).

[3]**Pink,** *v.a.* ausschneiden, auszacken. *Comp.* **—ing-iron,** *s.* das Auszackeisen.

Pinnace, *s.* die Pinasse.

Pinn—acle, *s.* die Zinne; der Gipfel (*fig.*). **—ate,** *adj.* gefiedert. **—atifid,** *adj.* halbgefiedert. **—atiped,** *adj.* schwimmfüßig. **—er,** *s.* der Nadler (*obs.*); das Vorstecklätzchen. **—ers,** *pl.* die Flügelhaube. **—iped,** *s.* der Floßfüßler.

Pint, *s.* die Pinte, der Schoppen (= 0,577 Liter).

Pioneer, I. *s.* der Schanzgräber, Pionier (*Mil.*); der Bahnbrecher, Vorkämpfer (*fig.*). II. *v.a.* den Weg bahnen.

Pious, *adj.*, **—ly,** *adv.* fromm; liebevoll, kindlich, pflichtgetreu (*towards parents, etc.*).

[1]**Pip,** *s.* das Auge (*on cards*).

[2]**Pip,** *s.* der Obstkern, Kern (*of apples*). **—pin,** *s.* der Obstkern; (an apple of various kinds) der Pipin.

[3]**Pip,** *s.* der Pips (*in fowls*).

[1]**Pip—e,** I. *s.* die Pfeife (*also Mus.*); das Rohr, die Röhre (*for gas*); das Pfeifen (*of birds*); die Stimme. II. *v.n. & a.* auf der Pfeife, Flöte &c., spielen; pfeifen; (squeak) quieken; put that in your —e and smoke it, laß dir das gesagt sein. **—eful,** *s.* eine Pfeife (voll). **—er,** *s.* der Pfeifer; to pay the —er, die Zeche bezahlen, die Kosten tragen. **—ing,** I. *adj.* pfeifend, heulend; friedlich, matt; wallend, siedend; —ing hot, brühheiß. II. *s.* das Röhrenwerk; der Schnurbesatz, die Einlegborte (*Tailor.*). **—kin,** *s.* das Töpfchen. *Comp.* **—e-bowl,** *s.* der Pfeifenkopf. **—e-clay,** *s.* der Pfeifenton. **—e-stem,** *s.* das Pfeifenrohr.

[2]**Pipe,** *s.* die Pipe (*of wine*).

Pipit, *s.* der Pieper, die Pieplerche.

Piqu—ancy, *s.* das Beißende, Scharfe, die Schärfe; das Pikante (*fig.*). **—ant,** *adj.*, **—antly,** *adv.* pikant (*also fig.*), prickelnd, scharf. **—e,** I. *s.* der Groll; der Sechziger (*in Piquet*); —e of honour, der Ehrenpunkt. II. *v.a.* (an)reizen; (irritate) ärgern, kränken; to —e o.s. upon a th., sich (*dat.*) etwas auf eine Sache zu gute tun, seine Ehre darin suchen. **—et,** *s.* das Piquetspiel.

Pira—cy, *s.* die Seeräuberei; der literarische Diebstahl (*fig.*). **—te,** I. *s.* der Seeräuber; der literarische Dieb, Nachdrucker. II. *v.a.* ausschreiben, nachdrucken; —ted edition, unrechtmäßiger Nachdruck. **—tical,** *adj.* (see)räuberisch; Nachdrucks=; —tical edition, printer, der Nachdruck, Nachdrucker.

Pirouette, I. *s.* der Kreisschwung, die Pirouette. II. *v.n.* sich schnell im Kreise drehen, pirouettieren.

Pisc—ary, I. *adj.* zu den Fischen gehörig. II. *s.* das Recht zu fischen. **—atorial, —atory,** *adj.* Fisch=, Fischer=. **—es,** *pl.* die Fische (*Astr.*). **—ina,** *s.* der Wasserbecken. **—ivorous,** *adj.* fischfressend.

Pisé, *s.* der Pisé; building in —, Pisébau.

Pish, I. *int.* pfui! II. *v.n.* Pfui ausrufen *or* sagen.

Pis—mire, *s.* die Ameise, Seichameise. **—s,** I. *s.* der Harn. II. *v.n.* harnen, pissen.

Pistachio, *s.* der Grünmandelbaum, die Pistazie.

Pist—il, *s.* das Pistill, der Stempel (*Bot.*). **—on,** *s.* der Kolben. *Comp.* **—on-rod,** *s.* die Kolbenstange (*Locom.*).

Pistol, *s.* die Pistole. *Comp.* **—-case,** *s.* der Pistolenkasten. **—-duel,** *s.* das Pistolenduell, das Duell auf Pistolen. **—-shot,** *s.* der Pistolenschuß; within —-shot, in Pistolenschuß=Weite.

Pit, I. *s.* die Grube (*Min., Anat., etc.*); das Loch, die Tiefe (*in the earth*); (abyss) der Abgrund; das Grab (*B.*); die Hölle (*fig. & B.*); (cock-—) der Kampfplatz; das Parterre (*Theat.*); — of the stomach, Herzgrube; the bottomless —, der Abgrund der Hölle, der Höllenschlund. II. *v.a.* vergraben (*potatoes, etc.*); mit Narben zeichnen; feindlich gegenüberstellen; —ted with smallpox, blatternarbig. *Comp.* **—-coal,** *s.* die Steinkohle. **—fall,** *s.* die Fallgrube, Falle. **—-man,** *s.* der Bergmann.

Pitapat, *adv.* ticktack; tripptrapp.

[1]**Pitch,** I. *s.* das Pech; mineral —, Erdpech. II. *v.a.* (ver)pichen; teeren (*a ship*). **—, —y,** *adj.* pechig, pechicht; pechschwarz (*fig.*); — dark, pechfinster. *Comp.* **—-pine,** *s.* die Pechtanne.

[2]**Pitch,** I. *s.* der Wurf; (point) der Punkt, Grad, die Stufe; (height) die Höhe; die Tonhöhe (*Mus.*); die Pfeilhöhe (*of an arch*); der Abhang, die Neigung (*of a hill*); die Steigung (*of a screw*); die Schräge (*of a roof*); concert —, die Normalstimmung; to the highest —, auf das Äußerste; to play at — and toss, Kopf oder Schrift spielen. II. *v.a.* werfen, schleudern; (set up) feststecken; aufschlagen (*a camp, tent, etc.*); den Grundton angeben (*Mus.*); stimmen (*Mus.*); gabeln, mit einer Heugabel werfen (*hay, etc.*); —ed battle, regelmäßige Schlacht. III. *v.n.* sich niederlassen; (encamp) sich lagern; (fall) niederstürzen, niederfallen; stampfen (*Naut.*); to — at anchor, stampfreiten; to — and toss, stampfen (*Naut.*); to — **into,** herfallen über (*acc.*) (*fam.*); to — **upon,** wählen, sich entscheiden für; —ed work, die Steinpackung, das Packwerk. **—ing,** *s.* das Stampfen (*Naut.*); die Steinpackung (*Hydr.*); das Pflastern mit Steinen (*a street*). *Comp.* **—-accent,** *s.* musikalischer Akzent, die Tonhöhe. **—fork,** I. *s.* die Heugabel; die Stimmgabel (*Mus.*). II. *v.a.;* mit der Heugabel werfen *or* stechen; he was —forked into the place, er wurde Hals über Kopf zu dem Posten befördert.

Pitcher, *s.* der Krug; little —s have long ears, kleine Leutchen haben lange Ohren (*prov.*).

Pit—eous, *adj.*, **—eously,** *adv.* kläglich, traurig. **—eousness,** *s.* die Kläglichkeit, Traurigkeit. **—iable,** *adj.*, **—iably,** *adv.* bemitleidenswert, (miserable) kläglich, elend. **—iful,** *adj.*, **—ifully,** *adv.* mitleidig; *see* —iable; (paltry) jämmerlich, verächtlich. **—ifulness,** *s.* die Erbärmlichkeit; mitleidsvolles Wesen. **—iless,** *adj.*, **—ilessly,** *adv.* erbarmungslos, unbarmherzig, gefühllos. **—ilessness,** *s.* die Hartherzigkeit, Unbarmherzigkeit. **—y,** I. *s.* das Mitleid, Erbarmen; der Schade(n); what a —y! wie schade! it is a thousand —ies that . . ., es ist ewig schade, daß . . .; to have *or* take —y on, Mitleid haben mit . . .; for —y's sake, um Gottes willen; the more's the —y, desto schlimmer (*coll.*). II *v.a.* bemitleiden, bedauern.

Pith, *s.* das Mark (*also Bot.*); das Innere, der Kern (*fig.*); (force) die Kraft, Stärke; (importance) das Gewicht; (essence) das Mark. **—iness,** *s.* die Markigkeit, Kraft. **—y,** *adj.*, **—ily,** *adv.* markig, kernig, kräftig; a —y saying, ein Kernspruch.

Pittance, *s.* (dole) die Portion; der kleine Teil, Anteil; (livelihood) armseliges Auskommen; a mere —, ein armseliges Sümmchen.

Pituitary, *adj.* schleimabsondernd, Schleim=.
Pivot, *s.* der Drehpunkt, Zapfen, Stift; der Angel=, Stütz=, Schwenkungs=punkt (*also fig.*), der Flügelmann (*Mil.*). *Comp.* **—-gun**, *s.* die Drehbasse. **—-man**, *s.* der Flügelmann.
Pix—ie, —y, *s.* die Fee, Elfe. *Comp.* **—ie-led**, *adj.* von Elfen geleitet, behext.
Pizzle, *s.* die Rute (*of certain quadrupeds*).
Placab—ility, —leness, *s.* die Versöhnlichkeit. **—le**, *adj.*, **—ly**, *adv.* versöhnlich.
Placard, I. *s.* der Anschlagzettel, das Plakat. II. *v.a.* öffentlich anschlagen.
Place, I. *s.* der Platz, Raum; der Platz (*in a city, etc.*); (locality) der Ort; (town) die Stadt; abode) der Aufenthaltsort, Wohnort, Wohnsitz; (spot) die Stelle, der Ort, Platz; (situation) die Stelle, der Dienst; (office) das Amt; (rank) der Stand, Rang; *see* Stead; die Stelle (*in a book*); der Stand (*Astr.*); der höchste Flug eines Raubvogels (*Sport.*); (fort) die Festung; the other —, die Hölle (*fam.*); Cambridge is an interesting —, Cambridge ist ein interessanter Ort, eine interessante Stadt; — of refuge, Zufluchtsort; at this —, hier; in the first, second, last —, erstens, zweitens, letztens; in some —, irgendwo; in another —, anderswo; in your —, an deinem Platze (*in the spot where you stand*); an deiner Stelle (*if I were you*); in deiner Stellung (*in your position*); in its, his —, an seiner Stelle; in the wrong —, am unrichtigen Orte, an der falschen Stelle; of this —, hiesig(en Ortes); of that —, dort(ig); out of —, am unrechten Orte, ungelegen (*fig.*); außer Diensten (*of servants, etc.*); out of — here, (hier) nicht hergehörig; to give —, Platz machen; nachgeben; to hold a —, eine Stelle bekleiden; to know one's —, wissen was sich ziemt; to take —, stattfinden, geschehen; to take a p.'s —, jemandes Stelle einnehmen. II. *v.a.* (an einen Platz) stellen, legen, setzen; anbringen (*money*); aufpflanzen (*a gun*); to — to s.o.'s account, auf jemandes Rechnung setzen; to — to a p.'s credit, einem gutschreiben; to be —d, sich befinden; to — confidence in a p., Vertrauen setzen auf einen. *Comp.* **—-hunter**, *s.* der Stellenjäger, Streber. **—-hunting**, *s.* die Stellenjägerei, das Strebertum. **—-man**, *s.* der Angestellte. **—-name**, *s.* der Ortsname.
Placenta, *s.* der Mutterkuchen, die Nachgeburt; der Samenträger (*Bot.*). **—l**, *adj.* die Nachgeburt betreffend.
Plac—able, *see* Placab—. **—et**, *s.* das Ja (bei akademischen Abstimmungen zu Oxford und Cambridge), die Genehmigung; *non —et*, die Ablehnung eines Universitäts=Gesetzentwurfes durch den akademischen Senat. **—id**, *adj.*, **—idly**, *adv.* sanft, mild; (calm) ruhig. **—idity, —idness**, *s.* die Sanftheit, Milde; die Ruhe.
Placket, *s.* der Schlitz (an Weiberröcken); der Unterrock.
Plagiar—ism, *s.* das Plagiat, literarischer Diebstahl. **—ist**, *s.* der Bücherausschreiber, Abschreiber, der literarische Dieb. **—ize**, *v.a.* ausschreiben. **—y**, *see* —ism.
Plague, I. *s.* die Pest, Seuche; die Plage, der Quälgeist (*fig.*); — take it! das soll der Teufel holen! the ten —s of Eygpt, die zehn Landplagen Ägyptens; having the —, mit der Pest behaftet. II. *v.a.* plagen, quälen. *Comp.* **—-spot**, *s.* die Pestbeule; der Schandfleck (*fig.*).
Plaice, *s.* die Scholle, Platteise, der Plattfisch.
Plaid, I. *s.* der Mantel der Bergschotten; karriertes Wollenzeug (*C.L.*); (wrap) das Plaid, Umschlagetuch. II. *adj.* gestreift, bunt gewürfelt.
Plain, I. *adj. & adv.*, **—ly**, *adv.* eben, platt, flach; (simple) einfach, schlicht; (unadorned) schmucklos; (without a pattern, *etc.*) glatt, ungemustert; (of one colour) einfarbig; nicht hübsch (*as a face*); glatt, ungereiht (*as a bodice*); rein, nackt, bar (*as truth*); (clear) klar, verständlich; (open) offen; (easily seen) deutlich; (evident) offenbar; (homely) ungelehrt, einfach, schlicht; (blunt) derb, barsch; to tell in — terms, frei heraussagen; to make —, ebnen (*lit.*); deutlich *or* klar machen (*fig.*); to be — with a p., use — language towards a p., einem seine Meinung offen, rund heraussagen; she is very —, sie ist ziemlich häßlich; — cooking, einfache bürgerliche Küche — sewing, die Weißnäherei, das Weißnähen. II. *s.* die Ebene, Fläche. **—ness**, *s.* die Ebenheit; die Glätte; die Einfachheit, Schlichtheit; die Klarheit, Deutlichkeit; die Geradheit, Offenheit, Redlichkeit. *Comp.* **—-chant, —-song**, *s.* der Choralgesang. **—-clothes**, I. *s.* der Zivilanzug. II. *adj.*; —-clothes officer, der Geheimpolizist. **—-dealing**, I. *adj.* redlich, offen. II. *s.* gerade, ehrliche Handlungsweise. **—-speaking**, *s.* offnes Aussprechen, deutliche *or* unumwundene Meinungsäußerung. **—-spoken**, *adj.* offen herausredend; a —-spoken man, einer, der seine Meinung gerade heraussagt.
Plaint, *s.* die Klage, Beschwerde. **—iff**, *s.* der (die) Kläger(in). **—ive**, *adj.*, **—ively**, *adv.* kläglich. **—iveness**, *s.* die Kläglichkeit.
Plait, I. *s.* die Falte (*in dresses, etc.*); die Flechte (*of hair*); das Geflecht (*of straw*). II. *v.a.* falten; flechten. **—er**, *s.* der Faltende, Flechtende; der Faltenleger (*Sew.-mach.*).
Plan, I. *s.* der Plan, Entwurf, Riß (*Surv., etc.*); der Plan (*fig.*). II. *v.a.* einen Plan machen zu, abreißen; entwerfen, projektieren; to draw a —, einen Grundriß entwerfen; to make —s, Pläne schmieden, entwerfen *or* machen. **—ary**, *adj.* Plan=, Flächen=. **—chet**, *s.* die Platte (*Min.*). **—chette**, *s.* das Brettchen. **—e**, *see* [1]Plane. **—imeter**, *s.* der Flächen(inhalts)messer, der *and* das Planimeter. **—imetry**, *s.* die Flächenmeßkunde; die Flächenmessung, Planimetrie. **—ing**, *s.* das Hobeln, Behobeln. **—ipenn(at)es**, *pl.* Glattflügler (*Entom.*). **—ish**, *v.a.* glätten, planieren; glattstreichen (*Pott.*); hammerstrecken (*Metall.*). **—isher**, *s.* der Glätter, Planierer. **—isphere**, *s.* der Planiglob, die Erd=, Himmels=kugelkarte. **—ner**, *s.* der Planmacher. **—ometer**, *s.* der Planometer, die Prüfplatte für Ebenen. *Comp.* **—ing-bench**, *s.* die Hobelbank. **—ishing-hammer**, *s.* der Planierhammer. **—o-concave**, *adj.* plankonkav. **—o-convex**, *adj.* plankonvex.
[1]**Plane**, I. *adj.* eben, flach. II. *s.* der Hobel; die Fläche, Ebene (*Geom.*); inclined —, schiefe Ebene; — of projection, reflection, Projektionsebene, Zurückwerfungsebene; vertical —, senkrechte (Vertikal)ebene; — of direction, die Visierebene (*Artill.*). III. *v.a.* ebnen, glätten; (ab)hobeln (*Carp.*); bestoßen (*Typ.*); to — **down**, die Form klopfen (*Typ.*); to — **off**, abhobeln.
[2]**Plane**, *s.* (—-tree) die Platane.
Planet, *s.* der Planet, Wandelstern. **—arium**, *s.* das Planetarium. **—ary**, *adj.* Planeten=; von Planeten herrührend; planetarisch; (—-like) planetenartig; umherirrend (*fig.*).
Plank, I. *s.* die Planke, Bohle; die Stütze (*fig.*); to walk the —, ertränkt werden (*obs.*). II. *v.a.* mit Planken belegen, dielen. **—s**, *pl.* Dielen.
Plant, I. *s.* die Pflanze, das Gewächs, Kraut; die Gerätschaften, Betriebsanlage (*of a factory, etc.*); fixed —, feste Anlage; border —s, Pflanzen zur Einfassung. II. *v.a.* pflanzen; stiften, anlegen (*colonies*); (auf)pflanzen, aufstecken (*a flag, etc.*); einführen (*a religion*); aufpflanzen (*guns*); aufstellen (*an instrument, etc.*); (an)pflanzen, bepflanzen (*a garden, ground, etc.*); (set up) feststellen, einrichten; to — o s., sich hinpflanzen *or* festsetzen. **—ation**, *s.* die Pflanzung (*also fig.*); die Anlage; young —ation, die Schonung; —ation song, das Negerlied. **—er**, *s* der Pflanzer; der (erste) Ansiedler, Gründer, Pflanzer (*in a colony*). **—ing**, *s.* das Pflanzen, Anlegen von Baumpflanzungen; *see* —ation. *Comp.* **—-louse**, *s.* die Blattlaus.

[1]**Plantain**, *s.* der Wegerich (*Bot.*); water —, der Wasserwegerich.
[2]**Plantain**, *s.*, (— tree) der Pisang(baum).
Plantigrade, I. *adj.* auf den Fußsohlen gehend. II. *s.* der Sohlengänger.
Plaque, *s.* die Schnalle, Agraffe; das Metallplättchen als Zierat, Anhängsel.
[1]**Plash**, I. *s.* der zum Flechten halb eingeschnittene Zweig. II. *v.a.* die Zweige biegen, flechten, in einander schlingen.
[2]**Plash**, *v.n. see* Splash. —**y**, *adj.* putschig, schlammig.
Plasm, *s.* die (Guß=)Form. —(**at**)**ic**(**al**), *adj.* bildend, Gestalt gebend; die farblose Blutflüssigkeit betreffend.
Plasma, *s.* der lauchgrüne Chalcedon, Plasma (*Min.*); das Blutplasma.
Plast—er, I. *s.* das Pflaster (*Pharm.*); der Mörtel, Bewurf, die Tünche (*Build.*); —er of Paris, der Stuck, feine Gipsmörtel. II. *v.a.* bepflastern; (—er over) über=ziehen, =tünchen; tünchen, bewerfen, vergipsen (*Build.*). —**erer**, *s.* der Gipser, Gips=, Stuck=arbeiter; —erer's trowel, die Gipserkelle. —**ering**, *s.* die Stuckaturarbeit; der Gipsanwurf, Bewurf; (act of —ering) das Bewerfen, Tünchen. —**ic**, *adj.* plastisch, bildend; formbar, bildungsfähig (*as clay, etc.*); *see* Pliable; —ic art, die bildende Kunst, Bildhauerei, Skulptur, Plastik; —ic clay, der Töpferton. —**icity**, *s.* die bildende Kraft; die Gestaltungsfähigkeit.
[1]**Plat**, *see* Plait.
[2]**Plat**, *see* Plot. —**an**, *see* Plane tree. —**e**, *see* Plate. —**eau**, *s.* das Hochland, die Hochebene, das Plateau. —**ing**, *s.* die Plattierung (*Metall.*); (silver- —ing) die Versilberung; (coat) die Plattierung; die Bekleidung, Verplattung (*of a ship*); electro- —ing, galvanische Versilberung. —**inum**, *s.* das Platin. —**itude**, *s.* die Plattheit (*fig.*); (stupid remark) der Gemeinplatz. —**ter**, *s.* große, flache Schüssel. *Comp.* —**band**, *s.* das schmale Beet, Einfassungsbeet (*Hort.*); der Streifen, Borstims, die Borte (*Arch.*); (lintel) der Tür=, Fenster=sturz. —**form**, *s.* die Platform, das platte Dach, der Altan (*Arch.*); die Bettung (*Artil.*); die (Redner= 2c.) Bühne, das Podium (*in halls, etc.*); der Bahnsteig (*Railw.*); die Politik, das Programm (*of a party, etc.*); that is a plank of the Liberal —form, das gehört zu den Grundsätzen, auf welchen die Liberalen fußen.
Plate, I. *s.* die Platte (*of metal, etc.*); die Platte, der Stich (*Engr.*); (silver) das Silber= (Gold=) Geschirr; die Platte, Tafel (*Glassw.*); (dinner *etc.* —) der Teller; der Einsatz (*at races*); der Silberpfennig (*Her.*). II. *v.a.* plattieren, überziehen; (silver- —) versilbern; panzern; —d ware, goods, plattiertes Geschirr; electro- —d, galvanisch versilbert. —**ful**, *s.* der Teller voll. *Comp.* —**-armour**, *s.* die Plattenpanzerung. —**-basket**, *s.* der Teller=korb, (— bucket) =einsatz; der Besteckkorb (*for silver*). —**-glass**, *s.* das Spiegelglas. —**-layer**, *s.* der Schienenleger (*Railw.*). —**-rack**, —**-drainer**, *s.* das Tellergestell, Tellerbrett. —**-powder**, *s.* das Putzpulver. —**-rails**, *pl.* die Flachschienen. —**-warmer**, *s.* der Tellerwärmer.
Platoni—c, *adj.*, —**cally**, *adv.* platonisch. —**sm**, *s.* der Platonismus. —**st**, *s.* der Platoniker.
Platoon, I. *s.* das Peloton, die Rotte. II. *attrib.;* — firing, das Rottenfeuer, Pelotonfeuer.
Plau—dit, *s.* der laute Beifall. —**sibility**, *s.* die Wahrscheinlichkeit, Glaubwürdigkeit (*of a notion, etc.*); die Beredsamkeit, Gefälligkeit. —**sible**, *adj.*, —**sibly**, *adv.* triftig, einleuchtend, wahrscheinlich, annehmlich; überzeugend, beredt, *see* Fair-spoken, Specious.
Play, I. *v.n.* spielen (*also fig.*); (dally) tändeln; to — fast and loose with, ein zweideutiges Spiel treiben; to — fair, ehrlich spielen; to — a p. false, einen hintergehen, täuschen, falsches Spiel mit einem treiben; to — a losing game, ohne Aussicht auf Gewinn spielen; to — **at**, spielen; to — **away**, (— on) weiterspielen; to — **into** the hands of, (einem) in die Hände spielen; to — into one another's hands, einander in die Hände arbeiten; to — to a p., einem vorspielen (*Mus.*), zuspielen, invitieren (*Cards*); to — out, ausspielen; is Latin —ed out? hat das Latein seine Rolle ausgespielt? to — **upon** (words, the harp, etc.), spielen (mit Worten, auf der Harfe 2c.). II. *v.a.* spielen; vorstellen, spielen (*Theat.*); to — the devil with, schändlich zurichten, zerstören (*sl.*); to — the fool, sich albern stellen; we —ed that school, wir spielten gegen die Schule; to — truant, die Schule schwänzen; to — the woman, sich wie ein Weib benehmen; —! los! Achtung! (*Tennis*). III. *s.* das Spiel; das Schauspiel (*Theat.*); (pastime) der Zeitvertreib; (scope) der Spielraum; das Spiel (*of the piston, etc.*); fair (foul) —, (un)ehrliches Spiel, (un)redliches Verfahren; — of colours, das Farbenspiel; — upon words, das Wortspiel; to bring into —, hereinziehen; in Gang bringen. —**er**, *s.* der Spieler; der Schauspieler. —**ful**, *adj.*, —**fully**, *adv.* spielend, scherzhaft, mutwillig. —**fulness**, *s.* der Mutwille, die Scherzhaftigkeit. —**ing**, I. *adj.* spielend. II. *attrib.;* —ing cards, Spielkarten. III. *s.* das Spielen. *Comp.* —**bill**, *s.* der Theaterzettel. —**-book**, *s.* das Textbuch; das Bilderbuch. —**fellow**, *s.* der Spielgefährte, Gespiele, die Gespielin. —**goer**, *s.* der Theaterbesucher. —**going**, *adj.* das Theater häufig *or* regelmäßig besuchend. —**ground**, *s.* der Spielplatz. —**house**, *s.* das Schauspielhaus. —**mate**, *see* —fellow. —**thing**, *s.* das Spielzeug. —**time**, *s.* die Spielzeit. —**wright**, —**-writer**, *s.* der Schauspielschreiber, Bühnenschriftsteller.
Plea, *s.* die Ausrede, Entschuldigung, der Vorwand; (entreaty) das Gesuch, die dringende Bitte; (action) der Rechtshandel, Prozeß; die Verteidigungsrede, Einrede (*Law*); — in bar, peremptorische Einrede; to put in a —, eine Einrede vorbringen; on the — of, unter dem Vorwande von. —**d**, *v.* I. *n.* vor Gericht reden, rechten, antworten; plaidieren, einen Prozeß als Advokat führen; (defend) verteidigen; to —d for, sprechen für; to —d guilty, sich schuldig bekennen, die Berechtigung der Klage anerkennen. II. *a.* (discuss, argue) erörtern, verteidigen; (Prozesse) führen (*Law*); (allege) sich berufen auf (*acc.*) (—d as excuse) vorschützen; sich entschuldigen mit (*ignorance, sickness, etc.*); (allege in proof) als Beweisgrund vorbringen; to —d against, entgegenstellen. —**der**, *s.* der Advokat, Verteidiger. —**ding**, I. *adj.* bittend. II. *s.* die Verteidigung; *see* Defence; das Gesuch; die Führung einer Rechtssache (*Law*). —**dings**, *pl.* gerichtliche Verhandlungen.
Pleas—ant, *adj.*, —**antly**, *adv.* angenehm; freundlich (*as a room*); (lively) froh, munter heiter; (jocular) scherzhaft. —**antness**, *s.* di Annehmlichkeit, Anmut; die Freundlichkeit, Liebenswürdigkeit, das angenehme Wesen; die Munterkeit. —**antry**, *s.* der Scherz, Spaß, Witz, lustige Einfall; (gaiety) die Lustigkeit, muntere Laune. —**e**, *v.* I. *n.* gefallen; (seem good to) belieben; if you —e, wenn es Ihnen gefällt, gefälligst, bitte; —e be seated, setzen Sie sich gefälligst, bitte nehmen Sie Platz; as you —e, wie es Ihnen gefällt, wie Sie wollen; —e God, so Gott will; a little more soup? —e, ist Ihnen noch etwas Suppe gefällig? ja, bitte *or* wenn ich bitten darf. II. *a.* gefallen, Freude machen; (content) befriedigen; belieben; may it —e your majesty, Euere Majestät wollen geruhen; the king has been graciously —ed, Seine Majestät der König haben geruht, der König hat geruht; to —e everybody, es allen recht machen; hard to —e, schwer zu befriedigen; —e yourself, tun Sie, wie es Ihnen beliebt *or* nach Belieben; to be —ed with, Gefallen, sein Vergnügen finden an (*dat.*);

you are —ed to say so, das beliebt Ihnen zu sagen. —**ed**, *adj.* erfreut, zufrieden. —**ing**, *adj.*, —**ingly**, *adv.* gefällig, angenehm, hold. —**urable**, *adj.*, —**urably**, *adv.* angenehm, ergötzlich. —**ure**, *s.* das Vergnügen, die Freude, Lust; *see* Favour; (will) das Belieben, Gutdünken; at —ure, nach Belieben; what is your —ure? was beliebt? to take —ure in, Vergnügen haben *or* finden (an einer S.). *Comp.* —**ant-spoken**, *adj.* angenehm redend. —**ure-boat**, *s.* das Vergnügungsboot. —**ure-ground**, *s.* der Vergnügungsplatz, Rasenplatz. —**ure-grounds**, *pl.* die Anlagen. —**ure-loving**, *adj.* vergnügungssüchtig. —**ure-party**, *s.* die Lustpartie. —**ure-seeker**, *s.* der Vergnügungssüchtige. —**ure-trip**, *s.* die Vergnügungstour, der Ausflug (to, nach).

Plebeian, I. *adj.* gemein, plebejisch. II. *s.* der Plebejer, gemeine Mann. —**ism**, *s.* das pöbelhafte Wesen, Plebejertum.

Plebiscite, *s.* der Volksbeschluß, das Plebiszit.

Pledge, I. *s.* das Pfand, Unterpfand; (surety) die Bürgschaft; (hostage) der Bürge, Geisel; das Zutrinken (*in drinking*); (toast) der Bescheid; to take the —, ein Gelübde der Mäßigkeit ablegen; to hold in —, als Unterpfand in Händen haben. II. *v.a.* verpfänden; (guarantee) verbürgen; (bind) verpflichten; (gage) zum Pfande setzen; (einem) zutrinken, Bescheid tun. —**r**, *s.* der Verpfänder; der Zutrinkende.

Pleiades, *pl.* das Siebengestirn.

Plen—ariness, *s.* die Fülle. —**ary**, *adj.* völlig, vollständig; —ary indulgence, der vollkommene Ablaß. —**ipotentiary**, I. *adj.* bevollmächtigt. II. *s.* der Bevollmächtigte. —**itude**, *s.* die Fülle, Vollständigkeit, Vollkommenheit; —itude of power, die Machtvollkommenheit. —**teous**, *adj.*, —**teously**, *adv.* voll, ergiebig, reich(lich). —**teousness**, *s.* die Fülle, Reichlichkeit, der Überfluß. —**tiful**, *adj.*, —**tifully**, *adv.* reichlich, voll, im Überfluß vorhanden. —**tifulness**, *s.* die Fülle; die Fruchtbarkeit (*of a harvest, etc.*). —**ty**, I. *s.* die Fülle, Menge, der Überfluß, Reichtum; (fruitfulness) die Fruchtbarkeit; —ty (of), vollauf, genug; to have —ty of, reichlich versehen sein mit; we had —y of provisions, wir waren mit Vorräten reichlich versehen; he has —ty of money, er hat sehr viel Geld; have you enough money? (I have) —ty, hast du genug Geld? (ich habe) reichlich *or* völlig genug; in —ty, im Überfluß, in Hülle und Fülle; the horn of —ty, das Füllhorn. II. *adj.* im Überfluß vorhanden (*coll.*).

Pleonas—m, *s.* die Überfülle des Ausdrucks, der Wortüberfluß. —**tic**, *adj.*, —**tically**, *adv.* überflüssig gesetzt, überladen, pleonastisch.

Plethor—a, *s.* die Vollblütigkeit (*Med.*); die Überfülle (*fig.*). —**ic**, *adj.* vollblütig, vollsäftig.

Pleur—a, *s.* das Brustfell. —**isy**, *s.* die Brustfellentzündung, Rippenfellentzündung.

Pli—ability, *s.* die Biegsamkeit. —**able**, *adj.*, —**ably**, *adv.* biegsam; geschmeidig, fügsam, schmiegsam (*fig.*). —**ableness**, —**ancy**, *s.* die Biegsamkeit. —**ant**, *adj.*, —**antly**, *adv. see* —able. —**ca-polonica**, *s.* der Weichselzopf.

Pliers, *pl.* die Zange.

[1]**Plight**, *s.* der Zustand; (sad —) mißliche *or* traurige Lage.

[2]**Plight**, I. *s.* das Treuversprechen, die feierliche Verpflichtung. II. *v.a.* verpfänden; to — one's faith, sein Wort geben, versprechen; to — one's troth (to a p.), (einem) Treue schwören; sich verloben (mit einem); —ed troth, gelobte Treue.

Plinth, *s.* die Säulenplatte, Tafel, Plinthe.

Pliocene, I. *s.* das obere Tertiärgebirge, Pliozän. II. *adj.* pliozän, Pliozän=.

Plod, *v.n. & a.* langsam, mühsam gehen; (toil) sich anstrengen, sich placken, sich abmühen; büffeln *or* ochsen (*sl.*) (*of students*). —**der**, *s.* der sauer Arbeitende, Büffler. —**ding**, I. *adj.*, —**dingly**, *adv.* arbeitsam, sauer arbeitend. II. *s.* das saure Arbeiten, Büffeln.

Plosive, *adj.* explosiv, Geräusch=; — consonant, der Verschlußlaut.

[1]**Plot**, *s.* der Fleck, das Stück (Land); *see* Plan (*Surv.*); das Plätzchen, der Platz (*in a garden*); — of building ground, der Bauplatz, das Grundstück; grass —, der Rasenplatz. —**ting**, *s.* das Auf=tragen, =zeichnen. *Comp.* —**ing-scale**, *s.* verjüngter Maßstab.

[2]**Plot**, I. *s.* der Plan, Anschlag; (intrigue) die Intrigue; (conspiracy) die Verschwörung; die Verwickelung, Handlung (*of a play, etc.*); to lay a —, ein Komplott schmieden. II. *v.a.* an=stiften, =zetteln, sinnen (auf, *acc.*). III. *v.n.* Anschläge machen, intriguieren. —**ter**, *s.* der Anstifter, Ränkemacher; der Verschwörer.

[1]**Plough**, I. *s.* der Pflug; (—ed land) das Ackerland; der (Beschneide=)Hobel (*Bookb.*); der Nuthobel (*Carp.*); das Pohlmesser (*Weav.*); to put one's hand to the —, Hand ans Werk legen. II. *v.a.* pflügen; behobeln; durchfurchen (*the sea*); to — up, ausackern (*a crop, etc.*), umpflügen (*land*). —**ing**, *s.* das Pflügen. *Comp.* —**boy**, *s.* der Ackerknecht; der Bauernlümmel (*fig.*). —**-iron**, *s.* das Pflugeisen. —**man**, *s.* der Pflüger; der Landmann. —**share**, *s.* die Pflugschar.

[2]**Plough**, *v.a.* abweisen, durchfallen lassen (*sl.*); to be —ed, durchfallen (in einer Prüfung).

Plover, *s.* der Kiebitz, Regenpfeifer.

Pluck, I. *v.a.* (ab)pflücken, abbrechen; rupfen (*birds*); reißen (from, von); (pull) zerren, zupfen; durchfallen lassen (*sl.*); to have a crow to — with s.o., mit einem ein Hühnchen zu rupfen haben; to — **asunder**, auseinanderreißen; to — **away**, wegreißen; to — **down**, niederreißen; to — **off**, abpflücken, abreißen; to — **out**, ausreißen; to — **up**, (snatch) aufraffen; (— out) ausreißen; (root out) ausrotten; to — up courage, Mut fassen. II. *v.n.* zupfen, raufen (at, an). III. *s.* der Zug, das Rupfen, Ziehen; das Geschlinge (*of an animal, etc.*); die Beherztheit, der Mut (*coll.*); he wants —, er ist feige. —**ily**, *adv.*, —**y**, *adj.* mutig, beherzt, herzhaft (*coll.*).

Plug, I. *s.* der Pflock, Stöpsel, Pfropf(en), Zapfen; (barrel —) der Faßspund; der Pfropf (*Gunn.*); die Prieme (*of tobacco*); fire-—, der Feuerhahn an Wasserleitungen. II. *v.a.* zupflöcken verstopfen, einpflöcken.

Plum, *s.* die Pflaume; (raisin) die Rosine; £100,000 (*C. L.*); French —s, getrocknete Zwetsch(g)en. *Comp.* —**-cake**, *s.* der Rosinenkuchen. —**-pudding**, *s.* der Rosinenpudding, Plumpudding. —**-tart**, *s.* die Pflaumenpastete. —**-tree**, *s.* der Pflaumenbaum.

Plum—age, *s.* das Gefieder. —**e**, I. *s.* (feather) die Feder; (ostrich —e) die Straußenfeder; (tuft) der Federbusch. II. *v.a.* (sich) die Federn putzen (*as birds*); mit Federn schmücken, befiedern; to —e o.s. on a th., sich (einer S.) rühmen. —**eless**, *adj.* federlos. —**elet**, *s.* die kleine Feder. —**iped**, *s.* der Federfüßler. —**ose**, —**ous**, *adj.* federig. —**ule**, *s.* das Blattfederchen. —**y**, *adj.* befiedert.

Plumb, I. *s.* (plummet) das Senkblei, Lot; die Seigerschnur (*Surv.*). II. *adj. & adv.* senkrecht, lotrecht. III. *adv.* gerade, stracks. IV. *v.a.* lotrecht machen, nach der Bleiwage richten; (sound) sondieren. —**ago**, *s.* das Reißblei, der Graphit; das Bleiwurz (*Bot.*). —**er**, *s.* der Blei=arbeiter, =gießer, Bleiröhrenleger. —**ic**, *adj.* Blei=. —**ing**, *s.* die Bleiarbeit; die Bleiröhren &c. (*in a house, etc.*). *Comp.* —**-line**, *s.* die Bleischnur. —**-rule**, *s.* das Richtscheit.

Plumm—et, *s.* das Senkblei, Lot; levelling —et die Bleiwage. —**ing**, *s.* das Bohren (*Min.*).

[1]**Plump**, I. *adj.* dick, fett, rundlich; plump, derb, grob (*fig.*). II. *v.n.*; to — one's vote, bei Parlamentswahlen von zwei Kandidaten nur einem

ſeine Stimme geben (*Pol.*); aufſchwellen, dick und fett werden. —**er**, *s.* der Bauſch. —**ness**, *s.* die Beleibtheit, Rundlichkeit.

[2]**Plump**, I. *v.a.* hinplumpen, plump hinſetzen. II. *v.n.* wie ein Stein fallen; to — down, hinplumpſen (*vulg.*). III. *adj. & adv.* plump, platſch; (blunt) derb; — and plain, gerade heraus. IV. *s.* der Platzregen (*dial.*). —**er**, *s.* derbe, grobe Lüge; ungeteilte Wahlſtimme (*sl.*); einer, der nur für einen Kandidaten ſtimmt (*sl.*).

Plunder, I. *s.* die Beute, der Raub. II. *v.a.* plündern, (be)rauben. —**er**, *s.* der Plünderer.

Plung—e, I. *v.a.* tauchen (*into water, etc.*); ſtoßen (*a sword, etc.*); ſtürzen (*fig.*). II. *v.n.* (unter)tauchen, auf= und niedertauchen, ſinken; ſich ſtürzen; ſpringen und ausſchlagen (*as a horse*). III. *s.* das Eintauchen, Stürzen; der Sturz; das Ausſchlagen; to take a —e, ſich ſtürzen (ins Waſſer); to make the —e, den entſcheidenden Schritt tun. —**er**, *s.* der Taucher; der Kavalleriſt (*sl.*); (better) waghalſiger Wetter (*sports' sl.*); der Taucherkolben (*Mach.*). —**ing**, *adj.*; —ing battery, die Tauchbatterie; —ing fire, der Senkſchuß (*Mil.*).

Pluperfect, *s.* (— tense) die Vorvergangenheit, das Plusquamperfektum.

Plural, *s.* (— number) die Mehrzahl. —**ist**, *s.* der Beſitzer mehrerer Pfründen. —**ity**, *s.* die Mehrheit, Vielheit; —ity of gods, of wives, die Vielgötterei, Vielweiberei; die größte Zahl, Mehrzahl; das Innehaben mehrerer Pfründen.

Plus, I. *adv.* mehr. II. *s.* das Mehr, Plus.

Plush, *s.* der Plüſch. —**y**, *adj.* plüſchartig.

Plut—archy, —**ocracy**, *s.* die Geldherrſchaft, Herrſchaft des Reichtums; die Geldleute.

Pluvi—al, *adj.* regneriſch, Regen=. —**ometer**, *s.* der Regenmeſſer.

Ply, I. *v.a.* fleißig, eifrig anwenden, handhaben; (solicit) anliegen (a p., einem); (einem) zuſetzen (*with questions*); (supply) reichlich, immer wieder verſehen mit; to — with flattery, mit Schmeicheleien überhäufen; to — one's needle, fleißig nähen. II. *v.n.* beſchäftigt ſein; regelmäßig fahren, ſegeln, verkehren (*as 'buses, vessels*); to — to windward, den Wind abkneifen. III. *s.* die Falte; die Strähne (*in a rope*); (bias) der Hang; three-—, dreiſträhnig, (threefold) dreifaltig.

Pneumat—ic, *adj.* pneumatiſch, Luft=; aus Luft beſtehend, luftartig, gasartig; —ic engine, die Luftpumpe; —ic post, die Rohrpoſt; —ic tire, der Luftreifen (für Fahrräder). —**ics**, *s.* die Pneumatik. —**ology**, *s.* die Luftbewegungslehre; die Geiſterlehre (*obs.*).

Pneumoni—a, *s.* die Lungenentzündung. —**c**, I. *adj.* Lungen=. II. *s.* das Lungenmittel.

[1]**Poach**, *v.a.*; —ed eggs, Setzeier, verlorene Eier.

[2]**Poach**, *v.* I. *a.* plündern; Jagd machen auf (*acc.*). II. *n.* Wilddieberei treiben; auf dem Gebiete eines anderen jagen. —**er**, *s.* der Wilddieb. —**ing**, *s.* die Wilddieberei.

[3]**Poach**, *v.a.* eintreten (*soft ground*).

Pock, *s.* die Pocke, Blatter. —**et**, I. *s.* die Taſche; das Loch (*Bill.*); der Sack (*of hops, wool, etc.*); to be (in) out of —et by, verlieren, (gewinnen) an (*dat.*); out of —et expenses, Barauslagen. II. *v.a.* in die Taſche ſtecken; einſtecken (*also fig.*); machen (*Bill.*); to —et a shilling, an affront, einen Schilling, eine Beleidigung einſtecken. —**eting**, *s.* das Einſtecken. *Comp.* —**et-book**, *s.* das Taſchenbuch, die Brieftaſche. —**et-dictionary**, *s.* das Taſchenwörterbuch. —**et-edition**, *s.* die Taſchenausgabe. —**et-handkerchief**, *s.* das Taſchentuch. —**et-knife**, *s.* das Taſchenmeſſer. —**et-money**, *s.* das Taſchengeld. —**et-pistol**, *s.* die Taſchenpiſtole, das Terzerol; (flask) kleine Flaſche (*sl.*). —-**mark**, *s.* die Blatternarbe. —-**marked**, —-**pitted**, *adj.* blatternarbig.

Pod, I. *s.* die Hülſe, Schote. II. *v.n.* ſich hülſen, Hülſen bekommen. —**ded**, *adj.* mit Schoten, Hülſen verſehen. —**gy**, *adj.* kurz und dick (*coll.*).

Pod—agra, *s.* die Fußgicht, das Podagra. —**osperm**, *s.* die Nabelſchnur, der Keimgang (*Bot.*).

Poe—m, *s.* das Gedicht. —**sy**, *s.* die Dichtung, Poeſie; die Dichtkunſt. —**t**, *s.* der Dichter; —t laureate, (engliſcher) Hofdichter; minor —, weniger bedeutender Dichter, Dichter zweiten Ranges. —**taster**, *s.* der Dichterling. —**tess**, *s.* die Dichterin. —**tical**, *adj.*, —**tically**, *adv.* dichteriſch, poetiſch. —**tics**, *s.* die Lehre von der Dichtkunſt, Poetik. —**tize**, *v.a.* dichten; poetiſch darſtellen, dichteriſch verherrlichen. —**try**, *s.* die Dichtkunſt; (—ms) die Dichtungen, Gedichte; (the —tic) das Dichteriſche.

Poignan—cy, *s.* das Stechende, Scharfe, Beißende. —**t**, *adj.*, —**tly**, *adv.* ſtechend, ſcharf, beißend; heftig, durchdringend (*as pain, grief*).

Point, I. *s.* die Spitze; die Landzunge, Landſpitze, ins Meer weit vorſpringender Felſen (*Geog.*); die Radiernadel (*Eng.*); (— la e) genähte Spitzen; der Punkt, Tüpfel (*Bot.*); das Interpunktionszeichen (*Typ.*); (stop) der Punkt; (pith) die Pointe, Schärfe, Spitze; der Stachel (*of an epigram, etc.*); (aim) die Abſicht, der (End=)Zweck; (question) der Punkt, Satz, die Frage; (main subject) die Sache; (degree) der Grad, die Stufe; der Punkt (*Mus., Geom., Astr., Phys., Mech.*); der Grad (*Astr.*); das Stehen (*of a dog*); (spot) der Fleck, kleine Raum; das Auge (*on dice, etc.*); (characteristic) der Zug; (pin) die Ahle, Punktur (*Typ.*); —s, die Weichen (*Railw.*); vowel —s, Vokalzeichen; black —s, ſchwarze Extremitäten (*nose, etc., of horses*); boiling —, Siedepunkt; cardinal —s, die (vier) Himmelsgegenden; range of —s, die Punktreihe; — of the compass, der Kompaßſtrich; — of contact, Berührungspunkt; — of controversy, Streitpunkt; — of intersection, Durchſchnittspunkt; at the — of death, im Sterben; she was on the — of going out, ſie war (eben) im Begriff auszugehen; — of sight, Augen=, Geſichts=punkt; — of time, der Zeitpunkt Augenblick; to carry, gain one's —, ſeinen Zweck erreichen; to the —! zur Sache! to come to the —, zur Sache kommen; auf den Kern der Sache kommen; when it came to the —, als es zur Entſcheidung kam *or* Ernſt wurde; he spoke to the —, er ſprach ſachlich; that's the —, darauf kommt es an! das iſt es ja *or* gerade! that is not to the —, das gehört nicht hierher *or* zur Sache; in — of, in Hinſicht auf, was betrifft; in — of fact, tatſächlich; the case in —, der vorliegende Fall; a case in —, ein hergehöriger Fall, ein treffendes, paſſendes Beiſpiel; to make a —, einen Treffer machen, ins Schwarze treffen; to make a — of a th., es ſich (*dat.*) zur Pflicht *or* Aufgabe machen, es ſich (*dat.*) vornehmen; to prove one's —, ſeinen Satz beweiſen; to pursue one's —, ſein Vorhaben eifrig verfolgen; to strain *or* stretch a —, ein Übriges tun, fünf gerade ſein laſſen; to wander from the —, von der Hauptſache abſchweifen; the —s of a horse, die körperlichen Vorzüge eines Pferdes; that was a good — in his character, das war ein guter Zug in ſeinem Charakter; from this — of view, von dieſem Geſichtspunkt aus; these different —s of view, dieſe verſchiedenen Geſichtspunkte; armed at all —s, völlig geharniſcht; to end in a —, ſich zuſpitzen. II. *v.a.* (zu)ſpitzen; (— out) zeigen, bezeichnen, hinweiſen (auf, *acc.*); (aim) richten, ſtellen; (inter)punktieren; mit Punkten verſehen (*Mus.*); richten, anſchlagen (*a gun*); to — the finger at, mit Fingern weiſen (auf, *acc.*); (— with scorn) verhöhnen; to — a moral, eine Nutzanwendung ziehen, eine Moral anhängen, eine Lehre geben. III. *v.n.* ſtehen (*of dogs*); nachweiſen, zeigen; to — at, weiſen auf (*acc.*). —**ed**, *adj.*, —**edly**, *adv.* ſpitzig; beißend, ſarkaſtiſch, ſpitzfindig (*fig.*); *see* Epigrammatic; auf einen *or* etwas gerichtet, gemünzt; the remark was rather —ed, die Bemerkung war etwas anzüglich; —ed arch, der Spitzbogen; —ed style, der Spitzbogenſtil, gotiſcher

Stil. —**edness**, *s.* die Spitzigkeit; die Schärfe, das Beißende, Pikante. —**er**, *s.* der Zuspitzer; (indicator) der Zeiger, Weiser; der Zeigestock, Demonstrierstock; der Vorsteh- *or* Hühner-hund (*Zool.*); der Weichenhebel (*Railw.*). —**ing**, *s.* das Spitzen ꝛc.; die Interpunktion; die Richtung (*of guns*); das Stehen (*of a dog*). —**less**, *adj.*, —**lessly**, *adv.* stumpf; stumpf, nicht beißend, nicht passend; zwecklos. *Comp.* —**-blank**, *adj.* & *adv.* schnurgerade (*as a shot*); geradezu, unverhohlen, frei heraus (*fig.*); —-blank refusal, entschiedene Weigerung; to refuse —-blank, rundweg abschlagen; —-blank range, die Kernschußweite. —**-lace**, *s.* genähte Spitzen (*pl.*). —**sman**, *s.* der Weichenwärter.

Poise, I. *s.* (weight) das Gewicht; (counter—) das Gleichgewicht. II. *v.a.* (ab)wägen; im Gleichgewicht erhalten; a well —d head, ein gut auf den Schultern sitzender Kopf. —**r**, *s.* der Schwingkolben.

Poison, I. *s.* das Gift. II. *v.a.* vergiften. —**er**, *s.* der (die) Giftmischer(in). —**ous**, *adj.*, —**ously**, *adv.* giftig (*also fig.*). —**ousness**, *s.* die Giftigkeit. *Comp.* —**-fang**, *s.* der Giftzahn. —**-nut**, *s.* die Brechnuß.

¹**Poke**, *s.* die Tasche; der Heuschober (*Agr.*); to buy a pig in a —, die Katze im Sacke kaufen.

²**Pok—e**, I. *s.* der Stoß, Puff; *see* Loafer (*Amer.*); eine Vorrichtung, um Vieh zu hindern, über Zäune zu springen ꝛc. II. *v.a.* aufrühren, aufstöbern; stoßen; stecken (the nose into, die Nase in eine S.); schüren (*the fire*); hervorstecken (*the head forward, etc.*); to —e fun at a p., an einem einen Scherz auslassen, einen aufziehen, sich über einen lustig machen; to —e up, aufregen. III. *v.n.* tappen, tasten, herumfühlen. —**er**, *s.* der Feuerhaken, die Schürstange, das Schüreisen; einer, der schürt. —**ing**, *adj.* gemein (*coll.*); *see* —(e)y. —(**e**)**y**, *adj.* eng, klein, lumpig (*coll.*); (shabby) erbärmlich; *see* Dull.

¹**Poker**, *s.* eine Art Hasardspiel.

²**Poker**, *s.* — work, die Brandmalerei.

Polar, *adj.* Polar-, Pol-; polarisch (*Phys.*); — axis, die Polarachse; — bear, der Eisbär; — circles, Polarkreise; — star, der Polarstern, Nordstern. —**ity**, *s.* die Polarität. —**ization**, *s.* die Polarisation; —ization of light, Lichtpolarisation. —**ize**, *v.a.* polarisieren.

¹**Pole**, *s.* der Pol (*Astr.*, *Magnet.*, *Elec.*); positive —, positiver Pol, die Anode.

²**Pole**, I. *s.* der Pfahl, die Stange; die Gardinenstange; (balancing —) die Balanzierstange; die Deichsel (*Carr.*); englische Rute (= 5½ Yard); (square —) Quadratrute (= 30¼ Quadratellen); die Meßstange, der größere Absteckstab (*Surv.*); die Springstange (*Gym.*); telegraph —, Telegraphenstange; tent —, Zeltstange; under bare —s, vor Topp und Takel (*Naut.*). II. *v.a.* mit Stangen fort-stoßen, -schieben (*Naut.*). III. *v.n.* sich mit Stangen fortbewegen (*Naut.*). *Comp.* —**-pin**, *s.* der Deichselbolzen.

³**Pole**, *see under* Polar.

Poleax(e), *s.* die Streitaxt; das Enterbeil (*Naut.*).

Polecat, *s.* der Iltis.

Polem—ic, I. *adj.*, —**ical**, *adj.* streitsüchtig, feindselig, polemisch. II. *s.* der gelehrte Streiter, Polemiker. —**ics**, *s.* der Federkrieg, die Polemik.

Polic—e, *s.* die Polizei; secret —e, die Geheimpolizei; member of the secret —e, der Geheimpolizist. —**y**, *s.* die Politik; (prudence) die (Welt)klugheit; *see* Self-interest; (diplomacy) die Diplomatie; such a course is bad —y, ein solches Verfahren ist eine schlechte Politik *or* sehr undiplomatisch; to do from motives of —y, aus kluger Rücksicht tun; honesty is the best —y, ehrlich währt am längsten (*prov.*). *Comp.* —**e-constable**, *s.* der Konstabler; (—eman) der Schutzmann. —**e-court**, *s.* das Polizeigericht. —**e-inspector**, *s.* der Polizeikommissär. —**eman**, *s.* der Schutzmann, Polizist; mounted —e(men), berittene Schutzleute. —**e-office**, *s.* das Polizeiamt, die Polizei. —**e-officer**, *s.* der Polizeibeamte; —e-officer in plain clothes, der Geheimpolizist. —**e-station**, *s.* die Polizei(wache).

¹**Policy**, *s.* der Versicherungsschein; die Police (*C.L.*); —of (fire) insurance, Assekuranz-(Feuerversicherungs)police; floating —, Police auf Waren ohne Wertangabe; marine —, Schiffspolice; valued (open) —, (un)taxierte Police. *Comp.* —**-holder**, *s.* der Inhaber einer Police.

²**Policy**, *see under* Police.

Polish, I. *s.* die Glätte, Politur, der Glanz; die Geschliffenheit (*fig.*); — of manner, das feine Wesen; furniture- —, die Möbelpolitur. II. *v.a.* glätten, polieren, glänzend machen; bohnen (*with wax*); bilden, verfeinern, glätten (*fig.*); to — off, wegputzen (*vulg.*). III. *v.n.* glatt werden, Glanz annehmen. —**ed**, *adj.* glatt, poliert; gesittet, höflich; fein (*as manners*). —**ing**, I. *s.* das Polieren ꝛc. II. *attrib.*; —ing brush, die Glanzbürste; —ing paste, die Glanzwichse (für Leder); die Möbelpolitur; —ing powder, das Putzpulver.

Polite, *adj.*, —**ly**, *adv.* fein, gebildet, höflich, artig; — literature, die schönen Wissenschaften. —**ness**, *s.* die Höflichkeit, Artigkeit, Verbindlichkeit.

Polit—ic, *adj.* politisch; weltklug, schlau (*fig.*); body —ic, der Staatskörper. —**ical**, *adj.*, —**ically**, *adv.* politisch; staatskundig; Staats-; (science of) —ical economy, die Volkswirtschaft(slehre), Staatswirtschaft; —ical history, die Staatengeschichte; from —ical motives, for —ical reasons, aus Gründen der Staatsklugheit, politischen Gründen; —ical maxim, der Staatsgrundsatz. —**ician**, *s.* der Staatsmann, Politiker; pothouse —ician, politischer Kannegießer. —**ics**, *s.* die Politik, Staatswissenschaft. —**y**, *s.* die Verfassung, Regierungsform; ecclesiastical —y, kirchliche Hierarchie.

Polka, *s.* die Polka.

¹**Poll**, I. *s.* (back of head) der (Hinter)Kopf, Schädel; der Kopf (*fig.*), die Person; (register) die Namenliste; die Wahlliste (*Parl.*); (voting) die Abstimmung; (—ing-place) der Wahlort; (votes) die Stimmenzahl; at the close of the —, am Schlusse der namentlichen Abstimmung; how does the — stand? wie sieht es mit der Abstimmung aus? to be at the head of the —, die meisten Wahlstimmen erhalten haben; to go to the —, zur Wahlurne gehen. II. *v.a.* kappen, köpfen, stutzen; behauen (*trees, etc.*); abschneiden (*the hair*); Namen, Stimmen eintragen (*Parl.*); to — so many votes, so und so viele Stimmen erhalten. III. *v.n.*; to — for, stimmen für. IV. *v.a.* Stimmen erhalten; he —ed 4000 votes, 4000 Stimmen wurden für ihn abgegeben, fielen auf ihn. —**ard**, *s.* (— tree) der gekappte Baum; der Hirsch, der sein Geweih abgeworfen hat (*Sport.*); das Kleienmehl. —**ed**, *adj.* gekappt ꝛc.; ungehörnt (*as oxen*). —**er**, *s.* der Stimmende. —**ing**, *s.* das Stimmen, Wählen, die Abstimmung, der Wahlakt. *Comp.* —**-book**, *s.* die Liste der Wahlmänner, Wählerliste. —**-cattle**, *s.* das Rindvieh ohne Hörner. —**-evil**, *s.* die Kopfgeschwulst (*Vet.*). —**ing-booth**, *s.* die Wahlbude, das Wahllokal. —**ing-day**, *s.* der Wahltag. —**ing-district**, *s.* der Wahlbezirk. —**-tax**, *s.* das Kopfgeld.

²**Poll** (*only in compounds*): —**-degree**, *s.* der gewöhnliche Grad eines B. A. (*in Cambridge*) ohne besondere Auszeichnung. —**-examination**, *s.* die leichtere Prüfung zur Erlangung des Bachelor-Grades (an der Universität Cambridge; die höhere Prüfung heißt Tripos). —**man**, *s.* ein Student, welcher sich auf die leichtere Prüfung vorbereitet oder sie bestanden hat (Gegensatz: honours man).

Pollen, *s.* der Blütenstaub.

Pollut—e, *v.a.* beflecken (*also fig.*), verunreinigen; (dishonour) schänden; entweihen (*vessels, etc.*). —**er**, *s.* der Verunreiniger, Beflecker. —**ion**, *s.* die Befleckung, Verunreinigung; die Entweihung.

Polo, *s.* das Poloſpiel, Schlagballſpiel zu Pferde.
Poltroon, I. *s.* der Feigling, die Memme. II. *adj.* feig, erbärmlich. **—ery**, *s.* die Feigheit.
Poly— (*in many compds.* = viel); **—acoustic**, *adj.* den Schall vermehrend *or* erhöhend. **—adelphian**, *adj.* vielbrüderig. **—andrian**, **—androus**, *adj.* vielmännerig (*Bot.*). **—andry**, *s.* die Vielmännerei. **—anthus**, *s.* die (hohe) Primel; die Tazette. **—carpous**, *adj.* vielfrüchtig; wiederholt blühend. **—chord**, *adj.* vielſaitig. **—gamist**, *s.* der Polygamiſt, Anhänger der Vielweiberei. **—gamy**, *s.* die Vielweiberei. **—glot**, I. *adj.* vielſprachig (*—glot Bible, etc.*). II. *s.* die Polyglotte. **—gon**, *s.* das Vieleck (*Math.*); das Polygon (*Fort.*). **—gonal**, **—gonous**, *adj.* vieleckig, Polygonal=. **—hedron**, *s.* das Vielflach; *see* —scope. **—morphic**, **—morphous**, *adj.* vielgeſtaltig. **—nomial**, *adj.*; —nomial theorem, polynomiſcher Lehrſatz. **—p**, *s.* der Polyp. **—phonic**, *adj.* vieltönig. **—podium**, **—pody**, *s.* der Tüpfelfarn, Engelfuß. **—pous**, *adj.* polypenartig. **—pus**, *s.* der Polyp (*also Med.*). **—syllabic**, *adj.* mehrſilbig, vielſilbig. **—syllable**, *s.* vielſilbiges Wort. **—technic**, I. *adj.* polytechniſch. II. *s.* die Gewerbehochſchule, techniſche Hochſchule, das Polytechnikum. **—theism**, *s.* die Vielgötterei. **—theist**, *s.* der Polytheiſt. **—theistic(al)**, *adj.* polytheiſtiſch.
Pom—ade, **—atum**, *s.* die Pomade. **—aceous**, *adj.* Äpfel=. **—e**, *s.* die Kern=, Apfel=frucht. **—egranate**, *s.* der Granatapfel; der Granatapfelbaum. **—mel**, I. *s.* der (Degen=, Sattel=) Knopf (*of a sword, a saddle*); der Turmknopf (*Arch.*). II. *v.a.* ſchlagen; puffen, knuffen (*fam.*). *Comp.* **—e-water**, *s.* der Königsapfel.
Pomp, *s.* der Pomp, Prunk, das Gepränge. **—osity**, *s.* die Prahlerei, das Hochtrabende; *see* —ousness. **—ous**, *adj.*, **—ously**, *adv.* prunkvoll, pomphaft; (pretentious) prahleriſch, hochtrabend, wichtigtuend. **—ousness**, *s.* die Pomphaftigkeit, der Prunk.
Pompon, *s.* der Büſchel, das Nationale (*Mil.*).
Pond, *s.* der Teich, Weiher. *Comp.* **—lily**, *s.* die Waſſerlilie. **—-weed**, *s.* das Laichkraut.
Ponder, I. *v.a.* erwägen, bedenken. II. *n.* nachſinnen (on, over a th., über eine S.). **—ability**, *s.* die Wägbarkeit. **—able**, *adj.* wägbar. **—er**, *s.* der Nachdenkende, Überlegende. **—ing**, *adj.*, **—ingly**, *adv.* erwägend, nachdenklich. **—osity**, *see* —ousness. **—ous**, *adj.*, **—ously**, *adv.* ſchwer, gewichtig; (momentous) wichtig; ſchwerfällig, plump. **—ousness**, *s.* das Gewicht, die Schwere; die Schwerfälligkeit, Plumpheit.
Pongee, *s.* geringe chineſiſche Seide.
Poniard, I. *s.* der Dolch. II. *v.a.* erdolchen.
Pont—iff, *s.* der Hohepriester; (Roman —iff) der Papſt. **—ifical**, I. *adj.* oberprieſterlich; (papal) päpſtlich. II. *s.* das Pontifikale. **—ificals**, *pl.* prieſterliche Amtstracht. **—ificate**, *s.* das Hoheprieſtertum; die päpſtliche Würde; (papal reign) das Pontifikat. **—levis**, *s.* die Zugbrücke; das kerzengrade Aufbäumen eines Pferdes. **—on(n)eer**, *s.* der Pontonier. **—oon**, *s.* der Ponton (*Mil.*); der Bullen, Kiellichter (*for ships*). *Comp.* **—oon-bridge**, *s.* die Schiffbrücke, Pontonbrücke. **—oon-train**, *s.* der Pontontrain, Brückenzug.
Pony, *s.* das kleine Pferd, der (das) Pony; 25 Pfund Sterling (*sl.*); die Klatſche, Eſelsbrücke (*sl.*). *Comp.* **—-chaise**, **—-phaeton**, *s.* kleine Chaiſe. **—-engine**, *s.* die Rangierlokomotive (*Railw.*).
Poodle, *s.* der Pudel; two —s, zwei Pudel.
Pooh, *int.* pah! to — —, über die Achſel anſehen, verachten; to — — a p. down, einen geringſchätzig behandeln.
[1]**Pool**, *s.* der Pfuhl, Teich; die Lache (*of blood*).
[2]**Pool**, *s.* der Satz, Einſatz (*at games*); das Pouleſpiel (*Bill.*).
Poop, I. *s.* die Kampanje, die Hütte (*Naut.*). II. *v.a.* von hinten faſſen, das Achterſchiff treffen; to be —ed, eine Sturzſee von hinten bekommen. *Comp.* **—-lantern**, *s.* die Hinterlaterne.
Poor, I. *adj.* arm; (needy) dürftig; (sorry) erbärmlich, elend; (paltry) armſelig, gering; (worthless) ſchlecht; dürr, mager (*as soil*); taub (*Min.*); ſchlecht (*as a crop*); unruhig, ſchlecht (*as a night, etc.*); — health, ſchwache Geſundheit; — Fred, der arme Fritz; — little thing! armes kleines Ding! — me! ich Armer! a — look-out, eine traurige *or* ſchlechte Ausſicht; to make but a — shift, ſich kümmerlich behelfen; a — dinner, ein ſchlechtes Mittagseſſen; you have made a — breakfast, Sie haben ſehr wenig zum Frühſtück gegeſſen; to have but a — head for . . ., keinen Kopf *or* wenig Begabung haben für . . .; to have a (very) — opinion of a p., (ſehr) wenig von einem halten. II. *s.* der (die) Arme; the —, die Armen; the — in spirit, die da geiſtlich arm ſind; the aged —, die alten Armen. **—ly**, I. *adv.* *see* Poor. II. *adj.* unwohl, unpäßlich (*fam.*). **—ness**, *s.* die Armut (*also fig.*); die Dürftigkeit; die ſchlechte Beſchaffenheit; die Armſeligkeit; die Unfruchtbarkeit (*of soil*); die Beſchränktheit (*of the understanding*). *Comp.* **—-box**, *s.* die Armenbüchſe. **—house**, *s.* das Armenhaus. **—-law**, I. *s.* das Armengeſetz. II. *attrib.*; —-law elections, die Wahlen der Armenpfleger. **—-rate**, *s.* die Armenſteuer. **—-spirited**, *adj.* verzagt, feig. — relief, *s.* die Armenpflege, Armenfürſorge.
Pop, I. *s.* der Paff, Klatſch; ginger —, das Ingwerbier (*fam.*). II. *adv.* plötzlich. III. *int.* paff! IV. *v.n.* paffen, puffen, ſchnalzen; (dart) ſich ſchnell bewegen, huſchen; to — **along**, forthuſchen; to — **in**, herein=, hinein=fahren, plötzlich eintreten; to — **off**, entwiſchen; (die) ſterben; to — **up**, in die Höhe fahren, aufſchnellen; plötzlich erſcheinen, ſich zeigen (*sl.*); to — **upon**, plötzlich ſtoßen auf (*acc.*). V. *v.a.* plötzlich bringen, ſtoßen; to — the question, (einer Dame) einen Antrag machen, ſich erklären (*coll.*); to — **in**, hineinſtecken. *Comp.* **—gun**, *s.* die Knallbüchſe, kleine Piſtole.
Pop—e, *s.* der Papſt; the —e's gardens, die päpſtlichen Gärten; —e's eye, der Pfaffenſchnitt (am Braten); —e Joan, Päpſtin Johanna; ein Kartenſpiel; to kiss the —e's toe, dem Papſt den Pantoffel küſſen. **—edom**, **—ery**, *s.* das Papſttum; die Papiſterei (*contempt.*). **—ish**, *adj.*, **—ishly**, *adv.* papiſtiſch.
Popinjay, *s.* der kleine grüne Papagei, Sittich; der Grünſpecht; der Abſchießvogel, der Geck (*fig.*).
Poplar, *s.* die Pappel; black —, Schwarzpappel.
Poplin, *s.* der iriſche Pop(e)linſtoff, die Wollſeide.
Poppet, *s.* der Schlittenſtänder; die Docke der Drehbank; *see* Puppet.
Poppy, *s.* der Mohn.
Popul—ace, *s.* der Pöbel, das (gemeine) Volk. **—ar**, *adj.*, **—arly**, *adv.* Volks=, zum Volke gehörig, volksmäßig; (simple) gemein, verſtändlich, leichtfaßlich, leichtanſprechend; (generally liked) volkstümlich, beim Volke beliebt, populär; (widespread) unter dem Volke herrſchend, volkstümlich; —ar epic, das Volksepos; —ar government, die Volksherrſchaft; —ar writer, allgemein beliebter Schriftſteller, Volksſchriftſteller; —ar song, volkstümliches Lied, Volkslied; —ar tradition, volkstümliche Überlieferung. **—arity**, *s.* die Volksgunſt, Volkstümlichkeit, allgemeine Beliebtheit. **—arize**, *v.a.* gemeinverſtändlich, nützlich machen, unter dem Volke *or* in den weiteſten Kreiſen verbreiten, unter das Volk bringen, leichtfaßlich darſtellen. **—ate**, *v.a.* bevölkern. **—ation**, *s.* die Bevölkerung. **—ous**, *adj.*, **—ously**, *adv.* volkreich, ſtark *or* dicht bevölkert. **—ousness**, *s.* ſtarke *or* dichte Bevölkerung.
Porcelain, I. *s.* das Porzellan. II. *adj.* Porzellan=.
Porch, *s.* die Vorhalle, Halle; das Schutzdach.

Porc—ine, *adj.* Schwein=. **—upine**, *s.* das Stachelschwein; der Igel (*Spin.*). *Comp.* —**upine-fish**, *s.* der Igelfisch. **—upine-quill**, *s.* der Stachelschweinkiel.

[1]**Por—e**, *s.* die Pore. **—ite**, *s.* die Porenkoralle. **—osity**, **—ousness**, *s.* die Löcherigkeit, Durchlässigkeit; Porosität. **—ous**, *adj.* löcherig, porös.

[2]**Pore**, *v.n.* seine Gedanken richten (auf eine S.), emsig studieren, brüten, büffeln (over a th., über einer S.).

Pork, *s.* das Schweinefleisch. **—er**, *s.* das (Mast=) Schwein. *Comp.* **—-butcher**, *s.* der Schweineschlächter. **—-pie**, *s.* die Schweinefleischpastete.

Porphyr—itic, *adj.* porphyrhaltig, Porphyr=. **—y**, I. *s.* der Porphyr. II. *attrib.;* —y shell, die Porphyrschnecke.

Porpoise, *s.* das Meerschwein, der Tümmler.

Porri—dge, *s.* (oatmeal —dge) der Hafer(grützen)brei, Haferschleim; (soup) die Suppe. **—nger**, *s.* der Suppennapf.

[1]**Port**, I. *s.* der Hafen; — of entry, Einlaufhafen; to clear a —, (aus einem Hafen) auslaufen. II. *attrib.;* — charges, Hafengebühren.

[2]**Port**, *s.* das Tragen, die Haltung, der Anstand. **—able**, *adj.* tragbar; beweglich; —able chair, der Rollstuhl. **—age**, *s. see* —erage; die Tragstelle (zwischen schiffbaren Gewässern). **—er**, *s.* der Last=, Packträger; der Türhüter, Hausmann; der Portier (*Hotel*); der Gepäckträger (*Railw.*); das Porter=(Bier); town —er, der Dienstmann. **—erage**, *s.* das Tragen; die Zustellungsgebühr (*of telegrams, etc.*). **—liness**, *s.* die Stattlichkeit; *see* Corpulence. **—ly**, *adj.* stattlich; wohlbeleibt. *Comp.* **—-crayon**, *s.* der Stifthalter, die Reißfeder. **—folio**, *s.* die Mappe; das (Minister=)Portefeuille. **—manteau**, *s.* der Mantelsack; das Felleisen; der Handkoffer.

[3]**Port**, *s.* die Pforte, Pfortluke (*Naut.*); chase-—s, Jagdpforten; gun-—, Stückpforte. **—al**, *s.* das Portal (*Arch.*); der Haupteingang (*of a building*); die Pforte, das Tor (*fig.*). **—cullis**, *s.* das Fall=, Schutz=gatter. **—e**, *s.;* the Sublime —e, die hohe Pforte. **—er**, *s.* der Türhüter, Torwart, Torwächter, Pförtner, Portier; —er's lodge, die Pförtnerwohnung, Portierloge. **—ico**, *s.* der Portikus, die Säulenhalle. **—ress**, *s.* die Türsteherin, Pförtnerin. *Comp.* **—fire**, *s.* das Zündlicht. **—-hole**, *s.* die Pfortenöffnung, Stückpforte (*Shipb.*); der Dampfweg (*Locom.*).

[4]**Port**, I. *s.* das Backbord. II. *v.a.;* — the helm! backbord das Ruder!

[5]**Port**, *s.* der Portwein, Wein von Oporto.

Porten—d, *v.a.* vorbedeuten, verkündigen. **—t**, *s.* die Vorbedeutung, das (böse) Vorzeichen. —**tous**, *adj.*, **—tously**, *adv.* Unglück bedeutend *or* vorhersagend, Unheil verkündend, verhängnisvoll.

Portion, I. *s.* der Teil; (share) der Anteil; (legacy) das Erbteil; (dowry) das Heiratsgut. II. *v.a.* teilen; (— off) aus=steuern, =statten; (— out) austeilen. **—less**, *adj.* ohne Aussteuer.

Portrait, *s.* das Bild(nis), Porträt. **—ist**, *s.* der Porträtmaler. **—ure**, *s.* das Bild(nis), Porträt; die Abbildung (*fig.*); die Porträtmalerei.

Portray, *v.a.* abbilden, (ab)malen; malen, schildern (*fig.*). **—al**, *s.* die (bildliche) Darstellung; die Schilderung (*fig.*). **—er**, *s.* der Maler; der Schilderer (*fig.*).

Pos—e, I. *s.* die Stellung, Haltung, Pose, Positur. II. *v.a.* stutzig, verlegen machen, (durch schwierige Fragen) in Verlegenheit bringen; stellen, Stellungen geben (*Paint.*). III. *v.n.* sich (*dat.*) eine gekünstelte Haltung geben; auftreten als, (etwas) vorstellen wollen; posieren (*Paint.*). **—é**, *adj.* mit allen Füßen auf der Erde stehend (*Her.*). **—er**, *s.* der Examinator (*at Eton*); schwierige, im Augenblick verblüffende Frage, harte Nuß (*coll.*). **—ition**, *s.* die Stellung, Lage; (rank) der Stand; (post) die Stellung; (state) die Lage; die Regel Falsi (*Arith.*); die Lage der Hand (*on a violin, etc.*); angle of —ition, der Positionswinkel (*Astr.*); financial —ition, die Vermögensverhältnisse, Finanzlage; critical —ition, bedenkliche Lage; in my —ition, in meiner Stellung; to hold a —ition, eine Stelle bekleiden; to take up one's —ition, Aufstellung nehmen; to define one's —ition, seinen Standpunkt darlegen. **—itive**, I. *adj.*, **—itively**, *adv.* festgestellt; (explicit) ausdrücklich, bestimmt; (absolute) absolut, feststehend, sicher; (certain) bestimmt, sicher, gewiß, wahr, wirklich; (confident) sicher, gewiß, fest überzeugt; (decisive) entscheidend; (dogmatical) rechthaberisch, eigensinnig; positiv (*Math.*, *Philos.*, *Elect.*); (downright) unbedingt offen(bar), positiv, bar; —itive degree, der Positiv (*Gram.*); we have —itive orders, wir haben gemessenen Befehl; —itive quantity, positive (mit dem Pluszeichen versehene) Größe; —itive theology, die Dogmatik; I am —itive of it, ich bin fest davon überzeugt; to be —itive in, (etwas) gewiß behaupten; I am not —itive as to this point, hinsichtlich dieses Punktes kann ich nichts Bestimmtes behaupten; to be too —itive, in einem allzu entschiedenem Tone sprechen. II. *s.* das Positive, Gesetzte, Bestimmte; der Positiv (*Gram.*); das Positiv (*Phot.*). **—itiveness** *s.* das Positive; die Bestimmtheit; die Wirklichkeit; die Hartnäckigkeit, Rechthaberei. **—itivism**, *s.* die positivistische Philosophie (Comtes). **—itivity**, *s.* die Wirklichkeit.

Poss—e, *s.* (—e comitatus) die bewaffnete Macht einer Grafschaft, der Landsturm; die Schar, der Haufe(n), die Masse (*coll.*). **—ess**, *v.a.* besitzen, im Besitz haben, inne haben; (be master of) beherrschen; in Besitz setzen (*obs.*); to —ess o.s. of (a th.), sich (einer Sache) bemächtigen; to —ess one's soul in patience, sich in Geduld fassen; —essed, (von einem bösen Geiste) besessen; to be —essed of, im Besitze sein von; she is —essed with the idea that . . ., sie hat die fixe Idee, sie glaubt steif und fest, daß . . . **—ession**, *s.* der Besitz; (property) das Besitztum, Gut; die Besitzung; die Besitzergreifung; die Besessenheit; to be in —ession of the House, das Wort haben (*Parl.*); to give —ession, in Besitz setzen; to take, have —ession of, Besitz ergreifen von einer S., sich im Besitz einer S. befinden; the taking —ession of a th., die Übernahme, Besitzergreifung einer S.; immediate —ession, sofort zu beziehen *or* beziehbar (*C.L.*). **—essive**, I. *adj.* besitzanzeigend. II. *s.* (—essive case) der Genitiv. **—essor**, *s.* der Besitzer. **—ibility**, *s.* die Möglichkeit. **—ible**, *adj.* möglich. **—ibly**, *adv.* möglicherweise, vielleicht; if I —ibly can, wenn ich irgend kann.

Posset, *s.* (Bier=, Wein=)Molken (*pl.*).

[1]**Post**, I. *s.* der Pfahl, Ständer, Pfosten (*Build. etc.*); die Stange, Säule (*Tele.*); der Hintersteven (*Naut.*); (winning-—) das Ziel; as deaf (stupid) as a —, stocktaub (stockdumm). **—er**, *s.* der Plakatanschläger; der Anschlagzettel, das Plakat. II. *v.a.* (— up) an einem Pfosten anschlagen (*bills*).

[2]**Post**, *s.* der Posten (*Mil.*); (situation) die Stelle, das Amt, der Posten; (letter, *etc.* —) die Post; (stage) die Poststation; (courier) der Eilbote; (—-horse) das Eilpferd; der Rechnungsartikel, Posten (*C.L.*); to go by —, mit der Post reisen; general —, (game) das Plätzewechseln; by to-day's —, mit der heutigen Post; by return of —, mit wendender Post, umgehend. II. *adv.* eilig, in Eile; to ride —, schnell *or* Kurier reiten; to travel —, mit der Post reisen. III. *v.a.* eintragen, einschreiben (*C.L.*); auf die Post geben, aufgeben (*a letter*); aufstellen, postieren (*soldiers, etc.*); to — (up) books, die Bücher ins Reine schreiben; to — a letter in the box, einen Brief in den Briefkasten werfen; to be thoroughly —ed (up) in a subject, in einer Sache gründlich beschlagen sein. IV. *v.n.* mit der Post reisen; eilen (*fig.*); to — away, — off, forteilen. **—age**, I. *s.* das Porto; –

age free, portofrei. II. *attrib.;* —age stamp, die Briefmarke. —**al**, *adj.* Post=; —al card, die Postkarte; —al clerk, der Postbeamte; —al directory, das Postadreßbuch; —al order, der Postscheck der Postzahlschein; —a' privilege, der Postzwang; —al Union, der Weltpostverein; —al wrapper, das Kreuzband, Streifband. —**er**, *s.* das Postpferd. —**ilion**, *s.* der Postillon, Vorreiter. —**ing**, *s.* das Reisen mit der Post; das Eintragen ins Hauptbuch (*C.L.*). *Comp.* —**al-car**, *s.* der Eisenbahnpostwagen (*Amer.*). —**-bag**, *s.* der Briefbeutel. —**-bill**, *s.* das Briefverzeichnis (*at post-offices*); übertragbare Note der englischen Bank (*C.L.*). —**boy**, *s.* der Postreiter. —**-card**, *s.* (—al card) die Postkarte; pictorial —-card, die Ansichtspostkarte. —**-chaise**, *s.* der Postwagen. —**-day**, *s.* der Posttag. —**-free**, *adj.* franko, frankiert. —**-haste**, *adv.* in größter Eile. —**-horn**, *s.* das Posthorn. —**-horse**, *s.* das Postpferd. —**ing-house**, *s.* die Poststation. —**man**, *s.* der Briefträger; —man on the walk, der Revierbriefträger; rural —man, der Landbriefträger. —**mark**, I. *s.* das Postzeichen, der Poststempel. II. *v.a.;* abstempeln; to —mark a letter, einem Brief den Tagesstempel aufdrucken; —marking stamp, der Entwertungsstempel; Tagesstempel (*Amer.*). —**master**, *s.* der Postmeister; der Stipendiat (*of Merton Coll. Oxford*). —**master-general**, *s.* der Generalpostdirektor. —**mastership**, *s.* die Stelle eines Postmeisters; das Stipendium in Merton College (*Oxford*). —**mistress**, *s.* die Vorsteherin eines Postamts. —**-office**, I. *s.* das Postamt; general —-office (G.P.O.), das Hauptpostamt, die Hauptpost; branch —-office, das Zweigpostamt; local —-office, das Ortspostamt; travelling —-office, das Reisepostamt. II. *attrib.;* —-office counter *or* window, der Postschalter; —-office savings-bank, die Postsparkasse. —**-paid**, *adj.* franko, frei. —**-road**, *s.* die Poststraße. —**-town**, *s.* die Stadt mit einem Hauptpostamt. —**-waggon**, *s.* der Postwagen.

Post—date, *v.a.* nachdatieren. —**-dental**, *adj.* hinter den Zähnen liegend. —**diluvian**, I. *adj.*, —**diluvial**, *adj.* nachsündflutlich. II. *s.* der Nachsündflutliche. —**erior**, *adj.* später, nachkommend; *see* Hinder. —**eriors**, *pl.* das Hinterteil, der Hintere. —**erity**, *s.* die Nachkommenschaft; die Nachwelt. —**ern**, *s.* (—ern-gate) das Türchen, die Hinter=, Seiten=türe; das Ausfallpförtchen (*Fort.*). —**-graduate**, I. *s.* einer der nach Erlangung seines ersten akademischen Grades noch weiter studiert. II. *adj.* für vorgeschrittenere Studenten berechnet; —-graduate studies, höhere Studien. —**humous**, *adj.*, —**humously**, *adv.* nach des Vaters Tode geboren; hinterlassen, nachgelassen (*as writings*); nach dem Tode; —humous fame, der Nachruhm. —**il**, *s.* die Randglosse; die Postille, erklärende Predigt nach Lesung des Evangeliums. —**-meridian**, I. *adj.* nachmittägig, Nachmittags=. II. *s.* (*abbr.* P. M.) Nachmittags=. —**-mortem**, *adj.* nach dem Tode; (—-mortem examination) die Leichen=schau, =öffnung. —**-nuptial**, *adj.* nach der Verheiratung geschehend. —**-obit**, I. *adj. see* —humous. II. *s.* die nach dem Tode einer gewissen Person zahlbare Verschreibung. —**pone**, *v.a.* auf=, verschieben; (set below) nachsetzen. —**ponement**, *s.* der Aufschub, die Verschiebung. —**poner**, *s.* der Verschiebende. —**-positive**, *adj.* nachgestellt (*Gram.*). —**-prandial**, *adj.* nach dem Mittagsessen geschehend, Nachmittags=. —**scenium**, *s.* die Hinterbühne. —**script**, *s.* die Nachschrift.

Poste restante, *adj.* & *adv.* postlagernd.

Postula—nt, *s.* der Ansucher, Kandidat. —**te**, I. *s.* das Postulat, die Grundvoraussetzung, der Heischesatz (*Log.*); der Zwischensatz (*Geom.*). II. *v.a.* fordern; (assume) voraussetzen, als wahr annehmen; postulieren. —**tion**, *s.* das Gesuch; die Postulation (*Log., etc.*). —**tory**, *adj.* postulierend, voraussetzend (*Log.*); vorausgesetzt (*Log.*); fordernd (*Log.*).

Posture, *s.* die körperliche Stellung, Haltung; —of defence, die Verteidigungsstellung. *Comp.* —**-master**, *s.* der Gymnastiker.

Posy, *s.* der Sinnspruch, das Motto (auf Ringen); der kleine Blumenstrauß, das Bouquet.

Pot, I. *s.* der Topf (*also as measure*); der Tiegel, Kessel (*of metal*); the — calls the kettle black, ein Esel schimpft den andren Langohr (*prov.*). II. *v.a.* in einen Topf tun; in Töpfe setzen (*plants*); (in Töpfe 2c.) einmachen (*meat, etc.*); —ted meats, Fleischkonserven in Töpfen oder Büchsen. —**tage**, *s.* die dicke Suppe. —**ter**, *s.* der Töpfer; —ter's clay, der Töpferton; —ter's wheel, die Töpferscheibe. —**tery**, *s.* die Töpferware; (—tery factory) die Töpferei, Steingutfabrik. —**tle**, *s.* (2 quarts) das Maß, der Maßkrug, die große Flasche, Kanne (*obs.*). *Comp.* —**-belly**, *s.* der Dickbauch (*vulg.*). —**-boiler**, *s.* die nur des Geldes wegen unternommene Arbeit, Lohnarbeit (*coll.*). —**boy**, *s.* der Kellner in einem Bierhause (*obs.*). —**ful**, *s.* ein Topf voll, eine Kanne voll. —**-hanger**, *s.* der Kesselhaken. —**herb**, *s.* das Küchenkraut. —**-hole**, *s.* durch Stromsteine ausgewaschene Rundung (im Flußbett). —**-hook**, *s.* der Topfhenkel; der Kesselhaken; (—-hooks) Krähenfüße, Krikelkrakel. —**house**, *s.* das Bierhaus. —**-hunter**, *s.* einer der nur des Gewinns wegen jagt, Sport treibt oder studiert. —**-ladle**, *s.* der Kochlöffel. —**-lid**, *s.* der Deckel. —**-luck**, *s.* das Topfglück; to take —-luck, essen, was die Kelle giebt, fürliebnehmen. —**sherd**, *s.* die Scherbe. —**-valiant**, *adj.* vom Trinken mutig.

Pot—able, *adj.* trinkbar. —**ation**, *s.* das Zechen; (—**ion**, *s.*) der Trank; love —ion, der Liebestrank.

Potash, I. *s.* die Pottasche, das Kali; caustic —, die Kalilauge. II. *attrib.;* — soap, die Kaliseife.

Potassi—c, *adj.;* —c salts, Kalisalze. —**um**, *s.* das Kalium.

Potato, *s.* die Kartoffel. *Comp.* —**-disease**, *s.* die Kartoffelkrankheit. —**-flour**, *s.* das Kartoffelmehl. —**-skin**, *s.* die Kartoffelschale.

Poten—cy, *s.* die Macht, Stärke; (efficacy) die Wirksamkeit, Kraft; der Einfluß (*fig.*). —**t**, I. *adj.*, —**tly**, *adv.* mächtig, stark; stark (*as spirits*); wirksam, einflußreich, gewaltig. II. *s.* der Mächtige (*obs.*). —**tate**, *s.* der Machthaber. —**tial**, I. *adj.*, —**tially**, *adv.* möglich; potentiell (*Phys.*); —tial mood, der Potentialis. II. *s.* das Potential. —**tiality**, *s.* die Möglichkeit; (inherent power) die innere Kraft, das einwohnende Vermögen.

Pother, I. *s.* der Lärm, Wirrwarr, das Getümmel. II. *v.n.* lärmen, viel Wesens machen. III. *v.a.* plagen.

Potter, *v.n.* (— about) müssig einhergehen, herumbummeln, herumpusseln (*fam.*).

Pouch, *s.* die Tasche (*also Bot.*), der kleine Sack; der Tabaksbeutel; die Patrontasche (*Mil.*); der Beutel (*also Zool.*). —**ed**, *adj.* Beutel=. *Comp.* —**-belt**, *s.* der Patrontaschenriemen.

Poult—erer, *s.* der Geflügelhändler. —**ry**, *s.* das Federvieh. *Comp.* —**ry-market**, *s.* der Geflügelmarkt. —**ry-yard**, *s.* der Hühnerhof.

Poultice, I. *s.* der Breiumschlag. II. *v.a.* einen (warmen) Umschlag auflegen.

[1]**Pounce**, I. *s.* die Klaue, Kralle; das Locheisen. II. *v.n.;* to — upon, herfallen über (*acc.*), herabschießen auf (*acc.*). III. *v.a.* mit den Krallen packen. —**d**, *adj.* punktiert; —d design, Papier, auf welchem durch Stiche eine Zeichnung hergestellt ist.

[2]**Pounce**, I. *s.* das Bimsteinpulver; das Radierpulver; (—-bag) die Bausche. II. *v.a.* mit Bimsteinpulver abreiben; durchstäuben. *Comp.* —**-box**, *s.* die Streubüchse. —**-paper**, *s.* das (ohne Öl zubereitete) Pauspapier.

Pound, *s.* (lb.) das Pfund; (£ = 20 s.) das Pfund Sterling; — avoirdupois, englisches Handelspfund (= 0,4534 kg.); — troy, das Troypfund (= 0,3731 kg.); to pay 20 shillings in the —, voll bezahlen. **—age**, *s.* der Pfundzoll; die Provision per Pfund (*C.L.*). **—er**, *s.* der Pfünder; six- —er, Sechspfünder. *Comp.* **—-foolish**, *see* Penny-wise.

[2]**Pound**, I. *s.* die Hürde, der Pfandstall. II. *v.a.* einpferchen. **—age**, *s.* das Pfänden, Einsperren; das Pfandgeld. *Comp.* **—-keeper**, *s.* der Pfandstallaufseher.

[3]**Pound**, *v.* I. *a.* stoßen; (bray) zerstoßen; ausschlagen (*ore*); (beat) schlagen. II. *n.*; to — away, darauf losfeuern. *Comp.* **—ing-machine**, *s.* das Pochwerk.

Pour, I. *v.a.* gießen, schütten (from, out of, aus; in, into, in; on, upon, auf, *acc.*); to — water upon a drowned mouse, sich an einem Toten rächen; to — **forth**, ausströmen lassen; to — **off**, abgießen; to — **out**, einschenken (*tea, wine, etc.*), ausschütten (*one's heart, grief, etc.*). II. *v.n.* gießen, heftig strömen; heftig regnen; (rush) mit Heftigkeit dahinstürzen; to — **down**, herabstürzen; to — **in**, stark einlaufen; it never rains but it —s, ein Unglück kommt selten allein (*prov.*). III. *s.* (down—) der Regenguß. **—er** *s.* der Gießer, Einschenker.

Pout, I. *v.n.* schmollen; (protrude) hervorragen. II. *v.a.*; to — the lips, schmollen. III. *s.*; to be in a —, schmollen. **—er**, *s.* der Schmoller; (—er pigeon) die Kropftaube. **—ing**, I. *adj.*, **—ingly**, *adv.* schmollend; aufgeworfen, aufgestülpt, dick (*as lips*). II. *s.* das Schmollen.

Poverty, *s.* die Armut. *Comp.* **—-stricken**, *adj.* verarmt.

Powder, I. *s.* (dust) der Staub; der Puder (*for the face, hair, etc.*); das Pulver (*Gun., Med.*); effervescing —, Brausepulver; priming —, Knallpulver. II. *v.a.* zu Staub machen, zerreiben, pulvern; pudern; (salt) einsalzen; —ed sugar, gestoßener Zucker. **—y**, *adj.* staubig, pulverartig; (friable) zerreibbar. *Comp.* **—-barrel**, *s.* das Pulverfaß. **—-flask**, **—-horn**, *s.* die Pulverflasche, das Pulverhorn. **—-hose**, *s.* der Sprengpulverschlauch. **—-magazine**, *s.* das Pulvermagazin. **—-mill**, *s.* die Pulvermühle. **—-puff**, *s.* die Puderquaste. **—-room**, *s.* die Pulverkammer (*Naut.*).

Power, *s.* das Vermögen, die Kraft; die (bewegende) Kraft (*Mech.*); (authority, *etc.*) die Macht, Gewalt, Herrschaft; (influence) der Einfluß (with, bei); (—fulness) die Kraftfülle; (political —) die Macht; die Potenz (*Math.*); attorney under —, bevollmächtigter Rechtsanwalt; military —, Kriegsmacht; belligerent —s, kriegführende Mächte; vital —, die Lebenskraft, lebenspendende Gewalt; effective —, mechanical —, Nutzleistung; —s of the mind, Geisteskräfte; reasoning —, die Urteilskraft; —s of conversation, das Unterhaltungstalent; horse —, steam —, Pferde-, Dampf-kraft; illuminating —, die Leuchtkraft; resisting —, die Widerstandskraft; men in —, Gewalthaber; the great European —s, die europäischen Großmächte; the —s that be, die himmlischen Mächte; die gegenwärtigen Machthaber (*of people*); second (third) —, zweite (dritte) Potenz, das Quadrat (der Kubus); a — of, viel (*vulg.*). **—ful**, *adj.*, **—fully**, *adv.* kräftig, mächtig, gewaltig; einflußreich; (effective) wirksam. **—fulness**, *s.* die Kraft(-fülle), Stärke; die Macht, Gewalt, Wirksamkeit. **—less**, *adj.* kraftlos, machtlos. **—lessness**, *s.* die Kraftlosigkeit, Ohnmacht. *Comp.* **—-loom**, *s.* der mechanische Webstuhl.

Pow-wow, *s.* indianischer Priester; indianischer Kriegstanz; (conjuration) lärmende Krankheitsbeschwörung; lärmende politische Versammlung (*Amer.*).

Pox, I. *s.* (small- —) die Pocken; (French —) die Lustseuche; small- —, die (echten) Blattern; chicken- —, die Windpocken. II. *interj.* zum Henker!

Practic—able, *adj.*, **—ably**, *adv.* tunlich, ausführbar, möglich; (passable) gangbar, fahrbar; brauchbar (*for use*); erstürmbar (*as a breach*). **—ableness**, **—ability**, *s.* die Tunlichkeit. **—al**, *adj.*, **—ally**, *adv.* tatsächlich, wirklich; erfahren; praktisch; —al chemist, technischer Chemiker; —al chemistry, angewandte, praktische Chemie; —al falsehood, eine durch die Tat bewiesene Unwahrheit; —al geometry, angewandte Geometrie; —al joke, handgreiflicher Spaß, Possen, Schabernack; —al politics, das (politisch) Erreichbare; —al utility, die Anwendbarkeit. **—ality**, **—alness**, *s.* das Praktische.

Practice, *s.* die Praxis (*also Med.*); (doing, action) das Verfahren, die Verfahrungsweise; (usage) die Gewohnheit, der Gebrauch; (exercise) die Anwendung, Ausübung; die Praxis; (doctors' —) die Kundschaft, Praxis; die wälsche Praxis (*Arith.*); — makes perfect, Übung macht den Meister (*prov.*); in (out of) —, in (außer) Übung; to put into —, in Ausübung bringen; target —, das Scheibenschießen (*Mil.*); — of the court, der Gerichtsbrauch, Rechtsgang (*Law*); to make it a —, es sich (*dat.*) zur Gewohnheit machen; to have a large —, eine große Praxis haben; corrupt —s (in an election), Unregelmäßigkeiten (bei einer Wahl); foul —s, schändliche Anschläge, niedrige Mittel, Ränke.

Practise, *v.* I. *a.* in Ausübung bringen, (aus-)üben (*virtues, etc.*); begehen, verüben (*wickedness*); ausüben (*a profession, etc.*); einüben, einstudieren. II. *n.* sich üben, üben; Schieß-ꝛc.-Übungen abhalten; spielen, üben (*Mus.*); (negotiate) sich heimlich verstehen mit; to — on, Versuche machen an (*dat.*); to — as a doctor, (als Arzt) praktizieren. **—d**, *adj.* geübt, bewandert. **—r**, *s.* der Ausüber; *see* Practitioner.

Practitioner, *s.* der Praktiker, der Praktikant; (medical —) der praktische Arzt.

Prae—munire, *s.* (writ) schriftlicher Erlaß; (offence) das Verbrechen, weshalb er ergeht; (penalty) die verwirkte Strafe (*Law*).

Pragmatic, **—al**, *adj.*, **—ally**, *adv.* pragmatisch; (busy) geschäftig; (officious) auf-, zu-dringlich, sich in fremde Sachen mischend, naseweis; — sanction, pragmatische Sanktion (1724); —al fellow, der Vorwitzige, vorwitzige Bursche.

Prairie, *s.* die große Grasebene, Prärie. *Comp.* **—-dog**, *s.* der Präriehund. **—-warbler**, *s.* die amerikanische Grasmücke. **—-wolf**, *s.* der Präriewolf.

Praise, I. *s.* das Lob, der Preis; to say in a p.'s —, einem etwas zum Lobe sagen. II. *v.a.* loben, preisen (for, wegen); to — s.o. to the sky, in den Himmel erheben, mit Lobpreisungen überschütten. **—r**, *s.* der Preisende. *Comp.* **—worthy**, *adj.*, **—worthily**, *adv.* lobenswert. **—worthiness**, *s.* die Preiswürdigkeit.

[1]**Pram**, *s.* der Prahm, das flache Boot; die schwimmende Batterie (*Mil.*).

[2]**Pram**, *coll. for* Perambulator.

Pran—ce, *v.n.* sich bäumen (*as horses*); (ride) prunkend reiten; (strut) stolzieren, sich brüsten. **—k**, I. *s.* der Possen, Streich; to play —ks on s.o., mit einem Possen *or* sein Spiel treiben. II. *v.a.* schmücken, zieren, putzen. III. *v.n.* prunken.

Prandial, *adj.* sich auf die Mahlzeit beziehend.

Prase, *s.* der Chrysopras; der Prasem (*Min.*).

Prat—e, I. *v.n.* schwatzen, plappern. II. *v.a.* albern äußern, heraus plappern. III. *s.* das Geschwätz. **—er**, *s.* der Schwätzer. **—ing**, I. *adj.*, **—ingly**, *adv.* schwatzhaft. II. *s.* das Schwatzen, Geschwätz. **—tle**, I. *v.n.* schwatzen, plaudern. II. *s.* das Geschwätz. **—tler**, *s.* der Schwätzer, Plauderer. **—tling**, I. *adj.* schwatzhaft; plätschernd (*as a brook*). II. *s. see* —tle.

Prawn, *s.* die Steingarneele, große Garneele.
Pray, *v.* I. *n.* beten (to, zu; for, um, für); (beg) bitten; — tell me . . ., bitte, sagen Sie mir . . .; — don't mention it, o, bitte! (es ist) gern geschehen, es ist nicht der Rede wert! II. *a.* bitten, ersuchen (um eine S.). **—er**, *s.* das Gebet; die Bitte, das Gesuch; to say one's —ers, beten, sein Gebet verrichten; morning —ers, die Morgenandacht; Lord's —er, das Vaterunser; the book of Common —er, das Gebetbuch der englischen Hochkirche. **—erful**, *adj.* andächtig, vielbetend. **—erfully**, *adv.* unter vielem Gebet. **—erless**, *adj.* ohne Gebet. **—ing**, I. *adj.* betend; bittend. II. *s.* das Beten; Bitten. *Comp.* **—er-book**, *s.* das Gebetbuch; die Agende. **—er-meeting**, *s.* die Versammlung zum Gebet, Betstunde.
Preach, *v.a.* & *n.* predigen; (exhort) ermahnen, lehren; to — **down**, eifern, predigen gegen, niederpredigen. **—er**, *s.* der Prediger. **—ify**, *v.n.* salbungsvolle Reden halten, salbadern (*fam.*). **—ing**, *s.* das Predigen. **—ment**, *s.* die lange Predigt, das Geschwätz von der Kanzel, die Salbaderei.
Preadami—te, I. *adj.*, **—c**, **—tic**, *adj.* präadamitisch. II. *s.* der Präadamit.
Preamble, *s.* die Einleitung, der Eingang.
Prebend, *s.* die Pfründe, Präbende. **—al**, *adj.* Pfründen-. **—ary**, *s.* der Pfründner, Stifts-, Domherr (welcher einen bestimmten Teil der Einkünfte einer Kathedrale bezieht); *see* Prebend.
Precarious, *adj.* von der Willkür eines anderen abhängig; widerruflich; unsicher, schwankend, prekär (*fig.*); — state of health, in einem bedenklichen Gesundheitszustand. **—ly**, *adv.* ungewiß. **—ness**, *s.* die Ungewißheit, Unsicherheit.
Precaution, *s.* die Vorsicht; die Vorsichtsmaßregel; to take —s, Vorsichtsmaßregeln treffen. **—ary**, *adj.* warnend; vorbeugend, Vorsichts-; —ary measure, die Vorsichtsmaßregel.
Preced—e, *v.* I. *a.* vorher-, voraus-gehen; (einem) vorgehen, den Vorrang haben vor (einem) (*in rank*); it is usual to —e hostilities by a . . ., gewöhnlich läßt man Feindseligkeiten eine . . . vorangehen; the corruption of morals —es the ruin of a state, dem Verfall eines Staates geht der Sittenverfall vorher. II. *n.*; the day —ing, am Tage vorher, den Tag vor (*a battle, etc.*). — **ence**, **—ency**, *s.* das Vorhergehen; der Vortritt, Vorrang; (superiority) der Vorzug, die Überlegenheit. **—ent**, I. *adj.* vorhergehend. II. *s.* der frühere, ähnliche Fall, Präzedenzfall (*also Law*); die Vorschrift, Richtschnur; to be without a —ent, beispiellos sein; to create a dangerous —ent, einen gefährlichen Präzedenzfall abgeben; to be recorded for a —ent, als Richtschnur für künftige Fälle aufgeschrieben werden.
Precentor, *s.* der Vorsänger. **—ship**, *s.* das Vorsängeramt.
Precept, *s.* die Vorschrift, Regel; *see* Maxim; der schriftliche Befehl (*Law*). **—or**, *s.* der Lehrer, Hauptlehrer; College of —ors, ein (große Prüfungen abhaltender und Diplome verleihender) englischer Lehrerverein mit Sitz in London. — **orial**, *adj.* einem Lehrer gehörig. **—ory**, *s.* der Tempelhof (*of the Knights Templars*). **—ress**, *s.* die Lehrerin.
Precession, *s.* das Vorrücken (der Nachtgleichen).
Precinct, *s.* der Bezirk, Bereich; —s, die Grenzen.
Precious, I. *adj.*, **—ly**, *adv.* kostbar (*also iron.*), edel (*of stones, metals, etc.*); a — scoundrel, ein Erzspitzbube (*fam.*). II. *adv.*; — dear, schauderhaft teuer (*sl.*). **—ness**, *s.* die Kostbarkeit.
Precipi—ce, *s.* der Abgrund, die jähe Tiefe. — **table**, *adj.*; — table substance, die präzipitable Substanz (*Chem.* & *Bact.*). **—tance**, **—tancy**, *s.* die Hast, Übereilung. **—tant**, *s.* das Fällungsmittel (*Chem.*). **—tate**, I. *v.a.* jählings herab-, hinab-stürzen; zu sehr beschleunigen, (über-) stürzen, übereilen (*fig.*); niederschlagen, fällen (*Chem.*). II. *v.n.* sich setzen, niederfallen. III. *adj.*, **—tately**, *adv.* herabstürzend; rasch, jählings, übereilt. IV. *s.* das Präzipitat, der Niederschlag. **—tation**, *s.* das Herabstürzen, der Sturz; die Hast, Übereilung, Überstürzung; die Niederschlagung. **—tous**, *adj.*, **—tously**, *adv.* jäh, steil abfallend; rasch, übereilt, vorschnell. — **tousness**, *s.* die Steilheit, der jähe Absturz; die Übereilung, das Ungestüm.
Precis, *s.* (— writing) die gedrängte Darstellung; die Abfassung eines Auszugs *or* einer gedrängten Übersicht.
Precis—e, *adj.*, **—ely**, *adv.* bestimmt, genau; (formal) förmlich, steif, pedantisch, pünktlich, umständlich. **—eness**, *s.* die Bestimmtheit, Genauigkeit; die ängstliche Pünktlichkeit, Steifheit. **—ian**, *s.* der Rigorist, pedantische Mensch. **—ion**, *s.* *see* —eness; instrument of —, das Präzisions-Instrument; weapon of —, die Präzisions-Waffe.
Preclu—de, *v.a.* ausschließen; (obviate) vorbeugen. **—sion**, *s.* die Ausschließung.
Precoc—ious, *adj.*, **—iously**, *adv.* frühreif, frühzeitig; altklug, vorlaut (*fig.*). **—iousness**, — **ity**, *s.* die Frühzeitigkeit, Frühreife; die Vorzeitigkeit (*fig.*).
Preconc—eive, *v.a.* zum Voraus auffassen; —eived opinions, vorgefaßte Meinungen. **—eption**, *s.* die vorgefaßte Meinung.
Preconcert, *v.a.* vorher verabreden; —ed, vorher verabredet *or* abgemacht; —edly, nach vorheriger Abrede *or* Abmachung.
Precursor, *s.* der Vorläufer, Vorbote, Verkün(dig)er. **—y**, *adj.* verkündend, vorläufig, einleitend.
Predatory, *adj.* räuberisch, Raub-.
Predeceased, *adj.* vorher verstorben; his — wife, seine vor ihm verstorbene Frau.
Predecessor, *s.* der Vorgänger (*in office, etc.*).
Predestin—arian, *s.* der Anhänger der Prädestinationslehre. **—ate**, *v.a.* vorherbestimmen. **—ation**, *s.* die Vorherbestimmung; die Gnadenwahl (*Theol.*). **—ator**, *s.* der Vorherbestimmende. **—e**, *v.a.* vorherbestimmen.
Predetermin—able, *adj.* vorher bestimmbar. **—ate**, *adj.* vorher bestimmt. **—ation**, *s.* die Vorherbestimmung, der Vorbeschluß. **—e**, *v.a.* vorher bestimmen *or* beschließen *or* festsetzen.
Predic—ability, *s.* die Aussagbarkeit, Prädikabilität. **—able**, *adj.* aussagbar, beilegbar. **—ament**, *s.* (state) die Lage; schlimme Lage, die Verlegenheit (*fig.*); das Prädikament, die Kategorie, Klasse (*Log.*); to be in a pretty —ament, schön daran sein. **—ate**, I. *v.a.* & *n.* aussagen; gründen (*Amer.*). II. *s.* das Prädikat, die Aussage; das Aussagewort (*Gram.*). **—ation**, *s.* das Aussagen. **—ative**, *adj.* prädikativ. **—t**, *v.a.* vorher-, weis-sagen. **—tion**, *s.* die Vorhersage, Weissagung.
Predilection, *s.* die Vorliebe (für eine S.).
Predispos—e, *v.n.* zuvor geneigt machen (zu einer S. *or* für eine S.); (adapt) empfänglich machen (für), vorbereiten (auf eine S.). **—ition**, *s.* die Geneigtheit, Neigung; die Empfänglichkeit (*Med.*, *fig.*).
Predomina—nce, *s.* das Übergewicht, Vorherrschen. **—nt**, *adj.* vorherrschend. **—te**, *v.n.* vorherrschen. **—ting**, *adj.* vorherrschend, überwiegend.
Pre-eminen—ce, *s.* das Hervorragen, die Vorzüglichkeit (in einer S.), der Vorrang (vor einer S.); die Überlegenheit (über einen), der Vorzug (vor einem); die Obergewalt, überlegene Macht. **—t**, *adj.* hervor-ragend, -stechend, vorzüglich. **—tly**, *adv.* hervor-ragend, -stechend, vorzüglich, in hohem Grade, vor allen, über alle Maßen.
Pre-emption, *s.* der Vorkauf; das Vorkaufsrecht (*Amer.*).
Preen, *v.a.* (das Gefieder eines Vogels) ausputzen, in Ordnung legen (*of birds*).
Pre-engage, *v.a.* zum voraus verbinden, verpflichten, bestellen. **—ment**, *s.* die frühere Verbindung, das vorhergegangene Versprechen.

Pre-exist, *v.n.* vorher da sein, früher existieren. **—ence**, *s.* das frühere Dasein, die Präexistenz. **—ent**, *adj.* früher vorhanden.

Prefa—ce, I. *s.* die Vorrede, das Vorwort. II. *v.a.* mit einer Vorrede, Einleitung versehen, bevorworten; (introduce) einleiten, einführen. **—tory**, *adj.* einleitend, Einleitungs=.

Prefect, *s.* der Präfekt; der Schüler der höchsten Klasse an vielen großen public schools mit gewisser Aufsichts= und Straf=gewalt über die jüngeren Schüler. *See* Monitor, Prepositor. **—ure**, *s.* die Präfektur; die Präfektenstelle (*in France*).

Prefer, *v.a.* vorbringen, vorlegen (*a request*); (advance) erheben, befördern; (like better) vorziehen, bevorzugen; to — a charge against a p., eine Klage wider einen einreichen; I — it to everything, ich ziehe es allem andern vor; he has been —red to me, er ist mir vorgezogen; —red shares, Stammprioritätsaktien. **—able**, *adj.* vorzuziehen; vorzüglicher (to, als). **—ence**, I. *s.* der Vorzug; by —ence, mit besonderer Vorliebe, besonders gern; from —ence, mit Vorliebe; to give the —ence to, (einem, einem anderen, etwas, etwas anderem) den Vorzug geben. II. *attrib.*; —ence stock, Vorzugspapiere. **—ment**, *s.* die Beförderung, Erhebung; das Ehrenamt (*Eccl.*). **—rer**, *s.* der Anbringer (*Law*); der Beförderer.

Prefigure, *v.a.* vorbilden, vorher darstellen. **—ment**, *s.* die Vorhersagung.

Prefix, I. *v.a.* vor(an)setzen. II. *s.* die Vorsilbe, das Präfix.

Pregnan—cy, *s.* die Schwangerschaft; das Gedankenreiche, Inhaltschwere (*fig.*); (inventiveness) der Erfindergeist, die Schöpferkraft. **—t**, *adj.* schwanger (*of women*); trächtig (*of animals*); inhaltschwer, fruchtbar (*fig.*); reich (with, an, *dat.*).

Prehens—ile, *adj.* greifend, fassend, zum Greifen geeignet. **—ion**, *s.* das Fassen, Ergreifen.

Prehistoric, *adj.* vorgeschichtlich, urgeschichtlich.

Prejud—ge, *v.a.* ohne vorherige Prüfung entscheiden, vorher beurteilen; zum Voraus verurteilen. **—ice**, I. *s.* das Vorurteil; (injury) der Abbruch, Schaden, Nachteil. II. *v.a.* vorgefaßte Meinungen, Vorurteile beibringen, vorher einnehmen (against, gegen); (einer Sache 2c.) schaden, Eintrag tun; —iced, eingenommen (gegen), voreingenommen. **—icial**, *adj.*, **—icially**, *adv.* voreingenommen; schädlich, nachteilig, beeinträchtigend.

Prela—cy, *s.* die Prälatur; *see* Episcopacy; (—tes) die Prälaten. **—te**, *s.* der Prälat. **—tic(al)**, *adj.* Prälaten=, bischöflich.

Prelect—ion, *s.* die Vorlesung. **—or**, *s.* der Vorleser; der Prälektor (*a title e.g. at Trinity Coll. Cambridge*).

Preliminar—y, I. *adj.* vorläufig, vorgängig, einleitend; —y examination, die Aufnahmeprüfung (an einigen Universitäten); —y steps, vorläufige Schritte. II. *s.* das Vorläufige, Vorspiel, die Einleitung. **—ies**, *pl.* die Vorverhandlungen, die einleitenden Verhandlungen, die ersten Schritte.

Prelude, I. *s.* das Vorspiel; das Präludium, Vorspiel (*Mus.*); die Einleitung. II. *v.a.* einleiten; (*also v.n.*) präludieren, ein Vorspiel beginnen.

Premature, *adj.*, **—ly**, *adv.* früh=zeitig, =reif; (untimely) unzeitig, vorzeitig, verfrüht; (too hasty) voreilig, übereilt, vorschnell. **—ness**, *s.* die Frühreife; die Vorzeitigkeit; die Unzeitigkeit; die Voreiligkeit, das Verfrühte.

Premeditat—e, *v.a.* vorher überlegen, bedenken. **—ed**, *adj.*, **—edly**, *adv.* vorbedacht, vorher zurechtgelegt; vorsätzlich, mit Vorbedacht. **—ion**, *s.* der Vorbedacht.

Premier, I. *adj.* erst. II. *s.* der erste Minister, Premierminister, Ministerpräsident. **—ship**, *s.* das Amt, die Würde eines Premierministers *or* Ministerpräsidenten.

Premis—e, I. *v.a. & n.* vorangehen lassen, vorläufig erwähnen. II. *s. see* —s. **—es**, *pl.* das Haus nebst Zugehör, die Wohnung, Gebäude, Grundstücke; die Prämissen, Vordersätze (eines Schlusses, *Log.*); das Vorhererwähnte, Obenbemerkte (*Law*); on the —es, im Hause (selbst). **—s**, *s.* die Prämisse, der Vordersatz.

Premium, *s.* die Prämie, Belohnung, der Preis; das Agio, Aufgeld (*C. L.*); (fee) das Aufgeld; das Lehrgeld (des Lehrlings in technischen 2c. Geschäften); die Prämie (*of insurance, etc.*); *see* Bonus; at a —, über Pari; sehr hoch, gesucht (*fig.*).

Premonit—ion, *s.* die Warnung. **—ory**, *adj.* warnend, vorhergehend, verkündigend; —ory symptoms, Symptome, die Vorläufer einer Krankheit sind; warnende *or* erste Anzeichen.

Premonstrants, *pl.* Prämonstratenser(=mönche).

Prentice, *see* Apprentice.

Preoccup—ancy, *s.* die frühere Besitzergreifung; das Recht, vor anderen Besitz zu nehmen. **—ation**, *s.* die frühere Besitznahme; (bias) das Vorurteil, die Voreingenommenheit, die vorgefaßte Meinung; das Vorwegnehmen; mental —ation, die Befangenheit; die Zerstreutheit. **—y**, *v.a.* vorher *or* vor einem andern in Besitz nehmen; ausschließlich beschäftigen; to be —ied, in Gedanken *or* nachdenklich sein; to have a —ied air, zerstreut, sinnend, nachdenklich aussehen.

Preordain, *v.a.* vorher bestimmen, anordnen.

Prepar—ation, *s.* die Vorbereitung; die Zubereitung (*of food, etc.*); das Präparat, Arzneimittel (*Pharm.*); —ation for an examination, Vorbereitung auf eine Prüfung. **—ative**, I. *adj. see* —atory. II. *s.* die Vorbereitung; die Anstalt (to, zu). **—atory**, *adj.* vorbereitend, Vorbereitungs=; —atory department, die Vorschule (in einer höheren Schule); —atory school, eine Vorbereitungsschule (auf die großen englischen public schools); —atory to, als Vorbereitung auf (*acc.*). **—e**, *v.* I. *a.* vorbereiten (for, zu, auf); (zu)rüsten (*for war, etc.*); (dispose) veranstalten; (zu)bereiten; zurichten (*a table, etc.*); vorbereiten (*Mus.*); einrichten (*a horse, etc.*); präparieren (*Pharm.*); to —e the way for, (einer S. *or* einem) Bahn brechen, den Weg öffnen; to —e a boy for the university, einen Knaben auf die (*or* zum Besuch der) Hochschule vorbereiten; to be —ed for a th. (the worst), auf eine S. (das Schlimmste) vorbereitet sein *or* sich auf eine S. (das Schlimmste) gefaßt machen; they must be —ed for the same punishment, sie haben die gleiche Strafe zu gewärtigen. II. *n.* (—e, be —ing for) (auf eine S.) sich vorbereiten, sich rüsten, (für) sich gefaßt machen (auf, *acc.*). **—edness**, *s.* die Bereitschaft. **—er**, *s.* der Vorbereitende; der Bereiter; der Verfertiger.

Prepay, *v.a.* vorausbezahlen, im voraus bezahlen. **—ment**, *s.* die Vorausbezahlung.

Prepense, *adj.* vorbedacht, vorsätzlich; malice —, die böswillige Absicht, vorsätzliche Bosheit.

Prepondera—nce, *s.* das Übergewicht. **—nt**, *adj.* überwiegend. **—te**, *v.n.* überwiegen, vorherrschen.

Preposit—ion, *s.* das Verhältniswort, die Präposition. **—ional**, *adj.* Präpositions=. **—ive**, I. *adj.* vor(an)gesetzt. II. *s.* die vorgesetzte Partikel. **—or**, *s.* der Schüler der höchsten Klasse in einigen großen englischen public schools (z. B. Rugby), der eine gewisse Disziplinargewalt über die jüngeren Knaben ausübt; *see* Prefect.

Prepossess, *v.a.* vorher einnehmen, voreinnehmen, für sich gewinnen; —ed with, voreingenommen von. **—ing**, *adj.*, **—ingly**, *adv.* einnehmend, angenehm. **—ion**, *s.* die Voreingenommenheit, vorgefaßte Meinung.

Preposterous, *adj.*, **—ly**, *adv.* verkehrt, widersinnig, =natürlich. **—ness**, *s.* die Verkehrtheit, Widersinnigkeit.

Prerogative, *s.* das Vorrecht, Prärogativ.

Presage, I. *s.* die Vorbedeutung, das Vorzeichen, (foreboding) die Ahnung; (prediction) die Weissagung. II. *v.a.* vorbedeuten; vorherverkünden.

Presbyter, *s.* der Kirchenälteste, Kirchenvorsteher. **—ian**, I. *adj.* presbyterianisch. II. *s.* der Presbyterianer. **—ianism**, *s.* der Presbyterianismus. **—y**, *s.* das Presbyterium, die Kirchenältesten; die presbyterianische Synode; die Kirchenregierung durch Älteste.

Prescien—ce, *s.* das Vorherwissen. **—t**, *adj.* vorkundig, vorherwissend.

Prescri—be, *v.* I. *a.* & *n.* vorschreiben, verordnen (*rules, etc.*); verschreiben (*Med.*). II. *n.* (sich) verjähren (*Law*); (claim by —ption) den Anspruch der Verjährung machen (auf eine S.). **—ption**, *s.* die Vorschrift, Verordnung; das Rezept (*Med.*); die Verjährung. **—ptive**, *adj.*; —ptive property, (alt)verjährtes Eigentum; —ptive right, das Verjährungsrecht.

Presen—ce, *s.* die Gegenwart, Anwesenheit; (society) die Gegenwart, Nähe; (noble company) die (vor einer hohen Person versammelten) Anwesenden; (appearance) das Äußere, die Persönlichkeit; (air) das Benehmen, der Anstand; —ce of mind, die Geistesgegenwart; he lost his —ce of mind, er verlor den Kopf; in the —ce of a notary, im Beisein eines Notars; in the —ce of witnesses, in Gegenwart von Zeugen; in the —ce of these dangers, angesichts dieser Gefahren; page of the —ce, der Leibpage. **—t**, I. *adj.* gegenwärtig, anwesend, zugegen; jetzig, gegenwärtig; (actual) vorhanden; laufend (*of the year, etc.*); vorliegend, in Frage stehend; —t tense, die Gegenwart, das Präsens; —t time, gegenwärtige Zeit; the —t writer, der Schreiber dieses; to be —t at a th., einer S. beiwohnen; in the —t case, im vorliegenden Falle; —t! hier! always —t to my mind, mir immer gegenwärtig; the —t crisis, die jetzige Krisis; my brother was —t, mein Bruder war anwesend *or* zugegen. II. *s.* die Gegenwart, gegenwärtige Zeit; die Gegenwart, das Präsens (*Gram.*); by these —ts, durch Gegenwärtiges; at —t, jetzt; for the —t, für jetzt, vorläufig. **—ly**, *adv.* sogleich, gleich; (soon) bald, kurz darauf. *Comp.* **—ce-chamber**, *s.* das Audienzzimmer.

[1]**Present**, *see under* Presence.

[2]**Present**, *v.a.* darstellen, zeigen; (introduce) vorstellen, einführen (to, bei); gewähren, bieten (*a spectacle, etc.*); vorschlagen (to a benefice, etc., zu einer Pfründe, &c.); vorzeigen (a bill for acceptance, etc., einen Wechsel zur Annahme, &c.); (über die Taufe) halten (for baptism); (point) vorhalten; präsentieren (*arms*); (hand over) überreichen; einreichen (*a petition, memorial, etc.*); (give) (be)schenken; (offer) darbieten; darlegen (*one's ideas*); to — arms, das Gewehr präsentieren; —, fire! legt an, Feuer! to — one's compliments to a p., sich einem empfehlen; to — s.o. with a th., einem etwas schenken, einen mit einer S. beschenken; that —s difficulties, das bietet Schwierigkeiten dar; to — o.s., (vor einem) erscheinen. **—ability**, *s.* die Vorstellbarkeit. **—able**, *adj.* in einem Zustande, um sich, sehen lassen zu können, vorstellbar, präsentabel. **—ation**, I. *s.* die Präsentation; die Vorstellung (*Psych.*); der Vorschlag (zu einer Pfründe, to a benefice); (right of —ation) das Vorschlagsrecht, die Präsentation; die Eingabe, Einreichung; (gift) die Schenkung; die Überreichung; die Vorzeigung (*C. L.*); die Vorstellung (*at court*); on —ation, bei Vorzeigung. II. *attrib.*; —ation copy, das Freiexemplar; das Dedikationsexemplar. **—ment**, *s. see* —ation; die Darstellung, Vorstellung; (conduct) das Benehmen; eine ohne Denunziation unmittelbar von der Anklagejury erhobene Kriminalklage.

[3]**Present**, *s.* das Geschenk; to make a p. a — of, einem ein Geschenk machen mit; he made me a — of that book, er schenkte mir das Buch, gab mir das Buch zum Geschenk.

Presentiment, *s.* die Vorempfindung, Vorahnung, das Vorgefühl.

Preserv—ation, *s.* die Be-, Ver-wahrung (from, vor); die Erhaltung (*in good condition, etc.*); (saving) die Rettung; in good —ation, gut erhalten *or* in gutem Zustande. **—ative**, I. *adj.* verwahrend, erhaltend. II. das Verwahrungsmittel, Schutzmittel (against, gegen); das Konservierungsmittel; the best —atives of health, die besten Mittel, die Gesundheit zu bewahren. **—e**, I. *v.a.* bewahren, behüten (from, vor); erhalten (*in health, etc.*); (protect) schützen; einmachen (*fruit, etc.*); (lay up) (auf)bewahren; (keep) behalten; to —e one's gravity, ernst bleiben; to —e silence, still bleiben, Stillschweigen beobachten; to —e game, Wild hegen; Heaven —e me from that! der Himmel bewahre mich davor! II. *s.* das Gehege (*Sport.*); (—**es**, *pl.*) das Eingemachte. **—er**, *s.* der Beschützer, Retter; der Erhalter; der Einmachende.

Preside, *v.n.* vorsitzen, den Vorsitz führen; die Aufsicht führen (over, über); to — at (a dinner), bei (einem Festessen) den Vorsitz führen; to — over (a court, etc.), Vorsitzender (eines Gerichtshofs) sein; the meeting was —d over by . . ., in der Versammlung führte . . . den Vorsitz. **—ncy**, *s.* der Vorsitz; die Oberaufsicht; (—nt's office period of, etc.)) das Vorsitzeramt, die Präsidentschaft. **—nt**, *s.* der Vorsitzende, Vorsitzer, der Präsident (*also of a republic*); der Vorsteher; der zweite Vorsteher (*in some colleges the head of which is called Master*); der Präses (*in some students' clubs*); —nt of the Council, Vorsitz(end)er des geheimen Rates; election of a —nt, die Wahl eines Vorsitzenden, Vorsitzers, die Vorsitzerwahl. **—ntial**, *adj.* Präsidenten-; —ntial address, die Ansprache des Vorsitzenden (zur Eröffnung einer Versammlung oder Sitzung); —ntial chair, der Präsidentenstuhl. **—ntship**, *s.* das Vorsitzeramt (*of a club*); die Präsidentschaft.

Press, I. *v.a.* pressen, drücken; (crowd) drängen, treiben; (aus)pressen, keltern (*grapes*); pressen (*cloth, etc., also sailors or soldiers*); (ply hard) bedrängen, in die Enge treiben; (beg, urge) inständig bitten, nötigen; antreiben; to — a p. to . . ., einen (dringend) bitten, in einen dringen zu . . .; —ed beef, das Büchsenfleisch; to be —ed for time, es eilig haben, pressiert sein; to — on, (vorwärts) drängen, treiben; to — s.th. upon a p.'s acceptance, einem etwas aufdringen, aufnötigen; to be hard —ed, in (großer) Verlegenheit sein; to — sail, (carry a — of sail), alle Segel beisetzen. II. *v.n.* drücken, pressen; sich drängen, eilen, eilig sein, es eilig haben, pressieren; (be —ing) schleunige Hilfe erfordern, drängen; the matter is not —ing, die Sache hat keine Eile; to — **for**, sich eifrig bewerben, bemühen um; to — **forward**, vorwärts drängen, weiter eilen *or* stürmen, dringen (to, nach); to — a th. forward, eine S. durch-setzen *or* -drücken wollen; to — **on**, vorwärts, weiter eilen; to — **upon**, eindringen auf (*acc.*), eilen zu, (urge) dringen in (*acc.*), nötigen; to — **round**, sich drängen um. III. *s.* das Zeitungswesen, der Journalismus, die Presse (*Print.; also for wine, oil etc.*); der Schrank (*for linen, etc.*); das Gedränge (*of people*); (—ing) das Drängen, der Drang, Andrang (*of business, etc.*); das Matrosenpressen; liberty of the —, die Preßfreiheit; in the —, unter der Presse, im Druck (befindlich); to go, send to —, in Druck gehen, geben; —! druckfertig! Imprimatur! to pass a proof for —, einem Druckbogen das Imprimatur erteilen; daily —, Tages-Presse; steam —, Schnellpresse. **—er**, *s.* der Presser, Drücker; cloth-—er, Stoffdrücker (*Sew.-m.*). **—ing**, I. *adj.*, **—ingly**, *adv.*, dringend, dringlich; eilig; —ing need, dringendes Bedürfnis. II. *s.* das Pressen, Drücken. **—ure**, *s.* der Druck (*also fig.*); der Drang, die Klemme, Drangsal (*fig.*); —ure of business, der Drang der Geschäfte; —ure of the hand, Händedruck; —ure for money, die Geldnot. *Comp.* **—man**, *s.* der Drucker; der Zeitungsschreiber. **—mark**, *s.* die Bibliotheksnummer eines Buches. **—reader**, *s.* der Korrektor. **—room**, *s.* das Druckerzimmer. **—stick**, *s.* der Preßbengel (*Bookb.*). **—work**, *s.* die Druckerarbeit.

Prestige, *s.* das Ansehen, der Nimbus.
Presto, *adv. & interj.* schnell, geschwind.
Presum—able, *adj.*, **—ably**, *adv.* vermutlich, mutmaßlich. **—e**, *v.* I. *a.* voraussetzen, vermuten. II. *n.* vermuten; (venture) sich erkühnen, sich (*dat.*) herausnehmen, wagen; (—e on) sich verlassen auf (*acc.*); (—e upon, on) etwas voraussetzen; (be forward) sich (*dat.*) anmaßen; as I —e, wie ich annehme, wie mich dünkt; to —e too much on *or* upon, sich (*dat.*) zu viel einbilden auf (*acc.*); sich (*dat.*) zu viel herausnehmen mit. **—ing**, *adj.* anmaßend, vermessen. **—ption**, *s.* die Voraussetzung; (ground of —ption) die Wahrscheinlichkeit; (assurance) die Vermessenheit, Anmaßung; (self-sufficiency) der Eigendünkel. **—ptive**, *adj.* mutmaßlich; heir —ptive, Präsumptiv-Erbe; —ptive evidence, der Indizienbeweis. **—ptuous**, *adj.*, **—ptuously**, *adv.* dünkelhaft; anmaßend, vermessen. **—ptuousness**, *s.* der Dünkel; die Vermessenheit.
Presuppos—e, *v.a.* voraussetzen, zur Voraussetzung haben. **—ition**, *s.* die Voraussetzung.
Preten—ce, *s.* der Vorwand, Schein; *see* Pretext; under false —ces, unter falscher Vorspiegelung; under the —ce of, unter dem Scheine von (*friendship*), unter der Maske von (*patriotism*). **—d**, *v.* I. *a.* vorgeben; heucheln (*zeal, friendship, etc.*). II. *a. & n.* sich stellen, sich ausgeben für, sich (*dat.*) den Schein geben; (claim) Anspruch machen auf (*acc.*); to —d to be, sich ausgeben für; I don't —d to be an orator, ich bilde mir nicht ein, ein Redner zu sein. **—ded**, *adj.* vorgeblich, verstellt; (ostensible) angeblich; (supposed) vermeintlich. **—der**, *s.* der Vorschützende; (claimant) einer, der Anspruch macht (auf eine S.); der Bewerber (*to a lady's hand, etc.*), Freier; —der to a crown, Thronbewerber, der Prätendent (*Hist.*). **—sion**, *s.* der Anspruch (to, auf eine S.); die Anmaßung; not without, of no mean —sions (to ability), nicht ohne Talent. **—tious**, *adj.*, **—tiously**, *adv.* anspruchsvoll, anmaßlich, prätensiös; prunkhaft (*as a house, etc.*). **—tiousness**, *s.* die Anmaßlichkeit, das anspruchsvolle Wesen.
Preter—ite, *s.* (—ite tense) das Präteritum, die vergangene Zeit. **—ite-present**, *s.* das Präterito-Präsens, starkes Zeitwort dessen Vergangenheitsform Präsensbedeutung angenommen hat (z.B. ich weiß, darf, kann, muß). **—mission**, *s.* die Unterlassung. **—natural**, *adj.* über das Natürliche hinausgehend, abnorm.
Pretext, *s.* der Vorwand, das Vorgeben; to make a — of a th., eine S. vorschützen, vorgeben; under the — of, unter dem Vorwande.
Pretonic, *adj.* vortonig, vor dem Akzent.
Pretor, *s.* der Prätor. **—ian**, I. *adj.* prätorianisch; —ian guards, die Prätorianer. II. *s.* der Prätorianer. **—ship**, *s.* das Prätoramt.
Prett—ily, *adv.* niedlich, artig, nett. **—iness**, *s.* die Niedlichkeit, Nettigkeit; die Artigkeit (*of behaviour*). **—y**, I. *adj.* hübsch, niedlich, nett; he has played me a —y trick, er hat mir einen schönen Streich gespielt (*fam.*). II. *adv.* ziemlich, einigermaßen; —y considerable, ziemlich beträchtlich; I was —y near losing myself, ich war nahe daran, mich zu verirren; —y much the same thing, ungefähr dasselbe.
Prevail, *v.n.* die Oberhand haben, herrschen, vorwalten; häufig vorkommen, üblich sein; (obtain) vorherrschen; I could not — on myself, ich vermochte es nicht über mich, ich konnte es nicht übers Herz bringen *or* über mich gewinnen; to — **over**, die Oberhand bekommen, den Sieg davon tragen; to — **upon**, vermögen (zu), überwinden (o.s.), bereden, bewegen (a p.); to — **with** (a p. for a th.), (einen zu einer S.) vermögen *or* veranlassen; this —ed with him, dies gab bei ihm den Ausschlag. **—ing**, *adj.* überwiegend, (vor)herrschend, allgemein geltend *or* angenommen
Prevalen—ce, **—cy**, *s.* das Herrschen (*of a disease*); das Vorherrschen, Überhandnehmen (*of opinions, etc.*). **—t**, *adj.* überwiegend, vorherrschend; mächtig, wirksam; weit *or* überall verbreitet.
Prevaricat—e, *v.n.* Ausflüchte brauchen, um die Wahrheit herum gehen. **—ion**, *s.* die Umgehung der Wahrheit, Verdrehung, Ausflucht; die Kollusion (*Law*). **—or**, *s.* der Ausflüchte Gebrauchende.
Prevent, *v.a.* (einer Sache) zuvorkommen, vorbeugen; (hinder) (ver)hindern. **—able**, *adj.* verhütbar, zu verhüten. **—ative**, I. *adj.*; to be —ative of a th., eine S. verhindern. II. *s.* das Vorbauungsmittel (of, gegen); die Vorkehrung, das Schutzmittel. **—er**, *s.* der Zuvorkommende, Verhinderer; das Borg-tau, -holz ꝛc. (*Naut.*). **—ion**, *s.* die Verhinderung, Verhütung; society for the —ion of cruelty to animals, der Tierschutzverein, Verein gegen Tierquälerei; society for the —ion of cruelty to children, der Kinderschutzverein. **—ive**, *see* —ative.
Previous, *adj.*, **—ly**, *adv.* vorhergehend, vorläufig; — to, vor; — examination, die Aufnahmeprüfung (an d. Universität Cambridge); to move the — question, das Übergehen zur Tagesordnung beantragen (*Parl.*).
Prevision, *s.* das Vorher-, Voraus-sehen.
Prey, I. *s.* der Raub, die Beute; bird of —, der Raubvogel; to fall a — to . . ., (einem ꝛc.) zur Beute fallen *or* werden. II. *v.n.* auf Beute ausgehen, Beute machen; to — on, fressen, nagen (*fig.*), (plunder) plündern, (devour) fressen; it —ed on his mind, es lag ihm schwer im Sinn.
Price, I. *s.* der Preis; der Wert; to give a great — for, teuer kaufen; to set a — on, einen Preis setzen auf (*acc.*); statement of —s, die Preisangabe; I must have it at any —, ich muß es um jeden Preis haben; I cannot do it at any —, ich kann es unmöglich tun; cost —, Selbstkostenpreis; reduced —, die Preisermäßigung, Preisherabsetzung; — of labour, der Arbeitslohn; —s quoted, notierte, angegebene Preise. II. *v.a.* zu einem gewissen Preise anschlagen *or* ansetzen; nach dem Preis fragen (*coll.*); —d catalogue, der Katalog mit Preisangaben. **—less**, *adj.* unschätzbar. *Comp.* **—-list**, **—-current**, *s.* die Preisliste.
Prick, I. *v.a.* stechen; (spur) spornen, stacheln; (sting) stacheln, prickeln; (— down) bezeichnen, aufzeichnen, durch Punkte angeben (*sheriffs' names, etc.*); durchstechen (*a pattern, paper, etc.*); vernageln (*a horse*); to — a chart, die Karte pricken, passen; to — one's finger, sich in den Finger stechen; he was —ed to the heart, es ging ihm durchs Herz; his conscience —s him, das Gewissen schlägt ihm, er verspürt Gewissensbisse; to — up one's ears, die Ohren spitzen. II. *v.n.* stacheln, prickeln, die Sporen geben; heransprengen (*obs., poet.*). III. *s.* (goad) der Stachel; der Stich (*of an insect, a needle, etc.*); (point, dot) der Punkt; (result of —) stechender Schmerz; der Stachel, (Gewissens) Biß (*of conscience*). **—er**, *s.* der Pfriem; die Raumnadel (*Artil.*). **—le**, *s.* der Stachel, Dorn. **—liness**, *s.* die Stacheligkeit. **—ly**, *adj.* stachelig, Stachel-; —ly pear, indianische Feige. *Comp.* **—-punch**, *s.* der Dorn.
Pride, I. *s.* der Stolz, Hochmut, Übermut; (glory) die Pracht, Herrlichkeit; (arrogance) der Übermut; (cause of —) der Schmuck, Stolz, die Zierde; to take a — in, stolz sein auf (*acc.*); —-of-India, der Paternosterbaum; London —, eine Art des Steinbrechs (*Bot.*); — goes before a fall, Hochmut kommt vor dem Fall (*prov.*). II. *v.r.* stolz sein (auf eine S.); he —s himself much upon it, er tut sich viel darauf zu gute, brüstet sich damit.
Prier, *s.* der Späher, Gucker.
Priest, *s.* der Priester, Geistliche; der Pfaffe (*in contempt*). **—ess**, *s.* die Priesterin. **—hood**, *s.* das Priester-tum, -amt; (—s) die Priester-

ſchaft. **—liness,** *s.* die Prieſterlichkeit. **—ly,** *adj.* prieſterlich, Prieſter⸗; —ly office, das Prieſteramt. *Comp.* **—craft,** *s.* der Pfaffentrug; die Pfaffenpolitik. **—ridden,** *adj.* von Pfaffen regiert, den Pfaffen ergeben; pfäffiſch.

Prig, I. *s.* eingebildeter Fant; nüchterner pedantiſcher Tugendheld, Laffe; der Dieb (*sl.*). II. *v.a.* mauſen. **—gish,** *adj.*, **—gishly,** *adv.* vorlaut, geckenhaft, dünkelhaft; diebiſch. **—gishness,** *s.* die Eingebildetheit, Geckenhaftigkeit.

Prim, *adj.*, **—ly,** *adv.*, ſauber, fein; zimperlich, ſteif, geziert. **—a,** *s.* die Prima (*Typ.*). **—acy,** *s.* das Primat. **—a-donna,** *s.* die erſte Sängerin (*Theat.*). **—a-facie,** *adv.* auf den erſten Blick, von vornherein. **—age,** *s.* das Primgeld. **—arily,** *adv.* zuerſt, anfänglich. **—ary,** *adj.* erſt; (original) urſprünglich, Ur⸗, Grund⸗, Haupt⸗; Elementar⸗ (*as schools*); —ary colours, Grundfarben; of —ary importance, von höchſter Wichtigkeit; —ary instruction, der Volksſchulunterricht; —ary planets, Hauptplaneten; —ary rocks, das Urgebirge; —ary school, die Volksſchule. **—ate,** *s.* der Primas; das Oberhaupt der engliſchen Staatskirche; —ate of England, Titel des Erzbiſchofs von York; —ate of all England, der Erzbiſchof von Canterbury; —ate of Ireland, der Erzbiſchof von Dublin; —ate of all Ireland, der Erzbiſchof von Armagh. **—ates,** *pl.* die Primaten (*Zool.*). **—ateship,** *s.* das Primat. **—e,** *adj.* erſt, urſprünglich (*in time*); erſt, vornehmſt, vorzüglichſt (*in excellence, dignity, etc.*); (principal) hauptſächlich; (excellent) vorzüglich, vortrefflich; —e cost, der Einkaufspreis; —e entry, vorläufige Zollangabe; —e minister, der Miniſterpräſident; —e mover, der Haupthebel; —e number, die Primzahl. II. *s.* (—e of life) die Blüte, Jugendfriſche, Lebenskraft, volle Manneskraft; (the best) das Erſte, Beſte; der Kern; (perfection) höchſte Vollkommenheit; erſtes Stunden⸗Gebet (*R. C.*); die Prime (*Arith., Fenc.*). III. *v.a.* Pulver auf die Pfanne ſchütten (*of a gun*); grundieren (*Paint.*); anſtechen (*a pump*); to —e a p., einen in Bereitſchaft ſetzen (zum Handeln ꝛc.); betrunken machen (*sl.*). **—er,** I. *adj.* erſt (*obs.*). II. *s.* das Elementarbuch, *see* Reader. die Antiquaſchrift (*Typ.*); great —er, die Tertia (*Typ.*); long —er, die Korpusſchrift (*Typ.*); —er of geography, die Anfangsgründe der Geographie, Erſter Leitfaden der Erdkunde; German —er, das Elementarbuch der deutſchen Sprache. **—eval,** *adj.* uranfänglich, Ur⸗. **—itive,** I. *adj.* erſt, urſprünglich; Ur⸗ (*of rocks, etc.*); Stamm⸗ (*of words*); (old-fashioned) altertümlich, altväteriſch; einfach, primitiv; (*also* **—itively,** *adv.*) primitiv (*as colours*). II. *s.* das Stammwort. **—itiveness,** *s.* die Urſprünglichkeit; die Altertümlichkeit; die Einfachheit. **—ness,** *s.* die Ziererei; (prudishness) die Sprödigkeit. **—ogeniture,** *s.* die Erſtgeburt; das Erſtgeburtsrecht (*Law*). **—ordial,** I. *adj.* urſprünglich, uranfänglich; Primordial⸗, Erſtlings⸗ (*Bot.*). II. *s.* der Uranfang. *Comp.* **—rose,** I. *s.* die Schlüſſelblume, Primel; bläßlich gelbgrüne Farbe. II. *attrib.*; —rose League, der Primelbund (konſervativer Klub). III. *adj.* blaßgelb.

Prim—e, *v.a.* mit Zündpulver verſehen (*guns*); grundieren, gründen (*Paint.*). **—er,** *s.* der Zünddraht, die Zündnadel; der (die) Grundierende, Vorbereitende. **—ing,** *s.* die Grundierung (*Paint.*); die Gründung (*Gild.*); die Zündung; (combustible) das Zündkraut; die Vorbereitung (*fig.*); (—ing composition) der Zündſatz, das Sprudeln, Spuken (*Locom.*); das Leitfeuer (*of mines*). **—ing-colour,** *s.* die Grundierfarbe. **—ing-horn,** *s.* das Pulverhorn. **—ing-needle,** *s.* der Zünddraht. **—ing-powder,** *s.* das Zündpulver.

Prince, *s.* der (regierende) Fürſt; der Fürſt (*as a title*); der Prinz, Königsſohn, Herrſcherſohn; — of the blood, Prinz von Geblüt; the youngest —, der jüngſte Prinz; — Bismark, Fürſt Bismarck; Frederick was a great —, Friedrich war ein großer Fürſt *or* Herrſcher; the Black —, der ſchwarze Prinz; — consort, der Prinz⸗Gemahl; — Eugene of Savoy, Prinz Eugen von Savoyen; the merchant —, der reiche und einflußreiche Kaufherr; the poet —, der fürſtliche Dichter; our sailor —, unſer Flottenprinz; the — of darkness, der Höllenfürſt; the — of Peace, der Friedefürſt. **—liness,** *s.* das Fürſtliche, fürſtliche Weſen. **—ly,** *adj.* fürſtlich; prinzlich. **—ss,** *s.* die (regierende) Fürſtin; die Fürſtin (*title*); die Prinzeſſin, Königstochter; —ss Charlotte, Prinzeſſin Charlotte; —ss Reuss, Fürſtin Reuß. *Comp.* **—like,** *adj.* fürſtlich. **—-regent,** *s.* der Prinz⸗Regent.

Princip—al, I. *adj.*, **—ally,** *adv.* vorzüglich, hauptſächlich, Haupt⸗; Grund⸗, General⸗ (*Mus.*); —al arguments, Hauptbeweiſe; —al business, das Hauptgeſchäft (*C. L.*); —al creditor, der Hauptgläubiger; —al librarian, der Oberbibliothekar; —al subject, der Hauptgegenſtand; —al towns, die bedeutendſten Städte, Hauptorte. II. *s.* die Hauptperſon; (governor) der Vorſteher, Direktor; der Prinzipal, Chef, Handelsherr (*of a business*); Lady —al, die Vorſteherin; das Kapital, die Hauptſumme (*C. L.*); (*opp. to* Agent) der Prinzipal; das Prinzipale (*Org.*); (*opp. to* Second) der Duellant; —al and interest, Kapital und Zinſen. **—ality,** *s.* das Fürſtentum. **—le,** *s.* der Urſtoff; der (Grund) Beſtandteil (*Chem.*); (cause) die (Grund⸗)Urſache; (motive) der Beweggrund; (tenet) der Grundſatz, Grundgedanke, die Grundregel; a man of —le, *see* high-—led; on —le, aus Grundſatz, grundſätzlich. **—led,** *adj.*; a high-—led man, ein Mann von (edeln) Grundſätzen.

Print, I. *v.a.* drucken; (imprint) aufdrucken; (stamp) einprägen; to have —ed, in Druck geben. II. *n.* drucken; (publish) drucken laſſen, herausgeben. III. *s.* der Druck, Abdruck; der Abdruck (*Phot.*); (trace) die Spur, das Zeichen; der Stich, Schnitt (*Engr.*); der Schnitt, die Strieme, das Mal (*of the teeth, nails, etc.*); (form) das Modell, die Form, Stempel; (—ing, letters, what is —ed) der Druck (*Typ.*); (cotton) das Druckzeug; butter —, Buttermodel; — of butter, Stück geformter Butter; coloured —, farbiger Stich; in —, gedruckt; out of —, (beim Verleger) vergriffen, im Buchhandel nicht mehr zu haben *or* erhältlich; to appear in —, herausgegeben werden. IV. *attrib.*; —dress, das Kattunkleid. **—ed,** *adj.*; —ed goods, Druckzeuge; —ed matter, papers, die Druckſache. **—er,** *s.* der (Buch⸗, Kupfer⸗, Stein⸗, Kattun⸗) Drucker; the —er's devil, der Setzerjunge, der Laufburſche aus der Druckerei. **—ing,** *s.* das Drucken, die Druckerei, der Druck; block —ing, Handdruck. **—s,** *pl.* auf der Rückſeite bedruckte Wollenſtoffe, bedruckte Kalikos. *Comp.* **—ing-block,** *s.* die Druckform. **—ing-house,** **—ing-office,** *s.* die Buchdruckerei, (lithographic) Steindruckerei. **—ing-ink,** *s.* die Druckerſchwärze. **—ing-press,** *s.* die Druckerpreſſe; die Druckerei. **—ing-telegraph,** *s.* der Drucktelegraph. **—ing-types,** *pl.* die Lettern. **—-seller,** *s.* der Kunſthändler. **—-shop,** *s.* die Kunſthandlung.

Prior, I. *adj.* früher; — claim, das Vorgangsrecht, das nähere Anrecht (to, auf, *acc.*). II. *adv.*; — to, vor (*dat.*). III. *s.* der Prior. **—ess,** *s.* die Priorin. **—i,** *adv.*; a —i, von vornherein, aus Vernunftgründen. **—ity,** *s.* die Priorität; precedence) der Vorrang; das Vorgangsrecht (to, vor); —ity of birth, die Erſtgeburt. **—y,** *s.* die Priorei.

Prism, *s.* das Prisma. **—atic,** *adj.* prismatiſch. **—oid,** *s.* das Prismoid.

Prison, I. *s.* das Gefängnis; der Kerker (*high style*); to put *or* cast into —, ins Gefängnis werfen, feſtſetzen. II. *v.a. see* Imprison. **—er,**

s. der, die Gefangene; to take —er, gefangen nehmen; she was made —er, sie wurde zur Gefangenen gemacht *or* gefangen genommen; in the —ers' dock, vor den Schranken (des Gerichts). *Comp.* **—er's-base**, *s.* der Barlauf, das Barlaufen. **—-house**, *see* Prison.

Pristine, *adj.* ursprünglich, vormalig.

Prithee, *abbr.* ich bitte (dich)! bitte! (*obs.*).

Priv—acy, *s.* die Heimlichkeit; (seclusion) die Zurückgezogenheit. **—ate**, I. *adj.*, **—ately**, *adv.* heimlich, geheim, verborgen; (personal) Privat= (*as debts, concerns, correspondence, expenses, interest, purse, room, tutor, etc.*), privat, eigen, persönlich; (not in office) amtlos, Privat=; (non-official) nicht öffentlich, nicht amtlich, außeramtlich, Privat=; —ate and confidential, vertraulich, in strengstem Vertrauen; —ate account, das Geheimkonto; —ate adventure school, die Privatschule; —ate chapel, die Hauskapelle; to sell by —ate contract, unter der Hand verkaufen; —ate ends, Privatzwecke; —ate gentleman, der Privatmann; —ate information, vertrauliche Mitteilung; —ate means, eigenes Geld, das Privatvermögen; —ate property, das Privat=Vermögen; —ate road, ruhige Straße, keine Verkehrsstraße; —ate staircase, die geheime Treppe; —ate tutor, der Privatlehrer (Hauslehrer); —ate way, der Privatweg; to keep —, geheim halten. II. *s.* (—ate soldier) der Gemeine; in —ate, insgeheim, unter vier Augen. **—ateer**, *s.* der Kaper; (ship) das Kaperschiff. **—ateering**, *s.* die Kaperei. **—ateness**, *s.* die Heimlichkeit. **—ates**, *pl.* die Geschlechtsteile. **—ation**, *s.* die Entziehung; (destitution) die Entbehrung, Not; (want, absence) der Mangel. **—ative**, I. *adj.* beraubend, ausschließend, privativ; (negative) verneinend, negativ. II. *s.* die Verneinungs=partikel (*Gram.*). **—ilege**, I. *s.* das Vorrecht, Privilegium, die Gerechtsame. II. *v.a.* einem ein Vorrecht *or* Vorrechte einräumen, einen bevorrechten, privilegieren. **—ily**, *adv.* heimlich. **—ity**, *s.* das Mitwissen; with his —ity and consent, mit seinem Wissen und Willen. **—y**, I. *adj.* geheim, heimlich; mitwissend; mitschuldig; to be —y to, mit um (eine Sache) wissen; —y Chamber, das geheime Kabinett (des Königs); —y Council, der Staatsrat; —y Councillor, der geheime Rat, Geheimrat, Staatsrat; —y parts, Schamteile, Geschlechtsteile; —y purse, die Privatkasse; —y seal, das Geheimsiegel; Lord —y Seal, der Geheimsiegelbewahrer. II. *s.* der Mitinteressent (*Law*); der Abtritt.

Privet, *s.* die Rainweide, der Liguster.

[1]**Prize**, *s.* der Preis; die Prämie; die Beute, Prise (*at sea*); der (Lotterie) Gewinn; to carry off the —, to take the —, den Preis davontragen, mit dem Preise gekrönt werden; the —s of a profession, die besten in einem Beruf erreichbaren Stellen. *Comp.* **—-court**, *s.* das Prisengericht. **—-essay**, *s.* die Preisaufgabe. **—-fighter**, *s.* der Preiskämpfer. **—-fighting**, *s.* der Wettkampf um einen Preis. **—-list**, *s.* das Verzeichnis der gewonnenen Preise. **—-man**, *s.* ein Preisgekrönter. **—-money**, *s.* die Prisengelder. **—-subject**, *s.* die Preisaufgabe.

[2]**Prize**, *v.a.* (hoch) schätzen, würdigen.

[3]**Prize**, *v.a.* (— open) mit einem Hebel heben.

Pro = für; the —s and cons, das (*or* die Gründe) Für und Wider. *Comp.* **—-Boer**, I. *s.* der Burenfreund. II. *adj.* burenfreundlich. **—-forma**, *adj.* der Form wegen, um der Form zu genügen. **—-proctor**, *s.* der Vizeproktor. **—-rata**, *adj. & adv.* pro rata, nach Verhältnis.

Proa, *s.* das malaiische Segelkanoe.

Probab—ilism, *s.* die Wahrscheinlichkeitslehre, der Probabilismus. **—ilist**, *s.* der Anhänger der Wahrscheinlichkeitslehre, der Probabilist. **—ility**, *s.* die Wahrscheinlichkeit. **—le**, *adj.*, **—ly**, *adv.* wahrscheinlich, mutmaßlich.

Probat—e, I. *s.* die Bestätigung (*of a will*); der Bestätigungsschein. II. *attrib.*; —e Court, das Erbbestätigungsgericht; —e duty, die Erbschaftssteuer. **—ion**, *s.* die Probe, Prüfung; die Probezeit, das Noviziar; year of —ion, das Probejahr. **—ionary**, *adj.* zur Probe, Prüfung dienend, Probe=. **—ioner**, *s.* der Novize; (candidate) der Kandidat; der Predigtamtskandidat (*Scotch*).

Probe, I. *s.* die Probe; die Sonde (*Surg.*). II. *v.a.* sondieren (*also fig.*); gründlich untersuchen (*fig.*). *Comp.* **—e-scissors**, *pl.* die Wundschere.

Probity, *s.* die Rechtschaffenheit, Biederkeit.

Problem, *s.* die Aufgabe, das Problem. **—atic(al)**, *adj.* fraglich, ungewiß, zweifelhaft, dunkel.

Probosci—date, *adj.* mit einem Rüssel (versehen). **—deans**, *pl.* Rüsseltiere. **—s**, *s.* der Rüssel.

Procedure, *s.* das Verfahren; (mode of —) die Handlungsweise, die Art des Verfahrens; judicial —, gerichtliches Verfahren.

Proceed, *v.n.* vorwärts gehen, fort=schreiten, =rücken, schreiten (to, zu); sich begeben; fort=fahren, =reisen; to — with a journey, eine Reise fortsetzen; ausgehen (from, von); (arise) herkommen, hervorgehen, herrühren (from, von); (go on) von statten gehen; fortführen (*a narrative, etc.*); (act) handeln, verfahren; he was about to — to his country seat, er war im Begriff sich auf seinen Landsitz zu begeben; the vessel —ed on her voyage, das Schiff segelte weiter; they now — to ballot for a jury, man schreitet jetzt zur Auslosung der Geschworenen; to — upon a principle, einen Grundsatz befolgen; to — against s.o., gerichtlich gegen einen einschreiten; to — to the attack, zum Angriff schreiten; to — to business, ans Werk gehen. **—ing**, *s.* das Fortschreiten; das Verfahren, die Handlung. **—ings**, *pl.* gerichtliches Verfahren, der Rechtsgang (*Law*), die Verhandlungen, Sitzungsberichte (*of a society, etc.*); (record of —ings) protokollierte Verhandlungen. **—s**, *pl.* der Ertrag, Erlös, Gewinn; net —s of the sale, der Reinertrag aus dem Verkauf.

Process, I. *s.* das Fortschreiten; (course, proceeding) das Verfahren, die Methode; der Verlauf (*of time*); der Prozeß (*Chem., Law*); der Knochenfortsatz (*Anat.*); negative —, negatives Verfahren (*Photo.*); — of decomposition, der Verwesungsprozeß; in — of time, mit der Zeit. II. *v.a.* gerichtlich verfolgen. **—ion**, *s.* der feierliche Zug, die Prozession; die Betfahrt; das Ausgehen (*of the Holy Ghost*). **—ional**, I. *adj.* Prozessions=. II. *s.* das Prozessionsbuch; das Prozessionslied. *Comp.* **—-server**, der Gerichtsvollzieher.

Proclaim, *v.a.* öffentlich ausrufen, bekannt machen, verkünden; (manifest) kundgeben; in die Acht erklären (*a district, etc.*); the dress —s the man, Kleider machen Leute (*prov.*). **—er**, *s.* der Herold, öffentliche Ausrufer.

Proclamation, *s.* die Proklamation (*of a king, etc.*); feierliche Verkündigung, Bekanntmachung; royal —, königliche Erklärung, Verordnung; — of war, die Kriegserklärung; to issue a —, eine öffentliche Bekanntmachung erlassen.

Proclitic, I. *adj.* vorn (an ein andres Wort) angelehnt, proklitisch. II. *s.* proklitisches Wort.

Proclivity, *s.* die Neigung, Geneigtheit, der Hang (to, zu); (facility) die Anlage, Leichtigkeit zum Lernen.

Proconsul, *s.* der Prokonsul. **—ar**, *adj.* prokonsularisch. **—ate**, *s.* das Prokonsulat.

Procrastinat—e, *v.* I. *a.* aufschieben. II. *v.n.* zögern. **—ion**, *s.* der Aufschub, das Verschieben, die Verzögerung; das unentschlossene Wesen. **—or**, *s.* der Aufschieber, Zögerer.

Procreat—e, *v.a.* (er)zeugen. **—ion**, *s.* die Zeugung. **—ive**, *adj.* zeugungsfähig, zeugend. **—iveness**, *s.* die Zeugungskraft.

Proc—tor, *s.* der Geschäftsführer; der Sachwalter, Anwalt (*Law*); der Proktor, Disziplinarbeamte (*Univ.*); —tor's man, der Pedell. **—torise**, *v.a.*; to be —torised, in Ordnungs=

strafe genommen werden (*Univ. sl.*). **—torship,** *s.* das Proktoramt. **—urable,** *adj.* zu verschaffen, erlangbar. **—uration,** *s.* die Besorgung, Verwaltung (of another's business, einer Sache für andere); (written —uration) die Prokura, Vollmacht; die Kuppelei; by —uration, per Prokura (*C.L.*). **—urations,** *pl.* das Visitationsgeld (*Eccl.*). **—urator,** *s.* der Verwalter, Bevollmächtigte; (representer) der Stellvertreter. **—ure,** *v.* I. *a.* ver=, an=schaffen, besorgen; (get) erlangen, erwerben, ermitteln; herbeiführen, bewirken (*advantages, etc.*); to —ure the necessary capital, das erforderliche Kapital beschaffen; to —cure a prompt sale, einen raschen Verkauf bewirken. II. *n.* kuppeln. **—urement,** *s.* die Verschaffung, die Vermittelung. **—urer,** *s.* der Verschaffende; (go-between) der Vermittler; der Kuppler. **—uress,** *s.* die Kupplerin.

Prod, I. *s.* der Stachelstock; die Ahle. II. *v.a.* stechen, (kleine Löcher) bohren.

Prodigal, I. *adj.*, **—ly,** *adv.* verschwenderisch; —son, *see* —II. II. *s.*; —son, der verlorene Sohn (*B.*); der Taugenichts (*fig.*). **—ity,** *s.* die Verschwendung, Üppigkeit.

Prodig—ious, *adj.* ungeheuer, erstaunlich, außerordentlich groß. **—iously,** *adv.* sehr, ungeheuer. **—y,** *s.* das Wunder; (monster) das Ungeheuer.

Produce, I. *v.a.* vor=, ein=führen; beibringen (*witnesses, etc.*), anführen, vorbringen (*reasons, etc.*); (show) aufweisen, darstellen; (cause) verursachen, bewirken; erzeugen, hervorbringen (*Agr.*); eintragen, einbringen (*interest, etc.*); verlängern, ausdehnen (*Geom.*); hervorbringen (*great men, etc.*); verfassen, schreiben (*poetry, books*); schaffen, verfertigen, hervorbringen (*manufactures, works of art, etc.*); the ticket must be —d on demand, das Billet muß auf Verlangen vorgezeigt werden; he has —d a fine novel, er hat einen prächtigen Roman geschrieben *or* verfaßt; he has —d several fine female characters, er hat einige herrliche Frauencharaktere geschaffen; a photograph —d by my brother, eine von meinem Bruder gemachte Photographie. II. *s.* das Erzeugnis, Produkt; der Ertrag; —of the country, Landesprodukte; net —, der Reinertrag. **—r,** *s.* der Hervorbringer, Verfertiger; (*opp. to* Consumer) der Produzent.

Producible, *adj.* erzeugbar; hervorbringbar; vorführbar, aufweisbar.

Product, *s.* das Erzeugnis, Produkt; das Produkt (*Arith.*); (—ion) das Werk; (result) das Ergebnis, die Frucht. **—ion,** *s.* das Hervorbringen, die Vorführung, Vorlegung, Beibringung; die Produktion (*Pol. Econ.*); das Erzeugnis, Produkt (*of Nature, the earth, etc.*); das Werk, die Schöpfung, Frucht (*of the mind, etc.*); die Verlängerung (*of a line*). **—ive,** *adj.* hervorbringend, schaffend; (fertile) fruchtbar; (creative) schöpferisch; produktiv (*Pol. Econ.*). **—iveness, —ivity,** *s.* die Fruchtbarkeit.

Proem, *s.* die Vorrede, Einleitung.

Profan—ation, *s.* die Entweihung. **—e,** I. *adj.*, **—ely,** *adv.* unheilig, profan; weltlich, profan (*as history*); (impious) gottlos, ruchlos; (irreverent) unehrerbietig; *see* Blasphemous. II. *v.a.* entweihen, entheiligen, herabwürdigen; entadeln (*poet.*). **—eness, —ity,** *s.* die Gott=, Ruch=losigkeit. **—er,** *s.* der Entweiher; der Schänder; *see* Blasphemer. **—ing,** *s.* die Entweihung, Schändung (*of the Sabbath*).

Profess, *v.a.* (acknowledge) (öffentlich) bekennen; sich bekennen zu (*a religion, etc.*); behaupten, (laut) erklären, versichern (*an opinion*); (aus)üben, treiben (*a profession*); to — friendship, freundschaftliche Gefühle vorgeben; he —es to come from India, er behauptet aus Indien zu kommen, seiner Aussage nach kommt er aus Indien. **—ed,** *adj.*, **—edly,** *adv.* von Profession; bekannt, erklärt, offen, abgesagt (*as an enemy*). **—ion,** *s.* das Bekenntnis; die Erklärung, Versicherung; der Profeß (*of a nun, etc.*); der Beruf, (gelehrte) Stand; by —ion, von Beruf; —ion of arms, der Beruf eines Soldaten, der Soldatenstand; —ion of friendship, die Freundschaftsversicherung. **—ional,** I. *adj.*, **—ionally,** *adv.* berufsmäßig, Berufs= (*duties, etc.*), Amts= (*dignity, etc.*), Standes= (*promotion, etc.*); Advokaten= (*Law*); ärztlich (*Med.*); in a —ional way, berufsmäßig, als Broterwerb; —ional attendance, ärztliche Behandlung (*Med.*); —ional men, Männer von Fach, Ärzte, Advokaten, etc.; —ional gambler *or* player, der Spieler von Profession; —ional school, die Fachschule; —ional skill, die Berufsgeschicklichkeit; of a —ional nature, fachlich. II. *s.* der Fachmann, Kundige; der Berufskünstler, Schauspieler *or* Musiker von Fach. **—or,** *s.* der (Glaubens=)Bekenner (*obs.*); der (Universitäts=)Professor; —or of English, Professor des Englischen; —or of music, der Musiklehrer; —or's chair, der Lehrstuhl, (das) Katheder (*lit. & fig.*); full —or, ordentlicher Professor, Professor ordinarius; assistant —or, außerordentlicher Professor (*Amer.*). **—orial,** *adj.* Professor=; —orial chair, *see* —or's chair. **—oriate,** *s.* der Lehrkörper, die Professorschaft, die Professoren. **—orship,** *s.* die Professur, das Lehramt, der Lehrauftrag; —orship of German, Professur für Deutsch; a full —orship, eine ordentliche Professur, ein Ordinariat.

Proffer, I. *v.a.* anbieten. II. *s.* das Anerbieten.

Proficien—cy, *s.* die Tüchtigkeit. **—t,** I. *adj.* tüchtig, bewandert; —t in music, tüchtiger Musiker. II. *s.* der Meister; to be a —t in, es weit gebracht haben, bewandert sein in (*dat.*).

Profile, *s.* das Profil, Halbgesicht; das Profil, der Durchschnitt (*Arch.*); in —, im Profil.

Profit, I. *s.* der Vorteil, Nutzen, Gewinn; der Gewinn, Profit (*C.L.*); to derive — from, Nutzen, Vorteil ziehen aus; to leave a —, Gewinn abwerfen (*C.L.*); account of — and loss, das Gewinn= und Verlust=Konto; clear —, der Reingewinn. II. *attrib.*; on the half-— system, mit Teilung des Gewinns zu gleichen Teilen; — assurance, die Versicherung mit Gewinnanteil. III. *v.n.*; to — by, gewinnen durch, benutzen, Vorteil ziehen aus, sich (*dat.*) zu Nutze machen; he —s nothing thereby, er spinnt keine Seide dabei (*coll.*). III. *v.a.* nützen (einem), Nutzen bringen; what have your teachings —ed me? was haben mir Ihre Lehren genützt? **—able,** *adj.*, **—ably,** *adv.* vorteilhaft, einträglich. **—ableness,** *s.* die Nützlichkeit, Einträglichkeit. **—less,** *adj.*, **—lessly,** *adv.* nutzlos.

Profliga—cy, *s.* die Verworfenheit, Ruchlosigkeit. **—te,** I. *adj.* verworfen, ruchlos, liederlich. II. *s.* der Bösewicht, liederliche Gesell.

Profound, *adj.*, **—ly,** *adv.* tief (*also fig.*); (not superficial) tiefgründig; (—ly learned) grundgelehrt, gründlich; (weighty) inhaltschwer; —ignorance, krasse Unwissenheit; — reverence, tiefe Verbeugung, Ehrfurcht. **—ness,** *see* Profundity.

Profus—e, *adj.*, **—ely,** *adv.* überflüssig, allzu reichlich; (lavish) verschwenderisch, (allzu) freigebig; —ely illustrated, reich illustriert, mit zahlreichen Abbildungen; to be —e in apologies, sich wortreich entschuldigen. **—eness,** *see* —ion; die verschwenderische Freigebigkeit. **—ion,** *s.* der Überfluß, die Überfülle; in —ion, überreich(lich), im Überflusse.

Prog, I. *s.* (erbettelte) Lebensmittel; *see* Tramp. II. *v.n.* betteln; (steal) mausen (*sl.*). III. *v.a.* *see* Proctorise (*Univ. sl.*).

Progen—itor, *s.* der Vorfahr, Ahn. **—iture,** *s.* das Zeugen; (birth) die Geburt. **—y,** *s.* die Nachkommenschaft, Abkömmlinge; (young) die Brut (*of beasts*), Kinder (*of human beings*).

Prognostic, I. *adj.* vorbedeutend, vorher anzeigend. II. *s.* das Anzeichen, die Vorbedeutung; die ärztliche Voraussage, Prognose (*Med.*). **—ate,** *v.* I. *a.* vorandeuten; (predict) vorhersagen. II. *n.* weissagen. **—ation,** *s.* die Vorhersagung;

das Vorzeichen, die Vorandeutung. **—ator**, *s.* der Wahrsager, Verkündiger.

Programme, *s.* die Ordnung, Festordnung, das Programm; der Theaterzettel, Konzertplan; — of study (work), der Lehrplan; — of the government, die leitenden Grundsätze der Regierung.

Progress, I. *s.* das Vorschreiten, Vorrücken, der Lauf, Gang; (advancement) der Fortschritt; die festliche Rundreise, Prunkreise (*of a prince, etc.*); das Vordringen (*of an army*); to make —, fortschreiten, Fortschritte machen (in); in —, im Werden; Pilgrim's —, die Pilgerfahrt. II. *v.n.* fortschreiten, weiterrücken; fortschreiten (*fig.*), *see* To make —. **—ion**, *s.* das Fortschreiten (*also Mus.*), (Vor-)Gehen; die Progression (*Math.*); harmonical —ion, harmonische Reihe (*Math.*). **—ionist**, *s.* der Fortschrittler. **—ive**, *adj.*, vor-rückend, -schreitend; fortschreitend (*fig.*); (increasing) nach und nach zunehmend; fortschrittlich, freisinnig (*Pol.*); —ive assimilation, vorwärtswirkende Angleichung (*Gram.*). — **ively**, *adv.* stufenweise, nach und nach.

Prohibit, *v.a.* verbieten; (hinder) verhindern; smoking strictly —ed, das Rauchen ist streng verboten. **—ion**, *s.* das Verbot; writ of —ion, das Prohibitorium. **—ionist**, *s.* der Schutzzöllner; der Verfechter des Verbots alkoholischer Getränke (*Amer.*). **—ive**, **—ory**, *adj.* verbietend, prohibitiv; —ory duty, der Schutzzoll.

Project, I. *v.a.* (vorwärts) werfen, schleudern; entwerfen (*Draw.*); projizieren (*Geom.*); entwerfen, ersinnen (*a plan*). II. *v.n.* vorragen, hervorstehen, ausladen (*Arch.*). III. *s.* der Entwurf, Plan, Anschlag, das Projekt; (idle —) leeres, eitles Projekt. **—ile**, I. *adj.* vorwärts treibend; (impelled) geworfen, gestoßen; —ile force, die Wurfkraft; —ile motion, die Wurf-, Stoß-bewegung. II. *s.* fortgeschleuderter Körper; das Projektil, (Wurf-)Geschoß (*Artil.*); theory of —iles, die Geschoßlehre. **—ion**, *s.* das Werfen, Schleudern, Schießen; der Wurf, Stoß; das Vorspringen, Ausladen (*Arch.*); (—ed part) der Vorsprung, Überhang; die Projektion (*Geom.*, *Astr.*, *Draw.*); der Entwurf; plane of —ion, die Projektionsebene. **—or**, *s.* der Planmacher, Pläneschmied.

Prolaps—e, I. *v.a.* vorfallen. II. *s.*, **—us**, *s.* der Vorfall.

Prolegomen—on, *s.* (*pl.* —a) das Vorwort.

Prolep—sis, *s.* das Zuvorkommen; Vorausbeantwortung möglicher Einwürfe (*Rhet.*); das Vorgreifen in der Zeitrechnung (*Chron.*); die Prolepsis (*Gram.*). **—tic**, *adj.* proleptisch; vorläufig; vorrückend (*Med.*).

Proletaria—n, I. *adj.* Proletarier-, besitzlos, unbemittelt. II. *s.* der Besitzlose, Proletarier. **—t**, *s.* die besitzlose Bevölkerung, das Proletariat.

Prolific, *adj.* fruchtbar (*also fig.*); (fertilizing) befruchtend; — of evil consequences, böse Folgen hervorbringend, unheilschwanger.

Prolix, *adj.* weitläufig, weitschweifig. **—ity**, *s.* die Weitläufigkeit, Weitschweifigkeit.

Prolocutor, *s.* der Wortführer, Sprecher, Vorsitzer (der geistlichen Synode).

Prologue, *s.* der Vorspruch, Prolog; die Einleitung, das Vorwort.

Prolong, *v.a.* verlängern, länger machen; länger dauern lassen, in die Länge ziehen, hinziehen; hinausschieben; prolongieren (*the payment of a bill*). **—ation**, *s.* die Verlängerung; der Aufschub.

Promenade, I. *s.* der Spaziergang; (place of —) der Spazierplatz, Spazierweg, die Anlagen. II. *v.n.* spazieren, auf und ab gehen.

Prominen—ce, *s.* das Hervorragen (*also fig.*); hervorragender Teil, Vorsprung. **—t**, *adj.*, **—tly**, *adv.* hervor-ragend (*also fig.*), -stechend; ausgezeichnet (*fig.*); —t eyes, Glotzaugen.

Promiscuous, *adj.*, **—ly**, *adv.* gemischt, vermengt, nicht gesondert, durch einander; (common) mehreren gemein, gemeinschaftlich; ununterschieden, ohne Unterschied; men of all classes —ly assembled, ein buntes Gemisch von Männern aus allen Ständen. **—ness**, *s.* die unterschiedslose Vermischung, Gemischtheit.

Promis—e, I. *s.* das Versprechen, Wort, die Zusage; (what is —ed) die Verheißung, das Versprochene; land of —e, das gelobte Land; a harvest of great —e, —ing harvest, eine vielversprechende Ernte; a youth of great —e, ein vielversprechender *or* hoffnungsvoller Jüngling. II. *v.a. & n.* versprechen, geloben, verheißen; Hoffnungen erwecken, versprechen, hoffen lassen; (threaten) drohen; (assure) versichern (*coll.*); the wheat —es to be a good crop, der Weizen läßt sich gut an. III. *v.r.* sich (*dat.*) versprechen hoffen. **—er**, *s.* der Versprecher. **—ing**, *adj.*, **—ingly**, *adv.* vielversprechend, Hoffnung erweckend; —ing youth, vielversprechender Jüngling, ein junger Mann, der zu den schönsten Hoffnungen berechtigt; to be in a —ing state, einen guten Ausgang hoffen lassen (*as a business*); auf dem Wege der Besserung sein (*as a patient*). **—sory**, *adj.* versprechend; —sory note, der Hand-schein, -wechsel.

Promontory, *s.* das Vorgebirge, die Klippe.

Promot—e, *v.a.* befördern, begünstigen; befördern, erheben (*in rank, etc.*); gründen (*a company, etc.*). **—er**, *s.* der Beförderer; der Anstifter (*of a plot, etc.*); der Gründer (*of a company*). **—ion**, *s.* die Förderung; die Beförderung, Standeserhöhung. **—ive**, *adj.* befördernd.

Prompt, I. *adj.*, **—ly**, *adv.* schnell, rasch; (ready) gleich zur Hand *or* bereit, schnell fertig; (immediate) unverzüglich; (willing) geneigt, willfährig; pünktlich. II. *v.a.* zuflüstern, soufflieren; (dictate) eingeben; (urge) anreizen, erregen; antreiben (to, zu); to be —ed by, angetrieben werden durch, bewogen von. **—er**, *s.* der Eingeber; der Souffleur (*Theat.*); der Anreizer. **—itude**, **—ness**, *s.* die Schnelligkeit, Geschwindheit; die Unverzüglichkeit; die Pünktlichkeit, Promptheit; (willingness) die Bereitwilligkeit.

Promulgat—e, *v.a.* (öffentlich) bekannt machen, verkündigen, verbreiten. **—ion**, *s.* die öffentliche Bekanntmachung *or* Bekanntgebung.

Pron—ator, *s.* der Vorbeuger der Hand (*Anat.*). **—e**, *adj.* vorwärts geneigt; (lying —e) hingestreckt, mit dem Gesichte auf der Erde liegend; —e to, geneigt zu; —e to anger, jähzornig. **—eness**, *s.* das Liegen mit dem Gesichte auf der Erde; die Neigung, Geneigtheit, der Hang (zu einer S.).

Prong, *s.* spitziges Werkzeug; (tine) die Zinke, Zacke. **—ed**, *adj.* mit Zacken versehen, zackig, gezackt. *Comp.* **—-hoe**, *s.* die Hacke mit Zinken.

Pronominal, *adj.*, **—ly**, *adv.*, pronominal.

Pronoun, *s.* das Fürwort, Pronomen.

Pronounc—e, *v.* I. *a.* aussprechen; aussprechen, verkünden (*sentence of death, etc.*); halten, vortragen (*a speech*); erklären für; he —ed the book to be a libel, er erklärte das Buch für eine Schmähschrift. II. *n.* aussprechen; seine Meinung sagen, sich aussprechen. **—ed**, *adj.* ausgesprochen; entschieden, hervortretend (*Paint., etc.*); bestimmt (*fig.*). **—eable**, *adj.* aussprechbar, auszusprechen. **—ing**, I. *adj.* die Aussprache lehrend, Aussprache- (*as a dictionary*). II. *s. see* Pronunciation; das Aussprechen.

Pronunciation, *s.* die Aussprache; speaking —, die Sprechsprache, Gehörsprache; spelling —, die Schreibsprache, Buchsprache.

Proof, I. *s.* die Probe, der Versuch; (trial) die Prüfung; (evidence) der Beweis; die Probe (*of spirit, etc.*); der (Probe-)Abzug (*Phot., etc.*); der Korrekturbogen (*Typ.*); die Festigkeit, Stärke (*fig.*); — before letter, der Abzug vor der Schrift; artist's —s, erste Abzüge von Kupferstichen; clean —, Revision(-sbogen); under —, schwächer als die Normalstärke von 0,920; to put to the —, auf die Probe stellen; in — of, zum Beweise von. II. *adj.* undurchdringlich; — against, probehaltig, stichhaltig; fest, gefeit (gegen); (steady) standhaft; — against entreaty, unerbittlich; — against bribes, unbestechlich; — against bullets, kugelfest; bomb, fire —, bomben-, feuer-fest; my boots are water—, meine Stiefel sind wasserdicht. *Comp.* **—-reader**, *s.* der Korrektor. **—-sheet**, *s.* der Korrektur-, Aushängebogen. **—-spirit**, *s.* der Normalweingeist.

Prop, I. *s.* die Stütze (*also fig.*), der Pfahl; vine —, Weinpfahl. II. *v.a.* (— up) (unter)stützen; pfählen (*vines, etc.*).

Propaga—nda, *s.* die Bekehrungsgesellschaft; Bekehrungsanstalt(en); die Propaganda; to make —nda for a th., für die Ausbreitung von . . . Anhänger werben, für eine S. kräftig auftreten, Propaganda machen für eine S. **—ndist**, *s.* das Mitglied des Bekehrungsvereins; der Wühler (für), Propagandist. **—te**, *v.a.* weiter fortpflanzen (*also fig.*); erzeugen; (diffuse) verbreiten, ausbreiten, vermehren; to —te vines, junge Reben einlegen. **—tion**, *s.* die Fortpflanzung (*also fig.*); die Verbreitung. **—tor**, *s.* der Fortpflanzer; der Verbreiter.

Propel, *v.a.* vorwärts-, fort-treiben, fortstoßen; umtreiben (*a wheel*). **—ler**, *s.* der Fortstoßer, Treiber; screw —ler, die Schiffsschraube; der Schraubendampfer. *Comp.* **—ler-blade**, *s.* die Schrauben-schaufel (für Dampfer).

Propensity, *s.* die Neigung, der Hang (zu); with a — to, geneigt zu.

Proper, *adj.*, **—ly**, *adv.* eigentümlich (real) eigentlich; (natural) natürlich; (suitable) passend, schicklich, anständig, tauglich, geeignet (to, for, zu, für); (correct) richtig, genau; (good-looking) ansehnlich, hübsch, nett; — name *or* noun, Eigenname; to think —, für gut halten; do as you think —, handeln Sie, wie Sie es für gut finden; it is — for him, es ziemt sich für ihn; — fraction, eigentlicher Bruch (*Math.*); —ly speaking, im eigentlichen Sinne; the garden —, der eigentliche Garten. **—tied**, *adj.* besitzend. **—ties**, *pl.* Requisiten (*Theat.*) **—ty**, *s.* das Eigentum, Besitztum; (landed —ty) das Gut, die Ländereien; (quality) die Eigentümlichkeit, Eigenschaft; das Eigentumsrecht (*Law*); personal —ty, bewegliche Habe; literary —ty, literarisches Eigentumsrecht. *Comp.* **—ty-man**, *s.* der Requisitenmeister. **—ty-qualification**, *s.* die Wahlbefähigung. **—ty-tax**, *s.* die Vermögenssteuer, Steuer auf Vermögen.

Prophe—cy, *s.* die Prophezeiung. **—sy**, *v.a.* & *n.* prophezeien, weissagen. **—t**, *s.* der Weissager, Prophet; no man is a —t in his own country, ein Prophet gilt nichts in seinem Vaterlande. **—tess**, *s.* die Prophetin. **—tic**, *adj.*, **—tically**, *adv.* vorahnend, prophetisch.

Prophylactic, I. *adj.* vorbeugend, prophylaktisch. II. *s.* das Vorbeugungsmittel.

Propinquity, *s.* die Nähe (*in place, time*); die nahe Verwandtschaft.

Propiti—ate, *v.a.* günstig stimmen, geneigt machen; besänftigen; versöhnen. **—ation**, *s.* die Besänftigung, Versöhnung; (—atory sacrifice) das Sühnopfer. **—ator**, *s.* der Versöhner. **—atory**, *adj.* versöhnend; *see* —ation. **—ous**, *adj.*, **—ously**, *adv.* günstig; (favourably disposed) geneigt. **—ousness**, *s.* die günstige Beschaffenheit (*of the season, etc.*).

Proportion, I. *s.* das Verhältnis, Maß; (symmetry) das Eben-, Gleich-maß; (share) der Anteil; die Proportion (*Arith., Math., Chem.*); der Tonverhalt, das Tonverhältnis (*Mus.*); continual —, stetiges Verhältnis; inverse —, umgekehrtes Verhältnis; in due (out of) —, (un)verhältnismäßig; rule of —, Regel de tri. II. *v.a.* abmessen, in Verhältnis bringen (to, mit). **—able**, *adj.*, **—ably**, *adv.* (—able to, —ably to) im Verhältnisse, entsprechend (*dat.*). **—al**, I. *adj.*, **—ally**, *adv.* verhältnismäßig, Verhältnis-; —al numbers, Proportionalzahlen. II. *s.* die (mean, mittlere) Proportionale. **—ate**, *adj.*, **—ately**, *adv.* angemessen, entsprechend, im Verhältnis.

Propos—al, *s.* der Vorschlag, Antrag; (—al of marriage) Heiratsantrag. **—e**, *v.* I. *a.* vorschlagen, antragen auf (*acc.*); (offer) antragen; ausbringen (*a toast*); to —e s.th. to o.s., etwas beabsichtigen, sich (*dat.*) eine S. vornehmen. II. *n.* beabsichtigen; anhalten (to, for, um), einen Heiratsantrag machen; to —e to a girl, einem Mädchen einen Antrag machen, um ein Mädchen anhalten; man —es, God disposes, der Mensch denkt, Gott lenkt (*prov.*). **—er**, *s.* der Antragsteller, Vorschlagende. **—ition**, *s.* der Antrag, Vorschlag; der Satz, die Behauptung (*Log.*); die Aufgabe, der Satz (*Math.*); das Thema. **—itional**, *adj.* als Satz, Satz-.

Propound, *v.a.* vortragen; vorlegen, vorstellen (*a question*). **—er**, *s.* der Vortragende.

Propriet—ary, I. *adj.* einem Eigentümer gehörig; Eigentums-; —ary school, die Korporationsschule, von einer (Aktien-)Gesellschaft gegründete (höhere) Schule. II. *s.* der Eigentümer, Besitzer; der Eigentumsherr (*Eccl.*). **—or**, *s.* der Eigentümer, Besitzer, Inhaber. **—orship**, *s.* das Eigentumsrecht. **—ress**, *s.* die Eigentümerin. **—y**, *s.* die Schicklichkeit; die Richtigkeit, Angemessenheit (*of language*); —y of conduct, anständiges Betragen; all agreed as to the —y of . . ., alle stimmten darin überein, daß es schicklich sei . . .; I played —y, ich blieb um das Dekorum zu wahren da; the —ies, das, was sich schickt.

Prorog—ation, *s.* die Vertagung, Prorogation (*of Parliament, etc.*). **—ue**, *v.a.* vertagen.

Pros—aic, *adj.*, **—aically**, *adv.* prosaisch; alltäglich, gemein (*fig.*). **—e**, I. *s.* die Prosa; die Hinübersetzung; I have to do a German —e, ich muß eine Übersetzung ins Deutsche machen (*school sl.*). II. *adj.* prosaisch (*as a translation, etc.*); Prosa-; —e writer, der Prosaiker, Prosaschriftsteller. III. *v.n.* langweilig schreiben *or* erzählen. **—er**, *s.* langweiliger Erzähler. **—ing**, *s.* langweilige Erzählung. **—y**, *adj.* langweilig, ledern (*fig.*).

Proscenium, *s.* das Proszenium.

Proscri—be, *v.a.* ächten; (banish) verbannen; *see* Interdict. **—ption**, *s.* die Acht, Achtserklärung; die Ausschließung, Verbannung (*also fig.*).

Prosecut—e, *v.a.* verfolgen, fortsetzen (*a subject, studies, etc.*); gerichtlich verfolgen *or* belangen (*Law*). **—ion**, *s.* die Verfolgung, Fortsetzung; die gerichtliche Verfolgung. **—or**, *s.* der Verfolger; der Kläger (*Law*); public —or, der Staatsanwalt. **—rix**, *s.* die Klägerin.

Proselyt—e, *s.* der Übergetretene, Proselyt. **—ism**, *s.* der Bekehrungseifer. **—ize**, *v.a.* Anhänger werben, Proselyten machen (für eine S.). **—izer**, *s.* der Proselytenmacher.

Prosody, *s.* die Silbenmessung(slehre), Prosodie.

Prospect, I. *s.* die Aussicht (*also fig.*); (scenery) der Anblick, die Landschaft; (expectation) die Anwartschaft; der Schurf (*Min.*); there is a — of its succeeding, es ist Aussicht auf Gelingen der Sache vorhanden; pleasures in —, Freuden in Aussicht; to have in —, im Auge haben; to hold out a —, in Aussicht stellen. II. *v.n.* Umschau halten; schürfen (*Min.*). **—ive**, *adj.* vorsichtig; (in —) zu gewärtigen; (*opp. to* Retrospective) in Beziehung auf die Zukunft. **—us**, *s.* die Ankündigung eines litterarischen oder erziehlichen Unternehmens, der Prospekt, das Programm.

Prosper, *v.* I. *a.* beglücken, gedeihen lassen; O Lord, — them, O Herr, verleihe ihnen Glück, segne sie. II. *n.* gedeihen, fortkommen; gelingen, glücken (*as an undertaking*); things — with him, alles glückt ihm. **—ity**, *s.* das Gedeihen; die Wohlfahrt, der Wohlstand (*of a nation, etc.*). **—ous**, *adj.*, **—ously**, *adv.* gedeihlich, glücklich.

Prostate, *adj.*; — gland, die Vorsteherdrüse.

Prostitut—e, I. *v.a.* feil bieten *or* geben; zur Schändung ausbieten; (use unworthily) herabwürdigen, hergeben (to, zu), mißbrauchen, entehren (*talents, etc.*). II. *s.* feile Dirne, Hure; (base hireling) der feile Mensch, Mietling. **—ion**, *s.*

das Feil-geben, -bieten; (life of —ion) unzüchtiges Leben, das Dirnenleben; (lewdness) die Unzucht; (degradation) die Entehrung.

Pro(s)the—sis, *s.* die Vorsetzung einer Silbe, eines Buchstabens, einer Vorsatzsilbe ꝛc. (*Philol.*); künstliche Ansetzung eines Glieds (*Surg.*). **—tic**, *adj.* vorgesetzt, Vorsetz-.

Prostrat—e, I. *adj.* hingestreckt am Boden; entkräftet, hinfällig; niedergeworfen (*in humility*); fußfällig (*as a suppliant*); to fall —e before a p., einem zu Füßen fallen; —e with grief, vor Kummer schwer gebeugt. II. *v.a.* nieder-, hinwerfen; zerstören, vernichten, zu Grunde richten (*fig.*); to —e o.s. before . . ., niederfallen, einen Fußfall tun vor . . . **—ion**, *s.* das Nieder-werfen, -schlagen; das Niederknieen, der Fußfall (*in reverence, etc.*); die Niedergeschlagenheit (*of the spirits*); die Schwäche, das Darniederliegen der Körperkräfte (*Med.*).

Protagonist, *s.* der Vorkämpfer, Führer; der Held.

Protasis, *s.* der Vordersatz (*Rhet.*, *Gram.*); die Exposition, der Eingang (*of a drama*).

Protect, *v.a.* (— from, against) beschützen (vor, gegen), (be)schirmen (vor); einen Schutzzoll auferlegen (*Pol.*). **—ing**, *adj.*, **—ingly**, *adv.* schützend, Schutz-. **—ion**, *s.* der Schutz; die Beförderung; der Zollschutz (*C. L.*); —ion of animals, der Tierschutz; society for the —ion of animals, der Tierschutzverein; writ of —ion, der Schutzbrief, Paß. **—ionist**, I. *s.* der Verteidiger des Schutzzollsystems, Schutzzöllner. II. *attrib.*; schutzzöllnerisch; Bismarck's —ionist fiscal policy, Bismarcks schutzzöllnerische Staatspolitik. **—ive**, *adj.* schützend, Schutz-; —ive duties, Schutzzölle; —ive system, das Schutzzollsystem. **—or**, *s.* der Beschützer; der Schutz-, Schirm-herr (*also Law*); der Protektor, Reichsverweser (*in England*); der Kardinal-Protektor (*R. C.*). **—orate**, *s.* die Schutzherrschaft; Cromwell's —orate, Cromwells Regierung. **—orship**, *s.* die Reichsverweserschaft. **—ress**, *s.* die Beschützerin.

Protégé, *s.* der Schützling, der, die Schutzbefohlene.

Proteine, *s.* das Protein (*Chem.*).

Protest, I. *s.* die Einrede, der Einspruch, Protest; der (Wechsel-)Protest (*C. L.*); der Seeprotest (*Naut.*); to enter a —, Verwahrung einlegen gegen. II. *v.a.* beteuern; protestieren (lassen) (*a bill*). III. *v.n.* Einrede, Einspruch tun, sich verwahren (against, gegen, wider). **—ant**, I. *adj.* protestantisch. II. *s.* der (die) Protestant(in). **—antism**, *s.* der Protestantismus. **—ation**, *s.* die Beteurung, feierliche Versicherung; die Protestation, Einrede, Gegenrede. **—er**, *s.* der Beteurer; der Protestierende (*C. L.*). **—ingly**, *adv.* unter Verwahrung, unter Protest.

Prothonotary, *s.* erster Sekretär, Protonotar.

Proto, *pref.* = first, erst; erste, unterste Stufe (der Oxydation, Schwefelung ꝛc.). **—col**, *s.* das Protokoll. **—gine**, *s.* das Protogin. **—martyr**, *s.* der erste Märtyrer. **—plasm**, *s.* das Protoplasma, Urgebilde. **—type**, *s.* das Ur-, Vorbild. **—zoa**, *pl.* Urtierchen. **—zoic**, *adj.* Urtierchen betreffend; protozoisch (*Geol.*).

Protract, *v.a.* in die Länge ziehen; (delay) aufschieben; auftragen (*Surv.*). **—ed**, *adj.*, **—edly**, *adv.* lang; langwierig; weitschweifig; *see* Protract. **—ion**, *s.* das in-die-Länge-Ziehen, Hinausschieben; die Verzögerung. **—or**, *s.* der Gradbogen, Transporteur (*Draw.*).

Protru—de, *v.* I. *a.* vorstoßen, vorschieben. II. *n.* hervor-ragen, -stehen, vordringen. **—sion**, *s.* das Vordringen; das Hervorstehen; —sion of the lips, die Lippenründung.

Protuberan—ce, *s.* die Erhöhung, Ausbauchung, der Auswuchs; die Protuberanz (*Astr.*). **—t**, *adj.* hervorragend; hervorschwellend, knotig (*Bot.*).

Proud, *adj.*, **—ly**, *adv.* stolz (of a th., auf eine S.); (haughty) hochmütig; (splendid) stolz, prächtig, (spirited) kühn; faul (*as flesh*).

Prov—able, *adj.* erweislich, beweisbar. **—e**, *v.* I. *a.* (test) prüfen, erproben; (evince) be-, erweisen, dartun; (establish) bestätigen; die Probe machen auf (*Arith.*); beurkunden, beglaubigen (*a will*). II. *n.* sich ausweisen, sich ergeben, sich bewähren; ausfallen, werden; to —e true (false), sich (nicht) bestätigen *or* bewähren; it —ed to be . . ., es ergab sich, fand sich, stellte sich heraus, daß es . . . war; did I not tell you it would —e so? sagte ich Ihnen nicht, daß es so kommen würde? he will —e a good father, er wird noch einen guten Vater abgeben; he —ed himself a good son, er erwies sich als einen guten Sohn; er bewies, daß er ein guter Sohn war. **—en**, *adj.* (*incorr. p.p. of* Prove), erwiesen; not —en, nicht überführt, Schuldbeweis nicht erbracht (*Scotch*). **—er**, *s.* der Beweisende, Beweisführende.

Provender, *s.* das Futter, der Proviant.

Proverb, *s.* das Sprichwort. **—s**, *pl.* die Sprüche Salomonis. **—ial**, *adj.*, **—ially**, *adv.* sprichwörtlich. **—ialism**, *s.* sprichwörtliche Redensart.

Provide, *v.* I. *a.* versehen, versorgen (with, mit); (— against, for) zum Voraus anschaffen, verschaffen (gegen, für); (stipulate) vorbehalten, ausbedingen, stipulieren; it is —d by law, es ist durch das Gesetz vorgesehen. II. *n.* sorgen, Vorsorge tragen (for, für); sich verwahren *or* versichern, Anstalten treffen (against, gegen); to be well —d for, (gut) versorgt sein; —d that, vorausgesetzt daß . . ., wenn nur; I must — against that, dagegen muß ich Maßnahmen ergreifen. **—nce**, *s.* (preparation) die Vorbereitung, Vorsehung; (prudence) die Vorsicht, Vorsorge; (göttliche) Vorsehung (*Theol.*). **—nt**, *adj.*, **—ntly**, *adv.* vorsichtig; (economical) haushälterisch, sorgsam, sparsam; —nt society, die wirtschaftliche Genossenschaft, Wirtschaftsgenossenschaft, der Konsumverein. **—ntial**, *adj.*, **—ntially**, *adv.* durch die (göttliche) Vorsehung bewirkt (*as an escape, etc.*); God's —ntial care, die Fürsorge Gottes. **—r**, *s.* der Fürsorger; der Lieferant (*C. L.*).

Provinc—e, *s.* die Provinz; (department) das Gebiet; (sphere) der Bereich, Beruf, das Amt, Fach, die Pflicht; that is not within my —e, das liegt mir ganz fern, schlägt nicht in mein Fach; it is the —e of . . ., es ziemt *or* betrifft . . . **—ial**, I. *adj.* zur Provinz gehörig, Provinzial-, provinziell; (countrified) kleinstädtisch. II. *s.* der Provinzler, Provinzbewohner; —ial Board of School Inspectors, das Provinzialschulkollegium; —ial theatre, journal, das Provinz-theater, -blatt. **—ialism**, *s.* der mundartliche Ausdruck.

Provis—ion, I. *s.* die Vorkehrung, Anstalt; (measure) die Verordnung, Maßregel; (store) der Vorrat, Proviant; *see* —o. II. *v.a.* mit Proviant *or* Lebensmitteln versehen. **—ional**, *adj.*, **—ionally**, *adv.* vorläufig, bis auf Weiteres, provisorisch (*as a government*). **—ions**, *pl.* Lebensmittel, Mundvorräte. **—o**, *s.* der Vorbehalt, die Bedingung. **—or**, *s.* der Provisor. **—ory**, *see* —ional. *Comp.* **—ion-dealer**, **—ion-merchant**, *s.* der Kolonialwarenhändler, Groß-Viktualienhändler.

Provo—cation, *s.* die (An-)Reizung, Herausforderung; without —cation, ohne Anlaß. **—cative**, I. *adj.* (an)reizend, herausfordernd (of, zu). II. *s.* das Reizmittel, der Reiz. **—ke**, *v.a.* anregen, (an-)reizen; (call forth) hervorbringen; (challenge) herausfordern; (cause) erregen, veranlassen, verursachen; erzürnen, aufbringen; to —ke to anger, zum Zorn reizen. **—king**, *adj.*, **—kingly**, *adv.* herausfordernd; ärgerlich.

Provost, *s.* der Oberbürgermeister (*Scotch*); der Vorsteher (in einigen engl. Colleges); der Propst (*Eccl.*); — marshal, Generalprofoß.

Prow, *s.* das Vorschiff, der Schiffsschnabel.

Prowess, *s.* die Tapferkeit; der Heldenmut.

Prowl, *v.n.* umher-streichen, -schleichen.

Proxim—ate, *adj.*, **—ately**, *adv.* nächst, unmittelbar. **—ity**, *s.* die Nähe; close —ity, unmit-

telbare Nähe. **—o** (*abbrev.* prox.), nächsten Monats (*C. L.*).
Proxy, *s.* der (bevollmächtigte) Stellvertreter; (document) die Vollmacht; die Stellvertretung; stellvertretende Wahl (*Amer.*); *see* Procuration; by —, durch einen Stellvertreter, durch Vollmacht.
Prud—e, *s.* die Spröde. **—ery**, *s.* die Sprödigkeit; das Sprödetun. **—ish**, *adj.*, **—ishly**, *adv.* spröde; zimperlich, geziert.
Pruden—ce, *s.* die Klugheit, Vorsicht, Bedachtsamkeit; *see* Providence. **—t**, *adj.*, **—tly**, *adv.* klug, vorsichtig; sparsam. **—tial**, *adj.*, **—tially**, *adv.* Klugheits-; —tial considerations, Klugheitsrücksichten.
[1]**Prun—e**, *v.a.* beschneiden, stutzen; ausputzen (*vines, etc.*); putzen, glätten (*as birds*). **—ing**, *s.* das Ausputzen, Beschneiden. *Comp.* **—ing-knife**, **—ing-hook**, *s.* das Gartenmesser.
[2]**Prune**, *s.* (gedörrte) Pflaume. **—llo**, *s.* (*also* **—lla**) die Prunelle; die Brunelle (*Bot.*).
Pruri—ence, **—ency**, *s.* das Jucken, der Kitzel; heftige, unordentliche Begierde (*fig.*). **—ent**, *adj.* juckend; vom Kitzel gestochen (*fig.*); (lewd) unzüchtig. **—go**, *s.* die Krätze, die Juckblattern.
Pry, *v.n.* (— into) spähen, zu erforschen suchen, eindringen in (*acc.*); seine Nase stecken in (*acc.*); to — into other people's secrets, die Geheimnisse anderer Leute herausbekommen wollen. **—ing**, *adj.*, **—ingly**, *adv.* spähend, forschend; neugierig.
Psal—m, *s.* der Psalm. **—mist**, *s.* der Psalmist. **—mody**, *s.* das Psalmsingen; (—ter) die in Musik gesetzten Psalmen. **—ter**, *s.* der Psalter, das Psalmenbuch. **—tery**, *s.* der Psalter.
Pseudo (*in comp.* =) Pseudo-, Schein-, After-, falsch. **—nym**, *s.* falscher Name, das Pseudonym. **—nymous**, *adj.* pseudonym. **—philosophy**, *s.* die Afterphilosophie.
Pshaw, *int.* pah!
Psor—a, *s.* die Krätze. **—iasis**, *s.* die Schuppenflechte, trockene Flechte. **—ic**, *adj.* krätzig.
Psych—ic(al), *adj.* psychisch; —ical research, die Seelenforschung, Seelenkunde. **—ological**, *adj.*, **—ologically**, *adv.* psychologisch. **—ologist**, *s.* der Psycholog. **—ology**, *s.* die Seelenlehre, Psychologie.
Ptarmigan, *s.* das Schneehuhn.
Pteropod, *s.* der Flossenfüßer.
Ptomaine, *s.* das Ptomain.
Pub—erty, *s.* die Mannbarkeit, Geschlechtsreife; age of —erty, heiratsfähiges Alter. **—es**, *s.* der Flaum (*Bot.*); das Flaumhaar (*Physiol.*); die Schamgegend (*Anat.*). **—is**, *s.* das Schambein.
Public, I. *adj.*, **—ly**, *adv.* Staats-, öffentlich; (notorious) allgemein bekannt, offenkundig; — appointment, die Staatsanstellung; — auction, — sale, öffentlicher Verkauf; — conveyance, öffentliches Fuhrwerk; — credit, öffentlicher Kredit; — dinner, das Zweckessen; the — good, das allgemeine Beste, Gemeinwohl; — house, das Wirtshaus, die Schenke; — library, die öffentliche Bücherhalle, Volksbücherhalle; —man, die politische Persönlichkeit, Mann, der im öffentlichen Leben eine Rolle spielt; — money, Staats-, Gemeinde-gelder; — property, öffentliches Eigentum; — prosecutor, der Staatsanwalt; — school, teure exklusive Knabenschule ersten Ranges, Gelehrtenschule für die Söhne der bessern Stände (häufig Internatsschule) (*Eng.*), Elementarschule (*Amer.*); — spirit, der Gemeinsinn. II. *s.* das Publikum; die Leute (*pl.*), die Welt; *see* — house; in —, vor der Welt, öffentlich. **—an**, *s.* der Schenkwirt; der Zöllner (*B.*). **—ation**, *s.* die öffentliche Bekanntmachung, Verkündigung; die Herausgabe, Veröffentlichung (*of a work*); (book, *etc.*) das (herausgegebene) Werk, die Schrift; list of new —ations, das Verzeichnis neu erschienener Werke; monthly —ation, die Monatsschrift. **—ity**, *s.* die Öffentlichkeit, Offenkundigkeit; no —ity, strengste Diskretion. *Comp.* **—-spirited**, *adj.* gemeinsinnig, patriotisch.

Publish, *v.a.* bekannt machen, verkündigen, veröffentlichen; herausgeben, verlegen (*a book, etc.*); not yet —ed, noch unveröffentlicht; to — the banns of matrimony, ein Brautpaar (von der Kanzel) abkündigen. **—er**, *s.* der Herausgeber, Verleger; der Verkündiger (*of news*). **—ing**, *adj.*; —ing business, der Verlagshandel; —ing house, die Verlags(buch)handlung.
Puce, *adj.* braunrot, dunkelbraun, flohfarben.
Puck, *s.* der Kobold.
Pucker, I. *s.* der (Falten-)Bausch, die Falte; all in a —, außer sich vor Verlegenheit (*coll.*). II. *v.a.* falten, runzeln; beim Nähen einhalten, zusammenziehen (*Sew.*). III. *v.n.* sich falten.
Pudding, *s.* der Pudding; die süße Speise, Mehlspeise (*Cook.*); (sausage) die Wurst; black —, Blutwurst; (gut) der Darm, die Gedärme. *Comp.* **—-cloth**, *s.* das Puddingtuch.
Puddl—e, I. *s.* der Pfuhl, die Pfütze, Lache; *see* Pisé; der Lehmschlag. II. *v.a.* puddeln (*Metall.*); verfüllen (*Build.*); anmachen; —ed clay, der Lehmschlag. **—er**, *s.* der Schlämmer (*Agr.*); der Puddler (*Metall.*). **—ing**, *s.* das Verfüllen (*Build.*); das Puddeln (*Metall.*); —ing furnace, der Puddel-Eisenfrisch-Ofen.
Pudenda, *pl.* die Schamteile, Geschlechtsteile.
Pudgy, *adj.* patschig, feist; kurz und dick.
Puer—ile, *adj.* knabenhaft, kindisch. **—ility**, *s.* das kindische Wesen; —ilities, Kindereien. **—peral**, *adj.* Kindbett-.
Puff, I. *s.* der Hauch; der Windstoß; das Ausströmen (*of steam, etc.*); das Aufgeblasene, Leichte (*fig.*); der Bausch (*in dresses*); die Puffe (*as trimming*); (powder —) der Puderquast; der Blätterkuchen, leichtes Backwerk mit Obst (*Cook.*); die Aufbauschung; marktschreierische Anzeige, der Puff, die Reklame (*in newspapers*); the —s of his pipe, die Paffs seiner Pfeife. II. *v.n.* blasen; pusten, schnaufen, keuchen; aufbauschen (*fig.*); to — and blow, schnauben, keuchen; to — at, blasen, paffen an (*dat.*) (*a cigar*). III. *v.a.* (— up) aufblasen, aufblähen (*also fig.*); in die Höhe treiben (*at auctions*); prahlerisch ankündigen, anpreisen, Reklame machen (für eine S.) (*in newspapers, etc.*); to — away, fortblasen, verwehen; to be —ed up with pride, von Stolz aufgeblasen sein; —ed sleeve, der Bauschärmel. **—er**, *s.* der Blasende, Keuchende; der Prahler, Anpreiser (*fig.*). **—in**, *s.* der Larven-, Sturm-taucher (*Orn.*). **—iness**, *s.* die Aufgeblasenheit. **—ing**, *s.* die Prahlerei, Reklame. **—y**, *adj.* aufgeblasen; aufgedunsen. *Comp.* **—-ball**, *s.* der Bovist. **—-paste**, *s.* der Blätterteig. **—y-faced**, *adj.* mit aufgedunsenem Gesicht.
Pug, *s.* (—-dog) der Mops; der Fuchs (*dial.*). *Comp.* **—-faced**, *adj.* mit einem Affengesichte. **—-mill**, *s.* die Mörtelmühle. **—-nose**, *s.* die Stumpfnase. **—-nosed**, *adj.* stumpfnasig.
Pugging, *s.* die Lehmarbeit, das Lehmstampfen.
Pug—ilism, *s.* das Faustkämpfen, Boxen. **—ilist**, *s.* der Klopffechter, Faustkämpfer, Boxer. **—ilistic**, *adj.* zum Faustkampfe gehörig, Box-. **—nacious**, *adj.*, **—naciously**, *adv.* kampflustig, streitsüchtig. **—nacity**, *s.* die Kampflust, Streitsucht.
Puisne, I. *adj.* jünger, Unter-. II. *s.* (— judge) der Unterrichter.
Puissan—ce, *s.* die Macht, Gewalt, Herrschaft. **—t**, *adj.* mächtig, gewaltig.
Puke, *v.n.* sich erbrechen, krank *or* übel sein.
Pul—e, *v.n.* winseln. **—ing**, I. *adj.* winselnd. II. *s.* das Gewinsel.
Pull, I. *s.* der Zug, das Ziehen; der Zug (*of a bell, etc.*); der Griff (*of a door, etc.*); die Ruderfahrt (*Naut.*); der Satz (*Typ.*); der Vorteil (*sl.*); to take a — at the bottle, einen Zug aus der Flasche tun (*sl.*). II. *v.a.* ziehen, zerren; pflücken (*fruit*); abbrechen (*pears, etc.*); raufen (*flax*); abziehen (a proof, einen Druckbogen);

rudern (*Naut.*); to — the trigger, das Gewehr abdrücken; to — the bell, die Glocke ziehen, läuten; to — **along**, fortschleppen; to — **asunder**, aus-einander-ziehen, -zerren; to — **away**, weg-reißen, -ziehen; to — **down**, niederreißen (*a house, etc.*), schwächen, entkräften (*the strength, etc.*); to — **in**, anziehen (*a horse*), hineinziehen; to — **off**, abziehen (*a hat, etc.*), ausziehen (*clothes*); abreißen; to — **on**, fortziehen; to — **out**, ausziehen, (tear) ausraufen; to — **through**, durchziehen; durchhelfen, herausreißen; to — **up**, aufziehen; (stop) anhalten. III. *v.n.* ziehen, reißen; rudern (*Naut.*); to — **through**, sich erholen; — **up!** halt! —**ing**, das Raufen (*of flax*); der Ballenschlag (*Typ.*); —ing down, der Abbruch (*of houses*).

Pullet, *s.* das Hühnchen.

Pulley, I. *s.* die Rolle, Flasche, der Kloben; a set of —s, der Flaschenzug. II. *attrib.*; — door, selbstschließende Tür.

Pulmon—aria, *s.* das Lungenkraut. —**ary**, —**ic**, *adj.* Lungen-; —ary disease, die Lungensucht, -krankheit.

Pulp, *s.* breiige Masse, der Brei; das Mark (*in fruit, teeth, etc.*); das Ganzzeug, der Lumpenbrei (*Pap.*). —**iness**, *s.* die breiige Beschaffenheit. —**y**, *adj.* breiig, breiartig, weichmarkig.

Pulpit, I. *s.* die Kanzel; (rostrum) das Katheder. II. *attrib.*; — eloquence, die Kanzelberedsamkeit; — orator, der Kanzelredner.

Puls—ate, *v.n.* schlagen, pochen. —**atile**, *adj.* Schlag- (*Mus.*); pochend (*Med.*). —**ation**, *s.* das Schlagen, Klopfen. —**e**, *s.* der Puls; *see* —ation; to feel a p.'s —e, einem den Puls fühlen (*Med.*); einem auf den Zahn fühlen (*fig.*). —**eless**, *adj.* ohne Puls.

[1]**Pulse**, *see under* Puls—ate.

[2]**Pulse**, *s.* die Hülsenfrüchte.

Pulver—ization, *s.* das Pulvern, Pulverisieren. —**ize**, *v.a.* zu Pulver reiben, pulvern, pulverisieren. —**ulent**, *adj.* staubig.

Puma, *s.* der Silberlöwe, Puma, Kuguar.

Pumice-stone, *s.* der Bimsstein.

[1]**Pump**, I. *s.* die Pumpe; chain —, die Kettenpumpe. II. *v.a.* pumpen; ausforschen (*fig.*); to — a p. for a th., einen über eine S. ausforschen (*fam.*). —**ed**, *adj.* erschöpft, atemlos (*sl.*). *Comp.* —**-chamber**, *s.* der Pumpenstiefel. —**-handle**, *s.* der Pumpenschwengel. —**-room**, *s.* die Trinkhalle, der Kursaal. —**-staff**, *s.* der Pumpenstock. —**-water**, *s.* das Pumpenwasser.

[2]**Pump**, *s.* der Tanzschuh. —**ed**, *adj.* mit Tanzschuhen versehen, in Ballschuhen.

Pumpkin, *s.* der Kürbis.

Pun, I. *s.* das Wortspiel. II. *v.n.* mit Worten spielen, witzeln. —**ner**, —**ster**, *s.* der Wortspielmacher, Witzling. —**ning**, I. *adj.* witzelnd, mit Worten spielend. II. *s.* das Witzeln.

[1]**Punch**, *s.* der Hanswurst, der Kasperle (*in* — and Judy show, das Kasperle-Theater); (London comic paper) der Punch. —**inello**, *s.* der Hanswurst.

[2]**Punch**, *s.* der Punsch. *Comp.* —**-bowl**, *s.* der Punschnapf; die Punschbowle. —**-ladle**, *s.* der Punschlöffel.

[3]**Punch**, I. *s.* der Stoß, Puff. II. *v.a.* stoßen, knuffen. *Comp.* —**-ball**, *s.* der Stoßball.

[4]**Punch**, *s.* der Stöpsel, Purzel, kleine dicke Kerl; (horse) starkes, untersetztes Pferd. —**y**, *adj.* kurz und dick, untersetzt.

[5]**Punch**, I. *s.* das Locheisen (*Saddl.; smiths, etc.*); der Durchschlag, Punzen (*for leather, etc.*); der Pfriem; der Stiel, die Stütze (*Carp.*); der Stechbeitel (*for driving nails*); der Stempel, die Patrize (*Tech.*); die Laubrolle (*Bookb.*); der Dorn, Punzen (*Gun.*); die Stanze (*Mint.*). II. *v.a.* durchbohren, durchlochen (*tickets*); lochen (*a horse-shoe*). —**eon**, *s.* der Durchschlag; der Stiel (*Carp.*); starkbauchiges Faß, die Tonne (80-120 Gallonen). —**er**, *s.* der Lochstecher; der Schläger, Knuffer (*coll.*).

Punct—ilio, *s.* zarter Punkt, kleiner Umstand; with proper —ilio, mit schicklicher Förmlichkeit; nice about —ilios, *see* —ilious. —**ilious**, *adj.*, —**iliously**, *adv.* krittlig, spitzfindig, häkelig, genau, zeremoniös. —**iliousness**, *s.* ängstliche Pünktlichkeit, übertriebene Genauigkeit. —**ual**, *adj.*, —**ually**, *adv.* pünktlich; to be —ual in keeping an appointment, sein Versprechen pünktlich halten. —**uality**, *s.* die Pünktlichkeit, Genauigkeit. —**uate**, *v.a.* punktieren; interpunktieren. —**uation**, *s.* die Interpunktion. —**ure**, I. *s.* der Stich, die Punktur; das durch Aufritzen entstandene kleine Loch im Luftreifen eines Fahrrads. II. *v.a.* stechen; —uring the thorax, die Durchstechung des Brustkorbes.

Pundit, *s.* der gelehrte Brahmine, indische Rechtsgelehrte; der Scheingelehrte (*fam.*); our educational —s, unsere gelehrten Pädagogen.

Pungen—cy, *s.* das Stechende, Beißende. —**t**, *adj.*, —**tly** *adv.* stechend, beißend.

Pun—iness, *s.* die Winzigkeit, Schwächlichkeit. —**y**, *adj.* winzig und schwach; kümmerlich.

Punish, *v.a.* (be)strafen (for, wegen, um); züchtigen (für), abstrafen (wegen). —**able**, *adj.* strafbar. —**er**, *s.* der Strafende. —**ment**, *s.* die Strafe, Bestrafung; to bring to —ment, zur Strafe ziehen; capital —ment, die Todesstrafe.

Punitive, *adj.* strafend, Straf-; — expedition, der Strafzug, Feldzug zur Bestrafung.

[1]**Punk**, *s.* faules Holz; der Zündschwamm.

[2]**Punk**, I. *s.* der Faustschlag. II. *v.a.* mit der Faust schlagen (*Amer. sl.*).

Punkah, *s.* der Federfächer.

Punt, I. *s.* die Schauke; fishing, *etc.* —, das kleine Fischerfahrzeug, der Kahn. II. *v.a.* mit Ruderstangen fortbewegen, staken. III. *v.n.* auf einer Schauke, in einem Fischerkahn fahren.

Pup, *s. short for* Puppy; *slang for* Pupil.

Pupa, *s.* die Puppe.

[1]**Pupil**, *s.* der Augenstern, die Pupille (*Anat.*).

[2]**Pupil**, *s.* der (die) Schüler(in), Zögling, Pflegling; (ward) die, der Mündel (*obs.*). —**age**, *s.* die Zöglingsjahre, der Schülerstand, die Minderjährigkeit, der Mündelstand (*Law*). —**lary**, *adj.* Augapfel-, Pupillen- (*Anat.*); pupillarisch, Mündel- (*Law*). *Comp.* —**-teacher**, *s.* der (die) Lehrschüler(in), älterer Schüler, der zugleich jüngere lehrt; der Lehramts-Aspirant.

Puppet, *s.* die (Draht-)Puppe, Marionette; das Püppchen, Werkzeug (*fig.*); das Spulholz (*Weav.*); die Docke (*Turn.*). *Comp.* —**-play**, *s.* das Puppenspiel. —**-show**, *s.* das Puppentheater, Marionettentheater.

Puppy, I. *s.* der junge Hund; der Laffe, Geck (*fig.*). II. *attrib.*; — biscuit, der Hundekuchen. —**ism**, *s.* die Flegelei, das Laffentum.

Purblind, *adj.* blödsichtig; kurzsichtig (*fig.*).

Purchasable, *adj.* käuflich.

Purchase, I. *v.a.* (er)kaufen, einkaufen; (*opp. to* Inherit); erwerben, erlangen; to — from a p., einem (etwas) abkaufen; to — on speculation, auf Spekulation kaufen. II. *s.* die Erwerbung; (An-, Ein-)Kauf; (what is —d) der Kauf; der Halt, Griff (*in lifting heavy things*); die Hebekraft (*Mech.*); die Erwerbung (*Law*); die Auswirkung (*of a writ*); by —, käuflich; at 20 years' —, zum Zwanzigfachen des Jahresertrags. —**r**, *s.* der Käufer; der Abnehmer, Kunde, Käufer (*C. L.*); to meet with a —r, einen Käufer finden. *Comp.* —**-money**, *s.* das Kaufgeld. —**-price**, *s.* der Kaufpreis, Einkaufspreis.

Pure, *adj.*, —**ly**, *adv.* rein, lauter; (genuine) echt, gediegen, eitel; (chaste) keusch; (mere) rein, völlig, nichts als; — gold, feines Gold; — mathematics, reine Mathematik; — silk, die Ganzseide; — wool, die Ganzwolle; —ly invented, rein erfunden. —**ness**, *s.* die Reinheit.

Purg—ation, *s.* die Reinigung; die Abführung (*Med.*); die Rechtfertigung (*Law*). —**ative**, I. *adj.* purgierend. II. *s.* das Abführ(ungs)mittel. —**atorial**, *adj.*; —atorial fire, das Fegefeuer.

—atory, *s.* das Fegefeuer. **—e**, I. *v.a.* reinigen (*also fig.*), säubern; läutern, klären (*liquids*); rechtfertigen (*from a charge*); (*also* II. *v.n.*) purgieren, abführen (*Med.*). III. *s.* das Abführ(ungs)mittel.

Pur—ge, *see under* Purg—ation. **—ification**, *s.* die Reinigung. **—ifier**, *s.* der Reiniger, Läuterer; das Reinigungsmittel. **—ify**, *v.a.* reinigen; läutern, klären (*fluids*). **—ifying**, *s.* die Reinigung. **—ism**, *s.* der Purismus. **—ist**, *s.* der Sprachreiniger um jeden Preis, Purist. **—itan**, I. *s.* der Puritaner. II. *adj.*, **—itanical**, *adj.* puritanisch. **—itanism**, *s.* der Puritanismus; das Puritanertum. **—ity**, *s.* die Reinheit, Fleckenlosigkeit; (innocence) die Unschuld.

[1]**Purl**, *s.* krause Borte, der gestickte Rand (*of a cuff, etc.*); Ansetzspitzen (*of lace*); die Latzmasche (*in knitting*); (gold wire) der Golddraht.

[2]**Purl**, I. *s.* das Rieseln, Murmeln (*of a brook*); (eddy) der Wirbel, Strudel; der Kreis auf der Oberfläche des Wassers. II. *v.n.* rieseln, murmeln, sanft rauschen; sich wellenförmig erheben; sich kräuseln; umkippen (*of a boat, sl.*).

[3]**Purl**, *s.* das Kräuter-, Wermut-bier (*rare*).

Purlieu, *s.* der Bezirk. **—s**, *pl.* die Umgebungen.

Purloin, *v.a. & n.* entwenden, stehlen, mausen. **—er**, *s.* der Dieb.

Purp—le, I. *s.* der Purpur; *see* Cardinalate; die Herrscher-, fürstliche Würde (*fig.*). II. *adj.* purpurn, purpurfarben; purpurrot. III. *v.n.* sich purpurn färben. **—lish**, *adj.* purpurfarbig. **—uric**, *adj.*; —uric acid, die Purpursäure. *Comp.* **—le-emperor**, *s.* der Schillerfalter (*Ent.*).

Purport, I. *s.* der Zweck; (tenor) der Inhalt, Sinn. II. *v.a.* enthalten, bedeuten; (be)sagen. III. *v.n. see* Signify; zum Inhalte haben, meinen, besagen; —ing, des Inhalts.

Purpose, I. *s.* der Vorsatz; (intention) die Absicht, der Zweck; (subject) die Sache; (purport) der Inhalt, Sinn; (effect) der Erfolg, die Wirkung; for this, that —, in dieser Absicht, deshalb; for what —? wozu? for the — of, um zu . . .; on —, absichtlich, vorsätzlich, mit Willen; on — to annoy me, in der Absicht, mich zu ärgern; of set —, recht mit Fleiß; to the —, zweck-, sachdienlich, passend; with a —, mit bestimmter Absicht verfaßt, Tendenz-; it is to no — that. ., es ist vergeblich, daß . .; he spoke pretty much to the same —, er sagte fast ebendasselbe; to all intents and —s, in jeder Hinsicht, in jedem Betracht. II. *v.a.* beabsichtigen, sich (*dat.*) vor-nehmen, -setzen. **—less**, *adj.* zwecklos; (vain) ohne Erfolg. **—ly**, *adv.* vorsätzlich, mit Fleiß.

Purr, I. *v.n.* schnurren, the cat —s, die Katze schnurrt. II. *s.* das Schnurren, Geschnurre.

Purse, I. *s.* der Geldbeutel, die Börse; der Preis; public —, der Staatsschatz; long —, wohlgefüllte Börse; to bear the —, Herr im Hause sein; to make up a — for, Geld sammeln für; to have a common —, gemeinschaftliche Kasse machen; shepherd's —, das Hirtentäschelkraut (*Bot.*). II. *v.a.*; to — up, (wie einen Beutel) zusammenziehen, spitzen (the lips, den Mund). **—r**, *s.* der Proviant-, Zahl-meister (*Naut.*). *Comp.* **—proud**, I. *adj.* geldstolz. II. *s.* der Geldprotz. *Comp.* **—-string**, *s.* die Beutelschnur; the person that holds the —-strings, derjenige, welcher die Hand auf dem Beutel hält; to keep a tight hand on the —-strings, geizig sein, den Knopf auf dem Beutel halten.

Purs—iness, *s.* die Kurzatmigkeit. **—y**, *adj.* kurz und dick, (fett und) kurzatmig; aufgeblasen.

Purslane, *s.* der Portulak.

Pursu—ance, *s.* die Verfolgung, Fortsetzung; in —ance of an order, einem Befehle gemäß; in —ance of which, zufolge dessen. **—ant**, *adj.*; — to, **—antly**, *adv.* infolge, gemäß, nach. **—e**, *v.* I. *a.* verfolgen, nachsetzen (a p., einem); verfolgen (*one's course, conversation, a plan, etc.*); (carry on) fortsetzen, weiter verfolgen, fortfahren in; (strive after) streben nach; to —e a course, einen Weg einschlagen. II. *n.* fortfahren. **—er**, *s.* der Verfolger. **—it**, *s.* die Verfolgung; die Jagd; das Streben, Trachten; —it of knowledge, der Drang nach Wissen. **—its**, *pl.* die Geschäfte, Arbeiten, Studien; mercantile —its, der Handelsbetrieb. **—ivant**, *s.* der Unterherold (*obs.*); *see* Attendant.

Purulen—ce, **—cy**, *s.* das Eitern. **—t**, *adj.* eiternd, eiterig.

Purvey, *v.* I. *a.* sorgen für; (procure) beschaffen, anschaffen. II. *n.* Vorräte anschaffen. **—ance**, *s.* die Anschaffung (von Vorräten); der Vorrat, die Lebensmittel (*pl.*). **—or**, *s.* der Lieferant; —or to the King, königlicher Hoflieferant.

Purview, *s.* der verfügende Teil eines Statuts (*Law*); (sphere) der Wirkungskreis, die Sphäre.

Pus, *s.* der Eiter.

Push, I. *v.a.* stoßen, drängen, drücken, rücken; (drive) treiben, schieben; (press) hart zusetzen, dringen in; treiben (*fig.*); energisch (durch alle möglichen Mittel) betreiben (*a business*); to — one's fortune, sein Glück machen; to be —ed for, gedrängt werden um; to — **away**, fort-, weg-stoßen; to — **back**, zurückstoßen; (overcome) zurückdrängen; to — **down**, niederstoßen; to — **forward**, fortschieben; to — o.s. forward, sich (unbescheiden) vordrängen; to — **in**, hineintreiben, -stoßen; to — **on**, fort-, an-treiben, (further) befördern; to — **out**, hinausstoßen, fortjagen; to — **up**, in die Höhe treiben. II. *v.n.* stoßen; sich vordrängen; to — **on**, vordringen, vorwärtsdrängen; to — **off**, in See stechen. III. *s.* der Stoß; (shove) das Schieben, der Schub; (emergency) dringender Fall, die Not; die Energie, Aufdringlichkeit (*coll.*); he has plenty of —, er ist sehr keck; to make a — for, eine gewaltige Anstrengung machen, um zu (einer S.) zu gelangen; to give a p. a —, einem einen Stoß geben; to bring to the last —, aufs äußerste treiben. **—ing**, *adj.*, **—ingly**, *adv.* unternehmend, strebsam; zu-, vor-dringlich, keck, unbescheiden. *Comp.* **—-pin**, *s.* das Nadelschieben.

Pusillanim—ity, *s.* der Kleinmut. **—ous**, *adj.*, **—ously**, *adv.* kleinmütig, verzagt, feig.

Pustule, *s.* die Pustel, das Eiterbläschen.

Put, *ir.v.* I. *a.* legen, setzen, stellen, stecken (on, auf; to, an); tun (to, an); stellen, vorlegen (*questions*); setzen (the case, den Fall); setzen (*s.o. in a place*); werfen, schleudern (*stone, hammer*); *see* Weight; to — one's hand in one's pocket, die Hand in die Tasche stecken; to — the glass on the table, das Glas auf den Tisch stellen; to — the book on the table, das Buch auf den Tisch legen; to — the glass down, das Glas hinsetzen *or* hinstellen; to — **about**, herumschicken, herumgehen lassen (*the bottle, etc.*), umlegen (*a ship*); in Umlauf setzen (rumour); to — o.s. about, sich plagen, sich beunruhigen; to — s.o. about, einen in Verlegenheit bringen, verwirren; to — **aside**, bei Seite legen, setzen, zurücklegen; to — **asunder**, trennen; to — a horse **at**, ein Pferd setzen lassen über (*acc.*); to — **away**, weg-legen, -tun; (divorce) verstoßen (*B.*); (discard) fahren lassen (*B.*), verbannen (*care*); to — **back**, zurück-schieben (*a thing, etc.*), -stellen (*a clock, etc.*); (replace) wiederhinstellen; (delay) aufschieben; zurückversetzen (*in schools*); to — **before**, stellen, legen vor; to — a p. **beside** himself, einen außer sich bringen; to — **between**, dazwischen stellen, legen, setzen; (insert) einschieben; to — **beyond** a doubt, außer Zweifel setzen; to — **by**, bei Seite legen, aufbewahren (*money, etc.*), bei Seite schieben (*s.th. offered*); (parry) abwenden, ablenken; to — **down**, (lay down) nieder-setzen, -legen, aus der Hand legen; (write down) niederschreiben; (charge) anrechnen, ein-, zu-schreiben; (degrade) absetzen; (abolish) abschaffen, außer Gebrauch setzen; (crush) unterdrücken; (snub) **ab-**

fertigen, zurechtsetzen, einen Verweis geben; (silence) zum Schweigen bringen; (humble) demütigen; this boy must be — down, dieser Knabe muß (in eine niedere Schulklasse) zurückversetzt werden; that will be — down to my account, das wird auf meine Rechnung gesetzt werden, mir in die Schuhe geschoben werden; — it down to my account, stellen Sie es mir in Rechnung, schreiben *or* setzen Sie es auf meine Rechnung; — me down for 20 marks, führen Sie mich im Verzeichnis auf mit einem Beitrage von 20 Mark; to — it down to a p.'s ignorance, es der Unwissenheit einer Person zuschreiben; to — one's name down for a lecture, eine Vorlesung belegen; to — **forth**, hervor-, hinaus-, heraus-setzen, -legen, -stellen, -tun; (stretch forth) ausstrecken (*the hand, etc.*); treiben (*buds, etc.*); herausgeben (*a book*); aufbieten (*one's strength*); to — **forward**, vorbringen (*an opinion, etc.*), zum Vorschein bringen; to — o.s. forward, sich hervor-tun, -drängen (*fig.*); to — **in**, hineinsetzen (*a th. in a place*); hineinstecken (*one's money in an enterprise, etc.*), einstecken (*a th. in one's pocket, a p. in prison*); einlegen (*a good word for a p.*); einspannen (*horses*); einrücken (*an advertisement, etc.*); einschieben (*a clause*); leisten, stellen (*bail*); bringen (in order, in practice, in Ordnung, in Ausübung); einsegeln (*Naut.*); to — in (*or* forward) a claim to, etwas in Anspruch nehmen, Anspruch auf eine S. machen; to — in mind of, erinnern an eine S. (*coll.*); to — in force, *see* Enforce; to — in a passion, aufbringen; he has — his foot in it nicely! er hat sich eine schöne Suppe eingebrockt! to — in one's oar, sich in eine Sache (ein)mischen; allow me to — in a word, erlauben Sie mir, ein Wort mitzusprechen; to — in(to) a good temper, in gute Laune versetzen; to — **into** a p.'s hands (s.o.'s head), einem in die Hände geben (in den Kopf setzen); to — **off**, ablegen, abtun, ausziehen (*clothes*); abnehmen (*one's hat*); (*also v.n.*) abstoßen, absetzen (*from shore*); einen hinhalten, abfertigen, abspeisen (*with promises, etc.*); (delay) aufschieben, verschieben, verlängern, auf die lange Bank schieben; to — off with a jest, (etwas) mit einem Scherz abtun; to — **on**, antun, anlegen (*clothes*); aufsetzen (*one's hat*); ansetzen (*flesh*); (feign) heucheln (*vulg.*); vorrichten, vorrücken (*a clock, etc.*); auferlegen (*a burden*); (impute) anrechnen; to — the blame on s.o., einem die Schuld beimessen; (cheat) betrügen; to — a construction (upon s. th.), (einer Sache) eine Auslegung geben; *see* — to; to — on the shelf, an den Nagel hängen (*fig.*); to — a good face on a bad business, gute Miene zum bösen Spiel machen; to — **out**, hinaus-setzen, -stellen (*a thing*); ausstrecken (*the hand*); aufstecken (*a flag*); treiben (*leaves, etc.*); herausgeben (*a book*), anlegen, ausleihen, austun (*money*); austreiben, vertreiben (*of a place*); absetzen (*of an office*); auslöschen (*fire, a candle, etc.*); ausstreichen (*a word, etc.*); irre machen, stören (*in reading, speaking, etc.*); schlagen (*a horse, in racing*); ausrenken (*one's shoulder, etc.*); aus-geben, -tun (to nurse, in die Pflege), außer dem Hause machen, besorgen lassen (*work, etc., washing*); ausstechen (*a p's eyes*); bringen (out of order, aus der Ordnung); to — a p. out of countenance, einen aus der Fassung bringen; he was greatly — out at this news, diese Nachricht verstimmte ihn sehr; to — it out of s.o.'s power to do s.th., einem die Macht benehmen etwas zu tun; this dish always —s my stomach out of order, dieses Gericht verdirbt mir stets den Magen; to — **through**, durch-stechen, -stecken; durchsetzen, beendigen; to — **to**, (join, add) hinzu-legen, -setzen, -fügen, -tun; (yoke) anspannen, anschirren; (help) anlegen, Hand (an eine S.) legen; to — a p. to it, einem zusetzen, einen hart drängen: he was hard — to it to . . ., es kostete ihn viel Mühe, zu . . .; I have been hard — to it, ich habe es sehr schwer gefunden, es ist mir sehr schwer geworden; to — to the blush, schamrot machen; to — to expense, (einem) Unkosten machen; to — to a business, in ein(em) Geschäft einstellen; to — to the sword, über die Klinge springen lassen; to — to the vote, über (eine S.) abstimmen lassen; to — to a (*or* on) trial, vor Gericht bringen; (test) auf die Probe stellen; to — it to a p., es einem anheim-geben *or* -stellen, vorlegen; to — to death, hinrichten; to — an end to, (einer Sache) ein Ende machen; to — to flight, in die Flucht schlagen; to — one's hand to the plough, seine Hand an den Pflug legen, energisch zugreifen; to — a question to, eine Frage an (einen) richten; to — to rights, zurechtsetzen, wieder in Ordnung bringen; to — to shame, beschämen; to — **together**, zusammensetzen; to — two and two together, zwei Dinge zusammen halten und daraus seine Schlüsse ziehen; to — **up**, einstecken (*one's sword*); aufstellen (*machines*); aufschlagen (*beds*); setzen (*stoves, etc.*); aufstecken (*one's hair*); aufmachen (*curtains*); beiseite-, weg-legen (*books, work, etc.*); anheften, anschlagen (*a placard, etc.*); einpacken (*one's clothes, etc.*); verpacken (*goods*); aufjagen (*game*); ausstellen (*to auction*); vorbringen, -richten (*prayers*); (gastlich) aufnehmen; to — a p. up to a th., einen zu etwas anstiften; the horse was to be — up at Mr. N.'s, das Pferd sollte bei Herrn N. abgegeben *or* eingestellt werden; to — s.o.'s back up, einen ärgern, verdrießlich machen (*coll.*); to — **upon**, (einem) auf(er)legen; to — it upon, es auf (eine S.) ankommen lassen; if you — it upon that ground, wenn Sie es so nehmen. II. *n.*; to — **back**, zurück-laufen, -kehren, -fahren (*Naut.*); to — **forth**, auslaufen (*Naut.*); to — **in**, antun, einlaufen (*at a port*); to — **to** sea, auslaufen; to — **up** at, einkehren, absteigen in (einem Gasthause); to — up for, als Bewerber auftreten; to — up with, einstecken (*an insult*); geduldig ertragen, sich (*dat.*) (etwas) gefallen lassen; to — **upon** a p., einem (zu) viel zumuten (*coll.*). **—ting**, *s.* das Werfen, Fortschleudern (of a stone, eines Steines). *Comp.* **—log**, *s.* der Netzriegel, das Rüstholz.

Putative, *adj.* vermeintlich, mutmaßlich.

Putr—efaction, *s.* die Fäulnis, faule Gährung. **—efactive**, *adj.* Fäulnis verursachend, faulmachend. **—efy**, *v.* I. *a.* faul machen, in Fäulnis bringen; (poison) verpesten. II. *n.* in Fäulnis geraten, verfaulen, verwesen. **—escence**, *s.* die Fäulnis. **—escent**, *adj.* faulend. **—escible**, *adj.* der Fäulnis unterworfen. **—id**, *adj.* faul; —id fever, das Faulfieber. **—idity**, *s.* die Fäulnis, Fäule.

Puttock, *s.* die Gabelweihe; der Bussard (*dial.*).

Putty, I. *s.* der Kitt, Glaserkitt. II. *v.a.* (ver-)kitten. *Comp.* **—faced**, *adj.* blaß im Gesicht.

Puzzl—e, I. *s.* die schwierige Frage, der Knoten, das Rätsel; (perplexity) die Verlegenheit, Verwirrung; (game) das Vexierspiel. II. *v.a.* verwirren, irre machen; to —e one's brains over a th., sich (*dat.*) über eine S. den Kopf zerbrechen. III. *v.n.* verwirrt, in Verlegenheit sein. **—er**, *s.* der, das Verwirrende; schwere Frage (*fig.*); that's a —er for him, das wird ihm viel Kopfzerbrechen machen! (*fam.*). **—ing**, *adj.* verwirrend. *Comp.* **—e-headed**, *adj.* konfus.

Pygm—ean, *adj.* pygmäisch, zwerghaft, winzig. **—y**, *s.* der Pygmäe, Zwerg, das winzige Geschöpf.

Pyjamas, *pl.* der Schlafanzug für Herren.

Pylorus, *s.* untere Magenöffnung.

Pyramid, *s.* die Pyramide. **—al**, *adj.* pyramidenhaft, pyramidal.

Pyr—e, *s.* der Scheiterhaufen, Holzstoß. **—etic**, *adj.* gut gegen das Fieber, fiebervertreibend. **—ites**, *s.* der Eisenkies, Strahlenkies.

Pyriform, *adj.* birnförmig.

Pyro—graphy, *s.* die Brandmalerei, die Pokerarbeit. **—latry**, *s.* die Feueranbetung. **—ligneous**, *adj.*; —ligneous acid, der Holzessig. **—mania**, *s.* der Brandstiftungstrieb. **—meter**, *s.* der Hitzegradmesser. **—technic**, *adj.* pyrotechnisch. **—technics**, *s.* die Feuerwerkskunst. **—technist**, *s.* der Kunstfeuerwerker.
Pyrrhonism, *s.* der Skeptizismus.
Pyx, *s.* die Monstranz; die Büchse, in der Proben von neugeprägten Münzen aufbewahrt werden (*Mint.*).

Q

Q, q, *s.* Q, q. *For abbreviations see the end of the English-German part.*
[1]**Quack**, I. *v.n.* (wie eine Ente) quaken, quäken. II. *s.* das Quaken, Gequake (der Ente).
[2]**Quack**, I. *v.n.* quacksalbern, den Marktschreier machen; ein großes Geschrei machen (of, von, mit). II. *v.a.* pfuscherhaft behandeln. III. *s.* der Quacksalber; der Marktschreier, Pfuscher; der Schwindler. IV. *adj.*; — doctor, *see* — III; — medicines, Quacksalberarzneien, Wundermittel. **—ery**, *s.* die Quacksalberei, Kurpfuscherei.
Quad, *short for* Quadrangle.
Quadr—agesima, *s.* die Fasten. **—agesimal**, *adj.* Fasten=. **—angle**, *s.* das Viereck; der viereckige von Gebäuden umgebene Hof; der College=Hof (*often abbreviated:* quad). **—angular**, *adj.* viereckig. **—ant**, *s.* der Quadrant (*Math.*, *Astr.*, *Naut.*); gunner's —ant, Stangenquadrant. **—at**, *s.* das Quadrat (*Geom.*, *Print.*). **—ate**, I. *v.n.* passen, stimmen (zu, with), entsprechen (*dat.*). II. *v.a.* in Stellung bringen, passen. III. *adj.* viereckig, geviert, quadratisch, Quadrat=; billig, passend (*fig.*). IV. *s.* das Quadrat (*also Mus.*); *see* Quartile (*Astr.*). **—atic**, I. *adj.* quadratisch. II. *s.* die quadratische Gleichung. **—ature**, *s.* die Vierung, Quadratur (*Math.*, *Astr.*). **—ennial**, *adj.* vierjährlich, alle vier Jahre stattfindend; (of four years) vierjährig. **—ifid**, *adj.* vierspaltig. **—ilateral**, I. *adj.* vierseitig. II. *s.* vierseitige Figur, das Viereck. **—ille**, *s.* der Vierer=(reigen), die Quadrille; —ille à la cour, der Hofreigen, Hoftanz. **—illion**, *s.* die Quadrillion. **—inomial**, *adj.* viergliederig. **—ipartite**, *adj.* in vier Teile geteilt; vierteilig (*Bot.*). **—oon**, *s.* das Kind einer Mulattin und eines Weißen oder umgekehrt, der Quarterone. **—umana**, *pl.* Vierhänder (*Zool.*). **—umanous**, *adj.* vierhändig. **—uped**, I. *s.* das vierfüßige Tier, Landsäugetier. II. *adj.* vierfüßig. **—uple**, I. *adj.* vierfach. II. *s.* das Vierfache. III. *v.a.* vervierfachen. **—uplicate**, I. *v.a.*, *see* —uple III. II. *adj.* & *s.*, *see* —uple I. & II. III. *s.* eins von vier gleichen Dingen.
Quaff, *v.* I. *a.* trinken, hinunterstürzen. II. *n.* zechen.
Quag, *s.*, **—mire**, *s.* der Sumpfboden. **—gy**, *adj.* sumpfig.
Quagga, *s.* das Quagga.
Quaich, *s.* flache Schale (*Scot.*).
[1]**Quail**, *s.* die Wachtel (*Orn.*); the — calls, die Wachtel schlägt.
[2]**Quail**, *v.n.* verzagen, den Mut verlieren; (tremble) zittern und zurückbeben (vor Angst).
Quaint, *adj.*, **—ly**, *adv.* altmodisch; (curious) seltsam, wunderlich, drollig. **—ness**, *s.* die Seltsamkeit; das Altmodische.
Quak—e, I. *v.n.* zittern und beben; to —e in one's shoes, vor Angst außer sich sein. II. *s.* das Zittern, Beben, die Erschütterung. **—er**, *s.* der Quäker. **—eress**, *s.* die Quäkerin; —er oats, englische Hafergrütze. **—erism**, *s.* das Quäkertum. **—ing**, I. *adj.* zitternd. II. *s.* das Zittern. *Comp.* **—ing-grass**, *s.* das Zittergras.
Quali—fication, *s.* die (necessary, erforderliche) Eigenschaft, Berechtigung, Befähigung, Fähigkeit; mental —fications, Geistesfähigkeiten; my —fications for this post are . . ., das was mich für diese Stelle befähigt, ist. . . **—fied**, *adj.* (fitted) geeignet, befähigt; berechtigt, fähig; (*Law*) qualifiziert; (modified) bedingt, eingeschränkt; näher bestimmt (*Gram.*). **—fy**, *v.* I. *a.* befähigen, geeignet machen; (entitle) berechtigen; (modify) beschränken, mildern, mäßigen, modifizieren; näher bestimmen (*Gram.*). II. *n.* sich befähigt machen. **—tative**, *adj.* qualitativ (*as an analysis*). **—ty**, *s.* die Beschaffenheit, Eigenschaft, Art; die Qualität (*C.L.*); (virtue) der Wert; *see* Capacity; (high rank) vornehmer Stand; the —ty, vornehme Leute (*archaic*); people of every —ty, Leute aus allen Ständen; a person of —ty, die Standesperson.
Qualm, I. *s.* die Anwandlung von Übelkeit *or* von einer Krankheit; (twinge) der Gewissensskrupel. **—ish**, *adj.*; I am —ish, mir wird übel.
Quandary, *s.* die Verlegenheit, Ungewißheit; to be in a —, sich weder zu raten noch zu helfen wissen.
Quant—itative, *adj.* dem Umfang nach, umfänglich; quantitativ. **—ity**, *s.* die Menge, Quantität; der große Teil; die Größe (*Math.*); das Zeitmaß, die Quantiät (*Pros.*); die Kategorie (*Log.*); blackberries in —ities, Brombeeren in großer Menge; a —ity of, viele; eine Menge (von). **—um**, *s.* das Maß; das Quantum.
Quarantine, I. *s.* die Quarantäne, Isolierung; to perform, suffer —, die Quarantäne halten, isolieren. II. *v.a.* (einem) Quarantäne auferlegen.
[1]**Quarrel**, I. *s.* der Streit, Zwist; (brawl) lärmender Streit, Zank, Hader; *see* Contest, Dispute; (cause of —) die Ursache, der Grund (des Streites); to pick a — with, Händel suchen mit. II. *v.n.* streiten, zanken; *see* Cavil. **—some**, *adj.* zänkisch, streitsüchtig. **—someness**, *s.* die Streitsucht.
[2]**Quarrel**, *s.* die viereckige Fensterscheibe; der Glaserdiamant.
Quarr—ier, *s.* der Steinbrecher. **—y**, I. *s.* der Steinbruch; slate —y, der Schieferbruch. II. *v.a.* (aus einem Steinbruch) brechen. *Comp.* **—yman**, *see* —ier. **—y-stone**, *s.* der Bruchstein.
[1]**Quarry**, *see under* Quarr—ier.
[2]**Quarry**, *s.* die Jagdbeute (der Hunde und Stoßvögel); das (bes. vom Falken) verfolgte Wild; der Fang, die Beute; der gesuchte Gegenstand (*fig.*).
Quart, I. *s.* das Quart (= ¼ Gallone). II. *attrib.*; — bottle, die Quartflasche. **—an**, *adj.* viertägig; —an ague, viertägiges Fieber. **—er**, I. *s.* das Viertel (*of an hour*, *year*, *etc.*, *of mutton*, *etc.*, *of the moon*, *the heavens*, *etc.*); das Vierteljahr, Quartal; (region) die (Himmels=)Gegend; (source) die Quelle; das Stadtviertel (*in a town*); das englische Malter, Quart; (= 8 bushels) der Viertelzentner; das (Wappen=)Feld, Quartier (*Her.*); die Gnade, der Pardon (*Mil.*); die Schonung, Nachsicht (*fig.*); *see* —ers; a —er of a pound, ein Viertelpfund; to strike the —ers, die Viertel schlagen; to call for —er, um Pardon bitten (*Mil.*); to give —er, Pardon geben, das Leben schenken; to give little or no —er, wenig oder nichts schonen, geringe oder keine Schonung geben; in this —er, hier, hierzulande; from all —ers, von allen Seiten (her); the wind blows from another —er, der Wind bläst aus einer andern Richtung *or* (*coll.*) aus einem andern Loche; I have it from that —er, ich weiß es von jener Seite. II. *v.a.* vierteln (*also Her.*); vierteilen (*a criminal*, *etc.*); (shelter) beherbergen, unterbringen; einquartieren (*Mil.*); to be —ered upon (at), im Quartier liegen, (in Garnison liegen) bei; to —er o.s. upon a p., sich bei einem einquartieren. **—ering**, *s.* das Vierteilen; die Schildteilung (*Her.*); die Einquartierung (*Mil.*). **—erly**, I. *adj.* & *adv.* vierteljährlich, alle Vierteljahre. II. *s.* die Vierteljahrschrift. **—ern**, I. *s.* das Quartierchen. II. *attrib.*; **—ern loaf,**

vierpfündiges Brot. —**ers**, *pl.* das Nachtlager; (abode) die Wohnung, der Aufenthalt; das Quartier (*Mil.*); (station) die Militärstation; to take up one's —ers at a friend's, sein Quartier bei einem Freunde aufschlagen; to have free —ers, umsonst wohnen; to change one's —ers, seine Wohnung wechseln, umziehen; the fore, (hind) —ers, die Vor-, (Nach-)hand (*of a horse*); at quite close —ers, aus allernächster Nähe; to come to close —ers with a p., einem zu Leibe gehen *or* rücken, mit einem handgemein werden. —**et(te)**, *s.* das Quartett. —**ile**, *s.* der Geviertschein. —**o**, *s.* das Quartformat. *Comp.* —**erday**, *s.* der Vierteljahrstag, das Quartal. —**erdeck**, *s.* die Schanze, das Quarterdeck (*Naut.*). —**ermaster**, *s.* der Quartiermeister (*Mil.*); der Schiemann (*Naut.*). —**ermaster-general**, *s.* der Generalquartiermeister. —**er-point**, *s.* der Viertelstrich (*Naut.*). —**er-sessions**, *pl.* die vierteljährlichen Plenarversammlungen aller Friedensrichter einer englischen Grafschaft, Quartalgerichte. —**erstaff**, *s.* kurzer, dicker Stab.

Quartz, *s.* der Quarz.

Quash, *v.a.* zermalmen, zerschmettern; zerdrücken, zerquetschen; unterdrücken (einen Aufruhr); aufheben, annullieren (ein Urteil); kassieren, verwerfen (eine Anklage).

Quasi, *pref.* Quasi-, Schein-, eine Art von . . .; — crime, — delict, unvorsätzliches Vergehen. —**modo**, *s.* der erste Sonntag nach Ostern.

Quassia, *s.* die Quassia, der Bitterholzbaum.

Quat—ernary, I. *adj.* aus vier bestehend; *see* —ernate (*Bot.*); Quaternär- (*Geol.*). II. *s.* die Vier-zahl, -heit. —**ernate**, *adj.* vierzählig; zu je Vieren vorhanden (*Bot.*). —**ernion**, *s.* die Vier. —**ernity**, *s.* die Vierzahl, Gruppe von vier. —**rain**, *s.* die vierzeilige Strophe (meist mit überschlagenden Reimen). —**refoil**, *s.* das Vierblatt (*Arch.*).

Quaver, I. *v.n.* zittern; Triller schlagen, trillern (*Mus.*). II. *v.a.* tremulierend singen. III. *s.* (shake) der Triller; die Achtelnote (*Mus.*).

Quay, *s.* der Kai, Quai, Staden, die Ufermauer; die Uferstraße.

Quean, *s.* das Mädchen (*Scotch*); (hussy) die Vettel, Metze.

Queas—iness, *s.* die Übelkeit; der Ekel; übertriebene Empfindlichkeit. —**y**, *adj.* übel, zum Erbrechen geneigt; empfindlich.

Queen, I. *s.* die Königin (*also at Cards, etc. & of bees*); his —, seine königliche Gemahlin; the king and his —, der König und seine Gemahlin; —'s evidence, (*now* King's evidence) der Kronzeuge; — of Hearts, die Herzkönigin; — of Heaven, die Himmelskönigin; — Mab, die Elfenkönigin; — of the May, die Maikönigin; — of the meadows, das Mehlkraut; — of the North, Edinburgh; the —'s shilling, das Handgeld, Werbegeld (*Mil.*); to get a —, in die Dame ziehen (*Draughts*). II. *v.a.* zur Königin machen (*Chess*). —**hood**, *s.* der Rang *or* die Stellung einer Königin. —**like**, *adj.* wie eine Königin, königlich. —**ly**, *adj.* wie eine Königin. *Comp.* —**-apple**, *s.* die Renette. —**-bee**, *s.* die Bienenkönigin. —**-consort**, *s.* die Königsgemahlin. —**-dowager**, *s.* die Königin-Witwe. —**-mother**, *s.* die Königin-Mutter. —**-post**, *s.* die Hängesäule. —**-regent**, *s.* die Königin-Regentin. —**-regnant**, *s.* die regierende Königin. —**'s-Bench**, *s.* das Oberhofgericht, der höchste Gerichtshof Englands in Strafsachen (*now* King's-Bench). —**'s-metal**, *s.* das Weißmetall. —**'s-ware**, *s.* das gelbe Steingut.

Queer, *adj.*, —**ly**, *adv.* seltsam, wunderlich, eigentümlich; (sick) übel, krank (*coll.*); (bad) schlecht, falsch (*sl.*); a — fellow, ein Sonderling.

Quell, *v.a.* unterdrücken, bezwingen; (allay) zähmen, dämpfen. —**er**, *s.* der Bezwinger.

Quench, *v.a.* (aus)löschen; löschen, dämpfen, stillen (*thirst, etc.*); (stifle) ersticken, unterdrücken. —**less**, *adj.* unauslöschlich, unstillbar.

Quern, *s.* die Handmühle.

Querulous, *adj.*, —**ly**, *adv.* unzufrieden, klagsüchtig; kläglich und mürrisch (*as a voice*). —**ness**, *s.* die Klagsucht.

Query, I. *s.* die Frage; das Fragezeichen; —, will he go? ob er gehen wird, das ist eben die Frage. II. *v.a.* aus-, be-fragen; (doubt) bezweifeln; mit einem Fragezeichen versehen (*a word, etc.*). III. *v.n.* fragen, zweifeln.

Quest, *s.* das Suchen, die Nachforschung; to be in — of, suchen nach; to go in — of, aufsuchen. —**ion**, I. *s.* die Frage; (inquiry) die Untersuchung; (subject of dispute) die Streitfrage, der Streitpunkt; (doubt) der Zweifel; die Interpellation (*Parl.*); die Aufgabe (*Arith.*); leading —ion, die Suggestivfrage; to ask —ions, Fragen stellen; beyond all —ion, unzweifelhaft; to call in —ion, in Zweifel ziehen, bezweifeln; the —ion is, es handelt sich darum; the matter in —ion, die vorliegende Sache, der fragliche Gegenstand; the lady in —ion, die bewußte Dame; to beg the —ion, das erst zu Beweisende als bereits entschieden voraussetzen; to pop the —ion, sich (einem Mädchen) erklären, einen Antrag machen (*coll.*); that is out of the —ion, das steht außer Frage, kommt nicht in Betracht; that is foreign to the —ion, das gehört nicht zur Sache *or* hierher; to move the previous —ion, *see* Previous. II. *v.a.* befragen; (doubt) bezweifeln. —**ionable**, *adj.*, —**ionably**, *adv.* fraglich, zweifelhaft, ungewiß, streitig; (suspicious) fragwürdig, bedenklich, verdächtig, zweideutig. —**ionableness**, *s.* die Zweifelhaftigkeit, Fraglichkeit, Bedenklichkeit, Verdächtigkeit. —**ioner**, *s.* der Frager. —**ioning**, *s.* das Fragen. —**or**, *s.* der Quästor. —**orship**, *s.* das Quästoramt, die Quästur.

Queue, I. *s.* die Reihe, Queue; der Perückenzopf; *see* Cue. II. *v.a.* in einen Zopf flechten.

Quibble, I. *s.* die Ausflucht, Spitzfindigkeit, Sophisterei; (pun) das Witzwort, Wortspiel. II. *v.n.* (einer Frage) ausweichen, Zweideutigkeiten gebrauchen; witzeln. —**r**, *s.* der Wortspieler, Wortwitzler, Sophist.

Quick, I. *adj. & adv.* rasch (*as a movement, walk, step, etc.*), schnell, behend, hurtig, geschwind, munter; frisch, lebhaft, regsam (*fig.*); (too —) voreilig; (hasty) hitzig, (prompt) unverzüglich, gleich; scharf, fein (*as the ear*); lebhaft, scharf (*as the understanding*); (live) lebendig; — with child, (hoch)schwanger; be —! frisch! munter! mach schnell! — anatomy, die Vivisektion; — eye, scharfes Auge; — of apprehension, schnell von Begriff. II. *s.* das lebendige Fleisch (*B.*); (*opp. to* Dead) die Lebenden; the — of the nail, der weiche Teil des Nagels; to the —, ins Fleisch; ins Herz, in die Seele, tief (*fig.*); cut to the —, ins Fleisch getroffen; to cut a p. to the —, einen aufs empfindlichste kränken; — at meat, — at work, wie einer ißt, so arbeitet er auch; *see* —set hedge; double- —, der Geschwindschritt. —**en**, *v.* I. *a.* beleben; lebendig machen (*B.*); beschleunigen (*the pace, etc.*). II. *n.* Leben fühlen (*Med.*). —**ener**, *s.* der, das Belebende. —**ly**, *adv.* geschwind, schnell, hurtig; gleich. —**ness**, *s.* die Schnelligkeit, Raschheit (*of movements, etc.*); die Lebhaftigkeit, Schärfe, Feinheit (*of wit, imagination, etc.*); (sensitiveness) die Empfindsamkeit; —ness of parts, die schnelle Fassungskraft, Scharfsinnigkeit; —ness at repartee, die Schlagfertigkeit. *Comp.* —**-firing**, *adj.*; —-firing gun, das Schnellfeuer-Geschütz. —**lime**, *s.* ungelöschter Kalk, Ätzkalk. —**-match**, *s.* die Zündschnur, der Ludelfaden (*Artil., Min.*); —-match tube, das Schlagröhrchen. —**sand**, *s.* der Flugsand. —**set**, *s.* der Setzling, Hagedorn; (—set hedge) die (der) lebendige Hecke (Zaun). —**-sighted**, *adj.* scharfsichtig. —

sightedness, *s.* die Scharfsichtigkeit. —**silver**, *s.* das Quecksilber. —**step**, *s.* der Geschwindschritt. —**-tempered**, *adj.* heißblütig, reizbar. —**-witted**, *adj.* von raschem Witze, schlagfertig, scharfsinnig, schlau.

[1]**Quid**, *s.* die Prieme (Tabak) (*sl.*); *see* Cud.

[2]**Quid**, *s.* = 20 shillings (*sl.*).

Quid—dity, *s.* das Wesen (einer Sache), die Quiddität (*Log.*); (quibble) die Spitzfindigkeit. —**dle**, *v.n.* tändeln, sich mit unbedeutenden Dingen beschäftigen. —**nunc**, *s.* der Neuigkeitskrämer; der (politische) Kannegießer. —**-pro-quo**, *s.* die Gegenleistung; das Äquivalent; der Mißverstand, das Mißverständnis, die Verwechselung.

Quiescen—ce, *s.* die Ruhe; das Stummsein (*Gram.*). —**t**, *adj.*, —**tly**, *adv.* ruhend, still; ruhig (*fig.*); stumm (*Gram.*).

Quiet, I. *adj.*, —**ly**, *adv.* ruhig (*as the sea, air, etc., a person, colours, etc.*); geräuschlos; ruhig, still (*as one's life, a place, a period, etc.*); ruhig, sanft, friedlich (*as the disposition*); (calm) ruhig, gelassen; (undisturbed) ruhig, ungestört; be —, sei ruhig! still! schweig! II. *s.* die Ruhe. III. *v.a.* beruhigen, stillen, besänftigen. —**ism**, *s.* der Quietismus. —**ist**, *s.* der Quietist. —**ness**, *s.* die Gemütsruhe; (—ude) die Ruhe, Stille, Friedlichkeit. —**ude**, *see* —ness. —**us**, *s.* die Ruhe, der Tod (*obs.*); die Endquittung, Schlußentlastung.

Quill, I. *s.* (— pen) der Federkiel; (goose's —) die Federpose; die Feder (*fig.*); der Stachel (*of a porcupine*); das Glöckchen (*of a frill, etc.*); to drive the —, schreiben; hero of the —, der Federheld; brother of the —, der Genosse von der Feder. II. *v.a.* in Falten, Glöckchen legen, fälteln, glocken. —**ing**, *s.* die Rüsche. *Comp.* —**-driver**, *s.* der Federfuchser. —**-driving**, *s.* die Federfuchserei. —**-feathers**, *pl.* Schwungfedern.

Quilt, I. *s.* die (gesteppte) Bettdecke, Steppdecke. II. *v.a. & n.* steppen; —ed petticoat, wattierter Unterrock. —**ing**, *s.* das Steppen von Wattiersachen; die Stepperei. *Comp.* —**ing-guide**, *s.* das Wattierlineal (*Sew-mach.*).

Quin—ary, *adj.* gefünft, aus fünf bestehend. —**cuncial**, *adj.* zu fünf über Kreuz stehend; —cuncial æstivation, geschindelte *or* dachige Blütendecklage (*Bot.*). —**cunx**, *s.* das Gefünfte, geschobene Viereck, der Quincunx. —**decagon**, *s.* das Fünfzehneck. —**decemvir**, *s.* der Quindezemvir. —**quagesima**, *s.* der Quinquagesima(sonntag). —**que**, *pref.* = fünf=. —**queliteral**, *adj.* fünfbuchstabig. —**quennial**, *adj.* fünfjährlich, alle fünf Jahre wiederkehrend. —**tain**, *s.* die Quintane; (sport) das Quintanrennen. —**tessence**, *s.* die Quintessenz, der Kraftauszug (*also fig.*); der Kern (*fig.*). —**tet(te)**, *s.* das Quintett. —**tile**, *s.* der Gefünftschein. —**tillion**, *s.* die Quintillion. —**tuple**, I. *adj.* fünffach. II. *v.a.* verfünffachen.

Quince, *s.* die Quitte. *Comp.* —**-marmalade**, *s.* das Quittengelee.

Quinine, *s.* das Chinin; ammoniated —, Chinin mit Ammonia.

Quinsy, *s.* die (Hals)Bräune.

Quip, *s.* der Stich, Hieb; die Stichelei.

[1]**Quire**, *see* Choir.

[2]**Quire**, *s.* das Buch (Papier).

Quirk, *s.* die plötzliche Wendung, das Abspringen von einem Punkte; die Witzelei; der Einfall, die Grille; *see* Quip; die Einzahnung, Hohlkehle (*Arch.*); abgesonderter Platz (*from a ground-plan*). *Comp.* —**(ed)-moulding**, *s.* der Sims in Kegelschnittform.

Quit, I. *v.a.* verlassen; lossprechen, befreien; *see* Remit; verzichten (auf), ablassen (von); to — o. s., *see* Acquit; to — scores, sich ausgleichen. II. *adj.* (—s) quitt, nichts schuldig; frei, ledig, los; to be —s, (mit einem) quitt sein; doubles or —s! doppelt oder nichts! *Comp.* —**e**, *see* Quite. —**rent**, *s.* der Erbzins. —**tance**, *s.* die Quittung.

Quitchgrass, *s.* das Queckengras.

Quite, *adv.* ganz, völlig, durchaus.

[1]**Quiver**, *s.* der Köcher.

[2]**Quiver**, I. *v.n.* beben, zucken, zittern. II. *s.* das Zucken, Zittern, Beben. —**ing**, *adj.*, —**ingly**, *adv.* bebend, zitternd, zuckend.

Qui vive, *s.*; to be on the —, auf der Hut sein, scharf aufpassen.

Quiz, I. *s.* lächerliche, seltsame Person *or* Sache; die Rätselfrage, Falle, Neckerei; der Necker, Spötter, Rätselaufgeber; die Prüfung zum Zweck des Einpaukens, das Einpauken (*Amer.*). II. *v.a.* necken, aufziehen; zum Zweck des Einpaukens ausfragen *or* prüfen (*Amer.*). —**zical**, *adj.* spöttisch; höhnisch, zum Necken geneigt; (droll) komisch. *Comp.* —**zing-glass**, *s.* das Einglas, Monocle (*fam.*)

Quodlibet, *s.* das Quodlibet, Allerlei, Gemisch.

Quoin, I. *s.* die (ausspringende) Ecke; der Eckstein (*Arch.*); der Richtkeil (*Mil.*); der Keil (*Typ.*). II. *v.a.* (ein)keilen (die Form, *Typ.*).

Quoit, *s.* der Wurfring, die Wurfscheibe. —**s**, *pl.* das Wurf=ring *or* =scheibenspiel.

Quondam, I. *adj.* ehemalig, weiland. II. *s.* jemand, der früher ein höheres Amt bekleidete (*obs.*).

Quorum, *s.* beschlußfähige Anzahl (*of a board*).

Quot—a, *s.* der verhältnismäßige Teil, Anteil, Beitrag, die Quote. —**able**, *adj.* anführbar, anzuführen. —**ation**, *s.* die Anführung, (—ed passage) die angeführte Stelle, das Zitat; die Preisangabe, Preisnotierung (*C. L.*); —ations of specie, etc., der Geldkurszettel; familiar —ations, geflügelte Worte. —**e**, *v.a.*, anführen, zitieren; berechnen, notieren (*C. L.*); to be —ed at . . ., notiert sein mit . . .; at the price —ed, zu dem verzeichneten Preise. —**er**, *s.* der Zitator. —**idian**, I. *adj.* täglich. II. *s.* das tägliche Fieber. —**ient**, *s.* der Quotient.

Quoth, *obs. imperf.*; — **I**, — **he**, sagte ich, sagte er.

R

R, r, *s.* R, r; to know the three —'s (reading, writing, arithmetic), Elementarbildung besitzen. *For abbreviations see the List of abbreviations at the end of the English-German part.*

Rabbet, I. *s.* die Fuge, Nut, der Falz; die Spündung (*Shipb.*). II. *v.a.* falzen; (unite) (ein)fügen, einfalzen. *Comp.* —**-joint**, *s.* das Blatt, die Spündung. —**-plane**, *s.* der Nuthobel.

Rabbi, *s.* der Rabbiner. —**nical**, *adj.* rabbinisch. —**nism**, *s.* der Rabbinismus.

Rabbit, *s.* das Kaninchen; Welsh — (*for* rarebit), gerösteter Käse, in zerlassener Butter auf geröstetem Brot. *Comp.* —**-hutch**, *s.* der Kaninchenstall. —**-warren**, *s.* das Kaninchengehege.

Rabble, *s.* lärmender Haufe; the —, der Pöbel.

Rabid, *adj.*, —**ly**, *adv.* wütend, toll. —**ness**, *s.* die Wut.

Rabies, *s.* die Hundswut, Tollwut.

Raccoon, *s.* der Waschbär.

[1]**Rac—e**, *s.* das Geschlecht, der Stamm; die Rasse, Art, der Schlag (*of beasts*). —**ial**, *adj.* die Rasse betreffend, einen Volksstamm betreffend, Rassen=; —ial animosities, der Rassenhaß. —**iness**, *s.* das Pikante. —**y**, *see* Racy.

[2]**Rac—e**, I. *s.* der Lauf; (contest) der Wettlauf, die Wettfahrt, das Wett=rennen; the boat- —e, die Ruderwettfahrt; (current) der Strom, die Strömung; der Lauf, die Laufbahn (*fig.*); mill —e, das Mühlwasser, Mühlgerinne; head, (tail) —e, Ober=, (Unter=)graben. II. *v.n.* rennen; wettrennen, =fahren, =laufen; (keep —e-horses) Rennpferde halten. III. *v.a.* rennen lassen. —**er**, —**-horse**, *s.* das Rennpferd. —**es**, *pl.* das Pferdewettrennen, das Rennen. —**ing**, *s.* das Welt=rennen, =laufen; —ing boat, das Rennboot; —ing in sacks, das Sacklaufen. *Comp.* —**e-course**, *s.* die Rennbahn.

Racem—e, *s.* die Blütentraube. —**ous**, —**ose**, *adj.* Trauben=.

Rachis, *s.* die Spindel.

Rachitis, *s.* die englische Krankheit, Rachitis.

[1]Rack, I. *s.* das Reck; (torture —) die Folter; (framework) das Gestell, Gerüst; der Rechen (*for clothes, etc., also Horol.*); die Raufe (*in stables*); toast —, der Toasthalter; luggage —, das Gepäcknetz; — and pinion, Zahnstange und Getriebe. II. *v.a.* recken; foltern, quälen, martern; (strain) aufs Höchste spannen; in einen Flaschenbehälter tun (*bottles*); to — one's brains, sich (*dat.*) den Kopf zerbrechen; —ed with pain, von Schmerzen gefoltert, gequält. *Comp.* **—-rent**, I. *s.* eine so hoch wie möglich gesteigerte Miete, unerschwingliche Pacht. II. *v.a.* eine kaum erschwingliche Pacht auferlegen. **—-renter**, *s.* der Gutsbesitzer, der die Pachtzinse ungebührlich steigert. **—-wheel**, *s.* das Sperrad. **—work**, *s.* das Zahnwerk.

[2]Rack, *s.* der Nacken und Rücken, das Halsstück (*of veal and mutton*).

[3]Rack, I. *s.* ziehendes Gewölk, der Wolkendunst. II. *v.n.* ziehen, vom Winde getrieben werden.

[4]Rack, I. *s.* der schnelle Paßgang. II. *v.n.*; to go at a —ing pace, in vollem Laufe hinstürmen.

Rack, *s.* (= Wrack); to go to — and ruin, ganz und gar zu Grunde gehen.

Rack, *v.a.* abziehen, läutern (*wine*).

[1]Racket, *s.* der Schläger, Ballschläger, das Schlagnetz, Rakett (*for tennis, etc.*). **—s**, *pl.* das Rakettspiel, eine Art Rasenballspiel. *Comp.* **—-court**, *s.* der zum Rakettspiel eingerichtete Hof.

[2]Racket, I. *s.* der Lärm, das Getöse, der Spektakel. II. *v.n.* lärmen. **—(t)y**, *adj.* lärmend.

Racy, *adj.* einen starken Grundgeschmack habend; eigenartig, geistreich (*style*), gewürzt, pikant (*fig.*).

Raddle, I. *v.a.* verflechten. II. *s.* der Zaunstecken; (hedge) der geflochtene Zaun (*prov.*).

Radi—al, *adj.* strahlig (*Geom.*); Speichen- (*Anat.*). **—ance**, **—ancy**, *s.* das Strahlen, der Glanz. **—ant**, I. *adj.*, **—antly**, *adv.* strahlend (*also fig.*); —ant matter, strahlenwerfender Stoff; *see* —ate II. II. *s.* der Strahlpunkt. **—ata**, *pl.* Strahltiere. **—ate**, I. *v.n.* strahlen, glänzen; sich von einem Punkte nach allen Richtungen hin verbreiten (*also fig.*). II. *adj.* strahlenförmig (*Anat.*); strahlig, strahlblütig (*Bot.*); (—ated) Strahl-, strahlig (*Min.*); —ate animals, Strahltiere. **—ation**, *s.* das Strahlen, die Ausstrahlung. **—ator**, *s.* der Ausstrahlapparat, (Hitze ausstrahlende) Zimmerofen. **—i**, *pl. see* —us. **—ometer**, *s.* der Strahlenmesser (*Phys.*); der Jakobsstab (*Astr.*). **—o-telegraphy**, die Funkentelegraphie. **—us**, *s.* der Halbmesser, Radius: der Strahl (*Bot.*); die Speiche, Armspindel (*Anat.*); —us of curvature, Krümmungshalbmesser; —us of explosion, Wirkungsradius; —us vector, Leitstrahl (*of a point*).

Radi—cal, I. *adj.*, **—cally**, *adv.* wurzelhaft, Wurzel- (*also Alg., Gram., Bot.*); eingewurzelt, gründlich, Grund (*fig.*); (natural) angeboren, natürlich; wesentlich, inner; Grund- (*Chem.*); radikal, rücksichtslos bis zum Äußersten gehend (*Pol.*); —cal sign, das Wurzelzeichen; —cal quantities, Wurzelgrößen; —cal truth (error), Grund-wahrheit (-irrtum); a —cal difference of opinion, eine Grundverschiedenheit in den Meinungen. II. *s.* der Radikale; (—cal letter) der Wurzelbuchstabe; (—cal word) das Wurzelwort; das Radikal (*Chem.*). **—calism**, *s.* der Radikalismus. **—calness**, *s.* die Gründlichkeit, Ursprünglichkeit. **—cle**, *s.* das Würzelchen; *see* —cal (*Chem.*). **—sh**, *s.* der Rettig. **—x**, *s.* die Wurzel (*Zool., Anat.*).

Raff, *s.*; the riff-—, das Gesindel, die Hefe des Volkes. **—le**, I. *v.a.* ausspielen, verlosen. II. *v.n.* würfeln, losen (for, um). III. *s.* das Würfel-, Pasch-spiel, die Lotterie; (—ling) das Auswürfeln, Ausspielen. **—ler**, *s.* der Würfler.

Raft, I. *s.* das Floß; die Baumstauung (*in rivers, Amer.*); temporary —, das Notfloß. II. *v.a.* flößen. **—er**, *s.* der Sparren; —ers, das Sparrenwerk. *Comp.* **—sman**, *s.* der Flößer.

Rag, I. *s.* der Lumpen, Fetzen; der Skandal, Radau (*sl.*); coral —, der Korallensandstein; to be in —s, ganz zerlumpt *or* abgerissen sein; it is to him like a red — to a bull, das wirkt auf ihn wie auf einen Stier das rote Tuch. II. *v.n.* zerlumpt werden; Radau *or* Skandal machen (*sl.*). III. *v.a.* zerreißen; einen uzen, mit einem feinen Ulk treiben (*sl.*). **—amuffin**, *s.* der Lump. **—ged**, *adj.* zerrissen, abgerissen; (in —s) zerlumpt, lumpig; (uneven) rauh, uneben. **—gedness**, *s.* die Zerlumptheit; die Rauheit. **—ging**, *s* die Radaumacherei; der Radau, Skandal. *Comp.* **—-book**, *s.* unzerreißbares Bilderbuch für kleine Kinder. **—-cutting**, *adj.*; —-cutting machine, die Lumpenschneid(e)maschine. **—-fair**, *s.* der Trödelmarkt. **—-gatherer**, **—man**, **—-picker**, *s.* der Lumpensammler. **—ged-school**, *s.* die Schule für Bettel- *or* arme Kinder. **—stone**, *s.* der Sandstein. **—(tag) and bobtail**, *s.* Krethi und Plethi.

Rag—e, I. *s.* die Wut, Raserei; der Zorn, Grimm, die Wut (*fig.*); die Heftigkeit, das Toben; die Sucht, Manie, Gier, Leidenschaft (*for something*); (rapture) die Begeisterung, Ekstase, das Entzücken; (vogue) die Mode; all the —e, ganz in der Mode; —e for building, Bauwut; —e for collecting, Sammelwut. II. *v.n.* wüten, rasen, toben. **—ing**, *adj.*, **—ingly**, *adv.* wütend.

Ragout, *s.* das Würzfleisch, Mischgericht, Ragout.

Raid, I. *s.* der feindliche Einfall, Raubzug, Beutezug. II. *v.a.* einen Raub- und Beute-zug unternehmen. **—er**, *s.* einer, der einen feindlichen Einfall macht, an einem Raubzuge teilnimmt.

[1]Rail, I. *s.* das Querholz, der Riegel; die Reling, Bordwand; die Leiste (*for pictures*); *see* —ing; die Schiene, das Geleise (*Railw.*); der Schienenstrang, die Eisenbahn (*fig.*); by —, mit der (per) Bahn; to go off the —s, entgleisen; die Regeling (*Naut.*); hand-—, die Handleiste eines Geländers. II. *v.a.* mit Pfosten und Querhölzern umgeben, einfriedigen; mit einem Geländer *or* Gitter versehen; mit der Bahn schicken; to — off, durch ein Geländer absondern. **—ing**, *s.* das Geländer, Staket, der Lattenzaun, die (aus Pfosten und Querbalken bestehende) Einfriedigung. *Comp.* **—-fence**, *s.* (high fence) das Geländer; (low fence) der Zaun. **—road**, **—way**, I. *s.* der Schienenweg, die Eisenbahn; der Bahnkörper. II. *attrib.*; —way accident, das Eisenbahnunglück; —way fare, das (Eisenbahn-)Fahrgeld; —way junction, der Eisenbahnknotenpunkt; —way line, die (Eisen-)Bahnlinie; —way plant, das Betriebsmaterial (einer Eisenbahn); —way porter, der Gepäckträger, Kofferträger; —way share, die Eisenbahnaktie; —way station, der Bahnhof; —way ticket, die (Eisenbahn-)Fahrkarte, der Fahrschein, das Billet. *Comp.* **—way-carriage**, *s.* der Eisenbahnwagen. **—way-company**, *s.* die Eisenbahngesellschaft. **—way-crossing**, *s.* der Bahnübergang. **—way-train**, *s.* der (Eisenbahn-)Zug.

[2]Rail, *v.n.*; to — at, (scoff) spotten über (*acc.*), losziehen gegen; *see* Revile. **—er**, *s.* der Spötter, Schmäher. **—ing**, I. *adj.*, **—ingly**, *adv.* spöttisch, spottend; schmähend. II. *s.* das Schmähen. **—lery**, *s.* der Spott, die Neckerei.

[3]Rail, *s.* die Ralle, der Wiesenläufer.

Raiment, *s.* die Kleidung; der Anzug.

Rain, I. *s.* der Regen. II. *v.n.* regnen; it is —ing, es regnet; it is going to —, es will regnen, sieht regnerisch aus; it never —s but it pours, ein Unglück kommt selten allein (*prov.*); it —s cats and dogs, es regnet in Strömen, es gießt mit Mollen; it —s hard, es regnet heftig *or* stark. **—iness**, *s.* das Regnerische; the —iness of the weather obliges me to . . ., das Regenwetter nötigt mich, . . . **—y**, *adj.* regnerisch, Regen-; —y day, der Regentag; eine Zeit der Not (*fig.*); to lay s.th. by for a —y day, einen Notpfennig aufsparen; —y season, the —s, die Regenzeit.

Comp. —**bow**, *s.* der Regenbogen. —**bow-tinted**, *adj.* regenbogenfarbig. —**fall**, *s.* der Regen(fall), die Regenmenge. —**-gauge**, *s.* der Regenmesser. —**-water**, *s.* das Regenwasser.

Raise, I. *v.a.* (in die Höhe) heben, erheben, aufheben; (exert) auf-stellen, -richten, -setzen; (rouse) erwecken, erregen, in Bewegung setzen; (advance) erheben, befördern; (found) erbauen, stiften; (originate) ins Dasein rufen; erhöhen (*the ground; prices; one's courage, spirits, etc.*); ziehen (*plants, beasts; blisters*); bauen (*wheat etc.*); treiben, springen lassen (*water*); aufwirbeln (*dust*); erheben (*taxes; the voice*); erregen, erwecken (*passions*); in Umlauf setzen, verbreiten (*reports*); aufwiegeln (to revolt, etc., zum Aufruhr 2c.); anstiften (*sedition, etc.*); auftreiben, aufbringen, flüssig machen (*money, etc.*); erwecken (expectations, Erwartungen); erwecken (from the dead, vom Tode); zitieren (*spirits*); to — a cry, ein Geschrei erheben; to — the eyes, die Augen aufschlagen; to — one's hat, den Hut lüften; to — a hue and cry, Lärm schlagen; to — a loan, eine Anleihe machen; to — the nap of cloth, das Tuch aufrauhen; to — objections to, Einwendungen, Einwürfe gegen (eine S.) erheben; to — paste or dough, den Teig angehen, gären lassen; to — a siege, eine Belagerung aufheben; to — the skin, die Haut zerreißen; to — a shout, aufschreien; to — steam, Dampf aufmachen; to — troops, Truppen aufbringen; to — a wall, eine Mauer aufführen; to — a wish, einen Wunsch rege machen; to — the wind, sich (*dat.*) Geld verschaffen (*sl.*); with (in a) —ed voice, mit erhobener Stimme. II. *s.* die Höhe eines Bergrückens (*dial.*). —**ed**, *adj.* erhaben; —ed work, erhabene *or* Relief-Arbeit. —**r**, *s.* der Pflanzer; der Züchter (*of cattle*); der Stifter; *see* Riser (*Carp.*).

Raisin, *s.* die Rosine; Corinthian —, die Korinthe.

Raising, *s.* das Heben 2c.; *see* Raise.

Rajah, *s.* der Rajah, indischer Fürst.

[1]**Rake**, I. *s.* der Rechen, die Harke. II. *v.a.* harken, rechen (*Agr., Hort.*); (— together) zusammenschüren; verscharren, bedecken (*the fire*); *see* Stir; der Länge nach beschießen, bestreichen (*Mil., Naut., also with a glass*); to — out, auseinanderwerfen, zum Ausgehen bringen (*a fire*); to — up, aufwühlen, aufrühren (*an old story, etc.*). III. *v.n.* harken; kratzen; to — for, suchen nach . . .

[2]**Rak—e**, *s.* das Überhangen; das Ausschießen (*of a ship*); aft —e, der Fall des Achterstevens. —**ish**, *adj.* überhängend, ausschießend.

[3]**Rak—e**, I. *s.* der Wüstling. II. *v.n.* ein wüstes Leben führen. —**ish**, *adj.*, —**ishly**, *adv.* wüst, liederlich, ausschweifend; *see* Fast.

[1]**Rally**, I. *v.a.* wieder sammeln, in Ordnung bringen; zum Stehen bringen (*Mil.*). II. *v.n.* sich wieder sammeln, zur Ordnung zurückkehren (*as troops*); sich erholen (*after an illness or a commercial depression*). III. *s.* die Sammlung; das Signal zum Sammeln; der Gang (Tennis); to sound the —, zum Sammeln blasen. *Comp.* —**ing-point**, *s.* der Sammelplatz. —**ing-word**, *s.* das Losungswort.

[2]**Rally**, I. *v.a.*; to — s.o. upon a th., einen aufziehen mit, sich über einen lustig machen wegen. II. *v.n.* scherzen.

Ram, I. *s.* der Widder (*Zool., Astr., Naut.*); (—mer) die Ramme; (battering- —) der Widder, Sturmbock; (ship with a —) das Rammschiff. II. *v.a.* rammen; (mit dem Widder, Sporn) rammen (*Naut.*); to — **down** (the charge), (die Ladung) fest ansetzen; to — **in**, einrammen. —**mer**, *s.* der Pflasterstößel, die Ramme; der Ansetzer, Setzer (*Artil.*); *see* —rod. *Comp.* —**rod**, *s.* der Ladestock.

Rambl—e, I. *v.n.* umher-streifen, -streichen, -schweifen, -wandern; abschweifen (*in speaking*); he —es, er bleibt nicht bei seinem Gegenstand. II. *s.* das Umherstreifen, die Wanderung; (trip) der Streifzug. —**er**, *s.* der Umher-streicher, -schwärmer, Wanderer; crimson —er, eine hochrote Kletterose. —**ing**, I. *adj.*, —**ingly**, *adv.* weitschweifig, planlos, umherschweifend; abschweifend (*as a discourse*). II. *s.* das Umherschweifen.

Ram—eous, *adj.* ästig, verzweigt. —**ification**, *s.* die Verzweigung, Verästelung (*also Anat., Bot. & fig.*); —ifications, Äste, Zweige. —**ify**, *v.* I. *a.* verzweigen, in Äste *or* Zweige zerteilen. II. *n.* sich verzweigen (*also fig.*). —**ose**, —**ous**, *adj.* astreich, ästig.

Ramp, I. *v.n.* gewaltig springen, *see* Bound; sich zum Sprunge erheben; toben, wüten. II. *s.* die Rampe (*Fort., Build.*). —**acious**, *coll. for* —ageous. —**age**, I. *v.n.* lärmend oder wütend umher schweifen (*coll.*). II. *s.*; to be on the —age, sich austoben. —**ageous**, —**agious**, *adj.* wild umherspringend, tobend (*fam.*). —**ancy**, *s.* die Üppigkeit, das Überhandnehmen, Wuchern; —ancy of vice, das Umsichgreifen, Fortwuchern des Lasters. —**ant**, *adj.*, —**antly**, *adv.* überhandnehmend, wuchernd, üppig, um sich greifend; (wild) mutwillig, ausgelassen; aufgerichtet, steigend (*Her.*); lion —ant, aufgerichteter Löwe.

Rampart, *s.* der Wall, Haupt-, Festungs-wall (*Fort.*); die Brustwehr (*fig.*).

Ramshackle(d), *adj.* baufällig (*coll.*).

Ran, *imperf. sing. of* Run.

Ranch, *s.* der große Grundbesitz für Viehzucht, die Viehwirtschaft; die Viehweide (*Amer.*).

Ranc—id, *adj.* ranzig, stinkend. —**idity**, —**idness**, *s.* die Ranzigkeit. —**orous**, *adj.*, —**orously**, *adv.* voller Groll, boshaft. —**our**, *s.* der Groll, die Erbitterung, Boshaftigkeit.

Random, I. *s.*; at —, aufs Geratewohl. II. *adj.* zufällig, aufs Geratewohl; — shot, der Schuß ins Blaue, aufs Geratewohl; to talk at —, in den Tag hineinreden.

Rang, *imperf. of* Ring.

Range, I. *v.a.* reihen, ordnen, in Reihen stellen; *see* Arrange; durch-streifen, -laufen (*a place*); to — the coast, längs der Küste hinfahren. II. *v.n.* umherstreifen, herum-streifen, -wandern; (lie) in einer gewissen Richtung liegen, sich erstrecken; (sail, pass along) vorbei, entlang segeln, fahren; the age of the children —s from 6 to 16, das Alter der Kinder steigt von 6 bis auf 16. III. *s.* die Reihe; die (Hügel-)Kette (*of hills*); (roving) die Wanderung, der Ausflug, Lauf; (space) der Raum; der Umfang, Kreis, Bereich (*of ideas, observation, etc.*); die Schußweite (*Artil.*); der Spielraum; (compass) der Umfang; das Steigen und Fallen (*of a thermometer*); (kitchen —) der Kochherd; die Sprosse (*of a ladder*); großer Weideplatz; die Ausdehnung, Fläche (*fig.*); shooting —, der Schießplatz; — of thought, der Ideenkreis; to give one's fancy free —, seiner Einbildungskraft freien Lauf lassen; to take a wider —, sich ausbreiten, zu höherer Stufe aufsteigen; to determine the — of a fire-arm, ein Gewehr einschießen; at a — of 1000 yards, auf eine Entfernung von 1000 Schritt; at close —, aus nächster Nähe; point blank *or* right level —, die Kern-, Horizontal-schußweite; extreme —, äußerste Schußweite. —**r**, *s.* der Herumstreifer; der Förster; der Jäger (*Mil.*); der Aufseher (*in parks*); —r of Richmond Park, der Oberjägermeister.

[1]**Rank**, I. *s.* (row) die Reihe (*also Mil.*); (class) die Klasse; (grade) der Rang, Stand; das Glied; — and file, Reihe und Glied, gemeine Soldaten, die Mannschaft; to raise from the —s, vom Gemeinen zum Offizier befördern; to quit the —s, aus dem Gliede treten; desertieren; to reduce to the —s, (einen Offizier zum gemeinen Soldaten) degradieren; he was raised to the — of prince, er wurde in den Fürstenstand erhoben; keep your —s! bleibt im Gliede! all —s and classes, alle Stände und Klassen; the upper —s,

die bessern Stände; a writer of the first —, ein Schriftsteller ersten Ranges; man (lady) of —, Mann (Dame) von Stand; to take — of, den Vorrang haben vor. II. *v.a.* in eine Reihe stellen, reihen, ordnen; (class) rechnen, zählen (with, zu). III. *v.n.* sich reihen, sich ordnen; gezählt werden, sich rechnen (with, zu); he —s (takes —) with a major, er hat den Rang eines Majors; to — against, gegenüberstehen; to — high, hoch stehen, eine hohe Stellung einnehmen; to — next to, im Range gleich nach . . . kommen.

[2]**Rank**, *adj.*, **—ly**, *adv.* üppig, geil wachsend; fruchtbar, fett (*as soil*); stark, kräftig (*as poison*); arg, grob, Erz= (*as sedition, etc.*); *see* Rancid; — taste, starker Geschmack. **—le**, *v.n.* sich entzünden, eitern, um sich fressen; um sich fressen, nagen (*fig.*); envy's —ling sting, des Neides verderblicher Stachel. **—ness**, *s.* der üppige Wuchs, die Üppigkeit; der starke, üble Geruch *or* Geschmack. *Comp.* **—-scented**, *adj.* übelriechend.

Ransack, *v.a.* durchwühlen, durchsuchen; plündern.

Ransom, I. *s.* das Lösegeld; die Erlösung (*Theol.*). II. *v.a.* auslösen, loskaufen; erlösen (*B.*).

Rant, I. *s.* die Schwulst, Schwülstigkeit; das leere Geschrei, lärmende Geschwätz. II. *v.n.* hochtrabend reden; (bluster) toben, schreien, lärmen. **—er**, *s.* der polternde Redner, schwülstige Schwätzer, Kanzelpauker, Kulissenreißer; der Ranter (*Theol.*). **—ipole**, I. *adj.* wild, ausgelassen. II. *s.* der Ausgelassene, Wüstling. **—y**, *adj.* wild.

Ranunculus, *s.* die Ranunkel.

Ranz, *s.*; — des vaches, der Kuhreihen.

[1]**Rap**, I. *s.* der Schlag, Tapp, das Klopfen; there is a — at the door, man klopft (an die Tür); — on the knuckles, ein Schlag auf die Knöchel (*lit.*), ein Verweis (*fig.*); — on the nose, der Nasenstüber. II. *v.n.* schlagen, klopfen, pochen (at, an). III. *v.a.*; to — a p.'s fingers, einem auf die Finger klopfen. **—per**, *s.* der Türklopfer; der Geisterklopfer.

[2]**Rap**, *s.* der falsche (irische) Halbpfennig; der Heller, Deut; I don't care a —, das ist mir ganz gleichgültig *or* egal.

[3]**Rap**, *v.a.* fortreißen; to — and rend, ergreifen, erhaschen, erraffen. **—acious**, *see* Rapacious. **—e**, *s.* der Raub; die Entführung (*of Proserpine, etc.*); die Notzucht (*Law*); —e of the forest, der Waldfrevel; to commit a —e, Notzucht begehen. **—t**, *adj.* hingerissen, entzückt, außer sich. **—ture**, *s.* die Entzückung, Ekstase, Begeisterung; she is in —tures, sie ist außer sich vor Entzücken (über, *acc.*). **—turous**, *adj.*, **—turously**, *adv.* entzückend, hinreißend, leidenschaftlich, stürmisch.

Rap—acious, *adj.*, **—aciously**, *adv.* raub=gierig, =süchtig (*also Zool.*), räuberisch; (greedy) gierig; Raub= (*Zool.*). **—acity**, **—aciousness**, *s.* die Raub=gier, =sucht, *see* Greediness. **—id**, *adj.*, **—idly**, *adv.* schnell, geschwind, rasch (*as growth*); reißend (*as water*); —id fire, das Schnellfeuer (*Mil.*); —id speaker, einer, der geschwind spricht, der Schnellredner; —id decline, galoppierende Schwindsucht. **—idity**, *s.* die Geschwindigkeit, Schnelligkeit, Raschheit, der Ungestüm. **—ids**, *pl.* die Stromschnelle, der Strudel. **—ine**, *s.* der Raub, die Plünderung. **—tores**, *pl.* Raubvögel. **—torial**, *adj.* Raub=.

[1]**Rape**, *s.* (—-seed) der Rübsamen, (Kohl=)Raps. *Comp.* **—-cake**, *s.* der Rapskuchen. **—-seed**, I. *s.* der Rübsamen. II. *attrib.*; —-seed oil, das Rüböl, Rapsöl.

[2]**Rape**, *s.* das Reibeisen, die Raspel, Reibe.

[3]**Rape**, *s.* der Traubenkamm, Rapp. **—s**, *pl.* die ausgepreßten Traubenschalen, Trester; lose Weinbeeren. *Comp.* **—-wine**, *s.* der Tresterwein.

[4]**Rape**, *see* [3]Rap.

Rapier, *s.* der Stoßdegen, das Rapier.

Rappee, *s.* der Rapé (Tabak).

Rapscallion, *s.* der Lumpenkerl; *see* Rascallion.

Rapt, *imperf. & p.p. of* [1]Rap & [3]Rap.

Rar—a avis, *s.* seltene Erscheinung, besondere Person. **—e**, *adj.*, **—ely**, *adv.* selten, rar; (—ely equalled) selten, unvergleichlich, ausgezeichnet; locker, dünn, verdünnt, fein (*Phys., etc.*); (sparse) einzeln. **—efaction**, *s.* die Verdünnung. **—efy**, *v.a.* verdünnen. **—eness**, *s.* die Dünnheit, Dünne; die Seltenheit; die Kostbarkeit (*fig.*). **—ity**, *s. see* —eness; die Kostbarkeit, kostbare Sache. *Comp.* **—ebit**, *see* Rabbit (Welsh). **—ee-show**, *s.* der Guck=, Raritäten=kasten.

[1]**Rare**, *see under* Rar—a.

[2]**Rare**, *adj.* nicht ausgekocht, nicht durchgebraten (*Amer.*).

Rascal, I. *s.* der Schuft, Spitzbube; young —, kleiner Schelm, Schalk. II. *adj.* mager (*as a deer*); nichtswürdig. **—ity**, *s.* die Schurkerei, Büberei. **—lion**, *s.* der Lump, gemeine Kerl. **—ly**, *adv.* gemein, schuftig; erbärmlich.

Ras—e, *see* Raze. **—orial**, *adj.* hühnerartig. **—ure**, *see* Erasure.

[1]**Rash**, *adj.*, **—ly**, *adv.* hastig, voreilig; (headlong) unbesonnen, übereilt, tollkühn. **—er**, *s.* die gebratene Speckschnitte. **—ness**, *s.* die Voreiligkeit, Unbesonnenheit, der Ungestüm.

[2]**Rash**, *s.* der Hautausschlag.

Rasp, I. *s.* die Raspel; *see* —berry. II. *v.a.* raspeln; verletzen (*also fig.*). **—er**, *s.* der Schaber; das Schab=, Kratz=eisen. **—ing**, I. *s.* das raspeln; —ings, Raspelspäne. II. *adj.* raspelnd; —ing sound, kratzender Ton. *Comp.* **—berry**, *s.* die Himbeere. **—berry-bush**, der Himbeerbusch. **—berry-vinegar**, *s.* der Himbeeressig.

Rat, I. *s.* die Ratte; der politische Überläufer (*Pol., fam.*); der um geringeren Lohn Arbeitende, einer der an einem Streik sich nicht beteiligt (*sl.*); to smell a —, den Braten riechen, etwas merken (*sl.*). II. *v.n.* von einer Partei zur andern übertreten (*Pol., fam.*); um geringern Lohn arbeiten (*sl.*); Ratten fangen. **—ten**, *v.a.* mißliebige Arbeiter bei einem Ausstand einschüchtern. **—ter**, *s.* der Rattenfänger (*also of dogs*). **—ting**, *s. see* — II. *Comp.* **—-catcher**, *see* —ter. **—lines**, *pl.* die Webeleinen (*Naut.*). **—sbane**, *s.* das Rattengift. **—-tail**, *s.* der Rattenschwanz (*Vet.*); —-tail file, der Rattenschwanz; —-tail spoon, der (silberne) Löffel mit rattenschwanzartiger Fortsetzung des Griffs auf der Rückseite des Löffels. **—-trap**, *s.* die Rattenfalle.

Rat—able, *adj.* zu schätzen (at, auf (*acc.*)), wert; steuerbar, steuerpflichtig, zollpflichtig (*Law*). **—e**, I. *s.* das Verhältnis, der Maßstab, Maß; (price) der Preis; (value) die (Kommunal-) Abschätzung; (*tax*) die Gemeindesteuer, Ortssteuer, Kommunalabgabe; der Zinsfuß, Wechsel=Kurs (*C.L.*); (proportion) die Rate, der verhältnismäßige Anteil; (degree) der Grad; der Rang (*Naut.*); —e (*of going etc.*), die Schnelligkeit; —es and taxes, Kommunalabgaben und Staatssteuern; at the —e of, zu dem Preise von . . .; at the —e of 3 per cent per annum, zu 3 Prozent jährlich; at a —e of 7 knots, mit einer Geschwindigkeit von 7 Knoten (*Naut.*); at the —e at which he is (now) going, so wie er es (jetzt) macht, treibt, fährt, reitet; at a cheap —e, wohlfeil, billig; at a great —e, übermäßig, auf außergewöhnliche Weise, (quickly) sehr schnell; at any —e, auf jeden Fall, in jedem Falle; at this —e, solchergestalt, auf diese Weise; —e of interest, der Zinsfuß; —e of wages, der Lohnsatz; —e of currency, of exchange, der (Geld=)Kurs; —e of combustion, der Brennmaterialkonsum; a first- — opportunity, eine Gelegenheit ersten Ranges; the hotel was only second- —, der Gasthof war nur mäßig *or* zweiten Ranges; at the same —e, in demselben Maße; *see* First- —e. II. *v.a.* schätzen, veranschlagen; (assess) (ein)schätzen für städtische Steuern. **—er**, *s.* der Schätzer. **—ification**, *s.* die Bestätigung, Bekräftigung. **—ifier**, *s.* der Gutheißende, Bestätigende. **—ify**, *v.a.* bestätigen, gutheißen, vollziehen. **—ing**, *s.* die Einschätzung für städtische Steuern. **—io**, *s.* das Verhältnis; to be in the inverse —io, sich umgekehrt verhalten (to, wie). **—iocination**, *s.* vernünftiges Urteilen, Schließen; der Vernunftschluß. **—iocinative**, *adj.* schluß-, vernunfts-mäßig. **—ion**, *s.* die Ration (*Mil.*). **—ional**, *see* Rational. *Comp.* **—e-payer**, *s.* der Steuerzahler.

[2]**Rat—e**, *v.* I. *a.* heftig ausschelten, (einem etwas) derb verweisen, (einem) Verweise geben (for, about, wegen). II. *n.* schelten, schimpfen (at, über, *acc.*). **—er**, *s.* der Ausscheltende. **—ing**, *s.* das Schelten, to give a p. a good —ing, einen tüchtig ausschelten.

Ratafia, *s.* der Fruchtliqueur, Ratafia.

Rat(t)an, *s.* das indische Rohr, der Rotang; (cane) der Rohrstock.

Ratch, *s.* die gezahnte Sperrstange (*Mach.*); das Schöpfrad, die Auslösung (*Horol.*); circular —, *see* —et-wheel. **—et**, *s.* der Sperr-kegel, -haken, die Sperrklinke. *Comp.* **—et-wheel**, *s.* das Sperrad (mit Sperrklinke).

Ratel, *s.* der Honigfresser (*Orn.*).

Rather, *adv.* eher, lieber; vielmehr; (somewhat) einigermaßen, ziemlich, etwas; or —, oder vielmehr; I had —, ich wollte lieber, lieber wollte ich; the —, um so mehr; (especially) besonders; — a long time, eine recht lange Zeit, recht lange; (do you like him?) —! (haben Sie ihn gern?) ob ich ihn gern habe! das sollte ich meinen! freilich!

Rational, *adj.*, **—ly**, *adv.* vernunftgemäß, beweisfähig; vernünftig, mit Vernunft begabt (*as a being*); rational (*Math.*); — horizon, der wahre Horizont; — dress, die Reformkleidung; — dress association, der Verein zur Verbesserung der Frauenkleidung. **—e**, *s.* der Daseinsgrund; die wohlbegründete Erklärung. **—ism**, *s.* der Rationalismus, Vernunftglaube. **—ist**, *s.* der Rationalist. **—istic**, *adj.* rationalistisch. **—ity**, *s.* die Vernunft, das Denkvermögen; (reasonableness) die Vernünftigkeit. **—ize**, *v.* I. *a.* vernunftmäßig machen *or* prüfen *or* erklären. II. *n.* vernunftgemäß vorgehen; rationalistisch denken. **—ness**, *s.* die Vernunftmäßigkeit.

Ratoon, *s.* der Zuckerrohrschößling.

Rattl—e, I. *v. n.* rasseln, klappern; (chatter) plappern, herauspoltern; to —e **along, off,** dahin-, fort-rasseln. II. *v.a.* rasseln mit; to —e **off**, herrasseln; to —e **out**, herauspoltern. III. *s.* das Gerassel; das Geplapper; (death —e) das Röcheln (eines Sterbenden); (chatterer) *see* —er; die Schnarre, Rassel, Klapper; the watchman sprung his —e, der Nachtwächter drehte seine Schnarre. **—er**, *s.* die lärmende Person; der Schwätzer; derber Schlag (*sl.*); derbe Lüge (*sl.*); die Klapperschlange (*Amer.*). **—ing**, *adj.* rasselnd, prasselnd; schwatzhaft; to go at a —ing pace, in voller Karriere fahren; *see* Large, Fine (*coll.*); (lively) lebhaft (*fam.*). *Comp.* **—e-brain, —e-head, —e-pate**, *s.* der Schwindelkopf. **—-brained**, *adj.* lärmend, geschwätzig; unbesonnen, windig. **—esnake**, *s.* die Klapperschlange.

Rauc—ity, *s.* die Heiserkeit (*of the voice*); die Rauheit (*of tone*). **—ous**, *adj.* heiser, rauh.

Raught, (*obs.*) *imperf. & p.p. of* Reach.

Rav—age, I. *s.* die Verwüstung, Verheerung, Zerstörung; —ages of time, der Zahn der Zeit. II. *v.a.* verwüsten, verheeren. **—ager**, *s.* der Verwüster, Verheerer. **—en**, *v.n.* raubgierig sein, *see* Prey. **—ener**, *s.* der Räuber; der Raubvogel (*Orn.*). **—ening**, I. *adj.* verschlingend; raubend, plündernd; —ening wolves, reißende Wölfe (*B.*). II. *s. see* Rapacity. **—enous**, *adj.*, **—ly**, *adv.* gefräßig; heißhungrig; —enous appetite, der Heißhunger. **—enousness**, *s. see* Rapacity, Voracity; die Freßwut, Gefräßigkeit; der Heißhunger. **—ine**, *s.* die Bergschlucht; der Graben (*Mount.*). **—ish**, *v.a.* mit Gewalt wegnehmen; (violate) schänden, notzüchtigen; hinreißen, entzücken (*fig.*). **—isher**, *s.* der Räuber; der Notzüchtiger; der Entzücker. **—ishing**, *adj.*, **—ishingly**, *adv.* hinreißend, entzückend. **—ishment**, *s.* der (Frauen-, Kinder-)Raub, die Entführung; die Schändung, Notzucht; die Entzückung.

Rav—e, *v.n.* rasen; phantasieren (*Med.*); to —e about, wahnsinnig lieben, schwärmen für; aberwitzig reden, faseln über (*acc.*). **—ing**, I. *adj.* rasend; faselnd. II. *s.* das Rasen, Faseln.

Ravel, *v.* I. *a.* verwirren, verwickeln; to — out, auf-flechten, -drehen, -fasern, -trennen. II. *n.* sich auf-drehen, -fasern.

Ravelin, *s.* der Halbmond, das Ravelin (*Fort.*).

[1]**Raven**, *see under* Rav—age.

[2]**Raven**, *s.* der Rabe; the — croaks, der Rabe krächzt; black as a —, rabenschwarz.

Raw, I. *adj.*, **—ly**, *adv.* roh (*also of materials, products, etc.*); *see* Undiluted; (crude) unreif; rauh, wund (*as flesh*); rauh (*as weather*); (in the natural state) unbearbeitet; roh, unerfahren, ungeübt (*fig.*); a — climate, ein rauhes, unfreundliches Klima; — meat, rohes Fleisch; — sugar, der Rohzucker; — troops, unerfahrene Truppen. II. *s.* wund geriebene Stelle; to touch on the —, an einen wunden Fleck rühren. **—ness**, *s.* die Roheit; die Rauhigkeit; die Unerfahrenheit, Ungeschicklichkeit. *Comp.* **—-boned**, *adj.* mager, fleischlos. **—-head (and bloody bones)**, *s.* der Popanz. **—hide**, *s.* die Riemenpeitsche.

[1]**Ray**, I. *s.* der (Licht-)Strahl, Streifen; der Strahl (*Bot., also fig.*); — of heat, Wärmestrahl; luminous —, leuchtender Strahl; visual —, Seh-, Gesichts-strahl. II. *v.n.* strahlen. **—ed**, *adj.* gestrahlt, Strahl-. **—less**, *adj.* strahlenlos.

[2]**Ray**, *s.* der Roche (*Icht.*).

Raz—e, *v.a.* aus-kratzen, -löschen, -radieren; (demolish) zerstören, vernichten, dem Boden gleich machen; (destroy) vertilgen. **—ee**, *s.* das rasierte Kriegsschiff. **—or**, *s.* das Rasiermesser; here —ors are ground and set, hier werden Rasiermesser geschliffen und abgezogen; safety —or, das Sicherheitsrasiermesser. *Comp.* **—or-bill**, *s.* der Schermesserschnäbler, Tordalk. **—or-fish**, *s.* der Schermesserfisch. **—or-strop**, *s.* der Streichriemen, das Abziehleder.

[1]**Re**, *s.* der zweite Ton der diatonischen Tonleiter (*Mus.*).

[2]**Re**; *in re* (*Lat.*), in Sachen, in der Angelegenheit.

[3]**Re—**, *prefix* = wieder, nochmals, noch einmal. *For verbs, etc., compounded with this prefix and not given in the following lists see the simple verbs, etc.*

Reabsor—b, *v.a.* wieder-einsaugen, -einschlucken. **—ption**, *s.* das Wieder-einsaugen, -einschlucken.

Reach, I. *v.n.* reichen, sich erstrecken, langen, sich ausdehnen (to, bis); to — **after**, streben nach; to — **into**, eindringen (in eine S.); to — **to** a th., eine Sache erreichen; to — **out**, ausholen. II. *v.a.* reichen, langen; strecken (out, aus); (hand over) über-, hin-reichen, hergeben; (touch) treffen, erreichen; (overtake) einholen, erreichen; (arrive at) ankommen, anlangen in; (attain to) erlangen, erreichen; zukommen, zu Handen kommen (*as a letter*); your letter —ed me this morning, Ihr Brief traf heute früh bei mir ein *or* kam in meine Hände; when this —es you, wenn Sie dies erhalten; to — the bottom, den Grund finden; to — down (forth), herunter-holen, -langen (ausstrecken); this may not perhaps — your case, dies erstreckt sich vielleicht nicht auf Ihren Fall. III. *s.* das Reichen, Erreichen; (distance) die Weite, Entfernung; (power of —ing) die Tragweite, der Bereich; (ability) das Vermögen, die Fähigkeit, Kräfte, Fassungskraft; (— of water) die Breite; die Stromstrecke zwischen zwei Krümmungen; within — of gunshot, bis auf Flintenschußweite; (out of) within —, (un)erreichbar; he used all the means within his —, er wandte alle ihm zu Gebote stehenden Mittel an; to keep out of the — of danger, sich gegen Gefahr sichern; I advise him not to come within — of me, ich rate ihm mir nicht zu nahe zu kommen.

React, *v.a.* gegen=, (zu)rück=wirken, auf einander einwirken (*also fig.*); reagieren (*Chem.*); *see* Resist. **—ion**, *s.* die Rück=, Gegen=wirkung; die Reaktion (*Pol.*, *Chem.*), Gegenwirkung (*Mach.*, *Chem.*); period of —ion, die Periode der rückläufigen Bewegung (*also fig.*); a —ion set in, ein Rückschlag trat ein. **—ionary**, I. *adj.* reaktionär. II. *s.* der Reaktionär.

Read, I. *ir.v.a.* lesen (*also fig.*); to — the character, den Charakter durchschauen *or* erfassen; to — a paper (at a conference), einen Vortrag halten; to — **aloud**, laut (vor=)lesen; to — **off**, ablesen, vom Blatte lesen; to — **on**, fort=, weiter=lesen; to — **out**, *see* to — aloud, zu Ende lesen; to — **over**, durchlesen, überlesen; to — **to** s. o., einem vorlesen; to — to o.s., für sich lesen; to — **up**, sich (in ein Fach) einarbeiten, seine Kenntnisse auffrischen. II. *ir.v.n.* lesen, studieren; (sich) lesen; to — for an examination, sich auf eine Prüfung vorbereiten; to — for the press, Korrekturen lesen; a —ing man, ein fleißig Studierender; ein Bücherwurm; he is well —, er ist sehr belesen, von umfassender Belesenheit; it —s well, es liest sich gut; it —s like fact, es liest sich, als wäre es wahr. III. *adj.;* well —, belesen. **—able**, *adj.* lesbar. **—ableness**, *s.* die Lesbarkeit. **—er**, *s.* der (die) Leser(in); der (die) Vorleser(in); der Vorleser (*in church*); der Korrektor (*Typ.*); das Lesebuch; der Professor (an einigen englischen Universitäten für gewisse Fächer); German —er, zweites Elementarbuch der deutschen Sprache; —er in Germanic, der Universitätsprofessor für germanische Philologie; the general —er, das große Publikum. **—ership**, *s.* das Vorleseramt; die Professur (*Univ.*). **—ing**, I. *adj.* lesend; studierend. II. *s.* das Lesen; das Vorlesen; die Lektüre; die Leseprobe (*Theat.*); (way of —ing) die Art zu lesen, Auffassung, Deutung; die Lesart; various —ings, die Varianten; der angezeigte Stand (*of the barometer, thermometer*); die Korrektur (*Typ.*); die Belesenheit; a man of wide —ing, ein Mann von umfassender Belesenheit; her —ing of Beethoven's sonata, ihre Wiedergabe *or* Auffassung von Beethovens Sonate. *Comp.* **—ing-book**, *s.* das Lesebuch. **—ing-desk**, *s.* das Lesepult. **—ing-glasses**, *pl.* die Lesebrille. **—ing-lamp**, *s.* die Studierlampe. **—ing-party**, *s.* für Zwecke gemeinsamen Studiums gebildete kleine (Studenten=)Gesellschaft (in den Ferien an der See oder in den Bergen mit oder ohne Lehrer). **—ing-room**, *s.* das Lesezimmer.

Read—ily, *adv.* bereit, schnell, sogleich; (willingly) bereitwillig, gern; *see* —y. **—iness**, *s.* die Bereitschaft; die Schnelligkeit, Raschheit; die Bereitwilligkeit; (facility) die Fertigkeit, Gewandtheit; —iness for war, die Kriegsbereitschaft; to be in —iness (be —y) to, bereit sein zu; to set in —iness, in Bereitschaft setzen, bereiten; —iness of speech, die Redefertigkeit, Schlagfertigkeit; —iness of mind *or* wit, die Geistesgegenwart; schnelle Fassungsgabe; der schlagfertige Witz. **—y**, I. *adj.* bereit, gerüstet, fertig; bereitwillig, geneigt; (about to) im Begriffe, auf dem Punkte; (prompt) schnell, rasch; (apt) gewandt, geschickt, fähig; glücklich (*as the memory*); (easy) bequem, leicht; (convenient) nahe, gleich zur Hand; kurz (*as a way*); bar, prompt (*C.L.*); klar, bereit (*Naut.*); —y! alles fertig! not —y! noch nicht! (*Tennis*); —y money, bares Geld, Bargeld; a —y money article, ein Artikel gegen Barzahlung; to meet with a —y sale, schnellen Absatz finden; to get —y, bereiten, sich vorbereiten; (dress) sich anziehen; to get dinner —y, das Mittagessen bereiten, fertig machen; the —iest way . . ., die leichteste Art; she was —y to faint, sie war nahe daran ohnmächtig zu werden; —y wit, die Geistesgegenwart. II. *adv.* bereit. *Comp.* **—y-made**, *adj.;* —y-made clothes, fertige Kleidungsstücke. **—y-witted**, *adj.* schnell besonnen, von schneller Auffassung.

Readjust, *v. a.* wieder in Ordnung bringen. **—ment**, *s.* die Wiederherstellung.

Readmi—ssion, **—ttance**, *s.* die Wiederzulassung. **—t**, *v.a.* wiederzulassen.

Reaffirm, *v.a.* nochmals versichern.

Reagent, *s.* das Reagens.

[1]**Real**, *adj.* wahrhaft, echt, unverfälscht; Sach=, wesentlich (*Phil.*); (actual) wirklich, tatsächlich, faktisch, reell; unbeweglich, liegend (*Law*); — estate, — property, der Grundbesitz; — presence, die wirkliche Gegenwart Christi im Abendmahle. **—ism**, *s.* der Realismus. **—ist**, *s.* der Realist. **—istic**, *adj.* realistisch. **—ity**, *s.* die Wirklichkeit, Tatsächlichkeit, Wahrheit; (sincerity) die Wahrhaftigkeit, Aufrichtigkeit; in —ity, *see* —ly. **—izable**, *adj.* zu verwirklichen; zu verwerten, verwertbar. **—ization**, *s.* die Verwirklichung, Wirklichmachung; die Verwertung, Realisierung (*C.L.*); die Anlegung des Geldes in Ländereien. **—ize**, *v.a.* verwirklichen, realisieren; gewinnen, aufbringen (*a profit*); (appreciate, feel as) sich (*dat.*) vorstellen, sich (*dat.*) einer S. bewußt sein, sich (*dat.*) eine S. vergegenwärtigen, etwas in seiner ganzen Stärke fühlen; zu Geld machen (*stocks, etc.*); Waren verwerten, absetzen (*C. L.*); realisieren (*C. L.*); (—ize in land) in Ländereien anlegen; to —ize a fortune, sich (*dat.*) ein Vermögen erwerben. **—ly**, *adv.* wirklich, tatsächlich; in der Tat. **—ty**, *s.* die unbewegliche Habe.

[2]**Real**, *s.* (Spanish coin, about 2¼ d.) der Real.

Realm, *s.* das Reich, Königreich; Peer of the —, englischer Pair, das Mitglied des Oberhauses.

[1]**Ream**, *s.* das Ries (Papier).

[2]**Ream**, *v.a.* aufräumen.

Reanimat—e, *v.a.* wiederbeleben. **—ion**, *s.* die Wiederbelebung, Neubelebung.

Reannex, *v.a.* wiederhinzufügen, neu annektieren.

Reap, *v.a.* schneiden (corn with a sickle, Korn mit der Sichel); (ab)ernten (*a crop*); (ein)ernten (*fig.*); to — advantage from, Nutzen ziehen von *or* aus einer S. **—er**, *s.* der Schnitter, die Schnitterin; die Mähmaschine. **—ing**, *s.* das Ernten. *Comp.* **—ing-hook**, *s.* die Sichel. **—ing-machine**, *s.* die Ernte=, Mäh=maschine.

Reappear, *v.n.* wiedererscheinen. **—ance**, *s.* die Wiedererscheinung, das Wiedererscheinen.

Reapplication, *s.* wiederholte Anwendung.

Reappoint, *v.a.* wiederanstellen. **—ment**, *s.* die Wiederanstellung.

[1]**Rear**, I. *s.* der Hintergrund; der Nachtrab (*Mil.*); to bring up the —, den Zug beschließen (*Mil.*); die Nachhut befehligen (*Mil.*), zuletzt kommen (*fig.*). II. *adj.* hinter=, Nach=. **—ward**, I. *adj.* hinter. II. *s.* der Nachtrab, die Nachhut; das Ende, der Schwanz (*fig.*). *Comp.* **—-admiral**, *s.* der Konteradmiral. **—-guard**, *s.* die Nachhut, der Nachtrab. **—-line**, *s.* das Hintertreffen. **—-rank**, *s.* das hintere Glied. **—-wheel**, *s.* das Hinterrad.

[2]**Rear**, *v.* I. *a.* erheben, aufheben, aufrichten; errichten (*an edifice*); erziehen, großziehen (*children*); ziehen (*plants and animals*). II. *n.* sich bäumen, sich aufbäumen, sich emporrichten.

Rearrange, *v.a.* wiedereinrichten, neu ordnen. **—ment**, *s.* die Neuordnung, neue Anordnung.

Reascend, *v.n.* wiederaufsteigen.

Reason, I. *s.* die Vernunft; (understanding) der Verstand; (cause) die Ursache, der (Beweg=) Grund; (fairness) das Recht, die Billigkeit; by — of, wegen; in (all) —, mit (gutem) Recht; to bring to —, zur Vernunft bringen, einem den Kopf zurecht setzen; to listen to —, Vernunft annehmen; it stands to —, es versteht sich (von selbst); with still greater —, mit noch größerem Rechte, um so mehr; there is — for supposing, es ist Grund zur Vermutung vorhanden; to give one's —s, seine Gründe angeben; there is — in all that he says, alles was er sagt, hat Hand und Fuß. II. *v.n.* vernünftig denken, urteilen, schließen; (argue, debate) sprechen, reden, debattieren; (expostulate) rechten (mit) (*B.*); to — with o.s., mit sich selbst rechten, sich (*dat.*) Vernunft einreden; to — with a p., mit einem sprechen, einen durch Beweisgründe zu überzeugen suchen. III. *v.a.* durchdenken, besprechen, erörtern; durch Beweisgründe überzeugen, bewegen, zu etwas bringen; to — **away**, wegräsonnieren; to — **down**, durch (Vernunft-)Gründe nieder-kämpfen, -schlagen; to — **into**, durch Gründe zu (etwas) bringen; to — a p. **out** of a th., einem (etwas) ausreden. —**able**, *adj.*, —**ably**, *adv.* vernünftig, verständig; vernünftig, billig (*as an offer, demand, etc.*); (in accordance with —) vernunftgemäß, vernunftmäßig; (moderate) mäßig; billig (*in price*); —ably, ziemlich, leidlich. —**er**, *s.* der Denker, Dialektiker; subtle —er, scharfer Denker, feiner *or* kritischer Kopf. —**ing**, *s.* das Urteilen, Schließen, der Schluß; (argumentation) die Beweisführung.

Reassembl—e, *v.a.*(*n.*) (sich) wiederversammeln. —**ing**, *s.* der Wiederzusammentritt (des Parlaments).

Reassert, *v.a.* wiederbehaupten. —**ion**, *s.* die wiederholte Behauptung.

Reassur—ance, *s.* die Wiederversicherung. —**e**, *v.a.* aufs neue versichern.

Rebapti—sm, *s.* die Wiedertaufe. —**ze**, *v.a.* wiedertaufen.

¹**Rebate**, I. *v.a.* abschlagen; abziehen, ablassen (*from price*). II. *s.*, —**ment**, *s.* der Verminderung; der Rabatt, Nachlaß, Abzug (*C.L.*).

²**Rebate**, *see* Rabbet.

Rebel, I. *s.* der Empörer, Rebell. II. *adj. see* —lious. III. *v.n.* sich empören, sich auflehnen (against, gegen); (oppose) sich (einem) widersetzen. —**lion**, *s.* die Auflehnung, Empörung, der Aufstand, Aufruhr. —**lious**, *adj.*, —**liously**, *adv.* aufrührerisch, rebellisch; (intractable) widerspenstig. —**liousness**, *s.* die Widerspenstigkeit, Neigung zur Empörung.

Reboil, *v.a.* wiederkochen.

Rebound, I. *v.n.* zurückprallen. II. *s.* das Zurückprallen, der Rückprall; der Umschwung (*fig.*).

Rebuff, *s.* der Rückstoß, Rückschlag; to meet with a —, kurz abgewiesen werden, eine barsche, abschlägige Antwort bekommen; den kürzeren ziehen.

Rebuild, *v.a.* wieder(auf)bauen.

Rebuke, I. *s.* der Tadel, Vorwurf, Verweis. II. *v.a.* zurecht-, ver-weisen, ausschelten; to — a p. for, einem Vorwürfe machen wegen; to administer a —, einen Verweis geben. —**r**, *s.* der Verweisende, Tadler.

Rebus, *s.* das Rebus, Bilderrätsel; redendes Wappen (*Her.*).

Rebut, *v.a.* zurück-schlagen, -weisen.

Recalcitrant, *adj.* widerspenstig.

Recall, I. *v.a.* zurückrufen (*a person*); widerrufen (*a statement*); (remember) in das Gedächtnis zurückrufen; to — to one's mind, sich (*dat.*) ins Gedächtnis zurückrufen; kündigen (*money lent, etc.*). II. *s.* die Zurückrufung, der Widerruf; past —, unwiderruflich, unwiderbringlich, nicht zu ändern.

Recant, *v.* I. *a. & n.* widerrufen. II. *n.* zurücktreten. —**ation**, *s.* der Widerruf.

Recapitulat—e, *v.a.* in Kürze wiederholen. —**ion**, *s.* kurze Wiederholung. —**ory**, *adj.* wiederholend.

Recapture, I. *s.* die Wiedernahme; (what is —d) wiedergenommene Prise. II. *v.a.* wiedernehmen.

Recast, *v.a.* umgießen, umformen; aufs neue *or* neu (die Rollen) verteilen (*Theat.*).

Recede, *v.a.* zurück-gehen, -treten, abweichen; **to — from s.th.**, Verzicht liesten auf eine S.

Recei—pt, I. *s.* der Empfang (*of a letter, etc.*); (prescription) das Rezept, die Vorschrift; die Empfangsbescheinigung, Quittung, der Empfangsschein (*C. L.*); die Einnahmestätte (*B.*); to give a —pt, eine Empfangsbescheinigung ausstellen; on —pt of this, bei (nach) Empfang dieses; remit me the amount on —pt, remittieren Sie mir den Betrag nach Eingang; —pts and expenditures, Einnahme und Ausgabe; to be in —pt of, (etwas) empfangen haben. II. *v.a.* quittieren, eine Quittung geben. —**vable**, *adj.* annehmbar. —**ve**, *v.a.* empfangen, bekommen, erhalten (*a book, a parcel, news*); einnehmen (*money*); aufnehmen (*into a community, class*); empfangen, aufnehmen (*as guest*); (mentally —ve) (auf)fassen; (recognize) annehmen, anerkennen; (accept) annehmen; a —ved tradition, eine (allgemein) angenommene Überlieferung; —ved odds, Plus-Vorgaben (*Tennis*); to —ve the communion, das heilige Abendmahl empfangen *or* nehmen. —**ver**, *s.* der Empfänger; der Einnehmer (*of customs, etc.*); der Aufnehmende; der empfangende Teil; der Kommunikant, Abendmahlsgenosse; der Rezipient, Kondensator (*Phys., Chem.*); der Hörtrichter (*Teleph.*); —ver (of stolen goods, Diebs-)Hehler. —**ving**, *s.* der Empfang. *Comp.* —**pt-book**, *s.* das Quittungsbuch (*C.L.*); das Rezeptbuch. —**pt-stamp**, *s.* der Quittungsstempel.

Recen—cy, *s.* die Neuheit, Frische. —**t**, *adj.* neu, frisch, erst entstanden; neu geschehen (*as an event*); —t intelligence, frische *or* neueste Nachrichten; of —t date, von neuestem Datum. —**tly**, *adv.* neulich, unlängst, vor Kurzem; —tly returned from, eben (erst) zurückgekehrt von. —**tness**, *s.* die Frische, Neuheit.

Recension, *s.* die Prüfung, Durchsicht, Revision.

Recept—ability, *s.* die Empfänglichkeit, Aufnehmbarkeit. —**acle**, *s.* der Behälter, das Behältnis, der Aufbewahrungsort; der Fruchtboden (*Bot.*). —**acular**, *adj.* Fruchtboden-. —**ion**, *s.* der Empfang, die Aufnahme (*also of a book*); die Annahme (*of a play, a theory, etc.*); a channel for the —ion of water, eine Rinne, um Wasser aufzunehmen; to give a p. a gracious —ion, einen freundlich aufnehmen; there is a —ion at the palace to-day, im Palast findet heute großer Empfang statt. —**ive**, *adj.* aufnehmefähig, empfänglich (für); to be —ive of a th., etwas fassen können. —**ivity**, *s.* die Aufnahmefähigkeit, Empfänglichkeit (für). *Comp.* —**ion-room**, *s.* das Empfangszimmer.

Recess, *s.* das Zurückgehen; die (Parliaments-)Ferien (*Parl.*); (holidays) die Ferien; (retirement) die Abgeschiedenheit, der abgeschiedene Ort; die Vertiefung, Nische, Blende (*in a room, etc.*). —**es**, *pl.* die Winkel, Falten, Tiefen (*fig.*) (*of the heart*). —**ion**, *s.* das Zurückgehen; *see* Precession. —**ional**, *adj.* mit dem Weggehen verbunden; —ional hymn, der Gesang beim Weggang der Gemeinde.

Rechristen, *v.a.* umtaufen, anders nennen.

Recip—e, *s.* das Rezept. —**ient**, *s.* der Empfänger.

Reciproc—al, I. *adj.*, —**ally**, *adv.* wechsel-, gegen-, beider-seitig; reziprok (*Math., Log., Gram.*); —al action, die Wechselwirkung; —al ratio, umgekehrtes Verhältnis. II. *s.* das Gegenstück; der reziproke Wert (*Math.*). —**ate**, *v.* I. *n.* abwechselnd wirken, abwechseln. II. *a.* erwidern; austauschen; good wishes heartily —ated, herzlich erwiderte gute Wünsche; —ated favours, gegenseitig erfüllte Vergünstigungen. —**ating**, *adj.* abwechselnd; —ating motion, hin- und her-gehende, auf- und nieder-gehende Bewegung; —ating engine, die Dampfmaschine mit hin- und her-gehendem Kolben. —**ation**, *s.* die Hin- und Herbewegung; die Wechselwirkung, wechselseitige Einwirkung; der Austausch, die Erwiderung. —**ity**, *s.* gegenseitige Beziehung, Wechselwirkung.

Recit—al, *s.* das Vorlesen (*of laws, etc.*), Hersagen, Vortragen; (enumeration) die Aufzählung; (narration) die Erzählung; musical —al, musikalischer Vortrag; organ —al, das Orgelkonzert. **—ation**, I. *s.* das Hersagen (*of lessons*); der Vortrag, das Vortragen (eines Gedichtes, Musikstücks). II. *attrib.*; —ation room, der Hörsaal. **—ative**, I. *adj.* rezitativartig. II. *s.* der Redegesang, das Rezitativ. **—e**, *v.* I. *a.* aufsagen, hersagen, lesen (*a lesson, etc.*); vortragen (*a poem, etc.*); (narrate) erzählen. II. *n.* vortragen, deklamieren. **—er**, *s.* der Vortragende, Deklamator; der Erzähler.

Reck, *v.a. & n.* Sorge tragen, berücksichtigen, sich kümmern. **—less**, *adj.*, **—lessly**, *adv.* sorglos, achtlos, unbekümmert, rücksichtslos (gegen die Folgen); (rash) tollkühn, verwegen. **—lessness**, *s.* die Rücksichtslosigkeit, Verwegenheit.

Reckon, *v.* I. *a.* rechnen, zählen; (estimate) schätzen, ansehen als, halten für; (impute) zu-, an-rechnen (to a p. for, einem als); to — **up**, zusammen-rechnen, -zählen. II. *n.* rechnen; (think) meinen, denken, vermuten (*Amer.*); to — without one's host, die Rechnung ohne den Wirt machen; to — **on, upon**, rechnen, zählen, sich verlassen auf (*acc.*); to — **with**, abrechnen mit, Rechenschaft geben (von). **—er**, *s.* der Rechner; ready —er, der Schnellrechner, das Hülfsrechenbuch. **—ing**, *s.* das Rechnen; die Rechnung (*at an inn, etc.*); (calculation) die Berechnung; (settlement) die Ab-, Zusammen-rechnung; das Urteil, Erachten, Dafürhalten; dead —ing, ungefähre Berechnung, Gissung (*Naut.*); to be out in one's —ing, sich verrechnen *or* verrechnet haben; according to my —ing, meines Erachtens.

Reclaim, *v. a.* zurück-bringen, -leiten, -lenken (*fig.*); (convert) bekehren, bessern; kulturfähig *or* urbar machen (*land*); zurückfordern, reklamieren. **—able**, *adj.* verbesserungsfähig.

Reclamation, *s.* das Zurückbringen, die Besserung; die Zurückforderung; der Einspruch, die Beschwerde; die Nutzbarmachung, Urbarmachung (*of land*).

Reclin—ation, *s.* die Reklination (*Astr., Surg.*). **—e**, *v.n.* (sich) lehnen, anlehnen, zurücklehnen ruhen. *Comp.* **—ing-chair**, *s.* der Lehnstuhl. **—ing-dial**, *s.* reklinierende Sonnenuhr.

Reclose, *v.a.* wieder schließen *or* zumachen.

Recluse, I. *adj.* abgeschieden, einsam. II. *s.* der Einsiedler, Klausner.

Recogni—tion, *s.* die (Wieder-)Erkennung (*of a p., etc.*); (acknowledgement) die Anerkennung. **—zable**, *adj.* erkennbar, zu erkennen. **—zance**, *s.* das Erkenntnis (*of a jury*); to enter into —zances, sich gerichtlich verbindlich machen. **—ze**, *v.a.* (wieder)erkennen; grüßen (*in the street, etc.*); anerkennen.

Recoil, I. *v.n.* zurück-prallen, -springen; zurückfahren (from fear, aus Furcht), zurück-beben, -schaudern (at, vor); (shrink) zurückweichen. II. *s.* das Zurückspringen (*Horol.*); der Rückstoß (*of a gun*); der Rücklauf (*of a cannon*); das Zurückprallen (*fig.*); das Zurückschrecken. *Comp.* **—-escapement**, *s.* zurückspringende Hemmung.

Recoin, *v.a.* umprägen. **—age**, *s.* die Umprägung.

Recollect, *v.a.* sich erinnern (einer Person *or* Sache), sich (*dat.*) ins Gedächtnis zurückrufen; wieder sammeln; to — o.s., sich sammeln *or* fassen. **—ion**, *s.* die Erinnerung, *see* Reminiscence; das Gedächtnis; these events are beyond my —ion, dieser *or* an diese Ereignisse kann ich mich nicht mehr erinnern.

Recolonization, *s.* neue Kolonisierung.

Recommence, *v.a.* wiederbeginnen.

Recommend, *v.a.* empfehlen; young men were —ed to read Goethe, man empfahl jungen Leuten *or* es wurde jungen Leuten empfohlen Goethe zu lesen. **—ation**, *s.* die Empfehlung; (cause of —ation) der Empfehlungsgrund; letter of —ation, das Empfehlungsschreiben. **—atory**, *adj.* empfehlend, Empfehlungs-.

Recommission, *v.a.* neu beauftragen, wiederanstellen; wieder dienstbereit machen.

Recommit, *v.a.* wiederverhaften; abermals einer Kommission übergeben.

Recompense, I. *v.a.* ausgleichen, ersetzen, entschädigen; (reward) belohnen; (requite) vergelten, vergüten; to — a p. for kindness, einem seine Güte vergelten. II. *s.* der Ersatz, die Vergütung, Belohnung; *see* Reward.

Recompose, *v.a.* neu zusammensetzen; neu setzen (*Typ.*); (quiet) wieder beruhigen.

Reconcil—able, *adj.* versöhnbar; vereinbar, verträglich (with, mit). **—e**, *v.a.* ver-, aus-söhnen (*enemies, etc.*); vereinbaren, in Einklang bringen (with, to, mit); to —e o.s., become —ed to, sich fügen in (*acc.*). **—er**, *s.* der Versöhner. **—iation**, *s.* die Wiederaussöhnung, Versöhnung.

Recondensation, *s.* die Wiederverdichtung.

Recondite, *adj.* verborgen; (abstruse) tief, dunkel.

Reconduct, *v.a.* zurückführen.

Reconn—aissance, —oissance, *s.* prüfende Besichtigung; die Rekognoszierung (*Mil.*); —aissance in force, gewaltsame Rekognoszierung. **—oitre, —oiter**, *v.a.* besichtigen, auskundschaften; rekognoszieren (*Mil.*); —oitring party, die Rekognoszierungsabteilung.

Reconque—r, *v.a.* wiedererobern. **—st**, *s.* die Wiedereroberung.

Reconsider, *v.a.* wiedererwägen, überlegen. **—ation**, *s.* nochmalige Überlegung; on —ation, bei nochmaliger Überlegung *or* Erwägung.

Reconstruct, *v.a.* wieder(auf)bauen. **—ion**, *s.* die Wiederaufrichtung, Wiederherstellung.

Record, I. *v.a.* aufzeichnen, niederschreiben; tief einprägen (*obs. fig.*). II. *s.* die Urkunde, das Verzeichnis, Protokoll; schriftlicher Bericht; die Höchstleistung, Glanzleistung, der Vorsprung; their — is far from blameless, ihre Vergangenheit ist weit davon entfernt tadelfrei zu sein; he has left a good —, er hat ein gutes Andenken hinterlassen; it is *or* has been left upon —, es ist aufgezeichnet, ist eine historische Tatsache; phonographic —, das Hineinsprechen eines Stückes in Vers oder Prosa in einen Phonographen; die Wiedergabe eines solchen Stückes durch den Phonographen; die Walze oder Platte, welche ein solches Stück enthält; to beat the —, die bisherige Höchstleistung übertreffen. **—er**, *s.* der Registrator, Protokollant; die erste Gerichtsperson (*of certain towns*); registrierender, aufzeichnender Apparat (*Mach.*). **—ership**, *s.* die Stelle eines Urkundenbewahrers, Archivars, Registrators. **—s**, *pl.* Geschichtsbücher, Papiere, das Archiv. *Comp.* **—-maker**, *s.* einer, der Stücke zur Wiedergabe durch den Phonographen in das Instrument spricht. **—-office**, *s.* das Staats-Archiv.

Recount, *v.a.* aufzählen, herzählen, erzählen.

Recoup, *v.* I. *a.* abziehen; wieder vollständig einbringen. II. *n.* sich schadlos halten.

Recourse, *s.* die Zuflucht; to have — to a p., seine Zuflucht nehmen zu einem.

[1]**Recover**, *v.* I. *a.* wieder erlangen *or* bekommen; wiedererobern (*territory, etc.*); (retrieve) wieder einbringen *or* gut machen; eintreiben (*debts*); to — damages, Schadenersatz erhalten. II. *n.* besser werden, sich erholen, genesen; seinen Prozeß gewinnen. **—able**, *adj.* eintreibbar, wieder zu erlangen. **—y**, *s.* die Wiedererlangung; die Wiederherstellung, Genesung; die Erlangung; —y of damages, der Schadenersatz (*Law*); past —y, unwiederbringlich verloren; unheilbar.

[2]**Recover**, *v.a.* neu überziehen (*umbrellas*).

Recrean—cy, *s.* die schmähliche Verzagtheit; die Abtrünnigkeit. **—t**, I. *adj.* abtrünnig; (craven) feig. II. *s.* der Abtrünnige; der Feigling; der Bösewicht.

Recreat—e, *v.a.* neu schaffen; to —e o.s., sich er-

quicken or erfrischen or erholen. —ion, s. die Erholung, Erquickung, Erfrischung; (diversion) die Ergötzung, Ergötzlichkeit; das Wiederschaffen. —ive, adj. erquickend, erfrischend, erheiternd.
Recrement, s., —s, pl. ausgeschiedene Säfte.
Recriminat—e, v.n. Gegenbeschuldigungen vorbringen. —ion, s. die Gegenbeschuldigung; die Gegenklage (Law). —ory, adj. eine Gegenbeschuldigung enthaltend or machend.
Recross, v.a. wieder überschreiten, zurückfahren über (acc.), wieder übersetzen über (acc.).
Recrudescen—ce, s. der Wiederaufbruch, das Wiederaufbrechen (of a wound), das Wiederschlimmerwerden. —t, adj. wieder aufbrechend.
Recruit, I. v.a. (durch neuen Zusatz) wiederherstellen, ergänzen; wieder vollzählig machen, ergänzen (an army, etc.). II. v.a. & n. sich erholen, sich stärken. III. v.n. (an)werben (Mil.). IV. s. die Ergänzung, der neue Vorrat; der Rekrut (Mil.). Comp. —ing-officer, s. der Werbeoffizier. —ing-sergeant, s. der Werbesergeant.
Rect—angle, s. das Rechteck. —angular, adj. rechtwinklig. —ifiable, adj. verbesserbar, zu berichtigen. —ification, s. die Berichtigung (also C. L.); die Rektifikation (Geom., Chem.). —ifier, s. der Berichtiger; der Rektifikator (Chem.); das Deklinatorium. —ify, v.a. berichtigen; verbessern; rektifizieren (Geom.); rektifizieren, läutern (spirits, etc.). —ilinear, —ilineal, adj. geradlinig. —itude, s. die Geradheit; die Redlichkeit, Geradheit, Rechtschaffenheit (fig.). —um, s. der Mastdarm.
Rector, s. der Pfarrherr; der Oberpfarrer; der Vorsteher, Rektor (Scotch Univ., also of a Jesuitical college); der Direktor (einer öffentlichen Schule, Scotch). —ate, s. das Pfarramt; das Rektorat. —ial, adj. pfarrherrlich; Rektor-; —ial address, die Rektoratsrede. —ship, s. see —ate. —y, s. die Pfarre, das Pastorat; das Pfarrhaus.
Recumbent, adj., —ly, adv. lehnend, liegend.
Recuperat—e, v.n. sich erholen. —ive, adj. zur Wiedererlangung gehörig or dienlich; —ive power, die Wiedererholungsfähigkeit; France showed a great —ive power, Frankreich bewies, daß es sich sehr schnell erholen konnte.
Recur, v.n. zurückkehren (to the mind, ins Gedächtnis), einfallen; wieder zurückkommen auf (acc.) (to a subject); (periodisch) wiederkommen, wiederkehren. —rence, s. die Wiederkehr. —rent, adj. wiederkehrend; zurücklaufend (as nerves). —ring, adj. zurücklaufend; periodisch (of decimals); —ring series, zurücklaufende Reihen.
Recurv—ate, adj. zurückgekrümmt (Bot.). —irostér, s. der Säbelschnäbler.
Recus—ancy, s. die Weigerung; die Widerspenstigkeit. —ant, I. adj. sich weigernd, widerspenstig; sich weigernd, die Oberherrschaft des Königs in Religionssachen anzuerkennen. II. s. der Abweichende, Widerspenstige; der Nonkonformist, Katholik, &c. —e, v.a. verwerfen (Law).
[1]**Red**, I. adj. rot; bright —, hellrot; — chalk, der Rötel; — currant, die Johannisbeere; — herring, der Pökelhering; — men, die Rothäute, Indianer; — murrain, das Blutharnen; — ochre, der Roteisenoker. II. s. das Rot. —den, v. n. rot werden, sich röten; erröten. —dish, adj. rötlich. —ness, s. die Röte. Comp. —-Book, s. das Staatsadreßbuch; der Adelskalender. —breast, s. das Rotkehlchen. —-chalk, s. der Rötel, Rotstift. —coat, s. der Rotrock, englische Soldat. —-cross, I. s. das rote Kreuz. II. adj. ein rotes Kreuz tragend; —-Cross Society, der Verein vom Roten Kreuz, die Gesellschaft zur Pflege Verwundeter im Kriege. —-deer, s. der Rothirsch. —-faced, adj. rot aussehend. —-haired, adj. rothaarig. —-handed, adj. mit roten, blutigen Händen; to be taken —-handed, auf frischer Tat ertappt werden. —-hot, adj. feuerrot, glühend; hitzig, heftig (sl.): to be —-hot, glühen. —-lane, s. die Kehle, Gurgel (sl.). —-lead, s. der Mennig. —-letter, adj.; —-letter day, glücklicher Tag. —-nosed, adj. rotnasig. —pole, s. der Bluthänfling. —skin, s. die Rothaut, der Indianer. —start, s. das Rotschwänzchen. —-tape, see Tape. —-tapism, s. pedantischer Bureaugeist, die Beamtenwirtschaft. —-tapist, s. der Autokrat vom grünen Tisch. —-water, s. blutartiges Harnen (des Viehs). —wing, die Rotdrossel.
[2]**Red**, v.a. ordnen, zurechtmachen (Scotch).
Redact, v.a. redigieren. —ion, s. die Redaktion.
Redan, I. s. der Redan, die Flesche. II. attrib.; — system, die Zangenbefestigung.
Redd—endum, s. die Reservationsklausel. —itive, adj. erwidernd (Gram.); entsprechend.
Reddle, s. der Rötel, Rotstein.
Rede, v.a. & n. raten (obs.).
Redecorate, v.a. neu schmücken or dekorieren.
Redeem, v.a. wieder-, zurück-kaufen; loskaufen, auslösen (captives, etc.); einlösen (a pledge); amortisieren (Law, C. L.); erfüllen (a promise); erlösen (Theol.); (atone for) büßen, wieder gut machen; (compensate) ersetzen, erstatten; wiedereinbringen (the time); the —ing feature in a character, das was uns mit einem Charakter wieder aussöhnt; no —ing qualities, keine Eigenschaften, welche einen das Schlechte vergessen lassen. —able, adj. wiederkäuflich; tilgbar, einlösbar (C. L.); loskäuflich; wieder einzubringen. —er, s. der Einlösende; der Erlöser (B.).
Redeliver, v.a. wieder abliefern.
Redempt—ion, s. der Wieder-, Rück-kauf; die Amortisation, Tilgung (C.L.); die Loskaufung, Auslösung (of captives, etc.); die Erlösung (Theol.). —orist, s. der Redemptorist.
Redintegrat—e, v.a. wiederherstellen, wiedererneuern. —ion, s. die Wiederherstellung, Erneuerung, Ergänzung.
Redistribut—e, v.a. wiederverteilen. —ion, s. die Wiederverteilung, Neuverteilung.
Redolen—ce, s. der Wohlgeruch. —t, adj. wohlriechend; —t of, riechend nach; einen Anstrich habend von (fig.).
Redouble, v. I. a. verdoppeln. II. n. sich verdoppeln.
Redoubt, **Redout**, s. die (geschlossene) Schanze, Redoute.
Redound, v.n. gereichen (zu), beitragen (zu).
Redraft, I. s. der neue Riß, Entwurf; der Rückwechsel, die Rücktratte (C.L.). II. v.a. wieder or von neuem entwerfen, neu zeichnen or abreißen.
Redraw, v.a. see Redraft II.; zurücktrassieren (on a p., auf einen).
Redress, I. s. die Abhülfe, Abstellung; (reparation) die Wiedergutmachung; to obtain —, Abhilfe finden (für). II. v.a. abstellen, abhelfen; to — grievances, Beschwerden (dat.) abhelfen.
Reduc—e, v.a. zurück-bringen, -führen; verwandeln (to s.th. else, in eine S.); versetzen, bringen (to poverty, in Armut); bringen (to a system, in ein System &c.); (diminish) vermindern, verkleinern, verringern; herabsetzen (prices); (subdue) bezwingen, unterwerfen; (degrade) heruntersetzen; verjüngen, in verjüngtem Maßstabe darstellen (a drawing, etc.); reduzieren (fractions, equations, also Chem.); einrichten, wiedereinrenken (Surg.); degradieren (Mil.); to —e whole numbers to fractions, die Ganzen zu Brüchen machen; to —e shillings to pence, die Schillinge in Pence verwandeln; to —e a proposition to its simplest form, einen Satz auf seinen einfachsten Ausdruck zurückführen; to —e to order, in Ordnung bringen, to —e to practice, praktisch anwenden; to —e one's expenses, sich einschränken; the illness has —ed him greatly, die Krankheit hat ihn sehr mitgenommen; in —ed circumstances, in heruntergekommenen Vermögensumständen; at —ed prices, zu herabgesetzten Preisen; to —e a fortress, eine

Festung zur Übergabe zwingen. —**er**, *s.* der Zurück-bringende, -führende; der Bezwinger. —**ible**, *adj.* zurückführbar, zurückzu-führen, -bringen; to be —ible into, sich verwandeln lassen in; —ible to practice, ausführbar. —**tion**, *see under* Reductio. *Comp.* —**ing-agent**, *s.* das Reduktionsmittel. —**ing-compass**, *see* —tion-compasses. —**ing-scale**, *s.* der verjüngte Maßstab.

Reductio, *s.*; — ad absurdum, der Beweis der Unmöglichkeit, Nötigung, die Ungereimtheit zuzugeben. —**n**, *s.* die Zurück-führung, -bringung, Verwandlung (into, in); die Reduktion (*Arith.*, *Astr.*, *Chem.*, *Metall.*); die Auflösung, Reduzierung (*Alg.*); die Wiedereinrenkung (*Surg.*); die Preis-herabsetzung, -ermäßigung (*C. L.*); die Verminderung, Verringerung; die Unterwerfung; die Verjüngung (*of a drawing*); die Zerteilung in andere Figuren (*Geom.*); —n of a fraction, die Auflösung eines Bruches. *Comp.* —**n-compasses**, *pl.* der Reduktionszirkel.

Redundan—ce, —**cy**, *s.* die Überfülle; der Überfluß (an Worten ꝛc.). —**t**, *adj.*, —**tly**, *adv.* überflüssig, übersprudelnd; weitschweifig.

Reduplication, *s.* die Verdoppelung; die Reduplikation (*Gram.*).

Re-echo, *v.a. & n.* widerhallen (with, von).

Reed, *s.* das Rohr, Schilfrohr; (pipe) die Rohrpfeife, -flöte; das Rohr, Mundstück (*of the clarionet, etc.*); das Rohr (*Org.*); das Wetterblatt, Riet (*Weav.*). —**s**, *see* —ing. —**ed**, *adj.* mit Rohr *or* Schilf bedeckt; (—y) rohrähnlich. —**y**, *adj.* schilfig, rohrartig; schnarrend (*as a voice*). *Comp.* —**-bank**, —**-bed**, *s.* das Röhricht. —**-bunting**, *s.* der Rohrsperling. —**-grass**, *s.* das Riedgras. —**-organ**, *s.* die Zimmerorgel. —**-pipe**, *s.* die Rohrpfeife (*Org.*). —**-sparrow**, *see* —-bunting. —**-stop**, *s.* das Rohr-, Schnarr-werk (*Org.*).

Re-edit, *v.a.* wiederherausgeben.

[1]**Reef**, *s.* das Felsenriff. —**y**, *adj.* voll Felsenriffe.

[2]**Reef**, I. *s.* das Reef, Reff. II. *v.a.* reffen (*a sail*), einziehen, verkürzen; ein Reff einstecken. —**er**, *s.* der Einreffer. *Comp.* —**-tackle**, *s.* die Reeftalje.

Reek, I. *s.* der Rauch, Dampf. II. *v.n.* dampfen, rauchen, dunsten (with, von). —**y**, *adj.* räucherig, dunstig; verräuchert.

[1]**Reel**, I. *s.* der Haspel; das Garnröllchen, die Rolle (für Nähgarn); der rotierende Zylinder (*Bak.*); die Rolle (*of anglers*); die Mehlmaschine (*Mill.*); der Haspel (*of rope-makers*); die Spule, der Haspel, die Weife (*Spinn.*, *Silkm.*); die Walze, Rolle (*Tele.*); — of the log, die Logrolle (*Naut.*). II. *v.n.* (im Gehen) taumeln, wanken; *see* Whirl; my head —s, mir schwindelt der Kopf. III. *v.a.* (ab)haspeln, weifen; to — off, abwinden. *Comp.* —**-cotton**, *s.* das Nähgarn auf Röllchen.

[2]**Reel**, *s.* schottischer lebhafter Tanz.

Re-elect, *v.a.* wiederwählen. —**ion**, *s.* die Wiederwahl.

Re-eligible, *adj.* wiederwählbar.

Re-emerge, *v.n.* wieder auftauchen.

Re-enact, *v.a.* wiederverordnen; wieder in Kraft (in Szene (*Theat.*)) setzen.

Re-engage, *v.a.* wieder in Dienst nehmen, dingen; den Kampf erneuern *or* wiederaufnehmen.

Re-enlist, *v.n.* sich aufs neue anwerben lassen, kapitulieren (*Mil.*).

Re-enter, *v.* I. *a.* wiederbetreten, eintreten in (*acc.*). II. *n.* die Linien vertiefen (*Engr.*). —**ing**, I. *adj.* einspringend. II. *s.* das Eindrucken (*Calico-Print.*); das Vertiefen der Linien; —ing angle, einspringender, eingehender Winkel.

Re-establish, *v.a.* wiederherstellen. —**ment**, *s.* die Wiederherstellung.

[1]**Reeve**, *s.* der Vogt, Schultheiß (*obs.*).

[2]**Reeve**, *s.* das Kampfhuhn; *see* Ruff.

[3]**Reeve**, *v.a.* einscheren (*Naut.*).

Re-examin—ation, *s.* abermalige Untersuchung, neue Prüfung. —**e**, *v.a.* neu untersuchen, aufs neue *or* wieder prüfen.

Re-exchange, *s.* der abermalige Tausch; der Rückwechsel, die Ritratte (*C.L.*); account of —, die Rückwechselrechnung.

Re-export, I. *v.a.* wieder ausführen. II. *s.* die wieder ausgeführte Ware. —**ation**, *s.* die Wiederausfuhr.

Refashion, *v.a.* neu formen, ummodeln.

Refasten, *v.a.* wieder befestigen.

Refect—ion, *s.* die Erfrischung, Labung; das Erquickungsmahl (*in convents*). —**ory**, *s.* der Speisesaal (*in convents, etc.*).

Refer, *v.* I. *a.* beziehen (to, auf (*acc.*); verweisen an (*for information, etc.*); verweisen (the reader to a note etc., den Leser auf eine Anmerkung ꝛc.); (hand over to) über-lassen, -geben, (der Entscheidung jemandes) anheimstellen *or* anheimgeben; (assign) zählen, rechnen (to, zu); auf weitern Bescheid aussetzen (*Law*); to — o.s., sich beziehen auf (*acc.*). II. *n.* sich beziehen (auf), (allude) anspielen (auf), meinen; (appeal) sich berufen, es ankommen lassen (to, auf (*acc.*)); (— to) nachschlagen in (einem Wörterbuch)). —**able**, *adj.* bezüglich (to, auf (*acc.*)). —**ee**, *s.* der Berichterstatter, Referent; der Schiedsrichter. —**ence**, I. *s.* die Verweisung, Nachweisung, der Nachweis; der Bezug, die Anspielung, Bezugnahme; die Referenz, Verweisung (to a p., auf einen); (person —red to) der Auskunfterteiler; (direction) die Hinweisung; die Verweisung einer Sache an einen Schiedsrichter; das Zeugnis (*of servants*); in —ence to, in Beziehung auf (*acc.*), in Betreff, hinsichtlich (einer Sache); —ence five years, fünf Jahre in der letzten Stelle (*in servants' advertisements*); works of —ence, Nachschlagewerke; to have no —ence to, sich nicht beziehen auf (*acc.*); he made no —ence to what had occurred, er machte keine Anspielung auf das Vorgefallene; on —ence to the work itself, I found . . ., als ich das Werk selbst nachschlug, fand ich . . . II. *attrib.*; —ence Bible, die Konkordanzbibel; —ence library, die Handbibliothek; —ence library for advanced students at a university, die Seminarbibliothek. —**ences**, *pl.* die Auskunft (über eine S.); to give —ences, Adressen geben zur Auskunfterteilung. —**endum**, *s.* das Plebiszit; ad —endum, zur Berichterstattung; to leave ad —endum, unentschieden lassen.

Refill, *v.a.* wiederfüllen; wiederstopfen (*a pipe*).

Refine, *v.* I. *a.* feiner machen, verfeinern; raffinieren (*petroleum, pig-iron, steel, sugar*); läutern (*glass, liquids*); rektifizieren, läutern (*Dist.*); läutern, raffinieren (*Chem.*); treiben, scheiden (*gold or silver*); flößen, pauschen (*tin*); verfeinern (*fig.*); läutern, veredeln, bilden (*the taste, mind, etc.*); refining furnace, der Treibherd, Abwerfofen; —d manners, habits, verfeinerte Sitten; —d iron, steel, Gareisen, gegerbter Stahl. II. *n.* sich verfeinern, vervollkommnen; grübeln, klügeln; to — on a th., etwas verbessern, verfeinern. —**ment**, *s.* die Verfeinerung, Bildung (*also of language, mind, etc.*); das Raffinieren, Reinigen ꝛc.; (purity) die Reinheit, Lauterkeit; (nicety) die Gesuchtheit, Spitzfindigkeit; —ments of cunning, durchtriebene Kniffe (Kunstgriffe), Spitzfindigkeiten. —**r**, *s.* der Läuterer; der Verfeinerende, Reiniger (*fig.*); der Frischer, Abtreiber (*Metall.*); der Raffineur, Sieder (*of sugar, saltpetre, etc.*); (subtle reasoner, *etc.*) der Grübler, Klügler. —**ry**, *s.* das Frischfeuer, der Treibherd, die Abtreibhütte; die Siederei (*for sugar*). *Comp.* —**ry-furnace**, *s.* der Raffinier-ofen, -herd.

Refining, I. *p. see* Refine. II. *s.* das Reinigen; das Raffinieren (*of metals, sugar, etc.*); die Destillation (*of petroleum*); das Gerben (*of steel*); das (Ab)Treiben (*of gold, etc.*).

Refit, *v.* I. *a.* wiederausrüsten, wiederherstellen; II. *n.* sich (ein Schiff) ausbessern lassen.

Reflect, *v.* I. *a.* zurückwerfen (*light, etc.*); to — credit upon, (einem) Ehre machen; to — disgrace on, Schande bringen über (*acc.*); to be —ed, sich spiegeln, zurückgeworfen werden. II. *n.* zurück-prallen, -fallen, -strahlen; nachdenken (on, über (*acc.*)); überlegen (*fig.*); (consider) Rücksicht nehmen auf (*acc.*); (blame) hämisch anspielen (auf (*acc.*)), tadelnd auftreten (gegen). **—ed**, *adj.* zurückgeworfen, reflektiert. **—ing**, *adj.* zurückwerfend, Reflexions-; —ing circle, der Reflexionskreis; —ing galvanometer, Spiegelgalvanometer; —ing telescope, das Spiegelteleskop, der Reflektor. **—ingly**, *adv.* nachdenkend; tadelnd. **—ion**, *s.* die Zurückwerfung, Reflexion, das Zurück-prallen, -strahlen, -fallen; (—ed ray, *etc.*) der Widerschein, Abglanz; das Nachdenken, die Überlegung, Erwägung, Betrachtung (*fig.*); (result of —ion) die Betrachtung, Bemerkung; (blame) der Tadel, Vorwurf; angle of —ion, der Reflexionswinkel; plane of —ion, die Reflexionsebene; power of —ion, —ive faculty, das Reflexions-, Vergleichungs-vermögen; on —ion, bei näherer Überlegung; in saying that, you cast —ions upon my honour, indem Sie so sprechen, werfen Sie einen Schatten auf meine Ehre. **—ive**, *adj.* zurückwerfend; nachdenkend, überlegend, *see* —ion. **—or**, *s.* der Reflektor, Strahlenwerfer; der Schallreflektor.

Reflex, I. *adj.* zurückstrahlend; zurückgebogen (*Bot.*); vom Widerschein erleuchtet (*Paint.*); rückwärts gerichtet (*fig.*); — action, die Reflex-Bewegung. II. *s.* der Widerschein, Reflex. **—ive**, *adj.* zurückwirkend, auf etwas Vergangenes bezüglich; (zu)rückbezüglich, reflexiv (*Gram.*); —ive verb, rückbezügliches Zeitwort. **—ively**, *adv.* rückwirkend, zurückfallend; reflexiv (*Gram.*).

Refloat, *v.a.* wieder flott machen.

Reflux, *s.* der Rückfluß; die Ebbe (*of tides*).

Refold, *v.a.* wieder zusammenfalten.

Reform, I. *v.a.* umgestalten; (ver)bessern, reformieren (*fig.*); (re-form) neu bilden, neu formieren (*Mil.*). II. *v.n.* sich (ver)bessern (*fig.*); (reform) sich wieder bilden *or* ordnen. III. *s.* die Verbesserung, Besserung. IV. *attrib.*; — movement, die Reformbewegung; die neuere Richtung (*e. g. in modern language teaching*). **—ation**, *s.* die Besserung, Sinnesänderung; die Umgestaltung, Umbildung; the —ation (of the Church), die Reformation. **—ative**, *adj.* umbildend; *see* —atory. **—atory**, I. *adj.* zur Besserung dienend, reformatorisch. II. *s.* die Besserungsanstalt, das Rettungshaus. **—ed**, *adj.* gebessert, verbessert; reformiert (*Eccl.*). **—er**, *s.* der Verbesserer, Reformator.

Refortify, *v.a.* wieder *or* aufs neue befestigen.

Refound, *v.n.* umgießen, neu gießen.

Refract, *v.a.* brechen (rays of light, Strahlen); —ed, gebrochen; —ing, brechend; double-—ing crystal, der Doppelspat; —ing telescope, der Refraktor; —ed angle, der Brechungswinkel. **—ion**, *s.* die (Strahlen-)Brechung; index of —ion, (—ive index) der Brechungsapparat. **—ive**, *adj* brechend, Brechungs-. **—or**, *see* —ing telescope. **—oriness**, *s.* die Widerspenstigkeit; die Strengflüssigkeit (*of minerals, etc.*) **—orily**, *adv.*, **—ory**, *adj.* widerspenstig, widersetzlich, ungehorsam; strengflüssig (*Chem.*); hart, hartflüssig (*Min.*); feuerbeständig (*as stones*).

[1]**Refrain**, *v.* I. *n.* sich enthalten. II. *n.* zurückhalten.

[2]**Refrain**, *s.* der Kehrreim, die Kehrzeile(n).

Refrangib—ility, *s.* die Brechbarkeit (*Opt.*). **—le**, *adj.* brechbar.

Refresh, *v.a.* erfrischen, erquicken; (freshen up) auffrischen. **—er**, *s.* der, die, das Erfrischende, Erquickende; ein dem plaidierenden Anwalt im voraus gegebenes Honorar (*Law*) (*fam.*). — **ing**, *adj.*, **—ingly**, *adv.* erfrischend, erquickend. **—ment**, I. *s.* die Erfrischung, Erquickung. II. *attrib.*; —ment rooms, die (Bahnhofs-)Restauration, das Buffet.

Refrigera—nt, I. *adj.* kühlend. II. *s.* der Kühltrank. **—te**, *v.a.* kühlen. **—tion**, *s.* die Abkühlung; das Kühlen der Würze (*Brew.*). — **tive**, *see* —nt I. & II. **—tor**, *s.* der Kühler, das Kühlgefäß, Kühlfaß; der Eisschrank.

Re-front, *v.a.*; to — old shirts, alte Hemden mit neuen Einsätzen versehen.

Reft, *p.p. see* Bereft.

Refuge, *s.* die Zuflucht; (place of —) der Zufluchtsort, die Freistatt; (expedient) das Hilfs-, Not-mittel; to take — with a p., seine Zuflucht nehmen zu einem. **—e**, *s.* der Flüchtling.

Refulgen—ce, **—cy**, *s.* der Glanz. **—t**, *adj.*, **—tly**, *adv.* glänzend, leuchtend.

Refund, *v.a.* zurück-zahlen, -geben, erstatten, ersetzen; to — o.s., sich bezahlt machen.

Refurbish, *v.a.* wiederaufputzen, aufpolieren.

Refurnish, *v.a.* neu möblieren.

Refus—al, *s.* die abschlägige Antwort, Verweigerung; (right of —al) die Vorhand, der Vorkauf; to meet with a —al, eine abschlägige Antwort (einen Korb) bekommen; in case of —al, im Weigerungsfalle; to have the —al of, die Vorhand haben, wählen *or* ablehnen dürfen. **—e**, I. *v.a.* verweigern (*obedience, etc.*), abschlagen; (decline) zurück-, ab-weisen, von der Hand weisen, ausschlagen; (deny) versagen; my pen —es to describe, meine Feder sträubt sich zu schildern; that is not to be —ed, das nehme ich mit Vergnügen an; he —ed to accept the money, er weigerte sich das Geld anzunehmen, er verweigerte die Annahme des Geldes; he —ed the money, er schlug das Geld aus; to —e absolutely, rundweg abschlagen. II. *v.n.* sich weigern, nicht tun wollen; (not accept) ausschlagen. III. *adj.* verworfen, wertlos. IV. *s.* der Ausschuß, Abfall, die Ausschußware; der Auswurf (*fig.*).

Refut—able, *adj.* widerlegbar. **—ation**, *s.* die Widerlegung. **—e**, *v.a.* widerlegen.

Regain, *v.a.* wieder-gewinnen, -erlangen, -erreichen.

Regal, *adj.*, **—ly**, *adv.* königlich. **—ia**, *pl.* Zeichen der königlichen Würde; (royal privileges) die Hoheitsrechte; die Abzeichen (of freemasons).

Regale, *v.a.* (festlich) bewirten; erquicken (*the eye, ear, etc.*); ergötzen (*fig.*).

Regard, I. *v.a.* ansehen; (heed) achten; (consider) berücksichtigen; (honour) (hoch)achten; (look on) betrachten; to — with kindness, warme, freundschaftliche Gefühle hegen für; to be —ed as, gelten für (*an enemy, etc.*), betrachtet werden als, angesehen werden für; as regards . . ., was . . . (an)betrifft. II. *s.* der Blick, die Achtung, Aufmerksamkeit; die Rücksicht; die (Hoch-)Achtung; (repute) das Ansehen; with — to, in Hinsicht auf, hinsichtlich, in Betreff (einer Sache); to have no — to, keine Rücksicht nehmen auf (*acc.*); nicht berücksichtigen; to send one's —s to, einen grüßen lassen; with our united kind —s to all of you, mit den herzlichsten Grüßen von Haus zu Haus. **—ant**, *adj.* anblickend (*Her.*). **—ing**, *prep.* hinsichtlich, in Betreff. **—less**, *adj.*, **—lessly**, *adv.* achtlos, rücksichtslos, unbekümmert; to be —less of the future, in den Tag hinein leben; we must not be —less of that, wir dürfen das nicht außer Acht lassen *or* in den Wind schlagen.

Regatta, *s.* die Bootwettfahrt, Regatta.

Regen—cy, *s.* die Regentschaft, Reichsverwesung; der Regierungs-Bezirk (eines Vizeregenten); (council of —cy) die Regentschaft.

Regenerat—e, I. *v.a.* wiedererzeugen, neu hervorbringen; (bessernd) umbilden (*fig.*). II. *adj.* wiedergeboren. **—ion**, *s.* die Wiederherstellung; die Wiedergeburt (*Theol.*).

Regent, I. *adj.* herrschend, regierend; reichsverwesend; queen —, die Königin-Regentin. II. *s.*

der Regent, Reichsverweser; Schul- und Kollegien-Inspektor (*New York*). —**ship**, *s.* die Regentschaft.

Regi—cide, *s.* der Königsmörder; (act of —cide) der Königsmord. —**men**, *s.* die Verwaltung; die Lebensordnung, Diät, Kost (*Med.*); die Regierung; (word, *etc.*, governed) der regierte Fall, das Objekt (*Gram.*). —**ment**, *s.* das Regiment (*Mil.*); die Schar (*fig.*). —**mental**, *adj.* Regiments-. —**mentals**, *pl.* die Uniform. —**on**, *see* Region.

Region, *s.* die Region, Gegend, das Gebiet; die Gegend (*of the body*); (sky) der Himmels-strich, -raum; (rank) die Sphäre; airy —s, der Luftkreis; heavenly —s, Himmelsgegend; those are unknown —s to you, das sind für Sie böhmische Dörfer.

Regist—er, I. *s.* das Verzeichnis, Register; (—ry of servants) der Stellennachweis; (records) das Protokoll; das Schiffszertifikat (*Naut.*); der Zugschieber, das Register (*Org.*, *Typ.*, *Locom.*, *for warm air*); das Register, der Umfang (*of a voice, etc.*); der Registrierapparat (*Tele.*); die Zeilengleichheit (*of 2 sheets, Typ.*); die Wahlliste (*Pol.*); parish —er, das Kirchenbuch; University —er, die Universitätsmatrikel. II. *v.a.* (in ein Register) eintragen, einschreiben, protokollieren; patentieren, gesetzlich schützen; anzeigen (*Mach.*); in das Register bringen (*Typ.*); einprägen (*in one's memory*); einschreiben (lassen) (*a letter*). —**ered**, *p.p. & adj.* eingeschrieben (*on letters*); patentiert, gesetzlich geschützt; —ered company, eingetragene Genossenschaft; —ered luggage, eingeschriebenes Gepäck; —ered trade-mark, eingetragene Schutzmarke. —**rar**, *s.* der Registrator; —rar's office, die Registratur. —**ration**, *s.* die Registrierung (*also of voters*), Protokollierung, das Einschreiben; —ration of luggage, die Einschreibung des Gepäcks; —ration of teachers, die Ausstellung eines offiziellen Verzeichnisses von als geeignet anerkannten Lehrern und Lehrerinnen. —**ry**, *s.* die Eintragung; das Verzeichnis, Protokoll; (—ry office) die Registratur; das Gesinde-Vermietungs-Kontor; University —ry, die Universitätskanzlei. *Comp.* —**er-grate**, *s.* der Registerofen. —**er-office**, *s.* das Einschreibeamt. —**er-thermometer**, *s.* der Thermometrograph. —**ration-fee**, *s.* die Einschreibegebühr. —**ration-stamp**, *s.* die Einschreibebriefmarke.

Regius, *adj.* königlich; vom König ernannt.

Reglet, *s.* der Steg, Zurichtespan (*Typ.*); das Leistchen (*Arch.*).

Regnant, *adj.* regierend; queen —, die regierende Königin.

Regraft, *v.a.* wieder pfropfen.

Regression, *s.* die Rückkehr.

Regret, I. *s.* das Bedauern; schmerzliches Vermissen; (sorrow) der Kummer; (remorse) die Reue. II. *v.a.* bedauern; bereuen; vermissen; verlangen nach (*something lost*); I — to see, ich sehe mit Bedauern. —**ful**, *adj.*, —**fully**, *adv.* mit Bedauern, ungern. —**table**, *adj.* bedauerlich.

Regul—ar, I. *adj.*, —**arly**, *adv.* ordentlich; (according to rule) regelmäßig (*also Gram.*); regelrecht, genau, pünktlich; (thorough) gehörig, tüchtig (*sl.*); regulär (*Geom.*, *Mil.*); —ar clergy, die Ordensgeistlichkeit. II. *s.* der reguläre Körper; der Linien-Soldat; der Ordensgeistliche (*Eccl.*); —ars, reguläre Truppen. —**arity**, *s.* die Regelmäßigkeit; die Richtigkeit, Ordnung. —**ate**, *v.a.* regeln, ordnen, einrichten; regulieren, stellen (*clocks, etc.*). —**ation**, I. *s.* die Ordnung, Einrichtung, Regulierung; (direction) die Verordnung, Anordnung, Vorschrift; —ations, Statuten. II. *attrib.* vorschriftsmäßig, Kommiß- (*Mil.*); —lation boot, der Kommißstiefel; —lation cap, die Kommißmütze. —**ative**, *adj.* ordnend. —**ator**, *s.* der Regler, Ordner, Anordner, Einrichtende; der Regulator (*Mach.*); die Klappe, das Register (*of a stove, etc.*); die Steuerung (*Hydr.*); der Regulator, die Spiralfeder (*Horol.*). —**us**, *s.* Regulus (*Astr.*); der König (*Chem.*); das Goldhähnchen (*Ornith.*).

Regurgitat—e, *v.* I. *a.* wiederausstoßen. II. *n.* wieder zurückfließen. —**ion**, *s.* das Wiederausstoßen; (reabsorption) das Wiedereinschlucken; das Zurückströmen (*Med.*).

Rehabilitat—e, *v.a.* wieder in frühere Rechte setzen; wieder zu Ehren bringen. —**ion**, *s.* die Wiedereinsetzung in frühere Rechte ꝛc.; die Ehrenrettung, Rehabilitation.

Rehears—al, *s.* die Wiederholung; (narration) die Erzählung; die Probe (*Mus.*, *Theat.*). —**e**, *v.* I. *a.* wiederholen; erzählen; probieren; besingen (*Poet.*). II. *n.* Probe halten. —**er**, *s.* der Erzähler; der, welcher die Probe abhält.

Reign, I. *v.n.* regieren, herrschen; *see* Predominate; he resolved to rule as well as to —, er beschloß nicht nur König zu heißen, sondern selbst zu herrschen. II. *s.* die Regierung; die Herrschaft (*fig.*); the — of King William, die Regierung König Wilhelms; the — of Terror, die Schreckensherrschaft.

Reimburse, *v.a.* wieder bezahlen *or* erstatten, zurückzahlen (*the outlay*); entschädigen (*a p.*); decken (*C. L.*); to — o.s. (at the expense of . . .), sich wieder bezahlt machen (bei . . .). —**ment**, *s.* die Rückzahlung; die Deckung; die Entschädigung.

Re-imprison, *v.a.* wiedereinkerkern.

Rein, I. *s.* der Zügel, Zaum (*also fig.*); to give —, the —s, die Zügel schießen lassen; to assume *or* take the —s (of government), die Zügel (der Regierung) ergreifen. II. *v.a.*; to — up (in), die Zügel anziehen (zum Anhalten), zügeln.

Reindeer, *s.* das Renntier.

Reinforce, I. *v.a.* verstärken. II. *s.* die Verstärkung; das Kammerstück (*Mil.*); first, second —, das Boden-, Zapfen-feld. —**ments**, *pl.* die Verstärkungstruppen, der Nachschub.

Reins, *pl.* die Nieren; das Innere, Herz (*B.*).

Re-insert, *v.a.* wiedereinrücken.

Reinstate, *v.a.* (reinstall) wiedereinsetzen; wiederherstellen.

Reinsure, *v.a.* nochmals versichern.

Re-introduc—e, *v.a.* wiedereinführen. —**tion**, *s.* die Wiedereinführung.

Reinvest, *v. a.* wiedereinsetzen; wiederanlegen (*money*). —**ment**, *s.* die Wiederanlegung.

Reissue, I. *v.a.* wiederausgeben. II. *s.* die Wiederausgabe.

Reiterat—e, *v. a.* wiederholen. —**ion**, *s.* die Wiederholung.

Reject, *v.a.* verwerfen, verstoßen; ausschlagen (*an offer*); (spurn) verschmähen; to be —ed, abgewiesen werden, einen Korb bekommen (von einer Dame), in einer Prüfung durchfallen. —**er**, *s.* der Ausschlagende. —**ion**, *s.* die Auswerfung; die Ausstoßung, Verwerfung, Ausschlagung.

Rejoic—e, *v.* I. *a.* erfreuen, Freude machen. II. *n.* sich freuen, erfreut sein; I am —ed at, ich freue mich über (*acc.*), es freut mich, daß; to —e in, seine Freude haben an (*dat.*), sich freuen über (*acc.*). —**er**, *s.* der sich Freuende. —**ing**, I. *adj.* sich freuend, froh. II. *s.* die Freude, das Frohlocken; —ings, Freudenbezeigungen, Lustbarkeiten (*pl.*).

Rejoin, *v.* I. *a.* (reunite) wieder zusammenfügen, wieder vereinigen; (join, meet) sich wieder vereinigen (mit), wieder kommen *or* stoßen (zu), (einen) wieder treffen, (mit einem) wieder zusammentreffen; (reply) erwidern, antworten, versetzen. II. *n.* erwidern, versetzen. —**der**, *s.* die Erwiderung.

Rejuven—ate, *v.a.* verjüngen. —**ation**, —**escence**, *s.* die Verjüngung; well of —escence, der Jungbrunnen, Quell der Verjüngung.

Rekindle, *v.* I. *a.* wieder-entzünden, -anzünden. II. *n.* (sich) wieder entflammen (*fig.*).

Relapse, I. *v.n.* zurückfallen; einen Rückfall bekommen (*Med. etc.*). II. *s.* der Rückfall.

Relat—e, *v.* I *a.* berichten, erzählen, melden; zuschreiben; in Beziehung bringen zu (*dat.*). II. *n.* sich beziehen (to a th., auf eine S.); to be —ed, verwandt sein (to, mit); —ing to, in Beziehung *or* mit Bezug auf. **—er**, *s.* der Erzähler. **—ion**, *s.* die Erzählung; (reference) die Beziehung, Bezugnahme; (connection) das Verhältnis (*also Geom.*); Verhältnis zu einem, mit einem; (kinship) die Verwandtschaft; (person —ed) der, die Verwandte; in —ion to, in Beziehung auf. **—ionship**, *s.* die Verwandtschaft. **—ive**, I. *adj.*, **—ively**, *adv.* sich beziehend, bezüglich, in Beziehung (to, auf); bezüglich, Beziehungs= (*Gram.*); —ive term, das Beziehungswort; the —ive value, der relative Wert. II. *s.* das Beziehliche; das bezügliche Fürwort, Relativum (*Gram.*); der, die Verwandte.

Relax, *v.* I. *a.* schlaff machen, erschlaffen; (open out) locker machen, öffnen, auflösen; (modify) mildern, mäßigen, vermindern; nachlassen (in energy, severity, etc., in Eifer, Strenge, 2c.); abspannen, erfrischen (*the mind*); öffnen, laxieren (*Med.*). II. *n.* erschlaffen; nachlassen von seiner Strenge, milder werden; sich (*dat.*) Erholung gewähren, ausruhen. **—ation**, *s.* die Erschlaffung, Verminderung der Spannung, Abspannung (*of the nerves, etc.*); das Nachlassen; die Erheiterung, Zerstreuung, Erholung, Ruhe (*fig.*). **—ed**, *adj.* schlaff, matt. **—ing**, *adj.* erschlaffend, weich.

[1]**Relay**, *s.* der Vorrat; Unterleg=, Wechsel=pferde; die Ablösung, das Eintreten neuer Arbeitskräfte (*of workmen, etc.*); das Relais (*Tele.*).

[2]**Relay**, *v.a.* umlegen, neu legen (*a pavement, etc.*).

Release, I. *v.a.* ent=, los=lassen, befreien; erlösen (from, von); aufgeben (*a right*); to — s. o. from his promise, einen seines Versprechens entbinden. III. *s.* die Entlassung, Los=, Freilassung; die Befreiung, Erlassung (*fig.*); die Verzichtleistung, Aufgebung; die Verzicht=Urkunde (*Law*).

Relegat—e, *v.a.* verweisen, relegieren. **—ion**, *s.* die Verweisung.

Relent, *v.n.* sich erweichen lassen, nachgeben, weich, milder werden. **—less**, *adj.*, **—lessly**, *adv.* nicht zu erweichen, unnachgiebig, hart, fühllos. **—lessness**, *s.* die Unnachgiebigkeit, Fühllosigkeit.

Relet, *v.a.* wieder vermieten *or* verpachten.

Relevan—cy, *s.* die Erheblichkeit. **—t**, *adj.* erheblich, passend; anwendbar (to, auf, *acc.*).

Relia—bility, —bleness, *s.* die Zuverlässigkeit. **—ble**, *adj.* zuverlässig. **—nce**, *s.* der Verlaß, das Vertrauen, die Zuversicht; to place —nce on, (sein) Vertrauen setzen au (*acc.*). **—nt**, *adj.* vertrauensvoll, sich verlassend auf (*acc.*); self-—nt, voll Selbstvertrauen.

Relic, *s.* der Rest, das Überbleibsel; die Reliquie (*of a saint, etc.*). **—t**, *s.* der (die) Hinterbliebene; die (der) Witwe(r).

Relie—f, *s.* die Erleichterung, Linderung (*of pain, etc.*); (help) die Hilfe; die Unterstützung (*of the poor*); (release) die Befreiung, Erlösung; die Ablösung (einer Schildwache); der Entsatz (*of a garrison, etc.*); erhabene Arbeit, das Relief (*Sculpt. etc.*); das Hervortreten, die Erhabenheit (*Paint.*); die Rechts=, gerichtliche Hilfe (*Law*); das Hervorheben (*fig.*); to throw into —f, hervortreten lassen, hervorheben; in the boldest —f, in den klarsten Umrissen. **—vable**, *adj.* der Abhilfe fähig. **—ve**, *v.a.* erleichtern, lindern, mindern; helfen, unterstützen; ablösen (*Mil.*); entsetzen; abhelfen (*wants*), Abhilfe gewähren; (ease, free) befreien, lindern, einer S. entheben; (hervor)heben; erhöhen; angenehm unterbrechen (*fig.*); beruhigen (*one's mind*). **—ver**, *s.* der Abhelfer, die Abhilfe; der Ablöser. **—ving**, *adj.* erleichternd; —ving tackle, die Nottalje; —ving officer, der Armenpfleger. **—vo**, *s.* das Relief.

Religio—n, *s.* die Religion. **—sity**, *s.* die Religiosität. **—us**, *adj.* religiös, Religions=; (pious) fromm, gottesfürchtig; kirchlich, gottesdienstlich (*as a service*); (*opp. to* Secular) (ordens)geistlich, Ordens=; —us house, ein Ordenshaus; —us orders, geistliche Orden. **—usly**, *adv. see* —us; pünktlich; (conscientiously) gewissenhaft. **—usness**, *s.* die Religiosität.

Relinquish *v.a.* verlassen; aufgeben, Verzicht leisten auf (*acc.*) (*a plan*). **—ment**, *s.* das Verlassen; die Aufgebung (von), der Verzicht (auf).

Reliquary, *s.* das Reliquienkästchen.

Relish, I. *s.* der Geschmack (*also fig.*); (savour) der Beigeschmack; to have no — for, keinen Geschmack finden an (einer S.); to eat with —, es sich (*dat.*) (gut) schmecken lassen. II. *v.a.* gern essen genießen, Geschmack finden an; genießen, Gefallen *or* finden an (*dat.*) (*fig.*); did you — your dinner, hat Ihnen Ihr Essen geschmeckt?

Reluctan—ce, —cy, *s.* die Abneigung, das Widerstreben, der Widerwille; with —ce, ungern, mit Widerstreben. **—t**, *adj.*, **—tly**, *adv.* unwillig, ungern, widerwillig, mit Widerstreben.

Rely, *v.n.* sich verlassen, vertrauen, bauen, zählen (auf einen *or* eine S.).

Remain, *v n.* (übrig) bleiben; (— behind) zurückbleiben; (continue) (ver)bleiben; to — till called for, postlagernd; to have —ing, übrig haben; I — your loving friend, etc., ich verbleibe deine dich liebende Freundin 2c.; it —s to be told, noch ist zu erzählen; what —s, das Übrige; this —s to be proved, dies bedarf noch des Beweises; to — on hand, auf Lager bleiben. **—der**, *s.* das Überbleibsel; der Rückstand (*of an account, etc.*); der Rest (*Arith.*). **—ing**, *adj.* übrig (geblieben). **—s**, *pl.* das Überbleibsel; die Asche, irdische Hülle (*fig.*); literary —s, der literarische Nachlaß.

Remake, *ir.v.a.* wiedermachen.

Remand, I. *v.a.* wiederkommen lassen; zurückverweisen, in Untersuchungshaft zurückschicken. II. *s.* die Zurücksendung in die Untersuchungshaft.

Remark, I. *s.* die An=, Be=merkung. II. *v.a.* bemerken, gewahr werden (einer S.), beobachten. III. *v.n.* bemerken, Bemerkungen machen (upon, über, zu). **—able**, *adj.*, **—ably**, *adv.* bemerkenswert, merkwürdig; (striking) auffallend; (distinguished) ausgezeichnet. **—ableness**, *s.* das Bemerkenswerte, die Merkwürdigkeit.

Remarry, *v.* I. *n.* wieder heiraten, sich wieder verheiraten. II. *a.* wieder verheiraten.

Remblai, *s.* die Aufschüttung, Erdaufschüttung.

Remed—ial, *adj.* Abhilfe gewährend, verbessernd. **—iless**, *adj.* unheilbar. **—y**, I. *s.* das Heilmittel; (help, cure) das Hilfs=, Rettungs=mittel, die Hilfe; —y of law, das Rechtsmittel. II. *v.a.* helfen; abhelfen (*an evil, etc.*); that is not to be —ied, dem ist nicht abzuhelfen, das läßt sich nicht abstellen.

Rememb—er, *v.* I. *a.* (recollect) sich erinnern (einer S. *or* an eine S.), sich besinnen auf (*acc.*); (bear in mind) im Gedächtnis *or* in der Erinnerung behalten, (einer Sache 2c.) gedenken *or* eingedenk sein; (*recall*) sich (*dat.*) eine S. ins Gedächtnis zurückrufen, sich (*acc.*) besinnen auf (*acc.*); (einen) bedenken (*with a present*); grüßen; —er me kindly to your sister, grüße deine Schwester freundlich von mir; he was —ered, man erinnerte sich seiner, er war unvergessen. II. *n.* gedenken, sich erinnern; do you —er, kannst du dich erinnern? weißt du noch? entsinnst du dich? — **rance**, *s.* die Erinnerung; (memory) das Gedächtnis; (memorial) das Andenken; in —rance of, zum Andenken an; give my kind —rances to him, grüßen Sie ihn bestens von mir. — **rancer**, *s.* der Mahner; der Sekretär der Schatzkammer.

Remind, *v.a.* erinnern, mahnen (of a th., an eine S.). **—er**, *s.* der Wink, die Mahnung.

Reminiscence, *s.* die (Rück=)Erinnerung.

Remiped, *s.* der Ruderfüßler.

Remise, I. *s.* die Rückerstattung, das Aufgeben (eines Anspruchs). II. *v.a.* zurückerstatten, aufgeben (*claims*).

Remiss, *adj.*, **—ly**, *adv.* nachlässig. **—ness**, *s.* die Nachlässigkeit. **—ion**, *s.* das Nachlassen, der Nachlaß; der Erlaß, die Vergebung (*Theol.*); (relaxation) die Erschlaffung, Abspannung.

Remit, *v.* I. *a.* über-senden, -machen, remittieren (*money, bills, etc.*); (abate) nachlassen, mäßigen; (forego) verzichten auf (*acc.*), abtreten; verzeihen, erlassen (*sins*). II. *n.* nachlassen, abnehmen. —**tance**, *s.* die Geldsendung, Übermachung, das Remittieren; (money —ted) der Wechsel, die Rimesse, Tratte; telegraphic —tance, die telegraphische Geldanweisung, Kabelrimesse. —**tent**, *adj.* nachlassend, remittierend (*as fever*). —**ter**, *s.* der Übermacher, Remittent; der Vergeber.

Remnant, *s.* das Überbleibsel, der Rest.

Remodel, *v.a.* umbilden, umwandeln, ummodeln.

Remollient, *adj.* erweichend.

Remonstra—nce, *s.* die Vorstellung, Ermahnung. **—nt**, I. *adj.* Vorstellungen machend. II. *s.* der Remonstrant. **—te**, *v.n.* (einem) Vorstellungen, Einwendungen machen (on s.th., über eine S.); *see* Expostulate. **—tive**, *adj.* zu (Gegen)Vorstellungen, Einwendungen geneigt. —**tion**, *s.* die (Gegen)Vorstellung, Einwendung.

Remorse, *s.* der Gewissensbiß, die Reue, Zerknirschung. **—ful**, *adj.*, **—fully**, *adv.* reuevoll; gefühlvoll. **—less**, *adj.*, **—lessly**, *adv.* reuelos, gefühllos; hartherzig. **—lessness**, *s.* die Gefühllosigkeit.

Remote, *adj.*, **—ly**, *adv.* entfernt, entlegen, fern, weit abliegend; fremd (*fig.*); — kinsmen, entfernte Verwandte; — resemblance, schwache Ähnlichkeit. **—ness**, *s.* die Entlegenheit, Entfernung, Ferne; the —ness of the deluge, der große Zeitraum, der uns von der Sündflut trennt.

Remount, I. *v.a. & n.* wiederaufsteigen; wiederbesteigen (*a horse*); wieder beritten machen; remontieren (*Mil.*). II. *s.* die Ergänzung der Kavalleriepferde, Pferdemusterung, Remonte (*Mil.*).

Remov—al, *s.* das Wegschaffen, die Beseitigung, Fortschaffung, Entfernung; die Hebung (*of a grievance, etc.*); die Entlassung, Absetzung (*from office*); die Wohnungsveränderung, der Umzug (*from a house, etc.*). **—e**, I. *v.a.* weg-, fort-schaffen, weg-rücken, -nehmen, -tun, entfernen, beseitigen; abnehmen (*a bandage, etc.*); verabschieden, entlassen (*an officer*); heben; versetzen (*plants, etc.*); (clear away) wegräumen, verrücken, versetzen (*a landmark*); vor ein anderes Gericht ziehen (*Law*); to —e the cloth, (den Tisch) abdecken; cousins twice —ed, Vettern im zweiten Gliede; Lieutenant Z. has been —ed from the army, Leutnant Z. hat seinen Abschied erhalten. II. *v.n.* aus-, um-ziehen, verziehen (*from a house*); sich wegbegeben, den Ort verändern; to —e from London to Paris, von London nach Paris ziehen. III. *s.* der Abstand, die Stufe, Abstufung; die Versetzung (*school*); der Name einer Mittelklasse an manchen höheren Schulen Englands; it is but a —e from nothing, es ist fast nichts. **—er**, *s.* einer, der wegschafft &c.; —er of furniture, der Möbelbeförderer.

Remunerat—e, *v.a.* belohnen, vergelten; lohnen, einen Ertrag gewähren. **—ion**, *s.* die Belohnung, Vergeltung, Vergütung. **—ive**, *adj.* (be-) lohnend, vergeltend; lohnend, einträglich.

Renaissance, *s.* die Renaissance.

Renal, *adj.* Nieren-.

Re-name, *v.a.* neu benennen, umtaufen.

Renascen—ce, *see* Renaissance; die Wiedergeburt. **—t**, *adj.* wiederwachsend, sich erneuernd; Renaissance-.

Rencounter, I. *s.* das Zusammenstoßen, der Zusammenstoß; das feindliche Zusammentreffen; (combat) das Gefecht; das Scharmützel (*Mil.*). II. *v.n.* feindlich zusammenstoßen.

Rend, *ir.v.a. & n.* reißen; zerreißen (*in pieces, also fig., etc.*); to — the air with cries, die Luft mit seinem Geschrei erfüllen.

Render, I. *v.a.* wieder-, zurück-geben; vergelten (*evil for good, etc.*); leisten (*a service*); gewähren (*help*); ablegen (*an account*); (interpret) übersetzen; vortragen (*a song, etc.*); angeben (*reasons*); abstatten (*thanks*); (make) machen; *see* Surrender; ausschmelzen (*fat*); bewerfen (*Build.*). II. *s.* die Pachtzahlung; (statement) der Bericht, die Angabe. **—ing**, *s.* das Wiedergeben; die Wiedergabe, Darstellung, der Vortrag; (interpretation) die Auslegung, Übersetzung; der erste Anwurf (*Build.*); das Ausschmelzen; —ing of thanks, die Danksagung.

Rendezvous, I. *s.* das Stelldichein; (place of —) der Zusammenkunftsort, Treffort; der Sammelplatz. II. *v.n.* sich einstellen (an einem Orte).

Rendition, *s.* die Übergabe; die Übersetzung; der Vortrag.

Renegade, *s.* der Abtrünnige, Glaubens-Verleugner, Renegat; der Überläufer, Deserteur (*Mil.*).

Renew, *v.a.* erneue(r)n; (revive) verjüngen; (repeat) wiederholen; neu bauen (*a house*); wieder anknüpfen (*an acquaintance, etc.*); prolongieren (*C. L.*). **—able**, *adj.* erneuerungsfähig; zu erneuern. **—al**, *s.* die Erneuerung. **—er**, *s.* der Erneuerer.

Reniform, *adj.* nierenförmig.

Rennet, I. *s.* das Lab. II. *v.a.* mit Lab behandeln.

Renounce, *v.* I. *a.* (einer S. (*dat.*)) entsagen, (auf eine S.) verzichten; (disown) verleugnen; abschwören; sich (*acc.*) lossagen von (einer S.); to — all joys, allen Freuden entsagen, auf alle Freuden verzichten. II. *n.* (die Farbe) nicht bekennen, abwerfen (*Cards*).

Renovat—e, *v.a.* erneue(r)n. **—ion**, *s.* die Erneu(er)ung. **—or**, *s.* der Erneuerer.

Renown, *s.* der Ruhm. **—ed**, *adj.* berühmt.

[1]**Rent**, I. *imperf. & p.p. see* Rend. II. *s.* der Riß, die Spalte; die Spaltung (*fig.*).

[2]**Rent**, I. *s.* die Miete, der Zins (*of a house, etc.*); die Pacht (*of a farm, etc.*); quit —, die Ablösungsrente. II. *v.a.* mieten, pachten; (let) vermieten, verpachten. **—al**, *s.* das Zins-buch, -register; der Mietertrag, Pachtertrag. **—er**, *s.* der Mieter. *Comp.* **—-charge**, *s.* der Erbzins. **—-free**, *adj.* zinsfrei. **—-roll**, *see* —al.

Renter, *v.a.* fein stopfen; anstoßen (seams).

Renunciation, *s.* die Entsagung, der Verzicht.

Reoccupy, *v.a.* wiederbesetzen.

Reopen, *v.* I. *a.* wieder öffnen; wieder eröffnen, aufs neue in Betrieb setzen. II. *n.* sich wieder öffnen, wieder anfangen.

Reorganiz—ation, *s.* die Neugestaltung. **—e**, *v.a.* wieder einrichten, neu gestalten.

Rep(p), *s.* der Rips.

Repack, *v.a.* umpacken.

Repaid, *imperf. & p.p. see* Repay.

[1]**Repair**, I. *s.* die Ausbesserung, Wiederherstellung; in good *or* thorough —, in gutem (baulichem) Zustande; out of —, baufällig, abgerissen. II. *v.a.* ausbessern, wiederherstellen; wiedergutmachen, ersetzen (*a loss, etc.*). **—er**, *s.* der Ausbesserer. **—s**, *pl.* die Ausbesserung, Instandsetzung, Reparatur; (costs) die Ausbesserungskosten; to be undergoing —s, (eben) ausgebessert werden.

[2]**Repair**, *v.n.*; to — to, hingehen, sich begeben nach einem Orte *or* an einen Ort.

Repara—ble, *adj.* auszubessern, verbesserlich; ersetzlich (*fig.*). **—tion**, *s.* die Wiederherstellung, Ausbesserung; (amends) die Entschädigung, Vergütung, Genugtuung, der Ersatz.

Repartee, *s.* schnelle, gewandte, schlagende Antwort; quick at —, schlagfertig.

Repass, *v.* I. *n.* zurückgehen. II. *a.* wieder vorbei gehen an (*dat.*).

Repast, *s.* die Mahlzeit, der Imbiß; (food) die Speise; to take a —, eine Mahlzeit einnehmen.

Repatriat—e, *v.a.* in die Heimat zurückbringen. **—ed**, in das Vaterland zurückgeführt. **—ion**, *s.* die Rücksendung in die Heimat.
Repay, *v.a.* zurückzahlen; (requite) vergelten, belohnen; (pay again) noch einmal bezahlen. — **able**, *adj.* zurückzubezahlen, rückzahlbar. — **ment**, *s.* die Rückzahlung.
Repeal, I. *v.a.* aufheben, abschaffen. II. *s.* die Aufhebung, Abschaffung (*of a law*). **—er**, *s.* der Abschaffende; der Gegner der Parlamentsvereinigung Irlands mit England (*Pol.*).
Repeat, I. *v.a.* wiederholen; herzählen, hersagen (*a poem, etc.*). II. *v.n.* repetieren (*Horol.*). III. *s.* das Wiederholungszeichen (*Mus.*). **—ed**, *adj.*, **—edly**, *adv.* wiederholt. **—er**, *s.* der Wiederholer; die Repetieruhr (*Horol.*); periodischer Dezimalbruch (*Arith.*); der Repetiteur (*Naut.*); das Repetiergewehr; *see* Relay (*Tele.*). **—ing**, *adj.* wiederholend; —ing decimal, —ing ship, —ing telegraph, *see* —er; —ing circle, der Repetitionskreis (*Astr.*).
Repel, *v.* I. *a.* zurückstoßen (*also fig.*), abstoßen (*fig.*); zurückweisen (*fig.*); to — one another, mutually —, einander abstoßen (*Phys.*); to — an attack, einen Angriff zurückschlagen. II. *n.* abstoßen. **—lent**, I. *adj.* zurück- ab-stoßend. II. *s.* zerteilendes Mittel.
[1]**Repent**, *adj.* kriechend (*Bot.*).
[2]**Repent**, *v.* I. *a.* bereuen; he —ed his folly, er bereute *or* ihn reute seine Torheit; it —ed him, es reute ihn, tat ihm leid (*obs. B.*). II. *n.* Reue empfinden; Buße tun (*B.*). **—ance**, *s.* die Reue, Buße. **—ant**, *adj.*, **—antly**, *adv.* reuig, bußfertig.
Repeople, *v.a.* wieder bevölkern.
Repercussion, *s.* der Rückstoß; das Zurückprallen; der Wiederschlag (*Mus.*).
Repertory, *s.* das wissenschaftliche Sachregister, Inhaltsverzeichnis, Nachschlagebuch, Repertorium; der Spielplan, das Repertoire (*Theat.*); die Fundgrube (*fig.*).
Reperus—al, *s.* das abermalige Durchlesen. **—e**, *v.a.* wieder *or* nochmals durchlesen.
Repet—end, *s.* die Periode (*of a decimal*). **—ition**, *s.* die Wiederholung; (reciting) das Hersagen, Rezitieren.
Repin—e, *v.n.* Verdruß empfinden, murren, unzufrieden sein (at a th. über eine S.). **—ing**, I. *adj.*, **—ingly**, *adv.* mürrisch, grämlich. II. *s.* das Murren, die Unzufriedenheit.
Replace, *v.a.* wieder an seinen Ort legen *or* stellen, wieder hinstellen; ersetzen (*in office, etc.*).
Replant, *v.a.* wiederpflanzen, verpflanzen.
Replenish, *v.a.* (wieder) anfüllen; to — one's (ammunition), sich wieder frisch mit (Schießbedarf) versehen.
Replet—e, *adj.* gefüllt (mit), voll (von). **—ion**, *s.* das Vollsein; (satiety) die Überfülle; die Vollblütigkeit (*Med.*).
Replev—in, *s.* die Klage auf Wiedererlangung eines unrechtmäßig vorenthaltenen Besitzes gegen Sicherstellung; die Wiedereinsetzung in gepfändetes Eigentum; der Befehl, durch welchen eine gerichtliche Beschlagnahme wieder aufgehoben wird (*Law*). **—y**, *v.a.* durch replevin wieder erlangen; gegen Sicherheit freigeben (*Law*).
Repli—ca, *s.* die Kopie eines Kunstwerkes durch den Künstler selbst. **—cate**, *adj.* zurückgeschlagen (*Bot.*). **—cation**, *s.* die Antwort (*obs.*); (echo) der Wiederhall (*obs.*); die Replik (*Law*). **—er**, *s.* der Antwortende.
Reply, I. *v.a. & n.* antworten, erwidern (to a question, auf eine Frage). II. *s.* die Antwort, Erwiderung; in — to, in Erwiederung auf (*acc.*). III. *attrib.*; — post card, die Postkarte mit Antwort.
Report, I. *s.* der Bericht, die Nachricht; (official —) amtlicher Bericht, die Berichterstattung; (rumour) das Gerücht; (name) der Ruf; der Knall, Schall (*of a gun, etc.*); newspaper —, der Zeitungsbericht; false newspaper —, die Zeitungsente, Ente; — of proceedings, Bericht über die Verhandlungen. II. *v.n.* (einen) Bericht abstatten, berichten. III. *v.a.* berichten; melden, Anzeige machen (von); (relate) erzählen; verbreiten, aussprengen (*news*); angeben, anzeigen (*a servant, schoolboy, etc.*); stenographieren, nachschreiben (*for the papers, etc.*); *see* Depict; I shall — you to the master, ich werde dich beim Lehrer anzeigen, melden; to — progress, über den Stand einer Sache berichten; it is —ed, man berichtet, man sagt, es heißt; to — o.s., sich melden (*Mil.*). **—er**, *s.* der Berichterstatter, Reporter; der Nachschreiber, Stenograph (*of speeches, etc.*). **—s**, *pl.* die Sammlung von Rechtssprüchen.
Repos—e, I. *s.* die Ruhe (*also fig.*), der Schlaf; die Harmonie der Farbentöne (*Paint.*); der Ruhepunkt (*Poet.*). II. *v.n.* ruhen, schlafen; (rest) liegen, ruhen; (rely) sich verlassen (on, auf (*acc.*)); beruhen auf (*dat.*) (*fig.*). **—eful**, *adj.* ruhevoll. **—itory**, *s.* der Verwahrungsort, die Niederlage; das Warenlager, der Laden.
Repossess, *v.r.* (— of) sich wieder in Besitz (einer S.) setzen.
Reprehen—d, *v.a.* tadeln, verweisen. **—sible**, *adj.*, **—sibly**, *adv.* tadelhaft, tadelnswert; strafbar. **—sibleness**, *s.* die Tadelhaftigkeit. — **sion**, *s.* der Verweis.
Represent, *v.a.* (portray) bildlich darstellen, abbilden, vorstellen; (describe) schildern, beschreiben; aufführen, geben (*Theat.*); (einem etwas) vorstellen, Vorstellungen machen, zu Gemüte führen (*the dangers of an undertaking, etc.*); vertreten (*s.o. or s.th. else*). **—ation**, *s.* die Vor-, Darstellung; das Bild, die Schilderung; die Vorstellung, Aufführung (*Theat.*); *see* Remonstrance; die Vertretung (*Law, Parl.*). **—ative**, I. *adj.* vorstellend; stellvertretend; vertretend, repräsentierend; (vor)bildlich; typisch; —ative government, die Repräsentativ-Verfassung. II. *s.* der Stellvertreter; der Vertreter (*Parl. etc.*). **—ativeness**, *s.* die Vorstellungskraft; die Bildlichkeit. **—er**, *s.* der Darsteller, Vertreter.
Repress, *v.a.* unterdrücken; (restrain) im Zaume halten, hemmen. **—ion**, *s.* die Unterdrückung, Hemmung. **—ive**, *adj.*, **—ively**, *adv.* unterdrückend; —ive measures, Unterdrückungsmaßregeln.
Reprieve, I. *s.* die Begnadigung; (respite) die Frist. II. *v.a.* eine Frist, einen Aufschub geben; (auf einige Zeit) befreien, retten; begnadigen.
Reprimand, I. *s.* der schwere Tadel, Verweis. II. *v.a.* verweisen, einen Verweis geben; he was —ed, er erhielt einen scharfen Verweis *or* (*sl.*) eine gehörige Nase.
Reprint, I. *v.a.* wieder abdrucken (*a book*); wiederaufprägen (*fig.*). II. *s.* die neue Ausgabe, der neue Abdruck, der Neudruck.
Reprisal, *s.* (—s) die Gegenmaßregel, Wiedervergeltung, Vergeltungsmaßregel; letters of marque and —, Repressalienbriefe; law of —, das Wiedervergeltungsrecht.
Reproach, I. *s.* der Vorwurf; (disgrace) die Schmach. II. *v.a.* vorwerfen, zum Vorwurf machen (s.o. with s.th., einem eine S.). **—er**, *s.* der Tadler, Vorwerfende. **—ful**, *adj.*, **—fully**, *adv.* vorwurfsvoll; (abusive) schmähend.
Reprobat—e, I. *adj.* verworfen, ruchlos; —e concerning the faith, untüchtig zum Glauben (*B.*). II. *s.* der Verworfene. **—ion**, *s.* die Verwerfung; die ewige Verdammnis (*Theol.*).
Reproduc—e, *v.a.* wiederhervorbringen, wiedergeben, wiederholen, reproduzieren. **—tion**, *s.* die Wiederhervorbringung; die Wiedergabe; die Reproduktion, Wiedererzeugung (*Physiol.*); das Nachdrucken (*of a book*). **—tive**, *adj.* reproduktiv, wiedererzeugend.
Reproof, *s.* der Tadel, Verweis, die Rüge.
Reprov—e, *v.a.* tadeln, verweisen, rügen; (serve as reproof) ein Vorwurf sein für. **—er**, *s.* der Tadler, Verweisende. **—ing**, *adj.*, **—ingly**, *adv.* tadelnd, verweisend, rügend.

Reptil—e, *s.* das Reptil; der kriechende Mensch, Kriecher (*fig.*). **—ian**, *adj.* zu den Reptilien gehörig.

Republic, *s.* die Republik; der Freistaat (*fig.*); — of letters, Gelehrtenrepublik, gelehrte Welt. **—an**, I. *adj.* republikanisch. II. *s.* der Republikaner. **—anism**, *s.* republikanische Gesinnung; (—an government) republikanische Regierungsform.

Republication, *s.* die Neuherausgabe, Wiederveröffentlichung.

Republish, *v.a.* wieder herausgeben.

Repudiat—e, *v.a.* nicht anerkennen (*debts*); (reject) verwerfen; verstoßen (*a wife*). **—ion**, *s.* die Verwerfung, Abweisung; die Nicht-Anerkennung (von Staatsschulden); die Verstoßung.

Repugnan—ce, **—cy**, *s.* die Abneigung, der Widerwille. **—t**, *adj.* zuwider, im Widerspruche stehend, unverträglich (to, mit); (distasteful) zuwider, widerlich; to be —t to, einen anwidern, einem widerwärtig sein.

Repuls—e, I. *s.* die Abweisung; die Zurücktreibung, das Zurückschlagen (*of the enemy*); (refusal) die abschlägige Antwort; to meet with a —e, zurückgeschlagen werden (*Mil.*); abgewiesen werden, eine abschlägige Antwort bekommen (*fig.*). II. *v.a.* zurück-schlagen, -treiben; abweisen (*fig.*). **—ion**, *s.* das Zurück-schlagen, -treiben; die Abstoßung (*Phys.*); (power of —ion) die Repulsions-, Abstoßungs-kraft. **—ive**, *adj.*, **—ively**, *adv.* zurück-schlagend, -treibend; abstoßend, ekelhaft, widerlich (*fig.*). **—iveness**, *s.* die Widerlichkeit, das Abstoßende.

Repurchase, I. *v.a.* wieder-, zurück-kaufen. II. *s.* der Wieder-, Zurück-kauf.

Reput—able, *adj.*, **—ably**, *adv.* anständig, angesehen, in gutem Rufe stehend; (creditable) ehrbar, anständig. **—ation**, *s.* der Ruf, gute Name, das Ansehen, die Ehre; to have the —ation of being . . ., den Ruf haben . . ., im Ruf stehen . . .; to ruin a p.'s —ation, einen um seinen guten Ruf *or* Namen bringen. **—e**, I. *v.a.* halten, achten für; schätzen; he is —ed to be rich, er gilt für reich. II. *s.* der Ruf; to be in high —e, in gutem Rufe stehen; of bad —e, von schlechtem Rufe. **—ed**, *adj.* vermeintlich. **—edly**, *adv.* dem Rufe nach, nach allgemeiner Annahme.

Request, I. *s.* das Gesuch, Ansuchen; (petition) die Bitte; *see* Demand; in —, gesucht, begehrt; (prized) geschätzt, in Ansehen; at the — of, auf das Gesuch des . . ., auf Anhalten von . . . II. *v.a.* bitten, ersuchen; earnestly —ed, dringend ersucht; to — a favour (of a p.), (einen) um eine Gefälligkeit ersuchen.

Requiem, *s.* die Seelenmesse, das Requiem.

Require, *v.a.* verlangen, erfordern; brauchen, haben müssen; (beg) ersuchen um; (exact) fordern, verlangen; the —d angle, der gesuchte Winkel; he does not — to be asked twice, er läßt sich nicht zweimal bitten. **—ment**, *s.* die Forderung; die Anforderung; (*need*) das Bedürfnis.

Requisit—e, I. *adj.* erforderlich, notwendig. II. *s.* das Erfordernis. **—ion**, I. *s.* die Forderung; die Requisition (*Law*); *see* Request, Demand; (formal call) schriftlicher Aufruf, die Einladung (zu Versammlungen &c.); to make —ions, to put into —ion, in Requisition setzen; *see* —ion II. II. *v.a.* requirieren, (zum Dienste des Staates) in Beschlag nehmen.

Requit—al, *s.* die Vergeltung, Belohnung. **—e**, *v.a.* vergelten, belohnen.

Reread, *v.a.* wieder lesen, noch einmal lesen.

Reredos, *s.* der Altarrücken, das Altarblatt.

Rescind, *v.a.* aufheben, umstoßen, für ungültig erklären (*ordinances*).

Rescission, *s.* die Aufhebung, Umstoßung.

Rescript, *s.* der amtliche Bescheid, Erlaß, die Verfügung, Verordnung.

Rescue, I. *v.a.* befreien; retten (*fig.*). II. *s.* die Befreiung, Rettung; die gewaltsame Befreiung (*of a prisoner*). **—r**, *s.* der Befreier, Retter.

Research, I. *v.a.* wiedersuchen; (examine) genau untersuchen, erforschen. II. *s.* die Untersuchung, (Nach)Forschung. **—er**, *s.* der Forscher. *Comp.* **—-degree**, *s.* der auf Grund einer Dissertation verliehene Universitätsgrad. **—-student**, *s.* ein vorgeschrittener Student, welcher eigene Forschungen anstellt.

Reseat, *v.a.* wieder setzen; mit neuen Sitzen versehen; be —ed, bitte, nehmen Sie wieder Platz.

Resell, *v.a.* wieder verkaufen.

Resembl—ance, *s.* die Ähnlichkeit. **—e**, *v.a.* (einem) gleichen, ähnlich sein *or* sehen.

Resend, *v.a.* wiederschicken, zurückschicken (*obs.*).

[1]**Resent**, *v.a.* übel aufnehmen; ahnden (*an insult, etc.*). **—ful**, *adj.*, **—fully**, *adv.* empfindlich, zum Groll geneigt, grollend. **—ment**, *s.* die Empfindlichkeit, der Verdruß, Groll, das Rachegefühl; starke Empfindung (*of a loss; obs.*).

[2]**Resent**, *past part. of* Resend.

Reserv—ation, *s.* der Rückhalt, Vorbehalt; (what is —ed) das Vorbehaltene, der Vorbehalt; das Reservatgebiet (*in America*); die Aufbewahrung, Verwahrung (*of the Eucharist*); mental —ation, Gedankenvorbehalt; der geistige Vorbehalt (*Theol.*); with a —ation, mit Vorbehalt. **—e**, I. *v.a.* aufsparen, bewahren; zurück-, vor-behalten; to —e to o.s., sich (*dat.*) vorbehalten, für sich behalten; all rights —ed, unter Vorbehaltung aller Rechte. II. *s. see* —ation; (store) der Vorrat; der Rückhalt, die Reserve (*Mil.*); die Zurückhaltung, Verschlossenheit, das zurückhaltende Wesen (*fig.*); (caution) die Vorsicht; with certain —es, unter gewissen Einschränkungen; without —e, ohne Einschränkung, rückhaltlos; to sell without —e, um jeden Preis verkaufen; in —e, im Rückhalt, im Vorrat; to keep in —e, aufsparen; the —es were called out, es wurde mobil gemacht; second —e, die Landwehr; third —e, der Landsturm. **—ed**, *adj.*, **—edly**, *adv.* zurückhaltend, verschlossen; vorsichtig; bestellt, belegt, vorgemerkt; —ed seat, numerierter Platz; —ed table, der bestellte Tisch; der Stammtisch. **—oir**, I. *s.* das Behältnis, der Behälter (*for water, fish, etc.*); das Auffangewerk (*Agr.*). II. *attrib.*; —oir pen, die Füllfeder. *Comp.* **—e-forces**, *pl.* die Reservemannschaft (*Mil.*). **—e-fund**, *s.* das Reservekapital (*C.L.*).

Reset, *v.a.* wiedereinfassen; neu einmauern (*a boiler*); wiedersetzen (*Typ.*).

Reshape, *v.a.* noch einmal bilden *or* gestalten.

Reship, *v.a.* wieder verschiffen.

Resid—e, *v.n.* wohnen, sich aufhalten. **—ence**, *s.* der Aufenthalt, das Wohnen; (place of —ence) der Wohnort; (house, *etc.*) die Wohnung, das Haus; der Sitz; die Residenz; der beständige Aufenthalt (*of a rector, etc.*); official —ence, die Amtswohnung. **—ent**, I. *adj.* wohnhaft, bleibend, sich aufhaltend; im Hause oder in der Anstalt wohnend (*of masters, etc.*). II. *s.* (dweller) der Bewohner; der Minister-Resident (*at foreign courts*); lady —ent, die Vorsteherin des Hauses. **—ential**, *adj.* wohnend; Residenten-. **—entiary**, *adj.* seßhaft, wohnhaft. **—ual**, I. *adj* übrig. II. *s.* (—ual quantity) die Differenz. **—uary**, *adj.* übrig (geblieben); —uary legatee, der Haupterbe, Universalerbe. **—ue**, *s.* der Rest, Überrest; *see* —uum (*Law*); electric —ue, elektrischer Rückstand, das Residuum. **—uum**, *s.* der Rückstand; der reine Erbnachlaß.

Resign, *v.a.* aufgeben, verzichten auf (eine S.); (hand over) überlassen; (relinquish) zurücktreten (von); to — one's place, abdanken; to — o.s. to, sich ergeben in (*acc.*) (to the will of God, dem Willen Gottes). **—ation**, *s.* die Abtretung, Verzichtleistung (auf eine S.), Entsagung (*dat.*); die Hin-, Er-gebung (in), Unterwerfung (unter *e.g.* den Willen Gottes). **—ed**, *adj.*, **—edly**, *adv.* ergeben; mit Ergebung.

Resilien—ce, —cy, *s.* das Zurück-springen, -prallen. **—t,** *adj.* zurückspringend, abprallend.

Resin, I. *s.* das Harz; das Geigenharz, Kolophonium. II. *attrib.;* — soap, die Harzseife. **—o-lectric,** *adj.* negativ elektrisch. **—o-electricity,** *s.* die Harzelektrizität. **—ous,** *adj.* harzig.

Resist, *v.a. & n.* widerstehen (einem), sich (einem) widersetzen. **—ance,** *s.* der Widerstand (*also Phys. & Elec.*). **—ant,** I. *adj.* widerstehend. II. *s.* der Widerstehende. **—er,** *s.* einer, der Widerstand leistet; passive —er, einer, welcher gewissen ihm unliebsamen Verordnungen der Behörden keine Beachtung schenkt. **—less,** *adj.* unwiderstehlich; (unresisting) ohne Widerstand. *Comp.* **—ance-coil,** *s.* die Widerstandsrolle.

Resolut—e, *adj.*, **—ely,** *adv.* entschlossen, entschieden, fest. **—eness,** *s.* die Entschlossenheit, Festigkeit, Standhaftigkeit. **—ion,** *s.* die Entschlossenheit, Festigkeit, der Mut; die Auflösung (*Phys., Mech., Mus.*); die Auflösung, Zerteilung (*of a tumour, etc.*); die (Auf-)Lösung, Hebung (*of difficult questions*); die Entscheidung (*Law*); (resolve) der Entschluß (zu einer S.); der (die) Beschluß(fassung) (*Parl.*); to form a —ion, einen Vorsatz fassen; to propose a —ion, einen Beschluß beantragen (*Parl.*); a —ion of congratulation, eine Glückwunschadresse; —ion of forces, die Zerlegung der Kräfte.

Resolv—able, *adj.* auflösbar. **—e,** I. *v.a.* auflösen (into, in); erweichen, zerteilen (*Med.*); auflösen (*Chem., Math.*); lösen (*questions*); heben (*doubts, difficulties*); (decide) entscheiden; to —e an equation, eine Gleichung auflösen. II. *v.r.* sich auflösen, sich bilden (*into a committee, etc.*). III. *v.n.* (—e on) beschließen, einen Beschluß fassen; (decide) sich entschließen; they —ed, sie beschlossen, sie entschlossen sich; to —e on a th., sich zu einer S. entschließen, eine Sache (fest) beschließen. IV. *s.* der Entschluß, Beschluß. **—ed,** *adj.* entschlossen. **—end,** *s.* der Resolvend (*Math.*). **—ent,** *s.* das Auflösungsmittel.

Resonan—ce, *s.* der Widerklang, die Resonanz. **—t,** *adj.* widerhallend. *Comp.* **—ce-chamber,** *s.* der Resonanzboden.

Resort, I. *s.* der Zusammenfluß, das Zusammenlaufen; (place of —) der Zusammenkunftsort; die Zuflucht (*fig.*); der Sammelplatz; health —, der Kurort, die Sommerfrische; as a last —, als letzte Zuflucht. II. *v.n.* sich begeben, kommen, gehen; (frequent) oft besuchen; to — to, seine Zuflucht nehmen zu (*fig.*).

Resound *v.* I. *a.* wiederhallen; ertönen lassen. II. *n.* wiederhallen, nachhallen. **—ing,** *adj.*, **—ingly,** *adv.* wieder-, nachhallend.

Resource, *s.* die Hilfsquelle, Zuflucht, das Hilfsmittel. —s, *pl.* Geldmittel; Fähigkeiten, Gaben. *Comp.* **—ful,** *adj.* nie um einen Ausweg verlegen.

Respect, I. *v.a.* berücksichtigen; (esteem) (hoch-) achten, schätzen, ehren, in Ehren halten; (refer to) betreffen, sich beziehen auf (*acc.*); a man who —s himself, ein Mann, der Selbstachtung hat, der etwas auf sich hält. II. *s.* die Rücksicht, Hinsicht, der Betracht; die Achtung, Hochachtung, Verehrung, Ehrerbietung; (point) der Umstand, Punkt; in — of, with — to, in Beziehung auf (*acc.*); hinsichtlich (*gen.*); in all —s, in every —, in jeder Hinsicht; in many (some) —s, in vieler (mancher) Hinsicht; to show — to, (einem) ehrerbietig begegnen; to have a — for, Ehrfurcht haben vor; to pay one's —s to s.o., sich einem gehorsamst empfehlen; (visit) einem seine Aufwartung machen. **—ability,** *s.* die Achtbarkeit, Achtungswürdigkeit; die Anständigkeit; die Solidität (*C. L.*). **—able,** *adj.*, **—ably,** *adv.* achtbar, achtenswert, ehrenwert, angesehen; (decent) anständig; (middling) erträglich, leidlich, nicht übel; solid, reell, gut (*C. L.*). **—er,** *s.* einer, der Achtung fühlt, Rücksicht nimmt. **—ful,** *adj.*, **—fully,** *adv.* ehrerbietig, ehrfurchtsvoll, höflich; yours —fully, Ihr ganz Ergebener, ergebenst, hochachtungsvollst. **—fulness,** *s.* die Ehrerbietigkeit, Ehrerbietung. **—ing,** *prep.* in Betreff, in Beziehung auf (*acc.*), hinsichtlich (*gen.*). **—ive,** *adj.* sich beziehend, bezüglich, relativ; (particular) besonder, sich (auf jeden im Einzelnen) beziehend, respektiv; they departed to their —ive homes, sie trennten sich und gingen jeder nach seinem eignen Hause. **—ively,** *adv.* beziehungsweise.

Respir—ation, *s.* das Atmen, die Atmung. **—ator,** *s.* der Atem-, Lungen-schützer. **—atory,** *adj.* Atmungs-, zum Atmen dienend; —atory organs, Atmungswerkzeuge. **—e,** *v.n.* atmen, Atem holen; den Atem ziehen (*high style*).

Respite, I. *s.* die Frist (*Law*). II. *v.a.* (— a criminal) die Vollstreckung des Urteils über einen Verbrecher verschieben (*Law*); (einem) eine Frist geben, gewähren; Ruhe gewähren.

Resplenden—ce, —cy, *s.* der Glanz; die Pracht (*fig.*). **—t,** *adj.*, **—tly,** *adv.* glänzend.

Respon—d, *v.* I. *n.* antworten; respondieren; (einer S.) entgegenkommen eingehen auf (*acc.*) (*fig.*); haften (*Amer.*); to —d to a letter, einen Brief beantworten; to —d to a call, einem Rufe Folge leisten. II. *a.* Genüge leisten (*Law*). III. *s.* die kurze Motette, Antwort des Chors (*Eccl.*). **—dent,** I. *adj.* antwortend, entsprechend. II. *s.* der, die Angeklagte (*Law*); (disputant) der Respondent. **—dentia,** *s.* (—dentia bond) der Bodmereibrief. **—se,** *s.* die Antwort (*also of an oracle*); die Erwiderung (*in a formal dispute*); das Responsorium (*in church*); die Wiederkehr eines fugierten Themas in einer andern Stimme (*Mus.*). **—sibility,** *s.* die Verantwortlichkeit; die Zahlungsfähigkeit. **—sible,** *adj.* verantwortlich; (able to pay) zahlungsfähig. **—sions,** *pl.*, die Aufnahmeprüfung an der Universität Oxford; *see* Little-go. **—sive,** *adj.* antwortend; (corresponding) entsprechend; (sympathetic) entgegenkommend. **—siveness,** *s.* das Entsprechende. **—sory,** I. *adj.* antwortend. II. *s.* das Responsorium.

[1]**Rest,** I. *s.* die Ruhe, Rast; der Friede (*fig.*); (sleep) der Schlaf; der Tod (*fig.*); (—ing place) der Ruheplatz; (support) die Stütze; der Schuh (*of a lance*); der Ruhepunkt, die Zäsur (*Pros.*); die Pause, Fermate (*Mus.*); das Pausezeichen (*Mus.*); die Handscheide (*in turning*); day of —, der Ruhetag; in —, eingelegt (*as a lance*); to retire to —, sich zur Ruhe begeben, schlafen gehen; to set at —, beruhigen; to be at —, ruhig sein; tot sein. II. *v.n.* rasten, (aus)ruhen; schlafen; (remain) sein, bleiben, verharren; (lean) lehnen, sich stützen (on, auf (*acc.*)); (be supported) beruhen, gegründet sein (auf (*acc.*)); (rely) sich verlassen, zählen (on, auf); the fault —s with you, die Schuld liegt an Ihnen; the matter now —s with him, jetzt bleibt die Sache ihm überlassen, sie liegt in seinen Händen, hängt von ihm ab; you may — assured that . . ., du kannst dich darauf verlassen, daß . . .; to — from one's labours, von seiner Arbeit ausruhen; the truth of religion —s on . . ., die Wahrheit der Religion beruht auf (*dat.*). . . III. *v.a.* ruhen lassen, zur Ruhe bringen; God — his soul! Gott hab' ihn selig! to — one's elbows, *etc.*, on, stützen auf (*acc.*). **—ful,** *adj.*, **—fully,** *adv.* ruhig; beruhigend. **—ing,** *s.* das Ruhen. **—less,** *adj.*, **—lessly,** *adv.* rastlos, ruhelos; unruhig (*in disposition*); aufrührerisch (*as a people*); (ever-moving) unstät. **—lessness,** *s.* die Rastlosigkeit, Unruhe. *Comp.* **—ing-place,** *s.* der Ruheplatz; der Absatz (*on a staircase*).

[2]**Rest,** I. *s.* der Rest, Überrest; (— capital) der Rechnungssaldo; der Gang (*Tennis*); —s, die Übrigen; — of a debt, der Rückstand einer Schuld; among the —, unter anderm; for the —, übrigens, im Übrigen. II. *v.n.* übrig bleiben.

Restate, *v.a.* noch einmal feststellen, darlegen.

Restaura—nt, *s.* die Wirtschaft, das Speisehaus, Restaurant. **—teur**, *s.* der Speisewirt.

Restitution, *s.* die Wiederherstellung; (indemnification) die Wiedererstattung, der Ersatz; to make —, Ersatz leisten.

Restive, *adj.*, **—ly**, *adv.* störrisch, widerspenstig, stetig; — to the rein, sich gegen den Zügel sträubend (*of horses*); *see* Refractory. **—ness**, *s.* die Störrigkeit, Stetigkeit (eines Pferdes); die Widerspenstigkeit, der Starrsinn.

Restor—ation, *s.* die Wiederherstellung; die Wiedereinsetzung; die Erneuerung, Restauration (*Hist.*). **—ative**, I. *adj.* wiederherstellend, stärkend. II. *s.* das Stärkungsmittel. **—e**, *v.a.* wiederherstellen; wieder einsetzen; (return) erstatten, wiedergeben; zurückführen (*to the paths of virtue*); to —e a p. to health (to liberty), einem die Gesundheit (die Freiheit) wiederverschaffen; to —e to life, ins Leben zurückrufen. **—er**, *s.* der Wiederhersteller.

Restrain, *v.a.* zurück-, ab-halten, in Schranken halten; (einem) Einhalt tun; verhindern; (repress) unterdrücken; —ing grace, die bewahrende Gnade. **—edly**, *adv.* mit Einschränkung. **—t**, *s.* die Zurückhaltung; (retention) die Gefangenschaft, Haft; (restriction) die Einschränkung, Hemmung, das Hindernis, der Zwang.

Restrict, *v.a.* be-, ein-schränken. **—ion**, *s.* die Einschränkung; die Beschränkung (on trade, des Handels); der Vorbehalt. **—ive**, *adj.* be-, einschränkend.

Result, I. *s.* das Ergebnis, Resultat, die Folge; das Fazit (*Arith.*); the general —, das Gesamtergebnis. II. *v.n.* als Folge entstehen, sich ergeben, herrühren (from, von); hinauslaufen (in, auf eine S.); to — in a th., eine S. zur Folge haben. **—ant**, I. *adj.* entstehend, aus (etwas) hervorgehend. II. *s.* die Resultante (*Math.*, *Mech.*).

Resum—e, *v.a.* wiedernehmen; (begin again, *also v.n.*) wieder anfangen, fortsetzen; wieder aufnehmen; wieder übernehmen (*an office, the reins of government, etc.*); to —e a discourse, auf ein Gespräch zurückkommen; reason —ed her sway, die Vernunft trat wieder in ihre Rechte. **—é**, *s.* die kurze Wiederholung, Zusammenfassung; das Resumé. **—ption**, *s.* die Wiederaufnahme; (taking back) die Zurücknahme.

Resurrection, *s.* die Auferstehung; das Wiedererstehen (*fig.*). **—ist**, (**—-man**), *s.* der Leichendieb.

Resuscitat—e, *v.* wiedererwecken *or* beleben, ins Leben zurückrufen. **—ion**, *s.* die Wieder-belebung, -erweckung. **—ive**, *adj.* wiederbelebend. **—or**, *s.* der Erwecker, Wiederbelebende.

Ret, *v.a.* rösten (*flax*). **—ting**, *s.* die Röste, das Rösten.

Retail, I. *v.a.* im Kleinen, im Detail verkaufen (*C.L.*); (sell at second-hand) wiederverkaufen; umständlich erzählen, wiederholen (*fig.*). II. *s.* der Kleinhandel, das Detailgeschäft; by —, stückweise; to sell by —, im Kleinen verkaufen, (Ellenwaren) ausschneiden. III. *adj.*; — business, der Kleinhandel; — dealer, der Kleinhändler; — price, der Detailpreis; — establishment, — shop, der Kramladen; das Ausschnittgeschäft. **—er**, *s.* der Kleinhändler, Wiederverkäufer.

Retain, *v.a.* behalten (*in the memory, etc.*); bestellen, vorher nehmen, sich (*dat.*) vormerken lassen belegen (*places, etc.*); bestellen, annehmen (*counsel, Law*). **—able**, *adj.* zu behalten. **—er**, *s.* der Anhänger, Gefolgsmann, (—ers, *pl.*) das Gefolge; (servant) der Bediente, Lakei; das feste Honorar, Anstellungshonorar (*for counsel, Law*). **—ing**, *adj.*; —ing fee, *see* —er (*Law*); —ing wall, die Stütz-, Futter-mauer.

Retake, *ir.v.a.* wiedernehmen.

Retaliat—e, *v.* I. *n.* & *a.* mit Gleichem vergelten, wiederzurückgeben, wettmachen. II. *n.* Wiedervergeltung üben (upon a p., an einem). **—ion**, *s.* die Wiedervergeltung, Rache; fiscal —ion, der Zollschutz gegenüber Ländern mit Schutzzoll. **—ory**, *adj.*; —ory duty, der Vergeltungszoll auf Waren aus Ländern mit Schutzzoll.

Retard, *v.a.* verspäten, aufhalten, verzögern; (impede) hindern, hemmen; —ed motion, —ed velocity, verzögerte Bewegung, verlangsamte Geschwindigkeit. **—ation**, *s.* die Verzögerung, das Aufhalten; das Hindern; (delay) der Verzug, Aufschub; die Aufhaltung (*Mus.*); die Verlangsamung, Verzögerung (*Phys.*). **—ment**, *s.* die Verspätung, das Hindern.

Retch, *v.n.* (sich) würgen, sich erbrechen wollen.

Retell, *v.a.* noch einmal erzählen.

Retent—ion, *s.* die Zurückhaltung; die Verhaltung (*of the urine*); die Retention (*Law*); die Beibehaltung (*of customs*). **—ive**, *adj.* zurückhaltend; leicht behaltend, treu (*as the memory*); —ive faculty, die Gedächtniskraft. **—iveness**, *s.* die Treue (des Gedächtnisses), Gedächtniskraft; behaltende Kraft.

Reticen—ce, *s.* die Verschwiegenheit; die Verschweigung. **—t**, *adj.* verschwiegen; schweigsam; zurückhaltend.

Reti—cular, *adj.* netzförmig. **—culate(d)**, *adj.* netzartig; netzartig durchbrochen; —culated moulding, die Netzverzierung, (—culated work) das Netzwerk. **—cule**, *s.* der (Damen-)Arbeits-, Strick-beutel; das Fadennetz, das Dreieck (in Fernrohren); *see* —culum. **—culum**, *s.* das Netzchen, Reticulum. **—form**, *adj.* netzförmig. **—na**, *s.* die Netzhaut (des Auges).

Retinue, *s.* das Gefolge.

Retir—ade, *s.* der Zufluchtsort, die Verschanzung (*Fort.*). **—e**, *v.* I. *a.* zurückziehen; einlösen (*a bill*); abdanken, pensionieren (*an officer*). II. *n.* sich zurückziehen; (go away) sich wegbegeben, fortgehen; sich entfernen (from, aus); to —e from business, sich vom Geschäft zurückziehen; to —e into the country, aufs Land ziehen; to —e from active service, seinen Abschied aus dem aktiven Dienst nehmen; to —e to rest, schlafen gehen. **—ed**, *adj.*, **—edly**, *adv.* zurückgezogen, einsam; (secret) verborgen; —ed list, die Pensionsliste; a —ed life, ein stilles, zurückgezogenes, abgeschiedenes Leben; —ed battery, die Kehlbatterie. **—edness**, *s.* die Eingezogenheit. **—ement**, *s.* das Sich-zurückziehen; (seclusion) die Zurückgezogenheit; the —ement of a partner, der Austritt eines Geschäftsteilhabers. **—ing**, *adj.* zurückhaltend, bescheiden, schüchtern; —ing allowance, das Ruhegehalt, die Pension.

Retort, I. *v.a.* zurückwerfen (*rare*); zurückgeben, erwidern (upon a p., einem). II. *v.n.* eine Beschuldigung zurückgeben, scharf erwidern *or* entgegnen. III. *s.* die Erwiderung, der zurückgegebene Vorwurf; die Retorte, der Kolben (*Chem.*).

Retouch, *v. a.* überarbeiten, auffrischen; aufstechen (*Engr.*); retouchieren (*Phot.*). **—ed**, *p.p.* & *adj.* nachgraviert (*of postage stamps*).

Retrace, *v.a.* zurückgehen auf (*acc.*); nochmals zeichnen (*Draw.*); zurückverfolgen (*also fig.*).

Retract, *v.a.* (withdraw) zurückziehen (*also v.n.*); (recall) widerrufen, zurücknehmen. **—able**, **—ile**, *adj.* zurück-, ein-ziehbar. **—ation**, **—ion**, *s.* die Zurücknahme, Widerrufung; die Zurücknahme (*of a claim, etc.*); der Widerruf. **—or**, *s.* der zurückziehende Muskel.

Retransfer, *v.a.* wieder auf einen Namen überschreiben, nochmals übertragen.

Retransla—te, *v.a.* (zu)rückübersetzen; wieder *or* noch einmal übersetzen. **—tion**, *s.* die Rückübersetzung.

Retreat, I. *s.* der Rückzug (*also Mil.*); (seclusion) die Zurückgezogenheit (refuge) der Zufluchtsort, die Zuflucht, das Asyl; der Zapfenstreich (*Mil.*); to beat the (a) —, den Zapfenstreich schlagen (*Mil.*), (sich zurückziehen, *fig.*); to sound the —, zum Rückzuge blasen; to beat a hasty —, sich eiligst aus dem Staube machen (*coll.*). II. *v.n.* sich zurückziehen.

Retrench, *v.* I. *a.* ab=, ver=kürzen, weglassen; einschränken, vermindern (*expenses*); *see* Intrench. II. *n.* seine Ausgaben vermindern, beschränken. **—ment,** *s.* die Verkürzung, Verminderung, Einschränkung; die Verschanzung (*Fort.*).

Retribut—ion, *s.* die Vergeltung, Vergütung, Wiederbezahlung. **—ive,** *adj.* vergeltend, Wiedervergeltungs=.

Retriev—able, *adj.* wiederbringlich, ersetzlich. **—e,** *v.* I. *a.* wiederauffinden, apportieren (*of dogs*); (recover) wiedereinbringen; wiedergutmachen; to —e a loss, sich entschädigen; to —e one's character, sich (*dat.*) wieder seinen vorigen Ruf gewinnen. II. *n.* wiederauf=finden, =jagen. **—er,** *s.* der Stöber(hund), Apportierhund.

Retro—action, *s.* die Rückwirkung. **—active,** *adj.*, **—actively,** *adv.* rückwirkend. **—cede,** *v.* I. *n.* zurückgehen. II. *a.* wiederabtreten (*an estate, etc.*). **—cession,** *s.* das Zurückgehen; die Wiederabtretung (*Law*); *see* Precession. **—gradation,** *s.* der Rückgang; die (scheinbar) rückläufige Bewegung (*Astr.*). **—grade,** I. *adj.* rückgängig, rückläufig; —grade motion, rückgängige, =läufige Bewegung. II. *v.n.* zurück=, rückwärts=gehen; zurückgehen (*fig.*). **—gression,** *s.* das Rückwärtsgehen; *see* —gradation (*Astr.*). **—gressive,** *adj.* rückwärtsgehend; —gressive assimilation, rückwärtswirkende Angleichung (*Gram.*). **—spect, —spection,** *s.* der Rückblick; —spection, die Rückerinnerung. **—spective,** *adj.*, **—spectively,** *adv.* zurückblickend; beziehlich, wechselseitig; *see* —active; not to have a —spective effect, not to be —spective, keine rückwirkende Kraft haben, nicht zurückwirken (*as a law*). **—version,** *s.* die Rückwärtswendung; die Gebärmutterbeugung.

Return, I. *v.n.* zurück=kehren, =kommen; (recur) wiederzurückkommen auf (*acc.*); wiederanheimfallen (an einen), zufallen (einem) (*to a former owner*); (reply) entgegnen, erwidern; to — home, nach Hause zurück=gehen, =reisen 2c. II. *v.a.* zurück=, wieder=geben; erstatten, abstatten, aussprechen (*one's thanks*); zurückgeben (*an accusation*); nachspielen (*Cards*); (bring back) zurückbringen; (send back) zurück=stellen, =senden, =schicken; abgeben, aussprechen (*a verdict*); wieder zustellen, einsenden, überweisen (to a tribunal, *etc.*, einem Gerichte); (give a list of) berichten, angeben; (answer) erwidern, antworten; (transmit) über=machen, =liefern; ins Parlament schicken, (als Vertreter *or* zum Abgeordneten) wählen (*a candidate*) (*Parl.*); to — a compliment, ein Kompliment erwidern; to — a visit, einen Gegenbesuch abstatten. III. *s.* die Rückkehr; (periodical —) periodische Wiederkehr; der Umlauf, Wechsel (*of the seasons, etc.*); das Zurückschlagen (*of a ball*); der Rückfall (*of a disease, etc.*); (the giving back) die Rückgabe; (repayment) die Rückzahlung; die Erwiderung (*of a kindness, etc.*); (requital) die Vergeltung, der Ersatz; das Wiedereinkommen (*of outlay*), der Umsatz (*C. L.*); (profit) der Gewinn, Ertrag, Nutzen; der (amtliche) Bericht; der Wahlbericht (*Parl.*); (answer) die Erwiderung, Antwort; der Seitenflügel (*Build.*); in —, dafür, dagegen, als Vergeltung; to wish a p. many happy —s (of the day), einem viel Glück wünschen *or* einem seine herzlichsten Glückwünsche schicken (zum Geburtstag 2c.); — of a writ, die Übermachung eines Gerichts=, Vollziehungs=befehls; — of affection, die Gegenliebe; — of health, die wiederkehrende Gesundheit; by — of post *or* mail, mit umgehender *or* wendender Post, postwendend; at the — of the year, wenn das Jahr wieder um ist; — of a salute, der Gegengruß. **—able,** *adj.* zurückstellbar. **—er,** *s.* der Zurückkehrende; der Heimbezahlende (*of money*). **—ing,** *p. see* Return. **—s,** *pl.* die Einnahme (*C. L.*); statistical —s, statistische Aufstellungen. *Comp.* **—-cargo,** *s.* die Rückladung. **—-freight,** *s.* die Rückfracht. **—ing-officer,** *s.* der Wahlkommissär. **—-match,** *s.* die Revanche=Partie. **—-ticket,** *s.* die Rückfahrkarte, der Rückfahrschein.

Reun—ion, *s.* die Wiedervereinigung; (party) die Gesellschaft. **—ite,** *v.a.* (& *n.* sich) wiedervereinigen; wiederversöhnen.

Revaccinate, *v.a.* wiederimpfen.

Revaluation, *s.* die abermalige Schätzung.

Reveal, *v.a.* entdecken; offenbaren (*also Theol.*); verraten (*secrets*); —ed religion, die geoffenbarte *or* Offenbarungs=Religion. **—able,** *adj.* enthüllbar. **—er,** *s.* der Offenbarer.

Reveille, *s.* die Reveille, der Weckruf (*Mil.*).

Revel, I. *s.* das Gelage, die Lustbarkeit; master of the —s, *see* Lord of Misrule. II. *v.n.* Gelage halten, schwärmen, jubeln, schmausen; (luxuriate) schwelgen; to — and riot, in Saus und Braus leben. **—ler,** *s.* der Schwelger, Teilnehmer an einer Lustbarkeit. **—ry,** *s.* wilde Lustbarkeit, das Jubeln, der Saus und Braus.

Revelation, *s.* die Offenbarung; — of St. John, die Offenbarung Johannis.

Revenge, I. die Rache, Ahndung; die Revanche (*Cards, etc.*); *see* —fulness. II. *v.a.* rächen, Rache nehmen (für); ahnden (*high style*); I'll be —d on him, ich werde mich an ihm zu rächen wissen. III. *v.r.* sich rächen, Rache nehmen (on a p., an einem). **—ful,** *adj.*, **—fully,** *adv.* rachgierig, rachsüchtig. **—fulness,** *s.* die Rachgier, Rachsucht. **—r,** *s.* der Rächer.

Revenue, *s.* das Einkommen, die Einkünfte; public —, Staatseinkünfte; board of —, die Finanzkammer. *Comp.* **—-cutter,** *s.* die Zolljacht, das Zollschiff. **—-officer,** *s.* der Zollbeamte.

Reverbera—nt, *adj.* widerhallend. **—te,** *v.* I. *a.* zurückwerfen. II. *n.* zurückstrahlen; widerhallen. **—tion,** *s.* das Zurück=prallen, =werfen; das Widerhallen; (re-echo) der Widerhall. **—tory,** *adj.* zurück=werfend, =strahlend; —tory furnace, der Flammofen.

Revere, *v.a.* (ver)ehren. **—nce,** I. *s.* die Ehrerbietung, Ehrfurcht, Achtung; (obeisance) die Verbeugung; your —nce, Euer Ehrwürden; saving your —nce, mit Erlaubnis zu sagen. II. *v.a.* ehren (einen), Ehrfurcht erweisen (einem). **—nd,** *adj.* ehrwürdig (*in titles*); Right —nd, Hoch(ehr)würdig. **—nt,** *adj.*, **—ntly,** *adv.* ehrerbietig, erfurchtsvoll; (humble) demütig. **—ntial,** *adj.*, **—ntially,** *adv.* ehrerbietig. **—r,** *s.* der Verehrer.

Reverie, *s.* die Träumerei, der wach(end)e Traum.

Revers—al, *s.* die Umkehrung; die Umstoßung, Umänderung (*Law*); das Umsteuern (*Locom., etc.*).; —al of fortune, die Peripetie (eines Trauerspiels). **—e,** I. *v.a.* umkehren (*also a cone*), umstürzen, verkehren; auf den Kopf stellen (*also fig.*); aufheben, umstoßen (*a decree, judgment*); umsteuern (*engines*); to —e the order, die Reihenfolge umkehren; to —e the order of things, die Weltordnung umkehren; to —e arms, verkehrt schultern. II. *s.* die Rückseite (*of a coin, etc.*); die Rück=, Kehr=seite (*Typ.*); (opposite) das Gegenteil, Gegenstück, Widerspiel; der Wechsel (*of fortune, etc.*); der (Schicksals=)schlag; das Mißgeschick, die Niederlage; (the case is) quite the —e, (die Sache verhält sich) gerade umgekehrt; he has met with —es, er hat Unglück gehabt; er hat eine Schlappe erlitten. III. *adj.*, **—ely,** *adv.* umgekehrt, entgegengesetzt; —e current, der Gegenstrom; —e fire, das Rückenfeuer. **—ed,** *adj.* verkehrt; with arms —ed, mit umgekehrten Gewehren; —ed curve, die Gegenkrümmung. **—ible,** *adj.* umstößlich; umkehrbar; auf beiden Seiten zutragen (*as cloth*). **—ion,** I. *s.* die Umkehrung; der Rück=, Heimfall (an einen); die Anwartschaft, der Erbanspruch (auf eine S.) (*Law*); der Rückschlag (*to a former type, etc.*), die Umkehrung (*Math.*); **he has the —ion of his brother's office, er**

hat die Anwartschaft auf seines Bruders Amt; fortune in —ion, das zu erwartende Vermögen, der Erbfall. II. *attrib.*; —ion company, die Gesellschaft zur Vertretung von Erbansprüchen. —**ionary**, *adj.* anwartschaftlich; Anwartschafts-; he has a —ionary interest in the estate, er hat einen Rechtsanspruch auf das Erbe; —ionary additions to policies, die Erhöhung der Versicherungssumme (wenn die Auszahlung der Dividende nicht gewünscht wird); —ionary annuity, anwartschaftliche Leibrente; —ionary property, Anwartschaft auf späteren Besitz. *Comp.* —**ing-gear**, *s.* die Umsteuerung.

Revert, *v.n.* zurück-, wieder-kehren; zurückkommen (to a th., auf eine S.); heimfallen (*Law*).

Revetment, *s.* die Verkleidung (*also Railw.*), Futtermauer (*Fort.*).

Review, I. *v.a.* zurück-blicken, -sehen auf (die Vergangenheit *etc.*); wieder durchgehen, durchsehen, revidieren (*manuscripts, etc.*); (inspect) prüfen, durchgehen, durchsuchen; beurteilen, besprechen, rezensieren (*a book, etc.*); mustern, Musterung halten über (*acc.*) (*Mil.*); *see* Re-examine. II. *v.n.* rezensieren. III. *s.* neue, wiederholte, nochmalige Durchsicht, Untersuchung, Prüfung; die Besprechung, Rezension, Kritik (*of a book, etc.*); critical —, die Rundschau; military —, die große Parade, Truppenschau; naval —, die Flottenschau; to pass in —, *see* — I. (*Mil.*). —**er**, *s.* der Musternde, Durchsucher; der Rezensent.

Revil—e, *v.a.* schmähen, verunglimpfen; lästern (*B.*). —**er**, *s.* der Schmäher. —**ing**, I. *adj.*, —**ingly**, *adv.* schmähend. II. *s.* das Schmähen.

Revis—al, *s.* die Revision. —**e**, I. *v.a.* wieder durchsehen, revidieren (*a work*). II. *s.* die abermalige Prüfung; die zweite Korrektur (*Typ.*); last —e, letzte Korrektur (*Typ.*). —**ed**, *p.p. & adj.*; the —ed Version (of the Bible), die revidierte englische Bibelübersetzung. —**er**, *s.* der Nachprüfer; der Korrektor (*Typ.*). —**ing**, *adj.*; —ing barrister, der mit der Prüfung der Wahllisten beauftragte Beamte (*Eng.*). —**ion**, *s.* die Revision (*also Typ.*), nochmalige Durchsicht. —**ional**, —**ionary**, *adj.* Revisions-.

Revisit, *v.a.* wiederbesuchen, aufs neue besuchen.

Reviv—al, *s.* die Wieder-belebung, -herstellung; das Wieder-aufleben, -aufblühen (*of learning, etc.*); die Wiederbelebung, Erweckung (*Rel.*); —al of letters, *etc.*, die Renaissance. —**alism**, *s.* die auf Glaubenserweckung abzielende religiöse Richtung. —**alist**, *s.* der Erweckungsprediger. —**e**, *v.* I. *a.* neubeleben, wieder ins Leben zurückbringen; *see* Renovate; (re-introduce) wieder aufbringen *or* einführen; (encourage) erquicken; neuen Mut einflößen; wieder zur Sprache bringen (*a subject*); wieder auf die Bühne bringen (*a play, etc.*). II. *n.* wiederaufleben, neues Leben, neue Kraft gewinnen. —**er**, *s.* der, die, das Belebende. —**ify**, *v.a.* wiederbeleben. —**ing**, *adj.* neubelebend.

Revoca—ble, *adj.*, —**bly**, *adv.* widerruflich. —**tion**, *s.* die Zurückberufung; der Widerruf; die Zurücknahme, Aufhebung (*of an edict, etc.*).

Revoke, I. *v.a.* widerrufen, zurücknehmen; zurücknehmen, aufheben. II. *v.n.* eine Farbe nicht bekennen (*cards*). III. *s.* das Nichtbekennen.

Revolt, I. *s.* die Empörung, der Aufruhr; der Abfall (*from allegiance*). II. *v.n.* sich empören; abfallen (from, von). III. *v.a.* empören, abstoßen (*fig.*). —**ing**, *adj.*, —**ingly**, *adv.* aufrührerisch; empörend, ekelhaft.

Revolution, *s.* die Umwälzung, Umdrehung, der Umlauf, Kreislauf; die (Staats-)Umwälzung, Revolution (*fig.*). —**ary**, *adj.* revolutionär, Revolutions-; —ary spirit, war, Revolutionsgeist, -krieg. —**ist**, *s.* der Revolutionär. —**ize**, *v.a.* umwälzen; umgestalten; Shakspere —ized the stage, Shakespeare hat die Bühne völlig neugestaltet.

Revolv—e, *v.* I. *n.* sich umwälzen, sich drehen, (on an axis, round a centre, um eine Achse, um einen Mittelpunkt): umlaufen; voranschreiten (*as time*); each —ing year, jedes umlaufende Jahr. II. *a.* umdrehen; über-legen, -denken, erwägen (*in one's mind*). —**er**, *s.* der Revolver. —**ing**, *adj.* sich drehend, drehbar; —ing bookcase, drehbarer Bücherständer; —ing chair, der Drehstuhl; —ing light, das Dreh- *or* Blink-feuer (eines Leuchtturms).

Revuls—ion, *s.* die Abziehung; der Rückschlag, Umschwung (*of feeling, etc.*); die Ableitung (*Med.*). —**ive**, *adj.* abziehung; ableitend (*Med.*).

Reward, I. *s.* die Belohnung, Vergeltung, der Lohn. II. *v.a.* belohnen; (requite) vergelten. —**er**, *s.* der Belohner, Vergelter.

Rewrite, *ir.v.a.* nochmals schreiben.

Rhapsod—ic(al), *adj.* begeistert, rhapsodisch; abgerissen, unzusammenhängend. —**ist**, *s.* der Rhapsode (*in Greece, etc.*); einer, der schwärmerisch und unzusammenhängend redet. —**ize**, *v.n.* sich in feurigen Reden ergießen, mit großer Begeisterung reden. —**y**, *s.* die Rhapsodie; der unzusammenhängende, schwärmerisch abgefaßte Vortrag; he went into —ies over, er schwärmte für, er kam ganz in Feuer über (*acc.*).

Rhetoric, *s.* die Redekunst, Rhetorik. —**al**, *adj.*, —**ally**, *adv.*, rednerisch, rhetorisch. —**ian**, *s.* der Redekünstler, Rhetor; (orator) der Redner.

Rheum, *s.* die Feuchtigkeit aus Auge und Nase. —**atic**, *adj.* rheumatisch; the —atics (*vulg.*), *see* —atism. —**atism**, *s.* der Gliederfluß, Gliederschmerz, Rheumatismus.

Rhino—ceros, *s.* das Nashorn, Rhinozeros (*Zool.*). —**plastic**, *adj.* nasenbildend.

Rhizo—me, *s.* der Wurzelstock. —**phagous**, *adj.* wurzelfressend.

Rhododendron, *s.* die Alpenrose, das Rhododendron.

Rhomb, *s.* der Rhombus, die Raute. —**ic**, *adj.* rautenförmig. —**ohedral**, *adj.* rhomboedrisch, rautenförmig; —ohedral system, das hexagonale Krystallsystem. —**ohedron**, *s.* das Rhomboeder. —**oid**, I. *s.* das Rhomboid. II. *adj.*, —**oidal**, *adj.* rhomboedrisch, rhomboidalisch; —oid muscle, rautenförmiger Muskel. —**us**, *see* —.

Rhubarb, *s.* der Rhabarber.

Rhumb, *s.* der Kompaß-, Wind-strich; — line, die Loxodrome.

Rhym—e, I. *s.* der Reim; (short poem) das Gedichtchen; *see* Verse; neither —e nor reason, weder Sinn noch Verstand. II. *v.n.* (sich) reimen. III. *v.a.* in Reime bringen; Verse machen. —**eless**, *adj.* reimlos, ohne Reim. —(**st**)**er**, *s.* der Versemacher, Reimschmied.

Rhythm, *s.* das Gleich-, Zeit-maß, der Rhythmus. —**ic**, —**ical**, *adj.*, —**ically**, *adv.* rhythmisch.

Rib, I. *s.* die Rippe (*Anat., Arch., Carp., Shipb., Weav., etc.*); die Schiene (*of umbrellas*); der Streifen (*in cloth*); —s of a ship, die Inhölzer, Spanten. II. *v.a.* rippen; streifen (*Agr.*). —**bed**, *adj.* mit Rippen, gerippt. —**bing**, *s.* die Rippen einer Wölbung. —**less**, *adj.* rippenlos. *Comp.* —**-grass**, —**wort**, *s.* der Wegerich.

Ribald, I. *adj.* wüst, liederlich. II. *s.* der Wüstling. —**ry**, *s.* gemeine, unzüchtige Rede, Zoten; (lewdness) die Liederlichkeit.

Riband, *see* Ribbon.

Ribbon, *s.* das Band, Seidenband; die Leiste (*Naut.*); (shred) der Fetzen; the —s, die Zügel (*Sport.*); to handle the —s, selbst fahren. II. *attrib.*; — agate, der Bandachat. —**ism**, *s.* das Bandmännerwesen. *Comp.* —**-fish**, *s.* der Bandfisch. —**-loom**, *s.* der Bandwebstuhl. —**-manufacture**, *s.* die Bandfabrik. —**men**, *pl.* Bandmänner; *see* Whiteboys. —**-trade**, *s.* der Bandhandel.

Rice, *s.* der Reis. *Comp.* —**-flour**, *s.* das Reismehl. —**-paper**, *s.* das Reispapier. —**-pudding**, *s.* der Reispudding.

Rich, *adj.*, —**ly**, *adv.* reich (in, an); üppig, ergiebig, fruchtbar (*as soil*); (abundant) reichhaltig, reichlich; (costly) prächtig, kostbar, glänzend; wohlklingend, volltönig (*as a voice*); glänzend, lebhaft (*as a colour*); fett (*as food*); kräftig, würzig (*as wine*); prächtig (*as a joke*); inhaltsreich (*fig.*); — in titles, reich an Titeln; the —, die Reichen. **—es**, *pl.* der Reichtum, die Reichtümer. **—ly**, *adv.* reich; reichlich; you have —ly deserved it, Sie haben es reichlich verdient. **—ness**, *s.* der Reichtum; die Reichhaltigkeit; die Fruchtbarkeit, Üppigkeit; das Fette; (abundance) die Fülle; die Volltönigkeit; die Pracht, Köstlichkeit, Kostbarkeit (*of a dress*); das Reichhaltige (*of a description*); die Ergiebigkeit (*of a mine*); die Güte (*of milk*); die Fettigkeit (*of food*).

Rick, I. *s.* der Schober, Heuschober. II. *attrib.;* — cloth, das Schoberdecktuch.

Ricket—s, *s.* die englische Krankheit, Rhachitis. **—(t)y**, *adj.* rhachitisch; (shaky) wackelig, baufällig; (weak) gebrechlich; schwach (*fig.*).

Ricochet, I. *s.* (— fire) der Prellschuß. II. *v.n.* rikoschettieren, aufschlagend abprallen.

[1]**Rid**, I. *ir.v.a.* wegschaffen; to — of, befreien, frei machen von; to — o.s. (of a th.), sich (*dat.*) (etwas) vom Halse schaffen. II. *adj.;* to be — of, (einer Sache) los sein; to get — of, (eine Sache) los werden. **—dance**, *s.* die Befreiung; die Wegräumung; to make a clear —dance, gänzlich wegräumen (of a th., eine S.), reines Feld machen (*coll.*).

[2]**Rid**, (*obs.*) *imperf. & p.p. of* Ride.

Rid—den, *p.p.* of —e; to be wife- —den, unter dem Pantoffel stehen. **—e**, I. *ir.v.n.* reiten; fahren (*in a carriage, etc.*); nicht Linie halten (*Typ.*); (rest) getragen werden, ruhen; to —e in a perambulator, im Kinderwagen ausfahren *or* ausgefahren werden; to —e a bicycle, Zweirad fahren, radeln; are you going to —e backwards? wollen Sie rückwärts fahren *or* sitzen? to —e at a walking pace, Schritt reiten; to —e at anchor, vor Anker liegen; to —e for a fall, wagehalsig reiten; bei einem Unternehmen vermutlich zu Schaden kommen; the rope —es, das Tau läuft unklar; —e with caution! vorsichtig fahren! (*Cycl.*); to —e **away**, fortreiten; to —e **behind**, hinter einem herreiten; hinten aufsitzen (*on the same horse*); to —e **by**, vorbeireiten; to —e **hard**, stark, geschwind reiten; to —e **out**, ausreiten; to —e **over**, reiten über (*acc.*) (*lit.*), beherrschen, tyrannisieren (*fig.*); to —e **up** to, hinreiten zu. II. *ir.v.a.* reiten; tyrannisieren, beherrschen (*fig.*); to —e a race, in die Wette reiten; to —e **down**, nieder-, um-reiten; to —e **out** a gale, einen Sturm vor Anker aushalten. III. *s.* der Ritt; die Fahrt (*in a train, a carriage*); der Reitweg, die Reitbahn; to go for a —e, spazieren reiten; to take a —e, aus-reiten, -fahren. **—er**, *s.* der Reiter; der Fahrende; das Beiblatt, der Zusatz (*manuscripts or documents*); —er to a bill, der Zusatz zu einem Gesetz-Entwurf; der Zusatz zu einer mathematischen Aufgabe, die Zusatzaufgabe (*Math.*); —ers, Radsporen (*Shipb.*). **—erless**, *adj.* reiterlos. **—ing**, *s.* das Reiten; —ing at the ring, das Ringelrennen. *Comp.* **—ing-boots**, *pl.* Reitstiefel. **—ing-cloak** (*or* **-coat**), *s.* der Reitmantel, (-rock). **—ing-habit**, *s.* das Reitkleid. **—ing-hat**, *s.* der Reithut. **—ing-hood**, *see Index of Names.* **—ing-master**, *s.* der Reitlehrer; der Stallmeister. **—ing-school**, *s.* die Reitschule. **—ing-whip**, *s.* die Reit-gerte, -peitsche.

[1]**Riddle**, *s.* das Rätsel; to give, propose (solve) a —, ein Rätsel aufgeben (lösen).

[2]**Riddle**, I. *s.* das grobe (Korn-)Sieb. II. *v.a.* sieben; durchlöchern (*with balls or shot*).

Ridge, I. *s.* der Rücken, der Kamm, Grat; (elevation) die Erhöhung; der Rain, die Rinne, Furche (*Agr.*); der Giebelrücken, (Dach-)First (*Build.*); die Naht (*Fort.*). II. *v.a.* furchen. *Comp.* **—-piece**, *s.* die Firstpfette. **—-plough**, *s.* der Häufelpflug. **—-tile**, *s.* der Firstziegel.

Ridicul—e, I. *s.* das Lächerliche; der Spott; to turn into —e, ins Lächerliche ziehen. II. *v.a.* verspotten, bespötteln, ins Lächerliche ziehen. **—er**, *s.* der Bespöttelnde, Spötter. **—ous**, *adj.*, **—ously**, *adv.* lächerlich. **—ousness**, *s.* die Lächerlichkeit.

Riding, *s.* (*for* Thridding, *a third part*) der Bezirk (*in Yorkshire; e. g.* the West —).

Rife, *adj.*, **—ly**, *adv.* häufig, herrschend, weitverbreitet; rumours were —, Gerüchte waren im Schwange. **—ness**, *s.* die Allgemeinheit.

Riff-raff, *s.* der Auswurf; (mob) das Gesindel.

[1]**Rifle**, *v.a.* berauben, plündern.

[2]**Rifl—e**, I. *v.a.* riffe(l)n, ziehen (*gun-barrels*). II. *s.* das gezogene Gewehr, die Büchse; —es, *see* —emen; breech-loading —e, der Hinterlader; double-barrelled —e, der Doppelstutzen. **—ed**, *adj.* gezogen (*Mil.*). **—ing**, *s.* der Zug, die Züge. *Comp.* **—e-barrel**, *s.* gezogener Flintenlauf. **—e-brigade**, *s.* die Schützenbrigade. **—e-butts**, *s.* der Schießstand. **—e-corps**, *s.* das Schützenkorps. **—emen**, *pl.* Jäger; Schützen; mounted —emen *or* —es, berittene Jäger *or* Schützen. **—e-pit**, *s.* der Schützengraben. **—e-range**, *s.* der Schießplatz, Schießstand.

Rift, I. *s.* die Ritze, der Spalt. II. *v.a.* spalten.

[1]**Rig** (*Scotch*), *see* Ridge.

[2]**Rig**, *s.;* to run a —, einen lustigen Streich begehen.

[3]**Rig**, I. *s.* die besondere Art des Takelns, die Takelung; (dress) der Putz. II. *v.a.* auftakeln, ausrüsten (*a ship*); den Markt künstlich vorbereiten (für Aktien, 2c., *sl.*); to — **in**, einholen; to — **out**, ausholen (*a mast*); auftakeln (*a p.*); to — the capstan, das Spill klar machen. **—ger**, *s.* der Takler; der Tambour (*Mach.*). **—ging**, *s.* das Takel-, Tau-werk, die Takelage.

Rigg, *s.* (*dial.*) *see* Ridge.

Right, I. *adj. & adv.*, **—ly**, recht (*also of angles, lines, the hand, side, etc.*); (correct) richtig; (properly done, *etc.*) in Ordnung, der Ordnung gemäß, wohlgeordnet; (genuine) echt; (fit) schicklich, passend; (lawful) recht(mäßig); recht, gerade (*as a way*); (— hand, *etc.*) die rechte Hand, Seite; to be —, Recht haben; he is not quite — (not in his — mind), er ist nicht ganz bei Verstande, nicht bei vollem Verstande (*fam.*); I don't feel quite —, mir ist nicht ganz wohl; all —! Alles in Ordnung! Gut! Schön! Sehr wohl! Abgemacht! on the — side of 40, noch nicht 40 Jahre alt; to go the — way to work, es recht angreifen; to set —, ordnen; (s.o., einen) zurechtweisen, aufklären; to set a p. — with, einen wieder versöhnen mit; if —, nach Richtig befinden; it is — for you to . . ., Sie tun recht, wenn Sie . . .; I think it — to tell you . . ., ich halte es für meine Pflicht, Ihnen zu sagen . . .; one's — hand, die rechte Hand (*lit.*); der treue Beistand, die Hauptstütze (*fig.*). II. *adv.* sehr, hoch (*before titles*); — ahead, geradeaus; — about *or* turn! rechts um! to send to the — about, kurz abweisen; — away, sogleich; los! — on, gerade-aus *or* -zu; we are —ly served, es geschieht uns recht. III. *s.* das Recht; gegründeter Anspruch (to a th., auf eine S.); (one's due) das Eigentum; (prerogative) das Vorrecht, Privilegium; — of possession, Eigentumsrecht; — of trial by jury, das Recht, vor ein Geschwornengericht gestellt zu werden; — of way, das Wegerecht; in — of his mother, von Seiten seiner Mutter; in his own —, durch Geburt; to have a — to, ein Recht *or* Anrecht haben auf (*acc.*), Recht haben zu; on the —, zur Rechten; to the —! rechts, auf der rechten *or* die rechte Seite; keep to the —, rechts fahren, rechts halten, rechts ausweichen! to get the —s of a story, den wahren Sachverhalt erfahren; by —(s), eigentlich, von Rechtswegen; to set, put to —s, zurechtmachen, wieder in Ordnung bringen, wieder herstellen; the —s and wrongs of a matter, die Sache von allen Seiten betrachtet (*coll.*). IV. *v.a.* Recht wiverfahren lassen (a p., einem); aufrichten (*a ship*); to — o.s., sich (*dat.*) selbst Recht verschaffen. V. *v.n.* aufstehen (*Naut.*). **—eous**, *adj.*, **—eously**, *adv.* gerecht, rechtschaffen. **—eousness**, *s.* die Rechtschaffenheit. **—ful**, *adj.*, **—fully**, *adv.* recht(mäßig); (just) gerecht. **—ness**, *s.* die Richtigkeit; die Geradheit (*of a line*). *Comp.* **—-angled**, *adj.* rechtwinklig. **—-hand**, *adj.* rechtsstehend; —-hand man, der rechte Nebenmann; die rechte Hand (*fig.*). **—-handed**, *adj.* die rechte Hand brauchend; he is —-handed, er ist rechts. **—-lined**, *adj.* rechtlinig. **—-minded**, *adj.* rechtschaffen. **—-mindedness**, *s.* die Rechtschaffenheit.

Rigid, *adj.*, **—ly**, *adv.* steif, starr, unbeugsam (*also fig.*); hart, streng (*fig.*). **—ity**, *s.* die Steife, Steifheit; die Strenge, Härte, Schärfe.

Rigmarole, *s.* das leere Geschwätz, Gewäsch (*coll.*); a long —, eine endlose Geschichte.

Rigor, *s.* die Starrheit, Erstarrung; der kalte Schauer, der Schüttelfrost (*Med.*); *see* Rigour. **—ism**, *s.* der Rigorismus. **—ist**, *s.* der Rigorist. **—ous**, *adj.*, **—ously**, *adv.* streng, hart; (exact) scharf, genau; —ous discipline, strenge Zucht; —ous winter, harter Winter.

Rigour, *s.* die Strenge, Härte; *see* **Rigor.**

Rile, *v.a.* ärgern, aufbringen (*coll.*).

Rill, *s.* das Bächlein.

Rim, I. *s.* der Rand, Reif(en); die Krempe (*of a hat*); der (Radfelgen)kranz (*of a wheel*) II. *v.a.* mit einem Reifen versehen.

[1]**Rim—e**, *s.* der Reif. **—y**, *adj.* voll Reif, bereift.

[2]**Rime**, *see* Rhyme.

Rimple, *v.a. see* Rumple.

Rind, *s.* die (harte Baum=)Rinde; die Käserinde.

Rinderpest, *s.* die Rinderpest.

[1]**Ring**, I. *s.* der Ring (*also Geom. & fig.*); (circle) der Ring, Kreis; der Reif (*Artil.*); der runde Platz, die Schranke, der Ringplatz (*for games, boxing, etc.*); (clique) der Ring; the —, (*pl.*) die Buchmacher; die Boxer; wedding —, der Trauring. II. *v.a.* (be)ringen; ringeln (*pigs, etc.*). **—let**, *s.* der Ringel, die Haarlocke. *Comp.* **—-dove**, *s.* die Ringeltaube. **—ed-plover**, *s.* der Halsbandregenpfeifer. **—-fence**, *s.* die Umzäunung rings um ein Gut. **—-finger**, *s.* der Ring=, Gold=finger. **—leader**, *s.* der Rädelsführer. **—-streaked**, *adj.* ringförmig gestreift, geringelt. **—worm**, *s.* fressende Flechte.

[2]**Ring**, I. *s.* der Klang, Schall; das Klingeln (*for the maid, etc.*); — of bells, das Glocken=geläute, =spiel; there is a —, man *or* es läutet. II. *ir. v.n.* läuten (*as a bell*) (for church, zur Kirche); klingen (*as coins*); erklingen, erschallen (with, von); does this bell —? läutet diese Glocke? — for the maid, klingeln Sie der Magd; the whole town —s with his fame, die ganze Stadt ist seines Ruhmes voll; my ears still — with the noise, noch klingen mir die Ohren von dem Lärm; the forest rang with the clamour of the huntsmen, die Wälder erschollen vom Getöse der Jäger. III. *v.a.* klingen lassen; läuten (*bells*); to — money, Geld nach seinem Klange prüfen; to — the changes on, wechselläuten (*lit.*); nach allen Richtungen *or* in der verschiedensten Weise behandeln (*fig.*); to — a p. up, einen anklingeln, einen durch den Fernsprecher anrufen (*Tele.*); to — a peal, die Glocken kunstvoll läuten; to — the knell of a th., etwas zu Grabe läuten. **—er**, *s.* der Glockenläuter. **—ing**, I. *adj.* klingend, schallend. II. *s.* das Klingen.

Rink, *s.* die Rollschlittschuhbahn; künstliche Eisbahn.

Rins—e, *v.a.* spülen; to —e out, ausspülen. **—ing**, *s.* das (Aus=)Spülen; die Aussüßung (*Chem.*); —ings, das Spülicht.

Riot, I. *s.* der Lärm; der Aufruhr, Aufstand, Tumult (*Law*); (revelling) die Schwelgerei, Ausschweifung; to run —, schwärmen, ausschweifen; (upon ...) sich seiner Neigung für ganz überlassen. II. *v.n.* schwelgen; in Saus und Braus leben, ausschweifen; lärmen; einen Aufruhr erregen. **—er**, *s.* der Aufrührer, Meuterer. **—ous**, *adj.*, **—ously**, *adv.* lärmend; schwelgerisch; aufrührerisch; to lead a —ous life, in Saus und Braus leben. **—ousness**, *s.* das aufrührerische Wesen; das Lärmen; die Schwelgerei.

Rip, I. *v.a.* (auf)trennen (*a seam, etc.*); to — **off**, abtrennen; to — **open**, aufreißen; to — **up**, aufschneiden, aufreißen. III. *s.* der Riß.

Ripe, *adj.* reif, zeitig, fertig; (consummate) vollkommen, vollendet; of —r age, in reif(er)en Jahren; when the time is —, wenn die rechte Zeit gekommen ist; — cheese, alter Käse; — scholar, Mann von vollendeter Gelehrsamkeit; — wine, flaschenreifer, trinkbarer Wein; a girl — for marriage, ein mannbares Mädchen. **—ly**, *adv.* reiflich, rechtzeitig. **—n**, *v.* I. *n.* reifen. II. *a.* zeitigen, reif machen, zur Reife bringen. **—ness**, *s.* die Reife; die Rechtzeitigkeit.

[1]**Ripple**, I. *v.n.* kleine Wellen schlagen, sich kräuseln, rieseln. II. *v.a.* kräuseln (*water*). III. *s.* kleine, krause Welle; (murmur) das Geriesel *Comp.* **—-mark**, *s.* das Wellenzeichen.

[2]**Ripple**, I. *v.a.* riffeln (*flax*). II. *s.* der Riffelkamm.

Rise, I. *ir.v.n.* aufstehen, sich erheben (*from a seat, bed, etc.*), emporsteigen; in die Höhe gehen, steigen (*in price, to a place; of water, temperature, etc.; of tones, etc.*); aufschlagen (*of prices*); aufsteigen (*of exhalations, stars, the sun, wind, etc., of a thought, etc.*); aufgehen (*as the sun, stars, etc.; of dough*); aufkeimen (*as anger*); (increase) wachsen, zunehmen; auseinandergehen, aufbrechen, die Sitzung schließen (*as an assembly*); sich erheben, sich empören (against, gegen); sich erheben (*as mountains*); auferstehen (from the dead, vom Tode); the thought rose to my mind, es drängte sich mir der Gedanke auf; to — in blisters, auffahren, kleine Blasen bekommen; angry words rose to my lips, mir kamen zornige Worte auf die Lippen; to — **up**, sich erheben, aufstehen, emporsteigen; to — up in arms, zu den Waffen greifen; the castle —s **upon** the view, das Schloß zeigt sich dem Auge. II. *s.* das Steigen (*in price, to a place, of the voice*), Aufsteigen; der Aufschlag (*in price*); der Aufgang (*of the sun*); das Anschwellen (*of the water, etc.*); (elevation) die Erhöhung; *see* Rising ground; (increase) der Zuwachs, die Zunahme; (origin) der Ursprung, die Entstehung; der Anbiß (*of fish*); die Erhöhung (*of the temperature*); to give — to, hervorrufen; (occasion) Anlaß *or* Gelegenheit geben, veranlassen; to get a — out of s.o., einen ärgerlich machen (*sl.*); einen lächerlich machen (*sl.*). **—n**, *p.p. of* Rise; the —n Master, der auferstandene Herr (Jesus). **—r**, *s.* der Aufstehende; die Steigung, Ansichtsfläche (*Build.*); die Futterstufe (*of a wooden step*); an early —r, ein Frühaufsteher.

Risib—ility, *s.* das Lachvermögen; (proneness to laugh) die Lachlust. **—le**, *adj.*, **—ly**, *adv.* des Lachens fähig; (laughable) lächerlich, possierlich· Lach= (faculty, *etc.*).

Rising, I. *p. & adj.*; — ground, die Anhöhe; — generation, das heranwachsende Geschlecht; — stress, steigender Akzent; — sun, aufgehende Sonne. II. *s.* das (Auf=)Steigen, Emporsteigen; das Auseinandergehen, Aufbrechen (*of an assembly*); (insurrection) die Empörung, der Aufruhr; das Sich=Erheben (*of a people*); die Auferstehung (*from the dead*); — of a vault, die Wölb=, Pfeil=höhe.

Risk, I. *s.* die Gefahr, das Wagnis; das Risiko (*C. L.*); at all —s, aufs Geratewohl; at the — of hurting his feelings, auf die Gefahr hin, ihn zu verletzen; to run a —, Gefahr laufen. II. *v.a.* wagen, in Gefahr, aufs Spiel setzen; to do a th. at one's own —, eine S. auf eigene Faust tun, seine Haut bei einem Unternehmen zu Markte tragen. **—y**, *adj.* gefährlich, gewagt.

Risorial, *adj.* das Lachen betreffend; — muscles, Lachmuskeln.

Rissole, *s.* das gebratene Fleisch- *or* Fisch-klößchen.

Rit—e, *s.* der Ritus, feierliche Gebrauch; funeral —es, die Totenfeier; nuptial —es, die Hochzeitsgebräuche. **—ual**, I. *adj.* ritualmäßig; Kirchengebräuche vorschreibend; —ual observances, kirchliche Gebräuche. II. *s.* das Ritual, die Kirchenordnung, Agende. **—ualism**, *s.* die Ritualistik; der Ritualismus (*in England, etc.*). **—ualist**, *s.* der Ritualist. **—ualistic**, *adj.* ritualistisch, streng auf Beobachtung des Rituals haltend.

Ritornello, *s.* das Ritornell.

Rival, I. *s.* der (die) Nebenbuhler(in), Mitbewerber, Rival(in), Konkurrent. II. *adj.* wetteifernd, nebenbuhlerisch; — firm, das Konkurrenzgeschäft. III. *v.a.* wetteifern mit, nacheifern, zu übertreffen suchen, (einem) Konkurrenz machen. **—ry**, *s.* die Nebenbuhlerei, Nebenbuhlerschaft; (emulation) der Wetteifer; (competition) der Wettbewerb, die Mitbewerbung, Konkurrenz.

Rive, *ir.v.* I. *a.* (zer)spalten, zerreißen (*also fig.*). II. *n.* spalten. **—n**, *p.p. of* Rive.

Riv—er, *s.* der Fluß, der Strom (*also fig.*); —ers, das Gewässer (*Geog.*); up (down) the —, stromauf(wärts), stromab(wärts). **—ulet**, *s.* das Flüßchen. *Comp.* **—er-bed**, *s.* das Flußbett. **—er-channel**, *s.* das Fahrwasser in einem Flusse. **—erhead**, *s.* die Flußquelle. **—er-horse**, *s.* das Flußpferd. **—er-lamprey**, *s.* das Neunauge. **—er-navigation**, *s.* die Flußschiffahrt. **—erside**, *s.* das Flußufer, die Flußgegend.

Rivet, I. *v.a.* (fest)nieten, vernieten; (stark) befestigen, fesseln, fest richten (*fig.*). II. *s.* das Niet, der Nietnagel; countersunk —, versenktes Niet. **—ing**, I. *s.* das Nieten. II. *adj.* (*in comp.*) Niet-.

Rix-dollar, *s.* der Reichstaler (*obs.*).

Roach, *s.* das Rotauge (*Icht.*).

Road, *s.* die (Land-)Straße; die Straße, der Weg (*fig.*); *see* —stead; on the —, unterwegs; to take to the —, ein Herumtreiber werden; the high — to success, der sichere Weg zum Erfolg; royal —, *see* Royal. **—stead**, *s.* die Reede. **—ster**, *s.* das Reisepferd; das auf der Reede liegende Schiff; das Tourenrad (*Cycl.*). *Comp.* **—-book**, *s.* das Reise-Handbuch. **—-engine**, *s.* die Straßenlokomotive. **—-making**, *s.* der Weg(e)bau. **—man**, *s.* der Straßenwärter. **—-metal**, *s.* die Straßenbeschläge. **—-racer**, *s.* der Straßenrenner (*Cycl.*). **—-side**, I. *s.* die Straßenseite. II. *attrib.*; —side inn, das Gasthaus an der Landstraße. **—-surveyor**, *s.* der Straßeninspektor. **—way**, *s.* die Landstraße; der Fahrweg.

Roam, I. *v.n.* umherstreifen, schweifen; to — through, durchstreifen. II. *v.a.* durchstreifen. **—er**, *s.* der Herumstreifer, Wanderer, Durchstreifer. **—ing**, *s.* die Streiferei, das Durchstreifen.

Roan, I. *adj.* graurötlich. II. *s.* (— horse) der Rotschimmel; saffianähnliches Schafleder.

Roar, I. *s.* das Gebrüll, Brüllen (*of beasts*); das laute Geschrei; das Brausen (*of water*); das Heulen (*of the wind*); das Krachen, Rollen (*of thunder*); der Donner (*of cannon*); der Schall (*of trumpets*); — of laughter, schallendes Gelächter; to set the company in a —, die Gesellschaft zu lautem Lachen bringen. II. *v.n.* brüllen; laut schreien; heulen; brausen; krachen; donnern; laut lachen; heulen, laut weinen (*as a child*). **—er**, *s.* der Brüller, Schreihals; das keuchende Pferd. **—ing**, I. *adj.* brüllend, außerordentlich, ungeheuer (*fam.*); a —ing trade, ein kapitales Geschäft (*vulg.*); —ing fire, kolossales Feuer (*coll.*). II. *s.* das Brüllen, Heulen, Brausen &c.; das Keuchen (*of horses*).

Roast, I. *v.a.* braten, rösten; backen (*metal*); brennen (*coffee*); aufziehen (*sl.*). II. *s.* der Braten; to rule the —, herrschen, das Kommando führen. III. *adj.* gebraten; gebrannt (*coffee*); — beef, Rinderbraten; — meat, der Braten, das gebratene Fleisch. **—er**, *s.* der Bratende; das Spanferkel (*for roasting*); *see* —ing-jack. *Comp.* **—ing-jack**, *s.* der Bratenwender.

Rob, *v.a.* (be)rauben, bestehlen; to — s.o. of s.th., einen einer S. berauben, einem eine S. rauben; to — Peter to pay Paul, hier borgen um dort zu zahlen (*coll.*). **—ber**, I. *s.* der Räuber, Dieb; highway —ber, der Straßenräuber. II. *attrib.*; —ber knight, der Raubritter. **—bery**, *s.* der Raub, Diebstahl; die Räuberei.

Rob—e, I. *s.* das (lange Ober-)Kleid; (official —e) Amtskleid; zubereitetes Büffelfell; state —es, Staatskleid; gentlemen of the long —e, Advokaten, Richter; master of the —es, der Oberkämmerer; mistress of the —es, die erste Hofdame; long —es, das Tragekleidchen (*of a baby*); academic —es, akademischer Ornat, Barett und Talar. II. *v.a.* bekleiden; schmücken, zieren (*fig.*). *Comp.* **—e-maker**, *s.* der Kleidermacher. **—ing-room**, *s.* das Ankleidezimmer.

[1]**Robin**, *s.* das Rotkehlchen.

[2]**Robin**, *s.*; round-—, einer von jedermann unterzeichnete Denk- *or* Bitte-schrift.

Robust, *adj.*, **—ly**, kräftig, stark, rüstig; fest (*as health*); schwer (*as work*). **—ness**, *s.* die Kraft, Stärke; die Festigkeit.

Rochet, *s.* der Chorrock (of bishops).

[1]**Rock**, *s.* der Fels, Felsen; die Klippe. **—ery**, *s.* die Farrenpflanzung (auf Gestein); *see* —-work. **—iness**, *s.* felsige Beschaffenheit, das Felsige, der Klippenreichtum. **—y**, *adj.* felsig, felsicht; (hard) felsenhart. *Comp.* (*gen'lly* Fels-). **—-alum**, *s.* der Steinalaun. **—-badger**, *s.* der Klippdachs. **—-bound**, *adj.* felsumgürtet. **—-cut**, *adj.* in den Fels gehauen; —-cut tomb, das Felsengrab. **—-oil**, *s.* das Steinöl. **—-plants**, *pl.* Alpenpflanzen. **—-ray**, *s.* der Kaulenroche. **—-work**, *s.* künstliches Felsen-, Grotten-Werk.

[2]**Rock**, *s.* der (Spinn-)Rocken.

[3]**Rock**, *v.* I. *a.* rütteln, schaukeln; wiegen (*a cradle*), einwiegen (*to sleep*). II. *n.* schwanken, [illegible]eln. **—er**, *s.* der Wiegende; die gekrümmte Kufe (*of a cradle or chair*). *Comp.* **—ing-chair**, *s.* der Schaukelstuhl. **—ing-horse**, *s.* das Schaukelpferd.

[1]**Rocket**, I. *s.* die Rakete (*Firew.*, *Mil.*). II. *attrib.*; — case, die Raketenhülse.

[2]**Rocket**, *s.* die Rauke (*Bot.*).

Rococo, I. *s.* das Rokoko, der Zopfstil. II. *adj.* Rokoko-, zopfig.

Rod, *s.* die Rute, Gerte, der Stab; die Stange (*Mach.*); die Meß-Rute (= 5½ yards *or* 5,029 Meter); fishing-—, die Angelrute; I have a — in pickle for you, ich habe einen Schinken für dich im Salze; connecting —s, die Träger (*Locom.*). *Comp.* **—-iron**, *s.* das Stangen-, Zain-eisen.

Rode, *imperf. of* Ride.

Rodent, I. *s.* das Nagetier. II. *adj.* nagend.

Rodomontade, *s.* die Prahlerei, Aufschneiderei.

[1]**Roe**, *s.* der (Fisch-)Rogen; hard (soft) —, der Laich, Rogen (die Milch). *Comp.* **—-stone**, *s.* der Rogenstein.

[2]**Roe**, *s.* das Reh; die Hirschkuh. **—buck**, *s.* der Rehbock.

Rogation, *s.* öffentliches Gebet (*Eccl.*). *Comp.* **—-days**, *pl.* drei Bettage vor Christi Himmelfahrt. **—-week**, *s.* die Betwoche, Himmelfahrtswoche.

Rogu—e, *s.* der Schelm, Schalk; (scoundrel) der Schurke, Spitzbube; (vagrant) der Landstreicher. **—ery**, *s.* die Spitzbüberei, der Spitzbubenstreich; die Schelmerei. **—ish**, *adj.*, **—ishly**, *adv.* schelmisch, schalkhaft; schurkisch.

Roister, *v.a.* lärmen, poltern, toben. **—er**, *s.* der Polterer. **—ing**, *adj.* tobend, lärmend.

Roll, I. *v.a.* rollen, wälzen; rollen (*the eyes, etc.*); walzen (*roads, metals*); (turn round) (um-)drehen, umwälzen; to — **away**, wegrollen; to —

out, ausrollen (*dough*); to — **up**, aufrollen (*a curtain, etc.*), einwickeln (*in a parcel*). II. *v.n.* rollen (*also of thunder, the eyes, of a carriage, etc.*); abrollen, ablaufen (*as time*); sich wälzen, sich drehen (*in an orbit, etc.*); (auf der Trommel) wirbeln (*Mil., etc.*); rollen, schlingern (*as a ship*); rauschend fließen (*as a river*); to — **in** wealth, steinreich sein, Geld wie Heu haben; to — **up**, sich zusammenrollen. III. *s.* die Rolle (*of tobacco, of parchment, papers, etc.*); die Locke (*of wool, etc.*) der Wirbel (*of drums*); das Schlingern (*of a ship*); das runde Brötchen, die Semmel (*Bak.*); (list) die Rolle, das Verzeichnis; (document) die Urkunde; die Schnecke, der Schnörkel (*Arch.*); die Walze, Rolle (*Mach.*); Master of the —s, der (englische) Reichsarchivar; music —, das Rollfutteral. **—er**, *s.* die Rolle, Walze, Welle (*Mach.*); (bandage) die (Roll=)Binde; das Wickelband (*for infants*); *see* —ing-pin; die Rolle (*for moving heavy bodies, etc., also for chairs, blinds, etc.*); die (field, *etc.*, Acker=, road, Chaussee=)Walze; (wave) schwere Woge; das Schlingern (*Naut.*). **—ers**, *pl.* das Walzwerk. **—ey**, *s.* der Förderwagen (*Min.*). **—ick**, *v.n.* hin und her taumeln, lärmen, toben. **—icking**, *adj.* lärmend; (merry) ausgelassen, lustig. **—ing**, I. *s.* das Rollen, Walzen, Strecken. II. *p. & adj.* rollend; wellenförmig, a —ing stone gathers no moss, ein rollender Stein setzt kein Moos an, ein unsteter Mensch bringt nichts vor sich (*prov.*); —ing capital, das Betriebskapital. *Comp.* **—-call**, *s.* der Appell (*Mil.*). **—er-chain**, *s.* die Rollenkette (*Cycl.*). **—er-gin**, *s.* die Walzenegrenier=maschine. **—er-skate**, *s.* der Rollschlittschuh. **—er-towel**, *s.* das Rollhandtuch, die Quehle. **—ing-friction**, *s.* die Schienenreibung. **—ing-pin**, *s.* das Rollholz. **—ing-stock**, *s.* das Betriebs=gerät, =material. **—-top**, *adj.*; —-top desk, das Zylinderbureau.

Rollock, *see* Rowlocks.

Roly-poly, I. *s.* (— pudding) der Rollkuchen. II. *adj.* rund und dick.

Rom—ance, I. *s.* der Roman; (ballad) die Romanze; die romantische Dichtung; (fiction) die Erdichtung, das Märchen; (the —antic) das Romantische; a hero of popular —ance, ein Sagenheld, sagenhafter Held; writer of —ances, der Romanschreiber. II. *v.n.* erdichten, Erdichtungen erzählen, aufschneiden. III. *adj.; see the Index of Names.* **—ancer**, *s.* der Romandichter; der Aufschneider, Lügner (*fig.*). **—antic**, *adj.*, **—antically**, *adv.* romantisch; malerisch (*Paint.*); romanhaft, abenteuerlich. **—anticism**, *s.* das Romantische; das Romanhafte; (—antic school, *etc.*) die Romantik.

Romp, I. *s.* die Range, das wilde, ausgelassene Mädchen; (—ing game) ausgelassenes, lärmendes Spiel. II. *v.n.* herumtoben, sich umhertummeln, sich herumbalgen. **—ish**, *adj.* wild, ausgelassen.

Rond—eau, **—o**, *s.* das Rondeau. **—el**, *s.* das Rondo (*Poet.*); das Rondel (*Fort.*).

Rood, *s.* das Kreuz; *see* Rod; — of land, englische Rute Land (= 1210 Quadrat=Yards). *Comp.* **—-loft**, *s.* der Lettner, die Chorbühne. **—-screen**, *s.* das Heiligengitter.

Roof, I. *s.* das Dach (*also fig.*); der Himmel (*of a coach*); — of heaven, das Himmelsgewölbe; — of the mouth, der Gaumen. II. *v.a.* mit einem Dache versehen; to — over, überdachen. **—ing**, *s.* das Dach(=Werk), die Dachung; iron —ing, Eisendachung; corrugated —ing, das Wellblech für Dächer. **—less**, *adj.* ohne Dach; (shelterless) obdachlos, ohne Obdach. *Comp.* **—ing-felt**, *s.* der Dachfilz, die Dachpappe. **—(ing)-slate**, *s.* der Dachschiefer. **—-tree**, *s.* der Firstbalken; das Dach (*fig.*).

[1]**Rook**, I. *s.* die Saatkrähe (*Orn.*); der Gauner, Betrüger (*fig.*); the — caws, die Dohle krächzt. II. *v.a.* betrügen. **—ery**, *s.* das Krähengenist(e), Brütplatz von Saatkrähen; die Brutstätte (*fig.*).

[2]**Rook**, *s.* der Turm, Roche (*Chess*).

Room, *s.* (space) der Raum, Platz; (chamber) das Zimmer, die Stube, (scope) der Raum, Anlaß, die Gelegenheit; (cause) die Veranlassung; (stead) die Stelle, Statt; in the — of, an der Stelle von, statt; there is no — for hope, es ist nichts zu hoffen, es ist keine Hoffnung mehr; thus there will be no — left for complaint, also wird man sich über nichts zu beklagen haben; to make — (for a p.), (einem) Platz machen; in the next —, im Nebenzimmer; come to my —s, komm in meine Wohnung. **—ed**, *adj.;* a four-—ed house, ein Haus mit vier Zimmern. **—ful**, *s.* das Zimmervoll. **—ily**, *adv.* geräumig. **—iness**, *s.* die Geräumigkeit. **—y**, *adj.* geräumig, weit.

Roost, I. *s.* der Schlafsitz (*of birds*); (perch) die Aufsetzstange; (fowls) zusammensitzende Vögel; to rule the —, herrschen, das Kommando führen; at —, ruhend, schlafend. II. *v.n.* aufsitzen, sitzend schlafen; hausen (*coll.*). **—er**, *s.* der Hahn.

[1]**Root**, I. *s.* die Wurzel (*also fig. & Math.*); (source) die Wurzel, Quelle, der Ursprung; das Stamm=, Wurzel=wort (*Gram.*); —s, die Wurzel (*of the nails, hair, teeth*); square, cube —, Quadrat=, Kubik=wurzel; to take (strike) —, Wurzel fassen, sich einwurzeln; — and branch, mit Stumpf und Stiel, ganz und gar, gänzlich; to go to the — of a th., einer S. (*dat.*) auf den Grund gehen. II. *v.a.* Wurzel fassen; Wurzel schlagen. **—ed**, *adj.* eingewurzelt, tief. **—edness**, *s.* das Eingewurzeltsein. **—let**, *s.* die kleine Wurzel, Wurzelfaser. *Comp.* **—-grafting**, *s.* das Wurzelpfropfen. **—-leaf**, *s.* das Wurzelblatt. **—stock**, *s.* der Wurzelschößling.

[2]**Root**, *v.* I. *a.* (wie ein Schwein mit dem Rüssel) aufwühlen; umwühlen, reuten, roden; (— out) ausjäten, ausroden; vertilgen, zerstören (*fig.*); (— up) ausreißen, ausrotten; to — from one's heart, sich (*dat.*) aus dem Herzen reißen. II. *n.* wühlen (*as pigs*), brechen (*as wild boars*). **—ing**, *s.* das Gebreche (*Hunt.*).

Rop—e, I. *s.* das Seil, Tau, der Strick; die Schnur (*of beads, onions, etc.*); das Reep (*Naut.*); —es, (*pl.*) das Tauwerk; —e of sand, schwaches lockeres Band (*fig.*); to give a p. —e, einen gewähren lassen, einem die Zügel schießen lassen. II. *v.a.* mit Stricken binden, befestigen; zusammenbinden, anseilen (*mountain climbers*). III. *v.n.* sich in Fäden ziehen. **—iness**, *s.* die Zähigkeit; das Kahmigwerden (*of wine*). **—y**, *adj.* strickartig; klebrig, zäh. *Comp.* **—e-dancer**, *s.* der (die) Seiltänzer(in). **—e-ladder**, *s.* die Strickleiter. **—e-maker**, *s.* der Seiler. **—e-making**, *s.* die Seilerei; das Reepschlagen. **—e's-end**, I. *s.* loses Ende. II. *v.a.* mit dem Tau=Ende strafen; durchbleuen (*coll.*). **—e-walk**, *s.* die Seilerbahn; die Reeperbahn (*Naut.*). **—e-yarn**, *s.* das Kabelgarn.

Roric, *adj.* tauig, betaut, Tau=.

Ros—aceous, *adj.* rosenartig. **—ary**, *s.* der Rosenkranz (*Rel.*); das Rosenbeet (*Hort.*). [1]**—e**, *s.* die Rose; die Brause (*of a watering-can*); under the —e, unter der Rose, im Vertrauen; standard and dwarf —es, hochstämmige und wurzelechte Rosen. **—eate**, *adj.* rosig. **—eola**, *s.* die Röteln. **—ette**, *s.* die Rosette (*also Arch.*). **—iness**, *s.* das Rosige, die rosige Färbung. **—y**, *see* Rosy. *Comp.* **—e-bud**, *s.* die Rosenknospe. **—e-bush**, *s.* der Rosenstrauch, Rosenstock. **—e-coloured**, *adj.* rosenfarbig, rosenfarben. **—e-diamond**, *s.* der rosenförmige Diamant. **—e-leaves**, *pl.* Rosenblätter. **—e-lake**, **—e-madder**, *s.* der Rosenlack. **—e-nursery**, *s.* die Rosenzüchterei. **—e-tree**, *s.* der Rosenstrauch, Rosenstock. **—e-water**, *s.* das Rosenwasser. **—e-window**, *s.* das Rosettenfenster. **—ewood**, *s.* das Rosenholz, Palisanderholz.

[2]**Rose**, *imperf.* (*& obs. p.p.*) *of* Rise.

Rosemary, *s.* der Rosmarin.

Rosin, I. *s.* das (Geigen)Harz, Kolophonium. II. *v.a.* mit Kolophonium einreiben (den Bogen), mit (Geigen) Harz bestreichen. **—y**, *adj.* harzig.

Roster, *s.* die Kommandierliste (*Mil.*).

Rostr—al, *adj.* schnabelartig. **—ate**, *adj.* geschnäbelt. **—um**, *s.* der Schnabel; (platform) die Rednerbühne; die Schnabelzange (*Surg.*).

Rosy, *adj.* rosig, rosenrot. **—y-fingered**, *adj.* rosenfingerig. **—y-tinted**, *adj.* rosenfarben.

Rot, *v.* I. *n.* (ver)faulen, verwesen, vermodern; to — off, wegfaulen. II. *a.* faul machen; *see* Ret. III. *s.* die Fäulnis; die Fäule (*in sheep*); dry —, trockene Fäulnis, Trockenfäule; what —! welcher Blödsinn! —! Blödsinn! Gewäsch! (*sl.*). **—ten**, *adj.* verfault, faul; angefressen, wurmstichig, morsch, mürbe (*as ice*); verdorben, verrottet, verfallen (*fig.*); brandig, stockig (*as wood*); (unsafe) betrügerisch; (bad) schauderhaft, grundschlecht, scheußlich (*sl.*); —ten eggs, faule Eier; —ten at the core, ins Mark hinein verdorben. **—tenness**, *s.* die Fäulnis, Fäule.

Rot—a, *s.* regelmäßiges Verfahren; päpstliches Appellationsgericht, die Rota (in Rome); *see* Roster; das Verzeichnis, die Liste. **—ary**, *adj.* sich drehend, kreisend; rotierend (*Mach.*); —ary motion, die Kreisbewegung. **—ate**, *v.n.* sich herumdrehen, im Kreise drehen. **—ation**, *s.* die Umdrehung, der Kreis-, Um-lauf; der Wechsel, die Abwechselung; —ation of office, der Amtswechsel; by —ation, nach der Reihe, abwechselnd; bestimmungsgemäß; —ation of crops, der (die) Frucht-wechsel (-folge). **—ator**, *s.* der Umdreher; der Umdrehmuskel (*Anat.*). **—atory**, *adj. see* —ary; abwechselnd; —atory storm, der Wirbelsturm. **—ifer**, *s.* das Räder-, Wirbeltierchen. **—und**, *adj.* rund; kugelig (*Bot.*) **—unda**, *s.* die Rotunde. **—undity**, *s.* die Rundung.

Rote, *s.* die Übung, Routine; by —, aus Übung, (by heart) auswendig; to learn by —, durch bloße Übung lernen, mechanisch auswendig lernen.

Rotten, *p.p. of* Rot.

Roué, *s. see* [3]Rake.

Rouge, I. *adj.* rot (*Her.*). II. *s.* die Schminke, das Rot. III. *v.a.* (*& n.* sich) schminken.

Rough, I. *adj.*, **—ly**, *adv.* rauh; (coarse) rauh, unhöflich, grob, schroff, derb; roh, ungebildet; wild, ungestüm; (shaggy) rauh, zottig; uneben, holperig (*as a road*); (harsh) streng; — or smooth? rauh oder glatt? (*Tennis*); through — and smooth, durch dick und dünn; — balance, rohe Bilanz; a — calculation, der Überschlag; die ungefähre, flüchtige Berechnung; — copy, der erste Entwurf, das Unreine, die Kladde; — customer, grober Gesell; diamond, ungeschliffener Diamant; — sea, das stürmische, bewegte Meer; a — sketch, eine flüchtige Skizze; — and ready, ins Grobe gearbeitet, (unpolished) ungeschliffen, herb in der Form. II. *s.* das Rauhe, Grobe; in the —, im (aus dem) Groben; der grobe Gesell, Knote, Lümmel, Flegel; town —, brutaler Straßenlümmel. III. *v.a.* schärfen (*horse-shoes*); to — it, sich (*dat.*) Entbehrungen gefallen lassen, Beschwerden *or* ein hartes Leben ertragen; I do not mind —ing it, ich mache mir nichts daraus, wenn es hart und mühselig ist. **—en**, *v.* I. *a.* rauh machen. II. *n.* rauh werden. **—ish**, *adj.* etwas rauh. **—ness**, *s.* die Rauheit; die Roheit; die Herbheit, Härte; das Ungestüm, die wilde Bewegung (*of the sea*). *Comp.* **—-cast**, I. *v.a.* aus dem Groben bilden; flüchtig entwerfen; mit grobem Mörtel bewerfen. II. *s.* der rohe Entwurf; der Spritzbewurf, Anwurf von Mörtel. **—-hew**, *v.a.* aus dem Groben (aus-)hauen; bearbeiten (*fig.*). **—-rider**, *s.* der Bereiter. **—-shod**, *adj.* mit scharfen Hufeisen versehen; to ride —-shod over (a p.), (einen) rücksichtslos *or* unbarmherzig behandeln, einen anfahren.

Roulette, *s.* das Rollrädchen, das Roulettespiel; die Punktiermaschine; der Durchstich (*stamps*).

[1]**Round**, I. *adj.*, **—ly**, *adv.* rund; in — terms, rundweg; to go at a good — pace, einen guten Schritt gehen; a — answer, eine aufrichtige Antwort; a — dance, ein Rundtanz; a — game, ein Gesellschaftsspiel; a — hand, ausgeschriebene Hand; a — sum, beträchtliche Summe; — Table, die Tafelrunde (of Arthur, des Königs Artus). II. *adv.* rings(um); (in circumference) herum, in der Runde, im Kreise; the country — (about), die umliegende Gegend; all the year —, das ganze Jahr (hin-)durch; all —, ringsum, ringsumher (*lit.*); durch die Bank, ohne Unterschied (*fig.*); to go —, herumgehen; kreisen (*as a bottle*); einen Umweg machen; to go — to a p., bei einem vorsprechen, bei einem Besuch machen; to come —, herumkommen (*lit.*); sich bessern, sich erholen (*from illness*); wieder zu sich kommen; sich beruhigen; umschlagen (*fig.*); to bring *or* get s.o. —, einen wieder zu sich bringen, einen besänftigen, umstimmen; to turn —, herumdrehen (*lit.*); umkehren, sich ändern; — about, rund, ringsherum; to go — about, umgehen. III. *prep.* rings(um), um, um . . . herum; to sail — . . ., um . . . segeln; to come, get — a p., einen überlisten, gewinnen, sich einschmeicheln. IV. *s.* die Runde (*also of soldiers, policemen, etc.*); die (Leiter-)Sprosse (*of a ladder*); die Scheibe (*of beef*); (circle) das Rund, der Kreis, Zirkel; der Rundgesang, Kanon (*Mus.*); der Kreis, Kreislauf (*of labours, etc.*); *see* Rotation; (bout) der Gang; — of applause, die Beifalls-Salve; — of ammunition, die Ladung (für einen Schuß), der Schuß; to fire five —s, fünf Schüsse abgeben; fünfmal feuern; — of case-shot, der Kartätschenschuß; to go the —s, to make the —s, die Runde machen (*also fig.*). V. *v.a.* runden (*also Paint.*); fließend gestalten (*style*); to — off, abrunden; a —ed figure, rundliche Gestalt; —ed vowels, gerundete (geründete) Vokale. VI. *v.n.* rund werden, sich runden; sich umdrehen; umfahren, umschiffen. **—el**, *s.* das Rondell (*Fort.*, *Hort.*); *see* —elay. **—elay**, *s.* das Ringelgedicht; der Rundgesang. **—ers**, *s.* der Kreislauf (bei einer Art Fußballspiel). **—ing**, *s.* die Rundung, Abrundung; Rundung, Ründung, Labialisierung (*Gram.*); die Ausbiegung des Rückens (*Bookb.*). **—ish**, *adj.* rundlich. **—ishness**, *s.* die Rundlichkeit. **—ness**, *s.* die Rundung; die Bestimmtheit (*of an answer, etc.*). *Comp.* **—about**, I. *adj.* weit-läufig, -schweifig; umgehend; —about way, der Umweg. II. *s.* der Umschweif, Umweg; *see* Merry-go-round. **—-backed**, **—-shouldered**, *adj.* rundschulterig. **—-hand**, *s.* die Rundschrift. **—head**, *s.* der Stutzkopf; der Puritaner. **—house**, *s.* das Wacht-Haus; die Hütte (*Naut.*). **—-robin**, *s.* die Bittschrift mit den Unterschriften aller Beteiligten.

[2]**Round**, *v.n.* raunen (*obs.*); to — on, (einen Helfershelfer) angeben, (abuse) derb anfahren.

Roup, *s.* die Darre.

Rous—e, I. *v.a.* auf-, er-wecken (*from sleep, etc.*); aufregen (*fig.*); aufmuntern, anreizen (*to revenge, etc.*); aufjagen (*game*); to —e o.s., sich ermannen, aufraffen, aufrappeln; to —e a p.'s anger, einen aufbringen. II. *v.n.* aufwachen. III. *s. see* Reveille. **—ing**, *adj.*, **—ingly**, *adv.* aufregend; (great) gewaltig (*sl.*).

[1]**Rout**, I. *s.* die Rotte, Bande, der Trupp; der gemeine Haufe, das Volk, der Pöbel; der Auflauf; die Zusammenrottung (*Law*); der große Empfang, die große vornehme Abendgesellschaft (*obs.*). II. *v.n.* sich lärmend versammeln (*obs.*); (— together) sich zusammenrotten.

[2]**Rout**, I. *s.* die Verwirrung, ungeordnete wilde Flucht; to put to (the) —, *see* II. II. *v.a.* in Verwirrung setzen; in wilde Flucht jagen, auseinandersprengen; (expel) hinausjagen. III. *v.n.* fortgescheucht werden, sich plötzlich aus dem Staube machen.

[3]**Rout**, I. *v.n.* lärmen, brüllen; schnarchen (*obs.*). II. *s.* der Lärm, Spektakel.

[4]**Rout**, *v.* I. *a.* vertiefen, aushöhlen. II. *n.* herumstöbern.

Rout—e, *s.* der Weg; die Marschroute (*Mil.*). **—ine**, *s.* die Gewohnheit, handwerksmäßige Gewandtheit, Routine; (old way) der (alte) Schlendrian; —ine business, die Geschäftsroutine.

[1]**Rov—e**, *v.n.* umher-schweifen, -schwärmen. **—er**, *s.* der Herumstreicher, Durchschweifer, Durchwanderer, Wanderer; der Seeräuber (*rare*). **—ing**, I. *adj.*, **—ingly**, *adv.* umherschweifend, herumstreichend. II. *s.* das Umherschweifen.

[2]**Rov—e**, *v.a.* durch eine Öse *or* Öffnung ziehen; *see* Ravel. **—ing**, *s.* das Vorspinnen; das grobe Vorgespinnst. *Comp.* **—ing-frame**, **—ing-machine**, *s.* die Vorspinnmaschine.

[1]**Row**, *s.* die Reihe; die Reihe Häuser.

[2]**Row**, *v.a.* & *n.* rudern; rojen; to — a long stroke, lang rojen; to — together, zugleich rojen; to — in the same boat, mit einem unter einer Decke stecken (*fig.*). **—er**, *s.* der Ruderer, Rojer. **—ing**, *s.* das Rudern. *Comp.* **—boat**, *s.* das Ruderboot. **—ing-match**, *s.* das Wettrudern. **—locks**, *pl.* die Ruderklampen, Gabeln.

[3]**Row**, I. *s.* der Lärm, Spektakel, Auflauf; to kick up a —, einen Auflauf verursachen (*sl.*); what's the —? was ist los? (*coll.*). II. *v.a. see* Scold. **—dy**, I. *s.* der Lärmer, Spektakelmacher, Strolch, Raufbold, gewalttätige Mensch. II. *adj.* lärmend; händelsüchtig. **—dyism**, *s.* das raufboldartige Benehmen, die Brutalität, das gewalttätige Wesen.

Rowan-tree, *s.* die Eberesche.

Rowel, I. *s.* das Spornrädchen; der Buckel (*in a horse's bit*); das Haarseil (*Vet.*). II. *v.a.* ein Haarseil durchziehen.

Rowen, *s.* das Stoppelfeld; das Nachheu.

Royal, I. *adj.*, **—ly**, *adv.* königlich, Königs-; (princely) fürstlich; erlaucht; prächtig, edel (*fig.*); — Prince, der Prinz von königlichem Geblüt; Prince —, der Kronprinz; Princess —, die Kronprinzessin; — assent, königliche Einwilligung; — antelope, die Zwergantilope; — antler, dritte Sprosse eines Hirschgeweihes; — blue, das Königsblau; — oak, die Königs-Eiche; — road, die Königsstraße; der besonders bequeme Weg (*fig.*); there is no — road to knowledge, ohne Fleiß, kein Preis (*prov.*); — Academy, die Akademie der Künste; — Society, die (englische) Akademie der (mathematischen und naturwissenschaftlichen) Wissenschaften. II. *s.* das Royalpapier; das Oberbramsegel (*Naut.*); kleiner Mörser (*Artil.*); das Hirschgeweih mit zwölf Sprossen; *see* — antler. **—ism**, *s.* die Königstreue, der Royalismus. **—ist**, *s.* der Königlichgesinnte, Royalist. **—ty**, *s.* das Königtum; (— dignity) die Königswürde; der (die) König(in) (*fig.*); zum königlichen Hause gehörige Person; (— right) königliches Vorrecht; (— manor) das Krongut, die Domäne; (— tax) die Abgabe an die Krone; (inventor's —ty) die einem Patentinhaber für Benutzung des Patentes bezahlten Gebühren; author's —ty, der Anteil des Verfassers an dem Ertrage seines Werkes; die Tantième (*Theat.*).

Rub, I. *s.* das Reiben, die Reibung; der Anstoß (*fig.*); (impediment) das Hindernis; (difficulty) die Schwierigkeit; (jibe) der Stich; *see* —ber; there's the —! da steckt der Knoten! da liegt der Hase im Pfeffer! (*coll.*). II. *v.a.* reiben; (chafe) abreiben; (clean) wischen, scheuern, putzen; (wax) bohne(r)n; (polish) schleifen, polieren; to — **down**, abreiben, striegeln (*horses*); to — **off**, weg-, ab-wischen; to — **out**, ausstreichen, verlöschen; to — **up**, polieren (*lit.*); erneuern, auffrischen (*fig.*); sich abgeben mit (*fig.*); reizen, ärgern (*a p.*). III. *v.n.* sich reiben, to — **along**, sich durch-drängen, -helfen. **—ber**, I. *s.* der Reiber, Frottierer; grobe Schürze (*for servants, etc.*); die Reibfläche (*on match-boxes*); das Reib-zeug, -kissen (*Elect.*); *see* Whetstone; das Frottierhandtuch (*for —bing*); der Rubber (*Cards*); India —ber, der Kautschuk, Gummi. II. *attrib.* Gummi-; —ber tire, der Gummireif (*Cycl.*); —ber tired, mit Gummireifen versehen. **—bing**, I. *adj.*; —bing cloth, das Reibtuch. II. *s.* die Reibung.

Rub-a-dub, *s.* der Trommelwirbel.

Rubb—ish, *s.* der Schutt; der Abfall, Auswurf, Kehricht; der Schund; all —ish! dummes Zeug! **—ishy**, *adj.* lumpig. **—le**, *s. see* —ish; der Steinschutt, Kalkschutt (*Build.*). *Comp.* **—ish-heap**, *s.* der Schutthaufen. **—le-stone**, *s.* der Rollstein. **—le-wall**, *s.* rauhes Mauerwerk. **—le-work**, *s.* das Bruchsteinmauerwerk.

Rubeola, *s.* die Masern (*Med.*).

Rubescen—ce, *s.* das Rotwerden, Erröten. **—t**, *adj.* rötlich.

Rub—icund, *adj.* rötlich, rot. **—ied**, *adj.* rubinrot, hochrot. **—ric**, I. *s.* die Rubrik (*Typ.*); die liturgische Vorschrift, Rubrik (*Eccl.*) II. *adj.* rot. **—ricate**, *v.a.* rot bezeichnen. **—y**, I. *s.* der Rubin; (—y colour) die Rubinfarbe, das Weinrot, Rot; *see* Carbuncle (*Med.*); die Pariserschrift (*Typ.*). II. *adj.* rubinrot.

Ruch—e, **—ing**, *s.* die Rüsche.

[1]**Ruck**, I. *s.* die Runzel, Falte. II. *v.a.* runzeln, zerknüllen. III. *v.n.* sich runzeln, zerknüllen; to — up, zerknittern; sich ärgern (*coll.*).

[2]**Ruck**, *s.* der Haufe; der Pöbel.

[3]**Ruck**, *v.n.* sitzen, hocken (wie ein Vogel auf der Stange) (*prov.*).

Rudd—iness, *s.* die Röte. **—le**, *s. see* Reddle. **—y**, *adj.*, **—ily**, *adv.* rot, rötlich.

Rudder, *s.* das (Steuer-)Ruder. *Comp.* **—bands**, *s.* die Ruderscheren.

Rude, *adj.*, **—ly**, *adv.* ungebildet; roh; (impolite) unhöflich, unartig; (rough) grob; *see* Clownish; (violent) heftig, ungestüm, stark; hart, rauh, streng (*as climate*); kunstlos (*as language*); roh, ungebildet (*as art, a people, etc.*); — health, derbe, kernige Gesundheit. **—ness**, *s.* die Roheit, Rauheit; das Wilde (*of a landscape*); die Grobheit (*of a nature, a work, etc.*); die Unhöflichkeit; (rusticity) die Roheit, Einfalt; die Kunstlosigkeit, Grobheit; die Rauhigkeit, Strenge (*of a winter, etc.*); —ness must be met with —ness, auf einen groben Klotz gehört ein grober Keil.

Rudiment, *s.* die Grundlage, der Anfang; die Anlage, der Anfang (*of an organ*); der Ansatz (*Bot.*); —s, Anfangsgründe. **—al**, **—ary**, *adj.* Anfangs-, Elementar-; rudimentär.

[1]**Rue**, *v.a.* bereuen, beklagen. **—ful**, *adj.*, **—fully**, *adv.* reuig; (sad) traurig, kläglich. **—fulness**, *s.* die Traurigkeit, der Gram.

[2]**Rue**, *s.* die Raute (*Bot.*).

[1]**Ruff**, *s.* der Halskragen, die Krause; der Streit-, Kampf-hahn (*Orn.*). **—ian**, *see* Ruffian. **—le**, I. *s.* die Krause; (frill) der Busenstreif; die Aufregung. II. *v.a.* in Falten legen, falten, krausmachen; (disorder) in Unordnung bringen, verwirren; (agitate) aufregen, in Aufruhr bringen; (rumple) zerknittern; (adorn with —les) mit Krausen versehen; to —le a p.'s feathers, (einen) aufbringen.

[2]**Ruff**, **—le**, *s.* kurzer Trommelwirbel.

[3]**Ruff**, I. *s.* das Abstechen, Trumpfen. II. *v.a.* & *n.* abstechen, trumpfen.

Ruffian, I. *adj.* wüst, roh. II. *s.* der Raufbold, brutale Mensch. **—ism**, *s.* das wüste Wesen; rohes Treiben; piece of —ism, die gemeine Gewalttätigkeit, Abscheulichkeit. **—ly**, *adj.* wüst, roh, wild, ruchlos.

Ruffler, *s.* der Prahler, Renommist.

Rug, *s.* grobwollene, rauhe Decke; das Plaid; die Decke, kleiner Teppich; railway, travelling —, die Reisedecke, das Reiseplaid. **—ged**, *adj.*, **—gedly**, *adv.* rauh, uneben, holperig, zackig; rauh, schroff (*fig.*); *see* Shaggy. **—gedness**, *s.* die Rauheit, Schroffheit. *Comp.* —**-work**, *s.* eine Art Wollstickerei.

Rugose, *adj.* runzelig.

Ruin, I. *s.* der Einsturz; der Verfall, Untergang (*fig.*); die Ruine (*of a castle, etc.*); —s, Trümmer, Ruinen; to be the — of (a p.), (einen) zu Grunde richten, verderben; to go to —, verfallen. II. *v.a.* zu Grunde richten, verderben, zerstören; verführen (*a girl*); zerrütten (*one's health*); to — o.s., sich ins Verderben stürzen. —**ation**, *s.* die Zerstörung, Verwüstung; das Verderben (*fam.*). —**ous**, *adj.*, —**ously**, *adv.* baufällig, den Einsturz drohend; unglücklich, verderbenbringend (*fig.*); a —ous undertaking, ein halsbrecherisches Unternehmen. —**ousness**, *s.* die Baufälligkeit; die Verderblichkeit (*fig.*).

Rul—**e**, I. *s.* die Regel (*also Arith.*); die Richtscheit, das Lineal (*T.*); (regulation, law) die Regel, Vorschrift, Ordnung, Richtschnur, Norm, der Grundsatz; (sway) die Herrschaft; (custom) der Gebrauch; das Kolumnenmaß (*Typ.*); —e of three, Regel de Tri; hard and fast —es, durchaus (*or* ohne Unterschied) bindende Regeln; to break a —e, eine Regel verletzen, gegen eine Regel verstoßen; to lay down a —e, eine Regel aufstellen; to make it a —e, es zur Regel machen; it is a —e with me, ich habe es mir zur Regel gemacht; as a — e, in der Regel; to have —e over, beherrschen; folding —e, die Schmiege; parallel —e, Parallellineal; —e of thumb, eine auf Erfahrung begründete Regel. II. *v.a.* liniieren (*paper, etc.*); (settle) ausmachen, abmachen; I have —ed, ich habe die Regel gemacht; verordnen, entscheiden (*Law*); (— over) beherrschen, regieren; he —es over the Empire, er herrscht über das Reich, er beherrscht das Reich; be —ed by me, laßt euch von mir raten *or* leiten. III. *v.n.* herrschen, sich behaupten (*as prices*). —**ed**, *adj.* liniert, mit Linien. —**er**, *s.* der Herrscher, Regierer; das Lineal. —**ing**, I. *adj.* herrschend; bestehend (*C.L.*). II. *s.* das Liniieren; die Entscheidung des Gerichts.

[1]**Rum**, *s.* der Rum.

[2]**Rum**, —**my**, *adj.* wunderlich, seltsam (*sl.*).

Rumb, *see* Rhumb.

Rumbl—**e**, I. *s.* das Rumpeln, dumpfe Getöse; (—e tumble) der Bedientensitz (*in a carriage*). II. *v.n.* rummeln, rumpeln, rasseln, poltern, dröhnen; rollen (*of thunder*). —**ing**, I. *adj.* rummelnd, rasselnd, rollend. II. *s.* das Rummeln.

Rumina—**nt**, I. *adj.* wiederkäuend. II. *s.* der Wiederkäuer. —**te**, *v.n.* wiederkäuen; grübeln, nachsinnen, überlegen. —**tion**, *s.* das Wiederkäuen; das Nachgrübeln. —**tor**, *s.* der Nachdenkliche, Nachsinnende, Grübler.

Rummage, *v.* I. *n.* suchen, stöbern. II. *a.* (— through) durch-suchen, -stöbern. III. *s.* der Wirrwarr.

Rummer, *s.* der Pokal, Römer.

Rumo(u)r, I. *s.* das Gerücht; the — is current, das Gerücht geht (um). II. *v.a.* ausbreiten als Gerücht; it is —ed, es geht das Gerücht.

Rump, I. *s.* der Steiß, Bürzel; (back) das Kreuz; das Schwanzstück (*Butch.*). II. *attrib.*; — Parliament, das Rumpfparlament. *Comp.* —**-bone**, *s.* das Steißbein. —**-steak**, *s.* die Fleischschnitte vom Lendenbraten, das Rumpfstück.

Rumple, I. *v.a.* runzeln, verkrümpeln. II. *s.* die Falte.

Rumpus, *s.* der Lärm, Spektakel (*coll.*).

Run, *ir.v.* I. *n.* rennen, laufen; (hasten) eilen; *see* Race; laufen (*as bills, etc.*); sich drehen (*as wheels*); in Betrieb sein (*as an engine*); verfließen, dahinschwinden (*as time*); mit einem Vorstich nähen (*Sew.*); eitern (*as a sore*); zerfließen, schmelzen (*as metals*); auftauen (*as ice*); laufen (*as a candle*); (— away) davonlaufen, fliehen; (be in operation) in Kraft sein; two days —ning, zwei auf einander folgende Tage, zwei Tage nach einander; this bill has 30 days to —, dieser Wechsel hat (noch) 30 Tage zu laufen (ehe er zahlbar wird); the piece ran for 100 nights, das Stück wurde 100 Mal gegeben (*Theat.*); there are trains —ning 6 times a day, es gehen 6 Züge täglich ab; packets — between Bremen and London, es fahren Packetboote zwischen Bremen und London; my garden —s north, mein Garten hat eine nördliche Richtung; thus —s the order, so lautet die Verordnung; to — **about**, umher-laufen, -rennen; to — **after**, nach-jagen, -laufen; he is greatly — after, er ist sehr gesucht, hat starken Zulauf (*of a clergyman*); to — **against**, laufen gegen, anlaufen (an, *acc.*); (oppose) zuwidersein; to — **aground**, stranden; to — **amuck**, einen Anfall von Mordraserei haben; to — **ashore**, auf den Strand laufen, auflaufen; to — **at**, laufen gegen, an (*acc.*), (attack) losstürzen auf (*acc.*); to — **away**, davon-, weg-laufen; (elapse) dahinschwinden; (— off) durchgehen (*as horses*); sich entfernen (from, von), abschweifen (*from a subject*); to — away with, wegführen; (elope) entführen; (carry away) hin-, fort-reißen; (adopt hastily) sich (*dat.*) in den Kopf setzen; (— off) durchgehen mit; to — **back**, zurücklaufen; to — **before**, voran-, voraus-eilen; to — before the wind, vor dem Winde segeln; to — **down**, herab-, hinab-, hinunter-laufen (*as tears, etc.*); the clock has — down, die Uhr ist abgelaufen; to — **for**, (— for s.th.), nach einer S. laufen, wett-laufen, -rennen (*for a prize*); to — for one's life, um sein Leben laufen; — for your life! laufen Sie, so lieb Ihnen Ihr Leben ist! you must — for it if . . ., Sie müssen tüchtig laufen, wenn . . .; to — **foul of**, anlaufen, fahren auf (*acc.*) (*lit.*); angreifen (*fig.*), über-, an-segeln, in den Grund segeln (*a ship*); to — **from**, fortlaufen von (*a p.*); übergehen (*from topic to topic*); to — **high**, hoch-, hohl-gehen (*Naut.*); words ran high, es wurden zornige Worte (zwischen ihnen) gewechselt; to — **in**, herein-laufen, -rennen, -fließen; it —s in the blood, es steckt im Geblüte; it —s in my head, es geht mir im Kopfe herum; to — in upon, zu-laufen, -segeln auf (*acc.*); to — **into**, laufen, rennen in (*lit.*); geraten, stürzen in; to — in(to) debt, sich in Schulden stürzen; to — into a port, einen Hafen ansegeln; the colours — into one another, die Farben laufen, fließen ineinander; pride is apt to — into . . ., der Stolz steigert sich leicht bis zur . . .; to — **low**, auf die Neige gehen; to — **off**, davon-gehen, -laufen, fortlaufen; to — off the rails, entgleisen (*Railw.*); to — off with, *see* — away with; to — **on**, fortlaufen, -gehen; (continue) fortfahren; (chatter) unablässig reden, schwatzen, fortplaudern; to — on one's sword, sich in sein Schwert stürzen; to — **out**, heraus-laufen, -rennen, -fließen; (let through) auslaufen (*as a vessel*), ablaufen, zu Ende gehen (*as time*); treiben (*suckers*), absegeln aus (*of a port*), *see* — over; to — **over**, überlaufen (*also Typ.*); to — over to . . ., hinüberlaufen zu . . ., sich nach . . . hinüberbegeben; to — **riot**, unbändig sein, sich (*dat.*) die Zügel schießen lassen; to — **short**, auf die Neige gehen, spärlich werden; to — short of money, knapp bei Gelde sein; to — **smoothly**, leicht, ohne Hindernis laufen (*lit.*); fließen (*fig.*); to — **through**, laufen, rennen durch (*lit.*); durchlaufen, -machen (*fig.*); to — through one's property, sein Vermögen durchbringen; to — **to** seed, in Samen schießen (*lit.*); alt, schäbig werden, vergehen (*fig.*); to — **up**, hinauf-laufen, -gehen; (shrink) einlaufen, eingehen; (amount) hinauflaufen, sich belaufen (to, auf, *acc.*); to — up against s.o., einen zufällig begegnen *or* treffen; to — **upon**, rennen, losgehen auf (*lit.*); sich beschäftigen mit (*fig.*); bestürmen (*a bank*); his thoughts *or* his mind ran upon this subject, all sein Denken war auf diesen Gegenstand gerichtet.

II. *a.* rennen, laufen; verfolgen, einschlagen (*a course*); (wett)rennen lassen (*a horse*); wettfahren lassen (*vessels*); gehen lassen (*trains*); ergießen, mit sich führen (*blood, wine, gold, etc.*); schmelzen; gießen (*bullets*); (pursue) verfolgen, nehmen; (force) zwingen; setzen (*a ship ashore, etc.*); *see* Manage, Conduct, Carry on (*Amer.*); he ran for the Presidency, *etc.*, er wurde für die Präsidentschaft in Vorschlag gebracht; to — a race, wettrennen; to — the gauntlet, Spießruten laufen; to — **down**, nieder rennen (*lit.*); herunter *or* schlecht machen (*fig.*); abjagen, zu Tode hetzen (*a stag*); in den Grund bohren *or* segeln (*a ship*); to — **hard**, (einen) in die Enge treiben; to — **in**, hineinlaufen lassen (*a boat, etc.*), hinein-stecken, -tun (*a ribbon in a dress, etc.*); einholen (*the guns*); einstecken (*a prisoner*) (*sl.*); to — **into**, hinreißen zu, bringen, führen (*a state or condition*); to — a nail into one's foot, (a needle into one's finger) sich (*dat.*) einen Nagel in den Fuß treten (eine Nadel in den Finger stechen *or* bekommen); to — **off**, ablaufen lassen; to — **out**, hinausstoßen (*a p., etc.*); an die Stückpforten fahren (*guns*); ausfahren (*Typ.*); to — **over**, durch-laufen, -gehen, flüchtig ansehen; (recount) in Kürze erzählen, schnell über (*acc.*) . . . hingehen; (glance, *etc.*) überblicken, durchsehen; to — **through**, durchlaufen; (bore) durchbohren; to — **to** ground, (einen Fuchs) in sein Lager zurücktreiben; to — **up**, hinauflaufen lassen; (build) schnell und leicht aufbauen (*houses*); in die Höhe treiben (*prices*); auflaufen, anwachsen lassen (*an account*); to — up bills, Schulden machen. III. *s.* das Laufen, Rennen, der Lauf; der Lauf, Gang, Fortgang (*fig.*); (trip) die Fahrt, Reise; die Reise, (ununterbrochene) Fahrt (*of a vessel*); das Zuströmen (*of custom*); (stream) der Bach; der Fluß (*also of verses*); die Trift (*for cattle, etc.*); der Mühlgang (*Mill.*); der Läufer (*Mus.*); the common —, der gewöhnliche Schlag; the common — of mankind, die Menschheit im allgemeinen; there has been a great — upon this article, es war starke Nachfrage nach diesem Artikel; this piece has had a — of 40 nights, dieses Stück wurde 40 Mal nach einander gegeben; to have the — of a garden, jederzeit freien Zutritt zu einem Garten haben; a — against, ein Geschrei gegen (*a measure, etc.*); a — upon a bank, das Bestürmen einer Bank (um deren Noten gegen klingende Münze einzuwechseln); a — of customers, viele Kundschaft; a — of luck, fortdauerndes Glück; in the long —, auf die Länge, auf die Dauer; am Ende; to be in the —, (bei einer Wahl) in Frage kommen; to be out of the —, nicht mehr in Frage kommen. **—let, —nel**, *see* Rivulet. **—ner**, *s.* der Renner, Läufer; der Bote; die (Schlitten-)Kufe, Läufer (*for sledges*); der Schieber (*of an umbrella*); der Ausläufer (*Bot.*); scarlet —ner, die türkische Bohne. **—ning**, *adj.* laufend, fließend, strömend; (in succession) nach, hinter einander, auf einander folgend; eiternd (*as a sore*); —ning account, laufende, offene Rechnung; a —ning hand, eine fließende, geläufige Hand(schrift); 5 times —ning, 5 Mal hinter einander; to keep up a —ning commentary, fortlaufende Bemerkungen einschalten; —ning days, Extraliegetage; —ning fire, das Lauffeuer; (*also* of questions, von Fragen); —ning footman, der Läufer; —ning knot, die Schleife, Schlinge; —ning title, der Kolumnentitel. *Comp.* **—away**, I. *adj.* flüchtig geworden, entlaufen; —away match, die Heirat nach vorheriger Entführung. II. *s.* der Flüchtling, Ausreißer.

Runcinate, *adj.* schrotsägenförmig.

Run—e, *s.* die Rune. **—ic**, *adj.* runisch, Runen-.

[1]**Rung**, *s.* der Knüttel (*dial.*): (rundle) die Sprosse (*of a ladder*); lowest —, unterste Stufe (*fig.*).

[2]**Rung**, *imperf. & p.p. of* Ring.

Runnet, *see* Rennet.

Runt, *s.* das verbuttete Tier; der Zwerg (*also fig.*), spanische Taube (*Orn.*).

Rupee, *s.* die Rupie (brittisch-indische Münze von schwankendem Werte, etwas unter 2 Schilling).

Rupture, I. *s.* das Brechen; der Bruch (*also Med.*); der Friedensbruch (*fig.*). II. *v.a.* brechen, sprengen (*a blood-vessel, etc.*). III. *v.n.* einen Bruch bekommen. **—d**, *p.p. & adj.* brüchig.

Rural, *adj.*, **—ly**, *adj.* ländlich; Land-; — dean, der Landdekan; — excursion, die Landpartie; — poetry, die Dorfpoesie, Idylle. **—ize**, I. *v.a.* einen ländlichen Charakter geben. II. *v.n.* aufs Land gehen, ein ländliches Leben führen.

Ruse, *s.* die List; — de guerre, Kriegslist.

[1]**Rush**, *s.* die Binse; I don't care a — about it, ich frage gar nichts danach. **—y**, *adj.* voller Binsen; aus Binsen, Binsen-. *Comp.* **—bottomed**, *adj.*; —-bottomed chairs, Binsenstühle. **—light**, *s.* das Binsen-, Nacht-licht. **—mat**, *s.* die Binsen-, Schilf-matte.

[2]**Rush**, I. *s.* das Rauschen, Toben (*of the waves, etc.*); (—ing) das Stürzen, Stoßen; (run) der Andrang, das Gedränge; there was a — for seats, man drängte sich um Plätze. II. *v.n.* mit Ungestüm anlaufen, angelaufen kommen, stürzen, schießen, fliegen; rauschen, sausen (*as wind*); sich stürzen (forward, vorwärts; in, hinein *or* herein; out, hinaus *or* heraus); to — **forth**, hervor-, los-stürzen; to — **into** print, vorschnell (mit etwas) vor die Öffentlichkeit treten; to — **on** *or* **to** certain death, einem gewissen Tode entgegenrennen. III. *v.a.*; to — a bill through Parliament, in aller Eile einen Gesetzentwurf durchbringen; to — a camp, ein Lager durch einen plötzlichen Überfall *or* Handstreich nehmen.

Rusk, *s.* der Zwieback.

Russet, I. *adj.* braunrot; bäuerisch, schlicht (*fig.*). II. *s.* das Braunrot; die Bauernkleidung; (apple) der Rötling.

Rust, I. *s.* der Rost (*also fig. & Bot.*); der Brand (*of wheat*). II. *v.n.* rosten, verrosten. III. *v.a.* rostig machen; abstumpfen, schwächen (*fig.*). **—iness**, *s.* die Rostigkeit; die Ungeläufigkeit aus Mangel an Übung. **—y**, *adj.* rostig, schimmelig; rostfarben (*also Bot.*); verrostet, halb vergessen, ungeläufig (*fig.*); (surly) mürrisch, versauert; my German has become rather —y, mein Deutsch ist etwas eingerostet, ich habe mein Deutsch etwas *or* ein bißchen vergessen.

Rustic, I. *adj.*, **—ally**, *adv.* ländlich, Land-; (simple) ländlich, einfach, schlicht; (rude) bäuerisch, roh; — work, die Rustik (*Arch.*); (— chairs, *etc.*) aus Baumästen hergestellte Gartenmöbel. II. *s.* der Landmann, Bauer. **—ate**, *v.* I. *n.* auf dem Lande leben. II. *a.* auf das Land verweisen; von der Universität fortschicken, relegieren (*Univ.*). **—ation**, *s.* das Landleben; die Relegation, Verweisung von der Universität; *see* — work. **—ity**, *s.* die Ländlichkeit; die ländliche Einfachheit; die Ungehobeltheit.

Rustl—e, *v.n.* rascheln, rasseln, rauschen. **—ing**, I. *adj.* rauschend. II. *s.* das Rauschen, Gerassel.

[1]**Rut**, I. *s.* die Brunst. II. *v.n.* in Brunst stehen. III. *v.a.* bedecken. **—ting**, *s.* die Brunst. **—tish**, *adj.* brünstig, geil (*of animals*).

[2]**Rut**, I. *s.* das (Wagen-)Geleise, die Spur; to go on in the same old —, immer im alten Geleise bleiben. II. *v.a.* Geleise fahren; eine Linie einstechen (*with a spade*). **—ty**, *adj.* voller Geleise, ganz ausgefahren.

Ruth, *s.* das Mitleid, Erbarmen (*obs.*). **—less**, *adj.*, **—lessly**, *adv.* erbarmungslos, grausam, hart. **—lessness**, *s.* die Unbarmherzigkeit.

Rye, *s.* der Roggen; die Kreidekrankheit (*Orn.*). *Comp.* **—bread**, *s.* das Roggenbrot. **—grass**, *s.* das Raigras, Haargras.

Ryot, *s.* der ostindische Pächter

S

S, s, *s*, S, s. *For abbreviations see the Index at the end of the English-German part.*

Sabbat—arian, *s.* der Sabbatarier. **—arianism**, *s.* die Lehre der Sabbatarier. **—h**, *s.* der Sabbat. **—ic(al)**, *adj.* sabbatisch, Sabbat=. *Comp.* **—h-breaker**, *s.* der Sabbatschänder. **—h-breaking**, *s.* die Entheiligung des Sabbats.

Sable, I. *s.* der Zobel; (— fur) das Zobelfell, der Zobelpelz; das Schwarz (*fig. & Her.*); a suit of —s, schwarzer Anzug. II. *adj.* Zobel=; (—-coloured) schwarz, dunkelfarbig; (sad) düster.

Sabre, I. *s.* der Säbel. II. *v.a.* niedersäbeln. **—tache**, *s.* die Säbeltasche.

Sabulous, *adj.* sandig, griesig.

Sac, *s.* der Sack, Beutel.

Saccade, *s.* der Ruck mit dem Zügel; der starke Druck des Bogens auf die Saiten (*Viol.*).

Sacchar—ify, *v.a.* in Zucker verwandeln. **—ine**, *adj.* zuckerartig, zuckerhaltig, Zucker=; —ine principle, der Zuckerstoff. **—ometer**, *s.* der Zuckergehaltsmesser.

Sacerdotal, *adj.* priesterlich, Priester=. **—ism**, *s.* das Priestertum.

Sachem, *s.* der Indianerhäuptling.

[1]**Sack**, I. *s.* der Sack, die Tasche; das Maß von 3-5 Buscheln; a — of wool, ein Sack Wolle; to get the —, entlassen werden, den Laufpaß bekommen (*vulg.*); to give a p. the —, einem den Abschied geben, einen vor die Tür setzen (*vulg.*). II. *v.a.* (ein)sacken, in einen Sack tun; entlassen (*sl.*). **—ful**, *s.* einen Sack voll. **—ing**, *s. see* —cloth. *Comp.* **—cloth**, *s.* die Sackleinwand. **—-race**, *s.* das Sacklaufen.

[2]**Sack**, I. *s.* die Plünderung, Erstürmung. II. *v.a.* plündern. **—er**, *s.* der Erstürmer, Plünderer.

[3]**Sack, Seck**, I. *s.* süßer (spanischer u. Kanar=) Wein (*obs.*); der Sekt. II. *attrib.*; —-posset, Sektmolken.

[4]**Sack**, *s.* der kurze, weite Mantel; (sacque) der Überwurf; der schoßlose Rock.

Sackbut, *s.* die Posaune.

Sacr—ament, *s.* das Sakrament; (Lord's supper) das heilige Abendmahl. **—amental**, *adj.* sakramentlich, Sakrament=; —amental wafers, (wine), Oblaten, (Abendmahlswein). **—amentarian**, *adj.* Abendmahls=; —amentarian controversy, die Abendmahlsstreitigkeit. **—ed**, *adj.*, **—edly**, *adv.* heilig; geheiligt, geweiht (to the memory, dem Andenken); (venerable) heilig, ehrwürdig; (religious) kirchlich, geistlich, Kirchen=; (inviolate) unverbrüchlich; —ed music, Kirchenmusik; —ed college, das heilige Kollegium. **—edness**, *s.* die Heiligkeit, Ehrwürdigkeit. **—ifice**, I. *s.* das Opfer (*also fig.*); —ifice of time and money, Opfer von Zeit und Geld; to make a —ifice of, (etwas) aufopfern, zum Opfer bringen. II. *v.a. & n.* opfern. **—ificer**, *s.* der Opferer. **—ificial**, *adj.* zum Opfer gehörig, Opfer= (rites, etc., =gebräuche 2c.). **—ilege**, *s.* die Entweihung, Gotteslästerung; der Kirchenraub (*in churches*). **—ilegious**, *adj.*, **—ilegiously**, *adv.* ruchlos, frevelhaft, entheiligend. **—istan**, *s.* der Kirchendiener, *see* Sexton. **—isty**, *s.* die Sakristei.

Sad, *adj.*, **—ly**, *adv.* traurig, trüb; (heavy) schwerfällig; schwer (*as bread*); fest (*as soil*); (serious) ernst; dunkel (*as colours*); (vexatious, bad) böse, schlimm, arg; to be —ly in want of food, an Nahrungsmitteln starken Mangel leiden; — havoc, arge Verwüstung. **—den**, *v.* I. *a.* betrüben, traurig machen. II. *n.* sich betrüben; fest *or* hart werden (*soil*). **—ness**, *s.* die Trauer, Schwermut, der Ernst; die Traurigkeit (*of a tale, etc.*).

Saddle, I. *s.* der Sattel; das Sattelstück (*of mutton*); die Klampe (*Naut.*); to put the — upon the right horse, die Schuld auf den rechten Mann schieben. II. *v.a.* (auf)satteln; belasten, beschweren, (einem eine S.) aufhalsen (*fig.*); to — o.s. with a th., etwas auf sich (*acc.*) nehmen. **—r**, *s.* der Sattler. **—ry**, *s.* Sattlerwaren; das Sattlerhandwerk. *Comp.* **—-back**, *s.* konvexe Mauerabdeckung (*Build.*); sattelförmiger Berg. **—-backed**, *adj.* hohlrückig, mit Sattelrücken. **—-bag**, *s.* die Satteltasche. **—-bow**, *s.* der Sattelbogen. **—-cloth**, *s.* die Satteldecke. **—-girth**, *s.* der Sattelgurt **—-horse**, *s.* das Reitpferd. **—-like**, **—-shaped**, *adj.* sattelförmig. **—-pillar**, *s.* die Sattelstütze (*Cycl.*). **—-rug**, *s.* die Satteldecke.

Safe, I. *adj.*, **—ly**, *adv.* sicher; (uninjured) unversehrt, wohlbehalten, unverletzt; glücklich (*as an arrival, journey, etc.*); (out of danger) außer Gefahr; (secured) nicht länger gefährlich, tot, festgenommen; (to be trusted) zuverlässig; — and sound, frisch und gesund; it is not — for us to stay here, wir sind hier nicht sicher; with a — conscience, mit ruhigem *or* gutem Gewissen. II. *s.* der Speiseschrank (*for meat, etc.*); (iron —) der feuerfeste (Geld=)Schrank, Kassenschrank. **—ness**, *s.* die Sicherheit. **—ty**, *s.* die Sicherheit; die Unverletztheit; *see* —-keeping; in —ty, in Sicherheit; (—ly) wohlbehalten; place of —ty, der Sicherheitsort, Zufluchtsort; to flee for —ty to, sich flüchten nach, zu. *Comp.* **—-conduct**, *s.* das Sicherheitsgeleit; (pass) der Schutz=, Geleits=brief. **—guard**, I. *s.* der Schutz; *see* —-conduct; die Sicherheitsschiene (*Railw.*); *see* Cow-catcher; die Warneidechse (*Zool.*). II. *v.a.* sicheres Geleit geben; beschützen; verwahren. **—-keeping**, *s.* die sichere Aufbewahrung, der sichere Gewahrsam. **—ty-bicycle**, *s.* das Niederrad (*Cycl.*). **—ty-cage**, *s.* der Fahr=, Sicherheits=korb (*Min.*). **—ty-chain**, *s.* die Notkette. **—ty-lamp**, *s.* die Sicherheitslampe. **—ty-matches**, *pl.* (schwedische) Sicherheitszündhölzchen. **—ty-pin**, *s.* die Sicherheitsnadel. **—ty-valve**, *s.* das Sicherheitsventil.

Saf—flower, *s.* der Saflor. **—fron**, I. *s.* der Safran. II. *adj.* (—fron-coloured) safrangelb.

Sag, *v.n.* niederhängen; to — to leeward, nach Lee treiben (*Naut.*).

Saga, *s.* die Heldengeschichte, Heldensage.

Sagac—ious, *adj.*, **—iously**, *adv.* klug, scharfsinnig. **—ity**, *s.* der Scharfsinn.

[1]**Sage**, I. *adj.*, **—ly**, *adv.* weise, klug, verständig. II. *s.* der Weise. **—ness**, *s.* die Weisheit, Klugheit.

[2]**Sage**, *s.* der (*also* die) Salbei (*Bot.*).

Sagitta, *s.* der Pfeil (*Astr.*). **—l**, *adj.* pfeilartig; Pfeil=. **—ria**, *s.* das Pfeilkraut. **—rius**, *s.* der Schütze (*Astr.*). **—te**, *adj.* pfeilförmig.

Sago, I. *s.* der Sago. II. *attrib.*; — powder, das Sagomehl.

Sahib, *s.* Herr (indische Anrede).

Said, I. *imperf. & p.p. of* Say; he is — to have been . . ., er soll . . . gewesen sein, es heißt, daß er . . . gewesen ist. II. *adj.* vorerwähnt, besagt, obbemeldet.

Sail, I. *s.* das Segel; das Schiff (*fig.*); die Fahrt (*on the sea, etc.*); der Flügel (*of a windmill*); das Segeln, die Segelpartie; ten — of frigates, zehn Fregatten; to set (up) one's — to every wind, den Mantel nach dem Winde hängen; to get under —, sich segelfertig machen; to set —, unter Segel gehen. II. *v.n.* (ab)segeln, schiffen, fahren (for, nach), unter Segel gehen, auslaufen; fliegen, segeln (*in the air*); schwimmen, dahinschweben (*fig.*); to — along the coast, die Küste entlang segeln; to — back, out, zurück=, aus=segeln; to — close to the wind, nah am Winde segeln (*lit.*); sich unnötiger Gefahr aussetzen; sich mit größter Vorsicht bewegen (*fig.*); ready to —, segelfertig. III. *v.a.* durchsegeln, befahren; segeln (*a ship; so many knots*). **—er**, *s.* der Segler; she is a fast —er, es ist ein Schnellsegler

—ing, I. *adj.* segelnd, Segel-. II. *s.* das Segeln. **—less**, *adj.* segellos. **—or**, I. *s.* der Matrose, Seemann; is she is a good —or? wird sie leicht seekrank? kann sie die Seefahrt gut vertragen? he is an excellent —or, er wird nie seekrank; —or's knot, der Schifferknoten. II. *attrib.;* —or hat, der Matrosenhut, breitkrämpiger Strohhut mit Band. *Comp.* **—cloth**, *s.* das Segeltuch. **—ing-match**, *s.* das Wettsegeln. **—ing-order**, *s.* die Marsch-, Segel-ordnung. **—ing-orders**, *pl.* der Befehl zum Auslaufen. **—ing-trim**, *s.* die Segelbereitschaft. **—-maker**, *s.* der Segelmacher. **—or-like**, *adj.* wie ein Matrose, matrosenmäßig.

Sainfoin, *s.* der Wickenklee; die Esparsette.

Saint, I. *s.* der, die Heilige; Sankt-; der (die) Scheinheilige, der (die) Frömmler(in) (*fig. contempt.*); patron —, der (die) Schutzheilige; — Anthony's fire, die Rose; — Vitus's Dance, der Veitstanz; All —s' day, Allerheiligen. II. *v.a.* heilig sprechen, kanonisieren; to — (it), den Heiligen spielen, frömmeln. **—ed**, *adj.* heilig; (dead) verklärt, selig (verstorben). **—liness**, *s.* das heilige Wesen, die Heiligkeit. **—ly**, (**—like**,) *adj.* heilig, fromm. **—ship**, *s.* die Würde und Eigenschaft eines Heiligen.

Sake, *s.* die bewegende Ursache; for the — of, um . . . willen *or* wegen; for his —, um seinetwegen; for their —s, um ihretwillen; for the — of peace, um des lieben Friedens willen.

Sal, *s.* das Salz (*Chem.*); —ammoniac, das salzsaure Ammoniak, Chlorammonium; — volatile, das Riechsalz. **—ad**, *s.* der Salat. **—aried**, *adj.* besoldet. **—ary**, *s.* der Jahresgehalt, die Besoldung. **—ine**, I. *adj.* Salz-; (—ty) salzig. II. *s.* die Salzquelle. **—miac**, *s.* der Salmiak. **—t**, *see* Salt. *Comp.* **—ad-dish**, *s.* die Salatschüssel. **—ad-oil**, *s.* das Salatöl.

Salaam, *s.* I. der feierliche Gruß (der Orientalen). II. *v.a. & n.* (nach orientalischer Weise) feierlich grüßen.

Salable, *see* Sale.

Salacious, *adj.* wollüstig, brünstig, geil.

Salamander, *s.* der Salamander (*Zool.*); großes Schüreisen, runde Eisenschaufel (*Cook.*).

Sale, *s.* der Verkauf; (*also* —s) der Um-, Absatz; (public —) die Auktion; — by arbitration, Verkauf durch Kompromiß; for —, zu verkaufen; to put up for —, feilbieten; to meet with a ready —, guten Absatz finden; cheap —, der Ausverkauf (zu herabgesetzten Preisen); bill of —, die Verkaufsrechnung, der Kaufkontrakt. **—able**, *adj.* verkäuflich, gangbar. **—ableness**, *s.* die Verkäuflichkeit, Gangbarkeit. *Comp.* **—-price**, *s.* der Verkaufspreis. **—-room**, *s.* das Auktionslokal; *see* Shop, Warehouse. **—sman**, (**—swoman**,) *s.* der (die) Verkäufer(in); der (die) Ladendiener(in).

Salic, *adj.* salisch; — law, salisches Gesetz.

Salic—in, *s.* das Salizin (*Chem.*). **—ylic**, *adj.;* —ylic acid, die Salizylsäure.

Salient, *adj.* springend, hüpfend; hervorragend (*Arch.; fig.*); — angle, ausspringender Winkel.

Saliva, *s.* der Speichel. **—ry**, *adj.* Speichel-. **—te**, *v.a.* durch den Speichelfluß reinigen. **—tion**, *s.* die Speichelbildung, der Speichelfluß; die Speichelkur.

[1]**Sallow**, *s.* die Salweide.

[2]**Sallow**, *adj.* bleich und gelblich. **—ness**, *s.* die gelbliche Farbe, Blässe.

Sally, I. *s.* der Ausfall (*of the besieged*); der witzige, sinnreiche Einfall, Witzfunken (*fig.*); der Vorsprung, Auslauf (*Arch.*). II. *v.n.;* to — **forth**, vorbrechen, herausbrechen; (start) sich auf den Weg machen; to — **out**, einen Ausfall machen. *Comp.* **—-port**, *s.* das Ausfallstor, die Ausfallspforte.

Sally-Lunn, *s.* süßer, lockerer Kuchen, Art Teekuchen.

Salmagundi, *s.* das Ragout; der Mischmasch.

Salmon, *s.* der Lachs, Salm; (— colour) die blaßrötliche Lachsfarbe. **—et**, *s.* der kleine Lachs. *Comp.* **—-trout**, *s.* die Lachsforelle.

Saloon, *s.* der große Saal, Gesellschaftssaal, Salon; die erste Klasse (auf Schiffen); die Trinkstube (*Amer.*). *Comp.* **—-car**, *s.* der Salonwagen (*Amer.*).

Salt, I. *s.* das Salz (*also fig.*); die Würze (*fig.*); (sailor) alter Seebär; Attic —, attisches Salz; table —, das Tafelsalz; — of lemons, — of sorrel, das Sauerkleesalz, saure, oxalsaure Kali; *see* —-marsh; above (below) the —, am obern (untern) Ende der Tafel; he's not worth his —, er ist nicht einmal das Salz zu seiner Suppe wert; to eat a p.'s —, jemandes Gast sein; to take with a grain of —, mit einiger Vorsicht, *or*, *cum grano salis*, aufnehmen. II. *adj.* salzig, gesalzen; — beef, das Pökelfleisch; — butter, gesalzene Butter; — meat, das Salzfleisch; — provisions, eingesalzene Lebensmittel; — sea, — water, die Salzsee, das Meer. III. *v.a.* salzen; einsalzen, pökeln (*meat, etc.*); Salz zu lecken geben (*cattle, etc.*); in Salzwasser tränken (*timber*). IV. *v.n.* Salz niederschlagen, ansetzen. **—er**, *s.* der Einsalzer, der Salzhändler; *see* Drysalter. **—ern**, *s.* das Salzwerk. **—ing**, *s.* das Salzen; das Pökeln, Einsalzen. **—less**, *adj.* ungesalzen. **—ness**, *s.* die Salzigkeit. **—s**, *pl.* die Salze; votatile —s, flüchtige Salze. **—y**, *adj.* (etwas) salzig. *Comp.* **—-box**, *s.* die Salzmäste. **—-cellar**, *s.* das Salzfäßchen. **—-fish**, *pl.* gesalzene Fische. **—ing-tub**, *s.* das Pökelfaß. **—-lick**, *s.* die Salzlecke (*Amer.*). **—-marsh**, *s.* der Salzmorast, die Salzlache. **—-mine**, *s.* die Salzgrube. **—petre**, *s.* der Salpeter. **—petre-manufactory**, *s.* die Salpetersiederei. **—-spring**, *s.* die Salzquelle. **—-tax**, *s.* die Salzsteuer, Steuer auf Salz. **—-water**, *s.* das Salzwasser. **—-works**, *s.* das Salzwerk.

Salt—ant, *adj.* springend, hüpfend. **—ation**, *s.* das Springen. **—atory**, *adj.* springend, Sprung-. **—igrade**, I. *adj.* springend.

Saltire, *s.* das schräge Kreuz, Andreaskreuz.

Salu—brious, *adj.*, **—briously**, *adv.* heilsam, gesund. **—brity**, *s.* die Heilsamkeit, Zuträglichkeit. **—tariness**, *s. see* —brity. **—tary**, *adj.* heilsam, gesund. **—tation**, *s.* der Gruß, die Begrüßung. **—tatory**, *adj.* grüßend, Begrüßungs-; —tatory oration, die Eröffnungsrede (*Amer. Univ.*). **—te**, I. *s.* der Gruß, die Begrüßung; (kiss) der Kuß; das Salutieren, der Salutschuß (*Mil.*); royal —te, königlicher Salut, Salutschüsse zu Ehren des Königs. II. *v.a.* (be)grüßen; küssen; salutieren (*Mil., Naut.*) III. *v.n.* grüßen; salutieren.

Salv—age, *s.* das Bergen, die Bergung (*of a ship's cargo, etc.*); (—age money) das Bergegeld. **—ation**, *s.* die Rettung; die Erlösung, Seligmachung (*Theol.*); to work out one's own —ation, sein Seelenheil erringen (*B.*); auf eigne Faust selig werden (*fig.*); —ation Army, die Heilsarmee. **—ationist**, *s.* das Mitglied der Heilsarmee. **—e**, *v.a.* retten, bergen (*Naut.*). **—er**, *s.* der Präsentierteller. **—o**, *s.* die Salve (*Mil.*); der Vorbehalt. **—or**, *s.* der Berger.

[1]**Salve**, *v.a. see* Salv—age.

[2]**Salve**, I. *s.* die Salbe, der Balsam; das Linderungs-, Rettungs-mittel (*fig.*); die Schmeichelei (*sl.*). II. *v.a.* mit Salbe einreiben, heilen; heilen, abhelfen (einer S.).

Same, *adj.* selb; the —, der-, die-, das-selbe; the very —, self—, eben der; much the —, (so) ziemlich dasselbe; at the — time, at the — moment, zur selben Zeit, zur gleichen Zeit; (also) zugleich, ebenfalls; all the —, durchaus dasselbe; (nevertheless) dennoch, gleichwohl, trotzdem. **—ness**, *s.* die Einerleiheit, die Gleichheit, Identität; *see* Monotony.

Sample, I. *s.* die Probe, das Muster (*C.L.*); (specimen) das Exemplar; according to —, nach Probe; as per —, laut Probe; —s, — post, Muster ohne Wert. II. *v.a.* Probe nehmen, eine Probe zeigen. —**r**, *s.* das Stickmuster, Muster.

Sanat—ive, *adj.* heilend, heilkräftig. —**orium**, *s.* die Heilanstalt, das Genesungsheim, Kurhaus. —**y**, *adj.* heilsam, heilend.

Sanct—ification, *s.* die Heiligmachung, Heiligung; (consecration) die Weihe. —**ifier**, *s.* der Heiliger. —**ify**, *v.a.* heiligen. —**imonious**, *adj.*, —**imoniously**, *adv.* scheinheilig. —**imoniousness**, —**imony**, *s.* die Scheinheiligkeit. —**ion**, I. *s.* die Bestätigung, Genehmigung, das Gutheißen; die Weihe; (authority) die Autorität. II. *v.a.* (to give —ion to a th. *or* an act) etwas gutheißen, genehmigen, bestätigen. —**ity**, *s.* die Heiligkeit; die Unverletzlichkeit; die Reinheit, Unschuld. —**uary**, *s.* das Heiligtum; der heilige Schutzort, die Freistätte, Freistatt (*fig.*); der Tempel (*at Jerusalem*); *see* Church; das Sanktuarium, Allerheiligste (*in churches*). —**um**, *s.* das Heiligtum; der Zufluchtsort; das Privatzimmer, Studierzimmer (*fam.*).

Sand, I. *s.* der Sand; to make ropes of —, leeres Stroh dreschen. II. *v.a.* mit Sand bestreuen. —**ed**, *adj.* besandet, versandet, Sand=; *see* —y. —**iness**, *s.* sandige Beschaffenheit; die Sandfarbe. —**s**, *pl.* das Sandufer; die Sandbank; (desert) die Sandwüste; die Augenblicke (*pl. poet.*); his —s are run (out), seine Zeit ist vorbei *or* dahin. —**y**, *adj.* sandig, voll Sand; (—-coloured) sandfarben, rötlich; (—like) sandartig. *Comp.* —**-bag**, *s.* der Sandsack. —**-bank**, *s.* die Sandbank. —**-drift**, *s.* der Treibsand. —**-glass**, *s.* die Sanduhr. —**-hill**, *s.* der Sandhügel; die Düne. —**-martin**, *s.* die Uferschwalbe. —**paper**, *s.* das Sandpapier. —**piper**, *s.* der Wasserläufer. —**-pit**, *s.* die Sandgrube. —**stone**, *s.* der Sandstein; old red —stone, alter Devonischer Rotsandstein; new red —stone, Buntsandstein; silicious —stone, Kieselsandstein. —**y-haired**, *adj.* rothaarig.

[1]**Sandal**, *s.* die Sandale. —**ed**, *adj.* in Sandalen. *Comp.* —**-shoon**, *pl.* Sandalen.

[2]**Sandal**, —**wood**, *s.* das Sandelholz.

Sandever, Sandiver, *s.* die Glasgalle.

Sandwich, I. *s.* das belegte Butterbrot; die Butterbemme, Butterstulle. II. *v.a.* dünne Butterbrote schneiden (aus); einlegen, einpferchen, einschieben (between, zwischen) (*fig.*). *Comp.* —**-box**, *s.* die Zinnkapsel für belegte Butterbrote. —**-man**, *s.* der Plakatträger, das wandelnde Plakat.

San—e, *adj.* geistig gesund, bei gesundem Verstande; (*also* —**ely**, *adv.*) vernünftig (*as an answer*). —**eness**, *s.* der gesunde Verstand. —**itary**, *adj.* Gesundheits= (*measures, etc.*); gesundheitlich; —itary Board, das Gesundheitsamt; the —itary arrangements, die Sanitätsvorrichtungen. —**ity**, *s.* die Gesundheit; der gesunde Verstand; die Vernunft.

Sang, *imperf. of* Sing.

Sangfroid, *s.* die Kaltblütigkeit, Geistesgegenwart.

Sanguin—ary, *adj.*, —**arily**, *adv.* blutig; (cruel) blutgierig, blutdürstig. —**e**, *adj.* blutreich, vollblütig (*Med.*); leichtblütig, sanguinisch (*fig.*); (hopeful, confident) zuversichtlich, hoffnungsvoll; (red) blutrot; it has succeeded even beyond the most —e expectations, sein Erfolg hat selbst die kühnsten Erwartungen übertroffen; —e of success, voller Hoffnung auf Erfolg; a —e habit of body, sanguinische Leibesbeschaffenheit. —**eous**, *adj.* Blut=; (plethoric) blutreich, sanguinisch; (red) blutfarben.

Sanhedrim, Sanhedrin, *s.* der Sanhedrin, hohe Rat der Juden; die Ratsversammlung (*fig.*).

Sani—es, *s.* dünner Eiter. —**ous**, *adj.* dünneiterig.

Sank, *imp. of* Sink.

Sans, *prep.* ohne. —**-culotte**, *s.* der Ohnehose(n), Sansculotte, der extreme Republikaner. —**-culottism**, *s.* das Sansculottentum.

[1]**Sap**, *s.* der Saft (*in plants*); das Mark, die Kraft (*fig.*). —**less**, *adj.* saftlos; ohne Saft und Kraft (*fig.*). —**ling**, *s.* das Bäumchen, der Schößling; (young plant) das Pflänzchen; der junge Windhund. —**piness**, *s.* die Saftigkeit. —**py**, *adj.* saftig; jung, schwach (*fig.*).

[2]**Sap**, I. *s.* der Laufgraben, die Sappe (*Fort.*). II. *v.a.* untergraben (*also fig.*), sappieren, (unter)minieren. —**per**, *s.* der Schanzgräber, Sappeur; —pers and miners, Pioniere.

[3]**Sap**, I. *s.* der Büffler (*sl.*). II. *v.n.* büffeln, ochsen (*sl.*).

Sapid, *adj.* schmackhaft. —**ity**, *s.* die Schmackhaftigkeit.

Sapien—ce, *s.* die Weisheit. —**t**, *adj.*, —**tly**, *adv.* weise.

Sapon—aceous, *adj.* seifenartig. —**ification**, *s.* die Seifenbildung. —**ify**, *v.a.* verseifen. —**ite**, *s.* der Seifenstein.

Sapphire, I. *s.* der Saphir; das Saphir=Blau. II. *adj.* saphiren, von Saphir; blau (*Her.*).

Saraband, *s.* die Sarabande (Tanz und Musik).

Sarc—asm, *s.* der beißende, bittere Spott, Sarkasmus. —**astic**, *adj.*, —**astically**, *adv.* beißend, sarkastisch. —**ology**, *s.* die Lehre vom Fleische. —**oma**, *s.* das Fleischgewächs. —**ophagous**, *adj.* fleischfressend. —**ophagus**, *s.* der Sarkophag.

Sarcenet, *s.* der dünne Taffet, Sarsenet.

Sard, *s.* der Karneol. —**onyx**, *s.* der Sardonyx.

Sardine, *s.* die Sardine; packed as close as —s, eng gedrängt wie Heringe, zusammengepfercht wie Schafe.

Sardonic, *adj.* sardonisch; hämisch, bitter; — laughter, höhnisches Lachen, sardonisches Gelächter.

Sark, *s.* das Hemd (*Scotch*).

Sarment, —**um**, *s.* der Ausläufer (*Bot.*). —**ose**, —**ous**, *adj.* wurzel=rankig, =rankend.

Sarsenet, *see* Sarcenet.

Sartori—al, *adj.* Schneider=; den Schneidermuskel betreffend. —**us**, *s.* der Schneidermuskel.

[1]**Sash**, *s.* die Schärpe, Leibbinde; die Feldbinde (*Mil.*).

[2]**Sash**, I. *s.* der Fensterrahmen (eines Schieb=, Aufzieh=fensters); das Fenster (*fig.*). II. *v.a.* mit einem Rahmen *or* Schiebfenster versehen. *Comp.* —**-bar**, *s.* der Fensterstab. —**-bolt**, *s.* der Fensterriegel. —**-fastener**, *s.* der Fensterwirbel. —**-frame**, *s.* der Schiebrahmen. —**-pulley**, *s.* die Schiebfensterrolle. —**-window**, *s.* das Schiebfenster, Ziehfenster.

Sassafras, *s.* der Sassafras.

Sat, *imperf. & p.p. of* Sit.

Satchel, *s.* die Schulmappe, Büchertasche, der Schulranzen.

[1]**Sate**, (*obs.*) *imperf. & p.p. of* Sit.

[2]**Sat—e**, *v.a. see* —iate. —**eless**, *adj.* unersättlich. —**iate**, I. *v.a.* sättigen; (glut) übersättigen. II. *adj.* satt, gesättigt. —**iation**, *s.* die Sättigung; die Übersättigung. —**iety**, *s.* die Sättigung; die Sattheit, der Überdruß, Ekel.

Sat—een, *s.* der satinierte Baumwollstoff, das englische Leder. —**in**, I. *s.* der Atlas. II. *v.a.* satinieren, glätten. —**inet**, *s.* der Satinet. —**iny**, *adj.* satinartig, glatt. *Comp.* —**in-ribbon**, *s.* das Atlasband. —**in-wood**, *s.* das Atlasholz.

Satellite, *s.* der Anhänger, Satellit, Trabant (*also Astr.*); der Mond (eines Planeten).

Satir—e, *s.* die Satire, Spottrede, Spottschrift; das Spottgedicht. —**ic**, *adj.*, —**ical**, *adj.*, —**ically**, *adv.* satirisch. —**ist**, *s.* der Satiriker. —**ize**, *v.a.* verspotten, bespötteln.

Satis—faction, *s.* die Genugtuung, Befriedigung; (contentment) die Zufriedenheit, Freude; die Sühnung, Genugtuung, Bezahlung; (conviction) die Überzeugung, Gewißheit. —**factoriness**, *s.* das Befriedigende. —**factory**, *adj.*, —**factorily**, *adv.* befriedigend. —**fier**, *s.* der Genugtuende. —**fy**, *v.* I. *a.* befriedigen (*a* *passion, wish, etc.*); (suffice) genügen; (content) Genüge tun (einem), (einen) zufriedenstellen, befriedigen; bezahlen (*a debtor*); (convince) Gewißheit geben (of, über, *acc.*), überzeugen (of, von); sättigen (*one's appetite*); to —fy o.s., sich überzeugen (von einer S.); to —fy a want, einem Mangel abhelfen; to —fy certain requirements, gewissen Anforderungen genügen. II. *n.* Genüge leisten (einem); sättigen. **—fying**, *adj.* sättigend, nahrhaft; genügend, hinlänglich.

Satrap, *s.* der Satrap. **—y**, *s.* die Satrapie.

Satura—ble, *adj.* zu sättigen. **—nt**, I. *adj.* sättigend. II. *s.* das neutralisierende, Säuren absorbierende Mittel. **—te**, *v.a.* sättigen (*Chem.* & *fig.*). **—tion**, *s.* die Sättigung.

Saturday, *s.* der Samstag, Sonnabend.

Satyr, *s.* der Satyr, Waldgott. **—ic**, *adj.* satyrartig, Satyr-.

Sauc—e, I. *s.* die Soße, Brühe, Tunke; die Würze (*fig.*); die Unverschämtheit (*sl.*); what is — for the goose is — for the gander, was dem einen recht ist, ist dem andern billig (*prov.*); hunger is the best —, Hunger ist der beste Koch (*prov.*); to serve a p. with the same —, einem Gleiches mit Gleichem vergelten. II. *v.a.* würzen; frech reden mit, mit frechen Reden anfallen. **—er**, *s.* die Untertasse. **—ily**, *adv. see* —y. **—iness**, *s.* die Frechheit, Unverschämtheit. **—y**, *adj.* frech, keck, naseweis; unverschämt. *Comp.* **—e-boat**, *s.* die Soßenschale, der Soßennapf. **—e-pan**, *s.* die Schmorpfanne, Bratpfanne.

Sauciss—e, —on, *s.* die Zündwurst (*Mil.*).

Saunter, I. *s.* das Schlendern, gemächliche Wanderung; (—ing place) der Schlenderplatz. II. *v.n.* schlendern; to — about, herumschlendern. III. *v.a.;* to — away, vergeuden (*the time, etc.*). **—er**, *s.* der Schlenderer. **—ing**, *s.* das Schlendern, der Müßiggang.

Saurian, *s.* der Saurier, die Eidechse.

Sausage, *s.* die Wurst, Bratwurst.

Savable, *adj.* rettbar. **—ness**, *s.* die Rettbarkeit.

Savage, I. *adj.*, **—ly**, *adv.* wild, ungebildet; (fierce) grausam, roh, unbändig, barbarisch; (uncultivated) wüst, unbebaut. II. *s.* der Wilde, Barbar. **—ness**, *s.* die Wildheit; die Grausamkeit. **—ry**, *s.* die Wildheit, Barbarei.

Savanna, *s.* die Savanne, baumlose Grasfläche.

Savant, *s.* der Gelehrte; a —, ein Gelehrter.

Sav—e, I. *v.a.* (er)retten; selig machen, erlösen (*Theol.*); bergen (*Naut.*); ein-bringen, -fahren (*hay, etc.*); (keep) aufbewahren, erhalten; ersparen (a p. expense, shame, *etc.*, einem Kosten, Schande 2c.); (be —ing of) sparen; to —e appearances, (um) den Schein (zu) retten; you have —ed me a long journey, Sie haben mir einen weiten Weg erspart; (in order) to —e time, um keine Zeit zu verlieren; God —e the King, Gott erhalte den König, Heil unserm König, Heil! to —e one's credit, seinen Kredit retten; to —e from, retten von *or* aus, sichern vor; to —e up, aufsparen. II. *v.n.* Kosten (er)sparen; (be —ing) sparsam sein. III. *prep.* & *conj.* außer, ausgenommen; —e that, außer daß; the last —e one, der Vorletzte. **—er**, *s.* der (Er-)Retter, Erhalter; der Sparer. **—ing**, I. *adj.*, **—ingly**, *adv.* erlösend, seligmachend (*Theol.*); (protecting) vor Verlust sichernd; (economical) sparsam; to be —ing of, sparsam mit (einer Sache) umgehen; —ing clause, der Vorbehalt, die Klausel. II. *s.* die Rettung; *see* Preservation. III. *prep.* außer, ausgenommen; —ing your presence *or* reverence, *see* Reverence. **—ingness**, *s.* das Seligmachende; die Sparsamkeit, Kargheit. **—ings**, *pl.* die Ersparnisse, Sparpfennige. **—iour**, *s.* der Retter; der Erlöser, Heiland (*Theol.*). *Comp.* **—e-all**, *s.* der Lichtsparer. **—ings-bank**, I. *s.* die Sparkasse. II. *attrib.;* —ings-bank book, das Sparkassenbuch.

Savoir—faire, *s.* die Geschicklichkeit, Gewandtheit. **—vivre**, *s.* die Lebensart.

Savour, I. *s.* der Geschmack; (smell) der Geruch, Duft. II. *v.n.* schmecken, riechen (of, nach); to — of, riechen nach; einen Anstrich haben von, aussehen wie (*fig.*). III. *v.a.;* thou —est not the things that be of God, du meinest nicht, was göttlich ist (*B.*). **—iness**, *s.* die Schmackhaftigkeit; der Wohlgeruch. **—less**, *adj.* geschmacklos. **—y**, I. *adj.* schmackhaft, duftend (*also fig.*). II. *s.* (*also plur.* —ies) eine Schüssel appetitreizender Kleinigkeiten gegen Ende eines Diners.

Savoy, *s.* der Savoyer Kohl, Wirsingkohl.

[1]**Saw**, *imperf. of* See.

[2]**Saw**, *s.* der Spruch, das Sprichwort.

[3]**Saw**, I. *s.* die Säge. II. *v.a.* sägen; to — **down** a tree, einen Baum umsägen; to — **off**, absägen; to — **out**, ausstückeln; to — **through**, durchsägen; to — **up**, ansägen, zurichten. **—ed**, **—n**, *p.p. of* —. **—yer**, *s.* der (Holz-, Brett-)Säger. *Comp.* **—dust**, *s.* die Sägespäne (*pl.*). **—fish**, *s.* der Sägefisch. **—ing-jack**, *s.* der Sägebock. **—mill**, *s.* die Sägemühle. **—pit**, *s.* die Sägegrube.

Saxifrage, *s.* der Steinbrech (*Bot.*).

Saxophon—e, *s.* klarinettartiges Blechinstrument. **—ist**, *s.* der Saxophonbläser.

[1]**Say**, I. *ir.v.a.* sagen; hersagen (*one's lesson*); (tell) erzählen, berichten; I am sorry to —, es tut mir leid, sagen zu müssen; to — mass, die Messe lesen; — that . . ., angenommen, gesetzt (daß) . . .; I — ! Du! hör' mal! (*in calling to a p.*); na aber! potztausend! (*expressing astonishment*); that is —ing a great deal, das ist viel gesagt, das will viel sagen; that is to —, das ist, das heißt; I will have nothing to — to him, ich will nichts mit ihm zu tun, zu schaffen haben; what have you to — for yourself? was kannst du zu deiner Rechtfertigung sagen? does that mean to say . . .? soll das heißen *or* bedeutet das, daß . . .? do you — so? ist das wirklich Ihre Meinung? ist das Ihr Ernst? you don't — so! was Sie (nicht) sagen! das wäre! — the word! schlag ein! there were — 100 men present, es waren etwa 100 Mann anwesend; to — nay, verweigern, abschlagen; . . . to — nothing of her beauty, . . . ihrer Schönheit ganz zu geschweigen; never — die! nur nicht verzagt! II. *s.* das, was man zu sagen hat; der Ausspruch; let him have his —, laß ihn auch mitsprechen, seine Meinung äußern, sich aussprechen. **—ing**, *s.* die Rede; die Redensart; das Gerede; *see* Saw; as the —ing is, wie man zu sagen pflegt; that goes without —ing, das versteht sich von selbst.

[2]**Say**, *s.* die Probe, das Muster (*obs.*).

Scab, *s.* die Kruste, der Grind (*Med.*); der Schorf (*in wounds*); die Räude (*in sheep, etc.*). **—bed**, **—by**, *adj.* schäbig, grindig; räudig. **—biness**, *s.* das Grindige; die Räudigkeit. **—ious**, I. *adj.* krätzig, räudig; (leprous) aussätzig. II. *s.* der Sternkopf, die Skabiose (*Bot.*). **—rous**, *adj.* holperig. **—wort**, *s.* der Garten-Alant.

Scabbard, I. *s.* die (Degen-)Scheide, (Säbel-Scheide. II. *v.a.* in die Scheide stecken.

Scaffold, I. *s.* das Gerüst, Baugerüst; das Blutgerüst, Schafott; (stand) die Bühne, das Gestell, Gerüst; to erect a —, ein Gerüst aufschlagen (*Build.*). II. *v.n.* ein Gerüst errichten. **—ing**, *s.* das (Bau-)Gerüst; (materials) das Rüstzeug. *Comp.* **—ing-pole**, *s.* die Rüststange.

Scal—able, *adj.* ersteigbar. —e, *etc.*, *see* [1]Scale.

[1]**Scald**, I. *s.* die Brandwunde. II. *v.a.* (durch heißes Wasser 2c.) verbrennen *or* verbrühen; (ab)brühen (*vegetables, clothes, etc.*); — not your lips with other folks' broth, was dich nicht brennt, das blase nicht (*prov.*). **—ing**, I. *adj.* brühend; —ing hot, brühheiß. II. *s.* das Brühen; das Verbrennen; letzte Bäuche (*in washing*).

[2]**Scald**, *s.* der Schorf, Grind.

[3]**Scald**, *s.* der Skalde, Barde. **—ic**, *adj.* skaldisch; —ic poetry, die Skaldendichtung.

[1]**Scale**, I. *s.* die Schale, Hülse; die Schale (*of a*

knife); (splinter) das Blättchen, der Splitter; die Schuppe (*of fish, serpents, etc.*); (scurf) die Schuppe; —es of iron, der Hammerschlag; (boiler) —e, der Kesselstein. II. *v.a.* (ab)schuppen (*fishes, etc.*); (—e off, pare) abschälen, ablösen, abschaben, abschiefern; ausbrennen, abblasen (*guns*); streuen (*manure*). III. *v.n.* sich schuppen, sich schilfern, sich abblättern. **—ed**, *adj.* schuppig. **—eless**, *adj.* schuppenlos. **—iness**, *s.* das Schuppige, Blätterige. **—ing**, *s.* das Abschuppen; das Glühen der Blechtafeln (*Metall.*). **—y**, *adj.* schuppig; (—e-like) schuppicht, Schuppen= (*armour, etc.*). *Comp.* **—y-lizard**, *s.* das Schuppentier.

[2]**Scale**, I. *s.* die Wagschale; (*usually pl.* —s *or* pair of —s) die Wage; die Wage (*Astron.*); to turn the —s, den Ausschlag geben; to put in the — against, abwägen gegen. II. *v.a.* abwägen; abmessen, vergleichen (mit); (weigh) wiegen. *Comp.* **—beam**, *s.* der Wagebalken. **—sugar**, *s.* der Zucker zum Auswägen.

[3]**Scal—e**, I. *s.* die Leiter (*rare*); (series) die Stufenfolge, Abstufung; die Tonleiter (*Mus.*); der Maßstab, die Skala (*Geom., Surv., etc.*); der Zollstock (*Build.*); das Maß, der Maßstab (*fig.*); das Kolumnenmaß (*Typ.*); diatonic (descending) —e, diatonische (absteigende) Tonleiter; —e of notation, arithmetische Reihe, Progression; reduced (enlarged) —e, verjüngter (vergrößerter) Maßstab; plain —e, natürliche Größe (*Draw.*); on a large —e, im Großen, auf großem Fuße; to play —es, Tonleitern spielen. II. *v.a.* ersteigen, erklettern; stürmen (*Mil.*). III. *v.n.* *see* Ascend. **—ing**, *adj.* ersteigend. *Comp.* **—ing-ladder**, *s.* die Sturmleiter.

Scalene, I. *adj.* ungleichseitig. II. *s.* das ungleichseitige Dreieck.

Scall, I. *s.* der Grind. **—ed**, *adj.* grindig, schorfig; schäbig (*fig.*). **—op**, I. *s.* der Ausschnitt, Wellenschnitt (*on papers, etc.*); rund ausgeschnittene Zacke (*on dresses*); die Kammuschel; die Guirlande (*postage stamps*); kleine flache Pfanne *or* Schüssel (*Cook.*). II. *v.a.* auszacken, kerben; in der Schale, mit Butter, Brosamen 2c. zubereiten (*oysters*).

Scallion, *s.* die Schalotte.

Scalp, I. *s.* (skull) die Hirnschale; die Schädelhaube, Hirnschalenhaut (*Anat.*); der Skalp. II. *v.a.* abhäuten, skalpieren. *Comp.* **—ing-knife**, *s.* das Skalpiermesser.

Scalpel, *s.* das Skalpell.

Scambler, *s.* der Schmarotzer (*obs.*).

Scammony, *s.* die Purgierwinde; das Skammonium (*Pharm.*).

Scamp, I. *s.* der Schuft, Schurke; der Taugenichts, Tunichtgut, Lump. II. *v.n.* oberflächlich ausführen, liederlich arbeiten; pfuschen. **—er**, *s.* der schwindelhafte Arbeiter, Pfuscher. **—ish**, *adj.*, **—ishly**, *adv.* schurkisch.

[1]**Scamper**, *see* Scamp.

[2]**Scamper**, I. *v.n.*; to —er **about**, sich umhertummeln; to — **away**, **off**, ausreißen, davon laufen. II. *s.* der Lauf, das Laufen; to go for a —, ausgehen, um sich zu tummeln.

Scan, *v.* I. *a.* skandieren (*verses*); forschen; *see* Scrutinize. II. *n.* sich skandieren lassen. **—sion**, *s.* das Skandieren. **—sores**, *pl.* Klettervögel. **—sorial**, *adj.* Kletter=.

Scandal, *s.* (offence) der Anstoß, das öffentliche Ärgernis; die Verleumdung, Lästerung; (shame) die Unehre, Schmach; School for —, die Lästerschule; to cause —, Ärgernis geben; to bring — upon, Schande bringen über (*acc.*). **—ize**, *v.a.* ärgern, Ärgernis, Anstoß geben; to be —ized at *or* by, sich über (eine S.) ärgern, an (einer S.) Anstoß nehmen. **—ous**, *adj.*, **—ously**, *adv.* anstößig, ärgerlich; (shameful) schimpflich, entehrend, schändlich; (defamatory) verleumderisch. **—ousness**, *s.* die Anstößigkeit, das Skandalöse; die Niederträchtigkeit, Schändlichkeit. *Comp.* **—monger**, *s.* der (die) Verleumder(in), das Lästermaul, die Klatschbase.

Scant, I. *adj.*, **—ily**, *adv.* knapp, kärglich, ungenügend; Mangel leidend (of, an); schral(end), (of wind, *Naut.*); (stingy) karg. II. *v.a.* einschränken, knapphalten, verkürzen. **—iness**, *s.* die Knappheit; (insufficiency) die Beschränktheit, Unzulänglichkeit. **—ness**, *s.* die Knappheit, Enge. **—y**, *adj.* knapp; (narrow) enge; mager, arm, dürftig (of, an, *dat.*); (insufficient) unzureichend.

Scantle, I. *v.a.* beschränken; zerstückeln, zuschneiden. II. *v.n.* knapp werden, mangeln. III. *s.* das Schieferdeckermaß.

Scantling, *s.* das kleine Stück (*rare*); das Maß (*Carp.*); das Faßgestell (*for casks*); die Materialstärke (*Shipb.*); (sketch) der Riß. **—s**, *pl.* die kleineren Verbandstücke (*Carp.*).

[1]**Scape**, *s.* & *v.a.* *see* Escape. **—ment**, *see* Escapement. *Comp.* **—goat**, *s.* der Sündenbock. **—grace**, *s.* der Taugenichts, Tunichtgut.

[2]**Scape**, *s.* der Säulenschaft; der Schaft, Stiel (*Bot.*). **—less**, *adj.* schaftlos, stiellos.

Scaphoid, *adj.* kahnförmig; — bone, das Kahnbein.

Scapula, *s.* das Schulterblatt. **—r(y)**, I. *adj.* Schulterblatt=. II. *s.* das Skapulier (*Eccl.*).

[1]**Scar**, I. *s.* die Schramme, Narbe, Scharte; die Narbe (*Bot.*); der Schandfleck (*fig.*). II. *v.a.* schrammen; ritzen. III. *v.n.* vernarben. **—red**, *adj.* genarbt, narbig.

[2]**Scar**, *s.* der steile Abhang, die Klippe.

Scarab, *s.* der Käfer; *see* —ee; die Skarabäen=Gemme. **—ee**, *s.* der Skarabäuskäfer.

Scaramouch, *s.* der Hanswurst; der Bramarbas (*fig.*).

Scarc—e, I. *adj.* selten, rar; money is —e, das Geld ist knapp; to be —e of money, schlecht bei Kasse sein (*fam.*); to make o.s. —e, sich rar machen; sich wegstehlen, davonlaufen. II. *adv.* **—ely**, *adv.* kaum; (hardly) schwerlich. **—eness**, **—ity**, *s.* (want) der Mangel; die Spärlichkeit, Seltenheit.

Scare, I. *v.a.* (— away) (ver)scheuchen; (alarm) erschrecken; to — away, wegscheuchen. II. *s.* der Schrecken, die Panik. *Comp.* **—crow**, *s.* die Vogelscheuche (*also fig.*); das Schreckbild, der Popanz.

[1]**Scarf**, I. *s.* (sash) die Schärpe, Binde; die Halsbinde. II. *attrib.*; — pin, die Schlipsnadel.

[2]**Scarf**, I. *s.* (— joint) schräges Blatt. II. *v.a.* zusammenblatten (*Carp.*); splissen (*Shipb.*).

Scarif—ication, *s.* das Schröpfen. **—icator**, *s.* das Schröpfeisen, der Schröpfschnäpper. **—ier**, *s.* der Schröpfer; der Skarifikator (*Agr.*). **—y**, *v.a.* schröpfen, skarifizieren.

Scarl—atina, *s.* das Scharlachfieber. **—et**, I. *adj.* scharlachrot; —let hat, der Kardinalshut. II. *s.* der Scharlach. *Comp.* **—et-day**, *s.* der Festtag, an dem die Doktoren der Universität Scharlachtalare tragen (*Oxf., Cambr.*). **—et-fever**, *see* —atina. **—et-runner**, *s.* die Feuer=, Scharlach=bohne, türkische Bohne.

Scarp, I. *s.* die Böschung, Abdachung; die Eskarpe. II. *v.a.* (ab)böschen, abdachen.

Scath(e), I. *s.* der Schade(n), Nachteil. II. *v.a.* beschädigen. **—ing**, *adj.* verletzend, scharf. **—less**, *adj.* unbeschädigt; harmlos.

Scatter, *v.* I. *a.* ausstreuen, verbreiten (*seed, etc.*); (dispel) zerstreuen; (— about) umherstreuen. II. *n.* sich zerstreuen. **—ed**, *adj.* zerstreut (*as one's senses, etc.*); zerstreut liegend (*as houses, etc.*). **—ing**, *s.* das Zerstreuen. *Comp.* **—brain**, *s.* der Windbeutel, Spatzenkopf (*fam.*). **—brained**, *adj.* leichtsinnig, flatterhaft.

Scaup, *s.* die Reiherente.

Scaur, *see* [2]Scar.

Scavenger, *s.* der Straßenkehrer.

Scen—e, *s.* die Szene; der Auftritt, die Szene (*in a play*); *see* Landscape; (place where something occurs) der Schauplatz; (stage) die (Schau=)

bühne; (play) das Stück, die Bühnenhandlung; —es, die Szenerie, Kulissen; behind the —es, hinter den Kulissen (*lit. & fig.*); drop —e, Schlußszene; the —e closes, der Vorhang fällt; the —e lies, das Stück spielt; sylvan —e, Waldszene; I had a nice —e with her, ich hatte eine nette Szene mit ihr; to appear on the —e, auftreten (*of an actor*); plötzlich erscheinen. **—ery**, *s.* die Landschaft, Gegend; das Gemälde; die Szenerie, Dekoration (*Theat.*); woodland —ery, die Waldlandschaft. **—ic(al)**, *adj.* theatralisch, dramatisch, Bühnen=. **—ographic**, *adj.* perspektivisch. **—ography**, *s.* perspektivische Abbildung eines Körpers, die Perspektivmalerei. *Comp.* **—e-painter**, *s.* der Dekorationsmaler. **—e-painting**, *s.* die Dekorationsmalerei. **—e-shifter**, *s.* der Koulissenrücker, Maschinist.

Scent, I. *s.* (power of —) der Geruch; (smell) der Duft, Geruch; (perfume) die Parfümerie, der Wohlgeruch; die Witterung, Fährte (*Sport.*); (track) die Spur; on *or* upon the —, auf der Fährte *or* Spur; a dog of quick —, ein guter Spürhund; to put a p. on the wrong —, throw s.o. off the —, (einen) auf falsche Spur bringen, von der Spur abbringen; to get — of, Wind bekommen von. II. *v.a.* riechen; wittern; parfümieren, durchdüften. **—ed**, *adj.* wohlriechend, duftend; —ed soap, parfümierte Seife. **—less**, *adj.* geruchlos. *Comp.* **—-bottle**, *s.* das Riechfläschchen.

Sceptic, *s.* der Zweifler, Skeptiker. **—al**, *adj.*, **—ally**, *adv.* zweifelnd, skeptisch. **—ism**, *s.* die Zweifelsucht, der Skeptizismus.

Sceptre, *s.* das Zepter, Szepter; königliche Macht (*fig.*). **—d**, *adj.* mit einem Zepter, Szepter (versehen), bezeptert. **—less**, *adj.* ohne Zepter (Szepter), zepterlos.

Schedule, I. *s.* der Zettel, die Liste, das Verzeichnis; der Zusatzzettel, die Zusatzurkunde. II. *v.a.* aufzeichnen; inventieren.

Schem—atic, *adj.* schematisch. **—e**, I. *s.* (system) das System, Schema; die Gestalt, Form (*of things*); (plan) der Entwurf, Plan; die Figur (*Astr.*); to form a —e, einen Plan machen, entwerfen; some —e is afloat, etwas ist im Werke. II. *v.n.* Pläne machen *or* schmieden; Ränke schmieden. **—er**, *s.* der Planmacher, Projektmacher; (plotter) der Pläneschmied, Ränkemacher, Intrigant. **—ing**, *adj.* Pläne machend; intrigant.

Schism, *s.* die (Kirchen)spaltung, das Schisma. **—a**, *s.* kleines Intervall (*Mus.*). **—atic**, I. *adj.* schismatisch. II. *s.* der Schismatiker.

Schist, *s.* der Schiefer, Schist. **—ose, —ous**, *adj.* schieferig.

Scholar, *s.* der (die) Schüler(in); (learned man) der studierte Mann, Gelehrte; (learner) der fleißig Lernende; der Stipendiat (*Univ.*); she is an excellent German —, sie ist im Deutschen vortrefflich beschlagen; he is a classical —, er ist ein (gründlicher) Kenner der klassischen Sprachen; she is a mathematical —, sie hat Mathematik gründlich studiert; ihr Fach ist die Mathematik; to be bred a —, studiert haben; eine gelehrte Erziehung genossen haben. **—ly**, *adj.* wie ein Gelehrter; gelehrt (*as education*); —ly edition, gelehrte, gründliche Ausgabe. **—ship**, *s.* die Gelehrsamkeit; das Stipendium; classical —ship, die Vertrautheit mit den alten Sprachen und Fertigkeit in ihrem schriftlichem Gebrauch; entrance —ship, ein beim Eintritt in die Schule oder ein College auf Grund einer guten Aufnahmeprüfung verliehenes Stipendium; leaving —ship, ein durch gute Schlußprüfung beim verlassen einer höheren Schule erworbenes Stipendium; travelling —ship, das Reisestipendium.

Scholastic, I. *adj.*, **—al**, *adj.*, **—ally**, *adv.* schulmäßig, gelehrt, scholastisch, Schul=; (like a school) Schul=; — agency, die Schulagentur; — divinity, scholastische Theologie; — institution, die Schulanstalt; — learning, die Schulgelehrsamkeit; — philosophy, die Scholastik; the — profession, der Lehr(er)stand, Lehrberuf, das Schulamt; to enter the — profession, Lehrer werden; a — vacancy, eine freie Lehrerstelle; the — world, die Schulwelt, Lehrerwelt, der Lehrstand. II. *s.* der Scholastiker, Schulgelehrte. **—ism**, *s.* die Scholastik.

Scholi—ast, *s.* der Scholiast. **—um**, *s.* die Erklärung, Scholie.

School, I. *s.* die Schule (*also fig.*); die Lehre; die Sekte; (—-house) die Schule, das Schulgebäude; (instruction) der Unterricht; der höhere Unterrichtskursus an der Universität Oxford; the —s, die Hörsäle (*obs.*); die höchsten Universitätsprüfungen (*Oxf.*); to send to —, in die Schule schicken; to keep —, Schule halten; — of theology, theologische Schule; board —, die Volksschule; endowed —, die Stiftungsschule, Stiftsschule; girls' —, die Töchterschule; grammar —, die Lateinschule, Gelehrtenschule, höhere (Knaben)Schule; high —, die höhere Schule; high — for girls, höhere Töchterschule; non provided —, staatlich nicht unterstützte Schule; primary —, die Volksschule, Elementarschule; public —, *see* Public; Sunday —, die Kinderlehre; die Bibelschule; — of mines, die Bergakademie; — of Modern Languages (at Oxford), das höhere wissenschaftliche (zu einem Universitätsgrad führende) Studium der Neueren Sprachen (an der Universität Oxford). II. *v.a.* schulen, unterrichten, in (die) Zucht nehmen; Verweise geben (*fig.*); —ed by adversity, in der Schule der Trübsal erzogen. **—ing**, *s.* der Schulunterricht; (— money) das Schulgeld; das Zureiten (*of horses*). *Comp.* **—-board**, *see* Board. **—-boy**, *s.* der Schulknabe, Schuljunge. **—-days**, *pl.* die Schulzeit, die Schuljahre. **—-divinity**, *s.* scholastische Theologie. **—-fellow**, *s.* der Schulgenosse, Mitschüler; we were —-fellows, wir waren zusammen auf der Schule, wir besuchten dieselbe Schule. **—-girl**, *s.* das Schulmädchen. **—-house**, *s.* das Schulgebäude. **—-magazine**, *s.* die Schulzeitung (von Schülern verfaßt). **—man**, *s.* der Scholastiker. **—-manager**, *s.* der Volksschuldirektor. **—master**, *s.* der Schulmeister, Lehrer. **—mate**, *s.* der (die) Mitschüler(in). **—mistress**, *s.* die Schullehrerin. **—-room**, *s.* das Klassenzimmer, Schulzimmer, die Klasse. **—-time**, *s.* die Schulzeit. **—-treat**, *s.* das Schulfest.

Schooner, *s.* der Schoner.

Schorl, *s.* der Schörl.

Sciagraphy, *s.* die Schattenriß=Zeichenkunst.

Sciatic, *adj.* Hüft=. **—a**, *s.* das Hüftweh, die Ischias.

Scien—ce, I. *s.* die Wissenschaft, Kunde, Lehre; (natural —ce) die Naturwissenschaft(en); (knowledge) das Wissen, die Kenntnis; man of —ce, der Gelehrte; doctor of —ce, der Doktor der Naturwissenschaften; moral —ce, die Ethik, Moralphilosophie; natural —ce, die Naturwissenschaften; —ce of economics, die Volkswirtschaftslehre; —ce of medicine, die Heilkunde, medizinische Wissenschaft, Medizin. II. *attrib.*; —ce reader, das Handbuch der Naturwissenschaften, naturwissenschaftliches Elementarbuch. **—tial**, *adj.* wissenschaftlich. **—tific**, *adj.*, **—tifically**, *adv.* wissenschaftlich, gelehrt; naturwissenschaftlich; work of a —tific character, das Werk von wissenschaftlichem Gepräge; a primer of —tific German, ein Elementarbuch der deutschen naturwissenschaftlichem Sprache. **—tist**, *s.* der Gelehrte, Forscher; der Naturwissenschaftler.

Scimitar, *s.* krummer türkischer Säbel.

Scintilla—nt, *adj.* Funken sprühend, funkelnd. **—te**, *v.n.* funkeln; Funken sprühen. **—tion**, *s.* das Funkeln; das Funkensprühen.

Sciolis—m, *s.* die Halbwisserei. **—t**, *s.* der Halbwisser.

Scio—machy, —graphy, *s.* der Scheinkampf mit dem eignen Schatten, die Spiegelfechterei

Scion, *s.* der Ableger; der Sprößling, Sproß (*fig.*).

Scioptic, *adj.;* — ball, die Schattenspielkugel, stellbare Linse der camera obscura.

Scirrhous, *adj.* verhärtet, skirrhös.

Sciss—ion, *s.* das Zerspalten, der Schnitt. **—ors**, *pl.* (pair of —ors) die Schere. *Comp.* **—ors-case**, *s.* das Scherenfutteral. **—ors-grinder**, *s.* der Scherenschleifer.

Sclero—sis, *s.* die (Zellen)Verhärtung (*Med.*). **—tic**, I. *adj.* hart. II. *s.* (—tic membrane, —tic coat) harte *or* weiße Augenhaut.

Scoff, I. *s.* der Spott, Hohn. II. *v.n.* (— at) (ver=) spotten; (scorn) (ver)höhnen. **—er**, *s.* der Spötter. **—ing**, *adj.*, **—ingly**, *adv.* spöttisch, höhnisch.

Scold, I. *v.a. & n.* (aus)schelten. II. *s.* die Zänkerin, das böse Weib. **—er**, *s.* der Schelter. **—ing**, I. *adj.*, **—ingly**, *adv.* scheltend; (railing) zänkisch. II. *s.* das Schelten; to give a p. a good —ing, einen tüchtig ausschelten.

Scollop, *see* Scallop.

[1]**Sconce**, I. *s.* die Verschanzung; die Schutzwehr (*fig.*); der Kopfschutz, Helm; der Kopf, Schädel; der Verstand, die Grütze (*obs.*); die Geldstrafe (per Kopf). II. *v.a.* verschanzen; per Kopf besteuern.

[2]**Sconce**, *s.* die Blendlaterne; die Laterne; die Röhre eines Leuchters; der Wandleuchter.

Scone, *s.* der weiche Hafer= *or* Weizen=mehlkuchen.

Scoop, I. *s.* die Schippe, Schöpfkelle, Schaufel; (boat's —) das Öhrfaß; der Spatel (*Surg.*). II. *v.a.* ausschöpfen, ausschaufeln; (— out) aushöhlen; (— up) zusammenscharren. *Comp.* **—-net**, *s.* das Streichnetz.

Scope, *s.* (view) der Gesichtskreis, die Ausdehnung; (end) das Ziel, der (End=)Zweck, die Absicht; (play) der (Spiel=)Raum, die Freiheit; full, free —, freier Spielraum; to have more —, mehr Spielraum haben, freier handeln können.

Scorbutic, *adj.* skorbutisch.

Scorch, *v.* I. *a.* sengen, brennen, dörren. II. *n.* (aus)dörren; dahinrasen (*Cycl. sl.*). **—er**, *s.* der Sengende; to-day was a —er, heute war ein sehr heißer Tag; der schnell Fahrende (*Cycl.*); der Draufgänger. **—ing**, *adj.* sengend.

Score, I. *s.* (notch) die Kerbe, der Einschnitt; (20) zwanzig (Stück); (account) die Rechnung, Zeche; die Rechnung (*Cards, Tennis, etc.*); der Grund, die Ursache (*fig.*); die Partitur (*Mus.*); —s, viele; three —, sechzig; four —, achtzig; to run up —s, Schulden machen; to quit —s, völlig bezahlen, *see* Quit; upon the — of, wegen; upon what —? aus welchem Grunde? she will put that down to my —, sie wird das auf meine Rechnung schreiben; what's the —? wie steht das Spiel, wie steht's? (*Cards, Tennis, etc.*). II. *v.a.* (ein)kerben, einschneiden, furchen; (record) anschreiben; anlegen (*at whist, etc.*), anschreiben, markieren (*at games*); (set down to) auf (die) Rechnung setzen, aufschreiben, ansetzen, anrechnen; (attribute) beimessen, zuschreiben; in Partitur bringen (*Mus.*); to — a success *or* victory, einen Erfolg davontragen; to — a goal, ein Tor gewinnen *or* zählen (*Footb.*); to — **out**, ausstreichen; to — **up**, anschreiben, bezeichnen. III. *v.n.* zahlen, mitgerechnet *or* angeschrieben werden; machen, gewinnen (*at games*); (make a hit) richtig treffen; that —s for me, das zählt zu meinen Gunsten; he —d heavily, er hat viel gemacht *or* gewonnen.

Scori—a, *s.* die Schlacke (*of metal*). **—aceous**, *adj.* schlackig; Schlacken= (lava, =lava). **—fy**, *v.a.* zu Schlacken machen.

Scorn, I. *s.* die Verachtung; (derision) der Spott, Hohn; to laugh to —, verlachen; to treat with —, verächtlich behandeln. II. *v.a.* verachten, verschmähen; I should — to . . ., ich würde es verschmähen, zu . . . **—er**, *s.* der Spötter; der Verächter, Verschmäher. **—ful**, *adj.*, **—fully**, *adv.* verächtlich, verachtend; (insolent) übermütig; —ful of, (eine Sache) nicht achtend, (einer S.) trotzend *or* zum Trotz. **—fulness**, *s.* das Verächtliche, Übermütige; der Übermut.

Scorpion, *s.* der Skorpion; (whip) die Skorpiongeißel. *Comp.* **—-fly**, *s.* die Skorpionsfliege.

[1]**Scot**, *s.* der Schoß, die Steuer; — and lot, ordentliche Gemeindeabgaben; to pay — and lot, alles auf Heller und Pfennig bezahlen. *Comp.* **—-free**, *adj.* schoß=, steuer=frei; (safe) unverletzt, sicher.

[2]**Scot**, *see* Proper Names.

[1]**Scotch**, I. *s.* der Einschnitt, die Kerbe; eingegrabene Linie, Ritze, Furche (*in the ground*). II. *v.a.* ein=schneiden, =kerben; (notch) zacken; leicht verwunden (*a snake*). *Comp.* **—ed-, —-collops**, *pl.* geschmorte Fleischschnitten. **—-hop**, *s.* das Hüpfespiel.

[2]**Scotch**, I. *v.a.* keilhemmen, aufhalten (*a wheel*). II. *s.* der Unterleg=, Hemm=keil.

Scotia, *s.* die Skotie (*Arch.*).

Scoundrel, *s.* der Schuft, Schurke. **—ly**, *adj.* schurkisch. **—ism**, *s.* die Schuftigkeit.

[1]**Scour**, *v.* I. *a.* scheuern, putzen, blank machen; (clean) säubern, reinigen; waschen, entfetten (*wool*); kochen, entschälen (*silk*); schrubben, scheuern (*the deck*); schnell dahinfahren, fegen (*the sea, etc.*), durchstreifen (*the country*). II. *n.* scheuern. **—er**, *s.* der Scheuerer, Feger, Reiniger. **—ing**, *s.* das Scheuern; das Ausschwemmen (*Hydr.*).

[2]**Scour**, *v.* I. *n.* schnell laufen, rennen, fliegen, fahren; to — along, streifen längs (einer Küste); to — about, umher streifen. II. *a.* durchstreifen, über (*acc.*) hinstreifen; —ing party, die Streifpartie. **—er**, *s.* der Umherstreifer, Renner.

Scourge, I. *v.a.* peitschen, geißeln; züchtigen, plagen (*fig.*). II. *s.* die Peitsche, Geißel; die Plage (*fig.*). **—r**, *s.* der Geißler; der Geißelbruder (*Rel.*).

[1]**Scout**, I. *s.* der Späher, Kundschafter; (lookout) die Lauer, Warte; der Stiefelfuchs, Aufwärter (*Oxford Univ. sl.; see* Gyp); *see* Fielder (*Cricket*); der Spähkreuzer (*Naut.*). II. *v.n.* spähen, auskundschaften; durch Plänkler absuchen, rekognoszieren (*Mil.*); —ing party, das Streifkorps.

[2]**Scout**, *v.a.* spotten, sticheln auf (einen), verächtlich abweisen.

Scow, *s.* das Fährboot, Lichterschiff.

Scowl, I. *v.n.* die Stirne runzeln, finster blicken; to — at a p., einen finster ansehen. II. *s.* der finstere Blick. **—ing**, *adj.*, **—ingly**, *adv.* finster; mürrisch.

Scrabble, *v.* I. *n.* kritzeln; krabbeln, sich balgen. II. *a.* bekritzeln; zusammenscharren.

Scrag, *s.* eingeschrumpfte, hagere Person, das Gerippe (*vulg.*); etwas Dürres, Dünnes, Höckeriges; — (end) of mutton, der Hammelhals. **—giness**, *s.* das Hagere, Höckerige. **—gy**, *adj.* schrundig, hager, rauh.

Scrambl—e, I. *s.* das Klettern; das begierige Greifen (for, nach); das Gereiße, Grapsen, die Balgerei (for, um). II. *v.n.* grapsen, sich reißen um; (climb) klettern. III. *v.a.;* to —e eggs, Rühreier machen; —ed eggs, Rühreier. **—er**, *s.* der sich Balgende, Haschende, der Aufraffende; der Kletterer. **—ing**, *adj.*, **—ingly**, *adv.* unordentlich, hastig, aufs Geratewohl.

Scrap, *s.* das Stückchen, Bruchstück; (cutting) das Exzerpt; das Bild, der Ausschnitt; — of paper, der Papierschnitzel. **—e**, *see* Scrap—e. **—py**, *adj.* bruchstückartig, zusammengestoppelt; —py bits, Brocken. **—s**, *pl.* Brocken (*of French, etc.*); Bruchstücke (*of poetry*); die (Fett=)Griebe (*Cook.*). *Comp.* **—-book**, *s.* das Sammelbuch, Einklebebuch. **—-iron**, *s.* das Abfall=, Ramaß=, Alt=eisen.

Scrap—e, I. *s.* das Scharren, Kratzen; (bow, *etc.*) der Kratzfuß; die Not, Klemme, Patsche (*fig.*); to get into a —e, in die Klemme geraten. II. *v.a.* schrapen, schaben, scharren, kratzen; kratzen, schlecht geigen; to bow and —e, dienern und Kratzfüße machen; to —e **off**, abschaben, abkratzen; to —e **together**, to —e **up**, zusammenscharren, aufsammeln, ersparen; to —e acquaintance **with** (a p.), mit (einem) Bekanntschaft suchen, sich bei (einem) einzuschmeicheln suchen. III. *v.n.* scharren; kratzen (*on the violin*); einen Kratzfuß machen. **—er**, *s.* der Scharrende, Kratzende rc.; (miser) der Geizhals; der schlechte Geiger; (door—er) der (Fuß-)Abstreicher; das Kratz-, Schabeisen (*Engr.*); der Schraper (*Naut.*); das Schabeisen (*Metall.*). **—ing**, *s.* (act of —ing) das Scharren; das Schabsel. **—ings**, *pl.* das Gekrätz, die Krätze; das mühsam Ersparte (*fig.*).

Scratch, I. *s.* der Ritz; die Schramme, Ritze, der Ritz (*of the skin, etc.*); leichte Wunde (*fig.*); der Pfannenstein, das Bodensalz (*of sea water*); der Strich durch den Ring (*for boxers*); die Normalklasse, Klasse 0 (*Tennis*); die Mauke (*Vet.*); to come up to the —, beim Treffen erscheinen, seinen Mann stehen. II. *adj.* dem Zufall nach zusammen gebracht (*as a team in cricket, etc.*). III. *v.a.* (zer)kratzen, ritzen; leicht verwunden; scharren, kratzen (*holes, etc.*); (write) kratzen, kritzeln; to — out, streichen, ausstreichen (*a name, etc.*); auskratzen, ausradieren; to — a p.'s eyes out, einem die Augen auskratzen (*fig.*). IV. *v.n.* kratzen. **—er**, *s.* der Kratzer, Schaber; der Scharrvogel (*as a hen*). *Comp.* **—-race**, *s.* der Wettlauf, der keinem einen Vorsprung giebt; *see* — II. **—-work**, *s.* die Sgraffitomalerei.

Scrawl, I. *v.a. & n.* kritzeln, schmieren. II. *s.* das Gekritzel, Geschmiere. **—er**, *s.* der Kritzler.

Screak, *v.n. see* Screech; *see* Creak.

Scream, I. *s.* der grelle, laute Schrei, Angstschrei. II. *v.n.* schreien; kreischen; to — out, aufschreien. III. *v.a.* schreien. **—er**, *s.* der Schreier, Schreiende; das Straußhuhn. **—ing**, *adj.* kreischend; schallendes Gelächter erregend (*sl.*); a —ing farce, eine tolle Posse, ein Stück zum Totlachen.

Scree, *s.* das Geröll.

Screech, *see* Scream I., II. & III.; pfeifen (*of engines*). *Comp.* **—-owl**, *s.* die Baumeule, Knarreule; das Käuzchen.

Screed, I. *s.* (scrap) der lange Streifen; der Mörtelstreifen; die lange Rede, Tirade (*coll.*). II. *v.a. & n.* reißen (*prov.*).

Screen, I. *s.* der Schirm; der Feuer-, Ofen-, Windschirm; (folding —, Japanese —) die spanische Wand; die Schranke, Kanzelle (*Arch.*); (riddle) das Sieb. II. *v.a.* (be)schirmen, (be)schützen, decken; durchsieben (*corn, etc.*); separieren (*Min.*); to — from, verwahren vor; to — from justice, der Gerechtigkeit entziehen.

Screw, I. *s.* die Schraube; (niggard) der Geizhals; die Pfennigdüte (of tobacco, Tabak); (pressure) der Druck; der Gehalt, Lohn (*sl.*); there is a — loose somewhere, es muß irgendwo eine Schraube los sein, es ist nicht ganz richtig; he has a — loose, er hat einen Sparren zu viel (*fam.*); male, female, perpetual —, die Patrize *or* Schraubenspindel, Schraubenmutter, endlose Schraube; Archimedean —, *see* —-propeller. II. *v.a.* schrauben; (— in) einschrauben; drücken, schrauben (*fig.*); to — **down**, to — **tight**, zu-, fest-schrauben; to — **out**, ausschrauben; to — out of s.o., aus einem herauspressen; to — one's face **up**, sein Gesicht verziehen; to — up one's courage, Mut *or* sich (*dat.*) ein Herz fassen. *Comp.* **—-compasses**, *pl.* der Schraubenzirkel. **—-driver**, *s.* der Schraubenzieher. **—-nail**, *s.* der Schraubennagel. **—-nut**, *s.* die Schraubenmutter. **—-propeller**, *s.* die Schraube (*Naut.*); die Wasserschraube. **—-steamer**, *s.* das Schraubendampfer. **—-vice**, *s.* der Schraubstock. **—-wrench**, *s.* der Schraubenschlüssel.

Scribbl—e, I. *v.a. & n.* kritzeln, schmieren; to —e over, überkritzeln. II. *s.* das Gekritzel, Geschmiere. **—er**, *s.* der Schmierer (*also fig.*). **—ing**, I. *adj.* kritzelnd. II. *s.* das Schmieren, die Kritzelei, Schmiererei.

Scribe, *s.* der Schreiber; der Schriftgelehrte (*B.*).

Scrimmage, *s.* der Aufruhr, das Getümmel, der Krawall; das Handgemenge; der Nahkampf im Fußballspiel.

Scrimp, I. *v.a.* knapp halten; knapp messen, knausern mit. II. *v.n.* knausern. III. *adj.* knapp. IV. *s.* der Knauser.

[1]**Scrip**, *s.* das Ränzel, die Tasche.

[2]**Scrip**, *s.* der (beschriebene) Zettel; der Interimsanleiheschein. **—t**, I. *s. see* Scrip; die Handschrift; Schrift; phonetic —t, Lautschrift. II. *attrib.*; —t type, die Schreibschrift. **—torium**, *s.* das Schreibzimmer (*in convents*). **—tural**, *adj.* schriftmäßig, biblisch. **—ture**, I. *s.* die heilige Schrift; (*pl.*) die Bibel. III. *attrib.*; —ture proofs, Schriftbeweise. *Comp.* **—ture-reader**, *s.* der Bibelleser; jemand welcher den Armen und Unwissenden die Bibel vorliest.

Scrivener, *s.* der öffentliche Schreiber, Notar; der Geldmakler (*C.L.*).

Scroful—a, *s.* die Skrofeln. **—ous**, *adj.* skrofelartig, skrofulös.

Scroll, *s.* die (Papier-)Rolle; (list) die Liste; der Schnörkel, die Schnecke (*Arch., Viol.*); (flourish) der Namenszug; das Siegelzeichen (*Law*). *Comp.* **—work**, *s.* die Arabeskenverzierung.

Scrot—al, *adj.* Hodensack-. **—ocele**, *s.* der Hodenbruch. **—um**, *s.* der Hodensack.

[1]**Scrub**, I. *v.a.* abschrubben, (ab)scheuern, schrubben (*Naut.*). II. *v.n.* schrubben, scheuern; (—ard) sich schinden (*for a living*) (*fam.*). III. *s.* der Besenstumpf; (niggard) der Knauser. **—by**, *adj.* elend, armselig, schäbig; (stunted) zwergig. *Comp.* **—bing-brush**, *s.* die Schrubbürste.

[2]**Scrub**, *s.* das Gestrüpp, Buschwerk, Unterholz; das im Wachstum Verkümmerte; der abgenutzte stumpfe Besen; der kleine Knirps. **—by**, *adj.* im Wachstum verkümmert, zwergig, klein, niedrig; elend, schäbig.

Scrummage, *s. see* Scrimmage.

Scrumptious, *adj.* nett, vortrefflich; eigen, wählerisch (*sl.*).

Scrunch, I. *v.a.* zerkauen, zermalmen. II. *v.n.* krachen, knirschen. III. *s.* das Krachen, Knirschen.

Scrup—le, I. *s.* der Skrupel (= 20 Gran); der Zweifel, die Bedenklichkeit, der Skrupel; to make no —le, kein Bedenken tragen, keinen Anstand nehmen. II. *v.n.* Bedenken tragen, Anstand nehmen, sich (*dat.*) ein Gewissen (aus einer S.) machen. **—ulosity**, *s.* die Bedenklichkeit, Gewissenhaftigkeit; (preciseness) die Ängstlichkeit, Genauigkeit. **—ulous**, *adj.*, **—ulously**, *adv.* bedenklich; gewissenhaft, ängstlich; genau.

Scrutin—ize, *v.a.* durchforschen, untersuchen, prüfen; to —ize closely, genau untersuchen. **—y**, *s.* die Nachforschung, Untersuchung, genaue Prüfung; (—y of votes) die Wahlprüfung.

Scud, I. *s.* die vom Wind gejagte Wolke; der schnelle Läufer (*sl.*). II. *v.n.* laufen, eilen, fliehen; treiben, lenzen (*Naut.*); to — along, to — away, fort-laufen, -eilen, -fliehen.

Scuffle, I. *s.* die Balgerei, das Handgemenge, Gewühl. II. *v.n.* sich balgen, sich raufen, handgemein werden. **—r**, *s.* der Raufbold.

Scuffler, *s.* die Pflugscharegge, der Räumpflug.

Scull, I. *s.* das kurze Ruder, Skull. II. *v.a. & n.* skullen (*with sculls*); wricken (*with one oar*). **—er**, *s.* der Skuller; der Wricker.

Scull—ery, *s.* die Spülküche. **—ion**, *s.* der Küchenjunge. *Comp.* **—ery-maid**, *s.* die Scheuer-, Spül-magd.

Sculpt—or, *s.* der Bildhauer. **—ural**, *adj.* bildhauerisch, Bildhauer-. **—ure**, I. *s.* die Bildhauerkunst. II. *v.a.* schnitzen, aushauen.

Scum, I. *s.* der Schaum; der Abschaum, Auswurf (*fig.*); — of society, Abschaum der Menschheit. II. *v.a.* abschäumen. **—mer**, *see* Skimmer.

Scupper, *s.* (— hole) das Speigatt.

Scurf, *s.* der Schorf, Grind. —**iness**, *s.* die Schorfigkeit. —**y**, *adj.* schorfig, grindig.

Scurril—ity, *s.* die Possenreißerei, der niedrige Scherz; die Gemeinheit; (obscenity) Zotenreißerei; (invective) die Schimpfrede, Beschimpfung. —**ous**, *adj.*, —**ously**, *adv.* grob scherzend; grob verletzend; gemein, niedrig; zotig. —**ousness**, *see* —ity.

Scurry, I. *v.n.* (fort)eilen, weglaufen. II. *s.* die Eile, Hast; der Wirbel (von Festlichkeiten); die unruhige stürmische Zeit; der kurze Wettlauf.

Scurv—ily, *adv.* gemein, elend, niederträchtig. —**iness**, *s.* die Gemeinheit, Grobheit, Niederträchtigkeit. —**y**, I. *adj.* schorfig, grindig; (base) *see* —ily. II. *s.* der Skorbut (*Med.*). *Comp.* —**y-grass**, *s.* das Löffelkraut.

Scut, *s.* kurzer Schwanz.

Scutage, *s.* die Lehensdienstpflicht; das Dienstgeld (als Ablösung der kriegerischen L.).

Scutch, I. *v.a.* schwingen (*flax*). II. *s.* die Flachsschwinge, das Schwingmesser. *Comp.* —(**ing**)-**mill**, *s.* die Schlag-, Klopf-maschine.

Scutcheon, *s. see* Escutcheon; (— of a keyhole) das Schloßblech, Schlüssellochschild; (nameplate) das Namenschild.

Scutiform, *adj.* schildförmig.

[1]**Scuttle**, *s.* der flache Korb; coal —, der Kohlenkasten, Kohlenbehälter (in Zimmern).

[2]**Scuttle**, I. *v.a.* Löcher einschneiden in (*a ship*). II. *s.* die Springluke (*Naut.*).

[3]**Scuttle**, I. *v.n.*; to — away, forteilen. II. *s.* der eilige Lauf, der flinke, trippelnde Gang.

Scythe, *s.* die Sichel, Sense. *Comp.* —**cradle**, *s.* das Sensengerüst. —**handle**, *s.* der Sensenbaum.

Sea, *s.* die See, das Meer; die See, hohe Welle, Woge (*Naut.*); die Flut, das Meer (*fig.*); at —, auf der See (*lit.*); in Verwirrung, ratlos, (*fig.*); by —, zur See, zu Wasser; to go to —, zur See gehen, Seemann werden; (put to —) in See stechen; a heavy — was running, die See ging sehr hoch, das Meer war sehr aufgeregt; beyond the —(s), über See, übers Meer; on the high —s, auf hoher See; half —s over, benebelt (*sl.*). *Comp.* (*in comp. gen'lly* = See-) —-**bathing**, *s.* das Seebaden, Baden in der See. —-**beach**, *s.* der (Meeres-)Strand. —-**beat(en)**, *adj.* meerbespült. —**board**, *s.* die Küstenlinie, Seeküste. —-**borne**, *adj.* von der See getragen; —-borne trade, der Seehandel. —-**breeze**, *s.* der Seewind. —-**calf**, *s.* das Seekalb, der gemeine Seehund. —-**chart**, *s.* die Seekarte. —-**coast**, *s.* die Meeresküste. —-**devil**, *s.* der Meerteufel. —-**eagle**, *s.* der Beinbrecher (*Icht.*); der Seeadler (*Orn.*). —**farer**, der Seefahrer. —**faring**, *adj.* seemännisch, seefahrend. —-**fowl**, *s.* der Seevogel. —-**gate**, *s.* das Docktor, Seetor. —-**girt**, *adj.* seeumgürtet. —-**going**, *adj.* die See befahrend, See- (*ship, etc.*). —-**green**, I. *s.* das Meergrün. II. *adj.* meergrün. —-**gull**, *s.* die Seemöve. —-**horse**, *s.* das Seepferdchen (*Icht.*); das Walroß. —-**kale**, *s.* der Seekohl. —-**kings**, *see* Vikings. —-**legs**, *pl.* Seemannsbeine (*pl.*), die Fähigkeit bei unruhiger See auf dem Verdeck zu gehen (*coll.*). —-**level**, *s.* der Meeresspiegel. —-**lion**, *s.* der Seelöwe. —**man**, *s.* (sailor) der Seemann, der Matrose; able(-bodied) —man, der Vollmatrose. —**manlike**, *adj.* seemännisch. —**manship**, *s.* die Seemanns-, Seefahrer-kunst. —-**mark**, *s.* das Seezeichen. —-**monster**, *s.* das Meerungeheuer; die Seekatze (*Zool.*). —**port**, *s.* der Seehafen, Hafenplatz; (—port town) die Hafenstadt. —-**room**, *s.* die Räumte; to get —-room, die hohe See gewinnen. —-**rover**, *s.* der Seeräuber. —-**salt**, *s.* das See-, Meer-salz. —-**serpent**, *s.* die Seeschlange. —-**shore**, *s.* das Seeufer. —**sick**, *adj.* seekrank. —**sickness**, *s.* die Seekrankheit. —**side**, I. *s.* die (Meeres-)Küste; to go to the —side, to live at the —side, an die See gehen, an der See wohnen. II. *adj.* an der Küste gelegen; Küsten-, Strand-. —-**swallow**, *s.* die Meerschwalbe. —**ward(s)**, I. *adv.* seewärts. II. *adj.* nach der See gerichtet. —-**water**, *s.* das Seewasser. —-**weed**, *s.* die Alge, der Seetang. —**worthiness**, *s.* die Seetüchtigkeit. —**worthy**, *adj.* seefest, seetüchtig. —-**wrack**, *s.* das Seegras

[1]**Seal**, *s.* der Seehund, (die) Robbe. —**ing**, *s.* der Robbenfang, Seehundsfang. *Comp.* —-**blubber**, *s.* das Robbenfett. —-**fishing**, —-**fishery**, *see* —ing. —-**oil**, *s.* der Robbentran. —**skin**, *s.* das Seehundsfell.

[2]**Seal**, I. *s.* das Siegel, Petschaft; (stamp) der Stempel; die Bestätigung (*fig.*); to affix (put) one's — to a document, einer Urkunde sein Siegel aufdrücken, sie (unter)siegeln; under hand and —, unter Brief und Siegel, under the —, unter dem Siegel (*of secrecy, the confession, etc.*). II. *v.a.* (zu)siegeln (*letters, etc.*); (confirm) besiegeln, bestätigen; (attest) besiegeln (*with one's blood*); to — up, versiegeln (a p.'s lips, einem die Lippen), zusiegeln; eingießen, befestigen (*with lead, cement, etc.*), zuschmelzen (*a glass tube*); to — hermetically, hermetisch verschließen. *Comp.* —-**engraver**, *s.* der Petschaftstecher. —**ing-wax**, *s.* der Siegellack. —-**ring**, *s.* der Siegelring.

Seam, I. *s.* der Saum, die Naht (*Sew.*); das Lager, (der) Flöz, die Schicht, Ader (*Geol.*); (work) die Hand-, Näh-arbeit (*Amer.*); (scar) die Narbe; coal —, die Kohlenschicht; flat —, run and fell —, Kappnaht; — of the trousers, die Hosennaht; middle finger touching the —, Hand an der Hosennaht. II. *v.a.* zusammen nähen; narben. —**less**, *adj.* ohne Naht, nahtlos, ungenäht. —**stress**, *s.* die Näherin. —**y**, *adj.* eine Naht habend; —y side, die Nahtseite (*lit.*); die unangenehme Seite, Schattenseite (*fig.*).

[1]**Sear**, I. *adj.* trocken, dürr, welk. II. *v.a.* dörren; (burn) versengen, brennen; (brand) brandmarken; (cicatrize) vernarben; verhärten (*the conscience*). III. *s.* die Trockenheit, Dürre. —**ed**, *adj.* versengt; verwelkt, dürr; verhärtet. *Comp.* —**ing-iron**, *s.* das Brenneisen.

[2]**Sear**, *s.* die Stange, der Stengel.

Search, I. *v.a.* suchen, forschen nach; (seek through) unter-, durch-suchen; (examine) untersuchen, prüfen, genau ansehen; to — **out**, erforschen, ausfindig machen. II. *v.n.* suchen, forschen; to — **after**, forschen nach; to — **for**, suchen nach, sich umsehen nach; to — **into**, Untersuchungen anstellen über (*acc.*); untersuchen, ergründen. III. *s.* das Suchen, Aufsuchen, Durchsuchen; die Untersuchung; (exploration) die Forschung, das Forschen; to go in — of (a p.), (einen) aufsuchen, (einem) nachforschen; right of —, das Durchsuchungsrecht; after a long — for the boy, nachdem man lange nach dem Knaben gesucht hatte; in — of truth, beim *or* im Forschen nach Wahrheit. —**er**, *s.* der Sucher; der Erforscher; der Untersucher, Prüfer; der Güterbeschauer (*at the Custom-house*); das Visitiereisen (*Customs, Artil.*). —**ing**, I. *adj.* tief eindringend, gründlich. II. *s.* das Suchen; die Durchsuchung; —ing of hearts, die Prüfung der Herzen. —**ingness**, *s.* die Schärfe, Eindringlichkeit, Genauigkeit der Prüfung. *Comp.* —-**light**, *s.* der Scheinwerfer. —-**warrant**, *s.* der Haus-, Durch-suchungsbefehl.

Season, I. *s.* die Jahreszeit, Zeit; (right time) passende, rechte Zeit; (bathing —) Badezeit, Kurzeit, Saison; (theatrical —) Theaterzeit; die Saison (*in London, etc.*); *see* —ing; the height of the —, die Hochsaison; dead —, die Sauregurkenzeit; for a —, für ein Weilchen, eine Zeit lang; in (due) —, zu rechter Zeit; everything in its —, alles zu seiner Zeit; out of —, der Jahreszeit nicht angemessen; zur Unzeit; ungelegen, unpassend; caviare is now out of —, Kaviar ist jetzt nicht zu haben, die Kaviarzeit ist vorüber; with the compliments of the —, fröhliche Weihnachten! ein glückliches neues Jahr! to send a p. the compliments of the —, einem zu Weihnachten, Neujahr, Ostern, Glück wünschen. II. *v.a.* zeitigen; würzen; angenehm, schmackhaft machen (*fig.*); to — with salt, salzen; to become —ed, sich gewöhnen (*to a climate*); zum Gebrauche tauglich werden, die gehörige Reife erhalten; —ed timber, lufttrocknes Bauholz; —ed cask, weingrünes Faß; —ed stomach, ausgepichter Magen. III. *v.n.* reifen, zeitigen; trocknen, auswittern (*as wood*). —**able**, *adj.*, —**ably**, *adv.* zeitgemäß, gelegen, passend. —**ableness**, *s* das Zeitgemäße, das Günstige, Gelegene; die rechte Zeit. —**er**, *s.* der, die, das Würzende. —**ing**, *s.* die Würze; *see* Stuffing (*Cook.*). *Comp.* —**ticket**, *s.* die Jahreskarte, Zeitkarte.

Seat, I. *s.* der Sitz (*also fig.*); (chair, *etc.*) der Sessel, Stuhl; (bench) die Bank; (residence) der Wohnsitz, Sitz; (country-seat) der Landsitz, das Lustschloß; (scene) der Schauplatz; der Sitz (*on horseback, in an assembly, in Parliament, etc.*); das Gesäß, der Sitz (*of trousers, of a chair, etc., of a closet, etc.*); — of judgment, der Richterstuhl; — in church, der Kirchenstuhl, -platz; — of commerce, der Sitz des Handels; — of war, der Kriegsschauplatz; keep your —, bleiben Sie sitzen; take a —, setzen Sie sich, nehmen Sie Platz; take your —s! einsteigen! (*Railw.*). II. *v.a.* (hin)setzen; (ein-)setzen, erheben (*on a throne, etc.*); mit Stühlen versehen (*a church*); mit Sitzen &c. versehen (*people*); ein neues Gesäß einsetzen (*trousers*); to — o.s., sich setzen; they were —ed, sie saßen; I had not been —ed many minutes, ich hatte eben erst Platz genommen; to — a chair, einen Sitz an einem Stuhl anbringen.

Sebac—eous, *adj.* talgartig, Talg-. —**ic**, *adj.* Talg-, Fett-; —ic acid, Fettsäure.

Secant, I. *adj.* schneidend. II. *s.* die Sekante.

Seccotine, *s.* der Porzellan-, Glas-klebestoff.

Secede, *v.n.* sich zurückziehen, sich trennen. —**r**, *s.* einer, der sich zurückzieht *or* trennt, Separatist; —rs, die Dissidenten (*in the Scotch Church*).

Secern, *v.n.* ausschzeiden, absondern.

Secession, *s.* die Abscheidung, das Abgehen, Sich-Zurückziehen; kirchliche Spaltung; die künstlerische Loslösung (von einer herrschenden Partei); War of —, der Bürger- *or* Sezessions-Krieg (1861-65). —**ist**, *s.* der Teilnehmer an einer Trennung, Separatist, Sezessionist; der Sonderbündler (*Pol.*).

Seclu—de, *v.a.* abschließen, ausschließen. —**ded**, *adj.*, —**dedly**, *adv.* abgeschlossen, zurückgezogen, einsam. —**sion**, *s.* die Abgeschiedenheit.

Second, I. *adj.* zweit, ander; (next) nächst, folgend; (inferior) geringer, schlechter, niedriger stehend, nicht so gut (to, wie); to be, stand — (to a p.) (einem) nachstehen; he is — to none, er steht keinem nach; upon — thoughts, bei nochmaliger, besserer Überlegung; every — year, ein Jahr ums andere; — best, zweitbest, nächstbest, minder, Neben-; to come off — best, im Wettstreit der zweitbeste sein; — class, zweiten Ranges, zweiter Klasse; — class matter, Postsachen zweiter Ordnung, Zeitungen, Zeitschriften (*Amer.*); — cousins, Kinder der Geschwisterkinder, Vettern im zweiten Grade *or* Gliede; to play — fiddle, die Nebenrolle, zweite Rolle spielen; — captain, der Hauptmann zweiter Klasse; — lieutenant, der Leutnant (*German army*); der Unterleutnant; — mate, zweiter Steuermann; — mourning, die Halbtrauer; — quality, mittelgut, zweiter Qualität; — sight, zweites Gesicht; a — time, zum zweitenmale. II. *s.* der, die, das Nächste, Zweite; der Sekundant (*in duels*); (helper) der Beistand; die Sekunde (*of time, also Mus. & Fenc.*); — of exchange, die Sekunda, der Sekunda-Wechsel; — in command, der Unterbefehlshaber; to act as —, sekundieren; to take the —, die begleitende Stimme übernehmen (*Mus.*); my —, mein Zweites (*in charades*); mein Sekundant. III. *v.a.* (einem) beistehen, helfen, (einen) unterstützen (*a p.*); (einem) sekundieren (*in a duel*); befördern (*an undertaking, etc.*); unterstützen (a motion, einen Antrag). —**arily**, *adv.* zunächst, nebenbei, nebenher, untergeordnet. —**ariness**, *s.* das Sekundäre, Untergeordnete, der zweite Grad *or* Rang. —**ary**, I. *adj.* nächstfolgend, in zweiter Linie stehend, zweiten Grades *or* Ranges, zweiter Sorte, unter-, bei-geordnet; sekundär (*also Med.*); (derived) entlehnt, abgeleitet, Neben-; sekundär, Flöz- (*Geol.*); Abänderungs- (*Crystall.*); —ary accent, der Nebenton; —ary cause, die Nebenursache; —ary education, das höhere Schulwesen, das Mittelschulwesen; —ary fever, das Fieber nach einer Krise; —ary proposition, der Nebensatz; —ary school, die höhere Schule (*Prussia*), Mittelschule (*Austria and parts of Germany; Amer.*). II. *s.* der Stellvertreter; der untergeordnete Gerichtsbeamte, Untersheriff (*in the City of London*); (—ary circle) der Nebenkreis; (—ary colour) die Mittelfarbe, zusammengesetzte Farbe; hintere Schwungfeder (*Orn.*). —**er**, *s.* der Unterstützende. —**ly**, *adv.* zweitens. *Comp.* —**hand**, I. *s.* der Besitz aus zweiter Hand; (—s-hand) der Sekundenzeiger. II. *adj.* aus zweiter Hand; (not new) alt, schon gebraucht; (not original) nicht ursprünglich, von andern entlehnt, aufgewärmt; antiquarisch (*of books*); —-hand bookseller, der Antiquar; to have a thing at —hand, etwas erst aus der zweiten Hand wissen. —**-rate**, *adj.* zweiten Ranges, zweiter Güte, mittelmäßig, mittelgut.

Secre—cy, *s.* die Heimlichkeit, Verborgenheit; (discretion) die Verschwiegenheit. —**t**, I. *adj.*, —**tly**, *adv.* geheim, heimlich, verborgen; verschwiegen; (lonely) einsam; *see* Privy; to keep —t, geheimhalten; —t society, die geheime Gesellschaft, der Geheimbund. II. *s.* das Geheimnis; in —t, insgeheim, heimlich; to be in the —t, um das Geheimnis wissen; to let a p. into the —t, einen in das Geheimnis einweihen; to make no —t of, kein Hehl machen aus. —**tarial**, *adj.* Sekretär-. —**tary**, *s.* der Geheimschreiber; der Schriftführer, Schriftwart, Sekretär; —tary of State, der (englische) Minister; der Minister des Äußern (*Amer.*); —tary of State for War, der Kriegsminister; —tary of War, der Kriegsminister (*Amer.*). —**taryship**, *s.* das Schriftführeramt, die Stelle des Schriftwarts. —**te**, *v.a.* verbergen, verstecken; absondern, ausscheiden (*Phys.*); to —te o.s., sich verbergen. —**tion**, *s.* die Absonderung. —**tive**, *adj.* verheimlichend. —**tiveness**, *s.* der Heimlichkeitstrieb. —**tness**, *s.* die Heimlichkeit, Verborgenheit. *Comp.* —**tary-bird**, *s.* der Schlangenadler.

Sect, *s.* die Sekte, Partei. —**arian**, I. *adj.* sektiererisch, Sekten-; konfessionell (*with a sense of blame*). II. *s.* der Sektierer, Anhänger einer Sekte. —**arianism**, *s.* die Sektiererei, das Sektentum. —**ary**, *see* —arian II. —**ile**, *adj.* spaltbar. —**ion**, *s.* die Durchschneidung, der Schnitt; die Öffnung, Sektion (*Surg.*); (portion) der Teil; der Schnitt (*Draw., Arch.*); (division) der Abschnitt, die Abteilung, der Paragraph (*also in books*); der Schnitt, Durchschnitt (*Geom.*); der Absatz (*Typ.*); (sign) das Abschnittszeichen, der Paragraph (*Typ.*); das Stück Staatsland von 640 Acker (*Amer.*); der Halbzug, die Sektion (*Mil.*); das Profil, die Durchschnittsansicht (*Arch.*); —ion of a railway, das Bahnprofil; cross, lateral, transverse —ion, der Querschnitt, das Querprofil; *see* Conic. —**ional**, *adj.* zu einem besonderen Teile eines größeren Körpers *or* Territoriums gehörig, partikularistisch, Teil-, Sekten-; —ional elevation, (plan), der Länge-, Quer-(Horizontal-)schnitt. —**or**, *s.* der Sektor, Kreisausschnitt (*Geom.*); der Proportionalzirkel

(*Draw.*); der Kreissektor (*Surv.*); (—or wheel) das Sektorrad.

Secular, I. *adj.* weltlich; weltgeistlich; säkular (*Astr.*, *etc.*); hundertjährig; — clergy, die Weltgeistlichkeit; — poem, das weltliche Gedicht. II. *s.* der Weltgeistliche; der Laie; nicht geweihter, kirchlicher Beamter. **—ity**, *s.* die Weltlichkeit, der Weltsinn. **—ize**, *v.a.* säkularisieren; (geistliche Güter) einziehen; verweltlichen (*fig.*).

Secund, *adj.* einseitig (*Bot.*). **—ine**, *s.*, **—ines**, *pl.* die Nachgeburt.

Secur—e, I. *adj.*, **—ely**, *adv.* sicher (from, vor); (without care) sich sicher fühlend, sorglos; (certain) zuversichtlich, gewiß (of a th., einer Sache). II. *v.a.* sichern, bewahren, schützen (from, against, vor); (make certain) gewiß machen; verschließen (*a door*); festnehmen (einen Dieb), sich versichern (eines Diebes); in sichern Gewahrsam bringen, hinter Schloß und Riegel setzen; sicherstellen (*a debt*); (warrant) Sicherheit geben; sich (*dat.*) sichern (*a seat*, *etc.*); to —e places, Plätze (vorher) belegen. **—ity**, *s.* (confidence) die Ruhe, Sorglosigkeit; (safety) die Sicherheit; die Zuversicht, Gewißheit; (defence) der Schutz; (guarantee) die Versicherung, Bürgschaft, Kaution, das Unterpfand, der Bürge; to give —ity, Bürgschaft leisten, sich verbürgen (*Law*, *etc.*); Delkredere stehen (*C. L.*); —ities, Pfänder, Wertpapiere; collateral —ities, mittelbare Sicherheit; public —ities, fundierte Staatsschulden.

Sedan, *attrib.*; — chair, die Sänfte, der Tragsessel.

Sed—ate, *adj.*, **—ately**, *adv.* gesetzt, ruhig, still. **—ateness**, *s.* die Gesetztheit, Ruhe, der Ernst. **—ative**, I. *adj.* beruhigend, besänftigend. II. *s.* beruhigendes *or* niederschlagendes Mittel. **—entariness**, *s.*; the —entariness of their life, ihre sitzende Lebensart. **—entary**, *adj.* sitzend; to lead a —entary life, eine sitzende Lebensweise führen. **—erunt**, *s.* die Sitzung.

Sedg—e, *s.* die Binse, das Schilfgras. **—ed**, *adj.* Schilf-, aus Schilf. **—y**, *adj.* schilfig.

Sediment, *s.* der (Boden-)Satz, Niederschlag, die Hefe. **—ary**, *adj.* Niederschlags-; angeschwemmt (*Geol.*); —ary rocks, das Flözgebirge.

Seditio—n, *s.* der Aufruhr, Aufstand. **—nary**, *s.* der Aufrührer, Meuterer. **—us**, *adj.*, **—usly**, *adv.* aufrührerisch, meuterisch. **—usness**, *s.* das Aufrührerische, der aufrührerische Geist.

Seduc—e, *v.a.* verführen. **—ement**, *s. see* —tion; der verführerische Reiz. **—er**, *s.* der Verführer. **—ible**, *adj.* verführbar. **—ing**, *see* —tive. **—tion**, *s.* die Verführung, Verleitung. **—tive**, *adj.* verführerisch.

Sedulous, *adj.*, **—ly**, *adv.* emsig. **—ness**, *s.* die Emsigkeit.

[1]**See**, *ir.v.* I. *n.* sehen; einsehen (*fig.*); I —, ich verstehe (schon); don't you —, verstanden? Nicht wahr? he —s which way the wind blows, er weiß, was die Uhr geschlagen hat; to — **about** *or* to, eine S. besorgen, Sorge tragen für eine S.; to — **into**, hineinblicken in (eine Sache, sie) durchschauen; to — **through** a th., eine S. durchschauen; to — **to** s.o.'s affairs, the house, the children, seine Geschäfte besorgen, aufs Haus, auf die Kinder achten; — to it! sorgen Sie dafür! achten Sie darauf! **II.** *a.* sehen; (perceive) einsehen, verstehen, begreifen, gewahr werden; (experience) erfahren, erleben; (witness) ansehen; zusehen, Sorge tragen (that s. th. is done, daß etwas geschehe); besuchen (*patients*); to — company, Besuche annehmen, Gesellschaften geben; to — no company, keinen Menschen bei sich empfangen, ein eingezogenes Leben führen; to — justice done to a p., dafür sorgen, daß einem Gerechtigkeit widerfahre; to let s.o. —, einem zeigen; to go to — a p., einen besuchen; to — a lady home (to her carriage), eine Dame nach Hause begleiten (bis an ihren Wagen führen); to — fair play, darauf achten, daß alles gehörig zugeht, den Schiedsrichter machen; to live to —, erleben, erfahren, to — out, zu Ende führen, (bei einer S.) ausharren; to — a p. out, einen zur Tür begleiten; to — a p. away *or* off, einen abreisen sehen, einen an die Eisenbahn, aufs Schiff bringen; to — a th. through, eine S. durchführen, zu Ende führen; I cannot — my way to . . ., ich kann mir noch nicht recht denken, wie ich . . .; now I — my way clearly, jetzt sehe ich meinen Weg klar vor mir, weiß ich, was ich zu tun habe. **—ing**, I. *p. see* See. II. *conj.*; —ing that, weil, da, weil nun einmal; —ing it is so, da es nun einmal so ist. III. *s.* das Sehen; worth —ing, sehenswert; —ing is believing, was man sieht, das glaubt man. **—n**, *p.p. of* See. **—r**, *s.* der Sehende; (prophet) der Seher.

[2]**See**, *s.* der (bischöfliche, erzbischöfliche) Sitz, das (Erz-)Bistum; holy —, päpstlicher Stuhl.

Seed, I. *s.* die Saat, der Same; (offspring) die Nachkommenschaft; (first principle) der Keim, Ursprung; to sow the —s of discord, Zwietracht säen, Unfrieden stiften. II. *v.n.* in Samen schießen. III. *v.a.* (sow) säen; besäen. **—iness**, *s.* die Schäbigkeit; das Sichelendfühlen (*coll.*). **—ling**, *s.* das Samengewächs, der Sämling. **—y**, *adj.* voller Samen, in Samen schießend; mit einem Beigeschmack (*of cognac*); (shabby) schäbig, fadenscheinig; (wretched) katzenjämmerlich, elend (*sl.*); —y looking, von schäbigem Aussehen; he looks rather —y, er sieht elend aus, sieht aus, als ob er einen Katzenjammer hätte; I feel rather —y, ich bin nicht recht auf dem Damm, nicht gut zu Wege. *Comp.* **—-cake**, *s.* der Kümmelkuchen. **—-leaves**, **—-lobes**, *pl.* Samenblätter. **—-pearls**, *pl.* Samen-, Staub-perlen. **—sman**, *s.* der Samenhändler. **—-time**, *s.* die Säe-, Saat-zeit. **—-vessel**, *s.* die Fruchthülle.

Seek, *ir.v.* I. *a.* suchen; (— out) aufsuchen, auffinden; (desire) begehren, verlangen; (strive after) streben, trachten nach; to — a p.'s life, einem nach dem Leben trachten; he sought her in marriage, er hielt um sie an; to — out, aussuchen, ausfindig machen; there is s.th. to — in our methods, unsere Methoden lassen noch zu wünschen übrig. II. *n.* suchen; to — after, for, (etwas) suchen, nach (einer S.) suchen, trachten, streben, um (eine S.) ansuchen, anhalten. **—er**, *s.* der Sucher, (die) Suchende; —er after truth, der Wahrheitsuchende; —er for office, der Stellenbewerber, Stellensuchende.

[1]**Seel**, *v.a.* blenden, verhüllen (*fig.*).

[2]**Seel**, *v.n.* schlingern (*of ships*).

Seem, *v.* I. *n.* scheinen; (einem) erscheinen; all —ed pleased, allen schien es zu gefallen; it —s, (wie) es scheint, dem Anschein nach; it —s to me that . . ., mich dünkt, daß . . . II. *a. see* Beseem. **—ing**, I. *adj.* anscheinend, scheinbar. II. *s.* der Anschein, Schein, das Aussehen. **—ingly**, *adv.* anscheinend, scheinbar; zum Schein. **—ingness**, *s.* die Scheinbarkeit. **—liness**, *s.* die Schicklichkeit, der Anstand. **—ly**, *adv.* geziemend, schicklich.

Seen, *p.p. of* See.

See-saw, I. *s.* die Wippe; die Schaukel; (— motion) das Schaukeln, Schwanken; die Mühle (*Cards*); to play at —, sich wippen, schaukeln. II. *v.n.* wippen, schaukeln.

Seeth—e, *v.a. & n.* sieden, kochen; aufwallen; siedend heiß sein; einweichen. *Comp.* **—ing-pot**, *s.* der Kochtopf.

Seggar, **Saggar**, *s.* die Brennkapsel, der Koker.

Segment, *s.* der Abschnitt, das Segment; — of a circle (a sphere), der Kreisabschnitt, Kreisausschnitt. **—al**, *adj.* Stich-.

Segregat—e, *v.a.* absondern, trennen. **—ion**, *s.* die Absonderung.

Seign—eurial, *adj.* grundherrlich, herrschaftlich; (independent) unabhängig. **—ior**, *s.* der Herr (*in Spain*, *etc.*); der Lehnsherr (*of a fief*);

grand —ior, der Groß=herr, =sultan. **—iorage,** *s.* die königliche Münzgebühr; *see* Royalty (of authors). **—iorial,** *see* —eurial.

Seine, *s.* das Schlagnetz, Schleppnetz.

Seism—ic, *adj.* Erdbeben=; —ic disturbances, Erderschütterungen. **—ologist,** *s.* der Erdbebenforscher. **—ometer,** *s.* der Erdbebenmesser.

Seiz—able, *adj.* ergreifbar, greifbar. **—e,** *v.* I. *a.* ergreifen, fassen, packen; (take possession of) sich (einer S.) bemächtigen, (eine S.) ergreifen; an=fallen (*also of diseases*); verhaften, in Beschlag nehmen, mit Beschlag belegen (*Law*); begreifen, erfassen (*with the mind*); befestigen, anschlagen, bindseln (*Naut.*); —ed of, im Besitz von; to be —ed with, ergriffen werden von. II. *n.*; to —e upon, sich (einer Sache, jemandes) bemächtigen. **—er,** *s.* der Ergreifende; der mit Beschlag belegt. **—in,** *s.* die (in deed, wirkliche; in law, rechtliche) Besitzergreifung (*Law*); die Besitznahme; (possession) der Besitz. **—ing,** *s.* das Ergreifen 2c.; das Bindsel, Sorrtau (*Naut.*). **—ure,** *s.* das Ergreifen, die Ergreifung; die Verhaftung, Festnahme; (possession) der Besitz; plötzlicher Anfall (*of sickness*); to be under —ure, mit Beschlag belegt sein.

Sej(e)ant, *adj.* sitzend (*Her.*).

Seldom, *adv.* selten.

Select, I. *v.a.* aus=lesen, =wählen. II. *adj.* aus=erlesen, =erwählt, erkoren; — circle, gewählter Kreis. **—ed,** *adj. see* —. **—ion,** *s.* die Aus=lesung, =lese, =wahl; (choice) die Wahl; natural —ion, die natürliche Zuchtwahl. **—ive,** *adj.* auswählend, Auswahls=.

Selen—itic, *adj.* den Mond betreffend, selenitisch. **—ography,** *s.* die Mondbeschreibung.

Self, I. *s.* das Selbst, Ich; the love of —, die Selbst= Eigen=liebe: I look upon him as my other —, ich betrachte ihn als mein zweites Ich; your worthy —, Ihre werte Person; my poor *or* humble—, meine Wenigkeit. II. *adj.* selb, selbig, nämlich III. *pronom. adj.* selbst, selber; I my—, ich selber *or* selbst; he him—, er selbst; one('s)—, sich selbst; she is kindness it—, sie ist die Güte selbst; you said it your—, Sie haben es selbst gesagt; know thy—, erkenne dich selbst, he forgot him—, er vergaß sich; er vergaß sich selbst. **—ish,** *adj.*, **—ishly,** *adv.* selbstisch. **—ishness,** *s.* die Selbstsucht. *Comp.* (*gen'lly* = Selbst=.) **—-abandonment,** *s.* die Selbstvergessenheit, Hingabe. **—-abasement,** *s.* die Selbsterniedrigung. **—-accusing,** *adj.* sich selbst anklagend. **—-acting,** *adj.* selbstwirkend, sich selbst regulierend. **—-aggrandizement,** *s.* die Selbsterhebung. **—-assertion,** das Bestehen auf seinem Recht, die Anmaßung. **—-assertive,** *adj.* sich selbst gern zur Geltung bringend, anmaßend. **—-assurance,** *s.* die Zuversicht(lichkeit). **—-assured,** *adj.* zuversichtlich. **—-coloured,** *adj.* in Naturfarbe; einfarbig. **—-command,** *s.* die Selbstbeherrschung. **—-complacent,** *adj.* selbstgefällig, selbstzufrieden. **—-conceit,** *s.* der Eigendünkel. **—-conceited,** *adj.* dünkelhaft; eingebildet. **—-confidence,** *s.* das Selbstvertrauen. **—-conscious,** *adj.* selbstbewußt. **—-constituted,** *adj.* selbsternannt. **—-contained,** *see* Reserved; —-contained flats, (für sich) abgeschlossene Etagen. **—-contradiction,** *s.* der Selbstwiderspruch. **—-contradictory,** *adj.* sich (*dat.*) selbst widersprechend. **—-control,** *see* —-command. **—-deception,** *s.* die Selbsttäuschung. **—-defence,** *s.* die Selbstverteidigung, Notwehr; in —-defence, aus Notwehr, zur Selbstverteidigung. **—-denial,** *s.* die Selbstverleugnung. **—-denying,** *adj.* selbstverleugnend. **—-educated,** *adj.* durch sich selbst gebildet. **—-elected,** *adj.* selbsterwählt. **—-evident,** *adj.* selbstverständlich, einleuchtend, augenscheinlich. **—-examination,** *s.* die Selbstprüfung. **—-existence,** *s.* die Selbstexistenz. **—-existent,** *adj.* selbstexistierend. **—-feeder,** *s.* der Füllofen, Selbstfütterer (*Mach.*). **—-feeding,** *adj.* sich selbst speisend *or* regelnd, selbst regulierend. **—-fitting,** *adj.* von selbst sich anschließend (*candles*). **—-governed,** *adj.* selbstregiert. **—-government,** *s.* die Selbstverwaltung. **—-gratulation,** die Selbstbeglückwünschung. **—-importance,** *s.* das Selbstgefühl, der Eigendünkel. **—-indulgence,** *s.* die Nachsicht gegen sich selbst; zügellose Genußsucht. **—-indulgent,** *adj.* bequem, schwach gegen sich selbst; seinen Leidenschaften nachgebend. **—-inflicted,** *adj.* selbstauferlegt; selbstgeschlagen (*as a wound*). **—-interest,** *s.* der Eigennutz. **—-love,** *s.* die Selbstsucht, Eigenliebe. **—-made,** *adj.* selbstgemacht; a —-made man, ein durch sich selbst emporgekommener Mann, ein Mann aus eigner Kraft. **—-opinionated,** *adj.* dünkelhaft; eigensinnig. **—-possessed,** *adj.* gefaßt, gelassen; Selbstbeherrschung besitzend. **—-possession,** *s.* die Selbstbeherrschung; (calm) die Fassung, Ruhe; to regain one's —-possession, sich wieder fassen *or* sammeln. **—-praise,** *s.* das Selbst=, Eigenlob. **—-preservation,** *s.* die Selbsterhaltung. **—-registering,** *adj.* selbst registrierend. **—-regulating,** *adj.* sich selbst regulierend. **—-reliance,** *s.* das Selbstvertrauen. **—-respect,** *s.* die Selbstachtung. **—-restraint,** *s.* die Selbstbeschränkung, =beherrschung. **—-righteous,** *adj.* selbstgerecht. **—-righteousness,** *s.* die Selbstgerechtigkeit. **—-sacrificing,** *adj.* sich selbst aufopfernd. **—-same,** *adj.*; the —same, eben der=, die=, das=selbe *or* nämliche, ein und der= 2c. selbe. **—-satisfied,** *adj.* selbstbefriedigt. **—-seeking,** *adj.* selbstsüchtig. **—-styled,** *adj.* sich selbst so nennend, selbstbenannt; anmaßlich. **—-sufficiency,** *s.* dünkelhafte Selbstgenügsamkeit. **—-sufficient,** *adj.* selbstgenügsam. **—-sufficing,** *adj.* selbstgenügsam; von sich selbst eingenommen, eitel, dünkelhaft. **—-supporting,** *adj.* sich selbst erhaltend. **—-taught,** *adj.* selbstgelehrt. **—-tormentor,** *s.* der Selbstquäler. **—-torture,** *s.* die Selbstquälerei. **—-will,** *s.* der Eigenwille. **—-willed,** *adj.* eigenwillig, =sinnig.

Sell, I. *ir.v.a.* verkaufen (*also fig.*); to — a p., einen anführen (*sl.*); to — one's country, sein Vaterland verraten; sold! angeführt! (*sl.*); to — **off, out,** ausverkaufen; to — a p. **up,** einen auspfänden. II. *ir. v. n.* handeln; sich verkaufen, Absatz finden, abgehen (*as goods*); to — well, readily, sich gut, leicht verkaufen, schnellen Absatz finden; to — **out,** seine Offiziersstelle verkaufen (*Mil.*); seinen Abschied nehmen (*fig.*). III. *s.* der Trug (*sl.*). **—er,** *s.* der Verkäufer; der vom Verkäufer geforderte Preis (*C.L.*). **—ing,** I. *adj.*; —ing price, der Verkaufspreis. II. *s.* das Verkaufen, der Verkauf; —ing off, der Ausverkauf.

Selvage, Selvedge, *s.* das Sahlband, die Sahlleiste, Borte, Kante; die Egge.

Semantics, *s.* die Lehre vom Bedeutungswandel, die Bedeutungslehre.

Semaphore, I. *s.* der Flügel=, Küsten=Telegraph, optische Telegraph, Semaphor. II. *v.a.* durch optische Telegraphie übermitteln.

Semasiolog—ical, *adj.* die Bedeutungslehre betreffend; —ical studies, Studien über Bedeutungslehre und den Bedeutungswandel. **—y,** *s.* die Bedeutungslehre. *See* Semantics.

Semblance, *s.* die Ähnlichkeit; (exterior) der Anschein, das Aussehen; (image) die Gestalt, das (Eben)bild.

Semi, *pref.* = Halb=, halb=. **—-barbarous,** *adj.* halbbarbarisch. **—circle,** *s.* der Halbkreis. **—circular,** *adj.* halbkreisförmig. **—-circumference,** *s.* der halbe Umfang. **—-classical,** *adj.* halbklassisch; nur Latein (nicht Griechisch) lehrend; (first grade) —-classical school, das Realgymnasium. **—colon,** *s.* der Strichpunkt, das Semikolon. —-**detached**, *adj.* halb getrennt; —-detached house, an einer Seite angebautes Haus. —**diameter**, *s.* der Halbmesser. —-**official**, *adj.* halbamtlich. —**ped**, *s.* der halbe Versfuß. —**quaver**, *s.* die Sechszehntelnote. —**tone**, *s.* der Halbton. —-**transparent**, *adj.* halb- *or* unvollkommen durchsichtig. —-**vowel**, *s.* der Halbvokal (j *and* w).

Semina—l, *adj.* Samen-; ursprünglich. —**rist**, *s.* der Seminarist, Alumnus (*R. C.*). —**ry**, I. *s.* die Pflanzschule; (school) die Erziehungsanstalt; das Seminar (*also R. C.*). II. *adj.* Seminar-.

Semolina, *s.* der (Weizen-)Gries. *Comp.* —-**pudding**, *s.* der Griespudding.

Sempiternal, *adj.* immerwährend, ewig.

Sempstress, *s.* die Näherin.

Senat—e, *s.* der Senat, die Ratsversammlung. —**or**, *s.* der Ratsherr, Senator. —**orial**, *adj.* senatorisch, Senator-; zur Wahl eines Senators berechtigt (*Amer.*). —**orship**, *s.* die Senatorwürde. *Comp.* —**e-chamber**, *s.* der Saal des Senats. —**e-house**, *s.* das Senatsgebäude.

Send, *ir.v.a.* senden, schicken; übersenden, zuschicken, zukommen lassen (a p. money, etc., einem Geld &c.); (despatch, depute) absenden; Heaven — thee good fortune! möge der Himmel dir beistehen! God — him a speedy release, möge der liebe Gott ihn baldigst erlösen! to — a stone through a window, einen Stein durch ein Fenster werfen; he sent it flying, er warf es in die Luft; he sent him staggering, er stieß ihn fort, so daß er schwankte; to — one's kind regards to, (einen) bestens, herzlich, vielmals, *etc.*; grüßen lassen; to — s.o. packing, einen fortjagen; he sent me word, er ließ mir sagen, ließ mich wissen; to — a message, eine (mündliche) Bestellung machen lassen; to — a p. on errands, einen ausschicken um Botschaften auszurichten; to — to prison, verhaften lassen ins Gefängnis schicken; to — **abroad**, ins Ausland schicken; to — **away**, fort-, weg-schicken; (turn out) abfertigen; to — **down**, schicken; (zeitweise) relegieren (*Univ. sl.*); to — **for**, nach einem schicken, einen holen *or* kommen lassen; to — **forth**, fortschicken, in die Welt senden; von sich geben, auswerfen, verbreiten; to — **in**, hineinschicken, zuführen; to — in one's name, sich melden; to — in one's name for an examination, sich zu einer Prüfung melden; to — **out**, herausschicken, hinausschicken, aussenden; to — **round**, umherschicken, umlaufen lassen. —**er**, *s.* der Schickende, (Ab-)Sender. *Comp.* —-**off**, *s.* die Abschiedsfeier, das (feierliche) Lebewohl (*coll.*).

Seneschal, *s.* der Seneschall. —**ship**, *s.* das Seneschallamt.

Seni—le, *adj.* greisenhaft. —**lity**, *s.* das hohe Alter; die Greisenhaftigkeit. —**or**, I. *adj.* älter; senior (*in office*); —or partner, älterer Associé; —or classic (wrangler), der Erste in der höchsten altsprachlichen (mathematischen) Schlußprüfung (*Cambridge*). II. *s.* der Ältere; der Senior (*also Amer. Univ.*); he is my —or by five years, er ist fünf Jahr älter als ich; he is my —or in office, er geht mir im Dienstalter vor. —**ority**, *s.* das höhere (Jahres-, Dienst-)Alter.

Senna, *s.* die Senna, Sennen-Kassie, der Sennes-Strauch (*Bot.*); das Sennesblatt (*Pharm., Med.*).

Sennet, *s.* das Signal (zum Auftreten der Schauspieler), der Trompetenstoß (*obs.*).

Sennight, *s.* acht Tage, eine Woche; this day —, heute vor acht Tagen; heute über acht Tage (*obs.*).

Sens—ate, *adj.* durch die Sinne empfunden. —**ation**, *s.* die Empfindung, das Gefühl; der Eindruck; das Aufsehen; to make *or* create a —ation, Aufsehen erregen. —**ational**, *adj.*, —**ationally**, *adv.* Aufsehen erregend, überraschend, sensationell; sinnlich, Empfindungs- (*Psych.*); —ational novel, der Sensationsroman. —**ationalism**, *s.* die Effekthascherei, sensationelle Richtung. —**ationalist**, *s.* der Sensualphilosoph (*Phil.*); der Effekthascher. —**e**, *s.* der Sinn; die Empfindung; *see* —ation; (understanding) die Vernunft, der Verstand; der Sinn, die Bedeutung (*of a word*); (feeling) das Gefühl; the five —es, die fünf Sinne; —e of taste, Geschmacks-sinn; —e of humour, Sinn für Humor; common —e, der gesunde Menschenverstand; good (sound) —e, vernünftiges, richtiges Gefühl; a man of —e, ein verständiger Mann; out of one's —es, außer sich, verrückt; to talk —e, vernünftig reden; to have a just —e of, (eine Sache) richtig nehmen, den rechten Begriff (davon) haben; to take the —e of the House upon, die Ansicht des Parlaments (Kongresses) über . . . durch Abstimmung ermitteln; figurative, literal, proper, strict —e, bildlicher Sinn, buchstäbliche Bedeutung, eigentliche Bedeutung, engerer Sinn. —**eless**, *adj.*, —**elessly**, *adv.* sinnlos, unvernünftig; *see* Insensible. —**elessness**, *s.* die Unvernünftigkeit; *see* Insensibility. —**ibility**, *s.* das Empfindungsvermögen; die Empfindlichkeit (*of body & mind; also of a balance*); exquisite —ibility, äußerst zartes, feines Gefühl. —**ible**, *adj.*, —**ibly**, *adv.* spürbar, fühlbar, merkbar; (appreciable) schätzbar, bemerkbar; *see* —itive; (prudent, judicious) verständig, vernünftig, klug, gescheit; fühlbar (*Phys.*); empfindlich, fein (*as a thermometer*); to be —ible of a th., für eine S. empfänglich sein *or* Gefühl haben, (etwas) empfinden, fühlen, merken; to make (a p.) —ible of, (einem) etwas begreiflich machen; —ible loss, empfindlicher Verlust; —ible note, große Septime (*Mus.*); *see* Horizon. —**ibleness**, *s.* die Vernünftigkeit, Verständigkeit; *see* —ibility, —itiveness; die Spürbarkeit. —**itive**, *adj.*, —**itively**, *adv.* empfindungsfähig, Empfindungs-; (of fine —ibility) fein-, zart-fühlend, empfindlich (*also Phys.*); —itive plant, die Sinnpflanze, Mimose; —itive soul, empfindsame Seele. —**itiveness**, *s.* die Empfindlichkeit (*also Phys.*); das Zartgefühl; die Empfindungsfähigkeit. —**itize**, *v.a.* präparieren (*paper*). —**orial**, *adj.* Sinnes-. —**orium**, —**ory**, *s.* der Sitz der Empfindung, das Sensorium. —**ual**, *adj.*, —**ually**, *adv.* sinnlich; (voluptuous) wollüstig; —ual love, sinnliche Liebe. —**ualism**, *s.* der Sensualismus; (voluptuousness) die Sinnlichkeit. —**ualist**, *s.* der Sensualist (*also Phil.*); der sinnliche Mensch. —**uality**, *s.* die Sinnlichkeit. —**ualize**, *v.a.* sinnlich machen, zur Sinnlichkeit reizen. —**ualness**, *see* —uality. —**uous**, *adj.* die Sinne betreffend; sinnlich, den Sinnen dienend, sinnlichen Lüsten sich hingebend.

Sent, *imperf. & p.p. of* Send.

Senten—ce, I. *s.* der Satz, die Periode (*Gram.*); der Rechtsspruch, Richterspruch, das Urteil (*Law*); (opinion) das Urteil; to pass —ce upon a p., *see* —ce II.; —ce of death, Todesurteil. II. *v.a.* ein Urteil fällen über (*acc.*), verurteilen; to be —ced to 7 years' penal servitude, zu sieben Jahren Zuchthaus verurteilt werden. —**tious**, *adj.*, —**tiously**, *adv.* kurz, bündig, kräftig; sentenzenreich. —**tiousness**, *s.* die kräftige Kürze, Bündigkeit, Gedrungenheit.

Sentient, *adj.* empfindend, empfindungsfähig.

Sentiment, *s.* das Gefühl (*of gratitude, etc.*); *see* Sensibility; (thought) die Meinung, Gesinnung; der Gedanke (*opp. to* the words); man of —, Mann von Gefühl, zartfühlender Mensch. —**al**, *adj.*, —**ally**, *adv.* gefühlvoll, empfindsam, sentimental; (affectedly —al) empfindelnd, sentimental; —al journey, empfindsame Reise; —al novel, gefühlvoller Roman. —**alism**, —**ality**, *s.* das gefühlvolle Wesen, die Empfindelei, Sentimentalität. —**alist**, *s.* der empfindsame Mensch. —**alize**, *v.a.* empfindeln, sentimental sein *or* reden *or* schreiben.

Sent—inel, —**ry**, I. *s.* die Schildwache; to stand —inel, Schildwache stehen; to go on —ry, auf

Wache ziehen; to keep —ry over, bewachen. II. *v.a.* mit einer Schildwache *or* Schildwachen besetzen (*Mil.*). *Comp.* **—ry-box,** *s.* das Schilderhaus.

Sepal, *s.* das Kelchblatt. **—oid,** *adj.* kelchblattartig.

Separa—bility, *s.* die Trennbarkeit. **—ble,** *adj.*, **—bly,** *adv.* trennbar. **—bleness,** *s.* die Trennbarkeit. **—te,** I. *v.a.* absondern, (zer)trennen (*also fig.*); scheiden (*husband & wife; also Chem.*). II. *v.n.* sich trennen; sich scheiden. III. *adj.*, **—tely,** *adv.* abgesondert, getrennt, abgeschieden, einzeln genommen, besonder, für sich; —te account, die Separat-Rechnung; —te maintenance, die Alimente der geschiedenen Frau; (—tely) besonders. **—ting,** *p. see* —te; Scheide- (*Chem., etc.*). **—tion,** *s.* die Absonderung, Trennung, Scheidung; (state of —tion) die Getrenntheit, Abgeschiedenheit; die Scheidung (*Chem.*); die Ehescheidung (*Law*); —tion a mensa et thoro, die Trennung von Tisch und Bett. **—tism,** *s.* der Absonderungsgeist in Glaubenssachen, Separatismus. **—tist,** der Sonderling in Glaubenssachen, Separatist; Irish —tist, Irischer Nationalist, welcher Irland von England zu trennen wünscht. **—tive,** *adj.* zur Trennung geeignet. **—tor,** *s.* der Riet-, Scheide-, Schlichtkamm; die Scheidemaschine. **—tory,** I. *adj.* Absonderungs-. II. *s.* das Scheidemesser (*Surg.*).

Sepia, *s.* der Tintenfisch; die Sepia, das Tintenfischbraun.

Sepoy, *s.* der Sepoy, als englischer Soldat dienende eingeborene Ostindier.

Sept—angle, *s.* das Siebeneck. **—angular,** *adj.* siebenwink(e)lig. **—ember,** *s.* der September. **—enary,** *adj.* aus sieben bestehend; *see* —ennial. **—ennial,** *adj.* siebenjährig, sieben Jahre dauernd; (every 7th year) siebenjährlich, alle sieben Jahre. **—et,** *s.* das Septett. **—entrional,** *adj.* nördlich. **—i,** *in many cpds.* = sieben. **—ifolious,** *adj.* siebenblätterig. **—uagenarian,** *s.* der Siebzigjährige. **—uagesima,** *s.* Septuagesimä. **—uagint,** *s.* die Septuaginta.

Septic, I. *adj.* Fäulnis bewirkend, septisch. II. *s.* der Fäulnis bewirkende Stoff. **—ity,** *s.* die Neigung zur Fäulnis.

Septum, *s.* die Scheidewand (*Anat.*); die Kammer (*Bot.*).

Sepul—chral, *adj.* Grab-, Begräbnis-; —chral stone, der Leichenstein, Grabstein. **—chre,** *s.* das Grab, die Grabstätte. **—ture,** *s.* die Beerdigung.

Seque—l, *s.* die Folge; (result) der Erfolg; die Folgerung, Schlußfolge; in the —l, nachher, in der Folge. **—nce,** *s.* die Folge, Stufen-, Reihen-folge; (order) die Ordnung, Methode; die Sequenz (*Cards*); die Sequenz (*Mus., R. C.*). **—nt,** I. *adj.* auf einander folgend. II. *s.* der, die, das Folgende.

Sequest—er, *v.* I. *a.* absondern, entfernen; arm machen (*fig.*); sequestrieren (*Law*). II. *r.* sich zurückziehen. III. *n.* sich der Ansprüche begeben, verzichten auf (*acc.*) (*property*). **—ered,** *adj.* abgeschieden, zurückgezogen, einsam. **—rate,** *v.a.* sequestrieren. **—ration,** *s.* die Absonderung, Entfernung; *see* Seclusion; die Sequestration; besondere Verwaltung mit Beschlag belegter Güter (*Law*). **—rator,** *s.* der Sequestrator.

Sequin, *s.* die Zechine.

Seraglio, *s.* das Serail (der türkische Palast); der Harem.

Serai, *s.* die Karavanenherberge; der Harem.

Seraph, *s.* der Seraph. **—ic,** *adj.*, **—ically,** *adv.* seraphisch. **—im,** *pl. of* Seraph. **—ina,** *s.* die Seraphine (*Mus.*).

Sere, *adj. see* Sear.

Seren—ade, I. *s.* das Ständchen, die Nachtmusik, Serenade. II. *v.a.* (einem) ein Ständchen bringen. **—ader,** *s.* einer, der ein Ständchen bringt. **—e,** *adj.*, **—ely,** *adj.* heiter, klar, hell; (calm) ungetrübt, gelassen, ruhig; durchlauchtig (*as title*); most —e, durchlauchtigst; —e drop, der schwarze Star; Your (His) —e Highness, Euer (Seine) Durchlaucht. **—ity,** *s.* die Heiterkeit; die Gemütsruhe, Gelassenheit; your —ity, Euer Durchlaucht.

Serf, *s.* der Sklave, die Sklavin, der *and* die Leibeigene. **—dom,** *s.* die Leibeigenschaft.

Serge, *s.* die Serge, Sersche, Sarsche.

Sergeant, *s.* (bailiff) der Gerichtsdiener, Häscher; (police-constable) der Polizeidiener, Konstabler; *see* Serjeant; der Sergeant (*Mil.*); colour —, der Feldwebel; drill —, der Exerzierunteroffizier; pay —, Zahlmeistersergeant; quartermaster —, der Unterquartiermeister. *Comp.* **—-major,** *s.* der höchste Unteroffizier des Regiments. **—ship,** *s.* die Sergeantenstelle; der Sergeantendienst.

Seri—al, I. *adj.* zu einer Reihe gehörig, in Lieferungen, periodisch *or* heftweise erscheinend. II. *s.* (—al publication) das in Lieferungen, Heften erscheinende Werk. **—es,** *s.* die Reihe (*also Math.*); die Serie, Reihe(n-folge); die Reihe (*Math.*); (class) die Abteilung. **—ate,** *adj.*, **—ately,** *adv.* in Serien, in Reihen. **—atim,** *adv.* reihenweise, der Reihe nach.

Seri—ceous, *adj.* seidenartig (*of leaves*) (*Bot.*). **—culture,** *s.* die Seidenwürmerzucht.

Serio—comic(al), *adj.* ernst-komisch. **—us,** *adj.*, **—usly,** *adv.* ernst, ernsthaft, ernstlich; (important) bedeutend, wichtig; (solemn) feierlich; (religious) religiös, fromm; I am quite —us, es ist mein völliger Ernst; a —us matter, eine ernste Sache *or* Sache von Wichtigkeit; a —us illness, eine schwere Krankheit. **—usness,** *s.* die Ernsthaftigkeit, das ernsthafte Wesen; der Ernst; die Wichtigkeit; die Frömmigkeit.

Serjeant, *s. see* Sergeant; —-at-arms, — of the mace, der Stab-, Zepter-träger (*Parl.*); — at law, der Rechtskundige ersten Ranges, geheimer Justizrat.

Sermon, *s.* die Predigt. **—ize,** *v.* I. *n.* predigen, im Predigerton sprechen; Predigten schreiben. II. *a.* (einem) vorpredigen, (einen) hofmeistern.

Ser—osity, *s.* das Serum, die Serosität. **—ous,** *adj.* wässerig; serös; —ous membranes, vessels, seröse Häute, Gefäße. **—um,** *s.* das Blutwasser; das Heilserum.

Serpent, *s.* die Schlange (*also fig.*); der Serpent (*Mus.*). **—arius,** *s.* der Schlangenträger (*Astr.*). **—ine,** I. *adj.* schlangenartig, Schlangen-; (winding) sich schlängelnd, geschlängelt; Schlangen- (*stone, tongue, verse*). II. *s.* der Schlangenstein. *Comp.* (*in cdps. usually* = Schlangen-). **—-charmer,** *s.* der Schlangenbeschwörer. **—-eater,** *see* Secretary-bird. **—-like,** *adj.* schlangenartig.

Serpigo, *s.* die fressende Flechte (*Med.*).

Serrat—ed, *adj.* gezackt, zackig, sägenartig; gesägt, sägezähnig (*Bot.*). **—ion, —ure,** *s.* sägeartiger Einschnitt, die Auszähnung.

Serried, *adj.* gedrängt, dicht.

Serval, *s.* die Tigerkatze, Pantherkatze.

Serv—ant, *s.* der Knecht, Diener; (maid) die Magd, Dienerin; der Diener (*fig.*); der Beamte; civil —ant, der Zivilbeamte, im Zivildienst; general —ant, das Mädchen für alles; the —ants, das Gesinde; man —ant, der Bediente; your obedient —ant, Ihr gehorsamer Diener, ergebenst (*in letters*); your humble —ant, meine Wenigkeit (*coll., hum.*). **—e,** *v.* I. *a.* dienen (God, a p., a th., Gott, einem, einer Sache); bedienen (*a p., customers, the guns, a church*); anbieten, vorlegen (*food*); (—e up) auftragen; verwalten (*an office*); (satisfy) befriedigen; (treat) behandeln, (einem) begegnen; (be instead of) statt einer andern Sache dienen; erfüllen (*one's purpose*); (help) helfen, nützen, dienlich sein, (be)fördern; ausdienen (*one's time, etc.*); bekleiden (*ropes, rigging, etc.*); to —e in Parliament, im Parlament sitzen; to —e the ball, den Ball aufschlagen, anschlagen (*Tennis*); to —e an execution, einen Vollziehungsbefehl ausführen; to —e a notice or summons upon (a p.), (einen) vorladen, vor Gericht zitieren; to —e a process, (einem) eine gerichtliche Eröffnung machen, wodurch ein Beklagter gezwungen werden soll, sich vor Gericht zu stellen; to —e s. o.'s purpose, jemandes Zwecke (Vorhaben) günstig sein, ihn (es) fördern; to —e no purpose, zu nichts dienen; to —e quarantine, Quarantäne halten; that —es him right, das geschieht ihm recht; to —e a p. a trick, einem einen Streich spielen; it —es our turn, es paßt sich gerade für uns; when his turn is —ed, wenn seine Wünsche erfüllt sind; he —ed me ungratefully (very badly), er hat mir mit Undank gelohnt, (sich sehr schlecht gegen mich benommen); to —e a warrant, einen Verhaftsbefehl verlesen und vollstrecken; to —e a writ upon, (dem Beklagten) einen richterlichen Befehl vorlesen *or* zustellen; to —e a writ of attachment, in Beschlag nehmen (*goods, etc.*); verhaften (*a p.*); first come, first —ed, wer zuerst kommt, mahlt zuerst (*prov.*); to —e **out**, austeilen, reichen, geben (*supplies, etc.*); ausdienen, -stehen (*an apprenticeship*); mit gleicher Münze bezahlen; to —e **up**, auftragen; dinner is —ed (up), das Essen ist aufgetragen *or* steht auf dem Tisch. II. *n.* dienen, dienstbar sein; dienen (*Mil.*); in Diensten stehen bei (*as a servant, etc.*); aufwarten, servieren (*at table*); (suit) nützen, passen, günstig sein; (suffice) reichen, hinlänglich sein, genügen; (answer for) dienen (zu, statt), geeignet sein; that will —e to convince him, das wird dazu dienen, ihn zu überzeugen; the rug —ed as a carpet, die Decke diente als Teppich. **—er**, *s.* der Aufschläger, Anschläger (*Tennis*). **—ice**, *s.* der Dienst; (use) der Nutzen, Vorteil; (kind act) der Dienst, die Dienstleistung, Gefälligkeit; der Gang (*of dishes*); das Tafel-gerät, -zeug (*of china, etc.*); die Aufwartung, Bedienung (*in a hotel, etc.*); die Bedienung (*Artil.*); der Aufschlag, Anschlag (*Tennis, etc.*); civil, military, naval, public —ice, Zivil-, Kriegs-, See-, Staats-dienst; active military —ice, Dienst bei der Fahne; Indian civil —ice, der Staatsdienst in Ostindien; universal military —ice, die allgemeine Wehrpflicht; —ice abroad, der Auslandsdienst; baptismal, church, divine, funeral, marriage, solemn —ice, die Taufhandlung, der Kirchendienst, die Trauhandlung, die Seelenmesse (*R. C.*); (book) das Gebet- und Gesang-buch *or* die Kirchenagende, der Gottesdienst, das Totenamt; night —ice, der Nachtdienst (*Railw.*); passenger —ice, die Personenbeförderung; postal —ice, der Postdienst; to be at, in —ice, in Diensten sein, stehen; to be on —ice, Dienst haben; to go out to —ice, in Dienst gehen, Dienst annehmen; out of —ice, außer Dienst; your —ice, Sie schlagen an (*Tennis*); underhand(-twist) —ice, der Tiefaufschlag (mit Drehball) (*Tennis*); to see —ice, vor dem Feinde stehen, Pulver riechen; to be of —ice to, (einem) nützlich sein, nützen; to be at a p.'s —ice, einem zu Diensten stehen; to do s.o. a —ice, einem einen Gefallen erweisen, einen Dienst leisten; he came to offer me his —ices, er kam, um mir seine Dienste anzubieten. **—iceable**, *adj.* dienlich, nützlich; (fit for use) zu gebrauchen, brauchbar; dienstfertig (*Shakes.*). **—iceableness**, *s.* die Zweckdienlichkeit, Nützlichkeit. **—ile**, *adj.*, **—ilely**, *adv.* sklavisch, dienend; knechtisch; unterwürfig; (cringing) kriechend; niedrig (*as obedience, fear, etc.*). **—ility**, *s.* die Sklaverei; das knechtische Wesen; der Knechtsinn, die Kriecherei. **—itor**, *s.* der Diener, der Stipendiat der zweiten Klasse (*obs., Oxford Univ.*). **—itude**, *s.* die Dienstbarkeit, Knechtschaft, die Sklaverei; die Servitut (*Law*); penal —itude, die Zwangsarbeit, Zuchthausstrafe. *Comp.* **—ant-maid, —ing-maid**, *s.* die Magd. **—ice-line**, *s.* die Auf-, An-schlagslinie (*Tennis*). **—ice-(side-)line**, *s.* die Aufschlags(seiten)linie (*Tennis*). **—ice-pipe**, *s.* das Zweig-, Neben-rohr. **—ing-man**, *s.* der Diener; der Aufwärter.

Service—-berry, *s.* die Sperlingsbeere. **—-tree**, *s.* die zahme Eberesche.

Serviette, *s.* die Serviette.

Sesame, *s.* der Sesam; open —! Sesam, Sesam, tu dich auf!

Sesqui, *in cpds.* anderthalb. **—alteral, —alterate**, *adj.* anderthalbmal so viel. **—duplicate**, *s.* das Verhältnis von 2½ zu 1 oder 5 zu 2 andeutend. **—pedalian**, *adj.* anderthalbfüßig; übertrieben lang (*hum.*). **—plicate**, *adj.* das Verhältnis von 1½ zu 1 bezeichnend.

Sess—ile, *adj.* sitzend, stiellos (*Bot.*). **—ion**, *s.* die Sitzung, Gerichtssitzung (*Law*); die Sitzungsperiode; das Semester (*Americ.*); —ions of the peace, Sitzungen der Friedensrichter. **—ional**, *adj.* Sitzungs-.

Sestet, *s.* das Sextett, sechsstimmige Tonstück.

Sestine, *s.* die sechszeilige Stanze, Sestine.

Set, I. *ir.v.a.* setzen, stellen; (lay) legen; (adjust) (ein)richten; stecken, legen (*potatoes, etc.*); setzen, pflanzen (*trees, etc.*); setzen (to music, etc., in Musik ꝛc.); stellen (*a watch, clock*); ausstellen (*a watch, Mil.*); beisetzen (*one's seal or name*); hinstellen (*an example*); angeben, einführen (*a fashion*); festaufsetzen (*stakes*); fassen (*guns*); besetzen, fassen (*with stones, etc.*); aussetzen (*the sails*); gerinnen machen (*milk*); erstarren machen (*metals*); einrichten, einsetzen (*a broken limb*); schärfen, schleifen (*edged tools, razors*); richten (*a file*); schränken (*a saw*); festsetzen, bestimmen (*a time*); richten (one's mind on, die Gedanken auf (*acc.*)); (vor)stehen (*birds, Sport.*); (embarrass) ängstigen, bedrängen; to — free, befreien, in Freiheit setzen, fliegen lassen (*of birds*); to — in order, ordnen; bestellen (*one's house*); to — sail, unter Segel gehen; he — me a subject for an essay, er gab mir ein Thema für einen Aufsatz; to — a p. a task, einem eine Aufgabe stellen; to — an (examination) paper, einen Fragebogen (für eine Prüfung) aufstellen *or* verfassen; to — a trap, eine Falle stellen; to — the teeth, mit den Zähnen knirschen; he — his teeth hard, er biß die Zähne zusammen; to — **afloat**, verbreiten (*a rumour*); to — **against**, entgegensetzen; to — a p. against a th., einen gegen etwas einnehmen; to — **(a-)going**, in Gang, Umlauf bringen; to — a mill (a-)going, eine Mühle anlassen; to — **apart**, besonders stellen (*lit.*); beiseite legen, auf die Seite legen; bei Seite schieben; to — **aside**, bei Seite setzen; (reject) verwerfen; (annul) aufheben, umstoßen; to — **at** defiance, (einem) Trotz bieten; to — at ease *or* rest, beruhigen; to — at naught, nicht achten; to — at variance, entzweien; to — at work, beschäftigen, zur Arbeit anstellen; to — **back**, zurücksetzen; to — **before**, (einem) vorsetzen, vorlegen; to — **behind**, hintan-, nach-setzen; to — store **by**, Wert legen auf (*acc.*); to — **down**, niedersetzen (*a th.*); absetzen (*out of a carriage*); nieder-, auf-schreiben (*in writing*); zuschreiben (*to a p.*); — it down to my account, schreiben Sie es auf meine Rechnung, setzen (stellen) Sie es mir auf (in) Rechnung; it was — down to me, die Schuld wurde mir zugeschrieben; — me down at No. 22, lassen Sie mich bei Nro. 22 aussteigen; to give s.o. a —ting down, einem einen derben Verweis erteilen, ihn demütigen (*coll.*); to — s.o. (a th.) down to *or* as, einen (eine Sache) erklären für; he — down their fears to female timidity, er schrieb ihre Befürchtungen weiblicher Zaghaftigkeit zu; to — **forth**, kundtun, zeigen; (dispose) stellen, ordnen; to — **off**, hervorheben, (stark) hervortreten lassen; to — **on**, (incite) antreiben; (employ) anstellen; to — on shore, ans Land setzen; to — eyes on, sehen; to — on foot, in Gang bringen; to — on high, on edge, on fire, erheben, (die Zähne) stumpf machen, (ein Haus ꝛc.) in Brand stecken;

to — **out**, aussetzen; vorzeigen, vorstellen; (mark out) abstecken (*houses, etc.*); anlegen (*a garden*); (embellish) schmücken, herausputzen; herausstreichen (*fig.*); (equip) ausrüsten; (publish) bekanntmachen; (assign) zuteilen; (show) darstellen; (prove) beweisen; (state) auseinandersetzen; to — pen **to** paper, die Feder ansetzen; to — one's hand to, Hand an (eine S.) legen, (eine Urkunde) unterschreiben; to — to rights, in Ordnung bringen, ordnen; (repair) reparieren; to — **up**, auf=stellen, =richten, =pflanzen, errichten; (print) (auf, in Druck) setzen (*Typ.*); sich (*dat.*) anschaffen (*a carriage*); aufstellen, vorbringen (*doctrines*); ausstoßen (*a shout*); (einen) erheben, (einem) aufhelfen (*a person*); anfangen (*a business*); he — his son up in business, er verschaffte seinem Sohn ein Geschäft. II. *ir.v.n.* (congeal, *etc.*) gerinnen, erstarren; fließen, laufen (*as a current*); untergehen (*as the sun, etc.*); the tide —s to the south, die Flut läuft südwärts; to — to partners, den Schwebeschritt machen; to — **about**, sich (*dat.*) vornehmen, anfangen; I don't know how to — about it, ich weiß nicht, wie ich es anfangen soll; to — **forth**, sich aufmachen, aufbrechen; to — forth on a journey, eine Reise antreten; to — **forward**, sich auf den Weg machen, weiter reisen; to — **in**, beginnen; a southern monsoon — in, es trat ein südlicher Monsun ein; to — **on** *or* **upon**, anfangen; (attack) angreifen; to — upon a p., über einen herfallen; to — **out**, abreisen, aufbrechen, sich auf den Weg machen; (take its rise) ausgehen (from, von); to — **up**, sich niederlassen, sich selbständig machen (*in business, etc.*), anfangen (ein Geschäft); to — up for, sich ausgeben für; I never — up for a saint, ich habe nie für einen Heiligen gelten wollen; to — up for o.s., ein eigenes Geschäft anfangen, sein eigenes *or* sich (*dat.*) ein Hauswesen gründen; auf eigne Faust handeln. III. *p.p. & adj.* fest, unbeweglich, starr; (prescribed) vorgeschrieben; (in due form) förmlich; (intent) versessen (auf eine S.), entschlossen (zu); fest (*as prices; a determination, etc.*); I was hard —, ich war in großer Not; sharp —, heißhungrig; at — distances, in gewissen, bestimmten Entfernungen; — form, das Formular; — purpose, fester Vorsatz; a — speech, eine wohlüberlegte, wohldurchdachte Rede; with — teeth, mit zusammengebissenen Zähnen. IV. *s.* eine Anzahl zusammengehöriger oder zu einander passender Dinge einer Art, die Reihe, Folge, Sammlung; der Untergang (*of the sun*); der Vorstand, das Stehen (*of a dog*); der Satz (*of boxes, balls, chessmen, instruments, weights, etc.*); das Besteck (*of instruments*); (clique) die Gesellschaft, Clique; (pack, lot) die Sippschaft, Rotte, Bande, das Pack; die Garnitur (*of ribbons, etc.*); der Guß (*of letters*); die Sammlung (*of engravings, etc.*); das Carré (*Danc.*); der Aufsatz, das Service (*of china, etc.*); der Setzling (*Hort.*); die Unterabteilung einer Schulklasse; (stake) der Satz; (bent, direction) die Richtung; (game) die Partie; der Schnitt (*of a dress, etc.*); the skirt has got a wrong —, der Rock fällt schlecht; — of teeth, das Gebiß; — of features, die Gesichtszüge; a — of fools, eine Narrengesellschaft; to make a dead — upon, at a p., von einem durchaus nicht loslassen wollen; he has got into a bad —, er ist in schlechte Gesellschaft geraten; — of quadrilles, die Quadrille. —**tee**, *s.* das Kanapee, kleine Sofa (mit hohem Rücken und zwei Lehnen). —**ter**, *s.* der Hühnerhund, Vorstehhund; der Setzer (*in stones, etc.*); —ter up, Auf=richter, =steller. —**ting**, *s.* das Setzen; die Fassung (*of a jewel, etc.*); der Untergang (*of the sun, etc.*); die Richtung (*of a current, etc.*); das Hartwerden (*of a semi-fluid*); das Erstarren (*of iron*); —ting up in business, die Selbständigmachung, Geschäftsgründung. —**tle**, *etc.*, *see* Settl—e. *Comp.* —**-down**, *s.* der derbe Verweis. —**-fair**, *s.* schön Wetter (*on barometers*); zweiter Abputz (*Mason.*). —**-off**, *s.* der Abstich, starke Gegensatz; (adornment) der Schmuck, die Zierde; die Gegen=forderung, =rechnung (*C. L.*); die Gegenforderung (*Law*). —**ting-board**, *s.* das Schmetterlingsbrett. —**ting-rule**, *s.* die Setzlinie (*Typ.*). —**ting-stick**, *s.* der Winkelhaken (*Typ.*). —**-to**, *s.* der (Wort=)Streit, die Schlägerei.

Settl—e, I. *s.* der Sessel, Sitz, die Ruhebank. II. *v.n.* sich setzen; sich ansiedeln *or* niederlassen (*in a place*); (marry, *etc.*) sich verheiraten und häuslich niederlassen; (—e in business) ein Geschäft gründen; (become solid) Festigkeit gewinnen (*also fig.*); (decide) sich fest bestimmen, entscheiden; sich senken (*as walls*); sich setzen (*as a fluid*); sich niederschlagen (*as sediment*); sich aufklären *or* beständig werden (*as weather*); nachlassen, sich legen (*as fury*); sich ausgleichen, sich arrangieren (*with one's creditors*); to —e down, sich häuslich einrichten; sich beruhigen; the wind came round and —ed **in** the west, der Wind drehte sich und wehte beständig aus Westen; to —e **into**, allmählich in einen Zustand übergehen; to —e **on** something, sich entschließen *or* entscheiden (für, zu); to —e **to** something, sich zu etwas bestimmen. III. *v.a.* (fest=)setzen, feststellen; (arrange) ordnen, in Ordnung bringen; zu Ende bringen (*a matter*); abführen (*a debt*); abschließen, abmachen (*accounts*); (pay) bezahlen; beilegen, ausgleichen, schlichten (*disputes, etc.*); (calm) in Ruhe bringen; (colonize) kolonisieren, ansiedeln; versorgen (*one's children*); verheiraten (*daughters*); selbständig machen, etablieren (*a p. in business*); aussetzen (*an annuity upon, etc.*); klären (*fluids*); nieder, zu Boden schlagen (*sl.*); to —e the price (points of law, *etc.*), den Preis (Rechtspunkte) festsetzen; to —e the succession to the throne, die Thronfolge bestimmen *or* festsetzen; he has —ed £300 a year upon her, er hat ihr eine Leibrente von 300 Pfund jährlich ausgesetzt. —**ed**, *adj.* fest, bestimmt; (methodical) geordnet; (decided) entschieden; (steady) beständig (*as wind, weather*); —ed abode, fester Wohnort; —ed account, abgemachte Rechnung; —ed conviction, feste Überzeugung; —ed habit, eingewurzelte Gewohnheit; —ed opinions, bestimmte, unumstößliche Meinungen. —**edness**, *s.* der Zustand. —**ement**, *s.* das Festsetzen, die Festsetzung, Bestimmung, endgültige Entscheidung; (dregs) der Satz; das Setzen, Senken, Sacken (*Railw.*); die Niederlassung (*in a place*); (establishment in life, *etc.*) die Gründung eines Hausstandes, eines Geschäftes; die Verheiratung; die Versorgung (*of children*); (colonization) die Niederlassung, Ansiedelung; (colony) die Niederlassung, Kolonie; das Leibgeding, die Leibrente; das Anstellungsgeld (*of an American pastor*); (—ing) die Beruhigung, Schlichtung, Übereinkunft, Ausgleichung, der Vergleich; die Ausgleichung, Saldierung, der Abschluß (*of an account*); act, bill of —ement, die Thronfolge-Akte; deed of —ement, die Gründungsurkunde; to come to a —ement, sich vergleichen, einen Vergleich abschließen; to make a —ement upon, einem etwas aussetzen. —**er**, *s.* der Ansiedler, Pflanzer; das entscheidende Wort, der entscheidende Schritt, das Entscheidende (*coll.*); (blow) der derbe Schlag (*sl.*). —**ing**, *s.* das sich Setzen (*of dregs, etc.*); die Ansiedelung (*of a country*); die Abmachung (*of disputes*); die Abrechnung, Berechnung (*C. L.*). *Comp.* —**ing-day**, der Abrechnungstag.

Seven, *num. adj.* sieben; (— o'clock) sieben Uhr; — Years' War, der Siebenjährige Krieg. —**fold**, *adj. & adv.* siebenfach, siebenfältig. —**night**, *see* Sennight. —**teen**, *num. adj.* siebzehn. —**teenth**, *adj.* siebzehnt. —**th**, I. *adj.* siebent. II. *s.* das Siebentel; die Septime (*Mus.*). —**thly**, *adv.* siebentens. —**tieth**, *adj.* siebzigst.

—ty, I. *num. adj.* siebzig. II. *s.* die (Zahl) Siebzig; the —ty, die 70 Verfasser der Septuaginta. *Comp.* **—-hilled,** *adj.* siebenhügelig. **—-leagued,** *adj.;* —-leagued boots, Siebenmeilenstiefel.

Sever, *v.* I. *a.* trennen, sondern. II. *n.* sich trennen, sich scheiden. **—al,** I. *adj.* besonder, einzeln; (different) verschieden, unterschieden; (divers) mehrere, verschiedene; (separate) getrennt, geteilt; —al large ships, mehrere große Schiffe; each —al ship, jedes einzelne Schiff; three —al armies, drei verschiedene Heere; each —al part, jeder Teil im Besondern; joint and —al note, solidarisch verbürgter Schuldschein. II. *s.* das Einzelding (*obs.*); der Einzelne (*obs.*); (*pl.*) mehrere, einige; in —al, insbesondre, besonders. **—ally,** *adv.* besonders, einzeln; jointly and —ally bound, solidarisch verbunden; jointly and —ally responsible, einzeln und zusammen verantwortlich. **—ance,** *s.* die Trennung, Scheidung, Absonderung.

Sever—e, *adj.*, **—ely,** *adv.* streng (*as a judge, words, treatment, etc.*); streng, hart (*as the winter*); heftig (*as pain*); ernst, schmucklos (*in style*); ernst, streng (*of the countenance*); genau, kritisch (*as a test*); schlimm, schwer (*as an accident or wound*); (rigid) hart, streng; to be —e upon a p., strenge mit einem verfahren. **—ity,** *s.* die Strenge, Schärfe, Härte; die Ernsthaftigkeit; die Heftigkeit (*of pain*); the —ity of a test, die Gründlichkeit einer Prüfung.

Sew, *v.* I. *a.* nähen; heften, broschieren (*a book*); to — **on,** annähen; to — **together,** zusammennähen; to — **up,** zunähen. II. *n.* nähen. **—er,** *s.* der, die Nähende, die Näherin. **—ing,** *s.* das Nähen, die Näherei. *Comp.* **—ing-case,** *s.* das Nähkästchen. **—ing-desk,** *s.* das Nähtischchen, Nähpult. **—ing-machine,** I. *s.* die Nähmaschine. II. *attrib.;* —ing-machine attachments, die an eine Nähmaschine anzuschraubenden Apparate. **—ing-needle,** *s.* die Nähnadel. **—ing-silk** *or* **-thread,** *s.* die Nähseide, das Nähgarn.

Sew—age, *s.* das Kloaken=, Siel=wasser. **—er,** *s.* der Abzugskanal, die Abzucht, Kloake. **—erage,** *s.* der Kanalbau, die Gesammtheit der Abzugskanäle, das Kloakensystem.

Sex, *s.* das Geschlecht; the fair —, das schöne Geschlecht; of both —es, beiderlei Geschlechts. **—less,** *adj.* geschlechtslos. **—ual,** *adj.*, **—ually,** *adv.* geschlechtlich, Geschlechts=, Sexual=; —ual disease, die Geschlechtskrankheit; —ual intercourse, geschlechtlicher Umgang; —ual system, das Sexualsystem (*Bot.*). **—ualist,** *s.* der Sexualist (*Bot.*). **—uality,** *s.* die Geschlechtlichkeit.

Sex—agenarian, *s.* der, die Sechzigjährige. **—agenary,** *adj.* sechzigjährig; —agenary arithmetic, die Sexagesimalrechnung. **—agesima,** *s.* der Sonntag Sexagesima. **—agesimal,** I. *adj.* sechzigst; Sexagesimal= (*arithmetic, etc.*). II. *s.* der Sexagesimalbruch. **—angle,** *s.* das Sechseck. **—ennial,** *adj.* sechsjährig; alle sechs Jahre wiederkehrend. **—fid,** *adj.* sechsspaltig (*Bot.*). **—tant,** *s.* der Sextant. **—tile,** *s.* der Gesechstschein. **—tuple,** *adj.* sechsfach.

Sextain, *s.* die sechszeilige Strophe.

Sexton, *s.* der Küster; (grave-digger) der Totengräber. *Comp.* **—-beetle,** *s.* der Aaskäfer.

Shabb—ily, *adv.*, **—y,** *adj.* schäbig, abgetragen, fadenscheinig (*as clothes*); (mean) elend, niederträchtig, gemein, schuftig; —y trick, ein elender Streich; —y finery, armseliger Putz; —ily dressed man, ein armselig gekleideter Mann. **—iness,** *s.* die Schäbigkeit, Lumpigkeit. *Comp.* **—y-genteel,** *adj.* ärmlich=fein, schäbig=nobel.

Shabrack, *s.* die Schabracke.

Shackle, I. *v.a.* fesseln, hemmen (*also fig.*). II. *s.* das Kettenglied; der bewegliche eiserne Bügel. **—s,** *pl.* Fesseln (*also fig.*); Hand= *or* Bein=schellen. *Comp.* **—-bone, —-joint,** *s.* das Handgelenk.

Shad, *s.* die Alse, Else (*Icht.*).

Shad—e, I. *s.* der Schatten (*also fig., Art, etc.*); (shelter) der Schutz, Schatten; (—y spot) der Schatten, schattige Platz; (—ing) die Schattierung; die Abtönung, Nüance (*of colours*), der Farbenton; der (Licht=, Feuer= 2c.) Schirm (*for lamps, fires, etc.*); (ghost) der Schatten, das Gespenst; —e for the eyes, der Augenschützer; the —es, die Dunkelheit; die Manen (*pl.*); (realm of —s) das Schattenreich; to cast in (throw into) the —e, (einen) in Schatten stellen, verdunkeln, ausstechen; a —e higher, um eine Kleinigkeit höher; glass —e, der Glassturz, die Glasglocke. II. *v.a.* be=, um=schatten; schützen (*from light, heat, etc.*), bergen; in Schatten stellen, verdunkeln (*fig.*); schattieren, schatten (*Paint.*); (darken) in dunkeln Farben malen; to —e **away,** vermindern; to —e **off,** abschattieren. **—ed,** *adj.* abgetönt. **—eless,** *adj.* schattenlos. **—ily,** *adv.* schattig. **—iness,** *s.* das Schattige, der Schatten. **—ing,** *s.* das Schattieren; das Abtönen (der Farben). **—ow,** I. *s.* der Schatten; der Schatten, unzertrennliche Begleiter (*fig.*); der Schatten, das Vorbild, Bild (*fig.*); die Maske, der Vorwand (*fig.*); das Dunkel, der Schatten (*Paint.*); der Geheimpolizist (*Amer.*); to be afraid of one's own —ow, vor seinem eignen Schatten erschrecken; darkness and the —ow of death, Finsternis und Dunkel (*B.*). II. *v.a.* verdunkeln; (—ow forth) vorbilden, (vor)bildlich darstellen; (indicate) andeuten, undeutlich darstellen; (a p., einem) auf dem Fuße folgen; a criminal —owed by a detective, ein Verbrecher, dem ein Geheimpolizist wie sein Schatten *or* auf dem Fuße folgt(e). **—owless,** *adj.* schattenlos. **—owy,** *adj.* schattig, dunkel; (spiritlike) schattenhaft; (dim) dämmerig; (unreal) wesenlos. **—y,** *adj. see* —owy; (sheltered) geschützt; dunkel, zweideutig, anrüchig, verrufen; bedenklich (*fig.*); on the —y side of fifty, über die Fünfzig hinaus; a —y trick, ein böser Streich. *Comp.* **—e-temperature,** *s.* die Temperatur im Schatten.

Shaft, *s.* der Schaft (*Arch., Weav., of an arrow, tree, etc.*); die Spindel (*of a tower*); der Kasten (*of a chimney*), Kaminschacht; die Welle, der Wellbaum (*Mach.*); der Helm, Stiel (*of a hammer, etc.*); die Stange, der Schaft (*Gun.*); die Deichsel (*Carr.*); (arrow) der Pfeil; der Schacht (*Min.*); to sink a —, einen Schacht abteufen. **—s,** *pl.* die Scherendeichsel, Gabel (*of a carriage*); the —s of ridicule, die Pfeile des Spottes. *Comp.* **—-horse,** *s.* das Gabelpferd.

Shag, I. *s.* die Zotte, rauhes zottiges Haar; das rauhe Haar am Tuche; der Plüsch; das abgesetzte Stück; das Gerstenstroh (*Agr.*); der langfaserige Kraus=, Krull=tabak; der Seerabe (*Orn.*). II. *v.a.* zottig, rauh machen; (deform) entstellen. III. *v.n.* zottig herabhängen. **—giness,** *s.* das Zottige. **—gy,** *adj.* zottig.

Shagreen, *s.* der Chagrin, das genarbte Leder.

Shah, *s.* der Schah (von Persien, of Persia).

Shak—e, I. *ir.v.a.* schütteln; (jolt, rock) rütteln; zittern machen; ausschütteln (*carpets, etc.*); trillern (*Mus.*); (er)schüttern (*the nerves, etc.*); (endanger) erschüttern, gefährden; to —e hands, sich (*dat.*) die Hände schütteln, geben; let us —e hands over it! gieb mir die Hand darauf! he shook him cordially by the hand, er schüttelte ihm herzlich die Hand; he shook the dust from off his feet, er schüttelte den Staub von seinen Füßen; to be very much —en, stark erschüttert werden; not to be —en, unerschütterlich; to —e **down,** herabschütteln; to —e **off,** abschütteln (*a yoke, etc.*); sich losmachen von (a p.); to —e **to pieces,** entzweischütteln; to —e **out,** herausschütteln, ausschütten; to —e **up,** zusammen=, auf=schütten. II. *ir.v.n.* zittern, beben, schüttern (with, at, vor); trillern (*Mus.*); to —e with laughter, sich vor Lachen schütteln. III. *s.* das Schütteln; das Schüttern; der Triller (*Mus.*); der Kernriß (*in *wood*); —e of the hand, —e-hands, der Händedruck; no great —es, nichts Besonderes (*sl.*). —**en**, I. *p.p. of* —e. II. *adj.* erschüttert. —**er**, *s.* der Schüttler, Rüttler; das Zittergras (*Bot.*); the —ers, die Schakers, Zitterer (*Rel.*). —**iness**, *s.* die Wackligkeit; die Gebrechlichkeit. —**ing**, I. *adj.* schüttelnd. II. *s.* das Schütteln; das Zittern, Beben; die Erschütterung. —**y**, *adj.* zitternd, unsicher; (unreliable) unzuverlässig; (weak) wackelig, schwach; gebrechlich; kernrissig (*as wood*); the firm is —y, das Haus wankt *or* steht auf schwachen Füßen. *Comp.* —**e-down**, *s.* eine Schütte Stroh; das Lager auf dem Boden *or* auf Stühlen (*fig.*).

Shako, *s.* der Tschako.

[1]**Shale**, I. *s.* die Schale. II. *v.a.* schälen, aushülsen.

[2]**Shale**, *s.* der Schieferton, Bandschiefer.

Shall, *ir. aux. v.* werden; (must, ought, *etc.*) sollen; werden, wollen (*in pure questions*); sollen (*with questions asking permission, direction, etc.*); — I fetch it for you? soll ich es dir holen? will you do it? I —, werden Sie es tun? Ja; — we go for a walk, wollen wir spazieren gehen?

Shallop, *s.* die Schaluppe.

Shal(l)ot, *s.* die Schalotte (*Bot.*).

Shallow, I. *adj.* seicht, nicht tief; seicht, oberflächlich (*fig.*); *see* —-brained. II. *s.* die Untiefe. —**ness**, *s.* die Seichtigkeit, Untiefe; die Oberflächlichkeit. *Comp.* —-**brained**, —-**pated**, *adj.* seichtköpfig, oberflächlich, albern.

Sham, I. *s.* der Trug, der leere Schein; die Lüge, Täuschung. II. *v.a. see* Feign; betrügen. III. *v.n.* sich stellen, heucheln. IV. *adj.* falsch, unecht; (counterfeit) nachgemacht; (pretended) angeblich, scheinbar; — fight, das Scheingefecht; — title-page, der Schmutztitel; — window, blindes Fenster. —**mer**, *s.* der Betrüger.

Shambl—e, *v.n.* schlenkern; linkisch, schleppend gehen. —**ing**, *adj.* schlenkernd, schlotternd.

Shambles, *s.* die Schlachtbank, das Schlachthaus.

Shame, I. *s.* die Scham, das Schamgefühl, die Bescheidenheit, Sittsamkeit; (disgrace) die Schande; for —! pfui! schäme dich! schämt euch! to cry — upon, sich aufhalten über (*acc.*); to put to —, beschämen; I take — to myself that . . ., ich gestehe zu meiner Schande, daß . . . II. *v.a.* beschämen, schamrot machen; to — a p. into . . ., einen durch Beschämung dazu bringen zu . . .; tell the truth and — the devil, rede die Wahrheit und lache den Teufel aus! —**ful**, *adj.*, —**fully**, *adv.* schändlich, schmachvoll; (indecent) unanständig. —**fulness**, *s.* die Schändlichkeit. —**less**, *adj.*, —**lessly**, *adv.* schamlos, schändlich (*as a deed*). —**lessness**, *s.* die Schamlosigkeit. *Comp.* —**faced**, *adj.*, —**facedly**, *adv.* schamhaft, verschämt, blöde. —**facedness**, *s.* die Schamhaftigkeit.

Shammy, *s.* das Sämischleder, Waschleder.

Shampoo, I. *v.a.* kneten (*the body*); waschen (the hair, den Kopf). II. *s.* (—ing) das Waschen und Kneten des Kopfes.

Shamrock *s.* der kriechende Weißklee; das Kleeblatt, Nationalzeichen der Irländer.

Shandygaff, *s.* eine Mischung von ginger-beer und ale.

Shank, *s.* der Schenkel; der Stengel, Stiel (*of plants*); der Schaft, das Rohr (*of a key*); das Öhr (*of a button*); der Schaft (*of a column*); to ride —'s mare, auf Schusters Rappen reiten. —**ed**, *adj.* mit Schenkeln 2c.

Shanty, *s.* die Hütte, der Schuppen.

Shape, I. *s.* die Gestalt, Form, Bildung; (being) die Gestalt; (figure) der Wuchs, die Taille; die Hutform (*of milliners, etc.*); (mould) die Form; der feste Pudding (*Cook.*); to put out of —, aus der Form *or* Fasson bringen; to take —, eine Form bekommen, sich gestalten; to lick into —, manierlich machen; in the — of a man, in der Gestalt eines Mannes. II. *v.a.* bilden, formen, gestalten; (adjust) einrichten, anordnen; richten (*one's course, etc.*). —**less**, *adj.* formlos, ungestalt. —**liness**, *s.* die Wohlgestalt. —**ly**, *adj.* wohlgestaltet; ebenmäßig (*as a column*). —**n**, *p.p. & adj.* gestaltet; —n in iniquity, aus sündlichem Samen gezeugt (*B.*).

Shard, *s.* die Scherbe; die Schale (*of an egg, o snail*); harte Flügeldecke (*of a beetle*).

[1]**Share**, I. *s.* der Teil, Anteil; der Beitrag (*towards something*); der Anteilschein, die Aktie (*in a joint-stock company*); der Kux (*in a mine*); ordinary —, die Stammaktie; preferred —, die Stammprioritätsaktie; the —s are (selling) at . . ., die Aktien stehen auf . . .; to have a — in, teil-haben, -nehmen an einer S.; to fall to one's —, einem zuteil werden; to go —s in, teilen mit, teilnehmen an (*dat.*); he bears his — of, er trägt seinen Anteil an; but a small — of good sense, nur wenig Verstand; — and — alike, zu gleichen Teilen. II. *v.a.* (ver)teilen, austeilen (amongst, unter, *acc.*); (divide) zerteilen; to — with a p., mit einem teilen; to — s.o.'s joy, jemandes Freude teilen; I — the common fate, ich teile das allgemeine Schicksal. III. *v.n.* teilhaben (in a th., an einer S.). —**r**, *s.* der Teiler, Verteiler; (partaker) der Teil-haber, -nehmer, Mitinteressent. *Comp.* —-**bone**, *s.* das Schambein (*Anat.*). —-**broker**, *s.* der Aktienmakler. —**holder**, *s.* der Aktieninhaber, Aktionär.

[2]**Share**, *s.* die Pflugschar (*Agr.*).

Shark, *s.* der Hai(fisch); der Beutelschneider, Betrüger (*fig.*).

Sharp, I. *adj.*, —**ly**, *adv.* scharf (*lit. & fig.*); scharf, schneidend (*as the air*); durchdringend, heftig, scharf (*as pain*); scharf, hart, bitter (*as words*); heftig, hitzig (*as a quarrel*); (clever, witty) scharf(sinnig), sinnreich; (subtle) scharf, spitzfindig, verschlagen; (wide-awake) scharf, munter, aufgeweckt; hart, streng (*as a sentence*); *see* Hungry; (quick) rasch; (eager) gierig; a — contest, ein scharfer Streit; she sings —, sie singt falsch (zu hoch); look —! paß' auf! aufgepaßt! (quick!) schnell, geschwind! — features, scharfe Gesichtszüge; C —, Cis (*Mus.*). II. *s.* das Kreuz (♯); die durch ein Kreuz erhöhte Note (*Mus.*); der Gauner, Schwindler (*sl.*). —**en**, *v.a.* schärfen, schleifen, wetzen; (whet) zuspitzen, schärfen; (excite) antreiben, aufregen; reizen (*the appetite*); schärfer machen (*a tone*); durch ein Kreuz erhöhen (*a note*); spitzen (*a pencil*). —**er**, *s.* der Gauner, Schwindler, Betrüger. —**ness**, *s.* die Schärfe (*also fig.*); die Schärfe, Säure (*of a sauce, etc.*); (pungency) die Schärfe, das Beißende; die Strenge, Härte (*of words, etc.*); das Beißende (*of satire*); die Heftigkeit (*of pain*); (intelligence) die Aufgewecktheit, der Scharfsinn; (subtleness) die Feinheit, Gewandtheit, Pfiffigkeit. *Comp.* —-**edged**, *adj.* scharf, schneidig. —-**eyed**, *adj.* scharfsichtig. —-**faced**, *adj.* schmalbäckig, mit scharfen Zügen. —-**set**, *adj.* hungrig; erpicht (on, auf eine S.). —-**shooter**, *s.* der Scharfschütze. —-**shooting**, *s.* das Büchsen-, Scharf-schießen. —-**sighted**, *adj.* scharfsichtig. —-**witted**, *adj.* scharfsinnig.

Shatter, *v.* I. *a.* zerbrechen, zerschmettern, zertrümmern; zertrümmern, vernichten, zerstören (*hopes, etc.*); zerstören, zerrütten (*the constitution, health, etc.*). II. *n.* zerbrechen. *Comp.* —**brained**, *see* Scatter-brained.

Shav—e, I. *v.a.* rasieren, barbieren; abfalzen (*skins*); (graze) streifen, hinstreichen an (*dat.*); (fleece) wuchern, plündern; to get —ed, sich rasieren lassen; to —e up, gegen den Strich rasieren. II. *v.n.* sich rasieren. III. *s.*; give me a —e, bitte rasieren Sie mich! it was a close —e, es wäre um ein Haar geschehen, ich bin nur eben mit heiler Haut davongekommen. —**en**, *adj.*; a —en head, ein geschorener Kopf; clean —en, glattrasiert. —**er**, *s.* der Bartscherer; der Wucherer, Leuteschinder (*fig.*); cunning —er, listiger Schelm, Pfiffikus; young —er, *see*

Youngster; a close —er, ein Pfennigfuchser. **—ing**, I. *p.* Rasier=, Barbier=. II. *s.* das Rasieren; der Span. **—ings**, *pl.* die Späne, Schnitzel, Abschabsel. *Comp.* **—ing-brush**, *s.* der Rasierpinsel. **—ing-case**, *s.* das Rasierzeug.

Shawl, *s.* das Umschlagetuch, der Schal.

Shawm, Shalm, *s.* die Rohrpfeife, Schalmei.

She, I. *pers. pron.* sie; es (*referring to ships, names of countries, etc.*); — bear, die Bärin; — devil, ein Teufel von einem Weibe, eine Teufelin, eine böse Sieben; — dog, die Hündin. II. *s.* das weibliche Tier, Weibchen; das Weib (*vulg.*).

Sheaf, *s.* die Garbe; (bundle) das Bund, Bündel.

Shealing, *s.* die Schäferhütte (*Scotch*).

Shear, I. *ir.v.a.* (ab)scheren; (reap) (ab)mähen; (cut down) zerschneiden; scheren, rupfen (*fig.*). II. *s.* die Schur (*of a sheep*); die große Schere. **—er**, *s.* der Scherer; der Schnitter (*Scotch*). **—ing**, *s.* das Scheren, die Schur; das Mähen; wool of the second —ing, zweischürige Wolle. **—ings**, *pl.* die Scherwolle. **—ling**, *s.* der einmal geschorne Widder. *Comp.* **—ing-time**, *s.* die Schafschur. **—water**, *s.* der Sturmtaucher (*Orn.*).

Sheath, *s.* die Scheide (*also Bot.*); die Flügeldecke (*Ent.*). **—e**, *v.a.* in die Scheide stecken, einstecken (*the sword*); (cover) bedecken, überziehen, bekleiden; (hide) einschließen; verhäuten (*a ship*). **—ing**, *s.* das Einstecken; die Haut, Verhäutung (*of a ship*). **—less**, *adj.* ohne Scheide; bloß (*as swords*). *Comp.* **—-winged**, *adj.* mit Flügeldecken.

Sheave, *s.* die Rolle, Scheibe (*Mech.*).

[1]**Shed**, I. *ir.v.a.* ausgießen (*the Holy Spirit*); vergießen (*tears, blood, etc.*); verbreiten (light upon a th., Licht über eine S.); abwerfen (*horns, leaves*); verlieren (*teeth*); ausbreiten (*perfumes*). II. *s. see* Bloodshed, Watershed. **—der**, *s.* der Vergießende. **—ding**, *s.* das Vergießen, *c.

[2]**Shed**, *s.* der Schuppen (*for carts, engines, etc.*); (hut) die Hütte; das Wetter=, Schirm=dach (*on a wharf, etc.*); das Fach (*Weav.*).

Sheeling, *see* Shealing.

Sheen, *s.* der Schein, Glanz (*poet.*).

Sheep, *s.* (*also pl.*) das Schaf (*also fig.*); the — bleats (says baa), das Schaf blökt (sagt Bä); —'s eye, das Schafsauge; der schüchtern=verliebte Blick (*fig.*); to cast —'s eyes at a girl, ein Mädchen schmachtend anblicken, einem Mädchen verliebte Augen machen. **—ish**, *adj.*, **—ishly**, *adv.* schafsmäßig, einfältig; (silly) scheu, blöde; to look —ish, blöde aussehen. **—ishness**, *s.* die Blödigkeit. *Comp.* **—cot(e)**, *s.* die Schafhürde. **—-dog**, *s.* der Schäferhund. **—-farm**, *s.* die Schäferei. **—fold**, **—-pen**, *s. see* —cote. **—-shearing**, *s.* die Schafschur. **—skin**, *s.* das Schaffell; das Schafleder. **—-stealing**, *s.* der Schafdiebstahl. **—walk**, *s.* die Schafweide.

[1]**Sheer**, I. *adj.* lauter, rein, bloß; — nonsense, barer Unsinn. II. *adv.* gänzlich.

[2]**Sheer**, I. *v.n.* abstechen, gieren; to — **off**, sich fortmachen; to — **up**, angieren (*Naut.*). II. *s.* der Spring (*of the deck*), die Form, Linien (*pl.*) (*of a ship*). **—s**, *pl.* der Mastenkrahn.

Sheet, *s.* die Breite, Fläche (*of water, etc.*); die Platte, Tafel, das Blatt (*of iron, copper, etc.*); die Tafel, Scheibe (*of glass*); das Bettuch, Leintuch (*of linen, etc.*); der Bogen (*of paper*); (sail) das Segel; in —s, uneingebunden (*Bookb.*); —s, die Schoten (*Naut.*); (pamphlet, *etc.*) die Flugschrift; to come down in —s, in Strömen fallen (*of rain*); a — of flame, eine Feuermasse, ein Flammenmeer; — of pins, der Brief Stecknadeln; three —s in the wind, benebelt (*sl.*). **—ed**, *adj.* (im Leichentuch) eingehüllt. **—ing**, *s.* die Leinwand zu Bettüchern. *Comp.* **—-anchor**, *s.* der Pflicht=, Not=anker; die Zuflucht (*fig.*). **—-glass**, *s.* das Tafel=, Scheibenglas. **—-iron**, *s.* das dünne Eisenblech. **—-lightning**, *s.* das Wetterleuchten.

Sheik, *s.* der Scheik.

Shekel, *s.* der Sekel.

Sheldrake, *s.* die Brandente.

Shelf, *s.* der Sims, das Brett, Regal, (Bücher=) Gestell; das Fach (*in a cabinet, bookcase, shop, etc.*); das Riff, die Sandbank; das Brett (*in a kitchen, etc.*); — of rock, die Felsenplatte; to put, lay on the —, bei Seite legen *or* schieben, aufs Ungewisse verschieben, unberücksichtigt lassen; on the —, auf lange verschoben, abgetan.

Shell, I. *s.* die Schale, Rinde, Hülse (*of eggs, crabs, cocoa, nuts, etc., also fig.*); (coffin) roher Sarg; das Gerippe, Gerüste (*of a house, etc.*); die Bombe, Sprengkugel (*Mil.*); die Mittelklasse an einigen höheren Knabenschulen, Tertia (*Eng.*); die Muschel; characteristic —, die Leitmuschel. II. *v.a.* schälen, aushülsen (*nuts, peas, etc.*); beschießen, bombardieren (*a town*). **—ed**, *adj.* schalig. *Comp.* **—-almonds**, *pl.* Knackmandeln. **—-fish**, *s.* das Schaltier. **—-work**, *s.* das Muschelwerk.

Shellac, *s.* der Schellack.

Shelter, I. *s.* das Obdach, der Schirm, Schutz; der Schuppen, das Schutzdach; to take — from, Schutz suchen vor; to fly to a p. for —, Zuflucht bei einem suchen; under —, unter Dach und Fach. II. *v.a.* (be=)schützen, (be)=schirmen (from, vor); (einem) Zuflucht gewähren (*as a rock, etc.*). III. *v.r.* & *n.* Schutz suchen. **—ed**, *adj.* geschützt. **—er**, *s.* der Beschützende, Beherberger, Obdachgeber. **—less**, *adj.* obdachlos, schutzlos.

[1]**Shelv—e**, *v.a.* auf ein Brett *c. legen; mit Brettern versehen (*a cupboard, etc.*); bei Seite legen, beseitigen, unberücksichtigt lassen, auf die lange Bank schieben (*fig.*). **—es**, *pl. see* Shelf; set of —es, das Regal.

[2]**Shelv—e**, *v.n.* sich neigen, abschüssig sein. **—ing**, *adj.* abschüssig, abhängig; land —ing to the sea, nach der See hin abfallendes Land.

Shepherd, I. *s.* der Schäfer, Hirte; —'s crook, der Schäferstab; —'s dog, der Schäferhund; —'s plaid, ein schwarz und weiß gewürfelter Wollstoff, der Schäferschawl; —'s pouch, —'s purse, das Hirtentäschelkraut; —'s weatherglass, das Gauchheil. II. *attrib.*; — boy, der Hirtenknabe; — spider, die Afterspinne. III. *v.a.* wie ein Schäfer hüten; sorglich im Auge behalten. **—ess**, *s.* die Schäferin, Hirtin.

Sherbet, *s.* das Sorbett, Scherbett, Gefrorene.

Shereef, Sherif, *s.* der Scherif, Heilige, Fürst (Titel der Nachkommen Muhameds). **—ian**, *adj.* dem Emir von Mekka *or* dem Sultan von Marokko angehörig.

Sheriff, *s.* der Sheriff, erste Grafschaftsbeamte. **—alty**, **—ship**, *see* Shrievalty.

Sherry, *s.* der Xereswein.

Shew, *see* Show. **—ed**, (*obs.*) *p.p. of* —, *see* Shown. **—n**, *see* Shown.

Shibboleth, *s.* das Erkennungszeichen, Losungswort, Schibboleth.

Shield, I. *s.* der Schild (*also fig.*), das Wappenschild. II. *v.a.* beschilden, schirmen, bedecken, behüten (from, vor, gegen). *Comp.* **—-bearer**, *s.* der Schildträger. **—-fern**, *s.* der Schildfarn (*Bot.*). **—less**, *adj.* schildlos; schutzlos (*fig.*).

Shift, I. *v.a.* schieben, bewegen; verschieben; wegschieben; (move) wenden, umlegen; verändern (one's ground, den Standpunkt); verlegen, vertauschen (the scene, den Schauplatz); wechseln (*clothes*); schieben (the blame on others, den Tadel auf andere). II. *v.n.* den Ort verändern; umspringen, umlaufen (*as wind*); über=gehen, =schießen (*as ballast*); (manage) sich durchschlagen, sich heraushelfen; to — for o.s., für sich selbst sorgen, sich selbst helfen; to — about, *see* Vacillate; übergehen. III. *s.* das Übergreifen (*Mus.*); (change) die Veränderung, das Wenden; der Wechsel (*of clothing, etc.*); (chemise) das Frauenhemd; (resource) die Ausflucht, das Notmittel, der Behelf; (trick) die List, der Kunstgriff, Kniff; die Schicht (*of work*); *see* Rotation; day (night) —, Tag-, (Nacht-)arbeit; to make —, sich durcharbeiten, sich behelfen; I can make — without it, ich kann mich auch so behelfen. **—er**, *s.* der Schiebende; der Schlaukopf; der unzuverlässige Mensch; der Kochgehilfe (*Naut.*, *obs.*). **—ing**, *adj.* sich wendend; listig, schlau, verschmitzt; —ing beach, der Treibsandgrund; —ing sand, der Treibsand. **—less**, *adj.* ohne Mittel, hilflos, ungeschickt; gedankenlos, sorglos; zwecklos. **—lessness**, *s.* die Hilflosigkeit. **—y**, *adj.* veränderlich; gewandt, verschmitzt, schlau; unzuverlässig wetterwendisch.

Shillelagh, *s.* der eichene Knüttel (*Irish*).

Shilling, *s.* der Schilling (= etwa eine Mark); the King's (Queen's) —, das Handgeld, Werbegeld; a — in the pound, 5 Prozent; a —'s worth of butter, für einen Schilling Butter.

Shilly-shally, I. *s.* die Unentschlossenheit. II. *adj.* unentschlossen. III. *v.n.* tändeln, zögern.

Shimmer, I. *v.n.* schimmern. II. *s.* der Schimmer.

Shin, I. *s.* das Schienbein. II. *v.a.* erklimmen. III. *v.n.* hinaufklettern.

Shindy, *s.* der Aufruhr, Tumult, Lärm.

Shin—e, I. *s.* der Schein, Glanz; to take the —e out of a p., einen überstrahlen, ausstechen, in den Schatten stellen (*coll.*). II. *ir.v.n.* scheinen, leuchten, glänzen, funkeln; glänzen (*fig.*); to —e forth, — out, hervorleuchten; love in her person shone, Liebe strahlte aus ihrer Erscheinung hervor. **—er**, *s.* das Goldstück (*sl.*); der Barsch. **—ey**, *s.* das Geld (*sl.*). **—ing**, I. *adj.* glänzend (*also fig.*); —ing instances, glänzende Beispiele; he is a —ing light, er ist ein großes Licht. II. *s.* der Glanz. **—y**, *adj.* hell, glänzend; *see* Glossy.

[1]**Shingl—e**, I. *s.* die (Dach-)Schindel. II. *v.a.* mit Schindeln decken. **—ing**, *s.* die Schindelbedachung. *Comp.* **—e-roofed**, *adj.* mit Schindeln gedeckt.

[2]**Shingl—e**, *s.* der Meerkies, Singel, kleine Steine. **—y**, *adj.* grobkiesig, voller Kiesel; —y beach, der Kieselstrand, aus Kieseln bestehende Strand.

Shingles, *s.* die Gürtelrose (*Med.*).

Shintoism, *s.* die Sinto-Religion (der Japaner).

Ship, I. *s.* das Schiff; das Vollschiff, dreimastige Schiff (*Naut.*); — of the line, das Linienschiff; to take —, sich einschiffen (for, nach); —'s armour, der Schiffspanzer; —'s carpenter, der Schiffszimmermann; —'s chandler, der Schiffslieferant; —'s husband, der Besteder, Bestader; a fine —, she sails to-morrow, ein stolzes Schiff, es geht morgen unter Segel; sales from —'s side, Verkauf direkt aus dem Schiff. II. *v.a.* an Bord bringen, einschiffen; (— off) verschiffen, absenden; (in das Schiff) bekommen (*a heavy sea*); mieten, dingen, heiern (*sailors*); klarmachen (*oars*); (make fast) befestigen (an). III. *v.n.* sich als Matrose verdingen. **—ment**, *s.* die Verschiffung, Verladung; (goods —ped) die Ladung. **—per**, *s.* der Verschiffende, Verlader, Befrachter, Schiffer. **—ping**, I. *s.* das Einschiffen; die Schiffe; die Flotte (*of a country*); to take —ping, sich einschiffen; ready for —ping, zur Verladung bereit; the harbour is crowded with —ping, es liegen sehr viele Schiffe im Hafen. II. *adj.;* —ping business, concerns, charges *or* expenses, interests, intelligence, Seegeschäfte, das Schiffswesen, die Verschiffungsspesen, Verladungsangelegenheiten, Schiffsnachrichten; —ping interest, der Seehandelsstand, die Reederei. *Comp.* **—board**, *s.;* on —board, auf dem Schiffe, an Bord; (on board —, an Bord). **—-builder**, *s.* der Schiffsbaumeister. **—-building**, *s.* der (die) Schiffbau(kunst). **—-money**, *s.* die Schiffssteuer. **—-owner**, *s.* der Reeder. **—ping-agent**, *s.* der Schiffsagent. **—ping-charges**, *pl.* Verschiffungskosten. **—ping-house**, *s.* die Seehandlung. **—ping-office**, *s.* das Speditionsbureau (für Transporte zur See). **—shape**, *adj.* nach Schiffsart; gehörig, richtig. **—-worm**, *s.* der Bohrwurm. **—wreck**, I. *s.* der Schiffbruch; to suffer *or* make —wreck, Schiffbruch leiden, scheitern, stranden, verunglücken (*also fig.*); to make —wreck of a th., eine S. vernichten, zerstören (*fig.*) II. *v.a.* scheitern lassen; an den Strand werfen; to be —wrecked, scheitern. III. *v.n.* scheitern, verunglücken, Schiffbruch leiden. **—wright**, *s.* der Schiffszimmermann, Schiffsbauer.

Shire, *s.* die Grafschaft. *Comp.* **—-hall**, *s.* die Grafschaftshalle, das Assisengericht der Grafschaft. **—-horse**, *s.* schweres Lastpferd. **—-mote**, *s.* das Grafschaftsgericht (*obs.*).

Shirk, *v.a.* vermeiden, ausweichen (einer S.); sich drücken (um eine S.) (*sl.*).

Shirr, *s.* die Gummikordel. **—ed**, *adj.* aus Gummikordel, gerippt; —ed goods, Gurtwaren (*C.L.*).

Shirt, *s.* das (Mannes-)Hemd; — of mail, Panzerhemd. **—ing**, I. *s.* der Hemdenkattun, Schirting (*Manuf.*). II. *attrib.;* —ing flannel, der Hemdenflanell. **—less**, *adj.* ohne Hemd. *Comp.* **—-cuffs**, *pl.* Manschetten. **—-front**, *s.* das Vorhemd. **—-maker**, *s.* der Hemdenmacher. **—-pin**, *s.* die Vorstecknadel, Busennadel. **—-sleeve**, *s.* der Hemdärmel; in o.'s —-sleeves, in Hemdärmeln. **—-stud**, *s.* der (lose, einzufügende) Hemdknopf.

[1]**Shiver**, I. *v.a.* zerbrechen, zertrümmern, zersplittern. II. *v.n.* in Stücke gehen, zerbrechen, zerschellen. III. *s.* kleines *or* Bruch-stück, der Splitter; der Schiefer (*Min.*).

[2]**Shiver**, I. *s.* der Schauer. II. *v.n.* schauern, zittern; to — and shudder, zittern und beben. **—ing**, I. *adj.*, **—ingly**, *adv.* schauernd; —ing fits, der Schüttelfrost, Fieberschauer. II. *s.* das Schauern, der Schauer. **—y**, *adj.* fröstelnd; I feel —y, mich fröstelt, ich habe Schüttelfrost.

[1]**Shoal**, *s.* die Menge, der Schwarm, Haufe; der Zug (*of fishes*).

[2]**Shoal**, I. die Untiefe; die Sandbank. II. *v.n.* untief, seichter werden. III. (**—y**) *adj.* untief, seicht. **—iness**, *s.* das Flachwasser.

[1]**Shock**, I. *s.* der Haufe (Garben), die Mandel (*of sheaves*). II. *v.n.* in Garben, Mandeln setzen, mandeln.

[2]**Shock**, I. *s.* der Stoß, Anstoß, Schlag; (collision) der Zusammenstoß; (violent shake) die Erschütterung; (attack) der Angriff, Anfall, Zusammenstoß; (offence) der Anstoß, Verdruß, das Ärgernis; (alarm) der Schrecken; (agitation) die Erschütterung; to give a — to a p.'s feelings, einen tief verletzen; to stand the —, dem Angriff widerstehen. II. *v.a.* (an)stoßen, einen Stoß geben; Anstoß erregen *or* geben, Ärgernis geben, anstößig sein; erschrecken; to be —ed at, ergriffen, verletzt, betroffen sein durch, empört sein über (*acc.*); I was —ed to see, mit Abscheu *or* Entsetzen sah ich; I was —ed at the sight of so much misery, der Anblick so vielen Elends flößte mir Entsetzen ein. **—ing**, *adj.*, **—ingly**, *adv.* verletzend, empörend, unerhört, schrecklich; anstößig.

[3]**Shock**, *s.;* — of hair, der dichte Haarschopf. *Comp.* **—-headed**, *adj.* mit struppigem Haar; zottelhaarig; —-headed Peter, der Struwelpeter.

Shod, *imperf. & p.p. of* Shoe.

Shoddy, I. *s.* die Trümmer-, Lumpen-wolle; der Schund (*fig.*). II. *adj.* lumpen-wollen; unecht, wertlos, erbärmlich (*fig.*).

Shoe, I. *s.* der Schuh (*also of a pole, a scabbard, etc.*); das Hufeisen (*of horses*); der Beschlag (*of a skate*); (drag) der Hemmschuh; to wait for dead men's —s, auf jemandes Tod warten; I should not like to be in your —s, ich möchte nicht in deiner Haut stecken; to shake in one's —s, (vor Angst *or* Aufregung) zittern. II. *ir.v.a.* beschuhen; beschlagen (*horses*); beschienen, beschlagen (*wheels*). —**r**, *s.* der Hufschmied. —**ing**, *s.* das Beschuhen; der Hufbeschlag. II. *adj.;* —ing tools, das Beschlagzeug. —**less**, *adj.* ohne Schuhe; ohne Hufbeschlag. *Comp.* —**-black**, *s.* der Schuhputzer. —**-blacking**, *s.* die Schuhwichse. —**-buckle**, *s.* die Schuhschnalle. —**-horn**, *s.* der Schuhanzieher. —**ing-smith**, *s.* der Hufschmied. —**-lace**, *s.* der Schuhriemen, das Schuhband. —**-latchet**, *s.* der Schuhriemen. —**-leather**, *s.* *s.* das Schuhleder; to save —-leather, einen Gang sparen (*fam.*). —**maker**, *s.* der Schuhmacher, Schuster; —maker's thread, der Pechdraht. —**making**, I. *s.* das Schuhmachen, Schustern. II. *attrib.;* —making trade, die Schusterei, das Schusterhandwerk. —**-scraper**, *s.* das Schuheisen. —**-string**, *s.* das Schuhband.

Shone, *imperf.* & *p.p.* *of* Shine.

Shook, *imperf.* *of* Shake.

Shoot, I. *ir.v.n.* schießen; ein-, durch-dringen (*fig.*); (fly) schießen, fliegen; (rush) stürzen; strömen, fallen; keimen, sprossen, ausschlagen (*plants*); stechen, prickeln (*pain*); to — true, gut treffen; to — **ahead**, voran eilen; to — ahead of, hinter sich lassen, (outsail) tot segeln; to — **at**, schießen nach; to — **forth**, keimen, ausschlagen; to — **up**, aufschießen, heranwachsen. II. *ir.v.a.* schießen (*also fig.*), treiben, schnellen; abschießen, abfeuern (*guns*), entsenden (*arrows, etc.*); vorschieben (*a bolt*); stürzen (*a cart*); schroten (*casks*); to — a bridge, unter einer Brücke durchfahren; to — rapids, über Stromschnellen fahren. III. *s.* *see* Shot; der Schoß, Sprößling (*Hort.*); der Schuß *or* Stoß aufs Tor (*Footb.*). —**er**, *s.* der Schießende; (sharp- —er) der Schütze. —**ing**, I. *s.* das Schießen; die Jagd; to go (for a day's *etc.*) —ing, (einen Tag) auf die Jagd gehen. II. *adj.* stechend (*as pain*). *Comp.* —**ing-boots**, *pl.* Jagdstiefel. —**ing-box**, *s.* das Jagdhäuschen. —**ing-party**, *s.* die Jagdgesellschaft. —**ing-star**, *s.* die Sternschnuppe.

Shop, I. *s.* der Laden, das Gewölbe, Geschäftslokal; *see* Workshop; das Fach, der Beruf (*coll.*); barber's —, die Barbierstube; to talk —, fachsimpeln. II. *v.n.* Einkäufe machen, Kaufläden besuchen; to go —ping, die Läden besuchen, ausgehen um Einkäufe zu machen. —**ping**, *s.* der Ladenbesuch, das Einkäufe-Machen. —**py**, *adj.* voll von Läden (*coll.*); krämerhaft, philisterhaft (*coll.*). *Comp.* —**-boy**, *s.* der Ladenbursche. —**-fittings**, *pl.* die Ladeneinrichtungen. —**-front**, *s.* das Schaufenster. —**keeper**, *s.* der Ladeninhaber, Krämer. —**keeping**, *s.* der Klein-Handel, das Detailgeschäft. —**lifter**, *s.* der Ladendieb. —**lifting**, *s.* der Ladendiebstahl. —**man**, *s.* der Ladendiener. —**-walker**, *s.* der Ladenaufseher. —**-window**, *s.* das Ladenfenster, die Auslage. —**-woman**, *s.* die Verkäuferin, das Ladenfräulein.

[1]**Shore**, *also* **Sheared**, *imperf.* *of* Shear.

[2]**Shore**, *s.* das Ufer, Gestade, die Küste; (strand) der Strand. —**less**, *adj.* uferlos. —**ward**, *adv.* uferwärts. *Comp.* —**-anchor**, *s.* der Wallanker. —**-battery**, *s.* die Küstenbatterie. —**-painter**, *s.* das Spanntau.

[3]**Shore**, I. *s.* die Stütze, Strebe, der Strebbalken. II. *v.a.;* to — up, (unter-)stützen.

[4]**Shore**, *see* Sewer.

Shorl, *s.* der Schörl.

Shorn, *also* **Sheared**, I. *p.p.* *of* Shear. II. *adj.;* — of, beraubt (*gen.*).

Short, I. *adj.* & *adv.* kurz (*also fig.*); klein (*in figure*); abgekürzt (*Bot.*); brüchig, mürbe (*as cakes, pie-crust*); schwach, schlecht (*as memory*); (— of) dürftig, knapp, mangelhaft; in —, kurz(um); in a — time, in kurzer Zeit, in Kurzem; — and sweet, kurz und gut at — notice, binnen kurzer Zeit; — bills, Wechsel auf kurze Sicht; — of breath, kurzatmig; — of money *or* means, knapp bei Geld *or* Kasse; — of our expectations, unseren Erwartungen nicht entsprechend; to be —, sich kurz fassen; to be — with a p., take s.o. up —, einen kurz abfertigen; nothing — of the severest measures, nichts als die strengsten Maßregeln; no remedy — of, kein Mittel außer; to come *or* fall — of, nicht erreichen, zurückbleiben hinter, nicht entsprechen; to cut —, plötzlich unterbrechen; to fall —, ausgehen (*as provisions*); to give a p. a — answer, einem kurz, unehrerbietig antworten; to keep s.o. on — allowance, einen kurz halten; to stop —, plötzlich stille stehen, stehen bleiben; auf einmal kurz abbrechen, innehalten; to make — work of, es kurz machen mit; six miles — of the town, sechs Meilen von der Stadt. II. *s.* kurze Silbe (*Pros.*); *see* Summary; the long and the — of it is, die Sache ist in Kürze diese, kurz, das Ende vom Liede ist (*fam.*). —**age**, *s.* der Mangel (of, an, *dat.*). —**en**, *v.* I. *a.* (ver)kürzen; (curtail) abkürzen; stutzen (*hair*); (lessen) vermindern, schmälern, beschränken; *see* — coat; einziehen (*sail*); abkürzen (*time*). II. *n.* kürzer werden; abnehmen (*as days*); sich zusammenziehen (*as metals*). —**ening**, *s.* die Verkürzung; Butter oder Fett zum Backen (*Cook.*). —**ish**, *adj.* etwas kurz. —**ly**, *adv.* bald, in kurzem; (briefly) kurz, in kurzen Worten. —**ness**, *s.* die Kürze; die Schwäche (*of the memory*); (want) die Mangelhaftigkeit. —**s**, *pl.* die Kniehosen (*coll.*). *Comp.* —**-bread**, *s.* schottisches süßes sehr trocknes Gebäck. —**-coated**, *adj.* mit kurzem Röckchen, in kurzem Kleidchen; kurzhaarig. —**coming**, *s.* die Schwäche, der Fehler, Mangel; die Pflichtversäumnis. —**-cut**, *s.* der Richteweg. —**-dated**, *adj.* auf kurze Sicht. —**hand**, *s.* die Kurzschrift, Stenographie, Geschwindschrift. —**-handed**, *adj.;* to be —-handed, Mangel an Arbeitern *or* an Hilfskräften haben. —**hand-writer**, *s.* der Stenograph. —**horns**, *pl.* kurzhörniges Rindvieh. —**-leg**, *s.* der Schrägab (*Cricket*). —**-legged**, *adj.* kurzbeinig. —**-lived**, *adj.* kurzlebig, von kurzer Dauer, vergänglich. —**-sighted**, *adj.* kurzsichtig. —**-sightedness**, *s.* die Kurzsichtigkeit (*also fig.*). —**-tempered**, *adj.* heftig, reizbar. —**-waisted**, *adj.* kurzleibig. —**-winded**, *adj.* kurzatmig.

[1]**Shot**, I. *imperf.* & *p.p.* *of* Shoot. II. *adj.* schillernd, changierend; — silk, schillernde Seide.

[2]**Shot**, *s.* der Schuß; (shooter) der Schütze; das Geschoß, die Kugel (*for guns*); small —, das Schrot; — of distress, das Notsignal; — with ball, der scharfe Schuß; to exchange —s, Schüsse wechseln, auf einander schießen; within gun—, innerhalb Schußweite; within ear—, in Hörweite; point-blank —, Visier-, Kern-schuß; to make a —, ins Blaue hinein raten, aufs Geratewohl annehmen; to make a bad —, einen Fehlschuß tun; falsch raten (*fig.*); he is a good —, er schießt vorzüglich; he is a dead —, er ist ein nie fehlender Schütze, er trifft mit unfehlbarer Sicherheit; like a —, sofort, unverzüglich, ohne langes Besinnen. *Comp.* —**-mould**, *s.* die Gußschale. —**-tower**, *s.* der Schrotturm.

[3]**Shot**, *s.* die Zeche, Rechnung.

Shotten, (*obs.*) *p.p.* *of* Shoot, & *adj.* gelaicht habend, ausgeleert; — herring, der Schuß-, Hohl-hering.

Should, *imperf.* *of* Shall; if I —, sollte ich; — I do that, wenn ich das täte; whom — I meet but . . . ? wen anders sollte ich treffen als gerade . . . ?

Shoulder, I. *s.* die Schulter (*also of a horse*), Achsel; der Vorderbug, das Vorderviertel (*of quadrupeds*); das Schulterstück (*Butch.*); die Schulter (*of a bastion*); (prominence) das Hervor-ragende, -springende, der Auslauf; — to —, Schulter an Schulter; to give a p. the cold —, einen links liegen lassen; to put one's — to the wheel, etwas fest angreifen. II. *v.a.* mit der Schulter drücken, stoßen; to — one's way through, sich durchdrängen; — arms! Gewehr auf! *Comp.* —**-belt**, *s.* das Schulter-, Degen-

Wehr-gehenk. —**blade**, *s.* das Schulterblatt. —**-knot**, *s.* das Achselband; das Achselstück, die Epaulette (*Mil.*). —**-piece**, *s.* das Schulterstück. —**-straps**, *pl.* die Schulterbänder (*on stays, etc.*); die Achselklappen (*Mil.*).

Shout, I. *s.* der laute Schrei, das Geschrei. II. *v.n.* laut schreien; to — for joy, laut jauchzen; to — **at**, zurufen; ein Geschrei erheben über (*acc.*); to — **to**, zurufen (einem). —**er**, *s.* der Schreier; der Jauchzer. —**ing**, *s.* das Geschrei.

Shove, I. *v.a.* schieben, stoßen; to — aside, away, on, weg-, beiseite-, weiter-schieben; to — off, abstoßen. II. *v.n.;* to — off, abstoßen (*from the shore*). III. *s.* der Schub, Stoß. —**l**, I. *s.* die Schaufel. II. *v.a.* schaufeln. —**lful**, *s.* eine Schaufel voll. *Comp.* —**l-board**, *s.* die Beilketafel. —**l-hat**, *s.* der Schaufelhut (der engl. Geistlichen).

Show, I. *ir.v.a.* zur Schau stellen; (point out) sehen lassen, zeigen, weisen; (prove) beweisen, dartun; erzeigen, erweisen (*kindness, etc.*); zeigen, führen (*the way*); angeben (*cause*); to — fight, sich kampflustig zeigen; never — your face again! laß dich nie wieder sehen! to — dirt, leicht schmutzen; to — the white feather, sich feige benehmen; to — **forth**, verkündigen; to — **in**, hereinführen, eintreten lassen; to — **off**, in vollem Glanze erscheinen lassen, hervorheben; to — **up**, heraufführen (*lit.*); im wahren Lichte zeigen, entlarven, der Verachtung bloßstellen (*a person, faults, etc.*). II. *ir.v.n.* erscheinen, beweisen; time will —, die Zeit wird es lehren; to — **off**, ab-, hervor-stechen, in vollem Glanze erscheinen; she likes to — off, sie tut gern groß. III. *s.* die Schau (*also fig.*); die Ausstellung; die Schaubude (*at a fair, etc.*); (appearance) der Anschein, Anblick; to be only for —, nur zur Schau dienen; to make a — of, zur Schau tragen, sehen lassen; (pretend) sich (*dat.*) den Anschein geben von; to make a — of anger, sich zornig stellen; to make a fine —, prächtig aussehen; to run the —, einer Sache vorstehen (*coll.*); dumb —, stumme Geberde; — of hands, Aufheben der Hände (bei Wahlen); on —, zur Ansicht, zu besehen; — of tulips, der Tulpenflor. IV. *attrib.;* — pupil, der Paradeschüler. —**er**, *s.* der Zeigende. —**ily**, *adv.*, —**y**, *adj.* prunkhaft, prahlend. —**iness**, *s.* der Prunk. —**ing**, *s.* das Zeigen, die Dartuung. *Comp.* —**-bill**, *s.* das ausgehängte Warenverzeichnis. —**bread**, *s.* das (jüdische) Schaubrot. —**-card**, *s.* die Musterkarte; die Geschäftsanzeige. —**-case**, *s.* das Schaukästchen. —**man**, *s.* der Schausteller. —**-place**, *s.* der Schauplatz (*obs.*). —**-room**, *s.* das Ausstellungszimmer. —**-window**, *s.* das Schaufenster.

Shower, I. *s.* der (Regen-)Guß; das Schauer; der Überfluß, die Fülle (*of gifts, etc.*); der Hagel (*of arrows*). II. *v.a.* (— down on) herabschütten auf (*acc.*), überschütten mit. —**iness**, *s.* das Regnerische. —**y**, *adj.* regnerisch; —y weather, das Regenwetter. *Comp.* —**-bath**, *s.* das Sturzbad, Brausenduschenbad. —**-proof**, *adj.* wasserdicht.

Shown, *p.p. of* Show.

Shrank, *p.p. of* Shrink.

Shrapnel-shell, *s.* die Granat-Kartätsche, der, das Schrapnell.

Shred, I. *s.* der Fetzen, das Schnitzel. II. *v.a.* zerfetzen, in schmale Streifen zerschneiden; schneiden (*vegetables*).

[1]**Shrew**, *s.* das böse Weib, die Zänkerin; Taming of the —, der Widerspenstigen Zähmung. —**d**, *adj.*, —**ly**, *adv.* scharf-sinnig, -sichtig, klug; to have a —d guess, stark vermuten. —**dness**, *s.* der Scharfsinn, die Scharfsinnigkeit. —**ish**, *adj.* zänkisch.

[2]**Shrew**, —**-mouse**, *s.* die Spitzmaus.

Shriek, I. *s.* der (grelle) Schrei, Angstschrei; das Gekreisch(e); —s of laughter, wieherndes Gelächter. II. *v.n.* (laut auf-)schreien, kreischen. —**er**, *s.* der Schreier, Schreihals.

Shrievalty, *s.* die Scheriffs-würde, -gerichtsbarkeit.

Shrift, *s.* die (Ohren-)Beichte; die Absolution.

Shrike, *s.* der Würger (*Orn.*).

Shrill, I. *adj.*, —**y**, *adv.* gellend, grell, scharf, schrill, durchdringend. II. *v.a.;* to — forth, gellend äußern; ausgellen lassen. —**ness**, *s.* das Gellende, Schrille. *Comp.* —**-voiced**, *adj.* mit gellender Stimme.

Shrimp, I. *s.* die Garneele; der Knirps, Zwerg (*fig.*). II. *v.a.* Garneelen fischen.

Shrine, *s.* der Heiligen- (for relics, Reliquien-)schrein; (altar) der Altar.

Shrink, *ir.v.* I. *n.* (ein-, zusammen-)schrumpfen, sich zusammenziehen, einlaufen, eingehen; (recoil) zurückfahren; to — **at**, sich entsetzen vor; to — **back**, zurückfahren; to — **from**, zurückschaudern vor, sich (einer S.) entziehen, einer S. ausweichen, nicht daran wollen; he shrank from exposing his poverty, es war ihm zuwider, seine Armut zu verraten. II. *a.* einschrumpfen machen, einlaufen lassen. —**age**, *s.* das Einlaufen, Eingehen (*of cloth, etc.*); das Sich-Setzen (*Build.*); das Schwinden (*of wood*); die Verminderung, Abnahme (*fig.*). —**ing**, I. *adj.* einschrumpfend. II. *s.* die Zusammenziehung; das Ausweichen; das Zurückfahren.

Shriv—e, *ir.v.* I. *a.* (einem) die Beichte abnehmen; Buße auferlegen. —**ing**, *s.* das Beichten.

Shrivel, *v.* I. *n.* einschrumpfen, sich zusammenziehen, runzelig werden. II. *a.* zusammenziehen, runzelig machen; zerknittern, zerknüllen.

[1]**Shroud**, I. *s.* die Hülle; die Leichenhülle, das Leichenkleid, Sterbekleid. II. *v.a.* decken; (wrap up) (ein)hüllen, einwickeln; einhüllen, in das Sterbekleid hüllen (*the dead*).

[2]**Shroud**, *s.* das Wanttau, Hauptau. —**s**, *pl.* die Wanten.

Shrove, *imperf. see* Shrive *Comp.* —**tide**, I. *s.* die Fastenzeit. II. *attrib.;* —tide custom, der Fastenbrauch. —**-Tuesday**, *s.* die Fastnacht.

[1]**Shrub**, *s.* die Staude, der Strauch, Busch; (dwarf tree) der Zwergbaum. —**bery**, *s.* die Anpflanzung von Staudengewächsen, das Ziergebüsch. —**by**, *adj.* strauchig, buschig; (full of —s) voller Gesträuch; —by plant, das Staudengewächs.

[2]**Shrub**, *s.* eine Art Punsch.

Shrug, I. *s.* das Achselzucken. II. *v.a. & n.;* to — (the shoulders), (die Achseln) zucken.

Shrunk, *imperf. & p.p. of* Shrink. —**en**, (*rare*) *p.p. of* Shrink, & *adj.* zusammengeschrumpft; —en form, abgemagerte Gestalt; —**en** cheeks, eingefallene Wangen.

Shudder, I. *v.n.* schaudern, schauern, zittern. II. *s.* der Schauder, das Zittern. —**ing**, I. *adj.*, —**ingly**, *adv.* schaudernd, zitternd, mit Zittern. II. *s.* das Schaudern, Zittern.

Shuffl—e, I. *v.a.* mischen (*cards*); to —e **away**, unvermerkt fortschaffen, gewandt wegbringen; to —e **off**, von sich schieben; when we have —ed off this mortal coil, wenn wir diese sterbliche Hülle abgestreift haben. II. *v.n.* (die Karten) mischen; schlurfen, die Füße nachschleppen (*in walking*); mit den Füßen scharren; Ausflüchte machen, nicht aufrichtig sein *or* handeln &c. (*fig.*); to —e along, fortwackeln; to —e off, aus dem Zimmer schlurfen. III. *s.* das Mischen (*of cards*); die Ausflucht, der Kunstgriff. —**er**, *s.* der Mischer; einer, der Ausflüchte sucht, Winkelzüge gebraucht. —**ing**, I. *adj.*, —**ingly**, *adv.* ausweichend; (dishonest) unredlich; —ing gait, schlurfender, schleppender Gang; —ing excuse, leere Ausflucht, faule Ausrede. II. *s.* das Kartenmischen; der Winkelzug, die Ausflucht. *Comp.* —**e-board**, *see* Shovelboard.

Shun, *v.a.* meiden, fliehen (*s.o.*); ausweichen (p. or th., einer Person oder Sache).

Shunt, I. *v.a.* auf ein Seitengleis bringen, rangieren (*Railw.*); to — s.th. on to s.o., einem etwas aufhalsen (*fam.*). II. *v.n.* auf ein Nebengleis fahren, einlenken. III. *s.* die Nebenschließung eines elektrischen Stromkreises (*Elect.*, *Tele.*); das Seitengleis, die Weiche (*Railw.*); to do a —, sich heimlich aus dem Staube machen (*sl.*). *Comp.* —**ing-station**, *s.* der Rangierbahnhof.

Shut, *ir.v.* I. *a.* (ver)schließen, zumachen; to — the door in a p.'s face, einem die Tür vor der Nase zuschlagen; to — **in**, einschließen, einsperren; (hide the view) die Aussicht versperren; to — **out**, aus-schließen, -sperren; to — **up**, verschließen, versperren; (— in) einsperren; (close) sperren (*a part*); zumachen (*a knife*); to — up shop, den Laden zumachen (*lit.*); den Handel aufgeben (*fig. sl.*). II. *n.* sich schließen; the door does not — easily, die Tür geht schwer zu; — **up**! still! halt den Mund! (*coll.*). —**ter**, *s.* einer, der schließt, zumacht rc.; (window —ter) der Fensterladen; revolving (sliding) —ter, der Roll-(Schieb-)laden. —**terless**, *adj.* ohne Fensterladen. *Comp.* —**ter-bolt**, *s.* der Schubriegel.

Shuttle, *s.* das Schiffchen (*also Sew-Mach.*), Weberschiff(chen), die Schütze (*Weav.*); hand —, die Handschütze. *Comp.* —**cock**, *s.* der Federball.

[1]**Shy**, I. *adj.*, —**ly**, *adv.* scheu (*also of beasts*), schüchtern; (cautious) behutsam, vorsichtig; (reserved) zurückhaltend; (suspicious) mißtrauisch, argwöhnisch; to fight — of, vermeiden (*coll.*); he fights — of me, er meidet mich, so viel er nur kann. II. *v.n.* scheu sein *or* werden; to — at, (sich) scheuen vor. —**er**, *s.* das scheue Pferd. —**ness**, *s.* die Scheu, Schüchternheit; die Behutsamkeit; der Argwohn.

[2]**Shy**, I. *v.a.* werfen, schleudern (*sl.*). II. *s.* der Wurf; der Hieb, Schlag.

Si, *s.* H (*Mus.*).

Sibila—nt, I. *adj.* zischend. II. *s.* der Zischlaut. —**tion**, *s.* das Zischen.

Siccative, *adj.* trocknend.

Sick, I. *adj.* nicht wohl; (ill) krank; müde, überdrüssig (of life, flattery, etc., des Lebens, der Schmeichelei rc.); (feeling nausea) übel; I feel —, mir ist übel; it makes me —, es macht mir übel, mir wird übel dabei; (pains me) mir wird weh (at the sight of, beim Anblicke von); — with fear, (joy,) vor Furcht (vor Freude) krank; to be — and tired of a th., etwas gründlich satt haben (*fam.*); to fall —, krank werden. II. *s.*; the —, die Kranken. —**en**, *v.* I. *n.* siechen, erkranken, krank werden; Ekel empfinden (at, vor). II. *a.* Übelkeit erregen; anekeln (*fig.*); it is —ening, es ist widerwärtig. —**ish**, *adj.* zur Übelkeit geneigt. —**liness**, *s.* die Kränklichkeit; die Ungesundheit (*of a climate*). —**ly**, I. *adj.* kränklich; (weak) siech, schwächlich; (unhealthy) ungesund; krankhaft, schmerzlich (*as a smile*); to be —ly, kränkeln. II. *v.a.*; —lied o'er, angekränkelt. —**ness**, *s.* die Krankheit; (nausea) die Übelkeit; (plague) die Pest. *Comp.* —-**bed**, *s.* das Krankenbett. —-**leave**, *s.* der Urlaub wegen Krankheit; on —-leave, wegen Krankheit beurlaubt. —-**list**, *s.* die Krankenliste. —-**room**, *s.* die Krankenstube.

Sickle, *s.* die Sichel. *Comp.* —**man**, *s.* der Schnitter.

Side, I. *s.* die Seite; die Abteilung; die Partei, Faktion (*fig.*); das Ufer, der Rand (*of a river, etc.*); der Abhang (*of a hill*); no —! keine Gegenpartei, Spiel aus, fertig! (*Sport.*); near, off —, die linke, rechte Seite (*of a horse*); bright —, die Lichtseite; dark, shady —, die Schattenseite; by his —, ihm zur Seite, an seiner Seite; on this — of the water, hier zu Lande; on this — of the Rhine, diesseits des Rheins; on this — of 50, unter 50 Jahren; on yonder —, jenseits; by the — of, zur Seite von, neben; on the road- —, an der Heerstraße, am Wege; by the mother's —, von mütterlicher Seite her, mütterlicherseits; on all —s *or* every —, auf, von allen Seiten; on the other —, auf der andern Seite; anderseits; on my —, meinerseits; as noted on the other —, wie umstehend bemerkt (*C. L.*); classical, modern —, die Gymnasial-, Real-abteilung (*in secondary schools*); — by —, nebeneinander; to change —s, sich zu einer andern Partei schlagen; to take a p.'s —, take —s with s.o., Partei für einen nehmen, jemandes Partei ergreifen; to shake, split one's —s with laughing, sich (*dat.*) vor Lachen die Seiten halten (*vulg.*). II. *adj.* Seiten-; — elevation, der Seitenaufriß; — face, das Profil; — gable, der Seitengiebel; — glance, der Seitenblick; — issue, der nebensächliche Punkt; — motion, die Seitenbewegung; — pocket, die Seitentasche; — view, die Seitenansicht; — scenes, die Seitenwände, Kulissen. III. *v.n.* Partei nehmen (with, für; against, gegen); to — with the Tories, auf der Seite der Tories sein; (take the — of) sich zu den Tories schlagen, für die Tories Partei ergreifen. —**d**, *adj.* -seitig. —**ling**, *adv.* see under Sid—ing. *Comp.* —-**aisle**, *s.* das Seitenschiff. —-**arms**, *pl.* das Seitengewehr (*Mil.*). —**board**, *s.* der Anrichte-, Kredenz-tisch, das Büffet. —-**dish**, *s.* das Nebengericht. —-**light**, *s.* das Seitenlicht; (window) das Seitenfenster. —**long**, *adj.* & *adv.* seitwärts, schief. —-**rail**, *s.* die Brückenlehne; (—-rails, *pl.*) Seitenschienen (*Railw.*). —**sman**, *s.* der Parteigenosse (*obs.*); der Beistand (*Eccl.*). —-**saddle**, *s.* der Frauen-, Quer-sattel. —-**table**, *s.* der Seiten-, Neben-tisch. —**walk**, *s.* der Bürgersteig. —**ways**, —**wise**, *adv.* seitwärts, von der Seite.

Sidereal, *adj.* Sternen-, Stern-; (starry) gestirnt; — year, das Sternjahr.

Sider—ite, *s.* der Magnetstein; der Eisenstein (*Min.*). —**ography**, *s.* die Stahlstechkunst.

Sid—ing, *s.* der Ausweicheplatz, das Nebengeleise (*Railw.*); das Parteinehmen, die Parteinahme. —**le**, *v.n.* sich mit der Seite voran bewegen; to —le **off**, seitwärts fortwischen; to —le **up** to a p., sich einem verstohlen nähern.

Siege, *s.* die Belagerung; to lay — to, belagern (*lit.*); (einem) zusetzen (*fig.*); to raise the —, die Belagerung aufheben. *Comp.* —-**artillery**, *s.* das Belagerungsgeschütz. —-**carriage**, *s.* die Belagerungslaffe(t)te. —-**gun**, *s.* das Belagerungsgeschütz. —-**park**, —-**train**, *s.* der Belagerungspark.

Sienna, *s.* die Sienaerde.

Siesta, *s.* die Mittagsruhe, Siesta.

Sieve, *s.* das Sieb; der gehäufte Scheffel; hair —, Haarsieb.

Sift, *v.a.* sieben, sichten; prüfen, erforschen (*fig.*); to — out, ausforschen, herausbringen; to — to the bottom, aufs genaueste untersuchen; to — the chaff from the wheat, die Spreu von dem Weizen sondern (*also fig.*). —**er**, *s.* der Sieber, Sichter; der Erforscher. —**ing**, *s.* das Sieben; das Prüfen.

Sigh, I. *s.* der Seufzer. II. *v.n.* seufzen (after, for, nach). III. *v.a.* beseufzen; to — **forth**, ausseufzen; to — **out**, — **away**, unter Seufzen aushauchen (*one's soul*).

Sight, *s.* das Gesicht, die Sehkraft; das Auge (*fig.*); (view) der Anblick, die Ansicht; (spectacle) das Schauspiel, die Erscheinung; das Zerrbild, die Fratze; das Visier (*also on a helmet*); fore-, back-sight, das (Richt-)Korn, Visier (*on a rifle*); die Sicht (*C.L.*); second —, zweites Gesicht, das Hellsehen; at —, auf, nach Sicht, bei Ansicht dieses (*C.L.*); vom Blatte (*Mus.*); at first —, beim ersten Anblick; in the — of, vor den Augen von; out of —, aus den Augen, nicht mehr sichtbar; out of —, out of mind, aus den Augen, aus dem Sinn (*proverb*); to be (with-)in —, in Sicht sein; to come in —, in Sicht kommen; as soon as we came in — of the mountains, so bald uns die Berge zu Gesicht kamen; to gain, get a — of a th., etwas zu Gesicht bekommen; to know by —, von Ansehn kennen; to hate the — of, nicht ausstehen können; to lose — of a p., einen aus dem Gesichte verlieren; to take —, das Visier einstellen, visieren; the gunners had got their —s, die Kanoniere hatten die Visiere eingestellt; what a — you look! wie Sie aussehen! this bonnet makes me quite a —! dieser Hut entstellt mich schrecklich! (*coll.*); a precious — of, eine ganze Masse (*vulg.*). **—ed**, *adj.* =sichtig. **—less**, *adj.* blind. **—lessness**, *s.* die Blindheit. **—liness**, *s.* die Wohlgestalt. **—ly**, *adj.* wohlgestalt(et), schön. *Comp.* **—-hole**, *s.* das Sehloch. **—-seeing**, *s.* das Beschauen der Merkwürdigkeiten. **—-seer**, *s.* der Schaulustige. **—-singing**, *s.* das Singen vom Blatt.

Sigmoid(al), *adj.* sigmaförmig.

Sign, I. *s.* das Zeichen; (nod, *etc.*) der Wink; (mark) das Kennzeichen, Abzeichen, Merkmal; (—-board) das Schild; (omen) das Vorzeichen; das Zeichen, Wunder (*B.*); (symbol) das Vorbild, Symbol; conventional —s, übliche Zeichen (*Tele.*, *etc.*); — of exclamation, interrogation, das Ausrufungs=, Frage=zeichen; — of the cross, Zeichen des Kreuzes; the —s of the Zodiac, die Zeichen des Tierkreises; — manual, das Handzeichen, die eigenhändige Unterschrift; to look upon as a good —, als (eine) gute Vorbedeutung, ein gutes Zeichen betrachten. II. *v.a.* unterzeichnen, =schreiben; —ed and sealed, unterschrieben und besiegelt. III. *v.n.* ein Zeichen geben, winken (to s.o., einem). **—al**, I. *s.* das Signal (*Naut.*, *Railw.*); das Signal, die Losung (*Mil.*); —al of distress, Notsignal; fog —als, Nebelsignale; code of —s, das Signalreglement. II. *adj.*, **—ally**, *adv.* bemerkenswert, wichtig, außerordentlich, merkwürdig; —al defeat, eine gänzliche Niederlage; to fire —al guns, Signalschüsse abfeuern. III. *v.n.* Signale geben, durch Signale anzeigen. **—alize**, *v.a.* auszeichnen; an den Tag legen, zuerkennen geben; Signale geben (*Naut.*); to —alize o.s. by, sich auszeichnen, hervortun durch. **—atory**, I. *adj.* Siegel=. II. *s. see* —er. **—ature**, *s.* eigenhändige Unterschrift; das Handlungszeichen, die Marke (*C.L.*); die Signatur (*Typ.*, *Mus.*). **—er**, *s.* der Unter=zeichner, =zeichnende. **—et**, *s.* das Siegel; (privy seal) königliches Handsiegel; writer to the —et, (*abbrev.* W. S.) der Rechtsanwalt (*Scotch*). **—ify**, *etc.*, *see under* Signif—icance. *Comp.* **—al-box**, *s.* das Signalhäuschen. **—al-gun**, *s.* der Signalschuß. **—alling-apparatus**, *s.* der Signalapparat. **—al-man**, *s.* der Bahnwärter. **—-board**, *s.* das (Aushänge=)schild; die Tafel. **—et-ring**, *s.* der Siegelring. **—-painter**, *s.* der Schildmaler. **—-post**, *s.* der Schildpfosten; der Wegweiser.

Signif—icance, **—icancy**, *s.* (meaning) die Bedeutung, der Sinn; (importance) die Wichtigkeit; Bedeutsamkeit; (emphasis) die Kraft, der Nachdruck. **—icant**, *adj.*, **—icantly**, *adv.* (—icant of) bedeutsam, bezeichnend; bedeutungsvoll, bedeutsam; nachdrücklich. **—ication**, *s.* der Sinn, die Bedeutung. **—icative**, *adj.* bezeichnend; *see* —icant. **—icatory**, *adj.* bezeichnend. **—y**, *v.* I. *a.* bezeichnen, andeuten, anzeigen; (make known) zu verstehen geben, zu erkennen geben, kund tun, bekanntmachen; (mean) bedeuten; what does it —y? was liegt daran . . .? II. *n.*; it doesn't —y, es tut *or* macht nichts, hat nichts zu bedeuten, hat nichts auf sich.

Silen—ce, I. *s.* das (Still=)Schweigen; (oblivion) die Vergessenheit; (quiet) die Ruhe, Stille; (secrecy) die Verschwiegenheit; to keep —ce, still schweigen; to pass over in —ce, mit Stillschweigen übergehen; —ce gives consent, wer schweigt, willigt ein (*prov.*). II. *int.* still! Ruhe! Silentium! (*students' sl.*). III. *v.a.* zum Schweigen bringen (*also a battery*); suspendieren (*a clergyman*). **—t**, *adj.*, **—tly**, *adv.* still, schweigend; (quiet) ruhig; (of few words) schweigsam; stumm (*Gram.*); be —t! schweig (still)!

Silhouette, *s.* der Schattenriß.

Silic—a, *s.* die Kieselerde. **—ate**, I. *s.* kieselsaure Verbindung, das Silikat. II. *attrib.*, —ate cotton, die Schlackenwolle. **—ious**, *adj.* kiesel=artig, =haltig.

Silk, I. *s.* die Seide; (— stuff) der Seidenstoff, das Seidenzeug; raw —, Rohseide; sewing —, Nähseide; Tussah —, rohe Seide; he has got his —, er ist zum Staatsanwalt (King's Counsel) ernannt worden; he took —, er wurde Doktor. II. *adj.* seiden; — ribbon, das Seidenband; — embroidery, die Seidenstickerei; — gown, seidenes Kleid; — lace, die Blonden; — net, der Seidentüll; — twist, der Seidenzwirn. **—en**, *adj.* seiden; *see* —y; —en lashes, seidene Wimpern. **—iness**, *s.* das Seidenartige; (softness) die Weichheit. **—y**, *adj.* seidig, seidenartig, (seiden)weich. *Comp.* **—-mercer**, *s.* der Seidenhändler. **—worm**, *s.* die Seidenraupe.

Sill, *s.* die Schwelle, Sohlbank (*of a door*, *etc.*), das Gesims, Fensterbrett (*of a window*).

Sillabub, *s.* süßer Trank aus Wein und Milch.

Sill—ily, *adv.*, **—y**, *adj.* albern, einfältig, töricht, dumm; —y season, die Sauregurkenzeit. **—iness**, *s.* die Albernheit, das dumme Benehmen.

Silt, I. *s.* der Schlamm, Kot; der Triebsand (*Min.*, *etc.*). II. *v.a.* durch Schlamm verstopfen.

Silur—e, *s.* der Wels. **—ian**, *adj.* silurisch, Silur=. **—oid**, *adj.* welsartig, zu den Welsen gehörig.

Silvan, *see* Sylvan.

Silver, I. *s.* das Silber; (— money) das Silbergeld; (plate) das Silberzeug; German —, das Neusilber. II. *adj.* silbern; she was born with a — spoon in her mouth, sie ist ein Glückskind. III. *v.a.* ver=, über=silbern; mit Folie belegen (*a mirror*, *etc.*). **—ing**, *s.* das Versilbern; die Belegung. **—y**, *adj.* silbern, Silber=; klangvoll, wie Silber klingend (*as the voice*). *Comp.* **—-fir**, *s.* die Edeltanne, Weißtanne, Silbertanne. **—-gilt**, *s.* vergoldetes Silber. **—-gray**, *adj.* silbergrau. **—-haired**, *adj.* silberhaarig. **—-lace**, *s.* die Silbertresse. **—-leaf**, *s.* das Blattsilber. **—-mounted**, *adj.* silberbeschlagen. **—-paper**, *s.* das Staniolpapier. **—-plating**, *s.* die Silberplattierung. **—smith**, *s.* der Silber=arbeiter, =schmied. **—y-toned**, *adj.* silbern klingend, silbertönig.

Silviculture, *s.* der Waldbau.

Simil—ar, *adj.*, **—arly**, *adv.* ähnlich, gleich; (of like nature) gleichartig. **—arity**, *s.* die Ähnlichkeit, Gleichartigkeit. **—e**, *s.* das Gleichnis, die Vergleichung. **—itude**, *s.* die Ähnlichkeit; *see* —e.

Simmer, *v.n.* gelinde kochen, wallen; —ing rebellion, gährender Aufstand.

Simony, *s.* der Pfründenschacher, die Simonie.

Simoom, *s.* der Giftwind, Samum.

Simper, I. *s.* das gezierte *or* einfältige Lächeln. II. *v.n.* geziert, affektiert, einfältig lächeln. **—er**, *s.* einer, der albern, geziert lächelt. **—ing**, I. *see* — I. II. *adj.*, **—ingly**, *adv.* einfältig *or* geziert lächelnd.

Simpl—e, I. *adj.* einfach (*also fig.*, *Bot.*, *Chem.*); (plain) schlicht, einfach; (foolish) einfältig; —e body, das Element (*Chem.*); he is very —e, er ist ein Einfaltspinsel. II. *s.* das Simplum; (herb) das (einfache) Heilkraut. **—es**, *pl.* die einfachen Arzneipflanzen, Heilkräuter. **—eton**, *s.* der Einfaltspinsel, Tropf. **—icity**, *s.* die Einfachheit; die Schlichtheit, Einfachheit; die Einfachheit, Einfalt (*of manners, customs*, *etc.*); die Einfachheit, Deutlichkeit (*of a doctrine*, *etc.*); die Einfältigkeit, Arglosigkeit, Naivetät; *see* Sincerity. **—ification**, *s.* die Vereinfachung. **—ify**, *v.a.* vereinfachen; (make easier) erleichtern. **—y**, *adv.* einfach; schlicht; (merely) bloß, nur, einzig und allein; (plainly) schlechthin. *Comp.* **—e-minded**, *adj.* arglos, offenherzig. **—e-mindedness**, *s.* die Arglosigkeit, Herzenseinfalt, Schlichtheit.

Simul—ate, *v.a.* nachmachen, vorgeben, zum Schein tun; (pretend) (er)heucheln, sich stellen als ob; a feeling that —ated love, ein Gefühl, das Liebe schien, das den Anschein der Liebe hatte. **—ated**, *adj.* nachgemacht, geheuchelt. **—ation**, *s.* die Verstellung, Heuchelei. **—taneous**, *adj.*, **—taneously**, *adv.* gleichzeitig. **—taneousness**, *s.* die Gleichzeitigkeit.

Sin, I. *s.* die Sünde; besetting —, die Gewohnheitssünde, Schoßsünde; original —, die Erbsünde (*Theol.*). II. *v.n.* sündigen, sich vergehen (against a p., an einem, gegen einen); a man more —ned against than —ning, ein Mann, an dem mehr gesündigt worden ist, als er gesündigt hat. III. *v.a.;* to — a —, eine Sünde begehen. **—ful**, *adj.*, **—fully**, *adv.* sündhaft, sündig; sündlich (*as an action, etc.*). **—fulness**, *s.* die Sündhaftigkeit; die Sündlichkeit. **—less**, *adj.*, **—lessly**, *adv.* sündenfrei, sünd(en)los, unschuldig. **—lessness**, *s.* die Sündlosigkeit, Unschuld. **—ner**, *s.* der (die) Sünder(in); (criminal) der Verbrecher. *Comp.* **—-offering**, *s.* das Sündopfer.

Sinapism, *s.* das Senfpflaster.

Since, I. *adv.* seitdem; two years —, vor zwei Jahren; long —, lange her; how long —? seit wann? seit wie lange? how long is it —? wie lange ist es her, seitdem? II. *prep.* seit; — that time, seit dieser Zeit. III. *conj.* da (einmal), weil; seit(dem); — you are determined to . . ., da Sie einmal entschlossen sind, zu . . .; it is not a week — I saw him, es ist keine Woche her, seitdem ich ihn sah.

Sincer—e, *adj.*, **—ely**, *adv.* aufrichtig, wahr, redlich; (serious) im Ernst; it gives me —e pleasure, es gewährt mir ein wahres Vergnügen; yours —ely, aufrichtig der Ihrige, Ihr (aufrichtig) ergebener; yours very —ely, Dein (Ihr) treuer. **—ity**, *s.* die Aufrichtigkeit, Redlichkeit.

Sinciput, *s.* das Vorderhaupt.

[1]**Sin—e**, *s.* der Sinus (*Geom.*). **—ical**, *adj.;* —ical quadrant, der Reduktionsquadrant.

[2]**Sine**, *prep.* ohne; — die, auf unbestimmte Zeit; — qua non, unerläßliche Bedingung. **—cure**, *s.* das Amt ohne Arbeit, einträgliches Ruheamt, die fette Pfründe, Sinekure. **—curist**, *s.* der Inhaber einer Sinekure.

Sinew, *s.* die Sehne, Flechse; die Stärke, Hauptstütze, der Nerv (*fig.*); the —s of war, der Nerv des Krieges (das Geld). **—less**, *adj.* kraftlos. **—y**, *adj.* sehnig; nervig, sehnig, stark (*fig.*).

Sing, *ir.v.a. & n.* singen; dichten, singen (*as a poet*); to — **off**, vom Blatte singen; **to — off** key *or* **out** of tune, unrein *or* nicht rein singen; **to** — out, aufsingen (*Naut.*); aufschreien, ausrufen (*sl.*); to — **to**, vorsingen; to — a child to sleep, ein Kind einsingen, in den Schlaf singen; to — **over**, absingen. **—er**, *s.* der (die) Sänger(in). **—ing**, I. *adj.* singend. II. *s.* das Singen, der Gesang; —ing in the ears, das Ohrenbrausen, Ohrensausen. *Comp.* **—ing-bird**, *s.* der Singvogel. **—ing-master**, *s.* der Singlehrer, Gesanglehrer. **—-song**, I. *s.* der Singsang. II. *adj.* singsangartig, eintönig.

Sing—le, I. *adj.* einzig; (individual) einzeln; (simple) einfach; (unmarried) unverheiratet, ledig; —le bill, Sola-Wechsel; to live in a state of —le blessedness, ledig sein; —le combat, der Zweikampf; bookkeeping by —le entry, einfache Buchhaltung; —le file, der Gänsemarsch; —le house, ein Haus mit Zimmern nach einer Seite des Ganges; —le man, der Junggeselle, Hagestolz; —le woman, lediges, alleinstehendes Frauenzimmer. II. *v.a.* (—le out) aus-lesen, -wählen, -sondern. **—leness**, *s.* die Vereinzelung, Einfachheit; die Aufrichtigkeit, Redlichkeit (*of heart, of purpose*). **—ly**, *adv.* einzeln, vereinzelt, besonders, stückweise; (alone) allein. **—ular**, I. *adj.*, **—ularly**, *adv.* seltsam; (unusual) ungewöhnlich; (odd) sonderbar, eigentümlich, eigen; (wonderful) ausgezeichnet. II. *s.* (—ular number) die Einzahl, der Singular. **—ularity**, *s.* die Sonderbarkeit, Eigentümlichkeit; (rarity) die Seltenheit; *see* Oddity. *Comp.* **—le-breasted**, *adj.* einreihig (*coat*). **—le-court**, *s.* das Einzelspielfeld (*Tennis*). **—le-handed**, *adj.* einhändig; (alone) einzeln, einzig, allein; ohne Unterstützung, auf eigne Faust; —le-handed game, das Einzelspiel. **—le-hearted**, **—le-minded**, *adj.* aufrichtig, redlich. **—le-heartedness**, **—le-mindedness**, *s.* die Redlichkeit, Aufrichtigkeit. **—le-needle**, *adj.;* —le-needle instrument, der Zeigerapparat (*Tele.*). **—le-stick**, *s.* der Fechtstock mit Korbgeflecht.

Singe, I. *v.a.* (ver)sengen, brennen; to — off, absengen. II. *s.* der (leichte) Brandschaden.

Sinister, *adj.* link, zur Linken; (evil) böse, schlimm, schlecht; (dishonest) unrecht, unredlich; (unlucky) unglücklich, unglückbedeutend; unheilvoll, finster, unheildrohend.

Sink, I. *ir.v.n.* sinken; (— down) niedersinken; (settle) sich senken; (— below) untergehen; (be swallowed up) versinken; (give way) ein-sinken, -fallen; eindringen (*into one's heart, etc.*); erliegen (beneath, unter der Last von); sinken, abnehmen (*fig.*); the patient's strength is fast —ing, die Kräfte des Kranken nehmen sichtlich ab; he is —ing fast, er ist an Todes Enden, liegt im Sterben (*coll.*); the nobles were sunk in apathetic sloth, der Adel war in teilnahmlose Trägheit versunken; sunken eyes, eingefallene Augen; to — **back**, zurücksinken in (*acc.*); to — **down**, niedersinken; to — **in** price, im Preise fallen; to — **into** oblivion (absurdity), in Vergessenheit geraten (in das Abgeschmackte verfallen); to — **under** the weight of years, unter der Last der Jahre erliegen. II. *ir.v.a.* (ver)senken; abteufen, absenken (*a shaft, etc.*); graben, bohren (*a well*); abtragen (*capital*); anlegen (*money*); tilgen (*a debt*); vertiefen (*a picture*); ins Verderben stürzen, verderben (*fig.*); to — differences *or* quarrels, Streitigkeiten beilegen; to — ditches, Gräben ziehen; to — a ship, ein Schiff versenken, in den Grund bohren. III. *s.* die Senkgrube; der Guß-, Gossen-stein (*in a kitchen, etc.*); — of corruption *or* iniquity, der Sündenpfuhl. **—er**, *s.* der Schachtarbeiter (*Min.*). **—ing**, *s.* das Sinken, Untergehen; das Einsinken (*Build.*); well- —ing, das Brunnenbohren. *Comp.* **—ing-fund**, *s.* der Tilgungs-Fonds.

Sinu—ate, *adj.* buchtig (*Bot.*). **—osity**, *s.* die Krümmung, Wellenförmigkeit. **—ous**, *adj.* gewunden, krumm, wellig. **—s**, *s.* die Krümmung; (bay) die Bucht; die Höhle (*Anat.*); der Sinus, die Winkelstütze (*Geom.*).

Sip, I. *s.* der Nipp, das Schlückchen. II. *v.a.* nippen; schlürfen (*as bees, also fig.*). **—pet**, *s.* das Eingetunkte, Eingeweichtes Brot.

Siphon *or* **Syphon**, *s.* der (Saug-)Heber; die Druckflasche, die Siphonflasche (*for soda-water*).

Sir, *s.* Herr (*in addressing*); Sir (*as title*); yes, —, ja, Herr Müller; jawohl, Herr Doktor; jawohl, gnädiger Herr (*but not:* ja, mein Herr); —? wie beliebt? was befehlen Sie? wie (sagten Sie)? go out, —! marsch! hinaus! (*to a dog*). **—e**, *s.* Sire (*in addressing a sovereign, etc.*); (parent) der Vater; (ancestor) der Vorfahr(e), Ahn(e); der Vater, männliche Stamm (*of horses, dogs, etc.*). **—rah**, *s.* du da! Junge!

Sirdar, *s.* der Sirdar, ostindische Häuptling; der Oberbefehlshaber des anglo-ägyptischen Heeres.

Siren, I. *s.* die Sirene (*also Acoust., etc., fig.*); der Armmolch, die Sirene (*Zool.*). II. *adj.* Sirenen-, verführerisch.

Sirloin, *s.* das (Rinder-)Lendenstück.

Sirocco, *s.* der Sirokko, heiße Südostwind.

Sirup, *see* Syrup.

Siskin, *s.* der Zeisig.

Sister, I. *s.* die Schwester (*also fig.*); (nun) die Nonne; your —, Ihre Schwester, Ihr Fräulein Schwester, Ihre Frau Schwester; **—s of mercy**, barmherzige Schwestern. II. *attrib.* Schwester=; — country, das Schwesterland. —**hood**, *s.* die Schwesterschaft; klösterliche Genossenschaft. —**ly**, *adj.* schwesterlich. *Comp.* —**-in-law**, *s.* die Schwägerin.

Sit, *ir.v.* I. *n.* sitzen (*also Sport.*); Sitzung(en) halten, versammelt sein, sitzen (*as Parliament*); beraten (upon a th., über eine S.); Mitglied sein (upon a commission, etc., einer Kommission ꝛc.), im Rate sitzen; (rest) ruhen, liegen; brüten, sitzen (*as birds*); sitzen, kleiden, anstehen (*as clothes*); to — close, enge sitzen *or* anliegen; to — still, ruhig, still sitzen; the wind —s fair, der Wind sitzt gut; to — in judgment upon, zu Gericht sitzen über (*acc.*); to — **at** table, bei Tische sitzen; come and — **by** me, komm', setze dich zu mir *or* an meine Seite; to — **down**, niedersitzen, sich setzen; she sat down at our table, sie setzte sich an unsern Tisch, nahm an unserm Tische Platz; to — down and do nothing, die Hände in den Schoß legen; the Hon. Member who has just sat down, der geehrte Herr Vorredner (*Parl.*); to — down to meals, sich zu Tische setzen; to — down before, belagern; to — **for** one's picture, sich malen lassen, dem Maler sitzen; to — for one's degree, sich einer Prüfung unter=werfen *or* =ziehen; to — **on**, *see* — upon; to — on horseback, zu Pferde sitzen; to — heavy on, schwer lasten auf (*dat.*); to — **out**, aus=, müßig sitzen (*at Whist, etc.*); vorübergehen lassen (a dance, einen Tanz), (dabei) sitzen bleiben; to — **to** an artist, einem Maler sitzen; to — **up**, sich aufrichten, (not go to bed) aufbleiben, die Nacht hinbringen (at, mit); wachen (with a sick person, bei einem Kranken); to — **upon**, sitzen auf einer S. (*lit.*), Gericht halten über einen (*fig.*); to — upon thorns, wie auf Kohlen sitzen; to — upon a p., einen anfahren, anschnauzen, herrisch behandeln, tyrannisieren (*sl.*). II. *a.* sitzen; to — a horse well, gut zu Pferde sitzen; to — a p. out, länger bleiben *or* aushalten als einer; to — a piece out, ein Stück zu Ende hören. —**ter**, *s.* der, die Sitzende; die Brüthenne; der brütende Vogel. —**ting**, I. *s.* das Sitzen, Brüten; die Sitzung; (seat) der Sitz. II. *adj.* sitzend (*also Bot.*); the —ting member for, der gegenwärtige Abgeordnete des Wahlkreises (von). *Comp.* —**-down**, *adj.*; —-down supper, Abendessen, wobei man an der Tafel sitzt und nicht nur an Tischen steht. —**ting-room**, *s.* das Wohnzimmer.

Sit—e, *s.* die Lage, Situation; der Bauplatz; plan of —e, der Situationsplan. —**uate(d)**, *adj.* liegend, gelegen; —uated, befindlich; think how I am —uated with respect to . . ., denke an meine Lage . . . gegenüber; —uated in the northeast of, nordöstlich von. —**uation**, *s.* die Lage; die Lage, der Zustand (*fig.*); die Situation, Lage (*Theat.*); (place) die Stelle, Anstellung.

Six, I. *num. adj.* sechs; sechs Uhr. II. *s.* die Sechs; all at —es and sevens, in größter Unordnung, in völliger Verwirrung. —**fold**, *adj.* sechsfach. —**teen**, *adj.* sechzehn. —**teenth**, I. *adj.* sechzehnt. II. *s.* das Sechzehntel. —**th**, I. *adj.* sechst. II. *s.* das Sechstel; die Sexte (*Mus.*). —**thly**, *adv.* sechstens, an sechster Stelle. —**tieth**, *adj.* sechzigst. —**ty**, *s.* die Sechzig. *Comp.* —**pence**, —**penny-piece**, *s.* das 6=Pence=Stück. —**penny**, *adj.* 6 Pence an Wert. —**pennyworth**, *s.*; a —pennyworth of sugar, Zucker für sechs pence *or* für 6p. Zucker. —**-pounder**, *s.* der Sechspfünder. —**-sided**, *adj.* sechsseitig.

Siz—ar, *s.* besonders armer tüchtiger Student (*in Cambridge*), welcher in seinem College weniger bezahlt als der gewöhnliche Student (pensioner). —**e**, *s.* (bulk, *etc.*) der Umfang, die Größe; das Format (*of a book*); die Stich, die Nummer, Größe (*gloves, boots*); die Gestalt (*fig.*); für einen farthing Brot oder Getränk (*obs.*); life —e, Lebensgröße; quarter —e, Viertelgröße; —ings, Rationen (*Univ., obs.*). —**ed**, *adj.*; middle-—ed, von mittlerer Größe. *Comp.* —**arship**, *s.* die Stellung und Vergünstigungen eines Sizar, das Collegestipendium (*Cambridge*).

[1]**Size**, *see under* Siz—ar.

[2]**Siz—e**, I. *s.* der Leim; das Planierwasser (*Bookb.*). II. *v.a.* leimen, planieren. —**ing**, *s.* das Leimen (*also Paint.*), Planieren, der Kleister; das Stärken (*Weav.*).

Sjambok, *s.* die Nilpferdpeitsche.

Skald, *s.* der Barde.

[1]**Skat—e**, I. *s.* der Schlittschuh; rinking —e, der Rollschlittschuh. II. *v.n.* Schlittschuh laufen *Comp.* —**ing-rink**, *s.* die Rollschlittschuhbahn.

[2]**Skate**, *s.* der Glattroche (*Icht.*).

Skean-dhu, *s.* der schottische **Dolch**.

Skedaddle, *v.n.* ausreißen (*coll.*).

Skee, I. *s.* der Ski. II. *v.n.* auf Skien laufen. —**ing**, *s.* das Skilaufen.

Skein, *s.* das Gebinde, der Strähn, Strang; — of silk, der Strang Seide.

Skeleton, I. *s.* das Gerippe (*also Carp.*), Skelett; das Gestell (*of an umbrella, a hat, etc.*); — in the cupboard, das Gespenst im Hause, verborgener häuslicher Kummer. II. *attrib.*; — army, die Skelett=Armee; — bills, bonds, letters, unausgefüllte Formulare von Wechseln, Schuldverschreibungen, *etc.*; — corps, der Stamm *or* Rahmen eines Truppenkörpers; — enemy, der markierte Feind (*Milit.*); — key, der Dietrich.

Skerry, *s.* felsige Insel.

Sketch, I. *s.* die Skizze, der Entwurf; die Aufnahme (*Surv.*); rough —, erster, flüchtiger Entwurf. II. *v.a.* skizzieren, entwerfen; flüchtig aufnehmen (*Surv.*). III. *v.n.* Skizzen entwerfen, zeichnen. —**er**, *s.* der Skizzierer, Skizzenzeichner. —**iness**, *s.* das Skizzenartige; das Oberflächliche, leicht Hingeworfene (*fig.*). —**y**, *adj.* skizzenhaft. *Comp.* —**-book**, *s.* das Skizzenbuch.

Skew, *adj. see* Askew. *Comp.* —**-bridge**, *s.* schiefe Brücke.

Skewer, I. *s.* der Speiler, Fleischspieß. II. *v.a.* speilern.

Skid, I. der Hemmschuh, die Hemmkette; das Reibholz (*Naut.*). II. *v.a.* hemmen. III. *v.n.* ausrutschen, seitwärts ausgleiten (*Cycl.*).

Skies, *pl. see* Sky.

Skiff, *s.* das Schiffchen, der Kahn.

Skiing, *s. see* Skee—.

Skil—ful, *adj.*, —**fully**, *adv.* geschickt, gewandt, kunstfertig, erfahren. —**l**, (—**fulness**,) *s.* die Geschicklichkeit, Gewandtheit, Kunstfertigkeit, Kenntnis; to show one's —l, seine Geschicklichkeit zeigen; he has no —l in, er versteht sich nicht auf (*acc.*). —**led**, *adj.* geschickt, erfahren, geübt, bewandert (in einer S.); —led hands, geschickte Hände (*lit.*); eingeschulte, gelernte Handwerker (*fig.*). —**lless**, *adj.* ungeschickt.

Skillet, *s.* der kleine Kessel, Tiegel.

Skim, I. *v.a.* abschäumen, abrahmen (*milk, etc.*); (— over) streifen, leicht berühren; oberflächlich lesen, flüchtig durchblättern (*a book*). II. *s.* der Schaum; *see* Scum (*fig.*). —**mer**, *s.* der Abschöpfende; (—ming-ladle) der Rahm=, Schaumlöffel. —**mingly**, *adv.* leicht hinfahrend. —**mings**, *pl.* das Abgeschäumte. *Comp.* —**-milk**, *s.* abgerahmte **Milch**, Magermilch.

Skin, I. *s.* die Haut (*of men and beasts*); das Fell (*of beasts*); (fur) der Pelz; die Schale, Hülse (*Bot.*); der Wasser=, Wein=schlauch; he is nothing but — and bone, an ihm ist nichts als Haut und Knochen; I should not like to be in his —, ich möchte nicht in seiner Haut stecken; to have a thick (thin) —, dickfellig, unempfindlich (feinfühlig) sein. II. *v.a.* häuten, abziehen, abstreifen; (peel) schälen. III *v.n.* sich häuten —**ned**, *adj.* =häutig. —**ner**, *s.* der Rauchwaren=, Pelz=händler. —**niness**, *s.* die Magerkeit. —**ny**, *adj.* häutig; (thin) fleischlos, mager;

geizig, filzig (*coll.*). *Comp.* —**-deep**, *adj.* oberflächlich. —**flint**, *s.* der Geizige, Geizhals (*sl.*).

Skip, I. *v.a.* über-springen, -hüpfen; auslassen. II. *v.n.* Seil-hüpfen, -springen; (leap) hüpfen (for joy, vor Freude); to — over, *see* — I. III. *s.* der Hupf, Sprung; by —s, sprungweise. —**per**, *s.* der Hüpfer, Springer; der, die Seilspringende (*with a rope*); die Käsemilbe (*Ent.*). —**ping**, *s.* das (Seil-)Springen ꝛc. *Comp.* —**jack**, *s.* der Hüpfer; der Springkäfer; der Emporkömmling (*fig.*). —**ping-rope**, *s.* das Springseil (*for children*).

[1]**Skipper**, *see under* Skip.

[2]**Skipper**, *s.* der Schiffer, Schiffsherr, Kapitän.

Skirmish, I. *s.* das Scharmützel, das Geplänkel; das Schützengefecht. II. *v.n.* scharmützeln. —**er**, *s.* der Plänkler.

Skirt, I. *s.* der (Unter-)Rock (*of a woman's dress*); der Schoß (*of a coat*); der Saum, Rand (*of a wood, etc.*); (outskirts) das Ende (*of the town*); divided —, der geteilte Rock, Reformrock. II. *v.a.* am Rande, an der Grenze sein; (*also v.n.* to — **along**) den Saum entlang laufen. —**ing**, *s.* die Fußleiste. *Comp.* —**-dance**, *s.* der Serpentintanz. —**-dancer**, *s.* die Serpentintänzerin. —**ing-board**, *s.* die Scheuerleiste, Wandleiste.

Skit, *s.* (squib) die Stichelei, Spott-rede, -schrift. —**tish**, *adj.*, —**tishly**, *adv.* scheu, stätisch; (wanton) leichtfertig, ausgelassen; (volatile) wankelmütig, unstät. —**tishness**, *s.* das scheue, stätische Wesen, die Sprödigkeit; die Leichtfertigkeit; die Unbeständigkeit.

Skittle, *s.* der Kegel. —**s**, *pl.* das Kugelwerfen, eine Art Kegelspiel. *Comp.* —**-alley** *or* —**-ground**, *s.* die Kegelbahn.

Skulk, *v.n.* lauern; (hide) sich verstecken; (sneak) schleichen. —**er**, *s.* der Laurer, Schleicher. —**ing**, *adj.*, —**ingly**, *adv.* lauernd, sich versteckend.

Skull, *s.* die Hirnschale, der Hirnschädel. *Comp.* —**-cap**, *s.* die Kappe, Becken-, Pickel-haube.

Skunk, *s.* amerikanisches Stinktier.

Sky, I. *s.* der Wolken-, Luft-himmel, Luftraum; (weather) das Wetter, Klima; to praise a p. up to the skies, einen bis in den Himmel erheben. II. *v.a.* zu hoch hängen (*a picture*); —ed, (skied,) himmelhoch. —**ward**, *adv.* himmelwärts. *Comp.* —**-blue**, *adj.* himmelblau. —**lark**, *s.* die Feldlerche. —**larking**, *s.* das Possenreißen; tolle Streiche. —**light**, *s.* das Oberlicht; das Dachfenster, Schrägfenster. —**-scraper**, *s.* das Schei-, Oberbramlee-segel (*Naut.*); der Wolkenkratzer (*Amer.*).

Slab, *s.* die (Stein-, Marmor-)Platte; die Schwarte (*of wood*).

Slabber, *see* Slobber.

Slack, I. *adj.*, —**ly**, *adv.* schlaff, locker; schlaff, nachlässig, träge (*fig.*); flau (*C.L.*); — rope, schlaffes Tau, das Schlappseil (*of rope-dancers*); — water, das Totwasser. II. *s.* die Staubkohle, das Kohlenklein, der Kohlengrus; *see* Slake. III. *see* —en. —**en**, *v.* I. *n.* schlaff werden, erschlaffen; erschlaffen, nachlassen, nachlässig werden (*fig.*); langsamer werden (*as a current, etc.*); flau werden (*C. L.*); the demand —ens, die Nachfrage läßt nach (*C.L.*); the wind —ens, der Wind wird schwächer. II. *a.* schlaff machen, nachlassen (*a rope*); (loosen) locker, los machen; to —en speed, die Geschwindigkeit vermindern (*of an engine*); *see* Relax. —**ness**, *s.* die Schlaffheit; die Flauheit (*of business*); (remissness) die Nachlässigkeit, Saumseligkeit.

Slag, *s.* die Schlacke (*of metals, etc.*); *see* Slack II. —**gy**, *adj.* schlackig.

Slain, *p.p. of* Slay.

Slake, *v.a.* löschen, stillen (*thirst*); löschen (*lime*); ablassen (*fire*); —d lime, gelöschter Kalk.

Slam, I. *v.a.* zuwerfen, zuschlagen (*a door, etc.*); (strike down) hinwerfen, hinschmeißen; einen schlemm machen (*at Whist*); to — a door in a p.'s face, einem die Tür vor der Nase zuschlagen. II. *v.n.* heftig zuschlagen, (sich) mit Geräusch schließen. III. *s.* das Zuwerfen; der Schlemm (*Cards*).

Slander, I. *s.* die Verleumdung. II. *v.a.* verleumden, verunglimpfen. —**er**, *s.* der Verleumder, Lästerer. —**ous**, *adj.*, —**ously**, *adv.* verleumderisch, Läster-.

[1]**Slang**, I. *s.* die Kunstsprache (eines Standes, des Sports), das Slang; das Rotwelsch; thieves' —, Gaunersprache. II. *adj.* der Kunstsprache eines Standes oder Faches angehörig. III. *v.a.* einen schlecht machen, herunterreißen, ausschimpfen (*coll.*). —**y**, *adj.* zum Slang gehörig; derb, unfein; Slang-Ausdrücke gebrauchend.

[2]**Slang**, (*obs.*) *imperf. of* Sling.

Slank, (*obs.*) *imperf. of* Slink.

Slant, I. *v.a.* eine schiefe *or* schräge Richtung geben. II. *v.n. see* Slope. III. *s.* die Schräge, die schiefe Richtung. —**ing**, *adj.*, —**ingly**, *adv.*, —**wise**, *adv.* schief, schräg.

Slap, I. *s.* die Schlappe, der Schlag, Klaps. II. *v.a.* klapsen, schlagen. *Comp.* —**-bang**, *int.* pauz! pardauz! plumps! —**-dash**, I. *s.* der rauhe Anwurf. II. *adv.* plötzlich; (wildly) übereilt, überhudelt (*vulg.*).

Slash, I. *v.a.* aufschlitzen, zerfetzen, zerschneiden; —ed sleeve, der Schlitzärmel. II. *v.n.* (um sich) hauen. III. *s.* der Hieb, Streich; (cut) die Schramme, Wunde, der Schnitt; der Schlitz (*in a dress*). —**ing**, *adj.* schneidig, scharf; urwüchsig (*sl.*); —ing criticism, vernichtende Kritik. *Comp.* —**-sword**, I. *s.* der Haudegen; (straight-bladed) —-sword, das Rappier, der Mensurschläger. II. *attrib.*; —-sword duel, die Schlägermensur.

Slat, *s.* dünne Schiene, Leiste (*of Venetian blinds, etc.*). —**e**, I. *s.* der Schiefer; die Schiefertafel (*for children, etc.*). II. *v.a.* mit Schiefer decken. III. *adj.* Schiefer-, schieferfarbig; —e pencil, der Schieferstift; —e quarry, der Schieferbruch; —e roof, das Schieferdach. —**er**, *s.* der Schieferdecker; die gemeine Mauerassel (*Ent.*). —**ing**, *s.* die Schiefereindeckung. —**y**, *adj.* schieferartig.

[1]**Slate**, *see under* Slat.

[2]**Slate**, I. *v.a.* ausschelten, abkanzeln, heruntermachen (*sl.*). II. *s.* die Schimpfrede (*sl.*).

Slattern, *s.* die Schlumpe. —**liness**, *s.* schlumpiges Wesen. —**ly**, *adj.* schlumpig.

Slaughter, I. *s.* das Schlachten, Gemetzel, Blutbad; (murder) die Ermordung; — of cattle, Viehschlachten. II. *v.a.* schlachten (*also cattle*); (nieder)metzeln. —**er**, *s.* der Schlächter; der Mörder. —**ous**, *adj.*, —**ously**, *adv.* mörderisch. *Comp.* —**-house**, *s.* das Schlachthaus.

Slav—e, I. *s.* der (die) Sklav(in); der Knecht (*fig.*); *see the Index of names.* II. *v.n.* wie ein Sklave arbeiten, sich placken. —**er**, *s.* das Sklavenschiff. —**ery**, *s.* die Sklaverei, Knechtschaft; der Sklavendienst (*fig.*). —**ey**, *s.* der (männliche oder weibliche) Dienstbote, das Mädchen für alles (*sl.*). —**ish**, *adj.*, —**ishly**, *adv.* sklavisch, knechtisch. —**ishness**, *s.* sklavisches Wesen. *Comp.* —**e-dealer**, *s.* der Sklavenhändler. —**e-driver**, *s.* der Sklavenaufseher; der Leuteschinder (*fig.*). —**e-hunter**, *s.* der Sklavenjäger. —**e-market**, *s.* der Sklavenmarkt. —**e-trade**, *s.* der Sklavenhandel; white —e-trade, der [Mädchenhandel.

[1]**Slaver**, *see* Slav—.

[2]**Slaver**, I. *s.* der Geifer. II. *v.a.* begeifern. —**er**, *s.* der Geiferer.

[1]**Slay**, *ir.v.a.* erschlagen, töten; vernichten (*fig.*); the slain, die Erschlagenen, Toten. —**er**, *s.* der Totschläger.

[2]**Slay**, **Sley**, *s.* der Weberkamm.

Sleave, *s.* das Verworrenes, Verfitztes; (— silk) aufgewundene Docken-Seide; — of care, der Sorgenknäuel (*fig.*).

[1]**Sledg—e**, I. *s.* der Schlitten. II. *v.n. see* Sleigh. *Comp.* —**e-carriage**, *s.* die Schlittenlafette (*Artil.*). —**ing-party**, *s.* die Schlittenpartie.

[2]**Sledge**, *s.*, —**-hammer**, *s.* der Schmiedehammer; with a —, gewaltsam.

Sleek, I. *adj.* schlicht, glatt. II. *v.a.* glatt machen; streichen (*hair*); to — over, *see* Smooth. —**ness**, *s.* die Glätte. *Comp.* —**-haired**, *adj.* glatthaarig.

Sleep, I. *ir.v.n.* schlafen (*also fig.*); (go to —) einschlafen; (be dead) entschlafen sein; to be —ing, schlafen, träumen, unaufmerksam sein; I will — upon it, ich will darüber schlafen; the bed has been slept in, in dem Bette ist geschlafen worden. II. *ir.v.a.* schlafen (the — of the dead, den Todesschlaf); to — a dog's sleep, sich stellen, als ob man schlafe; to — away, off, verschlafen (*the time or a headache*); to — o.s. sober, seinen Rausch verschlafen. III. *s.* der Schlaf. —**er**, *s.* der Schläfer; die Schwelle (*Railw.*); der Rost (*Glassw.*). —**ily**, *adv.*, —**y**, *adj.* schläfrig; schwerfällig, stumpfsinnig (*fig.*); einschläfernd; überreif (*fruit*). —**iness**, *s.* die Schläfrigkeit. —**ing**, *p.* & *adj.*; —ing partner, der stille Teilhaber. —**less**, *adj.*, —**lessly**, *adv.* schlaflos; ruhelos (*fig.*). —**lessness**, *s.* die Schlaflosigkeit. *Comp.* —**ing-carriage** *or* **-car**, *s.* der Schlafwagen. —**-walker**, *s.* der Nachtwandler. —**-walking**, I. *s.* das Nachtwandeln. II. *adj.* nachtwandelnd. —**yhead**, *s.* die Schlafmütze (*coll.*).

Sleet, I. *s.* die Schloßen, Graupeln; mit Schnee untermischter Regen; der Hagel (von Pfeilen) (*fig.*). II. *v.n.* graupeln, zu gleicher Zeit regnen und schneien. —**y**, *adj.* Graupel-.

Sleeve, I. *s.* der Ärmel; to laugh in one's —, sich (*dat.*) ins Fäustchen lachen; to hang one's judgment on the — of a p., der Meinung jemands blindlings folgen; to wear one's heart on one's —, seine Gedanken zur Schau tragen. II. *v.a.* mit Ärmeln versehen. —**less**, *adj.* ohne Ärmel. *Comp.* —**-link**, *s.* der Manschettenknopf.

Sleigh, *s.* der Schlitten. —**ing**, I. *s.* das Schlittenfahren. II. *adj.*; —ing party, *see* Sledging party. *Comp.* —**-bells**, *pl.* das Schlittengeläute. —**-ride**, *s.* die Schlittenfahrt.

Sleight, *s.* der Kunstgriff, die List; — of hand, das Kunststück, der Taschenspielerstreich.

Slender, *adj.*, —**ly**, *adv.* schlank; (thin) mager, dünn; karg, spärlich (*as means*); schwach, gering (*as hopes*). —**ness**, *s.* die Schlankheit; die Geringfügigkeit; die Spärlichkeit.

Slept, *imperf. of* Sleep.

Sleuth, *s.* die Spur, Fährte (*dial.*). *Comp.* —**-hound**, *s.* der Spürhund, Bluthund.

Slew, *imperf. of* Slay.

Slice, I. *s.* der Schnitt, die Schnitte, Scheibe, das Stück; der Spatel (*Pharm.*); das Farb-, Streicheisen (*Typ.*); fish-—, die Fischkelle; a — of bread, of meat, ein Stück Brot, Fleisch. II. *v.a.* in flache, dünne Scheiben, Schnitten schneiden; (cut up) zerschneiden; (— off) abschneiden.

Slid, *imperf.*, —**den**, (*rare*) *p.p. of* —e. —**e**, I. *ir.v.n.* gleiten, schlüpfen; gleiten, glitschen (*on the ice, etc.*); (slip) ausgleiten; to —e down, herabgleiten. II. *ir.v.a.* gleiten, schlüpfen lassen. III. *s.* die Schleifbahn; die Rutsche (*for wood, etc.*); leichter Übergang (*of the voice*); der Zug (*of a flute, etc.*); der Schieber (*of a belt, etc., of a lock*). —**er**, *s.* der Gleitende, Glitschende; der Schieber (*of an umbrella, instrument, etc.*). —**ing**, I. *adj.* gleitend; —ing door, die Schiebetür; —ing knot, die Schleife, Schlinge; —ing rule, der Zollstock mit Auszug; —ing sash, das Schiebfenster; —ing scale, die bewegliche (Lohn-, Preis-)Skala; —ing seat, der Rollsitz. II. *s.* das Gleiten; das Vergehen, der Fehltritt. *Comp.* —**e-rail**, *s.* die Weichschiene. —**e-rule**, *s.*; *see* —ing rule. —**er-wine-bin**, *s.* verschiebbares Flaschengestell.

Slight, I. *adj.*, —**ly**, *adv. see* Slender; (weak) schwach; (inconsiderable) gering, klein, unbedeutend; — of frame, von zartem Körperbau; a — effort, eine leichte Anstrengung; — illness, die Unpäßlichkeit; — scratch, die Schramme. II. *v.a.* geringschätzig behandeln; (neglect) vernachlässigen. III. *s.* die Geringschätzung, Verachtung. —**er**, *s.* der Geringschätzende, Verächter. —**ingly**, *adv.* geringschätzig. —**ness**, *s.* die Schlankheit; die Schwäche; die Geringfügigkeit; die Dünnheit.

Slily, *adv. see* Sly.

Slim, *adj.*, —**ly**, *adv.* schmächtig, schlank. —**ness**, *s.* die Schmächtigkeit.

Slim—e, *s.* der Schlamm. —**iness**, *s.* das Schlammige; das Schleimige. —**y**, *adj.* schlammig; (mucous) schleimig.

Sling, I. *s.* die Schlinge, Binde (*Surg.*, *etc.*); die Schleuder (*for hurling, also Surg.*, *Agr.*); (throw) der Wurf; der Gewehr-, Schulter-riemen; arm in a —, Arm in einer Binde. II. *ir.v.a.* schleudern, werfen; schlingen (over one's shoulder, über die Schulter); anschnüren, anhängen (*hammocks*); to — up, aufhissen.

[1]**Slink**, I. *ir.v.n.* schleichen; to — off, sich wegschleichen *or* davonmachen. II. *s.* der Schleicher, Betrüger (*prov.*).

[2]**Slink**, I. *v.a.* & *n.* zu früh (Junge) werfen. II. *s.* zu früh geworfenes Tier. III. *adj.* frühzeitig geworfen.

Slip, I. *s.* das (Aus-)Gleiten, (Ab-)Glitschen; (false step) der Fehltritt (*also fig.*); (mistake) das Versehen, der Flüchtigkeitsfehler; (land —) der (Erd-)Sturz, Erdrutsch; der Streifen, das Stückchen (*of paper, etc.*); (— proof) der Fahnenabzug (*Print.*); der Setzling, Zweig, das Setzreis (*Hort.*); der Abkömmling, Sproß, Sprößling; die Leine (*for dogs*); der Überzug (*of a pillow*); (pinafore) das Lätzchen; das Unterkleid (*for ladies*); die Fahne (*Typ.*); die Rippe, Schnur (*Bookb.*); a — of a girl, schmächtiges, junges Mädchen (*fam.*); the —s, die Seitengänge (*Theat.*); to make a —, einen Fehler machen, sich versehen; einen Fehltritt begehen; — of the pen, der Schreibfehler; it was a — of the tongue, es entfuhr mir unversehens; there is many a —'twixt the cup and the lip, zwischen Lipp' und Kelchesrand schwebt der finstern Mächte Hand; to give a p. the —, einem heimlich entwischen, ihn im Stiche lassen (*coll.*). II. *v.a.* schlüpfen, gleiten lassen; unbemerkt hineinbringen, -tun, -schieben, -stecken; loslassen (*dogs*); schlippen lassen (*a cable*); to — **in**, einfließen lassen, dazwischenwerfen (*a word, etc.*); to — money into s.o.'s hand, einem Geld in die Hand drücken; to — **on**, to — **off**, hurtig (an)ziehen, ausziehen (*clothes, etc.*); to — **out**, ausziehen (*one's neck out of the collar*); to let a word — (out), ein Wort fallen lassen. III. *v.n.* schlüpfen, gleiten; (blunder) fehlen, sich (im Reden) verschnappen; (escape) entschlüpfen; ausgleiten (*in walking, etc.*); to let an opportunity —, sich (*dat.*) eine Gelegenheit entgehen lassen; to — **away**, sich fortschleichen, sich wegstehlen; (elapse) verstreichen; to — **down**, hinunterschlüpfen; to — **in**, (hin)einschleichen; to — **into** one's clothes, schnell in die Kleider schlüpfen; to — **off**, entwischen; to — **out**, hinausgleiten, entschlüpfen; to — out of a p.'s hands, den Händen entschlüpfen; to — **up**, im Irrtum sein, auf dem Holzwege sein; to — up to, sich hinaufschleichen zu. —**per**, *s.* der Pantoffel. —**pered**, *adj.* mit Pantoffeln versehen. —**periness**, *s.* die Schlüpfrigkeit (*also fig.*). —**pery**, *adj.* schlüpfrig, glatt; ungewiß, unzuverlässig (*fig.*). *Comp.* —**-carriage**, *s.* Eisenbahnwagen, der während der Fahrt abgekoppelt werden kann und auf einer Station zurückbleibt, während der Zug ohne zu halten durchfährt. —**-knot**, *s.* verlorener Knoten. —**per-bath**, *s.* die pantoffelförmige Badewanne. —**shod**, *adj.* in niedergetretenen Schuhen; nachlässig (*of style*).

Slish, *s.* der Hieb (*rare*); —, slash! ritsch, ratsch!

Slit, I. *ir.v.a.* auf-schlitzen, -spalten, -ritzen. II. *v.n.* sich spalten. III. *s.* der Schlitz, die Spalte. —**ting**, *p.*; —ting mill, das Schneidewerk.

Slither, *v.n.* die Füße nachziehen; ausgleiten

(*prov.*); to — along, nachlässig dahinschlurfen (*prov.*).

Sliver, I. der Splitter, das abgeschnittene Stück. II. *v.a.* zerschlitzen, zerspalten; abreißen.

Slobber, *v.* I. *n.* schlabbern, geifern. II. *a.* begeifern. **—er**, *s.* der Geiferer; der Schlabberer (*fig.*). **—y**, *adj.* feucht. *Comp.* **—ing-bib**, *s.* das Geiferlätzchen, der Pichel.

Sloe, *s.* die Schlehe; der Schwarzdorn, Schlehdorn; black as a —, pechschwarz.

Slogan, *s.* das Kriegsgeschrei (*of Highlanders*).

Sloop, *s.* die Schaluppe, das einmastige Fahrzeug; — of war, die Korvette.

[1]**Slop**, I. *s.*; (puddle) die Pfütze, Lache; to make a —, Flüssigkeit verschütten. II. *v.a.* verschütten (*water, etc.*). **—s**, *pl.* leichte, flüssige Speisen, Krankensuppen; (dirty water, *etc.*) schmutziges Wasser, das Spülicht. **—py**, *adj.* naß, schmutzig. *Comp.* **—-basin**, *s.* der Spülnapf, die Schale zum Ausleeren der Teetassen. **—-pail**, *s.* der Spüleimer.

[2]**Slop**, *s.* der Kittel, die Bluse. **—s**, *pl.* fertige Kleider (und Bettzeug, *Naut.*); (trousers) die Schifferhose. *Comp.* **—-shop**, *s.* Laden mit billigen fertigen Kleidern.

Slop—e, I. *s.* die Schräge; der Abhang (*of a hill, etc.*); die Gehre (*Carp., also of a dress, etc.*); die Böschung, der Abhang (*Fort., Build., etc.*). II. *v.n.* sich neigen, schräg abgehen, abhängen; weglaufen (*sl.*). III. *v.a.* abschüssig machen; abböschen (*Fort., Build.*); (incline) neigen, senken; to —e out, ausschneiden; —e arms! Gewehr über! (*Mil.*). **—ewise**, *adv.* schräg, abschüssig. **—ing**, *adj.*, **—ingly**, *adv.* schräg, abschüssig.

Slot, *s.* hölzerner Riegel; die Fährte (*Sport.*).

Sloth, *s.* das Faultier (*Zool.*); *see* —fulness. **—ful**, *adj.*, **—fully**, *adv.* träge, faul. **—fulness**, *s.* die Trägheit, Faulheit.

Slouch, I. *s.* das Schlotterige im Gange. II. *attrib.*; — hat, der Schlapphut. III. *v.n.* schlaff niederhängen (z. B. Hutkrempen); den Kopf hängen lassen; schlaff einhergehen, latschen, schlottern. IV. *v.a.* nieder=, hinein=drücken (*one's hat, etc.*).

[1]**Slough**, *s.* der feuchte, sumpfige Ort, Morast; — of despond, der Sumpf der Verzweiflung. **—y**, *adj.* kotig, sumpfig, morastig.

[2]**Slough**, I. *s.* der Balg, die abgestreifte, leere Haut (*of a serpent*); der Schorf (*of a wound*). II. *v.n.* (— off) sich ablösen (*from the sound flesh*); sich häuten (*as serpents, etc.*).

Sloven, *s.* der Schmutzhammel, Schmutzfink. **—liness**, *s.* die Nachlässigkeit, das schlotterige Wesen. **—ly**, *adj.* unordentlich, schlumpig, liederlich.

Slow, I. *adj.*, **—ly**, *adv.* langsam; (tardy) spät; (inactive) träg, untätig; schleichend, langsam (*as fevers*); — to wrath, geduldig; langsam zum Zorn (*B.*); — of speech, von schwerer Zunge; my watch is —, meine Uhr geht nach; they were not — to act, sie handelten schnell; ihre Wirkung ließ nicht lange auf sich warten; the vessel was going dead —, das Schiff fuhr sehr langsam. II. *v.n.* langsam gehen, fahren. **—ness**, *s.* die Langsamkeit; die Trägheit, Untätigkeit; *see* Unwillingness; (dulness) die Stumpfsinnigkeit; (hesitation) das Zögern; das Nachgehen (*of a watch, etc.*); the —ness of the clock made me . . ., das Nachgehen der Uhr ließ mich . . . *Comp.* **—-coach**, *s.* langsamer Mensch, langweiliger Gesell. **—-match**, *s.* die Lunte (*Artil.*). **—-witted**, *adj.* von langsamem Verstande. **—-worm**, *s.* die Blindschleiche.

Sloyd, I. *s.* die Handfertigkeit. II. *attrib.*; — schools, Schulen zur Erteilung des Handfertigkeitsunterrichts, Handfertigkeitsschulen.

Sludge, *s.* der Schlamm, Kot.

[1]**Slug**, *s.* die Wegschnecke; der Faulenzer. **—gard**, I. *s.* der Faulenzer. II. *adj.* träg, faul. **—gish**, *adj.*, **—gishly**, *adv.* träg, schwerfällig. **—gishness**, *s.* die Trägheit, Faulheit, Schwerfälligkeit, Langsamkeit.

[2]**Slug**, *s.* der Posten, die Kugel; halbgeröstetes Erz (*Metall.*).

Sluice, I. *s.* die Schleuse, das Siel; der aus einer Schleuse ausfließende Strom; (flood-gate) das Schleusentor; das Tor, die Quelle (*fig.*). II. *v.a.* durch eine Schleuse abfließen lassen.

Slum, I. *s.* der schmutzige Schlupfwinkel, das Hintergäßchen; —s, verrufene Stadtgegend. II. *v.n.* die schmutzigen Schlupfwinkel (von London 2c.) bewohnen *or* besuchen.

Slumber, I. *s.* der Schlummer. II. *v.n.* schlummern. III. *v.a.*; to — away, verschlummern. **—er**, *s.* der Schlummerer. **—ingly**, *adv.* schlummernd. **—ous**, *adj.* einschläfernd.

[1]**Slump**, I. *v.n.* plötzlich hinplumpsen, in das Wasser oder den Schmutz fallen, einbrechen, einsinken; durchfallen (*fig.*). II. *s.* der Mißerfolg; das Sinken der Preise.

[2]**Slump**, I. *v.a.* auf einen Haufen zusammenwerfen. II. *s.* die ganze Masse; — sum, die Bauschsumme; in the —, im Ramsch, in Bausch und Bogen.

Slung, *imperf. & p.p. of* Sling.

Slunk, *imperf. & p.p. of* Slink.

Slur, I. *s.* der Flecken, Vorwurf; das Schleif=, Winde=zeichen (*Mus.*); unreiner Druck (*Typ.*); to cast a — upon a p., einem einen Schandfleck anhängen. II. *v.a.* besudeln, beflecken; schleifen (*Mus.*); kneipen (*dice* (*sl.*)); to — over, leicht übergehen; (im Reden) undeutlich aussprechen.

Slush, *s.* der weiche Kot, Schlamm; (snow —) das Schneewasser. **—y**, *adj.* schlackerig, naß und kotig.

Slut, *s.* die Schlumpe; das schmutzige Weib. **—tish**, *adj.* schlumpig, schmutzig.

Sly, *adj.*, **—ly**, *adv.* schlau, listig, verschlagen; on the —, insgeheim (*coll.*). **—ness**, *s.* die Schlauheit, Verschlagenheit. *Comp.* **—-boots**, *s.* schlauer Fuchs (*fam.*).

[1]**Smack**, I. *s.* der (Bei)geschmack; (pleasing taste) der Wohlgeschmack (*rare*); (a little) das Bißchen, wenig; der (kleine) Anstrich (*of learning, etc.*). II. *v.n.* schmecken; to — of, schmecken nach, etwas an sich (*dat.*) haben *or* einen Anstrich haben von.

[2]**Smack**, *s.* die Schmack(e) (*Naut.*).

[3]**Smack**, I. *s.* das Schmatzen (*with the lips*); (kiss) der Schmatz; (blow) der Schlag, Schmitz, Patsch. II. *v.a.* schmatzen; (beat) schlagen, patschen. III. *int.* patsch! **—ing**, I. *adj.* heftig, frisch (*of a breeze*). II. *s.* Schläge (*pl.; vulg.*).

Small, I. *adj.* klein; (slight) dünn; (narrow) schmal; (weak) schwach; (of little moment) geringfügig, unbedeutend, klein; to look —, beschämt aussehen, kleinlaut werden; to make a p. feel —, einen beschämen; — beer, dünnes Bier; — coal, die Schmiedekohle; — fry, kleines Volk, Kinder (*coll.*); — hours, frühen Stunden (nach Mitternacht); a — matter, eine Kleinigkeit, geringfügige Sache; — money, das Kleingeld, die Scheidemünze. II. *s.* schmaler, dünner Teil; das (Rück=) Kreuz, der untere Teil (*of the back*). **—ish**, *adj.* ziemlich klein, ziemlich dünn. **—ness**, *s.* die Kleinheit 2c. *Comp.* **—-arms**, *pl.* kleine (Schuß=) Waffen. **—clothes**, *pl.* Beinkleider. **—pox**, *s.* die Pocken, Blattern. **—-talk**, *s.* leichte Unterhaltung, das Geschwätz, Geplauder. **—-tooth(ed)**, *s.* (*adj.*); —-tooth(ed) comb, der Staubkamm.

Smalt, *s.* die Schmalte.

Smaragd—ine, *adj.* smaragden. **—us**, *s.* der Smaragd.

Smart, I. *adj.*, **—ly**, *adv.* heftig, lebhaft (*as pain, a combat, a blow*); (lively) munter, lebhaft, aufgeweckt, gewandt; witzig (*of people, words, etc.*); frisch (*as a breeze*); (pungent) beißend, stechend, scharf; (spruce) geputzt, schmuck, schneidig, fein, elegant, patent (*coll.*); — reply, spitzige Antwort. II. *s.* der Schmerz. III. *v.n.* schmerzen, weh tun (*as a wound*); (suffer) leiden, büßen; you shall — for it, du sollst es büßen. **—en**, *v.a.*; to —en up, auf=, heraus=putzen (*coll.*). —**ness**, *s.* das Beißende, die Schärfe (*of wit, etc.*); die Aufgewecktheit, Schneidigkeit (*of people*); die Schmuckheit.

Smash, I. *v.a.* zerschmettern, zerschmeißen. II. *v.n.* zusammenbrechen; to — up, Bankerott machen (*sl.*). III. *s.* das Zerschmeißen; (fall) der Fall, Schmiß; (failure) das Fallissement, der Bankerott; der Gewaltschlag (*Tennis*); all to —, in tausend Stücken (*vulg.*); (to go) (to) —, Bankerott machen (*sl.*), in Stücke gehen.

Smatter—er, *s.* der Halbwisser, seichte Kenner. —**ing**, *s.* oberflächliche Kenntnis; die Halbwisserei.

Smear, I. *v.a.*; to — (with), beschmieren (mit). II. *s.* der Fettfleck; die Schmiererei; die Schmiere.

Smell, I. *s.* der Geruch, Geruchssinn; der Geruch, Duft. II. *ir.v.a.* riechen (eine S., an einer S.); aufspüren, auswittern (*fig.*); to — a rat, den Braten *or* die Lunte riechen. III. *ir.v.n.* riechen (of, nach). —**er**, *s.* der Riechende; der Riecher, die Nase (*sl.*). —**ing**, *s.* das Riechen; der Geruch. *Comp.* —**ing-bottle**, *s.* das Riechfläschchen. —**ing-salts**, *pl.* die Riechsalze.

[1]**Smelt**, *imperf. & p.p. of* Smell.

[2]**Smelt**, *v.a.* schmelzen. —**er**, *s.* der Schmelzarbeiter. *Comp.* —**ing-furnace**, *s.* der Schmelzofen.

[3]**Smelt**, *s.* der Stint (*Icht.*).

Smerlin, *s.* die Schmerle (*Icht.*).

Smil—e, I. *s.* das Lächeln; der holde, freundliche Blick (*fig.*). II. *v.n.* lächeln; she —ed to see, sie lächelte als sie sah . . .; to —e **at**, (einen) an- *or* (einem) zu-lächeln; lächeln über (*acc.*); to —e **upon** a p., einen anlächeln (*lit.*); einem günstig sein (*fig.*); to —e **through** one's tears, unter Tränen lächeln. III. *v.a.* (zu) lächeln (*approval, etc.*); to —e **away** *or* **off**, weglächeln. —**ing**, I. *adj.*, —**ingly**, *adv.* lächelnd; freundlich, heiter. II. *s.* das Lächeln.

Smirch, I. *v.a.* beschmutzen, beschmieren; verunglimpfen (*fig.*). II. *s.* der Schmier, Schmutz; die Beschmutzung.

Smirk, I. *s.* das Schmunzeln, gezierte Lächeln. II. *v.n.* schmunzeln, geziert lächeln.

Smit, —**ten**, *p.p. of* —e. —**e**, *ir.v.* I. *a.* schlagen; (kill) erschlagen; (fell) hinstrecken; (chastise) züchtigen; ergreifen, rühren (*fig.*); entflammen, einnehmen (*with love, etc.*); his conscience smote him, er fühlte Gewissensbisse. II. *n.* schlagen; to —e together, zusammenschlagen, schlottern. —**ten**, *p.p.* getroffen, bezaubert (with her beauty, von ihrer Schönheit), ergriffen (von); —ten with amazement, von Erstaunen ergriffen; betroffen.

Smith, *s.* der Schmied; (blacksmith) der Grobschmied. —**y**, *s.* die Schmiede.

Smithers, Smithereens, *s.* kleine Stücke, Fetzen (*sl.*); to knock to —, zerschlagen (*sl.*); gone to —, entzwei, kaputt (*sl.*).

Smock, I. *s.* das Frauenhemd. II. *v.a.* mit einem Weiberhemd *or* Arbeitskittel versehen; fälteln (*a kind of stitch in sewing*). *Comp.* —**frock**, *s.* der Arbeitskittel, die Bluse.

Smok—e, I. *v.n.* rauchen; (steam, fume) dampfen; Tabak rauchen. II. *v.a.* rauchen (*tobacco*); räuchern (*hams, etc.*); schrauben (*a person*); durchprügeln (*sl.*); to —e out, ausrauchen (*a pipe*), ausräuchern. III. *s.* der Rauch; das Rauchen; have a —e with me! rauchen Sie mit mir! no —e without fire, wo Rauch ist, muß auch Feuer sein (*prov.*); to end in —e, zu Wasser werden. —**eless**, *adj.* rauchlos; —eless fuel, rauchlose Heizstoffe, der Glühstoff. —**er**, *s.* der Raucher; der (Fleisch-)Räucherer. —**ily**, *adv.*, —**y**, *adj.* rauchig, voll Rauch; —y chimney, ein rauchiger Kamin. —**iness**, *s.* das Rauchige. —**ing**, I. *s.*; no —ing allowed! das Rauchen ist verboten! II. *adj.* dampfend, rauchend; —ing hot, brühheiß. *Comp.* —**e-black**, *s.* die Rußschwärze. —**e-consuming**, *adj.* rauchverzehrend. —**e-dried**, *adj.* geräuchert. —**e-helmet**, *s.* der Rauchhelm (*fire brig.*). —**e-** *or* —**ing-room**, *s.* das Rauchzimmer. —**e-stained**, *adj.* verräuchert. —**ing-car**, —**ing-carriage**, *s.* der Wagen für Raucher, Rauchwagen. —**ing-coat**, *s.* die Hausjacke (mit breitem Kragen und Aufschlägen an den Ärmeln). —**ing-compartment**, *s.* das Rauchcoupé, der Abteil für Raucher. **non-—ing-compartment**, *s.* (Abteil) für Nichtraucher. —**ing-concert**, *s.* das Konzert, bei dem geraucht wird, Rauchkonzert. —**ing-jacket**, *s. see* —ing-coat.

Smooth, I. *adj.*, —**ly**, *adv.* glatt (*Bot.; materials etc.*); sanft fließend (*as water*); fließend (*as verses, style, etc.*); (bland) sanft, mild; (flattering) schmeichelnd; to make —, *see* — II; to file —, schlicht feilen. II. *v.a.* glätten, ebnen; (polish) polieren; (iron) bügeln, glätten; glatt hobeln (*wood*); to — the way, den Weg bahnen *or* ebnen; to — **away**, heben, entfernen (*difficulties*); to — **down**, glatt streichen (*lit.*); mildern (*fig.*); to — **over**, beschönigen (*faults*). —**er**, *s.* der Glätter. —**ing**, I. *adj.* glättend. II. *s.* das Glätten. —**ness**, *s.* die Glätte (*also fig.*). *Comp.* —**-faced**, *adj.* mit glattem Antlitz; freundlich aussehend. —**-haired**, *adj.* glatthaarig. —**ing-iron**, *s.* das Plätt-, Bügel-eisen. —**-tongued**, *adj.* glattzüngig, schmeichlerisch.

Smote, *imperf. &* (*obs.*) *p.p. of* Smite.

Smother, *v.* I. *a.* ersticken (*also fig.*); unterdrücken (*rage, etc.*); schmoren (*Cook.*); —ed in *or* with, bedeckt mit. II. *n.* ersticken. —**er**, *s.* der Ersticker, Unterdrücker.

Smoulder, *v.n.* schwelen; glimmen (*also fig.*).

Smudg—e, I. *s.* der Schmutzfleck. II. *v.a.* beschmutzen, beschmieren. —**ed**, —**y**, *adj.* beschmiert, schmutzig.

Smug, I. *adj.* schmuck; spießbürgerlich. II. *s.* der gezierte, geschniegelte Mensch; der Ochser, Büffler (*Univ. sl.*). III. *v.n.*; to — up, sich herausputzen.

Smuggl—e, *v.a.* schmuggeln, Schleichhandel treiben; to —e in, einschmuggeln (*also fig.*). —**er**, *s.* der Schmuggler, Schleichhändler. —**ing**, *s.* die Schmuggelei, der Schleichhandel.

Smut, I. *s.* der Schmutz, Rußfleck; (spot) der schmutzige Fleck; der Brand (*Bot.*); —s, Rußflecken; to talk —, zoten. II. *v.a.* beschmutzen, berußen; brandig machen. —**ch**, I. *v.a.* beschmutzen. II. *s.* der schmutzige Fleck. —**tiness**, *s.* die Schmutzigkeit; das Zotige (*vulg.*). —**ty**, *adj.* schmutzig, rußig; brandig; (obscene) zotig.

Snack, *s.* der Imbiß; to go —s, teilen (*coll.*).

Snaffle, *s.* die Trense. *Comp.* —**-bit**, *s.* das Trensengebiß.

Snag, I. *s.* die Knagge, der Knorren, Knoten; der Baumstamm in Flüssen (*Amer.*); (—-tooth) der Raffzahn. II. *v.a.* behauen. —**ged**, *adj.* knotig, knorrig (*said of boats*); gegen einen Baumstamm ꝛc. gelaufen (*Amer.*).

Snail, *s.* die Schnecke; at a —'s pace, im Schneckengang, sehr langsam. *Comp.* —**-shell**, *s.* das Schneckenhaus.

Snak—e, *s.* die Schlange; the —e hisses, die Schlange zischt. —**y**, *adj.* schlangenartig. *Comp.* —**e-bird**, *s.* der gemeine Wendehals. —**e-bite**, *s.* der Schlangenbiß. —**e-fish**, *s.* der Schlangenfisch. —**estone**, *s.* der Ammonit. —**e-weed**, *s.* der Wiesenknöterich, die Schlangenwurz.

Snap, I. *v.n.* schnappen (at, nach); (break) (zer-)springen, kurz abbrechen; to — **at** a p., *see* — a p. up (*fig.*). II. *v.a.* schnappen; (seize) gacken, haschen, erschnappen; (crack) klatschen; to — one's fingers **at** (a p.), (einem) ein Schnippchen schlagen; to — **away**, wegschnappen; to — **off**, abschnappen, abbrechen; to — **up**, auffessen (*food*), aufschnappen; to — a p. up (short), einen scharf *or* barsch anfahren. III. *s.* der Schnapp, Biß; (—ping noise) der Knack, Klatsch; (crack) der Sprung, Bruch; der Knall (*of a whip*); das Schloß, der Schnepper (*of bracelets, etc.*); das Schnippchen; not worth a —, wertlos. —

per, *s.* der Schnappende; —per up, der Aufraffer. —**pish**, *adj.*, —**pishly**, *adv.* bissig, beißend (*as dogs*); schnippisch, auffahrend (*fig.*). —**pishness**, *s.* das auffahrende, schnippische Wesen. *Comp.* —**dragon**, *s.* das Löwenmaul (*Bot.*); ein Weihnachts-Spiel. —**shot**, *s.* die Augenblicksphotographie, das Augenblicksbild. —**shotting**, *s.* die Aufnahme von Augenblicksbildern *or* Momentphotographien.

Snare, I. *s.* die Schlinge, der Fallstrick. II. *v.a.* verstricken, fangen. —**r**, *s.* der Fallensteller; der Schlingenleger.

Snarl, *v.n.* knurren (*as a dog*); brummen, murren (*fig.*). —**er**, *s.* der Knurrende; der Murrkopf. —**ing**, *adj.* knurrend, mürrisch.

Snatch, I. *s.* das Haschen, der Schnapp, rasche Griff; (fragment) das Bißchen, Stückchen, der Bissen; by —es, dann und wann, in Absätzen, ruckweise; —es of sunshine, kurze Sonnenblicke; the music rose in —es, die Musik ließ sich abgebrochen vernehmen. II. *v.n.* schnappen, haschen (at, nach). III. *v.a.* schnell, begierig ergreifen, erschnappen, erhaschen; (— away) weg-reißen, -schnappen, -raffen; (— up) schnell aufraffen, aufnehmen; to — a kiss, einen Kuß rauben; to — a th. from (a p.), (einem) etwas entreißen; to — a th. from a p.'s hand, einem etwas aus der Hand reißen.

Sneak, I. *s.* der Schleicher, Kriecher; der Angeber, Petzer. II. *v.n.* schleichen, kriechen; angeben, petzen; to — away, — off, sich fortschleichen. —**ing**, *adj.*, —**ingly**, *adv.* kriechend, schleichend, niedrig; —ing fellow, der Schleicher —**ingness**, *s.* die Kriecherei.

Sneer, I. *s.* das Hohnlächeln; (ridicule) der Spott, Hohn. II. *v.n.* (— at) höhnisch *or* verächtlich lachen, hohnlächeln (über einen); die Nase rümpfen (at a p., über einen). III. *v.a.* verlachen, verhöhnen. —**er**, *s.* der Hohnlachende, Spötter. —**ing**, I. *adj.* höhnisch. II. *s.* das Hohnlachen, Naserümpfen, Sticheln. —**ingly**, *adv.* höhnisch; mit Hohnlachen, Naserümpfen, bitterm Spott.

Sneeze, I. *s.* das Niesen. II. *v.n.* niesen.

Snick, I. *v.a.* hacken, schneiden; den Ball noch eben parieren (*Cricket*). II. *v.n.* knipsen, schnippen. III. *s.* der Einschnitt, die Kerbe; der eben noch berührte Ball (*Cricket*); der schlechte Schlag.

Sniff, I. *v.a. & n.* schnuffeln, schnüffeln, schnuppern; to — at a th., über eine S. verächtlich die Nase rümpfen (*fig.*); to — about, herumspionieren. II. *s.* das Schnüffeln. *Comp.* —**levalve**, *s.* das Schnarr-, Schnüffel-ventil.

Snigger, Sniggle, I. *v.n.* kichern; sich ins Fäustchen lachen. II. *s.* das Kichern, Gekicher.

Snip, I. *v.a.* schnippen, schneiden; to — **off**, abschneiden; to — **up**, aufschneiden. II. *s.* der Schnipps, Schnitt; (shred) das Schnitzel. —**per**, *s.* der Schnitzer. —**pets**, kleine Stückchen (*pl.*); education of —pets, die Schnitzel-, Schnipfelbildung. —**pings**, *pl.* die Schnitzel.

Snipe, I. *s.* die Schnepfe; der Tropf (*fig.*). II. *v.a.* aus dem Hinterhalt schießen, einzeln aus großer Entfernung wegschießen (*Mil.*); Schnepfen aus weiter Entfernung schießen. *Comp.* —**-shooting**, *s.* die Schnepfenjagd.

Snivel, *v.n.* schnüffeln, den Nasenschleim hinaufziehen; (whine) wimmern, weinen, greinen. —**ler**, *s.* der weinerliche Mensch. —**ling**, I. *adj.* triefnasig; weinend, weinerlich; jämmerlich (*fig.*). II. *s.* das Greinen, Heulen.

Snob, *s.* Mensch, der vornehmes Wesen nachäfft, der Vornehmtuer, der Philister (*Univ. sl.*); *see* Shoemaker. —**bery**, *s.* die Nachäfferei vornehmen Wesens, eitles Vornehmtun. —**bish**, *adj.*, —**bishly**, *adv.* vornehm tuend, aufgeblasen. —**bishness**, *s.* die Vornehmtuerei.

Snood, *s.* die Haarbinde (*Scotch*).

Snooze, I. das Schläfchen. II. *v.n.* schlafen, ein Schläfchen halten (*coll.*).

Snore, I. *s.* das Schnarchen. II. *v.n.* schnarchen. —**r**, *s.* der Schnarcher.

Snort, *v.n.* schnauben, schnaufen (*as horses*). —**er**, *s.* der Schnaufer.

Snot, *s.* der Rotz (*vulg.*). —**ty**, *adj.* (*vulg.*) rotzig; schmutzig, gemein (*fig.*).

Snout, *s.* die Schnauze (*of dogs*); der Rüssel (*of pigs and elephants*); (nozzle) die Schnauze, Spitze, der Schnabel.

Snow, I. *s.* der Schnee; white as —, schneeweiß. II. *v.n.* schneien; to — (a p.) up, (einen) einschneien; to be —ed up, eingeschneit sein, im Schnee stecken bleiben. —**y**, *adj.* schneeig; (—white) schneeweiß. *Comp.* (*usually* = Schnee-), —**ball**, I. *s.* der Schneeball; *see* Guelder-rose. II. *v.a.* schneeballen, (einander) mit Schneebällen werfen. —**-broth**, *s.* das Schneewasser. —**-bunting**, *s.* die Schneeammer. —**-capped**, *adj.* schneegekrönt. —**drift**, *s.* die Schneewehe. —**drop**, *s.* das Schneeglöckchen. —**flake**, *s.* die Schneeflocke. —**-line**, *s.* die Schnee-linie, -grenze. —**-plough**, *s.* der Schneepflug. —**-storm**, *s.* der Schneesturm.

Snub, I. *v.a.* abschnippen, stutzen; derb verweisen (*fig.*); (rebuff) abweisen. II. *s.* der Rückstoß, die derbe Rüge. *Comp.* —**-nose**, *s.* die Stumpfnase. —**-nosed**, *adj.* stumpfnasig.

Snuff, I. *s.* der Schnupftabak; die Schnuppe (*of a candle*); to be up to —, wissen, wo Bartel den Most holt (*vulg.*); to take —, schnupfen; to take a pinch of —, sich (*dat.*) eine Prise nehmen; to take — at a th., eine Sache übelnehmen (*coll.*). II. *v.n.* schnauben, schnaufen; (take —) (Tabak) schnupfen; to — at, die Nase rümpfen über (*acc.*). III. *v.a.* (— up) (ein)schnupfen, einatmen; (smell) (be)schnüffeln, riechen; (ein **Licht**) putzen (*a candle*); to — out, ausputzen (*a candle*); auslöschen, sterben (*fig.*). —**er**, *s.* der Schnupfende. —**ers**, *pl.* die Licht-schere, -putze. —**ing**, *s.* das Tabakschnupfen. —**le**, I. *v.n.* schnüffeln, schnuppern; durch die Nase reden. II. *s.* das Näseln. —**y**, *adj.* nach Schnupftabak riechend, mit Schnupftabak besudelt; empfindlich (*fig.*). *Comp.* —**-box**, *s.* die Schnupftabaksdose. —**-coloured**, *adj.* rotbräunlich, zimmtfarben. —**-taker**, *s.* der Schnupfer.

Snug, *adj.*, —**ly**, *adv.* angeschmiegt; (close) dicht, eng; (comfortable) bequem, behaglich, gemütlich, gut eingerichtet; (concealed) versteckt; (closed in) eingehüllt, eingeschlossen, warm; to lie —, warm liegen; gut zugedeckt sein (*lit.*), still liegen (*fig.*). —**gery**, *s.* trauliche, behagliche Wohnung; das Boudoir; warmes Nest (*fig.*). —**gle**, *v.n.* sich anschmiegen, sich einhüllen. —**ness**, *s.* die Behaglichkeit.

So, I. *adv.* so; (thus) also, auf diese Art; not — rich as, nicht so reich wie; be — kind as to lend me . . ., sei so gut und leihe mir, bitte leihe mir (doch) . . .; — beautiful a day, ein so schöner Tag; his speech was — much nonsense, seine Rede war lauter Unsinn; — much the better, um so besser; — early as Monday, schon am Montag; — —, so so, so ziemlich, so leidlich, passabel; a score or —, etwa 20; — be it, wohl, gut; if it be —, wenn dem so ist; how —? wie so? wie das? she is pretty, but her sister is more —, sie ist hübsch, ihre Schwester ist es aber noch mehr; I told him —, das sagte ich ihm; I think —, ich denke; I should think —, das sollte ich meinen, ich glaube wohl; I shall write to him, if you wish me to do —, ich werde ihm schreiben, wenn Sie es wünschen; he was great ere fortune made him —, er war groß, ehe das Glück ihn dazu machte *or* ihm Größe verlieh; you are tired; — am I, du bist müde; ich auch. II. *conj.* so; (provided that) wofern, wenn nur; —that, damit; — then, also, darum, daher; — far from blaming him I praise his behaviour, weit entfernt ihn zu tadeln lobe ich sein Verhalten. *Comp.* —**-and-**—, *s.* so und so; Mr. —-and-—, Herr Soundso. —**-called**, *adj.* sogenannt.

Soak, *v.* I. *a.* einweichen, durchweichen, (wet

thoroughly) durch=nässen, =feuchten; to — up, in sich saugen, einsaugen; to — in lime water, ein=kalken. II. *n.* ein=, durch=dringen; weichen (*as skins*); (drink) saufen (*vulg.*); to — in, einschla=gen (*Paint.*, *etc.*). **—ed, —ing,** *adj.*; —ed with rain, —ing wet, vom Regen durchnäßt, trief=naß, naß bis auf die Haut. **—er,** *s.* der Säufer (*vulg.*). *Comp.* **—ing-pit,** *s.* die Treibgrube.

Soap, I. *s.* die Seife; soft —, die Schmierseife; cake of —, das Stück Seife. II. *v.a.* (ein)seifen, beseifen. **—y,** *adj.* seifig; (like —) seifenartig. *Comp.* (*in cpds. usually* Seifen=). **—-ball,** *s.* die Seifenkugel; das Stück Toilettenseife. **—-boiler,** *s.* der Seifensieder. **—-boiling,** *s.* die Seifensiederei. **—-bubble,** *s.* die Seifenblase. **—-case,** *s.* die Seifenbüchse. **—-dish,** *s.* das Seifenschälchen. **—-house,** *s.* die Seifensiederei. **—-maker,** *s.* der Seifensieder. **—stone,** *s.* der Seifenstein. **—-suds,** *s.* die Seifenlauge.

Soar, *v.n.* sich erheben, hoch fliegen; sich auf=schwingen, hoch emporschwingen (*fig.*); (be lofty) in der Höhe schweben; to — above, sich er=heben über (*acc.*). **—ing,** *adj.* hochfliegend.

Sob, I. *v.n.* schluchzen. II. *v.a.* (— out) schluch=zend äußern, herausschluchzen. III. *s.* das Schluchzen. **—bing,** *s.* das Schluchzen.

Sob—er, I. *adj.*, **—erly,** *adv.* nüchtern; (temper-ate) mäßig; (serious) ernsthaft; vernünftig, besonnen (*as judgment*); gesund (*as senses*); in —er earnest, in vollem Ernste; as —er as a judge, vollkommen nüchtern. II. *v.a.* nüchtern machen, dämpfen. **—riety, —erness,** *s.* die Nüchternheit, Mäßigkeit; die Mäßigung, Beson=nenheit (*fig.*); der Ernst, die Ernsthaftigkeit. *Comp.* **—er-minded,** *adj.* mäßig; (calm) be=sonnen, ruhig; (chaste) züchtig. **—er-suited,** *adj.* ehrbar und schlicht gekleidet.

Sobriquet, *s.* der Spitzname, Beiname.

[1]**Soc,** *s.* der Standarten=, Lanzen=schuh (*Mil.*).

[2]**Soc, Soke,** *s.* die Gerichtsbarkeit, der Gerichts=bezirk; die Fronfreiheit; der Mühlzwang.

Socage, *s.* der Frondienst(besitz), das Bauernlehen. **—r,** *s.* der Inhaber eines Bauernlehens, Dienst=mann, Fröner.

Soci—ability, —ableness, *s.* die Geselligkeit, der Geselligkeitstrieb. **—able,** I. *adj.*, **—ably,** *adv.* gesellig, umgänglich. II. *s.* der offne vier=räderige Wagen; (tricycle) das Sociable; (couch) eine Art Polsterstuhl. **—al,** *adj.*, **—ally,** *adv.* gesellschaftlich, Gesellschafts=, sozial; (friendly) gesellig; —al democrat, der Sozialdemokrat; —al evening, geselliger Abend; —al gathering, ge=sellige Zusammenkunft; —al intercourse, gesell=schaftlicher Verkehr; —al philosopher, der Na=tionalökonom; —al philosophy, die Volkswirt=schaftslehre. **—alism,** *s.* der Sozialismus; die Sozialdemokratie. **—alist,** *s.* der Sozialist; der Sozialdemokrat; Christian —alists, christlich=soziale Partei. **—alistic,** *adj.* sozialistisch. **—alize,** *v.a.* gesellig machen. **—ety,** *s.* die Ge=sellschaft (*also C. L.*); (union) der Verein; (com-munity) die Gemeinde; *see* Fraternity; to go into —ety, in Gesellschaft gehen. **—ology,** *s.* die Gesellschaftslehre, Sozialwissenschaft. **—ologi-cal,** *adj.* die Gesellschaftslehre betreffend; —ological problem, Frage der Gesellschaftslehre.

[1]**Soc—k,** *s.* die Socke; (sole) innere Sohle; der Sokkus (*Greek Theat.*); das Lustspiel (*fig.*). **—ket,** *s.* die Dille (*of a candlestick*); die Röhre (*of tools*); die Höhle, Höhlung (*of the eyes, teeth, etc.*). **—le,** *s.* der Sockel, Untersatz.

[2]**Sock,** *s.* die Pflugschar, das Pflugeisen.

[1]**Sod,** I. *s.* der Rasen, Deckrasen, das Stück Rasen: beneath the —, im Grabe; to cut the first —, das erste Stück Rasen abstechen. II. *v.a.* mit Rasen belegen. *Comp.* **—-cutter,** *s.* der Rasenstecher.

[2]**Sod,** (*obs.*) *imperf. of* Seethe.

Sod—a, *s.* die Soda. **—ium,** *s.* das Sodium. *Comp.* **—a-water,** *s.* das Sodawasser.

Sodden, *p.p. of* Seethe, & *adj.* nicht aufgegangen (*as bread*); verkocht (*as meat*); aufgedunsen (*fig.*).

Soever, *adv.* auch immer, auch nur.

Sofa, *s.* das Sofa, Ruhebett; *in comp.* = Sofa=.

Soffit, *s.* die Gewölbdecke. **—s,** *pl.* Soffiten.

Soft, I. *adj.*, **—ly,** *adv.* sanft, weich (*to the touch, the ear, etc.*); mild (*also of wine, etc.*), gelinde, lind (*as the air*); sachte, leise (*as a tread*); sanft (*in colour and disposition*); (yielding) nachgiebig; (gentle) zart, zärtlich; (effeminate) weich(lich); (silly) schwachköpfig, einfältig; ver=liebt (on, in, *acc.*, *sl.*); — answer, milde Ant=wort; — goods, Tuchwaren; —er sex, zarteres Geschlecht; — nothings, verliebter Unsinn (*sl.*); to have a — place (in one's head), einen Sparren haben; to have a — spot in one's heart for a p., einem besonders zugetan sein; — water, weiches Wasser; das Regenwasser; — soap, die Kaliseife, Schmierseife (*lit.*), die Schmeichelei (*fig.*, *vulg.*); — and fair goes far, Eile mit Weile (*prov.*). II. *int.*, —ly! sachte! still! halt! **—en,** *v.* I. *a.* weich machen, erweichen; mildern, lindern (*pain*); verschmelzen (*colouring*); (enervate) weichlich machen, schwächen, entkräften; mildern (*an ex-pression, etc.*); to —en a fault, einen Fehler (zu) mildern (suchen). II. *n.* weich(er) werden; sanft(er) werden; sich erweichen, sich besänftigen lassen. **—ener,** *s.* der Milderende, Besänfti=gende; (—ening stuff) das Erweichungsmittel; die Linderung (*of pain*). **—ening,** I. *adj.* er=weichend. II. *s.* das Erweichen; —ening of the brain, die Gehirnerweichung. **—ness,** *s.* die Sanftheit, Weichheit; die Sanftmut, Milde, Freundlichkeit (*of disposition*); die Milde (*of the climate*); die Weichlichkeit; die Einfalt; die Schwäche (for a p., für einen); —ness of manners, das sanfte Wesen. *Comp.* **—-brained,** *adj.* dumm, albern, läppisch. **—-eyed,** *adj.* sanft=äugig. **—-headed,** *adj.* einfältig. **—-hearted,** *adj.* weichherzig. **—-heartedness,** *s.* die Weich=herzigkeit. **—-spoken,** *adj.* sanftredend. **—-voiced,** *adj.* von sanfter Stimme.

Soho, *int.* hollo!

Soi-disant, *adj.* angeblich.

[1]**Soil,** I. der Boden, Grund, die Erde; der Boden, das Erdreich; das Land (*fig.*); one's native —, der Heimatboden, das Heimatland, die Heimat.

[2]**Soil,** I. *s.* der Fleck, Schmutz. II. *v.a.* besudeln, beschmutzen; beflecken (*fig.*); (manure) düngen (*fields*). III. *n.* schmutzig werden, fleckig werden.

[3]**Soil,** *v.a.* Vieh mit frischem Grase füttern, mit Grünfutter mästen. **—ing,** *s.* die Stallfütterung.

Soirée, *s.* die Abendgesellschaft, Soirée.

Sojourn, I. *s.* der Aufenthalt, das Verweilen. II. *v.n.* sich aufhalten, verweilen. **—er,** *s.* der Ver=weilende, Gast, Fremde, Fremdling.

Solace, I. *s.* der Trost, die Beruhigung. II. *v.a.* trösten; (cheer) erheitern, besänftigen, mildern. **—ment,** *s.* die Tröstung.

Solar, *adj.* zur Sonne gehörig, von der Sonne kommend, Sonnen=; — myth, der Sonnen=mythus; — system, das Sonnensystem.

Sold, *imperf.* & *p.p. of* Sell.

Solder, I. *s.* das Lot, die Löte. II. *v.a.* (zu=sammen)löten, verlöten. **—ing,** I. *s.* das Löten, die Lötung. II. *adj.* lötend. *Comp.* **—ing-iron,** *s.* der Lötkolben.

Soldier, I. *s.* der Soldat; der Krieger, Kriegs=mann (*high style*); good —, der tüchtige Soldat; poor —, schlechter Soldat; common —, gemeiner Soldat. II. *v.n.* den Soldaten machen *or* spielen. **—like, —ly,** *adj.* soldatenhaft, sol=datisch. **—ship,** *s.* der Soldatenstand, Solda=tenberuf; die soldatische Tüchtigkeit. **—y,** *s.* das Kriegsvolk, Militär, die Soldateska.

[1]**Sole,** *adj.* allein, einzig; ledig (*Law*). **—ly,** *adv.* allein, einzig; (only) nur. **—ness,** *s.* das Alleinsein.

[2]**Sole,** I. die Sohle (*of the foot, shoe, etc.*); — of the foot, Fußsohle. II. *v.a.* besohlen.

Sole, *s.* die Seezunge, Scholle (*Ichth.*); lemon —, gewöhnlichere Schollenart zwischen Scholle und Plattfisch.

Solecism, *s.* der Sprachfehler; der Verstoß, die Ungeschicklichkeit (*in conduct, etc.*); die Widersinnigkeit.

Solemn, *adj.*, **—ly**, feierlich; (serious) ernst; — oath, feierlicher Eid. **—ity**, *s.* die Feierlichkeit; der feierliche Ernst; (formality) die Steifheit. **—ize**, *v.a.* feiern. **—ization**, *s.* die Feier.

Sol-fa, I. *v.n.* solfeggieren. II. *attrib.*; — system, die Solfeggier-Schule.

Solferino, *s.* das Lilarot.

Solicit, *v.a.* anhaltend *or* dringend bitten, ansuchen. **—ant**, *s.* der Bittsteller. **—ation**, *s.* das Anhalten, Ansuchen; (supplication) das (dringende) Bitten; (invitation) die Aufforderung. **—or**, *s.* der Anhaltende, Ansuchende; der Sachwalter, (nicht vor Gericht selbst plaidierende) Anwalt; —or general, der Kronanwalt, Oberstaatsanwalt. **—ous**, *adj.* sorgfältig; (anxious) besorgt, bekümmert; to be —ous for, besorgt sein um, streben nach; men are often more —ous to obtain favour than to . . ., die Menschen bemühen sich oft mehr um Gunst, als um . . . *or* als daß sie . . . **—ousness**, **—ude**, *s.* die Sorge, Sorgfalt; die Besorgnis, Ängstlichkeit; to feel —ude for, besorgt sein um.

Solid, I. *adj.*, **—ly**, *adv.* fest (*also fig.*); (strong) stark, fest, dauerhaft; (profound, sound) gründlich; (true) wahrhaft, reell; (massive) gediegen; körperlich, kubisch (*Geom.*); kernhaft, echt, wahrhaft, zuverlässig (*fig.*); — angle, körperlicher Winkel; — contents, das Volumen; — geometry, die Stereometrie; — square, das geschlossene Karré (*Mil.*); — food *or* sustenance, feste Nahrung. II. *s.* der feste Körper (*Phys.*); der Körper (*Geom.*); feste Speise (*Cook.*). **—arity**, *s.* die gemeinsame Verpflichtung, gegenseitige Verbindlichkeit; der Zusammenschluß; die Solidarität. **—ification**, *s.* die Verdichtung; das Festwerden. **—ify**, *v.* I. *a.* fest machen, verdichten. II. *n.* sich verdichten. **—ity**, *s.* die Festigkeit, Dichtheit; die Echtheit, Wahrheit; die Gültigkeit (*of reasons, etc.*); die Gründlichkeit; die Solidität (*C. L., Geom.*). **—ungulate**, *s.* der Einhufer (*Zool.*). **—ungulous**, *adj.* einhufig.

Sol—ifidian, I. *adj.* zu der Lehre gehörig, daß der Glaube allein selig macht. II. *s.* der Anhänger dieser Lehre. **—iloquist**, *s.* der ein Selbstgespräch führt. **—iloquize**, *v.n.* mit sich selbst reden, ein Selbstgespräch führen. **—iloquy**, *s.* das Selbstgespräch, der Monolog. **—iped**, *s.* der Einhufer. **—itaire**, *s.* der Solitär (*Jewelry*); (game) das Grillenspiel, Solitaire. **—itariness**, *s.* die Einsamkeit. **—itary**, *adj.*, **—itarily**, *adv.* einsam; (single) einzeln (*also Bot.*); (living alone) alleinstehend; —itary confinement, die Einzelhaft. **—itude**, *s.* die Einsamkeit; (desert) die Einöde. **—o**, *s.* das Solo. **—oist**, *s.* der Solist, Solosänger, Solospieler.

Solsti—ce, *s.* die Sonnenwende. **—tial**, *adj.* die Sonnenwende betreffend, Sonnenwende- (points, etc., Punkte 2c.); Sonnenstillstands- (elevation, etc., -höhe 2c.); —tial heat, die Sommerhitze.

Sol—ubility, **—ubleness**, *s.* die Auflösbarkeit, Löslichkeit. **—uble**, *adj.*, **—ubly**, *adv.* (auf)löslich; to be —uble, sich auflösen (in, in). **—ution**, *s.* die (Auf-)Lösung (*also Geom. & Alg.*); die Lösung, Auflösung (*Chem.*); das Aufgelöste (*Chem.*); die Beseitigung (*of difficulties*); —ution of continuity, die Trennung zusammenhängender Körper. **—vable**, *adj.* auflösbar; erklärbar; (payable) zahlbar, was bezahlt werden kann. **—ve**, *v.a.* (auf)lösen (*problems, riddles, difficulties, doubts, etc.*); lösen (*Chem.*); aufklären (*a matter*); (remove) heben, beseitigen; the problem to be —ved, die zu lösende Aufgabe. **—vency**, *s.* die Zahlungsfähigkeit, Solvenz. **—vend**, *s.* das Aufzulösende. **—vent**, I. *adj.* auflösend; zahlungsfähig (*C.L.*); the estate is —vent, die Masse ist zahlungsfähig, Aktiva decken die Passiva. II. *s.* das Auflösungsmittel. **—ver**, *s.* der, die Auflösende.

Somatology, *s.* die Lehre vom menschlichen Körper.

Somb—er, **—re**, *adj.* düster, finster, dunkel; trüb, traurig, schwermütig, mürrisch. **—erness**, *s.* die Düsterkeit.

Sombrero, *s.* der breitkrämpige Hut.

Some, I. *adj.* ein, irgend ein, (irgend) etwas; — person, irgend eine Person, irgend jemand; give me — bread, gieb mir etwas Brot; — time, einige Zeit; — nine persons, etwa neun Personen; there are — people who, es giebt Leute, welche; he has — ability, er hat Anlage; — one, jemand, irgend einer; — one or other has, irgend jemand *or* einer hat; — time or other, irgend einmal; to — extent, bis zu einem gewissen Grade; — 70 miles distant, einige siebzig Meilen entfernt; — few, einige wenige; — such, solcher, solch ein(e). II. *pron.* einige; etwas, ein Teil von; will you allow me to send you —, wollen Sie mir erlauben, Ihnen einige *or* (*coll.*) welche zu schicken; to forego — of one's right, einen Teil seines Rechtes aufgeben; — of these days, an einem der nächsten Tage. *Comp.* **—body**, *s.* irgend einer, jemand; eine bedeutende Person (*fig.*); he thinks himself —body, er dünkt sich etwas Rechtes. **—how**, *adv.* auf irgend eine Weise, irgendwie; —how or other, auf die eine oder die andere Weise. **—thing**, I. *s.* das Etwas; a certain —thing, ein gewisses Etwas. II. *pron. & adv.* etwas, ein wenig, einigermaßen; —thing yet of doubt remains, noch bleibt einiger Zweifel bestehen. **—time**, I. *adv.* noch einmal, einst, dereinst, eines Tages. II. *adj.* ehemalig, einstig. **—times**, *adv.* zu-, bis-weilen, dann und wann. **—what**, I. *s.* etwas. II. *adv.* etwas, ein wenig. **—where**, *adv.* irgend wo(hin).

Somers—ault, **—et**, *s.* der Burzelbaum; to turn a —ault, einen Burzelbaum schlagen.

Somn—ambulation, *s.* das Schlafwandeln. **—ambulism**, *s.* der Somnambulismus. **—ambulist**, *s.* der (die) Nachtwandler(in). **—iferous**, *adj.* schlafbringend. **—ipathy**, *s.* der mesmerische Schlaf. **—olence**, **—olency**, *s.* die Schlafsucht. **—olent**, *adj.*, **—olently**, *adv.* schlafsüchtig.

Son, *s.* der Sohn; every mother's —, jeder Muttersohn; —-in-law, der Schwiegersohn; —s of God, die Kinder Gottes, die Frommen. **—ship**, *s.* die Sohnschaft.

Sonance, *s.* der Klang, Schall (*obs.*); das Signal (*obs.*).

Sonant, I. *adj.* tönend, stimmhaft (*Phonet.*). II. *s.* der stimmhafte, tönende Laut; (*esp'lly*) der tönende Verschlußlaut, Sonant (*Phonet.*).

Sonata, *s.* die Sonate (*Mus.*).

Soncy, **Sonsy**, *adj.* glücklich, angenehm; aufgeräumt (*dial.*).

Song, *s.* der Sang, Gesang; (poem, *etc.*) das Lied; (poetry) die Poesie; die Kleinigkeit (*fig.*); sacred —, das geistliche Lied; to give a —, ein Lied vortragen; give us a —! laß uns ein Lied hören! sing uns ein Lied! for a (mere *or* an old) —, spottbillig; drinking —, Trinklied; — of joy, Freudengesang; — of Songs, das Hohe Lied (Salomonis). **—ster**, *s.* der Sänger; *see* —-bird. **—stress**, *s.* die Sängerin. *Comp.* **—-bird**, *s.* der Singvogel. **—-book**, *s.* das Liederbuch. **—-thrush**, *s.* die Sang-, Singdrossel. **—-writer**, *s.* der Liederdichter. **—-writing**, *s.* die Liederdichtung.

Sonnet, *s.* das Sonett; cycle of —s, der Sonettenkranz. **—(t)eer** (*also:* **—-writer**), *s.* der Sonettendichter; der Verseschmied, Dichterling (*fig.*). **—ize**, *v.a.* Sonette dichten; in Sonetten besingen.

Sono—meter, *s.* der Tonmesser. **—rity**, *s.* die Schallfülle, Vernehmlichkeit. **—rous**, *adj.*, **—rously**, *adv.* (voll)tönend, klingend; (clear-

high-sounding) klangvoll, hellklingend. **—rousness**, *s.* die Volltönigkeit; der Wohlklang.
Soon, *adv.* bald; (early) früh; (readily) gern; as — as, so bald als; I would as — remain as go, ich möchte ebensogern bleiben wie gehen (*coll.*). **—er**, *comp. of* Soon; eher; früher; lieber; —er or later, früher oder später; no —er had he, kaum hatte er; no —er said than done, gesagt, getan; *see* Rather.
Soot, *s.* der Ruß. **—iness**, *s.* die Rußigkeit. **—y**, *adj.* rußig, berußt; (—like) rußartig.
Sooth, *s.* die Wahrheit (*obs.*); for —, in —, in Wahrheit, traun, fürwahr; — to say, die Wahrheit zu sagen. *Comp.* **—say**, *v.n.* wahrsagen, weissagen, prophezeien. **—sayer**, *s.* der Wahrsager, Prophet.
Sooth—e, *v.a.* besänftigen; (flatter) schmeicheln; (allay) lindern. **—er**, *s.* der Besänftigende; der Schmeichler. **—ing**, *adj.*, **—ingly**, *adv.* lindernd, besänftigend, schmeichelnd.
Sop, I. *s.* der eingetunkte Bissen; das Besänftigungsmittel (*fig.*); — for Cerberus, die Bestechung für einen Gefängniswärter (*coll.*). II. *v.a.* eintunken, einweichen. **—py**, *adj.* eingeweicht, weich.
Soph, *s. see* —ister. **—ism**, *s.* der Trugschluß. **—ist**, *s.* der Sophist. **—ister**, *s.* der Student, (junior) im zweiten, (senior) im dritten Jahre (*Cambridge*). **—istical**, *adj.*, **—istically**, *adv.* spitzfindig, trügerisch, sophistisch. **—isticate**, *v.a.* sophistisch darstellen, verdrehen; verfälschen. **—isticated**, *adj.* verfälscht; den Rummel verstehend. **—istication**, *s.* der Trugschluß; die Verfälschung. **—istry**, *s.* die Spitzfindigkeit, Sophisterei. **—omore**, *s.* Student im zweiten Jahre seines Studiums, in der zweiten Klasse (*Amer.*).
Soporif—erous, *adj.* einschläfernd. **—ic**, I. *adj.* einschläfernd. II. *s.* das Schlafmittel.
Sopran—ist, *s.* der Sopransänger, die Sopransängerin, Sopranistin. **—o**, *s.* der Sopran.
Sorb, *s.* zahme Eberesche; (fruit) die Vogelbeere, der Sorbapfel. **—ic**, *adj.*; —ic acid, die Sorbeisäure.
Sorcer—er, *s.* der Zauberer. **—ess**, *s.* die Zauberin, Hexe. **—y**, *s.* die Zauberei, Zauberkunst.
Sordid, *adj.*, **—ly**, *adv.* gemein, niedrig; (miserly) schmutzig, filzig. **—ness**, *s.* die Gemeinheit, Niederträchtigkeit; die Filzigkeit.
Sore, I. *adj.*, **—ly**, *adv.* schmerzhaft, wund; böse (*as the eyes, a finger, etc.*); heftig, schwer (*as a calamity*); (susceptible) empfindlich, reizbar; that is a — point with him, das ist ein wunder *or* heikler Punkt bei ihm, seine wunde Stelle. II. *s.* wunde Stelle, das Geschwür; that is an eye-— to him, das ist ihm ein Dorn im Auge. III. —, **—ly**, *adv.* schwer, arg; —ly tried, schwer geprüft; —ly grieved, tief betrübt; —ly vexed, sehr ergrimmt (*obs.*); —ly against my will, durchaus wider meinen Willen. **—ness**, *s.* die Schmerzhaftigkeit, das Wehe; die Empfindlichkeit, Reizbarkeit (*fig.*).
Sorites, *s.* der Kettenschluß.
Sororicide, *s.* der Schwester-mord *or* -mörder.
[1]**Sorrel**, *s.* der Sauerampfer.
[2]**Sorrel**, *adj.* rötlich; — horse, der Rotfuchs.
Sorr—iness, *s.* die Armseligkeit. **—ow**, I. *s.* der Kummer, Gram, die Trauer, Betrübnis, das Leid; to my —ow! zu meinem Leidwesen, leider. II. *v.n.* trauern, sich grämen *or* härmen (for, um). **—owful**, *adj.*, **—owfully**, *adv.*, kummervoll, betrübt, traurig; (mournful) kläglich. **—owfulness**, *s.* die Traurigkeit, der Kummer. **—ows**, *pl.*, die Leiden. **—y**, *adj.* bekümmert, betrübt; (pitiful) erbärmlich, kläglich; I am —y for it, es tut mir leid; I am —y for him, er tut mir leid; I am —y for you, ich bedaure Sie, es tut mir leid um Sie; I am —y to say, leider *or* zu meinem Leidwesen muß ich sagen; —y excuse, klägliche *or* jämmerliche Entschuldigung; to make a —y appearance, traurig *or* kläglich aussehen. *Comp.* **—ow-laden**, *adj.* sorgenschwer. **—ow-stricken**, *adj.* von Kummer gebeugt.
Sort, I. *s.* die Art, Gattung, Sorte, Qualität; (class) die Klasse; (manner) die Art, Weise; he is a good —, er ist ein gutmütiger Mensch, ein guter Kerl (*coll.*); he is a strange — of man, er ist ein sonderbarer Mann; all —s of people, allerlei Leute; that — of thing, so etwas, etwas Derartiges; and that — of thing, und dergleichen; the common —, das gemeine Volk; the better —, die höheren Stände; in some —, gewissermaßen; out of —s, unpäßlich; übelgelaunt, verstimmt, verdrießlich (*coll.*). II. *v.a.* sortieren; assortieren (*C. L.*); to — out, aussuchen. III. *v.n.* sich verbinden, sich vereinigen (with, mit); (suit) sich schicken, passen, angemessen sein. **—able**, *adj.* sortierbar.
Sortie, *s.* der Ausfall.
Sot *s.* der Trunkenbold, Säufer. **—tish**, *adj.*, **—tishly**, *adv.* versoffen; (stupid) dumm. **—tishness**, *s.* die Dummheit; die Versoffenheit.
Sotnia, *s.* die Sotnie, Schwadron (Kosaken).
Sotto voce, *adv.* mit gedämpfter Stimme.
Soufflé, *s.* der (Eier)auflauf.
Sough, I. *s.* das Pfeifen, Heulen. II. *v.n.* pfeifen, heulen.
Sought, *imperf. & p.p. of* Seek.
Soul, *s.* (*opp. to* Body) die Seele; (mind) der Geist, das Herz; das Feuer, der Mut (*fig.*); die Seele, der Kern, Leiter, Führer (*of an undertaking*); All —s' day, Allerseelen(tag); poor —! armer Wicht! a good —, eine gute Seele *or* treue Haut; not a — was to be seen, keine Menschenseele war zu sehen; nobility of —, der Seelenadel; with heart and —, von ganzer Seele, mit Leib und Seele; to have a — for, Sinn haben für. **—less**, *adj.*, **—lessly**, *adv.* seelenlos; gefühllos, niederträchtig (*fig.*). *Comp.* **—stirring**, *adj.* herzergreifend.
[1]**Sound**, I. *adj.*, **—ly**, *adv.* gesund (*as a tooth, a limb, a body, also fig.*); (whole) unversehrt, unbeschädigt, fehlerfrei (*as a horse*); (stout) stark, kräftig, fest; fest, stark (*as sleep*); kräftig, tüchtig, derb (*as a blow*); wohlbegründet, tüchtig, richtig (*as principles*); — sense, gesunder Menschenverstand; safe and —, frisch und gesund. II. *adv.*; — asleep, in tiefem Schlafe. **—ness**, *s.* die Gesundheit; die Unversehrtheit; die Tüchtigkeit, Gründlichkeit; die Richtigkeit, Reinheit (*of one's belief*); the —ness of his constitution, seine gesunde Leibesbeschaffenheit; the —ness of his principles, der gesunde Charakter seiner Grundsätze; the —ness of a firm, die Solidität eines Geschäftes, Hauses. *Comp.* **—hearted**, *adj.* von gesundem Herzen.
[2]**Sound**, *s.* der Sund, die Meerenge; die Fischblase (*Icht.*).
[3]**Sound**, I. *v.a.* schallen, ertönen, erklingen lassen; schmettern (*the trumpet*); hören lassen (*a letter, etc.*); blasen (*the charge, etc.*); to — abroad, ausposaunen (*iron.*), erschallen lassen. II. *v.n.* schallen, tönen, klingen, lauten; (resound) ertönen, erklingen, erschallen; that does not — well, das klingt nicht gut; he —s his own trumpet, er posaunt seinen eigenen Ruhm aus; to — the march, zum Aufbruch blasen. III. *s.* der Schall, Ton, Laut, Klang; (noise) das Geräusch; table of —s, die Lauttafel (*Phonet.*). **—ing**, I. *adj.* klingend; *see* Sonorous. II. *s.* das Blasen (*Mil.*); —ing of the charge, das Signal zum Angriff. **—less**, *adj.* tonlos. *Comp.* **—board**, **—ing-board**, *s.* der Resonanzboden (*Mus.*); das Schallbrett (*Org.*); der Schalldeckel (*on a pulpit*). **—chart**, *s.* die Lauttafel. **—hole**, *s.* das F-Loch (*Viol.*). **—post**, *s.* die Stimme.
[4]**Sound**, I. *v.a.* sondieren, peilen (*Naut.*); sondieren, mit der Sonde untersuchen (*Surg.*); aushorlen, (einem) auf den Zahn fühlen (*fig.*). II. *s.* die Sonde. **—ing**, *s.* das Erforschen, Sondieren. **—ings**, *pl.* der Ankergrund, die lotbare Wasser-

tiefe. *Comp.* **—ing-lead**, *s.* das Senkblei, Lot. **—ing-line**, *s.* die Lotleine, Senkschnur. **—ing-rod**, *s.* die Sondierstange.
Soup, *s.* die Suppe, Fleischbrühe. *Comp.* **—kitchen**, *s.* die Suppenanstalt, Volksküche. **—ladle**, *s.* der Vorlege=, Suppen=löffel. **—plate**, *s.* der Suppenteller, tiefe Teller. **—tureen**, *s.* die Suppen=schüssel, =terrine.
Sour, I. *adj.*, **—ly**, *adv.* sauer, herb, scharf; sauer, bitter (*fig.*); sauer(töpfisch), mürrisch (*as looks*); to turn —, sauer werden; to grow —, mürrisch, bitter werden. II. *v.a.* sauer machen, säuern; erbittern, bitter machen (*fig.*). III. *v.n.* sauer werden; mürrisch, verdrießlich, bitter werden (*fig.*). **—ish**, *adj.* säuerlich. **—ness**, *s.* die Säure; die Herbheit, Bitterkeit (*fig.*).
Source, *s.* die Quelle, der Ursprung; to draw from a —, aus einer Quelle schöpfen.
[1]**Souse**, I. *s.* die Salzbrühe; die eingepökelten Ohren und Füße (of pigs, von Schweinen). II. *v.a.* (ein)pökeln, einsalzen; (plunge) ins Wasser werfen, durchs Wasser ziehen, einweichen.
[2]**Souse**, I. *s.* das Herabstürzen, Herabstoßen (auf eine S.); der schwere Schlag *or* Fall. II. *v.n.* mit Heftigkeit fallen, niederschießen, herabstoßen (auf, *acc.*). III. *v.a.* heftig schlagen *or* treffen. IV. *adv.* mit plötzlichem Herabstoß, stracks.
South, I. *s.* der Süden; der Süd (*poet.*); die Südseite; from the —, von Süden. II. *adj. & adv.* südlich, südwärts; — sea, die Südsee; — wind, der Südwind. **—erly**, *adj.* südlich, Süd=. **—ern**, *adj.*, **—ernly**, *adv. see* —erly. **—erner**, *s.* der Südländer; der Südstaatler (*in America*). **—(ern)most**, *adj.* südlichst. **—ing**, *s.* südliche Richtung; der Durchgang durch die Mittagslinie, die Kulmination (*of the moon, etc.*). **—ward**, *adv.* südwärts. *Comp.* **—east**, I. *adj.* (—eastern) südöstlich. II. *s.* der Südost. **—west**, I. *adj.* (—western) südwestlich. II. *s.* der Südwest. **—wester**, *s.* der Südwestwind; (cap) die Sturmkappe.
Souvenir, *s.* das Andenken, Memento.
Sovereign, I. *adj.* oberherrlich, allerhöchst, unumschränkt; *see* Supreme; unübertrefflich (*fig.*); unfehlbar (*as a remedy*); — contempt, tiefste Verachtung; — imagination, allumfassende Einbildungskraft; our — lady, Queen Alexandra, Ihre Majestät die Königin A.; — poet, der Dichterfürst. II. *s.* der (die) Herr(in), Herrscher(in), Fürst(in); (pound) das 20=Schilling=Stück, der Sovereign. **—ty**, *s.* unumschränkte Staatsgewalt; die Oberherrschaft; *see* Supremacy.
[1]**Sow**, *s.* die Sau, das Mutterschwein; die Sau (*of iron*); *in comp.* Sau=.
[2]**Sow**, *v.a. & n.* (*p.p. also* —n) säen, ausstreuen; besäen (*a field, etc.*); verbreiten (*fig.*); to — one's wild oats, sich (*dat.*) die Hörner ablaufen. **—er**, *s.* der Sämann, Säer; der Verbreiter, Anstifter (*fig.*). **—ing**, *s.* das Säen. *Comp.* **—ing-machine**, *s.* die Sämaschine.
Sowans, Sowens, *pl.* der saure Haferbrei.
Sowar, *s.* eingeborener Reiter (*in India*).
Sown, *p.p. of* Sow.
Spa, *s.* das Mineralwasser; (spring) der Sauerbrunnen; der Kurort, Badeort, das Bad.
Spac—e, I. *s.* der Raum; (—e between) der Zwischenraum, Abstand; (interval) der Zeitraum; (time) die Zeit, Frist; die Fläche (*Geom.*); das Spatium (*Typ.*); der Raum zwischen den Notenlinien (*Mus.*). II. *v.a.* die Spatien *or* Füllstifte einsetzen (*Typ.*); to —e out, sperren. **—ed**, *p.p. & adj.* gesperrt (*Typ.*). **—eless**, *adj.* raumlos, unendlich. **—er**, *s.* die Taste, die die Zwischenräume zwischen den Wörten bewirkt (*Typewrit.*). **—ing**, *s.* die Räumung, Aussetzung (*Typ.*). **—ious**, *adj.*, **—iously**, *adv.* geräumig, weit, umfangreich. **—iousness**, *s.* die Geräumigkeit, Weite, der Umfang.
[1]**Spade**, I. *s.* der Spaten, das Grabscheit; to call a — a —, das Kind beim rechten Namen nennen. II. *v.a.* mit dem Spaten graben. **—ful**, *s.* einen Spaten voll.
[2]**Spade**, *s.* (*usually pl.* —s) die (*pl.*) Schüppen, das Pik; ten of —s, die Pikzehn.
[3]**Spade**, *s.* das verschnittene Tier, der Geltling.
Spadix, *s.* der Kolben (*Bot.*).
Spake, *obs. imperf. of* Speak.
[1]**Span**, I. *s.* die Spanne (*also fig.*); das Gespann (*of horses*); — of an arch, die Spannung, Spannweite eines Bogens; — of a bridge, die Brückenweite. II. *v.a.* (um=, über=)spannen; (measure) (aus)messen. **—drel**, *s.* die Bogen=Hintermauerung, der Zwickel zwischen den Bogenschenkeln. **—ner**, *s.* der Spanner, Schlüssel, Hahn, Schraubenzieher.
[2]**Span**, (*obs.*) *imperf. of* Spin.
Spangle, I. *s.* der Flitter, Flimmer. II. *v.a.* beflittern; —d heavens, gestirnter Himmel; star —d banner, das Sternenbanner (*Amer.*).
Spaniel, *s.* der Wachtelhund.
[1]**Spank**, *v.n.* tüchtig zuschreiten; schnell dahintraben. **—er**, *s.* einer, der gewaltige Schritte macht; das Giekfegel, der Besan (*Naut.*). **—ing**, *adj.* schnell laufend *or* dahinfahrend; stark, tüchtig, derb; —ing breeze, lebhafte Brise (*Naut.*).
[2]**Spank**, *v.a.* mit flacher Hand schlagen, klapsen.
[1]**Spar**, *s.* der Spat. **—ry**, *adj.* spatähnlich; Spat=; —ry iron ore, der Spateisenstein.
[2]**Spar**, *s.* die Spiere, der Sparren (*Naut.*).
[3]**Spar**, I. *v.n.* Scheinhiebe machen; boxen; *see* [2]Box II.; zanken; streiten (*fig.*). II. *s.* der Scheinhieb; (—ring match) das Faustkampfspiel; der Streit, Zank, Hader.
Spar—e, I. *adj.*, **—ely**, *adv.* (—ing) sparsam; (scanty) spärlich; (lean) mager; (to —e) überzählig, übrig, vorrätig, zur Not; —e anchor, der Reserveanker; —e bed, das Gastbett; ein Bett übrig; —e diet, magere, schmale Kost; —e horse, das Reservepferd; —e hours, Mußestunden; —e money, der Sparpfennig; —e pole, die Vorratsdeichsel; —e rigging, das Reservetauwerk; —room, das Gastzimmer; —e time, die Mußezeit. II. *v.a.* (use —ingly) sparen; (save) ersparen, erübrigen; (lay by) übrig behalten, aufsparen; (treat tenderly) (ver)schonen, nachsehen, nachsichtig behandeln; (do without) entbehren, missen; fristen, erhalten (*one's life, etc.*); —e my blushes, schonen Sie mein Zartgefühl; I have none to —e, ich habe keine übrig; enough and to —e, vollauf, mehr als nötig; he —es no expense, er scheut keine Kosten; he —es no pains, er läßt sich keine Mühe verdrießen; we might have —ed ourselves the trouble of coming, wir hätten uns die Mühe des Kommens ersparen können; if God —e me, wenn Gott mich am Leben läßt. III. *v.n.* sparen, sparsam sein; (forbear) Nachsicht haben; —ing towards, nachsichtig gegen. **—eness**, *s.* die Magerkeit. **—ing**, *adj.*, **—ingly**, *adv.* sparsam, schonend (of, mit); (scanty) spärlich, mager, knapp; —ing of one's words, wortkarg. **—ingness**, *s.* die Sparsamkeit. *Comp.* **—e-rib**, *s.* das Schweinsrippchen, Rippespeer.
[1]**Spark**, *s.* flotter, munterer Gesell; der Stutzer; (lover) der Liebhaber.
[2]**Spark**, I. *s.* der Funke(n) (*also fig.*). II. *v.n.* Funken sprühen. **—le**, I. *s.* der Funke; der Glanz, Schimmer (*fig.*). II. *v.n.* funkeln, blitzen, Funken sprühen; glänzen; perlen (*as wine*); her eyes —led with joy, ihre Augen strahlten vor Freude. **—ling**, *adj.* funkelnd, glänzend; perlend; —ling wine, der Schaumwein.
Sparling, *s.* der Stintfisch.
Sparrow, *s.* der Sperling; the — twitters, der Sperling zwitschert, priestert. *Comp.* **—hawk**, *s.* der Sperber.
Sparse, *adj.*, **—ly**, *adv.* dünn gesät, zerstreut; *see* Scanty. **—ness**, *s.* die Zerstreutheit.
Spasm, *s.* der Krampf. **—odic**, I. *adj.*, **—odically**, *adv.* krampfhaft; stoßweise. II. *s.* das Krampfmittel.

[1]**Spat**, *s.* junges Schaltier, der Laich. **—s**, *pl.* kurze Gamaschen. **—ter**, *v.n.* (be)spritzen, aussprudeln. **—terdashes**, *pl.* Gamaschen.

[2]**Spat**, *imperf. & p.p. of* Spit.

Spatch-cock, *s.* das eben geschlachtete und zubereitete Huhn (*Cook.*).

Spath—e, *s.* die Blütenscheide, der Löffel. [1]**—ose**, *adj.* blumenscheidenartig (*Bot.*).

Spath—ic, *adj.* blätterig. [2]**—ose**, *see* Sparry.

Spatula, *s.* der Spatel. **—te**, *adj.* spatelförmig.

Spavin, *s.* der Spat. **—ed**, *adj.* spatig (*Vet.*).

Spawn, I. *s.* der Laich (*of fishes and frogs*); der Rogen (*of fishes*); die Brut, das Gezücht (*fig.*); die weiße Wurzelfaser (*of fungi*). II. *v.a. & n.* laichen, streichen; ausbrüten. **—er**, *s.* der Rogenfisch, Rogner. **—ing**, *s.* das Laichen. *Comp.* **—ing-time**, *s.* die Laichzeit.

Speak, *ir.v.* I. *n.* sprechen, reden; (an)sprechen, erklingen (*Mus.*); to — **about**, (discuss) über (eine Sache) sprechen, (eine Sache) besprechen; (talk about) von (einer Sache) sprechen; he was —ing **against** time, er mußte mit seiner Rede die Zeit auskaufen; to — **for**, ein gutes Wort einlegen für; it—s well for him, es spricht für ihn; to — **of**, *see* To — about; nothing to — of, nichts von Bedeutung; not to — of, geschweige; to — **on**, weiter sprechen; to — **out**, laut sprechen; to — **up**, frei heraussprechen; — up! (sprich) lauter! to — **to**, sprechen (*acc.*); he wished to — to me, er wünschte mich zu sprechen. II. *a.* sprechen; äußern, aussagen (*one's mind, etc.*); anzeigen (*fig.*); einsprechen (*comfort, peace, etc.*); to — **a** p. fair, einem gute Worte geben; to — a ship, ein Schiff anrufen, (an)preien (*Naut.*). **—er**, *s.* der (die) Sprecher(in); der Sprecher, Vorsitzende des englischen oder amerikanischen Unterhauses (*Parl.*). **—ing**, I. *adj.* sprechend; a —ing acquaintance, oberflächliche Bekanntschaft; —ing likeness, sprechend ähnliches Bild; to be on —ing terms, (mit einem) oberflächlich bekannt sein. *Comp.* **—ing-trumpet**, *s.* das Sprachrohr.

Spear, I. *s.* der Speer, Spieß; (lance) die Lanze. II. *v.a.* spießen, mit einem Speer durchbohren, durchstechen. *Comp.* **—head**, *s.* die Speerspitze, Lanzenspitze. **—man**, *s.* der Speerreiter, Lanzenträger. **—shaped**, *adj.* lanzettförmig.

Spec (*vulg.*) *see* —ulation. **—s**, *see* —tacles.

Speci—al, I. *adj.*, **—ally**, *adv.* besonder, eigen; speziell, Spezial- (*Law*); ausdrücklich (*as orders*); Gattungs- (*Philos.*); (—ally) besonders; —al edition, die Sonderausgabe, das Extrablatt; —al knowledge, eingehende Kenntnis, Fachkenntnis; —al train, der Sonderzug; —al verdict, das Urteil der Jury in Bezug auf die Tatsachen allein. II. *s.* der außerordentliche Konstabler. **—alist**, I. *s.* der Spezialist, der Fachmann; der Spezialarzt. II. *attrib.*; —alist teacher, der Fachlehrer. **—ality**, *s.* das Einzelfach, Lieblingsfach, Spezialfach; *see* —alty. **—alize**, *v.* I. *n.* einer S. ein besonders eingehendes Studium widmen; to —alize in history, Geschichte als Spezialfach studieren. II. *a.* einzeln erwähnen, einzeln anführen; auf den Artunterschied zurückführen. **—alization**, *s.* die Spezialisation; das Arbeiten auf einem Sondergebiete, das gründliche Studium eines Faches; too early —alization, allzu frühes Spezialisieren. **—alty**, *s.* die Besonderheit, Spezialität; (bond) der gerichtlich vollzogene Kontrakt, Schuldschein 2c. **—e**, *s.* das Metallgeld, bare Geld; to make a consignment in —e, eine Barsendung machen. **—es**, *s.* die Art, Gattung, Spezies, Sorte; die Art, Gattung (*Zool., Bot., Log.*); human —es, menschliche Gattung; a —es of, eine Art von. **—fic**, I. *adj.*, **—fically**, *adv.* eigen(artig), spezifisch; (definite) bestimmt; —fic character, spezifischer *or* Art-Charakter; —fic gravity, das spezifische Gewicht; —fic name, der Artname, Gattungsname. II. *s.* das Eigenmittel. **—fication**, *s.* die Spezifizierung; das genaue Verzeichnis, die stückweise Angabe und Berechnung (*Arch., etc.*); die Erwähnung (*of particulars*). **—fy**, *v.a.* spezifizieren, besonders bezeichnen, erwähnen; sum —fied, einzeln angegebene Summe; —fied books, besonders bezeichnete (zum Studium vorgeschriebene) Bücher. **—men**, I. *s.* das Probestück, die Probe; das Exemplar (*fig., Bot.*); die Ansichtssendung. II. *attrib.*; —men copy (*book*), das Musterexemplar; das Freiexemplar. **—ous**, *adj.* gut aussehend, dem Auge gefällig; (showy) oberflächlich. **—ously**, *adv.* scheinbar (wahr, gerecht 2c.), Schein- (*as reason, arguments, etc.*). **—ousness**, *s.* die Scheinbarkeit.

Speck, *s.* der Fleck; das Stückchen; — of dust, der Staubfleck, das Stäubchen. **—le**, I. *s.* der kleine, bunte Fleck. II. *v.a.* flecken, sprenkeln. **—led**, *adj.* gefleckt, gesprenkelt, bunt.

Spec—tacle, *s.* das Schauspiel; (sight) der Anblick; a shocking —tacle, ein widriger Anblick. **—tacled**, *adj.* brillentragend. **—tacles**, *pl.* (pair of —tacles) die Brille. **—tacular**, *adj.* schauspielmäßig. **—tator**, *s.* der Zuschauer. **—tral**, *adj.* geisterhaft; Spektral- (*Opt.*). **—tre**, *s.* die Erscheinung, das Gespenst. **—troscope**, *s.* das Spektroskop, der Spektralapparat. **—trum**, *s.* das Farbenbild, Spektrum (*Phys.*); solar —trum, Sonnenspektrum; —trum analysis, die Spektralanalyse. **—ular**, *adj.* spiegelartig, spiegelnd; (assisting sight) zum Sehen dienlich; —ular iron, das Spiegeleisen. **—ulate**, *v.n.* nachdenken, -sinnen (upon, über eine S.); spekulieren (*C.L.*). **—ulation**, *s.* die Betrachtung, Grübelei, das Nach-sinnen, -forschen; die Spekulation, das Unternehmen. **—ulative**, *adj.* forschend, tiefsinnig, spekulativ; unternehmend, spekulierend (*C.L.*). **—ulator**, *s.* der Forscher, Beobachter; der Spekulant (*C. L.*). **—ulum**, *s.* der Metallspiegel. *Comp.* **—tacle-case**, *s.* das Brillenfutteral. **—tacle-frame**, *s.* das Brillengestell.

Sped, *imperf. & p.p. of* Speed.

Speech, I. *s.* die Sprache; (faculty of —) das Sprechen, Sprachvermögen; (oration) die Rede; — from the throne, die Thronrede; to make a —, eine Rede halten; connected —, das Sprachgefüge. II. *attrib.*; — sounds, die Sprachlaute. **—ify**, *v.n.* eine lange Rede halten, viele Worte machen. **—less**, *adj.* sprachlos, stumm. **—lessness**, *s.* die Sprachlosigkeit. *Comp.* **—day**, *s.* der Schulaktus, das Schulfest. **—maker**, *s.* der Fest-Redner.

Speed, I. *ir.v.n.* sich sputen, eilen; (fare) gedeihen, fahren. II. *v.a.* eiligst fortschicken; (cause to succeed) (be)fördern, helfen, Glück verleihen; God — thee! Gott schütze, geleite dich! how have you sped? wie ist es dir gelungen? III. *s.* die Eile, Schnelligkeit, (Fahr)Geschwindigkeit; (progress) der Forigang, Ausgang, Erfolg, das Glück; with all possible —, mit möglichster Eile; at full —, mit verhängtem Zügel (*as a horse*), mit voller Geschwindigkeit (*Locom.*); aus Leibeskräften; at half —, mit halber Geschwindigkeit. **—ily**, *adv.*, **—y**, *adj.* eilig, eilfertig, schnell. **—iness**, *s.* die Eile, Eilfertigkeit, Geschwindigkeit. **—well**, *s.* der Ehrenpreis (*Bot.*).

[1]**Spell**, *s.* die Ablösung, Abwechselung, Reihe (*at work*); (time) die kurze Zeit, Frist, das Weilchen; to take a — at, in seiner Reihe an . . . arbeiten; we have had a long — of fine weather, wir haben eine lange Weile gutes Wetter gehabt.

[2]**Spell**, I. *s.* der Zauber; der Zauberspruch. II. *v.a. & n.* (*imperf. & p.p. also* Spelt) buchstabieren; sprachrichtig schreiben; bedeuten (*coll.*); how do you — this word? wie schreibt man das Wort? to — out, herausbuchstabieren, entziffern; Greek —s culture, das Griechische bedeutet *or* steht für Kultur. **—er**, *s.* der Orthograph; he is a bad —er, er schreibt nicht orthographisch, nicht sprachrichtig. **—ing**, *s.* das Buchstabieren; (orthography) die Rechtschreibung. *Comp.* **—bound**, *adj.* bezaubert, festgebannt. **—ing-bee**,

s. die Buchstabierversammlung, Buchstabiergesellschaft. **—ing-book,** *s.* das Abc-Buch, die Fibel.
[1]**Spelt,** (*also* **Spelled,**) *imperf. & p.p. of* Spell.
[2]**Spelt,** *s.* der Spelt, Spelz, Dinkel(weizen).
Spencer, *s.* das Schnausegel, Gaffelsegel (*Naut.*).
Spen—d, *ir.v.* I. *a.* aufwenden, ausgeben (*money, etc.*); (employ) verwenden, anlegen (upon, auf, *acc.*); anwenden, hin-, zu-bringen (*time*); durchbringen (*a fortune*); erschöpfen (*balls*). II. *n.* Aufwand machen, Geld ausgeben; (be —t) verwendet, verbraucht werden (*rare*). **—der,** *s.* der Aufwandmacher. **—t,** I. *imp. & p.p. of* —d. II. *adj.* erschöpft, entkräftet (*with watching, etc.*); matt (*as a ball or a bullet*); — horse, abgetriebenes Pferd. *Comp.* **—thrift,** I. *s.* der Verschwender. II. *adj.* verschwenderisch.
Sperm, *s.* der Same (der Tiere). **—aceti,** *s.* der Walrat. **—atic,** *adj.* aus männlichem tierischen Samen bestehend, Samen enthaltend; —atic vessels, Samengefäße. **—atize,** *v.n.* Samen absondern. **—atocele,** *s.* der Samenbruch. **—atozoa,** *pl.* Samentierchen. **—oderm,** *s.* die Samenhülle.
Spew, *v.* I. *a.* aus-speien, -werfen. II. *n.* speien.
Sphacelate, *v.n.* brandig werden.
Sphenoid(al), *adj.* keilartig, Keil- (bone, -bein).
Spher—e, *s.* die Kugel; der Himmelskörper (*Astr.*); künstliche Erd- oder Himmels-kugel (*for schools*); der Kreislauf, die Bahn (*of a planet, etc.*); die Sphäre, der (Denk-)Kreis, Bereich, Umfang (*fig.*); —e of activity, Wirkungskreis; persons belonging to a higher —e, Leute, die sich in höheren Kreisen bewegen; music of the —es, die Sphärenmusik, Harmonie der Sphären; that is out of (beyond) his —e, das geht über seine Begriffe. **—ic, —ical,** *adj.*, **—ically,** *adv.* kugelrund, sphärisch; —ical angle, sphärischer Winkel; —ical trigonometry, sphärische Trigonometrie. **—icalness, —icity,** *s.* die Kugelgestalt, Rundung. **—icle,** *s.* die kleine Kugel. **—ics,** *s.* die Kugellehre, Sphärik. **—oid,** *s.* das Sphäroid, Drehungsellipsoid. **—oidal,** *adj.* sphäroidisch. **—ule,** *s.* das Kügelchen. *Comp.* **—e-descended,** *adj.* aus den Sphären herab gestiegen.
Sphincter, *s.* der Schließmuskel (*Anat.*).
Sphragistics, *s.* die Siegelkunde.
Spic—e, I. *s.* das Gewürz, die Würze; der (Bei-)Geschmack, (An-)Strich (*fig.*); —es, Gewürz. II. *v.a.* würzen. **—ily,** *adv.*, **—y,** *adj.* gewürzreich, würzig; (—e-like) gewürzhaft; stark gewürzt, gepfeffert, pikant (*fig.*). **—iness,** *s.* die Würzigkeit; die Gewürztheit; das Duftige; das Pikante. *Comp.* **—e-cake,** *s.* eine Art Pfefferkuchen.
Spick-and-span, *adj.* blitzblank, funkelnagelneu, wie aus dem Ei gepellt.
Spicule, *s.* die (Eis- *etc.*)Nadel.
Spider, *s.* die Spinne; —'s web, das Spinnengewebe. *Comp.* **—line,** *s.* die Spinnenlinie.
Spigot, *s.* der Zapfen.
Spik—e, I. *s.* der Spiker, Bolzen, lange Nagel (*Carp. etc.*); die Ähre (*Agr.*); der Zündlochnagel (*for —ing guns*); die Ähre, Granne (*Bot.*); der Dorn, Stachel. II. *v.a.* mit eisernen Spitzen versehen; vernageln (*a gun, etc.*). **—elet,** *s.* das Ährchen. **—y,** *adj.* spitzig. *Comp.* **—e-iron,** *s.* das Spikereisen. **—e-oil, —enard,** *s.* das Lavendelöl, Nardenöl.
Spile, I. *s.* der Spund, Pflock; (stake) der Pfahl. II. *v.a.* spünden, mit Pflöcken versehen.
[1]**Spill,** *s.* der Fidibus.
[2]**Spill,** I. *v.a.* (*imperf. & p.p. also* Spilt) verschütten (*water, etc.*); vergießen (*blood*); abwerfen (*from horseback*), umwerfen (*a carriage*). II. *v.n.* verschüttet werden. III. *s.* die Verschüttung; das Um-, Ab-werfen (*sl.*).
Spillikin, *s.* das lange schmale Stäbchen aus Holz, Bein, oder Elfenbein; the game of —s, das Federspiel, Beilkespiel.
Spilt, (*also* **Spilled,**) *imperf. & p.p. of* Spill.
Spin, *ir.v.* I. *a.* spinnen; wirbeln, herumdrehen; kreiseln (*a top*); to — the top, den Kreisel schlagen; to — **out,** in die Länge ziehen (*a story, etc.*). II. *n.* spinnen; to — **along,** sich schnell bewegen, (roll) rollen (*as carriages*); to — **round,** sich herumdrehen; herumtanzen; herumwirbeln; my head —s round, der Kopf schwindelt mir. III. *s.* das (Herum)-Wirbeln, -Drehen; die schnelle Bewegung *or* Fahrt; a — on a bicycle, eine schnelle Fahrt auf dem Rade. **—dle,** *s.* die Spindel; die Schnecke (*Horol.*); die Zunge (*Shipb.*); die Pinne (*of a capstan*). **—ner,** *s.* der (die) Spinner(in). **—ster,** I. *s.* die Spinnerin (*obs.*); das Mädchen, ledige Frauenzimmer; she is a —ster, sie ist (noch) unverheiratet. II. *attrib.*; —ster aunt, unverheiratete Tante. *Comp.* **—dle-shanks,** *pl.* die Spindelbeine (*vulg.*). **—ning-jenny,** *s.* die Feinspinnmaschine. **—ning-mill,** *s.* die Spinnmühle, Spinnerei. **—ning-wheel,** *s.* das Spinnrad.
Spin—ach, *s.* der Spinat. **—al,** *adj.* Rückgrat(s)-, zum Rückgrat gehörig; —al curvature, die Rückgratsverkrümmung; —al marrow, das Rückenmark. **—e,** *s.* der Dorn; das (der) Rückgrat (*Anat.*). **—et,** *s.* das Spinett (*Mus.*). **—osity,** *s.* das Dornige. **—ous,** *adj.* dornig, stachelig. **—y,** *adj. see* —ous; häkelig (*fig.*).
Spir—acle, *s.* das Luftloch. **—it,** *see* Spirit, etc.
Spiræa, *s.* die Spierstaude, Spiräe.
Spir—al, I. *adj.*, **—ally,** *adv.* spiral-, schneckenförmig; Spiral-, Schnecken-; —al line, die Schneckenlinie, Spirallinie; —al staircase, die Wendeltreppe. II. *s.* die Spirale (*Geom. etc.*). **—e,** *s. see* [2]Spire. **—y,** *adj.* spiralförmig.
Spirant, *s.* der Reibelaut, Hauchlaut, die Spirans (*Phonet.*); the voiceless labial —, der tonlose Lippen-Reibelaut (f). **—ic,** *adj.* einen Reibelaut verursachend, Hauch-, gehaucht; —ic sounds, Hauchlaute, Reibelaute.
[1]**Spire,** *s.* der Spitzturm, die Turmspitze; (church —) Kirchturmspitze; der Halm (*of grass, etc.*).
[2]**Spire,** *s.* die Schneckenlinie; *see* Wreath.
Spirit, I. *s.* (life) das Leben, der Lebenshauch; (*opp. to* Body) der Geist, die Seele; (ghost) der Geist, das Gespenst; (person) der Geist; (disposition) das Gemüt, Gefühl, die Gemütsart, Gesinnung, der Charakter; (courage, fire) der Geist, Mut, das Feuer, Leben, die Lebhaftigkeit; der Geist, Spiritus (*Chem. etc.*); good, high, flow of —s, die Heiterkeit, Munterkeit, der Frohsinn; low, depressed —s, die Niedergeschlagenheit; in good (bad) —s, heiter, wohlgemut, aufgelegt, (niedergeschlagen); to put into good —s, revive a p.'s —s, einen aufheitern; — of the age, der Zeitgeist; out of a — of charity, aus christlicher Liebe; in the — of a true diplomatist, in echt diplomatischem Sinne; Holy —, der heilige Geist. II. *v.a.*; to — away, verschwinden lassen; weglocken. **—ed,** *adj.* lebhaft, munter, voll Leben; (fiery) mutig, kühn, angefeuert, feurig; high—ed, stolz, hochgemut, mit hohem Geist *or* Sinn. **—edness,** *s.* das Feuer, der Mut. **—ism,** *s.* der Spiritismus. **—ist,** *s.* der Spiritist. **—less,** *adj.*, **—lessly,** *adv.* leblos; (depressed) niedergeschlagen; mutlos, kleinlaut, kleinmütig. **—lessness,** *s.* die Mutlosigkeit, der Kleinmut. **—s,** *pl.* (ardent —s) geistige Getränke; —s of wine, der Weingeist; —s of turpentine, Terpentingeist. **—ual,** *adj.*, **—ually,** *adv.* (immaterial) geistig, unkörperlich; (intellectual) geistig; (not temporal, divine) geistlich; (ecclesiastical) kirchlich; Lords temporal and —ual, die geistlichen und weltlichen Lords; —ual life, das geistliche (*Rel.*), geistige Leben; —ual songs, geistliche Lieder. **—ualism,** *s.* der Spiritualismus. **—ualist,** *s.* der Spiritualist. **—ualities,** *pl.* die Gebühren, Einkünfte eines Geistlichen (*Eccl.*). **—uality,** *s.* die Geistigkeit (*also Rel.*); geistige Natur. **—ualization,** *s.* die Vergeistigung. **—ualize,**

v.a. vergeistigen (*fig. & Chem.*). **—uous**, *adj.* geistig; —uous liquors, geistige Getränke. *Comp.* **—-lamp**, *s.* die Spirituslampe. **—-level**, *s.* die Nivellierwage. **—-licence**, *s.* die Erlaubnis zum Kleinverkauf von geistigen Getränken. **—-like**, *adj.* geisterähnlich. **—-rapping**, *s.* das Geisterklopfen. **—-stirring**, *adj.* geist=, muter=regend. **—ually-minded**, *adj.* geistlich gesinnt, religiös.

¹Spirt, I. *v.n. & a.* spritzen; to — out, heraus=spritzen. II. *s.* das Hervorspritzen, der Strahl; plötzlicher Anstoß.

²Spirt, *s.* plötzliche Anstrengung, der Ruck; to put on a —, eine plötzliche Anstrengung machen.

¹Spit, I. *s.* der (Brat=)Spieß; die Landzunge (*Geog.*). II. *v.a.* an den Bratspieß stecken.

²Spit, I. *s.* der Speichel. II. *ir.v.a.* speien; (— forth, out) ausspeien. III. *ir.v.n.* speien; to — **at**, anspeien; to — **upon**, bespeien. IV. (*also* **—ted**,) *imperf. & p.p.*, **—ten**, (*obs.*) *p.p. of* —. **—ter**, *s.* einer der speit, spuckt. **—tle**, *s.* der Speichel. **—toon**, *s.* der Spucknapf. *Comp.* **—fire**, *s.* der Hitzkopf, Brausekopf.

Spite, I. *s.* der Ärger, Verdruß; die Bosheit, der Haß; in — of, trotz (*gen.*), ungeachtet (*gen.*); in — of you, dir zum Trotz; to do out of —, einem andern zum Ärger tun. II. *v.a.* ärgern, kränken, quälen, erzürnen. **—ful**, *adj.*, **—fully**, *adv.* boshaft, gehässig. **—fulness**, *s.* die Bosheit.

Splash, I. *v.a.* bespritzen, patschen. II. *v.n.* spritzen, patschen. III. *s.* der Spritzer (von Straßenkot 2c.). **—er**, *s.* der Raddeckel; der Tapetenschützer (am Waschtisch). **—y**, *adj.* naß, schlammig. *Comp.* **—-board**, *s.* das Spritz=brett. **—(ing)-leather**, *s.* das Spritzleder.

Splay, I. *adj.* auswärts gebogen. II. *s.* die schiefwinklige Fläche. III. *v.a.* ausschrägen (*Arch.*); (einem Pferde die Schulter) verrenken, (es) buglahm machen. **—ed**, *adj.* schief. *Comp.* **—-footed**, *adj.* mit auswärts gebogenen Füßen. **—-mouth**, *s.* schiefes Maul.

Spleen, *s.* die Milz (*Anat.*); die Milzsucht (*Med.*); der Spleen (*fig.*); (ill-humour) die Galle, üble Laune; (anger) der Groll; *see* Whim. **—ful**, **—y**, *adj.* milzsüchtig; launisch.

Splend—ent, *see* Resplendent. **—id**, *adj.*, **—idly**, *adv.* glänzend; prächtig, herrlich. **—our**, *s.* der helle Glanz; der Glanz, die Pracht, Herr=lichkeit (*fig.*).

Splen—etic, I. *adj.*, **—etically**, *adv.* milzsüchtig, spleenig; mürrisch, reizbar. II. *s.* der Milz=süchtige. **—ic**, *adj.* Milz=.

Splic—e, I. *s.* die Splissung; die Einfalzung (*Carp.*). II. *v.a.* splissen, einfügen (*ropes*); einfalzen (*Carp.*); in den Spalt pfropfen (*Hort.*). **—ing**, *s.* das Splissen. *Comp.* **—ing-hammer**, *s.* der Splißhammer.

Splint, I. *s. see* —er I.; die Schiene (*Surg.*); in —s, geschient, in Schienen (*Surg.*). II. *v.a.* schienen. **—er**, I. *s.* der Splitter, Span (*of wood, bone, etc.*); das Granatstück (*Mil.*). II. *v.a.* (zer)splittern, schiefern. III. *v.n.* sich split=tern. *Comp.* **—-coal**, *s.* die Schieferkohle.

Split, I. *s.* der Spalt, Riß; die Spaltung (*also fig.*). II. *ir.v.a.* (*also pret. & p.p.*) spalten; beleidigen (*the ears, fig.*); unter zwei Kandidaten teilen (*a vote*); let us — the difference, wir wollen uns in die streitige Summe teilen *or* jeder die Hälfte nachgeben; to — one's sides with laugh-ing, vor Lachen bersten wollen. III. *ir.v.n.* sich spalten, bersten; sich entzweien *or* trennen (*fig.*); —ing headache, rasender Kopfschmerz, als ob einem der Kopf springen wollte. IV. (*rarely* **—ted**,) *imperf. & p.p. of* —. **—ter**, *s.* der Spaltende.

Splutter, I. *s.* der Lärm, das Wesen. II. *v.n.* hastig und verworren reden, heraussprudeln (beim Reden), schlabbern; spritzen (*as a pen*). III. *v.a.*; . . . he —ed out, . . . sprudelte er heraus.

Spoil, I. *v.a.* berauben (einen einer S.); plün=dern; verderben, vernichten, zerstören, zu Grunde richten; verderben (die Augen, gute Sitten); ver=ziehen, verwöhnen (Kinder); vereiteln (Pläne); to — a p.'s plans, einem einen Strich durch die Rechnung machen. II. *v.n.* rauben, plündern; to — for a th., nach einer S. schmachten (*sl.*). III. *s.* die Beute, der Raub; die Ausbeute, Er=rungenschaft (*fig.*). **—er**, *s.* der Berauber, Plünderer; der Zerstörer, Vernichter; der Ver=zieher (*of children*).

¹Spoke, *imperf. & (obs. & vulgar) p.p.*, **—n**, *p.p. of* Speak. **—sman**, (**—swoman**,) *s.* der (die) Wortführer(in).

²Spoke, *s.* die Speiche (*of a wheel*); (rung) die Leitersprosse; —s, die Spaken (*Naut.*); to put a — in a p.'s wheel, einem ein Bein stellen (*coll.*).

Spoliat—e, *v.a. & n.* plündern. **—ion**, *s.* die Plünderung; die Spoliation (*Law*).

Spond—aic, *adj.* spondäisch. **—ee**, *s.* der Spon=däus, der aus zwei Längen bestehende Versfuß.

Spondulics, *pl.* das Geld (*sl.*).

Spondyle, *s.* der Rückgratswirbel (*Anat.*).

Spong—e, I. *s.* der Schwamm (*also fig.*); der Wischer (*Artil.*); die Stolle (*Vet.*); to throw up the —e, sich für besiegt erklären (*sl.*). II. *v.n.* sich vollsaugen, sich füttern lassen, schmarotzen (upon a p., bei einem). III. *v.a.* mit einem Schwamme wischen; auswischen (*Artil.*). **—er**, *s.* der Wischer (*Artil.*); der Schmarotzer. **—iness**, *s.* die Schwammigkeit. **—iole**, *s.* das Schwämmchen (*Bot.*). **—y**, *adj.* schwammig, schwammicht; einsaugend (*fig.*). *Comp.* **—e-bag**, *s.* der Schwammbeutel (von Wachstuch). **—e-bath**, *s.* das Sitzbad. **—e-cake**, *s.* eine Art lockerer Kuchen. **—e-glove**, *s.* der Wasch=handschuh. **—ing-house**, *s.* vorläufiger Ge=wahrsam beim Gerichtsdiener (*obs.*).

Spon—sal, *adj.* bräutlich, hochzeitlich. **—sor**, *s.* der Bürge; der Pate (*for a child*); to stand —sor to, Gevatter *or* Paten stehen bei. **—sorial**, *adj.* bürgschaftsmäßig; Paten=. **—sorship**, *s.* die Patenstelle; Stelle des Bürgen. **—taneous**, *adj.*, **—taneously**, *adv.* freiwillig, von selbst, aus eignem Antriebe (handelnd); wildwachsend (*Bot.*); (produced of itself) von selbst entstanden, natürlich, spontan; —taneous combustion, die Selbstverbrennung; —taneous generation, die Urzeugung. **—taneousness**, **—taneity**, *s.* die Freiwilligkeit, Spontaneität.

Spontoon, *s.* der Sponton (*Mil.*).

Spool, I. *s.* die Spule. II. *v.a.* spulen. *Comp.* **—-stand**, **—-holder**, *s.* der Zwirnhalter.

¹Spoon, *s.* der Löffel; apostle —, Löffel mit Apostelkopf am Griffende; wooden —, der Stu=dent, welcher die höchste mathematische Schluß=prüfung am schlechtesten besteht und einen riesigen hölzernen Löffel bei Verkündigung der Prüfungs=ergebnisse von den Mitstudenten erhält; *see* Senior Wrangler (*Cambridge Univ. sl.*). **—ful**, *s.* der Löffelvoll. *Comp.* **—-bill**, *s.* der Löffler. **—-drift**, *s.* der Schaum von der Meeresfläche bei Stürmen. **—-meat**, *s.* die Löffelspeise.

²Spoon, I. *s.* der Einfaltspinsel, Tropf; der Ver=liebte. II. *v.a.* den Hof machen (einem Mädchen) (*sl.*). III. *v.n.* närrisch verliebt sein (*sl.*). **—(e)y**, *adj.* sehr verliebt, töricht zärtlich (*sl.*).

Spor—adic, *adj.* sporadisch; —adic vowel, der Sproßvokal. **—e**, **—ule**, *s.* das Keimpulver.

Sporran, *s.* die Vorhänge=Tasche der Bergschotten.

Sport, I. *s.* das Spiel; (fun) der Scherz, Spaß; (diversion) die Belustigung, der Zeitvertreib; der Sport; *see* Hunting, Fishing, Racing, Cricket, etc.; —s, Spiele, Turnspiele; inter-university —s, die großen alljährlichen Wettkämpfe zwischen Studenten von Oxford und Cambridge, oder von amerikanischen Universitäten; we have had cap-ital —, wir haben eine vortreffliche Jagd gehabt; wir haben uns köstlich amüsiert; in —, for —, zum Spaß, aus Scherz; the — of every wind, das Spiel eines jeden Windes; to spoil a p.'s —, einem den Spaß verderben; to make —, scher=

zen, Spaß treiben; to make — of, einen zum besten haben, sich über einen lustig machen. II. *v.a.* zur Schau tragen sehen lassen, paradieren mit (*coll.*). III. *v.n.* spielen, sich belustigen; den Vergnügungen im Freien nachgehen; sein Spiel treiben (with, mit); to — one's door *or* oak, die äußere Wohnungstür (aus Eichenholz) von innen schließen, sein, sich gegen jedermann absperren (*Univ. sl.*). **—ful**, *adj.*, **—fully**, *adv.* lustig; (playful) scherzhaft. **—fulness**, *s.* die Lustigkeit; die Scherzhaftigkeit. **—ing**, *p.*; —ing man, ein dem Sport huldigender Mann, Liebhaber der Jagd, des Wettrennens &c; —ing world, die Welt des Sports. **—ive**, *adj.*, **—ively**, *adv.* scherzhaft, lustig, spaßhaft; —ive humour, scherzhafte Laune. **—iveness**, *s.* die Scherzhaftigkeit, Lustigkeit, der Scherz. *Comp.* **—sman**, *s.* der Sportsmann, Freund des Sports, der Jäger, Fischer, Vogelsteller aus Liebhaberei. **—smanlike**, *adj.* wie ein Jäger, &c., weidmännisch. **—smanship**, *s.* die Jägerkunst, Jägerei. **—swoman**, *s.* dem Sport huldigende Frau weiblicher Sportsman.

Spot, I. *s.* der Flecken (*also on the sun*), Makel; (place) der Fleck, Ort, die Stelle; der Flecken, Fehler (*fig.*); der Punkt (*Bill.*); on *or* upon the —, an Ort und Stelle; (at once) auf der Stelle, sogleich. II. *attrib.*; — price, Preis bei sofort auszuführendem Auftrag (*C.L.*). III. *v.a.* flecken; (mark with —s) sprenkeln, tüpfeln; besudeln, beflecken (*also the reputation, etc.*); (note) bemerken; anhauen (*timber*). **—less**, *adj.* fleckenlos. **—lessness**, *s.* die Fleckenlosigkeit, Unbeflecktheit. **—ted**, *adj.* getüpfelt; *see* —ty; —ted fever, das Fleckfieber. **—tiness**, *s.* die Fleckigkeit. **—ty**, *adj.* fleckig, gefleckt.

Spous—al, *adj.* hochzeitlich, ehelich. **—als**, *pl.* die Hochzeit; (marriage) die Ehe. **—e**, *s.* der Gatte, Gemahl; die Gattin, Gemahlin (*high style, poet.*). **—eless**, *adj.* gattenlos.

Spout, I. *s.* der Ausguß (*also of a gutter*); die Ausgußröhre (*of a pump, etc.*); die Schnauze (*in jugs, etc.*); (gutter) die Dachrinne. II. *v.a.* (aus)spritzen; deklamieren (*verses, etc.; fam.*). III. *v.n.* (— out, heraus-, hervor-)spritzen, sprudeln; deklamieren (*fam.*). **—er**, *s.* der Deklamator (*coll.*). *Comp.* **—ing-club**, *s.* der Deklamierverein (*coll.*).

Sprain, I. *s.* die Verrenkung. II. *v.a.* verrenken; I —ed my foot, ich verrenkte mir den Fuß.

Sprang, (*obs.*) *imperf. of* Spring.

Sprat, *s.* die Sprotte.

Sprawl, *v.n.* sich der Länge nach ausstrecken, sich spreizen; sich unordentlich ausdehnen; —ing charge, die Schwärmattacke (*Mil.*); to lie —ing, mit gespreizten Beinen auf dem Boden liegen.

[1]**Spray**, *s.* der Zweig (*of holly, etc.*), das Reis; — of flowers, das Sträußchen.

[2]**Spray**, *s.* der Sprühregen; die Staubdusche, feine Dusche; (sea —) der Sprühregen von Seeschaum.

Spread, I. *ir.v.a.* (*also imperf. & p.p.*) spreiten, breiten (on, auf); ausbreiten, (aus)spannen (*sails*); verbreiten, aussprengen (*a report, etc.*); (cover) (be)decken, überziehen; to — the cloth, den Tisch decken; the peacock —s his tail, der Pfau schlägt ein Rad. II. *ir.v.n.* sich ausbreiten, sich verbreiten; sich dehnen (*as metals*). III. *s.* die Ver-, Aus-breitung; (compass) der Umfang. IV. *adj.*; — eagle, aufgespaltener und gebratener Vogel (*Cook.*). **—er**, *s.* einer, der aus-, ver-breitet &c. **—ing**, I. *adj.* ausgebreitet, weit. II. *s.* das Aus-, Ver-breiten, &c. *Comp.* **—eagle**, *adj.* prahlerisch, anmaßend (*fig.*).

Spree, *s.* das Vergnügen, der Spaß, die Lustbarkeit; das Zechen; on a —, beim Zechen, fidel; to go on a —, auf den Bummel gehen.

Sprig, I. *v.a.* mit kleinen Zweigen verzieren; sticken. II. *s.* der Sproß, das Reis; der Stift (*Naut., Carp.*); der Sprößling (*fig.*). *Comp.* **—crystal**, *s.* der Bergkrystall. **—ged**, *p.p. & adj.* verzweigt; beblümt, bunt bemalt.

Sprightl—iness, *s.* die Lebendigkeit, Munterkeit. **—y**, *adj.* lebhaft, munter.

Spring, I. *ir.v.n.* springen; (arise) entspringen, quellen (from, aus), herkommen (from, von); to — **at**, losspringen auf (*acc.*); to — **back**, zurückspringen; to — **forth**, hervor-springen, -schießen; to — **forwards**, vorwärts springen, sich stürzen (auf einen); to — **in**, hinein-springen, -stürzen; to — **into** existence, (plötzlich) entstehen; to — **on**, **upon**, springen auf (*acc.*), anfallen; to — **over**, springen, setzen über (*acc.*); to — **up**, aufspringen; aufkommen (*of ideas*); the wind —s up, der Wind springt auf; to — up like mushrooms, wie Pilze aus der Erde schießen; a well of —ing water, ein Brunnen lebendigen Wassers. II. *ir.v.a.* sprengen, springen lassen, spielen lassen (*mines, etc.*); schnarren machen (*a rattle*); (ein Leck) bekommen, (leck) werden (*a leak*); sprengen (*a ball, Bill.*); (produce suddenly) plötzlich, unerwartet hervorbringen, hervorrufen; auf-treiben, -jagen (*game*); to — a surprise upon a p., einen höchlich überraschen. III. *s.* der Springquell, Springbrunnen, die Quelle; (source) der Quell, Ursprung, Anfang; (jump) der Sprung, Satz; (elasticity) die Spring-, Schnell-, Feder-kraft, Elastizität; die (Spring-, Trieb-)Feder (*Mach.*); (—ing back) das Zurück-springen, -schnellen; (motive) der Anlaß, Beweggrund; (dawn) der Anbruch des Tages; (season of —) der Lenz, Frühling; der Sprung (*in a mast*); der Spalt (*in a plank, etc.*); —s, das Getriebe; main —, die Haupt-, Schlag-feder; hot —, heiße Quelle; —s of action, die Triebfedern; — of a vault, der Gewölb-anfang, -anfall. **—e**, I. *s.* die Schlinge, der Sprenkel. II. *v.a.* in einer Schlinge fangen; verstricken (*fig.*). **—er**, *s.* der Treiber (*Sport.*); *see* Grampus; *see* —bok; der Anlauf (*Arch.*); (—ing stone) der Gewölbanfangstein. **—iness**, *s.* die Springkraft, Elastizität. **—ing**, *s.* das Springen. **—y**, *adj.* elastisch, prall; naß, quellenreich (*as land*). *Comp.* **—back**, *s.* loser Rücken (*Bookb.*). **—balance**, *s.* die Federwage. **—board**, *s.* das Sprungbrett; das Federbrett. **—bok**, *s.* der Springbock. **—bolt**, *s.* der Federriegel. **—braces**, *pl.* Federriemen. **—carriage**, *s.* der in Federn hängende Wagen. **—tide**, *s.* die Frühlingszeit, der Lenz. **—tide**, *s.* die Springflut. **—time**, *s.* der Frühling. **—tree**, *adj.*; —tree bar, die Wage (am Wagen).

Sprinkl—e, I. *v.a.* sprenkeln, überfäen; (be)sprengen (clothes, etc., Wäsche &c.); besprengen, bestreuen (with, mit); book with —ed edges, das Buch mit gesprenkeltem Schnitt. II. *v.n.* sprühen. **—ing**, *s.* das Sprengen, Gesprenge; —ing of, ein Wenig, ein Anstrich *or* Anflug von (*fam. fig.*); —ing of rain, der Sprühregen.

Sprint, I. *s.* kurzer, schneller Wettlauf. II. *v.n.* schnell laufen. **—er**, *s.* der Renner.

Sprit, *s.* das Spriet. *Comp.* **—sail**, *s.* das Sprietsegel.

Sprite, *s.* der Geist; (elf) der Kobold, Schrat; die Naiade; mountain —, der Bergschrat.

Sprout, I. *v.n.* (—up, auf-)sprossen; keimen (*Brew.*). II. *s.* die Sprosse, der Sprößling; —s, die Kohlsprossen; Brussels —s, der Brüsseler Kohl, der Rosenkohl.

[1]**Spruce**, *adj.*, **—ly**, *adv.* sauber, geputzt, geleckt **—ness**, *s.* die Sauberkeit, der Putz.

[2]**Spruce**, *s.* die Fichte, Rottanne, picea excelsa, der Tannenbaum; — fir, Norway —, *see* —. *Comp.* **—beer**, *s.* das Sprossenbier.

Sprung, *imperf. & p.p. of* Spring.

Spry, *adj.* flink, hurtig, rüstig, wacker (*coll.*).

Spud, *s.* die Gäthacke, das Stoßeisen.

Spum—e, *s.* der Schaum. **—ous**, **—y**, *adj.* schaumig, schäumend.

Spun, *imperf. & p.p. of* Spin; — **gold**, **der** Goldfaden; — silk, das Seidengarn; — **out**, **in** die Länge gezogen (*a story*).

Spunge, *see* Sponge.
Spunk, *s.* der Zündschwamm; der Mut (*vulg.*).
Spur, I. *s.* der Sporn (*Mil.*, *etc.*, *Bot.*, *Zool.*); die Strebe, Gewölbstütze (*Arch.*); das Vorwerk (*Fort.*); der Sporn, Antrieb (*fig.*); der Ausläufer (*of a mountain*); on the — of the moment, unter dem ersten Eindrucke, der ersten Eingebung folgend; to clap, put, set —s to one's horse, seinem Pferde die Sporen geben. II. *v.a.* mit Sporen versehen; die Sporen geben, anspornen; to — **on**, anspornen, antreiben, anstacheln. III. *v.n.* die Sporen geben, spornen; to — **after**, sprengen nach; to — **on**, forteilen. —**n**, *see* Spurn. —**red**, *adj.* gespornt (*also Bot.*). *Comp.* —**-gall**, *s.* der Spornstich.
Spurge, *s.* die Wolfsmilch. *Comp.* —**-laurel**, *s.* der lorbeerblättrige Seidelbast.
Spurious, *adj.*, —**ly**, *adv.* unecht, falsch (*as coins, documents, etc.*); untergeschoben (*as writings*); (illegitimate) unehelich. —**ness**, *s.* die Unechtheit.
Spurn, *v.a.* mit dem Fuße (weg)stoßen, treten; von sich werfen *or* weisen, zurückweisen (*fig.*); (scorn) verschmähen.
Spurry, *s.* der Ackerspergel.
Spurt, *see* Spirt.
Sputter, I. *v.n. see* Splutter; sprühen. II. *v.a.* aussprudeln. III. *s.* das Gesprudel. —**er**, *s.* der Sprudler.
Spy, I. *s.* der Kundschafter, Späher, Spion. II. *v.a.* (er)spähen; to — **out**, erspähen, auskundschaften (*lit.*); erspähen, entdecken (*fig.*). III. *v.n.* spionieren; gucken (*in children's games*); to — **into**, (einer Sache) nachspähen, nachspüren. —**ing**, *s.* das Spionieren, die Spioniererei. *Comp.* —**-glass**, *s.* das Fern=glas, =rohr.
Squab, I. *s.* die kurze, dicke Person; der ausgepolsterte niedrige Sessel; das Polsterkissen. II. *adj.* wabbelig, fleischig, dick und fett. III. *adv.* schwapp(s), plumps; to come down —, himplumpsen.
Squabble, I. *v.n.* hadern, streiten, zanken. II. *s.* der Hader, Zank. —**r**, *s.* der Zänker.
Squad, *s.* die Rotte, Korporalschaft (*Mil.*); der Haufe. —**ron**, *s.* die Schwadron (*Mil.*); das Geschwader (*Naut.*).
Squal—id, *adj.*, —**idly**, *adv.* schmutzig, garstig; in —id poverty, im Schmutz des Elends. —**or**, *s.* der Schmutz, die Unreinlichkeit.
[1]**Squall**, *s.* der plötzliche heftige Windstoß, die Bö (*Naut.*); sudden —s, plötzliche Windstöße. —**y**, *adj.* stürmisch, windig; —y weather, stürmisches, mit Böen vermischtes, Wetter.
[2]**Squall**, I. *v.n.* laut schreien, aufschreien. II. *s.* der laute Schrei, Aufschrei. —**er**, *s.* der Schreier, Schreihals.
Squam—ipennate, *adj.* mit schuppenartigen Federn. —**ous**, —**ose**, *adj.* schuppig.
Squander, *v.a.* verschwenden, verschleudern, vergeuden. —**er**, *s.* der Verschwender.
Square, I. *adj.*, —**ly**, *adv.* viereckig; Geviert=, Quadrat= (*foot, mile, etc.*); ehrlich (*fig.*); (suitable) genau passend, angemessen; quitt, gleich; abgeschlossen (*as accounts*); *see* —-built, —-set; — dealing, ehrliches Verfahren; — mile, die Quadratmeile; — number, die Quadratzahl; — pianoforte, tafelförmiges Klavier; — roof, das Winkeldach; — root, die Quadratwurzel; to make all —, alles in Richtigkeit bringen. II. *s.* das rechtwinklige, regelmäßige Viereck, Quadrat (*Geom.*); das Quadrat, die Quadratzahl (*Arith.*); der freie (von Häusern umgebene) Platz (*in a city*); die Säulenplatte (*Arch.*); der Winkel(haken), das Winkeleisen (*Carp.*, *etc.*); das Winkellineal (*Draw.*); das Karree (*Mil.*); die Scheibe (*of glass*); das Ebenmaß, Verhältnis, die Gleichheit, Ordnung (*fig.*); das Feld (*on a chess-board, etc.*); viereckiger Halsausschnitt (*in dresses*); on the —, ehrlich, geradezu, in Ordnung (*sl.*); hollow —, offenes Karree; *see* Quartile. III. *v.a.* vieren, viereckig machen; abvieren, vierkantig behauen (*timber*); ausgleichen (*an account*); zum Quadrat erheben, quadrieren (*a number, etc.*); auf den Winkel prüfen (*Carp.*, *etc.*); (adjust) einrichten, regeln; (suit) anpassen; to — one's shoulders, sich in die Brust werfen; to — a p., einen bestechen, auf seine Seite bringen. IV. *v.n.* passen, stimmen (with, zu). —**ness**, *s.* das Viereckige. *Comp.* —**-built**, —**-set**, *adj.* viereckig gebaut; vierschrötig (*fig.*). —**-faced**, *adj.* mit vierschrötigem Gesicht. —**-rigged**, *adj.* mit Raaen getakelt. —**-sail**, *s.* das Raasegel. —**-toes**, *s.* der altmodische, gezierte Mensch (*coll.*).
Squash, I. *s.* das Breiartige; der Quatsch; lemon —, die Zitronen=Limonade; (squash-rackets) eine Art Rackets=Spiel; zwanglose Abendgesellschaft (mit leichten Erfrischungen) (*sl.*). II. *v.a.* (zer)quetschen, weich schlagen. —**y**, *adj.* quatschig, weich und naß.
Squat, I. *v.n.* sich niedersetzen, niederkauern, hocken; (settle) sich auf fremdem Boden niederlassen. II. *adj.* kauernd, hockend; kurz und dick, stämmig (*as a figure*). —**ter**, *s.* der Hockende; der Ansiedler auf fremdem Grund und Boden.
Squaw, *s.* das Weib (der Indianer).
Squeak, I. *s.* das Geknarre, das Quieken. II. *v.n.* quieken (*as pigs*); knarren (*as a door, a wheel*); —ing pig, quiekendes Ferkel. —**er**, *s.* einer, der quiekt. —**y**, *adj.* quiekend.
Squeal, *v.n.* schreien, quieken (*as pigs*).
Squeamish, *adj.*, —**ly**, *adv.* ekel, Ekel empfindend; wählerisch, eigen, heikel, zimperlich (*fig.*); übertrieben ängstlich, gewissenhaft (*fig.*). —**ness**, *s.* das Gefühl des Unbehagens, Ekels, die Übelkeit, die übertriebene Empfindlichkeit, Zimperlichkeit, das wählerische Wesen.
Squeez—able, *adj.* zusammen=drückbar, =preßbar; dem Drucke nachgebend (*fig.*). —**e**, I. *s.* der Druck, die Quetschung; der kräftige Händedruck; (embrace) innige Umarmung. II. *v.a.* drücken, (aus)pressen; (crush) (be)drücken, drängen; (hug) in die Arme schließen; to —e **out**, auspressen; to —e **up**, zusammenpressen. III. *v.n.* dringen, drängen; to —e **through**, sich durchdrängen. —**er**, *s.* der Drücker, Presser; die Auspreßmaschine; lemon —er, die Zitronenpresse.
Squib, *s.* die Rakete, der Handschwärmer (*Firew.*); das Spottgedicht, Pasquill.
Squid, I. *s.* der Tintenfisch; der künstliche Köder, Angelhaken mit Köder. II. *v.n.* mit künstlichem Köder fischen.
Squill, *s.* die Meerzwiebel (*Bot.*, *Pharm.*).
Squint, I. *adj.* schielend. II. *s.* der schielende Blick; das Guckloch; der Blick (*fig.*). III. *v.n.* schielen. —**ing**, I. *adj.*, —**ingly**, *adv.* schielend. II. *s.* das Schielen. *Comp.* —**-eyed**, *adj.* schieläugig.
Squire, I. *s.* der Schildknappe (*obs.*); der Squire (*as a title*); der Gutsbesitzer, Rittergutsbesitzer; der Landjunker; der Friedensrichter (*Amer.*). II. *v.a.*; to — a lady, einer Dame den Hof machen. —**archy**, *s.* die Junkerherrschaft. —**en**, *s.* das (irische) Junkerchen, der kleine Gutsbesitzer.
Squirm, *v.n.* sich wie ein Wurm bewegen, sich winden, sich krümmen.
Squirrel, I. *s.* das Eichhörnchen. II. *attrib.*; — skin, das Eichhörnchenfell, Grauwerk.
Squirt, I. *s.* die Spritze. II. *v.a.* spritzen. III. *v.n.*; to — out, hervorsprudeln. *Comp.* —**ing-cucumber**, *s.* die Spritz=, Esels=gurke.
Stab, I. *s.* der Stich, Stoß; (wound) die (Stoß=) Wunde; hinterlistiger Streich (*fig.*). II. *v.a.* (run through) (durch)stechen; erstechen, erdolchen (*a person*); verwunden (*fig.*); it will — her to the heart, es wird ihr das Herz brechen. III. *v.n.* stechen. —**ber**, *s.* der Stecher; das Locheisen (*Saddl.*); der Pricker (*Naut.*).
Stab—ility, *s.* die Beständigkeit, Dauerhaftigkeit, Stabilität (*Phys. etc.*); die Standhaftigkeit (*fig.*). —**le**, I. *adj.* fest, dauerhaft, haltbar,

ſtark; (durable) beſtändig, ſtandhaft. II. *s.* der Stall. III. *v.a.* einſtallen. **—leness**, *see* —ility. **—ling**, *s.* die Einſtallung; (—le-room) die Stallung. **—lish**, *v.a.* feſt machen; *see* Establish. *Comp.* **—le-boy**, *s.* der Stalljunge. **—le-call**, *s.* das Signal zum Pferdeputzen (*Mil.*). **—le-door**, *s.* die Stalltür; to shut the —le-door when the horse is stolen, den Brunnen zudecken, wenn das Kind ertrunken iſt. **—le-keeper**, *s.* der Stallhalter; der Pferdeverleiher. **—le-man**, *s.* der Stallknecht. **—le-yard**, *s.* der Stallhof, Viehhof.

Stack, I. *s.* der Schober (*of hay, etc.*); der Stoß (*of wood*); die Schornſtein-reihe, -gruppe (*Build.*); — of arms, die Gewehrpyramide; — of bricks, der Stapel. II. *v.a.* aufſchichten, in Schober ſetzen (*hay, etc.*); aufſtapeln, aufſtellen (*arms, etc.*). *Comp.* **—-cover**, *s.* das Schoberdach. **—-yard**, *s.* der Hof für Schober.

Staddle, *s.* die Stütze, der Pfahl; (crutch) die Krücke. *Comp.* **—-roof**, *see* Stack-cover.

Stadtholder, *s.* der (Erb-)Statthalter. **—ship**, *s.* die Statthalterſchaft.

Staff, I. *s.* der Stab, Stock; (prop) die Stütze; die Notenlinien, das Notenſyſtem (*Mus.*); der Stab (*Mil., also of office*); medical — (of a hospital), das Ärztepersonal; (Army Med. Corps) die Militärärzte; editorial — (of a paper), die Schriftleitung (eines Blattes); the whole — of teachers, das ganze Lehrerkollegium, der Lehrkörper (einer Anſtalt); regimental —, der Regimentsſtab; officers of the —, Stabsoffiziere; ensign —, der Flaggenſtock (hinten am Schiff); flag—, der Flaggenſtock (am Topp der Maſten); — of life, das Brot. II. *v.a.* mit einem Stocke, Stabe verſehen; mit einem Beamtenkörper verſehen; the school is well —ed (under —ed), die Schule hat eine (keine) genügende Anzahl von Lehrern. *Comp.* **—-officer**, *s.* der Stabsoffizier. **—-surgeon**, *s.* der Stabsarzt.

Stag, *s.* der (Edel-)Hirſch; the — bellows, der Hirſch ſchreit *or* röhrt; the — sobs, der Hirſch klagt; warrantable —, 5jähriger Hirſch; das männliche junge Tier (*dial.*). **—gart**, *s.* 4jähriger Hirſch. *Comp.* **—-beetle**, *s.* der Hirſchkäfer. **—hound**, *s.* der Hetzhund zur Parforcejagd auf Rotwild (Hirſche). **—-hunt**, *s.* die Hirſchjagd.

Stage, *s.* das Gerüſt; die Bühne (*Theat.*); die (Poſt)Station (*on a journey*); die Etappe (*Mil.*); *see* —-coach; (degree of progress) der Fortgang, Verlauf; der Zuſtand, Grad, die Stufe, das Stadium (*of a disease, dramatic action, etc.*); to bring on the —, auf die Bühne bringen; to go off, leave the —, abtreten; to go on the —, Schauſpieler(in) werden; to be on the —, Schauſpieler(in) ſein; to have a clear —, freies Feld haben. **—r**, *s.;* old —r, erfahrener Mann, alter Praktikus. **—y, Stagy**, *adj.* theatraliſch. *Comp.* **—-box**, *s.* die Proſzeniumsloge. **—-coach**, *s.* der Poſtwagen, die Poſtkutſche, Landkutſche. **—-directions**, *pl.* Bühnenanweiſungen. **—-effect**, *s.* die Bühnenwirkung. **—-manager**, *s.* der Theaterdirektor. **—-practice**, *s.* die Theaterroutine. **—-property**, *s.* Theater-Requiſiten (*pl.*). **—-whisper**, *s.;* in a —-whisper, im Theaterflüſterton. **—-writer**, *s.* der Schauſpieldichter, Bühnenſchriftſteller.

Stagger, I. *v.n.* ſchwanken, taumeln, wanken; ſtutzen (*fig.*). II. *v.a.* wankend, ſtutzig machen; verblüffen. **—ing**, *adj.* wankend, taumelnd. **—s**, *pl.* der Schwindel (*of horses*); die Drehkrankheit (*of sheep*).

Stagna—ncy, *s.* die Stockung, das Stillſtehen. **—nt**, *adj.* (ſtill)ſtehend, ſtockend, ſtagnierend; flau (*C.L.*). **—te**, *v.a.* ſtillſtehen, ſtocken; flau ſein (*C.L.*). **—tion**, *s.* das Stillſtehen, die Stockung (*of the blood, water, etc.*); die Stockung, Flauheit (*of business*).

[1]**Staid**, *adj.*, **—ly**, *adv.* geſetzt, ruhig. **—ness**, *s.* die Geſetztheit, Ruhe.

[2]**Staid**, (*also* **Stayed**,) *imperf. & p.p. of* Stay.

Stain, I. *s.* der Fleck(en); der Flecken, Makel, Schandfleck (*fig.*). II. *v.a.* beflecken (*also fig.*); färben, bemalen; —ed glass, buntes Glas; —ed paper, buntes Papier; —ed windows, Fenſter mit (eingebrannten) Glasmalereien, bunte Fenſter; —ed wood, gebeiztes Holz. **—er**, *s.* der Färber, Farbenbeizer. **—ing**, *s.;* —ing of glass, die Glasmalerei. **—less**, *adj.* ohne Flecken, ungefleckt; unbefleckt, fleckenlos, makellos (*fig.*).

Stair, *s.* die Stufe, Staffel, der Tritt; (*flight of*) —s, die Treppe, Stiege; up one pair of —s, eine Treppe hoch; down —s, unten; herunter, hinunter; below —s, im Erdgeſchoß; go down —s, geh hinunter; up *or* above —s, oben; it is up —s, es iſt oben; bring it up —s, bringen Sie es herauf; high life below —s, das feine Leben der Dienſtboten (*hum.*). *Comp.* **—case**, *s.* das Treppenhaus; (—s) die Treppe; to live on the same —case, Zimmernachbarn ſein (*Univ.*); servants' *or* back-—cases, Nebentreppen, Hintertreppen. **—-carpet**, *s.* der Treppenläufer. **—-landing**, *s.* der Treppenabſatz. **—-rod**, *s.* die Läuferſtange.

Stake, I. *s.* die Stange, der (kleine) Pfahl; der Abſteckſtab, die Abſteckſtange (*Surv.*); (martyr's —) der Märtyrerpfahl; das Märtyrertum (*fig.*); der Einſatz (*in gaming*); das Spiel; to be at —, auf dem Spiele ſtehen; to have at —, auf dem Spiele ſtehen haben, zu verlieren haben; he has no — in the country, er hat keine Intereſſen in dem Lande. II. *v.a.* bepfählen; umpfählen (*ground, etc.*); (pierce) mit einem Pfahle durchbohren; zum Pfande ſetzen (one's honour, ſeine Ehre); (ein)ſetzen (*at play*); aufs Spiel ſetzen, wagen (*fig.*); to — out, abſtecken, abpfählen.

Stal—actite, *s.* der Tropfſtein, (Kalk-)Sinter. **—actitic**, *adj.* tropfſteinartig. **—agmite**, *s.* der Stalagmit, von unten nach oben wachſende Tropfſteinart.

[1]**Stale**, *adj.* ſchal, matt, abgeſtanden (*of beer, etc.*); hart, altbacken (*bread*); verlegen (*merchandise*); abgenutzt, ſtumpf, veraltet (*fig.*); — news, veraltete Neuigkeiten; to grow —, alt werden, abgelagert ſein; den Reiz der Neuheit verlieren (*fig.*). **—ness**, *s.* die Schalheit, Abgenutztheit.

[2]**Stale**, *s.*, **—mate**, I. *s.* das Patt (*Chess*). II. *v.a.* patt ſetzen *or* machen.

[3]**Stale**, I. *v.n.* ſtallen, harnen (*of horses, etc.*). II. *s.* der Harn (*of horses, etc.*).

[4]**Stale**, (*obs.*) *imperf. of* Steal.

[1]**Stalk**, I. *s.* der Stengel, Stiel; der Halm (*of corn*). **—ed**, *adj.* ſtielig. **—less**, *adj.* ſtiellos. **—y**, *adj.* ſtengelartig.

[2]**Stalk**, I. *v.n.* heimlich gehen, ſich vorſichtig heranſchleichen; ſich anpirſchen (an Wild); hinter einem (Verſteck-)Pferde hergehen; ſtolz einherſchreiten. II. *v.a.* beſchleichen (*game*). III. *s.* das Heranſchleichen, Beſchleichen; der große, weite, ſtolze Schritt. **—er**, *s.* der Einherſchreitende; deer —er, der Pirſchjäger. *Comp.* **—ing-horse**, *s.* das Verſteckpferd (für den lauernden Jäger); der Deckmantel (*fig.*).

Stall, I. *s.* der (Pferde-)Stand (*in a stable, etc.*); der Verkaufsſtand, die Marktbude; der Stiftsherrnſtuhl, erhöhte Kirchenſtuhl (*Eccl.*); der Sperrſitz, Parkettſitz (*Theat.*); to keep a —, an einem Stand feil halten; book-—, Bücher(verkaufs-)ſtand; finger-—, der Fingerling. II. *v.a.* einſtallen. **—age**, *s.* die Standgerechtigkeit; (— rent) das Standgeld, der Budenzins. **—ion**, *s.* der Zuchthengſt. *Comp.* **—-fed**, *adj.* im Stalle gefüttert, gemäſtet. **—-feed**, *ir.v.a.* mäſten.

Stalwart, *adj.* ſtark, kräftig, handfeſt.

Stam—en, *s.* der Staubfaden (*Bot.*). **—ina**, I. *pl. see* —en. II. *s.* der Urſtoff; die Haupt-ſtärke, -ſtütze; die Ausdauer (*fig.*). **—inal**, *adj.* die Staubgefäße betreffend. **—iniferous**, *adj.* Staubgefäße tragend, ſtaubfädentragend; **—iniferous flower**, männliche Blüte.

Stammer, I. *v.n.* stammeln, stottern. II. *s.* das Stammeln, Stottern. **—er**, *s.* der Stotterer, Stammler. **—ing**, *adj.*, **—ingly**, *adv.* stammelnd, stotternd.

Stamp, I. *s.* das Stampfen (*with the foot*); (mark) der Stempel; der Pochstempel (*Mining*); das Gepräge (*on a coin, etc.*); (postage —) die (Brief-)Marke, das Postwertzeichen; (—ing tool) der Stempel; (character) die Art, der Schlag, Charakter; a man of his —, ein Mann seines Schlages; a man of the old —, ein Mann von altem Schrot und Korn; of the right —, von gutem Schlage, unverfälscht; to bear the — of, das Gepräge tragen; adhesive —, gummiertes Postwertzeichen. II. *v.a.* stampfen; stempeln; prägen, münzen (*money*); stampfen (*ore*); drucken (*cloths, etc.*); to — on one's memory, dem Gedächtnisse einprägen; that —ed him in my eyes, das charakterisierte ihn in meinen Augen; to — out, austreten (*a fire*); ausrotten (*fig.*); to — out a revolt, einen Aufstand gewaltsam unterdrücken. **—ede**, I. *s.* die plötzliche Furcht, welche Herden auf den Prairien erfaßt; wilde Flucht. II. *v.n.* durchgehen (*of mules, horses*). **—er**, *s.* der Stampfer; der Stempel. *Comp.* **—-act**, *s.* die Stempelakte. **—-duty**, *s.* die Stempelsteuer, -abgabe. **—ing-mill**, *s.* das Pochwerk. **—ing-press**, *s.* das Präg(e)werk. **—-office**, *s.* das Stempelamt.

Stanch, I. *v.a.* hemmen, stillen (*blood*). II. *adj.* (*often spelt* Staunch) wasserdicht; dicht, fest, tüchtig; zuverlässig, standhaft, treu. **—er**, *s.* das Hemmende, das blutstillende Mittel. **—ion**, I. *s.* die Stütze, der Pfosten, Pfeiler; die Fensterstange, der Gitterstab. II. *v.a.* an einen Pfosten binden. **—less**, *adj.* unstillbar; unersättlich (*fig.*). **—ness**, **Staunchness**, *s.* die Dichtigkeit, Festigkeit, gute Beschaffenheit; die Treue, Standhaftigkeit, Zuverlässigkeit (*fig.*).

Stand, I. *ir.v.n.* stehen; als Kandidat auftreten (für), sich bewerben (um) (*Parl., etc.*); (be) sein, sich befinden, gelegen sein; (last) dauern, sich halten; (persist) bestehen, beharren; (not move) stehen bleiben, stillstehen; steuern, segeln (*Naut.*); (stagnate) stocken, nicht fließen; he —s about 5 feet 10 inches, er ist etwa 5 Fuß 10 Zoll groß; the house —s by itself, das Haus steht allein; to — fast, feststehen; to — first, zuerst kommen, obenan stehen; to — a p.'s friend, einen unterstützen, sich als Freund gegen einen beweisen; to — godfather to, Gevatter stehen (zu einem Kinde), (ein Kind) über die Taufe heben; to — good, gültig sein; the enemy will not —, der Feind wird nicht stand halten; to know how matters —, die Lage der Dinge kennen; to — **about**, umherstehen; to — **against**, bestehen gegen, (einem) widerstehen; to — **aloof**, sich fernhalten; to — **aside**, auf die Seite treten, aus dem Wege gehen; to — **back**, zurücktreten; to — **between**, dazwischen stehen (*lit.*); die Mittelsperson abgeben (*fig.*); to — **by**, dabei stehen *or* sein (*lit.*); (einem) zur Seite stehen, beistehen (*fig.*); stehen bleiben bei (*Naut.*); to — **for**, als Kandidat auftreten *or* sich als Kandidaten aufstellen lassen für (*a borough, etc.*); (denote) bedeuten, anzeigen; (steer towards) zu-steuern, -segeln; to — **forth**, hervortreten, sich zeigen; to — **in**, stehen in; (be in) da sein; tears stood in her eyes, Tränen standen ihr in den Augen; to — in awe, danger, dread of, in Furcht sein, in Gefahr schweben vor, Angst haben vor; to — in (good) stead, zu statten kommen, nützlich sein; to — in stead of, dienen als; to — in need (of a th., eine S.) nötig haben bedürfen; to — in a p.'s way, einem im Wege stehen; to — in for, (das Land ꝛc.) antun (*Naut.*); to — **off**, abstehen, sich entfernt halten (von), zurücktreten (von); to — off from the shore, seewärts anliegen; we stood off the Cape of Good Hope, wir waren auf der Höhe des Vorgebirges der guten Hoffnung; — off! weg da! to — **on**, fußen auf (*dat.*); to — on end, zu Berge stehen (*as hair*), aufrechtstehen; to — on record, als bemerkenswert aufgezeichnet sein; to — **out**, heraus-, hervor-stehen, hervorragen; (hold out) aushalten, standhalten (against, gegen), nicht nachgeben, bestehen (for, auf, *dat.*); rückständig sein; he —s out, er sticht hervor, steht uns vor Augen; to — out to sea, die See halten, auf die hohe See fahren; to — **over**, liegen *or* aufgeschoben bleiben (*as a case, etc.*); to — **to**, bleiben bei, beharren bei; he still —s to it that, er bleibt noch immer dabei, daß; to — to a p., einen unterstützen (*coll.*); it —s to reason that . . ., es ist natürlich *or* selbstverständlich, daß . . ., es leuchtet ein, daß . . .; they stood to their guns, sie hielten sich schießbereit; sie blieben ihrer Fahne treu; sie hielten an ihrer Ansicht fest (*fig.*); — to the guns! an die Geschütze! (*Mil.*); to — **together**, neben einander bestehen; übereinstimmen; to — **up**, aufstehen (*from a seat, etc.*), sich aufrichten; to — up against, bekämpfen, sich erheben wider; to — up for, verteidigen; to — up to, es aufnehmen mit; to — **upon**, stehen auf (*dat.*); (insist) bestehen auf (*dat.*); to — upon one's guard (defence), auf seiner Hut sein, (sich verteidigen); to — upon ceremony, Umstände machen; he has not a leg to — upon, er hat keine Ausflucht mehr (*fig.*); to — well **with** s.o., gut mit einem stehen. II. *ir.v.a.* aushalten, ertragen, leiden; stellen, lehnen; do not — bicycles against this wall, Fahrräder dürfen nicht gegen diese Wand gestellt *or* gelehnt werden; to — fire, das Feuer aushalten; to teach a horse to — fire, ein Pferd an das Feuer gewöhnen; to — one's ground, seinen Platz behaupten; to — a p. a dinner, einem ein Mittagessen spendieren (*sl.*); I shan't — such goings on, ein solches Verfahren dulde ich nicht (*coll.*); he could not — it any longer, er konnte es nicht mehr aushalten; there's no —ing his impudence, seine Unverschämtheit ist unerträglich; to — the test, die Probe bestehen. III. *s.* der Stand, das Stehen; (post) der Standpunkt, Posten, die Stelle; (pause) der Stillstand; (resistance) der Widerstand; die Tribüne, das Holzgerüst (*for spectators*); der Ständer, Untersetzer, das Gestell (*for things to stand on*); (stall) die Bude, der Krämerstand; der Untersatz (*for a dish, etc.*); das Stativ (*for a microscope, etc.*); das Regal (*Typ.*); der Verschlag (*in a stable, etc.*); — of arms, das Gewehr mit allem Dazugehörigen; vollständige Ausrüstung; candle —, der Leuchterstuhl; folding —, zusammenlegbarer (Musik-)Ständer, das Notenpult; — for bottles (casks), Flaschenständer, (Tonnengestell); to make a —, Halt machen (*lit.*); Widerstand leisten, sich widersetzen (*fig.*). **—ard**, I. *s.* die Standarte, Fahne; der freistehende hochstämmige (rose, Rosenbaum-)Stamm, (fruit-tree, Obst-)Baum (*Hort.*); der Pfosten, die Riegelsäule (*Carp.*); das aufrechte Fenstereisen (*Build.*); der Ständer (*of mills, machinery, etc.*); (—ard value) feste, beständige Valuta; (—ard price) der Normalpreis; (—ard measure) das Normal-, Eich-maß, der Eichstab; der Maßstab, die Richtschnur; der Münzfuß, die Währung (*Mint.*); above (below) —ard, übergut (geringhaltig); is the —ard (*of an examination*) high? sind die Anforderungen hoch?; his —ard is not a high one, er hat kein hohes Ideal; —ard of living, die Lebenshaltung, Lebensführung, das Lebensideal; —ard of value, der Wert-Regulator. II. *adj.* musterhaft, maßgebend, Normal-; —ard author, maßgebender Schriftsteller, Klassiker; —ard gauge, die Spurlehre (*Railw.*), Normallehre; —ard gold, das Probegold; —ard lamp, aufrecht stehende Lampe; —ard measure, das Normalmaß; —ard rose, hochstämmige Rose; —ard weight, das Normalgewicht; —ard works (books), Musterwerke, klassische Werke. **—er**, *s.*; —er-by, der Dabeistehende. **—ing**, I. *adj.*

stehend (*of water; of an army*); stehend, haltbar (*as colours*); fest, bestimmt (*as an order*); (lasting) bleibend; —ing committee, der stehende Ausschuß; —ing corn, Getreide auf dem Halme; a —ing danger, eine dauernde, bleibende, ewige Gefahr; —ing dish, das stehende, gewöhnliche Gericht; —ing joke, der Meidinger; —ing orders, die Geschäftsordnung (*Parl.*); a —ing puzzle, eine immer wiederkehrende schwierige Frage. II. *s.* das Stehen; (—ing place) der Stand, Posten; *see* Stall; (post) die Stelle; (rank) der Rang, Stand, die Würde; der bewährte Ruf; there is no —ing here, hier kann man nicht bleiben; our friendship is of 10 years' —ing, unsere Freundschaft besteht (nun schon) seit 10 Jahren; of long —ing, von lange(r Zeit) her, alt; a weighty question of long —ing, eine wichtige längst aufgeworfene Frage; the —ing of a commercial house, der (bewährte) Ruf eines Handelshauses. *Comp.* **—ard-bearer,** *s.* der Fähn(d)rich, Fahnenträger, Standartenträger. **—ing-room,** *s.* der Stehplatz. **—still,** *s.* das Stillstehen; to be at a —still, stocken; (be perplexed) in Verlegenheit sein; to come to a —still, ins Stocken kommen, anhalten, stehen bleiben. **—-up,** *adj.;* —-up collar, der Stehkragen; —-up fight, regelrechter Kampf.

Stang, (*obs.*) *imperf. & p.p. of* Sting.

Stank, (*obs.*) *imperf. & p.p. of* Stink.

Stann—ate, *s.* zinnsaures Salz. **—ic,** *adj.;* —ic acid, der Zinnsäure.

Stanza, *s.* die Strophe. **—ic,** *adj.* aus Strophen bestehend.

[1]Staple, I. *s.* das Haupterzeugnis (*of a country*); (thread) der Stapel; die Beschaffenheit (of land, des Landes); der Hauptgegenstand (*fig.*). II. *adj.* bestimmt, im Handel hergebracht; Stapel=; — commodities, Stapelwaren. **—r,** *s.* der (wool-, Woll=)Händler.

[2]Staple, *s.* die Krampe, der Riegelhaken.

Star, I. *s.* der Stern (*also Typ.*), das Gestirn (*Astr.*); (fate) der Stern, das Geschick; der (die) große Künstler(in), Schauspieler(in), die Kraft ersten Ranges, der Virtuos; (decoration) der Ordensstern; the —s and stripes, das Sternenbanner (der nordamerikanischen Union); to thank one's —s that . . ., sich glücklich schätzen, daß . . .; my — has set, mein Glücksstern ist untergegangen. II. *v.a.* besternen; — it, (*or* III. *v.n.*) glänzen, figurieren; Gastrollen geben (*Theat.*). **—less,** *adj.* sternenlos. **—like,** *adj.* sternengleich. **—red,** *adj.* besternt. **—riness,** *s.* die Sternenhelle. **—ring,** *s.* das Gastspielgeben, =reisen; —ring tour, die Gastspielreise. **—ry,** *adj.* sternenhell, Sternen=; —ry sky, gestirnter Himmel. *Comp.* **—-Chamber,** *s.* die Sternkammer; der heimliche Gerichtshof (*fig.*). **—fish,** *s.* der Seestern. **—-gazer,** *s.* der Sterngucker, Astrolog. **—-gazing,** *s.* das Sterngucken. **—light,** I. *s.* das Sternenlicht. II. *adj.*, **—lit,** *adj.* sternenhell. **—-spangled,** *adj.* sternbesät.

Starboard, I. *s.* das Steuerbord. II. *v.t.;* — the helm! Ruder am Steuerbord!

Starch, I. *s.* die Stärke; das Steife (*fig.*); das Stärkemehl (*Chem.*). II., **—y,** *adj.*, **—ily,** *adv.* steif, förmlich; stärkehaltig. III. *v.a.* stärken. **—ed,** *see* — II. **—er,** *s.* der Stärkende. **—iness,** *s.* die Stiefheit. *Comp.* **—-flour,** *s.* das Stärkemehl.

Star—e, I. *s.* das Starren, der Starrblick. II. *v.n.* starren, stieren; (—e with surprise) große Augen machen; to —e at, anstarren. III. *v.a.* starren; to —e out of countenance, durch Anstarren aus der Fassung bringen; to —e a p. in the face, einem vor Augen stehen; death —ed the men in the face, die Männer hatten den Tod vor Augen; failure —ed him in the face, er sah sein Verderben deutlich vor sich. **—er,** *s.* der Anstarrer, Anstauner. **—ing,** *adj.*, **—ingly,** *adv.* starrend, stier.

Stark, *adj. & adv.* steif; völlig; — mad, rein toll, ganz verrückt; — naked, splitternakt.

[1]Starling, *s.* der Star.

[2]Starling, *s.* das Pfeilerhaupt, der Eisbrecher.

Start, I. *v.n.* (auf)springen; auslaufen, ansetzen, anrennen (*on a race*); abgehen (*as a carriage*); aufbrechen, abreisen, sich auf den Weg machen (*on a journey*); (set out) ausgehen, beginnen (*fig.*); (move suddenly) sich schnell, plötzlich bewegen; zusammenfahren, auffahren, aufschrecken, aufspringen (*in alarm, etc.*); (— back) zurückfahren, =springen; (— forward) fort=, vorwärts=schießen; (— up) sich plötzlich erheben, auffahren, aufsteigen, plötzlich entstehen; (wince, shrink) stutzen, erbeben (at, bei), stutzig werden (at, vor); (— aside) abspringen, abweichen; to — in the world, eine Laufbahn beginnen; we are at the very spot we —ed **from,** wir sind auf demselben Flecke, von welchem wir ausgingen; capital to — **with,** ein Kapital zum Anfange(n). II. *v.a.* hervortreiben; auf=jagen, =treiben (*game*); aufrufen (*spirits*); gründen, anfangen (*a business*); erregen, hervorrufen, anfangen (*a quarrel*); in Gang bringen, anlassen (*machinery*); verziehen (*a sinew*); vor=, auf=bringen (*a theory, etc.*); aufwerfen (*a question*); auf die Bahn bringen (*a subject, etc.*); machen (a project, einen Anschlag; an objection, einen Einwurf); anbieten (*at auctions*); *see* —le. III. *s.* der Sprung, Satz, Ruck; das Auffahren, Stutzen (*from fright, etc.*); der Anfang, Anlauf (*of a race, etc.*); (commencement) der Anfang; der Vorsprung, Vorzug (*fig.*); der Aufbruch (*on a journey, etc.*); by fits and —s, ruckweise, sprungweise; to get the — of a p., einem den Vorsprung abgewinnen, einem zuvorkommen; he received 200 points —, er erhielt 200 vorgegeben; *see* Up—. **—er,** *s.* der Anreger, Urheber, einer, der vor=, auf=bringt; der Auftreiber (*of game, etc.*); derjenige, der das Zeichen zum Ablaufen der Pferde giebt (*Rac.*); das mitrennende Pferd (*Rac.*). **—ing,** *s.* das Ablaufen; at —ing, beim Ablauf, am Anfang. **—le,** *v.a.* (unangenehm) überraschen; (alarm) erschrecken, in Furcht setzen. **—ling,** *adj.* erschreckend, ergreifend; Aufsehen erregend. *Comp.* **—ing-place,** *s.* der Ausgangsort, Aufbruchsplatz. **—ing-point,** *s.* der Ausgangspunkt.

Starv—ation, *s.* das Verhungern. **—e,** *v.* I. *n.* verhungern, Hunger leiden. II. *a.* verhungern lassen, aushungern; to —e a p. to death, einen Hungers sterben lassen; to —e **into,** durch Hunger dazu bringen, zwingen zu; to —e **out,** aushungern. **—eling,** I. *s.* das (die) ausgehungerte Tier (Pflanze); der Hungerleider. II. *adj.* hungrig, ausgehungert. **—ing,** *p.;* —ing system, die Hungerkur.

State, I. *s.* der Zustand; der Stand (*of a question*); die Lage (*of affairs*); (political body) der Staat, das Reich, Gemeinwesen; (civil power) die Regierung; (pomp) die Pracht, der Pomp, Staat, Gepränge; (rank) der Stand, Rang; (dignity) die Würde; the — of affairs, die Sachlage, Lage der Dinge; die Geschäftslage (*C.L.*); the — of his health, sein Gesundheitszustand; no — with me! keine Umstände mit mir! to be in a —, sehr aufgeregt sein; to live in great —, großen Staat machen; to lie in —, auf dem Paradebette liegen; chair of —, der Prachtsessel; in a — of nature, im Naturzustande, nackt; affair of —, die Staats=sache, =angelegenheit; Secretary of —, der Staatssekretär; der (englische) Minister; Secretary of — for Foreign Affairs, der Minister des Äußeren. II. *v.a.* angeben, erklären, aussagen, erwähnen, darlegen, auseinandersetzen, melden; aufstellen (*one's views, a proposition in Euclid, etc., a rule, etc.*). **—d,** I. *p.p.;* as —d, wie erwähnt; angeblich. II. *adj.* bestimmt, fest; (regular) regelmäßig; —d salary, festes Gehalt. **—liness,** *s.* die Stattlichkeit, Hoheit; (dignity) die Würde, vornehmes Wesen; (pomp) die Pracht, das Gepränge. **—ly,** *adj.* stattlich;

würdevoll; prächtig; (elevated) erhaben. —ment, s. die Darstellung, Auseinandersetzung, Darlegung; (narrative) die Erzählung; (account) die Angabe, Aussage; (report) der Bericht, die Berichterstattung; die Aufstellung (*of facts, of the balance, etc.*); (specification) das Verzeichnis; (—ment of prices) die Preisliste; der Tarif (*of duties*); die Aufstellung (*of a proposition*); der Ansatz, die Anordnung (*of an account, etc.*); —ment of account-current, der Rechnungsabschluß. —**s**, *pl.* die (Land=)Stände; United —s, die Vereinigten Staaten von Nord=Amerika. *Comp.* —**craft**, *s.* die Politik, Staats=klugheit. —-**criminal**, *s.* der Staatsverbrecher. —-**papers**, *pl.* Staats=akten, =papiere. —-**prisoner**, *s.* der Staatsgefangene. —-**prosecution**, —-**trial**, *s.* der Staatsprozeß. —-**room**, *s.* das Staatszimmer; die Kajüte für Passagiere (*Naut.*). —**s-General**, *s.* General=staaten. —**sman**, *s.* der Staatsmann, Diplomat; our —smen, unsere Staatsmänner. —**s-manlike**, *adj.* staatsmännisch. —**smanship**, *s.* die Staatsmannskunst.

Stat—e, *see* State. —**ic**, *adj.* statisch. —**ics**, *s.* die Gleichgewichtslehre, Statik. —**ion**, *see* Station. —**ist**, *s.* der Staatsmann (*obs.*); der Statistiker. —**istic(al)**, *adj.* zahlenmäßig erwiesen, statistisch. —**istician**, *s.* der Statistiker. —**istics**, *s.* die Statistik, zahlenmäßige Nachweisung.

Station, I. *s.* der Stand; (situation) die Stelle; (position) die Stellung; die Station (*Mil., Naut., Railw., R. C.*); (rank) der Stand, Rang; (—-house) der Bahnhof (*Railw.*); (stopping-place) die Station, der Stand(ort), Aufenthalts=ort; der (scheinbare Still=)Stand (*Astr.*); der Stand=, Stütz=punkt (*Surv.*); der Amtsort, Posten (*in India*); die Garnison (*in India, Mil.*). II. *v.a.* aufstellen, postieren; to be —ed, postiert sein; leben, sich aufhalten. —**al**, *adj.* eine Stelle betreffend. —**ary**, *adj.* stillstehend (*also Astr. & fig.*); bleibend, feststehend, stationär (*Mach., etc.*); —ary engine, eine stillstehende (Dampf=)Maschine, die Lokomobile; to be —ary, unbeweglich auf der Stelle bleiben, sich nicht vom Platze rühren *or* bewegen; to remain —ary, nicht weiter kommen. —**er**, *s.* der Papier=, Schreibwaren=händler; —er's Hall, die Buch=händlerbörse. —**ery**, *s.* Schreibwaren, Papier= und Papp=waren. *Comp.* —-**house**, *s.* die Polizeiwache; das Bahnhofsgebäude. —-**master**, *s.* der Stationsvorsteher.

Statu—ary, I. *s.* die Bildhauerkunst; (sculptor) der Bildhauer; Bildhauerarbeiten, Standbilder, Statuen. II. *adj.* Statuen=; —ary marble, der Bildsäulenmarmor. —**e**, *s.* die Bildsäule, das Standbild, die Statue. —**esque**, *adj.* bildsäulenartig. —**ette**, *s.* kleine Statue, das Stand=bildchen, die Statuette. —**re**, *s.* die Leibesgröße, Statur, der Wuchs. —**s**, *s.* der Zustand, die Stellung, Lage; the —s of newspapers, die anerkannte Stellung der Presse. —**te**, *s.* das Statut, (Grund=, Landes=)Gesetz, die Verordnung, Satzung; —te of limitations, Verjährungsgesetz. —**tory**, *adj.* gesetzlich, statutarisch; —tory holidays, staatlich freie Tage. *Comp.* —**e-founder**, *s.* der Bildgießer. —**te-book**, *s.* das geschriebene Landrecht, das Verordnungs=recht. —**te-labour**, *s.* der Frondienst. —**te-law**, *s.* das Landrecht, positive Recht.

Staunch, *see* Stanch.

Staurolite, *s.* der Kreuzstein, Staurolit.

Stave, I. *s.* die Faßdaube; der Stab (*Metre, Music*). II. *ir.v.a.;* to — **in**, einschlagen; to — **off**, abhalten, abwehren; aufschieben, verzögern. —**s**, *pl. see* Staff.

[1]**Stay**, I. *v.n.* stehen bleiben; bleiben, verweilen, sich aufhalten (*at a place*); to come to —, sich einbürgern; to — **away**, wegbleiben; to — for a p., auf einen warten; to — **in**, zu Hause bleiben; to — **to** dinner, zum Mittagessen bleiben; to — **up**, aufbleiben. II. *v.a.* zurückhalten, hemmen; (support) aufrecht halten, (unter)stützen; stillen (*hunger*); abwarten (*supper, etc.*). III. *s.* das Bleiben, Verweilen, der Aufenthalt; (prop) die Stütze (*fig.*). —**s**, *pl.* das Korsett. *Comp.* —-**at-home**, I. *s.* der Stubenhocker, der in der Heimat Bleibende. II. *adj.* häuslich, solid. —-**busk**, *s.* das Blankscheit. —-**lace**, *s.* das Schnürband. —-**maker**, *s.* der (die) Korsett=macher(in).

[2]**Stay**, I. *s.* das Stag, das (dicke) Tau (zur Befestigung des Mastes); das Stütztau (*of a telegraph pole, etc.*); der Steg (*of an anchor-chain*). —**s**, *pl.;* in —s, in der Wendung (*Naut.*); to miss —s, die Wendung versagen, das Wenden versehen (*Naut.*). II. *v.a.* (einen Mast) stagen; (ein Schiff) in den Wind bringen. III. *v.n.* wenden (*Naut.*). *Comp.* —-**sail**, *s.* das Stag=segel.

Stead, *s.* die Statt, Stelle, Stätte; in — of, anstatt, statt; in — of him, anstatt seiner, statt seiner; in — of writing, statt zu schreiben; it stood me in good —, es kam mir wohl zu statten. —**fast**, *adj.*, —**fastly**, *adv.* fest, unentwegt, standhaft; unverwandt (*look*). —**fastness**, *s.* die Festigkeit, Stetigkeit, Beständigkeit, Pflichttreue. —**iness**, *s.* die Festigkeit (*also fig.*); —iness of mind, fester Sinn. —**y**, I. *adj.*, —**ily**, *adv.* fest; fest, standhaft, beständig (*fig.*); (respectable) solid, gesetzt; beständig, fest (*as prices, the wind, etc.*); —y friendship, beständige treue Freundschaft; with —y toil, mit anhaltender Mühe; is the table —y? steht der Tisch fest? II. *v.a.* fest, sicher machen; zur Vernunft bringen (*a person*). III. *v.n.* fest werden; eine feste Stellung behaupten.

Steak, *s.* die (gebratene *or* zu bratende) Fleisch=schnitte; das Beefsteak.

Steal, *ir.v.* I. *a.* stehlen (*also fig.*), entwenden; to — a march upon (a p.); (einem) zuvorkommen, unvermerkt einen Vorsprung abgewinnen; to — a glance, einen verstohlenen Blick tun. II. *n.* stehlen; (slip) schleichen; to — **away**, — **off**, sich wegstehlen; to — **behind** s.o., sich hinter einen schleichen; to — **into**, sich einschleichen in; to — **upon**, beschleichen, überfallen. —**er**, *s.* der Dieb. —**ing**, *s.* das Stehlen. —**th**, *s.* die heimliche List, Heimlichkeit; by —th, verstohlenerweise. —**thily**, *adv.*, —**thy**, *adv.* verstohlen, heimlich. —**thiness**, *s.* die Heimlichkeit.

Steam, I. *s.* der Dampf; (fume) der Dunst. II. *v.n.* dampfen (*also fig.*). III. *v.a.* aus=dünsten; im Dampfe kochen, dämpfen (*Cook.*); dekatieren (*cloth*). —**er**, *s. see* —boat, —ship; der Dampfkochtopf. —**iness**, *s.* der dunstartige Zustand, die Dunstigkeit. —**y**, *adj.* dampfig, dunstig, feucht. *Comp.* (*gen'lly* = Dampf=). —**boat**, *s.* das Dampfboot. —-**engine**, *s.* die Dampfmaschine; die Lokomotive (*Railw.*). —-**launch**, *s.* die Dampfpinasse. —-**laundry**, *s.* die Dampfwaschanstalt. —-**lift**, —-**hoist**, *s.* der Dampfaufzug. —-**navigation(-company)**, *s.* die Dampfschifffahrts(=Gesellschaft). —-**plough**, *s.* der Dampfpflug. —-**roller**, *s.* die Dampfwalze. —**ship**, *s.* das Dampfschiff, der Dampfer. —-**tug**, *s.* der Schleppdampfer.

Steari—c, *adj.* Stearin=. —**n**, I. *s.* das Stearin. II. *attrib.;* —n candle, die Stearinkerze.

Steed, *s.* das Roß, Streitroß, Schlachtroß.

Steel, I. *s.* der Stahl (*also fig.*); true as —, echt wie Gold; cast —, der Gußstahl. II. *adj.* stählern, stahlartig; — pen, die Stahlfeder. III. *v.a.* (ver)stählen; stählen, verhärten (*fig.*). —**y**, *adj.* stählern, stahlhart. *Comp.* —-**clad**, *adj.* stahlbepanzert. —-**engraver**, *s.* der Stahl=stecher. —-**engraving**, *s.* die Stahlstecherkunst; der Stahlstich. —-**plated**, *adj.* stahlplattiert. —-**topped**, *adj.;* —-topped rail, die Stahlkopf=schiene (*Rail.*).

Steelyard, *s.* die Schnellwage, Balkenwage.

[1]**Steep**, I. *adj.*, **—ly**, *adv.* steil, jäh, abschüssig. II. *s.* jäher Abhang. **—ness**, *s.* die Steilheit.

[2]**Steep**, I. *s.* das Weichwasser; die Lauge, Beuche (*for clothes*); das Bad (*Dyer*); die Röste (*for flax*); to put the clothes in —, die Wäsche in die Lauge einwerfen. II. *v.a.* einweichen (*Brew.*), (dip in) eintauchen, tunken; wässern, rösten (*flax*).

Steeple, *s.* der Kirchturm, Glockenturm. *Comp.* **—-chase**, *s.* das Hindernisrennen.

[1]**Steer**, *s.* der junge verschnittene Ochs.

[2]**Steer**, *v.a. & n.* steuern, lenken, leiten, führen; to — (one's course) by, seine Fahrt richten auf (*acc.*) *or* nach. **—able**, *adj.* lenkbar. **—age**, I. *s.* die Steuerung, Lenkung; das Zwischendeck. II. *attrib.*; —age passenger, der Zwischendecks=passagier. **—ing**, *s.* die Steuermannskunst. *Comp.* **—age-way**, *s.* die Steuer=kraft, =macht. **—ing-wheel**, *s.* das Steuerrad. **—sman**, *s.* der Steuermann.

Steganography, *s.* die Geheimschreibekunst.

Stell—ar, *adj.* Sternen= (regions, etc., =regionen ꝛc.); *see* Starry. **—ate**, *adj.* sternig, sternförmig; —ate flower, die Strahlenblume. **—ular**, *adj.* sternchenförmig, wie Sternchen.

[1]**Stem**, I. *s.* der Stamm (*of a tree*); der Stengel, Stiel (*of a plant, fruit*); der Stamm (*of a family, of a word*); der Notenschwanz (*Mus.*); der Grundstrich (*Typ.*). II. *v.a.* abstengeln, vom Stengel befreien.

[2]**Stem**, *s.* der Vordersteven; der Schiffsschnabel, das Schiffsvorderteil (*Naut.*); from — to stern, vom Vorder= bis zum Hintersteven, von vorn bis hinten.

[3]**Stem**, *v.a.* stemmen, eindämmen, zurückstauen (*water*); aufhalten, hemmen, zurückdrängen (*fig.*); to — the tide, den Strom totsegeln (*Naut.*); to — the tide of misfortune, dem einbrechenden Unglück Halt gebieten.

Stench, *s.* der Gestank. **—y**, *adj.* stinkend (*obs.*).

Stencil, I. *s.* (—-plate) die Schablone, Patrone. II. *v.a.* mit Schablonen, Patronen malen ꝛc.

Stenograph, I. *s.* das Stenogramm. II. *v.a.* in Schnellschrift schreiben, mit Kurzschrift nachschreiben, stenographieren. **—er**, *s.* der Stenograph. **—ic**, *adj.* kurzschriftlich, in Kurzschrift, stenographisch. **—y**, *s.* die Kurzschrift, Schnellschrift, Stenographie.

[1]**Step**, I. *s.* der Schritt (*also fig.*), Tritt; (foot—) die Fußstapfe; die Stufe, Staffel (*of stairs, etc.*); die Sprosse (*of a ladder*); die Türschwelle (*at a door*); der Wagentritt (*of a carriage*); eine kurze Strecke; to bend one's —s to, seine Schritte lenken nach; to make, take a —, einen Schritt tun; to make a false —, einen Fehltritt tun; — by —, Schritt für Schritt. II. *v.n.* schreiten; (walk) gehen, treten; to — **after**, (einem) folgen, hinter einem herschreiten; to — **aside**, bei Seite treten, ausweichen; to — **back**, zurücktreten; to — **down**, hinuntergehen; to — **forth**, hervortreten; to — **forward**, vor=treten, =schreiten; to — **in**, hinein=gehen, =treten; to — **into**, treten in (*acc.*); (get) gelangen zu; to — **out**, hinaustreten; lange Schritte machen; to — **up**, hinaufgehen, heraufkommen; to — up to a p., auf einen zugehen, zutreten. III. *v.a.* (pace) abschreiten; einsetzen (*a mast*). **—ping**, *s.* das Schreiten, Gehen; das Abschreiten. **—s**, *pl.* die Stufen=, Treppen=leiter; die Maßregeln; stone —s, die Steintreppen, Freitreppe (before a door, vor einer Tür); to take the necessary —s, die nötigen Maßregeln ergreifen *or* Maßnahmen treffen. *Comp.* **—ping-stone**, *s.* der Schrittstein (in Wasser, Schmutz, *etc.*); das (zur Erreichung eines höheren Ziels behülfliche) Mittel (*fig.*); der erste Schritt zu.

[2]**Step**, (*in comp.* =) Stief= (*mother, brother, etc.*).

Steppe, *s.* die Steppe. II. *attrib.*; — murrain, die Rinderpest.

Stereo—graphy, *s.* die Stereographie. **—metry**, *s.* die Stereometrie. **—scope**, *s.* das Stereoskop. **—scopic**, *adj.* körperlich erscheinend, stereoskopisch. **—type**, I. *s.* die Stereotypie; (—type plate) die Stereotype, Stereotypplatte; in —type, stereotypiert. II. *adj.* mit feststehender Schrift gedruckt, stereotypisch, Stereotyp= (*also fig.*); unabänderlich (*fig.*); —type edition, die Stereotypausgabe; —type printing, der Stereotypdruck. III. *v.a.* stereotypieren, mit Stereotypplatten drucken; (einer Sache) eine unabänderliche *or* bleibende Form geben (*fig.*). **—typed**, *adj. see* —type II.; —typed phrase, stets wiederkehrende, sich stets gleichbleibende Redensart. **—typography**, *s.* der Stereotypendruck.

Steril—e, *adj.* unfruchtbar (*also fig.*); (desert) öde; nutzlos, hohl, leer (*fig.*). **—ity**, *s.* die Unfruchtbarkeit. **—ize**, *v.a.* unfruchtbar machen; ausmergeln (*soil*). **—ized**, *adj.* entkeimt, keimfrei; —ized milk, sterilisierte, keimfreie Milch.

Sterling, *adj.* nach dem gesetzlichen Münzfuße, Sterling; echt, bewährt, probehaltig; a pound —, ein Pfund Sterling; of — worth, von erprobtem Wert; a man of — worth, ein Mann von gutem (*or* echtem) Schrot und Korn.

[1]**Stern**, I. *s.* das Heck, der Spiegel, das Hinterschiff; too much by the —, achter=, steuer=lastig. II. *attrib.*; — chase, die Spiegeljagd (bei welcher das verfolgende Schiff genau im Fahrwasser des verfolgten fährt); — chaser, das Heckgeschütz. *Comp.* **—board**, *s.* die Rückwärtsbewegung (des Schiffes). **—-ports**, *pl.* die Hinter=, Kreuz=pforten.

[2]**Stern**, *adj.*, **—ly**, *adv.* ernst (*as a look, etc.*); (severe) streng, hart, grausam. **—ness**, *s.* der Ernst, die Strenge, Härte.

Sternum, *s.* das Brustbein.

Sternuta—tion, *s.* das Niesen. **—tory**, I. *adj.* Niesen erregend. II. *s.* das Niesmittel.

Stertorous, *adj.* schnarchend.

Stethoscop—e, *s.* das Horchrohr, Stethoskop (*Med.*). **—ic**, *adj.* vermittelst des Horchrohrs, stethoskopisch.

Stevedore, *s.* der Stauer, (Aus=)Lader.

Stew, I. *v.a. & n.* dämpfen, in Dampf kochen, langsam kochen, schmoren; —ed apples with cream, gedämpfte Äpfel mit Sahne. II. *s.* das Schmorgericht; gedämpftes, geschmortes Fleisch; (Irish —) gedämpftes Gericht aus Hammelfleisch, Kartoffeln, Zwiebeln ꝛc. (*Cook.*); die Verwirrung (*vulg.*); (brothel) das Bordell (*obs.*); to get into a — about . . ., in Aufregung geraten über (*acc.*) (*coll.*). *Comp.* **—-pan**, *s.* die Schmorpfanne.

Steward, *s.* der Verwalter (*of estates*); der Haushofmeister (*in princely, etc., houses*); der Proviant=meister, =verwalter (*Naut.*); der Aufwärter auf Personenschiffen; der College=Küchenverwalter (*Univ.*); der Aufseher, Festordner (*at races, etc.*); —'s room, die Mundvorratskammer, Bottlerei; Lord High —, der Großhofmeister von England. **—ess**, *s.* die Aufwärterin (*on board ship*). **—ship**, *s.* das Verwalteramt.

Stich—ic, *adj.* aus einzelnen Verszeilen bestehend, stichisch. **—ometry**, *s.* das Abschätzen durch Zeilenzählung. **—omythia**, *s.* die lebhafte Unterhaltung, der Redekampf im Drama, wo ein jeder Redner in einer oder zwei Zeilen spricht, die Stychomythie.

[1]**Stick**, I. *s.* der Stock; (staff) der Stab; das Scheit, Stück (*for firing*); die Stange (*of sealing wax*); das Richtscheit (*Carp.*); der Steg (*Typ.*); small —s, die Reiser, das Reisholz; composing —, der Winkelhaken; the devil on two —s, der hinkende Teufel. II. *v.a.* mit einem Stocke *or* mit Stäben versehen; in den Winkelhaken nehmen (*Typ.*).

[2]**Stick**, *ir.v.* I. *a.* stechen, durchstoßen, spießen; abstechen, schlachten (*a pig, etc.*); stecken (*pins into a cushion, etc.*); (fasten) stecken, befestigen, heften, ankleben; — no bills, Anschläge sind nicht gestattet, das Anschlagen von Plakaten ist verboten; to — **on**, anstecken (*with pins, etc.*), aufkleben; to — **out**, herausstecken; to — **up**, auf-

stecken, -kleben, -heften. II. *ir.v.n.* feststecken, kleben bleiben, sich anhängen; (hold) (fest)halten; (stop) stecken bleiben, stocken (*in a speech*); (scruple) sich stoßen (at, an, *dat.*), sich (*dat.*) ein Gewissen machen (at, aus); he —s at nothing, ihn hält nichts auf, er nimmt keine Rücksicht, macht sich (*dat.*) aus nichts ein Gewissen; to — **by**, ankleben, anhängen; to — by a p., einem anhangen, ihn nicht verlassen (*lit.*), ihm treu bleiben *or* zur Seite stehen (*fig.*); the word stuck **in** my throat, das Wort blieb mir im Halse stecken; to — in the mud, im Kot stecken bleiben; to — **to**, (einem) anhangen, festhalten an (*dat.*); to — to one's work, bei der Arbeit bleiben, unablässig arbeiten; to — to one's friends, sich an seine Freunde halten; to — **together**, an einander hängen; to — **up**, aufrechtstehen; to — up for a p., jemandes Partei nehmen, einen verteidigen (*coll.*). —**iness**, *s.* die Klebrigkeit. —**y**, *adj.* klebrig, zäh. *Comp.* —**-fast**, *s.* der Klebegummi, Kleister. —**ing-plaster**, *s.* das Heftpflaster. —**-in-the-mud**, *s.* der Knirps (*coll.*); der Faulenzer (*coll.*).

Stickle, *v.n.* zwischen Kämpfende als Schiedsrichter treten (*obs.*); to — for a p., für einen Partei nehmen; to — for a th., nachdrücklich für eine S. eintreten, eifrig um eine S. streiten; von einer Partei zur andern übergehen. —**r**, *s.* der Eiferer, Streiter (for, für), der eifrige Vertreter (einer S.); —r for trifles, der Pedant.

Stickleback, *s.* der Stichling (*Icht.*).

Stiff, *adj.*, —**ly**, *adv.* steif; (rigid) starr, straff; steif, gezwungen, pedantisch (*fig.*); (stubborn) steif, eigensinnig, hartnäckig, unbeugsam; (strong) stark, kräftig; my legs are —, ich habe steife Beine; a — glass of brandy and water, ein Glas starken Branntweins mit Wasser; — neck, steifer Hals; — breeze, steife Brise. —**en**, *v.* I. *a.* steif, starr machen; steifen (*cloth, etc.*). II. *n.* steif(er) werden, erstarren. —**ener**, *s.* die Einlage (in einer Halsbinde, einem Muff ꝛc.). —**ening**, *s.* das Steifen (*of clothes, etc.*); die Steife, Einlage. —**ish**, *adj.* etwas steif. —**ness**, *s.* die Steifheit, Steife, Unbiegsamkeit; die Steifheit, Gezwungenheit (*fig.*). *Comp.* —**-necked**, *adj.* hartnäckig, halsstarrig.

¹**Stifle**, *v.a.* ersticken; erdrücken (*with kisses, etc.*); unterdrücken (*resentment, etc.*).

²**Stifle**, *s.* die Kniescheibe (*of a horse*); die (Fluß-)Galle (*Vet.*).

Stigma, *s.* das Brandmal (*obs.*); das Brandmal, der Schandfleck (*fig.*); das Stigma (*Bot.*). —**ta**, *pl. see* —; die Wundmale (*of Christ*); die Luftlöcher (der Insekten). —**tize**, *v.a.* brandmarken.

Stile, *s.* der Zauntritt, Zaunübergang.

Stiletto, *s.* das Stilett, der kleine Dolch; der Stecker (*Sew.*).

¹**Still**, I. *v.a.* beruhigen, stillen. II. *adj.* still, ruhig; (motionless) bewegungslos, regungslos; be —! sei ruhig! to stand —, stillstehen; — life, das Stilleben (*Paint.*); — waters run deep, stille Wasser sind tief (*prov.*). III. *adv.* stets, immer; (after that) noch immer, (immer) noch, bis jetzt; — more, noch mehr. IV. *conj.* doch, dennoch, indessen, bei alledem. —**er**, *s.* der Beruhiger. —**ness**, *s.* die Stille, Ruhe. —**y**, I. *adj.* still, ruhig. II. *adv.* leise, geräuschlos. *Comp.* —**-birth**, *s.* die Totgeburt. —**-born**, *adj.* totgeboren.

²**Still**, *s. see* Alembic, der Brennkessel, Destillierapparat; die Brennerei. *Comp.* —**-room**, I. *s.* die Hausbrennerei; (Raum in dem Kaffee, Tee *etc.* bereitet werden) die Milchkammer, Vorratskammer. II. *attrib.;* —-room maid, das Vorratskammer-Mädchen.

Stilt, *s.* die Stelze. —**ed**, *adj.* hochtrabend; gespreizt; (stiff) steif.

Stilton, *s.* (— cheese) der Stiltonkäse.

Stimul—ant, I. *s.* das Reizmittel. II. *adj.* reizend, anregend; stimulierend. —**ate**, *v.a.* reizen; stimulieren (*Med.*); anreizen, (an-)spornen (*fig.*). —**ation**, *s.* das (An-)Spornen, die Reizung, der Antrieb. —**ative**, I. *adj.* (an-)spornend, reizend, antreibend. II. *s.* die Anreizung. —**us**, *s.* der Sporn, Antrieb (to, zu); das Reizmittel (*Med.*); die Brennspitze (*Bot.*).

Sting, I. *ir.v.a.* stechen, stacheln, anstacheln (*also fig.*); (pain) verwunden, schmerzen, tief kränken (*fig.*); stung with remorse, von Gewissensbissen gepeinigt. II. *s.* der Stachel (*of insects*); der Stich, Biß (*inflicted by insects*); der Stich (*fig.*); die Schärfe, Spitze (*of a remark*); — of death, der Stachel des Todes. —**ing**, *adj.*, —**ingly**, *adv.* stachelnd, stechend. —**less**, *adj.* stachellos.

Sting—ily, *adv.*, —**y**, *adj.* geizig, filzig; (scanty) karg, kärglich, knapp; to be —y, knausern. —**iness**, *s.* die Kargheit; die Filzigkeit, Knauserei.

Stink, I. *ir.v.n.* stinken. II. *s.* der Gestank. —**ard**, *s.* der Stinkdachs, Telagon. —**ing**, *adj.*, —**ingly**, *adv.* stinkend; schmutzig, elend (*fig.*). *Comp.* —**-trap**, *s.* der Wasserverschluß (für Wasserklosets, ꝛc.).

Stint, I. *v.a.* ein-, be-schränken, verkürzen; knapp halten (*in food*). II. *v.n.* sich einschränken, sparen. III. *s.* die Einschränkung; (limit) das Maß. —**ed**, *adj.* knapp, beschränkt.

Stipend, *s.* die Besoldung, das Gehalt; der Sold, Lohn, das Stipendium. —**iary**, I. *adj.* besoldet. II. *s.* der Besoldete, Söldner, Söldling.

Stipple, *v.a.* in gepunkteter Manier stechen, punktieren, tüpfeln (*Paint.*, *Engr.*).

Stipul—ate, *v.a. & n.* verabreden, festsetzen, bedingen; at the time —ated, zur festgesetzten Zeit. —**ation**, *s.* die Übereinkunft, Festsetzung; (condition) die Bedingung. —**ator**, *s.* der Kontrahent. —**e**, *s.* das Nebenblättchen (*Bot.*).

Stir, I. *v.a.* (move) rühren, bewegen, regen; (um)rühren (*sauce, etc.*); schüren (*the fire*); (incite) aufregen, anfeuern; to — up, aufrühren; aufrütteln, reizen, aufhetzen (*fig.*); he —red up the people to rebellion, er wiegelte die Leute zur Empörung auf. II. *v.n.* sich regen, sich rühren; (get up) aufstehen; to be —ring, auf sein; (be in motion) im Gange, im Umlauf sein; don't —! rühre dich nicht! (*coll.*); to — abroad, — out, ausgehen; there is not a breath —ring, es regt sich kein Lüftchen. III. *s.* die Bewegung; (tumult) der Aufruhr; (bustle) das Getümmel, Geräusch; (agitation) die Aufregung. —**ring**, *adj.* aufregend; begeisternd; tätig, rührig; unruhig; —ring times, unruhige Zeiten. *Comp.* —**about**, *s.* der Haferbrei.

Stirk, *s.* das junge Rind, junger Ochse, junge Kuh.

Stirrup, *s.* der Steigbügel. *Comp.* —**-cup**, *s.* der Abschiedstrunk. —**-leather**, *s.* der Steigriemen.

Stitch, I. *s.* der Stich; die Masche (*in knitting, etc.*); der Stich, das Stechen (*in the side, etc.*); back, cross, chain *or* looped, herring-bone, running —, Stepp-, Kreuz-, Ketten-, Gräten-, Vorder-stich; to drop (pick up) a —, eine Masche fallen lassen (aufnehmen); every — of canvas, alle Segel. II. *v.a. & n.* steppen; (sew) nähen, heften; broschieren, heften (*Bookb.*); —ed book, geheftetes Buch. —**er**, *s.* der (die) Näher(in). —**ing**, *s.* die Näherei; das Steppen; das Heften.

Stithy, *s.* der Amboß.

Stiver, *s.* der Stüber, Stüver.

Stoat, *s.* das Hermelin.

Stoccade, *see* Stockade.

Stock, I. *s.* der Stock, Stengel, Strunk (*of plants, etc.*); der Stamm (*of a tree*); (block) der Stock, Block, Klotz; der Stock (*of tools, etc.*); der Schaft (*of a gun*); (race) das Geschlecht, der Stamm; die Levkoje (*Bot.*); (neck-tie) die Halsbinde; (store) der Vorrat, das Quantum, Lager; (capital) das Stammkapital; der Anteil, die Aktie (*of a bank, etc.*); das lebendige Inventur, der Viehstand (*of cattle*); der Stand (*of bees*); die Fleischbrühe (*Cook.*); over — and stone, über Stock und Stein; to take —, das Lager, die Inventur aufnehmen; to take — of one's own soul, mit sich selbst zu Rate gehen; — (of goods) on hand, der Warenvorrat, Lagervorrat; — in trade, das Stammkapital; in —, vorrätig; — of learning, der Schatz von Kenntnissen; — of books, Büchervorrat; floating —, zirkulierendes Kapital; rolling —, das Betriebsmaterial (*Railw.*). II. *adj.* auf Lager, bereit; stehend, ständig (*fig.*); — piece *or* play, das Repertoire- *or* Kassen-stück; — tale, ständige Geschichte. III. *v.a.* versehen; (— with) füllen (mit); bereichern (*the mind with learning*); besetzen (*a park with deer*); schäften (*a gun*); stocken (*an anchor*); vorrätig *or* auf Lager haben; to — a farm, a pond, ein Landgut mit Vieh, einen Teich mit Fischen besetzen. **—s**, *pl.* der Stock, Fuß-, Zwang-block; der Stapel (*Naut.*); die Staats-aktien, -papiere, der Fonds (*C.L.*). **—ade**, *s.* das Staket, Pfahlwerk, die Estakade (*Fort.*). **—inet**, *s.* das Trikot. **—ing**, *s.* der Strumpf; woven —ing, gewirkter Strumpf. **—ish**, *adj.* verstockt. *Comp.* **—-account**, *s.* das Kapitalkonto. **—-book**, *s.* das Lagerbuch. **—-broker**, *s.* der Börsenmakler, Effektenhändler. **—-dove**, *s.* die Holztaube. **—-exchange**, *s.* die Börse für Staats- und andere Papiere, Fondsbörse; der Geldmarkt; —-exchange news, der Fondsbericht, Börsenbericht. **—-fish**, *s.* der Stockfisch. **—-gilliflower**, *s.* die Levkoje. **—holder**, *s.* der Aktionär. **—ing-frame**, *s.* der Strumpfwirkerstuhl. **—ing-knitter**, *s.* der Strumpfstricker. **—ing-yarn**, *s.* das Strickgarn. **—-jobber**, *s.* der Börsenspekulant, Börsenmakler (von den —broker's benutzter Zwischenhändler), Agioteur. **—-jobbing**, *s.* das Börsenspiel. **—-taking**, *s.* die Inventuraufnahme. **—still**, *adj.* stockstill, mäuschenstill.

Stodg—e, I. *v.a.* vollstopfen. II. *v.n.* sich vollfressen. III. *s.* der Milchbrei; das Futter. **—y**, *adj.* stopfend, den Magen füllend *or* beschwerend; dick, fett, plump, unverdaulich.

Stoke, *v.a.* stochern, schüren. **—r**, *s.* der Schürer, Heizer. *Comp.* **—-hole**, *s.* das Schürloch.

[1]**Stole**, *s.* die Stola (*Eccl.*); der Ausläufer (*Bot.*).

[2]**Stole**, *imperf.* (& *obs. p.p.*), **—n**, *p.p.*, *of* Steal.

Stolid, *adj.*, **—ly**, *adv.* tölpelhaft, albern, schwerfällig, stumpf, unempfindlich; (stupid) dumm. **—ity**, *s.* die Unempfindlichkeit, Schwerfälligkeit, der Stumpfsinn.

Stolon, *s.* der Schößling, Ausläufer (*Bot.*).

Stomach, I. *s.* der Magen; (appetite) die Eßlust; die Neigung, Lust (*fig.*); der Mut (*obs.*); to have no — for, keine Lust haben zu; that goes against his —, das widert ihn an; to turn a p.'s —, Erbrechen verursachen (*vulg.*). II. *v.a.* sich (*dat.*) gefallen lassen, geduldig ertragen, einstecken (*an affront*). **—er**, *s.* das Brusttuch, der Latz. **—ic**, I. *adj.* magenstärkend, Magen-. II. *s.* das Magenmittel. *Comp.* **—-ache**, *s.* der Leibschmerz, das Magendrücken.

Ston—e, I. *s.* der Stein (*also fig.*, *Med.* & *as weight*); der Fels, Felsen; der Stein, Kern (*of fruit*); die Hode (*Anat.*); (grave-—e) der Grabstein; to leave no —e unturned, alles aufbieten, nichts unversucht lassen; within a —e's throw, in Steinwurfweite. II. *adj.* von Stein, steinern. III. *v.a.* steinigen. **—er**, *s.* der Steiniger. **—iness**, *s.* das Steinige; die Hartherzigkeit. **—y**, *adj.* steinig, steinicht, versteinert, (stein)hart (*fig.*); —y ground, der Steinboden. *Comp.* **—e-blind**, *adj.* stockblind. **—e-bottle**, *s.* der Steinkrug. **—e-coloured**, *adj.* steinfarben. **—crop**, *s.* der Mauerpfeffer, die Fetthenne (*Bot.*). **—e-cutter**, *s.* der Steinhauer; der Steinschleifer (*Jewelry*). **—e-deaf**, *adj.* stocktaub. **—e-fruit**, *s.* das Steinobst. **—e-jug**, *s.* steinerner Krug. **—e-mason**, *s.* der Steinmetz. **—e-quarry**, *s.* der Steinbruch. **—e-ware**, *s.* das Steingut. **—ework**, *s.* das Mauerwerk. **—y-hearted**, *adj.* stein-, hart-herzig.

Stood, *imperf.* & *p.p.* *of* Stand.

Stook, I. *s.* der Haufe von (12) Garben. II. *v.a.* in Haufen setzen. III. *v.n.* Garbenhaufen machen.

Stool, *s.* der Stuhl, Sessel; (office —) der Kontorstuhl; (foot—) der Schemel; (close —) der Nachtstuhl; der Stuhlgang (*Med.*); — of repentance, die Bußbank, der Bußschemel.

Stoop, I. *v.n.* sich bücken, sich beugen, sich neigen; krumm gehen (*in walking, etc.*); sich beugen, sich herablassen *or* demütigen; sich niederlassen (*as a bird*); she —s to conquer, sie beugt sich, um zu siegen. II. *s.* das Beugen, Bücken, Neigen; (swoop) das Niederschießen; to have a —, sich krumm halten; to walk with a —, gebückt gehen. **—ing**, *s.* das Bücken; die gebückte Haltung.

Stop, I. *v.a.* (auf)halten (*in running, etc.*); stillen (*blood*); (ver)sperren (*a way, etc.*); (— up) (ver-, zu-)stopfen, zumachen; *see* put a — to; niederschlagen (proceedings, das Verfahren); greifen (*strings, Mus.*); interpunktieren (*writing*); stopfen (*a leak, etc.*); zurückhalten (*out of wages*); einstellen (*payment*); to — a p.'s mouth, einem den Mund stopfen; —ped consonant, der Verschlußlaut, die Muta. II. *v.n.* (an)halten, stille stehen, stehen bleiben; (stay) sich aufhalten, bleiben, logieren; (cease) aufhören, innehalten; —! halt! stopp! (*Boat.*); to — **for**, warten auf (*acc.*); to — **to** supper, zum Abendessen bleiben. III. *s.* der Halt, Einhalt; (interruption) die Pause; (obstruction) die Aufhaltung, Hemmung, Sperrung; (cessation) das Aufhören, Ende; (full —) der Punkt; die Klappe, das Ventil (*on wind instruments*); das Register, die Stimme (*Org.*); der Griff (*on a violin, lute, etc.*); die Sperre (*Horol.*); der Verschlußlaut, die Muta (*Phonet.*); to make a —, come to a —, Halt machen, einhalten; to put a full —, einen Punkt machen; to put a — to a th., einer Sache Einhalt tun. **—page**, *s.* das (Ver-)Stopfen; das Anhalten (*of a vehicle*); der Aufenthalt (*on journeys*); (—ping) die Hemmung, Sperrung, der Einhalt, das Hindernis; der Abzug (from wages, etc., am Gehalte ꝛc.); die Zahlungseinstellung; die Verstopfung (*in the bowels, etc.*); die Hemmung (*of the circulation, etc.*). **—per**, I. *s.* der Anhaltende; (—per-up) der (Ver-)Stopfende; der Stöpsel, Pfropf (*of a bottle*); die Hemmfeder (*Horol.*). II. *v.a.* verstopfen, zustöpseln. **—ping**, *s.* die Plombe, Zahnfüllung. **—ple**, *s.* der Stöpsel, Pfropf, Spund. *Comp.* **—-cock**, *s.* der Sperrhahn. **—-consonant**, *s.* der Verschlußlaut. **—-gap**, *s.* der Lückenbüßer, Notbehelf. **—-lock**, *s.* das Sicherheitsschloß. **—ping-place**, *s.* der Anhalteplatz, die Haltestelle. **—-press**, *adj.*; —-press news, nach Schluß der Redaktion eingelaufene Nachrichten.

Stor—age, *s.* das Lagern (*of goods*); (cost of —age) das Lagergeld. **—e**, I. *s.* der Vorrat; die Fülle, der Schatz (*of knowledge, etc.*); (warehouse) das Gewölbe, (Waren-)Lager; (shop) der Laden (*Amer.*); co-operative —e(s), das Kaufhaus, der Spar- und Konsum-Laden, der Konsumverein (*C. L.*), das Genossenschaftsgeschäft (*Pol. Econ.*); —es, (*pl.*) die Kriegs-, Schiffsvorräte; in —e, vorrätig, auf Lager; to be in —e for, aufgehoben sein für, warten auf (*acc.*), erwarten; to set great —e by, großen Wert legen auf (*acc.*), hochachten. II. *v.a.* aufspeichern, (ein-)lagern; verproviantieren (*a ship*); versehen, versorgen (with, mit); (—e up) aufhäufen, aufspeichern, sammeln; to —e one's mind with knowledge, sich (*dat.*) Kenntnisse sammeln; to —e away, unterbringen. **—er**, *s.* der Sammler, Aufhäufer. *Comp.* **—e-house**, *s.* das Vorrats-, Lager-haus, Magazin; der große Vorrat (*fig.*). **—e-keeper**, *s.* der Magazinverwalter. **—e-room**, *s.* die Vorratskammer. **—e-ship**, *s.* das Proviantschiff.

[1]**Stor—ied**, *adj.* mit Erzählungen versehen, geschichtlich berühmt, sagenreich; mit Geschichtsbildern verziert (*as windows*). **—y**, *see* Story.

[2]**Stor—ied**, *adj.* mit Stockwerken, -stöckig; three—ied, dreistöckig. **—(e)y**, *see* [2]Story.

Stork, *s.* der Storch; the — chatters, der Storch klappert. *Comp.* **—'s-bill**, *s.* der Reiherschnabel.

Storm, I. *s.* der Sturm (*also Mil. & fig.*); (thunder—) das Gewitter; to take by —, mit stürmender Hand nehmen (*Mil.*); im Sturm erobern (*fig.*); — of musket shot, der Kugelregen; — of wind, der Sturmwind; —and Stress Period, die Sturm- und Drangperiode. II. *v.a.* (be)stürmen; (take by —) erstürmen. III. *v.n.* stürmen, toben, wüten (at, gegen, über (*fig.*)). **—iness**, *s.* das Ungestüm. **—ing**, I. *adj.* stürmend. II. *s.* das Sturmlaufen, die Erstürmung (*Mil.*); —ing board, das Sturmbrett (*Gym.*). **—y**, *adj.*, **—ily**, *adv.* stürmisch; —y petrel, die Sturmschwalbe. *Comp.* **—-cloud**, *s.* die Sturmwolke. **—-staysail**, *s.* die Sturmfock. **—-tossed**, *adj.* vom Sturm umhergeschleudert *or* umhergetrieben. **—-vexed**, *adj.* von Stürmen geplagt.

[1]**Story**, *s.* die Geschichte; (narrative) die Erzählung, das Geschichtchen; (tale) das Märchen, die Novelle; (lie) die Erfindung, Lüge, Finte; as the —y goes, wie man sagt, wie es heißt; always the same old —y, immer die alte Leier; to make a long —y short, um es kurz zu sagen. *Comp.* **—y-book**, *s.* das Geschichten-, Märchen-buch. **—y-teller**, *s.* der (die) Erzähler(in); der (die) Märchen-, Novellen-schreiber(in); der (die) Lügner(in) (*coll.*). **—y-telling**, *s.* das Erzählen; das Fintenmachen, Lügen.

[2]**Story**, *s.* das Stock(werk), Geschoß.

Stoup, *s.* das Weihwasserbecken (*Scotch*).

Stout, I. *adj.*, **—ly**, *adv.* stark, stämmig, rüstig, (hand)fest; (brave) wacker, mannhaft; (thick, fat) dick, stark; fest, stark (*as ships*); —ly built, starkgebaut; — resistance, tapfrer Widerstand; a — gentleman, ein dicker Herr. II. *s.* ein starkes Bier. **—ish**, *adj.*, ziemlich stark. **—ness**, *s.* die Stärke. *Comp.* **—-hearted**, *adj.* herzhaft.

[1]**Stove**, I. *s.* der Ofen; das Treibhaus (*Hort.*). II. *v.a.* ins Treibhaus setzen (*plants*); *see* Stew. *Comp.* **—-grate**, *s.* der Ofenrost. **—-heated**, *adj.* durch einen Ofen geheizt. **—-plant**, *s.* die Treibhauspflanze, das Treibhausgewächs.

[2]**Stove** (*also* **Staved**), *imperf. & p.p. of* Stave.

Stow, *v.a.* stauen, packen; to — away, unterbringen, hinstecken. **—age**, *s.* das Stauen, Packen; (room) der Stau-, Pack-raum. *Comp.* **—away**, *s.* ein auf einem Schiff Versteckter, heimlich Mitreisender, blinder Passagier.

Strabism, *s.* das Schielen.

Straddle, *v.* I. *n.* sich spreizen, sperrbeinig gehen, grätscheln. II. *a. see* Bestride. *Comp.* **—-legged**, *adj.* grätschbeinig.

Straggl—e, *v.n.* zerstreut, einzeln liegen, stehen; (roam) umherschweifen; (—e off) abweichen; (go —ing) zerstreut, einzeln gehen; wuchern, unordentlich hervorschießen (*as plants*). **—er**, *s.* der Herum-streifer, -streicher; der Nachzügler (*Mil.*); einzeln stehendes Ding; der Schößling, wilde Schuß (*Hort.*). **—ing**, *adj.* umherschweifend; einzeln stehend, zerstreut liegend.

Straight, I. *adj.*, **—ly**, *adv.* gerade (*also fig.*); ehrlich, rechtschaffen (*sl.*); *see* Strait; — as a rush, kerzengerade; to make things —, die Sachen in Ordnung bringen; she keeps him —, sie hält ihn fest im Zaume. II. *adv.* stracks, geradeswegs; (directly) sogleich; — out, gerade heraus. **—en**, *v.* I. *a.* gerade machen, straff ziehen; *see* Straiten. II. *n.* gerade werden. **—ener**, *s.* einer, der gerade macht. **—ness**, *s.* die Geradheit. *Comp.* **—-edge**, *s.* das Richtscheit. **—forward**, *adj.*, **—forwardly**, *adv.* gerade; geradsinnig, aufrichtig, redlich (*fig.*). **—forwardness**, *s.* die Redlichkeit, Aufrichtigkeit. **—way**, *adv.* stracks, geradeswegs, flugs.

[1]**Strain**, I. *v.a.* anstrengen, straff anziehen, spannen, dehnen; anstrengen, anspannen, zwingen (*fig.*); (squeeze) zusammenziehen; verrenken, verstauchen (*a muscle, etc.*); drücken, pressen (*to one's heart, etc.*); durch-pressen, -schlagen, -seihen (*milk, etc.*); to — a meaning, (einer Äußerung) einen gezwungenen Sinn geben; to — every nerve, jeden Nerv anspannen, alles aufbieten; the relations between G. & B. are somewhat —ed, die Beziehungen zwischen G. und B. sind etwas gespannt; —ed interpretation, gezwungene Auslegung. II. *v.n.* sich anstrengen *or* bestreben; durchsickern; to — at a gnat, bei Kleinigkeiten Umstände machen. III. *s.* die Anstrengung, Spannung; (pressure) der Druck; die Verrenkung, Verstauchung (*Surg.*); (tone) der Ton; (lay) das Gedicht; die Weise, der Ton, Gesang (*Mus.*); (way) die Weise, Art, Manier; (way of acting) die Handlungsweise; (style) der Stil, die Schreibart; to take too high a —, die Saiten zu hoch spannen (*fig.*); a lofty —, ein erhabener (insolent, hochfahrender) Ton. **—er**, *s.* die Seihe, der Durchschlag, Filter, das Seihetuch; das Teesieb. **—ing**, *s.* das Haschen (*after effect*); das Durchseihen; das Pressen &c.

[2]**Strain**, *s.* die Linie, Abkunft, das Geschlecht; *see* Kind, Sort; (tendency) der Hang.

Strait, I. *adj.*, **—ly**, *adv.* eng, schmal; (difficult) schwierig; streng, genau. II. *s.* die Landenge; (—s) die Meerenge, Straße; die Enge, Klemme, Not (*fig.*); —s of Gibraltar, die Meerenge *or* Straße von Gibraltar; to reduce to great —s, stark in die Enge treiben. **—en**, *v.a.* enge machen, verengen; spannen (*a rope, etc.*); beengen, beschränken, in Verlegenheit setzen; to be —ened for money, in Geldverlegenheit sein; to be in —ened (—ened in one's) circumstances, in beschränkten Umständen leben. **—ness**, *s.* die Enge, Beschränktheit; die Not; die Peinlichkeit, Strenge. *Comp.* **—-laced**, *adj.* enggeschnürt; steif, streng; pietistisch. **—-waistcoat**, *s.* die Zwangsjacke.

[1]**Strake**, *s.* der Streifen, Strich (*obs.*); die Radschiene.

[2]**Strake**, (*obs.*) *imperf. of* Strike.

[1]**Strand**, I. *s.* der Strand, die Küste, das Ufer. II. *v.a.* auf den Strand setzen, treiben; stranden lassen (*fig.*). III. *v.n.* stranden; to be left —ed, auf dem Trocknen sitzen (*fig.*).

[2]**Strand**, *s.* die (Tau-)Litze, Ducht; die Strähne, die Faser.

Strange, *adj.*, **—ly**, *adv.* fremd; (unusual) unbekannt, neu, ungewöhnlich, unerhört, befremdlich; (wonderful) seltsam, sonderbar, wunderlich, auffallend; to look — on, kalt ansehen; — (to say), sonderbar, merkwürdig(erweise); — looking, sonderbar aussehend. **—ness**, *s.* die Fremdheit, das Fremde, Ausländische; die Seltsamkeit, das Wunderbare, Auffällige; (shyness) das Fremdtun. **—r**, *s.* der (die) Fremde, Ausländer(in); der (die) Unbekannte; (novice) der Neuling, Unerfahrene; (guest, *etc.*) der Reisende, Gast; he is a (perfect) —r to me, er ist mir (völlig) fremd; to make a (no) —r of a p., einen wie einen Fremden (als Familienglied) behandeln.

Strang—le, *v.a.* erwürgen, erdrosseln; unterdrücken (*fig.*). **—ler**, *s.* der Erwürger. **—les**, *s.* die Druse (*Vet.*). **—ulated**, *adj.* eingeschnürt (*Med.*). **—ulation**, *s.* die Erwürgung; die Zuschnürung der Kehle (*Med.*). **—ury**, *s.* der Harnzwang.

Strap, I. *s.* der Riemen; (belt) der (die) Gurt(e); die Strippe (*on trousers*); (strop) der Streichriemen (*of a razor*); die Achselschnur (*Mil.*). II. *v.a.* mit einem Riemen befestigen, umschnüren; (beat) mit Riemen peitschen (*vulg.*). **—pado**, I. *s.* das Wippen. II. *v.a.* wippen. **—per**, *s.* große, starke Person, der Dragoner. **—ping**, *adj.* groß und stark, stämmig. *Comp.* **—-hinges**, *pl.* lange Türbänder.

Strat—a, *pl. see* —um. **—ification**, *s.* die Schichtung; (strata) die (Schichten-)Lage. **—ified**, *adj.* aufgeschichtet, schichtenförmig. **—iform**, *adj.* schichtenförmig. **—ify**, *v.a.* schichten. **—igraphical**, *adj.* schichtenbeschreibend. **—um**, *s.* die Schicht, Lage.

Strat—agem, *s.* der Kriegsplan, die Kriegslist (*Mil.*); die List, der Kunstgriff. **—egic**, *adj.* strategisch. **—egist**, *s.* der Stratege. **—egy**, *s.* die Feldherrnkunst, Strategie; die List (*fig.*).

Strathspey, *s.* lebhafter, schottischer Tanz.

Stratus, *s.* die Schichtwolke (*Meteorol.*).

Strave, (*obs.*) *imperf. of* Strive.

Straw, I. *s.* das Stroh; (— stalk) der Strohhalm; die Kleinigkeit (*fig.*); not worth a —, keinen Heller wert; man of —, der Strohmann (*lit. & fig.*); the last — that breaks the camel's back, der Tropfen, der das Faß zum Überlaufen bringt. II. *v.a.* mit Stroh versehen *or* binden. III. *adj.*; — mattress, die Strohmatratze, der Strohsack. *Comp.* **—berry**, *s.* die Erdbeere. **—coloured**, *adj.* strohfarbig, strohfarben.

Stray, I. *v.n.* in der Irre gehen, (sich ver)irren; abweichen, abschweifen (from, von); (wander) umher-streifen, -schweifen; (wind) sich schlängeln; frei hinziehen (*as wind*). II. *adj.* verirrt, verlaufen; (odd) zufällig; — thoughts, Gedankensplitter. III. *s.* das verlaufene Tier. **—er**, *s.* der Herumstreicher, Stromer.

Streak, I. *s.* der Streifen, Strich; der Erdgang (*Min.*). II. *v.a.* streifen. **—y**, *adj.* streifig.

Stream, I. *s.* der Bach; der Strom (*also fig.*); das Fahrwasser, die Strömung (*of a river*); to go with the —, dem Strome folgen; down (up) —, strom-abwärts (-aufwärts); — of words, der Wortschwall. II. *v.n.* strömen, fließen; strahlen (*as light*); flattern (*as a flag*); with —ing hair, mit fliegendem *or* aufgelöstem Haar; with —ing eyes, mit tränenden Augen. III. *v.a.* auswerfen (*a buoy*). **—er**, *s.* die Fahne, der Wimpel; (ribbon) fliegendes Band; der Lichtstrahl (*of the Aurora Borealis*). **—let**, *s.* das Bächlein. *Comp.* **—anchor**, *s.* der Wurfanker.

Street, I. *s.* die Straße, Gasse. II. *attrib.*; — Arab, der Straßenjunge. *Comp.* **—car**, *s.* der Straßenbahnwagen (*Amer.*). **—door**, I. *s.* die Haustür. II. *attrib.*; —door bell, die Haustürklingel. **—lighting**, *s.* die Straßenbeleuchtung. **—walker**, *s.* die Gassendirne.

Strength, *s.* die Kraft, Stärke (*also fig.*); (firmness) die Festigkeit; die Haltbarkeit (*of a fortress, etc.*); die (Truppen-, Heeres-)Macht (*Mil.*); to gather —, wieder zu Kräften kommen; upon the — of, kraft, vermöge, auf (*acc.*) . . . hin. **—en**, *v.* I. *n.* stärken, kräftigen; (confirm) bestärken, bekräftigen. II. *n.* erstarken, stark *or* stärker werden. **—ener**, *s.* die Stärkung.

Strenuous, *adj.*, **—ly**, *adv.* tätig, emsig, eifrig; (bold) kühn, tapfer, tüchtig; ruhelos (*as a life*). **—ness**, *s.* die Tätigkeit, Emsigkeit, der Eifer.

Stress, *s.* das Gewicht, der Nachdruck, Drang; (importance) die Wichtigkeit; (emphasis) die Betonung; by — of weather, durch das ungestüme Wetter; storm and —, Sturm und Drang; to lay — upon, Gewicht legen auf (*acc.*); under the — of circumstances, unter dem Druck der Umstände. *Comp.* **—group**, *s.* die Akzentgruppe, Tongruppe.

Stretch, I. *v.a.* strecken, recken; (extend) (aus-)dehnen, spannen, ausbreiten; (reach out) ausstrecken; zu weit ausdehnen, über-treiben, -schreiten (*fig.*); über den Leisten schlagen (*a boot*); to — a point, ein Übriges tun, fünf gerade sein lassen. II. *v.n.* sich (er)strecken, sich dehnen; (— a point) sich anstrengen; (exaggerate) aufschneiden. III. *s.* die Strecke, Weite; (strain) die Spannung, Anstrengung, Kraft; (course) der Lauf, die Richtung; at a —, in einem Zuge, auf einmal; (in case of need) im Notfalle; 4 hours at a —, 4 Stunden hintereinander; by a — of imagination, durch eine Anstrengung der Einbildungskraft; to be on the —, in peinlicher Ungewißheit sein; to keep on the —, in Spannung erhalten. **—er**, *s.* einer, der streckt &c.; der Handschuhweiter (*for gloves*); die Rippe, der Spannstab (*of an umbrella*); der Fußstock, die Fußlade (*in a boat*); der Richtleisten (*for shoes, etc.*); die Tragbahre (*for the sick, etc.*); das Streck-, Quer-holz, der Läufer(stein) (*Build.*); die Übertreibung, Aufschneiderei (*coll.*). *Comp.* **—er-bearer**, *s.* der Krankenträger.

Strew, *v.a.* bestreuen, bedecken; (— about, umher-)streuen. **—n**, *imperf. & p.p. of* —.

Stri—ae, *pl.* Streifen; Riefen (*on pillars*). **—ate(d)**, *adj.* gestreift; gerieft.

Stricken, I. (*rare*) *p.p. of* Strike. II. *adj.*; — in years, hochbejahrt; alt und hochbetagt (*B.*).

Strict, *adj.*, **—ly**, *adv.* streng; (exact) genau; stark, groß, fest; a — love of justice, eine starke Gerechtigkeitsliebe; to keep a — watch upon, über (einen) streng wachen; in the — sense (of the word), streng genommen, im engeren Sinne; — order, ausdrücklicher *or* gemessener, strenger Befehl. **—ness**, *s.* die Strenge, Schärfe; die Genauigkeit, Pünktlichkeit. **—ure**, *s.* die Anspielung, kritische Bemerkung; die Vereng(er)ung (*Med.*).

Strid, (*obs.*) *imperf. of* —e. **—den**, *p.p. of* —e. **—e**, I. *s.* der (weite) Schritt; (progress) der Fortschritt. II. *ir.v.n.* (—e along, dahin-)schreiten; *see* Straddle.

Strid—ent, *adj.* knarrend, quietschend, schneidend, grell (*sound*). **—ulous**, *adj. see* —ent; quiekend (*as a voice*).

Strife, *s.* das Bemühen; der Wettstreit; der Streit; der Widerspruch; das Widerstreben; der Hader; der Kampf, Krieg.

Strike, I. *ir.v.a.* schlagen; (hit) stoßen, schlagen, treffen; (ein)schlagen (*root*); schlagen (*the hours, etc.*); prägen, münzen (*coin, etc.*); streichen (*a flag, sails, etc.*); abbrechen (*a tent*); einstellen (work, die Arbeit); (touch) rühren, ergreifen, auffallen; (ab)schließen (*a bargain*); anschlagen, spielen (*a guitar, etc.*); auffallen (the eye, dem Auge); machen (blind, blind); anzünden, machen (a light, Licht); to — an attitude, eine (theatralische) Stellung annehmen; to — a balance, den Saldo ziehen *or* ausgleichen; to — a blow, einen Schlag tun *or* versetzen; to — dead, töten; to — dumb, verstummen machen; to — hands, einander die Hände reichen (*coll.*); to — hard, heftig treffen; to — home, (einem) einen empfindlichen Schlag versetzen, (einen) empfindlich treffen; — while the iron is hot, man muß das Eisen schmieden, solange es warm ist (*prov.*); to — oil, eine Ölquelle finden; es gut treffen (*coll.*); to — the sands, stranden; it struck me, mir fiel auf; the thought struck me, mir kam der Gedanke; I was struck by this remark, ich wurde von dieser Bemerkung betroffen; to — **asunder**, entzweischlagen; to — **down**, nieder-, zu Boden schlagen, fällen; to — **in**, hineinschlagen (in eine S.); to — **off**, abschlagen, abhauen; (print) abziehen, abdrucken; (erase) ausstreichen; to — off a p.'s head, einem den Kopf abschlagen, einen köpfen; to — **out**, ausstreichen (*a name, etc.*); herausschlagen (*sparks, etc.*), entwerfen, erfinden (*a course, plan, etc.*); to — **up**, in die Höhe schlagen; (play) aufspielen, anstimmen (*a tune*); rühren (*the drum*); to — **upon**, schlagen auf (*acc.*); to — **with** awe, surprise, mit Ehrfurcht, mit Bestürzung erfüllen; to — with alarm, (einem) Furcht einjagen. II. *ir.v.n.* schlagen; (auf den Grund) stoßen, geraten auf (*acc.; Naut.*); (— colours) die Flagge streichen; die Arbeit einstellen, streiken; schlagen (*as clocks*); einschlagen (*of lightning*); to — **against**, schlagen, stoßen an an (eine S.); to — **at**, schlagen nach; to — **in**, hineinschlagen; to — **into**, sich wenden in (eine Straße, *etc.*); to — **on**, fallen, treffen auf (*acc.*) (*as light*); to — **up**, anspielen; to — upon the ear, das Ohr treffen. III. *s.* der (Arbeiter-)Ausstand, Streik. **—r**, *s.* der Schläger; der ausständische Streiker (*of work*); —er out, der Rückschläger (*Tennis*).

Striking, I. *p. of* Strike; without —ing a blow, ohne einen Schlag zu tun. II. *adj.*, **—ingly**, *adv.* in die Augen fallend, auffallend, treffend; —ing likeness, treffende, überraschende *or* sofort in die Augen fallende Ähnlichkeit.

String, I. *s.* die Schnur, das Band, der Bindfaden; die Sehne (*of a bow*); die Saite (*Mus.*); die Fiber, Faser (*Bot.*); a — of, eine Schnur (*beads, pearls, etc.*); a long — of nonsense, ein Langes und Breites von Unsinn; — of arguments, eine Reihe, Folge von Gründen; to be always harping on the same —, immer auf der alten Leier spielen; to have two —s to one's bow, zwei Mittel in Bereitschaft haben. II. *ir. v.a.* (auf)reihen; besaiten, mit Saiten beziehen (*Mus.*); beziehen (*an instrument*); abziehen (*beans*); a highly strung nature, eine hochgespannte, feinbesaitete Natur; to — up, aufziehen, hängen; —ed instrument, das Saiteninstrument. III. *ir.v.n.;* to — for lead, losen um den Beginn (*Bill.*). —**iness**, *s.* die Faserigkeit. —**less**, *adj.* unbesaitet. —**s**, *pl.* Saiteninstrumente. —**y**, *adj.* faserig, zaserig; klebrig, zähe. *Comp.* —**-band**, *s.* die Kapelle von Saiteninstrumenten. —**-box**, *s.* der Saitenbehälter, die Saitenkapsel. —**-halt**, *s.* der Hahnenschritt (*Vet.*).

Stringen—cy, *s.* die Strenge, Knappheit (*of money, etc.*); die Bündigkeit, Härte. —**t**, *adj.*, —**tly**, *adv.* streng, kräftig, nachdrücklich; —t rule, feste Regel.

Strip, I. *v.a.* abstreifen, abziehen; (ab)schälen (*bark, etc.*); ausmelken (*cows*); abschälen, streifen (*Agr.*); abtakeln (*ships*); (divest) entblößen, ausziehen, berauben; to — a p. of a th., einem etwas entziehen; to — naked, nackt ausziehen. II. *v.n.* sich ausziehen (*coll.*). III. *s.* der (schmale) Streifen, das Streifchen. —**e**, I. *s.* der Streifen, Strich; (wale) der Striemen, Hieb, die Wunde; (stroke) der Schlag; the stars and —es, die Flagge der nordamerikanischen Union; to get his —es, die Tressen erhalten (*Mil.*). II. *v.a.* streifen. —**ed**, *adj.* gestreift, streifig. —**ling**, I. *s.* der junge Mensch, das Bürschchen. II. *adj.* jugendlich, Jugend-.

Strive, *ir.v.n.* (sich be)streben, sich anstrengen *or* bemühen; (contend) sich sträuben, streiten, kämpfen, ringen; (vie) wetteifern; to — for the mastery, um den Vorzug streiten. —**n**, *p.p. of* —. —**r**, *s.* der Strebende.

Strode, *imperf. of* Stride.

Stroke, I. *s.* der (Feder-, Pinsel-)Strich, Zug; (blow) der Schlag, Streich, Hieb; der Stoß (*Bill.*); der Schlag (*of a hammer, bell, clock, etc.*); der Strich (*Engr.*); der Schlag (*of calamity; of an oar*); der Stich (*of the sun*); der (Schlag-)Anfall (*Med.*); der Hub, Schlag (*of the piston, etc.*); der Strauch (*of a mill-wheel*); der Zug (*of business*); (—sman) der Vormann; bold —, kühner Zug; — of genius, das Meisterstück, geniale Leistung; a great — of statecraft, ein großer staatsmännischer Zug; upon the — of three, auf den Schlag drei; down (up) —, Grund-, (Haar-)Strich; to row with a long —, lang rojen; to pull —, den Takt beim Rudern angeben; to keep —, Takt schlagen. II. *v.a.* streiche(l)n. *Comp.* —**-bell**, *s.* die Schlagglocke (*Cycl.*). —**-oar**, *s.* der Vormann.

Stroll, I. *s.* das Herumziehen, Schlendern; to go for a —, einen kleinen Spaziergang machen. II. *v.n.* (— about) herum-streichen, -schlendern, -wandern; to — **out**, hinausschlendern; to — **up and down**, hin- und her-schlendern; —ing actor, player, umherziehender Schauspieler. —**er**, *s.* der Strolch; der Dorfkomödiant.

Strong, *adj.*, —**ly**, *adv.* stark; (powerful) kräftig, gewaltig; (firm) fest, stark, dauerhaft; stark, derb (*as food*); stark, berauschend (*as wine*); stark, ranzig (*as a smell, taste, etc.*); (numerous) zahlreich, mächtig; stark, voll (*as a voice, a pulse*); stark, hell, grell (*as light*); (ardent) eifrig; stark, ablautend, unregelmäßig (*Gram.*); — argument, starker Beweis, schwerwiegender Grund (für); — constitution, kräftige Leibesbeschaffenheit; — conviction, feste *or* unerschütterliche Überzeugung; to use — language, sich stark ausdrücken; fluchen; with a — hand, mit Gewalt; 6000 —, 6000 Mann stark; — on the wing, schon gut flügge (*of young birds*); — impression, starker, tiefer Eindruck; — will, fester, unbeugsamer Wille; — wind, stetiger Wind; their proposals savour —ly of, ihre Vorschläge schmecken stark nach; I feel very —ly about it, es liegt mir sehr am Herzen, mir liegt sehr viel daran. *Comp.* —**-backed**, *adj.* mit starkem Rücken. —**-bodied**, *adj.* stark (*also of wine*). —**hold**, *s.* die Festung, Feste; das Bollwerk (*fig.*). —**-limbed**, *adj.* starkgliederig. —**-minded**, *adj.* geistesstark, von großem Geist. —**-room**, *s.* feuerfester, diebessicherer Kassenraum. —**-willed**, *adj.* von starker Willenskraft.

Strook, (*obs.*) *imperf. of* Strike.

Strop, I. *s.* der Streichriemen, Abzieher (*for razors*). II. *v.a.* streichen.

Stroph—e, *s.* die Strophe, der Vers(ab)satz. —**ic**, *adj.* strophisch, aus Strophen bestehend.

Strove, *imperf.* (*& obs. p.p.*) *of* Strive.

Strown, *p.p. of* Strow.

Struck, *imperf. & p.p. of* Strike; betroffen, bestürzt. —**en**, (*obs. dial.*) *p.p. of* Strike.

Structur—al, *adj.* den Bau betreffend, baulich; organisch. —**e**, *s.* (building) der Bau, das Gebäude; die Bauart, die Zusammensetzung, Fügung; das Gefüge; —e of sentences, das Satzgefüge, der Satzbau.

Struggle, I. *s.* das heftige Mühen, Ringen, Sträuben; (fight) der Kampf; — for existence, Kampf ums Dasein. II. *v.n.* sich anstrengen, sich abmühen, sich winden, sich sträuben; (— against) ringen, kämpfen (against, gegen, with, mit); ankämpfen, anstreben (wider); zappeln (*in a net, etc.*); to — out of, sich losringen von. —**r**, *s.* der Kämpfer, Ringer. —**s**, *pl.* Zuckungen, Verzerrungen.

Strum, *v.n.* klimpern, schlecht spielen (auf einem Instrument).

Strum—a, *s.* der Kropf (*Med., Bot.*). —**ous**, *adj.* kropfartig, kröpfig.

Strumpet, *s.* die Dirne, das gemeine Weibsbild.

Strung, *imperf. & p.p. of* String.

Strut, I. *v.n.* strotzen, sich brüsten, stolzieren. II. *s.* das Sich-Brüsten, Stolzieren; der stolze Gang; die Strebe (*Build.*). —**ter**, *s.* der Stolzierende; der Großtuer, Prahler. —**ting**, *adj.*, —**tingly**, *adv.* stolzierend.

Struthious, *adj.* straußartig, den Strauß betreffend.

Strychnine, *s.* das Strychnin.

Stub, I. *s.* der (Baum-)Stumpf, Stock. II. *v.a.* (— up) entwurzeln, ausreißen. —**ble**, *s.* die Stoppel. —**bly**, *adj.* stoppelig, stoppelartig. —**born**, *adj.*, —**bornly**, *adv.* steif, starr, unbiegsam, hart; (obstinate) hartnäckig, widerspenstig, halsstarrig; (persistent) beharrlich, ausdauernd; stet; (steady) standhaft; strengflüssig (*Metall.*). —**bornness**, *s.* die Unbiegsamkeit, Hartnäckigkeit; die Strengflüssigkeit. —**by**, *adj.* kurz und dick, untersetzt. *Comp.* —**ble-field**, *s.* das Stoppelfeld. —**-nail**, *s.* der Kupp(en)nagel.

Stucco, I. *s.* der Stuck, Gipsmörtel; (— work) die Stuck(atur)arbeit; — ornaments, *pl.* Stuckverzierungen. II. *v.a.* mit Stuck überziehen.

Stuck, *imperf. & p.p. of* Stick.

Stuck-up, *adj.* eingebildet, steif, hochnäsig.

[1]**Stud**, *s.* das Gestüt; (horses) die Anzahl Pferde. *Comp.* —**-book**, *s.* das Zuchtbuch; das (Pferde- *etc.*) Stammbuch. —**-horse**, *s.* der Zuchthengst.

[2]**Stud**, I. *s.* der Stift, Knauf, plattierte Beschlag-Nagel; (shirt, *etc.*, —) der (Hemden- 2c.) Knopf; der Ständer (*Build.*). II. *v.a.* beschlagen, verzieren (*with nails, etc.*); besetzen, besäen; —ded with trees, mit Bäumen besetzt. *Comp.* —**ding-sail**, *s.* das Leesegel.

Stud—ent, *s.* der (die) Student(in) (*Univ.*); der Lernende, Forschende, Studierende; der Forscher, Gelehrte; a close —ent, ein anhaltend, fleißig, emsig Studierender; —ent of nature, die Naturforscher; —ent of psychology, der Psycholog, Seelenforscher; —ent teacher, der Kandidat des höheren Lehramts während seines Seminarjahrs; —ent's dictionary, das Handwörterbuch; he is a real —ent, er studiert aus Liebe zur Sache. **—entship**, *s.* das Stipendium; the travelling —entship, das Reisestipendium. **—ied**, *adj.* durchdacht, studiert; (learned) belesen, gelehrt; (deliberate) vorbedacht, vorsätzlich, absichtlich; (affected) gesucht, erkünstelt; a —ied reserve, eine angenommene Zurückhaltung. **—io**, *s.* das Atelier. **—ious**, *adj.*, **—iously**, *adv.* dem Studium obliegend; (industrious) fleißig, emsig; bedacht, aufmerksam (of, auf eine S.); beflissen, bemüht (to please, zu gefallen); to lead a —ious life, fleißig studieren. **—iousness**, *s.* der Fleiß im Studieren; die Liebe zur Wissenschaft. **—y**, I. *s.* das Studieren, Forschen, Lernen, Studium, das Eindringen *or* Sichversenken (in eine S.); (object of —y) das Studium; die Wissenschaft; (diligence) das eifrige Streben, die fleißige Bemühung; (room) die Studierstube, das Arbeitszimmer; das Studienstück, Vorlegeblatt; he makes it his —y to, er bemüht sich, legt sich darauf, zu . . .; the Scriptures are her daily —y, die heilige Schrift ist ihr tägliches Studium. II. *v.n.* studieren, den Wissenschaften obliegen; (ponder) nachdenken, sinnen; streben, sich bemühen *or* befleißigen; to —y for, auf (eine S. hin) studieren. III. *v.a.* studieren; (learn) (ein)lernen, einstudieren; betreiben, studieren (*languages*); (ponder) durchdenken, erforschen, genau untersuchen, nachdenken (über, *acc.*), sinnen (auf, *acc.*).

Stuff, I. *s.* der Stoff, die Materie, Masse; der Stoff, das Wesentliche (*fig.*); das Zeug, Gewebe, der Stoff (*Weav.*); der Arzneistoff (*Med.*); dummes Zeug, der Unsinn; die Salbe, Schmiere (*Naut.*); das Geld (*sl.*); he has the — of an artist in him, er hat das Zeug zu einem Künstler; — and nonsense! dummes Zeug! good —, etwas Delikates (*coll.*); household —, Hausgerät(e). II. *v.a.* (voll)stopfen, (an)füllen; überladen (*fig.*); füllen (*Cook.*); ausstopfen (*birds, etc.*); polstern (*chairs*); to — up, zu-, ver-stopfen. III. *v.n.* sich vollstopfen (mit Speise), viel essen. **—iness**, *s.* die Dumpfigkeit, Schwüle. **—ing**, *s.* die Füllung; das Füllhaar (*for chairs*); das Füllsel, die Farce (*Cook.*). **—y**, *adj.* dick (air); dumpfig (a room); schwül (weather).

Stultify, *v.a.* wertlos machen; für wahnwitzig erklären; to — o.s., sich (*dat.*) widersprechen.

Stumbl—e, I. *v.n.* stolpern, straucheln, fehl treten; to —e **over**, wegfallen über (*acc.*); to —e **upon**, zufällig stoßen auf (*acc.*), antreffen, geraten auf (*acc.*), finden. II. *s.* das Stolpern; der Fehltritt (*fig.*). **—er**, *s.* der, die Stolpernde. **—ing**, I. *adj.*, **—ingly**, *adv.* stolpernd. II. *s.* das Stolpern; der Fehltritt. **—y**, *adj.* leicht stolpernd. *Comp.* **—ing-block**, *s.* das Hindernis. **—ing-stone**, *s.* der Stein des Anstoßes; das Hindernis (für) (*fig.*).

Stump, I. *s.* der (Baum-, Zahn-, Arm- &c.) Stumpf (*of a tree, a tooth, an arm, etc.*); der Stab (*Cricket*); der Wischer (*Draw.*); to stir one's —s, sich auf die Beine machen (*sl.*); to be on the —, *see* to — the country, zum Volke reden. II. *v.a.* (ab)stumpfen; (puzzle) verblüffen (*coll.*); das Ballgestell niederwerfen (*Cricket*); to — the country, Wahlreden haltend im Land herumziehen; to — it, sich aus dem Staube machen (*sl.*); to — a boy in an examination, einen Jungen in einer Prüfung hereinlegen (*sl.*). III. *v.n.* schwerfällig gehen; to — up, bar bezahlen (*sl.*). **—ed**, *adj.* geldlos (*vulg.*). **—er**, *s.* einer, der Wahlreden hält (*sl.*); die verblüffende Frage (*sl.*). **—y**, *adj.* kurz und dick. *Comp.* **—orator**, *s.* der Redner bei Wahlen, Volksredner. **—oratory**, *s.* die Wahlredekunst.

Stun, *v.a.* betäuben; bestürzt machen (*fig.*). **—ner**, *s.* der, die, das Wunderbare, Famose (*sl.*). **—ning**, *adj.* famos (*vulg.*).

Stung, *imperf. & p.p. of* Sting.

Stunk, *imperf. & p.p. of* Stink.

Stunt, *v.a.* am Wachstum hindern. **—ed**, *adj.* verkürzt, im Wuchs verkümmert.

Stupe, *v.a.* der warme Umschlag. II. *v.a.* bähen.

Stup—efaction, *s.* die Betäubung; (dulness) der Stumpfsinn. **—efy**, *v.a.* betäuben; bestürzt machen; (make —id) verdummen. **—endous**, *adj.*, **—endously**, *adv.* erstaunlich (*coll.*). **—endousness**, *s.* das Erstaunliche. **—id**, *adj.*, **—idly**, *adv.* (—efied) betäubt, verblüfft; (silly, dull) dumm, einfältig, albern, geistlos, blöde; —id rimes, fade Reime; —id fellow, der Dummkopf. **—idity**, *s.* die Dummheit, der Stumpfsinn (*fig.*). **—or**, *s.* die Betäubung, Erstarrung; das Erstaunen; —or of the limbs, das Eingeschlafensein der Glieder; —or of the mind, der Stumpfsinn.

Sturd—ily, *adv.*, **—y**, *adj.*, stark, handfest, kräftig; (bold) derb, dreist. **—iness**, *s.* die Stärke, Festigkeit, Derbheit.

Sturgeon, *s.* der Stör.

Stutter, *v.n.* stottern, stammeln. **—er**, *s.* der Stotterer, Stammler.

[1]**Sty**, I. *s.* (*pl.* Sties) der (Schweine-)Stall. II. *v.a.* in einen Schweinestall sperren; einsperren (*fig.*). III. *v.n.* in einem Schweinestall leben (*also fig.*).

[2]**Sty(e)**, *s.* das Gerstenkorn.

[1]**Styl—e**, I. *s.* der Stichel (*Engr.*); die Sonde (*Surg.*); der Stilus, Griffel (*of the ancients*); die Rede-, Ausdrucks-weise, der Stil (*fig.*); der Stil (*Arch., Paint., Mus., Chron.*); (way) die Art, Weise; (title) die Benennung, der Titel; judicial —e, der Kanzleistil; in —e, prunkhaft, hochtrabend; in first-rate —e, herrlich, prächtig, nach neuestem Geschmack; to live in —e, ein großes Haus machen, Aufwand machen; in bad (good) —e, in schlechtem (gutem) Geschmack. II. *v.a.* (be)nennen, betiteln. **—et**, *s.* das Stilett. **—ish**, *adj.*, **—ishly**, *adv.* modisch (*as dress*); flott, wobei es hoch hergeht (*as a way of living, etc.*); (showy) prunkhaft. **—ishness**, *s.* die Eleganz, das feine modische Wesen. **—ist**, *s.* der Stilist, Meister des feinen Stils. **—istic**, *adj.* stilistisch. **—ographic**, *adj.* stylographisch; —ographic pen, die Griffelfeder. **—ography**, *s.* die Stylographie, Griffel-Schreibekunst.

[2]**Styl—e**, *s.* die Säule, der Pfeiler; der Zeiger (*of a sun-dial*); der Blumengriffel (*Bot.*). **—ite**, *s.* der Säulenheilige.

Styptic, I. *adj.* blutstillend. II. *s.* blutstillendes Mittel.

Suasion, *s.* die Beredung, Überredung.

Suav—e, *adj.*, **—ely**, *adv.* angenehm, sanft, gewinnend. **—ity**, *s.* die Lieblichkeit, Anmut, Sanftmut; das Verbindliche (*of manners*).

Sub, I. *pref.* = unter. II. *s. see* —altern I., —ordinate II. *Comp.* (*generally* = unter). —**acid**, I. *s.* säuerliche Substanz. II. *adj.* säuerlich; beißend (*fig.*). **—altern**, I. *s.* der Subalternoffizier. II. *adj.* untergeordnet, Unter-. —**axillary**, *adj.* unter der Achselhöhle; Unterachsel- (*Bot.*). **—carbonate**, *s.*; —carbonate of soda, das einfach kohlensaure Natron. —**commissioner**, *s.* der Unterkommissär. —**committee**, *s.* der Unterausschuß. **—contrary**, *adj.* subkonträr (*Log.*); —contrary section, der Wechselschnitt (*Geom.*). **—costal**, *adj.* unter den Rippen. **—cutaneous**, *adj.* unter der Haut, unterhäutig. **—dean**, *s.* der Unter-Dechant, -Dekan. **—divide**, *v.a.* Unterabteilungen machen. **—division**, *s.* die Unterabteilung. **—dominant**, *s.* die Unter-, Sub-Dominante (*Mus.*). **—due**, *v.a.* unterwerfen, bezwingen, überwältigen, überwinden, besiegen (*also fig.*); besiegen, unterdrücken (*passions*); kreuzigen (*one's flesh*); mildern, dämpfen (*light, colours, etc.*); —dued colours, matte Farben; —dued voice, gedämpfte Stimme. —**generic**, *adj.* zu einer Untergattung gehörig. —**genus**, *s.* die Untergattung. —**inspector**, *s.* der Unterinspektor. —**jacent**, *adj.* darunter *or* tiefer liegend. —**ject**, I. *adj.* unter=geben, =worfen, =tan, dienstbar; (liable) aus=gesetzt, unterworfen; (obedient) gehorsam (*B.*); —ject matter, der Gegenstand, Hauptinhalt (*of a discourse*); —ject to the regulations, gemäß den gesetzlichen Bestimmungen; —ject to my order, nach meinem Geheiß, zu meiner Verfügung. II. *s.* der Untertan; der Gegenstand (*of discourse, etc.*); das Fach; das Subjekt (*Log., Philos., Gram.*); die Leiche, der Kadaver (*Anat.*); die Person, Versuchsperson (*Med.*); der Hauptsatz, das Thema (*Mus.*); compulsory —jects, obligatorische Fächer; optional —jects, wahlfreie, fakultative Fächer; chief —ject, der Hauptgegenstand; das Hauptfach; additional —ject, das Nebenfach; British —jects, Britische Untertanen; English —jects, Englische Fächer in der Schule, d. h. Englische Sprache, Geschichte, Geographie, und auch Religion; the —ject treated of, die behandelte Sache. III. *v.a.* legen unter, unterlegen; *see* —due; (expose) bloßstellen, aussetzen (*dat.*). —**jection**, *s.* das Unterwerfen; (state of —jection) die Unterwerfung (to, unter), das Unterworfensein; (dependence) die Abhängigkeit; to bring into —jection, unterwerfen. —**jective**, *adj.*, —**jectively**, *adv.* subjektiv. —**jectiveness**, —**jectivity**, *s.* die Subjektivität. —**join**, *v.a.* noch hinzufügen. —**jugate**, *v.a.* unterjochen (*also fig.*). —**jugation**, *s.* die Unterjochung. —**junctive**, *s.* (—junctive mood) der Konjunktiv. —**let**, *v.a.* aftervermieten, weitergeben. —**librarian**, *s.* der Unterbibliothekar. —**lieutenant**, *s.* der Unterleutnant. —**limate**, I. *s.* das Sublimat. II. *v.a.* sublimieren. —**limation**, *s.* die Sublimation. —**lime**, I. *adj.*, —**limely**, *adv.* erhaben, hehr, hoch; —lime Porte, Hohe Pforte. II. *s.* das Erhabene, der erhabene Stil. —**limity**, *s.* die Erhabenheit. —**lingual**, *adj.* Unterzungen=. —**lunar(y)**, *adj.* unter dem Monde (befindlich), irdisch. —**marine**, I. *adj.* unterseeisch. II. *s.* das Unterseeboot. —**mediant**, *s.* die Submediante (*Mus.*). —**merge**, *v.a.* unter Wasser setzen, überschwemmen (*land, etc.*); (*also v.n.*) untertauchen. —**mergence**, *s.* das Unter=tauchen, =sinken; die Überschwemmung. —**mersion**, *s.* die Untertauchung; die Überschwemmung. —**mission**, *s.* die Unterwerfung, Ergebung (to the will of another, in den Willen eines andern); (—missiveness) die Unter=würfigkeit, =tänigkeit; (obedience) der Gehorsam. —**missive**, *adj.*, —**missively**, *adv.* unter=würfig, =tänig; gehorsam; (humble) demütig. —**missiveness**, *s.* die Unterwürfigkeit, Demut. —**mit**, *v.a.* überlassen, anheim=geben, =stellen; (lay before) vor=, dar=legen; to —mit o.s., sich (einem) unterwerfen; untertan sein (*B.*). II. *n.* sich ergeben, sich gefangen geben; *see* Yield; sich fügen (to, in eine S.). —**multiple**, *s.* der in einer Zahl gewisse Male enthaltene Faktor. —**ordinate**, I. *adj.*, —**ordinately**, *adv.* untergeordnet, Unter=; —ordinate sentence, abhängiger Satz. II. *s.* der Untergeordnete. III. *v.a.* unterordnen; (subject) unterwerfen. —**ordination**, *s.* die Unterordnung; die Unterwerfung; (obedience) der (Dienst=)Gehorsam. —**orn**, *v.a.* (zur Ablegung eines falschen Zeugnisses) verleiten. —**ornation**, *s.* die Erkaufung falscher Zeugen (*Law*). —**orner**, *s.* der Verführer (zum Meineid). —**pœna**, I. *s.* die Vorladung (bei Strafe). II. *v.a.* bei Strafe vorladen, zitieren. —**scribe**, *v.* I. *a.* unter=schreiben, =zeichnen; zeichnen (*ten pounds, etc.*). II. *n.* abonnieren (to, auf eine S.); (agree) einwilligen (to, in eine S.), beipflichten (to a th., einer Sache), sich verstehen (to, zu); to —scribe to the 39 Articles, sich zu den 39 Artikeln bekennen; risk —scribed, übernommene Gefahr (*C.L.*); to —scribe for 1000 copies, 1000 Exemplare fest bestellen. —**scriber**, *s.* der Unterzeichner; der Subskribent, Abonnent; list of —scribers, die Subskriptions=, Abonnenten=liste. —**scription**, *s.* das Unterschreiben, die Unterzeichnung; (signature) die Unterschrift; das Abonnement; (amount —scribed) gezeichnete Summe; —scriptions may be sent, Vorbestellungsgelder können geschickt werden *or* sind zu richten an (*acc.*); yearly —scription, der Jahresbeitrag, Preis des Jahrgangs. —**sequence**, *s.* das Später=Eintreffen, =Eintreten. —**sequent**, *adj.* (nach)folgend, nachherig; —sequent to that period, nach dieser Zeit; —sequent clause, der Zusatzartikel. —**sequently**, *adv.* hernach, darauf, später. —**serve**, *v.a.* förderlich *or* dienlich sein, befördern. —**servience**, —**serviency**, *s.* die Dienlichkeit, Förderlichkeit; die Unterwürfigkeit; in —servience to our wishes, aus Willfährigkeit gegen unsere Wünsche. —**servient**, *adj.* (useful) dienlich, nützlich, förderlich; (subordinate) untergeordnet, dienend. —**side**, *v.n.* sich setzen (*also Chem.*), sich senken, sinken; (settle down) sich legen (*also of wind*), nachlassen; allmählich werden (into, zu); a tunnel —sided, ein Tunnel senkte sich. —**sidence**, *s.* das Sich=Setzen, =Senken, die Abnahme (*fig.*). —**sidiaries**, *pl.* Hilfstruppen. —**sidiary**, *adj.* Hilfe leistend, behilflich, zur Aushilfe dienend, mitwirkend; Hilfs= (-treaty, -troops, =vertrag, =truppen); —sidiary subject, das Nebenfach. —**sidies**, *pl.* Hilfsgelder. —**sidize**, *v.a.* Hilfsgelder zahlen, mit Hilfsgeldern unterstützen. —**sidy**, *s.* das Hilfsgeld; (tax) die Hilfs=Beisteuer. —**sist**, *v.n.* sein; bestehen, Bestand haben; to —sist on, leben *or* sich ernähren von. —**sistence**, *s.* (existence) das Dasein; der Unterhalt, die Nahrung, das Auskommen; (inherence) das Inwohnen, die Inhärenz. —**sistent**, *adj.* bestehend; *see* Inherent. —**soil**, *s.* der Untergrund. —**species**, *s.* die Unterart. —**stance**, *s.* die Substanz; (real thing) das Wesen, Ding; (essence) das Wesentliche; (important element) der Hauptinhalt, wesentliche Teil, Inhalt; (reality) die Wirklichkeit; (solidity) die Festigkeit, der Körper; (strength) die Kraft, das Mark, der Kern; (means) die Habe, das Vermögen; (stuff) der Stoff, die Substanz; in —stance, im Wesentlichen; we are exhausting our —stance, wir erschöpfen unser Vermögen; the —stance of his remarks, der Hauptinhalt seiner Bemerkungen (hieß 2c.); to sacrifice the —stance to the shadow, das Wesen dem (bloßen) Scheine opfern. —**stantial**, I. *adj.*, —**stantially**, *adv.* wesentlich; (real) wirklich, wahrhaft; (corporeal) körperlich, materiell; (solid, strong) stark, fest (*also fig.*), dicht; nahrhaft, kräftig (*as food, a meal*); wohlhabend; —stantial damages, wesentliche Entschädigung; —stantial lessees, zuverlässige Mieter; —stantial meal, ein kräftiges Mahl, eine tüchtige Mahlzeit. II. *s.* das (wirkliche) Ding; der Hauptpunkt, wesentliche Teil. —**stantiality**, —**stantialness**, *s.* die Wesentlichkeit; die Materialität; die Stärke, Festigkeit; die Nahrhaftigkeit. —**stantiate**, *v.a.* beweisen, erhärten, bestätigen. —**stantive**, I. *adj.*, —**stantively**, *adv.* als Hauptwort (gebraucht), substantivisch; —stantive verb, das Zeitwort „sein." II. *s.* (noun —stantive) das Hauptwort, Substantiv. —**stitute**, I. *v.a.* an eines andern Stelle (ein=) setzen, unterschieben. II. *s.* der Stell=, Amtsvertreter; (thing —stituted) das Ersatzmittel. —**stitution**, *s.* die Einsetzung eines Stellvertreters, Unterschiebung; (state of —stituting) die Stellvertretung; die Substitution, Vertauschung (*Alg.*); die Syllepsis (*Gram.*); die Aftereinsetzung (*Law*). —**stratum**, *s.* die Unterlage; (layer) die Schicht; die Substanz (*Log.*). —

structure, *s.* der Unterbau. —**tend**, *v.a.* gegenüberliegen, sich hinziehen unter (*dat.*). —**terfuge**, *s.* die leere Ausflucht. —**terranean**, —**terraneous**, *adj.* unterirdisch. —**tile**, *adj.* fein, dünn, zart; *see* —tle. —**tility**, *s.* die Feinheit. —**tilization**, *s.* die Verfeinerung, Verdünnung; die Verfeinerung, Spitzfindigkeit (*fig.*). —**tilize**, *v.* I. *a.* verfeinern (*also fig.*). II. *n.* spitzfindig sein, grübeln. —**tle**, *adj.*, —**tly**, *adv.* fein; *see* Artful; fein, scharfsinnig (*as a thought, etc.*). —**tlety**, *s.* die Feinheit; die Subtilität, Spitzfindigkeit (*fig.*); *see* Artfulness. —**tract**, *v.a.* abziehen, subtrahieren. —**traction**, *s.* das Abziehen, die Subtraktion. —**trahend**, *s.* der Subtrahend (*Arith.*). —**urb**, *s.* die Vorstadt, der Vorort. —**urban**, *adj.* vorstädtisch, in der Vorstadt. —**vene**, *v.n.* hinzukommen, zu Hilfe kommen, (einem) beistehen. —**vention**, *s.* die Beisteuer, Hilfe. —**version**, *s.* der Umsturz. —**versive**, *adj.* umstürzend, zerstörend; to be —versive of a th., etwas umstürzen, umwerfen. —**vert**, *v.a.* um-kehren, -stoßen, -stürzen; (pervert) ver-kehren, -führen, -derben. —**verter**, *s.* der Zerstörer. —**vertible**, *adj.* umstürzbar. —**way**, *s.* unterirdischer Gang *or* Weg; die Unterführung, Straßenunterführung.

Succeed, *v.* I. *n.* folgen; nachfolgen (on the throne, auf dem Throne; to an office, in einem Amte); glücken, gelingen, Erfolg haben, von statten gehen; he —s in everything, alles gelingt, glückt ihm; if I — in my undertaking, wenn mein Unternehmen mir gelingt; I have —ed in this, es ist mir hierin gelungen; I have —ed in drawing attention to this, es ist mir gelungen, die Aufmerksamkeit hierauf zu richten; to — with a p., es bei einem durchsetzen. II. *a.* (einem) (nach)folgen; to — a p., einem folgen. —**ing**, *adj.* nachfolgend.

Success, *s.* (result) der Ausgang, Erfolg; der glückliche Erfolg, das Gelingen, Glück; to wish a p. — in, einem Glück wünschen zu; he was a great —, er hatte großen Erfolg, er gewann allgemeinen Beifall. —**ful**, *adj.*, —**fully**, *adv.* erfolgreich, glücklich; the —ful candidates, die Durchgekommenen; die Angenommenen. —**ion**, *s.* die Reihe(nfolge); die Nachfolge (*in office, etc.*); (—ion to the throne) die Thronfolge; (order of —ion) die Erbfolge, Linie; (heirs) die Nachkommenschaft; by order of —ion, nach der Erbfolgeordnung; in —ion, nach, auf, hintereinander; right of —ion, das Erbfolgerecht; apostolical —ion, ununterbrochene apostolische Nachfolge; —ion of octaves, die Oktavengänge; war of —ion, Erbfolge-, Thronfolge-krieg. —**ional**, *adj.* Sukzessions-. —**ive**, *adj.* aufeinander folgend. —**ively**, *adv.* nach einander, der Reihe nach. —**or**, *s.* der Nachfolger; —or to the throne, Thronfolger.

Succinct, *adj.*, —**ly**, *adv.* kurz, bündig. —**ness**, *s.* die Kürze, Bündigkeit.

Succory, *see* Chicory.

Succour, I. *s.* die Hilfe, Unterstützung; *see* —er; Hilfstruppen, der Entsatz (*Mil.*). II. *v.a.* (einem) helfen, beispringen, zu Hilfe kommen, (einen) unterstützen; he has —ed her, er hat ihr geholfen. —**er**, *s.* der Helfer, Beistand.

Succulen—ce, *s.* die Saftigkeit. —**t**, *adj.* saftig.

Succumb, *v.n.*, unterliegen, erliegen.

Such, I. *adj. or pron.* solch; so; so groß, der Art; — another, eben ein solcher; auch so einer; — a one, so einer; at — a time, zu solcher *or* einer solchen Zeit; — are . . ., zum Beispiel, der Art sind . . .; — as, die(jenigen), welche; — books as contribute, solche Bücher, die dazu beitragen; his bravery was — as to, — was his bravery that . . ., so groß war seine Tapferkeit, daß . . .; at — time as you think proper, zu der Zeit, welche Sie für passend halten; — as you, (solche) Leute wie Sie; — and —, der und der, so einer; — creatures! welche (elende &c.) Geschöpfe! he did no — thing, er tat nichts dergleichen, das hat er wohl bleiben lassen; — like, dergleichen; — is my feeling, das ist mein Gefühl, so fühle ich; — is life, so geht es in der Welt. II. *adv.* so; es; you are happy now, I hope you will remain —, Sie sind jetzt glücklich; ich hoffe, Sie werden es bleiben.

Suck, I. *v.a. & n.* (ein)saugen; to — one's thumbs, sich (*dat.*) die Daumen lutschen; little —-a-thumb, der Daumenlutscher; to — **in**, — **out**, ein-, aus-saugen; to — **up**, einsaugen; to be —ed, geprellt werden (*sl.*). II. *s.* die Muttermilch; to give —, *see* —le; die Prellerei (*sl.*). —**er**, *s.* der Sprößling (*Hort.*); das Saugleder, die Sauge (*Mech.*); (—er pipe) das Saugrohr; der Lump, Bauchsauger (*Icht.*). —**ing**, I. *p.* saugend, Saug-; —ing bottle, das Saugfläschchen; —ing pig, das Spanferkel; —ing pump, *see* Suction pump. II. *s.* das Saugen, Einsaugen. —**le**, *v.a.* säugen, stillen. —**ling**, *s.* das Säugen; (infant) der Säugling.

Suct—ion, *s.* das Säugen; —ion pipe, valve, pump, das Saugrohr, Saugventil, die Saugpumpe. —**orial**, *adj.*, zum Saugen geschickt, Saug-. —**oria(ns)**, *pl.* Saugmäuler (*Icht.*).

Sud—atorium, —**atory**, *s.* das Schwitzbad. —**orific**, I. *adj.* schweißtreibend. II. *s.* das Schweißmittel.

Sudden, *adj.* (on a —), —**ly**, *adv.* plötzlich; hastig, vorschnell. —**ness**, *s.* die Plötzlichkeit.

Suds, *pl.* das Seifenwasser, die Seifenlauge.

Sue, *v.* I. *a.* gerichtlich verfolgen *or* belangen; (petition for) anhalten um; to — a p. for damages, einen auf Schadenersatz verklagen. II. *n.* klagen (for, auf eine S.), nachsuchen, bitten, werben (for, um), mit Bitten, Forderungen angehen.

Suet, *s.* das Nierenfett; der Talg.

Suffer, *v.* I. *a.* ertragen, aushalten, erdulden, ausstehen; (allow) (zu)lassen, gestatten, erlauben; (undergo) erleiden; to — a loss, einen Verlust erleiden; he —ed himself to be imposed on, er ließ sich anführen; this is not to be —ed, dies ist unerträglich. II. *n.* leiden; (sustain injury) Schaden leiden; (die) den Tod erleiden; to — for, büßen für; to — from, an (einer S.) leiden. —**able**, *adj.*, —**ably**, *adv.* erträglich, leidlich, zu erdulden. —**ableness**, *s.* die Erträglichkeit. —**ance**, *s.* das Leiden; die Duldung, Geduld, Toleranz; der Zollerlaubnisschein zur Ausfuhr (*C. L.*); on —ance, (nur eben) geduldet. —**er**, *s.* der, die Leidende; der, die Gestattende, Zulassende; one of the —ers, einer der Verunglückten; to be a —er by, leiden durch, verlieren bei. —**ing**, I. *adj.*, —**ingly**, *adv.* leidend. II. *s.* das Leiden; die Zulassung.

Suffic—e, *v.* I. *n.* genug sein, genügen; —e it to say, es möge hinreichen zu sagen. II. *a.* genug sein lassen; *see* Satisfy. —**iency**, *s.* die Hinlänglichkeit, Genüge; (competence) das Auskommen; (ability) die Fähigkeit, Tauglichkeit; self-—iency, (dünkelhafte) Selbstgenügsamkeit. —**ient**, *adj.*, —**iently**, *adv.* hinlänglich, genug; (able) fähig; to be —ient, genügen; to be —ient for, taugen, tüchtig sein zu; —ient unto the day is the evil thereof, es ist genug, daß ein jeglicher Tag seine Plage habe (*B.*), jeder Tag hat seine Plage; to have —ient, genug haben.

Suffix, I. *s.* die Nachsilbe, das Suffix. II. *v.a.* am Ende anhängen, anheften.

Suffocat—e, *v.a. & n.* ersticken. —**ing**, *adj.* erstickend. —**ingly**, *adv.* zum Ersticken. —**ion**, *s.* die Erstickung; death by —ion, der Erstickungstod. —**ive**, *adv.* erstickend.

Suffrag—an, I. *adj.* beistehend, Hilfs-. II. *s.* der Suffraganbischof. —**e**, *s.* die (Wahl-)Stimme; die Abstimmung; das Stimmrecht, Wahlrecht; woman's —e, das Frauenstimmrecht; universal —e, allgemeines Wahlrecht. —**ette**, —**ist**, *s.* die Frauenrechtlerin.

Suffus—e, *v.a.* übergießen; überziehen; —ed with blushes, with tears, mit Schamröte bedeckt, mit Tränen überströmt. —**ion**, *s.* die Ergießung; —ion of blood in the eye, das Blutauge.

Sugar, I. *s.* der Zucker; — of lead, Bleizucker. II. *v.a.* zuckern, versüßen; to — over, überzuckern. **—iness**, *s.* die Zuckersüßigkeit; die zuckerartige Beschaffenheit. **—less**, *adj.* zuckerlos. **—y**, *adj.* zuckerig, zuckersüß; (fond of —) das Süße liebend. *Comp.* **—-basin**, *s.* die Zucker-büchse, -dose. **—-bounty**, *s.* die Zuckerprämie. **—-box**, *s.* die Zuckerdose. **—-candy**, *s.* der Kandis(-zucker). **—-cane**, *s.* das Zuckerrohr. **—-caster**, *s.* die Zuckerstreubüchse. **—-coated**, *adj.* verzuckert, mit Zuckerguß. **—-loaf**, *s.* der Zuckerhut. **—-maple**, *s.* der Zuckerahorn. **—-plantation**, *s.* die Zuckerpflanzung, Zuckerplantage. **—plum**, *s.* das Bonbon; etwas besonders Süßes, Angenehmes (*fig.*). **—-refiner**, *s.* der Zuckersieder. **—-sifter**, *s.* der Zuckerstreuer. **—-tongs**, *pl.* die Zuckerzange.

Suggest, *v.a.* eingeben, in den Sinn geben, beibringen, einblasen, (Worte &c.) in den Mund legen (*words, etc.*); vorschlagen; hinweisen auf (*acc.*); suggerieren (*Hypnot.*); he —ed to me the propriety of . . ., er gab mir zu verstehen, daß es schicklich sein würde, wenn ich . . .; it —s, es legt nahe. **—er**, *s.* der, welcher eingiebt, einbläst. **—ion**, *s.* die Eingebung, Einflüsterung; (proposal) der Vorschlag; (hint) der (zarte) Wink; (instigation) die Anregung, der Antrieb; unbeeidigte Anzeige; die Suggestion (*Hypnot.*); at the —ion . . ., auf Anraten . . . **—ive**, *adj.*, **—ively**, *adv.* einen Wink, eine Andeutung enthaltend, andeutend, anregend; verführerisch (*fig.*); (weighty) voller Deutung, inhaltsschwer; to be —ive of, andeuten, auf die Vermutung bringen, daß . . .; —ive epithet, gedankenreiches Beiwort. **—iveness**, *s.* das Gedankenanregende, Stoffreiche.

Suicid—al, *adj.*, **—ally**, *adv.* selbstmörderisch. **—e**, *s.* der Selbstmord; der Selbstmörder.

Suit, I. *s.* (petition) das Gesuch, die Bitte, Bittschrift; (wooing) die Werbung; (series) die Folge, Reihe; *see* —e; (— of clothes) der Anzug; (set) der Satz, Besatz, die Garnitur; die Farbe (*Cards*); die Klage, der Prozeß, Rechtshandel (*Law*); — of armour, vollständige Rüstung; to follow —, Farbe bekennen (*cards*); tun was die andern tun, sich anschließen (*fig.*). II. *v.a.* (adapt) anpassen, anbequemen, einrichten nach; (become) anstehen, passen; angenehm, passend, angemessen sein (*one's taste, etc.*); kleiden, (einem gut) stehen (*as a bonnet, etc.*); to — a p.'s purpose, seinem Zwecke entsprechen; to — the action to the word, dem Worte die Tat folgen lassen, gesagt, getan. III. *v.n.* übereinstimmen, passen; ill —ed, schlecht geeignet (*for s.th.*); he is well —ed, er ist gut versorgt (mit), gut untergebracht; the servant is —ed, das Dienstmädchen hat eine Stelle (gefunden). **—ability**, **—ableness**, *s.* die Angemessenheit, Übereinstimmung, Schicklichkeit, das Passende, Schickliche. **—able**, *adj.*, **—ably**, *adv.* passend, angemessen, geeignet, gemäß, entsprechend; to be —able to *or* for, einer Sache gemäß sein, anstehen, übereinstimmen mit. **—e**, *s.* das Gefolge (*of a prince, etc.*); die Reihe (of rooms, Zimmer); die Saite (*Mus.*). **—ings**, *pl.* Tuche für ganze Anzüge aus einem Stoff. **—or**, *s.* der Bittsteller; der Bewerber, Freier; der Prozessierende, Kläger (*Law*).

Sulk, *v.n.* schmollen, mürrisch, verdrießlich, übler Laune sein. **—ily**, *adv. see* —y. **—iness**, *s.* das mürrische Wesen, Schmollen. **—s**, *pl. see* —iness; to be in the —s, *see* —. **—y**, I. *adj.* mürrisch, verdrießlich, übler Laune. II. *s.* leichter, einsitziger Wagen.

Sullen, *adj.*, **—ly**, *adv.* düster, finster, mürrisch; (obstinate) starrköpfig. **—ness**, *s.* finsteres, mürrisches Wesen; die Halsstarrigkeit.

Sully, *v.* I. *a.* besudeln, beschmutzen, beflecken. II. *n.* schmutzen, Schmutz annehmen. III. *s.* der Schmutzfleck; der Makel (*fig.*).

Sulph—ate, *s.* schwefelsaures Salz; —ate of soda, schwefelsaures Natron. **—ide**, *s.* das Sulfid, die Schwefelverbindung. **—ite**, *s.* schwefligsaures Salz; —ite of, schwefligsauer. **—ur**, I. *s.* der Schwefel; flowers of —ur, die Schwefelblumen; milk of —ur, die Schwefelmilch; stick —, Stangenschwefel. II. *attrib.*; —ur spring, die Schwefelquelle. **—urate**, *v.a.* (ein)schwefeln; —urated match, der Schwefelfaden. **—uration**, *s.* das Schwefeln. **—ureous**, *adj.* schweflig. **—uret**, *s.* die Schwefelverbindung. **—uretted**, *adj.* geschwefelt; —uretted hydrogen, der Schwefelwasserstoff. **—uric**, *adj.*; —uric acid, die Schwefelsäure. **—urization**, *s.* die Schwefelung. **—urize**, *v.a.* schwefeln, vulkanisieren. **—urous**, *adj.* schweflig, schwefelhaltig, Schwefel-; —urous acid, schweflige Säure.

Sultan, *s.* der Sultan. **—a**, *s.* die Sultanin; die Sultans-Rosine, Sultanine.

Sultr—iness, *s.* die Schwüle. **—y**, *adj.* schwül.

Sum, I. *s.* die Summe (*also Arith.*); (— and substance) die Summe, der Inbegriff, (Haupt-) Inhalt, Abriß; (— of money) die Geldsumme; (problem) das Exempel (*Arith.*); — total, die Gesammtsumme, der Gesammtbetrag; to do a —, ein Exempel rechnen. II. *v.a.* zusammenrechnen -zählen; to — up, zusammen-rechnen; kurz zusammenfassen *or* wiederholen. **—marily**, *adv.* kurz, in Kürze, mit wenig Worten, ohne Umstände. **—mary**, I. *adj.* kurz (gefaßt), summarisch; summarisch (*Law*). II. *s.* der kurze Auszug, Begriff, Hauptinhalt, das Kompendium. **—mation**, *s.* die Summierung (of a series, einer Zahlenreihe). **—mit**, *s.* die Höhe, Spitze, der Gipfel; der Gipfel; Höhepunkt (*fig.*).

[1]**Summer**, I. *s.* der Sommer; das Jahr (*poet.*). II. *adj.* Sommer-; —('s) day, der Sommertag; — lightning, das Wetterleuchten; — solstice, die Sommersonnenwende. III. *v.n.* den Sommer zubringen, übersommern. IV. *v.a.* durchsommern, Vieh den Sommer über auf die Weide lassen. *Comp.* **—-house**, *s.* das Gartenhaus, die Laube, der Gartenpavillon.

[2]**Summer**, *s.* der Trägerbalken; (—tree) der Stützbalken. **—ing**, *s.* flache Querbalken zwischen den Backsteinlagen eines Gewölbes.

Summon, *v.a.* auffordern, aufrufen, einladen; (send for) (herbei)rufen; vor-fordern, -laden, zitieren (*Law*); to — up, aufbieten (*fig.*); to — up courage, sich (*dat.*) ein Herz fassen, Mut fassen. **—er**, *s.* der Vorlader, Gerichtsbote. **—s**, *s.* die Aufforderung; die Vorladung, das Vorfordern (*Law*); —ses were issued, Aufforderungen wurden erlassen.

Sump, *s.* der Sumpf (*also Min.*).

Sumpter, I. *s.* das Saumroß, Packtier. II. *attrib.*; — mule, das Saumtier; — saddle, der Saumsattel.

Sumptu—ary, *adj.* den Aufwand betreffend; —ary laws, Aufwandgesetze. **—ous**, *adj.*, **—ously**, *adv.* kostbar, prächtig. **—ousness**, *s.* der Prachtaufwand, die Pracht.

Sun, I. *s.* die Sonne; der Sonnenschein; from — to —, den ganzen Tag; under the —, unter der Sonne; the — (he) rises, sets, die Sonne (sie) geht auf, geht unter. II. *v.n.* (& *r.* sich) sonnen. **—less**, *adj.* sonnenlos. **—niness**, *s.* die Sonnigkeit; das sonnige, freundliche Wesen (*fig.*). **—ny**, *adj.* sonnig; golden, glänzend; freundlich. *Comp.* (*in cpds. usually* = Sonnen-). **—-and-planet wheels**, *pl.* das Laufgetriebe. **—beam**, *s.* der Sonnenstrahl. **—-blind**, *s.* das (Fenster-) Rouleau. **—-bonnet**, *s.* der leichte luftige Frauenhut. **—-bright**, *adj.* sonnenhell. **—-bronzed**, *adj.* sonnengebräunt. **—burn**, I. *v.a.* bräunen. II. *s.* der Sonnenbrand. **—burns**, *pl.* die Sommersprossen. **—burned**, **—burnt**, *adj.* sonnenverbrannt, braun. **—burning**, *s.* der Sonnenbrand. **—burst**, *s.* der plötzliche Durchbruch der Sonne. **—day**, *see* Sunday. **—-dial**, *s.* die

Sonnenuhr. —**-down**, *s.* der Sonnenuntergang; der Abend (*fig.*); at —down, bei Sonnenuntergang. —**-dried**, *adj.* an *or* von der Sonne getrocknet. —**flower**, *s.* die Sonnenblume. —**light**, *s.* das Sonnenlicht. —**lit**, *adj.* sonnenerhellt. —**-lounge**, *s.* das Sonnenbad. —**-ray**, *s.* der Sonnenstrahl. —**rise**, *s.* der Sonnenaufgang; at —rise, bei Sonnenaufgang. —**set**, *s.* der Sonnenuntergang. —**shade**, *s.* der Sonnenschirm. —**shine**, *s.* der Sonnenschein. —**shiny**, *adj.* sonnig, heiter. —**-spot**, *s.* der Sonnenfleck. —**stroke**, *s.* der Sonnenstich.

Sunday, I. *s.* der Sonntag. II. *attrib.* Sonntags-; — clothes, Sonntagskleider; — school, die Sonntagsschule, Kinderlehre.

Sunder, I. *v.a.* sondern, trennen; entzweien (*fig.*). II. *v.n.* auseinandergehen (*rare*). III. *s.; in* —, entzwei.

Sundr—ies, *pl.* verschiedenartige Gegenstände, Waren; Spesen (für allerlei). —**y**, *adj.* verschiedene, mehrere.

Sung, *imp. & p.p. of* Sing.

Sunk, *imperf. & p.p. of* Sink; —fence, das Aha. —**en**, (*rare p.p. of* Sink, *&*) *adj.* eingesunken; —en eyes, eingefallene Augen; his eyes are —en in their sockets, die Augen liegen ihm tief im Kopfe; —en rocks, blinde Klippen; —en battery, versenkte Batterie.

Sup, I. *s.* der Schluck-, Mund-voll. II. *v.a.* schlürfen, schlucken; (— up) einschlürfen; (experience) erleiden, erleben. III. *v.n.* zu Abend essen; (sip) schlürfen. —**per**, *see* Supper. —**ping**, *s.* das Abendessen.

Super, I. *s.* die stumme Person, der Statist (*Theat.*). II. *pref.* (*in cpds. generally* = über-). *Comp.* —**abound**, *v.n.* überreichlich vorhanden sein; Überfluß haben (with, an einer S.). —**abundance**, *s.* großer Überfluß, die Überfülle. —**abundant**, *adj.*, —**abundantly**, *adv.* überreichlich, -flüssig; (exuberant) überschwenglich. —**add**, *v.a.* noch hinzu-tun, -fügen. —**annuate**, *v.a.* in den Ruhestand versetzen; —annuated, verjährt, veraltet; alt (*fig.*); —annuated soldier, ausgedienter Soldat. —**annuation**, I. *s.* die Dienstunfähigkeit wegen hohen Alters; (—annuating) die Pensionierung (*in England* meist mit 65 Jahren); (pension) die Pension. II. *attrib.;* —annuation bill, der Gesetzentwurf über Verabschiedung und Pensionierung. —**b**, *see* Superb. —**cargo**, *s.* der Supercargo. —**cilious**, *adj.*, —**ciliously**, *adv.* stolz, hochmütig, anmaßend, gebieterisch. —**ciliousness**, *s.* der Stolz, Hochmut, die Anmaßung. —**dominant**, *s.* die Oberdominante (*Mus.*). —**erogation**, *s.* die Übergebühr; works of —erogation, die freiwilligen *or* überflüssig guten Werke. —**erogatory**, *adj.* übergebührlich, ungeboten. —**excellence**, *s.* hohe Vortrefflichkeit. —**excellent**, *adj.* höchst vortrefflich. —**fetation**, —**fœtation**, *s.* die Überschwängerung. —**ficial**, *adj.*, —**ficially**, *adv.* oberflächlich. —**ficiality**, *s.* die Oberflächlichkeit. —**ficies**, *s.* die Oberfläche. —**fine**, *adv.* extra-fein, hochfein, sehr fein. —**fluity**, *s.* der Überfluß, das Zuviel. —**fluous**, *adj.*, —**fluously**, *adv.* überflüssig, reichlich; —fluous interval, das übermäßige (um einen halben Ton erhöhte) Intervall (*Mus.*). —**glottal**, *adj.* über *or* vor der Stimmritze liegend; —glottal passages, der über der Stimmritze liegende Teil des Mundkanals. —**human**, *adj.* übermenschlich. —**impose**, *v.a.* auf *or* über (eine S.) legen; über ein bestimmtes Maß hinaus auferlegen. —**incumbent**, *adj.* darauf-, darüber-liegend. —**induce**, *v.a.* hin-zulegen, -fügen, oben auflegen. —**intend**, *v.a.* die Aufsicht haben über, beaufsichtigen, verwalten. —**intendence**, *s.* die Oberaufsicht; die Superintendentur (*Eccl.*). —**intendent**, *s.* der Oberaufseher, Inspektor, der Superintendent; —intendent of the line, der Betriebsdirektor (*Railw.*). —**lative**, I. *adj.* höchst; unübertrefflich. II. *s.* (—lative degree) der höchste Grad, Superlativ. —**latively**, *adv.* höchst, äußerst, im höchsten Grade. —**lativeness**, *s.* der höchste Grad. —**man**, *s.* der Übermensch. —**natural**, *adj.*, —**naturally**, *adv.* übernatürlich; supernaturalistisch (*Rel.*). —**naturalism**, *s.* der Supernaturalismus. —**numerary**, I. *adj.* überzählig. II. *s.* der, die, das Überzählige; *see* Super I. —**oxide**, *s.* das Superoxyd. —**phosphate**, *s.* doppeltphosphorsaures Salz. —**pose**, *see* —impose. —**position**, *s.* die Schichtung (*Geol.*). —**scribe**, *v.a.* überschreiben; (address) adressieren. —**scription**, *s.* die Überschrift, Aufschrift. —**sede**, *v.a.* bei Seite setzen, aufheben; aufschieben, aussetzen; (displace) ersetzen, verdrängen, um die Stelle bringen; to be —seded in the command, im Oberbefehl ersetzt werden (by, durch). —**sensual**, *adj.* übersinnlich. —**stition**, *s.* der Aberglaube. —**stitious**, *adj.*, —**stitiously**, *adv.* abergläubisch. —**stratum**, *s.* obere Schicht. —**struction**, *s.* die Überbauung; der obere Bau, Oberbau. —**structure**, *s.* der Oberbau. —**vene**, *v.n.* dazu *or* dazwischen kommen; *see* Occur. —**vention**, *s.* die Dazukunft; das unvermutete Eintreten; die Überraschung. —**vise**, *v.a.* über eine S. die Aufsicht führen, eine S. beaufsichtigen; eine S. prüfend besichtigen. —**vision**, *s.* die Beaufsichtigung; die (Ober)aufsicht. —**visor**, *s.* der Aufseher; der Prüfer; der Inspektor. —**visory**, *adj.* die (Ober)Aufsicht betreffend.

Superb, *adj.*, —**ly**, *adv.* prächtig, herrlich.

Superior, I. *adj.* ober; höher, vorzüglicher, vortrefflicher (*fig.*); — to, (einem) überlegen; to be — to, erhaben sein über (*acc.*); of — understanding, von überlegenem Verstande; — officer, der Vorgesetzte, der höhere Offizier; of — quality, von vorzüglicher *or* besonders guter Beschaffenheit. II. *s.* der Obere, Höhere, Vorgesetzte; der (die) Superior(in) (*in convents*). —**ity**, *s.* die Übermacht, Überlegenheit, das Übergewicht, der Vorzug, Vorrang.

Supine, I. *adj.*, —**ly**, *adv.* rückwärts, auf dem Rücken liegend; (sloping) rückwärts gebogen; träg, nachlässig, sorglos (*fig.*). II. *s.* das Supinum (*Gram.*). —**ness**, *s.* das Rückwärtsliegen; die Nachlässigkeit, Sorglosigkeit, Untätigkeit.

Supper, *s.* das Abendessen, Abendbrot; to have (take) —, zu Abend essen; to partake of the Lord's —, zum heiligen Abendmahl gehen, das H. Abendmahl nehmen. —**less**, *adj.* ohne Abendessen, ohne zu Abend gegessen zu haben.

Supplant, *v.a.* (einem) ein Bein stellen (*obs.*); (displace) ausstechen, verdrängen, stürzen. —**er**, *s.* der Verdränger, (einen andern) Ausstechende.

Suppl—e, I. *adj.* biegsam, geschmeidig. II. *v.a.* biegsam machen. —**eness**, *s.* die Biegsamkeit, Geschmeidigkeit. —**iant**, I. *adj.* demütig, bittend, flehend. II. *s.* der Bittsteller, Bittende, Supplikant. —**icant**, *s.* der Bittsteller. —**icat**, *s.* die Bittschrift, das Gesuch. —**icate**, *v.a. & n.* demütig bitten, anflehen, ersuchen. —**icating**, *adj.*, —**icatingly**, *adv.* bittend. —**ication**, *s.* demütige Bitte, das Anflehen; (request) das Gesuch, Ansuchen, die Bittschrift. —**icatory**, *adj.* bittend, Bitt-.

Suppl—ement, I. *s.* die Ergänzung, der Nachtrag; die Beilage (*to a newspaper, etc.*); das Supplement (*Geom.*). II. *v.a.* ergänzen, hinzufügen. —**emental**, —**ementary**, *adj.* ergänzend, Ergänzungs-, nachträglich, als Beitrag (to, zu); —ementary arc, der Supplementärbogen. —**ier**, *s.* der Verschaffende; der Lieferant (*C.L.*). —**ies**, *pl.* (money) Hilfsgelder; (provisions, *etc.*) Mund- und Kriegs-vorrat; Hilfstruppen (*Mil.*); Zufuhren (*C. L.*). —**y**, I. *v.a.* versehen, verschaffen, versorgen (with, mit); (give) darreichen, geben; (furnish) liefern; ausfüllen, vertreten (a p.'s place, jemandes Stelle), ersetzen (the want of, den Mangel an einer Sache); to —y with provisions, mit Mundvorräten versehen, verproviantieren; —y the place of, (etwas) ersetzen, anstatt (einer Sache) dienen. II. *s.* (grant) die Hilfe, Beisteuer, der Beitrag; (store) der Vorrat; der Proviant (*of water, etc.*); das Ausgabebudget (*Pol.*); *see* —ies; der Stellvertreter (*Scotch*); —y of, die Verstärkung an (men, Mannschaft), der Zuschuß an (money, Geld); —y and demand, Angebot und Nachfrage.

Support, I. *v.a.* (unter)stützen; (prop up) tragen, (aufrecht)halten; (bear) ertragen; (maintain, aid, succour, favour, bear out, second) unterstützen; verteidigen (*a cause*); behaupten (*an opinion, a dignity*); unterhalten (*a person, a war, an army, a contest, debate, etc.*); erhalten, unterhalten (*o.s., a family, life, a good character*); he —s the character of Hamlet, er giebt *or* spielt den Hamlet (*Theat.*); — arms! Gewehr in Arm! II. *s.* das (Unter-)Stützen; (prop) die Stütze; (stand) das Stativ, der Untersatz; (—er) die Stütze; (that which —s) der Unterhalt, Lebensbedarf, die Nahrung; (livelihood, means) das Auskommen, Mittel; (aid) der Beistand, die Hilfe, die Unterstützung, Stütze; in — of, zur Bestätigung (*an opinion, etc.*); zur Unterstützung; line of —, das zweite Treffen, die Aufnahmetruppen. —**able**, *adj.*, —**ably**, *adv.* erträglich, leidlich; (maintainable) haltbar. —**er**, *s.* einer, der stützt, aufrecht erhält; der (Unter)Stützende, Beistehende, der Beistand, Helfer, Beschützer (*fig.*); *see* Adherent; der Verteidiger, Verfechter (*of an opinion, etc.*); der Schildhalter (*Her.*); der Träger (*Arch.*).

Suppos—e, *v.a.* (pre—e) voraussetzen; (assume) den Fall setzen, annehmen; (imagine) vermuten, halten, sich (*dat.*) denken; she is —ed to be very clever, sie gilt *or* man hält sie für sehr klug; he is —ed to know all about it, man denkt *or* man nimmt an, daß er von allem unterrichtet ist; I —e you are aware . . ., Sie wissen vermutlich; —ing it to be true, angenommen, es wäre wahr; —e we didn't do it, gesetzt, wir täten es nicht; they are soldiers, I —e, es werden wohl Soldaten sein. —**ed**, *adj.* eingebildet; mutmaßlich, vermeintlich. —**ition**, *s.* die Voraussetzung, Annahme; (surmise) die Vermutung, Meinung. —**itional**, *adj.* angenommen. —**ititious**, *adj.*, —**ititiously**, *adv.* untergeschoben, unecht. —**itory**, *s.* das Stuhlzäpfchen.

Suppress, *v.a.* unterdrücken; (restrain) zurückhalten, hemmen; (crush) überwältigen, unterdrücken; (conceal) verheimlichen, verhehlen, vertuschen; stillen, verstopfen (*hemorrhage*); (absichtlich) auslassen (*a word*); aufheben (*convents, etc.*); verbeißen (*anger, rage*); to — a book, die Herausgabe eines Buches verbieten. —**ion**, *s.* die Unterdrückung (*of a riot, rumour, book, the truth, etc.*); die Aufhebung; die Zurückhaltung, Verheimlichung, Verhehlung; die Überwältigung; die Aus-, Weglassung (*of a word*); die Aufhebung; die Verhaltung (*of the urine*). —**ive**, *adj.* unterdrückend.

Suppurat—e, *v.n.* eitern. —**ion**, *s.* die Eiterung; (matter) das Eiter. —**ive**, *adj.* die Eiterung befördernd.

Supra, *pref.* (= Super). —**axillary**, *adj.* oberwinkelständig (*Bot.*). —**clavicular**, *adj.* über dem Schlüsselbein befindlich. —**dorsal**, *adj.* über *or* auf dem Rücken befindlich. —**lapsarian**, I. *adj.* dem Sündenfall vorhergehend. II. *s.* der Supralapsarier. —**mundane**, *adj.* überweltlich; himmlisch. —**naturalism**, *s. see* Supernaturalism.

Suprem—acy, *s.* die Obergewalt, höchste Gewalt; das Supremat (*of the sovereign in church matters*); oath of —acy, der Suprematseid. —**e**, *adj.*, —**ely**, *adv.* höchst (*in dignity, power, rank, worth, etc.*); größt; (most excellent) erhabenst; —e folly, die größte Torheit; —e Being, das höchste Wesen; —e command, der Oberbefehl; —e court, das Oberlandesgericht.

Sur, *pref.* (= Super). —**base**, *s.* der Kragen, Kranz, Rand des Postaments (*Arch.*). —**cease**, *v.n.* aufhören. —**charge**, I. *v.a.* überladen (*also fig.*); *see* Overcharge; übertreiben (*pasture*). II. *s.* die Über-bürdung, -last, zu große Bürde; die Überforderung (*C.L.*); das Zuschlagsporto (*Post Off.*); der Überdruck, Aufdruck (*postage stamps*). —**charged**, *adj.* aufgedruckt. —**coat**, *s.* der kurze Oberrock; der Waffen-, Wappen-rock. —**face**, I. *s.* die Oberfläche, Außenseite; on the —face, it seems . . ., oberflächlich betrachtet, scheint es . . . II. *adj.* oberflächlich, äußerlich. *Comp.* —face printing, der Haut-Reliefwalzendruck; —face water, das Straßen-Abwasser. —**feit**, I. *v.a.* über-laden, -füllen, -sättigen; (cloy) Überdruß erregen. II. *v.n.* sich über-laden, -füllen. III. *s.* die Überladung (*of the stomach*), Übersättigung; (satiety) der Überdruß; (disgust) der Ekel. —**loin**, *see* Sirloin. —**mise**, I. *v.a.* vermuten, mutmaßen; (suspect) argwöhnen. II. *s.* die Vermutung, Mutmaßung, Einbildung; der Argwohn. —**mising**, *s.* das Vermuten 2c. —**mount**, *v.a.* überragen; übersteigen, überwinden, besiegen (*fig.*). —**mountable**, *adj.* übersteigbar, überwindlich, zu überwinden. —**mounted**, *adj.* überragt; überdeckt (*Her.*); überhöht (*Arch.*). —**name**, I. *s.* der Geschlechts-, Familien-name; (nickname, *etc.*) der Beiname. II. *v.a.* einen Zunamen geben. —**pass**, *v.a.* über-steigen, -treffen. —**passing**, *adj. & adv.*, —**ingly**, *adv.* vortrefflich, ausgezeichnet, außerordentlich. —**plice**, *s.* das Chorhemd; die Stola (*R.C.*). —**pliced**, *adj.* ein Chorhemd tragend. —**plus**, I. *s.* der Überschuß, Rest; der Überrest (*of an estate*). II. *adj.* übrig(bleibend); —plus value, der Mehrwert. —**plusage**, *s. see* —plus; das Überflüssige, Unnötige (*Law*). —**prise**, I. *v.a.* über-raschen, -rumpeln, hereinbrechen über (*acc.*); (astonish) in Erstaunen setzen, befremden; (perplex) bestürzt machen, verwirren. II. *s.* die Über-raschung, -rumpelung, der Überfall; das Erstaunen, die Bestürzung. —**prising**, *adj.*, —**prisingly**, *adv.* überraschend, erstaunlich, wunderbar. —**prisingness**, *s.* das Überraschende. —**rebutter**, *s.* die Quintuplik (*Law*). —**rejoinder**, *s.* die Triplik (*Law*). —**render**, I. *v.a.* übergeben, ausliefern; (cede) abtreten (to, an, *acc.*); (resign) aufgeben; to —render at discretion, auf Gnade und Ungnade sich ergeben. II. *v.r.* sich stellen, sich gefangen geben (*as a prisoner*); sich hingeben *or* überlassen (*to grief, etc.*). III. *v.n.* sich ergeben. IV. *s.* die Übergabe, Ergebung, Überlieferung (to, an, *acc.*); die Güterabtretung (*Law*). —**round**, *v.a.* umgeben, umringen, einschließen. —**rounding**, *adj.* umgebend. —**roundings**, *pl.* die Umgebung. —**solid**, *s.* fünfte Potenz (*Math.*). —**tout**, *s.* der Überrock, Überzieher (*obs.*). —**vey**, I. *v.a.* über-blicken, -schauen; (inspect) mustern, besichtigen; aus-, ver-messen (*land*); aufnehmen (*a coast*); peilen (*a harbour, etc.*); markscheiden (*underground*). II. *s.* der Überblick; die Besichtigung; das Feldmessen, die Vermessung, Aufnahme (*Surv.*); (plan) der Plan, Abriß; to make a —vey of, aufnehmen; geological —vey, geologische Aufnahme. —**veying**, *s.* das Aufnehmen, Vermessen; (art) die Meßkunst; die Besichtigung, Inspektion; geodetic, marine, plane —veying, die Geodäsie, die Seeaufnahme *or* das Peilen, die Feldmeßkunst. —**veyor**, *s.* der Besichtiger, Beschauer; *see* Overseer; der Feldmesser (*Surv.*). —**veyorship**, *s.* das Amt eines Feldmessers 2c. —**vival**, *s.* das Überleben; —vival of the fittest, das Überbleiben der Lebenskräftigsten (im Kampf ums Dasein). —**vive**, *v.* I. *a.* überleben.

II. *v.n.* am Leben bleiben, übrig bleiben. **—vivor,** *s.* der Überlebende, Hinterbliebene. *Comp.* —**veying-instruments,** *pl.* Meßinstrumente. —**veyor-general,** *s.* der Oberlandmesser (*Amer.*); der Generalaufseher (*of the royal parks, etc.*).

Surd, I. *adj.* unhörbar; stimmlos (*Phonet.*); irrational, unnennbar (*Math.*). II. *s.* der stimmlose Laut, Laut ohne Stimmton; die Irrationalzahl.

Sure, I. *adj.* sicher, gewiß, zweifellos, zuverlässig; (safe) in Sicherheit, außer Gefahr, gesichert; (reliable) zuverlässig, wahrlich, treu, fest; to be —! versteht sich! freilich! be — you wake me, wecke mich ganz gewiß; to feel —, sicher *or* gewiß sein; I am — of it, ich weiß es ganz gewiß; as — as I live! so wahr ich lebe! you may be —, du kannst dich darauf verlassen (daß ...); I'm — I don't know, ich weiß es wahrhaftig nicht; to make — of (a th.), sich (einer Sache) vergewissern; (a p.) sich des Beistandes (jemandes) versichern, sich (einer Person) bemächtigen. II. *adv.;* = —ly, (*coll.*) doch; — you won't go? du willst doch nicht gehen? III. —, **—ly,** *adv.* sicher; sicherlich; (assuredly) wahrhaftig. **—ness,** *s.* die Sicherheit. **—ty,** *s.* die Sicherheit; Gewißheit; (safety) die Sicherheit; (security) die Bürgschaft; (hostage) der (Wechsel)bürge, die Geißel; of a —ty, ganz gewiß, ohne Zweifel. *Comp.* **—-footed,** *adj.* fest auf den Füßen.

Surf, *s.* die Brandung, Widersee.

Surg—e, I. *s.* hohe Welle, Woge, See. II. *v.n.* aufschwellen, wogen; schricken (*Naut.*). III. *v.a.* aufschricken (*Naut.*). **—ing,** *adj.* brandend, hoch wogend, ungestüm.

Surg—eon, *s.* der Arzt für äußere Krankheiten, Chirurg, Wundarzt; (doctor) der Arzt, der Schiffsarzt; —eon general, der General(stabs)arzt; —eon major, der Stabsarzt. **—ery,** *s.* die Wundarzneikunst, Chirurgie. **—ical,** *adj.* wundärztlich, chirurgisch.

Surl—ily, *adv.*, **—y,** *adj.* mürrisch, sauertöpfisch; rauh; schroff, grob (*as an answer, etc.*). **—iness,** *s.* das mürrische, finstere Wesen; die Rauheit, Schroffheit.

Surreptitious, *adj.*, **—ly,** *adv.* heimlich getan, erschlichen, verstohlen; — edition, der Nachdruck.

Surrogate, *s.* das Surrogat, der Stellvertreter; eine Art Nachlaßrichter (*Amer.*).

Suscepti—bility, —veness, *s.* die Empfänglichkeit, Empfindlichkeit. **—ble, —ve,** *adj.*, **—bly,** *adv.* empfänglich; (sensitive) empfindlich.

Suspect, I. *v.a.* (be)argwöhnen, im Verdacht haben (of, wegen); (distrust) mißtrauen, zweifeln an (*dat.*); (imagine) vermuten; he is —ed of theft (of having stolen), er steht im Verdacht des Diebstahls (gestohlen zu haben). II. *adj. see* —ed (*obs.*). III. *s.* der Verdächtige, Beargwöhnte. **—ed,** *adj.* verdächtig, im Verdacht stehend.

Suspen—d, *v.a.* (hang) aufhängen; (put off) verschieben, aussetzen, anstehen lassen; einstellen (*payment, etc.*); zurückhalten mit (one's judgment, seinem Urteil); suspendieren, vorläufig absetzen (*clergymen, etc.*); suspendieren (*a law*). **—der,** *s.* einer, der aufschiebt rc.; das Bruchband (*Surg.*). **—ders,** *pl.* Hosenträger; Tragbänder (*for stockings*). **—se,** *s.* die Ungewißheit, Spannung; tortured with —se, in peinlicher Ungewißheit. **—sion,** *s.* das (Auf-)hängen; die Zurückhaltung, Verschiebung, der Aufschub (*of judgment*); der Stillstand (*from activity, etc.*); einstweilige Entsetzung (*from office*), Suspension; der Aufschub (*of the execution of a sentence*); einstweilige Aufhebung, Suspension (*of a law*); das Spannen der Erwartung (*Rhet.*); die Hemmung, der Vorhalt, die Aufhaltung (eines Akkords rc., *Mus.*); die Auflösung (*of a fluid*), Suspension (*Chem.*); to be held in —sion, schwimmend erhalten werden; —sion of payment, die Zahlungseinstellung (*C.L.*); —sion of hostilities, der Waffenstillstand; points of —sion, die Aufhängepunkte. **—sor,** *s.* der Tragbeutel, das Tragband (*Surg.*). **—sory,** I. *adj.* hängend, schwebend; (—ding) einstellend. II. *s. see* —sor. *Comp.* **—sion-bridge,** *s.* die Hänge-, Ketten-brücke. **—sion-lamp,** *s.* die Hängelampe. **—sion-railway,** *s.* die schwebende Eisenbahn. Schwebebahn.

Suspicio—n, *s.* der Verdacht, Argwohn, Wahn (*all three have no plural*); my worst —ns, meine schlimmsten Vermutungen. **—us,** *adj.*, **—usly,** *adv.* argwöhnisch, mißtrauisch; (raising —n) verdachterregend, verdächtig. **—usness,** *s.* argwöhnisches Wesen; die Verdächtigkeit.

Suspire, *v.n.* seufzen, stöhnen, tief atmen.

Sustain, *v.a.* (aufrecht)halten, tragen; (prop) stützen; (support) erhalten, unterhalten, ernähren; (aid) unterstützen, (einem) beistehen, helfen; (bear) aushalten, ertragen; aufrecht halten (*a charge, etc.*); (confirm) bekräftigen, bestätigen; stärken (*as food*); aushalten (*a note, Mus.*); to — a loss, einen Verlust erleiden; to — an injury, sich verletzen, zu Schaden kommen. **—able,** *adj.* haltbar (*as a charge*).

Susten—ance, *s.* die Unterstützung; (support) der Unterhalt, die Beköstigung; (food) die Lebensmittel (*pl.*), Nahrung. **—tation,** *s.* das Halten, die Haltung; *see* —ance.

Sutler, *s.* der (die) Marketender(in). *Comp.* **—-woman,** *s.* die Marketenderin.

Suttee, *s.* die Sutti; die Hinduwitwe, welche sich auf dem Scheiterhaufen ihres Gatten verbrennt; der freiwillige Feuertod einer Hinduwitwe.

Sutur—al, *adj.* Naht-. **—e,** *s.* die Naht.

Suzerain, *s.* der Oberlehnsherr; der tributäre Fürst. **—ty,** *s.* die Oberlehnsherrlichkeit.

Swab, I. *s.* der Kehrwisch; der Schwabber (*Naut.*); *see* Sponge (*Artill.*). II. *v.a.* schwabbern, schrubben (*Naut.*).

Swaddl—e, I. *s.* das Wickelband. II. *see* Swathe. *Comp.* **—ing-clothes,** *pl.* Windeln.

Swagger, I. *v.n.* prahlen, großtun, bramarbasieren. II. *s.* die Großtuerei, Prahlerei. —**er,** *s.* der Prahler, Bramarbas, Renommist. **—ing,** I. *adj.*, **—ingly,** *adv.* prahlerisch, aufgebläht. II. *s.* die Aufschneiderei; *see* — II.

Swain, *s.* der Bauernbursch, Schäfer, Bursche; der Liebhaber; amorous —, verliebter Schäfer.

[1]**Swallow,** *s.* die Schwalbe; the — twitters, die Schwalbe zwitschert; one — does not make a summer, eine Schwalbe macht keinen Sommer (*prov.*). *Comp.* **—tail,** *s.* der Schwalbenschwanz (*Bot., Fort., Carp.*); (coat) der Frack. **—-tailed,** *adj.* schwalbenschwanzartig; —-tailed coat, der Frack.

[2]**Swallow,** I. *s.* der Schlund, die Kehle, Gurgel; (voracity) die Freßgier. II. *v.a.* (ver-)schlucken, verschlingen, niederschlucken; verschlingen, verzehren (*fig.*); unterdrücken; einstecken (*an insult*); begierig aufnehmen, einsaugen, für bare Münze nehmen (*statements, opinions, etc.*); zurücknehmen, widerrufen (one's words, seine Aussage); to — one's vexation, seinen Ärger verschlucken. III. *v.n.* schlucken.

Swam, *imperf.* (*& obs. p.p.*) *of* Swim.

Swamp, I. *s.* der Sumpf, Morast. II. *v.a.* versenken, sinken machen; (outbalance) überfüllen; (plunge into difficulties) in endlose Schwierigkeiten stürzen. **—y,** *adj.* sumpfig, morastig.

Swan, *s.* der Schwan; the — sings, der Schwan singt; — of Avon, Shakespeare; all his geese are —s, er erhebt alles ihm Gehörige bis in den Himmel (*prov.*). *Comp.* **—'s-down,** *s.* die Schwanendaunen (*pl.*). **—-song,** der Schwanengesang, das Schwanenlied.

Swang, (*obs.*) *imperf. of* Swing.

Swap, *see* Swop.

Sward, *s.* der Rasen; the green—, der Rasenteppich. *Comp.* **—-cutter,** *s.* der Rasenstecher.

Sware, (*obs.*) *imperf. of* Swear.

[1]**Swarm,** I. *s.* der Schwarm (*of bees, etc.*); das Gewimmel, der Haufen (*fig.*). II. *v.n.* schwä-

men; to — (with), wimmeln (von); sich drängen, sich häufen.
²Swarm, *v.n.* klettern (up, hinauf, *acc.*).
Swarth, **—y**, (**Swart**,) *adj.* schwarz-, dunkelbraun, schwärzlich. **—iness**, *s.* schwärzliche, braune (Gesichts-)Farbe.
Swash, I. *s.* das Rauschen, der Guß. II. *v.a. & n.* schwappen (*of liquids*); rasseln, klappern, mit dem Schwert (auf den Schild) schlagen; prahlen. *Comp.* **—-buckler**, *s.* der Säbelrassler, Eisenfresser, Prahlhans.
Swate, (*obs.*) *imperf. of* Sweat.
Swath, *s.* der Schwaden (*of cut grass*); der Sensenhieb.
Swathe, *v.a.* wickeln, windeln; einhüllen.
Sway, I. *v.a.* schwingen, schwenken (*also a sword, etc.*); (weigh down) überwiegen; (govern) leiten, lenken, regieren; to — the sceptre, das Szepter führen, regieren. II. *v.n.* schwanken, sich schwingen; sich wiegen (*as branches*); (lean) sich neigen; (have —) herrschen, Gewicht *or* Einfluß haben. III. *s.* der Schwung; (preponderance) das Übergewicht, der Aufschlag; der Einfluß (*fig.*); (rule) die Gewalt, Herrschaft, Macht; to bear —, herrschen, (die) Gewalt haben.
Sweal, *v.* I. *n.* schmelzen, laufen (*as candles*); sich verzehren. II. *a.* sengen.
Swear, *ir.v.* I. *n.* schwören, beteuern, eidlich aussagen; beschwören (to a th., etwas); (blaspheme) fluchen; to — at, Flüche ausstoßen gegen (einen ꝛc.), einen mit Verwünschungen überhäufen; to — by a p. or a th., auf einen oder eine S. schwören; to — to a p., jemandes Persönlichkeit eidlich feststellen; I would — to it, ich möchte darauf schwören. II. *a.* schwören, durch einen Schwur bekräftigen; (— to) beschwören; to — a p., vereidigen, (einem) einen Eid abnehmen; to be sworn, vereidet werden, (into office, den Amtseid) ablegen; to — (a p.) in, (einen) vereidigen, in Eid nehmen; the new ministers were sworn in, die neuen Minister wurden vereidigt, legten den Amtseid ab; I'll be sworn, ich wollte darauf schwören; to — away, durch einen Eid um eine S. bringen; sworn enemy, geschworener *or* abgesagter Feind; sworn narrative, beschworene Erzählung. **—er**, *s.* der Schwörende; der Flucher; der Vereidigende.
Sweat, I. *s.* der Schweiß. II. *v.n.* schwitzen; verringern (*coin*); to — out, ausschwitzen, durch Schwitzen vertreiben. III. *v.a.* aussaugen, für schwere Arbeit jämmerlich bezahlen. IV. —, **—ed**, *imperf. of* — III.; —ed articles, für Hungerlöhne hergestellte Waren. **—en**, (*obs.*) *p.p. of* — III. **—er**, *s.* einer, der schwitzt; *see* Sudorific II.; wollene Jacke, Überziehjacke (*of athletes*); (employer) der Schinder, habgierige Arbeitsgeber *or* Brotherr. **—iness**, *s.* der schweißig Zustand. **—y**, *adj.* schweißig. *Comp.* **—ing-bath**, *s.* das Schwitzbad. **—ing-price**, *s.* der Hungerlohn, Schindpreis. **—ing-sickness**, *s.* das Schweißfieber; der englische Schweiß. **—ing-system**, *s.* das Aussaugesystem, das Kaufen guter Arbeit zu Schindpreisen. **—ing-terms**, *pl.* der Schindpreis, Hungerlohn.
Sweep, I. *ir.v.a.* fegen, kehren; (graze) streifen, bestreichen; treiben, jagen (*as wind*); wehen (*as a breeze*); (drag) schleppen, streichen (*a harp, etc.*); besichtigen (*the horizon*); to — away *or* off, wegkehren (*lit.*), weg-, mit sich fort-reißen, wegraffen (*fig.*); to — the board, alles wegnehmen; alle Preise bekommen (*coll.*); to — (the bottom) for an anchor, nach einem Anker dreggen; to — a chimney, den Schornstein fegen, kehren. II. *ir.v.n.* (— along, dahin-)schweifen, fegen, fahren, schießen, jagen, wischen; (— past) schnell vorübergehen, vorüberfahren; she swept through the court, sie zog prunkend, majestätisch durch den Hof einher. III. *s.* das Fegen, Kehren; (chimney—) der Schornsteinfeger; das Streifen, der Strich (*of a door, etc.*); (reach) der Bereich; (range) der Schwung, Spielraum; (curve) die Krümmung, Kurve; (carriage-drive) der halbkreisförmige Weg zum Anfahren (vor Häusern); der Schwengel (*of a pump*); der Schlagbalken (*of a drawbridge*); die Patsche, langes Ruder (*of a boat*), der Flügel (*of a windmill*); — of the tiller, der Leuwagen des Ruders; *see* —stakes; to make a clean —, alles auskehren, vollständig aufräumen *or* reinen Tisch machen (mit). **—er**, *s.* der Feger. **—ing**, *adj.*, **—ingly**, *adv.* durchgreifend, allumfassend, radikal, unbedingt (*as a declaration*); (overwhelming) reißend, gewaltsam; —ing statements, allzu weit ausgreifende, zu allgemeine Behauptungen. **—ings**, *pl.* das Fegsel, Kehricht. *Comp.* **—ing-machine**, *s.* (—er) die Kehrmaschine. **—-net**, *s.* das Schleppnetz. **—stake**, *s.* der Gewinner des ganzen Einsatzes (*Rac.*). **—stakes**, *s.* die Einsätze der Wettenden; ein Wettrennen, wo die Prämie aus den Einsätzen der Wettenden besteht.
Sweet, I. *adj.*, **—ly**, *adv.* süß (*also fig.*); (fresh) süß, frisch; sanft, lieb, hold, artig (*in character*); to smell (taste) —, gut (süß) riechen (schmecken); — almond oil, das Süßmandelöl; — herbs, Küchengewächse; — seventeen, das holde Mädchen von siebzehn Jahren; das liebliche Mädchenalter von siebzehn Jahren; — tooth, der Leckerzahn; — upon, verliebt in (*vulg.*). II. *s.* das Süße; das Liebchen (*fig.*). **—en**, *v.a.* (ver-)süßen, süß machen (*tea, etc.*); wieder frisch machen (*butter, etc.*); wohlriechend machen (*the breath, etc.*); versüßen, angenehm machen (*life*). **—ish**, *adj.* süßlich. **—ness**, *s.* die Süßigkeit; der Wohlgeruch; die Liebenswürdigkeit (*fig.*); die Anmut (*of manners, etc.*); die Sanftheit (*of temper*); die Verliebtheit (*obs.*). **—s**, *pl.* Bonbons, Konditoreisachen, süße Speise, der Pudding; —s of life, Annehmlichkeiten des Lebens. *Comp.* **—bread**, *s.* das Bröschen. **—-brier**, *s.* die Heckenrose, wilde Rose. **—heart**, *s.* das Herzchen, Schätzchen, der, die Geliebte. **—meat**, *s.* das Zuckerwerk, (der) Bonbon. **—-natured**, *adj.* liebreich, hold. **—-oil**, *s.* das Baumöl. **—-pea**, *s.* wohlriechende Wicke. **—-potato**, *s.* die Batate. **—-scented**, *adj.* wohlriechend. **—-spoken**, *adj.* lieblich sprechend; schmeichlerisch. **—-tempered**, *adj.* sanft, mild, hold. **—-toned**, *adj.* süßtönend. **—-tongued**, *adj.* süßzungig. **—-violet**, *s.* das Märzveilchen. **—-voiced**, *adj.* mit lieblicher Stimme. **—-william**, *s.* die Bartnelke.
Swell, I. *ir.v.n.* (an-, auf-)schwellen; (bulge) sich puffen, bauschen; (be inflated) sich blähen, sich aufblähen; (increase) anwachsen (*also of water*), sich steigern, sich vergrößern; (multiply) sich vermehren; anschwellen, dick werden (*as a book*); anschwellen, anlaufen (*as water*); auf-schwellen, -laufen (*as wounds*); anschwellen, stärker werden (*as a sound*); an-, auf-laufen (*as debts, money, etc.*); swollen vein, die Adergeschwulst; to — with rage (pride), vor Wut bersten, (sich stolz aufblähen); —ing like a turkey-cock, aufgeblasen wie ein Puter. II. *ir.v.a.* (an)schwellen (*water*); aufschwellen (*sails*), aufblähen, auftreiben; (increase) erhöhen, vermehren. III. *s.* das Schwellen, die Anschwellung (*of a song, etc.*); die Dünung (*of the sea*); (hill) der Hügel; der Schweller (*Org.*); der Stutzer, Modeherr (*sl.*); the — of the organ, die anschwellenden Töne der Orgel; all the big —s, die ganze feine Gesellschaft; alle großen Tiere (*coll.*). IV. *adj.* vornehm fein, elegant (*sl.*); prunkend, aufgedonnert (*sl.*); — mob, vornehmes Diebsgesindel; — neighbourhood, hochfeine Gegend; — organ, die Schwellorgel. **—ed**, *p.p. of* —. **—ing**, I. *adj.* (an)schwellend; (inflated) aufgeblasen; a —ing heart, ein kummerbeladenes Herz; —ing sails, schwellende Segel. II. *s.* die Geschwulst, Anschwellung.
Swelter, *v.n.* vor Hitze vergehen, schmachten; (sweat) schwitzen.
Swept, *imperf. & p.p. of* Sweep.

Swerve, *v.n.* abweichen; einen Seitensprung machen (*a horse*); abschweifen (*from one's purpose*), das Ziel aus den Augen verlieren.

Swift, I. *adj.*, **—ly**, *adv.* schnell, geschwind, hurtig, rasch, flüchtig; — of foot (—-footed), schnellfüßig; — of wing, leichtbeschwingt; — to mischief, geneigt, Böses zu tun. II. *s.* die Turmschwalbe (*Orn.*); die Eidechse (*Zool.*). **—ness**, *s.* die Schnelligkeit, Geschwindigkeit.

Swig, *v.n. & a.* in großen Zügen trinken (*vulg.*).

Swill, I. *v.a. see* Swig; berauschen; spülen, abwaschen (*the decks*). II. *v.n. see* Swig; sich betrinken. III. *s.* tüchtiger Schluck; das Gesöff (*fig.*); der Spültrank (*for pigs*). **—er**, *s.* der Säufer.

Swim, I. *ir.v.n.* schwimmen (*also fig.*); (overflow) überfließen; to — with the tide, mit dem Strome schwimmen; my head —s, es schwimmt mir vor den Augen, der Kopf schwindelt mir. II. *ir.v.a.* durchschwimmen, hinüberschwimmen (über, *acc.*); schwimmen lassen (*horses, etc.*); eintauchen, ins Wasser tun; (drench) schwemmen. III. *s.* das Schwimmen; to have *or* take a —, schwimmen; in the —, mitten im Strome, eingeweiht sein; mit dem Geschäftsgange vertraut. **—mer**, *s.* der Schwimmer; der Schwimmvogel (*Orn.*). **—ming**, I. *adj.* schwimmend; gleitend; —ming gait, schwimmender Gang. II. *s.* das Schwimmen; (—ming of the head) der Schwindel. **—mingly**, *adv.* leicht, glatt, von selbst, nach Wunsch, glücklich (*sl.*). *Comp.* **—ming-bath**, *s.* das Schwimmbad. **—ming-belt**, *s.* der Schwimmgürtel. **—ming-jacket**, *s.* die Schwimmjacke. **—ming-lesson**, *s.* die Schwimmstunde; to take —ming-lessons, Schwimmunterricht nehmen *or* haben. **—ming-master**, *s.* der Schwimmlehrer.

Swindl—e, I. *v.a.* beschwindeln, betrügen (out of, um). II. *s.* der Betrug. **—er**, *s.* der Schwindler, Gauner. **—ing**, I. *adj.*; —ing transactions, Schwindeleien. II. *s.* das Schwindeln, der Schwindel.

Swin—e, I. *s.* das Schwein (*also fig.*). II. *pl.* Schweine; to cast one's pearls before —e, Perlen vor die Säue werfen (*B.*). **—ish**, *adj.*, **—ishly**, *adv.* schweinisch. *Comp.* **—e-bread**, *s.* die Trüffel. **—eherd**, *s.* der Schwein(e)hirt. **—e-sty**, *s.* der Schwein(e)stall, Schwein(e)koben.

Swing, I. *ir.v.n.* schwingen, schwanken; (hang —ing) baumeln; sich schaukeln (*on a swing*); schwaien, vor einem Anker aufdrehen (*Naut.*); — open, auffliegen, sich auftun, sich öffnen (*as doors*); he may — for it, er kann deswegen an den Galgen kommen (*vulg.*); let her —! fall ab! (*Naut.*). II. *ir.v.a.* schwingen, schwenken; schwingen, schlenkern (*one's arms, etc.*); schaukeln; to — about, herum-schwingen, -drehen. III. *s.* das Schwingen, die Schwingung, der Schwung; die Schaukel; der freie Gang, Lauf, Spielraum (*fig.*); let him have his —, laß ihn seiner Neigung folgen; in full —, in vollem Gange, gut im Zuge. **—e**, *v.a.* peitschen. **—er**, *s.* der Schwingende, Schaukler. **—ing**, I. *adj.* schwankend, schwingend. II. *s.* das Schwingen. **—le**, I. *v.a.* brechen, schwingen (*flax, etc.*). II. *s.* die Schwinge. *Comp.* **—-door**, *s.* die Schwingtür, Drehtür. **—-gate**, *s.* das Drehtor. **—ling-knife**, *s.* das Schwingmesser.

Swipe, *v.a.* weit ausholend kräftig schlagen; hastig hinuntertrinken (*obs.*). **—r**, *s.* der tüchtige Schläger (*Cricket*). **—s**, *pl.* das schlechte, dünne Bier (*sl.*).

Swirl, I. *v.n.* sich im Kreise herumdrehen; wirbeln. II. *s.* der Wirbel, Strudel.

Switch, I. *s.* die Gerte, Rute; die Weiche (*Railw.*); der Kommutator (*Tele.*); der Zopf (*of hair*). II. *v.a.* peitschen; rangieren (*Railw.*); umschalten (*Elect.*); to — on (off) the electric light, das elektrische Licht an- (ab-)drehen. *Comp.* **—-back**, *s.* die Rutschbahn, Berg-Talbahn.

Swivel, *s.* der Drehring; der Riemenbügel (*Artill.*); (— gun) die Drehbasse.

Swollen (*also* **Swoln**), *p.p. of* Swell.

Swoon, I. *s.* die Ohnmacht. II. *v.n.* in Ohnmacht fallen, ohnmächtig werden; she —ed, sie wurde ohnmächtig; ihr vergingen die Sinne (*poet.*). **—ing**, I. *adj.* ohnmächtig. II. *s.* das Ohnmächtigwerden.

Swoop, I. *v.n.* (nieder) schießen, (sich) stürzen. II. *v.a.*; to — up, wegschnappen, aufraffen. III. *s.* der Sturz, Schuß, Stoß; at one fell —, mit einem grimmigen Anlauf; mit gewaltigem Sturz.

Swop, *v.a.* (ver)tauschen (*coll.*).

Sword, *s.* das Schwert, der Säbel, Degen; das Seitengewehr; to put to the —, über die Klinge springen lassen; fix —s! das Seitengewehr pflanzt auf! *Comp.* **—-arm**, *s.* rechter Arm. **—-bayonet**, *s.* das Haubajonett, Säbelbajonett. **—-bearer**, *s.* der Schwertträger. **—-belt**, *s.* das Degengehenk. **—-cane**, *s.* der Stockdegen. **—-cut**, *s.* der Säbelhieb. **—-cutler**, *s.* der Schwertfeger. **—-exercise**, *s.* das Fechten. **—fish**, *s.* der Schwertfisch. **—-hilt**, *s.* der Degengriff. **—-knot**, *s.* die Degenquaste. **—-lily**, *s.* die Schwertlilie. **—sman**, *s.* der Fechter. **—smanship**, *s.* die Fechtkunst, Geschicklichkeit im Fechten. **—-stick**, *see* —-cane.

Swor—e, *imperf.* (*& obs. p.p.*) *of* Swear. **—n**, I. *p.p. of* Swear. II. *adj.*; — enemy (friend), der Todfeind (erklärte Freund).

Swum, *imperf. & p.p. of* Swim.

Swung, *imperf. & p.p. of* Swing.

Sycamore, Sycomore, *s.* (— fig) wilder Feigenbaum; (plane tree) der Bergahorn.

Sycophan—cy, *s.* die Fuchsschwänzerei. **—t**, *s.* der Schmeichler, Schmarotzer; (informer) der Angeber. **—tic**, *adj.* sykophantisch, angeberisch.

Syll—abic, *adj.* syllabisch, Silben-. **—able**, I. *s.* die Silbe; there is not a —able of truth in it, es ist kein wahres Wort daran. II *v.a.* in Silben bringen, syllabieren; (utter) aussprechen. **—abled**, *adj.* -silbig. **—abus**, *s.* der kurze Inbegriff, das kurze Verzeichnis; der Unterrichtsplan; —abus of lectures, der Vorlesungsplan, das Programm, der Prospekt; der Syllabus (*R. Cath.*). **—epsis**, *s.* die Syllepsis.

Syllogis—m, *s.* der Vernunftschluß. **—tical**, *adj.*, **—tically**, *adv.* syllogistisch, in Schlußform.

Sylph, *s.* der Luftgeist, Sylph. **—id**, *s.* die Sylphide. **—like**, *adj.* sylphengleich.

Sylv—an, *adj.* waldig, Wald-. **—iculture**, *s. see* Silviculture.

Symbol, *s.* das Sinnbild, Symbol. **—ic(al)**, *adj.*, **—ically**, *adv.* sinnbildlich, symbolisch; to be —ical of, sinnbildlich andeuten. **—ics**, *s.* die Symbolik. **—ism**, *s.* die sinnbildliche Darstellung; der Symbolismus. **—ization**, *s.* die Versinnlichung; *see* —ism. **—ize**, *v.n.* versinnbildlichen, sinnbildlich darstellen, symbolisieren.

Symmetr—ical, *adj.*, **—ically**, *adv.* gleich-, ebenmäßig, symmetrisch; symmetrisch (*Math.*). **—y**, *s.* das Ebenmaß, die Symmetrie.

Sympath—etic, *adj.*, **—etically**, *adv.* mitfühlend, teilnehmend, mitleidend; harmonierend, seelenverwandt; geheimwirkend (*Phys.*); sympathetisch (*as a cure, as ink*); —etic nerve, sympathetischer Nerv. **—ize**, *v.n.* mitfühlen, mitleiden, sympathisieren; (agree) übereinstimmen. **—y**, *s.* die Mitempfindung, Sympathie, das Mitgefühl; die Mitleidenschaft (*Med.*); die Sympathie, geheime Wechselbeziehung (*Phys.*); (dividing interest) der Anteil, die Teilnahme; (compassion) das Mitleid; to feel —y for, Teilnahme fühlen für, Anteil nehmen (an, *dat.*).

Symphon—ic, *adj.* symphonisch; gleichklingend. **—ious**, *adj.* zusammenstimmend, harmonisch (to, mit). **—y**, *s.* die Symphonie.

Symphysis, *s.* die Bein-, Knochen-fügung.

Symposi—arch, *s.* der Vorsitzende bei einem Gastmahl. **—um**, *s.* das Gastmahl, Gelage; die Gesellschaft von Freunden *or* Gleichdenkenden (*fig.*).

Symptom, *s.* das Zeichen, Symptom (*in illness*); das (Kenn-, Vor-)Zeichen. —**atic**, *adj.* symptomatisch; anzeigend. —**atology**, *s.* die Lehre von den Krankheitszeichen.

Synagogue, *s.* die Synagoge.

Synchron—**al**, *adj.* gleichzeitig. —**ism**, *s.* die Gleichzeitigkeit; (table) synchronistische Zusammenstellung *or* Tabelle. —**ize**, I. *v.n.* gleichzeitig sein. II. *v.a.* als gleichzeitig zusammenstellen; übereinstimmend machen (*clocks*). —**ous**, *adj.* gleichzeitig.

Syncop—**ate**, *v.a.* verkürzen (*words*); den Rhythmus verrücken (*of notes*); synkopieren. —**ation**, *s.* das Synkopieren. —**e**, *s.* die Ohnmacht (*Med.*); die Synkope, der Ausfall eines Inlauters, die Wortverkürzung im Inlaut (*Gram.*).

Syndic, *s.* der Syndikus; (magistrate) der Schultheiß. —**ate**, *s.* der Rat, Ausschuß.

Syne, *adv.* vorher; auld lang —, die alte vergangene *or* längstvergangne Zeit (*dial.*).

Synecdoche, *s.* die Wortvertauschung (*Rhet.*).

Synod, *s.* die Kirchenversammlung, Synode. —**al**, —**ic**(**al**), *adj.* Synodal-; synodisch (*Astr.*).

Synonym, *s.* das sinnverwandte Wort, Synonym. —**ous**, *adj.* sinnverwandt, synonym.

Synop—**sis**, *s.* die Übersicht, Synopsis. —**tic**(**al**), I. *adj.* synoptisch, übersichtlich; —tic gospels, die synoptischen Evangelien (nach Matthäus, Markus, Lukas). II. *s.* der Synoptiker, Verfasser eines der synoptischen Evangelien.

Synovia, *s.* der Gelenkschleim. —**l**, *adj.*; —l glands, Gelenkdrüsen.

Synta—**ctical**, *adj.*, —**ctically**, *adv.* syntaktisch. —**x**, *s.* die Satzlehre, Lehre von der Satzbildung, Wortfügung, die Syntax.

Synthe—**sis**, *s.* die Synthese, Zusammen-fügung, -setzung (*Log.*, *Math.*, *Surg.*, *Chem.*). —**tic**(**al**), *adj.*, —**tically**, *adv.* verbindend, zusammenfügend, synthetisch.

Syphili—**s**, *s.* die Lustseuche, Syphilis. —**tic**, *adj.* geschlechtskrank, syphilitisch; —ic diseases, Geschlechtskrankheiten.

Syphon, *see* Siphon.

Syring—**a**, *s.* der Flieder. —**e**, I. *s.* die Spritze. II. *v.a.* einspritzen (in, *acc.*), Einspritzungen machen, eine Wunde ausspritzen. —**otomy**, *s.* der Fistelschnitt.

Syrup, *s.* der Sirup; golden —, gereinigter hellgelber Sirup. —**y**, *adj.* süß, wie Sirup.

System, *s.* das System (*Astr.*, *Philos.*, *Phys.*, *Med.*, *etc.*); — of government, Regierungssystem. —**atic**(**al**), *adj.*, —**atically**, *adv.* planmäßig, zielbewußt, systematisch. —**atist**, *s.* der Systematiker. —(**at**)**ization**, *s.* die Systematisierung. —**atize**, *v.a.* systematisieren, wissenschaftlich ordnen.

Systile, *s.* nahesäulige Ordnung (*Arch.*).

Systole, *s.* die Zusammenziehung (*of the heart*), Systole; die Systole (*Gram.*).

T

T, **t**, I. *s.* T, t; to a —, auf ein Haar, bis aufs Haar, ganz genau (*fam.*). II. *attrib.*; — bandage, die T-Binde; — ruler, — square, das Anschlaglineal; *for abbreviations see the Index at the end of the English-German part.*

Tab, *s.* die Latsche (*Shoem.*); *see* Tag.

Tabard, *s.* der (Wappen-)Mantel, Heroldsrock.

Tabby, I. *s.* gewässertes, moiriertes Zeug, der Mohr (*Weav.*); eine Art Mörtel, der steinhart wird; (— cat) die (bunte) Katze; alte Jungfer, Klatschbase (*fig.*, *fam.*). II. *adj.* gewässert, gestreift, scheckig. III. *v.a.* wässern.

Tabernac—**le**, I. *s.* das Zelt; die Stiftshütte (*B.*); das Tabernakel, Sakramentshäuschen (*R. C.*); der Altaraufsatz, die verzierte Nische, das Schutzdach für Heiligenbilder, *etc.* (*R. C.*); feast of —les, das Laubhüttenfest. II. *v.n.* wohnen. —**ular**, *adj.* gegittert; —ular work, das Gitterwerk.

Tabes, *s.* die Auszehrung; die Rückenmarkschwindsucht.

Tab(**b**)**inet**, *s.* der Tabinet.

Tab—**lature**, *s.* die Tabulatur (*Mus.*); die Decken- *or* Wand-malerei (*Paint.*); die Teilung des Schädels in zwei Hälften (*Anat.*). —**le**, *see* Table. —**leau**, *s.* das Gemälde; das Bild (*Theat.*); —leaux vivants, lebende Bilder. —**let**, *s.* das Täfelchen; Stückchen (*of soap*, *etc.*); (—lets) die Schreibtafel. —**loid**, *s.* das Täfelchen, Plätzchen, Arznei in kleinen Tafeln (*Med.*). —**ula**, *s.*; —ula rasa, unbeschriebenes Blatt, reiner Tisch. —**ular**, *adj.* tafelförmig; (in laminae) blätterig; (scheduled) tabellarisch, in Tafeln gebracht; in Tabellen berechnet. —**ulate**, *v.a.* täfeln; (—le) in Tabellen bringen, tabellarisieren.

Table, I. *s.* der Tisch, die Tafel; die Kost (*fig.*); (diners, *etc.*) die Tischgesellschaft; der Spieltisch (*Cards*); (index, *etc.*) das Verzeichnis, Register; die Tafel, Platte (*Build.*); die Tabelle (*Math.*, *Phys.*, *etc.*); — on casters, Rolltisch; — of contents, das Inhaltsverzeichnis; — d'hôte, die gemeinschaftliche Mittagstafel im Gasthaus, die Table d'hôte; folding —, der Klapptisch; —s of the Law, Gesetzestafeln (*B.*); — of interest, Zinstabelle; loo —, kleiner runder Tisch; the holy —, the Lord's —, Gottes Tisch, der Tisch des Herrn, das heilige Abendmahl; multiplication —, das Einmaleins; occasional —, der kleine Seitentisch; Round —, die Tafelrunde; time —, der Fahrplan; time —s, das Kursbuch; — of wages, Lohntabelle; to lay a bill on the —, eine Vorlage auf den Tisch des Hauses legen (*Parl.*); to turn the —s, einer Sache eine andre Wendung geben, den Spieß umdrehen; the —s are turned, das Blatt hat sich gewendet; to keep a good —, einen guten Tisch führen; to lay *or* spread the —, den Tisch decken; to sit at —, zu Tisch sitzen, beim Essen sein; to wait at —, bei Tische aufwarten; to put upon the —, auftragen; to serve —s, die Armen speisen (*B.*). II. *v.a.* tabellarisch verzeichnen. *Comp.* —-**beer**, *s.* das Tischbier. —-**book**, *s.* das Rechenbuch. —-**centre**, *s.* der Tischläufer. —**cloth**, *s.* das Tischtuch. —-**cover**, *s.* die Tischdecke. —-**fork**, *s.* die Tischgabel. —-**fruit**, *s.* das Tafelobst. —-**knife**, *s.* das Tischmesser —**land**, *s.* das Tafelland, die Hochebene. —-**leaf**, *s.* die Tischklappe. —-**linen**, *s.* das Tischzeug. —-**mat**, *s.* die Tischmatte, der Untersatz. —-**plate**, *s.* das (silberne) Tafelgeschirr. —-**rapping**, *s.* das Geisterklopfen. —-**salt**, *s.* das Tafelsalz. —-**spoon**, *s.* der Eßlöffel. —-**talk**, *s.* das Tischgespräch; Luther's —-talk, Luthers Tischreden. —-**tennis**, *s.* das Zimmernetzball. —-**tipping**, —-**turning**, *s.* das Tischrücken. —-**top**, *s.* das Tischblatt.

Taboo, I. *s.* der Priesterbann (*in Polynesia*, *etc.*). II. *adj.* verboten, untersagt, in Verruf. III. *v.a.* den Gebrauch verbieten; ausstoßen (aus der Gesellschaft), verstoßen (aus dem Gebrauche); in den Bann tun.

Tabor, —**et**, *s.* die Handtrommel.

Tabouret, *s.* *see* Taboret; der Sessel; der Stickrahmen.

Tacit, *adj.*, —**ly**, *adv.* stillschweigend. —**urn**, *adj.*, —**urnly**, *adv.* schweigsam, wortkarg. —**urnity**, *s.* die Schweigsamkeit, Verschlossenheit, Wortkargheit.

Tack, I. *v.a.* (an)heften, anschlagen; (mit Stiften) befestigen, anheften (*Carp.*, *etc.*); anschließen, anheften, verbinden (*fig.*); (— to) verbinden (mit), anschließen; to — together, zusammenheften. II. *v.n.* wenden, lavieren (*Naut.*); to — about, umlegen, lavieren; to be on the wrong —, auf dem Holzwege sein (*fam.*); to get on a new —, neue Mittel ersinnen (*fam.*). III. *s.* der kleine Nagel, Stift, Tapeziernagel, die Zwecke, Zwicke (*Carp.*, *etc.*); (rope) das Geitau (*Naut.*); der Hals (*of a sail*); der Gang (beim Lavieren); up —s and sheets! stich auf Halsen und Schoten! —**ing**, *s.* das Lavieren.

Tackl—e, I. *s.* der Flaschenzug, Rollenzug, Kloben (*Mach.*); die Talje, das Takel (*Naut.*); (ropes, *etc.*) das Tau- und Takel-werk (*Naut.*); das Gerät(e), die Gerätschaften; fishing —e, Fisch(erei)gerät; hoisting —e, Flaschenzug; running —e, der Aufzug; steering —e, Rudertalje. II. *v.a.* (an-, auf-)takeln; ernstlich angreifen, in die Hand nehmen, anfangen; fertig werden (mit) (*fig.*). —**ing**, *s.* das Takelwerk, die Takelage.

Tact, *s.* der Takt, die Feinfühligkeit, das Schicklichkeitsgefühl; der Takt(schlag) (*Mus.*). —**ile**, *adj.* fühlbar. —**less**, *adj.* taktlos, nicht feinfühlig. —**lessness**, *s.* die Taktlosigkeit.

Tactic—ian, *s.* der Taktiker. —**s**, *s.* die Kriegskunst, Taktik (*also fig.*).

Tadpole, *s.* der Kaulfrosch, die Kaulquappe.

Tænia, *s.* der Bandwurm; schmaler Streif.

Taffet—a, —**y**, I. der Taft; watered —a, der Mohr, Moiré. II. *adj.* taften.

Taffrail, *s.* das Hack-, Heck-bord (*Naut.*).

Tag, I. *s.* der Senkelstift, die Schnürnadel; das Anhängsel, der Zipfel; der angehängte Zettel, gepäckzettel (*on parcels, etc.*); —, rag and bobtail, Krethi und Plethi; das Lumpenpack. II. *v.a.* einen Stift machen an (*acc.*); (add on) verbrämen, anhängen.

Tail, I. *s.* der Schwanz, Schweif; (end) das Ende, der Schluß; der Schwanz (*of letters, notes, etc.*); der Schoß (*of a coat, shirt, etc.*); der Avers (*of coins*); das Ende (*of a storm*); der Schweif (*of a comet*); der Anhang, Schweif (*of a party*); die Sterze (*of a plough*); to turn —, davonlaufen. II. *v.a.* (— in) in eine Mauer einlassen. —**ed**, *adj.* geschwänzt. —**less**, *adj.* schwanzlos, ohne Schwanz. *Comp.* —**-coat**, *s.* der Leibrock; *see* Swallow—. —**-end**, *s.* das Schwanzende; das Ende, der Schluß (*fig.*). —**-piece**, *s.* der Finalstock (*Print.*); der Saitenhalter (*Mus.*). —**-pin**, *s.* das Bodenstück (am Geschütz); der Saitenhalter (*Violin*). —**race**, *s.* das Schußwasser; der Abzugskanal (*Hydr.*). —**-rime**, I. *s.* der Schweifreim. II. *attrib.*; —-rime stanza, die Schweifreimstrophe. —**-water**, *s.* abfließendes Wasser; das Stauwasser.

Tailor, I. *s.* der Schneider; —'s goose, großes Bügeleisen; —'s spasm, der Schneiderkrampf. II. *v.n.* schneidern. —**ess**, *s.* die Schneiderin. —**ing**, I. *s.* die Schneiderei. II. *attrib.*; —ing business, das Schneidergeschäft. *Comp.* —**-made**, *adj.* (Frauenkleider) vom Schneider gemacht.

Taint, I. *v.a.* vergiften, anstecken; infizieren (*Med.*); (corrupt) verderben; beflecken, besudeln. II. *v.n.* verderben. III. *s.* das (Ansteckungs-) Gift; die Infektion; der Flecken, Makel; hereditary —, erbliche Belastung.

Take, *ir.v.* I. *a.* nehmen; (accept, assume) annehmen; befragen um (*a p.'s opinion*); annehmen (*advice, a bribe, an impression*); ergreifen (*measures, a step, an opportunity*); sich (*dat.*) gefallen lassen, einstecken (*an insult, etc.*); (seize) anfallen (*as an illness*), ergreifen, fassen; fangen (*fishes, foxes, etc.*); machen (a trick, einen Stich); (ein)nehmen, erobern (*a fortress, etc.*); nehmen, aufbringen (*a ship*); einnehmen (*a meal, medicine*); zu sich nehmen, genießen (*food*); trinken (*wine*); (require) erfordern, in Anspruch nehmen, kosten; wegnehmen (*time*); schlagen (*Pawns, Chess, etc.*); photographieren (a p.'s likeness, einen); (über-)nehmen (*a part, the treble, etc.*); nehmen, mieten, pachten (*a house, etc.*); nehmen, einschlagen (*a road, etc.*); (understand) verstehen; (interpret) aufnehmen, auffassen, auslegen; (consider) halten, ansehen (for, für); wegnehmen (*a piece at Chess, etc.*); it will — (me) some years to complete this work, ich werde einige Jahre nötig haben, um dies Werk zu vollenden; to — amiss *or* ill, übel aufnehmen, übelnehmen; to — a (deep) breath, (tief) aufatmen; to — care, sich in Acht nehmen; to — one's chance of (a seat, *etc.*), es darauf ankommen lassen sich auf den Zufall verlassen; to — a class, Schule halten; it —s so much cloth to make a coat, so viel Tuch ist zu einem Rock nötig; — whichever you please, wählen Sie nach Belieben; to — compassion on, sich erbarmen (*gen. or* über einen); to — one's death of cold, sich (*dat.*) eine tödliche Erkältung zuziehen (*coll.*); to — the dimensions of, ausmessen; to — effect, in Kraft treten; to — exercise, sich (*dat.*) Bewegung machen; to — a last farewell, den letzten Abschied nehmen; to — fire, Feuer fangen; to — flight, fliehen; to — s.o. by the hand, einen an (bei) der Hand nehmen (*lit.*); (einen) beschützen; (einem) beistehen (*fig.*); to — in hand, unternehmen; to — a p. in hand, sich eines Menschen annehmen; einen bearbeiten *or* beeinflussen; to — heart, sich (*dat.*) ein Herz fassen; to — to heart, sich (*dat.*) zu Herzen nehmen; to — a hedge, über eine Hecke setzen; to — hold (of a p.), (einen) anfassen; to — horse, sich zu Pferde setzen; she took the head of the table, sie setzte sich oben an am Tische, nahm den Ehrenplatz bei Tische ein; to — infection, angesteckt werden; to — liberties, sich (*dat.*) Freiheiten herausnehmen; to — the lead, den Ton angeben; to — s.o.'s measure, einem das Maß nehmen; it —s its name from, es leitet seinen Namen her von; to — a newspaper, eine Zeitung halten; — notice! kund und zu wissen sei; to — occasion, die Gelegenheit benutzen; to — parts, mehrstimmig singen; — your places, setzen Sie sich; to — place, stattfinden, sich ereignen; to — post, Post(-Pferde) nehmen; to — rank, rangieren, auf gleicher Stufe stehen (mit); to — rest, ausruhen; to — shelter, sich schützen (from, vor); to — ship, sich einschiffen nach; to — snuff, schnupfen; to — one's stand, seinen Stand einnehmen; to — steps, Maßregeln ergreifen; to — a stick to, prügeln; to — a survey of, überblicken (*lit. & fig.*); to — tea with a p., Tee bei einem trinken; that —s time, das erfordert, bedarf, *or* kostet Zeit; to — the time, sich (*dat.*) die Zeit nehmen, geben; to — trouble, sich (*dat.*) Mühe geben; to — a turn, sich wenden *or* ändern; (walk out) einen kleinen Spaziergang machen; (dance) eine Tour tanzen; to — one's turn, der Reihe nach eintreten *or* etwas tun; to — the veil, den Schleier nehmen, Nonne werden; to — a walk, einen Spaziergang machen; to — warning, sich warnen lassen (by, von); to — the water, ins Wasser gehen; to — the waters, Brunnen trinken; to — one's way to, sich begeben nach; to — wing, davonfliegen; to — **about**, umherführen; to — **along** with, mitnehmen; to — **aside**, bei Seite nehmen *or* ziehen; to — **away**, wegnehmen, entziehen (einem etwas); (remove) abräumen (the things, den Tisch); that —s my breath away, dies benimmt mir den Atem, überrascht mich aufs höchste; to — **by** surprise, überraschen; to — **down**, herunter-, ab-nehmen (*walls, pictures, etc.*); abrüsten (*a scaffolding*); abreißen (*a house*); demütigen (*pride*); niederschreiben, niedersetzen (*in writing*); to — **for**, nehmen, halten für, ansehen für; to — **from**, wegnehmen, abziehen von; — 5 from 9 and 4 remains, (zieht) 5 von 9 (ab, so) bleibt 4; to — **in**, einziehen, einnehmen, bergen (*sails, etc.*); einnehmen (*cargo*); (receive) einnehmen; (tighten) einnähen, enger machen (*a dress*), abnehmen (*in knitting*); (tuck in) einschlagen; (harbour) beherbergen (*a traveller, etc.*), (zu sich, ins Haus) nehmen, aufnehmen (*a guest, etc.*); annehmen (*work, etc.*); einlegen (*supplies*); halten (*a newspaper*); (comprise) einschließen, in sich fassen; (understand) geistig aufnehmen, begreifen; (cheat) anführen, hinters Licht führen, betrügen; to — **off**, abnehmen (*a limb, one's hat, etc.*); aufheben (*a tax*); ausziehen (*clothes*); (— away) weg=, ab=nehmen; (remove) fortführen, schaffen; (carry off) wegnehmen, dahinraffen; (mimic) nachäffen (*coll.*); aufheben (*an embargo*); I am —ing a day or two off with a friend, ich mache mir mit einem Freunde ein paar Tage Ferien, ich habe ein paar Tage ausgespannt (*coll.*); to — the edge off, (ab)stumpfen; to — the edge off one's appetite, den ersten Hunger stillen; to — s.th. off s.o.'s hands, (einem etwas) abnehmen; to — the skin off, die Haut abziehen (*dat. or* von), enthäuten; to — off the spell, entzaubern; to — o.s. off, sich aus dem Staube machen, sich fortmachen; to — **out**, heraus=nehmen, =holen, =bringen, =ziehen; (remove) (her)ausmachen (*stains*), sich (*dat.*) auswirken, nehmen (*a licence, patent*), ausführen (*children, horses, etc.*), ausziehen (*a cork*), entpfropfen, entkorken (a cork out of a bottle, eine Flasche); to — the creases out of cloth, die falschen Falten, die Striche aus dem Tuche nehmen; to — it out of s.o., sich an einem bezahlt machen; einem stark zusetzen; to — a p. out of himself, einen über sich selbst erheben; einen von sich selbst abziehen; to — **over**, mit sich hinüber nehmen; übernehmen; to — **to** pieces, auseinandernehmen, zerlegen (*lit.*); genau besehen, bekritteln (*fig.*); to — to wife, zur Frau nehmen, heiraten; they took to the boats, sie begaben sich in die Boote; to — **up**, auf=nehmen, =heben (*also Typ.*); ergreifen (*arms*); in Verhaft *or* festnehmen (*a prisoner*); aufreißen (*a pavement*); aufbrechen (*a floor*); annehmen (*a challenge, etc.*); aufnehmen, akzeptieren (a bill, einen Wechsel); sich (a quarrel, eines Streites) annehmen; anfangen (*business*); aufnehmen (*a stitch*); wegnehmen, kosten (*time, room*); (understand) begreifen (*Scotch*); to — up one's abode, sich einquartieren; to — **upon** o.s., unternehmen, auf *or* über sich nehmen; to be —n **with** a fever, ein (schleichendes 2c.) Fieber bekommen. II. *n.* (— effect) wirken, Eindruck machen; (please) Beifall finden, gefallen; (be fixed) sich festsetzen, fangen; fangen (*fire*); empfangen, trächtig werden (*as mares, etc.*); he was vaccinated, but the virus did not —, er wurde geimpft aber die Lymphe schlug nicht an; do you — well? sind Sie leicht zu photographieren? haben Sie ein gutes Photographiergesicht? (*Phot.*); to — **after**, (einem) nacharten; ähneln; to — **from**, abziehen von; (derogate from) (einer Sache) Abbruch tun, nachteilig sein; (lessen) verringern; to — **on**, heftig gerührt sein, wüten; (grieve) sich grämen (*vulg.*); to — **to**, sich begeben nach (*a place*), auf (*acc.*) (*the road*); (— a liking to) liebgewinnen; (occupy o.s. with) sich legen auf (*acc.*); to — to study, sich dem Studium widmen; to — to drinking, sich dem Trunke ergeben, zu trinken anfangen, an den Trunk kommen; to — kindly to a p. (a th.), sich leicht *or* schnell an einen (eine S.) gewöhnen; I don't — kindly to this way of living, ich kann mich nicht gut an diese Lebensweise gewöhnen; to — to the water, gern ins Wasser gehen (*as a dog*); sich ins Wasser flüchten; he has of late —en **up** with bad company, er hat sich in der letzten Zeit mit schlechter Gesellschaft eingelassen; to — **with**, (einem) gefallen; that won't — with me, das billige ich nicht. —**n**, *p.p.;* to be —n, besetzt sein; to be (greatly) —n with, entzückt sein von; to be —n ill, krank werden; —n in, betrogen; to be —n up with, beschäftigt sein mit. —**r**, *s.* der Nehmer, Abnehmer; —r of a bill, der Wechselkäufer. *Comp.* **—-in**, *s.* der Betrug (*coll.*). **—-off**, *s.* die Nachahmung, Karikatur; der Absprung.

Taking, I. *p. see* Take. II. *adj.*, **—ly**, *adv.* einnehmend, anziehend, reizend. III. *s.* das Nehmen 2c. —**s**, *pl.* die Einnahmen (*C.L.*). **—ness**, *s.* das Einnehmende.

Talc, *s.* der Talk.

Tale, *s.* die Erzählung, der Bericht; das Märchen, die Sage; *see* Novel; (number) die Zahl; to tell —s, ein Geheimnis ausplaudern; to tell —s out of school, aus der Schule schwatzen; thereby hangs a —, daran knüpft sich eine Geschichte. *Comp.* **—bearer**, *s.* der Zuträger, Angeber. **—bearing**, *s.* die Angeberei, Ohrenbläserei. **—teller**, *s.* der Geschichtenerzähler; der Angeber, Verräter.

Talent, *s.* die Gabe, Anlage, Begabung, Fähigkeit, das Talent; das Talent (*of gold, silver, etc.*); man of —(s), ein talentvoller Mann; he has a — for drawing, er hat Anlage, Talent zum Zeichnen. **—ed**, *adj.* begabt, befähigt, talentvoll.

Tal—esman, *s.* der Ersatzmann einer Jury. **—ion**, *s.* die Wiedervergeltung (*Law*).

Talisman, *s.* der Talisman, Schutzzauber, das zauberhafte Schutzmittel. **—ic**, *adj.* zauberisch.

Talk, I. *v.a. & n.* sprechen, reden; to — to the purpose, zur Sache, vernünftig reden; to — nonsense, Unsinn schwatzen; to — **away**, herschwatzen; to — away the time, die Zeit verplaudern; to — **down**, niederreden; to — **of**, besprechen; to — (o.s.) **out**, (sich) ausreden; to — a p. out of s.th., einem eine S. abschwatzen; to — **over**, durchsprechen; to — a p. over, einen überreden; to — a matter over, eine Angelegenheit (mit einem) besprechen. II. *s.* das Gespräch; (idle —) das Geschwätz, Gerede; (report) das Gerücht; öffentliche Verhandlung (*of the Indians*); I must have a little — with him, ich muß ein Wörtchen mit ihm sprechen; small —, die leichte Unterhaltung, das Geplauder; that is idle —, das ist leeres Geschwätz; — of the town, das Stadtgespräch; der Stadtklatsch; der Gegenstand der allgemeinen Unterhaltung. **—ative**, *adj.*, **—atively**, *adv.* gesprächig, redselig, geschwätzig, plauderhaft. **—ativeness**, *s.* die Gesprächigkeit, Redseligkeit. **—er**, *s.* der Schwätzer, Plauderer, die Plaudertasche. **—ing**, *s.* das Geplauder. *Comp.* **—ing-to**, *s.;* to give s.o. a —ing-to, einen ausschelten.

Tall, *adj.* lang, groß; hoch (*as trees, houses, etc.*); — talk, die Prahlerei. **—ness**, *s.* die Länge, Höhe, Größe. *Comp.* **—-boy**, *s.* hohes Stengelglas (*obs.*); hohe Kommode (*coll.*).

Tallow, *s.* der Talg. **—y**, *adj.* talgig. *Comp.* **—-candle**, *s.* das Talglicht. **—-chandler**, *s.* der Licht=zieher, =gießer.

[1]**Tally**, I. *s.* das Kerbholz; das Seiten=, Gegenstück. II. *v.a.* anholen, einziehen (*Naut.*); aufs Kerbholz schneiden. III. *v.n.;* to — with, passen zu, stimmen mit. *Comp.* **—-system**, **—-trade**, *s.* das Abzahlungs=system *or* =geschäft.

[2]**Tally**, **—ho**, I. *int.* ho! hallo! II. *s.* der Weidruf, das Weidgeschrei.

Talmud, *s.* der Talmud.

Talon, *s.* die Klaue, Kralle (der Raubvögel).

Talus, *s.* das Sprungbein (*Anat.*); die Böschung, Abdachung (*Anat., Fort.*); die Abdachung (*Geol.*).

Tam—able, *adj.* (be)zähmbar. **—ableness**, *s.* die (Be=)Zähmbarkeit. **—e**, I. *v.a.* zähmen (*also beasts*); bezähmen, bändigen. II. *adj.*, **—ely**, *adv.* zahm; (spiritless) mutlos, leblos, demütig; (insipid) geistlos, matt; to submit —ly to, sich (in eine S.) ohne Widerspruch fügen. **—eness**, *s.* die Zahmheit; die Mutlosigkeit; (insipidity) die Geschmacklosigkeit. **—er**, *s.* der Bezähmer, Bändiger.

Tamarin, *s.* der Tamarinaffe.

Tamarind, *s.* die Tamarinde; —s, eingemachte Tamarinden (*C.L.*).

Tamarisk, *s.* die Tamariske, der Tamariskenbaum.

Tambour, I. *s.* das Tamburin, die Handtrommel; (— work) tamburierte Stickerei; die Säulentrommel, der Kelch, die Glocke (*of a column*); der zylinderförmige Teil einer Kuppel (*Arch.*); der Tambour, die Trommel (*Fort.*). II. *v.a.* tamburieren, sticken. **—ine**, *s.* das Tamburin.

Comp. **—-frame**, *s.* der Stick-, Trommel-rahmen. **—-needle**, *s.* die Tamburiernadel.
Tamin(**e**), **Tammy**, *s.* der Etamin, Stamin.
Tam-o'-Shanter, *s.* (— cap) eine Art wollene Mütze mit Quastenknopf oben in der Mitte.
Tamp, *v.a.* (die Öffnung des Bohrlochs mit Lehm rc.) verstopfen; einschlagen. **—ion**, *s.* der Stöpsel; der Mundpfropf, Stückzapfen (*Artil.*); der Hut, Deckel (*Org.*).
Tamper, *v.n.* (meddle) sich abgeben, sich einlassen (with, mit); quacksalbern (*with a disease*); (intrigue) heimlich unterhandeln, intriguieren; (bribe) bestechen; to — with a p., einen zu gewinnen suchen; to — with a lock, versuchen ein Schloß aufzubrechen.
Tan, I. *s.* die Lohe; die gelbliche Farbe der Haut. II. *v.a.* lohen, gerben; (sunburn) bräunen. **—ned**, *adj.* lohgar; lohfarben, gebräunt, sonnenverbrannt. **—ner**, *s.* der (Loh-, Rot-) Gerber. **—nery**, *s.* die Gerberei. **—nic**, *adj.*; —nic acid (**—nin**), die Gerbsäure, das Tannin. **—ning**, *s.* das Lohgerben, die Lohgerberei. *Comp.* **—-bark**, *s.* die Lohe. **—-pit**, *s.* die Lohgrube. **—-yard**, *s.* die Gerberei.
Tandem, I. *s.* zweispänniger Wagen, bei dem die Pferde vor einander gespannt sind, das Tandem; (— bicycle) das Fahrrad mit zwei oder mehr Sitzen hintereinander, das Tandem (*Cycl.*). II. *adv.*; to drive —, mit voreinander gespannten Pferden fahren.
[1]**Tang**, *s.* der Beigeschmack, Nachgeschmack (*fig.*).
[2]**Tang**, *s.* der schrille Ton, Klang.
[3]**Tang**, *s.* die Angel (*of a knife, chisel, etc.*); der Heftzapfen, der Dorn, die Zunge (*of a buckle*); die Angel, der Dorn (*of a sword-blade*).
[4]**Tang**, *s.* der Seetang. **—le**, I. *s.* das Gewirr, der Knoten. II. *v.a. & n. see* Entangle.
Tang—ency, *s.* die Berührung. **—ent**, I. *s.* die Berührungslinie, Tangente; to fly off at a —ent, vom Gegenstande abspringen. II. *adj.*, **—ent**(**i**)**al**, *adj.* tangentenartig; —ent plane, die Berührungs-, Tangential-ebene; —ential co-ordinates, Linienkoordinaten; —ential force, Tangentialkraft. **—ibility**, *s.* die Berührbarkeit, Fühlbarkeit. **—ible**, *adj.*, **—ibly**, *adv.* fühlbar, greifbar; (real) wirklich, zu verwirklichen; *see* Palpable. *Comp.* **—ent-compass**, *s.* die Tangentenbussole.
Tank, *s.* der Behälter, Teich, die Zisterne, das große Bassin. *Comp.* **—-engine**, *s.* die Tendermaschine.
Tankard, *s.* die Kanne, der Deckelkrug, Römer
Tansy, *s.* der Rainfarn.
Tantaliz—e, *v.a.* quälen, (bis aufs Blut *or* aufs äußerste) peinigen, (einem) Tantalusqualen bereiten. **—ing**, *adj.*, **—ingly**, *adv.* quälend, peinigend.
Tantamount, *adj.*; — to, gleich, ebensoviel wie, gleichbedeutend mit.
Tantrum, *s.* die Grille, Laune; to be in a —, übler Laune *or* aufgebracht sein.
[1]**Tap**, I. *v.a. & n.* sanft schlagen, leise klopfen. II. *s.* der gelinde Schlag. **—per**, *s.* der Klopfende. **—ping**, *s.* das leise Klopfen.
[2]**Tap**, I. *v.a.* zapfen; anzapfen (*a cask, a tree, a dropsical person*); to — the wire, a telegraph line, sich einen Teil des elektrischen Stromes unbefugterweise aneignen, fremde Telegramme abfangen und lesen. II. *s.* der Zapfen, Hahn (*of a barrel, etc.*); die Wasserleitung (*in houses, etc.*); (liquor) das Getränk; *see* —-room; (borer) der Schraubenbohrer; on —, vom Faß (*as beer*), angezapft. **—ster**, *s.* der Kellner. *Comp.* **—-room**, *s.* die Trink-, Schenk-stube. **—-root**, *s.* die Pfahlwurzel.
Tape, *s.* das Zwirn-, Leinen-band; der sich selbst abrollende schmale Papierstreifen beim Telegraphieren; red —, die Bureaukratie vom grünen Tisch (*fig.*). **—ism**, *s.*; red-—ism, die Verwaltung vom grünen Tisch. *Comp.* **—-line**, *s.* die Meßschnur (*Survey.*). **—-measure**, *s.* das Bandmaß, Metermaß (*of tailors*). **—worm**, *s.* der Bandwurm.
Taper, I. *s.* die Wachskerze. II. *adj.* spitz (zulaufend); — fingers, lange schmal zulaufende Finger. III. *v.a.* zuspitzen, abschärfen. IV. *v.n.* spitz zulaufen. **—ing**, I. *adj. see* — II. II. *s.* das Spitzzulaufen.
Tapestry, I. *s.* gewirkte Tapete, Teppichtapete, Tapezierung, der Wandteppich. II. *v.a.* mit Tapeten schmücken. *Comp.* **—-frame**, *s.* der Stickrahmen. **—-maker**, *s.* der Tapeten-weber, -wirker. **—-needle**, *s.* die Tapeziernadel.
Tapioca, *s.* die Tapioka.
Tapir, *s.* der Tapir (*Zool.*).
Tar, I. *s.* der Teer; Jack —, die Teerjacke, der Matrose; an old —, ein alter Seebär. II. *v.a.* teeren; to — over, beteeren; to — and feather, beteeren und in Federn stecken. **—paulin**, *see* Tarpaulin. **—ry**, *adj.* teerig.
Tarant—ella, *s.* der Tarantellatanz. **—ism**, *s.* die Tanzwut. **—ula**, *s.* die Tarantel; like one stung by a —ula, wie von der Tarantel gestochen.
Tarboosh, *s.* der Tarbusch, die türkische Mütze.
Tard—igrade, *s.* das Faultier. **—iness**, *s.* die Langsamkeit, Säumigkeit. **—ily**, *adv.*, **—y**, langsam, säumig; (late) spät.
[1]**Tare**, *s.* die Wicke (*Agr.*); das Unkraut.
[2]**Tare**, *s.* die Tara, Verpackung (*C. L.*).
[3]**Tare**, *obs. imperf. of* Tear.
Target, *s.* die (Schieß-)Scheibe; (shield) die Tartsche (*obs.*). *Comp.* **—-practice**, *s.* das Scheibenschießen, die Schießübung.
Tariff, *s.* der Tarif; (customs —) Zolltarif. *Comp.* **—-war**, *s.* der Zollkrieg, Zollkampf.
Tarlatan, *s.* der Tarlatan.
Tarn, *s.* der kleine Bergsee; (bog) der Sumpf.
Tarnish, *v.* I. *a.* trüben, matt machen; (soil) beschmutzen, beflecken. II. *n.* den Glanz verlieren, matt werden.
Taro, *s.* eßbarer Arum, eßbare Zehrwurzel.
Tarpaulin, *s.* die Persenning, Presenning, das geteerte Segeltuch (*Naut.*); geteerte Wagendecke (*for waggons, etc.*); der Matrosenhut aus geteertem Segeltuch.
Tarry, *v.* I. *n.* verweilen, warten; (delay) zögern, säumen, zaudern. II. *a.* abwarten. **—ing**, *s.* das Säumen, Weilen.
[1]**Tart**, *adj.*, **—ly**, *adv.* scharf, sauer, herb; schroff, bissig (*fig.*). **—ish**, *adj.* etwas derb, säuerlich. **—ness**, *s.* die Schärfe (*also fig.*).
[2]**Tart**, *s.* die Torte, das Pasteichen. **—let**, *s.* das Törtchen.
Tartan, I. *s.* buntgewürfelter schottischer Wollstoff, der Tartan; buntgewürfeltes schottisches Plaid. II. *adj.* buntgewürfelt.
[1]**Tart—ar**, *s.* der Weinstein (*also of the teeth*); cream of —ar, der Weinsteinrahm; —ar emetic, Brechweinstein. **—aric**, *adj.*; —aric acid, die Weinsteinsäure. **—rate**, *s.* weinsteinsaures Salz.
[2]**Tartar**, *s. see the Index of Names.*
Task, I. *s.* die Aufgabe, aufgegebene Arbeit; (work) die Beschäftigung, das Tagewerk, Geschäft; to take a p. to — for, einen zur Rede stellen, einen vornehmen *or* einem einen Verweis geben wegen. II. *v.a.* eine Arbeit aufgeben, beschäftigen; (tax) anstrengen. **—er**, *see* —master. *Comp.* **—master**, *s.* der Arbeitsgeber; der (strenge) Zuchtmeister, gestrenge Herr (*also fig.*). **—-work**, *s.* die Akkordarbeit. **—-worker**, *s.* der Akkordarbeiter.
Tassel, *s.* die Troddel, Quaste. **—ed**, *adj.* betroddelt, mit einer Troddel (versehen).
Tast—e, I. *v.a.* kosten, schmecken; (try) versuchen, probieren; fühlen, empfinden (*fig.*); (enjoy) genießen. II. *v.n.* kosten (of, von); schmecken (of, nach). III. *s.* der Geschmack (*also fig.*); (specimen) der Bissen zum Kosten; (little piece) das Bischen, Tröpfchen; (liking) die Neigung, Lust (for, zu), Vorliebe (für); in good —e, von feinem

Takt, Geschmack; that was very bad —e, das war sehr unfein; there is no accounting for —es, über den Geschmack läßt sich nicht streiten; —es differ, die Geschmäcke sind verschieden; to take a —e of, ein wenig versuchen, kosten (*coll.*). —**ed**, *adj.* =schmeckend. —**eful**, *adj.*, —**efully**, *adv.* schmackhaft; geschmackvoll (*fig.*). —**efulness**, *s.* die Schmackhaftigkeit; der feine Geschmack. —**eless**, *adj.* geschmacklos. —**elessness**, *s.* die Geschmacklosigkeit. —**er**, *s.* der Koster, Schmecker. —**ily**, *adv.*, —**y**, *adj.* (*coll.*) schmackhaft.

[1]**Tat**, *s.*; tit for —, wie du mir, so ich dir; Wurst wider Wurst; to give tit for —, mit gleicher Münze bezahlen.

[2]**Tat**, *v.a.* & *n.* Frivolitäten anfertigen. —**ting**, *s.* die Frivolitäten (eine Art Spitzen).

Ta-ta, *interj.* Adieu (*children's lang.*).

Tatter, *v.a.* zerreißen, zerfetzen; —ed, zerlumpt, zerfetzt; all —ed and torn, ganz zerlumpt und abgerissen. —**demalion**, *s.* der Lumpenkerl. —**s**, *pl.* Lumpen; Fetzen (*fig.*); in —s, ganz zerlumpt, völlig abgerissen.

Tattl—e, I. *s.* das Geschwätz. II. *v.n.* schwatzen, plaudern. —**er**, *s.* der Schwätzer, Plauderer. —**ing**, I. *s.* das Geschwätz. II. *adj.* schwatzhaft.

[1]**Tattoo**, *s.* der Zapfenstreich (*Mil.*); devil's —, das Trommeln mit den Fingern (*fam.*).

[2]**Tattoo**, *v.a.* (& *r.* sich) tätowieren.

Taught, *imperf.* & *p.p.* of Teach.

Taunt, I. *s.* die Stichelei, böswillige Neckerei; der spöttische Vorwurf, Stich. II. *v.a.* (ver=)höhnen; *see* Reproach; (einen mit etwas) aufziehen. —**er**, *s.* der Höhner, Stichler. —**ing**, *adj.*, —**ingly**, *adv.* höhnisch, spöttisch.

Taurine, I. *adj.* Stier=. II. *s.* das Taurin (*Chem.*).

Taut, *adj.* steif, straff.

Tautolog—ical, *adj.*, —**ically**, *adv.* tautologisch; der Wortschwall. —**ist**, *s.* der Tautolog. —**y**, *s.* die Tautologie, dasselbe besagend.

Tavern, *s.* die Schenke, das Weinhaus; (inn) das Wirtshaus. *Comp.* —-**bill**, *s.* die Wirtshausrechnung. —-**keeper**, *s.* der Schenkwirt.

[1]**Taw**, *v.a.* (weiß oder sämisch) gerben. —**er**, *s.* der Weißgerber. —**ery**, *s.* die Weißgerberei.

[2]**Taw**, *s.* die Murmel; das Murmelspiel.

Tawdr—y, *adj.*, —**ily**, *adv.* flitterhaft; —y finery, verkommener, unordentlicher Flitterstaat. —**iness**, *s.* das Flitterhafte, der verkommene Flitterstaat.

Tawn—iness, *s.* die Lohfarbe, das Gelbbraune. —**y**, *adj.* lohfarben, gelbbraun (*also wines*).

Taws(e), *s.* die Peitsche, Geißel, Fuchtel.

Tax, I. *s.* die Staatssteuer, Auflage; die Last, Bürde (*fig.*); rates and —es, örtliche und staatliche Abgaben. II. *v.a.* taxieren, schätzen (at, auf, *acc.*); (impose a — on) besteuern; ansetzen (*costs*); in Anspruch nehmen (*one's energies*); to — a p. with, einen einer Sache beschuldigen, (ihm etwas) vorwerfen. —**able**, *adj.* steuerbar, steuerpflichtig. —**ableness**, *s.* die Steuerbarkeit. —**ation**, *s.* die Schätzung, Besteuerung; (tax) die Steuer; die Ansetzung der Gerichtskosten (*Law*). —**i(meter)cab**, *s.* die Taxameterdroschke. —**imeter**, *s.* der Taxameter. *Comp.* —-**collector**, *s.* der Steuereinnehmer. —-**payer**, *s.* der Steuerzahler.

Taxiderm—ic, *adj.* taxidermisch. —**ist**, *s.* der Tierausstopfer. —**y**, *s.* die Kunst, Tiere auszustopfen, die Ausbalgekunst.

Tea, *s.* der Tee; high —, frühes Abendbrot (5-6 Uhr Nachm.) mit Tee; to blend —, Teesorten mischen; to take — with a p., mit einem Tee trinken. *Comp.* —-**blender**, *s.* der Teemischer; *see* —-dealer. —-**caddy**, —-**canister**, *s.* die Teebüchse. —-**chest**, *s.* die Teekiste. —-**cup**, *s.* die Teetasse. —-**dealer**, *s.* der Teehändler. —-**gown**, *s.* leichtes, nicht eng anschließendes Damenkleid (für) Teegesellschaften. —**kettle**, *s.* der Teekessel. —-**leaf**, *s.* das Teeblatt. —-**party**, *s.* die Teegesellschaft, Gesellschaft zum Tee. —-**pot**, *s.* die Teekanne, der Teetopf. —-**rose**, *s.* die Teerose. —-**service**, *s.* das Teeservice. —-**spoon**, *s.* der Teelöffel. —**spoonful**, *s.* ein Teelöffelvoll; three —spoonfuls, drei Teelöffelvoll. —-**table**, *s.* der Teetisch. —-**things**, *pl.* das Teegeschirr. —-**tray**, *s.* das Teebrett. —-**urn**, *s.* die Tee=urne, =maschine.

Teach, *ir.v.a.* & *n.* lehren, unterrichten, unterweisen; abrichten (*animals*); to — a p. how to do a th., einem zeigen, wie eine Sache zu machen ist; I will — you to laugh at me, ich will dir das Lachen vertreiben. —**able**, *adj.* lernfähig; (docile) gelehrig. —**ableness**, *s.* die Lernfähigkeit; die Gelehrigkeit. —**er**, *s.* der (die) Lehrer(in); secondary —er, Lehrer an einer höheren Schule. —**ing**, *s.* das Lehren; die Lehre, der Unterricht.

Teak, *s.* der Teakbaum, Tiekbaum.

Teal, *s.* die Krickente (*Orn.*).

Team, *s.* das Gespann, der Zug (*of horses, etc.*); die Gesellschaft, Gruppe (*of workmen, cricketers, etc.*); a good —, eine gute Mannschaft *or* Spielgesellschaft. —**ster**, *s.* der Fuhrmann.

[1]**Tear**, I. *ir.v.a.* reißen, zerren; zerreißen (*one's clothes, etc.*); ausraufen (*one's hair*); (scratch) ritzen, verwunden (*the skin*); to — **asunder**, auseinanderreißen, gewaltsam trennen; to — **down**, herunterreißen; to — **from** a p., einem ent=, weg=reißen; to — **off**, ab=reißen, =zerren; to — **out**, ausreißen; to — **in** *or* **to** pieces, in Stücke reißen; to — **up**, auf=, zer=reißen. II. *v.n.* stürzen, stürmen; wüten, rasen (*fam.*); he tore upstairs, er stürzte hinauf; he tore about the room, er rannte wütend im Zimmer auf und ab. III. *s.* der Riß (*in clothes*); wear and —, die Abnutzung (durch den Gebrauch). —**er**, *s.* einer, der (zer)reißt. —**ing**, *adj.* leicht zerreißbar; rasend, tobend, ausgelassen; äußerst, stark, heftig; in a —ing passion, höchst aufgebracht (*coll.*); in a —ing hurry, in kolossaler Eile (*coll.*); —ing goods, leicht zerreißbare Zeuge (*C.L.*). *Comp.* —-**off**, *adj.*; —-off calendar, der Abreißkalender.

[2]**Tear**, *s.* die Träne; to shed —s, Tränen vergießen, weinen; to reduce to —s, zu Tränen bringen. —**ful**, *adj.*, —**fully**, *adv.* tränenvoll. —**less**, *adj.* tränenlos. *Comp.* —-**stained**, *adj.* tränenfeucht.

Teas—e, I. *v.a.* kämmen, krempeln, kratzen (*wool*); (auf)rauhen (*cloth*); necken, hänseln, ärgern, quälen (*fig.*); he was —ed into consenting, er wurde so gequält, daß er einwilligte. II. —**e**, (—**er**,) *s.* der Quälende, Quälgeist, Necker. —**ing**, *adj.* quälerisch.

Teasel, (**Teazel**,) I. *s.* die Kardendistel (*Bot.*); die Karde, Rauhmaschine. II. *v.a.* Tuch rauhen, kardätschen.

Teat, *s.* die Zitze, Brustwarze; soothing —, der Lutschbeutel.

Tech—iness, *s.* die Verdrießlichkeit, Reizbarkeit. —**ily**, *adv.*, —**y**, *adj.* verdrießlich, reizbar. *See* Touchy.

Techn—ic, I. *adj. see* —ical. II. *s.* die Kunstfertigkeit, Technik; (*often* —ics) die Kunstlehre. —**ical**, *adj.*, —**ically**, *adv.* kunstmäßig, kunstgerecht, technisch; —ical term, der Kunstausdruck, Fachausdruck; —ical language, die Kunstsprache, Fachsprache. —**icality**, *s.* das Technische, Kunstgerechte; die technische Eigentümlichkeit. —**ics**, *pl.* die technischen Dinge, Ausdrücke, Methoden. —**ological**, *adj.*, —**ologically**, *adv.* technologisch; —ological institute, die Kunst= und Gewerbeschule. —**ology**, *s.* die Gewerbekunde.

Te Deum, *s.* das Tedeum; der Dankgottesdienst.

Tedi—ous, *adj.*, —**ously**, *adv.* langweilig; (fatiguing) ermüdend, lästig. —**ousness**, *s.* die Langweiligkeit; (prolixity) die Weitschweifigkeit; das Ermüdende. —**um**, *s.* die Langeweile, der Überdruß, Ekel.

Tee, I. *s.* das Ziel (bei Wurf= und Ball=Spielen); der Sandhaufen, von dem der Golfball geschlagen

wird (*Golf*). II. *v.a.* den Golfball zum Schlagen auf den Sandhaufen setzen.
Teem, *v.n.* voll sein, wimmeln (with, von); schwanger sein, gehen (with, mit); (bring forth) werfen (*as beasts*); gebären; (be prolific) fruchtbar sein. **—ing**, *adj.* fruchtbar.
Teens, *pl.* Lebensjahre die sich auf zehn endigen (von 13–19); still in one's —, noch nicht 20 Jahre alt; a miss in her —, ein Backfisch.
Teeth, I. *pl. of* Tooth. II. —, **—e**, *v.n.* zahnen. **—ing**, *s.* das Zahnen.
Teetotal, *adj.* Enthaltsamkeits=, Mäßigkeits=. **—(l)er**, *s.* das Mitglied eines Mäßigkeitsvereins, der Temperänzler, Mäßigkeitsvereinler. **—ism**, *s.* die gänzliche Enthaltsamkeit von allen geistigen Getränken.
Teetotum, *s.* das Drehrädchen.
Tegument, *s.* die Hülle, Decke. **—ary**, *adj.* Decken=, Hüllen=.
Telamones, *s.* Tragsäulen in Männergestalt.
Tele—gram, *s.* das Telegramm, der Drahtbericht, die (telegraphische) Depesche, Drahtnachricht, Drahtung; wireless —gram, drahtlose Depesche. **—graph**, I. *v.a. & n.* drahten, telegraphieren. II. *s.* der Telegraph. III. *attrib.*; —graph office, das Telegraphenamt. **—graphic**, *adj.*, — **graphically**, *adv.* telegraphisch. **—graphy**, *s.* die Telegraphie; wireless —graphy, drahtlose Telegraphie. **—ological**, *adj.* teleologisch. **—ology**, *s.* die Teleologie. **—pathy**, *s.* die seelische Fernwirkung, Gedanken=Übertragung, Telepathie. **—phone**, I. *s.* der Fernsprecher, das Telephon; connection by —phone, die Telephonverbindung. II. *attrib.*; —phone office, das Fernsprechamt, die Fernsprechstelle. — **phonic**, *adj.* telephonisch. **—phonist**, *s.* der (die) Telephonist(in). **—phony**, *s.* die Fernsprechung. **—scope**, I. *s.* das Fernrohr, Teleskop. II. *v.a.* (*& n.*) (sich) ineinanderschieben (*railway collision*). **—scopic**, *adj.* teleskopisch.
Tell, *ir.v.* I. *a.* (count) zählen; (relate) berichten, sagen, mitteilen, erzählen; (disclose) entdecken; (bid) heißen, befehlen; experience —s us, die Erfahrung lehrt uns; I have been told, mir ist gesagt worden; ich habe mir sagen lassen; to — a p. of his faults, einen auf seine Fehler aufmerksam machen; to — stories, Geschichtchen erzählen; (— lies) lügen; to — tales, flunkern; den Angeber spielen; that told a tale, das verriet viel, enthielt eine ganze Geschichte; to — a p. the plain truth, einem reinen Wein einschenken; I could — a tale of it, ich weiß ein Lied davon zu singen; I cannot — the one from the other, ich kann die beiden nicht unterscheiden; to — **again**, wiedersagen; to — **off**, abzählen; a number of men were told off (to) . . ., eine Anzahl Männer wurde ausgewählt (zu) . . . II. *n.* erzählen, sprechen (of, von); (produce effect) Eindruck machen, seine Wirkung tun, treffen; sich geltend machen; every shot told, jede Kugel traf; every word —s, jedes Wort ist von Wirkung; this must — in the long run, am Ende muß es doch seinen Zweck erreichen; peace —s for righteousness, Friede befördert Rechtlichkeit; it —s heavily against a p., es fällt schwer gegen einen ins Gewicht; this told most of all on classics, dies traf die alten Sprachen in erster Linie; her cares have told heavily upon her, ihre Sorgen haben sie sehr mitgenommen; you yourself can best —, Sie selbst wissen am besten; to — **of**, zeugen von, verkünden (*want, etc.*); to — **of** *or* **on**, angeben. **—er**, *s.* der Erzähler; der Zähler; der Stimmenzähler (*at elections*); der Kassengehilfe (*in banks*). **—ing**, *adj.* wirkungsvoll, eindrucksvoll, effektvoll. *Comp.* **—tale**, I. *s.* der Angeber, Ohrenbläser. II. *adj.* schwatzhaft; —tale looks, verräterische Blicke.
Telluri—c, *adj.* irdisch; —c acid, die Tellursäure. **—on**, *s.* das Tellurium. **—um**, *s.* das Tellur(metall).
Telpher, *adj.* zur elektrischen Lastenbeförderung dienend. **—age**, *s.* die elektrische Lastenbeförderung.
Temerity, *s.* die Verwegenheit, Tollkühnheit.
Temper, I. *v.a.* in das gehörige Maß, Verhältnis bringen, mischen; (moderate) mäßigen, mildern, lindern, besänftigen; temperieren (*Mus.*); (mit Wasser) anmachen (*colours*); anmachen, anrühren (*lime*); adoucieren (*cast iron*); anlassen, härten, tempern (*steel*). II. *s.* richtige Mischung; die Härte (*of needles, etc.*); der Härtegrad (*Metall.*); die Beschaffenheit (*of the body*), Körperanlage, das Temperament; das Gemüt, Naturell (*fig.*); die Stimmung, Laune; die Reizbarkeit, Heftigkeit; moral —, die Gemütsbeschaffenheit; in a good (bad) —, in guter (übler) Laune; to be out of —, übler Laune sein; to be in a —, aufgebracht sein; to get out of — with, ungehalten werden über (*acc.*); to keep (lose) one's —, an sich halten (heftig werden); to put out of —, übel gelaunt machen. **—a (painting)**, *s.* die Tempera (Malerei). **—ament**, *s.* die Beschaffenheit, das Temperament; die Temperatur (*Mus.*). **—ance**, I. *s.* die Mäßigung; die Mäßigkeit (*in eating, etc.*); die Enthaltsamkeit (in drinking, von geistigen Getränken). II. *attrib.*; —ance hotel, der Mäßigkeits=Gasthof (in dem keine geistigen Getränke verabreicht werden); —ance Society, der Mäßigkeits=verein. **—ate**, *adj.*, **—ately**, *adv.* gemäßigt (*as a climate, also fig.*); mäßig (*in eating, etc.*); (calm) gelassen, ruhig; —ate language, maßvolle Sprache; —ate zones, gemäßigte Zonen. **—ature**, *s.* die Temperatur, der Wärmestand. **—ed**, *adj.*; even-—ed, gleichmütig; good-, ill-—ed, gut, schlecht gelaunt.
Tempest, *s.* der Sturm(wind); das Unwetter, Gewitter; der Sturm (*fig.*). **—uous**, *adj.* stürmisch, ungestüm. **—uousness**, *s.* das Ungestüm. *Comp.* **—-tossed**, *adj.* von Sturm umhergeworfen *or* umhergetrieben.
Templar, *s.* der Tempel=ritter, =herr; (student) der Student der Rechte (im Londoner Tempel).
[1]**Temple**, *s.* die Schläfe.
[2]**Temp—le**, *s.* der Tempel, die Kirche; der Temple (*in London*); master of the —le, erster Pfarrer der Londoner Temple=Kirche; student of the —le, *see* —lar. **—let**, *s.* die Schablone, Lehre; das Lehrbrett (*Mas.*). **—oral**, *adj.*, **—orally**, *adv.* zeitlich; (*opp. to* Spiritual) weltlich. **—oralities**, *pl.* die Temporalien, zeitlichen Güter. **—orality**, *s.* die Weltlichkeit. **—orary**, *adj.*, **—orarily**, *adv.* einstweilig, zeitweilig, vorübergehend; (for a time) auf einige Zeit; —orary stoppage, zeitweilige Stockung. **—orariness**, *s.* zeitweilige Dauer. **—orization**, *s.* das Zaudern, Zeitabwarten. **—orize**, *v.n.* die Zeit abwarten, sich in die Zeit schicken, den Mantel nach dem Winde hängen; (delay) zögern, zaudern. **—orizer**, *s.* einer, der den Mantel nach dem Winde hängt *or* sich nach den Umständen richtet.
Tempt, *v.a.* reizen (zu einer S.), versuchen, verlocken, in Versuchung führen. **—ation**, *s.* die Versuchung, Reizung. **—er**, **—ress**, *s.* der (die) Versucher(in), Verführer(in). **—ing**, *adj.*, — **ingly**, *adv.* verführerisch, reizend **—ingness**, *s.* das Verführerische, Reizende.
Ten, *num. adj.* zehn. **—fold**, *adj.* zehnfach. **—th**, I. *adj.* zehnt. II. *s.* das Zehntel; die Dezime (*Mus.*). **—thly**, *adv.* zehntens.
Ten—able, *adj.* haltbar. **—ableness**, *s.* die Haltbarkeit. **—acious**, *adj.*, **—aciously**, *adv.* festhaltend (of, an einer S.); beharrlich, zäh; treu (*of memory*); to be —acious (of one's opinion, of life, (sich nicht umstimmen lassen,) ein zähes Leben haben. **—aciousness**, **—acity**, *s.* die Zähigkeit (des Festhaltens); die Treue, (Gedächtnis=)Stärke; die Hartnäckigkeit (*fig.*). — **aille**, I. *s.* das Zangenwerk, Scherenwerk (*Fort.*). II. *attrib.*; —aille system, die Zangenbefesti=

gung. —**ancy**, *s.* der einstweilige Besitz, Pacht-, Miet-besitz; —ancy at will, nach Willkür kündbare Pachtung. —**ant**, I. *s.* der Pächter (eines Gutes), Mieter (eines Hauses, einer Wohnung); (occupier) der Bewohner, Insasse; der Lehnsmann (*Law*); —ant at will, nach Willkür kündbarer Pächter. II. *v.a.* bewohnen. —**antable**, *adj.* mietbar; (habitable) bewohnbar. —**antless**, *adj.* unvermietet, unbewohnt. —**antry**, *s.* die Pächter (eines Gutes). —**ement**, I. *s.* das Haus, die Wohnung, der Wohnsitz; jedes beständige Besitztum. II. *attrib.*; —ement house, das von mehreren Familien bewohnte Miethaus, die Mietkaserne. —**emental**, *adj.* Pacht-. —**esmus**, *s.* der Stuhlzwang (*Med.*). —**et**, *s.* der Grund-, Lehr-satz; socialistic —ets, sozialistische Lehren *or* Grundsätze. —**nis**, *s.* das Tennis. —**on**, *s.* der Zapfen. —**or**, *s.* der Fortgang, (Ver-)Lauf; (purport) der Sinn, Inhalt; die Tenorstimme (*Mus.*); (—or singer) der Tenor; of the same —or, gleichlautend; even —or, die Gleichförmigkeit. —**ure**, *see* Tenure. *Comp.* —**ant-right**, *s.* das Pachtrecht. —**nis-court**, *s.* das Spielfeld (für Tennis). —**nis-racket**, *s.* der Tennisschläger.

Tench, *s.* die Schleie (*Ichth.*).

[1]**Tend**, *v.n.* sich richten, wenden (towards, nach); (aim at) hinarbeiten (auf eine S.), abzielen (auf eine S.), bezwecken; (contribute) beitragen (zu einer S.); these things — to draw away, diese Dinge ziehen leicht ab. —**ency**, *s.* die Richtung (auf eine S.), Neigung (zu), der Hang (zu); die Tendenz, Richtung (*of books, etc.*); —ency of blood, der Blutandrang (*Med.*); he has a —ency to, er ist geneigt zu. —**er**, I. *s.* (offer) das Anerbieten; das Gebot (auf Submission), der Antrag, Kostenanschlag, die Bedingungen (*for work, etc.*); legal —er, gesetzliches Zahlungsmittel; to make a —er of (to —er), (etwas) anbieten; to make a —er for, zur Übernahme von (etwas) seine Bedingungen einreichen. II. *v.a.* darreichen, an-, dar-bieten; zuschieben (*an oath*). —**on**, *s.* die Sehne, Flechse. —**ril**, I. *s.* die zarte Ranke, Wickelranke, Gabel. II. *attrib.* rankend, Ranken-.

[2]**Tend**, *v.a.* aufwarten, bedienen; bewachen, hüten, pflegen. —**er**, *s.* der Wärter, Pfleger; der Tender (*Railw.*); der Lichter, das Beischiff, der Tender (*Naut.*).

[1]**Tender**, *adj.*, —**ly**, *adv.* zart (*as a flower, age, conscience*); weich, schonend, sorgsam (*as flesh, the heart, etc.*); zärtlich (*as love*); (weak) weichlich, schwach; empfindlich (*as a wound*); to leave a p. to the — mercies of, einen schutzlos den Händen von . . . überlassen. —**ness**, *s.* die Zartheit; die Weichheit; (love) die Zärtlichkeit, Liebe; die Empfindlichkeit (*of a wound, etc.*). *Comp.* —**-eyed**, *adj.* sanftäugig; schwachsichtig. —**-hearted**, *adj.* weichherzig. —**-mouthed**, *adj.* weichmäulig.

[2]**Tender**, *see under* [2]Tend.

Tenebrous, *adj.* dunkel, finster.

[1]**Tens**—**e**, *adj.*, —**ely**, *adv.* gespannt, straff. —**eness**, —**ity**, *s.* die Gespanntheit, Straffheit. —**ible**, —**ile**, *adj.* dehnbar. —**ion**, *s.* die Spannung, Streckung, Spannkraft. —**or**, *s.* der Spannmuskel.

[2]**Tense**, *s.* die Zeitform, das Tempus.

[1]**Tent**, *s.* das Zelt; to pitch one's —, sein Zelt aufschlagen; sich häuslich niederlassen (*also fig.*). —**acle**, *s.* der Fühlfaden (*Ent.*). —**acular**, *adj.* Fühlfaden-. —**ative**, I. *adj.* versuchend, probend. II. *s.* der Versuch. —**er**, *s.* der Spannrahmen; to be on —ers *or* —er-hooks, gespannt *or* auf der Folter sein, wie auf Kohlen sitzen (*fig.*). *Comp.* —**-bed**, *s.* das Zeltbett. —**er-hook**, *s.* der Spannhaken; *see* —er. —**-pegs**, *pl.* Zeltpflöcke. —**-pole**, *s.* die Zeltstange.

[2]**Tent**, I. *s.* die Wieke (*Surg.*). II. *v.a.* sondieren, untersuchen; eine Wieke in eine Wunde legen (*Surg.*).

[3]**Tent**, *s.* der Tintowein.

Tenu—**ity**, *s.* die Dünnheit; die Zartheit, Feinheit. —**ous**, *adj.*, —**ously**, *adv.* dünn, fein, zart; geringfügig.

Tenure, *s.* Art des Besitzes; (holding) der Besitz; his — of life is an uncertain one, mit seiner Lebensfähigkeit ist es schlecht bestellt.

Tep—**efy**, *v.a.* lau machen. —**id**, *adj.* lau. —**idness**, —**idity**, *s.* die Lauheit.

Terce, *see* Tierce. —**l**, *s.* der Terz, das Falkenmännchen (*Ornith.*). —**ntenary**, I. *adj.* 300-jährig. II. *s.* das dreihundertjährige Jubelfest, Jubiläum, der dreihundertjährige Gedenktag.

Tergiversation, *s.* die Ausflucht, Finte, der Winkelzug; (fickleness) der Wankelmut.

Term, I. *s.* die bestimmte Zeit, Frist; die Zeit der Sitzung, Session (*of a law-court, of parliament*); der Termin, das Ziel (*for payment, etc.*); (end) das Ziel, Ende; der Jahresabschnitt; das Quartal, Trimester (*in schools, universities*); (expression) das Wort, der Ausdruck; die Grenzsäule, Terme (*Arch.*); das Glied (*Alg., Arith., Log.*); — of office, die Amtsdauer, Amtszeit; technical —, der Kunst-, Fach-ausdruck; for a —, (auf) eine Zeit lang; — of life, die Lebenszeit; to keep one's —s, die erforderliche Anzahl von Tagen in jedem Trimester (auf der Universität) verbringen. II. *v.a.* (be)nennen. —**inable**, *adj.* begrenzbar; zu Ende gehend, auf eine bestimmte Anzahl von Jahren laufend, lösbar, kündbar, sich endigend (*as a contract, etc.*); the lease is —inable at any time, die Pacht kann zu jeder Zeit aufgekündigt werden. —**inal**, *adj.* die Spitze bildend; gipfelständig (*Bot.*). —**inate**, *v.* I. *a.* begrenzen; (end) enden, (be)endigen; schließen (*a letter*); aus-machen, -gleichen (*quarrels*). II. *n.* endigen; auslaufen (in eine Spitze, in a point, *etc.*); (sich) endigen (in, auf eine S.). —**ination**, *s.* der Ausgang, das Ende; die Endung (*Gram.*). —**inology**, *s.* die Terminologie, Fachsprache; die Fach-, Kunst-ausdrücke (*collect.*). —**inus**, I. *s.* die Endstation (*Railw.*). II. *attrib.*; —inus hotel, das Eisenbahnhotel, der Gasthof im oder gegenüber dem Bahnhof. —**s**, *pl.* Bedingungen; (relations) das Verhältnis, der Fuß; to come to —s, übereinkommen, sich einigen, sich abfinden (with, mit); at your own —s, deinen eignen Bedingungen gemäß; on reasonable (favourable) —s, zu billigem Preise, (unter günstigen Bedingungen); upon no —s, unter keiner Bedingung; by the —s of the contract, nach Wortlaut des Kontrakts; —s of sale, Verkaufsbedingungen; to be on good (bad) —s with, gut, (schlecht,) auf gutem (schlechtem) Fuße stehen mit; to meet a p. on equal —s, einem gleichberechtigt gegenübertreten; to be on —s of intimacy with a p., mit einem auf vertrautem Fuße stehen; we are on the best of —s, wir stehen sehr gut mit einander; in plain —s, rund heraus (gesagt). *Comp.* —**-day**, *s.* der Zieltag. —**-fee**, *s.* die Gebühr an den Advokaten für jeden Termin, während dessen eine Sache anhängig ist.

Termagant, I. *s.* der Termagant; der Zankteufel, Hausdrache, das Mannweib. II. *attrib.*; a — wife, ein Hausdrache, eine böse Sieben, Xantippe.

Tern, *s.* die Seeschwalbe, Meerschwalbe.

Terna—**ry**, I. *adj.* aus drei bestehend. II. *s.* die Zahl Drei. —**te**, *adj.* dreizählig.

Terr—**a**, *s.* die Erde; —a firma, das feste Land; —a incognita, unbekanntes Land. —**ace**, I. *s.* die Terrasse, Erdstufe; (roof) das platte Dach; der Häuserkomplex, die Häuserreihe (*in towns*). II. *v.a.* in Terrassen aufführen, terrassieren. —**aced**, *adj.* terrassiert; —aced walk, der Terrassengang. —**aqueous**, *adj.* aus Land und Wasser bestehend. —**arium**, *s.* das Terrarium. —**ene**, *adj.* irdisch. —**estrial**, *adj.* zur Erde gehörig, Erden-, Erd-; (earthly) irdisch; —estrial globe, der Erdball. **—ier**, *s.* der Terrier; das Lebensregister, Grundbuch (*Law*); fox —ier, der Fuchsterrier. **—itorial**, *adj.* den Grund und Boden, das Gebiet betreffend, Landes=; —itorial jurisdiction, die Territorialgerichtsbarkeit. **—itory**, *s.* das Gebiet, der Bezirk. *Comp.* **—acotta**, *s.* gebrannte Erde, Terracotta; die Terracottafigur.

Terr—ible, *adj.*, **—ibly**, *adv.* schrecklich, entsetzlich, fürchterlich. **—ibleness**, *s.* die Schrecklichkeit, Furchtbarkeit. **—ific**, *adj.*, **—ifically**, *adv.* fürchterlich. **—ify**, *v.a.* erschrecken, entsetzen. **—or**, *s.* der Schrecken, das Entsetzen. **—orism**, *s.* die Schreckensherrschaft, der Terrorismus. **—orist**, *s.* der Terrorist (*Hist.*). **—orize**, *v.a.* durch Schrecken vergewaltigen, terrorisieren, durch Gewaltmaßregeln einschüchtern. *Comp.* **—orstricken**, *adj.* von Schrecken ergriffen.

Terse, *adj.*, **—ly**, *adv.* bündig und geglättet. **—ness**, *s.* die Bündigkeit.

Tertia—n, *adj.* dreitägig ; —n ague *or* fever, das Tertianfieber. **—ry**, *adj.* dritt, tertiär ; —ry formation, —ries (*pl.*), die Tertiärformation, tertiäre Gebilde.

Tesselat—e, *v.a.* würfeln; mit Würfeln auslegen ; —ed pavement, der Mosaikfußboden. **—ion**, *s.* die Mosaikarbeit.

Test, I. *s.* die Probe, der Versuch, das Experiment; die Untersuchung; (means of —) das Reagens (*Chem.*); to put to the —, auf die Probe stellen ; to stand the —, die Probe aushalten *or* bestehen ; religious —s, Glaubensprüfungen. II. *attrib.;* — Act, die Testakte (*Engl. Hist. 1673–1828*). III. *v.a.* prüfen; untersuchen. **—aceous**, *adj.* hartschalig ; —aceous animals, Schaltiere. **—er**, *s.* der Himmel (*of a bed, etc.*). **—iness**, *s.* die Reizbarkeit. **—y**, *adj.*, **—ily**, *adv.* mürrisch, reizbar. **—udinal**, *adj.* schildkrötenartig. **—udo**, *s.* die Schildkrötengeschwulst (*Med.*). *Comp.* **—-paper**, *s.* das Reagenzpapier (*Chem.*); (unseen —) das Extemporale, die unvorbereitete Prüfungsarbeit. **—-tube**, *s.* die Probierröhre (*Chem.*).

Test—ament, *s.* das Testament. **—amentary**, *adj.* testamentarisch; (by will) im Testament, letztwillig. **—ator**, *s.* der Erblasser. **—atrix**, *s.* die Erblasserin. **—icle**, *s.* die Hode. **—ifier**, *s.* der Zeuge. **—ify**, *v.* I. *a.* bezeugen. II. *n.* Zeugnis ablegen. **—imonial**, *s.* das schriftliche Zeugnis, Attestat. **—imony**, *s.* das Zeugnis; (proof) der Beweis ; to bear —imony, Zeugnis ablegen; in —imony whereof, urkundlich dessen.

Tetanus, *s.* der Starrkrampf.

Tête-de-pont, *s.* der Brückenkopf (*Mil.*).

Tether, I. *s.* das Spannseil; der Spielraum (*fig.*) ; I am at the end of my —, hier geht mein Latein *or* mein Witz zu Ende, weiter kann ich nicht gehen. II. *v.a.* anbinden.

Tetra—chord, *s.* der Intervall von 4 Tönen (*Mus.*) ; (lyre, *etc.*) viersaitiges Instrument. **—dactyl**, *s.* vierzehiges Tier. **—gon**, *s.* das Viereck. **—gonal**, *adj.* viereckig. **—hedral**, *adj.* vierflächig. **—hedron**, *s.* das Vierflach. **—logy**, *s.* die Tetralogie. **—meter**, *s.* der Tetrameter. **—petalous**, *adj.* vierkronenblätterig. **—rch**, *s.* der Vierfürst. **—rchate**, *s.* das Vierfürstentum. **—syllabic**, *adj.* viersilbig. **—syllable**, *s.* viersilbiges Wort.

Tetter, *s.* der Bläschenausschlag (*Med.*).

Text, *s.* der Text (*of a book, a sermon, an opera, etc., also Typ.*). **—ile**, *adj.* gewebt; webbar; —ile industry, die Textilindustrie. **—ual**, *adj.* zum Texte dienend; —ual reading, die Lesart des Textes. **—ualist**, *s.* einer, der sich an den Text hält, der Bibelkundige (*rare*). **—ure**, *s.* das Gefüge, die Textur ; (web) das Gewebe; der Bau (*of the body*) ; die Struktur (*of minerals*) ; die Dichtigkeit (*of paper, etc.*); cloth of fine —ure, Tuch von feinem Gewebe. *Comp.* **—-book**, *s.* der Leitfaden, das Textbuch.

Than, *conj.* (*usually after comparatives*) als ; denn (*poet., obs.*).

Thane, *s.* der Degen, Recke; der Than (*as a title*). **—dom**, *s.* die Gerichtsbarkeit eines Than.

Thank, *v.a.* (einem) danken ; — you, (ich) danke (dir *or* Ihnen) ; yes, — you, bitte, wenn ich bitten darf ; no, — you, danke, (ich) danke schön ; I'll — you for the salt, bitte um das Salz (*fam.*); you may — yourself if . . ., Sie haben es sich selbst zu danken, wenn . . . **—s**, *pl.* der Dank, die Danksagung; to return —s, danken, Dank abstatten; —s, *see* — you; no —s to you ! ohne Ihnen dafür zu Dank verpflichtet zu sein; —s be to God ! Gott sei Dank ! —s to you I can walk again, Ihnen danke ich es, daß ich wieder gehen kann. **—ful**, *adj.*, **—fully**, *adv.* dankbar, erkenntlich. **—fulness**, *s.* die Dankbarkeit, Erkenntlichkeit. **—less**, *adj.*, **—lessly**, *adv.* undankbar. *Comp.* **—-offering**, *s.* das Dankopfer. **—sgiving**, I. *s.* die Danksagung ; (festival) das Dankfest; autumn —sgiving, das Erntedankfest. II. *attrib.;* —sgiving sermon, die Dankpredigt. **—worthy**, *adj.* dankenswert.

That, I. *dem., adj. & pron.* jen=er, =e, =es, dieser, =e, =es, dies, der, die, das(=jenige); — is, das ist, das heißt ; what book is — ? was ist das für ein Buch? I saw it would come to —, ich sah wohl ein, das es dahin kommen würde ; I am responsible for —, ich bin dafür verantwortlich; in — you are right, darin hast du Recht ; see you to —, da siehe du zu ! at — time, zu jener Zeit. II. *rel. pron.* der, die, das, welcher, welche, welches ; so (*obs.*) ; the best — I have, das Beste, das ich habe; the girl — has done it, das Mädchen, welches es getan hat; the people — sat in darkness have seen a great light, das Volk, so im Finstern wandelt, siehet ein großes Licht (*B.*). III. *conj.* daß ; (in order —) damit; seeing —, insofern als, weil ; not but — I prefer the other, nicht etwa, daß ich das andere nicht vorziehe ; it is not — I love you less, nicht weil ich Sie weniger liebe ; now — you are young, jetzt weil ihr (noch) jung seid ; now — the day has come, nun (da) der Tag gekommen ist.

Thatch, I. *s.* das Strohdach; (roof) das Dach; (—ing) das Dach=stroh, =schilf 2c. II. *v.a.* mit Stroh 2c. decken, überdachen ; —ed roof, das Strohdach. **—er**, *s.* der Strohdecker.

Thaumaturg—ical, *adj.* wundertätig; magisch. **—ist**, *s.* der Wundertäter. **—y**, *s.* das Wundertun; die Zauberei.

Thaw, I. *s.* das Tauwetter, (Auf=)Tauen. II. *v.a. & n.* auftauen, schmelzen.

The, *def. art.* der, die, das ; je, desto, um so (*old instrumental, before comparatives*) ; — more, — better, je mehr, desto besser; so much — more, um so viel mehr; — most we can do is to . . ., alles, was wir tun können, ist . . .; all — men do it, alle Männer tun es ; all — men who escaped, alle die Männer, welche entkamen ; all — world, die ganze Welt.

Theatr—e, *s.* das Schauspielhaus, Theater; der Schauplatz (*fig.*) ; das Disputationslokal (*Univ.*); anatomical —e, anatomischer Saal. **—ic(al)**, *adj.*, **—ically**, *adv.* bühnenmäßig, theatralisch. **—icality**, *s.* das theatralische, affektierte Wesen. **—icals**, *pl.* (Bühnen=)Aufführungen ; private —icals, Liebhaberaufführungen.

Thee, I. *pron.* dich; (to —) dir; of —, deiner, von dir; I love —, ich liebe dich; I told —, ich sagte dir; we thought of —, wir dachten dein(er), an dich; we spoke of —, wir sprachen von dir. II. *v.a.;* to — and thou, duzen.

Theft, *s.* der Diebstahl.

Theine, *s.* das Tein, der Teestoff.

Their, *poss. adj.* ihr(e). **—s**, *poss. pron.* der, die, das ihrige, ihr, ihre, ihres ; the fault was —s, die Schuld lag an ihnen.

Theis—m, *s.* der Theismus. **—t**, *s.* der Theist. **—tic(al)**, *adj.* theistisch.

Them, *pers. pron.* sie; (to —) ihnen; we told —, wir sagten ihnen. **—selves**, *pron.* sie selbst; (*used reflexively*) sich selbst; they —selves, sie selbst; things in —selves innocent, Dinge, welche an und für sich unschuldig sind; to —selves, ihnen selbst, sich selbst.

Them—atic, *adj.* thematisch. **—e**, *s.* das Thema, der Gegenstand; der Aufsatz; der Hauptsatz (*Mus.*).

Then, I. *adv.* (at that time) damals; (after that) dann, alsdann, darauf; — and not till —, damals und nicht eher; there and —, auf der Stelle, sogleich; what —? was dann? was weiter? nun, was wollen Sie damit sagen? till —, bis damals. II. *adj.;* the — king, der damalige König. III. *conj.* denn, also, folglich; he breathes, — he is alive, er atmet, also lebt er. IV. *expletive;* now —, nun denn, wohlan denn. **—ce**, I. *adv.* daher, daraus, darum; (from —ce) von da, dort *or* dannen. II. *conj.* daher; —ce it came to pass, daher geschah es. **—ceforth**, **—ceforward**, *adv.* von da (der Zeit) an, seit der Zeit, seitdem.

Theo—cracy, *s.* die Gottesherrschaft, Theokratie. **—cratic**, *adj.* theokratisch. **—dolite**, *s.* der Theodolit (*Surv.*). **—gony**, *s.* die Theogonie. **—logian**, *s* der Theolog. **—logical**, *adj.*, **—logically**, *adv.* theologisch. **—logist**, *s.* der Theolog. **—logy**, *s.* die Gottesgelehrtheit, Theologie. **—machy**, *s.* der Kampf gegen die Götter. **—phany**, *s.* die Gottes-Erscheinung. **—sophic**, *adj.* theosophisch. **—sophist**, *s.* der Gottesschwärmer, Theosoph. **—sophy**, *s.* die Theosophie; Gottesschwärmerei, das Eindringen in die Geheimnisse Gottes.

Theor—em, *s.* der Lehrsatz, das Theorem. **—etic(al)**, *adj.*, **—etically**, *adv.* theoretisch. **—ist**, *s.* der Theoretiker. **—ize**, *v.n.* Theorien bilden, spekulieren. **—y**, *s.* die Theorie.

Therapeutics, *s.* die Heilkunde, Heilkunst.

There, *adv.* da, dort, daselbst; (thither) dahin, dorthin; we were —, wir waren da; we went —, wir gingen dorthin; — he is, da ist er; down —, da unten; in —, da drin, out —, da draußen; — is, are, es giebt, es ist, es sind; — is no saying . . ., es läßt sich nicht sagen . . .; —'s a good boy! so ist es recht! (*coll.*); where — is wit — is . . ., wo Witz ist, da ist auch . . .; once upon a time — was, es war einmal; — was a king, es gab einen König, es war (einmal) ein König; — are kings who . . ., es giebt Könige, die . . .; — was a day when I . . ., es gab einen Tag, wo ich . . .; — spoke the king, das war wie ein König gesprochen. *Comp.* **—about(s)**, *adv.* da herum; (about that) ungefähr so viel. **—after**, *adv.* da(r)nach. **—at**, *adv.* dabei, darauf. **—fore**, *adv. & conj.* deswegen, deshalb, darum, dafür; deshalb, also, folglich. **—from**, **—of**, *adv.* davon; dessen, deren. **—in**, *adv.* darin. **—upon**, *adv.* darauf; deshalb, darum. **—with**, *adv.* damit; gleich darauf. **—withal**, *adv.* damit; (besides) überdies.

Therm—al, *adj.* Thermal-. **—o-electricity**, *s.* die Wärme-Elektrizität. **—ometer**, *s.* das Thermometer. **—ometrical**, *adj.* thermometrisch. **—oscope**, *s.* der Wärmezeiger.

These, *pl. of* This; diese; — are the joys of . . ., dies sind die Freuden der . . .; I have not seen him — last few days, ich habe ihn in den letzten paar Tagen nicht gesehen; it has been there — 9 years, es ist seit den letzten 9 Jahren dort gewesen; I shall not be ready — 5 years, ich werde in (den nächsten) 5 Jahren noch nicht fertig werden.

Thesis, *s* der (Streit)satz, Leitsatz, die These; die These (*Log.*, *Mus.*, *Pros.*).

Thews, *pl.* Muskeln; die Sehnen (*fig.*).

They, *pers. pron.* sie; — who, die(jenigen), welche; — say, man sagt.

Thick, I. *adj.* dick; (stout) stark, dick; trüb, dick (*as fluids*); dicht (*as fog*); (crowded) dick, dicht, gedrängt; dick, vertraut (*vulg.*); — soup, dicke Suppe; — fog, dichter Nebel; 7 inches —, 7 Zoll dick. II. *adv.* dick, dicht; to speak —, eine schwere Zunge haben. III. *s.* das Dickste; der schwierigste Teil; through — and thin, durch dick und dünn; in the — of the fight, im dichtesten Schlachtgewühl. **—en**, *v.* I. *a.* dick machen, verdicken; (inspissate) eindicken; (make stouter) verstärken. II. *n.* dicker werden, sich verdicken; sich verdichten; the combat —ens, der Kampf wird hitziger; the crowd —ens, das Gedränge nimmt zu. **—et**, *s.* das Dickicht. **—ly**, *see* — II. **—ness**, *s.* die Dicke, Dichtheit; die Trübheit; die Dichtigkeit. *Comp.* **—-headed**, *adj.* dickköpfig. **—-lipped**, *adj.* dicklippig. **—ly-planted**, *adj* dicht gepflanzt. **—-set**, I. *adj.* untersetzt; dicht bepflanzt II. *s.* dichte Hecke. **—-skinned**, *adj.* dickhäutig (*also fig.*). **—-skulled**, *adj.* dickköpfig.

Thie—f, *s.* der (die) Dieb(in); der Räuber (*in the candle*) (*prov.*); opportunity makes the —f, Gelegenheit macht Diebe (*Prov.*); to set a —f to catch a —f, den Bock zum Gärtner machen. **—ve**, *v.n.* stehlen. **—very**, *s.* die Dieberei. **—ves**, *pl. of* —f. **—vish**, *adj.* diebisch (*also fig.*). **—vishly**, *adv.* diebischerweise. **—vishness**, *s.* der Diebssinn, Hang zum Stehlen; das Diebische (*of a look, etc.*).

Thigh, *s* der Schenkel, die Lende *Comp.* **—-bone**, *s.* das Schenkelbein.

Thill, *s.* die (Gabel-)Deichsel.

Thimble, *s.* der Fingerhut; der Stemmring (*Shoem.*); die Kausche (*Naut.*). **—ful**, *s.* sehr geringe Quantität. *Comp.* **—rig**, *v.a. & n.* durch einen Taschenspielerstreich täuschen; betrügen (*fig.*).

Thin, I. *adj.*, **—ly**, *adv.* dünn; leicht (*in texture*); schwach (*in tone*); (not thick) dünn, leicht; dünn. mager; to grow —, dünn, mager werden; a — house, ein leeres Haus; a — crop, eine spärliche Ernte. II. *v.a.* dünn machen, verdünnen; lichten (*wood, the ranks of an army, etc.*); to — out, ausheben, lichten (*plants, etc.*). III. *v.n.;* to — out, allmählich abnehmen. **—ness**, *s.* die Dünnheit; die Leichtigkeit, Dünnheit; die Magerkeit. *Comp.* **—-faced**, *adj.* mit magerem Gesichte. **—ly-clad**, *adj.* dünn-, leicht-gekleidet. **—-skinned**, *adj.* dünnhäutig; empfindlich (*fig.*).

Thine, I. *poss. pron.* der, die, das Deinige, dein-er, -e, -es. II. *poss. adj.* dein.

Thing, *s.* das Ding (*also fig.*); die Sache; (being) das Wesen, Geschöpf, Etwas; a — of nought, little —, ein Nichts; —s, Sachen, Kleider; Sachen, Angelegenheiten; that's the —! so ist's! that's another —, das ist ganz (et)was Anderes; this is (quite) the —, das ist das Rechte, Passende (*sl.*); I am not quite the —, ich bin nicht ganz wohl, nicht ganz auf dem Damm; the — is that . . ., die Sache ist die, daß . . .; to make a good — of, Nutzen *or* Gewinn ziehen aus; any—, irgend etwas; any— but, alles nur nicht, nichts weniger als; the first —, zu allererst; above all —s, vor allen Dingen, vor allem; not an earthly —, nichts von dieser Welt.

Think, *ir.v.* I. *n.* denken; denken (of, an einen, etwas; von einer P. oder S.; auf eine S.); nachdenken (upon, über eine S.); sich besinnen (of, auf eine S.); (believe) meinen, glauben (of, von); (intend) gedenken, beabsichtigen; *see* Remember; I did not — of it, ich dachte nicht daran; what do you — of it? was halten Sie davon? only — (of it)! denken Sie sich nur! to — much of, viel auf (*acc.*) halten; I should — so, das sollte ich meinen (*coll.*); he —s nothing of walking twenty miles a day, er macht sich nichts daraus, täglich zwanzig Meilen zu gehen; to — good, für gut halten; to — to o.s., bei sich denken; I must — it over, ich muß es überlegen; what in the world were you —ing of, that you . . .! was in aller Welt dachten Sie, daß Sie . . .? II. *a.* denken, urteilen, meinen, glauben, vermuten, halten für; he —s himself clever, er hält sich für klug; do you — it advisable? halten Sie es für angebracht, scheint es Ihnen rätlich? to — scorn, verschmähen, verachten; (einen Gedanken) entrüstet von sich weisen; to — shame of s.th., etwas für schimpflich halten; to — out, aussinnen, sich (*dat.*) ausdenken; to — away, mit Nachdenken zubringen. **—er**, *s.* der Denker. **—ing**, I. *adj.* denkend, vernünftig. II. *s.* das Denken; die Meinung; to my —ing, nach meiner Meinung *or* meinem Dafürhalten.

Thir—d, I. *adj.* dritt. II. *s.* der, die, das Dritte; (—d part) das Drittel; die Tertie, Terz (*Mus.*). **—dly**, *adv.* drittens. **—teen**, *num.adj.* dreizehn. **—teenth**, I. *adj.* dreizehnt; one —teenth, ein Dreizehntel. II. *s.* der, die, das Dreizehnte. **—tieth**, I. *adj.* dreißigst; one —tieth, ein Dreißigstel. II. *s.* der, die, das Dreißigste. **—ty**, *num. adj.* dreißig; dreißig Jahre. *Comp.* **—d-rate**, *adj.* dritten Ranges.

Thirst, I. *s.* der Durst (*also fig.*). II. *v.n.* dürsten, dursten (for, after, nach). **—ily**, *adv.* durstig. **—iness**, *s.* die Durstigkeit, der Durst. **—y**, *adj.* durstig (*also fig.*); dürr, versengt (*as soil*).

This, I. *dem. adj.* dies=er, =e, =es, dies; laufend (*C.L.*); — morning, heute morgen; for *or* during — last month, in dem letzten Monat; in — country, hier zu Lande; to — day, noch heute; — day week, heute über 8 Tage; I shan't be ready — half hour (yet), ich werde in der nächsten halben Stunde noch nicht fertig (*coll.*). II. *dem. pron. see* — I.; between — and that, bis dahin; by —, hierdurch; (by — time) indessen, inzwischen.

Thistl—e, *s.* die Distel. **—y**, *adj.* voll Disteln. *Comp.* **—e-down**, *s.* die Distelwolle.

Thither, *adv.* dorthin, dahin. **—wards**, *adv.* dorthin.

[1]**Thole**, *s.* der Dolle, der Ruderpflock eines Bootes.

[2]**Thole**, *v.a.* (*& n.* sich ge=)dulden; geduldig ertragen (*obs., dial.*).

Thong, *s.* der Riemen, Gurt, Peitschenriemen.

Thora—cic, *adj.* Brust=. **—x**, *s.* die Brust; das Bruststück (*Ent.*); der Brustharnisch.

Thoral, *adj.* das Ehebett betreffend; — separation, die Scheidung vom Bett; — line, die Venuslinie in der Hand.

Thorn, *s.* der Dorn, Stachel; white —, Weißdorn; — in the flesh, der Pfahl im Fleische; a — in a p.'s side, einem ein Dorn im Auge sein; to sit upon —s, wie auf Kohlen sitzen. **—less**, *adj.* dornenlos. **—y**, *adj.* dornig, stachelig; beschwerlich, häklig, dornig (*fig.*). *Comp.* **—hedge**, *s.* die Dornenhecke.

Thorough, *adj.* durchgehend, durch und durch, gänzlich, vollständig; (perfect) vollendet, vollkommen, gründlich, gediegen. **—ly**, *adv.* durchaus, völlig, gänzlich, gründlich; a —ly good-natured fellow, ein durch und durch gutmütiger Mensch. **—ness**, *s.* die Vollständigkeit, Gründlichkeit. *Comp.* **—-bass**, *s.* der Generalbaß. **—bred**, I. *adj.* vollblütig, von reiner Rasse. II. *s.* das Vollblut(=Pferd). **—fare**, *s.* der Durchgang, die Durchfahrt; no —fare, verbotene Durchfahrt, verbotener Durchgang. **—-going**, **—-paced**, *adj.* vollendet, vollkommen; ausgemacht, durchtrieben, Erz= (*thief, scoundrel*); —-going partisan, der Draufgänger, ein durch dick und dünn folgender Parteigänger.

Those, *pl. of* That, *dem.* I. *adj.* jene, diejenigen. II. *pron.* die(jenigen), solche; what (sort of) books are —? was sind das für Bücher?

Thou, *pers. pron.* du; *see* Thee.

Though, *conj.* ob=schon, =gleich, =wohl, wenn auch, wenngleich; (nevertheless) doch; zwar, freilich, allerdings; I see him —, ich sehe ihn dennoch; as —, als ob, als wenn; he acts as — he did not see it, er handelt, als sähe er es nicht; — I say it, ohne mich zu rü[illegible]men.

Thought, I. *imperf. & p.p. see* Think. II. *s.* der Gedanke; (reflection) das Denken; (notion) der Begriff; (idea) der Einfall, die Meinung; (solicitude) die Sorge; I had some —s of . . ., ich habe daran gedacht . . .; want of —, die Gedankenlosigkeit; a — browner, ein wenig brauner (*coll.*); take no — for the morrow, sorge nicht für morgen; on second —, bei näherer *or* nochmaliger Überlegung. **—ful**, *adj.*, **—fully**, *adv.* gedankenvoll, nachdenkend, tiefsinnig; (considerate) bedacht (of, auf), zuvorkommend, taktvoll; (attentive) aufmerksam. **—fulness**, *s.* tiefes Nachdenken, die Tiefsinnigkeit; die Zuvorkommenheit, Aufmerksamkeit; (carefulness) die Sorgfalt. **—less**, *adj.*, **—lessly**, *adv.* gedankenlos; (careless) achtlos, sorglos (of, um); (irreflective) leichtfertig, unbesonnen. **—lessness**, *s.* die Gedankenlosigkeit, Unbesonnenheit. *Comp.* **—-reading**, *s.* das Gedankenlesen.

Thousand, I. *num. adj.* tausend. II. *s.* das Tausend. **—th**, I. *adj.* tausendst. II. *s.* das Tausendstel, Tausendteil.

Thral—dom, *s.* die Knechtschaft, Sklaverei. **—l**, *s.* der Knecht, Sklave. **—lful**, *adj.* unterjocht.

Thrash, *v.a.* (— out, aus=)dreschen; (beat) (durch)-prügeln. **—ing**, *s.* das Dreschen; die tüchtige Tracht Prügel. *Comp.* **—ing-floor**, *s.* die Dreschtenne. **—ing-machine**, *s.* die Dreschmaschine.

Thread, I. *s.* der Faden (*also fig.*); (linen —) der Zwirn; das Gewinde (*of a screw*); to resume the — of one's discourse, den Faden seiner Rede wieder aufnehmen. II. *v.a.* einfädeln (*a needle*); anreihen (*beads*); sich winden; to — one's way, seinen Weg mühsam ziehen (durch). *Comp.* **—bare**, *adj.* fadenscheinig; (worn out) abgenutzt. **—bareness**, *s.* die Fadenscheinigkeit. **—-paper**, *s.* der Zwirnwickel.

Threat, I. *s.* die Drohung; — of, Androhung von. II. —, **—en**, *v.a. & n.* bedrohen, (einem) drohen (mit). **—ening**, *adj.*, **—eningly**, *adv.* drohend; —ening letter, der Drohbrief.

Three, I. *num. adj.* drei. II. *s.* die Drei; (figure —) die Drei; by —s, zu Dreien; diary of — children, das Tagebuch dreier Kinder. *Comp.* **—-cornered**, *adj.* dreieckig. **—-decker**, *s.* der Dreidecker. **—fold**, *adj.* dreifach. **—-handed**, *adj.* (game), (Spiel) zu dreien (*Tennis*). **—-inch**, *adj.* drei Zoll hoch *or* lang. **—-legged**, *adj.* dreibeinig. **—pence**, *s.* drei Pence; das Dreipence=Stück. **—penny**, *adj.* um drei Pence, drei Pence wert. **—-ply**, *adj.* dreimal, dreifach gefaltet. **—-pronged**, *adj.* dreizinkig. **—-quarter**, *adj.* dreiviertel; —-quarter back, der Dreiviertel= *or* Hinter=spieler (*Footb.*). **—score**, *adj.* sechzig. **—-sided**, *adj.* dreiseitig. **—-storied**, *adj.* dreistöckig.

Thren—etic, *adj.* klagend. **—ody**, *s.* das Klagelied.

Thresh, *see* Thrash.

Threshold, *s.* die Schwelle, der Eingang (*also fig.*).

Threw, *imperf. of* Throw.

Thrice, *adv.* dreimal, dreifach; — noble lord, höchst edler Herr.

Thrift, *s.* die Wirtschaftlichkeit; (economy) die Sparsamkeit; die Standnelke (*Bot.*). **—ily**, *adv.*, **—y**, *adj.* haushälterisch, wirtschaftlich; sparsam; (thriving) gedeihlich, im Wohlstand zunehmend. **—iness**, *s.* die Wirtschaftlichkeit. **—less**, *adj.*, **—lessly**, *adv.* ungedeihlich; verschwenderisch; nicht haushälterisch (*as a wife, etc.*); he is a —less fellow, er kommt auf keinen grünen Zweig.

Thrill, I. *s.* der Schauer, das Durchschauern; das Erbeben. II. *v.a.* durch=bohren, =dringen, =schauern. III. *v.n.* schauern, zittern, beben. **—ing**, *adj.*, **—ingly**, *adv.* durchdringend, gellend; erschütternd, ergreifend (*as a tale*).

Thriv—e, *ir.v.n.* gedeihen, fortkommen, wachsen (*as plants*); gedeihen, fort=, auf=kommen, Glück haben; a —ing trade, ein gedeihliches Geschäft; —ing town, blühende Stadt; he will never —e, er wird nie auf einen grünen Zweig kommen. —**ed**, *rare imperf. & p.p. of* —e. —**en**, *p.p. of* —e. —**ing**, *adj.*, —**ingly**, *adv.* gedeihlich, emporkommend.

Throat, *s.* die Gurgel, Kehle, der Schlund; (neck) der Hals; to have a sore —, Halsweh haben; he cut his —, er schnitt sich (*dat.*) die Gurgel durch *or* den Hals ab; to cut a person's —, einem den Hals abschneiden.

Throb, I. *s.* der (Puls=)Schlag (of the heart, des Herzens); das Stampfen (*of an engine*). II. *v.n.* schlagen, pochen, klopfen; —bing heart, pochendes, hochklopfendes Herz.

Throe, *s.* der Schmerz. —**s**, *pl.* die Schmerzen; (birth —s) die Geburtswehen; last —s, die Todesangst.

Throne, I. *s.* der Thron; to mount, ascend the —, den Thron besteigen. II. *v.a.* auf den Thron setzen. —**d**, *adj.* thronend.

Throng, I. *s.* das Gedränge (*of people*); der Zulauf; (number) die Menge, Schar. II. *v.n.* sich drängen, in Menge zuströmen; to — upon, bedrängen. III. *v.a.* drängen, mit Gedränge füllen; —ed, gedrängt voll.

Throstle, *s.* die Drossel (*Orn.*); der Drosselstuhl (*Spin.*).

Throttle, I. *s.* die Luftröhre; das Drosselventil (*Eng.*). II. *v.a.* erdrosseln; drosseln (*an engine*).

Through, I. *prep.* durch; (because of) aus, vor; (by means of) mittelst; — fear, aus Furcht; to fall asleep — weakness, vor Mattigkeit einschlafen. II. *adv.* durch; (at an end) zu Ende; to go — with, aus=, durch=führen; to fall —, nicht zustande kommen; — and —, durch und durch. *Comp.* —**-carriage**, *s.* durchgehender Wagen. —**-train**, *s.* durchgehender Zug. —**-ticket**, *s.* durchgehender Fahrschein. —**ly**, *see* Thoroughly. —**out**, I. *prep.* ganz (hin=)durch, durch . . . hin; — out the year, das Jahr hindurch; —out the whole course of his life, während seines ganzen Lebens. II. *adv.* durchaus, in jeder Beziehung; (everywhere) überall.

Throve, *imperf. of* Thrive.

Throw, I. *ir.v.a.* werfen, schleudern; gießen, schütten (*water*); abwerfen (as a horse his rider, wie ein Pferd seinen Reiter); (zu Boden) werfen (*wrestling*); zwirnen (*silk*); to — **aside**, bei Seite werfen; to — **at**, werfen nach, auf (*acc.*); to — **away**, wegwerfen; (reject) verwerfen; (waste) vergeuden; to — o.s. away, sich wegwerfen; to — **by**, bei Seite legen, werfen; to — **down**, niederwerfen; to — **in**, hineinwerfen (*lit.*), hereinbringen, einschalten (*a remark, etc.*); dazu tun, mit in den Kauf geben; to — in a p.'s face, einem (etwas) vorwerfen; to — into prison, ins Gefängnis werfen; to — in s.o.'s way, einem (etwas) zustecken, zuwerfen; to — forward, vorwerfen (*Footb.*); to — **into** raptures, in Entzücken versetzen; to — into the shade, in den Schatten stellen; to — **off**, loslassen (*dogs*); ablegen (*all shame, a disguise, one's clothes*); sich frei machen von (*a restraint, etc.*); to — a train off the line, einen Zug zum Entgleisen bringen; that threw me off the scent, das machte, daß ich die Spur verlor; to — **out**, (hin)auswerfen (*lit.*); von sich geben (*light, heat*); verwerfen (*a bill*); zu verstehen geben, fallen lassen (*a hint*); hereinwerfen (*Footb.*); to — out of gear, in Unordnung bringen; to — **over**, aufgeben (*a friend*); to — a bridge over (across) a river, eine Brücke über einen Fluß schlagen; to — **up**, aufwerfen (*also Fort.*); in die Höhe werfen (*lit.*); errichten (*barricades*); aufgeben (*an office, a game, etc.*); *see* Vomit. II. *ir.v.n.* werfen; würfeln (*with dice*). III. *s.* der Wurf; stone's —, ein Steinwurf. —**er**, *s.* der Werfende. —**ing**, *s.* das Werfen. *Comp.* —**n-silk**, *s.* gezwirnte, moulinierte Seide.

[1]**Thrum**, I. *s.* das Trumm, der Drohm, Saum (*of linen*); grobes Garn. II. *v.a.* befransen; spicken (*sails, etc.*).

[2]**Thrum**, *v.n.* (*& a.*) klimpern (auf einem Instrument).

[1]**Thrush**, *s.* die Drossel.

[2]**Thrush**, *s.* der Mundschwamm (*Med.*); der Hufgrind, die Strahlfäule (*Vet.*).

Thrust, I. *ir.v.a.* stoßen; to — **away**, wegstoßen; to — **down**, nieder=, hinunter=, hinab=stoßen; to — **in**, ein=stoßen, =treiben, =keilen; to — **into**, hinein=stoßen, =schlagen; to — o.s. into, sich drängen in (*acc.*); to — **on**, vorwärtsstoßen; (incite) antreiben; to — **out**, (her)ausstoßen; (put out) herausstrecken (*the tongue*); *see* To — away; to — **through**, durch=stoßen, =stechen. II. *ir.v.n.* stoßen (at, nach). III. *s.* der Stoß, Stich; der Schub, Druck (*Arch.*). *Comp.* —**-and-cut**, *adj.*; —-and-cut duel, die Hieb= und Stoß=Mensur. —**-sword**, *s.* der Stoßdegen.

Thud, I. *v.a.* dumpf aufschlagen; dröhnen. II. *s.* dumpfe Schlag; — of hoofs, dröhnender Hufschlag.

Thumb, I. *s.* der Daumen; by rule of —, erfahrungsmäßig, auf dem Wege praktischer Erfahrung; under one's —, unter den Fingern, in der Gewalt. II. abgreifen, (durch den Gebrauch) beschmutzen. —**ed**, *adj.* mit Daumen; well —ed volumes, abgegriffene Bände. *Comp.* —**-mark**, *s.* der Abdruck des Daumens (auf Papier, *etc.*). —**-piece**, *s.* der Angriff (*Typ.*). —**-ring**, *s.* der Schlagring (am Daumen des Zitherspielers). —**-screw**, *s.* die Daumenschraube. —**-stall**, *s.* der Däumling, die Daumkappe.

Thump, I. *s.* der Schlag, Puff. II. *v.a. & n.* schlagen, puffen. —**er**, *s.* der Schlagende; etwas Erstaunliches (*coll.*); derbe Lüge (*vulg.*). —**ing**, *adj.* dick, derb (*vulg.*).

Thunder, I. *s.* der Donner; the — roars *or* rolls, der Donner rollt. II. *v.n.* donnern. III. *v.a.*; to — forth, — out, hervordonnern (*a reply, etc.*); schleudern (*excommunication*). —**er**, *s.* der Donnernde; (Zeus) der Donnerer. —**ing**, *adj.*, —**ingly**, *adv.* donnernd; —ing voice (voice of —), die Donnerstimme. —**y**, *adj.* gewitterhaft. *Comp.* —**bolt**, *s.* der Donnerkeil, der Blitzstrahl. —**clap**, *s.* der Donnerschlag. —**-cloud**, *s.* die Gewitterwolke. —**-shower**, *s.* der Gewitterregen. —**-storm**, *s.* das Gewitter. —**struck**, *adj.* wie vom Donner gerührt; heftig erschrocken.

Thursday, *s.* der Donnerstag; on —s, every —, Donnerstags, jeden Donnerstag.

Thus, *adv.* so, daher; so, bis zu diesem Grade.

Thwack, I. *v.a.* schlagen, durchwalken. II. *s.* der Puff, Schlag.

Thwaite, *s.* die Lichtung, Reutung (*dial.*).

[1]**Thwart**, I. *adj.* quer, schräg. II. *v.a.* durchkreuzen, vereiteln, widerstehen, in die Quere kommen.

[2]**Thwart**, *s.* die Sitzbank, Ducht (*Naut.*).

Thy, *poss. adj.* dein(e). —**self**, *pron.* du (selbst); dir, dich.

Thym—e, *s.* der Thymian. —**y**, *adj.* voll Thymian.

Thyrsus, *s.* der Thyrsus(stab).

Tiara, *s.* die Tiara; die päpstliche Würde (*fig.*).

Tibia, *s.* das Schienbein. —**l**, *adj.* Schienbein=.

Tic—-douloureux, *s.* der nervöse Gesichtsschmerz, das Gesichts=Zucken. —**k**, *see* [4]Tick.

[1]**Tick**, *s.* die Schecke, Schaflaus.

[2]**Tick**, *s.* (bed-—, die Bett=)Zieche. —**ing**, *s.* der Drillich.

[3]**Tick**, *s.*; upon —, auf Borg (*sl.*). —**et**, I. der Zettel; der Fahrschein, die Fahrkarte (*Railw.*); die Eintrittskarte, das Billet (*Theat.*) *see* Railway—et; die Etikette (*on goods, etc.*); die Kandidatenliste (*Pol., Amer.*); lottery —et, das Lotterielos; —et of leave, der Entlassungsschein; —et of leave man, vorläufig entlassener Sträfling; to issue —ets, Fahrkarten, Eintrittskarten, Bil-

lets ausgeben. II. *v.a.* bezetteln, mit Etiketten und Preisen versehen (*goods*). *Comp.* **—et-clerk**, *s.* der Fahrscheinausgeber, Billetverkäufer. **—et-collector**, *s.* der Billeteinnehmer, Kontrolleur. **—et-office**, *s.* die Fahrkartenausgabe, der Schalter. **—et-porter**, *s.* der konzessionierte Gepäckträger. **—et-window**, *s.* der Schalter.

[2]**Tick**, I. *s.* das Ticken; der Punkt, das Vermerkzeichen. II. *v.n.* ticken, picken (*as a clock*). III. *v.a.;* to — off, punktieren. **—er**, *s.* die Uhr, Ticktack (*coll.*). **—le**, *v.* I. *a.* kitzeln (*also fig.*); amüsieren, belustigen (*coll.*); schmeicheln. II. *n.* Kitzeln, Kitzel verursachen. **—ler**, *s.* der, die, das Kitzelnde. **—ling**, *s.* das Kitzeln. **—lish**, *adj.* kitzlig; kritisch (*as times, etc.*). **—-tack**, I. *s.* das Ticktack. II. *adv.* ticktack.

Tid—al, *adj.* Flut=; Ebbe und Flut bezeichnend (*as a chart*); der Ebbe und Flut unterworfen; —al basin, das Flutdock; —al harbour, der Guthafen; —al wave, die Flutwelle; —al rivers, Flüsse, in welche die Flut dringt. **—e**, I. *s.* die Zeit (*obs. poet., and especially as the second part of comp'ds*); die Ebbe und Flut (*of the sea*); die Gezeit (*Naut.*); der Lauf (*of the times*); der Strom (*of the blood*); die bestimmte Arbeitszeit, Schicht; to swim with (against) the —e, mit dem (gegen den) Strom schwimmen; the —e is going out (coming in), die Flut verläuft, ebbt, strömt ab, es tritt Ebbe ein (die Flut kommt, tritt ein); high —e, die Flutzeit; to drop down a river with the —e, auf einem Flusse absacken; turn of the —e, der Flutenwechsel (*lit.*); der Glückswechsel (*fig.*); even—e, die Abendzeit; —e of events, die Zeitströmung. II. *v.a.* mit dem Strome treiben; to —e over difficulties, über Schwierigkeiten glücklich hinüberkommen. **—eless**, *adj.* ohne Ebbe und Flut. **—y**, I. *adj.*, **—ily**, *adv.* sauber, wohlgeordnet, ordentlich; nett, niedlich (*fig.*). II. *s.* das Schutzdeckchen für Möbel. III. *v.a.* (—y up) nett und sauber machen, in Ordnung bringen. **—iness**, *s.* die Sauberkeit; die Ordnung. **—ings**, *pl.* die Nachrichten, Neuigkeiten; glad —ings, frohe Botschaft. *Comp.* **—e-gate**, *s.* das Flut=tor, =gatter. **—e-** (*or* **—al-**) **harbour**, *s.* der Guthafen. **—e-tables**, *pl.* Fluttabellen. **—e-waiter**, *s.* der Zollbeamte im Hafen.

Tie, I. *v.a.* binden; (unite) verknüpfen; binden, schleifen (*Mus.*); to — a knot, einen Knoten schlagen, machen; to — **down**, hinunterbinden (*lit.*); festbinden (*fig.*); — it **in** a bow, machen Sie eine Schleife damit, to — **up**, zu=, auf=, zusammen=binden. II. *s.* das Band, die Schleife, Binde (*for the neck, etc.*); die Bindung (*Mus.*); gleiche Zahl, Gleichheit (of votes, etc., der Stimmenzahl 2c.); das unentschiedene Spiel (*Tennis, etc.*). *Comp.* **—-wig**, *s.* die Knotenperücke.

Tier, *s.* die Reihe, Lage; die Sitzreihe, der Rang (*Theat.*); in —s, lagenweise; guns in —s, Stockwerksbatterien, ein Batteriestockwerk.

Tierce, *s.* die Tertie, Terz (*Mus., Fenc., Cards*). **—l(et)**, *s. see* Tercel.

Tiers-état, *s.* der dritte Stand, der Nährstand.

Tiff, *s.* das Schmollen, die üble Laune (*fam.*).

Tiffin, *s.* das Gabelfrühstück (*in India*).

Tig, *s.* das Berühr=, Anschlag=spiel.

Tig—er, *s.* der Tiger; (servant) der kleine (Livree=)Bediente. **—erish**, *adj.* tigerhaft. **—ress**, *s.* die Tigerin.

Tight, *adj.*, **—ly**, *adv.* dicht, fest; (taut) gespannt, straff; (narrow) eng; (not leaky) dicht, nicht leck; (spare) knapp; genau (*as a bargain*); dicht, knapp anliegend, anschließend (*as a jacket, etc.*); — fit, enges Anliegen; die Klemme (*fig.*); — rope, straffes Seil; — waistcoat, die Zwangsjacke. **—en**, *v.a.* zusammen=heften, =ziehen, enger machen, schnüren, verengen. **—ness**, *s.* die Dichtheit; die Festigkeit; die Straffheit; die Enge, Knappheit; die Genauigkeit. **—s**, *pl.* knapp anliegende Hosen; das Trikot. *Comp.* **—-fitting**, *adj.* knapp anliegend. **—-laced**, *adj.* festgeschnürt; engherzig, pedantisch (*fig.*).

Tilbury, *s.* zweiräderiger, offener Wagen.

Til—e, I. *s.* der (roof, Dach=)Ziegel; (drain —e) Drainziegel; Dutch —e, die Kachel. II. *v.a.* mit Ziegeln decken. **—er**, *s.* der Ziegeldecker. **—ing**, *s.* das Ziegeldach; (—es) die Ziegel. *Comp.* **—e-clay**, *s.* die Ziegelerde. **—e-floor**, *s.* der Fliesen=Fußboden. **—e-hanging**, *s.* die Ziegelverkleidung (eines Hauses). **—e(d)-roof**, *s.* das Ziegeldach.

[1]**Till**, *conj. & prep.* bis (zu), bis (auf); — now, bisjetzt, bisher, bislang.

[2]**Till**, *s.* die Geldschublade, Ladentischkasse.

[3]**Till**, *v.a.* bebauen, ackern, pflügen. **—age**, *s.* der Acker=, Feld=bau. **—er**, *s.* der Ackersmann, Landmann.

Tiller, *s.* der Helmstock, die Ruderpinne. *Comp.* **—-rope**, *s.* das Steuerreep.

[1]**Tilt**, *s.* das Zelt, Obdach; die Plane (*of a cart, boat, etc.*).

[2]**Tilt**, I. *s.* (slope) die Neigung; (thrust) der Stoß; das Lanzen=brechen, =stechen (*of knights*); a-—, abwärts geneigt; to run full — against s.o., in vollem Stoß auf einen losrennen. II. *v.a.* neigen, kippen (*a barrel, etc.*); einlegen (*the lance*); hämmern (*steel, etc.*). III. *v.n.* Lanzen brechen, turnieren; to — **at**, stoßen nach (einem), sich stürzen auf (einen); to — **up**, sich kippen, sich neigen. **—er**, *s.* der Lanzenstecher, Turnierer; die Unterlage (*for casks, etc.*). **—ing**, I. *adj.* Turnier= II. *s.* das Lanzenbrechen, Ritterspiel.

Tilth, *s.* das Pflügen, Bauen, der Ackerbau; the land is in good —, das Land ist gut angebaut.

Timbal, *s. see* Tymbal.

Timber, I. *s.* das Zimmer=, Nutz=, Bau=holz; (tree) der Baumstamm; —s, Inhölzer, Spannten, das Rippenwerk (*of a ship*). II. *attrib.;* — bridge, hölzerne Brücke. III. *v.a.* (aus) zimmern. **—ed**, *adj.* aus Holz gebaut; bewaldet; well —ed park, gut mit Bäumen bestandener Park. **—ing**, *s.* die Zimmerung. *Comp.* **—-merchant**, *s.* der Bauholzhändler. **—-trade**, *s.* der Holzhandel. **—-work**, *s.* das Zimmerwerk; das Dachgespärre (*of a roof*). **—-yard**, *s.* der Zimmer=, Bau=hof.

Timbre, *s.* der Klang, die Klangfarbe, Tonfarbe (*Phonet., Mus.*).

Timbrel, *s.* die kleine (türkische) Trommel, Schellentrommel.

Time, I. *s.* die Zeit; der Takt, das Tempo (*Danc.*); der Takt, Zeitschlag, das Zeitmaß; das Mal; — essay, der Klassenaufsatz; — paper, das Extemporale; — past, present and to come, vergangene, gegenwärtige und zukünftige Zeit; every —, allemal, jedesmal; many a —, manchmal; three —s, dreimal; many —s, oft, häufig; all that —, die ganze Zeit; the — has come, es ist Zeit, es ist an der Zeit, die Zeit ist da; half —, die Pause (*games*); to speak against —, mit knapper Zeit, äußerst schnell sprechen; at all —s, stets, immer; at another —, ein anderes mal; at any —, zu jeder Zeit, (always) stets, immer; at no —, zu keiner Zeit; at the same — (= at the same moment), zur selben Zeit, zu gleicher Zeit; (= also), zugleich, ebenfalls; the train and the coach arrived at the same — der Zug und der Wagen kamen zur gleichen Zeit an; he is an officer and at the same — an author, er ist Offizier und zugleich Schriftsteller; at this —, zu dieser Zeit; at what — soever, zu irgend einer Zeit; behind —, verspätet; behind the —s, veraltet; to bid a person the — of day, einem die Tageszeit bieten; by that —, zu der Zeit; (mean—) unterdessen, bis dahin; by the —, bis dahin; by this —, jetzt; for a —, eine Zeitlang; for the —, für den Augenblick; for the — being, für den Augenblick, unter gegen=

wärtigen (*or* damaligen) Umständen; for that —, für damals; in —, zur Zeit, zu seiner Zeit; you have come just in —, Sie sind gerade zur rechten Zeit gekommen; in good —, gerade recht, zu guter Zeit; in the day- —, bei Tage; in the mean —, mittlerweile, unterdessen; in no —, in kürzester Zeit; in —s of old *or* yore, in alten Zeiten, vormals; in — to come, in der Zukunft; in the — of, zur (Lebens-)Zeit von; in proper — and place, zu seiner Zeit und an seinem Orte; — out of mind, vor *or* seit unvordenklicher Zeit; —s without number, unzählige Male; in quick —, im Geschwindschritt (*Mil.*); sehr schnell; she is near her —, sie ist ihrer Entbindung nahe; to keep —, Takt, Schritt halten; to keep good —, richtig gehen; to lose —, nachgehen (*as a clock*); Zeit verlieren; to mark —, auf der Stelle treten; abwarten (*fig.*); can you tell me the right —? können Sie mir sagen, wieviel Uhr es ist? out of —, aus dem Takte, Schritte, (prematurely) zur Unzeit; to be out of one's —, aus-gedient, -gelernt haben; this — twelve months, heute übers Jahr; take your own —, nehmen Sie sich (*dat.*) Zeit; once upon a — there was, es war einmal; to watch one's —, den günstigen Augenblick abpassen; to watch the —, viel auf die Uhr sehen; —! Schluß (der Debatte)! (*Parl.*); the Times, die (Zeitung) 'Times'; the Times has printed, die Times hat gedruckt. II. *v.a.* der Zeit gemäß einrichten, den Verhältnissen anpassen, etwas zur richtigen Zeit tun; nach der Zeit, dem Takt (*Mus.*) abmessen, taktmäßig begleiten; die Zeit bestimmen; to — o.s., sich (*dat.*) eine Zeit festsetzen *or* erlauben; sehen, wieviel Zeit man zu einer S. gebraucht; to — a matter well, die rechte Zeit für eine S. wählen; to — one's words ill, seine Worte zur Unzeit anbringen. III. *v.n.* Takt halten; zusammenstimmen (mit). **—liness**, *s.* die Rechtzeitigkeit. **—ly**, *adj.* (recht)zeitig. *Comp.* **—-expired**, *adj.* ausgedient (*of soldiers*). **—-honoured**, *adj.* altehrwürdig. **—keeper**, *s.* das Chronometer; der Aufseher (*in factories, etc.*). **—piece**, *s.* die Uhr. **—-sanctioned**, *adj.* durch die Zeit geheiligt. **—-server**, *s.* der, welcher sich in die Zeit schickt, der Achselträger. **—-serving**, I. *adj.* achselträgerisch, der Gewalt dienend, knechtisch. II. *s.* die Achselträgerei. **—-table**, *s.* der Fahrplan (*Railw.*); der Stundenplan (*in schools, for examinations*); —-tables, das Kursbuch, der Eisenbahnführer (*Railw.*). **—-worn**, *adj.* veraltet, abgenutzt.

Tim—id, *adj.*, **—idly**, *adv.* furchtsam, schüchtern, blöde, zaghaft. **—idness**, **—idity**, *s.* die Furchtsamkeit, Schüchternheit, Zaghaftigkeit. **—orous**, *adj.*, **—orously**, *adv.* furchtsam, schüchtern. **—orousness**, *s.* die Furchtsamkeit.

Timist, *s.* einer, der gut Takt hält.

Tin, I. *s.* das Zinn; (—ware) das Weißblech; (—box) die Blechbüchse; das Geld (*sl.*). II. *v.a.* ver-, über-zinnen; im Blechbüchsen verpacken; —ned meat, fruit, konserviertes *or* Büchsen-Fleisch, Obst. *Comp.* **—foil**, *s.* das Blattzinn, Stanniol. **—ware**, *s.* das Weißblech. **—works**, *s.* die Zinnhütte.

Tincal, *s.* unreiner Borax.

Tincture, I. *s.* die Farbe; die Tinte (*Paint.*); die Tinktur (*Chem.*); der Anstrich, die Beimischung, der (Bei-)Geschmack (*fig.*). II. *v.a.* färben, einen Anstrich geben.

Tinder, *s* der Zunder; German —, der Feuerschwamm. **—y**, *adj.* zunderhaft. *Comp.* **—box**, *s.* das Feuerzeug. **—-like**, *adj.* zunderartig, leicht entzündbar.

Tine, *s.* die Zinke, Zacke. **—d**, *adj.* zinkig.

Ting, I. *interj.* kling! II. *s.* das Klingen.

Tinge, I. *s.* die Farbe, Färbung; der Anstrich, Beigeschmack (*fig.*). II. *v.a.* färben; einen Anstrich, einen Geschmack geben.

Tingl—e, *v.n.* klingen, summen, tönen; prickeln, stechen (*as pain*); the pain —es up to my little finger, der Schmerz durchzuckt mich bis in den kleinen Finger; my ears —e, mir klingen die Ohren **—ing**, *s.* das Klingen; das Prickeln, Stechen.

Tink, *v.n.* klingen (*rare*). **—er**, I. *s.* der Klempner, der Kesselflicker; der Pfuscher (*coll.*). II. *v.a.*; to —er up, zusammenflicken; it is no good —ering, halbe Maßregeln können nichts nützen. **—ering**, *s.* das Kesselflicken. **—le**, *v.* I. *n.* klingen. II. *a.* klingen machen.

Tinsel, I. *s.* das Rausch-, Flitter-gold *or* -silber; falscher Glanz, Flitterglanz. II. *adj.* Flitter-, Schein-, flimmernd. III. *v.a.* mit Flitterwerk schmücken, zieren; —ed paper, getöntes Papier.

Tint, I. *s.* die Farbe, der Anstrich. II. *v.a.* färben, einen Anstrich geben; —ed paper, das Tonpapier.

Tintinnabul—ary, **—ous**, *adj.* klingelnd. **—ation**, *s.* das Klingeln, Klingen, Tönen, Schellen.

Tiny, *adj.* winzig, klein.

Tip, I. *s.* die Spitze (*of the ear, nose, tongue, a spear*); die Zwinge (*of an umbrella, etc.*); (feather —) kurze Feder; — of the tongue, die Zungenspitze; der Wink, die Andeutung (*coll.*); das Trinkgeld (*coll.*). II. *v.a.* an der Spitze versehen mit; beschlagen (*a stick, etc.*); (— up) (um-)kippen; stürzen (*a cart, etc.*); ein Trinkgeld geben (*sl.*); we —ped the driver, wir gaben dem Kutscher ein Trinkgeld. **—pet**, *s.* der (fur, Pelz-)Kragen, die Pelerine. **—ple**, *v.n.* trinken, saufen, zechen. **—pler**, *s.* der Säufer, Trunkenbold. **—sy**, *adj.* betrunken, berauscht, bezecht. *Comp.* **—-cat**, *s.* ein Knabenspiel. **—staff**, *s.* mit Silber beschlagener Stab; (constable, *etc.*) der Gerichtsdiener. **—sy-cake**, *s.* mit Wein gesättigter Kuchen *or* Pudding. **—toe**, *s.* die Spitze der Zehe; to stand on —toe, auf den Zehen stehen; on —toe, (with curiosity, *etc.*) voller Erwartung. **—top**, I. *s.* höchster Grad, das Höchste (*fam.*). II. *adj.* höchst; ausgezeichnet, herrlich; in —top style, im Prunkstil, ausgezeichnet, tadellos (*vulg.*).

Tir—ade, *s.* die Tirade; der Strom (*of abuse, etc.*). **—ailleur**, *s.* der Tirailleur, Plänkler. **—e**, I. *v.a.* putzen. II. *s.* der Kopfputz, die Haartracht. *Comp.* **—ing-room**, *s.* das Ankleidezimmer.

[1]**Tire**, *see* Tir—ade.

[2]**Tire**, *v.* I. *a.* müde machen, ermüden; to — out, gänzlich ermüden. II. *n.* müde werden. **—d**, müde, angegriffen, abgespannt; —d of, (einer Sache) überdrüssig; to be —d of a th., einer Sache (*gen.*) satt sein, eine Sache (*acc.*) satt haben. **—dness**, *s.* die Ermüdung, Müdigkeit; der Überdruß. **—less**, *adj.* unermüdlich. **—some**, *adj.*, **—somely**, *adv.* ermüdend; (boring) langweilig; (annoying) verdrießlich (*coll.*). **—someness**, *s.* das Langweiligkeit.

[3]**Tire**, *s.* die Radschiene, der Rad-reif, -mantel, Schlauch; pneumatic —, der Luftreif, elastische Gummireif (um Fahrräder); *see* Tyre.

Tirwit, *s.* der Kiebitz.

Tisic, *see* Phthisic.

Tissue, *s.* das Gewebe (*also fig.*); gold, silver —, der Gold-, Silber-stoff; cellular —, das Zellengewebe; — paper, das Seidenpapier.

Tit, *s.* kleines Pferd; *see* —mouse; — for tat, *see* Tat. **—ling**, *s.* der Pieper; *see* —mouse. *Comp.* **—bit**, *s.* der Leckerbissen. **—lark**, *s.* die Wiesenlerche. **—mouse**, *s.* die Meise. **—tle**, *s.* das Pünktchen, Jota; not a jot nor —tle, nicht ein Jota *or* Tüttelchen, nicht das Geringste. **—tle-tattle**, I. *s.* das Geschwätz. II. *v.n.* schwatzen.

Tith—able, *adj.* zehnt-bar, -pflichtig. **—e**, I. *s.* das Zehntel (*tax*); der Zehnte. II. *v.a.* den Zehnten auflegen, zehnten (*a people, etc.*); (pay —e) zehnten. **—ing**, *s.* das Zehnten; die Zehntschaft (*Hist.*).

Titillat—e, *v.a.* kitzeln. **—ion**, *s.* das Kitzeln, die Kitzelung; der Kitzel, das Vergnügen (*fig.*).

Titivate, *v.* I. *a.* aufputzen, nett machen (*sl.*). II. *n.* sich hübsch machen, Toilette machen (*sl.*).

Tit—le, I. *s.* der (Buch=)Titel; die Überschrift (*of a chapter, etc.*); *see* Appellation; der (Ehren=) Titel (*as Earl, etc.*); (right) der (Rechts=)Titel, Anspruch, das (Besitz=)Recht; clear —le, unbestreitbares Besitzrecht, Anrecht, (auf eine S.); to have a —le to, berechtigt sein zu. II. *v.a.* betiteln, nennen; —led, betitelt, einen Titel führend. **—ular**, *adj.*, **—ularly**, *adv.* dem Titel nach, nominell. **—ulary**, I. *adj.* Titular=. II. *s.* der Titular. *Comp.* **—le-deed**, *s.* die (Eigentums=)Urkunde. **—le-page**, *s.* das Titelblatt.

Titter, I. *v.n.* kichern. II. *s.* das Kichern, Gekicher.

To, I. *part.* (sign of the inf., Zeichen des Infinitivs) zu. II. *prep. & adv.* zu; (*indicating direction towards*) zu, gegen, nach, an, in, auf; (towards, in comparison with, in presence of, for) gegen; (according —) nach; (in order —) um zu; (up —, as far, high, etc., as) bis (zu, in, an, nach, auf); (about —) bis zu, bis an; (*indicating end, aim, or effect*) zu; (for) für; — me, you, him, etc. (*forming the dat.*) mir, Ihnen, ihm, &c.; it is known — you, es ist dir bekannt; she gave it — me, sie gab es mir; he came — me, er kam zu mir; it happened — me, es geschah mir; he spoke — me, er sprach zu mir; he said — me, er sagte mir; add — that, dazu kommt noch; as —, mit Rücksicht auf (*acc.*); attentive —, aufmerksam, bedacht auf (*acc.*); where are you going —? wo gehen Sie hin? — my knowledge, meines Wissens; lost — all sense of . . ., gegen alles Gefühl von . . . stumpf; deaf — entreaty, unerbittlich; alive —, lebhaft fühlend; our duty —, unsere Pflicht gegen; to have a dislike —, Widerwillen haben gegen; he was a friend — me in . . ., er war mir ein (treuer) Freund in . . .; cousin —, Vetter des (Königs &c.); secretary —, Sekretär des; an enemy — vice, ein Feind des Lasters; tired — death, totmüde; — my taste, nach meinem Geschmacke *or* Sinne; — all appearance, dem Anscheine nach; ungrateful —, undankbar gegen; — the last man, bis auf den letzten Mann; — within 3 inches, bis auf 3 Zoll; to live — a great age, ein hohes Alter erreichen; to press — one's heart, an sein Herz drücken; keep that — yourself, behalte das für dich; I weep — think of it, ich weine, wenn ich daran denke; — his cost, auf seine Kosten; — the prejudice of, zum Nachteile des; this is nothing — what, dies ist nichts im Vergleich mit dem, was; five — one, fünf gegen eins; 2 is — 4 as 4 is — 8, 2 verhält sich zu 4 wie 4 zu 8; what is that — you? was geht Sie das an? here's — you! (hier trinke ich) auf Ihr Wohlsein! put the horses —, spann' an; — and fro, hin und her, auf und ab; — the end that, damit. **—-day**. **—-morrow**, *etc.*, *see* To-day, Tomorrow, *etc.* **—do**, **—gether**, *see* Ado, Together.

Toad, *s.* die Kröte. **—y**, I. *s.* der Speichellecker, Schmarotzer, niedrige Schmeichler. II. *v.a.* niedrig schmeicheln, den Speichellecker machen bei. **—ying**, **—yism**, *s.* die Speichelleckerei, niedrige Schmeichelei. *Comp.* **—-eater**, *s.* der Speichellecker. **—-eating**, I. *adj.* speichelleckerisch. II. *s.* die Speichelleckerei. **—stool**, *s.* der Giftschwamm, (giftiger) Pilz.

[1]**Toast**, I. *s.* die geröstete (Weiß=)Brotschnitte. II. *v.a.* rösten; (warm) durchwärmen. *Comp.* **—ing-fork**, *s.* die Röstgabel. **—-rack**, *s.* das Gestell für geröstete Brotschnitten.

[2]**Toast**, I. *s.* der Trinkspruch, Toast, die ausgebrachte Gesundheit; das (Lebe)Hoch; Person oder Sache, auf die eine Gesundheit ausgebracht wird; standing —, stehende, übliche Gesundheit; reigning —, stets in Trinksprüchen gefeierte Person; loyal —s, Gesundheiten auf Herrscher und Herrscherhaus; to propose a —, eine Gesundheit ausbringen. II. *v.a.* eine Gesundheit ausbringen auf (*acc.*), trinken auf (*acc.*).

Tobacco, *s.* der Tabak. **—nist**, *s.* der Tabak und Zigarren=händler; (— -maker) der Tabaksfabrikant. *Comp.* **—-pipe**, *s.* die Tabakspfeife. **—-pouch**, *s.* der Tabaksbeutel.

Toboggan, I. *s.* der Rodelschlitten. II. *v.a.* rodeln, schlitteln. **—ing**, *s.* das Rodeln, Schlitteln. **—ist**, *s.* der (die) Rodler(in), Schlittler(in). *Comp.* **—-run**, *s.* die Rodelbahn.

Tocsin, *s.* die Sturmglocke.

Tod, I. *s.* der Busch (*obs.*); 28 Pfund (Wolle) (*obs.*). II. *v.a.* 28 Pfund wiegen, liefern (*obs.*).

To-day, I. *adv.* heute. II. *s.* der heutige Tag.

Toddle, *v.n.* wie ein kleines Kind gehen, zotteln, watscheln; to — off, abschieben, sich (fort)trollen.

Toddy, *s.* süßer Grog.

Toe, *s.* die Zehe; to tread on a p.'s —s, einem auf die Füße *or* Hühneraugen treten (*fig.*). **—d**, *adj.* mit Zehen, =zehig.

Toffy, Taffy, *s.* Backwerk aus Zucker und Butter.

Together, *adv.* zusammen, mit einander; beisammen; (at the same time) zugleich; three days —, drei Tage nach einander; for days —, tagelang.

Toggery, *s.* die Kleidung, der Anzug (*sl.*).

[1]**Toil**, I. *s.* die Mühe, Arbeit, Plackerei. II. *v.n.* sich abmühen, sich placken, sich abarbeiten, sich anstrengen. **—er**, *s.* einer der sich abarbeitet, abmüht, plackt. **—some**, *adj.*, **—somely**, *adv.* mühsam, mühselig. **—someness**, *s.* die Mühsamkeit, das Mühselige.

[2]**Toil**, *s.*, **—s**, *pl.* das Netz; in the —s of, umgarnt *or* umstrickt von. **—et(te)**, *s.* der Putz; (dress) die Toilette; to make one's —et, sich anziehen. *Comp.* **—et-glass**, *s.* der Toilettenspiegel. **—et-paper**, *s.* das Klosettpapier. **—et-table**, *s.* der Putztisch.

Token, *s.* das Zeichen; (memorial) das Andenken; (coin) (von Privaten geprägte) Münze; in — of, zum Zeichen von.

Told, *imperf. & p.p. of* Tell; all —, alles in allem.

Tolera—ble, *adj.*, **—bly**, *adv.* leidlich, erträglich; (middling) leidlich, ziemlich. **—bleness**, *s.* die Erträglichkeit, Leidlichkeit. **—nce**, *s.* die Duldung; die Duldsamkeit, Toleranz (*in religion, etc.*). **—nt**, *adj.*, **—ntly**, *adv.* duldsam; —nt of, nachsichtig gegen. **—te**, *v.a.* dulden, ertragen, leiden. **—tion**, *s.* die Duldung, Nachsicht, Toleranz; act of —tion, das Toleranzedikt.

[1]**Toll**, *s.* der Zoll; das Wege=, Brücken=geld (*for right of passage*). *Comp.* **—-bar**, *s.* der Schlagbaum. **—-bridge**, *s.* die Zollbrücke. **—-keeper**, *s.* der Zoll=, Wegegeld=einnehmer. **—-gate**, *s.* das Zolltor.

[2]**Toll**, *v.a. & n.* in langen Zwischenräumen läuten (the funeral bell, die Totenglocke).

Tomahawk, I. *s.* die Streitaxt (*of American Indians*); to bury the —, das Kriegsbeil begraben, Frieden schließen. II. *v.a.* mit der Streitaxt töten.

Tomato, I. *s.* die Tomate, der Liebesapfel. II. *attrib.*; — sauce, die Tomatensoße.

Tomb, *s.* das Grab, Grabmal, die Gruft. *Comp.* **—stone**, *s.* der Grabstein.

Tombac, *s.* der Tombak.

Tom—boy, *s.* die Range, das wilde Mädchen. **—-cat**, *s.* der Kater. **—fool**, *s.* der Tropf. **—foolery**, *s.* die Narretei, Albernheit, die Narrenspossen (*pl.*). **—foolish**, *adj.* albern, närrisch. **—tit**, *s.* die Meise.

Tome, *s.* das Band, das Buch (*of a work*).

To-morrow, I. *adv.* morgen; — morning, morgen früh; the day after —, übermorgen. II. *s.* morgender Tag.

Tommy-rot, *s.* das Blech, der Blödsinn (*sl.*).

Tom-tom, *s.* das Tamtam.

[1]**Ton**, I. *s.* herrschender Ton, die Mode; bon —, feine Lebensart. **—e**, I. *s.* der Ton (*in speaking, also Med., Mus., Paint.*); der Klang, Laut; intellectual —e, der geistige Ton. II. *v.a.* Ton *or* Färbung geben; abtönen (*Phot.*); *see* Intone; to —e down, herabstimmen, mildern. **—ed**, *adj.* tönend; abgetönt (*Phot.*). **—eless**, *adj.* tonlos **—ic**, I. *adj.* tonisch (*Mus., Med.*); —ic stress der Hauptton. II. *s.* nervenstärkendes beruhi·

gendes Mittel (*Med.*); die Tonika, der Grundton (*Mus.*); hair —ic, das Haarwasser.

²Ton, *s.* die Tonne, halbe Last (= 2000 Pfd. oder 2240 Pfd. avoirdupois); die Tonnenlast (*Naut.*); a ship of 400 —s burden, ein Schiff von 200 Last. **—nage**, *s.* die Tragfähigkeit, Lastigkeit, der Tonnengehalt (*of a ship*); (duty) das Tonnengeld; Schiffe (*C.L.*).

Tongs, *pl.* (a pair of —) die Zange; (fire —) die Feuerzange.

Tongue, *s.* die Zunge; die Sprache (*fig.*); die Zunge (*of land etc.*); slip of the —, der Sprachfehler; das entschlüpfte Wort; a slip of the — betrayed her, ein unvorsichtiges Wort verriet sie; to hold one's —, den Mund halten; to give —, anschlagen, bellen (*as dogs*); schwatzen (*as people*); (scold) schelten; I had the word on the tip of my —, das Wort schwebte mir auf der Zunge; gift of —s, die Gabe mit Zungen zu reden (*B.*); das Sprachtalent. **—d**, *adj.* mit einer Zunge; long—d, schwatzhaft. **—less**, *adj.* ohne Zunge. *Comp.* **—-shaped**, *adj.* zungenförmig. **—-tied**, *adj.* an der Zunge gelähmt, mundfaul, stumm (*fig.*). **—-valiant**, *adj.* tapfer mit der Zunge; a —-valiant person, ein Zungenheld, Maulheld.

To-night, I. *adv.* zur Nacht, heute abend. II. *s.* der heutige Abend.

Tonsil, *s.* die (Hals)mandel. **—lar**, *adj.* Mandel-. **—litis**, *s.* die Mandelentzündung.

Tons—orial, *adj.* Barbier-. **—ure**, *s.* die Tonsur (*also of priests*); die Platte (*of priests*). **—ured**, *adj.* mit einer Tonsur *or* Platte.

Too, *adv.* (all)zu; noch dazu, auch, ebenfalls.

Took, *imperf. of* Take.

Tool, I. *s.* das Werkzeug (*also fig.*). II. *v.a.* abdrücken, abstempeln (*Bookb.*). III. *v.n.* mit einem Werkzeug arbeiten; mit gepreßten Verzierungen versehen (*Bookb.*). **—s**, *pl.* das Gerät(e), die Gerätschaften, das Handwerkszeug. *Comp.* **—-chest**, **—-box**, *s.* der Werkzeugkasten. **—-house**, *s.* das Geräthaus.

Toot, **—le**, *v.* I. *n.* tuten, blasen, dudeln. II. *a.* blasen, tuten. III. *s.* das Tuten; —-—, —le—le, das Getute.

Tooth, (*pl.* Teeth) I. *s.* der Zahn; der Zacken, Zahn (*Mach.*); to cut teeth, zahnen, Zähne bekommen; to have a sweet —, lecker sein; to go at it — and nail, etwas mit aller Kraft angreifen (*vulg.*); to show one's teeth, (einem) die Zähne weisen, drohen; in the teeth of a determined opposition, einem entschlossenen Widerstande gegenüber; in one's teeth, gerade entgegen (*as wind*); to a p.'s teeth, einem offen ins Gesicht; to cast s.th. in a p.'s teeth, einem etwas vorwerfen; to set the teeth on edge, die Zähne zusammenbeißen. II. *v.a.* zahnen. **—ed**, *adj.* gezähnt, zähnig; —ed wheel, das Zahnrad. **—ing**, *s.* die Verzahnung; die Zahnung (*of a saw*). **—less**, *adj.* zahnlos. **—some**, *adj.* schmackhaft. **—someness**, *s.* die Schmackhaftigkeit. *Comp.* **—ache**, *s.* der Zahnschmerz, das Zahnweh. **—brush**, *s.* die Zahnbürste. **—-drawing**, *s.* das Zahnausziehen. **—pick**, *s.* der Zahnstocher. **—-powder**, *s.* das Zahnpulver. **—-work**, *s.* die Verzahnung.

¹Top, I. *s.* der Kopf, Wipfel (*of a tree*); der Giebel, der (die) First(e) (*of a house*); die Koppe, Kuppe, der Gipfel (*of a hill*); der Gipfel, die Krone, der höchste Grad (*fig.*); (— place) die Spitze; der Kopf, das Kraut (*of turnips*); das Mars (*Naut.*); der Scheitel (*of the head*); (head) das Haupt, der Erste; die Kappe, der Deckel (*of utensils*); die Stulpe (*of a — boot*); der Himmel (*of a canopied bed*); — of the water, die Oberfläche des Wassers; at the — of his voice, so laut er konnte; from — to bottom, von oben bis unten; from — to toe, von Kopf zu Fuß; on the — of, oben auf; (at the) — of one's class *or* form, der Erste in der Klasse; to the — of one's bent, bis aufs äußerste Maß. II. *adj.* oberst, Haupt-; —stone, oberster Stein. III. *v.n.* steigen, sich emporheben; hervorragen (*as mountains*). IV. *v.a* (oben) bedecken, bekränzen, krönen; (rise above) sich erheben über, überragen; über-treffen, -steigen (*fig.*); (clip) beschneiden; bekappen (*a boot*). **—per**, *s.* der Hauptkerl (*sl.*). **—ple**, *v.a.* & *n.* (—ple down *or* over) niederstürzen. **—sy-turvy**, *adv.* das Oberste zu unterst; alles unter einander, verkehrt (*fig.*). *Comp.* **—-beam**, *s.* der Hahnbalken am Dachstuhl. **—-boots**, *pl.* Stulpenstiefel. **—-boy**, *s.* der Primus (einer Klasse). **—-coat**, *s.* der Über-rock, -zieher. **—-draining**, *s.* die Trockenlegung der Bodenfläche (*Agr.*). **—-dressing**, *s.* obere breitwürfige Düngung. **—gallant**, *s.* (sail) das Bramsegel. **—-hat**, *s.* der Zylinder(hut). **—-heavy**, *adj.* oben schwerer als unten. **—-knot**, *s.* die Kopfschleife. **—mast**, *s.* der oberste *or* Top-Mast. **—most**, *adj.* höchst, oberst. **—sail**, *s.* das Mars-, Top-segel.

²Top, *s.* der Kreisel; to spin a —, den Kreisel schlagen.

Topaz, *s.* der Topas.

Tope, *v.n.* zechen, saufen. **—r**, *s.* der Säufer.

Top—ic, *s.* der Gegenstand, das Thema; the —ic is dismissed, der Gegenstand wird fallen gelassen. **—ical**, *adj.*, **—ically**, *adv.* topisch; (local) örtlich. **—ographical**, *adj.*, **—ographically**, *adv.* topographisch. **—ography**, *s.* die Ortsbeschreibung, Topographie.

Toque, *s.* eine Art Barett (für Frauen).

Tor, *s.* der hohe, spitzige Felsen.

Torch, *s.* die Fackel. *Comp.* **—-light**, I. *s.* das Fackellicht. II. *attrib.*; —-light procession, der Fackelzug.

Tore, *imperf.* & (*obs.*) *p.p. of* Tear.

Torment, I. *s.* die Pein, Qual; (person) die Plage. II. *v.a.* martern, quälen, peinigen. **—illa**, *s.* die Tormentille. **—ing**, *adj.*, **—ingly** *adv.* quälend. **—or**, *s.* der Peiniger, Quäler.

Torn, *p.p. of* Tear.

Tornado, *s.* der Wirbelsturm.

Torp—edo, I. *s.* der Zitterroche (*Icht.*); der Torpedo (*Naut.*); das Torpedogeschoß (*Naut.*). II. *v.a.* mittelst eines Torpedo leck machen *or* in die Luft sprengen. **—id**, *adj.*, **—idly**, *adv.* starr, erstarrt, betäubt; gefühllos (*fig.*); (sluggish) träge. **—idity**, **—idness**, **—itude**, *s.* die Erstarrung; der Stumpfsinn. **—ids**, *pl.* Ruderwettfahrten im Frühling (*Oxford sl.*). **—or**, *s.* die Gefühl-, Reizlosigkeit; *see* —idity. *Comp.* **—edo-boat**, *s.* das Torpedoboot. **—edo-catcher**, **—(-boat)-destroyer**, *s.* das auf Torpedoboote Jagd machende Schiff, der Torpedobootzerstörer. **—edo-tube**, *s.* das (Torpedo-)Lancierrohr.

Torr—efaction, *s.* das Rösten. **—efy**, *v.a.* dörren, rösten. **—ent**, *s.* der Gießbach; (river) reißender Strom; der Strom (*fig.*); —ents of rain, Regengüsse. **—ential**, *adj.* strömend, reißend; überwältigend; wortreich (*fig.*). **—id**, *adj.* dörrend; (hot) brennend, heiß; —id heat, brennende Hitze; —id regions, zone, heiße Gegenden, die heiße Zone; die Tropen (*pl.*).

Torsion, *s.* das Drehen; die Drehung, Torsion (*Phys.*). **—al**, *adj.*; —al strength, die Torsionsfestigkeit.

Torso, *s.* der Torso, Rumpf (of a statue, einer Bildsäule); der Rumpf.

Tort, *s.* das Unrecht, die Schädigung, Beleidigung (*Law*); law of —s, das Beleidigungsrecht. *Comp.* **—feasor**, *s.* der Missetäter.

Tort—ile, *adj.* gedreht, gewunden. **—oise**, *s.* die Schildkröte (*also Mil.*). **—uous**, *adj.*, **—uously**, *adv.* gewunden, schlangenartig; winkelzügig, versteckt (*fig.*). **—uousness**, **—uosity**, *s.* das Gewundene. **—ure**, I. *s.* die Folter, Marter (*also fig.*); to put to the —ure, auf die Folter spannen. II. *v.a.* foltern, martern. **—urer**, *s.* der Folterer; der Peiniger (*fig.*). **—uring**, *adj.*, **—uringly**, *adv.* folternd, quälend. *Comp.* **—oise-shell**, I. *s.* die Schildkrötenschale, das Schildpatt. II. *attrib.*; —oise-shell box, comb, die Dose aus

Schildpatt, der Schildpattkamm; —oise-shell cat (butterfly), dreifarbige Katze (kleiner Fuchs).

Tory, I. *s.* der englische Konservative, Tory. II. *adj.* Tory=. **—ism**, *s.* Grundsätze *rc.* der Tories, der Konservatismus.

Toss, I. *v.a.* (*p.p. also* Tost) emporschleudern (*as bulls, etc.*); (shake) hin= und herbewegen, schütteln, prellen; (fling) werfen, schleudern; auslosen (*tennis, etc.*); to — hay, Heu wenden; to — oars, Riemen picken (*Naut.*); to — **off**, hinunterstürzen; to — **up**, in die Höhe werfen, schleudern; das Los werfen. II. *v.n.* sich (unruhig) bewegen *or* hin und her wälzen (*in sleep*); treiben; to — **for**, losen um. III. *s.* der Wurf, Stoß, das Werfen; das Zurückwerfen (*of the head*); to win the —, beim Losen (durch Emporschnellen einer Münze) gewinnen. *Comp.* **—-up**, *s.* (reiner) Zufall.

[1]**Tot**, *v.a.;* to — up, zusammenrechnen. **—al**, I. *adj.*, **—ally**, *adv.* ganz, gänzlich, völlig. II. *s.* das Ganze, der Gesammtbetrag; (sum —al) die Gesammtsumme. III. *v.n.* sich belaufen auf. **—ality**, *s.* das Ganze; die Vollständigkeit.

[2]**Tot**, *s.* kleines Kind, kleines Mädchen.

Totem, *s.* das Totem, Familiensymbol (*of North American Indians*).

Totter, *v.n.* wanken, wackeln; schwanken (*fig.*). **—er**, *s.* der Wankende. **—ing**, *adj.*, **—ingly**, *adv.* (sch)wankend, wackelig.

Touch, I. *v.a.* be=, an=rühren, angreifen, anstoßen, stoßen an (*acc.*); (feel) an=fühlen, =tasten; (reach) erreichen; *see* to — upon; (affect) bewegen, rühren; to — with pity, Mitleid einflößen; to — one's hat to a p., einen grüßen; they cannot — me for . . ., sie können mich wegen . . . nicht verhaften; to — glasses, anstoßen; to — the wind, sich dicht am Winde halten (*Naut.*); they that — pitch will be defiled, wer Pech angreift, besudelt sich (*prov.*); that —es the pocket, das reißt in den Beutel (*coll.*); a little —ed, ein wenig angegangen (*as meat*); verrückt (*of people*); to — up, auffrischen (*a picture, etc.*), aufputzen. II. *v.n.* sich berühren; to — and go, kurz verweilen und gleich weitergehen; to — **at**, ankommen, anlanden; to — at a port, in einen Hafen einlaufen; to — down, anhalten, die Hand auflegen (*Footb.*); to — **for** the king's evil, die Skrofeln berühren (heilen); to — **upon**, berühren, kommen auf (*acc.*). III. *s.* die Berührung; der Anfall (*of illness*); (dash) der Anflug, Anstrich, Hauch; der Anschlag (*Mus.*); der (Pinsel=) Strich (*Draw., etc.*); (sense of —), der Tastsinn; das Mark, die Seitenlinie (*Footb.*); — of red, rötlicher Schimmer; to give the finishing — to a th., die letzte Hand an eine S. legen; to keep —, in Berührung sein *or* bleiben; to keep in — with, Fühlung behalten mit. **—ily**, *adv.*, **—y**, *adj.* empfindlich, reizbar. **—iness**, *s.* die Empfindlichkeit, Reizbarkeit. **—ing**, I. *adj.*, **—ingly**, *adv.* rührend. II. *s.* das Berühren. III. *prep.* betreffend, in Betreff. *Comp.* **—-and-go**, I. *adj.* gewagt (*sl.*); leichtfertig, oberflächlich. II. *s.* knappes Entkommen; gewagte Sache. **—-hole**, *s.* das Zündloch. **—-in-goal**, *s.* das Markmal (*Footb.*). **—-judges**, *s.* Linien=, Seiten=richter (*pl.*). **—-line**, *s.* die Marklinie, Seitengrenze (*Footb.*). **—-needle**, *s.* die Probiernadel. —**stone**, *s.* der Probierstein; der Prüfstein (*fig.*).

Tough, *adj.*, **—ly**, *adv.* zäh(e) (*also fig.*); — customer, eigenwilliger Mensch, der Grobian. —**en**, *v.* I. *a.* zäh(e) machen. II. *n.* zäh(e) werden. **—ness**, *v.* die Zähigkeit.

Toupe—e, —t, *s.* das Toupet, Stirnhaar.

Tour, I. *s.* die (Rund=)Reise, der Ausflug; walking —, die Fußreise; to make the grand —, eine Reise durch Europa machen. II. *v.n.* reisen. **—ist**, I. *s.* der Reisende; der Reiseanzug (*coll.*). II. *attrib.;* —ist club, der Touristenklub. —**nament, —ney**, *s.* das Turnier. **—niquet**, *s.* die Aderpresse (*Surg.*). **—nure**, *s.* die Figur; der Bausch, die Wulst, Tournüre; die Haltung.

Tous(l)e, *v.a.* (zer)zausen (*prov.*).

Tout, I. *v.n.* Kunden zutreiben *or* suchen; tradesmen are —ing, Geschäftsleute suchen nach Kunden, Kundschaft; Spionierdienste verrichten (*Rac. sl.*). II. *s.* der Kundensucher.

[1]**Tow**, I. *v.a.* (am Seile nach=)schleppen, bugsieren. II. *s.* das Schlepptau; to take in —, ins Schlepptau nehmen. **—age**, *s.* (—ing) das Bugsieren; der Bugsierlohn. *Comp.* **—boat**, *s.* das Schleppboot. **—(ing)-path**, *s.* der Leinpfad, Treidelweg, Schleppweg. **—line, —rope**, *s.* das Schlepptau.

[2]**Tow**, *s.* das Werg, die Hede.

Toward, I., **—s**, *prep.* gegen, nach . . . zu; —s the right hand, nach der rechten Hand hin; his heart relented —s her, sein Herz wurde milder gegen sie; to grow —s manhood, sich dem Mannesalter nähern. II. *adj.*, **—ly**, *adv.* geneigt, willig, lenksam. III. *adv.* (nearly) ungefähr, (ready) bereit. **—ness**, *s.* die Gelehrigkeit; die Bereitschaft, das Bereitsein.

Towel, *s.* das Handtuch; die Binde (*Med.*). —**ling**, *s.* das Handtuchzeug. *Comp.* **—-horse, —-rack**, *s.* der Handtuchständer.

Tower, I. *s.* der Turm (*also Fort.*); *see* Fortress; der Hort (*fig.*). II. *v.n.* sich emportürmen, sich erheben. **—ed**, *adj.* be=, ge=türmt. **—ing**, *adj.* turmhoch; *see* Soaring; (elevated) erhaben, sehr hoch; in a —ing passion, in fürchterlicher Wut.

Town, *s.* die Stadt; (inhabitants) die Bewohner der Stadt; das Stadtgebiet, die territoriale Unterabteilung eines Distriktes (*Amer.*); die politische Unterabteilung eines Staates (*Amer.*); in —, in der Stadt, in London; man about —, der Modeherr, Lebemann, Roué; woman of the —, das Freudenmädchen; the — of Berlin, die Stadt Berlin; — and gown, Philister und Studenten. **—ship**, *s.* der Stadtbezirk, die Stadtgemeinde (*Law*); das Stadtgebiet, die territoriale Unterabteilung eines Distriktes (*Amer.*); das Dorf (*Austral.*). *Comp.* **—-bred**, *adj.;* —bred child, das Stadtkind. **—-clerk**, *s.* der Stadtschreiber. **—-council**, *s.* der Stadtrat, Magistrat. **—-councillor**, *s.* der Stadtrat. **—-crier**, *s.* öffentlicher Ausrufer. **—-hall**, *s.* das Rathaus. **—-house**, *s.* das Haus in der Stadt. **—-life**, *s.* das Stadtleben. **—-porter**, *s.* der Dienstmann. **—-rough**, *s.* brutaler Straßenlümmel. **—sfolk**, *s.* Stadtleute, Städter (*pl.*). **—sman**, *s.* der Bürger; der Philister (*Univ.*); fellow —sman, der Mitbürger. **—-talk**, *s.* das Stadtgespräch. **—-wall**, *s.* die Stadtmauer.

Toxicolog—ical, *adj.* toxikologisch. **—ist**, *s.* der Giftkundige. **—y**, *s.* die Giftkunde.

Toxophilite, *s.* der eifrige Pfeilschütze.

Toy, I. *s.* das Spielzeug; der Tand. II. *v.n.* tändeln. **—ing**, *s.* die Tändelei. *Comp.* —-**book**, *s.* das Bilderbuch; movable —-book, das Ziehbilderbuch. **—man**, *s.* der Spielzeughändler **—-railway**, *s.* die Kleinbahn. **—-shop**, *s.* der Spielwarenladen. **—-symphony**, *s.* die Kindersinfonie.

[1]**Trac—e**, I. *s.* die Spur (*also fig.*); der Spurpunkt (*Math.*). II. *v.a.* zeichnen, skizzieren (*an outline, etc.*); nach=spüren, =gehen, =ziehen (a p., einem); abstecken (*Surv., Mil.*); aufzeichnen (*a plan*); to —e a th. to its original cause, etwas auf seine Grundursache zurückführen *or* zurückverfolgen; to —e out, aus=forschen, =spüren. **—eable**, *adj.* ausspürbar; herzuleiten; zurückzuverfolgen. **—er**, *s.* der Ausspürer. **—eried**, *adj.* mit Maßwerk versehen. **—ery**, *s.* das Maßwerk, die Schenkelverzierungen (*in Gothic architecture*). **—ing**, *s.* das (Durch=)Zeichnen, Durchpausen; der Aufriß (*Build. etc.*). **—k, —t**, *see* Track, Tract, etc. *Comp.* **—ing-paper**, *s.* das Papier zum Durchzeichnen, Ölpapier, das Pauspapier.

[2]**Trace**, *s.* der Strang, Zugriemen, das Zugtau; to kick over the —s, über die Stränge schlagen (*fig.*).

Trache—a, *s.* die Luftröhre. **—al**, *adj.* Luftröhren=. **—ocele**, *s.* das Luftröhrenbruch. **—otomy**, *s.* der Luftröhrenschnitt.

Track, I. *s.* die Spur; (path) die Bahn, der Pfad; das Geleise (*of a carriage wheel*); der Schienenweg, das Geleise (*Railw.*); die Fährte (*Sport.*). II. *v.a.* der Spur folgen; (pursue) verfolgen; to — out, ausspüren. **—er**, *s.* der Spürhund; der Verfolger. **—less**, *adj.* spurlos, pfadlos. **—lessness**, *s.* die Pfadlosigkeit.

[1]**Tract**, *s.* die Strecke, der Strich (*of country*), die Gegend; der Verlauf, Fortgang.

[2]**Tract**, *s.* der Traktat, die Abhandlung; —s for the times, zeitgemäße Traktate. **—able**, *adj.*, **—ably**, *adv.* lenk=, folg=sam. **—ableness**, **—ability**, *s.* die Lenksamkeit. **—arian**, *s.* der Traktätchenschreiber, Traktarianer. **—arianism**, *s.* der Puseyismus. **—ate**, *s. see* [1]—. **—ile**, *adj.* dehn=, streck=bar. **—ility**, *s.* die Dehnbarkeit. **—ion**, *s.* das Ziehen, der Zug; electric —ion, elektrische Fortbewegung. **—ive**, *adj.* ziehend, Zieh=; —ive power, die Zugkraft. **—or**, *s.* der Zieher, die Ziehkraft, das Zugmittel. *Comp.* **—ion-engine**, *s.* die Zugmaschine, nicht auf Schienen laufende Straßenlokomotive.

Trad—e, I. *s.* der Handel; die Geschäftswelt; (business) das Geschäft, Gewerbe; (handicraft) das Handwerk; (habit) die Gewohnheit; book—e, der Buchhandel; carrying —e, Fracht=, Speditions=handel; free —e, der Freihandel; fair —e, der Handel unter billigen Bedingungen; inland —e, der Binnenhandel; retail —e, der Kleinhandel, Einzelverkauf; wholesale —e, der Großhandel; board of —e, das Handelsamt, Handelsministerium; president of the board of —e, der (englische) Handelsminister. II. *v.a.* handeln, Handel treiben (with, mit); to —e on *or* upon a p.'s kindness, aus jemandes Güte Vorteil ziehen; to —e in bills of exchange, Wechselreiterei treiben; to —e away, verhandeln. **—er**, *s.* der Handelsmann, Händler; das Handelsschiff, Kauffahrteischiff (*Naut.*). **—ing**, *p. & adj.* handeltreibend, Handels=; —ing interest, das Handelsinteresse; der Handelsstand; —ing ports, Handelshäfen; —ing place, der Handelsplatz; —ing nation, handeltreibende Nation. *Comp.* **—e-mark**, *s.* die Schutzmarke, Etikette; registered —e-mark, eingetragene Schutzmarke. **—e-notes**, *s.* Handelsnachrichten (*pl.*). **—e-price**, *s.* der Handels=, Engros=preis. **—esman**, *s.* der Kleinhändler, Krämer; (mechanic) der Handwerker; —esmen's entrance, Nebeneingang für Geschäftsleute. **—espeople**, *pl.* Geschäfts=, Handelsleute. **—e(s)-union**, *s.* der Gewerkverein. **—e(s)-unionism**, *s.* die Gewerkschaftsvereinigung; die Gewerkvereine (*collect.*). **—e(s)-unionist**, *s.* der Gewerkvereinler. **—e-winds**, *pl.* Passatwinde.

Tradition, *s.* die mündliche Überlieferung, Sage; (custom) alter Brauch, das Herkommen; die Tradition (*Rel.*); popular —, die Volksüberlieferung, Volkssage. **—al**, **—ary**, *adj.* mündlich überliefert; auf Sagen gegründet; herkömmlich; —al custom, altherkömmlicher Brauch. **—ally**, *adv.* durch Überlieferung, der Sage nach.

Traduce, *v.a.* verleumden. **—r**, *s.* der Verleumder.

Traffic, I. *s.* der Handel, Verkehr; der Verkehr (*on railways, etc.*). II. *v.n.* handeln, Handel treiben (in with, mit); (chaffer) schachern, markten. IV. *v.a. see* Exchange. **—ker**, *s.* der Handelsmann. *Comp.* **—-manager**, *s.* der Betriebsinspektor. **—-returns**, *s.* Betriebs=, Verkehrs=Nachrichten *or* =Berichte (*pl.*).

Trag—edian, *s.* der Trauerspieldichter, Tragiker; (actor) der tragische Schauspieler. **—edy**, *s.* das Trauerspiel; tragische Begebenheit der erschütternde Unglücksfall (*fig.*); domestic —edy, das bürgerliche Trauerspiel. **—ic(al)**, *adj.*, **—ically**, *adv.* tragisch; traurig, unselig (*fig.*). **—icalness**, *s.* das Tragische. **—icomedy**, *s.* die Tragikomödie. **—icomic**, *adj.* tragikomisch.

Trail, I. *v.a.* (nach)schleppen; auf der Spur verfolgen (*Sport.*); to — arms, das Gewehr zur Seite *or* in die rechte Hand nehmen. II. *v.n.* kriechen (*plants*); to — along, sich hinschleppen. III. *s.* die Witterung, Fährte; (train) die Schleppe; der (Lafetten=)Schwanz (*Artil.*). **—er**, *s.* der leichte Anhängewagen an ein Zweirad. **—ing**, *adj.* gestreckt, auf der Erde liegend; wagerecht; —ing arbutus, kriechender Grindstrauch, —(ing) net, das Schleppnetz.

Train, I. *v.a.* abrichten, dressieren (*animals*); (auf=)erziehen (*children, etc.*); ausbilden (*teachers*); (ein)exerzieren (*recruits*); (form) bilden; ziehen (*plants, trees, etc.*); trainieren (*athletes, horses*); richten (*a gun*). II. *v.n.* üben, drillen, exerzieren; sich üben, sich trainieren; sich ausbilden; to — (it), mit der Eisenbahn fahren (*sl.*). III. *s.* die Schleppe (*of a dress*); (procession, string) der Zug; der Zug (*Railw., Mil.*); (retinue) das Gefolge, die Begleitung; (series) die Reihe, Folge; die Zündlinie, das Leitfeuer (*Mil., etc.*); — of thought, die Gedankenfolge; — of artillery, der Artillerietrain; armoured —, Panzerzug; corridor —, Durchgangszug; excursion —, Vergnügungszug, Extrazug; fast —, Schnellzug; goods —, Güterzug; slow —, Bummelzug; passenger —, Personenzug; special —, Sonderzug; Victoria —, der Zug nach Victoria; city —, der Zug nach der City; up (down) —, nach London fahrender (von L. fortfahrender) Zug; to catch one's —, den Zug erreichen, den Anschluß bekommen; to miss one's —, den Zug versäumen, den Anschluß nicht erreichen; to change —s, umsteigen; to leave the —, aussteigen; to travel by —, mit der Bahn fahren. **—ed**, *adj.* ausgebildet; abgerichtet (*animals*). **—er**, *s.* der Abrichter, Zureiter, Traineur (*of horses*); einer, der dressiert (*dogs*); der Erzieher. **—ing**, *s.* die Erziehung; die Ausbildung; die Abrichtung, das Zureiten, Trainieren; das Einexerzieren. *Comp.* **—-bearer**, *s.* der Schleppenträger. **—ing-college**, *s.* das Lehrerseminar; —ing-college for women teachers, das Lehrerinnenseminar. **—ing-school**, *s.* die Ausbildungsanstalt, das Seminar. **—ing-ship**, *s.* das Schulschiff. **—-oil**, *s.* der (Fisch=)Tran.

Trait, *s.* der Zug, Charakterzug.

Trait—or, *s.* der Verräter, Treulose. **—orous**, *adj.*, **—orously**, *adv.* verräterisch. **—ress**, *s.* die Verräterin.

Traject, I. *v.a.* durchwerfen. II. *s.* die Überfahrt, Fähre. **—ory**, *s.* die Kegelschnittlinie, Wurf= *or* Flug=bahn.

Tram, *s.* die Grubenschiene (*Min.*); der Laufkarren, Forderwagen (*Min.*); *see* —-car. *Comp.* **—-car**, *s.* der Straßenbahnwagen; der Pferdebahnwagen. **—-line**, *s. see* —way. **—-rail**, *s.* die Falzschiene. **—way**, *s.* die Straßen=, Pferdebahn; electric —way, elektrische Straßenbahn.

Trammel, I. *s.* der Spannriemen (*for horses*); (net) das Garn; die Fessel (*fig.*). II. *v.a.* hindern, hemmen, fesseln. **—led**, *adj.* gefesselt.

Tramontane, *adj.* jenseits der Alpen wohnend, überalpisch.

Tramp, I. *v.n.* derb auftreten, trampeln; (walk) gehen, zu Fuß reisen. II. *v.a.* treten, trampeln auf; das Land zu Fuß durchstreifen; to — down, niedertreten. III. *s.* das Getrampel; — of horses, das Pferdegetrappel; (vagrant) der Landstreicher, Vagabund, Bettler; die Fuß=reise *or* =wanderung; to go on the —, Arbeit suchen; on the —, zu Fuße. **—le**, *v.a. & n.* trampeln; treten; to —le under foot, niedertreten, mit Füßen treten (*fig.*).

Trance, *s.* die Verzückung; der hypnotische Schlaf; der Scheintod, die Starrsucht (*Med.*).

Tranquil, *adj.*, **—ly**, *adv.* ruhig, still. **—lity**, *s.* die Ruhe, Stille; die Gelassenheit (*fig.*). **—lization**, *s.* die Beruhigung. **—lize**, *v.a.*, beruhigen, stillen. —**lizer**, *s.* der, welcher, *or* das, was beruhigt.

Trans—act, *v.a.* verrichten, abmachen, durchführen; to —act business (with), Geschäfte machen (in Geschäftsverbindung stehen mit). —**action**, *s.* die Verrichtung, Verhandlung (*of a business*); (affair) das Geschäft, die Sache, der Vorfall. —**actions**, *pl.* Verhandlungen (*of learned bodies, etc.*); Abhandlungen (*published by learned bodies*); during these —actions, unterdessen. —**actor**, *s.* der Verrichtende, Unterhandelnde. —**alpine**, *adj.* jenseits der Alpen, transalpinisch. —**atlantic**, *adj.* transatlantisch. —**cend**, *v. a* übersteigen, =schreiten; (excel) übertreffen. —**cendency**, *s.* ungemeine Überlegenheit *or* Vortrefflichkeit, hervorragende Größe, Erhabenheit. —**cendent**, *adj.*, —**cendently**, *adv.* höchst vortrefflich, =züglich; *see* —cendental. —**cendental**, *adj.* tran(s)szendental (*Philos.*); tran(s)szendent (*Math.*). —**cendentalism**, *s.* der Tran(s)szendentalismus. —**cendentalist**, *s.* der Tran(s)szendental=Philosoph. —**cribe**, *v.a.* abschreiben; umschreiben (in eine andere Sprache oder Mundart). —**criber**, *s.* der Abschreiber. —**cript**, *s.* die Abschrift; (copy) die Kopie. —**cription**, *s.* das Abschreiben; die Umschrift. —**ept**, *s.* der Kreuzflügel, das Kreuzschiff. —**fer**, I. *v.a.* übertragen; versetzen, verlegen (*to another place*); abtreten, übergeben (to a p., einem); abschreiben, (einen Rechnungsposten) versetzen (*C.L.*); übertragen, umdrucken (*a print, etc.*). II. *s.* (change of place) die Verlegung, Versetzung; die Übertragung, Abtretung (*of a right, etc.*); der Übertrag (*C. L.*); der Abzug, Umdruck (*Print., Engr., etc.*); —fer of balance, der Saldoübertrag; school —fer, die Abtretung, Übertragung einer Schule. —**ferability**, *s.* die Versetzbarkeit, Übertragbarkeit. —**ferable**, *adj.* versetzbar; übertragbar. —**feree**, *s.* der Annehmer der Zession. —**ference**, *s.* die Übertragung. —**ferrer**, *s.* der Übertragende. —**figuration**, *s.* die Umgestaltung; die Verklärung (*B.*). —**figure**, *v.a.* umgestalten, umbilden; verklären. —**fix**, *v.a.* durch=stechen, =bohren. —**form**, *v. a.* umgestalten (*also Alg.*), umbilden; (change) verwandeln, umwandeln. —**formation**, *s.* die Um=bildung, =gestaltung; die Verwandlung, Umwandlung. —**formative**, *adj.* umgestaltend. —**fuse**, *v. a.* umgießen; überleiten (blood). —**fusible**, *adj.* mitteilbar. —**fusion**, *s.* das Umgießen; das Überleiten. —**gress**, *v.* I. *a.* überschreiten; über=schreiten, =treten, verstoßen gegen (*fig.*). II. *n.* sich vergehen. —**gression**, *s.* die Über=schreitung, =tretung, Vergehung. —**gressor**, *s.* der Übertreter, Sünder. —**hip**, *v.a.* umladen, aus einem Schiff ins andere laden. —**hipment**, I. *s.* die Umladung. II. *attrib.*; —hipment port, der Umladehafen, Umschlagsplatz. —**ient**, *adj.*, —**iently**, *adv.* vorübergehend; vergänglich, flüchtig (*fig.*). —**ientness**, *s.* die Flüchtigkeit, Vergänglichkeit. —**it**, *s.* der Durchgang. —**ition**, *s.* der Übergang; —ition period, die Übergangszeit. —**itional**, *adv.* Übergangs=. —**itive**, *adj.* übergehend (*also fig.*); transitiv (*Gram.*). —**itorily**, *adv.*, —**itory**, *adj. see* —ient. —**itoriness**, *s.* die kurze Dauer, Flüchtigkeit. —**itu**, *s.*; in —itu, im Transitverkehr, durchgehend (*C. L.*). —**latable**, *adj.* übersetzbar. —**late**, *v.a.* versetzen (*a bishop, etc.*); in den Himmel versetzen (*B.*); übersetzen, übertragen (*a language*). —**lation**, *s.* die Versetzung (*also* in den Himmel); die Übertragung, Übersetzung; German —lation, Übersetzung aus dem Deutschen; —lation at sight, unvorbereitete Übersetzung. —**lator**, *s.* der Übersetzer. —**literation**, *s.* die Transskription. —**lucency**, —**lucence**, *s.* die Durchsichtigkeit. —**lucent**, *adj.* durchscheinend, durchsichtig; hell (*fig.*). —**marine**, *adj.* überseeisch. —**migrate**, *v.n.* fort=, auswandern, übersiedeln; hinübergehen, übersiedeln (*fig.*). —**migration**, *s.* die Über=, Auswanderung, Übersiedelung; der Übergang (*into another state, etc.*), die Umwandlung; —migration of souls, die Seelenwanderung. —**migratory**, *adj.* wegziehend, wandernd. —**missible**, *adj.* übertragbar, übersendbar; fortpflanzbar (*as light, heat, etc.*). —**mission**, *s.* die Überschickung, =sendung, =machung; die (Waren=) Versendung, Spedition (*C.L.*); die Durchlassung, Fortpflanzung, Leitung (*Phys.*); die Vererbung (*of qualities, etc.*). —**mit**, *v.a.* über=schicken, =senden, =liefern; durchlassen, fortpflanzen (*Phys.*); fortpflanzen, vererben (to a p., auf einen); on —mitting the invoice, bei Einsendung der Faktura. —**mitter**, *s.* der Übersender; der Fortpflanzende. —**mutability**, *s.* die Verwandelbarkeit. —**mutable**, *adj.*, —**mutably**, *adv.* verwandelbar. —**mutation**, *s.* die Ver=, Um=wandlung. —**muter**, *s.* der Verwandler. —**om**, *s.* das Querholz, der Querbalken. —**parency**, *s.* die Durchsichtigkeit; das Transparent (*for windows, etc.*); das Durchsichtsbild. —**parent**, *adj.*, —**parently**, *adv.* durchsichtig, klar, hell; leicht zu erraten, ohne Heimlichkeit (*fig.*). —**pierce**, *v.a.* durchbohren. —**pire**, *v.n.* ausdünsten; verlauten, bekannt werden (*fig.*). —**plant**, *v.a.* ver=pflanzen, =setzen. —**plantation**, *s.* die Verpflanzung, Versetzung. —**port**, I. *v.a.* über=fahren, =setzen; (send away) fort=schaffen, =bringen, versetzen; (send across) übersenden; transportieren, deportieren (*criminals, etc.*); außer sich bringen, hinreißen, entzücken (*fig.*); he is —ported with love, er ist vor Liebe außer sich; —ported by passion, von Leidenschaft hingerissen. II. *s.* das Fortschaffen; die Fortschaffung, Überfahrt, der Transport; das Transportschiff; der Ausbruch, Anfall (*of passion, etc.*), die Entzückung (*of joy, etc.*); —ports (of joy), der Freudentaumel. —**portable**, *adj.* versendbar. —**portation**, *s.* die Fortschaffung, Versendung, Verschiffung; die Transportation, Landesverweisung. —**porting**, *adj.* entzückend, hinreißend. —**pose**, *v.a.* versetzen (*also Typ.*); transponieren (*Mus.*). —**position**, *s.* die Versetzung; das Transponieren (*Mus.*). —**ubstantiate**, *v.a.* verwandeln. —**ubstantiation**, *s.* die (Substanzver=)Wandlung; die Transubstantiation (*Eccl.*). —**versal**, I. *adj.* überzwerch, quer, schräg, Quer=; transversal (*Math.*). II. *s.* die Transversale. —**verse**, *adj.* querlaufend, durchgehend. *Comp.* —**ferbook**, *s.* das Umschreibungsbuch. —**ferpaper**, *s.* das Überdruckpapier. —**it-duty**, *s.* der Durchgangszoll. —**it-instrument**, *s.* das Passageinstrument, Meridianfernrohr.

[1]**Trap**, I. *s.* die Falle; die Falle, Schlinge, der Fallstrick (*fig.*); (ambush) der Hinterhalt; der Wasserverschluß (*for drains, etc.*); der offne leichte Wagen; pony —, das Ponywägelchen. II. *v.a.* fangen; ertappen (*fig.*); mit einem Wasserverschluß versehen. —**an**, (**Trepan**), I. *s.* die Falle, Schlinge, List. II. *v.a.* fangen, bestricken, überlisten. —**anner**, *s.* der Verführer, einer der Fallstricke legt. —**per**, *s.* der Fallensteller, Pelzjäger. *Comp.* —**-ball**, *s.* der Schlagball. —**-door**, *s.* die Klappe, Falltür.

[2]**Trap**, I. *v.a.* aufputzen, anschirren. II. *s.* die Pferdedecke (*obs.*). —**s**, *pl.* das Zubehör, Gepäck, die Siebensachen. —**pings**, *pl.* der Putz, Schmuck; das Pferdegeschirr, der Pferdeschmuck (*of horses*).

[3]**Trap**, *s.* der Trapp; (— rocks) Trappgebirge.

Trapez—e, —**ium**, *s.* das Trapez (*Math.*); das Schwebereck, Trapez (*Gymn.*); viereckiger Handwurzelknochen (*Anat.*). —**iform**, *adj.* trapezförmig. —**oid**, *s.* das verschobene Viereck, Trapezoid

Trash, I. *s.* der Schofel, die Lumperei; (refuse) der Abfall, Auswurf; der Unsinn, das Blech. II. *v.a.* kappen, beschneiden. **—y**, *adj.* nichtswürdig, wertlos, schofel, schlecht.
Travail, I. *v.n.* sich mühen, sich placken; in Kindesnöten sein, kreißen. II. *s.* mühevolle Arbeit; (labour) die Kindesnöte, Wehen.
Trave, *s.* der Querbalken (*rare*); der Notstall (*for horses*).
Travel, I. *v.n.* reisen; sich schnell bewegen; to — through, over, durch-wandern, -reisen, bereisen. II. *v.a.*; to — 20 miles in one day, 20 Meilen in einem Tage zurücklegen. III. —, *s.*, **—s**, *pl.* die Reise(n); book of —s, die Reisebeschreibung. **—led**, *adj.* weit gereist, weit gewandert. **—ler**, *s.* der Reisende; a —ler, ein Reisender; —ler on foot, der Fußreisende, Wanderer; commercial —ler, der Geschäftsreisende; —lers' guide, das Reisehandbuch. —lers' room, das Gastzimmer für Handlungsreisende. **—ling**, I. *adj.* Reise-; —ling preacher, der Reiseprediger, Wanderprediger. II. *s.* das Reisen. *Comp.* **—ling-expenses**, *s.* Reisekosten. **—ling-scholarship**, *s.* das Reisestipendium.
Travers—able, *adj.* einen Rechtseinwand zulassend. **—e**, I. *adj.* quer, überzwerch. II. *s.* das Quer-stück, -holz, der Quer-riegel, -balken; der Quergang, die Gallerie (*Arch.*); die Traverse, der Querwall (*Fort.*); der Rechtseinwand; (turn) die Biegung, Krümmung; der Querstrich (*fig.*). III. *v.a.* quer, mitten durch-gehen, -reiten, -fahren ꝛc.; durchreisen (*a country, etc.*); durchgehen, durchforschen (*fig.*); durchkreuzen (*a project*); (ab)leugnen, Einwendungen machen gegen (*Law*); drehen, wenden, richten (*guns*). IV. *v.n.* traversieren (*Fenc., also in riding*); (turn) sich (wie auf einem Zapfen) drehen. **—er**, *s.* der Durchziehende; einer, der ein Rechtsmittel gegen ein Urteil einwendet (*Law*). *Comp.* **—e-beam**, *s.* die Querschwelle. **—e-gallery**, *s.* der Querminengang. **—e-sailing**, *s.* der Koppelkurs, schiefe Lauf. **—e-table**, *s.* die Logtafel. **—ing-platform**, *s.* bewegliche Bettung, das Rahmengestell (*Artil.*). **—ing-table**, *s.* die Schiebebühne (*Railw.*).
Travesty, I. *s.* die Travestie. II. *v.a.* travestieren.
Trawl, *v.n.* mit dem Schleppnetz fischen. **—er**, *s.* der (das) Schleppnetzfischer(boot).
Tray, *s.* das (Tee-, Kaffee- ꝛc.)Brett; der Präsentierteller, das Tablett.
Treacher—ous, *adj.*, **—ously**, *adv.* verräterisch, treulos, falsch, hinterlistig; untreu (*as memory*). **—ousness**, *s.* die Treulosigkeit. **—y**, *s.* der Verrat, die Falschheit.
Treacle, *s.* der (Deck-)Sirup; der Theriak (*Pharm.*); das Universal(heil)mittel (*fig.*).
Tread, I. *ir.v.n.* treten, den Fuß setzen, gehen (upon, auf); (walk) einhertreten; sich begatten, treten (*as fowls*); to — (**up**)**on**, treten auf, (trample) mit Füßen treten; to — on a p.'s heels, einem auf der Ferse nachfolgen. II. *ir.v.a.* (be)treten, beschreiten; tanzen (*a minuet, etc.*); treten (*a hen*); to — **down**, niedertreten; to — **under** foot, mit Füßen treten, niedertreten. III. *s.* der Tritt, Schritt; die Trittstufe (*of stairs*). **—er**, *s.* der Treter. **—le**, *s.* der Tritt; der Hahnentritt (*in eggs*); das Pedal (*Cycl.*). *Comp.* **—mill**, *s.* die Tretmühle.
Treason, *s.* der Verrat, die Verräterei; high —, Hochverrat. **—able**, *adj.*, **—ably**, *adv.* verräterisch. **—ableness**, *s.* das Verräterische.
Treasur—e, I. *s.* der Schatz. II. *v.a.* (—e up) aufbewahren; (hoard) sammeln, aufhäufen. **—er**, *s.* der Schatzmeister, Kassenwart (*of societies*); (Lord) High —er, Lord-Oberschatzmeister. **—ership**, *s.* das Schatzmeisteramt. **—y**, *s.* die Schatz-, Finanz-kammer; First Lord of the —y, Secretary to the —y, erster Lord des Schatzes, Finanzminister; Junior Lord of the —y, der Kommissär des Finanzministeriums; Secretary of the —y, der Finanzminister (*Amer.*). *Comp.* **—e-house**, *s.* das Schatzhaus. **—e-trove**, *s.* verborgen gefundener Schatz. **—y-bench**, *s.* der Sitz des (Finanz-)Ministeriums im Parlament. **—y-bill**, *s.* die Kassenanweisung, der Schatzkammer-, Kassen-schein. **—y-bond**, *s.* der (nicht fundierte) Schatzschein. **—y-department**, *s.* das Schatzkammeramt, Finanzministerium. **—y-note**, *s.* der Schatz(kammer)schein. **—y-office**, *s.* das Schatzamt.
Treat, I. *v.a.* behandeln, (mit einem) umgehen; (entertain) bewirten; freihalten. II. *v.n.*; to — **of**, handeln von (einem Gegenstande), (einen G.) behandeln; to — **with**, unterhandeln, in Unterhandlung treten mit. III. *s.* die Bewirtung, der Schmaus; der (Hoch-)Genuß; to stand (a) —, traktieren, bewirten (*vulg.*); it is **a** — to hear him, es ist ein wahrer Genuß (ein Hochgenuß), ihn zu hören. **—er**, *s.* der Abhandelnde; der Bewirtende. **—ise**, *s.* die Abhandlung (über eine S.). **—ment**, *s.* die Behandlung. **—y**, *s.* die Unterhandlung; (compact) der Vertrag; to be in —y for, in Unterhandlung stehen wegen.
Trebl—e, I. *adj.*, **—y**, *adv.* dreifach; Diskant-; —e clef, der Diskantschlüssel. II. *s.* der Diskant (*Mus.*); (—e singer) der Sopran, Sopransänger. III. *v.a.* (*& n.* sich) verdreifachen.
Tree, *s.* der Baum; fruit —, Obstbaum; genealogical —, Stammbaum. **—less**, *adj.* baumlos. *Comp.* **—-frog**, *s.* der Laubfrosch. **—nail**, *s.* der Dübel, Döbel, lange hölzerne Nagel.
Trefoil, *s.* der Klee; das Kleeblatt (*Arch.*).
Trek, *v.n.* (mit Ochsenwagen als Kolonisten) ziehen; they —ked southwards, sie zogen nach Süden. *Comp.* **—-oxen**, *pl.* Zugochsen.
Trellis, I. *s.* das Gitter, Gatter. II. *v.a.* vergittern; an Spalieren ziehen (*Hort.*); —ed window, das Gitterfenster. *Comp.* **—-work**, *s.* das Gitterwerk.
Trem—ble, I. *v.n.* zittern (at, with, vor); to —ble all over, am ganzen Leibe zittern. II. *s.*; in a —ble, zitternd. **—bling**, I. *adj.*, **—blingly**, *adv.* zitternd. II. *s.* das Zittern, Beben. **—endous**, *adj.*, **—endously**, *adv.* furchtbar, fürchterlich; ungeheuer, kolossal (*coll.*); a —endous crowd, eine kolossale Menge Menschen. **—olo**, *s.* das Tremolo (*Mus.*). **—or**, *s.* das Zittern, Beben. **—ulous**, *adj.*, **—ulously**, *adv.* zitternd, bebend. **—ulousness**, *s.* das Zittern.
Trenail, *s. see* Treenail, *under* Tree.
Trench, I. *v.a.* mit Gräben durchziehen, rajolen; verschanzen (*Mil.*). II. *v.n.*; to — upon, *see* Encroach. III. *s.* der Graben, die Rinne; der Laufgraben (*Fort.*); to mount (relieve) the —es, die Wache in den Laufgräben beziehen (ablösen). **—ant**, *adj.*, **—antly**, *adv.* schneidend, scharf. **—er**, *s.* das Tranchier-, Schneide-brett; die Tafel (*fig.*). *Comp.* **—er-cap**, *s.* viereckige steife mit einer Troddel in der Mitte versehene Kopfbedeckung der Studenten und Dozenten in Oxford und Cambridge sowie der Schüler einiger größeren Knabenschulen. **—er-friend**, **—er-knight**, *s.* der Tafelfreund, Tellerheld, Schmarotzer. **—(ing)-plough**, *s.* der Rajolpflug.
Trend, I. *s.* die Neigung, geneigte Richtung; der Ankerhals (*Naut.*); the — of his argument was seine Beweisführung lief darauf hinaus; the general — of public opinion, die allgemeine Richtung der öffentlichen Meinung. II. *v.n.* sich neigen, sich strecken; —ed coast, gewundene Küste.
[1]**Trepan**, *see* Trapan.
[2]**Trepan**, I. *s.* der Schädelbohrer. II. *v.a.* trepanieren. **—ner**, *s.* der Trepanierer.
Trephine, I. *s.* die Trepaniersäge, Trephine (*Surg.*). II. *v.a.* trepanieren.
Trepidation, *s.* das Zittern, Beben; die Angst, Bestürzung; in —, zitternd, ängstlich; in great —, mit Zittern und Zagen, mit Furcht und Zittern.

Trespass, I. *v.n.* sich vergehen, sündigen (against, wider) übertreten; unbefugt fremdes Eigentum betreten; to — upon a p.'s good-nature, auf jemands Gutmütigkeit hin sündigen; to — upon a p.'s time, jemandes Zeit zu sehr in Anspruch nehmen. II. *s.* unbefugtes Betreten fremden Eigentums, die Eigentums=, Personen=, Rechts=verletzung, der Eingriff; (sin) das Vergehen, die Übertretung, Sünde. **—er**, *s.* der Übertreter, Rechtsverletzer; —ers will be prosecuted, Unbefugten ist der Eintritt untersagt.

Tress, *s.* die (Haar=)Flechte, Locke.

Trestle, *s.* das Gestell, der Bock; das Tischgestell (*of a table*).

Tret, *s.* die Gewichtsvergütung, Refaktie (*C.L.*).

Tri—ad, *s.* die Drei=heit, =einigkeit. **—angle**, *s.* das Dreieck; der Triangel (*Mus.*). **—angular**, *adj.* drei=eckig, =seitig; —angular numbers, Dreieckszahlen. **—as**, *s.* der Trias (*Geol.*). **—bal**, *etc. see* Tribal. **—car**, *s.* das Dreirad mit Motormaschine (*Mot.*). **—cennial**, *adj.* dreißig=jährig. **—chord**, *adj.* dreichörig. **—colo(u)r**, *s.* die dreifarbige Fahne, Trikolore. **—coloured**, *adj.* dreifarbig. **—cycle**, *s.* das Dreirad; to ride a —cycle, Dreirad fahren. **—cyclist**, *s.* der (die) Dreiradfahrer(in). **—dent**, *s.* der Dreizack. **—ennial**, *adj.*, **—ennially**, *adv.* dreijährig; (every 3 years) alle 3 Jahre (wiederkehrend), dreijährlich. **—erarch**, *s.* der Trierarch. **—fallow**, *v.a.* dreibrachen, zum dritten Male pflügen. **—foliate**, *adj.* dreiblätterig. **—furcated**, *adj.* dreigabelig. **—glyph**, *s.* der Dreischlitz, die Triglyphe (*Arch.*). **—gonometrical**, *adj.* trigonometrisch. **—gonometry**, *s.* die Trigonometrie. **—gynian**, *adj.* dreiweibig. **—hedral**, *adj.* drei=flächig, =seitig. **—hedron**, *s.* das Dreiflach. **—lateral**, *adj.*, **—laterally**, *adv.* dreiseitig. **—llion**, *s.* die Trillion. **—lobate**, *adj.* dreilappig. **—logy**, *s.* die Trilogie. **—mester**, *s.* das Trimester. **—meter**, *s.* der Trimeter. **—nal**, *adj.* dreifach, dreifältig. **—ne**, I. *adj. see* —nal; gedritt. II. *s.* der gedritte Schein. **—nitarian**, I. *adj.* trinitarisch. II. *s.* der Dreieinigkeitsbekenner, Trinitarier. **—nitarianism**, *s.* die Dreieinigkeitslehre. **—nity**, I. *s.* die Dreieinigkeit. II. *attrib.;* —nity Sunday, Sonntag Trinitatis; —ity term, das Sommersemester (*Law*). **—nomial**, I. *adj.* dreigliederig. II. *s.* dreiteilige Größe. **—o**, *s.* das Trio. **—olet**, *s.* das Triolett. **—partite**, *adj.* dreiteilig; (divided in 3) dreigeteilt. **—petalous**, *adj.* drei(kronen)blättrig. **—phthong**, *s.* der Dreilaut, Triphthong. **—phthongal**, *adj.* triphthongisch. **—ple**, I. *adj.* dreifach; dreimal; —ple Alliance, der Dreibund; —ple time, der Tripeltakt. II. *v.a.* verdreifachen. **—plet**, *s.* drei Dinge oder Personen derselben Art, das Trio; die Triole (*Mus.*); der Dreireim (*Poet.*); —plets, die Drillinge. **—plicate**, *adj.* dreifach. **—plication**, *s.* die Verdreifachung. **—pod**, *s.* der Dreifuß. **—pos**, I. *s.* die höhere Abgangsprüfung in den verschiedenen Fächern, deren Bestehen dem Studenten den 'Honour degree' eines B. A. verleiht (*Cambr. Univ.*); medieval and modern languges —pos, das wissenschaftliche Studium der neueren Sprachen an der Universität Cambridge. II. *attrib.;* a —pos man, ein Student, welcher sich auf eine der höchsten Cambridger Prüfungen vorbereitet oder eine bestanden hat. **—reme**, *s.* dreiruderige Galeere. **—sect**, *v.a.* in drei gleiche Teile teilen. **—section**, *s.* die Dreiteilung. **—syllabic(al)**, *adj.* dreisilbig. **—syllable**, *s.* dreisilbiges Wort. **—theism**, *s.* die Drei=Gottheitslehre. **—umvir**, *s.* der Triumvir. **—umvirate**, *s.* das Triumvirat. **—une**, *adj.* dreieinig. **—vet**, *s.* der Dreifuß. **—vial**, *see* Trivial, etc.

Trial, I. *s.* der Versuch; (test) die Probe, Prüfung; das Verhör, die gerichtliche Untersuchung; die Versuchung, Anfechtung (*fig.*); — by jury, das Geschwornengericht; by way of —, zum Versuch, zur Probe; to bring to —, vor Gericht bringen; the hour of —, die Prüfungsstunde; to make — of, eine Probe (mit etwas) machen; on —, zur Probe; he is a great — to us, er macht uns schwere Sorgen (*coll.*). II. *attrib.;* — lesson, die Probelektion; — sermon, die Probepredigt; — trip, die Probefahrt.

Trib—al, *adj.* zu einem Stamme gehörig. **—e**, *s.* der Stamm; (race) der Volksstamm, das Geschlecht; die Zunft (*in Rome, etc., also fig.*); (horde) die Horde. **—unal**, *s.* der Richterstuhl; (court of justice) das Gericht. **—une**, *s.* der Volkstribun. **—uneship**, *s.* das Tribunat.

Tribulation, *s.* die Trübsal, Drangsal.

Tribut—ariness, *s.* die Zinsbarkeit. **—ary**, I. *adj.*, **—arily**, *adv.* zinspflichtig; (subject) untertan, unterwürfig; —ary streams, Nebenflüsse; the Ohio has many —ary streams and is itself —ary to the Mississippi, viele große Flüsse ergießen sich in den Ohio und er selbst fällt in den *or* ist ein Nebenfluß des Mississippi. II. *s.* der Zinspflichtige; der Nebenfluß. **—e**, *s.* der Tribut, Zins; *see* Contribution; —e of respect, die Achtungsbezeugung. *Comp.* **—e-money**, *s.* der Zinsgroschen.

Trice, *s.* der Augenblick; in a —, im Nu, sofort.

[1]**Trick**, I. *s.* der Trug, Kniff, Pfiff; der Streich, Spaß, die Posse; (clever contrivance) der Kunstgriff; das (Karten=)Kunststück (*with cards*); der (Karten=)Stich (*at whist, etc.*); (habit) die Eigenheit, Art, Gewohnheit; to play s.o. a —, einem einen Streich spielen; odd —, der Trick; to be up to a p.'s —s, jemandes Streiche durchschauen (*vulg.*). II. *v.a.* betrügen; to — a p. out of, einen um (eine S.) betrügen. **—ery**, *s.* die Betrügerei. **—iness**, *s.* die Verschmitztheit, Gaunerhaftigkeit. **—ish**, *adj.* verschmitzt, listig, tückisch. **—siness**, *s.* die Mutwilligkeit, Scherzhaftigkeit. **—ster**, *s.* der Betrüger. **—sy**, *adj. see* —y. **—y**, *adj.* verschmitzt, listig, schlau; schelmisch, schalkhaft.

[2]**Trick**, *v.a.;* to — out, aufputzen, schmücken.

Trickle, *v.n.* tröpfeln, träufeln, rieseln.

Tri—ed, *imperf. p.p. see* Try. **—er**, *s.* einer, der versucht, probiert oder richtet.

Trifl—e, I. *s.* der Tand, die Kleinigkeit, Lappalie; eine Art Auflauf (*Cook.*). II. *v.a. & n.* tändeln, scherzen; kindisch reden oder handeln; to —e with a p.'s feelings, mit jemandes Gefühlen sein Spiel treiben; you —e away your time, Sie vertändeln Ihre Zeit; he is not to be —ed with, mit ihm ist nicht zu spaßen. **—er**, *s.* der Tändler. **—ing**, I. *adj.*, **—ingly**, *adv.* tändelnd, spielend; (of little value) geringfügig, wertlos, unbedeutend. II. *s.* das Tändeln; das Nichtstun, die Spielerei. **—ingness**, *s.* die Geringfügigkeit; die Leichtfertigkeit, Albernheit.

Trig, *v.a.* hemmen (*wheels*). **—ger**, *s.* der Hemmschuh, Radschuh, die Bremse; der Drücker (am Gewehr).

Trill, I. *s.* der Triller. II. *v.a. & n.* trillern, Triller schlagen; rollen (ein r); —ed r, gerolltes r, Zungen=r.

Trim, I. *adj.*, **—ly**, *adv.* ordnungsmäßig, geputzt, hübsch, nett. II. *s.* die Ausrüstung; (dress) der (Auf=)Putz, Staat; die Gleichgewichtslage (*of a ship*); die vorteilhafteste Lage, Stellung (*of sails, masts, etc.*); in sailing —, segelfertig. III. *v.a.* ordnen; besetzen, garnieren, ausputzen (*dresses, hats, etc.*); stutzen (*the beard, hair, etc.*); beschneiden (*hedges, etc.*); (an)schüren (*the fire*); zurecht machen (*a lamp*); stellen (*sails*); ins Gleichgewicht setzen (*Naut.*); — the boat! gerade das Boot! to — up, ausputzen. IV. *v.n.* die Mitte halten, es bald mit der einen, bald mit der andern Partei halten. **—mer**, *s.* der Wetterhahn (*fig.*); *see* Temporizer; (—mer up) der Staffierer. **—ming**, *s.* das Aufputzen; der Ausputz, Besatz, die Garnitur (*for hats, etc.*);

—mings, die Ausstaffierung; Besatzartikel für Damenkleider; —mings manufacturer, der Posamentier. **—ness**, *s.* die gute Ordnung, Nettigkeit, Niedlichkeit.

Trinket, *s.* die Schmucksache, das Geschmeide.

Trip, I. *s.* das Stolpern, Trippeln; der Fehltritt, Fehler (*fig.*); (excursion) kleine (Luft-)Reise, der Ausflug, Abstecher; (sea —) die kurze Seereise; to take a — to, einen Ausflug machen nach. II. *v.a.* (— up) (einem) ein Bein stellen; (catch) ertappen. III. *v.n.* straucheln, stolpern, ausgleiten; sich irren, fehlen (*fig.*); (move with short steps) trippeln, hüpfen; einen Ausflug, einen Abstecher machen; to catch a p. —ping, einen auf einem Fehler *or* Irrtum ertappen; to — along, dahintrippeln. **—per**, *s.* der Ausflügler (*fam.*). **—ping**, I. *adj.*, **—pingly**, *adv.* hüpfend, munter; (*adv.*) leichthin, frischweg. II. *s.* das Hüpfen; das Beinstellen (*Footb.*).

Tripe, *s.* das Gedärme, die Kaldaunen; die Flecke (*Cook.*).

Tripoli, *s.* die Trippelerde.

Trit—e, *adj.*, **—ely**, *adv.* abgedroschen, platt, gemein. **—eness**, *s.* die Abgenutztheit, Plattheit, das Gemeine. **—urable**, *adj.* zerreiblich. **—urate**, *v.a.* zerreiben. **—uration**, *s.* die Zerpulverung; die Zerreibung zu feinem Pulver.

Triumph, I. *s.* der Triumph, Siegeszug; die Siegesfreude; (victory) der Triumph, Sieg. II. *v.n.* den Sieg davon tragen, siegen; (exult) frohlocken, jubeln; to — over, überwinden, siegen, (exult) sich erheben über, triumphieren über (*acc.*); to cause justice to —, dem Rechte zum Siege verhelfen. **—al**, *adj.* Triumph-, Sieges-; —al arch, der Triumphbogen; —al car, der Siegeswagen; —al march, der Siegesmarsch. **—ant**, *adj.*, **—antly**, *adv.* triumphierend; siegreich.

Trivial, *adj.*, **—ly**, *adv.* (trifling) gering(fügig), unbedeutend; (common) gemein, alltäglich. **—ity**, *s.* die Geringfügigkeit, Unbedeutendheit.

Troch—aic, *adj.* trochäisch. **—e**, *s.* das Kügelchen. **—ee**, *s.* der Trochäus. **—ilus**, *s. see* Humming-bird; die Hohlkehle (*Arch.*).

Troglodyt—e, *s.* der Höhlenbewohner, Troglodyt. **—ic**, *adj.* Höhlenmenschen betreffend, troglodytisch.

[1]**Troll**, *s.* der Erdgeist, das Erdmännchen.

[2]**Troll**, *v.* I. *a.* rollen (lassen); die Runde machen lassen; (ein Lied) trällern, einen Rundgesang anstimmen; fischen. II. *n.* rollen, sich umdrehen, sich schnell bewegen; trällern; angeln. III. *s.* der Kreislauf, die Runde; der Rundgesang; die Rolle an der Angelrute. **—(e)y**, *s.* der Rollwagen, die Draisine; (coal, etc., —ey) der Förderkarren, der Hund (*Min.*); Metallrolle zur Zuführung des Stroms (*Electr.*). **—op**, I. *v.n.* schlampig herabhängen; schlampig, nachlässig gehen (*Scotch*). II. *s.* die Schlumpe, die Dirne.

Trombone, *s.* die Posaune.

Troop, I. *s.* der Trupp, Haufe, die Schar, Truppe; — of actors, die Schauspielergesellschaft; — of horse, der Trupp Reiter, die Reiter-schar, -kompagnie; —s (of the line, Linien-)Truppen. II. *v.n.* sich scharen, sich sammeln, in Scharen ziehen; to — away, off, sich davon machen; they — to their standard, sie scharen sich um ihre Fahne. III. *v.a.* in Truppen formieren; —ing the colours, die Fahnenparade. **—er**, *s.* der Kavallerist; der gemeine Soldat (*Mil.*); —er's horse, das Kavalleriepferd; to swear like a —er, fluchen wie ein Reitknecht. *Comp.* **—-ship**, *s.* das Truppen-Transportschiff.

Trop—e, *s.* die Trope, der bildliche Ausdruck (*Rhet.*). **—hy**, *see* Troph—. **—ic**, *s.* der Wendekreis (of Cancer, des Krebses, of Capricorn, des Steinbocks). **—ic(al)**, *adj.*, **—ically**, *adv.* tropisch, Wendekreis-; figürlich, bildlich (*Rhet.*); —ical heat, die Tropenhitze; —ical plants, tropische Pflanzen. **—ics**, *pl.* die Wendekreise, Tropen. **—ology**, *s.* bildliche Sprechweise.

Troph—ied, *adj.* mit Trophäen geschmückt. **—y**, *s.* die Trophäe (*also Arch.*), das Siegeszeichen.

Trot, I. *s.* der Trott, Trab; at a —, im Trabe. II. *v.n.* trotten, traben, Trab reiten; to — off, davonreiten. III. *v.a.* trotten lassen. **—ter**, *s.* der Trotter, Traber. *Comp.* **—ting-match**, *s.* das Trabrennen.

Troth, *s.* das Treuegelöbnis; die Verlobung; to plight one's —, sein Wort geben; sich verloben; by my —, bei meiner Treu'! auf mein Wort! **—-plight** *Comp.* (**to**), *adj.* verlobt (mit).

Troubadour, *s.* der Troubadour, Trobador.

Trouble, I. *v.a.* (disturb) stören, beunruhigen, belästigen; trüben (*waters*); (pain, grieve) betrüben, quälen, ängstigen, (einem) Kummer, Sorge, Verdruß bereiten; (inconvenience) (einem) Mühe machen; to — a p. for, einen bemühen, bitten um (*acc.*); don't — (yourself), bemühe dich nicht; to be —d in mind, sehr beunruhigt sein; he is —d with the gout, die Gicht nimmt ihn sehr mit, er wird von der Gicht geplagt. II. *s.* die Unruhe, Störung, Verwirrung; (vexation) der Kummer, Verdruß; (inconvenience, *etc.*) die Mühe, Beschwerde, Not; to take (the) —, sich (*dat.*) (die) Mühe geben; do not take the — to answer this, bemühe dich nicht, dies zu beantworten; to put s.o. to —, to give a p. —, einem Mühe machen; to bring — upon, Unheil über (einen) bringen; to be a — to a p., einem zur Last fallen. **—r**, *s.* der Störer, Unruhestifter. **—some**, *adj.*, **—somely**, *adv.* störend, unruhig; (importunate) beschwerlich, lästig; unbequem, unangenehm; (vexatious) verdrießlich, peinlich. **—someness**, *s.* (difficulty) die Mühsamkeit; die Lästigkeit, Beschwerlichkeit; die Verdrießlichkeit.

Troublous, *adj.* unruhig, beunruhigend; verworren.

Trough, *s.* der Trog, die Mulde; der Graben; das Gerinne (*of mills, etc.*); — of the sea, das Wellental.

Trounce, *v.a.* derb prügeln, durchwichsen (*sl.*).

Trouser—ings, *pl.* Hosenstoffe. **—s**, *pl.*; a pair of —s, ein Paar Beinkleider, die Hosen.

Trousseau, *s.* die Aussteuer, Ausstattung.

Trout, *s.* die Forelle. *Comp.* **—-fishing**, *s.* der Forellenfang. **—-stream**, *s.* der Forellenbach.

Trover, *s.*; action of —, die Klage auf Zurückgabe.

Trow, *v.n.* glauben, meinen (*obs., poet.*).

Trowel, *s.* die Mauerkelle; der Hohlspatel, die Gartenschaufel (*Hort.*).

Troy, *attrib.*; — weight, das Troy- (Gold-, Silber-, Juwelen- und Apotheker-)gewicht.

Truant, I. *adj.*, **—ly**, *adv.* müßiggängerisch, träge, faul; — children, schulschwänzende Kinder. II. *s.* der Schulschwänzer; to play (the) —, die Schule schwänzen, hinter die Schule gehen (*lit.*); das Geschäft versäumen.

Truce, *s.* der Waffenstillstand, die Ruhe; — of God, der Gottesfriede; a — to *or* with . . ., still von . . ., hör auf mit . . .! to make a — with, Waffenstillstand schließen mit.

[1]**Truck**, I. *v.n.* (*& a.* aus-, ver-)tauschen. II. *s.* (—age) der Tausch(handel). III. *attrib.*; — system, das Tauschwertsystem, die Auslöhnung der Arbeiter durch Waren. **—le**, *v.n.* sich unterwerfen, sklavische Unterwürfigkeit zeigen.

[2]**Truck**, *s.* das Blockrad; (— cart) der Handwagen; der Schleppwagen (*Mil.*); der, die Lori, der Lastwagen (*Railw.*). **—le**, *s.* das Laufrädchen, -röllchen. *Comp.* **—le-bed**, *s.* das Roll-, Schiebe-bett.

Truculen—ce, **—cy**, *s.* die Grausamkeit. **—t**, *adj.*, **—tly**, *adv.* wild, roh; (cruel) grausam; (destructive) zerstörend.

Trudge, *v.n.* zu Fuß wandern; to — along, schwerfällig gehen, sich mühsam fortschleppen.

Tru—e, *adj.* wahr(haft); (real) echt, wirklich; (honest) redlich, aufrichtig, treu; (trusty) zuverlässig; (straight, exact) regelrecht, genau, recht; gerade (*as a line*); (rightful) rechtmäßig;

—e to one's word *or* promise, seinem Worte, seinem Versprechen treu; —e copy, getreue, richtige Abschrift; —e friend, echter, treuer Freund; —e man, ehrlicher Mann; —e story, wahre Geschichte; —e strength, wirkliche Stärke; to prove —e, sich bewahrheiten; it is —e (that), zwar; —e bill, für begründet erklärte Anklage; —e to myself, mir selbst treu; to shoot —e, gut treffen. **—eness**, *s.* die Treue Aufrichtigkeit, Redlichkeit; (faithfulness) die Treue, Anhänglichkeit; die Echtheit, Wirklichkeit; die Richtigkeit. **—ism**, *s.* augenscheinliche, von selbst einleuchtende Wahrheit; *see* Platitude. **—ly**, *adv.* aufrichtig; offen; (really) wirklich, in der Tat; wahrhaft; yours —ly, der Ihrige, ergebenst (*at close of letters*). **—th**, *see* Truth. *Comp.* **—e-blue**, I. *adj.* wasch-echt; beständig, treu. II. *s.* ein Mann von Grundsätzen; ehrlicher Matrose. **—e-born**, *adj.* echt (von Geburt); —e-born gentleman, echter Gentleman. **—e-hearted**, *adj.* treuherzig, aufrichtig, ehrlich. **—e-heartedness**, *s.* die Treuherzigkeit, Redlichkeit. **—e-love**, *s.* das Lieb, Liebchen, der (die) Geliebte. **—e-lover's knot**, *s.* der Liebesknoten.

Truffle, *s.* die Trüffel.

[1]**Trump**, I. *s.* der Trumpf (*Cards*); guter, braver Kerl (*fig.*); all his cards are —s, er ist ein Glückspilz. II. *v.a.* abtrumpfen, (ab)stechen. III. *v.n.* Trumpf spielen, trumpfen.

[2]**Trump**, *v.a.*; to — up, erdichten, schmieden, zusammenraffen. **—ery**, I. *s.* die Lumperei, der Trödelkram. II. *adj.* wertlos, Lumpen-.

[3]**Trump**, *s.* die Trompete. **—et**, I. *s.* die Trompete; die Posaune (*B.*); to blow one's own —et, sich selbst loben. II. *v.a. & n.* trompeten; (—et forth) ausposaunen, laut verkünden; the crane (elephant) —ets, der Kranich (Elefant) trompetet. **—eter**, *s.* der Trompeter; der Ausposauner (*fig.*); (pigeon) die Trommeltaube. *Comp.* **—et-call**, *s.* der Trompetenruf. **—et-clangour**, *s.* der Trompetenklang. **—et-tongued**, *adj.* mit Posaunenstimme.

Truncat—e, I. *v.a.* verstümmeln, stutzen. II. *adj.* gestutzt. **—ion**, *s.* die Stutzung, Verstümmelung.

Truncheon, I. *s.* der Knüttel; (baton) der Feldherrnstab. II. *v.a.* durchprügeln.

Trundle, I. *v.a.* rollen, wälzen; schlagen (*a hoop*). II. *s.* die Rolle, das kleine Rad. *Comp.* **—bed**, *s.* das Rollbett.

Trunk, *s.* der (Baum-)Stamm; der Rumpf (*of men, etc.*); der Rüssel (*of the elephant*); (travelling —) der große Koffer, die Kiste; der Schaft (*of a column*). *Comp.* **—fish**, *s.* der Kofferfisch. **—hose**, *s.* die Pumphosen. **—line**, *s.* die Haupt-, Stamm-linie (*Railw.*). **—maker**, *s.* der Koffermacher.

Trunnion, *s.* der Zapfen; der Schildzapfen (*Mil.*). *Comp.* **—hole**, *s.* das Schildzapfenlager. **—plate**, *s.* die Schildzapfenpfanne.

Truss, I. *s.* das Bund; das Bruchband (*Surg.*); das Racktau (*Naut.*); das Hängewerk (*Build.*); — of hay (straw), ein Gebund Heu, (Bund Stroh). II. *v.a.* packen; (auf)zäumen, zum Braten zurechtmachen *or* dressieren (*a fowl*); to — up, aufschürzen, -binden, -schlagen; to — a roof, ein Hängewerk anlegen, aufrichten. *Comp.* **—frame**, *s.* das Hänge-, Spreng-werk; —frame bridge, die Sprengwerkbrücke. **—post**, *s.* die Hängesäule.

Trust, I. *s.* das Vertrauen; (faith) der Glaube; der (Unternehmer-)Ring, Trust (*C. L.*); (credit) der Kredit, Borg; (something entrusted) das Anvertraute, Pfand; das Depositum, anvertraute Gut (*Law*); (care, charge) die Verwahrung, Obhut; breach of —, der Treubruch, Mißbrauch des Vertrauens; place of —, der Vertrauensposten; on —, auf Kredit; to put great — in, großes Vertrauen auf (einen) setzen; there is no — to be placed in . . ., man kann sich nicht auf . . . verlassen; to hold in — for, in Verwaltung haben, verwalten für. II. *attrib.*: — funds, funds on —, — money, anvertrautes Geld; Stiftungsgelder, Mündelgelder. III. *v.a.* (ver)trauen; glauben; anvertrauen; to — a p. with, einem (etwas) anvertrauen, in Verwahrung geben, einen mit etwas betrauen; I don't — him, ich traue ihm nicht; he cannot be —ed, man darf ihm nicht trauen, kann sich nicht auf ihn verlassen; he cannot be —ed with so large a sum, man darf ihm eine so große Summe nicht anvertrauen. IV. *v.n.* vertrauen, sein Vertrauen setzen, sich verlassen (in, to, on, auf einen); (hope) hoffen, zuversichtlich erwarten; we — that the gloves will give satisfaction, wir geben uns der Hoffnung hin, daß die Handschuhe Ihren Beifall finden werden; to know what one has to — to, wissen, was man zu erwarten hat; — me for that! verlaß dich nur auf mich! to — in God, sein Vertrauen auf Gott setzen. **—ee**, *s.* der Vertrauensmann, Bevollmächtigte (*Law*); der Verwahrer; der Verwalter (*of public or of other people's money*); board of —ees, das Kuratorium. **—eeship**, *s.* die Bevollmächtigung, Sachwalterschaft. **—ful**, *adj.*, **—fully**, *adv.* vertrauensvoll. **—fulness**, *s.* das Vertrauensvolle. **—ily**, *adv.*, **—y**, *adj.* treu, zuverlässig, getreu, sicher. **—iness**, *s.* die Treue, Redlichkeit, die Zuverlässigkeit. **—ing**, *adj.*, **—ingly**, *adv.* vertrauensvoll. *Comp.* **—worthiness**, *s.* die Zuverlässigkeit, Vertrauenswürdigkeit. **—worthy**, *adj.* zuverlässig, vertrauenswürdig.

Truth, *s.* die Wahrheit; (reality) die Wirklichkeit; (veracity) die Wahrhaftigkeit; (honesty) die Ehrlichkeit, Redlichkeit; die Richtigkeit; in —, of a —, in Wahrheit, wahrhaftig; there is no — in it, daran ist nichts Wahres *or* kein wahres Wort. **—ful**, *adj.*, **—fully**, *adv.* wahrhaft(ig). **—fulness**, *s.* die Wahrhaftigkeit. *Comp.* **—loving**, *adj.* wahrheitsliebend.

Try, I. *ir.v.a.* versuchen, probieren, erproben, auf die Probe stellen; berichtigen (*weights, etc.*); probieren, reinigen (*metals*); untersuchen, verhören, vor Gericht stellen (*Law*); angreifen, anstrengen (*the eyes*); to — conclusions, Versuche machen, es versuchen (with, mit; on, an (*dat.*)); sich messen (mit); to be tried on a charge, infolge einer Anklage vor Gericht gestellt werden; to — on, an-probieren, -passen (*a coat, etc.*), versuchen: to — one's luck, sein Glück versuchen; to — by . . ., erproben, messen an (*dat.*). II. *ir.v.n.* versuchen; sich bemühen (for, um), trachten (for, nach). III. *s.* der Versuch (*coll. & Footb.*). **—ing**, *adj.* bedenklich, schwierig; mißlich, peinlich; —ing position, bedenkliche Lage. *Comp.* **—sail**, *s.* das Schnausegel.

Tryst, *s.* verabredete Zusammenkunft, das Stelldichein. *Comp.* **—ing-place**, *s.* der Zusammenkunftsort, Ort des Stelldicheins.

Tsar, *s.* der Zar. **—evitch**, *m.* der Zarewitsch. **—ina**, *s.* die Zarin(a), Zaritza.

T-square, *s.* der Anschlagwinkel, die Reißschiene.

Tub, I. *s.* der Zuber, Kübel, die Bütte, das Faß; (bath) die Badewanne; der Kübel (*for plants*); das Übungsboot (*Rowing*). II. *v.a.* in Kübel setzen (*plants*); baden (*children*); im Übungsboot rudern lassen, im Rudern unterrichten. **—by**, *adj.* faßartig, tonnenförmig.

Tub—e, *s.* die Röhre (*also Bot. & Anat.*), das Rohr; der Vorstoß (*of a retort, etc.*); india-rubber —e, der Gummischlauch; speaking —e, Sprachrohr; *see* Two-penny —e. **—ing**, *s.* das Material zu Röhren; (—es) das Röhrenwerk. **—iporite**, *s.* fossile Röhrenkoralle. **—ular**, *adj.* röhrenförmig, Röhren-; —ular bridge, die Röhrenbrücke. **—ulated**, *adj.* tubuliert (*Chem.*).

Tuber, *s.* der Knollen, die Knolle. **—cle**, *s.* (pimple) der Knoten, das (Eiter-)Bläschen; kleine, harte Geschwulst; die (Lungen-)Tuberkel (*on the lungs*); die Knolle, Warze (*Bot.*). **—cular**, *adj.* warzig, höckerig, knotig; Tuberkel-, tuberkulös. **—culine**, *s.* das Tuberkulin, Mittel gegen die Lungensucht. **—culization**, *s.* die

(Lungen=)Knoten=Bildung. **—culosis**, *s.* die Lungensucht; bovine —culosis, die Rinderlungenseuche. **—ose**, *s.* die Tuberose. **—osity**, *s.* das Knotige, Höckerige. **—ous**, *adj.* knotig, knollig.

Tuck, I. *s.* die (Quer=)Falte (*in dresses, etc.*). II. *v.a.* einschlagen, Falten nähen in (*acc.*); to — **in**, einschlagen (*cloth, etc.*); to — **up**, auf=schürzen, =schlagen; to — up one's sleeves, sich (*dat.*) die Ärmel aufstreifen; to — **a p. up in bed**, einen gut in Bettdecken einwickeln. III. *v.n.* sich zusammenziehen, einschrumpfen; to — in, schmausen (*vulg.*). **—er**, *s.* der Brust=, Hals=streifen. *Comp.* **—-shop**, *s.* der Konditorladen (*sl.*).

Tuesday, *s.* der Dienstag.

Tuf—f (Tufa), *s.* der Tuff(stein). **—aceous**, *adj.* tuff(artig).

Tuft, *s.* der Busch, Büschel; — of hair, der Haarbüschel, Haarschopf. *Comp.* **—ed-lark**, *s.* die Haubenlerche. **—-hunter**, *s.* einer, der den Adeligen und Vornehmen nachläuft, der Schmarotzer, Speichellecker.

Tug, I. *s.* der Zug, das Zerren; die Anstrengung, Mühe (*fig.*); das Schleppboot (*Naut.*); the — of war, der heftigste Kampf, das Heldenringen um den Preis; das Seilziehen (*Gymn.*); I had a hard — of it, das hat mir viele Mühe gekostet. II. *v.a.* ziehen, schleppen, zerren; zausen (*one's hair, etc.*). III. *v.n.* stark, heftig ziehen; sich anstrengen (*fig.*).

Tuition, *s.* der Unterricht; die Anleitung; die Aufsicht, Obhut (*fig.*); private —, der Privatunterricht, die Privatstunden; (fee for —) das Unterrichtshonorar; she is under my —, ich erteile ihr Unterricht, sie ist meine Schülerin. *Comp.* **—-fee**, *s.* das Privatstundengeld.

Tulip, *s.* die Tulpe. *Comp.* **—-root**, *s.* die Tulpenzwiebel. **—-tree**, *s.* der Tulpenbaum.

Tulle, *s.* der Tüll.

Tulwar, *s.* indischer Säbel.

Tumb—le, I. *v.n.* fallen, stürzen, ein=, nieder=fallen; (roll, —le about) rollen, sich wälzen; springen, gaukeln (*as mountebanks*); to —le down, einstürzen; (roll down) herabrollen; to —le to pieces, in Stücke fallen; to —le out of bed, aus dem Bette heraus=fallen, =plumpsen (*in the morning*). II. *v.a.* (—le down) zu Fall bringen, (um)stürzen; (rumple) in Unordnung bringen, zerknittern, zerkrümpeln; to —le out, hinauswerfen. III. *s.* der Sturz, Fall; (somersault) der Purzelbaum. **—ler**, *s.* der Springer, Gaukler; (glass) das Trinkglas, Wasserglas; das Stehaufglas; der Clown; die Tummlertaube (*Orn.*); die Nuß (*on guns*); die Zuhaltung (*of locks*). **—rel**, *s.* der Schutt=, Stürz=karren; der Munitionskarren (*Artil.*). *Comp.* **—le-down**, *adj.* baufällig, einfallend. **—lerful**, *s.* das Wasserglas voll.

Tum—efaction, *s.* das Aufschwellen; (—our) die Geschwulst. **—efy**, *v.a. & n.* (auf)schwellen. **—id**, *adj.*, **—idly**, *adv.* geschwollen, schwellend; schwülstig (*fig.*). **—idity**, **—idness**, *s.* die Geschwollenheit; die Schwülstigkeit. **—o(u)r**, *s.* die Schwellung; die Geschwulst. **—ular**, *adj.* hügelförmig. **—ult**, *s.* der Lärm, das Getöse, Getümmel; (uproar) der Auflauf, Aufruhr. **—ultuous**, *adj.*, **—ultuously**, *adv.* lärmend, tobend, ungestüm, aufrührerisch. **—ultuousness**, *s.* das lärmende Wesen, Treiben; *see* Turbulence. **—ulus**, *s.* der Grabhügel.

Tun, *s.* die Tonne, das (Stück=)Faß; die Tonne (= 252 Gallonen Wein); *see* Ton. **—nel**, I. *s.* der Trichter; der Tunnel (*Build.*). II. *v.a.* einen Tunnel führen durch, durchtunneln. **—nelling**, *s.* der Tunnelbau.

Tun—able, *adj.* stimmbar; wohlklingend. **—e**, I. *s.* die Singweise, Weise, Melodie, das Tonstück; (richtige) Stimmung (*of a piano, etc., also fig.*); **in —e**, gestimmt (*lit.*); bei Stimmung, bei Laune, aufgelegt; out of —e, verstimmt, nicht bei Laune; to play out of —e, falsch, unrein spielen (*Mus.*); to change one's —e, aus einem andern Tone reden. II. *v.a.* stimmen; (—e up) stimmen, vorbereiten (*coll.*); to be —ed to the same pitch, zusammenstimmen. III. *v.n.* ein Lied singen; to —e up, zu singen anfangen, anstimmen (*sl.*). **—eful**, *adj.*, **—efully**, *adv.* sangreich; (melodious) wohlklingend, melodisch. **—efulness**, *s.* das Melodische, der süße Klang, Wohlklang. **—eless**, *adj.* unmelodisch; (silent) stumm. **—er**, *s.* der (Klavier=)Stimmer. *Comp.* **—ing-fork**, *s.* die Stimmgabel.

Tungst—ate, *s.* wolframsaures, schelsaures Salz. **—en**, *s.* der Wolfram, Schel.

Tunic, *s.* die Tunika; der Waffenrock; der Arbeitsrock (*Mil.*); die Haut, das Häutchen (*Anat., Bot.*).

Tunny, *s.* der Thunfisch.

Tup, I. *s.* der Widder. II. *v.a.* bespringen.

Turban, *s.* der Turban (*also for women*); das Gewinde (*of shells*). **—ed**, *adj.* beturbant.

Turbary, *s.* der Torfgrund; das Recht, auf eines andern Mannes Land Torf zu stechen.

Turb—id, *adj.* trüb, dick, hefig; verworren (*fig.*). **—idness**, *s.* das Trübe, Dicke. **—ulence**, **—ulency**, *s.* die Unruhe, Verwirrung, das Ungestüm. **—ulent**, *adj.*, **—ulently**, *adv.* unruhig, stürmisch, ungestüm.

Turbine. *s.* (— wheel) das Kreiselrad, die Turbine. *Comp.* **—-steamer**, der Turbinendampfer.

Turbot, *s.* der Steinbutt.

Turd, *s.* der Dreck, Menschenkot (*vulg.*).

Tureen, *s.* die tiefe Suppenschüssel, Terrine.

Turf, I. *s.* der Rasen; (peat) der (Brenn=)Torf; a —, ein Stück Torf; the —, das Pferderennen; (gentlemen of the —) Freunde der Wettrennen. II. *v.a.* mit Rasen belegen. **—iness**, *s.* der Rasenreichtum; das Torfartige. **—y**, *adj.* rasenreich; (—like) torfartig.

Turg—ent, *see* —id. **—escence**, *s.* die Aufgedunsenheit; die Schwulst, der Bombast (*fig.*). **—escent**, *adj.* schwellend, geschwollen. **—id**, *adj.*, **—idly**, *adv.* geschwollen; (bloated) aufgedunsen; schwülstig, aufgeblasen (*fig.*). **—idity**, **—idness**, *see* —escence.

Turkey, *s.* (—-cock) der Truthahn; (—-hen) die Truthenne; the — gobbles, der Truthahn kollert.

Turmoil, *s.* die Plackerei; (tumult) der Aufruhr.

Turn, I. *v.a.* drehen (*a wheel, etc.*); (direct) richten; (change the position of) drehen, wenden, kehren, richten; wenden, richten (*one's thoughts, etc.*); (change) (ver)ändern, ver=, um=wandeln (into, in); (divert) abwenden, abbringen (from, von); (guide) leiten, lenken; wenden (*a dress, etc.*); stumpf machen (*the edge of a tool, etc.*); gerinnen, sauer machen (*milk, etc.*); übersetzen, übertragen (*into English, etc.*); (shape) formen, bilden; drechseln (*on a lathe*); runden (*a sentence*); schwindlig machen, berauschen, verwirren (*the head*); her brain is —ed, sie ist verrückt; to — one's coat, abtrünnig werden (*coll.*); to — a corner, um eine Ecke biegen; to — the enemy's flanks, den Feind umgehen; he —ed his head and there . . ., er sah sich um und da . . .; to — the key (*in a door, etc.*), den Schlüssel drehen, auf= *or* zu=schließen; to — loose, fahren lassen, loslassen; to — an honest penny, ein Stückchen Geld redlich verdienen; to — the scale, (der Wagschale) den Ausschlag geben; to — s.o.'s stomach, Übelkeit erregen; to — tail, davonlaufen; to — upside down, das Oberste zu unterst kehren; to — (the) wrong side out, die unrichtige Seite nach außen kehren; to — **about**, umdrehen; to — **adrift**, fortjagen, dem Winde und den Wellen preisgeben; to — s.o. **against**, einen gegen (einen andern *or* etwas) verstimmen, aufbringen; to — **aside**, abwenden; to — **away**, weg=, ab=wenden (*also wrath, evil, etc.*); (send away) weg=, fort=schicken; to — **back**, zurück=schicken, =weisen; to — **down**, einschlagen (*a page of a book*); herunterschrauben, klein stellen (*the gas*); to — down a bed, die Bettdecke zurückschlagen; to — **from**, abwenden von; to — the thoughts from . . . to . . ., die Gedanken von . . . auf (*acc.*) . . . richten; to — **in**, einschlagen (*also Sew.*); einwärts wenden, einbiegen; to — **into**, (verse, in Verse) verwandeln; (money, zu Geld) machen, versilbern; (ridicule, lächerlich) machen; to — night into day, die Nacht zum Tage umwandeln; to — **off**, ab-, um-leiten (*lit.*); ab-lenken, -ziehen, -leiten, -wenden (*fig.*); (send away) fort-schicken, -jagen, verabschieden; umgehen (*a question*); to — the water off (on), den Zufluß des Wassers abschneiden (andrehen), den Hahn zudrehen, absperren (andrehen, öffnen); to — a th. off with a laugh, über eine Sache mit einem Scherz hinweggehen; to be —ed off, seines Dienstes entlassen, abgesetzt werden; to — **out**, auswärts wenden *or* drehen, herauskehren; (send away) hinaustreiben, fortjagen; (produce) hervorbringen, herauskommen lassen; (send out) hinaustreiben, auf die Weide tun (*cattle*); to — out a room, ein Zimmer gründlich reinmachen; to — out into the world, in die weite Welt schicken; — him out! werft ihn zur Türe hinaus! to — out one's toes, die Füße nach außen *or* auswärts setzen; to — **over**, um-wenden, -schlagen (*a page, etc.*); über-tragen, -geben (*fig.*); (overturn) umkehren, -werfen, -stürzen; please, — over (*abbr.* P. T. O.), bitte umzuwenden! to — over articles (*in a shop, etc.*), Gegenstände besichtigen; to — over a new leaf, ein neues Blatt aufschlagen; ein neues Leben anfangen, sich bessern (*fig.*); he was —ed over to . . ., er wurde an . . . verwiesen; in his business he —s over £500 a week, er setzt wöchentlich £500 in seinem Geschäfte um; to — **round**, herumdrehen; to — **to**, richten (*one's attention*); to — to good (account), vorteilhaft verwenden, Nutzen ziehen aus; to — **towards**, richten nach; to — **up**, umwenden, umschlagen (*a card*); aufschlagen (*the eyes*); aufdrehen (*gas, etc.*); aufschlagen (*one's sleeves, the brim of a hat*); aufheben (*a dress*); zusammenschlagen (*chairs, etc.*); to — up one's nose at a th., über eine S. die Nase rümpfen; to — the tables **upon**, (einem) Gleiches mit Gleichem vergelten; to — one's back upon, einem den Rücken kehren. II. *v.n.* sich drehen, sich wenden; (— round) sich um-drehen, -wenden, -kehren; sich herumwenden (*in bed, etc.*); (change) sich (ver)ändern, sich verwandeln; gerinnen, sauer werden (*as milk*); I know not where to —, ich weiß nicht, wohin ich mich wenden soll; to be —ed fifty, über fünfzig Jahre alt sein; to — bankrupt, Bankrott machen; to — Christian, Christ werden; to — gray, grau werden; to — homewards, nach Hause zurückkehren; to — soldier, Soldat werden; to — sour, sauer werden; the tide has —ed, die Flut ist umgeschlagen (*lit.*); das Blatt hat sich gewendet (*fig.*); to — **about**, sich um-wenden, -kehren, sich herumdrehen; to — **away**, sich wegwenden; to — away from, verlassen; to — **back**, zurückgehen, -kehren, umkehren; (— backwards) sich zurückwenden; (give up) etwas Begonnenes wieder aufgeben (*fig.*); to — **down** (the road), umbiegen; to — **from**, sich wenden von; to — **in**, sich einwärts kehren, sich einbiegen; (go in) einkehren, hineingehen; (go to bed) zu Bett gehen (*fam.*); to — **into**, sich verwandeln in (*acc.*), werden zu; to — **off**, ablenken, abgehen, sich seitwärts wenden *or* schlagen; to — **on**, sich drehen um, (depend) abhängen von (*fig.*); to — **out**, sich heraus-drehen, -wenden, -kehren; (strike work) die Arbeit einstellen; (appear) hervortreten; (end) ausfallen, enden; (happen) sich ereignen; (get up) aufstehen (of bed, in the morning, vom Bette, des Morgens) (*fam.*); ausrücken (*Mil.*); to — out well, gut ausschlagen *or* ausfallen; — out guard! Wache heraus! it —ed out to be a wreck, es stellte sich heraus, daß es ein Wrack war, es erwies sich als ein Wrack; to — **over**, sich (her-)umwenden; to — **round**, sich herum-drehen, -wenden; my head —s round, der Kopf schwindelt mir; to — **to**, sich wenden nach, zu; sich verwandeln in; (have recourse to) seine Zuflucht nehmen zu; to — to oil, zu Öl werden; — to the left! links wenden! the road —s to the right, die Straße biegt rechts ab; to — **up**, sich aufwärts drehen, wenden; (stick up) sich aufrichten; (appear) sich zeigen, zum Vorschein kommen; he has —ed up at last, endlich ist er gekommen; to — **upon**, sich wenden auf (*acc.*), *see* — on; sich wenden gegen, (einen) anfallen; the conversation —ed upon, das Gespräch kam auf (*acc.*); to — upon one's heel, sich auf den Absätzen herumdrehen. III. *s.* das (Um-)Drehen, die (Um-)Drehung, der Umschwung; (direction) die Wendung, Richtung, der Lauf, Weg; (taste, tendency) herrschende Richtung, Neigung, der Hang; (place of —ing) die Wendung; (bend) die Krümme, Krümmung; (change) der Wechsel, die Veränderung; (short walk) der Gang; (form) die Form, Gestalt, Bildung; (manner) die Art, Beschaffenheit; (order) die Reihe(nfolge); (service) der Dienst; die ganze Umdrehung (*of a wheel*); der Schwung (*of a period*); at every —, alle Augenblicke; by —s, in —, der Reihe nach, abwechselnd, umschichtig; it is (now) my —, ich bin an der Reihe; when it comes to my —, wenn die Reihe an mich kommt, wenn ich daran *or* an die Reihe komme; to take one's —, etwas tun wenn die Reihe einen trifft; to take —s (at), mit einander abwechseln; to a —, aufs Haar; to have a — for books, politics, eine Vorliebe für Bücher haben, Neigung zur Politik; her virtues are of a domestic —, ihre Tugenden haben eine häusliche Richtung; he took two or three —s up and down the room, er ging zwei-, dreimal im Zimmer auf und ab; let us take a — round the garden, laßt uns die Runde durch den Garten machen, im Garten herumgehen; a friendly —, ein Freundschaftsdienst; to do a p. a good —, einem einen Dienst *or* eine Gefälligkeit erweisen; one good — deserves another, eine Liebe ist der andern wert (*prov.*); he will serve my —, er wird meinen Zwecken dienen; to give a certain — to, (einer Sache) eine gewisse Wendung geben; the affair took an unexpected —, die Sache nahm eine unerwartete Wendung; — of mind, die Denkart; — of the scale, der Ausschlag. **—er**, *s.* der Drechsler (*of wood, etc.*). **—ery**, *s.* die Drechslerarbeit. **—ing**, *s.* das Drehen, Drechseln; (bend) die Krümmung, Windung; die Abweichung (*from the path of duty, etc.*); —ing movement, die Umgehung (*Mil.*); 't is a long lane that has no —ing, das größte Unglück dauert nicht ewig (*prov.*); take the next —(ing) to the left, biege in die nächste Querstraße links. *Comp.* **—coat**, *s.* der Abtrünnige, Achselträger, Überläufer, Renegat. **—(ed)-down**, *adj.*; —-down collar, der Klappkragen. **—ed-up**, *adj.*; —-up nose, die Stülpnase. **—ing-lathe**, *s.* die Dreh-, Drechsel-bank. **—ing-point**, *s.* der Entscheidungs-, Wendepunkt. **—(ing)-table**, *s.* die Drehscheibe. **—key**, *s.* der Schließer, Gefangenwärter. **—-out**, *s.* die äußere Erscheinung; der Putz; die Schaustellung; der Aufzug; die Equipage (*vulg.*); *see* Strike; die Gesammtproduktion (*C. L.*); die Ausweichestelle (*Rail.*). **—over**, *s.* halbrundes Törtchen; der Umsatz (*C. L.*). **—pike**, *s.* der Schlag-, Chaussee-baum. **—pike-man** *or* **-keeper**, *s.* der Chausseegeldeinnehmer. **—pike-road**, *s.* die Kunststraße, Chaussee. **—spit**, *s.* der Bratenwender. **—stile**, *s.* das Drehkreuz (auf Fußwegen), der Drehzähler.

Turnip, *s.* die Rübe. *Comp.* **—-cabbage**, *s.* der Kohlrabi. **—-cutter**, *s.* die Rübenschneidemaschine. **—-radish**, *s.* der Rüben-Rettig. **—-tops**, *pl.* das Kraut der Rübe.

Turpentine, *s.* der Terpentin.

Turpitude, *s.* die Verworfenheit, moralische Schlechtigkeit, Schändlichkeit.

Turquoise, *s.* der Türkis.
Turret, *s.* das Türmchen; das Belagerungstürmchen (*Mil.*); der Ventilationsaufsatz (*Railw.*, *etc.*). **—ed**, *adj.* betürmt.
[1]**Turtle**, *s.* die (Meer=)Schildkröte. *Comp.* **—-soup**, *s.* die Schildkrötensuppe.
[2]**Turtle, —dove**, *s.* die Turteltaube.
Tush, *int.* pah!
Tusk, *s.* der Fang=, Hau=zahn; der Hakenzahn (*of horses*); der Hauer, das Gewehr (*of a wild boar*); der Stoßzahn (*of an elephant*); der Zahn (*fig.*). **—ed**, *adj.* mit Fangzähnen.
Tussle, I. *s.* der Kampf, die Balgerei. II. *v.n.* kämpfen, ringen.
Tut, *int.* pfui! fort! weg damit!
Tut—elage, *s.* die Unmündigkeit, der Mündelstand; (guardianship) die Vormundschaft; die Leitung (*fig.*). **—elary**, *adj.* schützend, Schutz=; —elary deity, der Schutzgott. **—or**, I. *s.* der Vormund; (teacher) der Lehrer, Privatlehrer; private —or, Privatlehrer (für einzelne Fächer); Hauslehrer, Erzieher; college —or, der Tutor, Berater eines Studenten in seinem College=Repetent (*Oxf.*, *Cambr.*). II. *v.a.* (be)lehren; erziehen (*also fig.*, *one's heart*, *etc.*). **—orage**, *s.* die Aufsicht; das Wächteramt, die Hofmeisterstelle; die Vormundschaft (*Law*). **—orial**, *adj.* Vormunds=; Lehrer=. **—orship**, *s.* die Hauslehrerstelle; die Repetentenstelle.
Twaddle, I. *s.* albernes Geschwätz. II. *v.n.* schwatzen. **—r**, *s.* alberner Schwätzer.
Twain, *s.* zwei; das Paar (*obs. & poet.*); in —, entzwei.
Twang, I. *s.* gellender, scharfer Ton, das Schwirren; das Näseln, die näselnde Aussprache (*in speaking*); to speak with a —, durch die Nase reden. II. *v.n.* (*& a.*) schwirren (lassen).
Tweak, *v.a.* zwicken.
Tweed, *s.*, **—s**, *pl.* eine Art Halbtuch.
Tweezers, *pl.* (pair of —) das (Haar=)Zängelchen.
Twel—fth, I. *adj.* zwölft. II. *s.* der, die, das Zwölfte; (—fth part) das Zwölftel. **—ve**, I. *num. adj.* zwölf; —ve score, zwölfmal zwanzig. II. *s.* die Zwölf; das Duodez (*Typ.*). *Comp.* **—fth-night**, *s.* der Dreikönigsabend. II. *attrib.*; the —fth-night cake, der Dreikönigskuchen. **—vemonth(s)**, *s.*; this day —vemonth(s), heute über ein Jahr.
Twent—ieth, I. *adj.* zwanzigst. II. *s.* der, die, das Zwanzigste; (—ieth part) das Zwanzigstel. **—y**, I. *num. adj.* zwanzig. II. *s.* die Zwanzig.
Twice, *adv.* zweimal; doppelt; — the amount, der doppelte Betrag, noch einmal so viel; — told, zweimal erzählt; doppelt gezählt.
Twiddle, *v.a.*; to — one's thumbs, mit den Daumen spinnen; die Hände in den Schoß legen (*fig.*).
Twifallow, *v.a.* zum zweiten Male pflügen.
[1]**Twig**, *s.* der Zweig, die Rute; die Wünschelrute, der Zauberstab; to work the —, die Wünschelrute gebrauchen.
[2]**Twig**, *v.a.* verstehen, begreifen; aufpassen auf (*acc.*); begreifen, einsehen (*coll.*).
[3]**Twig**, *v.a.* zwicken, zupfen, ziehen (*obs. dial.*).
Twilight, I. *s.* das Zwielicht. II. *adj.* im Zwielicht gesehen, getan &c.; dämmernd, dunkel.
Twill, I. *s.* der Köper, das geköperte Zeug. II. *v.a.* köpern. **—ed**, *adj.* geköpert, Köper=.
Twin, *s.* der Zwilling. II. *adj.* Zwillings=; doppelt, gepaart (*Bot.*, *etc.*); — brother, der Zwillings=bruder. **—ling**, *s.* das Zwillingslamm. *Comp.* **—-screw**, *s.* die Doppelschraube; —-screw steamer, der Doppelschraubendampfer.
Twin—e, I. *s.* der Bindfaden, die Kordel; die Schnur, das Garn, der Zwirn; (—ing) die Windung. II. *v.a.* zwirnen (*threads*, *etc.*); (—e together) flechten, zusammenschlingen; (—e about) umwinden. III. *v.n.* einander umschlingen, sich verflechten; *see* Wind; to —e about, sich herumwinden. **—ing**, I. *adj.* sich windend (*Bot.*). II. *s.* das Zwirnen (*Manuf.*). *Comp.* **—ing-machine**, *s.* die Zwirnmaschine.
Twinge, I. *s.* der Stich, Zwick, stechende Schmerz, das Stechen; —s of conscience, Gewissensbisse. II. *v.a. & n.* stechen.
Twinkl—e, I. *v.n.* blinzeln (*of the eyes*); flimmern, funkeln (*also fig.*), blitzen (*as stars*). II. *s.* das Blinzeln, Zwinkern; a merry —e, ein lustiges Zwinkern (mit den Augen). **—ing**, *s. see* —e II.; in the —ing of an eye, im Nu, in einem Nu, im Augenblick.
Twirl, I. *s.* schnelle Umdrehung, der Wirbel. II. *v.a.* herumdrehen. III. *v.n.* sich schnell umdrehen. *Comp.* **—ing-stick**, *s.* der Quirl.
Twist, I. *v.a.* (zusammen)drehen, (ver)flechten; winden (*the body*); spinnen (*tobacco*, *oakum*); flechten (*the hair*); zwirnen (*thread*, *silk*, *etc.*); verdrehen (*a passage in an author*, *etc.*); to — about, umdrehen; —ed barrel, der gezogene Lauf, der Damast (*of a gun*); to — round one's finger, um den Finger wickeln (*fig.*). II. *v.n.* sich drehen. III. *s.* die Drehung, Windung, Verflechtung; der Twist, das Maschinengarn (*Spin.*); die Flechte (*of hair*, *etc.*); *see* Twine; kleine Rolle (*of tobacco*); silk —, die Maschinenseide; it has got a —, es ist schief, krumm (geworden); he has got a — in his character, er hat etwas Schiefes in seinem Wesen. **—ing**, *s.* das Drehen. *Comp.* **—ing-machine**, *s.* die Drehmaschine.
Twit, *v.a.*; to — s.o. with, einem (etwas) vorwerfen. **—tingly**, *adv.* vorwurfsweise.
Twitch, I. *v.a.* zwicken, zupfen. II. *v.n.* zucken (*Med.*). III. *s.* schneller Ruck, das Zupfen; das nervöse Zucken; die Zuckung (*Med.*).
Twitter, I. *s.* das Gezwitscher; das (leichte Nerven=)Zittern; das Beben (*fam.*); in a —, in Furcht, Angst, Schreck. II. *v.n.* zwitschern; (tremble) zittern. **—ing**, I. *adj.* zwitschernd. II. *s.* das Gezwitscher.
Two, I. *num. adj.* zwei; in a day or —, in ein paar Tagen; — and —, paarweise; a marble statue or —, einige Marmorbildsäulen. II. *s.* die Zwei; the —, die beiden; they came out in —s and threes, sie kamen zu zweien und dreien heraus. *Comp.* **—-decker**, *s.* der Zweidecker. **—-edged**, *adj.* zweischneidig. **—-faced**, *adj.* falsch, doppelzüngig. **—fold**, *adj.* zweifach; zweifältig (*B.*); doppelt. **—-handed**, *adj.* zweihändig. **—-headed**, *adj.* zweiköpfig. **—-legged**, *adj.* zweibeinig. **—penny**, *adj.* zwei Pence kostend; gering (*fig.*); —penny tube, die unterirdische elektrische Londoner Stadtbahn (*sl.*). **—-ply**, *adj.* zweischäftig (*of ropes*); —-ply carpet, doppelter Teppich. **—-pronged**, *adj.* zweizinkig. **—-wheeled**, *adj.* zweirädrig.
Tymbal, *s.* die Kesselpauke.
Tympan, *s.* der Preßdeckel (*Print.*); *see* —um. **—um**, *s.* das Trommelfell (*Anat.*); die Trommel (*Anat.*); das Stirn=, Bogen=giebelfeld (*Arch.*); —um of a door, das Türbogenfeld. **—y**, **—ites**, *s.* die Trommelsucht.
Typ—e, I. *s.* das Urbild, der Typus; (figure of something to come) das Vorbild; (emblem) das Sinnbild; (sign) das Zeichen; die Grundform, der Typus (*Nat. Hist.*); (image, copy) der Abdruck, die Abbildung; der Charakter, Typus (*Med.*); die Type, Letter; (the —es) die Schrift, Lettern; in —e, gesetzt; spaced —e, gesperrter Druck; German —e, die Fraktur; Roman —e, die Antiqua; Italic —e, der Kursivdruck. II. *v.a. & n. see* —e-write. **—ical**, *adj.*, **—ically**, *adv.* (vor)bildlich; typisch, exemplarisch (*as a case*); to be —ical of, das Ur=, Vor=, Muster=bild einer Sache sein; this is a —ical case, dieser Fall ist typisch, stellt eine Gattung dar (*Med.*, *etc.*). **—ify**, *v.a.* bildlich darstellen, vorbilden. **—ographer**, *s.* der Buchdrucker. **—ographic(al)**, *adj.*, **—ographically**, *adv.* buchdruckerisch, typographisch; —ographic error, der Druckfehler.

—**ography**, *s.* die Buchdruckerkunst, Typographie. *Comp.* —**e-founder**, *s.* der Schriftgießer. —**e-founding**, *s.* das Schriftgießen. —**e-foundry**, *s.* die Schriftgießerei. —**e-metal**, *s.* das Schriftmetall. —**e-write**, *v.a. & n.* mit der Schreibmaschine schreiben. —**e-writer**, *s.* die Schreibmaschine; der (die) Maschinenschreiber(in).
Typh—litis, *s.* die Blinddarmentzündung. —**oid**, —**ous**, *adj.* typhusartig, typhös; —oid fever, der Unterleibstyphus. —**us**, *s.* der Typhus.
Typhoon, *s.* der Taifun, chinesischer Orkan.
Typist, *s. see* Type-writer.
Typographer, *etc. see under* Type.
Tyran—nic(al), *adj.*, —**nically**, *adv.* tyrannisch. —**nicalness**, *s.* das Tyrannische. —**nicide**, *s.* der Tyrannenmord; (murderer) der Tyrannenmörder. —**nize**, *v.n.* grausam, tyrannisch herrschen; to —nize over, tyrannisieren. —**nous**, *adj.*, —**nously**, *adv.* tyrannisch; (cruel) grausam. —**ny**, *s.* die Tyrannei (*also fig.*); die Willkürherrschaft, Tyrannis (*Hist.*). —**t**, *s.* der Tyrann (*also fig. & Hist.*).
Tyre, *s.* der Radreif(en); pneumatic —, der Luftreifen (*Cycl.*). *See* ³Tire.
Tyro, *s.* der Anfänger, Neuling, Lehrling.

U

U, **u**, *s.* U, u. *For abbreviations see the Index at the end of the English-German Part.*
Ubiquit—ous, *adj.*, —**ously**, *adv.* überall befindlich, allgegenwärtig. —**y**, *s.* die Allgegenwart.
Udder, *s.* das Euter.
Udometer, *s.* der Regenmesser.
Ugh, *interj.* hu! (Schauder); hu, sch (Scheuchlaut).
Ugl—iness, *s.* die Häßlichkeit, Garstigkeit; die Widerwärtigkeit. —**y**, *adj.* häßlich, garstig; (suspicious) bedenklich; (dangerous) gefährlich, bösartig.
Ukase, *s.* der Ukas.
Ulcer, *s.* das Geschwür; (malignant —) der Krebs. —**ate**, *v.n.* schwären. —**ation**, *s.* das Schwären; (—) das Geschwür. —**ed**, *adj.* schwärend, eiterig. —**ous**, *adj.* voller Geschwüre; eiterig; *see* —ed. —**ousness**, *s.* der Zustand der Eiterung.
Ullage, *s.* die in einem Fasse durch das Lecken verloren gegangene Menge Flüssigkeit; der in den Gläsern zurückgebliebene Wein (*sl.*); —s, nicht ganz volle Fässer (*C.L.*).
Ulmic, *adj.;* — acid, die Ulminsäure.
Ulster, *s.* der Havelok, der Pelerinen-Mantel, langer bis auf die Füße gehender Überzieher.
Ult, *see* —imo. —**erior**, *adj.* jenseitig; weiter (*as a motive*); anderweitig, sonstig, nachträglich. —**imate**, *adj.* (aller-)letzt, endlich. —**imately**, *adv.* zuletzt, endlich, zum Schluß. —**imatum**, *s.* das Ultimatum, die letztmalige Aufforderung. —**imo** (*abbrev.* ult. *read:* of last month), *adv.* im letzten Monat; your favour of the 23d ult., Ihr geschätztes Schreiben vom 23. vorigen Monats.
Ultra, *adj.* übermäßig. *Comp.* —**liberal**, *adj.* ultraliberal. —**marine**, I. *adj.* jenseits des Meers, überseeisch. II. *s.* das Ultramarin. —**montane**, I. *adj.* jenseits der Gebirge (Alpen) liegend; ultramontan, päpstlich gesinnt (*fig.*). II. *s.; see* —montanist. —**montanism**, *s.* der Ultramontanismus. —**montanist**, *s.* der Ultramontane, Erzkatholik.
Umbel, *s.* die Dolde. —**lar**, *adj.* doldig. —**liferous**, *adj.* doldentragend, Dolden-.
Umber, *s.* das Umbra, die Umbererde.
Umb—el, *see* Umbel. —**rage**, *s.* der Schatten, das Laubwerk (*of trees*); (suspicion of injury) der Verdacht, Argwohn; der Anstoß, Ärger; to give —rage, beleidigen; to take —rage at, Anstoß nehmen an (einer S.), (eine S.) übel nehmen. —**rageous**, *adj.* schattig, schattenreich. —**rageousness**, *s.* der Schattenreichtum. —**rella**, *s.* der Regenschirm. *Comp.* —**rella-case**, *s.* das Schirmfutteral. —**rella-stand**, *s.* das Regenschirmgestell. —**rella-stick**, *s.* der Schirmstock.
Umb—ilic(al), *adj.* zum Nabel gehörig, Nabel-; —ilical cord, die Nabelschnur. —**o**, *s.* der Schildnabel.
Umpire, I. *s.* der Obmann, Unparteiische, Schiedsrichter. II. *v.n.* den Schiedsrichter machen, Unparteiischer sein.
Un— *in numerous compds.* = Un-, nicht. *For words not given in the following lists see the simple words.*
Unabashed, *adj.* uneingeschüchtert.
Unabated, *adj.* unvermindert, ungeschwächt.
Unabbreviated, **Unabridged**, *adj.* unverkürzt, nicht abgekürzt.
Unable, *adj.* unfähig, unvermögend; to be —, nicht können; nicht imstande *or* in der Lage sein.
Unaccented, *adj.* unbetont.
Unaccommodating, *adj.* unnachgiebig; unverträglich, ungefällig.
Unaccompanied, *adj.* unbegleitet.
Unaccountable, *adj. see* Inexplicable; (strange) sonderbar; unverantwortlich; he is an — fellow, man kann nicht klug aus ihm werden.
Unaccustomed, *adj.* ungewohnt (*to*); (new) ungewöhnlich, neu.
Unacknowledged, *adj.* nicht anerkannt; (unconfessed) nicht zugestanden.
Unacquainted, *adj.* unbekannt (mit), unkundig (einer Sache).
Unadorned, *adj.* ungeschmückt, nicht ausgeschmückt.
Unaffected, *adj.*, —**ly**, *adv.* unberührt; ungerührt (*fig.*); (natural) ungekünstelt, unbefangen, natürlich, schlicht, einfach.
Unaided, *adj.* ununterstützt; unbewaffnet, bloß (*of the eye*).
Unalloyed, *adj.* ohne Beimischung, unvermischt; rein, lauter.
Unalterabl—e, *adj.*, —**y**, *adv.* unveränderlich. —**eness**, *s.* die Unveränderlichkeit.
Unambitious, *adj.* nicht ehrgeizig; nicht begierig (of, nach); (modest) anspruchslos.
Unamenable, *adj.* unwillfährig.
Unamiable, *adj.* unliebenswürdig.
Unanim—ity, *s.* die Einmütigkeit, Einstimmigkeit. —**ous**, *adj.*, —**ously**, *adv.* einmütig, einstimmig.
Unanswerabl—e, *adj.*, —**y**, *adv.* unwiderlegbar. —**eness**, *s.* die Unwiderlegbarkeit.
Unappalled, *adj.* unerschrocken.
Unappeas—able, *adj.* nicht zu besänftigen. —**ed**, *adj.* unbesänftigt; (unreconciled) unversöhnt.
Unapproachable, *adj.* unnahbar.
Unappropriated, *adj.* unverwendet, nicht zugewiesen, herrenlos.
Unapproved, *adj.* nicht gebilligt; unbewährt.
Unarmed, *adj.* unbewaffnet, waffenlos.
Unashamed, *adj.* nicht beschämt, schamlos.
Unasked, *adj.* unverlangt, ungebeten, unaufgefordert.
Unassailable, *adj.* unangreifbar.
Unassisted, *adj.* ununterstützt, ohne Beistand.
Unassuming, *adj.* nicht anmaßend, bescheiden, anspruchslos.
Unattached, *adj.* nicht verbunden, nicht anhängend; zur Disposition (*Mil.*); freistehend; zu keinem College gehörend, extern (*Univ.*).
Unattainable, *adj.* unerreichbar.
Unattempted, *adj.* unversucht.
Unattended, *adj.* unbegleitet.
Unattractive, *adj.* reizlos, nicht anziehend.
Unauthorized, *adj.* unbefugt, unerlaubt.
Unavailing, *adj.* vergeblich, nutzlos.
Unavenged, *adj.* ungerächt.
Unavoidabl—e, *adj.*, —**y**, *adv.* unvermeidlich.
Unaware, *adj.;* to be — (of a th.), (eine S.) nicht vermuten, nicht wissen. —**s**, *adv.* unversehens, unvermutet; (suddenly) plötzlich.
Unawed, *adj.* nicht eingeschüchtert, nicht zurückgehalten.

Unbalanced, *adj.* nicht im Gleichgewicht.
Unbaptized, *adj.* nicht getauft, ungetauft.
Unbar, *v.a.* auf-, ent-riegeln, aufschließen.
Unbearabl—e, *adj.*, **—y**, *adv.* unerträglich.
Unbecoming, *adj.*, **—ly**, *adv.* schlecht kleidend; (unsuitable) ungeziemend ; (improper) unanständig ; her bonnet is very —, ihr Hut steht ihr sehr schlecht. **—ness**, *s.* die Unschicklichkeit.
Unbefriended, *adj.* freundlos, alleinstehend; hilflos.
Unbelie—f, *s.* der Unglaube, schwache Glaube; das Mißtrauen, der Zweifel. **—ver**, *s.* der Ungläubige. **—ving**, *adj.*, **—vingly**, *adv.* ungläubig.
Unbend, *ir.v.* I. *a.* abspannen (*a bow*), nachlassen; abschlagen (*sails*); erschlaffen lassen, nachlassen (*fig.*); to — one's mind, ausruhen, seinen Geist ruhen lassen. II. *n.* sich herablassen, gemütlich werden. **—ing**, *adj.*, **—ingly**, *adv.* unbeugsam; fest, entschlossen (*fig.*).
Unbestowed, *adj.* nicht vergeben, unvergeben.
Unbiassed, *adj.* uneingenommen, vorurteilslos, unbefangen.
Unbidden, *adj.* uneingeladen, unaufgefordert; freiwillig.
Unbind, *ir.v.a.* losbinden; (loose) lösen.
Unbleached, *adj.* ungebleicht.
Unblemished, *adj.* unbefleckt, rein.
Unblest, *adj.* ungesegnet.
Unblushing, *adj.*, **—ly**, *adv.* schamlos.
Unbolt, *see* Unbar.
Unborn, *adj.* (noch) ungeboren, zukünftig.
Unbosom, *v.r.* sein Herz ausschütten (einem).
Unbound, *adj.* ungebunden, geheftet, brochiert.
Unbounded, *adj.* unbeschränkt, schrankenlos.
Unbrace, *v.a.* losspannen, auf-schnallen, -binden; abspannen (*fig.*).
Unbreeched, *adj.* hosenlos, ohne Hosen.
Unbridled, *adj.* ungezäumt, zügellos.
Unbroached, *adj.* unangezapft; unbesprochen (*a subject*).
Unbroken, *adj.* ungebrochen; (continuous) ununterbrochen.
Unbrotherly, *adj.* unbrüderlich.
Unbuckle, *v.a.* losschnallen, aufschnallen.
Unburden, **Unburthen**, *v.a.* entlasten, erleichtern (sein Herz gegen einen).
Unburied, *adj.* unbegraben.
Unburnt, *adj.* ungebrannt, unverbrannt.
Unbusinesslike, *adj.* nicht geschäftsmäßig; nachlässig (*fig.*).
Unbutton, *v.a.* los-, auf-knöpfen.
Uncalled, *adj.* nicht eingefordert; capital —, gezeichnetes, aber noch einzuzahlendes Aktienkapital ; — for, unverlangt, unnötig, überflüssig, unangebracht.
Uncandid, *adj.*, **—ly**, *adj.* unaufrichtig.
Uncanny, *adj.* unheimlich, nicht geheuer.
Uncared-for, *adj.* unversorgt, vernachlässigt.
Uncarpeted, *adj.* ohne Teppich.
Unceasing, *adj.*, **—ly**, *adv.* unaufhörlich.
Unceremonious, *adj.*, **—ly**, *adv.* nicht umständlich, ohne Umstände, einfach, schlicht; to be —, kurz angebunden sein, nicht viel Umstände machen.
Uncertain, *adj.* unsicher ; (doubtful) ungewiß ; (fickle) unzuverlässig, unstät, veränderlich ; to be — of, einer Sache nicht gewiß sein ; — weather, unbeständiges Wetter. **—ty**, *s.* die Ungewißheit; die Unzuverlässigkeit.
Uncertified, *adj.* unbeglaubigt, nicht attestiert.
Unchain, *v.a.* entfesseln, von der Kette lösen.
Unchang—eable, *adj.*, **—eably**, *adv.* unveränderlich. **—eableness**, *s.* die Unveränderlichkeit. **—ed**, *adj.* unverändert. **—ing**, *adj.*, **—ingly**, *adv.* wechsellos, bleibend.
Uncharitabl—e, *adj.*, **—y**, *adv.* unbarmherzig. hartherzig, lieblos; (evil-thinking) übeldenkend. **—eness**, *s.* die Lieblosigkeit.
Unchartered, *adj.* ohne Freibrief.
Unchaste, *adj.*, **—ly**, *adv.* unkeusch. **—ned**, *adj.* ungezüchtigt; nicht geläutert, nicht rein.
Unchecked, *adj.* ungehemmt, ungehindert.
Unchivalrous, *adj.* unritterlich, grob.
Unchrist—ened, *adj.* ungetauft. **—ian**, *adj.*, **—ianly**, *adv.*, **—like**, *adj.* unchristlich.
Uncial, *adj.* Unzial-; — letter, der Unzialbuchstabe
Uncircumcis—ed, *adj.* unbeschnitten. **—ion** *s.* die Nichtbeschneidung; die Heidenwelt (*fig.*).
Uncivil, *adj.* unhöflich.
Unclaimed, *adj.* nicht beansprucht, nicht verlangt; unanbringbar (*as letters*).
Unclasp, *v.a.* loshaken, aufhaken; öffnen.
Unclassed, *adj.* nicht in Klassen geordnet; in der Prüfung durchgefallen (*Univ.*).
Uncle, *s.* der Onkel, Oheim; der Pfandverleiher (*sl.*).
Unclean, *adj.*, **—ly**, *adv.* unrein, unsauber. **—ness**, *s.* die Unreinheit; die Unkeuschheit (*fig.*).
Unclerical, *adj.* dem geistlichen Stande nicht geziemend, ungeistlich.
Uncloak, *v.a.* (einen) des Mantels berauben, (einem) den Mantel nehmen; *see* Unmask.
Unclose, *v.a.* aufmachen, öffnen.
Unclothe, *adj.* entkleiden, auskleiden.
Unclouded, *adj.* wolkenlos; heiter (*fig.*).
Uncocked, *adj.* ungespannt.
Uncoil, *v.a.* auf-winden, -wickeln.
Uncollected, *adj.* nicht gesammelt.
Uncomfortabl—e, *adj.*, **—y**, *adv.* unbehaglich, ungemütlich, unbequem ; (unpleasant) unangenehm. **—eness**, *s. see* Discomfort.
Uncommon, *adj.*, **—ly**, *adv.* ungewöhnlich, selten, ungemein ; sehr (*adv.*). **—ness**, *s.* die Ungewöhnlichkeit, Seltenheit.
Uncommunicative, *adj.* nicht mitteilsam, (in sich) verschlossen.
Uncomplaining, *adj.*, **—ly**, *adv.* nicht klagend, ohne Beschwerden, klaglos. **—ness**, *s.* die Klaglosigkeit, Geduld, Ergebung.
Uncompromising, *adj.*, **—ly**, *adv.* keinen Vergleich eingehend, nicht nachgebend.
Unconcern, *s.* die Gleichgültigkeit. **—ed**, *adj.*, **—edly**, *adv.* gleichgültig, sorglos.
Unconditional, *adj.*, **—ly**, *adv.* unbedingt, absolut; to surrender —ly, sich auf Gnade und Ungnade ergeben.
Unconfessed, *adj.* nicht bekannt; ohne bekannt zu haben, ohne Beichte (*R. C.*).
Unconfined, *adj.* unbeschränkt.
Unconfirmed, *adj.* unbestätigt; nicht eingesegnet, nicht konfirmiert; nicht fest, schwankend.
Uncongenial, *adj.* ungleichartig, nicht zusagend, unsympathisch, nicht geistesverwandt.
Unconnected, *adj.* unverbunden, ohne Verbindung; (loose) unzusammenhängend.
Unconquer—able, *adj.*, **—ably**, *adv.* unbezwinglich. **—ed**, *adj.* unbesiegt, unbezwungen.
Unconscientious, *adj.*, **—ly**, *adv.* gewissenlos.
Unconscionabl—e, *adj.*, **—y**, *adv.* gewissenlos; übertrieben, enorm (*fam.*).
Unconscious, *adj.*, **—ly**, *adv.* unbewußt ; bewußtlos ; ohnmächtig ; to be — of, sich (einer Sache) nicht bewußt sein. **—ness**, *s.* die Bewußtlosigkeit, Ohnmacht.
Unconsecrated, *adj.* ungeweiht.
Unconstitutional, *adj.*, **—ly**, *adv.* verfassungswidrig.
Unconstrained, *adj.*, **—ly**, *adv.* ungezwungen.
Uncontaminated, *adj.* unbefleckt.
Uncontested, *adj.*, **—ly**, *adv.* unbestritten; offenbar, unbestreitbar ; — election, eine Wahl, bei welcher die Gegenpartei keinen Kandidaten aufstellt.
Uncontrollabl—e, *adj.*, **—y**, *adv.* unbeherrschbar, unbändig; (wild) wild, zügellos.
Unconventional, *adj.*, **—ly**, *adv.* natürlich ; formlos, frei und ungebunden, zwanglos.
Unconverted, *adj.* unbekehrt ; nicht konvertier (*C.L.*).
Unconvinc—ed, *adj.* unüberzeugt, nicht überzeugt **—ing**, *adj.*, **—ingly**, *adv.* nicht überzeugend

Uncord, *v.a.* aufbinden, losbinden.
Uncork, *v.n.* entkorken, aufkorken.
Uncorrected, *adj.* unverbessert.
Uncorrupted, *adj.*, **—ly**, *adv.* unverdorben; unbestochen. **—ness**, *s.* die Unverdorbenheit: die strenge Rechtlichkeit.
Uncouple, *v.a.* loskoppeln, lösen.
Uncouth, *adj.* ungeschlacht, roh; (awkward) linkisch, tölpisch; (odd) wunderlich.
Uncovenanted, *adj.* nicht bundesgemäß; durch keine Übereinkunft verpflichtet.
Uncover, *v.* I. *a.* aufdecken, entblößen; to — o.s., *see* II. *n.* II. *n.* das Haupt entblößen, den Hut *or* die Kopfbedeckung abnehmen.
Uncritical, *adj.*, **—ly**, *adv.* unkritisch.
Unct—ion, *s.* die Salbung; (ointment) die Salbe; die Inbrunst, Salbung (*in speaking, etc.*); with —ion, salbungsvoll; extreme —ion, letzte Ölung. **—uous**, *adj.* ölig, fettig; salbungsvoll (*fig.*).
Uncultivated, *adj.* unangebaut (*as land*); (rude) ungebildet, roh.
Uncured, *adj.* ungeheilt; ungesalzen, nicht eingemacht.
Uncurl, *v.a.* (*& n.* sich) entkräuseln.
Uncut, *adj.* ungeschnitten; unabgeschnitten, ungestutzt (*as hair, nails, etc.*); (untouched) unangeschnitten; nicht aufgeschnitten (*as books*).
Undamaged, *adj.* unbeschädigt, ohne Datum.
Undated, *adj.* undatiert.
Undaunted, *adj.* unerschrocken, unverzagt.
Undecanted, *adj.* nicht abgegossen (in eine Karaffe).
Undecay—ed, *adj.* nicht verfallen, unzerstört, frisch. **—ing**, *adj.* unverwelklich, unvergänglich.
Undeceive, *v.a.* enttäuschen, (einem) die Augen öffnen.
Undecided, *adj.* unentschieden.
Undefended, *adj.* unverteidigt.
Undefiled, *adj.* unbefleckt, makellos.
Undefined, *adj.* unbestimmt, nicht begrenzt.
Undemonstrative, *adj.* ruhig, kalt, verschlossen, zurückhaltend.
Undeniabl—e, *adj.*, **—y**, *adv.* unleugbar.
Undenominational, *adj.* keiner Konfession ausschließlich angehörend; — school, die Simultanschule.
Under, I. *adv.* unten; (—neath) darunter; to keep —, im Gehorsam, in Unterwürfigkeit erhalten. II. *prep.* unter; from — . . ., unter (*dat.*) . . . hervor; — age, unmündig; — arms, unter den Waffen; a man — authority, ein Untertan der Obrigkeit; — one's breath, mit zurückgehaltenem Atem; — a p.'s care, unter jemandes Aufsicht; — command, befehligt; the matter is still — consideration, die Sache ist noch immer in Überlegung; I speak — correction, nach meiner unmaßgeblichen Meinung; — date of the 2d inst., unterm 2ten dieses; — the direction of, nach Anweisung von; — fire, im feindlichen Feuer; — 15 years of age, unter fünfzehn Jahren; — ground, unter dem Boden, unter der Erde, unterirdisch; — one's own hand, eigenhändig; a deed — his hand and seal, eine von ihm unterschriebene und gesiegelte Urkunde; — a heavy load, schwerbelastet; to be *or* labour — a mistake, sich in einem Irrtum befinden; — way, auf dem Wege; to be — the necessity of, genötigt sein zu; — an obligation, verbunden; — pain of death, bei Todesstrafe; — protest, mit *or* unter Protest; — restraint, nicht frei, gezwungen; — sail, unter (im) Segel(n); — sentence of, zu . . . verurteilt; to lie — the table, unter dem Tische liegen; to throw — the table, unter den Tisch werfen; to be — treatment, in Behandlung sein. *Comp.* **—bid**, *v.a.* unterbieten. **—bred**, *adj.* nicht fein, ungebildet, (von Haus aus) gemein. **—clothing**, *s.* das Unterzeug, die Unterkleidung, Leibwäsche. **—current**, *s.* die Unterströmung, Strömung in der Tiefe; —current of sadness, der Untergrund von Trauer. **—done**, *adj.* noch nicht gar, ungar. **—estimate**, *v.a.* unterschätzen. **—fed**, *adj.* nicht gehörig gefüttert, ungenügend genährt. **—go**, *ir.v.a.* (er)leiden, ertragen, aushalten, sich (einer Sache) unterziehen. **—graduate**, *s.* der Student (welcher den Grad des B. A. noch nicht erreicht hat) (*Univ.*). **—ground**, *adj. & adv.* unterirdisch; —ground (railway), die unterirdische Eisenbahn, (Londoner) Stadtbahn; —ground story, das Erd-, Keller-geschoß. **—growth**, *s.* das Unterholz, Gebüsch. **—hand**, *adj. & adv.* heimlich, versteckt, listig; —hand dealings, listiges Verfahren, versteckte (unehrliche) Handlungsweise; —hand service, der Tiefaufschlag; —hand-twist service, Tiefaufschlag mit Drehball (*Tennis*). **—hung**, *adj.* über den Oberkiefer hervorragend; mit hervorragendem Oberkiefer; auf einer Schiene ruhend (*Mach.*). **—-jaw**, *s.* der Unterkinnbacken. **—-jersey**, *s.* dünne Wolljacke. **—lie**, *ir.v.n.* zu Grunde liegen. **—line**, *v.a.* unterstreichen. **—-linen**, *s.* die Leibwäsche. **—ling**, *s.* der untergeordnete Gehilfe, Untergebene. **—-lip**, *s.* die Unterlippe. **—lying**, *adj.* zu Grunde liegend (*of principles, etc.*); —lying idea, der Grundgedanke. **—manned**, *adj.* nicht genügend bemannt. **—mentioned**, *adj.* unten erwähnt. **—mine**, *v.a.* untergraben; zerstören, schwächen (*the health*). **—most**, I. *adj.* unterst. II. *adv.* zu unterst. **—neath**, I. *adv.* unterwärts, unten. II. *prep.* unter. **—paid**, *adj.* ungenügend *or* schlecht bezahlt. **—part**, *s.* die Nebenrolle, untergeordnete Rolle. **—-petticoat**, *s.* der Unterrock. **—pin**, *v.a.* den Grund unterbauen, unterfahren, stützen (*a house, etc.*). **—pinning**, *s.* der Grundbau. **—rate**, *v.a.* unterschätzen. **—score**, *v.a.* unterstreichen. **—-secretary**, *s.* der Untersekretär. **—sell**, *ir.v.a.* wohlfeiler verkaufen als (*another person*); unter dem Werte (*of an article*) verkaufen. **—shot**, *adj.* unterschlächtig (*of mills*). **—signed**, *s.* der Unterzeichnete. **—sized**, *adj.* unter der gewöhnlichen Größe. **—skirt**, *s.* der Unterrock. **—sleeve**, *s.* der Unterärmel. **—-staffed**, *adj.*; the school is —-staffed, das Lehrerpersonal an der Schule ist nicht genügend. **—stand**, *ir.v.* I. *a.* verstehen; (hear) vernehmen; (comprehend) begreifen, fassen, einsehen; (know how to) kennen, wissen, sich verstehen auf (*acc.*); to give a p. to —stand, einem zu verstehen geben; to —stand by, ersehen aus, darunter verstehen; he —stands horses, er versteht sich auf Pferde; be it —stood, wohlverstanden; let it be an —stood thing, wir wollen es als abgemachte Sache betrachten. II. *n.* verstehen, vernehmen; fassen. **—standing**, *s.* der Verstand; (agreement) das Verständnis, Einvernehmen; to come to an —standing with, sich verständigen, verabreden mit; there is a good —standing between them, zwischen ihnen besteht ein gutes Einvernehmen; with this —standing, unter dieser Voraussetzung. **—state**, *v.a.* zu gering angeben, nicht entsprechend darstellen. **—study**, I. *s.* der Schauspieler welcher die Rolle eines anderen nebenher einstudiert, um den gewöhnlichen Spieler im Notfall vertreten zu können. II. *v.a.*; to —study a part, eine von einem anderen gespielte Rolle nebenher einstudieren. **—take**, *ir.v.a.* unternehmen; (take upon o.s., assume) übernehmen. **—taker**, *s.* der Unternehmer; der Leichenbestatter; der Arbeitsgeber, Kapitalist; der Bürge (*obs.*); —taker's man, der Leichenträger. **—taking**, *s.* die Unternehmung; general —taking, das Hauptunternehmen. **—tone**, *s.* leiser Ton; niedriger Ton (*Mus.*). **—value**, *v.a.* unter dem Werte schätzen, zu niedrig einschätzen, unterschätzen; (despise) geringschätzen, verachten. **—wear**, *s.* das Unterzeug, die Leibwäsche. **—wood**, *s.* das Gestrüpp, Unterholz. **—-world**, *s.* die Unterwelt. **—write**, *ir.v.a.* versichern, assekurieren (*C. L.*). **—writer**, *s.* der Versicherer, Assekurant, Assekurateur.

Underogatory, *adj.* nicht schmälernd, nicht nachteilig (einer S.), keinen Eintrag tuend (*dat.*).
Undeserv—ed, *adj.*, **—edly**, *adv.* unverdient. **—ing**, *adj.* verdienstlos, unwert.
Undesigned, *adj.*, **—ly**, *adv.* unbeabsichtigt, unvorsätzlich.
Undesirable, *adj.* nicht wünschenswert.
Undeterred, *adj.* nicht abgeschreckt.
Undeveloped, *adj.* unentwickelt.
Undeviating, *adj.* nicht abweichend, gerade.
Undigested, *adj.* unverdaut.
Undignified, *adj.* ohne Würde, würdelos.
Undiluted, *adj.* unverdünnt, nicht verdünnt.
Undiminished, *adj.* unvermindert.
Undimmed, *adj.* unverdunkelt.
Undiscern—ed, *adj.* unbemerkt. **—ing**, *adj.* einsichtslos, ohne Einsicht.
Undisciplined, *adj.* zuchtlos, ohne Mannszucht; ungeübt, ungeschult, unausgebildet.
Undiscover—able, *adj.* unentdeckbar. **—ed**, *adj.* unentdeckt.
Undiscriminating, *adj.* keinen Unterschied machend
Undisguised, *adj.* unverkleidet, unverhüllt, offen.
Undismayed, *adj.* unerschrocken.
Undisputed, *adj.* unbestritten.
Undistributed, *adj.* unverteilt.
Undisturbed, *adj.* ungestört; ungetrübt (*mirror*).
Undivided, *adj.* ungeteilt (*attention, etc.*).
Undo, *ir.v.a.* aufmachen (*a parcel, a knot, etc.*); auflösen (*a knot, string, etc.*); auftrennen (*a seam*); rückgängig, ungeschehen machen (*s.th. done*); (ruin) vernichten, zu Grunde richten, unglücklich machen. **—ing**, *s.* das Aufmachen 2c.; das Verderben. **—ne**, *adj.* vernichtet, hin, verloren; I am —ne, es ist um mich geschehen, es ist aus mit mir; to come —ne, aufgehen; to leave —ne, ungetan *or* unvollendet lassen.
Undoubted, *adj.*, **—ly**, *adv.* unbezweifelt; unstreitig, gewiß, ohne Zweifel.
Undraped, *adj.* nicht behangen; nackt (*Draw.*).
Undreamt-of, *adj.* ungeträumt, ungeahnt.
Undress, I. *v.a.* auskleiden, entkleiden, ausziehen. II. *v.r. & n.* sich entkleiden. III. *s.* das Hauskleid, Negligé; die Halbuniform (*Mil.*). **—ed**, *adj.* unbekleidet; unzubereitet (*as salad*); nicht verbunden (*of wounds*); ungegerbt (*as leather*).
Undried, *adj.* ungetrocknet, ungedörrt; grün; naß.
Undrinkable, *adj.* nicht trinkbar.
Undu—e, *adj.*, **—ly**, *adv.* ungebührend, ungehörig, übertrieben, unangemessen.
Undulat—e, *v.n.* sich wellenförmig bewegen, wallen, wogen. **—ing**, *adj.* wallend, sich wellenförmig bewegend; (wave-like) wellenförmig, wellig. **—ion**, *s.* wellenförmige Bewegung, Wellenbewegung. **—ory**, *adj.* wellenförmig; —ory theory, die Undulationstheorie, Wellentheorie.
Undutiful, *adj.*, **—ly**, *adv.* pflichtvergessen, ungehorsam. **—ness**, *s.* die Pflichtwidrigkeit, Pflichtvergessenheit, der Ungehorsam.
Undying, *adj.* unsterblich, unvergänglich.
Unearned, *adj.* unverdient.
Unearth, *v.a.* aus dem Loch treiben, ausgraben (*beasts*); ans Licht ziehen, auftreiben, aufgabeln, aufstöbern (*fig.*). **—ly**, *adj.* überirdisch; unheimlich, gräßlich (*fig.*).
Uneas—iness, *s.* die Unruhe, Ängstlichkeit; (discomfort) das Mißbehagen; to cause a p. —iness, einem Beschwerden verursachen. **—ily**, *adv.*, **—y**, *adj.* unbequem; unbehaglich; unruhig, ängstlich (*about something*).
Uneat—able, *adj.* nicht eßbar, nicht genießbar. **—en**, *adj.* ungegessen, unverzehrt.
Uneducated, *adj.* ungebildet, ohne Erziehung.
Unembarrassed, *adj.* nicht verlegen.
Unemotional, *adj.* leidenschaftslos; nicht leicht *or* gern Gefühle zeigend; nicht aufregend, das Gefühl nicht ergreifend.
Unemployed, *adj.* unbeschäftigt, müßig; tot (*as capital*); the —, die Arbeitslosen. **—ment**, *s.* die Arbeitslosigkeit.
Unenclosed, *adj.* unein-geschlossen, -gefriedigt.
Unencumbered, *adj.* unbelastet, frei.
Unending, *adj.* endlos, nicht endend.
Unendowed, *adj.* ohne Mitgift; undotiert (*as churches*); unbegabt (with, mit); — schools, Schulen ohne Stiftungsvermögen.
Unendurable, *adj.* unerträglich.
Unenlightened, *adj.* unaufgeklärt.
Unenlivened, *adj.* unbelebt.
Unenterprising, *adj.* nicht unternehmend *or* unternehmungslustig.
Unenviable, *adj.* nicht beneidenswert.
Unequal, *adj.*, **—ly**, *adv.* ungleich; (disproportionate) ungleich-, unverhältnis-mäßig; unangemessen, nicht gemäß; — to, (einem 2c.) nicht gewachsen. **—led**, *adj.* unvergleichlich, unübertroffen, unerreicht.
Unequivocal, *adj.* unzweideutig.
Unerring, *adj.*, **—ly**, *adv.* nicht irrend; (certain) unfehlbar, gewiß; unfehlbar (treffend) (*arrow*).
Unessential, *adj.*, **—ly**, *adv.* unwesentlich.
Uneven, *adj.*, **—ly**, *adv.* uneben, ungleich; ungerade (*as a number*). **—ness**, *s.* die Ungerad-, Ungleich-, Uneben-heit.
Uneventful, *adj.* ereignislos; still (*fig.*).
Unexampled, *adj.* beispiellos, ohne Beispiel.
Unexceptionable, *adj.* unverwerflich, tadellos.
Unexhausted, *adj.* nicht erschöpft.
Unexpected, *adj.*, **—ly**, *adv.* unerwartet, unvermutet, unvorhergesehen.
Unexplored, *adj.* unerforscht.
Unexpressed, *adj.* nicht ausgedrückt.
Unfad—ed, *adj.*, unverwelkt; nicht verschossen *or* verblaßt (*as colours*). **—ing**, *adj.*, **—ingly**, *adv.* unverwelklich, nie verblassend.
Unfailing, *adj.*, **—ly**, *adv.* unfehlbar, gewiß; — courtesy, nie versagende Höflichkeit.
Unfair, *adj.*, **—ly**, *adv.* unredlich, unehrlich, unbillig; ungehörig (*Footb.*); — competition, unlauterer Wettbewerb. **—ness**, *s.* die Unbilligkeit.
Unfaithful, *adj.*, **—ly**, *adv.* ungetreu, treulos; (undutiful) pflichtvergessen. **—ness**, *s.* die Treulosigkeit, Untreue.
Unfaltering, *adj.* nicht schwankend. **—ly**, *adv.* ohne Zaudern; fest, mutig, unerschrocken.
Unfamiliar, *adj.* unbekannt, nicht vertraut; ungewöhnlich. **—ity**, *s.* die Unvertrautheit.
Unfashionabl—e, *adj.*, **—y**, *adv.* aus der Mode, nicht modisch, unmodisch, unmodern. **—eness**, *s.* das Unmodische.
Unfasten, *v.a.* los-binden, -machen, aufmachen.
Unfatherly, *adj.* unväterlich.
Unfathomable, *adj.* unergründlich, unerforschlich; *see* Immeasurable.
Unfavo(u)rabl—e, *adj.*, **—y**, *adv.* ungünstig, nicht günstig; (disadvantageous) unvorteilhaft; ungünstig (*as wind*). **—eness**, *s.* das Ungünstige; die Ungunst (*of circumstances*).
Unfeeling, *adj.*, **—ly**, *adv.* gefühllos.
Unfeigned, *adj.*, **—ly**, *adv.* unverstellt, wahr.
Unfelt, *adj.* unempfunden, nicht gefühlt.
Unfermented, *adj.* ungegoren.
Unfettered, *adj.* ungefesselt, fessellos, ungezwungen.
Unfilial, *adj.* unkindlich.
Unfinished, *adj.* unvollendet, nicht fertig.
Unfit, I. *adj.*, **—ly**, *adv.* untauglich, unpassend. II. *v.a.* untauglich machen (für eine S.). **—ness**, *s.* die Untauglichkeit.
Unfix, *v.a.* losmachen; — bayonets! Bajonett ab!
Unflagging, *adj.* nicht erschlaffend, unermüdlich.
Unflattering, *adj.* nicht schmeichelhaft, ungeschmeichelt, ungeschminkt.
Unfledged, *adj.* ungefiedert; zart, jung (*fig.*).
Unflinching, *adj.*, **—ly**, *adv.* nicht wankend, nicht weichend; fest entschlossen, unentwegt.
Unfold, *v.a.* entfalten, aufschlagen, ausbreiten; entdecken, offenbaren, erzählen (*fig.*).
Unforbidden, *adj.* unverboten.
Unforced, *adj.* ungezwungen, natürlich.

Unforeseen, *adj.* unvorhergesehen.
Unforgiving, *adj.* nicht vergebend, nachtragend. unversöhnlich.
Unforgotten, *adj.* unvergessen.
Unformed, *adj.* ungeformt, nicht gebildet; unausgebildet (*fig.*).
Unforsaken, *adj.* nicht verlassen *or* aufgegeben.
Unfortified, *adj.* unbefestigt.
Unfortunate, *adj.* unglücklich. **—ly**, *adv.* unglücklicherweise zum Unglück, leider.
Unfought, *adj.* ungekämpft.
Unfounded, *adj.* ungegründet; unbegründet, grundlos (*fig.*).
Unfrequented, *adj.* unbesucht, einsam, verlassen.
Unfriend—ed, *adj.* freundlos (*rare*). **—liness**, *s.* die Unfreundlichkeit. **—ly**, *adj.* unfreundlich.
Unfrock, *v.a.* die geistliche Tracht *or* die Mönchskutte ausziehen.
Unfruitful, *adj.* unfruchtbar. **—ness**, *s.* die Unfruchtbarkeit.
Unfulfilled, *adj.* unerfüllt.
Unfurl, *v.a.* entfalten, auseinanderbreiten; losmachen (*sails*); entfalten, wehen lassen (*a flag*).
Unfurnished, *adj.* nicht ausgerüstet *or* versehen; unmöbliert (*as houses*).
Ungainl—iness, *s.* die Plumpheit, das linkische Wesen. **—y**, *adj.* linkisch; (clumsy) plump.
Ungallant, *adj.* unritterlich, ungalant.
Ungenerous, *adj.*, **—ly**, *adv.* nicht freigebig; (not magnanimous) unedel, ungroßmütig.
Ungent—eel, *adj.* unfein, unhöflich, unartig. **—le**, *adj.*, **—ly**, *adv.* unsanft, rauh, hart, roh.
Ungentlemanl—y, *adj.* eines anständigen und gebildeten Menschen unwürdig, ungesittet, ungebildet. **—iness**, *s.* das Ungebildete, Unanständige, eines anständigen und gebildeten Mannes unwürdige Benehmen.
Un-get-at-able, *adj.* unerreichbar, unerlangbar.
Ungird, *v.a.*(*p.p.* Ungirt) losgürten, lose schürzen.
Unglazed, *adj.* ohne Glas; unglasiert.
Ungloved, *adj.* ohne Handschuhe.
Ungodl—iness, *s.* die Gottlosigkeit. **—y**, *adj.* gottlos, verrucht.
Ungovern—able, *adj.* unlenksam, zügellos, unbändig. **—ed**, *adj.* ohne Regierung; ungezähmt, wild (*fig.*).
Ungrac—eful, *adj.*, **—efully**, *adv.* nicht graziös; (unlovely) anmutslos, reizlos. **—efulness**, *s.* der Mangel an Grazie *or* Anmut. **—ious**, *adj.*, **—iously**, *adv.* ungnädig; unhold; *see* Unfriendly. **—iousness**, *s.* das unfreundliche Wesen, die Unfreundlichkeit, Ungnädigkeit.
Ungrammatical, *adj.*,**—ly**, *adv.* ungrammatisch.
Ungrateful, *adj.*, **—ly**, *adv.* undankbar. **—ness**, *s.* die Undankbarkeit.
Ungratified, *adj.* unbefriedigt.
Ungrounded, *adj.* ungegründet, unbegründet, grundlos.
Ungrudging, *adj.*, **—ly**, *adv.* bereitwillig, willig, gern, ohne Murren.
Unguarded, *adj.*, **—ly**, *adv.* unbewacht, unbeschützt; unvorsichtig; in an — moment, in einem unbewachten Augenblick.
Unguent, *s.* die Salbe.
Ungula, *s.* die Hufe (*Geom.*). **—te**, *adj.* hufförmig.
Unhallowed, *adj.* nicht geweiht, ungeheiligt, unheilig, gottlos.
Unhampered, *adj.* ungehindert, frei.
Unhand, *v.a.* loslassen. **—ily**, *adv.*, **—y**, *adj.* unbequem; (awkward) ungeschickt. **—iness**, *s.* die Unbequemlichkeit. **—some**, *adj.* unfein, unschön, unedel (*behaviour*).
Unhapp—ily, *adv.* unglücklicherweise, zum Unglück; *see* —y. **—iness**, *s.* das Unglück; (misery) das Elend, die Unglückseligkeit; —iness of mind, das Sichunglücklichfühlen. **—y**, *adj.* unglücklich, elend, traurig; unglückselig, unheilvoll.
Unharmed, *adj.* unversehrt, unbeschädigt.
Unharness, *v.a.* abschirren, ausspannen.
Unhealth—ful, *adj.*, **—fully**, *adv.* ungesund. **—iness**, *s.* die Ungesundheit. **—y**, *adj.* ungesund, kränklich; krankhaft.
Unheard, *adj.* ungehört; — of, unerhört.
Unheed—ed, *adj.* unbeachtet, unbemerkt. **—ing**, *adj.*, **—ingly**, *adv.* unachtsam, sorglos, nachlässig.
Unhesitating, *adj.*, **—ly**, *adv.* ohne Zaudern, ohne Weiteres, ohne Anstand zu nehmen.
Unhinge, *v.a.* zerrütten; verwirren, aus der Fassung bringen (*fig.*); I feel quite —d, ich bin ganz aus der Fassung gebracht, aus den Fugen; his mind is —d, sein Verstand ist zerrüttet.
Unhitch, *v.a.* loshaken.
Unholy, *adj.* unheilig, ungeweiht; gottlos.
Unhonoured, *adj.* nicht geehrt, ungeehrt.
Unhook, *v.a.* auf-, aus-haken.
Unhoped-for, *adj.* ungehofft, unverhofft.
Unhorse, *v.a.* aus dem Sattel heben, abwerfen.
Unhouse, *v.a.* aus dem Hause jagen; vertreiben.
Unhurt, *adj.* unbeschädigt, unverletzt.
Uni—corn, *s.* das Einhorn. **—fication**, *s.* die Einigung. **—form**, I. *adj.*, **—formly**, *adv.* ein-, gleich-förmig; gemäß. II. *s.* die Uniform (*also Mil.*), der bunte Rock (*coll.*); die Amtstracht. **—formity**, *s.* die Ein-, Gleich-förmigkeit; —formity of opinion, die Übereinstimmung; act of —formity, die Uniformitätsakte. **—fy**, *v.a.* vereinen. **—lateral**, *adj.* einseitig. **—on**, I. *s.* die Vereinigung, Verbindung; (concord) die Eintracht; (society) der Verein; (marriage) eheliches Band, die Ehe; die Übereinstimmung (*Paint.*, *Arch.*); die Union (*Pol.*); der Armenhausbezirk (*for the care of the poor*), das Armenhaus; art —on, Kunstverein; trade(s)- —on, der Gewerkverein, die Gewerkschaft; —on is strength, Eintracht hat große Macht (*prov.*). II. *attrib.*; —on jack, die Rotkreuzflagge, die britische Nationalflagge; —on society, die akademische Lesehalle (*at Oxf. & Camb.*). **—onist**, *s.* der Verteidiger der Union; liberal —onist, Liberaler welcher Irland nicht von England (durch Verleihung von Home Rule) zu trennen wünscht. **—que**, *adj.* einzig in seiner Art. **—sexual**, *adj.* eingeschlechtig. **—son**, *s.* der Ein-, Gleich-klang; die Übereinstimmung (*fig.*). **—sonous**, *adj.* gleichtönend. **—t**, *etc.*, *see* Unit, *etc.* **—valve**, I. *adj.* einschalig. II. *s.* das Einschaltier. **—vers—**, *see* Univers—.
Unilluminated, *adj.* unerleuchtet.
Unimagina—ble, *adj.* undenkbar, nicht vorstellbar. **—tive**, *adj.* ohne Einbildungskraft, phantasielos.
Unimpaired, *adj.* unvermindert, ungeschwächt.
Unimpassioned, *adj.* leidenschaftslos.
Unimpeachable, *adj.* vorwurfsfrei, unanfechtbar, unantastbar.
Unimpeded, *adj.* ungehindert.
Unimportant, *adj.* unwichtig.
Unimproved, *adj.* unverbessert; unbebaut, wild (*land*); unbenutzt.
Uninclosed, *see* Unenclosed.
Uninfluenced, *adj.* unbeeinflußt, uneingenommen; — by passion, leidenschaftslos; — by personal considerations, durch persönliche Neigungen *or* Rücksichten nicht beeinflußt.
Uninformed, *adj.* ununterrichtet.
Uninhabit—able, *adj.* unbewohnbar. **—ed**, *adj.* unbewohnt.
Uninitiated, *adj.* uneingeweiht.
Uninjured, *adj.* unbeschädigt, unverletzt.
Uninspired, *adj.* nicht begeistert, uneingegeben
Uninstructed, *adj.* ununterrichtet; (without instructions) ohne Verhaltungsbefehle.
Unintelligib—le, *adj.*, **—ly**, *adv.* unverständlich. **—ility**, *s.* die Unverständlichkeit.
Uninten—ded, *adj.* unbeabsichtigt. **—tional**, *adj.*, **—tionally**, *adv.* unabsichtlich, unvorsätzlich.
Uninteresting, *adj.* uninteressant, nicht anziehend, langweilig.

Unintermitt—ed, **—ing**, *adj.* ununterbrochen, unaufhörlich, beständig, unausgesetzt.
Uninterrupted, *adj.*, **—ly**, *adv.* ununterbrochen.
Unintoxicating, *adj.* nicht berauschend.
Uninvit—ed, *adj. see* Unbidden. **—ing**, *adj.* nicht einladend.
Union, *see* Uni—.
Uniparous, *adj.* nur ein Junges auf einmal gebärend.
Unit, *s.* der Einer, die Einheit. **—arian**, I. *s.* der Unitarier. II. *adj.* unitarisch. **—arianism**, *s.* die Lehre der Unitarier. **—e**, *v.* I. *a.* vereinigen, verbinden. II. *n.* sich vereinigen, sich verbinden; (agree) einstimmen. **—y**, *s.* die Einheit (*also Math.*, *etc.*); (agreement) die Eintracht, Übereinstimmung; —y is strength, Einigkeit macht stark (*prov.*); the 3 —ties, die 3 (dramatischen) Einheiten.
Univers—al, I. *adj.*, **—ally**, *adv.* allgemein; (comprising all) allumfassend, gesamt, das Ganze betreffend; —al joint, das Universalgelenk; —al history, die Weltgeschichte; —al Postal Union, der Weltpostverein. II. *s.* das Allgemeine, der allgemeine Satz. **—alism**, *s.* der Universalismus. **—alist**, *s.* der Universalist. **—ality**, *s.* die Allgemeinheit. **—e**, *s.* das Weltall. **—ity**, I. *s.* die Hochschule, Universität; to enter a —ity, eine Universität beziehen; to study at the —ity, an *or* auf der Universität studieren, die Universität besuchen; the —ity of Berlin, die Universität Berlin, die Berliner Hochschule. II. *attrib.* Universitäts=; —ity education, die Hochschulbildung; —ity extension, die Volkshochschule; —ity extension meeting, volkstümliche Hochschulkurse; —ity extension movement, das Volkshochschulwesen; —ity intelligence, Hochschulnachrichten, Universitätsbericht; —ity man, das Mitglied einer Universität; der Mann mit Universitätsbildung; —ity ordinances, von der Universität selbständig erlassene (und von ihr ohne Weiteres zurücknehmbare) Verordnungen; —ity lecturer, außerordentlicher Professor (*not* Lektor); —ity register, die Universitätsmatrikel; —ity statutes, für die Universität gemachte Grundgesetze, welche nur durch Parlamentsbeschluß abänderlich sind.
Unjust, *adj.*, **—ly**, *adv.* ungerecht, unbillig. **—ifiable**, *adj.*, **—ifiably**, *adv.* nicht zu rechtfertigen, unverantwortlich.
Unkempt, *adj.* ungekämmt; unordentlich; roh.
Unkind, *adj.*, **—ly**, *adv.* ungütig, unfreundlich, lieblos; to take —ly to, sich schwer gewöhnen an (*acc.*), sich nicht aussöhnen mit. **—ness**, *s.* die Unfreundlichkeit, Ungefälligkeit, Härte.
Unknot, *v.a.* aufknüpfen, aufmachen.
Unknow—ingly, *adv.* unwissentlich. **—n**, *adj.* unbekannt; unbewußt; (strange) ungekannt, ungewöhnlich; —n to me, ohne mein Wissen; he is —n to me, ich kenne ihn nicht, er ist mir fremd.
Unlace, *v.a.* aufschnüren, lösen.
Unlade, *v.a.* ausladen, löschen (*goods*); ausladen, entladen (*ships*).
Unladylike, *adj.* nicht wie eine feine Dame.
Unlamented, *adj.* unbeklagt, unbeweint.
Unlatch, *v.a.* aufklinken.
Unlawful, *adj.*, **—ly**, *adv.* ungesetzlich, unerlaubt, unrechtmäßig; —ly born, von unehelicher Geburt. **—ness**, *s.* die Ungesetzlichkeit.
Unlearn, *v.a.* verlernen, vergessen. **—ed**, *adj.* nicht erlernt; (ignorant) unwissend, ungelehrt.
Unleavened, *adj.* ungesäuert.
Unless, *conj.* wofern *or* wenn nicht, ausgenommen, außer, es sei denn daß; damit nicht (*obs.*).
Unlettered, *adj.* ungelehrt, unwissend.
Unlicensed, *adj.* unberechtigt, ohne Erlaubnis, ohne Konzession.
Unlicked, *adj.* ungeleckt; — cub, roher Bengel.
Unlike, *adj.* unähnlich; ungleich; that is quite — him, das ist gar nicht seine Art, das sieht ihm gar nicht ähnlich. **—lihood**, *s.* die Unwahrscheinlichkeit. **—ly**, *adv.* unwahrscheinlich.
Unlimber, *v.a.* abprotzen (*Mil.*).
Unlimited, *adj.* unbegrenzt, unbeschränkt.
Unlined, *adj.* ohne Futter; ohne Linien.
Unliquidated, *adj.* nicht abgemacht, nicht berichtigt, nicht bezahlt.
Unload, *v.a.* ent=, ab=, aus=laden; *see* Unburden; entladen (*guns*).
Unlock, *v.a.* aufschließen (*also Print.* & *fig.*), öffnen; to — the form, das Format abschlagen. **—ed**, *adj.* unverschlossen.
Unlooked-for, *adj.* unerwartet, überraschend.
Unloose, *v.a.* auflösen, loslassen.
Unlov—able, *adj.* nicht liebenswürdig, unliebenswürdig. **—ed**, *adj.* ungeliebt. **—ely**, *adj.* reizlos. **—ing**, *adj.* lieblos, unfreundlich.
Unluck—ily, *adv.* unglücklicherweise. **—y**, *adj.* unglücklich; (ill-omened) unheilbringend.
Unmade, *adj.* ungemacht; nicht fertig.
Unmaidenly, *adj.* nicht mädchenhaft, nicht jungfräulich.
Unmake, *ir.v.a.* zerstören; absetzen (*kings*).
Unman, *v.a.* entmannen (*also fig.*); (discourage) entmutigen; der Mannschaft berauben (*Naut.*). **—liness**, *s.* die Unmännlichkeit. **—ly**, *adj.* unmännlich. **—ned**, *adj.* entmutigt; entmannt.
Unmanageable, *adj.* unlenksam, unleitbar, widerspenstig. **—ness**, *s.* die Unlenksamkeit.
Unmanner—liness, *s.* das unmanierliche Wesen, rohe unfeine Benehmen. **—ly**, *adj.* ungesittet, unmanierlich, roh.
Unmarked, *adj.* unbezeichnet; unbemerkt.
Unmarri—ageable, *adj.* nicht heiratsfähig. **—ed**, *adj.* unverheiratet, ledig.
Unmask, *v.a.* & *n.* (einem) die Maske abnehmen; (einen) entlarven (*fig.*); enthüllen (*fig.*).
Unmatched, *adj.* ungepaart; unvergleichlich.
Unmeaning, *adj.* nichtssagend, bedeutungslos; (silly) albern.
Unmeasured, *adj.* ungemessen; unermeßlich.
Unmeet, *adj.* ungeziemend; ungeeignet.
Unmelodious, *adj.* unmelodisch, mißtönend.
Unmentionable, *adj.* nicht zu erwähnen, unnennbar. **—s**, *pl.* die Unaussprechlichen (*vulg.*).
Unmerciful, *adj.*, **—ly**, *adv.* unbarmherzig. **—ness**, *s.* die Unbarmherzigkeit.
Unmerited, *adj.* unverdient.
Unmindful, *adj.*, **—ly**, *adv.* unbedachtsam; to be — of, vergessen, nicht achten auf (*acc.*), sich (*dat.*) nichts machen aus, nicht denken an (*acc.*).
Unmistakabl—e, *adj.*, **—y**, *adv.* unverkennbar.
Unmitigated, *adj.* ungemildert, ungelindert; arg (*fig.*); — scoundrel, der Erzschurke.
Unmix—ed, **—t**, *adj.* ungemischt, unvermischt.
Unmodified, *adj.* nicht abgeändert; — vowels, unumgelautete Vokale, reine Vokale (*Gram.*).
Unmolested, *adj.* unbelästigt, ungestört.
Unmoor, *v.a.* von den Tauen losmachen (*a ship*).
Unmortgaged, *adj.* unverpfändet.
Unmotherly, *adj.* unmütterlich.
Unmourned, *adj.* unbetrauert, unbeweint.
Unmoved, *adj.* unbewegt, ungerührt (*also fig.*); (firm) fest, standhaft.
Unmusical, *adj.* unmusikalisch; übelklingend.
Unmuzzle, *v.a.* den Maulkorb abnehmen (*dat.*).
Unnameable, *adj.* unnennbar.
Unnatural, *adj.* unnatürlich.
Unnavigable, *adj.* unschiffbar.
Unnecessar—ily, *adv.* unnötigerweise. **—y**, *adj.* unnötig, überflüssig.
Unneighbourly, *adj.* unnachbarlich.
Unnerve, *v.a.* entnerven, entkräften, schwächen.
Unnot—ed, *adj.* nicht bezeichnet; unbemerkt. **—iced**, *adj.* unbemerkt, unbeachtet; (neglected) vernachlässigt.
Unnumbered, *adj.* ungezählt, zahllos.
Unobjectionable, *adj.* untadelhaft.
Unobserv—ant, *adj.* unaufmerksam. **—ed**, *adj.* nicht beachtet, unbemerkt.

Unobtainable, *adj.* nicht erhältlich, nicht zu haben.
Unobtrusive, *adj.*, **—ly**, *adv.* nicht zudringlich, bescheiden. **—ness**, *s.* die Bescheidenheit.
Unoccupied, *adj.* unbesetzt, uneingenommen; (idle) unbeschäftigt, müßig.
Unoffending, *adj.* unanstößig, harmlos.
Unopened, *adj.* ungeöffnet; unaufgeschnitten (*of books*).
Unopposed, *adj.* ungehindert; einspruchslos, ohne Gegenkandidaten; — by, ohne Widerstand seitens (*gen.*).
Unorthodox, *adj.* nicht rechtgläubig.
Unostentatious, *adj.*, **—ly**, *adv.* nicht prahlerisch, bescheiden; ohne Prunk *or* Schaustellung.
Unpack, *v.a.* ab=, aus=packen.
Unpaid, *adj.* unbezahlt; *see* Unrewarded.
Unpalatable, *adj.* unschmackhaft; widrig (*fig.*).
Unparalleled, *adj.* unvergleichlich, beispiellos.
Unpardonabl—e, *adj.*, **—y**, *adv.* unverzeihlich, nicht zu vergeben.
Unparliamentary, *adj.* unparlamentarisch.
Unpatriotic, *adj.* unvaterländisch, unpatriotisch.
Unpaved, *adj.* ungepflastert.
Unperceived, *adj.* unbemerkt, unbeachtet.
Unperformed, *adj.* unvollführt, unerfüllt.
Unperturbed, *adj.* ungestört, unbeirrt.
Unperused, *adj.* undurchlesen, ungelesen.
Unphilosophic, *adj.*, **—al**, *adj.*, **—ally**, *adv.* unphilosophisch.
Unpicked, *adj.* ungepflückt; nicht ausgelesen.
Unpin, *v.a.* losheften, die Stecknadeln herausnehmen (aus einer S.).
Unpitying, *adj.* unbarmherzig, grausam.
Unplaced, *adj.* ohne Platz gelassen, unangestellt; the horse was —, das Pferd war nicht unter den drei Ersten (*Rac.*).
Unpleasant, *adj.*, **—ly**, *adv.* unangenehm, mißfällig. **—ness**, *s.* die Unannehmlichkeit.
Unpoetic, *adj.*, **—ally**, *adv.* undichterisch.
Unpolished, *adj.* unpoliert; ungebildet (*fig.*).
Unpolluted, *adj.* unbefleckt.
Unpopular, *adj.* (beim Volke) nicht beliebt, unbeliebt, nicht volkstümlich. **—ity**, *s.* die Unbeliebtheit (beim Volk), der Mangel an Volkstümlichkeit.
Unpractical, *adj.* unpraktisch.
Unpractised, *adj.* ungeübt.
Unprecedented, *adj.* beispiellos, ohne Vorgang, noch nie dagewesen, unerhört.
Unprejudiced, *adj.* vorurteils=los, =frei, unbefangen.
Unpremeditated, *adj.*, **—ly**, *adv.* unüberlegt, nicht vorbedacht; aus dem Stegreif; *see* Unintentional.
Unprepared, *adj.* unvorbereitet; nicht bereit.
Unprepossessing, *adj.* nicht einnehmend.
Unpresentable, *adj.* nicht vorstellbar, nicht vorzeigbar; nicht gesellschaftsfähig.
Unpretending, *adj.* nicht anmaßlich, bescheiden.
Unprincipled, *adj.* ohne feste Grundsätze; (bad) unsittlich, gewissenlos, lasterhaft; ruchlos.
Unproductive, *adj.* unfruchtbar, unergiebig; (unprofitable) uneinträglich. **—ness**, *s.* die Unfruchtbarkeit, Unergiebigkeit.
Unprofessional, *adj.*, **—ly**, *adv.* nicht professionell; nicht berufsmäßig, Laien=; *see* Nonprofessional.
Unprofitabl—e, *adj.*, **—y**, *adv.* keinen Vorteil *or* Gewinn bringend; unvorteilhaft, uneinträglich; (useless) nutzlos, unnütz. **—eness**, *s.* die Nutzlosigkeit.
Unpromising, *adj.* nicht viel versprechend.
Unpronounceable, *adj.* unaussprechlich.
Unpropitious, *adj.* ungeneigt, ungünstig, unglücklich, ungnädig.
Unprotected, *adj.* ungeschützt, schutzlos.
Unprovided, *adj.* nicht versehen, unversorgt.
Unprovoked, *adj.* nicht herausgefordert; (uncaused) nicht veranlaßt, ohne Veranlassung.
Unpublished, *adj.* unveröffentlicht.
Unpunctual, *adj.*, **—ly**, *adv.* unpünktlich. **—ity**, *s.* die Unpünktlichkeit.
Unpunished, *adj.* ungestraft.
Unqualified, *adj.* ungeeignet, unbefähigt; (— by oath) unbeeidigt, unberechtigt; (unlimited) unbeschränkt, unbedingt.
Unquenchable, *adj.* unlöschbar, unauslöschlich, unersättlich.
Unquestion—able, *adj.*, **—ably**, *adv.* unfraglich, unzweifelhaft. **—ing**, *adj.* nicht in Frage stellend; *see* Unhesitating.
Unravel, *v.* I. *a.* auf=fase(r)n, =ziehen; entwickeln, lösen (*a plot*). II. *n.* sich auffase(r)n.
Unread, *adj.* ungelesen; unbelesen, unwissend. **—able**, *adj.* unleserlich, undeutlich; unlesbar.
Unread—ily, *adv.*, **—y**, *adj.* nicht bereit, nicht fertig, ungerüstet; (slow) langsam; (awkward) linkisch, ungeschickt. **—iness**, *s.* die Unbereitschaft; die Unbereitwilligkeit.
Unreal, *adj.* nicht wirklich, unwesentlich. **—ity**, *s.* die Nichtwirklichkeit, Wesenlosigkeit.
Unreason—able, *adj.*, **—ably**, *adv.* unvernünftig; (unjust) unbillig, grundlos; (immoderate) unmäßig. **—ableness**, *s.* die Unvernünftigkeit; die Unbilligkeit; die Unmäßigkeit (*of a demand, etc.*). **—ing**, *adj.* vernunftlos; passiv (*as obedience*).
Unrebuked, *adj.* ungetadelt.
Unreclaim—able, *see* Irreclaimable. **—ed**, *adj.* ungebessert; unangebaut (*as land*).
Unrecogniz—able, *adj.* nicht wiederzuerkennen. **—ed**, *adj.* nicht (an)erkannt.
Unrecompensed, *adj.* unbelohnt.
Unrecorded, *adj.* unaufgezeichnet.
Unrecovered, *adj.* nicht wieder erlangt.
Unredeemed, *adj.* nicht losgekauft, nicht erlöst; ungemildert (by, durch, *fig.*); ungetilgt (*as debts*); uneingelöst (*as stocks, bills, etc.*).
Unredressed, *adj.* ungesühnt, nicht gutgemacht.
Unrefined, *adj.* nicht gereinigt, nicht raffiniert; nicht verfeinert, unveredelt, ungebildet (*fig.*).
Unreflecting, *adj.* nicht (Strahlen) zurückwerfend; nicht überlegend; unüberlegt.
Unrefresh—ed, *adj.* unerquickt. **—ing**, *adj.* nicht erquickend, unerquicklich.
Unregarded, *adj.* unberücksichtigt; unbeachtet, vernachlässigt.
Unregenera—cy, *s.* die Nichtwiedergeburt (*Theol.*). **—te**, *adj.* nicht wiedergeboren (*Theol.*).
Unregretted, *adj.* unbedauert, unbeklagt.
Unrelenting, *adj.* unerweichbar; gefühllos, hart.
Unreliable, *adj.* unzuverlässig.
Unrelieved, *adj.* unerleichtert, ungelindert.
Unremitting, *adj.* unablässig.
Unrepealed, *adj.* unwiderrufen, unaufgehoben.
Unrepented, *adj.* unbereut.
Unrepining, *adj.* ohne Klage, klaglos, gelassen.
Unrepresented, *adj.* unvertreten, ohne Vertreter; nicht dargestellt.
Unrequited, *adj.* unvergolten.
Unreserved, *adj.*, **—ly**, *adv.* nicht zurückgehalten; nicht numeriert (*seats at a theatre*); (open) nicht zurückhaltend, offen.
Unresisting, *adj.* widerstandslos.
Unrest, *s.* die Unruhe. **—ing**, *adj.* ruhelos.
Unrestrained, *adj.* *see* Unrestricted; zügellos.
Unrestricted, *adj.* unbeschränkt, uneingeschränkt.
Unreturned, *adj.* nicht zurückgegeben; nicht erwidert; nicht gewählt (*Parl.*).
Unrevealed, *adj.* nicht geoffenbart, nicht entdeckt.
Unrevenged, *adj.* ungerächt.
Unrewarded, *adj.* unbelohnt.
Unrhymed, Unrimed, *adj.* ungereimt, reimlos.
Unrighteous, *adj.*, **—ly**, *adv.* ungerecht (*also Theol.*); unredlich. **—ness**, *s.* die Ungerechtigkeit, Sündigkeit.
Unrip, *v.a.* auftrennen.
Unripe, *adj.* unreif, unzeitig. **—ned**, *adj.* nicht gereift. **—ness**, *s.* die Unreife.
Unrivalled, *adj.* ohne Nebenbuhler; ohne Gleichen, unvergleichlich, beispiellos.
Unroll, *v.a.* entfalten, aufrollen, herauswickeln.

Unromantic, *adj.* unromantisch.
Unround, *v.a.* entrunden, entründen; —ed vowels, entrundete Vokale. —**ing**, *s.* die Entründung.
Unruffled, *adj.* glatt, still, ruhig; gleichmütig.
Unrul—ed, *adj.* nicht liniert; unregiert. —**iness**, *s.* die Unlenksamkeit, Wildheit, Widerspenstigkeit. —**y**, *adj.* unlenksam, widerspenstig, unbändig, wild.
Unsabbatic(al), *adj.* nicht sabbatmäßig.
Unsaddle, *v.a.* absatteln.
Unsafe, *adj.*, —**ly**, *adv.* unsicher, nicht sicher. —**ness**, *s.* die Unsicherheit.
Unsaid, *adj.* ungesagt.
Unsaleable, *adj.* unverkäuflich.
Unsancti—fied, *adj.* ungeheiligt, ungeweiht. —**oned**, *adj.* nicht gebilligt; —oned by custom, nicht durch den Gebrauch geheiligt.
Unsatisf—actoriness, *s.* das Unbefriedigende; die Unzulänglichkeit. —**actorily**, *adv.*, —**actory**, *adj.* unbefriedigend. —**ying**, *adj.* unbefriedigend; nicht sättigend (*of food*); (insufficient) unzulänglich.
Unsavoury, *adj.* unschmackhaft; (ill-smelling) übelriechend, widrig.
Unsay, *ir.v.a.* zurücknehmen, widerrufen.
Unscathed, *adj.* unbeschädigt, unversehrt.
Unscholarly, *adj.* unwissenschaftlich.
Unschooled, *adj.* ungeschult, ungeübt; ungelehrt, ungebildet.
Unscientific, *adj.*, —**ally**, *adv.* unwissenschaftlich.
Unscratched, *adj.* unzerkratzt, unzerrissen.
Unscrew, *v.a.* auf=, ab=, zurück=schrauben.
Unscriptural, *adj.* nicht schriftgemäß, unbiblisch.
Unscrupulous, *adj.*, —**ly**, *adv.* unbedenklich, gewissenlos. —**ness**, *s.* die Gewissenlosigkeit.
Unseal, *v.a.* entsiegeln.
Unsearchable, I. *adj.* unerforschlich; unergründlich. II. *s.* das Unerforschliche.
Unseason—able, *adj.* der Jahreszeit nicht gemäß, unzeitig; ungelegen (*fig.*). —**ableness**, *s.* die Unzeitigkeit; die Ungelegenheit. —**ed**, *adj.* nicht getrocknet oder ausgewittert (*as wood*); ungewohnt, nicht abgehärtet (*fig.*); (unspiced) ungewürzt.
Unseat, *v.a.* vom Sitze werfen; aus dem Sattel heben; abwerfen; des *or* seines Sitzes berauben (*in Parliament*).
Unseaworth—iness, *s.* die Untauglichkeit zum Seedienst. —**y**, *adj.* zum Seedienst untauglich.
Unsectarian, *adj* nicht sektiererisch, frei von Sektiererei.
Unseeml—iness, *s.* die Unziemlichkeit —**y**, *adj.* unziemlich.
Unseen, I. *adj.* ungesehen, unsichtbar. II. *s.* das Jenseits.
Unselfish, *adj.*, —**ly**, *adv.* uneigennützig, selbstlos. —**ness**, *s.* die Uneigennützigkeit, Selbstlosigkeit.
Unsentimental, *adj.* nicht empfindsam, nicht sentimental, frei von Empfindsamkeit.
Unserviceable, *adj.* undienlich; unhaltbar (*as stuffs, colours, etc.*). —**ness**, *s.* die Undienlichkeit, Nutzlosigkeit.
Unsettle, *v.a.* von seinem Platze bewegen; (confuse) verwirren, in Unordnung bringen; ungewiß, schwankend machen (*in mind*). —**d**, *adj.* (not fixed) nicht festgesetzt, unbestimmt; unbezahlt (*as an account*); (restless) unstät; (changeable) unbeständig, veränderlich; unreguliert (*as claims*); schwankend, veränderlich (*as prices*); —d weather, unbeständiges Wetter.
Unsex, *v.a.* des Geschlechtes berauben; entweiben; to — o.s., ihr Geschlecht aufgeben, sich emanzipieren (*of women*).
Unshaded, *adj.* unbeschattet, schattenlos.
Unshaken, *adj.* unerschüttert.
Unshape—ly, —**n**, *adj.* ungestalt.
Unshaven, *adj.* unrasiert.
Unsheath, *v.a.* aus der Scheide ziehen, entblößen; to — the sword, vom Leder ziehen, Krieg beginnen.
Unshed, *adj.* unvergossen.
Unsheltered, *adj.* ungeschützt, ohne Schutz.
Unship, *v.a.* aus=schiffen, =laden, löschen.
Unshod, *adj.* unbeschuht; unbeschlagen (*as horses*).
Unshorn, *adj.* unbeschnitten, ungeschoren.
Unshrink—able, *adj.* nicht einlaufend. —**ing**, *adj* nicht zurückweichend, unverzagt.
Unsightl—iness, *s.* die Häßlichkeit, Unansehnlichkeit. —**y**, *adj.* häßlich.
Unskil—ful, *adj.*, —**fully**, *adv.* ungeschickt. —**led**, *adj.* unerfahren, unbewandert (*as workmen, etc.*); —led labour, nur körperliche Arbeit.
Unslackened, *adv.* nicht nachgelassen.
Unslaked, *adj.* ungelöscht, nicht gelöscht (*fig.*).
Unslumbering, *adj.* nie schlummernd, ewig wach.
Unsocia—ble, *adj.* ungesellig. —**l**, *adj.* gesellschaftswidrig.
Unsold, *adj.* nicht verkauft, auf Lager.
Unsoldierl—ike, —**y**, *adj.* unsoldatisch, unkriegerisch.
Unsolicited, *adj.* nicht angefleht; freiwillig gegeben, unaufgefordert ausgestellt (*testimonial*); unerbeten.
Unsolved, *adj.* ungelöst, unerklärt.
Unsophisticated, *adj.* unverfälscht, unverdorben, wahr, natürlich.
Unsought, *adj.* ungesucht; unerbeten.
Unsound, *adj.*, —**ly**, *adv.* ungesund (*in health, etc.*); (spoiled) angegangen, verdorben; (worm-eaten) faul, wurmstichig; nicht rechtgläubig (*in faith*); — argument, nicht stichhaltiger Beweisgrund; of — mind, nicht recht bei Verstande; — doctrine, die Irrlehre (*Theol.*). —**ness**, *s.* die Verdorbenheit; die Unrichtigkeit, Unechtheit, Unwahrheit; die Faulheit.
Unsparing, *adj.*, —**ly**, *adv.* freigebig, nicht sparsam; schonungslos.
Unspeakabl—e, *adj.*, —**y**, *adv.* unsäglich, unsagbar, unaussprechlich.
Unspecified, *adj.* nicht besonders bemerkt, nicht besonders angegeben *or* vorgeschrieben.
Unspent, *adj.* unverbraucht; unerschöpft.
Unspoiled, *adj.* unverdorben.
Unspoken, *adj.* ungesagt.
Unsportsmanlike, *adj.* nicht sportmäßig; unweidmännisch.
Unspotted, *adj.* unbefleckt, fleckenlos.
Unstable, *adj.* wankend, schwankend, unbeständig.
Unstatesmanlike, *adj.* unstaatsmännisch.
Unstead—iness, *s.* die Unstätigkeit, das Schwanken. —**ily**, *adv.*, —**y**, *adj.* unstät, schwankend, unbeständig; liederlich (*in character*).
Unstint—ed, *adj.* unverkürzt, unbeschränkt. —**ing**, *adj.* nicht geizend, freigebig, reichlich.
Unstratified, *adj.* ungeschichtet.
Unstrung, *adj.* ungespannt; abgereiht (*pearls*); abgespannt (*fig.*).
Unstudied, *adj.* ungekünstelt, leicht, natürlich.
Unsubdued, *adj.* ununterjocht, unbesiegt.
Unsubmissive, *adj.*, —**ly**, *adv.* nicht unterwürfig; *see* Refractory.
Unsubstantial, *adj.* unwesentlich, unkörperlich; (not solid) nicht stark *or* solid; gehaltlos.
Unsuccessful, *adj.*, —**ly**, *adv.* erfolg=, frucht=los; *see* Unfortunate; — candidates, durchgefallene Examinanden, zurückbewiesene Bewerber. —**ness**, *s.* der üble Erfolg, der schlechte Ausgang, die Erfolglosigkeit.
Unsuit—ability, *s.* das Unpassende, die Unangemessenheit. —**able**, *adj.*, —**ably**, *adv.* unpassend, ungeeignet; *see* Unbecoming; ungeschickt (for, zu). —**ed**, *adj.* ungeeignet; ohne Stelle.
Unsullied, *adj.* unbefleckt.
Unsummoned, *adj.* unaufgefordert.
Unsung, *adj.* ungesungen; unbesungen.
Unsuppressed, *adj.* ununterdrückt.
Unsurpass—able, *adj.* unübertrefflich. —**ed**, *adj.* unübertroffen.
Unsusp—ected, *adj.* unverdächtig. —**ecting**, —**icious**, *adj.* arglos, nicht argwöhnisch.

Unsweetened, *adj.* unversüßt.
Unswerving, *adj.* nicht abweichend, fest.
Unsymmetrical, *adj.*, **—ly**, *adv.* nicht ebenmäßig, ungleichmäßig, unsymmetrisch.
Unsympath—etic, (**—izing**,) *adj.* gefühllos, teilnahmlos; nicht geistesverwandt.
Unsystematic, *adj.* unsystematisch.
Untainted, *adj.* unangesteckt, unverdorben; *see* Unspotted.
Untam—able, *adj.* unbezähmbar, unbezwinglich. **—ed**, *adj.* unbezähmt.
Untanned, *adj.* ungegerbt.
Untarnished, *adj.* ungetrübt, glänzend.
Untasted, *adj.* ungekostet; ungenossen (*fig.*).
Untaught, *adj.* ungelehrt, ununterrichtet.
Untena—ble, *adj.* unhaltbar. **—nted**, *adj.* unbewohnt, unvermietet.
Untended, *adj.* ungepflegt; ohne Bedienung.
Unthinking, *adj.*, **—ly**, *adv.* gedankenlos.
Unthought, *adj.* ungedacht; — of, unvermutet.
Unthread, *v.a.* ausfädeln; ausfasern; auflösen (*fig.*); sich (*dat.*) einen Weg bahnen durch (*fig.*).
Unthrifty, *adj.* nicht haushälterisch, verschwenderisch.
Untid—ily, *adv.*, **—y**, *adj.* unordentlich. **—iness**, *s.* die Unordnung.
Untie, *v.a.* lösen, aufmachen (*a knot, etc.*); aufknüpfen (*a bow*).
Until, I. *prep.* bis. II. *conj.* bis (daß); it was not — (he fell, that I saw . . .), erst als (er fiel sah ich . . .).
Untilled, *adj.* unbebaut.
Untimel—iness, *s.* die Unzeitigkeit. **—y**, *adj.* unzeitig, unpassend, ungehörig.
Untiring, *adj.* unermüdlich.
Unto, *see* To.
Untold, *adj.* unerzählt; (unnumbered) ungezählt.
Untouched, *adj.* unberührt; ungerührt (*fig.*).
Untoward, *adj.* widerwärtig, verdrießlich; (awkward) verkehrt, ungeschickt. **—ness**, *s.* die Verdrießlichkeit, Widrigkeit.
Untractable, *adj.* schwer zu bewältigen, schwierig zu behandeln; *see* Unruly.
Untrained, *adj.* unabgerichtet, ungeschult, nicht ausgebildet, ungeübt, unerzogen, ungebildet.
Untrammelled, *adj.* ungehindert, ungefesselt.
Untranslat—able, *adj.* unübersetzbar. **—ed**, *adj.* unübersetzt, nicht übertragen.
Untravelled, *adj.* ungereist, der nie gereist ist, der daheim geblieben ist; unbereist (*as a land*).
Untraversed, *adj.* nicht durchschritten, nicht durchzogen, nicht durchreist.
Untried, *adj.* unversucht; (untested) unerprobt; unverhört, ununtersucht (*Law*).
Untrimmed, *adj.* unausgeputzt, unbesetzt.
Untrodden, *adj.* unbetreten.
Untroubled, *adj.* ungetrübt; (calm) ungestört, ruhig, still.
Untru—e, *adj.* unwahr, falsch; (faithless) treulos. **—ly**, *adv.* unwahr. **—th**, *s.* die Unwahrheit; to tell an —th, die Unwahrheit sagen, lügen. **—thful**, *adj.*, **—thfully**, *adv.* unwahr, falsch. **—thfulness**, *s.* die Unwahrheit.
Untrustworth—iness, *s.* die Unzuverlässigkeit. **—y**, *adj.* Vertrauens unwert, unzuverlässig.
Unturned, *adj.* ungewendet; to leave no stone —, nichts unversucht lassen, Himmel und Erde in Bewegung setzen.
Untutored, *adj.* unerzogen, ungebildet, roh.
Untwine, **Untwist**, *v.a.* auf-drehen, -flechten; losmachen.
Unus—ed, *adj.* (not used) ungebraucht; (unaccustomed) nicht gewöhnt. **—ual**, *adj.* ungewöhnlich, selten. **—ualness**, *s.* die Seltenheit.
Unutter—able, *adj.*, **—ably**, *adv.* unaussprechlich. **—ed**, *adj.* unausgesprochen.
Unvalued, *adj.* nicht geachtet, ungeschätzt.
Unvar—ied, *adj.* unverändert, einförmig. **—ying**, *adj.* unveränderlich, unwandelbar; sich nicht verändernd, beständig.
Unvarnished, *adj.* ungefirnißt; ungeschminkt, ungeschmückt, schlicht.
Unveil, *v.a.* entschleiern, enthüllen.
Unvisited, *adj.* unbesucht, unbetreten.
Unvoiced, *adj.* nicht ausgesprochen; stimm-, tonlos, ohne Stimmton (*consonants*).
Unwar—ily, *adv.*, **—y**, *adj.* unachtsam, unvorsichtig, nicht behutsam. **—iness**, *s.* die Unbehutsamkeit, Unbedachtsamkeit.
Unwarlike, *adj.* unkriegerisch.
Unwarrant—able, *adj.*, **—ably**, *adv.* nicht zu rechtfertigen, unverantwortlich; (unsuitable) ungebührlich. **—ableness**, *s.* die Unverantwortlichkeit. **—ed**, *adj.* ungerechtfertigt, unverantwortlich.
Unwashe—d, **—n**, *adj.* ungewaschen; the great —d, der Pöbel (*coll.*).
Unwavering, *adj.* nicht wankend, standhaft, fest.
Unwear—ied, *adj.*, **—iedly**, *adv.* unermüdet. **—ying**, *adj.* nicht ermüdend, unermüdlich.
Unwedded, *adj.* unverheiratet, ledig.
Unwelcome, *adj.* unwillkommen.
Unwell, *adj.* unwohl, nicht wohl.
Unwept, *adj.* unbeweint.
Unwholesome, *adj.* ungesund; (injurious) schädlich. **—ness**, *s.* die Ungesundheit, Schädlichkeit.
Unwield—iness, *s.* die Schwerfälligkeit. **—y**, *adj.* unbehülflich, schwerfällig.
Unwilling, *adj.*, **—ly**, *adv.* un-, wider-willig, abgeneigt; to be —, nicht wollen; I am — to (admit), ich (gebe) ungern (zu); willing or —, man (er, sie, *etc.*) mag wollen oder nicht. **—ness**, *s.* der Widerwille, die Abgeneigtheit.
Unwind, *ir.v.* I. *a.* los-, ab-winden. II. *n.* sich abwinden.
Unwise, *adj.*, **—ly**, *adv.* unweise, unklug, töricht.
Unwished, *adj.* ungewünscht; — for, unerwünscht.
Unwithered, *adj.* unverwelkt.
Unwitting, *adj.*, **—ly**, *adv.* unwissentlich.
Unwomanl—iness, *s.* die Unweiblichkeit. **—y**, *adj.* unweiblich.
Unwonted, *adj.* ungewohnt; (unusual) ungewöhnlich.
Unwooed, *adj.* ungefreit, ohne Freier.
Unworkmanlike, *adj.* ungeschickt, stümperhaft.
Unworldl—iness, *s.* die Unweltlichkeit, das Freisein von weltlicher Gesinnung. **—y**, *adj.* ohne weltliche Gesinnung.
Unworth—ily, *adv.*, **—y**, *adj.* unwürdig; *see* Worthless. **—iness**, *s.* die Unwürdigkeit.
Unwounded, *adj.* unverwundet, unverletzt.
Unwrap, *v.a.* auf-wickeln, -schlagen, enthüllen.
Unwrinkled, *adj.* ungerunzelt.
Unwritten, *adj.* ungeschrieben (*as a letter*); unbeschrieben (*as a page*).
Unwrought, *adj.* unbearbeitet; (raw) roh.
Unyielding, *adj.* nicht weichend, unnachgiebig, unbeugsam.
Unyoke, *v.a.* vom Joche losspannen, ausspannen.
Up, I. *adv.;* (— at) auf (*dat.*); (—wards, ascending) auf (*acc.*), in die Höhe, empor, aufwärts; (towards the speaker) herauf; (away from the speaker) hinauf; (aloft) oben, in der Höhe; (risen) auf(gestanden); aufgegangen (*as the sun, plants, etc.*); abgelaufen (*as time*); (in excitement) in Aufregung; —! gut; not —! tot (*Tennis*); to be — in arms, unter den Waffen stehen, zu den Waffen gegriffen haben (*lit.*); sich auf die Hinterbeine stellen (*fig.*); his blood was —, sein Blut kochte *or* war in Wallung; he is not — yet, er ist noch nicht aufgestanden; — and down, auf und nieder, auf und ab; (hither and thither) hin und her; to be — and doing, rege, tätig sein; prices are going —, die Preise gehen in die Höhe; hard —, in schlechten Umständen, in der Klemme sein; from my youth —, von Jugend auf; — to, bis an, bis auf; settled — to the end of last year, bis ultimo vorigen Jahres abgeschlossen; — to this day, bis auf den

heutigen Tag; — to the chin, bis ans Kinn; — to date, bis heute; modern, zeitgemäß; to feel — to a th., sich einer S. gewachsen fühlen; — to the mark, den Anforderungen, Erwartungen entsprechend; I feel not quite — to the mark, ich fühle mich nicht ganz wohl; what are you — to there? was macht ihr da? what is —? was ist los? (*sl.*); he's always — to some mischief, er sinnt immer auf Unfug; to be — to a p.'s tricks, hinter jemandes Schliche kommen, *see* Trick; to act — to, gemäß handeln, handeln nach; to be — to a thing or two, pfiffig sein; to be well — in a subject, in einem Gegenstande gut beschlagen (*or* gut bewandert) sein; to give o.s. — to a th., sich einer Sache hingeben, widmen; to take a p. —, einen vor Gericht ziehen; — with, auf gleicher Höhe, Linie mit; it's all — with him, es ist aus mit ihm. II. *int.* auf! herauf! heran! — and away, auf und davon! heads —! Köpfe hoch! hands —! Hände hoch! ergebt euch! (*mil.*). III. *prep.* hinauf, auf; — the country, landeinwärts; — the hill, den Berg hinauf, bergan; — the river (Rhine), den Fluß hinauf, flußaufwärts (Rheinaufwärts). IV. *absol.;* then — and spake, dann erhob sich und sprach (*poet.*). V. *s.;* the —s and downs, die Wippe (*lit.*); the —s and downs of life, die Wechselfälle des Lebens. **—braid**, *see* Upbraid. **—per**, *adj.* ober, höher, Ober=; —per air, höhere Luft; —per hand, die Oberhand; —per house, das Oberhaus (*Parl.*); —per jaw, oberer Kinnbacken; —per lip, die Oberlippe; —per part, der (das) Oberteil; —per room, die Oberstube; —per story, oberes Stockwerk; the —per ten (thousand), die höheren *or* bessern Stände. **—permost**, *adj.* höchst, oberst; to say whatever comes —permost, sagen, was einem auf die Zunge kommt. **—pish**, *adj.* stolz, anmaßend (*coll.*). **—ward**, I. *adj.* nach oben gerichtet; *see* Heavenward(s). II. *adv.*, **—wards**, *adv.* aufwärts, in die Höhe, himmelwärts; (over) darüber(hinaus); —wards of, mehr als; 20 and —wards, 20 und darüber. *Comp.* **—-bow**, *s.* der Hinaufstrich (*Viol.*). **—cast**, *adj.* aufgeschlagen, emporgerichtet; —cast shaft, der Ausfahrschacht. **—heaval**, *s.* die Er=, Empor=hebung. **—heave**, *v.a.* emporheben. **—hill**, I. *adj.* den Berg hinauf, bergauf (gehend); beschwerlich, mühsam, anstrengend (*fig.*). II. *adv.* berg=auf, =an, aufwärts. **—hold**, *ir. v.a.* auf(recht) halten; (support) halten, stützen; aufrecht erhalten, verteidigen (*fig.*); to —hold a principle, sich zu einem Grundsatze bekennen, an einem Grundsatze festhalten. **—holder**, *s.* die Stütze; der Erhalter (*fig.*); (defender) der Verteidiger. **—holsterer**, *s.* der Tapezier(er), Möbelhändler. **—holstery**, *s.* das Zimmergerät, die Möbel, die Tapezier=Arbeit; (—holstery business) das Tapezier=Geschäft. **—keep**, *s.* die Instandhaltung (*of a building*). **—land**, I. *s.* das Hochland. II. *adj.* Hochlands=, hochgelegen. **—lift**, *v.a.* auf=, hoch=, er=, empor=heben. **—on**, *prep.* (oben) auf; *see* On; —on this, hierauf, darauf; —on inquiry, nach geschehener Nachfrage; my blood be —on your head, mein Blut komme über euer Haupt; to live —on, leben, sich ernähren von; to run —on, einfallen (in); to rush —on, sich werfen auf (*acc.*); —on his leaving the room, bei seinem Weggehen aus dem Zimmer; —on my word, bei meinem Worte, auf mein Wort. **—-platform**, *s.* der Bahnsteig für ankommende Züge (*or* für Züge nach London). **—raise**, *v.a.* erheben, erhöhen. **—rear**, *v.a.* aufrichten. **—right**, I. *adj.*, **—rightly**, *adv.* aufrecht, gerade; (honest) aufrichtig, gerade, ehrlich, bieder. II. *s.* der Ständer (*Carp., etc.*). **—rightness**, *s.* die Geradheit; die Aufrichtigkeit, Biederkeit, Rechtschaffenheit (*fig.*). **—rising**, *s.* das Aufstehen; das Aufgehen, der Aufgang (*of the sun*); das Ansteigen (*of a hill*); (revolt) die Erhebung, der Aufstand. **—roar**, *s.* der Aufruhr, Lärm, das Getümmel. **—roarious**, *adj.*, **—roariously**, *adv.* lärmend, tobend. **—root**, *v.a.* entwurzeln, ausreißen. **—set**, I. *v.a.* umwerfen, umstürzen; *see* Discompose. II. *s.* der Umsturz. III. *adj.;* —set price, der Anschlagspreis (*at auctions*). — **shot**, *s.* der Ausgang, das Ende, die Folge. — **side**, *adv.;* —side down, drunter und drüber, das Oberste zu unterst gekehrt. **—-stairs**, *adv.* (above) oben; to go —-stairs, die Treppe hinauf gehen. **—start**, I. *s.* der Emporkömmling. II. *adj.* emporkömmlingsartig. **—-stream**, *adv.* stromauf(wärts). **—-stroke**, *s.* der feine Strich, Haar=Strich (*in writing*); —stroke of a piston, der Kolbenaufgang. **—-train**, *s.* der nach London gehende Zug. **—turn**, *v.a.* aufwerfen, in die Höhe werfen.

Upas, *s.* (— tree) der Giftbaum.

Upbraid, *v.a.* vor=werfen, =halten (a p. with s. th., einem eine S.); *see* Chide. **—ing**, I. *adj.* vorwurfsvoll. II. *s.* der Tadel, Vorwurf.

Uran—ium, *s.* das Uran(ium). **—ography**, *s.* die Himmelsbeschreibung. **—us**, *s.* der Uranus.

Urban, *adj.* Stadt=, städtisch. **—e**, *adj.* höflich, artig. **—ity**, *s.* die Höflichkeit, Artigkeit.

Urchin, *s.* loses Kind, der Balg, kleine Schelm; der Igel (*obs.*); sea —, der Seeigel.

Ure, Ure-ox, Urus, *s.* der Auerochs.

Ur—ea, *s.* der Harnstoff. **—eter**, *s.* der Harngang. **—ethra**, *s.* die Harnröhre. **—ic**, *adj.;* —ic acid, die Harnsäure. **—inal**, *s.* der Harnbehälter; das Pissoir. **—inary**, I. *adj.* den Harn betreffend. II. *s.* das Pissoir. **—inate**, *v.n.* harnen. **—ine**, *s.* der Urin, Harn. **—inometer**, *s.* der Urinmesser.

Urge, *v.a.* (— on) drängen, (an)treiben; (press) pressen, nötigen, (in einen) dringen, (einem) anliegen, zusetzen; to — upon, dringen auf (*acc.*), Nachdruck legen auf (*acc.*), vorbringen, vorhalten; to — upon a p. the necessity of (haste), auf (Eile) bei einem dringen; to — s. th. upon s.o.'s acceptance, einem etwas aufdringen. **—ncy**, *s.* die Dringlichkeit, Not, der (Not=)Drang; (prayer) dringende Bitte. **—nt**, *adj.*, **—ntly**, *adv.* dringend, dringlich; *see* Earnest; to be in —nt need of, (etwas) höchst nötig brauchen; to be —nt for s. th., heftig auf eine S. dringen.

Urn, *s.* die Urne, der (*also* Aschen=)Krug; tea —, der Teekessel, die Teemaschine. *Comp.* **—stand**, *s.* das Gestell für den Teekessel.

Urs—a, *s.* der Bär (*Astr.*). **—ine**, *adj.* bärenartig.

Us, *pron.* (*acc. of* We), uns; to — (*dat. of* We), uns; of —, unser; all of —, wir alle.

Us—age, *s.* der Gebrauch, die Gewohnheit, Sitte, das Herkommen; (treatment) die Behandlung, das Verfahren; commercial —age, der Handelsbrauch, die Usance. **—ance**, *s.* der Gebrauch, der Uso, die Wechselfrist (*C.L.*); der Zins (*obs.*); Zinsen; *see* —ury; bill of —ance, der Usowechsel. **—e**, I. *s.* der Gebrauch, die Benutzung, Anwendung; (enjoyment) der Genuß, die Nutznießung; (custom) der Gebrauch, die Gewohnheit, Sitte; (advantage) der Nutzen, Vorteil; (need) das Bedürfnis; for —e in schools, für den Schulgebrauch; to make —e of, gebrauchen, Gebrauch machen von, anwenden; to make —e of a p.'s name, sich auf einen berufen; in —e, gebräuchlich (*as words*), in Gebrauch, (usual) üblich; out of —e, ungebräuchlich, außer Gebrauch; of —e, nützlich; of no —e, nutzlos, unnütz; of what —e is it to . . . ? what is the —e of . . . ? was nützt *or* hilft es? it is of no —e for you to . . ., es hilft Ihnen nichts zu . . .; there is no —e in . . ., it is of no —e to . . ., es ist unnütz *or* vergeblich zu . . .; to have no further —e for s. th., eine S. nicht mehr brauchen. II. *v.a.* (ge)brauchen, sich (einer Sache ꝛc.) bedienen, benutzen, anwenden; (practise) (aus)üben; (treat) behandeln, (einem) begegnen, (mit einem) verfahren; (accustom) gewöhnen; to — due diligence, das Erforderliche beobachten; to —e strong language, fluchen, schimpfen; to —e severity, Strenge gebrauchen; to —e up, verbrauchen, abnutzen; —ed up, abgenutzt, blasiert; to be —ed (to), (eine S.) gewohnt, (an eine S.) gewöhnt sein. III. *v.n.* gewohnt sein, pflegen; he —ed to say, er pflegte zu sagen. —**eful**, *adj.*, —**efully**, *adv.* nützlich, nutzbar. —**efulness**, *s.* die Nützlichkeit. —**eless**, *adj.*, —**elessly**, *adv.* nutzlos, unnütz. —**elessness**, *s.* die Nutzlosigkeit. —**er**, *s.* der Brauchende, Nutznießer, Benutzer. —**ual**, *adj.* gewöhnlich, gebräuchlich, üblich; (frequent) häufig, gemein. —**ually**, *adv.* gewöhnlich, meistens. —**ufruct**, *s.* die Nutzung, Nutznießung. —**ufructuary**, *s.* der Nutznießer. —**urer**, *s.* der Wucherer. —**urious**, *adj.*, —**uriously**, *adv.* wucher-isch, -haft. —**uriousness**, *s.* das Wucherische. —**urp**, *see* Usurp. —**ury**, *s.* der Wucher.

Usher, I. *s.* der Zeremonienmeister, Pedell, Türsteher, Einführer (*in Parliament, etc.*); der Unterlehrer, Aufseher (*in schools, etc.*) (*obs.*); der Gerichtsdiener (*of a court of justice*). II. *v.a.* (— in) einführen, anmelden; (precede) vorangehen, ankündigen, einleiten.

Usurp, *v.a.* an sich reißen, sich (*dat.*) widerrechtlich zueignen, sich (*dat.*) anmaßen, mit Gewalt nehmen, sich (einer S.) bemächtigen. —**ation**, *s.* die rechtswidrige Besitznahme, Aneignung, Anmaßung. —**er**, *s.* der unrechtmäßige Machthaber, rechtswidriger Throninhaber, Thronräuber; der widerrechtlich Besitznehmende. —**ing**, *adj.*, —**ingly**, *adv.* angemaßt, widerrechtlich.

Utensil, *s.* das Gerät, Geschirr, Handwerkszeug.

Uter—ine, *adj.* Gebärmutter-, Mutter-; von derselben Mutter geboren (*Law*); —ine complaints, Gebärmutterbeschwerden; —ine fury, die Mutterwut; —ine brother, der Halbbruder; —ine brothers and sisters, Halbgeschwister, Geschwister von der Mutterseite. —**us**, *s.* die Gebärmutter. *Comp.* —**o-gestation**, *s.* die Schwangerschaft (*Med.*).

Utili—tarian, I. *adj.* die Nützlichkeit befördernd, den Nutzen ins Auge fassend, utilitarisch, Nützlichkeits-. II. *s.* der nur auf den Nutzen Bedachte, Utilitarier. —**tarianism**, *s.* die Nützlichkeitslehre. —**ty**, *s.* die Nützlichkeit, der Nutzen, Vorteil. —**zation**, *s.* die Nutzbarmachung, Nutzanwendung, Benutzung. —**ze**, *v.a.* benutzen, ausnutzen, nutzbar machen.

Utmost, I. *adj.* höchst, äußerst; — misery, das tiefste Elend. II. *s.* das Äußerste, Höchste, Möglichste; to do one's —, sein Möglichstes tun; to the —, bis zum Äußersten; to the — of my power, mit äußerster Kraftanstrengung.

Utric—le, *s.* der Schlauch. —**ular**, *adj.* schlauchartig.

Utter, I. *adj.* äußerst; — ruin, gänzlicher Ruin; an — stranger, ein völlig Fremder, ganz fremd. II. *v.a.* äußern, aus-sprechen, -drücken, -stoßen, hervorbringen; veräußern (*Law*); in Umlauf bringen, setzen (*coin, etc.*); to — a shriek, einen Schrei ausstoßen; the last words he —ed were, seine letzten Worte waren. —**ance**, *s.* das Aussprechen, die Aussprache, die Sprechart; die Ausgabe (*of coin, etc.*); die Äußerung (*of words*). —**er**, *s.* einer, der etwas äußert, in Umlauf setzt &c. —**ly**, *adv.* durchaus, gänzlich, völlig. —**most**, *see* Utmost.

Uvula, *s.* das Zäpfchen. —**r**, *adj.* am Zäpfchen befindlich, zum Zäpfchen gehörig; am Zäpfchen gebildet; —r r, das Zäpfchen-r.

Uxorious, *adj.*, —**ly**, *adv.* der Gattin sehr ergeben, in sie übertrieben verliebt. —**ness**, *s.* die übertriebene Liebe zur Gattin.

V

V, **v**, *s.* V, v; V = 5. *For abbreviations see the Index at the end of the English-German part.*

Vac—ancy, *s.* die Leere, der leere Raum; (gap) die Lücke, der Spalt, Zwischenraum; das Unbesetztsein, Freiwerden (*of a post*); (opening) erledigte Stelle; scholastic —ancy, die freie Lehrerstelle; —ancy of mind, die Gedankenleere. —**ant**, *adj.*, —**antly**, *adv.* leer, erledigt, ledig, unbesetzt, vakant, offen, leer (*as an office*); unbewohnt, herrenlos (*as a house*); gedankenleer, geistlos; to stare in —ant stupidity, gedankenlos vor sich hinstarren; to fall —ant, vakant werden, zu besetzen sein; —ant space, leerer, unbesetzter Raum. —**ate**, *v.a.* erledigen (*a throne, office, etc.*), niederlegen (*employment, an office, etc.*). —**ation**, *s.* die Ferien (*in schools, etc.*); (—ating) die Erledigung; the long —ation, die großen Ferien, Sommerferien. —**uity**, *s.* die Leere. —**uo**, *abl. sing. of* -uum; in —uo, in luftleerem Raume. —**uous**, *adj.* leer; ausdruckslos (*fig.*). —**uum**, *s.* die Leere, der leere Raum; der luftleere Raum, das Vacuum; (gap) die Lücke.

Vaccin—ate, *v.a.* impfen. —**ation**, *s.* die Kuhpockenimpfung, Einimpfung der Kuhpocken. —**ator**, *s.* der Impfarzt. —**e**, *adj.* Kuhpocken-, Impf-; der Impfstoff, die Lymphe; —e matter, der Kuhpocken-, Impf-stoff.

Vacillat—e, *v.n.* schwanken, wankelmütig, unschlüssig sein. —**ing**, *adj.*, —**ingly**, *adv.* schwankend, wankelmütig. —**ion**, *s.* das Schwanken; der Wankelmut, die Unentschlossenheit.

Vade-mecum, *s.* das Handbuch, Vademecum.

Vag—abond, I. *s.* der Landstreicher, Vagabund, umherziehende Bettler. II. *adj.* herumschweifend; *see* Dissolute. —**ary**, *s.* die Grille, Schrulle. —**rancy**, *s.* die Landstreicherei. —**rant**, *adj. see* —abond I. & II.; —rant act, das Gesetz gegen Landstreicherei. —**ue**, *adj.*, —**uely**, *adv.* unbestimmt, ungewiß; —ue ideas, unbestimmte Begriffe, unklare Vorstellungen; —ue report, dunkles Gerücht; —ue suspicion, entfernter, dunkler Verdacht. —**ueness**, *s.* die Unbestimmtheit, Ungewißheit.

Vagin—a, *s.* die Mutterscheide, Scheide (*Anat.*); die Scheide (*Bot.*). —**al**, *adj.* scheidenförmig, zur Mutterscheide gehörig, Scheiden-. —**ate(d)**, *adj.* scheiden-artig, -förmig. —**itis**, *s.* die Scheidenentzündung.

Vain, *adj.*, —**ly**, *adv.* eitel, eingebildet, stolz; (futile) eitel, nichtig, fruchtlos, vergeblich, unnütz; (unreal) leer, wesenlos, eitel; (showy) prahlerisch; in —, umsonst, vergebens; to take the name of the Lord in —, den Namen Gottes unnützlich führen *or* mißbrauchen; — hopes, leere Hoffnungen; — show, die Prahlerei; — wish, eitler Wunsch. *Comp.* —**glorious**, *adj.*, —**gloriously**, *adv.* großsprecherisch, prahlerisch, ruhmredig. —**glory**, *s.* die Großsprecherei, Prahlerei; (pride) die Hoffart.

Valance, *s.* die Bettgardine.

Vale, *s.* das Tal.

Valedict—ion, *s.* der Abschied, das Lebewohl. —**ory**, *adj.* Abschieds- (address, etc., -rede &c.), zum Abschiede.

Valerian, *s.* der Baldrian.

Valet, *s.* der Bediente, (Kammer-)Diener; — de place, der Lohndiener, Fremdenführer.

Valetudinarian, I. *adj.* kränkelnd, kränklich. II. *s.* kränkliche Person.

Vali—ant, *adj.*, —**antly**, *adv.* tapfer, mutig, kühn; —ant trencher man, starker Esser. —**d**, *adj.*, —**dly**, *adv.* rechtskräftig, gültig; bündig, triftig (*as arguments*); to be —d, gelten; a judgment becomes —d, ein Urteil wird rechtskräftig, erlangt Rechtskraft. —**dity**, *s.* die Rechtskräftigkeit, Gültigkeit, Geltung; die Tüchtigkeit.

Valise, *s.* das Felleisen, der Reisesack.

Valley, *s. see* Vale; die Dachkehle (*Build.*).

Valor, **Valour**, *s.* die Tapferkeit; der Wert (*obs.*). —**ous**, *adj.*, —**ously**, *adj.* tapfer, kühn.

Valu—able, *adj.* wertvoll; (costly) kostbar.

teuer; (estimable) schätzbar. —**ation**, *s.* die Abschätzung, Wertbestimmung, Veranschlagung. —**ator**, *s.* der Taxator, Schätzer. —**e**, I. *s.* der Wert (*also fig.*); die Valute, Währung (*C. L.*); die Geltung (*of a note, of a word, of a coin*); —e as per invoice, Wert in Faktura; —e received, Wert empfangen; intrinsic —e, innerer Wert; to set a great —e upon, großen Wert auf (eine S.) legen. II. *v.a.* schätzen, (ver=) anschlagen; (prize) schätzen, hochachten, wert=halten, beachten; not to —e money, nicht viel Wert auf das Geld legen, sich (*dat.*) nichts aus dem Gelde machen; to —e o.s. upon, sich (*dat.*) etwas einbilden *or* zu gute tun auf (*acc.*). —**e-less**, *adj.* wertlos. —**er**, *s.* der Schätzer, Ein=schätzer, Taxator.

Valv—e, *s.* die Klappe (*also Anat. & Bot.*), das Ventil; safety- —e, das Sicherheitsventil. —**u-lar**, *adj.* klappig.

Vamp, *s.* das Oberleder (*on shoes*).

Vampire, *s.* (— bat) der Vampir (*also fig.*); der Blutsauger.

[1]**Van**, *s.* die Vorhut, der Vortrab; to lead the —, die Vorhut führen; leading the —, im Vorder=treffen. *Comp.* —**guard**, *s.* das Vordertreffen, die Vorhut (*Mil.*); das Vorgeschwader (*Naut.*).

[2]**Van**, I. *s.* die (Getreide=)Schwinge; die Schwinge, der Flügel (*Orn.*). II. *v.a.* (Erze) schwingen *or* waschen.

[3]**Van**, *s.* der große, gedeckte (Möbeltransport=) Wagen; (luggage —) der Gepäckwagen (*Railw.*).

Vandyke, I. *s.* das Zackenmuster, die Zackenspitze. II. *adj.*; — collar, ausgezackter, überschlagener Halskragen.

Vane, *s.* der Wetterhahn, die Wetterfahne; (sight —) das Visier, der Schieber, Diopter; der Flügel (*on masts; of wind-mills*).

Vanilla, *s.* die Vanille.

Vanish, *v.n.* (ver=)schwinden, vergehen; to — from (a p.'s) sight, (einem) aus den Augen entschwin=den; —ing line (plane), die Flucht=linie (=ebene) (*Draw. etc.*); —ing point, der Fluchtpunkt.

Vanity, *s.* die Eitelkeit; (worthlessness) die Nich=tigkeit, Eitelkeit; — fair, der Eitelkeitsmarkt; Titel einer englischen satirischen Zeitung.

Vanquish, *v.a.* besiegen, über=wältigen, =winden; widerlegen. —**er**, *s.* der Besieger, Überwinder.

Vantage, *s. see* Advantage. *Comp.* —**-ground**, *s.* die günstige Stellung, Überlegenheit.

Vap—id, *adj.*, —**idly**, *adv.* schal, geistlos, fade. —**orize**, *v.n.* verdampfen. —**orous**, *adj.* dun=stig, dampfig; nebelhaft, nichtig (*fig.*); (affected with —ours) grillenhaft. —**or**, —**our**, I. *s.* der Dunst, Dampf; watery —our, der Wasser=dampf; to pass off in —our, *see* Evaporate I.; to have the —ours, Grillen haben. II. *v.n.* dunsten, dampfen; *see* Evaporate; prahlen (*fig.*). *Comp.* —**our-bath**, *s.* das Dampfbad.

Vari—able, I. *adj.*, —**ably**, *adv.* veränderlich, abwechselnd; (unsteady) unbeständig. II. *s.* veränderliche Größe (*Math.*). —**ableness**, *s.* die Veränderlichkeit; die Unbeständigkeit, der Wankelmut. —**ance**, *s.* die Veränderung, der Widerspruch; (disagreement) die Uneinigkeit, der Zwist; to be at —ance, uneinig sein; (be con-tradictory) sich widersprechen; to set at —ance, uneinig machen, Zwietracht stiften (zwischen). —**ation**, *s.* die Veränderung, Abwechselung; (difference) der Unterschied, die Verschiedenheit; die Biegung (*Gram.*); die Abweichung (*Phys., Naut., fig.*); die Variation (*Mus., Astr., Math.*); line of no —ation, agonische Linie. —**ed**, *adj.* mannigfaltig, abwechselnd, bunt. —**egate**, *v.a.* vielfarbig, mannigfaltig *or* bunt machen. —**egated**, *adj.* bunt(scheckig), gefleckt. —**egation**, *s.* die Viel=, Bunt=farbigkeit; das Buntmachen. —**ety**, *s.* die Mannigfaltigkeit, Abwechselung, Ver=schiedenheit; die Abart, Spielart, Varietät (*Nat. Hist.*); (number) die Auswahl, Menge; 20 —e-**ties**, 20 verschiedene Arten; a —ety of good things, allerlei gute Dinge. —**olite**, *s.* der Blatter=, Pocken=stein. —**orum**, *attrib.*; —orum edition, die Ausgabe mit Anmerkungen verschie=dener Herausgeber. —**ous**, *adj.*, —**ously**, *adv.* mannigfaltig; (different) verschieden(artig).

Varicose, *adj.* krampfaderig; — vein, die Krampf=ader.

Varlet, *s.* der Knappe; (rascal) der Schuft, Kerl.

Varnish, I. *s.* der Firnis, Lack; die Glasur (*of earthenware*); äußerer glänzender Anstrich (*fig.*). II. *v.a.* mit Firniß überziehen (*pictures, etc.*), (über=)firnissen; glasieren; (einer S.) einen An=strich geben, (eine S.) überfirnissen, bemänteln (*fig.*). —**er**, *s.* der Lackierer, Firnisser. *Comp.* —**ing-brush**, *s.* der Firnispinsel.

Varsity, (*Univ. sl.*) *for* University.

Vary, *v.* I. *a.* Abwechselung, Verschiedenheit bringen (in eine S.), wechseln, verändern, vari=ieren. II. *n.* sich verändern, variieren, (ab=) wechseln; (differ) sich unterscheiden, verschieden sein (from, von); veränderlich sein (*as wind*); to — from, abweichen, abgehen von; men — in opinion, die Menschen gehen in den Ansichten auseinander, haben verschiedene Meinungen. —**ing**, *adj.* abwechselnd, veränderlich.

Vas—cular, *adj.* Gefäß=; —cular system, das Gefäßsystem (*Physiol.*). —**e**, *s.* die Vase, das (Kunst=)Gefäß; die Trommel, Glocke (*of capitals*).

Vaseline, *s.* das Vaselin.

Vassal, *s.* der Lehnsmann, Vasall. —**age**, *s.* die Lehnbarkeit, Lehnsmannschaft, der Vasallen=stand, das Vasallentum.

Vast, *adj.* groß, unermeßlich, weit (ausgedehnt) ungeheuer; vielumfassend (*fig.*); a — deal, ge=waltig viel (*vulg.*); — majority, überwiegende Mehrzahl. —**ly**, *adv.* ungeheuer, in hohem Grade, gewaltig. —**ness**, *s* ungeheure Aus=dehnung, ungeheure Größe, Unermeßlichkeit; (greatness) die Großartigkeit. —**y**, *adj.* un=geheuer (*obs.*)

Vat, *s.* das große Faß, die Kufe; die Küpe (*Dyer.*); der Trog (*Pap.*); die Grube (*Tan.*).

Vaticination, *s.* die Weissagung.

[1]**Vault**, I. *s.* das Gewölbe, die Wölbung; (cellar) (das) der Keller(gewölbe); (grave) das Toten=gewölbe, die Gruft; — of heaven, Himmels=gewölbe. II. *v.a.* ein Gewölbe aufführen, wöl=ben; (arch over) überwölben. —**ed**, *adj.* gewölbt. —**ing**, *s.* die Wölbung.

[2]**Vault**, I. *v.n.* springen, sich schwingen (on, upon, auf, *acc.*); Kunstsprünge machen, voltigieren; Bogensprünge machen (*Riding*); to — into the saddle, in den Sattel springen, sich in den Sattel schwingen. II. *v.n.* über (eine S.) hinüber=springen. III. *s.* der Sprung Satz, das Über=springen (mit Aufstützen der Hände oder Benut=zung einer Stange).

Vaunt, I. *v.a.* rühmen, anpreisen. II. *v.n.* prahlen, sich rühmen. III. *s. see* Boast. —**er**, *s.* der Prahler. —**ing**, I. *s.* die Prahlerei. II. *adj.*, —**ingly**, *adv.* prahlerisch.

Vaward, *s. see* Vanguard.

Veal, *s.* das Kalbfleisch; roast (of) —, der Kalbs=braten; — cutlets, Kalbs=rippchen, =koteletten.

Vedette, *s.* der Kavalleriepòsten, die Vedette.

Veer, *v.* I. *n.* sich drehen; sich umwenden, fieren (*as wind*); to — **about**, umspringen; to — **aft**, räumen (*said of the wind*). II. *a.* drehen, (um=) wenden; halsen (*a ship*); abfieren (*a cable*); to — **away**, ausstechen.

Vegeta—ble, I. *s.* die Pflanze; (*also* —bles) das Gemüse. II. *adj.* vegetabilisch, Pflanzen=, Ge=wächs=; —ble chemistry (dye), die Pflanzen=chemie (=farbe); —ble food, die Pflanzennahrung; —ble ivory, vegetabilisches Elfenbein; —ble marrow, kürbisartiges Gewächs; —ble kingdom, das Pflanzenreich. —**rian**, *s.* einer, der sich aus=schließlich von Pflanzenkost nährt, der Vegetari=(an)er. —**rianism**, *s.* der Vegetari(an)ismus. —**te**, *v.n.* wachsen; ein Pflanzenleben führen

(*fig.*). —**tion**, *s.* der Pflanzenwuchs, die Vegetation; die Pflanzenwelt. —**tive**, *adj.* pflanzlich, wie Pflanzen wachsend; (growth-producing) den Pflanzenwuchs befördernd.
Vehemen—ce, *s.* die Heftigkeit, das Ungestüm; (fervour) das Feuer, die Hitze. —**t**, *adj.*, —**tly**, *adv.* heftig, hitzig, leidenschaftlich; gewaltig, hinreißend.
Vehic—le, *s.* das Fuhrwerk, Gefährt, der Wagen; das Hilfsmittel, Vehikel (*fig.*). —**ular**, *adj.* zu einem Führwerke gehörig.
Vehm—e, *s.* (—ic court) das Femgericht.
Veil, I. *s.* der Schleier, die Hülle (*also fig.*); to take the —, Schleier nehmen, Nonne werden. II. *v.a.* verschleiern; verhüllen, bemänteln (*fig.*).
Vein, *s.* die (Blut=)Ader; die Ader (*in wood, stones, etc., also Min. & fig.*); der Hang, die Neigung, Stimmung, Laune (*fig.*); — of wit, humour, Ader des Witzes, Humors; to be in the — for, aufgelegt sein zu. —**ed**, *adj.* geadert, äderig, aderig, marmoriert, gemasert (*also Bot.*). —**ing**, *s.* die Aderung. —**less**, *adj.* ungerippt.
Vel—ar, *adj.* zum Gaumensegel gehörig, am weichen Gaumen gesprochen, velar. —**um** (**palati**), *s.* das Gaumensegel, der weiche Gaumen.
Velleity, *s.* das kraftlose Wollen, die (Willens=) Anwandlung, Regung, das bloße Gelüst.
Vellum, *s.* das Schreib=, Jungfern=pergament, Velin; on —, auf Pergament; bound in —, der Pergamentband. *Comp.* —**-paper**, das Velin=(papier).
Veloci—pede, *s.* das Fahrrad, Veloziped. —**pedist**, *s.* der Velozipedfahrer, Radfahrer, Radler. —**ty**, *s.* die Geschwindigkeit.
Velvet, I. *s.* der Sammet, Samt. II. *adj.* Samt=; (—y) samten, samtweich. —**een**, *s.* der Baumwollsamt, Manchester. —**y**, *see* — II. *Comp.* —**-brush**, *s.* die Samtbürste.
[1]**Venal**, *adj.* venös.
[2]**Venal**, *adj.* verkäuflich, feil. —**ity**, *s.* die Verkäuflichkeit, Feilheit, die Bestechlichkeit.
Vend, *v.a.* verkaufen, feilbieten. —**er**, —**or**, *s.* der Verkäufer. —**ible**, *adj.* verkäuflich, gangbar. —**ue**, *s.* öffentliche Steigerung. *Comp.* —**ue-master**, *s.* der Auktionator.
Veneer, I. *s.* das Furnier, Furnierblatt. II. *v.a.* furnieren, auslegen (*fig.*). —**ing**, *s.* die Furnierung, furnierte *or* ausgelegte Arbeit; der äußere Anstrich (*fig.*).
Venera—ble, *adj.* ehr=, achtungs=würdig. —**bleness**, *s.* die Ehrwürdigkeit. —**te**, *v.a.* (ver)ehren. —**tion**, *s.* die Verehrung, Hochachtung, Ehrfurcht. —**tor**, *s.* der Verehrer.
Venereal, *adj.* den geschlechtlichen Verkehr, Liebesgenuß betreffend, geschlechtlich; venerisch (*also Med.*); — disease, die Geschlechtskrankheit; — pleasure, der Geschlechtsgenuß.
[1]**Venery**, *s.* die Fleischeslust, der Liebesgenuß.
[2]**Venery**, *s.* die Jägerei, Jagd.
Ven—esection, *s.* das Aderlassen. —**ous**, *adj.* venös, zu den Venen gehörig, aderreich.
Venetian, *adj.* venetianisch; —blind, die Jalousie.
Venge—ance, *s.* die Rache, Strafe; to take — ance on, Rache nehmen, sich rächen an (einem); with a —ance, gewaltig, tüchtig, ganz gehörig, daß es eine Art hat (*fam.*). —**ful**, *adj.*, —**fully**, *adv.* rachsüchtig.
Venial, *adj.*, —**ly**, *adv.* verzeihlich, erläßlich. —**ity**, —**ness**, *s.* die Erläßlichkeit, Verzeihlichkeit.
Venison, *s.* das Wildbret, Hochwild.
Venom, *s.* das (tierische) Gift; das Gift (*fig.*). —**ed**, *adj.* vergiftet; giftig. —**ous**, *adj.*, —**ously**, *adv.* giftig. —**ousness**, *s.* die Giftigkeit.
Vent, I. *s.* die Öffnung; das Zwickloch (*of a cask*); das Zünd=loch, =korn (*of guns*); der After (*of birds and fishes*); (passage) der Ausweg; to give — to one's anger, etc., seinem Zorn ꝛc. Luft machen *or* freien Lauf lassen. II. *v.a.* lüften, auslassen, Luft machen.
Ventilat—e, *v.a.* ventilieren, lüften, die Luft erneuern, mit frischer Luft versehen; Luftlöcher anbringen (*Build.*); erörtern, verhandeln (*fig.*). —**ion**, *s.* die Luftreinigung, Lüftung, Reinigung durch Luftzug; die Wetter=Führung, =losung (*Min.*); die Äußerung (*of views*); die Erörterung (*fig.*). —**or**, *s.* der Ventilator, Windfang; (wheel —or) das Windrad.
Ventr—al, *adj.* Bauch=. —**icle**, *s.* die Höhle, Kammer (*Anat.*). —**icular**, *adj.* Höhlen=, Kammer=. —**iloquial**, *adj.* bauchrednerisch. —**iloquism**, *s.* die Bauchrednerei. —**iloquist**, *s.* der Bauchredner. —**iloquize**, *v.n.* bauchreden.
Ventur—e, I. *s.* das Wagnis; (something —ed) der Einsatz; (enterprise) das Unternehmen, die Spekulation; (chance) das Geratewohl; at a —e, aufs Geratewohl, auf gut Glück. II. *v.a.* wagen, aufs Spiel setzen; auf gut Glück versenden (*goods, etc.*); nothing —e, nothing have, wer nichts wagt, gewinnt nichts, frisch gewagt ist halb gewonnen (*prov.*). III. *v.n.* sich erkühnen *or* erdreisten; (run the risk) wagen, sich der Gefahr aussetzen; to —e upon a th., sich wagen an eine S., etwas unternehmen; I —e to ask, ich erlaube mir zu fragen, ich gestatte mir die Anfrage; he —ed to promise, kühn versprach er. —**esome**, *adj.*, —**esomely**, *adv.* kühn, verwegen. —**esomeness**, *s.* die Kühnheit, Verwegenheit. —**ous**, *see* —esome.
Venue, *s.* der Ort der Handlung; zuständiger Gerichtsort (dem Tatort benachbart) (*Law*).
Veraci—ous, *adj.* wahrhaft, wahrheitsliebend, wahr. —**ty**, *s.* die Wahrhaftigkeit, Glaubwürdigkeit; (truth) die Wahrheit.
Veranda, *s.* der Vorbau, die Vorhalle, Veranda.
Verb, *s.* das Zeitwort, Verbum. —**al**, I. *adj.*, —**ally**, *adv.* wörtlich; mündlich; Verbal= (*Gram.*); —al acceptance, mündliche Annahme; —al memory, das Wortgedächtnis. II. *s.* (—al noun) das Verbal=Hauptwort. —**alist**, *s.* der Wortkrämer. —**alize**, *v.a.* in ein Zeitwort verwandeln. —**atim**, *adv.* Wort für Wort. —**iage**, *s.* der Wortschwall. —**ose**, *adj.* wortreich. —**osity**, *s. see* —iage; die Wortfülle, Weitschweifigkeit.
Verbena, *s.* die Verbene, das Eisenkraut.
Verd—ancy, *s.* das Grüne. —**ant**, *adj.*, —**antly**, *adv.* grün, frisch; blühend (*fig.*); unerfahren, grün (*fig.*). —**igris**, *s.* der Grünspan. —**ure**, *s.* das Grün.
Verdict, *s.* der Spruch, Urteilspruch, das Verdikt (der Geschwornen); (judgment) das Urteil, die Entscheidung.
[1]**Verge**, *s.* der (Amts=)Stab. —**r**, *s.* der Stabträger; der Kirchendiener, Meßner (*in churches*).
[2]**Verge**, I. *s.* der Rand; on the — of bankruptcy (ruin), dem Bankerott nahe, (am Rande des Verderbens). II. *v.n.* sich (hin=)neigen, sich nähern, sinken (*also fig.*); to — on, streifen an (*acc.*); verging on . . ., an (*acc.*) . . . grenzend.
Veri—est, *adj.* ärgst, ausgemachtest. —**fiable**, *adj.* erweislich, beweisbar. —**fication**, *s.* die Bewahrheitung, Beurkundung, Bewährung; in —fication of which, zur Urkunde dessen. —**fier**, *s.* der Beglaubiger, Untersucher. —**fy**, *v.a.* die Wahrheit, Echtheit einer Sache prüfen; bewahrheiten, beurkunden, erhärten, als wahr erweisen; wahr machen, bestätigen, erfüllen (*a prediction, etc.*); *see* Prove. —**ly**, *adv.* wahrlich, fürwahr; (really) wirklich, wahrhaftig. —**similitude**, *s.* die Wahrscheinlichkeit. —**table**, *adj.*, —**tably**, *adv.* wahr(haftig). —**ty**, *s.* die Wahrheit.
Verjuice, *s.* der herbe Wein, Sauerwein.
Vermi—celli, *s.* Fadennudeln (*pl.*). —**cular**, *adj.* wurmförmig. —**culate**, I. *v.a.* wurmlinig furnieren, einlegen; —culated work, die wurmlinig eingelegte Arbeit. II. *adj. see* —cular. —**form**, *adj.* wurmförmig. —**fuge**, *s.* das Wurmmittel. —**lion**, *s.* der Zinnober; hochrote Farbe. —**n**, *s.* das Ungeziefer; die Brut, das Gesindel, Geschmeiß (*fig.*).

Vernacular, I. *adj.* einheimisch, vaterländisch. II. *s.* die Landessprache, Muttersprache.
Vernal, *adj.* zum Frühlinge gehörig, Frühlings=; — equinox, Frühlings=Tag= und Nacht=gleiche.
Vernier, *s.* der Vernier, Nonius, Zehntelzeiger.
Veronica, *s.* der Ehrenpreis.
Vers—atile, *adj.* (changeable) veränderlich; (unsteady) unbeständig, wankelmütig; (clever) gewandt, vielseitig, geschmeidig (*fig.*). **—atility,** *s.* die Veränderlichkeit, Unbeständigkeit; die Geschmeidigkeit, Gewandtheit. **—e,** *s.* der Vers (*also B.*), die Strophe; (poetry) die Poesie, Dicht=, Vers=kunst; blank —e, reimlose Verse. **—ed,** *adj.* erfahren, bewandert; —ed in the ways of the world, welterfahren. **—ification,** *s.* das Versmachen, der Versbau; (art) die Verskunst. **—ify,** *v.* I. *n.* Verse machen, reimen. II. *a.* in Verse bringen; in Versen erzählen, besingen (*a tale, etc.*). **—ion,** *s.* die Übersetzung; (account) die Darstellung, Erklärung; die Lesart; die Auffassung(sweise). **—us,** *prep.* gegen (*Law*).
Verst, *s.* die Werst.
Vert—ebra, *s.* (*pl.* —ebrae) der Rückenwirbel, das Wirbelbein. **—ebral,** *adj.* zu den Wirbelbeinen gehörig, Wirbel(bein)=; —ebral column, die Wirbelsäule, (der) das Rückgrat. **—ebrate,** I. *adj.*, **—ebrated,** *adj.* mit Rückenwirbeln versehen, gewirbelt. II. *s.* (—ebrate animal) das Wirbeltier. **—ex,** *s.* der Scheitel(punkt); (top) die Spitze; der Zenit (*Astr.*). **—ical,** *adj.*, **—ically,** *adv.* senkrecht, scheitelrecht, lotrecht, vertikal; —ical angle, Scheitel=, Vertikal=winkel; —ical line, Scheitellinie. **—igo,** *s.* der Schwindel.
Vervain, *s.* das Eisenkraut.
Verve, *s.* künstlerische Begeisterung, das Feuer, die Kraft, der Schwung.
Very, I. *adv.* sehr. II. *adj.* wahrhaftig; (actual) wirklich, echt; the — same, derselbe, der nämliche; a — fool, ein ausgemachter Narr; in the — act, auf frischer Tat; the — devil, der leibhaftige Teufel; to the — bone, bis auf den Knochen; that's the — reason, das ist gerade der Grund; the — air you breathe, selbst die Luft, die ihr einatmet; the — thought, schon der, *or* der bloße, Gedanke; the — next morning, schon den folgenden Morgen; on the — (same) day, an dem nämlichen Tage, noch an demselben Tage; the — man, gerade derselbe Mann; the — best, last, das aller=beste, =letzte.
Vesic—ation, *s.* das Blasenziehen. **—atory,** *s.* das Blasen=, Zug=pflaster. **—le,** *s.* das Bläschen. **—ular,** **—ulous,** *adj.* voll Bläschen, mit Bläschen besetzt.
Vesper, I. *s.* der Abend (*Poet.*); der Abendstern. II. *adj.* Abend=. **—s,** *pl.* die Vesper, Abendbetstunde (*R. C.*).
Vessel, *s.* das Gefäß (*also Anat., Bot., fig.*); das Fahrzeug, Schiff (*Naut.*); chosen —, ein Auserwählter; weak —, ein schwankes Rohr (*coll.*); no — till Monday, Schiff unmöglich vor Montag (*C. L.*).
Vest, I. *s.* das Gewand (*obs.*); die Unterjacke; das Wams, die Weste. II. *v.a.* bekleiden; belehnen (*Law*); verleihen, festsetzen (*Law*); to — **in,** in Besitz setzen, einsetzen, bekleiden; the supreme executive power is —ed in the king, die höchste vollziehende Gewalt komm dem König zu; to — **with,** bekleiden, belehnen mit; —ed interests, rechtlich begründete Interessen; —ed priest, der Priester in langem Gewande; —ed rights, altbegründete Rechte. II. *v.n.* übergehen, fallen (in, an, *acc.*). **—ment,** *s.* das Gewand, Kleid. **—ry,** *s.* die Sakristei; (—ry board) das Kirchenkollegium, die Gemeindevertretung. **—ure,** *s.* Kleider (*pl.*). *Comp.* **—ry-clerk,** *s.* der Kirchspielschreiber. **—ryman,** *s.* der Kirchen=älteste, =vorsteher. **—ry-meeting,** *s.* die Versammlung der Kirchenvorsteher.
Vesta, *s.*; wax —, das Wachszündhölzchen.
Vestibule, I. *s.* der Vor=hof, =saal, die Vorhalle. II. *attrib.*; — car, der Korridorwagen; — **train,** der D=Zug, Durchgangszug, (*coll.*) Harmonikazug.
Vestige, *s.* die Spur.
Vetch, *s.* die Wicke. **—ling,** *s.* die Platterbse.
Veteran, I. *adj.* alt, gedient, erfahren. II. *s.* der altgediente *or* ausgediente Soldat, Veteran.
Veterinary, I. *adj.* tierärztlich; — art, die Tierarzneikunde; — surgeon, der Tierarzt. II. *s.* der Tier=, Roß=arzt.
Veto, I. *s.* das Verwerfungsrecht, Veto, Verbot. II. *v.a.*; (to put one's — upon) sein Veto einlegen gegen, gegen eine S. stimmen *or* sich erklären.
Vex, *v.* I. *a.* plagen, quälen; (annoy) ärgern; (disquiet) beunruhigen, beängstigen. II. *n.* sich quälen, ärgern. **—ation,** *s.* die Beunruhigung; die Plage, Plackerei, Qual, der Kummer, Verdruß, Ärger. **—atious,** *adj.*, **—atiously,** *adv.* drückend, quälerisch, verdrießlich; *see* Distressing; —atious wars, bedrückende Kriege; —atious suit, vexatorischer Prozeß. **—atiousness,** *s.* das Quälende, Plagende, die Verdrießlichkeit, Ärgerlichkeit. **—ed,** *adj.* verdrießlich, ärgerlich; Streit veranlassend; —ed question, die schwierige, vielumstrittene Frage, Streitfrage. **—ing,** *adj. see* —atious.
Via, *prep.* über; — London, über London. **—duct,** *s.* der Viadukt. **—ticum,** *s.* der Reisebedarf; der Reisepfennig; das Zehrgeld (*R. C.*).
Vial, *see* Phial.
Viands, *pl.* die Lebensmittel, (Fleisch=)Speisen.
Vibrat—e, *v.* I. *n.* schwingen, zittern, vibrieren; it —es still in his ear, das klingt ihm noch in den Ohren nach. II. *a.* schwingen lassen. **—ion,** *s.* die Schwingung, Vibration. **—ive,** **—ory,** *adj.* schwingend, Schwingungs=; —ory motion, die Schwingungsbewegung.
Vicar, *s.* der Stellvertreter, Amtsverweser; der Pfarrverweser, Vikar, (Unter=)Pfarrer; — general, General=Vikar. **—age,** *s.* die Pfarrverweserstelle, Vikarpfründe; (house) die Wohnung des Vikars, die Pfarre. **—ious,** *adj.*, **—iously,** *adv.* stellvertretend.
[1]**Vice,** *s.* das Laster; (defect) der Fehler, die Unart.
[2]**Vice,** *s.* der Schraubstock.
[3]**Vice,** an Stelle von; (*in comp.* =) Unter=, Vize=. **—-admiral,** *s.* der Vizeadmiral. **—-chancellor,** *s.* der Vizekanzler, Rektor magnificus (*Univ.*). **—gerency,** *s.* die Statthalterschaft, Verwesung. **—gerent,** I. *adj.* stellvertretend. II. *s.* der Stellvertreter, Verweser. **—-president,** *s.* der stellvertretende Vorsitzer, Vizepräsident. **—regal,** *adj.* vizeköniglich. **—roy,** *s.* der Vizekönig. **—royalty,** *s.* das Vizekönigtum. **—-versa,** *adv.* umgekehrt, im entgegengesetzten Falle.
Vicin—age, *s.* die Nachbarschaft, Nähe. **—al,** *adj.* benachbart, nahe. **—ity,** *s. see* —age.
Vicious, *adj.*, **—ly,** *adv.* lasterhaft; fehlerhaft; (impure) unrein, schlecht; — horse, bösartiges Pferd, Pferd das Mucken hat; — circle, der Zirkelschluß. **—ness,** *s.* die Lasterhaftigkeit, Schlechtigkeit; die Bösartigkeit (*of horses*).
Vicissitude, *s.* die Abwechselung, der Wechsel.
Victim, *s.* das Opfer (*also fig.*); to fall a — to one's own excesses, seinen eigenen Ausschweifungen zum Opfer fallen; to be the — of one's own imagination, sich durch seine eigene Einbildungskraft betrügen lassen. **—ize,** *v.a.* (hin=)opfern, zum Schlachtopfer machen, quälen.
Victor, *s.* der Sieger. **—ia,** *s.* die Viktoriachaise, leichter Einspänner. **—ious,** *adj.*, **—iously,** *adv.* siegreich, siegend; Sieges=. **—y,** *s.* der Sieg; to get the —y, to be —ious, den Sieg davontragen (over, über einen).
Victual, I. *v.a.* mit Lebensmitteln versehen, verproviantieren. II. *s.*, **—s,** *pl.* Lebensmittel, der Mundvorrat, Proviant. **—ing,** I. *adj.* Proviant=. II. *s.* die Verproviantierung. **—ler,** *m.*

der Verkäufer von Lebensmitteln, Lieferant; licensed —ler, konzessionierter Verkäufer geistiger Getränke, Schankwirt.

Vicugna, Vicuña, I. *s.* das Vikunja. II. *attrib.*; — wool, die Vikunjenwolle, Vigognewolle.

Vide, (*Lat.*) *interj.* sieh, vergleiche.

Videlicet, (*abbr.* **viz.**; *read:* namely, that is) *adv.* nämlich, das heißt.

Vie, *v.n.* wetteifern, es (mit einem) aufnehmen.

View, I. *v.a.* besehen, besichtigen, betrachten; (examine) untersuchen, mustern. II. *s.* der Blick, Anblick; (prospect) die Aussicht; (reach of sight) das Auge, die Sehweite; (point of —) der Gesichts-, Stand-punkt; (intention) der Zweck, die Absicht; (opinion) die Meinung, Ein-, Ansicht; my own — is, meine eigene Ansicht ist; die Ansicht (*Draw.*); front —, Vorderansicht; dissolving —s, Nebelbilder, Wandelbilder; at first —, beim ersten Anblick; to be in —, vor Augen liegen; to command a — of (over), die Aussicht haben nach; to have in —, vor Augen haben (*lit.*); beabsichtigen, bezwecken (*fig.*); to keep in —, im Auge behalten (*lit.*); berücksichtigen (*fig.*); to take a — of, in Augenschein nehmen; with a — to, in Absicht auf (*acc.*); with that —, in dieser Absicht; the end in —, der beabsichtigte Zweck; on —, (ausgestellt) zur Besichtigung, zur Ansicht; broad —s on a subject, aufgeklärte weitherzige Ansichten über einen Gegenstand. **—er,** *s.* der Beschauer. *Comp.* **—-finder,** *s.* der Sucher (*Phot.*).

Vigil, *s.* das Wachen; der heilige Abend (*of a festival*); (fast) das Fasten vor einem Festtage. **—ance,** *s.* die Wachsamkeit, Vorsicht, Sorgfalt. **—ant,** *adj.*, **—antly,** *adv.* wachsam, sorgsam. **—s,** *pl.* die Vigilien (*R. C.*).

Vignette, *s.* das Zierbild, die Vignette, der Buchdruckerstock.

Vigor, *see* Vigour. **—ous,** *adj.*, **—ously,** *adv.* stark, kräftig, frisch; (lively) frisch, munter; kernhaft; nachdrücklich (*fig.*).

Vigour, *s.* die Lebens-kraft, -frische, Regsamkeit, Kraft, Energie; der Nachdruck (*fig.*); — of mind, die Geistesstärke.

Viking, I. *s.* der Wiking, nordische Seeheld. II. *attrib.*; a — ship, ein Wikingerschiff; the old — spirit, der alte Wikingergeist.

Vil—e, *adj.*, **—ely,** *adv.* verächtlich, wertlos; (mean) gering, niedrig; (bad) schlecht, ruchlos, nichtswürdig. **—eness,** *s.* die Gemeinheit, Niederträchtigkeit; die Wertlosigkeit; die Schlechtigkeit. **—ification,** *s.* das Herabsetzen, Schmähen. **—ifier,** *s.* der Beschimpfer, Schmäher, Lästerer. **—ify,** *v.a.* schmähen, verrufen. **—ipend,** *v.a.* verachten.

Vill—a, *s.* das Landhaus, die Villa. **—age,** *s.* das Dorf. **—ager,** *s.* der Dorfbewohner, Dörfler. **—ain,** *s.* der Schurke, Bösewicht; (serf) der Leibeigne, Bauer (*obs.*). **—ainous,** *adj.*, **—ainously,** *adv.* schändlich, schurkisch, abscheulich. **—ainy,** *s.* die Schurkerei, Schlechtig-, Schändlich-keit; (piece of —ainy) der Schurkenstreich. **—anage,** — **einage,** *s.* die Leibeigenschaft, Frone. **—eggiatura,** *s.* der Landaufenthalt, die Sommerfrische.

Vin—aceous, *adj.* Wein-; (rot)weinfarbig. — **aigrette,** *s.* das Riechfläschchen. **—e,** *see* Vine. **—osity,** *s.* der Gehalt an Weingeist; die Weinartigkeit. **—ous,** *adj.* weinig; weinartig; —ous smell, der Weingeruch; —ous fermentation, weinige Gärung. **—tage,** *s.* die Weinlese; (harvest time) die Zeit der Weinlese, der Herbst; (produce) der geerntete Wein, Jahrgang. — **tager,** *s.* der Winzer, Weinleser. **—tner,** *s.* der Weinhändler; (tavern-keeper) der Weinwirt.

Vindic—able, *adj.* zu verteidigen *or* rechtfertigen. **—ate,** *v.a.* rechtfertigen; (defend) schützen, verteidigen; behaupten; to —ate the law, dem Gesetze Achtung verschaffen. **—ation,** *s.* die Rechtfertigung; die Verteidigung, Ehrenrettung; die Behauptung (*of opinions*). **—atory,** *adj.* verteidigend, rechtfertigend; bestrafend, rächend. — **tive,** *adj.*, **—tively,** *adv.* rachsüchtig. **—tiveness,** *s.* die Rachsucht.

Vine, *s.* der Weinstock, Rebstock, die Rebe; to prune a —, einen Rebstock beschneiden. **—gar,** I. *s.* der (Wein-)Essig. II. *attrib.*; —gar bottle *or* cruet, das Essigfläschchen. III. *v.a.* Essig tun (an); in Essig legen, marinieren. **—ry,** *s.* das Treibhaus für Weintrauben. **—yard,** *s.* der Wein-garten, -berg. *Comp.* **—-branch,** *s.* die Weinrebe, der Rebschoß. **—-clad,** *adj.* rebenbedeckt. **—-dresser,** *s.* der Weingärtner. **—-leaf,** *s.* das Wein-, Reben-blatt. **—-leaves,** *pl.* das Weinlaub. **—-louse,** *s.* die Reblaus. **—-prop,** *s.* der Weinpfahl. **—-shoot,** *s.* der Rebenschößling, die Ranke.

Viol, —a, *s.* die Viole, Bratsche; —a di gamba, kleine Baßgeige. **—in,** I. *s.* die Geige, Violine; to play the —in, Geige spielen, geigen. II. *attrib.*; —in blanket, die Geigendecke; —in bow, der Geigenbogen; —in case, der Geigenkasten, das Violinfutteral; —in clef, der Violinschlüssel; —in player, der Geiger, Geigenspieler. **—inist,** *s.* der Geiger, Violinspieler. **—ist,** *s.* der Bratschenspieler. **—oncellist,** *s.* der Violoncellist, Cellist. **—oncello,** *s.* das Violoncell, Cello.

Viol—able, *adj.* verletzlich. **—ate,** *v.a.* verletzen, freveln an (*dat.*), entweihen; (transgress) übertreten; brechen (*an oath, etc.*); schänden, entehren, notzüchten (*women*). **—ation,** *s.* die Verletzung; die Entehrung, Schändung; der (Eides-, Bundes-, Friedens-) Bruch (*of an oath, a contract, peace, etc.*). **—ator,** *s.* der Verletzer, Übertreter; der Schänder, Ehrenräuber. **—ence,** *s.* die Gewaltsamkeit, Heftigkeit, das Ungestüm; (act of —ence) die Gewalt(tat); to do —ence to, (einem) Gewalt antun; to offer —ence to, gewalttätig behandeln; (—ate) notzüchtigen wollen (*a woman*). **—ent,** *adj.*, **—ently,** *adv.* heftig (*as a blow, wind, language, a fight, etc.*), ungestüm, stark; (passionate) heftig, hitzig; (produced by force) gewalt-sam (*as a death*), -tätig; to lay —ent hands on o.s., Hand an sich legen.

Violet, I. *s.* das Veilchen. II. *adj.* (— blue) veilchenblau.

Viper, *s.* die Viper, Natter (*also fig.*), Otter; to nourish a — in one's bosom, eine Schlange am Busen hegen. **—ine,** I. *adj.* viperartig, Viper-. II. *s.* die Viper. **—ous,** *adj.* viperartig, giftig (*also fig.*).

Vir—ago, *s.* das Mannweib; der Dragoner, die böse Sieben (*fig.*). **—ile,** *adj.* männlich, mannhaft; mannbar. **—ility,** *s.* die Männlichkeit, Mannhaftigkeit; (procreative power) die Manneskraft, männliche Kraft, Zeugungskraft. **—tue,** *see* Virtu—.

Virelay, *s.* das Ringellied, Zweireimgedicht.

Virg—in, I. *s.* die Jungfrau, Jungfer; die Jungfrau (*Astron.*); der, die Unverheiratete (*B.*); blessed —in Mary, die heilige Jungfrau, gebenedeite Jungfrau Maria. II. *adj.* jungfräulich; (chaste) keusch, züchtig; (pure) rein; frisch, neu, ungebraucht (*fig.*); gediegen (*Metall.*); —in earth, die Jungfernerde; —in forest, der Urwald; —in gold, das Jungfern-, gediegenes Gold; —in honey, der Jungfernhonig; —in soil, noch ungepflügtes Land, unbebauter Boden; unerforschtes, noch nicht bearbeitetes Gebiet (*fig.*); jungfräulicher Boden (*poet.*); —in worship, der Marienkultus, die Marienverehrung. **—inal,** I. *adj.* jungfräulich; madonnenhaft. II. *s.* (*usually pl.* —inals) das Clavicymbel, Dockenklavier, Spinett. III. *attrib.*; —inal book, das Notenbuch für ein Spinett. **—inian,** *adj.* virginisch; —inia(n) creeper, virginische Waldrebe, der wilde Wein. **—inity,** *s.* die Jungfern-, Jungfrau-schaft. **—o,** *s.* die Jungfrau (*Astr.*). *Comp.* **—in-like,** *adj.* jungfräulich.

Virid—escence, *s.* das Grünwerden. **—escent,** *adj.* grünlich. **—ity,** *s.* das Grüne.

Virtu (*also* Vertu), *s.* die Liebe zu den schönen Künsten, der Geschmack an Kunstsachen; articles of —, Kunstgegenstände; Kuriositäten. **—al,** *adj.*, **—ally,** *adv.* fähig zu wirken; im Grunde genommen, eigentlich, so gut als, dem Wesen nach; —al power, das Wirkungsvermögen, die Wirkungskraft; —al velocity, virtuelle Geschwindigkeit. **—e,** *s.* die Tugend; die Sittsamkeit, Keuschheit (*of women*); (power) die Kraft, Wirksamkeit; (excellence) die Vorzüglichkeit, der Wert; to make a —e of necessity, aus der Not eine Tugend machen; by *or* in —e of, kraft, vermöge; in —e whereof, urkundlich dessen. **—oso,** *s.* (*opp. to* Dilettante), der Virtuos, große Künstler, die Virtuosin (*Mus., etc.*); der Kunstkenner, Kunstliebhaber (*rare*). **—ous,** *adj.*, **—ously,** *adv.* tugendhaft; keusch, sittsam; vortrefflich, vorzüglich; kräftig, wirksam, heilkräftig (*obs.*).

Viru—lence, —lency, *s.* das Gift; die Giftigkeit, Bosheit, der Ingrimm (*fig.*). **—lent,** *adj.*, **—lently,** *adv.* giftig; ansteckend, bösartig; boshaft (*fig.*). **—s,** *s.* das Gift, der Giftstoff; die Giftigkeit (*also fig.*).

Vis, *s.*; — inertiae, das Beharrungsvermögen, die Trägheitskraft.

Visage, *s.* das Gesicht, Antlitz, Angesicht. **—d,** *adj.*; long- —d, mit einem langen Gesicht.

Vis-à-vis, I. *adv.* gegenüber. II. *s.* das Gegenüber, Vis-à-vis.

Viscera, *pl.* Eingeweide. **—l,** *adj.* Eingeweide-, innerlich.

Visc—id, *adj.* klebrig. **—idity,** *s.* die Klebrigkeit, Dickflüssigkeit. **—ous,** *adj.* klebrig, zäh.

Viscount, (**—ess,**) *s.* der (die) Vicomte(-sse).

Visib—ility, *s.* die Sichtbarkeit. **—le,** *adj.*, **—ly,** *adv.* sichtbar; (obvious) augenscheinlich, offenbar.

Vision, *s.* das Sehen; (power of —) die Sehkraft, das Gesicht; (apparition) die Erscheinung; (dream, *etc.*) das Traumgesicht, Traumbild, die Vision; (imaginary appearance) das Hirngespinnst. **—ariness,** *s.* die Träumerei. **—ary,** I. *adj.* eingebildet, geträumt, nur in der Einbildung existierend, phantastisch. II. *s.* der (die) Geisterseher(in), Träumer(in), Schwärmer(in).

Visit, I. *v.a.* besuchen; (inspect) besichtigen, visitieren, unter-, durch-suchen, in Augenschein nehmen; heimsuchen (*B.*); visitieren (*Mil.*); to — one's indignation upon a p., seinen Zorn auslassen an einem. II. *v.n.* Besuche machen; we don't —, wir haben keinen Umgang mit einander; she —s there, sie kommt oft dahin. III. *s.* der Besuch, die Visite; to pay a p. a —, einem einen Besuch abstatten; to pay a flying —, einen kurzen Besuch machen; —to Weimar, ein Besuch in Weimar; we shall pay a — to Munich, wir werden München besuchen. **—ant,** I. *s.* der Besucher, Besuch; der Strichvogel (*Ornith.*). II. *adj.* besuchend. **—ation,** *s.* der Besuch; (— of inspection) die Visitation, Besichtigung, Untersuchung; die (göttliche) Heimsuchung (*of God*), Schickung; —ation of our Lady, Mariä Heimsuchung. **—ing,** I. *adj.* Besuchs-; —ing card, die Visitenkarte; —ing committee, der Untersuchungsausschuß; —ing day, der Besuchstag; —ing governor, ein nicht an einem Orte residierender Statthalter; to take —ing lessons at a school, an einer Schule hospitieren; —ing list, die Besuchsliste; —ing mistress, —ing teacher, Lehrer(in), welche(r) ins Haus (oder in die Schule) kommt; —ing officer, visitierender Offizier; to be on —ing terms, auf Besuchsfuß stehen. II. *s.* das Besuchen; die Heimsuchung. **—or,** *s.* der Besuchende, Besuch(er); (inspector) der Inspektor; —ors' book, die Besuchsliste; das Fremdenbuch. **—(at)orial,** *adj.* Visitations-.

Visor, Vizor, *s.* das Visi(e)r (eines Helmes); (mask) die Maske. **—ed,** *adj.* maskiert.

Vista, *s.* die Aussicht, Durchsicht, (durch einen Baumgang); die Aussicht (*fig.*).

Visual, *adj.* zum Sehen, zum Gesichte gehörig; — angle, der Seh-, Gesichts-winkel; — field, das Sehfeld; — line, die Gesichtslinie; — nerve, (ray,) der Seh-nerv (-strahl). **—ize,** *v.a. & n.* (sich) im Geiste vor Augen stellen; reproduzierte Gesichtsvorstellungen bilden (*Psych.*).

Vital, *adj.* zum Leben gehörig, Lebens-; (essential) höchst notwendig, wesentlich; — energy, die Lebenskraft; — interests are at stake, Lebensinteressen stehen auf dem Spiele; — parts, edle Teile (*of the body*); — power, Lebenskraft; — question, die Lebensfrage; — spark, der Lebensfunken. **—ity,** *s.* die Lebens-kraft, -fähigkeit; (life) das Leben. **—ization,** *s.* die Belebung. **—ize,** *v.a.* beleben. **—s,** *pl.* die zum Leben notwendigen *or* Lebens-Teile; das Leben, Herz (*fig.*).

Vitiat—e, *v.a.* verderben; ungültig machen (*Law*); entheiligen, schänden; verfälschen; (nullify) entkräften, vernichten, untauglich machen; —ed air, schlechte, verdorbene Luft. **—ion,** *s.* die Verderbung; die Vernichtung; die Ungültigmachung; die Schändung, Verfälschung.

Vitr—eous, *adj.* gläsern; (glass-like) glasartig; (pertaining to glass) Glas-; —eous electricity, Glaselektrizität; —eous humour, —eous body, der Glaskörper (*of the eye*). **—escent, —escible,** *adj.* verglasbar. **—ifaction,** *s.* die Verglasung. **—ify,** *v.a.* (*& n.* sich) verglasen, schmelzen. **—iol,** *s.* (der) das Vitriol; —iol of lead, schwefelsaures Bleivitriol; oil of —iol, die Schwefelsäure. **—iolic,** *adj.* vitriolhaltig, Vitriol-; beizend, ätzend (*fig.*).

Vituperat—e, *v.a.* (schmähend) tadeln, schelten. **—ion,** *s.* der beschimpfende Tadel, die Beschimpfung. **—ive,** *adj.* schmähend.

Viv—acious, *adj.*, **—aciously,** *adv.* lebhaft, munter. **—acity, —aciousness,** *s.* die Lebhaftigkeit, Munterkeit, das (jugendliche) Feuer. **—at,** *s.* der Hochruf, das Lebehoch. **—a-voce,** *adv.* mündlich. **—id,** *adj.*, **—idly,** *adv.* lebhaft, lebendig (*as the imagination, colour, etc.*); —id flash of lightning, helleuchtender Blitzstrahl; —id narrative, lebendige Erzählung. **—idness,** *s.* die Lebhaftigkeit, Lebendigkeit. **—ify,** *v.a.* beleben. **—iparous,** *adj.* lebendige Junge gebärend. **—isection,** *s.* die Vivisektion.

Vixen, *s.* die Füchsin; die Zänkerin, böse Sieben (*fig.*). **—ish,** *adj.* zänkisch, keifend.

Viz., *see* Videlicet.

Vizier, *s.* der Vezier.

Voc—able, *s.* das Wort, die Vokabel. **—abulary,** *s.* das Wörterverzeichnis, Vocabularium; der Wortschatz (beim Reden). **—al,** *adj.* (with a voice) stimmbegabt, Stimmen-; Vokal-; laut, mündlich; —al with, tönend von; —al chords, Stimmbänder; —al concert, die Gesangsaufführung; —al music, die Vokalmusik, der Gesang. **—alist,** *s.* der (die) Sänger(in). **—alization,** *s.* das Aussprechen der Vokale; das Vokalisieren, Skalasingen. **—alize,** I. *v.a.* zum Laute bilden, tönend machen; vokalisieren (*Mus.*); mit Vokalen versehen (*in Semitic languages*). II. *v.n.* sprechen, singen. **—ally,** *adv.* mittelst der Stimme, durch Laute. **—ation,** *s.* der (innere) Beruf; (taste, talent) die Anlage, Neigung, der Ruf; (occupation) der Beruf, das Geschäft, die Beschäftigung. **—ative,** I. *adj.* rufend. II. *s.* (—ative case) der Vokativ. **—iferate,** *v.* I. *n.* heftig schreien, brüllen. II. *a.* laut (aus-)rufen. **—iferation,** *s.* das laute Geschrei, der Lärm. **—iferous,** *adj.*, **—iferously,** *adv.* schreiend, lärmend; aus vollem Halse.

Vogue, *s.* die Mode, Beliebtheit; to be in —, in der Mode, im Schwange sein; ziehen; to bring into —, in Aufnahme bringen.

Voic—e, I. *s.* die Stimme; innere Regung, Stimme (*fig.*); (speech) die Rede, Sprache; (vote) die (Wahl-)Stimme; to give —e to a thought, einem Gedanken Ausdruck verleihen; in —e, bei Stimme; active (passive) —e, die Tätigkeitsform, das Aktivum (die Leideform, das Passivum); at the top of one's —e, aus vollem Halse. II. *v.a.* stimmen, regulieren, probieren (*the pipes of an organ*); äußern, ausdrücken, Stimme verleihen; stimmhaft aussprechen; —ing of consonants, die stimmhafte Aussprache der Konsonanten. **—ed**, *adj.* stimmhaft; —ed stop, stimmhafter Verschlußlaut, Media. **—eless**, *adj.* ohne Stimme, stimmlos; ohne Wahlstimme; —eless stop, stimmloser Verschlußlaut, Tenuis.

Void, I. *adj.* leer; *see* Vacant; (null) nichtig, ungültig; — of, arm an, leer an, ohne, (free) frei von; — of sense, sinnlos; — of reason, unvernünftig; — of interest, uninteressant, langweilig; — of offence, schuldlos; null and —, null und nichtig; to make —, ungültig machen, aufheben (*Law, etc.*). II. *s.* der leere Raum, die Leere; to fill a —, eine Lücke ausfüllen. III. *v.a.* leeren; (quit) räumen, verlassen; (evacuate) ausspeien, von sich geben. **—able**, *adj.* ausleerbar; aufhebbar, aufzuheben. **—ance**, *s.* die Ausleerung; das Ausspeien ꝛc.; die Ausstoßung aus einer Pfründe. **—ness**, *s.* die Leere, Leerheit; die Nichtigkeit, Ungültigkeit.

Vol—ant, *adj.* fliegend (*Her.*). **—atile**, *adj.* fliegend; flüchtig, verfliegend (*Chem.*); flüchtig, lebendig, flatterhaft; —atile oils, ätherische Öle; sal —atile, kohlensaures Ammoniak; —atile salt, das Riechsalz. **—atileness**, **—atility**, *s.* die Flüchtigkeit (*also fig.*); (unsteadiness) die Unbeständigkeit. **—atilization**, *s.* die Verflüchtigung. **—ley**, I. *s.* die Salve, Ladung; der Ausbruch, Strom (*fig.*); der Flugschlag (*Tennis*); firing in —leys, die Salvenabgabe, das Salvenfeuer, Rottenfeuer. II. *attrib.*; —ley firing, das Rottenfeuer. III. *v.a.* abschießen, ausstoßen; den Ball vor dem Aufprallen zurückschlagen (*Tennis*). IV. *v.n.* sich plötzlich entladen, krachen; einen Ball im Fluge zurückschlagen (*Tennis*).

Volcan—ic, *adj.* vulkanisch. **—o**, *s.* der Vulkan, feuerspeiende Berg.

[1]**Vole**, *s.* der Schlemm, alle Stiche im Kartenspiel.

[2]**Vole**, *s.* die Wühlmaus.

Volition, *s.* das Wollen; (power of —) die Willenskraft, das Willensvermögen.

Volt, *s.* die Wendung (*Fenc.*); die Volte (*of horses*).

Voltai—c, *adj.* voltaisch; —c electricity, *see* —sm; —c pile, voltaische Säule. **—sm**, *s.* die Berührungselektrizität, der Galvanismus.

Volu—bility, *s.* die Beweglichkeit, der Wechsel; die Geläufigkeit (der Zunge), die Zungenfertigkeit. **—ble**, *adj.*, **—bly**, *adv.* geläufig, fließend; (fluent in speech) zungenfertig. **—me**, *s.* der Band (*of a book*); das Volumen, der körperliche Inhalt (*Phys., etc.*); die Stärke, der Umfang (*of the voice*); —mes, viel, Massen; —mes of smoke, Rauchmassen, dicke Rauchwolken. **—metric**, *adj.*; —metric analysis, die Maßanalyse. **—minous**, *adj.*, **—uminously**, *adv.* umfangreich, voluminös, dick; bändereich; —minous writer, fruchtbarer Schriftsteller.

Volunt—arily, *adv.* aus freien Stücken. **—ariness**, *s.* die Freiwilligkeit. **—ary**, I. *adj.* freiwillig; willkürlich; vorsätzlich; selbstbestimmend; —ary system, das Freiwilligkeitssystem (wodurch die Gemeinde ihren Geistlichen selbst wählt und unterhält). II. *s.* das freie Vor=, Zwischen=spiel (auf der Orgel). **—eer**, I. *s.* der Freiwillige; —eers, das Freiwilligenkorps, die freiwillige Reserve und Landwehr. II. *adj.* freiwillig dienend. III. *v.n.* als Freiwilliger eintreten; freiwillig dienen (*also Mil.*). IV. *v.a.* aus freien Stücken, eignem Antriebe bieten (*one's services, etc.*).

Voluptu—ary, *s.* der Wollüstling. **—ous**, *adj.*, **—ously**, *adv.* wollüstig, üppig. **—ousness**, *s.* die Wollust, Üppigkeit.

Volute, *s.* die Schnecke (*Arch.*); die Walzenschnecke (*Mollusc.*). **—d**, *adj.* schneckenförmig.

Vomi—c, *adj.* eiterig (*rare*). **—t**, I. *v.a.* (—t forth, up) aus=brechen, =werfen, =speien; aus=stoßen, =werfen (*fig.*). II. *v.n.* (sich er=)brechen, sich übergeben. III. *s.* das Gespieene, Ausgebrochene; (—tory) das Brechmittel. **—tory**, I. *s.* *see* —t III; der Hauptausgang (eines Theaters ꝛc.). II. *adj.* Brechen erregend, Brech=. *Comp.* **—c-nut**, *s.* (Nux vomica) die Brechnuß.

Voraci—ous, *adj.*, **—ously**, *adv.* gefräßig, gierig. **—ty**, **—ousness**, *s.* die Gefräßigkeit.

Vortex, *s.* (*pl.* Vortices) der Wirbel, Strudel.

Vot—ary, *s.* der Geweihte; (worshipper) der Verehrer, Anbeter; her —aries, ihre Getreuen; —ary of music, einer, der sich der Musik gewidmet hat. **—e**, I. *s.* die (Wahl=)Stimme, das Votum; die Abstimmung; to put to the —e, abstimmen lassen, zur Abstimmung bringen; casting —e, die entscheidende *or* ausschlaggebende Stimme; to pass a —e of thanks, ein Dankvotum beschließen; —e of confidence, Vertrauensvotum; —e of censure, Mißtrauensvotum. II. *v.n.* (ab)stimmen, seine Stimme abgeben; to —e by ballot, in geheimer Wahl (ab)stimmen; to abstain from —ing, sich der Abstimmung enthalten; to —e down, überstimmen. III. *v.a.* durch Abstimmen erwählen, ernennen; (propose) vorschlagen; beschließen (*an address of thanks, etc.*); (—e for) votieren, durch Abstimmung genehmigen (*a bill, etc.*); halten für (*sl.*). **—er**, *s.* der Stimmgeber, Wahlmann. **—ing**, I. *p. & adj.*; stimmend, Stimm=. II. *s.* das (Ab=)Stimmen. **—ive**, *adj.* geweiht, Votiv=. *Comp.* **—ing-paper**, *s.* der Stimmzettel.

Vouch, I. *v.n.* Zeugnis ablegen, Bürge sein, sich verbürgen, stehen (for, für). II. *s.* das Zeugnis, die Beteuerung. **—er**, *s.* der Zeuge; (written —er) das Zeugnis, die Urkunde, der (Beleg=)Schein; die Interimskarte; die Einlaßkarte (*Theat., etc.*); die Vorladung zur Begründung von Rechtsansprüchen. **—safe**, *v.* I. *a.* gewähren, verstatten; —safe, O Lord, verleih, *or* gieb, o Herr! II. *n.* geruhen, sich herablassen.

Voussoir, *s.* der Wölb=, Schluß=, Kiel=stein.

Vow, I. *v.a.* (an)geloben, feierlich versprechen, schwören; (devote) widmen; geloben. II. *v.n.* geloben, schwören. III. *s.* das (heilige) Gelübde; das Angelöbnis (of fidelity, etc., der ehelichen Treue ꝛc.); to make a —, etwas feierlich geloben; to take a —, ein Gelübde tun *or* ablegen (*of a Jesuit*); to take the —s, das Ordensgelübde ablegen, Profeß tun.

Vowel, I. *s.* der Vokal, Selbstlauter; oral — (without nasal resonance), reiner Vokal; front —, palataler Vokal; back —, Gutturalvokal; nasal —, Nasal(vokal); modified —, umgelauteter Vokal; rounded —, der geründete Vokal. II. *adj.* vokalisch. *Comp.* **—-gradation**, *s.* der Ablaut. **—-lengthening**, *s.* die Vokaldehnung; compensatory —-lengthening, die Ersatzdehnung. **—-modification**, **—-mutation**, *s.* der Umlaut.

Voyage, I. *s.* die Seereise; große lange Reise; — out and home, die Hin= und Her=reise. II. *v.n.* zur See reisen. III. *v.a.* bereisen, befahren. **—r**, *s.* der, die (See=)Reisende.

Vulcani—te, *s.* der Hartgummi, Ebonit. **—ze**, *v.a.* vulkanisieren.

Vulgar, I. *adj.*, **—ly**, *adv.* gemein; (low) niedrig, pöbelhaft; (recognized) allgemein anerkannt; (common, usual) gewöhnlich, landesüblich, volkstümlich; — fractions, gemeine, gewöhnliche Brüche; — tongue, die Volkssprache, lebende Sprache; — minds, gemeine, niedrige Seelen. II. *s.*; the —, gemeine Leute, das gemeine Volk, der gemeine Haufen, Pöbel; die Volkssprache. **—ian**, *s.* der Gemeine, gemeine Mensch. **—ism**, *s.* der gemeine Ausdruck. **—ity**, *s.* die Gemeinheit, Niedrigkeit, Pöbelhaftigkeit **—ize**, *v.a* gemein machen, herabwürdigen.

Vulnera—bility, *s.* die Verwundbarkeit, Verletzlichkeit. **—ble**, *adj.* verwundbar, verletzlich·

—ble spot, verwundbare Stelle. —**ry**, *adj.* Wunden heilend, Wund=.
Vulpine, *adj.* Fuchs=; schlau (*fig.*).
Vultur—e, *s.* der Geier. —**ine**, *adj.* geierartig.
Vulva, *s.* äußere weibliche Genitalien, die weibliche Scham.
Vying, *see* Vie.

W

W, w, *s.* W, w. *For abbreviations see the Index at the end of the English-German part.*
Wabbl—e, I. *v.n.* wackeln, watscheln, schlottern, wanken; schwatzen, plappern (*Amer.*). II. *v.a.* wanken *etc.* machen; to —e the head, mit dem Kopfe wackeln, den Kopf schütteln. —**y**, *adj.* wackelig, watschelig; unsicher, zitternd.
Wad, I. *s.* die Schütte, das Bündel (*of hay, etc.*); die Vorladung, der Pfropf (*Artil.*); der Ladepfropf (*of guns*). II. *v.a.* (aus)stopfen; wattieren (*a mantle, etc.*). —**ding**, *s.* die Wattierung, Watte.
Waddl—e, *v.n.* watscheln. —**er**, *s.* der Watschler. —**ing**, *adj.*, —**ingly**, *adv.* watschelig.
Wade, I. *v.n.* waten; to — through, durchwaten (*lit.*); sich durcharbeiten durch, eindringen in (*fig.*). II. *v.a.* durchwaten; sich hindurcharbeiten durch (*fig.*). —**r**, *s.* einer, der watet; der Watvogel, Stelzenläufer (*Orn.*).
Waf—er, *s.* die Waffel; die Oblate (*for letters, etc., also R. C.*); consecrated —er, die Hostie (*R. C.*). —**fle**, *s.* die Waffel.
Waft, I. *v.a.* wehen, tragen; (— towards) zuwehen. II. *s.* das Wehen; to hoist with a —, (die Fahne) im Schau wehen lassen (*Naut.*).
[1]**Wag**, I. *v.a.* schütteln (*the head*); wedeln (mit dem Schwanze); to — the tongue, die Zunge rühren, schwatzen. II. *s.* das Schütteln, die Schwingung. —**gle**, *v.n.* wackeln. *Comp.* —**tail**, *s.* die Bachstelze.
[2]**Wag**, *s.* der Spaßvogel; (wit) der Witzling, Schalk. —**gery**, *s.* der Spaß. —**gish**, *adj.*, —**gishly**, *adv.* schelmisch, possierlich. —**gishness**, *s.* die Schalkhaftigkeit.
Wage, I. *v.a.* wetten; zu unternehmen wagen, auf sich nehmen; to — war, Krieg führen. II. *s.*, —**s**, *pl.* der (Dienstboten=, Arbeits=)Lohn; der Lohn (*fig.*); agricultural —s, ländliche Arbeitslöhne. —**r**, I. *s.* die Wette; der Entscheidungseid (*Law*); das Unterpfand; to lay a —r, eine Wette machen, wetten; name your —r, was gilt die Wette? II. *v.a. & n.* wetten. —**rer**, *s.* der Wettende.
Waggon, *s.* der Wagen; der Güterwagen (*Railw.*). —**er**, *s.* der (Fracht=)Fuhrmann. —**ette**, *s.* großer offener Wagen für Ausflüge.
Waif, *s.* herrenlose Sache, das verlorene Gut *or* Vieh; (street Arab) verwahrlostes, verwildertes Kind; —s and strays, verwahrloste und heimatlose Kinder; verlaufenes Gesindel.
Wail, I. *s.* die Wehklage. II. *v.n.* wehklagen, sich beklagen. III. *v.a.* wehklagen, jammern; *see* Bewail. —**ing**, I. *adj.*, —**ingly**, *adv.* klagend. II. *s.* das Wehklagen, Jammern.
Wain, *s.* der Wagen; Charles' —, der große Bär (*Astr.*). *Comp.* —**wright**, *s.* der Wagenbauer.
Wainscot, I. *s.* das Tafelwerk, Getäfel, die Wandbekleidung. II. *v.a.* (über)täfeln, (mit Tafelwerk) verkleiden. —**ing**, *see* — I.
Waist, *s.* die Taille; die Schweifung (*of bells*); die Kuhl (*of a ship*). *Comp.* —**band**, *s.* der Hosenbund; das Gürtelband (*of a dress*). —**belt**, *s.* der Leibgürtel (*for a dress*); die Degenkoppel (*Mil.*). —**coat**, *s.* die Weste; die lose Jacke, das Wams, Kamisol.
Wait, I. *v.n.* warten, bleiben; to — **for**, auf (einen) warten, (einen) erwarten; to — **on, upon**, (einem) aufwarten; (pay respects to) (einem) seine Aufwartung machen; (visit) besuchen; (nurse) pflegen; (escort) begleiten, folgen; to keep —ing, (einen) warten lassen. II. *v.a. see* Await; to — dinner (coffee) for s.o., mit dem Essen (Kaffee) auf einen warten. III. *s.*; to lie in — for, (einem) auflauern, nachstellen. —**er**, *s.* der Kellner, Aufwärter; (tray) der Präsentierteller; dumb- —er, stummer Diener, drehbares Präsentierbrett auf der Mitte des Eßtisches; head —er, der Oberkellner. —**ress**, *s.* die Aufwärterin; die Kellnerin (*in a hotel, etc.*). —**ing**, *s.* die Aufwartung, Bedienung; der Dienst (*at court, etc.*); lady in —ing, die Hofdame; lord in —ing, diensttuender Kammerherr. —**s**, *pl.* Stadtmusikanten; Musikanten, welche zur Weihnachtszeit während der Nacht spielen. *Comp.* —**ing-girl**, —**ing-maid**, *s.* die Aufwärterin, das Schenkmädchen; das Kammermädchen. —**ing-room**, *s.* der Wartesaal (*Railw.*); das Wartezimmer. —**ing-woman**, *s.* die Kammerfrau.
Waive, *v.a.* verzichten auf (*acc.*), aufgeben.
[1]**Wak—e**, I. *ir.v.n.* wachen; (awake, wake up) erwachen; I woke at 6, ich erwachte um 6 Uhr. II. *ir.v.a.* (—e up) er=, auf=wecken; erwecken (*fig.*); auferwecken (*from the dead*); —e me at 7, wecke mich um 7; to —e a corpse, bei einer Leiche wachen; ein Leichenfest halten (*Irish*). III. *s.* die Toten, Leichen=feier, Totenwache; (church —e) das Kirchweihfest, die Kirmeß. —**eful**, *adj.*, —**efully**, *adv.* wachend, schlaflos; (vigilant) wachsam. —**efulness**, *s.* die Schlaflosigkeit; die Wachsamkeit. —**en**, *v.* I. *n.* (er)wachen. II. *a.* auf=, er=wecken; erwecken, erregen, rege machen (*fig.*). —**ener**, *s.* der Erwecker. —**ing**, I. *p.*; —ing hours, wache Stunden. II. *s.* das Wachen, Erwachen.
[2]**Wake**, *s.* das Kielwasser; in the — of s.o., unmittelbar hinter einem, einem auf dem Fuße (*fig.*).
Wale, *s.* die Sahlleiste, das Sahlband (*of cloth*); die Schwiele, Strieme (*given by a rod, etc.*); das Berg=, Krumm=holz (*Naut.*).
Walk, I. *v.n.* gehen; (take a —) spazieren gehen, sich (*dat.*) Bewegung machen; wandeln, leben (*fig.*); umgehen, spuken (*as ghosts*); Schritt gehen (*as a horse*); to — in one's sleep, nachtwandeln, im Schlaf wandeln; to — **about**, umhergehen; to — **along**, weiter gehen; I will tell you as we — along, unterwegs will ich es Ihnen sagen; to — **back**, zurückgehen; to — **backwards**, rücklings, hinter sich gehen; to — **by**, vorübergehen; to — **down**, hinuntergehen; to — **forwards**, vorwärts=, weiter=gehen; to — **in**, hineingehen, hereinkommen; — in, gentlemen! treten Sie ein, meine Herren! to — **into**, losgehen auf, herfallen über (einen) (*sl.*); to — **on**, fortwandern; — on! weiter! to — **out**, hinausgehen; to — out with her young man, mit dem Schatz spazieren gehen (*of servant girls*); to — **up**, hinaufgehen, heraufkommen; to — up to s.o., auf einen zugehen. II. *v.a.* im Schritt gehen lassen (*a horse*); spazieren führen (*a person*); durchschreiten (*a room*); tanzen (*a minuet*); (zu Fuß) machen (*a long way*); to — off, durch Gehen vertreiben (*a headache*); to — one's clothes dry, die Kleider im Gehen trocknen; to — the rounds, die Runde machen; to — the streets, die Straßen durchstreifen; to — the hospitals, die Krankenhäuser besuchen. III. *s.* das Gehen, der Gang; der Spaziergang (*in the air, etc.*); der Schritt (*in driving, etc.*); (path, *etc.*) der Spazier=weg, =gang; (way) der Weg; die Laufbahn, der Lebensgang (*fig.*); die Weide, Hut (*for sheep, etc.*); — of life, der Beruf, das Fach, die Lebensstellung; the higher —s of society, die höheren Kreise, Klassen der Gesellschaft; to go for a —, to take a —, einen Spaziergang machen, spazieren gehen. —**er**, *s.* der Fuß=, Spazier=gänger; to be a good —er, gut zu Fuß sein. —**ing**, I. *adj.* gehend; —ing boots, Ausgehstiefel; —ing dress, der Ausgehanzug; —ing tour, die Fußreise, Fußtour; —ing machine, der Gehstuhl (für kleine Kinder). II. *s.* das Wandeln, Gehen; das Gehen, Spazie=

ren. *Comp.* **—ing-stick**, *s.* der Spazierstock. **—over**, *s.* die Übertragung eines Spielers auf die nächste Runde (*Tennis*); leichter Sieg (*Sport.*).

Wall, I. *s.* die Wand, Mauer; within the —s, innerhalb der Stadt *or* Festung, to go to the —, unterliegen; zu Grunde gehen; Bankrott machen (*C.L.*); blank *or* dead —, blinde Mauer (ohne Fenster und Türen); — of rock, Felsenwand; to give (a person) the —, (einem) den Vorrang lassen (*fig.*). II. *v.a.* (enclose) mit einer Mauer umgeben, mit Mauern versehen, umwallen; to — up, zu=, ver=mauern. *Comp.* **—-eyed**, *adj.* glas=; weißäugig (*of horses*). **—-fern**, *s.* der Tüpfelfarn. **—flower**, *s.* der Goldlack, die gelbe Levkoje; das Mauerblümchen, eine Dame, die nicht zum Tanzen kommt (*fig.*). **—-fruit**, *s.* das Spalierobst. **—-map**, *s.* die Wandkarte (*in schools*). **—-painting**, *s.* die Wandmalerei; das Wandgemälde. **—-paper**, *s.* die Tapete.

Wallet, *s.* der Beutel; der Rucksack, Quersack.

Wallow, *v.n.* sich wälzen; schwelgen in (*dat.*) (*fig.*). **—er**, *s.* einer, der sich wälzt.

Walnut, *s.* die Walnuß, welsche Nuß; der Walnußbaum; (*in comp.* =) Walnuß=.

Walrus, *s.* das Walroß.

Waltz, I. *s.* der Walzer. II. *v.n.* walzen. **—er**, *s.* der Walzende. **—ing**, *s.* das Walzertanzen.

Wampum, *s.* der Wampum.

Wan, *adj.* bleich, blaß, kränklich aussehend. **—e**, I. *v.n.* abnehmen (*as the moon, time, etc.*); abnehmen, sinken, (ver)welken (*fig.*). II. *s.* die Abnahme (*also fig.*). **—ing**, I. *adj.* abnehmend. II. *s.* das Abnehmen, Verfallen. **—ness**, *s.* die Bleiche, Blässe. **—t**, *see* Want.

Wand, *s.* die Rute, Gerte; der Stab; conjurer's —, divining —, der Zauberstab, die Zauberrute.

Wander, *v.n.* wandern; (— about) umherschweifen, =streifen, =irren; (— from) abweichen (von); phantasieren (*fig.*); his mind —s, er phantasiert, faselt; to — through, durchwandern. **—er**, *s.* der Wanderer, Umherschweifer. **—ing**, I. *adj.* wandernd; (scattered) zerstreut; —ing Jew, der ewige Jude. II. *s.* das Wandern, Umherstreifen; (going astray) die Abweichung, Verirrung; das Irrereden, die Phantasie.

Want, I. *s.* der Mangel; das Bedürfnis; (poverty) die Armut, Not; to be in — of, bedürfen, nötig haben, Mangel leiden an (*dat.*); for — of, aus Mangel an (*dat.*); in Ermangelung von; — of money, die Geldnot; — of spirit, die Mutlosigkeit. II. *v. a.* bedürfen, nötig haben, brauchen; (be without) ermangeln; fehlen, ohne (eine S.) sein; (desire) wünschen, verlangen; I — to know why, ich möchte gern den Grund wissen *or* wissen warum; he is —ed, man sucht ihn, man wünscht ihn zu sprechen; you are —ed, ich verhafte Sie, im Namen des Gesetzes (*words spoken by way of quiet arrestation in the street by the constable*); he —s a hat, er braucht einen Hut, muß einen Hut haben; he —s knowledge, es fehlt ihm an Kenntnissen; I know what you —, ich weiß, was du willst; the piano —s tuning, das Klavier muß gestimmt werden; what do you — with me? was wollen Sie von mir? he —s me to do it, er will, daß ich es tue; who —s you to do such a thing? wer verlangt so etwas von Ihnen? it —s 10 minutes to 9, es fehlen 10 Minuten an 9 Uhr, es ist 10 Minuten vor Neun; the story —s confirmation, die Geschichte bedarf der Bestätigung. III. *v.n.* fehlen, mangeln, es fehlen lassen (in, an einer S.); Mangel haben, Not leiden; he is —ing in energy, es fehlt ihm an Tatkraft; I shall not be —ing for my part, an mir soll es nicht fehlen; I shall not be —ing in exertion, ich werde mich bestens bemühen. **—age**, *s.* der Fehlbetrag, das Defizit.

Wanton, I. *adj.*, **—ly**, *adv.* (roguish) mutwillig; (unrestrained) lose, leichtfertig, zügellos; (luxuriant) üppig; (licentious) lüstern, liederlich, ausschweifend; in — sport, aus reinem Mutwillen. II. *s.* der Wollüstling, Wüstling; fröhlicher Mensch, ausgelassenes Mädchen. III. *v.n.* flattern, im Winde spielen; (frolic) sich belustigen; (to be licentious) der Wollust pflegen. **—ness**, *s.* der Mutwille; die Leichtfertigkeit, Ausgelassenheit; die Üppigkeit, Geilheit.

Wapentake, *s.* der Gau, Hundertbezirk (*Yorks.*).

War, I. *s.* der Krieg; at —, im Kriege, kriegführend; to levy, wage — against, make — upon, Krieg führen gegen, mit Krieg überziehen; to go to — with, Krieg anfangen mit *or* gegen; the fortune, chances of —, das Kriegsglück; council of —, der Kriegsrat; man of —, der Krieger (*Mil.*); man-of- —, das Kriegsschiff (*Naut.*); tug of —, das Seilziehen (*Gymn.*); heißester Kampf (*fig.*); industrial —, Industriekrieg; tariff —, Zollkrieg; — to the knife, der Krieg bis aufs Messer, Vernichtungskrieg. II. *attrib.*; — footing, der Kriegsfuß. III. *v.n.* kriegen; streiten, kämpfen (*fig.*). **—fare**, *s.* der Kriegsdienst, das Kriegsleben; (war) der Krieg; (struggle) der Kampf. **—rior**, *see* Warrior. *Comp.* **—-cry**, *s.* das Kriegsgeschrei; der Schlachtruf. **—-department**, *s.* das Kriegsministerium. **—-horse**, *s.* das Schlachtroß. **—like**, *adj.* kriegerisch, Kriegs=. **—-office**, *s.* das (englische) Kriegsministerium. **—-paint**, *s.* die Kriegsschminke; der Putz, Staat (*fig.*). **—-path**, *s.* der Kriegspfad.

Warbl—e, *v.* I. *n.* wirbeln, trillern; schmettern, schlagen (*as birds*); (sing) singen. II. *a.* trillern; singen; —ing of larks, das Lerchengewirbel, Lerchengeschmetter. **—er**, *s.* der Sänger; der Singvogel.

[1]**Ward**, I. *v.a.* bewahren; to — off, abwehren, abwenden, parieren (*a blow, etc.*). II. *s.* die Wehr, Wache, Hut, Verwahrung; *see* —en; (guardianship) die Aufsicht, Vormundschaft; die Parade (*Fenc.*); das Eingerichte, Gewirre (*of a lock*); der Einstrich (*of a key*); das Gefängniszimmer (*of a prison*); die Abteilung (of a hospital, in einem Krankenhause); das Mündel, der, die Minderjährige; der Stadtbezirk (*of a town*); —s in Chancery, Minderjährige, welche unter dem Schutze des Lordkanzlers stehen; casual —, das Asyl für Obdachlose; watch and —, die Wache. **—en**, *s.* der Hüter, Aufseher; der Gouverneur (of the Cinque Ports, der Fünfhäfen); der Vorsteher (*Freem.*); der Rektor (*of some Oxford colleges*); church—en, Kirchenvorsteher. **—enship**, **—enry**, *s.* das Amt *or* die Gerichtsbarkeit eines Vorstehers. **—er**, *s.* der Wärter, Hüter, Wächter, Gefängniswärter. *Comp.* **—-mote**, *s.* die Bezirksversammlung; das Bezirksgericht (*Law*). **—robe**, *s.* der Kleiderschrank, das Kleiderspind; der Kleiderraum, die Garderobe. **—-room**, *s.* große Kajüte; das Bezirkszimmer, Wahlzimmer eines Stadtbezirks (*Amer.*).

[2]**Ward**, *adv.* =wärts; heaven—, dem Himmel zu, himmelwärts.

[1]**Ware**, *see* Beware.

[2]**Ware**, *s.* die Ware; das Geschirr; china (Delft) —, das Porzellan (Delfter Geschirr, Steingut); earthen—, irdenes Geschirr; fancy —, buntes Geschirr; potter's —, Töpferwaren; small —(s), Kurzwaren. *Comp.* **—house**, I. *s.* das Warenlager, Magazin, die Niederlage; bonded — house, der Packhof. II. *v.a.* auf (das) Lager bringen, auf=, ein=speichern; in Zollverschluß tun; I had my furniture —housed, ich ließ mein Mobiliar auf Lager bringen. *Comp.* **—house-account**, *s.* das Lagerkonto. **—house-clerk**, *s.* der Lagerdiener. **—houseman**, *s.* der Kaufmann im Großen, Großhändler. **—housing-system**, *s.* das Zollverschlußsystem.

War—ily, *adv.* vorsichtig, bedachtsam. **—iness**, *s.* die Vorsicht, Behutsamkeit. **—y**, *adj.* vorsichtig, behutsam, bedachtsam.

Warlock, *s.* der Zauberer, Hexenmeister (*obs.*).

Warm, I. *adj.*, **—ly**, *adv.* warm, heiß; heiß, hart

(*as work*); warm, hitzig, eifrig (*fig.*); (enthusiastic) lebhaft, enthusiastisch. II. *s.* die Erwärmung (*coll.*). III. *v.a.* (er)wärmen (*also fig.*); (thrash) prügeln (*vulg.*); to — up, aufwärmen. IV. *v.n.* warm werden; sich erwärmen *or* interessieren (to, für). **—ing**, I. *adj.* wärmend. II. *s.* die Züchtigung (*vulg.*). **—th**, *s.* die Wärme; die Lebhaftigkeit (*of colour*); die Wärme, Hitze, das Feuer, der Eifer. *Comp.* **—-hearted**, *adj.* warmherzig. **—ing-pan**, *s.* die Wärmpfanne.

Warn, *v.a.* warnen; (admonish) ermahnen; (give notice of) vorher benachrichtigen, (einem) zu wissen tun, (einem) anzeigen; (einem Dienstboten) (auf=) kündigen; he —ed him of it, er gab ihm einen Wink davon; the troops have been —ed to hold themselves in readiness, die Truppen sind angewiesen, sich bereit zu halten. **—er**, *s.* der Ermahner, Warner. **—ing**, I. *p.*, **—ingly**, *adv.* warnend, ermahnend. II. *s.* die Warnung, Mahnung; (notice) die Voranzeige, der Bescheid; die Kündigung; by way of —ing, um anzudeuten *or* darauf aufmerksam zu machen; to give —ing, (einen) warnen; (einem den Dienst) kündigen; I have given you fair —ing, ich habe dich ausdrücklich gewarnt; to take —ing by, sich warnen lassen von; at a minute's —ing, in kürzester Frist, jeden Augenblick.

Warp, I. *s.* die Kette, der Zettel, Aufzug (*Weav.*); das, die Werptroß (*Naut.*); with a high —, hochkettig; — and woof, Zettel und Einschlag. II. *v.a.* krumm machen (*wood, etc.*); die Kette (an)scheren, (an)zetteln (*Weav.*); anscheren (*a rope*); bugsieren (*Naut.*); (turn aside) ablenken, ableiten; beeinflussen, verleiten (*the judgment, etc.*); mit Seewasser überschwemmen (*land*); zu früh werfen (*calves, etc.*). III. *v.n.* sich werfen, sich krümmen; werpen, warpen (*Naut.*); (swerve) abweichen, schwanken; (bend) sich neigen; verwerfen (*as cattle*). *Comp.* **—ing-frame**, *s.* der Scher=, Zettel=rahmen. **—ing-post**, *s.* der Anscherpfahl.

Warrant, I. *s.* die Bürgschaft, Gewähr, Versicherung; (commission) die Ermächtigung, Befugnis, Vollmacht; (writ of arrest) der Verhaftsbefehl; der Lagerschein (*C. L.*); — of distress, das Pfändungsmandat (*Law*). II. *v.a.* Gewähr, Bürgschaft leisten für; (bail) verbürgen, stehen für, garantieren; (maintain) behaupten; (assure) versichern; (empower) bevollmächtigen, ermächtigen, Befugnis erteilen; all stamps —ed genuine, für die Echtheit aller Marken wird gebürgt; I — you, ich versichere Sie; I'll — (me), dafür bürge ich, das kannst du glauben. **—able**, *adj.* zu rechtfertigen. **—ably**, *adj.* rechtmäßig, billigerweise. **—ed**, *adj.* garantiert. **—er**, *s.* der Gewährsmann, Bürge. **—y**, *s.* die Garantie, der Bürgschafts=vertrag, =schein; (authority) die Vollmacht. *Comp.* **—-officer**, *s.* der (Subaltern)Offizier, Feldwebelleutnant (*Mil.*); der Deckoffizier (*Naut.*).

Warren, *s.* das (Kaninchen=)Gehege.

Warrior, *s.* der Krieger, Kriegsmann.

Wart, *s.* die Warze; die Mauke (*Vet.*). **—y**, *adj.* warzig; (—-like) warzenartig.

War—y, *see* —ily.

Was, *imperf. see* Be; he — to have come, er hätte kommen sollen; that — to be expected, das war zu erwarten, ließ sich erwarten.

Wash, I. *v.a.* waschen; (aus)spülen (*glasses, etc.*); abspülen (*a deck, etc.*); waschen, schlämmen (*ore*); benetzen, bespülen (*as rivers*); waschen, tuschen (*Paint.*); dünn überziehen, plattieren (*with gold*); den ersten Leimgrund auftragen (*in gilding*); to — one's hands of, nichts zu schaffen haben wollen mit; I — my hands of it, ich wasche meine Hände in Unschuld, will nichts damit zu tun haben; to — **away**, weg=, ab=waschen; (undermine) wegspülen; to — **down**, niederspülen; to — **off**, to — **out**, *see* To — away; auswaschen; to — **over**, überwaschen; (cover over) über=streichen, =tünchen; to — **up**, aufwaschen (*vessels*); (— ashore) ans Ufer spülen. II. *v.n.* waschen; (— oneself) sich waschen; to — off, sich auswaschen, durch Waschen ausgehen; to — **up**, Geschirr spülen; —ing fabrics, Stoffe, die sich waschen lassen, waschechte Stoffe. III. *s.* die Handlung des Waschens, das Waschen, die Ausspülung; der Wellenschlag; die Wäsche; (shallow of a river, *etc.*) der seichte Teil eines Flusses oder Meeresarmes, die flache Meereseinbuchtung; großer Meerbusen in Südostengland bei Lynn; (lotion) das (Wasch=, Schönheits= 2c.) Wasser; (waste liquor) das Spülwasser, Spülicht; leicht aufgetragene Farbe, Tusche (*Paint.*); (plating) der Metallüberzug, die Plattierung; to have a —, sich waschen (*coll.*). **—able**, *adj.* (ab=) waschbar. **—er**, *s.* der Waschapparat; *see* —er-woman, —ing-machine; die Unterlags=, Dichtungs=scheibe, das Mutterblech (*under a screw*). **—ing**, *s.* das Waschen, Reinigen; (linen) die Wäsche; die Anspülung; die Tuschung. **—y**, *adj.* wässerig; (weak) weichlich, schwach. *Comp.* **—-board**, *s.* die Fußleiste, Fußlambrerie (*Build.*); das Setzbord (*Naut.*); das Waschbrett. **—-erwoman**, *s.* die Waschfrau, Wäscherin. **—-(hand)basin**, *s.* das Waschbecken. **—-house**, *s.* das Waschhaus. **—ing-bill**, *s.* der Waschzettel. **—ing-day**, *s.* der Waschtag. **—ing-machine**, *s.* die Waschmaschine. **—-leather**, *s.* das Waschleder. **—stand**, *s.* der Waschtisch. **—-tub**, *s.* das Waschfaß, der Waschkübel.

Wasp, *s.* die Wespe; —s nest, das Wespennest; sting of a —, der Wespenstich. **—ish**, *adj.*, **—ishly**, *adv.* wespenartig; verdrießlich, leicht reizbar. **—ishness**, *s.* die Reizbarkeit.

Wassail, *s.* ein Getränk aus Äpfeln, Zucker und Ale; (drinking bout) das Trinkgelage. **—er**, *s.* der Zecher. *Comp.* **—-cup**, *s.* der Humpen.

Waste, I. *v.a.* verwüsten, veröden, verheeren, zerstören; *see* Squander; ab=, ver=zehren (*as a fever*); to — one's money (time) in gambling, sein Geld verspielen, (seine Zeit mit Spielen verbringen). II. *v.n.* sich leichter werden lassen, im Gewicht heruntergehn (*Sport.*); to — away, hinschwinden, sich verzehren, vergehen. III. *adj.* wüst, öde; (unused) unbenutzt, nicht verwendet, überflüssig; (worthless) wertlos; to lay —, verwüsten, verheeren; — cotton, der Abfall von Baumwolle; — paper, das Ausschußpapier, die Makulatur. IV. *s.* die Vergeudung, Verschwendung (*of money, time, etc.*); (desert) die Wüste, Einöde; (loss) der Verlust, Abgang, Abfall; *see* —-pipe; to go to —, verfallen; to let a garden run to —, einen Garten verwildern lassen. **—ful**, *adj.*, **—fully**, *adv.* verwüstend, verheerend; (spendthrift) verschwenderisch. **—fulness**, *s.* die Verschwendung. **—r**, *s.* der Verwüster, der Verschwender; der Tunichtgut (*sl.*). *Comp.* **—-(paper-)basket**, *s.* der Papierkorb. **—-pipe**, *s.* das Abzugsrohr (*also Locom.*), die Ablaufröhere. **—-water**, *s.* das Ablaufwasser.

Wastrel, *s.* der Abfall; unbenutztes Land; verwahrlostes Kind; der arbeitsscheue Lump.

Watch, I. *v.n.* (wake) wachen, aufbleiben; Wache halten, wachen (with, bei, over, über einen); (take care) Acht geben (auf, *acc.*); to — for, warten auf (*acc.*), lauern. II. *v.a.* (guard) bewachen, hüten; (observe) beobachten, ein wachsames Auge haben auf, beobachtend folgen, zusehen; (take care) Acht geben auf; abpassen (*an opportunity*). III. *s.* die Wache, das Wachen; die Wache (*Mil., etc.*); die Aufmerksamkeit, Acht, Wachsamkeit (*fig.*); (spy) heimlicher Beobachter; die Taschenuhr (*Horol.*); horizontal —, die Zylinderuhr; lever —, die Ankeruhr; to be upon the —, auf der Lauer liegen; keep a — upon, habt Acht auf (*acc.*); to keep a — upon a p., einen heimlich beobachten (lassen); to be upon the — for, (einem) auflauren, aufpassen; to relieve the —, die Wache ablösen; to set the —, die Wache ausstellen; to set a —, eine Uhr stellen; morning —, Tag=, Morgen=wache. **—er**, *s.* der, welcher wacht *or* aufbleibt; (nurse) der Krankenwärter. **—ful**, *adj.*, **—fully**, *adv.* wachsam, achtsam; to be —ful of, beobachten. **—fulness**, *s.* die Wachsamkeit, Achtsamkeit. **—ing**, *s.* das Wachen; das Aufpassen. *Comp.* **—-case**, *s.* das Uhrgehäuse. **—-chain**, *s.* die Uhrkette. **—-dog**, *s.* der Kettenhund. **—-key**, *s.* der Uhrschlüssel. **—maker**, *s.* der Uhrmacher. **—man**, *s.* der Wächter, die Wache; (night —) der Nachtwächter. **—-pocket**, *s.* die Uhrtasche. **—-stand**, *s.* das Uhrgestell, der Uhrhalter. **—-tower**, *s.* der Wachtturm. **—word**, *s.* die Losung.

Water, I. *s.* das Wasser (*also Pharm., fig., etc.*); to drink the —s, (den) Brunnen trinken; of the first —, vom reinsten Wasser (*as a diamond, etc.*); ersten Schlages, erster Art (*as a man, etc.*); to go to —, zu Wasser werden, ins Wasser fallen, scheitern (*of plans*); to get into hot —, in Verlegenheit geraten (*fig.*); high (low) —, der Hoch= (Tief=)stand des Wassers; to be in low —, auf dem Trocknen sitzen (*fig.*); to hold —, wasserdicht sein (*lit.*); stichhaltig sein (*fig.*); to cast one's bread upon the —s, sein Hab und Gut vergeuden; to fish in troubled —s, im Trüben fischen; to take to the —, ins Wasser gehen, das Wasser lieben; to throw cold — over a p., einen mit kaltem Wasser übergießen, einen gründlich ernüchtern (*fig.*); —'s edge, das Ufer; die Wasserkante (*dial.*); still —s run deep, stille Wasser sind tief (*prov.*). II. *v.a.* (be=)wässern, benetzen, begießen; schwemmen, tränken (*horses*); wässern, flammen, moirieren (*silk, etc.*). III. *v.n.* wässern; tränen (*as the eyes*); to make a p.'s mouth —, einem den Mund wässerig machen; his mouth —s, ihm wässert der Mund. **—iness**, *s.* die Wässerigkeit. **—ing**, *s.* die Handlung des Wässerns, das Wässern, Begießen, Besprengen (*streets*). **—y**, *adj.* wässerig (*as potatoes, etc., also fig.*); (containing —) wasserhaltend, Wasser=; (moist) feucht, naß; (—-like) wasserartig, wässerig; —y eyes, nasse, tränende Augen; a —y sky, ein Regenhimmel; —y waste, die Wasserwüste. *Comp.* (*gen'lly* = Wasser=). **—-beetle**, *s.* der Schwimmkäfer. **—-bottle**, *s.* die Wasser=flasche, =karaffe; hot —-bottle, die Wärmflasche. **—-cart**, *s.* der Wasserwagen, Sprengwagen. **—-closet**, *s.* der Abtritt mit Wasserverschluß, das Wasser=klosett. **—-colours**, *pl.* die Wasser=, Aquarell=farben; das Aquarellgemälde; painting in —-colours, die Malerei mit Wasserfarben, Aquarellmalerei. **—-communication**, *s.* die Verbindung zu Wasser. **—-conduit**, *s.* die Wasserröhre. **—-cress**, *s.* die Brunnenkresse. **—-cure**, *s.* die Wasserkur. **—fall**, *s.* der Wasserfall. **—fowl**, *s.* das Wassergeflügel. **—-gruel**, *s.* der Haferschleim. **—head**, *s.* das Ende eines Landsees. **—hen**, *s.* graufüßiges Rohrhuhn. **—ing-can** *or* **-pot**, *s.* die Gießkanne. **—ing-place**, *s.* der Badeort, Gesundbrunnen; die Schwemme (*for horses, etc.*); —ing-places, Badeorte, Bäder. **—-lily**, *s.* die Wasserlilie. **—-line**, *s.* (*also* Loadline) die Wasserlinie (*on ships*). **—-locked**, *adj.* vom Wasser eingeschlossen. **—-logged**, *adj.* voll Wasser (*of ships*). **—man**, *s.* der Fährmann, Bootsführer. **—manship**, *s.* die Wassertüchtigkeit, Rudergewandtheit. **—-mark**, *s.* die Wassermarke; das Wasserzeichen (*Pap.*); high-—-mark, das Flutzeichen; der Höhepunkt, Hochstand (*fig.*); low-—-mark, der Tiefstand (*fig.*). **—-marked**, *adj.* mit Wasserzeichen. **—-mill**, *s.* die Wassermühle. **—-parting**, *see* —-shed. **—-pipe**, *s.* die Wasserröhre. **—-plantain**, *s.* der Wasserwegerich. **—-pot**, *s.* der Wasserkrug. **—-power**, *s.* die Wasserkraft. **—-proof**, I. *adj.* wasserdicht. II. *s.* der Regen=, Gummi=mantel. **—-rat**, *s.* die Wasserratte. **—-rate**, *s.* die Abgabe für häuslichen Wasserverbrauch. **—shed**, *s.* die Wasserscheide. **—spout**, *s.* die Abtraufe, Speiröhre (*of a roof*); die Wasserhose (*Phys.*). **—-supply**, *s.* die Wasserversorgung. **—-tight**, *adj.* wasserdicht. **—-wagtail**, *s.* die Bachstelze. **—way**, *s.* die Wasserstraße; der Flutraum (*of a bridge*); das Leibholz, der Wassergang (*Shipb.*). **—-wheel**, *s.* das Wasserrad. **—works**, *pl.* das Wasserwerk, die Wasserkunst; die Wasserleitung (*of a town, etc.*).

Wattl—e, I. *s.* das Geflecht, Flechtwerk, die Hürde, Umzäunung; they built with —e and daub, sie bauten ihre Häuser aus mit Lehm beworfenem Flechtwerk. II. *v.a.* mit Zweigen, Ruten binden, flechten. **—es**, *pl.* der Bart, Fleischlappen (*of a cock*). **—ing**, *s.* das Geflecht, Flechtwerk.

Wav—e, I. *s.* die Welle, Woge; (streak) die Welle; —e of the hand, der Wink mit der Hand. II. *v.n.* wogen; schwanken, wehen, flattern (*in the wind, etc.*); zuwinken (*to a p.*). III. *v.a.* wellenförmig machen; (brandish) schwingen, schwenken; (sign to) (einem) (zu)winken. **—eless**, *adj.* wellenlos, glatt. **—elet**, *s.* kleine Welle, das Wellchen. **—er**, *v.n.* wanken, schwanken, unschlüssig sein. **—erer**, *s.* der Schwankende, Unschlüssige. **—ering**, I. *adj.*, **—eringly**, *adv.* schwankend, unschlüssig. II. *s.* das Schwanken, die Unschlüssigkeit. **—eringness**, *s.* die Unschlüssigkeit. **—iness**, *s.* das Wellige. **—y**, *adj.* wogig, wogend; (—e-like) wellenförmig, wellig; —y lines, die Wellenlinien. *Comp.* **—e-offering**, *s.* das Webeopfer (*Jewish Relig.*).

[1]**Wax**, I. *s.* das Wachs; *see* Sealing- —; shoemaker's —, das Schuhmacherpech; — of the ears, das Ohrenschmalz. II. *v.a.* mit Wachs bestreichen, wichsen (*boots*), bohnen (*floors*). III. *adj.*; — doll, die Wachspuppe; — vestas, Wachsstreichhölzchen. **—en**, *adj.* wächsern, Wachs=. **—y**, *adj.* wächsern; (soft) weich. *Comp.* **—-candle**, *s.* das Wachslicht. **—-end**, *s.* der Pechdraht. **—-light**, *s.* die Wachskerze, das Wachslicht. **—work**, *s.* die Wachsfigur; —works, das Wachsfigurenkabinett.

[2]**Wax**, *v.n.* wachsen, zunehmen, werden; to — indignant, aufgebracht werden.

Way, *s.* der Weg; (road) die Straße; (path) die Bahn; (direction) die Richtung; (means) der Weg, das Mittel; (distance) die Strecke, Weite; (manner) die Art, Weise, Manier; das Wesen, die Fahrt, der Lauf (*of a ship*); the ship is under —, das Schiff läuft; — in (out), Ein=(Aus=)gang; this —, hier=her, =durch; in this —, auf diese Weise, in dieser Weise; in a —, gewisserweise; if my mother was out of the —, wenn meine Mutter nicht in der Nähe wäre, mir nicht in die Quere kommen könnte; —s and means, Mittel und Wege; committee of —s and means, ein zur Beratung der Staats=Einkünfte und Finanzen niedergesetzter Ausschuß; which — did he go? wohin ging er? I don't know which — to turn, ich weiß nicht, wohin ich mich wenden soll; any — you please, ganz wie Sie wollen; some — or (an)other, auf irgend eine Weise; a great — off, eine gute Strecke weit entfernt; it will go a great — towards, es wird viel dazu beitragen, um; by the —, im Vorbeigehen, beiläufig (gesagt); (*also* on the —) unterwegs; by — of, über; by — of excuse, als Entschuldigung, um sich zu entschuldigen; by — of jest, im Scherz; by — of proof, als Beweis, um etwas zu beweisen; a bottle by — of a candlestick, eine Flasche anstatt eines Leuchters (*coll.*); to ask one's —, sich nach dem Wege erkundigen; out of the —, abgelegen; (unusual) außer=gewöhnlich, =ordentlich; (make —!) Platz da! to ask an out-of-the-— price, einen übermäßigen Preis fordern; to be in the —, im Wege sein, stören, genieren; in the family —, guter Hoffnung; to be of a p.'s — of thinking, jemandes Denkungsweise, An=

sichten, Meinung teilen; to be out of the —, nicht bei der Hand sein; to bring a p. on his —, einen eine Strecke Weges begleiten; that is always the — with her, so macht sie es immer; (that always happens to her) so geht es ihr immer; that's the — of the world, so geht es in der Welt; to come in s.o.'s —, einem in den Weg, unter die Augen kommen; to get out of the —, sich davon machen; to give —, weichen, nachgeben; the props gave —, die Stützen brachen ein; to go one's —, seinen Weg gehen; to go out of one's —, ein Übriges tun, sich (*dat.*) besondere Mühe geben; you go the wrong — to work, Sie greifen die Sache verkehrt an; go your —s! geh' deiner Wege! to go a long — round, einen weiten Umweg machen; let her have her own —, laß sie ihren eigenen Weg gehen; you let the children have their own — too much, Sie sind zu nachsichtig gegen die Kinder, lassen ihnen zu sehr ihren eignen Willen; if I had my own —, wenn es nach mir ginge; he will have everything his own —, er will in allen Stücken seinen Kopf durchsetzen; to keep out of the —, (sich) verstecken, sich fern halten; to lead the —, vorangehen; to lose one's —, den Weg verlieren, vom Wege abkommen, sich verirren; to make one's —, durchdringen; to make the best of one's — (to), so schnell wie möglich gehen; to make — for, Platz machen für; to put, throw a thing in a p.'s —, einem etwas zukommen lassen; to put s.o. in the — to, einem verhelfen zu; to put out of the —, aus dem Wege räumen, wegstellen; to stand (*or* be) in s.o.'s —, einem im Wege stehen, hinderlich sein; to work one's — to, sich (*dat.*) einen Weg öffnen zu, eine S. mühsam erreichen. **—ward**, *adj.*, **—wardly**, *adv.* launisch, eigensinnig. **—wardness**, *s.* der Eigensinn, die Launenhaftigkeit. *Comp.* **—-bill**, *s.* der Frachtbrief. **—farer**, *s.* der Wanderer, Reisende. **—faring**, *adj.* wandernd, reisend, Reise=. **—lay**, *v.a.* (einem) auflauern, den Weg verlegen. **—-leave**, *s.* das Wegerecht. **—side**, I. *s.* die Seite am Wege *or* an der Straße. II. *adj.* am Wege; —side inn, der Gasthof an der Straße. **—worn**, *adj* weg(e)müde, von der Reise ermüdet.

We, *pers. pron.* wir.

Weak, *adj.*, **—ly**, *adv.* schwach, kraftlos (*also fig.*); schwächlich; kränklich; one's — side, jemandes schwache Seite, Schwäche. **—en**, *v.a.* schwächen. **—ling**, *s.* der Schwächling. **—ly**, *adj.* schwächlich, schwach. **—ness**, *s.* die Schwäche, Schwachheit; to have a —ness for, eine kleine Schwäche für (einen, eine S.) haben. *Comp.* **—-minded**, *adj.* schwachsinnig; charakterschwach.

[1]**Weal**, *s.* das Wohl, die Wohlfahrt; public —, das Gemeinwohl. **—th**, *s.* der Wohlstand, Reichtum. **—thy**, *adj.* reich, begütert, wohlhabend.

[2]**Weal**, *s.* die Schwiele, Strieme.

Wean, *v.a.* (Kinder) entwöhnen; abgewöhnen, abbringen, entwöhnen (from, von, *fig.*); to — o.s. from a th., sich (*dat.*) eine S. abgewöhnen.

Weapon, *s.* die Waffe; (gun) das Gewehr. **—less**, *adj.* waffenlos, ohne Waffe.

Wear, I. *ir.v.a.* anhaben, tragen (*a dress, crown, sword, etc.*); zeigen, annehmen (*a smile*); to — **away**, ab=tragen, =nutzen, zerstören; constant dripping will — away a stone, steter Tropfen höhlt den Stein (*prov.*); to — **off**, abnutzen; to — **out**, abtragen, abnutzen; (destroy) zerstören, zerrütten; (exhaust) erschöpfen, ermüden (*a p.'s patience, etc.*); (weary) ermüden. II. *ir.v.n.* sich tragen, sich halten; sich abtragen; to — well, sich gut tragen (*as clothes*); sich gut konservieren (*as people*); to — **away**, abnehmen, vergehen; *see* — on; to — **off**, abnehmen; (pass off) vorübergehen; to — **on**, hinschwinden, vergehen; to — **out**, sich abnutzen, sich abtragen. III. *s.* das Tragen; it is good enough for everyday —, es ist noch gut genug, um am Alltage getragen zu werden; — and tear, die gewöhnliche Abnutzung. **—able**, *adj.* tragbar, zu tragen. **—er**, *s.* der (Kleider &c. an sich) Tragende. **—ily**, *see* Wear—ily. **—ing**, I. *p.;* —ing apparel, Kleidungsstücke. II. *s.* das Tragen; the —ing out, das Abtragen.

Wear—ily, *adv.* müde. **—iness**, *s.* die Müdigkeit, Ermüdung; (disgust) der Überdruß. **—isome**, *adj.*, **—isomely**, *adv.* ermüdend, mühsam; (tedious) langwierig, langweilig; (burdensome) lästig. **—isomeness**, *s.* die Mühsamkeit, Lästigkeit. **—y**, I. *adj.* müde (with, von); überdrüssig (of a th., einer S.); (tiresome) ermüdend; lästig. II. *v.a.* ermüden; (bore) langweilen; erschöpfen (*s.o.'s patience*). III. *v.n.* müde werden.

Weasel, *s.* das Wiesel.

Weather, I. *s.* das Wetter, die Witterung; pleasant — for walking, gutes Ausgehwetter; (wind and) — permitting, bei günstiger Witterung, wenn es das Wetter erlaubt. II. *v.a.* dem Wetter, der Gefahr trotzen; (bear) ausdauern, aushalten, sich mit Mühe durcharbeiten; umschiffen (*a cape*), luvwärts vorübersegeln (*a point*); to — out, aushalten (*a storm*), überstehen (*dangers, etc.*). **—ed**, *adj.* verwittert (*Geol.*). **—ly**, *adj.* luvwärts. *Comp.* **—-beaten**, *adj.* wetterhart, abgehärtet. **—-board**, *s.* die Wind=, Luv=seite. **—-bound**, *adj.* durch schlechtes Wetter am Auslaufen verhindert. **—cock**, *s.* der Wetterhahn (*also fig.*). **—-forecast**, *s.* der Wetterbericht, die (*pl.*) Wetteraussichten. **—-gauge**, *s.* die Luvseite, der Vorteil des Windes. **—-glass**, *s.* das Wetterglas, Barometer. **—-side**, *s.* die Luvseite. **—-tight**, *adj.* wetter=dicht, =fest. **—-tiling**, *s.* die Ziegelverkleidung (*of a house*). **—-wise**, *adj.* wetterkundig.

Weav—e, *ir.v.* I. *a.* weben; (twine together) wirken, flechten; (—e up) einweben (into, in), verweben (with, mit). II. *n.* weben. **—er**, *s.* der Weber, Wirker; der Weber (*Manuf.*); —er's loom, der Webstuhl. **—ing**, *s.* das Weben, die Weberei; art of —ing, die Webekunst.

Weazen, *adj.* dünn, dürr. *Comp.* **—-faced**, *adj.* schmalbäckig.

Web, *s.* das Gewebe (*also fig.*); die Webe (*of linen, prov.*); die Schwimmhaut; endless — of paper, der Streifen von endlosem Papier. **—bed**, *adj.* mit einer Schwimmhaut versehen. **—bing**, *s.* das Gurtband, der Gurt. *Comp.* **—-footed**, *adj.* mit Schwimmfüßen.

Wed, *v.* I. *a.* heiraten; to be —ded to, verheiratet sein an (*acc.*) (*lit.*); hängen, gefesselt *or* gebunden sein an (einen) (*fig.*); he is —ded to his opinion, er ist von seiner Meinung sehr eingenommen. II. *n.* sich verheiraten. **—ding**, *s.* die Hochzeit. *Comp.* **—ding-day**, *s.* der Hochzeitstag. **—ding-feast**, *s.* der Hochzeitsschmaus. **—ding-garment**, *s.* das Hochzeitskleid. **—ding-march**, *s.* der Hochzeitsmarsch. **—ding-ring**, *s.* der Trauring. **—ding-tour**, **—ding-trip**, *s.* die Hochzeitsreise. **—lock**, *s.* die Ehe, der Ehestand; joined in —lock, ehelich verbunden, verheiratet.

Wedge, I. *s.* der Keil; der Klumpen (*of gold, etc.*); the thin end of the —, das dünne (*or* schmale) Ende des Keils (*also fig.*). II. *v.a.* (ver)keilen, eindrängen; to — in, ein=keilen, =drängen, =zwängen. *Comp.* **—-shaped**, *adj.* keilförmig.

Wednesday, *s.* der Mittwoch; on —s, Mittwochs.

Wee, *adj.* klein, winzig (*Scotch*).

[1]**Weed**, I. *s.* das Unkraut; (tobacco) der Tabak; ill —s grow apace, Unkraut vergeht nicht (*prov.*). II. *v.a.* jäten; befreien von (*fig.*); to — **out**, ausjäten; to — **up**, ausroden, ausrotten. **—er**, *s.* der Jäter, Ausjäter. **—y**, *adj.* voller Unkraut; verwildert, verwachsen (*fig.*). *Comp.* **—ing-fork**, *s.* die Jätgabel.

[2]**Weed**, *s.* das Gewand; (widow's) —s, die (Witwen=)Trauer=kleider.

Week, *s.* die Woche; by the —, wochenweise; this day —, heute über acht Tage. **—ly**, I. *adj.*

wöchentlich; —ly paper, das Wochenblatt. II. *s.* das Wochenblatt. *Comp.* **—-day,** *s.* der Wochentag. **—-end,** I. *s.* das Ende der Woche. II. *attrib.;* —-end ticket, der Fahrschein von Freitag bis Dienstag *or* Sonnabend bis Montag.

Ween, *v.n.* wähnen, glauben, denken (*obs.*).

Weep, *ir.v.* I. *n.* weinen; to — **for,** beweinen, um einen weinen; to — for joy, vor Freude weinen; to — **over,** Tränen vergießen über (*acc.*). II. *a.* vergießen (tears, etc., Tränen 2c.). **—er,** *s.* der Weinende, Klagende; —ers, weiße Trauerschleifen. **—ing,** I. *s.* das Weinen; to fall a-—ing, in Tränen ausbrechen. II. *adj.,* **—ingly,** *adv.* weinend; —ing birch, die Hängebirke; —ing willow, die Trauerweide.

Weevil, *s.* der Kornwurm, Rüsselkäfer.

Weft, *s.* der Ein-schlag, -schuß, -trag.

Weigh, *v.* I. *a.* wägen; (— out s.th. to a p., einem etwas) zuwägen; abwägen; (er)wägen, prüfen (*fig.*); lichten (*the anchor*); to — down, überwiegen; to be —ed down with age and sorrow, von Alter und Kummer niedergebeugt sein. II. *n.* wiegen, schwer sein; to — with, Gewicht haben, gelten bei. III. *s. see* Weight; to be under — *or* way, im Gange sein (*lit. & fig.*); to get under — (*or* way), abfahren. **—able,** *adj.* wägbar. **—er,** *s.* der Wäger; (public —er) der Wag(e-)meister; letter-—er, die Briefwage. **—t,** I. *s.* das Gewicht (*of a weighing machine, a clock, etc.*); das Gewicht, Ansehen, die Wichtigkeit (*fig.*); die Last (*of years, etc.*); (pair of) —ts, die Wage; full —t, vollwichtig; up to —, kräftig, imstande ein großes Gewicht zu tragen (*of a horse*); a matter of great —t, eine höchst wichtige Sache; to carry great —t, viel gelten *or* vermögen, von großer Wichtigkeit sein; that adds —t to his words, das gibt seinen Worten Gewicht; to put the —t *or* stone, das Gewicht *or* den Stein emporheben und schleudern; dead —t, das Eigengewicht; die schwere, drückende Last; die tote Last (*Railw.*); letter —t, der Briefbeschwerer. II. *v.a.* belasten, beschweren. **—tiness,** *s.* die Schwere, das Gewicht; das Gewicht, die Wichtigkeit (*fig.*). **—ty,** *adj.,* **—tily,** *adv.* gewichtig, schwer; wichtig, erheblich (*fig.*). *Comp.* **—-house,** *s.* das Wagehaus. **—-bridge, —ing-machine,** *s.* die Brückenwage.

Weir, *s.* das Wehr, der Wehrdamm; das Teichgitter, die Fischreuse (*for fish*).

Weird, *adj.* in Zauberkünsten erfahren; zauberhaft, geheimnisvoll; ungewöhnlich, merkwürdig, seltsam (*coll.*); — sisters, Schicksalsschwestern.

Wel—come, I. *adj.* willkommen; angenehm, willkommen (*as news*); to bid, make a p. —come, einen willkommen heißen; you are —come to come or go, es steht Ihnen frei, zu kommen oder zu gehen; you are —come to it, ich gebe es gern, es steht Ihnen zu Diensten; es ist gern geschehen. II. *s.* der Willkomm, die Bewillkommnung, freundliche Aufnahme; to outstay one's —come, zu lange bleiben. III. *v.a.* bewillkommnen, willkommen heißen. IV. *int.* willkommen! **—comeness,** *s.* das Willkommensein. **—comer,** *s.* der Bewillkommner. **—fare,** *s.* die Wohlfahrt, das Wohlergehen.

Weld, *v.a.* (— together, zusammen-)schweißen.

Welkin, *s.* der (Wolken-)Himmel, das Firmament.

[1]**Well,** I. *s.* die Quelle (*Poet.*); der Brunnen; der Pumpensod (*in a ship*); der Wasserbehälter (*Locom., etc.*); das Treppenhaus (*of stairs*); der Gepäckraum, Flaschenkeller (*in cars*); draw —, Ziehbrunnen; petroleum —, Petroleumquelle; to sink a —, einen Brunnen bohren *or* graben. II. *v.n.* (— forth, hervor-, — up, herauf-)quellen *or* sprudeln. **—s,** *pl.* Heilquellen, Brunnen. *Comp.* **—-sinking,** *s.* das Brunnengraben. **—spring,** *s.* die Quelle, der Urquell.

[2]**Well,** I. *adv.* wohl, gut; (cleverly) geschickt, tüchtig, gut; (quite) gänzlich, völlig; — and good, sehr wohl, mir ganz recht! — done! bravo! gut! vorzüglich! — enough, ziemlich gut; — off, in guten Verhältnissen, wohlhabend; as — as, so gut wie; to be —, gesund, wohl sein; all's — that ends —, Ende gut, alles gut (*prov.*); let — (enough) alone, was dich nicht brennt, das blase nicht (*prov.*); before he was — out of the room, ehe er noch ganz aus dem Zimmer war; to take a thing —, etwas gut aufnehmen; I don't — know how to . . ., ich weiß nicht recht wie . . .; I cannot — go, ich kann nicht wohl gehen; to speak — of a p., Gutes von einem reden, einen loben; and — it might, wie zu erwarten war. II. *adj.* wohl, gesund; that's —, das ist gut; it is — for us that we . . ., es ist gut, daß wir . . . III. *part.;* — then! nun gut! wohlan! —! nun, wohlan! —? nun, und (was) dann, und nachher? —-a-day! ach! leider! *Comp.* (*gen'lly,* wohl-, gut-). **—-affected,** *adj.* wohlgesinnt, zugetan. **—-appointed,** *adj.* wohlausgerüstet. **—-balanced,** *adj.* gut abgewogen; wohlgeordnet. **—-behaved,** *adj.* wohlerzogen, wohlgesittet. **—-being,** *s.* die Wohlfahrt. **—-born,** *adj.* wohlgeboren, edel. **—-bred,** *adj.* wohlerzogen, artig; (gentlemanly, *etc.*) feingebildet. **—-chosen,** *adj.* gut ausgewählt *or* auserlesen. **—-couched,** *adj.* wohlabgefaßt. **—-deserved,** *adj.* wohlverdient. **—-doing,** *s.* gute Werke, das Wohltun. **—-dressed,** *adj.* gut gekleidet. **—-earned,** *adj.* wohlverdient. **—-educated,** *adj.* wohlerzogen. **—-favoured,** *adj.* gut aussehend. **—-fed,** *adj.* gut genährt. **—-informed, —-instructed,** *adj.* wohlunterrichtet. **—-intentioned,** *adj. see* —-meaning; wohlgemeint (*as a rebuke, etc.*). **—-known,** *adj.* wohlbekannt. **—-lighted,** *adj.* wohlerleuchtet. **—-loved,** *adj.* vielgeliebt, teuer. **—-made,** *adj.* wohlgebaut (*as men*); gut gemacht (*as clothes*). **—-meaning,** *adj.* wohlmeinend. **—-meant,** *adj.* wohlgemeint. **—-met,** I. *adj.;* they are —-met, sie passen für einander. II. *int.* gut getroffen! **—-nigh,** *adv.* fast, beinah. **—-ordered,** *adj.* wohlgeordnet; gut regiert. **—-pleasing,** *adj.* wohlgefällig. **—-proportioned,** *adj.* wohlproportioniert. **—-read,** *adj.* belesen. **—-regulated,** *adj.* wohlgeordnet. **—-seasoned,** *adj.* gut getrocknet. **—-shaped,** *adj.* wohl-gestaltet, -gebildet. **—-spent,** *adj.* wohlangewandt; a life —-spent, ein wohlangewendetes Leben. **—-thumbed,** *adj.* recht abgegriffen. **—-timed,** *adj.* zu rechter Zeit angebracht; gut Takt haltend. **—-to-do,** *adj.* in guten Verhältnissen, wohlhabend, reich. **—-wisher,** *s.* der Gönner, Freund. **—-wooded,** *adj.* wohlbestanden. **—-worn,** *adj.* abgetragen, ausgetreten; abgedroschen (*of arguments*).

Welt, I. *s.* der Saum; der Rahmen (*of a shoe*). II. *v.a.* säumen, umfassen.

Welter, *v.n.* sich wälzen; schwimmen (*in blood*).

Wen, *s.* die Balg-, Fett-geschwulst.

Wench, I. *s.* das Mädchen, die Dirne; (strumpet) die Buhldirne. II. *v.n.* Dirnen nachgehen.

Wen—d, I. *ir.v.n.* gehen, sich wenden. II. *v.a.* wenden; to —d one's way to, seinen Weg nehmen *or* seine Schritte lenken nach. **—t,** *imperf. of* Go.

Were, *imperf. of* Be; as it —, gleichsam, sozusagen; as you —! Griff zurück! Zurück! (*Mil.*).

Wer(e)wolf, *s.* der Werwolf.

West, *s.* der Westen; der West (*Poet. & Naut.*); — by north, (south), West zum Norden (Süden); — variation, die Nordwestering; — End (of London), das Westende (Londons); das vornehme Viertel (*fig.*). **—erly,** *adj.* westlich. **—ern,** I. *adj.* westlich, abendlich, West-; abendländisch. II. *s.* der Abendländer. **—erner,** *s.* der Bewohner des Westens; Bewohner der nordamerikanischen Weststaaten. **—ernmost,** *adj.* westlichst. **—ward,** *adv.* westlich. **—wards,** *adj.* westwärts. *Comp.* **—-ender,** *s.* der Bewohner des Westendes.

Wet, I. *adj.* naß, feucht; regnerisch (*as weather*); — with tears, tränenfeucht, von Tränen benetzt; — through, völlig durchnäßt; — weather, nasses

Wetter, Regenwetter. II. *s.* die Nässe, Feuchtigkeit; das Regenwetter. III. *v.a.* naß machen, benetzen, anfeuchten. —**ness**, *s.* die Nässe, Feuchtigkeit. —**ting**, *s.* das Naßmachen. —**tish**, *adj.* ziemlich feucht, näßlich, etwas naß. *Comp.* —**-dressing**, *s.* der feuchte kalte Umschlag (*Med.*). —**-nurse**, *s.* die (Säug-)Amme.

Wether, *s.* der Hammel, Schöps.

Wey, *s.* Maß = 40 Buschel (*of corn or salt*), 182 Pfund (*of wool*), 48 Buschel (*of oats or barley*).

Whack, I. *s.* derber Schlag. II. *v.a.* schlagen, durchprügeln (*coll.*). —**er**, *s.* etwas Großartiges (*sl.*); derbe Lüge (*sl.*). —**ing**, I. *s.* tüchtige Tracht Prügel. II. *adj.* kolossal (*coll.*).

Whal—e, *s.* der Walfisch. —**er**, *s.* der Walfischfänger (*Naut.*). —**ing**, *s.* der Walfischfang; —ing expedition, die Fahrt auf den Walfischfang. *Comp.* —**e-boat**, *s.* das Walfischboot. —**ebone**, *s.* das Fischbein. —**e-fishery**, *s.* der Walfischfang. —**e-oil**, *s.* der Walfischtran.

Wharf, *s.* der Kai, die (das) Werft, die Schiffslande. —**age**, *s.* der Anlageplatz, die Ladestelle, Werft und Lagerplatz; das Werftgeld. —**inger**, *s.* der Kaimeister. *Comp.* —**-charges**, *s.* das Werft-, Kai-geld.

What, I. *rel. pron.* was; — is right, was recht ist; that is nothing to — I, etc., das ist nichts im Vergleich zu dem, was ich &c.; cheap for — it is, billig für das, was es ist, verhältnismäßig billig; (*used as adj.*) he gave away — money he had about him, er gab das *or* alles Geld her, das er bei sich hatte; we got together — few things were left us, wir brachten die wenigen Sachen zusammen, die uns geblieben waren; see — colours, etc., sieh, welche Farben &c.; that shows — sort of a man he is, das zeigt, was für ein Mensch er ist; — a man! was für ein Mann! — a to-do, welch' ein Spektakel! — virtue! was für eine Tugend! (*used as s.*); — not, alles Mögliche; I know —'s —, ich weiß, wo der Bartel Most holt, ich bin nicht auf den Kopf gefallen; I 'll tell you —, ich will dir was sagen. II. *inter. pron.* was? wie? wie viel? — next? was nun? was wird nun kommen? — are you, that . . .? wer bist du, der du . . .? — of that? was liegt daran? was tut's? —'s the news? was giebt's Neues? for —? wofür? of —? wovon? Mr. —'s his name, der Herr Dings-da, -hausen. III. *adv.;* — with . . . — with . . ., teils durch . . . und (teils durch) . . .; — though, wenn auch, obgleich; — though he come, und wenn er auch käme. *Comp.* —**ever**, —**soever**, I. *rel. pron.* was auch (immer), was nur, alles was. II. *adj.* welch(-er, -e, -es) immer. —**-not**, der Nipptisch, die Etagere.

Wheat, *s.* der Weizen. —**en**, *adj.* Weizen-.

Wheedl—e, *v.a. & n.* schmeicheln; *see* Coax, Cajole; to —e a p. into . . ., einen durch glatte Worte, Schmeichelei, Liebkosungen zu . . . bewegen *or* beschwatzen. —**er**, *s.* der Schmeichler. —**ingly**, *adv.* mit Schmeicheln.

Wheel, I. *s.* das Rad; (spinning-—) das Spinnrad; (bicycle) das Fahrrad; (turn) die Umdrehung; free — cycles, Freilaufräder; to be fond of the —, gerne radeln; to break upon the —, rädern; to break a fly on the —, kleiner Zwecke wegen große Mittel aufbieten (*fig.*); —s within —s, verwickelte Verhältnisse (*fig.*). II. *v.n.* rollen, sich drehen; sich schwenken (*Mil.*). III. *v.a.* rollen, schieben (*a chair, etc.*); (auf Rädern) fortbewegen, führen, fahren. —**ed**, *adj.* mit Rädern, Räder-. —**ers**, *pl.* Stangenpferde. —**ing**, *s.* die Beförderung auf der Achse; die Schwenkung (*Mil.*). *Comp.* —**barrow**, *s.* der Schubkarren. —**chair**, *s.* der Rollstuhl, Fahrsessel. —**man**, *s.* der Steuermann. —**work**, *s.* das Räderwerk. —**wright**, *s.* der Radmacher.

Wheez—e, I. *v.n.* schnaufen, keuchen. II. *s.* keuchender Ton; der Scherz; der Kniff (*sl.*). —**y**, *adj.* keuchend, schnaubend.

[1]Whelk, *s.* die Anschwellung, Pustel, der Auswuchs.

[2]Whelk, *s.* die Trompetenschnecke.

Whelm, *v.a.* verschütten, überdecken; zermalmen (*fig.*).

Whelp, I. *s.* das Junge. II. *v.n.* Junge werfen.

When, I. *inter. adv.* wann. II. *conj. & rel. adv.* wenn, da, als; (whilst) während; — due, bei Verfall, zur Verfallzeit; — received, nach Empfang; just —, gerade wenn; eben als; — a man leaves home for the first time, wenn ein Mann seine Heimat zum ersten Male verläßt; — we left Germany we felt very sorry, als wir Deutschland verließen, waren wir sehr traurig; about the time — the grapes are ripening, um die Zeit, wenn die Trauben reifen. —**ce**, I. *inter. & rel. adv.* woher, woraus, von wo(her); —ce come you? wo kommen Sie her? II. *conj.* daher. *Comp.* —(**so**)**ever**, *conj.* wenn auch immer, so oft als.

Where, I. *inter. adv.* wo. II. *rel. adv. & conj.*, wo; da; (— to) wohin; before they know — they are, ehe sie wissen, woran sie sind. *Comp.* —**abouts**, I. *adv.* wo herum, wo da, wo ungefähr. II. *s.* der Aufenthalt, Wohnort. —**as**, *conj.* da hingegen, da sonst, da doch; da nun, weil, da (*Parl., Law*). —**at**, *rel. adv. & conj.* wobei, worüber; worauf. —**by**, *rel. adv. & conj.* wodurch, womit, wovon, wobei. —**ever**, *see* —**ver**. —**fore**, I. *adv. & conj.* weshalb, weswegen; (und) daher. II. *inter. adv.* weshalb, warum, wozu. —**in**, *adv. & conj.* worin. —**-is-it**, *s.* das Privatadreßbuch, der Notiz-Adreßkalender. —**of**, *adv. & conj.* wovon, woraus; the crime —of we are accused, das Verbrechen, dessen man uns beschuldigt. —**on**, *rel. adv. & conj.* worauf, woran, auf dem *or* der. —**soever**, *rel. adv.* wo auch nur; *see* Whithersoever. —**upon**, *rel. adv. & conj.* worauf; (after which) wonach. —**to**, —**unto**, *rel. adv. & conj.* wozu, wohin. —**ver**, *rel. adv.* wo auch nur, wo auch immer, überall wo. —**with**, *rel. adv. & conj.* womit, wovon. —**withal**, I. *rel. adv.* womit auch. II. *s.* das Erforderliche, die Mittel (*pl.*); he had not the —withal, er hatte nicht das nötige Geld (*sl.*).

Wherry, *s.* die Fähre; der Ewer, Lichter, die Jolle.

Whet, I. *v.a.* wetzen, schärfen, schleifen; reizen (*the appetite*). II. *s.* das Wetzen; (that which —s) die Reizung; das (Appetit-)Reizmittel. *Comp.* —**stone**, *s.* der Wetz-, Abzieh-, Schleif-stein.

Whether, I. *pron.* welcher, welches, wer von beiden II. *conj.* ob; — it be true or not, ob es wahr ist oder nicht; — or no, er mag wollen oder nicht.

Whew, *interj.* huh! uff!

Whey, *s.* die Molken. —**ish**, *adj.* molkenartig. *Comp.* —**-faced**, *adj.* blaß wie Molken.

Which, I. *rel. pron.* der, die, das, welcher, welche, welches; was; our Father, — art in Heaven, unser Vater, der du bist im Himmel (*B.*); to — (of them)? an welchen? take — you will, nehmen Sie, welches Sie wollen; I don't know — is —, ich kann sie nicht unterscheiden; (they declared him to be innocent) — he is not, was er nicht ist; the crime — you accuse him of, is . . ., das Verbrechen, dessen Sie ihn beschuldigen, ist . . .; he reminded him of that — justice demands, er erinnerte ihn an das, was die Gerechtigkeit fordert. II. *inter. pron.* welcher, welche, welches; — of you convinceth me of sin? welcher unter euch kann mich einer Sünde zeihen? (*B.*). III. *inter. adj.* welch; — actor pleased you best? welcher Schauspieler gefiel Ihnen am meisten? *Comp.* —**ever**, *rel. pron.* welches auch (immer).

Whiff, I. *s.* der Piff, Paff, Hauch; to take — at one's pipe, einen Zug aus der Pfeife tun. II. *v.a.* paffen.

Whil—e, I. *s.* die Weile, Zeit; a little —e ago *or* since, vor kurzem, kürzlich, unlängst; a long —e ago, längst, schon lange her; between —es, dann und wann, zuweilen; worth —e, der Mühe wert; once in a —e, dann und wann. II. *v.a.;* to —e away, verbringen, vertändeln. III., **—st**, *conj.* während, so lange als; (as) indem; —e *or* —st I write, während ich schreibe; —e there 's life, there 's hope, solange Leben da ist, ist auch Hoffnung da. **—om**, I. *adj.* vormalig. II. *adv.* vormals, weiland (*obs.*).

[1]**Whim**, *s.* der Einfall, die Grille; full of —s, voller Grillen. **—sical**, *adj.*, **—sically**, *adv.* grillenhaft, wunderlich, launisch. **—sicalness**, **—sicality**, *s.* die Wunderlichkeit, das grillenhafte Wesen.

[2]**Whim**, *s.* der Göpel, Haspel (*Mach.*). *Comp.* **—-engine**, *s.* die Göpelkunst.

Whimper, I. *v.n.* wimmern, winseln. II., **—ing**, *s.* das Gewimmer, Gewinsel.

[1]**Whin**, *s.* der Stechginster. **—ny**, *adj.* viel Stechginster enthaltend. *Comp.* **—chat**, *s.* das Braunkehlchen.

[2]**Whin**, *s.* (—stone) der Basalt. **—ny**, *adj.* basaltartig, voll Basalt.

Whin—e, I. *v.n.* winseln, wimmern, weinen. II. *s.* das Gewinsel. **—er**, *s.* der Winseler **—ing**, *adj.*, **—ingly**, *adv.* wimmernd, winselnd; kläglich (*fig.*).

Whinny, I. *v.n.* wiehern. II. *s.* das Gewieher.

Whip, I. *v.a.* (*p.p.* —ped *and* —t) peitschen, züchtigen, geißeln; treiben, schlagen (*tops*); leicht übernähen (*Sew.*); schlagen (*cream*); —ped cream, die Schlagsahne; —ped seam, überschlagene Naht; to — the stream, die Angelschnur vor sich ins Wasser werfen; to — **away**, schnell wegnehmen; to — **in**, Parteimitglieder (im Parlament) behufs einer Abstimmung zusammenbringen, zusammentrommeln (*coll.*); to — **off**, schnell wegtun; to — **on**, geschwind überwerfen *or* anziehen; to — **up**, zupeitschen, antreiben (*horses*), schnell aufnehmen, aufraffen (*a thing*); zusammentrommeln. II. *v.n.* sich schnell bewegen, hüpfen, springen, schnellen. III. *s.* die Peitsche, Geißel; (driver) der Kutscher; (parliamentary —) der Zusammentrommler der Parlamentsmitglieder für wichtige Abstimmungen; (Liberal) —, der Sekretär (der liberalen Partei). **—per**, *s.* der Peitschende. **—ping**, *s.* das Peitschen, Züchtigen. **—ster**, *s.* der Springinsfeld. *Comp.* **—-cord**, *s.* die Peitschenschnur. **—-hand**, *s.* rechte Hand; to have the —-hand of a p., die Oberhand, den Vorteil über einen haben. **—handle**, *s.* der Peitschenstiel. **—-lash**, *s.* die Peitschenschmitze. **—per-in**, *s.* der Jäger, der die Jagdhunde zusammenhält; *see* Parliamentary —. **—per-snapper**, *s.* der nichtssagende nichtsnutzige Mensch, das freche Bürschchen, der Gelbschnabel. **—ping-post**, *s.* der Schandpfahl, die Stäupsäule. **—(ping)-top**, *s.* der Kreisel.

Whir, I. *v.n.* schwirren. II. *s.* das Schwirren, Geschwirre. **—l**, I. *v.a.* (*& n.*) wirbeln, (sich) drehen; to —l off, away, fort-wirbeln, -eilen, schnell davonrollen. II. *s.* der Wirbel, Strudel; —l of gaiety, Strudel der Vergnügungen. **—ligig**, *s.* der Kreisel. **—ling**, I. *adj.* wirbelnd. II. *s.* das Wirbeln. **—ring**, *s.* das Schwirren. *Comp.* **—lpool**, *s.* der Strudel, Wirbel. **—lwind**, *s.* der Wirbelwind; der Sturm (*fig.*).

Whisk, I. *s.* der (Stroh-)Wisch, Besen, die Bürste; der Schlägel (*for eggs*); schnelle, plötzliche Bewegung (*of the tail, etc.*); clothes —, Kleiderbesen. II. *v.a.* fegen, kehren, bürsten; schlagen (*eggs*); to — away, schnell wegtun. III. *v.n.* huschen; to — away, to — off, weghuschen. **—er**, *s.*, *usually* **—ers** (*pl.*), der Backenbart; —ers, der Bart (*of cats, etc.*). **—ered**, *adj.* backenbärtig.

Whisk(e)y, *s.* der Whisky. *Comp.* **—-money**, *s.* das Whiskygeld (zur Beförderung der technischen Erziehung), *see* Beer-money.

Whisper, I. *s.* das Geflüster. II. *v.n.* flüstern, wispern, leise reden. III. *v.a.* (zu-, ins Ohr) flüstern; it is —ed (that . . .), man raunt sich ins Ohr (daß . . .), man munkelt (davon); —ed sounds, Flüsterlaute. **—er**, *s.* der Flüsterer; der Zuträger, Ohrenbläser (*fig.*). **—ing**, I. *adj.*, **—ingly**, *adv.* wispernd, flüsternd, leise. II. *s.* das Geflüster.

[1]**Whist**, *int.* still! bst!

[2]**Whist** (*older* **Whisk**), *s.* das Whist(spiel).

Whistl—e, I. *v.a. & n.* pfeifen; to —e for, vergeblich nach (etwas) suchen, trachten (*coll.*); now he may —e for them, jetzt kann er ihnen nachflöten, jetzt mag er sehen, wie er sie kriegt (*coll.*). II. *s.* das Pfeifen, der Pfiff; (instrument) die Pfeife; (throat) die Kehle (*vulg.*); to wet one's —e, sich (*dat.*) die Kehle anfeuchten; to —e before one is out of the wood, den Tag vor dem Abend loben. **—er**, *s.* der Pfeifer. **—ing**, I. *adj.* pfeifend. II. *s.* das Pfeifen.

Whit, *s.* das Jota, der Punkt; not a —, nicht ein Jota, durchaus das Geringste; I am not a — the wiser for it, ich bin dadurch um nichts klüger; she is every — as bad as . . ., sie ist in jeder Hinsicht ebenso schlecht wie . . . **—tle**, *see* Whittle.

White, I. *adj.* weiß; (pale) bleich, blaß; grau, weiß (*of hair*); (pure) rein; — bear, der Eisbär; — friar, der Karmeliter; — heat, die Weißglühhitze; — hot, weißglühend; — lie, kleine Lüge, Notlüge; — owl, die Schleiereule; — paint, die Bleiweißfarbe; — pine, der Weymouths-, weiße Kiefer; — squall, leichte Bö; — swelling, weiße Gelenkgeschwulst; — wine, der Weißwein; — as snow, schneeweiß; to show the — feather, sich feige zeigen. II. *s.* die, das Weiße, das Weiß; das Schminkweiß (*for the face, etc.*); die Lücke (*Typ.*); das Weiße (of the eye, im Auge); — of egg, das Eiweiß; dressed in —, weiß gekleidet, in weißem Kleide; the —s, die Weißen (*opp. to negroes, etc.*); der weiße Fluß (*Med.*). **—n**, *v.* I. *a.* weißen; (bleach) bleichen; decken, terrieren (*sugar*). II. *n.* weiß werden; bleichen. **—ner**, *s.* der Weißputzer, Tüncher. **—ness**, *s.* die Weiße; (paleness) die bleiche Farbe. **—ning**, *s.* die Schlemmkreide. *Comp.* **—bait**, *s.* der kleine Weißfisch der Themse, Breitling (*Icht.*); —bait dinner, das Essen der Englischen Staatsminister in Greenwich vor Parlamentsschluß. **—boy**, *s.* der Weißbube, irische Ruhestörer (1762). **—faced**, *adj.* weißaussehend. **—-lead**, *s.* das Bleiweiß. **—-livered**, *adj.* feige. **—-smith**, *s.* der Weißblechschmied. **—wash**, I. *s.* (weiße) Tünche. II. *v.a.* (aus-) weißen, übertünchen. **—washer**, *s.* der Tüncher, Anstreicher. **—y-brown**, *adj.* bräunlichweiß.

Whither, *rel. & inter. adv.* wohin. *Comp* **—soever**, *rel. adv.* wohin auch nur.

Whit—ing, spanische Kreide; der Weißfisch (*Icht.*). **—ish**, *adj.* weißlich. **—monday**, *s.* Pfingstmontag, der 2te Pfingstag. **—sun**, *adj.* zur Pfingstfeier gehörig, Pfingst-; —sun holidays, *see* —suntide. **—sunday**, *s.* der Pfingst(sonn)tag. **—suntide**, I. *s.* (—sun holidays) die Pfingstzeit, (das) Pfingsten. II. *attrib.* Pfingst-; —suntide holidays *or* recess, die Pfingstferien.

Whitlow, *s.* das Nagelgeschwür.

Whittl—e, *v.a.* I. *s.* das Schnitzmesser. II. schneiden, schnitzeln. **—ing**, *s.* das Schnitzeln, Schnitzwerk.

Whiz, I. *v.n.* zischen, sausen, schwirren. II. *s.* das Zischen, Sausen.

Who, I. *rel. pron.* der, die, das, welcher, welche, welches, —'s, —, Wer ist's? alphabetisch geordnetes Jahrbuch bekannter Zeitgenossen; as — should say, wie wenn einer sagte; he — lies would also steal, wer lügt, der stiehlt auch. II. *inter. pron.* wer; — goes there? wer da? **—m**, I. *obj. of* — I. welchen, welche, welches, den, die, das; to —m, welchem, welcher, dem, der, (*pl.*) welchen, denen; the woman —m thou gavest me, das Weib, das Du mir zugesellt hast (*B.*). II. *obj. of* — II. wen; to —m?

wem? —**se**, I. *poss. of* — I. dessen, deren, dessen, (*pl.*) deren; the man —se house I bought, der Mann, dessen Haus ich kaufte; the ladies —se brother we know, die Damen, deren Bruder wir kennen. II. *poss. of* — II. wessen; —se book is this? wessen Buch ist das? wem gehört dies Buch? *Comp.* —**se-soever**, *rel. pron.* wessen auch. —**so**, —(**so**)**ever**, *rel. pron.* wer nur, wer auch immer, jeder der.

Whoa, *interj.* brr! halt!

Whole, I. *adj.* ganz; (complete) vollkommen, völlig, vollständig; (sound) heil, gesund; in a — skin, mit heiler Haut. II. *s.* das Ganze; upon the —, im ganzen, überhaupt. —**some**, *adj.*, —**somely**, *adv.* heilsam, gesund; nützlich, zweckmäßig (*as advice, doctrine, etc.*). —**someness**, *s.* die Gesundheit, Heilsamkeit; die Nützlichkeit, Zweckmäßigkeit. *Comp.* —**sale**, I. *adj.* im Großen; (general) allgemein, unterschiedslos; —sale business, das Großgeschäft, Geschäft en gros; —sale dealer *or* merchant, der Großhändler, Großkaufmann. II. *s.* der Verkauf, Handel im großen, Großhandel.

Wholly, *adv.* ganz, gänzlich, völlig, durchaus.

Whoop, I. *s.* lautes Geschrei; *see* Hoopoe; war —, Kriegsgeschrei. II. *v.n.* laut aufschreien. —**ing-cough**, *s.* der Stickhusten, Keuchhusten.

Whop, *see* Whap.

Whor—e, *s.* die Hure, Dirne, Prostituirte, das Freudenmädchen. —**emonger**, *s.* der Dirnenjäger. —**eson**, *adj.* Dirnen=; niedrig, gemein (*fig.*). —**ish**, *adj.* hurerisch, unzüchtig.

Whorl, *s.* der Quirl, Wirbel (*Bot.*); das Gewinde (*of a snail*).

Whortleberry, *s.* die Heidelbeere; red —, die Preißelbeere, Kronsbeere, rote Heidelbeere.

Whose, **Whoso**, *etc. see* Who.

Why, I. *adv.* warum; for —, weshalb; — so? warum denn? wie so? the reason —, der Grund dafür. II. *int. & part.* ei! nun, nun ja, na ja; —, to be sure, ja freilich! III. *s.*; the — and the wherefore, das Wie und das Warum.

Wick, *s.* der Docht.

Wicked, *adj.*, —**ly**, *adv.* (spiteful) boshaft; (bad) gottlos, verrucht, schlecht, böse; (naughty) lose, schalkhaft. —**ness**, *s.* die Gottlosigkeit, Bosheit; (act of —ness) verruchte Tat.

Wicker, *adj.* (von Weidenzweigen) geflochten; — basket, der Weidenkorb; — cage, geflochtener Käfig; — chair, geflochtener Stuhl, der Korbstuhl. *Comp.* —**work**, *s.* das Flechtwerk.

Wicket, *s.* (— gate) das Pförtchen; der Dreistab (*Cricket*). *Comp.* —-**keeper**, *s.* der Verteidiger des Dreistabes.

Wide, *adj. & adv.*, —**ly**, *adv.* weit, breit; fern, weit (of the mark, vom Ziele); — awake, völlig wach *or* munter; — difference, großer Unterschied; 3 inches —, 3 Zoll breit. —**n**, *v.a.* (*& n.* sich) erweitern, ausdehnen. —**ness**, *s.* die Weite, Breite, Ausdehnung. —**ning**, *s.* die Erweiterung. *Comp.* —-**awake**, I. *adj.* hellsehend, schlau, verschmitzt (*sl.*). II. *s.* breitkrempiger, weicher Hut. —-**mouthed**, *adj.* mit breitem Munde. —**spread**, *adj.* weit ausgebreitet, weitverbreitet.

Widow, *s.* die Witwe; grass-—, — bewitched, die Strohwitwe; —s' fund, die Wittwenkasse; —'s weeds, die Witwentracht, Trauertracht. —**ed**, *adj.* verwitwet; verwaist (*fig.*). —**er**, *s.* der Witwer. —**erhood**, *s.* der Witwerstand. —**hood**, *s.* der Witwenstand. *Comp.* —-**hunter**, *s.* einer, der auf reiche Witwen Jagd macht.

Width, *s* die Weite, Breite.

Wield, *v.a.* handhaben, schwingen; to — the sceptre, das Zepter führen, regieren.

Wife, *s.* (*pl.* Wives) das (Ehe=)Weib, die Gattin, (Ehe=)Frau; my —, meine Frau. —**ly**, *adj.* (—like) einer Frau geziemend.

Wig, *s.* die Perrücke; big —, der Oberbeamte, Vornehme (*sl.*). *Comp.* —-**block**, *s.* der Perrückenstock. —-**maker**, *s.* der Perrückenmacher.

Wigging, *s.* das Ausschelten (*sl.*).

Wight, *s.* der Wicht, Kerl, das Geschöpf.

Wigwam, *s.* die Indianerhütte, der Wigwam.

Wild, I. *adj.*, —**ly**, *adv.* wild (*as beasts, weather, ideas, looks, passions, land, plants, etc.*); (fantastic) wild, abenteuerlich, phantastisch; (unsteady) liederlich; — beast, das wilde Tier; — boar, der Eber, das Wildschwein; — fancies, tolle Einfälle; — goose, wilde Gans; — goose chase, vergebliche Jagd (*fig.*); — oats, der Wildhafer; to sow one's — oats, sich austoben, sich (*dat.*) die Hörner ablaufen; — plum, die Schlehe; — scheme, abenteuerliches Projekt; the — man of the woods, der wilde Mann; to run —, wild wachsen; ins Kraut schießen. II. *s.*, —**s**, *pl.* die Wildnis, Wüste, Einöde. —**er**, *see* Bewilder. —**erness**, *s.* die Wildnis, Wüste; a howling —erness, die Einöde, da es heulet (*B.*); watery —erness, Wasserwüste. —**ing**, *s.* der Wildling; (—apple) der Holzapfel. —**ness**, *s.* die Wildheit. *Comp.* —-**cat**, *s.* die Wildkatze. —-**fire**, *s.* das griechische (unauslöschliche) Feuer; der Sprühteufel; to spread like —-fire, sich wie ein Lauffeuer verbreiten. —-**fowl**, *s.* wildes Geflügel.

Wil—e, I. *s.* die List; —es, Kniffe, Ränke, Schliche (*pl.*). II. *v.a.* an=, ver=locken; to —e away, vertändeln (*time*). —**ily**, *adv. see* —y. —**iness**, *s.* die List, Arglist, Verschlagenheit. —**y**, *adj.* listig, schlau, verschlagen.

Wilful, *adj.*, —**ly**, *adv.* eigen=willig, =sinnig, halsstarrig; stätisch (*as a horse*); *see* Intentional; —ly, mit Fleiß. —**ness**, *s.* der Eigensinn.

Will, I. *s.* der Wille; (pleasure) die Willkür, der Wille; (power) die Willkür, Macht, Gewalt; (wish) der Wille, Wunsch; (last —) letzter Wille, das Testament; good —, das Wohlwollen; ill —, das Übelwollen, die Abneigung; at —, nach Belieben; with a —, energisch; to hold at the — of the proprietor, (eine Pachtung) innehaben, deren Pacht von dem Grundbesitzer beliebig aufgehoben werden kann; what is your —? was wollen Sie? to put a p. in one's —, einen in seinem Testamente bedenken; where there's a —, there's a way, frisch gewagt ist halb gewonnen (*prov.*). II. *ir.v.a.* wollen; (wish) wünschen, begehren; durch Testament verfügen, testieren; pflegen; let the circumstances be what they —, die Verhältnisse mögen sein, wie sie wollen; would to God! wollte Gott! he that — not when he may, when he — he shall have nay, wer nicht will, wenn er kann, soll nicht können, wenn er will; — he, nil he, —y nilly, er mag wollen oder nicht. III. *ir.v.aux.* werden, wollen; I —, ja. —**ed**, *adj.*; self-—, eigen=willig, =sinnig. —**ing**, I. *p.*; God —ing, so Gott will. II. *adj.* willig, bereit(willig); I am —ing to do it, ich bin bereit, es zu tun; I am —ing to believe, ich glaube gern, ich will gern glauben. —**ingly**, *adv.* gern; (voluntarily) aus freien Stücken. —**ingness**, *s.* die Bereitwilligkeit.

Will-o'-the-wisp, *s.* das Irrlicht.

Willow, *s.* die Weide; der Wolf, Teufel (*for wool*); der Zauseler (*for cotton*); to wear the —, um die (den) Geliebte(n) trauern; weeping —, die Trauerweide. II. *attrib.*; — pattern, das Weidenmuster. —**y**, *adj.* wie eine Weide. *Comp.* —-**herb**, *s.* der Weiderich (*Bot.*). —-**tree**, *s.* der Weidenbaum. —-**wren**, *s.* der Weidenzeisig.

Wilton, *attrib.*; — carpet, der Plüschteppich.

Wimble, *s.* (*obs.*) *see* Gimlet.

Wimple, I. *s.* der Schleier um Kopf und Hals bis über das Kinn, das Hals= und Kopf=tuch; der Schleier (*B.*). II. *v.a.* verschleiern, mit einem Schleier bedecken; sich schlängeln (*dial.*).

Win, *ir.v.* I. *a.* gewinnen (*a battle, prize, money, etc.*); erlangen (*fig.*); to — a p. over (to), einen gewinnen (für). II. *n.* siegen, den Sieg davontragen; gewinnen (*at play, etc.*); (— **upon**) einnehmen, gewinnen.

Wince—e, I. *v.n.* zurück=weichen, =fahren; zusammenzucken. II. *s.* das Zusammenfahren, Zurückfahren, Zucken. **—h**, *s.* der Haspel, die Winde; die Kurbel (*of a wheel, etc.*).

[1]**Wind**, *s.* der Wind; die Blähung, der Wind (*Med.*); die Lunge (*of a horse*); der Atem (*fig.*); the four —s of heaven, die vier Himmelsgegenden; the — is very high, es geht ein starker Wind; shot between — and water, der Schuß, welcher die Schiffsseite gerade im Wasserspiegel trifft; to get — of, Wind bekommen von, hören von; to get the — of a ship, einem Schiffe den Wind abgewinnen; to take the — out of a p.'s sails, einem das Wort aus dem Munde nehmen; einem alles vorweg nehmen; in the —'s eye, in the teeth of the —, dem Winde gerade entgegen; there is something in the —, es ist etwas in der Luft *or* im Werk; to raise the —, sich (*dat.*) Geld verschaffen (*sl.*); to break a horse's —, ein Pferd überreiten; it's an ill — that blows nobody good, zu etwas ist ein Unglück immer gut (*prov.*). **—age**, *s.* der Spielraum (*of a gun*). **—iness**, *s.* die Windigkeit; die Aufgeblasenheit (*fig.*). **—less**, *adj.* ohne Wind. **—ow**, *s.* das Fenster; bow *or* bay, French, sash —ow, rundes oder viereckiges Erker=, Flügel=, Schieb=fenster. **—owed**, *adj.* mit Fenstern versehen. **—owless**, *adj.* fensterlos. **—ward**, I. *adj. & adv.* windwärts. II. *s.* die Wind=, Luv=seite; to ply to —ward, den Wind abkneifen. **—y**, *adj.* windig, Wind=; (stormy) stürmisch; blähend (*Med.*); windig, luftig; leer; aufgeblasen (*fig.*). *Comp.* **—bag**, *s.* der Windbeutel, leere Schwätzer. **—bound**, *adj.* von widrigem Wind aufgehalten. **—fall**, *s.* das Fallobst; der Glücksfall (*fig.*); a great —fall of money, ein großer unerwarteter Geldregen. **—-flower**, *s.* das Windröschen. **—-instrument**, *s.* das Blasinstrument. **—mill**, *s.* die Windmühle. **—ow-bar**, *s.* die Fensterstange. **—ow-blind**, *s.* die Jalousie, das Rouleau. **—ow-case**, *s.* die Fenstereinfassung. **—ow-curtain**, *s.* der Fenstervorhang, die Fenstergardine. **—ow-frame**, *s.* der Fensterrahmen. **—ow-hangings**, *pl.* Fenstervorhänge. **—ow-pane**, *s.* die Fensterscheibe. **—ow-sash**, *s.* der (meist verschiebbare) Rahmen für Fensterscheiben. **—ow-sill**, *s.* der Fenstersims, das Fensterbrett; (wooden sill) das Gesims. **—pipe**, *s.* die Luftröhre. **—-row**, *s.* der Schwaden (*of hay*); die Reihe (of turf, Torfstücke) zum Trocknen; an einander aufgestapelte Getreidegarben.

[2]**Wind**, *ir.v.a.* I. winden; (meander) schlängeln; blasen (*a horn*); (turn round) wenden, drehen; (— round, change) verändern, wenden; wickeln (*wool*); (screw) schrauben; to — a rope **into** a coil, ein Tau aufschlagen; to — o.s. into a p.'s favour, sich bei einem einschmeicheln; to — **off**, ab=winden, =wickeln; to — **up**, aufwinden, aufwickeln (*thread, etc., a weight*); aufziehen (*a watch, clock*); ordnen, abschließen (*affairs, etc.*); abschließen (*an account*); ordnen, abmachen (*a business*). II. *n.* sich winden, sich schlängeln. **—er**, *s.* einer, der windet; (reel) der, die Haspel, Winde. **—ing**, I. *adj.* sich windend; (crooked) schief, krumm; —ing curve, die Wellenlinie; —ing stairs, die Wendeltreppe. II. *s.* das Winden, Spulen; die Windung, Krümmung, Wendung; —ing up, das Aufziehen, Aufwinden (*lit.*), der Abschluß (*fig.*). **—lass**, *s.* der Haspel, die (Hebe=) Winde, der Krahn; das Bratspill (*Naut.*). *Comp.* **—ing-sheet**, *s.* das Grabtuch, Totenhemd. **—-up**, *s.* das Ende, der Abschluß.

Wine, *s.* der Wein; when the — is in, the wit is out, wenn Wein eingeht, geht Witz aus; good — needs no bush, gute Ware braucht keine Empfehlung (*prov.*); to take — with a p., mit einem ein Gläschen trinken. *Comp.* **—bibber**, *s.* der Weinsäufer. **—-bin**, *s.* das Weinflaschengestell; slider —-bin, verschiebbares Flaschengestell. **—bottle**, *s.* die Weinflasche. **—-cask**, *s.* das Weinfaß. **—-cellar**, *s.* der Weinkeller. **—-cooler**, *s.* der Weinkühler. **—-glass**, *s.* das Weinglas. **—-merchant**, *s.* der Weinhändler. **—-press**, *s.* die Weinpresse, die Kelter. **—-trade**, *s.* der Weinhandel. **—-vault**, *see* —-cellar.

Wing, I. *s.* der Flügel (*of a bird, seed, an army, a fleet, a house, etc.*), Fittich, die Schwinge; to take —, weg=, auf=fliegen; to be upon the —, im Fluge sein, fliegen (*as birds*); sich regen, sich rühren (*fig.*); to clip a p.'s —s, einem die Flügel beschneiden; on the —s of love, auf Fittichen der Liebe; on the —s of the wind, mit Windeseile. II. *v.a.* (be)flügeln; mit Flügeln versehen (*an army, etc.*); the bird —s its way towards, der Vogel richtet seinen Flug nach. **—ed**, *adj.* beflügelt, geflügelt; beschwingt (*poet.*); geflügelt, gefiedert (*Bot.*); schnell, flüchtig (*fig.*); —ed creation, das Geflügel; —ed words, geflügelte Worte. **—less**, *adj.* flügellos. *Comp.* **—-case**, *s.* die Flügeldecke.

Wink, I. *s.* das Auf= und Nieder=schlagen der Augenlider, Blinzeln; (hint) der Wink (mit den Augen); not to get a — of sleep, kein Auge zutun (*colloq.*). II. *v.n.* winken, blinzeln; to — at *or* to (s.o., einem) zuwinken; to — at (a th.), ein Auge zudrücken bei, (bei einer S.) durch die Finger sehen; he —ed at it, er sah es ihm *or* ihr nach. **—er**, *s.* der Blinzelnde; das Scheuleder, die Scheuklappe (*for horses*). **—ing**, *s.* das Winken, Blinzeln.

Winkle, *s. short for* Periwinkle.

Winn—er, *s.* der Gewinner; he is the —er, er hat gewonnen. **—ing**, I. *adj.*, **—ingly**, *adv.* einnehmend, gewinnend; —ing way(s), einnehmendes, gewinnendes Wesen. II. *s.* das Gewinnen. **—ings**, *pl.* der Gewinn. *Comp.* **—ing-post**, *s.* das Ziel.

Winnow, *v.a.* wannen, schwingen, worfeln; sondern, sichten (*fig.*). **—er**, *s.* der Kornschwinger. **—ing**, *s.* das Kornschwingen, Wannen. *Comp* **—ing-fan**, *s.* die Worfschaufel. **—ing-machine**, *s.* die Kornreinigungs=maschine.

Winsome, *adj.* anziehend, reizend. **—ness**, *s.* der Reiz.

Winter, I. *s.* der Winter; hard —, strenger Winter. II. *attrib.*; — crop, die Winterfrucht; —quarters, die Winterquartiere. III. *v.n.* überwintern, den Winter zubringen. **—ly**, **—y**, (**Wintry**,) *adj.* winterlich, Winter=; frostig, kalt.

Wipe, I. *v.a.* (ab)wischen (*also one's shoes, etc.*); (dry) trocknen; (clean) reinigen; to — one's nose, sich (*dat.*) die Nase putzen; to — **away**, wegwischen; to — **down**, abwischen; to — **off**, abwischen (*lit.*); bezahlen (*an account*); to — **out**, aus=, ver=wischen; zerstören, vernichten (*fig.*). II. *s.* das (Ab=)Wischen, Reinigen; der Wischer, Stich (*fig.*); to give a —, (eine S.) oberflächlich abwischen. **—r**, *s.* der Wischer.

Wire, I. *s.* der Draht; das Telegramm, die Drahtnachricht; answer by —, die Drahtantwort; to transmit by —, drahtlich übermitteln; barbed —, der Stachelzaundraht. II. *adj.* drahten; Draht=; — fence, der Drahtzaun; — gauze, die Drahtgaze; — netting, das Drahtnetz; — rope, das Drahtseil; — sieve, das Drahtsieb; — spring, die Drahtfeder. III. *v.a.* mit Draht befestigen; (für elektrische Leitung) mit einem Draht versehen (*a lamp*). IV. *v.n.* telegraphieren, drahten (*Tele.*); he —d back, er antwortete telegraphisch *or* telegraphierte zurück. **—less**, *adj.*; —less telegraphy, die Funkentelegraphie, drahtlose Depeschensendung; —less telegraphy station, die Funkspruchstation. *Comp.* **—draw**, *v.a.* (zu) Draht ziehen; in die Länge ziehen, ausdehnen (*fig.*). **—drawer**, *s.* der Drahtzieher. **—drawing**, *s.* das Drahtziehen; das In=die=Länge=ziehen (*fig.*). **—-haired**, *adj.* mit borstigen Haaren. **—-puller**, *s.* der Marionettenspieler; der Drahtzieher, bezahlter Agitator; der Intrigant, heimliche Agent (*fig.*). **—-pulling**, *s.* das Ziehen der Drähte für Marionetten; das Ränkeschmieden; die heimliche Leitung. **—worm**, *s.* der Drahtwurm, die schädliche Raupe. **—-wove(n)**, *adj.* aus Draht geflochten; —-wove(n) mattress, die Springfedermatratze.

Wiry, *adj.* drahtähnlich; sehnig, zäh, gedrungen (*of the frame of the body*); borstig (*as hair*).

Wisdom, *s.* die Weisheit; (prudence) die Klugheit; (knowledge) die Einsicht, Erfahrung. *Comp.* **—-tooth**, *s.* der Weisheitszahn.

[1]**Wise**, *adj.*, **—ly**, *adv.* weise, vernünftig, verständig; (prudent) klug, weise; (learned) weise, gelehrt; I am none the —r, ich bin um nichts klüger *or* so klug wie zuvor; they managed it without our being any the —r, sie taten es unter sich, ohne daß irgend einer von uns darum wußte; **—man** (woman), der (die) Wahrsager(in). *Comp.* **—acre**, *s.* der Weisheitsprediger, Gelehrttuende.

[2]**Wise**, *s.* die Weise, Art und Weise; in no —, auf keine Weise, keineswegs; in, on this —, auf diese Art, in dieser Weise; in any —, auf welche Art auch.

Wish, I. *v.a.* wünschen; (desire) ersuchen, verlangen; to — a p. joy of, (einem) Glück wünschen zu. II. *v.n.* wünschen; to — for, sich (*dat.*) (etwas) wünschen, sich sehnen nach; we do not — for war, wir wünschen keinen Krieg; as heart could —, nach Herzenswunsch; I — to God he had never come, wollte Gott, er wäre nie gekommen! III. *s.* der Wunsch, das Verlangen, Begehren; to breathe a —, einen Wunsch äußern; he has got his —, sein Wunsch ist erfüllt; —ed for, ersehnt. **—er**, *s.* der Wünschende. **—ful**, *adj.*, **—fully**, *adv.* wünschend, sehnlich, sehnsüchtig. **—fulness**, *s.* die Sehnsucht. *Comp.* **—bone**, **—ing-bone**, *s.* das gabelförmige Brustbein des Geflügels. **—ing-cap**, *s.* das Wünschelhütlein. **—ing-rod**, *s.* die Wünschelrute.

Wish—wash, *s.* dünnes schlechtes Getränk (*fam.*). **—y-washy**, *adj.* wässerig (*lit.*); saft- und kraft-los, läppisch, geringfügig (*fig.*).

Wist, *obs. imperf.* (*of the obs.* Wot) wußte, wußtet, wußten.

Wistful, *adj.*, **—ly**, *adv.* sehnlich, sehnsüchtig; (earnest) ernst, gedankenvoll. **—ness**, *s.* die Nachdenklichkeit, Aufmerksamkeit.

Wit, I. *s.* der Witz; (understanding) der Witz, Verstand, Kopf; (—ty person) der witzige Kopf; (clever man) der Schöngeist, sinnreiche Kopf; he was a noted —, er war ein bekannter Schöngeist; mother —, Mutterwitz; a piece of —, witziger Einfall, Gedanke; —s, der Verstand, (*pl.*) geistige Fähigkeiten; to be at one's —s' end, mit seinem Witz zu Ende sein, sich (*dat.*) nicht zu raten noch zu helfen wissen; I feel at my —s' end, mir steht der Verstand stille; to be out of one's —s, den Verstand verloren haben; to frighten a p. out of his —s, einen vor Schreck außer sich bringen; to have one's —s about one, seinen Verstand *or* seine fünf Sinne beisammen haben; to live by one's —s, sich (*dat.*) durch seinen Kopf sein Brot verdienen; to learn —, klug werden (*coll.*); to teach a p. —, einem Klugheit beibringen. II. *v.n.;* to —, nämlich, das heißt. **—less**, *adj.*, **—lessly**, *adv.* ohne Verstand; (thoughtless) gedankenlos; (silly) einfältig. **—ling**, *s.* der Witzling. **—ness**, *see* Witness. **—ticism**, **—tingly**, *see* Witt—ed.

Witch, *s.* die Hexe, Zauberin. **—craft**, *s.* die Hexerei, Zauberkraft. **—ery**, *s.* der Zauber; *see* —craft. **—ing**, *adj.;* —ing hour, die Gespensterstunde, Geisterstunde. *Comp.* **—-hazel**, *s.* der virginische Zauberstrauch. **—-meal**, *s.* das Hexenmehl.

Witenagemot(e), *s.* der Rat der Weisen, die alte Ratsversammlung der Angelsachsen.

[1]**With**, *prep.* (together —) mit, nebst; (in the house of) bei; (having, along —) mit; (by means of) mit; (at, through, by, owing to) mit, über, durch, von, vor; (*with verbs denoting emotion*) vor; she came — her brother, sie kam mit ihrem Bruder; he lives — me, er wohnt bei mir; what do you want — me? was wollen Sie von mir? he is one — us, er ist mit uns einig; his influence — the king, sein Einfluß auf den (bei dem) König(e); to ingratiate o.s. —, sich einschmeicheln bei; ; it is just so — me, es geht mir geradeso; it rests — you, es steht bei Ihnen; she wept — joy, sie weinte vor Freude; he trembled — emotion, er zitterte vor Aufregung; mad — joy, vor Freude toll; stiff — cold, steif vor Kälte; did that affair succeed — him? gelang ihm jene Sache? unpopular — the country, im Lande nicht beliebt; it is usual — the French, es ist bei den Franzosen üblich; that is usual — him das ist das Gewöhnliche bei ihm; one — another, eins ins andre (gerechnet); to be out of conceit —, nicht mehr Gefallen finden an (*dat.*); to trust a p. —, (einem) anvertrauen; — this, hiermit, hierauf; — all speed, in aller Eile; — pleasure, mit Vergnügen, sehr gern; to write, cut, cover, draw, sew, etc. —, schreiben, schneiden, bedecken, zeichnen, nähen *2c.* mit; angry —, böse auf (*acc.*); pleased —, zufrieden mit; thirsty — walking, durstig vom Gehen; to cure — fasting, durch Fasten heilen; the hall resounded — the clash of arms, die Halle erdröhnte vom Waffengeklirr. **—al**, *adv.* zugleich, daneben, dabei, übrigens. *Comp.* **—draw**, *ir.v.*I.*a.* zurückziehen, entziehen; (recall) widerrufen, zurücknehmen; to —draw one's assistance from, seine Hand abziehen von. II. *n.* sich zurückziehen, sich entfernen. **—drawal**, *s.* die Zurückziehung; die Entziehung (*of capital*); die Zurücknahme (*of an order, etc.*). **—drawing**, *adj.;* —ing room, *see* Drawing-room. **—hold**, *ir.v.a.* (hinder) zurückhalten, verhindern; (keep from) vorenthalten; to —hold a th. from a p., einem etwas versagen *or* vorenthalten. **—in**, I. *adv.* im Innern, drin(nen), darin; from —in, von innen; is your mistress —in? ist Ihre Herrin zu Hause? II. *prep.* innerhalb, binnen, in; —in doors, im Hause; they came —in a mile of . . ., sie kamen bis auf eine Meile von . . .; well —in the time, völlig in der festgesetzten Zeit; —in a few steps of him, einige Schritte von ihm; —in our memory, soweit wir zurückdenken können; —in a fortnight, in(nerhalb) *or* binnen vierzehn Tagen; —in call, im Bereich der Stimme; keep —in your income, richte dich nach deinem Einkommen; he was —in an ace of being killed, er war nahe daran, getötet zu werden; the crime falls —in that statute, das Verbrechen fällt unter jene Gesetzesbestimmung. **—out**, I. *adv.* außen, draußen; (towards outside) hinaus; (outside) äußerlich; from —out, von außen. II. *prep.* außerhalb; (wanting) ohne; —out book, auswendig, ohne Buch; —out delay, ohne Verzug; —out doubt, ohne Zweifel; —out more ado, ohne weitere Umstände. III. —out that, *conj.* wenn nicht, außer wenn (*rare*). **—stand**, *ir.v.a.* (einem) widerstehen, sich (einem) widersetzen; he —stood the temptation, er widerstand der Versuchung.

[2]**With**, **—e**, **—y**, *s.* die Weidenrute; der Weidenzweig.

[1]**Wither**, *v.* I. *a.* verwelken, verdorren machen, welk machen (*fig.*). II. *n.* (ver)welken, verdorren, vergehen (*fig.*). **—ed**, *adj.* welk, verdorrt. **—edness**, *s.* die Verwelktheit, das Welksein. **—ing**, *adj.*, **—ingly**, *adv.* dörrend, vertrocknend; niederschlagend, vernichtend (*as a glance*).

[2]**Wither**, *s.*, **—s**, *pl.* der Widerrist (*in horses*). *Comp.* **—-wrung**, *adj.* am Widerriste verletzt.

Witness, I. *s.* der Zeuge; (evidence) das Zeugnis; to call, take to —, zum Zeugen auf-, anrufen; to examine the —es, die Zeugen abhören; in — whereof, zum Zeugnis *or* urkundlich dessen; to bear — (to), Zeugnis ablegen (von), (eine S.), bezeugen. II. *v.a.* bezeugen; (see) (Augen-) Zeuge sein von. *Comp.* —**-box,** *s.* der Zeugenstand.

Witt—ed, *adj.*, half (quick)-—ed, halbklug, einfältig, albern, (scharfsinnig, geistreich). —**i-cism,** *s.* der Witz, witzige Einfall. —**ily,** *adj.*, —**y,** *adj.* witzig, sinnreich; to be —y at a p.'s expense, auf jemands Kosten Witze machen. —**iness,** *s.* der Witz. —**ingly,** *adv.* wissentlich, geflissentlich, vorsätzlich, mit Fleiß.

Witwall, *s.* der Grünspecht, die Goldamsel.

Wive, I. *v.n.* sich verheiraten, sich beweiben. II. *v.a.* heiraten, zur Frau nehmen. —**s,** *pl. see* Wife.

Wizard, *s.* der Zauberer, Hexenmeister.

Wizen(ed), *adj.* eingeschrumpft.

Woad, *s.* der Waid.

Wobble, *v.n.* wackeln.

Woe, I. *s.* das Weh, Leid; — is me! wehe mir! — worth the day! Wehe über *or* treffe den Tag; —s, die Leiden (*pl.*), das Leiden. II. *int.* wehe! —**ful, Woful,** *adj.*, —**fully, Wofully,** *adv.* jammervoll, elend, traurig. —**fulness, Wofulness,** *s.* der Jammer, das Elend. *Comp.* —**begone,** *adj.* leiderfüllt, trauervoll. —**-worn,** *adj.* abgehärmt.

Wold, *s.* freie, hügelige Gegend; (wood) der Wald.

Wolf, *s.* der Wolf (*also Surg.*); the — howls, der Wolf heult; she-—, die Wölfin; to cry —, blinden Lärm machen; to keep the — from the door, sich durchschlagen, so daß man nicht verhungert. —**ish,** *adj.*, —**ishly,** *adv.* wölfisch, wolfsartig; gefräßig (*fig.*). *Comp.* —**-dog,** *s.* der Wolfs-hund, -spitz.

Wolve—rine, *s.* der braune Vielfraß. —**s,** *pl. see* Wolf.

Woman, *s.* (*pl.* Women) das Weib, Frauenzimmer, die Frau; (low —, female) das Weibsbild; — of the world, die Weltdame; — in white, die weiße Frau; to play the —, sich weibisch benehmen; women students (teachers), Studentinnen (Lehrerinnen). —**hood,** *s.* der Frauenstand; die Weiblichkeit; to reach —hood, erwachsen sein; mannbar werden. —**ish,** *adj.*, —**ishly,** *adv.* weibisch. —**liness,** *s.* die Weiblichkeit. —**ly,** *adj.* weiblich; mannbar. *Comp.* —**folk,** —**kind,** *s.* das weibliche Geschlecht, die Frauen und Mädchen, die Frauensleute (*coll.*). —**-hater,** *s.* der Weiberfeind. —**like,** *adj.* weiblich; weibisch. —**-servant,** *s.* die Magd.

Womb, *s.* der (Mutter)leib, Schoß; — of futurity, der Zukunft dunkler Schoß.

Wombat, *s.* das Wombat, Beutelmurmeltier.

Won, *imperf. & p.p. of* Win.

Wonder, I. *s.* das Wunder(werk); (surprise) das Wunder, Staunen, die Verwunderung; to do —s, Wunder tun, wirken; in the name of —! um des Himmels willen! to promise —s, goldene Berge versprechen; 'tis a nine days'—, es wird bald Gras darüber wachsen. II. *v.n.* sich (ver)wundern (at a th., über eine S.); (*also v.a.*) wissen mögen, neugierig sein (if, ob); I — if . . ., ich bin doch neugierig ob . . .; I — why, ich bin erstaunt *or* verwundert, warum. —**ful,** *adj.*, —**fully,** *adv.* wunder-voll, -bar, erstaunlich; (strange) außerordentlich. —**fulness,** *s.* das Wunderbare. —**ing,** I. *adj.*, —**ingly,** *adv.* staunend, verwundert. II. *s.* die Verwunderung. —**ment,** *s.* das Erstaunen. *Comp.* —**land,** *s.* das Wunderland; in —land, im Wunderland. —**-working,** *adj.* wundertuend, wundertätig.

Wondrous, *adj. & adv.*, —**ly,** *adv.* wundersam, erstaunlich, ungemein.

Won't, *abbr. of* Will not; it — do, es hilft nichts, es geht nicht.

Wont, I. *s.* die Gewohnheit; as is his —, wie er pflegt. II. *adj.* gewohnt; to be —, pflegen. —**ed,** *p.p. & adj.* gewohnt, gewöhnlich.

Woo, *v.* I. *a.* sich bewerben, freien, werben (um); to — sleep, den Schlaf suchen, sich bemühen zu schlafen; *see* Court. II. *n.* freien, auf Freiersfüßen gehen, werben. —**er,** *s.* der Freier, Bewerber. —**ing,** *s.* das Freien, Werben; to go a —ing, auf Freiersfüßen *or* auf die Freite gehen.

Wood, I. *s.* der Wald, die Waldung, das Gehölz; (timber) das Holz; (barrel) das Faß. II. *v.a.* mit Holz versehen; drawn from the —, frisch vom Faß. —**ed,** *adj.* waldig, bewaldet; well, richly —ed, waldreich; soft-—ed, weichholzig. —**en,** *adj.*, —**enly,** *adv.* (of —) hölzern, Holz-; steif, klotzig (*fig.*); —en shoes, Holzschuhe; —en spoon, der Cambridger Student, welcher in der jährlichen höchsten mathematischen Abschlußprüfung am schlechtesten bestanden hat; *see* Wrangler. —**iness,** *s.* die Waldigkeit. —**less,** *adj.* holzarm. —**y,** *adj.* waldig, Wald-; holzig, Holz-. *Comp.* —**-anemone,** *s.* die Waldanemone, das Windröschen. —**-ashes,** *pl.* Holzasche. —**bine,** *s.* das (gemeine) Geißblatt; die Heckenlilie. —**-carver,** *s.* der Holzschneider, Bildschnitzer. —**-carving,** *s.* die Holzschnitzerei, Bildschnitzerei; das Holzschnitzwerk. —**cock,** *s.* die Waldschnepfe. —**cut,** *s.* der Holzschnitt. —**cutter,** *s.* der Holz-fäller, -hauer. —**-engraver,** *s.* der Holzschneider. —**-engraving,** *s.* die Holzschneidekunst; *see* —cut. —**land,** I. *s.* das Holzland, die Waldung. II. *adj.* waldig, Wald-; —land scenery, die Waldlandschaft. —**lark,** *s.* die Baum-, Heide-lerche. —**man,** *s.* der Holzfäller, -hauer; (forest officer) der Jäger, Waldmann; (ranger) der Forstbeamte. —**-nymph,** *s.* die Waldnymphe. —**(en)-pavement,** *s.* das Holzpflaster. —**pecker,** *s.* der Baumhacker, Specht; the —pecker pecks, der Specht pickt. —**-pigeon,** *s.* die Holztaube. —**roof,** —**ruff,** *s.* der Waldmeister. —**-sorrel,** *s.* der Sauerklee. —**work,** *s.* das Holzwerk (*of a house*); die Holzarbeit. —**-yard,** *s.* der Holzhof.

Woof, *s.* der Einschlag, Einschuß; das Gewebe.

Wool, *s.* die Wolle (*also Bot.*); wolliges Haar (*fam.*). —**len,** I. *adj.* wollen; —len cloth, das wollene Zeug, Wollenzeug; —len yarn, das Wollengarn. II. *s.* die Wollenware. —**lens,** *pl.* Wollenstoffe; fancy —lens, wollene Modeartikel. —**liness,** *s.* die Wolligkeit. —**ly,** *adj.* wollig; (—-like) woll(en)artig. *Comp.* —**-comb,** *s.* der Wollkamm. —**-dyed,** *adj.* in der Wolle gefärbt. —**-gathering,** I. die Zerstreutheit. II. *adj.* zerstreut; to be —-gathering, seinen Gedanken nachhängen. —**-grower,** *s.* der Wollproduzent, Schafzüchter. —**len-draper,** *s.* der Wollenhändler. —**-sack,** *s.* der Wollsack (*seat of the Lord Chancellor*). —**-stapler,** *s.* der Wollgroßhändler; der Wollsortierer. —**-winder,** *s.* der Wollpacker. —**-work,** *s.* die Wollstickerei.

Word, I. *s.* das Wort; (information) die Nachricht; (watch—) die Losung; (promise) das Versprechen, die Zusage; (saying) der Spruch; (short conversation) das Wort, Wörtchen; das Wort (*Theol.*); — of God, Wort Gottes; —s, (*pl.*) Wörter (*viewed singly*), Worte (*viewed with regard to their meaning*), der Wortwechsel (*fig.*), der Text (*of a song, of an opera*); songs without —s, Lieder ohne Worte; to come to high —s, sich leidenschaftlich zanken; to bring —, Nachricht bringen; to eat one's —s, sein Wort zurücknehmen müssen; to put in a good — for, ein gutes Wort einlegen für; by — of mouth, mündlich; an honest man is as good as his —, ein Mann, ein Wort (*prov.*); he is a man of his —, *or* as good as his —, er ist ein Mann von Wort; — for —, Wort für Wort; upon my —, auf mein Wort; to take a p. at his —, einen beim Wort nehmen; to pass one's —, sein Wort geben; to be as good as one's —, Wort halten; money's the —! Geld ist die Losung; mum's the —, nichts gesagt (*coll.*); too funny for —s, unsagbar komisch; to leave — with, (einem) Bescheid zurücklassen;

to send — to, (einem) sagen, lassen, (einem) Nachricht geben; in a —, mit einem Worte, kurz; to take s.o.'s — for it, einem aufs Wort glauben; (let me have) a — with you! auf ein Wort! II. *v.a.* in Worte fassen, in Worten schildern, ausdrücken, abfassen. —**ily**, *adv.* wortreich. —**iness**, *s.* die Wortfülle, Weitschweifigkeit. —**ing**, *s.* das Ausdrücken in Worten, Abfassen; (style) der Stil, Ausdruck, die Fassung. —**less**, *adj.* wortlos, stumm. —**y**, *adj.* wortreich; (diffuse) weitschweifig; (in —s) Wort-. *Comp.* —**-book**, *s.* das Wörterbuch. —**-building**, —**-formation**, *s.* die Wortbildung.

Wore, *imperf. of* Wear.

Work, I. *v.n.* (*p.p. also* Wrought) arbeiten; arbeiten, gähren (*as wine*); (take effect) wirken, wirksam sein; in heftiger Bewegung sein, ungestüm sein; this wood —s easily, dies Holz läßt sich leicht bearbeiten; to — hard, fleißig, eifrig, schwer arbeiten, es sich (*dat.*) sauer werden lassen; to — against time, aus allen Kräften arbeiten, um zur rechten Zeit fertig zu sein; to — **away** at, darauf losarbeiten; to — **out**, sich herausarbeiten, herauskommen; to — **to** windward, beim Winde aufstechen; to — **up**, sich emporarbeiten; to — **upon**, Einfluß ausüben auf (*acc.*). II. *v.a.* (effect) (be)wirken, hervorbringen, verrichten; bearbeiten (*a business, profession, etc.*); bauen (*land*); ausbeuten (*mines*); wirken (*dough*); bearbeiten (*fields, iron, a literary subject*); lösen (*an account, Arith.*); (sew, make) machen, sticken, nähen; regieren, führen (*a ship*); arbeiten lassen (*a horse*); (conduct) leiten, führen; to — **in**, eintragen (*Weav.*), hineinarbeiten; to — **off**, verarbeiten; form —ed off, ausgedruckte Form (*Typ.*); to — **out**, ausarbeiten, vollenden, zustande bringen; (solve) lösen; to — out for o.s., sich (*dat.*) selbst erringen; to — **over**, überarbeiten; to — over again, auf neue durcharbeiten; to — **up**, erhöhen; entflammen (*passions*); verarbeiten (into, zu), verbrauchen (*materials*); bearbeiten, studieren (*a subject, etc.*); sich einarbeiten in (*a science, etc.*). III. *s.* das Werk; (act) das Werk, die Tat, Handlung, Arbeit; (product) das Erzeugnis; die (Hand-)Arbeit (*Sew.*); (literary —. — of art, Schrift-, Kunst-)Werk; Festungswerk (*Fort.*); at —, bei der Arbeit (*as people*); im Gang (*as machinery*); out of —, arbeitslos; hard —, schwere Arbeit; to cut out — for, (einem) viel zu schaffen machen; to fall to —, sich an die Arbeit machen; to go to —, an die Arbeit, ans Werk gehen; to make sad — of it, etwas Schönes anrichten; to make short — with, mit einem *or* einer S. nicht viel Federlesen(s) machen; to set (o.s.) to —, sich an die Arbeit begeben; to strike —, die Arbeit einstellen; to throw out of —, außer Arbeit setzen. —**able**, *adj.* bearbeitbar, bearbeitungsfähig. —**er**, *s.* der (die) Arbeiter(in); der Urheber, Bewirker (*fig.*); —ers of iniquity, Übeltäter (*B.*). —**ing**, I. *s.* das Wirken, die Wirkung (*fig.*); das Arbeiten, die Gärung; der Betrieb (*of a business, etc.*); der Gang, das Spiel (*Mach.*); der Bau (*Min., Agr.*); the —ing of the Chinese mind, der Gedankenprozeß *or* die Vorstellungsweise eines Chinesen. II. *adj.;* —ing expenses, Betriebskosten; —ing theory, eine Theorie, mit der sich arbeiten läßt; —ing vocabulary, ein genügender Wortschatz. —**s**, *pl.* das (Uhr-)Werk (*Horol.*); das Getriebe, Werk (*Mach.*); die Hütte, das Hüttenwerk (*Chem., Manuf., etc.*); (factory) die Fabrik. *Comp.* —**-a-day**, *adj.;* the —-a-day world, die Alltagswelt. —**bag**, *s.* der Arbeitsbeutel. —**basket**, *s.* der Arbeitskorb. —**house**, *s.* das Armenhaus. —**ing-drawing**, *s.* der Riß, die Detailzeichnung. —**ing-day**, *s.* der Werktag, Alltag. —**ing-classes**, *pl.* arbeitende Klassen, die Arbeiterbevölkerung. —**ingman**, *s.* der Arbeiter. —**man**, *s.* der Arbeiter, Handwerk‴. —**manlike**, (—**manly**,) *adj.* geschickt, kunstmäßig. —**manship**, *s.* (geschickte) Arbeit; (manner of —ing) die (Art der) Arbeit; (— done) das Werk. —**-people**, *pl.* Arbeitsleute, Arbeiter. —**shop**, *s.* die Werkstatt, Werkstätte. —**-table**, *s.* das Arbeitstischchen. —**woman**, *s.* die Näh(t)erin.

World, *s.* die Welt; the — to come, next —, other —, die andere Welt, das Jenseits; all the — over, in der ganzen Welt; a — of care, eine Welt voll Sorgen; he has not a farthing in the —, er hat nichts zu nagen und zu beißen; a — of faults, eine Menge Fehler; a — too wide, um vieles zu weit; — without end, von Ewigkeit zu Ewigkeit; the great, learned, polite —, die große Welt *or* die Vornehmen, die gelehrte, die feine Welt; knowledge of the —, die Weltkenntnis *or* -erfahrung; man of the —, der Weltmann; ways of the —, der Weltlauf, Lauf der Welt; that is the way of the —, so wags the — away, so geht es in der Welt; all the — and his wife, jedermann; for all the —, gerade, durchaus, ebenso; not for all the —, um alles in der Welt nicht, um keinen Preis; to begin the —, in die Welt eintreten, das Leben *or* seine Laufbahn beginnen; to come into the —, auf die Welt kommen, geboren werden. —**liness**, *s.* die Weltlichkeit, Weltklugheit; *see* —ly-mindedness. —**ling**, *s.* der Weltmensch, das Weltkind. —**ly**, *adj.* weltlich, Welt-; (earthly) zeitlich, irdisch. *Comp.* —**ly-minded**, *adj.* weltlich gesinnt. —**ly-mindedness**, *s.* der Weltsinn, die Weltliebe, das Weltlichgesinntsein. —**ly-wise**, I. *adj.* weltklug, welterfahren; not —ly-wise, unweltläufig. II. *pl.* die Weltweisen. —**-wide**, *adj.* weitverbreitet; allgemein anerkannt; of —-wide reputation, von Weltruf.

Worm, I. *s.* der Wurm (*also fig.*); die Raupe, Made, Larve; das Gewinde (*of a screw*); die Schlange (*Chem., Dist.*); der Krätzer (*Gun.*); das Zungenband, der Tollwurm (*of dogs*); der Lumpenzieher (*Artil.*); —s, Würmer, die Wurmkrankheit (*Med.*). II. *v.a.* trensen (*Naut.*); den Wurm nehmen (a dog, einem Hunde); putzen (*a gun*); to — a secret out of, (einem) ein Geheimnis ab- *or* entlocken; to — o.s. into favour, sich in jemandes Gunst einschleichen. —**y**, *adj.* wurmig. *Comp.* —**-eaten**, *adj.* wurmstichig. —**-like**, *adj.* wurmähnlich.

Wormwood, *s.* der Wermut; die Bitterkeit (*fig.*).

Worn, *p.p. of* Wear; — into holes, durchlöchert; — out, abgenutzt, abgetragen, verbraucht; —-out constitution, zerrüttete Gesundheit.

Worr—ier, *s.* der Quäler, Placker. —**y**, I. *v.a.* würgen, zerreißen, zerren, zausen; quälen, plagen (*fig.*); to —y a p. into, einen durch Plagen bewegen zu; to —y s. th. out of s.o., einem etwas durch Quälereien abringen, abpressen. II. *s.* die Qual, Plage. —**ying**, *adj.*, —**yingly**, *adv.* plagend, quälend.

Wors—e, *adj. & adv.* (*comp. of* Bad, Ill, Evil) schlechter, schlimmer; kränker (*Med., etc.*); ärger (*fig.*); from bad to —e, aus dem Regen in die Traufe; —e and —e, immer schlimmer; so much the —e, um so schlimmer; to be none the —e, nicht übler daran sein; you shall be none the —e for me, mit mir sollst du nicht schlimmer daran sein, an mir sollst du nicht verlieren; am I the —e for it? stehe ich mich dabei schlimmer? (a little) the —e for drink, (etwas) berauscht *or* betrunken; (and) to make it —e, das Unglück vollzumachen; —e luck, unglücklicherweise (*coll.*). —**t**, *see* Worst.

Worship, I. *s.* die Verehrung, Anbetung; der Gottesdienst (*Rel.*); der Kult(us); your —, Eure Hochwürden; place of —, das Bethaus, die Kirche. II. *v.a.* ehren, achten, anbeten (*God, etc.*); (pay homage to) huldigen (einem), (einen) verehren. —**ful**, *adj.* ehrwürdig, angesehen, ehrsam, achtbar. —**per**, *s.* der Verehrer, Anbeter; the —pers, die Andächtigen; —per of idols, der Götzendiener

Worst, I. *sup. adj.* schlimmst, schlechtest, ärgst; the —t of men, der schlechteste Mensch. II. *s.;* the —t, das Schlimmste, Ärgste &c.; to be at the —t, aufs Höchste gestiegen, aufs Äußerste, zum Schlimmsten gekommen sein; the —t is yet to come, das Schlimmste kommt noch; at the —t, when the —t comes to the —t, im schlimmsten Fall; to have the —t of it, am schlimmsten wegkommen, den Kürzeren ziehen bei; the —t is past, das Schlimmste ist überstanden, vorüber; do your —t! tut euer Ärgstes! macht, was ihr wollt! to do one's —t, es so arg machen, wie man kann. III. *v.a.* überwältigen, besiegen.

Worsted, I. *s.* das Kammgarn, die Kammwolle; das Kammwollzeug (*Manuf.*). II. *adj.* wollen, aus Kammwolle gefertigt; — **stockings**, wollene Strümpfe; — yarn, Kammgarn.

[1]**Wort**, *s.* die Wurz, das Kraut.

[2]**Wort**, *s.* die (Bier-)Würze.

Worth, I. *adj.* wert; it is not — powder and shot, es ist keinen Schuß Pulver wert; he is said to be — £10,000 a year, seine Einkünfte sollen sich auf jährlich zehntausend Pfund belaufen; he is — £10,000, er ist seine 10,000 Pfund Sterling wert; — reading, lesenswert; — seeing, sehenswert; it is — doing, es lohnt sich es zu tun, ist der Mühe wert; it is not — speaking of, es ist nicht der Rede wert; it is not — while (*or* the trouble), es ist nicht der Mühe wert; to be — one's weight in gold, wert sein, mit Gold aufgewogen zu werden; it is — to me . . ., es bringt mir ein . . .; take all I'm —, nimm alles, was ich habe; a bird in the hand is — two in the bush, ein Sperling in der Hand ist besser als eine Taube auf dem Dach (*prov.*). —**ily**, *adv.* würdig, nach Verdienst. —**iness**, *s.* die Würdigkeit. —**less**, *adj.*, —**lessly**, *adv.* wertlos; nichtswürdig (*fig.*). —**lessness**, *s.* die Wertlosigkeit; die Nichtswürdigkeit, Schlechtigkeit. —**y**, I. *adj.* würdig, wert; (estimable) verdienstvoll, schätzbar, tugendhaft; trefflich, sauber (*iron.*); —y of death, todeswürdig. II. *s.* der große, höchst verdienstvolle Mann; der Held; the 9 —ies, die 9 Würdenträger.

Wot, (*obs.*) 1 *pers. sing. pres. ind.* ich weiß.

Would, *imperf. of* Will; — to God! wollte Gott! I — fain know, ich möchte gern wissen; she — often say, oft pflegte sie zu sagen; every afternoon at 2 he — go for a walk, jeden Nachmittag um 2 Uhr pflegte er einen Spaziergang zu machen; he then — think, dann dachte er wohl; I — rather not, lieber möchte ich nicht; with him this — seem to be, es hatte offenbar den Anschein, als ob er; I — have you know that . . ., ich muß Ihnen sagen, daß . . .; I — have you go early, ich wollte, daß ihr frühe ginget. *Comp.* —-**be**, *adj.;* vorgeblich, angeblich, Schein-, After-; a —-be wit, der Witzling, Witzreißer; the —-be assassin, der, welcher den Mord plante, den Mordversuch machte; the —-be painter, der vorgebliche Maler.

Wouldn't, *abbrev. for* Would not.

[1]**Wound**, I. *s.* die Wunde (*also fig.*), Verwundung; die Kränkung (*fig.*). II. *v.a.* verwunden (to the quick, aufs schmerzlichste).

[2]**Wound**, *imperf. see* [1]Wind.

Wove, I. *imperf. see* Weave. II. *adj.;* — paper, das Velinpapier.

[1]**Wrack**, *s.* der Seetang, Tang.

[2]**Wrack**, *s.* das ziehende Gewölk, die windzerrissene eilende Wolke; *see* Rack.

Wraith, *s.* die Erscheinung einer bald sterbenden oder eben gestorbenen Person, das Gespenst.

Wrangl—e, I. *v.n.* zanken, streiten. II. *s.* der Zank, Streit, Hader. —**er**, *s.* der Zänker; senior —er, Student zu Cambridge, der in der jährlichen höchsten mathematischen Konkurrenzprüfung am besten bestanden hat; *see* Wooden spoon. —**ing**, I. *adj.* zänkisch. II. *s.* das Zanken.

Wrap, *v.a.* wickeln; to — up (in), — in, einwickeln, einhüllen; he is completely —ped up in her, er ist vollständig für sie eingenommen, sie macht sein ganzes Glück aus. —**per**, *s.* der Umschlag, die Hülle, Decke; (morning, *etc.* —per) der Morgenrock; das Deckblatt (*of a cigar*); der Umschlag (*of a book, etc.*); postal —, das Kreuzband, Streifband; under —per, unter Kreuzband; —pers, ungebunden (*of a book*). *Comp.* —**ping-paper**, *s.* das Packpapier.

Wrath, *s.* der Zorn, Grimm, die Wut. —**ful**, *adj.*, —**fully**, *adv.* zornig, grimmig, wütend.

Wreak, *v.a.* wirken, ausüben; to — one's anger upon a p., seinen Zorn auslassen *or* sein Mütchen kühlen an einem; to — vengeance upon, seine Rache auslassen an (*dat.*).

Wreath, *s.* das Gewinde; (garland) der Kranz; — of smoke, das Rauchwölkchen; — of snow, die Schneewehe. —**e**, *v.a.* winden, flechten; (be-) kränzen.

Wreck, I. *s.* das Wrack, die Schiffstrümmer; (ship—) der Schiffbruch; die Zerstörung, das Verderben (*fig.*). II. *v.a.* zertrümmern; to — a train, einen Zug zum Entgleisen bringen; to be —ed, scheitern, stranden; the ship has been —ed, das Schiff ist gestrandet. —**age**, *s.* die Schiffstrümmer. —**er**, *s.* der Wracker, Stranddieb.

Wren, *s.* der Zaunkönig.

Wrench, I. *s.* der heftige Ruck; (sprain) die Verrenkung, Verstauchung. II. *v.a.* mit Gewalt reißen, winden; entwinden, entreißen (from s.o., einem); verrenken, verstauchen; to — **out**, herausreißen; to — **open**, mit Gewalt öffnen, aufsprengen.

Wrest, *v.a.* reißen; verdrehen (the meaning, den Sinn); to — from, entreißen, entwinden, abpressen; it was —ed from him, es wurde ihm entrissen *or* entwunden. —**er**, *s.* der Entreißer; der Verdreher. —**le**, *v.n.* ringen, kämpfen. —**ler**, *s.* der Ringer; der Wettkämpfer (*at —ling matches*). —**ling**, I. *p.* ringend; —ling match, der Ringkampf. II. *s.* der Kampf, Streit.

Wretch, *s.* der Elende; (worthless —) der Wicht, Lump, Tropf. —**ed**, *adj.*, —**edly**, *adv.* elend, unglücklich, jämmerlich; (worthless) nichtswürdig, ärmlich, lumpig, verächtlich. —**edness**, *s.* das Elend; (paltriness) die Erbärmlichkeit.

Wriggl—e, I. *v.a.* (& *n.* sich) hin und her bewegen, biegen, schlängeln, winden. —**ing**, *adj.* sich windend, sich biegend, sich krümmend.

Wright, *s.* der Arbeiter, Handwerker; (*in compds.*) der Verfertiger, -macher.

Wring, *ir.v.a.* ringen (*one's hands*), winden; (— out) herauswinden, aus(w)ringen (*clothes*); drücken, martern, quälen (*the heart*); to — **from**, (einem) entreißen; to — **off**, abdrehen (*the neck of a fowl, etc.*). —**er**, *s.* der (die) Aus(w)ringer(in); (—ing machine, clothes —er) die Auswinde-, Wring-maschine. —**ing**, *s.* das (Aus-) Ringen, Wringen, Auswinden. *Comp.* —**ing-wet**, *a.* zum Aus(w)ringen naß.

[1]**Wrinkle**, I. *s.* die Runzel, Falte; (unevenness) die Unebenheit. II. *v.a.* runzeln, in Falten ziehen. III. *v.n.* sich runzeln, Falten schlagen. —**d**, *adj.* runzelig, voll Runzeln.

[2]**Wrinkle**, *s.* der gute Einfall, gute Wink, die neue Idee; der Kniff (*obs.*).

Wrist, *s.* das Handgelenk; bridle-—, die linke Faust; — drop, die Handgelenkslähmung; — touch, der Anschlag aus dem Handgelenk (*Mus.*). *Comp.* —**band**, *s.* das Preischen *or* Prieschen (am Hemdärmel); die Hemdmanchette.

Writ, *s.* die Schrift; schriftlicher, obrigkeitlicher Befehl an den Sheriff &c., eine amtliche Handlung vorzunehmen (*Law*); die Vorladung (*Law*); der Wahlbefehl (*sent by the Lord Chancellor*); — to apprehend the body, Verhaftsbefehl; —s for an election, Wahl-Ausschreiben (*pl.*); — for the new parliament, das Ausschreiben zu den Parlamentswahlen; — of error, Revisionsbefehl wegen Formfehler. —**e**, I. *ir.v.a.* schreiben;

(—e down) auf-, nieder-schreiben, aufzeichnen (*in a notebook, etc.*), niederschreiben (*fig.*), (injure, *etc.*) durch Schreiben vernichten, herabsetzen; to —e to a p., einem *or* an einen schreiben; to —e o.s. *or* one's name, sich schreiben; to —e against time, in der größtmöglichen Eile schreiben; to —e **off**, schreiben und absenden (*a letter, etc.*), abschreiben (*C.L.*); to —e **out**, aus-, ab-schreiben; to —e o.s. out, sich ausschreiben; to —e **up**, durch Schreiben in die Höhe bringen, anrühmen; to —e **to** *or* **at** a p.'s dictation, jemandes Diktat nachschreiben. II. *n.* schreiben (—e books, *etc.*) schriftstellern; (relate) erzählen; (—e letters) Briefe schreiben; to —e **for**, bestellen, kommen lassen; to —e for a journal, *etc.*, für eine Zeitschrift schreiben; to —e **off**, schreiben und absenden; to —e **on**, fortschreiben. **—er**, *s.* einer der schreibt, der Schreiber (*of a letter, a book*); der Verfasser (*of a book, a poem, etc.*); (bad —er) der Skribent; der Schriftsteller (*used absolutely*); a great —er, ein großer Schriftsteller; the —er of 'Esmond,' der Verfasser des Esmond; —er's cramp, der Schreibkrampf; —er to the signet, der Advokat (*Scotch*). **—ership**, *s.* die Schreiber-, Beamten-stelle. **—ing**, I. *p.* schreibend. II. *s.* das Schreiben, die Schrift; (hand—ing) Handschrift; (—ten article) der Aufsatz; die Schrift, das Buch, Werk; (style of —ing) der Stil; (document) die Urkunde; in —ing, schriftlich; —ings, die Schriften, Werke; vertical —ing, die Steilschrift; slanting —ing, die Schrägschrift. —**ten**, *p.p. & adj.*; —ten evidence, der Urkundenbeweis; —ten law, geschriebenes, positives Recht. *Comp.* **—ing-case**, *s.* das Schreibzeug. **—ing-desk**, *s.* das Schreib(e)pult. **—ing-paper**, *s.* das Schreibpapier. **—ing-school**, *s.* die Schreibschule. **—ing-table**, *s.* der Schreibtisch.

Writhe, *v.n.* sich winden, sich krampfhaft krümmen (with pain, vor Schmerz).

Wrong, I. *adj. & adv.* unrecht, verkehrt; (not correct) unrichtig; (not right) unrecht, unbillig; to be —, Unrecht haben, im Irrtum sein, sich im Irrtum befinden; to get —, sich irren; the — glove, der unrechte Handschuh; — letter, verwechselter, falscher Buchstabe; to hit upon the — person, an den Unrechten kommen; on the — side of 30, über 30 Jahre alt; right or —, mit Recht oder Unrecht. II. *v.a.* (einem) Unrecht tun, benachteiligen, (einem) schaden; I am —ed, mir geschieht Unrecht. III. *s.* das Unrecht, die Unbill; (injury) die Kränkung; to be in the —, Unrecht haben. **—er**, *s.* einer, der einem andern Unrecht tut. **—ful**, *adj.*, **—fully**, *adv.* ungerecht, beleidigend, kränkend, nachteilig. **—ly**, *adv.* verkehrt, auf ungerechte Weise. **—ness**, *s.* die Verkehrtheit. *Comp.* **—doing**, *s.* die Übeltat, das Unrechttun. **—headed**, *adj.* querköpfig, verschroben, verkehrt. **—headedness**, *s.* die Verschrobenheit.

Wroth, *adj.* ergrimmt, erzürnt (with a p., auf einen).

Wrought, *imperf. of* Work; — iron, das Schmiede-, Stab-eisen.

Wry, *adj.* schief, krumm, verdreht; to make — faces, Gesichter schneiden. *Comp.* **—-mouthed**, *adj.* schiefmäulig. **—-necked**, *adj.* krummhalsig.

Wych-elm, *s.* die Bergrüster, Bergulme.

Wyvern, Wiver(n), *s.* eine Art Drache (*Her.*).

X

X, x, *s.* X, x; *as numeral* X = 10; Xmas = Christmas, Weihnachten.

Xebec, *s.* kleiner Dreimaster (*in the Mediterranean*).

Xenia, *pl.* die Gastgeschenke, Xenien.

Xero— (*in cpds.* = trocken). **—phagy**, *s.* die trockene Kost. **—phthalmy**, *s.* die trockene Augenentzündung.

X-rays, *s.* X- *or* Röntgen-strahlen (*pl.*).

Xylo—glyph, *s.* der Holzschneider, Bildschnitzer. **—glyphic**, *adj.* Holzschnitz-. **—glyphy**, *s.* die Holzschnitzerei. **—grapher**, *s.* der Holzschneider, Holzschnitzer. **—graphic(al)**, *adj.* die Holzschneidekunst betreffend; —graphic impression, der Holzschnitt. **—graphy**, *s.* die Holzschneidekunst. **—phon**, *s.* die Strohfiedel, das Xylophon.

Y

Y, y, *s.* Y, y.

Y— (*in obsolete cpds., orig. the prefix of the p.p. of weak verbs*). *See* Yclad, Yclept.

Yacht, I. *s.* die Jacht. **—ing**, *s.* das Segeln auf einer Jacht; der Segelsport. II. *v.n.* auf einer Jacht umherfahren. *Comp.* **—-club**, *s.* der Jachtklub, Klub für Wettsegeln mit Jachten. **—sman**, *s.* der Jachtfahrer, einer, der sich eine Jacht hält.

Yak, *s.* der Yak, Grunzochs.

Yam, *s.* die Yamswurzel.

Yankee, *s.* der Neuengländer; der Nordamerikaner der Vereinigten Staaten. *Comp.* **—-doodle**, *s.* der Yankeedoodle (amerikanisches Volkslied) **—ism**, *s.* das Wesen *or* die Spracheigentümlichkeit eines Yankee.

Yap, I. *v.n.* kläffen, bellen. II. *s.* der Kläffer, das Hündchen.

[1]**Yard**, *s.* die Rute; die Yard (3 englische Fuß = 0,9144 Meter); die Segelstange, Raa (*Naut.*); das männliche Glied, der Penis (*Anat.*); pocket — (measure), das Taschenmetermaß. *Comp.* **—-arm**, *s.* der Nock, Arm einer Raa. **—stick, —-wand**, *s.* der Ellenstock.

[2]**Yard**, *s.* der Hof(raum). *Comp.* **—-dog**, *s.* der Kettenhund. **—-gate**, *s.* das Hoftor.

Yarn, I. *s.* das Garn (*also Naut.*); die Geschichte (*Naut. & coll.*); to spin a long (tough) —, eine lange (unglaubliche) Geschichte erzählen; woollen (worsted) —, das Wollen-(Kamm-)garn. II. *v.n.* Geschichten erzählen.

Yarrow, *s.* die Schafgarbe (*Bot.*).

Yataghan, *s.* langes gekrümmtes (türkisches) Dolchmesser (ohne Heft).

Yawl, *s.* die Jolle; kleines Segelschiff mit größerem Mast vorn und kleinem ganz hinten.

Yawn, I. *s.* das Gähnen. II. *v.n.* gähnen; gähnen, sich weit auftun *or* öffnen (*fig.*). **—ing**, I. *adj.* gähnend; —ing gulf, gähnender Abgrund. II. *s.* das Gähnen; —ing is catching, Gähnen steckt an.

Yclad, *adj.* gekleidet (*obs.*).

Yclept, *adj.* genannt (*obs.*).

Ye, *old-fashioned for* þe, the, *def. art.*, der, die, das.

Ye, *pers. pron.* (*nom.*) ihr; (*rarely acc. dat.*) euch.

Yea, I. *adv.* ja, wahrhaftig; by — and nay, auf Ja und Nein. II. *s.* das Ja; the —s have it, der Antrag ist angenommen (*Parl.*).

Yean, *v.n.* lammen, werfen. **—ling**, *s.* das Lämmchen.

Year, *s.* das Jahr; —s, Jahre, das Alter; a —, ein Jahr; (—ly) das Jahr, jährlich; a — and a day, Jahr und Tag; — by —, Jahr für Jahr; — in — out, Jahr aus Jahr ein; one — with another, ein Jahr ins andere (gerechnet); every —, jährlich, jedes Jahr; every other —, alle zwei Jahre; once a —, einmal im Jahr; half —, das Halbjahr, Semester (*Univ.*); New —, das Neujahr, das neue Jahr; with all good wishes for the New —, die besten Wünsche zum Jahreswechsel; —s of discretion, das gesetzte Alter, Schwabenalter; to get into —s, alt werden; well(-stricken) in —s, hochbetagt, hochbejahrt. **—ling**, *s.* der Jährling; —ling heifer, einjährige Färse. **—ly**, *adj.* jährlich. *Comp.* **—-book**, *s.* das Jahrbuch.

Yearn, *v.n.* sich sehnen, schmachten (for, nach); his bowels —ed towards his brother, sein Herz entbrannte ihm gegen seinen Bruder (*obs.*); her heart —s towards you, ihr Herz fühlt Mitleid mit euch, neigt sich euch zu. **—ing**, I. *adj.*, — **ingly**, *adv.* sehnsüchtig. II. *s.* die Sehnsucht.

Yeast, *s.* die Hefe. **—y**, *adj.* hefig.

Yell, I. *s.* der laute, gellende Schrei; der Kriegsruf, das Feldgeschrei. II. *v.n.* gellen; laut aufschreien, heulen. III. *v.a.;* to — (out), mit Geschrei *or* gellend ausstoßen.

Yellow, I. *adj.* gelb; — amber, der Bernstein; — fever, das gelbe Fieber; the — peril, die gelbe Gefahr, Gefahr des Mongolentums; — **press**, die Hetzpresse. II. *s.* das Gelb; **—s**, die Gelbsucht (*Bot.*). III. *v.a.* gelb färben. **—ish**, *adj.* gelblich. **—ness**, *s.* das Gelbe. *Comp.* **—hammer**, *s.* die Goldammer. **—-haired**, *adj.* goldhaarig.

Yelp, I. *v.n.* bellen, kläffen, II. *s.* das Gekläff.

Yeoman, *s.* der Freisasse; der niedere Hofbeamte, der Hofbediente (*of the royal household*) (*obs.*); — of the guard, königlicher Leibgardist. **—ly**, I. *adj.* vom Range eines Freibauern; schlicht, einfach. II. *adv.* männlich, tapfer. **—ry**, *s.* die Freisassen; (—ry troops, imperial —ry), die berittene Miliz, (freiwillige) Landwehrkavallerie.

Yes, I. *adv.* ja. II. *s.* das Ja.

Yester, *adj.* gestrig; — sun, gestrige Sonne. — **day**, I. *s.* der gestrige Tag. II. *adv.* gestern. **—eve(n)**, I. *s.* der gestrige Abend. II. *adv.* gestern abend. **—night**, I. *s.* die letzte Nacht. II. *adv.* gestern abend.

Yet, I. *adv.* jetzt noch; (till now) bis jetzt; (still) noch; (even) selbst, sogar; as —, bis jetzt, bisher; not —, noch nicht; — a moment, nur noch einen Augenblick; — blacker, noch abscheulicher. II. *conj.* doch, dennoch, gleichwohl.

Yew, *s.* die Eibe. **—en**, *adj.* von Eibenholz. *Comp.* **—-tree**, *s. see* —. **—-wood**, *s.* das Eibenholz.

Yiddish, I. *adj.* jüdisch-englisch. II. *s.* die Judensprache.

Yield, I. *v.a.* hergeben, (ein)tragen, einbringen, abwerfen; (produce) hervorbringen, geben, liefern; tragen (*crops*); (— up) aufgeben (*the ghost*), her-, hin-geben; (— up, — over) übergeben, ausliefern; (admit) zugestehen, einräumen. II. *v.n.* sich ergeben, sich unterwerfen; nachgeben, weichen (to a p. *or* th., einer Person *or* Sache); nachgeben, sinken (*as walls*); eingehen (to conditions, auf Bedingungen); to — to the current of public opinion, dem Strome der öffentlichen Meinung folgen. III. *s.* der Ertrag; die Ausbeute (*Min.*); die Nutzung (*Forestry*). **—er**, *s.* der Nachgiebige, der sich Ergebende; —er up, der Aufgebende. **—ing**, *adj.*, **—ingly**, *adv.* willfährig, nachgiebig. **—ingness**, *s.* die Nachgiebigkeit, Willfährigkeit.

Yoke, I. *s.* das Joch (*also fig.*); das Paar (*of oxen*). II. *v.a. & n.* ins Joch spannen, anjochen; (join) paaren, verbinden; (enslave) unterjochen. *Comp.* **—fellow**, **—-mate**, *s.* der Gefährte; (spouse) der Gatte, die Gattin; der Lebensgefährte, die Lebensgefährtin.

Yokel, *s.* der Landmann; country —, der Bauernlümmel, -tölpel, dumme Bauer.

Yolk, *s.* das (Ei-)Dotter.

Yon, *adj.* jen(-er, -e, -es) (*Poet.*). **—der**, I. *adj. see* Yon. II. *adv.* drüben, dort.

Yore, *s.;* (in days) of —, ehemals, vor alten Zeiten, weiland.

You, *pers. pron.* ihr; Sie, du; man; I tremble only for —, — dull fools, ich zittre nur für euch, ihr blöden Toren; as — approach, — see, wie man näher kommt, sieht man. **—r**, *poss. adj.* Euer, Ihr, dein; that is —r affair, das ist Ihre Sache; it is —r own fault, es ist deine eigne Schuld. **—rs**, *poss. pron.* euer, dein, Ihr; der, die, das Eurige, Deinige, Ihrige; this is —rs, dies gehört Ihnen; —rs truly, achtungsvoll zeichnet (*C. L.*), Ihr ergebener; give me —rs, gebt mir das Eurige; this moment is —rs, dieser Augenblick ist euer. **—rself**, *pron.* (*pl.* —rselves) (ihr, Sie, du) selbst, euch, Sie, dich (selbst), sich selbst; you must do it —rself, Sie müssen es selbst tun; you love only —rself, Sie lieben nur sich selbst; what will you do with —rself this evening? was fangen Sie diesen Abend an; be but —rself, sei nur du selbst!

Young, I. *adj.* jung; (inexperienced) unerfahren; — in years, jung an Jahren; — one, das Junge; her — man, ihr Schatz (*of girls of the lower classes*); — people, junge Leute, die Jugend; — person, das junge Mädchen; — shoot, der Schößling; to grow — again, sich verjüngen, wieder jung werden; to be the —er hand, die Hinterhand haben (im Spiel); — Men's Christian Association, der Verein christlicher Jünglinge, Jünglingsverein. II. *pl.* die Jungen; with —, trächtig (*of animals*). **—ish**, *adj.* ziemlich *or* etwas jung. **—ster**, *s.* der junge Mensch, Jüngling; das Kind.

Youth, *s.* die Jugend; die Jugendlichkeit; (lad) der Jüngling, junge Mann *or* Mensch; (young people) junge Leute, die Jugend; in —, in der Jugend. **—ful**, *adj.*, **—fully**, *adv.* jugendlich, Jugend-. **—fulness**, *s.* die Jugendlichkeit, Jugendfülle.

Yule, I. *s.* Weihnachten. II. *attrib.;* Jul-, Weihnachts-; — log, der Weihnachtsklotz, Julblock; — song, das Weihnachtslied. *Comp.* **—-tide**, *s.* die Weihnachtszeit.

Ywis, *adv.* gewiß, sicherlich (*obs.*).

Z

Z, **z**, *s.* Z, z.

Zany, *s.* der Hanswurst, Possenreißer.

Zariba, *s.* das afrikanische befestigte Lager.

Zeal, *s.* der Eifer; full of —, sehr eifrig, voll(er) Eifer; — for truth, Wahrheitseifer. **—ot**, *s.* der Glaubenseiferer, Zelot. **—otical**, *adj.* übertrieben eifrig, zelotisch. **—otism**, *s.* der übertriebene Glaubenseifer. **—ous**, *adj.*, **—ously**, *adv.* eifrig, hitzig, warm. **—ousness**, *s.* der Eifer, die (große) Wärme.

Zebra, *s.* das Zebra.

Zechin, *s.* die Zechine.

Zenana, *s.* das Frauengemach (in Indien).

Zenith, I. *s.* der Zenit, Scheitelpunkt; der Höhepunkt (*fig.*). II. *attrib.;* — distance, die Zenitdistanz (*Astr.*).

Zephyr, *s.* der Westwind, Zephyr.

Zero, *s.* die Null; der Nullpunkt; der Gefrierpunkt (*on all thermometers except Fahrenheit's*); below —, unter Null.

Zest, *s.* die Würze, der erhöhte Geschmack, das Pikante; his presence gave a — to the enjoyment, seine Gegenwart verlieh der Lustbarkeit ihre Würze, erhöhte noch mehr das Vergnügen; the highest —, der höchste Reiz (*fig.*).

Zigzag, I. *s.* das Zickzack. II. *adj.* im Zickzack laufend, Zickzack-.

Zinc, I. *s* das Zink. II. *v.a.* verzinken. **—ography**, *s.* die Zinkographie. *Comp.* **—-white**, *s.* das Zink-weiß, -oxyd. **—-works**, *pl.* die Zinkwerke, Zinkhütte.

Zither, *s.* die Zither; to play the —, Zither spielen; die Zither schlagen (*high style*).

Zodiac, *s.* der Tier-, Sonnen-kreis; signs of the —, die Zeichen des Tierkreises. **—al**, *adj.* zum Tierkreise gehörig, Zodiakal- (light, etc., -licht 2c.).

Zone, *s.* der Gürtel (*also Med.*); die Zone, der Erdgürtel (*Geog.*); der Erdstrich, das Gebiet (*fig.*); die Zone, der Himmelsgürtel (*Astr.*); temperate (torrid) —, die gemäßigte (heiße) Zone. **—d**, *adj.* gegürtelt.

Zoo—geography, *s.* die Kunde von der Verbreitung der Tiere über die Erde. **—grapher**, *s.* der Tierbeschreiber. **—graphy**, *s.* die Zoographie, Tierbeschreibung. **—lite,** *s.* der Zoolith, das versteinerte Tier. **—logical,** *adj.*, **—logically,** *adv.* zoologisch; —logical garden (*abbrev.* Zoo), der zoologische Garten. **—logist,** *s.* der Zoolog. **—logy,** *s.* die Tierkunde, Zoologie. **—nomy,** *s.* Gesetze des Tierlebens. **—phagous,** *adj.* fleischfressend. **—phorus,** *s.* der mit Tierbildern verzierte Fries. **—phyte,** *s.* die Tierpflanze, das Pflanzentier. **—phytic,** *adj.* zoophytisch. **—tomy,** *s.* die Tierzergliederung.

Zouave, *s.* der Zuave.

Zounds, *int.* Potztausend! Sapperment! Donnerwetter!

Zygomatic, *adj.* zum Jochbein gehörig.

Zymo—logy, *s.* die Gärungslehre. **—tic,** *adj.* Gärung erregend.

INDEX OF NAMES.

GEOGRAPHICAL AND OTHER PROPER NAMES.

In the subjoined list of Geographical, Historical, and other Proper Names the following classes of words have been omitted, unless there was a special reason for including certain words:—

1. Those in which the English and German forms correspond exactly: e. g. Alexander, Alexander; Alexandra, Alexandra; Alfred, Alfred; Dora, Dora; Berlin, Berlin; London, London; Europa, Europa, etc., etc.

2. Those names of countries in which the English terminations -ia, -ica, correspond to the German -ien, -ika: e. g. Africa, Afrika; Attica, Attika; Asia, Asien; India, Indien; Scandinavia, Skandinavien, etc., etc.

3. Those adjectives and nouns derived from names of men and countries in which the English terminations -ic and -ism correspond to the German -isch and -ismus; e. g. Anacreontic, anakreontisch; Buddhistic, buddhistisch; Homeric, homerisch; Platonic, platonisch; etc. etc.; and Buddhism, Buddhismus; Calvinism, Calvinismus; Latinism, Latinismus; Plutonism, Plutonismus, etc. etc.

Names of the more important rivers in which the English and German forms correspond exactly have been included in the following lists in order to show their German gender.

In cases where the spellings of German names given in Part I. and Part II. are not the same, those given in Part II. (representing the latest spellings) should be preferred. Those found in Part I. are in that case those usually found in the older German books.

For the accentuation of the German words and other points of interest, also for words not included in the Index to Part II., reference should be made to the Index of German names at the end of Part I., pp. 771–785.

A

Aar R., Aar (*f.*).
Abigail, Abigail (*f.*); Kammerjungfer (*f.*), zanksüchtige Dienerin, böses Weib (*n.*).
Abra(ha)m, (Abe,) Abraham (*m.*); —'s bosom, Abrahams Schoß (*m.*).
Abruzzi, die Abruzzen (*pl.*).
Abyssini—a, Abessinien (*n.*). **—an**, Abessinier (*m.*); Abessinierin (*f.*); abessinisch (*adj.*).
Acadia (*old poetic name for* **Nova Scotia**), Neuschottland (*n.*).
Achaean, Achaian, achäisch (*adj.*); Achäer (*m.*).
Achilles, Achill(es) (*m.*); tendon of —, Achillessehne, Achillesferse (*f.*).
Acre, Akka (*n.*); Akkon (*n.*) (*Medieval hist.*).
Ada (*for* **Adelaide**), Ada (*f.*).
Adam, Adam (*m.*); —'s-apple, Adamsapfel (*m.*); Adam's wine (*or* ale), Gänsewein (*m.*), Wasser (*n.*); not to know a p. from —, keine blasse Ahnung haben, wer jemand ist (*coll.*). **—itic**, Adams-; —itic attire, Adamskostüm (*n.*).
Addy, Adel (*for* **Adela**), Adelinchen (*n.*).
Adela, Adelaide, Adelheid (*f.*)
Adelina, Adeline, Adeline (*f.*).
Adige R., Etsch (*f.*).
Adolph, Adolphus, Adolf (*m.*).
Adonijah, Adonia (*m.*).
Adrian, adrianisch (*adj.*); (*the emperor*) Hadrian (*m.*).
Adrianople, Adrianopel (*n.*).
Adriatic, adriatisch (*adj.*); — (Sea), Adriatisches Meer (*n.*).
Aegades, die Egadi Inseln (*pl.*); Ägatische Inseln (*pl.*) (*Anc. hist.*).
Aegean Sea, Ägäisches Meer (*n.*).
Aeneid, die Äneide (*f.*).
Aeoli—an, —c, äolisch (*adj.*); —an harp, Äolsharfe (*f.*).
Aesculapius, Äskulap (*m.*).
Afghan, afghanisch (*adj.*); Afghane (*m.*).
Africa, Afrika (*n.*); Central —, Binnenafrika (*n.*). **—n**, afrikanisch (*adj.*); Afrikaner (*m.*); Afrikanerin (*f.*).
Agatha, Agathe (*f.*).
Aggy (*dim. of* **Agnes**), Amsel (*f.*), Amselchen (*n.*).
Ahasuerus, Ahasver (*m.*).

Aix-la-Chapelle, Aachen (*n.*).
Aladdin, Aladin (*m.*).
Alan, Alanus; Alane (*m.*).
Alaric(k), Alarich (*m.*).
Albanian, albanisch (*adj.*); Alban(i)er, Albanese (*m.*).
Alberic(k), Alberich (*m.*).
Albert, Albert, Albrecht (*m.*).
Albigenses, die Albigenser (*pl.*).
Albina, Alwine (*m.*).
Albion, Albion, Name der großbritannischen Insel; (*usually*) England (*n.*).
Alcides, der Alcide (Herkules).
Alec(k), Alick (*dim. of* **Alexander**), Alex (*m.*).
Alemanni, die Alemannen (*pl.*). **—c**, alemannisch; badisch-schweizerisch (*adj.*).
Alexandrian, alexandrinisch (*adj.*).
Alf (*dim. of* **Alfred**), Alfred (*m.*).
Alger—ia, Algerien (*n.*). **—ian, —ine**, algerisch (*adj.*); Algierer, Bewohner von Algier (*pl.*).
Algiers, Algier (*n.*).
Alice, Alicia, Alice, Alexia (*f.*).
Alic(k) (*dim. of* **Alexander**), Alex (*m.*).
Aller R., Aller (*f.*).
Alphonso, Alfonso, Alfons (*m.*).
Alp—ine, alpinisch (*adj.*), Alpen- (*in compounds*). **—s**, die Alpen (*pl.*).
Alsace, Alsatia, Elsaß (*n.*); **Alsatian**, elsässisch (*adj.*); Elsässer (*m.*); Elsässerin (*f.*).
Alva, Duke of —, der Herzog von Alba.
Amazon, Amazone (*f.*); (*river*) Amazonenstrom (*m.*).
Ambros—e, Ambrosius (*m.*). **—ian**, ambrosianisch (*adj.*); —ian hymn, der ambrosianische Lobgesang.
Amelia, Amalia, Amalie (*f.*); Malchen (*n.*).
America, Amerika (*n.*). **—n**, amerikanisch (*adj.*); Amerikaner (*m.*); Amerikanerin (*f.*).
Amperian, Ampèresch (*adj.*); the — currents, die Ampèreschen Ströme (*Magnet.*).
Amy (*dim. of* **Amelia**), Malchen (*n.*).
Anak, Enak (*m.*); son of —, Enakssohn (*m.*).
Andes, die Anden (*pl.*).
Andrew, Andreas (*m.*); Merry —, der Hanswurst; St. —'s Saltire, Andreaskreuz (*n.*).
Angelo; Castle of St. —, Engelsburg (*f.*).
Angevin dynasty, das Herrscherhaus Anjou; the Angevins, die Anjous (*pl.*).

Angle, der Bewohner von Angeln, Angel (*m.*); the —s, die Angeln (*pl.*).
Anglia, Angeln, England (*n.*); East —, Ostangeln, Ostanglien (*n.*).
Anglican, anglikanisch (*adj.*); Anglikaner (*m.*). —**ism**, Verfassung (*f.*) *or* Ritus (*m.*) der englischen Hochkirche.
Anglici—sm, Anglizismus (*m.*). —**ze**, englisch machen, anglisieren.
Anglo—-German, deutsch-englisch (*adj.*); the —-German agreement, der deutsch-englische Vertrag. —**mania**, übertriebene Bewunderung Englands, Engländerei, Anglomanie (*f.*). —**-Norman**, anglo-normannisch (*adj.*); Anglo-Normanne (*m.*). —**phile**, Engländerfreund, Bewunderer Englands (*m.*). —**phobia**, Engländerhaß (*m.*), Abneigung (*f.*) gegen England und Engländer, Anglophobie. —**-Saxon**, angelsächsisch (*adj.*); Angelsachse (*m.*).
Ann(a), **Anne**, Anna (*f.*); Ännchen (*n.*), Annette, Nannette, Nanni (*f.*), Nettchen (*n.*) (*dim.*).
Annamese, annamitisch (*adj.*), Annamese (*m.*).
Annie (*dim. of* **Anna**), Ännchen (*n.*), Nanni (*f.*), Nettchen (*n.*).
Antarctic, antarktisch (*adj.*); — circle, der südliche Polarkreis; the — ocean, das südliche Eismeer.
Ant(h)ony, Anton, Antonius, Toni (*m.*); St. —'s fire, das Antoniusfeuer, die Rose.
Anti-Lebanon, der Antilibanon.
Antilles, die Antillen (*pl.*); Greater *or* Larger —, die großen Antillen; Lesser *or* Smaller —, die kleinen Antillen.
Antiochian, antiochenisch (*adj.*).
Antwerp, Antwerpen (*n.*).
Apennines, die Apenninen (*pl.*).
Appalachian Mountains, die Appalachen (*pl.*).
Appian Way, die appische Straße (*f.*).
Aquitani—a, **Aquitaine**, Aquitanien (*n.*). —**an**, aquitanisch (*adj.*); Aquitanier (*m.*).
Arabia, Arabien (*n.*); — deserta, felix, petræa, das wüste, glückliche, steinige, Arabien. —**n**, arabisch (*adj.*); Araber (*m.*); —Nights' Entertainment, die Tausendundeine Nacht (*f.*).
Aragon, **Arragon**, Aragonien (*n.*).
Arcadia, Arkadien (*n.*); das Hirten- und Schäferland, idyllisches Land der stillen Zufriedenheit (*fig.*). —**n**, arkadisch; ländlich, hirtenmäßig, idyllisch (*adj.*) (*fig.*).
Archipelago, Archipel(agus) (*m.*).
Arctic, arktisch (*adj.*); — circle, der nördliche Polarkreis; — Ocean, das nördliche Eismeer.
Arden; Forest of —, der Ardenner-Wald. —**nes**, die Ardennen (*pl.*).
Arelate, (The,) Arelatum, das arelatische Reich.
Areopagus, der Areopag.
Argand-lamp, die Argandsche Lampe.
Argentine Republic, die argentinische Republik
Argive, argivisch (*adj.*); Argiver (*m.*).
Argonauts, die Argonauten (*pl.*).
Argonne; Forest of —, Argonnerwald (*m.*).
Argovia, Aargau (*m.*). —**n**, Aargauer (*m.*).
Argus; the eyes of —, Argusaugen, scharfe Augen (*pl.*). —**-eyed**, argusäugig (*adj.*).
Arian, arianisch (*adj.*); Arianer, Anhänger des Arius (*m.*). —**ism**, der Arianismus.
Aristot—le, Aristoteles (*m.*). —**elian**, aristotelisch (*adj.*); Aristoteliker (*m.*).
Arminian, arminianisch (*adj.*); Arminianer (*m.*).
Arminius the Cheruscan, Hermann der Cherusker.
Armoric(an), armorisch, armorikanisch (*adj.*); Armorikaner (*m.*).
Arno R., Arno (*m.*).
Artesian well, der artesische Brunnen, Bohrbrunnen.
Arthur, Arthur (*m.*); King —, der König Artus; —'s Round Table, die Tafelrunde; —'s chase, das wilde *or* wütende Heer. —**ian**, den König Artus betreffend (*adj.*); —ian legend, Artussage (*f.*).
Aryan, (**Arian**,) arisch (*adj.*); indo-germanisch (*adj.*) (*in a wider sense including European languages*); Arier (*m.*).
Ashanti, **Ashantee**, (*country*) Aschanti (*n.*); (*inhabitant*) Aschanti (*m.*).
As(h)taroth, **As(h)tareth**, Astarte (*f.*).
Asia, Asien (*n.*); — Minor, Kleinasien (*n.*); Central —, Mittelasien (*n.*). —**tic**, asiatisch (*adj.*); the —tic, der Asiat, die Asiatin. —**tics**, die Asiaten (*pl.*).
Asshur, Assur (*n.*) *also* = **Assyria** (Assyrien).
Assyrian, assyrisch (*adj.*); Assyr(i)er (*m.*).
Astrachan, Astrachan (*n.*). —(**ese**), astrachanisch (*adj.*); der Einwohner von A.
Astrophel, Dichtername des Sir Philip Sidney.
Asturia—s, Asturien (*n.*); Prince of the —s, Prinz von Asturien. —**n**, asturisch (*adj.*); Asturier, Bewohner (*m.*) von Asturien.
Athanasian, athanasianisch (*adj.*); — Creed, athanasianisches Glaubensbekenntnis.
Athenian, athenisch (*adj.*); Athener (*m.*)
Athens, Athen (*n.*).
Atkins; Tommy —, der englische gemeine Soldat.
Atlantic (Ocean), der atlantische Ozean.
Atlas Mountains, der Atlas.
Attila, Attila (*m.*) (*Hist.*); Etzel (*m.*) (*legend*).
Audrey (*for* **Etheldred**), Etheldred (*m.*).
Augean, augeisch (*adj.*); to cleanse the — stable, des Augias Stall *or* den Augiasstall reinigen.
Augusta, Augusta (*high style*), Auguste (*ord. style*) (*f.*). —**n**, *adj.*; —n age, das augusteische, klassische Zeitalter; das klassische Zeitalter, die Blütezeit (*generally*); —n Confession, die Augsburgische Konfession (1530).
Augustin(e); — friar, Augustinermönch (*m.*); — nun, Augustinernonne (*f.*).
Augustus, (*Christian name*) August (*m.*); (*the Roman emperor*) Augustus (*m.*).
Aurora, *s.* die (Göttin der) Morgenröte, Aurora; — borealis, das Nordlicht; — australis, das Südlicht.
Austin (*for* **Augustine**), Augustin (*m.*); — friars, — nuns, *see* Augustine.
Australasia, Australien (*n.*) und Neuseeland (*n.*). —**n**, australisch-neuseeländisch (*adj.*).
Australian, australisch (*adj.*); Australier (*m.*).
Austria, Österreich (*n.*). —**n**, österreichisch (*adj.*); Österreicher (*m.*); Österreicherin (*f.*); —-Hungary, Österreich-Ungarn (*n.*); Austro-Hungarian, österreichisch-ungarisch (*adj.*).
Avars, Avaren (*pl.*).
Aventine; Mount —, der aventinische Hügel, der Aventin.
Avon, Avon (*m.*); on —, am Avon; Sweet Swan of —, Shakespeare (*m.*).
Azov; Sea of —, das Asowsche Meer.
Azores, die Azoren (*pl.*).
Aztec, Azteke (*m.*).

B

Bab(bie) (*dim. of* **Barbara**), Bärbchen, Bärbelchen (*n.*).
Babel; Tower of —, Babylonischer Turm (*m.*), *or* Turmbau (*m.*) zu Babel.
Babylonian, babylonisch (*adj.*); Babylonier (*m.*).
Bactria, Baktrien (*n.*) (*now* Balkh). —**n**, Baktrer (*m.*).
Baden, (*Grand-Duchy*) Baden (*n.*); (*town*) Baden-Baden (*n*); badisch (*adj.*).
Balaam, Bileam (*m.*).
Balaton; Lake —, der Plattensee.
Baldur, **Balder**, Balder (*m.*).
Baldwin, Balduin (*m.*).
Bâle, **Basle**, Basel (*n.*).
Balearic Islands *or* **Isles**, die Balearen (*pl.*).
Balkan; — Peninsula, Balkanhalbinsel (*f.*); the —s, (*mountains*) das Balkangebirge; die Balkanländer (*pl.*).
Ballon d'Alsace, Elsässer Belchen (*m.*).

Balthazar, Balthasar (*m.*); Balzer (*m.*) (*coll.*).
Baltic, baltisch (*adj.*); — (Sea), die Ostsee (*f.*), Belt (*m.*) (*poet.*); — **Provinces**, die Ostseeprovinzen (*pl.*).
Barbado(e)s, Barbados (*n.*).
Barbary, die Berberei (*f.*); — horse, Berberroß (*n.*); — States, Barbaresken-Staaten (*pl.*).
Barmecide, Barmakide (*m.*), Barmecide (*m.*), einer der Scheinnahrung gibt, Scheinwohltaten erweist; — feast, Barmecidenschmaus (*m.*), Scheinmahlzeit (*f.*).
Barnaby, Barnabas (*m.*).
Bartholomew, Bartholomäus; Barthel, Berthel (*m.*) (*dim.*); St. —'s Eve, St. —'s Massacre, Bartholomäusnacht (*f.*), Pariser Bluthochzeit (*f.*) (*Aug. 23d-24th, 1572*).
Basil, Basilius (*m.*).
Basque, baskisch, biscayisch (*adj.*); Baske (*m.*).
Batavian, batavisch (*adj.*); Bataver, Holländer (*m.*).
Bath; — brick, Ziegelstein, Putzstein (*m.*); — bun, Rosinenkuchen (*m.*); — chair, Rollstuhl (*m.*).
Bathsheba, Bathseba (*f.*).
Bavaria, Bayern (*n.*); Upper —, Oberbayern (*n.*). —**n**, bayrisch (*adj.*); Bayer (*m.*); Bay(e)rin (*f.*); —n electorate, Kurbayern (*n.*).
Beatrice, **Beatrix**, Beatrice (*f.*).
Beattie (*dim. of* **Beatrice**), Beate.
Beauty; Sleeping —, Dornröschen (*n.*).
Bechuanaland, Betschuanenland (*n.*).
Becky (*dim. of* **Rebecca**), Beckchen (*n.*).
Bede, Beda (*m.*).
Bedouin, Beduine (*m.*); Bedawin, Beduinen (*pl.*).
Behring Strait, die Behring-Straße.
Belgi—an, belgisch (*adj.*); Belgier (*m.*); Belgierin (*f.*). —**c**, belgisch (*adj.*). —**um**, Belgien (*n.*).
Belgrade, Belgrad (*n.*).
Belisarius, Belisar (*m.*).
Bell(a) (*dim. of* **Arabella, Isabella**), Bella (*f.*).
Belshazzar, Belsazar (*m.*).
Ben, Benny (*dim. of* **Benjamin**), Ben(jamin) (*m.*). (Ben *has many different etymologies.*)
Benedick, Benedict, Benedikt (*m.*); junger Ehemann, bekehrter Hagestolz.
Benedictine (monk), der Benediktiner (Mönch); dem Benediktiner-Orden angehörig (*adj.*).
Bengal, Bengalen (*n.*); bengalisch (*adj.*); Bay of —, der Bengalische Meerbusen; — cane, spanisches Rohr; bengalisch (*adj.*); — fire, das bengalische Feuer (*pl.*); — lights, bengalische Flammen (*pl.*). —**i**, Bengale (*m.*); bengalische Sprache (*f.*); Bengalisch (*n.*).
Bennet (*dim. of* **Benedict**), Benedikt (*m.*).
Berlin work, Wollstickerei (*f.*).
Bermudas, die Bermudas-Inseln (*pl.*).
Bernard, Bernhard (*m.*); St. — dog, Bernhardiner (*m.*); —ine monk, Bernhardinermönch (*m.*) *or* Cistercienser (*m.*).
Bern—(e), Bern (*n.*); Bernese, bernisch (*adj.*); Berner (*m.*); Bernerin (*f.*). —**ese Alps**, das Berner Oberland.
Bertie (*dim. of* **Albert, Ethelbert**), Albertchen (*n.*), lieber Albert.
Bess(ie) (*dim. of* **Elizabeth**), Betty (*f.*), Lieschen, Elschen (*n.*).
Bethany, Bethanien (*n.*).
Betsy, Betty (*dim. of* **Elizabeth**), Betty (*f.*), Lieschen, Elschen (*n.*).
Beyrout, Beirut (*n.*).
Biddy (*dim. of* **Bridget**), Brigitte, Gitta, Breite (*f.*).
Bill(y) (*dim. of* **William**), Willy (*m.*); Miss —, weiblicher Stutzer.
Billingsgate, Londoner Fischmarkt; — language, die gemeine Sprache der Fischweiber.
Birmingham ware, Englische Kurzwaren (*pl.*).
Biscay, Biscaya *or* Viscaya (*f.*); Bay of —, Meerbusen von Biscaya (*m.*). —**an**, biscayisch (*adj.*); Biscayer (*m.*).
Blackfoot Indians, die Schwarzfüßler (*pl.*).
Black Forest, Schwarzwald (*m.*).
Black Prince, der schwarze Prinz, Eduard, Sohn König Eduards III.
Black Sea, das Schwarze Meer.
Blaise, Blasius (*m.*) (*dim. coll.* Blasi).
Blanch(e), Blanka (*f.*).
Blenheim, Blindheim (*n.*); battle of —, Schlacht (*f.*) bei Höchstädt (*1704*).
Blucher, Blücher (*m.*); — boots, starke Halbstiefel (*pl.*) mit Klappen zum Zuschnüren.
Bluebeard, Blaubart (*m.*).
Bob(by), *dim. of* **Robert**; (**Bobby**) (*sl.*) Polizist (*m.*).
Bœotia, Böotien (*n.*). —**n**, böotisch (*adj.*); dumm, stumpfsinnig, indolent (*fig.*); Böotier (*m.*).
Boer, Bur, Boer (*m.*); Burin (*f.*), Burenweib (*n.*); — war, Burenkrieg (*m.*).
Bohemia, Böhmen (*n.*). —**n**, böhmisch; ungebunden (*fig.*) (*adj.*); Böhme (*m.*); Zigeuner (*m.*); leichtlebiger Mensch (*m.*); —n Forest, Böhmerwald (*m.*).
Bohemond, Bohemund (*m.*).
Bokhara, Bukhara, die Bucharei (*f.*); the Ameer of —, der Amir der Bucharei.
Bologna; inhabitant of —, Bologneser (*m.*); — sausage, Bologneser Wurst (*f.*); Cervelatwurst (*f.*). *See* **Polony**.
Boney, *hum. for* **Bonaparte** (Napoleon I).
Boniface, Bonifacius. Bonifaz (*m.*).
Benonian, (**Bolognese**,) bolognesisch (*adj.*).
Bosnia—n, —c, bosnisch, bosniakisch (*adj.*); Bosnier, Bosniake (*m.*).
Bosp(h)or—ian, bosporisch (*adj.*); Bosporaner (*m.*). —**us**, Bosporus (*m.*).
Bothni—a, Botten (*n.*); Gulf of —a, Bottnischer Meerbusen (*m.*). —**an, —c**, bottnisch (*adj.*).
Bradshaw('s railway guide), (Englisches) Eisenbahnkursbuch (*n.*).
Brahmin, (**Brahman**,) der Brahmane, Brahmine. —**ic**, (**Brahmanic**), brahminisch (*adj.*). —**ism** Brahminentum (*n.*); Brahmaismus (*m.*).
Bramah-lock, Sicherheitsschloß (*n.*).
Brazil, Brasilien (*n.*). —**ian**, brasilianisch (*adj.*); Brasilianer (*m.*); — nut, Paranuß (*f.*); — wood, rotes Brasilienholz (*m.*); Fernambukholz (*n.*).
Bride (*dim. of* **Bridget**), Breite, Gitta (*f.*).
Bridget, Brigitte (*f.*).
Bright's disease, Brightsche Nierenkrankheit (*f.*).
Britain, Britannien (*n.*); Great —, Großbritannien (*n.*); Greater —, Großbritannien und seine Kolonien.
Britann—ia, Britannien (*n.*); —ia-metal, das Britanniametall (*s.*). —**ic**, britannisch, brittisch (*adj.*); His —ic Majesty, Seine Majestät der König von Großbritannien und Irland.
Brit—ish, brit(t)isch (*adj.*); the —ish, die Brit(t)en (*pl.*). —**isher**, Engländer (*m.*) (*Amer.*). —**on**, Brit(t)e (*m.*).
Brittany, (**Britan(n)y**,) die Bretagne (*f.*); in —, in der Bretagne.
Brobdingnagian, riesig (*adj.*); Riese (*m.*).
Brocken, Brocken (*m.*); — spectre, Brockengespenst (*n.*).
Brown, Jones & Robinson, Meyer, Müller, und Schulze.
Bruges, Brügge (*n.*).
Bruin, (Meister) Braun (*m.*), der Bär.
Brum(m)agem (*for* **Birmingham**); — (goods), minderwertige, billige und nachgemachte Waren (*pl.*).
Brunswick, Braunschweig (*n.*); — green, Braunschweiger Grün (*n.*).
Brussels, Brüssel (*n.*); — carpet, Brüsseler Teppich; — lace, Brüsseler Spitzen (*pl.*); — sprouts, Rosenkohl (*m.*), Brüsseler Kohl.
Bucharest, Bukarest (*n.*).
Buda, Ofen (*n.*).
Burgund—ian, burgundisch (*adj.*); Burgunder

(*m.*); Burgunderin (*f.*). **—y**, Burgund (*n.*); (*wine*) Burgunder (*m.*)
Burm—a, Birma, Barma (*n.*). **—an, —ese**, birmanisch, barmanisch (*adj.*); Birmane, Barmane (*m.*).
Bushmen, die Buschmänner (*pl.*).
Byzant—ium, Byzanz (*n.*). **—ian, —ine**, byzantinisch (*adj.*); Byzantiner (*m.*).

C

Cadmus, Kadmos (*n.*).
Cædmon, Kädmon (*m.*).
Cæsar, Cäsar (*m.*). **—ean**, cäsarisch (*adj.*).
Caffraria, Kaffernland (*n.*).
Caiaphas, Kaiphas (*m.*).
Cain, Kain (*m.*).
Cairo, Kairo (*n.*).
Calabrian, kalabresisch (*adj.*); Kalabrese (*m.*).
Caleb, Kaleb (*m.*).
Caledonia, Kaledonien, Schottland (*n.*). **—n**, Kaledonier, Schotte (*m.*), Schottin (*f.*); kaledonisch, schottisch (*adj.*).
California, Kalifornien (*n.*). **—n**, Kalifornier (*m.*); kalifornisch (*adj.*).
Caliph, Kalif (*m.*). **—ate**, Kalifat (*n.*).
Calmuck, Kalmücke (*m.*); kalmückisch (*adj.*).
Calvary, Golgatha (*n.*), Schädelstätte (*f.*) der Kalvarienberg, Leidensweg (*m.*) (*fig.*).
Cambodia, Kambodscha, Kambodja (*f.*).
Cambria, *see* **Wales**. **—n**, wallisisch, Walliser (*adj.*).
Cambyses, Kambyses (*m.*).
Cameroons, (The), Kamerun, Kamerun (*n.*).
Camford, Name einer idealen englischen Universität [aus Cam(bridge) und (Ox)ford], Versteckname für Cambridge oder Oxford. *See* **Oxbridge**.
Canaan, Kanaan (*n.*). **—ite**, Kananiter (*m.*); Simon the —ite, Simon (*m.*) von Kana. **—itish**, kanaanitisch (*adj.*).
Canad—a, Kanada (*n.*). **—ian**, Kanadier (*m.*); Kanadierin (*f.*); kanadisch (*adj.*).
Canary (Islands), Canaries, Kanarische Inseln (*pl.*); (*bird*) Kanarienvogel (*m.*); (*wine*) Kanariensekt (*m.*).
Cancer; Tropic of —, Wendekreis (*m.*) des Krebses.
Candia, Kandia (*n.*).
Cantab—(rigian), Cambridger (*m.*). **The —s**, die Cambridger Studenten.
Canterbury, Canterbury (*n.*); elegantes Notenregal. **—bell**, Glockenblume (*f.*).
Canton, Kanton (*n.*).
Canute, Knut (*m.*).
Cape; — Colony, Kapkolonie (*f.*), Kapland (*n.*); — Town, Kapstadt (*f.*); — of Good Hope, Kap (*n.*) der guten Hoffnung.
Capetians, Capetinger (*pl.*).
Capitol, Kapitol (*n.*), Capitolium (*n.*). *See p.* 69.
Capricorn; Tropic of —, Wendekreis (*m.*) des Steinbocks.
Cardigan (jacket), gestickte wollene Jacke (*f.*).
Carey; Mother —'s chicken, Petersvogel (*m.*).
Carib—bean Sea, karaibisches Meer, Antillenmeer (*n.*). **—(bee)**, Karaibe (*m.*).
Carinthia, Kärnten (*n.*). **—n**, kärntnisch (*adj.*).
Carlist, Karlist (*m.*); karlistisch (*adj.*).
Carlo—man, Karlmann (*m.*). **—vingian**, Karolinger (*m.*); karolingisch (*adj.*)
Carmelite, Karmeliter (*m.*); — nun, Karmeliterin (*f.*).
Carniola, Krain (*n.*). **—n**, krainisch (*adj.*); Krainer (*m.*).
Caroline Islands, die Karolinen (*pl.*).
Carolingian, *see* **Carlovingian**.
Carpathian Mts., die Karpathen (*pl.*).
Carrie (*dim. of* **Caroline**), Lina, Line (*f.*).
Carthag—e, Karthago (*n.*). **—inian**, Karthager (*m.*); karthagisch (*adj.*).
Carthusian (friar), Kartäuser(mönch) (*m.*).
Cashmere, Kaschmir (*n.*).
Casimir, Kasimir (*m.*).
Caspian Sea, Kaspisches Meer (*n.*).
Cassiterides, Zinninseln (*pl.*).
Castil—e, Kastilien (*n.*). **—ian**, Kastilianer (*m.*); kastil(ian)isch (*adj.*).
Catalaunian Fields, Katalaunische Gefilde (*pl.*) (*battle of A. D. 451*).
Catharine, Catherine, Katharine, Kathrine, Käthe (*f.*), Käthchen (*n.*); —wheel, Katharinenrad (*n.*).
Catholic, katholisch (*adj.*); Katholik (*m.*); Roman —, Katholik (*m.*); (römisch-)katholisch (*adj.*).
Catiline, Katilina (*m.*); conspiracy of —, katilinarische Verschwörung (*f.*).
Catullus, Catull (*m.*).
Caucas—us, Kaukasus (*m.*). **—ian**, Kaukasier (*m.*); Kaukasierin (*f.*); kaukasisch (*adj.*).
Caudine Forks, caudinische Pässe (*pl.*).
Cecilia, Cecily, Cäcilie (*f.*).
Celestine, Cölestin (*m.*); Cölestina (*f.*); (*friar*) Cölestiner(mönch) (*m.*).
Celt, der Kelte. **—ic**, keltisch (*adj.*); Keltisch (*n.*).
Celtiberian, Keltiberier (*m.*) (Mischvolk von Kelten und Iberiern im alten Spanien); keltiberisch (*adj.*)
Cevennes, Cevennen (*pl.*).
Chald—æa, Chaldäa (*n.*). **—æan, (—ee,)** Chaldäer (*m.*); chaldäisch (*adj.*).
Champagne, (*country*) die Champagne; (*wine*) Champagner (*m.*), (französischer) Sekt (*m.*).
Channel; the English —, Kanal (*m.*), Ärmelmeer (*n.*); — Islands, die Kanal-Inseln (*pl.*); — passage, die Überfahrt über den Kanal.
Chanticleer, Henning der Hahn.
Charles, (Charlie,) Karl (*m.*), (Karlchen (*n.*)); King —'s dog, Bologneserhündchen (*n.*); —'s Wain, der große Bär.
Charlemagne, Karl der Große.
Charlotte, Charlotte (*f.*); apple —, Apfeltorte (*f.*); — russe, mit Eierrahm gefüllte Sandtorte.
Chelsea, the Sage of, Thomas Carlyle.
Cherethites and Pelethites, Krethi und Plethi (*pl.*).
Chersonese, Chersones (*m.*).
Cherusc—an, Cherusker (*m.*); cheruskisch (*adj.*). **—i**, Cherusker (*pl.*).
Cheshire cheese, Chesterkäse (*m.*).
Chil—ian, Chilene (*m.*); chilenisch (*adj.*).
Chiltern Hundreds, ein Bezirk in Buckinghamshire, dessen Verwaltung nominell als königliches Amt denen übergeben wird, die ihren Sitz im Parlament aufgeben wollen; to accept the (stewardship of the) — —, seinen Sitz im Parlament aufgeben.
Chin—a, China (*n.*). **—ee, (John —aman,)** (*coll. Amer.*), **—ese**, Chinese (*m.*); Chinesin (*f.*); chinesisch (*adj.*); —ese lantern, Papierlaterne (*f.*), Lampion (*m.*); —ese puzzle, Vexierspiel, Mosaikspiel (*n.*); —ese shades, chinesisches Schattenspiel.
Chris (*dim. of* **Christopher**), Christoph, Töffel (*m.*).
Chrissie (*dim. of* **Christiana, Christina**), *s.* Christiane, Christinchen, Stinchen (*n.*).
Christ, Christus (*m.*). **—ian**, Christ (*m.*); Christin (*f.*); christlich (*adj.*); **—ian name**, Taufname, Vorname, Rufname (*m.*).
Christiana, Christiane (*f.*).
Christiania, Kristiania (*n.*).
Christina, Christine (*f.*); Stinchen, Tinchen (*n.*) (*dim.*).
Christopher, Christy, Christoph, Stoffel, Töffel (*m.*).
Cicely, *see* **Cecilia**.
Ciceronian, ciceronisch (*adj.*); im Stile Ciceros.
Cimbri, die Cimbern (*pl.*). **—c Chersonese**, Schleswig und Jütland.
Cinderella, Aschenputtel, Aschenbrödel (*n.*).
Cinque Ports, die fünf Häfen (Sandwich, Dover, Hythe, Romney, Hastings), welche Wilhelm der

Eroberer zum Schutz der englischen Südküste dem Lord Warden of the — — unterordnete.
Circassia, Tscherkessien (*n.*). **—n**, Tscherkesse (*m.*); Tscherkessin (*f.*); tscherkessisch (*adj.*).
Cis—alpine, cisalpinisch (*adj.*). **—leithan**, cisleithanisch, österreichisch (*adj.*). **—padane**, cispadanisch (*adj.*).
Cistercian (monk), Cistercienser(mönch) (*m.*).
Clar—a, **—e**, Klara (*f.*).
Clarrie (*dim. of* **Clara**), Klärchen, Kläre (*n.*).
Claus; Santa —, Knecht Ruprecht; Weihnachtsmann (*m.*).
Clement, Clemens (*m.*).
Cleopatra, Kleopatra (*f.*).
Cleves, Cleve (*n.*).
Clio, Klio (*f.*).
Clovis, Chlodwig, Chlodowech (*m.*).
Cluniac (monk), Cluniacenser (*m.*).
Clyde R., Clyde (*m.*).
Coblence, **Coblenz**, Koblenz (*n.*).
Cocaigne, land of —, das Schlaraffenland.
Cochin-China, Kochinchina, Kotschinchina (*n.*).
Cockney, Londoner (*m.*); Sprache (*f.*) des richtigen Londoners. **—ism**, Londoner Spracheigenheit (*f.*).
Cologne, Köln (*n.*); Eau de —, kölnisches Wasser.
Colosseum, Kolosseum (*n.*).
Colossians, Kolosser (*pl.*).
Columbia, Kolumbien (*n.*).
Como; Lake —, Comersee, Como See (*m.*).
Confuci—us, Konfutse (*m.*); **—an**, konfutsisch.
Congo R., Kongo (*m.*).
Connie (*dim. of* **Constance**), Stanze (*f.*).
Conrad(e), Konrad (*m.*).
Constance, (*town*) Konstanz (*n.*); (*name*) Konstanze (*f.*); Lake of —, Bodensee (*m.*).
Constantin—e, Konstantin (*m.*). **—ople**, Konstantinopel (*n.*).
Copenhagen, Kopenhagen (*n.*).
Copernican, kopernikanisch (*adj.*).
Copt, Kopte (*m.*); Koptin (*f.*). **—ic**, koptisch (*adj.*).
Cordilleras, Kordilleren (*pl.*).
Cordova, Kordova (*n.*). **—n**, korduanisch (*adj.*).
Corea, Korea (*n.*).
Corfu, Korfu (*n.*).
Corinth, Korinth (*n.*). **—ian**, Korinther (*m.*); korinthisch (*adj.*); —ian order, korinthische Säulenordnung (*f.*).
Coriolanus, Coriolan (*m.*).
Cornelia, Kornelie (*f.*).
Corn—ish, cornisch (*adj.*), aus *or* von Cornwall. **—wall**, Cornwall(is) (*n.*).
Corsica, Korsika (*n.*). **—n**, Korse (*m.*); Korsin (*f.*); korsisch, korsikanisch (*adj.*).
Cossack, Kosak (*m.*); kosakisch (*adj.*).
Courland, Kurland (*n.*). **—er**, Kurländer (*m.*).
Coventry; to send a p. to —, einen in Verruf erklären, nicht mit einem sprechen und verkehren (*school sl.*).
Craco—w, Krakau (*n.*). **—vian**, Krakauer (*m.*); krakauisch (*adj.*).
Crapaud, *see* **Johnny**.
Creole, Kreole (*m.*); Kreolin (*f.*); kreolisch (*adj.*).
Cret—e, Kreta (*n.*). **—an**, Kreter (*m.*); kretisch (*adj.*).
Crimea, die Krim (*f.*); —n war, Krimkrieg (*m.*).
Croat—ia, Kroatien (*n.*). **—ian**, Kroat (*m.*); Kroatin (*f.*); kroatisch (*adj.*).
Crœsus, Krösus (*m.*).
Cuba, Kuba (*n.*). **—n**, Kubaner (*m.*); kubanisch (*adj.*).
Cunegund, Kunigunde (*f.*).
Cupid, Cupido (*m.*).
Cyclades, Cykladen (*pl.*).
Cypr—us, Cypern (*n.*). **—iot(e)**, Cypriot (*m.*). **—ian**, cyprisch (*adj.*); — plum, Cyperpflaume (*f.*); — wine, Cyperwein (*m.*).
Cyril, Cyrill (*m.*).
Czech, Tscheche (*m.*); Tschechin (*f.*); tschechisch (*adj.*).

D

Dahomey, Dahome (*n.*).
Dalai Lama, (**Grand Llama**,) Dalai Lama (*m.*).
Damas—cus, Damaskus (*n.*); —cus blade, die Damaszener Klinge; —cus raisins, die Zibeben (*pl.*). **—cene**, **—k**, damaszenisch (*adj.*); Damaszener (*m.*).
Danai, die Danaer (*pl.*).
Dan—e, *s.* Däne (*m.*); Dänin (*f.*). **—egelt**, Dänensteuer (*f.*), Dänengeld (*n.*). **—ish**, dänisch (*adj.*); —ish war, der Dänenkrieg.
Daniel, **Dan(ny)**, Daniel (*m.*).
Dantzic, **Dantzig**, Danzig (*n.*).
Danub—e R., Donau (*f.*). **—ian principalities**, Donaufürstentümer (*pl.*).
Darby and Joan, ein glückliches altes Ehepaar.
Dardanelles, die Dardanellen (*pl.*).
Darwinian, darwinisch, darwinistisch (*adj.*); — theory, darwinische Abstammungslehre, Deszendenztheorie (*f.*).
David, David (*m.*).
Davy, Davidchen (*n.*) (*dim.*); — Jones's locker, die See (*fig.*); — lamp, Sicherheitslampe (*f.*).
Dead Sea, das Tote Meer.
Debora(h), **Deb**, Debora (*f.*).
Delaware R., Delaware (*m.*).
Delft (Dutch) ware, Delfter Geschirr (*n.*).
Delilah, Delila (*f.*).
Delphi—an, **—c**, delphisch (*adj.*).
Denis, **Dennis**, Dionys (*m.*).
Denmark, Dänemark (*n.*).
Derby(shire) neck, Kropfgeschwulst (*f.*).
Derrick (*dim. of* **Theodoric**), Dietrich (*m.*).
Dervish, Derwisch (*m.*).
Di (*for* **Diana** *and* **Dinah**), Di(a)na (*f.*).
Dick (*dim. of* **Richard**); Tom, —, and Harry, Hans und Kunz, Hinz und Kunz.
Dick(e)y (*dim. of* **Richard**); — (bird), Matz (*m.*), Mätzchen (*n.*).
Dinah, Dina (*f.*).
Dionysius, Dionysius, Dionys (*m.*).
Dioscuri, die Dioskuren (*pl.*); Zwillinge (*pl.*) (*Astron.*).
Dizzy, *hum. for* **Disraeli**.
Dnieper R., Dniepr (*m.*).
Dniester R., Dniestr (*m.*).
Dobbin, **Dob(by)** (*dim. of* **Robert**), (*name of a cart-horse*) Hans (*m.*).
Doll(y) (*dim. of* **Dorothy**), Dortchen, Dorchen, Dorle, Dürten (*n.*).
Dominic; St. —, der heilige Dominicus. **—an**, Dominikaner (*m.*).
Don R., Don (*m.*); — Cossacks, die donischen Kosaken (*pl.*).
Dora (*short for* **Dorothea**, **Theodora**), Dora (*f.*).
Dorcas Society, (der Armen Kleider 2c. spendende (Frauen)Verein) Nähverein (*m.*).
Dorothea, **Dorothy**, Dorothea (*f.*); Dorette (*f.*), Dorchen, Dortchen, Dürten (*n.*) (*dim.*).
Dot(ty) (*dim. of* **Dorothy**), Dorchen, Dortchen, Dorle, Dürten (*n.*).
Douro R., (*Spanish name*) Duero (*m.*), (*Portuguese name*) Douro (*m.*).
Dover Straits, Straße (*f.*) von Dover, *Pas de Calais* (*m.*).
Downing Street, das (englische) Ministerium des Äußeren (befindet sich hier). *Cp.* Wilhelmstraße.
Drave R., Drau (*f.*).
Dresden china, Meißner Porzellan (*n.*).
Druid, Druide (*m.*). **—ess**, Druidin (*f.*) **—ical**, druidisch (*adj.*). **—ism**, Druidentum (*n.*).
Dunkirk, Dünkirchen (*n.*).
Dutch, holländisch (*adj.*); the —, die Holländer (*pl.*). **—man**, Holländer (*m.*); the flying — man, (*legendary captain*) der fliegende Holländer; Blitzzug (*m.*). **—woman**, Holländerin (*f.*).
Dwina; North — River, Dwina (*f.*); Western —, Düna (*f.*).

E

East, Osten (*m.*); the —, Morgenland (*n.*), Orient (*m.*); the Far —, Ostasien (*n.*); the Near —, die Balkanhalbinsel und Kleinasien (*n.*); the Far —ern question, die ostasiatische Frage; — Indies, Ostindien (*n.*); — India Company, Ostindische Kompanie; — Indiaman, Ostindienfahrer (*m.*).
Ebro R., Ebro (*m.*).
Ecclesiastes, der Prediger Salomo.
Eden, Eden (*n.*), Paradies (*n.*).
Edin—burgh, **—boro'**, Edinburg (*n.*).
Edith, Edith, Editha (*f.*).
Edward, Eduard (*m.*); — the Confessor, Eduard der Bekenner.
Edwin and Angelina, ein glückliches junges Paar.
Egadi Is. (*or obs.*) **Egates**, Egadi, (*or obs. and hist.*) Ägatische Inseln (*pl.*).
Egra, Eger (*n.*).
Egypt, Ägypten (*n.*). **—ian**, ägyptisch (*adj.*); Ägypter (*m.*); (*gipsy*) Zigeuner (*m.*) (*obs.*); Lower —, Unterägypten (*n.*); Upper —, Oberägypten (*n.*). **—ology**, Ägyptenforschung, Ägyptologie (*f.*). **—ologist**, Ägyptolog (*m.*).
Eider, Eider (*f.*); — Danes, (*Danish Chauvinists, especially 1864, see Part I, p. 774*) Eiderdänen (*pl.*); —-duck, Eiderente (*f.*); —-down, Eiderdunen, Eiderdaunen (*f.pl.*).
Elbe R., Elbe (*f.*).
Eleanor, **Elinor**, Eleonore, Le(o)nore (*f.*).
Eleazer, Eleasar (*m.*).
Eleusinian, eleusinisch (*adj.*); — festival, eleusisches Fest; — mysteries, eleusinische Mysterien.
Elia—h, **—s**, Elia, Elias (*m.*).
Elijah, Elias (*m.*).
Elisha, Elisa (*m.*).
Eliza, Elise (*f.*).
Elizabeth, Elisabeth (*f.*); Betty, Else, Elsbeth (*f.*), Elschen (*n.*), Ilse (*f.*), Li(e)schen (*n.*), Li, Liese(l), Lisabeth (*f.*) (*dim.*). **—an**, zur Zeit der (Königin) Elisabeth; the —ans, die Männer (besonders Dichter) zur Zeit Elisabeths; —an poet, Dichter aus dem Zeitalter der Königin Elisabeth; —an style, Elisabethstil (*1550-1600*).
Ella, **Ellen**, **Ellie** (*dim. of* **Helena** *or* **Eleanor**), Lene (*f.*), Lenchen (*n.*), Lore (*f.*), Lorchen.
(St.) Elmo's-fire, St. Elmsfeuer (*n.*).
Elsa, **Elsie**, (*dim. of* **Elizabeth**), Else (*f.*), Elschen (*n.*), Liese (*f.*), Lieschen (*n.*).
Elsinore, Helsingör (*n.*).
Elster R., Elster (*f.*).
Elysi—an, elys(ä)isch (*adj.*). **—um**, Elysium (*n.*).
Em (*dim. of* **Emma**), Emmchen (*n.*).
Emerald Isle, die Smaragd-Insel (Irland).
Emery, Emmerich (*m.*).
Emily, Emilie (*f.*).
Emmanuel, Emanuel (*m.*).
Emmy (*dim. of* **Emma**, **Em(m)eline**), Emmi (*f.*), Emmchen (*n.*).
Ems R., Ems (*f.*).
England, England (*n.*); Church of —, die Anglikanische Kirche, Englische Hochkirche.
English, englisch (*adj.*); Englisch (*n.*), englische Sprache (*f.*); the —, die Engländer (*pl.*); she is —, sie ist eine Engländerin; — subjects (in schools), englische Sprache und Litteratur, Geschichte und Geographie, Religion; — Channel, Ärmelmeer (*n.*); King's (Queen's) —, das reine mustergültige Englisch; to murder the King's —, die englische Sprache radebrechen; Old —, altenglisch (*adj.*); Old — type, Frakturschrift (*f.*); to —, ins Englische übersetzen *or* übertragen (*v.a.*). **—man**, Engländer (*m.*). **—woman**, Engländerin (*f.*).
Ephesian, ephesisch (*adj.*); Epheser (*m.*).
Epicur—e, Epikur (*m.*); Feinschmecker (*m.*), Leckermaul (*n.*) (*fig.*). **—ean**, epikur(e)isch; schwelgerisch, sinnlich, genußsüchtig (*adj.*) (*fig.*); Epikureer (*m.*); Lebemann, Genußmensch (*m.*) (*fig.*). **—eanism**, Lehre (*f.*) Epikurs, Epikureismus (*m.*). **—ism**, Hang (*m.*) zum Wohlleben.
Epicurus, Epikur (*m.*).
Epsom salts, englisches Salz, Bittersalz (*n.*).
Equator, Äquator (*m.*). **—ial**, äquatorial, unter dem Äquator liegend (*adj.*).
Eric, Erich (*m.*).
Erin, (*poetical name for*) Irland (*n.*).
Ernest, (**Ernie**,) Ernst (*m.*), (Ernstchen (*n.*)).
Erse, ersisch (*adj.*); irische Volkssprache (*f.*).
Erinnys, Erinnye, Furie (*f.*).
Eskimo, **Esquimau**, Eskimo (*m.*) (*pl.* Eskimos).
Essenes, die (Sekte (*f.*) der) Essener (*pl.*).
Esthonia, Esthland (*n.*). **—n**, esthnisch (*adj.*); Esthe (*m.*).
Ethelbert, Adalbert (*m.*).
Ethiop, Äthiopier, Mohr (*m.*), Mohrin (*f.*). **—ia**, Äthiopien, Abessinien, Mohrenland (*n.*). **—ian**, äthiopisch; mohrenschwarz (*adj.*); Äthiopier (*m.*).
Etna, Ätna (*m.*).
Etonian, Eton betreffend, zu Eton gehörig (*adj.*); Schüler (*m.*) von Eton.
Etrurian, **Etruscan**, etrurisch, etruskisch (*adj.*); Etrurier, Etrusker (*m.*).
Euclid, Euklid (*m.*); Geometrie (*f.*) (*fig.*). **—ian**, euklidisch (*adj.*).
Eugene, Eugen (*m.*).
Euphrates, Euphrat (*m.*).
Eurasian, europäisch-asiatisch, halbasiatisch (*adj.*); in Asien geborenes Kind eines Europäers und einer Asiatin, Halbeuropäer, Halbasiat (*m.*).
Europe, Europa (*n.*). **—an**, europäisch (*adj.*); Europäer (*m.*).
Eustace, Eustachius (*m.*).
Eustachian (valve) tube, eustachische Klappe, Röhre (*f.*).
Euxine, das Schwarze Meer.
Eva, (**Eve**, **Evy**,) Eva (*f.*), (Evchen (*n.*)).
Evan (*Welsh*), Johann, Hans (*m.*).
Eveline, **Evelyn**, (*dim. of* **Eva**), Eveline (*f.*), Evchen (*n.*).
Everard (*dim.* **Evvy**), Eberhard (*m.*).
Everest (Mt.), Gaurisankar (*m.*).
Ezekiel, Ezechiel, Hesekiel (*m.*).
Ezra, Esra (*m.*).

F

Fabii, Fabier (*pl.*).
Fan(ny) (*dim. of* **Frances**), Fanny (*f.*).
Faröe Islands, Faröer, (Far-Öer-) Inseln (*pl.*).
Faroese, faröisch (*adj.*).
Faustus, Faust (*m.*).
Fenian, fenisch (*adj.*); Fenier (*m.*). **—ism**, Feniertum (*n.*).
Fiji Islands, Fiji (Fidschi) Inseln (*pl.*).
Filipino, Bewohner (*m.*) der Philippinen.
Fin—(n), **—lander**, Finne, Finnländer (*m.*). —(**n**), **—nish**, finnisch (*adj.*). **—land**, Finnland (*n.*); Gulf of —land, finnischer (Meer)busen.
Fir Mountains, Fichtelgebirge (*n.*).
Flanders, Flandern (*n.*).
Flem—ing, Flam(l)änder (*m.*). **—ish**, flämisch, flandrisch (*adj.*).
Flibbertigibbet, ein böser Geist.
Flo, **Flora**, **Florrie**, **Florence**, Flora, Florentia (*f.*).
Floren—ce, (*city*) Florenz (*n.*). **—tine**, florentinisch (*adj.*); Florentiner (*m.*); —tine work, florentinische Arbeit, Mosaik (*f.*).
Flossie, **Floxie**, (*dim. of* **Flora**), Florchen (*n.*).
Flushing, Vlissingen (*n.*); via —, über Vlissingen.
Forth R., Forth (*m.*).
Fortunatus, Fortunat (*m.*); —'s purse, Glücksäckel (*m.*); —'s wishing-cap, Fortunats Wünschelhütlein (*n.*).
France, Frankreich (*n.*).
Frances, Franziska (*f.*); Fränzchen (*n.*) (*dim.*).
Francis, Franz (*m.*); St. —, der heilige Franciscus; der heilige Franz von Assisi.

Franciscan (friar), Franziskaner(mönch) (*m.*).
Franco-German, deutsch-französisch (*adj.*).
Franconia, Franken (*n.*); Lower —, Unterfranken (*n.*). **—n**, fränkisch (*adj.*); Franke (*m.*); —n emperors, fränkische *or* salische Kaiser (*Hist.*).
Frank (*for* **Francis**), (*Christian name*) Franz (*m.*); (*name of an old German tribe*) Franke (*m.*). **—ish**, fränkisch (*adj.*).
Frankfort, Frankfurt (*n.*); — on the Main, Frankfurt am Main; — fair, Frankfurter Messe (*f.*).
Fred, Fritz (*m.*); —'s father, Fritzens Vater (*m.*). **—dy**, Fritzchen (*n.*). **—eric(k)**, Friedrich (*m.*).
Frederica, Friederike (*f.*); Rickchen (*n.*) (*dim.*).
French, französisch (*adj.*); she is —, sie ist eine Französin; the —, die Franzosen (*pl.*); — bean, welsche Bohne, Säbelbohne (*f.*); — brandy, Cognac (*m.*); — briar, die englische kurze Pfeife, Stummelpfeife; — casement, Fensterflügel (*pl.*); — chalk, Schneiderkreide (*f.*); — horn, Waldhorn (*n.*); — polish, Schellakpolitur (*f.*); — slops, Pluderhosen (*pl.*); — window, Flügelfenster (*n.*); — windows, bis auf den Boden reichende Fensterflügel, (Salon-)Glastür (*f.*); to take — leave, sich heimlich entfernen, sich unbemerkt drücken (*v.n.*) (*sl.*). **—ify**, französisch machen, französieren (*v.a.*). **—man**, Franzose (*m.*). **—woman**, Französin (*f.*).
Friendly Islands, Freundschaftsinseln (*pl.*)
Frisia, Friesland (*n.*). **—n**, friesisch (*adj.*); Friese (*m.*); Friesin (*f.*).
Frieslander, Friese (*m.*); Friesin (*f.*).,
Friuli, Friaul (*n.*).
Fuegian, Feuerländer (*m.*); feuerländisch (*adj.*).
Fulda R., Fulda (*f.*).
Fyen, Fünen (*n.*).

G

Gabriella, Gabrielle, Gabriele (*f.*).
Gael, Gäle (*m.*). **—ic**, gälisch (*adj.*).
Galatians, Galater (*pl.*).
Galen(us), Galen (*m.*).
Galicia, Galizien (*n.*).
Galilea, (Galilee,) Galiläa (*n.*). **—n**, galiläisch (*adj.*); Galiläer (*m.*).
St. Gall, (*place*) Sankt Gallen (*n.*); (*person*) der heilige Gallus.
Gallic, gallisch (*adj.*). **—an**, gallikanisch (*adj.*). **—ism**, Gallizismus (*m.*).
Gallo—mania, Französelei (*f.*). **—phil**, franzosenfreundlich (*adj.*). **—phobe**, Franzosenfeind, Franzosenfresser (*m.*); franzosenfeindlich (*adj.*). **—phobia**, Franzosenhaß (*m.*), Franzosenfresserei (*f.*).
Ganges R., Ganges (*m.*).
Ganymede, Ganymed (*m.*).
Garonne R., Garonne (*f.*).
Gascon, gasconisch (*adj.*); Gascogner (*m.*). **—y**, die Gascogne (*f.*).
Gaspar(d), Kaspar (*m.*); Kasperle (*m.*) (*dim.*).
Gaul, (*country*) Gallien (*n.*); (*inhabitant*) Gallier (*m.*). **—ish**, gallisch (*adj.*).
Gauntgrim, Isegrim (*m.*).
Genev—a, Genf (*n.*); der Wachholderbranntwein; Lake of —a, Genfer See (*m.*). **—ese**, Genfer (*m.*).
Geno—a, Genua (*n.*). **—ese**, genuesisch (*adj.*); Genueser (*m.*).
Ge(o)ffrey, Gottfried (*m.*).
Geor—ge, (—die, —gie,) Georg (*m.*); yellow —ge, Guinee (*f.*) (*coll.*). **—gian**, georgisch (*adj.*).
Georgiana, Georgie, Georgina, Georgine (*f.*).
Ger, Gerald, Gerard, Gerhard (*m.*).
German, deutsch (*adj.*); Deutsche (*m. f. n.*); the —, der Deutsche, die Deutsche; a —, ein Deutscher, eine Deutsche; the —s, die Deutschen; we —s, wir Deutsche; in good —, auf gut deutsch; he (she) is —, er ist ein Deutscher, sie ist eine Deutsche; he speaks — well, er spricht gut deutsch; — band, fremde herumziehende Musikanten (*pl.*); — black, Frankfurter Schwarz (*n.*); — clock, Schwarzwälder Uhr (*f.*); — Confederation, Deutscher Bund (*m.*) (*1815-66*); — measles, Röteln (*pl.*); — Ocean, Nordsee (*f.*); — silver, Neusilber (*n.*); — steel, Rohstahl, Schmelzstahl (*m.*); — text, Frakturschrift (*f.*); — tinder, Zündschwamm (*m.*); — tongue, deutsche Zunge *or* Sprache (*f.*), Deutsch (*n.*); — toys, Nürnberger Spielsachen (*pl.*); High —, hochdeutsch (*adj.*); Low —, plattdeutsch, niederdeutsch (*adj.*); Middle High —, mittelhochdeutsch (*adj.*); New High —, neuhochdeutsch (*adj.*); Old High —, althochdeutsch (*adj.*).
Germanic, germanisch (*adj.*).
Germany, Deutschland (*n.*); Lower —, Niederdeutschland (*n.*); Upper —, Oberdeutschland (*n.*); the whole of —, ganz Deutschland.
Gerry (*dim. of* **Gerald**), Gerhard (*m.*).
Gertrude, (Gerty,) Gertrud (*f.*), (Trudchen (*n.*), Trudel (*f.*)).
Gervase, Gervasius (*m.*).
Getae, Geten (*pl.*).
Ghent, Gent (*n.*).
G(h)ibel(l)ine, G(h)ibelline, Waiblinger (*m.*).
Giant's Causeway, Riesendamm (*m.*).
Gibraltar; Straits of —, Straße (*f.*) von Gibraltar.
Giles, Ägidius.
Gill(ian), Julchen (*n.*); every Jack has his Gill, jeder Hans hat seine Grete. *See* **Jill**.
Gipsy, Zigeuner (*m.*).
Girtonian, Studentin von Girton College (*Cambridge ladies' college*).
Gladstone (bag), Reise-Handtasche (*f.*).
Glauber's salt, Glaubersalz (*n.*).
Goddard, Gotthard (*m.*).
Godfrey, Gottfried (*m.*).
Goethean, goethesch (*adj.*).
Golgotha, Golgatha (*n.*).
Good Hope; Cape of — —, Kap (*m.*) der guten Hoffnung.
Gordian, gordisch (*adj.*); to cut the — knot, den gordischen Knoten durchhauen.
Gorgon, Gorgone (*f.*).
Goshen; in the land of —, im Lande Gosen.
Goth, Gote (*m.*); Barbar, roher Mensch (*fig.*); East —, Ostgote (*m.*). **—ic**, gotisch (*adj.*); —ic letters, Frakturschrift (*f.*); —ic people, Gotenvolk (*n.*), Goten (*pl.*).
Gotham, Abdera, Krähwinkel (*n.*). **—ite** *or* **Wise man of —**, Abderit, Krähwinkler, Schildbürger.
Gothard; the St. —, der Sankt Gotthard-Tunnel oder -Paß.
Gracchi, Gracchen (*pl.*).
Grac—e, —ie, Gratia (*f.*); the —es, die drei Grazien (*pl.*).
Grail; the Holy —, der Heilige Gral; Knight of the Holy —, Gralsritter (*m.*); legend of the Holy —, Gralsage (*f.*).
Grain Coast, Pfefferküste (*f.*).
Grecian, *see* Greek.
Greece, Griechenland (*n.*).
Greek, Grieche (*m.*); Griechin (*f.*); griechisch (*adj.*); der Hellenist; ancient —, altgriechisch (*adj.*); a —, ein Grieche; that is — to me, das sind mir böhmische Dörfer, das kommt mir spanisch vor.
Greenland, Grönland (*n.*). **—er**, der Grönländer.
Gregor—y, Gregor, Gregorius (*m.*). **—ian**, gregorianisch (*adj.*).
Grimalkin, alte Katze (*f.*).
Grimm's law, das Gesetz der (germanischen und hochdeutschen) Lautverschiebung (*f.*).
Griselda, Griseldis (*f.*).
Grison, Graubündner (*m.*); Graubündnerin (*f.*); graubündnerisch (*adj.*). **—s**, Graubünden (*pl.*).
Grissel, Grizel (*dim. of* **Griselda**), Griseldis (*f.*)
Grub Street, früherer Name der Milton Street in London, in welcher arme Schriftsteller zu wohnen pflegten.
Grundy; what will Mrs. — say? was wird Tante Anstand (*or* die Welt) sagen?

Guadalquivir R., Guadalquivir (*m.*).
Guelders, Guelderland, Geldern (*n.*).
Guelph, Welfe (*m.*). **—ic**, welfisch, Welfen= (*adj.*).
Gueux, Geusen (*pl.*).
Guinea; — fowl, — hen, Perlhuhn (*n.*); — pepper, spanischer Pfeffer; — pig, Meerschweinchen.
Gulf Stream, Golfstrom (*m.*).
Gunther, Günther (*m.*).
Gunther's chain, Gunthersche Maßkette.
Gus(sie), *for* **Augustus, Augusta**, Gustel.
Guy, Veit, Guido (*m.*).
Gwalia, *for* **Wales**.

H

Hades, Hades (*m.*), Unterwelt (*f.*).
Haff, Haff (*n.*).
Hague; the —, der Haag.
Hainault, Hennegau (*m.*).
Hal (*dim. of* **Henry**), Heinz, Heini (*m.*).
Hamelin, Hameln (*n.*); Pied Piper of —, Rattenfänger (*m.*) von Hameln.
Hanover, Hannover (*n.*). **—ian**, Hannoveraner (*m.*); Hannoveranerin (*f.*); hannöversch, hannoversch (*adj.*) (*the latter form is spoken and written in the town of Hanover itself*).
Hansard, Hanseat (*m.*).
Hanse, (**Hansa**,) Hanse, Hansa (*f.*); — towns, Hansestädte (*pl.*). **—atic**, hansisch *or* hanseatisch (*adj.*); —atic League, Hansebund (*m.*).
Hapsburg, Habsburg (*m.*); the **—s**, die Habsburger.
Harriet (*dim. of* **Henrietta**), Jettchen (*n.*), Jette (*f.*).
Harrovian, Harrow betreffend, zu Harrow gehörig (*adj.*); Schüler (*m.*) von Harrow School.
Harry (*for* **Henry**), Heinz, Heini; Old —, der Teufel.
Hartz Mts., Harzgebirge (*n.*), Harz (*m.*).
Hatty (*dim of* **Henrietta**), Jettchen (*n.*).
Havana, Havanna, (*city*) Havanna; Havannazigarre (*f.*).
Havel R., Havel (*f.*).
Hebrai—c, hebräisch (*adj.*). **—sm**, hebräische Spracheigentümlichkeit. **—st**, Kenner (*m.*) des Hebräischen.
Hebrew, Hebräer (*m.*); Hebräisch (*n.*); hebräisch (*adj.*); — Jew, Stockjude, Erzjude (*m.*).
Hebrid—es, Hebriden (*pl.*). **—ian, —ean**, hebridisch (*adj.*).
Hector, Hektor (*m.*).
Hed—da, —dy, —wig, Hedwig (*f.*); Hedchen (*n.*), Hedde (*f.*) (*dim.*).
Hegelian, hegelsch (*adj.*); Hegelianer (*m.*); — philosophy, Hegelsche Philosophie.
Hegira, Hedschra (*f.*).
Helen(a), Helene (*f.*); Lenchen (*m.*) (*dim.*); — of Troy, die schöne Helena, Helena (*f.*) aus Griechenland.
Heligoland, Helgoland (*n.*).
Helleni—c, hellenisch (*adj.*). **—sm**, der Hellenismus, das Hellenentum. **—st**, der Hellenist, Kenner des Hellenentums. **—stic**, *adj.* hellenistisch. **—ze**, *v.a.* hellenisieren.
Hellespont, Hellespont (*m.*).
Helvet—ia, Helvetien (*n.*), die Schweiz (*f.*). **—ic**, helvetisch, schweizerisch (*adj.*); —ic Confederation, Eidgenossenschaft (*f.*), Schweizerbund (*m.*).
Henrietta (*dim.* **Henny**), Henriette, (Jette (*f.*), Jettchen (*n.*)).
Henry, Heinrich; — the Fowler, Heinrich der Finkler *or* der Vogelsteller († *936*); — the Navigator, Heinrich der Seefahrer.
Heraclitus, Heraklit (*m.*).
Hercule—s, Herkules (*m.*); Pillars of —s, Säulen (*pl.*) des Herkules. **—an**, herkulisch (*adj.*).
Hercynian Forest, herzynischer Wald, mitteldeutsches Waldgebirge (vom Rhein bis zu den Karpathen).
Herman, Hermann (*m.*).
Hermione, Hermine (*f.*); Minchen (*n.*) (*dim.*).
Herod, Herodes (*m.*); —ian disease, Läusekrankheit (*f.*); to out- — —, alles überbieten, Wagner überwagnern.
Hesper, *usually* **—us**, Hesperus (*m.*), der Abendstern. **—ian**, *adj.* hesperisch. **—ides**, Hesperiden (*pl.*).
Hess—e, Hessen (*n.*). **—ian**, Hesse (*m.*), hessisch (*adj.*); —ian boots, über die Hosen getragene Stiefel, Kurierstiefel, Schaftstiefel (*pl.*).
Hest(h)er, Hetty, *for* **Esther**, Esther.
Hetty (*dim. of* **Henrietta**), Jettchen (*n.*).
Hezekiah, Hiskia(s) (*m.*).
Hiberni—a, Irland, Hibernien (*n.*). **—an**, Irländer (*m.*); Irländerin (*f.*); irländisch, irisch (*adj.*). **—cism**, irländische Spracheigenheit (*f.*).
Highland—er, Bergschotte (*m*). **—s**, Hochlande (*pl.*); das schottische Hochland.
Hilary, Hilarius (*m.*); — term, Quartal (*n.*) von etwa Mitte Januar bis Mitte März (*Oxford Univ.*); einer der vier englischen Gerichtstermine (*11-31 January*).
Hilda, Hilde (*f.*).
Hindoo, Hindu, Hindu (*m.f.*).
Hindustan, Hindustan (*n.*), (Vorderindien (*n.*)). **—i**, hindustanisch (*adj.*); Hindi (*n.*).
Hob(by), *dim. of* **Robert**.
Hobson's choice, keine Wahl (*f.*), Zwang (*m.*); he gave us — —, er ließ uns keine Wahl *or* freie Hand.
Hock, Hochheimer Rheinwein.
Hodge; Farmer —, biedrer Landmann (*m.*).
Hodge, Hodgkin, *for* **Roger**.
Holland, Holland (*n.*); brown —, ungebleichte Leinwand.
Holsatia, Holstein (*n.*). **—n**, der Holsteiner; Holste (*m.*) (*high style*).
Honour, Honoria (*f.*).
Hora—ce, Horaz (*m.*). **—tian**, horazisch (*adj.*).
Horatii, Horatier (*pl.*).
Hospital(l)er, Hospitaliter, Johanniter (*m.*).
Hottentot, Hottentott(e) (*m.*); Hottentottin (*f.*).
Howleglass, (Till) Eulenspiegel (*m.*).
Hudibrastic, satirisch, knittelversartig (*adj.*).
Hugh, Hugo, Hugo (*m.*).
Huguenot, Hugenott(e) (*m.*); Hugenottin (*f.*).
Humber R., Humber (*m.*).
Humphrey, Humfried (*m.*).
Hun, Hunne (*m.*); Hunnin (*f.*). **—, —nic**, hunnisch (*adj.*).
Hundsruck, Hundsrück (*m.*).
Hungar—y, Ungarn (*n.*). **—ian**, Ungar (*m.*); Ungarin (*f.*); ungarisch (*adj.*).
Huron, Hurone (*m.*). **—ian**, huronisch (*adj.*).
Hussite, Hussit (*m.*); — war, der Hussitenkrieg (*1419-34*).
Hyades, (*daughters of Atlas*) die Hyaden (*pl.*).

I

Iberia, Iberien, Spanien (*n.*). **—n**, Iberer (*m.*); iberisch (*adj.*); —n Peninsula, Pyrenäische Halbinsel.
Icarian, ikarisch; abenteuerlich (*adj.*) (*fig.*).
Iceland, Island (*n.*); — spar, — crystal, isländischer Doppelspat (*m.*). **—er**, Isländer (*m.*); Isländerin (*f.*). **—ic**, isländisch (*adj.*).
Ignatius, Ignatius, Ignaz, Nazi (*m.*) (*dim.*).
Iliad, Ilias, Iliade (*f.*).
Ill R., Ill (*f.*).
Iller R., Iller (*f.*).
Illyrian, Illyrier (*m.*); illyrisch (*adj.*); — Alps, Illyrische Alpen (*pl.*).
Ilm R., Ilm (*f.*).
Inca, Inka (*m.*).
India, (Ost)Indien (*n.*); — House, das alte Geschäftshaus der ostindischen Gesellschaft in London; —man, (Ost)Indienfahrer (*m.*); — paper, Chinesisches Papier (*n.*); —-rubber, (Radier)gummi (*n.*); Kautschuk (*m.*); East- — Company,

Ostindische Gesellschaft (*f.*); East- —man, Ostindienfahrer (*m.*); Further —, Hinterindien (*n.*).
Indian, (*American red*) Indianer (*m.*), Indianerin (*f.*), indianisch (*adj.*); (*Asiatic*) Inder, Indier (*m.*), Inderin, Indierin (*f.*); indisch (*adj.*); — bark, Kaskarillrinde (*f.*); — corn, Mais, türkischer Weizen (*m.*); — file, Gänsemarsch, Rottenmarsch (*m.*); — ink, chinesische Tusche (*f.*); — meal, Maismehl (*n.*); — summer, Nachsommer (*m.*), Spätsommer (*m.*).
Indies; East —, Ostindien (*n.*); West —, Westindien (*n.*); in the West —, in Westindien.
Indo; —-China, Hinterindien (*n.*); —-Chinese, hinterindisch (*adj.*); —-European, **indoeuropäisch** (*adj.*); —-Germanic, **indogermanisch** (*adj.*).
Indus R., Indus (*m.*).
Inn, Inn (*m.*).
Innocent, Innocenz (*m.*).
Ionian, Ionic, ionisch (*adj.*); Ionier (*m.*); — Sea, ionisches Meer.
Ireland, Irland (*n.*).
Irish, irisch, irländisch, ersisch (*adj.*); Irländer, Iren (*pl.*); irische Sprache (*f.*); she is —, sie ist eine Irin *or* Irländerin; — bull, witzige, komisch klingende Bemerkung, die einen Widersinn enthält oder in der zwei Metaphern vermischt werden; — stew, gedämpftes Fleisch mit Kartoffeln und Zwiebeln. **—ism**, irländische Spracheigenheit (*f.*). **—man**, Irländer (*m.*). **—woman**, Irländerin (*f.*). **—ry**, irländisches Volk (*n.*) (*coll.*).
Iroquois, Irokese (*m.*); irokesisch (*adj.*).
Isaac, Isaak (*m.*).
Isabel(la), Isabelle (*f.*).
Isaiah, Jesaias (*m.*).
Isar R., Isar (*f.*).
Iscariot, Ischarioth (*m.*).
Isengrim, Isegrim (*m.*) (**Wolf in der Tierfabel**).
Ishmael, Ismael (*m.*). **—ite**, Ismaelit (*m.*).
Isidore, Isidor (*m.*).
Islam, Islam (*m.*). **—ism**, Islamismus (*m.*). **—itic**, islamitisch (*adj.*).
Israelit—e, Israelit (*m.*); Israelitin (*f.*). **—ic**, israelitisch (*adj.*).
Italian, Italiener (*m.*); Italienerin (*f.*); italienisch (*adj.*); das Italienische; — warehouseman, Materialwarenhändler (*m.*).
Italic, italisch (*adj.*). **—s**, — characters, Kursivschrift (*f.*), Kursivdruck (*m.*). **—ize**, *v.a.* in Kursivschrift schreiben *or* drucken; —ized, kursiv (*adj.*) (gedruckt).
Italy, Italien (*n.*); North —, Oberitalien (*n.*).

J

Jack(y), *for* **James** (**Jacobus**).
Jack, Hans; Bube, Scherwenzel (*m.*) (*Cards*); — Frost, Winter (*m.*); künstlicher Reif als Schmuck des Weihnachtsbaums; — in the box, Schachtelmännchen (*n.*); — and Jill, Hans und Grete; — Ketch, Meister Hämmerlein, Henker (*m.*); — of all trades, Hans Dampf in allen Gassen; Tausendkünstler (*m.*); — of all work, Factotum (*n.*), Scherwenzel (*m.*); — o' lantern, Irrlicht (*n.*); — Pudding, Hanswurst, Kasperle (*m.*); — Rake, Hans Liederlich (*m.*); — Sauce, Naseweis (*m.*); — Sprat, Dreikäsehoch (*m.*); — Straw, nichtiger Mensch (*m.*); — tar, Matrose (*m.*), Teerjacke (*f.*); before you could say — Robinson, im Umsehn, im Handumdrehn (*n.*); yellow —, gelbes Fieber (*n.*); all work and no play makes — a dull boy, immer daran verdirbt am Ende Roß und Mann (*prov.*); Union —, brittische Nationalflagge (*f.*). **—anapes**, Naseweis (*m.*); Schelm (*m.*). **—ass**, männlicher Esel; Dummkopf (*m.*). **—boots**, hohe Stiefel, Wasserstiefel (*m.*); Kanonenstiefel (*m.*). **—daw**, Dohle (*f.*). **—knife**, großes Klappmesser.
Jacob, Jakob (*m.*); —'s ladder, Jakobsleiter (*f.*). **—ean**, unter der Regierung Jakobs des Ersten geschehen *or* gemacht (*adj.*). **—in**, Jakobiner (*m.*). **—ine**, Jakobine (*f.*). **—ite**, Jakobit (*m.*); jakobitisch (*adj.*). **—itism**, Grundsätze *or* Wesen der Jakobiten (*pl.*).
Jamaica, Jamaika (*n.*). **—n**, jamaikanisch (*adj.*); Bewohner von Jamaika (*m.*).
James, Jakob (*m.*).
Jane, Johanna, Johanne (*f.*); **Hanne** (*f.*), Hannchen (*n.*) (*dim.*).
January, Januar (*m.*).
Japan, Japan (*n.*); japanisch (*adj.*). **—ese**, Japaner (*m.*); Japanerin (*f.*); the —ese (*coll.* the Japs), die Japaner, (*pl.*) japanisch (*adj.*); Japanisch (*n.*), japanische Sprache (*f.*); —ese paper, Büttenpapier (*n.*).
Jarvey, Jarvis, Gervasius (*m.*).
Jaspar, Kasp—ar, —er (*m.*); **Kasperle** (*m.*) (*dim.*).
Java, Java (*n.*). **—nese**, Javane (*m.*), Java-n(er)in (*f.*); Javaner (*pl.*).
Jeames, der Bediente.
Jeff(ery), Gottfried (*m.*).
Jehoshaphat, Josaphat (*m.*).
Jehovah, Jehova (*m.*).
Jehu, Jehu, Wagenlenker (*m.*); **Droschkenkutscher** (*m.*) (*sl.*).
Jem(my) (*dim. of* **James**), Jaköbchen (*n.*).
Jena; inhabitant of —, Jenenser (*m.*).
Jenny (*dim. of* **Jane**), Hannchen (*n.*).
Jeremia—h, Jeremias (*m.*). **—d**, **Jeremiade** (*f.*), Klagelied (*n.*).
Jeremy, *for* **Jeremiah**, Jeremias.
Jericho; to go to —, zum Henker *or* ins Pfefferland gehen; to wish s. o. at —, einen auf den Blocksberg wünschen *or* dahin, wo der Pfeffer wächst; tell him to go to —, sage ihm, er solle sich zum Teufel scheren.
Jeroboam, Jerobeam (*m.*).
Jerome, Hieronymus (*m.*).
Jerry, kleiner Jeremias; — builder, habsüchtiger Bauspekulant; —-built, unsolide *or* zu leicht gebaut (*adj.*); —-sneak, Pantoffelheld (*m.*) (*vulg.*).
Jersey, die Insel Jersey; (*wool*) feines Wollgarn, (*n.*); (*vest*) knapp anliegende wollene Tricotjacke (*f.*).
Jerusalem, Jerusalem (*n.*); — pony, Esel (*m.*).
Jessie, Jessika (*f.*).
Jesuit, Jesuit (*m.*); — convent, Jesuitenkloster (*n.*). **—ical**, (**—ically**), jesuitisch (*adj.*) ((*adv.*)). **—ism, —ry**, Jesuitismus (*m.*); **Verschlagenheit** (*f.*).
Jesus, Jesus (*m.*); in the name of — (Christ), im Namen Jesu (Christi).
Jew, Jude (*m.*); Jüdin (*f.*); —'s harp, Maultrommel (*f.*); Hebrew —, Erzjude (*m.*); Wandering —, der Ewige Jude; as rich as a —, steinreich (*adj.*); — baiting, Judenhetze (*f.*). **—ess**, Jüdin (*f.*). **—dom**, Judentum (*n.*); Judenschaft (*f.*). **—ish**, (**Judaic**,) jüdisch (*adj.*); —ish Christian, Judenchrist (*m.*); —ish slang, Judendeutsch, Judenenglisch (*n.*), Judensprache (*f.*). **—ry**, Judenschaft (*f.*), Judenviertel (*n.*), Judenland (*n.*).
Jezebel, Isebel (*f.*).
Jiddish, *see* **Yiddish**.
Jill, Julchen (*n.*), junges lustiges Mädchen; leichtsinniges Mädchen. *See* **Jack**.
Jim(my), *for* **James**, Jakob.
Jingo, Chauvinist (*m.*); the — party, die politischen Heißsporne, die Säbelraßler, Hurrapatrioten; by —! (*for* by Jove), Donnerwetter! **—ism**, Chauvinismus, Hurrapatriotismus (*m.*).
Jinny (*for* **Jane**), Hannchen (*f.*).
Joan, *see* **Jane**; — of Arc, Jungfrau (*f.*) von Orleans; Pope —, die Päpstin Johanna.
Job, Hiob (*m.*); —'s comforter, Hiobströster (*m.*), schlechter Tröster; —'s patience, Engelsgeduld (*f.*); the Book of —, das Buch Hiob (*B.*).
Jocelin, Jocelyn, Jodokus (*m.*); Jodoka (*f.*).

Joe(y) (*dim. of* **Joseph**), Seppi, Sepperl, Sepp (*m.*); Joe Miller, Meidinger (*m.*).
John, Johann(es), Hans (*m.*), Häns̈chen (*n.*), Hansel, Jan (*m.*); St. —, der heilige Johannes; — a dreams, Hansträumer (*m.*); — the Baptist, Johannes der Täufer; — Bull, der Engländer, das englische Volk; — Chinaman, der Chinese; — Lackland, Johann (*m.*) ohne Land; St. —'s day, Johannisfest (*n.*); Knight of St. —, Johanniter (*m.*).
Johnny (*for* **John**), Hänschen (*n.*); — Crapaud, der Franzose.
Jonah, Jonas, Jonas (*m.*).
Jonathan, Jonathan (*m.*); Brother —, der (Nord) Amerikaner; das Volk der Vereinigten Staaten.
Jordan R., Jordan (*m.*).
Joseph, Joseph (*m.*); Sepperl, Seppi, Sepp (*m.*) (*dim.*). —**a**, Josephe (*f.*); Sephchen (*n.*) (*dim.*).
Joshua, Josua (*m.*).
Josiah, Josias (*m.*).
Jove (*for* **Jupiter**), Jupiter (*m.*); **by —**, beim Zeus! wahrhaftig!
Joyce, Jodokus (*m.*); Jodoka (*f.*).
Judaea, Judea, Judäa (*n.*).
Judah, Juda (*m.*).
Judai—sm, Judaismus (*m.*), Judentum (*n.*). —**ze**, judaisieren.
Judas, Judas, Verräter (*m.*); — Iscariot, Judas Ischariot; — hole, Guckloch (*n.*) in Kerkertüren.
Jude, Juda (*m.*).
Judith, Ju(dy), Judith (*f.*).
Judy, Weib (*n.*) des Punch im Marionettentheater. *See* **Punch**.
Juli—a(na), Julie, (Juliane) (*f.*); Jule (*f.*), Julchen (*n.*) (*dim.*). —**et**, Julchen, Jule; Romeo and —et, Romeo und Julie.
Julian, julianisch (*adj.*); — Alps, Julische Alpen (*pl.*).
July, Juli (*m.*).
June, Juni (*m.*).
Juno-like, junonisch (*adj.*).
Jutland, Jütland (*n.*); of —, (Jutish,) jütisch (*adj.*). —**er**, Jüte, Jütländer (*m.*); Jütin, Jütländerin (*f.*).

K

Kaff—ir, Kaffer (*m.*). —**raria**, Kaffer(n)land (*n.*).
Kamchatca, Kamtschatka (*n.*). —**n**, Kamtschadale (*m.*); Kamtschadalin (*f.*); kamtschadalisch (*adj.*).
Kantian, kantisch (*adj.*); der Kantianer, Anhänger (*m.*) der kantischen Philosophie.
Kate(y) (*dim. of* **Katharine**), Käthchen (*n.*), Käthe, Trine (*f.*).
Katharine, Katherine, Katharine, Kathrine (*f.*).
Kathleen, Kathy, Katie, *see* **Katharine**.
Khalifa, Kalif (*m.*).
Kiev, Kiew (*n.*).
Kirghi—z, —**se**, Kirgise (*m.*). —**se**, kirgisisch (*adj.*).
Kit (*dim. of*) **Christopher**, Töffel.
Kitty (*dim. of* **Kate, Katherine**), Käthchen (*n.*).
Kremlin, Kreml (*m.*).
Kremnitz white, Kremser Weiß (*n.*).
Kurd, Kurde (*m.*), Kurdin (*f.*). —**ish**, kurdisch (*adj.*). —**istan**, Kurdistan (*n.*).

L

Lacedæmon, Lacedämon (*n.*).
Lacedemonia, Lacedämonien (*n.*). —**n**, Lacedämonier (*m.*); lacedämonisch (*adj.*).
Laconi—a, Lakonien (*n.*). —**an**, Lakonier (*m.*); Lakonierin (*f.*). —**c**, lakonisch, wortkarg, knapp (*adj.*).
Lahn R., Lahn (*f.*).
Lambert, Lambert, Lamprecht (*m.*).
Lammas, (Petri) Kettenfeier (*f.*).
Langobard (*see* **Lombard**), Longobarde (*m.*).
Lapland, Lappland (*n.*) —**er**, Lappe, Lappländer (*m.*); Lappländerin (*f.*). —**ish**, lappländisch (*adj.*).
Lateran, Lateran (*m.*); — councils, lateranische Konzilien (*pl.*).
Latin, Latein (*n.*); lateinisch (*adj.*); dog —, Küchenlatein (*n.*); Low —, Vulgärlatein (*n.*). —**ism**, *s.* der Latinismus. —**ity**, *s.* die Latinität. —**ize**, ins Lateinische übertragen *or* übersetzen (*v.a.*); latinisieren (*v.n.*).
Latter-day-Saints, Mormonen (*pl.*).
La(u)nce (*short for* **La(u)ncelot**), Lanzelot (*m.*).
Laurence, Lawrence, Lorenz, St. Lawrence, St. Laurentius (*m.*); St. Lawrence R., Lorenzstrom (*m.*).
Lebanon, Libanon (*m.*).
Lech R., Lech (*m.*).
Leeward Islands, die westlichen *or* kleinen Antillen (*pl.*).
Leghorn, Livorno (*n.*); — **hat**, italienischer Strohhut (*f.*).
Leine R., Leine (*f.*).
Leipsic, Leipzig, Leipzig (*n.*); — **-fair**, Leipziger Messe (*f.*).
Leman (Lake), Genfersee (*m.*).
Lena (*short for* **Helena, Magdalene**), Lene (*f.*), Lenchen (*n.*).
Leonard, Len(nie), Leonhard (*m.*).
Leonora, Lenore (*f.*); Lore (*f.*), Lorchen (*n.*) (*dim.*).
Leopold, Leopold, Liutpold (*m.*).
Lepontine Alps, Lepontische Alpen (*pl.*).
Letitia (Lettie, Lettice), Lätitia (*f.*).
Lett—s, Letten (*pl.*). —**ic**, lettisch (*adj.*).
Levant, Levante (*f.*). —**ine**, levant(in)isch (*adj.*).
Levit—e, Levit (*m.*). —**ical**, levitisch (*adj.*). —**icus**, *s.* das dritte Buch Mosis.
Lewis, Ludwig (*m.*).
Leyden-jar, Leydener *or* elektrische Flasche (*f.*).
Leys, *short for* Wesley's, wesleyanisch (*adj.*).
Libyan, Libyer (*m.*); Libyerin (*f.*); libysch (*adj.*).
Liddy, *for* **Lydia**.
Liège, Lüttich (*n.*).
Ligurian Sea, Ligurisches Meer.
Lilian, Lilias, Lil(y), Lil(l)i (*f.*).
Lilliputian, Liliputer (*m.*); liliput(an)isch, winzig.
Limerick, Vers aus fünf Kurzzeilen (*a a b b a*).
Linnean, *adj.*; — system, Linnésches System.
Lipari Islands, Liparische Inseln (*pl.*).
Lippe R., Lippe (*f.*); belonging to the Count of —, lippisch (*adj.*).
Lisbon, Lissabon (*n.*).
Lithuania, Litauen (*n.*). —**n**, Litauer (*m.*); Litauerin (*f.*); litauisch (*adj.*).
Livonia, Livland (*n.*). —**n**, Livländer (*m.*); Livländerin (*f.*); livländisch (*adj.*).
Livy, Livius (*m.*).
Liz(zie) (*dim. of* **Elizabeth**), Lieschen, Liesel (*n.*), Liese, Li (*f.*).
Lloyd's, Zimmer (*n.*) in der Königl. Börse zu London, wo alle den Seeverkehr betreffenden Angelegenheiten verhandelt werden.
Lofoden Islands, Lofoten (*pl.*).
Loire R., Loire (*f.*).
Lollard—s, Lollarden (*pl.*). —**y**, *s.* das Lollardentum.
Lombard, Lombarde (*m.*); Lombardin (*f.*). —, —**ic**, lombardisch (*adj.*). —**y**, die Lombardei (*f.*).
London, London (*n.*); londonisch, Londoner (*adj.*); — train, Londoner Zug, Zug (*m.*) von *or* nach London; — pride, Porzellanblümchen (*n.*), Schatten-Steinbrech (*m.*).
Loo, *for* **Louisa**.
Lora (*dim. of* **Leonora**), Lore (*f.*), Lorchen (*n.*).
Loreley, Lorelei (*f.*).
Lorraine, Lothringen (*n.*); men of —, Lothringer (*pl.*); lothringisch, Lothringer (*adj.*).
Lothario, Lothar (*m.*); gay —, Frauenjäger (*m.*).
Lothringian, Lothringer (*m.*); lothringisch (*adj.*).
Lottie (*dim. of* **Charlotte**), Lottchen (*n.*), Lotti (*f.*).
Lou(ie), *for* **Louisa**.
Louis, Ludwig (*m.*).

Louisa, Luise (*f.*).
Louvain, Löwen (*n.*).
Low Countries, Niederlande (*pl.*).
Lowlands, die Niederlande (*usually poet.*).
Lubberland, Schlaraffenland (*n.*).
Lubeck, Lübeck (*n.*); lübisch, Lübecker (*adj.*).
Lucas, Lukas (*m.*).
Lucchese, Bewohner (*m.*) von Lucca, aus Lucca.
Lucerne, (*town*) Luzern (*n.*); inhabitant of —, Luzerner (*m.*); lake of —, Vierwaldstättersee (*m.*).
Lucifer, Lucifer, Satan (*m.*); Morgenstern (*m.*); — match, Streichholz, Zündhölzchen (*n.*).
Lucrece, Lucretia, Lukrezia (*f.*).
Lucreti—an, auf den Dichter Lucretius *or* Lukrez bezüglich (*adj.*). **—us**, Lucretius, Lukrez (*m.*).
Lucy, Luc(i)e, Lucie, Luzie (*f.*).
Luke, Lukas (*m.*); St. —, der heilige Lukas.
Lusatia, Lausitz (*f.*). **—n**, Lausitzer (*m.*); Lausitzerin (*f.*); lausitzisch (*adj.*).
Lusitania (Portugal), Lusitanien, Portugal (*n.*). **—n**, lusitanisch, portugiesisch (*adj.*).
Lutheran, lutherisch (*adj.*); Lutheraner (*m.*). **—ism**, Luthertum (*n.*).
Luxembourg, Luxemburg (*n.*); luxemburgisch (*adj.*); inhabitant of —, Luxemburger (*m.*).
Lycurgus, Lykurg (*m.*).
Lydia, (*person*) Lydia (*f.*); (*country*) Lydien (*n.*). **—n**, lydisch (*adj.*); Lydier (*m.*).
Lyons, Lyon (*n.*).

M

Maccabees, Makkabäer (*pl.*).
Macedonia, Macedonien (*n.*). **—n**, Macedonier (*m.*); macedonisch (*adj.*).
Machiavellian, machiavelli(sti)sch (*adj.*).
Madagascan, *see* **Malagasy**.
Maddie, Madeline, Madge (*dim. of* **Magdalene**), Magda (*f.*).
Madge (*dim. of* **Margaret**), Gretchen (*n.*).
Mæcenas, Mäcen (*m.*).
Maelstrom, Mahlstrom (*m.*), Strudel (*m.*).
Magdalen(e), Magdalene (*f.*); Lene (*f.*), Lenchen (*n.*) (*dim.*); die reuige Sünderin (*fig.*).
Mag(gie) (*dim. of* **Margaret**), Gretchen (*n.*).
Magi, Magier (*pl.*).
Mahomet, Muhammed, Mohammed (*m.*). **—an**, Mohammedan, Mohammedaner (*m.*); Mohammedanerin (*f.*); mohammedanisch (*adj.*).
Mahratta States, Mahrattenstaaten (*pl.*).
Main R., Main (*m.*); on the —, am Main.
Malacca, Malakka (*n.*).
Malachi, Maleachi (*m.*).
Malagasy, madegassisch (*adj.*); Madegasse (*m.*); Madegassin (*f.*); Madegassisch (*n.*).
Malay, Malaie (*m.*). **—an**, malaiisch (*adj.*); — Archipelago, Malaien-Inseln (*pl.*).
Maldive Islands, Malediven (*pl.*).
Malines (*see* **Mechlin**), Mecheln (*n.*).
Malt—a, Malta (*n.*). **—ese**, Malteser (*m.*); maltesisch (*adj.*); —ese Cross, Malteserkreuz (*n.*); Knight of—a, —ese knight, Malteser(ritter) (*m.*).
Mamaluke, Mameluke, Mameluck (*m.*).
Man, Isle of, die Insel Man.
Manasseh, Manasse (*m.*).
Manchu, (**Manchoo**,) Mandschu (*m.*). **—ria**, die Mandschurei (*f.*). **—rian**; —rian railway, mandschurische Eisenbahn.
Manich—æan, **—ee**, Manichäer (*m.*). **—æan**, manichäisch (*adj.*). **—æism**, Manichäismus (*m.*). **—eeism**, Mänichäertum (*n.*).
Manx, die Insel Man betreffend; der Insel Man gehörig *or* angehörig; die auf Man gesprochene Sprache. **—man**, Bewohner (*m.*) der Insel Man.
Margaret, (**Margery**,) Marg(a)rete (*f.*)(Grete(l), Gret(el)chen (*n.*) (*dim.*)).
Maria, Maria, Marie (*f.*); — Theresa, Maria Theresia (*n.*).
Marian, Marianne (*f.*); marianisch (*adj.*).
Marjory (*see* **Margaret**), Gretchen (*n.*).
Mark, Markus (*m.*).
Marmora; Sea of —, Marmarameer (*n.*).
Marne R., Marne (*f.*).
Marseilles, Marseille (*n.*), Piqué (*n.*); — quilt, Steppdecke (*f.*).
Martha, Marthe (*f.*); Märtchen, Märtel (*n.*) (*dim.*).
Martin; St. —'s summer, Altweibersommer, Spätsommer (*m.*).
Mary, Marie (*f.*); — Ann, Marianne (*f.*), (*servant*) Dienstmädchen (*n.*); Bloody —, die Blutige Maria; Virgin —, die Jungfrau Maria; St. —'s Church, Marienkirche, Frauenkirche (*f.*).
Mastersingers, Meistersänger (*pl.*).
Mat(h)ilda, Mathilde, Mechthild (*f.*); Tilde (*f.*), Tildchen (*n.*).
Matthew, Matthäus (*Rel.*); Matthias, Matthes (*m.*); Matz (*m.*), Mätzchen (*n.*) (*dim.*).
Matthias, (**Matty**,) Matthias, (Hiesel) (*m.*).
Maud (*dim. of* **Matilda**), Tildchen (*n.*), Tilde (*f.*).
Maudlin (*see* **Magdalene**), Lenchen (*n.*).
Maurice, Moritz (*m.*).
Maxim, Maxim (*m.*); — gun, Maximkanone (*f.*).
May (*dim. of* **Mary**), Mariechen, Miechen (*n.*), Mieze (*f.*).
Mayence, Mainz (*n.*).
Mazur, Masure (*m.*); Masurin (*f.*).
Meander R., Mäander (*m.*); — pattern, Mäander, Kettenzug (*m.*).
Mecca, Mekka (*n.*).
Mechlin, Mecheln (*n.*); — lace, Mechelner Spitzen (*pl.*).
Med—e, Meder (*m.*). **—ian**, medisch (*adj.*).
Medici; Venus of —, die mediceische Venus.
Mediterranean (Sea), mittelländisches Meer.
Meg(gy) (*dim. of* **Margaret**), Lenchen (*n.*).
Melancthon, Melanchthon (*m.*).
Melanesia, Melanesien (*n.*) (die westliche Inselgruppe von Ozeanien, von Neuguinea bis Fiji).
Memel R., Memel (*f.*).
Mercury, Merkur (*m.*).
Merovingian, Merowinger (*m.*); merowingisch (*adj.*).
Mersey R., Mersey (*m.*).
Messia—d, Messiade (*f.*). **—h**, Messias (*m.*). **—hship**, Würde (*f.*) *or* Amt (*n.*) des Messias. **—nic**, messianisch (*adj.*).
Meta (*dim. of* **Margaret**), Meta (*f.*).
Methuselah, Methusalem (*m.*); as old as —, steinalt (*adj.*).
Meuse R., Maas (*f.*).
Mexic—o, Mexiko (*n.*). **—an**, Mexikaner (*m.*); Mexikanerin (*f.*); mexikanisch (*adj.*).
Micah, Micha (*m.*).
Michael, Mick(y), Mike, Mich(a)el (*m.*).
Milan, Mailand (*n.*). **—ese**, Mailänder (*m.*); Mailänderin (*f.*); mailändisch (*adj.*).
Milky Way, Milchstraße (*f.*).
Miller; a Joe —, ein Meidinger (*m.*).
Minna, (**Minnie**,) Minna (*f.*)., (Minchen (*n.*)).
Minnesingers, Minnesinger, Minnesänger (*pl.*).
Misnia, Meißen (*n.*). **—n**, Meißner, meißnisch (*adj.*).
Moabit—e, Moabiter (*m.*). **—ish**, moabitisch (*adj.*).
Mocha, Mokka (*n.*).
Mœsogoth, Mösogote (*m.*). **—ic**, mösogotisch (*adj.*).
Mohammed, *see* **Mahomet**. **—an**, Mohammedaner (*m.*); mohammedanisch (*adj.*). **—anism**, Mohammedanismus (*m.*).
Moldavia, die Moldau (*f.*). **—n**, Moldauer (*m.*); moldauisch (*adj.*).
Moll(y), *see* **Mary**.
Moluccas, Molukken (*pl.*).
Mongolia, die Mongolei (*f.*). **—n**, Mongole (*m.*); Mongolin (*f.*); mongolisch (*adj.*).
Montenegrin, Montenegriner (*m.*); montenegrinisch (*adj.*).

Moor, Maure, Berber (*m.*); **Mohr** (*m.*). **—ish**, maurisch (*adj.*).
Moravia, Mähren (*n.*). **—n**, Mähre (*m.*); (*member of —n sect*) Herrnhuter, mährischer Bruder (*m.*); mährisch (*adj.*); —n Brethren, Herrnhuter (*pl.*). **—nism**, Herrnhutertum (*n.*).
Moresque, maurisch, moresk, arabeskisch (*adj.*).
Mormon, Mormone (*m.*); Mormonin (*f.*); mormonisch (*adj.*). **—ism**, Mormonentum (*n.*).
Morocc—o, Marokko (*n.*); —o leather, Marokkoleder, Saffian (*m.*). **—an**, Marokkaner (*m.*); marokkanisch (*adj.*).
Morris, *see* **Maurice**.
Morse code, Morsesches Zeichenalphabet.
Mosaic(**al**), mosaisch (*adj.*).
Moscow, Moskau (*n.*).
Moselle R., Mosel (*f.*).
Moslem, *see* **Mussulman**.
Mother; — Carey's chicken, Sturmschwalbe (*f.*), Petersvogel (*m.*); — Carey is plucking her geese, es schneit (*sailors' sl.*); — Goose, angebliche Verfasserin von Kinderreimen.
Mudie, (*—'s Library*) Londons größte Leihbibliothek.
Mulatt—o, Mulatte (*m.*). **—ress**, Mulattin (*f.*).
Munich, München (*n.*); Münchener (*adj.*).
Muscov—y, (*obs.*) Fürstentum Moskovien (*n.*), (*now in a wider sense*) Rußland (*n.*); —y duck, türkische Ente (*f.*). **—ite**, Moskowit(er), Russe (*m.*); Moskowitin, Russin (*f.*); moskowitisch (*adj.*).
Mussulman, Muselmann (*m.*); Muselmännin (*f.*); muselmännisch (*adj.*).
Mycen—æ, **—e**, Myzen (*n.*). **—æan**, myzenisch, mykenisch (*adj.*).

N

Nan, **Nancy**, **Nannie**, Anne (*f.*), Ännchen, Annchen (*n.*); Miss Nancy, Muttersöhnchen (*n.*).
Naples, Neapel (*n.*).
Nathaniel, **Nat**(**ty**), Nathanael (*m.*).
Navigator Islands, Schifferinseln (*pl.*).
Nawab, Nabob (*m.*).
Nazar—ene, Nazaräer, Nazarener (*m*); nazarenisch (*adj.*). **—ite**, Nasiräer (*m.*).
Neapolitan, Neapolitaner (*m.*); Neapolitanerin (*f.*); neapolitanisch (*adj.*).
Nebuchadnezzar, Nebukadnezar (*m.*).
Neckar R., Neckar (*m.*).
Ned(**dy**) (*dim. of* **Edward**), Edu (*m.*); (*pet name for a donkey*) Grauchen (*n.*).
Negr—o, Neger (*m.*). **—ess**, Negerin (*f.*).
Nehemiah, Nehemia (*m.*).
Nell(**ie**) (*dim. of* **Helen**), Lenchen (*n.*), Lene (*f.*).
Nemean, nemeisch (*adj.*).
Neo-Latin nations, Neulateiner, Romanen (*pl.*).
Neptun—e, Neptun (*m.*). **—ian**, neptunisch (*adj.*).
Nervii, Nervier (*pl.*).
Netherland—s, Niederlande (*pl.*). **—ish**, niederländisch (*adj.*).
Newcastle; to carry coals to —, **Wasser** (*n.*) **ins Meer** (*or* **Eulen** (*pl.*) **nach Athen**) **tragen**.
New England, Neuengland (*n.*).
Newfoundland, Neufundland (*n.*); (*dog*) Neufundländer(hund) (*m.*).
New South Wales, Neusüdwales (*n.*).
New York, Neu-York (*n.*).
New Zealand, Neuseeland (*n.*); **neuseeländisch** (*adj.*). **— —er**, Neuseeländer (*m.*).
Newnhamite, Studentin (*f.*) von Newnham College (*Camb. ladies' college*) (*Univ. sl.*).
Nibelung, Nibelung (*f.*); Song *or* Lay of the —s, Nibelungenlied (*n.*); treasure of the —s, Nibelungenhort (*m.*).
Nice, Nizza (*n.*). **—a**, Nicäa, Nikäa (*n.*). **—ne**, nicäisch, nikäisch (*adj.*); —ne creed, nicäisches *or* nikäisches Glaubensbekenntnis (*n.*).
Nicholas, (**Nick**,) Nikola(u)s, (Kla(u)s) (*m.*); St. —, Santa Klaus, der Weihnachtsmann; Old Nick, der Teufel (*m.*).
Niger R., Niger (*m.*). **—ia**, Nigerien (*n.*).
Nigritia, Negerland (*n.*).
Nil—e R., Nil(strom) (*m.*). **—e-bird**, **Ibis(vogel)** (*m.*). **—ometer**, Nilmesser (*m.*).
Nimeguen, Nimwegen (*n.*).
Nineveh, Ninive (*n.*).
Noll, *dim. of* **Oliver**.
Nonconformist, ein nicht der englischen Hochkirche angehöriger englischer Protestant, protestantischer Sektirer; nonkonformistisch (*adj.*).
Nora (*dim. of* **Leonora**), Nora, Lore (*f.*).
Norman, Normanne (*m.*); Normannin (*f.*); normannisch (*adj.*). **—dy**, Normandie (*f.*)
Norse, nordisch (*adj.*); Old —, altnordisch (*adj.*); original —, urnordisch. **—man**, Nordmann, alter Skandinavier, Wiking (*m.*).
North; — Cape, Nordkap (*n.*); — Sea, Nordsee (*f.*). **—man**, Nordmann, Wiking (*m.*).
Norw—ay, Norwegen (*n.*); —ay spruce fir, Edeltanne (*f.*). **—egian**, Norweger (*m.*); Norwegerin (*f.*); norwegisch (*adj.*).
Nova; — **Scotia**, Neuschottland (*n.*). — **Zembla**, die Insel Nowaja Semlja.
Nubian, Nubier (*m.*); nubisch (*adj.*).
Number Nip, Rübezahl (*but see the note on* Rübezahl *on p. 782 of Part I.*).
Numidian, Numidier (*m.*); **numidisch** (*adj.*); — crane, Jungfernkranich (*m.*).
Nuremberg, Nürnberg (*n.*).

O

Obadiah, Obadja, Obadias (*m.*).
Oceania, Ozeanien (*i. e.* **Polynesien und Melanesien** zusammen).
Oder R., Oder (*f.*); on the —, **an der Oder**.
Odoacer, Odovakar, Odoakar (*m.*).
Odyssey, Odyssee (*f.*).
Olives; Mt. of —, **Olivet**, Ölberg (*m.*).
Olymp—iad, Olympiade (*f.*). **—ian**, **Olympier** (*m.*), (**—ic**,) olympisch (*adj.*). **—ics**, **die olympischen Spiele**. **—us**, Olymp (*m.*).
Orange, Oranien (*n.*); Prince of —, **Prinz** (*m.*) von Oranien; — Free State, Orange-Freistaat (*m.*), *now* Orangefluß-Kolonie (*f.*); — R., Orangefluß (*m.*). **—ism**, **die Oranierpartei**. **—man**, irländischer Protestant, Orangist (*m.*).
Orcades, *see* **Orkney Islands**.
Orestes, Orest (*m.*).
Orinoco R., Orinoko (*m.*).
Orkney Islands, Orkney-Inseln (*pl.*).
Orlando, Roland (*m.*).
Orleans, Maid of, Jungfrau (*f.*) **von Orleans**.
Orph—ean, **—ic**, orphisch (*adj.*).
Oscar, Oskar (*m.*).
Ostend, Ostende (*n.*).
Ostrogoth, Ostgote (*m.*). **—ic**, **ostgotisch** (*adj.*).
Otho, **Otto**, Otto (*m.*); the emperors —, **die** Ottonen (*936-1002*).
Otranto Channel, Straße (*f.*) **von Otranto**.
Ottilia, Ottilie (*m.*).
Ottoman, Ottomane (*m.*); **ottomanisch** (*adj.*).
Owlglass, *see* **Howleglass**.
Oxbridge, *see* **Camford**.
Oxon(**ian**), Oxforder (*m.*); **Oxforder**, **oxfordisch** (*adj.*); the Oxonians, **die Oxforder Studenten**.

P

Pacific Ocean, **Stiller** *or* **Großer Ozean**.
Paddy (*dim. of* **Patrick**), (*Irishman*) **Irländer** (*m.*); —'s land, Irland (*n.*).
Palatinate, Pfalz (*f.*); Pfalzgrafschaft (*f.*); Upper —, Oberpfalz (*f.*); Rhenish —, Rheinpfalz (*f.*).
Palatine, pfälzisch, zur (Rhein-)Pfalz **gehörig** (*adj.*); County —, Pfalz(grafschaft) (*f.*); Count —, Pfalzgraf (*m.*); Countess —, Pfalzgräfin (*f.*); Elector —, Kurfürst (*m.*) **von der Pfalz**.
Palestin—e, Palästina (*n.*). **—ian**, **palästinisch** (*adj.*).

Palsgrav—e, Pfalzgraf (*m.*). **—ine**, Pfalzgräfin (*f.*).
Pan, Pan (*m.*); —'s pipes, —dean pipes, die Pansflöte, Panspfeife (*f.*).
Panslavi—c, panslavisch (*adj.*). **—sm**, Panslavismus (*m.*).
Papal States, Kirchenstaat (*m.*).
Parcae, Parzen, Schicksalsgöttinnen (*pl.*).
Parian, parisch (*adj.*).
Paris, (*city*) Paris (*n.*). **—ian**, Pariser (*m.*); Pariserin (*f.*); parisisch (*adj.*); plaster of —, Stuck, Gipsmörtel (*m.*). **—ienne**, Pariserin (*f.*).
Parmesan, Parmesaner (*m.*), parmesanisch (*adj.*); — cheese, Parmesankäse (*m.*).
Parnass—us, Parnaß (*m.*). **—ian**, parnassisch (*adj.*).
Parsee, Parse (*m.*). **—ism**, Parsentum (*n.*).
Parthian, Parther (*m.*); parthisch (*adj.*); — arrow *or* shaft, Partherpfeil (*m.*).
Partlett; Dame —, (Frau) Kratzefuß (*f.*) (die Henne in der Tiersage).
Pat (*dim. of* **Paddy**), Patrick (*m.*).
Patrick, Patricius (*m.*).
Patsy, **Patty** (*dim. of* **Martha**), Märtchen (*n.*).
Paul, Paul(us) (*m.*); — Pry, Hans Dampf in allen Gassen; St. —, der heilige Paulus; St. Paul's (cathedral), Paulskirche (*f.*). **—ina**, Pauline (*f.*). **—ine**, paulinisch (*adj.*).
Paynim, Heidentum (*n.*); Heide (*m.*); Heidin (*f.*); heidnisch (*adj.*) (*high style*).
Pegasus, Pegasus (*m.*); Musenroß (*n.*).
Peg(gy), **Peggoty** (*dim. of* **Margaret**), Gretchen, Gretel(chen) (*n.*).
Pegnitz R., Pegnitz (*f.*).
Pehlevi, Pali (*n.*).
Pekin, Peking (*n.*).
Pelagian, pelagianisch (*adj.*); Pelagianer (*m.*).
Pelasgi(ans), Pelasger (*pl.*).
Peloponnes—e, **—us**, Peloponnes (*m.*).
Penniless; Miss —, Jungfer (*f.*) Habenichts, Fräulein (*n.*) von Habenichts.
Percival, Parzival (*m.*).
Peregrine, Peregrinus (*m.*).
Pericles, Perikles (*m.*).
Perkin (*dim. of* **Peter**) Peterchen, Peterle (*n.*).
Pernambuco, Fernambuk, Pernambuco (*n.*).
Perry, *see* **Peregrine**.
Persi—an, Perser (*m.*); Perserin (*f.*); Persienne (*f.*) (*C.L.*); die persische Sprache; persisch (*adj.*); —an berries, Avignonkörner (*pl.*); —an wars, Perserkriege (*pl.*). **—c**, persisch (*adj.*).
Pert; Miss —, Jungfer Naseweis (*f.*).
Peruvian, Peruaner (*m.*); Peruanerin (*f.*); peruanisch (*adj.*); — bark, Chinarinde (*f.*).
Peter, Peter (*m.*); Petrus (*m.*); — Grievous, Herr Griesgram, Heulemeier (*m.*); —'s pence, Peterspfennige (*pl.*); Peterspfennig (*m.*) (*collect.*); — the Great, Peter der Große; St. —, der heilige Petrus; St. —'s (Church), Peterskirche (*f.*); to rob — to pay Paul, ein Loch aufreißen um das andere zuzustopfen. **—kin**, Peterchen, Peterle (*n.*).
Petrarch, Petrarca (*m.*).
Phaeacia, Phäakien, Phäakenland (*n.*). **—n**, Phäake (*m.*); phäakisch (*adj.*).
Pharis—ee, Pharisäer (*m.*). **—aical**, pharisäisch (*adj.*). **—aism**, Pharisäertum (*n.*), Scheinheiligkeit (*f.*).
Pharaoh, Pharao (*m.*); —'s chicken, Ägyptischer Geier (*m.*).
Philip, Philipp, (Lips) (*m.*). **—pa**, Philippine (*f.*). **—pians**, Philipper (*pl.*). **—pic**, Standrede, Philippika (*f.*). **—pine Islands**, Philippinen (*pl.*). **—popolis**, Philippopel (*n.*).
Philistine, Philister (*m.*); beschränkter Spießbürger (*fig.*).
Phoci—an, Phokier (*m.*); phokisch (*adj.*). **—s**, Phokis (*n.*).
Phoebe, Phöbe, Luna (*f.*).
Phoenician, Phönizier (*m.*); phönizisch (*adj.*).
Phoenix, der (Vogel) Phönix.
Phrygian, phrygisch (*adj.*); Phrygier (*m.*).
Pict, Pikte (*m.*); —s' Wall, Piktenwall (*m.*). **—ish**, piktisch (*adj.*).
Piedmont, Piemont (*n.*). **—ese**, Piemontese (*m.*); piemontesisch (*adj.*).
Piers Plowman, Peter der Pflüger.
Pilate, Pilatus (*m.*).
Pippin, Pipin (*m.*).
Piraeus, Piräus (*m.*).
Pityusae Isles, Pityusen (*pl.*).
Plataea, Platää (*n.*).
Plate R., (**La Plata**, **Rio Plata**,) Platafluß (*m.*).
Platonist, Platoniker (*m.*).
Pleisse R., Pleiße (*f.*).
Pliny, Plinius (*m.*); — the Elder, der ältere Plinius.
Plutoni—an, plutonisch (*adj.*); Plutonist (*m.*). **—c**, plutonisch (*adj.*). **—sm**, der Plutonismus (*s.*).
Po R., Po (*m.*); the river —, der Po.
Pol—and, Polen (*n.*). **—e**, Pole (*m.*); Polin (*f.*). **—ish**, polnisch (*adj.*). **—onaise**, die Polonaise, der Rundgang, Aufmarsch, polnischer Tanz.
Polar Sea, Eismeer (*n.*).
Poll(y) (*dim. of* **Mary**), Molly (*f.*), M(ar)iechen (*n.*), Mieze (*f.*).
Polony, Bologneser Wurst (*f.*) (*coll.*).
Polycrates, Polykrates (*m.*).
Polynesia, Polynesien (*n.*) (östlich von Melanesien, die östliche Gruppe der ozeanischen Inseln). **—n**, polynesisch (*adj.*).
Pomerania, Pommern (*n.*); Further —, Hinterpommern (*n.*). **—n**, Pommer (*m.*); pommersch (*adj.*); —n dog, Spitz (*m.*).
Pompe—ian, Pompejaner (*m.*); pompejanisch (*adj.*). **—ii**, Pompeji (*n.*). **—y**, Pompejus (*m.*).
Pontine; — Sea, Pontus Euxinus (*m.*), Schwarzes Meer (*n.*); — marshes, pontinische Sümpfe (*pl.*).
Porte; the Sublime —, die Hohe Pforte.
Portug—al, Portugal (*n.*). **—uese**, Portugiese (*m.*); Portugiesin (*f.*); portugiesisch (*adj.*).
Prague, Prag (*n.*).
Pregel R., Pregel (*m.*).
Premonstrant (friar), Prämonstratenser(**mönch**).
Pre-Raphaelite, Präraphaelit (*m.*).
Priam, Priamus, (*poet.*) Priam (*m.*).
Procopius, Prokop (*m.*).
Procrustean bed, Prokrustesbett (*n.*).
Promethean, prometheisch (*adj.*).
Propertius, Properz (*m.*).
Protean, proteisch, proteusartig (*adj.*).
Protestant, Protestant (*m.*); Protestantin (*f.*); protestantisch (*adj.*). **—ism**, Protestantismus (*m.*).
Proven—çal, Provenzale (*m.*); provenzalisch (*adj.*) **—ce**, Provence (*f.*).
Prudence, Prudentia (*m.*).
Prussi—a, Preußen (*n.*). **—an**, Preuße (*m.*); Preußin (*f.*); preußisch (*adj.*); —an blue, Berlinerblau (*n.*). **—ianism**, Preußentum (*n.*), preußisches Wesen. **—c**; —c acid, (Berliner-)blausäure, Blausäure (*f.*).
Pruth R., Pruth (*m.*).
Ptolem—y, Ptolemäus (*m.*). **—ies**, Ptolemäer (*pl.*). **—aic**, ptolemäisch (*adj.*).
Puck, Elf, Kobold, Puck (*m.*).
Pullman car, (Pullmanscher) Salonwagen.
Punch, **—inello**, Kasperle, Polichinell (*m.*); — and Judy, Kasperle und Käthchen (*n.*); — and Judy show, Kasperle-Theater (*n.*).
Puni—an, Punier (*m.*). **—c**, punisch (*adj.*); trügerisch (*adj.*) (*fig.*).
Punjab, **Panjab**, Pandschab (*n.*).
Puritan, Puritaner (*m.*); Puritanerin (*f.*); puritanisch (*adj.*).
Pusey—ism, Puseyismus (*m.*). **—ite**, Anhänger (*m.*) der Lehre Puseys, Puseyit (*m.*).

Puss(y); —-cat, Mieʒ(chen) (*n.*); (*hare*) Lampe (*m.*); —-in-Boots, der Gestiefelte Kater.
Pyrenees, Pyrenäen (*pl.*).
Pyrrhic victory, der Pyrrhussieg.
Pythagorean, pythagoräisch (*adj.*); Pythagoräer (*m.*).
Pyth—ian, pythisch (*adj.*). **—on**, Python (*m.*). **—oness**, Priesterin zu Delphi, Wahrsagerin (*f.*).

Q

Quaker, Quäker (*m.*); Quäkerin (*f.*); — city, Philadelphia (*f.*) (*Amer.*); — oats, Hafermehl (*n.*). **—ism**, Quäkertum (*n.*).
Quentin, Quintin (*n.*).
Quixot—e, (Don) Quichotte (*m.*). **—ic**, donquichotisch; übertrieben ritterlich (*adj.*). **—ism**, Donquichotterie (*f.*); übertrieben ritterliches Gefühl (*n.*).

R

Rachel, Rahel (*f.*).
Rafe, *see* **Ralph**.
Rajpoot, Radschput (*m.*).
Ralph, Raphe, Rudolf, Rudi (*m.*).
Ratisbon, Regensburg (*n.*).
Ravenna, (*battle*) Schlacht bei Ravenna (*f.*); Rabenschlacht (*f.*) (*poet.*).
Raym—ond, —und, Raimund (*m.*).
Rebecca, Rebekka (*f.*).
Red Riding Hood (Little), Rotkäppchen (*n.*).
Red Sea, Rotes Meer.
Redskins, Rothäute (*pl.*).
Reformist, (*Calvinist*) Reformierte (*m.*).
Regen R., Regen (*m.*).
Reginald, Reggie, Reinhold, Reinwald (*m.*).
Rehoboam, Rehabeam (*m.*).
Reuben, Ruben (*m.*).
Reuss R., Reuß (*f.*).
Reynard, Reinhard (*m.*); — the Fox, Reineke Fuchs (*m.*).
Reynold, *see* **Reginald**.
Rhenish, rheinisch (*adj.*); — wine, Rheinwein (*m.*); — Franconia, Rheinfranken (*n.*) (*or* Rheno-); — Franconian, Rheno-Franconian, Rheinfranke (*m.*); rheinfränkisch (*adj.*).
Rhine R., Rhein (*m.*); — lands, Rheinlande (*pl.*); — province, Rheinprovinz (*f.*); Confederation of the —, Rheinbund (*m.*); Falls of the —, Rheinfall (*m.*); Lower —, Niederrhein (*m.*); Palatinate of the —, Rheinpfalz (*f.*); Upper —, Oberrhein (*m.*); castle on the —, Schloß (*n.*) am Rhein; boat on the —, Boot (*n.*) auf dem Rhein.
Rhodes, (*island*) Rhodus (*n.*).
Rhone R., Rhone (*f.*).
Richard, Richard (*m.*); — Cœur de Lion, Richard Löwenherz.
Riding, einer der drei Bezirke, in welche die Grafschaft York eingeteilt ist (Riding = Thrid-ing); the West — of Yorkshire, der Westbezirk von Yorkshire.
Riga, Riga (*n.*); Gulf of —, Rigischer Busen.
Ripuarian, ripuarisch (*adj.*).
Robert, Rob(bie), Robert, Ruprecht (*m.*).
Robin, *see* **Robert**; — Goodfellow, guter Hauskobold; — Redbreast, Rotkehlchen (*n.*). **—son**; before one could say Jack —son, ehe man sich's versah.
Roc, (*bird*) Vogel Rock (*m.*).
Rocky Mountains, Felsengebirge (*n.*).
Roderick, Rod(e)rigo, Roderich (*m.*).
Ro(d)ger, Rüdiger (*m.*); Sir — (de Coverley), alter englischer Tanz (in 2 langen Reihen).
Roland, Roland; to give a — for an Oliver, mit gleicher Münze bezahlen.
Romaic, romaisch, neugriechisch (*adj.*).
Roman, Römer (*m.*); Römerin (*f.*); römisch (*adj.*); — balance, Schnellwage (*f.*); — candle, Leuchtkugel (*f.*); — Catholic, Katholik (*m.*); (römisch-)katholisch (*adj.*); **— characters**, lateinische Buchstaben (*pl.*), Antiquaschrift (*f.*); — nose, Adlernase (*f.*); — order, römische Säulenordnung; — road, Römerstraße (*f.*).
Romance, romanisch (*adj.*); — nations, Romanen (*pl.*); — philology, romanische Philologie; student *or* teacher of — philology, Romanist (*m.*).
Romani—st, Römling, Anhänger Roms (*m.*). **—ze**, romanisieren, zur römisch-katholischen Kirche bekehren; zur römischen Kirche *or* nach Rom hinneigen. **—zer**, zum Übertritt in die römisch-katholische Kirche Bekehrender.
Romanesque, romanesk, romanisch (*adj.*); romantisch, phantastisch (*Paint.*); early — style, frühromanischer Baustil; das Romanische.
Romano-British, römisch-brittisch (*adj.*).
Romansh, Rhätoromanisch, Romaunsch (*n.*).
Romany, Zigeuner (*m.*); Zigeunerin (*f.*); zigeunerisch (*adj.*); (*speech*) Kauderwelsch, Zigeunerisch (*n.*).
Rome, Rom (*n.*); — was not built in a day, Rom ist nicht an einem Tage gebaut (*prov.*); do in — as the Romans do, mit den Wölfen muß man heulen (*prov.*).
Romish, römisch(-katholisch) (*adj.*).
Rosa, (Ros(i)e), Rosa (*f.*), (Röschen (*n.*)). **—lind**, Rosalinde (*f.*). **—mond**, Rosamunde (*f.*).
Rosicrucian, Rosenkreuzer (*m.*).
Rotten Row, Korso (*m.*) im Hyde Park, Sammelplatz (*m.*) der feinen Welt Londons in der Season.
Roumania, Rumänien (*n.*). **—n**, Rumäne (*m.*); Rumänin (*f.*); rumänisch (*adj.*).
Roumelia, Rumelien (*n.*). **—n**, rumelisch (*adj.*).
Rowland, *see* **Roland**.
Rubicon R., Rubikon (*m.*); to pass the —, den R. überschreiten; einen entscheidenden Schritt tun.
Rudolph(us), Rudolf (*m.*).
Ruhr R., Ruhr (*f.*).
Rupert, Ruprecht (*m.*).
Russia, Rußland (*n.*); Little —, Kleinrußland (*n.*); Autocrat of all the —s (*not* —ns), Selbstherrscher (*m.*) aller Reußen; — leather, Juchten (*m.*), Juchtenleder (*n.*). **—n**, Russe (*m.*); Russin (*f.*); russisch (*adj.*); **—nize**, russifizieren (*f.*).
Russo—phile, Russenfreund (*m.*); russenfreundlich (*adj.*). **—phobe**, Russenfeind (*m.*); russenfeindlich (*adj.*). **—Turkish**, russisch-türkisch.

S

Saale R., Saale (*f.*).
Sabaoth, Zebaoth (*m.*); Lord God of —, Herr Zebaoth.
Sabine, Sabiner (*m.*); sabinisch, Sabiner (*adj.*); rape of the —s, Raub (*m.*) der Sabinerinnen.
Sadducee, Sadduzäer (*m.*). **—ism**, Sadduzäertum (*n.*).
Sadowa, (*battle*) (Schlacht (*f.*) bei) Königgrätz (*n.*).
Saguntum, Sagunt (*n.*).
Sahara, Sahara (*f.*).
Sal—ian, Salier (*m.*). **—ic**, salisch (*adj.*).
Sall(y), *for* **Sarah**; Aunt —, ein Wurfspiel (mit Kugeln um Kokosnüsse). (Ursprünglich hatte Tante Sally eine Tonpfeife im Munde, die man mit einer Kokosnuß treffen mußte.)
Sam, *see* **Samuel**; Uncle —, Nord-Amerikaner (*m.*); die Vereinigten Staaten (*pl.*) von N. A.
Samaritan, Samariter (*m.*); Samariterin (*f.*); samariterhaft, barmherzig (*adj.*); the good —, der barmherzige Samariter.
Samnite, Samniter (*m.*); samnitisch (*adj.*).
Samoan, Samoaner (*m.*); — Islands, Samoa-Inseln (*pl.*).
Samoied, Samoyed(e), Samojede (*m.*); samojedisch (*adj.*).
Samson, Simson (*m.*).
Sandhurst, englische Militärakademie für Infanterie und Kavallerie.
Sandy, *for* **Alexander**. **—(man)**, Schotte (*m.*).
Sangraal, Sangreal, der heilige Gral.

Sanscrit, Sanskrit (*n.*); sanskritisch (*adj.*); professor of —, Professor des *or* für Sanskrit.
Santa Claus, der heilige Nikolas, Knecht Ruprecht, Weihnachtsmann (*m.*).
Sapphic, sapphisch (*adj.*); sapphisches Versmaß.
Saracen, Sarazene (*m.*); Sarazenin (*f.*); sarazenisch (*adj.*).
Sarah, Sara (*f.*).
Sardanapalus, Sardanapal (*m.*).
Sardian, Sarde (*m.*); sardisch (*adj.*).
Sardinian, Sardinier (*m.*); sardinisch (*adj.*).
Sarmatian, Sarmate (*m.*); sarmatisch (*adj.*).
Sassanidæ, Sassaniden (*pl.*).
Sassenach, der (Angel) Sachse, Engländer (*a Celtic appellation*).
Satan, Satan (*m.*). **—ic**, satanisch, teuflisch (*adj.*); his —ic Majesty, S. Majestät der Teufel.
Saturn, Saturn (*m.*); Schwarz (*n.*) (*Herald.*). **—alia**, Saturnalien, Schwelgereien (*pl.*), Trinkgelage (*n.*). **—ian**, saturnisch, glücklich, golden (*adj.*) (*fig.*). **—ine**, melancholisch, mürrisch (*adj.*). **—us**, *see* —.
Save R., Sau (*f.*).
Saverne, Zabern (*n.*).
Savoy, Savoyen (*n.*). **—ard**, Savoyard(e) (*m.*); savoyardisch (*adj.*).
Saxe; **— -Coburg**, Sachsen-Koburg (*n.*). **— -Coburg-Gotha**, Sachsen-Koburg-Gotha (*n.*). **— -Meiningen**, Sachsen-Meiningen (*n.*). **— -Weimar**, Sachsen-Weimar (*n.*).
Saxon, Sachse (*m.*); Sächsin (*f.*); sächsisch (*adj.*); Old —, altsächsisch, altniederdeutsch (*adj.*). **—y**, Sachsen(land) (*n.*); Electorate of —y, Kursachsen (*n.*); Kingdom of —y, Königreich (*n.*) Sachsen, Obersachsen (*n.*). **—ys**, Stoffe (*pl.*) aus sächsischen Wollen, Streichwollen (*pl.*).
Scandinavia, Skandinavien (*n.*). **—n**, Skandinavier (*m.*); Skandinavierin (*f.*); skandinavisch (*adj.*).
Scania, Schonen (*n.*).
Scheldt R., Schelde (*f.*).
Scot, der Schotte (*unusual in conversation of Englishmen, but often used by Scotchmen of one another, and usually implying a certain warmth of feeling. Also in one or two phrases, like* a hungry —). **—ch**, schottisch (*adj.*); Schotte (*m.*); Schottin (*f.*); (*the adj. is generally used in easy and colloquial language, and always with regard to things of everyday life that are not specially dignified, e. g. banks, barley, broth, express, newspapers, nursery rimes, railways, whisky, caution, thrift etc.*); they are —ch, sie sind Schotten; he has a —ch accent, er spricht mit schottischem Akzent; —ch fir, Kiefer (*f.*); —ch heather, Hochlandsheide (*f.*); —ch Highlander, Bergschotte (*m.*); —ch mist, Staubregen (*m.*); —ch pearls, Barockperlen (*pl.*); —ch pebble, schottischer Achat; —ch rose, Heiderose (*f.*). **—chie**, Schottchen (*n.*), kleiner Schotte (*sometimes humorous, usually disparaging*). **—ia, —land**, Schottland (*n.*); —land Yard, Hauptpolizeiamt in London. **—chman**, Schotte (*m.*); Flying —chman, schottischer Eilzug; —chmen, Schotten (*pl.*). **—chwoman**, Schottin (*f.*). **—s**, schottisch (*adj.; it is archaic and now only used in a few set phrases such as* —s law, guards, worthies); —s Greys, die schottische berittene Leibwache; Schottisch (*n.*); specimens of Middle —s, Proben des Mittelschottischen. **—sman**, Schotte (*m.*). (Scotsman *and* Scotsmen *are archaic and seldom used in conversation, although they are sometimes written.* 'The Scotsman' *is the title of an important Edinburgh newspaper*). **—ticism**, schottische Spracheigenheit. **—tish**, schottisch (*adj.*). (Scottish *is more formal than* Scotch, *and being more dignified and literary, occurs especially in written and printed texts, in higher prose and in serious poetry. It is used in connection with words such as crown, king, army, valour, standard, minstrel, poetry, theology, Parliament, border, victories etc. In many cases* Scotch *may be used in writing as well as* Scottish, *e. g. with ancestors, ballads, character, church, customs, parents, scenery, soldiers, etc. No definite rule can be given. In conversation, however,* Scotch *is generally preferred.*)
Scythian, Skythe (*m.*); skythisch (*adj.*).
Seine R., Seine (*f.*).
Seljuk, Seldschuke (*m.*); Seldschukin (*f.*).
Seltzer water, Selterswasser (*n.*).
Semit—e, Semit (*m.*). **—ic**, semitisch (*adj.*).
Sennacherib, Sanherib (*m.*).
Seoul, Söul (*n.*).
Serb, *see* **Servian**.
Servia, Serbien (*n.*). **—n**, Serbe (*m.*); Serbin (*f.*); Serbier (*m.*); Serben (*pl.*); serbisch (*adj.*).
Severn R., Severn (*m.*), Saverne (*f.*).
Sevill—e, Sevilla (*n.*). **—ian**, sevillanisch (*adj.*).
Seychelles (Islands), Seschellen (*pl.*).
Shalmaneser, Salmanassar (*m.*).
Sheba, Saba (*n.*).
Shechem, Sichem (*n.*).
Sheffield-ware, feine Messerschmiedwaren (*pl.*).
Shem, Sem (*m.*) (son of Noah).
Shiraz, Schiras (*n.*).
Siamese, siamesisch (*adj.*); Siamese (*m.*); Siamesin (*f.*); — twins, Siamesische Zwillinge (*pl.*).
Sib, *short for* **Sibyl**.
Siberia, Sibirien (*n.*) **—n**, Sibirier (*m.*); sibirisch (*adj.*).
Sibyl, (**—la**,) Sibylle. **—line**, sibyllinisch (*adj.*).
Sicil—y, Sizilien (*n.*). **—ian**, Sizili(an)er (*m.*); sizil(ian)isch (*adj.*).
Sienn—a, Siena (*n.*). **—ese**, Sienese (*m.*); sienesisch (*adj.*).
Sigismond, Sigismund, Siegmund (*m.*).
Sikh, S(e)ikh (*m.*) (brittisch-indischer Soldat).
Silesia, Schlesien (*n.*); schlesische Leinwand (*C L.*). **—n**, Schlesier (*m.*); schlesisch (*adj.*).
Silurian, silurisch (*adj.*).
Sim, Simeon, *see* **Simon**.
Simon, Simon (*m.*); — the Canaanite, Simon von Kana; Simple —, Dummrian, Einfaltspinsel.
Singapore, Singapur (*n.*).
Sing(h)alese, Sing(h)alese (*m.*); sing(h)alesisch.
Sistine, sixtinisch (*adj.*).
Slav, Slawe (*m.*). **—ic**, slawisch (*adj.*). **—ism**, Slawentum (*n.*). **—onian, —onic**, slawisch (*adj.*). **—ophil**, Slawenfreund (*m.*); slawenfreundlich (*adj.*). **—ophobe**, Slawenhasser (*m.*); slawenfeindlich (*adj.*).
Slave Coast, Sklavenküste (*f.*).
Slovac, Slowake (*m.*); slowakisch (*adj.*).
Sleswig, Schleswig (*n.*); Schleswiger, schleswig(i)sch (*adj.*).
Slovene, Slowene (*m.*).
Smalcald—en, Schmalkalden (*n.*). **—ic**, schmalkaldisch (*adj.*).
Smyrnian, Smyrner (*m.*); smyrnisch (*adj.*).
Snip, Master, Meister Zwirn (*m.*) (*hum.*).
Society Islands, die Gesellschaftsinseln (*pl.*).
Socinian, Sozinianer (*m.*); sozinianisch (*adj.*).
Socrat—es, Sokrates (*m.*). **—ic(al)**, sokratisch (*adj.*). **—ist**, Sokratiker (*m.*).
Solomon, Sol, Salomo(n) (*m.*); Song of Solomon, das hohe Lied Salomonis.
Somerset House, am Strand von London gelegenes Staatsarchiv, wo alle Testamente aufbewahrt werden.
Sophia, Sophy, Sophie (*f.*); Fiekchen (*n.*) (*dim.*).
Soudan, Sudan (*m.*). **—ese**, Sudanese (*m.*), Bewohner (*m.*) des Sudan; sudanesisch (*adj.*).
Sound; the —, der Sund.
South Sea, Südsee (*f.*); — — Islands, Südseeinseln (*pl.*), Ozeanien (*n.*).
Spa, Spa(a) (*n.*).
Spain, Spanien (*n.*).
Span—iard, Spanier (*m.*); Spanierin (*f.*). —

ish, spanisch (*adj.*); —ish juice, —ish liquorice, Lakritzensaft (*m.*), Lakritze (*f.*); —ish leather, Korduan, Saffian (*m.*).
Spartan, Spartaner (*m.*); spartanisch (*adj.*); hart (*adj.*) (*fig.*).
Sphinx, Sphinx (*f.*), Nachtfalter (*m.*) (*Entom.*).
Spice Islands, Gewürzinseln, Molukken (*pl.*).
Spire(s), Speier (*n.*).
Spitsbergen, Spitzbergen, Spitzbergen (*n.*).
Sporades, Sporaden (*pl.*).
Spree R., Spree (*f.*).
Stamboul, Stambul (*n.*).
Stationers' Hall, die Buchbörse (*in London*).
Stauf(f)er(s), Staufer, Hohenstaufen (*pl.*).
Steelyard, Staalhof (*m.*) in London (*Hist.*).
Stentorian voice, Stentorstimme, weitschallende Stimme (*f.*).
Stephen, (Stephano,) Stephan (*m.*).
Stoic, Stoiker (*m.*); stoisch (*adj.*). **—ism**, Stoizismus (*m.*).
Strasburg, Straßburg (*n.*); — pie, (Straßburger) Gänseleberpastete (*f.*).
Sty—gian, stygisch (*adj.*); —gian shore, Unterwelt (*f.*), Reich (*n.*) der Schatten. **—x**, Styx (*m.*).
Styria, Steiermark (*f.*). **—n**, Steiermärker (*m.*); steiermärkisch, steirisch (*adj.*).
Sudetic Mts., Sudeten (*pl.*).
Suevi, Sueven (*pl.*).
Suleyman, Suleiman, Soliman (*m.*).
Sumatran, sumatranisch (*adj.*), aus Sumatra.
Susan(nah), (Susie,) Susanne (*f.*), (Suschen (*n.*), Suse (*f.*)).
Swabia, Schwaben(land) (*n.*). **—n**, Schwabe (*m.*); Schwäbin (*f.*); schwäbisch (*adj.*); —n emperors, Schwabenkaiser (*pl.*); —n Sea (*obs.*), schwäbisches Meer (*n.*), Bodensee (*m.*).
Swed—e, Schwede (*m.*); Schwedin (*f.*); (*—ish turnip*) (schwedische) Kohlrübe (*f.*). **—en**, Schweden (*n.*). **—ish**, schwedisch (*adj.*); —ish drill, schwedisches Turnen (*n.*); —ish gymnastics, schwedische Heilgymnastik (*f.*).
Swedenborgian, Swedenborgianer (*m.*); swedenborgianisch (*adj.*). **—ism**, die Lehre Swedenborgs (*f.*).
Swiss, Schweizer (*m.*); Schweizerin (*f.*); schweizerisch, Schweizer (*adj.*); — cottage, Schweizerhäuschen (*n.*); — journey, Schweizerreise, Reise (*f.*) in die Schweiz; — nation, Schweizervolk (*n.*).
Swithin; St. —, der Heilige Swithun; der Wetterheilige; St. —'s Day, der 15. Juli.
Switzerland, die Schweiz (*f.*); in —, in der Schweiz; to —, in die Schweiz; French —, die französische Schweiz (*f.*).
Sybarit—e, Sybarit, Schwelger, Wollüstling (*m.*) (*fig.*). **—ism**, Sybaritismus (*m.*).
Sybilline, *see* **Sibylline**.
Syracus—e, Syrakus (*n.*). **—an**, Syrakusaner (*m.*); syrakus(an)isch (*adj.*).
Syria, Syrien (*n.*). **—c, —n**, Syr(i)er (*m.*); syrisch (*adj.*); syrische Sprache (*f.*), Syrisch (*n.*).
Syro—-Egyptian, syrisch-ägyptisch (*adj.*). **—-Phœnician**, syrisch-phönizisch (*adj.*).
Syrtis, Syrte (*f.*); — Major (Minor), die Große (Kleine) Syrte.

T

Taal, Burensprache (*f.*), Taal (*n.*).
Table-Mountain, Tafelberg (*m.*).
Taffy, *for* **David**, Walliser (*m.*).
Tagus R., Tajo (*m.*) (*in Spain*), Tejo (*m.*) (*in Portugal*). *See* **Douro**.
Tahitian, Otahaitier (*m.*); otahaitisch (*adj.*).
Tam(mie), *for* **Thomas**.
Tamburlaine, Tamerlane, Tamerlan (*m.*).
Tamil, Tamule (*m.*); tamulisch (*adj.*).
Tammany; — Hall, Logenhaus (*n.*) der — Society; demokratische Partei in New York (*fig.*); — Society, geheimer 1789 zu New York gegründeter Orden.
Tangerine, aus Tanger (*adj.*); kleine Orange (aus Tanger) (*f.*).
Tangier(s), Tanger (*n.*).
Tannhauser, Tannhäuser (*m.*).
Tantalus' cup, Tantalusbecher, Vexierbecher (*m.*).
Tar; Jack —, Hans Teerjacke, alter Seebär (*m.*).
Taranto, Tarent (*n.*).
Tarpeian, tarpejisch (*adj.*); — Rock, tarpejischer Fels.
Tarsian, Tarser (*m.*); tarsisch (*adj.*).
Tartar, Ta(r)tar (*m.*); wilder Mensch, Hitzkopf, Brausekopf (*fig.*); tatarisch (*adj.*); little —, kleiner Rüpel, Taugenichts (*vulg.*); to catch a —, übel ankommen, an den Unrechten kommen (*coll.*). **—ean, —ic**, ta(r)tarisch (*adj.*). **—y**, Ta(r)tarei (*f.*).
Tasmanian, Tasmane, Vandiemensländer (*m.*).
Tauric Chersonese, taurische Halbinsel (*f.*), (*Hist.; but now usually*) Krim (*f.*).
Taurus, der Stier (*Astr.*).
Tchech, Tscheche (*m.*); Tschechin (*f.*); tschechisch (*adj.*).
Ted(dy) (*dim. of* **Edward**), Edchen (*n.*), Edu (*m.*).
Teenie (*dim. of* **Christina**), Stine (*f.*), Stinchen (*n.*).
Telemachus, Telemach (*m.*).
Templar, Knight —, Tempelritter, Templer (*m.*).
Teneriffe, Teneriffa (*n.*).
Terence, Terenz (*m.*).
Terry (*dim. of* **Theresa**), Resi, Resel (*f.*).
Teuton, Germane, Teutone (*m.*). **—ic**, germanisch, teutonisch (*adj.*); —ic Order, Deutscher Orden, Deutschritterorden (*m.*); Knights of the —ic Order, Deutschherrn (*pl.*).
Texan, Texaner (*m.*); aus Texas, texanisch (*adj.*).
Thames R., Themse (*f.*); he will not set the — on fire, er wird die Welt nicht aus den Angeln heben, er hat das Pulver nicht erfunden.
Theb—es, Theben (*n.*). **—an**, Thebaner (*m.*); thebanisch (*adj.*). **—aid**, (*epic*) Thebaide (*f.*).
Theo, *see* **Theobald, Theodore, Theophilus.**
Theo(bald), (Tybalt, Tibald,) Theobald (*m.*).
Theocritus, Theokrit (*m.*).
Theo(dora), Theodora, Dora, Thea (*f.*).
Theo(dore), Theodor, Theo (*m.*).
Theodoric, Theodorik, Theodorich, Dietrich (*m.*); — of Verona, Dietrich von Bern (*in legend*); Theodorich der Große (*in history*, † 526).
Theo(philus), Gottlieb (*m.*).
Theresa, Therese (*f.*); Maria —, Maria Theresia (*f.*).
Thessal—y, Thessalien (*n.*). **—ian**, Thessalier (*m.*); thessalisch (*adj.*). **—onian**, Thessalonicher (*m.*); Epistle to the —onians, Brief (*f.*) an die Thessalonicher. **—onica**, Thessalonich (*n.*).
Thingamy, Mr., Herr Dings(da), Herr Dingskirchen, Herr Dingerich (*m.*).
Thrac—e, Thrazien (*n.*). **—ian**, Thrazier (*m.*); thrazisch (*adj.*).
Thurgovia, Thurgau (*m.*)
Thuringia, Thüringen (*n.*); forest of —, Thüringerwald (*m.*). **—n**, Thüringer (*m.*); thüringisch (*adj.*).
Tiber R., Tiber (*f. & m.*).
Tibullus, Tibull (*m.*).
Ticino R., Tessin (*m.*).
Tierra del Fuego, Feuerland (*n.*).
Tigris R., Tigris (*m.*).
Tilda, Tilly (*dim. of* **Matilda**), Tildchen (*n.*).
Tim(othy), Timotheus (*m.*).
Tina, Tiny (*dim. of* **Christina**), Stinchen, Tinchen (*n.*), Tine (*f.*).
Titan, (*giant*) Titan(e); (*god*) Titan. **—ic**, riesenhaft, titanisch (*adj.*); —ic acid, die Titansäure (*f.*).
Tobiah, Tobias, Toby, Tobit, Tobias (*m.*); Book of Tobit, das Buch Tobiä.
Tokay (wine), Tokaier (*m.*).
Tom, *for* **Thomas**; — and Tib, Hans und Grete; — Tell-Truth, ehrliche Haut (*f.*); — **Thumb**,

(der kleine) Däum(er)ling; Dreikäsehoch (*m.*); — Tug, Fährmann (*m.*); Uncle —'s cabin, Onkel Toms Hütte (*f.*). **—boy**, Range (*f.*), ausgelassenes, jungenhaftes Mädchen. **—-fool**, **—-noddy**, Dummerjan, Hans Narr (*m.*). **—-foolery**, Unsinn (*m.*), dummes Zeug.

Tommy, *for* **Thomas**; — Atkins, (englischer) gemeiner Soldat, (*especially*) Infanterist (*m.*).

Tonquin, Tonkin (*n.*). **—ese**, Tonkinese (*m.*); tonkinesisch (*adj.*).

Tony (*dim. of* **Anthony**), Toni (*m.*).

Trans—alpine, trans-alpinisch, nördlich der Alpen (von Rom aus) (*adj.*). **—atlantic**, transatlantisch (*adj.*). **—caspian**, transkaspisch (*adj.*). **—caucasian**, transkaukasisch (*adj.*). **—leithanian**, transleithanisch (*adj.*), jenseits der Leitha (von Wien aus) gelegen, ungarisch (*adj.*). **—pacific**, den Stillen Ozean durchquerend. **—padane**, jenseits (nördlich) des Po gelegen, transpadanisch (*adj.*). **—pontine**, südlich von der Themse stattfindend (*of certain melodramatic plays*), volkstümlich-rührselig, melodramatisch (*Theatr.*). **—rhenish**, überrheinisch (*adj.*). **—-siberian**, transsibirisch, Sibirien durchquerend (*adj.*). **—vaal**; the —, Transvaal (*m.*); in the —vaal, in Transvaal. **—ylvania**, Siebenbürgen (*n.*). **—ylvanian**, Siebenbürge (*m.*); Siebenbürgin (*f.*); siebenbürgisch (*adj.*).

Trappist, Trappist (*m.*). **—s**, Trappisten (*pl.*).

Trebizond, Trapezunt (*n.*).

Trent R., Trent (*m.*); on —, am Trent.

Trent, Trient, Trident (*n.*); Council of —, Tridentiner Konzil (*n.*).

Trèv—es, Trier (*n.*). **—iran**, trierisch (*adj.*).

Tricksie, *for* **Beatrix**, **Beatrice**, Beate.

Triest(e), Triest (*n.*).

Trinitarian, Dreieinigkeitsbekenner (*m.*).

Tripoli, Tripolis (*n.*). **—tan**, Tripolitaner (*m.*); tripolitanisch (*adj.*).

Tristram, Tristan (*m.*).

Trix(ie), *see* **Beatrice**.

Tro—ad, Troas (*n.*). **—jan**, Trojaner (*m.*); der Kerl, der lustige Gesell (*coll.*); like a —jan, wie ein Held (*coll.*), trojanisch (*adj.*); —jan war, Trojanerkrieg (*m.*).

Troy, Troja (*n.*).

Tudor; — blood, Tudorblut (*n.*); — line, Linie (*f.*) der Tudors, Tudordynastie (*f.*); — sovereigns, Herrscher (*pl.*) aus dem Hause Tudor.

Tull—y, Tullius (*m.*). **—ian**, tullianisch (*adj.*).

Tunis—ian, **—ine**, Tunesier (*m.*); tunesisch (*adj.*).

Turco, *see* **Turk—o**.

Turcoman, Turkomane (*m.*).

Turinese, Turiner (*m.*); turinisch (*adj.*).

Turk, Türke (*m.*); Türkin (*f.*); wilder Mensch (*fig.*); Grand —, Großtürke (*m.*). **—estan**, Turkestan (*n.*). **—ey**, die Türkei (*f.*); —ey carpet, türkischer Teppich, Smyrna-Teppich; —ey cock, Truthahn, kalekutischer Hahn, Puter (*m.*); —ey hen, Truthenne (*f.*); the —ey gobbles, der Truthahn kollert; —ey in Asia, die asiatische Türkei; —ey red, Türkischrot (*n.*). **—o**, Turko (*m.*). **—o-Egyptian**, türkisch-ägyptisch (*adj.*).

Tuscan, Toskaner (*m.*); toskanisch (*adj.*). **—y**, Toskana (*n.*).

Tweed R., Tweed (*m.*).

Tybalt, *see* **Theobald**.

Tyne R., Tyne (*m.*); on —, am Tyne.

Tyr—e, Tyrus (*n.*). **—ian**, Tyr(i)er (*m.*); tyrisch (*adj.*).

Tyrol; the — Tirol (*n.*); in the —, in Tirol. **—ese**, Tiroler (*m.*); tirolisch, Tiroler- (*adj.*).

Tyrrhene, **Tyrrhenian Sea**, tyrrhenisches Meer (*n.*), Tyrrhener Meer (*poet.*) (*m.*).

U

Uckermark, Uckermark (*f.*).

Ukraine R., Ukraine (*f.*).

Ulric, **Ulrich** (*m.*); **Uli** (*m.*) (*dim.*). **—a**, **Ul**[illegible]**ke**.

Umbrian, Umbrier (*m.*); umbrisch (*adj.*).

United States (*in Engl. occasionally used as a singular*), Vereinigte Staaten (*pl.*).

Ural; — Mts., Uralgebirge (*n.*); — **R.**, Ural (*m.*).

Uriah, Uria(s) (*m.*).

Ursuline, Ursulinerin (*f.*); ursulinisch (*adj.*).

Uruguay R., Uruguay (*m.*); die Republik U.

Utopia, Utopien, Nirgendheim, Land des Ideals. (*n.*).

V

Valais, Wallis (*n.*). **—an**, (Schweizer) Walliser (*m.*); wallisisch (*adj.*)

Valentine, Valentin (*m.*); zum Valentinstage (*Feb. 14*) geschriebenes scherzhaftes Liebesbriefchen (*n.*); (*sweetheart*) Liebchen (*n.*).

Valeria, Valerie (*f.*).

Valhalla, Walhalla (*f.*).

Valkyrie, Walküre (*f.*).

Vandal, Vandale (*m.*). **—(ian)**, **—(ic)**, vandalisch (*adj.*). **—ism**, Vandalismus (*m.*); Roheit (*f.*); Zerstörungswut (*f.*).

Vatican, Vatikan (*m.*); vatikanisch (*adj.*).

Vaud, Waadt(land) (*n.*). **—ois**, Waadtländer (*m.*); waadtländisch (*adj.*).

Venetia, Venetien (*n.*). **—n**, Venetianer (*m.*); venetianisch, venedisch (*adj.*); —n blinds, Fensterjalousien (*pl.*); —n boat, Gondel (*f.*); —n door, Glastür (*f.*).

Venice, Venedig (*n.*); — of the North, Stockholm (*n.*).

Verde, Cape, Grünes Vorgebirge (*n.*).

Vesta, Vesta (*f.*). **—l**, Vestalin, vestalische Jungfrau (*f.*); vestalisch, keusch, jungfräulich (*adj.*).

Vesuvi—an, vesuvisch (*adj.*); der Zünder (*for cigars*); der Vesuvian (*Min.*). **—us**, Vesuv (*m.*).

Vic(ky), *see* **Victoria**.

Victoria, Viktoria (*f.*); — cross, Viktoriakreuz (*n.*); —n age, Zeitalter (*m.*) Victorias *or* der Königin Victoria.

Vienn—a, Wien (*n.*). **—ese**, Wiener (*m.*), wienerisch, Wiener (*adj.*).

Viking, Wiking (*m.*); time of the —s, Wikingerzeit (*f.*).

Vin(cent), Vincenz (*m.*).

Virginia, (*state*) Virginien (*n.*); (*name*) Virginie (*f.*); — creeper, wilder Wein (*m.*).

Virgil(ius), Vergil (*m.*).

Vishnu, Wischnu (*m.*).

Visigoth, Westgote (*m.*). **—ic**, westgotisch (*adj.*).

Vistula R., Weichsel (*f.*).

Vitus, Veit (*m.*); St. —'s dance, Veitstanz (*m.*).

Volga R., Wolga (*f.*).

Vosges, Vogesen (*pl.*); Waskenwald (*obs. poet.*).

Vulgate, Vulgata, Lateinische Bibelübersetzung (aus dem Ende des vierten Jahrhunderts) (*f.*).

W

Wagnerite, Wagnerianer (*m.*).

Waldenses, Waldenser (*pl.*).

Wales, Wales (*n.*); of —, *see* **Welsh**.

Wallachia, die Walachei (*f.*). **—n**, Walache (*m.*); walachisch (*adj.*).

Walloon, Wallone (*m.*); wallonisch (*adj.*).

Walter (Walt), Walter, Walther, (Walt, Wälti (*m.*), Waltchen (*n.*)).

Warsaw, Warschau (*n.*).

Wash, The, Arm der Nordsee zwischen Norfolk und Lincolnshire.

Wat(tie), *see* **Walter**.

Waterloo, Battle of, Schlacht (*f.*) bei Waterloo.

Wayland (Smith), Wieland der Schmied.

Wedgewood (ware), Wedgewoodporzellan (*n.*).

Weimar; inhabitant of —, Weimaraner (*m.*).

Wellington boot, Schaftstiefel (*m.*).

Welsh, wallisisch, Walliser- (*adj.*); die Walliser (*pl.*); — rabbit (*for* rarebit), warmer Käse auf geröstetes Brot gebreitet. **—man**, Walliser (*m.*). **—woman**, Walliserin (*f.*).

Wenceslas, Wenzel (*m.*).
Wend, Wende (*m.*); Wendin (*f.*); wendisch (*adj.*)
Werra R., Werra (*f.*).
Weser R., Weser (*f.*).
Wesleyan, wesleyanisch (*adj.*); Wesleyaner (*m.*).
West Indies, Westindien (*n.*).
Westphalia, Westfalen (*n.*); Peace of —, der westfälische Friede. **—n**, Westfale (*m.*); Westfälin (*f.*); westfälisch (*adj.*).
Westrick, Neustrien, Westr(e)ich (*n.*) (*Hist.*).
Weyland, *see* **Wayland**.
Whitehall, Straße (*f.*) der Engl. Ministerien; englisches Unterrichtsministerium.
White Sea, Weißes Meer (*n.*).
Wight, Isle of, die Insel Wight.
Wilfred, Wilfried (*m.*).
Wilhelmina, Wilhelmine (*f.*); Minchen (*n.*) (*dim.*).
Will, *see* **William**; — o'-the-wisp, Irrlicht (*n.*).
William, Wilhelm (*m.*); Willi (*m.*) (*dim.*); — the Conqueror, Wilhelm der Eroberer; — Rufus, Wilhelm der Rote; sweet-—, Bartnelke (*f.*).
Will—ie, —y, (*dim. of* **William**,) Willi (*m.*).
Winfr—ed, —id, Winfried (*f.*).
Winifred, Winnie, Winfreda (*f.*).
Wiseacre, Mr., (**Miss**,) Herr (*m.*) (Jungfer (*f.*)) Naseweis *or* Überklug.
Woden, Wodan (*m.*); cult of —, Wodanskult (*m.*).
Woolwich, englische Militärakademie für Ausbildung der Ingenieuroffiziere und Artilleristen.
Wupper R., Wupper (*f.*).
Wurtemberg, Würtemberg (*n.*). **—ian**, Würtemberger (*m.*); würtembergisch (*adj.*).
Wurzburg, Würzburg (*n.*).

X

Xantippe, Xanthippe (*f.*).
Xavier, Xaver (*m.*).

Y

Yang-tse-kiang R., Yangtsekiang (*m.*).
Yankee, Yankee, Neu-Engländer (*m.*); Nordamerikaner (der Vereinigten Staaten) (*m.*). — **Doodle**, Yankee-Doodle (*n.*), ein Nationallied der Nordamerikaner (*n.*); Yankee, typischer Nordamerikaner (*m.*); Tölpel (*m.*). **—fied**, yankeeartig, zum Yankee geworden (*adj.*) (*coll.*). — **ism**, Yankee-Wesen (*n.*), nordamerikanische Art (*f.*); nordamerikanische Spracheigentümlichkeit (*f.*). — **States**, die neuenglischen Staaten Neuengland (*n.*).
Yellow Sea, Gelbes Meer (*n.*).
Yemen, Jemen (*n.*) (*S.W. coast of Arabia*).
Yenisei R., Jenisei (*m.*).
Yiddish, die Sprache der ungebildeten Juden.
Ypres, Ypern (*n.*); — lace, feinste Spitzen (*pl.*).
Yssel R., Yssel (*f.*).
Yukon R., Yukon (*m.*).
Yvetot; King of —, Duodezfürst (*m.*).

Z

Zaccheus, Zachäus (*m.*).
Zach(ariah), **Zacky**, Zacharias (*m.*)
Zambesi R., Sambesi (*m.*).
Zamiel, Samiel (*m.*).
Zanzibar, Sansibar (*n.*).
Zealand, Seeland (*n.*) **—er**, Seeländer (*m.*). **New** —, Neuseeland (*n.*).
Zebed—iah, —ee, Zebedäus (*m.*).
Zend, Zendsprache (*f.*). **—s**, Zendvolk (*n.*).
Zouave, Zuave (*m.*).
Zuleikah, Suleika (*f.*).
Zurich, Zürich (*n.*); Lake of —, Zür(i)cher See.
Zuyder Zee, Zuidersee (*m.*).

INDEX OF THE MORE COMMON ENGLISH ABBREVIATIONS.

A

A., amateur, Liebhaber; associate, außerordentliches Mitglied.
A. *or* **Ans.**, answer, Antwort.
A 1, first class (of ships); erste Klasse (von Schiffen); this is — —, das ist tadellos (*sl.*).
A. A. C., anno ante Christum, (im Jahre) vor Christi Geburt.
A. B., able-bodied seaman, dienstfähiger Matrose; Artium Baccalaureus (*usually* B. A.).
Abb., abbess, Äbtissin; abbot, Abt; abbey, Abtei.
abbr. *or* **abbrev.**, abbreviated *or* abbreviation, abgekürzt *or* Abkürzung.
A. B. C., Aerated Bread Company, *see Part II, p. 8.*
A. B. C. F. M., American Board of Commissioners for Foreign Missions.
abd., abdicated, abgedankt.
Abp., archbishop, Erzbischof.
abr., abridged, abgekürzt.
A. B. S., American Bible Society.
A. C., ante Christum, vor Christi Geburt.
acad., academy, Akademie.
acc. *or* **acct.**, account *or* accountant, Rechnung oder Rechnungsführer.
A. D., Anno Domini, im Jahres des Herrn.
A. D. C., Aide-de-camp, Adjutant; Amateur Dramatic Club, Liebhabertheater-Klub.
ad fin., ad finem, am Ende *or* bis ans Ende.
ad inf., ad infinitum, bis ins Unendliche.
ad init., ad initium, im Anfang.
ad int., ad interim, unterdessen.
Adjt., adjutant, Adjutant.
Adjt.-Gen., Adjutant-General, Generaladjutant.
ad lib., ad libitum, nach Belieben.
ad loc., ad locum, zur Stelle.
Adm., Admiral, Admiral.
Adv., Advent.
adv., advocate, adversus, gegen; adverb.
ad val., ad valorem, dem Werte gemäß.
advt., advertisement, Anzeige.
æ. *or* **æt.**, ætatis, aged (so many years), im Alter von (so und so viel Jahren).
A. F. B. S., American and Foreign Bible Society.
A. G., Attorney-General, Oberstaatsanwalt; Adjutant-General, Generaladjutant.
Ag., Argentum, Silber.
Agr., **Agric.**, Agriculture, Ackerbau.
Agt., agent, Agent.
a. h. l., ad hunc locum, zu dieser Stelle.
A. H. S., anno humanæ salutis, im Jahre des Heils.
A. I. C. E., Associate of the Institute of Civil Engineers.
Ald., alderman, Ratsherr.
Alg., Algebra.
alt., alternate, abwechselnd; altitude, Höhe.
A. M., Artium Magister (*usually* M. A.); ante meridiem, before noon, Morgens (v. 12 Uhr nachts bis 12 Uhr mittags); Associate Member, Außerordentliches Mitglied.
Am. *or* **Amer.**, America *or* American, Amerika, Amerikaner, amerikanisch.
A. M. A., American Missionary Association, Amerikanischer Missionsverein.
amt., amount, Summe.
an., anno, im Jahre.
anal., analysis, Analyse.
anat., anatomy *or* anatomical, Anatomie *or* anatomisch.
anc., ancient, alt.
Ang., Anglice, auf Englisch.
Anon., anonymous, anonym, namenlos.
ant. *or* **antiq.**, antiquities, Altertümer.
A. O. F., Ancient Order of Foresters, Verein zu Geselligkeit- und Unterstützungs-zwecken.
Ap., **Apl.**, **Apr.**, April, April.
app., appendix, Anhang; apprentice, Lehrling.
aq., aqua, Wasser.
A. R., anno regni, im Jahre der Regierung.
A. R. A., Associate of the Royal Academy, korrespondierendes Mitglied der kgl. Akademie.
arch., archaic, veraltet.
arch., **archit.**, architecture, Baukunst.
Archd., Archdeacon, Archidiakonus.
Arg., Argentum, Silber.
A. R. H. A., Associate of the Royal Hibernian Academy, korrespondierendes Mitglied der kgl. Irischen Akademie.
A. R. I. B. A., Associate of the Royal Institute of British Architects, Mitglied des Kgl. Britischen Architektenvereins.
arith., arithmetic, Arithmetik.
arr., arrival, Ankunft.
A. R. S. A., Associate of the Royal Scottish Academy, korrespondierendes Mitglied der kgl. Schottischen Akademie.
A. R. S. L., Associate of the Royal Society of Literature.
A. R. S. M., Associate of the Royal School of Mines.
A. R. S. S., Antiquariorum Regiæ Societatis Socius, Fellow of the Royal Society of Antiquaries, Mitglied der Königlichen Gesellschaft der Altertumsforscher.
Art., article, Artikel; artist, Künstler.
A. S., Anglo-Saxon, Angelsächsisch.
Ass., **Assoc.**, Association, Verein.
asst., assistant, Gehilfe, Hilfs-.
Astr., **Astron.**, astronomer, Astronom.
Att., **Atty.**, attorney, Rechtsanwalt.
Atty.-Gen., Attorney-General, Oberstaatsanwalt (1611).
Aug., augmentative, vermehrend; August, August.
A. V., Authorized Version, die autorisierte Bibelübersetzung (1611); Artillery Volunteers, freiwillige Artillerie.
Av., average, Durchschnitt; Avenue, Allee.
Avoir., **Avdp.**, avoirdupois, das gemeine englische Gewicht.
ax., axiom, Axiom, Grundsatz.

B

b., born, geboren.
B., **Bk.**, book, Buch.
B., **Brit.**, British, britisch.
B. A., Baccalaureus Artium, Bachelor of Arts, Baccalaureus der freien Künste; Brit(ish) Ass(ociation), große, besonders naturwissenschaftliche, Gesellschaft, mit jährlichen Zusammenkünften; British America; British Academy.
Bach., Bachelor, Baccalaureus.
bal., balance, Überschuß.
Bap., **Bapt.**, Baptist.
Bar., Barometer, Barometer; Barrister, Advokat.
Bart., **Bt.**, Baronet, Baronet, erblicher Ritter.
Bat., **Batt.**, Battalion, Battalion; Battery, Batterie.
bbl(s)., barrel(s), Faß (Fässer).
B. C., before Christ, vor Christi Geburt.

B. C. L., Bachelor of Civil Law.
B. D., Bachelor of Divinity.
bd., bound (for), bestimmt (nach); bound, eingebunden.
bds., boards, (in) Pappband, kartonniert.
b. e., bill of exchange, Wechsel.
Beds., Bedfordshire.
bef., before, vor, vorher.
Belg., Belgian, belgisch.
Ben., **Benj.**, Benjamin, Benjamin.
B. Eng., Bachelor of Engineering.
Berks., Berkshire.
bet., between, zwischen.
Bib., Bible, Bibel.
Biog., Biography, Biographie.
Biol., Biology, Biologie.
bk., book, Buch; Bank, Bank.
Bkg., Banking.
bkt., basket, Korb.
B. L., Bachelor of Letters *or* Laws; bill of lading, Frachtbrief.
bl., barrel, Faß; bale, Ballen.
B. M., Bachelor of Medicine, Baccalaureus der Medizin; of blessed memory, selig.
B. Mus., Bachelor of Music, Bacc. der Musik.
Bn., Battalion, Battalion; Baron, Baron.
b. o., branch office, Zweiggeschäft; buyer's option, Wahl des Käufers.
Bomb. C. S., Bombay Civil Service.
Bomb. S. C., Bombay Staff Corps.
Bor., Borough, Wahlbezirk.
Bot., Botany, Botanik
Bp., Bishop, Bischof.
b. p., bill of parcels, Warenrechnung; bills payable, zahlbare Wechsel.
bpl., birthplace, Geburtsort.
Br., **Bro.**, Brother, Bruder; **Bros.**, Gebrüder; **Cook Bros.**, Gebrüder Cook.
Braz., Brazil, Brasilien.
Brev., Brevet, Offizierspatent.
Brig., Brigadier, Brigadier.
Brig.-Gen., Brigadier-General, Brigadegeneral.
Brit., Britain, Britannia, Brittannien, British, brittisch.
b. s., bill of sale, Kaufbrief.
B. S. C., Bengal Staff Corps.
B. Sc., Bachelor of Science, Baccalaureus der Naturwissenschaften.
B. S. L., Botanical Society of London.
Bt., Baronet, Baronet.
bu., **bush.**, bushel, Scheffel.
Bucks., Buckinghamshire.
Bulg., Bulgaria(n), Bulgarien (bulgarisch).
B. V., Blessed Virgin, heilige Jungfrau.
B. V. M., Blessed Virgin Mary, heilige Jungfrau Maria.
B. W. T. A., British Women's Temperance Association, Mäßigkeitsverein der englischen Frauen.

C

C., cent (*Amer.*); Centigrade, Centigrad-Thermometer; Catholic, katholisch; Consul, Konsul; Church, Kirche; Chancellor, Kanzler; Conservative, Konservativer.
C., **Cap.**, caput, chapter, Kapitel.
C. A., Chief Accountant, erster Buchhalter; Commercial Agent, Handelsvertreter eines Volkes im Auslande; Confederate Army, verbündetes Heer; Südstaatenheer (*Amer. Hist.*); Schweizerheer.
ca., circa, about, ungefähr, etwa.
Ca., **Cal.**, California, Kalifornien.
Cam., **Camb.**, Cambridge; **Cambs.**, Cambridgeshire.
Can., Canon, Kanonikus; Canto, Gesang (eines Gedichtes).
Cant., Canterbury; **Canticles**, **das Hohe Lied Salomos.**
Cantab., Cantabrigiensis, von Cambridge, Cambridger; **the Cantabs**, **Cambridger Studenten.**
Cantuar., Cantuaria, Canterbury; Cantuariensis, Erzbischof von Canterbury.
Cap., **Capt.**, Captain, Kapitän; Anführer, Leiter
Caps., Capitals, Majuskeln, große Buchstaben.
Car., Carat, Karat.
Card., Cardinal, Kardinal.
Cath., Catherine, Katharine; Catholic, katholisch.
C. B., Companion of the Most Honourable Order of the Bath, Ritter des Bathordens.
C. C., County Council, Grafschaftsrat; County Clerk, Grafschaftssekretär; Cricket Club, Cricket Klub; Catholic Clergyman, Priester.
C. C. C., Corpus Christi College; Christ's College, Cambridge.
C. D. Acts, Contagious Diseases Acts, Gesetze gegen ansteckende Krankheiten.
C. E., Church of England, englische Staatskirche; der engl. Staatskirche angehörig; Civil Engineer.
Cel., Celsius; celebrated, berühmt.
Cent., Century, Jahrhundert; Central, zentral.
Centig., Centigrade, Celsiusches (100 teiliges) Thermometer.
Cert., **Certif.**, Certificate, Beglaubigungsschein; certify, bescheinigen.
C. E. T. S., Church of England Temperance Society, Anglikanischer Mäßigkeitsverein.
C. F., Chaplain to the Forces, Feldprediger.
Cf., confer, compare, vergleiche, vgl.
c. f. & i., cost, freight & insurance, Kosten, Fracht und Versicherung.
cg., Centigram, Centigramm.
C. G., Captain-General, Oberbefehlshaber; Captain of the Guard, Gardehauptmann; Coastguard, Küstenzollaufseher; Commissary-General, Generalkriegskommissar; Consul General, Generalkonsul.
C. G. H., Cape of Good Hope, Kap der Guten Hoffnung.
C. H., Custom House, Zollamt.
Ch., Church, Kirche; Chapter, Kapitel; Chief, Vorsteher, Chef.
Chamb., Chamberlain, Kammerherr.
Chanc., Chancellor, Kanzler.
Chap., Chaplain, Kaplan; Chapter, Kapitel.
Chas., Charles, Karl.
Ch. B., Chirurgiæ Baccalaureus.
Ch. C.; **Ch. Ch.**, Christ Church (Oxford).
Chem., Chemistry, Chemie; Chemical, chemisch.
Chin., China, China, Chinese, chinesisch.
Chr., Christ, Christus; Christian, christlich.
Chron., Chronicles, Chroniken; Chronology, Chronologie.
C. I., (Imperial Order of the) Crown of India, Indischer Kronenorden.
C. I. E., Companion (of the Most Eminent Order of the) Indian Empire.
cir., **circ.**, circa, circiter, about, ungefähr, etwa.
cit., citation, Anführung, Zitat; citizen, Bürger.
C. I. V., City Imperial Volunteers, Londoner Freiwilligenkorps.
Civ., civil, bürgerlich, Zivil-, Staats-; civilian, Bürgerlicher, Zivilist.
C. J., Chief Justice, Oberrichter.
C. M., **Cor. Mem.**, Corresponding Member, Korrespondierendes Mitglied.
C. M., Chirurgiæ Magister, Master in Surgery.
c. m., causa mortis, by reason of death, durch Versterben.
C. M. G., Companion (of the Order of) St. Michael and St. George.
C. M. S., Church Missionary Society, anglikanische Missionsgesellschaft.
C. O., Colonial Office, Kolonialministerium.
Co., Company, Gesellschaft; County, Grafschaft.
c/o, Care of, per Adresse, mit Briefen des Herrn.
C. O., Commanding Officer, Oberbefehlshaber.
Cod., Codex, Handschrift; **Codd.**, **Codices**, **Handschriften.**

C. O. D., cash on delivery, zahlbar bei Sicht.
Col., Colonel, Oberst; column, Bildsäule; Colossians, Kolosser.
Coll., College, College; colloquial, familiär, der Umgangssprache angehörig.
collat., collateral, parallel, entsprechend.
colloq., colloquially, *see* **Coll.**
Col. Sergt., Colour Sergeant, Fahnenunteroffizier, Feldwebel.
Com., Commander, Befehlshaber; Committee, Ausschuß.
com., common, gewöhnlich.
Commn., Commission, Auftrag.
Commy., Commissary, Kommissär.
comp., comparative, vergleichend; compare, vergleiche; compound, zusammengesetzt.
compar., comparative, vergleichend.
Con., Consul, Konsul.
con., contra, against, gegen; Gegengrund.
Cong., Congress, Kongreß; Congregation, Gemeinde.
Conn., **Ct.**, Connecticut.
cons., consonant, Konsonant.
con. sec., conic section, Kegelschnitt.
consols, Consolidated Funds, Staatspapiere.
Cor., Corinthians, Korinther; coroner, Leichenbeschauer.
Corn., Cornish, cornisch; Cornwall, Cornwallis.
corr., corrupted, verderbt.
C. O. S., Charity Organization Society, Verein gegen Hausbettelei.
cos., cosine, Kosinus.
cot., cotangent, Kotangente.
C. P., Clerk of the Peace, Grafschaftssekretär; Common Pleas (Court of), (Gerichtshof für) Privatsachen.
C. P. C., Clerk of the Privy Council, Sekretär des Staatsrates.
C. P. R., Canadian Pacific Railway.
Cres., Crescent, halbmondförmige Häuserreihe.
C. S. U., Christian Social Union, Christlich-sozialer Verein.
C. T. C., Cyclists' Touring Club, Radfahrerverein.
C. U., Cambridge University, der Universität Cambridge (angehörig) (*before many clubs*).
C. V. O., Commander of Victorian Order.
cwt., hundredweight, der Zentner.

D

d., dele(te), zu streichen; dead *or* died, gestorben; denarius *or* denarii, a penny *or* pence, Pfennig *or* Pfennige.
Dan., Danish, dänisch.
D. C., Da Capo, zu wiederholen.
D. C. L., Doctor of Civil Law, Doktor der Jurisprudenz.
D. D., Doctor of Divinity, Doktor der Theologie.
D. D. D., dat, dicat, dedicat, schenkt, stiftet; dono dedit, dedicavit, hat gestiftet, geschenkt.
Dea., Deacon, Diakonus.
Dec., December, Dezember; declaration, Bekanntmachung; declension, Deklination.
deft., defendant, Angeklagter.
deg., degree, degrees, Grad, Grade.
Del., Delaware; delegate, Abgeordneter.
del., **delt.**, delineavit, er hat es gezeichnet.
dent., dental, zu den Zähnen gehörig, Zahn-.
Dep., Department, (also **Dept.**), Bezirk; Deputy, Abgeordneter.
der., derivation, Ableitung; derived, abgeleitet.
D. F., Defender of the Faith, Schützer des Glaubens; Dean of the Faculty, Dekan der Fakultät.
dft., defendant, Angeklagter; draft, Wechsel.
D. G., deo gratia, by the grace of God, von Gottes Gnaden.
diam., diameter, Durchmesser.
Dict., Dictator, Diktator; dictionary, Wörterbuch.
Dir., Director, Direktor, Leiter.
disc., discount, Rabatt.
diss., dissertation, Dissertation.
dist., distance, Entfernung.
div., divide, teilen.
D. Litt. (*also* **Litt. D.**), Doctor of Literature, Doktor der Litteratur.
D. L. O., Dead-Letter Office, Postamt für unbestellbare Briefe.
do., ditto, the same, dasselbe.
dolls., dollars, Dollars, Taler.
doz., dozen, Dutzend.
D. P. H., Department of Public Health, Öffentliches Gesundheitsamt.
Dpt., Department, Abteilung.
Dr., Debtor, Schuldner; Doctor, Doktor.
D. Sc., Doctor of Science, Doktor der Naturwissenschaften oder Mathematik.
D. S. O., Distinguished Service Order, Verdienstorden für Heer und Flotte.
D. S. P., decessit sine prole, ohne Nachkommen gestorben *or* verstorben.
Dunelm., Dunelmensis, Bischof von Durham.
D. V., Deo volente, wenn Gott will.
dwt., pennyweight (**d.** penny; **wt.** weight).

E

E., East, Osten; English, englisch.
ea., each, jedes.
Ebor., Eboracum, York; Eboracensis, Erzbischof von York.
E. C., Eastern Central, Östlich Zentral, die östliche Hälfte der Mitte Londons, die Hauptgeschäftsgegend.
Eccl., **Eccles.**, Ecclesiastes, der Prediger (Salomo); ecclesiastical, geistlich, Kirchen-.
Ecclus., Ecclesiasticus, das Buch Jesus Sirach.
E. C. U., English Church Union, Englischer Kirchenverein.
Ed., **Edit.**, Editor, Herausgeber; Edition, Auflage; edited, herausgegeben.
Ed., **Edw.**, Edward, Eduard.
Edin., Edinburgh, Edinburg.
E. D. S., English Dialect Society, Englischer Dialektverein.
E. E., errors excepted, Fehler ausgenommen.
E. E. T. S., Early English Text Society, Gesellschaft zur Herausgabe altenglischer Denkmäler.
e. g., **ex. gr.**, exempli gratia, zum Beispiel.
E. I., East Indies, Ostindien.
E. I. C., East India Company, die Ostindische Gesellschaft.
ejusd., ejusdem, derselben Art.
Elis., **Eliz.**, Elisabeth, Elizabeth.
Elz., Elzevir.
Emp., Emperor, Kaiser; Empress, Kaiserin.
Ency., **Encyc.**, Encyclopædia, Konversationslexikon.
Ens., Ensign, Fähnrich.
Ent., **Entom.**, Entomology, Insektenlehre.
Ent. Sta. Hall, Entered at Stationers' Hall, auf der Buchhändlerbörse eingetragen.
Ep., Epistle, Epistel.
Eph., Ephesians, Epheser.
Epis., **Episc.**, Episcopal, bischöflich.
Epit., Epitaph, Grabschrift.
eq., equal, gleich.
esp., **espec.**, especially, besonders.
Esq., Esquire, Wohlgeb(oren).
Est., Established, gegründet.
et. al., et alibi, und an andern Orten; et alii, et alia, und andere.
etc., **&c.**, et cetera, und so weiter, und so fort.
et seq., **et sq.**, **et sqq.**, et sequentes *or* sequentia, und die folgenden, und folgende.
Ex., Example, Beispiel; Exodus, das zweite Buch Mose.
Exc., Excellency, Exzellenz; except, ausgenommen; exception, Ausnahme.
Exon., Exonia, Exeter; Exoniensis, von Exeter; **Cod. Exon.**, Codex Exoniensis, das Exeterbuch.

Exp., Export, Ausfuhr.
Ez., Ezra.
Ezek., Ezekiel.
E. & O. E., errors and omissions excepted.

F

f., following, folgend; farthing, Heller; fathom, Faden; foot, Fuß.
F., Fellow, Mitglied (gelehrter Gesellschaften).
F., **Fahr.**, Fahrenheit.
F. A., Football Association.
Fam., familiar, familiär.
F. A. S., Fellow of the Antiquarian Society; Fellow of the Society of Arts.
F. B., Fenian Brotherhood, Fenierbund.
F. B. A., Fellow of the British Academy.
F. B. S., Fellow of the Botanical Society.
F. C., Free Church (of Scotland), Freie Kirche (von Schottland); Football Club, Fußballverein.
F. C. P., Fellow of the College of Preceptors.
fcp., **flp.**, foolscap, Propatriapapier.
F. C. S., Fellow of the Chemical Society.
F. D., Fidei Defensor, Schützer des Glaubens.
Feb., February, Februar.
fec., fecit, (er) hat es gemacht.
feud., feudal, feudal, Lehns=.
F. F. A., Fellow of the Faculty of Actuaries.
F. G. S., Fellow of the Geological Society.
F. I. A., Fellow of the Institute of Actuaries.
fig., figure, Bild; figuratively, bildlich.
F. K. C. P. I., Fellow of the King's College of Physicians in Ireland.
fl., floruit, lebte.
F. L. S., Fellow of the Linnæan Society.
F. M., Field Marshal, Feldmarschall.
fm., fathom, Faden.
F. O., Field-officer, Stabsoffizier; Foreign Office, Ministerium des Äußeren.
fo., **fol.**, folio, Folio.
Fr., France, Frankreich; French, französisch; friar, Mönch; Friday, Freitag.
F. R. A. S., Fellow of the Royal Astronomical Society, or of the Asiatic Society.
F. R. C. P., Fellow of the Royal College of Physicians.
F. R. C. S., Fellow of the Royal College of Surgeons.
Fred., Frederick, Friedrich.
F. R. G. S., Fellow of the Royal Geographical Society.
F. R. H. S., Fellow of the Royal Horticultural Society.
F. R. I. B. A., Fellow of the Royal Institute of British Architects.
F. R. S., Fellow of the Royal Society (M. d. kgl. Akademie der [Natur=]Wissenschaften).
F. R. S. E., Fellow of the Royal Society, Edinburgh.
F. R. S. L., Fellow of the Royal Society of Literature.
F S. A., Fellow of the Society of Arts; Fellow of the Society of Antiquaries.
ft., foot, feet, Fuß; Fort, Festung.
fth., **fthm.**, fathom, Klafter.
fur., furlong, 200 Meter, Achtelmeile.
F. Z. S., Fellow of the Zoological Society.

G

G., Great, Groß, *e.g.* **G. E. R.**, Great Eastern Railway, Große Ostbahn.
Gal., Galatians, Galater.
Gam., Gamut, Tonleiter.
G. B., Great Britain, Großbritannien.
G. B. & I., Great Britain & Ireland.
G. C., Grand Cross, Großkreuz.
G. C. B., Knight Grand Cross of the Most Honourable the Order of the Bath.
Gen., **Genl.**, General, General.
Gen., gender, Geschlecht; genus, **Art**; **Genesis**, das erste Buch Mose.
Gent., Gentleman, Herr; Gentlemen, **Herren**.
Geo., George, Georg.
Geol., Geology, Geologie.
Geom., Geometry, Geometrie.
G. F. S., Girls' Friendly Society, **Mädchen=Schutz= und Unterstützungs=Verein.**
G. L., Grand Lodge, Großloge.
Glos., Gloucestershire.
G. M. T., Greenwich Mean Time, **Mittlere Greenwicher Zeit.**
G. O., General Order, **Allgemeiner Befehl**; **grand** organ, große Orgel.
Gov., Government, Regierung; Governor, **Gouverneur.**
G. P., General Practitioner, **praktischer Arzt**; Gloria Patri, dem Herrn die Ehre.
G. P. O., General Post Office, **Hauptpostamt.**
Gr., grain, Korn, Gran.
Gram., Grammar, Grammatik.
gs. guineas, Guineen.

H

h., **hr.**, hour, Stunde; **hrs.**, **hours, Stunden.**
Hab., Habakkuk, Habakuk.
hab., habitat, Wohnort.
Hag., Haggai.
Hants., Hampshire.
Har., Harold.
H. B. M., His (*or* Her) **Britannic Majesty, Seine** (Ihre) **Majestät der König (die Königin) von** Großbritannien.
h. e., hic est, die ist; hoc est, **das ist.**
Heb., Hebrews, Hebräer.
hf., half, halb; **hf.-bd.**, **Halbfranzband, in Halbleder**; **hf.-cf.**, half calf, Halbfranzband.
H. G., His Grace, S. **Durchlaucht**; Horse Guards, Gardekavallerie.
hhd., hogshead, Oxhoft.
H. I. H., His (Her) Imperial Highness, Seine (Ihre) Kaiserliche Hoheit.
Hist., History, Geschichte.
H. M., His (*or* Her) Majesty, Seine (od. Ihre) Majestät.
H. M. C., His (*or* Her) Majesty's Customs.
H. M. I. S., His (*or* Her) Majesty's Inspector of Schools.
H. M. S., His Majesty's Ship, Seiner Majestät Schiff; His Majesty's Service, **in Königl. Dienst,** Regierungssache.
Ho., house, Haus.
Hon., Honourable, ehrenwert (*in titles*).
Hor., Horizon, Horizont; Horology, Zeitmessungslehre.
Hort., **Hortic.**, Horticulture, Gartenbau.
Hos., Hosea, Hoseas.
H. P., horse power, **Pferdekraft, Pferdestärke**; half-pay, halber Sold.
hr., hour, Stunde.
H. R. E., Holy Roman Empire, **Heiliges Römisches** Reich (800-1806).
H. R. H., His (*or* Her) Royal Highness, Seine (*or* Ihre) Königliche Hoheit.
H. S., High School, Höhere Schule.
H. S. H., His Serene Highness, **Seine Durchlaucht.**
Hy., Henry, Heinrich.

I

ib., **ibid.**, ibidem, am selben Orte.
I. C. E., Institute of Civil Engineers.
Ich., **Ichth.**, Ichthyology, Fischkunde.
Icon., Iconography, Ikonographie.
I. C. S., Indian Civil Service, **Indischer Staatsdienst.**
id., idem, dasselbe.
i. e., id est, das ist.
ign., ignotus, **unbekannt.**

I. H. P., Indicated Horse Power, angezeigte Pferdekraft.
I. H. S., Jesus Hominum Salvator, Heiland.
ill., illustration, Illustration; illustrated, illustriert.
Imp., Imperial, kaiserlich; Imperator, Kaiser; imprimatur, druckfertig.
I. M. S., Indian Medical Service, Indischer Sanitätsdienst.
in., inches, Zoll.
inc., **incorp.**, incorporated, einverleibt.
incog., incognito, inkognito.
indef., indefinite, unbestimmt.
Ind. Ter., Indian Territory, Indisches Gebiet.
inf., infra, unten.
in loc. cit., in loco citato, am angeführten Orte.
inst., instant, of the present month, dieses Monats, d. M.; Institute, Institut.
Int., Interior, innere; Interest, Zins.
interrog., interrogation, Ausfrage; interrogative(ly), fragend.
in trans., in transitu, unterwegs.
introd., introduction, Einleitung.
inv., invenit, erfand; inventor, Erfinder; invented, erfunden.
I. O., Independent Order, Freie Vereinigung (*especially:* I. O. O. F., Independent Order of Odd Fellows).
I. of M., Isle of Man, Insel Man.
I. of W., Isle of Wight, Insel Wight.
I. O. U., I owe you, ich bin Ihnen schuldig, *i.e.*, Schuldverschreibung, Schuldschein.
i. q., idem quod, dasselbe wie.
Is., **Isa.**, Isaiah, Jesias.
Is., **Isab.**, Isabella, Isabella.
I. S. C., Indian Staff Corps.
It., **Ital.**, Italian, italienisch.
ital., italics, Kursivdruck.

J

J. A., Judge Advocate, Auditor, Militärrichter.
Jan., January, Januar.
Jas., James, Jakob.
J. C., Juris Consultus, Rechtsanwalt.
Jno., John, Johann.
Jo., Joel.
Jos., Josiah, Josias, Joseph.
Josh., Joshua.
J. P., Justice of the Peace, Friedensrichter.
Jul., July, Juli.
Junc., Junction.

K

Kan., **Ks.**, Kansas.
K. B., Knight of the Bath, Ritter des Bathordens; King's Bench, Oberhofgericht.
K. C., Knight Commander (*of various orders*), Komtur, Großmeister; King's Counsel, Geh. Justizrat; King's College (Cambridge, London).
K. C. B., Knight Commander of the Most Honourable Order of the Bath.
K. G., Knight of the (Most Noble Order of the) Garter, Ritter des Hosenbandordens.
K. G. C., Knight of the Grand Cross.
K. G. C. B., Knight of the Grand Cross of the Bath.
K. G. F., Knight of the Golden Fleece, Ritter des goldenen Vlieses.
kilo., kilogramme, Kilo(gramm).
Kit, Christopher, Christoph.
K. M., Knight of Malta, Malteser(ritter).
Km., Kingdom, Reich; kilometre, Kilo(meter).
Knt., **Kt.**, Knight, Ritter.
K. of L., Knight(s) of Labour, Ritter der Arbeit, Arbeiterbildungsverein (*Amer.*).
K. P. S., Keeper of the Privy Seal, Geheimsiegelbewahrer.
K. S. I., Knight of the Star of India.
K. T., Knight of the Order of the Thistle.
Ky., **Ken.**, Kentucky.

L

L., 50; Lake, der See; Latin, lateinisch; Liberal, Liberal; Libra (£), Pfund (£30, 30 Pfund Sterling); Latitude, Breite; League, Verein, Verbindung, Liga; London, *e. g.* L. & N. W. R., London and Northwestern Railway.
La., Louisiana.
Lam., Lamentations, Klagelieder Jeremiä.
Lang., Language, Sprache.
Lat., Latitude, Breite; Latin, Latein(isch).
Lb., Libra, Pfund.
l. c., lower case (in printing), Kleinletterkasten; loco citato, am angeführten Orte; left centre, linkes Zentrum; letter of credit, Kreditbrief.
L. C., Lower Canada, Unter-Kanada; Lord Chancellor, Großkanzler; Lord Chamberlain, Großkämmerer; Oberzeremonienmeister.
L. C. C., London County Council, Londoner Grafschaftsrat.
L. C. J., Lord Chief Justice, Lord Oberrichter.
L. C. P., Licentiate of the College of Preceptors.
L. D., Lady Day, Mariä Verkündigung (25 März); Light Dragoons, leichte Dragoner.
Ld., Lord.
Ldp., **Lp.**, Lordship, Lordschaft, Herrlichkeit.
L. D. S., Licentiate in Dental Surgery, Approbierter Zahnarzt.
Leg., legal, gerichtlich; Legate, Legat; Legislature, Gesetzgebung.
Lev., **Levit.**, Leviticus, das dritte Buch Mose.
Lex., Lexicon, Wörterbuch.
l. h., left hand, linke Seite.
L. I., Long Island; Light Infantry, leichte Infanterie.
Lib., Liber, Buch.
Lib. Cat., Library Catalogue, Bibliotheks-Verzeichnis.
Lieut., **Lt.**, Lieutenant, Leutnant.
Linn., Linnæus, Linnæan.
liq., liquid, flüssig, Flüssigkeit.
lit., literally, wörtlich; literature, Litteratur.
Litt. D. *See* D. Litt.
LL. B., Legum Baccalaureus, Baccalaureus der Rechte.
LL. D., Legum Doctor, Doktor beider Rechte.
L. M. S., London Missionary Society, Londoner Missionsverein.
Loc. cit., loco citato, am angeführten Orte.
log., logarithm, Logarithmus.
Lon., **Long.**, longitude, Länge.
loq., loquitur, spricht.
Lou., **La.**, Louisiana.
L. P., Lord Provost, Oberbürgermeister (*Scott.*).
L. R. C. P., Licentiate of the Royal College of Physicians.
L. R. C. S., Licentiate of the Royal College of Surgeons.
L. S., left side, linke Seite; Linnæan Society; loco sigilli, an (der) Stelle des Siegels.
L. S. A., Licentiate of the Society of Apothecaries.
L. S. D., libræ, solidi, denarii, pounds, shillings, pence, Pfunde, Schillinge und Pence.
Ltd., limited (liability company), (Gesellschaft mit) beschränkter (Haftung).
L. U., Liberal Unionist, *see Part II, pp. 274–275.*
LXX., Septuagint Version of the Bible, Septuaginta.

M

M., mille, tausend; married, verheiratet; masculine, männlich; meridiem, Mittag; metre, Metrum.
M. A., Master of Arts, Magister (der freien Künste).
Mac., **Macc.**, Maccabees, Makkabäer.
Mach., Machinery, Maschinen.
Mad., Madam, gnädige Frau.
Mag., Magazine, Zeitschrift.

Maj., Major, Major.
Mal., Malachi, Maleachi.
Mar., March, März.
marg., margin, Rand.
Marq., Marquis, Marquis.
Mas., **Masc.**, Masculine, männlich.
Mass., Massachusetts.
Math., **Maths.**, Mathematics, Mathematik.
Matt., Matthew, Matthäus.
M. B., Medicinæ Baccalaureus, Baccalaureus der Medizin.
M. C., Member of Congress, Kongreßmitglied, Abgeordneter; Master of Ceremonies, Oberhofmeister; Member of Council, Ratsherr.
M. C. C., Member of County Council.
M. C. P., Member of the College of Preceptors.
M. C. S., Madras Civil Service.
Md., Maryland.
M. D., Medicinæ Doctor, Dr. Med.
Mdlle., **Mlle.**, Mademoiselle, Fräulein.
Mdm., Madam, Frau.
Me., Maine.
M. E., Most Excellent, Erzellenz; Middle English, Mittelenglisch; Mining Engineer, Bergingenieur.
M. E. C., Member of the Executive Council, Mitglied des geschäftsführenden Ausschusses.
med., medical, medizinisch; medicine, Medizin; medieval, mittelalterlich.
mem., memorandum, Memorandum.
Messrs., Messieurs, Herren.
Met., **Metaph.**, Metaphysics, Metaphysik.
Metal., **Metall.**, Metallurgy, Erzscheidekunst, Hüttenkunde.
Meteor., Meteorology, Wetterkunde.
mfd., manufactured, angefertigt, fabriziert.
mfrs., manufacturers, Fabrikanten.
M. F. H., Master of Foxhounds.
Mgr., monseigneur, Monsignor.
M. H. R., Member of the House of Representatives, Abgeordneter.
M. I. C. E., Member of the Institute of Civil Engineers.
Mich., Michigan.
Min., mineralogy, Mineralogie.
Minn., Minnesota.
Mis., Missouri.
misc., miscellaneous, Vermischtes.
mil., **milit.**, military, militärisch; militia, Miliz, Landwehr.
Miss., Mississippi.
M. L. A., Member of the Legislative Assembly.
M. L. C., Member of the Legislative Council.
Mme., Madame.
M. N. S., Member of the Numismatical Society.
mo., **mos.**, month, months, Monat, Monate.
mod., modern, modern.
Mods., Moderations, *see Part II, p. 301.*
Monsig., Monsignor (*title of high dignitaries of the Rom. Cath. Church*).
morn., morning, Morgen.
M. P., Member of Parliament, Parlamentsmitglied, Abgeordneter.
M. P. S., Member of the Philological *or* of the Pharmaceutical Society.
M. R., Master of the Rolls, Staatsarchivar.
Mr., Master, Mister, Herr.
M. R. A. S., Member of the Royal Asiatic Society *or* of the Royal Academy of Sciences.
M. R. C. C., Member of the Royal College of Chemistry.
M. R. C. P., Member of the Royal College of Physicians *or* Preceptors.
M. R. C. S., Member of the Royal College of Surgeons.
M. R. C. V. S., Member of the Royal College of Veterinary Surgeons.
M. R. G. S., Member of the Royal Geographical Society.
M. R. I., Member of the Royal Institution.
M. R. I. A., Member of the Royal Irish Academy.
Mrs., Mistress, Frau.
MS., Manuscript, **Handschrift**; **MSS.**, Manuscripts, Handschriften.
M. S., Master in Surgery; Memoriæ sacrum, dem Andenken geweiht.
m. s., months (after) sight, Monate (nach) Sicht.
M. Sc., Master of Science, Magister der Naturwissenschaften.
M. S. C., Madras Staff Corps.
m. s. l., mean sea-level, mittlerer Meeresspiegel.
Mt., **Mts.**, Mount, Mountains, Berg, Gebirge.
mth., month, Monat.
Mus., Music, Musik; Museum, Museum.
Mus. B., Bachelor of Music, Baccalaureus der Tonkunst.
Mus. D., **Doc.**, **Doct.**, Doctor of Music, **Doktor** der Tonkunst.
M. V. O., Member of the (Royal) Victorian Order.
Myth., Mythology, Mythologie.

N

N., North, Nord, **Norden**; nitrogen, **Stickstoff**; natus, **geboren**; neuter, sächlich; noon, Mittag.
N. A., North America, Nord-Amerika.
Na., Nebraska.
Nah., Nahum.
Nat., national, national.
Nat. Hist., Natural History, Naturgeschichte.
nat. ord., natural order, natürliche **Reihenfolge**.
naut., nautical, Schiffsausdruck.
nav., naval, Flottenausdruck.
Nav., navigation, Schiffahrt.
N. B., New Brunswick, Neubraunschweig; North Britain, **Schottland**; **nota bene**, **Merkzeichen** wobei wohl zu **merken** *or* **nicht** zu vergessen.
N. C., North Carolina.
N. C. U., National Cyclists' Union, Nationaler Radlerverein.
N. D., no date, not dated, **ohne Jahr**, **undatiert**.
N. Dak., North Dakota.
N. E., northeast, Nordost; New England, Neuengland.
Neb., **Nebr.**, Nebraska.
neg., negative, verneinend.
Neh., Nehemiah, Nehemia.
nem. con., nemine contradicente, **einspruchslos**, ohne Widerspruch.
nem. diss., nemine dissentiente, **einspruchslos**.
Nept., Neptune, Neptun.
net., **nett.**, netto, netto, rein.
Neth., Netherlands, **Niederlande**.
neut., neuter, sächlich.
N. F., Newfoundland, **Neufundland**; Norman French, normannisch.
N. H., New Hampshire.
N. J., New Jersey.
n. l., non licet, es ist **unerlaubt**; non liquet, es ist unklar; non longe, **nicht** weit.
N. N. E., north-northeast, Nord-Nordost.
N. N. W., north-northwest, Nord-Nordwest.
N. O., New Orleans; natural order, **natürliche Reihenfolge**.
no., numero, Nummer.
non con., non content, **unzufrieden**.
non obst., non obstante, **nichtsdestoweniger**.
non seq., non sequitur, es folgt **nicht**.
n. o. p., not otherwise provided, **nicht anderweit** vorgesehen.
Northants, Northamptonshire.
Northumb., Northumberland.
nos., numbers, Nummern.
Notts., Nottinghamshire.
Nov., November, November.
N. P., Notary Public, öffentlicher Notar.
N. S., New Style, **neuen Stils**; Nova Scotia, Neuschottland.

n. s., not specified, nicht angegeben.
N. S. W., New South Wales, Neusüdwales.
n. u., name unknown, Name unbekannt.
Num., **Numb.**, Numbers, Numeri, das vierte Buch Mose.
Numis., **Numism.**, Numismatics, Münzkunde.
N. U. T., National Union of Teachers, Verein der englischen Elementarlehrer.
N. V., New Version, Neue Version *or* Übertragung.
N. W., northwest, nordwest.
N. W. P., Northwest Provinces (India).
N. W. T., Northwest Territory.
N. Y., New York, Neu York.
N. Z., New Zealand, Neuseeland.

O

O., Ohio; Oxygen, Sauerstoff.
o., only, nur.
o/a, on account of, wegen.
ob., obiit, gestorben.
Ob., **Obad.**, Obadiah, Obadja.
obdt., obedient, gehorsam.
obj., object, Objekt; objective, Objektiv.
obl., oblong, länglich; oblique, schräg.
obs., observation, Bemerkung; obsolete, veraltet.
Obstet., Obstetrics, Entbindungskunst.
Oc., Ocean, Ozean.
Oct., October, Oktober.
O. E., Old English, Altenglisch.
O. F., Odd Fellow, Mitglied des Ordens der Odd Fellows; Old French, altfranzösisch.
off., official, amtlich.
O. H. G., Old High German, Althochdeutsch.
O. H. M. S., On His Majesty's Service, in Sr. Majestät Dienst, amtlich.
O. M., Old Measurement, altes Maß; Order of Merit, Verdienstorden.
Onomat., Onomatopœia, Wortnachahmung.
o/o, per cent, prozent, vom Hundert.
O. P., old price, alter Preis.
Op., Opera, Oper; opposite, gegenüber; Opus, Werk, Opus (*Mus.*).
Or., Oregon.
Ord., ordained, ordiniert; Order, Ordnung; ordinary, gewöhnlich; Ordnance, Artillerie.
O. S., Old Style, alten Stils.
O. S. A., Ordinis Sancti Augustini, Augustiner.
O. S. B., Ordinis Sancti Benedicti, Benediktiner.
O. S. F., Ordinis Sancti Francisci, Franziskaner.
O. T., Old Testament, Altes Testament.
Oxf., Oxford.
Oxon., Oxonia, Oxford; Oxoniensis, von Oxford, Oxforder; the Oxons, die Oxforder Studenten.
oz., ounce, Unze.
O. & O., Oriental and Occidental Steamship Company.
O. S. N. C., Oriental Steam Navigation Company.
O. U., Oxford University, der Universität Oxford zugehörig, Oxforder (*before the names of many clubs*).

P

p., page, Seite; participle, Partizip.
p. a., participial adjective, Partizipialadjektiv.
Pa., **Penn.**, Pennsylvania, Pennsylvanien.
Pac. Oc., Pacific Ocean, Stiller Ozean.
Paint., Painting, Malerei.
Pal., Palestine, Palästina; Palæontology, Petrefaktenkunde.
pam., pamphlet, Flugschrift, Flugblatt.
Pan., Panama.
par., paragraph, Abschnitt; parallel, gleichlaufend; parish, Gemeinde.
Pat., **Pk.**, Patrick.
Pat. Off., Patent Office, Patentamt.
P. C., Privy Councillor, Geheimer Rat; Police Constable, Schutzmann.
P. C., **p. c.**, post-card, Postkarte.
pd., paid, bezahlt.
P. E. I., Prince Edward Island.
Pen., Peninsula, Halbinsel.
Pent. Pentecost, Pfingsten.
per., period, Periode.
per., **pers.**, person, Person.
per an., per annum, jährlich.
per cent., **per ct.**, per centum, prozent.
Pg., Portugal.
phar., **pharm.**, pharmaceutical, pharmazeutisch.
Phil., Philip, Philipp; Philippians, Philipper.
Phila., Philadelphia.
Philem., Philemon.
Phil. Trans., Philosophical Transactions.
Phon., **Phonet.**, Phonetics, Phonetik.
Phonog., Phonography, Phonographie.
Phot., Photography, Photographie.
Phys., Physiology, Physiologie; Physics, Physik; Physician, Arzt.
pinx., **pxt.**, pinxit, er (*or* sie) hat es gemalt.
P. M., Post Meridiem, nachmittags; Post Mortem (examination), Leichenschau.
pm., premium, Prämie.
P. M. G., Postmaster General, Oberpostdirektor.
p. n., promissory note, Schuldschein.
P. O., Post-Office, Postamt.
P. & O. *or* **P. O. C.**, Peninsular and Oriental Company, Italienisch-orientalische Dampfschiffahrtsgesellschaft (nach Indien).
p. o. d., pay on delivery, zahlbar bei Ablieferung.
P. O. O., Post Office Order, Postanweisung.
pop., population, Bevölkerung; popular, volkstümlich.
pos., **posit.**, positive, positiv.
pp., pages, Seiten.
P. P. C., pour prendre congé, um Abschied zu nehmen.
P. R., Porto Rico.
pr., pair, Paar; per, present, gegenwärtig; pronoun, Fürwort; price, Preis.
P. R. A., President of the Royal Academy.
P. R. B., Pre-Raphaelite Brotherhood.
Preb., Prebendary, Pfründner, Domherr.
pref., preface, Vorwort.
Pres., **Preses.**, President, Vorsitz(end)er.
P. R. I. B. A., President of the Royal Institute of British Architects.
pro., professional, von Beruf, Berufs-.
Prot., Protestant.
pro-tem., pro tempore, zeitweilig.
Prov., Proverbs, Sprüche (Salomos).
prox., proximo, nächst; nächsten Monats.
P. R. S. (E.), President of the Royal Society (of Edinburgh).
P. R. S. A., President of the Royal Scottish Academy.
P. S., postscriptum, Nachschrift.
Ps., **Psa.**, Psalms, Psalmen.
P. S. N. C., Pacific Steam Navigation Company.
pt., pint, Liter.
P. T., post town, Poststadt; pupil teacher, *see Part II, p. 364.*
Pte., private, gewöhnlicher Soldat, Gemeiner.
P. T. O., please turn over, bitte (umzu)wenden.
Pub. Doc., public document, öffentliche Urkunde.
P. W. D., Public Works Department, Abteilung für öffentliche Arbeiten.

Q

Q., Queen, Königin; quadrans, farthing, Heller; query, Frage.
Q., **Qu.**, query, question, Frage.
Q. A. B., Queen Anne's Bounty.
Q. B., Queen's Bench, *see K. B.*
Q. C., Queen's Counsel, der königliche Anwalt, Kronanwalt; Queen's College (*in various places*).
Q. E. D., quod erat demonstrandum, was zu beweisen war.

Q. M., quartermaster, Quartiermeister.
qm., quomodo, auf welche Weise, wie.
Q. M. G., Quartermaster-general, Generalquartiermeister.
qr., quarter, Viertel; Quartal (*C.L.*).
Q. S., Quarter Sessions, *see Part II, p. 368;* quantum sufficit, genügend.
qt., quantity, Menge, Anzahl; quart, Quart(maß); **qts.**, quarts.
qto., quarto, Quartformat.
Qu., Queen, Königin; question, Frage.
quar., **qu.**, quart, Quart(maß); quarterly, vierteljährlich.
Queensl., Queensland.
Q. U. I., Queen's University in Ireland.
Q. V., quod vide, welches nachzusehen; quantum vis, soviel du willst, nach Belieben.

R

R., Rex, Regina.
R. A., Royal Academy, kgl. Akademie.
rabb., rabbinical, rabbinisch.
R.A.C., Royal Agricultural College, Kgl. Ackerbauakademie.
rad., radical, radikal.
R. A. M., Royal Academy of Music, Kgl. Musikakademie.
R. A. S., Royal Asiatic Society.
R. B., Rifle Brigade, Schützenbrigade.
R. B. A., Royal Society of British Artists, Kgl. Britischer Künstlerverein.
R. C., Roman Catholic, katholisch; Red Cross, Rotes Kreuz.
R. C. M., Royal College of Music.
R. C. P., Royal College of Physicians.
R. C. S., Royal College of Surgeons.
R. D., Rural Dean, Landdekan; Royal Dragoons, Kgl. Dragoner.
Rec., recipe, nimm!
recd., received, erhalten.
recpt., receipt, Quittung.
Rect., Rector, Rektor, Pfarrer.
R. E., Royal Engineer, Militäringenieur.
Ref. Ch., Reformed Church, reformierte Kirche.
Reg. Prof., Regius Professor, von der Krone ernannter Professor (*in Oxford and Cambridge*).
Regt., Regiment, Regiment.
Rep., Representative, Vertreter; Republic, Republik; Report, Bericht.
rept., receipt, Quittung.
retd., returned, zurück.
Rev., Revise; Revision; Revelation, Offenbarung.
Rev., **Revd.**, Reverend, Ehrwürden.
Rev. Ver., Revised Version.
R. G. S., Royal Geographical Society.
r. h., right hand, rechte Hand.
R. H., Royal Highness, Königliche Hoheit; Royal Highlanders, Kgl. Bergschottische Regimenter.
R. H. A., Royal Horse Artillery, Reitende Artillerie.
Rhet., Rhetoric, Rhetorik.
R. H. S., Royal Humane Society, Gesellschaft zur Rettung im Wasser Verunglückter; Royal Horticultural Society, Kgl. Gartenbaugesellschaft; Royal Historical Society, Kgl. Historische Gesellschaft.
R. I., Rhode Island.
R. I. B. A., Royal Institute of British Architects.
R. I. P., requiescat in pace, er (sie) ruhe in Frieden, Friede seiner (ihrer) Asche.
R. M., Royal Mail, kgl. Post(dienst); Royal Marines, kgl. Seetruppen.
R. M. A., Royal Marine Artillery, Kgl. Marineartillerie.
R. M. L. I., Royal Marine Light Infantry, Kgl. Marineinfanterie.
R. M. S., Royal Mail Steamer, kgl. Postdampfer.
R. N., Royal Navy, Kgl. Marine.
R. N. R., Royal Naval Reserve, Kgl. Seereservetruppen.
Rob., Robt., Robert.
Rom., Romans, Römer.
Rom. Cath., Roman Catholic, römisch-katholisch.
R. P., Reformed Presbyterian; Regius Professor, *see* Reg. Prof.; Reply paid, Rückantwort bezahlt.
R. R., Right Reverend, hoch(ehr)würdig (*title of bishops*) Seine *or* Ew. Hochehrwürden.
R. S., Royal Society, Kgl. Akademie der (Natur-) Wissenschaften.
R. S. A., Royal Society of Antiquaries; Royal Scottish Academy.
R. S. D., Royal Society of Dublin.
R. S. E., Royal Society of Edinburgh.
R. S. L., Royal Society of London.
R. S. M., Royal School of Mines, Kgl. Bergakademie.
R. S. O., Railway Sub-Office, Eisenbahn-Unterbureau.
R. S. S., *or* **S. R. S.**, Regiæ Societatis Socius, Fellow of the Royal Society, *see* F. R. S.
R. S. V. P., répondez, s'il vous plaît, um Antwort wird gebeten, U. A. w. g.
Rt. Hon., Right Honourable, Hochwohlgeboren.
Rt. Rev., Right Reverend, hoch(ehr)würdig.
R. T. S., Religious Tract Society, Gesellschaft zur Verbreitung religiöser Flugschriften.
R. U., Rugby Union, Gesellschaft zur Beförderung des Rugby-Fußballspiels.
R. U. I., Royal University of Ireland.
R. V., Rifle Volunteers, freiwillige Jäger (*Mil.*); Revised Version, Revidierte engl. Bibelübersetzung (1881–85).
Rt. W., **Rt. Wpful**, Right Worshipful, *or* Right Worthy, hochwürdig (*in many titles*).
rx., tens of rupees.
Ry., Railway, Eisenbahn, Bahn.

S

S., South, Süd; Saint, Sankt; Seconds, Sekunden; Society, Verein.
S. A., South Africa, Südafrika; South America, Südamerika; South Australia, Südaustralien.
Sa., **Sat.**, Saturday, Samstag, Sonnabend.
s.a., secundum artem, der Kunst gemäß; sine anno, ohne Zeitangabe, ohne Jahr.
Sam., Samuel.
Sarum., Salisbury, aus Salisbury.
S. A. S., Societatis Antiquariorum Socius, *see* F. A. S.
S. C., South Carolina.
s. c., **s. caps**, **sm. caps.**, small capitals, Kapitälchen.
sc., **scil.**, scilicet, nämlich.
sc., **sculp.**, **sculpt.**, sculpsit, hat gemeißelt.
Sc. B., Scientiæ Baccalaureus, *see* B. Sc.
Sc. D., Scientiæ Doctor, *see* D. Sc.
S. C. L., Student of Civil Law.
Scot., Scotland, Schottland; Scotch, schottisch.
Script., Scriptures, die heilige Schrift.
S. D., South Dakota; Senior Dea(co)n, älterer Dekan; salutem dicit, läßt grüßen.
s. d., sine die, without day, ohne Tag.
S. E., southeast, südost.
sec., second, Sekunde; section, Abteilung.
Sec., **Secy.**, Secretary, Sekretär.
sec. leg., secundum legem, dem Gesetz gemäß.
sec. reg., secundum regulam, der Regel gemäß.
sect., section, Abteilung.
sem., seminary, Seminar; Semitic, semitisch.
Sen., Senator.
Sep., **Sept.**, September; Septuagint, Septuaginta (Bibel).
seq., sequentes *or* sequentia, die folgenden.
ser., series, Reihe, Serie; sermon, Predigt.
Serg., **Sergt.**, **Serj.**, **Serjt.**, Sergeant.

Sess., session, Sitzungsperiode.
S. G., Solicitor-General, *see Part II, p. 429.*
s. g., specific gravity, spezifisches Gewicht.
sh., shilling, Schilling.
s. h. v., sub hoc verbo, unter diesem Worte.
S. J., Society of Jesus, Gesellschaft Jesu, Jesuiten(orden).
S. L., Solicitor at Law, Sachwalter.
S. l., **S. lat.**, south latitude, südliche Länge.
sld., sailed, fuhr ab.
s. l. p., sine legitima prole, ohne gesetzliche Nachkommenschaft.
S. M., Sa Majesté, Seine (*or* Ihre) Majestät.
Smith. Inst., Smithsonian Institute.
S. M. Lond. Soc., Societatis Medicæ Londiniensis Socius, *see* F. L. M. S.
S. M. M., Sancta Mater Maria, Heilige Mutter Maria.
s. m. p., sine mascula prole, ohne männliche Nachkommenschaft.
s. n., secundum naturam, der Natur gemäß.
S. O., sub-office, Unteramt, Nebenamt.
s. o., seller's option, Recht des Verkäufers, Papiere zum vereinbarten Kurse zu liefern.
Soc., society, Verein.
sol., solution, Lösung.
Sol., **Solr.**, Solicitor. Rechtsanwalt.
Sol.-Gen., Solicitor-General.
sop., soprano, Sopran.
s. p., sine prole, ohne Nachkommenschaft.
S. P. C. A., Society for the Prevention of Cruelty to Animals, Tierschutzverein.
S. P. C. C., Society for the Prevention of Cruelty to Children, Kinderschutzverein.
S. P. C. K., Society for Promoting Christian Knowledge.
S. P. G., Society for the Propagation of the Gospel, anglikanischer Missionsverein.
sport., sporting, den Sport betreffend.
s. p. s., sine prole superstite, ohne überlebenden Erben.
spt., seaport, Seehafen.
Sq., Square, Quadrat.
sq., sequens, das folgende.
S. R. I., Sacrum Romanum Imperium, das Heilige Römische Reich (deutscher Nation) (800–1806).
Ss., Saints, die Heiligen.
S. S., steamship, Dampfer, screw steamer, Schraubendampfer.
S. S. C., Solicitor before the Supreme Court; Societas Sanctae Crucis, Verbindung des heiligen Kreuzes.
SS. D., Sanctissimus Dominus.
S. S. E., south-southeast, Süd-Südost.
S. S. W., south-southwest, Süd-Südwest.
St., Saint, der Heilige; Street, Straße; Strait, Straße (von).
Ste., Sainte, die Heilige.
Ster., **Stereo.**, Stereotype, Stereotyp.
ster., **stg.**, sterling.
S. T. P., Sanctæ Theologiæ Professor.
Su., Sunday, Sonntag.
sub., subject, Gegenstand, Subjekt; suburb, Vorstadt, Vorort.
subj., subject, Subjekt; subjunctive, Konjunktiv.
subst., substitute, Stellvertreter; substantive, Hauptwort.
suf., **suff.**, suffix.
sup., superfine, sehr fein; superior, höher; supreme, höchst.
Sup. Ct., Supreme Court, höchster Gerichtshof.
supp., supplement, Ergänzung(s-Band, -s-Heft).
Supt., superintendent, Oberaufseher.
Surg., Surgery, Chirurgie; surgeon, Chirurg.
Surv.-Gen., Surveyor-General, Generalinspektor; Oberlandvermesser.
S. V., Sancta Virgo, Heilige Jungfrau; Sanctitas Vestra, Eure Heiligkeit.
s. v., sub voce, unter dem Worte.
sym., symbol, Symbol; symbolisch.
syn., synonym, sinnverwandt.
synop., synopsis, zusammenfassender Überblick.
syst., system; systematic, systematisch.

T

tan., tangent, Tangente.
Tasm., Tasmania.
tc., tierce, Drittel, Drittelpipe (*of wine*).
T. C. D., Trinity College, Dublin.
Te., tellurium.
Tech., technically, technisch; technology, Gewerbekunde.
tel., **teleg.**, telegram, Telegramm; telegraph, Telegraph.
temp., temporal, zeitlich, weltlich; tempore, zur Zeit von.
Ten., Tenor.
Ten., **Tenn.**, Tennessee.
Ter., **Terr.**, Territory, Gebiet.
term., termination, Endung.
Tex., Texas.
Text. Rec., Textus Receptus, angenommene Lesung.
theat., theatrical, theatralisch.
Theol., theologian, Theolog(e); Theology, Theologie.
Theos., Theosophy.
Therap., Therapeutics, Heilkunde.
Thess., Thessalonians, Thessalonicher (*Bibl.*).
Tho., **Thos.**, Thomas.
Tim., Timothy, Timotheus.
Tit., Titus.
tn., ton, Tonne.
T. O., turn over, umschlagen; Telegraph Office, Telegraphenamt.
tom., tome *or* volume, Band; **toms.**, Bände.
tp., township, Stadtbezirk.
tr., transpose, umzusetzen.
Tr., Transactions, Verhandlungen; Translator, Übersetzer; Trustee, Kurator.
trans., transitive, transitiv.
transf., transferred, übertragen.
T. R. C., Thames Rowing Club, Themse-Ruderklub.
Treas., Treasurer, Kassenwart, Schatzmeister.
T. R. H., Their Royal Highnesses, Ihre Königlichen Hoheiten.
Trig., Trigonometry, Trigonometrie.
Trin., Trinity, Dreieinigkeit.
Trop., Tropic, tropisch.
T. S. O., Town Sub-office, städtisches Nebenamt.
Tu., **Tues.**, Tuesday, Dienstag.
Typo., **Typ.**, Typographer, Buchdrucker, Schriftsetzer; Typography, Buchdruckerkunst.

U

U. C., Upper Canada, Ober-Kanada.
U. K., United Kingdom, das Vereinigte Königreich.
ult., ultimo, letzten *or* vorigen Monats.
Unit., Unitarian, Unitarier.
Univ., University, Universität.
Up., Upper, Ober.
U. S., United States, Vereinigte Staaten; United Service, Heer und Flotte.
U. S. A., United States of America, die Vereinigten Staaten von Nordamerika; United States Army, das Heer der Vereinigten Staaten (von Nordamerika).
U. S. C., United States of Colombia.
U. S. N., United States Navy, Marine der Vereinigten Staaten (von Nordamerika).
U. S. S., United States ship *or* steamer, Schiff oder Dampfer der Vereinigten Staaten.
u. s., ut supra, wie oben.
usu., usually, gewöhnlich.
ut. sup., ut supra, wie oben.
ux., uxor, Ehefrau.

V

v., versus, gegen; vide, man sehe; verb, Zeitwort; verse, Vers; volume, Band.
V., Viscount, Vicomte (*between rank of earl and that of baron*).
V. A., Royal Order of Victoria & Albert, Victoria und Albertorden (für Frauen); Vicar Apostolic, Großvikar, Vikar des Papstes.
Va., Virginia.
val., value, Wert.
var. lect., varia lectio, abweichende Lesart, Variante.
Vat., Vatican.
vb., verb, Zeitwort.
V. C., Victoria Cross, Viktoriakreuz; Vice-Consul, Vizekonsul; Vice-Chancellor, Vizekanzler, Prorektor (einer englischen Universität).
V. D. M., Verbi Dei Minister, Prediger des (göttlichen) Wortes.
Ven., Venerable, Ehrwürdig.
Venet., Venetian, venezianisch.
Vert., Vertebrata, Wirbeltiere.
ves., vessel, Schiff.
Vet., **Veter.**, Veterinary, tierärztlich.
Vet. Surg., Veterinary Surgeon, Tierarzt.
V. G., Vicar General, Generalvikar.
v. g., verbi gratia, zum Beispiel.
Vic., Vicar, Landprediger; Vicarage, Landpfarre.
vid., vide, man sehe, vgl.
v. imp., verb impersonal, unpersönliches Zeitwort.
v. irr., verb irregular, unregelmäßiges Zeitwort.
Vis., **Visc.**, Viscount, Vicomte.
viz., videlicet, nämlich.
v. n., verb neuter, intransitives Zeitwort.
vocab., vocabulary, Glossar.
Vol., Volunteer, Freiwilliger.
vol., **vols.**, volume, Band; volumes, Bände.
Volc., Volcano, Vulkan.
V. P., Vice-President, stellvertretender Vorsitzer.
V. R., Victoria Regina, Königin Victoria.
v. r., verb reflexive, zurückbezügliches Zeitwort.
V. R. I., Victoria Regina et Imperatrix, Victoria, Königin von Großbritannien und Kaiserin von Indien.
V. O., Victorian Order.
V. S., Veterinary Surgeon, Tierarzt.
v. t., verb transitive, transitives Zeitwort.
Vul., **Vulg.**, Vulgate, Vulgata.
vul., vulgar, gemein.
vv. ll., variæ lectiones, Varianten, abweichende Lesarten.

W

W., west, Westen; Warden, *see Part II, p. 503*; week, Woche; Welsh, wallisisch.
W. A., West Africa, Westafrika; West Australia, Westaustralien.
Wal., Walloon, Wallone.
Wash., Washington.
W. B., way-bill, Frachtbrief; Passagierzettel.
W. C., watercloset, Abtritt; Western Central, die westliche Hälfte der Mitte Londons, die Gegend um das britische Museum.
W., **Wed.**, Wednesday, Mittwoch.
w. f., wrong font, falsche Schriftart.
W. I., West Indies, Westindien.
Winton., Wintoniensis, von Winchester.
Wis., Wisconsin.
wk., week, Woche.
Wm., William, Wilhelm.
W. N. W., west-northwest, West-Nordwest.
W. O., War Office, Kriegsministerium.
Wp., **Wpfl.**, Worshipful, verehrlich.
W. R., West Riding, *see Part II, p. 389.*
W. S., Writer to the Signet, *see Part II, p. 420.*
W. S. W., west-southwest, West-Südwest.
wt., weight, Gewicht.
W. Va., West Virginia.

X

X, **Xt.**, Christ, Christus (X, *Gr.* χ).
Xm., **Xmas.**, Christmas, Weihnachten.
Xn., **Xtian**, Christian, christlich, Christ.

Y

y., **yr.**, year, Jahr.
y., **yd.**, yard, Meter.
ye, the (y *for Old English* þ, th), der, die, das.
Y. M. C. A. (*or* **S.**), Young Men's Christian Association (*or* Society), Verein christlicher Jünglinge, Jünglingsverein.
Yorks., Yorkshire.
yr., **your**, Ihr; younger, jünger.
Y. W. C. A. (*or* **S.**), Young Women's Christian Association (or Society), Verein christlicher Jungfrauen, Jungfrauenverein.

Z

Zn., Zinc, Zink.
Zech., Zechariah, Zacharias.
Zeph., Zephaniah, Zephania.

STRONG AND ANOMALOUS VERBS.

* = archaic. *A = archaic, but still used adjectivally. † = becoming archaic. ‡ = colloquial.
R = rare. S = slang.

Pres. Infin.	Imperf. Indic.	Past Part.
abide	abode	abode
arise	arose	arisen
awake	awoke	awaked
	*awaked	
bake	baked	baked
		*baken
be *Pres. Ind.* am	was	been
bear	bore	borne
bear	*bare	born
beat	beat	beaten
		*beat
become	became	become
beget	begot	begotten
	*begat	*begot
begin	began	begun
	*begun	
bend	bent	bent
	*bended	*A bended [1]
bereave	bereft	bereft
	bereaved	bereaved
beseech	besought	besought
	R beseeched	R beseeched
*bestead	*bestead	*bestead
	*bested	*bested
bestride	bestrode	bestridden
	*bestrid	*bestrid
bid	bade	bidden
	† bid	*bid
bind	bound	bound
		*A bounden [2]
bite	bit	bitten
		*bit
bleed	bled	bled
blow	blew	blown
		S blowed
break	broke	broken
	*brake	S *broke
breed	bred	bred
bring	brought	brought
build	built	built
	*builded	*builded
burn	burnt	burnt
	burned	burned
burst	burst	burst
		*bursten
buy	bought	bought
Pres. Ind. can	could	——
cast	cast	cast
catch	caught	caught
	*catched	*catched
chide	chid	chidden
		*chid
choose	chose	chosen
cleave	cleft	cleft
	*clove	*A cloven [3]
	*clave	cleaved
cleave	cleaved	cleaved
	*clave	
cling	clung	clung
clothe	† clad	† clad
	clothed	clothed
come	came	come
cost	cost	cost
creep	crept	crept

Pres. Infin.	Imperf. Indic.	Past Part.
crow	crowed	crowed
	*crew	
cry	cried	cried
cut	cut	cut
dare	durst	
	dared	dared
deal	dealt	dealt
	*dealed	*dealed
dig	dug	dug
	*digged	*digged
R ding	R *dung	R *dung
	R dinged	R dinged
do	did	done
draw	drew	drawn
dream	dreamt	dreamt
	dreamed	dreamed
drink	drank	drunk
	*drunk	*A drunken [4]
drive	drove	driven
dwell	dwelt	dwelt *dwelled
eat	ate, eat	eaten
		*eat
fall	fell	fallen
feed	fed	fed
feel	felt	felt
fight	fought	fought
		*foughten
find	found	found
flee	fled	fled
fling	flung	flung
fly	flew	flown
forbear	forebore	forborne
	*forebare	
forbid	forebade, forbad	forbidden
	*forbid	*forbid
forget	forgot	forgotten
	*forgat	*forgot
forgive	forgave	forgiven
forsake	forsook	forsaken
		*forsook
freeze	froze	frozen
geld	gelded	gelded
	gelt	gelt
get	got	got
	*gat	*A gotten [5]
gild	*gilt	*A gilt [6]
	gilded	gilded
gird	girt	girt
	girded	girded
give	gave	given
go	went	gone
(en)grave	(en)graved	*A (en)graven [7]
		(en)graved
grind	ground	ground
grow	grew	grown
hang	hung	hung
have	had	had
hear	heard	heard
heave	*hove	*hoven, hove
	heaved	heaved
help	*holp	*holpen
	helped	helped
hew	hewed	hewn
		hewed
hide	hid	hidden *hid

[1] Cp. "On *bended* knees." [2] Cp. "It is his *bounden* duty." [3] Cp. "*Cloven* hoof."
[4] Cp. "A *drunken* man." [5] "Ill-*gotten* gains." [6] "*Gilt*-edged." [7] "A *graven* image."

PRES. INFIN.	IMPERF. INDIC.	PAST PART.
hit	hit	hit
hold	held	held
		* holden
hurt	hurt	hurt
keep	kept	kept
kneel	knelt	knelt
	* kneeled	* kneeled
knit	* knit	*A knit [1]
	knitted	knitted
know	knew	known
lade	laded	laded
		*A laden [2]
lay	laid	laid
lead	led	led
lean	leant	leant
	* leaned	† leaned
leap	leapt	leapt
	leaped	leaped
learn	learnt	learnt learned
	learned	*A learnéd [3]
leave	left	left
lend	lend	lent
let	let	let
lie	lay	lain
light	lit	lit
	lighted	lighted
load	loaded	loaded
		* loaden
lose	lost	lost
make	made	made
Pres. Ind. may	might	——
mean	meant	meant
meet	met	met
melt	melted	melted
		*A molten [4]
mix	R mixt	R mixt
	mixed	mixed
mow	mowed	mowed
		mown
nip	nipped	nipped
	R nipt	R nipt
Pres. Ind. must [5]	——	——
owe	owed	owed
	ought	
pay	paid	paid
pen	penned	penned
	pent	pent
plead	pleaded	pleaded
	* pled	* pled
put	put	put
quit	quit	quit
	quitted	quitted
——	† quoth	
rap	rapped	rapped
	R rapt	R rapt
reach	reached	reached
	* raught	* raught
read	read	read
rend	rent	rent
rid	rid	rid
ride	rode	ridden
	* rid	* rid
		* rode
ring	rang	rung
	* rung	
rise	rose	risen
rive	rived	rived
		riven
rot	rotted	rotted
		*A rotten [6]
run	ran	run

PRES. INFIN.	IMPERF. INDIC.	PAST PART.
saw	sawed	sawn
		sawed
say	said	said
see	saw	seen
seek	sought	sought
seethe	seethed	seethed
	* sod	*A sodden
		R * sod
sell	sold	sold
send	sent	sent
set	set	set
shake	shook	shaken
		* shook
		* shaked
Pres. Ind. shall [7]	should [7]	——
shape	shaped	shaped
		* shapen
shear	sheared	sheared
	* shore	*A shorn [8]
shed	shed	shed
* shend	* shent	* shent
shew, show	shewed, showed	shewn, shown
		showed
shine	shone	shone
shoe	shod	shod
shoot	shot	shot
shred	shred	shred
	shredded	shredded
shrink	shrank	shrunk
	shrunk	* shrunken
shut	shut	shut
sing	sang	sung
	† sung	
sink	sank	sunk
	† sunk	* sunken [9]
sit	sat	sat
	* sate	* sate
slay	slew	slain
sleep	slept	slept
slide	slid	slid
		* slidden
sling	slung	slung
slink	* slank	slunk
	slunk	
slit	slit	slit
	R slitted	R slitted
smell	smelled	smelled
	smelt	smelt
smite	smote	smitten
		* smote
sow	sowed	sowed
		sown
speak	spoke	spoken
	* spake	* spoke
speed	sped	sped
	* speeded	* speeded
spell	spelt	spelt
	spelled	spelled
spend	spent	spent
spill	spilt	spilt
	spilled	spilled
spin	spun	spun
	* span	
spit	spit † spat	spit
[spit = to put on a spit	spitted	spitted]
split	split	split
	R splitted	R splitted
spread	spread	spread
spring	sprang	sprung
	R sprung	
spy	spied	spied

[1] "Well-*knit*." [2] "*Laden* with corn." [3] "A *learnéd* man." [4] "*Molten* metal." [5] Used as an auxiliary verb only, and has no inflections. [6] "A *rotten* concern" (*sl.*). [7] Used as auxiliaries only. [8] "A *shorn* sheep." [9] "*Sunken* cheeks."

Pres. Infin.	Imperf. Indic.	Past Part.	Pres. Infin.	Imperf. Indic.	Past Part.
stand	stood	stood	tell	told	told
stave	stove	stove	think	thought	thought
	staved	staved	thrive	throve	thriven
stay	* staid	* staid		R thrived	R thrived
	stayed	stayed	throw	threw	thrown
steal	stole	stolen	thrust	thrust	thrust
	* stale	* stole	tread	trod	trodden S trod
stick	stuck	stuck		* trode	* trode
sting	* stang	stung	try	tried	tried
	stung		wake	woke	waked
stink	† stank	stunk		waked	woke
	stunk		wax	* wax, wox(e)	* waxen
strew	strewed	strewed		waxed	waxed
		*A strewn	wear	wore	worn
stride	strode * strid	stridden		* ware	* wore
strike	struck	*A stricken [1]	weave	wove	woven
	* strake	struck		R weaved	R weaved
string	strung	strung			* wove [3]
		R stringed	weep	wept	wept
strive	strove	striven	wet	* wet	* wet
	* strived	* strove		wetted	wetted
strow [2]	strowed	strown *and*	will	would	———
		strowed [2]	win	won * wan	won
swear	swore	sworn	wind	wound	wound
	* sware	* swore		R winded	R winded
sweat	‡ sweat	‡ sweat	wont	* wont	† wont
	sweated	sweated			*A wonted
sweep	swept	swept	work	worked	worked
swell	swelled	swollen		wrought	wrought
		R swoln	wrap	wrapped	wrapped
		swelled		wrapt	wrapt
swim	swam	swum	wreathe	wreathed	wreathed
	* swum				R wreathen
swing	swang	swung	wring	* wrang wrung	wrung
	swung			R wringed	R wringed
take	took	taken	write	wrote	written
teach	taught	taught		* writ	† writ *wrote
tear	tore	torn	writhe	writhed	writhed
	* tare	* tore			R writhen

1 "Well-*stricken* in years." 2 *Strow*, with imperf. *strowed*, p.p. *strowed* and *strown*, is the archaic form of *strew*. 3 "Vellum-*wove* paper."

PRINTED AT
THE CHAPEL RIVER PRESS,
KINGSTON, SURREY.

100.11.31